SCOTT

2003 STANDARD POSTAGE STAMP CATALOGUE

ONE HUNDRED AND FIFTY-NINTH EDITION IN SIX VOLUMES

VOLUME 5

COUNTRIES OF THE WORLD

P-SI

EDITOR	James E. Kloetzel
ASSOCIATE EDITOR	William A. Jones
ASSISTANT EDITOR /NEW ISSUES & VALUING	Martin J. Frankevicz
VALUING ANALYSTS	Leonard J. Gellman
	Rich Wolff
EDITORIAL ASSISTANT	Beth Brown
DESIGN MANAGER	Teresa M. Wenrick
IMAGE COORDINATOR	Nancy S. Martin
ELECTRONIC MEDIA MANAGER	Mark Kaufman
MARKETING/SALES DIRECTOR	William Fay
ADVERTISING	Renee Davis
CIRCULATION / PRODUCT PROMOTION MANAGER	Tim Wagner
EDITORIAL DIRECTOR/AMOS PRESS INC.	Michael Laurence

Released August 2002

Includes New Stamp Listings through the July, 2002 *Scott Stamp Monthly* Catalogue Update

Scott Publishing Co.

911 Vandemark Road, Sidney, OH 45365-0828

A division of AMOS PRESS, INC., publishers of *Scott Stamp Monthly, Linn's Stamp News, Coin World* and *Cars & Parts* magazine.

Table of Contents

On the Cover: This year's theme for the catalogue covers is the Centennial of Powered Flight.

A special thank you to Eric Kindig for allowing us to photograph his 1941 North American T-6 "Texan"

See Volume 1 for United States, United Nations and Countries of the World A-B.
See Volumes 2, 3, 4, 6 for Countries of the World C-O, So-Z.

Volume 2: C-F
Volume 3: G-I
Volume 4: J-O
Volume 6: So-Z

Scott Publishing Mission Statement

The Scott Publishing Team exists to serve the recreational, educational and commercial hobby needs of stamp collectors and dealers.

We strive to set the industry standard for philatelic information and products by developing and providing goods that help collectors identify, value, organize and present their collections.

Quality customer service is, and will continue to be, our highest priority. We aspire toward achieving total customer satisfaction.

ISBN 0-89487-287-7

Library of Congress Card No. 2-3301

You'll meet all kinds of interesting people inside the pages of Scott Stamp Monthly!

ENTERTAINING

INFORMATIVE

PROVOCATIVE

12 ISSUES ONLY $23.95

Every month you'll find:

- Entertaining and informative articles written by the hobby's leading authors and columnists.
- The very latest information on the world's new stamps in the Catalogue Update. Each month you get Scott numbers and photos for nearly 1,000 stamps.
- A magazine that serves an important function in the hobby, providing the latest information on new stamp issues, including illustrations and other details not available in other philatelic publications.
- Automatic enrollment into the Amos Advantage Program that can save you up 30% off stamp supplies, accessories, supplements, books and catalogues!

Order online at:

www.scottonline.com

Call toll-free:

1-800-448-3611

write:

P.O. Box 828, Sidney, OH 45365-0828

AMOS HOBBY PUBLISHING

(Offer valid only for U.S. subscribers. Canadian and International subscribers add $15.00 for postage.)

SCOTT

Scott Publishing Co.

SCOTT 911 VANDEMARK ROAD, SIDNEY, OHIO 45365 937-498-0802

Dear Scott Catalogue User:

In the Editor's Letter for last year's Scott Volume 5, we announced the beginning of a new phase of our project for digitally scanning all the stamp images in the catalogs. This new phase involved the scanning of early stamps from the large unused collection owned by a Scott friend from Ohio. This collection beautifully complemented the more modern Scott reference collection. For the 2002 Volume 4-6 catalogs, we were able to scan our friend's early stamps, and this scanning continued through the 2003 Scott Volume 3 that was released in June 2002.

More than 110,000 stamps have been scanned for the catalogs, but we still are missing scanned stamp images for somewhat more than 6,000 stamps. For these, we are temporarily using black and white scanned images of the old velox prints that previously appeared in the catalogs for all stamp designs.

We call the scanning of the stamps from the Scott reference collection Phase 1 of the scanning project. Phase 2 was the scanning of our friend's more classic unused stamps. We have now begun Phase 3 of the scanning project, which is to locate, borrow and scan the 6,000+ remaining stamps. Many collectors and dealers have offered to loan us many of the needed stamps, and we have begun contacting these individuals. We appreciate their spirit of cooperation in helping us complete this mammoth task. The quality of the new scanned stamp images is apparent to all, and we appreciate the good words that we have received.

What about value changes in the 2003 Volume 5?

Almost 12,000 value changes appear in this year's Volume 5 of the *2003 Scott Standard Postage Stamp Catalogue.* Volume 5 contains listings for countries of the world P-Sl. The stamps of the Philippines lead the way with almost 2,000 value changes, followed by Portugal with almost 1,600, Russia with more than 1,300, and Romania with almost 1,000. Additional countries that also record large numbers of value changes are Saar, Sierra Leone and Singapore. All told, 27 of the 61 countries listed in Volume 5 have had more than 100 values changed.

What's going up, and what's coming down?

For the stamps of the Philippines, many value adjustments continue last year's strong upward trend for stamps of the Republic from 1946 to the present. Most increases are in the range of 10-15 percent, though many used values show changes in the opposite direction. An example of this mixed trend is the 1947 seven-stamp set of definitives, Scott 504-510, which this year rises to $8.75 mint, never hinged from a value of $7.55 in the 2002 catalogue, while at the same time the used value falls to $2.10 from $2.75. In addition, a large number of value increases have been brought forward from Volume 1 of the 2003 catalog for those stamps issued under the U.S. Administration from 1899-1946.

In Western Europe, the stamps of Portugal prior to 1976 exhibit a strong upward value trend. The increase is also true for Portuguese stamps from 1960 to 1992 devoted to the subject of Europa. For most of the later Europa issues, the major increases occur in the souvenir sheets that accompany the stamps. The 1977 two-stamp Europa issue picturing landscapes, Scott 1332-1333, moves upward to $3.25 mint, never hinged in 2003 from $2.75 in 2002, while the used value remains unchanged. However, the souvenir sheet, Scott 1333a, doubles its value to $50 mint, never hinged and $45 used this year, from $25 both ways last year.

Russia is another country showing very strong upward movement in the issues from 1950-60. Pre-WWII stamps also show strong value increases, with the greatest increases appearing in the mint, never hinged values. For the stamps of Romania, issues of the late nineteenth and early twentieth century show decreases. However, an examination of semi-postals and airmails shows rather large increases.

Continuing the review of the German area begun in Volume 3, the stamps of the Saar between the two World Wars received a detailed examination. Decreases generally in the range of 10-15 percent are the rule. Frequently, however, values for minor varieties defy this trend and show increases. As an example, the vertical tête bêche pair of the 15-centime surcharge on the 40-pfennig definitive issued in 1921, Scott 88a, climbs to $72.50 unused and $250 used in 2003, from $67.50 unused and $190 used in 2002.

For the stamps of Singapore during the 1970s, there are value changes in both directions. On balance, the trend does appear to be upward, especially among used material, and many changes are quite large. The four-stamp set issued in 1975 picturing Birds, Scott 236-239, jumps to $26 mint, never hinged and used, from $23.35 mint, never hinged and $11.15 used last year. In 2003, Sierra Leone also sees a number of very strong value increases among its stamps issued between 1985-1990. One of the largest increases is for the set of 15 butterflies issued in 1987, Scott 859-873. The set climbs to $47.50 mint, never hinged and $34.25 used in 2003, from $16 both ways in 2002.

Where are the editorial enhancements?

The major editorial changes to Volume 5 are in the Philippines. The 1856 1r gray green and 2r carmine picturing Queen Isabella II have been reinstalled as Scott 8 and 9. These two stamps can only be distinguished from Cuba Nos. 2 and 3 by their cancellations, as they were issued for use in more than one Spanish colony. The used values of $75 and $100, respectively, are for stamps with identifiable Philippines cancellations of the period. A new six-stamp set and souvenir sheet recognizing the 1984 Los Angeles Summer Olympics has been added as Scott 1699-1705. A new minor with a green color, Scott 34a, has been added to the 1868-74 definitive set of "Habilitado por la Nacion" overprints, Scott 25-38. A number of other editorial changes and additions have been made in the Philippines listings.

In the stamps of Slovakia, the Castles & Churches set issued from 1995-2001 has been closed and renumbered as Scott 218-227. For Papua New Guinea, two new minor varieties have been added to identify errors. Scott 720a is the 20-toea double surcharge on the 17-toea Fish series issued in 1989, and Scott 867a is the 50-toea inverted surcharge on the Gogodala Dance Mask issued in 1994.

For Portuguese India, a recently identified 100-reis stamp of the 1872 issue on thick, soft-wove paper is now a major number, Scott 7A. And for Portuguese Guinea, a new minor variety has been added to identify a tête bêche pair for the Postal Tax stamp issued in 1934 picturing the Coat of Arms, Scott RA4a. In St. Lucia, a new lettered minor has been added to complete the sideways watermark varieties for the set of coil stamps of the Arms of St. Lucia definitives issued in 1973. This stamp is the 25-cent claret, Scott 336a.

For Saudi Arabia, a new minor variety has been added for the 1925 issue to identify the stamp with a gold-on-blue overprint, Scott L61a. In addition, a number of editorial changes and additions also have been made.

For Russia, a 1964 souvenir sheet containing six 10-kopek stamps and celebrating the Conquest of Space has been added as Scott 2930A, including a minor, Scott 2930Ab. This listing was previously only given the status of a footnote.

A number of listings for never-hinged stamps have been added after unused, hinged sets throughout Volume 5, and a number of footnotes throughout the catalog have been added or modified.

Happy collecting,

James E. Kloetzel

James E. Kloetzel/Catalogue Editor

Acknowledgments

Our appreciation and gratitude go to the following individuals who have assisted us in preparing information included in the 2003 Scott Catalogues. Some helpers prefer anonymity. These individuals have generously shared their stamp knowledge with others through the medium of the Scott Catalogue.

Those who follow provided information that is in addition to the hundreds of dealer price lists and advertisements and scores of auction catalogues and realizations that were used in producing the catalogue values. It is from those noted here that we have been able to obtain information on items not normally seen in published lists and advertisements. Support from these people goes beyond data leading to catalogue values, for they also are key to editorial changes.

A special acknowledgment to Liane and Sergio Sismondo of The Classic Collector for their extraordinary assistance and knowledge sharing that has aided in the preparation of this year's Standard and Classic Specialized Catalogues.

Dr. Karl Agre
Donald R. Alexander (China Stamp Society)
A. R. Allison (Orange Free State Study Circle)
B. J. Ammel (The Nile Post)
Robert Ausubel (Great Britain Collectors Club)
John Barone (Stamptracks)
Jack Hagop Barsoumian (International Stamp Co.)
William Batty-Smith (Sarawak Specialists' Society)
Jules K. Beck (Latin American Philatelic Society)
Vladimir Berrio-Lemm (CEFIN_PANAMA)
John D. Bowman (Carriers and Locals Society)
Chris Brainard (B&S Stamp Bourse)
Jeff Brasor (Honduras Coll. Club, Associated Coll. of El Salvador)
Roger S. Brody
Keith & Margie Brown
Mike Bush (Joseph V. Bush, Inc.)
Peter Bylen
Nathan Carlin
Henry Chlanda
Bob Coale
Laurie Conrad
Leo Constantinides
Frank D. Correl
Andrew Cronin (Canadian Society of Russian Philately)
William T. Crowe (The Philatelic Foundation)
Tony L. Crumbley (Carolina Coin & Stamp, Inc.)
Norman S. Davis
Tom Derbyshire (University Stamp Co.)
John DeStefanis (Matthew Bennett, Inc.)
Bob Dumaine (Sam Houston Duck Co.)
William S. Dunn
Esi Ebrani
Paul G. Eckman
Peter R. Feltus
Karol Fercák (Karol Fercák International)
Leon Finik (Loral Stamps)
Joseph E. Foley (Eire Philatelic Association)
Nicholas Follansbee
Robert S. Freeman
Richard Friedberg
Bob Genisol (Sultan Stamp Center)
Henry L. Gitner
Daniel E. Grau
Michael H. Grollnek (Mid South Stamp Co.)
Harry Hagendorf
Erich E. Hamm (Philactica)
Jerone Hart (Aden & Somaliland Study Group)
Bruce Hecht (Bruce L. Hecht Co.)
Clifford O. Herrick (Fidelity Trading Co.)
Lee H. Hill, Jr.
John-Paul Himka (Lemberg Stamps & Covers)
Wilson Hulme
Kalman V. Illyefalvi (Society for Hungarian Philately)
Eric Jackson
John I. Jamieson (Saskatoon Stamp Centre)
Peter C. Jeannopoulos
Richard A. Johnson
Allan Katz (Ventura Stamp Company)
Stanford M. Katz
Lewis Kaufman
Patricia A. Kaufmann
Dr. James W. Kerr
Charles F. Kezbers
Dr. Thomas C. Kingsley
Juri Kirsimagi
Janet Klug
William V. Kriebel
William Langs
Frederick P. Lawrence
John R. Lewis (The William Henry Stamp Co.)
Ulf Lindahl (Ethiopian Philatelic Society)
William A. Litle
Gary B. Little (Luxembourg Collectors Club)
Pedro Llach (Filatelia Llach S.L.)
William Thomas Lockard (Liberian Philatelic Society)
Dennis Lynch
Larry Lyons (Carriers and Locals Society)
David MacDonnell
Nick Markov (Italia Stamp Co.)
Marilyn R. Mattke
James Mazepa (Mexico-Elmhurst Philatelic Society)
Gary N. McLean (Korean Philately)
Dr. Hector R. Mena (Society for Costa Rica Collectors)
Mark S. Miller
Allen Mintz (United Postal Stationery Society)
Jack E. Molesworth (Jack E. Molesworth, Inc.)
Chuck O. Moo
Gary M. Morris (Pacific Midwest Co.)
Peter Mosiondz, Jr.
Bruce M. Moyer (Moyer Stamps & Collectibles)
Richard H. Muller (Richard's Stamps)
Naya Nicolins (Indigo)
Robert Odenweller
Victor Ostolaza
Dr. Everett L. Parker (St. Helena, Ascension & Tristan da Cunha Philatelic Society)
John E. Pearson (Pittwater Philatelic Service)
John Pedneault
Donald J. Peterson (International Philippine Philatelic Society)
Stanley M. Piller (Stanley M. Piller & Associates)
Todor Drumev Popov
Peter W. W. Powell
Stephen Radin (Albany Stamp Co.)
Siddique Mahmudur Rahman (Bangladesh Institute of Philatelic Studies)
Ghassan D. Riachi
Omar Rodriguez
Michael Rogers (Michael Rogers, Inc.)
Jon W. Rose
Michael Ruggiero
Frans H.A. Rummens (American Society for Netherlands Philately)
Theodosios Sampson
Jacques C. Schiff, Jr. (Jacques C. Schiff, Jr., Inc.)
Bernard Seckler (Fine Arts Philatelists)
F. Burton Sellers
J. Randall Shoemaker (Professional Stamp Experts, Inc.)
Charles F. Shreve (Shreves Philatelic Galleries, Inc.)
Jeff Siddiqui (Pakistan Philatelic Study Circle)
Sergio & Liane Sismondo (The Classic Collector)
Richard Stambaugh
Frank J. Stanley, III
Philip & Henry Stevens (postalstationery.com)
Mark Stucker
Glenn Tjia (Quality Philatelics)
A. John Ultee (Iran Philatelic Study Circle)
Xavier Verbeck (American Belgian Philatelic Society)
Hal Vogel (American Society of Polar Philatelists)
Philip T. Wall
Daniel C. Warren
Richard A. Washburn
Giana Wayman (Asociacion Filatélica de Costa Rica)
William R. Weiss, Jr. (Weiss Philatelics)
Ed Wener (Indigo)
Hans A. Westphal
Don White (Dunedin Stamp Centre)
John M. Wilson (Wilson Stamps)
Kirk Wolford
David Wood (Premier Philately Auctions)
Robert F. Yacano (K-Line Philippines)
Ralph Yorio
Val Zabijaka
Dr. Michal Zika (Album)
Alfonso G. Zulueta, Jr.

Addresses, Telephone Numbers, Web Sites, E-Mail Addresses of General & Specialized Philatelic Societies

Collectors can contact the following groups for information about the philately of the areas within the scope of these societies, or inquire about membership in these groups. Aside from the general societies, we limit this list to groups that specialize in particular fields of philately, particular areas covered by the Scott Standard Postage Stamp Catalogue, and topical groups. Many more specialized philatelic societies exist than those listed below. These addresses were compiled in January 2002, and are, to the best of our knowledge, correct and current. Groups should inform the editors of address changes whenever they occur. The editors also want to hear from other such specialized groups not listed.

Unless otherwise noted all website addresses begin with http://

American Philatelic Society
PO Box 8000
State College PA 16803
Ph: (814) 237-3803
www.stamps.org
E-mail: relamb@stamps.org

American Stamp Dealers' Association
Joseph Savarese
3 School St.
Glen Cove NY 11542
Ph: (516) 759-7000
www.asdaonline.com
E-mail: asda@erols.com

International Society of Worldwide Stamp Collectors
Anthony Zollo
PO Box 150407
Lufkin TX 75915-0407
www.iswsc.org
E-mail: stamptmf@frontiernet.net

Junior Philatelists of America
Jennifer Arnold
PO Box 2625
Albany OR 97321
www.jpastamps.org
E-mail: exec.sec@jpastamps.org

Royal Philatelic Society
41 Devonshire Place
London, United Kingdom W1G 6JY

Royal Philatelic Society of Canada
PO Box 929, Station Q
Toronto, ON, Canada M4T 2P1
Ph: (888) 285-4143
www.rpsc.org
E-mail: info@rpsc.org

Groups focusing on fields or aspects found in world-wide philately (some may cover U.S. area only)

American Air Mail Society
Stephen Reinhard
PO Box 110
Mineola NY 11501
ourworld.compuserve.com/home pages/ aams/
E-mail: sr1501@aol.com

American First Day Cover Society
Douglas Kelsey
PO Box 65960
Tucson AZ 85728-5960
Ph: (520) 321-0880
www.afdcs.org
E-mail: afdcs@aol.com

American Revenue Association
Eric Jackson
PO Box 728
Leesport PA 19533-0728
Ph: (610) 926-6200
www.revenuer.org
E-mail: eric@revenuer.com

American Topical Association
Paul E. Tyler
PO Box 50820
Albuquerque NM 87181-0820
Ph: (505) 323-8595
home.prcn.org/~pauld/ata/
E-mail: ATAStamps@juno.com

Errors, Freaks and Oddities Collectors Club
Jim McDevitt
PO Box 1126
Kingsland GA 31548
Ph: (912) 729-1573
E-mail: cwouscg@aol.com

Fakes and Forgeries Study Group
Anthony Torres
107 Hoover Rd.
Rochester NY 14617-3611
E-mail: ajtorres@rochester.rr.com

First Issues Collectors Club
Kurt Streepy
608 Whitethorn Way
Bloomington IN 47403
Ph: (812) 339-6229
E-mail: kstreepy@msn.com

International Philatelic Society of Joint Stamp Issues Collectors
Richard Zimmermann
124, Avenue Guy de Coubertin
Saint Remy Les Chevreuse, France F-78470
perso.clubinternet.fr/rzimmerm/index.htm
E-mail: rzimmerm@club-internet.fr

National Duck Stamp Collectors Society
Anthony J. Monico
PO Box 43
Harleysville PA 19438-0043
www.hwcn.org/link/ndscs
E-mail: ndscs@hwcn.org

No Value Identified Club
Albert Sauvanet
Le Clos Royal B, Boulevard des Pas Enchantes
St. Sebastien-sur Loire, France 44230
E-mail: alain.vailly@irin.univ_nantes.fr

The Perfins Club
Bob Szymanski
10 Clarridge Circle
Milford MA 01757
E-mail: perfinman@attbi.com

Post Mark Collectors Club
David Proulx
7629 Homestead Drive
Baldwinsville NY 13027
E-mail: stampdance@baldcom.net

Postal History Society
Kalman V. Illyefalvi
8207 Daren Court
Pikesville MD 21208-2211
Ph: (410) 653-0665
Precancel Stamp Society
176 Bent Pine Hill
North Wales PA 19454
Ph: (215) 368-6082
E-mail: abentpine1@aol.com

United Postal Stationery Society
Cora Collins
PO Box 1792
Norfolk VA 23501-1792
Ph: (757) 420-3487
www.upss.org
E-mail: poststat@juno.com

Groups focusing on U.S. area philately as covered in the Standard Catalogue

Canal Zone Study Group
Richard H. Salz
60 27th Ave.
San Francisco CA 94121

Carriers and Locals Society
John D. Bowman
PO Box 382436
Birmingham AL 35238-2436
Ph: (205) 967-6200
www.pennypost.org
E-mail: jdbowman@premierhome.net

Confederate Stamp Alliance
Richard L. Calhoun
PO Box 581
Mt. Prospect IL 60056-0581

Hawaiian Philatelic Society
Kay H. Hoke
PO Box 10115
Honolulu HI 96816-0115
Ph: (808) 521-5721
E-mail: bannan@pixi.com

Plate Number Coil Collectors Club
Gene C. Trinks
3603 Bellows Court
Troy MI 48083
www.pnc3.org
E-mail: gctrinks@sprynet.com

United Nations Philatelists
Blanton Clement, Jr.
292 Springdale Terrace
Yardley PA 19067-3421
www.unpi.com
E-mail: bclemjr@aol.com

United States Stamp Society
Executive Secretary
PO Box 6634
Katy TX 77491-6631
www.usstamps.org

U.S. Cancellation Club
Roger Rhoads
3 Ruthana Way
Hockessin DE 19707
www.geocities.com/athens/2088/uscchome.htm
E-mail:rrrhoads@aol.com

U.S. Philatelic Classics Society
Mark D. Rogers
PO Box 80708
Austin TX 78708-0708
www.uspcs.org
E-mail: mrogers23@austin.rr.com

Groups focusing on philately of foreign countries or regions

Aden & Somaliland Study Group
Gary Brown
PO Box 106
Briar Hill, Victoria, Australia 3088
E-mail: garyjohn951@optushome.com.au

American Society of Polar Philatelists (Antarctic areas)
Alan Warren
PO Box 39
Exton PA 19341-0039
south-pole.com/aspp.htm
E-mail: alanwar@att.net

Albania Study Circle
Paul Eckman
PO Box 39880
Los Angeles CA 90039
members.netscapeonline.co.uk/johnsphipps/index.html
E-mail: peckman797@earthlink.net

Andorran Philatelic Study Circle
D. Hope
17 Hawthorn Dr.
Stalybridge, Cheshire, United Kingdom SK15 1UE
www.chy-an-piran.demon.co.uk/
E-mail: apsc@chy-an-piran.demon.co.uk

Australian States Study Circle
Ben Palmer
GPO 1751
Sydney, N.S.W., Australia 1043

Austria Philatelic Society
Ralph Schneider
PO Box 23049
Belleville IL 62223
Ph: (618) 277-6152
www.apsus.esmartweb.com
E-mail: rsstamps@aol.com

American Belgian Philatelic Society
Kenneth L. Costilow
621 Virginius Dr.
Virginia Beach VA 23452-4417
Ph: (757) 463-6081
groups.hamptonroads.com/ABPS
E-mail: kcos32@home.com

Bechuanalands and Botswana Society
Neville Midwood
69 Porlock Lane
Furzton, Milton Keynes, United Kingdom MK4 1JY
www.netcomuk.co.uk/~midsoft/bbsoc.html
E-mail: runnerpo@netcomuk.co.uk

Bermuda Collectors Society
Thomas J. McMahon
PO Box 1949
Stuart FL 34995

Brazil Philatelic Association
Kurt Ottenheimer
462 West Walnut St.
Long Beach NY 11561
Ph: (516) 431-3412
E-mail: oak462@juno.com

British Caribbean Philatelic Study Group
Dr. Reuben A. Ramkissoon
3011 White Oak Lane
Oak Brook IL 60523-2513

British North America Philatelic Society (Canada & Provinces)
H. P. Jacobi
5295 Moncton St.
Richmond, B.C., Canada V7E 3B2
www.bnaps.org
E-mail: beaver@telus.net

British West Indies Study Circle
W. Clary Holt
PO Drawer 59
Burlington NC 27216
Ph: (336) 227-7461

Burma Philatelic Study Circle
A. Meech
7208 91st Ave.
Edmonton, AB, Canada T6B 0R8
E-mail: ameech@telusplanet.net

Ceylon Study Group
R. W. P. Frost
42 Lonsdale Road, Cannington
Bridgewater, Somerset, United Kingdom TA5 2JS

China Stamp Society
Paul H. Gault
PO Box 20711
Columbus OH 43220
www.chinastampsociety.org
E-mail: secretary@chinastampsociety.org

Colombia/Panama Philatelic Study Group
PO Box 2245
El Cajon CA 92021
E-mail: jimacross@juno.com

Society for Costa Rica Collectors
Dr. Hector R. Mena
PO Box 14831
Baton Rouge LA 70808
www.socorico.org
E-mail: hrmena@aol.com

Croatian Philatelic Society (Croatia & other Balkan areas)
Ekrem Spahich
502 Romero, PO Box 696
Fritch TX 79036-0696
Ph: (806) 857-0129
www.croatianmall.com/cps/
E-mail: ou812@arn.net

Cuban Philatelic Society of America
Ernesto Cuesta
PO Box 34434
Bethesda MD 20827
www.philat.com/cpsa

Cyprus Study Circle
Jim Wigmore
19 Riversmeet, Appledore
Bideford, N. Devon, United Kingdom EX39 1RE
www.geocities.com/cyprusstudycircle
E-mail: istug@aol.com

Society for Czechoslovak Philately
Robert T. Cossaboom
PO Box 25332
Scott AFB IL 62225-0332
www.czechoslovakphilately.com
E-mail: klfck1@aol.com

Danish West Indies Study Unit of the Scandinavian Collectors Club
John L. Dubois
Thermalogic Corp.
22 Kane Industrial Drive
Hudson MA 01749
Ph: (800) 343-4492
dwi.thlogic.com
E-mail: jld@thlogic.com

East Africa Study Circle
Ken Hewitt
16 Ashleigh Road
Solihull, United Kingdom B91 1AE
E-mail: 106602.2410@compuserve.com

Egypt Study Circle
Mike Murphy
109 Chadwick Road
London, United Kingdom SE15 4PY
E-mail: egyptstudycircle@hotmail.com

Estonian Philatelic Society
Juri Kirsimagi
29 Clifford Ave.
Pelham NY 10803

Ethiopian Philatelic Society
Ulf Lindahl
640 S. Pine Creek Rd.
Fairfield CT 06430
Ph: (203) 255-8005
members.home.net/fbheiser/ethiopia5.htm
E-mail: ulindahl@optonline.net

Falkland Islands Philatelic Study Group
Carl J. Faulkner
Williams Inn, On-the-Green
Williamstown MA 01267-2620
Ph: (413) 458-9371

Faroe Islands Study Circle
Norman Hudson
28 Enfield Road
Ellesmere Port, Cheshire, United Kingdom CH65 8BY
www.pherber.com/fisc/fisc.html
E-mail: jntropics@hotmail.com

Former French Colonies Specialist Society
BP 628
75367 Paris Cedex 08, France
www.ifrance.com/colfra
E-mail: clubcolfra@aol.com

France & Colonies Philatelic Society
Walter Parshall
103 Spruce St.
Bloomfield NJ 07003-3514

Germany Philatelic Society
PO Box 779
Arnold MD 21012-4779
www.gps.nu
E-mail: germanyphilatelic@starpower.net

German Democratic Republic Study Group of the German Philatelic Society
Ken Lawrence
PO Box 8040
State College PA 16803-8040
Ph: (814) 237-3803
E-mail: apsken@aol.com

Gibraltar Study Circle
D. Brook
80 Farm Road
Weston Super Mare, Avon, United Kingdom BS22 8BD
www.abel.co.uk/~stirrups/GSC.HTM
E-mail: drstirrups@dundee.ac.uk

Great Britain Collectors Club
Parker A. Bailey, Jr.
PO Box 773
Merrimack NH 03054-0773
www.gbstamps.com/gbcc
E-mail: pbaileyjr@worldnet.att.net

Hellenic Philatelic Society of America (Greece and related areas)
Dr. Nicholas Asimakopulos
541 Cedar Hill Ave.
Wyckoff NJ 07481
Ph: (201) 447-6262

International Society of Guatemala Collectors
Mrs. Mae Vignola
105 22nd Ave.
San Francisco CA 94121

Haiti Philatelic Society
Ubaldo Del Toro
5709 Marble Archway
Alexandria VA 22315
E-mail: u007ubi@aol.com

Honduras Collectors Club
Jeff Brasor
PO Box 143383
Irving TX 75014

Hong Kong Stamp Society
Dr. An-Min Chung
3300 Darby Rd. Cottage 503
Haverford PA 19041-1064

Society for Hungarian Philately
Robert Morgan
2201 Roscomare Rd.
Los Angeles CA 90077-2222
www.hungarianphilately.org
E-mail: h.alanhoover@lycosemail.com

India Study Circle
John Warren
PO Box 7326
Washington DC 20044
Ph: (202) 564-6876
E-mail: warren.john@epa.gov

Indian Ocean Study Circle
K. B. Fitton
50 Firlands
Weybridge, Surrey, United Kingdom KT13 0HR
www.stampdomain.com/iosc
E-mail: keithfitton@intonet.co.uk

Society of Indo-China Philatelists
Norman S. Davis
PO Box 290406
Brooklyn NY 11229

Iran Philatelic Study Circle
Darrell R. Hill
1410 Broadway
Bethlehem PA 18015-4025
www.iranphilatelic.org
E-mail: d.r.hill@att.net

Eire Philatelic Association (Ireland)
Myron G. Hill III
PO Box 1210
College Park MD 20741-1210
eirephilatelicassoc.org
E-mail: mhill@radix.net

Society of Israel Philatelists
Paul S. Aufrichtig
300 East 42nd St.
New York NY 10017

Italy and Colonies Study Circle
Andrew D'Anneo
1085 Dunweal Lane
Calistoga CA 94515
E-mail: audanneo@napanet.net

International Society for Japanese Philately
Kenneth Kamholz
PO Box 1283
Haddonfield NJ 08033
www.isjp.org
E-mail: isjp@home.com

Korea Stamp Society
John E. Talmage
PO Box 6889
Oak Ridge TN 37831
www.pennfamily.org/KSS-USA
E-mail: jtalmage@usit.net

Latin American Philatelic Society
Piet Steen
197 Pembina Ave.
Hinton, AB, Canada T7V 2B2

Latvian Philatelic Society
Aris Birze
569 Rougemount Dr.
Pickering, ON, Canada L1W 2C1

Liberian Philatelic Society
William Thomas Lockard
PO Box 106
Wellston OH 45692
Ph: (740) 384-2020
E-mail: tlockard@zoomnet.net

Liechtenstudy USA (Liechtenstein)
Ralph Schneider
PO Box 23049
Belleville IL 62223
Ph: (618) 277-6152
www.rschneiderstamps.com/Liechtenstudy.htm
E-mail: rsstamps@aol.com

Lithuania Philatelic Society
John Variakojis
3715 W. 68th St.
Chicago IL 60629
Ph: (773) 585-8649
www.filatelija.lt/lps/
E-mail: variakojis@earthlink.net

Luxembourg Collectors Club
Gary B. Little
3304 Plateau Dr.
Belmont CA 94002-1312
www.luxcentral.com/stamps/LCC
E-mail: lcc@luxcentral.com

Malaya Study Group
Joe Robertson
12 Lisa Court
Downsland Road
Basingstoke, Hampshire, United Kingdom RG21 8TU
home.freeuk.net/johnmorgan/msg.htm

Malta Study Circle
Alec Webster
50 Worcester Road
Sutton, Surrey, United Kingdom SM2 6QB
E-mail: alecwebster50@hotmail.com

Mexico-Elmhurst Philatelic Society International
David Pietsch
PO Box 50997
Irvine CA 92619-0997
E-mail: mepsi@msn.com

Society for Moroccan and Tunisian Philately
206, bld. Pereire
75017 Paris, France
members.aol.com/Jhaik5814
E-mail: jhaik5814@aol.com

Nepal & Tibet Philatelic Study Group
Roger D. Skinner
1020 Covington Road
Los Altos CA 94024-5003
Ph: (650) 968-4163
fuchs-online.com/ntpsc/

American Society of Netherlands Philately
Jan Enthoven
221 Coachlite Ct. S.
Onalaska WI 54650
Ph: (608) 781-8612
www.cs.cornell.edu/Info/People/aswin/NL/neth
E-mail: jenthoven@centurytel.net

New Zealand Society of Great Britain
Keith C. Collins
13 Briton Crescent
Sanderstead, Surrey, United Kingdom CR2 0JN
www.cs.stir.ac.uk/~rgc/nzsgb
E-mail: rgc@cs.stir.ac.uk

Nicaragua Study Group
Erick Rodriguez
11817 S.W. 11th St.
Miami FL 33184-2501
clubs.yahoo.com/clubs/nicaraguastudygroup
E-mail: nsgsec@yahoo.com

Society of Australasian Specialists/Oceania
Henry Bateman
PO Box 4862
Monroe LA 71211-4862
Ph: (800) 571-0293
members.aol.com/stampsho/saso.html
E-mail: hbateman@jam.rr.com

Orange Free State Study Circle
J. R. Stroud
28 Oxford St.
Burnham-on-sea, Somerset, United Kingdom TA8 1LQ
www.ofssc.org
E-mail: jrstroud@classicfm.net

Pacific Islands Study Group
John Ray
24 Woodvale Avenue
London, United Kingdom SE25 4AE
www.pisc.org.uk
E-mail: john.ray@bigfoot.com

Pakistan Philatelic Study Circle
Jeff Siddiqui
PO Box 7002
Lynnwood WA 98046
E-mail: jeffsiddiqui@msn.com

Centro de Filatelistas Independientes de Panama
Vladimir Berrio-Lemm
Apartado 0835-348
Panama, 10, Panama
E-mail: filatelia@cwpanama.net

Papuan Philatelic Society
Steven Zirinsky
PO Box 49, Ansonia Station
New York NY 10023
E-mail: szirinsky@compuserve.com

International Philippine Philatelic Society
Robert F. Yacano
PO Box 100
Toast NC 27049
Ph: (336) 783-0768
E-mail: yacano@advi.net

Pitcairn Islands Study Group
Nelson A. L. Weller
2940 Wesleyan Lane
Winston-Salem NC 27106
Ph: (336) 724-6384
E-mail: nalweller@aol.com

Plebiscite-Memel-Saar Study Group of the German Philatelic Society
Clay Wallace
100 Lark Court
Alamo CA 94507
E-mail: wallacec@earthlink.net

Polonus Philatelic Society (Poland)
Arkadius Walinski
7414 Lincoln Ave. - D
Skokie IL 60076-3898
Ph: (847) 674-4286

International Society for Portuguese Philately
Clyde Homen
1491 Bonnie View Rd.
Hollister CA 95023-5117
www.portugalstamps.com
E-mail: cjh@hollinet.com

Rhodesian Study Circle
William R. Wallace
PO Box 16381
San Francisco CA 94116
www.rhodesianstudycircle.org.uk
E-mail: bwall8rscr@earthlink.net

Canadian Society of Russian Philately
Andrew Cronin
PO Box 5722, Station A
Toronto, ON, Canada M5W 1P2
Ph: (905) 764-8968
www3.sympatico.ca/postrider/postrider
E-mail: postrider@sympatico.ca

Rossica Society of Russian Philately
Gerald D. Seiflow
27 N. Wacker Drive #167
Chicago IL 60606-3203
www.rossica.org
E-mail: ged.seiflow@rossica.org

Ryukyu Philatelic Specialist Society
Carmine J. DiVincenzo
PO Box 381
Clayton CA 94517-0381

St. Helena, Ascension & Tristan Da Cunha Philatelic Society
Dr. Everett L. Parker
HC 76, Box 32
Greenville ME 04441-9727
Ph: (207) 695-3163
ourworld.compuserve.com/homepages/ ST_HELENA_ASCEN_TDC
E-mail: eparker@prexar.com

St. Pierre & Miquelon Philatelic Society
David Salovey
320 Knights Corner
Stony Point NY 10980
E-mail: jamestaylor@wavehome.com

Associated Collectors of El Salvador
Jeff Brasor
PO Box 143383
Irving TX 75014

Fellowship of Samoa Specialists
Jack R. Hughes
PO Box 1260
Boston MA 02117-1260
members.aol.com/tongaJan/foss.html

Sarawak Specialists' Society
Stu Leven
4031 Samson Way
San Jose CA 95124-3733
Ph: (408) 978-0193
www.britborneostamps.org.uk
E-mail: stulev@ix.netcom.com

Scandinavian Collectors Club
Donald B. Brent
PO Box 13196
El Cajon CA 92020
www.scc-online.org
E-mail: dbrent47@sprynet.com

Slovakia Stamp Society
Jack Benchik
PO Box 555
Notre Dame IN 46556

Philatelic Society for Greater Southern Africa
William C. Brooks VI
PO Box 4158
Cucamonga CA 91729-4158
Ph: (909) 484-2806
www.homestead.com/psgsa/index.html
E-mail: bbrooks@hss.co.sbcounty.gov

Spanish Philatelic Society
Robert H. Penn
1108 Walnut Drive
Danielsville PA 18038
Ph: (610) 767-6793

Sudan Study Group
Charles Hass
PO Box 3435
Nashua NH 03061-3435
Ph: (603) 888-4160
E-mail: hassstamps@aol.com

American Helvetia Philatelic Society (Switzerland, Liechtenstein)
Richard T. Hall
PO Box 15053
Asheville NC 28813-0053
www.swiss-stamps.org
E-mail: secretary@swiss-stamps.org

Tannu Tuva Collectors Society
Ken Simon
513 Sixth Ave. So.
Lake Worth FL 33460-4507
Ph: (561) 588-5954
www.seflin.org/tuva
E-mail: p003115b@pb.seflin.org

Society for Thai Philately
H. R. Blakeney
PO Box 25644
Oklahoma City OK 73125
E-mail:HRBlakeney@aol.com

Transvaal Study Circle
J. Woolgar
132 Dale Street
Chatham, Kent ME4 6QH, United Kingdom
www.transvaalsc.org

Ottoman and Near East Philatelic Society (Turkey and related areas)
Bob Stuchell
193 Valley Stream Lane
Wayne PA 19087
E-mail: president@oneps.org

Ukrainian Philatelic & Numismatic Society
George Slusarczuk
PO Box 303
Southfields NY 10975-0303
www.upns.org
E-mail: Yurko@warwick.net

Vatican Philatelic Society
Sal Quinonez
2 Aldersgate, Apt. 119
Riverhead NY 11901
Ph: (516) 727-6426

British Virgin Islands Philatelic Society
Roger Downing
PO Box 11156
St. Thomas VI 00801-1156
Ph: (284) 494-2762
www.islandsun.com/FEATURES/bviphil9198.html
E-mail: issun@candwbvi.net

West Africa Study Circle
Dr. Peter Newroth
33-520 Marsett Place
Victoria, BC, Canada V8Z 7J1
ourworld.compuserve.com/homepages/ FrankWalton

Western Australia Study Group
Brian Pope
PO Box 423
Claremont, Western Australia, Australia 6910

Yugoslavia Study Group of the Croatian Philatelic Society
Michael Lenard
1514 North 3rd Ave.
Wausau WI 54401
Ph: (715) 675-2833
E-mail: mjlenard@aol.com

Topical Groups

Americana Unit
Dennis Dengel
17 Peckham Rd.
Poughkeepsie NY 12603-2018
www.americanaunit.org
E-mail: info@americanaunit.org

Astronomy Study Unit
George Young
PO Box 632
Tewksbury MA 01876-0632
Ph: (978) 851-8283
www.fandm.edu/departments/astronomy/miscell/astunit.html
E-mail: george-young@msn.com

Bicycle Stamp Club
Norman Batho
358 Iverson Place
East Windsor NJ 08520
Ph: (609) 448-9547
members.tripod.com/~bicyclestamps
E-mail: normbatho@worldnet.att.net

Biology Unit
Alan Hanks
34 Seaton Dr.
Aurora, ON, Canada L4G 2K1
Ph: (905) 727-6993

Bird Stamp Society
G. P. Horsman
9 Cowley Drive, Worthy Down
Winchester, Hants., United Kingdom
SO21 2OW

Canadiana Study Unit
John Peebles
PO Box 3262, Station "A"
London, ON, Canada N6A 4K3
E-mail: john.peebles@odyssey.on.ca

Captain Cook Study Unit
Brian P. Sandford
173 Minuteman Dr.
Concord MA 01742-1923
www.captaincookstudyunit.com/
E-mail: USagent@captaincookstudyunit.com/

Casey Jones Railroad Unit
Oliver C. Atchison
PO Box 31631
San Francisco CA 94131-0631
Ph: (415) 648-8057
www.uqp.de/cjr/index.htm
E-mail: cjrrunit@aol.com

Cats on Stamps Study Unit
Mary Ann Brown
3006 Wade Rd.
Durham NC 27705

Chemistry & Physics on Stamps Study Unit
Dr. Roland Hirsch
20458 Water Point Lane
Germantown MD 20874
www.cpossu.org
E-mail: rfhirsch@cpossu.org

Chess on Stamps Study Unit
Anne Kasonic
7625 County Road #153
Interlaken NY 14847
www.iglobal.net/home/reott/stamps1.htm#cossu
E-mail: akasonic@epix.net

Christmas Philatelic Club
Linda Lawrence
312 Northwood Drive
Lexington KY 40505
Ph: (606) 293-0151
www.hwcn.org/link/cpc
E-mail: stamplinda@aol.com

Christopher Columbus Philatelic Society
Donald R. Ager
PO Box 71
Hillsboro NH 03244-0071
Ph: (603) 464-5379
E-mail: meganddon@conknet.com

Collectors of Religion on Stamps
Verna Shackleton
425 North Linwood Avenue #110
Appleton WI 54914
Ph: (920) 734-2417
www.powernetonline.com/~corosec/coros1.htm
E-mail: corosec@powernetonline.com

Dogs on Stamps Study Unit
Morris Raskin
202A Newport Rd.
Monroe Township NJ 08831
Ph: (609) 655-7411
www.dossu.org
E-mail: mraskin@nerc.com

Earth's Physical Features Study Group
Fred Klein
515 Magdalena Ave.
Los Altos CA 94024
www.philately.com/society_news/earths _physical.htm

Ebony Society of Philatelic Events and Reflections (African-American topicals)
Sanford L. Byrd
PO Box 8888
Corpus Christi, TX 78468-8888
www.slsabyrd.com/esper.htm
E-mail: esper@ibm.net

Embroidery, Stitchery, Textile Unit
Helen N. Cushman
1001 Genter St., Apt. 9H
La Jolla CA 92037
Ph: (619) 459-1194

Europa Study Unit
Hank Klos
PO Box 611
Bensenville IL 60106
E-mail: eunity@aol.com or klosh@clearnet.org

Fine & Performing Arts
Ruth Richards
10393 Derby Dr.
Laurel MD 20723
www.philately.com/society_news/fap.htm
E-mail: bersec@aol.com

Fire Service in Philately
Brian R. Engler, Sr.
726 1/2 W. Tilghman St.
Allentown PA 18102-2324
Ph: (610) 433-2782
E-mail: brenglersr@enter.net

Gay & Lesbian History on Stamps Club
Joe Petronie
PO Box 190842
Dallas TX 75219-0842
www.glhsc.org
E-mail: glhsc@aol.com

Gems, Minerals & Jewelry Study Group
George Young
PO Box 632
Tewksbury MA 01876-0632
Ph: (978) 851-8283
www.rockhounds.com/rockshop/gmjsuapp.txt
E-mail: george-young@msn.com

Graphics Philately Association
Mark Winnegrad
PO Box 380
Bronx NY 10462-0380

Journalists, Authors & Poets on Stamps
Sol Baltimore
28742 Blackstone Dr.
Lathrup Village MI 48076

Lighthouse Stamp Society
Dalene Thomas
8612 West Warren Lane
Lakewood CO 80227-2352
Ph: (303) 986-6620
www.lighthousestampsociety.org
E-mail: dalene1@wideopenwest.com

Lions International Stamp Club
John Bargus
304-2777 Barry Rd. RR 2
Mill Bay, BC, Canada V0R 2P0
Ph: (250) 743-5782

Mahatma Gandhi On Stamps Study Circle
Pramod Shivagunde
Pratik Clinic, Akluj
Solapur, Maharashtra, India 413101
E-mail: drnanda@bom6.vsnl.net.in

Mask Study Unit
Helen N. Cushman
1001 Genter St. Apt. 9H
La Jolla CA 92037
www.philately.com/philately/masks.htm
E-mail: kencar@vlnk.net

Masonic Study Unit
Stanley R. Longenecker
930 Wood St.
Mount Joy PA 17552-1926
E-mail: natsco@usa.net

Mathematical Study Unit
Estelle Buccino
5615 Glenwood Rd.
Bethesda MD 20817-6727
Ph: (301) 718-8898
www.math.ttu.edu/msu/
E-mail: m.strauss@ttu.edu

Medical Subjects Unit
Dr. Frederick C. Skvara
PO Box 6228
Bridgewater NJ 08807
E-mail: fcskvara@bellatlantic.net

Mesoamerican Archeology Study Unit
Chris Moser
PO Box 1442
Riverside CA 92502
www.masu.homestead.com/info.html
E-mail:cmoser@ci.riverside.ca.us

Napoleonic Age Philatelists
Ken Berry
7513 Clayton Dr.
Oklahoma City OK 73132-5636
Ph: (405) 721-0044
E-mail: krb2@earthlink.net

Old World Archeological Study Unit
Eileen Meier
PO Box 369
Palmyra VA 22963

Parachute Study Group
Bill Wickert
3348 Clubhouse Road
Virginia Beach VA 23452-5339
Ph: (757) 486-3614
E-mail: bw47psg@worldnet.att.net

Petroleum Philatelic Society International
Linda W. Corwin
5427 Pine Springs Court
Conroe TX 77304
Ph: (936) 441-0216
E-mail: corwin@pdq.net

Philatelic Computing Study Group
Robert de Violini
PO Box 5025
Oxnard CA 93031-5025
www.pcsg.org
E-mail: dviolini@west.net

Philatelic Lepidopterists' Association
Alan Hanks
34 Seaton Dr.
Aurora, ON, Canada L4G 2K1
Ph: (905) 727-6933

Philatelic Music Circle
Cathleen Osborne
PO Box 1781
Sequim WA 98382
Ph: (360) 683-6373
www.stampshows.com/pmc.html

Rainbow Study Unit
Shirley Sutton
PO Box 37
Lone Pine, AB, Canada T0G 1M0
Ph: (780) 584-2268
E-mail: george-young@msn.com

Rotary on Stamps Unit
Donald Fiery
PO Box 333
Hanover PA 17331
Ph: (717) 632-8921

Scouts on Stamps Society International
Carl Schauer
PO Box 526
Belen NM 87002
Ph: (505) 864-0098
www.sossi.org
E-mail: rfrank@sossi.org

Ships on Stamps Unit
Robert Stuckert
2750 Highway 21 East
Paint Lick KY 40461
Ph: (859) 925-4901
www.shipsonstamps.org

Space Unit
Carmine Torrisi
PO Box 780241
Maspeth NY 11378
Ph: (718) 386-7882
stargate.1usa.com/stamps/
E-mail: ctorrisi1@juno.com

Sports Philatelists International
Margaret Jones
5310 Lindenwood Ave.
St. Louis MO 63109-1758
www.geocities.com/colosseum/track/6279

Stamps on Stamps Collectors Club
William Critzer
1360 Trinity Drive
Menlo Park CA 94025
Ph: (650) 234-1136
www.stampsonstamps.org
E-mail: wllmcritz@aol.com

Windmill Study Unit
Walter J. Hollien
PO Box 346
Long Valley NJ 07853-0346

Wine on Stamps Study Unit
James D. Crum
816 Kingsbury Ct.
Arroyo Grande CA 93420-4517
Ph: (805) 489-3559
E-mail: jdakcrum@aol.com

Women on Stamps Study Unit
Hugh Gottfried
2232 26th St.
Santa Monica CA 90405-1902
Ph: (310) 452-1442
E-mail: hgottfri@lausd.k12.ca.us

Zeppelin Collectors Club
Cheryl Ganz
PO Box A3843
Chicago IL 60690-3843

Expertizing Services

The following organizations will, for a fee, provide expert opinions about stamps submitted to them. Collectors should contact these organizations to find out about their fees and requirements before submitting philatelic material to them. The listing of these groups here is not intended as an endorsement by Scott Publishing Co.

General Expertizing Services

American Philatelic Expertizing Service (a service of the American Philatelic Society)
PO Box 8000
State College PA 16803
Ph: (814) 237-3803
Fax: (814) 237-6128
www.stamps.org
E-mail: ambristo@stamps.org
Areas of Expertise: Worldwide

B. P. A. Expertising, Ltd.
PO Box 137
Leatherhead, Surrey, United Kingdom
KT22 0RG
E-mail: sec.bpa@tcom.co.uk
Areas of Expertise: British Commonwealth, Great Britain, Classics of Europe, South America and the Far East

Philatelic Foundation
501 Fifth Ave., Rm. 1901
New York NY 10017
Areas of Expertise: U.S. & Worldwide

Professional Stamp Experts
PO Box 6170
Newport Beach CA 92658
Ph: (877) STAMP-88
Fax: (949) 833-7955
www.collectors.com/pse
E-mail: pseinfo@collectors.com
Areas of Expertise: Stamps and covers of U.S., U.S. Possessions, British Commonwealth

Royal Philatelic Society Expert Committee
41 Devonshire Place
London, United Kingdom W1N 1PE
www.rpsl.org.uk/experts.html
E-mail: experts@rpsl.org.uk
Areas of Expertise: All

Expertizing Services Covering Specific Fields Or Countries

Canadian Society of Russian Philately Expertizing Service
PO Box 5722, Station A
Toronto, ON, Canada M5W 1P2
Fax: (416)932-0853
Areas of Expertise: Russian areas

China Stamp Society Expertizing Service
1050 West Blue Ridge Blvd
Kansas City MO 64145
Ph: (816) 942-6300
E-mail: hjmesq@aol.com
Areas of Expertise: China

Confederate Stamp Alliance Authentication Service
c/o Patricia A. Kaufmann
10194 N. Old State Road
Lincoln DE 19960-9797
Ph: (302) 422-2656
Fax: (302) 424-1990
www.webuystamps.com/csaauth.htm
E-mail: trish@ce.net
Areas of Expertise: Confederate stamps and postal history

Croatian Philatelic Society Expertizing Service
PO Box 696
Fritch TX 79036-0696
Ph: (806) 857-0129
E-mail: ou812@arn.net
Areas of Expertise: Croatia and other Balkan areas

Errors, Freaks and Oddities Collectors Club Expertizing Service
138 East Lakemont Dr.
Kingsland GA 31548
Ph: (912) 729-1573
Areas of Expertise: U.S. errors, freaks and oddities

Estonian Philatelic Society Expertizing Service
39 Clafford Lane
Melville NY 11747
Ph: (516) 421-2078
E-mail: esto4@aol.com
Areas of Expertise: Estonia

Hawaiian Philatelic Society Expertizing Service
PO Box 10115
Honolulu HI 96816-0115
Areas of Expertise: Hawaii

Hong Kong Stamp Society Expertizing Service
PO Box 206
Glenside PA 19038
Fax: (215) 576-6850
Areas of Expertise: Hong Kong

International Association of Philatelics Experts
United States Associate members:
Paul Buchsbayew
119 W. 57th St.
New York NY 10019
Ph: (212) 977-7734
Fax: (212) 977-8653
Areas of Expertise: Russia, Soviet Union

William T. Crowe
(see Philatelic Foundation)

John Lievsay
(see American Philatelic Expertizing Service and Philatelic Foundation)
Areas of Expertise: France

Robert W. Lyman
P.O. Box 348
Irvington on Hudson NY 10533
Ph and Fax: (914) 591-6937
Areas of Expertise: British North America, New Zealand

Robert Odenweller
P.O. Box 401
Bernardsville, NJ 07924-0401
Ph and Fax: (908) 766-5460
Areas of Expertise: New Zealand, Samoa to 1900

Alex Rendon
P.O. Box 323
Massapequa NY 11762
Ph and Fax: (516) 795-0464
Areas of Expertise: Bolivia, Colombia, Colombian States

Sergio Sismondo
10035 Carousel Center Dr.
Syracuse NY 13290-0001
Ph: (315) 422-2331
Fax: (315) 422-2956
Areas of Expertise: Cape of Good Hope, Canada, British North America

International Society for Japanese Philately Expertizing Committee
32 King James Court
Staten Island NY 10308-2910
Ph: (718) 227-5229
Areas of Expertise: Japan and related areas, except WWII Japanese Occupation issues

International Society for Portuguese Philately Expertizing Service
PO Box 43146
Philadelphia PA 19129-3146
Ph: (215) 843-2106
Fax: (215) 843-2106
E-mail: s.s.washburne@worldnet.att.net
Areas of Expertise: Portugal and colonies

Mexico-Elmhurst Philatelic Society International Expert Committee
PO Box 1133
West Covina CA 91793
Areas of Expertise: Mexico

Philatelic Society for Greater Southern Africa Expert Panel
13955 W. 30th Ave.
Golden CO 80401
Areas of expertise: Entire South and South West Africa area, Bechuanalands, Basutoland, Swaziland

Ryukyu Philatelic Specialist Society Expertizing Service
1710 Buena Vista Ave.
Spring Valley CA 91977-4458
Ph: (619) 697-3205
Areas of Expertise: Ryukyu Islands

Ukrainian Philatelic & Numismatic Society Expertizing Service
30552 Dell Lane
Warren MI 48092-1862
Ph: (810) 751-5754
Areas of Expertise: Ukraine, Western Ukraine

V. G. Greene Philatelic Research Foundation
Box 100, First Canadian Place
Toronto, ON, Canada M5X 1B2
Ph: (416) 863-4593
Fax: (416) 863-4592
Areas of Expertise: British North America

Information on Catalogue Values, Grade and Condition

Catalogue Value

The Scott Catalogue value is a retail value; that is, an amount you could expect to pay for a stamp in the grade of Very Fine with no faults. Any exceptions to the grade valued will be noted in the text. The general introduction on the following pages and the individual section introductions further explain the type of material that is valued. The value listed for any given stamp is a reference that reflects recent actual dealer selling prices for that item.

Dealer retail price lists, public auction results, published prices in advertising and individual solicitation of retail prices from dealers, collectors and specialty organizations have been used in establishing the values found in this catalogue. Scott Publishing Co. values stamps, but Scott is not a company engaged in the business of buying and selling stamps as a dealer.

Use this catalogue as a guide for buying and selling. The actual price you pay for a stamp may be higher or lower than the catalogue value because of many different factors, including the amount of personal service a dealer offers, or increased or decreased interest in the country or topic represented by a stamp or set. An item may occasionally be offered at a lower price as a "loss leader," or as part of a special sale. You also may obtain an item inexpensively at public auction because of little interest at that time or as part of a large lot.

Stamps that are of a lesser grade than Very Fine, or those with condition problems, generally trade at lower prices than those given in this catalogue. Stamps of exceptional quality in both grade and condition often command higher prices than those listed.

Values for pre-1900 unused issues are for stamps with approximately half or more of their original gum. Stamps with most or all of their original gum may be expected to sell for more, and stamps with less than half of their original gum may be expected to sell for somewhat less than the values listed. On rarer stamps, it may be expected that the original gum will be somewhat more disturbed than it will be on more common issues. Post-1900 unused issues are assumed to have full original gum. From breakpoints in most countries' listings, stamps are valued as never hinged, due to the wide availability of stamps in that condition. These notations are prominently placed in the listings and in the country information preceding the listings. Some countries also feature listings with dual values for hinged and never-hinged stamps.

Grade

A stamp's grade and condition are crucial to its value. The accompanying illustrations show examples of Very Fine stamps from different time periods, along with examples of stamps in Fine to Very Fine and Extremely Fine grades as points of reference.

FINE stamps (illustrations not shown) have designs that are noticeably off center on two sides. Imperforate stamps may have small margins, and earlier issues may show the design touching one edge of the stamp design. For perforated stamps, perfs may barely clear the design on one side, and very early issues normally will have the perforations slightly cutting into the design. Used stamps may have heavier than usual cancellations.

FINE-VERY FINE stamps may be somewhat off center on one side, or slightly off center on two sides. Imperforate stamps will have two margins of at least normal size, and the design will not touch any edge. For perforated stamps, the perfs are well clear of the design, but are still noticeably off center. *However, early issues of a country may be printed in such a way that the design naturally is very close to the edges. In these cases, the perforations may cut into the design very slightly.* Used stamps will not have a cancellation that detracts from the design.

VERY FINE stamps may be slightly off center on one side, but the design will be well clear of the edge. The stamp will present a nice, balanced appearance. Imperforate stamps will have three normal-sized margins. *However, early issues of many countries may be printed in such a way that the perforations may touch the design on one or more sides. Where this is the case, a boxed note will be found defining the centering and margins of the stamps being valued.* Used stamps will have light or otherwise neat cancellations. This is the grade used to establish Scott Catalogue values.

EXTREMELY FINE stamps are close to being perfectly centered. Imperforate stamps will have even margins that are larger than normal. Even the earliest perforated issues will have perforations clear of the design on all sides.

Scott Publishing Co. recognizes that there is no formally enforced grading scheme for postage stamps, and that the final price you pay or obtain for a stamp will be determined by individual agreement at the time of transaction.

Condition

Grade addresses only centering and (for used stamps) cancellation. *Condition* refers to factors other than grade that affect a stamp's desirability.

Factors that can increase the value of a stamp include exceptionally wide margins, particularly fresh color, the presence of selvage, and plate or die varieties. Unusual cancels on used stamps (particularly those of the 19th century) can greatly enhance their value as well.

Factors other than faults that decrease the value of a stamp include loss of original gum, regumming, a hinge remnant or foreign object adhering to the gum, natural inclusions, straight edges, and markings or notations applied by collectors or dealers.

Faults include missing pieces, tears, pin or other holes, surface scuffs, thin spots, creases, toning, short or pulled perforations, clipped perforations, oxidation or other forms of color changelings, soiling, stains, and such man-made changes as reperforations or the chemical removal or lightening of a cancellation.

Grading Illustrations

On the following two pages are illustrations of various stamps from countries appearing in this volume. These stamps are arranged by country, and they represent early or important issues that are often found in widely different grades in the marketplace. The editors believe the illustrations will prove useful in showing the margin size and centering that will be seen on the various issues.

In addition to the matters of margin size and centering, collectors are reminded that the very fine stamps valued in the Scott catalogues also will possess fresh color and intact perforations, and they will be free from defects.

Most examples shown are computer-manipulated images made from single digitized master illustrations.

Stamp Illustrations Used in the Catalogue

It is important to note that the stamp images used for identification purposes in this catlaogue may not be indicative of the grade of stamp being valued. Refer to the written discussion of grades on this page and to the grading illustrations on the following two pages for grading information.

Fine-Very Fine →

SCOTT CATALOGUES VALUE STAMPS IN THIS GRADE

Very Fine →

Extremely Fine →

Fine-Very Fine →

SCOTT CATALOGUES VALUE STAMPS IN THIS GRADE

Very Fine →

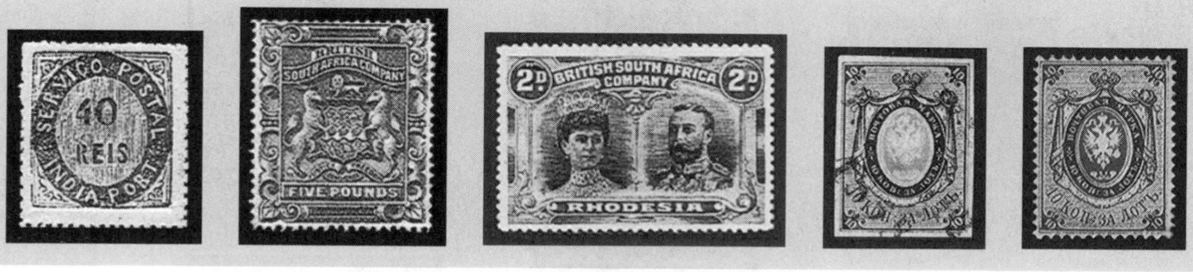

Extremely Fine →

Fine-Very Fine →

SCOTT CATALOGUES VALUE STAMPS IN THIS GRADE

Very Fine →

Extremely Fine →

Fine-Very Fine →

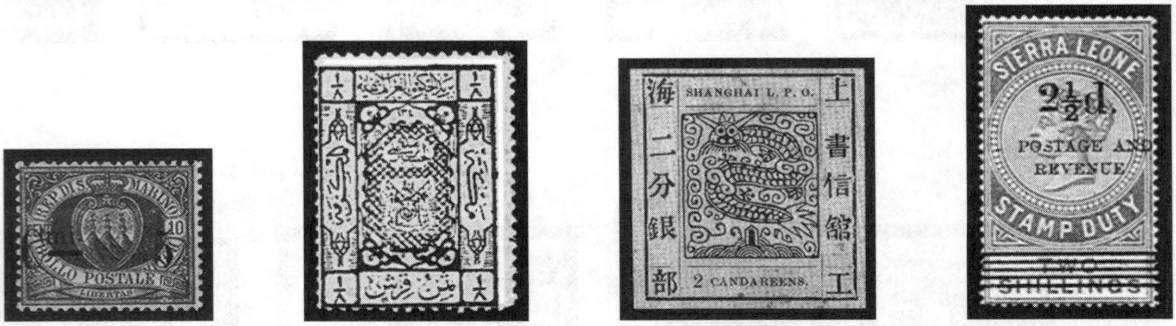

SCOTT CATALOGUES VALUE STAMPS IN THIS GRADE

Very Fine →

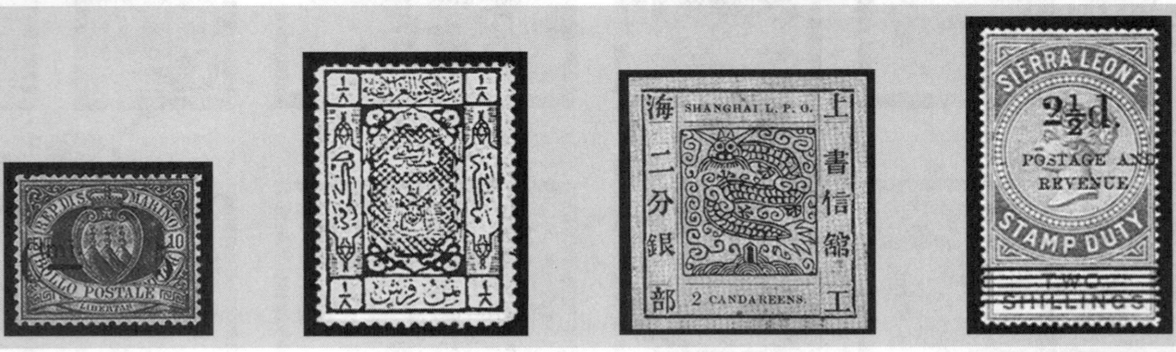

Extremely Fine →

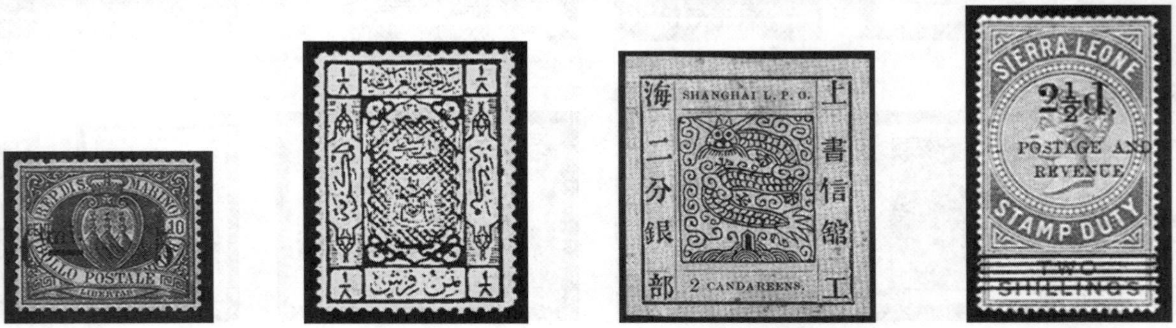

For purposes of helping to determine the gum condition and value of an unused stamp, Scott Publishing Co. presents the following chart which details different gum conditions and indicates how the conditions correlate with the Scott values for unused stamps. Used together, the Illustrated Grading Chart on the previous pages and this Illustrated Gum Chart should allow catalogue users to better understand the grade and gum condition of stamps valued in the Scott catalogues.

Gum Categories:	MINT N.H.	ORIGINAL GUM (O.G.)				NO GUM
	 **Mint Never Hinged** *Free from any disturbance*	 **Lightly Hinged** *Faint impression of a removed hinge over a small area*	 **Hinge Mark or Remnant** *Prominent hinged spot with part or all of the hinge remaining*	 **Large part o.g.** *Approximately half or more of the gum intact*	 **Small part o.g.** *Approximately less than half of the gum intact*	 **No gum** *Only if issued with gum*
Commonly Used Symbol:	★★	★	★	★	★	(★)
Pre-1900 Issues (Pre-1890 for U.S.)	*Very fine pre-1900 stamps in these categories trade at a premium over Scott value*			Scott Value for "Unused"		Scott "No Gum" listings for selected unused classic stamps
From 1900 to breakpoints for listings of never-hinged stamps	Scott "Never Hinged" listings for selected unused stamps	Scott Value for "Unused" (Actual value will be affected by the degree of hinging of the full o.g.)				
From breakpoints noted for many countries	Scott Value for "Unused"					

Never Hinged (NH; ★★): A never-hinged stamp will have full original gum that will have no hinge mark or disturbance. The presence of an expertizer's mark does not disqualify a stamp from this designation.

Original Gum (OG; ★): Pre-1900 stamps should have approximately half or more of their original gum. On rarer stamps, it may be expected that the original gum will be somewhat more disturbed that it will be on more common issues. Post-1900 stamps should have full original gum. Original gum will show some disturbance caused by a previous hinge(s) which may be present or entirely removed. The actual value of a post-1900 stamp will be affected by the degree of hinging of the full original gum.

Disturbed Original Gum: Gum showing noticeable effects of humidity, climate or hinging over more than half of the gum. The significance of gum disturbance in valuing a stamp in any of the Original Gum categories depends on the degree of disturbance, the rarity and normal gum condition of the issue and other variables affecting quality.

Regummed (RG; (★)): A regummed stamp is a stamp without gum that has had some type of gum privately applied at a time after it was issued. This normally is done to deceive collectors and/or dealers into thinking that the stamp has original gum and therefore has a higher value. A regummed stamp is considered the same as a stamp with none of its original gum for purposes of grading.

SUBSCRIBE TODAY!

Linn's Stamp News is the **indispensable** reading and entertainment guide for all the stamps you **want** and all the news you **need**. Each issue is jam packed with:

www.linns.com

Linn's Stamp News

WORLD'S LARGEST WEEKLY STAMP NEWS AND MARKETPLACE VOL. 74 ISSUE 3771 $2.00 U.S. FEBRUARY 5, 2001

34¢ Liberty, Flag, Four Flowers to be issued Feb. 7 in New York; no ceremony planned

Five semipostals for 2002-10; public will propose subjects

United Nations continues Endangered Species series

CONTENTS: PAGE 3

- All the latest-breaking news from our exclusive national and international sources.
- In-depth analysis from top authorities on all aspects of collecting, new issues, forgeries, security and more.
- Regular features you always looked forward to - *Stamp Market Tips* and *Tip of the Week, Collectors' Forum, Editor's Choice, Readers' Opinions, Postmark Pursuit, Collectors' Workshop, Refresher Course* and much more.
- The world's largest stamp market place. Listings of events, auctions and sales. Classified ads and readers' notices for buying, selling and trading.

Special Bonus: As a paid subscriber, you are automatically enrolled, at no extra cost to you, in the Amos Advantage Program. As a member, you can save up to 30% on catalogues, books, albums, accessories, supplements and supplies produced and distributed by Amos Hobby Publishing.

(Offer valid only for U.S. subscribers.
Canadian subscribers add $22.50 for postage.
International subscribers add $37.50 for postage.)

Order online at:

www.linns.com

or Call toll-free:

1-800-448-7293

or write:

P.O. Box 4315,
Sidney, OH 45365

Subscribe Today and take advantage of Linn's get acquainted offer:

6 months – 26 issues - $23.95!

AMOS HOBBY PUBLISHING

Catalogue Listing Policy

It is the intent of Scott Publishing Co. to list all postage stamps of the world in the *Scott Standard Postage Stamp Catalogue.* The only strict criteria for listing is that stamps be decreed legal for postage by the issuing country and that the issuing country actually have an operating postal system. Whether the primary intent of issuing a given stamp or set was for sale to postal patrons or to stamp collectors is not part of our listing criteria. Scott's role is to provide basic comprehensive postage stamp information. It is up to each stamp collector to choose which items to include in a collection.

It is Scott's objective to seek reasons why a stamp should be listed, rather than why it should not. Nevertheless, there are certain types of items that will not be listed. These include the following:

1. Unissued items that are not officially distributed or released by the issuing postal authority. If such items are officially issued at a later date by the country, they will be listed. Unissued items consist of those that have been printed and then held from sale for reasons such as change in government, errors found on stamps or something deemed objectionable about a stamp subject or design.

2. Stamps "issued" by non-existent postal entities or fantasy countries, such as Nagaland, Occusi-Ambeno, Staffa, Sedang, Torres Straits and others. Also, stamps "issued" in the names of legitimate, stamp-issuing countries that are not authorized by those countries.

3. Semi-official or unofficial items not required for postage. Examples include items issued by private agencies for their own express services. When such items are required for delivery, or are valid as prepayment of postage, they are listed.

4. Local stamps issued for local use only. Postage stamps issued by governments specifically for "domestic" use, such as Haiti Scott 219-228, or the United States non-denominated stamps, are not considered to be locals, since they are valid for postage throughout the country of origin.

5. Items not valid for postal use. For example, a few countries have issued souvenir sheets that are not valid for postage. This area also includes a number of worldwide charity labels (some denominated) that do not pay postage.

6. Intentional varieties, such as imperforate stamps that look like their perforated counterparts and are usually issued in very small quantities. Also, other egregiously exploitative issues such as stamps sold for far more than face value or stamps purposefully issued in artificially small quantities or only against advance orders. All of these kinds of items are usually controlled issues and/or are intended for speculation.

7. Items distributed by the issuing government only to a limited group, such as a stamp club, philatelic exhibition or a single stamp dealer, and later brought to market at inflated prices. These items normally will be included in a footnote.

The fact that a stamp has been used successfully as postage, even on international mail, is not in itself sufficient proof that it was legitimately issued. Numerous examples of so-called stamps from non-existent countries are known to have been used to post letters that have successfully passed through the international mail system.

There are certain items that are subject to interpretation. When a stamp falls outside our specifications, it may be listed along with a cautionary footnote.

A number of factors are considered in our approach to analyzing how a stamp is listed. The following list of factors is presented to share with you, the catalogue user, the complexity of the listing process.

Additional printings — "Additional printings" of a previously issued stamp may range from an item that is totally different to cases where it is impossible to differentiate from the original. At least a minor number (a small-letter suffix) is assigned if there is a distinct change in stamp shade, noticeably redrawn design, or a significantly different perforation measurement. A major number (numeral or numeral and capital-letter combination) is assigned if the editors feel the "additional printing" is sufficiently different from the original that it constitutes a different issue.

Commemoratives — Where practical, commemoratives with the same theme are placed in a set. For example, the U.S. Civil War Centennial set of 1961-65 and the Constitution Bicentennial series of 1989-90 appear as sets. Countries such as Japan and Korea issue such material on a regular basis, with an announced, or at least predictable, number of stamps known in advance. Occasionally, however, stamp sets that were released over a period of years have been separated. Appropriately placed footnotes will guide you to each set's continuation.

Definitive sets — Blocks of numbers generally have been reserved for definitive sets, based on previous experience with any given country. If a few more stamps were issued in a set than originally expected, they often have been inserted into the original set with a capital-letter suffix, such as U.S. Scott 1059A. If it appears that many more stamps than the originally allotted block will be released before the set is completed, a new block of numbers will be reserved, with the original one being closed off. In some cases, such as the U.S. Transportation and Great Americans series, several blocks of numbers exist. Appropriately placed footnotes will guide you to each set's continuation.

New country — Membership in the Universal Postal Union is not a consideration for listing status or order of placement within the catalogue. The index will tell you in what volume or page number the listings begin.

"No release date" items — The amount of information available for any given stamp issue varies greatly from country to country and even from time to time. Extremely comprehensive information about new stamps is available from some countries well before the stamps are released. By contrast some countries do not provide information about stamps or release dates. Most countries, however, fall between these extremes. A country may provide denominations or subjects of stamps from upcoming issues that are not issued as planned. Sometimes, philatelic agencies, those private firms hired to represent countries, add these later-issued items to sets well after the formal release date. This time period can range from weeks to years. If these items were officially released by the country, they will be added to the appropriate spot in the set. In many cases, the specific release date of a stamp or set of stamps may never be known.

Overprints — The color of an overprint is always noted if it is other than black. Where more than one color of ink has been used on overprints of a single set, the color used is noted. Early overprint and surcharge illustrations were altered to prevent their use by forgers.

Se-tenants — Connected stamps of differing features (se-tenants) will be listed in the format most commonly collected. This includes pairs, blocks or larger multiples. Se-tenant units are not always symmetrical. An example is Australia Scott 508, which is a block of seven stamps. If the stamps are primarily collected as a unit, the major number may be assigned to the multiple, with minors going to each component stamp. In cases where continuous-design or other unit se-tenants will receive significant postal use, each stamp is given a major Scott number listing. This includes issues from the United States, Canada, Germany and Great Britain, for example.

Understanding the Listings

On the opposite page is an enlarged "typical" listing from this catalogue. Below are detailed explanations of each of the highlighted parts of the listing.

1 Scott number — Scott catalogue numbers are used to identify specific items when buying, selling or trading stamps. Each listed postage stamp from every country has a unique Scott catalogue number. Therefore, Germany Scott 99, for example, can only refer to a single stamp. Although the Scott catalogue usually lists stamps in chronological order by date of issue, there are exceptions. When a country has issued a set of stamps over a period of time, those stamps within the set are kept together without regard to date of issue. This follows the normal collecting approach of keeping stamps in their natural sets.

When a country issues a set of stamps over a period of time, a group of consecutive catalogue numbers is reserved for the stamps in that set, as issued. If that group of numbers proves to be too few, capital-letter suffixes, such as "A" or "B," may be added to existing numbers to create enough catalogue numbers to cover all items in the set. A capital-letter suffix indicates a major Scott catalogue number listing. Scott uses a suffix letter only once. Therefore, a catalogue number listing with a capital-letter suffix will not also be found with the same letter (lower case) used as a minor-letter listing. If there is a Scott 16A in a set, for example, there will not also be a Scott 16a. However, a minor-letter "a" listing may be added to a major number containing an "A" suffix (Scott 16Aa, for example).

Suffix letters are cumulative. A minor "b" variety of Scott 16A would be Scott 16Ab, not Scott 16b.

There are times when a reserved block of Scott catalogue numbers is too large for a set, leaving some numbers unused. Such gaps in the numbering sequence also occur when the catalogue editors move an item's listing elsewhere or have removed it entirely from the catalogue. Scott does not attempt to account for every possible number, but rather attempts to assure that each stamp is assigned its own number.

Scott numbers designating regular postage normally are only numerals. Scott numbers for other types of stamps, such as air post, semi-postal, postal tax, postage due, occupation and others have a prefix consisting of one or more capital letters or a combination of numerals and capital letters.

2 Illustration number — Illustration or design-type numbers are used to identify each catalogue illustration. For most sets, the lowest face-value stamp is shown. It then serves as an example of the basic design approach for other stamps not illustrated. Where more than one stamp use the same illustration number, but have differences in design, the design paragraph or the description line clearly indicates the design on each stamp not illustrated. Where there are both vertical and horizontal designs in a set, a single illustration may be used, with the exceptions noted in the design paragraph or description line.

When an illustration is followed by a lower-case letter in parentheses, such as "A2(b)," the trailing letter indicates which overprint or surcharge illustration applies.

Illustrations normally are 70 percent of the original size of the stamp. An effort has been made to note all illustrations not illustrated at that percentage. Virtually all souvenir sheet illustrations are reduced even more. Overprints and surcharges are shown at 100 percent of their original size if shown alone, but are 70 percent of original size if shown on stamps. In some cases, the illustration will be placed above the set, between listings or omitted completely. Overprint and surcharge illustrations are not placed in this catalogue for purposes of expertizing stamps.

3 Paper color — The color of a stamp's paper is noted in italic type when the paper used is not white.

4 Listing styles — There are two principal types of catalogue listings: major and minor.

Major listings are in a larger type style than minor listings. The catalogue number is a numeral that can be found with or without a capital-letter suffix, and with or without a prefix.

Minor listings are in a smaller type style and have a small-letter suffix or (if the listing immediately follows that of the major number) may show only the letter. These listings identify a variety of the major item. Examples include perforation, color, watermark or printing method differences, multiples (some souvenir sheets, booklet panes and se-tenant combinations), and singles of multiples.

Examples of major number listings include 16, 28A, B97, C13A, 10N5, and 10N6A. Examples of minor numbers are 16a and C13Ab.

5 Basic information about a stamp or set — Introducing each stamp issue is a small section (usually a line listing) of basic information about a stamp or set. This section normally includes the date of issue, method of printing, perforation, watermark and, sometimes, some additional information of note. *Printing method, perforation and watermark apply to the following sets until a change is noted.* Stamps created by overprinting or surcharging previous issues are assumed to have the same perforation, watermark and printing method as the original. Dates of issue are as precise as Scott is able to confirm and often reflect the dates on first-day covers, rather than the actual date of release.

6 Denomination — This normally refers to the face value of the stamp; that is, the cost of the unused stamp at the post office at the time of issue. When a denomination is shown in parentheses, it does not appear on the stamp. This includes the non-denominated stamps of the United States, Brazil and Great Britain, for example.

7 Color or other description — This area provides information to solidify identification of a stamp. In many recent cases, a description of the stamp design appears in this space, rather than a listing of colors.

8 Year of issue — In stamp sets that have been released in a period that spans more than a year, the number shown in parentheses is the year that stamp first appeared. Stamps without a date appeared during the first year of the issue. Dates are not always given for minor varieties.

9 Value unused and Value used — The Scott catalogue values are based on stamps that are in a grade of Very Fine unless stated otherwise. Unused values refer to items that have not seen postal, revenue or any other duty for which they were intended. Pre-1900 unused stamps that were issued with gum must have at least most of their original gum. Later issues are assumed to have full original gum. From breakpoints specified in most countries' listings, stamps are valued as never hinged. Stamps issued without gum are noted. Modern issues with PVA or other synthetic adhesives may appear ungummed. Self-adhesive stamps are valued as appearing undisturbed on their original backing paper. For a more detailed explanation of these values, please see the "Catalogue Value," "Condition" and "Understanding Valuing Notations" sections elsewhere in this introduction.

In some cases, where used stamps are more valuable than unused stamps, the value is for an example with a contemporaneous cancel, rather than a modern cancel or a smudge or other unclear marking. For those stamps that were released for postal and fiscal purposes, the used value represents a postally used stamp. Stamps with revenue cancels generally sell for less. Scott values for used self-adhesive stamps are for examples either on piece or off piece.

10 Changes in basic set information — Bold type is used to show any changes in the basic data given for a set of stamps. This includes perforation differences from one stamp to the next or a different paper, printing method or watermark.

11 Total value of a set — The total value of sets of three or more stamps issued after 1900 are shown. The set line also notes the range of Scott numbers and total number of stamps included in the grouping. The actual value of a set consisting predominantly of stamps having the minimum value of twenty cents may be less than the total value shown. Similary, the actual value or catalogue value of se-tenant pairs or of blocks consisting of stamps having the minimum value of twenty cents may be less than the catalogue values of the component parts.

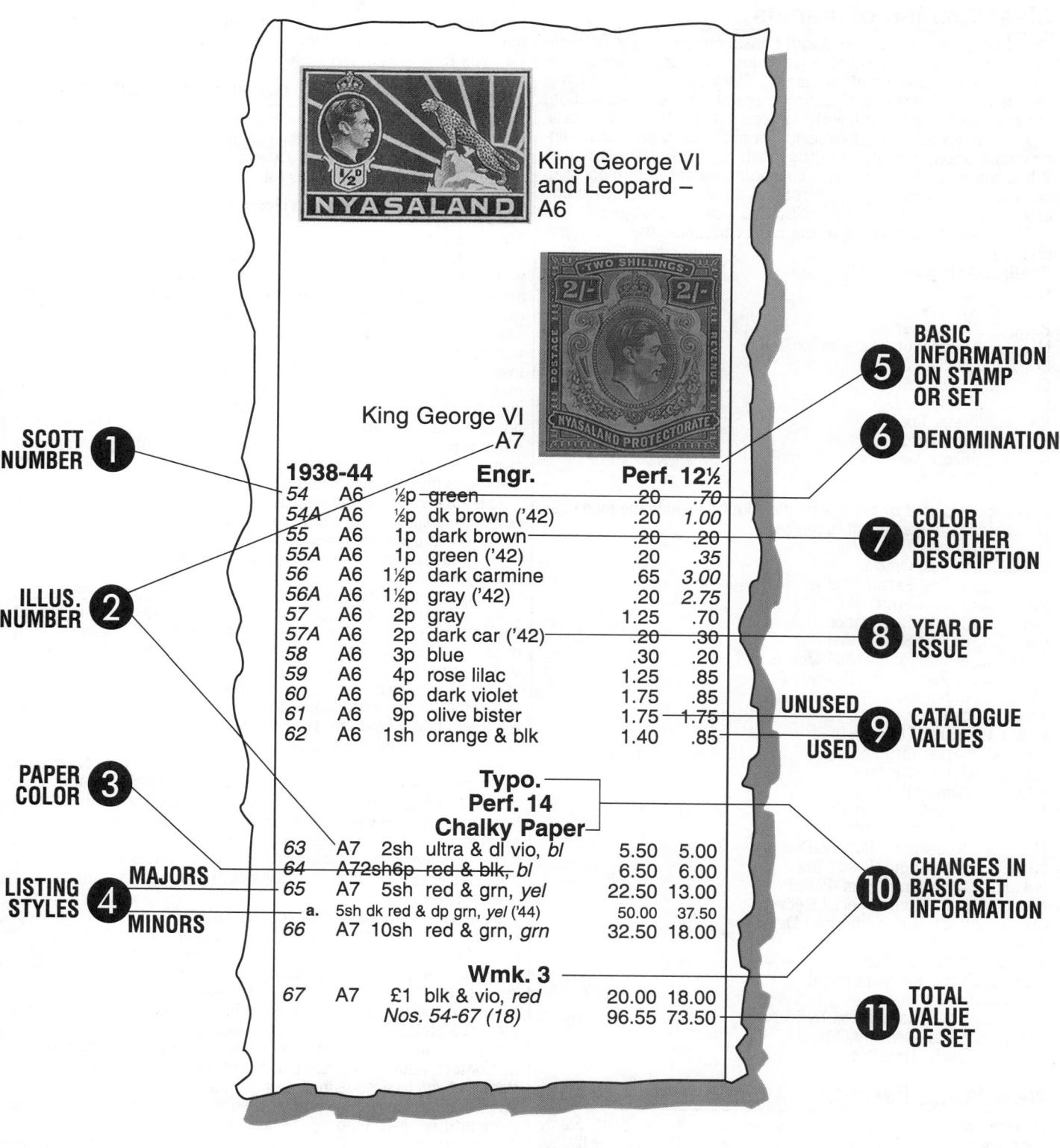

King George VI and Leopard – A6

King George VI – A7

1938-44 **Engr.** **Perf. 12½**

54	A6	½p	green	.20	*.70*
54A	A6	½p	dk brown ('42)	.20	*1.00*
55	A6	1p	dark brown	.20	.20
55A	A6	1p	green ('42)	.20	*.35*
56	A6	1½p	dark carmine	.65	*3.00*
56A	A6	1½p	gray ('42)	.20	*2.75*
57	A6	2p	gray	1.25	.70
57A	A6	2p	dark car ('42)	.20	.30
58	A6	3p	blue	.30	.20
59	A6	4p	rose lilac	1.25	.85
60	A6	6p	dark violet	1.75	.85
61	A6	9p	olive bister	1.75	1.75
62	A6	1sh	orange & blk	1.40	.85

Typo.
Perf. 14
Chalky Paper

63	A7	2sh	ultra & dl vio, *bl*	5.50	5.00
64	A7	2sh6p	red & blk, *bl*	6.50	6.00
65	A7	5sh	red & grn, *yel*	22.50	13.00
a.			5sh dk red & dp grn, *yel* ('44)	50.00	37.50
66	A7	10sh	red & grn, *grn*	32.50	18.00

Wmk. 3

67	A7	£1	blk & vio, *red*	20.00	18.00
			Nos. 54-67 (18)	96.55	73.50

1. SCOTT NUMBER
2. ILLUS. NUMBER
3. PAPER COLOR
4. LISTING STYLES — MAJORS / MINORS
5. BASIC INFORMATION ON STAMP OR SET
6. DENOMINATION
7. COLOR OR OTHER DESCRIPTION
8. YEAR OF ISSUE
9. CATALOGUE VALUES — UNUSED / USED
10. CHANGES IN BASIC SET INFORMATION
11. TOTAL VALUE OF SET

Special Notices

Classification of stamps

The *Scott Standard Postage Stamp Catalogue* lists stamps by country of issue. The next level of organization is a listing by section on the basis of the function of the stamps. The principal sections cover regular postage, semi-postal, air post, special delivery, registration, postage due and other categories. Except for regular postage, catalogue numbers for all sections include a prefix letter (or number-letter combination) denoting the class to which a given stamp belongs. When some countries issue sets containing stamps from more than one category, the catalogue will at times list all of the stamps in one category (such as air post stamps listed as part of a postage set).

The following is a listing of the most commonly used catalogue prefixes.

Prefix ...Category
C ....Air Post
M...........Military
P............Newspaper
N ....Occupation - Regular Issues
O ....Official
Q ....Parcel Post
J.............Postage Due
RA ....Postal Tax
B............Semi-Postal
E............Special Delivery
MR ....War Tax

Other prefixes used by more than one country include the following:
H ....Acknowledgment of Receipt
I.............Late Fee
CO.........Air Post Official
CQ.........Air Post Parcel Post
RAC ....Air Post Postal Tax
CF..........Air Post Registration
CB ....Air Post Semi-Postal
CBO.......Air Post Semi-Postal Official
CE ....Air Post Special Delivery
EY..........Authorized Delivery
S ....Franchise
G ....Insured Letter
GY ....Marine Insurance
MC ....Military Air Post
MQ........Military Parcel Post
NC.........Occupation - Air Post
NO.........Occupation - Official
NJ ....Occupation - Postage Due
NRA.......Occupation - Postal Tax
NB ....Occupation - Semi-Postal
NE ....Occupation - Special Delivery
QY ....Parcel Post Authorized Delivery
AR ....Postal-fiscal
RAJ ....Postal Tax Due
RAB ....Postal Tax Semi-Postal
F ....Registration
EB..........Semi-Postal Special Delivery
EO ....Special Delivery Official
QE ....Special Handling

New issue listings

Updates to this catalogue appear each month in the *Scott Stamp Monthly* magazine. Included in this update are additions to the listings of countries found in the *Scott Standard Postage Stamp Catalogue* and the *Specialized Catalogue of United States Stamps*, as well as corrections and updates to current editions of this catalogue.

From time to time there will be changes in the final listings of stamps from the *Scott Stamp Monthly* to the next edition of the catalogue. This occurs as more information about certain stamps or sets becomes available.

The catalogue update section of the *Scott Stamp Monthly* is the most timely presentation of this material available. Annual subscriptions to the *Scott Stamp Monthly* are available from Scott Publishing Co., Box 828, Sidney, OH 45365-0828.

Number additions, deletions & changes

A listing of catalogue number additions, deletions and changes from the previous edition of the catalogue appears in each volume. See Catalogue Number Additions, Deletions & Changes in the table of contents for the location of this list.

Understanding valuing notations

The *minimum catalogue value* of an individual stamp or set is 20 cents. This represents a portion of the cost incurred by a dealer when he prepares an individual stamp for resale. As a point of philatelic-economic fact, the lower the value shown for an item in this catalogue, the greater the percentage of that value is attributed to dealer mark up and profit margin. In many cases, such as the 20-cent minimum value, that price does not cover the labor or other costs involved with stocking it as an individual stamp. The sum of minimum values in a set does not properly represent the value of a complete set primarily composed of a number of minimum-value stamps, nor does the sum represent the actual value of a packet made up of minimum-value stamps. Thus a packet of 1,000 different common stamps — each of which has a catalogue value of 20-cents — normally sells for considerably less than 200 dollars!

The *absence of a retail value* for a stamp does not necessarily suggest that a stamp is scarce or rare. A dash in the value column means that the stamp is known in a stated form or variety, but information is either lacking or insufficient for purposes of establishing a usable catalogue value.

Stamp values in *italics* generally refer to items that are difficult to value accurately. For expensive items, such as those priced at $1,000 or higher, a value in italics indicates that the affected item trades very seldom. For inexpensive items, a value in italics represents a warning. One example is a "blocked" issue where the issuing postal administration may have controlled one stamp in a set in an attempt to make the whole set more valuable. Another example is an item that sold at an extreme multiple of face value in the marketplace at the time of its issue.

One type of warning to collectors that appears in the catalogue is illustrated by a stamp that is valued considerably higher in used condition than it is as unused. In this case, collectors are cautioned to be certain the used version has a genuine and contemporaneous cancellation. The type of cancellation on a stamp can be an important factor in determining its sale price. Catalogue values do not apply to fiscal, telegraph or non-contemporaneous postal cancels, unless otherwise noted.

Some countries have released back issues of stamps in canceled-to-order form, sometimes covering as much as a 10-year period. The Scott Catalogue values for used stamps reflect canceled-to-order material when such stamps are found to predominate in the marketplace for the issue involved. Notes frequently appear in the stamp listings to specify which items are valued as canceled-to-order, or if there is a premium for postally used examples.

Many countries sell canceled-to-order stamps at a marked reduction of face value. Countries that sell or have sold canceled-to-order stamps at *full* face value include Australia, Netherlands, France and Switzerland. It may be almost impossible to identify such stamps if the gum has been removed, because official government canceling devices are used. Postally used copies of these items on cover, however, are usually worth more than the canceled-to-order stamps with original gum.

Abbreviations

Scott Publishing Co. uses a consistent set of abbreviations throughout this catalogue to conserve space, while still providing necessary information.

COLOR ABBREVIATIONS

amb	amber	crim	crimson	ol	olive
anil	aniline	cr	cream	olvn	olivine
ap	apple	dk	dark	org	orange
aqua	aquamarine	dl	dull	pck	peacock
az	azure	dp	deep	pnksh	pinkish
bis	bister	db	drab	Prus	Prussian
bl	blue	emer	emerald	pur	purple
bld	blood	gldn	golden	redsh	reddish
blk	black	grysh	grayish	res	reseda
bril	brilliant	grn	green	ros	rosine
brn	brown	grnsh	greenish	ryl	royal
brnsh	brownish	hel	heliotrope	sal	salmon
brnz	bronze	hn	henna	saph	sapphire
brt	bright	ind	indigo	scar	scarlet
brnt	burnt	int	intense	sep	sepia
car	carmine	lav	lavender	sien	sienna
cer	cerise	lem	lemon	sil	silver
chlky	chalky	lil	lilac	sl	slate
cham	chamois	lt	light	stl	steel
chnt	chestnut	mag	magenta	turq	turquoise
choc	chocolate	man	manila	ultra	ultramarine
chr	chrome	mar	maroon	Ven	Venetian
cit	citron	mv	mauve	ver	vermilion
cl	claret	multi	multicolored	vio	violet
cob	cobalt	mlky	milky	yel	yellow
cop	copper	myr	myrtle	yelsh	yellowish

When no color is given for an overprint or surcharge, black is the color used. Abbreviations for colors used for overprints and surcharges include: "(B)" or "(Blk)," black; "(Bl)," blue; "(R)," red; and "(G)," green.

Additional abbreviations in this catalogue are shown below:

Adm. ....Administration
AFL ....American Federation of Labor
Anniv. ....Anniversary
APS ....American Philatelic Society
Assoc. ....Association
ASSR. ....Autonomous Soviet Socialist Republic
b.....................Born
BEP ....Bureau of Engraving and Printing
Bicent. ....Bicentennial
Bklt.................Booklet
Brit. ....British
btwn...............Between
Bur..................Bureau
c. or ca. ....Circa
Cat. ....Catalogue
Cent. ....Centennial, century, centenary
CIO ....Congress of Industrial Organizations
Conf. ....Conference
Cong...............Congress
Cpl. ....Corporal
CTO ....Canceled to order
d.....................Died
Dbl. ....Double
EKU................Earliest known use
Engr. ....Engraved
Exhib..............Exhibition
Expo. ....Exposition
Fed. ....Federation
GB..................Great Britain
Gen. ....General
GPO ....General post office
Horiz. ....Horizontal
Imperf.............Imperforate
Impt. ....Imprint
Intl. ....International
Invtd...............Inverted
L.....................Left
Lieut., lt. ....Lieutenant
Litho...............Lithographed
LL...................Lower left
LR ....Lower right
mm.................Millimeter
Ms. ....Manuscript
Natl. ....National
No. ....Number
NY..................New York
NYC ....New York City
Ovpt. ....Overprint
Ovptd. ....Overprinted
P.....................Plate number
Perf.................Perforated, perforation
Phil.................Philatelic
Photo..............Photogravure
PO ....Post office
Pr....................Pair
P.R..................Puerto Rico
Prec. ....Precancel, precanceled
Pres. ....President
PTT ....Post, Telephone and Telegraph
Rio..................Rio de Janeiro
Sgt. ....Sergeant
Soc. ....Society
Souv. ....Souvenir
SSR.................Soviet Socialist Republic, see ASSR
St....................Saint, street
Surch. ....Surcharge
Typo. ....Typographed
UL ....Upper left
Unwmkd. ....Unwatermarked
UPU ....Universal Postal Union
UR..................Upper Right
US ....United States
USPOD...........United States Post Office Department
USSR ....Union of Soviet Socialist Republics
Vert. ....Vertical
VP ....Vice president
Wmk. ....Watermark
Wmkd. ....Watermarked
WWI ....World War I
WWII ....World War II

Examination

Scott Publishing Co. will not comment upon the genuineness, grade or condition of stamps, because of the time and responsibility involved. Rather, there are several expertizing groups that undertake this work for both collectors and dealers. Neither will Scott Publishing Co. appraise or identify philatelic material. The company cannot take responsibility for unsolicited stamps or covers sent by individuals.

How to order from your dealer

When ordering stamps from a dealer, it is not necessary to write the full description of a stamp as listed in this catalogue. All you need is the name of the country, the Scott catalogue number and whether the desired item is unused or used. For example, "Japan Scott 422 unused" is sufficient to identify the unused stamp of Japan listed as "422 A206 5y brown."

Basic Stamp Information

A stamp collector's knowledge of the combined elements that make a given stamp issue unique determines his or her ability to identify stamps. These elements include paper, watermark, method of separation, printing, design and gum. On the following pages each of these important areas is briefly described.

Paper

Paper is an organic material composed of a compacted weave of cellulose fibers and generally formed into sheets. Paper used to print stamps may be manufactured in sheets, or it may have been part of a large roll (called a web) before being cut to size. The fibers most often used to create paper on which stamps are printed include bark, wood, straw and certain grasses. In many cases, linen or cotton rags have been added for greater strength and durability. Grinding, bleaching, cooking and rinsing these raw fibers reduces them to a slushy pulp, referred to by paper makers as "stuff." Sizing and, sometimes, coloring matter is added to the pulp to make different types of finished paper.

After the stuff is prepared, it is poured onto sieve-like frames that allow the water to run off, while retaining the matted pulp. As fibers fall onto the screen and are held by gravity, they form a natural weave that will later hold the paper together. If the screen has metal bits that are formed into letters or images attached, it leaves slightly thinned areas on the paper. These are called watermarks.

When the stuff is almost dry, it is passed under pressure through smooth or engraved rollers - dandy rolls - or placed between cloth in a press to be flattened and dried.

Stamp paper falls broadly into two types: wove and laid. The nature of the surface of the frame onto which the pulp is first deposited causes the differences in appearance between the two. If the surface is smooth and even, the paper will be of fairly uniform texture throughout. This is known as *wove paper*. Early papermaking machines poured the pulp onto a continuously circulating web of felt, but modern machines feed the pulp onto a cloth-like screen made of closely interwoven fine wires. This paper, when held to a light, will show little dots or points very close together. The proper name for this is "wire wove," but the type is still considered wove. Any U.S. or British stamp printed after 1880 will serve as an example of wire wove paper.

Closely spaced parallel wires, with cross wires at wider intervals, make up the frames used for what is known as *laid paper*. A greater thickness of the pulp will settle between the wires. The paper, when held to a light, will show alternate light and dark lines. The spacing and the thickness of the lines may vary, but on any one sheet of paper they are all alike. See Russia Scott 31-38 for examples of laid paper.

Batonne, from the French word meaning "a staff," is a term used if the lines in the paper are spaced quite far apart, like the printed ruling on a writing tablet. Batonne paper may be either wove or laid. If laid, fine laid lines can be seen between the batons. The laid lines, which are a form of watermark, may be geometrical figures such as squares, diamonds, rectangles or wavy lines.

Quadrille is the term used when the lines in the paper form little squares. *Oblong quadrille* is the term used when rectangles, rather than squares, are formed. See Mexico-Guadalajara Scott 35-37 for examples of oblong quadrille paper.

Paper also is classified as thick or thin, hard or soft, and by color if dye is added during manufacture. Such colors may include yellowish, greenish, bluish and reddish.

Brief explanations of other types of paper used for printing stamps, as well as examples, follow.

Pelure — Pelure paper is a very thin, hard and often brittle paper that is sometimes bluish or grayish in appearance. See Serbia Scott 169-170.

Native — This is a term applied to handmade papers used to produce some of the early stamps of the Indian states. Stamps printed on native paper may be expected to display various natural inclusions that are normal and do not negatively affect value. Japanese paper, originally made of mulberry fibers and rice flour, is part of this group. See Japan Scott 1-18.

Manila — This type of paper is often used to make stamped envelopes and wrappers. It is a coarse-textured stock, usually smooth on one side and rough on the other. A variety of colors of manila paper exist, but the most common range is yellowish-brown.

Silk — Introduced by the British in 1847 as a safeguard against counterfeiting, silk paper contains bits of colored silk thread scattered throughout. The density of these fibers varies greatly and can include as few as one fiber per stamp or hundreds. U.S. revenue Scott R152 is a good example of an easy-to-identify silk paper stamp.

Silk-thread paper has uninterrupted threads of colored silk arranged so that one or more threads run through the stamp or postal stationery. See Great Britain Scott 5-6 and Switzerland Scott 14-19.

Granite — Filled with minute cloth or colored paper fibers of various colors and lengths, granite paper should not be confused with either type of silk paper. Austria Scott 172-175 and a number of Swiss stamps are examples of granite paper.

Chalky — A chalk-like substance coats the surface of chalky paper to discourage the cleaning and reuse of canceled stamps, as well as to provide a smoother, more acceptable printing surface. Because the designs of stamps printed on chalky paper are imprinted on what is often a water-soluble coating, any attempt to remove a cancellation will destroy the stamp. *Do not soak these stamps in any fluid.* To remove a stamp printed on chalky paper from an envelope, wet the paper from underneath the stamp until the gum dissolves enough to release the stamp from the paper. See St. Kitts-Nevis Scott 89-90 for examples of stamps printed on this type of chalky paper.

India — Another name for this paper, originally introduced from China about 1750, is "China Paper." It is a thin, opaque paper often used for plate and die proofs by many countries.

Double — In philately, the term double paper has two distinct meanings. The first is a two-ply paper, usually a combination of a thick and a thin sheet, joined during manufacture. This type was used experimentally as a means to discourage the reuse of stamps.

The design is printed on the thin paper. Any attempt to remove a cancellation would destroy the design. U.S. Scott 158 and other Banknote-era stamps exist on this form of double paper.

The second type of double paper occurs on a rotary press, when the end of one paper roll, or web, is affixed to the next roll to save time feeding the paper through the press. Stamp designs are printed over the joined paper and, if overlooked by inspectors, may get into post office stocks.

Goldbeater's Skin — This type of paper was used for the 1866 issue of Prussia, and was a tough, translucent paper. The design was printed in reverse on the back of the stamp, and the gum applied over the printing. It is impossible to remove stamps printed on this type of paper from the paper to which they are affixed without destroying the design.

Ribbed — Ribbed paper has an uneven, corrugated surface made by passing the paper through ridged rollers. This type exists on some copies of U.S. Scott 156-165.

Various other substances, or substrates, have been used for stamp manufacture, including wood, aluminum, copper, silver and gold foil, plastic, and silk and cotton fabrics.

Wove Laid Granite

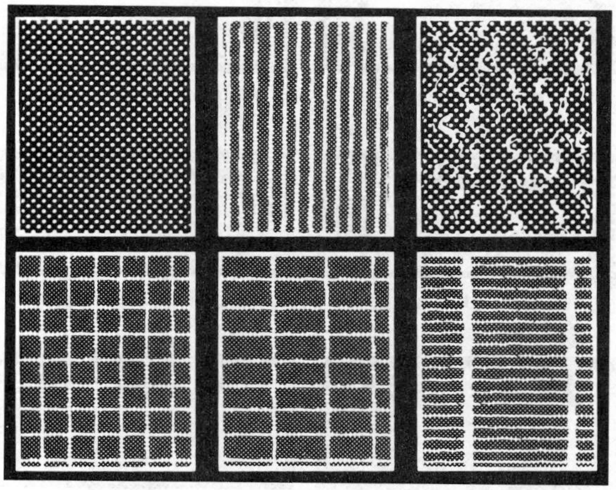

Quadrille Oblong Quadrille Batonne

Watermarks

Watermarks are an integral part of some papers. They are formed in the process of paper manufacture. Watermarks consist of small designs, formed of wire or cut from metal and soldered to the surface of the mold or, sometimes, on the dandy roll. The designs may be in the form of crowns, stars, anchors, letters or other characters or symbols. These pieces of metal - known in the paper-making industry as "bits" - impress a design into the paper. The design sometimes may be seen by holding the stamp to the light. Some are more easily seen with a watermark detector. This important tool is a small black tray into which a stamp is placed face down and dampened with a fast-evaporating watermark detection fluid that brings up the watermark image in the form of dark lines against a lighter background. These dark lines are the thinner areas of the paper known as the watermark. Some watermarks are extremely difficult to locate, due to either a faint impression, watermark location or the color of the stamp. There also are electric watermark detectors that come with plastic filter disks of various colors. The disks neutralize the color of the stamp, permitting the watermark to be seen more easily.

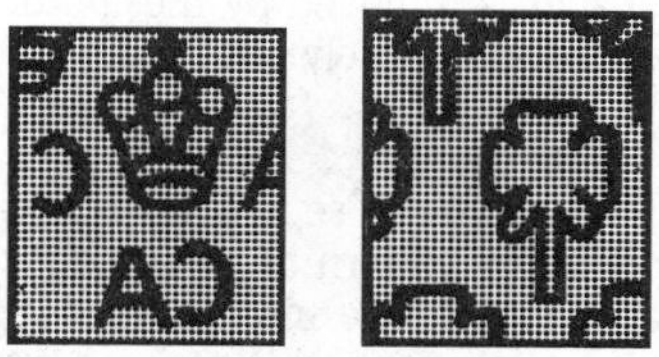

Multiple watermarks of Crown Agents and Burma

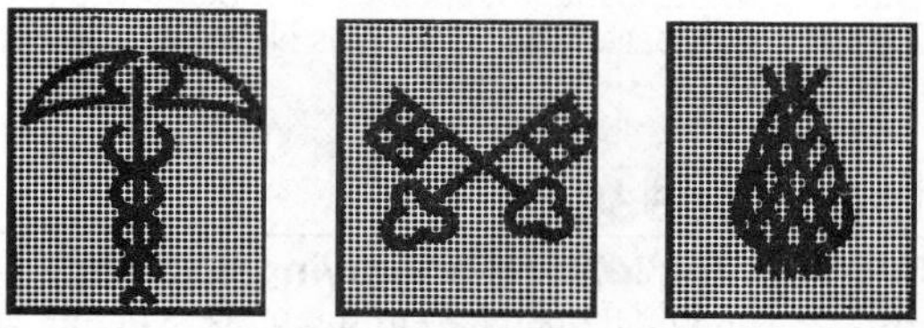

Watermarks of Uruguay, Vatican City and Jamaica

WARNING: Some inks used in the photogravure process dissolve in watermark fluids (Please see the section on Soluble Printing Inks). Also, see "chalky paper."

Watermarks may be found normal, reversed, inverted, reversed and inverted, sideways or diagonal, as seen from the back of the stamp. The relationship of watermark to stamp design depends on the position of the printing plates or how paper is fed through the press. On machine-made paper, watermarks normally are read from right to left. The design is repeated closely throughout the sheet in a "multiple-watermark design." In a "sheet watermark," the design appears only once on the sheet, but extends over many stamps. Individual stamps may carry only a small fraction or none of the watermark.

"Marginal watermarks" occur in the margins of sheets or panes of stamps. They occur on the outside border of paper (ostensibly outside the area where stamps are to be printed). A large row of letters may spell the name of the country or the manufacturer of the paper, or a border of lines may appear. Careless press feeding may cause parts of these letters and/or lines to show on stamps of the outer row of a pane.

Soluble Printing Inks

WARNING: Most stamp colors are permanent; that is, they are not seriously affected by short-term exposure to light or water. Many colors, especially of modern inks, fade from excessive exposure to light. There are stamps printed with inks that dissolve easily in water or in fluids used to detect watermarks. Use of these inks was intentional to prevent the removal of cancellations. Water affects all aniline inks, those on so-called safety paper and some photogravure printings - all such inks are known as *fugitive colors. Removal from paper of such stamps requires care and alternatives to traditional soaking.*

Separation

"Separation" is the general term used to describe methods used to separate stamps. The three standard forms currently in use are perforating, rouletting and die-cutting. These methods are done during the stamp production process, after printing. Sometimes these methods are done on-press or sometimes as a separate step. The earliest issues, such as the 1840 Penny Black of Great Britain (Scott 1), did not have any means provided for separation. It was expected the stamps would be cut apart with scissors or folded and torn. These are examples of imperforate stamps. Many stamps were first issued in imperforate formats and were later issued with perforations. Therefore, care must be observed in buying single imperforate stamps to be certain they were issued imperforate and are not perforated copies that have been altered by having the perforations trimmed away. Stamps issued imperforate usually are valued as singles. However, imperforate varieties of normally perforated stamps should be collected in pairs or larger pieces as indisputable evidence of their imperforate character.

PERFORATION

The chief style of separation of stamps, and the one that is in almost universal use today, is perforating. By this process, paper between the stamps is cut away in a line of holes, usually round, leaving little bridges of paper between the stamps to hold them together. Some types of perforation, such as hyphen-hole perfs, can be confused with roulettes, but a close visual inspection reveals that paper has been removed. The little perforation bridges, which project from the stamp when it is torn from the pane, are called the teeth of the perforation.

As the size of the perforation is sometimes the only way to differentiate between two otherwise identical stamps, it is necessary to be able to accurately measure and describe them. This is done with a perforation gauge, usually a ruler-like device that has dots or graduated lines to show how many perforations may be counted in the space of two centimeters. Two centimeters is the space universally adopted in which to measure perforations.

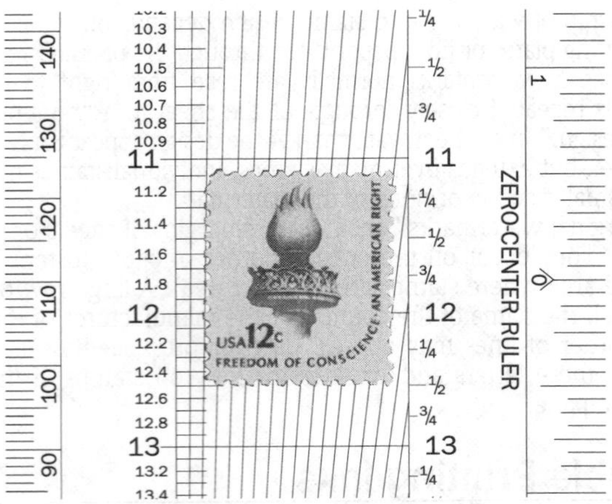

Perforation gauge

To measure a stamp, run it along the gauge until the dots on it fit exactly into the perforations of the stamp. If you are using a graduated-line perforation gauge, simply slide the stamp along the surface until the lines on the gauge perfectly project from the center of the bridges or holes. The number to the side of the line of dots or lines that fit the stamp's perforation is the measurement. For example, an "11" means that 11 perforations fit between two centimeters. The description of the stamp therefore is "perf. 11." If the gauge of the perforations on the top and bottom of a stamp differs from that on the sides, the result is what is known as *compound perforations.* In measuring compound perforations, the gauge at top and bottom is always given first, then the sides. Thus, a stamp that measures 11 at top and bottom and 10 1/2 at the sides is "perf. 11 x 10 1/2." See U.S. Scott 632-642 for examples of compound perforations.

Stamps also are known with perforations different on three or all four sides. Descriptions of such items are clockwise, beginning with the top of the stamp.

A perforation with small holes and teeth close together is a "fine perforation." One with large holes and teeth far apart is a "coarse perforation." Holes that are jagged, rather than clean-cut, are "rough perforations." *Blind perforations* are the slight impressions left by the perforating pins if they fail to puncture the paper. Multiples of stamps showing blind perforations may command a slight premium over normally perforated stamps.

The term *syncopated perfs* describes intentional irregularities in the perforations. The earliest form was used by the Netherlands from 1925-33, where holes were omitted to create distinctive patterns. Beginning in 1992, Great Britain has used an oval perforation to help prevent counterfeiting. Several other countries have started using the oval perfs or other syncopated perf patterns.

A new type of perforation, still primarily used for postal stationery, is known as microperfs. Microperfs are tiny perforations (in some cases hundreds of holes per two centimeters) that allows items to be intentionally separated very easily, while not accidentally breaking apart as easily as standard perforations. These are not currently measured or differentiated by size, as are standard perforations.

perce en arc

perce en lignes

perce en points

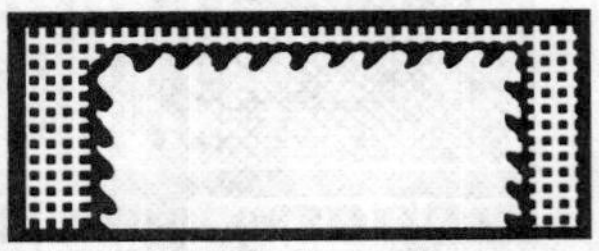

oblique roulette

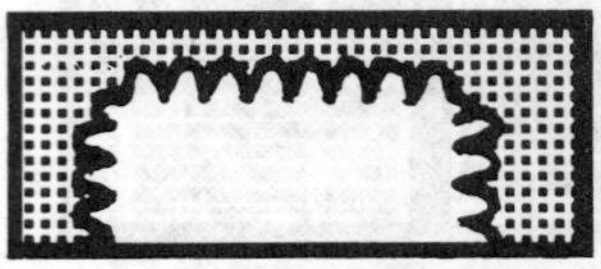

perce en scie

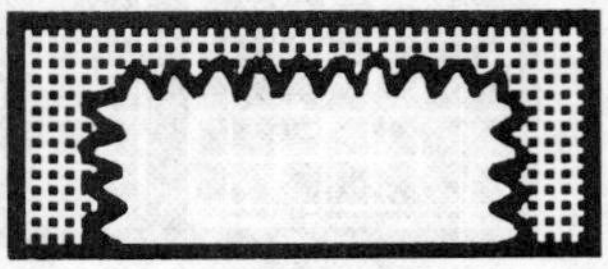

perce serpentin

ROULETTING

In rouletting, the stamp paper is cut partly or wholly through, with no paper removed. In perforating, some paper is removed. Rouletting derives its name from the French roulette, a spur-like wheel. As the wheel is rolled over the paper, each point makes a small cut. The number of cuts made in a two-centimeter space determines the gauge of the roulette, just as the number of perforations in two centimeters determines the gauge of the perforation.

The shape and arrangement of the teeth on the wheels varies. Various roulette types generally carry French names:

Perce en lignes - rouletted in lines. The paper receives short, straight cuts in lines. This is the most common type of rouletting. See Mexico Scott 500.

Perce en points - pin-rouletted. This differs from a small perforation because no paper is removed, although round, equidistant holes are pricked through the paper. See Mexico Scott 242-256.

Perce en arc and *perce en scie* - pierced in an arc or saw-toothed designs, forming half circles or small triangles. See Hanover (German States) Scott 25-29.

Perce en serpentin - serpentine roulettes. The cuts form a serpentine or wavy line. See Brunswick (German States) Scott 13-18.

Once again, no paper is removed by these processes, leaving the stamps easily separated, but closely attached.

DIE-CUTTING

The third major form of stamp separation is die-cutting. This is a method where a die in the pattern of separation is created that later cuts the stamp paper in a stroke motion. Although some standard stamps bear die-cut perforations, this process is primarily used for self-adhesive postage stamps. Die-cutting can appear in straight lines, such as U.S. Scott 2522, shapes, such as U.S. Scott 1551, or imitating the appearance of perforations, such as New Zealand Scott 935A and 935B.

Printing Processes

ENGRAVING (Intaglio, Line-engraving, Etching)

Master die — The initial operation in the process of line engraving is making the master die. The die is a small, flat block of softened steel upon which the stamp design is recess engraved in reverse.

Master die

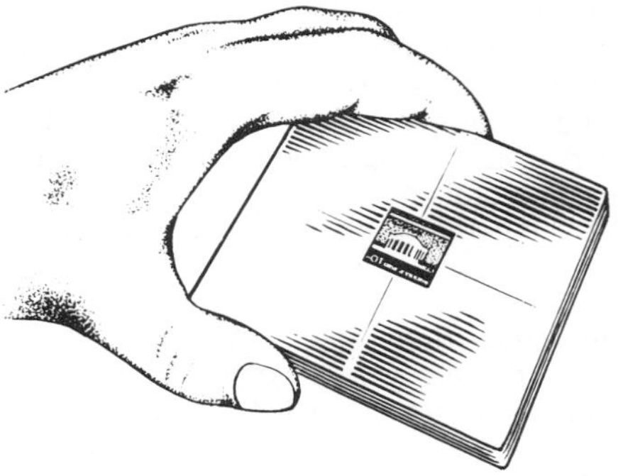

Photographic reduction of the original art is made to the appropriate size. It then serves as a tracing guide for the initial outline of the design. The engraver lightly traces the design on the steel with his graver, then slowly works the design until it is completed. At various points during the engraving process, the engraver hand-inks the die and makes an impression to check his progress. These are known as progressive die proofs. After completion of the engraving, the die is hardened to withstand the stress and pressures of later transfer operations.

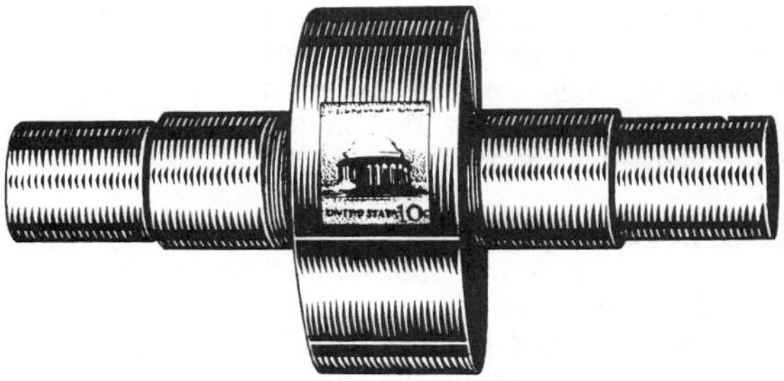

Transfer roll

Transfer roll — Next is production of the transfer roll that, as the name implies, is the medium used to transfer the subject from the master die to the printing plate. A blank roll of soft steel, mounted on a mandrel, is placed under the bearers of the transfer press to allow it to roll freely on its axis. The hardened die is placed on the bed of the press and the face of the transfer roll is applied to the die, under pressure. The bed or the roll is then rocked back and forth under increasing pressure, until the soft steel of the roll is forced into every engraved line of the die. The resulting impression on the roll is known as a "relief" or a "relief transfer." The engraved image is now positive in appearance and stands out from the steel. After the required number of reliefs are "rocked in," the soft steel transfer roll is hardened.

Different flaws may occur during the relief process. A defective relief may occur during the rocking in process because of a minute piece of foreign material lodging on the die, or some other cause. Imperfections in the steel of the transfer roll may result in a breaking away of parts of the design. This is known as a relief break, which will show up on finished stamps as small, unprinted areas. If a damaged relief remains in use, it will transfer a repeating defect to the plate. Deliberate alterations of reliefs sometimes occur. "Altered reliefs" designate these changed conditions.

Plate — The final step in pre-printing production is the making of the printing plate. A flat piece of soft steel replaces the die on the bed of the transfer press. One of the reliefs on the transfer roll is positioned over this soft steel. Position, or layout, dots determine the correct position on the plate. The dots have been lightly marked on the plate in advance. After the correct position of the relief is determined, the design is rocked in by following the same method used in making the transfer roll. The difference is that this time the image is being transferred from the transfer roll, rather than to it. Once the design is entered on the plate, it appears in reverse and is recessed. There are as many transfers entered on the plate as there are subjects printed on the sheet of stamps. It is during this process that double and shifted transfers occur, as well as re-entries. These are the result of improperly entered images that have not been properly burnished out prior to rocking in a new image.

Modern siderography processes, such as those used by the U.S. Bureau of Engraving and Printing, involve an automated form of rocking designs in on preformed cylindrical printing sleeves. The same process also allows for easier removal and re-entry of worn images right on the sleeve.

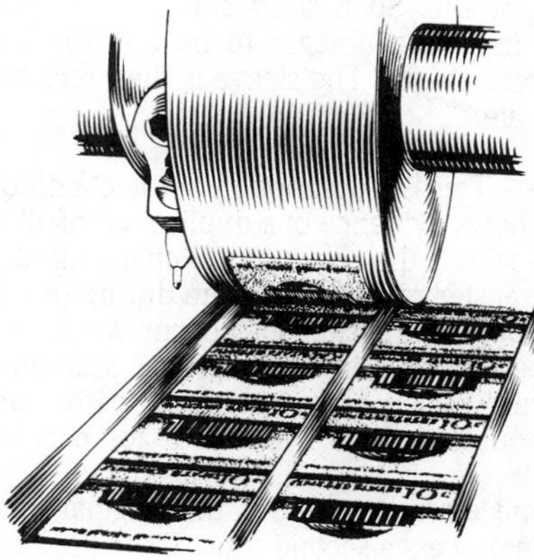

Transferring the design to the plate

Following the entering of the required transfers on the plate, the position dots, layout dots and lines, scratches and other markings generally are burnished out. Added at this time by the siderographer are any required *guide lines, plate numbers* or other *marginal markings.* The plate is then hand-inked and a proof impression is taken. This is known as a plate proof. If the impression is approved, the plate is machined for fitting onto the press, is hardened and sent to the plate vault ready for use.

On press, the plate is inked and the surface is automatically wiped clean, leaving ink only in the recessed lines. Paper is then forced under pressure into the engraved recessed lines, thereby receiving the ink. Thus, the ink lines on engraved stamps are slightly raised, and slight depressions (debossing) occur on the back of the stamp. Prior to the advent of modern high-speed presses and more advanced ink formulations, paper had to be dampened before receiving the ink. This sometimes led to uneven shrinkage by the time the stamps were perforated, resulting in improperly perforated stamps, or misperfs. Newer presses use drier paper, thus both *wet* and *dry printings* exist on some stamps.

Rotary Press — Until 1914, only flat plates were used to print engraved stamps. Rotary press printing was introduced in 1914, and slowly spread. Some countries still use flat-plate printing.

After approval of the plate proof, older *rotary press plates* require additional machining. They are curved to fit the press cylinder. "Gripper slots" are cut into the back of each plate to receive the "grippers," which hold the plate securely on the press. The plate is then hardened. Stamps printed from these bent rotary press plates are longer or wider than the same stamps printed from flat-plate presses. The stretching of the plate during the curving process is what causes this distortion.

Re-entry — To execute a re-entry on a flat plate, the transfer roll is re-applied to the plate, often at some time after its first use on the press. Worn-out designs can be resharpened by carefully burnishing out the original image and re-entering it from the transfer roll. If the original impression has not been sufficiently removed and the transfer roll is not precisely in line with the remaining impression, the resulting double transfer will make the re-entry obvious. If the registration is true, a re-entry may be difficult or impossible to distinguish. Sometimes a stamp printed from a successful re-entry is identified by having a much sharper and clearer impression than its neighbors. With the advent of rotary presses, post-press re-entries were not possible. After a plate was curved for the rotary press, it was impossible to make a re-entry. This is because the plate had already been bent once (with the design distorted).

However, with the introduction of the previously mentioned modern-style siderography machines, entries are made to the preformed cylindrical printing sleeve. Such sleeves are dechromed and softened. This allows individual images to be burnished out and re-entered on the curved sleeve. The sleeve is then rechromed, resulting in longer press life.

Double Transfer — This is a description of the condition of a transfer on a plate that shows evidence of a duplication of all, or a portion of the design. It usually is the result of the changing of the registration between the transfer roll and the plate during the rocking in of the original entry. Double transfers also occur when only a portion of the design has been rocked in and improper positioning is noted. If the worker elected not to burnish out the partial or completed design, a strong double transfer will occur for part or all of the design.

It sometimes is necessary to remove the original transfer from a plate and repeat the process a second time. If the finished re-worked image shows traces of the original impression, attributable to incomplete burnishing, the result is a partial double transfer.

With the modern automatic machines mentioned previously, double transfers are all but impossible to create. Those partially doubled images on stamps printed from such sleeves are more than likely re-entries, rather than true double transfers.

Re-engraved — Alterations to a stamp design are sometimes necessary after some stamps have been printed. In some cases, either the original die or the actual printing plate may have its "temper" drawn (softened), and the design will be re-cut. The resulting impressions from such a re-engraved die or plate may differ slightly from the original issue, and are known as "re-engraved." If the alteration was made to the master die, all future printings will be consistently different from the original. If alterations were made to the printing plate, each altered stamp on the plate will be slightly different from each other, allowing specialists to reconstruct a complete printing plate.

Dropped Transfers — If an impression from the transfer roll has not been properly placed, a dropped transfer may occur. The final stamp image will appear obviously out of line with its neighbors.

Short Transfer — Sometimes a transfer roll is not rocked its entire length when entering a transfer onto a plate. As a result, the finished transfer on the plate fails to show the complete design, and the finished stamp will have an incomplete design printed. This is known as a "short transfer." U.S. Scott No. 8 is a good example of a short transfer.

TYPOGRAPHY (Letterpress, Surface Printing, Flexography, Dry Offset, High Etch)

Although the word "Typography" is obsolete as a term describing a printing method, it was the accepted term throughout the first century of postage stamps. Therefore, appropriate Scott listings in this catalogue refer to typographed stamps. The current term for this form of printing, however, is "letterpress."

As it relates to the production of postage stamps, letterpress printing is the reverse of engraving. Rather than having recessed areas trap the ink and deposit it on paper, only the raised areas of the design are inked. This is comparable to the type of printing seen by inking and using an ordinary rubber stamp. Letterpress includes all printing where the design is above the surface area, whether it is wood, metal or, in some instances, hardened rubber or polymer plastic.

For most letterpress-printed stamps, the engraved master is made in much the same manner as for engraved stamps. In this instance, however, an additional step is needed. The design is transferred to another surface before being transferred to the transfer roll. In this way, the transfer roll has a recessed stamp design, rather than one done in relief. This makes the printing areas on the final plate raised, or relief areas.

For less-detailed stamps of the 19th century, the area on the die not used as a printing surface was cut away, leaving the surface area raised. The original die was then reproduced by stereotyping or electrotyping. The resulting electrotypes were assembled in the required number and format of the desired sheet of stamps. The plate used in printing the stamps was an electroplate of these assembled electrotypes.

Once the final letterpress plates are created, ink is applied to the raised surface and the pressure of the press transfers the ink impression to the paper. In contrast to engraving, the fine lines of letterpress are impressed on the surface of the stamp, leaving a debossed surface. When viewed from the back (as on a typewritten page), the corresponding line work on the stamp will be raised slightly (embossed) above the surface.

PHOTOGRAVURE (Gravure, Rotogravure, Heliogravure)

In this process, the basic principles of photography are applied to a chemically sensitized metal plate, rather than photographic paper. The design is transferred photographically to the plate through a halftone, or dot-matrix screen, breaking the reproduction into tiny dots. The plate is treated chemically and the dots form depressions, called cells, of varying depths and diameters, depending on the degrees of shade in the design. Then, like engraving, ink is applied to the plate and the surface is wiped clean. This leaves ink in the tiny cells that is lifted out and deposited on the paper when it is pressed against the plate.

Gravure is most often used for multicolored stamps, generally using the three primary colors (red, yellow and blue) and black. By varying the dot matrix pattern and density of these colors, virtually any color can be reproduced. A typical full-color gravure stamp will be created from four printing cylinders (one for each color). The original multicolored image will have been photographically separated into its component colors.

Modern gravure printing may use computer-generated dot-matrix screens, and modern plates may be of various types including metal-coated plastic. The catalogue designation of Photogravure (or "Photo") covers any of these older and more modern gravure methods of printing.

For examples of the first photogravure stamps printed (1914), see Bavaria Scott 94-114.

LITHOGRAPHY (Offset Lithography, Stone Lithography, Dilitho, Planography, Collotype)

The principle that oil and water do not mix is the basis for lithography. The stamp design is drawn by hand or transferred from engraving to the surface of a lithographic stone or metal plate in a greasy (oily) substance. This oily substance holds the ink, which will later be transferred to the paper. The stone (or plate) is wet with an acid fluid, causing it to repel the printing ink in all areas not covered by the greasy substance.

Transfer paper is used to transfer the design from the original stone or plate. A series of duplicate transfers are grouped and, in turn, transferred to the final printing plate.

Photolithography — The application of photographic processes to lithography. This process allows greater flexibility of design, related to use of halftone screens combined with line work. Unlike photogravure or engraving, this process can allow large, solid areas to be printed.

Offset — A refinement of the lithographic process. A rubber-covered blanket cylinder takes the impression from the inked lithographic plate. From the "blanket" the impression is *offset* or transferred to the paper. Greater flexibility and speed are the principal reasons offset printing has largely displaced lithography. The term "lithography" covers both processes, and results are almost identical.

EMBOSSED (Relief) Printing

Embossing, not considered one of the four main printing types, is a method in which the design first is sunk into the metal of the die. Printing is done against a yielding platen, such as leather or linoleum. The platen is forced into the depression of the die, thus forming the design on the paper in relief. This process is often used for metallic inks.

Embossing may be done without color (see Sardinia Scott 4-6); with color printed around the embossed area (see Great Britain Scott 5 and most U.S. envelopes); and with color in exact registration with the embossed subject (see Canada Scott 656-657).

HOLOGRAMS

For objects to appear as holograms on stamps, a model exactly the same size as it is to appear on the hologram must be created. Rather than using photographic film to capture the image, holography records an image on a photoresist material. In processing, chemicals eat away at certain exposed areas, leaving a pattern of constructive and destructive interference. When the phororesist is developed, the result is a pattern of uneven ridges that acts as a mold. This mold is then coated with metal, and the resulting form is used to press copies in much the same way phonograph records are produced.

A typical reflective hologram used for stamps consists of a reproduction of the uneven patterns on a plastic film that is applied to a reflective background, usually a silver or gold foil. Light is reflected off the background through the film, making the pattern present on the film visible. Because of the uneven pattern of the film, the viewer will perceive the objects in their proper three-dimensional relationships with appropriate brightness.

The first hologram on a stamp was produced by Austria in 1988 (Scott 1441).

FOIL APPLICATION

A modern tecnique of applying color to stamps involves the application of metallic foil to the stamp paper. A pattern of foil is applied to the stamp paper by use of a stamping die. The foil usually is flat, but it may be textured. Canada Scott 1735 has three different foil applications in pearl, bronze and gold. The gold foil was textured using a chemical-etch copper embossing die. The printing of this stamp also involved two-color offset lithography plus embossing.

COMBINATION PRINTINGS

Sometimes two or even three printing methods are combined in producing stamps. In these cases, such as Austria Scott 933 or Canada 1735 (described in the preceding paragraph), the multiple-printing technique can be determined by studying the individual characteristics of each printing type. A few stamps, such as Singapore Scott 684-684A, combine as many as three of the four major printing types (lithography, engraving and typography). When this is done it often indicates the incorporation of security devices against counterfeiting.

INK COLORS

Inks or colored papers used in stamp printing often are of mineral origin, although there are numerous examples of organic-based pigments. As a general rule, organic-based pigments are far more subject to varieties and change than those of mineral-based origin.

The appearance of any given color on a stamp may be affected by many aspects, including printing variations, light, color of paper, aging and chemical alterations.

Numerous printing variations may be observed. Heavier pressure or inking will cause a more intense color, while slight interruptions in the ink feed or lighter impressions will cause a lighter appearance. Stamps printed in the same color by water-based and solvent-based inks can differ significantly in appearance. This affects several stamps in the U.S. Prominent Americans series. Hand-mixed ink formulas (primarily from the 19th century) produced under different conditions (humidity and temperature) account for notable color variations in early printings of the same stamp (see U.S. Scott 248-250, 279B, for example). Different sources of pigment can also result in significant differences in color.

Light exposure and aging are closely related in the way they affect stamp color. Both eventually break down the ink and fade colors, so that a carefully kept stamp may differ significantly in color from an identical copy that has been exposed to light. If stamps are exposed to light either intentionally or accidentally, their colors can be faded or completely changed in some cases.

Papers of different quality and consistency used for the same stamp printing may affect color appearance. Most pelure papers, for example, show a richer color when compared with wove or laid papers. See Russia Scott 181a, for an example of this effect.

The very nature of the printing processes can cause a variety of differences in shades or hues of the same stamp. Some of these shades are scarcer than others, and are of particular interest to the advanced collector.

Luminescence

All forms of tagged stamps fall under the general category of luminescence. Within this broad category is fluorescence, dealing with forms of tagging visible under longwave ultraviolet light, and phosphorescence, which deals with tagging visible only under shortwave light. Phosphorescence leaves an afterglow and fluorescence does not. These treated stamps show up in a range of different colors when exposed to UV light. The differing wavelengths of the light activates the tagging material, making it glow in various colors that usually serve different mail processing purposes.

Intentional tagging is a post-World War II phenomenon, brought about by the increased literacy rate and rapidly growing mail volume. It was one of several answers to the problem of the need for more automated mail processes. Early tagged stamps served the purpose of triggering machines to separate different types of mail. A natural outgrowth was to also use the signal to trigger machines that faced all envelopes the same way and canceled them.

Tagged stamps come in many different forms. Some tagged stamps have luminescent shapes or images imprinted on them as a form of security device. Others have blocks (United States), stripes, frames (South Africa and Canada), overall coatings (United States), bars (Great Britain and Canada) and many other types. Some types of tagging are even mixed in with the pigmented printing ink (Australia Scott 366, Netherlands Scott 478 and U.S. Scott 1359 and 2443).

The means of applying taggant to stamps differs as much as the intended purposes for the stamps. The most common form of tagging is a coating applied to the surface of the printed stamp. Since the taggant ink is frequently invisible except under UV light, it does not interfere with the appearance of the stamp. Another common application is the use of phosphored papers. In this case the paper itself either has a coating of taggant applied before the stamp is printed, has taggant applied during the papermaking process (incorporating it into the fibers), or has the taggant mixed into the coating of the paper. The latter method, among others, is currently in use in the United States.

Many countries now use tagging in various forms to either expedite mail handling or to serve as a printing security device against counterfeiting. Following the introduction of tagged stamps for public use in 1959 by Great Britain, other countries have steadily joined the parade. Among those are Germany (1961); Canada and Denmark (1962); United States, Australia, France and Switzerland (1963); Belgium and Japan (1966); Sweden and Norway (1967); Italy (1968); and Russia (1969). Since then, many other countries have begun using forms of tagging, including Brazil, China, Czechoslovakia, Hong Kong, Guatemala, Indonesia, Israel, Lithuania, Luxembourg, Netherlands, Penrhyn Islands, Portugal, St. Vincent, Singapore, South Africa, Spain and Sweden to name a few.

In some cases, including United States, Canada, Great Britain and Switzerland, stamps were released both with and without tagging. Many of these were released during each country's experimental period. Tagged and untagged versions are listed for the aforementioned countries and are noted in some other countries' listings. For at least a few stamps, the experimentally tagged version is worth far more than its untagged counterpart, such as the 1963 experimental tagged version of France Scott 1024.

In some cases, luminescent varieties of stamps were inadvertently created. Several Russian stamps, for example, sport highly fluorescent ink that was not intended as a form of tagging. Older stamps, such as early U.S. postage dues, can be positively identified by the use of UV light, since the organic ink used has become slightly fluorescent over time. Other stamps, such as Austria Scott 70a-82a (varnish bars) and Obock Scott 46-64 (printed quadrille lines), have become fluorescent over time.

Various fluorescent substances have been added to paper to make it appear brighter. These optical brightners, as they are known, greatly affect the appearance of the stamp under UV light. The brightest of these is known as Hi-Brite paper. These paper varieties are beyond the scope of the Scott Catalogue.

Shortwave UV light also is used extensively in expertizing, since each form of paper has its own fluorescent characteristics that are impossible to perfectly match. It is therefore a simple matter to detect filled thins, added perforation teeth and other alterations that involve the addition of paper. UV light also is used to examine stamps that have had cancels chemically removed and for other purposes as well.

Gum

The Illustrated Gum Chart in the first part of this introduction shows and defines various types of gum condition. Because gum condition has an important impact on the value of unused stamps, we recommend studying this chart and the accompanying text carefully.

The gum on the back of a stamp may be shiny, dull, smooth, rough, dark, white, colored or tinted. Most stamp gumming adhesives use gum arabic or dextrine as a base. Certain polymers such as polyvinyl alcohol (PVA) have been used extensively since World War II.

The *Scott Standard Postage Stamp Catalogue* does not list items by types of gum. The *Scott Specialized Catalogue of United States Stamps* does differentiate among some types of gum for certain issues.

Reprints of stamps may have gum differing from the original issues. In addition, some countries have used different gum formulas for different seasons. These adhesives have different properties that may become more apparent over time.

Many stamps have been issued without gum, and the catalogue will note this fact. See, for example, United States Scott 40-47. Sometimes, gum may have been removed to preserve the stamp. Germany Scott B68, for example, has a highly acidic gum that eventually destroys the stamps. This item is valued in the catalogue with gum removed.

Reprints and Reissues

These are impressions of stamps (usually obsolete) made from the original plates or stones. If they are valid for postage and reproduce obsolete issues (such as U.S. Scott 102-111), the stamps are *reissues.* If they are from current issues, they are designated as *second, third,* etc., *printing.* If designated for a particular purpose, they are called *special printings.*

When special printings are not valid for postage, but are made from original dies and plates by authorized persons, they are *official reprints. Private reprints* are made from the original plates and dies by private hands. An example of a private reprint is that of the 1871-1932 reprints made from the original die of the 1845 New Haven, Conn., postmaster's provisional. *Official reproductions* or imitations are made from new dies and plates by government authorization. Scott will list those reissues that are valid for postage if they differ significantly from the original printing.

The U.S. government made special printings of its first postage stamps in 1875. Produced were official imitations of the first two stamps (listed as Scott 3-4), reprints of the demonetized pre-1861 issues (Scott 40-47) and reissues of the 1861 stamps, the 1869 stamps and the then-current 1875 denominations. Even though the official imitations and the reprints were not valid for postage, Scott lists all of these U.S. special printings.

Most reprints or reissues differ slightly from the original stamp in some characteristic, such as gum, paper, perforation, color or watermark. Sometimes the details are followed so meticulously that only a student of that specific stamp is able to distinguish the reprint or reissue from the original.

Remainders and Canceled to Order

Some countries sell their stock of old stamps when a new issue replaces them. To avoid postal use, the *remainders* usually are canceled with a punch hole, a heavy line or bar, or a more-or-less regular-looking cancellation. The most famous merchant of remainders was Nicholas F. Seebeck. In the 1880s and 1890s, he arranged printing contracts between the Hamilton Bank Note Co., of which he was a director, and several Central and South American countries. The contracts provided that the plates and all remainders of the yearly issues became the property of Hamilton. Seebeck saw to it that ample stock remained. The "Seebecks," both remainders and reprints, were standard packet fillers for decades.

Some countries also issue stamps *canceled-to-order (CTO),* either in sheets with original gum or stuck onto pieces of paper or envelopes and canceled. Such CTO items generally are worth less than postally used stamps. In cases where the CTO material is far more prevalent in the marketplace than postally used examples, the catalogue value relates to the CTO examples, with postally used examples noted as premium items. Most CTOs can be detected by the presence of gum. However, as the CTO practice goes back at least to 1885, the gum inevitably has been soaked off some stamps so they could pass as postally used. The normally applied postmarks usually differ slightly from standard postmarks, and specialists are able to tell the difference. When applied individually to envelopes by philatelically minded persons, CTO material is known as *favor canceled* and generally sells at large discounts.

Cinderellas and Facsimiles

Cinderella is a catch-all term used by stamp collectors to describe phantoms, fantasies, bogus items, municipal issues, exhibition seals, local revenues, transportation stamps, labels, poster stamps and many other types of items. Some cinderella collectors include in their collections local postage issues, telegraph stamps, essays and proofs, forgeries and counterfeits.

A *fantasy* is an adhesive created for a nonexistent stamp-issuing authority. Fantasy items range from imaginary countries (Occusi-Ambeno, Kingdom of Sedang, Principality of Trinidad or Torres Straits), to non-existent locals (Winans City Post), or nonexistent transportation lines (McRobish & Co.'s Acapulco-San Francisco Line).

On the other hand, if the entity exists and could have issued stamps (but did not) or was known to have issued other stamps, the items are considered *bogus* stamps. These would include the Mormon postage stamps of Utah, S. Allan Taylor's Guatemala and Paraguay inventions, the propaganda issues for the South Moluccas and the adhesives of the Page & Keyes local post of Boston.

Phantoms is another term for both fantasy and bogus issues.

Facsimiles are copies or imitations made to represent original stamps, but which do not pretend to be originals. A catalogue illustration is such a facsimile. Illustrations from the Moens catalogue of the last century were occasionally colored and passed off as stamps. Since the beginning of stamp collecting, facsimiles have been made for collectors as space fillers or for reference. They often carry the word "facsimile," "falsch" (German), "sanko" or "mozo" (Japanese), or "faux" (French) overprinted on the face or stamped on the back. Unfortunately, over the years a number of these items have had fake cancels applied over the facsimile notation and have been passed off as genuine.

Forgeries and Counterfeits

Forgeries and counterfeits have been with philately virtually from the beginning of stamp production. Over time, the terminology for the two has been used interchangeably. Although both forgeries and counterfeits are reproductions of stamps, the purposes behind their creation differ considerably.

Among specialists there is an increasing movement to more specifically define such items. Although there is no universally accepted terminology, we feel the following definitions most closely mirror the items and their purposes as they are currently defined.

Forgeries (also often referred to as *Counterfeits*) are reproductions of genuine stamps that have been created to defraud collectors. Such spurious items first appeared on the market around 1860, and most old-time collections contain one or more. Many are crude and easily spotted, but some can deceive experts.

An important supplier of these early philatelic forgeries was the Hamburg printer Gebruder Spiro. Many others with reputations in this craft included S. Allan Taylor, George Hussey, James Chute, George Forune, Benjamin & Sarpy, Julius Goldner, E. Oneglia and L.H. Mercier. Among the noted 20th-century forgers were Francois Fournier, Jean Sperati and the prolific Raoul DeThuin.

Forgeries may be complete replications, or they may be genuine stamps altered to resemble a scarcer (and more valuable) type. Most forgeries, particularly those of rare stamps, are worth only a small fraction of the value of a genuine example, but a few types, created by some of the most notable forgers, such as Sperati, can be worth as much or more than the genuine. Fraudulently produced copies are known of most classic rarities and many medium-priced stamps.

In addition to rare stamps, large numbers of common 19th- and early 20th-century stamps were forged to supply stamps to the early packet trade. Many can still be easily found. Few new philatelic forgeries have appeared in recent decades. Successful imitation of well-engraved work is virtually impossible. It has proven far easier to produce a fake by altering a genuine stamp than to duplicate a stamp completely.

Counterfeit (also often referred to as *Postal Counterfeit* or *Postal Forgery*) is the term generally applied to reproductions of stamps that have been created to defraud the government of revenue. Such items usually are created at the time a stamp is current and, in some cases, are hard to detect. Because most counterfeits are seized when the perpetrator is captured, postal counterfeits, particularly used on cover, are usually worth much more than a genuine example to specialists. The first postal counterfeit was of Spain's 4-cuarto carmine of 1854 (the real one is Scott 25). Apparently, the counterfeiters were not satisfied with their first version, which is now very scarce, and they soon created an engraved counterfeit, which is common. Postal counterfeits quickly followed in Austria, Naples, Sardinia and the Roman States. They have since been created in many other countries as well, including the United States.

An infamous counterfeit to defraud the government is the 1-shilling Great Britain "Stock Exchange" forgery of 1872, used on telegraph forms at the exchange that year. The stamp escaped detection until a stamp dealer noticed it in 1898.

Fakes

Fakes are genuine stamps altered in some way to make them more desirable. One student of this part of stamp collecting has estimated that by the 1950s more than 30,000 varieties of fakes were known. That number has grown greatly since then. The widespread existence of fakes makes it important for stamp collectors to study their philatelic holdings and use relevant literature. Likewise, collectors should buy from reputable dealers who guarantee their stamps and make full and prompt refunds should a purchased item be declared faked or altered by some mutually agreed-upon authority. Because fakes always have some genuine characteristics, it is not always possible to obtain unanimous agreement among experts regarding specific items. These students may change their opinions as philatelic knowledge increases. More than 80 percent of all fakes on the philatelic market today are regummed, reperforated (or perforated for the first time), or bear forged overprints, surcharges or cancellations.

Stamps can be chemically treated to alter or eliminate colors. For example, a pale rose stamp can be re-colored to resemble a blue shade of high market value. In other cases, treated stamps can be made to resemble missing color varieties. Designs may be changed by painting, or a stroke or a dot added or bleached out to turn an ordinary variety into a seemingly scarcer stamp. Part of a stamp can be bleached and reprinted in a different version, achieving an inverted center or frame. Margins can be added or repairs done so deceptively that the stamps move from the "repaired" into the "fake" category.

Fakers have not left the backs of the stamps untouched either. They may create false watermarks, add fake grills or press out genuine grills. A thin India paper proof may be glued onto a thicker backing to create the appearance an issued stamp, or a proof printed on cardboard may be shaved down and perforated to resemble a stamp. Silk threads are impressed into paper and stamps have been split so that a rare paper variety is added to an otherwise inexpensive stamp. The most common treatment to the back of a stamp, however, is regumming.

Some in the business of faking stamps have openly advertised foolproof application of "original gum" to stamps that lack it, although most publications now ban such ads from their pages. It is believed that very few early stamps have survived without being hinged. The large number of never-hinged examples of such earlier material offered for sale thus suggests the widespread extent of regumming activity. Regumming also may be used to hide repairs or thin spots. Dipping the stamp into watermark fluid, or examining it under longwave ultraviolet light often will reveal these flaws.

Fakers also tamper with separations. Ingenious ways to add margins are known. Perforated wide-margin stamps may be falsely represented as imperforate when trimmed. Reperforating is commonly done to create scarce coil or perforation varieties, and to eliminate the naturally occurring straight-edge stamps found in sheet margin positions of many earlier issues. Custom has made straight-edged stamps less desirable. Fakers have obliged by perforating straight-edged stamps so that many are now uncommon, if not rare.

Another fertile field for the faker is that of overprints, surcharges and cancellations. The forging of rare surcharges or overprints began in the 1880s or 1890s. These forgeries are sometimes difficult to detect, but experts have identified almost all. Occasionally, overprints or cancellations are removed to create non-overprinted stamps or seemingly unused items. This is most commonly done by removing a manuscript cancel to make a stamp resemble an unused example. "SPECIMEN" overprints may be removed by scraping and repainting to create non-overprinted varieties. Fakers use inexpensive revenues or pen-canceled stamps to generate unused stamps for further faking by adding other markings. The quartz lamp or UV lamp and a high-powered magnifying glass help to easily detect removed cancellations.

The bigger problem, however, is the addition of overprints, surcharges or cancellations - many with such precision that they are very difficult to ascertain. Plating of the stamps or the overprint can be an important method of detection.

Fake postmarks may range from many spurious fancy cancellations to a host of markings applied to transatlantic covers, to adding normally appearing postmarks to definitives of some countries with stamps that are valued far higher used than unused. With the increased popularity of cover collecting, and the widespread interest in postal history, a fertile new field for fakers has come about. Some have tried to create entire covers. Others specialize in adding stamps, tied by fake cancellations, to genuine stampless covers, or replacing less expensive or damaged stamps with more valuable ones. Detailed study of postal rates in effect at the time a cover in question was mailed, including the analysis of each handstamp used during the period, ink analysis and similar techniques, usually will unmask the fraud.

Restoration and Repairs

Scott Publishing Co. bases its catalogue values on stamps that are free of defects and otherwise meet the standards set forth earlier in this introduction. Most stamp collectors desire to have the finest copy of an item possible. Even within given grading categories there are variances. This leads to a controversial practice that is not defined in any universal manner: stamp *restoration.*

There are broad differences of opinion about what is permissible when it comes to restoration. Carefully applying a soft eraser to a stamp or cover to remove light soiling is one form of restoration, as is washing a stamp in mild soap and water to clean it. These are fairly accepted forms of restoration. More severe forms of restoration include pressing out creases or removing stains caused by tape. To what degree each of these is acceptable is dependent upon the individual situation. Further along the spectrum is the freshening of a stamp's color by removing oxide build-up or the effects of wax paper left next to stamps shipped to the tropics.

At some point in this spectrum the concept of *repair* replaces that of restoration. Repairs include filling thin spots, mending tears by reweaving or adding a missing perforation tooth. Regumming stamps may have been acceptable as a restoration or repair technique many decades ago, but today it is considered a form of fakery.

Restored stamps may or may not sell at a discount, and it is possible that the value of individual restored items may be enhanced over that of their pre-restoration state. Specific situations dictate the resultant value of such an item. Repaired stamps sell at substantial discounts from the value of sound stamps.

Terminology

Booklets — Many countries have issued stamps in small booklets for the convenience of users. This idea continues to become increasingly popular in many countries. Booklets have been issued in many sizes and forms, often with advertising on the covers, the panes of stamps or on the interleaving.

The panes used in booklets may be printed from special plates or made from regular sheets. All panes from booklets issued by the United States and many from those of other countries contain stamps that are straight edged on the sides, but perforated between. Others are distinguished by orientation of watermark or other identifying features. Any stamp-like unit in the pane, either printed or blank, that is not a postage stamp, is considered to be a *label* in the catalogue listings.

Scott lists and values booklet panes. Modern complete booklets also are listed and valued. Individual booklet panes are listed only when they are not fashioned from existing sheet stamps and, therefore, are identifiable from their sheet stamp counterparts.

Panes usually do not have a used value assigned to them because there is little market activity for used booklet panes, even though many exist used and there is some demand for them.

Cancellations — The marks or obliterations put on stamps by postal authorities to show that they have performed service and to prevent their reuse are known as cancellations. If the marking is made with a pen, it is considered a "pen cancel." When the location of the post office appears in the marking, it is a "town cancellation." A "postmark" is technically any postal marking, but in practice the term generally is applied to a town cancellation with a date. When calling attention to a cause or celebration, the marking is known as a "slogan cancellation." Many other types and styles of cancellations exist, such as duplex, numerals, targets, fancy and others. See also "precancels," below.

Coil Stamps — These are stamps that are issued in rolls for use in dispensers, affixing and vending machines. Those coils of the United States, Canada, Sweden and some other countries are perforated horizontally or vertically only, with the outer edges imperforate. Coil stamps of some countries, such as Great Britain and Germany, are perforated on all four sides and may in some cases be distinguished from their sheet stamp counterparts by watermarks, counting numbers on the reverse or other means.

Covers — Entire envelopes, with or without adhesive postage stamps, that have passed through the mail and bear postal or other markings of philatelic interest are known as covers. Before the introduction of envelopes in about 1840, people folded letters and wrote the address on the outside. Some people covered their letters with an extra sheet of paper on the outside for the address, producing the term "cover." Used airletter sheets, stamped envelopes and other items of postal stationery also are considered covers.

Errors — Stamps that have some major, consistent, unintentional deviation from the normal are considered errors. Errors include, but are not limited to, missing or wrong colors, wrong paper, wrong watermarks, inverted centers or frames on multicolor printing, inverted or missing surcharges or overprints, double impressions, missing perforations and others. Factually wrong or misspelled information, if it appears on all examples of a stamp, are not considered errors in the true sense of the word. They are errors of design. Inconsistent or randomly appearing items, such as misperfs or color shifts, are classified as freaks.

Overprints and Surcharges — Overprinting involves applying wording or design elements over an already existing stamp. Overprints can be used to alter the place of use (such as "Canal Zone" on U.S. stamps), to adapt them for a special purpose ("Porto" on Denmark's 1913-20 regular issues for use as postage due stamps, Scott J1-J7) or to commemorate a special occasion (United States Scott 647-648).

A *surcharge* is a form of overprint that changes or restates the face value of a stamp or piece of postal stationery.

Surcharges and overprints may be handstamped, typeset or, occasionally, lithographed or engraved. A few hand-written overprints and surcharges are known.

Precancels — Stamps that are canceled before they are placed in the mail are known as precancels. Precanceling usually is done to expedite the handling of large mailings and generally allow the affected mail pieces to skip certain phases of mail handling.

In the United States, precancellations generally identified the point of origin; that is, the city and state. This information appeared across the face of the stamp, usually centered between parallel lines. More recently, bureau precancels retained the parallel lines, but the city and state designations were dropped. Recent coils have a service inscription that is present on the original printing plate. These show the mail service paid for by the stamp. Since these stamps are not intended to receive further cancellations when used as intended, they are considered precancels. Such items often do not have parallel lines as part of the precancellation.

In France, the abbreviation *Affranchts* in a semicircle together with the word *Postes* is the general form of precancel in use. Belgian precancellations usually appear in a box in which the name of the city appears. Netherlands precancels have the name of the city enclosed between concentric circles, sometimes called a "lifesaver." Precancellations of other countries usually follow these patterns, but may be any arrangement of bars, boxes and city names.

Precancels are listed in the Scott catalogues only if the precancel changes the denomination (Belgium Scott 477-478); if the precanceled stamp is different from the non-precanceled version (such as untagged U.S. precancels); or if the stamp exists only precanceled (France Scott 1096-1099, U.S. Scott 2265).

Proofs and Essays — Proofs are impressions taken from an approved die, plate or stone in which the design and color are the same as the stamp issued to the public. Trial color proofs are impressions taken from approved dies, plates or stones in colors that vary from the final version. An essay is the impression of a design that differs in some way from the issued stamp. "Progressive die proofs" generally are considered to be essays.

Provisionals — These are stamps that are issued on short notice and intended for temporary use pending the arrival of regular issues. They usually are issued to meet such contingencies as changes in government or currency, shortage of necessary postage values or military occupation.

During the 1840s, postmasters in certain American cities issued stamps that were valid only at specific post offices. In 1861, postmasters of the Confederate States also issued stamps with limited validity. Both of these examples are known as "postmaster's provisionals."

Se-tenant — This term refers to an unsevered pair, strip or block of stamps that differ in design, denomination or overprint.

Unless the se-tenant item has a continuous design (see U.S. Scott 1451a, 1694a) the stamps do not have to be in the same order as shown in the catalogue (see U.S. Scott 2158a).

Specimens — The Universal Postal Union required member nations to send samples of all stamps they released into service to the International Bureau in Switzerland. Member nations of the UPU received these specimens as samples of what stamps were valid for postage. Many are overprinted, handstamped or initial-perforated "Specimen," "Canceled" or "Muestra." Some are marked with bars across the denominations (China-Taiwan), punched holes (Czechoslovakia) or back inscriptions (Mongolia).

Stamps distributed to government officials or for publicity purposes, and stamps submitted by private security printers for official approval, also may receive such defacements.

The previously described defacement markings prevent postal use, and all such items generally are known as "specimens."

Tete Beche — This term describes a pair of stamps in which one is upside down in relation to the other. Some of these are the result of intentional sheet arrangements, such as Morocco Scott B10-B11. Others occurred when one or more electrotypes accidentally were placed upside down on the plate, such as Colombia Scott 57a. Separation of the tete-beche stamps, of course, destroys the tete beche variety.

Currency Conversion

Country	Dollar	Pound	S Franc	Yen	HK Dollar	Euro	Cdn Dollar	Aus Dollar
Australia	1.8520	2.6824	1.1260	0.0142	0.2375	1.6517	1.1782	-----
Canada	1.5719	2.2767	0.9557	0.0121	0.2015	1.4019	-----	0.8488
European Union	1.1213	1.6241	0.6817	0.0086	0.1438	-----	0.7133	0.6055
Hong Kong	7.7994	11.297	4.7419	0.0599	-----	6.9557	4.9618	4.2113
Japan	130.31	188.74	79.225	-----	16.708	116.21	82.900	70.362
Switzerland	1.6448	2.3823	-----	0.0126	0.2109	1.4669	1.0464	0.8881
United Kingdom	0.6904	-----	0.4198	0.0053	0.0885	0.6157	0.4392	0.3728
United States	-----	1.4484	0.6080	0.0077	0.1282	0.8918	0.6362	0.5400

Country	Currency	U.S. $ Equiv.
Pakistan	rupee	.0167
Palau	US dollar	1.00
Palestinian Authority	Jordanian dinar	1.41
Panama	balboa	1.00
Papua New Guinea	kina	.2689
Paraguay	guarani	.0002
Penrhyn Island	New Zealand dollar	.4482
Peru	new sol	.2918
Philippines	peso	.0197
Pitcairn Islands	New Zealand dollar	.4482
Poland	zloty	.2485
Portugal	euro	.8918
Azores	euro	.8918
Madeira	euro	.8918
Qatar	riyal	.2746
Romania	leu	.00003
Russia	ruble	.0321
Rwanda	franc	.0022
St. Helena	British pound	1.4484
St. Kitts	East Caribbean dollar	.3745
St. Lucia	East Caribbean dollar	.3745
St. Pierre & Miquelon	euro	.8918
St. Thomas & Prince	dobra	.0001
St. Vincent	East Caribbean dollar	.3745
St. Vincent Grenadines	East Caribbean dollar	.3745
El Salvador	colon	.1143
Samoa	tala (dollar)	.2909
San Marino	euro	.8918
Saudi Arabia	riyal	.2666
Senegal	Community of French Africa (CFA) franc	.0014
Seychelles	rupee	.1780
Zil Elwannyen Sesel	rupee	.1780
Sierra Leone	leone	.0005
Singapore	dollar	.5493
Slovakia	koruna	.0214
Slovenia	tolar	.0040

Source: ***Wall Street Journal*** *April 22, 2002. Figures reflect values as of April 19, 2002.*

Common Design Types

Pictured in this section are issues where one illustration has been used for a number of countries in the Catalogue. Not included in this section are overprinted stamps or those issues which are illustrated in each country.

EUROPA

Europa, 1956

The design symbolizing the cooperation among the six countries comprising the Coal and Steel Community is illustrated in each country.

Belgium 496-497
France 805-806
Germany 748-749
Italy 715-716
Luxembourg 318-320
Netherlands 368-369

Europa, 1958

"E" and Dove CD1

European Postal Union at the service of European integration.

1958, Sept. 13

Belgium 527-528
France 889-890
Germany 790-791
Italy 750-751
Luxembourg 341-343
Netherlands 375-376
Saar 317-318

Europa, 1959

6-Link Endless Chain – CD2

1959, Sept. 19

Belgium 536-537
France 929-930
Germany 805-806
Italy 791-792
Luxembourg 354-355
Netherlands 379-380

Europa, 1960

19-Spoke Wheel – CD3

First anniverary of the establishment of C.E.P.T. (Conference Europeenne des Administrations des Postes et des Telecommunications.)

The spokes symbolize the 19 founding members of the Conference.

1960, Sept.

Belgium 553-554
Denmark 379
Finland 376-377
France 970-971
Germany 818-820
Great Britain 377-378
Greece 688
Iceland 327-328
Ireland 175-176
Italy 809-810
Luxembourg 374-375
Netherlands 385-386
Norway 387
Portugal 866-867
Spain 941-942
Sweden 562-563
Switzerland 400-401
Turkey 1493-1494

Europa, 1961

19 Doves Flying as One – CD4

The 19 doves represent the 19 members of the Conference of European Postal and Telecommunications Administrations C.E.P.T.

1961-62

Belgium 572-573
Cyprus 201-203
France 1005-1006
Germany 844-845
Great Britain 383-384
Greece 718-719
Iceland 340-341
Italy 845-846
Luxembourg 382-383
Netherlands 387-388
Spain 1010-1011
Switzerland 410-411
Turkey 1518-1520

Europa, 1962

Young Tree with 19 Leaves CD5

The 19 leaves represent the 19 original members of C.E.P.T.

1962-63

Belgium 582-583
Cyprus 219-221
France 1045-1046
Germany 852-853
Greece 739-740
Iceland 348-349
Ireland 184-185
Italy 860-861
Luxembourg 386-387
Netherlands 394-395
Norway 414-415
Switzerland 416-417
Turkey 1553-1555

Europa, 1963

Stylized Links, Symbolizing Unity – CD6

1963, Sept.

Belgium 598-599
Cyprus 229-231
Finland 419
France 1074-1075
Germany 867-868
Greece 768-769
Iceland 357-358
Ireland 188-189
Italy 880-881
Luxembourg 403-404
Netherlands 416-417
Norway 441-442
Switzerland 429
Turkey 1602-1603

Europa, 1964

Symbolic Daisy CD7

5th anniversary of the establishment of C.E.P.T. The 22 petals of the flower symbolize the 22 members of the Conference.

1964, Sept.

Austria 738
Belgium 614-615
Cyprus 244-246
France 1109-1110
Germany 897-898
Greece 801-802
Iceland 367-368
Ireland 196-197
Italy 894-895
Luxembourg 411-412
Monaco 590-591
Netherlands 428-429
Norway 458
Portugal 931-933
Spain 1262-1263
Switzerland 438-439
Turkey 1628-1629

Europa, 1965

Leaves and "Fruit" CD8

1965

Belgium 636-637
Cyprus 262-264
Finland 437
France 1131-1132
Germany 934-935
Greece 833-834
Iceland 375-376
Ireland 204-205
Italy 915-916
Luxembourg 432-433
Monaco 616-617
Netherlands 438-439
Norway 475-476
Portugal 958-960
Switzerland 469
Turkey 1665-1666

Europa, 1966

Symbolic Sailboat CD9

1966, Sept.

Andorra, French 172
Belgium 675-676
Cyprus 275-277
France 1163-1164
Germany 963-964
Greece 862-863
Iceland 384-385
Ireland 216-217
Italy 942-943
Liechtenstein 415
Luxembourg 440-441
Monaco 639-640
Netherlands 441-442
Norway 496-497
Portugal 980-982
Switzerland 477-478
Turkey 1718-1719

Europa, 1967

Cogwheels CD10

1967

Andorra, French 174-175
Belgium 688-689
Cyprus 297-299
France 1178-1179
Germany 969-970
Greece 891-892
Iceland 389-390
Ireland 232-233
Italy 951-952
Liechtenstein 420
Luxembourg 449-450
Monaco 669-670
Netherlands 444-447
Norway 504-505
Portugal 994-996
Spain 1465-1466
Switzerland 482
Turkey B120-B121

Europa, 1968

Golden Key with C.E.P.T. Emblem CD11

1968

Andorra, French 182-183
Belgium 705-706
Cyprus 314-316
France 1209-1210
Germany 983-984
Greece 916-917
Iceland 395-396
Ireland 242-243
Italy 979-980
Liechtenstein 442
Luxembourg 466-467
Monaco 689-691
Netherlands 452-453
Portugal 1019-1021
San Marino 687
Spain 1526
Turkey 1775-1776

Europa, 1969

"EUROPA" and "CEPT" – CD12

Tenth anniversary of C.E.P.T.

1969

Andorra, French 188-189
Austria 837
Belgium 718-719
Cyprus 326-328
Denmark 458
Finland 483
France 1245-1246
Germany 996-997
Great Britain 585
Greece 947-948
Iceland 406-407
Ireland 270-271
Italy 1000-1001
Liechtenstein 453
Luxembourg 474-475
Monaco 722-724
Netherlands 475-476
Norway 533-534
Portugal 1038-1040
San Marino 701-702
Spain 1567

Sweden 814-816
Switzerland 500-501
Turkey....1799-1800
Vatican 470-472
Yugoslavia....1003-1004

Europa, 1970

Interwoven Threads CD13

1970

Andorra, French 196-197
Belgium....741-742
Cyprus....340-342
France 1271-1272
Germany 1018-1019
Greece 985, 987
Iceland 420-421
Ireland....279-281
Italy....1013-1014
Liechtenstein....470
Luxembourg....489-490
Monaco....768-770
Netherlands....483-484
Portugal....1060-1062
San Marino....729-730
Spain....1607
Switzerland 515-516
Turkey....1848-1849
Yugoslavia....1024-1025

Europa, 1971

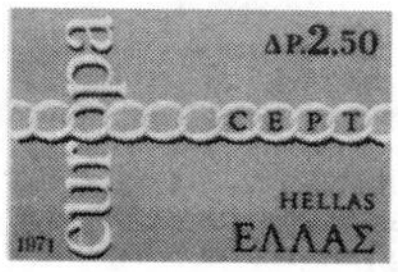

"Fraternity, Cooperation, Common Effort" – CD14

1971

Andorra, French 205-206
Belgium....803-804
Cyprus....365-367
Finland....504
France....1304
Germany 1064-1065
Greece....1029-1030
Iceland 429-430
Ireland....305-306
Italy....1038-1039
Liechtenstein....485
Luxembourg....500-501
Malta....425-427
Monaco....797-799
Netherlands....488-489
Portugal....1094-1096
San Marino....749-750
Spain....1675-1676
Switzerland 531-532
Turkey....1876-1877
Yugoslavia....1052-1053

Europa, 1972

Sparkles, Symbolic of Communications CD15

1972

Andorra, French 210-211
Andorra, Spanish 62
Belgium....825-826
Cyprus....380-382
Finland....512-513
France....1341
Germany 1089-1090
Greece....1049-1050
Iceland 439-440
Ireland....316-317
Italy....1065-1066
Liechtenstein....504
Luxembourg....512-513
Malta....450-453
Monaco....831-832
Netherlands....494-495
Portugal....1141-1143
San Marino....771-772
Spain....1718
Switzerland 544-545
Turkey....1907-1908
Yugoslavia....1100-1101

Europa, 1973

Post Horn and Arrows CD16

1973

Andorra, French 319-320
Andorra, Spanish 76
Belgium....839-840
Cyprus....396-398
Finland....526
France....1367
Germany 1114-1115
Greece....1090-1092
Iceland 447-448
Ireland....329-330
Italy....1108-1109
Liechtenstein....528-529
Luxembourg....523-524
Malta....469-471
Monaco....866-867
Netherlands....504-505
Norway....604-605
Portugal....1170-1172
San Marino....802-803
Spain....1753
Switzerland 580-581
Turkey....1935-1936
Yugoslavia....1138-1139

Europa, 2000

CD17

2000

Albania....2621-2622
Andorra, French....522
Andorra, Spanish....262
Armenia....610-611
Austria....1814
Azerbaijan....698-699
Belarus....350
Belgium....1818
Bosnia & Herzegovina (Moslem)....358
Croatia....428-429
Cyprus....959
Czech Republic....3120
Denmark....1189
Estonia....394
Faroe Islands....376
Finland....1129
Aland Islands....166
France....2771
Georgia....228-229
Germany....2086-2087
Gibraltar....837-840
Great Britain (Guernsey)....805-809
Great Britain (Jersey)....935-936
Great Britain (Isle of Man)....883
Greece....1959
Greenland....363
Hungary....3699-3700
Iceland....910
Ireland....1230-1231
Italy....2349
Latvia....504
Liechtenstein....1178
Lithuania....668
Luxembourg....1035
Macedonia....187
Malta....1011-1012
Moldova....355
Monaco....2161-2162
Poland....3519
Portugal....2358
Portugal (Azores)....455
Portugal (Madeira)....208
Romania....4370
Russia....6589
San Marino....1480
Slovakia....355
Slovenia....424
Spain....3036
Sweden....2394
Switzerland....1074
Turkey....2762
Turkish Republic of Northern Cyprus....500
Ukraine....379
Vatican City....1152

The Gibraltar stamps are similar to the stamp illustrated, but none have the design shown above. All other sets listed above include at least one stamp with the design shown, but some include stamps with entirely different designs. Bulgaria Nos. 4131-4132 are Europa stamps with completely different designs.

PORTUGAL & COLONIES

Vasco da Gama

Fleet Departing CD20

Fleet Arriving at Calicut CD21

Embarking at Rastello CD22

Muse of History – CD23

San Gabriel, da Gama and Camoens – CD24

Archangel Gabriel, the Patron Saint CD25

Flagship San Gabriel CD26

Vasco da Gama CD27

Fourth centenary of Vasco da Gama's discovery of the route to India.

1898

Azores....93-100
Macao....67-74
Madeira....37-44
Portugal....147-154
Port. Africa....1-8
Port. Congo....75-98
Port. India....189-196
St. Thomas & Prince Islands....170-193
Timor....45-52

Pombal

POSTAL TAX

POSTAL TAX DUES

Marquis de Pombal CD28

Planning Reconstruction of Lisbon,1755 CD29

Pombal Monument, Lisbon CD30

Sebastiao Jose de Carvalho e Mello, Marquis de Pombal (1699-1782), statesman, rebuilt Lisbon after earthquake of 1755. Tax was for the erection of Pombal monument. Obligatory on all mail on certain days throughout the year.

Postal Tax Dues are inscribed "Multa."

1925

Angola RA1-RA3, RAJ1-RAJ3
Azores....RA9-RA11, RAJ2-RAJ4
Cape Verde....RA1-RA3, RAJ1-RAJ3
Macao....RA1-RA3, RAJ1-RAJ3
Madeira RA1-RA3, RAJ1-RAJ3
Mozambique....RA1-RA3, RAJ1-RAJ3
Nyassa....RA1-RA3, RAJ1-RAJ3
Portugal RA11-RA13, RAJ2-RAJ4
Port. Guinea....RA1-RA3, RAJ1-RAJ3
Port. India....RA1-RA3, RAJ1-RAJ3
St. Thomas & Prince Islands....RA1-RA3, RAJ1-RAJ3
Timor....RA1-RA3, RAJ1-RAJ3

Vasco da Gama CD34

Mousinho de Albuquerque CD35

Dam CD36

Prince Henry the Navigator – CD37

Affonso de Albuquerque CD38

Plane over Globe CD39

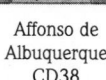

1938-39

Angola	274-291, C1-C9
Cape Verde	234-251, C1-C9
Macao	289-305, C7-C15
Mozambique	270-287, C1-C9
Port. Guinea	233-250. C1-C9
Port. India	439-453, C1-C8
St. Thomas & Prince Islands	302-319, 323-340, C1-C18
Timor	223-239, C1-C9

Lady of Fatima

Our Lady of the Rosary, Fatima, Portugal CD40

1948-49

Angola	315-318
Cape Verde	266
Macao	336
Mozambique	325-328
Port. Guinea	271
Port. India	480
St. Thomas & Prince Islands	351
Timor	254

A souvenir sheet of 9 stamps was issued in 1951 to mark the extension of the 1950 Holy Year. The sheet contains: Angola No. 316, Cape Verde No. 266, Macao No. 336, Mozambique No. 325, Portuguese Guinea No. 271, Portugese India Nos. 480, 485, St. Thomas & Prince Islands No. 351, Timor No. 254.

The sheet also contains a portrait of Pope Pius XII and is inscribed "Encerramento do Ano Santo, Fatima 1951." It was sold for 11 escudos.

Holy Year

Church Bells and Dove CD41

Angel Holding Candelabra CD42

Holy Year, 1950.

1950-51

Angola	331-332
Cape Verde	268-269
Macao	339-340
Mozambique	330-331
Port. Guinea	273-274
Port. India	490-491, 496-503
St. Thomas & Prince Islands	353-354
Timor	258-259

A souvenir sheet of 8 stamps was issued in 1951 to mark the extension of the Holy Year. The sheet contains: Angola No. 331, Cape Verde No. 269, Macao No. 340, Mozambique No. 331, Portuguese Guinea No. 275, Portuguese India No. 490, St. Thomas & Prince Islands No. 354, Timor No. 258, some with colors changed. The sheet contains doves and is inscribed "Encerramento do Ano Santo, Fatima 1951." It was sold for 17 escudos.

Holy Year Conclusion

Our Lady of Fatima CD43

Conclusion of Holy Year. Sheets contain alternate vertical rows of stamps and labels bearing quotation from Pope Pius XII, different for each colony.

1951

Angola	357
Cape Verde	270
Macao	352
Mozambique	356
Port. Guinea	275
Port. India	506
St. Thomas & Prince Islands	355
Timor	270

Medical Congress

CD44

First National Congress of Tropical Medicine, Lisbon, 1952.

Each stamp has a different design.

1952

Angola	358
Cape Verde	287
Macao	364
Mozambique	359
Port. Guinea	276
Port. India	516
St. Thomas & Prince Islands	356
Timor	271

POSTAGE DUE STAMPS

CD45

1952

Angola	J37-J42
Cape Verde	J31-J36
Macao	J53-J58
Mozambique	J51-J56
Port. Guinea	J40-J45
Port. India	J47-J52
St. Thomas & Prince Islands	J52-J57
Timor	J31-J36

Sao Paulo

Father Manuel de Nobrega and View of Sao Paulo CD46

Founding of Sao Paulo, Brazil, 400th anniv.

1954

Angola	385
Cape Verde	297
Macao	382
Mozambique	395
Port. Guinea	291
Port. India	530
St. Thomas & Prince Islands	369
Timor	279

Tropical Medicine Congress

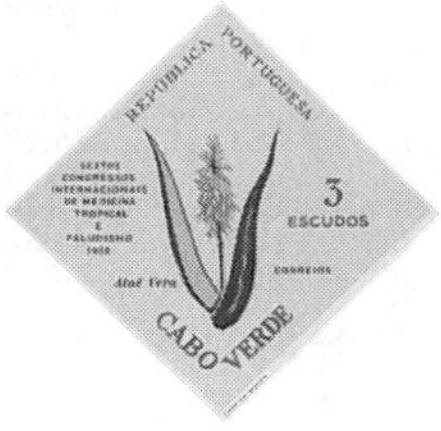

CD47

Sixth International Congress for Tropical Medicine and Malaria, Lisbon, Sept. 1958.

Each stamp shows a different plant.

1958

Angola	409
Cape Verde	303
Macao	392
Mozambique	404
Port. Guinea	295
Port. India	569
St. Thomas & Prince Islands	371
Timor	289

Sports

CD48

Each stamp shows a different sport.

1962

Angola	433-438
Cape Verde	320-325
Macao	394-399
Mozambique	424-429
Port. Guinea	299-304
St. Thomas & Prince Islands	374-379
Timor	313-318

Anti-Malaria

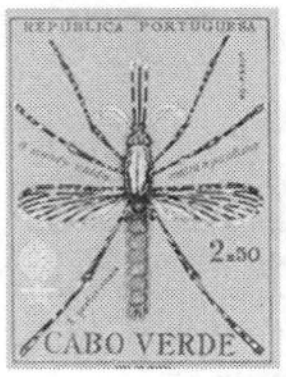

Anopheles Funestus and Malaria Eradication Symbol CD49

World Health Organization drive to eradicate malaria.

1962

Angola	439
Cape Verde	326
Macao	400
Mozambique	430
Port. Guinea	305
St. Thomas & Prince Islands	380
Timor	319

Airline Anniversary

Map of Africa, Super Constellation and Jet Liner CD50

Tenth anniversary of Transportes Aereos Portugueses (TAP).

1963

Angola	490
Cape Verde	327
Mozambique	434
Port. Guinea	318
St. Thomas & Prince Islands	381

National Overseas Bank

Antonio Teixeira de Sousa CD51

Centenary of the National Overseas Bank of Portugal.

1964, May 16

Angola	509
Cape Verde	328
Port. Guinea	319
St. Thomas & Prince Islands	382
Timor	320

ITU

ITU Emblem and the archangel Gabriel CD52

International Communications Union, Cent.

1965, May 17

Angola	511
Cape Verde	329
Macao	402
Mozambique	464
Port. Guinea	320
St. Thomas & Prince Islands	383
Timor	321

National Revolution

CD53

40th anniv. of the National Revolution.

Different buildings on each stamp.

1966, May 28

Angola	525
Cape Verde	338
Macao	403
Mozambique	465
Port. Guinea	329
St. Thomas & Prince Islands	392
Timor	322

Navy Club

CD54

Centenary of Portugal's Navy Club.

Each stamp has a different design.

1967, Jan. 31

Angola	527-528
Cape Verde	339-340
Macao	412-413
Mozambique	478-479
Port. Guinea	330-331
St. Thomas & Prince Islands	393-394
Timor	323-324

Admiral Coutinho

CD55

Centenary of the birth of Admiral Carlos Viegas Gago Coutinho (1869-1959), explorer and aviation pioneer.

Each stamp has a different design.

1969, Feb. 17

Angola	547
Cape Verde	355
Macao	417
Mozambique	484
Port. Guinea	335
St. Thomas & Prince Islands	397
Timor	335

Administration Reform

Luiz Augusto Rebello da Silva CD 56

Centenary of the administration reforms of the overseas territories.

1969, Sept. 25

Angola	549
Cape Verde	357
Macao	419
Mozambique	491
Port. Guinea	337
St. Thomas & Prince Islands	399
Timor	338

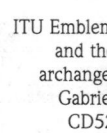

Marshal Carmona

CD57

Birth centenary of Marshal Antonio Oscar Carmona de Fragoso (1869-1951), President of Portugal.

Each stamp has a different design.

1970, Nov. 15

Angola	563
Cape Verde	359
Macao	422
Mozambique	493
Port. Guinea	340
St. Thomas & Prince Islands	403
Timor	341

Olympic Games

CD59

20th Olympic Games, Munich, Aug. 26-Sept. 11.

Each stamp shows a different sport.

1972, June 20

Angola	569
Cape Verde	361
Macao	426
Mozambique	504
Port. Guinea	342
St. Thomas & Prince Islands	408
Timor	343

Lisbon-Rio de Janeiro Flight

CD60

50th anniversary of the Lisbon to Rio de Janeiro flight by Arturo de Sacadura and Coutinho, March 30-June 5, 1922.

Each stamp shows a different stage of the flight.

1972, Sept. 20

Angola	570
Cape Verde	362
Macao	427
Mozambique	505
Port. Guinea	343
St. Thomas & Prince Islands	409
Timor	344

WMO Centenary

WMO Emblem
CD61

Centenary of international meterological cooperation.

1973, Dec. 15

Angola	571
Cape Verde	363
Macao	429
Mozambique	509
Port. Guinea	344
St. Thomas & Prince Islands	410
Timor	345

FRENCH COMMUNITY

Upper Volta can be found under Burkina Faso in Vol. 1

Madagascar can be found under Malagasy in Vol. 3

Colonial Exposition

People of French Empire CD70

Women's Heads CD71

France Showing Way to Civilization CD72

"Colonial Commerce" CD73

International Colonial Exposition, Paris.

1931

Cameroun	213-216
Chad	60-63
Dahomey	97-100
Fr. Guiana	152-155
Fr. Guinea	116-119
Fr. India	100-103
Fr. Polynesia	76-79
Fr. Sudan	102-105
Gabon	120-123
Guadeloupe	138-141
Indo-China	140-142
Ivory Coast	92-95
Madagascar	169-172
Martinique	129-132
Mauritania	65-68
Middle Congo	61-64
New Caledonia	176-179
Niger	73-76
Reunion	122-125
St. Pierre & Miquelon	132-135
Senegal	138-141
Somali Coast	135-138
Togo	254-257
Ubangi-Shari	82-85
Upper Volta	66-69
Wallis & Futuna Isls.	85-88

Paris International Exposition Colonial Arts Exposition

"Colonial Resources"
CD74 CD77

Overseas Commerce – CD75

Exposition Building and Women CD76

"France and the Empire" CD78

Cultural Treasures of the Colonies CD79

Souvenir sheets contain one imperf. stamp.

1937

Cameroun	217-222A
Dahomey	101-107
Fr. Equatorial Africa	27-32, 73
Fr. Guiana	162-168
Fr. Guinea	120-126
Fr. India	104-110
Fr. Polynesia	117-123
Fr. Sudan	106-112
Guadeloupe	148-154
Indo-China	193-199
Inini	41
Ivory Coast	152-158
Kwangchowan	132
Madagascar	191-197
Martinique	179-185
Mauritania	69-75
New Caledonia	208-214
Niger	72-83
Reunion	167-173
St. Pierre & Miquelon	165-171
Senegal	172-178
Somali Coast	139-145
Togo	258-264
Wallis & Futuna Isls.	89

Curie

Pierre and Marie Curie CD80

40th anniversary of the discovery of radium. The surtax was for the benefit of the Intl. Union for the Control of Cancer.

1938

Cameroun	B1
Cuba	B1-B2
Dahomey	B2
France	B76
Fr. Equatorial Africa	B1
Fr. Guiana	B3
Fr. Guinea	B2
Fr. India	B6
Fr. Polynesia	B5
Fr. Sudan	B1
Guadeloupe	B3
Indo-China	B14
Ivory Coast	B2
Madagascar	B2
Martinique	B2
Mauritania	B3
New Caledonia	B4
Niger	B1
Reunion	B4
St. Pierre & Miquelon	B3
Senegal	B3
Somali Coast	B2
Togo	B1

Caillie

Rene Caille and Map of Northwestern Africa - CD81

Death centenary of Rene Caillie (1799-1838), French explorer.

All three denominations exist with colony name omitted.

1939

Dahomey	108-110
Fr. Guinea	161-163
Fr. Sudan	113-115
Ivory Coast	160-162
Mauritania	109-111
Niger	84-86
Senegal	188-190
Togo	265-267

New York World's Fair

Natives and New York Skyline CD82

1939

Cameroun	223-224
Dahomey	111-112
Fr. Equatorial Africa	78-79
Fr. Guiana	169-170
Fr. Guinea	164-165
Fr. India	111-112
Fr. Polynesia	124-125
Fr. Sudan	116-117
Guadeloupe	155-156
Indo-China	203-204
Inini	42-43
Ivory Coast	163-164
Kwangchowan	121-122
Madagascar	209-210
Martinique	186-187
Mauritania	112-113
New Caledonia	215-216
Niger	87-88
Reunion	174-175
St. Pierre & Miquelon	205-206
Senegal	191-192
Somali Coast	179-180
Togo	268-269
Wallis & Futuna Isls.	90-91

French Revolution

Storming of the Bastille – CD83

French Revolution, 150th anniv. The surtax was for the defense of the colonies.

1939

Cameroun	B2-B6
Dahomey	B3-B7
Fr. Equatorial Africa	B4-B8, CB1
Fr. Guiana	B4-B8, CB1
Fr. Guinea	B3-B7
Fr. India	B7-B11
Fr. Polynesia	B6-B10, CB1
Fr. Sudan	B2-B6
Guadeloupe	B4-B8
Indo-China	B15-B19, CB1
Inini	B1-B5
Ivory Coast	B3-B7
Kwangchowan	B1-B5
Madagascar	B3-B7, CB1
Martinique	B3-B7
Mauritania	B4-B8
New Caledonia	B5-B9, CB1
Niger	B2-B6
Reunion	B5-B9, CB1
St. Pierre & Miquelon	B4-B8
Senegal	B4-B8, CB1
Somali Coast	B3-B7
Togo	B2-B6
Wallis & Futuna Isls.	B1-B5

Plane over Coastal Area CD85

All five denominations exist with colony name omitted.

1940

Dahomey	C1-C5
Fr. Guinea	C1-C5
Fr. Sudan	C1-C5
Ivory Coast	C1-C5
Mauritania	C1-C5
Niger	C1-C5
Senegal	C12-C16
Togo	C1-C5

Colonial Infantryman CD86

1941

Cameroun	B13B
Dahomey	B13
Fr. Equatorial Africa	B8B
Fr. Guiana	B10
Fr. Guinea	B13
Fr. India	B13
Fr. Polynesia	B12
Fr. Sudan	B12
Guadeloupe	B10
Indo-China	B19B
Inini	B7
Ivory Coast	B13
Kwangchowan	B7
Madagascar	B9
Martinique	B9
Mauritania	B14
New Caledonia	B11
Niger	B12
Reunion	B11
St. Pierre & Miquelon	B8B
Senegal	B14
Somali Coast	B9
Togo	B10B
Wallis & Futuna Isls.	B7

Cross of Lorraine & Four-motor Plane CD87

1941-5

Cameroun	C1-C7
Fr. Equatorial Africa	C17-C23
Fr. Guiana	C9-C10
Fr. India	C1-C6
Fr. Polynesia	C3-C9
Fr. West Africa	C1-C3
Guadeloupe	C1-C2
Madagascar	C37-C43
Martinique	C1-C2
New Caledonia	C7-C13
Reunion	C18-C24
St. Pierre & Miquelon	C1-C7
Somali Coast	C1-C7

Transport Plane CD88

Caravan and Plane CD89

1942

Dahomey	C6-C13
Fr. Guinea	C6-C13
Fr. Sudan	C6-C13
Ivory Coast	C6-C13
Mauritania	C6-C13
Niger	C6-C13
Senegal	C17-C25
Togo	C6-C13

Red Cross

Marianne CD90

The surtax was for the French Red Cross and national relief.

1944

Cameroun	B28
Fr. Equatorial Africa	B38
Fr. Guiana	B12
Fr. India	B14
Fr. Polynesia	B13
Fr. West Africa	B1
Guadeloupe	B12
Madagascar	B15
Martinique	B11
New Caledonia	B13
Reunion	B15
St. Pierre & Miquelon	B13
Somali Coast	B13
Wallis & Futuna Isls.	B9

Eboue

CD91

Felix Eboue, first French colonial administrator to proclaim resistance to Germany after French surrender in World War II.

1945

Cameroun	296-297
Fr. Equatorial Africa	156-157
Fr. Guiana	171-172
Fr. India	210-211
Fr. Polynesia	150-151
Fr. West Africa	15-16
Guadeloupe	187-188
Madagascar	259-260
Martinique	196-197
New Caledonia	274-275
Reunion	238-239
St. Pierre & Miquelon	322-323
Somali Coast	238-239

Victory

Victory – CD92

European victory of the Allied Nations in World War II.

1946, May 8

Cameroun	C8
Fr. Equatorial Africa	C24
Fr. Guiana	C11
Fr. India	C7
Fr. Polynesia	C10
Fr. West Africa	C4
Guadeloupe	C3
Indo-China	C19
Madagascar	C44
Martinique	C3
New Caledonia	C14
Reunion	C25
St. Pierre & Miquelon	C8
Somali Coast	C8
Wallis & Futuna Isls.	C1

Chad to Rhine

Leclerc's Departure from Chad – CD93

Battle at Cufra Oasis – CD94

Tanks in Action, Mareth – CD95

Normandy Invasion – CD96

Entering Paris – CD97

Liberation of Strasbourg – CD98

"Chad to the Rhine" march, 1942-44, by Gen. Jacques Leclerc's column, later French 2nd Armored Division.

1946, June 6

Cameroun	C9-C14
Fr. Equatorial Africa	C25-C30
Fr. Guiana	C12-C17
Fr. India	C8-C13
Fr. Polynesia	C11-C16
Fr. West Africa	C5-C10
Guadeloupe	C4-C9
Indo-China	C20-C25
Madagascar	C45-C50
Martinique	C4-C9
New Caledonia	C15-C20
Reunion	C26-C31
St. Pierre & Miquelon	C9-C14
Somali Coast	C9-C14
Wallis & Futuna Isls.	C2-C7

UPU

French Colonials, Globe and Plane CD99

Universal Postal Union, 75th anniv.

1949, July 4

Cameroun	C29
Fr. Equatorial Africa	C34
Fr. India	C17
Fr. Polynesia	C20
Fr. West Africa	C15
Indo-China	C26
Madagascar	C55
New Caledonia	C24
St. Pierre & Miquelon	C18
Somali Coast	C18
Togo	C18
Wallis & Futuna Isls.	C10

Tropical Medicine

Doctor Treating Infant CD100

The surtax was for charitable work.

1950

Cameroun	B29
Fr. Equatorial Africa	B39
Fr. India	B15
Fr. Polynesia	B14
Fr. West Africa	B3
Madagascar	B17
New Caledonia	B14
St. Pierre & Miquelon	B14
Somali Coast	B14
Togo	B11

Military Medal

Medal, Early Marine and Colonial Soldier CD101

Centenary of the creation of the French Military Medal.

1952

Cameroun	332
Comoro Isls.	39
Fr. Equatorial Africa	186
Fr. India	233
Fr. Polynesia	179
Fr. West Africa	57
Madagascar	286
New Caledonia	295
St. Pierre & Miquelon	345
Somali Coast	267
Togo	327
Wallis & Futuna Isls.	149

Liberation

Allied Landing, Victory Sign and Cross of Lorraine – CD102

Lberation of France, 10th anniv.

1954, June 6

Cameroun	C32
Comoro Isls.	C4
Fr. Equatorial Africa	C38
Fr. India	C18
Fr. Polynesia	C22
Fr. West Africa	C17
Madagascar	C57
New Caledonia	C25
St. Pierre & Miquelon	C19
Somali Coast	C19
Togo	C19
Wallis & Futuna Isls.	C11

FIDES

Plowmen CD103

Efforts of FIDES, the Economic and Social Development Fund for Overseas Possessions (Fonds d' Investissement pour le Developpement Economique et Social).

Each stamp has a different design.

1956

Cameroun	326-329
Comoro Isls.	43
Fr. Polynesia	181
Fr. West Africa	65-72
Madagascar	292-295
New Caledonia	303
Somali Coast	268
Togo	331

Flower

CD104

Each stamp shows a different flower.

1958-9

Cameroun	333
Comoro Isls.	45
Fr. Equatorial Africa	200-201
Fr. Polynesia	192
Fr. So. & Antarctic Terr.	11
Fr. West Africa	79-83
Madagascar	301-302

New Caledonia....304-305
St. Pierre & Miquelon....357
Somali Coast....270
Togo....348-349
Wallis & Futuna Isls....152

Human Rights

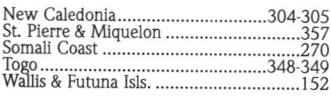

Sun, Dove and U.N. Emblem – CD105

10th anniversary of the signing of the Universal Declaration of Human Rights.

1958
Comoro Isls....44
Fr. Equatorial Africa....202
Fr. Polynesia....191
Fr. West Africa....85
Madagascar....300
New Caledonia....306
St. Pierre & Miquelon....356
Somali Coast....274
Wallis & Futuna Isls....153

C.C.T.A.

CD106

Commission for Technical Cooperation in Africa south of the Sahara, 10th anniv.

1960
Cameroun....335
Cent. Africa....3
Chad....66
Congo, P.R....90
Dahomey....138
Gabon....150
Ivory Coast....180
Madagascar....317
Mali....9
Mauritania....117
Niger....104
Upper Volta....89

Air Afrique, 1961

Modern and Ancient Africa, Map and Planes – CD107

Founding of Air Afrique (African Airlines).

1961-62
Cameroun....C37
Cent. Africa....C5
Chad....C7
Congo, P.R....C5
Dahomey....C17
Gabon....C5
Ivory Coast....C18
Mauritania....C17
Niger....C22
Senegal....C31
Upper Volta....C4

Anti-Malaria

CD108

World Health Organization drive to eradicate malaria.

1962, Apr. 7
Cameroun....B36
Cent. Africa....B1
Chad....B1
Comoro Isls....B1
Congo, P.R....B3
Dahomey....B15
Gabon....B4
Ivory Coast....B15
Madagascar....B19
Mali....B1
Mauritania....B16
Niger....B14
Senegal....B16
Somali Coast....B15
Upper Volta....B1

Abidjan Games

CD109

Abidjan Games, Ivory Coast, Dec. 24-31, 1961. Each stamp shows a different sport.

1962
Chad....83-84
Cent. Africa....19-20
Congo, P.R....103-104
Gabon....163-164, C6
Niger....109-111
Upper Volta....103-105

African and Malagasy Union

Flag of Union CD110

First anniversary of the Union.

1962, Sept. 8
Cameroun....373
Cent. Africa....21
Chad....85
Congo, P.R....105
Dahomey....155
Gabon....165
Ivory Coast....198
Madagascar....332
Mauritania....170
Niger....112
Senegal....211
Upper Volta....106

Telstar

Telstar and Globe Showing Andover and Pleumeur-Bodou – CD111

First television connection of the United States and Europe through the Telstar satellite, July 11-12, 1962.

1962-63
Andorra, French....154
Comoro Isls....C7
Fr. Polynesia....C29
Fr. So. & Antarctic Terr....C5
New Caledonia....C33
Somali Coast....C31
St. Pierre & Miquelon....C26
Wallis & Futuna Isls....C17

Freedom From Hunger

World Map and Wheat Emblem CD112

U.N. Food and Agriculture Organization's "Freedom from Hunger" campaign.

1963, Mar. 21
Cameroun....B37-B38
Cent. Africa....B2
Chad....B2
Congo, P.R....B4
Dahomey....B16
Gabon....B5
Ivory Coast....B16
Madagascar....B21
Mauritania....B17
Niger....B15
Senegal....B17
Upper Volta....B2

Red Cross Centenary

CD113

Centenary of the International Red Cross.

1963, Sept. 2
Comoro Isls....55
Fr. Polynesia....205
New Caledonia....328
St. Pierre & Miquelon....367
Somali Coast....297
Wallis & Futuna Isls....165

African Postal Union, 1963

UAMPT Emblem, Radio Masts, Plane and Mail CD114

Establishment of the African and Malagasy Posts and Telecommunications Union.

1963, Sept. 8
Cameroun....C47
Cent. Africa....C10
Chad....C9
Congo, P.R....C13
Dahomey....C19
Gabon....C13
Ivory Coast....C25
Madagascar....C75
Mauritania....C22
Niger....C27
Rwanda....36
Senegal....C32
Upper Volta....C9

Air Afrique, 1963

Symbols of Flight – CD115

First anniversary of Air Afrique and inauguration of DC-8 service.

1963, Nov. 19
Cameroun....C48
Chad....C10
Congo, P.R....C14
Gabon....C18
Ivory Coast....C26
Mauritania....C26
Niger....C35
Senegal....C33

Europafrica

Europe and Africa Linked CD116

Signing of an economic agreement between the European Economic Community and the African and Malagasy Union, Yaounde, Cameroun, July 20, 1963.

1963-64
Cameroun....402
Chad....C11
Cent. Africa....C12
Congo, P.R....C16
Gabon....C19
Ivory Coast....217
Niger....C43
Upper Volta....C11

Human Rights

Scales of Justice and Globe CD117

15th anniversary of the Universal Declaration of Human Rights.

1963, Dec. 10
Comoro Isls....58
Fr. Polynesia....206
New Caledonia....329
St. Pierre & Miquelon....368
Somali Coast....300
Wallis & Futuna Isls....166

PHILATEC

Stamp Album, Champs Elysees Palace and Horses of Marly – CD118

Intl. Philatelic and Postal Techniques Exhibition, Paris, June 5-21, 1964.

1963-64
Comoro Isls....60
France....1078
Fr. Polynesia....207
New Caledonia....341
St. Pierre & Miquelon....369
Somali Coast....301
Wallis & Futuna Isls....167

Cooperation

CD119

Cooperation between France and the French-speaking countries of Africa and Madagascar.

1964

Cameroun	409-410
Cent. Africa	39
Chad	103
Congo, P.R.	121
Dahomey	193
France	1111
Gabon	175
Ivory Coast	221
Madagascar	360
Mauritania	181
Niger	143
Senegal	236
Togo	495

ITU

Telegraph, Syncom Satellite and ITU Emblem CD120

Intl. Telecommunication Union, Cent.

1965, May 17

Comoro Isls.	C14
Fr. Polynesia	C33
Fr. So. & Antarctic Terr.	C8
New Caledonia	C40
New Hebrides	124-125
St. Pierre & Miquelon	C29
Somali Coast	C36
Wallis & Futuna Isls.	C20

French Satellite A-1

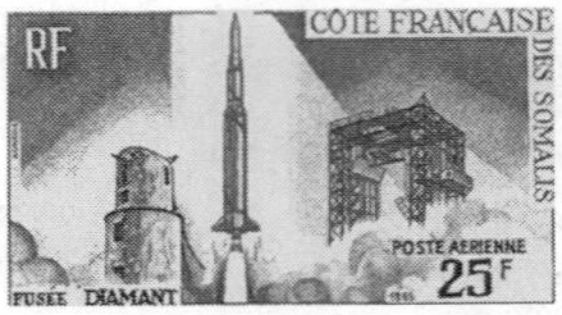

Diamant Rocket and Launching Installation – CD121

Launching of France's first satellite, Nov. 26, 1965.

1965-66

Comoro Isls.	C15-C16
France	1137-1138
Fr. Polynesia	C40-C41
Fr. So. & Antarctic Terr.	C9-C10
New Caledonia	C44-C45
St. Pierre & Miquelon	C30-C31
Somali Coast	C39-C40
Wallis & Futuna Isls.	C22-C23

French Satellite D-1

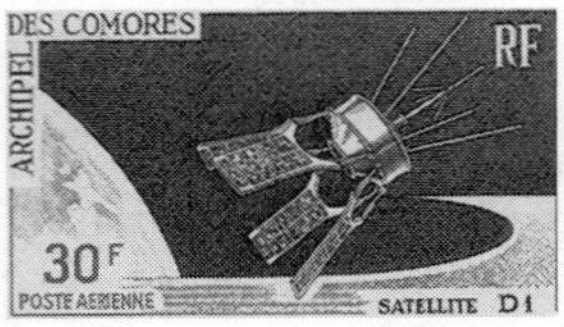

D-1 Satellite in Orbit – CD122

Launching of the D-1 satellite at Hammaguir, Algeria, Feb. 17, 1966.

1966

Comoro Isls.	C17
France	1148
Fr. Polynesia	C42
Fr. So. & Antarctic Terr.	C11
New Caledonia	C46
St. Pierre & Miquelon	C32
Somali Coast	C49
Wallis & Futuna Isls.	C24

Air Afrique, 1966

Planes and Air Afrique Emblem – CD123

Introduction of DC-8F planes by Air Afrique.

1966

Cameroun	C79
Cent. Africa	C35
Chad	C26
Congo, P.R.	C42
Dahomey	C42
Gabon	C47
Ivory Coast	C32
Mauritania	C57
Niger	C63
Senegal	C47
Togo	C54
Upper Volta	C31

African Postal Union, 1967

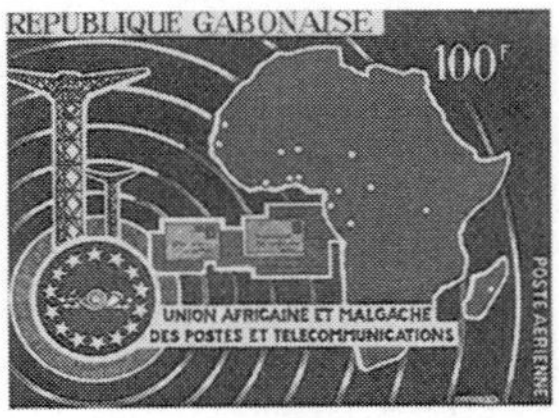

Telecommunications Symbols and Map of Africa – CD124

Fifth anniversary of the establishment of the African and Malagasy Union of Posts and Telecommunications, UAMPT.

1967

Cameroun	C90
Cent. Africa	C46
Chad	C37
Congo, P.R.	C57
Dahomey	C61
Gabon	C58
Ivory Coast	C34
Madagascar	C85
Mauritania	C65
Niger	C75
Rwanda	C1-C3
Senegal	C60
Togo	C81
Upper Volta	C50

Monetary Union

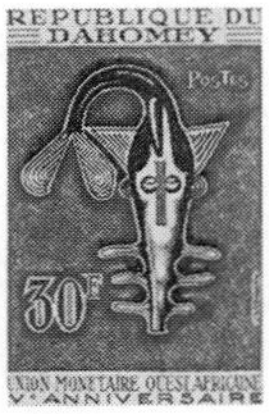

Gold Token of the Ashantis, 17-18th Centuries CD125

West African Monetary Union, 5th anniv.

1967, Nov. 4

Dahomey	244
Ivory Coast	259
Mauritania	238
Niger	204
Senegal	294
Togo	623
Upper Volta	181

WHO Anniversary

Sun, Flowers and WHO Emblem CD126

World Health Organization, 20th anniv.

1968, May 4

Afars & Issas	317
Comoro Isls.	73
Fr. Polynesia	241-242
Fr. So. & Antarctic Terr.	31
New Caledonia	367
St. Pierre & Miquelon	377
Wallis & Futuna Isls.	169

Human Rights Year

Human Rights Flame CD127

1968, Aug. 10

Afars & Issas	322-323
Comoro Isls.	76
Fr. Polynesia	243-244
Fr. So. & Antarctic Terr.	32
New Caledonia	369
St. Pierre & Miquelon	382
Wallis & Futuna Isls.	170

2nd PHILEXAFRIQUE

CD128

Opening of PHILEXAFRIQUE, Abidjan, Feb. 14. Each stamp shows a local scene and stamp.

1969, Feb. 14

Cameroun	C118
Cent. Africa	C65
Chad	C48
Congo, P.R.	C77
Dahomey	C94
Gabon	C82
Ivory Coast	C38-C40
Madagascar	C92
Mali	C65
Mauritania	C80
Niger	C104
Senegal	C68
Togo	C104
Upper Volta	C62

Concorde

Concorde in Flight CD129

First flight of the prototype Concorde supersonic plane at Toulouse, Mar. 1, 1969.

1969

Afars & Issas	C56
Comoro Isls.	C29
France	C42
Fr. Polynesia	C50
Fr. So. & Antarctic Terr.	C18
New Caledonia	C63
St. Pierre & Miquelon	C40
Wallis & Futuna Isls.	C30

Development Bank

Bank Emblem CD130

African Development Bank, fifth anniv.

1969

Cameroun	499
Chad	217
Congo, P.R.	181-182
Ivory Coast	281
Mali	127-128
Mauritania	267
Niger	220
Senegal	317-318
Upper Volta	201

ILO

ILO Headquarters, Geneva, and Emblem – CD131

Intl. Labor Organization, 50th anniv.

1969-70

Afars & Issas	337
Comoro Isls.	83
Fr. Polynesia	251-252
Fr. So. & Antarctic Terr.	35
New Caledonia	379
St. Pierre & Miquelon	396
Wallis & Futuna Isls.	172

ASECNA

Map of Africa, Plane and Airport – CD132

10th anniversary of the Agency for the Security of Aerial Navigation in Africa and Madagascar (ASECNA, Agence pour la Securite de la Navigation Aerienne en Afrique et a Madagascar).

1969-70

Cameroun	500
Cent. Africa	119
Chad	222
Congo, P.R.	197
Dahomey	269
Gabon	260
Ivory Coast	287
Mali	130
Niger	221
Senegal	321
Upper Volta	204

U.P.U. Headquarters

CD133

New Universal Postal Union headquarters, Bern, Switzerland.

1970

Afars & Issas	342
Algeria	443
Cameroun	503-504
Cent. Africa	125
Chad	225
Comoro Isls.	84
Congo, P.R.	216
Fr. Polynesia	261-262
Fr. So. & Antarctic Terr.	36
Gabon	258
Ivory Coast	295
Madagascar	444
Mali	134-135
Mauritania	283
New Caledonia	382
Niger	231-232
St. Pierre & Miquelon	397-398
Senegal	328-329
Tunisia	535
Wallis & Futuna Isls.	173

De Gaulle

CD134

First anniversary of the death of Charles de Gaulle, (1890-1970), President of France.

1971-72

Afars & Issas 356-357
Comoro Isls. 104-105
France 1322-1325
Fr. Polynesia 270-271
Fr. So. & Antarctic Terr. 52-53
New Caledonia 393-394
Reunion 377, 380
St. Pierre & Miquelon 417-418
Wallis & Futuna Isls. 177-178

African Postal Union, 1971

UAMPT Building, Brazzaville, Congo – CD135

10th anniversary of the establishment of the African and Malagasy Posts and Telecommunications Union, UAMPT.

Each stamp has a different native design.

1971, Nov. 13

Cameroun C177
Cent. Africa C89
Chad C94
Congo, P.R. C136
Dahomey C146
Gabon C120
Ivory Coast C47
Mauritania C113
Niger C164
Rwanda C8
Senegal C105
Togo C166
Upper Volta C97

West African Monetary Union

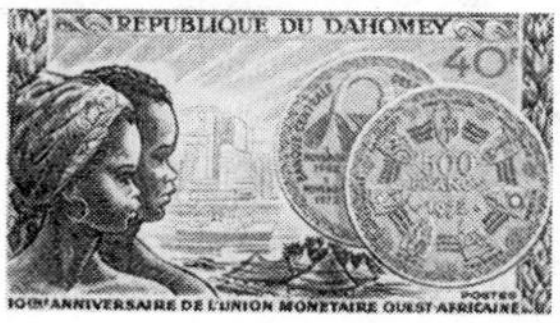

African Couple, City, Village and Commemorative Coin – CD136

West African Monetary Union, 10th anniv.

1972, Nov. 2

Dahomey 300
Ivory Coast 331
Mauritania 299
Niger 258
Senegal 374
Togo 825
Upper Volta 280

African Postal Union, 1973

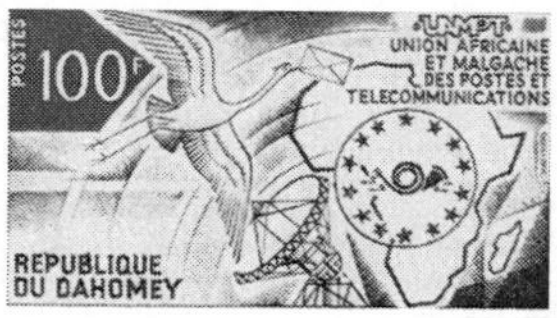

Telecommunications Symbols and Map of Africa – CD137

11th anniversary of the African and Malagasy Posts and Telecommunications Union (UAMPT).

1973, Sept. 12

Cameroun 574
Cent. Africa 194
Chad 294
Congo, P.R. 289
Dahomey 311
Gabon 320
Ivory Coast 361
Madagascar 500
Mauritania 304
Niger 287
Rwanda 540
Senegal 393
Togo 849
Upper Volta 297

Philexafrique II — Essen

CD138

CD139

Designs: Indigenous fauna, local and German stamps.

Types CD138-CD139 printed horizontally and vertically se-tenant in sheets of 10 (2x5). Label between horizontal pairs alternately commemoratives Philexafrique II, Libreville, Gabon, June 1978, and 2nd International Stamp Fair, Essen, Germany, Nov. 1-5.

1978-1979

Benin C285-C286
Central Africa C200-C201
Chad C238-C239
Congo Republic C245-C246
Djibouti C121-C122
Gabon C215-C216
Ivory Coast C64-C65
Mali C356-C357
Mauritania C185-C186
Niger C291-C292
Rwanda C12-C13
Senegal C146-C147
Togo C363-C364
Upper Volta C253-C254

BRITISH COMMONWEALTH OF NATIONS

The listings follow established trade practices when these issues are offered as units by dealers. The Peace issue, for example, includes only one stamp from the Indian state of Hyderabad. The U.P.U. issue includes the Egypt set. Pairs are included for those varieties issues with bilingual designs se-tenant.

Silver Jubilee

Windsor Castle and King George V CD301

Reign of King George V, 25th anniv.

1935

Antigua 77-80
Ascension 33-36
Bahamas 92-95
Barbados 186-189
Basutoland 11-14
Bechuanaland Protectorate 117-120
Bermuda 100-103
British Guiana 223-226
British Honduras 108-111
Cayman Islands 81-84
Ceylon 260-263
Cyprus 136-139
Dominica 90-93
Falkland Islands 77-80
Fiji 110-113
Gambia 125-128
Gibraltar 100-103
Gilbert & Ellice Islands 33-36
Gold Coast 108-111
Grenada 124-127
Hong Kong 147-150
Jamaica 109-112
Kenya, Uganda, Tanganyika 42-45
Leeward Islands 96-99
Malta 184-187
Mauritius 204-207
Montserrat 85-88
Newfoundland 226-229
Nigeria 34-37
Northern Rhodesia 18-21
Nyasaland Protectorate 47-50
St. Helena 111-114
St. Kitts-Nevis 72-75
St. Lucia 91-94
St. Vincent 134-137
Seychelles 118-121
Sierra Leone 166-169
Solomon Islands 60-63
Somaliland Protectorate 77-80
Straits Settlements 213-216
Swaziland 20-23
Trinidad & Tobago 43-46
Turks & Caicos Islands 71-74
Virgin Islands 69-72

The following have different designs but are included in the omnibus set:

Great Britain 226-229
Offices in Morocco 67-70, 226-229, 422-425, 508-510
Australia 152-154
Canada 211-216
Cook Islands 98-100
India 142-148
Nauru 31-34
New Guinea 46-47
New Zealand 199-201
Niue 67-69
Papua 114-117
Samoa 163-165
South Africa 68-71
Southern Rhodesia 33-36
South-West Africa 121-124
249 stamps

Coronation

Queen Elizabeth and King George VI CD302

1937

Aden 13-15
Antigua 81-83
Ascension 37-39
Bahamas 97-99
Barbados 190-192
Basutoland 15-17
Bechuanaland Protectorate 121-123
Bermuda 115-117
British Guiana 227-229
British Honduras 112-114
Cayman Islands 97-99
Ceylon 275-277
Cyprus 140-142
Dominica 94-96
Falkland Islands 81-83
Fiji 114-116
Gambia 129-131
Gibraltar 104-106
Gilbert & Ellice Islands 37-39
Gold Coast 112-114
Grenada 128-130
Hong Kong 151-153
Jamaica 113-115
Kenya, Uganda, Tanganyika 60-62
Leeward Islands 100-102
Malta 188-190
Mauritius 208-210
Montserrat 89-91
Newfoundland 230-232
Nigeria 50-52
Northern Rhodesia 22-24
Nyasaland Protectorate 51-53
St. Helena 115-117
St. Kitts-Nevis 76-78
St. Lucia 107-109
St. Vincent 138-140
Seychelles 122-124
Sierra Leone 170-172
Solomon Islands 64-66
Somaliland Protectorate 81-83
Straits Settlements 235-237
Swaziland 24-26
Trinidad & Tobago 47-49
Turks & Caicos Islands 75-77
Virgin Islands 73-75

The following have different designs but are included in the omnibus set:

Great Britain 234
Offices in Morocco 82, 439, 514
Canada 237
Cook Islands 109-111
Nauru 35-38
Newfoundland 233-243
New Guinea 48-51
New Zealand 223-225
Niue 70-72
Papua 118-121
South Africa 74-78
Southern Rhodesia 38-41
South-West Africa 125-132
202 stamps

Peace

King George VI and Parliament Buildings, London – CD303

Return to peace at the close of World War II.

1945-46

Aden 28-29
Antigua 96-97
Ascension 50-51
Bahamas 130-131
Barbados 207-208
Bermuda 131-132
British Guiana 242-243
British Honduras 127-128
Cayman Islands 112-113
Ceylon 293-294
Cyprus 156-157
Dominica 112-113
Falkland Islands 97-98
Falkland Islands Dep. 1L9-1L10
Fiji 137-138
Gambia 144-145
Gibraltar 119-120
Gilbert & Ellice Islands 52-53
Gold Coast 128-129
Grenada 143-144
Jamaica 136-137
Kenya, Uganda, Tanganyika 90-91
Leeward Islands 116-117
Malta 206-207
Mauritius 223-224
Montserrat 104-105
Nigeria 71-72
Northern Rhodesia 46-47
Nyasaland Protectorate 82-83
Pitcairn Island 9-10
St. Helena 128-129
St. Kitts-Nevis 91-92
St. Lucia 127-128
St. Vincent 152-153
Seychelles 149-150
Sierra Leone 186-187
Solomon Islands 80-81
Somaliland Protectorate 108-109
Trinidad & Tobago 62-63
Turks & Caicos Islands 90-91
Virgin Islands 88-89

The following have different designs but are included in the omnibus set:

Great Britain 264-265
Offices in Morocco 523-524
Aden
Kathiri State of Seiyun 12-13
Qu'aiti State of Shihr and Mukalla 12-13
Australia 200-202
Basutoland 29-31
Bechuanaland Protectorate 137-139
Burma 66-69
Cook Islands 127-130
Hong Kong 174-175
India 195-198
Hyderabad 51
New Zealand 247-257
Niue 90-93
Pakistan-Bahawalpur O16
Samoa 191-194
South Africa 100-102
Southern Rhodesia 67-70
South-West Africa 153-155
Swaziland 38-40
Zanzibar 222-223
164 stamps

Silver Wedding

King George VI and Queen Elizabeth
CD304 CD305

1948-49

Aden	30-31
Kathiri State of Seiyun	14-15
Qu'aiti State of Shihr and Mukalla	14-15
Antigua	98-99
Ascension	52-53
Bahamas	148-149
Barbados	210-211
Basutoland	39-40
Bechuanaland Protectorate	147-148
Bermuda	133-134
British Guiana	244-245
British Honduras	129-130
Cayman Islands	116-117
Cyprus	158-159
Dominica	114-115
Falkland Islands	99-100
Falkland Islands Dep.	1L11-1L12
Fiji	139-140
Gambia	146-147
Gibraltar	121-122
Gilbert & Ellice Islands	54-55
Gold Coast	142-143
Grenada	145-146
Hong Kong	178-179
Jamaica	138-139
Kenya, Uganda, Tanganyika	92-93
Leeward Islands	118-119
Malaya	
Johore	128-129
Kedah	55-56
Kelantan	44-45
Malacca	1-2
Negri Sembilan	36-37
Pahang	44-45
Penang	1-2
Perak	99-100
Perlis	1-2
Selangor	74-75
Trengganu	47-48
Malta	223-224
Mauritius	229-230
Montserrat	106-107
Nigeria	73-74
North Borneo	238-239
Northern Rhodesia	48-49
Nyasaland Protectorate	85-86
Pitcairn Island	11-12
St. Helena	130-131
St. Kitts-Nevis	93-94
St. Lucia	129-130
St. Vincent	154-155
Sarawak	174-175
Seychelles	151-152
Sierra Leone	188-189
Singapore	21-22
Solomon Islands	82-83
Somaliland Protectorate	110-111
Swaziland	48-49
Trinidad & Tobago	64-65
Turks & Caicos Islands	92-93
Virgin Islands	90-91
Zanzibar	224-225

The following have different designs but are included in the omnibus set:

Great Britain	267-268
Offices in Morocco	93-94, 525-526
Bahrain	62-63
Kuwait	82-83
Oman	25-26
South Africa	106
South-West Africa	159

138 stamps

U.P.U.

Mercury and Symbols of Communications – CD306

Plane, Ship and Hemispheres CD307

Mercury Scattering Letters over Globe CD308

U.P.U. Monument, Bern CD309

Universal Postal Union, 75th anniversary.

1949

Aden	32-35
Kathiri State of Seiyun	16-19
Qu'aiti State of Shihr and Mukalla	16-19
Antigua	100-103
Ascension	57-60
Bahamas	150-153
Barbados	212-215
Basutoland	41-44
Bechuanaland Protectorate	149-152
Bermuda	138-141
British Guiana	246-249
British Honduras	137-140
Brunei	79-82
Cayman Islands	118-121
Cyprus	160-163
Dominica	116-119
Falkland Islands	103-106
Falkland Islands Dep.	1L14-1L17
Fiji	141-144
Gambia	148-151
Gibraltar	123-126
Gilbert & Ellice Islands	56-59
Gold Coast	144-147
Grenada	147-150
Hong Kong	180-183
Jamaica	142-145
Kenya, Uganda, Tanganyika	94-97
Leeward Islands	126-129
Malaya	
Johore	151-154
Kedah	57-60
Kelantan	46-49
Malacca	18-21
Negri Sembilan	59-62
Pahang	46-49
Penang	23-26
Perak	101-104
Perlis	3-6
Selangor	76-79
Trengganu	49-52
Malta	225-228
Mauritius	231-234
Montserrat	108-111
New Hebrides, British	62-65
New Hebrides, French	79-82
Nigeria	75-78
North Borneo	240-243
Northern Rhodesia	50-53
Nyasaland Protectorate	87-90
Pitcairn Islands	13-16
St. Helena	132-135
St. Kitts-Nevis	95-98
St. Lucia	131-134
St. Vincent	170-173
Sarawak	176-179
Seychelles	153-156
Sierra Leone	190-193
Singapore	23-26
Solomon Islands	84-87
Somaliland Protectorate	112-115
Southern Rhodesia	71-72
Swaziland	50-53
Tonga	87-90
Trinidad & Tobago	66-69
Turks & Caicos Islands	101-104
Virgin Islands	92-95
Zanzibar	226-229

The following have different designs but are included in the omnibus set:

Great Britain	276-279
Offices in Morocco	546-549
Australia	223
Bahrain	68-71
Burma	116-121
Ceylon	304-306
Egypt	281-283
India	223-226
Kuwait	89-92
Oman	31-34
Pakistan-Bahawalpur	26-29, O25-O28
South Africa	109-111
South-West Africa	160-162

319 stamps

University

Arms of University College CD310
Alice, Princess of Athlone CD311

1948 opening of University College of the West Indies at Jamaica.

1951

Antigua	104-105
Barbados	228-229
British Guiana	250-251
British Honduras	141-142
Dominica	120-121
Grenada	164-165
Jamaica	146-147
Leeward Islands	130-131
Montserrat	112-113
St. Kitts-Nevis	105-106
St. Lucia	149-150
St. Vincent	174-175
Trinidad & Tobago	70-71
Virgin Islands	96-97

28 stamps

Coronation

Queen Elizabeth II CD312

1953

Aden	47
Kathiri State of Seiyun	28
Qu'aiti State of Shihr and Mukalla	28
Antigua	106
Ascension	61
Bahamas	157
Barbados	234
Basutoland	45
Bechuanaland Protectorate	153
Bermuda	142
British Guiana	252
British Honduras	143
Cayman Islands	150
Cyprus	167
Dominica	141
Falkland Islands	121
Falkland Islands Dependencies	1L18
Fiji	145
Gambia	152
Gibraltar	131
Gilbert & Ellice Islands	60
Gold Coast	160
Grenada	170
Hong Kong	184
Jamaica	153
Kenya, Uganda, Tanganyika	101
Leeward Islands	132
Malaya	
Johore	155
Kedah	82
Kelantan	71
Malacca	27
Negri Sembilan	63
Pahang	71
Penang	27
Perak	126
Perlis	28
Selangor	101
Trengganu	74
Malta	241
Mauritius	250
Montserrat	127
New Hebrides, British	77
Nigeria	79
North Borneo	260
Northern Rhodesia	60
Nyasaland Protectorate	96
Pitcairn	19
St. Helena	139
St. Kitts-Nevis	119
St. Lucia	156
St. Vincent	185
Sarawak	196
Seychelles	172
Sierra Leone	194
Singapore	27
Solomon Islands	88
Somaliland Protectorate	127
Swaziland	54
Trinidad & Tobago	84
Tristan da Cunha	13
Turks & Caicos Islands	118
Virgin Islands	114

The following have different designs but are included in the omnibus set:

Great Britain	313-316
Offices in Morocco	579-582
Australia	259-261
Bahrain	92-95
Canada	330
Ceylon	317
Cook Islands	145-146
Kuwait	113-116
New Zealand	280-284
Niue	104-105
Oman	52-55
Samoa	214-215
South Africa	192
Southern Rhodesia	80
South-West Africa	244-248
Tokelau Islands	4

106 stamps

Royal Visit 1953

Separate designs for each country for the visit of Queen Elizabeth II and the Duke of Edinburgh.

1953

Aden	62
Australia	267-269
Bermuda	163
Ceylon	318
Fiji	146
Gibraltar	146
Jamaica	154
Kenya, Uganda, Tanganyika	102
Malta	242
New Zealand	286-287

13 stamps

West Indies Federation

Map of the Caribbean CD313

Federation of the West Indies, April 22, 1958.

1958

Antigua	122-124
Barbados	248-250
Dominica	161-163
Grenada	184-186
Jamaica	175-177
Montserrat	143-145
St. Kitts-Nevis	136-138
St. Lucia	170-172
St. Vincent	198-200
Trinidad & Tobago	86-88

30 stamps

Freedom from Hunger

Protein Food CD314

U.N. Food and Agricultural Organization's "Freedom from Hunger" campaign.

1963

Aden	65
Antigua	133
Ascension	89
Bahamas	180
Basutoland	83
Bechuanaland Protectorate	194
Bermuda	192
British Guiana	271
British Honduras	179
Brunei	100
Cayman Islands	168
Dominica	181
Falkland Islands	146
Fiji	198

Gambia	172
Gibraltar	161
Gilbert & Ellice Islands	76
Grenada	190
Hong Kong	218
Malta	291
Mauritius	270
Montserrat	150
New Hebrides, British	93
North Borneo	296
Pitcairn	35
St. Helena	173
St. Lucia	179
St. Vincent	201
Sarawak	212
Seychelles	213
Solomon Islands	109
Swaziland	108
Tonga	127
Tristan da Cunha	68
Turks & Caicos Islands	138
Virgin Islands	140
Zanzibar	280

37 stamps

Red Cross Centenary

Red Cross and Elizabeth II – CD315

1963

Antigua	134-135
Ascension	90-91
Bahamas	183-184
Basutoland	84-85
Bechuanaland Protectorate	195-196
Bermuda	193-194
British Guiana	272-273
British Honduras	180-181
Cayman Islands	169-170
Dominica	182-183
Falkland Islands	147-148
Fiji	203-204
Gambia	173-174
Gibraltar	162-163
Gilbert & Ellice Islands	77-78
Grenada	191-192
Hong Kong	219-220
Jamaica	203-204
Malta	292-293
Mauritius	271-272
Montserrat	151-152
New Hebrides, British	94-95
Pitcairn Islands	36-37
St. Helena	174-175
St. Kitts-Nevis	143-144
St. Lucia	180-181
St. Vincent	202-203
Seychelles	214-215
Solomon Islands	110-111
South Arabia	1-2
Swaziland	109-110
Tonga	134-135
Tristan da Cunha	69-70
Turks & Caicos Islands	139-140
Virgin Islands	141-142

70 stamps

Shakespeare

Shakespeare Memorial Theatre, Stratford-on-Avon – CD316

400th anniversary of the birth of William Shakespeare.

1964

Antigua	151
Bahamas	201
Bechuanaland Protectorate	197
Cayman Islands	171
Dominica	184
Falkland Islands	149
Gambia	192
Gibraltar	164
Montserrat	153
St. Lucia	196
Turks & Caicos Islands	141
Virgin Islands	143

12 stamps

ITU

ITU Emblem CD317

Intl. Telecommunication Union, cent.

1965

Antigua	153-154
Ascension	92-93
Bahamas	219-220
Barbados	265-266
Basutoland	101-102
Bechuanaland Protectorate	202-203
Bermuda	196-197
British Guiana	293-294
British Honduras	187-188
Brunei	116-117
Cayman Islands	172-173
Dominica	185-186
Falkland Islands	154-155
Fiji	211-212
Gibraltar	167-168
Gilbert & Ellice Islands	87-88
Grenada	205-206
Hong Kong	221-222
Mauritius	291-292
Montserrat	157-158
New Hebrides, British	108-109
Pitcairn Islands	52-53
St. Helena	180-181
St. Kitts-Nevis	163-164
St. Lucia	197-198
St. Vincent	224-225
Seychelles	218-219
Solomon Islands	126-127
Swaziland	115-116
Tristan da Cunha	85-86
Turks & Caicos Islands	142-143
Virgin Islands	159-160

64 stamps

Intl. Cooperation Year

ICY Emblem – CD318

1965

Antigua	155-156
Ascension	94-95
Bahamas	222-223
Basutoland	103-104
Bechuanaland Protectorate	204-205
Bermuda	199-200
British Guiana	295-296
British Honduras	189-190
Brunei	118-119
Cayman Islands	174-175
Dominica	187-188
Falkland Islands	156-157
Fiji	213-214
Gibraltar	169-170
Gilbert & Ellice Islands	104-105
Grenada	207-208
Hong Kong	223-224
Mauritius	293-294
Montserrat	176-177
New Hebrides, British	110-111
New Hebrides, French	126-127
Pitcairn Islands	54-55
St. Helena	182-183
St. Kitts-Nevis	165-166
St. Lucia	199-200
Seychelles	220-221
Solomon Islands	143-144
South Arabia	17-18
Swaziland	117-118
Tristan da Cunha	87-88
Turks & Caicos Islands	144-145
Virgin Islands	161-162

64 stamps

Churchill Memorial

Winston Churchill and St. Paul's, London, During Air Attack – CD319

1966

Antigua	157-160
Ascension	96-99
Bahamas	224-227
Barbados	281-284
Basutoland	105-108
Bechuanaland Protectorate	206-209
Bermuda	201-204
British Antarctic Territory	16-19
British Honduras	191-194
Brunei	120-123
Cayman Islands	176-179
Dominica	189-192
Falkland Islands	158-161
Fiji	215-218
Gibraltar	171-174
Gilbert & Ellice Islands	106-109
Grenada	209-212
Hong Kong	225-228
Mauritius	295-298
Montserrat	178-181
New Hebrides, British	112-115
New Hebrides, French	128-131
Pitcairn Islands	56-59
St. Helena	184-187
St. Kitts-Nevis	167-170
St. Lucia	201-204
St. Vincent	241-244
Seychelles	222-225
Solomon Islands	145-148
South Arabia	19-22
Swaziland	119-122
Tristan da Cunha	89-92
Turks & Caicos Islands	146-149
Virgin Islands	163-166

136 stamps

Royal Visit, 1966

Queen Elizabeth II and Prince Philip CD320

Caribbean visit, Feb. 4 - Mar. 6, 1966.

1966

Antigua	161-162
Bahamas	228-229
Barbados	285-286
British Guiana	299-300
Cayman Islands	180-181
Dominica	193-194
Grenada	213-214
Montserrat	182-183
St. Kitts-Nevis	171-172
St. Lucia	205-206
St. Vincent	245-246
Turks & Caicos Islands	150-151
Virgin Islands	167-168

26 stamps

World Cup Soccer

Soccer Player and Jules Rimet Cup CD321

World Cup Soccer Championship, Wembley, England, July 11-30.

1966

Antigua	163-164
Ascension	100-101
Bahamas	245-246
Bermuda	205-206
Brunei	124-125
Cayman Islands	182-183
Dominica	195-196
Fiji	219-220
Gibraltar	175-176
Gilbert & Ellice Islands	125-126
Grenada	230-231
New Hebrides, British	116-117
New Hebrides, French	132-133
Pitcairn Islands	60-61
St. Helena	188-189
St. Kitts-Nevis	173-174
St. Lucia	207-208
Seychelles	226-227
Solomon Islands	167-168
South Arabia	23-24
Tristan da Cunha	93-94

42 stamps

WHO Headquarters

World Health Organization Headquarters, Geneva – CD322

1966

Antigua	165-166
Ascension	102-103
Bahamas	247-248
Brunei	126-127
Cayman Islands	184-185
Dominica	197-198
Fiji	224-225
Gibraltar	180-181
Gilbert & Ellice Islands	127-128
Grenada	232-233
Hong Kong	229-230
Montserrat	184-185
New Hebrides, British	118-119
New Hebrides, French	134-135
Pitcairn Islands	62-63
St. Helena	190-191
St. Kitts-Nevis	177-178
St. Lucia	209-210
St. Vincent	247-248
Seychelles	228-229
Solomon Islands	169-170
South Arabia	25-26
Tristan da Cunha	99-100

46 stamps

UNESCO Anniversary

"Education" – CD323

"Science" (Wheat ears & flask enclosing globe). "Culture" (lyre & columns).

20th anniversary of the UNESCO.

1966-67

Antigua	183-185
Ascension	108-110
Bahamas	249-251
Barbados	287-289
Bermuda	207-209
Brunei	128-130
Cayman Islands	186-188
Dominica	199-201
Gibraltar	183-185
Gilbert & Ellice Islands	129-131
Grenada	234-236
Hong Kong	231-233
Mauritius	299-301
Montserrat	186-188
New Hebrides, British	120-122
New Hebrides, French	136-138
Pitcairn Islands	64-66
St. Helena	192-194
St. Kitts-Nevis	179-181
St. Lucia	211-213
St. Vincent	249-251
Seychelles	230-232
Solomon Islands	171-173
South Arabia	27-29
Swaziland	123-125
Tristan da Cunha	101-103
Turks & Caicos Islands	155-157
Virgin Islands	176-178

84 stamps

Silver Wedding, 1972

Queen Elizabeth II and Prince Philip
CD324

Designs: borders differ for each country.

1972

Anguilla 161-162
Antigua 295-296
Ascension 164-165
Bahamas 344-345
Bermuda 296-297
British Antarctic Territory 43-44
British Honduras 306-307
British Indian Ocean Territory 48-49
Brunei 186-187
Cayman Islands 304-305
Dominica 352-353
Falkland Islands 223-224
Fiji 328-329
Gibraltar 292-293
Gilbert & Ellice Islands 206-207
Grenada 466-467
Hong Kong 271-272
Montserrat 286-287
New Hebrides, British 169-170
Pitcairn Islands 127-128
St. Helena 271-272
St. Kitts-Nevis 257-258
St. Lucia 328-329
St.Vincent 344-345
Seychelles 309-310
Solomon Islands 248-249
South Georgia 35-36
Tristan da Cunha 178-179
Turks & Caicos Islands 257-258
Virgin Islands 241-242
60 stamps

Princess Anne's Wedding

Princess Anne and Mark Phillips
CD325

Wedding of Princess Anne and Mark Phillips, Nov. 14, 1973.

1973

Anguilla 179-180
Ascension 177-178
Belize 325-326
Bermuda 302-303
British Antarctic Territory 60-61
Cayman Islands 320-321
Falkland Islands 225-226
Gibraltar 305-306
Gilbert & Ellice Islands 216-217
Hong Kong 289-290
Montserrat 300-301
Pitcairn Island 135-136
St. Helena 277-278
St. Kitts-Nevis 274-275
St. Lucia 349-350
St. Vincent 358-359
St. Vincent Grenadines 1-2
Seychelles 311-312
Solomon Islands 259-260
South Georgia 37-38
Tristan da Cunha 189-190
Turks & Caicos Islands 286-287
Virgin Islands 260-261
44 stamps

Elizabeth II Coronation Anniv.

CD326

CD327

CD328

Designs: Royal and local beasts in heraldic form and simulated stonework. Portrait of Elizabeth II by Peter Grugeon.

25th anniversary of coronation of Queen Elizabeth II.

1978

Ascension 229
Barbados 474
Belize 397
British Antarctic Territory 71
Cayman Islands 404
Christmas Island 87
Falkland Islands 275
Fiji 384
Gambia 380
Gilbert Islands 312
Mauritius 464
New Hebrides, British 258
St. Helena 317
St. Kitts-Nevis 354
Samoa 472
Solomon Islands 368
South Georgia 51
Swaziland 302
Tristan da Cunha 238
Virgin Islands 337
20 sheets

Queen Mother Elizabeth's 80th Birthday

CD330

Designs: Photographs of Queen Mother Elizabeth. Falkland Islands issued in sheets of 50; others in sheets of 9.

1980

Ascension 261
Bermuda 401
Cayman Islands 443
Falkland Islands 305
Gambia 412
Gibraltar 393
Hong Kong 364
Pitcairn Islands 193
St. Helena 341
Samoa 532
Solomon Islands 426
Tristan da Cunha 277
12 stamps

Royal Wedding, 1981

Prince Charles and Lady Diana
CD331

Wedding of Charles, Prince of Wales, and Lady Diana Spencer, St. Paul's Cathedral, London, July 29, 1981.

1981

Antigua 623-625
Ascension 294-296
Barbados 547-549
Barbuda 497-499
Bermuda 412-414
Brunei 268-270
Cayman Islands 471-473
Dominica 701-703
Falkland Islands 324-326
Falkland Islands Dep. 1L59-1L61
Fiji 442-444
Gambia 426-428
Ghana 759-761
Grenada 1051-1053
Grenada Grenadines 440-443
Hong Kong 373-375
Jamaica 500-503
Lesotho 335-337
Maldive Islands 906-908
Mauritius 520-522
Norfolk Island 280-282
Pitcairn Islands 206-208
St. Helena 353-355
St. Lucia 543-545
Samoa 558-560
Sierra Leone 509-517
Solomon Islands 450-452
Swaziland 382-384
Tristan da Cunha 294-296
Turks & Caicos Islands 486-488
Caicos Island 8-10
Uganda 314-316
Vanuatu 308-310
Virgin Islands 406-408

Princess Diana

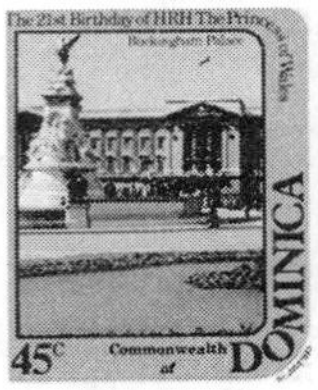

CD332

CD333

Designs: Photographs and portrait of Princess Diana, wedding or honeymoon photographs, royal residences, arms of issuing country. Portrait photograph by Clive Friend. Souvenir sheet margins show family tree, various people related to the princess. 21st birthday of Princess Diana of Wales, July 1.

1982

Antigua 663-666
Ascension 313-316
Bahamas 510-513
Barbados 585-588
Barbuda 544-546
British Antarctic Territory 92-95
Cayman Islands 486-489
Dominica 773-776
Falkland Islands 348-351
Falkland Islands Dep. 1L72-1L75
Fiji 470-473
Gambia 447-450
Grenada 1101A-1105
Grenada Grenadines 485-491
Lesotho 372-375
Maldive Islands 952-955
Mauritius 548-551
Pitcairn Islands 213-216
St. Helena 372-375
St. Lucia 591-594
Sierra Leone 531-534
Solomon Islands 471-474
Swaziland 406-409
Tristan da Cunha 310-313
Turks and Caicos Islands 530A-534
Virgin Islands 430-433

250th anniv. of first edition of Lloyd's List (shipping news publication) & of Lloyd's marine insurance.

CD335

Designs: First page of early edition of the list; historical ships, modern transportation or harbor scenes.

1984

Ascension 351-354
Bahamas 555-558
Barbados 627-630
Cayes of Belize 10-13
Cayman Islands 522-525
Falkland Islands 404-407
Fiji 509-512
Gambia 519-522
Mauritius 587-590
Nauru 280-283
St. Helena 412-415
Samoa 624-627
Seychelles 538-541
Solomon Islands 521-524
Vanuatu 368-371
Virgin Islands 466-469

Queen Mother 85th Birthday

CD336

Designs: Photographs tracing the life of the Queen Mother, Elizabeth. The high value in each set pictures the same photograph taken of the Queen Mother holding the infant Prince Henry.

1985

Ascension 372-376
Bahamas 580-584
Barbados 660-664
Bermuda 469-473
Falkland Islands 420-424
Falkland Islands Dep. 1L92-1L96
Fiji 531-535
Hong Kong 447-450
Jamaica 599-603
Mauritius 604-608
Norfolk Island 364-368
Pitcairn Islands 253-257
St. Helena 428-432
Samoa 649-653
Seychelles 567-571
Solomon Islands 543-547
Swaziland 476-480
Tristan da Cunha 372-376
Vanuatu 392-396
Zil Elwannyen Sesel 101-105

Queen Elizabeth II, 60th Birthday

CD337

1986, April 21

Ascension 389-393
Bahamas 592-596
Barbados 675-679
Bermuda 499-503
Cayman Islands 555-559
Falkland Islands 441-445
Fiji 544-548
Hong Kong 465-469
Jamaica 620-624
Kiribati 470-474
Mauritius 629-633
Papua New Guinea 640-644
Pitcairn Islands 270-274
St. Helena 451-455
Samoa 670-674
Seychelles 592-596
Solomon Islands 562-566
South Georgia 101-105
Swaziland 490-494
Tristan da Cunha 388-392
Vanuatu 414-418
Zambia 343-347
Zil Elwannyen Sesel 114-118

Royal Wedding

Marriage of Prince Andrew and Sarah Ferguson
CD338

1986, July 23

Ascension 399-400
Bahamas 602-603
Barbados 687-688
Cayman Islands 560-561
Jamaica 629-630
Pitcairn Islands 275-276
St. Helena 460-461
St. Kitts 181-182
Seychelles 602-603
Solomon Islands 567-568
Tristan da Cunha 397-398
Zambia 348-349
Zil Elwannyen Sesel 119-120

Queen Elizabeth II, 60th Birthday

Queen Elizabeth II Inspecting Guard, 1946
CD339

Designs: Photographs tracing the life of Queen Elizabeth II.

1986

Anguilla 674-677
Antigua 925-928
Barbuda 783-786
Dominica 950-953
Gambia 611-614
Grenada 1371-1374
Grenada Grenadines 749-752
Lesotho 531-534
Maldive Islands 1172-1175
Sierra Leone 760-763
Uganda 495-498

Royal Wedding, 1986

CD340

Designs: Photographs of Prince Andrew and Sarah Ferguson during courtship, engagement and marriage.

1986

Antigua 939-942
Barbuda 809-812
Dominica 970-973
Gambia 635-638
Grenada 1385-1388
Grenada Grenadines 758-761
Lesotho 545-548
Maldive Islands 1181-1184
Sierra Leone 769-772
Uganda 510-513

Lloyds of London, 300th Anniv.

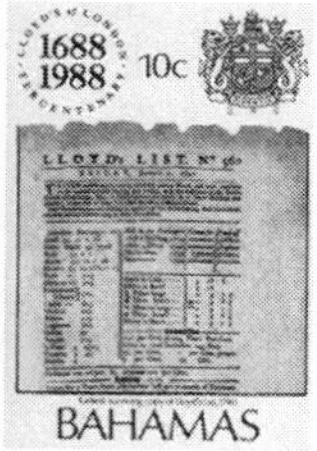

CD341

Designs: 17th century aspects of Lloyds, representations of each country's individual connections with Lloyds and publicized disasters insured by the organization.

1986

Ascension 454-457
Bahamas 655-658
Barbados 731-734
Bermuda 541-544
Falkland Islands 481-484
Liberia 1101-1104
Malawi 534-537
Nevis 571-574
St. Helena 501-504
St. Lucia 923-926
Seychelles 649-652
Solomon Islands 627-630
South Georgia 131-134
Trinidad & Tobago 484-487
Tristan da Cunha 439-442
Vanuatu 485-488
Zil Elwannyen Sesel 146-149

Moon Landing, 20th Anniv.

CD342

Designs: Equipment, crew photographs, spacecraft, official emblems and report profiles created for the Apollo Missions. Two stamps in each set are square in format rather than like the stamp shown; see individual country listings for more information.

1989

Ascension Is. 468-472
Bahamas 674-678
Belize 916-920
Kiribati 517-521
Liberia 1125-1129
Nevis 586-590
St. Kitts 248-252
Samoa 760-764
Seychelles 676-680
Solomon Islands 643-647
Vanuatu 507-511
Zil Elwannyen Sesel 154-158

Queen Mother, 90th Birthday

CD343 CD344

Designs: Portraits of Queen Elizabeth, the Queen Mother. See individual country listings for more information.

1990

Ascension Is. 491-492
Bahamas 698-699
Barbados 782-783
British Antarctic Territory 170-171
British Indian Ocean Territory 106-107
Cayman Islands 622-623
Falkland Islands 524-525
Kenya 527-528
Kiribati 555-556
Liberia 1145-1146
Pitcairn Islands 336-337
St. Helena 532-533
St. Lucia 969-970
Seychelles 710-711
Solomon Islands 671-672
South Georgia 143-144
Swaziland 565-566
Tristan da Cunha 480-481
Zil Elwannyen Sesel 171-172

Queen Elizabeth II, 65th Birthday, and Prince Philip, 70th Birthday

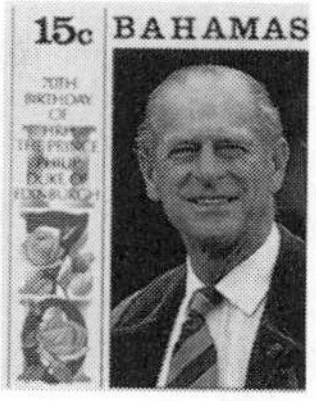

CD345 CD346

Designs: Portraits of Queen Elizabeth II and Prince Philip differ for each country. Printed in sheets of 10 + 5 labels (3 different) between. Stamps alternate, producing 5 different triptychs.

1991

Ascension Is. 505-506
Bahamas 730-731
Belize 969-970
Bermuda 617-618
Kiribati 571-572
Mauritius 733-734
Pitcairn Islands 348-349
St. Helena 554-555
St. Kitts 318-319
Samoa 790-791
Seychelles 723-724
Solomon Islands 688-689
South Georgia 149-150
Swaziland 586-587
Vanuatu 540-541
Zil Elwannyen Sesel 177-178

Royal Family Birthday, Anniversary

CD347

Queen Elizabeth II, 65th birthday, Charles and Diana, 10th wedding anniversary: Various photographs of Queen Elizabeth II, Prince Philip, Prince Charles, Princess Diana and their sons William and Henry.

1991

Antigua 1446-1455
Barbuda 1229-1238
Dominica 1328-1337
Gambia 1080-1089
Grenada 2006-2015
Grenada Grenadines 1331-1340
Guyana 2440-2451
Lesotho 871-875
Maldive Islands 1533-1542
Nevis 666-675
St. Vincent 1485-1494
St. Vincent Grenadines 769-778
Sierra Leone 1387-1396
Turks & Caicos Islands 913-922
Uganda 918-927

Queen Elizabeth II's Accession to the Throne, 40th Anniv.

CD348

CD349

Various photographs of Queen Elizabeth II with local Scenes.

1992 - CD348

Antigua 1513-1518
Barbuda 1306-1309
Dominica 1414-1419
Gambia 1172-1177
Grenada 2047-2052
Grenada Grenadines 1368-1373
Lesotho 881-885
Maldive Islands 1637-1642
Nevis 702-707
St. Vincent 1582-1587
St. Vincent Grenadines 829-834
Sierra Leone 1482-1487
Turks and Caicos Islands 978-987
Uganda 990-995
Virgin Islands 742-746

1992 - CD349

Ascension Islands 531-535
Bahamas 744-748
Bermuda 623-627
British Indian Ocean Territory 119-123
Cayman Islands 648-652
Falkland Islands 549-553
Gibraltar 605-609
Hong Kong 619-623
Kenya 563-567
Kiribati 582-586
Pitcairn Islands 362-366
St. Helena 570-574
St. Kitts 332-336
Samoa 805-809
Seychelles 734-738
Soloman Islands 708-712
South Georgia 157-161
Tristan da Cunha 508-512
Vanuatu 555-559
Zambia 561-565
Zil Elwannyen Sesel 183-187

Royal Air Force, 75th Anniversary

CD350

1993

Ascension 557-561
Bahamas 771-775
Barbados 842-846
Belize 1003-1008
Bermuda 648-651
British Indian Ocean Territory 136-140
Falkland Is. 573-577
Fiji 687-691
Montserrat 830-834
St. Kitts 351-355

Royal Air Force, 80th Anniv.

Design CD350 Re-inscribed

1998

Ascension 697-701
Bahamas 907-911
British Indian Ocean Terr 198-202
Cayman Islands 754-758
Fiji 814-818
Gibraltar 755-759
Samoa 957-961
Turks & Caicos Islands 1258-1265
Tuvalu 763-767
Virgin Islands 879-883

End of World War II, 50th Anniv.

CD351

CD352

1995

Ascension	613-617
Bahamas	824-828
Barbados	891-895
Belize	1047-1050
British Indian Ocean Territory	163-167
Cayman Islands	704-708
Falkland Islands	634-638
Fiji	720-724
Kiribati	662-668
Liberia	1175-1179
Mauritius	803-805
St. Helena	646-654
St. Kitts	389-393
St. Lucia	1018-1022
Samoa	890-894
Solomon Islands	799-803
South Georgia & S. Sandwich Is.	198-200
Tristan da Cunha	562-566

UN, 50th Anniv.

CD353

1995

Bahamas	839-842
Barbados	901-904
Belize	1055-1058
Jamaica	847-851
Liberia	1187-1190
Mauritius	813-816
Pitcairn Islands	436-439
St. Kitts	398-401
St. Lucia	1023-1026
Samoa	900-903
Tristan da Cunha	568-571
Virgin Islands	807-810

Queen Elizabeth, 70th Birthday

CD354

1996

Ascension	632-635
British Antarctic Territory	240-243
British Indian Ocean Territory	176-180
Falkland Islands	653-657
Pitcairn Islands	446-449
St. Helena	672-676
Samoa	912-916
Tokelau	223-227
Tristan da Cunha	576-579
Virgin Islands	824-828

Diana, Princess of Wales (1961-97)

CD355

1998

Ascension	696
Bahamas	901A-902
Barbados	950
Belize	1091
Bermuda	753
Botswana	659-663
British Antarctic Territory	258
British Indian Ocean Terr.	197
Cayman Islands	752A-753
Falkland Islands	694
Fiji	819-820
Gibraltar	754
Kiribati	719A-720
Namibia	909
Niue	706
Norfolk Island	644-645
Papua New Guinea	937
Pitcairn Islands	487
St. Helena	711
St. Kitts	437A-438
Samoa	955A-956
Seycelles	802
Solomon Islands	866-867
South Georgia & S. Sandwich Islands	220
Tokelau	253
Tonga	980
Niuafo'ou	201
Tristan da Cunha	618
Tuvalu	762
Vanuatu	719
Virgin Islands	878

Wedding of Prince Edward and Sophie Rhys-Jones

CD356

1999

Ascension	729-730
Cayman Islands	775-776
Falkland Islands	729-730
Pitcairn Islands	505-506
St. Helena	733-734
Samoa	971-972
Tristan da Cunha	636-637
Virgin Islands	908-909

1st Manned Moon Landing, 30th Anniv.

CD357

1999

Ascension	731-735
Bahamas	942-946
Barbados	967-971
Bermuda	778
Cayman Islands	777-781
Fiji	853-857
Jamaica	889-893
Kirbati	746-750
Nauru	465-469
St. Kitts	460-464
Samoa	973-977
Solomon Islands	875-879
Tuvalu	800-804
Virgin Islands	910-914

Queen Mother's Century

CD358

1999

Ascension	736-740
Bahamas	951-955
Cayman Islands	782-786
Falkland Islands	734-738
Fiji	858-862
Norfolk Island	688-692
St. Helena	740-744
Samoa	978-982
Solomon Islands	880-884
South Georgia & South Sandwich Islands	231-235
Tristan da Cunha	638-642
Tuvalu	805-809

Prince William, 18th Birthday

CD359

2000

Ascension	755-759
Cayman Islands	797-801
Falkland Islands	762-766
Fiji	889-893
South Georgia and South Sandwich Islands	257-261
Tristan da Cunha	664-668
Virgin Islands	925-929

SUBSCRIBE TODAY!

Linn's Stamp News is the **indispensable** reading and entertainment guide for all the stamps you **want** and all the news you **need**. Each issue is jam packed with:

www.linns.com

Linn's Stamp News

WORLD'S LARGEST WEEKLY STAMP NEWS AND MARKETPLACE VOL. 74 ISSUE 3771 $2.00 U.S. FEBRUARY 5, 2001

34¢ Liberty, Flag, Four Flowers to be issued Feb. 7 in New York; no ceremony planned

United Nations continues Endangered Species series

Five semipostals for 2002-10; public will propose subjects

CONTENTS: PAGE 3

- All the latest-breaking news from our exclusive national and international sources.
- In-depth analysis from top authorities on all aspects of collecting, new issues, forgeries, security and more.
- Regular features you always looked forward to - *Stamp Market Tips* and *Tip of the Week, Collectors' Forum, Editor's Choice, Readers' Opinions, Postmark Pursuit, Collectors' Workshop, Refresher Course* and much more.
- The world's largest stamp market place. Listings of events, auctions and sales. Classified ads and readers' notices for buying, selling and trading.

Special Bonus: As a paid subscriber, you are automatically enrolled, at no extra cost to you, in the Amos Advantage Program. As a member, you can save up to 30% on catalogues, books, albums, accessories, supplements and supplies produced and distributed by Amos Hobby Publishing.

(Offer valid only for U.S. subscribers.
Canadian subscribers add $22.50 for postage.
International subscribers add $37.50 for postage.)

Order online at:

www.linns.com

or Call toll-free:

1-800-448-7293

or write:

P.O. Box 4315,
Sidney, OH 45365

Subscribe Today and take advantage of Linn's get acquainted offer:

6 months - 26 issues - $23.95!

AMOS
HOBBY PUBLISHING

British Commonwealth of Nations

Dominions, Colonies, Territories, Offices and Independent Members

Comprising stamps of the British Commonwealth and associated nations.

A strict observance of technicalities would bar some or all of the stamps listed under Burma, Ireland, Kuwait, Nepal, New Republic, Orange Free State, Samoa, South Africa, South-West Africa, Stellaland, Sudan, Swaziland, the two Transvaal Republics and others but these are included for the convenience of collectors.

1. Great Britain

Great Britain: Including England, Scotland, Wales and Northern Ireland.

2. The Dominions, Present and Past

AUSTRALIA

The Commonwealth of Australia was proclaimed on January 1, 1901. It consists of six former colonies as follows:

New South Wales
Queensland
South Australia
Victoria
Tasmania
Western Australia

Territories belonging to, or administered by Australia: Australian Antarctic Territory, Christmas Island, Cocos (Keeling) Islands, Nauru, New Guinea, Norfolk Island, Papua New Guinea.

CANADA

The Dominion of Canada was created by the British North America Act in 1867. The following provinces were former separate colonies and issued postage stamps:

British Columbia and Vancouver Island
New Brunswick
Newfoundland
Nova Scotia
Prince Edward Island

FIJI

The colony of Fiji became an independent nation with dominion status on Oct. 10, 1970.

GHANA

This state came into existence Mar. 6, 1957, with dominion status. It consists of the former colony of the Gold Coast and the Trusteeship Territory of Togoland. Ghana became a republic July 1, 1960.

INDIA

The Republic of India was inaugurated on January 26, 1950. It succeeded the Dominion of India which was proclaimed August 15, 1947, when the former Empire of India was divided into Pakistan and the Union of India. The Republic is composed of about 40 predominantly Hindu states of three classes: governor's provinces, chief commissioner's provinces and princely states. India also has various territories, such as the Andaman and Nicobar Islands.

The old Empire of India was a federation of British India and the native states. The more important princely states were autonomous. Of the more than 700 Indian states, these 43 are familiar names to philatelists because of their postage stamps.

CONVENTION STATES

Chamba
Faridkot
Gwalior
Jhind
Nabha
Patiala

NATIVE FEUDATORY STATES

Alwar
Bahawalpur
Bamra
Barwani
Bhopal
Bhor
Bijawar
Bundi
Bussahir
Charkhari
Cochin
Dhar
Duttia
Faridkot (1879-85)
Hyderabad
Idar
Indore
Jaipur
Jammu
Jammu and Kashmir
Jasdan
Jhalawar
Jhind (1875-76)
Kashmir
Kishangarh
Las Bela
Morvi
Nandgaon
Nowanuggur
Orchha
Poonch
Rajpeepla
Sirmur
Soruth
Travancore
Wadhwan

NEW ZEALAND

Became a dominion on September 26, 1907. The following islands and territories are, or have been, administered by New Zealand:

Aitutaki
Cook Islands (Rarotonga)
Niue
Penrhyn
Ross Dependency
Samoa (Western Samoa)
Tokelau Islands

PAKISTAN

The Republic of Pakistan was proclaimed March 23, 1956. It succeeded the Dominion which was proclaimed August 15, 1947. It is made up of all or part of several Moslem provinces and various districts of the former Empire of India, including Bahawalpur and Las Bela. Pakistan withdrew from the Commonwealth in 1972.

SOUTH AFRICA

Under the terms of the South African Act (1909) the self-governing colonies of Cape of Good Hope, Natal, Orange River Colony and Transvaal united on May 31, 1910, to form the Union of South Africa. It became an independent republic May 3, 1961.

Under the terms of the Treaty of Versailles, South-West Africa, formerly German South-West Africa, was mandated to the Union of South Africa.

SRI LANKA (CEYLON)

The Dominion of Ceylon was proclaimed February 4, 1948. The island had been a Crown Colony from 1802 until then. On May 22, 1972, Ceylon became the Republic of Sri Lanka.

3. Colonies, Past and Present; ControlledTerritory and Independent Members of the Commonwealth

Aden
Aitutaki
Antigua
Ascension
Bahamas
Bahrain
Bangladesh
Barbados
Barbuda
Basutoland
Batum
Bechuanaland
Bechuanaland Prot.
Belize
Bermuda
Botswana
British Antarctic Territory
British Central Africa
British Columbia and Vancouver Island
British East Africa
British Guiana

British Honduras
British Indian Ocean Territory
British New Guinea
British Solomon Islands
British Somaliland
Brunei
Burma
Bushire
Cameroons
Cape of Good Hope
Cayman Islands
Christmas Island
Cocos (Keeling) Islands
Cook Islands
Crete,
British Administration
Cyprus
Dominica
East Africa & Uganda
Protectorates
Egypt
Falkland Islands
Fiji
Gambia
German East Africa
Gibraltar
Gilbert Islands
Gilbert & Ellice Islands
Gold Coast
Grenada
Griqualand West
Guernsey
Guyana
Heligoland
Hong Kong
Indian Native States
(see India)
Ionian Islands
Jamaica
Jersey
Kenya
Kenya, Uganda & Tanzania
Kuwait
Labuan
Lagos
Leeward Islands
Lesotho
Madagascar
Malawi
Malaya
Federated Malay States
Johore
Kedah
Kelantan
Malacca
Negri Sembilan
Pahang
Penang
Perak
Perlis
Selangor
Singapore
Sungei Ujong
Trengganu
Malaysia
Maldive Islands
Malta
Man, Isle of
Mauritius
Mesopotamia
Montserrat
Muscat
Namibia
Natal
Nauru
Nevis
New Britain
New Brunswick
Newfoundland
New Guinea
New Hebrides
New Republic
New South Wales
Niger Coast Protectorate
Nigeria
Niue
Norfolk Island
North Borneo
Northern Nigeria
Northern Rhodesia
North West Pacific Islands
Nova Scotia
Nyasaland Protectorate
Oman
Orange River Colony
Palestine
Papua New Guinea
Penrhyn Island
Pitcairn Islands
Prince Edward Island
Queensland
Rhodesia
Rhodesia & Nyasaland
Ross Dependency
Sabah
St. Christopher
St. Helena
St. Kitts
St. Kitts-Nevis-Anguilla
St. Lucia
St. Vincent
Samoa
Sarawak
Seychelles
Sierra Leone
Solomon Islands
Somaliland Protectorate
South Arabia
South Australia
South Georgia
Southern Nigeria
Southern Rhodesia
South-West Africa
Stellaland
Straits Settlements
Sudan
Swaziland
Tanganyika
Tanzania
Tasmania
Tobago
Togo
Tokelau Islands
Tonga
Transvaal
Trinidad
Trinidad and Tobago
Tristan da Cunha
Trucial States
Turks and Caicos
Turks Islands
Tuvalu
Uganda
United Arab Emirates
Victoria
Virgin Islands
Western Australia
Zambia
Zanzibar
Zululand

POST OFFICES IN FOREIGN COUNTRIES

Africa
East Africa Forces
Middle East Forces
Bangkok
China
Morocco
Turkish Empire

Colonies, Former Colonies, Offices, Territories Controlled by Parent States

Belgium

Belgian Congo
Ruanda-Urundi

Denmark

Danish West Indies
Faroe Islands
Greenland
Iceland

Finland

Aland Islands

France

COLONIES PAST AND PRESENT, CONTROLLED TERRITORIES

Afars & Issas, Territory of
Alaouites
Alexandretta
Algeria
Alsace & Lorraine
Anjouan
Annam & Tonkin
Benin
Cambodia (Khmer)
Cameroun
Castellorizo
Chad
Cilicia
Cochin China
Comoro Islands
Dahomey
Diego Suarez
Djibouti (Somali Coast)
Fezzan
French Congo
French Equatorial Africa
French Guiana
French Guinea
French India
French Morocco
French Polynesia (Oceania)
French Southern & Antarctic Territories
French Sudan
French West Africa
Gabon
Germany
Ghadames
Grand Comoro
Guadeloupe
Indo-China
Inini
Ivory Coast
Laos
Latakia
Lebanon
Madagascar
Martinique
Mauritania
Mayotte
Memel
Middle Congo
Moheli
New Caledonia
New Hebrides
Niger Territory
Nossi-Be
Obock
Reunion
Rouad, Ile
Ste.-Marie de Madagascar
St. Pierre & Miquelon
Senegal
Senegambia & Niger
Somali Coast
Syria
Tahiti
Togo
Tunisia
Ubangi-Shari
Upper Senegal & Niger
Upper Volta
Viet Nam
Wallis & Futuna Islands

POST OFFICES IN FOREIGN COUNTRIES

China
Crete
Egypt
Turkish Empire
Zanzibar

Germany

EARLY STATES

Baden
Bavaria
Bergedorf
Bremen
Brunswick
Hamburg
Hanover
Lubeck
Mecklenburg-Schwerin
Mecklenburg-Strelitz
Oldenburg
Prussia
Saxony
Schleswig-Holstein
Wurttemberg

FORMER COLONIES

Cameroun (Kamerun)
Caroline Islands
German East Africa
German New Guinea
German South-West Africa
Kiauchau
Mariana Islands
Marshall Islands
Samoa
Togo

Italy

EARLY STATES

Modena
Parma
Romagna
Roman States
Sardinia
Tuscany
Two Sicilies
  Naples
  Neapolitan Provinces
  Sicily

FORMER COLONIES, CONTROLLED TERRITORIES, OCCUPATION AREAS

Aegean Islands
  Calimno (Calino)
  Caso
  Cos (Coo)
  Karki (Carchi)
  Leros (Lero)
  Lipso
  Nisiros (Nisiro)
  Patmos (Patmo)
  Piscopi
  Rodi (Rhodes)
  Scarpanto
  Simi
  Stampalia
Castellorizo
Corfu
Cyrenaica
Eritrea
Ethiopia (Abyssinia)
Fiume
Ionian Islands
  Cephalonia
  Ithaca
  Paxos
Italian East Africa
Libya
Oltre Giuba
Saseno
Somalia (Italian Somaliland)
Tripolitania

POST OFFICES IN FOREIGN COUNTRIES

"ESTERO"*
Austria
China
  Peking
  Tientsin
Crete
Tripoli
Turkish Empire
  Constantinople
  Durazzo
  Janina
Jerusalem
Salonika
Scutari
Smyrna
Valona

*Stamps overprinted "ESTERO" were used in various parts of the world.

Netherlands

Aruba
Netherlands Antilles (Curacao)
Netherlands Indies
Netherlands New Guinea
Surinam (Dutch Guiana)

Portugal

COLONIES PAST AND PRESENT, CONTROLLED TERRITORIES

Angola
Angra
Azores
Cape Verde
Funchal
Horta
Inhambane
Kionga
Lourenco Marques
Macao
Madeira
Mozambique
Mozambique Co.
Nyassa
Ponta Delgada
Portuguese Africa
Portuguese Congo
Portuguese Guinea
Portuguese India
Quelimane
St. Thomas & Prince Islands
Tete
Timor
Zambezia

Russia

ALLIED TERRITORIES AND REPUBLICS, OCCUPATION AREAS

Armenia
Aunus (Olonets)
Azerbaijan
Batum
Estonia
Far Eastern Republic
Georgia
Karelia
Latvia
Lithuania
North Ingermanland
Ostland
Russian Turkestan
Siberia
South Russia
Tannu Tuva
Transcaucasian Fed. Republics
Ukraine
Wenden (Livonia)
Western Ukraine

Spain

COLONIES PAST AND PRESENT, CONTROLLED TERRITORIES

Aguera, La
Cape Juby
Cuba
Elobey, Annobon & Corisco
Fernando Po
Ifni
Mariana Islands
Philippines
Puerto Rico
Rio de Oro
Rio Muni
Spanish Guinea
Spanish Morocco
Spanish Sahara
Spanish West Africa

POST OFFICES IN FOREIGN COUNTRIES

Morocco
Tangier
Tetuan

PAKISTAN

ˈpa-ki-ˌstan

LOCATION — In southern, central Asia
GOVT. — Republic
AREA — 307,293 sq. mi.
POP. — 130,579,571 (1998)
CAPITAL — Islamabad

Pakistan was formed August 15, 1947, when India was divided into the Dominions of the Union of India and Pakistan, with some princely states remaining independent. Pakistan became a republic on March 23, 1956.

Pakistan had two areas made up of all or part of several predominantly Moslem provinces in the northwest and northeast corners of pre-1947 India. West Pakistan consists of the entire provinces of Baluchistan, Sind (Scinde) and "Northwest Frontier," and 15 districts of the Punjab. East Pakistan consisting of the Sylhet district in Assam and 14 districts in Bengal Province, became independent as Bangladesh in December 1971.

The state of Las Bela was incorporated into Pakistan.

12 Pies = 1 Anna
16 Annas = 1 Rupee
100 Paisa = 1 Rupee (1961)

Catalogue values for all unused stamps in this country are for Never Hinged items.

Watermarks

Wmk274

Wmk. 351-Crescent and Star Multiple

Stamps of India, 1937-43, Overprinted in Black:

PAKISTAN — Nos. 1-12
PAKISTAN — Nos. 13-19

Perf. 13½x14

1947, Oct. 1 **Wmk. 196**

1	A83	3p slate	.20	.20
2	A83	½a rose violet	.20	.20
3	A83	9p lt green	.20	.20
4	A83	1a carmine rose	.20	.20
4A	A84	1a3p bister ('49)	.90	1.60
5	A84	1½a dk purple	.20	.20
6	A84	2a scarlet	.20	.20
7	A84	3a violet	.20	.20
8	A84	3½a ultra	.70	2.00
9	A85	4a chocolate	.20	.20
10	A85	6a peacock blue	1.00	.75
11	A85	8a blue violet	.30	.55
12	A85	12a carmine lake	1.00	.20
13	A81	14a rose violet	2.25	1.40
14	A82	1r brn & slate	1.75	.75
a.		Inverted overprint	125.00	
b.		Pair, one without ovpt.	525.00	
15	A82	2r dk brn & dk vio	3.00	1.40
16	A82	5r dp ultra & dk grn	3.75	3.50
17	A82	10r rose car & dk vio	3.75	2.25
18	A82	15r dk grn & dk brn	50.00	67.50
19	A82	25r dk vio & bl vio	55.00	40.00
		Nos. 1-19 (20)	125.00	123.50
		Set, hinged	71.00	

The overprint on Nos. 14-19 is slightly smaller than the illustration.

Provisional use of stamps of India with handstamped or printed "PAKISTAN" was authorized in 1947-49. Nos. 4A, 14a 14b exist only as provisional issues.

Used values are for postal cancels. Telegraph cancels sell for much less.

Constituent Assembly Building, Karachi A1

Crescent and Urdu Inscription — A2

Designs: 2½a, Karachi Airport entrance. 3a, Lahore Fort gateway.

Unwmk.

1948, July 9 **Engr.** **Perf. 14**

20	A1	1½a bright ultra	.25	.20
21	A1	2½a green	.50	.20
22	A1	3a chocolate	.50	.20
		Perf. 12		
23	A2	1r red	1.75	.60
a.		Perf. 14	6.00	60.00
		Nos. 20-23 (4)	3.00	1.20

Pakistan's independence, Aug. 15, 1947.

For Nos. 23-23 and later issues, many "errors" exist from printer's waste.

Scales, Star and Crescent A3

Star and Crescent A4

Karachi Airport Building A5

Karachi Port Authority Building — A6

Khyber Pass — A7

2½a, 3½a, 4a, Ghulan Muhammed Dam, Indus River, Sind. 1r, 2r, 5r, Salimullah Hostel.

Perf. 12½, 14 (3a, 10a), 14x13½ (2½a, 3½a, 6a, 12a)

1948-57 **Unwmk.**

24	A3	3p org red, perf. 13½ ('54)	.20	.20
a.		Perf. 12½	.20	.20
25	A3	6p pur, perf. 12½	.55	.20
a.		Perf. 13½ ('54)	1.25	.30
26	A3	9p dk grn, perf. 12½	.30	.20
a.		Perf. 13½ ('54)	.50	.20
27	A4	1a dark blue	.20	.20
28	A4	1½a gray green	.20	.20
29	A4	2a orange red	.40	.25
30	A6	2½a green	1.75	2.50
31	A5	3a olive green	4.75	.20
32	A6	3½a violet blue	2.25	3.00
33	A6	4a chocolate	.30	.20
34	A6	6a deep blue	.30	.20
35	A6	8a black	.30	.20
36	A5	10a red	2.75	4.00
37	A6	12a red	4.00	.40
		Perf. 14		
38	A5	1r ultra	3.50	.20
a.		Perf. 13½ ('54)	15.00	3.00
39	A5	2r dark brown	12.00	.20
a.		Perf. 13½ ('54)	37.50	2.00
		Perf. 13½		
40	A5	5r car ('54)	9.25	.40
a.		Perf. 13½x14	13.00	.20
		Perf. 13		
41	A7	10r rose lilac ('51)	11.00	.20
a.		Perf. 14	8.00	10.00
b.		Perf. 12	80.00	7.50
42	A7	15r blue green ('57)	11.00	8.00
a.		Perf. 14	15.00	22.50
b.		Perf. 12	25.00	10.00
		Perf. 14		
43	A7	25r purple	35.00	20.00
a.		Perf. 13 ('54)	47.50	50.00
b.		Perf. 12	22.50	25.00
		Nos. 24-43 (20)	100.00	40.95
		Set, hinged	75.00	

See No. 259, types A9-A11. For surcharges and overprints see Nos. 124, O14-O26, O35-O37, O41-O43A, O52, O63, O68.

Imperfs of Nos. 24-43 are from proof sheets improperly removed from the printer's archives.

"Quaid-i-Azam" (Great Leader), "Mohammed Ali Jinnah" — A8

1949, Sept. 11 **Engr.** **Perf. 13½x14**

44	A8	1½a brown	1.25	.75
45	A8	3a dark green	1.25	.75
46	A8	10a blk *(English inscriptions)*	4.50	5.50
		Nos. 44-46 (3)	7.00	7.00

1st anniv. of the death of Mohammed Ali Jinnah (1876-1948), Moslem lawyer, pres. of All-India Moslem League.

Re-engraved (Crescents Reversed)

A9

A10

A11

Perf. 12½, 13½x14 (3a, 10a), 14x13½ (6a, 12a)

1949-53

47	A10	1a dk blue ('50)	3.25	.50
a.		Perf. 13 ('52)	3.50	.20
48	A10	1½a gray green	3.00	.50
a.		Perf. 13 ('53)	3.00	.20
49	A10	2a orange red	3.25	.20
a.		Perf. 13 ('52)	3.50	.20
50	A9	3a olive green	6.25	.40
51	A11	6a deep blue ('50)	7.00	.30
52	A11	8a black ('50)	3.75	.70
53	A9	10a red	11.50	1.00
54	A11	12a red ('50)	15.00	1.00
		Nos. 47-54 (8)	53.00	4.60

For overprints see #O27-O31, O38-O40.

Vase and Plate — A12

Star and Crescent, Plane and Hour Glass — A13

Moslem Leaf Pattern — A14

Arch and Lamp of Learning A15

1951, Aug. 14 **Engr.** **Perf. 13**

55	A12	2½a dark red	.80	.50
56	A13	3a dk rose lake	.45	.20
57	A12	3½a dp ultra (Urdu "½3")	.70	2.75
57A	A12	3½a dp ultra (Urdu "3½") ('56)	3.00	3.00
58	A14	4a deep green	.30	.20
59	A14	6a red orange	.40	.20
60	A15	8a brown	3.75	.20
61	A15	10a purple	.75	.75
62	A13	12a dk slate blue	.80	.20
		Nos. 55-62 (9)	10.95	8.00

Fourth anniversary of independence.

On No. 57, the characters of the Urdu denomination at right appears as "½3." On the reengraved No. 57A, they read "3½."

Issue date: Dec. 1956.

See Nos. 88, O32-O34.

For surcharges see Nos. 255, 257.

Scinde District Stamp and Camel Train A16

1952, Aug. 14

63	A16	3a olive green, *citron*	.75	.70
64	A16	12a dark brown, *salmon*	1.25	.20

5th anniv. of Pakistan's Independence and the cent. of the 1st postage stamps in the Indo-Pakistan sub-continent.

Peak K-2, Karakoram Mountains A17

1954, Dec. 25

65	A17	2a violet	.30	.25

Conquest of K-2, world's 2nd highest mountain peak, in July 1954.

Kaghan Valley — A18

Gilgit Mountains A19

Tea Garden, East Pakistan A20

Designs: 1a, Badshahi Mosque, Lahore. 1½a, Emperor Jahangir's Mausoleum, Lahore. 1r, Cotton field. 2r, River craft and jute field.

1954, Aug. 14 **Engr.**

66 A18 6p rose violet .20 .20
67 A19 9p blue 2.75 1.00
68 A19 1a carmine rose .20 .20
69 A18 1½a red .20 .20
70 A20 14a dark green .40 .20
71 A20 1r yellow green 9.00 .20
72 A20 2r orange 2.25 .20
Nos. 66-72 (7) 15.00 2.20

Seventh anniversary of independence.
Nos. 66, 69 exist in booklet panes of 4 torn from sheets.
For overprints & surcharges see #77, 101, 123, 126, O44-O50, O53-O56, O60-O62, O67, O69-O71.

Karnaphuli Paper Mill, East Pakistan (Urdu "½2") — A21

6a, Textile mill. 8a, Jute mill. 12a, Sui gas plant.

1955, Aug. 14 **Unwmk.** ***Perf. 13***

73 A21 2½a dk car (Urdu "½2") .40 .50
73A A21 2½a dk car (Urdu "2½") ('56) .30 .50
74 A21 6a dark blue .80 .20
75 A21 8a violet 3.00 .20
76 A21 12a car lake & org 3.00 .20
Nos. 73-76 (5) 7.50 1.60

Eighth anniversary of independence.
On No. 73, the characters of the Urdu denomination at right appear as "½2." On the reengraved No. 73A, they read "2½."
Issue date: Dec. 1956.
See No. 87. For overprints and surcharges see Nos. 78, 102-103, 256, O51, O58-O59.

Nos. 69 and 76 Overprinted in Ultramarine

TENTH ANNIVERSARY UNITED NATIONS

24. 10. 55.

1955, Oct. 24

77 A18 1½a red 1.60 3.00
78 A21 12a car lake & org .65 2.00

UN, 10th anniv.

Map of West Pakistan — A22

1955, Dec. 7 **Unwmk.** ***Perf. 13½x13***

79 A22 1½a dark green .20 .20
80 A22 2a dark brown .20 .20
81 A22 12a deep carmine .50 .20
Nos. 79-81 (3) .90 .60

West Pakistan unification, Nov. 14, 1955.

National Assembly A23

1956, Mar. 23 **Litho.** ***Perf. 13x12½***

82 A23 2a green .75 .20

Proclamation of the Republic of Pakistan, Mar. 23, 1956.

Crescent and Star — A24

Map of East Pakistan — A25

1956, Aug. 14 **Engr.** ***Perf. 13***

83 A24 2a red .60 .20

Ninth anniversary of independence.
For surcharges and overprints see Nos. 127, O57, O72-O73.

1956, Oct. 15 ***Perf. 13½x13***

84 A25 1½a dark green .50 *.75*
85 A25 2a dark brown .50 .20
86 A25 12a deep red .50 *.75*
Nos. 84-86 (3) 1.50 1.70

1st Session at Dacca (East Pakistan) of the National Assembly of Pakistan.

Redrawn Types of 1951, 1955 and

Orange Tree — A26

Perf. 13x13½, 13½x13

1957, Mar. 23 **Engr.**

87 A21 2½a dark carmine .20 .20
88 A12 3½a bright blue .25 .20
89 A26 10r dk green & orange .65 .40
Nos. 87-89 (3) 1.10 .80

Nos. 87-89 inscribed "Pakistan" in English, Urdu and Bengali. Denomination in English only.
Islamic Republic of Pakistan, 1st anniv.
See Nos. 95, 258, 475A. For surcharge and overprint see Nos. 159, O64.

Flag and Broken Chain — A27

1957, May 10 **Litho.** ***Perf. 13***

90 A27 1½a green .40 .20
91 A27 12a blue 1.10 .20

Cent. of the struggle for Independence (Indian Mutiny).

Industrial Plants and Roses as Symbols of Progress A28

1957, Aug. 14 **Unwmk.** ***Perf. 13½***

92 A28 1½a light ultra .20 .25
93 A28 4a orange vermilion .40 .45
94 A28 12a red lilac .40 .30
Nos. 92-94 (3) 1.00 1.00

Tenth anniversary of independence.

Type of 1957.

Design: 15r, Coconut Tree.

1958, Mar. 23 **Engr.** ***Perf. 13½x13***

95 A26 15r rose lilac & red 4.50 3.50

Issued to commemorate the second anniversary of the Islamic Republic of Pakistan.

Verse of Iqbal Poem A29

1958, Apr. 21 **Photo.** ***Perf. 14½x14***

Black Inscriptions

96 A29 1½a citron .50 .20
97 A29 2a orange brown .50 .20
98 A29 14a aqua .75 .20
Nos. 96-98 (3) 1.75 .60

20th anniv. of the death of Mohammad Iqbal (1877-1938), Moslem poet and philosopher.

Globe and Book — A30

1958, Dec. 10 **Litho.** ***Perf. 13***

99 A30 1½a Prus blue .20 .20
100 A30 14a dark brown .55 .20

10th anniv. of the signing of the Universal Declaration of Human Rights.

Nos. 66 and 75 Overprinted: "Pakistan Boy Scout 2nd National Jamboree Chittagong Dec. 58-Jan. 59"

1958, Dec. 28 **Engr.** ***Perf. 13***

101 A18 6p rose violet .20 .20
102 A21 8a violet .60 .25

2nd National Boy Scout Jamboree held at Chittagong, Dec. 28-Jan. 4.

No. 74 Overprinted in Red: "Revolution Day, Oct. 27, 1959."

1959, Oct. 27

103 A21 6a dark blue .65 .20

First anniversary of the 1958 Revolution.

Red Cross — A31

Engr.; Cross Typo.

1959, Nov. 19 **Unwmk.** ***Perf. 13***

104 A31 2a green & red .30 .20
105 A31 10a dk blue & red .60 .20

Armed Forces Emblem — A32

1960, Jan. 10 **Litho.** ***Perf. 13***

106 A32 2a blue grn, red & ultra .50 .20
107 A32 14a ultra & red 1.25 .20

Issued for Armed Forces Day.

Map Showing Disputed Areas A33

1960, Mar. 23 **Engr.** **Unwmk.**

108 A33 6p purple .40 .20
109 A33 2a copper red .50 .20
110 A33 8a green 1.10 .20
111 A33 1r blue 1.50 .20
Nos. 108-111 (4) 3.50 .80

Publicizing the border dispute with India over Jammu and Kashmir, Junagarh and Manavadar.
For overprints and surcharges see Nos. 122, 125, 128, 178, O65-O66, O74-O75.

Uprooted Oak Emblem — A34

1960, Apr. 7

112 A34 2a carmine rose .20 .20
113 A34 10a green .30 .20

Issued to publicize World Refugee Year, July 1, 1959-June 30, 1960.

House, Field and Column (Allegory of Democratic Development) A35

1960, Oct. 27 **Photo.** ***Perf. 13***

114 A35 2a brown, pink & grn .20 .20
a. Green & pink omitted 13.50
115 A35 14a multicolored .35 .30

Revolution Day, Oct. 27, 1960.
No. 114a is easily counterfeited.

Punjab Agricultural College, Lyallpur A36

Design: 8a, College shield.

1960, Oct. **Engr.** ***Perf. 12½x14***

116 A36 2a rose red & gray blue .20 .20
117 A36 8a lilac & green .20 .20

50th anniv. of the Punjab Agricultural College, Lyallpur.

Caduceus, College Emblem — A37

1960, Nov. 16 **Photo.** ***Perf. 13½x13***

118 A37 2a blue, yel & blk .50 .20
119 A37 14a car rose, blk & emerald 1.60 .40

King Edward Medical College, Lahore, cent.

Map of South-East Asia and Commission Emblem — A38

1960, Dec. 5 Engr. *Perf. 13*

120 A38 14a red orange .30 .20

Conf. of the Commission on Asian and Far Eastern Affairs of the Intl. Chamber of Commerce, Karachi, Dec. 5-9.

"Kim's Gun" and Scout Badge A39

Perf. 12½x14

1960, Dec. 24 Unwmk.

121 A39 2a dk green, car & yel .65 .20

3rd Natl. Boy Scout Jamboree, Lahore, Dec. 24-31.

No. 110 Overprinted in Red

LAHORE STAMP
EXHIBITION
1961

1961, Feb. 12

122 A33 8a green .90 *1.00*

10th Lahore Stamp Exhibition, Feb. 12.

New Currency

Nos. 24, 68-69, 83, 108-109 Surcharged with New Value in Paisa

1961 *Perf. 13*

123	A18	1p on 1½a red	.20	.20
124	A3	2p on 3p orange red	.20	.20
125	A33	3p on 6p purple	.20	.20
126	A19	7p on 1a car rose	.20	.20
127	A24	13p on 2a red	.20	.20
128	A33	13p on 2a copper red	.20	.20
		Nos. 123-128 (6)	1.20	1.20

Various violet handstamped surcharges were applied to a variety of regular-issue stamps. Most of these repeat the denomination of the basic stamp and add the new value. Example: "8 Annas (50 Paisa)" on No. 75. Many errors exist.

For overprints see Nos. O74-O75.

Khyber Pass — A40

Chota Sona Masjid Gate — A41

Design: 10p, 13p, 25p, 40p, 50p, 75p, 90p, Shalimar Gardens, Lahore.

Type I

Type II

Two types of 1p, 2p and 5p:

I - First Bengali character beside "N" lacks appendage at left side of loop.

II - This character has a downward-pointing appendage at left side of loop, correcting "sh" to read "p".

On Nos. 129, 130, 132 the corrections were made individually on the plates, and each stamp may differ slightly. On No. 131a, the corrected letter is more clearly corrected and is uniform throughout the plate.

1961-63 Engr. *Perf. 13½x14*

129	A40	1p violet (II)	.65	.20
a.		Type I	1.40	.20
130	A40	2p rose red (II)	.65	.20
a.		Type I	1.40	.20
131	A40	3p magenta	.25	.20
a.		Re-engraved die	5.00	5.00
132	A40	5p ultra (II)	2.75	.20
a.		Type I	2.10	.20
133	A40	7p emerald	1.10	.20
134	A40	10p brown	.20	.20
135	A40	13p blue vio	.20	.20
136	A40	25p dark blue ('62)	4.25	.20
137	A40	40p dull purple ('62)	1.40	.20
138	A40	50p dull green ('62)	.30	.20
139	A40	75p dk carmine ('62)	.35	.20
140	A40	90p lt olive grn ('62)	.45	.20

Perf. 13½x13

141	A41	1r vermilion ('63)	1.75	.20
142	A41	1.25r purple	.70	.40
143	A41	2r orange ('63)	5.00	.20
144	A41	5r green ('63)	5.50	1.50
		Nos. 129-144 (16)	25.50	4.70

See #200-203. For surcharge and overprints see Nos. 184, O76-O82, O85-O93A.

Designs Redrawn

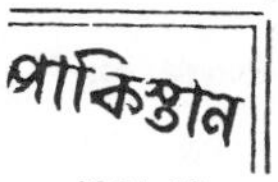
1961-62 Bengali Inscription

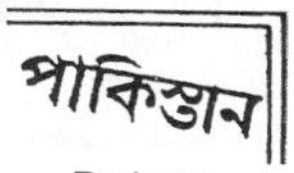
Redrawn Bengali Inscription

Bengali inscription redrawn with straight connecting line across top of characters. Shading of scenery differs, especially in Shalimar Gardens design where reflection is strengthened and trees at right are composed of horizontal lines instead of vertical lines and dots.

Designs as before; 15p, 20p, Shalimar Gardens.

1963-70 *Perf. 13½x14*

129b	A40	1p violet	.20	.20
130b	A40	2p rose red ('64)	.80	.20
131a	A40	3p magenta ('70)	4.25	2.10
132b	A40	5p ultra	.20	.20
133a	A40	7p emerald ('64)	5.00	2.10
134a	A40	10p brown	.20	.20
135a	A40	13p blue violet	.20	.20
135B	A40	15p rose lilac ('64)	.20	.20
135C	A40	20p dull green ('70)	.25	.20
136a	A40	25p dark blue	7.00	.20
137a	A40	40p dull purple ('64)	.20	.20
138a	A40	50p dull green ('64)	.20	.20
139a	A40	75p dark carmine ('64)	.25	.45
140a	A40	90p lt olive green ('64)	.25	.60
		Nos. 129b-140a (14)	19.20	7.25

For overprints see #174, O76b, O77b, O78a, O79b, O80a, O81a, O82a, O83-O84A, O85a, O86a.

Warsak Dam, Kabul River A42

1961, July 1 Engr. *Perf. 12½x13½*

150 A42 40p black & lt ultra .65 .20

Dedication of hydroelectric Warsak Project.

Symbolic Flower — A43

1961, Oct. 2 Unwmk. *Perf. 14*

151 A43 13p greenish blue .30 .20

152 A43 90p red lilac 1.00 .20

Issued for Children's Day.

Roses — A44

1961, Nov. 4 *Perf. 13½x13*

153 A44 13p deep green & ver .40 .20

154 A44 90p blue & vermilion 1.10 .30

Cooperative Day.

Police Crest and Traffic Policeman's Hand — A45

1961, Nov. 30 Photo. *Perf. 13x12½*

155 A45 13p dk blue, sil & blk .50 .20

156 A45 40p red, silver & blk 1.00 .25

Centenary of the police force.

"Eagle Locomotive, 1861" — A46

Design: 50pa, Diesel Engine, 1961.

1961, Dec. 31 *Perf. 13½x14*

157 A46 13p yellow, green & blk .75 .50

158 A46 50p green, blk & yellow 1.00 .75

Centenary of Pakistan railroads.

No. 87 Surcharged in Red with New Value, Boeing 720-B Jetliner and: "FIRST JET FLIGHT KARACHI-DACCA"

1962, Feb. 6 Engr. *Perf. 13*

159 A21 13p on 2½a dk carmine 1.25 .60

1st jet flight from Karachi to Dacca, Feb. 6, 1962.

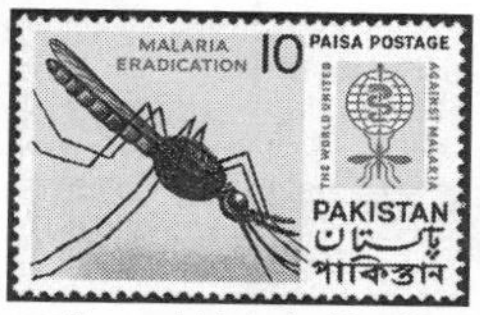

Mosquito and Malaria Eradication Emblem — A47

13p, Dagger pointing at mosquito, and emblem.

1962, Apr. 7 Photo. *Perf. 13½x14*

160 A47 10p multicolored .45 .20

161 A47 13p multicolored .45 .20

WHO drive to eradicate malaria.

Map of Pakistan and Jasmine — A48

1962, June 8 Unwmk. *Perf. 12*

162 A48 40p grn, yel grn & gray .95 .20

Introduction of new Pakistan Constitution.

Soccer A49

13p, Hockey & Olympic gold medal. 25p, Squash rackets & British squash rackets championship cup. 40p, Cricket & Ayub challenge cup.

1962, Aug. 14 Engr. *Perf. 12½x13½*

163	A49	7p blue & black	.20	.20
164	A49	13p green & black	.35	.25
165	A49	25p lilac & black	.20	.20
166	A49	40p brown org & blk	1.25	1.25
		Nos. 163-166 (4)	2.00	1.90

Marble Fruit Dish and Clay Flask — A50

13p, Sporting goods. 25p, Camel skin lamp, brass jug. 40p, Wooden powder bowl, cane basket. 50p, Inlaid box, brassware.

1962, Nov. 10 *Perf. 13½x13*

167	A50	7p dark red	.20	.20
168	A50	13p dark green	2.75	1.10
169	A50	25p bright purple	.20	.20
170	A50	40p yellow green	.20	.20
171	A50	50p dull red	.20	.20
		Nos. 167-171 (5)	3.55	1.90

Pakistan Intl. Industries Fair, Oct. 12-Nov. 20, publicizing Pakistan's small industries.

Children's Needs A51

1962, Dec. 11 Photo. *Perf. 13½x14*

172 A51 13p blue, plum & blk .35 .20

173 A51 40p multicolored .35 .20

16th anniv. of UNICEF.

No. 135a Overprinted in Red: "U.N. FORCE W. IRIAN"

1963, Feb. 15 Engr. Unwmk.

174 A40 13p blue violet .20 .20

Issued to commemorate the dispatch of Pakistani troops to West New Guinea.

Camel, Bull, Dancing Horse and Drummer A52

1963, Mar. 13 Photo. *Perf. 12*

175 A52 13p multicolored .20 .20

National Horse and Cattle Show, 1963.

Wheat and Tractor A53

Design: 50p, Hands and heap of rice.

1963, Mar. 21 Engr. *Perf. 12½x13½*

176 A53 13p brown orange 1.50 .20

177 A53 50p brown 3.00 .40

FAO "Freedom from Hunger" campaign.

No. 109 Surcharged with New Value and: "INTERNATIONAL/DACCA STAMP/EXHIBITION/1963"

1963, Mar. 23 *Perf. 13*

178 A33 13p on 2a copper red .55 .20

International Stamp Exhibition at Dacca.

Centenary Emblem — A54

Engr. and Typo.

1963, June 25 ***Perf. 13½x12½***
179 A54 40p dark gray & red 1.75 .20

International Red Cross, cent.

Paharpur Stupa A55

Designs: 13p, Cistern, Mohenjo-Daro, vert. 40p, Stupas, Taxila. 50pa, Stupas, Mainamati.

Perf. 12½x13½, 13½x12½

1963, Sept. 16 **Engr.** **Unwmk.**
180 A55 7p ultra .40 .20
181 A55 13p brown .40 .20
182 A55 40p carmine rose .75 .20
183 A55 50p dark violet .80 .20
Nos. 180-183 (4) 2.35 .80

No. 131 Surcharged and Overprinted: "100 YEARS OF P.W.D. OCTOBER, 1963"

1963, Oct. 7 ***Perf. 13½x14***
184 A40 13p on 3pa magenta .20 .20

Centenary of Public Works Department.

Atatürk Mausoleum, Ankara A56

1963, Nov. 10 ***Perf. 13x13½***
185 A56 50p red .75 .20

25th anniv. of the death of Kemal Atatürk, pres. of Turkey.

Globe and UNESCO Emblem A57

1963, Dec. 10 **Photo.** ***Perf. 13½x14***
186 A57 50p dk brn, vio blue & red .60 .20

15th anniv. of the Universal Declaration of Human Rights.

Multan Thermal Power Station A58

1963, Dec. 25 **Engr.** ***Perf. 12½x13½***
187 A58 13p ultra .20 .20

Issued to mark the opening of the Multan Thermal Power Station.

Type of 1961-63

Perf. 13½x13

1963-65 **Engr.** **Wmk. 351**
200 A41 1r vermilion .25 .20
201 A41 1.25r purple ('64) .75 .20
202 A41 2r orange .40 .20
203 A41 5r green ('65) 3.25 .40
Nos. 200-203 (4) 4.65 1.00

For overprints see Nos. O92-O93A.

A59

13p, Temple of Thot, Dakka, and Queen Nefertari with Goddesses Hathor and Isis. 50p, Ramses II, Abu Simbel, and View of Nile.

Perf. 13x13½

1964, Mar. 30 **Unwmk.**
204 A59 13p brick red & turq blue .35 .20
205 A59 50p black & rose lilac .65 .20

UNESCO world campaign to save historic monuments in Nubia.

Pakistan Pavilion and Unisphere A60

1.25r, Pakistan pavilion, Unisphere, vert.

Perf. 12½x14, 14x12½

1964, Apr. 22 **Engr.** **Unwmk.**
206 A60 13p ultramarine .20 .20
207 A60 1.25r dp orange & ultra .30 .25

New York World's Fair, 1964-65.

Mausoleum of Shah Abdul Latif — A61

Mausoleum of Jinnah — A62

1964, June 25 ***Perf. 13½x13***
208 A61 50p magenta & ultra 1.00 .20

Bicentenary (?) of the death of Shah Abdul Latif of Bhit (1689-1752).

1964, Sept. 11 **Unwmk.** ***Perf. 13***

Design: 15p, Mausoleum, horiz.

209 A62 15p green .50 .20
210 A62 50p greenish gray 1.50 .20

16th anniv. of the death of Mohammed Ali Jinnah (1876-1948), the Quaid-i-Azam (Great Leader), founder and president of Pakistan.

Bengali Alphabet on Slate and Slab with Urdu Alphabet A63

1964, Oct. 5 **Engr.**
211 A63 15p brown .20 .20

Issued for Universal Children's Day.

West Pakistan University of Engineering and Technology — A64

1964, Dec. 21 ***Perf. 12½x14***
212 A64 15p henna brown .20 .20

1st convocation of the West Pakistan University of Engineering & Technology, Lahore, Dec. 1964.

Eyeglasses and Book — A65

Perf. 13x13½

1965, Feb. 28 **Litho.** **Unwmk.**
213 A65 15p yellow & ultra .20 .20

Issued to publicize aid for the blind.

ITU Emblem, Telegraph Pole and Transmission Tower — A66

1965, May 17 **Engr.** ***Perf. 12½x14***
214 A66 15p deep claret 1.40 .25

Cent. of the ITU.

ICY Emblem A67

1965, June 26 **Litho.** ***Perf. 13½***
215 A67 15p blue & black .40 .20
216 A67 50p yellow & green 1.00 .30

International Cooperation Year, 1965.

Hands Holding Book — A68

50p, Map & flags of Turkey, Iran & Pakistan.

Perf. 13½x13, 13x12½

1965, July 21 **Litho.** **Unwmk.**

Size: 46x35mm

217 A68 15p org brn, dk brn & buff .20 .20

Size: 54x30½mm

218 A68 50p multicolored 1.00 .20

1st anniv. of the signing of the Regional Cooperation for Development Pact by Turkey, Iran and Pakistan.

Tanks, Army Emblem and Soldier — A69

Designs: 15p, Navy emblem, corvette No. O204 and officer. 50p, Air Force emblem, two F-104 Starfighters and pilot.

1965, Dec. 25 **Litho.** ***Perf. 13½x13***
219 A69 7p multicolored .60 .25
220 A69 15p multicolored 1.25 .20
221 A69 50p multicolored 2.25 .25
Nos. 219-221 (3) 4.10 .70

Issued to honor the Pakistani armed forces.

Emblems of Pakistan Armed Forces — A70

1966, Feb. 13 **Litho.** ***Perf. 13½x13***
222 A70 15p buff, grn & dk bl .50 .20

Issued for Armed Forces Day.

Atomic Reactor, Islamabad — A71

Unwmk.

1966, Apr. 30 **Engr.** ***Perf. 13***
223 A71 15p black .20 .20

Pakistan's first atomic reactor.

Habib Bank Emblem A72

Perf. 12½x13½

1966, Aug. 25 **Litho.** **Unwmk.**
224 A72 15p brown, org & dk grn .20 .20

25th anniversary of the Habib Bank.

Boy and Girl — A73

1966, Oct. 3 **Litho.** ***Perf. 13x13½***
225 A73 15p multicolored .20 .20

Issued for Children's Day.

UNESCO Emblem A74

1966, Nov. 24 Unwmk. ***Perf. 14***
226 A74 15p multicolored 2.25 .25

20th anniv. of UNESCO.

Secretariat Buildings, Islamabad, Flag and Pres. Mohammed Ayub Khan — A75

1966, Nov. 29 Litho. ***Perf. 13***
227 A75 15p multicolored .25 .20
228 A75 50p multicolored .50 .20

Publicizing the new capital, Islamabad.

Avicenna — A76

Mohammed Ali Jinnah — A77

1966, Dec. 3 ***Perf. 13½***
229 A76 15p sal pink & slate grn .45 .20

Issued to publicize the Health Institute.

Lithographed and Engraved
1966, Dec. 25 Unwmk. ***Perf. 13***

Design: 50p, Different frame.

230 A77 15p orange, blk & bl .20 .20
231 A77 50p lilac, blk & vio bl .50 .20

90th anniv. of the birth of Mohammed Ali Jinnah (1876-1948), 1st Governor General of Pakistan.

ITY Emblem — A78

1967, Jan. 1 Litho.
232 A78 15p bis brn, blue & blk .20 .20

International Tourist Year, 1967.

Red Crescent Emblem — A79

1967, Jan. 10 Litho. ***Perf. 13½***
233 A79 15p brn, brn org & red .20 .20

Tuberculosis eradication campaign.

Scout Sign and Emblem A80

Perf. 12½x13½
1967, Jan. 29 Photo.
234 A80 15p dp plum & brn org .25 .20

4th National Pakistan Jamboree. "Faisa" is a plate flaw, not an error.

Justice Holding Scales — A81

Unwmk.
1967, Feb. 17 Litho. ***Perf. 13***
235 A81 15p multicolored .20 .20

Centenary of High Court of West Pakistan.

Mohammad Iqbal — A82

1967, Apr. 21 Litho. ***Perf. 13***
236 A82 15p red & brown .20 .20
237 A82 1r dk green & brn .50 .20

90th anniv. of the birth of Mohammad Iqbal (1877-1938), poet and philosopher.

Flag of Valor — A83

1967, May 15 Litho. ***Perf. 13***
238 A83 15p multicolored .20 .20

Flag of Valor awarded to the cities of Lahore, Sialkot and Sargodha.

Star and "20" — A84

1967, Aug. 14 Photo. Unwmk.
239 A84 15p red & slate green .20 .20

20th anniversary of independence.

Rice Plant and Globe A85

Cotton Plant, Bale and Cloth — A86

Design: 50p, Raw jute, bale and cloth.

1967, Sept. 26 Photo. ***Perf. 13x13½***
240 A85 10p dk blue & yellow .20 .20

Perf. 13

241 A86 15p orange, bl grn & yel .20 .20
242 A86 50p blue grn, brn & tan .25 .20
Nos. 240-242 (3) .65 .60

Issued to publicize major export products.

Toys — A87

1967, Oct. 2 Litho. ***Perf. 13***
243 A87 15p multicolored .20 .20

Issued for International Children's Day.

Shah and Empress Farah of Iran — A88

Lithographed and Engraved
1967, Oct. 26 ***Perf. 13***
244 A88 50p yellow, blue & lilac .65 .20

Coronation of Shah Mohammed Riza Pahlavi and Empress Farah of Iran.

"Each for all, . . ." A89

1967, Nov. 4 Litho. ***Perf. 13***
245 A89 15p multicolored .20 .20

Cooperative Day, 1967.

Mangla Dam — A90

1967, Nov. 23 Litho. ***Perf. 13***
246 A90 15p multicolored .20 .20

Indus Basin Project, harnessing the Indus River for flood control and irrigation.

"Fight Against Cancer" — A91

Human Rights Flame — A92

1967, Dec. 26
247 A91 15p red & dk brown .70 .20

Issued to publicize the fight against cancer.

1968, Jan. 31 Photo. ***Perf. 14x12½***
248 A92 15p Prus green & red .20 .20
249 A92 50p yellow, silver & red .20 .20

International Human Rights Year 1968.

Agricultural University and Produce A93

1968, Mar. 28 Litho. ***Perf. 13½***
250 A93 15p multicolored .20 .20

Issued to publicize the first convocation of the East Pakistan Agricultural University.

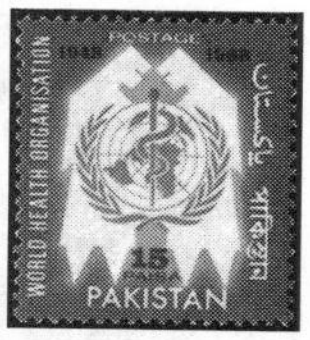

WHO Emblem — A94

1968, Apr. 7 Photo. ***Perf. 13½x12½***
251 A94 15p emerald & orange .20 .20
252 A94 50p orange & dk blue .20 .20

20th anniv. of WHO. "Pais" is a plate flaw, not an error.

Kazi Nazrul Islam A95

Lithographed and Engraved
1968, June 25 Unwmk. ***Perf. 13***
253 A95 15p dull yellow & brown .30 .20
254 A95 50p rose & brown .60 .20

Kazi Nazrul Islam, poet and composer.

Nos. 56, 61 and 74 Surcharged with New Value and Bars in Black or Red

1968, Sept. Engr. *Perf. 13*

255	A13	4p on 3a dk rose lake	.40	.75
256	A21	4p on 6a dk blue (R)	.60	.75
257	A15	60p on 10a purple (R)	.35	.25
a.		Black surcharge	.25	.50
		Nos. 255-257 (3)	1.35	1.75

Types of 1948-57

1968 Wmk. 351 Engr. *Perf. 13*

258	A26	10r dk green & orange	2.50	*3.00*
259	A7	25r purple	5.00	*7.00*

Children with Hoops A96

Unwmk.

1968, Oct. 7 Litho. *Perf. 13*

260	A96	15p buff & multi	.20	.20

Issued for International Children's Day.

Symbolic of Political Reforms — A97

Designs: 15p, Agricultural and industrial development. 50p, Defense. 60p, Scientific and cultural advancement.

1968, Oct. 27 Litho. *Perf. 13*

261	A97	10p multicolored	.20	.20
262	A97	15p multicolored	.20	.20
263	A97	50p multicolored	1.75	.20
264	A97	60p multicolored	.75	.30
		Nos. 261-264 (4)	2.90	.90

Development Decade, 1958-1968.

Chittagong Steel Mill — A98

1969, Jan. 7 Unwmk. *Perf. 13*

265	A98	15p lt gray grn, lt blue & blk	.20	.20

Opening of Pakistan's first steel mill.

Family of Four A99

1969, Jan. 14 Litho. *Perf. 13½*

266	A99	15p lt blue & plum	.20	.20

Issued to publicize family planning.

Hockey Player and Medal — A100

1969, Jan. 30 Photo. *Perf. 13½*

267	A100	15p green, lt bl, blk & gold	1.00	.40
268	A100	1r grn, sal pink, blk & gold	2.50	.75

Pakistan's hockey victory at the 19th Olympic Games in Mexico.

Mirza Ghalib — A101

1969, Feb. 15 Litho. *Perf. 13*

269	A101	15p blue & multi	.20	.20
270	A101	50p multicolored	.50	.20

Mirza Ghalib (Asad Ullab Beg Khan, 1797-1869), poet who modernized the Urdu language.

Dacca Railroad Station A102

1969, Apr. 27 Litho. *Perf. 13*

271	A102	15p yel, grn, blk & dull bl	.40	.20

Opening of the new railroad station in Kamalpur area of Dacca.

ILO Emblem and Ornamental Border — A103

1969, May 15 Litho. *Perf. 13½*

272	A103	15p brt grn & ocher	.20	.20
273	A103	50p car rose & ocher	.30	.20

50th anniv. of the ILO.

Lady on Balcony, Mogul Miniature, Pakistan A104

50p, Lady Serving Wine, Safavi miniature, Iran. 1r, Sultan Suleiman Receiving Sheik Abdul Latif, 16th cent. miniature, Turkey.

1969, July 21 Litho. *Perf. 13*

274	A104	20p multicolored	.20	.20
275	A104	50p multicolored	.20	.20
276	A104	1r multicolored	.25	.20
		Nos. 274-276 (3)	.65	.60

5th anniv. of the signing of the Regional Cooperation for Development Pact by Turkey, Iran and Pakistan.

Eastern Refinery, Chittagong A105

1969, Sept. 14 Photo. *Perf. 13½*

277	A105	20p yel, blk & vio bl	.20	.20

Opening of the 1st oil refinery in East Pakistan.

Children Playing — A106

1969, Oct. 6 *Perf. 13*

278	A106	20p blue & multi	.20	.20

Issued for Universal Children's Day.

Japanese Doll, Map of Dacca-Tokyo Pearl Route — A107

1969, Nov. 1 Litho. *Perf. 13½x13*

279	A107	20p multicolored	.60	.20
280	A107	50p ultra & multi	1.10	.30

Inauguration of the Pakistan International Airways' Dacca-Tokyo "Pearl Route."

Reflection of Light Diagram — A108

1969, Nov. 4 *Perf. 13*

281	A108	20p multicolored	.20	.20

Alhazen (abu-Ali al Hasan ibn-al-Haytham, 965-1039), astronomer and optician.

Vickers Vimy and London-Darwin Route over Karachi — A109

1969, Dec. 2 Photo. *Perf. 13½x13*

282	A109	50p multicolored	.90	.30

50th anniv. of the 1st England to Australia flight.

View of EXPO '70, Sun Tower, Flags of Pakistan, Iran and Turkey A110

1970, Feb. 15 Litho. *Perf. 13*

283	A110	50p multicolored	.25	.25

Issued to publicize EXPO '70 International Exhibition, Osaka, Japan, Mar. 15-Sept. 13.

UPU Headquarters, Bern — A111

1970, May 20 Litho. *Perf. 13½x13*

284	A111	20p multicolored	.20	.20
285	A111	50p multicolored	.25	.20

Opening of new UPU headquarters in Bern.

A souvenir sheet of 2 exists, inscribed "U.P.U. Day 9th Oct. 1971". It contains stamps similar to Nos. 284-285, imperf. Value, $25.

UN Headquarters, New York — A112

Design: 50p, UN emblem.

1970, June 26

286	A112	20p green & multi	.20	.20
287	A112	50p violet & multi	.20	.20

25th anniversary of the United Nations.

Education Year Emblem and Open Book — A113

1970, July 6 Litho. *Perf. 13*

288	A113	20p blue & multi	.20	.20
289	A113	50p orange & multi	.20	.20

International Education Year, 1970.

Saiful Malook Lake, Pakistan A114

Designs: 50p, Seeyo-Se-Pol Bridge, Esfahan, Iran. 1r, View, Fethiye, Turkey.

1970, July 21

290 A114 20p yellow & multi .20 .20
291 A114 50p yellow & multi .25 .20
292 A114 1r yellow & multi .30 .20
Nos. 290-292 (3) .75 .60

6th anniv. of the signing of the Regional Cooperation for Development Pact by Pakistan, Iran and Turkey.

Asian Productivity Year Emblem — A115

1970, Aug. 18 Photo. ***Perf. 12½x14***

293 A115 50p black, yel & grn .20 .20

Asian Productivity Year, 1970.

Dr. Maria Montessori A116

1970, Aug. 31 Litho. ***Perf. 13***

294 A116 20p red & multi .20 .20
295 A116 50p multicolored .20 .25

Maria Montessori (1870-1952) Italian educator and physician.

Tractor and Fertilizer Factory — A117

1970, Sept. 12

296 A117 20p yel grn & brn org .20 .20

10th Regional Food and Agricultural Organization Conf. for the Near East in Islamabad.

Boy, Girl, Open Book A118

Flag and Inscription A119

1970, Oct. 5 Photo. ***Perf. 13***

297 A118 20p multicolored .20 .20

Issued for Children's Day.

1970, Dec. 7 Litho. ***Perf. 13½x13***

298 A119 20p violet & green .20 .20
299 A119 20p brt pink & green .20 .20

No. 298 inscribed "Elections for National Assembly 7th Dec. 1970," No. 299 inscribed "Elections for Provincial Assemblies 17th Dec. 1970."

Emblem and Burning of Al Aqsa Mosque — A120

1970, Dec. 26 ***Perf. 13½x12½***

300 A120 20p multicolored .20 .20

Islamic Conference of Foreign Ministers, Karachi, Dec. 26-28.

Coastal Embankment — A121

1971, Feb. 25 Litho. ***Perf. 13***

301 A121 20p multicolored .20 .20

Development of coastal embankments in East Pakistan.

Men of Different Races — A122

1971, Mar. 21 Litho. ***Perf. 13***

302 A122 20p multicolored .20 .20
303 A122 50p lilac & multi .20 .20

Intl. Year against Racial Discrimination.

Cement Factory, Daudkhel — A123

1971, July 1 Litho. ***Perf. 13***

304 A123 20p purple, blk & brn .20 .20

20th anniversary of Colombo Plan.

Badshahi Mosque, Lahore — A124

Designs: 10pa, Mosque of Selim, Edirne, Turkey. 50pa, Religious School, of Chaharbagh, Isfahan, Iran, vert.

1971, July 21 Litho. ***Perf. 13***

305 A124 10p red & multi .20 .20
306 A124 20p green & multi .20 .20
307 A124 50p blue & multi .30 .40
Nos. 305-307 (3) .70 .80

7th anniversary of Regional Cooperation among Pakistan, Iran and Turkey.

Electric Train and Boy with Toy Locomotive — A125

1971, Oct. 4 Litho. ***Perf. 13***

308 A125 20p slate & multi 1.50 .40

Children's Day.

Messenger and Statue of Cyrus the Great — A126

1971, Oct. 15

309 A126 10p green & multi .40 .25
310 A126 20p blue & multi .50 .30
311 A126 50p red & multi .60 .50
Nos. 309-311 (3) 1.50 1.05

2500th anniversary of the founding of the Persian Empire by Cyrus the Great.

A souvenir sheet of 3 contains stamps similar to Nos. 309-311, imperf. Value, $25.

Hockey Player and Cup — A127

1971, Oct. 24

312 A127 20p red & multi 2.00 .50

First World Hockey Cup, Barcelona, Spain, Oct. 15-24.

Great Bath at Mohenjo-Daro — A128

1971, Nov. 4

313 A128 20p dp org, dk brn & blk .25 .25

25th anniv. of UNESCO.

UNICEF Emblem A129

1971, Dec. 11 Litho. ***Perf. 13***

314 A129 50p dull bl, org & grn .30 .40

25th anniv. of UNICEF.

King Hussein and Jordan Flag A130

1971, Dec. 25

315 A130 20p blue & multi .20 .20

50th anniversary of the Hashemite Kingdom of Jordan.

Pakistan Hockey Federation Emblem, and Cup — A131

1971, Dec. 31

316 A131 20p yellow & multi 2.50 .75

Pakistan, world hockey champions, Barcelona, Oct. 1971.

Arab Scholars A132

1972, Jan. 15 Litho. ***Perf. 13½***

317 A132 20p brown, blk & blue .20 .25

International Book Year 1972.

Angels and Grand Canal, Venice — A133

1972, Feb. 5 ***Perf. 13***

318 A133 20p blue & multi .30 .25

UNESCO campaign to save Venice.

ECAFE Emblem A134

1972, Mar. 28 Litho. ***Perf. 13***

319 A134 20p blue & multi .20 .25

Economic Commission for Asia and the Far East (ECAFE), 25th anniversary.

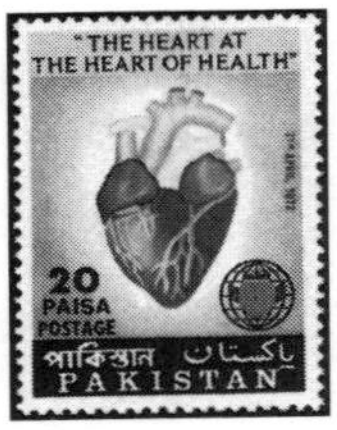

"Your Heart is your Health" — A135

1972, Apr. 7 *Perf. 13x13½*
320 A135 20p vio blue & multi .20 .25

World Health Day 1972.

"Only One Earth" A136

1972, June 5 Litho. *Perf. 12½x14*
321 A136 20p ultra & multi .20 .25

UN Conference on Human Environment, Stockholm, June 5-16.

Young Man, by Abdur Rehman Chughtai A137

Paintings: 10p, Fisherman, by Cevat Dereli (Turkey). 20p, Persian Woman, by Behzad.

1972, July 21 Litho. *Perf. 13*
322 A137 10p multicolored .20 .20
323 A137 20p multicolored .30 .25
324 A137 50p multicolored .50 .55
Nos. 322-324 (3) 1.00 1.00

Regional Cooperation for Development Pact among Pakistan, Turkey and Iran, 8th anniversary.

Jinnah and Independence Memorial A138

"Land Reforms" — A139

Designs: Nos. 326-329, Principal reforms. 60pa, State Bank, Islamabad, meeting-place of National Assembly, horiz.

Perf. 13 (A138), 13½x12½ (A139)
1972, Aug. 14
325 A138 10p shown .20 .20
326 A139 20p shown .20 .20
327 A139 20p Labor reforms .20 .20
328 A139 20p Education .20 .20
329 A139 20p Health care .20 .20
a. Vert. strip of 4, #326-329 .75
330 A138 60p rose lilac & car .25 .25
Nos. 325-330 (6) 1.25 1.25

25th anniversary of independence. No. 329a has decorative labels adjoining.

Blood Donor, Society Emblem — A140

1972, Sept. 6 Litho. *Perf. 14x12½*
331 A140 20p multicolored .25 .25

Pakistan National Blood Transfusion Service.

Census Chart A141

1972, Sept. 16 Litho. *Perf. 13½*
332 A141 20p multicolored .20 .20

Centenary of population census.

Children Leaving Slum for Modern City — A142

1972, Oct. 2 Litho. *Perf. 13*
333 A142 20p multicolored .20 .20

Children's Day.

Giant Book and Children A143

1972, Oct. 23
334 A143 20p purple & multi .20 .20

Education Week.

Nuclear Power Plant, Karachi A144

1972, Nov. 28 Litho. *Perf. 13*
335 A144 20p multicolored .25 .25

Pakistan's first nuclear power plant.

Copernicus in Observatory, by Jan Matejko — A145

1973, Feb. 19 Litho. *Perf. 13*
336 A145 20p multicolored .25 .25

Dancing Girl, Public Baths, Mohenjo-Daro — A146

1973, Feb. 23 *Perf. 13½x13*
337 A146 20p multicolored .20 .20

Mohenjo-Daro excavations, 50th anniv.

Radar, Lightning, WMO Emblem — A147

1973, Mar. 23 Litho. *Perf. 13*
338 A147 20p multicolored .25 .25

Cent. of intl. meteorological cooperation.

Prisoners of War — A148

1973, Apr. 18
339 A148 1.25r black & multi 1.50 1.75

A plea for Pakistani prisoners of war in India.

National Assembly, Islamabad A149

1973, Apr. 21 *Perf. 12½x13½*
340 A149 20p green & multi .45 .30

Constitution Week.

State Bank and Emblem — A150

1973, July 1 Litho. *Perf. 13*
341 A150 20p multicolored .20 .25
342 A150 1r multicolored .30 .35

State Bank of Pakistan, 25th anniversary.

Street, Mohenjo-Daro, Pakistan A151

Designs: 20p, Statue of man, Shahdad, Kerman, Persia, 4000 B.C. 1.25r, Head from mausoleum of King Antiochus I (69-34 B.C.), Turkey.

1973, July 21 *Perf. 13x13½*
343 A151 20p blue & multi .25 .20
344 A151 60p emerald & multi .50 .35
345 A151 1.25r red & multi .70 .75
Nos. 343-345 (3) 1.45 1.30

Regional Cooperation for Development Pact among Pakistan, Turkey and Iran, 9th anniversary.

Pakistani Flag and Constitution A152

1973, Aug. 14 Litho. *Perf. 13*
346 A152 20p blue & multi .20 .20

Independence Day.

Mohammed Ali Jinnah — A153

1973, Sept. 11 Litho. *Perf. 13*
347 A153 20p emerald, yel & blk .20 .20

Mohammed Ali Jinnah (1876-1948), president of All-India Moslem League.

Wallago Attu — A154

Fish: 20p, Labeo rohita. 60p, Tilapia mossambica. 1r, Catla catla.

1973, Sept. 24 Litho. *Perf. 13½*
348 A154 10p multicolored 1.10 1.10
349 A154 20p multicolored 1.10 1.10
350 A154 60p multicolored 1.40 1.40
351 A154 1r ultra & multi 1.40 1.40
a. Strip of 4, #348-351 5.00 5.00

Book, Torch, Child and School — A155

1973, Oct. 1
352 A155 20p multicolored .20 .20

Universal Children's Day.

Sindhi Farmer and FAO Emblem A156

1973, Oct. 15 Litho. *Perf. 13*
353 A156 20p multicolored .50 .30

World Food Organization, 10th anniv.

Kemal Ataturk and Ankara — A157

1973, Oct. 29
354 A157 50p multicolored .45 .30

50th anniversary of Turkish Republic.

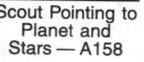

Scout Pointing to Planet and Stars — A158

Human Rights Flame, Sheltered Home — A159

Perf. 13½x12½

1973, Nov. 11 **Litho.**
355 A158 20p dull blue & multi 1.40 .40

25th anniversary of Pakistani Boy Scouts and Silver Jubilee Jamboree.

1973, Nov. 16
356 A159 20p multicolored .30 .25

25th anniversary of the Universal Declaration of Human Rights.

al-Biruni and Jhelum Observatory — A160

1973, Nov. 26 **Litho.** ***Perf. 13***
357 A160 20p multicolored .40 .20
358 A160 1.25r multicolored 1.10 .50

International Congress on Millenary of abu-al-Rayhan al-Biruni, Nov. 26-Dec. 12.

Dr. A. G. Hansen A161

1973, Dec. 29
359 A161 20p ultra & multi 1.10 .45

Centenary of the discovery by Dr. Armauer Gerhard Hansen of the Hansen bacillus, the cause of leprosy.

Family and WPY Emblem A162

1974, Jan. 1 **Litho.** ***Perf. 13***
360 A162 20p yellow & multi .20 .20
361 A162 1.25r salmon & multi .25 .25

World Population Year 1974.

Summit Emblem and Ornament — A163

Emblem, Crescent and Rays A164

1974, Feb. 22 ***Perf. 14x12½, 13***
362 A163 20p multicolored .20 .20
363 A164 65p multicolored .25 .40
a. Souvenir sheet of 2 2.50 3.00

Islamic Summit Meeting. No. 363a contains two stamps similar to Nos. 362-363 with simulated perforations.

Metric Measures A165

1974, July 1 **Litho.** ***Perf. 13***
364 A165 20p multicolored .20 .20

Introduction of metric system.

Kashan Rug, Lahore A166

Designs: 60p, Persian rug, late 16th century. 1.25r, Anatolian rug, 15th century.

1974, July 21
365 A166 20p multicolored .20 .20
366 A166 60p multicolored .40 .40
367 A166 1.25r multicolored .65 .75
Nos. 365-367 (3) 1.25 1.35

10th anniversary of the Regional Cooperation for Development Pact among Pakistan, Iran and Turkey.

Hands Protecting Sapling — A167

1974, Aug. 9 **Litho.** ***Perf. 13***
368 A167 20p multicolored .50 .40

Arbor Day.

Torch over Map of Africa with Namibia — A168

1974, Aug. 26
369 A168 60p green & multi .45 .40

Namibia (South-West Africa) Day. See note after United Nations No. 241.

Map of Pakistan with Highways and Disputed Area — A169

1974, Sept. 23
370 A169 20p multicolored .75 .40

Highway system under construction.

Child and Students A170

1974, Oct. 7 **Litho.** ***Perf. 13***
371 A170 20p multicolored .25 .25

Universal Children's Day.

UPU Emblem — A171

Liaqat Ali Khan — A172

2.25r, Jet, UPU emblem, mail coach.

1974, Oct. 9

Size: 24x36mm

372 A171 20p multicolored .25 .20

Size: 29x41mm

373 A171 2.25r multicolored .75 1.00
a. Souv. sheet of 2, #372-373, imperf. 3.00 4.00

Centenary of Universal Postal Union.

1974, Oct. 16 **Litho.** ***Perf. 13x13½***
374 A172 20p black & red .25 .25

Liaqat Ali Khan, Prime Minister 1947-1951.

Mohammad Allama Iqbal — A173

1974, Nov. 9 **Litho.** ***Perf. 13***
375 A173 20p multicolored .25 .25

Mohammad Allama Iqbal (1877-1938), poet and philosopher.

Dr. Schweitzer on Ogowe River, 1915 — A174

1975, Jan. 14 **Litho.** ***Perf. 13***
376 A174 2.25r multicolored 2.25 *2.50*

Dr. Albert Schweitzer (1875-1965), medical missionary, birth centenary.

Tourism Year 75 Emblem A175

1975, Jan. 15
377 A175 2.25r multicolored .50 .50

South Asia Tourism Year, 1975.

Flags of Participants, Memorial and Prime Minister Bhutto — A176

1975, Feb. 22 **Litho.** ***Perf. 13***
378 A176 20p lt blue & multi .50 .30
379 A176 1r brt pink & multi 1.00 1.00

2nd Lahore Islamic Summit, Feb. 22, 1st anniv.

IWY Emblem and Woman Scientist — A177

Design: 2.25r, Old woman and girl learning to read and write.

1975, June 15 **Litho.** ***Perf. 13***
380 A177 20p multicolored .20 .20
381 A177 2.25r multicolored 1.00 1.25

International Women's Year 1975.

Globe with Dates, Arabic "X" — A178

Camel Leather Vase, Pakistan A179

1975, July 14 Litho. *Perf. 13*

382 A178 20p multicolored .55 .40

International Congress of Mathematical Sciences, Karachi, July 14-20.

1975, July 21

60p, Ceramic plate and RCD emblem, Iran, horiz. 1.25r, Porcelain vase, Turkey.

383	A179	20p lilac & multi	.30	.25
384	A179	60p violet blk & multi	.55	.75
385	A179	1.25r blue & multi	.80	1.10
		Nos. 383-385 (3)	1.65	2.10

Regional Cooperation for Development Pact among Turkey, Iran and Pakistan.

Sapling, Trees and Ant — A180

Black Partridge A181

1975, Aug. 9 Litho. *Perf. 13x13½*

386 A180 20p multicolored .40 .30

Tree Planting Day.

1975, Sept. 30 Litho. *Perf. 13*

387	A181	20p blue & multi	1.25	.25
388	A181	2.25r yellow & multi	3.75	3.00

Wildlife Protection.

Girls — A182

1975, Oct. 6

389 A182 20p multicolored .30 .25

Universal Children's Day.

Hazrat Amir Khusrau, Sitar and Tabla — A183

1975, Oct. 24 Litho. *Perf. 14x12½*

390	A183	20p lt blue & multi	.25	.30
391	A183	2.25r pink & multi	.75	1.00

700th anniversary of Hazrat Amir Khusrau (1253-1325), musician who invented the sitar and tabla instruments.

Mohammad Iqbal — A184

1975, Nov. 9 *Perf. 13*

392 A184 20p multicolored .25 .20

Mohammad Allama Iqbal (1877-1938), poet and philosopher, birth centenary.

Wild Sheep of the Punjab — A185

1975, Dec. 31 Litho. *Perf. 13*

393	A185	20p multicolored	.40	.25
394	A185	3r multicolored	1.50	*2.00*

Wildlife Protection. See Nos. 410-411.

Mohenjo-Daro and UNESCO Emblem A186

View of Mohenjo-Daro excavations.

1976, Feb. 29 Litho. *Perf. 13*

395	A186	10p multicolored	.65	.65
396	A186	20p multicolored	.75	.75
397	A186	65p multicolored	.75	.75
398	A186	3r multicolored	.75	.75
399	A186	4r multicolored	.85	.85
a.		Strip of 5, #395-399	4.50	3.00

UNESCO campaign to save Mohenjo-Daro excavations.

Dome and Minaret of Rauza-e-Mubarak Mausoleum — A187

1976, Mar. 3 Photo. *Perf. 13½x14*

400	A187	20p blue & multi	.20	.20
401	A187	3r gray & multi	.80	.60

International Congress on Seerat, the teachings of Mohammed, Mar. 3-15.

Alexander Graham Bell, 1876 Telephone and Dial — A188

1976, Mar. 10 *Perf. 13*

402 A188 3r blue & multi 1.25 1.25

Centenary of first telephone call by Alexander Graham Bell, Mar. 10, 1876.

College Emblem — A189

1976, Mar. 15 Litho. *Perf. 13*

403 A189 20p multicolored .30 .30

Cent. of Natl. College of Arts, Lahore.

Peacock A190

1976, Mar. 31 Litho. *Perf. 13*

404	A190	20p lt blue & multi	1.00	.25
405	A190	3r pink & multi	3.25	3.25

Wildlife protection.

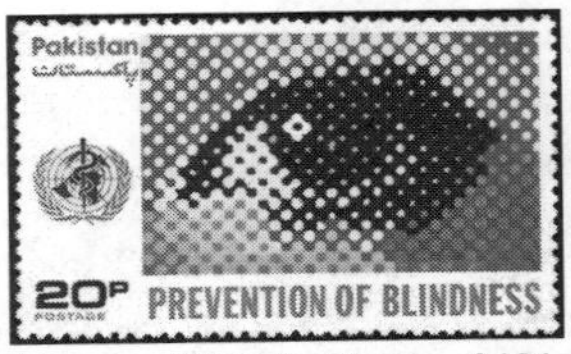

Eye and WHO Emblem — A191

1976, Apr. 7

406 A191 20p multicolored .70 .50

World Health Day: "Foresight prevents blindness."

Mohenjo-Daro, UNESCO Emblem, Bull (from Seal) — A192

1976, May 31 Litho. *Perf. 13*

407 A192 20p multicolored .30 .25

UNESCO campaign to save Mohenjo-Daro excavations.

Jefferson Memorial, US Bicentennial Emblem — A193

Declaration of Independence, by John Trumbull — A194

1976, July 4 *Perf. 13*

408 A193 90p multicolored .75 .40

Perf. 13½x13

409 A194 4r multicolored 2.75 *3.00*

American Bicentennial.

Wildlife Type of 1975

Wildlife protection: 20p, 3r, Ibex.

1976, July 12

410	A185	20p multicolored	.25	.25
411	A185	3r multicolored	1.50	1.50

Mohammed Ali Jinnah — A195

65p, Riza Shah Pahlavi. 90p, Kemal Ataturk.

1976, July 21 Litho. *Perf. 14*

412	A195	20p multicolored	.75	.50
413	A195	65p multicolored	.75	.50
414	A195	90p multicolored	.75	.50
a.		Strip of 3, #412-414	2.50	2.25

Regional Cooperation for Development Pact among Pakistan, Turkey and Iran, 12th anniversary.

Ornament A196

Jinnah and Wazir Mansion A197

Designs (Jinnah and): 40p, Sind Madressah (building). 50p, Minar Qarardad (minaret). 3r, Mausoleum.

1976, Aug. 14 Litho. *Perf. 13½*

415	A196	5p multicolored	.20	.20
416	A196	10p multicolored	.20	.20
417	A196	15p multicolored	.20	.20
418	A197	20p multicolored	.20	.20
419	A197	40p multicolored	.20	.20
420	A197	50p multicolored	.20	.20

421 A196 1r multicolored .30 .25
422 A197 3r multicolored .40 .40
a. Block of 8, #415-422 1.90 1.90

Mohammed Ali Jinnah (1876-1948), first Governor General of Pakistan, birth centenary. Horizontal rows of types A196 and A197 alternate in sheet.

Mohenjo-Daro and UNESCO Emblem — A198

1976, Aug. 31 ***Perf. 14***
423 A198 65p multicolored .45 .40

UNESCO campaign to save Mohenjo-Daro excavations.

Racial Discrimination Emblem — A199

Perf. 12½x13½
1976, Sept. 15 **Litho.**
424 A199 65p multicolored .30 .35

Fight against racial discrimination.

Child's Head, Symbols of Health, Education and Food — A200

1976, Oct. 4 ***Perf. 13***
425 A200 20p blue & multi .20 .20

Universal Children's Day.

Verse by Allama Iqbal A201

1976, Nov. 9 **Litho.** ***Perf. 13***
426 A201 20p multicolored .20 .20

Mohammed Allama Iqbal (1877-1938), poet and philosopher, birth centenary.

Scout Emblem, Jinnah Giving Salute — A202

Children Reading A203

1976, Nov. 20
427 A202 20p multicolored .60 .25

Quaid-I-Azam Centenary Jamboree, Nov. 1976.

1976, Dec. 15 **Litho.** ***Perf. 13***
428 A203 20p multicolored .25 .20

Books for children.

Mohammed Ali Jinnah — A204

Lithographed and Embossed

1976, Dec. 25 ***Perf. 12½***
429 A204 10r gold & green 2.25 2.50

Mohammed Ali Jinnah (1876-1948), 1st Governor General of Pakistan.

An imperf presentation sheet of 1 exists.

Farm Family and Village, Tractor, Ambulance A205

1977, Apr. 14 **Litho.** ***Perf. 13***
430 A205 20p multicolored .20 .20

Social Welfare and Rural Development Year, 1976-77.

Terracotta Bullock Cart, Pakistan — A206

Designs: 20p, Terra-cotta jug, Turkey. 90p, Decorated jug, Iran.

1977, July 21 **Litho.** ***Perf. 13***
431 A206 20p ultra & multi .35 .20
432 A206 65p blue green & multi .55 .25
433 A206 90p lilac & multi .80 1.00
Nos. 431-433 (3) 1.70 1.45

Regional Cooperation for Development Pact among Pakistan, Turkey and Iran, 13th anniversary.

Trees — A207

1977, Aug. 9 **Litho.** ***Perf. 13***
434 A207 20p multicolored .20 .20

Tree planting program.

Desert A208

1977, Sept. 5 **Litho.** ***Perf. 13***
435 A208 65p multicolored .30 .20

UN Conference on Desertification, Nairobi, Kenya, Aug. 29-Sept. 9.

"Water for the Children" — A209

1977, Oct. 3 **Litho.** ***Perf. 14x12½***
436 A209 50p multicolored .40 .25

Universal Children's Day.

Aga Khan III — A210

1977, Nov. 2 **Litho.** ***Perf. 13***
437 A210 2r multicolored .65 .65

Aga Khan III (1877-1957), spiritual ruler of Ismaeli sect, statesman, birth centenary.

Mohammad Iqbal — A211

20p, Spirit appearing to Iqbal, painting by Behzad. 65p, Iqbal looking at Jamaluddin Afghani & Saeed Halim offering prayers, by Behzad. 1.25r, Verse in Urdu. 2.25r, Verse in Persian.

1977, Nov. 9
438 A211 20p multicolored .35 .35
439 A211 65p multicolored .35 .35
440 A211 1.25r multicolored .40 .40
441 A211 2.25r multicolored .45 .45
442 A211 3r multicolored .55 .60
a. Strip of 5, #438-442 2.10 2.25

Mohammad Allama Iqbal (1877-1938), poet and philosopher, birth centenary.

Holy Kaaba, Mecca A212

1977, Nov. 21 ***Perf. 14***
443 A212 65p green & multi .30 .20

1977 pilgrimage to Mecca.

Healthy and Sick Bodies — A213

Woman from Rawalpindi-Islamabad — A214

1977, Dec. 19 **Litho.** ***Perf. 13***
444 A213 65p blue green & multi .35 .25

World Rheumatism Year.

1978, Feb. 5 **Litho.** ***Perf. 12½x13½***
445 A214 75p multicolored .30 .20

Indonesia-Pakistan Economic and Cultural Cooperation Organization.

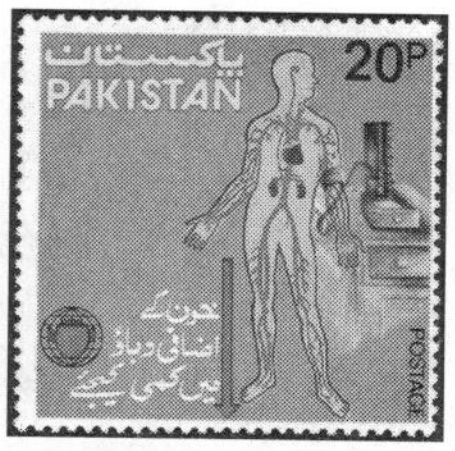

Blood Circulation and Pressure Gauge A215

1978, Apr. 20 **Litho.** ***Perf. 13***
446 A215 20p blue & multi .20 .20
447 A215 2r yellow & multi .60 .60

Campaign against hypertension.

Henri Dunant, Red Cross, Red Crescent A216

1978, May 8 ***Perf. 14***
448 A216 1r multicolored 1.00 .20

Henri Dunant (1828-1910), founder of Red Cross, 150th birth anniversary.

Red Roses, Pakistan — A217

90p, Pink roses, Iran. 2r, Yellow rose, Turkey.

1978, July 21 Litho. *Perf. 13½*

449 A217 20p multicolored .35 .20
450 A217 90p multicolored .50 .20
451 A217 2r multicolored .75 .35
a. Strip of 3, #449-451 1.75 1.00

Regional Cooperation for Development Pact among Turkey, Iran and Pakistan.

Hockey Stick and Ball, Championship Cup — A218

Fair Building, Fountain, Piazza Tourismo A219

1978, Aug. 26 Litho. *Perf. 13*

452 A218 1r multicolored 1.00 .20
453 A219 2r multicolored .50 .25

Riccione '78, 30th International Stamp Fair, Riccione, Italy, Aug. 26-28. No. 452 also commemorates Pakistan as World Hockey Cup Champion.

Globe and Cogwheels A220

1978, Sept. 3

454 A220 75p multicolored .25 .20

UN Conference on Technical Cooperation among Developing Countries, Buenos Aires, Argentina, Sept. 1978.

St. Patrick's Cathedral, Karachi A221

Design: 2r, Stained-glass window.

1978, Sept. 29 Litho. *Perf. 13*

455 A221 1r multicolored .20 .20
456 A221 2r multicolored .20 .20

St. Patrick's Cathedral, Karachi, centenary.

"Four Races" — A222

1978, Nov. 20 Litho. *Perf. 13*

457 A222 1r multicolored .20 .20

Anti-Apartheid Year.

Maulana Jauhar — A223

1978, Dec. 10 Litho. *Perf. 13*

458 A223 50p multicolored .30 .20

Maulana Muhammad Ali Jauhar, writer, journalist and patriot, birth centenary.

Type of 1957 and

Qarardad Monument A224

Tractor A225

Tomb of Ibrahim Khan Makli — A225a

Engr.; Litho. (10p, 25p, 40p, 50p, 90p)

1978-81 *Perf. 14*

459	A224	2p	dark green	.20	.20
460	A224	3p	black	.20	.20
461	A224	5p	violet blue	.20	.20
462	A225	10p	lt blue & blue ('79)	.20	.20
463	A225	20p	yel green ('79)	.40	.20
464	A225	25p	rose car & grn ('79)	.75	.20
465	A225	40p	carmine & blue	.20	.20
466	A225	50p	bl grn & vio ('79)	.25	.20
467	A225	60p	black	.20	.20
468	A225	75p	dull red	.50	.20
469	A225	90p	blue & carmine	.20	.20

Perf. 13½x13

Engr. Wmk. 351

470	A225a	1r	olive ('80)	.20	.20
471	A225a	1.50r	dp orange ('79)	.20	.20
472	A225a	2r	car rose ('79)	.20	.20
473	A225a	3r	indigo ('80)	.20	.20
474	A225a	4r	black ('81)	.20	.20
475	A225a	5r	dk brn ('81)	.20	.20
475A	A26	15r	rose lil & red ('79)	1.50	1.50
			Nos. 459-475A (18)	6.00	4.90

Lithographed stamps, type A225, have bottom panel in solid color with colorless lettering and numerals 2mm high instead of 3mm.

For overprints see Nos. O94-O110.

Tornado Jet Fighter, de Havilland Rapide and Flyer A — A226

Wright Flyer A and: 1r, Phantom F4F jet fighter & Tristar airliner. 2r, Bell X15 fighter & TU-104 airliner. 2.25r, MiG fighter & Concorde.

Unwmk.

1978, Dec. 24 Litho. *Perf. 13*

476 A226 65p multicolored 1.25 1.25
477 A226 1r multicolored 1.40 1.40
478 A226 2r multicolored 1.50 1.50
479 A226 2.25r multicolored 1.75 1.75
a. Block of 4, #476-479 6.25 6.25

75th anniv. of 1st powered flight.

Koran Lighting the World and Mohammed's Tomb — A227

1979, Feb. 10 Litho. *Perf. 13*

480 A227 20p multicolored .30 .20

Mohammed's birth anniversary.

Mother and Children A228

1979, Feb. 25

481 A228 50p multicolored .50 .20

APWA Services, 30th anniversary.

Lophophorus Impejanus — A229

Pheasants: 25p, Lophura leucomelana. 40p, Puccrasia macrolopha. 1r, Catreus walichii.

1979, June 17 Litho. *Perf. 13*

482 A229 20p multicolored 1.25 .40
483 A229 25p multicolored 1.25 .55
484 A229 40p multicolored 1.60 1.25
485 A229 1r multicolored 3.00 1.50
Nos. 482-485 (4) 7.10 3.70

For overprint see No. 525.

At the Well, by Allah Baksh — A230

Paintings: 75p, Potters, by Kamalel Molk, Iran. 1.60r, Plowing, by Namik Ismail, Turkey.

1979, July 21 Litho. *Perf. 14x13*

486 A230 40p multicolored .20 .20
487 A230 75p multicolored .20 .20
488 A230 1.60r multicolored .25 .20
a. Strip of 3, #486-488 .65 .65

Regional Cooperation for Development Pact among Pakistan, Iran and Turkey, 15th anniversary.

Guj Embroidery — A231

Handicrafts: 1r, Enamel inlay brass plate. 1.50r, Baskets. 2r, Peacock, embroidered rug.

1979, Aug. 23 Litho. *Perf. 14x13*

489 A231 40p multicolored .20 .20
490 A231 1r multicolored .25 .20
491 A231 1.50r multicolored .30 .20
492 A231 2r multicolored .35 .20
a. Block of 4, #489-492 1.10 1.10

Children, IYC and SOS Emblems — A232

1979, Sept. 10 Litho. *Perf. 13*

493 A232 50p multicolored .30 .25

SOS Children's Village, Lahore, opening.

Playground, IYC Emblem — A233

IYC Emblem and: Children's drawings.

1979, Oct. 22 *Perf. 14x12½*

494 A233 40p multicolored .20 .20
495 A233 75p multicolored .20 .20
496 A233 1r multicolored .20 .20
497 A233 1.50r multicolored .20 .20
a. Block of 4, #494-497 .85 .85

Souvenir Sheet

Imperf

498 A233 2r multi, vert. 1.75 1.75

IYC. For overprints see #520-523.

Fight Against Cancer A234

Unwmk.

1979, Nov. 12 Litho. *Perf. 14*

499 A234 40p multicolored	.65	.50

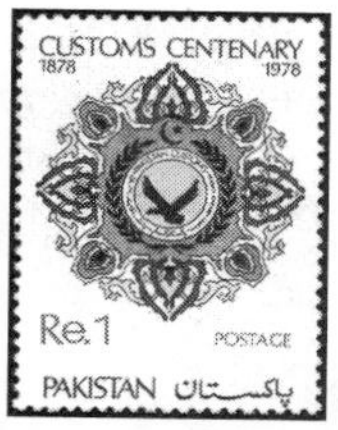

Pakistan Customs Service Centenary — A235

1979, Dec. 10 *Perf. 13x13½*

500 A235 1r multicolored	.25	.20

"1378" is a plate flaw, not an error.

Tippu Sultan Shaheed — A236

1979, Mar. 23 Wmk. 351 *Perf. 14*

501 A236 10r shown	.75	.90
502 A236 15r Syed Ahmad Khan	1.00	1.10
503 A236 25r Altaf Hussain Hali	1.25	1.25
a. Strip of 3, #501-503	3.25	3.50

See No. 699.

A237 A238

Ornament — A239

Perf. 12x11½, 11½x12

1980 Unwmk.

506 A237 10p dk grn & yel org	.20	.20
507 A237 15p dk grn & apple grn	.20	.20
508 A237 25p multicolored	.20	.25
509 A237 35p multicolored	.20	.25
510 A238 40p red & lt brown	.20	.20
511 A239 50p olive & vio bl	.20	.25
512 A239 80p black & yel grn	.20	.30
Nos. 506-512 (7)	1.40	1.65

Issued: 25, 35, 50, 80p, 3/10; others, 1/15.
See Nos. O111-O117.

Pakistan International Airline, 25th Anniversary — A240

1980, Jan. 10 Litho. *Perf. 13*

516 A240 1r multicolored	1.75	.75

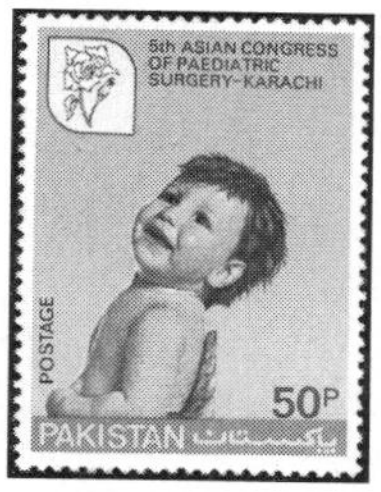

Infant, Rose — A241

1980, Feb. 16 *Perf. 13*

517 A241 50p multicolored	.75	1.25

5th Asian Congress of Pediatric Surgery, Karachi, Feb. 16-19.

Conference Emblem A242

1980, May 17 Litho. *Perf. 13*

518 A242 1r multicolored	.75	.40

11th Islamic Conference of Foreign Ministers, Islamabad, May 17-21.

Lighthouse, Oil Terminal, Map Showing Karachi Harbor — A243

1980, July 15 *Perf. 13½*

519 A243 1r multicolored	1.75	1.00

Karachi Port, cent. of independent management.

Nos. 494-497 Overprinted in Red: RICCIONE 80

1980, Aug. 30 Litho. *Perf. 14x12½*

520 A233 40p multicolored	.30	*.50*
521 A233 75p multicolored	.40	*.60*
522 A233 1r multicolored	.45	*.65*
523 A233 1.50r multicolored	.60	*.75*
a. Block of 4, #520-523	2.00	*3.00*

RICCIONE 80 International Stamp Exhibition, Riccione, Italy, Aug. 30-Sept. 2.

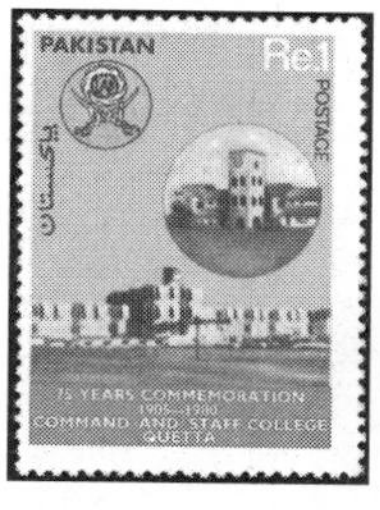

Quetta Command and Staff College, 75th Anniversary A244

1980, Sept. 18 Litho. *Perf. 13*

524 A244 1r multicolored	.20	.20

No. 485 Overprinted: "World Tourism Conference/Manila 80"

1980, Sept. 27

525 A229 1r multicolored	.60	.25

World Tourism Conf., Manila, Sept. 27.

Birth Centenary of Mohammed Shairani — A245

1980, Oct. 5 Litho. *Perf. 13*

526 A245 40p multicolored	.25	.45

Aga Khan Architecture Award — A246

1980, Oct. 23 Litho. *Perf. 13½*

527 A246 2r multicolored	.50	.45

Rising Sun A247

1981, Mar. 7 Litho. *Perf. 13*

Size: 30x41mm

528 A247 40p Hegira emblem	.20	.40

1980, Nov. 6 Litho. *Perf. 13*

529 A247 40p shown	.20	.25

Perf. 14

Size: 33x33mm

530 A247 2r Moslem symbols	.20	.35

Perf. 13x13½

Size: 31x54mm

531 A247 3r Globe, hands holding Koran	.25	.50
Nos. 528-531 (4)	.85	1.50

Souvenir Sheet

Imperf

532 A247 4r Candles	.65	.75

Hegira (Pilgrimage Year).

Airmail Service, 50th Anniversary — A248

Postal History: No. 533, Postal card cent. No. 534, Money order service cent.

1980-81 *Perf. 13*

533 A248 40p multi, vert.	.25	.35
534 A248 40p multi, vert.	.25	.35
535 A248 1r multi	.50	.20
Nos. 533-535 (3)	1.00	.90

Issued: #533, 12/27; #534, 12/20; #535, 2/15/81.

Heinrich von Stephan, UPU Emblem A249

1981, Jan. 7 *Perf. 13½*

536 A249 1r multicolored	.30	.20

Von Stephan (1831-97), founder of UPU.

Conference Emblem, Afghan Refugee A250

Conference Emblem, Flags of Participants, Men — A251

Conference Emblem, Map of Afghanistan — A252

Conference Emblem in Ornament A253

Conference Emblem, Flags of Participants A254

1981, Mar. 29 Litho. *Perf. 13*

537 A250 40p multicolored	.30	.20
538 A251 40p multicolored	.30	.20
539 A250 1r multicolored	.50	.20

540 A251 1r multicolored .50 .20
541 A252 2r multicolored .60 .35
Nos. 537-541 (5) 2.20 1.15

1981, Mar. 29 ***Perf. 13½***
542 A253 40p multicolored .20 .20
543 A254 40p multicolored .20 .20
544 A253 85p multicolored .20 .25
545 A254 85p multicolored .20 .25
Nos. 542-545 (4) .80 .90

3rd Islamic Summit Conference, Makkah al-Mukarramah, Jan. 25-28.

Kemal Ataturk (1881-1938), First President of Turkey — A255

1981, May 19 Litho. ***Perf. 13x13½***
546 A255 1r multicolored .35 .20

Green Turtle A256

1981, June 20 Litho. ***Perf. 12x11½***
547 A256 40p multicolored 1.25 .30

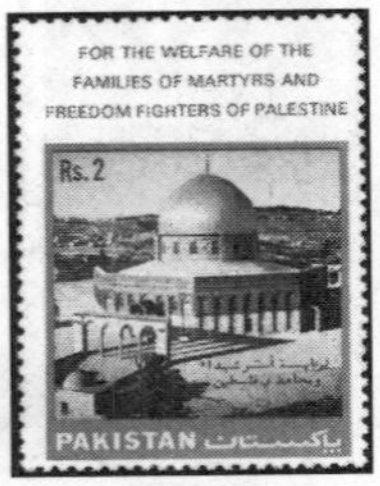

Palestinian Cooperation A257

1981, July 25 Litho. ***Perf. 13***
548 A257 2r multicolored .40 .25

Mountain Ranges and Peaks — A258

1981, Aug. 20 ***Perf. 14x13½***
549 40p Malubiting West, range .50 .30
550 40p Peak .50 .30
a. A258 Pair, #549-550 1.00
551 1r Mt. Maramosh, range .75 .50
552 1r Mt. Maramosh, peak .75 .50
a. A258 Pair, #551-552 1.50
553 1.50r K6, range 1.00 .60
554 1.50r Peak 1.00 .60
a. A258 Pair, #553-554 2.00
555 2r K2, range 1.25 1.00
556 2r Peak 1.25 1.00
a. A258 Pair, #555-556 2.50
Nos. 549-556 (8) 7.00 4.80

Inauguration of Pakistan Steel Furnace No. 1, Karachi A260

1981, Aug. 31 ***Perf. 13***
557 A260 40p multicolored .20 .20
558 A260 2r multicolored .50 .75

Western Tragopan in Summer A261

1981, Sept. 15 Litho. ***Perf. 14***
559 A261 40p shown 1.25 .50
560 A261 2r Winter 3.00 3.25

Intl. Year of the Disabled A262

1981, Dec. 12 Litho. ***Perf. 13***
561 A262 40p multicolored .30 .30
562 A262 2r multicolored 1.25 1.00

World Cup Championship A263

1982, Jan. 31 Litho. ***Perf. 13½x13***
563 A263 1r Cup, flags in arc 1.75 1.00
564 A263 1r shown 1.75 1.00
a. Pair, #563-564 3.50 2.00

Camel Skin Lampshade A264

1982, Feb. 20 Litho. ***Perf. 14***
565 A264 1r shown .75 .50
566 A264 1r Hala pottery .75 .50

See Nos. 582-583.

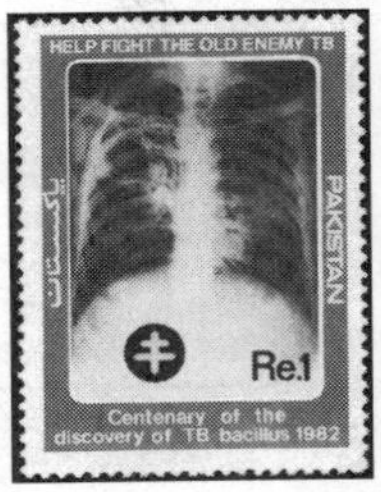

TB Bacillus Centenary A265

1982, Mar. 24
567 A265 1r multicolored 1.25 .60

Blind Indus Dolphin A266

1982, Apr. 24 Litho. ***Perf. 12x11½***
568 A266 40p Dolphin 2.00 .75
569 A266 1r Dolphin, diff. 3.50 1.50

Peaceful Uses of Outer Space — A267

1982, June 7 Litho. ***Perf. 13***
570 A267 1r multicolored 1.75 .75

50th Anniv. of Sukkur Barrage — A268

1982, July 17 Litho. ***Perf. 13***
571 A268 1r multicolored .25 .25

For overprint see No. 574.

Independence Day — A269

1982, Aug. 14
572 A269 40p Flag .20 .20
573 A269 85p Map .30 .30

No. 571 Overprinted: "RICCIONE-82/1932-1982"

1982, Aug. 28
574 A268 1r multicolored .30 .20

RICCIONE '82 Intl. Stamp Exhibition, Riccione, Italy, Aug. 28-30.

University of the Punjab Centenary — A270

1982, Oct. 14 Litho. ***Perf. 13½***
575 A270 40p multicolored .65 .25

Scouting Year — A271

1982, Dec. 23 Litho. ***Perf. 13***
576 A271 2r Emblem .50 .35

Quetta Natural Gas Pipeline Project A272

1983, Jan. 6 Litho. ***Perf. 13***
577 A272 1r multicolored .30 .20

Common Peacock A273

1983, Feb. 15 Litho. ***Perf. 14***
578 A273 40p shown 1.00 .20
579 A273 50p Common rose 1.25 .20
580 A273 60p Plain tiger 1.50 .40
581 A273 1.50r Lemon butterfly 2.25 1.50
Nos. 578-581 (4) 6.00 2.30

Handicraft Type of 1982

1983, Mar. 9
582 A264 1r Straw mats .20 .20
583 A264 1r Five-flower cloth design .20 .20

Opening of Aga Khan University — A274

1983, Mar. 16 ***Perf. 13½***
584 A274 2r multicolored .30 .25

Yak Caravan, Zindiharam-Darkot Pass, Hindu Kush Mountains — A275

1983, Apr. 28 Litho. ***Perf. 13***
585 A275 1r multicolored 1.75 .40

Marsh Crocodile
A276

1983, May 19 ***Perf. 13½x14***
586 A276 3r multicolored 3.75 1.25

1983, June 20 Litho. ***Perf. 14***
Size: 50x40mm
587 A276 1r Gazelle 2.25 1.25

36th Anniv. of Independence
A277

1983, Aug. 14 ***Perf. 13***
588 A277 60p Star .20 .20
589 A277 4r Torch .35 .30

25th Anniv. of Indonesia-Pakistan Economic and Cultural Cooperation Org. — A278

Weavings.

1983, Aug. 19 Litho. ***Perf. 13***
590 A278 2r Pakistani (geometric) .30 .20
591 A278 2r Indonesian (figures) .30 .20

Siberian Cranes — A279

1983, Sept. 8 ***Perf. 13½***
592 A279 3r multicolored 2.75 2.75

World Communications Year — A280

1983, Oct. 9 Litho. ***Perf. 13***
593 A280 2r multicolored .25 .20
Size: 33x33mm
594 A280 3r Symbol, diff. .30 .25

World Food Day
A281

1983, Oct. 24 Litho. ***Perf. 13***
595 A281 3r Livestock 1.50 1.25
596 A281 3r Fruit 1.50 1.25
597 A281 3r Grain 1.50 1.25
598 A281 3r Seafood 1.50 1.25
a. Strip of 4, #595-598 6.00 5.00

A282

A283

1983, Oct. 24 Litho. ***Perf. 13½***
599 A282 60p multicolored .20 .20

National Fertilizer Corp.

1983, Nov. 13 Litho. ***Perf. 13***
600 Strip of 6, View of Lahore City, 1852 3.00 2.50
a.-f. A283 60p any single .50 .40

PAKPHILEX '83 Natl. Stamp Exhibition.

Yachting Victory in 9th Asian Games, 1982 — A284

1983, Dec. 31 Litho. ***Perf. 13***
601 A284 60p OK Dinghy 1.50 1.50
602 A284 60p Enterprise 1.50 1.50

Snow Leopard — A285

1984, Jan. 21 ***Perf. 14***
603 A285 40p lt green & multi 1.50 .75
604 A285 1.60r blue & multi 4.50 4.50

Jehangir Khan (b. 1963), World Squash Champion
A286

1984, Mar. 17 Litho. ***Perf. 13***
605 A286 3r multicolored 2.00 1.00

Pakistan Intl. Airway China Service, 20th Anniv.
A287

1984, Apr. 29 Litho. ***Perf. 13***
606 A287 3r Jet 4.50 3.50

Glass Work, Lahore Fort — A288

Various glass panels.

1984, May 31 Litho. ***Perf. 13***
607 A288 1r green & multi .20 .20
608 A288 1r purple & multi .20 .20
609 A288 1r vermilion & multi .20 .20
610 A288 1r brt blue & multi .20 .20
Nos. 607-610 (4) .80 .80

Forts — A289

1984-88 Litho. ***Perf. 11***
613 A289 5p Kot Diji .20 .20
614 A289 10p Rohtas .20 .20
615 A289 15p Bala Hissar ('86) .20 .20
616 A289 20p Attock .20 .20
617 A289 50p Hyderabad ('86) .20 .20
618 A289 60p Lahore .20 .20
619 A289 70p Sibi ('88) .20 .20
620 A289 80p Ranikot ('86) .30 .20
Nos. 613-620 (8) 1.70 1.60

Issued: 5p, 11/1; 10p, 9/25; 80p, 7/1.
For overprints see Nos. O118-O124.

Shah Rukn-i-Alam Tomb, Multan — A290

1984, June 26 Litho. ***Perf. 13***
624 A290 60p multicolored 1.75 1.00

Aga Khan Award for Architecture.

Asia-Pacific Broadcasting Union, 20th Anniv. — A290a

1984, July 1 Litho. ***Perf. 13***
625 A290a 3r multicolored .80 .40

1984 Summer Olympics, Los Angeles — A291

1984, July 31
626 A291 3r Athletics 1.25 1.00
627 A291 3r Boxing 1.25 1.00
628 A291 3r Hockey 1.25 1.00
629 A291 3r Yachting 1.25 1.00
630 A291 3r Wrestling 1.25 1.00
Nos. 626-630 (5) 6.25 5.00

Issued in sheets of 10.

Independence, 37th Anniv. — A292

1984, Aug. 14
631 A292 60p Jasmine .20 .20
632 A292 4r Lighted torch .45 .35

Intl. Trade Fair, Sept. 1-21, Karachi
A293

1984, Sept. 1
633 A293 60p multicolored .65 .25

1984 Natl. Tourism Convention, Karachi, Nov. 5-8 — A293a

Shah Jahan Mosque: a, Main dome interior. b, Tile work. c, Entrance. d, Archways. e, Dome interior, diff.

1984, Nov. 5 Litho. ***Perf. 13½***
634 Strip of 5 2.50 2.00
a.-e. A293a 1r any single .50 .40

United Bank Limited, 25th Anniv.
A294

1984, Nov. 7
635 A294 60p multicolored .80 .50

UNCTAD, UN Conference on Trade and Development, 20th Anniv. — A294a

1984, Dec. 24 *Perf. 14½x14*

636 A294a 60p multicolored .70 .30

Postal Life Insurance, Cent. — A295

1984, Dec. 29 *Perf. 13½x14*

637 A295 60p multicolored .40 .20

638 A295 1r multicolored .50 .20

UNESCO World Heritage Campaign A296

1984, Dec. 31

639 A296 2r Unicorn, rock painting 1.50 .60

640 A296 2r Unicorn seal, round 1.50 .60

a. Pair, #639-640 3.00 1.25

Restoration of Mohenjo-Daro.

IYY, Girl Guides 75th Anniv. A297

1985, Jan. 5 *Perf. 13½*

641 A297 60p Emblems 2.50 1.00

Smelting A298

Pouring Steel — A299

1985, Jan. 15 *Perf. 13*

642 A298 60p multicolored .60 .20

643 A299 1r multicolored 1.00 .20

Referendum Reinstating Pres. Zia — A300

1985, Mar. 20 **Litho.** *Perf. 13*

644 A300 60p Map, sunburst .90 .40

Minar-e-Qarardad-e-Pakistan Tower — A301

Ballot Box A302

1985 Elections.

1985, Mar. 23

645 A301 1r multicolored .60 .20

646 A302 1r multicolored .60 .20

Mountaineering — A303

1985, May 27 **Litho.** *Perf. 14*

647 A303 40p Mt. Rakaposhi, Karakoram 1.75 .50

648 A303 2r Mt. Nangaparbat, Western Himalayas 3.75 3.50

Championship Pakistani Men's Field Hockey Team — A304

Design: 1984 Olympic gold medal, 1985 Dhaka Asia Cup, 1982 Bombay World Cup.

1985, June 5 **Litho.** *Perf. 13*

649 A304 1r multicolored 2.25 1.00

King Edward Medical College, Lahore, 125th Anniv. — A305

1985, July 28 **Litho.** *Perf. 13*

650 A305 3r multicolored 1.75 .50

Natl. Independence Day — A306

Designs: No. 651a, 37th Independence Day written in English. No. 651b, In Arabic.

1985, Aug. 14

651 Pair + 2 labels .30 .30

a.-b. A306 60p any single .30 .30

Printed in sheets of 4 stamps + 4 labels.

Sind Madressah-Tul-Islam, Karachi, Education Cent. — A307

1985, Sept. 1

652 A307 2r multicolored 1.75 .50

Mosque, Jinnah Avenue, Karachi — A308

1985, Sept. 14

653 A308 1r Mosque by day .75 .25

654 A308 1r At night .75 .25

35th anniv. of the Jamia Masjid Pakistan Security Printing Corporation's miniature replica of the Badshahi Mosque, Lahore.

Lawrence College, Murree, 125th Anniv. — A309

1985, Sept. 21

655 A309 3r multicolored 2.00 .50

UN, 40th Anniv. — A310

1985, Oct. 24 **Litho.** *Perf. 14x14½*

656 A310 1r UN building, sun .30 .20

657 A310 2r Building emblem .40 .20

10th Natl. Scouting Jamboree, Lahore, Nov. 8-15 — A311

1985, Nov. 8 *Perf. 13*

658 A311 60p multicolored 2.00 1.50

Islamabad and Capital Development Authority Emblem — A312

1985, Nov. 30 *Perf. 14½*

659 A312 3r multicolored 1.90 .30

Islamabad, capital of Pakistan, 25th anniv.

Flags and Map of SAARC Nations A313

Flags as Flower Petals A314

1985, Dec. 8 *Perf. 13½, 13*

660 A313 1r multicolored 1.75 *3.00*

661 A314 2r multicolored 1.25 *1.50*

SAARC, South Asian Assoc. for Regional Cooperation.

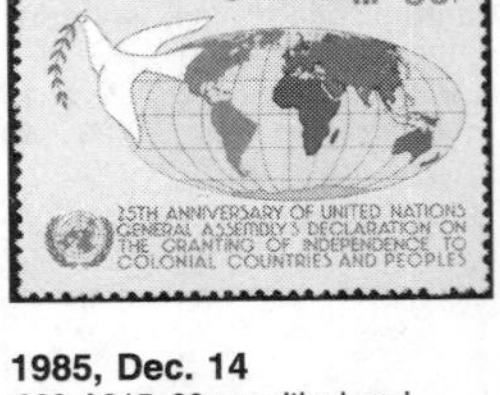

Dove and World Map A315

1985, Dec. 14 *Perf. 13*

662 A315 60p multicolored 1.10 .40

UN Declaration on the Granting of Independence to Colonial Countries and Peoples, 25th Anniv.

Shaheen Falcon — A316

1986, Jan. 20 ***Perf. 13½x14***
663 A316 1.50r multicolored 4.00 3.00

Agricultural Development Bank, 25th Anniv. — A317

1986, Feb. 18 Litho. ***Perf. 13***
664 A317 60p multicolored 1.00 .35

Sadiq Egerton College, Bahawalpur, Cent. — A318

1986, Apr. 25
665 A318 1r multicolored 1.50 .30

A319

A320

1986, May 11 ***Perf. 13½***
666 A319 1r multicolored 1.50 .25

Asian Productivity Organization, 25th anniv.

1986, Aug. 14 Litho. ***Perf. 14½x14***
667 A320 80p "1947-1986" .50 .20
668 A320 1r Urdu text, fireworks .50 .20

Independence Day, 39th anniv.

A321

A322

1986, Sept. 8 ***Perf. 13***
669 A321 1r Teacher, students .75 .25

Intl. Literacy Day.

1986, Oct. 28 Litho. ***Perf. 13½x13***
670 A322 80p multicolored 1.25 .20

UN Child Survival Campaign.

Aitchison College, Lahore, Cent. — A323

1986, Nov. 3 ***Perf. 13½***
671 A323 2.50r multicolored .35 .20

Intl. Peace Year — A324

1986, Nov. 20 ***Perf. 13***
672 A324 4r multicolored .50 .30

4th Asian Cup Table Tennis Tournament, Karachi A325

1986, Nov. 25 ***Perf. 14½***
673 A325 2r multicolored 2.00 .40

Marcopolo Sheep — A326

1986, Dec. 4 Litho. ***Perf. 14***
674 A326 2r multicolored 2.75 2.00

See No. 698.

Eco Philex '86 — A327

Mosques: No. 675a, Selimiye, Turkey. No. 675b, Gawhar Shad, Iran. No. 675c, Grand Mosque, Pakistan.

1986, Dec. 20 ***Perf. 13***
675 Strip of 3 4.00 3.00
a.-c. A327 3r any single 1.25 1.00

St. Patrick's School, Karachi, 125th Anniv. — A328

1987, Jan. 29 Litho. ***Perf. 13***
676 A328 5r multicolored 1.75 .60

Savings Bank Week — A329

Birds, berries and: a, National defense. b, Education. c, Agriculture. d, Industry.

1987, Feb. 21 Litho. ***Perf. 13***
677 Block of 4 + 2 labels 3.75 2.00
a.-d. A329 5r any single 1.10 .50

Parliament House Opening, Islamabad — A330

1987, Mar. 23
678 A330 3r multicolored .30 .20

Fight Against Drug Abuse A331

1987, June 30 Litho. ***Perf. 13***
679 A331 1r multicolored .50 .20

Natl. Independence, 40th Anniv. — A332

Natl. flag and: 80p, Natl. anthem, written in Urdu. 3r, Jinnah's first natl. address, the Minar-e-Qarardad-e-Pakistan and natl. coat of arms.

1987, Aug. 14 Litho. ***Perf. 13***
680 A332 80p multicolored .25 .20
681 A332 3r multicolored .60 .20

Miniature Sheet

Air Force, 40th Anniv. — A333

Aircraft: a, Tempest II. b, Hawker Fury. c, Super Marine Attacker. d, F86 Sabre. e, F104 Star Fighter. f, C130 Hercules. g, F6. h, Mirage III. i, A5. j, F16 Fighting Falcon.

1987, Sept. 7 Litho. ***Perf. 13½***
682 Sheet of 10 11.00 10.00
a.-j. A333 3r any single 1.25 1.00

Tourism Convention 1987 — A334

Views along Karakoram Highway: a, Pasu Glacier. b, Apricot trees. c, Highway winding through hills. d, Khunjerab peak.

1987, Oct. 1 ***Perf. 13***
683 Block of 4 2.00 1.25
a.-d. A334 1.50r any single .60 .30

Shah Abdul Latif Bhitai Mausoleum — A335

1987, Oct. 8 ***Perf. 13***
684 A335 80p multicolored .20 .20

D.J. Sind Government Science College, Karachi, Cent. — A336

1987, Nov. 7
685 A336 80p multicolored .20 .20

College of Physicians and Surgeons, 25th Anniv. — A337

1987, Dec. 9 Litho. ***Perf. 13***
686 A337 1r multicolored .20 .20

Intl. Year of Shelter for the Homeless A338

1987, Dec. 15
687 A338 3r multicolored .30 .25

Cathedral Church of the Resurrection, Lahore, Cent. — A339

1987, Dec. 20
688 A339 3r multicolored .30 .25

Natl. Postal Service, 40th Anniv. A340

1987, Dec. 28
689 A340 3r multicolored .30 .25

Radio Pakistan A341

1987, Dec. 31
690 A341 80p multicolored .20 .20

Jamshed Nusserwanjee Mehta (1886-1952), Mayor of Karachi, Member of the Sind Legislative Assembly — A342

1988, Jan. 7
691 A342 3r multicolored .30 .25

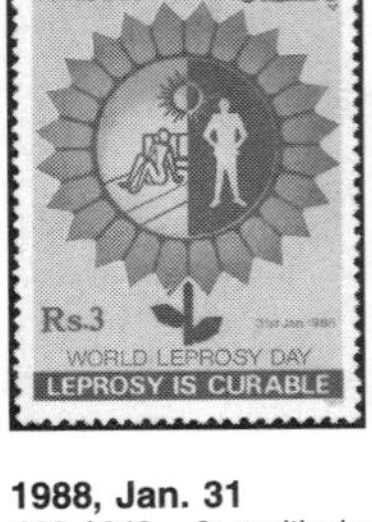

World Leprosy Day — A343

1988, Jan. 31
692 A343 3r multicolored .75 .25

World Health Organization, 40th Anniv. — A344

1988, Apr. 7 Litho. *Perf. 13*
693 A344 4r multicolored .50 .25

Intl. Red Cross and Red Crescent Organizations, 125th Annivs. — A345

1988, May 8
694 A345 3r multicolored .30 .25

Independence Day, 41st Anniv. — A346

1988, Aug. 14 Litho. *Perf. 13½*
695 A346 80p multicolored .20 .20
696 A346 4r multicolored .20 .25

Miniature Sheet

1988 Summer Olympics, Seoul — A347

Events: a, Discus, shot put, hammer throw, javelin. b, Relay, hurdles, running, walking. c, High jump, long jump, triple jump, pole vault. d, Gymnastic floor exercises, rings, parallel bars. e, Table tennis, tennis, field hockey, baseball. f, Volleyball, soccer, basketball, team handball. g, Wrestling, judo, boxing, weight lifting. h, Sport pistol, fencing, rifle shooting, archery. i, Swimming, diving, yachting, quadruple-sculling, kayaking. j, Equestrian jumping, cycling, steeplechase.

1988, Sept. 17 Litho. *Perf. 13½x13*
697 Sheet of 10+32 labels 10.00 7.50
a.-j. A347 10r any single 1.00 .75

Labels contained in No. 697 picture the Seoul Games character trademark or emblem. Size of No. 697: 251x214mm.

Fauna Type of 1986

1988, Oct. 29 Litho. *Perf. 14*
698 A326 2r Suleman markhor, vert. 1.00 .40

Pioneers of Freedom Type of 1979

1989, Jan. 23 Litho. Wmk. 351
699 A236 3r Maulana Hasrat Mohani .20 .20

Islamia College, Peshawar, 75th Anniv. — A348

1988, Dec. 22 Unwmk. *Perf. 13½*
700 A348 3r multicolored .30 .20

SAARC Summit Conference, Islamabad — A349

Designs: 25r, Flags, symbols of commerce. 50r, Globe, communication and transportation. 75r, Bangladesh #69, Maldive Islands #1030, Bhutan #132, Pakistan #403, Ceylon #451, India #580, Nepal #437.

1988, Dec. 29 *Perf. 13*
701 A349 25r shown 1.25 1.00

Size: 33x33mm

Perf. 14

702 A349 50r multicolored 3.00 2.00

Size: 52x28mm

Perf. 13½x13

703 A349 75r multicolored 3.75 3.00
Nos. 701-703 (3) 8.00 6.00

Adasia '89, 16th Asian Advertising Congress, Lahore, Feb. 18-22 — A350

1989, Feb. 18 Litho. *Perf. 13*
704 Strip of 3 2.00 1.50
a. A350 1r deep rose lilac & multi .65 .50
b. A350 1r green & multi .65 .50
c. A350 1r bright vermilion & multi .65 .50

Printed in sheets of 9.

Pres. Zulfikar Ali Bhutto (1928-1979), Ousted by Military Coup and Executed A351

Portraits.

1989, Apr. 4 Litho. *Perf. 13*
705 A351 1r shown .20 .20
706 A351 2r multi, diff. .25 .20

Submarine Operations, 25th Anniv. — A352

Submarines: a, *Agosta.* b, *Daphne.* c, *Fleet Snorkel.* Illustration reduced.

1989, June 1 Litho. *Perf. 13½*
707 Strip of 3 2.75 2.75
a.-c. A352 1r any single .90 .90

Oath of the Tennis Court, by David — A353

1989, June 24 Litho. *Perf. 13½*
708 A353 7r multicolored 1.75 .60

French revolution, bicent.

Archaeological Heritage — A354

Terra cotta vessels excavated in Baluchistan: a, Pirak, c. 2200 B.C. b, Nindo Damb, c. 2300 B.C. c, Mehrgarh, c. 3600 B.C. d, Nausharo, c. 2600 B.C.

1989, June 28 *Perf. 14½x14*
709 Block of 4 .75 .60
a.-d. A354 1r any single .20 .20

Asia-Pacific Telecommunity, 10th Anniv. — A355

1989, July 1 *Perf. 13½x14*
710 A355 3r multicolored .30 .20

Laying the Foundation Stone for the 1st Integrated Container Terminal, Port Qasim A356

1989, Aug. 5 Litho. *Perf. 14*
711 A356 6r Ship in berth 3.00 2.50

Mohammad Ali Jinnah — A357

Litho & Engr.

1989, Aug. 14 Wmk. 351 *Perf. 13*
712 A357 1r multicolored .25 .20
713 A357 1.50r multicolored .30 .20
714 A357 2r multicolored .40 .25
715 A357 3r multicolored .50 .30

716 A357	4r multicolored		.65	.35
717 A357	5r multicolored		.70	.40
	Nos. 712-717 (6)		2.80	1.70

Independence Day.

Abdul Latif Bhitai Memorial A358

1989, Sept. 16 Litho. Unwmk.

718 A358 2r multicolored .20 .20

245th death and 300th birth annivs. of Shah Abdul Latif Bhitai.

World Wildlife Fund A359

Himalayan black bears and WWF emblem: a, Bear on slope, emblem UR. b, Bear on slope, emblem UL. c, Bear on top of rock, emblem UR. d, Seated bear, emblem UL.

Perf. 14x13½

1989, Oct. 7 Litho. Unwmk.

719	Block of 4	3.50	3.00
a.-d.	A359 4r any single	.85	.75

World Food Day — A360

1989, Oct. 16 ***Perf. 14x12½***

720 A360 1r multicolored .35 .25

Quilt and Bahishiti Darwaza (Heavenly Gate) — A361

1989, Oct. 20 ***Perf. 13***

721 A361 3r multicolored .30 .20

800th Birth anniv. of Baba Farid.

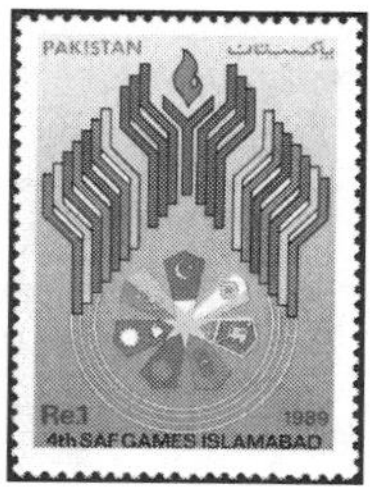

4th SAF Games, Islamabad A362

1989, Oct. 20

722 A362 1r multicolored .35 .25

Pakistan Television, 25th Anniv. A363

1989, Nov. 26 Litho. ***Perf. 13½***

723 A363 3r multicolored .30 .20

SAARC Year Against Drug Abuse and Drug Trafficking A364

1989, Dec. 8 ***Perf. 13***

724 A364 7r multicolored 1.25 .50

Murray College, Sialkot, Cent. A365

1989, Dec. 18 ***Perf. 14***

725 A365 6r multicolored .55 .40

Government College, Lahore, 125th Anniv. — A366

1989, Dec. 21 ***Perf. 13***

726 A366 6r multicolored .50 .50

Center on Integrated Rural Development for Asia and the Pacific (CIRDAP), 10th Anniv. — A367

1989, Dec. 31

727 A367 3r multicolored .60 .40

Organization of the Islamic Conference (OIC), 20th Anniv. — A368

1990, Feb. 9 Litho. ***Perf. 13***

728 A368 1r multicolored .50 .20

7th World Field Hockey Cup, Lahore, Feb. 12-23 — A369

Illustration reduced.

1990, Feb. 12 ***Perf. 14x13½***

729 A369 2r multicolored 3.75 2.50

A370

Pakistan Resolution, 50th Anniv. — A371

Designs: a, Allama Mohammad Iqbal addressing the Allahabad Session of the All-India Muslim League and swearing-in of Liat Ali Khan as league secretary-general. b, Freedom fighter Maulana Mohammad Ali Jauhar at Muslim rally and Mohammed Ali Jinnah at microphone. c, Muslim woman holding flag and swearing-in of Mohammed Ali Jinnah as governor-general of Pakistan, Aug. 14, 1947. 7r, English and Urdu translations of the resolution, natl. flag and Minar-e-Qarardade Pakistan.

1990, Mar. 23 Litho. ***Perf. 13***

730	Strip of 3	2.25	2.25
a.-c.	A370 1r any single	.75	.75

Size: 90x45mm

Perf. 13½

731 A371 7r multicolored 1.75 1.50

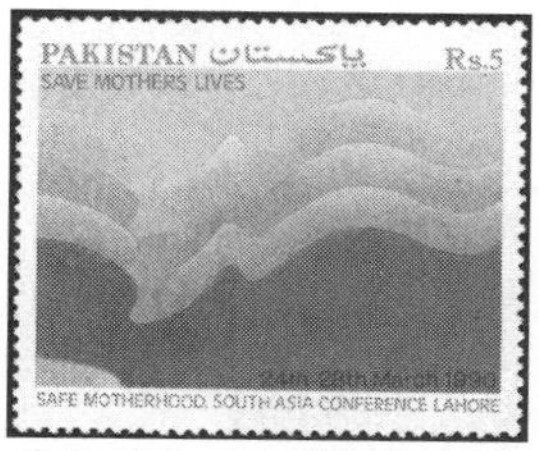

Safe Motherhood South Asia Conference, Lahore — A372

1990, Mar. 24 ***Perf. 13½***

732 A372 5r multicolored .75 .50

Calligraphic Painting of a Ghalib Verse, by Shakir Ali (1916-1975) — A373

1990, Apr. 19 Litho. ***Perf. 13½x13***

733 A373 1r multicolored 1.00 .50

See Nos. 757-758.

Badr-1 Satellite — A374

1990, July 26 Litho. ***Perf. 13***

734 A374 3r multicolored 1.50 1.50

Pioneers of Freedom A375

No. 735: a, Allama Mohammad Iqbal (1877-1938). b, Mohammad Ali Jinnah (1876-1948). c, Sir Syed Ahmad Khan (1817-98). d, Nawab Salimullah (1884-1915). e, Mohtarma Fatima Jinnah (1893-1967). f, Aga Khan III (1877-1957). g, Nawab Mohammad Ismail Khan (1884-1958). h, Hussain Shaheed Suhrawardy (1893-1963). i, Syed Ameer Ali (1849-1928).

No. 736: a, Nawab Bahadur Yar Jung (1905-44). b, Khawaja Nazimuddin (1894-1964). c, Maulana Obaidullah Sindhi (1872-1944). d, Sahibzada Abdul Qaiyum Khan (c. 1863-1937). e, Begum Jahanara Shah Nawaz (1896-1979). f, Sir Shulam Hussain Hidayatullah (1879-1948). g, Qazi Mohammad Isa (1913-76). h, Sir M. Shahnawaz Khan Mamdot (1883-1942). i, Pir Shaib of Manki Sharif (1923-60).

No. 737: a, Liaquat Ali Khan (1895-1951). b, Maulvi A.K. Fazl-Ul-Haq (1873-1962). c, Allama Shabbir Ahmad Usmani (1885-1949). d, Sardar Abdur Rab Nishtar (1899-1958). e, Bi Amma (c. 1850-1924). f, Sir Abdullah Haroon (1872-1942). g, Chaudhry Rahmat Ali (1897-1951). h, Raja Sahib of Mahmudabad (1914-73). i, Hassanally Effendi (1830-1895).

No. 737J: k, Maulana Zafar Ali Khan (1873-1956). l, Maulana Mohamed Ali Jauhar (1878-1931). m, Chaudhry Khaliquzzaman (1889-1973). n, Hameed Nizami (1915-62). o, Begum Ra'ana Liaquat Ali Khan (1905-90). p, Mirza Abol Hassan Ispahani (1902-81). q, Raja Ghazanfar Ali Khan (1895-1963). r, Malik Barkat Ali (1886-1946). s, Mir Jaffer Khan Jamali (c. 1911-67).

1990-91 Litho. ***Perf. 13***

Miniature Sheets

735	Sheet of 9	1.75	1.50
a.-i.	A375 1r any single	.20	.20
736	Sheet of 9	1.75	1.50
a.-i.	A375 1r any single	.20	.20
737	Sheet of 9	1.75	1.50
a.-i.	A375 1r any single	.20	.20
737J	Sheet of 9 ('91)	1.75	1.50
k.-s.	A375 1r any single	.20	.20
	Nos. 735-737J (4)	7.00	6.00

Issued: #735-737, Aug. 19; #737J, 1991.

See Nos. 773, 792, 804, 859-860, 865, 875-876, 922-924.

Indonesia Pakistan Economic and Cultural Cooperation Organization, 1968-1990 — A376

1990, Aug. 19

738 A376 7r multicolored .75 .60

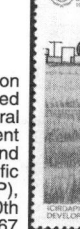

Intl. Literacy Year — A377

1990, Sept. 8
739 A377 3r multicolored 1.00 .75

A378

1990, Sept. 22
740 A378 2r multicolored .60 .35

Joint meeting of Royal College of Physicians, Edinburgh and College of Physicians and Surgeons, Pakistan.

World Summit for Children A379

1990, Sept. 19
741 A379 7r multicolored .65 .40

Year of the Girl Child A380

1990, Nov. 21 Litho. ***Perf. 13½***
742 A380 2r multicolored .75 .50

Security Papers Ltd., 25th Anniv. — A381

1990, Dec. 8 ***Perf. 13***
743 A381 3r multicolored .90 .75

Intl. Civil Defense Day — A382

1991, Mar. 1 Litho. ***Perf. 13***
744 A382 7r multicolored 1.25 1.00

South & West Asia Postal Union — A383

1991, Mar. 21
745 A383 5r multicolored 1.75 1.25

World Population Day — A384

1991, July 11
746 A384 10r multicolored 2.00 1.50

Intl. Special Olympics A385

1991, July 19
747 A385 7r multicolored 1.75 1.50

Habib Bank Limited, 50th Anniv. — A386

1991, Aug. 25 Litho. ***Perf. 13***
748 A386 1r brt red & multi .50 .20
749 A386 5r brt green & multi 2.00 1.50

St. Joseph's Convent School, Karachi — A387

1991, Sept. 8
750 A387 5r multicolored 1.75 1.50

Emperor Sher Shah Suri (c. 1472-1545) A388

1991, Oct. 5
751 A388 5r multicolored 1.25 1.25

Souvenir Sheet
Size: 90x81mm
Imperf

752 A388 7r multicolored 1.75 1.75

Pakistani Scientific Expedition to Antarctica — A389

1991, Oct. 28
753 A389 7r multicolored 2.50 2.00

Houbara Bustard — A390

1991, Nov. 4
754 A390 7r multicolored 2.00 1.50

Asian Development Bank, 25th Anniv. — A391

1991, Dec. 19 Litho. ***Perf. 13***
755 A391 7r multicolored 1.25 1.00

Hazrat Sultan Bahoo, 300th Death Anniv. A392

1991, Dec. 22
756 A392 7r multicolored .75 .50

Painting Type of 1990

Paintings and artists: No. 757, Village Life, by Allah Ustad Bux (1892-1978). No. 758, Miniature of Royal Procession, by Muhammad Haji Sharif (1889-1978).

1991, Dec. 24
757 A373 1r multicolored 1.00 .75
758 A373 1r multicolored 1.00 .75

American Express Travelers Cheques, 100th Anniv. — A393

Illustration reduced.

1991, Dec. 26 ***Perf. 13½***
759 A393 7r multicolored 2.00 1.50

Muslim Commercial Bank, First Year of Private Operation — A394

7r, City skyline, worker, cogwheels, computer operators.

1992, Apr. 8 Litho. ***Perf. 13***
760 A394 1r multicolored .20 .20
761 A394 7r multicolored .50 .40

Pakistan, 1992 World Cricket Champions — A395

World Cricket Cup and: 2r, Pakistani player, vert. 7r, Pakistan flag, fireworks, vert.

1992, Apr. 27
762 A395 2r multicolored .60 .50
763 A395 5r multicolored 1.40 1.00
764 A395 7r multicolored 1.60 1.25
Nos. 762-764 (3) 3.60 2.75

Intl. Space Year — A396

Design: 2r, Globe, satellite.

1992, June 7 Litho. ***Perf. 13***
771 A396 1r multicolored .20 .20
772 A396 2r multicolored .30 .20

30th anniv. of first Pakistani rocket (#771).

Pioneers of Freedom Type of 1990

Designs: a, Syed Suleman Nadvi (1884-1953). b, Nawab Iftikhar Hussain Khan Mamdot (1906-1969). c, Maulana Muhammad Shibli Naumani (1857-1914).

1992, Aug. 14 Litho. ***Perf. 13***
773 A375 1r Strip of 3, #a.-c. 2.25 2.25

World Population Day — A397

1992, July 25
774 A397 6r multicolored .80 .75

Medicinal Plants — A398

1992, Nov. 22 Litho. *Perf. 13*
775 A398 6r multicolored 1.50 1.50

See No. 791.

Extraordinary Session of Economic Cooperation Organization Council of Ministers, Islamabad — A399

1992, Nov. 28
776 A399 7r multicolored 1.00 .75

Intl. Conference on Nutrition, Rome A400

1992, Dec. 5 *Perf. 14*
777 A400 7r multicolored .75 .75

A401

A402

1992, Dec. 14 *Perf. 13*
778 A401 7r Alhambra, Spain .75 .75

Islamic cultural heritage.

1992, Aug. 23 *Perf. 14x12½*
779 A402 6r 6th Jamboree .60 .60
780 A402 6r 4th Conference .60 .60

Islamic Scouts, Islamabad.

Government Islamia College, Lahore, Cent. — A403

1992, Nov. 1 *Perf. 13*
781 A403 3r multicolored .35 .35

Industries A404

Designs: a, 10r, Surgical instruments. b, 15r, Leather goods. c, 25r, Sports equipment.

1992, July 5 Litho. *Perf. 13½x13*
782 A404 Strip of 3, #a.-c. 3.50 3.50

World Telecommunications Day — A405

1993, May 17 Litho. *Perf. 13*
783 A405 1r multicolored .60 .25

21st Islamic Foreign Ministers Conference A406

1993, Apr. 25
784 A406 1r buff & multi .40 .25
785 A406 6r green & multi 1.10 .75

A407

A408

Traditional costumes of provinces.

1993, Mar. 10
786 A407 6r Sindh 1.25 1.25
787 A407 6r North West Frontier 1.25 1.25
788 A407 6r Baluchistan 1.25 1.25
789 A407 6r Punjab 1.25 1.25
Nos. 786-789 (4) 5.00 5.00

1992, Dec. 31 *Perf. 14x13*

Birds: a, Gadwall. b, Common shelduck. c, Mallard. d, Greylag goose. The order of the birds is different on each row. Therefore the arc of the rainbow is different on each of the 4 Gadwalls, etc.

790 A408 5r Sheet of 16 8.50 8.50
a. oriz. strip of 4, #a-d 1.50 *4.00*

Medicinal Plants Type

1993, June 20 Litho. *Perf. 13*
791 A398 6r Fennel, chemistry equipment 1.00 .50

Pioneers of Freedom Type of 1990

Designs: a, Rais Ghulam Mohammad Bhurgri (1878-1924). b, Mir Ahmed Yar Khan, Khan of Kalat (1902-1977). c, Mohammad Abdul Latif Pir Sahib Zakori Sharif (1914-1978).

1993, Aug. 14 Litho. *Perf. 13*
792 A375 1r Strip of 3, #a.-c. 1.50 1.25

Gordon College, Rawalpindi, Cent. — A410

1993, Sept. 1
793 A410 2r multicolored 1.00 1.00

Juniper Forests, Ziarat — A411

1993, Sept. 30
794 A411 7r multicolored 1.75 1.25

See No. 827.

World Food Day — A412

1993, Oct. 16 *Perf. 14*
795 A412 6r multicolored 1.00 1.00

A413

A414

Wmk. 351

1993, Dec. 25 Litho. *Perf. 13½*
796 A413 1r multicolored .60 .25

Wazir Mansion, birthplace of Muhammad Ali Jinnah.

Perf. 13x13½

1993, Oct. 28 Unwmk.
797 A414 7r multicolored 1.50 1.50

Burn Hall Institutions, 50th anniv.

South & West Asia Postal Union — A415

1993, Nov. 18 *Perf. 13*
798 A415 7r multicolored 1.50 1.50

Pakistani College of Physicians & Surgeons, Intl. Medical Congress A416

1993, Dec. 10
799 A416 1r multicolored .60 .25

ILO, 75th Anniv. A417

1994, Apr. 11 Litho. *Perf. 13*
800 A417 7r multicolored .90 .90

Bio-diversity A418

a, Ratan jot, medicinal plant. b, Wetlands. c, Mahseer fish. d, Himalayan brown bear.

1994, Apr. 20 Litho. *Perf. 13½*
801 A418 6r Strip or block of 4, #a.-d. 1.50 1.50

Intl. Year of the Family — A419

1994, May 15 *Perf. 13*
802 A419 7r multicolored .50 .50

World Population Day — A420

1994, July 11 Litho. *Perf. 13*
803 A420 7r multicolored .50 .50

Pioneers of Freedom Type of 1990

Miniature Sheet of 8

Designs: a, Nawab Mohsin-Ul-Mulk (1837-1907). b, Sir Shahnawaz Bhutto (1888-1957).

c, Nawab Viqar-Ul-Mulk (1841-1917). d, Pir Ilahi Bux (1890-1975). e, Sheikh Sir Abdul Qadir (1874-1950). f, Dr. Sir Ziauddin Ahmed (1878-1947). g, Jam Mir Ghulam Qadir Khan (1920-88). h, Sardar Aurangzeb Khan (1899-1953).

1994, Aug. 14 Litho. *Perf. 13*
804 A375 1r #a.-h. + label 1.00 1.00

A421

A422

1994, Oct. 2 *Perf. 13x13½*
805 A421 2r multicolored .45 .25
First Intl. Festival of Islamic Artisans.

1994, Sept. 8
806 A422 7r multicolored .40 .40
Intl. Literacy Day.

Hyoscyamus Niger — A423

1994 *Perf. 13*
807 A423 6r multicolored .60 .50

Mohammed Ali Jinnah — A424

Litho. & Engr.
1994, Sept. 11 Wmk. 351 *Perf. 13*

808	A424	1r slate & multi	.20	.20
809	A424	2r claret & multi	.20	.20
810	A424	3r bright bl & multi	.20	.20
811	A424	4r emerald & multi	.20	.20
812	A424	5r lake & multi	.20	.20
813	A424	7r blue & multi	.30	.30
814	A424	10r green & multi	.50	.50
815	A424	12r orange & multi	.65	.65
816	A424	15r violet & multi	.80	.80
817	A424	20r rose & multi	1.00	1.00
818	A424	25r brown & multi	1.25	1.25
819	A424	30r olive brn & multi	1.50	1.50
		Nos. 808-819 (12)	7.00	7.00

2nd SAARC & 12th Natl. Scout Jamboree, Quetta — A425

1994, Sept. 22 Litho.
820 A425 7r multicolored .60 .40

Publication of Ferdowsi's Book of Kings, 1000th Anniv. — A426

1994, Oct. 27
821 A426 1r multicolored .25 .25

Indonesia-Pakistan Economic & Cultural Cooperation Organization — A427

1994, Aug. 19
822 A427 10r Hala pottery .60 .60
823 A427 10r Lombok pottery .60 .60
a. Pair, #822-823 1.25 1.25

See Indonesia Nos. 1585-1586.

Lahore Museum, Cent. — A428

Wmk. 351
1994, Dec. 27 Litho. *Perf. 13*
824 A428 4r multicolored .50 .50

Pakistan, 1994 World Cup Field Hockey Champions A429

1994, Dec. 31
825 A429 5r multicolored .50 .35

World Tourism Organization, 20th Anniv. — A430

1995, Jan. 2
826 A430 4r multicolored .40 .25

Juniper Forests Type of 1993
1995, Feb. 14 Litho. *Perf. 13*
827 A411 1r like #794 .40 .20

Third Economic Cooperation Organization Summit, Islamabad A431

1995, Mar. 14 Litho. *Perf. 14*
828 A431 6r multicolored .65 .65

Khushall Khan Khatak (1613-89) A432

1995, Feb. 28 *Perf. 13*
829 A432 7r multicolored .70 .70

Earth Day A433

Wmk. 351
1995, Apr. 20 Litho. *Perf. 13*
830 A433 6r multicolored .60 .60

Snakes A434

a, Krait. b, Cobra. c, Python. d, Viper.

1995, Apr. 15 Unwmk. *Perf. 13½*
831 A434 6r Block of 4, #a.-d. 3.00 3.00

Traditional Means of Transportation — A435

Wmk. 351
1995, May 22 Litho. *Perf. 13*
832 A435 5r Horse-drawn carriage .60 .60

Louis Pasteur (1822-95) A436

Wmk. 351
1995, Sept. 28 Litho. *Perf. 13*
833 A436 5r multicolored .55 .55

UN, FAO, 50th Anniv. A437

1995, Oct. 16
834 A437 1.25r multicolored .25 .20

Kinnaird College for Women, Lahore — A438

4th World Conference on Women, Beijing — A439

1995, Nov. 3 *Perf. 14x13*
835 A438 1.25r multicolored .25 .20

1995, Sept. 15 *Perf. 13*

Women in various activities: a, Playing golf, in armed forces, repairing technical device. b, Graduates, student, chemist, computer operator, reading gauge. c, At sewing machine, working with textiles. d, Making rugs, police woman, laborers.

836 A439 1.25r Strip of 4, #a.-d. .90 .90

Presentation Convent School, Rawalpindi, Cent. A440

Wmk. 351
1995, Sept. 8 Litho. *Perf. 13½*
837 A440 1.25r multicolored .40 .30

A440a

Panel colors: 5p, Orange. 15p, Violet. 25p, Red. 75p, Red brown.

1995-96 Litho. Unwmk. *Perf. 13½*
837A-837D A440a Set of 4 .25 .25

Issued: 5p, 15p, 10/10/95; 25p, 9/28/95; 75p, 5/15/96.

Liaquat Ali Khan (1895-1951) — A441

1995, Oct. 1 *Perf. 13*
838 A441 1.25r multicolored .25 .25

1st Conference of Women Parliamentarians from Muslim Countries — A442

Designs: No. 839, Dr. Tansu Ciller, Prime Minister of Turkey. No. 840, Mohtarma Benazir Bhutto, Prime Minister of Pakistan.

1995, Aug. 1 Unwmk.
839 A442 5r multicolored .60 .60
840 A442 5r multicolored .60 .60
a. Pair, #839-840 1.25 1.25

Intl. Conference of Writers and Intellectuals A443

Wmk. 351
1995, Nov. 30 Litho. *Perf. 14*
841 A443 1.25r multicolored .25 .25

Allama Iqbal Open University, 20th Anniv. — A444

1995, Dec. 16 *Perf. 13*
842 A444 1.25r multicolored .30 .30

Butterflies A445

Designs: a, Érasmie. b, Catogramme. c, Ixias. d, Héliconie.

Wmk. 351
1995, Sept. 1 Litho. *Perf. 13½*
843 A445 6r Strip of 4, #a.-d. 1.75 1.75

Fish — A446

Designs: a, Sardinella long. b, Tilapia mossambica. c, Salmo fario. d, Labeo rohita.

1995, Sept. 1
844 A446 6r Strip of 4, #a.-d. 1.75 1.75

SAARC, 10th Anniv. — A447

1995, Dec. 8 *Perf. 13*
845 A447 1.25r multicolored .25 .25

UN, 50th Anniv. — A448

Wmk. 351
1995, Oct. 24 Litho. *Perf. 13½*
846 A448 7r multicolored .50 .50

Karachi '95, Natl. Water Sports Gala — A449

Designs: a, Man on jet ski. b, Gondola race. c, Sailboard race. d, Man water skiing.

1995, Dec. 14 *Perf. 14x13*
847 A449 1.25r Block of 4, #a.-d. .75 .75

University of Baluchistan, Quetta, 25th Anniv. — A452

Wmk. 351
1995, Dec. 31 Litho. *Perf. 13*
850 A452 1.25r multicolored .25 .25

Zulfikar Ali Bhutto (1928-79), Politician, President — A455

Designs: 1.25r, Bhutto, flag, crowd of people, vert. 8r, like No. 855

Wmk. 351
1996, Apr. 4 Litho. *Perf. 13*
855 A455 1.25r multicolored .40 .25
856 A455 4r shown 1.00 .75

Size: 114x69mm
Imperf
857 A455 8r multicolored 1.50 1.50

Raja Aziz Bhatti Shaheed (1928-65) — A456

Wmk. 351
1995, Sept. 5 Litho. *Perf. 13*
858 A456 1.25r multicolored .75 .40

Pioneers of Freedom Type of 1990

#859, Maulana Shaukat Ali (1873-1938). #860, Chaudhry Ghulam Abbas (1904-67).

1995, Aug. 14 Unwmk. *Perf. 13*
859 A375 1r green & brown .35 .35
860 A375 1r green & brown .35 .35
a. Pair, #859-860 .70 .70

1996 Summer Olympic Games, Atlanta — A457

Design: 25r, #861-864 without denominations, simulated perfs, Olympic rings, "100," Atlanta '96 emblem. Illustration reduced.

Wmk. 351
1996, Aug. 3 Litho. *Perf. 13*
861 A457 5r Wrestling .40 .40
862 A457 5r Boxing .40 .40
863 A457 5r Pierre de Coubertin .40 .40
864 A457 5r Field hockey .40 .40
Nos. 861-864 (4) 1.60 1.60

Imperf
Size: 111x101mm
864A A457 25r multicolored 2.25 2.25

Pioneers of Freedom Type of 1990

Allama Abdullah Yousuf Ali (1872-1953).

Unwmk.
1996, Aug. 14 Litho. *Perf. 13*
865 A375 1r green & brown .25 .25

Restoration of General Post Office, Lahore A458

1996, Aug. 21 Wmk. 351 *Perf. 14*
866 A458 5r multicolored .35 .35

Intl. Literacy Day A459

1996, Sept. 8 Wmk. 351 *Perf. 13*
867 A459 2r multicolored .25 .25

Yarrow — A459a

Wmk. 351
1996, Nov. 25 Litho. *Perf. 13*
867A A459a 3r multicolored .60 .40

Faiz Ahmed Faiz, Poet, 86th Birthday A460

Unwmk.
1997, Feb. 13 Litho. *Perf. 13*
868 A460 3r multicolored .25 .25

Tamerlane (1336-1405) A461

Unwmk.
1997, Apr. 8 Litho. *Perf. 13*
869 A461 3r multicolored .25 .25

Famous Men — A462

Designs: No. 870, Allama Mohammad Iqbal. No. 871, Jalal-Al-Din Moulana Rumi.

1997, Apr. 21 *Perf. 13½*
870 A462 3r multicolored .20 .20
871 A462 3r multicolored .20 .20

Pakistani Independence, 50th Anniv. — A463

1997, Mar. 23 ***Perf. 13***
872 A463 2r multicolored .20 .20

Special Summit of Organization of Islamic Countries, Islamabad.

World Population Day — A464

Unwmk.
1997, July 11 Litho. ***Perf. 13***
873 A464 2r multicolored .25 .25

Intl. Atomic Energy Agency-Pakistan Atomic Energy Commission Cooperation, 40th Anniv. — A465

1997, July 29 ***Perf. 14***
874 A465 2r multicolored .25 .25

Pioneers of Freedom Type of 1990

#875, Begum Salma Tassaduq Hussain (1908-95). #876, Mohammad Ayub Khuhro (1901-80).

1997, Aug. 14 Litho. ***Perf. 13***
875 A375 1r green & brown .20 .20
876 A375 1r green & brown .20 .20

Fruits of Pakistan A466

1997, May 8
877 A466 2r Apples .25 .25

Independence, 50th Anniv. — A467

Designs: a, Allama Mohammad Iqbal. b, Mohammad Ali Jinnah. c, Liaquat Ali Khan. d, Mohtarma Fatima Jinnah.

1997, Aug. 14
Block of 4 + 2 Labels
878 A467 3r #a.-d. 1.00 .75

Lophophorus Impejanus A468

Wmk. 351
1997, Oct. 29 Litho. ***Perf. 13***
879 A468 2r multicolored .50 .25

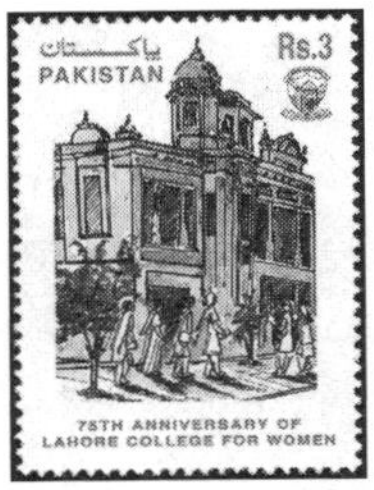

Lahore College for Women, 75th Anniv. — A469

1997, Sept. 23
880 A469 3r multicolored .35 .35

Intl. Day of the Disabled A470

Unwmk.
1997, Dec. 3 Litho. ***Perf. 13***
881 A470 4r multicolored .40 .40

Protection of the Ozone Layer — A471

1997, Nov. 15
882 A471 3r multicolored .35 .35

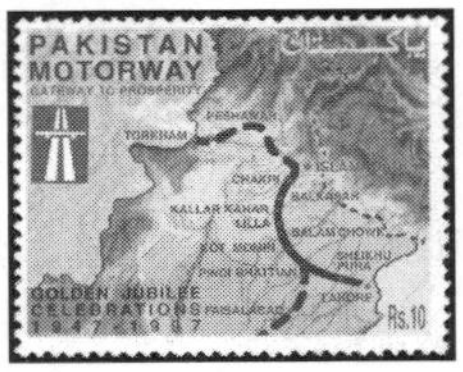

Pakistan Motorway, 50th Anniv. A472

1997, Nov. 26 ***Perf. 13½***
883 A472 10r multicolored .75 .75
a. Souvenir sheet of 1 1.60 1.60

No. 883a sold for 15r.

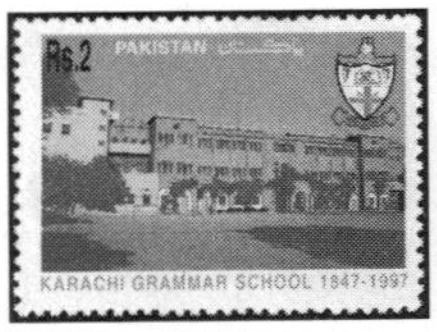

Karachi Grammar School, 150th Anniv. A473

1997, Dec. 30 Litho. ***Perf. 13½***
884 A473 2r multicolored .25 .25

Garlic A474

1997, Oct. 22 ***Perf. 13***
885 A474 2r multicolored .40 .20

Mirza Asad Ullah Khan Ghalib (1797-1869), Poet — A475

1998, Feb. 15
886 A475 2r multicolored .30 .30

Pakistan Armed Forces, 50th Anniv. A476

Wmk. 351
1997, Mar. 23 Litho. ***Perf. 13½***
887 A476 7r multicolored .50 .50

Sir Syed Ahmad Khan (1817-98), Educator, Jurist, Author — A477

1998, Mar. 27 ***Perf. 14***
888 A477 7r multicolored .40 .40

27th Natl. Games, Peshawar A478

Wmk. 351
1998, Apr. 22 Litho. ***Perf. 13***
889 A478 7r multicolored .40 .40

Jimsonweed A479

1998, Apr. 27
890 A479 2r multicolored .20 .20

Faisalabad Government College, Cent. (in 1997) — A480

1998, Aug. 14 Litho. ***Perf. 13***
891 A480 5r multicolored .25 .25

Pakistan Senate, 25th Anniv. A481

1998, Aug. 6 ***Perf. 13½***
892 A481 2r green & multi .20 .20
893 A481 5r blue & multi .25 .25

Mohammed Ali Jinnah — A482

Litho. & Engr.
1998-2001 Wmk. 351 ***Perf. 14***
893A A482 1r red & black .20 .20
894 A482 2r dk bl & red .20 .20
895 A482 3r slate grn & brn .20 .20
896 A482 4r dp vio blk & org .20 .20
897 A482 5r dp brn & grn .25 .25
898 A482 6r dp grn & bl grn .30 .30
899 A482 7r dp brn red & dp vio .35 .35
Nos. 894-899 (6) 1.50 1.50

Nos. 894 issued 8/14/98. No. 893A, 2001(?).

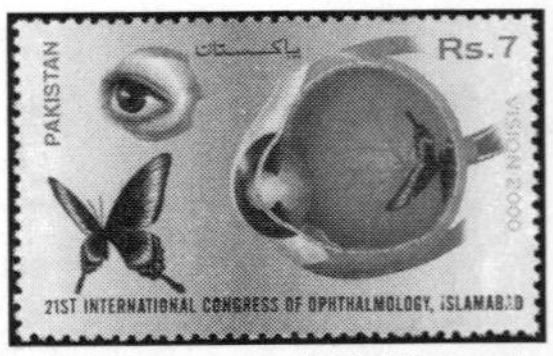

21st Intl. Congress of Ophthalmology, Islamabad — A483

Wmk. 351
1998, Sept. 11 Litho. ***Perf. 13***
900 A483 7r multicolored .30 .30

Syed Ahmed Shah Patrus Bukhari, Birth Cent. A484

1998, Oct. 1
901 A484 5r multicolored .25 .25

Philately in Pakistan, 50th Anniv. — A485

Various portions of stamps inside "50," #20-23.

1998, Oct. 4
902 A485 6r multicolored .30 .30

World Food Day A486

Wmk. 351

1998, Oct. 16 Photo. *Perf. 13*
903 A486 6r multicolored .30 .30

Mohammad Ali Jinnah (1876-1948) A487

Wmk. 351

1998, Sept. 11 Photo. *Perf. 13½*
904 A487 15r multicolored .65 .65
a. Souvenir sheet of 1, unwmk. .85 .85

No. 904a sold for 20r.

Universal Declaration of Human Rights, 50th Anniv. A488

Perf. 13x14

1998, Dec. 10 Wmk. 351
905 A488 6r multicolored .30 .30

Better Pakistan, 2010 A489

#906, Harvesting grain. #907, Health care. #908, Satellite dishes. #909, Airplane.

1998, Nov. 27 Unwmk.
906 A489 2r multicolored .20 .20
907 A489 2r multicolored .20 .20
908 A489 2r multicolored .20 .20
909 A489 2r multicolored .20 .20
Nos. 906-909 (4) .80 .80

Dr. Abdus Salam, Scientist A490

Unwmk.

1998, Nov. 21 Litho. *Perf. 13*
910 A490 2r multicolored .20 .20

See No. 916.

Qaumi Parcham March A491

1998, Dec. 16 Wmk. 351
911 A491 2r multicolored .20 .20

Intl. Year of the Ocean A492

1998, Dec. 15 *Perf. 14*
912 A492 5r multicolored .25 .25

UNICEF in Pakistan, 50th Anniv. A493

a, Distributing water. b, Child holding book. c, Girl. d, Child receiving oral vaccine.

1998, Dec. 15
913 A493 2r Block of 4, #a.-d. .40 .40

Kingdom of Saudi Arabia, Cent. — A494

Perf. 13½

1999, Jan. 27 Litho. Unwmk.
914 A494 2r Emblem on sand .20 .20
915 A494 15r Emblem on carpet .65 .65
a. Souvenir sheet of 1 .85 .85

No. 915a sold for 20r.

Scientists of Pakistan Type

Dr. Salimuz Zaman Siddiqui (1897-1994).

1999, Apr. 14 *Perf. 13*
916 A490 5r multicolored .25 .25

Pakistani Nuclear Test, 1st Anniv. — A495

1999, May 28 Litho. *Perf. 13*
917 A495 5r multicolored .25 .25

Completion of Data Darbar Mosque Complex — A496

1999, May 31 Litho. *Perf. 13*
918 A496 7r multicolored .30 .30

Fasting Buddha, c. 3-4 A.D. — A497

1999, July 21 Litho. *Perf. 13½x13¾*
919 A497 7r shown .35 .35
920 A497 7r Facing forward .35 .35
a. Souv. sheet of 2, #919-920 1.10 1.10

No. 920a sold for 25r. China 1999 World Philatelic Exhibition (No. 920a).

Geneva Conventions, 50th Anniv. — A498

Perf. 12¾x13¾

1999, Aug. 12 Litho.
921 A498 5r pink, black & red .25 .25

Pioneers of Freedom Type of 1990

Designs: No. 922, Chaudhry Muhammad Ali (1905-80), 1st Secretary General. No. 923, Sir Adamjee Haji Dawood (1880-1948), banker. No. 924, Maulana Abdul Hamid Badayuni (1898-1970), religious scholar.

1999, Aug. 14 Litho. *Perf. 13*
922 A375 2r green & brown .20 .20
923 A375 2r green & brown .20 .20
924 A375 2r green & brown .20 .20
Nos. 922-924 (3) .60 .60

Ustad Nusrat Fateh Ali Khan (1948-97), Singer — A499

1999, Aug. 16
925 A499 2r multicolored .20 .20

Islamic Development Bank, 25th Anniv. (in 2000) — A500

1999, Sept. 18
926 A500 5r multicolored .25 .25

People's Republic of China, 50th Anniv. — A501

1999, Sept. 21
927 A501 2r Gate of Heavenly Peace .20 .20
928 A501 15r Arms, Mao Zedong, horiz. .60 .60

A502

A503

No. 929: a, Enterprise class. b, 470 class. c, Optimist class. d, Laser class. e, Mistral class.

1999, Sept. 28 *Perf. 13½x13¼*
929 A502 2r Strip of 5, #a.-e. .40 .40

Ninth Asian Sailing Championship.

10th Asian Optimist Sailing Championships — A502a

1999, Oct. 7 Litho. *Perf. 13¾x13½*
929F A502a 2r multi + label .20 .20

1999, Oct. 9 *Perf. 14¼*
930 A503 10r multicolored .45 .45

UPU, 125th anniv.

Hakim Mohammed Said (1920-98), Physician
A504

1999, Oct. 17 **Litho.** ***Perf. 13***
931 A504 5r multicolored .25 .25

National Bank of Pakistan, 50th Anniv. — A505

Perf. 13¼x13¾

1999, Nov. 8 **Litho.** **Wmk. 351**
932 A505 5r multi .20 .20

Shell Oil in Pakistan, Cent. — A506

Perf. 13¼x13

1999, Nov. 15 **Wmk. 351**
933 A506 4r multi .20 .20

Rights of the Child, 10th Anniv. — A507

Perf. 13x13¼

1999, Nov. 20 **Unwmk.**
934 A507 2r multi .20 .20

Allam Iqbal Open University, Islamabad — A508

Designs: 2r, University crest, flasks, microphone, mortarboard, book, computer. 3r, Similar to 2r, crest in center. 5r, Crest, map, mortarboard, book.

Unwmk.

1999, Nov. 20 **Litho.** ***Perf. 13***
935 A508 2r bl grn & multi .20 .20
936 A508 3r multi .20 .20
937 A508 5r multi .20 .20
Nos. 935-937 (3) .60 .60

Shabbir Hassan Khan Josh Malihabadi (1898-1982), Poet — A509

1999, Dec. 5
938 A509 5r multi .20 .20

Dr. Afzal Qadri (1912-74), Entomologist — A510

1999, Dec. 6
939 A510 3r multi .20 .20

Ghulam Bari Aleeg (1907-49), Journalist
A511

1999, Dec. 10 **Litho.** ***Perf. 13***
940 A511 5r multi .20 .20

Plantain — A512

1999, Dec. 20
941 A512 5r multi .20 .20

Eid-Ul-Fitr — A513

Illustration reduced.

Perf. 13¾x13½

1999, Dec. 24 **Litho.**
942 A513 2r green & multi .20 .20
943 A513 15r blue & multi .60 .60

SOS Children's Villages of Pakistan, 25th Anniv. — A514

2000, Mar. 12 ***Perf. 13***
944 A514 2r multi .20 .20

International Cycling Union, Cent. — A515

Illustration reduced.

2000, Apr. 14 **Litho.** ***Perf. 13¼***
945 A515 2r multi .20 .20

Convention on Human Rights and Dignity — A516

Illustration reduced.

Perf. 13¼

2000, Apr. 21 **Litho.** **Unwmk.**
946 A516 2r multi .20 .20

Edwardes College, Peshawar, Cent. — A517

2000, Apr. 24 ***Perf. 13½***
947 A517 2r multi .20 .20

Mahomed Ali Habib (1904-59), Banker, Philantropist — A518

2000, May 15 **Litho.** ***Perf. 13***
948 A518 2r multi .20 .20

Institute of Cost and Management Accountants, 50th Anniv. — A519

Design: 15r, Globe.

2000, June 23 **Litho.** ***Perf. 13***
950 A519 15r multi

An additional stamp was issued in this set. The editors would like to examine it.

Ahmed E. H. Jaffer (1909-90), Politician
A520

2000, Aug. 9 **Litho.** ***Perf. 13***
951 A520 10r multi .40 .40

Creation of Pakistan, 53rd Anniv. — A521

a, No tree. b, Tree in foreground. c, Tree behind people, cart. d, Tree in distance.

2000, Aug. 14 **Litho.** ***Perf. 13***
952 A521 5r Strip of 4, #a-d .75 .75

Nishan-e-Haider Medal Type of 1995

Nishan-e-haider gallantry award winners: a, Capt. Muhammad Sarwar Shaheed (1910-48). b, Maj. Tufail Muhammad (1914-58).
Illustration reduced.

2000, Sept. 6 **Litho.** ***Perf. 13***
953 A456 5r Pair, #a-b .40 .40

2000 Summer Olympics, Sydney — A523

No. 954: a, Runners. b, Field hockey. c, Weight lifting. d, Cycling.
Illustration reduced.

2000, Sept. 20 ***Perf. 14¼***
954 A523 4r Block of 4, #a-d .65 .65

Natl. College of Arts, 125th Anniv. A524

2000, Oct. 28
955 A524 5r multi .20 .20

Creating the Future — A525

2000, Nov. 4 ***Perf. 13½x13¼***
956 A525 5r multi .20 .20

Intl. Defense Exhibition and Seminar — A526

2000, Nov. 14 **Litho.** ***Perf. 13***
957 A526 7r multi .30 .30

Licorice — A527

2000, Nov. 28 Litho. *Perf. 13*

958 A527 2r multi .20 .20

Rotary Intl. Campaign Against Polio — A528

2000, Dec. 13

959 A528 2r multi .20 .20

UN High Commissioner for Refugees, 50th Anniv. — A529

2000, Dec. 14

960 A529 2r multi .20 .20

Poets — A530

Design: 2r, Hafeez Jalandhri (1900-82).

2001 Litho. *Perf. 13*

961 A530 2r multi .20 .20
962 A530 5r multi .20 .20

Issued: 2r, 1/14. 5r, 9/25.

Habib Bank AG Zurich — A531

2001, Mar. 20 Litho. *Perf. 13*

963 A531 5r multi .20 .20

Chashma Nuclear Power Plant A532

2001, Mar. 29

964 A532 4r multi .20 .20

9th SAF Games, Islamabad A533

Background colors: No. 965, 4r, Light blue. No. 966, 4r, Lilac.

2001, Apr. 9 *Perf. 13½x13¼*

965-966 A533 Set of 2 .30 .30

Pakistan-People's Rep. of China Diplomatic Relations, 50th Anniv. — A534

Designs: No. 967, Yugur and Hunza women, flags.

No. 968 - Paintings by Yao Youdou: a, Ma Gu's Birthday Offering. b, Two Pakistani Women Drawing Water.

2001, May 12 *Perf. 13*

967 A534 4r multi .20 .20
968 A534 4r Horiz. pair, #a-b .30 .30

Mohammed Ali Jinnah (1876-1948) A535

2001, Aug. 14

969 A535 4r multi .20 .20

Sindh Festival A536

Unwmk.

2001, Sept. 22 Litho. *Perf. 13*

970 A536 4r multi .20 .20

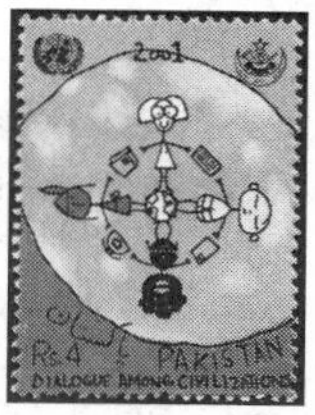

Year of Dialogue Among Civilizations A537

2001, Oct. 9 *Perf. 13½*

971 A537 4r multi .20 .20

Turkmenistan, 10th Anniv. of Independence A538

2001, Oct. 27 *Perf. 13*

972 A538 5r multi .20 .20

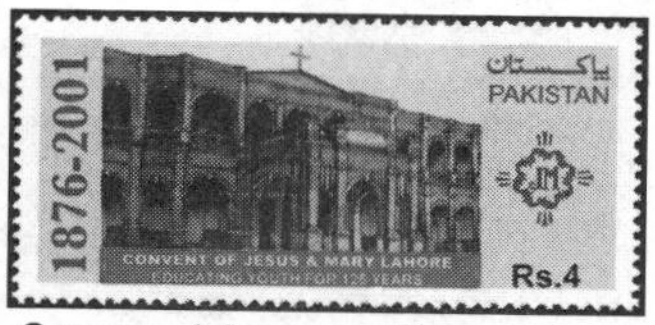

Convent of Jesus and Mary, Lahore, 125th Anniv. — A539

2001, Nov. 15 Wmk. 351

973 A539 4r multi .20 .20

Men of Letters Type of 1999

Design: 4r, Dr. Ishtiaq Husain Qureshi (1903-81), historian.

2001, Nov. 20 Unwmk.

974 A511 4r multi .20 .20

Birds — A540

No. 975: a, Blue throat. b, Hoopoe. c, Pin-tailed sandgrouse. d, Magpie robin.

2001, Nov. 26 *Perf. 13¼x13*

975 A540 4r Block of 4, #a-d .60 .60

Pakistan - United Arab Emirates Friendship, 30th Anniv. — A541

Designs: 5r, Flags, handshake, vert. 30r, Sheik Zaid bin Sultan al Nahayan, Mohammed Ali Jinnah.

2001, Dec. 2 *Perf. 13*

976-977 A541 Set of 2 1.40 1.40

Nishtar Medical College, Multan, 50th Anniv. — A542

2001, Dec. 20

978 A542 5r multi .20 .20

Quaid Year — A543

No. 979: a, Mohammed Ali Jinnah reviewing troops, 1948. b, Jinnah, soldiers, artillery gun, 1948.

No. 980, vert.: a, Jinnah taking oath as Governor General, 1947. b, Jinnah at opening ceremony of State Bank of Pakistan, 1948. c, Jinnah saluting at presentation of colors, 1948.

2001, Dec. 25 *Perf. 13*

979 Horiz. pair .30 .30
a.-b. A543 4r Any single .20 .20

Size: 33x56mm

Perf. 13x13¼

980 Horiz. strip of 3 .45 .45
a.-c. A543 4r Any single .20 .20

Pakistan Ordnance Factories, 50th Anniv. — A544

2001, Dec. 28 *Perf. 13¼x13½*

981 A544 4r multi .20 .20

Men of Letters Type of 1999

Design: 5r, Syed Imtiaz Ali Taj (1900-70), playwright.

2001 ? *Perf. 13*

982 A511 5r multi .20 .20

Nishan-e-Haider Type of 1995

No. 983: a, Maj. Mohammad Akram Shaheed (1938-71). b, Maj. Shabbir Sharif Shaheeb (1943-71).

2001 ? *Perf. 13*

983 Horiz. pair .30 .30
a.-b. A456 4r Any single .20 .20

Peppermint A545

Wmk. 351

2002, Feb. 15 Litho. *Perf. 13*

985 A545 4r multi .20 .20

OFFICIAL STAMPS

Official Stamps of India, 1939-43, Overprinted in Black **PAKISTAN**

1947-49 Wmk. 196 *Perf. 13½x14*

O1	O8	3p	slate	.70	.20
O2	O8	½a	dk rose vio	.25	.20
O3	O8	9p	green	3.00	.20
O4	O8	1a	carmine rose	.25	.20
O4A	O8	1a3p	bister ('49)	3.75	3.75
O5	O8	1½a	dull purple	.25	.20
O6	O8	2a	scarlet	.25	.20
O7	O8	2½a	purple	4.50	4.50
O8	O8	4a	dk brown	1.10	.20
O9	O8	8a	blue violet	1.40	.50

India Nos. O100-O103 Overprinted in Black **PAKISTAN**

O10	A82	1r	brown & slate	.70	.50
O11	A82	2r	dk brn & dk vio	3.25	.25
O12	A82	5r	dp ultra & dk grn	12.50	*50.00*
			Telegraph cancel		7.50

O13 A82 10r rose car & dk vio 32.50 *40.00*
Telegraph cancel *5.00*
Nos. O1-O13 (14) 64.40 100.90

Regular Issue of 1948 Overprinted in Black or Carmine **SERVICE**

Perf. 12½, 13, 13½x14, 14x13½

1948, Aug. 14 Unwmk.

O14 A3 3p orange red .20 .20
O15 A3 6p purple (C) .20 .20
O16 A3 9p dk green (C) .20 .20
O17 A4 1a dk blue (C) 3.50 .20
O18 A4 1½a gray grn (C) 3.25 .20
O19 A4 2a orange red 1.25 .20
O20 A5 3a olive green 17.50 4.50
O21 A6 4a chocolate .70 .20
O22 A6 8a black (C) 1.25 *4.50*
O23 A5 1r ultra .90 .20
O24 A5 2r dark brown 12.00 5.00
O25 A5 5r carmine 20.00 5.00
O26 A7 10r rose lil, perf. 14x13½ 12.00 *32.50*
a. Perf. 12 15.00 *30.00*
b. Perf. 13 13.00 *40.00*
Nos. O14-O26 (13) 72.95 53.10

Issued: #O26a, 10/10/51; #O26b, 1954(?).

Nos. 47-50 and 52 Overprinted Type "a" in Black or Carmine

1949-50 *Perf. 12½, 13½x14*

O27 A10 1a dark blue (C) .80 .20
O28 A10 1½a gray green (C) .25 .20
a. Inverted ovpt. 150.00 40.00
O29 A10 2a orange red .80 .20
O30 A9 3a olive grn ('49) 14.00 3.25
O31 A11 8a black (C) 21.00 11.00
Nos. O27-O31 (5) 36.85 14.85

Types of Regular Issue of 1951, "Pakistan" or "Pakistan Postage" Replaced by "SERVICE"

Unwmk.

1951, Aug. 14 Engr. *Perf. 13*

O32 A13 3a dark rose lake 4.00 *4.00*
O33 A14 4a deep green 1.00 .25
O34 A15 8a brown 5.00 1.75
Nos. O32-O34 (3) 10.00 *6.00*

Nos. 24-26, 47-49, 38-41 Overprinted in Black or Carmine

b **SERVICE**

1954

O35 A3 3p orange red .20 .20
O36 A3 6p purple (C) .20 .20
O37 A3 9p dk green (C) .20 .20
O38 A10 1a dk blue (C) .20 .20
O39 A10 1½a gray green (C) .20 .20
O40 A10 2a orange red .20 .20
O41 A5 1r ultra 7.00 2.00
O42 A5 2r dark brown 3.00 .20
O43 A5 5r carmine 20.00 10.00
O43A A7 10r rose lilac 18.00 *40.00*
Nos. O35-O43A (10) 49.20 *53.40*

Nos. 66-72 Overprinted Type "b" in Carmine or Black

1954, Aug. 14

O44 A18 6p rose violet (C) .20 *1.10*
O45 A19 9p blue (C) 1.60 *3.75*
O46 A19 1a carmine rose .25 *.95*
O47 A18 1½a red .25 *.95*
O48 A20 14a dk green (C) 1.10 *3.25*
O49 A20 1r yellow grn (C) 1.40 *.20*
O50 A20 2r orange 2.75 .20
Nos. O44-O50 (7) 7.55 *10.40*

No. 75 Overprinted in Carmine Type "b" Overprint: 13x2½mm

1955, Aug. 14 Unwmk. *Perf. 13*

O51 A21 8a violet .35 .20

Nos. 24, 40, 66-72, 74-75, 83, 89 Overprinted in Black or Carmine

c **SERVICE**

1957-61

O52 A3 3p org red ('58) .20 .20
O53 A18 6p rose vio (C) .20 .20
O54 A19 9p blue (C) ('58) .20 *.25*
O55 A19 1a carmine rose .20 .20
O56 A18 1½a red .20 .20
O57 A24 2a red ('58) .20 .20
O58 A21 6a dk bl (C) ('60) .20 .20
O59 A21 8a vio (C) ('58) .20 .20
O60 A20 14a dk grn (C) ('58) .40 *2.00*
O61 A20 1r yel grn (C) ('58) .40 .20
O62 A20 2r orange ('58) 5.00 .20
O63 A5 5r carmine ('58) 5.00 .20
O64 A26 10r dk grn & org (C) ('61) 6.00 6.00
Nos. O52-O64 (13) 18.40 10.25

For surcharges see Nos. O67-O73.

Nos. 110-111 Overprinted Type "c"

1961, Apr.

O65 A33 8a green .20 .20
O66 A33 1r blue .20 .20
a. Inverted overprint 7.50

New Currency

Nos. O52, O55-O57 Surcharged with New Value in Paisa

1961

O67 A18 1p on 1½a red .20 .20
a. Overprinted type "b" 3.00 1.25
O68 A3 2p on 3p orange red .20 .20
a. Overprinted type "b" 4.50 3.00
O69 A19 6p on 1a car rose
O70 A19 7p on 1a car rose .20 .20
a. Overprinted type "b" 5.00 5.00
O71 A18 9p on 1½a red
O72 A24 13p on 2a red ("PAISA") .20 .20
O73 A24 13p on 2a red ("Paisa")

Nos. O69, O71, O73 were locally overprinted at Mastung. On these stamps "paisa" is in lower case.

Forgeries of No. O73 abound.

Nos. 125, 128 Overprinted Type "c"

1961

O74 A33 3p on 6p purple .20 .20
O75 A33 13p on 2a copper red .20 .20

Various violet handstamped surcharges were applied to several official stamps. Most of these repeat the denomination of the basic stamp and add the new value. Example: "4 ANNAS (25 Paisa)" on No. O33.

Nos. 129-135, 135B, 135C, 136a, 137-140a Overprinted in Carmine

d

1961-78 *Perf. 13½x14*

O76 A40 1p violet (II) .20 .20
a. Type I .20 .20
O77 A40 2p rose red (II) .20 .20
a. Type I .20 .20
O78 A40 3p magenta .20 .20
O79 A40 5p ultra (II) .20 .20
a. Type I .20 .20
O80 A40 7p emerald .20 .20
O81 A40 10p brown .20 .20
O82 A40 13p blue violet .20 .20
O83 A40 15p rose lil (#135B; '64) .20 .20
O84 A40 20p dl grn (#135C; '70) .20 .20
O84A A40 25p dark blue (#136a; '77) .20 .20
O85 A40 40p dull pur ('62) .20 .20
O86 A40 50p dull grn ('62) .20 .20
O87 A40 75p dk car ('62) .20 .20
O88 A40 90p lt ol grn (#140a; '78) .30 .20
Nos. O76-O88 (14) 2.90 2.80

Designs Redrawn

1961-66

O76b A40 1p violet (#129b) ('63) .20 .20
O77b A40 2p rose red (#130b) ('64) .20 .20
O78a A40 3p mag (#131a) ('66) .20 .20
O79b A40 5p ultra (#132b) ('63) .20 .20
O80a A40 7p emerald (#133a) 2.00 .20
O81a A40 10p brown (#134a) ('64) .20 .20
O82a A40 13p blue vio (#135a) ('63) .20 .20
O85a A40 40p dull purple (#137a) .35 .20
O86a A40 50p dull grn (#138a) ('64) .20 .20
O87a A40 75p dark carmine (#139a)
Nos. O76b-O87a (9) 3.75 1.80

See Nos. O84A and O88 for other stamps with designs redrawn.

Nos. 141, 143-144 Overprinted Type "c" in Black or Carmine

1963, Jan. 7 Unwmk. *Perf. 13½x13*

O89 A41 1r vermilion .35 .20
O90 A41 2r orange 1.50 .25
O91 A41 5r green (C) 4.25 5.00
Nos. O89-O91 (3) 6.10 5.45

Nos. 200, 202-203 Overprinted Type "c"

1968-? Wmk. 351 *Perf. 13½x13*

O92 A41 1r vermilion 1.00 .20
O93 A41 2r orange 5.00 .50
O93A A41 5r green (C) 12.00 5.00
Nos. O92-O93A (3) 18.00 5.70

Nos. 459-468, 470-475 Overprinted Type "d" in Carmine or Black

1980-84

O94 A224 2p dark green .20 .20
O95 A224 3p black .20 .20
O96 A224 5p violet blue .20 .20
O97 A225 10p grnsh blue .20 .20
O98 A225 20p yel grn ('81) .20 .20
O99 A225 25p rose car & grn ('81) .20 .20
O100 A225 40p car & bl ('81) .25 .20
O101 A225 50p bl grn & vio .20 .20
O102 A225 60p black 1.00 .20
O103 A225 75p dp orange 1.00 .20
O105 A225a 1r olive ('81) 2.25 .20
O106 A225a 1.50r dp orange .20 .20
O107 A225a 2r car rose (B) .20 .20
O108 A225a 3r indigo ('81) .20 .20
O109 A225a 4r black ('84) 1.25 .25
O110 A225a 5r dk brn ('84) 1.25 .30
Nos. O94-O110 (16) 9.00 3.35

Types A237-A239 Inscribed "SERVICE POSTAGE"

1980 Litho. *Perf. 12x11½, 11½x12*

O111 A237 10p dk grn & yel org .90 .20
O112 A237 15p dk grn & ap grn .90 .20
O113 A237 25p dp vio & rose car .20 .20
O114 A237 35p rose pink & brt yel grn .20 .20
O115 A238 40p red & lt brn .90 .20
O116 A239 50p olive & vio bl .20 .20
O117 A239 80p blk & yel grn .25 .20
Nos. O111-O117 (7) 3.55 1.40

Issued: 10p, 15p, 40p, 1/15; others, 3/10.

Nos. 613-614, 616-620 Ovptd. "SERVICE" in Red

1984-87 Litho. *Perf. 11*

O118 A289 5p Kot Diji .20 .20
O119 A289 10p Rohtas .20 .20
O120 A289 20p Attock Fort .20 .20
O121 A289 50p Hyderabad .20 .20
O122 A289 60p Lahore ('86) .20 .20
O123 A289 70p Sibi .20 .20
O124 A289 80p Ranikot .20 .20
Nos. O118-O124 (7) 1.40 1.40

Issued: 10p, 9/25; 80p, 8/3/87.

No. 712 Ovptd. "SERVICE"

Litho. & Engr.

1989, Dec. 24 *Perf. 13*

O124A A357 1r multicolored 1.75 .50

National Assembly, Islamabad - O1

Wmk. 351

1991-99 Litho. *Perf. 13½*

O125 O1 1r green & red .20 .20
O126 O1 2r rose car & red .20 .20
O127 O1 3r ultra & red .20 .20
O128 O1 4r red brown & red .20 .20
O129 O1 5r rose lilac & red .20 .20
O130 O1 10r brown & red .30 .30
Nos. O125-O130 (6) 1.30 1.30

Issued: 10r, 2/6/99; others, 4/12/91.

1999 Unwmk.

O131 O1 2r rose car & red .20 .20

This is an expanding set. Numbers may change.

BAHAWALPUR

LOCATION — A State of Pakistan.
AREA — 17,494 sq. mi.
POP. — 1,341,209 (1941)
CAPITAL — Bahawalpur

Bahawalpur was a State of India until 1947. These stamps had franking power solely within Bahawalpur.

Seventeen King George VI stamps of India exist overprinted with star, cresent and a line of Arabic. These are not considered to be legitimate stamps.

Used values are for c-t-o or favor cancels.

Amir Muhammad Bahawal Khan I Abbasi — A1

Perf. 12½x12

1947, Dec. 1 Wmk. 274 Engr.

1 A1 ½a brt car rose & blk 1.25 *2.50*

Bicentenary of the ruling family.

Nawab Sadiq Muhammad Khan V Abbasi Bahadur — A2

Tombs of the Amirs — A3

Mosque, Sadiq Garh — A4

Fort Dirawar A5

Nur-Mahal Palace — A6

Palace, Sadiq Garh — A7

Nawab Sadiq Muhammad Khan V Abbasi Bahadur — A8

A9

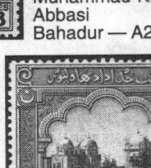

Perf. 12½ (A2), 12x12½ (A3, A5, A6, A7), 12½x12 (A4, A8), 13x13½ (A9)

1948, Apr. 1 Engr. Wmk. 274

2	A2	3p dp blue & blk	.60	2.50
3	A2	½a lake & blk	.60	2.50
4	A2	9p dk green & blk	.60	2.50
5	A2	1a dp car & blk	.60	2.50
6	A2	1½a violet & blk	.60	2.50
7	A3	2a car & dp grn	.85	2.50
8	A4	4a brn & org red	1.00	2.50
9	A5	6a dp bl & vio brn	1.00	2.50
10	A6	8a brt pur & car	1.00	2.50
11	A7	12a dp car & dk bl grn	1.25	2.50
12	A8	1r chocolate & vio	15.00	20.00
13	A8	2r dp mag & dk grn	30.00	32.50
14	A8	5r purple & black	30.00	42.50
15	A9	10r black & car	30.00	52.50
		Nos. 2-15 (14)	113.10	172.50

See #18-21. For overprints see #O17-O24.

Soldiers of 1848 and 1948 — A10

1948, Oct. 15 Engr. *Perf. 11½*

16	A10	1½a dp car & blk	.75	2.50

Centenary of the Multan Campaign.

Amir Khan V and Mohammed Ali Jinnah — A11

1948, Oct. 3 *Perf. 13x12½*

17	A11	1½a grn & car rose	.75	2.50

1st anniv. of the union of Bahawalpur with Pakistan.

Types of 1948

1948 *Perf. 12x11½*

18	A8	1r orange & dp grn	.90	2.50
19	A8	2r carmine & blk	1.10	2.50
20	A8	5r ultra & red brn	1.25	2.50
		Perf. 13½		
21	A9	10r green & red brn	1.50	2.50
		Nos. 18-21 (4)	4.75	10.00

Panjnad Weir — A12

1949, Mar. 3 *Perf. 14*

22	A12	3p shown	.20	2.50
23	A12	½a Wheat	.20	2.50
24	A12	9p Cotton	.20	2.50
25	A12	1a Sahiwal Bull	.20	2.50
		Nos. 22-25 (4)	.80	10.00

25th anniv. of the acquisition of full ruling powers by Amir Khan V.

UPU Monument, Bern — A13

1949, Oct. 10 *Perf. 13*

Center in Black

26	A13	9p green	.20	1.50
27	A13	1a red violet	.20	1.50
28	A13	1½a brown orange	.20	1.50
29	A13	2½a blue	.20	1.50
		Nos. 26-29 (4)	.80	6.00

UPU, 75th anniv. Exist perf 17½x17. Exist imperf.

For overprints see Nos. O25-O28.

OFFICIAL STAMPS

Panjnad Weir — O1

Camel and Colt — O2

Antelopes O3

Pelicans O4

Juma Masjid Palace, Fort Derawar O5

Temple at Pattan Munara O6

Red Overprint

Wmk. 274

1945, Jan. 1 Engr. *Perf. 14*

O1	O1	½a brt grn & blk	2.50	2.50
O2	O2	1a carmine & blk	3.50	3.00
O3	O3	2a violet & blk	3.25	3.00
O4	O4	4a olive & blk	7.50	6.75
O5	O5	8a brown & blk	17.00	8.75
O6	O6	1r orange & blk	17.00	8.75
		Nos. O1-O6 (6)	50.75	32.75

For types overprinted see Nos. O7-O9, O11-O13.

Types of 1945, Without Red Overprint, Surcharged in Black

1945 Unwmk.

O7	O5	½a on 8a lake & blk	3.75	3.00
O8	O6	1½a on 1r org & blk	30.00	12.50
O9	O1	1½a on 2r ultra & blk	110.00	45.00
		Nos. O7-O9 (3)	143.75	60.50

Camels - O7

1945, Mar. 10 Red Overprint

O10	O7	1a brown & black	32.50	35.00

Types of 1945, Without Red Overprint, Overprinted in Black

1945

O11	O1	½a carmine & black	1.25	2.50
O12	O2	1a carmine & black	2.00	2.50
O13	O3	2a orange & black	3.00	3.00
		Nos. O11-O13 (3)	6.25	8.00

Nawab Sadiq Muhammad Khan V Abbasi Bahadur — O8

1945

O14	O8	3p dp blue & blk	2.50	2.50
O15	O8	1½a dp violet & blk	14.00	5.25

Flags of Allied Nations O9

1946, May 1

O16	O9	1½a emerald & gray	2.00	2.50

Victory of Allied Nations in World War II.

Stamps of 1948 Overprinted in Carmine or Black

Perf. 12½, 12½x12, 12x11½, 13½

1948 Wmk. 274

O17	A2	3p dp bl & blk (C)	.70	2.50
O18	A2	1a dp carmine & blk	.70	2.50
O19	A3	2a car & dp grn	.70	2.50
O20	A4	4a brown & org red	.70	2.50
O21	A8	1r org & dp grn (C)	.70	2.50
O22	A8	2r car & blk (C)	.70	2.50
O23	A8	5r ultra & red brn (C)	.70	2.50
O24	A9	10r grn & red brn (C)	.70	2.50
		Nos. O17-O24 (8)	5.60	20.00

Same Ovpt. in Carmine on #26-29

1949 *Perf. 13, 18*

Center in Black

O25	A13	9p green	.20	2.50
O26	A13	1a red violet	.20	2.50
O27	A13	1½a brown orange	.20	2.50
O28	A13	2½a blue	.20	2.50
		Nos. O25-O28 (4)	.80	10.00

75th anniv. of the UPU. Exist perf 17½x17 and imperf.

PALAU

pə-'lau

LOCATION — Group of 100 islands in the West Pacific Ocean about 1,000 miles southeast of Manila
AREA — 179 sq. mi.
POP. — 18,467 (1999 est.)
CAPITAL — Koror

Palau, the western section of the Caroline Islands (Micronesia), was part of the US Trust Territory of the Pacific, established in 1947. By agreement with the USPS, the republic began issuing its own stamps in 1984, with the USPS continuing to carry the mail to and from the islands.

On Jan. 10, 1986 Palau became a Federation as a Sovereign State in Compact of Free Association with the US.

100 Cents = 1 Dollar

Catalogue values for all unused stamps in this country are for Never Hinged items.

Inauguration of Postal Service — A1

1983, Mar. 10 Litho. *Perf. 14*

1	A1	20c Constitution preamble	.50	.50
2	A1	20c Hunters	.50	.50
3	A1	20c Fish	.50	.50
4	A1	20c Preamble, diff.	.50	.50
a.		Block of 4, #1-4	2.00	2.00

Palau Fruit Dove — A2

1983, May 16 *Perf. 15*

5	A2	20c shown	.40	.40
6	A2	20c Palau morningbird	.40	.40
7	A2	20c Giant white-eye	.40	.40
8	A2	20c Palau fantail	.40	.40
a.		Block of 4, #5-8	1.60	1.60

Sea Fan — A3

1983-84 Litho. *Perf. 13½x14*

9	A3	1c shown	.20	.20
10	A3	3c Map cowrie	.20	.20
11	A3	5c Jellyfish	.20	.20
12	A3	10c Hawksbill turtle	.20	.20
13	A3	13c Giant Clam	.20	.20
a.		Booklet pane of 10	10.00	—
b.		Bklt. pane of 10 (5 #13, 5 #14)	11.00	—
14	A3	20c Parrotfish	.35	.35
b.		Booklet pane of 10	10.50	—
15	A3	28c Chambered Nautilus	.45	.45
16	A3	30c Dappled sea cucumber	.50	.50
17	A3	37c Sea Urchin	.55	.55
18	A3	50c Starfish	.80	.80
19	A3	$1 Squid	1.60	1.60
		Perf. 15x14		
20	A3	$2 Dugong	4.25	4.25
21	A3	$5 Pink sponge	10.50	10.50
		Nos. 9-21 (13)	20.00	20.00

See Nos. 75-85.

Humpback Whale, World Wildlife Emblem — A4

1983, Sept. 21 *Perf. 14*

24 A4 20c shown .50 .50
25 A4 20c Blue whale .50 .50
26 A4 20c Fin whale .50 .50
27 A4 20c Great sperm whale .50 .50
a. Block of 4, #24-27 2.00 2.00

Christmas 1983 — A5

Paintings by Charlie Gibbons, 1971.

1983, Oct. Litho. *Perf. 14½*

28 A5 20c First Child ceremony .50 .50
29 A5 20c Spearfishing from Red Canoe .50 .50
30 A5 20c Traditional feast at the Bai .50 .50
31 A5 20c Taro gardening .50 .50
32 A5 20c Spearfishing at New Moon .50 .50
a. Strip of 5, #28-32 2.50 2.50

A6

Capt. Wilson's Voyage, Bicentennial — A7

1983, Dec. 14 *Perf. 14x15*

33 A6 20c Capt. Henry Wilson .45 .45
34 A7 20c Approaching Pelew .45 .45
35 A7 20c Englishman's Camp on Ulong .45 .45
36 A6 20c Prince Lee Boo .45 .45
37 A6 20c King Abba Thulle .45 .45
38 A7 20c Mooring in Koror .45 .45
39 A7 20c Village scene of Pelew Islands .45 .45
40 A6 20c Ludee .45 .45
a. Block or strip of 8, #33-40 4.00 4.00

Local Seashells — A8

Shell paintings (dorsal and ventral) by Deborah Dudley Max.

1984, Mar. 15 Litho. *Perf. 14*

41 A8 20c Triton trumpet, d. .45 .45
42 A8 20c Horned helmet, d. .45 .45
43 A8 20c Giant clam, d. .45 .45
44 A8 20c Laciniate conch, d. .45 .45
45 A8 20c Royal cloak scallop, d. .45 .45
46 A8 20c Triton trumpet, v. .45 .45
47 A8 20c Horned helmet, v. .45 .45
48 A8 20c Giant clam, v. .45 .45
49 A8 20c Laciniate conch, v. .45 .45
50 A8 20c Royal cloak scallop, v. .45 .45
a. Block of 10, #41-50 4.50 4.50

Explorer Ships A9

1984, June 19 Litho. *Perf. 14*

51 A9 40c Oroolong, 1783 .85 .85
52 A9 40c Duff, 1797 .85 .85
53 A9 40c Peiho, 1908 .85 .85
54 A9 40c Albatross, 1885 .85 .85
a. Block of 4, #51-54 3.50 3.50

UPU Congress.

Ausipex '84 — A10

Fishing Methods.

1984, Sept. 6 Litho. *Perf. 14*

55 A10 20c Throw spear fishing .40 .40
56 A10 20c Kite fishing .40 .40
57 A10 20c Underwater spear fishing .40 .40
58 A10 20c Net fishing .40 .40
a. Block of 4, #55-58 1.75 1.75

Christmas Flowers — A11

1984, Nov. 28 Litho. *Perf. 14*

59 A11 20c Mountain Apple .40 .40
60 A11 20c Beach Morning Glory .40 .40
61 A11 20c Turmeric .40 .40
62 A11 20c Plumeria .40 .40
a. Block of 4, #59-62 1.75 1.75

Audubon Bicentenary — A12

1985, Feb. 6 Litho. *Perf. 14*

63 A12 22c Shearwater chick .85 .85
64 A12 22c Shearwater's head .85 .85
65 A12 22c Shearwater in flight .85 .85
66 A12 22c Swimming .85 .85
a. Block of 4, #63-66 3.50 3.50
Nos. 63-66,C5 (5) 4.50 4.50

Canoes and Rafts A13

1985, Mar. 27 Litho.

67 A13 22c Cargo canoe .55 .55
68 A13 22c War canoe .55 .55
69 A13 22c Bamboo raft .55 .55
70 A13 22c Racing/sailing canoe .55 .55
a. Block of 4, #67-70 2.25 2.25

Marine Life Type of 1983

1985, June 11 Litho. *Perf. 14½x14*

75 A3 14c Trumpet triton .30 .30
a. Booklet pane of 10 *8.00* —
76 A3 22c Bumphead parrotfish .55 .55
a. Booklet pane of 10 *10.00* —
b. Booklet pane, 5 14c, 5 22c *11.00* —

77 A3 25c Soft coral, damsel fish .60 .60
79 A3 33c Sea anemone, clownfish .80 .80
80 A3 39c Green sea turtle .95 .95
81 A3 44c Pacific sailfish 1.10 1.10

Perf. 15x14

85 A3 $10 Spinner dolphins 19.00 19.00
Nos. 75-85 (7) 23.30 23.30

This is an expanding set. Numbers will change if necessary.

A14

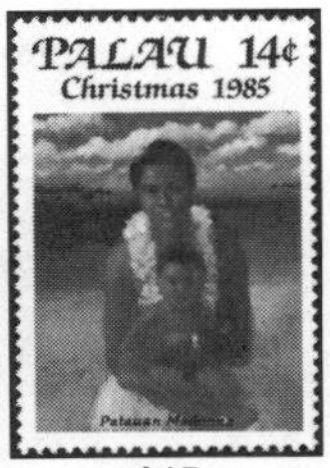

A15

IYY emblem and children of all nationalities joined in a circle.

1985, July 15 Litho. *Perf. 14*

86 A14 44c multicolored .80 .80
87 A14 44c multicolored .80 .80
88 A14 44c multicolored .80 .80
89 A14 44c multicolored .80 .80
a. Block of 4, #86-89 3.25 3.25

No. 89a has a continuous design.

1985, Oct. 21 Litho. *Perf. 14*

Christmas: Island mothers and children.

90 A15 14c multicolored .35 .35
91 A15 22c multicolored .50 .50
92 A15 33c multicolored .80 .80
93 A15 44c multicolored 1.10 1.10
Nos. 90-93 (4) 2.75 2.75

Souvenir Sheet

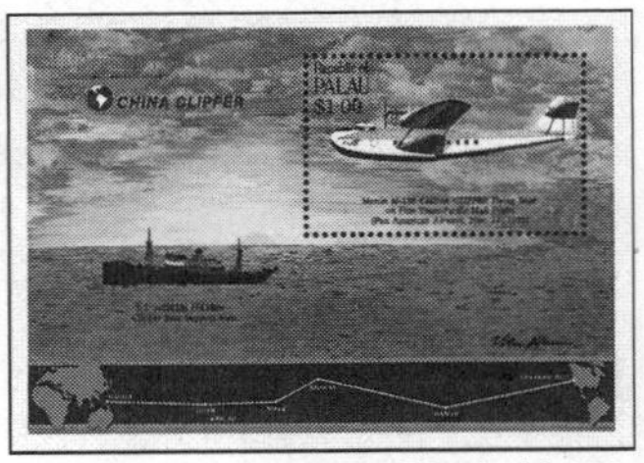

Pan American Airways Martin M-130 China Clipper — A16

1985, Nov. 21 Litho. *Perf. 14*

94 A16 $1 multicolored 2.50 2.50

1st Trans-Pacific Mail Flight, Nov. 22, 1935. See Nos. C10-C13.

Return of Halley's Comet A17

Fictitious local sightings.

1985, Dec. 21 Litho. *Perf. 14*

95 A17 44c Kaeb canoe, 1758 .75 .75
96 A17 44c U.S.S. Vincennes, 1835 .75 .75
97 A17 44c S.M.S. Scharnhorst, 1910 .75 .75
98 A17 44c Yacht, 1986 .75 .75
a. Block of 4, #95-98 3.00 3.00

Songbirds — A18

1986, Feb. 24 Litho. *Perf. 14*

99 A18 44c Mangrove flycatcher .85 .85
100 A18 44c Cardinal honeyeater .85 .85
101 A18 44c Blue-faced parrotfinch .85 .85
102 A18 44c Dusky and bridled white-eyes .85 .85
a. Block of 4, #99-102 3.50 3.50

World of Sea and Reef — A19

Designs: a, Spear fisherman. b, Native raft. c, Sailing canoes. d, Rock islands, sailfish. e, Inter-island boat, flying fish. f, Bonefish. g, Common jack. h, Mackerel. i, Sailfish. j, Barracuda. k, Triggerfish. l, Dolphinfish. m, Spear fisherman, grouper. n, Manta ray. o, Marlin. p, Parrotfish. q, Wrasse. r, Red snapper. s, Herring. t, Dugong. u, Surgeonfish. v, Leopard ray. w, Hawksbill turtle. x, Needlefish. y, Tuna. z, Octopus. aa, Clownfish. ab, Squid. ac, Grouper. ad, Moorish idol. ae, Queen conch, starfish. af, Squirrelfish. ag, Starfish, sting ray. ah, Lion fish. ai, Angel fish. aj, Butterfly fish. ak, Spiny lobster. al, Mangrove crab. am, Tridacna. an, Moray eel.

1986, May 22 Litho. *Perf. 15x14*

103 Sheet of 40 *37.50*
a.-an. A19 14c any single .25 .25

AMERIPEX '86, Chicago, May 22-June 1

Seashells — A20

1986, Aug. 1 Litho. *Perf. 14*

104 A20 22c Commercial trochus .55 .55
105 A20 22c Marble cone .55 .55
106 A20 22c Fluted giant clam .55 .55
107 A20 22c Bullmouth helmet .55 .55
108 A20 22c Golden cowrie .55 .55
a. Strip of 5, #104-108 2.75 2.75

See Nos. 150-154, 191-195, 212-216.

Intl. Peace Year A21

1986, Sept. 19 Litho.

109 A21 22c Soldier's helmet .55 .55
110 A21 22c Plane wreckage .55 .55
111 A21 22c Woman playing guitar .55 .55
112 A21 22c Airai vista .55 .55
a. Block of 4, #109-112 2.20 2.20
Nos. 109-112,C17 (5) 3.10 3.10

Reptiles A22

1986, Oct. 28 Litho. *Perf. 14*

113 A22 22c Gecko .60 .60
114 A22 22c Emerald tree skink .60 .60
115 A22 22c Estuarine crocodile .60 .60
116 A22 22c Leatherback turtle .60 .60
a. Block of 4, #113-116 2.40 2.40

Christmas — A23

Butterflies — A23a

Joy to the World, carol by Isaac Watts and Handel: No. 117, Girl playing guitar, boys, goat. No. 118, Girl carrying bouquet, boys singing. No. 119, Palauan mother and child. No. 120, Children, baskets of fruit. No. 121, Girl, fairy tern. Nos. 117-121 printed in a continuous design.

1986, Nov. 26 **Litho.**

117 A23 22c multicolored .40 .40
118 A23 22c multicolored .40 .40
119 A23 22c multicolored .40 .40
120 A23 22c multicolored .40 .40
121 A23 22c multicolored .40 .40
a. Strip of 5, #117-121 2.00 2.00

1987, Jan. 5 **Litho.** ***Perf. 14***

121B A23a 44c Tangadik, soursop .90 .90
121C A23a 44c Dira amartal, sweet orange .90 .90
121D A23a 44c Ilhuochel, swamp cabbage .90 .90
121E A23a 44c Bauosech, fig .90 .90
f. Block of 4, #121B-121E 3.75 3.75

See Nos. 183-186.

Fruit Bats A24

1987, Feb. 23 **Litho.**

122 A24 44c In flight .85 .85
123 A24 44c Hanging .85 .85
124 A24 44c Eating .85 .85
125 A24 44c Head .85 .85
a. Block of 4, #122-125 3.50 3.50

Indigenous Flowers — A25

1987-88 **Litho.** ***Perf. 14***

126 A25 1c Ixora casei .20 .20
127 A25 3c Lumnitzera littorea .20 .20
128 A25 5c Sonneratia alba .20 .20
129 A25 10c Tristellateria australasiae .20 .20
130 A25 14c Bikkia palauensis .20 .20
a. Booklet pane of 10 3.50 —
131 A25 15c Limnophila aromatica ('88) .25 .25
a. Booklet pane of 10 ('88) 3.00 —
132 A25 22c Bruguiera gymnorhiza .40 .40
a. Booklet pane of 10 6.50 —
b. Booklet pane, 5 each 14c, 22c 6.50 —
133 A25 25c Fagraea ksid ('88) .50 .50
a. Booklet pane of 10 ('88) 5.00 —
b. Booklet pane, 5 each 15c, 25c ('88) 5.00 —
134 A25 36c Ophiorrhiza palauensis ('88) .65 .65
135 A25 39c Cerbera manghas .70 .70
136 A25 44c Sandera indica .85 .85
137 A25 45c Maesa canfieldiae ('88) .85 .85
138 A25 50c Dolichandrone spathacea 1.00 1.00
139 A25 $1 Barringtonia racemosa 1.90 1.90
140 A25 $2 Nepenthes mirabilis 4.00 4.00
141 A25 $5 Dendrobium palawense 9.50 9.50

Size: 49x28mm

142 A25 $10 Bouquet ('88) 16.00 16.00
Nos. 126-142 (17) 37.60 37.60

Issued: 3/12; $10, 3/17; 15c, 25c, 36c, 45c, 7/1; #131a, 133a-133b, 7/5.

CAPEX '87 — A26

1987, June 15 **Litho.** ***Perf. 14***

146 A26 22c Babeldaob Is. .50 .50
147 A26 22c Floating Garden Isls. .50 .50
148 A26 22c Rock Is. .50 .50
149 A26 22c Koror .50
a. Block of 4, #146-149 2.00 2.00

Seashells Type of 1986

1987, Aug. 25 **Litho.** ***Perf. 14***

150 A20 22c Black-striped triton .55 .55
151 A20 22c Tapestry turban .55 .55
152 A20 22c Adusta murex .55 .55
153 A20 22c Little fox miter .55 .55
154 A20 22c Cardinal miter .55 .55
a. Strip of 5, #150-154 2.75 2.75

US Constitution Bicentennial A27

Excerpts from Articles of the Palau and US Constitutions and Seals.

1987, Sept. 17 **Litho.** ***Perf. 14***

155 A27 14c Art. VIII, Sec. 1, Palau .20 .20
156 A27 14c Presidential seals .20 .20
157 A27 14c Art. II, Sec. 1, US .20 .20
a. Triptych + label, #155-157 .60 .60
158 A27 22c Art. IX, Sec. 1, Palau .40 .40
159 A27 22c Legislative seals .40 .40
160 A27 22c Art. I, Sec. 1, US .40 .40
a. Triptych + label, #158-160 1.25 1.25
161 A27 44c Art X, Sec. 1, Palau .75 .75
162 A27 44c Supreme Court seals .75 .75
163 A27 44c Art. III, Sec. 1, US .75 .75
a. Triptych + label, #161-163 2.50 2.50
Nos. 155-163 (9) 4.05 4.05

Nos. 156, 159 and 162 are each 28x42mm. Labels picture national flags.

Japanese Links to Palau — A28

Japanese stamps, period cancellations and installations: 14c, No. 257 and 1937 Datsun sedan used as mobile post office, near Ngerchelechuus Mountain. 22c, No. 347 and phosphate mine at Angaur. 33c, No. B1 and Japan Airways DC-2 over stone monuments at Badrulchau. 44c, No. 201 and Japanese post office, Koror. $1, Aviator's Grave, Japanese Cemetary, Peleliu, vert.

1987, Oct. 16 **Litho.** ***Perf. 14x13½***

164 A28 14c multicolored .30 .30
165 A28 22c multicolored .45 .45
166 A28 33c multicolored .65 .65
167 A28 44c multicolored .85 .85
Nos. 164-167 (4) 2.25 2.25

Souvenir Sheet

Perf. 13½x14

168 A28 $1 multicolored 2.25 2.25

Christmas — A30

Symbiotic Marine Species — A31

Verses from carol "I Saw Three Ships," Biblical characters, landscape and Palauans in outrigger canoes.

1987, Nov. 24 **Litho.** ***Perf. 14***

173 A30 22c I saw... .45 .45
174 A30 22c And what was... .45 .45
175 A30 22c 'Twas Joseph... .45 .45
176 A30 22c Saint Michael... .45 .45
177 A30 22c And all the bells... .45 .45
a. Strip of 5, #173-177 2.25 2.25

1987, Dec. 15

#178, Snapping shrimp, goby. #179, Mauve vase sponge, sponge crab. #180, Pope's damselfish, cleaner wrasse. #181, Clown anemone fish, sea anemone. #182, Four-color nudibranch, banded coral shrimp.

178 A31 22c multicolored .50 .50
179 A31 22c multicolored .50 .50
180 A31 22c multicolored .50 .50
181 A31 22c multicolored .50 .50
182 A31 22c multicolored .50 .50
a. Strip of 5, #178-182 2.75 2.75

Butterflies and Flowers Type of 1987

Designs: No. 183, Dannaus plexippus, Tournefotia argentia. No. 184, Papilio machaon, Citrus reticulata. No. 185, Captopsilia, Crataeva speciosa. No. 186, Colias philodice, Crataeva speciosa.

1988, Jan. 25

183 A23a 44c multicolored .75 .75
184 A23a 44c multicolored .75 .75
185 A23a 44c multicolored .75 .75
186 A23a 44c multicolored .75 .75
a. Block of 4, #183-186 3.00 3.00

Ground-dwelling Birds — A32

1988, Feb. 29 **Litho.** ***Perf. 14***

187 A32 44c Whimbrel .75 .75
188 A32 44c Yellow bittern .75 .75
189 A32 44c Rufous night-heron .75 .75
190 A32 44c Banded rail .75 .75
a. Block of 4, #187-190 3.00 3.00

Seashells Type of 1986

1988, May 11 **Litho.** ***Perf. 14***

191 A20 25c Striped engina .50 .50
192 A20 25c Ivory cone .50 .50
193 A20 25c Plaited miter .50 .50
194 A20 25c Episcopal miter .50 .50
195 A20 25c Isabelle cowrie .50 .50
a. Strip of 5, #191-195 2.50 2.50

Souvenir Sheet

Postal Independence, 5th Anniv. — A33

FINLANDIA '88: a, Kaep (pre-European outrigger sailboat). b, Spanish colonial cruiser. c, German colonial cruiser SMS Cormoran, c. 1885. d, Japanese mailbox, WWII machine gun, Koror Museum. e, US Trust Territory ship, Malakal Harbor. f, Koror post office.

1988, June 8 **Litho.** ***Perf. 14***

196 A33 Sheet of 6 2.50 2.50
a.-f. 25c multicolored .40 .40

Souvenir Sheet

US Possessions Phil. Soc., 10th Anniv. — A34

PRAGA '88: a, "Collect Palau Stamps," original artwork for No. 196f and head of a man. b, Soc. emblem. c, Nos. 1-4. d, China Clipper original artwork and covers. e, Man and boy studying covers. f, Girl at show cancel booth.

1988, Aug. 26 **Litho.** ***Perf. 14***

197 A34 Sheet of 6 4.25 4.25
a.-f. 45c any single .70 .70

Christmas — A35

Hark! The Herald Angels Sing: No. 198, Angels playing the violin, singing and sitting. No. 199, 3 angels and 3 children. No. 200, Nativity. No. 201, 2 angels, birds. No. 202, 3 children and 2 angels playing horns. Se-tenant in a continuous design.

1988, Nov. 7 **Litho.** ***Perf. 14***

198 A35 25c multicolored .45 .45
199 A35 25c multicolored .45 .45
200 A35 25c multicolored .45 .45
201 A35 25c multicolored .45 .45
202 A35 25c multicolored .45 .45
a. Strip of 5, #199-202 2.25 2.25

Miniature Sheet

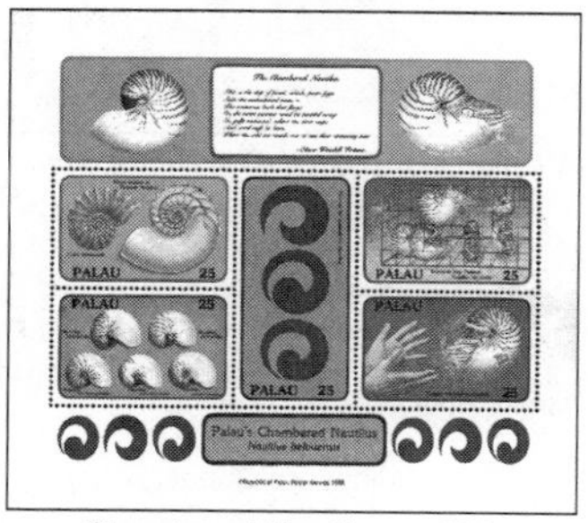

Chambered Nautilus — A36

Designs: a, Fossil and cross section. b, Palauan *bai* symbols for the nautilus. c, Specimens trapped for scientific study. d, *Nautilus belauensis, pompilius, macromphalus, stenomphalus* and *scrobiculatus.* e, Release of a tagged nautilus.

1988, Dec. 23 **Litho.** ***Perf. 14***

203 A36 Sheet of 5 3.00 3.00
a.-e. 25c multicolored .60 .60

Endangered Birds of Palau — A37

1989, Feb. 9 Litho. *Perf. 14*

204 A37 45c Nicobar pigeon	.75	.75
205 A37 45c Ground dove	.75	.75
206 A37 45c Micronesian megapode	.75	.75
207 A37 45c Owl	.75	.75
a. Block of 4, #204-207	3.00	3.00

Exotic Mushrooms — A38

1989, Mar. 16 Litho. *Perf. 14*

208 A38 45c Gilled auricularia	.80	.80
209 A38 45c Rock mushroom	.80	.80
210 A38 45c Polyporous	.80	.80
211 A38 45c Veiled stinkhorn	.80	.80
a. Block of 4, #208-211	3.25	3.25

Seashell Type of 1986

1989, Apr. 12 Litho. *Perf. 14x14½*

212 A20 25c Robin redbreast triton	.50	.50
213 A20 25c Hebrew cone	.50	.50
214 A20 25c Tadpole triton	.50	.50
215 A20 25c Lettered cone	.50	.50
216 A20 25c Rugose miter	.50	.50
a. Strip of 5, #212-216	2.50	2.50

Souvenir Sheet

A Little Bird, Amidst Chrysanthemums, 1830s, by Hiroshige (1797-1858) — A39

1989, May 17 Litho. *Perf. 14*

217 A39 $1 multicolored	1.90	1.90

Hirohito (1901-1989) and enthronement of Akihito as emperor of Japan.

Miniature Sheet

First Moon Landing, 20th Anniv. — A40

Apollo 11 mission: a, Third stage jettison. b, Lunar spacecraft. c, Module transposition *(Eagle).* d, *Columbia* module transposition (command module). e, *Columbia* module transposition (service module). f, Third stage burn. g, Vehicle entering orbit, Moon. h, *Columbia* and *Eagle.* i, *Eagle* on the Moon. j, *Eagle* in space. k, Three birds, Saturn V third stage, lunar spacecraft and escape tower. l, Astronaut's protective visor, pure oxygen system. m, Astronaut, American flag. n, Footsteps on lunar plain Sea of Tranquillity, pure oxygen system. o, Armstrong descending from *Eagle.* p, Mobile launch tower, Saturn V second stage. q, Space suit remote control unit and oxygen hoses. r, *Eagle* lift-off from Moon. s, Armstrong's first step on the Moon. t, Armstrong descending ladder, module transposition *(Eagle* and *Columbia).* u, Launch tower, spectators and Saturn V engines achieving thrust. v, Spectators, clouds of backwash. w, Parachute splashdown, U.S. Navy recovery ship and helicopter. x, Command module reentry. y, Jettison of service module prior to reentry.

1989, July 20 Litho. *Perf. 14*

218 A40 Sheet of 25	10.50	10.50
a.-y. 25c any single	.40	.40

Buzz Aldrin Photographed on the Moon by Neil Armstrong — A41

1989, July 20 *Perf. 13½x14*

219 A41 $2.40 multicolored	4.75	4.75

First Moon landing 20th anniv.

Literacy — A42

Imaginary characters and children reading: a, Youth astronaut. b, Boy riding dolphin. c, Cheshire cat in palm tree. d, Mother Goose. e, New York Yankee at bat. f, Girl reading. g, Boy reading. h, Mother reading to child. i, Girl holding flower and listening to story. j, Boy dressed in baseball uniform. Printed se-tenant in a continuous design.

1989, Oct. 13 Litho. *Perf. 14*

220 Block of 10	4.00	4.00
a.-j. A42 25c any single	.40	.40

No. 220 printed in sheets containing two blocks of ten with strip of 5 labels between. Inscribed labels contain book, butterflies and "Give Them / Books / Give Them / Wings."

Miniature Sheet

Stilt Mangrove Fauna — A43

World Stamp Expo '89: a, Bridled tern. b, Sulphur butterfly. c, Mangrove flycatcher. d, Collared kingfisher. e, Fruit bat. f, Estuarine crocodile. g, Rufous night-heron. h, Stilt mangrove. i, Bird's nest fern. j, Beach hibiscus tree. k, Common eggfly. l, Dog-faced watersnake. m, Jingle shell. n, Palau bark cricket. o, Periwinkle, mangrove oyster. p, Jellyfish. q, Striped mullet. r, Mussels, sea anemones, algae. s, Cardinalfish. t, Snapper.

1989, Nov. 20 Litho. *Perf. 14½*

221 A43 Block of 20	10.00	10.00
a.-t. 25c any single	.50	.50

Christmas — A44

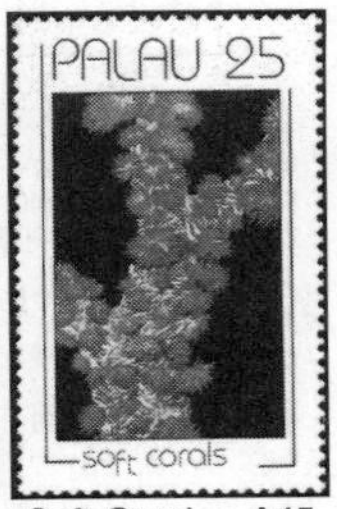

Soft Coral — A45

Whence Comes this Rush of Wings? a carol: No. 222, Dusky tern, Audubon's shearwater, angels, island. No. 223, Fruit pigeon, angel. No. 224, Madonna and Child, ground pigeons, fairy terns, rails, sandpipers. No. 225, Angel, blue-headed green finch, red flycatcher, honeyeater. No. 226, Angel, black-headed gulls. Printed se-tenant in a continuous design.

1989, Dec. 18 Litho. *Perf. 14*

222 A44 25c multicolored	.45	.45
223 A44 25c multicolored	.45	.45
224 A44 25c multicolored	.45	.45
225 A44 25c multicolored	.45	.45
226 A44 25c multicolored	.45	.45
a. Strip of 5, #222-226	2.25	2.25

1990, Jan. 3

227 A45 25c Pink coral	.50	.50
228 A45 25c Pink & violet coral	.50	.50
229 A45 25c Yellow coral	.50	.50
230 A45 25c Red coral	.50	.50
a. Block of 4, #227-230	2.00	2.00

Birds of the Forest A46

1990, Mar. 16

231 A46 45c Siberian rubythroat	.75	.75
232 A46 45c Palau bush-warbler	.75	.75
233 A46 45c Micronesian starling	.75	.75
234 A46 45c Cicadabird	.75	.75
a. Block of 4, #231-234	3.00	3.00

Miniature Sheet

State Visit of Prince Lee Boo of Palau to England, 1784 A47

Prince Lee Boo, Capt. Henry Wilson and: a, HMS *Victory* docked at Portsmouth. b, St. James's Palace, London. c, Rotherhithe Docks, London. d, Capt. Wilson's residence, Devon. e, Lunardi's Grand English Air Balloon. f, St. Paul's and the Thames. g, Lee Boo's tomb, St. Mary's Churchyard, Rotherhithe. h, St. Mary's Church. i, Memorial tablet, St. Mary's Church.

1990, May 6 Litho. *Perf. 14*

235 Sheet of 9	4.00	4.00
a.-i. A47 25c any single	.45	.45

Stamp World London '90.

Souvenir Sheet

Penny Black, 150th Anniv. — A48

1990, May 6

236 A48 $1 Great Britain #1	1.75	1.75

Orchids — A49

1990, June 7 *Perf. 14*

237 A49 45c *Corymborkis veratrifolia*	.75	.75
238 A49 45c *Malaxis setipes*	.75	.75
239 A49 45c *Dipodium freycinetianum*	.75	.75
240 A49 45c *Bulbophyllum micronesiacum*	.75	.75
241 A49 45c *Vanda teres* and *hookeriana*	.75	.75
a. Strip of 5, #237-241	3.75	3.75

Butterflies and Flowers A50

1990, July 6 Litho. *Perf. 14*

242 A50 45c Wedelia strigulosa	.70	.70
243 A50 45c Erthrina variegata	.70	.70
244 A50 45c Clerodendrum inerme	.70	.70
245 A50 45c Vigna marina	.70	.70
a. Block of 4, #242-245	2.80	2.80

Miniature Sheet

Fairy Tern, Lesser Golden Plover, Sanderling A51

Lagoon life: b, Bidekill fisherman. c, Sailing yacht, insular halfbeaks. d, Palauan kaeps. e, White-tailed tropicbird. f, Spotted eagle ray. g, Great barracuda. h, Reef needlefish. i, Reef blacktip shark. j, Hawksbill turtle. k, Octopus. l, Batfish. m, Lionfish. n, Snowflake moray. o, Porcupine fish, sixfeeler threadfins. p, Blue sea star, regal angelfish, cleaner wrasse. q, Clown triggerfish. r, Spotted garden eel and orange fish. s, Blue-lined sea bream, bluegreen chromis, sapphire damselfish. t, Orangespine unicornfish, white-tipped soldierfish. u, Slatepencil sea urchin, leopard sea cucumber. v, Partridge tun shell. w, Mandarinfish. x, Tiger cowrie. y, Feather starfish, orange-fin anemonefish.

1990, Aug. 10 Litho. *Perf. 15x14½*

246 A51 25c Sheet of 25, #a.-y.	12.00	12.00

Nos. 246a-246y inscribed on reverse.

Pacifica — A52

1990, Aug. 24 Litho. *Perf. 14*

247 A52 45c Mailship, 1890 1.00 1.00
248 A52 45c US #803 on cover, forklift, plane 1.00 1.00
a. Pair, #247-248 2.25 2.25

Christmas — A53

Here We Come A-Caroling: No. 250, Girl with music, poinsettias, doves. No. 251, Boys playing guitar, flute. No. 252, Family. No. 253, Three girls singing.

1990, Nov. 28

249 A53	25c	multicolored	.40	.40
250 A53	25c	multicolored	.40	.40
251 A53	25c	multicolored	.40	.40
252 A53	25c	multicolored	.40	.40
253 A53	25c	multicolored	.40	.40
a.		Strip of 5, #249-253	2.00	2.00

US Forces in Palau, 1944 A54

Designs: No. 254, B-24s over Peleliu. No. 255, LCI launching rockets. No. 256, First Marine Division launching offensive. No. 257, Soldier, children. No. 258, USS *Peleliu.*

1990, Dec. 7

254 A54	45c	multicolored	.85	.85
255 A54	45c	multicolored	.85	.85
256 A54	45c	multicolored	.85	.85
257 A54	45c	multicolored	.85	.85
a.		Block of 4, #254-257	3.50	3.50

Souvenir Sheet

Perf. 14x13½

258 A54 $1 multicolored 2.25 2.25

No. 258 contains one 51x38mm stamp.

See No. 339 for No. 258 with added inscription.

Coral — A55

1991, Mar. 4 Litho. *Perf. 14*

259 A55	30c	Staghorn	.55	.55
260 A55	30c	Velvet Leather	.55	.55
261 A55	30c	Van Gogh's Cypress	.55	.55
262 A55	30c	Violet Lace	.55	.55
a.		Block of 4, #259-262	2.25	2.25

Miniature Sheet

Angaur, The Phosphate Island — A56

Designs: a, Virgin Mary Statue, Nkulangelul Point. b, Angaur kaep, German colonial postmark. c, Swordfish, Caroline Islands No. 13. d, Phosphate mine locomotive. e, Copra ship off Lighthouse Hill. f, Dolphins. g, Estuarine crocodile. h, Workers cycling to phosphate plant. i, Ship loading phosphate. j, Hammerhead shark, German overseer. k, Marshall Islands No. 15. l, SMS Scharnhorst. m, SMS Emden. n, Crab-eating macaque monkey. o, Great sperm whale. p, HMAS Sydney.

1991, Mar. 14

263 A56 30c Sheet of 16, #a.-p. 9.00 9.00

Nos. 263b-263c, 263f-263g, 263j-263k, 263n-263o printed in continuous design showing map of island.

Birds — A57

Perf. 14½x15, 13x13½

1991-92 Litho.

266 A57	1c	Palau bush-warbler	.20	.20
267 A57	4c	Common moorhen	.20	.20
268 A57	6c	Banded rail	.20	.20
269 A57	19c	Palau fantail	.30	.30
b.		Booklet pane, 10 #269	3.00	—
		Complete booklet, #269b	3.00	
270 A57	20c	Mangrove flycatcher	.30	.30
271 A57	23c	Purple swamphen	.35	.35
272 A57	29c	Palau fruit dove	.45	.45
a.		Booklet pane, 5 each #270, #272	4.50	—
		Complete booklet, #272a	4.50	
b.		Booklet pane, 10 #272	4.50	—
		Complete booklet, #272b	4.50	
273 A57	35c	Great crested tern	.55	.55
274 A57	40c	Pacific reef heron	.60	.60
275 A57	45c	Micronesian pigeon	.70	.70
276 A57	50c	Great frigatebird	.75	.75
277 A57	52c	Little pied cormorant	.80	.80
278 A57	75c	Jungle night jar	1.10	1.10
279 A57	95c	Cattle egret	1.40	1.40
280 A57	$1.34	Great sulphur-crested cockatoo	2.00	2.00
281 A57	$2	Blue-faced parrotfinch	3.00	3.00
282 A57	$5	Eclectus parrot	7.75	7.75

Size: 52x30mm

283 A57	$10	Palau bush warbler	15.00	15.00
		Nos. 266-283 (18)	35.65	35.65

The 1, 6, 20, 52, 75c, $10 are perf. 14½x15.

Issued: 1, 6, 20, 52, 75c, $5, 4/6/92; $10, 9/10/92; #269b, 272a, 272b, 8/23/91; others, 4/18/91.

Miniature Sheet

Christianity in Palau, Cent. — A58

Designs: a, Pope Leo XIII, 1891. b, Ibedul Ilengelekei, High Chief of Koror, 1871-1911. c, Fr. Marino de la Hoz, Br. Emilio Villar, Fr. Elias Fernandez. d, Fr. Edwin G. McManus (1908-1969), compiler of Palauan-English dictionary. e, Sacred Heart Church, Koror. f, Pope John Paul II.

1991, Apr. 28 *Perf. 14½*

288 A58 29c Sheet of 6, #a.-f. 2.75 2.75

Miniature Sheet

Marine Life A59

Designs: a, Pacific white-sided dolphin. b, Common dolphin. c, Rough-toothed dolphin. d, Bottlenose dolphin. e, Harbor porpoise. f, Killer whale. g, Spinner dolphin, yellowfin tuna. h, Dall's porpoise. i, Finless porpoise. j, Map of Palau, dolphin. k, Dusky dolphin. l, Southern right-whale dolphin. m, Striped dolphin. n, Fraser's dolphin. o, Peale's dolphin. p, Spectacled porpoise. q, Spotted dolphin. r, Hourglass dolphin. s, Risso's dolphin. t, Hector's dolphin.

1991, May 24 Litho. *Perf. 14*

289 A59 29c Sheet of 20, #a.-t. 10.00 10.00

Miniature Sheet

Operations Desert Shield / Desert Storm — A60

Designs: a, F-4G Wild Weasel fighter. b, F-117A Stealth fighter. c, AH-64A Apache helicopter. d, TOW missle launcher on M998 HMMWV. e, Pres. Bush. f, M2 Bradley fighting vehicle. g, Aircraft carrier USS Ranger. h, Corvette fast patrol boat. i, Battleship Wisconsin.

1991, July 2 Litho. *Perf. 14*

290 A60 20c Sheet of 9, #a.-i. 3.25 3.25

Size: 38x51mm

291 A60 $2.90 Fairy tern, yellow ribbon 4.25 4.25

Souvenir Sheet

292 A60 $2.90 like #291 4.50 4.50

No. 291 has a white border around design. No. 292 printed in continuous design.

Republic of Palau, 10th Anniv. — A61

Designs: a, Palauan bai. b, Palauan bai interior, denomination UL. c, Same, denomination UR. d, Demi-god Chedechuul. e, Spider, denomination at UL. f, Money bird facing right. g, Money bird facing left. h, Spider, denomination at UR.

1991, July 9 *Perf. 14½*

293 A61 29c Sheet of 8, #a.-h. 4.00 4.00

See No. C21.

Miniature Sheet

Giant Clams A62

Designs: a, Tridacna squamosa, Hippopus hippopus, Hippopus porcellanus, and Tridacna derasa. b, Tridacna gigas. c, Hatchery and tank culture. d, Diver, bottom-based clam nursery. e, Micronesian Mariculture Demonstration Center.

1991, Sept. 17 Litho. *Perf. 14*

294 A62 50c Sheet of 5, #a.-e. 4.00 4.00

No. 294e is 109x17mm and imperf on 3 sides, perf 14 at top.

Miniature Sheet

Japanese Heritage in Palau A63

Designs: No. 295: a, Marine research. b, Traditional arts, carving story boards. c, Agricultural training. d, Archaeological research. e, Training in architecture and building. f, Air transportation. $1, Map, cancel from Japanese post office at Parao.

1991, Nov. 19

295 A63 29c Sheet of 6, #a.-f. 2.75 2.75

Souvenir Sheet

296 A63 $1 multicolored 1.50 1.50

Phila Nippon '91.

Miniature Sheet

Peace Corps in Palau, 25th Anniv. A64

Children's drawings: No. 297a, Flag, doves, children, and islands. b, Airplane, people being greeted. c, Red Cross instruction. d, Fishing industry. e, Agricultural training. f, Classroom instruction.

1991, Dec. 6 Litho. *Perf. 13½*

297 A64 29c Sheet of 6, #a.-f. 3.00 3.00

Christmas — A65

Silent Night: No. 298: a, Silent night, holy night. b, All is calm, all is bright. c, Round yon virgin, mother and Child. d, Holy Infant, so tender and mild. e, Sleep in heavenly peace.

1991, Nov. 14 *Perf. 14*

298 A65 29c Strip of 5, #a.-e. 2.25 2.25

Miniature Sheet

World War II in the Pacific A66

Designs: No. 299a, Pearl Harbor attack begins. b, Battleship Nevada gets under way. c, USS Shaw explodes. d, Japanese aircraft carrier Akagi sunk. e, USS Wasp sunk off Guadalcanal. f, Battle of the Philippine Sea. g, US landing craft approach Saipan. h, US 1st Cavalry on Leyte. i, Battle of Bloody Nose Ridge, Peleliu. j, US troops land on Iwo Jima.

1991, Dec. 6 *Perf. 14½x15*

299 A66 29c Sheet of 10, #a.-j. 5.00 5.00

See No. C22.

A67

A68

Butterflies: a, Troides criton. b, Alcides zodiaca. c, Papillio poboroi. d, Vindula arsinoe.

1992, Jan. 20 Litho. *Perf. 14*
300 A67 50c Block of 4, #a.-d. 3.00 3.00

1992, Mar. 11

Shells: a, Common hairy triton. b, Eglantine cowrie. c, Sulcate swamp cerith. d, Black-spined murex. e, Black-mouth moon.

301 A68 29c Strip of 5, #a.-e. 2.50 2.50

Miniature Sheet

Age of Discovery A69

Designs: a, Columbus. b, Magellan. c, Drake. d, Wind as shown on old maps.
Maps and: e, Compass rose. f, Dolphin, Drake's ship Golden Hinde. g, Corn, Santa Maria. h, Fish. i, Betel palm, cloves and black pepper. j, Victoria, shearwater and great crested tern. k, White-tailed tropicbird, bicolor parrotfish, pineapple and potatoes. l, Compass. m, Sea monster. n, Paddles and astrolabe. o, Parallel ruler, dividers and Inca gold treasures. p, Back staff.
Portraits: q, Wind, diff. r, Vespucci. s, Pizarro. t, Balboa.

1992, May 25 Litho. *Perf. 14*
302 A69 29c Sheet of 20, #a.-t. 10.50 10.50

Miniature Sheet

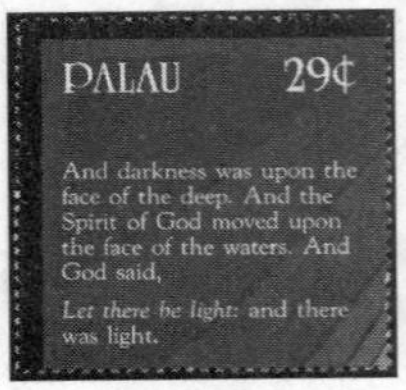

Biblical Creation of the World — A70

Designs: a, "And darkness was..." b, Sun's rays. c, Water, sun's rays. d, "...and it was good." e, "Let there be a..." f, Land forming. g, Water and land. h, "...and it was so." i, "Let the waters..." j, Tree branches. k, Shoreline. l, Shoreline, flowers, tree. m, "Let there be lights..." n, Comet, moon. o, Mountains. p, Sun, hillside. q, "Let the waters..." r, Birds. s, Fish, killer whale. t, Fish. u, "Let the earth..." v, Woman, man. w, Animals. x, "...and it was very good."

1992, June 5 *Perf. 14½*
303 A70 29c Sheet of 24, #a.-x. 13.00 13.00

Nos. 303a-303d, 303e-303h, 303i-303l, 303m-303p, 303q-303t, 303u-303x are blocks of 4.

Souvenir Sheets

1992 Summer Olympics, Barcelona — A71

1992, July 10 *Perf. 14*

304	A71	50c	Dawn Fraser	.90	.90
305	A71	50c	Olga Korbut	.90	.90
306	A71	50c	Bob Beamon	.90	.90
307	A71	50c	Carl Lewis	.90	.90
308	A71	50c	Dick Fosbury	.90	.90
309	A71	50c	Greg Louganis	.90	.90
			Nos. 304-309 (6)	5.40	5.40

Miniature Sheet

Elvis Presley A72

Various portraits.

1992, Aug. 17 *Perf. 13½x14*
310 A72 29c Sheet of 9, #a.-i. 6.00 6.00

See No. 350.

Christmas — A73

The Friendly Beasts carol depicting animals in Nativity Scene: No. 312a, "Thus Every Beast." b, "By Some Good Spell." c, "In The Stable Dark Was Glad to Tell." d, "Of The Gift He Gave Emanuel." e, "The Gift He Gave Emanuel."

1992, Oct. 1 Litho. *Perf. 14*
312 A73 29c Strip of 5, #a.-e. 2.50 2.50

Fauna A74

Designs: a, Dugong. b, Masked booby. c, Macaque. d, New Guinean crocodile.

1993, July 9 Litho. *Perf. 14*
313 A74 50c Block of 4, #a.-d. 3.25 3.25

Seafood A75

Designs: a, Giant crab. b, Scarlet shrimp. c, Smooth nylon shrimp. d, Armed nylon shrimp.

1993, July 22
314 A75 29c Block of 4, #a.-d. 2.00 2.00

Sharks A76

Designs: a, Oceanic whitetip. b, Great hammerhead. c, Leopard. d, Reef black-tip.

1993, Aug. 11 Litho. *Perf. 14½*
315 A76 50c Block of 4, #a.-d. 3.25 3.25

Miniature Sheet

World War II in the Pacific A77

Actions in 1943: a, US takes Guadalcanal, Feb. b, Hospital ship Tranquility supports action. c, New Guineans join Allies in battle. d, US landings in New Georgia, June. e, USS California participates in every naval landing. f, Dauntless dive bombers over Wake Island, Oct. 6. g, US flamethrowers on Tarawa, Nov. h, US landings on Makin, Nov. i, B-25s bomb Simpson Harbor, Rabaul, Oct. 23. j, B-24s over Kwajalein, Dec. 8.

1993, Sept. 23 Litho. *Perf. 14½x15*
316 A77 29c Sheet of 10, #a.-j. + label 6.00 6.00

See Nos. 325-326.

Christmas — A78

Christmas carol, "We Wish You a Merry Christmas," with Palauan customs: a, Girl, goat. b, Goats, children holding leis, prow of canoe. c, Santa Claus. d, Children singing. e, Family with fruit, fish.

1993, Oct. 22 Litho. *Perf. 14*
317 A78 29c Strip of 5, #a.-e. 2.50 2.50

Miniature Sheet

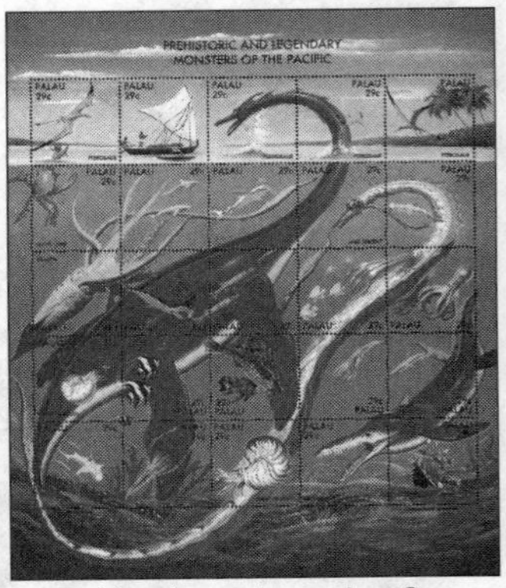

Prehistoric and Legendary Sea Creatures — A79

Illustration reduced.

1993, Nov. 26 Litho. *Perf. 14*
318 A79 29c Sheet of 25, #a.-y. 12.50 12.50

Miniature Sheet

Intl. Year of Indigenous People — A80

Paintings, by Charlie Gibbons: No. 319: a, After Child-birth Ceremony. b, Village in Early Palau.
Storyboard carving, by Ngiraibuuch: $2.90, Quarrying of Stone Money, vert.

1993, Dec. 8 *Perf. 14x13½*
319 A80 29c Sheet, 2 ea #a.-b. 2.00 2.00

Souvenir Sheet
Perf. 13½x14

320 A80 $2.90 multicolored 5.00 5.00

Miniature Sheet

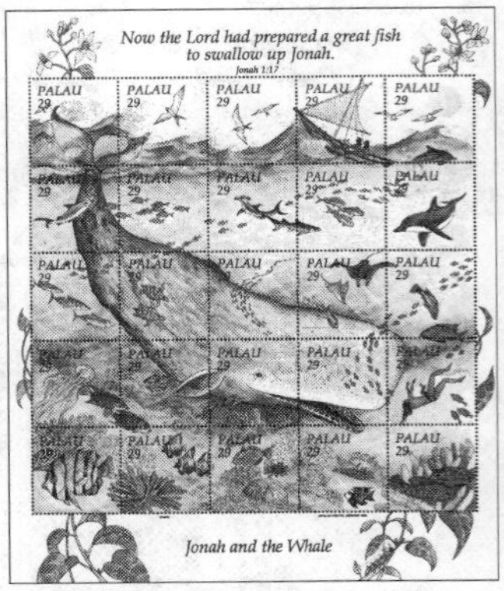

Jonah and the Whale — A81

Illustration reduced.

1993, Dec. 28 Litho. *Perf. 14*
321 A81 29c Sheet of 25, #a.-y. 13.00 13.00

Hong Kong '94 A82

Rays: a, Manta (b). b, Spotted eagle (a). c, Coachwhip (d). d, Black spotted.

1994, Feb. 18 Litho. *Perf. 14*

322 A82 40c Block of 4, #a.-d. 2.75 2.75

Estuarine Crocodile A83

Designs: a, With mouth open. b, Hatchling. c, Crawling on river bottom. d, Swimming.

1994, Mar. 14

323 A83 20c Block of 4, #a.-d. 2.00 2.00

World Wildlife Fund.

Large Seabirds — A84

a, Red-footed booby. b, Great frigatebird. c, Brown booby. d, Little pied cormorant.

1994, Apr. 22 Litho. *Perf. 14*

324 A84 50c Block of 4, #a.-d. 3.00 3.00

World War II Type of 1993
Miniature Sheets

Action in the Pacific, 1944: No. 325: a, US Marines capture Kwajalien, Feb. 1-7. b, Japanese enemy base at Truk destroyed, Feb. 17-18. c, SS-284 Tullibee participates in Operation Desecrate, March. d, US troops take Saipan, June 15-July 9. e, Great Marianas Turkey Shoot, June 19-20. f, Guam liberated, July-Aug. g, US troops take Peleliu, Sept. 15-Oct. 14. h, Angaur secured in fighting, Sept. 17-22. i, Gen. Douglas MacArthur returns to Philippines, Oct. 20. j, US Army Memorial, Palau, Nov. 27.

D-Day, Allied Invasion of Normandy, June 6, 1944: No. 326: a, C-47 transport aircraft dropping Allied paratroopers. b, Allied warships attack beach fortifications. c, Commandos attack from landing craft. d, Tanks land. e, Sherman flail tank beats path through minefields. f, Allied aircraft attack enemy reinforcements. g, Gliders deliver troops behind enemy lines. h, Pegasus Bridge, first French house liberated. i, Allied forces move inland to form bridgehead. j, View of beach at end of D-Day.

1994, May *Perf. 14½*

Sheets of 10

325 A77 29c #a.-j. + label 5.00 5.00
326 A77 50c #a.-j. + label 8.50 8.50

Pierre de Coubertin (1863-1937) — A85

Winter Olympic medalists: No. 328, Anne-Marie Moser, vert. No. 329, James Craig. No. 330, Katarina Witt. No. 331, Eric Heiden, vert. No. 332, Nancy Kerrigan. $2, Dan Jansen.

1994, July 20 Litho. *Perf. 14*

327 A85 29c multicolored .60 .60

Souvenir Sheets

328 A85 50c multicolored .85 .85
329 A85 50c multicolored .85 .85
330 A85 $1 multicolored 1.60 1.60
331 A85 $1 multicolored 1.60 1.60
332 A85 $1 multicolored 1.60 1.60
333 A85 $2 multicolored 3.25 3.25

Intl. Olympic Committee, cent.

Miniature Sheets of 8

PHILAKOREA '94 — A86

Wildlife carrying letters: No. 334: a, Sailfin goby. b, Sharpnose puffer. c, Lightning butterflyfish. d, Clown anemonefish. e, Parrotfish. f, Batfish. g, Clown triggerfish. h, twinspot wrasse.

No. 335a, Palau fruit bat. b, Crocodile. c, Dugong. d, Banded sea snake. e, Bottle-nosed dophin. f, Hawksbill turtle. g, Octopus. h, Manta ray.

No. 336: a, Palau fantail. b, Banded crake. c, Island swiftlet. d, Micronesian kingfisher. e. Red-footed booby. f, Great frigatebird. g, Palau owl. h, Palau fruit dove.

1994, Aug. 16 Litho. *Perf. 14*

334 A86 29c #a.-h. 4.75 4.75
335 A86 40c #a.-h. 6.50 6.50
336 A86 50c #a.-h. 8.00 8.00

No. 336 is airmail.

Miniature Sheet of 20

First Manned Moon Landing, 25th Anniv. — A87

Various scenes from Apollo moon missions.

1994, July 20

337 A87 29c #a.-t. 11.00 11.00

Independence Day — A88

#338: b, Natl. seal. c, Pres. Kuniwo Nakamura, Palau, US Pres. Clinton. d, Palau, US flags. e, Musical notes of natl. anthem.

1994, Oct. 1 *Perf. 14*

338 A88 29c Strip of 5, #a.-e. 2.50 2.50

No. 338c is 57x42mm.

No. 258 with added text
"50th ANNIVERSARY / INVASION OF PELELIU /
SEPTEMBER 15, 1944"

1994 Litho. *Perf. 14X13½*

339 A54 $1 multicolored 2.00 2.00

Miniature Sheet of 9

Disney Characters Visit Palau — A89

No. 340: a, Mickey, Minnie arriving. b, Goofy finding way to hotel. c, Donald enjoying beach. d, Minnie, Daisy learning the Ngloik. e, Minnie, Mickey sailing to Natural Bridge. f, Scrooge finding money in Babeldaob jungle. g, Goofy, Napoleon Wrasse. h, Minnie, Clam Garden. i, Grandma Duck weaving basket.

No. 341, Mickey exploring underwater shipwreck. No. 342, Donald visiting Airai Bai on Babeldaob. No. 343, Pluto, Mickey in boat, vert.

1994, Oct. 14 *Perf. 13½x14*

340 A89 29c #a.-i. 5.00 5.00

Souvenir Sheets

341-342 A89 $1 each 2.25 2.25

Perf. 14x13½

343 A89 $2.90 multicolored 6.25 6.25

Miniature Sheet of 12

Intl. Year of the Family — A90

Story of Tebruchel: a, With mother as infant. b, Father. c, As young man. d, Wife-to-be. e, Bringing home fish. f, Pregnant wife. g, Elderly mother. h, Elderly father. i, With first born. j, Wife seated. k, Caring for mother. l, Father, wife and baby.

1994, Nov. 1 Litho. *Perf. 14*

344 A90 20c #a.-l. 4.00 4.00

Christmas — A91

O Little Town of Bethlehem: a, Magi, cherubs. b, Angel, shepherds, sheep. c, Angels, nativity. d, Angels hovering over town, shepherd, sheep. e, Cherubs, doves.

1994, Nov. 23 Litho. *Perf. 14*

345 A91 29c Strip of 5 2.50 2.50

No. 345 is a continuous design and is printed in sheets containing three strips. The bottom strip is printed with se-tenant labels.

Miniature Sheets of 12

1994 World Cup Soccer Championships, US — A92

US coach, players: No. 346: a, Bora Milutinovic. b, Cle Kooiman. c, Ernie Stewart. d, Claudio Reyna. e, Thomas Dooley. f, Alexi Lalas. g, Dominic Kinnear. h, Frank Klopas. i, Paul Caligiuri. j, Marcelo Balboa. k, Cobi Jones. l, US flag, World Cup trohpy.

US players: No. 347a, Tony Meola. b, John Doyle. c, Eric Wynalda. d, Roy Wegerle. e, Fernando Clavijo. f, Hugo Perez. g, John Harkes. h, Mike Lapper. i, Mike Sorber. j, Brad Friedel. k, Tab Ramos. l, Joe-Max Moore.

No. 348: a, Babeto, Brazil. b, Romario, Brazil. c, Franco Baresi, Italy. d, Roberto Baggio, Italy. e, Andoni Zubizarreta, Spain. f, Oleg Salenko, Russia. g, Gheorghe Hagi, Romania. h, Dennis Bergkamp, Netherlands. i, Hristo Stoichkov, Bulgaria. j, Tomas Brolin, Sweden. k, Lothar Matthaus, Germany. l, Arrigo Sacchi, Italy, Carlos Alberto Parreira, Brazil, flags of Italy & Brazil, World Cup trophy.

1994, Dec. 23

346 A92 29c #a.-l. 6.25 6.25
347 A92 29c #a.-l. 6.25 6.25
348 A92 50c #a.-l. 10.50 10.50

Elvis Presley Type of 1992
Miniature Sheet

Various portraits.

1995, Feb. 28 Litho. *Perf. 14*

350 A72 32c Sheet of 9, #a.-i. 5.50 5.50

Fish — A93

1c, Cube trunkfish. 2c, Lionfish. 3c, Long-jawed squirrelfish. 4c, Longnose filefish. 5c, Ornate butterflyfish. 10c, Yellow seahorse. 20c, Magenta dottyback. 32c, Reef lizardfish. 50c, Multibarred goatfish. 55c, Barred blenny. $1, Fingerprint sharpnose puffer. $2, Longnose hawkfish. $3, Mandarinfish. $5, Blue surgeonfish. $10, Coral grouper.

1995, Apr. 3 Litho. *Perf. 14½*

351 A93 1c multicolored .20 .20
352 A93 2c multicolored .20 .20
353 A93 3c multicolored .20 .20
354 A93 4c multicolored .20 .20
355 A93 5c multicolored .20 .20
356 A93 10c multicolored .20 .20
357 A93 20c multicolored .30 .30
358 A93 32c multicolored .45 .45
359 A93 50c multicolored .70 .70
360 A93 55c multicolored .75 .75
361 A93 $1 multicolored 1.50 1.50
362 A93 $2 multicolored 3.00 3.00
363 A93 $3 multicolored 4.50 4.50
364 A93 $5 multicolored 7.75 7.75

Size: 48x30mm

365 A93 $10 multicolored 16.00 16.00
Nos. 351-365 (15) 36.15 36.15

Booklet Stamps

Size: 18x21mm

Perf. 14x14½ Syncopated

366 A93 20c multicolored .40 .40
a. Booklet pane of 10 3.50
Complete booklet, #366a 3.50
367 A93 32c multicolored .60 .60
a. Booklet pane of 10 5.50
Complete booklet, #367a 5.50
b. Booklet pane, 5 ea #366, 367 4.50
Complete booklet, #367b 4.50

Miniature Sheet of 18

Lost Fleet of the Rock Islands A94

Underwater scenes, silhouettes of Japanese ships sunk during Operation Desecrate, 1944: a, Unyu Maru 2. b, Wakatake. c, Teshio Maru. d, Raizan Maru. e, Chuyo Maru. f, Shinsei Maru. g, Urakami Maru. h, Ose Maru. i, Iro. j, Shosei Maru. k, Patrol boat 31. l, Kibi Maru. m, Amatsu Maru. n, Gozan Maru. o, Matuei Maru. p, Nagisan Maru. q, Akashi. r, Kamikazi Maru.

1995, Mar. 30 Litho. *Perf. 14*

368 A94 32c #a.-r. 10.00 10.00

Miniature Sheet of 18

Flying Dinosaurs A95

Designs: a, Pteranodon sternbergi. b, Pteranodon ingens (a, c). c, Pterodoctyls (b). d, Dorygnathus (e). e, Dimorphodon (f). f, Nyctosaurus (e, c). g, Pterodactylus kochi. h, Ornithodesmus (g, i). i, Diatryma (l). j, Archaeopteryx. k, Campylognathoides (l). l, Gallodactylus. m, Batrachognathus (j). n, Scaphognathus (j, k, m, o). o, Peteinosaurus (l). p, Ichthyorinis. q, Ctenochasma (m, p, r). r, Rhamphorhynchus (n, o, q).

1995 Litho. *Perf. 14*
369 A95 32c #a.-r. 10.00 10.00

Earth Day, 25th anniv.

Miniature Sheet

Research & Experimental Jet Aircraft — A96

Designs: a, Fairey Delta 2. b, B-70 "Valkyrie." c, Douglas X-3 "Stilletto." d, Northrop/NASA HL-10. e, Bell XS-1. f, Tupolev Tu-144. g, Bell X-1. h, Boulton Paul P.111. i, EWR VJ 101C. j, Handley Page HP-115. k, Rolls Royce TMR "Flying Bedstead." l, North American X-15.

$2, BAC/Aerospatiale Concorde SST.

1995 Litho. *Perf. 14*
370 A96 50c Sheet of 12, #a.-l. 10.00 10.00

Souvenir Sheet

371 A96 $2 multicolored 3.50 3.50

No. 370 is airmail. No. 371 contains one 85x29mm stamp.

Miniature Sheet of 18

Submersibles — A97

Designs: a, Scuba gear. b, Cousteau diving saucer. c, Jim suit. d, Beaver IV. e, Ben Franklin. f, USS Nautilus. g, Deep Rover. h, Beebe Bathysphere. i, Deep Star IV. j, DSRV. k, Aluminaut. l. Nautile. m, Cyana. n, FNRS Bathyscaphe. o, Alvin. p, Mir 1. q, Archimede. r, Trieste.

1995, July 21 Litho. *Perf. 14*
372 A97 32c #a.-r. 10.00 10.00

Singapore '95 — A98

Designs: a, Dolphins, diver snorkeling, marine life. b, Turtle, diver, seabirds above. c, Fish, coral, crab. d, Coral, fish, diff.

1995, Aug. 15 Litho. *Perf. 13½*
373 A98 32c Block of 4, #a.-d. 2.25 2.25

No. 373 is a continuous design and was issued in sheets of 24 stamps.

UN, FAO, 50th Anniv. A99

Designs: No. 374a, Outline of soldier's helmet, dove, peace. b, Outline of flame, Hedul Gibbons, human rights. c, Books, education. d, Outline of tractor, bananas, agriculture.

No. 375, Palau flag, bird, UN emblem. No. 376, Water being put on plants, UN emblem, vert.

1995, Sept. 15 Litho. *Perf. 14*
374 A99 60c Block of 4, #a.-d. 4.00 4.00

Souvenir Sheets

375 A99 $2 multicolored 3.25 3.25
376 A99 $2 multicolored 3.25 3.25

Independence, 1st Anniv. — A100

Palau flag and: a, Fruit doves. b, Rock Islands. c, Map of islands. d, Orchid, hibiscus.

32c, Marine life.

1995, Sept. 15 *Perf. 14½*
377 A100 20c Block of 4, #a.-d. 1.40 1.40
378 A100 32c multicolored .55 .55

No. 377 was issued in sheets of 16 stamps.

See US No. 2999.

Miniature Sheets

A101

End of World War II, 50th Anniv. — A102

Paintings by Wm. F. Draper: No. 379a, Preparing Tin-Fish. b, Hellcats Take-off into Palau's Rising Sun. c, Dauntless Dive Bombers over Malakai Harbor. d, Planes Return from Palau. e, Communion Before Battle. f, The Landing. g, First Task Ashore. h, Fire Fighters Save Flak-torn Pilot.

Paintings by Tom Lea: No. 379i, Young Marine Headed for Peleliu. j, Peleliu. k, Last Rites. l, The Thousand-Yard Stare.

Portraits by Albert Murray, vert.: No. 380a, Adm. Chester W. Nimitz. b, Adm. William F. Halsey. c, Adm. Raymond A. Spruance. d, Vice Adm. Marc A. Mitscher. e, Gen. Holland M. Smith, USMC.

$3, Nose art of B-29 Bock's Car.

1995, Oct. 18 *Perf. 14x13½*
379 A101 32c Sheet of 12, #a.-l 7.50 7.50

Perf. 13½x14

380 A101 60c Sheet of 5, #a.-e. 6.00 6.00

Souvenir Sheet

Perf. 14

381 A102 $3 multicolored 5.00 5.00

Christmas — A103

Native version of "We Three Kings of Orient Are:" a, Angel, animals. b, Two wise men. c, Joseph, Mary, Jesus in manger. d, Wise man, shepherd, animals. e, Girl with fruit, goat, shepherd.

1995, Oct. 31 Litho. *Perf. 14*
382 A103 32c Strip of 5, #a.-e. 2.75 2.75

No. 382 is a continuous design and was issued in sheets of 15 stamps + 5 labels se-tenant with bottom row of sheet.

Miniature Sheet of 12

Life Cycle of the Sea Turtle — A104

Small turtles, arrows representing routes during life cycle and: a, Large turtle. b, Upper half of turtle shell platter, Palau map. c, Rooster in tree, island scene. d, Native woman. e, Lower half of turtle shell platter, Palau map, island couple. f, Fossil, palm trees, native house

1995, Nov. 15 Litho. *Perf. 14*
383 A104 32c 2 each, #a.-f. 8.50 8.50

John Lennon (1940-80) — A105

1995, Dec. 8 Litho. *Perf. 14*
384 A105 32c multicolored 1.00 1.00

No. 384 was issued in sheets of 16.

Miniature Sheet

New Year 1996 (Year of the Rat) — A106

Stylized rats in parade: No. 385: a, One carrying flag, one playing horn. b, Three playing musical instruments. c, Two playing instruments. d, Family in front of house.

Mirror images, diff. colors: No. 386: a, Like #385c-385d. b, Like #385a-385b.

1996, Feb. 2 Litho. *Perf. 14*
385 A106 10c Strip of 4, #a.-d. 1.25 1.25

Miniature Sheet

386 A106 60c Sheet of 2, #a.-b. 2.50 2.50

No. 385 was issued in sheets of 2 + 4 labels like No. 386. Nos. 386a-386b are airmail and are each 56x43mm.

UNICEF, 50th Anniv. — A107

Three different children from Palau in traditional costumes, child in middle wearing: a, Red flowerd dress. b, Pink dress. c, Blue shorts. d, Red headpiece and shorts.

1996, Mar. 12 Litho. *Perf. 14*
387 A107 32c Block of 4, #a.-d. 2.50 2.50

No. 387 was issued in sheets of 4.

Marine Life — A108

Letter spelling "Palau," and: a, "P," fairy basslet, vermiculate parrotfish. b, "A," yellow cardinalfish. c, "L," Marten's butterflyfish. d, "A," starry moray, slate pencil sea urchin. e, "U," cleaner wrasse, coral grouper.

1996, Mar. 29 Litho. *Perf. 14*
388 A108 32c Strip of 5, #a.-e. 3.00 3.00

No. 388 was issued in miniature sheets of 3.

China '96, Intl. Stamp Exhibition, Beijing.

Sheets of 9

Capex '96 A109

Circumnavigators of the earth: No. 389: a, Ferdinand Magellan, ship Victoria. b, Charles Wilkes, ship Vincennes. c, Joshua Slocum, oyster boat Spray. d, Ben Carlin, amphibious vehicle Half-Safe. e, Edward L. Beach, submarine USS Triton. f, Naomi James, yacht Express Crusader. g, Sir Ranulf Fiennes, polar vehicle. h, Rick Hansen, wheel chair. i, Robin Knox-Johnson, catamaran Enza New Zealand.

No. 390: a, Lowell Smith, Douglas World Cruisers. b, Ernst Lehmann, Graf Zeppelin. c, Wiley Post, Lockheed Vega Winnie Mae. d, Yuri Gagarin, spacecraft Vostok I. e, Jerrie Mock, Cessna 180 Spirit of Columbus. f, Ross Perot, Jr., Bell Longranger III, Spirit of Texas. g, Brooke Knapp, Gulfstream III, The American Dream. h, Jeana Yeager, Dick Rutan, airplane Voyager. i, Fred Lasby, piper Commanche.

No. 391, Bob Martin, Mark Sullivan, Troy Bradley, Odyssey Gondola. No. 392, Sir Francis Chichester, yacht Gipsy Moth IV.

1996, May 3 Litho. *Perf. 14*
389 A109 32c #a.-i. 5.25 5.25
390 A109 60c #a.-i. 10.00 10.00

Souvenir Sheets

391-392 A109 $3 each 5.50 5.50

No. 390 is airmail.

Miniature Sheet

Disney Sweethearts — A110

1c, like #393a. 2c, #393c. 3c, #393d. 4c, like #393e. 5c, #393f. 6c, #393h.

#393: a, Simba, Nala, Timon. b, Bernard, Bianca, Mr. Chairman. c, Georgette, Tito, Oliver. d, Duchess, O'Malley, Marie. e, Bianca, Jake, Polly. f, Tod, Vixey, Copper. g, Robin Hood, Maiden Marian, Alan-a-Dale. h, Thumper, Flower, their sweethearts. i, Pongo, Perdita, puppies.

#394, Lady, vert. #395, Bambi, Faline.

1996, May 30 Litho. *Perf. 14x13½*

392A-392F A110 Set of 6 .75 .75

Sheet of 9

393 A110 60c #a.-i. 11.00 11.00

Souvenir Sheets

Perf. 13½x14, 14x13½

394-395 A110 $2 each 4.25 4.25

Jerusalem, 3000th Anniv. — A111

Biblical illustrations of the Old Testament appearing in "In Our Image," by Guy Rowe (1894-1969): a, Creation. b, Adam and Eve. c, Noah and his Wife. d, Abraham. e, Jacob's Blessing. f, Jacob Becomes Israel. g, Joseph and his Brethren. h, Moses and the Burning Bush. i, Moses and the Tablets. j, Balaam. k, Joshua. l, Gideon. m, Jephthah. n, Samson. o, Ruth and Naomi. p, Saul Anointed. q, Saul Denounced. r, David and Jonathan. s, David and Nathan. t, David Mourns. u, Solomon Praying. v, Solomon Judging. w, Elijah. x, Elisha. y, Job. z, Isaiah. aa, Jeremiah. ab, Ezekiel. ac, Nebuchadnezzar's Dream. ad, Amos.

1996, June 15 Litho. *Perf. 14*

396 A111 20c Sheet of 30 12.00 12.00

For overprint see No. 461.

1996 Summer Olympics, Atlanta A112

No. 397, Fanny Blankers Koen, gold medalist, 1948, vert. No. 398, Bob Mathias, gold medalist, 1948, 1952, vert. No. 399, Torchbearer entering Wembley Stadium, 1948. No. 400, Olympic flag, flags of Palau and U.K. before entrance to Stadium, Olympia, Greece.

Athletes: No. 401: a, Hakeem Olajuwan, US. b, Pat McCormick, US. c, Jim Thorpe, US. d, Jesse Owens, US. e, Tatyana Gutsu, Unified Team. f, Michael Jordan, US. g, Fu Mingxia, China. h, Robert Zmelik, Czechoslovakia. i, Ivan Pedroso, Cuba. j, Nadia Comaneci, Romania. k, Jackie Joyner-Kersee, US. l, Michael Johnson, US. m, Kristin Otto, E. Germany. n, Vitali Scherbo, Unified Team. o, Johnny Weissmuller, US. p, Babe Didrikson, US. q, Eddie Tolan, US. r, Krisztina Egerszegi, Hungary. s, Sawao Kato, Japan. t, Alexander Popov, Unified Team.

1996, June 17 Litho. *Perf. 14*

397 A112 40c multicolored .80 .80
398 A112 40c multicolored .80 .80
a. Pair, #397-398 1.60 1.60
399 A112 60c multicolored 1.25 1.25
400 A112 60c multicolored 1.25 1.25
a. Pair, #399-400 2.50 2.50
401 A112 32c Sheet of 20, #a.-t. 12.00 12.00

Nos. 398a, 400a were each issued in sheets of 20 stamps. No. 401 is a continuous design.

Birds Over Palau Lagoon A113

Designs: a, Lakkotsiang, female. b, Maladaob. c, Belochel (g). d, Lakkotsiang, male. e, Sechosech. f, Mechadelbedaoch (j). g, Laib. h, Cheloteachel. i, Deroech. j, Kerkirs. k, Dudek. l, Lakkotsiang. m, Bedaoch. n, Bedebedchaki. o, Sechou (gray Pacific reef-heron) (p). p, Kekereiderariik. q, Sechou (white Pacific reef-heron). r, Ochaieu. s, Oltirakladial. t, Omechederiibabad.

1996, July 10

402 A113 50c Sheet of 20, #a.-t. 19.00 19.00

Aircraft A114

Stealth, surveillance, and electronic warfare: No. 403: a, Lockheed U-2. b, General Dynamics EF-111A. c, Lockheed YF-12A. d, Lockheed SR-71. e, Teledyne-Ryan-Tiere II Plus. f, Lockheed XST. g, Lockhood ER-2. h, Lockheed F-117A Nighthawk. i, Lockheed EC-130E. j, Ryan Firebee. k, Lockheed Martin/Boeing "Darkstar." l, Boeing E-3A Sentry.

No. 404: a, Northrop XB-35. b, Leduc O.21. c, Convair Model 118. d, Blohm Und Voss BV 141. e, Vought V-173. f, McDonnell XF-85 Goblin. g, North American F-82B Twin Mustang. h, Lockheed XFV-1. i, Northrop XP-79B. j, Saunders Roe SR/A1. k, Caspian Sea Monster. l, Grumman X-29.

No. 405, Northrop B-2A Stealth Bomber. No. 406, Martin Marietta X-24B.

1996, Sept. 9 Litho. *Perf. 14*

403 A114 40c Sheet of 12, #a.-l. 9.50 9.50
404 A114 60c Sheet of 12, #a.-l. 14.40 14.40

Souvenir Sheets

405 A114 $3 multicolored 6.00 6.00
406 A114 $3 multicolored 6.00 6.00

No. 404 is airmail. No. 406 contains one 85x28mm stamp.

Independence, 2nd Anniv. — A115

Paintings, by Koh Sekiguchi: No. 407, "In the Blue Shade of Trees-Palau (Kirie). No. 408 "The Birth of a New Nation (Kirie).

1996, Oct. 1 Litho. *Perf. 14½*

407 20c multicolored .40 .40
408 20c multicolored .40 .40
a. A115 Pair, #407-408 .80 .80

#408a issued in sheets of 16 stamps.

Christmas — A116

Christmas trees: a, Pandanus. b, Mangrove. c, Norfolk Island pine. d, Papaya. e, Casuarina.

1996, Oct. 8 *Perf. 14*

409 A116 32c Strip of 5, #a.-e. 3.25 3.25

No. 409 was issued in sheets of 3.

Voyage to Mars — A117

No. 410: a, Viking 1 (US) in Mars orbit. b, Mars Lander fires de-orbit engines. c, Viking 1 symbol (top). d, Viking 1 symbol (bottom). e, Martian moon phobos. f, Mariner 9 in Mars orbit. g, Viking lander enters Martian atmosphere. h, Parachute deploys for Mars landing, heat shield jettisons. i, Proposed manned mission to Mars, 21st cent., US-Russian spacecraft (top). j, US-Russian spacecraft (botton). k, Lander descent engines fire for Mars landing. l, Viking 1 lands on Mars, July 20, 1976.

No. 411, NASA Mars rover. No. 412, NASA water probe on Mars. Illustration reduced.

1996, Nov. 8 Litho. *Perf. 14x14½*

410 A117 32c Sheet of 12, #a.-l. 7.75 7.75

Souvenir Sheets

411-412 A117 $3 each 6.00 6.00

No. 411 contains one 38x30mm stamp.

Souvenir Sheet

New Year 1997 (Year of the Ox) — A117a

Illustration reduced.

1997, Jan. 2 Litho. *Perf. 14*

412A A117a $2 multicolored 4.00 4.00

Souvenir Sheet

South Pacific Commission, 50th Anniv. — A118

Illustration reduced.

1997, Feb. 6 Litho. *Perf. 14*

413 A118 $1 multicolored 2.00 2.00

Hong Kong '97 — A119

Flowers: 1c, Pemphis acidula. 2c, Sea lettuce. 3c, Tropical almond. 4c, Guettarda. 5c, Pacific coral bean. $3, Sea hibiscus.

No. 420: a, Black mangrove. b, Cordia. c, Lantern tree. d, Palau rock-island flower.

No. 421: a, Fish-poison tree. b, Indian mulberry. c, Pacific poison-apple. d, Ailanthus.

1997, Feb. 12 *Perf. 14½, 13½ (#419)*

414-419 A119 Set of 6 6.25 6.25
420 A119 32c Block of 4, #a.-d. 2.50 2.50
421 A119 50c Block of 4, #a.-d. 4.00 4.00

Size of No. 419 is 73x48mm.

Nos. 420-421 were each issued in sheets of 16 stamps.

Bicent. of the Parachute A120

Uses of parachute: No. 422: a, Apollo 15 Command Module landing safely. b, "Caterpillar Club" flyer ejecting safely over land. c. Skydiving team formation. d, Parasailing. e, Military parachute demonstration teams. f, Parachute behind dragster. g, Dropping cargo from C-130 aircraft. h, "Goldfish Club" flyer ejecting safely at sea.

No. 423: a, Demonstrating parachute control. b, A.J. Gernerin, first successful parachute descent, 1797. c, Slowing down world land-speed record breaking cars. d, Dropping spies behind enemy lines. e, C-130E demonstrating "LAPES." f, Parachutes used to slow down high performance aircraft. g, ARD parachutes. g, US Army parachutist flying Parafoil.

No. 424 Training tower at Ft. Benning, Georgia. No. 425, "Funny Car" safety chute.

Perf. 14½x14, 14x14½

1997, Mar. 13 Litho.

422 A120 32c Sheet of 8, #a.-h. 5.25 5.25
423 A120 60c Sheet of 8, #a.-h. 9.75 9.75

Souvenir Sheets

Perf. 14

424-425 A120 $2 each 4.00 4.00

Nos. 422a-423a, 422b-423b, 422g-423g, 422h-423h are 20x48mm. No. 424 contains one 28x85mm, No. 425 one 57x42mm stamps.

No. 423 is airmail.

Postage Stamp Mega-Event, NYC, Mar. 1997 (#422-423).

Native Birds A121

a, Gray duck, banana tree. b, Red junglefowl, calamondin. c, Nicobar pigeon, fruited parinari tree. d, Cardinal honeyeater, wax apple tree. e, Yellow bittern, purple swamphen, giant taro, taro. f, Eclectus parrot, pangi football fruit tree. g, Micronesian pigeon, Rambutan. h, Micronesian starling, mango tree. i, Fruit bat, breadfruit tree. j, Collared kingfisher, coconut palm. k, Palau fruit dove, sweet orange tree. l, Chestnut mannikin, soursop tree.

1997, Mar. 27 Litho. *Perf. 13½x14*

426 A121 20c Sheet of 12, #a.-l. 4.75 4.75

UNESCO, 50th Anniv. — A122

Sites in Japan, vert: Nos. 427: a, c-h, Himeji-jo. b, Kyoto.

Sites in Germany: Nos. 428: a-b, Augustusburg Castle. c, Falkenlust Castle. d, Roman ruins, Trier. e, Historic house, Trier.

No. 429, Forest, Shirakami-Sanchi, Japan. No. 430, Yakushima, Japan.

Perf. 13½x14, 14x13½

1997, Apr. 7 **Litho.**

Sheets of 8 or 5 + Label

427 A122 32c #a.-h. 5.25 5.25
428 A122 60c #a.-e. 6.00 6.00

Souvenir Sheets

429-430 A122 $2 each 4.00 4.00

A123

A124

Paintings by Hiroshige (1797-1858): No. 431: a, Swallows and Peach Blossoms under a Full Moon. b, A Parrot on a Flowering Branch. c, Crane and Rising Sun. d, Cock, Umbrella, and Morning Glories. e, A Titmouse Hanging Head Downward on a Camellia Branch.

No. 432, Falcon on a Pine Tree with the Rising Sun. No. 433, Kingfisher and Iris.

1997, June 2 **Litho.** ***Perf. 14***

431 A123 32c Sheet of 5, #a.-e. 3.75 3.75

Souvenir Sheets

432-433 A123 $2 each 4.00 4.00

1997 **Litho.** ***Perf. 14***

Volcano Goddesses of the Pacific: a, Darago, Philippines. b, Fuji, Japan. c, Pele, Hawaii. d, Pare, Maori. e, Dzalarhons, Haida. f, Chuginadak, Aleuts.

434 A124 32c Sheet of 6, #a.-f. 3.75 3.75

PACIFIC 97.

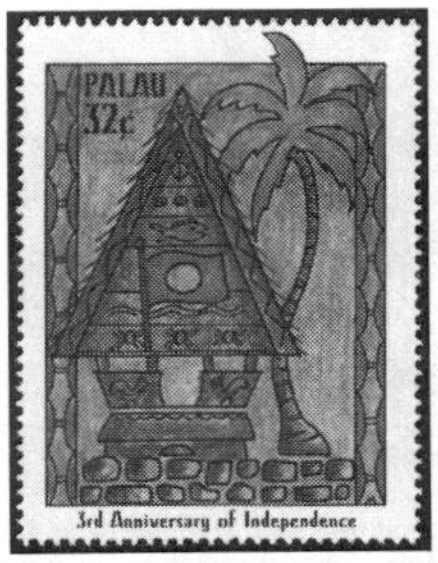

Independence, 3rd Anniv. — A125

1997, Oct. 1 **Litho.** ***Perf. 14***

435 A125 32c multicolored .65 .65

No. 435 was issued in sheets of 12.

Oceanographic Research — A126

Ships: No. 436: a, Albatross. b, Mabahiss. c, Atlantis II. d, Xarifa. e, Meteor. f, Egabras III. g, Discoverer. h, Kaiyo. i, Ocean Defender.

No. 437, Jacques-Yves Cousteau (1910-97). No. 438, Cousteau, diff., vert. No. 439, Pete Seeger, vert.

1997, Oct. 1 ***Perf. 14x14½, 14½x14***

436 A126 32c Sheet of 9, #a.-i. 5.75 5.75

Souvenir Sheets

437-439 A126 $2 each 4.00 4.00

Diana, Princess of Wales (1961-97) A127

1997, Nov. 26 **Litho.** ***Perf. 14***

440 A127 60c multicolored 1.25 1.25

No. 440 was issued in sheets of 6.

Disney's "Let's Read" — A128

Various Disney characters: 1c, like #447i. 2c, like #447d. 3c, like #447c. 4c, like #447f. 5c, #447b. 10c, like #447h.

No. 447: a, "Exercise your right to read." b, "Reading is the ultimate luxury." c, "Share your knowledge." d, "Start them Young." e, "Reading is fundamental." f, "The insatiable reader." g, "Reading time is anytime." h, "Real men read." i, "I can read by myself."

No. 448, Daisy, "The library is for everyone," vert. No. 449, Mickey, "Books are magical."

1997, Oct. 21 ***Perf. 14x13½, 13½x14***

441-446 A128 Set of 6 .50 .50

Sheet of 9

447 A128 32c #a.-i. 5.75 5.75

Souvenir Sheets

448 A128 $2 multicolored 4.00 4.00
449 A128 $3 multicolored 6.00 6.00

Christmas — A129

Children singing Christmas carol, "Some Children See Him:" No. 450: a, Girl, boy in striped shirt. b, Boy, girl in pigtails. c, Girl, boy, Madonna and Child. d, Girl, two children. e, Boy, girl with long black hair.

1997, Oct. 28 ***Perf. 14***

450 A129 32c Strip of 5, #a.-e. 3.25 3.25

No. 450 was issued in sheets of 3 strips, bottom strip printed se-tenant with 5 labels containing lyrics.

Souvenir Sheets

New Year 1998 (Year of the Tiger) — A130

Chinese toys in shape of tiger: No. 451, White background. No. 452, Green background.

Illustration reduced.

1998, Jan. 2 **Litho.** ***Perf. 14***

451 A130 50c multicolored 1.00 1.00
452 A130 50c multicolored 1.00 1.00

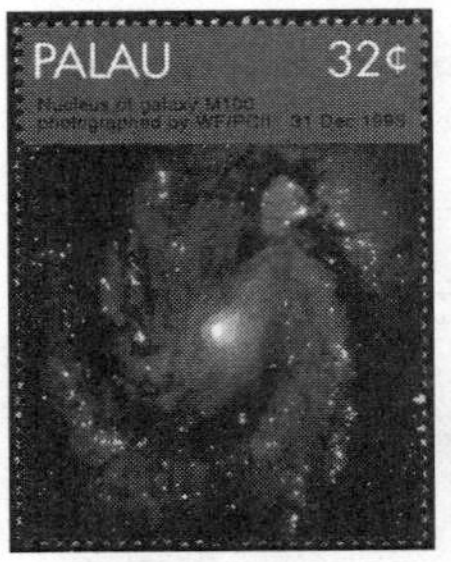

Repair of Hubble Space Telescope A131

No. 453: a, Photograph of nucleus of galaxy M100. b, Top of Hubble telescope with solar arrays folded. c, Astronaut riding robot arm. d, Astronaut anchored to robot arm. e, Astronaut in cargo space with Hubble mounted to shuttle Endeavor. f, Hubble released after repair.

No. 454, Hubble cutaway, based on NASA schematic drawing. No. 455, Edwin Hubble (1889-1953), astronomer who proved existence of star systems beyond Milky Way. No. 456, Hubble Mission STS-82/Discovery.

1998, Mar. 9 **Litho.** ***Perf. 14***

453 A131 32c Sheet of 6, #a.-f. 3.75 3.75

Souvenir Sheets

454-456 A131 $2 each 4.00 4.00

Mother Teresa (1910-97) — A132

Various portraits.

1998, Mar. 12 **Litho.** ***Perf. 14***

457 A132 60c Sheet of 4, #a.-d. 4.75 4.75

Deep Sea Robots A133

No. 458: a, Ladybird ROV. b, Slocum Glider. c, Hornet. d, Scorpio. e, Odyssey AUV. f, Jamstec Survey System Launcher. g, Scarab. h, USN Torpedo Finder/Salvager. i, Jamstec Survey System Vehicle. j, Cetus Tether. k, Deep Sea ROV. l, ABE. m, OBSS. n, RCV 225G Swimming Eyeball. o, Japanese UROV. p, Benthos RPV. q, CURV. r, Smartie.

No. 459, Jason Jr. inspecting Titanic. No. 460, Dolphin 3K.

1998, Apr. 21

458 A133 32c Sheet of 18, #a.-r. 11.50 11.50

Souvenir Sheets

459-460 A133 $2 each 4.00 4.00

UNESCO Intl. Year of the Ocean.

No. 396 Ovptd. in Silver

1998, May 13 **Litho.** ***Perf. 14***

461 A111 20c Sheet of 30, a.-ad. 12.00 12.00

No. 461 is overprinted in sheet margin, "ISRAEL 98 - WORLD STAMP EXHIBITION / TEL AVIV 13-21 MAY 1998." Location of overprint varies.

Legend of Orachel — A134

#462: a, Bai (hut), people. b, Bai, lake. c, Bai, lake, person in canoe. d, Bird on branch over lake. e, Men rowing in canoe. f, Canoe, head of snake. g, Alligator under water. h, Fish, shark. i, Turtle, body of snake. j, Underwater bai, "gods". k, Snails, fish, Orachel swimming. l, Orachel's feet, coral, fish.

1998, May 29 **Litho.** ***Perf. 14***

462 A134 40c Sheet of 12, #a.-l. 9.50 9.50

1998 World Cup Soccer Championships, France — A135

Players, color of shirt - #463: a, Yellow, black & red. b, Blue, white & red. c, Green & white. d, White, red & blue. e, Green & white (black shorts). f, White, red & black. g, Blue & yellow. h, Red & white.
$3, Pele.

1998, June 5

463 A135 50c Sheet of 8, #a.-h. 8.00 8.00

Souvenir Sheet

464 A135 $3 multicolored 6.00 6.00

4th Micronesian Games, Palau — A136

Designs: a, Spear fishing. b, Spear throwing. c, Swimming. d, Pouring milk from coconut. e, Logo of games. f, Climbing coconut trees. g, Canoeing. h, Husking coconut. i, Deep sea diving.

1998, July 31 Litho. *Perf. 14*

465 A136 32c Sheet of 9, #a.-i. 5.75 5.75

Rudolph The Red-Nosed Reindeer — A137

Christmas: a, Rudolph, two reindeer, girl. b, Two reindeer, girl holding flowers. c, Girl, two reindeer, boy. d, Two reindeer, girl smiling. e, Santa, children, Christmas gifts.

1998, Sept. 15 Litho. *Perf. 14*

466 A137 32c Strip of 5, #a.-e. 3.25 3.25

No. 466 is a continuous design and was issued in sheets of 15 stamps.

Disney/Pixar's "A Bug's Life" — A138

No. 467: a, Dot. b, Heimlich, Francis, Slim. c, Hopper. d, Princess Atta.
No. 468: Various scenes with Flik, Princess Atta.
No. 469, horiz.: a, Circus bugs. b, Slim, Francis, Heimlich. c, Manny. d, Francis.
No. 470: a, Slim, Flik. b, Heimlich, Slim, Francis performing. c, Manny, Flik. d, Gypsy, Manny, Rosie.
No. 471, Gypsy. No. 472, Princess Atta, Flik, horiz. No. 473, Slim, Francis, Heimlich, horiz. No. 474, Francis, Slim, Flik, Heimlich, horiz.

Perf. 13½x14, 14x13½

1998, Dec. 1 Litho.

Sheets of 4

467 A138 20c #a.-d. 1.60 1.60
468 A138 32c #a.-d. 2.50 2.50
469 A138 50c #a.-d. 4.00 4.00
470 A138 60c #a.-d. 4.75 4.75

Souvenir Sheets

471-474 A138 $2 each 4.00 4.00

Nos. 473-474 each contain one 76x51mm stamp.

John Glenn's Return to Space — A139

No. 475, Various photos of Project Mercury, Friendship 7 misssion, 1962.
No. 476, Various photos of Discovery Space Shuttle mission, 1998.
No. 477, Portrait, 1962. No. 478, Portrait, 1998.

1999, Jan. 7 Litho. *Perf. 14*

Sheets of 8

475-476 A139 60c #a.-h., each 9.50 9.50

Souvenir Sheets

477-478 A139 $2 each 4.00 4.00

Nos. 477-478 each contain one 28x42mm stamp.

Environmentalists — A140

a, Rachel Carson. b, J.N. "Ding" Darling, US Duck stamp #RW1. c, David Brower. d, Jacques Cousteau. e, Roger Tory Peterson. f, Prince Philip. g, Joseph Wood Krutch. h, Aldo Leopold. i, Dian Fossey. j, US Vice-President Al Gore. k, David Attenborough. l, Paul McCready. m, Sting (Gordon Sumner). n, Paul Winter. o, Ian MacHarg. p, Denis Hayes.

1999, Feb. 1 Litho. *Perf. 14½*

479 A140 33c Sheet of 16, #a.-p. 10.50 10.50

No. 479i shows Dian Fossey's name misspelled "Diane."

MIR Space Station A141

No. 480: a, Soyuz Spacecraft, Science Module. b, Specktr Science Module. c, Space Shuttle, Spacelab Module. d, Kvant 2, Scientific and Air Lock Module. e, Kristall Technological Module. f, Space Shutle, Docking Module.
No. 481, Astronaut Charles Precout, Cosmonaut Talgat Musabayev. No. 482, Cosmonaut Valeri Poliakov. No. 483, US Mission Specialist Shannon W. Lucid, Cosmonaut Yuri Y. Usachov. No. 484, Cosmonaut Anatoly Solovyov.

1999, Feb. 18 Litho. *Perf. 14*

480 A141 33c Sheet of 6, #a.-f. 3.75 3.75

Souvenir Sheets

481-484 A141 $2 each 4.00 4.00

Personalities — A142

1c, Haruo Remiliik. 2c, Lazarus Salil. 20c, Charlie W. Gibbons. 22c, Adm. Raymond A. Spruance. 33c, Kuniwo Nakamura. 50c, Adm. William F. Halsey. 55c, Col. Lewis "Chesty" Puller. 60c, Franklin D. Roosevelt. 77c, Harry S Truman. $3.20, Jimmy Carter.

1999, Mar. 4 *Perf. 14x15*

485	A142	1c green	.20	.20
486	A142	2c purple	.20	.20
487	A142	20c violet	.40	.40
488	A142	22c bister	.45	.45
489	A142	33c red brown	.65	.65
490	A142	50c brown	1.00	1.00
491	A142	55c blue green	1.10	1.10
492	A142	60c orange	1.25	1.25
493	A142	77c yellow brown	1.50	1.50
494	A142	$3.20 red violet	6.50	6.50
		Nos. 485-494 (10)	13.25	13.25

Nos. 485, 492 exist dated 2001.

Australia '99 World Stamp Expo A143

Endangered species - #495: a, Leatherback turtle. b, Kemp's ridley turtle. c, Green turtle. d, Marine iguana. e, Table mountain ghost frog. f, Spiny turtle. g, Hewitt's ghost frog. h, Geometric tortoise. i, Limestone salmander. j, Desert rain frog. k, Cape plantanna. l, Long-toed tree frog.
No. 496, Marine crocodile. No. 497, Hawksbill turtle.

1999, Mar. 19 Litho. *Perf. 13*

495 A143 33c Sheet of 12, #a.-l. 8.00 8.00

Souvenir Sheets

496-497 A143 $2 each 4.00 4.00

IBRA '99, Nuremburg — A144

No. 498, Leipzig-Dresden Railway, Caroline Islands Type A4. No. 499, Gölsdorf 4-8-0, Caroline Islands #8, 10.
$2, Caroline Islands #1.

1999, Apr. 27 Litho. *Perf. 14*

498-499 A144 55c Set of 2 2.25 2.25

Souvenir Sheet

500 A144 $2 multicolored 4.00 4.00

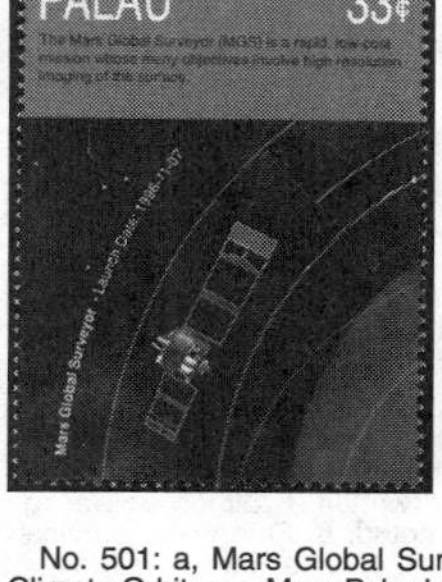

Exploration of Mars A145

No. 501: a, Mars Global Surveyor. b, Mars Climate Orbiter. c, Mars Polar Lander. d, Deep Space 2. e, Mars Surveyor 2001 Orbiter. f, Mars Surveyor 2001 Lander.
No. 502, Mars Global Surveyor. No. 503, Mars Climate Orbiter. No. 504, Mars Polar Lander. No. 505, Mars Surveyor 2001 Lander.

1999, May 10 Litho. *Perf. 14*

501 A145 33c Sheet of 6, #a.-f. 4.00 4.00

Souvenir Sheets

502-505 A145 $2 each 4.00 4.00

Nos. 502-505 each contain one 38x50mm stamp.
See Nos. 507-511.

Earth Day — A146

Pacific insects: a, Banza Natida. b, Drosophila heteroneura. c, Nesomicromus vagus. d, Megalagrian leptodemus. e, Pseudopsectra cookearum. f, Ampheida neacaledonia. g, Pseudopsectra swezeyi. h, Deinacrida heteracantha. i, Beech forest butterfly. j, Hercules moth. k, Striped sphinx moth. l, Tussock butterfly. m. Elytrocheilus. n, Bush cricket. o, Longhorn beetle. p, Abathrus bicolor. q, Stylagymnusa subantartica. r, Moth butterfly. s, Paraconosoma naviculare. t, Ornithoptera priamus.

1999, May 24

506 A146 33c Sheet of 20, #a.-t. 13.50 13.50

Space Type

International Space Station - #507: a, Launch 1R. b, Launch 14A. c, Launch 8A. d, Launch 1J. e, Launch 1E. f, Launch 16A.
No. 508, Intl. Space Station. No. 509, Cmdr. Bob Cabana, Cosmonaut Sergei Krikalev. No. 510, Crew of Flight 2R, horiz. No. 511, X-38 Crew Return Vehicle, horiz.

1999, June 12 Litho. *Perf. 14*

507 A145 33c Sheet of 6, #a.-f. 4.00 4.00

Souvenir Sheets

508-511 A145 $2 each 4.00 4.00

20th Century Visionaries A147

Designs: a, William Gibson, "Cyberspace." b, Danny Hillis, Massively Parallel Processing. c, Steve Wozniak, Apple Computer. d, Steve Jobs, Apple Computer. e, Nolan Bushnell, Atari, Inc. f, John Warnock, Adobe, Inc. g, Ken Thompson, Unix. h, Al Shugart, Seagate Technologies. i, Rand & Robyn Miller, "MYST." j, Nicolas Negroponte, MIT Media Lab. k, Bill Gates, Microsoft, Inc. l, Arthur C. Clarke, Orbiting Communications Satellite. m, Marshall Mcluhan, "The Medium is the Message." n, Thomas Watson, Jr., IBM. o, Gordon Moore, Intel Corporation, "Moore's Law." p, James Gosling, Java. q, Sabeer Bhatia & Jack Smith, Hotmail.com. r, Esther Dyson, "Release 2.0." s, Jerry Yang, David Filo, Yahoo! t, Jeff Bezos, Amazon.com. u, Bob Kahn, TCP-IP. v, Jaron Lanter, "Virtual Reality." w, Andy Grove, Intel Corporation. x, Jim Clark, Silicon Graphics, Inc., Netscape Communications Corp. y, Bob Metcalfe, Ethernet, 3com.

1999, June 30 Litho. *Perf. 14*

512 A147 33c Sheet of 25, a.-y. 17.00 17.00

Paintings by Hokusai (1760-1849) — A148

#513: a, Women Divers. b, Bull and Parasol. c, Drawings of Women (partially nude). d, Drawings of Women (seated, facing forward). e, Japanese spaniel. f, Porters in Landscape.

#514: a, Bacchanalian Revelry. b, Bacchanalian Revelry (two seated back to back). c, Drawings of Women (crawling). d, Drawings of Women (facing backward). e, Ox-Herd. f, Ox-Herd (man on bridge).
No. 515, Mount Fuji in a Thunderstorm, vert. No. 516, At Swan Lake in Shinano.

1999, July 20 *Perf. 14x13¾*

Sheets of 6

513-514 A148 33c #a.-f., each 4.00 4.00

Souvenir Sheets

515-516 A148 $2 each 4.00 4.00

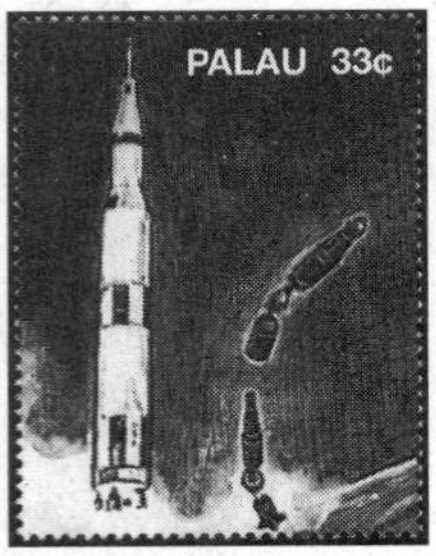

Apollo 11, 30th Anniv. A149

No. 517: a, Lift-off, jettison of stages. b, Earth, moon, capsule. c, Astronaut on lunar module ladder. d, Lift-off. e, Planting flag on moon. f, Astronauts Collins, Armstrong and Aldrin.
No. 518, Rocket on launch pad. No. 519, Astronaut on ladder, earth. No. 520, Lunar module above moon. No. 521, Capsule in ocean.

1999, July 20 Litho. *Perf. 13½x14*

517 A149 33c Sheet of 6, #a.-f. 4.00 4.00

Souvenir Sheets

518-521 A149 $2 each 4.00 4.00

Queen Mother (b. 1900) — A150

No. 522: a, In Australia, 1958. b, In 1960. c, In 1970. d, In 1987.
$2, Holding book, 1947.

Gold Frames

522 A150 60c Sheet of 4, #a.-d., + label 4.75 4.75

Souvenir Sheet

Perf. 13¾

523 A150 $2 black 4.00 4.00

No. 523 contains one 38x51mm stamp.
See Nos. 636-637.

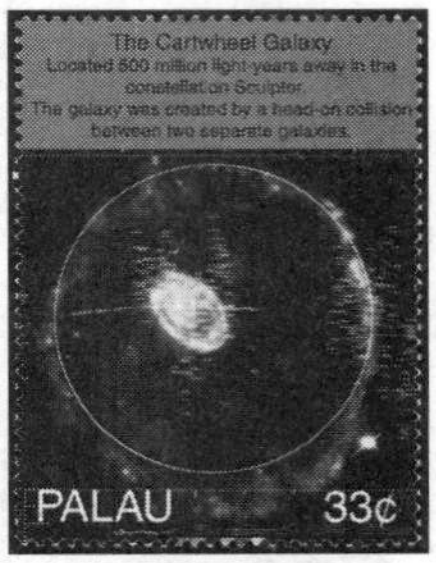

Hubble Space Telescope Images A151

No. 524: a, Cartwheel Galaxy. b, Stingray Nebula. c, NGC 3918. d, Cat's Eye Nebula (NGC 6543). e, NGC 7742. f, Eight-burst Nebula (NGC 3132).
No. 525, Eta Carinae. No. 526, Planetary nebula M2-9. No. 527, Supernova 1987-A. No. 528, Infrared aurora of Saturn.

1999, Oct. 15 Litho. *Perf. 13¾*

524 A151 33c Sheet of 6, #a.-f. 4.00 4.00

Souvenir Sheets

525-528 A151 $2 each 4.00 4.00

Christmas — A152

Birds and: a, Cows, chickens. b, Donkey, geese, rabbit. c, Infant, cat, lambs. d, Goats, geese. e, Donkey, rooster.

1999, Nov. 15 *Perf. 14*

529 A152 20c Strip of 5, #a.-e. 2.00 2.00

Love for Dogs — A153

No. 530: a, Keep safe. b, Show affection. c, A place of one's own. d, Communicate. e, Good food. f, Annual checkup. g, Teach rules. h, Exercise & play. i, Let him help. j, Unconditional love.
No. 531, Pleasure of your company. No. 532, Love is a gentle thing.

1999, Nov. 23 Litho. *Perf. 14*

530 A153 33c Sheet of 10, #a.-j. 6.75 6.75

Souvenir Sheets

531-532 A153 $2 each 4.00 4.00

Futuristic Space Probes A154

Text starting with - No. 533: a, Deep space probes like. . . b, This piggy-back. . . c, Deep space telescope. . . d, Mission planning. . . e, In accordance. . . f, Utilizing onboard. . .
No. 534, This secondary. . . No. 535, Deep space probes are an integral. . . No. 536, Deep space probes are our. . . , horiz. No. 537, With the. . . , horiz.

2000, Jan. 18 Litho. *Perf. 13¾*

533 A154 55c Sheet of 6, #a.-f. 3.50 3.50

Souvenir Sheets

534-537 A154 $2 each 4.00 4.00

Millennium A155

Highlights of 1800-50 - No. 538: a, Brazilian Indians. b, Haiti slave revolt. c, Napoleon becomes Emperor of France. d, Shaka Zulu. e, "Frankenstein" written. f, Simon Bolivar. g, Photography invented. h, First water purification works built. i, First all-steam railway. j, Michael Faraday discovers electromagnetism. k, First use of anesthesia. l, Samuel Morse completes first telegraph line. m, Women's rights convention in Seneca Falls, NY. n, Birth of Karl Marx. o, Revolution in German Confederation. p, Charles Darwin's voyages on the "Beagle" (60x40mm). q, Beijing, China.
Highlights of 1980-89 - No. 539; a, Lech Walesa organizes Polish shipyard workers. b, Voyager I photographs Saturn. c, Ronald Reagan elected US president. d, Identification of AIDS virus. e, Wedding of Prince Charles and Lady Diana Spencer. f, Compact discs go into production. g, Bhopal, India gas disaster. h, I. M. Pei's Pyramid entrance to the Louvre opens. i, Mikhail Gorbachev becomes leader of Soviet Union. j, Chernobyl nuclear disaster. k, Explosion of Space Shuttle "Challenger." l, Klaus Barbie convicted of crimes against humanity. m, Life of author Salman Rushdie threatened by Moslems. n, Benazir Bhutto becomes first woman prime minister of a Moslem state. o, Tiananmen Square revolt. p, Berlin Wall falls (60x40mm). q, World Wide Web.

2000, Feb. 2 Litho. *Perf. 12¾x12½*

Sheets of 17, #a.-q.

538-539 A155 20c each 7.00 7.00

Misspellings and historical inaccuracies abound on Nos. 538-539.
See No. 584.

New Year 2000 (Year of the Dragon) — A156

Illustration reduced.

2000, Feb. 5 *Perf. 13¾*

540 A156 $2 multi 4.00 4.00

US Presidents — A157

2000, Mar. 1 Litho. *Perf. 13½x13¼*

541 A157 $1 Bill Clinton 2.00 2.00
542 A157 $2 Ronald Reagan 4.00 4.00
543 A157 $3 Gerald Ford 6.00 6.00
544 A157 $5 George Bush 10.00 10.00

Size: 40x24mm

Perf. 14¾x14

545 A157 $11.75 Kennedy 22.50 22.50
Nos. 541-545 (5) 44.50 44.50

20th Century Discoveries About Prehistoric Life — A158

Designs: a, Australopithecines. b, Australopithecine skull. c, Homo habilis. d, Hand axe. e, Homo habilis skull. f, Lucy, Australopithecine skeleton. g, Archaic Homo sapiens skull. h, Diapithicine skull. i, Homo erectus. j, Wood hut. k, Australopithecine ethopsis skull. l, Dawn of mankind. m, Homo sapiens skull. n, Taung baby's skull. o, Homo erectus skull. p. Louis Leakey (1903-72), paleontologist. q, Neanderthal skull. r, Neandertahal. s, Evolution of the foot. t, Raymond Dart (1893-1988), paleontologist.

2000, Mar. 15 *Perf. 14¼*

546 A158 20c Sheet of 20, #a.-t. 8.00 8.00

Misspellings and historical inaccuracies are found on Nos. 546g, 546m, 546p, 546t and perhaps others.

2000 Summer Olympics, Sydney A159

Designs: a, Charlotte Cooper, tennis player at 1924 Olympics. b, Women's shot put. c, Helsinki Stadium, site of 1952 Olympics. d, Ancient Greek athletes.

2000, Mar. 31 *Perf. 14*

547 A159 33c Sheet of 4, #a.-d. 2.75 2.75

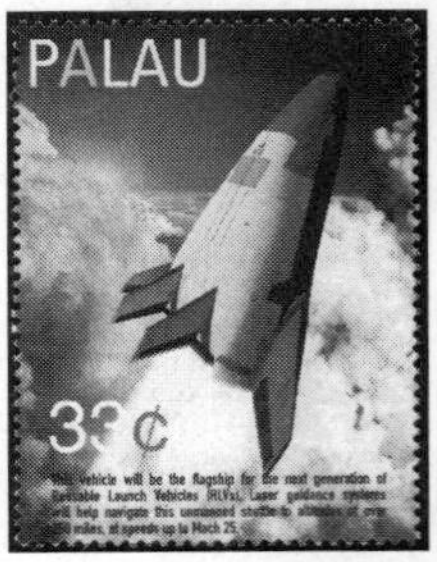

Future of Space Exploration A160

Text starting with - No. 548: a, This vehicle will be. . . b, This single stage. . . c, This robotic rocket. . . d, Dynamic. . . e, This fully. . . f, This launch vehicle. . .
No. 549, Increasingly, space travel. . . No. 550, Designed with projects. . ., horiz. No. 551, Design is currently. . ., horiz. No. 552, Inevitably, the future. . ., horiz.

2000, Apr. 10 *Perf. 13¾*

548 A160 33c Sheet of 6, #a.-f. 4.00 4.00

Souvneir Sheets

549-552 A160 $2 each 4.00 4.00

Birds — A161

No. 553: a, Slatey-legged crake. b, Micronesian kingfisher. c, Little pied cormorant. d, Pacific reed egret. e, Nicobar pigeon. f, Rufous night heron.
No. 554: a, Palau ground dove. b, Palau scops owl. c, Mangrove flycatcher. d, Palau bush warbler. e, Palau fantail. f, Morningbird.
No. 555, Palau fruit dove, horiz. No. 556, Palau white-eye, horiz.

2000, Apr. 14 Litho. *Perf. 14¼*

553 A161 20c Sheet of 6, #a.-f. 2.40 2.40
554 A161 33c Sheet of 6, #a.-f. 4.00 4.00

Souvenir Sheets

555-556 A161 $2 each 4.00 4.00

Visionaries of the 20th Century — A162

a, Booker T. Washington. b, Buckminster Fuller. c, Marie Curie. d, Walt Disney. e, F. D. Roosevelt. f, Henry Ford. g, Betty Friedan. h, Sigmund Freud. i, Mohandas Gandhi. j, Mikhail Gorbachev. k, Stephen Hawking. l, Martin Luther King, Jr. m, Toni Morrison. n, Georgia O'Keeffe. o, Rosa Parks. p, Carl Sagan. q, Jonas Salk. r, Sally Ride. s, Nikola Tesla. t, Wilbur and Orville Wright.
Illustration reduced.

2000, Apr. 28 Litho. *Perf. 14¼x14½*

557 A162 33c Sheet of 20, #a.-t. 13.50 13.50

20th Century Science and Medicine Advances — A163

No. 558: a, James D. Watson, 1962 Nobel laureate. b, Har Gobind Khorana and Robert Holley, 1968 Nobel laureates. c, Hamilton O. Smith and Werner Arber, 1978 Nobel laureates. d, Extraction fo DNA from cells. e, Richard J. Roberts, 1993 Nobel laureate.

No. 559: a, Francis Crick, 1962 Nobel laureate. b, Marshall W. Nirenberg, 1968 Nobel laureate. c, Daniel Nathans, 1978 Nobel laureate. d, Harold E. Varmus and J. Michael Bishop, 1989 Nobel laureates. e, Phillip A. Sharp, 1993 Nobel laureate.

No. 560: a, Maurice H. F. Wilkins, 1962 Nobel laureate. b, DNA strand. c, Frederick Sanger and Walter Gilbert, 1980 Nobel laureates. d, Kary B. Mullis, 1993 Nobel laureate. e, Two DNA strands.

No. 561: a, Four sheep, test tube. b, Two DNA strands, diagram of DNA fragments. c, Paul Berg, 1980 Nobel laureate. d, Michael Smith, 1993 Nobel laureate. e, Deer, DNA strands.

#562, Deer. #563, Dolly, 1st cloned sheep.

Illustration reduced.

2000, May 10 ***Perf. 13¾***

Sheets of 5, #a.-e.

558-561 A163 33c each 3.50 3.50

Souvenir Sheets

562-563 A163 $2 each 4.00 4.00

Nos. 562-563 each contain one 38x50mm stamp.

Marine Life — A164

No. 564: a, Prawn. b, Deep sea angler. c, Rooster fish. d, Grenadier. e, Platyberix opalescens. f, Lantern fish.

No. 565: a, Emperor angelfish. b, Nautilus. c, Moorish idol. d, Sea horse. e, Clown triggerfish. f, Clown fish.

No. 566, Giant squid. No. 567, Manta ray.

Illustration reduced.

2000, May 10 Litho. ***Perf. 14***

Sheets of 6, #a-f

564-565 A164 33c each 4.00 4.00

Souvenir Sheets

566-567 A164 $2 each 4.00 4.00

Millennium — A165

No. 568, horiz. - "2000," hourglass, and map of: a, North Pacific area. b, US and Canada. c, Europe. d, South Pacific. e, South America. f, Southern Africa.

No. 569 - Clock face and: a, Sky. b, Building. c, Cove and lighthouse. d, Barn. e, Forest. f, Desert.

Illustration reduced.

2000, May 25 ***Perf. 13¾***

568 A165 20c Sheet of 6, #a-f 2.40 2.40

569 A165 55c Sheet of 6, #a-f 6.75 6.75

The Stamp Show 2000, London.

New and Recovering Species — A166

No. 570: a, Aleutian Canada goose. b, Western gray kangaroo. c, Palau scops owl. d, Jocotoco antpitta. e, Orchid. f, Red lechwe.

No. 571: a, Bald eagle. b, Small-whorled pogonia. c, Arctic peregrine falcon. d, Golden lion tamarin. e, American alligator. f, Brown pelican.

No. 572, Leopard. No. 573, Lahontan cutthroat trout, horiz.

Illustration reduced.

2000, June 20 ***Perf. 14***

Sheets of 6, #a-f

570-571 A166 33c each 4.00 4.00

Souvenir Sheets

572-573 A166 $2 each 4.00 4.00

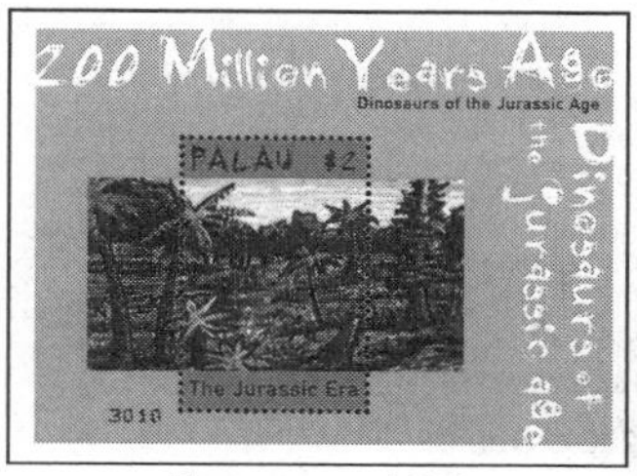

Dinosaurs — A167

No. 574: a, Rhamphorhynchus. b, Ceratosaurus. c, Apatosaurus. d, Stegosaurus. e, Archaeopteryx. f, Allosaurus.

No. 575: a, Parasaurolophus. b, Pteranodon. c, Tyrannosaurus. d, Triceratops. e, Ankylosaurus. f, Velociraptor.

No. 576, Jurassic era view. No. 577, Cretaceous era view.

Illustration reduced.

2000, June 20

574 A167 20c Sheet of 6, #a-f 2.40 2.40

575 A167 33c Sheet of 6, #a-f 4.00 4.00

Souvenir Sheets

576-577 A167 $2 each 4.00 4.00

Queen Mother, 100th Birthday — A168

No. 578, 55c: a, With King George VI. b, Wearing brown hat.

No. 579, 55c: a, Wearing green hat. b, Wearing white hat.

Illustration reduced.

2000, Sept. 1 Litho. ***Perf. 14***

Sheets of 4, 2 each #a-b

578-579 A168 Set of 2 9.00 9.00

Souvenir Sheet

580 A168 $2 Wearing yellow hat 4.00 4.00

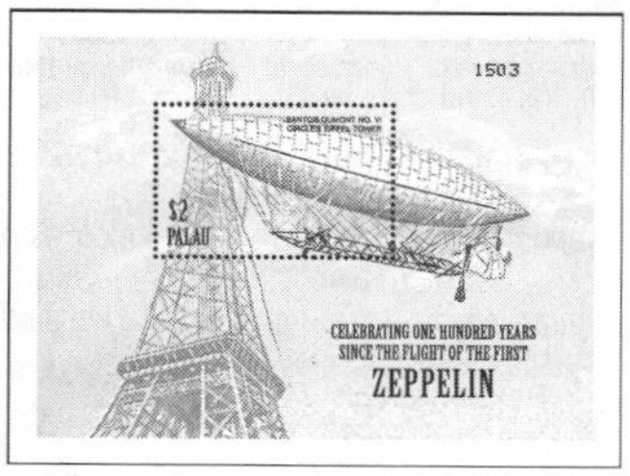

First Zeppelin Flight, Cent. — A169

No. 581: a, Le Jaune. b, Forlanini's Leonardo da Vinci. c, Baldwin's airship. d, Astra-Torres I. e, Parseval PL VII. f, Lebaudy's Liberte.

No. 582, $2, Santos-Dumont No. VI. No. 583, $2, Santos-Dumont Baladeuse No. 9.

Illustration reduced.

2000, Sept. 1

581 A169 55c Sheet of 6, #a-f 6.75 6.75

Souvenir Sheets

582-583 A169 Set of 2 8.00 8.00

Millennium Type of 2000

Sheet of 17

Undersea History and Exploration: a, Viking diver. b, Arab diver Issa. c, Salvage diver. d, Diver. e, Diving bell. f, Turtle. g, Siebe helmet. h, C.S.S. Hunley. i, Argonaut. j, Photosphere. k, Helmet diver. l, Bathysphere. m, Coelacanth. n, WWII charioteers. o, Trieste. p, Alvin visits geothermal vents (60x40mm). q, Jim suit.

2000, Oct. 16 ***Perf. 12¾x12½***

584 A155 33c #a-q + label 11.50 11.50

Photomosaic of Pope John Paul II — A170

Various photos with religious themes. Illustration reduced.

2000, Dec. 1 ***Perf. 13¾***

585 A170 50c Sheet of 8, #a-h 8.00 8.00

Souvenir Sheets

New Year 2001 (Year of the Snake) — A171

Snake color: #586, Black. #587, Red.

Illustration reduced.

2000, Dec. 1 ***Perf. 14¼***

586-587 A171 60c Set of 2 2.40 2.40

Pacific Ocean Marine Life — A172

No. 588: a, Scalloped hammerhead shark. b, Whitetip reef shark. c, Moon jellyfish. d, Lionfish. e, Seahorse. f, Spotted eagle ray.

Illustration reduced.

2000 ***Perf. 14½x14¼***

588 A172 55c Sheet of 6, #a-f 6.75 6.75

Atlantic Ocean Fish — A173

No. 589, horiz.: a, Reef bass. b, White shark. c, Sharptail eel. d, Sailfish. e, Southern stingray. f, Ocean triggerfish.

#590, Short bigeye. #591, Gafftopsail catfish.

Illustration reduced.

2000 ***Perf. 13¾***

589 A173 20c Sheet of 6, #a-f 2.40 2.40

Souvenir Sheets

590-591 A173 $2 Set of 2 8.00 8.00

Pacific Arts Festival — A174

No. 592: a, Dancers, by S. Adelbai. b, Story Board Art, by D. Inabo. c, Traditional Money, by M. Takeshi. d, Clay Lamp and Bowl, by W. Watanabe. e, Meeting House, by Pasqual Tiakl. f, Outrigger Canoe, by S. Adelbai. g, Weaver, by M. Vitarelli. h, Rock Island Scene, by W. Marcil. i, Contemporary Music, by J. Imetuker.

2000, Nov. 1 Litho. *Perf. 14¼*

592 A174 33c Sheet of 9, #a-i 6.00 6.00

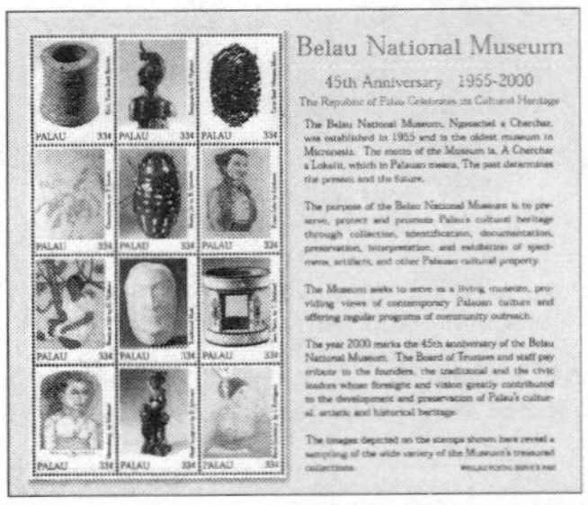

National Museum, 45th Anniv. — A175

No. 593: a, Klilt, turtle shell bracelet. b, Sculpture by H. Hijikata. c, Turtle shell women's money. d, Cherecheroi, by T. Suzuki. e, Money jar, by B. Sylvester. f, Prince Lebu by Ichikawa. g, Beach at Lild, by H. Hijikata. h, Traditional mask. i, Taro platter, by T. Rebluud. j, Meresebang, by Ichikawa. k, Wood sculpture, by B. Sylvester. l, Birth Ceremony, by I. Kishigawa.

2000, Nov. 1 *Perf. 14x14¾*

593 A175 33c Sheet of 12, #a-l 8.00 8.00

Butterflies A176

Designs: No. 594, 33c, Indian red admiral. No. 595, 33c, Fiery jewel. No. 596, 33c, Checkered swallowtail. No. 597, 33c, Yamfly.

No. 598, 33c: a, Large green-banded blue. b, Union Jack. c, Broad-bordered grass yellow. d, Striped blue crow. e, Red lacewing. f, Palmfly.

No. 599, 33c: a, Cairn's birdwing. b, Meadow argus. c, Orange albatross. d, Glasswing. e, Beak. f, Great eggfly.

No. 600, $2, Clipper. No. 601, $2, Blue triangle.

2000, Dec. 15 *Perf. 14*

594-597 A176 Set of 4 2.75 2.75

Sheets of 6, #a-f

598-599 A176 Set of 2 8.00 8.00

Souvenir Sheets

600-601 A176 Set of 2 8.00 8.00

Flora and Fauna — A177

No. 602, 33c: a, Giant spiral ginger. b, Good luck plant. c, Ti tree, coconuts. d, Butterfly. e, Saltwater crocodile. f, Orchid.

No. 603, 33c: a, Little kingfisher. b, Mangrove snake. c, Bats, breadfruit. d, Giant tree frog. e, Giant centipede. f, Crab-eating macaque.

No. 604, $2, Soft coral, surgeonfish. No. 605, $2, Land crab, vert.

2000, Dec. 29 *Perf. 14x14¼, 14¼x14*

Sheets of 6, #a-f

602-603 A177 Set of 2 8.00 8.00

Souvenir Sheets

604-605 A177 Set of 2 8.00 8.00

Personalities Type of 1999

Design: 11c, Lazarus Salil.

2001 Litho. *Perf. 14x14¾*

606 A142 11c purple .25 .25

Personalities Type of 1999

Designs: 70c, Gen. Douglas MacArthur. 80c, Adm. Chester W. Nimitz. $12.25, John F. Kennedy.

2001, June 10 Litho. *Perf. 14x14¾*

607 A142	70c lilac		1.40	1.40
608 A142	80c green		1.60	1.60
609 A142	$12.25 red		25.00	25.00
	Nos. 607-609 (3)		28.00	28.00

Phila Nippon '01, Japan — A178

No. 610, 60c: a, Ono no Komachi Washing the Copybook, by Kiyomitsu Torii. b, Woman Playing Samisen and Woman Reading al Letter, by School of Matabei Iwasa. c, The Actor Danjura Ichikawa V as a Samurai in a Wrestling Arena Striking a Pose on a Go Board, by Shunsho Katsukawa. d, Gentleman Entertained by Courtesans, by Kiyonaga Torii. e, Geisha at a Teahouse in Shinagawa, by Kiyonaga Torii.

No. 611, 60c: a, Preparing Sashimi, by Utamaro. b, Ichimatsu Sanogawa I as Sogo no Goro and Kikugoro Onoe as Kyo no Jiro in Umewakana Futaba Soga, by Toyonobu Ishikawa. c, Courtesan Adjusting Her Comb, by Dohan Kaigetsudo. d, The Actor Tomijuro Nakamura I in a Female Role Dancing, by Shunsho Katsukawa. e, Woman with Poem Card and Writing Brush, by Gakutei Yashima.

No. 612, Six panels of screen, Kitano Shrine in Kyoto, by unknown artist.

No. 613, $2, Raiko Attacks a Demon Kite, by Hokkei Totoya. No. 614, $2, Beauty Writing a Letter, by Doshin Kaigetsudo. No. 615, $2, Fireworks at Ikenohata, by Kiyochika Kobayashi.

2001, Aug. 13 Litho. *Perf. 14*

Sheets of 5, #a-e

610-611 A178 Set of 2 12.00 12.00

612 A178 60c Sheet of 6, #a-f 7.25 7.25

Souvenir Sheets

613-615 A178 Set of 3 12.00 12.00

Moths — A179

Designs: 20c, Veined tiger moth. 21c, Basker moth. 80c, White-lined sphinx moth. $1, Isabella tiger moth.

No. 620, 34c: a, Cinnabar moth. b, Beautiful tiger moth. c, Great tiger moth. d, Provence burnet moth. e, Jersey tiger moth. f, Ornate moth.

No. 621, 70c: a, Hoop pine moth. b, King's bee hawk moth. c, Banded bagnest moth. d, Io moth. e, Tau emperor moth. f, Lime hawkmoth.

No. 622, $2, Spanish moon moth. No. 623, $2, Owl moth.

2001, Oct. 15 Litho. *Perf. 14*

616-619 A179 Set of 4 4.50 4.50

Sheets of 6, #a-f

620-621 A179 Set of 2 12.50 12.50

Souvenir Sheets

622-623 A179 Set of 2 8.00 8.00

Nobel Prizes, Cent. — A180

Literature laureates - No. 624, 34c: a, Ivo Andric, 1961. b, Eyvind Johnson, 1974. c, Salvatore Quasimodo, 1959. d, Mikhail Sholokhov, 1965. e, Pablo Neruda, 1971. f, Saul Bellow, 1976.

No. 625, 70c: a, Boris Pasternak, 1958. b, Francois Mauriac, 1952. c, Frans Eemil Sillanpää, 1939. d, Roger Martin du Gard, 1937. e, Pearl Buck, 1938. f, André Gide, 1947.

No. 626, 80c: a, Karl Gjellerup, 1917. b, Anatole France, 1921. c, Sinclair Lewis, 1930. d, Jacinto Benavente, 1922. e, John Galsworthy, 1932. f, Erik. A. Karlfeldt, 1931.

No. 627, $2, Luigi Pirandello, 1934. No. 628, $2, Bertrand Russell, 1950. No. 629, Harry Martinson, 1974.

2001, Oct. 30

Sheets of 6, #a-f

624-626 A180 Set of 3 22.50 22.50

Souvenir Sheets

627-629 A180 Set of 3 12.00 12.00

2002 World Cup Soccer Championships, Japan and Korea — A181

No. 630, 34c - World Cup posters from: a, 1950. b, 1954. c, 1958. d, 1962. e, 1966. f, 1970.

No. 631, 80c - World Cup posters from: a, 1978. b, 1982. c, 1986. d, 1990. e, 1994. f, 1998.

No. 632, $2, World Cup poster, 1930. No. 633, $2, Head and globe from World Cup trophy.

2001, Nov. 29 *Perf. 13¾x14¼*

Sheets of 6, #a-f

630-631 A181 Set of 2 14.00 14.00

Souvenir Sheets

Perf. 14½x14¼

632-633 A181 Set of 2 8.00 8.00

Christmas — A182

Denominations: 20c, 34c.

2001, Nov. 29 *Perf. 14*

634-635 A182 Set of 2 1.10 1.10

Queen Mother Type of 1999 Redrawn

No. 636: a, In Australia, 1958. b, In 1960. c, In 1970. d, In 1987.

$2, Holding book, 1947.

2001, Dec. 13 *Perf. 14*

Yellow Orange Frames

636 A150 60c Sheet of 4, #a-d, + label 4.75 4.75

Souvenir Sheet

Perf. 13¾

637 A150 $2 black 4.00 4.00

Queen Mother's 101st birthday. No. 637 contains one 38x51mm stamp that is slightly darker than that found on No. 523. Sheet margins of Nos. 636-637 lack embossing and gold arms and frames found on Nos. 522-523.

Pasturing Horses, by Han Kan — A183

2001, Dec. 17 *Perf. 14x14¾*

638 A183 60c multi 1.25 1.25

New Year 2002 (Year of the Horse). Printed in sheets of 4.

Birds — A184

No. 639, 55c: a, Yellow-faced myna. b, Red-bellied pitta. c, Red-bearded bee-eater. d, Superb fruit dove. e, Coppersmith barbet. f, Diard's trogon.
No. 640, 60c: a, Spectacled monarch. b, Banded pitta. c, Rufous-backed kingfisher. d, Scarlet robin. e, Golden whistler. f, Jewel babbler.
No. 641, $2, Paradise flycatcher. No. 642, $2, Common kingfisher.

2001, Dec. 26 ***Perf. 14***

Sheets of 6, #a-f

639-640	A184	Set of 2	14.00 14.00

Souvenir Sheets
Perf. 14¾

641-642	A184	Set of 2	8.00 8.00

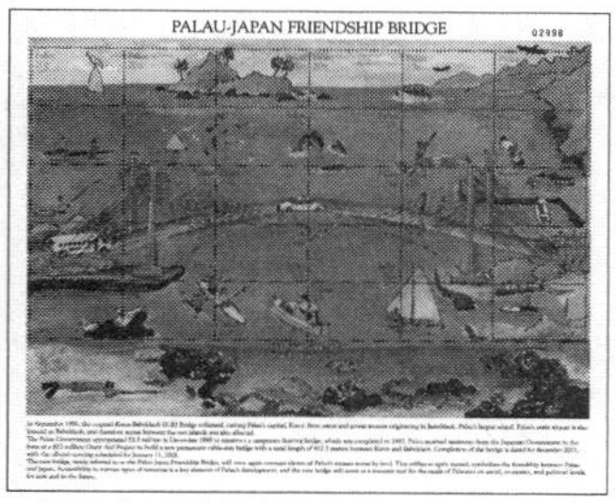

Opening of Palau-Japan Frendship Bridge — A185

No. 643, 20c; No. 644, 34c: a, Bird on orange rock. b, Island, one palm tree. c, Island, three palm trees. d, Rocks, boat prow. e, Boat, bat. f, Cove, foliage. g, Red boat with two people. h, Buoy, birds. i, Birds, dolphin's tail. j, Dolphins. k, Person on raft. l, Two people standing in water. m, Person with fishing pole in water. n, Bridge tower. o, Bicyclist, taxi. p, Front of taxi. q, People walking on bridge, bridge tower. r, Truck, boat. s, School bus. t, Base of bridge tower. u, Birds under bridge, oar. v, Birds under bridge. w, Base of bridge tower, tip of sail. x, Motorcyclist. y, Birds on black rock. z, Kayakers. aa, Kayak, boat. ab, Boat, sailboat. ac, Sailboat, jetty. ad, Jetski.

2002, Jan. 11 ***Perf. 13***

Sheets of 30, #a-ad

643-644	A185	Set of 2	32.50 32.50

United We Stand — A186

2002, Jan. 24 ***Perf. 14***

645	A186	$1 multi	2.00 2.00

Reign of Queen Elizabeth II, 50th Anniv. — A187

No. 646: a, In uniform. b, Wearing flowered hat. c, Prince Philip. d, Wearing tiara.
$2, Wearing white dress.

2002, Feb. 6 ***Perf. 14¼***

646	A187	80c Sheet of 4, #a-d	6.50 6.50

Souvenir Sheet

647	A187	$2 multi	4.00 4.00

Birds — A188

Designs: 1c, Gray-backed white-eye. 2c, Great frigatebird. 3c, Eclectus parrot. 4c, Red-footed booby. 5c Cattle egret. 10c, Cardinal honeyeater. 11c, Blue-faced parrot-finch. 15c, Rufous fantail. 20c, White-faced storm petrel. 21c, Willie wagtail. 23c, Black-headed gull. 50c, Sanderling. 57c, White-tailed tropicbird. 70c, Rainbow lorikeet. 80c, Moorhen. $1, Buff-banded rail. $2, Beach thick-knee. $3, Common tern. $3.50, Ruddy turnstone. $3.95, White-collared kingfisher. $5, Sulphur-crested cockatoo. $10, Barn swallow.

2002, Feb. 20 ***Perf. 14¼***

648	A188	1c	multi	.20 .20
649	A188	2c	multi	.20 .20
650	A188	3c	multi	.20 .20
651	A188	4c	multi	.20 .20
652	A188	5c	multi	.20 .20
653	A188	10c	multi	.20 .20
654	A188	11c	multi	.20 .20
655	A188	15c	multi	.30 .30
656	A188	20c	multi	.40 .40
657	A188	21c	multi	.40 .40
658	A188	23c	multi	.45 .45
659	A188	50c	multi	1.00 1.00
660	A188	57c	multi	1.10 1.10
661	A188	70c	multi	1.40 1.40
662	A188	80c	multi	1.60 1.60
663	A188	$1	multi	2.00 2.00
664	A188	$2	multi	4.00 4.00
665	A188	$3	multi	6.00 6.00
666	A188	$3.50	multi	7.00 7.00
667	A188	$3.95	multi	8.00 8.00
668	A188	$5	multi	10.00 10.00
669	A188	$10	multi	20.00 20.00
	Nos. 648-669 (22)			65.05 65.05

Flowers — A189

Designs: 20c, Euanthe sanderiana. 34c, Ophiorrhiza palauensis. No. 672, 60c, Cerbera manghas. 80c, Mendinilla pterocaula.
No. 674, 60c: a, Bruguiera gymnorhiza. b, Samadera indiccal. c, Maesa canfieldiae. d, Lumnitzera litorea. e, Dolichandrone palawense. f, Limnophila aromatica (red and white orchids).
No. 675, 60c: a, Sonneratia alba. b, Barringtonia racemosa. c, Ixora casei. d, Tristellateia australasiae. e, Nepenthes mirabilis. f, Limnophila aromatica (pink flowers).
No. 676, $2, Fagraea ksid. No. 677, $2, Cerbera manghas, horiz.

2002, Mar. 4 ***Perf. 14***

670-673	A189	Set of 4	4.00 4.00

Sheets of 6, #a-f

674-675	A189	Set of 2	14.50 14.50

Souvenir Sheets

676-677	A189	Set of 2	8.00 8.00

2002 Winter Olympics, Salt Lake City A190

Skier with: No. 678, $1, Blue pants. No. 679, $1, Yellow pants.

2002, Mar. 18 ***Perf. 14¼***

678-679	A190	Set of 2	4.00 4.00
679a		Souvenir sheet, #678-679	4.00 4.00

Cats and Dogs — A191

No. 680, 50c, horiz.: a, Himalayan. b, Norwegian forest cat. c, Havana. d, Exotic shorthair. e, Persian. f, Maine coon cat.
No. 681, 50c, horiz.: a, Great Dane. b, Whippet. c, Bedlington terrier. d, Golden retriever. e, Papillon. f, Doberman pinscher.
No. 682, $2, British shorthair. No. 683, $2, Shetland sheepdog.

2002, Mar. 18 **Litho.** ***Perf. 14***

Sheets of 6, #a-f

680-681	A191	Set of 2	12.00 12.00

Souvenir Sheets

682-683	A191	Set of 2	8.00 8.00

SEMI-POSTAL STAMPS

Olympic Sports SP1

1988, Aug. 8 **Litho.** ***Perf. 14***

B1	SP1	25c +5c Baseball glove, player	.50 .50
B2	SP1	25c +5c Running shoe, athlete	.50 .50
a.		Pair, #B1-B2	1.00 1.00
B3	SP1	45c +5c Goggles, swimmer	1.25 1.25
B4	SP1	45c +5c Gold medal, diver	1.25 1.25
a.		Pair, #B3-B4	2.50 2.50

AIR POST STAMPS

White-tailed Tropicbird — AP1

1984, June 12 **Litho.** ***Perf. 14***

C1	AP1	40c shown	.75 .75
C2	AP1	40c Fairy tern	.75 .75
C3	AP1	40c Black noddy	.75 .75
C4	AP1	40c Black-naped tern	.75 .75
a.		Block of 4, #C1-C4	3.00 3.00

Audubon Type of 1985

1985, Feb. 6 **Litho.** ***Perf. 14***

C5	A12	44c Audubon's Shearwater	1.10 1.10

Palau-Germany Political, Economic & Cultural Exchange Cent. — AP2

Germany Nos. 40, 65, Caroline Islands Nos. 19, 13 and: No. C6, German flag-raising at Palau, 1885. No. C7, Early German trading post in Angaur. No. C8, Abai architecture recorded by Prof. & Frau Kramer, 1908-1910. No. C9, S.M.S. Cormoran.

1985, Sept. 19 **Litho.** ***Perf. 14x13½***

C6	AP2	44c multicolored	.90 .90
C7	AP2	44c multicolored	.90 .90
C8	AP2	44c multicolored	.90 .90
C9	AP2	44c multicolored	.90 .90
a.		Block of 4, #C6-C9	3.75 3.75

Trans-Pacific Airmail Anniv. Type of 1985

Aircraft: No. C10, 1951 Trans-Ocean Airways PBY-5A Catalina Amphibian. No. C11, 1968 Air Micronesia DC-6B Super Cloudmaster. No. C12, 1960 Trust Territory Airline SA-16 Albatross. No. C13, 1967 Pan American Douglas DC-4.

1985, Nov. 21 **Litho.** ***Perf. 14***

C10	A16	44c multicolored	.85 .85
C11	A16	44c multicolored	.85 .85
C12	A16	44c multicolored	.85 .85
C13	A16	44c multicolored	.85 .85
a.		Block of 4, #C10-C13	3.50 3.50

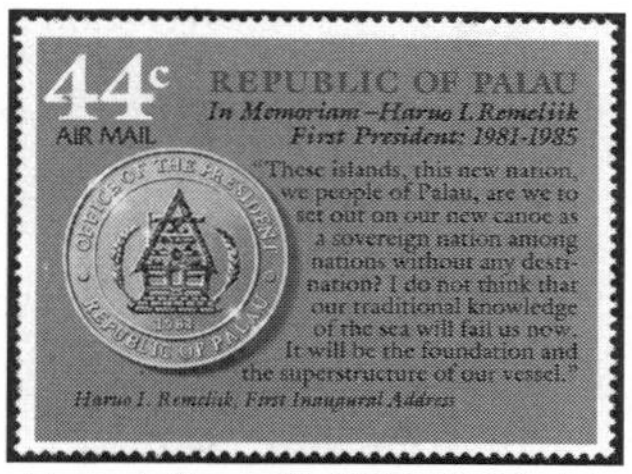

Haruo I. Remeliik (1933-1985), 1st President — AP3

Designs: No. C14, Presidential seal, excerpt from 1st inaugural address. No. C15, War canoe, address excerpt, diff. No. C16, Remeliik, US Pres. Reagan, excerpt from Reagan's speech, Pacific Basin Conference, Guam, 1984.

1986, June 30 **Litho.** ***Perf. 14***

C14	AP3	44c multicolored	1.10 1.10
C15	AP3	44c multicolored	1.10 1.10
C16	AP3	44c multicolored	1.10 1.10
a.		Strip of 3, #C14-C16	3.50 3.50

Intl. Peace Year, Statue of Liberty Cent. — AP4

1986, Sept. 19 **Litho.**

C17	AP4	44c multicolored	.90 .90

Aircraft — AP5

Birds — AP6

1989, May 17 Litho. ***Perf. 14x14½***

C18	AP5 36c Cessna 207 Skywagon	.65	.65
a.	Booklet pane of 10	6.50	—
C19	AP5 39c Embraer EMB-110 Bandeirante	.85	.85
a.	Booklet pane of 10	7.25	—
C20	AP5 45c Boeing 727	1.00	1.00
a.	Booklet pane of 10	8.00	—
b.	Booklet pane, 5 each 36c, 45c	7.50	—
	Nos. C18-C20 (3)	2.50	2.50

Palauan Bai Type

1991, July 9 Litho. ***Die Cut***

Self-Adhesive

C21	A61 50c like #293a	1.50	1.50

World War II in the Pacific Type

Miniature Sheet

Aircraft: No. C23: a, Grumman TBF Avenger, US Navy. b, Curtiss P-40C, Chinese Air Force "Flying Tigers." c, Mitsubishi A6M Zero-Sen, Japan. d, Hawker Hurricane, Royal Air Force. e, Consolidated PBY Catalina, Royal Netherlands Indies Air Force. f, Curtiss Hawk 75, Netherlands Indies. g, Boeing B-17E, US Army Air Force. h, Brewster Buffalo, Royal Australian Air Force. i, Supermarine Walrus, Royal Navy. j, Curtiss P-40E, Royal New Zealand Air Force.

1992, Sept. 10 Litho. ***Perf. 14½x15***

C22	A66 50c Sheet of 10, #a.-j.	10.00	10.00

1994, Mar. 24 Litho. ***Perf. 14***

a, Palau swiftlet. b, Barn swallow. c, Jungle nightjar. d, White-breasted woodswallow.

C23	AP6 50c Block of 4, #a.-d.	3.75	3.75

No. C23 is printed in sheets of 16 stamps.

PALESTINE

'pa-lə-ˌstin

LOCATION — Western Asia bordering on the Mediterranean Sea
GOVT. — Former British Mandate
AREA — 10,429 sq. mi.
POP. — 1,605,816 (estimated)
CAPITAL — Jerusalem

Formerly a part of Turkey, Palestine was occupied by the Egyptian Expeditionary Forces of the British Army in World War I and was mandated to Great Britain in 1923. Mandate ended May 14, 1948.

10 Milliemes = 1 Piaster
1000 Milliemes = 1 Egyptian Pound
1000 Mils = 1 Palestine Pound (1928)

Jordan stamps overprinted with "Palestine" in English and Arabic are listed under Jordan.

Watermark

Wmk33

Issued under British Military Occupation

For use in Palestine, Transjordan, Lebanon, Syria and in parts of Cilicia and northeastern Egypt

A1

Wmk. Crown and "GvR" (33)

1918, Feb. 10 Litho. ***Rouletted 20***

1	A1 1pi deep blue	190.00	100.00
2	A1 1pi ultra	2.75	2.75

Nos. 2 & 1 Surcharged in Black

1918, Feb. 16

3	A1 5m on 1pi ultra	6.00	4.25
a.	5m on 1pi gray blue	110.00	*700.00*

Nos. 1 and 3a were issued without gum. No. 3a is on paper with a surface sheen.

1918 Typo. ***Perf. 15x14***

4	A1	1m dark brown	.20	.20
5	A1	2m blue green	.20	.20
6	A1	3m light brown	.25	.30
7	A1	4m scarlet	.30	.35
8	A1	5m orange	.30	.30
9	A1	1pi indigo	.30	.20
10	A1	2pi olive green	.50	.40
11	A1	5pi plum	1.50	1.60
12	A1	9pi bister	2.50	3.50
13	A1	10pi ultramarine	2.50	3.50
14	A1	20pi gray	10.00	13.00
		Nos. 4-14 (11)	18.55	23.55

Many shades exist.

Nos. 4-11 exist with rough perforation.

Issued: 1m, 2m, 4m, 2pi, 5pi, 7/16; 5m, 9/25; 1pi, 11/9; 3m, 9pi, 10pi, 12/17; 20pi, 12/27.

Nos. 4-11 with overprint "O. P. D. A." (Ottoman Public Debt Administration) or "H.J.Z." (Hejaz-Jemen Railway) are revenue stamps; they exist postally used.

For overprints on stamps and types see #15-62 & Jordan #1-63, 73-90, 92-102, 130-144, J12-J23.

Issued under British Administration

Overprinted at Jerusalem

Stamps and Type of 1918 Overprinted in Black or Silver

1920, Sept. 1 Wmk. 33 ***Perf. 15x14***

Arabic Overprint 8mm long

15	A1	1m dark brown	1.25	1.25
16	A1	2m bl grn, perf 14	1.00	1.10
d.		Perf 15x14	7.00	4.00
17	A1	3m lt brown	3.00	3.25
d.		Perf 14	45.00	*40.00*
e.		Inverted overprint	400.00	*600.00*
18	A1	4m scarlet	1.25	1.50
19	A1	5m org, perf 14	1.25	.75
e.		Perf 15x14	10.00	4.00
20	A1	1pi indigo (S)	1.00	.60
21	A1	2pi olive green	1.75	1.75
22	A1	5pi plum	9.00	12.00
23	A1	9pi bister	10.00	14.00
24	A1	10pi ultra	10.00	13.50
25	A1	20pi gray	20.00	32.50
		Nos. 15-25 (11)	59.50	82.20

Forgeries exist of No. 17e.

Similar Overprint, with Arabic Line 10mm Long, Arabic "S" and "T" Joined, ".." at Left Extends Above Other Letters

1920-21 ***Perf. 15x14***

15a	A1	1m dark brown	.50	.75
e.		Perf. 14	625.00	750.00
g.		As "a," invtd. ovpt.		
16a	A1	2m blue green	2.25	2.75
e.		"PALESTINE" omitted	*2,500.*	*1,500.*
f.		Perf. 14	2.50	3.50
17a	A1	3m light brown	.50	.75
18a	A1	4m scarlet	.85	1.10
b.		Perf. 14	67.50	80.00
19a	A1	5m orange	1.75	.60
f.		Perf. 14	1.50	1.00
20a	A1	1pi indigo, perf. 14 (S) ('21)	25.00	1.75
d.		Perf. 15x14	650.00	30.00
21a	A1	2pi olive green ('21)	65.00	30.00
22a	A1	5pi plum ('21)	20.00	8.00
d.		Perf. 14	200.00	*750.00*
		Nos. 15a-22a (8)	115.85	45.70

This overprint often looks grayish to grayish black. In the English line the letters are frequently uneven and damaged.

Similar Overprint, with Arabic Line 10mm Long, Arabic "S" and "T" Separated and 6mm Between English and Hebrew Lines

1920, Dec. 6

15b	A1	1m dk brn, perf 14	22.50	30.00
17b	A1	3m lt brn, perf 15x14	27.50	35.00
19b	A1	5m orange, perf 14	400.00	30.00
d.		Perf. 15x14	*19,000.*	*17,500.*
		Nos. 15b-19b (3)	450.00	95.00

Overprinted as Before, 7½mm Between English and Hebrew Lines, ".." at Left Even With Other Letters

1921 ***Perf. 15x14***

15c	A1	1m dark brown	5.00	2.00
f.		1m dull brown, perf 14		*2,500.*
16c	A1	2m blue green	6.00	3.25
17c	A1	3m light brown	15.00	1.50
18c	A1	4m scarlet	12.00	1.50
19c	A1	5m orange	15.00	.75
20c	A1	1pi indigo (S)	15.00	.70
21c	A1	2pi olive green	20.00	5.00
22c	A1	5pi plum	17.00	8.00
23c	A1	9pi bister	30.00	*90.00*
24c	A1	10pi ultra	30.00	15.00
25c	A1	20pi pale gray	90.00	55.00
d.		Perf. 14	*17,500.*	*2,500.*
		Nos. 15c-25c (11)	255.00	*182.70*

Overprinted at London

Stamps of 1918 Overprinted

1921 ***Perf. 15x14***

37	A1	1m dark brown	.30	.25
38	A1	2m blue green	.30	.25
39	A1	3m light brown	.30	.25
40	A1	4m scarlet	1.00	.50
41	A1	5m orange	.30	.20
42	A1	1pi bright blue	.55	.20
43	A1	2pi olive green	1.10	.50
44	A1	5pi plum	5.00	5.50
45	A1	9pi bister	16.00	16.00
46	A1	10pi ultra	18.00	*750.00*
47	A1	20pi gray	47.50	*2,000.*
		Nos. 37-47 (11)	90.35	
		Nos. 37-45 (9)		23.65

The 2nd character from left on bottom line that looks like quotation marks consists of long thin lines.

Deformed or damaged letters exist in all three lines of the overprint.

Similar Overprint on Type of 1921

1922 Wmk. 4 ***Perf. 14***

48	A1	1m dark brown	.20	.20
a.		Inverted overprint		*15,000.*
b.		Double overprint	200.00	400.00
49	A1	2m yellow	.40	.20
50	A1	3m Prus blue	.25	.20
51	A1	4m rose	.20	.20
52	A1	5m orange	.35	.20
53	A1	6m blue green	.50	.20
54	A1	7m yellow brown	.60	.20
55	A1	8m red	.55	.20
56	A1	1pi gray	.55	.20
57	A1	13m ultra	.60	.20
58	A1	2pi olive green	1.00	.25
a.		Inverted overprint	325.00	*475.00*
b.		2pi yellow bister	*125.00*	*6.00*
59	A1	5pi plum	5.00	1.00
a.		Perf. 15x14	30.00	3.50

Perf. 15x14

60	A1	9pi bister	10.00	9.00
a.		Perf. 14	1,300.	200.00
61	A1	10pi light blue	9.00	5.00
a.		Perf. 14	25.00	9.00
62	A1	20pi violet	7.50	4.00
a.		Perf. 14	175.00	85.00
		Nos. 48-62 (15)	36.70	21.25

The 2nd character from left on bottom line that looks like quotation marks consists of short thick lines.

The "E. F. F." for "E. E. F." on No. 61 is caused by damaged type.

Rachel's Tomb — A3

Mosque of Omar (Dome of the Rock) — A4

Citadel at Jerusalem A5

Tiberias and Sea of Galilee A6

1927-42 Typo. ***Perf. 13½x14½***

63	A3	2m Prus blue	.20	.20
64	A3	3m yellow green	.20	.20
65	A4	4m rose red	1.10	.35
66	A4	4m violet brn ('32)	.20	.20
67	A5	5m brown org	.20	.20
c.		Perf. 14½x14 (coil stamp) ('36)	2.25	2.75
68	A4	6m deep green	.20	.20
69	A5	7m deep red	1.40	.25
70	A5	7m dk violet ('32)	.20	.20
71	A4	8m yellow brown	8.00	4.00
72	A4	8m scarlet ('32)	.25	.20
73	A3	10m deep gray	.20	.20
a.		Perf. 14½x14 (coil stamp) ('38)	2.50	3.00
74	A4	13m ultra	2.00	.20
75	A4	13m olive bister ('32)	.20	.20
76	A4	15m ultra ('32)	.20	.20
77	A5	20m olive green	.20	.20

Perf. 14

78	A6	50m violet brown	.50	.20
79	A6	90m bister	50.00	40.00
80	A6	100m bright blue	.60	.20
81	A6	200m dk violet	1.00	.55
82	A6	250m dp brown ('42)	2.00	1.00
83	A6	500m red ('42)	1.90	1.60
84	A6	£1 gray black ('42)	3.00	2.50
		Nos. 63-84 (22)	73.75	53.05

Issued: 3m, #74, 6/1; 2m, 5m, 6m, 10m, #65, 69, 71, 77-81, 8/14; #70, 72, 6/1/32; #75, 15m, 8/1/32; #66, 11/1/32; #82-84, 1/15/42.

POSTAGE DUE STAMPS

D1

1923 Unwmk. Typo. ***Perf. 11***

J1	D1	1m bister brown	12.50	*15.00*
b.		Horiz. pair, imperf. btwn.	1,300.	
J2	D1	2m green	8.00	8.00
J3	D1	4m red	7.00	*8.00*
J4	D1	8m violet	4.50	*6.00*
b.		Horiz. pair, imperf. btwn.		*1,800.*
J5	D1	13m dark blue	4.50	*5.00*
a.		Horiz. pair, imperf. btwn.	850.00	
		Nos. J1-J5 (5)	36.50	*42.00*

Imperfs. of 1m, 2m, 8m, are from proof sheets.

Values for Nos. J1-J5 are for fine centered copies.

D2

D3

1924, Dec. 1 **Wmk. 4**

J6	D2	1m brown	.90	.90
J7	D2	2m yellow	1.00	1.00
J8	D2	4m green	1.10	.90
J9	D2	8m red	1.50	.45
J10	D2	13m ultramarine	3.50	2.25
J11	D2	5pi violet	8.00	1.50
		Nos. J6-J11 (6)	16.00	7.00

1928-45 ***Perf. 14***

J12	D3	1m lt brown	.35	.30
a.		Perf. 15x14 ('45)	21.00	37.50
J13	D3	2m yellow	.45	.50
J14	D3	4m green	.50	.65
a.		4m bluish grn, perf. 15x14 ('45)	30.00	*45.00*
J15	D3	6m brown org ('33)	1.00	1.00
J16	D3	8m red	.65	.60
J17	D3	10m light gray	.65	.45
J18	D3	13m ultra	1.50	1.00
J19	D3	20m olive green	1.40	1.00
J20	D3	50m violet	1.50	1.00
		Nos. J12-J20 (9)	8.00	6.50

The Hebrew word for "mil" appears below the numeral on all values but the 1m.

Issued: 6m, Oct. 1933; others, Feb. 1, 1928.

PALESTINIAN AUTHORITY

LOCATION — Areas of the West Bank and the Gaza Strip.
AREA — 2,410 sq. mi.
POP. — 2,825,000 (2000 est.)

1000 Fils (Mils) = 5 Israeli Shekels
1000 Fils = 1 Jordanian Dinar (Jan. 1, 1998)

Catalogue values for all unused stamps in this country are for Never Hinged items.

Hisham Palace, Jericho A1

5m, 10m, 20m, Hisham Palace. 30m, 40m, 50m, 75m, Mosque, Jerusalem. 125, 150m, 250m, 300m, 500m, Flag. 1000m, Dome of the Rock.

1994 **Litho.** ***Perf. 14***

1	A1	5m multicolored	.20	.20
2	A1	10m multicolored	.20	.20
3	A1	20m multicolored	.20	.20
4	A1	30m multicolored	.20	.20
5	A1	40m multicolored	.25	.25
6	A1	50m multicolored	.30	.30
7	A1	75m multicolored	.35	.35
8	A1	125m multicolored	.40	.40
9	A1	150m multicolored	.50	.50
10	A1	250m multicolored	.90	.90
11	A1	300m multicolored	1.25	1.25

Size: 51x29mm

12	A1	500m multicolored	2.25	2.25
13	A1	1000m multicolored	4.00	4.00
		Nos. 1-13 (13)	11.00	11.00

Issued: 125m-500m, 8/15; others, 9/1.

Nos. 1-13 Surcharged "FILS" in English and Arabic in Black or Silver and with Black Bars Obliterating "Mils"

1995, Apr. 10 **Litho.** ***Perf. 14***

14	A1	5f multicolored	.20	.20
15	A1	10f multicolored	.20	.20
16	A1	20f multicolored	.20	.20
17	A1	30f multicolored (S)	.20	.20
18	A1	40f multicolored (S)	.20	.20
19	A1	50f multicolored (S)	.25	.25
20	A1	75f multicolored (S)	.35	.35
21	A1	125f multicolored	.50	.50
22	A1	150f multicolored	.60	.60
23	A1	250f multicolored	1.00	1.00
24	A1	300f multicolored	1.10	1.10

Size: 51x29mm

25	A1	500f multicolored	2.00	2.00
26	A1	1000f multicolored	3.50	3.50
		Nos. 14-26 (13)	10.30	10.30

Palestine No. 63 — A2

350f, Palestine #67. 500f, Palestine #72.

1995, May 17 **Litho.** ***Perf. 14***

27	A2	150f multicolored	.55	.55
28	A2	350f multicolored	1.25	1.25
29	A2	500f multicolored	1.90	1.90
		Nos. 27-29 (3)	3.70	3.70

Traditional Costumes — A3

Christmas — A4

Women wearing various costumes.

1995, May 31

30	A3	250f multicolored	.80	.80
31	A3	300f multicolored	.95	.95
32	A3	550f multicolored	1.75	1.75
33	A3	900f multicolored	2.75	2.75
		Nos. 30-33 (4)	6.25	6.25

1995, Dec. 18

Designs: 10f, Ancient view of Bethlehem. 20f, Modern view of Bethlehem. 50f, Entrance to grotto, Church of the Nativity. 100f, Yasser Arafat, Pope John Paul II. 1000f, Star of the Nativity, Church of the Nativity, Bethlehem.

10f, 20f, 100f, 1000f are horiz.

34	A4	10f multicolored	.20	.20
35	A4	20f multicolored	.20	.20
36	A4	50f multicolored	.20	.20
37	A4	100f multicolored	.40	.40
38	A4	1000f multicolored	3.50	3.50
		Nos. 34-38 (5)	4.50	4.50

Pres. Yasser Arafat — A5

1996, Mar. 20

39	A5	10f red violet & bluish black	.20	.20
40	A5	20f yellow & bluish black	.20	.20
41	A5	50f blue & bluish black	.20	.20
42	A5	100f apple grn & bluish blk	.40	.40
43	A5	1000f orange & bluish black	3.50	3.50
		Nos. 39-43 (5)	4.50	4.50

1996 Intl. Philatelic Exhibitions — A6

Exhibition, site: 20f, CHINA '96, Summer Palace, Beijing. 50f, ISTANBUL '96, Hagia Sofia. 100f, ESSEN '96, Villa Hugel. 1000f, CAPEX '96, Toronto skyline.

1996, May 18

44	A6	20f multicolored	.20	.20
45	A6	50f multicolored	.20	.20
46	A6	100f multicolored	.35	.35
47	A6	1000f multicolored	4.25	4.25
a.		Sheet, 2 each #44-47 + 2 labels	10.00	
		Nos. 44-47 (4)	5.00	5.00

Souvenir Sheet

1st Palestinian Parliamentary & Presidential Elections — A7

Illustration reduced.

1996, May 20

48	A7	1250f multicolored	4.75	4.75

1996 Summer Olympic Games, Atlanta — A8

Designs: 30f, Boxing. 40f, Medal, 1896. 50f, Runners. 150f, Olympic flame. 1000f, Palestinian Olympic Committee emblem.

1996, July 19 ***Perf. 13½***

49	A8	30f multicolored	.20	.20
50	A8	40f multicolored	.20	.20
51	A8	50f multicolored	.25	.25
52	A8	150f multicolored	.60	.60
a.		Sheet of 3, #49, 51-52	*5.00*	
53	A8	1000f multicolored	3.75	3.75
		Nos. 49-53 (5)	5.00	5.00

Flowers — A9

1996, Nov. 22

54	A9	10f Poppy	.20	.20
55	A9	25f Hibiscus	.20	.20
56	A9	100f Thyme	.50	.50
57	A9	150f Lemon	.60	.60
58	A9	750f Orange	3.00	3.00
		Nos. 54-58 (5)	4.50	4.50

Souvenir Sheet

59	A9	1000f Olive	4.25	4.25

Souvenir Sheet

Christmas A10

a, 150f, Magi. b, 350f, View of Bethlehem. c, 500f, Shepherds, sheep. d, 750f, Nativity scene.

1996, Dec. 14 ***Perf. 14***

60	A10	Sheet of 4, #a.-d.	6.00	6.00

Birds — A11

1997, May 29

61	A11	25f Great tit	.20	.20
62	A11	75f Blue rock thrush	.20	.20
63	A11	150f Golden oriole	.50	.50
64	A11	350f Hoopoe	1.10	1.10
65	A11	600f Peregrine falcon	1.90	1.90
		Nos. 61-65 (5)	3.90	3.90

Historic Views — A12

1997, June 19

66	A12	350f Gaza, 1839	1.25	1.25
67	A12	600f Hebron, 1839	2.25	2.25

Souvenir Sheet

Return of Hong Kong to China — A13

Illustration reduced.

1997, July 1

68	A13	225f multicolored	1.00	1.00

Friends of Palestine — A14

#69, Portraits of Yasser Arafat, Hans-Jürgen Wischnewski. #70, Wischnewski shaking hands with Arafat. #71, Mother Teresa. #72, Mother Teresa with Arafat.

1997 **Litho.** ***Perf. 14***

69	A14	600f multicolored	1.75	1.75
70	A14	600f multicolored	1.75	1.75
a.		Pair, #69-70	3.50	3.50
71	A14	600f multicolored	1.75	1.75
72	A14	600f multicolored	1.75	1.75
a.		Pair, #71-72	3.50	3.50
		Nos. 69-l72 (4)	7.00	7.00

#70a, 72a were issued in sheets of 4 stamps.

Issued: #69-70, 7/24; #71-72, 12/17.

Christmas A15

1997, Nov. 28

73		350f multicolored	1.10	1.10
74		700f multicolored	2.10	2.10
a.		A15 Pair, #73-74	3.25	3.25

Mosaics from Floor of Byzantine Church, Jabalia-Gaza A16

50f, Rabbit, palm tree. 125f, Goat, rabbit, dog. 200f, Basket, fruit tree, jar. 400f, Lion.

1998, June 22 Litho. *Perf. 13½*

75	A16	50f multicolored		.25	.25
76	A16	125f multicolored		.40	.40
77	A16	200f multicolored		.75	.75
78	A16	400f multicolored		1.00	1.00
		Nos. 75-78 (4)		2.40	2.40

Souvenir Sheet

Baal — A17

1998, June 15 *Perf. 14*

79	A17	600f multicolored	2.00	2.00

A18

Raptors A19

Medicinal plants.

1998, Sept. 30 Litho. *Perf. 14*

80	A18	40f Urginea maritima	.20	.20
81	A18	80f Silybum marianum	.30	.30
82	A18	500f Foeniculum vulgare	1.75	1.75
83	A18	800f Inula viscosa	2.75	2.75
		Nos. 80-83 (4)	5.00	5.00

1998, Nov. 12 Litho. *Perf. 14*

84	A19	20f Bonelli's eagle	.20	.20
85	A19	60f Hobby	.30	.30
86	A19	340f Verreaux's eagle	1.00	1.00
87	A19	600f Bateleur	1.50	1.50
88	A19	900f Buzzard	2.25	2.25
		Nos. 84-88 (5)	5.25	5.25

Souvenir Sheet

Granting of Additional Rights to Palestinian Authority's Observer to UN — A20

Illustration reduced.

1998, Nov. 12

89	A20	700f multicolored	2.50	2.50

Butterflies A21

Designs: a, 100f, Papilio alexanor. b, 200f, Danaus chrysippus. c, 300f, Gonepteryx cleopatra. d, 400f, Melanargia titea.

1998, Dec. 3

90	A21	Sheet of 4, #a.-d.	4.00	4.00

Souvenir Sheet

Christmas, Bethlehem 2000 — A22

Illustration reduced.

1998, Dec. 3

91	A22	1000f multicolored	4.00	4.00

Souvenir Sheet

Signing of Middle East Peace Agreement, Wye River Conference, Oct. 23, 1998 — A23

Palestinian Pres. Yasser Arafat and US Pres. Bil Clinton. Illustration reduced.

1999 Litho. *Perf. 14*

92	A23	900f multicolored	2.75	2.75

New Airport, Gaza A24

Designs: 80f, Control tower, vert. 300f, Airplane. 700f, Terminal building.

1999

93	A24	80f multicolored	.20	.20
94	A24	300f multicolored	.90	.90
95	A24	700f multicolored	2.10	2.10
		Nos. 93-95 (3)	3.20	3.20

Intl. Philatelic Exhibitions & UPU, 125th Anniv. — A25

a, 20f, Buildings, China 1999. b, 260f, Buildings, Germany, IBRA '99. c. 80f, High-rise buildings, Australia '99. d, 340f, Eiffel Tower, Philex France '99. e, 400f, Aerial view of countryside, denomination LR, UPU, 125th anniv. f, 400f, like #96e, denomination LL.

1999

96	A25	Block of 6, #a.-f.	4.50	4.50

A26

Hebron: a, 400f, Lettering in gold. b, 500f, Lettering in white.

1999, Aug. 20 Litho. *Perf. 14*

97	A26	Pair, #a.-b.	2.75	2.75

A27

1999, Apr. 27

Arabian Horses (Various): a, 25f. b, 75f. c, 150f. d, 350f. e, 800f.

98	A27	Strip of 5, #a.-e.	4.25	4.25

Souvenir Sheet

Palestinian Sunbird — A28

Illustration reduced.

1999 Litho. *Perf. 13¾*

99	A28	750f multi	2.25	2.25

A29

Christmas, Bethlehem 2000 — A30

Giotto Paintings (Type A30): 200f, 280f, 2000f, The Nativity. 380f, 460f, The Adoration of the Magi. 560f, The Flight into Egypt. Inscription colors: Nos. 108a, 110a, Black. Nos. 109a, 111a, White. No. 112a, Yellow. Nos. 108b-112b have silver inscriptions and frames.

1999, Dec. 8 Litho. *Perf. 13¼x13*

Background Color

100	A29	60f black	.20	.20
101	A29	80f light blue	.25	.25
102	A29	100f dark gray	.30	.30
103	A29	280f lilac rose	.85	.85
104	A29	300f green	.90	.90
105	A29	400f red violet	1.25	1.25
106	A29	500f dark red	1.50	1.50
107	A29	560f light gray	1.75	1.75

Perf. 13¼

108	A30	200f Pair, #a.-b	*1.25*	*1.25*
109	A30	280f Pair, #a.-b.	*1.75*	*1.75*
110	A30	380f Pair, #a.-b.	*2.25*	*2.25*
111	A30	460f Pair, #a.-b.	*2.75*	*2.75*
112	A30	560f Pair, #a.-b.	*3.50*	*3.50*

Litho. & Embossed Foil Application

113	A30	2000f multi	6.00	6.00
a.		Booklet pane of 1	6.00	
		Nos. 100-113 (14)	*24.50*	*24.50*

Nos. 108-112 each printed in sheets of 10 containing 9 "a" +1 "b." No. 113 printed in sheets of 4. Nos. 108a-112a also exist in sheets of 10.

Issued: No. 113a, 2000.

Easter — A31

Designs: 150f, Last Supper, by Giotto, white inscriptions. 200f, Last Supper, yellow inscriptions. 300f, Lamentation, by Giotto, white inscriptions. 350f, Lamentation, yellow inscriptions. 650f, Crucifix, by Giotto, orange frame. 2000f, Crucifix, gold frame.

2000 Litho. *Perf. 13¼*

114-118	A31	Set of 5	5.25	5.25

Souvenir Sheet

Litho. & Embossed Foil Application

119	A31	2000f multi	6.00	6.00
a.		Booklet pane of 1	6.00	

Christmas A32

Madonna of the Star by Fra Angelico.

Litho. & Embossed Foil Application

2000 ***Perf. 13¼***

120 A32 2000f Bkit. pane of 1 6.00
a. Miniature sheet of 1 6.00 6.00
Booklet, #113a, 119a, 120 18.00

Holy Land Visit of Pope John Paul II — A33

Designs: 500f, Pope, Yasser Arafat holding hands. 600f, Pope with miter. 750f, Pope touching Arafat's shoulder. 800f, Pope, creche. 1000f, Pope, back of Arafat's head.

2000 **Litho.** ***Perf. 13¾***

121-125 A33 Set of 5 9.50 9.50

Intl. Children's Year — A34

Designs: 50f, Landscape. 100f, Children. 350f, Domed buildings. 400f, Family.

2000

126-129 A34 Set of 4 3.00 3.00

Pres. Arafat's Visit to Germany A35

Arafat and: 200f, German Chancellor Gerhard Schröder. 300f, German President Johannes Rau.

2000 ***Perf. 14x14¼***

130-131 A35 Set of 2 1.50 1.50

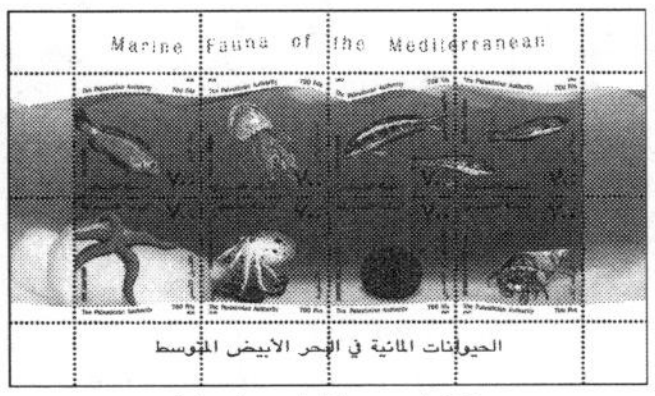

Marine Life — A36

No. 132: a, Parrotfish. b, Mauve stinger. c, Ornate wrasse. d, Rainbow wrasse. e, Red starfish. f, Common octopus. g, Purple sea urchin. h, Striated hermit crab.

2000 **Litho.** ***Perf. 13¾***

132 A36 700f Sheet of 8, #a-h 16.00 16.00

Souvenir Sheet

Blue Madonna — A37

2000 ***Perf. 14x13¾***

133 A37 950f multi 3.00 3.00

Christmas Type of 2000

Designs: No. 134, 100f, No. 138, 500f, Nativity, by Gentile da Fabriano, horiz. No. 135, 150f, Adoration of the Magi, by Fabriano, horiz. No. 136, 250f, Immaculate Conception, by Fabriano, horiz. No. 137, 350f, No. 139, 1000f, Like #120.

2000 **Litho.** ***Perf. 13¼***

134-139 A32 Set of 6 7.25 7.25

Easter Type of 2000

Designs: 150f, Christ Carrying Cross, by Fra Angelico, blue inscriptions. 200f, Christ Carrying Cross, white inscriptions. 300f, Removal of Christ from Cross, by Fra Angelico, yellow inscriptions. 350f, Removal of Christ from the Cross, white inscriptions.
2000f, Crucifix, by Giotto, vert.

2001 **Litho.** ***Perf. 13¼***

140-143 A31 Set of 4 2.75 2.75

Souvenir Sheet

Litho. & Embossed

144 A31 2000f gold & multi 5.75 5.75

A38

Palestinian Authority flag and flag of various organizations: 50f, 100f, 200f, 500f.

2001 **Litho.** ***Perf. 13¾***

145-148 A38 Set of 4 2.50 2.50

Souvenir Sheet

Art by Ibrahim Hazimeh — A39

No. 149: a, 350f, Jerusalem After Rain. b, 550f, Mysticism. c, 850f, Ramallah. d, 900f, Remembrance.

2001 ***Perf. 14x13¾***

149 A39 Sheet of 4, #a-d 8.00 8.00

Worldwide Fund for Nature (WWF) — A40

No. 150 - Houbara bustard, WWF emblem at: a, 350f, UR. b, 350f, LR. c, 750f, UL. d, 750f, LL.
Illustration reduced.

2001 **Litho.** ***Perf. 13¾x14***

150 A40 Block of 4, #a-d 9.50 9.50

Graf Zeppelin Over Holy Land — A41

Zeppelin and: 200f, Map of voyage. 600f, Hills.

2001 ***Perf. 13¾***

151-152 A41 Set of 2 2.40 2.40

Legends A42

Designs: 300f, Man with magic lamp, buildings. 450f, Eagle, snake, gemstones, man. 650f, Man and woman on flying horse. 800f, Man hiding behind tree.

2001 ***Perf. 13¾x14***

153-156 A42 Set of 4 6.75 6.75

Souvenir Sheet

Peace for Bethlehem — A43

2001 ***Perf. 14x13¾***

157 A42 950f multi 2.75 2.75

SEMI-POSTAL STAMPS

Souvenir Sheet

Gaza-Jericho Peace Agreement — SP1

Illustration reduced.

1994, Oct. 7 **Litho.** ***Perf. 14***

B1 SP1 750m +250m multi 3.50 3.50

For surcharge see No. B3.

Souvenir Sheet

Arab League, 50th Anniv. — SP2

Painting: View of Palestine, by Ibrahim Hazimeh.
Illustration reduced.

1995, Mar. 22 ***Perf. 13½***

B2 SP2 750f +250f multi 3.75 3.75

No. B1 Surcharged "FILS" in English & Arabic and with Added Text at Left and Right

1995, Apr. 10 **Litho.** ***Perf. 14***

B3 SP1 750f +250f multi 3.50 3.50

Honoring 1994 Nobel Peace Prize winners Arafat, Rabin and Peres.

OFFICIAL STAMPS

Natl. Arms — O1

1994, Aug. 15 **Litho.** ***Perf. 14***

O1	O1	50m	yellow	.20	.20
O2	O1	100m	green blue	.30	.30
O3	O1	125m	blue	.40	.40
O4	O1	200m	orange	.60	.60
O5	O1	250m	olive	.80	.80
O6	O1	400m	maroon	1.25	1.25
			Nos. O1-O6 (6)	3.55	3.55

Nos. O1-O6 could also be used by the general public, and non-official-use covers are known.

PANAMA

ˈpa-nə-ˌmä

LOCATION — Central America between Costa Rica and Colombia
GOVT. — Republic
AREA — 30,134 sq. mi.
POP. — 2,778,526 (1999 est.)
CAPITAL — Panama

Formerly a department of the Republic of Colombia, Panama gained its independence in 1903. Dividing the country at its center is the Panama Canal.

100 Centavos = 1 Peso
100 Centesimos = 1 Balboa (1904)

Catalogue values for unused stamps in this country are for Never Hinged items, beginning with Scott 350 in the regular postage section, Scott C82 in the airpost section, Scott CB1 in the airpost semi-postal section, and Scott RA21 in the postal tax section.

Watermarks

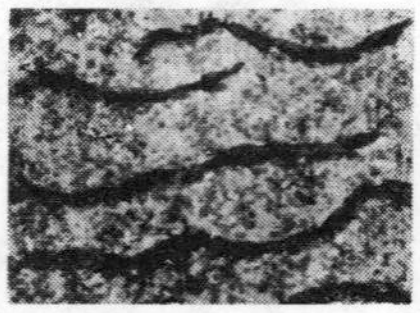
Wmk. 229- Wavy Lines

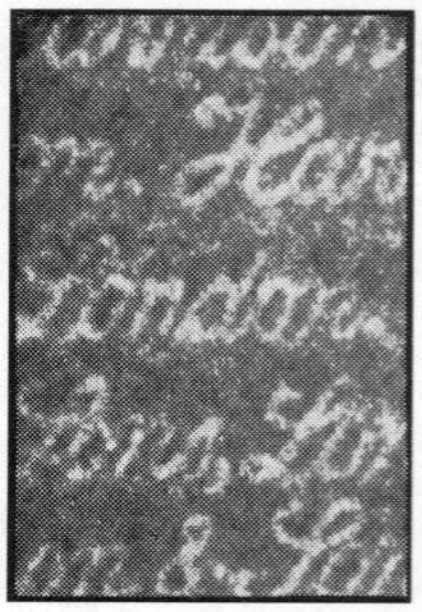
Wmk. 233- "Harrison & Sons, London." in Script

Wmk. 311- Star and RP Multiple

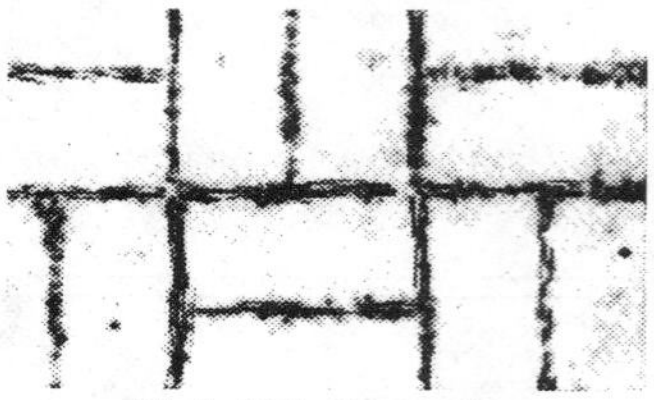
Wmk. 334- Rectangles

Wmk. 343- RP Multiple

Wmk. 365- Argentine Arms, Casa de Moneda de la Nacion & RA Multiple

Wmk. 377- Interlocking Circles

Wmk. 382- Stars

Wmk. 382 may be a sheet watermark. It includes stars, wings with sun in middle and "Panama R de P."

Issues of the Sovereign State of Panama Under Colombian Dominion

Valid only for domestic mail.

Coat of Arms
A1 A2

1878 Unwmk. Litho. *Imperf.*

Thin Wove Paper

1 A1 5c gray green 25.00 30.00
a. 5c yellow green 25.00 30.00
2 A1 10c blue 60.00 60.00
3 A1 20c rose red 40.00 32.50
Nos. 1-3 (3) 125.00

Very Thin Wove Paper

4 A2 50c buff *1,500.*

All values of this issue are known rouletted unofficially.

Medium Thick Paper

5 A1 5c blue green 25.00 30.00
6 A1 10c blue 65.00 70.00
7 A2 50c orange 13.00
Nos. 5-7 (3) 103.00

Nos. 5-7 were printed before Nos. 1-4, according to Panamanian archives.

Values for used Nos. 1-5 are for handstamped postal cancellations.

These stamps have been reprinted in a number of shades, on thin to moderately thick, white or yellowish paper. They are without gum or with white, crackly gum. All values have been reprinted from new stones made from retouched dies. The marks of retouching are plainly to be seen in the sea and clouds. On the original 10c the shield in the upper left corner has two blank sections; on the reprints the design of this shield is completed. The impression of these reprints is frequently blurred.

Reprints of the 50c are rare. Beware of remainders of the 50c offered as reprints.

Issues of Colombia for use in the Department of Panama

Issued because of the use of different currency.

Map of Panama
A3 A4

1887-88 ***Perf. 13½***

8 A3 1c black, *green* .90 .80
9 A3 2c black, *pink* ('88) 1.60 1.25
a. 2c black, *salmon* 1.60
10 A3 5c black, *blue* .90 .35
11 A3 10c black, *yellow* .90 .40
a. Imperf., pair
12 A3 20c black, *lilac* 1.00 .50
13 A3 50c brown ('88) 2.00 1.00
a. Imperf.
Nos. 8-13 (6) 7.30 4.30

See No. 14. For surcharges and overprints see Nos. 24-30, 107-108, 115-116, 137-138.

1892 **Pelure Paper**

14 A3 50c brown 2.50 1.10

The stamps of this issue have been reprinted on papers of slightly different colors from those of the originals.

These are: 1c yellow green, 2c deep rose, 5c bright blue, 10c straw, 20c violet.

The 50c is printed from a very worn stone, in a lighter brown than the originals. The series includes a 10c on lilac paper.

All these stamps are to be found perforated, imperforate, imperforate horizontally or imperforate vertically. At the same time that they were made, impressions were struck upon a variety of glazed and surface-colored papers.

Wove Paper

1892-96 **Engr.** ***Perf. 12***

15 A4 1c green .25 .25
16 A4 2c rose .40 .25
17 A4 5c blue 1.50 .50
18 A4 10c orange .35 .25
19 A4 20c violet ('95) .50 .35
20 A4 50c bister brn ('96) .50 .40
21 A4 1p lake ('96) 6.50 4.00
Nos. 15-21 (7) 10.00 6.00

In 1903 Nos. 15-21 were used in Cauca and three other southern Colombia towns. Stamps canceled in these towns are worth much more.

For surcharges and overprints see Nos. 22-23, 51-106, 109-114, 129-136, 139, 151-162, 181-184, F12-F15, H4-H5.

Nos. 16, 12-14 Surcharged:

a

HABILITADO.
1894
1
CENTAVO.
b

c

d

e

f

g

1894 **Black Surcharge**

22 (a) 1c on 2c rose .50 .40
a. Inverted surcharge 2.50 2.50
b. Double surcharge
23 (b) 1c on 2c rose .40 .50
a. "CCNTAVO" 2.50 2.50
b. Inverted surcharge 2.50 2.50
c. Double surcharge

Red Surcharge

24 (c) 5c on 20c black, *lil* 2.50 1.50
a. Inverted surcharge 12.50 12.50
b. Double surcharge
c. Without "HABILITADO"
25 (d) 5c on 20c black, *lil* 3.50 3.00
a. "CCNTAVOS" 7.50 7.50
b. Inverted surcharge 12.50 12.50
c. Double surcharge
d. Without "HABILITADO"
26 (e) 5c on 20c black, *lil* 6.00 5.00
a. Inverted surcharge 12.50 12.50
b. Double surcharge
27 (f) 10c on 50c brown 3.00 3.00
a. "1894" omitted
b. Inverted surcharge
c. "CCNTAVOS" 15.00
28 (g) 10c on 50c brown 12.50 12.50
a. "CCNTAVOS" 32.50
b. Inverted surcharge

Pelure Paper

29 (f) 10c on 50c brown 4.00 3.00
a. "1894" omitted 7.50
b. Inverted surcharge 12.50 12.50
c. Double surcharge
30 (g) 10c on 50c brown 10.00 10.00
a. "CCNTAVOS"
b. Without "HABILITADO"
c. Inverted surcharge 25.00 25.00
d. Double surcharge
Nos. 22-30 (9) 42.40 38.90

There are several settings of these surcharges. Usually the surcharge is about 15½mm high, but in one setting, it is only 13mm. All the types are to be found with a comma after "CENTAVOS." Nos. 24, 25, 26, 29 and 30 exist with the surcharge printed sideways. Nos. 23, 24 and 29 may be found with an inverted "A" instead of "V" in "CENTAVOS." There are also varieties caused by dropped or broken letters.

Issues of the Republic Issued in the City of Panama

Stamps of 1892-96 Overprinted

1903, Nov. 16

Rose Handstamp

51 A4 1c green 2.00 1.50
52 A4 2c rose 5.00 3.00
53 A4 5c blue 2.00 1.25
54 A4 10c yellow 2.00 2.00
55 A4 20c violet 4.00 3.50
56 A4 50c bister brn 10.00 7.00
57 A4 1p lake 50.00 40.00
Nos. 51-57 (7) 75.00 58.25

Blue Black Handstamp

58 A4 1c green 2.00 1.25
59 A4 2c rose 1.00 1.00
60 A4 5c blue 7.00 6.00
61 A4 10c yellow 5.00 3.50
62 A4 20c violet 10.00 7.50
63 A4 50c bister brn 10.00 7.50
64 A4 1p lake 50.00 42.50
Nos. 58-64 (7) 85.00 69.25

The stamps of this issue are to be found with the handstamp placed horizontally, vertically or diagonally; inverted; double; double, one inverted; double, both inverted; in pairs, one without handstamp; etc.

This handstamp is known in brown rose on the 1, 5, 20 and 50c, in purple on the 1, 2, 50c and 1p, and in magenta on the 5, 10, 20 and 50c.

Reprints were made in rose, black and other colors when the handstamp was nearly worn out, so that the "R" of "REPUBLICA" appears to be shorter than usual, and the bottom part of "LI" has been broken off. The "P" of "PANAMA" leans to the left and the tops of "NA" are broken. Many of these varieties are found inverted, double, etc.

Overprinted

1903, Dec. 3

Bar in Similar Color to Stamp

Black Overprint

65 A4 2c rose 2.50 2.50
a. "PANAMA" 15mm long 3.50
b. Violet bar 5.00
66 A4 5c blue 100.00
a. "PANAMA" 15mm long 100.00
67 A4 10c yellow 2.50 2.50
a. "PANAMA" 15mm long 6.00
b. Horizontal overprint 17.50

Gray Black Overprint

68 A4 2c rose 2.00 2.00
a. "PANAMA" 15mm long 2.50

Carmine Overprint

69 A4 5c blue 2.50 2.50
a. "PANAMA" 15mm long 3.50
b. Bar only 75.00 75.00
c. Double overprint
70 A4 20c violet 7.50 6.50
a. "PANAMA" 15mm long 10.00
b. Double overprint, one in black 150.00
Nos. 65,67-70 (5) 17.00 16.00

This overprint was set up to cover fifty stamps. "PANAMA" is normally 13mm long and 1¾mm high but, in two rows in each sheet, it measures 15 to 16mm.

This word may be found with one or more of the letters taller than usual; with one, two or three inverted "V's" instead of "A's"; with an inverted "Y" instead of "A"; an inverted "N"; an "A" with accent; and a fancy "P."

Owing to misplaced impressions, stamps exist with "PANAMA" once only, twice on one side, or three times.

Overprinted in Red

1903, Dec.

71 A4 1c green .75 .60
a. "PANAMA" 15mm long 1.25
b. "PANAMA" reading down 3.00 .75
c. "PANAMA" reading up and down 3.00
d. Double overprint 8.00
72 A4 2c rose .50 .40
a. "PANAMA" 15mm long 1.00
b. "PANAMA" reading down .75 .50
c. "PANAMA" reading up and down 4.00
d. Double overprint 8.00
73 A4 20c violet 1.50 1.00
a. "PANAMA" 15mm long 2.25
b. "PANAMA" reading down
c. "PANAMA" reading up and down 8.00 8.00
d. Double overprint 18.00 18.00
74 A4 50c bister brn 3.00 2.50
a. "PANAMA" 15mm long 5.00
b. "PANAMA" reading up and down 12.00 12.00
c. Double overprint 6.00 6.00
75 A4 1p lake 6.00 4.50
a. "PANAMA" 15mm long 6.25
b. "PANAMA" reading up and down 15.00 15.00
c. Double overprint 15.00
d. Inverted overprint 25.00
Nos. 71-75 (5) 11.75 9.00

This setting appears to be a re-arrangement (or two very similar re-arrangements) of the previous overprint. The overprint covers fifty stamps. "PANAMA" usually reads upward but sheets of the 1, 2 and 20c exist with the word reading upward on one half the sheet and downward on the other half.

In one re-arrangement one stamp in fifty has the word reading in both directions. Nearly all the varieties of the previous overprint are repeated in this setting excepting the inverted "Y" and fancy "P." There are also additional varieties of large letters and "PANAMA" occasionally has an "A" missing or inverted. There are misplaced impressions, as the previous setting.

Overprinted in Red

1904-05

76 A4 1c green .20 .20
a. Both words reading up 1.50
b. Both words reading down 2.75
c. Double overprint
d. Pair, one without overprint 15.00
e. "PANAAM" 20.00
f. Inverted "M" in "PANAMA" 5.00
77 A4 2c rose .20 .20
a. Both words reading up 2.50
b. Both words reading down 2.50
c. Double overprint 10.00
d. Double overprint, one inverted 14.00
e. Inverted "M" in "PANAMA" 5.00
78 A4 5c blue .30 .20
a. Both words reading up 3.00
b. Both words reading down 4.25
c. Inverted overprint 12.50
d. "PANAAM" 25.00
e. "PANANA" 8.00
f. "PAMANA" 5.00
g. Inverted "M" in "PANAMA" 5.00
h. Double overprint 20.00
79 A4 10c yellow .30 .20
a. Both words reading up 5.00
b. Both words reading down 5.00
c. Double overprint 15.00
d. Inverted overprint 6.75
e. "PAMANA" 8.00
f. Inverted "M" in "PANAMA" 15.00
g. Red brown overprint 7.50 3.50
80 A4 20c violet 2.00 1.00
a. Both words reading up 5.00
b. Both words reading down 10.00
81 A4 50c bister brn 2.00 1.60
a. Both words reading up 10.50
b. Both words reading down 10.00
c. Double overprint
82 A4 1p lake 5.00 5.00
a. Both words reading up 12.50
b. Both words reading down 12.50
c. Double overprint
d. Double overprint, one inverted 20.00
e. Inverted "M" in "PANAMA" 45.00
Nos. 76-82 (7) 10.00 8.40

This overprint is also set up to cover fifty stamps. One stamp in each fifty has "PANAMA" reading upward at both sides. Another has the word reading downward at both sides, a third has an inverted "V" in place of the last "A" and a fourth has a small thick "N." In a resetting all these varieties are corrected except the inverted "V." There are misplaced overprints as before.

Later printings show other varieties and have the bar 2½mm instead of 2mm wide. The colors of the various printings of Nos. 76-82 range from carmine to almost pink.

Experts consider the black overprint on the 50c to be speculative.

The 20c violet and 50c bister brown exist with bar 2½mm wide, including the error "PAMANA," but are not known to have been issued. Some copies have been canceled "to oblige."

Issued in Colon

Handstamped in Magenta or Violet

On Stamps of 1892-96

1903-04

101 A4 1c green .75 .75
102 A4 2c rose .75 .75
103 A4 5c blue 1.00 1.00
104 A4 10c yellow 3.50 3.00
105 A4 20c violet 8.00 6.50
106 A4 1p lake 80.00 70.00

On Stamps of 1887-92

Ordinary Wove Paper

107 A3 50c brown 25.00 20.00
Nos. 101-107 (7) 119.00 102.00

Pelure Paper

108 A3 50c brown 70.00

Handstamped in Magenta, Violet or Red

On Stamps of 1892-96

109 A4 1c green 5.50 5.00
110 A4 2c rose 5.50 5.00
111 A4 5c blue 5.50 5.00
112 A4 10c yellow 8.25 7.00
113 A4 20c violet 12.00 9.00
114 A4 1p lake 70.00 60.00

On Stamps of 1887-92

Ordinary Wove Paper

115 A3 50c brown 35.00 25.00
Nos. 109-115 (7) 141.75 116.00

Pelure Paper

116 A3 50c brown 50.00 37.50

The first note after No. 64 applies also to Nos. 101-116.

The handstamps on Nos. 109-116 have been counterfeited.

REPUBLICA DE PANAMA

Stamps with this overprint were a private speculation. They exist on cover. The overprint was to be used on postal cards.

Overprinted g

On Stamps of 1892-96

Carmine Overprint

129 A4 1c green .40 .40
a. Inverted overprint 6.00
b. Double overprint 2.25
c. Double overprint, one inverted 6.00
130 A4 5c blue .50 .50

Brown Overprint

131 A4 1c green 12.00
a. Double overprint, one inverted

Black Overprint

132 A4 1c green 60.00 30.00
a. Vertical overprint 42.50
b. Inverted overprint 42.50
c. Double overprint, one inverted 42.50
133 A4 2c rose .50 .50
a. Inverted overprint
134 A4 10c yellow .50 .50
a. Inverted overprint 4.00
b. Double overprint 16.00
c. Double overprint, one inverted 6.00
135 A4 20c violet .50 .50
a. Inverted overprint 4.00
b. Double overprint 5.50
136 A4 1p lake 16.00 14.00

On Stamps of 1887-88

Blue Overprint

Ordinary Wove Paper

137 A3 50c brown 3.00 3.00

Pelure Paper

138 A3 50c brown 3.00 3.00
a. Double overprint 14.00

This overprint is set up to cover fifty stamps. In each fifty there are four stamps without accent on the last "a" of "Panama," one with accent on the "a" of "Republica" and one with a thick, upright "i."

Overprinted in Carmine **REPUBLICA DE PANAMA.**

On Stamp of 1892-96

139 A4 20c violet *200.00*
a. Double overprint

Unknown with genuine cancels.

Issued in Bocas del Toro

Stamps of 1892-96 Overprinted

Handstamped in Violet R DE PANAMA

1903-04

151 A4 1c green 20.00 14.00
152 A4 2c rose 20.00 14.00
153 A4 5c blue 25.00 16.00
154 A4 10c yellow 15.00 8.25
155 A4 20c violet 50.00 30.00
156 A4 50c bister brn 100.00 55.00
157 A4 1p lake 140.00 110.00
Nos. 151-157 (7) 370.00 247.25

The handstamp is known double and inverted. Counterfeits exist.

Handstamped in Violet Panama

158 A4 1c green *100.00*
159 A4 2c rose *70.00*
160 A4 5c blue *80.00*
161 A4 10c yellow *100.00*
Nos. 158-161 (4) *350.00*

This handstamp was applied to these 4 stamps only by favor, experts state. Counterfeits are numerous. The 1p exists only as a counterfeit.

General Issues

A5

1905, Feb. 4 **Engr.** ***Perf. 12***

179 A5 1c green .60 .40
180 A5 2c rose .80 .50

Panama's Declaration of Independence from the Colombian Republic, Nov. 3, 1903.

Surcharged in Vermilion on Stamps of 1892-96 Issue:

1906

181 A4 1c on 20c violet .25 .25
a. "Panrma" 2.25 2.25
b. "Pnnama" 2.25 2.25
c. "Pauama" 2.25 2.25
d. Inverted surcharge 4.00 4.00
e. Double surcharge 3.50 3.50
f. Double surcharge, one inverted

182 A4 2c on 50c bister brn .25 .25
a. 3rd "A" of "PANAMA" inverted 2.25 2.25
b. Both "PANAMA" reading down 4.00 4.00
c. Double surcharge
d. Inverted surcharge 2.50

The 2c on 20c violet was never issued to the public. All copies are inverted. Value, 75c.

Carmine Surcharge

183 A4 5c on 1p lake .60 .40
a. Both "PANAMA" reading down 6.00 6.00
b. "5" omitted
c. Double surcharge
d. Inverted surcharge
e. 3rd "A" of "PANAMA" inverted 5.50 5.50

On Stamp of 1903-04, No. 75

184 A4 5c on 1p lake .60 .40
a. "PANAMA" 15mm long
b. "PANAMA" reading up and down
c. Both "PANAMA" reading down
d. Inverted surcharge
e. Double surcharge
f. 3rd "A" of "PANAMA" inverted
Nos. 181-184 (4) 1.70 1.30

National Flag — A6

Vasco Núñez de Balboa — A7

Fernández de Córdoba — A8

Coat of Arms — A9

Justo Arosemena A10

Manuel J. Hurtado A11

José de Obaldía — A12

Tomás Herrera — A13

José de Fábrega — A14

1906-07 **Engr.** ***Perf. 11½***

185 A6	½c orange & multi		.45	.35
186 A7	1c dk green & blk		.45	.35
187 A8	2c scarlet & blk		.60	.35
188 A9	2½c red orange		.75	.35
189 A10	5c blue & black		1.75	.35
a.	5c ultramarine & black		2.00	.50
190 A11	8c purple & blk		1.00	.65
191 A12	10c violet & blk		1.00	.50
192 A13	25c brown & blk		2.50	1.00
193 A14	50c black		6.50	3.50
	Nos. 185-193 (9)		15.00	7.40

Inverted centers exist of Nos. 185-187, 189, 189a, 190-193, Value, each $25. Nos. 185-193 exist imperf.

For surcharge see No. F29.

Map — A17

Balboa — A18

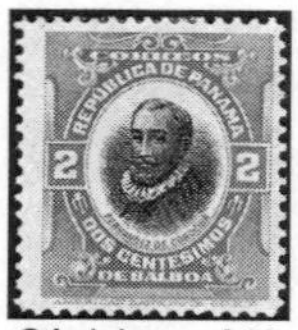
Córdoba — A19

Arms — A20

Arosemena A21

Obaldía A23

1909-15 ***Perf. 12***

195 A17	½c orange ('11)	.60	.30
a.	Booklet pane of 6		
196 A17	½c rose ('15)	.60	.60
197 A18	1c dk grn & blk	.80	.35
a.	Inverted center		
b.	Booklet pane of 6	*160.00*	
198 A19	2c red & blk	.60	.20
a.	Booklet pane of 6	*160.00*	
199 A20	2½c red orange	1.00	.20
a.	Booklet pane of 6		
200 A21	5c blue & blk	1.60	.20
a.	Booklet pane of 6	*160.00*	
201 A23	10c violet & blk	2.50	.80
a.	Booklet pane of 6		
	Nos. 195-201 (7)	7.70	2.65

For overprints and surcharges see #H23, I4-I7.

Balboa Sighting Pacific Ocean, His Dog "Leoncico" at His Feet — A24

1913, Sept.

202 A24	2½c dk grn & yel grn	.80	.65

400th anniv. of Balboa's discovery of the Pacific Ocean.

Panama-Pacific Exposition Issue

Chorrera Falls — A25

Map of Panama Canal A26

Balboa Taking Possession of the Pacific A27

Ruins of Cathedral of Old Panama A28

Palace of Arts — A29

Gatun Locks — A30

Culebra Cut — A31

Santo Domingo Monastery's Flat Arch — A32

1915-16 ***Perf. 12***

204 A25	½c ol grn & blk	.40	.30
205 A26	1c dk green & blk	.90	.30
206 A27	2c carmine & blk	.70	.30
a.	2c ver & blk ('16)	.70	.30
208 A28	2½c scarlet & blk	.90	.35
209 A29	3c violet & blk	1.50	.55
210 A30	5c blue & blk	2.00	.35
a.	Center inverted	750.00	650.00
211 A31	10c orange & blk	2.00	.70
212 A32	20c brown & blk	10.00	3.25
a.	Center inverted	275.00	
	Nos. 204-212 (8)	18.40	6.10

For surcharges and overprints see Nos. 217, 233, E1-E2.

Manuel J. Hurtado — A33

1916

213 A33	8c violet & blk	7.00	4.25

For surcharge see No. 30.

S. S. Panama in Culebra Cut Aug. 11, 1914 A34

S. S. Panama in Culebra Cut Aug. 11, 1914 A35

S. S. Cristobal in Gatun Lock — A36

1918

214 A34	12c purple & blk	15.00	5.75
215 A35	15c brt blue & blk	10.00	3.50
216 A36	24c yellow brn & blk	15.00	3.50
	Nos. 214-216 (3)	40.00	12.75

No. 208 Surcharged in Dark Blue

1919, Aug. 15

217 A28	2c on 2½c scar & blk	.30	.30
a.	Inverted surcharge	10.00	8.25
b.	Double surcharge	12.00	10.00

City of Panama, 400th anniversary.

Dry Dock at Balboa A38

Ship in Pedro Miguel Lock — A39

1920 **Engr.**

218 A38	50c orange & blk	30.00	22.50
219 A39	1b dk violet & blk	40.00	27.50

For overprint and surcharge see Nos. C6, C37.

Arms of Panama City — A40

José Vallarino — A41

"Land Gate" — A42

Simón Bolivar — A43

Statue of Cervantes — A44

Bolívar's Tribute — A45

Carlos de Ycaza — A46

Municipal Building in 1821 and 1921 — A47

Statue of Balboa — A48

Villa de Los Santos Church — A49

Herrera — A50

Fábrega — A51

1921, Nov.

220 A40	½c orange	.40	.25
221 A41	1c green	.55	.20
222 A42	2c carmine	.60	.25
223 A43	2½c red	1.40	1.10
224 A44	3c dull violet	1.40	1.10
225 A45	5c blue	1.40	.35
226 A46	8c olive green	5.00	2.75
227 A47	10c violet	3.25	1.25
228 A48	15c lt blue	4.00	1.60
229 A49	20c olive brown	7.00	3.25
230 A50	24c black brown	7.00	4.00
231 A51	50c black	12.00	6.00
	Nos. 220-231 (12)	44.00	22.10

Centenary of independence.

For overprints and surcharges see Nos. 264, 275-276, 299, 304, 308-310, C35.

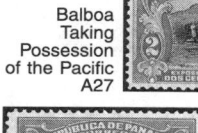

Hurtado — A52

Arms — A53

1921, Nov. 28
232 A52 2c dark green .50 .50

Manuel José Hurtado (1821-1887), president and folklore writer.
For overprints see Nos. 258, 301.

No. 208 Surcharged in Black

1923
233 A28 2c on 2½c scar & blk .35 .35

Surcharge varieties include wrong or omitted date, double surcharge and pair, one without surcharge. Value $2.50 each.
Two stamps in each sheet have a bar above "CENTESIMOS."

1924, May **Engr.**

234	A53	½c orange	.20	.20
235	A53	1c dark green	.20	.20
236	A53	2c carmine	.25	.20
237	A53	5c dark blue	.45	.20
238	A53	10c dark violet	.60	.20
239	A53	12c olive green	.75	.40
240	A53	15c ultra	.95	.40
241	A53	24c yellow brown	1.90	.60
242	A53	50c orange	4.50	1.10
243	A53	1b black	6.75	2.50
		Nos. 234-243 (10)	16.55	6.00

For overprints & surcharges see #277, 321A, 331-338, 352, C19-C20, C68, RA5, RA10-RA22.

Bolívar — A54

Statue of Bolívar — A55

Bolívar Hall — A56

1926, June 10 ***Perf. 12½***

244	A54	½c orange	.25	.25
245	A54	1c dark green	.25	.25
246	A54	2c scarlet	.35	.30
247	A54	4c gray	.45	.35
248	A54	5c dark blue	.70	.50
249	A55	8c lilac	1.10	.80
250	A55	10c dull violet	.80	.80
251	A55	12c olive green	1.25	1.00
252	A55	15c ultra	1.60	1.25
253	A55	20c brown	3.25	1.60
254	A56	24c black violet	4.00	2.00
255	A56	50c black	6.50	5.00
		Nos. 244-255 (12)	20.50	14.10

Bolivar Congress centennial.
For surcharges and overprints see Nos. 259-263, 266-267, 274, 298, 300, 302-303, 305-307, C33-C34, C36, C38-C39.

Lindbergh's Airplane, "The Spirit of St. Louis" — A57

Lindbergh's Airplane and Map of Panama — A58

1928, Jan. 9 **Typo.** ***Rouletted 7***
256 A57 2c dk red & blk, *salmon* .30 .25
257 A58 5c dk blue, *grn* .45 .40

Visit of Colonel Charles A. Lindbergh to Central America by airplane.
No. 256 has black overprint.

No. 232 Overprinted in Red

1928, Nov. 1 ***Perf. 12***
258 A52 2c dark green .25 .25

25th anniversary of the Republic.

No. 247 Surcharged in Black

1930, Dec. 17 ***Perf. 12½, 13***
259 A54 1c on 4c gray .25 .20

Centenary of the death of Simón Bolívar, the Liberator.

Nos. 244-246 Overprinted in Red or Blue

1932 ***Perf. 12½***

260	A54	½c orange (R)	.20	.20
261	A54	1c dark green (R)	.35	.20
a.		Double overprint	18.00	
262	A54	2c scarlet (Bl)	.35	.25

No. 252 Surcharged in Red

263	A55	10c on 15c ultra	1.00	.50
a.		Double surcharge	55.00	
		Nos. 260-263 (4)	1.90	1.15

No. 220 Overprinted as in 1932 in Black

1933 ***Perf. 12***

Overprint 19mm Long

264 A40 ½c orange .35 .20
a. Overprint 17mm long

Dr. Manuel Amador Guerrero — A60

1933, July 3 **Engr.** ***Perf. 12½***
265 A60 2c dark red .50 .20

Centenary of the birth of Dr. Manuel Amador Guerrero, founder of the Republic of Panama and its first President.

No. 251 Surcharged in Red

1933
266 A55 10c on 12c olive grn 1.25 .65

No. 253 Overprinted in Red

267 A55 20c brown 1.75 1.75

José Domingo de Obaldía — A61

Quotation from Emerson — A63

National Institute — A64

Designs: 2c, Eusebio A. Morales. 12c, Justo A. Facio. 15c, Pablo Arosemena.

1934, July **Engr.** ***Perf. 14***

268	A61	1c dark green	.70	.50
269	A61	2c scarlet	.70	.45
270	A63	5c dark blue	1.00	.80
271	A64	10c brown	2.75	1.50
272	A61	12c yellow green	5.00	2.00
273	A61	15c Prus blue	6.75	2.50
		Nos. 268-273 (6)	16.90	7.75

25th anniv. of the Natl. Institute.

Nos. 248, 227 Overprinted in Black or Red

1935-36 ***Perf. 12½, 12***
274 A54 5c dark blue .70 .30
275 A47 10c violet (R) ('36) 1.00 .60

No. 225 Surcharged in Red

1936 ***Perf. 11½***
276 A45 1c on 5c blue .40 .40
a. Lines of surcharge 1½mm btwn. 6.50

No. 241 Surcharged in Blue

1936, Sept. 24 ***Perf. 12***
277 A53 2c on 24c yellow brn .60 .50
a. Double surcharge 20.00

Centenary of the birth of Pablo Arosemena, president of Panama in 1910-12. See Nos. C19-C20.

Ruins of Custom House, Portobelo A67

Designs: 1c, Panama Tree. 2c, "La Pollera." 5c, Simon Bolivar. 10c, Cathedral Tower Ruins. Old Panama. 15c, Francisco Garcia y Santos, 20c, Madden Dam, Panama Canal. 25c, Columbus. 50c, Gaillard Cut. 1b, Panama Cathedral.

1936, Dec. **Engr.** ***Perf. 11½***

278	A67	½c yellow org	.40	.25
279	A67	1c blue green	.40	.20
280	A67	2c carmine rose	.40	.20
281	A67	5c blue	.70	.50
282	A67	10c dk violet	1.25	.75
283	A67	15c turq blue	1.25	.75
284	A67	20c red	1.60	1.50
285	A67	25c black brn	2.50	2.00
286	A67	50c orange	6.50	5.00
287	A67	1b black	15.00	12.00
		Nos. 278-287,C21-C26 (16)	50.65	39.90

4th Postal Congress of the Americas and Spain.

Stamps of 1936 Overprinted in Red or Blue

1937

288	A67	½c yellow org (R)	.30	.30
a.		Inverted overprint	18.00	
289	A67	1c blue green (R)	.35	.20
290	A67	2c car rose (Bl)	.35	.20
291	A67	5c blue (R)	.50	.25
292	A67	10c dk vio (R)	1.00	.35
293	A67	15c turq bl (R)	4.50	3.25
294	A67	20c red (Bl)	1.60	1.25
295	A67	25c black brn (R)	2.50	1.25
296	A67	50c orange (Bl)	6.75	6.00
297	A67	1b black (R)	12.00	10.00
		Nos. 288-297,C27-C32 (16)	64.25	54.05

Stamps of 1921-26 Overprinted in Red or Blue

1937, July ***Perf. 12, 12½***

298	A54	½c orange (R)	.80	.80
a.		Inverted overprint	30.00	
299	A41	1c green (R)	.25	.25
a.		Inverted overprint	30.00	

300	A54	1c dk green (R)	.25	.25
301	A52	2c dk green (R)	.35	.35
302	A54	2c scarlet (Bl)	.35	.35

Stamps of 1921-26 Surcharged in Red

303	A54	2c on 4c gray	.60	.45
304	A46	2c on 8c ol grn	.60	.60
305	A55	2c on 8c lilac	.60	.45
306	A55	2c on 10c dl vio	.60	.50
307	A55	2c on 12c ol grn	.60	.45
308	A48	2c on 15c lt blue	.60	.60
309	A50	2c on 24c blk brn	.60	.75
310	A51	2c on 50c black	.60	.35
		Nos. 298-310 (13)	6.80	6.15

Ricardo Arango A77

Juan A. Guizado A78

La Concordia Fire — A79

Modern Fire Fighting Equipment A80

Firemen's Monument A81

David H. Brandon A82

Perf. 14x14½, 14½x14

1937, Nov. 25 Photo. Wmk. 233

311	A77	½c orange red	.40	.35
312	A78	1c green	.40	.35
313	A79	2c red	.40	.25
314	A80	5c brt blue	.80	.50
315	A81	10c purple	1.50	1.25
316	A82	12c yellow grn	2.50	2.00
		Nos. 311-316,C40-C42 (9)	9.25	7.05

50th anniversary of the Fire Department.

Old Panama Cathedral Tower and Statue of Liberty Enlightening the World, Flags of Panama and US — A83

Engr. & Litho.

1938, Dec. 7 Unwmk. *Perf. 12½*

Center in Black; Flags in Red and Ultramarine

317	A83	1c deep green	.30	.25
318	A83	2c carmine	.40	.20
319	A83	5c blue	.65	.30
320	A83	12c olive	1.25	.75
321	A83	15c brt ultra	1.50	1.25
		Nos. 317-321,C49-C53 (10)	19.40	15.30

150th anniv. of the US Constitution.

No. 236 Overprinted in Black

1938, June 5 *Perf. 12*

321A	A53	2c carmine	.25	.25
b.		Inverted overprint	22.50	
		Nos. 321A,C53A-C53B (3)	1.05	1.05

Opening of the Normal School at Santiago, Veraguas Province, June 5, 1938.

Gatun Lake A84

Liberty A93

Designs: 1c, Pedro Miguel Locks. 2c, Allegory. 5c, Culebra Cut. 10c, Ferryboat. 12c, Aerial View of Canal. 15c, Gen. William C. Gorgas. 50c, Dr. Manuel A. Guerrero. 1b, Woodrow Wilson.

1939, Aug. 15 Engr. *Perf. 12½*

322	A84	½c yellow	.25	.20
323	A84	1c dp blue grn	.40	.20
324	A84	2c dull rose	.50	.20
325	A84	5c dull blue	.80	.20
326	A84	10c dk violet	1.00	.35
327	A84	12c olive green	1.00	.50
328	A84	15c ultra	1.00	.80
329	A84	50c orange	2.50	1.60
330	A84	1b dk brown	5.00	3.00
		Nos. 322-330,C54-C61 (17)	29.15	14.05

25th anniversary of the opening of the Panama Canal. For surcharges see Nos. C64, G2.

Stamps of 1924 Overprinted in Black or Red

1941, Jan. 2 *Perf. 12*

331	A53	½c orange	.25	.25
332	A53	1c dk grn (R)	.30	.30
333	A53	2c carmine	.30	.20
334	A53	5c dk bl (R)	.40	.30
335	A53	10c dk vio (R)	.65	.50
336	A53	15c ultra (R)	1.40	.65
337	A53	50c dp org	5.25	3.50
338	A53	1b blk (R)	12.00	6.00
		Nos. 331-338,C67-C71 (13)	40.95	27.35

New Panama constitution, effective 1/2/41.

Black Overprint

1942, Feb. 19 Engr.

339	A93	10c purple	1.00	1.00

Surcharged with New Value

340	A93	2c on 5c dk bl	1.25	.50
		Nos. 339-340,C72 (3)	5.25	4.00

Flags of Panama and Costa Rica A94

1942 Engraved and Lithographed

341	A94	2c rose red, dk bl & dp rose	.30	.25

1st anniv. of the settlement of the Costa Rica-Panama border dispute. See No. C73.

National Emblems — A95

Farm Girl in Work Dress — A96

Cart Laden with Sugar Cane (Inscribed "ACARRERO DE CAÑA") — A97

Balboa Taking Possession of the Pacific A98

Golden Altar of San José — A99

San Blas Indian Woman and Child — A101

Santo Tomas Hospital A100

Modern Highway A102

1942 Engr.; Flag on ½c Litho.

342	A95	½c dl vio, bl & car	.20	.20
343	A96	1c dk green	.20	.20
344	A97	2c vermilion	.20	.20
345	A98	5c dp bl & blk	.20	.20
346	A99	10c car rose & org	.35	.20
347	A100	15c lt bl & blk	.60	.50
348	A101	50c org red & ol blk	1.40	1.00
349	A102	1b black	2.00	1.00
		Nos. 342-349 (8)	5.15	3.50

See Nos. 357, 365, 376-377, 380, 395, 409.

For surcharges and overprints see Nos. 366-370, 373-375, 378-379, 381, 387-388, 396, C129-C130, RA23.

Catalogue values for unused stamps in this section, from this point to the end of the section, are for Never Hinged items.

Flag of Panama — A103

Arms of Panama — A104

Engraved; Flag on 2c Lithographed

1947, Apr. Unwmk. *Perf. 12½*

350	A103	2c car, bl & red	.20	.20
351	A104	5c deep blue	.20	.20

Natl. Constitutional Assembly of 1945, 2nd anniv.

No. 241 Surcharged in Black

1947 *Perf. 12*

352	A53	50c on 24c yel brn	1.50	1.50
a.		"Habiltada"	2.00	2.00

Nos. C6C, C75, C74 and C87 Surcharged in Black or Carmine

353	AP5	½c on 8c gray blk	.20	.20
a.		"B/.0.0½ CORREOS" (transposed)	2.50	2.50
354	AP34	½c on 8c dk ol brn & blk (C)	.20	.20
355	AP34	1c on 7c rose car	.20	.20
356	AP42	2c on 8c vio	.20	.20
		Nos. 352-356 (5)	2.30	2.30

Flag Type of 1942

1948 Engr. and Litho.

357	A95	½c car, org, bl & dp car	.20	.20

Monument to Firemen of Colon — A105

American-La France Fire Engine — A106

20c, Firemen & hose cart. 25c, New Central Fire Station, Colon. 50c, Maximino Walker. 1b, J. J. A. Ducruet.

1948 Engr.

Center in Black

358	A105	5c dp car	.35	.20
359	A106	10c orange	.60	.20
360	A106	20c gray bl	.90	.40
361	A106	25c chocolate	.90	.50
362	A105	50c purple	1.00	.50
363	A105	1b dp grn	2.50	1.50
		Nos. 358-363 (6)	6.25	3.30

50th anniversary of the founding of the Colon Fire Department.

For overprint see No. C125.

Cervantes A107

1948 Unwmk. *Perf. 12½*

364	A107	2c car & blk	.25	.20
		Nos. 364,C105-C106 (3)	.80	.65

Miguel de Cervantes Saavedra, novelist, playwright and poet, 400th birth anniv.

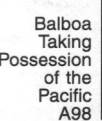

Oxcart Type of 1942 Redrawn
Inscribed: "ACARREO DE CANA"

1948 *Perf. 12*
365 A97 2c vermilion .60 .20

No. 365 Surcharged or Overprinted in Black

1949, May 23
366 A97 1c on 2c ver .20 .20
367 A97 2c vermilion .20 .20
a. Inverted overprint 3.00 3.00
Nos. 366-367,C108-C111 (6) 3.75 3.75

Incorporation of Chiriqui Province, cent.

Stamps and Types of 1942-48 Issues Overprinted in Black or Red

1949, Sept. **Engr.**
368 A96 1c dk green .20 .20
369 A97 2c ver (#365) .20 .20
370 A98 5c blue (R) .30 .20
Nos. 368-370,C114-C118 (8) 3.95 3.60

75th anniv. of the UPU.
Overprint on No. 368 is slightly different and smaller, 15½x12mm.

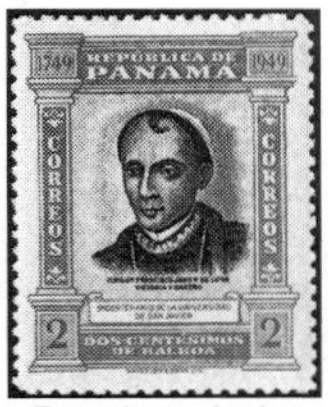
Francisco Javier de Luna — A108

Dr. Carlos J. Finlay — A109

1949, Dec. 7 *Perf. 12½*
371 A108 2c car & blk .25 .20

200th anniversary of the founding of the University of San Javier. See No. C119.

1950, Jan. 12 **Unwmk.** *Perf. 12*
372 A109 2c car & gray blk .35 .20

Issued to honor Dr. Carlos J. Finlay (1833-1915), Cuban physician and biologist who found that a mosquito transmitted yellow fever. See No. C120.

Nos. 343, 357 and 345, Overprinted or Surcharged in Carmine or Black

1950, Aug. 17
373 A96 1c dk green .20 .20
374 A95 2c on ½c car, org, bl & dp car (Bk) .20 .20
375 A98 5c dp bl & blk .30 .20
Nos. 373-375,C121-C125 (8) 4.30 3.60

Gen. José de San Martin, death cent.
The overprint is in four lines on No. 375.

Types of 1942

1950 **Engr.**
376 A97 2c ver & blk .20 .20
377 A98 5c blue .25 .20

No. 376 is inscribed "ACARREO DE CANA."

Nos. 376 and 377 Overprinted in Green or Carmine

1951, Sept. 26
378 A97 2c ver & blk (G) .20 .20
379 A98 5c blue (C) .25 .20

St. Jean-Baptiste de la Salle, 500th birth anniv.
The overprint exists (a) inverted on both stamps, (b) with top line omitted and second line repeated in its place. Value, each $12.50.

Altar Type of 1942

1952 **Engr.** *Perf. 12*
380 A99 10c pur & org .75 .25

No. 357 Surcharged "1952" and New Value in Black

1952
381 A95 1c on ½c multi .20 .20

Queen Isabella I and Arms — A110

1952, Oct. 20 **Engr.** *Perf. 12½*
Center in Black
382 A110 1c green .20 .20
383 A110 2c carmine .20 .20
384 A110 5c dk bl .20 .20
385 A110 10c purple .30 .30
Nos. 382-385,C131-C136 (10) 6.15 5.50

Queen Isabella I of Spain. 500th birth anniv.

No. 380 and Type of 1942 Surcharged "B/ .0.01 1953" in Black or Carmine

1953 *Perf. 12*
387 A99 1c on 10c pur & org .20 .20
388 A100 1c on 15c black (C) .20 .20

A similar surcharge on No. 346 was privately applied.

A111

A112

2c, Baptism of the Flag. 5c, Manuel Amador Guerrero & Senora de Amador. 12c, Santos Jorge A. & Jeronimo de la Ossa. 20c, Revolutionary Junta. 50c, Old city hall. 1b, Natl. coinage.

1953, Nov. 3 **Engr.** *Perf. 12*
389 A111 2c purple .20 .20
390 A112 5c red orange .25 .20
391 A112 12c dp red vio .55 .20
392 A112 20c slate gray 1.00 .25
393 A111 50c org yel 1.50 .60
394 A112 1b blue 2.50 1.25
Nos. 389-394 (6) 6.00 2.70

Founding of the Republic of Panama, 50th anniv.
See #C140-C145. For surcharge see #413.

Farm Girl Type of 1942

1954 **Unwmk.** *Perf. 12*
395 A96 1c dp car rose .20 .20

Surcharged with New Value
396 A96 3c on 1c dp car rose .20 .20

Monument to Gen. Tomas Herrera — A113

1954 **Litho.** *Perf. 12½*
397 A113 3c purple .20 .20
Nos. 397,C148-C149 (3) 2.90 2.65

Gen. Tomas Herrera, death cent.

Tocumen International Airport A114

1955
398 A114 ½c org brn .20 .20

For surcharges see Nos. 411-412.

General Remon Cantera, 1908-1955 — A115

1955, June 1
399 A115 3c lilac rose & blk .20 .20

See No. C153.

Victor de la Guardia y Ayala and Miguel Chiari A116

1955, Sept. 13
400 A116 5c violet .20 .20

Centenary of province of Coclé.

Ferdinand de Lesseps — A117

First Excavation of Panama Canal A118

Design: 50c, Theodore Roosevelt.

1955, Nov. 16
401 A117 3c rose brn, *rose* .35 .20
402 A118 25c vio bl, *lt bl* 1.25 .90
403 A117 50c vio, *lt vio* 1.90 1.00
Nos. 401-403,C155-C156 (5) 5.70 4.30

Ferdinand de Lesseps, 150th birth anniv., French promoter connected with building of Panama Canal. 75th anniv. of the 1st French excavations.
Imperfs exist, but were not sold at any post office.

Popes
A set of twelve stamps picturing various Popes exists. Value, approximately $75.

Arms of Panama City A119

Carlos A. Mendoza A120

Perf. 12½
1956, Aug. 17 **Litho.** **Unwmk.**
404 A119 3c green .20 .20

Sixth Inter-American Congress of Municipalities, Panama City, Aug. 14-19, 1956.
For souvenir sheet see C182a.

1956, Sept. 13 **Wmk. 311**
405 A120 10c rose red & dp grn .20 .20

Pres. Carlos A. Mendoza, birth cent.

National Archives A121

1956, Nov. 27
406 A121 15c shown .40 .20
407 A121 25c Pres. Belisario Porras .60 .50
Nos. 406-407,C183-C184 (4) 1.45 1.10

Centenary of the birth of Pres. Belisario Porras. For surcharge see No. 446.

Pan-American Highway, Panama — A122

1957, Aug. 1
408 A122 3c gray green .20 .20
Nos. 408,C185-C187 (4) 3.20 3.20

7th Pan-American Highway Congress.

Hospital Type of 1942

1957 **Unwmk.** **Engr.** *Perf. 12*
409 A100 15c black .60 .45

Manuel Espinosa Batista — A123

Flags of 21 American Nations — A124

Wmk. 311

1957, Sept. 20 Litho. *Perf. 12½*

410 A123 5c grn & ultra .20 .20

Centenary of the birth of Manuel Espinosa B., independence leader.

No. 398 Surcharged "1957" and New Value in Violet or Black

1957 Unwmk.

411 A114 1c on ½c org brn (V) .20 .20
412 A114 3c on ½c org brn .20 .20

No. 391 Surcharged "1958," New Value and Dots

1958 Engr. *Perf. 12*

413 A112 3c on 12c dp red vio .20 .20

Perf. 12½

1958, July 10 Litho. Unwmk.

Center yellow & black; flags in national colors

414 A124 1c lt gray .20 .20
415 A124 2c brt yel grn .20 .20
416 A124 3c red org .20 .20
417 A124 7c vio bl .25 .20
Nos. 414-417,C203-C206 (8) 3.75 3.40

Organization of American States, 10th anniv.

Brazilian Pavilion, Brussels Fair — A125

3c, Argentina. 5c, Venezuela. 10c, Great Britain.

1958, Sept. 8 Wmk. 311

418 A125 1c org yel & emer .20 .20
419 A125 3c lt bl & olive .20 .20
420 A125 5c lt brn & slate .20 .20
421 A125 10c aqua & redsh brn .20 .20
Nos. 418-421,C207-C209 (7) 3.10 3.05

World's Fair, Brussels, Apr. 17-Oct. 19.

Pope Pius XII as Young Man — A126

UN Headquarters Building — A127

Wmk. 311

1959, Jan. Litho. *Perf. 12½*

422 A126 3c orange brown .20 .20
Nos. 422,C210-C212 (4) 1.70 1.45

Pope Pius XII, 1876-1958. See #C212a.

1959, Apr. 14 Wmk. 311

Design: 15c, Humanity looking into sun.

423 A127 3c maroon & olive .20 .20
424 A127 15c orange & emer .35 .25
Nos. 423-424,C213-C217 (7) 3.40 3.10

10th anniv. (in 1958) of the signing of the Universal Declaration of Human Rights.
For overprints see Nos. 425-426, C219-C221.

Nos. 423-424 Overprinted in Dark Blue

1959, May 16

425 A127 3c maroon & olive .20 .20
426 A127 15c orange & emer .35 .20
Nos. 425-426,C218-C221 (6) 3.20 2.95

Issued to commemorate the 8th Reunion of the Economic Commission for Latin America.

Eusebio A. Morales — A128

National Institute A129

Wmk. 311

1959, July 27 Litho. *Perf. 12½*

427 A128 3c shown .20 .20
428 A128 13c Abel Bravo .25 .25
429 A129 21c shown .40 .25
Nos. 427-429,C222-C223 (5) 1.25 1.10

50th anniversary, National Institute.

Soccer — A130

Fencing — A131

1959, Oct. 26

430 A130 1c shown .20 .20
431 A130 3c Swimming .20 .20
432 A130 20c Hurdling .40 .40
Nos. 430-432,C224-C226 (6) 2.00 1.80

3rd Pan American Games, Chicago, 8/27-9/7/59.
For overprint and surcharge see #C289, C349.

Wmk. 343

1960, Sept. 22 Litho. *Perf. 12½*

433 A131 3c shown .20 .20
434 A131 5c Soccer .20 .20
Nos. 433-434,C234-C237 (6) 2.30 1.80

17th Olympic Games, Rome, 8/25-9/11.
For surcharges & overprints see #C249-C250, C254, C266-C270, C290, C298, C350, RA40.

Agricultural Products and Cattle A132

1961, Mar. 3 Wmk. 311 *Perf. 12½*

435 A132 3c blue green .20 .20

Issued to publicize the second agricultural and livestock census, Apr. 16, 1961.

Children's Hospital A133

1961, May 2

436 A133 3c greenish blue .20 .20
Nos. 436,C284-C286 (4) .80 .80

25th anniv. of the Lions Club of Panama. See #C245-C247.

Flags of Panama and Costa Rica A134

1961, Oct. 2 Wmk. 343 *Perf. 12½*

437 A134 3c car & bl .20 .20

Meeting of Presidents Mario Echandi of Costa Rica and Roberto F. Chiari of Panama at Paso Canoa, Apr. 21, 1961. See No. C251.

Arms of Colon — A135

Mercury and Cogwheel — A136

1962, Feb. 28 Litho. Wmk. 311

438 A135 3c car, yel & vio bl .20 .20

3rd Central American Municipal Assembly, Colon, May 13-17. See No. C255.

1962, Mar. 16 Wmk. 343

439 A136 3c red orange .20 .20

First industrial and commercial census.

Social Security Hospital A137

1962, June 1 *Perf. 12½*

440 A137 3c vermilion & gray .20 .20

Opening of the Social Security Hospital.
For surcharge see No. 445.

San Francisco de la Montana Church, Veraguas A138

Ruins of Old Panama Cathedral (1519-1671) A139

Designs: 3c, David Cathedral. 5c, Natá Church. 10c, Don Bosco Church. 15c, Church of the Virgin of Carmen. 20c, Colon Cathedral. 25c, Greek Orthodox Temple. 50c, Cathedral of Panama. 1b, Protestant Church of Colon.

1962-64 Litho. Wmk. 343

Buildings in Black

441 A138 1c red & bl .20 .20
441A A139 2c red & yel .20 .20
441B A138 3c vio & yel .20 .20
441C A139 5c rose & lt grn .20 .20
441D A139 10c grn & yel .25 .20
441E A139 10c red & bl ('64) .25 .20
441F A139 15c ultra & lt grn .30 .20
441G A139 20c red & pink .40 .25
441H A138 25c grn & pink .50 .45
441I A139 50c ultra & pink 1.00 .40
441J A138 1b lilac & yel 2.00 1.50
Nos. 441-441J (11) 5.50 4.00

Freedom of religion in Panama.
Issued: #441E, 6/4/64; others, 7/20/62.

See #C256-C265; souvenir sheet #C264a.
For surcharges and overprints see Nos. 445A, 451, 467, C288, C296-C297, C299.

Bridge of the Americas during Construction — A140

1962, Oct. 12 *Perf. 12½*

442 A140 3c carmine & gray .20 .20

Opening of the Bridge of the Americas (Thatcher Ferry Bridge), Oct. 12, 1962. See No. C273. For surcharge see No. 445B.

Fire Brigade Exercises, Inauguration of Aqueduct, 1906 — A141

Portraits of Fire Brigade Officials: 3c, Lt. Col. Luis Carlos Endara P., Col. Raul Arango N. and Major Ernesto Arosemena A. 5c, Guillermo Patterson Jr., David F. de Castro, Pres. T. Gabriel Duque, Telmo Rugliancich and Tomas Leblanc.

1963 Wmk. 311 *Perf. 12½*

443 A141 1c emer & blk .20 .20
443A A141 3c vio bl & blk .20 .20
444 A141 5c mag & blk .20 .20
Nos. 443-444,C279-C281 (6) 1.60 1.50

75th anniversary (in 1962) of the Panamanian Fire Brigade.
For surcharge see No. 445C.

Nos. 440, 441A, 442, 443A and 407 Surcharged "VALE" and New Value in Black or Red

1963 Wmk. 343 *Perf. 12½*

445 A137 4c on 3c ver & gray .20 .20
445A A138 4c on 3c vio & yel .20 .20
445B A140 4c on 3c car & gray .20 .20

Wmk. 311

445C A141 4c on 3c vio bl & blk .20 .20
446 A121 10c on 25c dk car rose & bluish blk (R) .35 .20
Nos. 445-446 (5) 1.15 1.00

1964 Winter Olympics, Innsbruck - 141a

Perf. 14x13½, 13½x14 (#447A, 447C)

1963, Dec. 20 Litho.

447 A141a ½c Mountains .20 .20
447A A141a 1c Speed skating .20 .20
447B A141a 3c like No. 447 .25 .20
447C A141a 4c like No. 447A .35 .20
447D A141a 5c Slalom skiing .45 .25
447E A141a 15c like No. 447D 1.10 .50
447F A141a 21c like No. 447D 2.10 1.00

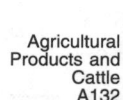

447G A141a 31c like No. 447D 2.75 1.25
h. Souv. sheet of 2, #447F-447G, perf. 13½x14 17.50 16.00

#447D-447G are airmail. #447Gh exists imperf., with background colors switched. Value, $17.50.

Pres. Francisco J. Orlich, Costa Rica — A142

Vasco Nuñez de Balboa — A143

Flags and Presidents: 2c, Luis A. Somoza, Nicaragua. 3c, Dr. Ramon Villeda M., Honduras. 4c, Roberto F. Chiari, Panama.

Perf. 12½x12

1963, Dec. 18 Litho. Unwmk.

Portrait in Slate Green

448 A142 1c lt grn, red & ultra .20 .20
448A A142 2c lt bl, red & ultra .20 .20
448B A142 3c pale pink, red & ultra .20 .20
448C A142 4c rose, red & ultra .25 .20
Nos. 448-448C,C292-C294 (7) 2.95 2.30

Meeting of Central American Presidents with Pres. John F. Kennedy, San José, Mar. 18-20, 1963.

1964, Jan. 22 Photo. *Perf. 13*

449 A143 4c green, *pale rose* .25 .20

450th anniv. of Balboa's discovery of the Pacific Ocean. See No. C295.

No. C231 Surcharged in Red: "Correos B/.0.10"

1964 Wmk. 311 Litho. *Perf. 12½*

450 AP74 10c on 21c lt bl .30 .20

Type of 1962 Overprinted in Red: "HABILITADA"

1964 Wmk. 343

451 A138 1b red, bl & blk 2.00 2.00

1964 Summer Olympics, Tokyo — A144

1964, Apr. *Perf. 13½x14*

452 A144 ½c shown .20 .20
452A A144 1c Torch bearer .20 .20

Perf. 14x13½

452B A144 5c Olympic stadium .30 .25
452C A144 10c like No. 452B .55 .30
452D A144 21c like No. 452B 1.10 .60
452E A144 50c like No. 452B 2.25 1.25
f. Souv. sheet of 1, perf. 13½x14 17.50 16.00

Nos. 452B-452E are airmail. No. 452Ef exists imperf. with different colors. Value, $17.50.

Space Conquest — A145

½c, Projected Apollo spacecraft. 1c, Gemini, Agena spacecraft. 5c, Astronaut Walter M. Schirra. 10c, Astronaut L. Gordon Cooper. 21c, Schirra's Mercury capsule. 50c, Cooper's Mercury capsule.

1964, Apr. 21 *Perf. 14x14x13½*

453 A145 ½c bl grn & multi .20 .20
453A A145 1c dk blue & multi .20 .20
453B A145 5c yel bis & multi .25 .25
453C A145 10c lil rose & multi .40 .30
453D A145 21c blue & multi 1.00 .75
453E A145 50c violet & multi 4.25 3.00
f. Souvenir sheet of 1 17.50 16.00

Nos. 453B-453E are airmail. No. 453Ef exists imperf. with different colors. Value, $17.50.

Aquatic Sports A146

1964, Sept. 2 *Perf. 14x13½, 13½x14*

454 A146 ½c Water skiing .20 .20
454A A146 1c Skin diving .20 .20
454B A146 5c Fishing .25 .20
454C A146 10c Sailing, vert. 1.50 .50
454D A146 21c Hydroplane racing 2.75 1.00
454E A146 31c Water polo 3.50 1.25
f. Souvenir sheet of 1 17.50 16.00

Nos. 454B-454E are airmail. Nos. 454-454Ef exists imperf. with different colors. Value, $17.50.

Eleanor Roosevelt - A147

Perf. 12x12½

1964, Oct. 9 Litho. Unwmk.

455 A147 4c car & blk, *grnsh* .30 .20

Issued to honor Eleanor Roosevelt (1884-1962). See Nos. C330-C330a.

Canceled to Order
Canceled sets of new issues have been sold by the government. Postally used copies are worth more.

1964 Winter Olympics, Innsbruck — A147a

Olympic medals and winners: ½c, Women's slalom. 1c, Men's 500-meter speed skating. 2c, Four-man bobsled. 3c, Women's figure skating. 4c, Ski jumping. 5c, 15km cross country skiing. 6c, 50km cross country skiing. 7c, Women's 3000-meter speed skating. 10c, Men's figure skating. 21c, Two-man bobsled. 31c, Men's downhill skiing.

Litho. & Embossed

Perf. 13½x14

1964, Oct. 14 Unwmk.

456 A147a ½c bl grn & multi .20 .20
456A A147a 1c dk bl & multi .20 .20
456B A147a 2c brn vio & multi .20 .20
456C A147a 3c lil rose & multi .20 .20
456D A147a 4c brn lake & multi .25 .20
456E A147a 5c brt vio & multi .45 .20
456F A147a 6c grn bl & multi .55 .25
456G A147a 7c dp vio & multi .65 .30
456H A147a 10c emer grn & multi .90 .40
456I A147a 21c ver & multi 1.40 .65
456J A147a 31c ultra & multi 2.50 1.00
k. Souv. sheet of 3, #456H-456J 17.50 16.00

Nos. 456E-456J are airmail. No. 456Jk exists imperf.
See Nos. 458-458J.

Satellites — A147b

Designs: ½c, Telstar 1. 1c, Transit 2A. 5c, OSO 1 Solar Observatory. 10c, Tiros 2 weather satellite. 21c, Weather station. 50c, Syncom 3.

1964, Dec. 21 *Perf. 14x14x13½*

457 A147b ½c ver & multi .40 .25
457A A147b 1c violet & multi .40 .25
457B A147b 5c lil rose & multi .40 .40
457C A147b 10c blue & multi .55 .25
457D A147b 21c bl grn & multi 1.50 1.25
457E A147b 50c green & multi 2.25 1.75
f. Souvenir sheet of 1 17.50 16.00

Nos. 457B-457E are airmail. No. 457Ef exists imperf with different colors. Value, $20.
For overprints see Nos. 489-489b.

1964 Olympic Medals Type

Summer Olympic Medals and Winners: ½c, Parallel bars. 1c, Dragon-class sailing. 2c, Individual show jumping. 3c, Two-man kayak. 4c, Team road race cycling. 5c, Individual dressage. 6c, Women's 800-meter run. 7c, 3000-meter steeplechase. 10c, Men's floor exercises. 21c, Decathlon. 31c, Men's 100-meter freestyle swimming.

Litho. & Embossed

1964, Dec. 28 *Perf. 13½x14*

458 A147a ½c orange & multi .20 .20
458A A147a 1c plum & multi .20 .20
458B A147a 2c bl grn & multi .20 .20
458C A147a 3c red brn & multi .20 .20
458D A147a 4c lilac rose & multi .25 .20
458E A147a 5c dull grn & multi .45 .20
458F A147a 6c blue & multi .55 .25
458G A147a 7c dk vio & multi .65 .30
458H A147a 10c ver & multi .90 .40
458I A147a 21c dl vio & multi 1.40 .65
458J A147a 31c dk bl grn & multi 2.50 1.00
k. Souv. sheet of 3, #458H-458J 20.00 17.50

#458E-458J are airmail. #458Jk exists imperf. Value, $21.

John F. Kennedy & Cape Kennedy — A147c

Designs: 1c, Launching of Titan II rocket, Gemini capsule. 2c, Apollo lunar module. 3c, Proposed Apollo command and service modules. 5c, Gemini capsule atop Titan II rocket. 6c, Soviet cosmonauts Komarov, Yegorov, Feoktistov. 11c, Ranger VII. 31c, Lunar surface.
Illustration reduced.

1965, Feb. 25 Litho. *Perf. 14*

459 A147c ½c vio bl & multi .20 .20
459A A147c 1c blue & multi .20 .20
459B A147c 2c plum & multi .20 .20
459C A147c 3c ol grn & multi .20 .20
459D A147c 5c lilac rose & multi .40 .30
459E A147c 10c dull grn & multi .65 .45
459F A147c 11c brt vio & multi 1.10 .75
459G A147c 31c green & multi 2.10 1.40
h. Souvenir sheet of 1 17.50 16.00

Nos. 459D-459G are airmail. No. 459Gh exists imperf. with different colors. Value, $17.50. For overprints see Nos. 491-491b.

Atomic Power for Peace — A147d

Designs: ½c, Nuclear powered submarine *Nautilus.* 1c, Nuclear powered ship *Savannah.* 4c, First nuclear reactor, Calderhall, England. 6c, Nuclear powered icebreaker *Lenin.* 10c, Nuclear powered observatory. 21c, Nuclear powered space vehicle.
Illustration reduced.

1965, May 12

460 A147d ½c blue & multi
460A A147d 1c green & multi
460B A147d 4c red & multi
460C A147d 6c dl bl grn & multi
460D A147d 10c blue grn & multi
460E A147d 21c dk violet & multi
f. Souv. sheet of 2, #460D-460E

Nos. 460B-460E are airmail. Nos. 460-460Ef exists imperf with different colors.

John F. Kennedy Memorial A147e

Kennedy and: ½c, PT109. 1c, Space capsule. 10c, UN emblem. 21c, Winston Churchill. 31c, Rocket launch at Cape Kennedy.

1965, Aug. 23 *Perf. 13½x13*

461 A147e ½c multicolored
461A A147e 1c multicolored
461B A147e 10c + 5c, multi
461C A147e 21c + 10c, multi
461D A147e 31c + 15c, multi
e. Souv. sheet of 2, #461A, 461D, perf. 12½x12

Nos. 461B-461D are airmail semipostal. Nos. 461-461De exist imperf with different colors.
For overprints see Nos. C367A-C367B.

Keel-billed Toucan A148

Song Birds: 2c, Scarlet macaw. 3c, Red-crowned woodpecker. 4c, Blue-gray tanager, horiz.

1965, Oct. 27 Unwmk. *Perf. 14*

462	A148 1c brt pink & multi		.20	.20
462A	A148 2c multicolored		.20	.20
462B	A148 3c brt vio & multi		.20	.20
462C	A148 4c org yel & multi		.20	.20
	Nos. 462-462C,C337-C338 (6)		1.25	1.20

Snapper — A149

1965, Dec. 7 Litho.

463	A149 1c shown	.20	.20
463A	A149 2c Dorado	.20	.20
	Nos. 463-463A,C339-C342 (6)	1.80	1.40

Pope Paul VI, Visit to UN — A149a

Designs: ½c, Pope on Balcony of St. Peters, Vatican City. 1c, Pope Addressing UN General Assembly. 5c, Arms of Vatican City, Panama, UN emblem. 10c, Lyndon Johnson, Pope Paul VI, Francis Cardinal Spellman. 21c, Ecumenical Council, Vatican II. 31c, Earlybird satellite.

1966 Apr. 4 *Perf. 12x12½*

464 A149a ½c multicolored
464A A149a 1c multicolored
464B A149a 5c multicolored
464C A149a 10c multicolored
464D A149a 21c multicolored
464E A149a 31c multicolored
f. Souv. sheet of 2, #464B, 464E, perf. 13x13½

Nos. 464B-464E are airmail. No. 464Ef exists imperf. with different margin color.
For overprints see Nos. 490-490B.

Famous Men — A149b

Designs: ½c, William Shakespeare. 10c, Dante Alighieri. 31c, Richard Wagner.

1966, May 26 *Perf. 14*

465 A149b ½c multicolored
465A A149b 10c multicolored
465B A149b 31c multicolored
c. Souv. sheet of 2, #465A-465B, perf. 13½x14

Nos. 465A-465B are airmail. No. 465Bc exists imperf. with different margin color.

Works by Famous Artists A149c

Paintings: ½c, Elizabeth Tucher by Durer. 10c, Madonna of the Rocky Grotto by Da Vinci. 31c, La Belle Jardiniere by Raphael.

1966, May 26

466 A149c ½c multicolored
466A A149c 10c multicolored
466B A149c 31c multicolored
c. Souv. sheet of 2, #466A-466B

Nos. 466A-466B are airmail. No. 466Bc exists imperf. with different margin color.

No. 441H Surcharged

1966, June 27 Wmk. 343 *Perf. 12½*

467	A138 13c on 25c grn & pink	.40	.25

The "25c" has not been obliterated.

A149d

A149e

1966, July 11 *Perf. 14*

468 A149d ½c shown
468A A149d .005b Uruguay, 1930, 1950
468B A149d 10c Italy, 1934, 1938
468C A149d 10c Brazil, 1958, 1962
468D A149d 21c Germany, 1954
468E A149d 21c Great Britain
f. Souv. sheet of 2, #468B, 468D
g. Souv. sheet of 2, #468, 468E, imperf.

World Cup Soccer Championships, Great Britain. Nos. 468B-468E are airmail. Imperfs. are different colors than perforated issues.
For overprints see Nos. 470-470g.

Perf. 12x12½, 12½x12

1966, Aug. 12

Italian Contributions to Space Research: ½c, Launch of Scout rocket, San Marco satellite. 1c, San Marco in orbit, horiz. 5c, Italian scientists, rocket. 10c, Arms of Panama, Italy, horiz. 21c, San Marco boosted into orbit, horiz.

469 A149e ½c multicolored
469A A149e 1c multicolored
469B A149e 5c multicolored
469C A149e 10c multicolored
469D A149e 21c multicolored
e. Souv. sheet of 2, #469C-469D, imperf.

Nos. 469B-469D are airmail.

Nos. 468-468g Ovptd.

1966, Sept. 28 *Perf. 14*

470 A149d ½c on #468
470A A149d .005b on #468A
470B A149d 10c on #468B
470C A149d 10c on #468C
470D A149d 21c on #468D
470E A149d 21c on #468E
f. on #468Ef
g. on #468Eg, imperf.

Nos. 470B-470E are airmail.

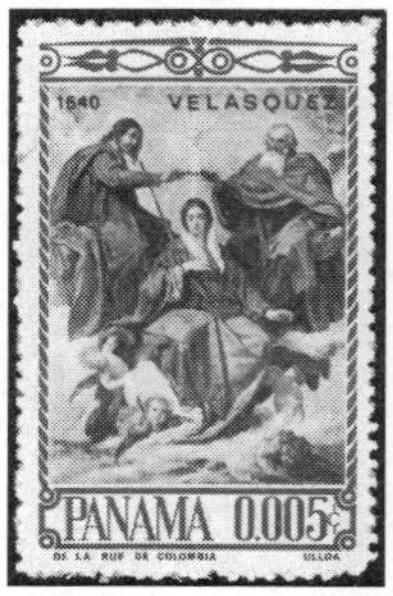

A149f

Religious Paintings A149g

Paintings: ½c, Coronation of Mary. 1c, Holy Family with Angel. 2c, Adoration of the Magi. 3c, Madonna and Child. No. 471D, The Annunciation. No. 471E, The Nativity. No. 471Fh, Madonna and Child.

1966, Oct. 24 *Perf. 11*

Size of No. 471D: 32x34mm

471 A149f ½c Velazquez
471A A149f 1c Saraceni
471B A149g 2c Durer
471C A149f 3c Orazio
471D A149g 21c Rubens
471E A149f 21c Boticelli

Souvenir Sheet

Perf. 14

471F Sheet of 2
g. A149f 21c like No. 471E, black inscriptions
h. A149f 31c Mignard

Nos. 471D-471F are airmail. All exist imperf. with different colors.

Sir Winston Churchill, British Satellites — A149h

Churchill and: 10c, Blue Streak, NATO emblem. 31c, Europa 1, rocket engine.

1966, Nov. 25 *Perf. 12x12½*

472 A149h ½c shown
472A A149h 10c org & multi
472B A149h 31c dk bl & multi
c. Souv. sheet of 2, #472A-472B, perf. 13½x14

Nos. 472A-472B are airmail. No. 472Bc exists imperf. with different colors.
For overprints see Nos. 492-492B.

John F. Kennedy, 3rd Death Anniv. — A149i

1966, Nov. 25 *Perf. 14*

473 A149i ½c shown
473A A149i 10c Kennedy, UN bldg.
473B A149i 31c Kennedy, satellites & map
c. Souv. sheet of 2, #473A-473B

Nos. 473A-473B are airmail. No. 473Bc exists imperf. with different colors.

Jules Verne (1828-1905), French Space Explorations — A149j

Designs: ½c, Earth, A-1 satellite. 1c, Verne, submarine. 5c, Earth, FR-1 satellite. 10c, Verne, telescope. 21c, Verne, capsule heading toward Moon. 31c, D-1 satellite over Earth.

1966, Dec. 28 *Perf. 13½x14*

474 A149j ½c bl & multi
474A A149j 1c bl grn & multi
474B A149j 5c ultra & multi
474C A149j 10c lil, blk & red
474D A149j 21c vio & multi
f. Souv. sheet of 2, #474C, 474D, imperf.
474E A149j 31c dl bl & multi
g. Souvenir sheet of 1

Nos. 474B-474E are airmail. All imperfs. are in different colors.

Hen and Chicks A150

Domestic Animals: 3c, Rooster. 5c, Pig, horiz. 8c, Cow, horiz.

1967, Feb. 3 Unwmk. *Perf. 14*

475	A150 1c multi	.20	.20
475A	A150 3c multi	.20	.20
475B	A150 5c multi	.20	.20
475C	A150 8c multi	.25	.20
	Nos. 475-475C,C353-C356 (8)	3.15	2.20

Easter A150a

Paintings: ½c, Christ at Calvary. 1c, The Crucifixion. 5c, Pieta, horiz. 10c, Body of Christ. 21c, The Arisen Christ. No. 476E, ChristAscending into Heaven. No. 476F, Christ on the Cross. No. 476G, Madonna and Child.

1967, Mar. 13 ***Perf. 14x13½, 13½x14***

476 A150a ½c Giambattista Tiepolo
476A A150a 1c Rubens
476B A150a 5c Sarto
476C A150a 10c Raphael Santi
476D A150a 21c Multscher
476E A150a 31c Grunewald

Souvenir Sheets

Perf. 12½x12x12½x13½

476F A150a 31c Van der Weyden

Imperf

476G A150a 31c Rubens

Nos. 476B-476G are airmail.

1968 Summer Olympics, Mexico City — A150b

Indian Ruins at: ½c, Teotihuacan. 1c, Tajin. 5c, Xochicalco. 10c, Monte Alban. 21c, Palenque. 31c, Chichen Itza.

1967, Apr. ***Perf. 12x12½***

477 A150b ½c plum & multi
477A A150b 1c red lilac & multi
477B A150b 5c blue & multi
477C A150b 10c ver & multi
477D A150b 21c green bl & multi
477E A150b 31c green & multi

Nos. 477B-477E are airmail.

New World Anhinga A151

Birds: 1c, Quetzals. 3c, Turquoise-browed motmot. 4c, Double-collared aracari, horiz. 5c, Macaw. 13c, Belted kingfisher. 50c, Hummingbird.

1967, July 20 ***Perf. 14***

478	A151	½c	lt bl & multi	.20	.20
478A	A151	1c	lt gray & multi	.20	.20
478B	A151	3c	pink & multi	.20	.20
478C	A151	4c	lt grn & multi	.20	.20
478D	A151	5c	buff & multi	.20	.20
478E	A151	13c	yel & multi	.50	.25
	Nos. 478-478E (6)			1.50	1.25

Souvenir Sheet

Perf. 14½

478F A151 50c Sheet of 1

No. 478A exists imperf. with blue background.

Works of Famous Artists A151a

Paintings: No. 479, Maiden in the Doorway. No. 479A, Blueboy. No. 479B, The Promise of Louis XIII. No. 479C, St. George and the Dragon. No. 479D, The Blacksmith's Shop, horiz. No. 479E, St. Hieronymus. Nos. 479F-479K, Self-portraits.

Perf. 14x13½, 13½x14

1967, Aug. 23

479 A151a 5c Rembrandt
479A A151a 5c Gainsborough
479B A151a 5c Ingres
479C A151a 21c Raphael
479D A151a 21c Velazquez
479E A151a 21c Durer

Souvenir Sheets

Various Compound Perfs.

479F A151a 21c Gainsborough
479G A151a 21c Rembrandt
479H A151a 21c Ingres
479I A151a 21c Raphael
479J A151a 21c Velazquez
479K A151a 21c Durer

Nos. 479C-479K are airmail.

Red Deer, by Franz Marc — A152

Animal Paintings by Franz Marc: 3c, Tiger, vert. 5c, Monkeys. 8c, Blue Fox.

1967, Sept. 1 ***Perf. 14***

480	A152	1c	multi	.20	.20
480A	A152	3c	multi	.20	.20
480B	A152	5c	multi	.20	.20
480C	A152	8c	multi	.25	.20
	Nos. 480-480C,C357-C360 (8)			2.30	1.80

Paintings by Goya A152a

Designs: 2c, The Water Carrier. 3c, Count Floridablanca. 4c, Senora Francisca Sebasa y Garcia. 5c, St. Bernard and St. Robert. 8c, Self-portrait. 10c, Dona Isabel Cobos de Porcel. 13c, Clothed Maja, horiz. 21c, Don Manuel Osoria de Zuniga as a child. 50c, Cardinal Luis of Bourbon and Villabriga.

1967, Oct. 17 ***Perf. 14x13½, 13½x14***

481 A152a 2c multicolored
481A A152a 3c multicolored
481B A152a 4c multicolored
481C A152a 5c multicolored
481D A152a 8c multicolored
481E A152a 10c multicolored
481F A152a 13c multi, horiz.
481G A152a 21c multicolored

Souvenir Sheet

481H A152a 50c multicolored

Nos. 481C-481H are airmail.

Life of Christ A152b

Paintings: No. 482, The Holy Family. No. 482A, Christ Washing Feet. 3c, Christ's Charge to Peter. 4c, Christ and the Money Changers in the Temple, horiz. No. 482D, Christ's Entry into Jerusalem, horiz. No. 482E, The Last Supper. No. 482Fl, Pastoral Adoration. No. 482Fm, The Holy Family. No. 482Gn, Christ with Mary and Martha. No. 482Go, Flight from Egypt. No. 482Hp, St. Thomas. No. 482Hq, The Tempest. No. 482Ir, The Transfiguration. No. 482Is, The Crucification. No. 482J, The Baptism of Christ, by Guido Reni. No. 482K, Christ at the Sea of Galilee, by Tintoretto, horiz.

1968, Jan. 10 ***Perf. 14x13½x13½x14***

482 A152b 1c Michaelangelo
482A A152b 1c Brown
482B A152b 3c Rubens
482C A152b 4c El Greco
482D A152b 21c Van Dyck
482E A152b 21c de Juanes

Souvenir Sheets

Various Perfs.

482F Sheet of 2
 l. A152b 1c Schongauer
 m. A152b 21c Raphael
482G Sheet of 2
 n. A152b 3c Tintoretto
 o. A152b 21c Caravaggio
482H Sheet of 2
 p. A152b 21c Anonymous, 12th cent.
 q. A152b 31c multicolored
482I Sheet of 2
 r. A152b 21c Raphael
 s. A152b 31c Montanez

Imperf

482J A152b 22c Sheet of 1
482K A152b 24c Sheet of 1

Nos. 482C-482K are airmail.

Butterflies — A152c

1968, Feb. 23 ***Perf. 14***

483 A152c ½c Apodemia albinus
483A A152c 1c Caligo ilioneus, vert.
483B A152c 3c Meso semia tenera
483C A152c 4c Pamphila epictetus
483D A152c 5c Entheus peleus
483E A152c 13c Tmetoglene drymo

Souvenir Sheet

Perf. 14½

483F A152c 50c Thymele chalco, vert.

Nos. 483D-483F are airmail. No. 483F exists imperf. with pink margin.

10th Winter Olympics, Grenoble — A152d

1968, May 7 ***Perf. 14x13½, 13½x14***

484 A152d ½c Emblem, vert.
484A A152d 1c Ski jumper
484B A152d 5c Skier
484C A152d 10c Mountain climber
484D A152d 21c Speed skater
484E A152d 31c Two-man bobsled

Souvenir Sheets

Perf. 14

484F Sheet of 2
 h. A152d 10c Emblem, snowflake
 i. A152d 31c Figure skater
484G Sheet of 2
 j. A152d 31c Biathlon
 k. A152d 10c Skier on ski lift

Nos. 484B-484G are airmail.

Sailing Ships — A152e

Paintings by: ½c, Gamiero, vert. 1c, Lebreton. 3c, Anonymous Japanese. 4c, Le Roi. 5c, Van de Velde. 13c, Duncan. 50c, Anonymous Portuguese, vert.

1968, May 7 ***Perf. 14***

485 A152e ½c multicolored
485A A152e 1c multicolored
485B A152e 3c multicolored
485C A152e 4c multicolored
485D A152e 5c multicolored
485E A152e 13c multicolored

Souvenir Sheet

Perf. 14½

485F A152e 50c multicolored

Nos. 485D-485E are airmail. No. 485F exists imperf. with light blue margin.

Tropical Fish — A152f

1968, June 26 ***Perf. 14***

486 A152f ½c Balistipus undulatus
486A A152f 1c Holacanthus ciliaris
486B A152f 3c Chaetodon ephippium
486C A152f 4c Epinephelus elongatus
486D A152f 5c Anisotremus verginicus
486E A152f 13c Balistoides conspicillum

Souvenir Sheet

Perf. 14½

486F A152f 50c Raja texana, vert.

Nos. 486D-486F are airmail. No. 486F exists imperf. with pink margin.

Olympic Medals and Winners, Grenoble — A152g

Olympic Medals and Winners: 1c, Men's giant slalom. 2c, Women's downhill. 3c, Women's figure skating. 4c, 5000-meter speed skating. 5c, 10,000-meter speed skating. 6c, Women's slalom. 8c, Women's 1000-

meter speed skating. 13c, Women's 1500-meter speed skating. 30c, Two-man bobsled. 70c, Nordic combined.

Litho. & Embossed

1968, July 30 ***Perf. 13½x14***

487	A152g	1c	pink & multi
487A	A152g	2c	vio & multi
487B	A152g	3c	grn & multi
487C	A152g	4c	plum & multi
487D	A152g	5c	red brn & multi
487E	A152g	6c	brt vio & multi
487F	A152g	8c	Prus bl & multi
487G	A152g	13c	bl & multi
487H	A152g	30c	rose lil & multi

Souvenir Sheet

487I A152g 70c red & multi

Nos. 487G-487H are airmail.

Miniature Sheet

Music — A152h

Paintings of Musicians, Instruments: 5c, Mandolin, by de la Hyre. 10c, Lute, by Caravaggio. 15c, Flute, by ter Brugghen. 20c, Chamber ensemble, by Tourmer. 25c, Violin, by Caravaggio. 30c, Piano, by Vermeer. 40c, Harp, by Memling.

1968, Sept. 11 Litho. ***Perf. 13½x14***

488 Sheet of 6
- *a.* A152h 5c multicolored
- *b.* A152h 10c multicolored
- *c.* A152h 15c multicolored
- *d.* A152h 20c multicolored
- *e.* A152h 25c multicolored
- *f.* A152h 30c multicolored

Souvenir Sheet

Perf. 14

488A A152h 40c multicolored

Nos. 457, 457E Ovptd. in Black

1968, Oct. 17

489 A147b ½c on No. 457
489A A147b 50c on No. 457E
b. Souv. sheet of 1, on No. 457Ef

Nos. 489-489A exist with gold overprint. Overprint differs on No. 489Ab.

Nos. 464, 464D & 464Ef Ovptd. in Black or Gold

1968, Oct. 18 ***Perf. 12x12½***

490 A149a ½c on No. 464
490A A149a 21c on No. 464D

Souvenir Sheet

Perf. 13x13½

490B on No. 464Ef (G)

Nos. 490A-490B are airmail. No. 490B exists imperf. with different colored border. Overprint differs on No. 490B.

Nos. 459, 459G-459Gh Ovptd. in Black

1968, Oct. 21 ***Perf. 14***

491 A147c ½c on No. 459
491A A147c 31c on No. 459G
b. on souv. sheet, No. 459Gh

Nos. 491A-491Ab are airmail. Nos. 491-491A exist overprinted in gold, and imperf., overprinted in gold. No. 491Ab exists imperf. with different colors and black or gold overprints.

Nos. 472-472A, 472Bc Overprinted in Black or Gold

1968, Oct. 22 ***Perf. 12x12½***

492 A149h ½c on No. 472
492A A149h 10c on No. 472A

Souvenir Sheet

Perf. 13½x14

492B on No. 472c

Nos. 492A-492B are airmail. No. 492B exists imperf with different colors.

Hunting on Horseback — A152i

Paintings and Tapestries: 1c, Koller. 3c, Courbet. 5c, Tischbein, the Elder. 10c, Gobelin, vert. 13c, Oudry. 30c, Rubens.

1968, Oct. 29 ***Perf. 14***

493	A152i	1c	multicolored
493A	A152i	3c	multicolored
493B	A152i	5c	multicolored
493C	A152i	10c	multicolored
493D	A152i	13c	multicolored
493E	A152i	30c	multicolored

Nos. 493D-493E are airmail.

Miniature Sheet

Famous Race Horses — A152j

Horse Paintings: a, 5c, Lexington, by Edward Troye. b, 10c, American Eclipse, by Alvan Fisher. c, 15c, Plenipotentiary, by Abraham Cooper. d, 20c, Gimcrack, by George Stubbs. e, 25c, Flying Childers, by James Seymour. f, 30c, Eclipse, by Stubbs.

1968, Oct. 29 ***Perf. 13½x14***

494 A152j Sheet of 6, #a.-f.

1968 Summer Olympics, Mexico City — A152k

Mexican art: 1c, Watermelons, by Diego Rivera. 2c, Women, by Jose Clemente Orozco. 3c, Flower Seller, by Miguel Covarrubias, vert. 4c, Nutall Codex, vert. 5c, Mayan statue, vert. 6c, Face sculpture, vert. 8c, Seated figure, vert. 13c. Ceramic angel, vert. 30c, Christ, by David Alfaro Siqueiros. 70c, Symbols of Summer Olympic events.

1968, Dec. 23 ***Perf. 13½x14, 14x13½***

495	A152k	1c	multicolored
495A	A152k	2c	multicolored
495B	A152k	3c	multicolored
495C	A152k	4c	multicolored
495D	A152k	5c	multicolored
495E	A152k	6c	multicolored
495F	A152k	8c	multicolored
495G	A152k	13c	multicolored
495H	A152k	30c	multicolored

Souvenir Sheet

Perf. 14

495I A152k 70c multicolored

Nos. 495G-495H are airmail.

First Visit of Pope Paul VI to Latin America A152l

Paintings: 1c-3c, 5c-6c, Madonna and Child. 4c, The Annunciation. 7c-8c, Adoration of the Magi. 10c, Holy Family. 50c, Madonna and Child, angel.

1969 ***Perf. 14***

496	A152l	1c	Raphael
496A	A152l	2c	Ferruzzi
496B	A152l	3c	Bellini
496C	A152l	4c	Portuguese School, 17th cent.
496D	A152l	5c	Van Dyck
496E	A152l	6c	Albani
496F	A152l	7c	Viennese master
496G	A152l	8c	Van Dyck
496H	A152l	10c	Portuguese School, 16th cent.

Souvenir Sheet

Perf. 14½

496I A152l 50c Del Sarto

Nos. 496E-496I are airmail.

Map of Americas and People — A153

5c, Map of Panama, People and Houses, horiz.

1969, Aug. Photo. Wmk. 350

500	A153	5c	violet blue	.20	.20
501	A153	10c	bright rose lilac	.30	.20

Issued to publicize the 1970 census.

Cogwheel A154

1969, Aug.

502 A154 13c yel & dk bl gray .35 .20

50th anniv. of Rotary Intl. of Panama.

Cornucopia and Map of Panama A155

Perf. 14½x15

1969, Oct. 10 Litho. Unwmk.

503 A155 10c lt bl & multi .25 .20

1st anniv. of the October 11 Revolution.

Map of Panama and Ruins — A156

Natá Church — A157

Designs: 5c, Farmer, wife and mule. 13c, Hotel Continental. 20c, Church of the Virgin of Carmen. 21c, Gold altar, San José Church. 25c, Del Rey bridge. 30c, Dr. Justo Arosemena monument. 34c, Cathedral of Panama. 38c, Municipal Palace. 40c, French Plaza. 50c, Thatcher Ferry Bridge (Bridge of the Americas). 59c, National Theater.

Perf. 14½x15, 15x14½

1969-70 Litho. Unwmk.

504	A156	3c	org & blk	.20	.20
505	A156	5c	lt bl grn ('70)	.20	.20
506	A157	8c	dl brn ('70)	.20	.20
507	A156	13c	emer & blk	.30	.20
508	A157	20c	vio brn ('70)	.50	.25
509	A157	21c	yellow ('70)	.50	.40
510	A156	25c	lt bl grn ('70)	.60	.25
511	A157	30c	black ('70)	.75	.40
512	A156	34c	org brn ('70)	.80	.50
513	A156	38c	brt bl ('70)	.85	.40
514	A156	40c	org yel ('70)	1.00	.60
515	A156	50c	brt rose lil & blk	1.10	.70
516	A156	59c	brt rose lil ('70)	1.40	.90
			Nos. 504-516 (13)	8.40	5.20

For surcharges see Nos. 541, 543, 545-547, RA78-RA80.

Stadium and Discus Thrower A158

Flor del Espiritu Santo — A159

Wmk. 365

1970, Jan. 6 Litho. *Perf. 13½*

517	A158	1c ultra & multi	.20	.20
518	A158	2c ultra & multi	.20	.20
519	A158	3c ultra & multi	.20	.20
520	A158	5c ultra & multi	.20	.20
521	A158	10c ultra & multi	.30	.20
522	A158	13c ultra & multi	.35	.20
523	A159	13c pink & multi	.40	.20
524	A158	25c ultra & multi	.85	.50
525	A158	30c ultra & multi	1.00	.75
		Nos. 517-525,C368-C369 (11)	5.00	3.70

11th Central American and Caribbean Games, Feb. 28-Mar. 14.

Office of Comptroller General, 1970 — A160

Designs: 5c, Alejandro Tapia and Martin Sosa, first Comptrollers, 1931-34, horiz. 8c, Comptroller's emblem. 13c, Office of Comptroller General, 1955-70, horiz.

1971, Feb. 25 Litho. Wmk. 365

526	A160	3c yel & multi	.20	.20
527	A160	5c brn, buff & gold	.20	.20
528	A160	8c gold & multi	.20	.20
529	A160	13c blk & multi	.25	.20
		Nos. 526-529 (4)	.85	.80

Comptroller General's Office, 40th anniv.

Indian Alligator Design A161

1971, Aug. 18 Wmk. 343 *Perf. 13½*

530	A161	8c multicolored	.20	.20

SENAPI (Servicio Nacional de Artesania y Pequeñas Industrias), 5th anniv.

Education Year Emblem, Map of Panama A162

1971, Aug. 19 Litho.

531	A162	1b multicolored	2.50	2.50

International Education Year, 1970.
For surcharge see No. 542.

Congress Emblem — A163

1972, Aug. 25

532	A163	25c multicolored	.75	.60

9th Inter-American Conference of Saving and Loan Associations, Panama City, Jan. 23-29, 1971.

UPU Headquarters, Bern — A164

Design: 30c, UPU Monument, Bern, vert.

1971, Dec. 14 Wmk. 343

533	A164	8c multicolored	.20	.20
534	A164	30c multicolored	.80	.60

Inauguration of Universal Postal Union Headquarters, Bern, Switzerland.
For surcharge see No. RA77.

Cow, Pig and Produce A165

1971, Dec. 15

535	A165	3c yel, brn & blk	.20	.20

3rd agricultural census.

Map of Panama and "4-S" Emblem A166

1971, Dec. 16

536	A166	2c multicolored	.20	.20

Rural youth 4-S program.

UNICEF Emblem, Children A167

Wmk. 365

1972, Sept. 12 Litho. *Perf. 13½*

537	A167	1c yel & multi	.20	.20
		Nos. 537,C390-C392 (4)	1.65	1.20

25th anniv. (in 1971) of UNICEF. See No. C392a.

Tropical Fruits A168

1972, Sept. 13

538	A168	1c shown	.20	.20
539	A168	2c Isla de Noche	.20	.20
540	A168	3c Carnival float, vert.	.20	.20
		Nos. 538-540,C393-C395 (6)	1.60	1.45

Tourist publicity.
For surcharges see Nos. RA75-RA76.

Nos. 516, 531 and 511 Surcharged in Red

Perf. 14½x15, 15x14½, 13½
Wmk. 343, Unwmkd.

1973, Mar. 16

541	A156	8c on 59c brt rose lil	.20	.20
542	A162	10c on 1b multi	.20	.20
543	A157	13c on 30c blk	.25	.25
		Nos. 541-543,C402 (4)	.95	.95

UN Security Council Meeting, Panama City, Mar. 15-21. Surcharges differ in size and are adjusted to fit shape of stamp.

José Daniel Crespo, Educator A169

Wmk. 365

1973, June 20 Litho. *Perf. 13½*

544	A169	3c lt bl & multi	.20	.20
		Nos. 544,C403-C413 (12)	5.45	3.85

For overprints and surcharges see Nos. C414-C416, C418-C421, RA81-RA82, RA84.

Nos. 511-512 and 509 Surcharged in Red

Perf. 15x14½, 14½x15

1974, Nov. 11 Unwmk.

545	A157	5c on 30c blk	.20	.20
546	A156	10c on 34c org brn	.20	.20
547	A157	13c on 21c yel	.25	.20
		Nos. 545-547,C417-C421 (8)	1.65	1.60

Surcharge vertical on No. 546.

Bolivar, Bridge of the Americas, Men with Flag — A170

Perf. 12½

1976, Mar. 30 Litho. Unwmk.

548	A170	6c multicolored	.20	.20
		Nos. 548,C426-C428 (4)	2.20	1.30

150th anniversary of Congress of Panama.

Evibacus Princeps A171

Marine life: 3c, Ptitosarcus sinuosus, vert. 4c, Acanthaster planci. 7c, Starfish. 1b, Mithrax spinossimus.

Perf. 12½x13, 13x12½

1976, May 6 Litho. Wmk. 377

549	A171	2c multi	.20	.20
550	A171	3c multi	.20	.20
551	A171	4c multi	.20	.20
552	A171	7c multi	.20	.20
		Nos. 549-552,C429-C430 (6)	1.70	1.50

Souvenir Sheet

Imperf

553	A171	1b multi	3.00	

Bolivar from Bolivar Monument A172

Bolivar and Argentine Flag A173

Stamps of design A172 show details of Bolivar Monument, Panama City; design A173 shows head of Bolivar and flags of Latin American countries.

Perf. 13½

1976, June 22 Unwmk. Litho.

554	A172	20c shown	.50	.50
555	A173	20c shown	.50	.50
556	A173	20c Bolivia	.50	.50
557	A173	20c Brazil	.50	.50
558	A173	20c Chile	.50	.50
559	A172	20c Battle scene	.50	.50
560	A173	20c Colombia	.50	.50
561	A173	20c Costa Rica	.50	.50
562	A173	20c Cuba	.50	.50
563	A173	20c Ecuador	.50	.50
564	A173	20c El Salvador	.50	.50
565	A173	20c Guatemala	.50	.50
566	A173	20c Guyana	.50	.50
567	A173	20c Haiti	.50	.50
568	A172	20c Assembly	.50	.50
569	A172	20c Liberated people	.50	.50
570	A173	20c Honduras	.50	.50
571	A173	20c Jamaica	.50	.50
572	A173	20c Mexico	.50	.50
573	A173	20c Nicaragua	.50	.50
574	A173	20c Panama	.50	.50
575	A173	20c Paraguay	.50	.50
576	A173	20c Peru	.50	.50
577	A173	20c Dominican Rep.	.50	.50
578	A172	20c Bolivar and flag bearer	.50	.50
579	A173	20c Surinam	.50	.50
580	A173	20c Trinidad-Tobago	.50	.50
581	A173	20c Uruguay	.50	.50
582	A173	20c Venezuela	.50	.50
583	A172	20c Indian delegation	.50	.50
a.		Sheet of 30, #554-583	15.00	15.00

Souvenir Sheet

584		Sheet of 3	2.25	2.25
a.	A172	30c Bolivar and flag bearer	.50	.50
b.	A172	30c Monument, top	.50	.50
c.	A172	40c Inscription tablet	.65	.65

Amphictyonic Congress of Panama, sesquicentennial. No. 584 comes perf. and imperf.

Nicanor Villalaz, Designer of Coat of Arms — A174

National Lottery Building, Panama City — A175

1976, Nov. 12 Litho. *Perf. 12½*

585	A174	5c dk blue	.20	.20
586	A175	6c multicolored	.20	.20

Contadora Island — A176

1976, Dec. 29 *Perf. 12½*

587	A176	3c multicolored	.20	.20

Pres. Carter and Gen. Omar Torrijos Signing Panama Canal Treaties — A177

Design: 23c, like No. 588. Design includes Alejandro Orfila, Secretary General of OAS.

1978, Jan. Litho. *Perf. 12*

Size: 90x40mm

588	A177	Strip of 3	2.00	2.00
a.		3c multicolored	.20	.20
b.		40c multicolored	.80	.50
c.		50c multicolored	1.00	.75

Perf. 14

Size: 36x26mm

589	A177	23c multicolored	.45	.20

Signing of Panama Canal Treaties, Washington, DC, Sept. 7, 1977.

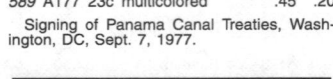

Pres. Carter and Gen. Torrijos Signing Treaties — A178

1978, Nov. 13 Litho. *Perf. 12*

590	A178	Strip of 3	2.00	2.00
a.		5c multi (30x40mm)	.20	.20
b.		35c multi (30x40mm)	.70	.35
c.		41c multi (45x40mm)	.80	.40

Size: 36x26mm

591	A178	3c Treaty signing	.20	.20

Signing of Panama Canal Treaties ratification documents, Panama City, Panama, June 6, 1978.

World Commerce Zone, Colon A179

1978 Litho. *Perf. 12*

592	A179	6c multicolored	.20	.20

Free Zone of Colon, 30th anniversary.

Melvin Jones, Lions Emblem A180

1978, Dec. 5

593	A180	50c multicolored	1.00	.75

Birth centenary of Melvin Jones, founder of Lions International.

Torrijos with Children, Ship, Flag A181

"75," Coat of Arms A182

Rotary Emblem, "75" A183

Gen. Torrijos and Pres. Carter, Flags, Ship A184

UPU Emblem, Globe — A185

Boy and Girl Inside Heart — A186

1979, Oct. 1 Litho. *Perf. 14*

594	A181	3c multicolored	.20	.20
595	A182	6c multicolored	.20	.20
596	A183	17c multicolored	.35	.30
597	A184	23c multicolored	.45	.20
598	A185	35c multicolored	.70	.60
599	A186	50c multicolored	1.00	.50
		Nos. 594-599 (6)	2.90	2.00

Return of Canal Zone to Panama, Oct. 1 (3c, 23c); Natl. Bank, 75th anniv.; Rotary Intl., 75th anniv.; 18th UPU Cong., Rio, Sept.-Oct., 1979; Intl. Year of the Child.

Colon Station, St. Charles Hotel, Engraving A187

Postal Headquarters, Balboa, Inauguration — A188

Return of Canal Zone to Panama, Oct. 1, 1979 — A189

Census of the Americas A190

Panamanian Tourist and Convention Center Opening — A191

Inter-American Development Bank, 25th Anniversary — A192

Canal Centenary A193

Olympic Stadium, Moscow '80 Emblem A194

1980, June 17 Litho. *Perf. 12*

600	A187	1c rose violet	.20	.20
601	A188	3c multicolored	.20	.20
602	A189	6c multicolored	.20	.20
603	A190	17c multicolored	.35	.25
604	A191	23c multicolored	.45	.20
605	A192	35c multicolored	.70	.30
606	A193	41c pale rose & blk	.90	.45
607	A194	50c multicolored	1.00	.50
		Nos. 600-607 (8)	4.00	2.30

Transpanamanian Railroad, 130th anniv. (1c); 22nd Summer Olympic Games, Moscow, July 19-Aug. 3 (50c).

La Salle Congregation, 75th Anniv. (1979) — A195

Louis Braille — A196

1981, May 15 Litho. *Perf. 12*

608	A195	17c multicolored	.35	.20

1981, May 15

609	A196	23c multicolored	.45	.20

Intl. Year of the Disabled.

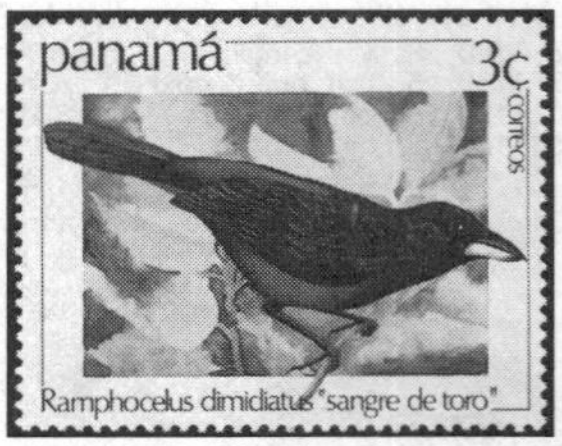

Bull's Blood — A197

1981, June 26 Litho. *Perf. 12*

610	A197	3c shown	.20	.20
611	A197	6c Lory, vert.	.20	.20
612	A197	41c Hummingbird, vert.	.90	.50
613	A197	50c Toucan	1.10	.40
		Nos. 610-613 (4)	2.40	1.30

Apparition of the Virgin to St. Catherine Laboure, 150th Anniv. — A198

1981, June 26 Litho. *Perf. 12*

614	A198	35c multicolored	.70	.35

Gen. Torrijos and Bayano Dam A199

Wmk. 311

1982, Mar. Litho. *Perf. 10½*

615	A199	17c multicolored	.35	.20

78th Anniv. of Independence Soldiers Institute — A200

1981, Nov. 30 Litho. *Perf. 10½*

616	A200	3c multicolored	.20	.20

First Death Anniv. of Gen. Omar Torrijos Herrera A201

1982, May 14 Litho. *Perf. 10½*

617	A201	5c Aerial view	.20	.20
618	A201	6c Army camp	.20	.20
619	A201	50c Felipillo Engineering Works	1.00	.40
		Nos. 617-619,C433-C434 (5)	2.90	1.60

Ricardo J. Alfaro (1882-1977), Statesman A202

1982, Aug. 18 Wmk. 382

620	A202	3c multicolored	.20	.20

See Nos. C436-C437.

1982 World Cup A203

1982, Dec. 27 Litho. *Perf. 10½*

621	A203	50c Italian team	1.00	.50

See Nos. C438-C440.

Expo Comer '83, Panama Intl. Commerce Exposition, Jan. 12-16 A204

1983 Litho. Wmk. 382 *Perf. 10½*

622	A204	17c multicolored	.40	.30

Visit of Pope John Paul II — A205

Bank Emblem — A206

Various portraits of the Pope. 35c airmail.

Perf. 12x11

1983, Mar. 1 Litho. Wmk. 382

623	A205	6c multicolored	.20	.20
624	A205	17c multicolored	.35	.25
625	A205	35c multicolored	.75	.25
		Nos. 623-625 (3)	1.30	.70

1983, Mar. 18

626	A206	50c multicolored	1.00	.40

24th Council Meeting of Inter-American Development Bank, Mar. 21-23.

Simon Bolivar (1783-1830) A207

1983, July 25 Litho. *Perf. 12*

627	A207	50c multicolored	1.00	.50

Souvenir Sheet

Imperf

628	A207	1b like 50c	2.00	.80

World Communications Year — A208

1983, Oct. 9 Litho. *Perf. 14*

629	A208	30c UPAE emblem	.60	.25
630	A208	40c WCY emblem	.80	.30
631	A208	50c UPU emblem	1.00	.40
632	A208	60c Dove in flight	1.25	.50
		Nos. 629-632 (4)	3.65	1.45

Souvenir Sheet

Imperf

633	A208	1b multicolored	2.00	2.00

No. 633 contains designs of Nos. 629-632 without denominations.

Freedom of Worship A209

1983, Oct. 21 Litho. *Perf. 11½*

634	A209	3c Panama Mosque	.20	.20
635	A209	5c Bahai Temple	.20	.20
636	A209	6c St. Francis Church	.20	.20
637	A209	17c Kol Shearit Israel Synagogue	.40	.25
		Nos. 634-637 (4)	1.00	.85

No. 637 incorrectly inscribed.

Ricardo Miro (1883-1940), Poet — A210

The Prophet, by Alfredo Sinclair — A211

Famous Men: 3c, Richard Newman (1883-1946), educator. 5c, Cristobal Rodriguez (1883-1943), politician. 6c, Alcibiades Arosemena (1883-1958), industrialist and financier. 35c, Cirilo Martinez (1883-1924), linguist.

1983, Nov. 8 Litho. *Perf. 14*

638	A210	1c multicolored	.20	.20
639	A210	3c multicolored	.20	.20
640	A210	5c multicolored	.20	.20
641	A210	6c multicolored	.20	.20
642	A210	35c multicolored	.70	.35
		Nos. 638-642 (5)	1.50	1.15

1983, Dec. 12 *Perf. 12*

#643, Village House, by Juan Manuel Cedeno. #644, Large Nude, by Manuel Chong Neto. 3c, On Another Occasion, by Spiros Vamvas. 6c, Punta Chame Landscape, by Guillermo Trujillo. 28c, Neon Light, by Alfredo Sinclair. 41c, Highland Girls, by Al Sprague. 1b, Bright Morning, by Ignacio Mallol Pibernat. Nos. 643-647, 650 horiz.

643	A211	1c multicolored	.20	.20
644	A211	1c multicolored	.20	.20
645	A211	3c multicolored	.20	.20
646	A211	6c multicolored	.20	.20
647	A211	28c multicolored	.55	.25
648	A211	35c multicolored	.70	.30
649	A211	41c multicolored	.80	.35
650	A211	1b multicolored	2.00	.80
		Nos. 643-650 (8)	4.85	2.50

Double Cup, Indian Period A212

Pottery: 40c, Raised dish, Tonosi period. 50c, Jug with face, Canazas period, vert. 60c, Bowl, Conte, vert.

1984, Jan. 16 Litho. *Perf. 12*

651	A212	30c multicolored	.90	.20
652	A212	40c multicolored	1.00	.30
653	A212	50c multicolored	1.25	.40
654	A212	60c multicolored	1.50	.55
		Nos. 651-654 (4)	4.65	1.45

Souvenir Sheet

Imperf

655	A212	1b like 30c	2.00	2.00

Pre-Olympics — A213

1984, June Litho. *Perf. 14*

656	A213	19c Baseball	.40	.35
657	A213	19c Basketball, vert.	.40	.35
658	A213	19c Boxing	.40	.35
659	A213	19c Swimming, vert.	.40	.35
		Nos. 656-659 (4)	1.60	1.40

Roberto Duran — A214

Paintings — A215

1984 Olympic Games — A214a

1984, June 14 Litho. *Perf. 14*

660	A214	26c multicolored	.60	.25

1st Panamanian to hold 3 boxing championships.

1984 Litho. *Perf. 14*

660A	A214a	6c Shooting	.20	.20
660B	A214a	30c Weight lifting	.60	.20
660C	A214a	37c Wrestling	.75	.30
660D	A214a	1b Long jump	2.00	1.50
		Nos. 660A-660D (4)	3.55	2.20

Souvenir Sheet

660E	A214a	1b Running	2.00	.80

Nos. 660B-660D are airmail. No. 660E contains one 45x45x64mm stamp.

1984, Sept. 17 Litho. *Perf. 14*

Paintings by Panamanian artists: 1c, Woman Thinking, by Manuel Chong Neto. 3c, The Child, by Alfredo Sinclair. 6c, A Day in the Life of Rumalda, by Brooke Alfaro. 30c, Highlands People, by Al Sprague. 37c, Intermission during the Dance, by Roberto Sprague. 44c, Punta Chame Forest, by Guillermo Trujillo. 50c, The Blue Plaza, by Juan Manuel Cedeno. 1b, Ira, by Spiros Vamvas.

661	A215	1c multi	.20	.20
662	A215	3c multi, horiz.	.20	.20
663	A215	6c multi, horiz.	.20	.20
664	A215	30c multi	.60	.20
665	A215	37c multi, horiz.	.75	.25
666	A215	44c multi, horiz.	.90	.35
667	A215	50c multi, horiz.	1.00	.40
668	A215	1b multi, horiz.	2.00	1.50
		Nos. 661-668 (8)	5.85	3.30

Postal Sovereignty — A216

1984, Oct. 1 Litho. *Perf. 12*

669	A216	19c Gen. Torrijos, canal	.40	.25

Fauna A217

1984, Dec. 5 Engr. *Perf. 14*

670	A217	3c Manatee	.20	.20
671	A217	30c Gato negro	.60	.25
672	A217	44c Tigrillo congo	.90	.40
673	A217	50c Puerco de monte	1.00	.40
		Nos. 670-673 (4)	2.70	1.25

Souvenir Sheet

674	A217	1b Perezoso de tres dedos, vert.	2.00	2.00

Nos. 671-673 are airmail.

Coins A218

Perf. 11x12

1985, Jan. 17 Litho. Wmk. 353

675	A218	3c 1935 1c	.20	.20
676	A218	3c 1904 10c	.20	.20
677	A218	6c 1916 5c	.20	.20
678	A218	30c 1904 50c	.60	.25

679 A218 37c 1962 half-balboa .75 .35
680 A218 44c 1953 balboa .90 .45
Nos. 675-680 (6) 2.85 1.65

Nos. 678-680 are airmail.

Contadora Type of 1985
Souvenir Sheet
Perf. 13½x13

1985, Oct. 1 Litho. Unwmk.
680A AP108 1b Dove, flags, map 2.00 2.00

Cargo Ship in Lock A219

1985, Oct. 16 ***Perf. 14***
681 A219 19c multicolored .40 .25

Panama Canal, 70th anniv. (1984).

UN 40th Anniv. A220

1986, Jan. 17 Litho. ***Perf. 14***
682 A220 23c multicolored .45 .35

Intl. Youth Year A221

1986, Jan. 17
683 A221 30c multicolored .60 .35

Waiting Her Turn, by Al Sprague (b.1938) — A222

Oil paintings: 5c, Aerobics, by Guillermo Trujillo (b. 1927). 19c, Cardboard House, by Eduardo Augustine (b. 1954). 30c, Door to the Homeland, by Juan Manuel Cedeno (b. 1914). 36c, Supper for Three, by Brooke Alfaro (b. 1949). 42c, Tenderness, by Alfredo Sinclair (b. 1915). 50c, Woman and Character, by Manuel Chong Neto (b. 1927). 60c, Calla lillies, by Maigualida de Diaz (b. 1950).

1986, Jan. 21
684 A222 3c multicolored .20 .20
685 A222 5c multicolored .20 .20
686 A222 19c multicolored .40 .20
687 A222 30c multicolored .60 .35
688 A222 36c multicolored .70 .45
689 A222 42c multicolored .85 .50
690 A222 50c multicolored 1.00 .60
691 A222 60c multicolored 1.25 .75
Nos. 684-691 (8) 5.20 3.25

Miss Universe Pageant A223

1986, July 7 Litho. ***Perf. 12***
692 A223 23c Atlapa Center .45 .30
693 A223 60c Emblem, vert. 1.25 .70

Halley's Comet A224

30c, Old Panama Cathedral tower, vert.

1986, Oct. 30 Litho. ***Perf. 13½***
694 A224 23c multicolored .45 .35
695 A224 30c multicolored .60 .35

Size: 75x86mm
Imperf
695A A224 1b multicolored 2.00

A225

A226

1986 World Cup Soccer Championships, Mexico: Illustrations from Soccer History, by Sandoval and Meron.

1986, Oct. 30
696 A225 23c Argentina, winner .45 .35
697 A225 30c Fed. Rep. of Germany, 2nd .60 .35
698 A225 37c Argentina, Germany .75 .60
Nos. 696-698 (3) 1.80 1.30

Souvenir Sheet
698A A225 1b Argentina, diff. 2.00

1986, Nov. 21
699 A226 20c shown .40 .25
700 A226 23c Montage of events .45 .35

15th Central American and Caribbean Games, Dominican Republic.

Christmas A227

1986, Dec. 18 Litho.
701 A227 23c shown .45 .30
702 A227 36c Green tree .70 .50
703 A227 42c Silver tree .85 .55
Nos. 701-703 (3) 2.00 1.35

Intl. Peace Year — A228

Tropical Carnival, Feb.-Mar. A229

1986, Dec. 30 ***Perf. 13½***
704 A228 8c multicolored .20 .20
705 A228 19c multicolored .40 .25

1987, Jan. 27 Litho. ***Perf. 13½***
706 A229 20c Diablito Sucio mask .40 .30
707 A229 35c Sun .70 .50

Size: 74x84mm
Imperf
708 A229 1b like 35c 2.00 1.50
Nos. 706-708 (3) 3.10 2.30

1st Panamanian Eye Bank — A230

1987, Feb. 17 Litho. ***Perf. 14***
709 A230 37c multicolored .75 .75

Panama Lions Club, 50th Anniv. (in 1985). Dated 1986.

Flowering Plants — A231

Birds A232

1987, Mar. 5
710 A231 3c Brownea macrophylla .20 .20
711 A232 5c Thraupis episcopus .20 .20
712 A231 8c Solandra grandiflora .20 .20
713 A232 15c Tyrannus melancholicus .30 .25
714 A231 19c Barleria micans .40 .35
715 A232 23c Pelecanus occidentalis .45 .35
716 A231 30c Cordia dentata .60 .45
717 A232 36c Columba cayennensis .75 .55
Nos. 710-717 (8) 3.10 2.55

Dated 1986.

Monument and Octavio Mendez Pereira, Founder A233

1987, Mar. 26 Litho. ***Perf. 14***
718 A233 19c multicolored .40 .30

University of Panama, 50th anniv. (in 1985). Stamp dated "1986."

UNFAO, 40th Anniv. (in 1985) A234

1987, Apr. 9 ***Perf. 13½***
719 A234 10c blk, pale ol & yel org .20 .20
720 A234 45c blk, dk grn & yel grn .90 .70

Natl. Theater, 75th Anniv. A235

Baroque composers: 19c, Schutz (1585-1672). 37c, Bach. 60c, Handel. Nos. 721, 723-724 vert.

1987, Apr. 28 ***Perf. 14***
721 A235 19c multicolored .35 .30
722 A235 30c shown .60 .45
723 A235 37c multicolored .75 .60
724 A235 60c multicolored 1.20 .90
Nos. 721-724 (4) 2.90 2.25

A236

A237

1987, May 13 Litho. ***Perf. 14***
725 A236 23c multicolored .50 .45

Inter-American Development Bank, 25th anniv.

1987, Nov. 28 Litho. ***Perf. 14***
726 A237 25c Fire wagon, 1887, and modern ladder truck .55 .40
727 A237 35c Fireman carrying victim .80 .60

Panama Fire Brigade, cent.

A238

A239

1987, Dec. 11

728 A238 15c Wrestling, horiz. .35 .25
729 A238 23c Tennis .50 .40
730 A238 30c Swimming, horiz. .65 .50
731 A238 41c Basketball .90 .70
732 A238 60c Cycling 1.25 1.00
Nos. 728-732 (5) 3.65 2.85

Souvenir Sheet

733 A238 1b Weight lifting 2.25 1.75

10th Pan American Games, Indianapolis.
For surcharges see Nos. 813, 817.

1987, Dec. 17

Christmas (Religious paintings): 22c, Adoration of the Magi, by Albrecht Nentz (d. 1479). 35c, Virgin Adored by Angels, by Matthias Grunewald (d. 1528). 37c, The Virgin and Child, by Konrad Witz (c. 1400-1445).

734 A239 22c multicolored .50 .35
735 A239 35c multicolored .80 .60
736 A239 37c multicolored .80 .60
Nos. 734-736 (3) 2.10 1.55

Intl. Year of Shelter for the Homeless A240

45c, by A. Sinclair. 50c, Woman, boy, girl, shack, housing in perspective by A. Pulido.

1987, Dec. 29 ***Perf. 14***

737 A240 45c multicolored 1.00 .75
738 A240 50c multicolored 1.10 .80

For surcharge see No. 814.

Reforestation Campaign A241

Say No to Drugs A242

1988, Jan. 14 Litho. ***Perf. 14½x14***

739 A241 35c dull grn & yel grn .80 .55
740 A241 40c red & pink .90 .70
741 A241 45c brn & lemon 1.00 .75
Nos. 739-741 (3) 2.70 2.00

Dated 1987. For surcharge see No. 816.

1988, Jan. 14

742 A242 10c org lil rose .25 .20
743 A242 17c yel grn & lil rose .40 .30
744 A242 25c pink & sky blue .55 .40
Nos. 742-744 (3) 1.20 .90

Child Survival Campaign A243

1988, Feb. 29 Litho. ***Perf. 14***

745 A243 20c Breast-feeding .45 .35
746 A243 31c Universal immunization .70 .60
747 A243 45c Growth and development, vert. 1.00 .90
Nos. 745-747 (3) 2.15 1.85

For surcharge see No. 816A.

Fish A244

1988, Mar. 14

748 A244 7c Myripristis jacobus .20 .20
749 A244 35c Pomacanthus paru .80 .60
750 A244 60c Holocanthus tricolor 1.25 1.00
751 A244 1b Equetus punctatus 2.25 1.60
Nos. 748-751 (4) 4.50 3.40

The 7c actually shows the Holocanthus tricolor, the 60c the Myripristis jacobus.
For surcharge see No. 819.

Girl Guides, 75th Anniv. — A245

1988, Apr. 14

752 A245 35c multicolored .80 .60

Christmas A246

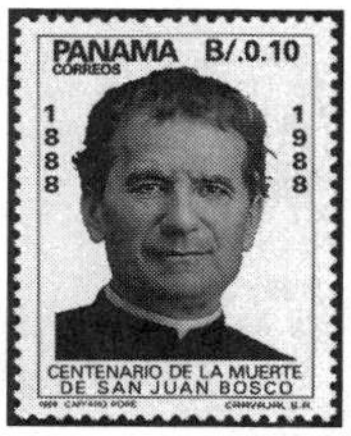

St. John Bosco (1815-1888) A247

Paintings: 17c, *Virgin and Gift-givers.* 45c, *Virgin of the Rosary and St. Dominic.*

1988, Dec. 29 Litho. ***Perf. 12***

753 A246 17c multicolored .40 .30
754 A246 45c multicolored 1.00 .75

See No. C446.

1989, Jan. 31

755 A247 10c Portrait .25 .20
756 A247 20c Minor Basilica .50 .35

1988 Summer Olympics, Seoul A248

Athletes and medals.

1989, Mar. 17 Litho. ***Perf. 12***

757 A248 17c Running .40 .30
758 A248 25c Wrestling .55 .40
759 A248 60c Weight lifting 1.25 1.00
Nos. 757-759 (3) 2.20 1.70

Souvenir Sheet

760 A248 1b Swimming, vert. 2.25 1.60

See No. C447.

A249

A250

1989, Apr. 12 Litho. ***Perf. 12***

761 A249 40c red, blk & blue 1.00 .75
762 A249 1b Emergency and rescue services 2.40 1.75

Intl. Red Cross and Red Crescent organizations, 125th annivs.

1989, Oct. 12 Litho. ***Perf. 12***

America Issue: Pre-Columbian artifacts.

767 A250 20c Monolith of Barriles 1.25 .40
768 A250 35c Vessel 2.25 .65

French Revolution, Bicent. A251

1989, Nov. 14 ***Perf. 13½***

769 A251 25c multicolored .60 .50
Nos. 769,C450-C451 (3) 2.60 2.00

Christmas — A252

17c, Holy family in Panamanian costume. 35c, Creche. 45c, Holy family, gift givers.

1989, Dec. 1

770 A252 17c multicolored .40 .30
771 A252 35c multicolored .90 .65
772 A252 45c multicolored 1.10 .85
Nos. 770-772 (3) 2.40 1.80

A253

A254

1990, Jan. 16

773 A253 23c brown .60 .45

Rogelio Sinan (b. 1902), writer.

1990, Mar. 14 Litho. ***Perf. 13½***

774 A254 25c blue & black .60 .45
775 A254 35c Experiment .80 .60
776 A254 45c Beakers, test tubes, books 1.00 .75
Nos. 774-776 (3) 2.40 1.80

Dr. Guillermo Patterson, Jr., chemist.

Fruits A255

1990, May 15 ***Perf. 13½***

777 A255 20c Byrsonima crassifolia .50 .35
778 A255 35c Bactris gasipaes .80 .60
779 A255 40c Anacardium occidentale 1.00 .70
Nos. 777-779 (3) 2.30 1.65

Tortoises A256

1990, July 17

780 A256 35c Pseudemys scripta .80 .60
781 A256 45c Lepidochelys olivacea 1.00 .75
782 A256 60c Geochelone carbonaria 1.40 1.00
Nos. 780-782 (3) 3.20 2.35

For surcharges see Nos. 815, 818.

Native American A257

1990, Oct. 12

783 A257 20c shown .65 .40
784 A257 35c Native, vert. 1.10 .85

Discovery of Isthmus of Panama, 490th Anniv. — A258

1991, Nov. 19 Litho. ***Perf. 12***

785 A258 35c multicolored .90 .65

St. Ignatius of Loyola, 500th Birth Anniv. — A259

1991, Nov. 29

786 A259 20c multicolored .50 .30
a. Tete beche pair 1.00 .65

Society of Jesus, 450th anniv.

Christmas A260

1991, Dec. 2

787 A260 35c Luke 2:14 .90 .65
788 A260 35c Nativity scene .90 .65
a. Pair, #787-788 1.80 1.30

Social Security Administration, 50th Anniv. — A261

Design: No. 790, Dr. Arnulfo Arias Madrid (1901-1988), Constitution of Panama, 1941.

1991 Litho. *Perf. 12*

789 A261 10c multicolored .25 .20
790 A261 10c multicolored .25 .20

Women's citizenship rights, 50th anniv. (No. 790).

Epiphany — A262

1992, Feb. 5 Litho. *Perf. 12*

791 A262 10c multicolored .25 .20
a. Tete beche pair .50 .30

New Life Housing Project — A263

1992, Feb. 17

792 A263 5c multicolored .20 .20
a. Tete beche pair .25 .20

Border Treaty Between Panama and Costa Rica, 50th Anniv. — A264

a, 20c, Hands clasped. b, 40c, Map. c, 50c, Pres. Rafael A. Calderon, Costa Rica, Pres. Arnulfo Arias Madrid, Panama.

1992, Feb. 20

793 A264 Strip of 3, #a.-c. 2.75 1.75

Causes of Hole in Ozone Layer — A265

1992, Feb. 24

794 A265 40c multicolored 1.00 .70
a. Tete beche pair 2.00 1.40

Expocomer '92, Intl. Commercial Exposition — A266

1992, Mar. 11

795 A266 10c multicolored .25 .20

A267

A268

Margot Fonteyn (1919-91), ballerina: a, 35c, Wearing dress. b, 45c, In costume.

1992, Mar. 12

796 A267 Pair, #a.-b. 1.90 1.40

1992, June 22 Litho. *Perf. 12*

797 A268 10c multicolored .25 .20
a. Tete beche pair .50 .30

Maria Olimpia de Obaldia (1891-1985), poet.

1992 Summer Olympics, Barcelona — A269

1992, June 24 Litho. *Perf. 12*

798 A269 10c multicolored .25 .20
a. Tete-beche pair .50 .35

Zion Baptist Church, Bocas del Toro, 1892 — A270

1992, Oct. 1 Litho. *Perf. 12*

799 A270 20c multicolored .50 .35
a. Tete beche pair 1.00 .70

Baptist Church in Panama, Cent.

Discovery of America, 500th Anniv. — A271

a, 20c, Columbus' fleet. b, 35c, Coming ashore.

1992, Oct. 12

800 A271 Pair, #a.-b. 1.40 .95

A272

A273

Endangered Wildlife: a, 5c, Agouti paca. b, 10c, Harpia harpyja. c, 15c, Felis onca. d, 20c, Iguana iguana.

1992, Sept. 23

801 A272 Strip of 4, #a.-d. 1.25 .90

1992, Dec. 21 Litho. *Perf. 12*

802 A273 10c multicolored .25 .20
a. Tete beche pair .50 .30

Expo '92, Seville.

A274

1992, Dec. 21

803 A274 15c multicolored .40 .30
a. Tete beche pair .80 .60

Worker's Health Year.

A275

1992, Dec. 21 Litho. *Perf. 12*

804 A275 10c multi + label .30 .20

Unification of Europe.

Christmas — A276

a, 20c, Angel announcing birth of Christ. b, 35c, Mary and Joseph approaching city gate.

1992, Dec. 21

805 A276 Pair, #a.-b. 1.25 .95

Evangelism in America, 500th Anniv. (in 1992) — A277

1993, Apr. 13 Litho. *Perf. 12*

806 A277 10c multicolored .25 .20
a. Tete beche pair .50 .30

Natl. Day for the Disabled A278

1993, May 10

807 A278 5c multicolored .20 .20
a. Tete beche pair .40 .30

Dr. Jose de la Cruz Herrera (1876-1961), Humanitarian A279

1993, May 26

808 A279 5c multicolored .20 .20
a. Tete beche pair .40 .30

1992 Intl. Conference on Nutrition, Rome — A280

1993, June 26 Litho. *Perf. 12*

809 A280 10c multicolored .25 .20
a. Tete beche pair .50 .30

Columbus' Exploration of the Isthmus of Panama, 490th Anniv. — A281

1994, June 2 Litho. *Perf. 12*

810 A281 50c multicolored 1.25 .95
a. Tete beche pair + 2 labels 2.50 2.00

Dated 1993.

Greek Community in Panama, 50th Anniv. A282

Designs: 20c, Greek influences in Panama, Panamanian flag, vert. No. 812a, Parthenon. No. 812b, Greek Orthodox Church.

1995, Feb. 16 Litho. *Perf. 12*

811 A282 20c multicolored .45 .30

Souvenir Sheet

812 A282 75c Sheet of 2, #a.-b. 3.25 2.50

Nos. 729, 731, 737, 741, 747, 750, 781-782 Surcharged

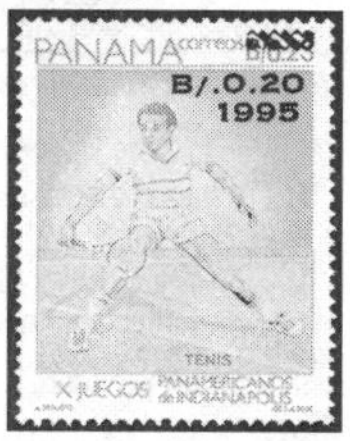

1995 *Perfs., Etc. as Before*

813	A238	20c on 23c #729	.45	.35
814	A240	25c on 45c #737	.60	.40
815	A256	30c on 45c #781	.70	.50
816	A241	35c on 45c #741	.80	.60
816A	A243	35c on 45c No. 747	.85	.65
817	A238	40c on 41c #731	.95	.70
818	A256	50c on 60c #782	1.40	1.00
819	A244	1b on 60c No. 750	2.50	2.00
		Nos. 813-819 (8)	8.25	6.20

Issued: #813-815, 816A-818, 5/6; #816, 819, 4/3.

First Settlement of Panama, 475th Anniv. (in 1994) — A283

Designs: 15c, Horse and wagon crossing bridge. 20c, Arms of first Panama City, vert. 25c, Model of an original cathedral. 35c, Ruins of cathedral, vert.

1996, Oct. 11 Litho. *Perf. 14*

820 A283	15c beige, black & brown	.40	.30
821 A283	20c multicolored	.50	.40
822 A283	25c beige, black & brown	.65	.45
823 A283	35c beige, black & brown	.95	.70
	Nos. 820-823 (4)	2.50	1.85

Endangered Species — A284

1996, Oct. 18 Litho. *Perf. 14*

824 A284 20c Tinamus major .50 .40

Mammals A285

a, Nasua narica. b, Tamandua mexicana. c, Cyclopes didactylus. d, Felis concolor.

1996, Oct. 18

825 A285 25c Block of 4, #a.-d. 2.50 1.90

A286

A287

1996, Oct. 22 Litho. *Perf. 14*

826 A286 40c multicolored 1.00 .75

Kiwanis Clubs of Panama, 25th anniv. (in 1993.)

1996, Oct. 17

827 A287 5b multicolored 12.50 9.50

Rotary Clubs of Panama, 75th anniv. (in 1994).

A288

A289

1996, Oct. 21

828 A288 45c multicolored 1.10 .85

UN, 50th anniv. (in 1995).

1996, Oct. 21

Design: Ferdinand de Lesseps (1805-94), builder of Suez Canal.

829 A289 35c multicolored .95 .70

Andrés Bello Covenant, 25th Anniv. (in 1995) — A290

1996, Oct. 23

830 A290 35c multicolored .95 .70

Chinese Presence in Panama A291

1996, June 10 *Perf. 14½*

831 A291 60c multicolored 1.50 1.10

Litho.

Imperf

Size: 80x68mm

Patterns depicting four seasons: 1.50b, Invierno, Primavera, Verano, Otono.

832 A291 1.50b multicolored 3.75 2.75

Radiology, Cent. (in 1995) — A292

1996, Oct. 23 Litho. *Perf. 14*

833 A292 1b multicolored 2.50 1.90

University of Panama, 60th Anniv. A293

1996, Oct. 14

834 A293 40c multicolored 1.00 .75

Christmas — A295

1996, Oct. 24 Litho. *Perf. 14*

836 A295 35c multicolored .95 .70

Mail Train A296

1996, Dec. 10 Litho. *Perf. 14*

837 A296 30c multicolored .60 .45

America issue.

Universal Congress of the Panama Canal A297

No. 838: a, Pedro Miguel Locks. b, Miraflores Double Locks. 1.50b, Gatún Locks.

1997, Sept. 9 Litho. *Perf. 14½x14*

838 A297 45c Pair, #a.-b. 2.25 2.25

Imperf

839 A297 1.50b multicolored 3.75 3.75

Perforated portion of No. 839 is 76x31mm.

Torrijos-Carter Panama Canal Treaties, 20th Anniv. — A298

Designs: 20c, Painting, "Panama, More Than a Canal," by C. Gonzalez P. 30c, "Curtain of Our Flag," by A. Siever M., vert. 45c, "Huellas Perpetuas," by R. Marinez R. 50c, 1.50b, #588.

1997, Sept. 9 *Perf. 14*

840 A298	20c multicolored	.50	.50
841 A298	30c multicolored	.75	.75
842 A298	45c multicolored	1.10	1.10
843 A298	50c multicolored	1.25	1.25
	Nos. 840-843 (4)	3.60	3.60

Imperf

844 A298 1.50b multicolored *3.75 3.75*

Perforated portion of No. 844 is 114x50mm.

India's Independence, 50th Anniv. — A299

1997, Oct. 2 *Perf. 14x14½*

845 A299 50c Mahatma Gandhi 1.25 1.25

Crocodylus Acutus A300

World Wildlife Fund: a, Heading right. b, Looking left. c, One in distance, one up close. d, With mouth wide open.

1997, Nov. 18 *Perf. 14½x14*

846 A300 25c Block of 4, #a.-d. 2.25 2.25

Christmas A301

1997, Nov. 18 Litho. *Perf. 14x14½*

847 A301 35c multicolored .90 .70

Colon Fire Brigade, Cent. A302

1997, Nov. 21 Litho. *Perf. 14½x14*

848 A302 20c multicolored .50 .50

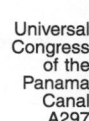

Frogs A303

Designs: a, Eleutherodactylus biporcatus. b, Hyla colymba. c, Hyla rufitela. d, Nelsonphryne aterrima.

1997, Nov. 21
849 A303 25c Block of 4, #a.-d. 2.50 2.50

National Costumes A304

1997, Nov. 25
850 A304 20c multicolored .50 .50

America issue.

Colon Chamber of Commerce, Agriculture and Industry, 85th Anniv. — A305

1997, Nov. 27 ***Perf. 14x14½***
851 A305 1b multicolored 2.50 2.50

Justo Arosemena, Lawyer, Politician, Death Cent. (in 1996) — A306

1997, Nov. 27
852 A306 40c multicolored 1.00 1.00

Panamanian Aviation Co., 50th Anniv. — A307

Designs: a, Douglas DC-3. b, Martin-404. c, Avro HS-748. d, Electra L-168. e, Boeing B727-100. f, Boeing B737-200 Advanced.

1997, Dec. 3 ***Perf. 14½x14***
853 A307 35c Block of 6, #a.-f. 5.25 5.25

Jerusalem, 3000th Anniv. — A308

20c, Jewish people at the Wailing Wall. 25c, Christians being led in worship at Church of the Holy Sepulchre. 60c, Muslims at the Dome of the Rock.

1997, Dec. 29 ***Perf. 14x14½***
854 A308 20c multicolored .50 .50
855 A308 25c multicolored .65 .65
856 A308 60c multicolored 1.50 1.50
Nos. 854-856 (3) 2.65 2.65

Imperf

857 A308 1.50b like #854-856 3.75 3.75

Perforated portion of No. 857 is 90x40mm.

Tourism A309

10c, Old center of town, Panama City. 20c, Soberania Park. 25c, Panama Canal. 35c, Panama Bay. 40c, Fort St. Jerónimo. 45c, Rafting on Chagres River. 60c, Beach, Kuna Yana Region.

Perf. 14x14½, 14½x14

1998, July 7 **Litho.**
858 A309 10c multi, vert .20 .20
859 A309 20c multi, vert .40 .40
860 A309 25c multi .50 .50
861 A309 35c multi .70 .70
862 A309 40c multi .80 .80
863 A309 45c multi .90 .90
864 A309 60c multi 1.25 1.25
Nos. 858-864 (7) 4.75 4.75

Organization of American States (OAS), 50th Anniv. — A310

1998, Apr. 30 ***Perf. 14½x14***
865 A310 40c multicolored .80 .80

Colón Free Trade Zone, 50th Anniv. — A311

Perf. 14x14½

1998, Feb. 2 **Litho.** **Unwmk.**
866 A311 15c multi .30 .30

Protection of the Harpy Eagle — A312

Contest-winning art by students: a, Luis Mellilo. b, Jorvisis Jiménez. c, Samuel Castro. d, Jorge Ramos.

1998, Jan. 20
867 A312 20c Block of 4, #a.-d. 1.60 1.60

Universal Declaration of Human Rights, 50th Anniv. — A313

1998, Feb. 10
868 A313 15c multi .30 .30

Panamanian Assoc. of Business Executives, 40th Anniv. — A314

1998, Jan. 28 ***Perf. 14½x14***
869 A314 50c multi 1.00 1.00

Beetles A315

Designs: a, Platyphora haroldi. b, Stilodes leoparda. c, Stilodes fuscolineata. d, Platyphora boucardi.

1998
870 A315 30c Block of 4, #a.-d. 2.40 2.40

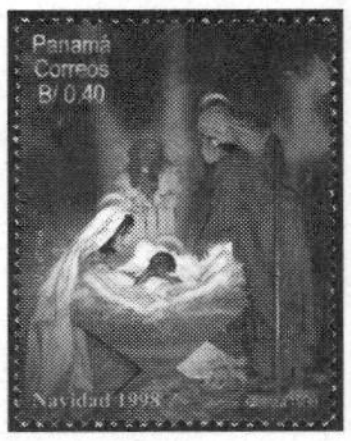
Christmas A316

1998, Jan. 14 **Litho.** ***Perf. 14x14½***
871 A316 40c multi .80 .80

Panama Pavilion, Expo '98, Lisbon A317

1998 **Litho.** ***Perf. 14½x14***
872 A317 45c multi .90 .90

Panama Canal, 85th Anniv. (in 1999) — A318

No. 873: a, Canal builders and crane on train trestle. b, Partially built structures, construction equipment.

2000, Sept. 7 **Litho.** ***Perf. 14½x14***
873 A318 40c Pair, #a-b 1.60 1.60

Souvenir Sheet

874 A318 1.50b Valley 3.00 3.00

No. 874 contains one label.

Reversion of Panama Canal to Panama (in 1999) A319

Various ships. Denominations: 20c, 35c, 40c, 45c.

2000, Sept. 7 ***Perf. 14½x14***
875-878 A319 Set of 4 2.75 2.75

Pres. Arnulfo Arias Madrid (1901-88) — A320

No. 879: a, 20c, Arias as medical doctor, with people. b, 20c, Arias giving speech, holding glasses.
No. 880, a, 30c, Arias in 1941, 1951 and 1969, Panamanian flag. b, 30c, Arias giving speech, crowd.
Illustration reduced.

2001, Aug. 14 **Litho.** ***Perf. 13x13½***
Horiz. pairs, #a-b
879-880 A320 Set of 2 2.00 2.00

Christmas — A321

2001, Dec. 4 **Litho.** ***Perf. 14x14½***
881 A321 35c multi .70 .70

Dated 1999.

Holy Year (in 2000) A322

2001, Dec. 4 ***Perf. 14½x14***
882 A322 20c multi .40 .40

Dated 2000.

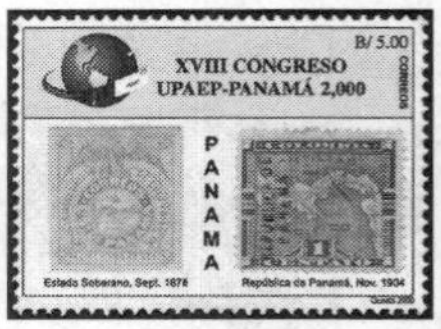
18th UPAEP Congress (in 2000) A323

2001, Dec. 4
883 A323 5b Nos. 7, 101 10.00 10.00

Dated 2000.

Dreaming of the Future — A324

Children's art by: No. 884, 20c, I. Guerra. No. 885, 20c, D. Ortega.
No. 886, horiz.: a, J. Aguilar P. b, S. Sittón.

2001, Dec. 4 ***Perf. 14x14½***
884-885 A324 Set of 2 .80 .80

Souvenir Sheet
Perf. 14½x14

886 A324 75c Sheet of 2, #a-b 3.00 3.00

Dated 2000.

Architecture of the 1990s — A325

Designs: No. 887, 35c, Los Delfines Condominium, by Edwin Brown. No. 888, 35c, Banco General Tower, by Carlos Medina.
No. 889, horiz.: a, Building with round sides, by Ricardo Moreno. b, Building with three peaked roofs, by Moreno.

2001, Dec. 4 ***Perf. 14x14½***
887-888 A325 Set of 2 1.40 1.40

Souvenir Sheet
Perf. 14½x14

889 A325 75c Sheet of 2, #a-b 3.00 3.00

Dated 2000.

Orchids A326

Designs: No. 890, 35c, Cattleya dowiana. No. 891, 35c, Psychopsis krameriana.
No. 892: a, Peristeria clata. b, Miltoniopsis roezlii.

2001, Dec. 4 ***Perf. 14½x14***
890-891 A326 Set of 2 1.40 1.40

Souvenir Sheet

892 A326 75c Sheet of 2, #a-b 3.00 3.00

Dated 2000.

AIR POST STAMPS

Special Delivery Stamp No. E3 Surcharged in Dark Blue

1929, Feb. 8 Unwmk. ***Perf. 12½***
C1 SD1 25c on 10c org 1.00 .80
a. Inverted surcharge 22.50 22.50

Nos. E3-E4 Overprinted in Blue

1929
C2 SD1 10c orange .50 .50
a. Inverted overprint 16.00 14.00
b. Double overprint 16.00 14.00

Some specialists claim the red overprint is a proof impression.

With Additional Surcharge of New Value

C3 SD1 15c on 10c org .50 .50
C4 SD1 25c on 20c dk brn 1.10 1.00
a. Double surcharge 14.00 14.00
Nos. C2-C4 (3) 2.10 2.00

No. E3 Surcharged in Blue

1930, Jan. 25
C5 SD1 5c on 10c org .50 .50

No. 219 Overprinted in Red

1930, Feb. 28 ***Perf. 12***
C6 A39 1b dk vio & blk 16.00 12.50

AP5

Airplane over Map of Panama — AP6

1930-41 Engr. ***Perf. 12***
C6A AP5 5c blue ('41) .20 .20
C6B AP5 7c rose car ('41) .25 .20
C6C AP5 8c gray blk ('41) .25 .20
C7 AP5 15c dp grn .30 .20
C8 AP5 20c rose .35 .20
C9 AP5 25c deep blue .65 .65
Nos. C6A-C9 (6) 2.00 1.65

See No. C112.
For surcharges and overprints see Nos. 353, C16-C16A, C53B, C69, C82-C83, C109, C122, C124.

1930, Aug. 4 ***Perf. 12½***
C10 AP6 5c ultra .20 .20
C11 AP6 10c orange .30 .20
C12 AP6 30c dp vio 5.50 4.00
C13 AP6 50c dp red 1.50 .50
C14 AP6 1b black 5.50 4.00
Nos. C10-C14 (5) 13.00 8.90

For surcharge and overprints see Nos. C53A, C70-C71, C115.

Amphibian AP7

1931, Nov. 24 Typo.
Without Gum

C15 AP7 5c deep blue .80 1.00
a. 5c gray blue .80 1.00
b. Horiz. pair, imperf. btwn. 50.00

For the start of regular airmail service between Panama City and the western provinces, but valid only on Nov. 28-29 on mail carried by hydroplane "3 Noviembre."
Many sheets have a papermaker's watermark "DOLPHIN BOND" in double-lined capitals.

No. C9 Surcharged in Red 19mm long

1932, Dec. 14 ***Perf. 12***
C16 AP5 20c on 25c dp bl 5.00 .50

Surcharge 17mm long

C16A AP5 20c on 25c dp bl 150.00 2.50

Special Delivery Stamp No. E4 Overprinted in Red or Black

1934 ***Perf. 12½***
C17 SD1 20c dk brn 1.00 .50
C17A SD1 20c dk brn (Bk) 75.00 55.00

Surcharged In Black

1935, June
C18 SD1 10c on 20c dk brn .80 .50

Same Surcharge with Small "10"

C18A SD1 10c on 20c dk brn 40.00 5.00
b. Horiz. pair, imperf. vert. 100.00

Nos. 234 and 242 Surcharged in Blue

1936, Sept. 24
C19 A53 5c on ½c org 225.00 250.00
C20 A53 5c on 50c org 1.00 .80
a. Double surcharge 60.00 60.00

Centenary of the birth of President Pablo Arosemena.
It is claimed that No. C19 was not regularly issued. Counterfeits of No. C19 exist.

Urracá Monument AP8

Human Genius Uniting the Oceans AP9

20c, Panama City. 30c, Balboa Monument. 50c, Pedro Miguel Locks. 1b, Palace of Justice.

1936, Dec. 1 Engr. ***Perf. 12***
C21 AP8 5c blue .55 .40
C22 AP9 10c yel org .70 .60
C23 AP9 20c red 1.65 1.50
C24 AP8 30c dk vio 3.00 2.50
C25 AP9 50c car rose 6.75 5.75
C26 AP9 1b black 8.00 6.00
Nos. C21-C26 (6) 20.65 16.75

4th Postal Congress of the Americas and Spain.

Nos. C21-C26 Overprinted in Red or Blue

1937, Mar. 29
C27 AP8 5c blue (R) .35 .30
a. Inverted overprint 35.00
C28 AP9 10c yel org (Bl) .55 .45
C29 AP9 20c red (Bl) 1.25 1.00
a. Double overprint 35.00
C30 AP8 30c dk vio (R) 3.25 3.25
C31 AP8 50c car rose (Bl) 13.00 13.00
a. Double overprint 120.00
C32 AP9 1b black (R) 16.00 13.00
Nos. C27-C32 (6) 34.40 31.00

Regular Stamps of 1921-26 Surcharged in Red

1937, June 30 ***Perf. 12, 12½***
C33 A55 5c on 15c ultra .75 .75
C34 A55 5c on 20c brn .75 .75
C35 A47 10c on 10c vio 1.75 1.50

Regular Stamps of 1920-26 Surcharged in Red

C36 A56 5c on 24c blk vio .75 .75
C37 A39 5c on 1b dk vio & blk .75 .50
C38 A56 10c on 50c blk 2.25 2.00
a. Inverted surcharge 20.00

No. 248 Overprinted in Red

C39 A54 5c dark blue .75 .75
a. Double overprint 18.00
Nos. C33-C39 (7) 7.75 7.00

Fire Dept. Badge AP14

Florencio Arosemena AP15

José Gabriel Duque — AP16

Perf. 14x14½
1937, Nov. 25 Photo. Wmk. 233
C40 AP14 5c blue .75 .60
C41 AP15 10c orange 1.00 1.00
C42 AP16 20c crimson 1.50 .75
Nos. C40-C42 (3) 3.25 2.35

50th anniversary of the Fire Department.

Basketball — AP17

Baseball
AP18

1938, Feb. 2 ***Perf. 14x14½, 14½x14***

C43 AP17	1c shown	.90	.20
C44 AP18	2c shown	.90	.20
C45 AP18	7c Swimming	1.25	.25
C46 AP18	8c Boxing	1.25	.25
C47 AP17	15c Soccer	3.00	1.25
a.	Souv. sheet of 5, #C43-C47	8.00	8.00
b.	As "a," No. C43 omitted	*2,500.*	
	Nos. C43-C47 (5)	7.30	2.15

4th Central American Caribbean Games.

US Constitution Type

Engr. & Litho.

1938, Dec. 7 **Unwmk.** ***Perf. 12½***

Center in Black, Flags in Red and Ultramarine

C49 A83	7c gray	.30	.25
C50 A83	8c brt ultra	.45	.35
C51 A83	15c red brn	.55	.45
C52 A83	50c orange	7.00	5.75
C53 A83	1b black	7.00	5.75
	Nos. C49-C53 (5)	15.30	12.55

Nos. C12 and C7 Surcharged in Red

1938, June 5 ***Perf. 12½, 12***

C53A AP6	7c on 30c dp vio	.40	.40
c.	Double surcharge	18.00	
d.	Inverted surcharge	27.50	
C53B AP5	8c on 15c dp grn	.40	.40
e.	Inverted surcharge	22.50	

Opening of the Normal School at Santiago, Veraguas Province, June 5, 1938. The 8c surcharge has no bars.

Belisario
Porras
AP23

Designs: 2c, William Howard Taft. 5c, Pedro J. Sosa. 10c, Lucien Bonaparte Wise. 15c, Armando Reclus. 20c, Gen. George W. Goethals. 50c, Ferdinand de Lesseps. 1b, Theodore Roosevelt.

1939, Aug. 15 **Engr.**

C54 AP23	1c dl rose	.35	.20
C55 AP23	2c dp bl grn	.35	.20
C56 AP23	5c indigo	.50	.20
C57 AP23	10c dk vio	.60	.20
C58 AP23	15c ultra	1.40	.35
C59 AP23	20c rose pink	3.50	1.40
C60 AP23	50c dk brn	4.00	.70
C61 AP23	1b black	6.00	3.75
	Nos. C54-C61 (8)	16.70	7.00

Opening of Panama Canal, 25th anniv.

For surcharges see Nos. C63, C65, G1, G3.

Flags of the
21 American
Republics
AP31

1940, Apr. 15 **Unwmk.**

C62 AP31	15c blue	.40	.35

Pan American Union, 50th anniversary.

For surcharge see No. C66.

Stamps of 1939-40 Surcharged in Black:

a

b

c

d

1940, Aug. 12

C63 AP23 (a)	5c on 15c lt ultra	.25	.25
a.	"7 AEREO 7" on 15c	40.00	40.00
C64 A84 (b)	7c on 15c ultra	.40	.25
C65 AP23 (c)	7c on 20c rose pink	.40	.25
C66 AP31 (d)	8c on 15c blue	.40	.25
	Nos. C63-C66 (4)	1.45	1.00

Stamps of 1924-30 Overprinted in Black or Red:

e

f

g

1941, Jan. 2 ***Perf. 12½, 12***

C67 SD1 (e)	7c on 10c org	.80	.80
C68 A53 (f)	15c on 24c yel brn (R)	2.00	2.00
C69 AP5 (g)	20c rose	1.60	1.60
C70 AP6 (g)	50c deep red	5.00	3.25
C71 AP6 (g)	1b black (R)	11.00	8.00
	Nos. C67-C71 (5)	20.40	15.65

New constitution of Panama which became effective Jan. 2, 1941.

Liberty — AP32

Black Overprint

1942, Feb. 19 **Engr.** ***Perf. 12***

C72 AP32	20c chestnut brn	3.00	2.50

Costa Rica - Panama Type

Engr. & Litho.

1942, Apr. 25 **Unwmk.**

C73 A94	15c dp grn, dk bl & dp rose	.55	.20

Swordfish
AP34

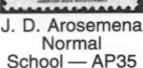

J. D. Arosemena Normal School — AP35

Alejandro Meléndez G. — AP40

Designs: 8c, Gate of Glory, Portobelo. 15c, Taboga Island, Balboa Harbor. 50c, Firehouse. 1b, Gold animal figure.

1942, June 4 **Engr.** ***Perf. 12***

C74 AP34	7c rose carmine	.50	.20
C75 AP34	8c dk ol brn & blk	.20	.20
C76 AP34	15c dark violet	.25	.20
C77 AP35	20c red brown	.35	.20
C78 AP34	50c olive green	.65	.40
C79 AP34	1b blk & org yel	1.60	.80
	Nos. C74-C79 (6)	3.55	2.00

See Nos. C96-C99, C113, C126. For surcharges and overprints see Nos. 354-355, C84-C86, C108, C110-C111, C114, C116, C118, C121, C123, C127-C128, C137.

1943, Dec. 16

Design: 5b, Ernesto T. Lefevre.

C80 AP40	3b dk olive gray	4.50	4.50
C81 AP40	5b dark blue	7.00	7.00

For overprint & surcharge see #C117, C128A.

Catalogue values for unused stamps in this section, from this point to the end of the section, are for Never Hinged items.

Nos. C6C and C7 Surcharged in Carmine

1947, Mar. 8 ***Perf. 12***

C82 AP5	5c on 8c gray blk	.20	.20
a.	Double overprint	25.00	
C83 AP5	10c on 15c dp grn	.50	.40

Nos. C74 to C76 Surcharged in Black or Carmine

C84 AP34	5c on 7c rose car (Bk)	.20	.20
a.	Double surcharge		*375.00*
C85 AP34	5c on 8c dk ol brn & blk	.20	.20
C86 AP34	10c on 15c dk vio	.25	.25
a.	Double surcharge	30.00	30.00
	Nos. C82-C86 (5)	1.35	1.25

National Theater — AP42

1947, Apr. 7 **Engr.** **Unwmk.**

C87 AP42	8c violet	.40	.25

Natl. Constitutional Assembly of 1945, 2nd anniv.

For surcharge see No. 356.

Manuel
Amador
Guerrero
AP43

Manuel
Espinosa
B. — AP44

5c, José Agustin Arango. 10c, Federico Boyd. 15c, Ricardo Arias. 50c, Carlos Constantino Arosemena. 1b, Nicanor de Obarrio. 2b, Tomas Arias.

1948, Feb. 11 ***Perf. 12½***

Center in Black

C88 AP43	3c blue	.30	.20
C89 AP43	5c brown	.30	.20
C90 AP43	10c orange	.30	.20
C91 AP43	15c deep claret	.30	.20
C92 AP44	20c deep carmine	.55	.55
C93 AP44	50c dark gray	1.00	.80
C94 AP44	1b green	3.00	2.50
C95 AP44	2b yellow	6.50	6.00
	Nos. C88-C95 (8)	12.25	10.65

Members of the Revolutionary Junta of 1903.

Types of 1942

1948, June 14 ***Perf. 12***

C96 AP34	2c carmine	.50	.20
C97 AP34	15c olive gray	.25	.20
C98 AP35	20c green	.25	.20
C99 AP34	50c rose carmine	4.00	3.00
	Nos. C96-C99 (4)	5.00	3.60

Franklin D.
Roosevelt
and Juan
D.
Arosemena
AP45

Four
Freedoms
AP46

Monument to F. D. Roosevelt — AP47

Map showing Boyd-Roosevelt Trans-Isthmian Highway — AP48

Franklin D. Roosevelt — AP49

1948, Sept. 15 ***Perf. 12½***

C100 AP45 5c dp car & blk .20 .20
C101 AP46 10c yellow org .30 .30
C102 AP47 20c dull green .35 .35
C103 AP48 50c dp ultra & blk .65 .60
C104 AP49 1b gray black 1.50 1.25
Nos. C100-C104 (5) 3.00 2.70

Franklin Delano Roosevelt (1882-1945).
For surcharges see Nos. RA28-RA29.

Monument to Cervantes
AP50

10c, Don Quixote attacking windmill.

1948, Nov. 15

C105 AP50 5c dk blue & blk .20 .20
C106 AP50 10c purple & blk .35 .25

400th anniv. of the birth of Miguel de Cervantes Saavedra, novelist, playwright and poet.

No. C106 Overprinted in Carmine

1949, Jan.

C107 AP50 10c purple & blk .60 .40
a. Inverted overprint *50.00*

José Gabriel Duque (1849-1918), newspaper publisher and philanthropist.

Nos. C96, C6A, C97 and C99 Overprinted in Black or Red

h

i

1949, May

C108 AP34(h) 2c carmine .20 .20
a. Double overprint 5.00
C109 AP5(i) 5c blue (R) .25 .25
C110 AP34(h) 15c olive gray (R) .65 .65
C111 AP34(h) 50c rose carmine 2.25 2.25
Nos. C108-C111 (4) 3.35 3.35

Centenary of the incorporation of Chiriqui Province.
No. C74 exists with this overprint.

Types of 1930-42

Design: 10c, Gate of Glory, Portobelo.

1949, Aug. 4 ***Perf. 12***

C112 AP5 5c orange .20 .20
C113 AP34 10c dk blue & blk .20 .20

For surcharge see No. C137.

Stamps of 1943-49 Overprinted or Surcharged in Black, Green or Red

1949, Sept. 9

C114 AP34 2c carmine .20 .20
a. Inverted overprint 17.50
b. Double overprint 22.50
C115 AP5 5c orange (G) .40 .25
a. Inverted overprint 9.00
b. Double overprint 20.00
c. Double ovpt., one inverted 20.00
C116 AP34 10c dk bl & blk (R) .40 .30
C117 AP40 25c on 3b dk ol gray (R) .50 .50
C118 AP34 50c rose carmine 1.75 1.75
Nos. C114-C118 (5) 3.25 3.00

75th anniv. of the UPU.
No. C115 has small overprint, 15½x12mm, like No. 368. Overprint on Nos. C114, C116 and C118 as illustrated. Surcharge on No. C117 is arranged vertically, 29x18mm.

University of San Javier
AP51

1949, Dec. 7 **Engr.** ***Perf. 12½***

C119 AP51 5c dk blue & blk .35 .20

See note after No. 371.

Mosquito — AP52

1950, Jan. 12 ***Perf. 12***

C120 AP52 5c dp ultra & gray blk 1.40 .65

See note after No. 372.

Nos. C96, C112, C113 and C9 Overprinted in Black or Carmine (5 or 4 lines)

1950, Aug. 17 **Unwmk.**

C121 AP34 2c carmine .35 .25
C122 AP5 5c orange .35 .35
C123 AP34 10c dk bl & blk (C) .50 .40
C124 AP5 25c deep blue (C) .80 .75

Same on No. 362, Overprinted "AEREO"

C125 A105 50c pur & blk (C) 1.60 1.25
Nos. C121-C125 (5) 3.60 3.00

Gen. José de San Martin, death cent.

Firehouse Type of 1942

1950, Oct. 30 **Engr.**

C126 AP34 50c deep blue 2.00 1.00

Nos. C113 and C81 Surcharged in Carmine or Orange

1952, Feb. 20

C127 AP34 2c on 10c .20 .20
a. Pair, one without surch. 250.00
C128 AP34 5c on 10c (O) .20 .20
b. Pair, one without surch. 250.00
C128A AP40 1b on 5b 20.00 20.00

The surcharge on No. C128A is arranged to fit stamp, with four bars covering value panel at bottom, instead of crosses.

Nos. 376 and 380 Surcharged "AEREO 1952" and New Value in Carmine or Black

1952, Aug. 1

C129 A97 5c on 2c ver & blk (C) .20 .20
a. Inverted surcharge 22.50
C130 A99 25c on 10c pur & org 1.00 1.00

Isabella Type of Regular Issue

Perf. 12½

1952, Oct. 20 **Unwmk.** **Engr.**

Center in Black

C131 A110 4c red orange .20 .20
C132 A110 5c olive green .20 .20
C133 A110 10c orange .20 .25
C134 A110 25c gray blue .65 .30
C135 A110 50c chocolate 1.00 .65
C136 A110 1b black 3.00 3.00
Nos. C131-C136 (6) 5.25 4.60

Queen Isabella I of Spain, 500th birth anniv.

No. C113 Surcharged "5 1953" in Carmine

1953, Apr. 22 ***Perf. 12***

C137 AP34 5c on 10c dk bl & blk .35 .20

Masthead of La Estrella — AP54

1953, July

C138 AP54 5c rose carmine .20 .20
C139 AP54 10c blue .25 .20

Panama's 1st newspaper, La Estrella de Panama, cent.
For surcharges see Nos. C146-C147.

Act of Independence
AP55

Senora de Remon and Pres. José A. Remon Cantera
AP56

Designs: 7c, Pollera. 25c, National flower. 50c, Marcos A. Salazar, Esteban Huertas and Domingo Diaz A. 1b, Dancers.

1953, Nov.

C140 AP55 2c deep ultra .20 .20
C141 AP56 5c deep green .20 .20
C142 AP56 7c gray .25 .20
C143 AP56 25c black 1.50 .65
C144 AP56 50c dark brown 1.00 .65
C145 AP56 1b red orange 2.50 1.00
Nos. C140-C145 (6) 5.65 2.90

Founding of republic, 50th anniversary.
For overprints see Nos. C227-C229.

Nos. C138-C139 Surcharged with New Value in Black or Red

1953-54

C146 AP54 1c on 5c rose car ('54) .20 .20
C147 AP54 1c on 10c blue (R) .20 .20

Gen. Herrera at Conference Table
AP57

Design: 1b, Gen. Herrera leading troops.

1954, Dec. 4 **Litho.** ***Perf. 12½***

C148 AP57 6c deep green .20 .20
C149 AP57 1b scarlet & blk 2.50 2.25

Death of Gen. Tomas Herrera, cent.
For surcharge see No. C198.

Rotary Emblem and Map — AP58

1955, Feb. 23

C150 AP58 6c rose violet .20 .20
C151 AP58 21c red .50 .35
C152 AP58 1b black 4.00 2.50
a. 1b violet black 4.50 3.75
Nos. C150-C152 (3) 4.70 3.05

Rotary International, 50th anniv.
For surcharge see No. C154.

Cantera Type

1955, June 1

C153 A115 6c rose vio & blk .20 .20

Issued in tribute to Pres. José Antonio Remon Cantera, 1908-1955.
For surcharge see No. C188.

No. C151 Surcharged

1955, Dec. 7

C154 AP58 15c on 21c red .40 .35

Pedro J. Sosa — AP60

First Barge Going through Canal and de Lesseps
AP61

Perf. 12½

1955, Nov. 22 **Unwmk.** **Litho.**

C155 AP60 5c grn, *lt grn* .20 .20
C156 AP61 1b red lilac & blk 2.00 2.00

150th anniversary of the birth of Ferdinand de Lesseps. Imperforates exist.

Pres. Dwight D. Eisenhower — AP62

Statue of Bolivar — AP63

Bolivar Hall AP64

Portraits-Presidents: C158, Pedro Aramburu, Argentina. C159, Dr. Victor Paz Estenssoro, Bolivia. C160, Dr. Juscelino Kubitschek O., Brazil. C161, Gen. Carlos Ibanez del Campo, Chile. C162, Gen. Gustavo Rojas Pinilla, Colombia. C163, Jose Figueres, Costa Rica. C164, Gen. Fulgencio Batista y Zaldivar, Cuba. C165, Gen. Hector B. Trujillo Molina, Dominican Rep. C166, José Maria Velasco Ibarra, Ecuador. C167, Col. Carlos Castillo Armas, Guatemala. C168, Gen. Paul E. Magloire, Haiti. C169, Julio Lozano Diaz, Honduras. C170, Adolfo Ruiz Cortines, Mexico. C171, Gen. Anastasio Somoza, Nicaragua. C172, Ricardo Arias Espinosa, Panama. C173, Gen. Alfredo Stroessner, Paraguay. C174, Gen. Manuel Odria, Peru. C175, Col. Oscar Osorio, El Salvador. C176, Dr. Alberto F. Zubiria, Uruguay. C177, Gen. Marcos Perez Jimenez, Venezuela. 1b, Simon Bolivar.

1956, July 18

C157	AP62	6c rose car & vio bl	.35	.35
C158	AP62	6c brt grnsh bl & blk	.25	.20
C159	AP62	6c bister & blk	.25	.20
C160	AP62	6c emerald & blk	.25	.20
C161	AP62	6c lt grn & brn	.25	.20
C162	AP62	6c yellow & grn	.25	.20
C163	AP62	6c brt vio & grn	.25	.20
C164	AP62	6c dl pur & vio bl	.25	.20
C165	AP62	6c red lil & sl grn	.25	.20
C166	AP62	6c citron & vio bl	.25	.20
C167	AP62	6c ap grn & brn	.25	.20
C168	AP62	6c brn & vio bl	.25	.20
C169	AP62	6c brt car & grn	.25	.20
C170	AP62	6c red & brn	.35	.25
C171	AP62	6c lt bl & grn	.25	.20
C172	AP62	6c vio bl & grn	.25	.20
C173	AP62	6c orange & blk	.25	.20
C174	AP62	6c bluish gray & brn	.25	.20
C175	AP62	6c sal rose & blk	.25	.20
C176	AP62	6c dk grn & vio bl	.25	.20
C177	AP62	6c dk org brn & dk grn	.25	.20
C178	AP63	20c dk bluish gray	.55	.55
C179	AP64	50c green	1.00	1.00
C180	AP63	1b brown	2.00	1.25
		Nos. C157-C180 (24)	9.00	7.20

Pan-American Conf., Panama City, July 21-22, 1956, and 130th anniv. of the 1st Pan-American Conf. Imperforates exist.

Ruins of First Town Council Building — AP65

Design: 50c, City Hall, Panama City.

1956, Aug. 17

C181	AP65	25c red	.50	.35
C182	AP65	50c black	1.00	.90
a.		Souv. sheet of 3, #404, C181-C182, imperf.	2.25	2.25

6th Inter-American Congress of Municipalities, Panama City, Aug. 14-19, 1956.

No. C182a sold for 85c.

For overprint see No. C187a.

Monument — AP66

St. Thomas Hospital AP67

1956, Nov. 27 **Wmk. 311**

C183	AP66	5c green	.20	.20
C184	AP67	15c dk carmine	.25	.20

Centenary of the birth of Pres. Belisario Porras.

Highway Construction AP68

20c, Road through jungle, Darien project. 1b, Map of Americas showing Pan-American Highway.

Wmk. 311

1957, Aug. 1 **Litho.** ***Perf. 12½***

C185	AP68	10c black	.20	.20
C186	AP68	20c lt blue & blk	.55	.55
C187	AP68	1b green	2.25	2.25
a.		AP65 Souvenir sheet of 3, unwmkd.	7.50	7.50
		Nos. C185-C187 (3)	3.00	3.00

7th Pan-American Highway Congress.

No. C187a is No. C182a overprinted in black: "VII degree CONGRESSO INTER-AMERICANO DE CARRETERAS 1957."

No. C153 Surcharged "1957" and New Value

1957, Aug. 13 **Unwmk.**

C188	AP59	10c on 6c rose vio & blk	.20	.20

Remon Polyclinic — AP69

Customs House, Portobelo AP70

Buildings: #C191, Portobelo Castle. #C192, San Jeronimo Castle. #C193, Remon Hippodrome. #C194, Legislature. #C195, Interior & Treasury Department. #C196, El Panama Hotel. #C197, San Lorenzo Castle.

Wmk. 311

1957, Oct. **Litho.** ***Perf. 12½***

Design in Black

C189	AP69	10c lt blue	.25	.20
C190	AP70	10c lilac	.25	.20
C191	AP70	10c gray	.25	.20
C192	AP70	10c lilac rose	.25	.20
C193	AP70	10c ultra	.25	.20
C194	AP70	10c brown ol	.25	.20
C195	AP70	10c orange yel	.25	.20
C196	AP70	10c yellow grn	.25	.20
C197	AP70	1b red	2.25	1.60
		Nos. C189-C197 (9)	4.25	3.20

No. C148 Surcharged with New Value and "1958" in Red

1958, Feb. 11 **Unwmk.**

C198	AP57	5c on 6c dp grn	.20	.20

United Nations Emblem — AP71

Flags of Panama and UN AP72

1958, Mar. 5 **Litho.** **Wmk. 311**

C199	AP71	10c brt green	.20	.20
C200	AP71	21c lt ultra	.35	.25
C201	AP71	50c orange	1.00	.85
C202	AP72	1b gray, ultra & car	2.00	1.60
a.		Souv. sheet of 4, #C199-C202, imperf.	4.50	4.50
		Nos. C199-C202 (4)	3.55	2.90

10th anniv. of the UN (in 1955).

The sheet also exists with the 10c and 50c omitted.

OAS Type of Regular Issue, 1958

Designs: 10c, 1b, Flags of 21 American Nations. 50c, Headquarters in Washington.

1958, July 10 **Unwmk.** ***Perf. 12½***

Center yellow and black; flags in national colors

C203	A124	5c lt blue	.20	.20
C204	A124	10c carmine rose	.20	.20
C205	A124	50c gray	.60	.60
C206	A124	1b black	1.90	1.60
		Nos. C203-C206 (4)	2.90	2.60

Type of Regular Issue

Pavilions: 15c, Vatican City. 50c, United States. 1b, Belgium.

1958, Sept. 8 **Wmk. 311** ***Perf. 12½***

C207	A125	15c gray & lt vio	.25	.20
C208	A125	50c dk gray & org brn	.65	.65
C209	A125	1b brt vio & bluish grn	1.40	1.40
a.		Souv. sheet of 7, #418-421, C207-C209	3.50	3.50
		Nos. C207-C209 (3)	2.30	2.25

No. C209a sold for 2b.

Pope Type of Regular Issue

Portraits of Pius XII: 5c, As cardinal. 30c, Wearing papal tiara. 50c, Enthroned.

1959, Jan. 21 **Litho.** **Wmk. 311**

C210	A126	5c violet	.20	.20
C211	A126	30c lilac rose	.50	.40
C212	A126	50c blue gray	.80	.65
a.		Souv. sheet of 4, #422, C210-C212, imperf.	1.90	1.90
		Nos. C210-C212 (3)	1.50	1.25

#C212a is watermarked sideways and sold for 1b. The sheet also exists with 30c omitted. #C212a with C.E.P.A.L. overprint is listed as #C221a.

Human Rights Issue Type

Designs: 5c, Humanity looking into sun. 10c, 20c, Torch and UN emblem. 50c, UN Flag. 1b, UN Headquarters building.

1959, Apr. 14 ***Perf. 12½***

C213	A127	5c emerald & bl	.20	.20
C214	A127	10c gray & org brn	.20	.20
C215	A127	20c brown & gray	.25	.20
C216	A127	50c green & ultra	.70	.65
C217	A127	1b red & blue	1.50	1.40
		Nos. C213-C217 (5)	2.85	2.65

Nos. C213-C215, C212a Overprinted and C216 Surcharged in Red or Dark Blue

1959, May 16

C218	A127	5c emer & bl (R)	.20	.20
C219	A127	10c gray & org brn (Bl)	.20	.20
C220	A127	20c brown & gray (R)	.35	.25
C221	A127	1b on 50c grn & ultra (R)	1.90	1.90
a.		Souvenir sheet of 4	4.00	4.00
		Nos. C218-C221 (4)	2.65	2.55

8th Reunion of the Economic Commission for Latin America.

This overprint also exists on Nos. C216-C217. These have been disavowed by Panama's postmaster general.

No. C221a is No. C212a with two-line black overprint at top of sheet: "8a. REUNION DE LA C.E.P.A.L. MAYO 1959."

Type of Regular Issue, 1959

Portraits: 5c, Justo A. Facio, Rector. 10c, Ernesto de la Guardia, Jr., Pres. of Panama.

Wmk. 311

1959, July 27 **Litho.** ***Perf. 12½***

C222	A128	5c black	.20	.20
C223	A128	10c black	.20	.20

Type of Regular Issue, 1959

1959, Oct. 26 **Wmk. 311** ***Perf. 12½***

C224	A130	5c Boxing	.20	.20
C225	A130	10c Baseball	.20	.20
C226	A130	50c Basketball	.80	.60
		Nos. C224-C226 (3)	1.20	1.00

For surcharge see No. C349.

Nos. C143-C145 Overprinted in Vermilion, Red or Black

Unwmk.

1960, Feb. 6 **Engr.** ***Perf. 12***

C227	AP56	25c black (V)	.75	.20
C228	AP56	50c dk brown (R)	1.00	.40
C229	AP56	1b red orange	1.75	1.25
		Nos. C227-C229 (3)	3.50	1.85

World Refugee Year, July 1, 1959-June 30, 1960.

The revenues from the sale of Nos. C227-C229 went to the United Nations Refugee Fund.

Administration Building, National University — AP74

Designs: 21c, Humanities building. 25c, Medical school. 30c, Dr. Octavio Mendez Pereria first rector of University.

Wmk. 311

1960, Mar. 23 **Litho.** ***Perf. 12½***

C230	AP74	10c brt green	.20	.20
C231	AP74	21c lt blue	.40	.20
C232	AP74	25c ultra	.50	.25
C233	AP74	30c black	.60	.35
		Nos. C230-C233 (4)	1.70	1.00

National University, 25th anniv.

For surcharges see Nos. 450, C248, C253, C287, C291.

Olympic Games Type

5c, Basketball. 10c, Bicycling, horiz. 25c, Javelin thrower. 50c, Athlete with Olympic torch.

1960, Sept. 22 Wmk. 343 *Perf. 12½*

C234 A131 5c orange & red .20 .20
C235 A131 10c ocher & blk .20 .20
C236 A131 25c lt bl & dk bl .50 .35
C237 A131 50c brown & blk 1.00 .65
a. Souv. sheet of 2, #C236-C237 2.25 2.25
Nos. C234-C237 (4) 1.90 1.40

For surcharges see Nos. C249-C250, C254, C266-C270, C290, C350, RA40.

Citizens' Silhouettes AP75

10c, Heads and map of Central America.

1960 Litho. Wmk. 229

C238 AP75 5c black .20 .20
C239 AP75 10c brown .20 .20

6th census of population and the 2nd census of dwellings (No. C238), Dec. 11, 1960, and the All America Census, 1960 (No. C239).

Boeing 707 Jet Liner AP76

1960, Dec. 1 Wmk. 343 *Perf. 12½*

C240 AP76 5c lt grnsh blue .20 .20
C241 AP76 10c emerald .20 .20
C242 AP76 20c red brown .40 .25
Nos. C240-C242 (3) .80 .65

1st jet service to Panama. For surcharge see No. RA41.

Souvenir Sheet

UN Emblem — AP77

Wmk. 311

1961, Mar. 7 Litho. *Imperf.*

C243 AP77 80c blk & car rose 1.60 1.60

15th anniv. (in 1960) of the UN. Counterfeits without control number exist.

No. C243 Overprinted in Blue with Large Uprooted Oak Emblem and "Ano de los Refugiados"

1961, June 2

C244 AP77 80c blk & car rose 2.50 2.50

World Refugee Year, July 1, 1959-June 30, 1960.

Lions International Type

Designs: 5c, Helen Keller School for the Blind. 10c, Children's summer camp. 21c, Arms of Panama and Lions emblem.

1961, May 2 Wmk. 311 *Perf. 12½*

C245 A133 5c black .20 .20
C246 A133 10c emerald .20 .20
C247 A133 21c ultra, yel & red .40 .25
Nos. C245-C247 (3) .80 .65

For overprints see Nos. C284-C286.

Nos. C230 and C236 Surcharged in Black or Red

1961 Wmk. 311 (1c); Wmk. 343

C248 AP74 1c on 10c .20 .20
C249 A131 1b on 25c (Bk) 2.00 2.00
C250 A131 1b on 25c (R) 2.00 2.00
Nos. C248-C250 (3) 4.20 4.20

Pres. Roberto F. Chiari and Pres. Mario Echandi AP78

Wmk. 343

1961, Oct. 2 Litho. *Perf. 12½*

C251 AP78 1b black & gold 2.00 1.25

Meeting of the Presidents of Panama and Costa Rica at Paso Canoa, Apr. 21, 1961.

Dag Hammarskjold AP79

1961, Dec. 27 *Perf. 12½*

C252 AP79 10c black .20 .20

Dag Hammarskjold, UN Secretary General, 1953-61.

No. C230 Surcharged

1962, Feb. 21 Wmk. 311

C253 AP74 15c on 10c brt grn .30 .20

No. C236 Surcharged

Wmk. 343

C254 A131 1b on 25c 2.00 1.25

City Hall, Colon — AP80

1962, Feb. 28 Litho. Wmk. 311

C255 AP80 5c vio bl & blk .20 .20

Issued to publicize the third Central American Municipal Assembly, Colon, May 13-17.

Church Type of Regular Issue, 1962

Designs: 5c, Church of Christ the King. 7c, Church of San Miguel. 8c, Church of the Sanctuary. 10c, Saints Church. 15c, Church of St. Ann. 21c, Canal Zone Synagogue (Now used as USO Center). 25c, Panama Synagogue. 30c, Church of St. Francis. 50c, Protestant Church, Canal Zone. 1b, Catholic Church, Canal Zone.

Wmk. 343

1962-64 Litho. *Perf. 12½*

Buildings in Black

C256 A138 5c purple & buff .20 .20
C257 A138 7c lil rose & brt pink .20 .20
C258 A139 8c purple & bl .20 .20
C259 A139 10c lilac & sal .20 .20
C259A A139 10c grn & dl red brn ('64) .20 .20
C260 A139 15c red & buff .30 .20
C261 A138 21c brown & blue .40 .40
C262 A138 25c blue & pink .50 .35
C263 A139 30c lil rose & bl .60 .40
C264 A138 50c lilac & lt grn 1.00 .65
a. Souv. sheet of 4, #441H-441J, C262, C264, imperf. 2.00 2.00
C265 A139 1b bl & sal 2.00 1.40
Nos. C256-C265 (11) 5.80 4.40

Freedom of religion in Panama. Issue dates: #C259A, June 4, 1964; others, July 20, 1962.

For overprints and surcharges see Nos. C288, C296-C297, C299.

Nos. C234 and C236 Overprinted and Surcharged "IX JUEGOS C.A. Y DEL CARIBE KINGSTON-1962" and Games Emblem in Black, Green, Orange or Red

1962 Wmk. 343 *Perf. 12½*

C266 A131 5c org & red .20 .20
C267 A131 10c on 25c (G) .20 .20
C268 A131 15c on 25c (O) .30 .30
C269 A131 20c on 25c (R) .40 .40
C270 A131 25c lt bl & dk bl .50 .50
Nos. C266-C270 (5) 1.60 1.60

Ninth Central American and Caribbean Games, Kingston, Jamaica, Aug. 11-25.

Nos. CB1-CB2 Surcharged

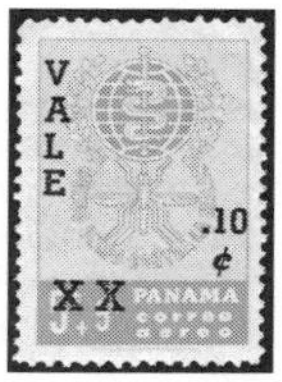

1962, May 3 Wmk. 311

C271 SPAP1 10c on 5c + 5c 1.00 .75
C272 SPAP1 20c on 10c + 10c 1.50 1.50

Type of Regular Issue, 1962

Design: 10c, Canal bridge completed.

1962, Oct. 12 Wmk. 343

C273 A140 10c blue & blk .20 .20

John H. Glenn, "Friendship 7" Capsule — AP81

UPAE Emblem — AP82

Designs: 10c, "Friendship 7" capsule and globe, horiz. 31c, Capsule in space, horiz. 50c, Glenn with space helmet.

1962, Oct. 19 Wmk. 311 *Perf. 12½*

C274 AP81 5c rose red .20 .20
C275 AP81 10c yellow .20 .20
C276 AP81 31c blue .80 .80
C277 AP81 50c emerald 1.00 1.00
a. Souv. sheet of 4, #C274-C277, imperf. 2.25 2.25
Nos. C274-C277 (4) 2.20 2.20

1st orbital flight of US astronaut Lt. Col. John H. Glenn, Jr., Feb. 20, 1962. No. C277a sold for 1b.

For surcharges see Nos. C290A-C290D, C367, CB4-CB7.

1963, Jan. 8 Litho. Wmk. 343

C278 AP82 10c multi .20 .20

50th anniversary of the founding of the Postal Union of the Americas and Spain, UPAE.

Type of Regular Issue

10c, Fire Engine "China", Plaza de Santa Ana. 15c, 14th Street team. 21c, Fire Brigade emblem.

1963, Jan. 22 Wmk. 311 *Perf. 12½*

C279 A141 10c orange & blk .20 .20
C280 A141 15c lilac & blk .30 .20
C281 A141 21c gold, red & ultra .50 .50
Nos. C279-C281 (3) 1.00 .90

"FAO" and Wheat Emblem — AP83

1963, Mar. 21 Litho.

C282 AP83 10c green & red .20 .20
C283 AP83 15c ultra & red .25 .20

FAO "Freedom from Hunger" campaign.

No. C245 Overprinted in Yellow, Orange or Green: "XXII Convención / Leonística / Centroamericana / Panamá, 18-21 / Abril 1963"

1963, Apr. 18 Wmk. 311 *Perf. 12½*

C284 A133 5c black (Y) .20 .20
C285 A133 5c black (O) .20 .20
C286 A133 5c black (G) .20 .20
Nos. C284-C286 (3) .60 .60

22nd Central American Lions Congress, Panama, Apr. 18-21.

No. C230 Surcharged:

1963, June 11

C287 AP74 4c on 10c brt grn .20 .20

Nos. 445 and 432 Overprinted "AEREO" Vertically

1963 Wmk. 343 *Perf. 12½*

C288 A139 10c green, yel & blk .20 .20

Wmk. 311

C289 A130 20c emerald & red brn .40 .25

No. C234 Overprinted: "LIBERTAD DE PRENSA 20-VIII-63"

1963, Aug. 20 Wmk. 343

C290 A131 5c orange & red .20 .20

Freedom of Press Day, Aug. 20, 1963.

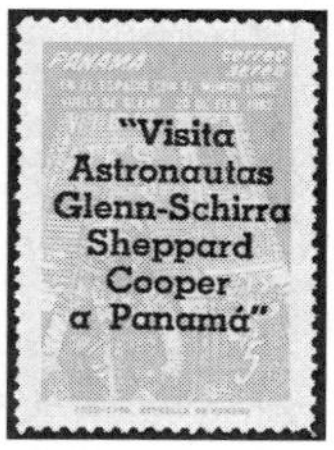

Nos. C274, C277a Overprinted or Surcharged - a

No. C274 Surcharged in Black - b

Wmk. 311

1963, Aug. 21 Litho. *Perf. 12½*

C290A AP81(a) 5c on #C274
C290B AP81(a) 10c on 5c #C274
C290C AP81(b) 10c on 5c #C274

Souvenir Sheet

Imperf.

C290D AP81(a) Sheet of 4, #C277a

Overprint on No. C290D has names in capital letters and covers all four stamps.

No. C232 Surcharged in Red: "VALE 10¢"

1963, Oct. 9 Wmk. 311 *Perf. 12½*

C291 AP74 10c on 25c ultra .20 .20

Type of Regular Issue, 1963

Flags and Presidents: 5c, Julio A. Rivera, El Salvador. 10c, Miguel Ydigoras F., Guatemala. 21c, John F. Kennedy, US.

Perf. 12½x12

1963, Dec. 18 Litho. Unwmk.

Portrait in Slate Green

C292 A142 5c yel, red & ultra .25 .20
C293 A142 10c bl, red & ultra .45 .30
C294 A142 21c org yel, red & ultra 1.40 1.00
Nos. C292-C294 (3) 2.10 1.50

Balboa Type of Regular Issue, 1964

1964, Jan. 22 Photo. *Perf. 13*

C295 A143 10c dk vio, *pale pink* .20 .20

No. C261 Surcharged in Red: "VALE B/.0.50"

1964 Wmk. 343 Litho. *Perf. 12½*

C296 A138 50c on 21c brn, bl & blk 1.00 .70

Type of 1962 Overprinted: "HABILITADA"

C297 A139 1b emer, yel & blk 2.00 2.00

Nos. 434 and 444 Surcharged: "Aéreo B/.0.10"

1964 Wmk. 343 *Perf. 12½*

C298 A131 10c on 5c bl grn & emer .20 .20
C299 A139 10c on 5c rose, lt grn & blk .20 .20

St. Patrick's Cathedral, New York - AP84

Cathedrals: #C301, St. Stephen's, Vienna. #C302, St. Sofia's, Sofia. #C303, Notre Dame, Paris. #C304, Cologne. #C305, St. Paul's, London. #C306, Metropolitan, Athens. #C307, St. Elizabeth's, Kosice, Czechoslovakia (inscr. Kassa, Hungary). #C308, New Delhi. #C309, Milan. #C310, Guadalupe Basilica. #C311, New Church, Delft, Netherlands. #C312, Lima. #C313, St. John's Poland. #C314, Lisbon. #C315, St. Basil's, Moscow. #C316, Toledo. #C317, Stockholm. #C318, Basel. #C319, St. George's Patriarchal Church, Istanbul. 1b, Panama City. 2b, St. Peter's Basilica, Rome.

Unwmk.

1964, Feb. 17 Engr. *Perf. 12*

Center in Black

C300 AP84 21c olive .90 .90
C301 AP84 21c chocolate .90 .90
C302 AP84 21c aqua .90 .90
C303 AP84 21c red brown .90 .90
C304 AP84 21c magenta .90 .90
C305 AP84 21c red .90 .90
C306 AP84 21c orange red .90 .90
C307 AP84 21c blue .90 .90
C308 AP84 21c brown .90 .90
C309 AP84 21c green .90 .90
C310 AP84 21c violet bl .90 .90
C311 AP84 21c dk slate grn .90 .90
C312 AP84 21c violet .90 .90
C313 AP84 21c black .90 .90
C314 AP84 21c emerald .90 .90
C315 AP84 21c dp violet .90 .90
C316 AP84 21c olive grn .90 .90
C317 AP84 21c carmine rose .90 .90
C318 AP84 21c Prus green .90 .90
C319 AP84 21c dark brown .90 .90
C320 AP84 1b dark blue 5.00 5.00
C321 AP84 2b yellow green 9.00 9.00
a. Souv. sheet of 6 9.00 9.00
Nos. C300-C321 (22) 32.00 32.00

Vatican II, the 21st Ecumenical Council of the Roman Catholic Church.

No. C321a contains 6 imperf. stamps similar to Nos. C300, C303, C305, C315, C320 and C321. Size: 198x138mm. Sold for 3.85b.

Six stamps of this set (Nos. C300, C305, C309. C319, C321a) were overprinted "1964." The overprint is olive bister on the stamps, yellow on the souvenir sheet. The overprint is reported to exist also in yellow gold on the same six stamps and in olive bister on the souvenir sheet.

World's Fair, New York AP84a

5c, 10c, 15c, Various pavilions. 21c, Unisphere.

1964, Sept. 14 Wmk. 311 *Perf. 12½*

C322 AP84a 5c yellow & blk
C323 AP84a 10c red & blk
C324 AP84a 15c green & blk
C325 AP84a 21c ultra & blk

Souvenir Sheet

Perf. 12

C326 AP84a 21c ultra & blk

No. C326 contains one 49x35mm stamp. Exists imperf.

AP84b

AP84c

Hammarskjold Memorial, UN Day: No. C327, C329a, Dag Hammarskjold. No. C328, C329b, UN emblem.

Perf. 13½x14

1964, Sept. 24 Unwmk.

C327 AP84b 21c black & blue
C328 AP84b 21c black & blue

Souvenir Sheet

Imperf

C329 Sheet of 2
a.-b. AP84b 21c blk & grn, any single

Nos. C327-C328 exist imperf. in black and green.

Roosevelt Type of Regular Issue

Perf. 12x12½

1964, Oct. 9 Litho. Unwmk.

C330 A147 20c grn & blk, *buff* .40 .30
a. Souv. sheet of 2, #455, C330, imperf. .55 .55

1964 *Perf. 13½x14*

C331 AP84c 21c shown
C332 AP84c 21c Papal coat of arms
a. Souv. sheet of 2, #C331-C332

Pope John XXIII (1881-1963). Nos. C331-C332 exist imperf in different colors.

Galileo, 400th Birth Anniv. — AP84d

21c, Galileo, studies of gravity. Illustration reduced.

1965 *Perf. 14*

C333 AP84d 10c blue & multi
C334 AP84d 21c green & multi
a. Souv. sheet of 2, #C333-C334

Nos. C333-C334a exist imperf. with different colors.

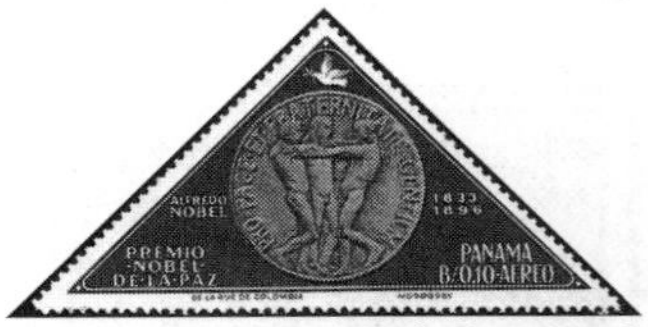

Alfred Nobel (1833-1896), Founder of Nobel Prize — AP84e

Illustration reduced.

1965 Litho. & Embossed

C335 AP84e 10c Peace Medal, rev.
C336 AP84e 21c Peace Medal, obv.
a. Souv. sheet of 2, #C335-C336

Nos. C335-C336a exist imperf. with different colors.

Bird Type of Regular Issue, 1965

Song Birds: 5c, Common troupial, horiz. 10c, Crimson-backed tanager, horiz.

1965, Oct. 27 Unwmk. *Perf. 14*

C337 A148 5c dp orange & multi .20 .20
C338 A148 10c brt blue & multi .25 .20
a. Souv. sheet of 6, #462-462C, C337-C338 .75 .75

Fish Type of Regular Issue

Designs: 8c, Shrimp. 12c, Hammerhead. 13c, Atlantic sailfish. 25c, Seahorse, vert.

1965, Dec. 7 Litho.

C339 A149 8c multi .20 .20
C340 A149 12c multi .30 .20
C341 A149 13c multi .30 .25
C342 A149 25c multi .60 .35
Nos. C339-C342 (4) 1.40 1.00

English Daisy and Emblem — AP85

Junior Chamber of Commerce Emblem and: #C344, Hibiscus. #C345, Orchid. #C346, Water lily. #C347, Gladiolus. #C348, Flor del Espiritu Santo.

1966, Mar. 16

C343 AP85 30c brt pink & multi .75 .35
C344 AP85 30c salmon & multi .75 .35
C345 AP85 30c pale yel & multi .75 .35
C346 AP85 40c lt grn & multi 1.00 .35
C347 AP85 40c blue & multi 1.00 .35
C348 AP85 40c pink & multi 1.00 .35
Nos. C343-C348 (6) 5.25 2.10

50th anniv. of the Junior Chamber of Commerce.

Nos. C224 and C236 Surcharged

1966, June 27 Wmk. 311 *Perf. 12½*

C349 A130 3c on 5c blk & red brn .20 .20

Wmk. 343

C350 A131 13c on 25c lt & dk bl .35 .25

The old denominations are not obliterated on Nos. C349-C350.

ITU Cent. AP85a

1966, Aug. 12 *Perf. 13½x14*

C351 AP85a 31c multicolored

Sovenir Sheet

Perf. 14

C352 AP85a 31c multicolored

No. C352 exists imperf. with blue green background.

Animal Type of Regular Issue, 1967

Domestic Animals: 10c, Pekingese dog. 13c, Zebu, horiz. 30c, Cat. 40c, Horse, horiz.

1967, Feb. 3 Unwmk. *Perf. 14*

C353 A150 10c multi .25 .20
C354 A150 13c multi .30 .20
C355 A150 30c multi .75 .45
C356 A150 40c multi 1.00 .55
Nos. C353-C356 (4) 2.30 1.40

Young Hare, by Durer AP86

10c, St. Jerome and the Lion, by Albrecht Durer. 20c, Lady with the Ermine, by Leonardo Da Vinci. 30c, The Hunt, by Delacroix, horiz.

1967, Sept. 1

C357 AP86 10c black, buff & car .20 .20
C358 AP86 13c lt yellow & multi .25 .20
C359 AP86 20c multicolored .40 .25
C360 AP86 30c multicolored .60 .35
Nos. C357-C360 (4) 1.45 1.00

Panama-Mexico Friendship — AP86a

Designs: 1b, Pres. Gustavo Diaz Ordaz of Mexico and Pres. Marco A. Robles of Panama, horiz.

1968, Jan. 20 *Perf. 14*

C361 AP86a 50c shown
C361A AP86a 1b multi
b. Souv. sheet of 2, #C361-C361A, imperf.

For overprints see Nos. C364-C364B.

Souvenir Sheet

Olympic Equestrian Events — AP86b

1968, Oct. 29 ***Imperf.***

C362 AP86b Sheet of 2
- *a.* 8c Dressage
- *b.* 30c Show jumping

Intl. Human Rights Year — AP86c

1968, Dec. 18 ***Perf. 14***

C363 AP86c 40c multicolored
- *a.* Miniature sheet of 1

Nos. C361-C361b Ovptd. in Red or Black

1969, Jan. 31

C364 AP86a 50c on #C361 (R)
C364A AP86a 1b on #C361A (B)

Souvenir Sheet

C364B on #C361a (R)

Intl. Philatelic and Numismatic Expo.
Overprint larger on No. C364A, larger and in different arrangement on No. C364B.

Intl. Space Exploration — AP86d

1969, Mar. 14

C365 Sheet of 6
- *a.* AP86d 5c France, Diadem I
- *b.* AP86d 10c Italy, San Marco II
- *c.* AP86d 15c Great Britain, UK 3
- *d.* AP86d 20c US, Saturn V/Apollo 7
- *e.* AP86d 25c US, Surveyor 7
- *f.* AP86d 30c Europe/US, Esro 2

Satellite Transmission of Summer Olympics, Mexico, 1968 — AP86e

1969, Mar. 14 ***Perf. 14½***

C366 AP86e 1b multi
- *a.* Miniature sheet of 1

Nos. CB4, 461B & 461C Surcharged

1969, Mar. 26 ***Perf. 13½x13***

C367 AP81 5c on 5c+5c
C367A A147e 5c on 10c+5c
C367B A147e 10c on 21c+10c

Games Type of Regular Issue and

San Blas Indian Girl — AP87

Design: 13c, Bridge of the Americas.

1970, Jan. 6 **Litho.** ***Perf. 13½***

C368	A158 13c multi		.40	.30
C369	AP87 30c multi		.90	.75
a.	"AEREO" omitted		*50.00*	*50.00*

See notes after No. 525.

Juan D. Arosemena and Arosemena Stadium — AP88

Designs: 2c, 3c, 5c, like 1c. No. C374, Basketball. No. C375, New Panama Gymnasium. No. C376, Revolution Stadium. No. C377, Panamanian man and woman in Stadium. 30c, Stadium, eternal flame, arms of Mexico, Puerto Rico and Cuba.

1970, Oct. 7 **Wmk. 365** ***Perf. 13½***

C370	AP88 1c pink & multi	.20	.20
C371	AP88 2c pink & multi	.20	.20
C372	AP88 3c pink & multi	.20	.20
C373	AP88 5c pink & multi	.20	.20
C374	AP88 13c lt blue & multi	.30	.20
C375	AP88 13c lilac & multi	.30	.20
C376	AP88 13c yellow & multi	.30	.20
C377	AP88 13c pink & multi	.30	.20
C378	AP88 30c yellow & multi	.85	.50
a.	Souv. sheet of 1, imperf.	1.50	1.50
	Nos. C370-C378 (9)	2.85	2.10

11th Central American and Caribbean Games, Feb. 28-Mar. 14.

US astronauts Charles Conrad, Jr., Richard F. Gordon, Jr. and Alan L. Bean. — AP89

EXPO '70 Emblem and Pavilion AP90

#C379, Astronaut on Moon.

1971 **Wmk. 343** ***Perf. 13½***

C379	AP89 13c gold & multi	.50	.35
C380	AP89 13c lt green & multi	.50	.35

Man's first landing on the moon, Apollo 11, July 20, 1969 (No. C379) and Apollo 12 moon mission, Nov. 14-24, 1969.
Issued: No. C379, Aug. 20; No. C380, Aug. 23.

1971, Aug. 24 **Litho.**

C381 AP90 10c pink & multi .25 .25

EXPO '70 International Exposition, Osaka, Japan, Mar. 15-Sept. 13.

Flag of Panama AP91

Design: 13c, Map of Panama superimposed on Western Hemisphere, and tourist year emblem.

1971, Dec. 11 **Wmk. 343**

C382	AP91 5c multi	.20	.20
C383	AP91 13c multi	.25	.25

Proclamation of 1972 as Tourist Year of the Americas.

Mahatma Gandhi AP92

1971, Dec. 17

C384 AP92 10c black & multi .60 .35

Centenary of the birth of Mohandas K. Gandhi (1869-1948), leader in India's fight for independence.

Central American Independence Issue

Flags of Central American States AP92a

1971, Dec. 20

C385 AP92a 13c multi .35 .25

160th anniv. of Central America independence.

AP93

AP94

1971, Dec. 21

C386 AP93 8c Panama #4 .25 .25

2nd National Philatelic and Numismatic Exposition, 1970.

1972, Sept. 7 **Wmk. 365**

C387 AP94 40c Natá Church .80 .60

450th anniversary of the founding of Natá.
For surcharges see Nos. C402, RA85.

Telecommunications Emblem — AP95

1972, Sept. 8

C388 AP95 13c lt bl, dp bl & blk .40 .40

3rd World Telecommunications Day (in 1971).

Apollo 14 — AP96

1972, Sept. 11

C389 AP96 13c tan & multi .65 .50

Apollo 14 US moon mission, 1/1-2/9/71.

Shoeshine Boy Counting Coins — AP97

1972, Sept. 12

C390	AP97 5c shown	.20	.20
C391	AP97 8c Mother & Child	.25	.25
C392	AP97 50c UNICEF emblem	1.00	.55
a.	Souv. sheet of 1, imperf.	1.25	1.25
	Nos. C390-C392 (3)	1.45	1.00

25th anniv. (in 1971) of the UNICEF.

San Blas Cloth, Cuna Indians
AP98

1972, Sept. 13

C393 AP98	5c shown	.20	.20
C394 AP98	8c Beaded necklace, Guaymi Indians	.25	.20
C395 AP98	25c View of Portobelo	.55	.45
a.	Souv. sheet of 2, #C393, C395, imperf.	1.00	1.00
	Nos. C393-C395 (3)	1.00	.85

Tourist publicity.
For surcharges see Nos. C417, RA83.

Baseball and Games' Emblem
AP99

Games' Emblem and: 10c, Basketball, vert. 13c, Torch, vert. 25c, Boxing. 50c, Map and flag of Panama, Bolivar. 1b, Medals.

Perf. 12½

1973, Feb. 9 Litho. Unwmk.

C396 AP99	8c rose red & yel	.20	.20
C397 AP99	10c black & ultra	.25	.20
C398 AP99	13c blue & multi	.35	.20
C399 AP99	25c blk, yel grn & red	.60	.25
C400 AP99	50c green & multi	1.25	.60
C401 AP99	1b multicolored	2.25	1.00
	Nos. C396-401 (6)	4.90	2.45

7th Bolivar Games, Panama City, 2/17-3/3.

No. C387 Surcharged in Red Similar to No. 542

1973, Mar. 16 Wmk. 365 *Perf. 13½*

C402 AP94	13c on 40c multi	.30	.30

UN Security Council Meeting, Panama City, Mar. 15-21.

Portrait Type of Regular Issue 1973

Designs: 5c, Isabel Herrera Obaldia, educator. 8c, Nicolas Victoria Jaén, educator. 10c, Forest Scene, by Roberto Lewis. No. C406, Portrait of a Lady, by Manuel E. Amador. No. C407, Ricardo Miró, poet. 20c, Portrait, by Isaac Benitez. 21c, Manuel Amador Guerrero, statesman. 25c, Belisario Porras, statesman. 30c, Juan Demostenes Arosemena, statesman. 34c, Octavio Mendez Pereira, writer. 38c, Ricardo J. Alfaro, writer.

1973, June 20 Litho. *Perf. 13½*

C403 A169	5c pink & multi	.20	.20
C404 A169	8c pink & multi	.20	.20
C405 A169	10c gray & multi	.20	.20
C406 A169	13c pink & multi	.35	.20
C407 A169	13c pink & multi	.35	.20
C408 A169	20c blue & multi	.50	.40
C409 A169	21c yellow & multi	.50	.40
C410 A169	25c pink & multi	.50	.40
C411 A169	30c gray & multi	.65	.35
C412 A169	34c lt blue & multi	.80	.60
C413 A169	38c lt blue & multi	1.00	.50
	Nos. C403-C413 (11)	5.25	3.65

Famous Panamanians.
For overprints and surcharges see Nos. C414-C416, C418-C421.

Nos. C403, C410, and C412 Overprinted in Black or Red

1973, Sept. 14 Litho. *Perf. 13½*

C414 A169	5c pink & multi	.20	.20
C415 A169	25c pink & multi	.60	.45
C416 A169	34c bl & multi (R)	.90	.75
	Nos. C414-C416 (3)	1.70	1.40

50th anniversary of the Isabel Herrera Obaldia Professional School.

Nos. C395, C408, C413, C412 and C409 Surcharged in Red

1974, Nov. 11 Litho. *Perf. 13½*

C417 AP98	1c on 25c multi	.20	.20
C418 A169	3c on 20c multi	.20	.20
C419 A169	8c on 38c multi	.20	.20
C420 A169	10c on 34c multi	.20	.20
C421 A169	13c on 21c multi	.20	.20
	Nos. C417-C421 (5)	1.00	1.00

Women's Hands, Panama Map, UN and IWY Emblems
AP100

Victoria Sugar Plant, Sugar Cane, Map of Veraguas Province
AP101

Perf. 12½

1975, May 6 Litho. Unwmk.

C422 AP100	17c blue & multi	.50	.20
a.	Souv. sheet, typo., imperf., no gum	1.00	1.00

International Women's Year 1975.

1975, Oct. 9 Litho. *Perf. 12½*

Designs: 17c, Bayano electrification project and map of Panama, horiz. 33c, Tocumen International Airport and map, horiz.

C423 AP101	17c bl, buff & blk	.35	.30
C424 AP101	27c ultra & yel grn	.50	.35
C425 AP101	33c bl & multi	.65	.45
	Nos. C423-C425 (3)	1.50	1.10

Oct. 11, 1968, Revolution, 7th anniv.

Bolivar Statue and Flags — AP102

Bolivar Hall, Panama City
AP103

Design: 41c, Bolivar with flag of Panama, ruins of Old Panama City.

1976, Mar.

C426 AP102	23c multi	.50	.20
C427 AP103	35c multi	.70	.30
C428 AP102	41c multi	.80	.60
	Nos. C426-C428 (3)	2.00	1.10

150th anniversary of Congress of Panama.
Issue dates: 23c, Mar. 15; others Mar. 30.

Marine Life Type of 1976

Marine life: 17c, Diodon hystrix, vert. 27c, Pocillopora damicornis.

Perf. 13x12½, 12½x13

1976, May 6 Litho. Wmk. 377

C429 A171	17c multi	.35	.30
C430 A171	27c multi	.55	.40

Cerro Colorado — AP104

1976, Nov. 12 Litho. *Perf. 12½*

C431 AP104	23c multi	.45	.20

Cerro Colorado copper mines, Chiriqui Province.

Gen. Omar Torrijos Herrera (1929-1981)
AP105

1982, Feb. Litho. *Perf. 10½*

C432 AP105	23c multi	.45	.20

Torrijos Type of 1982

Wmk. 311

1982, May 14 Litho. *Perf. 10½*

C433 A201	35c Security Council reunion, 1973	.70	.30
C434 A201	41c Torrijos Airport	.80	.50

Souvenir Sheet

Imperf

C435 A201	23c like #C432	2.00	2.00

No. C435 sold for 1b.

Alfaro Type of 1982

Photos by Luiz Gutierrez Cruz.

1982, Aug. 18 Wmk. 382

C436 A202	17c multi	.35	.20
C437 A202	23c multi	.45	.20

World Cup Type of 1982

1982, Dec. 27 Litho. *Perf. 10½*

C438 A203	23c Map	.60	.20
C439 A203	35c Pele, vert.	.80	.30
C440 A203	41c Cup, vert.	1.00	.40
	Nos. C438-C440 (3)	2.40	.90

1b imperf. souvenir sheet exists in design of 23c; black control number. Size; 85x75mm.

Nicolas A. Solano (1882-1943), Tuberculosis Researcher
AP106

Wmk. 382 (Stars)

1983, Feb. 8 Litho. *Perf. 10½*

C441 AP106	23c brown	.45	.20

World Food Day — AP107

Contadora Group for Peace — AP108

1984, Oct. 16 Litho. *Perf. 12*

C442 AP107	30c Hand grasping fork	.60	.20

1985, Oct. 1 Litho. *Perf. 14*

C443 AP108	10c multi	.20	.20
C444 AP108	20c multi	.40	.20
C445 AP108	30c multi	.60	.25
	Nos. C443-C445 (3)	1.20	.65

See No. 680A.

Christmas Type of 1988

1988, Dec. 29 Litho. *Perf. 12*

C446 A246	35c *St. Joseph and the Infant*	.80	.40

Olympics Type of 1989

1989, Mar. 17 Litho. *Perf. 12*

C447 A248	35c Boxing	.80	.40

Opening of the Panama Canal, 75th Anniv.
AP109

1989, Sept. 29 Litho. *Perf. 13½*

C448 AP109	35c *Ancon* in lock, 1914	.90	.65
C449 AP109	60c Ship in lock, 1989	1.50	1.10

Revolution Type of 1989

1989, Nov. 14 Litho.

C450 A251	35c Storming of the Bastille	.90	.65
C451 A251	45c Anniv. emblem	1.10	.85

French revolution, bicent.

AIR POST SEMI-POSTAL STAMPS

Catalogue values for unused stamps in this section are for Never Hinged items.

"The World Against Malaria" — SPAP1

Wmk. 311

1961, Dec. 20 Litho. *Perf. 12½*

CB1 SPAP1	5c + 5c car rose	.50	.50
CB2 SPAP1	10c + 10c vio bl	.50	.50
CB3 SPAP1	15c + 15c dk grn	.50	.50
	Nos. CB1-CB3 (3)	1.50	1.50

WHO drive to eradicate malaria.
For surcharges see Nos. C271-C272.

Nos. C274-C276 Surcharged in Red

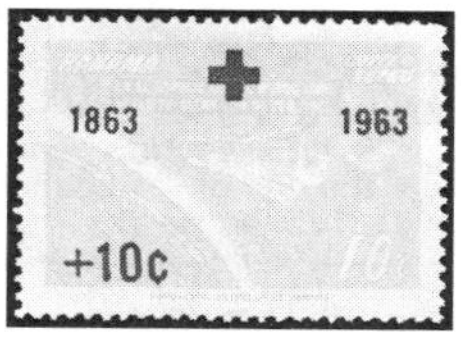

Wmk. 311

1963, Mar. 4 Litho. *Perf. 12½*

CB4 AP81 5c +5c on #C274
CB5 AP81 10c +10c on #C275
CB6 AP81 15c +15c on #C276

Surcharge on No. CB4 differs to fit stamp. See No. CB7.

No. CB4 Surcharged in Black

CB7 AP81 10c on 5c+5c

Intl. Red. Cross cent.

SPECIAL DELIVERY STAMPS

Nos. 211-212 Overprinted in Red

1926 Unwmk. *Perf. 12*

E1 A31 10c org & blk	7.50	3.25
a. "EXRPESO"	40.00	
E2 A32 20c brn & blk	10.00	3.25
a. "EXRPESO"	40.00	
b. Double overprint	35.00	35.00

Bicycle Messenger SD1

1929 Engr. *Perf. 12½*

E3 SD1 10c orange	1.25	1.00
E4 SD1 20c dk brn	4.75	2.50

For surcharges and overprints see Nos. C1-C5, C17-C18A, C67.

REGISTRATION STAMPS

Issued under Colombian Dominion

R1

1888 Unwmk. Engr. *Perf. 13½*

F1 R1 10c black, *gray*	8.00	5.25

Imperforate and part-perforate copies without gum and those on surface-colored paper are reprints.

R2

Magenta, Violet or Blue Black Handstamped Overprint

1898 *Perf. 12*

F2 R2 10c yellow	7.00	6.50

The handstamp on No. F2 was also used as a postmark.

R3

1900 Litho. *Perf. 11*

F3 R3 10c blk, *lt bl*	4.00	3.50

1901

F4 R3 10c brown red	30.00	20.00

R4

Blue Black Surcharge

1902

F5 R4 20c on 10c brn red	20.00	16.00

Issues of the Republic Issued in the City of Panama

Registration Stamps of Colombia Handstamped

R9

Handstamped in Blue Black or Rose — REPUBLICA DE PANAMA

1903-04 *Imperf.*

F6 R9 20c red brn, *bl*	45.00	42.50
F7 R9 20c blue, *blue* (R)	45.00	42.50

For surcharges and overprints see Nos. F8-F11, F16-F26.

Reprints exist of Nos. F6 and F7; see note after No. 64.

With Additional Surcharge in Rose

F8 R9 10c on 20c red brn, *bl*	60.00	55.00
b. "10" in blue black	60.00	55.00
F9 R9 10c on 20c bl, *bl*	60.00	45.00

Handstamped in Rose

F10 R9 10c on 20c red brn, *bl*	60.00	55.00
F11 R9 10c on 20c blue, *blue*	45.00	42.50

Issued in Colon

Regular Issues Handstamped "R/COLON" in Circle (as on F2) Together with Other Overprints and Surcharges

Handstamped

1903-04 *Perf. 12*

F12 A4 10c yellow	3.00	2.50

Handstamped PANAMA

F13 A4 10c yellow	22.50	

Overprinted in Red

F14 A4 10c yellow	3.00	2.50

Overprinted in Black — República de Panamá

F15 A4 10c yellow	7.50	5.00

The handstamps on Nos. F12 to F15 are in magenta, violet or red; various combinations of these colors are to be found. They are struck in various positions, including double, inverted, one handstamp omitted, etc.

Colombia No. F13 Handstamped Like No. F12 in Violet

Imperf

F16 R9 20c red brn, *bl*	60.00	55.00

Overprinted Like No. F15 in Black

F17 R9 20c red brn, *bl*	6.00	5.75

No. F17 Surcharged in Manuscript

F18 R9 10c on 20c red brn, *bl*	60.00	55.00

No. F17 Surcharged in Purple — 10

F19 R9 10c on 20c	82.50	80.00

No. F17 Surcharged in Violet — 10

F20 R9 10c on 20c	82.50	80.00

The varieties of the overprint which are described after No. 138 are also to be found on the Registration and Acknowledgment of Receipt stamps. It is probable that Nos. F17 to F20 inclusive owe their existence more to speculation than to postal necessity.

Issued in Bocas del Toro

Colombia Nos. F17 and F13 Handstamped in Violet

R DE PANAMA

1903-04

F21 R9 20c blue, *blue*	125.00	125.00
F22 R9 20c red brn, *bl*	125.00	125.00

No. F21 Surcharged in Manuscript in Violet or Red

F23 R9 10c on 20c bl, *bl*	150.00	140.00

Colombia Nos. F13, F17 Handstamped in Violet

Surcharged in Manuscript (a) "10" (b) "10cs" in Red

F25 R9 10 on 20c red brn, *bl*	70.00	65.00
F26 R9 10cs on 20c bl, *bl*	55.00	50.00
Nos. F21-F26 (5)	525.00	505.00

No. F25 without surcharge is bogus, according to leading experts.

General Issue

R5

1904 Engr. *Perf. 12*

F27 R5 10c green	1.00	.50

Nos. 190 and 213 Surcharged in Red

#F29-F30

#F29b

1916-17

F29 A11 5c on 8c pur & blk	3.00	2.25
a. "5" inverted	55.00	
b. Large, round "5"	50.00	
c. Inverted surcharge	12.50	11.00
d. Tête bêche surcharge		
F30 A33 5c on 8c vio & blk ('17)	3.50	.80
a. Inverted surcharge	10.00	8.25
b. Tête bêche surcharge		
c. Double surcharge		40.00

Stamps similar to No. F30, overprinted in green were unauthorized.

INSURED LETTER STAMPS

Stamps of 1939 Surcharged in Black

1942 Unwmk. *Perf. 12½*

G1 AP23 5c on 1b blk	.50	.50
G2 A84 10c on 1b dk brn	.80	.80
G3 AP23 25c on 50c dk brn	2.00	2.00
Nos. G1-G3 (3)	3.30	3.30

ACKNOWLEDGMENT OF RECEIPT STAMPS

Issued under Colombian Dominion

Experts consider this handstamp-"A.R. / COLON / COLOMBIA"-to be a cancellation or a marking intended for a letter to receive special handling. It was applied at Colon to various stamps in 1897-1904 in different colored inks for philatelic sale. It exists on cover, usually with the bottom line removed by masking the handstamp.

Nos. 17-18 Handstamped in Rose

1902

H4 A4 5c blue	5.00	5.00
H5 A4 10c yellow	10.00	10.00

This handstamp was also used as a postmark.

Issues of the Republic
Issued in the City of Panama
Colombia No. H3 Handstamped

AR2

Handstamped in Rose REPUBLICA DE PANAMA

1903-04 Unwmk. *Imperf.*
H9 AR2 10c blue, *blue* 10.00 8.00

Reprints exist of No. H9, see note after No. 64.

No. H9 Surcharged with New Value
H10 AR2 5c on 10c bl, *bl* 5.00 5.00

Colombia No. H3 Handstamped in Rose Panamá

H11 AR2 10c blue, *blue* 17.50 14.00

Issued in Colon

Handstamped in Magenta or Violet REPUBLICA DE PANAMA

Imperf
H17 AR2 10c blue, *blue* 15.00 15.00

Handstamped PANAMA

H18 AR2 10c blue, *blue* 82.50 70.00

Overprinted in Black

República de Panamá

H19 AR2 10c blue, *blue* 11.00 8.00

No. H19 Surcharged in Manuscript
H20 AR2 10c on 5c on 10c 100.00 82.50

Issued in Bocas del Toro
Colombia No. H3 Handstamped in Violet and Surcharged in Manuscript in Red Like Nos. F25-F26

1904
H21 AR2 5c on 10c blue, *blue*

No. H21, unused, without surcharge is bogus.

General Issue

AR3

1904 Engr. *Perf. 12*
H22 AR3 5c blue 1.00 .80

No. 199 Overprinted in Violet

1916
H23 A20 2½c red orange 1.00 .80
- *a.* "R.A." for "A.R." 50.00
- *b.* Double overprint 8.00
- *c.* Inverted overprint 8.00

LATE FEE STAMPS

Issues of the Republic
Issued in the City of Panama

LF3

Colombia No. I4 Handstamped in Rose or Blue Black REPUBLICA DE PANAMA

1903-04 Unwmk. *Imperf.*
I1 LF3 5c pur, *rose* 12.50 9.00
I2 LF3 5c pur, *rose* (Bl Blk) 17.50 12.50

Reprints exist of #I1-I2; see note after #64.

General Issue

LF4

1904 Engr. *Perf. 12*
I3 LF4 2½c lake 1.00 .65

No. 199 Overprinted with Typewriter Retardo

1910, Aug. 12
I4 A20 2½c red orange 125.00 100.00

Used only on Aug. 12-13.
Counterfeits abound.

Handstamped RETARDO

1910
I5 A20 2½c red orange 60.00 50.00

Counterfeits abound.

No. 195 Surcharged in Green

1917
I6 A17 1c on ½c orange .80 .80
- *a.* "UN CENTESIMO" inverted 50.00
- *b.* Double surcharge 10.00
- *c.* Inverted surcharge 6.50 6.50

Same Surcharge on No. 196

1921
I7 A17 1c on ½c rose 25.00 20.00

POSTAGE DUE STAMPS

San Lorenzo Castle Gate, Mouth of Chagres River
D1

Statue of Columbus
D2

Pedro J. Sosa — D4

D5

Design: 4c, Capitol, Panama City.

1915 Unwmk. Engr. *Perf. 12*

J1	D1	1c olive brown	3.00	.75
J2	D2	2c olive brown	4.50	.65
J3	D1	4c olive brown	6.00	1.25
J4	D4	10c olive brown	4.50	1.75
		Nos. J1-J4 (4)	18.00	4.40

Type D1 was intended to show a gate of San Lorenzo Castle, Chagres, and is so inscribed.

1930 *Perf. 12½*

J5	D5	1c emerald	.80	.60
J6	D5	2c dark red	.80	.60
J7	D5	4c dark blue	1.25	.80
J8	D5	10c violet	1.25	.80
		Nos. J5-J8 (4)	4.10	2.80

POSTAL TAX STAMPS

Pierre and Marie Curie — PT1

1939 Unwmk. Engr. *Perf. 12*

RA1	PT1	1c rose carmine	.50	.20
RA2	PT1	1c green	.50	.20
RA3	PT1	1c orange	.50	.20
RA4	PT1	1c blue	.50	.20
		Nos. RA1-RA4 (4)	2.00	.80

See Nos. RA6-RA18, RA24-RA27, RA30.

Stamp of 1924 Overprinted in Black

1940
RA5 A53 1c dark green 1.40 .75

Inscribed 1940

1941

RA6	PT1	1c rose carmine	.50	.20
RA7	PT1	1c green	.50	.20
RA8	PT1	1c orange	.50	.20
RA9	PT1	1c blue	.50	.20
		Nos. RA6-RA9 (4)	2.00	.80

Inscribed 1942

1942
RA10 PT1 1c violet .40 .20

Inscribed 1943

1943

RA11	PT1	1c rose carmine	.40	.20
RA12	PT1	1c green	.40	.20
RA13	PT1	1c orange	.40	.20
RA14	PT1	1c blue	.40	.20
		Nos. RA11-RA14 (4)	1.60	.80

Inscribed 1945

1945

RA15	PT1	1c rose carmine	.40	.20
RA16	PT1	1c green	.40	.20
RA17	PT1	1c orange	.40	.20
RA18	PT1	1c blue	.40	.20
		Nos. RA15-RA18 (4)	1.60	.80

Nos. 234 and 235 Surcharged in Black or Red

1946 Unwmk. *Perf. 12*
RA19 A53 1c on ½c orange .60 .20
RA20 A53 1c on 1c dk grn (R) .60 .20

Catalogue values for unused stamps in this section, from this point to the end of the section, are for Never Hinged items.

Same Surcharged in Black on Nos. 239 and 241

1947
RA21 A53 1c on 12c ol grn .40 .30
RA22 A53 1c on 24c yel brn .40 .30

Surcharged in Red on No. 342
RA23 A95 1c on ½c dl vio, bl & car .40 .20

Type of 1939
Inscribed 1947

1947

RA24	PT1	1c rose carmine	.40	.20
RA25	PT1	1c green	.40	.20
RA26	PT1	1c orange	.40	.20
RA27	PT1	1c blue	.40	.20
		Nos. RA24-RA27 (4)	1.60	.80

Nos. C100 and C101 Surcharged in Black

a

b

1949 Unwmk. *Perf. 12½*
RA28 AP45 (a) 1c on 5c .35 .20
- *a.* Inverted surcharge 10.00

RA29 AP46 (b) 1c on 10c yel org .35 .20

Type of 1939
Inscribed 1949

1949 *Perf. 12*
RA30 PT1 1c brown .50 .20

The tax from the sale of Nos. RA1-RA30 was used for the control of cancer.

Juan D. Arosemena Stadium
PT2

Torch Emblem
PT3

Discobolus
PT4

#RA33, Adan Gordon Olympic Swimming Pool.

1951 Unwmk. Engr. *Perf. 12½*

RA31	PT2	1c carmine & blk	.65	.20
RA32	PT3	1c dk bl & blk	.65	.20
RA33	PT2	1c grn & blk	.65	.20
		Nos. RA31-RA33 (3)	1.95	.60

1952

Design: No. RA34, Turners' emblem.

RA34 PT3 1c org & blk .65 .20
RA35 PT4 1c pur & blk .65 .20

The tax from the sale of Nos. RA31-RA35 was used to promote physical education.

Boys Doing Farm Work PT5

1958 Wmk. 311 Litho. Perf. 12½
Size: 35x24mm

RA36 PT5 1c rose red & gray .20 .20

Type of 1958
Inscribed 1959

1959 Size: 35x24mm

RA37 PT5 1c gray & emerald .20 .20
RA38 PT5 1c vio bl & gray .20 .20

Type of 1958
Inscribed 1960

1960 Litho. Wmk. 334 Perf. 13½
Size: 32x23mm

RA39 PT5 1c carmine & gray .20 .20

Nos. C235 and C241 Surcharged in Black or Red

1961 Wmk. 343 Perf. 12½

RA40 A131 1c on 10c ocher & blk .20 .20
RA41 AP76 1c on 10c emer (R) .20 .20
a. Inverted surcharge

Girl at Sewing Machine PT6

Wmk. 343
1961, Nov. 24 Litho. Perf. 12½

RA42 PT6 1c brt vio .20 .20
RA43 PT6 1c rose lilac .20 .20
RA44 PT6 1c yellow .20 .20
RA45 PT6 1c blue .20 .20
RA46 PT6 1c emerald .20 .20
Nos. RA42-RA46 (5) 1.00 1.00

1961, Dec. 1

Design: Boy with hand saw.

RA47 PT6 1c red lilac .20 .20
RA48 PT6 1c rose .20 .20
RA49 PT6 1c orange .20 .20
RA50 PT6 1c blue .20 .20
RA51 PT6 1c gray .20 .20
Nos. RA47-RA51 (5) 1.00 1.00

Boy Scout — PT7

Map of Panama, Flags — PT8

Designs: Nos. RA57-RA61, Girl Scout.

1964, Feb. 7 Wmk. 343

RA52 PT7 1c olive .20 .20
RA53 PT7 1c gray .20 .20
RA54 PT7 1c lilac .20 .20
RA55 PT7 1c carmine rose .20 .20
RA56 PT7 1c blue .20 .20
RA57 PT7 1c bluish green .20 .20
RA58 PT7 1c violet .20 .20
RA59 PT7 1c orange .20 .20
RA60 PT7 1c yellow .20 .20
RA61 PT7 1c brn org .20 .20
Nos. RA52-RA61 (10) 2.00 2.00

The tax from Nos. RA36-RA61 was for youth rehabilitation.

1973, Jan. 22 Unwmk.

RA62 PT8 1c black .20 .20

7th Bolivar Sports Games, Feb. 17-Mar. 3, 1973. The tax was for a new post office in Panama City.

Post Office — PT9

Designs: No. RA63, Farm Cooperative. No. RA64, 5b silver coin. No. RA65, Victoriano Lorenzo. No. RA66, RA69, Cacique Urraca. No. RA67, RA70, Post Office.

1973-75

RA63 PT9 1c brt yel grn & ver .20 .20
RA64 PT9 1c gray & red .20 .20
RA65 PT9 1c ocher & red .20 .20
RA66 PT9 1c org & red .20 .20
RA67 PT9 1c bl & red .20 .20
RA68 PT9 1c blue ('74) .20 .20
RA69 PT9 1c orange ('74) .20 .20
RA70 PT9 1c vermilion ('75) .20 .20
Nos. RA63-RA70 (8) 1.60 1.60

The tax was for a new post office in Panama City.

Stamps of 1969-1973 Surcharged in Violet Blue, Yellow, Black or Carmine

VALE 1¢
PRO EDIFICIO

1975

RA75 A168 1c on 1c (#538; VB) .20 .20
RA76 A168 1c on 2c (#539; Y) .20 .20
RA77 A164 1c on 30c (#534; B) .20 .20
RA78 A157 1c on 30c (#511; B) .20 .20
RA79 A156 1c on 40c (#514; B) .20 .20
RA80 A156 1c on 50c (#515; B) .20 .20
RA81 A169 1c on 20c (#C408; C) .20 .20
RA82 A169 1c on 25c (#C410; B) .20 .20
RA83 AP98 1c on 25c (#C395; B) .20 .20
RA84 A169 1c on 30c (#C411; B) .20 .20
RA85 AP94 1c on 40c (#C387; C) .20 .20
Nos. RA75-RA85 (11) 2.20 2.20

The tax was for a new post office in Panama City. Surcharge vertical, reading down on No. RA75 and up on Nos. RA76, RA78 and RA83. Nos. RA75-RA85 were obligatory on all mail.

PT10

PT11

1980, Dec. 3 Litho. Perf. 12

RA86 PT10 2c Boys .20 .20
RA87 PT10 2c Boy and chicks .20 .20
RA88 PT10 2c Working in fields .20 .20
RA89 PT10 2c Boys feeding piglet .20 .20
a. Souv. sheet of 4, #RA86-RA89 2.00
b. Block of 4, #RA86-RA89 .60

Tax was for Children's Village (Christmas 1980). #RA89a sold for 1b.

1981, Nov. 1 Litho. Perf. 12

RA90 PT11 2c Boy, pony .20 .20
RA91 PT11 2c Nativity .20 .20
RA92 PT11 2c Tree .20 .20
RA93 PT11 2c Church .20 .20
a. Block of 4, #RA90-RA93 .60

Souvenir Sheet

RA94 Sheet of 4 *7.50*
a.-d. PT11 2c, Children's drawings

Tax was for Children's Village. No. RA94 sold for 5b.

PT12

1982, Nov. 1 Litho. Perf. 13½x12½

RA95 PT12 2c Carpentry .20 .20
RA96 PT12 2c Beekeeping .20 .20
a. Pair, #RA95-RA96 .20
RA97 PT12 2c Pig farming, vert. .20 .20
RA98 PT12 2c Gardening, vert. .20 .20
a. Pair, #RA97-RA98 .20

Tax was for Children's Village (Christmas 1982).

Children's Drawings — PT13

Boy — PT14

1983, Nov. 1 Litho. Perf. 14½

RA99 PT13 2c Annunciation .20 .20
RA100 PT13 2c Bethlehem and Star .20 .20
RA101 PT13 2c Church and Houses .20 .20
RA102 PT13 2c Flight into Egypt .20 .20
Nos. RA99-RA102 (4) .80 .80

Nos. RA100-RA102 are vert.

Souvenir sheets exist showing undenominated designs of Nos. RA99, RA101 and Nos. RA100, RA102 respectively. They sold for 2b each.

1984, Nov. 1 Litho. Perf. 12x12½

RA103 PT14 2c White-collared shirt .20 .20
RA104 PT14 2c T-shirt .20 .20
RA105 PT14 2c Checked shirt .20 .20
RA106 PT14 2c Scout uniform .20 .20
a. Block of 4, #RA103-RA106 .60

Tax was for Children's Village. An imperf. souvenir sheet sold for 2b, with designs similar to Nos. RA103-RA106, exists.

Christmas 1985 — PT15

Inscriptions: No. RA107, "Ciudad del Nino es . . . mi vida." No. RA108, "Feliz Navidad." No. RA109, "Feliz Ano Nuevo." No. RA110, "Gracias."

1985, Dec. 10 Litho. Perf. 13½x13

RA107 PT15 2c multi .20 .20
RA108 PT15 2c multi .20 .20
RA109 PT15 2c multi .20 .20
RA110 PT15 2c multi .20 .20
a. Block of 4, #RA107-RA110 .60

Tax for Children's Village. A souvenir sheet, perf. and imperf., sold for 2b, with designs of Nos. RA107-RA110.

Children's Village, 20th Anniv. — PT16

Inscriptions and Embera, Cuna, Embera and Guaymies tribal folk figures: No. RA111, "1966-1986." No. RA112, "Ciudad del Nino es . . . mi vida." No. RA113, "20 anos de fundacion." No. RA114, "Gracias."

1986, Nov. 1 Litho. Perf. 13½

RA111 PT16 2c multi .20 .20
RA112 PT16 2c multi .20 .20
RA113 PT16 2c multi .20 .20
RA114 PT16 2c multi .20 .20
Nos. RA111-RA114 (4) .80 .80

Nos. RA111-RA114 obligatory on all mail through Nov., Dec. and Jan.; tax for Children's Village. Printed se-tenant. Sheets of 4 exist perf. and imperf. Sold for 2b. A sheet exists, perf and imperf, with one 58x68mm 2b stamp showing similar cahacters.

PAPUA NEW GUINEA

'pa-pyə-wə 'nü 'gi-nē

LOCATION — Eastern half of island of New Guinea, north of Australia
GOVT. — Independent state in British Commonwealth.
AREA — 185,136 sq. mi.
POP. — 4,705,126 (1999 est.)
CAPITAL — Port Moresby

In 1884 a British Protectorate was proclaimed over this part of the island, called "British New Guinea." In 1905 the administration was transferred to Australia and in 1906 the name was changed to Territory of Papua.

In 1949 the administration of Papua and New Guinea was unified, as the 1952 issue indicates. In 1972 the name was changed to Papua New Guinea. In 1974 came self-government, followed by independence on September 16, 1975.

Issues of 1925-39 for the mandated Territory of New Guinea are listed under New Guinea.

12 Pence = 1 Shilling
20 Shillings = 1 Pound
100 Cents = 1 Dollar (1966)
100 Toea = 1 Kina (1975)

Catalogue values for unused stamps in this country are for Never Hinged items, beginning with Scott 122 in the regular postage section and Scott J1 in the postage due section.

Watermarks

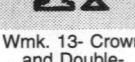

Wmk. 13- Crown and Double-Lined A

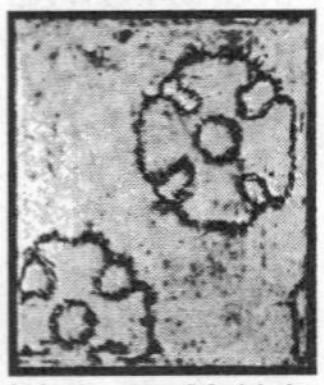

Wmk. 47- Multiple Rosette

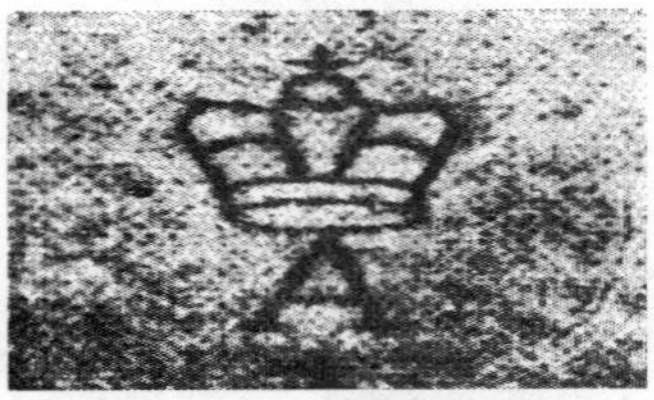

Wmk. 74- Crown and Single-Lined A Sideways

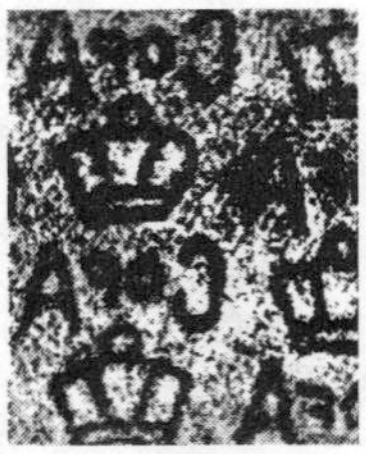

Wmk. 228- Small Crown and C of A Multiple

Wmk. 387

British New Guinea

Lakatoi — A1

Wmk. 47

1901, July 1 Engr. *Perf. 14*

Center in Black

1	A1	½p yellow green	4.25	3.75
2	A1	1p carmine	3.25	2.00
3	A1	2p violet	6.50	6.50
4	A1	2½p ultra	8.50	*8.50*
5	A1	4p black brown	30.00	*37.50*
6	A1	6p dark green	40.00	35.00
7	A1	1sh orange	52.50	*60.00*
8	A1	2sh6p brown ('05)	525.00	*500.00*
		Nos. 1-8 (8)	670.00	*653.25*

The paper varies in thickness and the watermark is found in two positions, with the greater width of the rosette either horizontal or vertical.

For overprints see Nos. 11-26.

Papua

Stamps of British New Guinea, Overprinted

1906, Nov. 8 Wmk. 47 *Perf. 14*

Center in Black

11	A1	½p yellow green	5.00	*18.50*
12	A1	1p carmine	8.50	*15.00*
13	A1	2p violet	5.50	4.00
14	A1	2½p ultra	4.00	*14.00*
15	A1	4p black brown	160.00	125.00
16	A1	6p dark green	26.00	*37.50*
17	A1	1sh orange	20.00	*35.00*
18	A1	2sh6p brown	125.00	*140.00*
		Nos. 11-18 (8)	354.00	*389.00*

Overprinted

1907 Center in Black

19	A1	½p yellow green	5.25	*6.50*
a.		Double overprint	1,650.	
20	A1	1p carmine	3.50	*4.75*
a.		Vertical overprint, up	1,800.	1,150.
21	A1	2p violet	4.25	2.50
22	A1	2½p ultra	8.00	17.50
a.		Double overprint		
23	A1	4p black brown	25.00	*40.00*
24	A1	6p dark green	25.00	*37.50*
a.		Double overprint	2,250.	*4,000.*
25	A1	1sh orange	25.00	*35.00*
a.		Double overprint	*6,250.*	*3,500.*
26	A1	2sh6p brown	32.50	*42.50*
b.		Vert. ovpt., down	*3,600.*	
d.		Double horiz. ovpt.		2,700.
		Nos. 19-26 (8)	128.50	*186.25*

A2

Small "PAPUA"

Perf. 11, 12½

1907-08 Litho. Wmk. 13

Center in Black

28	A2	1p carmine ('08)	4.50	3.50
29	A2	2p violet ('08)	6.50	4.50
30	A2	2½p ultra ('08)	14.50	*22.50*
31	A2	4p black brown	4.00	*7.50*
32	A2	6p dk green ('08)	11.00	*14.00*
33	A2	1sh orange ('08)	16.00	*19.00*
		Nos. 28-33 (6)	56.50	*71.00*

Perf. 12½

30a	A2	2½p	110.00	*125.00*
31a	A2	4p	8.00	*8.75*
33a	A2	1sh	55.00	*75.00*
		Nos. 30a-33a (3)	173.00	*208.75*

1909-10 Wmk. Sideways

Center in Black

34	A2	½p yellow green	2.50	*3.00*
a.		Perf. 11x12½	*2,250.*	*2,250.*
b.		Perf. 11	2.25	*6.00*
35	A2	1p carmine	6.00	*9.00*
a.		Perf. 11	9.00	9.00
36	A2	2p violet ('10)	5.00	*7.50*
a.		Perf. 11x12½	825.00	
b.		Perf. 11	6.00	*6.50*
37	A2	2½p ultra ('10)	5.00	*16.00*
a.		Perf. 12½	8.00	*20.00*
38	A2	4p black brn ('10)	4.75	*7.50*
a.		Perf. 11x12½	*6,750.*	
39	A2	6p dark green	10.00	10.00
a.		Perf. 12½	2,600.	*3,650.*
40	A2	1sh orange ('10)	16.00	*26.00*
a.		Perf. 11	40.00	*60.00*
		Nos. 34-40 (7)	49.25	*79.00*

One stamp in each sheet has a white line across the upper part of the picture which is termed the "rift in the clouds."

Large "PAPUA"

2sh6p:

Type I - The numerals are thin and irregular. The body of the "6" encloses a large spot of color. The dividing stroke is thick and uneven.

Type II - The numerals are thick and well formed. The "6" encloses a narrow oval of color. The dividing stroke is thin and sharp.

1910 Wmk. 13

Center in Black

41	A2	½p yellow green	3.75	*8.00*
42	A2	1p carmine	9.50	5.50
43	A2	2p violet	4.25	*4.50*
44	A2	2½p blue violet	4.75	*14.00*
45	A2	4p black brown	4.50	*8.00*
46	A2	6p dark green	8.00	*7.00*
47	A2	1sh orange	5.75	*14.00*
48	A2	2sh6p brown, type II	37.50	*37.50*
a.		Type I	42.50	*47.50*
		Nos. 41-48 (8)	78.00	*98.50*

Wmk. Sideways

49	A2	2sh6p choc, type I	50.00	*60.00*

1911 Typo. Wmk. 74 *Perf. 12½*

50	A2	½p yellow green	.90	*2.75*
51	A2	1p lt red	.65	.60
52	A2	2p lt violet	.65	.60
53	A2	2½p ultra	4.25	*6.75*
54	A2	4p olive green	2.00	*8.75*
55	A2	6p orange brown	3.25	*4.00*
56	A2	1sh yellow	8.00	*12.00*
57	A2	2sh6p rose	29.00	*30.00*
		Nos. 50-57 (8)	48.70	*65.45*

For surcharges see Nos. 74-79.

1915, June *Perf. 14*

59	A2	1p light red	6.00	2.00

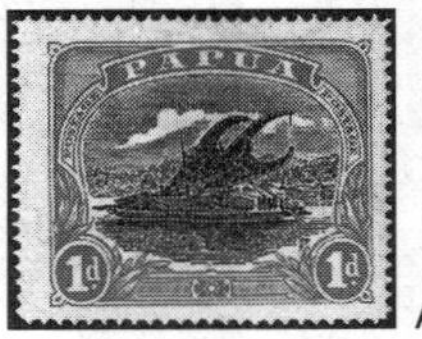

A3

1916-31

60	A3	½p pale yel grn & myr grn ('19)	.25	.25
61	A3	1p rose red & blk	.90	.90
62	A3	1½p yel brn & gray bl ('25)	.60	.60
63	A3	2p red vio & vio brn ('19)	2.50	1.00
64	A3	2p red brn & vio brn ('31)	3.25	2.25
a.		2p cop red & vio brn ('31)	35.00	7.50
65	A3	2½p ultra & dk grn ('19)	2.25	*2.50*
66	A3	3p emerald & blk	1.00	1.00
a.		3p dp bl grn & blk	4.50	3.50
67	A3	4p org & lt brn ('19)	3.75	3.75
68	A3	5p ol brn & sl ('31)	5.25	*6.00*
69	A3	6p vio & dl vio ('23)	2.25	*2.50*
70	A3	1sh ol grn & dk brn ('19)	3.00	*3.25*
71	A3	2sh6p rose & red brn ('19)	11.25	*13.50*
72	A3	5sh dp grn & blk	17.50	17.50
73	A3	10sh gray bl & grn ('25)	160.00	*190.00*
		Nos. 60-73 (14)	213.75	*245.00*

Type A3 is a redrawing of type A2.

The lines of the picture have been strengthened, making it much darker, especially the sky and water.

For surcharges & overprints see #88-91, O1-O10.

Stamps of 1911 Surcharged

1917 *Perf. 12½*

74	A2	1p on ½p yellow grn	.45	1.00
75	A2	1p on 2p lt violet	10.50	*10.00*
76	A2	1p on 2½p ultra	1.10	*4.50*
77	A2	1p on 4p olive green	1.50	*3.50*
78	A2	1p on 6p org brn	7.00	*12.50*
79	A2	1p on 2sh6p rose	1.25	*4.50*
		Nos. 74-79 (6)	21.80	*36.00*

No. 62 Surcharged

1931, Jan. 1 *Perf. 14*

88	A3	2p on 1½p yellow brn & gray blue	1.25	*1.75*

Nos. 70, 71 and 72 Surcharged in Black

1931

89	A3	5p on 1sh #70	1.00	1.75
90	A3	9p on 2sh6p #71	6.00	*10.00*
91	A3	1sh3p on 5sh #72	4.50	*9.00*
		Nos. 89-91 (3)	11.50	*20.75*

Type of 1916 Issue

1932 Wmk. 228 *Perf. 11*

92	A3	9p dp violet & gray	9.00	*27.50*
93	A3	1sh3p pale bluish green & grayish violet	11.00	*20.00*

For overprints see Nos. O11-O12.

Motuan Girl — A5

Bird of Paradise and Boar's Tusk — A6

Mother and Child — A7

Papuan Motherhood — A8

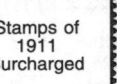

Dubu (Ceremonial Platform) — A9

Fire Maker — A10

Designs: 1p, Steve, son of Oala. 1½p, Tree houses. 3p, Papuan dandy. 5p, Masked dancer. 9p, Shooting fish. 1sh3p, Lakatoi. 2sh, Delta art. 2sh6p, Pottery making. 5sh, Sgt.-Major Simoi. £1, Delta house.

Unwmk.

1932, Nov. 14 Engr. Perf. 11

94	A5	½p	orange & blk	.90	1.75
95	A5	1p	yel grn & blk	1.10	.30
96	A5	1½p	red brn & blk	.75	3.75
97	A6	2p	light red	6.50	.20
98	A5	3p	blue & blk	2.25	3.50
99	A7	4p	olive green	3.75	4.50
100	A5	5p	grnsh sl & blk	1.75	1.50
101	A8	6p	bister brown	4.75	3.00
102	A5	9p	lilac & blk	6.50	11.00
103	A9	1sh	bluish gray	3.00	4.50
104	A5	1sh3p	brown & blk	10.25	13.00
105	A5	2sh	bluish slate & blk	10.25	12.50
106	A5	2sh6p	rose lilac & blk	18.00	20.00
107	A5	5sh	olive & blk	40.00	27.50
108	A10	10sh	gray lilac	60.00	42.50
109	A5	£1	lt gray & black	130.00	75.00
			Nos. 94-109 (16)	299.75	224.50

For overprints see Nos. 114-117.

Hoisting Union Jack at Port Moresby A21

H. M. S. "Nelson" at Port Moresby A22

1934, Nov. 6

110	A21	1p	dull green	.90	.90
111	A22	2p	red brown	1.10	1.10
112	A21	3p	blue	2.75	2.75
113	A22	5p	violet brown	6.25	6.25
			Nos. 110-113 (4)	11.00	11.00
			Set, never hinged	15.00	

Declaration of British Protection, 50th anniv.

Silver Jubilee Issue

Stamps of 1932 Issue Overprinted in Black:

a

b

1935, July 9

Glazed Paper

114	A5(a)	1p	yellow grn & blk	.65	1.60
115	A6(b)	2p	light red	1.75	1.60
116	A5(a)	3p	lt blue & blk	1.50	2.25
117	A5(a)	5p	grnsh slate & blk	2.10	2.50
			Nos. 114-117 (4)	6.00	7.95
			Set, never hinged	11.00	

25th anniv. of the reign of George V.

Coronation Issue

King George VI — A22a

Unwmk.

1937, May 14 Engr. Perf. 11

118	A22a	1p	green	.20	.20
119	A22a	2p	salmon rose	.20	.20
120	A22a	3p	blue	.25	.30
121	A22a	5p	brown violet	.35	.65
			Nos. 118-121 (4)	1.00	1.35
			Set, never hinged	2.00	

Catalogue values for unused stamps in this section, from this point to the end of the section, are for Never Hinged items.

Papua and New Guinea

Tree-climbing Kangaroo A23

Kiriwina Chief's House A24

Copra Making A25

Designs: 1p, Buka head-dress. 2p, Youth. 2½p, Bird of paradise. 3p, Policeman. 3½p, Chimbu headdress. 7½p, Kiriwina yam house. 1sh, Trading canoe. 1sh6p, Rubber tapping. 2sh, Shields and spears. 2sh6p, Plumed shepherd. 10sh, Map. £1, Spearing fish.

Unwmk.

1952, Oct. 30 Engr. Perf. 14

122	A23	½p	blue green	.20	.20
123	A23	1p	chocolate	.25	.20
124	A23	2p	deep ultra	.45	.20
125	A23	2½p	orange	2.00	.50
126	A23	3p	dark green	.75	.20
127	A23	3½p	dk carmine	.75	.20
128	A24	6½p	vio brown	2.00	.20
129	A24	7½p	dp ultra	3.75	1.50
130	A25	9p	chocolate	3.50	.75
131	A25	1sh	yellow green	2.25	.20
132	A24	1sh6p	dark green	8.00	1.00
133	A24	2sh	deep blue	6.00	.20
134	A25	2sh6p	dk red brown	5.00	.50
135	A25	10sh	gray black	40.00	12.50
136	A24	£1	chocolate	47.50	12.50
			Nos. 122-136 (15)	122.40	30.85
			Set, hinged	100.00	

See #139-141. For surcharges & overprints see #137-138, 147, J1-J3, J5-J6.

Nos. 125 and 131 Surcharged with New Values and Bars

1957, Jan. 29 Perf. 14

137	A23	4p on 2½p orange	.75	.20
138	A25	7p on 1sh yellow green	.50	.25

Type of 1952 and

Klinki Plymill A26

Designs: 3½p, Chimbu headdress. 4p, 5p, Cacao. 8p, Klinki Plymill. 1sh7p, Cattle. 2sh5p, Cattle. 5sh, Coffee, vert.

1958-60 Engr. Perf. 14

139	A23	3½p	black	6.50	1.00
140	A23	4p	vermilion	.75	.20
141	A23	5p	green ('60)	.75	.20
142	A26	7p	gray green	7.50	.20
143	A26	8p	dk ultra	1.00	1.00
144	A26	1sh7p	red brown	19.00	14.50
145	A26	2sh5p	vermilion	4.50	2.50
146	A26	5sh	gray olive & brn red	11.00	2.10
			Nos. 139-146 (8)	51.00	21.70

Issued: June 2, 1958, Nov. 10, 1960.

For surcharge see No. J4.

No. 122 Surcharged with New Value

1959, Dec. 1

147	A23	5p on ½p blue green	.75	.20

Council Chamber and Frangipani Flowers A27

1961, Apr. 10 Photo. Perf. 14½x14

148	A27	5p	green & yellow	1.00	.50
149	A27	2sh3p	grn & salmon	7.00	5.00

Reconstitution of the Legislative Council.

Woman's Head — A28

Red-plumed Bird of Paradise — A29

Port Moresby Harbor A30

Constable Ragas Amis Matia, Port Moresby A32

View of Rabaul, by Samuel Terarup Cham — A33

Woman Dancer A31

Elizabeth II A34

Designs: 3p, Man's head. 6p, Golden opossum. 2sh, Male dancer with drum. 2sh3p, Piaggio transport plane landing at Tapini.

Perf. 14 (A28, A31, A32), 11½ (A29, A33), 14x13½ (A30), 14½ (A34)

1961-63 Engr. Unwmk.

153	A28	1p	dk carmine	1.25	.20
154	A28	3p	bluish black	.30	.20
			Photo.		
155	A29	5p	lt brn, red brn, blk & yel	1.50	.20
156	A29	6p	gray, ocher & slate	.75	1.25
			Engr.		
157	A30	8p	green	.30	.20
158	A31	1sh	gray green	4.00	.20
159	A31	2sh	rose lake	.45	.20
160	A30	2sh3p	dark blue	.50	.40
161	A32	3sh	green	2.25	1.40
			Photo.		
162	A33	10sh	multicolored	12.50	10.00
163	A34	£1	brt grn, blk & gold	4.00	3.50
			Nos. 153-163 (11)	27.80	17.75

The 5p and 6p are on granite paper.

Issued: 3sh, 9/5/62; 10sh, 2/13/63: 5p, 6p, 3/27/63; 8p, 2sh3p, 5/8/63; £1, 7/3/63; others, 7/26/61.

Malaria Eradication Emblem — A35

1962, Apr. 7 Litho. Perf. 14

164	A35	5p	lt blue & maroon	.75	.40
165	A35	1sh	lt brown & red	1.40	.60
166	A35	2sh	yellow green & blk	1.60	1.75
			Nos. 164-166 (3)	3.75	2.75

WHO drive to eradicate malaria.

Map of Australia and South Pacific A36

1962, July 9 Engr. Unwmk.

167	A36	5p	dk red & lt grn	.85	.20
168	A36	1sh6p	dk violet & yel	2.25	.90
169	A36	2sh6p	green & lt blue	2.25	1.90
			Nos. 167-169 (3)	5.35	3.00

5th So. Pacific Conf., Pago Pago, July 1962.

High Jump — A37

Games Emblem - A38

1962, Oct. 24 Photo. Perf. 11½

Size: 26x21mm

Granite Paper

171	A37	5p	shown	.35	.25
172	A37	5p	Javelin	.35	.25
			Size: 32½x22½mm		
173	A37	2sh3p	runners	1.75	1.75
			Nos. 171-173 (3)	2.45	2.25

British Empire and Commonwealth Games, Perth, Australia, Nov. 22-Dec. 1.

Nos. 171 and 172 printed in alternating horizontal rows in sheet.

Red Cross Centenary Emblem — A38a

1963, May 1 Perf. 13½

174	A38a	5p blue grn, gray & red	.55	.20

1963, Aug. 14 Engr. Perf. 13½x14

176	A38	5p	olive bister	.20	.20
177	A38	1sh	green	.60	.25

So. Pacific Games, Suva, Aug. 29-Sept. 7.

Top of Wooden Shield — A39

Casting Ballot — A40

Various Carved Heads.

Perf. 11½

1964, Feb. 5 Unwmk. Photo.

Granite Paper

178 A39 11p multicolored .55 .20
179 A39 2sh5p multicolored .60 *1.00*
180 A39 2sh6p multicolored .60 .20
181 A39 5sh multicolored .75 .20
Nos. 178-181 (4) 2.50 1.60

1964, Mar. 4 Unwmk. *Perf. 11½*

Granite Paper

182 A40 5p dk brn & pale brn .20 .20
183 A40 2sh3p dk brn & lt bl .70 .40

First Common Roll elections.

A41

A42

Designs: 5p, Patients at health center clinic. 8p, Dentist and school child patient. 1sh, Nurse holding infant. 1sh2p, Medical student using microscope.

1964, Aug. 5 Engr. *Perf. 14*

184 A41 5p violet .20 .20
185 A41 8p green .20 .20
186 A41 1sh deep ultra .20 .20
187 A41 1sh2p rose brown .40 .30
Nos. 184-187 (4) 1.00 .90

Territorial health services.

1964-65 Unwmk. Photo. *Perf. 11½*

Designs: 1p, Striped gardener bower birds. 3p, New Guinea regent bower birds. 5p, Blue birds of paradise. 6p, Lawes six-wired birds of paradise. 8p, Sickle-billed birds of paradise. 1sh, Emperor birds of paradise. 2sh, Brown sickle-billed bird of paradise. 2sh3p, Lesser bird of paradise. 3sh, Magnificent bird of paradise. 5sh, Twelve-wired bird of paradise. 10sh, Magnificent rifle birds.

Birds in Natural Colors

Size: 21x26mm

188 A42 1p brt cit & dk brn .35 .20
189 A42 3p gray & dk brn .45 .20
190 A42 5p sal pink & blk .50 .20
191 A42 6p pale grn & sep .70 .20
192 A42 8p pale lil & dk brn 1.25 .20

Size: 25x36mm

193 A42 1sh salmon & blk 1.25 .20
194 A42 2sh blue & dk brn .70 .25
195 A42 2sh3p lt grn & dk brn .70 .70
196 A42 3sh yel & dk brn .70 *1.00*
197 A42 5sh lt ultra & dk brn 11.00 2.10
198 A42 10sh gray & dk blue 5.00 *8.25*
Nos. 188-198 (11) 22.60 13.50

Issued: 6p, 8p, 1sh, 10sh, 10/28/64; others, 1/20/65.

Carved Crocodile's Head — A43

Designs: Wood carvings from Sepik River Region used as ship's prows and as objects of religious veneration.

1965, Mar. 24 Photo. *Perf. 11½*

199 A43 4p multicolored .40 .20
200 A43 1sh2p gray brown, bister & dk brown 1.90 1.75
201 A43 1sh6p lil, dk brn & buff .40 .20
202 A43 4sh bl, dk vio & mar .80 .35
Nos. 199-202 (4) 3.50 2.50

"Simpson and His Donkey" by Wallace Anderson — A43a

1965, Apr. 14 *Perf. 13½x13*

203 A43a 2sh3p brt grn, sep & blk .50 .50

ANZAC issue. See note after Australia No. 387.

Urbanized Community and Stilt House — A44

Design: 1sh, Stilt house at left.

1965, July 7 Photo. *Perf. 11½*

204 A44 6p multicolored .20 .20
205 A44 1sh multicolored .20 .20

6th South Pacific Conf., Lae, July, 1965.

UN Emblem, Mother and Child A45

UN Emblem and: 1sh, Globe and orbit, vert. 2sh, Four globes in orbit, vert.

1965, Oct. 13 Unwmk. *Perf. 11½*

206 A45 6p brown, grnsh bl & dp bl .20 .20
207 A45 1sh dull pur, blue & org .20 .20
208 A45 2sh dp blue, pale grn & grn .20 .20
Nos. 206-208 (3) .60 .60

20th anniversary of the United Nations.

New Guinea Birdwing A46

Butterflies: 1c, Blue emperor, vert. 3c, White-banded map butterfly, vert. 4c, Mountain swallowtail, vert. 5c, Port Moresby terinos, vert. 12c, Blue crow. 15c, Euchenor butterfly. 20c, White-spotted parthenos. 25c, Orange Jezebel. 50c, New Guinea emperor. $1, Blue-spotted leaf-wing. $2, Paradise birdwing.

1966 Photo. *Perf. 11½*

Granite Paper

209 A46 1c salmon, blk & aqua .35 *.60*
210 A46 3c gray grn, brn & org .35 *.60*
211 A46 4c multicolored .35 *.60*
212 A46 5c multicolored .35 .20
213 A46 10c multicolored .45 .25
214 A46 12c salmon & multi 2.00 1.90
215 A46 15c pale vio, dk brn & buff 1.75 .70
216 A46 20c yel bister, dk brn & yel orange .65 .25
217 A46 25c gray, blk & yel 1.40 .90
218 A46 50c multicolored 9.00 1.10
219 A46 $1 pale blue, dk brn & dp org 3.50 1.40
220 A46 $2 multicolored 5.25 *7.00*
Nos. 209-220 (12) 25.40 *15.50*

In 1967 Courvoisier made new plates for the $1 and $2. Stamps from these plates show many minor differences and slight variations in shade.

Issued: 12c, 10/10; others, 2/14.

Molala Harai and Paiva Streamer — A47

Discus — A48

Myths of Elema People: 7c, Marai, the fisherman. 30c, Meavea Kivovia and the Black Cockatoo. 60c, Toivita Tapaivita (symbolic face decorations).

1966, June 8 Photo. *Perf. 11½*

Granite Paper

221 A47 2c black & carmine .20 .20
222 A47 7c blue, blk & yel .20 .20
223 A47 30c blk, yel grn & car .25 .20
224 A47 60c blk, org & car .60 .30
Nos. 221-224 (4) 1.25 .90

1966, Aug. 31 *Perf. 11½*

Granite Paper

225 A48 5c shown .20 .20
226 A48 10c Soccer .25 .20
227 A48 20c Tennis .35 .35
Nos. 225-227 (3) .80 .75

Second South Pacific Games, Noumea, New Caledonia, Dec. 8-18.

d'Albertis' Creeper — A49

Book and Pen ("Fine Arts") — A50

Flowers: 10c, Tecomanthe dendrophila. 20c, Rhododendron macgregoriae. 60c, Rhododendron konori.

1966, Dec. 7 Photo. *Perf. 11½*

228 A49 5c multicolored .20 .20
229 A49 10c multicolored .20 .20
230 A49 20c multicolored .50 .20
231 A49 60c multicolored 1.25 1.50
Nos. 228-231 (4) 2.15 2.10

1967, Feb. 8 Photo. *Perf. 12½x12*

3c, "Surveying," transit, view finder, pencil. 4c, "Civil Engineering," buildings, compass. 5c, "Science," test tubes, chemical formula. 20c, "Justice," Justitia, scales.

232 A50 1c orange & multi .20 .20
233 A50 3c blue & multi .20 .20
234 A50 4c brown & multi .20 .20
235 A50 5c green & multi .20 .20
236 A50 20c pink & multi .20 .20
Nos. 232-236 (5) 1.00 1.00

Issued to publicize the development of the University of Papua and New Guinea and the Institute of Higher Technical Education.

Leaf Beetle — A51

Hydroelectric Power — A52

Beetles: 10c, Eupholus schoenherri. 20c, Sphingnotus albertisi. 25c, Cyphogastra albertisi.

1967, Apr. 12 Unwmk. *Perf. 11½*

237 A51 5c blue & multi .20 .20
238 A51 10c lt green & multi .30 .25
239 A51 20c rose & multi .50 .30
240 A51 25c yellow & multi .55 .40
Nos. 237-240 (4) 1.55 1.15

1967, June 28 Photo. *Perf. 12x12½*

Designs: 10c, Pyrethrum (Chrysanthemum cinerariaefolium). 20c, Tea. 25c, like 5c.

241 A52 5c multicolored .20 .20
242 A52 10c multicolored .20 .20
243 A52 20c multicolored .30 .20
244 A52 25c multicolored .30 .20
Nos. 241-244 (4) 1.00 .80

Completion of part of the Laloki River Hydroelectric Works near Port Moresby, and the Hydrological Decade (UNESCO), 1965-74.

Battle of Milne Bay — A53

Designs: 5c, Soldiers on Kokoda Trail, vert. 20c, The coast watchers. 50c, Battle of the Coral Sea.

1967, Aug. 30 Unwmk. *Perf. 11½*

245 A53 2c multicolored .20 .35
246 A53 5c multicolored .20 .20
247 A53 20c multicolored .25 .20
248 A53 50c multicolored .45 .50
Nos. 245-248 (4) 1.10 1.25

25th anniv. of the battles in the Pacific, which stopped the Japanese from occupying Papua and New Guinea.

Pesquet's Parrot A54

Chimbu District Headdress A55

Parrots: 5c, Fairy lory. 20c, Dusk-orange lory. 25c, Edward's fig parrot.

1967, Nov. 29 Photo. *Perf. 12*

249 A54 5c multicolored .35 .20
250 A54 7c multicolored .40 .75
251 A54 20c multicolored .70 .20
252 A54 25c multicolored .70 .20
Nos. 249-252 (4) 2.15 1.35

Perf. 12x12½, 12½x12

1968, Feb. 21 Photo. Unwmk.

Headdress from: 10c, Southern Highlands District, horiz. 20c, Western Highlands District. 60c, Chimbu District (different from 5c).

253 A55 5c multi .20 .20
254 A55 10c multi .20 .20
255 A55 20c multi, horiz. .25 .20
256 A55 60c multi .75 .50
Nos. 253-256 (4) 1.40 1.10

Frogs — A56

1968, Apr. 24 Photo. *Perf. 11½*

257 A56 5c Tree	.35	.35
258 A56 10c Tree, diff.	.35	.20
259 A56 15c Swamp	.35	.20
260 A56 20c Tree, diff.	.45	.35
Nos. 257-260 (4)	1.50	1.10

Human Rights Flame and Headdress A57

Symbolic Designs: 10c, Human Rights Flame surrounded by the world. 20c, 25c, "Universal Suffrage" in 2 abstract designs.

1968, June 26 Litho. *Perf. 14x13*

261 A57 5c black & multi	.20	.20
262 A57 10c black & multi	.20	.20
263 A57 20c black & multi	.30	.30
264 A57 25c black & multi	.30	.30
Nos. 261-264 (4)	1.00	1.00

Issued for Human Rights Year, 1968, and to publicize free elections.

Frilled Clam — A58

Sea Shells: 1c, Egg cowry. 3c, Crested stromb. 4c, Lithograph cone. 5c, Marble cone. 7c, Orange-spotted miter. 10c, Red volute. 12c, Checkerboard helmet shell. 15c, Scorpion shell. 25c, Chocolate-flamed Venus shell. 30c, Giant murex. 40c, Chambered nautilus. 60c, Triton's trumpet. $1, Emerald snails. $2, Glory of the sea, vert.

Perf. 12½x12, 12x12½

1968-69 Photo.

Granite Paper

265 A58 1c multicolored	.20	.20
266 A58 3c multicolored	.25	.55
267 A58 4c multicolored	.20	.55
268 A58 5c multicolored	.20	.20
269 A58 7c multicolored	.30	.20
270 A58 10c multicolored	.35	.20
271 A58 12c multicolored	1.10	*1.40*
272 A58 15c multicolored	.50	*.65*
273 A58 20c multicolored	.55	.20
274 A58 25c multicolored	.55	.40
275 A58 30c multicolored	.55	*.75*
276 A58 40c multicolored	.60	*.75*
277 A58 60c multicolored	.55	.45
278 A58 $1 multicolored	1.10	1.00
279 A58 $2 multicolored	13.00	5.50
Nos. 265-279 (15)	20.00	13.00

Issued: 5c, 20c, 25c, 30c, 60c, 8/28/68; 3c, 10c, 15c, 40c, $1, 10/30/68; others, 1/29/69.

Legend of Tito-Iko — A59

Fireball Class Sailboat, Port Moresby Harbor — A60

Myths of Elema People: No. 281, 5c inscribed "Iko." No. 282, 10c inscribed "Luvuapo." No. 283, 10c inscribed "Miro."

#280 & 282:

Perf. 12½x13½xRoul. 9xPerf. 13½

#281 & 283:

Roul. 9 x Perf. 13½x12½x13½

1969, Apr. 9 Litho. Unwmk.

280 A59 5c black, yellow & red	.20	.20
281 A59 5c black, yellow & red	.20	.20
a. Vert. pair, #280-281	.40	.40
282 A59 10c black, gray & red	.25	.25
283 A59 10c black, gray & red	.25	.25
a. Vert. pair, #282-283	.50	.60
Nos. 280-283 (4)	.90	.90

Nos. 281a, 283a have continuous designs, rouletted between.

Perf. 14x14½, 14½x14

1969, June 25 Engr.

Designs: 10c, Games' swimming pool, Boroko, horiz. 20c, Main Games area, Konedobu, horiz.

284 A60 5c black	.20	.20
285 A60 10c bright violet	.20	.20
286 A60 20c green	.30	.30
Nos. 284-286 (3)	.70	.70

3rd S. Pacific Games, Port Moresby, Aug. 13-23.

Dendrobium Ostrinoglossum A61

Potter A62

Orchids: 10c, Dendrobium lawesii. 20c, Dendrobium pseudofrigidum. 30c, Dendrobium conanthum.

1969, Aug. 27 Photo. *Perf. 11½*

Granite Paper

287 A61 5c multicolored	.45	.25
288 A61 10c multicolored	.55	.50
289 A61 20c multicolored	.70	.75
290 A61 30c multicolored	.80	.50
Nos. 287-290 (4)	2.50	2.00

Issued to publicize the 6th World Orchid Conference, Sydney, Australia, Sept. 1969.

1969, Sept. 24 Photo. *Perf. 11½*

Granite Paper

291 A62 5c multicolored	.25	.20

50th anniv. of the ILO.

Bird of Paradise A63

Seed Pod Rattle (Tareko) A64

Coil Stamps

1969-71 *Perf. 14½ Horiz.*

291A A63 2c red, dp blue & blk	.20	.20
292 A63 5c orange & emerald	.20	.20

Issue dates: 5c, Sept. 24, 2c, Apr. 1, 1971.

1969, Oct. 29 Photo. *Perf. 12½*

Musical Instruments: 10c, Hand drum (garamut). 25c, Pan pipes (iviliko). 30c, Hourglass drum (kundu).

293 A64 5c multicolored	.20	.20
294 A64 10c multicolored	.20	.20
295 A64 25c multicolored	.30	.25
296 A64 30c multicolored	.70	.35
Nos. 293-296 (4)	1.40	1.00

Prehistoric Ambum Stone and Skull — A65

Designs: 10c, Masawa canoe of the Kula Circuit. 25c, Map of Papua and New Guinea made by Luis Valez de Torres, 1606. 30c, H.M.S. Basilisk, 1873.

1970, Feb. 11 Photo. *Perf. 12½*

297 A65 5c violet brown & multi	.20	.20
298 A65 10c ocher & multi	.20	.20
299 A65 25c org brn & multi	.45	.35
300 A65 30c olive green & multi	.65	.40
Nos. 297-300 (4)	1.50	1.15

King of Saxony Bird of Paradise — A66

Birds of Paradise: 10c, King. 15c, Augusta Victoria. 25c, Multi-crested.

1970, May 13 Photo. *Perf. 11½*

301 A66 5c tan & multi	.85	.20
302 A66 10c multicolored	.90	.50
303 A66 15c lt blue & multi	1.25	.90
304 A66 25c multicolored	1.50	.65
Nos. 301-304 (4)	4.50	2.25

Canceled to Order

Starting in 1970 or earlier, the Philatelic Bureau at Port Moresby began to sell new issues canceled to order at face value.

Douglas DC-3 and Matupi Volcano — A67

Aircraft: No. 305, DC-6B and Mt. Wilhelm. No. 306, Lockheed Mark II Electra and Mt. Yule. No. 307, Boeing 727 and Mt. Giluwe. No. 308, Fokker F27 Friendship and Manam Island Volcano. 30c, Boeing 707 and Hombom's Bluff.

1970, July 8 Photo. *Perf. 14½x14*

305 A67 5c "TAA" on tail	.30	.20
306 A67 5c Striped tail	.30	.20
307 A67 5c "T" on tail	.30	.20
308 A67 5c Red tail	.30	.20
a. Block of 4, #305-308	1.25	1.00
309 A67 25c multicolored	.70	.35
310 A67 30c multicolored	.70	.45
Nos. 305-310 (6)	2.60	1.60

Development of air service during the last 25 years between Australia and New Guinea.

Nicolaus N. de Miklouho-Maclay, Explorer, and Mask — A68

Designs: 10c, Bronislaw Kaspar Malinowski, anthropologist, and hut. 15c, Count Tommaso Salvadori, ornithologist, and cassowary. 20c, Friedrich R. Schlechter, botanist, and orchid.

1970, Aug. 19 Photo. *Perf. 11½*

311 A68 5c brown, blk & lilac	.20	.20
312 A68 10c multicolored	.25	.20
313 A68 15c dull lilac & multi	.45	.30
314 A68 20c slate & multi	.80	.30
Nos. 311-314 (4)	1.70	1.00

42nd Cong. of the Australian and New Zealand Assoc. for the Advancement of Science, Port Moresby, Aug. 17-21.

Wogeo Island Food Bowl — A69

Eastern Highlands Round House — A70

National Handicraft: 10c, Lime pot. 15c, Aibom sago storage pot. 30c, Manus Island bowl, horiz.

1970, Oct. 28 Photo. *Perf. 12½*

315 A69 5c multicolored	.20	.20
316 A69 10c multicolored	.30	.20
317 A69 15c multicolored	.30	.20
318 A69 30c multicolored	.40	.40
Nos. 315-318 (4)	1.20	1.00

1971, Jan. 27 Photo. *Perf. 11½*

Local Architecture: 7c, Milne Bay house. 10c, Purari Delta house. 40c, Sepik or Men's Spirit House.

319 A70 5c dark olive & multi	.25	.20
320 A70 7c Prus blue & multi	.25	.50
321 A70 10c deep org & multi	.25	.20
322 A70 40c brown & multi	.40	*.60*
Nos. 319-322 (4)	1.15	1.50

Spotted Cuscus — A71

Basketball A72

Animals: 10c, Brown and white striped possum. 15c, Feather-tailed possum. 25c, Spiny anteater, horiz. 30c, Good-fellow's tree-climbing kangaroo, horiz.

1971, Mar. 31 Photo. *Perf. 11½*

323 A71 5c blue green & multi	.35	.20
324 A71 10c multicolored	.50	.20
325 A71 15c multicolored	.90	.70
326 A71 25c dull yellow & multi	1.25	.70
327 A71 30c olive & multi	1.25	.45
Nos. 323-327 (5)	4.25	2.25

1971, June 9 Litho. *Perf. 14*

328 A72 7c shown	.20	.20
329 A72 14c Yachting	.35	.25
330 A72 21c Boxing	.35	.30
331 A72 28c Field events	.35	.35
Nos. 328-331 (4)	1.25	1.10

Fourth South Pacific Games, Papeete, French Polynesia, Sept. 8-19.

Bartering Fish for Coconuts and Taro — A73

Siaa Dancer — A74

Primary industries: 9c, Man stacking yams and taro. 14c, Market scene. 30c, Farm couple tending yams.

1971, Aug. 18 Photo. *Perf. 11½*

332 A73 7c multicolored .20 .20
333 A73 9c multicolored .25 .25
334 A73 14c multicolored .40 .20
335 A73 30c multicolored .60 .50
Nos. 332-335 (4) 1.45 1.15

1971, Oct. 27 Photo. *Perf. 11½*

Designs: 9c, Urasena masked dancer. 20c, Two Siassi masked dancers, horiz. 28c, Three Siaa dancers, horiz.

336 A74 7c orange & multi .20 .20
337 A74 9c yel green & multi .25 .25
338 A74 20c bister & multi .55 .55
339 A74 28c multicolored .90 .90
Nos. 336-339 (4) 1.90 1.90

Papua New Guinea and Australia Arms — A75

#341, Papua New Guinea & Australia flags.

1972, Jan. 26 *Perf. 12½x12*

340 A75 7c gray blue, org & blk .35 .30
341 A75 7c gray blue, blk, red & yel .35 .30
a. Pair, #340-341 .75 .75

Constitutional development for the 1972 House of Assembly elections.

Papua New Guinea Map, South Pacific Commission Emblem — A76

#343, Man's head, So. Pacific Commission flag.

1972, Jan. 26

342 A76 15c brt green & multi .50 .40
343 A76 15c brt green & multi .50 .40
a. Pair, #342-343 1.10 1.40

South Pacific Commission, 25th anniv.

Pitted-shelled Turtle — A77

Designs: 14c, Angle-headed agamid. 21c, Green python. 30c, Water monitor.

1972, Mar. 15 Photo. *Perf. 11½*

344 A77 7c multicolored .50 .20
345 A77 14c car rose & multi 1.25 1.00
346 A77 21c yellow & multi 1.25 1.25
347 A77 30c yel green & multi 1.60 1.00
Nos. 344-347 (4) 4.60 3.45

Curtiss Seagull MF 6 and Ship — A78

14c, De Havilland 37 & porters from gold fields. 20c, Junkers G 31 & heavy machinery. 25c, Junkers F 13 & Lutheran mission church.

1972, June 7

Granite Paper

348 A78 7c dp yellow & multi .30 .20
349 A78 14c dp orange & multi .85 1.00
350 A78 20c olive & multi 1.40 1.00
351 A78 25c multicolored 1.60 1.00
Nos. 348-351 (4) 4.15 3.20

50th anniv. of aviation in Papua New Guinea.

National Day Unity Emblem — A79

Designs: 10c, Unity emblem and kundu (drum). 30c, Unity emblem and conch.

1972, Aug. 16 *Perf. 12x12½*

352 A79 7c violet blue & multi .20 .20
353 A79 10c orange & multi .30 .20
354 A79 30c vermilion & multi .50 .50
Nos. 352-354 (3) 1.00 .90

National Day, Sept. 15, 1972.

Rev. Copland King — A80

Pioneering Missionaries: No. 356, Pastor Ruatoka. No. 357, Bishop Stanislaus Henry Verjus. No. 358, Rev. Dr. Johannes Flierl.

1972, Oct. 25 Photo. *Perf. 11½*

355 A80 7c dark blue & multi .30 .35
356 A80 7c dark red & multi .30 .35
357 A80 7c dark green & multi .30 .35
358 A80 7c dark olive bister & multi .30 .35
Nos. 355-358 (4) 1.20 1.40

Christmas 1972.

Relay Station on Mt. Tomavatur A81

1973, Jan. 24 Photo. *Perf. 12½*

359 A81 7c shown .30 .20
360 A81 7c Mt. Kerigomna .30 .20
361 A81 7c Sattelburg .30 .20
362 A81 7c Wideru .30 .20
a. Block of 4, #359-362 1.25 .85
363 A81 9c Teleprinter .40 .20
364 A81 30c Map of network 1.25 .85
Nos. 359-364 (6) 2.85 1.85

Telecommunications development 1968-1972. No. 362a has a unifying frame.

Queen Carol's Bird of Paradise — A82

Birds of Paradise: 14c, Goldie's. 21c, Ribbon-tailed astrapia. 28c, Princess Stephanie's.

1973, Mar. 30 Photo. *Perf. 11½*

Size: 22½x38mm

365 A82 7c citron & multi .75 .35
366 A82 14c dull green & multi 2.00 .90

Size: 17x48mm

367 A82 21c lemon & multi 2.25 1.25
368 A82 28c lt blue & multi 3.25 1.50
Nos. 365-368 (4) 8.25 4.00

Wood Carver, Milne Bay — A83

Designs: 3c, Wig makers, Southern Highlands. 5c, Bagana Volcano, Bougainville. 6c, Pig Exchange, Western Highlands. 7c, Coastal village, Central District. 8c, Arawe mother, West New Britain. 9c, Fire dancers, East New Britain. 10c, Tifalmin hunter, West Sepik District. 14c, Crocodile hunters, Western District. 15c, Mt. Elimbari, Chimbu. 20c, Canoe racing, Manus District. 21c, Making sago, Gulf District. 25c, Council House, East Sepik. 28c, Menyamya bowmen, Morobe. 30c, Shark snaring, New Ireland. 40c, Fishing canoes, Madang. 60c, Women making tapa cloth, Northern District. $1, Asaro mudmen, Eastern Highlands. $2, Sing festival, Enga District.

1973-74 Photo. *Perf. 11½*

Granite Paper

369 A83 1c multicolored .20 .20
370 A83 3c multi ('74) .35 .20
371 A83 5c multicolored .55 .20
372 A83 6c multi ('74) .75 .50
373 A83 7c multicolored .30 .20
374 A83 8c multi ('74) .35 .20
375 A83 9c multicolored .40 .20
376 A83 10c multi ('74) .55 .20
377 A83 14c multicolored .45 .50
378 A83 15c multicolored .50 .20
379 A83 20c multi ('74) 1.00 .30
380 A83 21c multicolored .50 .60
381 A83 25c multicolored .50 .50
382 A83 28c multicolored .50 .60
383 A83 30c multicolored .50 .50
385 A83 40c multicolored .50 .40
386 A83 60c multi ('74) .60 .75
387 A83 $1 multi ('74) .85 1.50
388 A83 $2 multi ('74) 3.50 4.50
Nos. 369-383,385-388 (19) 12.85 12.25

Issued: 1c, 7c, 9c, 15c, 25c, 40c, 6/13; 5c, 14c, 21c, 28c, 30c, Aug.

Papua New Guinea No. 7 — A84

1c, Ger. New Guinea #1-2. 6c, Ger. New Guinea #17. 7c, New Britain #43. 25c, New Guinea #1. 30c, Papua New Guinea #108.

Litho. (1c, 7c); Litho. & Engr. (others)

1973, Oct. 24 *Perf. 13½x14*

Size: 54x31mm

389 A84 1c gold, brn, grn & blk .20 .20
390 A84 6c silver, blue & indigo .25 .20
391 A84 7c gold, red, blk & buff .25 .25

Perf. 14x14½

Size: 45x38mm

392 A84 9c gold, org, blk & brn .30 .30
393 A84 25c gold & orange .70 .90
394 A84 30c silver & dp lilac .75 1.00
Nos. 389-394 (6) 2.45 2.85

75th anniv. of stamps in Papua New Guinea.

Masks — A85

1973, Dec. 5 Photo. *Perf. 12½*

Granite Paper

395 A85 7c multicolored .30 .20
396 A85 10c violet blue & multi .60 .60

Self-government.

Queen Elizabeth II A86

1974, Feb. 22 Photo. *Perf. 14x14½*

397 A86 7c dp carmine & multi .25 .20
398 A86 30c vio blue & multi .75 1.00

Visit of Queen Elizabeth II and the Royal Family, Feb. 22-27.

Wreathed Hornbill — A87

Size of No. 400, 32½x48mm.

Perf. 12, 11½ (10c)

1974, June 12 Photo.

Granite Paper

399 A87 7c shown 1.00 .75
400 A87 10c Great cassowary 2.00 *2.25*
401 A87 30c Kapul eagle 5.00 *6.00*
Nos. 399-401 (3) 8.00 9.00

Dendrobium Bracteosum — A88

Orchids: 10c, Dendrobium anosmum. 20c, Dendrobium smillieae. 30c, Dendrobium insigne.

1974, Nov. 20 Photo. *Perf. 11½*

Granite Paper

402 A88 7c dark green & multi .65 .20
403 A88 10c dark blue & multi .50 .40
404 A88 20c bister & multi .75 *1.00*
405 A88 30c green & multi 1.10 *1.40*
Nos. 402-405 (4) 3.00 3.00

Motu Lakatoi A89

Traditional Canoes: 10c, Tami two-master morobe. 25c, Aramia racing canoe. 30c, Buka Island canoe.

1975, Feb. 26 Photo. *Perf. 11½*

Granite Paper

406 A89 7c multicolored .25 .20
407 A89 10c orange & multi .45 .45
408 A89 25c apple green & multi .90 *1.75*
409 A89 30c citron & multi .90 *1.00*
Nos. 406-409 (4) 2.50 3.40

Paradise Birdwing Butterfly, 1t Coin — A90

Ornate Butterfly Cod on 2t and Plateless Turtle on 5t — A91

New coinage: 10t, Cuscus on 10t. 20t, Cassowary on 20t. 1k, River crocodiles on 1k coin with center hole; obverse and reverse of 1k.

Perf. 11, 11½ (A91)

1975, Apr. 21 Photo.

Granite Paper

410 A90	1t green & multi	.20	.20
411 A91	7t brown & multi	.45	.45
412 A90	10t violet blue & multi	.45	.45
413 A90	20t carmine & multi	.90	.90
414 A91	1k dull blue & multi	2.50	2.50
	Nos. 410-414 (5)	4.50	4.50

Ornithoptera Alexandrae — A92

Boxing and Games' Emblem — A93

Birdwing Butterflies: 10t, O. victoriae regis. 30t, O. allottei. 40t, O. chimaera.

1975, June 11 Photo. *Perf. 11½*

Granite Paper

415 A92	7t multicolored	.30	.20
416 A92	10t multicolored	.45	.40
417 A92	30t multicolored	1.25	1.50
418 A92	40t multicolored	1.75	2.25
	Nos. 415-418 (4)	3.75	4.35

1975, Aug. 2 Photo. *Perf. 11½*

Granite Paper

419 A93	7t shown	.25	.20
420 A93	20t Track and field	.45	.45
421 A93	25t Basketball	.50	*.60*
422 A93	30t Swimming	.50	*.75*
	Nos. 419-422 (4)	1.70	2.00

5th South Pacific Games, Guam, Aug. 1-10.

Map of South East Asia and Flag of PNG
A94

Design: 30t, Map of South East Asia and Papua New Guinea coat of arms.

1975, Sept. 10 Photo. *Perf. 11½*

Granite Paper

423 A94	7t red & multi	.20	.20
424 A94	30t blue & multi	.60	.60
a.	Souvenir sheet of 2, #423-424	1.50	1.50

Papua New Guinea independence, Sept. 16, 1975.

M. V. Bulolo
A95

Ships of the 1930's: 15t, M.V. Macdhui. 25t, M.V. Malaita. 60t, S.S. Montoro.

1976, Jan. 21 Photo. *Perf. 11½*

Granite Paper

425 A95	7t multicolored	.25	.20
426 A95	15t multicolored	.40	.30
427 A95	25t multicolored	.70	.45
428 A95	60t multicolored	1.65	1.75
	Nos. 425-428 (4)	3.00	2.70

Rorovana Carvings
A96

Bougainville Art: 20t, Upe hats. 25t, Kapkaps (tortoise shell ornaments). 30t, Carved canoe paddles.

1976, Mar. 17 Photo. *Perf. 11½*

Granite Paper

429 A96	7t multicolored	.25	.20
430 A96	20t blue & multi	.45	.45
431 A96	25t dp orange & multi	.50	.50
432 A96	30t multicolored	.55	.70
	Nos. 429-432 (4)	1.75	1.85

Houses
A97

1976, June 9 Photo. *Perf. 11½*

Granite Paper

433 A97	7t Rabaul	.20	.20
434 A97	15t Aramia	.30	.25
435 A97	30t Telefomin	.60	.50
436 A97	40t Tapini	.65	.90
	Nos. 433-436 (4)	1.75	1.85

Boy Scouts and Scout Emblem
A98

De Havilland Sea Plane, Map of Pacific — A99

Designs: 15t, Sea Scouts on outrigger canoe, Scout emblem. 60t, Plane on water.

1976, Aug. 18 Photo. *Perf. 11½*

Granite Paper

437 A98	7t multicolored	.35	.20
438 A99	10t lilac & multi	.35	.25
439 A98	15t multicolored	.45	.45
440 A99	60t multicolored	1.10	1.75
	Nos. 437-440 (4)	2.25	2.65

50th anniversaries: Papua New Guinea Boy Scouts; 1st flight from Australia.

Father Ross and Mt. Hagen
A100

1976, Oct. 28 Photo. *Perf. 11½*

Granite Paper

441 A100	7t multicolored	.40	.25

Rev. Father William Ross (1896-1973), American missionary in New Guinea.

Clouded Rainbow Fish — A101

Tropical Fish: 15t, Imperial angelfish. 30t, Freckled rock cod. 40t, Threadfin butterflyfish.

1976, Oct. 28

Granite Paper

442 A101	5t multicolored	.20	.20
443 A101	15t multicolored	.60	.40
444 A101	30t multicolored	1.25	.75
445 A101	40t multicolored	1.40	.95
	Nos. 442-445 (4)	3.45	2.30

Kundiawa Man — A102

Mekeo Headdress
A103

Headdresses: 5t, Masked dancer, East Sepik Province. 10t, Dancer, Koiari area. 15t, Hanuabada woman. 20t, Young woman, Orokaiva. 25t, Haus Tambaran dancer, East Sepik Province. 30t, Asaro Valley man. 35t, Garaina man, Morobe. 40t, Waghi Valley man. 50t, Trobriand dancer, Milne Bay. 1k, Wasara.

Perf. 12 (15, 25, 30t), 11½ (others)

1977-78 Photo.

Sizes: 25x30mm (1, 5, 20t),
26x26mm (10, 15, 25, 30, 50t),
23x38mm (35, 40t)

446 A102	1t multicolored	.20	.20
447 A102	5t multicolored	.20	.20
448 A102	10t multicolored	.25	.20
449 A102	15t multicolored	.25	.25
450 A102	20t multicolored	.40	.25
451 A102	25t multicolored	.30	.30
452 A102	30t multicolored	.35	.40
453 A102	35t multicolored	.55	.30
454 A102	40t multicolored	.50	.30
455 A102	50t multicolored	.80	.30

Litho.

Perf. 14½x14

Size: 28x35½mm

456 A102	1k multicolored	.80	1.40

Perf. 14½x15

Size: 33x23mm

457 A103	2k multicolored	1.40	2.75
	Nos. 446-457 (12)	6.00	6.85

Issued: #456-457, 1/12/77; #448, 450, 453, 455, 6/7/78; others, 3/29/78.

Elizabeth II and P.N.G. Arms
A104

Designs: 7t, Queen and P.N.G. flag. 35t, Queen and map of P.N.G.

1977, Mar. 16 Photo. *Perf. 15x14*

462 A104	7t multicolored	.30	.20
463 A104	15t multicolored	.40	.35
464 A104	35t multicolored	.60	.70
	Nos. 462-464 (3)	1.30	1.25

25th anniv. of the reign of Elizabeth II.

Whitebreasted Ground Dove — A105

Protected Birds: 7t, Victoria crowned pigeon. 15t, Pheasant pigeon. 30t, Orange-fronted fruit dove. 50t, Banded imperial pigeon.

1977, June 8 Photo. *Perf. 11½*

Granite Paper

465 A105	5t multicolored	.20	.20
466 A105	7t multicolored	.25	.20
467 A105	15t multicolored	.50	.50
468 A105	30t multicolored	1.00	.75
469 A105	50t multicolored	1.75	*2.25*
	Nos. 465-469 (5)	3.70	*3.90*

Girl Guides and Gold Badge
A106

Designs (Girl Guides): 15t, Mapping and blue badge. 30t, Doing laundry in brook and red badge. 35t, Wearing grass skirts, cooking and green badge.

1977, Aug. 10 Litho. *Perf. 14½*

470 A106	7t multicolored	.20	.20
471 A106	15t multicolored	.30	.20
472 A106	30t multicolored	.55	.40
473 A106	35t multicolored	.60	.50
	Nos. 470-473 (4)	1.65	1.30

Papua New Guinea Girl Guides, 50th anniv.

Legend of Kari Marupi — A107

Myths of Elema People: 20t, Savoripi Clan. 30t, Oa-Laea. 35t, Oa-Iriarapo.

1977, Oct. 19 Litho. *Perf. 13½*

474 A107	7t black & multi	.20	.20
475 A107	20t black & multi	.45	.35
476 A107	30t black & multi	.50	.60
477 A107	35t black & multi	.50	.60
	Nos. 474-477 (4)	1.65	1.75

Blue-tailed Skink
A108

Lizards: 15t, Green tree skink. 35t, Crocodile skink. 40t, New Guinea blue-tongued skink.

1978, Jan. 25 Photo. *Perf. 11½*

Granite Paper

478 A108	10t blue & multi	.30	.20
479 A108	15t lilac & multi	.40	.25
480 A108	35t olive & multi	.60	.75
481 A108	40t orange & multi	.80	.80
	Nos. 478-481 (4)	2.10	2.00

Roboastra Arika — A109

Sea Slugs: 15t, Chromodoris fidelis. 35t, Flabellina macassarana. 40t, Chromodoris trimarginata.

1978, Aug. 29 Photo. *Perf. 11½*

482 A109	10t multicolored	.30	.20
483 A109	15t multicolored	.40	.30
484 A109	35t multicolored	.65	.65
485 A109	40t multicolored	.75	.75
	Nos. 482-485 (4)	2.10	1.90

Mandated New Guinea Constabulary
A110

Constabulary and Badge: 10t, Royal Papua New Guinea. 20t, Armed British New Guinea. 25t, German New Guinea police. 30t, Royal Papua and New Guinea.

1978, Oct. 26 Photo. *Perf. 14½x14*

486 A110	10t multicolored	.20	.20
487 A110	15t multicolored	.30	.30
488 A110	20t multicolored	.35	.35

489 A110 25t multicolored .40 .40
490 A110 30t multicolored .50 .50
Nos. 486-490 (5) 1.75 1.75

Ocarina, Chimbu Province — A111

Prow and Paddle, East New Britain — A112

Musical Instruments: 20t, Musical bow, New Britain, horiz. 28t, Launut, New Ireland. 35t, Nose flute, New Hanover, horiz.

Perf. 14½x14, 14x14½

1979, Jan. 24 **Litho.**

491 A111 7t multicolored .20 .20
492 A111 20t multicolored .30 .30
493 A111 28t multicolored .40 .40
494 A111 35t multicolored .50 .50
Nos. 491-494 (4) 1.40 1.40

1979, Mar. 28 **Litho.** ***Perf. 14½***

Canoe Prows and Paddles: 21t, Sepik war canoe. 25t, Trobriand Islands. 40t, Milne Bay.

495 A112 14t multicolored .20 .20
496 A112 21t multicolored .30 .25
497 A112 25t multicolored .35 .30
498 A112 40t multicolored .45 .60
Nos. 495-498 (4) 1.30 1.35

Belt of Shell Disks — A113

Traditional Currency: 15t, Tusk chest ornament. 25t, Shell armband. 35t, Shell necklace.

1979, June 6 **Litho.** ***Perf. 12½x12***

499 A113 7t multicolored .20 .20
500 A113 15t multicolored .25 .25
501 A113 25t multicolored .45 .45
502 A113 35t multicolored .55 .65
Nos. 499-502 (4) 1.45 1.55

Oenetus A114

Moths: 15t, Celerina vulgaris. 20t, Alcidis aurora, vert. 25t, Phyllodes conspicillator. 30t, Nyctalemon patroclus, vert.

1979, Aug. 29 **Photo.** ***Perf. 11½***

503 A114 7t multicolored .20 .20
504 A114 15t multicolored .35 .35
505 A114 20t multicolored .40 .50
506 A114 25t multicolored .45 .65
507 A114 30t multicolored .60 .70
Nos. 503-507 (5) 2.00 2.40

Baby in String Bag Scale — A115

IYC (Emblem and): 7t, Mother nursing baby. 30t, Boy playing with dog and ball. 60t, Girl in classroom.

1979, Oct. 24 **Litho.** ***Perf. 14x13½***

508 A115 7t multicolored .20 .20
509 A115 15t multicolored .25 .25
510 A115 30t multicolored .35 .35
511 A115 60t multicolored .60 .60
Nos. 508-511 (4) 1.40 1.40

Mail Sorting, Mail Truck A116

UPU Membership: 25t, Wartime mail delivery. 35t, UPU monument, airport and city. 40t, Hand canceling, letter carrier.

1980, Jan. 23 **Litho.** ***Perf. 13½x14***

512 A116 7t multicolored .20 .20
513 A116 25t multicolored .30 .30
514 A116 35t multicolored .40 .40
515 A116 40t multicolored .50 .50
Nos. 512-515 (4) 1.40 1.40

Male Dancer, Betrothal Ceremony — A117

Third South Pacific Arts Festival, Port Moresby (Minj Betrothal Ceremony Mural): No. 516 has continuous design.

1980, Mar. 26 **Photo.** ***Perf. 11½***

Granite Paper

516 A117 Strip of 5 1.25 1.25
a. 20t single stamp .25 .25

National Census — A118

1980, June 4 **Litho.** ***Perf. 14***

517 A118 7t shown .20 .20
518 A118 15t Population symbol .20 .20
519 A118 40t P. N. G. map .55 .55
520 A118 50t Faces .75 .75
Nos. 517-520 (4) 1.70 1.70

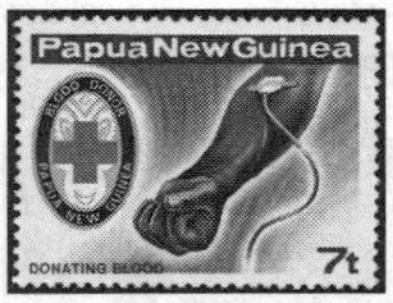

Blood Transfusion, Donor's Badge — A119

1980, Aug. 27 **Litho.** ***Perf. 14½***

521 A119 7t shown .20 .20
522 A119 15t Donating blood .20 .20
523 A119 30t Map of donation centers .45 .45
524 A119 60t Blood components and types .80 .80
Nos. 521-524 (4) 1.65 1.65

Dugong A120

1980, Oct. 29 **Photo.** ***Perf. 11½***

525 A120 7t shown .20 .20
526 A120 30t Native spotted cat, vert. .40 .40
527 A120 35t Tube-nosed bat, vert. .50 .50
528 A120 45t Raffray's bandicoot .75 .75
Nos. 525-528 (4) 1.85 1.85

Beach Kingfisher A121

Mask A122

1981, Jan. 21 **Photo.** ***Perf. 12***

Granite Paper

529 A121 3t shown .20 .20
530 A121 7t Forest kingfisher .20 .20
531 A121 20t Sacred kingfisher .50 .50

Size: 26x45½mm

532 A121 25t White-tailed paradise kingfisher .55 .55

Size: 26x36mm

533 A121 60t Blue-winged kookaburra 1.50 1.50
Nos. 529-533 (5) 2.95 2.95

Coil Stamps

Perf. 14½ Horiz.

1981, Jan. 21 **Photo.**

534 A122 2t shown .20 .20
535 A122 5t Hibiscus .20 .20

Defense Force Soldiers Firing Mortar — A123

1981, Mar. 25 **Photo.** ***Perf. 13½x14***

536 A123 7t shown .20 .20
537 A123 15t DC-3 military plane .25 .25
538 A123 40t Patrol boat Eitape .65 .65
539 A123 50t Medics treating civilians .80 .80
Nos. 536-539 (4) 1.90 1.90

For surcharge see No. 615.

Missionary Aviation Fellowship Plane — A124

Planes of Missionary Organizations: 15t, Holy Ghost Society. 20t, Summer Institute of Linguistics. 30t, Lutheran Mission. 35t, Seventh Day Adventist.

1981, June 17 **Litho.** ***Perf. 14***

540 A124 10t multicolored .20 .20
541 A124 15t multicolored .25 .25
542 A124 20t multicolored .30 .30
543 A124 30t multicolored .50 .50
544 A124 35t multicolored .55 .55
Nos. 540-544 (5) 1.80 1.80

Scoop Net Fishing A125

1981, Aug. 26

545 A125 10t shown .20 .20
546 A125 15t Kite fishing .25 .25
547 A125 30t Rod fishing .45 .45
548 A125 60t Scissor net fishing .95 .95
Nos. 545-548 (4) 1.85 1.85

Forcartia Buhleri A126

1981, Oct. 28 **Photo.** ***Perf. 12***

Granite Paper

549 A126 5t shown .20 .20
550 A126 15t Naninia citrina .30 .30
551 A126 20t Papuina adonis, papuina hermione .35 .35
552 A126 30t Papustyla hindei, papustyla novaepommeraniae .55 .55
553 A126 40t Rhynchotrochus strabo .70 .70
Nos. 549-553 (5) 2.10 2.10

75th Anniv. of Boy Scouts A127

1982, Jan. 20 **Photo.** ***Perf. 11½***

Granite Paper

554 A127 15t Lord Baden-Powell, flag raising .30 .30
555 A127 25t Leader, campfire .50 .50
556 A127 35t Scout, hut building .65 .65
557 A127 50t Percy Chatterton, first aid 1.00 1.00
Nos. 554-557 (4) 2.45 2.45

Wanigela Pottery A128

1982, Mar. 24 **Litho.** ***Perf. 14***

Size: 29x29mm

558 A128 10t Boiken, East Sepik .20 .20
559 A128 20t Gumalu, Madang .30 .30

Perf. 14½

Size: 36x23mm

560 A128 40t shown .60 .60
561 A128 50t Ramu Valley, Madang .75 .75
Nos. 558-561 (4) 1.85 1.85

Nutrition A129

1982, May 5 **Litho.** ***Perf. 14½x14***

562 A129 10t Mother, child .20 .20
563 A129 15t Protein .30 .30
564 A129 30t Fruits, vegetables .55 .55
565 A129 40t Carbohydrates .75 .75
Nos. 562-565 (4) 1.80 1.80

Coral A130

1982, July 21 **Photo.** ***Perf. 11½***

Granite Paper

566 A130 1t Stylophora sp. .20 .20
567 A130 5t Acropora humilis .20 .20
568 A130 15t Distichopora sp. .30 .30
569 A130 1k Xenia sp. 2.00 2.00
Nos. 566-569 (4) 2.70 2.70

See Nos. 575-579, 588-591, 614.

Centenary of Catholic Church in Papua New Guinea — A131

1982, Sept. 15 Photo. *Perf. 11½*
570 Strip of 3 .80 .80
a. A131 10t any single .25 .25

12th Commonwealth Games, Brisbane, Australia, Sept. 30-Oct. 9 — A132

1982, Oct. 6 Litho. *Perf. 14½*
571 A132 10t Running .20 .20
572 A132 15t Boxing .30 .30
573 A132 45t Shooting .90 .90
574 A132 50t Lawn bowling 1.00 1.00
Nos. 571-574 (4) 2.40 2.40

Coral Type of 1982

1983, Jan. 12 Photo. *Perf. 11½*
Granite Paper
575 A130 3t Dendrophyllia .20 .20
576 A130 10t Dendronephthya .20 .20
577 A130 30t Dendronephthya, diff. .65 .65
578 A130 40t Antipathes .90 .70
579 A130 3k Distichopora 7.00 7.00
Nos. 575-579 (5) 8.95 8.75

Nos. 575-579 vert.

Commonwealth Day — A133

1983, Mar. 9 Litho. *Perf. 14*
580 A133 10t Flag, arms .20 .20
581 A133 15t Youth, recreation .25 .25
582 A133 20t Technical assistance .30 .30
583 A133 50t Export assistance .85 .85
Nos. 580-583 (4) 1.60 1.60

World Communications Year — A134

1983, Sept. 7 Litho. *Perf. 14*
584 A134 10t Mail transport .20 .20
585 A134 25t Writing & receiving letter .50 .50
586 A134 30t Telephone calls .60 .60
587 A134 60t Family reunion 1.20 1.20
Nos. 584-587 (4) 2.50 2.50

Coral Type of 1982

1983, Nov. 9 Photo. *Perf. 11½*
588 A130 20t Isis sp. .60 .60
589 A130 25t Acropora sp. 1.00 1.00
590 A130 35t Stylaster elegans 1.50 1.50
591 A130 45t Turbinarea sp. 1.90 1.90
Nos. 588-591 (4) 5.00 5.00

Nos. 588-591 vert.

Turtles A135

1984, Feb. 8 Photo.
Granite Paper
592 A135 5t Chelonia depressa .20 .20
593 A135 10t Chelonia mydas .30 .30
594 A135 15t Eretkmochelys imbricata .50 .50
595 A135 20t Lepidochelys olivacea .60 .60
596 A135 25t Caretta caretta .80 .80
597 A135 40t Dermochelys coriacea 1.40 1.40
Nos. 592-597 (6) 3.80 3.80

Papua-Australia Airmail Service, 50th Anniv. — A136

Mail planes.

1984, May 9 Litho. *Perf. 14½x14*
598 A136 20t Avro X VH-UXX .45 .45
599 A136 25t DH86B VH-UYU Carmania .55 .55
600 A136 40t Westland Widgeon 1.00 1.00
601 A136 60t Consolidated Catalina NC777 1.40 1.40
Nos. 598-601 (4) 3.40 3.40

Parliament House Opening — A137

1984, Aug. 7 Litho. *Perf. 13½x14*
602 A137 10t multicolored .45 .45

Bird of Paradise A138

1984, Aug. 7 Photo. *Perf. 11½*
Granite Paper
603 A138 5k multicolored 9.50 9.50

Ceremonial Shield — A139

1984, Sept. 21
604 A139 10t Central Province .25 .25
605 A139 20t West New Britain .60 .60
606 A139 30t Madang .90 .90
607 A139 50t East Sepik 1.65 1.65
Nos. 604-607 (4) 3.40 3.40

See Nos. 677-680.

British New Guinea Proclamation Centenary — A140

1984, Nov. 6 Litho. *Perf. 14½x14*
608 A140 Pair .55 .55
a. 10t Nelson, Port Moresby, 1884 .25 .25
b. 10t Port Moresby, 1984 .25 .25
609 A140 Pair 2.50 2.50
a. 45t Rabaul, 1984 1.25 1.25
b. 45t Elizabeth, Rabaul, 1884 1.25 1.25

Chimbu Gorge A142

1985, Feb. 6 Photo. *Perf. 11½*
610 A142 10t Fergusson Island, vert. .30 .30
611 A142 25t Sepik River, vert. .80 .80
612 A142 40t shown 1.25 1.25
613 A142 60t Dali Beach, Vanimo 2.00 2.00
Nos. 610-613 (4) 4.35 4.35

Coral Type of 1982

1985, May 29 Photo. *Perf. 11½*
614 A130 12t Dendronephthya sp. .50 .50

For surcharge see No. 686.

No. 536 Surcharged

1985, Apr. 1 Litho. *Perf. 13½x14*
615 A123 12t on 7t multi .75 .75
a. Inverted surcharge —

Ritual Structures A143

Designs: 15t, Dubu platform, Central Province. 20t, Tamuniai house, West New Britain. 30t, Yam tower, Trobriand Island. 60t, Huli grave, Tari.

1985, May 1 *Perf. 13x13½*
616 A143 15t multicolored .50 .50
617 A143 20t multicolored .70 .70
618 A143 30t multicolored 1.00 1.00
619 A143 60t multicolored 1.75 1.75
Nos. 616-619 (4) 3.95 3.95

Indigenous Birds of Prey — A144

1985, Aug. 26 *Perf. 14x14½*
620 12t Accipiter brachyurus .50 .50
621 12t In flight .50 .50
a. A144 Pair, #629-621 1.00 1.00
622 30t Megatriorchis doriae 1.25 1.25
623 30t In Flight 1.25 1.25
a. A144 Pair, #622-623 2.50 2.50
624 60t Henicopernis longicauda 2.50 2.50
625 60t In flight 2.50 2.50
a. A144 Pair, #624-625 5.00 5.00
Nos. 620-625 (6) 8.50 8.50

Flag and Gable of Parliament House, Port Moresby — A145

1985, Sept. 11 *Perf. 14½x15*
626 A145 12t multicolored .50 .50

Post Office Centenary A146

Designs: 12t, No. 631a, 1901 Postal card, aerogramme, spectacles and inkwell. 30t, No. 631b, Queensland Type A15, No. 628. 40t, No. 631c, Plane and news clipping, 1885. 60t, No. 631d, 1892 German canceler, 1985 first day cancel.

1985, Oct. 9 *Perf. 14½x14*
627 A146 12t multicolored .35 .35
628 A146 30t multicolored .90 .90
629 A146 40t multicolored 1.25 1.25
630 A146 60t multicolored 1.90 1.90
Nos. 627-630 (4) 4.40 4.40

Souvenir Sheet

631 Sheet of 4 5.00 5.00
a. A146 12t multicolored .40 .40
b. A146 30t multicolored 1.00 1.00
c. A146 40t multicolored 1.40 1.40
d. A146 60t multicolored 2.00 2.00

Nombowai Cave Carved Funerary Totems — A147

1985, Nov. 13 *Perf. 11½*
632 A147 12t Bird Rulowlaw, headman .30 .30
633 A147 30t Barn owl Raus, headman .75 .75
634 A147 60t Melerawuk 1.50 1.50
635 A147 80t Cockerel, woman 2.00 2.00
Nos. 632-635 (4) 4.55 4.55

Conch Shells — A148

1986, Feb. 12 *Perf. 11½*
636 A148 15t Cypraea valentia .45 .45
637 A148 35t Oliva buelowi 1.10 1.10
638 A148 45t Oliva parkinsoni 1.40 1.40
639 A148 70t Cypraea aurantium 2.25 2.25
Nos. 636-639 (4) 5.20 5.20

Common Design Types pictured following the introduction.

Queen Elizabeth II 60th Birthday
Common Design Type

Designs: 15t, In ATS officer's uniform, 1945. 35t, Silver wedding anniv. portrait by Patrick Lichfield, Balmoral, 1972. 50t, Inspecting troops, Port Moresby, 1982. 60t, Banquet aboard Britannia, state tour, 1982. 70t, Visiting Crown Agents' offices, 1983.

Perf. 14½
1986, Apr. 21 Litho. Unwmk.
640 CD337 15t scar, blk & sil .30 .30
641 CD337 35t ultra & multi .70 .70
642 CD337 50t green & multi 1.00 1.00
643 CD337 60t violet & multi 1.10 1.10
644 CD337 70t rose vio & multi 1.40 1.40
Nos. 640-644 (5) 4.50 4.50

AMERIPEX '86 A149

Small birds.

1986, May 22 Photo. *Perf. 12½*
Granite Paper

645 A149 15t Pitta erythrogaster .65 .65
646 A149 35t Melanocharis striativentris 1.50 1.50
647 A149 45t Rhipidura rufifrons 1.90 1.90
648 A149 70t Poecilodryas placens, vert. 3.00 3.00
Nos. 645-648 (4) 7.05 7.05

Lutheran Church, Cent. — A150

1986, July 7 Litho. *Perf. 14x15*

649 A150 15t Monk, minister .55 .55
650 A150 70t Churches from 1886, 1986 2.50 2.50

Indigenous Orchids — A151

Folk Dancers — A152

1986, Aug. 4 Litho. *Perf. 14*

651 A151 15t Dendrobium vexillarius .65 .65
652 A151 35t Dendrobium lineale 1.50 1.50
653 A151 45t Dendrobium johnsoniae 1.90 1.90
654 A151 70t Dendrobium cuthbertsonii 3.00 3.00
Nos. 651-654 (4) 7.05 7.05

1986, Nov. 12 Litho. *Perf. 14*

655 A152 15t Maprik .65 .65
656 A152 35t Kiriwina 1.50 1.50
657 A152 45t Kundiawa 1.90 1.90
658 A152 70t Fasu 3.00 3.00
Nos. 655-658 (4) 7.05 7.05

Fish A153

Unwmk.

1987, Apr. 15 Litho. *Perf. 15*

659 A153 17t White-cap anemonefish .50 .50
660 A153 30t Black anemonefish .85 .85
661 A153 35t Tomato clownfish 1.00 1.00
662 A153 70t Spine-cheek anemonefish 2.00 2.00
Nos. 659-662 (4) 4.35 4.35

For surcharges see Nos. 720, 823, 868.

Ships — A154

1987-88 Photo. Unwmk. *Perf. 11½*
Granite Paper

663 A154 1t La Boudeuse, 1768 .20 .20
664 A154 5t Roebuck, 1700 .20 .20
665 A154 10t Swallow, 1767 .25 .25
666 A154 15t Fly, 1845 .35 .35
667 A154 17t like 15t .40 .40
668 A154 20t Rattlesnake, 1849 .45 .45
669 A154 30t Vitiaz, 1871 .75 .75
670 A154 35t San Pedrico, Zabre, 1606 .75 .75
671 A154 40t L'Astrolabe, 1827 .90 .90
672 A154 45t Neva, 1876 .90 .90
673 A154 60t Caravel of Jorge De Meneses, 1526 1.50 1.50
674 A154 70t Eendracht, 1616 1.50 1.50
675 A154 1k Blanche, 1872 2.75 2.75
676 A154 2k Merrie England, 1889 4.25 4.25
676A A154 3k Samoa, 1884 7.50 7.50
Nos. 663-676A (15) 22.65 22.65

Issued: 5, 35, 45, 70t, 2k, 6/15/87; 15, 20, 40, 60t, 2/17/88; 17t, 1k, 3/1/88; 1, 10, 30t, 3k, 11/16/88.

See Nos. 960-963. For surcharge see No. 824.

Shield Type of 1984

Perf. 11½x12

1987, Aug. 19 Photo. Unwmk.

War shields.

677 A139 15t Elema shield, Gulf Province, c. 1880 .30 .30
678 A139 35t East Sepik Province .75 .75
679 A139 45t Simbai region, Madang Province .95 .95
680 A139 70t Telefomin region, West Sepik 1.45 1.45
Nos. 677-680 (4) 3.45 3.45

Starfish A156

1987, Sept. 30 Litho. *Perf. 14*

682 A156 17t Protoreaster nodosus .40 .40
683 A156 35t Gomophia egeriae .90 .90
684 A156 45t Choriaster granulatus 1.10 1.10
685 A156 70t Neoferdina ocellata 1.75 1.75
Nos. 682-685 (4) 4.15 4.15

No. 614 Surcharged

1987, Sept. 23 Photo. *Perf. 11½*
Granite Paper

686 A130 15t on 12t multi .90 .90

Aircraft A157

Designs: 15t, Cessna Stationair 6, Rabaraba Airstrip. 35t, Britten-Norman Islander over Hombrum Bluff. 45t, DHC Twin Otter over the Highlands. 70t, Fokker F28 over Madang.

Unwmk.

1987, Nov. 11 Litho. *Perf. 14*

687 A157 15t multicolored .45 .45
688 A157 35t multicolored 1.00 1.00
689 A157 45t multicolored 1.25 1.25
690 A157 70t multicolored 2.00 2.00
Nos. 687-690 (4) 4.70 4.70

Royal Papua New Guinea Police Force, Cent. — A158

Historic and modern aspects of the force: 17t, Motorcycle constable and pre-independence officer wearing a lap-lap. 35t, Sir William McGregor, Armed Native Constabulary founder, 1890, and recruit. 45t, Badges. 70t, Albert Hahl, German official credited with founding the island's police movement in 1888, and badge, early officer.

Perf. 14x15

1988, June 15 Litho. Unwmk.

691 A158 17t multicolored .40 .40
692 A158 35t multicolored .75 .75
693 A158 45t multicolored 1.10 1.10
694 A158 70t multicolored 1.65 1.65
Nos. 691-694 (4) 3.90 3.90

Sydney Opera House and a Lakatoi (ship) — A159

Fireworks and Globes — A160

1988, July 30 Litho. *Perf. 13½*

695 A159 35t multicolored .80 .80
696 A160 Pair 1.60 1.60
a.-b. 35t any single .80 .80
c. Souvenir sheet of 2, #a.-b. 1.60 1.60

SYDPEX '88, Australia (No. 695); Australia bicentennial (No. 696).

World Wildlife Fund A161

Metamorphosis of a Queen Alexandra's birdwing butterfly.

1988, Sept. 19 *Perf. 14½*

697 A161 5t Courtship *.30 .30*
698 A161 17t Ovipositioning and larvae, vert. *1.00 1.00*
699 A161 25t Emergence from pupa, vert. *1.50 1.50*
700 A161 35t Adult male on leaf *2.00 2.00*
Nos. 697-700 (4) *4.80 4.80*

1988 Summer Olympics, Seoul A162

1988, Sept. 19 Litho. *Perf. 13½*

701 A162 17t Running .40 .40
702 A162 45t Weight lifting 1.10 1.10

Rhododendrons A163

Wmk. 387

1989, Jan. 25 Litho. *Perf. 14*

703 A163 3t *R. zoelleri* .20 .20
704 A163 20t *R. cruttwellii* .50 .50
705 A163 60t *R. superbum* 1.50 1.50
706 A163 70t *R. christianae* 1.75 1.75
Nos. 703-706 (4) 3.95 3.95

Intl. Letter Writing Week — A164

1989, Mar. 22 *Perf. 14½*

707 A164 20t Writing letter .40 .40
708 A164 35t Mailing letter .65 .65
709 A164 60t Stamping letter 1.10 1.10
710 A164 70t Reading letter 1.40 1.40
Nos. 707-710 (4) 3.55 3.55

Thatched Dwellings — A165

1989, May 17 Wmk. 387 *Perf. 15*

711 A165 20t Buka Is., 1880s .50 .50
712 A165 35t Koiari tree houses .90 .90
713 A165 60t Lauan, New Ireland, 1890s 1.50 1.50
714 A165 70t Basilaki, Milne Bay Province, 1930s 1.75 1.75
Nos. 711-714 (4) 4.65 4.65

Small Birds — A166

1989, July 12 Unwmk. *Perf. 14½*

715 A166 20t *Oreocharis arfaki* female, shown .60 .60
716 A166 20t Male .60 .60
a. Pair, #715-716 1.25 1.25
717 A166 35t *Ifrita kowaldi* 1.10 1.10
718 A166 45t *Poecilodryas albonotata* 1.40 1.40
719 A166 70t *Sericornis nouhuysi* 2.25 2.25
Nos. 715-719 (5) 5.95 5.95

No. 659 Surcharged

1989, July 12 Unwmk. *Perf. 15*

720 A153 20t on 17t multi .75 .75
a. Double surcharge 110.00

Traditional Dance — A167

Designs: 20t, Motumotu, Gulf Province. 35t, Baining, East New Britain Province. 60t, Vailala River, Gulf Province. 70t, Timbunke, East Sepik Province.

Perf. 14x14½

1989, Sept. 6 Litho. Wmk. 387

721 A167 20t multicolored	.60	.60
722 A167 35t multicolored	1.00	1.00
723 A167 60t multicolored	1.75	1.75
724 A167 70t multicolored	2.00	2.00
Nos. 721-724 (4)	5.35	5.35

For surcharge see No. 860.

Christmas A168

Designs: 20t, Hibiscus, church and symbol from a gulf gope board, Kavaumai. 35t, Rhododendron, madonna and child, and mask, Murik Lakes region. 60t, D'Albertis creeper, candle, and shield from Oksapmin, West Sepik highlands. 70t, Pacific frangipani, peace dove and flute mask from Chungrebu, a Rao village in Ramu.

Perf. 14x14½

1989, Nov. 8 Litho. Unwmk.

725 A168 20t multicolored	.55	.55
726 A168 35t multicolored	.90	.90
727 A168 60t multicolored	1.75	1.75
728 A168 70t multicolored	2.00	2.00
Nos. 725-728 (4)	5.20	5.20

Waterfalls — A169

Unwmk.

1990, Feb. 1 Litho. *Perf. 14*

729 A169 20t Guni Falls	.50	.50
730 A169 35t Rouna Falls	.85	.85
731 A169 60t Ambua Falls	1.50	1.50
732 A169 70t Wawoi Falls	1.65	1.65
Nos. 729-732 (4)	4.50	4.50

For surcharges see Nos. 866, 870.

Natl. Census A170

1990, May 2 *Perf. 14½x15*

733 A170 20t Three youths, form	.50	.50
734 A170 70t Man, woman, child, form	1.65	1.65

For surcharge see No. 869.

Gogodala Dance Masks — A171

1990, July 11 Litho. *Perf. 13½*

735 A171 20t shown	.50	.50
736 A171 35t multi, diff.	.85	.85
737 A171 60t multi, diff.	1.50	1.50
738 A171 70t multi, diff.	1.65	1.65
Nos. 735-738 (4)	4.50	4.50

For surcharges see Nos. 867, 871.

Waitangi Treaty, 150th Anniv. — A172

Designs: 20t, Dwarf Cassowary, Great Spotted Kiwi. No. 740, Double Wattled Cassowary, Brown Kiwi. No. 741, Sepik mask and Maori carving.

1990, Aug. 24 Litho. *Perf. 14½*

739 A172 20t multicolored	.50	.50
740 A172 35t multicolored	.80	.80
741 A172 35t multicolored	.80	.80
Nos. 739-741 (3)	2.10	2.10

No. 741 for World Stamp Exhibition, New Zealand 1990.
For surcharges see Nos. 862-863.

Birds A173

1990, Sept. 26 Litho. *Perf. 14*

742 A173 20t Whimbrel	.60	.60
743 A173 35t Sharp-tailed sandpiper	.95	.95
744 A173 60t Ruddy turnstone	1.90	1.90
745 A173 70t Terek sandpiper	2.00	2.00
Nos. 742-745 (4)	5.45	5.45

Musical Instruments A174

1990, Oct. 31 Litho. *Perf. 13*

746 A174 20t Jew's harp	.50	.50
747 A174 35t Musical bow	.80	.80
748 A174 60t Wantoat drum	1.45	1.45
749 A174 70t Gogodala rattle	1.65	1.65
Nos. 746-749 (4)	4.40	4.40

For surcharge see No. 861.

Snail Shells A174a

Designs: 21t, Rhynchotrochus weigmani. 40t, Forcartia globula, Canefriula azonata. 50t, Planispira deaniana. 80t, Papuina chancel, Papuina xanthocheila.

1991, Mar. 6 Litho. *Perf. 14x14½*

750 A174a 21t multicolored	.55	.55
751 A174a 40t multicolored	1.00	1.00
752 A174a 50t multicolored	1.25	1.25
753 A174a 80t multicolored	2.00	2.00
Nos. 750-753 (4)	4.80	4.80

For surcharge see No. 864.

A175

A176

1991-94 Litho. *Perf. 14½*

755 A175 1t Ptiloris magnificus	.20	.20
756 A175 5t Loria loriae	.20	.20
757 A175 10t Cnemophilus macgregorii	.20	.20
758 A175 20t Parotia wahnesi	.40	.40
759 A175 21t Manucodia chalybata	.45	.45
760 A175 30t Paradisaea decora	.60	.60
761 A175 40t Loboparadisea sericea	.80	.80
762 A175 45t Cicinnurus regius	.95	.95
763 A175 50t Paradigalla brevicauda	1.00	1.00
764 A175 60t Parotia carolae	1.30	1.30
765 A175 90t Paradisaea guilielmi	1.95	1.95
766 A175 1k Diphyllodes magnificus	2.00	2.00
767 A175 2k Lophorina superba	4.00	4.00
a. Strip of 4, #761, 763, 766-767 + label	8.00	8.00
768 A175 5k Phonygammus keraudrenii	10.00	10.00
Perf. 13		
769 A176 10k Paradisaea minor	21.00	21.00
Nos. 755-769 (15)	45.05	45.05

No. 767a for Hong Kong '94 and sold for 4k.
Stamps in No. 767a do not have "1992 BIRD OF PARADISE" at bottom of design.
Issued: 21t, 45t, 60t, 90t, 3/25/92; 5t, 40t, 50t, 1k, 2k, 9/2/92; 1t, 10t, 20t, 30t, 5k, 1993; 10k, 5/1/91; No. 767a, 2/18/94.
For surcharges see #878A, 878C.

Large T — A176a

1993 Litho. *Perf. 14½*

770A A176a 21T like #759	.50	.50
770B A176a 45T like #762	1.00	1.00
770C A176a 60T like #764	1.40	1.40
770D A176a 90T like #765	2.25	2.25
Nos. 770A-770D (4)	5.15	5.15

Originally scheduled for release on Feb. 19, 1992, #770A-770D were withdrawn when the denomination was found to have an upper case "T." Corrected versions with a lower case "T" are #759, 762, 764-765. A quantity of the original stamps appeared in the market and to prevent speculation in these items, the Postal Administration of Papua New Guinea released the stamps with the upper case "T."
For surcharges see #878B, 878D.

1991 South Pacific Games A177

1991, June 26 Litho. *Perf. 13*

771 A177 21t Cricket	.50	.50
772 A177 40t Running	.95	.95
773 A177 50t Baseball	1.20	1.20
774 A177 80t Rugby	1.90	1.90
Nos. 771-774 (4)	4.55	4.55

Anglican Church in Papua New Guinea, Cent. A178

Churches: 21t, Cathedral of St. Peter & St. Paul, Dogura. 40t, Kaieta Shrine, Anglican landing site. 80t, First thatched chapel, modawa tree.

1991, Aug. 7 Litho. *Perf. 14½*

775 A178 21t multicolored	.50	.50
776 A178 40t multicolored	.95	.95
777 A178 80t multicolored	1.90	1.90
Nos. 775-777 (3)	3.35	3.35

Traditional Headdresses A179

Designs: 21t, Rambutso, Manus Province. 40t, Marawaka, Eastern Highlands. 50t, Tufi, Oro Province. 80t, Sina Sina, Simbu Province.

1991, Oct. 16 Litho. *Perf. 13*

778 A179 21t multicolored	.50	.50
779 A179 40t multicolored	.95	.95
780 A179 50t multicolored	1.20	1.20
781 A179 80t multicolored	1.90	1.90
Nos. 778-781 (4)	4.55	4.55

Discovery of America, 500th Anniv. A180

1992, Apr. 15 Litho. *Perf. 14*

782 A180 21t Nina	.45	.45
783 A180 45t Pinta	.90	.90
784 A180 60t Santa Maria	1.30	1.30
785 A180 90t Columbus, ships	1.95	1.95
a. Souvenir sheet of 2, #784-785	2.75	2.75
Nos. 782-785 (4)	4.60	4.60

World Columbian Stamp Expo '92, Chicago. Issue date: No. 785a, June 3.

A181

A182

Papuan Gulf Artifacts: 21t, Canoe prow shield, Bamu. 45t. Skull rack, Kerewa. 60t, Ancestral figure, Era River. 90t, Gope (spirit) board, Urama.

1992, June 3 Litho. *Perf. 14*

786 A181 21t multicolored	.50	.50
787 A181 45t multicolored	1.00	1.00
788 A181 60t multicolored	1.40	1.40
789 A181 90t multicolored	2.25	2.25
Nos. 786-789 (4)	5.15	5.15

1992, July 22 Litho. *Perf. 14*

Soldiers from: 21t, Papuan Infantry Battalion. 45t, Australian Militia. 60t, Japanese Nankai Force. 90t, US Army.

790 A182 21t multicolored	.50	.50
791 A182 45t multicolored	1.00	1.00
792 A182 60t multicolored	1.40	1.40
793 A182 90t multicolored	2.25	2.25
Nos. 790-793 (4)	5.15	5.15

World War II, 50th anniv.

Flowering Trees — A183

1992, Oct. 28 Litho. *Perf. 14*

794 A183 21t Hibiscus tiliaceus	.50	.50
795 A183 45t Castanospermum australe	1.00	1.00
796 A183 60t Cordia subcordata	1.40	1.40
797 A183 90t Acacia auriculiformis	2.00	2.00
Nos. 794-797 (4)	4.90	4.90

Mammals A184

1993, Apr. 7 Litho. *Perf. 14*

798 A184 21t Myoictis melas	.50	.50
799 A184 45t Microperoryctes longicauda	1.10	1.10
800 A184 60t Mallomys rothschildi	1.50	1.50
801 A184 90t Pseudocheirus forbesi	2.25	2.25
Nos. 798-801 (4)	5.35	5.35

Small Birds — A185

1993, June 9 Litho. *Perf. 14*

802 A185 21t Clytomyias insignis	.45	.45
803 A185 45t Pitta superba	.95	.95
804 A185 60t Rhagologus leucostigma	1.25	1.25
805 A185 90t Toxorhamphus poliopterus	2.00	2.00
Nos. 802-805 (4)	4.65	4.65

Nos. 802-805 Redrawn with Taipei '93 emblem in Blue and Yellow

1993, Aug. 13 Litho. *Perf. 14*

806 A185 21t multicolored	.50	.50
807 A185 45t multicolored	1.10	1.10
808 A185 60t multicolored	1.40	1.40
809 A185 90t multicolored	2.25	2.25
Nos. 806-809 (4)	5.25	5.25

Freshwater Fish A186

Designs: 21t, Iriatherina werneri. 45t, Tateurndina ocellicauda. 60t, Melanotaenia affinis. 90t, Pseudomugil connieae.

1993, Sept. 29 Litho. *Perf. 14x14½*

810 A186 21t multicolored	.50	.50
811 A186 45t multicolored	1.00	1.00
812 A186 60t multicolored	1.40	1.40
813 A186 90t multicolored	2.00	2.00
Nos. 810-813 (4)	4.90	4.90

For surcharges see Nos. 876-878.

Air Niugini, 20th Anniv. A187

1993, Oct. 27 *Perf. 14*

814 A187 21t DC3	.50	.50
815 A187 45t F27	1.00	1.00
816 A187 60t Dash 7	1.40	1.40
817 A187 90t Airbus A310-300	2.00	2.00
Nos. 814-817 (4)	4.90	4.90

Souvenir Sheet

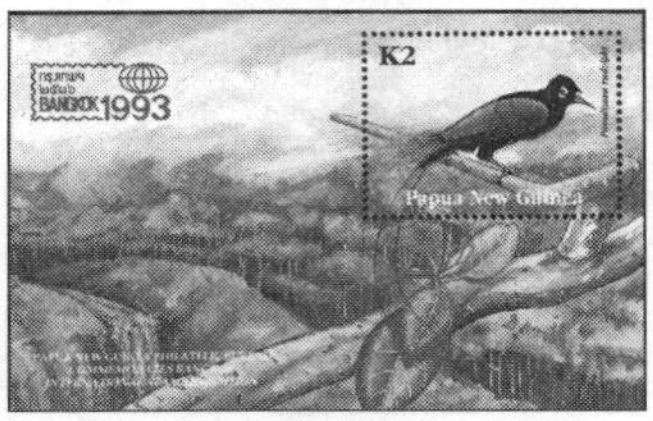

Paradisaea Rudolphi — A188

1993, Sept. 29 Litho. *Perf. 14*

818 A188 2k multicolored	5.25	5.25

Bangkok '93.

Huon Tree Kangaroo — A189

1994, Jan. 19 Litho. *Perf. 14½*

819 A189 21t Domesticated joey	.45	.45
820 A189 45t Adult male	1.00	1.00
821 A189 60t Female, joey in pouch	1.40	1.40
822 A189 90t Adolescent	1.90	1.90
Nos. 819-822 (4)	4.75	4.75

No. 661 Surcharged

No. 671 Surcharged

1994, Mar. 23

Perfs. and Printing Methods as Before

823 A153 21t on 35t multi	*8.50*	.40
824 A154 1.20k on 40t multi	*3.50*	1.00

No. 824 exists with double surcharge. Other varieties may exist.

Artifacts — A190

Designs: 1t, Hagen ceremonial axe, Western Highlands. 2t, Telefomin war shield, West Sepik. 20t, Head mask, Gulf of Papua. 21t, Kanganaman stool, East Sepik. 45t, Trobriand lime gourd, Milne Bay. 60t, Yuat River flute stopper, East Sepik. 90t, Tami island dish, Morobe. 1k, Kundu drum, Ramu River estuary. 5k, Gogodala dance mask, Western Province. 10k, Malanggan mask, New Ireland.

1994-95 Litho. *Perf. 14½*

825 A190 1t multicolored	.20	.20
826 A190 2t multicolored	.20	.20
828 A190 20t multicolored	.35	.35
829 A190 21t multicolored	.35	.35
833 A190 45t multicolored	.80	.80
835 A190 60t multicolored	1.10	1.10
836 A190 90t multicolored	1.65	1.65
837 A190 1k multicolored	1.65	1.65
839 A190 5k multicolored	9.00	9.00
840 A190 10k multicolored	15.00	15.00
Nos. 825-840 (10)	30.30	30.30

Issued: 21, 45, 60, 90t, 3/23; 1, 2, 20t, 5k, 6/29/94; 1k, 10k, 4/12/95.

This is an expanding set. Numbers may change.

Classic Cars A191

1994, May 11 Litho. *Perf. 14*

841 A191 21t Model T Ford	.50	.50
842 A191 45t Chevrolet 490	1.00	1.00
843 A191 60t Baby Austin	1.40	1.40
844 A191 90t Willys Jeep	2.00	2.00
Nos. 841-844 (4)	4.90	4.90

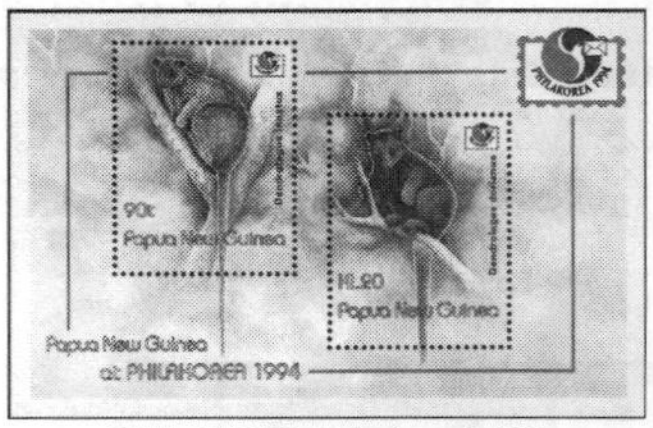

PHILAKOREA '94 — A192

Tree kangaroos: 90t, Dendrolagus inustus. 1.20k, Dendrolagus dorianus.

1994, Aug. 10 Litho. *Perf. 14*

845 A192 Sheet of 2, #a.-b.	4.50	4.50

Moths A193

Designs: 21t, Daphnis hypothous pallescens. 45t, Tanaorhinus unipuncta. 60t, Neodiphthera sciron. 90t, Parotis maginata.

1994, Oct. 26 Litho. *Perf. 14*

846 A193 21t multicolored	.45	.45
847 A193 45t multicolored	1.00	1.00
848 A193 60t multicolored	1.25	1.25
849 A193 90t multicolored	2.00	2.00
Nos. 846-849 (4)	4.70	4.70

Beatification of Peter To Rot — A194

1995, Jan. 11 Litho. *Perf. 14*

850 A194 21t Peter To Rot	.45	.45
851 A194 1k on 90t Pope John Paul II	2.25	2.25
a. Pair, #850-851 + label	2.75	2.75

No. 851 was not issued without surcharge.

Tourism A195

#852, Cruising. #853, Handicrafts. #854, Jet. #855, Resorts. #856, Trekking adventure. #857, White-water rafting. #858, Boat, diver. #859, Divers, sunken plane.

1995, Jan. 11

852 A195 21t multicolored	.45	.45
853 A195 21t multicolored	.45	.45
a. Pair, #852-853	.90	.90
854 A195 50t on 45t multi	1.10	1.10
855 A195 50t on 45t multi	1.10	1.10
a. Pair, #854-855	2.25	2.25
856 A195 65t on 60t multi	1.40	1.40
a. "65t" omitted	32.50	32.50
857 A195 65t on 60t multi	1.40	1.40
a. Pair, #856-857	2.75	2.75
858 A195 1k on 90t multi	2.25	2.25
859 A195 1k on 90t multi	2.25	2.25
a. Pair, #858-859	4.50	4.50
Nos. 852-859 (8)	10.40	10.40

Nos. 854-859 were not issued without surcharge.

Nos. 662, 722, 730, 732, 734, 736, 738, 740-741, 747, 753, 762, 765, 770B, 770D Surcharged

Thick "t" in Surcharge

1994 *Perfs., Etc. as Before*

860	A167	5t on 35t #722	1.75	1.00
861	A174	5t on 35t #747	*20.00*	*17.50*
862	A172	10t on 35t #740	*17.50*	*6.75*
863	A172	10t on 35t #741	*17.50*	*3.50*
864	A174a	21t on 80t #753	*20.00*	*1.50*
866	A169	50t on 35t #730	*25.00*	*17.50*
867	A171	50t on 35t #736	*42.50*	*17.50*
a.		Inverted surcharge	650.00	
868	A153	65t on 70t #662	2.75	1.75
869	A170	65t on 70t #734	2.75	1.75
870	A169	1k on 70t #732	*8.50*	*3.50*
871	A171	1k on 70t #738	3.50	2.50
		Nos. 860-871 (11)	*161.75*	*74.75*

Size, style and location of surcharge varies.

No. 861 exists in pair, one without surcharge. Other varieties exist.

Issued: #862, 8/23/94; #864, 8/28/94; #861, 863, 864, 10/3/94; #860, 871, 10/6/94; #866-868, 869-870, 11/28/94.

Mushrooms A196

25t, Lentinus umbrinus. 50t, Amanita hemibapha. 65t, Boletellus emodensis. 1k, Ramaria zippellii.

1995, June 21 Litho. *Perf. 14*
872 A196 25t multicolored .40 .40
Complete booklet, 10 #872 4.00
873 A196 50t multicolored .85 .85
Complete booklet, 10 #873 8.50
874 A196 65t multicolored 1.10 1.10
875 A196 1k multicolored 1.75 1.75
Nos. 872-875 (4) 4.10 4.10

1996 Litho. *Perf. 12*
875A A196 25t like #872 2.50 2.50

No. 875A has a taller vignette, a smaller typeface for the description, denomination, and country name and does not have a date inscription like #872.

Nos. 811-813 Surcharged Thick "t"
Nos. 762, 765, 770B, 770D
Surcharged Thin "t"

Thin "t" in Surcharge

See illustration above #860.

1995 Litho. *Perf. 14x14½*
876 A186 21t on 45t #811 1.00 .35
877 A186 21t on 60t #812 3.00 1.75
878 A186 21t on 90t #813 1.00 .70
878A A175 21t on 45t #762 1.75 .70
878B A176a 21t on 45T #770B 5.00 1.75
878C A175 21t on 90t #765 2.00 .70
878D A176a 21t on 90T #770D 10.00 1.75
Nos. 876-878D (7) 23.75 7.70

Nos. 878A-878D exist with thick surcharge. This printing of 3200 each does not seem to have seen much, if any, public sale.

#878A, 878C dated 1993. #878B, 878D dated 1992. #878A, 878C exist dated 1992

Issued: #876-878, 6/20; #878A-878B, 5/16; #878C, 3/27; #878D, 4/25.

Independence, 20th Anniv. — A197

Designs: 50t, 1k, "20" emblem.

1995, Aug. 30 *Perf. 14*
879 A197 21t shown .40 .40
880 A197 50t blue & multi .90 .90
881 A197 1k green & multi 1.75 1.75
Nos. 879-881 (3) 3.05 3.05

Souvenir Sheet

Singapore '95 — A198

Orchids: a, 21t, Dendrobium rigidifolium. b, 45t, Dendrobium convolutum. c, 60t, Dendrobium spectabile. d, 90t, Dendrobium tapiniense.

1995, Aug. 30 Litho. *Perf. 14*
882 A198 Sheet of 4, #a.-d. 4.50 4.50

No. 882 sold for 3k.

Souvenir Sheet

New Year 1995 (Year of the Boar) — A199

Illustration reduced.

1995, Sept. 14
883 A199 3k multicolored 4.50 4.50

Beijing '95.

Eruption of Rabaul Volcano, 1st Anniv. A200

1995, Sept. 19
884 A200 2k multicolored 3.00 3.00

Crabs A201

1995, Oct. 25 Litho. *Perf. 14*
885 A201 21t Zosimus aeneus .40 .40
886 A201 50t Cardisoma carnifex 1.00 1.00
887 A201 65t Uca tetragonon 1.30 1.30
888 A201 1k Eriphia sebana 2.00 2.00
Nos. 885-888 (4) 4.70 4.70

For surcharge see #939B.

Parrots — A202

Beetles — A203

Designs: 25t, Psittrichas fulgidas. 50t, Trichoglossus haemotodus. 65t, Alisterus chloropterus. 1k, Aprosmictus erythropterus.

1996, Jan. 17 Litho. *Perf. 12*
889 A202 25t multicolored .40 .40
890 A202 50t multicolored .75 .75
891 A202 65t multicolored 1.00 1.00
892 A202 1k multicolored 1.50 1.50
Nos. 889-892 (4) 3.65 3.65

1996, Mar. 20 Litho. *Perf. 12*

Designs: 25t, Lagriomorpha indigacea. 50t, Eupholus geoffroyi. 65t, Promechus pulcher. 1k, Callistola pulchra.

893 A203 25t multicolored .65 .65
894 A203 50t multicolored 1.30 1.30
895 A203 65t multicolored 1.70 1.70
896 A203 1k multicolored 2.60 2.60
Nos. 893-896 (4) 6.25 6.25

Souvenir Sheet

Zhongshan Memorial Hall, Guangzhou, China — A204

Illustration reduced.

1996, Apr. 22 Litho. *Perf. 14*
897 A204 70t multicolored 1.10 1.10

CHINA '96, 9th Asian Intl. Philatelic Exhibition.

1996 Summer Olympics, Atlanta A205

1996, July 24 Litho. *Perf. 12*
898 A205 25t Shooting .40 .40
899 A205 50t Track .75 .75
900 A205 65t Weight lifting 1.00 1.00
901 A205 1k Boxing 1.50 1.50
Nos. 898-901 (4) 3.65 3.65

Olymphilex '96.

Radio, Cent. A206

25t, Air traffic control. 50t, Commercial broadcasting. 65t, Gerehu earth station. 1k, 1st transmission in Papua New Guinea.

1996, Sept. 11 Litho. *Perf. 12*
902 A206 25t multicolored .40 .40
903 A206 50t multicolored .75 .75
904 A206 65t multicolored 1.00 1.00
905 A206 1k multicolored 1.50 1.50
Nos. 902-905 (4) 3.65 3.65

Souvenir Sheet

Taipei '96, 10th Asian Intl. Philatelic Exhibition — A207

a, Dr. Sun Yat-sen (1866-1925). b, Dr. John Guise (1914-91). Illustration reduced.

1996, Oct. 16 Litho. *Perf. 14*
906 A207 65t Sheet of 2, #a.-b. 2.00 2.00

Flowers A208

Designs: 1t, Hibiscus rosa-sinensis. 5t, Bougainvillea spectabilis. 65t, Plumeria rubra. 1k, Mucuna novo-guineensis.

1996, Nov. 27 Litho. *Perf. 14*
907 A208 1t multicolored .20 .20
908 A208 5t multicolored .20 .20
909 A208 65t multicolored 1.00 1.00
910 A208 1k multicolored 1.50 1.50
Nos. 907-910 (4) 2.90 2.90

Souvenir Sheet

Oxen and Natl. Flag — A209

1997, Feb. 3 Litho. *Perf. 14*
911 A209 1.50k multicolored 2.25 2.25

Hong Kong '97.

Boat Prows A210

1997, Mar. 19 Litho. *Perf. 14½x14*
912 A210 25t Gogodala .40 .40
913 A210 50t East New Britain .75 .75
914 A210 65t Trobriand Island 1.00 1.00
915 A210 1k Walomo 1.50 1.50
Nos. 912-915 (4) 3.65 3.65

Queen Elizabeth II and Prince Philip, 50th Wedding Anniv. — A211

#916, Princess Anne, polo players. #917, Queen up close. #918, Prince in riding attire. #919, Queen, another person riding horses. #920, Grandsons riding horses, Prince waving. #921, Queen waving, riding pony.

2k, Queen, Prince riding in open carriage.

1997, June 25 Litho. *Perf. 13½*
916 A211 25t multicolored .40 .40
917 A211 25t multicolored .40 .40
a. Pair, #916-917 .80 .80
918 A211 50t multicolored .75 .75
919 A211 50t multicolored .75 .75
a. Pair, #918-919 1.50 1.50
920 A211 1k multicolored 1.50 1.50
921 A211 1k multicolored 1.50 1.50
a. Pair, #920-921 3.00 3.00
Nos. 916-921 (6) 5.30 5.30

Souvenir Sheet

922 A211 2k multicolored 1.20 1.20

Souvenir Sheet

Air Niugini, First Flight, Port Moresby-Osaka — A212

Illustration reduced.

1997, July 19 Litho. *Perf. 12*
923 A212 3k multicolored 4.60 4.60

1997 Pacific Year of Coral Reef
A213

Designs: 25t, Pocillopora woodjonesi. 50t, Subergorgia mollis. 65t, Oxypora glabra. 1k, Turbinaria reinformis.

1997, Aug. 27 Litho. *Perf. 12*
924 A213 25t multicolored .40 .40
925 A213 50t multicolored .75 .75
926 A213 65t multicolored 1.00 1.00
927 A213 1k multicolored 1.50 1.50
Nos. 924-927 (4) 3.65 3.65

Flowers — A214

Designs: 10t, Thunbergia fragrans. 20t, Caesalpinia pulcherrima. 25t, Hoya. 30t, Heliconia. 50t, Amomum goliathensis.

1997, Nov. 26 Litho. *Perf. 12*
928 A214 10t multicolored .20 .20
929 A214 20t multicolored .30 .30
930 A214 25t multicolored .40 .40
931 A214 30t multicolored .45 .45
932 A214 50t multicolored .75 .75
Nos. 928-932 (5) 2.10 2.10

Birds
A215

Designs: 25t, Tyto tenebricosa. 50t, Aepypodius afrakiamus. 65t, Accipiter poliocephalus. 1k, Zonerodius heliosylus.

1998, Jan. 28 Litho. *Perf. 12*
933 A215 25t multicolored .40 .40
934 A215 50t multicolored .75 .75
935 A215 65t multicolored 1.00 1.00
936 A215 1k multicolored 1.50 1.50
Nos. 933-936 (4) 3.65 3.65

Diana, Princess of Wales (1961-97)
Common Design Type

Designs: a, In beige colored dress. b, In violet dress with lace collar. c, Wearing plaid jacket. d, Holding flowers.

1998, Apr. 29 Litho. *Perf. 14½x14*
937 CD355 1k Sheet of 4, #a.-d. 7.00 7.00

No. 937 sold for 4k + 50t with surtax from international sales being donated to the Princess Diana Memorial fund and surtax from national sales being donated to designated local charity.

Mother Teresa (1910-97)
A216

1998, Apr. 29 *Perf. 14½*
938 A216 65t With child 1.00 1.00
939 A216 1k shown 1.50 1.50
a. Pair, #938-939 2.50 2.50

No. 887 Surcharged

1998, May 28 Litho. *Perf. 14*
939B A201 25t on 65t multi .30 .30

Moths
A217

25t, Daphnis hypothous pallescens. 50t, Theretra polistratus. 65t, Psilogramma casurina. 1k, Meganoton hyloicoides.

1998, June 17 Litho. *Perf. 14*
940 A217 25t multicolored .40 .40
941 A217 50t multicolored .75 .75
942 A217 65t multicolored 1.00 1.00
943 A217 1k multicolored 1.50 1.50
Nos. 940-943 (4) 3.65 3.65

A218

A219

First Orchid Spectacular '98: 25t, Coelogyne fragrans. 50t, Den. cuthbertsonii. 65t, Den. vexillarius. 1k, Den. finisterrae.

1998, Sept. 15 Litho. *Perf. 14*
944 A218 25t multicolored .40 .40
945 A218 50t multicolored .75 .75
946 A218 65t multicolored 1.00 1.00
947 A218 1k multicolored 1.50 1.50
Nos. 944-947 (4) 3.65 3.65

1998, Oct. 5 Litho. *Perf. 14*

Sea Kayaking World Cup, Manus Island: 25t, Couple in kayak. 50t, Competitor running through Loniu Caves. 65t, Man standing in boat with sail, man seated in kayak. 1k, Competitor in kayak, bird of paradise silhouette.

948 A219 25t multicolored .40 .40
949 A219 50t multicolored .75 .75
950 A219 65t multicolored 1.00 1.00
951 A219 1k multicolored 1.50 1.50
Nos. 948-951 (4) 3.65 3.65

1998 Commonwealth Games, Kuala Lumpur — A220

1998, Sept. 30 Litho. *Perf. 14*
952 A220 25t Weight lifting .25 .25
953 A220 50t Lawn bowls .45 .45
954 A220 65t Rugby .60 .60
955 A220 1k Squash .95 .95
Nos. 952-955 (4) 2.25 2.25

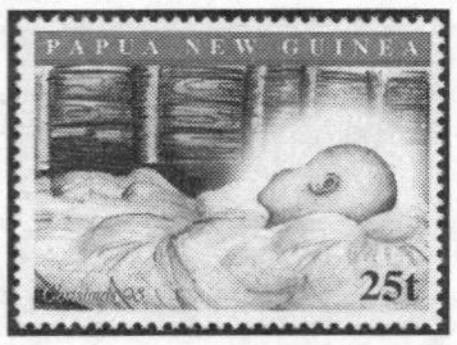

Christmas
A221

Designs: 25t, Infant in manger. 50t, Mother breastfeeding infant. 65t, "Wise men" in traditional masks, headdresses looking at infant. 1k, Map of Papua New Guinea.

1998, Nov. 18 Litho. *Perf. 14*
956 A221 25t multicolored .20 .20
957 A221 50t multicolored .40 .40
958 A221 65t multicolored .55 .55
959 A221 1k multicolored .85 .85
Nos. 956-959 (4) 2.00 2.00

Australia '99, World Stamp Expo — A222

Ships: 25t, "Boudeuse," 1768. 50t, "Neva," 1876. 65t, "Merrir England," 1889. 1k, "Samoa," 1884.

#964: a, 5t, Rattlesnake, 1849. b, 10t, Swallow, 1767. c, 15t, Roebeck, 1700. d, 20t, Blanche, 1872. e, 30t, Vitiaz, 1871. f, 40t, San Pedrico and Eabre, 1606. g, 60t, Jorge de Menesis, 1526. h, 1.20k, L'Astrolabe, 1827.

1999, Mar. 17
960 A222 25t multicolored .25 .25
961 A222 50t multicolored .50 .50
962 A222 65t multicolored .70 .70
963 A222 1k multicolored 1.00 1.00
Nos. 960-963 (4) 2.45 2.45

Sheet of 8
964 A222 #a.-h. 3.00 3.00

No. 964a is incorrectly inscribed "Simpson Blanche '1872."

IBRA '99, World Philatelic Exhibition, Nuremberg — A223

Exhibition emblem and: a, German New Guinea #17. b, German New Guinea #1, #2.

1999 Litho. *Perf. 14*
965 A223 1k Pair, #a.-b. 1.50 1.50

Millennium
A224

Map and: 25t, Stopwatch, computer keyboard. 50t, Concentric circles. 65t, Internet page, computer user. 1k, Computers, satellite dish.

1999 Litho. *Perf. 12¾*
966 A224 25t multicolored .20 .20
967 A224 50t multicolored .35 .35
968 A224 65t multicolored .50 .50
969 A224 1k multicolored .75 .75
Nos. 966-969 (4) 1.80 1.80

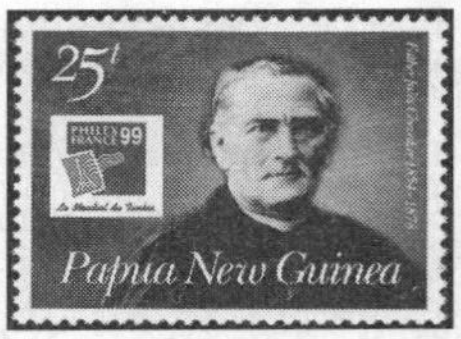

PhilexFrance '99 — A225

Frenchmen with historical ties to Papua New Guinea: 25t, Father Jules Chevalier. 50t, Bishop Alain-Marie. 65t, Chevalier D'Entrecasteaux. 1k, Count de Bougainville.

1999, Mar. 2 Litho. *Perf. 12¾*
970 A225 25t multi .20 .20
971 A225 50t multi .35 .35
972 A225 65t multi .45 .45
973 A225 1k multi .70 .70
Nos. 970-973 (4) 1.70 1.70

Hiri Moale Festival
A226

Designs: 25t, Clay pots, native. 50t, Hanenamo, native. 65t, Lakatoi, native. #977, 1k, Sorcerer, native.

No. 978: a, Sorcerer. b, Clay pots. c, Lakatoi.

1999, Sept. 8 *Perf. 12¾*
974 A226 25t multi .20 .20
975 A226 50t multi .35 .35
976 A226 65t multi .45 .45
977 A226 1k multi .70 .70
Nos. 974-977 (4) 1.70 1.70

Souvenir Sheet
978 A226 1k Sheet of 3, #a.-c. 2.10 2.10

Souvenir Sheet

Year of the Rabbit (in 1999) — A227

Color of rabbit: a, Gray. b, Tan. c, White. d, Pink.

Illustration reduced.

2000, Apr. 21 Litho. *Perf. 12¾*
979 A227 65t Sheet of 4, #a-d 1.60 1.60

Queen Mother, 100th Birthday
A228

Various photos. Color of frame: 25t, Yellow. 50t, Lilac. 65t, Green. 1k, Dull orange.

2000, Aug. 4 *Perf. 14*
980-983 A228 Set of 4 1.75 1.75

Shells
A229

Designs: 25t, Turbo petholatus. 50t, Charonia tritonis. 65t, Cassis cornuta. 1k, Ovula ovum.

2000, Feb. 23 Litho. *Perf. 14*
984-987 A229 Set of 4 1.75 1.75

Independence, 25th Anniv. — A230

Designs: 25t, Shell. 50t, Bird of Paradise. 65t, Ring. 1k, Coat of arms. Illustration reduced.

2000, June 21 *Perf. 14*

Stamps with se-tenant label

988-991 A230	Set of 4	1.75	1.75
991a	Souvenir sheet, #988-991, no labels	1.75	1.75

Strips with two stamps alternating with two different labels exist for Nos. 989 and 990.

2000 Summer Olympics, Sydney A231

Designs: 25t, Running. 50t, Swimming. 65t, Boxing. 1k, Weight lifting.

2000, July 12

992-995 A231	Set of 4	1.75	1.75

Souvenir Sheet

Olymphilex 2000, Sydney — A232

2000, July 12 *Perf. 14¼*

996 A232	3k multi	2.40	2.40

Sold for 3.50k.

Birds A233

Designs: 35t, Comb-crested jacana. 70t, Masked lapwing. 90t, White ibis. 1.40k, Black-tailed godwit.

2001, Mar. 21 Litho. *Perf. 14*

997-1000 A233	Set of 4	2.00	2.00

Mission Aviation Fellowship, 50th Anniv. in Papua New Guinea — A234

Designs: 35t, Cessna 170, pig, bird, Bibles. 70t, Harry Hartwig (1916-51), Auster Autocar. 90t, Pilot and Cessna 260. 1.40k, Twin Otter and plane mechanics.

2001, Oct. 17 *Perf. 13¼x13¾*

1001-1004 A234	Set of 4	2.00	2.00

Provincial Flags A236

2001, Dec. 12 Litho. *Perf. 14*

1013 A236	10t Enga	.20	.20
1014 A236	15t Simbu	.20	.20
1015 A236	20t Manus	.20	.20
1016 A236	50t Central	.25	.25
1017 A236	2k New Ireland	1.00	1.00
1018 A236	5k Sandaun	2.50	2.50
	Nos. 1013-1018 (6)	4.35	4.35

Reign Of Queen Elizabeth II, 50th Anniv. Issue

Common Design Type

Designs: Nos. 1019, 1023a, 1.25k, Princess Elizabeth with Queen Mother and Princess Margaret, 1941. Nos. 1020, 1023b, 1.45k, Wearing tiara, 1975. Nos. 1021, 1023c, 2k, With Princes Philip and Charles, 1951. Nos. 1022, 1023d, 2.65k, Wearing red hat. No. 1023e, 5k, 1955 portrait by Annigoni (38x50mm).

Perf. 14¼x14½, 13¾ (#1023e)

2002, Feb. 6 Litho. Wmk. 373

With Gold Frames

1019-1022 CD360	Set of 4	4.00	4.00

Souvenir Sheet

Without Gold Frames

1023 CD360	Sheet of 5, #a-e	6.75	6.75

AIR POST STAMPS

Regular Issue of 1916 Overprinted

AIR MAIL

1929 Wmk. 74 *Perf. 14*

C1 A3	3p blue grn & dk gray	1.25	6.00
b.	Vert. pair, one without ovpt.	3,000.	
c.	Horiz. pair, one without ovpt.	3,000.	
d.	3p blue grn & sepia blk	50.00	62.50
e.	Overprint on back, vert.	2,500.	

No. C1 exists on white and on yellowish paper, No. C1d on yellowish paper only.

Regular Issues of 1916-23 Overprinted in Red

1930, Sept. 15 Wmk. 74

C2 A3	3p blue grn & blk	1.00	5.00
a.	Yellowish paper	1,500.	2,500.
b.	Double overprint	1,400.	
C3 A3	6p violet & dull vio	5.00	7.50
a.	Yellowish paper	4.00	10.00
C4 A3	1sh ol green & ol brn	5.00	12.00
a.	Inverted overprint	4,000.	
b.	Yellowish paper	12.50	35.00
	Nos. C2-C4 (3)	11.00	24.50

Port Moresby AP1

Unwmk.

1938, Sept. 6 Engr. *Perf. 11*

C5 AP1	2p carmine	2.25	1.40
C6 AP1	3p ultra	2.25	1.40
C7 AP1	5p dark green	2.25	2.00
C8 AP1	8p red brown	6.25	8.50
C9 AP1	1sh violet	17.00	9.00
	Nos. C5-C9 (5)	30.00	22.30
	Set, never hinged	45.00	

Papua as a British possession, 50th anniv.

Papuans Poling Rafts — AP2

1939-41

C10 AP2	2p carmine	3.00	3.50
C11 AP2	3p ultra	3.00	6.00
C12 AP2	5p dark green	3.75	1.40
C13 AP2	8p red brown	6.75	2.25
C14 AP2	1sh violet	7.50	5.00
C15 AP2	1sh6p lt olive ('41)	22.50	25.00
	Nos. C10-C15 (6)	46.50	43.15
	Set, never hinged	67.50	

POSTAGE DUE STAMPS

Catalogue values for unused stamps in this section are for Never Hinged items.

Nos. 128, 122, 129, 139 and 125 Surcharged in Black, Blue, Red or Orange

1960 Unwmk. Engr. *Perf. 14*

J1 A24	1p on 6½p	7.00	7.00
J2 A23	3p on ½p (Bl)	8.25	5.00
a.	Double surcharge	600.00	
J3 A24	6p on 7½p (R)	25.00	12.00
a.	Double surcharge	600.00	
J4 A23	1sh3p on 3½p (O)	9.50	7.50
J5 A23	3sh on 2½p	25.00	15.00
	Nos. J1-J5 (5)	74.75	46.50

No. 129 Surcharged with New Value in Red

POSTAL CHARGES

6d.

IXIXIXIXIX

J6 A24	6p on 7½p	675.	375.
a.	Double surcharge	3,000.	1,750.

Surcharge forgeries exist.

D1

Perf. 13½x14

1960, June 2 Litho. Wmk. 228

J7 D1	1p orange	.70	.55
J8 D1	3p ocher	.75	.55
J9 D1	6p light ultra	.80	.30
J10 D1	9p vermilion	.80	1.25
J11 D1	1sh emerald	.80	.40
J12 D1	1sh3p bright violet	1.10	1.50
J13 D1	1sh6p light blue	5.00	4.50
J14 D1	3sh yellow	5.00	1.00
	Nos. J7-J14 (8)	14.95	10.05

OFFICIAL STAMPS

Nos. 60-63, 66-71, 92-93 Overprinted

1931 Wmk. 74 *Perf. 14½*

O1 A3	½p #60	.65	2.25
O2 A3	1p #61	.65	2.75
O3 A3	1½p #62	2.25	6.50
O4 A3	2p #63	2.75	8.25
O5 A3	3p #66	3.00	10.00
O6 A3	4p #67	3.00	10.00
O7 A3	5p #68	4.50	14.00
O8 A3	6p #69	5.00	10.00
O9 A3	1sh #70	6.50	14.00
O10 A3	2sh6p #71	27.50	52.50

1932 Wmk. 228 *Perf. 11½*

O11 A3	9p #92	25.00	50.00
O12 A3	1sh3p #93	25.00	52.50
	Nos. O1-O12 (12)	105.80	232.75

PARAGUAY

ˈpar-ə-ˌgwī

LOCATION — South America, bounded by Bolivia, Brazil and Argentina
GOVT. — Republic
AREA — 157,042 sq. mi.
POP. — 5,434,095 (1999 est.)
CAPITAL — Asuncion

10 Reales = 100 Centavos = 1 Peso
100 Centimos = 1 Guarani (1944)

Catalogue values for unused stamps in this country are for Never Hinged items, beginning with Scott 430 in the regular postage section, Scott B11 in the semi-postal section, and Scott C154 in the airpost section.

Watermarks

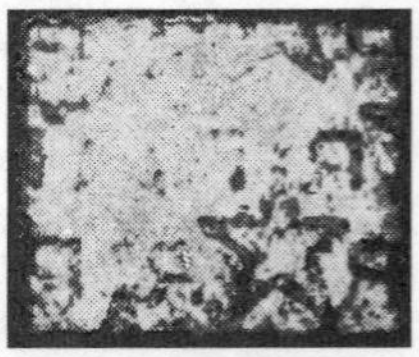

Wmk. 319 - Stars and R P Multiple

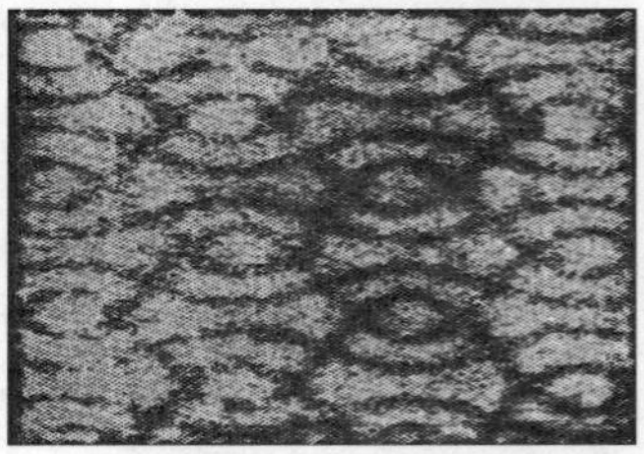

Wmk. 320 - Interlacing Lines

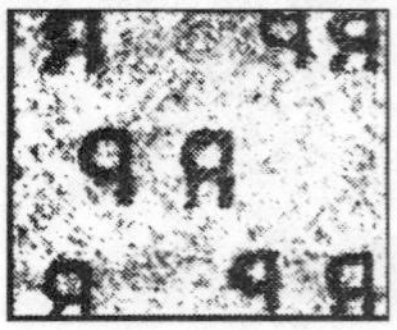

Wmk. 347 - RP Multiple

Vigilant Lion Supporting Liberty Cap

A1 A2

A3

Unwmk.

1870, Aug. 1 Litho. *Imperf.*

No.	Type	Description	Unused	Used
1	A1	1r rose	4.00	*8.00*
2	A2	2r blue	85.00	*100.00*
3	A3	3r black	175.00	*200.00*
		Nos. 1-3 (3)	264.00	*308.00*

Unofficial reprints of 2r in blue and other colors are on thicker paper than originals. They show a colored dot in upper part of "S" of "DOS" in upper right corner.

For surcharges see Nos. 4-9, 19.

Handstamp Surcharged

1878 Black Surcharge

No.	Type	Description	Unused	Used
4	A1	5c on 1r rose	75.00	*100.00*
5	A2	5c on 2r blue	325.00	300.00
5E	A3	5c on 3r black	450.00	450.00
		Nos. 4-5E (3)	850.00	850.00

Blue Surcharge

No.	Type	Description	Unused	Used
5F	A1	5c on 1r rose	75.00	*100.00*
5H	A2	5c on 2r blue	*1,000.*	*1,000.*
6	A3	5c on 3r black	425.00	425.00
		Nos. 5F-6 (3)	*2,500.*	*1,525.*

The surcharge may be found inverted, double, sideways and omitted.

The originals are surcharged in dull black or dull blue. The reprints are in intense black and bright blue. The reprint surcharges are over-inked and show numerous breaks in the handstamp.

Handstamp Surcharged

Black Surcharge

No.	Type	Description	Unused	Used
7	A2	5c on 2r blue	500.00	425.00
8	A3	5c on 3r black	425.00	425.00

Blue Surcharge

No.	Type	Description	Unused	Used
9	A3	5c on 3r black	250.00	250.00
a.		Dbl. surch., large & small "5"	—	
		Nos. 7-9 (3)	1,175.	1,100.

The surcharge on Nos. 7, 8 and 9 is usually placed sideways. It may be found double or inverted on Nos. 8 and 9.

Nos. 4 to 9 have been extensively counterfeited.

Two examples recorded of No. 9a, one without gum, the other with full but disturbed original gum.

A4 A4a

1879 Litho. *Perf. 12½*
Thin Paper

No.	Type	Description	Unused	Used
10	A4	5r orange	.60	
11	A4	10r red brown	.65	
a.		Imperf.		
b.		Horiz. pair, imperf. vert.	40.00	

Nos. 10 and 11 were never placed in use.

For surcharges see Nos. 17-18.

1879-81 Thin Paper

No.	Type	Description	Unused	Used
12	A4a	5c orange brown	2.50	2.00
13	A4a	10c blue grn ('81)	3.50	3.00
a.		Imperf., pair	10.00	*12.00*

Reprints of Nos. 10-13 are imperf., perf. 11½, 12, 12½ or 14. They have yellowish gum and the 10c is deep green.

A5 A6

A7

1881, Aug. Litho. *Perf. 11½-13½*

No.	Type	Description	Unused	Used
14	A5	1c blue	.80	.70
a.		Imperf., pair	—	
b.		Horiz. pair, imperf. btwn.	—	
15	A6	2c rose red	.80	*.70*
a.		2c dull orange red	1.00	.90
b.		Imperf., pair	—	
c.		Horiz. pair, imperf. vert.	25.00	25.00
d.		Vert. pair, imperf. horiz.	25.00	25.00
16	A7	4c brown	.80	*.70*
a.		Imperf., pair	—	
b.		Horiz. pair, imperf. vert.	25.00	25.00
c.		Vert. pair, imperf. horiz.	25.00	25.00

No. 11 Surcharged

Handstamped in Black or Gray

1881, July *Perf. 12½*

No.	Type	Description	Unused	Used
17	A4	1c on 10c blue grn	10.00	9.00
18	A4	2c on 10c blue grn	10.00	9.00

Gray handstamps sell for much more than black.

No. 1 Surcharged

1884, May 8 Handstamped *Imperf.*

No.	Type	Description	Unused	Used
19	A1	1c on 1r rose	4.50	4.00

The surcharges on Nos. 17-19 exist double, inverted and in pairs with one omitted. Counterfeits exist.

Seal of the Treasury
A11 A12

1884, Aug. 3 Litho. *Perf. 11½, 12½*

No.	Type	Description	Unused	Used
20	A11	1c green	.70	.65
21	A11	2c rose pink	.70	.65
22	A11	5c pale blue, *yellowish*	.70	.65
		Nos. 20-22 (3)	2.10	1.95

Shades exist.

For overprints see Nos. O1, O8, O15.

Imperf., Pairs

No.	Type	Description	Unused	Used
20a	A11	1c green	12.50	
21a	A11	2c rose red	16.00	
22a	A11	5c blue	16.00	
		Nos. 20a-22a (3)	44.50	

Perf. 11½, 11½x12, 12½x11½

1887 Typo.

No.	Type	Description	Unused	Used
23	A12	1c green	.25	.20
24	A12	2c rose	.25	.20
25	A12	5c blue	.35	.30
26	A12	7c brown	.45	.40
27	A12	10c lilac	.40	.30
28	A12	15c orange	.40	.30
29	A12	20c pink	.40	.30
		Nos. 23-29 (7)	2.50	2.00

See #42-45. For surcharges & overprints see #46, 49-50, 71-72, 167-170A, O20-O41, O49.

Symbols of Liberty from Coat of Arms — A13

1889, Feb. Litho. *Perf. 11½*

No.	Type	Description	Unused	Used
30	A13	15c red violet	2.50	2.00
a.		Imperf., pair	10.00	8.00

For overprints see Nos. O16-O19.

Overprint Handstamped in Violet

1892, Oct. 12 *Perf. 12x12½*

No.	Type	Description	Unused	Used
31	A15	10c violet blue	7.00	3.50

Discovery of America by Columbus, 400th anniversary. Overprint reads: "1492 / 12 DE OCTUBRE / 1892." Sold only on day of issue.

Juan G. González — A15

1c, Cirilo A. Rivarola. 2c, Salvador Jovellanos. 4c, Juan B. Gil. 5c, Higinio Uriarte. 10c, Cándido Bareiro. 14c, Gen. Bernardino Caballero. 20c, Gen. Patricio Escobar.

1892-96 Litho. *Perf. 12x12½*

No.	Type	Description	Unused	Used
32	A15	1c gray (centavos)	.20	.20
33	A15	1c gray (centavo) ('96)	.20	.20
34	A15	2c green	.20	.20
a.		Chalky paper ('96)	.20	.20
35	A15	4c carmine	.20	.20
a.		Chalky paper ('96)	.20	.20
36	A15	5c violet ('93)	.20	.20
a.		Chalky paper ('96)	.20	.20
37	A15	10c vio bl (punched) ('93)	.20	.20
		Unpunched ('96)	4.00	
38	A15	10c dull blue ('96)	.20	.20
39	A15	14c yellow brown	.45	.40
40	A15	20c red ('93)	.65	.40
41	A15	30c light green	1.00	.65
		Nos. 32-41 (10)	3.50	2.85

The 10c violet blue (No. 37) was, until 1896, issued punched with a circular hole in order to prevent it being fraudulently overprinted as No. 31.

Nos. 33 and 38 are on chalky paper.

For surcharge see No. 70.

Seal Type of 1887

1892 Typo.

No.	Type	Description	Unused	Used
42	A12	40c slate blue	1.75	.90
43	A12	60c yellow	.75	.40
44	A12	80c light blue	.65	.40
45	A12	1p olive green	.65	.40
		Nos. 42-45 (4)	3.80	2.10

No. 46

Nos. 47-48

1895, Aug. 1 *Perf. 11½x12*

No.	Type	Description	Unused	Used
46	A12	5c on 7c brown, #26	.40	.30

Telegraph Stamps Surcharged

1896, Apr. Engr. *Perf. 11½*
Denomination in Black

No.	Type	Description	Unused	Used
47		5c on 2c brown & gray	.50	.40
a.		Inverted surcharge	10.00	10.00
48		5c on 4c yellow & gray	.50	.40
a.		Inverted surcharge	7.50	7.50

Nos. 28, 42 Surcharged

1898-99 Typo.

No.	Type	Description	Unused	Used
49	A12	10c on 15c org ('99)	.45	.35
a.		Inverted surcharge	14.00	14.00
b.		Double surcharge	9.00	9.00
50	A12	10c on 40c slate bl	.20	.20

Surcharge on No. 49 has small "c."

Telegraph Stamps Surcharged

1900, May 14 Engr. *Perf. 11½*

50A		5c on 30c grn, gray & blk	1.25	.90
50B		10c on 50c dl vio, gray & blk	3.00	2.00

The basic telegraph stamps are like those used for Nos. 47-48, but the surcharges on Nos. 50A-50B consist of "5 5" and "10 10" above a blackout rectangle covering the engraved denominations.

A 40c red, bluish gray and black telegraph stamp (basic type of A24) was used provisionally in August, 1900, for postage. Value, postally used, $5.

Seal of the Treasury
A25

J. B. Egusquiza
A26

1900, Sept. Engr. *Perf. 11½, 12*

51	A25	2c gray	.20	.20
52	A25	3c orange brown	.20	.20
53	A25	5c dark green	.20	.20
54	A25	8c dark brown	.20	.20
55	A25	10c carmine rose	.20	.20
56	A25	24c deep blue	.30	.20
		Nos. 51-56 (6)	1.30	1.20

See Nos. 57-67. For surcharges see Nos. 69, 74, 76, 156-157.

1901, Apr. Litho. *Perf. 11½*

Small Figures

57	A25	2c rose	.20	.20
58	A25	5c violet brown	.20	.20
59	A25	40c blue	.70	.25
		Nos. 57-59 (3)	1.10	.65

1901-02

Larger Figures

60	A25	1c gray green ('02)	.20	.20
61	A25	2c gray	.20	.20
a.		Half used as 1c on cover		10.00
62	A25	4c pale blue	.20	.20
63	A25	5c violet	.20	.20
64	A25	8c gray brown ('02)	.20	.20
65	A25	10c rose red ('02)	.20	.20
66	A25	28c orange ('02)	.30	.20
67	A25	40c blue	.30	.20
		Nos. 60-67 (8)	1.80	1.60

1901, Sept. 24 Typo. *Perf. 12x12½*

Chalky Paper

68	A26	1p slate	.30	.20

For surcharge see No. 73.

No. 56 Surcharged

1902, Aug.

Red Surcharge

69	A25	20c on 24c dp blue	.25	.20
a.		Inverted surcharge	6.25	

Counterfeit surcharges exist.

Nos. 39, 43-44 Surcharged

No. 70

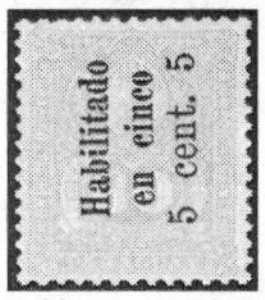

Nos. 71-72

1902, Dec. 22 *Perf. 12x12½*

70	A15	1c on 14c yellow brn	.20	.20
a.		No period after "cent"	.90	.75
b.		Comma after "cent"	.65	.50
c.		Accent over "Un"	.65	.50

1903 *Perf. 11½*

71	A12	5c on 60c yellow	.25	.20
72	A12	5c on 80c lt blue	.20	.20

Nos. 68, 64, 66 Surcharged

#73

#74

#76

1902-03 *Perf. 12*

73	A26	1c on 1p slate ('03)	.20	.20
a.		No period after "cent"	1.60	1.50

Perf. 11½

74	A25	5c on 8c gray brown	.25	.20
a.		No period after "cent"	.90	.75
b.		Double surcharge	3.50	3.00
76	A25	5c on 28c orange	.25	.20
a.		No period after "cent"	.90	.75
b.		Comma after "cent"	.40	.30
		Nos. 73-76 (3)	.70	.60

The surcharge on Nos. 73 and 74 is found reading both upward and downward.

Sentinel Lion with Right Paw Ready to Strike for "Peace and Justice"
A32 A33

Perf. 11½

1903, Feb. 28 Litho. Unwmk.

77	A32	1c gray	.20	.20
78	A32	2c blue green	.20	.20
79	A32	5c blue	.25	.20
80	A32	10c orange brown	.30	.20
81	A32	20c carmine	.30	.20
82	A32	30c deep blue	.40	.20
83	A32	60c purple	1.00	.65
		Nos. 77-83 (7)	2.65	1.85

For surcharges and overprints see Nos. 139-140, 166, O50-O56.

1903, Sept.

84	A33	1c yellow green	.20	.20
85	A33	2c red orange	.20	.20
86	A33	5c dark blue	.20	.20
87	A33	10c purple	.20	.20
88	A33	20c dark green	.65	.30
89	A33	30c ultramarine	.75	.20
90	A33	60c ocher	.80	.50
		Nos. 84-90 (7)	3.00	1.80

Nos. 84-90 exist imperf. Value for pairs, $3 each for 1c-20c, $4 for 30c, $5 for 60c.

The three-line overprint "Gobierno provisorio Ago. 1904" is fraudulent.

Sentinel Lion at Rest
A35 A36

Perf. 11½, 12, 11½x12

1905-10 Engr.

Dated "1904"

91	A35	1c orange	.20	.20
92	A35	1c vermilion ('07)	.20	.20
93	A35	1c grnsh bl ('07)	.20	.20
94	A35	2c vermilion ('06)	.20	.20
95	A35	2c olive grn ('07)	40.00	
96	A35	2c car rose ('08)	.20	.20
97	A35	5c dark blue	.20	.20
98	A35	5c slate blue ('06)	.20	.20
99	A35	5c yellow ('06)	.20	.20
100	A35	10c bister ('06)	.20	.20
101	A35	10c emerald ('07)	.20	.20
102	A35	10c dp ultra ('08)	.20	.20
103	A35	20c violet ('06)	.30	.20
104	A35	20c bister ('07)	.30	.20
105	A35	20c apple grn ('07)	.25	.20
106	A35	30c turq bl ('06)	.30	.20
107	A35	30c blue gray ('07)	.30	.20
108	A35	30c dull lilac ('08)	.40	.20
109	A35	60c chocolate ('07)	.25	.20
110	A35	60c org brn ('07)	3.50	1.25
111	A35	60c salmon pink ('10)	3.50	1.25
		Nos. 91-111 (21)	51.30	
		Nos. 91-94,96-111 (20)		6.10

All but Nos. 92 and 104 exist imperf. Value for pair, $10 each, except No. 95 at $35 and Nos. 109-111 at $15 each pair.

For surcharges and overprints see Nos. 129-130, 146-155, 174-190, 266.

1904, Aug. Litho. *Perf. 11½*

112	A36	10c light blue	.25	.20
a.		Imperf., pair	3.00	

No. 112 Surcharged in Black

1904, Dec.

113	A36	30c on 10c light blue	.40	.25

Peace between a successful revolutionary party and the government previously in power.

Governmental Palace, Asunción — A37

Dated "1904"

1906-10 Engr. *Perf. 11½, 12*

Center in Black

114	A37	1p bright rose	1.25	.75
115	A37	1p brown org ('07)	.50	.25
116	A37	1p ol gray ('07)	.50	.25
117	A37	2p turquoise ('07)	.25	.20
118	A37	2p lake ('09)	.25	.20
119	A37	2p brn org ('10)	.30	.20
120	A37	5p red ('07)	.75	.50
121	A37	5p ol grn ('10)	.75	.50
122	A37	5p dull bl ('10)	.75	.50
123	A37	10p brown org ('07)	.70	.50
124	A37	10p dp blue ('10)	.70	.50
125	A37	10p choc ('10)	.75	.50
126	A37	20p olive grn ('07)	1.75	1.60
127	A37	20p violet ('10)	1.75	1.60
128	A37	20p yellow ('10)	1.75	1.60
		Nos. 114-128 (15)	12.70	9.65

Nos. 94 and 95 Surcharged

1907

129	A35	5c on 2c vermilion	.20	.20
a.		"5" omitted	1.00	1.00
b.		Inverted surcharge	3.50	3.50
c.		Double surcharge		
d.		Double surcharge, one invtd.	1.00	1.00
e.		Double surcharge, both invtd.	6.00	6.00
130	A35	5c on 2c olive grn	.25	.20
a.		"5" omitted	1.00	1.00
b.		Inverted surcharge	1.00	1.00
c.		Double surcharge	2.00	2.00
d.		Bar omitted	2.00	2.00

Official Stamps of 1906-08 Surcharged

1908

131	O17	5c on 10c bister	.20	.20
a.		Double surcharge	3.00	3.00
132	O17	5c on 10c violet	.20	.20
a.		Inverted surcharge	2.25	2.25
133	O17	5c on 20c emerald	.20	.20
134	O17	5c on 20c violet	.20	.20
a.		Inverted surcharge	2.25	2.25
135	O17	5c on 30c slate bl	.65	.65
136	O17	5c on 30c turq bl	.65	.65
a.		Inverted surcharge		
b.		Double surcharge	6.00	6.00
137	O17	5c on 60c choc	.20	.20
a.		Double surcharge	6.00	6.00
138	O17	5c on 60c red brown	.20	.20
a.		Inverted surcharge	.40	.40
		Nos. 131-138 (8)	2.50	2.50

Same Surcharge on Official Stamps of 1903

139	A32	5c on 30c dp blue	1.25	1.10
140	A32	5c on 60c purple	.50	.30
a.		Double surcharge	2.50	2.50

Official Stamps of 1906-08 Overprinted

141	O17	5c deep blue	.20	.20
a.		Inverted overprint	1.50	1.50
b.		Bar omitted	4.50	4.50
c.		Double overprint	2.00	2.00
142	O17	5c slate blue	.25	.20
a.		Inverted overprint	2.00	2.00
b.		Double overprint	1.75	1.75
c.		Bar omitted	4.50	4.50
143	O17	5c greenish blue	.20	.20
a.		Inverted overprint	1.25	1.25
b.		Bar omitted	3.75	3.75
144	O18	1p brown org & blk	.25	.25
a.		Double overprint	1.00	1.00
b.		Double overprint, one inverted	1.25	1.25
c.		Triple overprint, two inverted	2.25	2.25
145	O18	1p brt rose & blk	.45	.35
a.		Bar omitted		
		Nos. 141-145 (5)	1.35	1.20

Regular Issues of 1906-08 Surcharged

1908

146	A35	5c on 1c grnsh bl	.20	.20
a.		Inverted surcharge	1.00	1.00
b.		Double surcharge	1.50	1.50
c.		"5" omitted	1.50	1.50
147	A35	5c on 2c car rose	.20	.20
a.		Inverted surcharge	1.75	1.75
b.		"5" omitted	2.00	2.00
c.		Double surcharge	3.50	3.50
d.		Double surcharge, one invtd.		
148	A35	5c on 60c org brn	.20	.20
a.		Inverted surcharge	2.50	2.50
b.		"5" omitted	1.00	1.00
149	A35	5c on 60c sal pink	.20	.20
a.		Double surcharge	.50	.50
b.		Double surcharge, one invtd.	3.50	3.50
150	A35	5c on 60c choc	.20	.20
a.		Inverted surcharge	5.00	5.00
151	A35	20c on 1c grnsh bl	.20	.20
a.		Inverted surcharge	1.50	1.50
152	A35	20c on 2c ver	6.00	5.00
153	A35	20c on 2c car rose	3.50	3.00
a.		Inverted surcharge	12.50	
154	A35	20c on 30c dl lil	.20	.20
a.		Inverted surcharge	1.50	1.50
b.		Double surcharge		
155	A35	20c on 30c turq bl	1.50	1.50
		Nos. 146-155 (10)	12.40	10.90

Same Surcharge on Regular Issue of 1901-02

156	A25	5c on 28c org	1.25	1.10
157	A25	5c on 40c dk bl	.40	.30
a.		Inverted surcharge	4.00	4.00

Same Surcharge on Official Stamps of 1908

158	O17	5c on 10c emer	.20	.20
a.		Double surcharge	7.00	
159	O17	5c on 10c red lil	.20	.20
a.		Double surcharge	2.00	2.00
b.		"5" omitted	1.50	1.50
160	O17	5c on 20c bis	.40	.30
a.		Double surcharge	1.25	1.25
161	O17	5c on 20c sal pink	.40	.30
a.		"5" omitted	1.75	1.75
162	O17	5c on 30c bl gray	.20	.20
163	O17	5c on 30c yel	.20	.20
a.		"5" omitted	1.50	1.50
b.		Inverted surcharge	1.25	1.25
164	O17	5c on 60c org brn	.20	.20
a.		Double surcharge	6.00	6.00
165	O17	5c on 60c dp ultra	.20	.20
a.		Inverted surcharge	2.50	2.50
b.		"5" omitted	1.50	
		Nos. 158-165 (8)	2.00	1.80

Same Surcharge on No. O52

166	A32	20c on 5c blue	1.25	1.00
a.		Inverted surcharge	3.00	3.75

Surcharged

1908

On Stamp of 1887

167 A12 20c on 2c car 2.50 2.00
a. Inverted surcharge 7.50

On Official Stamps of 1892

168 A12 5c on 15c org 2.50 1.75
169 A12 5c on 20c pink 40.00 32.50
170 A12 5c on 50c gray 17.50 12.50
170A A12 20c on 5c blue 1.50 1.25
b. Inverted surcharge 8.75 8.75
Nos. 167-170A (5) 64.00 50.00

Nos. 151, 152, 153, 155, 167, 170A, while duly authorized, all appear to have been sold to a single individual, and although they paid postage, it is doubtful whether they can be considered as ever having been placed on sale to the public.

Nos. O82-O84 Surcharged (Date in Red)

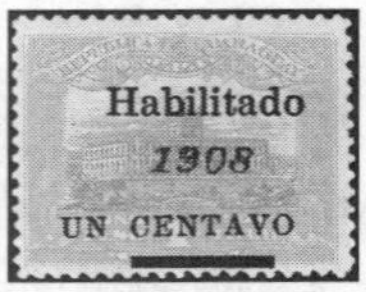

1908-09

171 O18 1c on 1p brt rose & blk .20 .20
172 O18 1c on 1p lake & blk .20 .20
173 O18 1c on 1p brn org & blk ('09) .90 .60
Nos. 171-173 (3) 1.30 1.00

Varieties of surcharge on Nos. 171-173 include: "CETTAVO"; date omitted, double or inverted; third line double or omitted.

Types of 1905-1910 Overprinted

1908, Mar. 5 ***Perf. 11½***

174 A35 1c emerald .20 .20
175 A35 5c yellow .20 .20
176 A35 10c lilac brown .20 .20
177 A35 20c yellow orange .20 .20
178 A35 30c red .25 .20
179 A35 60c magenta .20 .20
180 A37 1p light blue .20 .20
Nos. 174-180 (7) 1.45 1.40

Overprinted

1909, Sept.

181 A35 1c blue gray .20 .20
182 A35 1c scarlet .20 .20
183 A35 5c dark green .20 .20
184 A35 5c deep orange .20 .20
185 A35 10c rose .20 .20
186 A35 10c bister brown .20 .20
187 A35 20c yellow .20 .20
188 A35 20c violet .20 .20
189 A35 30c orange brown .30 .20
190 A35 30c dull blue .30 .20
Nos. 181-190 (10) 2.20 2.00

Counterfeits exist.

Coat of Arms above Numeral of Value A38

"The Republic" A39

1910-21 **Litho.** ***Perf. 11½***

191 A38 1c gray black .20 .20
192 A38 5c bright violet .20 .20
a. Pair, imperf. between 1.00 1.00
193 A38 5c blue grn ('19) .20 .20
194 A38 5c lt blue ('21) .20 .20
195 A38 10c yellow green .20 .20
196 A38 10c dp vio ('19) .20 .20
197 A38 10c red ('21) .20 .20
198 A38 20c red .20 .20
199 A38 50c car rose .30 .20
200 A38 75c deep blue .20 .20
a. Diag. half perforated ('11) .20 .20
Nos. 191-200 (10) 2.10 2.00

Nos. 191-200 exist imperforate.
No. 200a was authorized for use as 20c.
For surcharges see #208, 241, 261, 265.

1911 **Engr.**

201 A39 1c olive grn & blk .20 .20
202 A39 2c dk blue & blk .20 .20
203 A39 5c carmine & indigo .20 .20
204 A39 10c dp blue & brn .20 .20
205 A39 20c olive grn & ind .20 .20
206 A39 50c lilac & indigo .30 .20
207 A39 75c ol grn & red lil .30 .20
Nos. 201-207 (7) 1.60 1.40

Centenary of National Independence.
The 1c, 2c, 10c and 50c exist imperf. Value for pairs, $1.50 each.

No. 199 Surcharged

1912

208 A38 20c on 50c car rose .20 .20
a. Inverted surcharge 1.25 1.25
b. Double surcharge 1.25 1.25
c. Bar omitted 1.75 1.75

National Coat of Arms — A40

1913 **Engr.** ***Perf. 11½***

209 A40 1c gray .20 .20
210 A40 2c orange .20 .20
211 A40 5c lilac .20 .20
212 A40 10c green .20 .20
213 A40 20c dull red .20 .20
214 A40 40c rose .20 .20
215 A40 75c deep blue .20 .20
216 A40 80c yellow .20 .20
217 A40 1p light blue .20 .20
218 A40 1.25p pale blue .20 .20
219 A40 3p greenish blue .20 .20
Nos. 209-219 (11) 2.20 2.20

For surcharges see Nos. 225, 230-231, 237, 242, 253, 262-263, L3-L4.

Nos. J7-J10 Overprinted

1918

220 D2 5c yellow brown .20 .20
221 D2 10c yellow brown .20 .20
222 D2 20c yellow brown .20 .20
223 D2 40c yellow brown .20 .20

Nos. J10 and 214 Surcharged

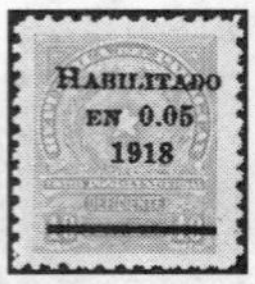

224 D2 5c on 40c yellow brn .20 .20
225 A40 30c on 40c rose .20 .20
Nos. 220-225 (6) 1.20 1.20

Nos. 220-225 exist with surcharge inverted, double and double with one inverted.
The surcharge "Habilitado-1918-5 cents 5" on the 1c gray official stamps of 1914, is bogus.

No. J11 Overprinted

1920

229 D2 1p yellow brown .20 .20
a. Inverted overprint .65 .65
e. as "g," "AABILITADO" .75 .75
f. as "g," "1929" for "1920" .75 .75
g. Overprint lines 8mm apart .20 .20

Nos. 216 and 219 Surcharged

230 A40 50c on 80c yellow .20 .20
231 A40 1.75p on 3p grnsh bl .75 .65

Same Surcharge on No. J12

232 D2 1p on 1.50p yel brn .25 .20
Nos. 229-232 (4) 1.40 1.25

Nos. 229-232 exist with various surcharge errors, including inverted, double, double inverted and double with one inverted. Those that were issued are listed.

Parliament Building A41

1920 **Litho.** ***Perf. 11½***

233 A41 50c red & black .25 .20
a. "CORRLOS" 1.50 1.50
234 A41 1p lt blue & blk .65 .30
235 A41 1.75p dk blue & blk .20 .20
236 A41 3p orange & blk 1.00 .20
Nos. 233-236 (4) 2.10 .90

50th anniv. of the Constitution.
All values exist imperforate and Nos. 233, 235 and 236 with center inverted. It is doubtful that any of these varieties were regularly issued.

No. 215 Surcharged

1920

237 A40 50c on 75c deep blue .30 .20

Nos. 200, 215 Surcharged

1921

241 A38 50c on 75c deep blue .20 .20
242 A40 50c on 75c deep blue .20 .20

A42

1922, Feb. 8 **Litho.** ***Perf. 11½***

243 A42 50c car & dk blue .20 .20
a. Imperf. pair .50
b. Center inverted 10.00 10.00
244 A42 1p dk blue & brn .20 .20
a. Imperf. pair .50
b. Center inverted 12.50 12.50

For overprints see Nos. L1-L2.

Rendezvous of Conspirators A43

1922-23

245 A43 1p deep blue .20 .20
246 A43 1p scar & dk bl ('23) .20 .20
247 A43 1p red vio & gray ('23) .20 .20
248 A43 1p org & gray ('23) .20 .20
249 A43 5p dark violet .40 .20
250 A43 5p dk bl & org brn ('23) .40 .20
251 A43 5p dl red & lt bl ('23) .40 .20
252 A43 5p emer & blk ('23) .40 .20
Nos. 245-252 (8) 2.40 1.60

National Independence.

No. 218 Surcharged "Habilitado en $1:-1924" in Red

1924

253 A40 1p on 1.25p pale blue .20 .20

This stamp was for use in Asunción. Nos. L3 to L5 were for use in the interior, as is indicated by the "C" in the surcharge.

Map of Paraguay — A44

1924 **Litho.** ***Perf. 11½***

254 A44 1p dark blue .20 .20
255 A44 2p carmine rose .20 .20
256 A44 4p light blue .20 .20
a. Perf. 12 .40 .20
Nos. 254-256 (3) .60 .60

#254-256 exist imperf. Value $3 each pair.
For surcharges and overprint see Nos. 267, C5, C15-C16, C54-C55, L7.

Gen. José E. Díaz — A45

Columbus — A46

1925-26 ***Perf. 11½, 12***

257 A45 50c red .20 .20
258 A45 1p dark blue .20 .20
259 A45 1p emerald ('26) .20 .20
Nos. 257-259 (3) .60 .60

#257-258 exist imperf. Value $1 each pair.
For overprints see Nos. L6, L8, L10.

1925 ***Perf. 11½***

260 A46 1p blue .20 .20
a. Imperf., pair 2.00

For overprint see No. L9.

Nos. 194, 214-215, J12 Surcharged in Black or Red

1926

261 A38 1c on 5c lt blue .20 .20
262 A40 7c on 40c rose .20 .20
263 A40 15c on 75c dp bl (R) .20 .20
264 D2 1.50p on 1.50p yel brn .20 .20
Nos. 261-264 (4) .80 .80

Nos. 194, 179 and 256 Surcharged "Habilitado" and New Values

1927

265 A38 2c on 5c lt blue .20 .20
266 A35 50c on 60c magenta .20 .20
a. Inverted surcharge 2.00
267 A44 1.50p on 4p lt blue .20 .20

Official Stamp of 1914 Surcharged "Habilitado" and New Value

268 O19 50c on 75c dp bl .20 .20
Nos. 265-268 (4) .80 .80

National Emblem — A47

Pedro Juan Caballero — A48

Map of Paraguay — A49

Fulgencio Yegros — A50

Ignacio Iturbe — A51

Oratory of the Virgin, Asunción — A52

Perf. 12, 11, 11½, 11x12

1927-38 Typo.

269 A47 1c lt red ('31) .20 .20
270 A47 2c org red ('30) .20 .20
271 A47 7c lilac .20 .20
272 A47 7c emerald ('29) .20 .20
273 A47 10c gray grn ('28) .20 .20
a. 10c light green ('31) .20 .20
274 A47 10c lil rose ('30) .20 .20
275 A47 10c light bl ('35) .20 .20
276 A47 20c dull bl ('28) .20 .20
277 A47 20c lil brn ('30) .20 .20
278 A47 20c lt vio ('31) .20 .20
279 A47 20c rose ('35) .20 .20
280 A47 50c ultramarine .20 .20
281 A47 50c dl red ('28) .20 .20
282 A47 50c orange ('30) .20 .20
283 A47 50c gray ('31) .20 .20
284 A47 50c brn vio ('34) .20 .20
285 A47 50c rose ('36) .20 .20
286 A47 70c ultra ('28) .20 .20
287 A48 1p emerald .20 .20
288 A48 1p org red ('30) .20 .20
289 A48 1p brn org ('34) .20 .20
290 A49 1.50p brown .20 .20
291 A49 1.50p lilac ('28) .20 .20
292 A49 1.50p rose red ('32) .20 .20
293 A50 2.50p bister .20 .20
294 A51 3p gray .20 .20
295 A51 3p rose red ('36) .20 .20
296 A51 3p brt vio ('36) .20 .20
297 A52 5p chocolate .20 .20
298 A52 5p violet ('36) .20 .20
299 A52 5p pale org ('38) .20 .20
300 A49 20p red ('29) 1.40 1.10
301 A49 20p emerald ('29) 1.40 1.10
302 A49 20p vio brn ('29) 1.40 1.10
Nos. 269-302 (34) 10.40 9.50

No. 281 is also known perf. 10½x11½.

Papermaker's watermarks are sometimes found on No. 271 ("GLORIA BOND" in double-lined circle) and No. 280 ("Extra Vencedor Bond" or "ADBANCE/M M C").

For surcharges and overprints see Nos. 312, C4, C6, C13-C14, C17-C18, C25-C32, C34-C35, L11-L30, O94-O96, O98.

Arms of Juan de Salazar de Espinosa A53

Columbus A54

1928, Aug. 15 ***Perf. 12***

303 A53 10p violet brown 1.75 1.25

Juan de Salazar de Espinosa, founder of Asunción.

A papermaker's watermark ("INDIAN BOND EXTRA STRONG S.&C") is sometimes found on Nos 303, 305-307.

1928 **Litho.**

304 A54 10p ultra .80 .50
305 A54 10p vermilion .80 .50
306 A54 10p deep red .80 .50
Nos. 304-306 (3) 2.40 1.50

For surcharge & overprint see #C33, L37.

President Rutherford B. Hayes of US and Villa Occidental — A55

1928, Nov. 20 ***Perf. 12***

307 A55 10p gray brown 5.00 2.25
308 A55 10p red brown 5.00 2.25

50th anniv. of the Hayes' Chaco decision.

Portraits of Archbishop Bogarin — A56

1930, Aug. 15

309 A56 1.50p lake 1.00 .75
310 A56 1.50p turq blue 1.00 .75
311 A56 1.50p dull vio 1.00 .75
Nos. 309-311 (3) 3.00 2.25

Archbishop Juan Sinforiano Bogarin, first archbishop of Paraguay.

For overprints see Nos. 321-322.

No. 272 Surcharged

Habilitado
en
CINCO

1930

312 A47 5c on 7c emer .20 .20

A57

1930-39 Typo. *Perf. 11½, 12*

313 A57 10p brown .50 .20
314 A57 10p brn red, *bl* ('31) .50 .20
315 A57 10p dk bl, *pink* ('32) .50 .20
316 A57 10p gray brn ('36) .40 .20
317 A57 10p gray ('37) .40 .20
318 A57 10p blue ('39) .20 .20
Nos. 313-318 (6) 2.50 1.20

1st Paraguayan postage stamp, 60th anniv.

For overprint see No. L31.

Gunboat "Humaitá" — A58

1931 ***Perf. 12***

319 A58 1.50p purple .40 .25
Nos. 319,C39-C53 (16) 6.40 6.10

Constitution, 60th anniv.

For overprint see No. L33.

View of San Bernardino — A59

1931, Aug.

320 A59 1p light green .25 .20

Founding of San Bernardino, 50th anniv.

For overprint see No. L32.

Nos. 309-310 Overprinted in Blue or Red

1931, Dec. 31

321 A56 1.50p lake (Bl) 1.00 1.00
322 A56 1.50p turq blue (R) 1.00 1.00

Map of the Gran Chaco A60

1932-35 Typo. *Perf. 12*

323 A60 1.50p deep violet .20 .20
324 A60 1.50p rose ('35) .20 .20

For overprints see Nos. L34-L36, O97.

Nos. C74-C78 Surcharged

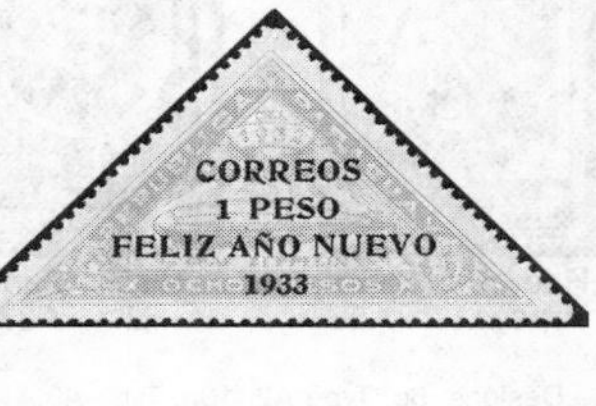

1933 **Litho.**

325 AP18 50c on 4p ultra .25 .20
326 AP18 1p on 8p red .50 .40
327 AP18 1.50p on 12p bl grn .50 .40
328 AP18 2p on 16p dk vio .50 .40
329 AP18 5p on 20p org brn 1.25 1.00
Nos. 325-329 (5) 3.00 2.40

Flag of the Race Issue

Flag with Three Crosses: Caravels of Columbus — A61

1933, Oct. 10 Litho. *Perf. 11*

330 A61 10c multicolored .20 .20
331 A61 20c multicolored .20 .20
332 A61 50c multicolored .20 .20
333 A61 1p multicolored .20 .20
334 A61 1.50p multicolored .20 .20
335 A61 2p multicolored .25 .25
336 A61 5p multicolored .50 .50
337 A61 10p multicolored .50 .50
Nos. 330-337 (8) 2.25 2.25

441st anniv. of the sailing of Christopher Columbus from the port of Palos, Aug. 3, 1492, on his first voyage to the New World.

Nos. 332, 334 and 335 exist with Maltese crosses omitted.

Monstrance A62

Arms of Asunción A63

1937, Aug. Unwmk. *Perf. 11½*

338 A62 1p dk blue, yel & red .20 .20
339 A62 3p dk blue, yel & red .20 .20
340 A62 10p dk blue, yel & red .20 .20
Nos. 338-340 (3) .60 .60

1st Natl. Eucharistic Congress, Asuncion.

1937, Aug.

341 A63 50c violet & buff .20 .20
342 A63 1p bis & lt grn .20 .20
343 A63 3p red & lt bl .20 .20
344 A63 10p car rose & buff .20 .20
345 A63 20p blue & drab .20 .20
Nos. 341-345 (5) 1.00 1.00

Founding of Asuncion, 400th anniv.

Oratory of the Virgin, Asunción — A64

Carlos Antonio Lopez — A65

José Eduvigis Diaz — A66

1938-39 Typo. *Perf. 11, 12*

346 A64 5p olive green .20 .20
347 A64 5p pale rose ('39) .25 .20
348 A64 11p violet brown .20 .20
Nos. 346-348 (3) .65 .60

Founding of Asuncion, 400th anniv.

1939 ***Perf. 12***

349 A65 2p lt ultra & pale brn .20 .20
350 A66 2p lt ultra & brn .20 .20

Reburial of ashes of Pres. Carlos Antonio Lopez (1790-1862) and Gen. José Eduvigis Diaz in the National Pantheon, Asuncion.

Pres. Patricio Escobar and Ramon Zubizarreta A67

Design: 5p, Pres. Bernardino Caballero and Senator José S. Decoud.

1939-40 Litho. ***Perf. 11½***
Heads in Black

351 A67 50c dull org ('40) .20 .20
352 A67 1p lt violet ('40) .20 .20
353 A67 2p red brown ('40) .20 .20
354 A67 5p lt ultra .25 .20
Nos. 351-354,C122-C123,O99-O104 (12) 9.40 9.30

Founding of the University of Asuncion, 50th anniv.

Varieties of this issue include inverted heads (50c, 1p, 2p); doubled heads; Caballero and Decoud heads in 50c frame: imperforates and part-perforates. Copies with inverted heads were not officially issued.

Coats of Arms — A69

Pres. Baldomir of Uruguay, Flags of Paraguay, Uruguay A70

Designs: 2p, Pres. Benavides, Peru. 3p, US Eagle and Shield. 5p, Pres. Alessandri, Chile. 6p, Pres. Vargas, Brazil. 10p, Pres. Ortiz, Argentina.

1939 Engr.; Flags Litho. ***Perf. 12***
Flags in National Colors

355 A69 50c violet blue .20 .20
356 A70 1p olive .20 .20
357 A70 2p blue green .20 .20
358 A70 3p sepia .25 .20
359 A70 5p orange .20 .20
360 A70 6p dull violet .50 .40
361 A70 10p bister brn .40 .25
Nos. 355-361,C113-C121 (16) 13.45 10.40

First Buenos Aires Peace Conference.
For overprint & surcharge see #387, B10.

Coats of Arms of New York and Asunción A76

1939, Nov. 30

362 A76 5p scarlet .20 .20
363 A76 10p deep blue .25 .20
364 A76 11p dk blue grn .35 .30
365 A76 22p olive blk .45 .40
Nos. 362-365,C124-C126 (7) 9.40 8.85

New York World's Fair.

Paraguayan Soldier — A77

Paraguayan Woman — A78

Cowboys — A79

Plowing — A80

View of Paraguay River — A81

Oxcart A82

Pasture A83

Piraretá Falls — A84

1940, Jan. 1 Photo. ***Perf. 12½***

366 A77 50c deep orange .20 .20
367 A78 1p brt red violet .20 .20
368 A79 3p bright green .20 .20
369 A80 5p chestnut .20 .20
370 A81 10p magenta .20 .20
371 A82 20p violet .40 .30
372 A83 50p cobalt blue .90 .45
373 A84 100p black 1.90 1.40
Nos. 366-373 (8) 4.20 3.15

Second Buenos Aires Peace Conference.
For surcharge see No. 386.

Map of the Americas — A85

1940, May Engr. ***Perf. 12***

374 A85 50c red orange .20 .20
375 A85 1p green .20 .20
376 A85 5p dark blue .25 .20
377 A85 10p brown .65 .50
Nos. 374-377,C127-C130 (8) 4.70 3.75

Pan American Union, 50th anniversary.

Reproduction of Type A1 — A86

Sir Rowland Hill — A87

Designs: 6p, Type A2. 10p, Type A3.

1940, Aug. 15 Photo. ***Perf. 13½***

378 A86 1p aqua & brt red vio .50 .25
379 A87 5p dp yel grn & red brn .65 .30
380 A86 6p org brn & ultra 1.50 .65
381 A86 10p ver & black 1.50 1.00
Nos. 378-381 (4) 4.15 2.20

Postage stamp centenary.

Dr. José Francia
A90 A91

1940, Sept. 20 Engr. ***Perf. 12***

382 A90 50c carmine rose .20 .20
383 A91 50c plum .20 .20
384 A90 1p bright green .20 .20
385 A91 5p deep blue .20 .20
Nos. 382-385 (4) .80 .80

Centenary of the death of Dr. Jose Francia (1766-1840), dictator of Paraguay, 1814-1840.

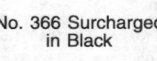

No. 366 Surcharged in Black

1940, Sept. 7 ***Perf. 12½***

386 A77 5p on 50c dp org .20 .20

In honor of Pres. Jose F. Estigarribia who died in a plane crash Sept. 7, 1940.

No. 360 Overprinted in Black

Visita al Paraguay
Agosto de 1941

1941, Aug. ***Perf. 12***

387 A70 6p multi .20 .20

Visit to Paraguay of Pres. Vargas of Brazil.

Nos. C113-C115 Overprinted "HABILITADO" and Bars in Blue or Red

1942, Jan. 17 ***Perf. 12½***

388 A69 1p multi (Bl) .20 .20
389 A69 3p multi (R) .20 .20
390 A70 5p multi (R) .20 .20
Nos. 388-390 (3) .60 .60

Coat of Arms — A92

1942-43 Litho. ***Perf. 11, 12, 11x12***

391 A92 1p light green .20 .20
392 A92 1p orange ('43) .20 .20
393 A92 7p light blue .20 .20
394 A92 7p yel brn ('43) .20 .20
Nos. 391-394 (4) .80 .80

Nos. 391-394 exist imperf.

The Indian Francisco — A93

Arms of Irala — A95

Domingo Martinez de Irala and His Vision A94

1942, Aug. 15 Engr. ***Perf. 12***

395 A93 2p green .65 .30
396 A94 5p rose .65 .30
397 A95 7p sapphire .65 .25
Nos. 395-397,C131-C133 (6) 7.95 5.85

400th anniversary of Asuncion.

Pres. Higinio Morinigo, Scenes of Industry & Agriculture A96

Christopher Columbus A97

1943, Aug. 15 ***Unwmk.***

398 A96 7p blue .20 .20

For surcharges see Nos. 404, 428.

1943, Aug. 15

399 A97 50c violet .20 .20
400 A97 1p gray brn .20 .20
401 A97 5p dark grn .45 .20
402 A97 7p brt ultra .25 .20
Nos. 399-402 (4) 1.10 .80

Discovery of America, 450th anniv.
For surcharges see Nos. 405, 429.

No. 296 Surcharged in Black

1944 ***Perf. 12, 11, 11½, 11x12***

403 A51 1c on 3p brt vio .20 .20

Nos. 398 and 402 Surcharged "1944 / 5 Centimos 5" in Red

1944 ***Perf. 12***

404 A96 5c on 7p blue .20 .20
405 A97 5c on 7p brt ultra .20 .20

Imperforates
Starting with No. 406, many Paraguayan stamps exist imperf.

Primitive Postal Service among Indians — A98

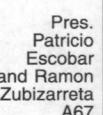

Ruins of Humaitá Church — A99

Locomotive of early Paraguayan Railroad — A100

Early Merchant Ship — A102

Marshal Francisco S. Lopez — A101

Port of Asunción — A103

Birthplace of Paraguay's Liberation — A104

Monument to Heroes of Itororó — A105

1944-45 Unwmk. Engr. *Perf. 12½*

406 A98	1c black	.20	.20
407 A99	2c copper brn ('45)	.20	.20
408 A100	5c light olive	1.00	.20
409 A101	7c light blue ('45)	.35	.25
410 A102	10c green ('45)	.45	.25
411 A103	15c dark blue ('45)	.45	.30
412 A104	50c black brown	.60	.40
413 A105	1g dk rose car ('45)	1.75	1.00
	Nos. 406-413 (8)	5.00	2.80
	Nos. 406-413,C134-C146 (21)	14.45	11.85

See #435, 437, 439, 441, C158-C162.
For surcharges see #414, 427.

No. 409 Surcharged in Red

1945

414 A101	5c on 7c light blue	.20	.20

Handshake, Map and Flags of Paraguay and Panama A106

Designs: 3c, Venezuela Flag. 5c, Colombia Flag. 2g, Peru Flag.

Engr.; Flags Litho. in Natl. Colors
1945, Aug. 15 Unwmk. *Perf. 12½*

415 A106	1c dark green	.20	.20
416 A106	3c lake	.20	.20
417 A106	5c blue blk	.20	.20
418 A106	2g brown	1.10	.75
	Nos. 415-418,C147-C153 (11)	7.00	6.65

Goodwill visits of Pres. Higinio Morinigo during 1943.

Nos. B6 to B9 Surcharged "1945" and New Value in Black

1945 Engr. *Perf. 12*

419 SP4	2c on 7p + 3p red brn	.20	.20
420 SP4	2c on 7p + 3p purple	.20	.20
421 SP4	2c on 7p + 3p car rose	.20	.20
422 SP4	2c on 7p + 3p saph	.20	.20
423 SP4	5c on 7p + 3p red brn	.20	.20
424 SP4	5c on 7p + 3p purple	.20	.20
425 SP4	5c on 7p + 3p car rose	.20	.20
426 SP4	5c on 7p + 3p saph	.20	.20

Similar Surcharge in Red on Nos. 409, 398 and 402

Perf. 12½, 12

427 A101	5c on 7c lt blue	.20	.20
428 A96	5c on 7p blue	.20	.20
429 A97	5c on 7p brt ultra	.20	.20
	Nos. 427-429 (3)	.60	.60

Nos. 427-429 exist with black surcharge.

Catalogue values for unused stamps in this section, from this point to the end of the section, are for Never Hinged items.

Coat of Arms ("U.P.U." at bottom) — A110

1946 Litho. *Perf. 11, 12, 11x12*

430 A110	5c gray	.20	.20

See Nos. 459-463, 478-480, 498-506, 525-536, 646-658.
For overprints see Nos. 464-466.

Nos. B6 to B9 Surcharged "1946" and New Value in Black

1946 *Perf. 12*

431 SP4	5c on 7p + 3p red brn	.30	.25
432 SP4	5c on 7p + 3p purple	.30	.25
433 SP4	5c on 7p + 3p car rose	.30	.25
434 SP4	5c on 7p + 3p saph	.30	.25
	Nos. 431-434 (4)	1.20	1.00

Types of 1944-45 and

First Telegraph in South America A111

Colonial Jesuit Altar — A113

Monument to Antequera A112

1946, Sept. 21 Engr. *Perf. 12½*

435 A102	1c rose car	.20	.20
436 A111	2c purple	.20	.20
437 A98	5c ultra	.20	.20
438 A112	10c org yel	.20	.20
439 A105	15c brn olive	.20	.20
440 A113	50c deep grn	.30	.20
441 A104	1g brt ultra	.65	.40
	Nos. 435-441 (7)	1.95	1.60

See Nos. C135-C138, C143.

Marshal Francisco Solano Lopez — A114

1947, May 15 *Perf. 12*

442 A114	1c purple	.20	.20
443 A114	2c org red	.20	.20
444 A114	5c green	.20	.20
445 A114	15c ultra	.20	.20
446 A114	50c dark grn	.25	.25
	Nos. 442-446,C163-C167 (10)	3.70	3.70

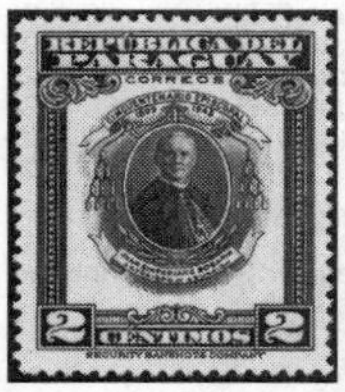

Juan Sinforiano Bogarin, Archbishop of Asunción — A115

Archbishopric Coat of Arms — A116

Projected Monument of the Sacred Heart of Jesus — A117

Vision of Projected Monument A118

1948, Jan. 6 Engr. *Perf. 12½*

447 A115	2c dark blue	.20	.20
448 A116	5c deep car	.20	.20
449 A117	10c gray blk	.20	.20
450 A118	15c green	.20	.20
	Nos. 447-450,C168-C175 (12)	4.45	4.45

Archbishopric of Asunción, 50th anniv.

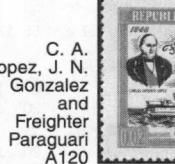

"Political Enlightenment" A119

1948, Sept. 11 Engr. & Litho.

451 A119	5c car red & bl	.20	.20
452 A119	15c red org, red & bl	.20	.20
	Nos. 451-452,C176-C177 (4)	2.90	2.65

Issued to honor the Barefeet, a political group.

C. A. Lopez, J. N. Gonzalez and Freighter Paraguari A120

1949 Litho.

Centers in Carmine, Black, Ultramarine and Blue

453 A120	2c orange	.20	.20
454 A120	5c blue vio	.20	.20
455 A120	10c black	.20	.20
456 A120	15c violet	.20	.20
457 A120	50c blue grn	.20	.20
458 A120	1g dull vio brn	.20	.20
	Nos. 453-458 (6)	1.20	1.20

Paraguay's merchant fleet centenary.

Type of 1946

1950 Unwmk. *Perf. 10½*

459 A110	5c red	.20	.20
460 A110	10c blue	.20	.20
461 A110	50c rose lilac	.20	.20
462 A110	1g pale violet	.20	.20

1951

Coarse Impression

463 A110	30c green	.20	.20
	Nos. 459-463 (5)	1.00	1.00

Blocks of Four of Nos. 459, 460 and 463 Overprinted in Various Colors

Illustration reduced one-half.

1951, Apr. 18

464 A110	5c red (Bk), block	.20	.20
465 A110	10c blue (R), block	.25	.20
466 A110	30c green (V), block	.40	.30

1st Economic Cong. of Paraguay, 4/18/51.

Columbus Lighthouse — A121

1952, Feb. 11 *Perf. 10*

467 A121	2c org brn	.20	.20
468 A121	5c light ultra	.20	.20
469 A121	10c rose	.20	.20
470 A121	15c light blue	.20	.20
471 A121	20c lilac	.20	.20

472 A121 50c orange .20 .20
473 A121 1g bluish grn .20 .20
Nos. 467-473 (7) 1.40 1.40

Silvio Pettirossi, Aviator — A122

1954, Mar. Litho. *Perf. 10*

474 A122 5c blue .20 .20
475 A122 20c rose pink .20 .20
476 A122 50c vio brn .20 .20
477 A122 60c lt vio .20 .20
Nos. 474-477,C201-C204 (8) 1.65 1.65

Arms Type of 1946

1954 *Perf. 11*

478 A110 10c vermilion .20 .20

Perf. 10

478A A110 10c ver, redrawn .20 .20
479 A110 10g orange .25 .20
480 A110 50g vio brn 1.25 1.00
Nos. 478-480 (4) 1.90 1.60

No. 478A measures 20½x24mm, has 5 frame lines at left and 6 at right. No. 478 measures 20x24½mm, has 6 frame lines at left and 5 at right.

Three National Heroes — A123

1954, Aug. 15 Litho. *Perf. 10*

481 A123 5c light vio .20 .20
482 A123 20c light blue .20 .20
483 A123 50c rose pink .20 .20
484 A123 1g org brn .20 .20
485 A123 2g blue grn .20 .20
Nos. 481-485,C216-C220 (10) 6.15 6.10

Marshal Francisco S. Lopez, Pres. Carlos A. Lopez and Gen. Bernardino Caballero.

Pres. Alfredo Stroessner and Pres. Juan D. Peron — A124

Photo. & Litho.

1955, Apr. Wmk. 90 *Perf. 13x13½*

486 A124 5c multicolored .20 .20
487 A124 10c multicolored .20 .20
488 A124 50c multicolored .20 .20
489 A124 1.30g multicolored .20 .20
490 A124 2.20g multicolored .20 .20
Nos. 486-490,C221-C224 (9) 1.80 1.80

Visit of Pres. Juan D. Peron of Argentina.

Jesuit Ruins, Trinidad Belfry A125

Santa Maria Cornice — A126

Jesuit Ruins: 20c, Corridor at Trinidad. 2.50g, Tower of Santa Rosa. 5g, San Cosme gate. 15g, Church of Jesus. 25g, Niche at Trinidad.

Perf. 12½x12, 12x12½

1955, June 19 Engr. Unwmk.

491 A125 5c org yel .20 .20
492 A125 20c olive bister .20 .20
493 A126 50c lt red brn .20 .20
494 A126 2.50g olive .20 .20
495 A125 5g yel brn .20 .20
496 A125 15g blue grn .25 .20
497 A126 25g deep grn .45 .25
Nos. 491-497,C225-C232 (15) 3.55 3.20

25th anniv. of the priesthood of Monsignor Rodriguez.

For surcharges see Nos. 545-551.

Arms Type of 1946

Perf. 10, 11 (No. 500)

1956-58 Litho. Unwmk.

498 A110 5c brown ('57) .20 .20
499 A110 30c red brn ('57) .20 .20
500 A110 45c gray olive .20 .20
500A A110 90c lt vio bl .20 .20
501 A110 2g ocher .20 .20
502 A110 2.20g lil rose .20 .20
503 A110 3g ol bis ('58) .20 .20
503A A110 4.20g emer ('57) .20 .20
504 A110 5g ver ('57) .20 .20
505 A110 10g lt grn ('57) .20 .20
506 A110 20g blue ('57) .30 .20
Nos. 498-506 (11) 2.30 2.20

No. 500A exists with four-line, carmine overprint: "DIA N. UNIDAS 24 Octubre 1945-1956". It was not regularly issued and no decree authorizing it is known.

Soldiers, Angel and Asuncion Cathedral — A127

#513-519, Soldier & nurse in medallion & flags.

Perf. 13½

1957, June 12 Photo. Unwmk.

Granite Paper

Flags in Red and Blue

508 A127 5c bl grn .20 .20
509 A127 10c carmine .20 .20
510 A127 15c ultra .20 .20
511 A127 20c dp claret .20 .20
512 A127 25c gray blk .20 .20
513 A127 30c lt blue .20 .20
514 A127 40c gray blk .20 .20
515 A127 50c dark car .20 .20
516 A127 1g bluish grn .20 .20
517 A127 1.30g ultra .20 .20
518 A127 1.50g dp claret .20 .20
519 A127 2g brt grn .20 .20
Nos. 508-519 (12) 2.40 2.40

Heroes of the Chaco war. See #C233-C245.

Statue of St. Ignatius (Guarani Carving) — A128

Blessed Roque Gonzales and St. Ignatius A129

1.50g, St. Ignatius and San Ignacio Monastery.

Wmk. 319

1958, Mar. 15 Litho. *Perf. 11*

520 A128 50c dk red brn .20 .20
521 A129 50c lt bl grn .20 .20
522 AP91 1.50g brt vio .20 .20
523 A128 3g light bl .20 .20
524 A129 6.25g rose car .20 .20
Nos. 520-524 (5) 1.00 1.00

St. Ignatius of Loyola (1491-1556).

See Nos. 935-935.

Arms Type of 1946

1958-64 Litho. *Perf. 10, 11*

525 A110 45c gray olive .20 .20
526 A110 50c rose vio .20 .20
527 A110 70c lt brn ('59) .20 .20
527A A110 90c vio blue .20 .20
528 A110 1g violet .20 .20
529 A110 1.50g lilac ('59) .20 .20
529A A110 2g bister ('64) .20 .20
530 A110 3g ol bis ('59) .20 .20
531 A110 4.50g lt ultra ('59) .20 .20
531A A110 5g rose red ('59) .20 .20
531B A110 10g bl grn ('59) .20 .20
532 A110 12.45g yel green .20 .20
533 A110 15g dl orange .20 .20
534 A110 30g citron .30 .20
535 A110 50g brown red .40 .30
536 A110 100g gray vio .85 .65
Nos. 525-536 (16) 4.15 3.75

Pres. Alfredo Stroessner A130

Wmk. 320

1958, Aug. 15 Litho. *Perf. 13½*

Center in Slate

537 A130 10c sal pink .20 .20
538 A130 15c violet .20 .20
539 A130 25c yel grn .20 .20
540 A130 30c light fawn .20 .20
541 A130 50c rose car .20 .20
542 A130 75c light ultra .20 .20
543 A130 5g lt bl grn .20 .20
544 A130 10g brown .20 .20
Nos. 537-544,C246-C251 (14) 4.80 4.80

Re-election of President General Alfredo Stroessner.

Nos. 491-497 Surcharged in Red

Perf. 12½x12, 12x12½

1959, May 14 Engr. Unwmk.

545 A125 1.50g on 5c org yel .20 .20
546 A125 1.50g on 20c ol bis .20 .20
547 A126 1.50g on 50c lt red brn .20 .20
548 A126 3g on 2.50g ol .20 .20
549 A125 6.25g on 5g yel brn .20 .20
550 A125 20g on 15g bl grn .25 .25
551 A126 30g on 25g dp grn .40 .40
Nos. 545-551,C252-C259 (15) 5.85 4.85

The surcharge is made to fit the stamps. Counterfeits of surcharge exist.

Goalkeeper Catching Soccer Ball — A131

WRY Emblem — A132

1960, Mar. 18 Photo. *Perf. 12½*

556 A131 30c brt red & bl grn .20 .20
557 A131 50c plum & dk bl .20 .20
558 A131 75c ol grn & org .20 .20
559 A131 1.50g dk vio & bl grn .20 .20
Nos. 556-559,C262-C264 (7) 1.60 1.60

Olympic Games of 1960.

1960, Apr. 7 Litho. *Perf. 11*

560 A132 25c sal & yel grn .25 .20
561 A132 50c lt yel grn & red org .25 .20
562 A132 70c lt brn & lil rose .30 .20
563 A132 1.50g lt bl & ultra .30 .20
564 A132 3g gray & bis brn .60 .45
Nos. 560-564,C265-C268 (9) 7.50 4.55

World Refugee Year, July 1, 1959-June 30, 1960 (1st issue).

UN Emblem and Dove — A133

Flags of UN and Paraguay and UN Emblem A134

UN Declaration of Human Rights: 3g, Hand holding seales. 6g, Hands breaking chains. 20g, Flame.

1960, Apr. 21 *Perf. 12½x13*

565 A133 1g dk car & bl .20 .20
566 A133 3g blue & org .20 .20
567 A133 6g gray grn & sal .25 .20
568 A133 20g ver & yel .35 .25
Nos. 565-568,C269-C271 (7) 2.20 2.05

Miniature sheets exist, perf. and imperf., containing one each of Nos. 565-568, all printed in purple and orange.

Perf. 13x13½

1960, Oct. 24 Photo. Unwmk.

569 A134 30c lt bl, red & bl .20 .20
570 A134 75c yel, red & bl .20 .20
571 A134 90c pale lil, red & bl .20 .20
Nos. 569-571,C272-C273 (5) 1.00 1.00

15th anniversary of the United Nations.

International Bridge, Arms of Brazil, Paraguay — A135

Truck Carrying Logs — A136

1961, Jan. 26 Litho. *Perf. 14*

572 A135 15c green .20 .20
573 A135 30c dull blue .20 .20
574 A135 50c orange .20 .20
575 A135 75c vio blue .20 .20
576 A135 1g violet .20 .20
Nos. 572-576,C274-C277 (9) 2.00 2.00

Inauguration of the International Bridge between Paraguay and Brazil.

Unwmk.

1961, Apr. 10 Photo. *Perf. 13*

90c, 2g, Logs on river barge. 1g, 5g, Radio tower.

577 A136 25c yel grn & rose car .20 .20
578 A136 90c blue & yel .20 .20
579 A136 1g car rose & org .20 .20
580 A136 2g ol grn & sal .20 .20
581 A136 5g lilac & emer .20 .20
Nos. 577-581,C278-C281 (9) 2.35 2.15

Paraguay's progress, "Paraguay en Marcha."

P. J. Caballero, José G. R. Francia, F. Yegros, Revolutionary Leaders — A137

1961, May 16 Litho. Perf. 14½

582 A137	30c	green	.20	.20
583 A137	50c	lil rose	.20	.20
584 A137	90c	violet	.20	.20
585 A137	1.50g	Prus bl	.20	.20
586 A137	3g	olive bis	.20	.20
587 A137	4g	ultra	.20	.20
588 A137	5g	brown	.20	.20
Nos. 582-588,C282-C287 (13)			3.25	3.20

150th anniv. of Independence (1st issue).

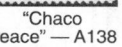

"Chaco Peace" — A138

Puma — A139

1961, June 12 Perf. 14x14½

589 A138	25c	vermilion	.20	.20
590 A138	30c	green	.20	.20
591 A138	50c	red brn	.20	.20
592 A138	1g	bright vio	.20	.20
593 A138	2g	dk bl gray	.20	.20
Nos. 589-593,C288-C290 (8)			2.30	2.20

Chaco Peace; 150th anniv. of Independence (2nd issue).

1961, Aug. 16 Unwmk. Perf. 14

594 A139	75c	dull vio	.35	.20
595 A139	1.50g	brown	.35	.20
596 A139	4.50g	green	.35	.20
597 A139	10g	Prus blue	.35	.25
Nos. 594-597,C291-C293 (7)			3.95	3.25

150th anniv. of Independence (3rd issue).

University Seal — A140

Hotel Guarani A141

1961, Sept. 18 Perf. 14x14½

598 A140	15c	ultra	.20	.20
599 A140	25c	dk red	.20	.20
600 A140	75c	bl grn	.20	.20
601 A140	1g	orange	.20	.20
Nos. 598-601,C294-C296 (7)			1.60	1.60

Founding of the Catholic University in Asuncion; 150th anniv. of Independence (4th issue).

1961, Oct. 14 Litho. Perf. 15

602 A141	50c	slate bl	.20	.20
603 A141	1g	green	.20	.20
604 A141	4.50g	lilac	.20	.20
Nos. 602-604,C297-C300 (7)			1.60	1.60

Opening of the Hotel Guarani; 150th anniv. of Independence (5th issue).

Tennis Racket and Balls in Flag Colors — A142

1961, Oct. 16 Litho. Perf. 11

605 A142	35c	multi	.20	.20
606 A142	75c	multi	.20	.20
607 A142	1.50g	multi	.20	.20
608 A142	2.25g	multi	.20	.20
609 A142	4g	multi	.20	.20
Nos. 605-609 (5)			1.00	

28th South American Tennis Championships, Asuncion, Oct. 15-23 (1st issue). Some specialists question the status of this issue. See Nos. C301-C303.

Imperforates exist in changed colors as well as two imperf. souvenir sheets with stamps in changed colors.

Limited Distribution Issues Beginning with No. 610, sets with limited distribution are not valued.

Alan B. Shepard, First US Astronaut A143

18.15g, 36g, 50g, Shepard, Saturn, horiz.

1961, Dec. 22 Litho. Perf. 11

610 A143	10c	blue & brown	.25	.20
611 A143	25c	blue & car rose	.25	.20
612 A143	50c	blue & yel org	.25	.20
613 A143	75c	blue & green	.25	.20
614 A143	18.15g	green & blue	6.50	6.50
615 A143	36g	orange & blue	6.50	6.50
616 A143	50g	car rose & blue	8.75	8.75
a.		Souvenir sheet of 1	—	—

Nos. 614-616a are airmail.

Uprooted Oak Emblem — A145

1961, Dec. 30 Unwmk. Perf. 11

619 A145	10c	ultra & lt bl	.20	.20
620 A145	25c	maroon & org	.20	.20
621 A145	50c	car rose & pink	.20	.20
622 A145	75c	dk bl & yel grn	.20	.20
Nos. 619-622 (4)			.80	

World Refugee Year, 1959-60 (2nd issue). Imperforates in changed colors and souvenir sheets exist. Some specialists question the status of this issue.

See Nos. C307-C309.

Europa A146

Design: 20g, 50g, Dove.

1961, Dec. 31

623 A146	50c	multicolored	.30	.20
624 A146	75c	multicolored	.30	.20
625 A146	1g	multicolored	.30	.20
626 A146	1.50g	multicolored	.30	.20
627 A146	4.50g	multicolored	.70	.70
a.		Souvenir sheet of 5, #623-627	—	—
628 A146	20g	multicolored	—	—
629 A146	50g	multicolored	—	—
a.		Souvenir sheet of 1	—	—

Nos. 628-629 are airmail.

Tennis Player — A147

1962, Jan. 5 Perf. 15x14½

630 A147	35c	Prussian bl	.20	.20
631 A147	75c	dark vio	.20	.20
632 A147	1.50g	red brn	.20	.20
633 A147	2.25g	emerald	.20	.20
634 A147	4g	carmine	.20	.20
635 A147	12.45g	red lil	.20	.20
636 A147	20g	bl grn	.35	.35
637 A147	50g	org brn	.55	.55
Nos. 630-637 (8)			2.10	2.10

28th South American Tennis Championships, 1961 (2nd issue) and the 150th anniv. of Independence (6th issue).

Nos. 634-637 are airmail.

Scout Bugler — A148

Lord Baden-Powell A148a

1962, Feb. 6 Perf. 11

Olive Green Center

638 A148	10c	dp magenta	.20
639 A148	20c	red orange	.20
640 A148	25c	dk brown	.20
641 A148	30c	emerald	.20
642 A148	50c	indigo	.20
643 A148a	12.45g	car rose & bl	.25
644 A148a	36g	car rose & emer	.75
645 A148a	50g	car rose & org yel	1.00
Nos. 638-645 (8)			3.00

Issued to honor the Boy Scouts. Imperfs. in changed colors exist and imperf. souvenir sheets exist. Some specialists question the status of this issue.

Nos. 643-645 are airmail.

Arms Type of 1946

1962-68 Litho. Wmk. 347

646 A110	50c	steel bl ('63)	.20	.20
647 A110	70c	dull lil ('63)	.20	.20
648 A110	1.50g	violet ('63)	.20	.20
649 A110	3g	dp bl ('68)	.20	.20
650 A110	4.50g	redsh brn ('67)	.20	.20
651 A110	5g	lilac ('64)	.20	.20
652 A110	10g	car rose ('63)	.20	.20
653 A110	12.45g	ultra	.20	.20
654 A110	15.45g	org ver	.20	.20
655 A110	18.15g	lilac	.20	.20
656 A110	20g	lt brn ('63)	.20	.20
657 A110	50g	dl red brn ('67)	.35	.20
658 A110	100g	bl gray ('63)	.70	.40
Nos. 646-658 (13)			3.25	2.80

Map and Laurel Branch — A149

UN Emblem A150

Design: 20g, 50g, Hands holding globe.

Perf. 14x14½

1962, Apr. 14 Unwmk.

659 A149	50c	ocher	.20	.20
660 A149	75c	vio blue	.20	.20
661 A149	1g	purple	.20	.20
662 A149	1.50g	brt grn	.20	.20
663 A149	4.50g	vermilion	.20	.20
664 A149	20g	lil rose	.20	.20
665 A149	50g	orange	.40	.40
Nos. 659-665 (7)			1.60	1.60

Day of the Americas; 150th anniv. of Independence (7th issue).

Nos. 664-665 are airmail.

1962, Apr. 23 Perf. 15

Design: #670-673, UN Headquarters, NYC.

666 A150	50c	bister brn	.20	.20
667 A150	75c	dp claret	.20	.20
668 A150	1g	Prussian bl	.20	.20
669 A150	2g	orange brn	.20	.20
670 A150	12.45g	dl vio	.20	.20
671 A150	18.15g	ol grn	.30	.30
672 A150	23.40g	brn red	.45	.45
673 A150	30g	carmine	.50	.50
Nos. 666-673 (8)			2.25	2.25

UN; Independence, 150th anniv. (8th issue).

Nos. 670-673 are airmail.

Malaria Eradication Emblem and Mosquito A151

Design: 75c, 1g, 1.50g, Microscope, anopheles mosquito and eggs. 3g, 4g, Malaria eradication emblem. 12.45g, 18.15g, 36g, Mosquito, UN emblem and microscope.

Perf. 14x13½

1962, May 23 Wmk. 346

674 A151	30c	pink, ultra & blk	.20
675 A151	50c	bis, grn & blk	.20
676 A151	75c	rose red, blk & bis	.20
677 A151	1g	brt grn, blk & bis	.20
678 A151	1.50g	dl red brn, blk & bis	.20
679 A151	3g	bl, red & blk	.20
680 A151	4g	grn, red & blk	.20
681 A151	12.45g	ol bis, grn & blk	.20
682 A151	18.15g	rose lil, red & blk	.40
683 A151	36g	rose red, vio bl & blk	1.00
Nos. 674-683 (10)			3.00

WHO drive to eradicate malaria. Imperforates exist in changed colors. Two souvenir sheets exist, one containing one copy of No. 683, the other an imperf. 36g in blue, red & black. Some specialists question the status of this issue.

Nos. 679-683 are airmail.

Stadium — A152

Soccer Players and Globe A152a

Perf. 13½x14

1962, July 28 Litho. Wmk. 346

684 A152 15c yel & dk brn .20
685 A152 25c brt grn & dk brn .20
686 A152 30c lt vio & dk brn .20
687 A152 40c dl org & dk brn .20
688 A152 50c brt yel grn & dk brn .20
689 A152a 12.45g brt rose, blk & vio .35
690 A152a 18.15g lt red brn, blk & vio .55
691 A152a 36g gray grn, blk & brn 1.10
Nos. 684-691 (8) 3.00

World Soccer Championships, Chile, May 30-June 17. Some specialists question the status of this issue. Imperfs. exist. A souvenir sheet contains one No. 691.
Nos. 689-691 are airmail.

Freighter A153

Ship's Wheel — A153a

Designs: Various merchantmen. 44g, Like 12.45g with diagonal colorless band in background.

Perf. 14½x15

1962, July 31 Unwmk.

692 A153 30c bister brn .20 .20
693 A153 90c slate bl .20 .20
694 A153 1.50g brown red .20 .20
695 A153 2g green .20 .20
696 A153 4.20g vio blue .20 .20

Perf. 15x14½

697 A153a 12.45g dk red .20 .20
698 A153a 44g blue .40 .30
Nos. 692-698 (7) 1.60 1.50

Issued to honor the merchant marine.
Nos. 697-698 are airmail.

Friendship 7 over South America — A154

Lt. Col. John H. Glenn, Jr., Lt. Cmdr. Scott Carpenter A154a

Perf. 13½x14

1962, Sept. 4 Litho. Wmk. 346

699 A154 15c dk bl & bis .20
700 A154 25c vio brn & bis .20
701 A154 30c dk sl grn & bis .20
702 A154 40c dk gray & bis .20
703 A154 50c dk vio & bis .20
704 A154a 12.45g car lake & gray .20
705 A154a 18.15g red lil & gray .20
706 A154a 36g dl cl & gray .40
Nos. 699-706 (8) 1.80

US manned space flights. Imperfs. in changed colors and two souvenir sheets exist. Some specialists question the status of this issue.
Nos. 704-706 are airmail.

Discus Thrower — A155

Olympic flame &: 12.45g, Melbourne, 1956. 18.15g, Rome, 1960. 36g, Tokyo, 1964.

1962, Oct. 1 Litho.

707 A155 15c blk & yel .20
708 A155 25c blk & lt grn .20
709 A155 30c blk & pink .20
710 A155 40c blk & pale vio .20
711 A155 50c blk & lt bl .20
712 A155 12.45g brt grn, lt grn & choc .20
713 A155 18.15g ol brn, yel & choc .20
714 A155 36g rose red, pink & choc .40
Nos. 707-714 (8) 1.80

Olympic Games from Amsterdam 1928 to Tokyo 1964. Each stamp is inscribed with date and place of various Olympic Games. Imperfs. in changed colors and two souvenir sheets exist. Some specialists question the status of this issue.
Nos. 712-714 are airmail.

Peace Dove and Cross A156

Dove Symbolizing Holy Ghost — A156a

Perf. 14½

1962, Oct. 11 Litho. Unwmk.

715 A156 50c olive .20 .20
716 A156 70c dark blue .20 .20
717 A156 1.50g bister .20 .20
718 A156 2g violet .20 .20
719 A156 3g brick red .20 .20
720 A156a 5g vio bl .20 .20
721 A156a 10g brt grn .20 .20
722 A156a 12.45g lake .20 .20
723 A156a 18.15g orange .25 .20
724 A156a 23.40g violet .30 .25
725 A156a 36g rose red .50 .35
Nos. 715-725 (11) 2.65 2.40

Vatican II, the 21st Ecumenical Council of the Roman Catholic Church, which opened Oct. 11, 1962.
Nos. 720-725 are airmail.

Europa A157

1962, Dec. 17 *Perf. 11*

726 A157 4g yel, red & brn
727 A157 36g multi, diff.
a. Souvenir sheet of 2, #726-727

No. 727 is airmail.

Solar System A158

12.45g, 36g, 50g, Inner planets, Jupiter & rocket.

Perf. 14x13½

1962, Dec. 17 Wmk. 346

728 A158 10c org & purple
729 A158 20c org & brn vio
730 A158 25c org & dark vio
731 A158 30c org & ultra
732 A158 50c org & dull green
733 A158 12.45g org & brown
734 A158 36g org & blue
735 A158 50g org & green
a. Souvenir sheet of 1

Nos. 733-735 are airmail.

The following stamps exist imperf. in different colors: Nos. 736-743a, 744-751a, 752-759a, 760-766a, 775-782a, 783-790a, 791-798a, 799-805a, 806-813a, 814-821a, 828-835a, 836-843, 841a, 850-857a, 858-865a, 871-878, 876a, 887-894a, 895-902, 900a, 903-910a, 911-918a, 919-926a, 927-934a, 943-950a, 951-958a, 959-966a, 978-985a, 986-993a, 994-1001a, 1002-1003, 1003d, 1004-1007a, 1051-1059, B12-B19.

Pierre de Coubertin (1836-1937), Founder of Modern Olympic Games — A159

Summer Olympic Games sites and: Nos. 12.45g, 18.15g, 36g, Torch bearer in stadium.

Perf. 14x13½

1963, Feb. 16 Wmk. 346

736 A159 15c Athens, 1896
737 A159 25c Paris, 1900
738 A159 30c St. Louis, 1904
739 A159 40c London, 1908
740 A159 50c Stockholm, 1912
741 A159 12.45g No games, 1916
742 A159 18.15g Antwerp, 1920
743 A159 36g Paris, 1924
a. Souvenir sheet of 1

Nos. 741-743a are airmail.

Walter M. Schirra, US Astronaut — A160

Design: 12.45g, 36g, 50g, Schirra.

1963, Mar. 16 *Perf. 13½x14*

744 A160 10c brn org & blk
745 A160 20c car & blk
746 A160 25c lake & blk
747 A160 30c ver & blk
748 A160 50c mag & blk
749 A160 12.45g bl blk & lake
750 A160 36g dl gray vio & lake
751 A160 50g dk grn bl & lake
a. Souvenir sheet of 1

Nos. 749-751a are airmail.

Winter Olympics A161

Games sites and: 12.45g, 36g, 50g, Snowflake.

1963, May 16 *Perf. 14x13½*

752 A161 10g Chamonix, 1924
753 A161 20c St. Moritz, 1928
754 A161 25c Lake Placid, 1932
755 A161 30c Garmisch-Partenkirchen, 1936
756 A161 50c St. Moritz, 1948
757 A161 12.45g Oslo, 1952
758 A161 36g Cortina d'Ampezzo, 1956
759 A161 50g Squaw Valley, 1960
a. Souvenir sheet of 1

Nos. 757-759a are airmail.

Freedom from Hunger A162

1963, May 31 *Perf. 13½x14, 14x13½*

760 A162 10c yel grn & brn
761 A162 25c lt bl & brn
762 A162 50c lt grn bl & brn
763 A162 75c lt lil & brn
764 A162 18.15g yel org & brn
765 A162 36g lt bl grn & brn
766 A162 50g bis & brn
a. Souvenir sheet of 1

#760-763 are vert. #764-766a are airmail.

Pres. Alfredo Stroessner A163

1963, Aug. 6 Wmk. 347 *Perf. 11*

767 A163 50c ol gray & sep .20 .20
768 A163 75c buff & sepia .20 .20
769 A163 1.50g lt lil & sep .20 .20
770 A163 3g emer & sepia .20 .20
771 A163 12.45g pink & claret .20 .20
772 A163 18.15g pink & grn .25 .20
773 A163 36g pink & vio .75 .50
Nos. 767-773 (7) 2.00 1.70

Third presidential term of Alfredo Stroessner. A 36g imperf. souvenir sheet exists.
Nos. 771-773 are airmail.

MUESTRA

Illustrations may show the word "MUESTRA." This means specimen and is not on the actual stamps. The editors would like to borrow copies so that replacement illustrations can be made.

Souvenir Sheet

Dag Hammarskjold, UN Secretary General — A164

1963, Aug. 21 Unwmk. *Imperf.*

774 A164 2g Sheet of 2

Project Mercury Flight of L. Gordon Cooper A165

12.45g, 18.15g, 50g, L. Gordon Cooper, vert.

Perf. 14x13½, 13½x14

1963, Aug. 23 Litho. Wmk. 346

775 A165 15c brn & orange
776 A165 25c brn & blue
777 A165 30c brn & violet
778 A165 40c brn & green
779 A165 50c brn & red vio
780 A165 12.45g brn & bl grn
781 A165 18.15g brn & blue
782 A165 50g brn & pink
a. Souvenir sheet of 1

Nos. 780-782 are airmail.

1964 Winter Olympics, Innsbruck A166

Design: 12.45g, 18.15g, 50g, Innsbruck Games emblem, vert.

Perf. 14x13½, 13½x14

1963, Oct. 28 Unwmk.

783 A166 15c choc & red
784 A166 25c gray grn & red
785 A166 30c plum & red
786 A166 40c sl grn & red
787 A166 50c dp bl & red
788 A166 12.45g sep & red
789 A166 18.15g grn bl & red
790 A166 50g tan & red
a. Souvenir sheet of 1

Nos. 788-790 are airmail.

1964 Summer Olympics, Tokyo — A167

12.45g, 18.15g, 50g, Tokyo games emblem.

1964, Jan. 8 *Perf. 13½x14*

791 A167 15c blue & red
792 A167 25c org & red
793 A167 30c tan & red
794 A167 40c vio brn & red
795 A167 50c grn bl & red
796 A167 12.45g vio & red
797 A167 18.15g brn & red
798 A167 50g grn bl & red
a. Souvenir sheet of 1

Nos. 796-798 are airmail.

Intl. Red Cross, Cent. A168

Designs: 10c, Helicopter. 25c, Space ambulance. 30c, Red Cross symbol, vert. 50c, Clara Barton, founder of American Red Cross, vert. 18.15g, Jean Henri Dunant, founder of Intl. Red Cross, vert. 36g, Red Cross space hospital, space ambulance. 50g, Plane, ship, ambulance, vert.

1964, Feb. 4 *Perf. 14x13½, 13½x14*

799 A168 10c vio brn & red
800 A168 25c bl grn & red
801 A168 30c dk bl & red
802 A168 50c ol blk & red
803 A168 18.15g choc, red, & pink
804 A168 36g grn bl & red
805 A168 50g vio & red
a. Souvenir sheet of 1

Nos. 803-805 are airmail.

Space Research A169

15c, 25c, 30c, Gemini spacecraft rendezvous with Agena rocket. 40c, 50c, Future Apollo and LunarModules. 12.45g, 18.15g, 50g, Telstar communications satellite, Olympic rings, vert.

1964, Mar. 11

806 A169 15c vio & tan
807 A169 25c grn & tan
808 A169 30c bl & tan
809 A169 40c brt bl & red
810 A169 50c sl grn & red
811 A169 12.45g dk bl & tan
812 A169 18.15g dk grn bl & tan
813 A169 50g dp vio & tan
a. Souvenir sheet of 1

1964 Summer Olympic Games, Tokyo (#811-813a). Nos. 811-813a are airmail.

Rockets and Satellites A170

15c, 25c, Apollo command module mock-up. 30c, Tiros 7 weather satellite, vert. 40c, 50c, Ranger 6. 12.45g, 18.15g, 50g, Saturn I lift-off, vert.

1964, Apr. 25

814 A170 15c brn & tan
815 A170 25c vio & tan
816 A170 30c Prus bl & lake
817 A170 40c ver & tan
818 A170 50c ultra & tan
819 A170 12.45g grn bl & choc
820 A170 18.15g bl & choc
821 A170 50g lil rose & choc
a. Souvenir sheet of 1

Nos. 819-821a are airmail.

Popes Paul VI, John XXIII and St. Peter's, Rome A171

Design: 12.45g, 18.15g, 36g, Asuncion Cathedral, Popes Paul VI and John XXIII.

1964, May 23 Wmk. 347

822 A171 1.50g claret & org .20 .20
823 A171 3g claret & dk grn .20 .20
824 A171 4g claret & bister .20 .20
825 A171 12.45g sl grn & lem .20 .20
826 A171 18.15g pur & lem .20 .25
827 A171 36g vio bl & lem 1.00 .80
Nos. 822-827 (6) 2.00 1.85

National holiday of St. Maria Auxiliadora (Our Lady of Perpetual Help).
Nos. 825-827 are airmail.

United Nations A172

Designs: 15c, John F. Kennedy. 25c, 12.45g, Pope Paul VI and Patriarch Atenagoras. 30c, Eleanor Roosevelt, Chairman of UN Commission on Human Rights. 40c, Relay, Syncom and Telstar satellites. 50c, Echo 2 satellite. 18.15g, U Thant, UN Sec. Gen. 50g, Rocket, flags of Europe, vert.

Perf. 14x13½, 14 (15c, 25c, 12.45g)

1964, July 30 Unwmk.

Size: 35x35mm (#830, 834), 40x29mm (#831-832, 835)

828 A172 15c blk & brn
829 A172 25c blk, bl & red
830 A172 30c blk & ver
831 A172 40c dk bl & sep
832 A172 50c vio & car
833 A172 12.45g blk, grn & red
834 A172 18.15g blk & grn

Perf. 13½x14

835 A172 50g multicolored
a. Souvenir sheet of 1

Nos. 833-835a are airmail.

Space Achievements — A173

Designs: 10c, 30c, Ranger 7, Moon, vert. 15c, 12.45+6g, Wernher von Braun looking through telescope, vert. 20c, 20+10g, John F. Kennedy, rockets, vert. 40c, 18.15+9g, Rockets, von Braun.

1964, Sept. 12 *Perf. 12½x12*

836 A173 10c bl & blk
837 A173 15c yel grn & brt pink
838 A173 20c yel org & bl
839 A173 30c mag & blk
840 A173 40c yel org, bl & blk
841 A173 12.45g +6g red & bl
a. Souvenir sheet of 2, #840-841
842 A173 18.15g +9g grn bl, brn & blk
843 A173 20g +10g red & bl

Nos. 841-843 are airmail.

Coats of Arms of Paraguay and France A174

Designs: 3g, 12.45g, 36g, Presidents Stroessner and de Gaulle. 18.15g, Coats of Arms of Paraguay and France.

1964, Oct. 6 Wmk. 347

844 A174 1.50g brown .20 .20
845 A174 3g ultramarine .20 .20
846 A174 4g gray .20 .20
847 A174 12.45g lilac .20 .20
848 A174 18.15g bl grn .20 .25
849 A174 36g magenta 1.00 .80
Nos. 844-849 (6) 2.00 1.85

Visit of Pres. Charles de Gaulle of France.
Nos. 847-849 are airmail.

Boy Scout Jamborees — A175

Designs: 15c, 18.15g, Lord Robert Baden-Powell (1857-1941), Boy Scouts founder. 20c, 30c, 12.45g, Boy Scout emblem, map, vert.

1965, Jan. 15 Unwmk. *Perf. 14*

850 A175 10c Argentina, 1961
851 A175 15c Peru, canceled
852 A175 20c Chile, 1959
853 A175 30c Brazil, 1954
854 A175 50c Uruguay, 1957
855 A175 12.45g Brazil, 1960
856 A175 18.15g Venezuela, 1964
857 A175 36g Brazil, 1963
a. Souvenir sheet of 1, perf. 12x12½

Nos. 855-857a are airmail.

A176

A177

Olympic and Paraguayan Medals: 25c, John F. Kennedy. 30c, Medal of Peace and Justice, reverse. 40c, Gens. Stroessner and DeGaulle, profiles. 50c, 18.15g, DeGaulle and Stroessner, in uniform. 12.45g, Medal of Peace and Justice, obverse.

Litho. & Embossed

1965, Mar. 30 *Perf. 13½x13*

858 A176 15c multicolored
859 A176 25c multicolored
860 A176 30c multicolored

Perf. 12½x12

861 A176 40c multicolored
862 A176 50c multicolored
863 A176 12.45g multicolored
864 A176 18.15g multicolored
865 A176 50g multicolored
a. Souv. sheet of 1, perf. 13½x13

Nos. 863-865a are airmail. Medal on No. 865a is gold foil.

Overprint: "Centenario de la Epopeya Nacional 1.864-1.870"

Design: Map of Americas.

1965, Apr. 26 Wmk. 347 *Perf. 11*

866 A177 1.50g dull grn .20 .20
867 A177 3g car red .20 .20
868 A177 4g dark blue .20 .20
869 A177 12.45g brn & blk .20 .20
870 A177 36g brt lil & blk .50 .35
Nos. 866-870 (5) 1.30 1.15

Centenary of National Epic. Not issued without overprint.
Nos. 869-870 are airmail.

Scientists — A178

Unwmk.

1965, June 5 Litho. *Perf. 14*

871	A178	10c	Newton
872	A178	15c	Copernicus
873	A178	20c	Galileo
874	A178	30c	like #871
875	A178	40c	Einstein
876	A178	12.45g	+6g like #873
a.			Souvenir sheet of 2, #875-876
877	A178	18.15g	+9g like #875
878	A178	20g	+10g like #872

Nos. 876-878 are airmail.

Cattleya Warscewiczii A179

Ceibo Tree — A179a

1965, June 28 Unwmk. *Perf. 14½*

879	A179	20c	purple	.20	.20
880	A179	30c	blue	.20	.20
881	A179	90c	bright mag	.20	.20
882	A179	1.50g	green	.20	.20
883	A179a	3g	brn red	.20	.20
884	A179a	4g	green	.20	.20
885	A179	4.50g	orange	.20	.20
886	A179a	66g	brn org	.75	.50
			Nos. 879-886 (8)	2.15	1.90

150th anniv. of Independence (1811-1961).
Nos. 883-884, 886 are airmail.

John F. Kennedy and Winston Churchill — A180

Designs: 15c, Kennedy, PT 109. 25c, Kennedy family. 30c, 12.45g, Churchill, Parliament building. 40c, Kennedy, Alliance for Progress emblem. 50c, 18.15g, Kennedy, rocket launch at Cape Canaveral. 50g, John Glenn, Kennedy, Lyndon Johnson examining Friendship 7.

1965, Sept. 4 *Perf. 12x12½*

887	A180	15c	bl & brn
888	A180	25c	red & brn
889	A180	30c	vio & blk
890	A180	40c	org & sep
891	A180	50c	bl grn & sep
892	A180	12.45g	yel & blk
893	A180	18.15g	car & blk
894	A180	50g	grn & blk
a.			Souvenir sheet of 1

Nos. 892-894a are airmail.

ITU, Cent. — A181

Satellites: 10c, 40c, Ranger 7 transmitting to Earth. 15c, 20g+10g, Syncom, Olympic rings. 20c, 18.15g+9g, Early Bird. 30c, 12.45g+6g, Relay, Syncom, Telstar, Echo 2.

1965, Sept. 30

895	A181	10c	dull bl & sep
896	A181	15c	lilac & sepia
897	A181	20c	ol grn & sep
898	A181	30c	blue & sepia
899	A181	40c	grn & sep
900	A181	12.45g	+6g ver & sep
a.			Souvenir sheet of 2, #899-900
901	A181	18.15g	+9g org & sep
902	A181	20g	+10g vio & sep

Nos. 900-902 are airmail.

Pope Paul VI, Visit to UN A182

Designs: 10c, 50c, Pope Paul VI, U Thant, A. Fanfani. 15c, 12.45g, Pope Paul VI, Lyndon B. Johnson. 20c, 36g, Early Bird satellite, globe, papal arms. 30c, 18.15g, Pope Paul VI, Unisphere.

1966, Nov. 19

903	A182	10c	multicolored
904	A182	15c	multicolored
905	A182	20c	multicolored
906	A182	30c	multicolored
907	A182	50c	multicolored
908	A182	12.45g	multicolored
909	A182	18.15g	multicolored
910	A182	36g	multicolored
a.			Souvenir sheet of 1

Nos. 908-910a are airmail.

Astronauts and Space Exploration — A183

15c, 50g, Edward White walking in space, 6/3/65. 25c, 18.15g, Gemini 7 & 8 docking, 12/16-18/65. 30c, Virgil I. Grissom, John W. Young, 3/23/65. 40c, 50c, Edward White, James McDivitt, 6/3/65. 12.45g, Photographs of lunar surface.

1966, Feb. 19 *Perf. 14*

911	A183	15c	multicolored
912	A183	25c	multicolored
913	A183	30c	multicolored
914	A183	40c	multicolored
915	A183	50c	multicolored
916	A183	12.45g	multicolored
917	A183	18.15g	multicolored
918	A183	50g	multicolored
a.			Souvenir sheet of 1

Nos. 916-918a are airmail.

Events of 1965 — A184

10c, Meeting of Pope Paul VI & Cardinal Spellman, 10/4/65. 15c, Intl. Phil. Exposition, Vienna. 20c, OAS, 75th anniv. 30c, 36g, Intl. Quiet Sun Year, 1964-65. 50c, 18.15g, Saturn rockets at NY World's Fair. 12.45g, UN Intl. Cooperation Year.

1965, Mar. 9

919	A184	10c	multicolored
920	A184	15c	multicolored
921	A184	20c	multicolored
922	A184	30c	multicolored
923	A184	50c	multicolored
924	A184	12.45g	multicolored
925	A184	18.15g	multicolored
926	A184	36g	multicolored
a.			Souvenir sheet of 1

Nos. 924-926a are airmail.

1968 Summer Olympics, Mexico City — A185

Perf. 12½x12 (Nos. 927, 929, 931, 933), 13½x13

1966, Apr. 1

927	A185	10c	shown
928	A185	15c	God of Death
929	A185	20c	Aztec calendar stone
930	A185	30c	like No. 928
931	A185	50c	Zapotec deity
932	A185	12.45g	like No. 931
933	A185	18.15g	like No. 927
934	A185	36g	like No. 929
a.			Souvenir sheet of 1

Nos. 932-934a are airmail.

St. Ignatius Type of 1958 and

St. Ignatius and San Ignacio Monastery A185a

1966, Apr. 20 Wmk. 347 *Perf. 11*

935	A129	15c	ultramarine	.20	.20
936	A129	25c	ultramarine	.20	.20
937	A129	75c	ultramarine	.20	.20
938	A129	90c	ultramarine	.20	.20
939	A185a	3g	brown	.20	.20
940	A185a	12.45g	sepia	.20	.20
941	A185a	18.15g	sepia	.20	.20
942	A185a	23.40g	sepia	.25	.20
			Nos. 935-942 (8)	1.65	1.60

350th anniv. of the founding of San Ignacio Guazu Monastery.
Nos. 939-942 are airmail.

German Contributors in Space Research — A186

Designs: 10c, 36g, Paraguay #835, C97, Germany #C40. 15c, 50c, 18.15g, 3rd stage of Europa 1 rocket, vert. 20c, 12.45g, Hermann Oberth, jet propulsion engineer, vert. 30c, Reinhold K. Tiling, builder of 1st German rocket, 1931, vert.

Perf. 12x12½ (Nos. 943, 950), 12½x12 (Nos. 945, 947, 949), 13½x13

1966, May 16 Unwmk.

943	A186	10c	multicolored
944	A186	15c	multicolored
945	A186	20c	multicolored
946	A186	30c	multicolored
947	A186	50c	multicolored
948	A186	12.45g	multicolored
949	A186	18.15g	multicolored
950	A186	36g	multicolored
a.			Souvenir sheet of 1, perf. 12x13½x13x13½

Nos. 948-950a are airmail.

Writers — A187

1966, June 11 *Perf. 12x12½*

951	A187	10c	Dante
952	A187	15c	Moliere
953	A187	20c	Goethe
954	A187	30c	Shakespeare
955	A187	50c	like #952
956	A187	12.45g	like #953
957	A187	18.15g	like #954
958	A187	36g	like #951
a.			Souvenir sheet of 1, perf. 13½x14

Nos. 956-958a are airmail.

Italian Contributors in Space Research — A188

10c, 36g, Italian satellite, San Marco 1. 15c, 18.15g, Drafting machine, Leonardo Da Vinci. 20c, 12.45g, Map, Italo Balbo (1896-1940), aviator. 30c, 50c, Floating launch & control facility, satellite.

1966, July 11

959	A188	10c	multicolored
960	A188	15c	multicolored
961	A188	20c	multicolored
962	A188	30c	multicolored
963	A188	50c	multicolored
964	A188	12.45g	multicolored
965	A188	18.15g	multicolored
966	A188	36g	multicolored
a.			Souvenir sheet of 1, perf. 13x13½

Nos. 964-966a are airmail.

Rubén Dario — A189

"Paraguay de Fuego" by Dario — A189a

1966, July 16 **Wmk. 347**

967	A189	50c	ultramarine	.20	.20
968	A189	70c	bister brn	.20	.20
969	A189	1.50g	rose car	.20	.20
970	A189	3g	violet	.20	.20
971	A189	4g	greenish bl	.20	.20
972	A189	5g	black	.20	.20
973	A189a	12.45g	blue	.20	.20
974	A189a	18.15g	red lil	.20	.20
975	A189a	23.40g	org brn	.25	.20
976	A189a	36g	brt grn	.40	.20
977	A189a	50g	rose car	.40	.20
	Nos. 967-977 (11)			2.65	2.20

50th death anniv. of Ruben Dario (pen name of Felix Rubén Garcia Sarmiento, 1867-1916), Nicaraguan poet, newspaper correspondent and diplomat.

Nos. 973-977 are airmail.

Space Missions — A190

1966, Aug. 25 **Unwmk.**

978	A190	10c	Gemini 8
979	A190	15c	Gemini 9
980	A190	20c	Surveyor 1 on moon
981	A190	30c	Gemini 10
982	A190	50c	like #981
983	A190	12.45g	like #980
984	A190	18.15g	like #979
985	A190	36g	like #978
a.			Souvenir sheet of 1, perf. 13x13½

Nos. 983-985a are airmail.

1968 Winter Olympics, Grenoble — A191

1966, Sept. 30 ***Perf. 14***

986	A191	10c	Figure skating
987	A191	15c	Downhill skiing
988	A191	20c	Speed skating
989	A191	30c	2-man luge
990	A191	50c	like #989
991	A191	12.45g	like #988
992	A191	18.15g	like #987
993	A191	36g	like #986
a.			Souvenir sheet of 1

Nos. 987, 992, World Skiing Championships, Portillo, Chile, 1966. Nos. 991-993a are airmail.

Pres. John F. Kennedy, 3rd Death Anniv. — A192

Perf. 12x12½, 13½x14 (#997-998, 1001)

1966, Nov. 7

994	A192	10c	Echo 1 & 2
995	A192	15c	Telstar 1 & 2
996	A192	20c	Relay 1 & 2
997	A192	30c	Syncom 1, 2 & 3, Early Bird
998	A192	50c	like #997
999	A192	12.45g	like #996
1000	A192	18.15g	like #995
1001	A192	36g	like #994
a.			Souvenir sheet of 1, perf. 13x14x13½x14

Nos. 999-1001a are airmail.

Paintings A193

Portraits of women by: No. 1002a, 10c, De Largilliere. b, 15c, Rubens. c, 20c, Titian. d, 30c, Hans Holbein. e, 50c, Sanchez Coello.

Paintings: No. 1003a, 12.45g, Mars and Venus with United by Love by Veronese. b, 18.15g, Allegory of Prudence, Peace and Abundance by Vouet. c, 36g, Madonna and Child by Andres Montegna.

1966, Dec. 10 ***Perf. 14x13½***

1002	A193	Strip of 5, #a.-e.	
1003	A193	Strip of 3, #a.-c.	
d.		Souvenir sheet of 1, #1003c	

Nos. 1003a-1003d are airmail. No. 1003d has green pattern in border and is perf. 12½x12.

Holy Week Paintings A194

Life of Christ by: No. 1004a, 10c, Raphael. b, 15c, Rubens. c, 20c, Da Ponte. d, 30c, El Greco. e, 50c, Murillo, horiz.

12.45g, G. Reni. 18.15g, Tintoretto. 36g, Da Vinci, horiz.

1967, Feb. 28 ***Perf. 14x13½, 13½x14***

1004	A194		Strip of 5, #a.-e.
1005	A194	12.45g	multicolored
1006	A194	18.15g	multicolored
1007	A194	36g	multicolored
a.			Souvenir sheet of 1

Nos. 1005-1007a are airmail. No. 1007a has salmon pattern in border and contains one 60x40mm, perf. 14 stamp.

Birth of Christ by Barocci A195

16th Cent. Paintings: 12.45g, Madonna and Child by Caravaggio. 18.15g, Mary of the Holy Family (detail) by El Greco. 36g, Assumption of the Virgin by Vasco Fernandes.

1967, Mar. 10 ***Perf. 14½***

1008	A195	10c	lt bl & multi
1009	A195	15c	lt grn & multi
1010	A195	20c	lt brn & multi
1011	A195	30c	lil & multi
1012	A195	50c	pink & multi
1013	A195	12.45g	lt bl grn & multi
1014	A195	18.15g	brt pink & multi
1015	A195	36g	lt vio & multi
a.			Souv. sheet of 1, sep & multi

Nos. 1013-1015a are airmail.

Exist imperf. with changed borders.

Globe and Lions Emblem — A196

Medical Laboratory "Health" A196a

Designs: 1.50g, 3g, Melvin Jones. 4g, 5g, Lions' Headquarters, Chicago. 12.45g, 18.15g, Library "Education."

1967, May 9 **Litho.** **Wmk. 347**

1016	A196	50c	light vio	.20	.20
1017	A196	70c	blue	.20	.20
1018	A196	1.50g	ultra	.20	.20
1019	A196	3g	brown	.20	.20
1020	A196	4g	Prussian grn	.20	.20
1021	A196	5g	ol gray	.20	.20
1022	A196a	12.45g	dk brn	.20	.20
1023	A196a	18.15g	violet	.20	.20
1024	A196a	23.40g	rose cl	.20	.20
1025	A196a	36g	Prus blue	.30	.20
1026	A196a	50g	rose car	.35	.20
	Nos. 1016-1026 (11)			2.45	2.20

50th anniversary of Lions International.

Nos. 1022-1026 are airmail.

Vase of Flowers by Chardin A197

Still Life Paintings by: No. 1027b, 15c, Fontanesi, horiz. c, 20c, Cezanne. d, 30c, Van Gogh. e, 50c, Renoir.

Paintings: 12.45g, Cha-U-Kao at the Moulin Rouge by Toulouse-Lautrec. 18.15g, Gabrielle with Jean Renoir by Renoir. 36g, Patience Escalier, Shepherd of Provence by Van Gogh.

1967, May 16 ***Perf. 12½x12***

1027	A197		Strip of 5, #a.-e.
1028	A197	12.45g	multicolored
1029	A197	18.15g	multicolored
1030	A197	36g	multicolored
a.			Souvenir sheet of 1, perf. 14x12x14x13½

Nos. 1028-1030a are airmail. No. 1030a has a green pattern in border.

Exist imperf. with changed borders.

Famous Paintings — A198

1967, July 16 ***Perf. 12x12½***

1031	A198	10c	Jan Steen

Perf. 14x13½, 13½x14

1032	A198	15c	Frans Hals, vert.
1033	A198	20c	Jordaens
1034	A198	25c	Rembrandt
1035	A198	30c	de Marees, vert.
1036	A198	50c	Quentin, vert.
1037	A198	12.45g	Nicolaes Maes, vert.
1038	A198	18.15g	Vigee-Lebrun, vert.
1039	A198	36g	Rubens, vert.

Souvenir Sheet

Perf. 12x12½

1040	A198	50g	G. B. Tiepolo

Nos. 1037-1039 are airmail. An imperf. souvenir sheet of 3, #1037-1039 exists with dark green pattern in border.

John F. Kennedy, 50th Birth Anniv. A199

Kennedy and: 10c, Recovery of Alan Shepard's capsule, Lyndon Johnson, Mrs. Kennedy. 15c, John Glenn. 20c, Mr. and Mrs. M. Scott Carpenter. 25c, Rocket 2nd stage, Wernher Von Braun. 30c, Cape Canaveral, Walter Schirra. 50c, Syncom 2 satellite, horiz. 12.45g, Launch of Atlas rocket. 18.15g, Theorized lunar landing, horiz. 36g, Portrait of Kennedy by Torres. 50g, Apollo lift-off, horiz.

Perf. 14x13½, 13½x14

1967, Aug. 19

1041	A199	10c	multicolored
1042	A199	15c	multicolored
1043	A199	20c	multicolored
1044	A199	25c	multicolored
1045	A199	30c	multicolored
1046	A199	50c	multicolored
1047	A199	12.45g	multicolored
1048	A199	18.15g	multicolored
1049	A199	36g	multicolored

Souvenir Sheet

1050	A199	50g	multicolored

Nos. 1047-1050 are airmail. An imperf. souvenir sheet of 3 containing #1047-1049 exists with violet border.

Sculptures A200

1967, Oct. 16 ***Perf. 14x13½***

1051	A200	10c	Head of athlete
1052	A200	15c	Myron's Discobolus
1053	A200	20c	Apollo of Belvedere
1054	A200	25c	Artemis
1055	A200	30c	Venus De Milo
1056	A200	50c	Winged Victory of Samothrace
1057	A200	12.45g	Laocoon Group
1058	A200	18.15g	Moses
1059	A200	50g	Pieta

Nos. 1057-1059 are airmail.

Mexican Art — A201

Designs: 10c, Bowl, Veracruz. 15c, Knobbed vessel, Colima. 20c, Mixtec jaguar pitcher. 25c, Head, Veracruz. 30c, Statue of seated woman, Teotihuacan. 50c, Vessel depicting a woman, Aztec. 12.45g, Mixtec bowl, horiz. 18.15g, Three-legged vessel, Teotihuacan, horiz. 36g, Golden mask, Teotihuacan, horiz. 50g, The Culture of the Totonac by Diego Rivera, 1950, horiz.

1967, Nov. 29 ***Perf. 14x13½***

1060	A201	10c	multicolored
1061	A201	15c	multicolored
1062	A201	20c	multicolored
1063	A201	25c	multicolored
1064	A201	30c	multicolored
1065	A201	50c	multicolored

Perf. 13½x14

1066	A201	12.45g	multicolored
1067	A201	18.15g	multicolored
1068	A201	36g	multicolored

Souvenir Sheet

Perf. 14

1069	A201	50g	multicolored

1968 Summer Olympics, Mexico City (#1065-1069).

Nos. 1066-1069 are airmail. An imperf. souvenir sheet of 3 containing #1066-1068 exists with green pattern in border.

Paintings of the Madonna and Child A202

1968, Jan. 27 ***Perf. 14x13½,13½x14***

1070	A202	10c	Bellini
1071	A202	15c	Raphael
1072	A202	20c	Correggio
1073	A202	25c	Luini
1074	A202	30c	Bronzino
1075	A202	50c	Van Dyck
1076	A202	12.45g	Vignon, horiz.
1077	A202	18.15g	de Ribera
1078	A202	36g	Botticelli

Nos. 1076-1078 are airmail and also exist as imperf. souvenir sheet of 3 with olive brown pattern in border.

Paintings of Winter Scenes — A203

1968 Winter Olympics Emblem A204

1968, Apr. 23 ***Perf. 13½x14, 14x13½***

1079	A203	10c	Pissarro
1080	A203	15c	Utrillo, vert.
1081	A203	20c	Monet
1082	A203	25c	Breitner, vert.
1083	A203	30c	Sisley
1084	A203	50c	Brueghel, vert.
1085	A203	12.45g	Avercampe, vert.
1086	A203	18.15g	Brueghel, diff.
1087	A203	36g	P. Limbourg & brothers, vert.

Souvenir Sheet

1088 Sheet of 2
a. A204 50g multicolored

Nos. 1087-1088, 1088a are airmail. No. 1088 contains #1088a and #1087 with red pattern.

Paraguayan Stamps, Cent. (in 1970) — A205

Perf. 13½x14, 14x13½

1968, June 3 **Litho.**

1089	A205	10c	#1, 4
1090	A205	15c	#C21, 310, vert.
1091	A205	20c	#203, C140
1092	A205	25c	#C72, C61, vert.
1093	A205	30c	#638, 711
1094	A205	50c	#406, C38, vert.
1095	A205	12.45g	#B2, B7
1096	A205	18.15g	#C10, C11, vert.
1097	A205	36g	#828, C76, 616

Souvenir Sheet

Perf. 14

1098 Sheet of 2
a. A205 50g #929 & #379

Nos. 1095-1098a are airmail. No. 1098 contains No. 1098a and No. 1097 with light brown pattern in border.

Paintings A206

#1099-1106, paintings of children. #1107-1108, paintings of sailboats at sea.

1968, July 9 ***Perf. 14x13½, 13½x14***

1099	A206	10c	Russell
1100	A206	15c	Velazquez
1101	A206	20c	Romney
1102	A206	25c	Lawrence
1103	A206	30c	Caravaggio
1104	A206	50c	Gentileschi
1105	A206	12.45g	Renoir
1106	A206	18.15g	Copley
1107	A206	36g	Sessions, horiz.

Souvenir Sheet

Perf. 14

1108 Sheet of 2
a. A206 50g Currier & Ives, horiz.

1968 Summer Olympics, Mexico City (Nos. 1107-1108).

Nos. 1106-1108a are airmail. No. 1108 contains No. 1108a and No. 1107 with a red pattern in border.

A207

WHO Emblem — A207a

1968, Aug. 12 **Wmk. 347** ***Perf. 11***

1109	A207	3g	bluish grn	.20	.20
1110	A207	4g	brt pink	.20	.20
1111	A207	5g	bister brn	.20	.20
1112	A207	10g	violet	.20	.20
1113	A207a	36g	blk brn	.30	.20
1114	A207a	50g	rose claret	.35	.25
1115	A207a	100g	brt bl	.75	.45
	Nos. 1109-1115 (7)			2.20	1.70

WHO, 20th anniv.; cent. of the natl. epic.

39th Intl. Eucharistic Congress A208

Paintings of life of Christ by various artists (except No. 1125a).

Perf. 14x13½

1968, Sept. 25 **Litho.** **Unwmk.**

1116	A208	10c	Caravaggio
1117	A208	15c	El Greco
1118	A208	20c	Del Sarto
1119	A208	25c	Van der Weyden
1120	A208	30c	De Patinier
1121	A208	50c	Plockhorst
1122	A208	12.45g	Bronzino
1123	A208	18.15g	Raphael
1124	A208	36g	Correggio

Souvenir Sheet

Perf. 14

1125 Sheet of 2
a. A208 36g Pope Paul VI
b. A208 50g Tiepolo

Pope Paul VI's visit to South America (No. 1125). Nos. 1122-1125b are airmail.

Events of 1968 — A209

Designs: 10c, Mexican 25p Olympic coin. 15c, Rentry of Echo 1 satellite. 20c, Visit of Pope Paul VI to Fatima, Portugal. 25c, Dr. Christian Barnard, 1st heart transplant. 30c, Martin Luther King, assasination. 50c, Pres. Alfredo Stroessner laying wreath at grave of Pres. Kennedy, vert. 12.45g, Pres. Stroessner, Pres. Lyndon B. Johnson. 18.15g, John F. Kennedy, Abraham Lincoln, Robert Kennedy. 50g, Summer Olympics, Mexico City, satellite transmissions, vert.

1968, Dec. 21 ***Perf. 13½x14, 14x13½***

1126	A209	10c	multicolored
1127	A209	15c	multicolored
1128	A209	20c	multicolored
1129	A209	25c	multicolored
1130	A209	30c	multicolored
1131	A209	50c	multicolored
1132	A209	12.45g	multicolored
1133	A209	18.15g	multicolored
1134	A209	50g	multicolored

Nos. 1132-1134 are airmail. Set exists imperf. in sheets of 3 in changed colors.

1968 Summer Olympics, Mexico City A210

Olympic Stadium A210a

Gold Medal Winners: 10c, Felipe Munoz, Mexico, 200-meter breast stroke. 15c, Daniel Rebillard, France, 4000-meter cycling. 20c, David Hemery, England, 400-meter hurdles. 25c, Bob Seagren, US, pole vault. 30c, Francisco Rodriguez, Venezuela, light flyweight boxing. 50c, Bjorn Ferm, Sweden, modern pentathlon. 12.45g, Klaus Dibiasi, Italy, platform diving. 50g, Ingrid Becker, West Germany, fencing, women's pentathlon.

1969, Feb. 13 ***Perf. 14x13½***

1135	A210	10c	multicolored
1136	A210	15c	multicolored
1137	A210	20c	multicolored
1138	A210	25c	multicolored
1139	A210	30c	multicolored
1140	A210	50c	multicolored
1141	A210	12.45g	multicolored
1142	A210a	18.15g	multicolored
1143	A210	50g	multicolored

Nos. 1141-1143 are airmail. Set exists imperf. in sheets of 3 in changed colors.

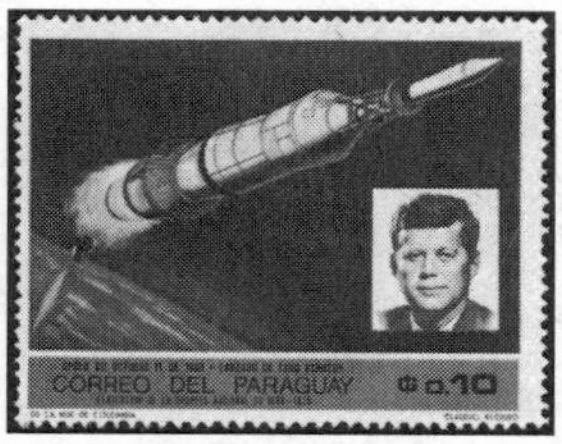

Space Missions — A211

Designs: 10c, Apollo 7, John F. Kennedy. 15c, Apollo 8, Kennedy. 20c, Apollo 8, Kennedy, diff. 25c, Study of solar flares, ITU emblem. 30c, Canary Bird satellite. 50c, ESRO satellite. 12.45g, Wernher von Braun, rocket launch. 18.15g, Global satellite coverage, ITU emblem. 50g, Otto Lilienthal, Graf Zeppelin, Hermann Oberth, evolution of flight.

1969, Mar. 10 ***Perf. 13½x14***

1144	A211	10c	multicolored
1145	A211	15c	multicolored
1146	A211	20c	multicolored
1147	A211	25c	multicolored
1148	A211	30c	multicolored
1149	A211	50c	multicolored
1150	A211	12.45g	multicolored
1151	A211	18.15g	multicolored
1152	A211	50g	multicolored

Nos. 1150-1152 are airmail. Set exists imperf. in sheets of 3 in changed colors.

"World United in Peace" — A212

1969, June 28 **Wmk. 347** ***Perf. 11***

1153	A212	50c	rose	.20	.20
1154	A212	70c	ultra	.20	.20
1155	A212	1.50g	light brn	.20	.20
1156	A212	3g	lil rose	.20	.20
1157	A212	4g	emerald	.20	.20
1158	A212	5g	violet	.20	.20
1159	A212	10g	brt lilac	.20	.20
	Nos. 1153-1159 (7)			1.40	1.40

Peace Week.

Birds A213

Designs: 10c, Pteroglossus viridis. 15c, Phytotoma rutila. 20c, Porphyrula martinica. 25c, Oxyrunchus cristatus. 30c, Spizaetus ornatus. 50c, Phoenicopterus ruber. 75c, Amazona ochrocephala. 12.45g, Ara ararauna, Ara macao. 18.15g, Colibri coruscans.

Perf. 13½x14, 14x13½

1969, July 9 **Unwmk.**

1160	A213	10c	multicolored
1161	A213	15c	multicolored
1162	A213	20c	multicolored
1163	A213	25c	multicolored
1164	A213	30c	multicolored
1165	A213	50c	multicolored
1166	A213	75c	multicolored
1167	A213	12.45g	multicolored
1168	A213	18.15g	multicolored

Nos. 1167-1168 are airmail. Nos. 1161, 1164-1168 are vert.

Fauna — A214

1969, July 9

1169	A214	10c	Porcupine
1170	A214	15c	Lemur, vert.
1171	A214	20c	3-toed sloth, vert.
1172	A214	25c	Puma
1173	A214	30c	Alligator
1174	A214	50c	Jaguar
1175	A214	75c	Anteater
1176	A214	12.45g	Tapir
1177	A214	18.15g	Capybara

Nos. 1176-1177 are airmail.

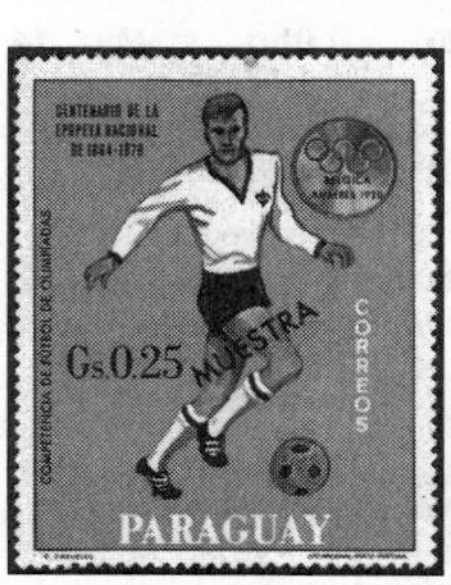

Olympic Soccer Champions, 1900-1968 A215

Designs: 10c, Great Britain, Paris, 1900. 15c, Canada, St. Louis, 1904. 20c, Great Britain, London, 1908 and Stockholm, 1912. 25c, Belgium, Antwerp, 1920. 30c, Uruguay, Paris, 1924 and Amsterdam, 1928. 50c, Italy, Berlin, 1936. 75c, Sweden, London, 1948; USSR, Melbourne, 1956. 12.45g, Yugoslavia, Rome, 1960. 18.15g, Hungary, Helsinki, 1952, Tokyo, 1964 and Mexico, 1968. 23.40g, Soccer ball, Mexico 1968 emblem.

1969, Nov. 26 ***Perf. 14***

1178	A215	10c	multicolored
1179	A215	15c	multicolored
1180	A215	20c	multicolored
1181	A215	25c	multicolored
1182	A215	30c	multicolored
1183	A215	50c	multicolored
1184	A215	75c	multicolored
1185	A215	12.45g	multicolored
1186	A215	18.15g	multicolored

Souvenir Sheet

1187	A215	23.40g	multicolored

Nos. 1185-1187 are airmail. No. 1187 contains one 49x60mm stamp.

A216

World Cup or South American Soccer Champions: 10c, Paraguay, 1953. 15c, Uruguay, 1930. 20c, Italy, 1934. 25c, Italy, 1938. 30c, Uruguay, 1950. 50c, Germany, 1954, horiz. 75c, Brazil, 1958. 12.45g, Brazil, 1962. 18.15g, England, 1966. No. 1198, Trophy. 23.40g, Soccer player, satellite.

1969, Nov. 26 ***Perf. 14***

1189	A216	10c	multicolored
1190	A216	15c	multicolored
1191	A216	20c	multicolored
1192	A216	25c	multicolored
1193	A216	30c	multicolored
1194	A216	50c	multicolored
1195	A216	75c	multicolored
1196	A216	12.45g	multicolored
1197	A216	18.15g	multicolored

Souvenir Sheets

Perf. 13½, Imperf(#1199)

1198	A216	23.40g	multicolored
1199	A216	23.40g	multicolored

Nos. 1196-1199 are airmail. No. 1198 contains one 50x60mm stamp. No. 1199 contains one 45x57mm stamp.

Paintings by Francisco de Goya (1746-1828) — A217

Designs: 10c, Miguel de Lardibazal. 15c, Francisca Sabasa y Gracia. 20c, Don Manuel Osorio. 25c, Young Women with a Letter. 30c, The Water Carrier. 50c, Truth, Time and History. 75c, The Forge. 12.45g, The Spell. 18.15g, Duke of Wellington on Horseback. 23.40g, "La Maja Desnuda."

1969, Nov. 29 **Litho.** ***Perf. 14x13½***

1200	A217	10c	multicolored
1201	A217	15c	multicolored
1202	A217	20c	multicolored
1203	A217	25c	multicolored
1204	A217	30c	multicolored
1205	A217	50c	multicolored
1206	A217	75c	multicolored
1207	A217	12.45g	multicolored
1208	A217	18.15g	multicolored

Souvenir Sheet

Perf. 14

1209	A217	23.40g	multicolored

Nos. 1207-1209 are airmail.

Christmas A218

Various paintings of The Nativity or Madonna and Child.

1969, Nov. 29 ***Perf. 14x13½***

1210	A218	10c	Master Bertram
1211	A218	15c	Procaccini
1212	A218	20c	Di Crediti
1213	A218	25c	De Flemalle
1214	A218	30c	Correggio
1215	A218	50c	Borgianni
1216	A218	75c	Botticelli
1217	A218	12.45g	El Greco
1218	A218	18.15g	De Morales

Souvenir Sheet

Perf. 13½

1219	A218	23.40g	Isenheimer Altar

Nos. 1217-1219 are airmail.

Souvenir Sheet

European Space Program — A219

1969, Nov. 29 **Litho.** ***Perf. 14***

1220	A219	23.40g	ESRO 1B

Imperf

1221	A219	23.40g	Ernst Stuhlinger

Francisco Solano — A220

1970, Mar. 1 **Wmk. 347** ***Perf. 11***

1222	A220	1g	bis brn	.20	.20
1223	A220	2g	violet	.20	.20
1224	A220	3g	brt pink	.20	.20
1225	A220	4g	rose claret	.20	.20
1226	A220	5g	blue	.20	.20
1227	A220	10g	bright grn	.20	.20
1228	A220	15g	lt Prus bl	.20	.20
1229	A220	20g	org brn	.20	.20
1230	A220	30g	gray grn	.25	.20
1231	A220	40g	gray brn	.30	.20
	Nos. 1222-1231 (10)			2.15	2.00

Marshal Francisco Solano Lopez (1827-1870), President of Paraguay. Nos. 1228-1231 are airmail.

1st Moon Landing, Apollo 11 — A221

Designs: 10c, Wernher von Braun, lift-off. 15c, Eagle and Columbia in lunar orbit. 20c, Deployment of lunar module. 25c, Landing on Moon. 30c, First steps on lunar surface. 50c, Gathering lunar soil. 75c, Lift-off from Moon. 12.45g, Rendevouz of Eagle and Columbia. 18.15g, Pres. Kennedy, von Braun, splashdown. No. 1241, Gold medal of Armstrong, Aldrin and Collins. No. 1242, Moon landing medal, Kennedy, von Braun. No. 1243, Apollo 12 astronauts Charles Conrad and Alan Bean on moon, and Dr. Kurt Debus.

1970, Mar. 11 **Unwmk.** ***Perf. 14***

1232	A221	10c	multicolored
1233	A221	15c	multicolored
1234	A221	20c	multicolored
1235	A221	25c	multicolored
1236	A221	30c	multicolored
1237	A221	50c	multicolored
1238	A221	75c	multicolored
1239	A221	12.45g	multicolored
1240	A221	18.15g	multicolored

Souvenir Sheets

1241	A221	23.40g	multicolored

Imperf

1242	A221	23.40g	multicolored
1243	A221	23.40g	multicolored

Nos. 1239-1243 are airmail. Nos. 1241-1242 contain one 50x60mm stamp, No. 1243 one 60x50mm stamp.

Easter — A222

Designs: 10c, 15c, 20c, 25c, 30c, 50c, 75c, Stations of the Cross. 12.45g, Christ appears to soldiers, vert. 18.15g, Christ appears to disciples, vert. 23.40g, The sad Madonna, vert.

1970, Mar. 11

1244 A222 10c multicolored
1245 A222 15c multicolored
1246 A222 20c multicolored
1247 A222 25c multicolored
1248 A222 30c multicolored
1249 A222 50c multicolored
1250 A222 75c multicolored
1251 A222 12.45g multicolored
1252 A222 18.15g multicolored

Souvenir Sheet

Perf. 13½

1253 A222 23.40g multicolored

Nos. 1251-1253 are airmail. No. 1253 contains one 50x60mm stamp.

Paraguay No. 2 — A223

Designs (First Issue of Paraguay): 2g, 10g, #1. 3g, #3. 5g, #2. 15g, #3. 30g, #2. 36g, #1.

1970, Aug. 15 Litho. Wmk. 347

1254	A223	1g	car rose	.20	.20
1255	A223	2g	ultra	.20	.20
1256	A223	3g	org brn	.20	.20
1257	A223	5g	violet	.20	.20
1258	A223	10g	lilac	.20	.20
1259	A223	15g	vio brn	.25	.20
1260	A223	30g	dp grn	.45	.40
1261	A223	36g	brt pink	.50	.40
	Nos. 1254-1261 (8)			2.20	2.00

Centenary of stamps of Paraguay.
#1259-1261 are airmail.

1972 Summer Olympics, Munich A224

No. 1262: a, 10c, Discus. b, 15c, Cycling. c, 20c, Men's hurdles. d, 25c, Fencing. e, 30c, Swimming, horiz.

50c, Shotput. 75c, Sailing. 12.45, Women's hurdles, horiz. 18.15g, Equestrian, horiz. No. 1267, Flags, Olympic coins. No. 1268, Frauenkirche Church, Munich. No. 1269, Olympic Village, Munich, horiz.

1970, Sept. 28 Unwmk. *Perf. 14*

1262 A224 Strip of 5, #a.-e.
1263 A224 50c multicolored
1264 A224 75c multicolored
1265 A224 12.45g multicolored
1266 A224 18.15g multicolored

Souvenir Sheets

Perf. 13½

1267 A224 23.40g multicolored

Imperf

1268 A224 23.40g multicolored
1269 A224 23.40g multicolored

Nos. 1265-1269 are airmail. Nos. 1267-1269 each contain one 50x60mm stamp.

Paintings, Pinakothek, Munich, 1972 A225

Nudes by: No. 1270a, 10c, Cranach. b, 15c, Baldung. c, 20c, Tintoretto. d, 25c, Rubens. e, 30c, Boucher, horiz. 50c, Baldung, diff. 75c, Cranach, diff.

12.45g, Self-portrait, Durer. 18.15g, Alterpiece, Altdorfer. 23.40g, Madonna and Child.

1970, Sept. 28 *Perf. 14*

1270 A225 Strip of 5, #a.-e.
1271 A225 50c multicolored
1272 A225 75c multicolored
1273 A225 12.45g multicolored
1274 A225 18.15g multicolored

Souvenir Sheet

Perf. 13½

1275 A225 23.40g multicolored

Nos. 1273-1275 are airmail. No. 1275 contains one 50x60mm stamp.

Apollo Space Program — A226

No. 1276: a, 10c, Ignition, Saturn 5. b, 15c, Apollo 1 mission emblem, vert. c, 20c, Apollo 7, Oct. 1968. d, 25c, Apollo 8, Dec. 1968. e, 30c, Apollo 9, Mar. 1969.

50c, Apollo 10, May 1969. 75c, Apollo 11, July 1969. 12.45g, Apollo 12, Nov. 1969. 18.15g, Apollo 13, Apr. 1970. No. 1281, Lunar landing sites. No. 1282, Wernher von Braun, rockets. No. 1283, James A. Lovell, John L. Swigert, Fred W. Haise.

1970, Oct. 19 *Perf. 14*

1276 A226 Strip of 5, #a.-e.
1277 A226 50c multicolored
1278 A226 75c multicolored
1279 A226 12.45g multicolored
1280 A226 18.15g multicolored

Souvenir Sheets

Perf. 13½

1281 A226 23.40g multicolored

Imperf

1282 A226 23.40g multicolored
1283 A226 23.40g multicolored

Nos. 1279-1283 are airmail. Nos. 1281-1283 each contain one 60x50mm stamp.

1970, Oct. 19 *Perf. 14*

Future Space Projects: No. 1284a, 10c, Space station, 2000. b, 15c, Lunar station, vert. c, 20c, Space transport. d, 25c, Lunar rover. e, 30c, Skylab.

50c, Space station, 1971. 75c, Lunar vehicle. 12.45g, Lunar vehicle, diff., vert. 18.15g, Vehicle rising above lunar surface. 23.40g, Moon stations, transport.

1284 A226 Strip of 5, #a.-e.
1285 A226 50c multicolored
1286 A226 75c multicolored
1287 A226 12.45g multicolored
1288 A226 18.15g multicolored

Souvenir Sheet

Perf. 13½

1289 A226 23.40g multicolored

Nos. 1287-1289 are airmail. No. 1289 contains one 50x60mm stamp. For overprints see Nos. 2288-2290, C653.

EXPO '70, Osaka, Japan A228

Paintings from National Museum, Tokyo: No. 1288a, 10c, Buddha. b, 15c, Fire, people. c, 20c, Demon, Ogata Korin. d, 25c, Japanese play, Hishikawa Moronobu. e, 30c, Birds.

50c, Woman, Utamaro. 75c, Samurai, Wantabe Kazan. 12.45c, Women Beneath Tree, Kano Hideroi. 18.15g, Courtesans, Torrii Kiyonaga. 50g, View of Mt. Fuji, Hokusai, horiz. No. 1296, Courtesan, Kaigetsudo Ando. No. 1297, Emblem of Expo '70. No. 1298, Emblem of 1972 Winter Olympics, Sapporo.

1970, Nov. 26 Litho. *Perf. 14*

1290 A228 Strip of 5, #a.-e.
1291 A228 50c multicolored
1292 A228 75c multicolored
1293 A228 12.45g multicolored
1294 A228 18.15g multicolored
1295 A228 50g multicolored

Souvenir Sheets

Perf. 13½

1296 A228 20g multicolored
1297 A228 20g multicolored
1298 A228 20g multicolored

Nos. 1293-1298 are airmail. Nos. 1296-1298 each contain one 50x60mm stamp.

Flower Paintings A229

Artists: No. 1299a, 10c, Von Jawlensky. b, 15c, Purrmann. c, 20c, De Vlaminck. d, 25c, Monet. e, 30c, Renoir.

50c, Van Gogh. 75, Cezanne. 12.45g, Van Huysum. 18.15g, Ruysch. 50g, Walscappelle. 20g, Bosschaert.

1970, Nov. 26 *Perf. 14*

1299 A229 Strip of 5, #a.-e.
1300 A229 50c multicolored
1301 A229 75c multicolored
1302 A229 12.45g multicolored
1303 A229 18.15g multicolored
1304 A229 50g multicolored

Souvenir Sheet

Perf. 13½

1305 A229 20g multicolored

Nos. 1302-1305 are airmail. No. 1305 contains one 50x60mm stamp.

Paintings from The Prado, Madrid — A230

Nudes by: No. 1306a, 10c, Titian. b, 15c, Velazquez. c, 20c, Van Dyck. d, 25c, Tintoretto. e, 30c, Rubens.

50c, Venus and Sleeping Adonis, Veronese. 75c, Adam and Eve, Titian. 12.45g, The Holy Family, Goya. 18.15g, Shepherd Boy, Murillo. 50g, The Holy Family, El Greco.

1970, Dec. 16 *Perf. 14*

1306 A230 Strip of 5, #a.-e.
1307 A230 50c multicolored
1308 A230 75c multicolored
1309 A230 12.45g multicolored
1310 A230 18.15g multicolored
1311 A230 50g multicolored

#1309-1311 are airmail. #1307-1311 are vert.

1970, Dec. 16

Paintings by Albrecht Durer (1471-1528): No. 1312a, 10c, Adam and Eve. b, 15c, St. Jerome in the Wilderness. c, 20c, St. Eustachius and George. d, 25c, Piper and drummer. e, 30c, Lucretia's Suicide.

50c, Oswald Krel. 75c, Stag Beetle. 12.45g, Paul and Mark. 18.15g, Lot's Flight. 50g, Nativity.

1312 A230 Strip of 5, #a.-e.
1313 A230 50c multicolored
1314 A230 75c multicolored
1315 A230 12.45g multicolored
1316 A230 18.15g multicolored
1317 A230 50g multicolored

Nos. 1315-1317 are airmail. See No. 1273.

Christmas A232

Paintings: No. 1318a, 10c, The Annunciation, Van der Weyden. b, 15c, The Madonna, Zeitblom. c, 20c, The Nativity, Von Soest. d, 25c, Adoration of the Magi, Mayno. e, 30c, Adoration of the Magi, Da Fabriano.

50c, Flight From Egypt, Masters of Martyrdom. 75c, Presentation of Christ, Memling. 12.45g, The Holy Family, Poussin, horiz. 18.15g, The Holy Family, Rubens. 20g, Adoration of the Magi, Giorgione, horiz. 50g, Madonna and Child, Batoni.

1971, Mar. 23

1318 A232 Strip of 5, #a.-e.
1319 A232 50c multicolored
1320 A232 75c multicolored
1321 A232 12.45g multicolored
1322 A232 18.15g multicolored
1323 A232 50g multicolored

Souvenir Sheet

Perf. 13½

1324 A232 20g multicolored

Nos. 1321-1324 are airmail. No. 1324 contains one 60x50mm stamp.

1972 Summer Olympics, Munich A233

Olympic decathlon gold medalists: No. 1325a, 10c, Hugo Wieslander, Stockholm 1912. b, 15c, Helge Lovland, Antwerp 1920. c, 20c, Harald M. Osborn, Paris 1924. d, 25c, Paavo Yrjola, Amsterdam 1928. e, 30c, James Bausch, Los Angeles 1932.

50c, Glenn Morris, Berlin 1936. 75c, Bob Mathias, London 1948, Helsinki 1952. 12.45g, Milton Campbell, Melbourne 1956. 18.15g, Rafer Johnson, Rome 1960. 50g, Willi Holdorf, Tokyo 1964. No. 1331, Bill Toomey, Mexico City 1968.

No. 1332, Pole vaulter, Munich, 1972.

1971, Mar. 23 *Perf. 14*

1325 A233 Strip of 5, #a.-e.
1326 A233 50c multicolored
1327 A233 75c multicolored
1328 A233 12.45g multicolored
1329 A233 18.15g multicolored
1330 A233 50g multicolored

Souvenir Sheets

Perf. 13½

1331 A233 20g multicolored
1332 A233 20g multicolored

Nos. 1328-1332 are airmail. Nos. 1331-1332 each contain one 50x60mm stamp.

Art — A234

Paintings by: No. 1333a, 10c, Van Dyck. b, 15c, Titian. c, 20c, Van Dyck, diff. d, 25c, Walter. e, 30c, Orsi.

50c, 17th cent. Japanese artist, horiz. 75c, David. 12.45g, Huguet. 18.15g, Perugino. 20g, Van Eyck. 50g, Witz.

1971, Mar. 26 ***Perf. 14***

1333 A234 Strip of 5, #a.-e.
1334 A234 50c multicolored
1335 A234 75c multicolored
1336 A234 12.45g multicolored
1337 A234 18.15g multicolored
1338 A234 50g multicolored

Souvenir Sheet

Perf. 13½

1339 A234 20g multicolored

Nos. 1336-1339 are airmail. No. 1339 contains one 50x60mm stamp.

Paintings from the Louvre, Paris

Portraits of women by: No. 1340a, 10c, De la Tour. b, 15c, Boucher. c, 20c, Delacroix. d, 25c, 16th cent. French artist. e, 30c, Ingres.

50c, Ingres, horiz. 75c, Watteau, horiz. 12.45g, 2nd cent. artist. 18.15g, Renoir. 20g, Mona Lisa, Da Vinci. 50g, Liberty Guiding the People, Delacroix.

1971, Mar. 26 ***Perf. 14***

1340 A234 Strip of 5, #a.-e.
1341 A234 50c multicolored
1342 A234 75c multicolored
1343 A234 12.45g multicolored
1344 A234 18.15g multicolored
1345 A234 50g multicolored

Souvenir Sheet

Perf. 13½

1346 A234 20g multicolored

Nos. 1343-1346 are airmail. No. 1346 contains one 50x60mm stamp.

Paintings A236

Artist: No. 1347a, 10c, Botticelli. b, 15c, Titian. c, 20c, Raphael. d, 25c, Pellegrini. e, 30c, Caracci.

50c, Titian, horiz. 75c, Ricci, horiz. 12.45g, Courtines. 18.15g, Rodas. 50g, Murillo.

1971, Mar. 29 ***Perf. 14***

1347 A236 Strip of 5, #a.-e.
1348 A236 50c multicolored
1349 A236 75c multicolored
1350 A236 12.45g multicolored
1351 A236 18.15g multicolored
1352 A236 50g multicolored

Nos. 1350-1352 are airmail.

Hunting Scenes — A237

Different Paintings by: No. 1353a, 10c, Gozzoli, vert. b, 15c, Velazquez, vert. c, 20c, Brun. d, 25c, Fontainebleau School, 1550, vert. e, 30c, Uccello, vert.

50c, P. De Vos. 75c, Vernet. 12.45g, 18.15g, 50g, Alken & Sutherland. No. 1359, Paul & Derveaux. No. 1360, Degas.

1971, Mar. 29

1353 A237 Strip of 5, #a.-e.
1354 A237 50c multicolored
1355 A237 75c multicolored
1356 A237 12.45g multicolored
1357 A237 18.15g multicolored
1358 A237 50g multicolored

Souvenir Sheets

Perf. 13½

1359 A237 20g multicolored
1360 A237 20g multicolored

Nos. 1356-1360 are airmail. Nos. 1359-1360 each contain one 60x50mm stamp.

Philatokyo '71 — A238

Designs: Nos. 1361a-1361e, 10c, 15c, 20c, 25c, 30c, Different flowers, Gukei. 50c, Birds, Lu Chi. 75c, Flowers, Sakai Hoitsu. 12.45g, Man and Woman, Utamaro. 18.15g, Tea Ceremony, from Tea museum. 50g, Bathers, Utamaro. No. 1367, Woman, Kamakura Period. No. 1368, Japan #1, #821, #904, #1023.

1971, Apr. 7 ***Perf. 14***

1361 A238 Strip of 5, #a.-e.
1362 A238 50c multicolored
1363 A238 75c multicolored
1364 A238 12.45g multicolored
1365 A238 18.15g multicolored
1366 A238 50g multicolored

Souvenir Sheets

Perf. 13½

1367 A238 20g multicolored
1368 A238 20g multicolored

Nos. 1364-1368 are airmail. Nos. 1367-1368 each contain one 50x60mm stamp.
See Nos. 1375-1376.

1972 Winter Olympics, Sapporo A239

Paintings of women by: No. 1369a, 10c, Harunobu. b, 15c, Hosoda. c, 20c, Harunobu, diff. d, 25c, Uemura Shoen. e, 30c, Ketao.

50c, Three Women, Torii. 75c, Old Man, Kakizahi. 12.45g, 2-man bobsled. 18.15g, Ice sculptures, horiz. 50g, Mt. Fuji, Hokusai, horiz. No. 1375, Skier, horiz. No. 1376, Sapporo Olympic emblems.

1971, Apr. ***Perf. 14***

1369 A239 Strip of 5, #a.-e.
1370 A239 50c multicolored
1371 A239 75c multicolored
1372 A239 12.45g multicolored
1373 A239 18.15g multicolored
1374 A239 50g multicolored

Souvenir Sheets

Perf. 14½

1375 A239 20g multicolored

Perf. 13½

1376 A239 20g multicolored

Nos. 1372-1376 are airmail. No. 1375 contains one 35x25mm stamp with PhilaTokyo 71 emblem. No. 1376 contains one 50x60mm stamp.

For Japanese painting stamps with white border and Winter Olympics emblem see #1409-1410.

UNESCO and Paraguay Emblems, Globe, Teacher and Pupil A240

Wmk. 347

1971, May 18 Litho. *Perf. 11*

1377 A240	3g	ultra	.20	.20
1378 A240	5g	lilac	.20	.20
1379 A240	10g	emerald	.20	.20
1380 A240	20g	claret	.20	.20
1381 A240	25g	brt pink	.20	.20
1382 A240	30g	brown	.20	.20
1383 A240	50g	gray olive	.35	.25
		Nos. 1377-1383 (7)	1.55	1.45

International Education Year.
Nos. 1380-1383 are airmail.

Paintings, Berlin-Dahlem Museum — A241

Artists: 10c, Caravaggio. No. 1385: a, 15c, b, 20c, Di Cosimo. 25c, Cranach. 30c, Veneziano. 50g, Holbein. 75c, Baldung. 12.45g, Cranach, diff. 18.15g, Durer. 50g, Schongauer.

1971, Dec. 24 Unwmk. *Perf. 14*

1384 A241 10c multicolored
1385 A241 Pair, #a.-b.
1386 A241 25c multicolored
1387 A241 30c multicolored
1388 A241 50c multicolored
1389 A241 75c multicolored
1390 A241 12.45g multicolored
1391 A241 18.15g multicolored
1392 A241 50g multicolored

Nos. 1390-1392 are airmail. No. 1385 has continuous design.

Napoleon I, 150th Death Anniv. A242

Paintings: No. 1393a, 10c, Desiree Clary, Gerin. b, 15c, Josephine de Beauharnais, Gros. c, 20c, Maria Luisa, Gerard. d, 25c, Juliette Recamier, Gerard. e, 30c, Maria Walewska, Gerard.

50c, Victoria Kraus, unknown artist, horiz. 75c, Napoleon on Horseback, Chabord. 12.45g, Trafalgar, A. Mayer, horiz. 18.15g, Napoleon Leading Army, Gautherot, horiz. 50g, Napoleon's tomb.

1971, Dec. 24

1393 A242 Strip of 5, #a.-e.
1394 A242 50c multicolored
1395 A242 75c multicolored
1396 A242 12.45g multicolored
1397 A242 18.15g multicolored
1398 A242 50g multicolored

Nos. 1396-1398 are airmail.

Locomotives — A243

Designs: No. 1399a, 10c, Trevithick, Great Britain, 1804. b, 15c, Blenkinsops, 1812. c, 20c, G. Stephenson #1, 1825. d, 25c, Marc Seguin, France, 1829. e, 30c, "Adler," Germany, 1835.

50c, Sampierdarena #1, Italy, 1854. 75c, Paraguay #1, 1861. 12.45g, "Munich," Germany, 1841. 18.15g, US, 1875. 20g, Japanese locomotives, 1872-1972. 50g, Mikado D-50, Japan, 1923.

1972, Jan. 6

1399 A243 Strip of 5, #a.-e.
1400 A243 50c multicolored
1401 A243 75c multicolored
1402 A243 12.45g multicolored
1403 A243 18.15g multicolored
1404 A243 50g multicolored

Souvenir Sheet

Perf. 13½

1405 A243 20g multicolored

Nos. 1402-1405 are airmail. No. 1405 contains one 60x50mm stamp.
See Nos. 1476-1480.

1972 Winter Olympics, Sapporo — A244

Designs: Nos. 1406a, 10c, Hockey player. b, 15c, Jean-Claude Killy. c, 20c, Gaby Seyfert. d, 25c, 4-Man bobsled. e, 30c, Luge.

50c, Ski jumping, horiz. 75c, Slalom skiing, horiz. 12.45g, Painting, Kuniyoshi. 18.15g, Winter Scene, Hiroshige, horiz. 50g, Ski lift, man in traditional dress.

1972, Jan. 6 ***Perf. 14***

1406 A244 Strip of 5, #a.-e.
1407 A244 50c multicolored
1408 A244 75c multicolored
1409 A244 12.45g multicolored
1410 A244 18.15g multicolored
1411 A244 50g multicolored

Souvenir Sheet

Perf. 13½

1412 A244 20g Skier
1413 A244 20g Flags

Nos. 1409-1413 are airmail. Nos. 1412-1413 each contain one 50x60mm stamp. For overprint see Nos. 2295-2297. For Winter Olympic stamps with gold border, see Nos. 1372-1373.

UNICEF, 25th Anniv. (in 1971) — A245

1972, Jan. 24

Granite Paper

1414 A245	1g	red brn	.20	.20
1415 A245	2g	ultra	.20	.20
1416 A245	3g	lil rose	.20	.20
1417 A245	4g	violet	.20	.20
1418 A245	5g	emerald	.20	.20
1419 A245	10g	claret	.20	.20
1420 A245	20g	brt bl	.20	.20
1421 A245	25g	lt ol	.20	.20
1422 A245	30g	dk brn	.20	.20
		Nos. 1414-1422 (9)	1.80	1.80

Nos. 1420-1422 are airmail.

Race Cars A246

No. 1423: a, 10c, Ferrari. b, 15c, B.R.M. c, 20c, Brabham. d, 25c, March. e, 30c, Honda.
50c, Matra-Simca MS 650. 75c, Porsche. 12.45g, Maserati-8 CTF, 1938. 18.15g, Bugatti 35B, 1929. 20g, Lotus 72 Ford. 50g, Mercedes, 1924.

1972, Mar. 20 Unwmk. *Perf. 14*

1423 A246		Strip of 5, #a.-e.
1424 A246	50c	multicolored
1425 A246	75c	multicolored
1426 A246	12.45g	multicolored
1427 A246	18.15g	multicolored
1428 A246	50g	multicolored

Souvenir Sheet

Perf. 13½

1429 A246 20g multicolored

Nos. 1426-1429 are airmail. No. 1429 contains one 60x50mm stamp.

Sailing Ships — A247

Paintings: No. 1430a, 10c, Holbein. b, 15c, Nagasaki print. c, 20c, Intrepid, Roux. d, 25c, Portuguese ship, unknown artist. e, 30c, Mount Vernon, US, 1798, Corne.
50c, Van Eertvelt, vert. 75c, Santa Maria, Van Eertvelt, vert. 12.45g, Royal Prince, 1679, Van Beecq. 18.15g, Van Bree. 50g, Book of Arms, 1497, vert.

1972, Mar. 29 *Perf. 14*

1430 A247		Strip of 5, #a.-e.
1431 A247	50c	multicolored
1432 A247	75c	multicolored
1433 A247	12.45g	multicolored
1434 A247	18.15g	multicolored
1435 A247	50g	multicolored

Nos. 1433-1435 are airmail.

Paintings in Vienna Museum A248

Nudes by: No. 1436a, 10c, Rubens. b, 15c, Bellini. c, 20c, Carracci. d, 25c, Cagnacci. e, 30c, Spranger.
50c, Mandolin Player, Strozzi. 75c, Woman in Red Hat, Cranach the elder. 12.45g, Adam and Eve, Coxcie. 18.15g, Legionary on Horseback, Poussin. 50g, Madonna and Child, Bronzino.

1972, May 22

1436 A248		Strip of 5, #a.-e.
1437 A248	50c	multicolored
1438 A248	75c	multicolored
1439 A248	12.45g	multicolored
1440 A248	18.15g	multicolored
1441 A248	50g	multicolored

Nos. 1439-1441 are airmail.

Paintings in Asuncion Museum A249

No. 1442: a, 10c, Man in Straw Hat, Holden Jara. b, 15c, Portrait, Tintoretto. c, 20c, Indians, Holden Jara. d, 25c, Nude, Bouchard. e, 30c, Italian School.
50c, Reclining Nude, Berisso, horiz. 75c, Carracci, horiz. 12.45g, Reclining Nude, Schiaffino, horiz. 18.15g, Reclining Nude, Lostow, horiz. 50g, Madonna and Child, 17th cent. Italian School.

1972, May 22

1442 A249		Strip of 5, #a.-e.
1443 A249	50c	multicolored
1444 A249	75c	multicolored
1445 A249	12.45g	multicolored
1446 A249	18.15g	multicolored
1447 A249	50g	multicolored

Nos. 1445-1447 are airmail.

Presidential Summit — A250

No. 1448: a, 10c, Map of South America. b, 15c, Brazil natl. arms. c, 20c, Argentina natl. arms. d, 25c, Bolivia natl. arms. e, 30c, Paraguay natl. arms.
50c, Pres. Emilio Garrastazu, Brazil. 75c, Pres. Alejandro Lanusse, Argentina. 12.45g, Pres. Hugo Banzer Suarez, Bolivia. 18.15, Pres. Stroessner, Paraguay, horiz. 23.40g, Flags.

1972, Nov. 18

1448 A250		Strip of 5, #a.-e.
1449 A250	50c	multicolored
1450 A250	75c	multicolored
1451 A250	12.45g	multicolored
1452 A250	18.15g	multicolored

Souvenir Sheet

Perf. 13½

1453 A250 23.40g multicolored

Nos. 1451-1453 are airmail. No. 1453 contains one 50x60mm stamp. For overprint see No. 2144.

Pres. Stroessner's Visit to Japan — A251

No. 1454: a, 10c, Departure of first Japanese mission to US & Europe, 1871. b, 15c, First railroad, Tokyo-Yokahama, 1872. c, 20c, Samurai. d, 25c, Geishas. e, 30c, Cranes, Hiroshige.
50c, Honda race car. 75c, Pres. Stroessner, Emperor Hirohito, Mt. Fuji, bullet train, horiz. 12.45g, Rocket. 18.15g, Stroessner, Hirohito, horiz. No. 1459, Mounted samurai, Masanobu, 1740. No. 1460, Hirohito's speech, state dinner, horiz. No. 1461, Delegations at Tokyo airport, horiz.

1972, Nov. 18 *Perf. 14*

1454 A251		Strip of 5, #a.-e.
1455 A251	50c	multicolored
1456 A251	75c	multicolored
1457 A251	12.45g	multicolored
1458 A251	18.15g	multicolored

Souvenir Sheets

Perf. 13½

1459 A251	23.40g	multicolored
1460 A251	23.40g	multicolored

Imperf

1461 A251 23.40g multicolored

Nos. 1457-1461 are airmail. Nos. 1459-1460 each contain one 50x60mm stamp. No. 1461 contains one 85x42mm stamp with simulated perforations. For overprints see Nos. 2192-2194, 2267.

Wildlife A252

Paintings - #1462: a, 10c, Cranes, Botke. b, 15c, Tiger, Utamaro. c, 20c, Horses, Arenys. d, 25c, Pheasant, Dietzsch. e, 30c, Monkey, Brueghel, the Elder. All vert.
50c, Deer, Marc. 75c, Crab, Durer. 12.45g, Rooster, Jakuchu, vert. 18.15g, Swan, Asselyn.

1972, Nov. 18 *Perf. 14*

1462 A252		Strip of 5, #a.-e.
1463 A252	50c	multicolored
1464 A252	75c	multicolored
1465 A252	12.45g	multicolored
1466 A252	18.15g	multicolored

Nos. 1465-1466 are airmail.

Acaray Dam A253

Designs: 2g, Francisco Solano Lopez monument. 3g, Friendship Bridge. 5g, Tebicuary River Bridge. 10g, Hotel Guarani. 20g, Bus and car on highway. 25g, Hospital of Institute for Social Service. 50g, "Presidente Stroessner" of state merchant marine. 100g, "Electra C" of Paraguayan airlines.

Perf. 13½x13

1972, Nov. 16 Wmk. 347

Granite Paper

1467 A253	1g	sepia	.20	.20
1468 A253	2g	brown	.20	.20
1469 A253	3g	brt ultra	.20	.20
1470 A253	5g	brt pink	.20	.20
1471 A253	10g	dl grn	.20	.20
1472 A253	20g	rose car	.20	.20
1473 A253	25g	gray	.20	.20
1474 A253	50g	violet	.35	.25
1475 A253	100g	brt lil	.70	.50
		Nos. 1467-1475 (9)	2.45	2.15

Tourism Year of the Americas.
Nos. 1472-1475 are airmail.

Locomotives Type

No. 1476: a, 10c, Stephenson's Rocket, 1829. b, 15c, First Swiss railroad, 1847. c, 20c, 1st Spanish locomotive, 1848. d, 2c, Norris, US, 1850. e, 30c, Ansaldo, Italy, 1859.
50c, Badenia, Germany, 1863. 75c, 1st Japanese locomotive, 1895. 12.45g, P.L.M., France, 1924. 18.15g, Stephenson's Northumbrian.

1972, Nov. 25 Unwmk. *Perf. 14*

1476 A243		Strip of 5, #a.-e.
1477 A243	50c	multicolored
1478 A243	75c	multicolored
1479 A243	12.45g	multicolored
1480 A243	18.15g	multicolored

Nos. 1479-1480 are airmail.

South American Wildlife — A254

No. 1481: a, 10c, Tetradactyla. b, 15c, Nasua socialis. c, 20c, Priodontes giganteus. d, 25c, Blastocerus dichotomus. e, 30c, Felis pardalis.
50c, Aotes, vert. 75c, Rhea americana. 12.45g, Desmodus rotundus. 18.15g, Urocyon cinereo-argenteus.

1972, Nov. 25

1481 A254		Strip of 5, #a.-e.
1482 A254	50c	multicolored
1483 A254	75c	multicolored
1484 A254	12.45g	multicolored
1485 A254	18.15g	multicolored

Nos. 1484-1485 are airmail.

OAS Emblem A255

Perf. 13x13½

1973 Litho. Wmk. 347

Granite Paper

1486 A255	1g	multi	.20	.20
1487 A255	2g	multi	.20	.20
1488 A255	3g	multi	.20	.20
1489 A255	4g	multi	.20	.20
1490 A255	5g	multi	.20	.20
1491 A255	10g	multi	.20	.20
1492 A255	20g	multi	.20	.20
1493 A255	25g	multi	.20	.20
1494 A255	50g	multi	.35	.25
1495 A255	100g	multi	.70	.50
		Nos. 1486-1495 (10)	2.65	2.35

Org. of American States, 25th anniv.
Nos. 1492-1495 are airmail.

Paintings in Florence Museum A256

Artists: No. 1496: a, 10c, Cranach, the Elder. b, 15c, Caravaggio. c, 20c, Fiorentino. d, 25c, Di Credi. e, 30c, Liss. f, 50c, Da Vinci. g, 75c, Botticelli.
No. 1497: a, 5g, Titian, horiz. b, 10g, Del Piombo, horiz. c, 20g, De Michelino, horiz.

1973, Mar. 13 Unwmk. *Perf. 14*

1496 A256	Strip of 7, #a.-g.
1497 A256	Strip of 3, #a.-c.

No. 1497 is airmail.

Butterflies — A257

#1498: a, 10c, Catagramma patazza. b, 15c, Agrias narcissus. c, 20c, Papilio zagreus. d, 25c, Heliconius chestertoni. e, 30c, Metamorphadido. f, 50c, Catagramma astarte. g, 75c, Papilio brasiliensis.

No. 1499a, 5g, Agrias sardanapalus. b, 10g, Callithea saphhira. c, 20g, Jemadia hospita.

1973, Mar. 13

1498 A257 Strip of 7, #a.-g.
1499 A257 Strip of 3, #a.-c.

No. 1499 is airmail.

Cats A258

Faces of Cats: No. 1500: a, 10c, b, 15c. c, 20c, d, 25c, e, 30c. f, 50c. g, 75c.

No. 1501a, 5g, Cat under rose bush, by Desportes. b, 10g, Two cats, by Marc, horiz. c, 20g, Man with cat, by Rousseau.

1973, June 29

1500 A258 Strip of 7, #a.-g.
1501 A258 Strip of 3, #a.-c.

No. 1500 is airmail. For other cat designs, see type A287.

Flemish Paintings A259

Nudes by: No. 1502: a, 10c, Spranger. b, 15c, Jordaens. c, 20c, de Clerck. d, 25c, Spranger, diff. e, 30c, Goltzius. f, 50c, Rubens. g, 75c, Vase of flowers, J. Brueghel.

No. 1503a, 5g, Nude, de Clerck, horiz. b, 10g, Woman with mandolin, de Vos. c, 20g, Men, horses, Rubens, horiz.

1973, June 29 Litho. *Perf. 14*

1502 A259 Strip of 7, #a.-g.
1503 A259 Strip of 3, #a.-c.

No. 1503 is airmail.

Hand Holding Letter — A260

EXPOPAR 73, Paraguayan Industrial Exhib. — A261

Wmk. 347

1973, July 10 Litho. *Perf. 11*

1504	A260	2g lil rose & blk	.20	.20

No. 1504 was issued originally as a nonobligatory stamp to benefit mailmen, but its status was changed to regular postage.

1973, Aug. 11 *Perf. 13x13½*

Granite Paper

1505	A261	1g	org brn	.20	.20
1506	A261	2g	vermilion	.20	.20
1507	A261	3g	blue	.20	.20
1508	A261	4g	emerald	.20	.20
1509	A261	5g	lilac	.20	.20
1510	A261	20g	lilac rose	.20	.20
1511	A261	25g	rose claret	.20	.20
			Nos. 1505-1511 (7)	1.40	1.40

Nos. 1510-1511 are airmail.

1974 World Cup Soccer Championships, Munich — A262

No. 1512: a, 10c, Uruguay vs. Paraguay. b, 15c, Crerand, England and Eusebio, Portugal. c, 20c, Bobby Charlton, England. d, 25c, Franz Beckenbauer, Germany. e, 30c, Erler, Germany and McNab, England. f, 50c, Pele, Brazil and Willi Schulz, Germany. g, 75c, Arsenio Erico, Paraguay.

5g, Brian Labone, Gerd Mueller, Bobby Moore. No. 1514a, 10g, Luigi Riva, Italy. No. 1514b, 20g, World Cup medals. No. 1515, World Cup trophy. 25g, Player scoring goal.

1973 Litho. Unwmk. *Perf. 14*

1512 A262 Strip of 7, #a.-g.
1513 A262 5g multicolored
1514 A262 Pair, #a.-b.

Souvenir Sheet

Perf. 13½

1515 A262 25g multicolored
1516 A262 25g multicolored

Nos. 1513-1516 are airmail. Issue dates: Nos. 1512-1514, 1516, Oct. 8. No. 1515, June 29. For overprint see No. 2131.

Paintings A263

Details from paintings, artist: No. 1517a, 10c, Lion of St. Mark, Carpaccio. b, 15c, Venus and Mars, Pittoni. c, 20c, Rape of Europa, Veronese. d, 25c, Susannah and the Elders, Tintoretto. e, 30c, Euphrosyne, Amigoni. f, 50c, Allegory of Moderation, Veronese. g, 75c, Ariadne, Tintoretto.

5g, Pallas and Mars, Tintoretto. No. 1519a, 10g, Portrait of Woman in Fur Hat, G.D. Tiepolo. b, 20g, Dialectic of Industry, Veronese.

1973, Oct. 8 *Perf. 14*

1517 A263 Strip of 7, #a.-g.
1518 A263 5g multicolored
1519 A263 Pair, #a.-b.

Nos. 1518-1519 are airmail.

Birds A264

No. 1520: a, 10c, Tersina viridis. b, 15c, Pipile cumanensis. c, 20c, Pyrocephalus rubinus. d, 25c, Andigena laminirostris. e, 30c, Xipholena punicea. f, 50c, Tangara chilensis. g, 75, Polytmus guainumbi.

5g, Onychorhynchus mexicanus, vert. No. 1522a, 10g, Rhinocrypta lanceolata, vert. b, 20g, Trogon collaris, vert. 25g, Colibri florisuga mellivora, vert.

1973, Nov. 14

1520 A264 Strip of 7, #a.-g.
1521 A264 5g multicolored
1522 A264 Pair, #a.-b.

Souvenir Sheet

Perf. 13½

1523 A264 25g multicolored

Nos. 1521-1523 are airmail. No. 1523 contains one 50x60mm stamp.

Space Exploration — A265

No. 1524a, 10c, Apollo 11. b, 15c, Apollo 12. c, 20c, Apollo 13. d, 25c, Apollo 14. e, 30c, Apollo 15. f, 50c, Apollo 16. g, 75c, Apollo 17.

5g, Skylab. No. 1526a, 10g, Space shuttle. b, 20g, Apollo-Soyuz mission. No. 1527, Pioneer 11, Jupiter. No. 1528, Pioneer 10, Jupiter, vert.

1973, Nov. 14 *Perf. 14*

1524 A265 Strip of 7, #a.-g.
1525 A265 5g multicolored
1526 A265 Pair, #a.-b.

Souvenir Sheet

Perf. 14½

1527 A265 25g multicolored

Perf. 13½

1528 A265 25g multicolored

#1525-1528 are airmail. #1527 contains on 35x25mm stamp, #1528 one 50x60mm stamp.

Souvenir Sheet

Women of Avignon, Pablo Picasso — A266

Illustration reduced.

1973, Nov. 14 *Perf. 13½*

1529 A266 25g multicolored

Traditional Costumes A267

No. 1530: a, 25c, Indian girl. b, 50c, Bottle dance costume. c, 75c, Dancer balancing vase on head. d, 1g, Dancer with flowers. e, 1.50g, Weavers. f, 1.75g, Man, woman in dance costumes. g, 2.25g, Musicians in folk dress, horiz.

1973, Dec. 30 *Perf. 14*

1530 A267 Strip of 7, #a.-g.

Flowers A268

Designs: No. 1531a, 10c Passion flower. b, 20c, Dahlia. c, 25c, Bird of paradise. d, 30c, Freesia. e, 40c, Anthurium. f, 50c, Water lily. g, 75c, Orchid.

1973, Dec. 31

1531 A268 Strip of 7, #a.-g.

Roses A269

Designs: No. 1532a, 10c, Hybrid perpetual. b, 15c, Tea scented. c, 20c, Japanese rose. d, 25c, Bouquet of roses and flowers. e, 30c, Rose of Provence. f, 50c, Hundred petals rose. g, 75c, Bouquet of roses, dragonfly.

1974, Feb. 2

1532 A269 Strip of 7, #a.-g.

Paintings in Gulbenkian Museum A270

Designs and artists: No. 1533a, 10c, Cupid and Three Graces, Boucher. b, 15c, Bath of Venus, Burne-Jones. c, 20c, Mirror of Venus, Burne-Jones. d, 25c, Two Women, Natoire. e, 30c, Fighting Cockerels, de Vos. f, 50c, Portrait of a Young Girl, Bugiardini. g, 75c, Madonna and Child, J. Gossaert.

5g, Outing on Beach at Enoshima, Utamaro. No. 1534a, 10g, Woman with Harp, Lowrence. b, 20g, Centaurs Embracing, Rubens.

1974, Feb. 4

1533 A270 Strip of 7, #a.-g.
1534 A270 5g multicolored
1535 A270 Pair, #a.-b.

Nos. 1534-1535 are airmail.

UPU Cent. A271

Horse-drawn mail coaches: No. 1536a, 10c, London. b, 15c, France. c, 20c, England. d, 25c, Bavaria. e, 30c, Painting by C.C. Henderson. f, 50c, Austria, vert. g, 75c, Zurich, vert.

5g, Hot air balloon, Apollo spacecraft, airplane, Graf Zeppelin. No. 1538a, 10g, Steam locomotive. b, 20g, Ocean liner, sailing ship. No. 1539, Airship, balloon. No. 1540, Mail coach crossing river.

1974, Mar. 20 ***Perf. 14***

1536 A271 Strip of 7, #a.-g.
1537 A271 5g multicolored
1538 A271 Pair, #a.-b.

Souvenir Sheets

Perf. 14½

1539 A271 15g multicolored

Perf. 13½

1540 A271 15g multicolored

Nos. 1537-1540 are airmail. No. 1539 contains one 50x35mm stamp, No. 1540 one 60x50mm stamp. Nos. 1539-1540 each include a 5g surtax for a monument to Francisco Solano Lopez. For overprint see No. 2127.

Paintings A272

Details from works, artist: No. 1541a, 10c, Adam and Eve, Mabuse. b, 15c, Portrait, Piero di Cosimo. c, 20c, Bathsheba in her Bath, Cornelisz. d, 25c, Toilet of Venus, Boucher. e, 30c, The Bathers, Renoir. f, 50c, Lot and his Daughters, Dix. g, 75c, Bouquet of Flowers, van Kessel.

5g, King's Pet Horse, Seele. No. 1543a, 10g, Woman with Paintbrushes, Batoni. b, 20g, Three Musicians, Flemish master.

1974, Mar. 20

1541 A272 Strip of 7, #a.-g.
1542 A272 5g multicolored
1543 A272 Pair, #a.-b.

Nos. 1542-1543 are airmail.

Sailing Ships — A272a

Designs: No. 1544a, 5c, Ship, map. b, 10c, English ship. c, 15c, Dutch ship. d, 20c, Whaling ships. e, 25c, Spanish ship. f, 35c, USS Constitution. g, 40c, English frigate. h, 50c, "Fanny," 1832.

1974, Sept. 13 ***Perf. 14½***

1544 A272a Strip of 8, #a.-h.

Strip price includes a 50c surtax.

Paintings in Borghese Gallery, Rome A273

Details from works and artists: No. 1545a, 5c, Portrait, Romano. b, 10c, Boy Carrying Fruit, Caravaggio. c, 15c, A Sybil, Domenichino. d, 20c, Nude, Titian. e, 25c, The Danae, Correggio. f, 35c, Nude, Savoldo. g, 40c, Nude, da Vinci. h, 50c, Nude, Rubens. 15g, Christ Child, Piero di Cosimo.

1975, Jan. 15 ***Perf. 14***

1545 A273 Strip of 8, #a.-h.

Souvenir Sheet

Perf. 14½

1546 A273 15g multicolored

No. 1546 is airmail and price includes a 5g surtax used for a monument to Francisco Solano Lopez.

Christmas A274

Paintings, artists: No. 1547a, 5c, The Annunciation, della Robia. b, 10c, The Nativity, G. David. c, 15c, Madonna and Child, Memling. d, 20c, Adoration of the Shepherds, Giorgione. e, 25c, Adoration of the Magi, French school, 1400. f, Madonna and Child with Saints, 35c, Pulzone. g, 40c, Madonna and Child, van Orley. h, 50c, Flight From Egypt, Pacher. 15g, Adoration of the Magi, Raphael.

1975, Jan. 17 ***Perf. 14***

1547 A274 Strip of 8, #a.-h.

Souvenir Sheet

Perf. 14½

1548 A274 15g multicolored

No. 1548 is airmail and price includes a 5g surtax for a monument to Francisco Solano Lopez.

"U.P.U.," Pantheon, Carrier Pigeon, Globe — A275

1975, Feb. Wmk. 347 ***Perf. 13½x13***

1549	A275	1g	blk & lilac	.20	.20
1550	A275	2g	blk & rose red	.20	.20
1551	A275	3g	blk & ultra	.20	.20
1552	A275	5g	blk & blue	.20	.20
1553	A275	10g	blk & lil rose	.20	.20
1554	A275	20g	blk & brn	.20	.20
1555	A275	25g	blk & emer	.20	.20
	Nos. 1549-1555 (7)			1.40	1.40

Centenary of Universal Postal Union. Nos. 1554-1555 are airmail.

Paintings in National Gallery, London A276

Details from paintings, artist: 5c, The Rokeby Venus, Velazquez, horiz. 10c, The Range of Love, Watteau. 15c, Venus (The School of Love), Correggio. 20c, Mrs. Sarah Siddons, Gainsborough. 25c, Cupid Complaining to Venus, L. Cranach the Elder. 35c, Portrait, Lotto. 40c, Nude, Rembrandt. 50c, Origin of the Milky Way, Tintoretto. 15g, Rider and Hounds, Pisanello.

1975, Apr. 25 Unwmk. ***Perf. 14***

1556 A276 5c multicolored
1557 A276 10c multicolored
1558 A276 15c multicolored
1559 A276 20c multicolored
1560 A276 25c multicolored
1561 A276 35c multicolored
1562 A276 40c multicolored
1563 A276 50c multicolored

Souvenir Sheet

Perf. 13½

1564 A276 15g multicolored

No. 1564 is airmail, contains one 50x60mm stamp and price includes a 5g surtax for a monument to Francisco Solano Lopez.

Dogs A277

1975, June 7 ***Perf. 14***

1565 A277 5c Boxer
1566 A277 10c Poodle
1567 A277 15c Basset hound
1568 A277 20c Collie
1569 A277 25c Chihuahua
1570 A277 35c German shepherd
1571 A277 40c Pekinese
1572 A277 50c Chow

Souvenir Sheet

Perf. 13½

1573 A277 15g Fox hound, horse

No. 1573 is airmail, contains one 39x57mm stamp and price includes a 5g surtax for a monument to Francisco Solano Lopez.

South American Fauna — A278

Designs: No. 1574a, 5c, Piranha (Pirana). b, 10c, Anaconda. c, 15c, Turtle (Tortuga). d, 20c, Iguana. e, 25c, Mono, vert. f, 35c, Mara. g, 40c, Marmota, vert. h, 50c, Peccary.

1975, Aug. 20 Litho. ***Perf. 14***

1574 A278 Strip of 8, #a.-h.

Souvenir Sheet

Perf. 13½

1575 A278 15g Aguara guazu

No. 1575 is airmail, contains one 60x50mm stamp, and price includes a 5g surtax for a monument to Francisco Solano Lopez.

For overprints see Nos. 2197.

Michelangelo (1475-1564), Italian Sculptor and Painter — A279

No. 1583: Statues, a, 5c, David. b, 10c, Aurora.

Paintings, c, 15c, Original Sin. d, 20c, The Banishment. e, 25c, The Deluge. f, 35c, Eve. g, 40c, Mary with Jesus and John. h, 50c, Judgement Day.

4g, Adam Receiving Life from God, horiz. No. 1585a, 5g, Libyan Sybil. b, 10g, Delphic Sybil. No. 1586, God Creating the Heaven and the Earth, horiz. No. 1587, The Holy Family.

1975, Aug. 23 Litho. ***Perf. 14***

1583 A279 Strip of 8, #a.-h.
1584 A279 4g multicolored
1585 A279 Pair, #a.-b.

Perf. 12

1586 A279 15g multicolored

Souvenir Sheet

Perf. 13½

1587 A279 15g multicolored

Nos. 1586-1587 sold for 20g with surtax for a monument to Francisco Solano Lopez. Nos. 1584-1587 are airmail.

Winter Olympics, Innsbruck, 1976 A280

#1597a, 2g, Slalom skier. b, 3g, Cross country skier. c, 4g, Pair figure skating. d, 5g, Hockey.

#1598a, 10g, Speed skater. b, 15g, Downhill skier.

1975, Aug. 27 Litho. ***Perf. 14***

1596 A280 1g Luge
1597 A280 Strip of 4, #a.-d.
1598 A280 Pair, #a.-b.
1599 A280 20g 4-Man bobsled

Souvenir Sheet

Perf. 13½

1600 A280 25g Ski jumper
1601 A280 25g Woman figure skater

Nos. 1596, 1598-1601 are horiz. Nos. 1598-1601 are airmail. Nos. 1600-1601 each contain one 60x50mm stamp.

Summer Olympics, Montreal, 1976
A281

No. 1606: a, 1g, Weightlifting. b, 2g, Kayak. c, 3g, Hildegard Flack, 800 meter run. d, Lasse Viren, 5,000 meter run.

No. 1607: a, 5g, Dieter Kottysch, boxing. b, 10g, Lynne Evans, archery. c, 15g, Akinori Kakayama, balance rings. 20g, Heide Rosendahl, broad jump. No. 1609, Decathlon. No. 1610, Liselott Linsenhoff, dressage, horiz.

1975, Aug. 28 *Perf. 14*

1606 A281 Strip of 4, #a.-d.
1607 A281 Strip of 3, #a.-c.
1608 A281 20g multicolored

Souvenir Sheets

Perf. 14½

1609 A281 25g multicolored
1610 A281 25g multicolored

Nos. 1607b-1610 are airmail.

US, Bicent. — A282

Ships.

Unwmk.

1975, Oct. 20 Litho. *Perf. 14*

1616 A282 5c Sachem, vert.
1617 A282 10c Reprisal, Lexington
1618 A282 15c Wasp
1619 A282 20c Mosquito, Spy
1620 A282 25c Providence, vert.
1621 A282 35c Yankee Hero, Milford
1622 A282 40c Cabot, vert.
1623 A282 50c Hornet, vert.

Souvenir Sheet

1624 A282 15g Montgomery

No. 1624 is airmail and contains one 50x70mm stamp.

US, Bicent. — A283

Details from paintings, artists: No. 1625a, 5c, The Collector, Kahill. b, 10c, Morning Interlude, Brackman, vert. c, 15c, White Cloud, Catlin, vert. d, 20c, Man From Kentucky, Benton, vert. e, 25c, The Emigrants, Remington. f, 35c, Spirit of '76, Willard, vert. g, John Paul Jones capturing Serapis, unknown artist. h, 50c, Declaration of Independence, Trumbull. 15g, George Washington, Stuart and Thomas Jefferson, Peale.

1975, Nov. 20 *Perf. 14*

1625 A283 Strip of 8, #a.-h.

Souvenir Sheet

Perf. 13½

1625A A283 15g multicolored

No. 1625A is airmail, contains one 60x50mm stamp and price includes a 5g surtax for a monument to Francisco Solano Lopez.

Institute of Higher Education — A284

Perf. 13½x13

1976, Mar. 16 Litho. Wmk. 347

1626 A284	5g vio, blk & red	.20	.20
1627 A284	10g ultra, blk & red	.20	.20
1628 A284	30g brn, blk & red	.25	.20
	Nos. 1626-1628 (3)	.65	.60

Inauguration of Institute of Higher Education, Sept. 23, 1974.

No. 1628 is airmail.

Rotary Intl., 70th Anniv. — A285

1976, Mar. 16 *Perf. 13x13½*

1629 A285	3g blk, bl & citron	.20	.20
1630 A285	4g car, bl & citron	.20	.20
1631 A285	25g emer, bl & lemon	.20	.20
	Nos. 1629-1631 (3)	.60	.60

No. 1631 is airmail.

IWY Emblem, Woman's Head — A286

1976, Mar. 16

1632 A286	1g ultra & brn	.20	.20
1633 A286	2g car & brn	.20	.20
1634 A286	20g grn & brn	.20	.20
	Nos. 1632-1634 (3)	.60	.60

Intl Women's Year (1975).

No. 1634 is airmail.

Cats
A287

Various cats: No. 1635a, 5c. b, 10c. c, 15c. d, 20c. e, 25c. f, 35c. g, 40c. h, 50c. 15g.

1976, Apr. 2 Unwmk. *Perf. 14*

1635 A287 Strip of 8, #a.-h.

Souvenir Sheet

Perf. 13½

1636 A287 15g multicolored

No. 1636 is airmail, contains one 50x60mm stamp and price includes a 5g surtax for a monument to Francisco Solano Lopez.

See Nos. 2132-2133, 2201-2202, 2274-2275. For overprint see No. 2212.

Railroads, 150th Anniv. (in 1975) — A288

Locomotives: 1g, Planet, England, 1830. 2g, Koloss, Austria, 1844. 3g, Tarasque, France, 1846. 4g, Lawrence, Canada, 1853. 5g, Carlsruhe, Germany, 1854. 10g, Great Sagua, US, 1856. 15g, Berga, Spain. 20g, Encarnacion, Paraguay. 25g, English locomotive, 1825.

1976, Apr. 2 *Perf. 13x13½*

1637 A288 1g multicolored
1638 A288 2g multicolored
1639 A288 3g multicolored
1640 A288 4g multicolored
1641 A288 5g multicolored
1642 A288 10g multicolored
1643 A288 15g multicolored
1644 A288 20g multicolored

Souvenir Sheet

1645 A288 25g multicolored

Nos. 1642-1645 are airmail. No. 1645 contains one 40x27mm stamp.

Painting by Spanish Artists — A289

Paintings: 1g, The Naked Maja by Goya. 2g, Nude by J. de Torres. 3g, Nude holding oranges by de Torres, vert. 4g, Woman playing piano by Z. Velazquez, vert. 5g, Knight on white horse by Esquivel. 10g, The Shepherd, by Murillo. 15g, The Immaculate Conception by Antolinez, vert. 20g, Nude by Zuloaga. 25g, Prince Baltasar Carlos on Horseback by D. Velasquez.

1976, Apr. 2 *Perf. 13x13½,13½x13*

1646 A289 1g multicolored
1647 A289 2g multicolored
1648 A289 3g multicolored
1649 A289 4g multicolored
1650 A289 5g multicolored
1651 A289 10g multicolored
1652 A289 15g multicolored
1653 A289 20g multicolored

Souvenir Sheet

1654 A289 25g multicolored

Nos. 1651-1654 are airmail. No. 1654 contains one 58x82mm stamp.

Butterflies — A290

No. 1655: a, 5c, Prepona praeneste. b, 10c, Prepona proschion. c, 15c, Pereute leucodrosime. d, 20c, Agrias amydon. e, 25c, Morpho aegea gynandromorphe. f, 35c, Pseudatteria leopardina. g, 40c, Morpho helena. h, 50c, Morpho hecuba.

1976, May 12 Unwmk. *Perf. 14*

1655 A290 Strip of 8, #a.-h.

Farm Animals — A291

1976, June 15

1656 A291 1g Rooster, vert.
1657 A291 2g Hen, vert.
1658 A291 3g Turkey, vert.
1659 A291 4g Sow
1660 A291 5g Donkeys
1661 A291 10g Brahma cattle
1662 A291 15g Holstein cow
1663 A291 20g Horse

Nos. 1661-1663 are airmail.

US and US Post Office, Bicent. — A292

Designs: 1g, Pony Express rider. 2g, Stagecoach. 3g, Steam locomotive, vert. 4g, American steamship, Savannah. 5g, Curtiss Jenny biplane. 10g, Mail bus. 15g, Mail car, rocket train. 20g, First official missile mail, vert. No. 1672, First flight cover, official missile mail. No. 1673, US #C76 tied to cover by moon landing cancel.

1976, June 18

1664 A292 1g multicolored
1665 A292 2g multicolored
1666 A292 3g multicolored
1667 A292 4g multicolored
1668 A292 5g multicolored
1669 A292 10g multicolored
1670 A292 15g multicolored
1671 A292 20g multicolored

Souvenir Sheets

Perf. 14½

1672 A292 25g multicolored
1673 A292 25g multicolored

Nos. 1669-1673 are airmail and each contain one 50x40mm stamp.

Mythological Characters — A293

Details from paintings, artists: No. 1674a, 1g, Jupiter, Ingres. b, 2g, Saturn, Rubens. c, 3g, Neptune, Tiepolo. d, 4g, Uranus and Aphrodite, Medina, horiz. e, 5g, Pluto and Prosperpine, Giordano, horiz. f, 10g, Venus, Ingres. g, 15g, Mercury, de la Hyre. 20g, Mars and Venus, Veronese.

25g, Viking Orbiter descending to Mars, horiz.

1976, July 18 *Perf. 14*

1674 A293 Strip of 7, #a.-g.
1675 A293 20g multicolored

Souvenir Sheet

Perf. 14½

1676 A293 25g multicolored

Nos. 1674f-1674g, 1675-1676 are airmail.

Sailing Ships — A294

Paintings: No. 1677a, 1g, Venice frigate of the Spanish Armada, vert. b, 2g, Swedish war ship, Vasa, 1628, vert. c, 3g, Spanish galleon being attacked by pirates by Puget. d, 4g, Combat by Dawson. e, 5g, European boat in Japan, vert. f, 10g, Elizabeth Grange in Liverpool by Walters. g, 15g, Prussen, 1903, by Holst. 20g, Grand Duchess Elizabeth, 1902, by Bohrdt.

1976, July 15 ***Perf. 14***

1677 A294 Strip of 7, #a.-g.
1678 A294 20g multicolored

Nos. 1677f-1678 are airmail.

German Sailing Ships — A295

Ship, artist: 1g, Bunte Kuh, 1402, Zeeden. 2g, Arms of Hamburg, 1667, Wichman, vert. 3g, Kaiser Leopold, 1667, Wichman, vert. 4g, Deutschland, 1848, Pollack, vert. 5g, Humboldt, 1851, Fedeler. 10g, Borussia, 1855, Seitz. 15g, Gorch Fock, 1958, Stroh, vert. 20g, Grand Duchess Elizabeth, 1902, Bohrdt. 25g, SS Pamir, Zeytline, vert.

Unwmk.

1976, Aug. 20 Litho. ***Perf. 14***

1685 A295 1g multicolored
1686 A295 2g multicolored
1687 A295 3g multicolored
1688 A295 4g multicolored
1689 A295 5g multicolored
1690 A295 10g multicolored
1691 A295 15g multicolored
1692 A295 20g multicolored

Souvenir Sheet

Perf. 14½

1693 A295 25g multicolored

Intl. German Naval Exposition, Hamburg; NORDPOSTA '76 (No. 1693). Nos. 1690-1693 are airmail.

US Bicentennial — A296

Western Paintings by: No. 1694a, 1g, E. C. Ward. b, 2g, William Robinson Leigh. c, 3g, A. J. Miller. d, 4g, Charles Russell. e, 5g, Frederic Remington. f, 10g, Remington, horiz. g, 15g, Carl Bodmer.

No. 1695, A. J. Miller. No. 1696, US #1, 2, 245, C76.

Unwmk.

1976, Sept. 9 Litho. ***Perf. 14***

1694 A296 Strip of 7, #a.-g.
1695 A296 20g multicolored

Souvenir Sheet

Perf. 13x13½

1696 A296 25g multicolored

Nos. 1694f-1694g, 1695-1696 are airmail. No. 1696 contains one 65x55mm stamp.

1976 Summer Olympics, Montreal — A297

Gold Medal Winners: No. 1703a, 1g, Nadia Comaneci, Romania, gymnastics, vert. b, 2g, Kornelia Ender, East Germany, swimming. c, 3g, Luann Ryan, US, archery, vert. d, 4g, Jennifer Chandler, US, diving. e, 5g, Shirley Babashoff, US, swimming. f, 10g, Christine Stuckelberger, Switzerland, equestrian. g, 15g, Japan, volleyball, vert.

20g, Annegret Richter, W. Germany, running, vert. No. 1705, Bruce Jenner, US, decathlon. No. 1706, Alwin Schockemohle, equestrian. No. 1707, Medals list, vert.

Unwmk.

1976, Dec. 18 Litho. ***Perf. 14***

1703 A297 Strip of 7, #a.-g.
1704 A297 20g multicolored

Souvenir Sheets

Perf. 14½

1705 A297 25g multicolored
1706 A297 25g multicolored
1707 A297 25g multicolored

Nos. 1703f-1703g, 1705-1707 are airmail. Nos. 1705-1706 each contain one 50x40mm stamp. No. 1707 contains one 50x70mm stamp.

Titian, 500th Birth Anniv. A298

Details from paintings: No. 1708a, 1g, Venus and Adonis. b, 2g, Diana and Callisto. c, 3g, Perseus and Andromeda. d, 4g, Venus of the Mirror. e, 5g, Venus Sleeping, horiz. f, 10g, Bacchanal, horiz. g, 15g, Venus, Cupid and the Lute Player. 20g, Venus and the Organist, horiz.

1976, Dec. 18 ***Perf. 14***

1708 A298 Strip of 7, #a.-g.
1709 A298 20g multicolored

No. 1708f-1708g, 1709 are airmail.

Peter Paul Rubens, 400th Birth Anniv. A299

Paintings: No. 1710a, 1g, Adam and Eve. b, 2g, Tiger and Lion Hunt. c, 3g, Bathsheba Receiving David's Letter. d, 4g, Susanna in the Bath. e, 5g, Perseus and Andromeda. f, 10g, Andromeda Chained to the Rock. g, 15g, Shivering Venus. 20g, St. George Slaying the Dragon. 25g, Birth of the Milky Way, horiz.

1977, Feb. 18

1710 A299 Strip of 7, #a.-g.
1711 A299 20g multicolored

Souvenir Sheet

Perf. 14½

1712 A299 25g multicolored

Nos. 1710f-1710g, 1711-1712 are airmail.

US, Bicent. — A300

Space exploration: No. 1713a, 1g, John Glenn, Mercury 7. b, 2g, Pres. Kennedy, Apollo 11. c, 3g, Wernher von Braun, Apollo 17. d, 4g, Mercury, Venus, Mariner 10. e, 5g, Jupiter, Saturn, Jupiter 10/11. f, 10g, Viking, Mars. g, 15g, Viking A on Mars. 20g, Viking B on Mars. No. 1715, Future space projects on Mars, vert. No. 1716, Future land rover on Mars.

1977, Mar. 3 ***Perf. 14***

1713 A300 Strip of 7, #a.-g.
1714 A300 20g multicolored

Souvenir Sheets

Perf. 13½

1715 A300 25g multicolored
1716 A300 25g multicolored

Nos. 1713f-1713g, 1714-1716 are airmail. No. 1715 contains one 50x60mm stamp, No. 1716 one 60x50mm stamp.

Olympic History A301

Designs: 1g, Spiridon Louis, marathon 1896, Athens, Pierre de Coubertin. 2g, Giuseppe Delfino, fencing 1960, Rome, Pope John XXIII. 3g, Jean Claude Killy, skiing 1968, Grenoble, Charles de Gaulle. 4g, Ricardo Delgado, boxing 1968, Mexico City, G. Diaz Ordaz. 5g, Hayata, gymnastics 1964, Tokyo, Emperor Hirohito. 10g, Klaus Wolfermann, javelin 1972, Munich, Avery Brundage. 15g, Michel Vaillancourt, equestrian 1976, Montreal, Queen Elizabeth II. 20g, Franz Klammer, skiing 1976, Innsbruck, Austrian national arms.

25g, Emblems of 1896 Athens games and 1976 Montreal games.

1977, June 7 ***Perf. 14***

1717 A301 1g multicolored
1718 A301 2g multicolored
1719 A301 3g multicolored
1720 A301 4g multicolored
1721 A301 5g multicolored
1722 A301 10g multicolored
1723 A301 15g multicolored
1724 A301 20g multicolored

Souvenir Sheet

Perf. 13½

1725 A301 25g multicolored

Nos. 1722-1725 are airmail. No. 1725 contains one 49x60mm stamp.

LUPOSTA '77, Intl. Stamp Exibition, Berlin A302

Graf Zeppelin 1st South America flight and: 1g, German girls in traditional costumes. 2g, Bull fighter, Seville. 3g, Dancer, Rio de Janeiro. 4g, Gaucho breaking bronco, Uruguay. 5g, Like #1530b. 10g, Argentinian gaucho. 15g, Ceremonial indian costume, Bolivia. 20g, Indian on horse, US.

No. 1734, Zeppelin over sailing ship. No. 1735, Ferdinand Von Zeppelin, zeppelin over Berlin, horiz.

1977, June 9 ***Perf. 14***

1726 A302 1g multicolored
1727 A302 2g multicolored
1728 A302 3g multicolored
1729 A302 4g multicolored
1730 A302 5g multicolored
1731 A302 10g multicolored
1732 A302 15g multicolored
1733 A302 20g multicolored

Souvenir Sheets

Perf. 13½

1734 A302 25g multicolored
1735 A302 25g multicolored

#1731-1735 are airmail. #1734 contains one 49x60mm stamp, #1735 one 60x49mm stamp.

Mburucuya Flowers A303

Weaver with Spider Web Lace — A304

Designs: 1g, Ostrich feather panel. 2g, Black palms. 20g, Rose tabebuia. 25g, Woman holding ceramic pot.

Perf. 13x13½

1977 Litho. Wmk. 347

1736	A304	1g multicolored		.20	.20
1737	A303	2g multicolored		.20	.20
1738	A303	3g multicolored		.20	.20
1739	A304	5g multicolored		.20	.20
1740	A303	20g multicolored		.25	.20
1741	A304	25g multicolored		.30	.20
		Set value		.75	.55

Issued: 2g, 3g, 20g, 4/25; 1g, 5g, 25g, 6/27.
Nos. 1740-1741 are airmail.

Aviation History — A305

Designs: No. 1742a, 1g, Orville and Wilbur Wright, Wright Flyer, 1903. b, 2g, Alberto Santos-Dumont, Canard, 1906. c, 3g, Louis Bleriot, Bleriot 11, 1909. d, 4g, Otto Lilienthal, Glider, 1891. e, 5g, Igor Sikorsky, Avion le Grande, 1913. f, 10g, Juan de la Cierva, Autogiro. g, 15g, Silvio Pettirossi, Deperdussin acrobatic plane. No. 1743, Concorde jet. No. 1744, Lindbergh, Spirit of St. Louis, Statue of Liberty, Eiffel Tower. No. 1745, Design of flying machine by da Vinci.

1977, July 18 Unwmk. ***Perf. 14***

1742 A305 Strip of 7, #a.-g.
1743 A305 20g multicolored

Souvenir Sheet

Perf. 14½

1744 A305 25g multicolored
1745 A305 25g multicolored

Nos. 1742f-1745 are airmail. No. 1745 contains one label.

Francisco Solano Lopez — A306

Perf. 13x13½

1977, July 24	**Litho.**		**Wmk. 347**
1752 A306	10g brown	.20	.20
1753 A306	50g dk vio	.50	.40
1754 A306	100g green	1.00	.75
Nos. 1752-1754 (3)		1.70	1.35

Marshal Francisco Solano Lopez (1827-1870), President of Paraguay.

Nos. 1753-1754 are airmail.

Paintings — A307

Paintings by: No. 1755a, 1g, Gabrielle Rainer Istvanffy. b, 2g, L. C. Hoffmeister. c, 3g, Frans Floris. d, 4g, Gerard de Lairesse. e, 5g, David Teniers I. f, 10g, Jacopo Zucchi. g, 15g, Pierre Paul Prudhon. 20g, Francois Boucher. 25g, Ingres. 5g-25g vert.

1977, July 25 ***Perf. 14***

1755 A307 Strip of 7, #a.-g.
1756 A307 20g multicolored

Souvenir Sheet

Perf. 14½

1757 A307 25g multicolored

Nos. 1755f-1757 are airmail.

German Sailing Ships — A308

Designs: No. 1764a, 1g, De Beurs van Amsterdam. b, 2g, Katharina von Blankenese. c, 3g, Cuxhaven. d, 4g, Rhein. e, 5g, Churprinz and Marian. f, 10g, Bark of Bremen, vert. g, 15g, Elbe II, vert. 20g, Karacke. 25g, Admiral Karpeanger.

Unwmk.

1977, Aug. 27 **Litho.** ***Perf. 14***

1764 A308 Strip of 7, #a.-g.
1765 A308 20g multicolored

Souvenir Sheet

Perf. 13½

1766 A308 25g multicolored

Nos. 1764f-1766 are airmail. No. 1766 contains one 40x30mm stamp.

Nobel Laureates for Literature — A309

Authors and scenes from books: No. 1773a, 1g, John Steinbeck, Grapes of Wrath, vert. b, 2g, Ernest Hemingway, Death in the Afternoon. c, 3g, Pearl S. Buck, The Good Earth, vert. d, 4g, George Bernard Shaw, Pygmalion, vert. e, 5g, Maurice Maeterlinck, Joan of Arc, vert. f, 10g, Rudyard Kipling, The Jungle Book. g, Henryk Sienkiewicz, Quo Vadis. 20g, C. Theodor Mommsen, History of Rome. 25g, Nobel prize medal.

1977, Sept. 5 ***Perf. 14***

1773 A309 Strip of 7, #a.-g.
1774 A309 20g multicolored

Souvenir Sheet

Perf. 14½

1775 A309 25g multicolored

Nos. 1773f-1775 are airmail.

1978 World Cup Soccer Championships, Argentina — A310

Posters and World Cup Champions: No. 1782a, 1g, Uruguay, 1930. b, 2g, Italy, 1934. c, 3g, Italy, 1938. d, 4g, Uruguay, 1950. e, 5g, Germany, 1954. f, 10g, Soccer player by Fritz Genkinger. g, 15g, Soccer player, orange shirt by Genkinger.

No. 1783a, 1g, Brazil, 1958. b, 2g, Brazil, 1962. c, 3g, England, 1966. d, 4g, Brazil, 1970. e, 5g, Germany, 1974. f, 10g, Player #4 by Genkinger. g, 15g, Player #1 by Genkinger, horiz.

No. 1784, World Cup Trophy. No. 1785, German players, Argentina '78. No. 1786, The Loser, by Genkinger. No. 1787, The Defender, (player #11) by Genkinger.

1977, Oct. 28 **Unwmk.** ***Perf. 14***

1782 A310 Strip of 7, #a.-g.
1783 A310 Strip of 7, #a.-g.
1784 A310 20g multicolored
1785 A310 20g multicolored

Souvenir Sheets

Perf. 14½

1786 A310 25g red & multi
1787 A310 25g black & multi

Nos. 1782f-1782g, 1783f-1783g, 1784-1787 are airmail.

Peter Paul Rubens, 400th Birth Anniv. A312

Details from paintings: No. 1788a, 1g, Rubens and Isabella Brant under Honeysuckle Bower. b, 2g, Judgment of Paris. c, 3g, Union of Earth and Water. d, 4g, Daughters of Kekrops Discovering Erichthonius. e, 5g, Holy Family with the Lamb. f, 10c, Adoration of the Magi. g, 15c, Philip II on Horseback.

20g, Education of Marie de Medici, horiz. 25g, Triumph of Eucharist Over False Gods.

1978, Jan. 19 **Unwmk.** ***Perf. 14***

1788 A312 Strip of 7, #a.-g.
1789 A312 20g multicolored

Souvenir Sheet

Perf. 14½

1790 A312 25g multicolored

Nos. 1788f-1788g, 1789-1790 are airmail. No. 1790 contains one 50x70mm stamp and exists inscribed in gold or silver.

1978 World Chess Championships, Argentina — A313

Paintings of chess players: No. 1791a, 1g, De Cremone. b, 2g, L. van Leyden. c, 3g, H. Muehlich. d, 4g, Arabian artist. e, 5g, Benjamin Franklin playing chess, E. H. May. f, 10g, G. Cruikshank. g, 15g, 17th cent. tapestry. 20g, Napoleon playing chess on St. Helena. 25g, Illustration from chess book, Shah Name.

1978, Jan. 23 ***Perf. 14***

1791 A313 Strip of 7, #a.-g.
1792 A313 20g multicolored

Souvenir Sheet

Perf. 14½

1793 A313 25g multicolored

Nos. 1791f-1791g, 1792-1793 are airmail. No. 1793 contains one 50x40mm stamp.

Jacob Jordaens, 300th Death Anniv. A314

Paintings: No. 1794a, 3g, Satyr and the Nymphs. b, 4g, Satyr with Peasant. c, 5g, Allegory of Fertility. d, 6g, Upbringing of Jupiter. e, 7g, Holy Family. f, 8g, Adoration of the Shepherds. g, 20g, Jordaens with his family. 10g, Meleagro with Atalanta, horiz. No. 1796, Feast for a King, horiz. No. 1797, Holy Family with Shepherds.

1978, Jan. 25 ***Perf. 14***

1794 A314 Strip of 7, #a.-g.
1795 A314 10g multicolored
1796 A314 25g multicolored

Souvenir Sheet

Perf. 14½

1797 A314 25g multicolored

Nos. 1795-1797 are airmail. No. 1797 contains one 50x70mm stamp.

Albrecht Durer, 450th Death Anniv. A315

Monograms and details from paintings: No. 1804a, 3g, Temptation of the Idler. b, 4g, Adam and Eve. c, 5g, Satyr Family. d, 6g, Eve. e, 7g, Adam. f, 8g, Portrait of a Young Man. g, 20g, Squirrels and Acorn. 10g, Madonna and Child. No. 1806, Brotherhood of the Rosary (Lute-playing Angel). No. 1807, Soldier on Horseback with a Lance.

1978, Mar. 10 ***Perf. 14***

1804 A315 Strip of 7, #a.-g.
1805 A315 10g multicolored
1806 A315 25g multicolored

Souvenir Sheet

Perf. 13½

1807 A315 25g blk, buff & sil

Nos. 1805-1807 are airmail. No. 1807 contains one 30x40mm stamp.

Francisco de Goya, 150th Death Anniv. A316

Paintings: No. 1814a, 3g, Allegory of the Town of Madrid. b, 4g, The Clothed Maja. c, 5g, The Parasol. d, 6g, Dona Isabel Cobos de Porcel. e, 7g, The Drinker. f, 8g, The 2nd of May 1908. g, 20g, General Jose Palafox on Horseback. 10g, Savages Murdering a Woman. 25g, The Naked Maja, horiz.

1978, May 11 ***Perf. 14***

1814 A316 Strip of 7, #a.-g.
1815 A316 10g multicolored
1816 A316 25g multicolored

Nos. 1815-1816 are airmail.

Future Space Projects — A317

Various futuristic space vehicles and imaginary creatures: No. 1816a, 3g. b, 4g. c, 5g. d, 6g. e, 7g. f, 8g. g, 20g.

1978, May 16

1817 A317 Strip of 7, #a.-g.
1818 A317 10g multicolored
1819 A317 25g multi, diff.

Nos. 1818-1819 are airmail.

Racing Cars — A318

No. 1820: a, 3g, Tyrell Formula I. b, 4g, Lotus Formula 1, 1978. c, 5g, McLaren Formula 1. d, 6g, Brabham Alfa Romeo Formula 1. e, 7g, Renault Turbo Formula 1. f, 8g, Wolf Formula 1. g, 20g, Porsche 935. 10g, Bugatti. 25g, Mercedes Benz W196, Stirling Moss, driver. No. 1823, Ferrari 312T.

1978, June 28 ***Perf. 14***

1820 A318 Strip of 7, #a.-g.
1821 A318 10g multicolored
1822 A318 25g multicolored

Souvenir Sheet

Perf. 14½

1823 A318 25g multicolored

Nos. 1821-1823 are airmail. No. 1823 contains one 50x35mm stamp.

Paintings by Peter Paul Rubens A319

3g, Holy Family with a Basket. 4g, Amor Cutting a Bow. 5g, Adam 7 Eve in Paradise. 6g, Crown of Fruit, horiz. 7g, Kidnapping of Ganymede. 8g, The Hunting of Crocodile & Hippopotamus. 10g, The Reception of Marie de Medici at Marseilles. 20g, Two Satyrs. 25g, Felicity of the Regency.

1978, June 30 ***Perf. 14***

1824	A319	3g	multicolored
1825	A319	4g	multicolored
1826	A319	5g	multicolored
1827	A319	6g	multicolored
1828	A319	7g	multicolored
1829	A319	8g	multicolored
1830	A319	10g	multicolored
1831	A319	20g	multicolored
1832	A319	25g	multicolored

Nos. 1830, 1832 are airmail.

National College A320

Perf. 13½x13

1978 **Litho.** **Wmk. 347**

1833	A320	3g claret		.20	.20
1834	A320	4g violet blue		.20	.20
1835	A320	5g lilac		.20	.20
1836	A320	20g brown		.20	.20
1837	A320	25g violet black		.20	.20
1838	A320	30g bright green		.25	.20
		Nos. 1833-1838 (6)		1.25	1.20

Centenary of National College in Asuncion.
Nos. 1836-1838 are airmail.

José Estigarribia, Bugler, Flag of Paraguay A321

1978 **Litho.** ***Perf. 13x13½***

1839	A321	3g multi	.20	.20
1840	A321	5g multi	.20	.20
1841	A321	10g multi	.20	.20
1842	A321	20g multi	.20	.20
1843	A321	25g multi	.20	.20
1844	A321	30g multi	.25	.20
		Nos. 1839-1844 (6)	1.25	1.20

Induction of Jose Felix Estigarribia (1888-1940), general and president of Paraguay, into Salon de Bronce (National Heroes' Hall of Fame).
Nos. 1842-1844 are airmail.

Queen Elizabeth II Coronation, 25th Anniv. A322

Flowers and: 3g, Barbados #234. 4g, Tristan da Cunha #13. 5g, Bahamas #157. 6g, Seychelles #172. 7g, Solomon Islands #88. 8g, Cayman Islands #150. 10g, New Hebrides #77. 20g, St. Lucia #156. 25g, St. Helena #139.
No. 1854, Solomon Islands #368a-368c, Gilbert Islands #312a-312c. No. 1855, Great Britain #313-316.

1978, July 25 **Unwmk.** ***Perf. 14***

1845	A322	3g	multicolored
1846	A322	4g	multicolored
1847	A322	5g	multicolored
1848	A322	6g	multicolored
1849	A322	7g	multicolored
1850	A322	8g	multicolored
1851	A322	10g	multicolored
1852	A322	20g	multicolored
1853	A322	25g	multicolored

Souvenir Sheets
Perf. 13½

1854	A322	25g	multicolored
1855	A322	25g	multicolored

Nos. 1851, 1853-1855 are airmail. Nos. 1854-1855 each contain one 60x40mm stamp.

Intl. Philatelic Exhibitions A323

Various paintings, ship, nudes, etc. for: No. 1856a, 3g, Nordposta '78. b, 4g, Riccione '78. c, 5g, Uruguay '79. d, 6g, ESSEN '78. e, 7g, ESPAMER '79. f, 8g, London '80. g, 20g, PRAGA '78. 10g, EUROPA '78. No. 1858, Eurphila '78.
No. 1859, Francisco de Pinedo, map of his flight.

1978, July 19 ***Perf. 14***

1856	A323		Strip of 7, #a.-g.
1857	A323	10g	multicolored
1858	A323	25g	multicolored

Souvenir Sheet
Perf. 13½x13

1859	A323	25g	multicolored

No. 1859 for Riccione '78 and Eurphila '78 and contains one 54x34mm stamp. Nos. 1857-1859 are airmail. Nos. 1856b-1858 are vert.

Intl. Year of the Child A324

Grimm's Snow White and the Seven Dwarfs: No. 1866a, 3g, Queen pricking her finger. b, 4g, Queen and mirror. c, 5g, Man with dagger, Snow White. d, 6g, Snow White in forest. e, 7g, Snow White asleep, seven dwarfs. f, 8g, Snow White dancing with dwarfs. g, 20g, Snow White being offered apple. 10g, Snow White in repose. 25g, Snow White, Prince Charming on horseback.

1978, Oct. 26

1866	A324		Strip of 7, #a.-g.
1867	A324	10g	multicolored
1868	A324	25g	multicolored

Nos. 1867-1868 are airmail.
See Nos. 1893-1896, 1916-1919.

Mounted South American Soldiers A325

No. 1869a, 3g, Gen. Jose Felix Bogado (1771-1829). b, 4g, Colonel, First Volunteer Regiment, 1806. c, 5g, Colonel wearing dress uniform, 1860. d, 6g, Soldier, 1864-1870. e, 7g, Dragoon, 1865. f, 8g, Lancer. g, 20g, Soldier, 1865. 10g, Gen. Bernardo O'Higgins, 200th birth anniv. 25g, Jose de San Martin, 200th birth anniv.

1978, Oct. 31

1869	A325		Strip of 7, #a.-g.
1870	A325	10g	multicolored
1871	A325	25g	multicolored

Nos. 1870-1871 are airmail.

1978 World Cup Soccer Championships, Argentina — A326

Soccer Players: No. 1872a, 3g, Paraguay, vert. b, 4g, Austria, Sweden. c, 5g, Argentina, Poland. d, 6g, Italy, Brazil. e, 7g, Netherlands, Austria. f, 8g, Scotland, Peru. g, 20g, Germany, Italy. 10g, Argentina, Holland. 25g, Germany, Tunisia.
No. 1875, Stadium.

1979, Jan. 9 ***Perf. 14***

1872	A326		Strip of 7, #a.-g.
1873	A326	10g	multicolored
1874	A326	25g	multicolored

Souvenir Sheet
Perf. 13½

1875	A326	25g	multicolored

Nos. 1873-1875 are airmail. No. 1875 contains one 60x40mm stamp.
For overprint see No. C610.

Christmas A327

Paintings of the Nativity and Madonna and Child by: No. 1876a, 3g, Giorgione, horiz. b, 4g, Titian. c, 5g, Titian, diff. d, 6g, Raphael. e, 7g, Schongauer. f, 8g, Muratti. g, 20g, Van Oost. 10g, Memling. No. 1878, Rubens.
No. 1879, Madonna and Child Surrounded by a Garland and Boy Angels, Rubens.

1979, Jan. 10 **Litho.** ***Perf. 14***

1876	A327		Strip of 7, #a.-g.
1877	A327	10g	multicolored
1878	A327	25g	multicolored

Souvenir Sheet
Photo. & Engr.
Perf. 12

1879	A327	25g	multicolored

Nos. 1877-1879 are airmail.

First Powered Flight, 75th Anniv. (in 1978) — A328

Airplanes: No. 1880a, 3g, Eole, C. Ader, 1890. b, 4g, Flyer III, Wright Brothers. c, 5g, Voisin, Henri Farman, 1908. d, 6g, Curtiss, Eugene Ely, 1910. e, 7g, Etrich-Taube A11. f, 8g, Fokker EIII. g, 20g, Albatros C, 1915. 10g, Boeing 747 carrying space shuttle. No. 1882, Boeing 707. No. 1883, Zeppelin flight commemorative cancels.

1979, Apr. 24 **Litho.** ***Perf. 14***

1880	A328		Strip of 7, #a.-g.
1881	A328	10g	multicolored
1882	A328	25g	multicolored

Souvenir Sheet
Perf. 14½

1883	A328	25g	blue & black

Nos. 1881-1883 are airmail. Nos. 1880-1883 incorrectly commemorate 75th anniv. of ICAO. No. 1883 contains one 50x40mm stamp.

Albrecht Durer, 450th Death Anniv. (in 1978) A329

Paintings: No. 1884a, 3g, Virgin with the Dove. b, 4g, Virgin Praying. c, 5g, Mater Dolorosa. d, 6g, Virgin with a Carnation. e, 7g, Madonna and Sleeping Child. f, 8g, Virgin Before the Archway. g, 20g, Flight Into Egypt. No. 1885, Madonna of the Haller family. No. 1886, Virgin with a Pear.
No. 1887, Lamentation Over the Dead Christ for Albrecht Glimm. No. 1888, Space station, horiz., with Northern Hemisphere of Celestial Globe in margin.

1979, Apr. 28 ***Perf. 14***

1884	A329		Strip of 7, #a.-g.
1885	A329	10g	multicolored
1886	A329	25g	multicolored

Souvenir Sheets
Perf. 13½

1887	A329	25g	multicolored
1888	A329	25g	multicolored

Intl. Year of the Child (#1885-1886).
Nos. 1885-1886, 1888 are airmail. No. 1887 contains one 30x40mm stamp, No. 1888 one 40x30mm stamp.

Sir Rowland Hill, Death Cent. — A330

Hill and: No. 1889a, 3g, Newfoundland #C1, vert. b, 4g, France #C14. c, 5g, Spain #B106. d, 6g, Similar to Ecuador #C2, vert. e, 7g, US #C3a. f, 8g, Gelber Hund inverted overprint, vert. g, 20g, Switzerland #C20a.
10g, Privately issued Zeppelin stamp. No. 1891, Paraguay #C82, #C96, vert. No. 1892, Italy #C49. No. 1892A, France #C3-C4.

1979, June 11 ***Perf. 14***

1889	A330		Strip of 7, #a.-g.
1890	A330	10g	multicolored
1891	A330	25g	multicolored

Souvenir Sheet

Perf. 13½x13

1892 A330 25g multicolored

Perf. 14½

1892A A330 25g multicolored

Issue dates: No. 1892A, Aug. 28. Others, June 11. Nos. 1890-1892A are airmail.

Grimm's Fairy Tales Type of 1978

Cinderella: No. 1893a, 3g, Two stepsisters watch Cinderella cleaning. b, 4g, Cinderella, father, stepsisters. c, 5g, Cinderella with birds while working. d, 6g, Finding dress. e, 7g, Going to ball. f, 8g, Dancing with prince. g, 20g, Losing slipper leaving ball.

10g, Prince Charming trying slipper on Cinderella's foot. No. 1895, Couple riding to castle. No. 1896, Couple entering ballroom.

1979, June 24 ***Perf. 14***

1893 A324 Strip of 7, #a.-g.
1894 A324 10g multicolored
1895 A324 25g multicolored

Souvenir Sheet

Perf. 13½

1896 A324 25g multicolored

Intl. Year of the Child.

Congress Emblem A331

1979, Aug. **Litho.** ***Perf. 13x13½***

1897 A331 10g red, blue & black .20 .20
1898 A331 50g red, blue & black .40 .30

22nd Latin-American Tourism Congress, Asuncion. No. 1898 is airmail.

1980 Winter Olympics, Lake Placid — A332

#1899: a, 3g, Monica Scheftschik, luge. b, 4g, E. Deufl, Austria, downhill skiing. c, 5g, G. Thoeni, Italy, slalom skiing. d, 6g, Canada Two-man bobsled. e, 7g, Germany vs. Finland, ice hockey. f, 8g, Hoenl, Russia, ski jump. g, 20g, Dianne De Leeuw, Netherlands, figure skating, vert.

10g, Hanni Wenzel, Liechtenstein, slalom skiing. No. 1901, Frommelt, Liechtenstein, slalom skiing, vert. No. 1902, Kulakova, Russia, cross country skier. No. 1903, Dorothy Hamill, US, figure skating, vert. No. 1904, Brigitte Totschning, skier.

1979 **Unwmk.** ***Perf. 14***

1899 A332 Strip of 7, #a.-g.
1900 A332 10g multicolored
1901 A332 25g multicolored

Souvenir Sheets

Perf. 13½

1902 A332 25g multicolored
1903 A332 25g multicolored
1904 A332 25g multicolored

#1900-1904 are airmail. #1902-1903 each contain one 40x30mm stamp, #1904, one 25x36mm stamp.

Issued: #1899-1902, 8/22; #1903, 6/11; #1904, 4/24.

Sailing Ships — A333

No. 1905: a, 3g, Caravel, vert. b, 4g, Warship. c, 5g, Warship, by Jan van Beeck. d, 6g, H.M.S. Britannia, vert. e, 7g, Salamis, vert. f, 8g, Ariel, vert. g, 20g, Warship, by Robert Salmon.

1979, Aug. 28 ***Perf. 14***

1905 A333 Strip of 7, #a.-g.
1906 A333 10g Lisette
1907 A333 25g Holstein, vert.

Nos. 1906-1907 are airmail.

Intl. Year of the Child A334

Various kittens: No. 1908a, 3g. b, 4g. c, 5g. d, 6g. e, 7g. f, 8g. g, 20g.

1979, Nov. 29 ***Perf. 14***

1908 A334 Strip of 7, #a.-g.
1909 A334 10g multicolored
1910 A334 25g multicolored

Nos. 1909-1910 are airmail.

Grimm's Fairy Tales Type of 1978

Little Red Riding Hood: No. 1916a, 3g, Leaving with basket. b, 4g, Meets wolf. c, 5g, Picks flowers. d, 6g, Wolf puts on Granny's gown. e, 7g, Wolf in bed. f, 8g, Hunter arrives. g, 20g, Saved by the hunter.

10g, Hunter enters house. No. 1918, Hunter leaves. No. 1919, Overall scene.

1979, Dec. 4 ***Perf. 14***

1916 A324 Strip of 7, #a.-g.
1917 A324 10g multicolored
1918 A324 25g multicolored

Souvenir Sheet

Perf. 14½

1919 A324 25g multicolored

Intl. Year of the Child. No. 1919 contains one 50x70mm stamp.

Greek Athletes A335

Paintings on Greek vases: No. 1926a, 3g, 3 runners. b, 4g, 2 runners. c, 5g, Throwing contest. d, 6g, Discus. e, 7g, Wrestlers. f, 8g, Wrestlers, diff. g, 20g, 2 runners, diff.

10g, Horse and rider, horiz. 25g, 4 warriors with shields, horiz.

1979, Dec. 20 ***Perf. 14***

1926 A335 Strip of 7, #a.-g.
1927 A335 10g multicolored
1928 A335 25g multicolored

Nos. 1927-1928 are airmail.

Electric Trains — A336

No. 1929: a, 3g, First electric locomotive, Siemens, 1879, vert. b, 4g, Switzerland, 1897. c, 5g, Model E71 28, Germany. d, 6g, Mountain train, Switzerland. e, 7g, Electric locomotive used in Benelux countries. f, 8g, Locomotive "Rheinpfeil," Germany. g, 20g, Model BB-9004, France.

10g, 200-Km/hour train, Germany. 25g, Japanese bullet train.

1979, Dec. 24 **Litho.** ***Perf. 14***

1929 A336 Strip of 7, #a.-g.
1930 A336 10g multicolored
1931 A336 25g multicolored

Nos. 1930-1931 are airmail.

Sir Rowland Hill, Death Cent. — A337

Hill and: No. 1938a, 3g, Spad S XIII, 1917-18. b, 4g, P-51 D Mustang, 1944-45. c, 5g, Mitsubishi A6M6c Zero-Sen, 1944. d, 6g, Deperdussin float plane, 1913. e, 7g, Savoia Marchetti SM 7911, 1936. f, 8g, Messerschmitt Me 262B, 1942-45. g, 20g, Nieuport 24bis, 1917-18.

10g, Zeppelin LZ 104-/l59, 1917. No. 1940, Fokker Dr-1 Caza, 1917. No. 1941, Vickers Supermarine "Spitfire" Mk.IX, 1942-45.

1980, Apr. 8 ***Perf. 14***

1938 A337 Strip of 7, #a.-g.
1939 A337 10g multicolored
1940 A337 25g multicolored

Souvenir Sheet

Perf. 13½

1941 A337 25g multicolored

Incorrectly commemorates 75th anniv. of ICAO. Nos. 1939-1941 are airmail. No. 1941 contains one 37x27mm stamp.

Sir Rowland Hill, Paraguayan Stamps — A338

Hill and: No. 1948a, 3g, #1. b, 4g, #5. c, 5g, #6. d, 6g, #379. e, 7g, #381. f, 8g, #C384. g, 20g, #C389.

10g, #C83, horiz. No. 1950, #C92, horiz. No. 1951, #C54, horiz. No. 1952, #C1, horiz.

1980, Apr. 14 **Litho.** ***Perf. 14***

1948 A338 Strip of 7, #a.-g.
1949 A338 10g multicolored
1950 A338 25g multicolored

Souvenir Sheets

Perf. 14½

1951 A338 25g multicolored
1952 A338 25g multicolored

#1949-1952 are airmail. #1951 contains one 50x40mm stamp. #1952 one 50x35mm stamp.

1980 Winter Olympics, Lake Placid A339

No. 1953: a, 3g, Thomas Wassberg, Sweden, cross country skiing. b, 4g, Scharer & Benz, Switzerland, 2-man bobsled. c, 5g, Annemarie Moser-Proll, Austria, women's downhill skiing. d, 6g, Hockey team, US. e, 7g, Leonhard Stock, Austria, men's downhill skiing. f, 8g, Anton (Toni) Innauer, Austria, ski jump. g, 20g, Christa Kinshofer, Germany, slalom skiing.

10g, Ingemar Stenmark, slalom, Sweden. No. 1955, Robin Cousins, figure skating, Great Britain. No. 1956, Eric Heiden, speed skating, US, horiz.

1980, June 4 ***Perf. 14***

1953 A339 Strip of 7, #a.-g.
1954 A339 10g multi, horiz.
1955 A339 25g multi, horiz.

Souvenir Sheet

Perf. 13½

1956 A339 25g multicolored

Nos. 1954-1956 are airmail. No. 1956 contains one 60x49mm stamp.

Composers and Paintings of Young Ballerinas A340

Paintings of ballerinas by Cydney or Degas and: No. 1957a, 3g, Gioacchino Rossini. b, 4g, Johann Strauss, the younger. c, 5g, Debussy. d, 6g, Beethoven. e, 7g, Chopin. f, 8g, Richard Wagner. g, 20g, Johann Sebastian Bach, horiz. 10g, Robert Stoltz. 25g, Verdi.

1980, July 1 ***Perf. 14***

1957 A340 Strip of 7, #a.-g.
1958 A340 10g multicolored
1959 A340 25g multicolored

Birth and death dates are incorrectly inscribed on 4g, 8g, 10g. No. 1957f is incorrectly inscribed "Adolph" Wagner. Nos. 1958-1959 are airmail. For overprints see Nos. 1998-1999.

Pilar City Bicentennial — A341

Perf. 13½x13

1980, July 17 **Litho.** **Wmk. 347**

1966 A341 5g multi .20 .20
1967 A341 25g multi .20 .20

No. 1967 is airmail.

Christmas, Intl. Year of the Child
A342

No. 1968: a, 3g, Christmas tree. b, 4g, Santa filling stockings. c, 5g, Nativity scene. d, 6g, Adoration of the Magi. e, 7g, Three children, presents. f, 8g, Children, dove, fruit. g, 20g, Children playing with toys. 10g, Madonna and Child, horiz. No. 1970, Children blowing bubbles, horiz. No. 1971, Five children, horiz.

1980, Aug. 4 Unwmk. *Perf. 14*

1968 A342 Strip of 7, #a.-g.
1969 A342 10g multicolored
1970 A342 25g multicolored

Souvenir Sheet

1971 A342 25g multicolored

Nos. 1969-1970 are airmail.

Ships
A343

Emblems and ships: No. 1972a, 3g, ESPAMER '80, Spanish Armada. b, 4g, NORWEX '80, Viking longboat. c, 5g, RICCIONE '80, Battle of Lepanto. d, 6g, ESSEN '80, Great Harry of Cruickshank. e, 7g, US Bicentennial, Mount Vernon. f, 8g, LONDON '80, H.M.S. Victory. g, 20g, ESSEN '80, Hamburg III, vert. 10g, ESSEN '80, Gorch Fock. 25g, PHILATOKYO '81, Nippon Maru, horiz.

1980, Sept. 15 *Perf. 14*

1972 A343 Strip of 7, #a.-g.
1973 A343 10g multicolored
1974 A343 25g multicolored

Nos. 1973-1974 are airmail. For overprint see No. 2278.

Souvenir Sheet

King Juan Carlos — A344

1980, Sept. 19 *Perf. 14½*

1975 A344 25g multicolored

Paraguay Airlines Boeing 707 Service Inauguration — A345

Perf. 13½x13

1980, Sept. 17 Litho. Wmk. 347

1976	A345	20g	multi	.20	.20
1977	A345	100g	multi	.80	.65

No. 1977 is airmail.

A346

World Cup Soccer Championships, Spain — A346a

Various soccer players, winning country: No. 1978a, 3g, Uruguay 1930, 1950. b, 4g, Italy 1934, 1938. c, 5g, Germany 1954, 1974. d, 6g, Brazil 1958, 1962, 1970. e, 7g, England, 1966. f, 8g, Argentina, 1978. g, 20g, Espana '82 emblem.

10g, World Cup trophy, flags. 25g, Soccer player from Uruguay.

1980, Dec. 10 Unwmk. *Perf. 14*

1978 A346 Strip of 7, #a.-g.
1979 A346 10g multicolored
1980 A346 25g multicolored

Souvenir Sheet

Perf. 14½

1981 A346a 25g Sheet of 1 + 2 labels

Nos. 1979-1981 are airmail.

1980 World Chess Championships, Mexico — A347

Illustrations from The Book of Chess: No. 1982a, 3g, Two men, chess board. b, 4g, Circular chess board, players. c, 5g, Four-person chess match. d, 6g, King Alfonso X of Castile and Leon. e, 7g, Two players, chess board, horiz. f, 8g, Two veiled women, chess board, horiz. g, 20g, Two women in robes, chess board, horiz.

10g, Crusader knights, chess board, horiz. 25g, Three players, chess board, horiz.

1980, Dec. 15 Litho. *Perf. 14*

1982 A347 Strip of 7, #a.-g.
1983 A347 10g multicolored
1984 A347 25g multicolored

Nos. 1983-1984 are airmail.

See Nos. C506-C510. Compare with illustration AP199.

1980 Winter Olympics, Lake Placid
A348

Olympic scenes, gold medalists: No. 1985a, 25c, Lighting Olympic flame. b, 50c, Hockey team, US. c, 1g, Eric Heiden, US, speed skating. d, 2g, Robin Cousins, Great Britain, figure skating. e, 3g, Thomas Wassberg, Sweden, cross country skiing. f, 4g, Annie Borckinck, Netherlands, speed skating. g, 5g, Gold, silver, and bronze medals.

No. 1986, Irene Epple, silver medal, slalom, Germany. 10g, Ingemar Stenmark, slalom, giant slalom, Sweden. 30g, Annemarie Moser-Proll, downhill, Austria. 25g, Baron Pierre de Coubertin.

1981, Feb. 4 Litho. *Perf. 14*

1985 A348 Strip of 7, #a.-g.
1986 A348 5g multicolored
1987 A348 10g multicolored
1988 A348 30g multicolored

Souvenir Sheet

Perf. 13½

1988A A348 25g multicolored

No. 1985 exists in strips of 4 and 3. Nos. 1986-1988A are airmail. No. 1988A contains one 30x40mm stamp.

Locomotives — A349

No. 1989, 25c, Electric model 242, Germany. b, 50c, Electric, London-Midlands-Lancashire, England. c, 1g, Electric, Switzerland. d, 2g, Diesel-electric, Montreal-Vancouver, Canada. e, 3g, Electric, Austria. f, 4g, Electric inter-urban, Lyons-St. Etienne, France, vert. g, 5g, First steam locomotive in Paraguay.

No. 1991, Steam locomotive, Japan. 10g, Stephenson's steam engine, 1830 England. No. 1993, Crocodile locomotive, Switzerland. 30g, Stephenson's Rocket, 1829, England, vert.

1981, Feb. 9 Litho. *Perf. 14*

1989 A349 Strip of 7, #a.-g.
1990 A349 5g multicolored
1991 A349 10g multicolored
1992 A349 30g multicolored

Souvenir Sheet

Perf. 13½x13

1993 A349 25g multicolored

Electric railroads, cent. (#1989a-1989f), steam-powered railway service, 150th anniv. (#1989g, 1990-1991), Liverpool-Manchester Railway, 150th anniv. (#1992). Swiss Railways, 75th anniv. (#1993).

Nos. 1990-1993 are airmail. No. 1993 contains one 54x34mm stamp.

Intl. Year of the Child
A350

Portraits of children with assorted flowers: No. 1994a, 10g. b, 25g. c, 50g. d, 100g. e, 200g. f, 300g. g, 400g.

1981, Apr. 13 Litho. *Perf. 14*

1994 A350 Strip of 7, #a.-g.
1995 A350 75g multicolored
1996 A350 500g multicolored
1997 A350 1000g multicolored

Nos. 1995-1997 are airmail.

Nos. 1957b and 1958 Overprinted in Red

1981, May 22

1998 A340 4g on #1957b
1999 A340 10g on #1958

No. 1999 is airmail.

The following stamps were issued in sheets of 8 with 1 label: Nos. 2001, 2013, 2037, 2044, 2047, 2055, 2140.

The following stamp was issued in sheets of 10 with 2 labels: No. 1994a.

The following stamps were issued in sheets of 6 with 3 labels: Nos. 2017, 2029, 2035, 2104, 2145.

The following stamps were issued in sheets of 3 with 6 labels: 2079, 2143.

The following stamps were issued in sheets of 5 with 4 labels: Nos. 2050-2051, 2057, 2059, 2061, 2067, 2069, 2077, 2082, 2089, 2092, 2107, 2117, 2120, 2121, 2123, 2125, 2129, 2135, 2138, 2142, 2146, 2148, 2151, 2160, 2163, 2165, 2169, 2172, 2176, 2179, 2182, 2190, 2196, 2202, 2204, 2214, 2222, 2224, 2232, 2244, 2246, 2248, 2261, 2263, 2265, 2271, 2273, 2275, 2277.

The following stamps were issued in sheets of 4 with 5 labels: Nos. 2307, 2310, 2313, 2316, 2324, 2329.

Royal Wedding of Prince Charles and Lady Diana Spencer — A351

Prince Charles, sailing ships: No. 2000a, 25c, Royal George. b, 50c, Great Britain. c, 1g, Taeping. d, 2g, Star of India. e, 3g, Torrens. f, 4g, Loch Etive. No. 2001, Medway.

No. 2002, Charles, flags, and Concorde. 10g, Flags, flowers, Diana, Charles. 25g, Charles, Diana, flowers, vert. 30g, Coats of arms, flags.

1981, June 27

2000 A351 Strip of 6, #a.-f.
2001 A351 5g multicolored
2002 A351 5g multicolored
2003 A351 10g multicolored
2004 A351 30g multicolored

Souvenir Sheet

Perf. 13½

2005 A351 25g multicolored

Nos. 2002-2005 are airmail. No. 2005 contains one 50x60mm stamp. For overprint see No. 2253.

Traditional Costumes and Itaipu Dam
A352

Women in various traditional costumes: a, 10g. b, 25g. c, 50g. d, 100g. e, 200g. f, 300g. g, 400g, President Stroessner, Itaipu Dam.

1981, June 30 ***Perf. 14***
2006 A352 Strip of 7, #a.-g.

For overprints see No. 2281.

UPU Membership Centenary — A353

1981, Aug. 18 Litho. ***Perf. 13½x13***

2007 A353	5g rose lake & blk	.20	.20
2008 A353	10g lil & blk	.20	.20
2009 A353	20g grn & blk	.20	.20
2010 A353	25g lt red brn & blk	.20	.20
2011 A353	50g bl & blk	.40	.30
Nos. 2007-2011 (5)		1.20	1.10

Peter Paul Rubens, Paintings A354

Details from paintings: No. 2012: a, 25c, Madonna Surrounded by Saints. b, 50c, Judgment of Paris. c, 1g, Duke of Buckingham Conducted to the Temple of Virtus. d, 2g, Minerva Protecting Peace from Mars. e, 3g, Henry IV Receiving the Portrait of Marie de Medici. f, 4g, Triumph of Juliers. 5g, Madonna and Child Reigning Among Saints (Cherubs).

1981, July 9 Litho. ***Perf. 14***
2012 A354 Strip of 6, #a.-f.
2013 A354 5g multicolored

Jean Auguste-Dominique Ingres (1780-1867), Painter — A355

Details from paintings: No. 2014: a, 25c, c, 1g, d, 2g, f, 4g, The Turkish Bath. b, 50c, The Water Pitcher. e, 3g, Oediphus and the Sphinx. g, 5g, The Bathing Beauty.

1981, Oct. 13
2014 A355 Strip of 7, #a.-g.

No. 2014f and 2014g exist in sheet of 8 (four each) plus label. For overprints see No. 2045.

Pablo Picasso, Birth Cent. — A356

Designs: No. 2015: a, 25c, Women Running on the Beach. b, 50c, Family on the Beach.

No. 2016: a, 1g, Still-life. b, 2g, Bullfighter. c, 3g, Children Drawing. d, 4g, Seated Woman. 5g, Paul as Clown.

1981, Oct. 19
2015 A356 Pair, #a.-b.
2016 A356 Strip of 4, #a.-d.
2017 A356 5g multicolored

Nos. 2015-2016 Ovptd. in Silver

1981, Oct. 22
2018 A356 on #2015a-2015b
2019 A356 on #2016a-2016d

Philatelia '81, Frankfurt.

Nos. 2015-2016 Ovptd. in Gold

1981, Oct. 25
2020 A356 on #2015a-2015b
2021 A356 on #2016a-2016d

Espamer '81 Philatelic Exhibition.

Royal Wedding of Prince Charles and Lady Diana A357

Designs: No. 2022a-2022c, 25c, 50c, 1g, Diana, Charles, flowers. d, 2g, Couple. e, 3g, Couple leaving church. f, 4g, Couple, Queen Elizabeth II waving from balcony. g, 5g, Diana. No. 2023, Wedding party, horiz. 10g, Riding in royal coach, horiz. 30g, Yeomen of the guard, horiz.

1981, Dec. 4 Litho. ***Perf. 14***
2022 A357 Strip of 7, #a.-g.
2023 A357 5g multicolored
2024 A357 10g multicolored
2025 A357 30g multicolored

Souvenir Sheets

Perf. 14½

2026 A357 25g like #2022d
2027 A357 25g Wedding portrait

No. 2022g exists in sheets of 8 plus label. Nos. 2023-2027 are airmail. Nos. 2026-2027 contain one each 50x70mm stamp.

Christmas A358

Designs: No. 2028a, 25c, Jack-in-the-box. b, 50c, Jesus and angel. c, 1g, Santa, angels. d, 2g, Angels lighting candle. e, 3g, Christmas plant. f, 4g, Nativity scene. 5g, Children singing by Christmas tree.

1981, Dec. 17 ***Perf. 14***
2028 A358 Strip of 6, #a.-f.

Size: 28x45mm

Perf. 13½

2029 A358 5g multicolored

Intl. Year of the Child (Nos. 2028-2029). For overprints see No. 2042.

Intl. Year of the Child A359

Story of Puss 'n Boots: No. 2030a, 25c, Boy, Puss. b, 50c, Puss, rabbits.
1g, Puss, king. 2g, Prince, princess, king. 3g, Giant ogre, Puss. 4g, Puss chasing mouse. 5g, Princess, prince, Puss.

1982, Apr. 16 Litho. ***Perf. 14***
2030 A359 Pair, #a.-b.
2031 A359 1g multicolored
2032 A359 2g multicolored
2033 A359 3g multicolored
2034 A359 4g multicolored
2035 A359 5g multicolored

#2031-2034 printed se-tenant with label.

Scouting, 75th Anniv. and Lord Baden-Powell, 125th Birth Anniv. — A360

No. 2036: a, 25c, Tetradactyla, Scout hand salute. b, 50c, Nandu (rhea), Cub Scout and trefoil. c, 1g, Peccary, Wolf's head totem. d, 2g, Coatimundi, emblem on buckle. e, 3g, Mara, Scouting's Intl. Communications emblem. f, 4g, Deer, boy scout.

No. 2037, Aotes, Den mother, Cub Scout. No. 2038, Ocelot, scouts cooking. 10g, Collie, boy scout. 30g, Armadillo, two scouts planting tree. 25g, Lord Robert Baden-Powell, founder of Boy Scouts.

1982, Apr. 21
2036 A360 Strip of 6, #a.-f.
2037 A360 5g multicolored
2038 A360 5g multicolored
2039 A360 10g multicolored
2040 A360 30g multicolored

Souvenir Sheet

Perf. 14½

2041 A360 25g multicolored

Nos. 2038-2041 are airmail. For overprint see No. 2140.

No. 2028 Overprinted with ESSEN 82 Emblem

1982, Apr. 28 ***Perf. 14***
2042 A358 on #2028a-2028f

Essen '82 Intl. Philatelic Exhibition.

Cats and Kittens — A361

Various cats or kittens: No. 2043a, 25c. b, 50c. c, 1g. d, 2g. e, 3g. f, 4g.

1982, June 7 ***Perf. 14***
2043 A361 Strip of 6, #a.-f.
2044 A361 5g multi, vert.

For overprints see Nos. 2054-2055.

Nos. 2014a-2014e Ovptd. PHILEXFRANCE 82 Emblem ans "PARIS 11-21.6.82" in Blue

1982, June 11
2045 A355 Strip of 5, #a.-e.

Philexfrance '82 Intl. Philatelic Exhibition. Size of overprint varies.

World Cup Soccer Championships, Spain — A362

Designs: 2046a, 25c, Brazilian team. b, 50c, Chilean team. c, 1g, Honduran team. d, 2g, Peruvian team. e, 3g, Salvadoran team. f, 4g, Globe as soccer ball, flags of Latin American finalists. No. 2047, Ball of flags. No. 2048, Austrian team. No. 2049, Players from Brazil, Austria. No. 2050, Spanish team. No. 2051, Two players from Argentina, Brazil, vert. No. 2052, W. German team. No. 2053, Players from Argentina, Brazil. No. 2053A, World Cup trophy, world map on soccer balls. No. 2053B, Players from W. Germany, Mexico, vert.

1982 Litho. ***Perf. 14***
2046 A362 Strip of 6, #a.-f.
2047 A362 5g multicolored
2048 A362 5g multicolored
2049 A362 5g multicolored
2050 A362 10g multicolored
2051 A362 10g multicolored
2052 A362 30g multicolored
2053 A362 30g multicolored

Souvenir Sheets

Perf. 14½

2053A A362 25g multicolored
2053B A362 25g multicolored

Issued: #2049, 2051, 2053, 2053A, 4/19; others, 6/13.

Nos. 2047 exists in sheets of 8 plus label. Nos. 2048-2053B are airmail.

For overprints see Nos. 2086, 2286, C593.

Nos. 2043-2044 Overprinted in Silver With PHILATECIA 82 and Intl. Year of the Child Emblems

1982, Sept. 12 ***Perf. 14***
2054 A361 Strip of 5, #a.-e.
2055 A361 5g on #2044

Philatelia '82, Hanover, Germany and Intl. Year of the Child.

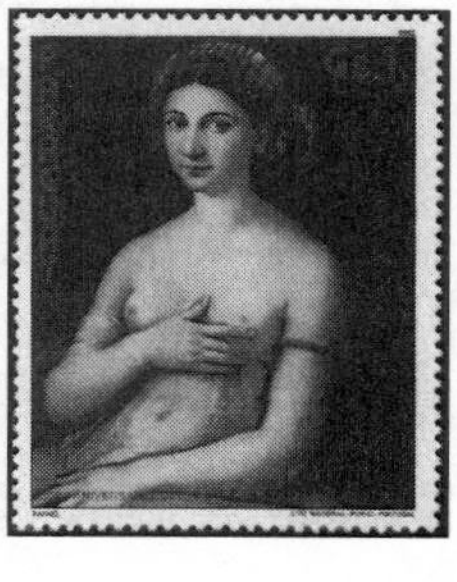

Raphael, 500th Birth Anniv. A363

Details from paintings: No. 2056a, 25c, Adam and Eve (The Fall). b, 50c, Creation of Eve. c, 1g, Portrait of a Young Woman (La Fornarina). d, 2g The Three Graces. e, 3g, f, 4g, Cupid and the Three Graces. 5g. Leda and the Swan.

1982, Sept. 27

2056 A363 Strip of 6, #a.-f.
2057 A363 5g multicolored

Nos. 2056e-2056f have continuous design.

Christmas A364

Entire works or details from paintings by Raphael: No. 2058a, 25c, The Belvedere Madonna. b, 50c, The Ansidei Madonna. c, 1g, La Belle Jardiniere. d, 2g, The Aldobrandini (Garvagh) Madonna. e, 3g, Madonna of the Goldfinch. f, 4g, The Alba Madonna. No. 2059, Madonna of the Grand Duke. No. 2060, Madonna of the Linen Window. 10g, The Alba Madonna, diff. 25g, The Holy Family with St. Elizabeth and the Infant St. John and Two Angels. 30g, The Canigiani Holy Family.

1982 ***Perf. 14, 13x13½ (#2061)***

2058 A364 Strip of 6, #a.-f.
2059 A364 5g multicolored
2060 A364 5g multicolored
2061 A364 10g multicolored
2062 A364 30g multicolored

Souvenir Sheet

Perf. 14½

2063 A364 25g multicolored

Issued: #2058-2059, 9/30; others, 12/17.
Nos. 2058a-2058f and 2059 exist perf. 13. Nos. 2060-2063 are airmail and have silver lettering. For overprint see No. 2087.

Life of Christ, by Albrecht Durer A365

Details from paintings: No. 2064a, 25c, The Flight into Egypt. b, 50c, Christ Among the Doctors. c, 1g, Christ Carrying the Cross. d, 2g, Nailing of Christ to the Cross. e, 3g, Christ on the Cross. f, 4g, Lamentation Over the Dead Christ. 5g, The Circumcision of Christ.

1982, Dec. 14 ***Perf. 14***

2064 A365 Strip of 6, #a.-f.

Perf. 13x13½

2065 A365 5g multicolored

For overprint see No. 2094.

South American Locomotives — A366

Locomotives from: No. 2066a, 25c, Argentina. b, 50c, Uruguay. c, 1g, Ecuador. d, 2g, Bolivia. e, 3g, Peru. f, 4g, Brazil. 5g, Paraguay.

1983, Jan. 17 **Litho.** ***Perf. 14***

2066 A366 Strip of 6, #a.-f.
2067 A366 5g multicolored

For overprint see No. 2093.

Race Cars A367

No. 2068: a, 25c, ATS-Ford D 06. b, 50c, Ferrari 126 C 2. c, 1g, Brabham-BMW BT 50. d, 2g, Renault RE 30 B. e, 3g, Porsche 956. f, 4g, Talbot-Ligier-Matra JS 19. 5g, Mercedes Benz C-111.

1983, Jan. 19 ***Perf. 14***

2068 A367 Strip of 6, #a.-f.

Perf. 13½x13

2069 A367 5g multicolored

For overprint see No. 2118.

Itaipua Dam, Pres. Stroessner — A368

1983, Jan. 22 **Litho.** **Wmk. 347**

2070 A368	3g	multi	.20	.20
2071 A368	5g	multi	.20	.20
2072 A368	10g	multi	.20	.20
2073 A368	20g	multi	.20	.20
2074 A368	25g	multi	.20	.20
2075 A368	50g	multi	.40	.30
Nos. 2070-2075 (6)			1.40	1.30

25th anniv. of Stroessner City.
Nos. 2073-2075 airmail.

1984 Winter Olympics, Sarajevo — A369

Ice skaters: No. 2076a, 25c, Marika Kilius, Hans-Jurgens Baumler, Germany, 1964. b, 50c, Tai Babilonia, Randy Gardner, US, 1976. c, 1g, Anett Poetzsch, E. Germany, 1980, vert. d, 2g, Tina Riegel, Andreas Nischwitz, Germany, 1980, vert. e, Dagmar Lurz, Germany, 1980, vert. f, 4g, Trixi Schuba, Austria, 1972, vert. 5g, Peggy Fleming, US, 1968, vert.

Perf. 13½x13, 13x13½

1983, Feb. 23 **Unwmk.**

2076 A369 Strip of 6, #a.-f.
2077 A369 5g multicolored

For overprints see Nos. 2177, 2266.

Pope John Paul II A370

#2078: a, 25c, Virgin of Caacupe. b, 50c, Cathedral of Caacupe. c, 1g, Cathedral of Asuncion. d, 2g, Pope holding crucifix. e, 3g, Our Lady of the Assumption. f, 4g, Pope giving blessing. 5g, Pope with hands clasped. 25g, Madonna & child.

1983, June 11 **Litho.** ***Perf. 14***

2078 A370 Strip of 6, #a.-f.
2079 A370 5g multicolored

Souvenir Sheet

Perf. 14½

2080 A370 25g multicolored

No. 2080 is airmail. For overprint see No. 2143.

Antique Automobiles — A371

No. 2081: a, 25c, Bordino Steamcoach, 1854. b, 50c, Panhard & Levassor, 1892. c, 1g, Benz Velo, 1894. d, 2g, Peugeot-Daimler, 1894. e, 3g, 1st car with patented Lutzmann system, 1898. f, 4g, Benz Victory, 1891-92. No. 2082, Ceirano 5CV. No. 2083, Mercedes Simplex PS 32 Turismo, 1902. 10g, Stae Electric, 1909. 25g, Benz Velocipede, 1885. 30g, Rolls Royce Silver Ghost, 1913.

1983, July 18 ***Perf. 14***

2081 A371 Strip of 6, #a.-f.
2082 A371 5g multicolored
2083 A371 5g multicolored
2084 A371 10g multicolored
2085 A371 30g multicolored

Souvenir Sheet

Perf. 14½

2085A A371 25g Sheet of 1 + label

Nos. 2083-2085A are airmail.

No. 2046 Ovptd. in Red, No. 2058 Ovptd. in Black with "52o CONGRESO F.I.P." and Brasiliana 83 Emblem

1983, July 27 ***Perf. 14***

2086 A362 Strip of 6, #a.-f.
2087 A364 Strip of 6, #a.-f.

Brasiliana '83, Rio de Janiero and 52nd FIP Congress. No. 2087 exists perf. 13.

Aircraft Carriers — A372

Carriers and airplanes: No. 2088a, 25c, 25 de Mayo, A-4Q Sky Hawk, Argentina. b, 50c, Minas Gerais, Brazil. c, 1g, Akagi, A6M3 Zero, Japan. d, 2g, Guiseppe Miraglia, Italy. e, 3g, Enterprise, S-3A Viking, US. f, 4g, Dedalo, AV-8A Matador, Spain. 5g, Schwabenland, Dornier DO-18, Germany. No aircraft on Nos. 2088b, 2088d.

25g, US astronauts Donn Eisele, Walter Schirra & Walt Cunningham, Earth & Apollo 7.

1983, Aug. 29 ***Perf. 14***

2088 A372 Strip of 6, #a.-f.
2089 A372 5g multicolored

Souvenir Sheet

Perf. 13½

2090 A372 25g multicolored

No. 2090 is airmail and contains one 55x45mm stamp.

Birds A373

#2091: a, 25c, Pulsatrix perspicillata. b, 50c, Ortalis ruficauda. c, 1g, Chloroceryle amazona. d, 2g, Trogon violaceus. e, 3g, Pezites militaris. f, 4g, Bucco capensis. 5g, Cyanerpes cyaneus.

1983, Oct. 22 ***Perf. 14***

2091 A373 Strip of 6, #a.-f.

Perf. 13

2092 A373 5g multicolored

No. 2066 Ovptd. for PHILATELICA 83 in Silver

1983, Oct. 28

2093 A366 Strip of 6, #a.-f.

Philatelia '83, Dusseldorf, Germany.

No. 2064 Overprinted in Silver for EXFIVIA - 83

1983, Nov. 5

2094 A365 Strip of 6, #a.-f.

Exfivia '83 Philatelic Exhibition, La Paz, Bolivia.

Re-election of President Stroessner — A374

10g, Passion flower, vert. 25g, Miltonia phalaenopsis, vert. 50g, Natl. arms, Chaco soldier. 75g, Acaray hydroelectric dam. 100g, Itaipu hydroelectric dam. 200g, Pres. Alfredo Stroessner, vert.

1983, Nov. 24 ***Perf. 14***

2095 A374 10g multicolored
2096 A374 25g multicolored
2097 A374 50g multicolored
2098 A374 75g multicolored

Perf. 13

2099 A374 100g multicolored
2100 A374 200g multicolored

#2099-2100 are airmail. #2096 exists perf 13. For overprint see #C577.

Montgolfier Brothers' 1st Flight, Bicent. — A375

No. 2101: a, 25c, Santos-Dumont's Biplane, 1906. b, 50c, Airship. No. 2102a, 1g, Paulhan's biplane over Juvisy. b, 2g, Zeppelin LZ-3, 1907. No. 2103a, 3g, Biplane of Henri Farman. b, 4g, Graf Zeppelin over Friedrichshafen. 5g, Lebaudy's dirigible. 25g, Detail of painting, Great Week of Aviation at Betheny, 1910.

1984, Jan. 7 ***Perf. 13***

2101 A375 Pair, #a.-b.
2102 A375 Pair, #a.-b.
2103 A375 Pair, #a.-b.

Perf. 14

2104 A375 5g multicolored

Souvenir Sheet

Perf. 13½

2105 A375 25g multicolored

No. 2105 is airmail and contains one 75x55mm stamp. For overprint see No. 2145.

Dogs A376

#2106: a, 25c, German Shepherd. b, 50c, Great Dane, vert. c, 1g, Poodle, vert. d, 2g, Saint Bernard. e, 3g, Greyhound. f, 4g, Dachshund. 5g, Boxer.

1984, Jan. 11 Litho. *Perf. 14*

2106 A376 Strip of 6, #a.-f.
2107 A376 5g multicolored

Animals, Anniversaries — A377

1984, Jan. 24 *Perf. 13*

2108 A377 10g Puma
2109 A377 25g Alligator
2110 A377 50g Jaguar
2111 A377 75g Peccary
2112 A377 100g Simon Bolivar, vert.
2113 A377 200g Girl scout, vert.

Simon Bolivar, birth bicent. and Girl Scouts of Paraguay, 76th anniv.
Nos. 2112-2113 are airmail.

Christmas A378

Designs: No. 2114a, 25c, Pope John Paul II. b, 50c, Christmas tree. c, 1g, Children. d, 2g, Nativity Scene. e, 3g, Three Kings. f, 4g, Madonna and Child. No. 2115, Madonna and Child by Raphael.

1984, Mar. 23 *Perf. 13x13½*

2114 A378 Strip of 6, #a.-f.
2115 A378 5g multicolored

Troubadour Knights A379

Illustrations of medieval miniatures: No. 2116a, 25c, Ulrich von Liechtenstein. b, 50c, Ulrich von Gutenberg. c, 1g, Der Putter. d, 2g, Walther von Metz. e, 3g, Hartman von Aue. f, 4g, Lutok von Seuen. 5g, Werner von Teufen.

1984, Mar. 27 *Perf. 14*

2116 A379 Strip of 6, #a.-f.

Perf. 13

2117 A379 5g multicolored

For overprint see No. 2121.

No. 2068 Ovptd. in Silver with ESSEN 84 Emblem

1984, May 10

2118 A367 Strip of 6, #a.-f.

Essen '84 Intl. Philatelic Exhibition.

Endangered Animals — A380

#2119: a, 25c, Priodontes giganteus. b, 50c, Catagonus wagneri. c, 1g, Felis pardalis. d, 2g, Chrysocyon brachyurus. e, 3g, Burmeisteria retusa. f, 4g, Myrmecophaga tridactyla. 5g, Caiman crocodilus.

1984, June 16 *Perf. 14*

2119 A380 Strip of 6, #a.-f.

Perf. 13

2120 A380 5g multicolored

For overprint see No. 2129.

No. 2117 Ovptd. in Silver with Emblems, etc., for U.P.U. 19th World Congress, Hamburg

1984, June 19 *Perf. 13*

2121 A379 5g on #2117

UPU Congress, Hamburg '84 — A381

Sailing ships: No. 2122a, 25c, Admiral of Hamburg. b, 50c, Neptune. c, 1g, Archimedes. d, 2g, Passat. e, 3g, Finkenwerder cutter off Heligoland. f, 4g, Four-masted ship. 5g, Deutschland.

1984, June 19 *Perf. 13*

2122 A381 Strip of 6, #a.-f.
2123 A381 5g multicolored

For overprints see Nos. 2146, 2279-2280.

British Locomotives — A382

No. 2124: a, 25c, Pegasus 097, 1868. b, 50c, Pegasus 097, diff. c, 1g, Cornwall, 1847. d, 2g, Cornwall, 1847, diff. e, 3g, Patrick Stirling #1, 1870. f, 4g, Patrick Stirling #1, 1870, diff. 5g, Stepney Brighton Terrier, 1872.

1984, June 20 *Perf. 14*

2124 A382 Strip of 6, #a.-f.

Perf. 13

2125 A382 5g multicolored

No. C486 Overprinted in Blue on Silver with UN emblem and "40o Aniversario de la / Fundacion de las / Naciones Unidas 26.6.1944"

1984, Aug. 1 Litho. *Perf. 14½*

2126 AP161 25g on No. C486

No. 1536 Ovptd. in Orange (#a.-d.) or Silver (#e.-g.) with AUSIPEX 84 Emblem and:

A383

1984, Aug. 21 *Perf. 14*

2127 A271 Strip of 7, #a.-g.

Souvenir Sheet

Perf. 14½

2128 A383 25g multicolored

Ausipex '84 Intl. Philatelic Exhibition, Melbourne, Australia. No. 2128 is airmail.

Nos. 2120 and C551 Ovptd. in Black and Red

1984 *Perf. 13*

2129 A380 5g on #2120

Perf. 14

2130 AP178 30g on #C551

Issued: #2129, Sept. 20; #2130, Aug. 30.
No. 2130 is airmail.

No. 1512 Ovptd. "VER STUTTGART CAMPEON NACIONAL DE FUTBOL DE ALEMANIA 1984" and Emblem

1984, Sept. 5 *Perf. 14*

2131 A263 Strip of 7, #a.-g.

VFB Stuttgart, 1984 German Soccer Champions.

Cat Type of 1976

Various cats: No. 2132: a, 25c. b, 50c. c, 1g. d, 2g. e, 3g. f, 4g.

1984, Sept. 10 *Perf. 13x13½*

2132 A287 Strip of 6, #a.-f.
2133 A287 5g multicolored

1984 Summer Olympics, Los Angeles — A384

Gold medalists: No. 2134a, 25c Michael Gross, W. Germany, swimming. b, 50c, Peter Vidmar, US, gymnastics. c, 1g, Fredy Schmidtke, W. Germany, cycling. d, 2g, Philippe Boisse, France, fencing. e, 3g, Ulrike Meyfarth, W. Germany, women's high jump. f, 4g, Games emblem. 5g, Mary Lou Retton, US, women's all-around gymnastics, vert. 30g, Rolf Milser, W. Germany, weight lifting, vert.

1985, Jan. 16 Litho. *Perf. 13*

2134 A384 Strip of 6, #a.-f.
2135 A384 5g multicolored

Souvenir Sheet

Perf. 13½

2136 A384 30g multicolored

No. 2136 is airmail and contains one 50x60mm stamp. For overprints see Nos. 2174, 2199, 2200. Compare with type A399.

Mushrooms A385

#2137: a, 25c, Boletus luteus. b, 50c, Agaricus campester. c, 1g, Pholiota spectabilis. d, 2g, Tricholoma terreum. e, 3g, Laccaria laccata. f, 4g, Amanita phalloides. 5g, Scleroderna verrucosum.

1985, Jan. 19 *Perf. 14*

2137 A385 Strip of 6, #a.-f.
2138 A385 5g multicolored

See Nos. 2166-2167.

World Wildlife Fund — A386

Endangered or extinct species: No. 2139a, 25c, Capybara. b, 50c, Mono titi, vert. c, 1g, Rana cornuda adornada. d, 2g, Priodontes giganteus, digging. e, 3g, Priodontes giganteus, by water. f, 4g, Myrmecophaga tridactyla. g, 5g, Myrmecophaga tridactyla, with young.

1985, Mar. 13 *Perf. 14*

2139 A386 Strip of 7, #a.-g.

See No. 2252.

No. 2037 Ovptd. in Red with ISRAPHIL Emblem

1985, Apr. 10

2140 A360 5g on No. 2037

Israel '85 Intl. Philatelic Exhibition.

John James Audubon, Birth Bicent. A387

Birds: No. 2141a, 25c, Piranga flava. b, 50c, Polyborus plancus. c, 1g, Chiroxiphia caudata. d, 2g, Xolmis irupero. e, 3g, Phloeoceastes leucopogon. f, 4g, Thraupis bonariensis. 5g, Parula pitiayumi, horiz.

1985, Apr. 18 ***Perf. 13***
2141 A387 Strip of 6, #a.-f.
2142 A387 5g multicolored

No. 2079 Ovptd. in Silver with Italia '85 Emblem

1985, May 20 ***Perf. 14***
2143 A370 5g on #2079

Italia '85 Intl. Philatelic Exhibition.

No. 1448e Ovptd. in Red on Silver

1985, June 12
2144 A250 30c on #1448e

No. 2104 Ovptd. in Silver and Blue with LUPO 85 Congress Emblem

1985, July 5
2145 A375 5g on No. 2104

LUPO '85, Lucerne, Switzerland.

No. 2123 Ovptd. in Silver and Blue with MOPHILA 85 Emblem and "HAMBURGO 11-12. 9. 85"

1985, July 5 ***Perf. 13***
2146 A381 5g on #2123

Mophila '85 Intl. Philatelic Exhibition, Hamburg.

Intl. Youth Year A388

Scenes from Tom Sawyer and Huckleberry Finn: No. 2147a, 25c, Mississippi riverboat. b, 50c, Finn. c, 1g, Finn and friends by campfire. d, 2g, Finn and Joe, sinking riverboat. e, 3g, Finn, friends, riverboat. f, 4g, Cemetery. 5g, Finn, Sawyer. 25g, Raft, riverboat.

1985, Aug. 5 ***Perf. 13½x13***
2147 A388 Strip of 6, #a.-f.
2148 A388 5g multicolored

Souvenir Sheet

Perf. 14½

2149 A388 25g multicolored

No. 2149 is airmail. For overprint see No. C612.

German Railroads, 150th Anniv. — A389

Locomotives: No. 2150a, 25c, T3, 1883. b, 50c, T18, 1912. c, 1g, T16, 1914. d, 2g, #01 118, Historic Trains Society, Frankfurt. e, 3g, #05 001 Express, Nuremberg Transit Museum. f, 4g, #10 002 Express, 1957. 5g, Der Adler, 1835. 25g, Painting of 1st German Train, Dec. 7, 1835.

1985, Aug. 8 ***Perf. 14***
2150 A389 Strip of 6, #a.-f.

Perf. 13

2151 A389 5g multicolored

Souvenir Sheet

Perf. 13½

2152 A389 25g multicolored

No. 2152 is airmail and contains one 75x53mm stamp. For overprint see No. 2165.

Development Projects — A390

Pres. Stroessner and: 10g, Soldier, map, vert. 25g, Model of Yaci Reta Hydroelectric Project. 50g, Itaipu Dam. 75g, Merchantman Lago Ipoa. 100g, 1975 Coin, vert. 200g, Asuncion Intl. Airport.

1985, Sept. 17 **Litho.** ***Perf. 13***
2153 A390 10g multicolored
2154 A390 25g multicolored
2155 A390 50g multicolored
2156 A390 75g multicolored
2157 A390 100g multicolored
2158 A390 200g multicolored

Chaco Peace Agreement, 50th Anniv. (#2153, 2157). Nos. 2157-2158 are airmail. For overprints see Nos. 2254-2259.

Nudes by Peter Paul Rubens A391

Details from paintings: No. 2159a, 25c, b, 50c, Venus in the Forge of Vulcan. c, 1g, Cimon and Iphigenia, horiz. d, 2g, The Horrors of War. e, 3g, Apotheosis of Henry IV and the Proclamation of the Regency. f, 4g, The Reception of Marie de Medici at Marseilles. 5g, Union of Earth and Water. 25g, Nature Attended by the Three Graces.

1985, Oct. 18 ***Perf. 14***
2159 A391 Strip of 6, #a.-f.

Perf. 13x13½

2160 A391 5g multicolored

Souvenir Sheet

Perf. 14

2161 A391 25g multicolored

No. 2161 is airmail.

1986, Jan. 16 ***Perf. 14***

Nudes by Titian: details from paintings. No. 2162a, 25c, Venus, an Organist, Cupid and a Little Dog. b, 50c, c, 1g, Diana and Actaeon. d, 2g, Danae. e, 3g, Nymph and a Shepherd. f, 4g, Venus of Urbino. 5g, Cupid Blindfolded by Venus, vert. 25g, Diana and Callisto, vert.

2162 A391 Strip of 6, #a.-f.

Perf. 13

2163 A391 5g multicolored

Souvenir Sheet

Perf. 13½

2164 A391 25g multicolored

No. 2164 is airmail and contains one 50x60mm stamp.

Nos. 2150 Ovptd. in Red

1986, Feb. 25 ***Perf. 14***
2165 A389 Strip of 6, #a.-f.

Essen '86 Intl. Philatelic Exhibition.

Mushrooms Type of 1985

Designs: No. 2166a, 25g, Lepiota procera. b, 50c, Tricholoma albo-brunneum. c, 1g, Clavaria. d, 2g, Volvaria. e, 3g, Licoperdon perlatum. f, 4g, Dictyophora duplicata. 5g, Polyporus rubrum.

1986, Mar. 17 ***Perf. 14***
2166 A385 Strip of 6, #a.-f.

Perf. 13

2167 A385 5g multicolored

Automobile, Cent. — A393

No. 2168: a, 25c, Wolseley, 1904. b, 50c, Peugeot, 1892. c, 1g, Panhard, 1895. d, 2g, Cadillac, 1903. e, 3g, Fiat, 1902. f, 4g, Stanley Steamer, 1898. 5g, Carl Benz Velocipede, 1885. 25g, Carl Benz (1844-1929), automotive engineer.

1986, Apr. 28 **Litho.** ***Perf. 13½x13***
2168 A393 Strip of 6, #a.-f.
2169 A393 5g multicolored

Souvenir Sheet

Perf. 13½

2170 A393 25g multicolored

No. 2170 is airmail and contains one 30x40mm stamp.

World Cup Soccer Championships, Mexico City — A394

Various match scenes, Paraguay vs.: No. 2171a, 25c, b, 50c, US, 1930. c, 1g, d, 2g, Belgium, 1930. e, 3g, Bolivia, 1985. f, 4g, Brazil, 1985.

5g, Natl. Team, 1986. 25g, Player, vert.

1986, Mar. 12 ***Perf. 13½x13***
2171 A394 Strip of 6, #a.-f.
2172 A394 5g multicolored

Souvenir Sheet

Perf. 14½

2173 A394 25g multicolored

No. 2173 is airmail. For overprints see Nos. 2283, 2287.

No. 2135 Ovptd. in Silver "JUEGOS / PANAMERICANOS / INDIANAPOLIS / 1987"

1986, June 9 ***Perf. 13***
2174 A384 5g on No. 2135

1987 Pan American Games, Indianapolis.

Maybach Automobiles — A395

#2175: a, 25c, W-6, 1930-36. b, 50c, SW-38 convertible. c, 1g, SW-38 hardtop, 1938. d, 2g, W-6/DSG, 1933. e, 3g, Zeppelin DS-8, 1931. f, 4g, Zeppelin DS-8, 1936. 5g, Zeppelin DS-8 aerodynamic cabriolet, 1936.

1986, June 19 ***Perf. 13½x13***
2175 A395 Strip of 6, #a.-f.
2176 A395 5g multicolored

No. 2077 Overprinted in Bright Blue with Olympic Rings and "CALGARY 1988"

1986, July 9 ***Perf. 13***
2177 A369 5g on #2077

1988 Winter Olympics, Calgary.

Statue of Liberty, Cent. — A396

Passenger liners: No. 2178a, 25c, City of Paris, England, 1867. b, 50c, Mauretania, England. c, 1g, Normandie, France, 1932. d, 2g, Queen Mary, England, 1938. e, 3g, Kaiser Wilhelm the Great II, Germany, 1897. f, 4g, United States, US, 1952. 5g, Bremen, Germany, 1928. 25g, Sailing ship Gorch Fock, Germany, 1976, vert.

1986, July 25 ***Perf. 13***
2178 A396 Strip of 6, #a.-f.
2179 A396 5g multicolored

Souvenir Sheet

Perf. 14½

2180 A396 25g multicolored

No. 2180 is airmail and contains one 50x70mm stamp.

Dog Type of 1984

#2181: a, 25c, German shepherd. b, 50c, Icelandic shepherd. c, 1g, Collie. d, 2g, Boxer. e, 3g, Scottish terrier. f, 4g, Welsh springer spaniel. 5g, Painting of Labrador retriever by Ellen Krebs, vert.

1986, Aug. 28 ***Perf. 13x13½***
2181 A376 Strip of 6, #a.-f.

Perf. 13½x13

2182 A376 5g multicolored

Paraguay Official Stamps, Cent. — A397

#2183-2185, #O1. #2186-2188, #O4.

1986, Aug. 28 **Litho.** ***Perf. 13x13½***

2183	A397	5g multi	.20	.20
2184	A397	15g multi	.20	.20
2185	A397	40g multi	.20	.20
2186	A397	65g multi	.20	.20
2187	A397	100g multi	.25	.20
2188	A397	150g multi	.40	.30
		Nos. 2183-2188 (6)	1.45	1.30

Nos. 2186-2188 are airmail.

Tennis Players A398

Designs: No. 2189a, Victor Pecci, Paraguay. b, 50c, Jimmy Connors, US. c, 1g, Gabriela Sabatini, Argentina. d, 2g, Boris Becker, W. Germany. e, 3g, Claudia Kohde, E. Germany. f, 4g, Sweden, 1985 Davis Cup team champions, horiz. 5g, Steffi Graf, W. Germany. 25g, 1986 Wimbledon champions Martina Navratilova and Boris Becker, horiz.

Perf. 13x13½, 13½x13

1986, Sept. 17 **Unwmk.**
2189 A398 Strip of 6, #a.-f.
2190 A398 5g multicolored

Souvenir Sheet

Perf. 13½

2191 A398 25g multicolored

No. 2191 is airmail and contains one 75x55mm stamp. For overprints see No. 2229.

Nos. 1454-1456 Ovptd. in Red or Silver (#2192c, 2192d): "Homenage a la visita de Sus Altezas Imperiales los Principees Hitachi --28.9-3.10.86"

1986, Sept. 28 ***Perf. 14***
2192 A251 Strip of 5, #a.-e.
2193 A251 50c on #1455
2194 A251 75c on #1456

1988 Summer Olympics, Seoul A399

Athletes, 1984 Olympic medalists: No. 2195a, 25c, Runner. b, 50c, Boxer. c, 1g, Joaquim Cruz, Brazil, 800-meter run. d, 2g, Mary Lou Retton, US, individual all-around gymnastics. e, 3g, Carlos Lopes, Portugal, marathon. f, 4g, Fredy Schmidtke, W. Germany, 1000-meter cycling, horiz. 5g, Joe Fargis, US, equestrian, horiz.

1986, Oct. 29 ***Perf. 13x13½,13½x13***
2195 A399 Strip of 6, #a.-f.
2196 A399 5g multicolored

For overprints see Nos. 2227-2228, 2230.

Nos. 1574c-1574g Ovptd. in Silver, Ship Type of 1983 Ovptd. in Red

1987, Mar. 20 **Litho.** ***Perf. 14***
2197 A278 Strip of 5, #a.-e.
2198 AP176 10g multicolored

500th Anniv. of the discovery of America and the 12th Spanish-American Stamp & Coin Show, Madrid.

Olympics Type of 1985 Overprinted in Silver with Olympic Rings and 500th Anniv. of the Discovery of America Emblems and "BARCELONA 92 / Sede de las Olimpiadas en el ano del 500o Aniversario del Descubrimiento de America"

Designs like Nos. 2134a-2134f.

1987, Apr. 24 ***Perf. 14***
2199 A384 Strip of 6, #a.-f.

1992 Summer Olympics, Barcelona and discovery of America, 500th anniv. in 1992.

No. 2135 Overprinted in Silver "ROMA / OLYMPHILEX" / Olympic Rings / "SEOUL / CALGARY / 1988"

1987, Apr. 30 ***Perf. 13***
2200 A384 5g on No. 2135

Olymphilex '87 Intl. Philatelic Exhibition, Rome.

Cat Type of 1976

Various cats and kittens: No. 2201: a, 1g. b, 2g. c, 3g. d, 5g. 60g, Black cat.

1987, May 22 ***Perf. 13x13½***
2201 A287 Strip of 4, #a.-d.
2202 A287 60g multicolored

No. 2202 also exists perf. 14. For overprint see No. 2212.

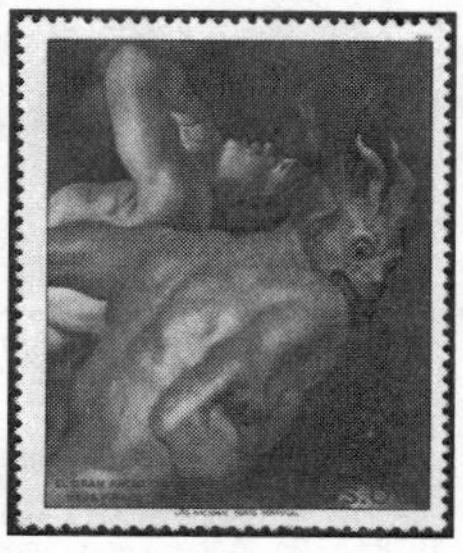

Paintings by Rubens A400

No. 2203: a, 1g, The Four Corners of the World, horiz. b, 2g, Jupiter and Calisto. c, 3g, Susanna and the Elders. d, 5g, Marriage of Henry IV and Marie de Medici in Lyon. 60g, The Last Judgment. 100g, The Holy Family with St. Elizabeth and John the Baptist. No. 2205A, War and Peace.

1987 **Litho.** ***Perf. 13x13½, 13½x13***
2203 A400 Strip of 4, #a.-d.
2204 A400 60g multicolored

Souvenir Sheets

2205 A400 100g multicolored
2205A A400 100g multicolored

Christmas 1986 (#2205).
Issued: #2204, May 25; #2205, May 26.
Nos. 2205-2205A are airmail and contain one 54x68mm stamp.

Places and Events — A401

10g, ACEPAR Industrial Plant. 25g, Franciscan monk, native, vert. 50g, Yaguaron Church altar, vert. 75g, Founding of Asuncion, 450th anniv. 100g, Paraguay Airlines passenger jet. 200g, Pres. Stoessner, vert.

1987, June 2 **Litho.** ***Perf. 13***
2206 A401 10g multicolored
2207 A401 25g multicolored
2208 A401 50g multicolored
2209 A401 75g multicolored
2210 A401 100g multicolored
2211 A401 200g multicolored

Nos. 2210-2211 are airmail. For overprints see Nos. 2225-2226, C685, C722.

No. 2201 Ovptd. in Blue

1987, June 12 ***Perf. 13x13½***
2212 A287 Strip of 4, #a.-d.

Discovery of America, 500th Anniv. (in 1992) — A402

Discovery of America anniv. emblem and ships: No. 2213a, 1g, Spanish galleon, 17th cent. b, 2g, Victoria, 1st to circumnavigate the globe, 1519-22. c, 3g, San Hermenegildo. 5g, San Martin, c.1582. 60g, Santa Maria, c.1492, vert.

1987, Sept. 9 ***Perf. 14***
2213 A402 Strip of 4, #a.-d.

Perf. 13x13½

2214 A402 60g multicolored

Colorado Party, Cent. — A403

Bernardino Caballero (founder), President Stroessner and: 5g, 10g, 25g, Three-lane highway. 150g, 170g, 200g, Power lines.

Perf. 13½x13

1987, Sept. 11 **Wmk. 347**

2215 A403	5g	multi	.20	.20
2216 A403	10g	multi	.20	.20
2217 A403	25g	multi	.20	.20
2218 A403	150g	multi	.35	.25
2219 A403	170g	multi	.40	.30
2220 A403	200g	multi	.45	.35
Nos. 2215-2220 (6)			1.80	1.50

Nos. 2218-2220 are airmail.

Berlin, 750th Anniv. — A404

Berlin Stamps and Coins: No. 2221: a, 1g, #9NB145. b, 2g, #9NB154. c, 3g, #9N57, vert. d, 5g, #9N170, vert. 60g, 1987 Commemorative coin, vert.

Perf. 13½x13, 13½x13

1987, Sept. 12 **Unwmk.**
2221 A404 Strip of 4, #a.-d.
2222 A404 60g multicolored

For overprints see Nos. 2239, 2294.

Race Cars A405

No. 2223: a, 1g, Audi Sport Quattro. b, 2g, Lancia Delta S 4. c, 3g, Fiat 131. d, 5g, Porsche 911 4x4. 60g, Lancia Rally.

1987, Sept. 27 ***Perf. 13***
2223 A405 Strip of 4, #a.-d.

Perf. 14

2224 A405 60g multicolored

Nos. 2209-2210 Ovptd. in Bright Blue

1987, Sept. 30 ***Perf. 13***
2225 A401 75g on #2209
2226 A401 100g on #2210

EXFIVIA '87 Intl. Philatelic Exhibition, LaPaz, Bolivia. No. 2226 is airmail.

Nos. 2195d-2195f, 2196 Overprinted in Black or Silver

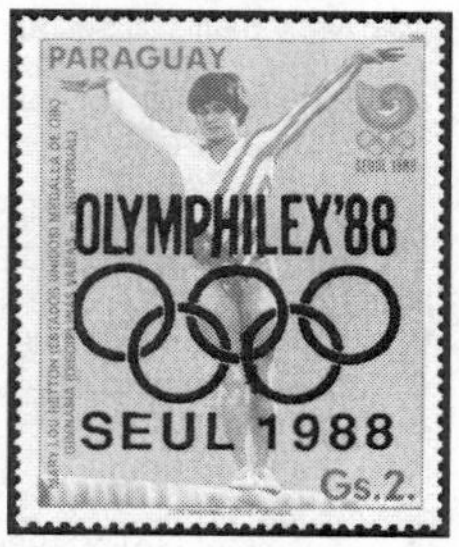

1987, Oct. 1 ***Perf. 13½x13***
2227 A399 Strip of 3, #a.-c.
2228 A399 5g on No. 2196 (S)

Olymphilex '87 Intl. Phil. Exhib., Seoul.

No. 2189 Ovptd. with Emblem and "PHILATELIA '87," etc.

1987, Oct. 15 ***Perf. 13x13½, 13½x13***
2229 A398 Strip of 6, #a.-f.

PHILATELIA '87 Intl. Phil. Exhib., Cologne. Size and configuration of overprint varies.

Nos. 2195a-2195b Ovptd. in Bright Blue for EXFILNA '87 and BARCELONA 92

1987, Oct. 24 ***Perf. 13x13½***
2230 A399 Pair, #a.-b.

Exfilna '87 Intl. Philatelic Exhibition.

Ship Paintings A406

No. 2231: a, 1g, San Juan Nepomuceno. b, 2g, San Eugenio. c, 3g, San Telmo. d, 5g, San Carlos. 60g, Spanish galleon, 16th cent. 100g, One of Columbus' ships.

1987 **Litho.** ***Perf. 14***
2231 A406 Strip of 4, #a.-d.

Perf. 13x13½

2232 A406 60g multicolored

Souvenir Sheet

Perf. 13½

2233 A406 100g multicolored

Discovery of America, 500th anniv. in 1992 (#2233). Issue dates: Nos. 2231-2232, Dec. 10. No. 2233, Dec. 12.
No. 2233 is airmail and contains one 54x75mm stamp.

1988 Winter Olympics, Calgary — A407

#2237: a, 5g, Joel Gaspoz. b, 60g, Peter Mueller.

1987, Dec. 31 ***Perf. 14***
2234 A407 1g Maria Walliser
2235 A407 2g Erika Hess
2236 A407 3g Pirmin Zurbriggen

Miniature Sheet

Perf. 13½x13

2237 A407 Sheet of 4 each #2237a, 2237b+label

Souvenir Sheet

Perf. 14½

2238 A407 100g Walliser, Zurbriggen

No. 2238 is airmail. For overprints see Nos. 2240-2242.

No. 2221 Ovptd. in Silver "AEROPEX 88 / ADELAIDE"

1988, Jan. 29 ***Perf. 13***
2239 A404 Strip of 4, #a.-d.

Aeropex '88, Adelaide, Australia.

Nos. 2234-2236 Ovptd. in Gold with Olympic Rings and "OLYMPEX / CALGARY 1988"

1988, Feb. 13 ***Perf. 14***
2240 A407 1g on #2234
2241 A407 2g on #2235
2242 A407 3g on #2236

Olympex '88, Calgary. Size and configuration of overprint varies.

1988 Summer Olympics, Seoul — A408

Equestrians: No. 2243a, 1g, Josef Neckermann, W. Germany, on Venetia. b, 2g, Henri Chammartin, Switzerland. c, 3g, Christine Stueckelberger, Switzerland, on Granat. d, 5g, Liselott Linsenhoff, W. Germany, on Piaff. 60g, Hans-Guenter Winkler, W. Germany.

1988, Mar. 7 ***Perf. 13***
2243 A408 Strip of 4, #a.-d.

Perf. 13½x13

2244 A408 60g multicolored

For overprint see No. 2291.

Berlin, 750th Anniv. A409

Paintings: No. 2245a, 1g, Virgin and Child, by Jan Gossaert. b, 2g, Virgin and Child, by Rubens. c, 3g, Virgin and Child, by Hans Memling. d, 5g, Madonna, by Albrecht Durer. 60g, Adoration of the Shepherds, by Martin Schongauer.

1988, Apr. 8 ***Perf. 13***
2245 A409 Strip of 4, #a.-d.
2246 A409 60g multicolored

Christmas 1987. See Nos. C727-C731.

Visit of Pope John Paul II A410

Religious art: No. 2247a, 1g, Pope John Paul II, hands clasped. b, 2g, Statue of the Virgin. c, 3g, Czestochowa Madonna. d, 5g, Our Lady of Caacupe. Nos. 2247a-2247d are vert.

1988, Apr. 11 ***Perf. 13***
2247 A410 Strip of 4, #a.-d.
2248 A410 60g multicolored

Visit of Pope John Paul II — A411

Rosette window and crucifix.

1988, May 5 **Litho.** ***Perf. 13x13½***

2249 A411	10g blue & blk	.20	.20
2250 A411	20g blue & blk	.20	.20
2251 A411	50g blue & blk	.25	.20
	Nos. 2249-2251 (3)	.65	.60

World Wildlife Fund Type of 1985

Endangered Animals: No. 2252a, 1g, like #2139g. b, 2g, like #2139f. c, 3g, like #2139d. d, 5g, like #2139e.

1988, June 14 **Unwmk.** ***Perf. 14***
2252 A386 Strip of 4, #a.-d.

Nos. 2252a-2252d have denomination and border in blue.

Nos. 2000a-2000d Ovptd. in Gold with Emblem and "Bicentenario de / AUSTRALIA / 1788-1988"

1988, June 17
2253 A351 Strip of 4, #a.-d.

Australia, bicent.

Types of 1985 Overprinted in 2 or 4 Lines in Gold "NUEVO PERIODO PRESIDENCIAL CONSTITUCIONAL 1988-1993"

1988, Aug. 12 ***Perf. 14***
2254 A390 10g like #2153
2255 A390 25g like #2154
2256 A390 50g like #2155
2257 A390 75g like #2156
2258 A390 100g like #2157
2259 A390 200g like #2158

Pres. Stroessner's new term in office. Nos. 2258-2259 are airmail.

Olympic Tennis, Seoul A412

Designs: No. 2260a, 1g, Steffi Graf, W. Germany. b, 2g, Olympic gold medal, horiz. c, 3g, Boris Becker, W. Germany. d, 5g, Emilio Sanchez, Spain. 60g, Steffi Graf, diff.

1988, Aug. 16 ***Perf. 13***
2260 A412 Strip of 4, #a.-d.
2261 A412 60g multicolored

1992 Summer Olympics, Barcelona — A413

Olympic medalists from Spain: No. 2262a, 1g, Ricardo Zamora, soccer, Antwerp, 1920, vert. b, 2g, Equestrian team, Amsterdam, 1928. c, 3g, Angel Leon, shooting, Helsinki, 1952. d, 5g, Kayak team, Montreal, 1976. 60g, Francisco Fernandez Ochoa, slalom, Sapporo, 1972, vert. 100g, Olympic Stadium, Barcelona, vert.

1989, Jan. 5 ***Perf. 14***
2262 A413 Strip of 4, #a.-d.

Perf. 13

2263 A413 60g multicolored

Souvenir Sheet

Perf. 13½

2264 A413 100g multicolored

Discovery of America 500th anniv. (in 1992). No. 2264 is airmail and contains one 50x60mm stamp. For overprint see No. 2293.

Columbus Space Station A414

1989, Jan. 7 **Litho.** ***Perf. 13x13½***
2265 A414 60g multicolored

Discovery of America 500th anniv. (in 1992).

No. 2076 Overprinted in Silver, Red and Blue with Olympic Rings, "1992" and Emblem

1989, Jan. 10 ***Perf. 13½x13, 13x13½***
2266 A369 Strip of 6, #a.-f.

1992 Winter Olympics, Albertville. Location and configuration of overprint varies.

No. 1454 Ovptd. in Silver "HOMENAJE AL EMPERADOR HIROITO DE JAPON 29.IV,1901-6.1.1989"

1989, Feb. 8 ***Perf. 14***
2267 A251 Strip of 5, #a.-e.

Death of Emperor Hirohito of Japan.

Formula 1 Drivers, Race Cars — A415

No. 2268: a, 1g, Stirling Moss, Mercedes W196. b, 2g, Emerson Fittipaldi, Lotus. c, 3g, Nelson Piquet, Lotus. d, 5g, Niki Lauda, Ferrari 312 B. 60g, Juan Manuel Fangio, Maserati 250F.

1989, Mar. 6 ***Perf. 13***
2268 A415 Strip of 4, #a.-d.
2269 A415 60g multicolored

Paintings by Titian A416

No. 2270: a, 1g, Bacchus and Ariadne (Bacchus). b, 2g, Bacchus and Ariadne (tutelary spirit). c, 3g, Death of Actaeon. d, 5g, Portrait of a Young Woman with a Fur Cape. 60g, Concert in a Field. 100g, Holy Family with Donor.

1989, Apr. 17 ***Perf. 13x13½***
2270 A416 Strip of 4, #a.-d.
2271 A416 60g multicolored

Souvenir Sheet

Perf. 13½

2271A A416 100g multicolored

No. 2271A is airmail and contains one 60x49mm stamp. Issue date: May 27.

1994 Winter Olympics, Lillehammer — A417

Athletes: No. 2272a, 1g, Torbjorn Lokken, 1987 Nordic combined world champion. b, 2g, Atle Skardal, skier, Norway. c, 3g, Geir Karlstad, Norway, world 10,000-meter speed skating champion, 1987. d, 5g, Franck Piccard, France, 1988 Olympic medalist, skiing. 60g, Roger Ruud, ski jumper, Norway.

1989, May 23 ***Perf. 13½x13***
2272 A417 Strip of 4, #a.-d.
2273 A417 60g multicolored

Cat Type of 1976

Various cats: #2274a, 1g. b, 2g. c, 3g. d, 5g.

1989, May 25 ***Perf. 13***
2274 A287 Strip of 4, #a.-d.
2275 A287 60g Siamese

Federal Republic of Germany, 40th Anniv. — A418

Famous men and automobiles: No. 2276a, 1g, Konrad Adenauer, chancellor, 1949-1963, Mercedes. b, 2g, Ludwig Erhard, chancellor, 1963-1966, Volkswagen Beetle. c, 3g, Felix Wankel, engine designer, 1963 NSU Spider. d, 5g, Franz Josef Strauss, President of Bavarian Cabinet, BMW 502. 60g, Pres. Richard von Weizsacker and Dr. Josef Neckermann.

1989, May 27 ***Perf. 13½x13***

2276 A418 Strip of 4, #a.-d.
2277 A418 60g multicolored

For overprints see No. 2369.

Ship Type of 1980 Overprinted with Discovery of America, 500th Anniv. Emblem in Red on Silver

1989, May 29 ***Perf. 14½***

Miniature Sheet

2278 A343 Sheet of 7+label, like #1972

Discovery of America 500th anniv. (in 1992).

No. 2122a Overprinted with Hamburg Emblem and Nos. 2122b-2122f, 2123 Ovptd. with Diff. Emblem in Red on Silver

1989, May 30 Litho. ***Perf. 13½x13***

2279 A381 Strip of 6, #a.-f.
2280 A381 5g on #2123

City of Hamburg, 800th anniv.

Nos. 2006a-2006b Ovptd. "BRASILIANA / 89"

1989, July 5 ***Perf. 14***

2281 A352 Pair, #a.-b.

No. 2171 Overprinted in Metallic Red and Silver with FIFA and Italia 90 Emblems and "PARAGUAY PARTICIPO EN 13 CAMPEONATOS MUNDIALES"

1989, Sept. 14 Litho. ***Perf. 13½x13***

2283 A394 Strip of 6, #a.-f.

Size and configuration of overprint varies.

Nos. C738, C753 Overprinted in metallic red with Italia '90 emblem and "SUDAMERICA-GRUPO 2 / PARAGUAY-COLOMBIA / PARAGUAY-ECUADOR / COLOMBIA-PARAGUAY / ECUADOR-PARAGUAY" and in metallic red on silver with FIFA emblem

1989, Sept. 14 Litho. ***Perf. 13***

2284 AP228 25g on #C738
2285 AP232 25g on #C753

Nos. 2046, 2172 Overprinted in Metallic Red and Silver "PARAGUAY CLASIFICADO EN 1930, 1950, 1958 Y 1986" and Emblems or "ITALIA '90"

1989, Sept. 15 Litho. ***Perf. 14***

2286 A362 Strip of 6, #a.-f.

Perf. 13½x13

2287 A394 5g multicolored

1990 World Cup Soccer Championships, Italy. Location and size of overprint varies.

Nos. 1284-1286 Ovptd. in Gold "...BIEN ESTUVIMOS EN LA LUNA AHORA NECESITAMOS LOS MEDIOS PARA LLEGAR A LOS PLANETAS" Wernher von Braun's Signature and UN and Space Emblems

1989, Sept. 16 ***Perf. 14***

2288 A226 Strip of 5, #a.-e.
2289 A226 50c multicolored
2290 A226 75c multicolored

Location, size and configuration of overprint varies.

Nos. 2243, C764 Overprinted in Silver or Gold with Emblem and "ATENAS 100 ANOS DE LOS JUEGOS OLIMPICOS 1896-1996"

1989, Sept. 18 ***Perf. 13***

2291 A408 Strip of 4, #a.-d.
2292 AP233 25g on #C764 (G)

1992 Summer Olympics Barcelona, Spain. Size and location of overprint varies.

Nos. 2262a-2262d Ovptd. in Silver with Heads of Steffi Graf or Boris Becker and: "WIMBLEDON 1988 / SEUL 1988 / WIMBLEDON 1989 / EL TENIS NUEVAMENTE EN / LAS OLIMPIADAS 1988-1992" or Similar

1989, Sept. 19 ***Perf. 14***

2293 A413 Strip of 4, #a.-d.

Addition of tennis as an Olympic sport in 1992. Size and configuration of overprint varies.

No. 2221 Ovptd. in Gold and Blue "PRIMER AEROPUERTO PARA / /COHETES, BERLIN 1930 OBERTH, / NEBEL, RITTER, VON BRAUN" space emblem and "PROF. DR. HERMANN / OBERTH 95o ANIV. / NACIMIENTO 25.6.1989"

Perf. 13½x13, 13x13½

1989, Sept. 20

2294 A404 Strip of 4, #a.-d.

Dr. Hermann Oberth, rocket scientist, 95th birth anniv. Overprint size, etc, varies.

Nos. 1406-1408 Ovptd. in Metallic Red and Silver with Emblems and "OLIMPIADAS / DE INVIERNO / ALBERTVILLE 1992" in 2 or 3 Lines

1989, Sept. 21 ***Perf. 14***

2295 A244 Strip of 5, #a.-e.
2296 A244 50c multicolored
2297 A244 75c multicolored

1992 Winter Olympics, Albertville. Size and configuration of overprint varies.

Nos. 2251, C724 Overprinted

Perf. 13½, 13½x13

1989, Oct. 9 Litho. Wmk. 347

2298 A411 50g on #2251
2299 AP226 120g on #C724

Parafil '89, Paraguay-Argentina philatelic exhibition.

Birds Facing Extinction — A419

Perf. 13½x13

1989, Dec. 19 Litho. Wmk. 347

2300	A419	50g	Ara chloroptera	.20	.20
2301	A419	100g	Mergus octosetaceus	.20	.20
2302	A419	300g	Rhea americana	.50	.40
2303	A419	500g	Ramphastos toco	.80	.65
2304	A419	1000g	Crax fasciolota	1.60	1.40
2305	A419	2000g	Ara araruna	3.25	2.50
			Nos. 2300-2305 (6)	6.55	5.35

Nos. 2302-2305 airmail. Nos. 2300 & 2305 vert. Frames and typestyles vary greatly. Watermark on 50g, 100g, 300g is 8mm high.

1992 Summer Olympics, Barcelona A420

Athletes: No. 2306a, 1g, A. Fichtel and S. Bau, W. Germany, foils, 1988. b, 2g, Spanish basketball team, 1984. c, 3g, Jackie Joyner-Kersee, heptathalon and long jump, 1988, horiz. d, 5g, L. Beerbaum, W. Germany, show jumping, team, 1988. 60g, W. Brinkmann, W. Germany, show jumping, team, 1988. 100g, Emilio Sanchez, tennis.

Unwmk.

1989, Dec. 26 Litho. ***Perf. 14***

2306 A420 Strip of 4, #a.-d.

Perf. 13

2307 A420 60g multicolored

Souvenir Sheet

Perf. 13½

2308 A420 100g multicolored

No. 2308 is airmail and contains one 47x57mm stamp.

World Cup Soccer Championships, Italy — A421

1986 World Cup soccer players in various positions: No. 2309a, 1g, England vs. Paraguay. b, 2g, Spain vs. Denmark. c, 3g, France vs. Italy. d, 5g, Germany vs. Morocco. 60g, Mexico vs. Paraguay. 100g, Germany vs. Argentina.

1989, Dec. 29 ***Perf. 14***

2309 A421 Strip of 4, #a.-d.

Perf. 13½

2310 A421 60g multicolored

Souvenir Sheet

Perf. 14½

2311 A421 100g multicolored

No. 2311 is airmail and contains one 40x50mm stamp.
For overprints see Nos. 2355-2356.

1992 Summer Olympics, Barcelona — A422

Barcelona '92, proposed Athens '96 emblems and: No. 2312a, 1g, Greece #128. b, 2g, Greece #126, vert. c, 3g, Greece #127, vert. d, 5g, Greece #123, vert. 60g, Paraguay #736. 100g, Horse and rider, vert.

1990, Jan. 4 ***Perf. 13½x13, 13x13½***

2312 A422 Strip of 4, #a.-d.
2313 A422 60g multicolored

Souvenir Sheet

Perf. 13½

2314 A422 100g multicolored

No. 2314 is airmail and contains one 50x60mm stamp and exists with either white or yellow border. Stamps inscribed 1989.
For overprints see No. 2357.

Swiss Confederation, 700th Anniv. — A423

#2315: a, 3g, Monument to William Tell. b, 5g, Manship Globe, UN Headquarters, Geneva. 60g, 15th cent. messenger, Bern. #2317, 1st Swiss steam locomotive, horiz. #2318, Jean Henri Dunant, founder of the Red Cross, horiz.

1990, Jan. 25 ***Perf. 14***

2315 A423 Pair, #a.-b.

Perf. 13

2316 A423 60g multicolored

Souvenir Sheets

Perf. 14½

2317 A423 100g multicolored
2318 A423 100g multicolored

Nos. 2317-2318 are airmail. For overprints see Nos. 2352-2354.

Wood Carving A424

Discovery of America, 500th anniv. emblem &: #2319: a, 1g, 1st cathechism in Guarani. b, 2g, shown. #2319 has continuous design.

1990, Jan. 26 ***Perf. 14***

2319 A424 Pair, #a.-b. + label

Organization of American States, Cent. — A425

Perf. 13½x13

1990, Feb. 9 Litho. Wmk. 347

2320	A425	50g	multicolored	.20	.20
2321	A425	100g	multicolored	.30	.25
2322	A425	200g	Map of Paraguay	.60	.45
			Nos. 2320-2322 (3)	1.10	.90

1992 Winter Olympics, Albertville — A426

Calgary 1988 skiers: No. 2323a, 1g, Alberto Tomba, Italy, slalom and giant slalom. b, 2g, Vreni Schneider, Switzerland, women's slalom and giant slalom, vert. c, 3g, Luc Alphand, France, skier, vert. d, 5g, Matti Nykaenen, Finland, ski-jumping.

60g, Marina Kiehl, W. Germany, women's downhill. 100g, Frank Piccard, France, super giant slalom.

1990, Mar. 7 Unwmk. *Perf. 14*

2323 A426 Strip of 4, #a.-d.

Perf. 13

2324 A426 60g multicolored

Souvenir Sheet

Perf. 14½

2325 A426 100g multicolored

No. 2325 is airmail, contains one 40x50mm stamp and exists with either white or yellow border.

Pre-Columbian Art, Customs A427

UPAE Emblem and: 150g, Pre-Columbian basket. 500g, Aboriginal ceremony.

1990, Mar. 8 Wmk. 347 *Perf. 13*

2326 A427 150g multicolored	.45	.40
2327 A427 500g multicolored	1.50	1.25

No. 2327 is airmail.
For overprints see Nos. 2345-2346.

First Postage Stamp, 150th Anniv. — A428

Penny Black, Mail Transportation 500th anniv. emblem and: No. 2328a, 1g, Penny Black on cover. b, 2g, Mauritius #1-2 on cover. c, 3g, Baden #4b on cover. d, 5g, Roman States #4 on cover. 60g, Paraguay #C38 and four #C54 on cover.

1990, Mar. 12 Unwmk. *Perf. 14*

2328 A428 Strip of 4, #a.-d.

Perf. 13½x13

2329 A428 60g multicolored

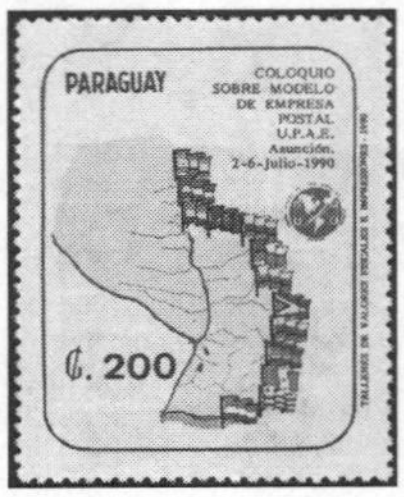

Postal Union of the Americas and Spain (UPAE) A429

1990, July 2 *Perf. 13x13½*

2330 A429 200g Map, flags	.35	.30
2331 A429 250g Paraguay #1	.40	.35
2332 A429 350g FDC of #2326-2327, horiz.	.60	.45
Nos. 2330-2332 (3)	1.35	1.10

National University, Cent. (in 1989) — A430

1990, Sept. 8

2333 A430 300g Future site	.90	.70
2334 A430 400g Present site	1.25	.95
2335 A430 600g Old site	1.75	1.50
Nos. 2333-2335 (3)	3.90	3.15

Franciscan Churches — A431

Perf. 13½x13

1990, Sept. 25 Litho. Wmk. 347

2336 A431 50g Guarambare	.20	.20
2337 A431 100g Yaguaron	.30	.25
2338 A431 200g Ita	.60	.45
Nos. 2336-2338 (3)	1.10	.90

For overprints see Nos. 2366-2368.

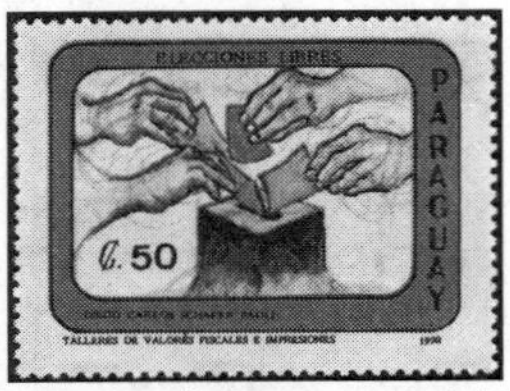

Democracy in Paraguay — A432

Designs: 100g, State and Catholic Church, vert. 200g, Human rights, vert. 300g, Freedom of the Press, vert. 500g, Return of the exiles. 3000g, People and democracy.

Perf. 13½x13, 13x13½

1990, Oct. 5 Litho. Wmk. 347

2339 A432 50g multicolored	.20	.20
2340 A432 100g multicolored	.20	.20
2341 A432 200g multicolored	.40	.35
2342 A432 300g multicolored	.60	.55
2343 A432 500g multicolored	1.00	.90
2344 A432 3000g multicolored	6.00	5.50
Nos. 2339-2344 (6)	8.40	7.70

Nos. 2343-2344 are airmail.

Nos. 2326-2327 Overprinted in Magenta

Visita de Sus
Majestades Los
Reyes de España
22-24 Octubre 1990

1990 Litho. Wmk. 347 *Perf. 13*

2345 A427 150g multicolored	.45	.40
2346 A427 500g multicolored	1.50	1.25

No. 2346 is airmail.

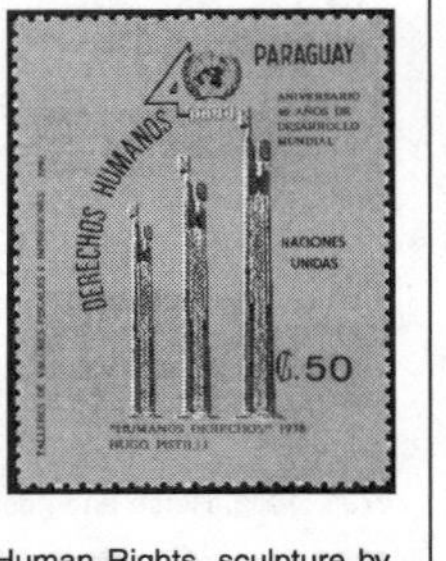

UN Development Program, 40th Anniv. — A433

Designs: 50m, Human Rights, sculpture by Hugo Pistilli. 100m, United Nations, sculpture by Hermann Guggiari. 150m, Miguel de Cervantes Literature Award, won by Augusto Roa Bastos.

1990, Oct. 26

2347 A433 50g lilac & multi	.20	.20
2348 A433 100g gray & multi	.30	.25
2349 A433 150g green & multi	.50	.40
Nos. 2347-2349 (3)	1.00	.85

America A434

50g, Paraguay River banks. 250g, Chaco land.

Perf. 13½x13

1990, Oct. 31 Wmk. 347

2350 A434 50g multicolored	.20	.20
2351 A434 250g multicolored	.50	.40

No. 2351 is airmail.

Nos. 2315-2316, 2318 Ovptd. in Metallic Red and Silver

Unwmk.

1991, Apr. 2 Litho. *Perf. 14*

2352 A423 Pair, #a.-b.

Perf. 13

2353 A423 60g on #2316

Souvenir Sheet

Perf. 14½

2354 A423 100g on #2318

Swiss Confederation, 700th anniv. and Red Cross, 125th anniv. No. 2354 is airmail. No. 2352 exists perf. 13. Location of overprint varies.

Nos. 2309-2310 Ovptd. in Silver

1991, Apr. 4 *Perf. 14*

2355 A421 Strip of 4, #a.-d.

Perf. 13x13½

2356 A421 60g on #2310

1994 World Cup Soccer Championships. Location of overprint varies.

Nos. 2312, C822, C766 Ovptd. in Silver

1991, Apr. 4 *Perf. 13*

2357 A422 Strip of 4, #a.-d.

2358 AP246 25g on #C822

Perf. 13x13½

2359 AP233 30g on #C766

Participation of reunified Germany in 1992 Summer Olympics. Nos. 2358-2359 are airmail. Location of overprint varies.

Professors A435

Designs: 50g, Julio Manuel Morales, gynecologist. 100g, Carlos Gatti, clinician. 200g, Gustavo Gonzalez, geologist. 300g, Juan Max Boettner, physician and musician. 350g, Juan Boggino, pathologist. 500g, Andres Barbero, physician, founder of Paraguayan Red Cross.

Perf. 13x13½

1991, Apr. 5 Wmk. 347

2360 A435 50g multicolored	.20	.20
2361 A435 100g multicolored	.20	.20
2362 A435 200g multicolored	.40	.35
2363 A435 300g multicolored	.60	.55
2364 A435 350g multicolored	.70	.60
2365 A435 500g multicolored	1.00	.90
Nos. 2360-2365 (6)	3.10	2.80

Nos. 2364-2365 are airmail.

Nos. 2336-2338 Ovptd. in Black and Red

1991 Wmk. 347 *Perf. 13½x13*

2366 A431 50g on #2336	.20	.20
2367 A431 100g on #2337	.20	.20
2368 A431 200g on #2338	.40	.35
Nos. 2366-2368 (3)	.80	.75

Espamer '91 Philatelic Exhibition.

Nos. 2276a-2276b Ovptd. in Silver

Nos. 2276c-2276d Ovptd. in Silver

1991 Unwmk. *Perf. 13*

2369 A418 Strip of 4, #a.-d.

Writers and Muscians — A436

Designs: 50g, Ruy Diaz de Guzman, historian. 100g, Maria Talavera, war correspondent, vert. 150g, Augusto Roa Bastos, writer, vert. 200g, Jose Asuncion Flores, composer, vert. 250g, Felix Perez Cardozo, harpist. 300g, Juan Carlos Moreno Gonzalez, composer.

Perf. 13½x13,13x13½

1991, Aug. 27 Litho. Wmk. 347

2373	A436	50g	multicolored	.20	.20
2374	A436	100g	multicolored	.25	.25
2375	A436	150g	multicolored	.40	.35
2376	A436	200g	multicolored	.50	.45
2377	A436	250g	multicolored	.60	.55
2378	A436	300g	multicolored	.75	.65
			Nos. 2373-2378 (6)	2.70	2.45

Nos. 2376-2378 are airmail.

America A437

100g, War of Tavare. 300g, Arrival of Spanish explorer Domingo Martinez de Irala in Paraguay.

Perf. 13x13½

1991, Oct. 9 Litho. Wmk. 347

2379	A437	100g	multicolored	.25	.25
2380	A437	300g	multicolored	.75	.65

No. 2380 is airmail.

Paintings A438

Designs: 50g, Compass of Life, by Alfredo Moraes. 100g, The Lighted Alley, by Michael Burt. 150g, Earring, by Lucy Yegros. 200g, Migrant Workers, by Hugo Bogado Barrios. 250g, Passengers Without a Ship, by Bernardo Ismachoviez. 300g, Native Guarani, by Lotte Schulz.

Perf. 13x13½

1991, Nov. 12 Litho. Wmk. 347

2381	A438	50g	multicolored	.20	.20
2382	A438	100g	multicolored	.25	.25
2383	A438	150g	multicolored	.40	.35
2384	A438	200g	multicolored	.50	.45
2385	A438	250g	multicolored	.60	.55
2386	A438	300g	multicolored	.75	.65
			Nos. 2381-2386 (6)	2.70	2.45

Nos. 2384-2386 are airmail.

Endangered Species — A439

Perf. 13x13½, 13½x13

1992, Jan. 28 Litho. Wmk. 347

2387	A439	50g	Catagonus wagneris, vert.	.20	.20
2388	A439	100g	Felis pardalis	.25	.25
2389	A439	150g	Tapirus terrestri	.40	.35
2390	A439	200g	Chrysocyon brachyurus	.50	.45
			Nos. 2387-2390 (4)	1.35	1.25

Tile Designs of Christianized Indians A440

Perf. 13x13½

1992, Mar. 2 Litho. Wmk. 347

2391	A440	50g	Geometric	.20	.20
2392	A440	100g	Church	.20	.20
2393	A440	150g	Missionary ship	.30	.25
2394	A440	200g	Plant	.40	.35
			Nos. 2391-2394 (4)	1.10	1.00

Discovery of America, 500th anniv.

Leprosy Society of Paraguay, 60th Anniv. — A441

Designs: 50g, Society emblem, Malcolm L. Norment, founder. 250g, Gerhard Henrik Armauer Hansen (1841-1912), discoverer of leprosy bacillus.

Perf. 13x13½

1992, Apr. 28 Litho. Wmk. 347

2395	A441	50g	multicolored	.20	.20
2396	A441	250g	multicolored	.60	.55

Earth Summit, Rio de Janeiro A442

Earth Summit emblem, St. Francis of Assisi, and: 50g, Hands holding symbols of clean environment. 100g, Butterfly, industrial pollution. 250g, Globe, calls for environmental protection.

1992, June 9

2397	A442	50g	multicolored	.20	.20
2398	A442	100g	multicolored	.25	.25
2399	A442	250g	multicolored	.55	.55
			Nos. 2397-2399 (3)	1.00	1.00

For overprints see Nos. 2422-2424.

Natl. Census A443

1992. July 30 *Perf. 13½x13, 13x13½*

2400	A443	50g	Economic activity	.20	.20
2401	A443	200g	Houses, vert.	.45	.45
2402	A443	250g	Population, vert.	.60	.55
2403	A443	300g	Education	.75	.65
			Nos. 2400-2403 (4)	2.00	1.85

1992 Summer Olympics, Barcelona — A444

1992, Sept. 1 *Perf. 13x13½, 13½x13*

2404	A444	50g	Soccer, vert.	.20	.20
2405	A444	100g	Tennis, vert.	.25	.25
2406	A444	150g	Running, vert.	.40	.35
2407	A444	200g	Swimming	.50	.40
2408	A444	250g	Judo, vert.	.60	.55
2409	A444	350g	Fencing	.85	.75
			Nos. 2404-2409 (6)	2.80	2.50

Evangelism in Paraguay, 500th Anniv. — A445

Designs: 50g, Friar Luis Bolanos. 100g, Friar Juan de San Bernardo. 150g, San Roque Gonzalez de Santa Cruz. 200g, Father Amancio Gonzalez. 250g, Monsignor Juan Sinforiano Bogarin, vert.

Rough Perf. 13½x13, 13x13½

1992, Oct. 9 Unwmk.

2410	A445	50g	multicolored	.20	.20
2411	A445	100g	multicolored	.25	.25
2412	A445	150g	multicolored	.40	.35
2413	A445	200g	multicolored	.50	.45
2414	A445	250g	multicolored	.60	.55
			Nos. 2410-2414 (5)	1.95	1.80

For overprints see Nos. 2419-2421.

America A446

Designs: 150g, Columbus, fleet arriving in New World. 350g, Columbus, vert.

Rough Perf. 13½x13, 13x13½

1992, Oct. 12

2415	A446	150g	multicolored	.40	.35
2416	A446	350g	multicolored	.85	.75

No. 2416 is airmail.

Ovptd. "PARAFIL 92" in Blue

1992, Nov. 9

2417	A446	150g	multicolored	.40	.35
2418	A446	350g	multicolored	.85	.75

No. 2418 is airmail.

Nos. 2410-2412 Ovptd. in Green

1992, Nov. 6 *Rough Perf. 13½x13*

2419	A445	50g	multicolored	.20	.20
2420	A445	100g	multicolored	.25	.25
2421	A445	150g	multicolored	.40	.35
			Nos. 2419-2421 (3)	.85	.80

Nos. 2397-2399 Ovptd. in Blue

Perf. 13x13½

1992, Oct. 24 Wmk. 347

2422	A442	50g	multicolored	.20	.20
2423	A442	100g	multicolored	.25	.25
2424	A442	250g	multicolored	.55	.55
			Nos. 2422-2424 (3)	1.00	1.00

Inter-American Institute for Cooperation in Agriculture, 50th Anniv. — A447

Designs: 50g, Field workers. 100g, Test tubes, cattle in pasture. 200g, Hands holding flower. 250g, Cows, corn, city.

Perf. 13x13½

1992, Nov. 27 Unwmk.

2425	A447	50g	multicolored	.20	.20
2426	A447	100g	multicolored	.25	.25
2427	A447	200g	multicolored	.50	.45
2428	A447	250g	multicolored	.60	.55
			Nos. 2425-2428 (4)	1.55	1.45

For overprints see Nos. 2461-2462.

Notary College of Paraguay, Cent. — A448

Designs: 50g, Yolanda Bado de Artecona. 100g, Jose Ramon Silva. 150g, Abelardo Brugada Valpy. 200g, Tomas Varela. 250g, Jose Livio Lezcano. 300g, Francisco I. Fernandez.

1992, Nov. 29 *Rough Perf. 13½x13*

2429	A448	50g	multicolored	.20	.20
2430	A448	100g	multicolored	.25	.25
2431	A448	150g	multicolored	.40	.35
2432	A448	200g	multicolored	.50	.45
2433	A448	250g	multicolored	.60	.55
2434	A448	300g	multicolored	.70	.65
			Nos. 2429-2434 (6)	2.65	2.45

Opening of Lopez Palace, Cent. A449

Paintings of palace by: 50g, Michael Burt. 100g, Esperanza Gill. 200g, Emili Aparici. 250g, Hugo Bogado Barrios, vert.

1993, Mar. 9 *Perf. 13½x13, 13x13½*

2435	A449	50g	multicolored	.20	.20
2436	A449	100g	multicolored	.25	.25
2437	A449	200g	multicolored	.50	.45
2438	A449	250g	multicolored	.60	.55
			Nos. 2435-2438 (4)	1.55	1.45

For overprints see Nos. 2453-2456.

Treaty of Asuncion, 1st Anniv. — A450

Rough Perf. 13x13½

1993, Mar. 10 **Wmk. 347**

2439 A450	50g	Flags, map	.20	.20
2440 A450	350g	Flags, globe	.85	.75

Santa Isabel Leprosy Assoc., 50th Anniv. — A451

Various flowers.

Perf. 13x13½

1993, May 24 **Unwmk.**

2441 A451	50g	multicolored	.20	.20
2442 A451	200g	multicolored	.50	.45
2443 A451	250g	multicolored	.60	.55
2444 A451	350g	multicolored	.85	.80
Nos. 2441-2444 (4)			2.15	2.00

Goethe College, Cent. — A452

Designs: 50g, Goethe, by Johann Heinrich Lips, inscription. 100g, Goethe (close-up), by Johann Heinrich Wilhelm Tischbein.

1993, June 18

2445 A452	50g	multicolored	.20	.20
2446 A452	200g	multicolored	.50	.45

For overprints see Nos. 2451-2452.

World Friendship Crusade, 35th Anniv. — A453

Designs: 50g, Stylized globe. 100g, Map, Dr. Ramon Artemio Bracho. 200g, Children. 250g, Two people embracing.

1993, July 1

2447 A453	50g	multicolored	.20	.20
2448 A453	100g	multicolored	.25	.25
2449 A453	200g	multicolored	.50	.45
2450 A453	250g	multicolored	.60	.55
Nos. 2447-2450 (4)			1.55	1.45

For overprint see No. 2486.

Nos. 2445-2446 Ovptd. "BRASILIANA 93"

1993, July 12

2451 A452	50g	multicolored	.20	.20
2452 A452	200g	multicolored	.50	.45

Nos. 2435-2438 Ovptd.

Perf. 13½x13, 13x13½

1993, Aug. 13

2453 A449	50g	multicolored	.20	.20
2454 A449	100g	multicolored	.25	.25
2455 A449	200g	multicolored	.50	.45
2456 A449	250g	multicolored	.60	.55
Nos. 2453-2456 (4)			1.55	1.45

Size of overprint varies.

Church of the Incarnation, Cent. — A454

Design: 50g, Side view of church, vert.

Unwmk.

1993, Oct. 8 **Litho.** ***Perf. 13***

2457 A454	50g	multicolored	.20	.20
2458 A454	350g	multicolored	.40	.35

Endangered Animals — A455

America: 50g, Myrmecophaga tridactyla. 250g, Speothos venaticus.

1993, Oct. 27

2459 A455	50g	multicolored	.20	.20
2460 A455	250g	multicolored	.30	.25

No. 2459 is airmail.

Nos. 2426-2427 Ovptd.

1993, Nov. 16 ***Perf. 13x13½***

2461 A447	100g	multicolored	.20	.20
2462 A447	200g	multicolored	.25	.20

Christmas A456

1993, Nov. 24

2463 A456	50g	shown	.20	.20
2464 A456	250g	Stars, wise men	.30	.25

Scouting in Paraguay, 80th Anniv. A457

50g, Girl scouts watching scout instuctor. 100g, Boy scouts learning crafts. 200g, Lord Robert Baden-Powell. 250g, Girl scout with flag.

1993, Dec. 30

2465 A457	50g	multicolored	.20	.20
2466 A457	100g	multicolored	.20	.20
2467 A457	200g	multicolored	.20	.20
2468 A457	250g	multicolored	.30	.25
Nos. 2465-2468 (4)			.90	.85

First Lawyers to Graduate from Natl. University of Asuncion, Cent. — A458

1994, Apr. 8 ***Perf. 13***

2469 A458	50g	Cecilio Baez	.20	.20
2470 A458	100g	Benigno Riquelme, vert.	.20	.20
2471 A458	250g	Emeterio Gonzalez	.30	.25
2472 A458	500g	J. Gaspar Villamayor	.50	.50
Nos. 2469-2472 (4)			1.20	1.15

Phoenix Sports Corporation, 50th Anniv. — A459

Designs: 50g, Basketball player, vert. 200g, Soccer players, vert. 250g, Pedro Andrias Garcia Arias, founder, tennis player.

1994, May 20 **Litho.** ***Perf. 13***

2473 A459	50g	multicolored	.20	.20
2474 A459	200g	multicolored	.25	.20
2475 A459	250g	multicolored	.30	.25
Nos. 2473-2475 (3)			.75	.65

1994 World Cup Soccer Championships, US — A460

Various soccer plays.

1994, June 2

2476 A460	250g	multicolored	.30	.25
2477 A460	500g	multicolored	.50	.50
2478 A460	1000g	multicolored	1.00	.85
Nos. 2476-2478 (3)			1.80	1.60

For overprints see Nos. 2483-2485.

Intl. Olympic Committee, Cent. — A461

Unwmk.

1994, June 23 **Litho.** ***Perf. 13***

2479 A461	350g	Runner	.40	.35
2480 A461	400g	Lighting Olympic flame	.45	.40

World Congress on Physical Education, Asuncion — A462

Designs: 1000g, Stylized family running to break finish line, vert.

Perf. 13½x13, 13x13½

1994, July 19 **Litho.**

2481 A462	200g	multicolored	.40	.30
2482 A462	1000g	multicolored	1.75	1.50

Nos. 2476-2478 Ovptd.

1994, Aug. 2 ***Perf. 13***

2483 A460	250g	multicolored	.45	.40
2484 A460	500g	multicolored	.90	.75
2485 A460	1000g	multicolored	1.75	1.50
Nos. 2483-2485 (3)			3.10	2.65

No. 2448 Ovptd.

1994, Aug. 3 ***Perf. 13x13½***

2486 A453	100g	multicolored	.20	.20

Agustin Pio Barrios Mangore (1885-1944), Musician A463

1994, Aug. 5 ***Perf. 13x13½***

2487 A463	250g	In tuxedo	.45	.40
2488 A463	500g	In traditional costume	.90	.75

Paraguayan Police, 151st Anniv. — A464

50g, 1913 Guardsman on horseback. 250g, Pedro Nolasco Fernandez, 1st capital police chief; Carlos Bernadino Cacabelos, 1st commissioner.

1994, Aug. 26 **Perf. 13x13½**

2489 A464 50g multicolored .20 .20
2490 A464 250g multicolored .45 .40

For overprint see Nos. 2569-2570.

Parafil '94 A465

Birds: 100g, Ciconia maquari. 150g, Paroaria capitata. 400g, Chloroceryle americana, vert. 500g, Jabiru mycteria, vert.

1994, Sept. 9 **Perf. 13**

2491 A465 100g multicolored .20 .20
2492 A465 150g multicolored .30 .25
2493 A465 400g multicolored .75 .60
2494 A465 500g multicolored .90 .75
Nos. 2491-2494 (4) 2.15 1.80

Solar Eclipse A466

Designs: 50g, Eclipse, Copernicus. 200g, Sundial, Johannes Kepler.

Unwmk.

1994, Sept. 23 **Litho.** **Perf. 13**

2495 A466 50g multicolored .20 .20
2496 A466 200g multicolored .40 .30

America Issue A467

1994, Oct. 11 **Perf. 13½**

2497 A467 100g Derelict locomotive .20 .20
2498 A467 1000g Motorcycle 2.00 1.60

Intl. Year of the Family — A468

1994, Oct. 25 **Perf. 13x13½**

2499 A468 50g Mother, child .20 .20
2500 A468 250g Family faces .50 .40

Christmas — A469

Ceramic figures: 150g, Nativity. 700g, Joseph, infant Jesus, Mary, vert.

1994, Nov. 4 **Perf. 13½**

2501 A469 150g multicolored .30 .25
2502 A469 700g multicolored 1.40 1.10

Paraguayan Red Cross, 75th Anniv. — A470

Designs: 150g, Boy Scouts, Jean-Henri Dunant. 700g, Soldiers, paramedics, Dr. Andres Barbero.

1994, Nov. 25 **Perf. 13½x13**

2503 A470 150g multicolored .30 .25
2504 A470 700g multicolored 1.40 1.10

A 500g showing "75" inside a red cross, with ambulance and emblem with black cross in center was part of thgis set. When it was discovered that the emblem contained a black instead of a red cross it was withdrawn. The editors are garthering information on this stamp.

San Jose College, 90th Anniv. — A471

Pope John Paul II and: 200g, Eternal flame. 250g, College entrance.

1994, Dec. 4

2505 A471 200g multicolored .40 .30
2506 A471 250g multicolored .50 .40

Louis Pasteur (1822-95) A472

1995, Mar. 24 **Litho.** **Perf. 13½**

2507 A472 1000g multicolored 1.50 1.00

Fight Against AIDS — A473

1995, May 4

2508 A473 500g Faces .75 .50
2509 A473 1000g shown 1.50 1.00

FAO, 50th Anniv. A474

1995, June 23

2510 A474 950g Bread, pitcher 1.40 1.00
2511 A474 2000g Watermelon 3.00 2.00

Fifth Neotropical Ornithological Congress — A475

1995, July 6

2512 A475 100g Parula pitiayumi .20 .20
2513 A475 200g Chirroxiphia caudata .30 .20
2514 A475 600g Icterus icterus .90 .60
2515 A475 1000g Carduelis magellanica 1.50 1.00
Nos. 2512-2515 (4) 2.90 2.00

Fifth Intl. Symposium on Municipalities, Ecology & Tourism A476

Designs: 1150g, Rio Monday rapids. 1300g, Areguá Railroad Station.

1995, Aug. 4 **Litho.** **Perf. 13½**

2516 A476 1150g multicolored 1.25 .85
2517 A476 1300g multicolored 1.40 .90

Volleyball, Cent. — A477

1995, Sept. 28

2518 A477 300g shown .30 .20
2519 A477 600g Ball, net .60 .40
2520 A477 1000g Hands, ball, net 1.00 .70
Nos. 2518-2520 (3) 1.90 1.30

America Issue A478

Preserve the environment: 950g, Macizo Monument, Achay. 2000g, Tinfunique Reserve, Chaco, vert.

1995, Oct. 12

2521 A478 950g multicolored 1.00 .65
2522 A478 2000g multicolored 2.00 1.40

UN, 50th Anniv. — A479

Designs: 200g, Flags above olive branch. 3000g, UN emblem, stick figures.

1995, Oct. 20

2523 A479 200g multicolored .20 .20
2524 A479 3000g multicolored 3.00 2.00

Christmas A480

1995, Nov. 7

2525 A480 200g shown .20 .20
2526 A480 1000g Nativity 1.00 .70

Jose Marti (1853-95) — A481

Designs: 200g, Hedychium coronarium, Marti, vert. 1000g, Hedychium coronarium, map & flag of Cuba, Marti.

1995, Dec. 19 **Litho.** **Perf. 13½**

2527 A481 200g multicolored .25 .20
2528 A481 1000g multicolored 1.10 .75

Lion's Clubs of South America & the Caribbean, 25th Anniv. — A482

1996, Jan. 11

2529 A482 200g Railway station .25 .20
2530 A482 1000g Viola House 1.10 .75

Orchids
A483

Designs: 100g, Cattleya nobilior. 200g, Oncidium varicosum. 1000g, Oncidium jonesianum, vert. 1150g, Sophronitis cernua.

Perf. 13½x13, 13x13½

1996, Apr. 22 **Litho.**

2531	A483	100g	multicolored	.20	.20
2532	A483	200g	multicolored	.20	.20
2533	A483	1000g	multicolored	1.00	.60
2534	A483	1150g	multicolored	1.10	.65
			Nos. 2531-2534 (4)	2.50	1.65

1996 Summer Olympic Games, Atlanta
A484

1996, June 6 ***Perf. 13½x13***

2535	A484	500g	Diving	.50	.30
2536	A484	1000g	Running	1.00	.60

Founding of Society of Salesian Fathers in Paraguay, Cent. — A485

Pope John Paul II, St. John Bosco (1815-88), and: 200g, Men, boys from Salesian Order, natl. flag. 300g, Madonna and Child, vert. 1000g, Map of Paraguay, man following light.

1996, July 22 ***Perf. 13½x13, 13x13½***

2537	A485	200g	multicolored	.20	.20
2538	A485	300g	multicolored	.30	.20
2539	A485	1000g	multicolored	1.00	.60
			Nos. 2537-2539 (3)	1.50	1.00

UNICEF, 50th Anniv. — A486

Children's paintings: 1000g, Outdoor scene, by S. Báez, 1300g, Four groups of children, by C. Pérez.

1996, Sept. 27 ***Perf. 13½x13***

2540	A486	1000g	multicolored	1.00	.60
2541	A486	1300g	multicolored	1.25	.85

Visit of Pope John Paul II to Caacupe, Site of Apparition of the Virgin — A487

Design: 200g, Pope John Paul II, church, Virgin of Caacupe, vert.

1996, Oct. 4 ***Perf. 13x13½, 13½x13***

2542	A487	200g	multicolored	.20	.20
2543	A487	1300g	multicolored	1.25	.85

Traditional Costumes
A488

America issue: 500g, Woman in costume. 1000g, Woman, man, in costumes.

1996, Oct. 11 ***Perf. 13x13½***

2544	A488	500g	multicolored	.50	.30
2545	A488	1000g	multicolored	1.00	.60

UN Year for Eradication of Poverty — A489

1996, Oct. 17 ***Perf. 13½x13, 13x13½***

2546	A489	1000g	Food products	1.00	.60
2547	A489	1150g	Boy, fruit, vert.	1.10	.75

Christmas
A490

Madonna and Child, by: 200g, Koki Ruíz. 1000g, Hernán Miranda.

1996, Nov. 7 ***Perf. 13x13½***

2548	A490	200g	multicolored	.20	.20
2549	A490	1000g	multicolored	1.00	.60

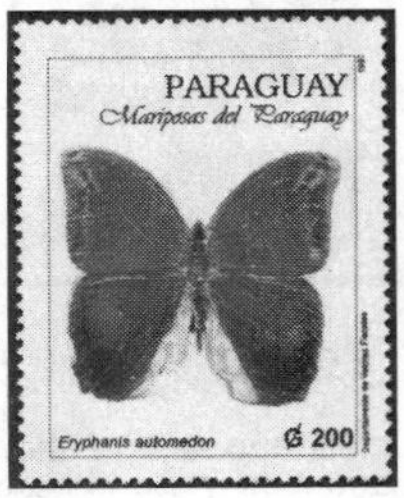

Butterflies
A491

Designs: 200g, Eryphanis automedon. 500g, Dryadula phaetusa. 1000g, Vanessa myrinna. 1150g, Heliconius ethilla.

1997, Mar. 5 **Litho.** ***Perf. 13x13½***

2550	A491	200g	multicolored	.20	.20
2551	A491	500g	multicolored	.50	.30
2552	A491	1000g	multicolored	.95	.55
2553	A491	1150g	multicolored	1.10	.65
			Nos. 2550-2553 (4)	2.75	1.70

Official Buildings — A492

200g, 1st Legistlature. 1000g, Postal Headquarters.

1997, May 5 ***Perf. 13½x13***

2554	A492	200g	multicolored	.20	.20
2555	A492	1000g	multicolored	1.10	.65

1997, Year of Jesus Christ — A493

1997, June 10 ***Perf. 13x13½***

2556	A493	1000g	Crucifix, Pope John Paul II	.95	.60

11th Summit of the Rio Group Chiefs of State, Asunción — A494

1997, Aug. 23 ***Perf. 13½x13***

2557	A494	1000g	multicolored	.95	.60

Environmental and Climate Change — A495

Flowers: 300g, Opunita elata. 500g, Bromelia balansae, 1000g, Monvillea kroenlaini.

Perf. 13½x13, 13x13½

1997, Aug. 25

2558	A495	300g	multi	.30	.20
2559	A495	500g	multi, vert.	.50	.30
2560	A495	1000g	multi	1.00	.60
			Nos. 2558-2560 (3)	1.80	1.10

1st Philatelic Exposition of MERCOSUR Countries, Chile and Bolivia — A496

Fauna: 200g, Felis tigrina. 1000g, Alouatta caraya, vert. 1150g, Agouti paca.

Perf. 13½x13, 13x13½

1997, Aug. 29

2561	A496	200g	multicolored	.20	.20
2562	A496	1000g	multicolored	.95	.60
2563	A496	1150g	multicolored	1.10	.65
			Nos. 2561-2563 (3)	2.25	1.45

MERCOSUR (Common Market of Latin America)
A497

1997, Sept. 26 ***Perf. 13x13½***

2564	A497	1000g	multicolored	.95	.60

See Argentina #1975, Brazil #2646, Urugray #1681.

America Issue — A498

Life of a postman: 1000g, Postman, letters going around the world, vert. 1150g, Window with six panes showing weather conditions, different roads, postman.

1997, Oct. 10 ***Perf. 13x13½, 13½x13***

2565	A498	1000g	multicolored	1.00	.60
2566	A498	1150g	multicolored	1.10	.65

Natl. Council on Sports, 50th Anniv. — A499

200g, Neri Kennedy throwing javelin. 1000g, Ramón Milciades Giménez Gaona throwing discus.

1997, Oct. 16 ***Perf. 13x13½***

2567	A499	200g	multicolored	.25	.20
2568	A499	1000g	multicolored	1.25	.75

Nos. 2489-2490 Ovptd. in Red

1997, Nov. 14

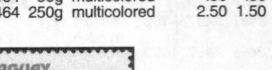

2569	A464	50g	multicolored	.50	.30
2570	A464	250g	multicolored	2.50	1.50

Christmas
A500

Paintings of Madonna and Child: 200g, By Olga Blinder. 1000g, By Hermán Miranda.

1997, Nov. 17

2571 A500 200g multicolored .20 .20
2572 A500 1000g multicolored 1.10 .65

UN Fund for Children of the World with AIDS — A501

Children's paintings: 500g, Boy. 1000g, Girl.

1997, Dec. 5

2573 A501 500g multicolored .50 .30
2574 A501 1000g multicolored 1.00 .60

Rotary Club of Asunción, 70th Anniv. — A502

1997, Dec. 11

2575 A502 1150g multicolored 1.10 .65

1998 World Cup Soccer Championships, France — A503

200g, Julio César Romero, vert. 500g, Carlos Gamarra, vert. 1000g, 1998 Paraguayan team.

1998, Jan. 22 Litho. *Perf. 13*

2576 A503 200g multicolored .20 .20
2577 A503 500g multicolored .50 .30
2578 A503 1000g multicolored 1.00 .60
Nos. 2576-2578 (3) 1.70 1.10

Fish A504

Designs: 200g, Tetrogonopterus argenteus. 300g, Pseudoplatystoma coruscans. 500g, Salminus brasiliensis. 1000g, Acestrorhynchus altus.

1998, Apr. 17 Litho. *Perf. 13½*

2579 A504 200g multicolored .20 .20
2580 A504 300g multicolored .25 .20
2581 A504 500g multicolored .40 .25
2582 A504 1000g multicolored .80 .50
Nos. 2579-2582 (4) 1.65 1.15

Contemporary Paintings — A505

200g, Hands, geometric shape, by Carlos Colombino. 300g, Mother nursing infant, by Félix Toranzos. 400g, Flowers, by Edith Giménez. 1000g, Woman lifting tray of food, by Ricardo Migliorisi.

1998, June 5

2583 A505 200g multi, vert. .20 .20
2584 A505 300g multi, vert. .25 .20
2585 A505 400g multi, vert. .35 .20
2586 A505 1000g multi .80 .50
Nos. 2583-2586 (4) 1.60 1.10

Mushrooms A506

400g, Boletus edulis. 600g, Macrolepiota procera. 1000g, Geastrum triplex.

1998, June 26

2587 A506 400g multicolored .35 .20
2588 A506 600g multicolored .50 .30
2589 A506 1000g multicolored .80 .50
Nos. 2587-2589 (3) 1.65 1.00

Organization of American States (OAS), 50th Anniv. — A507

Designs: 500g, Home of Carlos A. López, botantical and zooligical gardens, Asunción. 1000g, Palmerola Villa, Areguá.

1998, July 16

2590 A507 500g multicolored .40 .20
2591 A507 1000g multicolored .80 .50

Episcopacy of Hernando de Trejo y Sanabria, 400th Anniv. — A508

Pope John Paul II and : 400g, Sacrarium doors, Caazapá Church, vert. 1700g, Statue of St. Francis of Assisi, Atyrá Church.

Perf. 13x13½, 13½x13

1998, Sept. 5 Litho.

2592 A508 400g multi .30 .20
2593 A508 1700g multi 1.25 .75

Ruins of Jesuit Mission Church A509

1998, Sept. 16 Litho. *Perf. 13½x13*

2594 A509 5000g multicolored 3.50 2.00

Flowers A510

Designs: 100g, Acacia caven. 600g, Cordia trichotoma. 1900g, Glandularia sp.

1998, Sept. 16 Litho. *Perf. 13x13½*

2595 A510 100g multi .20 .20
2596 A510 600g multi .40 .40
2597 A510 1900g multi 1.40 1.40
Nos. 2595-2597 (3) 2.00 2.00

America Issue A511

Famous women and buildings: 1600g, Serafina Davalos (1883-1957), first woman lawyer, National College building. 1700g, Adela Speratti (1865-1902), director of Normal School.

1998, Oct. 12 Litho. *Perf. 13½x13*

2598 A511 1600g multi 1.10 .65
2599 A511 1700g multi 1.25 .75

Universal Declaration of Human Rights, 50th Anniv. — A512

Artwork by: 500g, Carlos Colombino. 1000g, Jose Filártiga.

1998, Oct. 23 *Perf. 13x13½*

2600 A512 500g multi .35 .25
2601 A512 1000g multi .70 .45

Christmas Creche Figures — A513

Perf. 13½x13, 13x13½

1998, Sept. 16 Litho.

2602 A513 300g shown .20 .20
2603 A513 1600g Stable, vert. 1.10 .65

Reptiles A514

Designs: 100g, Micrurus frontalis. 300g, Ameiva ameiva. 1600g, Geochelone carbonaria. 1700g, Caiman yacare.

1999, May 13 Litho. *Perf. 13½x13*

2604-2607 A514 Set of 4 2.50 2.50

Paintings — A515

Paintings by: 500g, Ignacio Nuñez Soler. 1600g, Modesto Delgado Rodas. 1700g, Jaime Bestard.

1999, June 23 Litho. *Perf. 13½x13*

2608 A515 500g multi .30 .30
2609 A515 1600g multi 1.00 1.00
2610 A515 1700g multi 1.10 1.10
Nos. 2608-2610 (3) 2.40 2.40

America Soccer Cup A516

Designs: 300g, Carlos Humberto Paredes, vert. 500g, South American Soccer Confederation Building, Luque. 1900g, Feliciano Cáceres Stadium, Luque.

Perf. 13x13½, 13½x13

1999, June 24

2611 A516 300g multi .20 .20
2612 A516 500g multi .30 .30
2613 A516 1900g multi 1.25 1.25
Nos. 2611-2613 (3) 1.75 1.75

SOS Children's Villages, 50th Anniv. — A517

1999, July 16 *Perf. 13½x13, 13x13½*

2614 A517 1700g Toucan 1.00 1.00
2615 A517 1900g Toucan, vert. 1.25 1.25

Protests of Assassination of Vice-President Luis Maria Argaña — A518

Designs: 100g, Protest at Governmental Palace. 500g, Argaña, vert. 1500g, Protest at National Congress.

1999, Aug. 26

2616 A518 100g multi .20 .20
2617 A518 500g multi .30 .30
2618 A518 1500g multi .90 .90
Nos. 2616-2618 (3) 1.40 1.40

Medicinal Plants — A519

Designs: 600g, Cochlospermum regium. 700g, Borago officinalis. 1700g, Passiflora cincinnata.

1999, Sept. 8 ***Perf. 13x13½***
2619 A519 600g multi .35 .35
2620 A519 700g multi .45 .45
2621 A519 1700g multi 1.00 1.00
Nos. 2619-2621 (3) 1.80 1.80

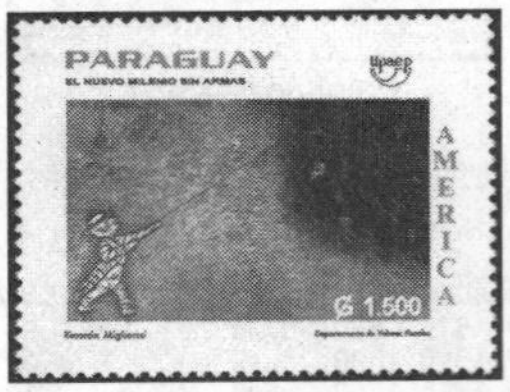

America Issue, A New Millennium Without Arms — A520

Various artworks by Ricardo Migliorisi.

Perf. 13½x13, 13x13½
1999, Oct. 12 **Litho.**
2622 A520 1500g multi .90 .55
2623 A520 3000g multi, vert. 1.90 1.25

Intl. Year of the Elderly A521

Artwork by: 1000g, Olga Blinder. 1900g, Maria de los Reyes Omella Herrero, vert.

Perf. 13½x13, 13x13½
1999, Oct. 20 **Litho.**
2624-2625 A521 Set of 2 1.75 1.75

Christmas A522

Artwork by: 300g, Manuel Viedma. 1600g, Federico Ordiñana.

1999, Nov. 11 **Litho.** ***Perf. 13x13½***
2626 A522 300g multi .20 .20
2627 A522 1600g multi .95 .60

City of Pedro Juan Caballero, Cent. — A523

Flowers: 1000g, Tabebuia impetiginosa. 1600g, Tabebuia pulcherrima, vert.

Perf. 13½x13, 13x13½
1999, Dec. 1 **Litho.**
2628 A523 1000g multi .60 .60
2629 A523 1600g multi 1.00 1.00

Inter-American Development Bank, 40th Anniv. — A524

Designs: 600g, Oratory of Our Lady of Asuncion and Pantheon of Heroes, Asuncion. 700g, Governmental Palace.

1999, Dec. 6 ***Perf. 13½x13***
2630 A524 600g multi .35 .35
2631 A524 700g multi .45 .45

Intl. Women's Day — A525

Carmen Casco de Lara Castro and sculpture: 400g, Conjunction, by Domingo Rivarola. 2000g, Violation, by Gustavo Beckelmann.

2000, Apr. 7 **Litho.** ***Perf. 13x13½***
2632-2633 A525 Set of 2 1.40 1.40

Expo 2000, Hanover A526

Designs: 500g, Yacyreta Dam and deer. 2500g, Itaipú Dam, tapir.

2000, May 5 ***Perf. 13½x13***
2634-2635 A526 Set of 2 1.75 1.75

Salesians in Paraguay, Cent. — A527

Madonna and Child, Pope John Paul II and: 600g, Salesians, vert. 2000g, College building.

Perf. 13x13½, 13½x13
2000, May 19 **Litho.**
2636-2637 A527 Set of 2 1.50 1.50

2000 Summer Olympics, Sydney — A528

Designs: 2500g, Soccer, vert. 3000g, Runner Francisco Rojas Soto.

2000, July 28 ***Perf. 13x13½, 13½x13***
2638-2639 A528 Set of 2 3.25 3.25

Rights of the Child A529

Designs: 1500g, Child between hands, vert. 1700g, Handprints.

Perf. 13x13½, 13½x13
2000, Aug. 16
2640-2641 A529 Set of 2 1.90 1.90

Fire Fighters A530

Designs: 100g, Fire fighters, white truck, vert. 200g, Fire fighter in old uniform, emblem, vert. 1500g, Fire fighters at fire. 1600g, Fire fighters, yellow truck.

Perf. 13x13½, 13½x13
2000, Sept. 28
2642-2645 A530 Set of 4 2.00 2.00

America Issue, Fight Against AIDS — A532

Designs: 1500g, Signs with arrows. 2500g, Tic-tac-toe game.

2000, Oct. 19 ***Perf. 13x13½***
2648-2649 A532 Set of 2 2.40 2.40

Christmas A534

Designs: 100g, Holy Family, sculpture by Hugo Pistilli. 500g, Poem by José Luis Appleyard. 2000g, Creche figures, horiz.

Perf. 13x13½, 13½x13
2000, Nov. 17 **Litho.**
2652-2654 A534 Set of 3 2.75 2.75

SEMI-POSTAL STAMPS

Red Cross Nurse SP1

Unwmk.
1930, July 22 **Typo.** ***Perf. 12***
B1 SP1 1.50p + 50c gray violet 1.25 .75
B2 SP1 1.50p + 50c deep rose 1.25 .75
B3 SP1 1.50p + 50c dark blue 1.25 .75
Nos. B1-B3 (3) 3.75 2.25

The surtax was for the benefit of the Red Cross Society of Paraguay.

College of Agriculture — SP2

1930
B4 SP2 1.50p + 50c blue, *pink* .30 .30

Surtax for the Agricultural Institute.
The sheet of No. B4 has a papermaker's watermark: "Vencedor Bond."
A 1.50p+50c red on yellow was prepared but not regularly issued. Value, 20 cents.

Red Cross Headquarters SP3

1932
B5 SP3 50c + 50c rose .30 .25

Our Lady of Asunción — SP4

1941 **Engr.**
B6 SP4 7p + 3p red brown .30 .25
B7 SP4 7p + 3p purple .30 .25
B8 SP4 7p + 3p carmine rose .30 .25
B9 SP4 7p + 3p sapphire .30 .25
Nos. B6-B9 (4) 1.20 1.00

For surcharges see Nos. 419-426, 431-434.

No. 361 Surcharged in Black

1944
B10 A70 10c on 10p multicolored .35 .25

The surtax was for the victims of the San Juan earthquake in Argentina.

Catalogue values for unused stamps in this section, from this point to the end of the section, are for Never Hinged items.

No. C169 Surcharged in Carmine "AYUDA AL ECUADOR 5 + 5"

1949 **Unwmk.** ***Perf. 12½***
B11 A117 5c + 5c on 30c dk blue .20 .20

Surtax for the victims of the Ecuador earthquake.

38th Intl. Eucharistic Congress, Bombay — SP5

Various coins and coat of arms.

Litho. & Engr.

1964, Dec. 11 *Perf. 12x12½*

B12 SP5 20g +10g multicolored
B13 SP5 30g +15g multicolored
B14 SP5 50g +25g multicolored
B15 SP5 100g +50g multicolored
a. Souvenir sheet of 4, #B12-B15

Buildings and Coats of Arms of Popes John XXIII & Paul VI — SP6

#B16, Dome of St. Peters. #B17, Site of Saint Peter's tomb. #B18, Saint Peter's Plaza. #B19,Taj Mahal .

1964, Dec. 12

B16 SP6 20g +10g multicolored
B17 SP6 30g +15g multicolored
B18 SP6 50g +25g multicolored
B19 SP6 100g +50g multicolored
a. Souvenir sheet of 4, #B16-B19

AIR POST STAMPS

Official Stamps of 1913 Surcharged

1929, Jan. 1 **Unwmk.** *Perf. 11½*

C1 O19 2.85p on 5c lilac	.75	.65
C2 O19 5.65p on 10c grn	.50	.40
C3 O19 11.30p on 50c rose	.75	.50
Nos. C1-C3 (3)	2.00	1.55

Counterfeits of surcharge exist.

Regular Issues of 1924-27 Surcharged as in 1929

1929, Feb. 26 *Perf. 12*

C4 A51 3.40p on 3p gray	1.75	1.10
a. Surch. "Correo / en $3.40 / Habilitado / Aereo"	8.75	
b. Double surcharge	8.75	
c. "Aéro" instead of "Aéreo"		
C5 A44 6.80p on 4p lt bl	1.75	1.10
a. Surch. "Correo / Aereo / en $6.80 / Habilitado"	8.75	
C6 A52 17p on 5p choc	1.75	1.10
a. Surch. "Correo / Habilitado / Habilitado / en 17p"	4.50	
b. Double surcharge	8.75	
Nos. C4-C6 (3)	5.25	3.30

Wings AP1

Pigeon with Letter AP2

Airplanes — AP3

1929-31 **Typo.** *Perf. 12*

C7 AP1 2.85p gray green	.50	.45
a. Imperf., pair	37.50	
C8 AP1 2.85p turq grn ('31)	.25	.20
C9 AP2 5.65p brown	.75	.35
C10 AP2 5.65p scar ('31)	.40	.25
C11 AP3 11.30p chocolate	.50	.35
a. Imperf., pair	37.50	
C12 AP3 11.30p dp blue ('31)	.25	.25
Nos. C7-C12 (6)	2.65	1.85

Sheets of these stamps sometimes show portions of a papermaker's watermark "Indian Bond C. Extra Strong."

Excellent counterfeits are plentiful.

Regular Issues of 1924-28 Surcharged in Black or Red

1929 *Perf. 11½, 12*

C13 A47 95c on 7c lilac	.20	.20
C14 A47 1.90p on 20c dull bl	.20	.20
C15 A44 3.40p on 4p lt bl (R)	.25	.20
a. Double surcharge	2.00	
C16 A44 4.75p on 4p lt bl (R)	.45	.40
a. Double surcharge	2.00	
C17 A51 6.80p on 3p gray	.50	.50
a. Double surcharge	3.00	
C18 A52 17p on 5p choc	1.50	1.50
a. Horiz. pair, imperf. between	25.00	
Nos. C13-C18 (6)	3.10	3.00

Six stamps in the sheet of No. C17 have the "$" and numerals thinner and narrower than the normal type.

Airplane and Arms — AP4

Cathedral of Asunción AP5

Airplane and Globe — AP6

1930 *Perf. 12*

C19 AP4 95c dp red, *pink*	.25	.25
C20 AP4 95c dk bl, *blue*	.25	.25
C21 AP5 1.90p lt red, *pink*	.25	.25
C22 AP5 1.90p violet, *blue*	.25	.25
C23 AP6 6.80p blk, *lt bl*	.25	.25
C24 AP6 6.80p green, *pink*	.25	.30
Nos. C19-C24 (6)	1.50	1.55

Sheets of Nos. C19-C24 have a papermaker's watermark: "Extra Vencedor Bond."

Counterfeits exist.

Stamps and Types of 1927-28 Overprinted in Red

1930

C25 A47 10c olive green	.20	.20
a. Double overprint	3.00	
C26 A47 20c dull blue	.20	.20
a. "CORREO CORREO" instead of "CORREO AEREO"	2.50	
b. "AEREO AEREO" instead of "CORREO AEREO"	2.50	
C27 A48 1p emerald	.50	.50
C28 A51 3p gray	.50	.50
Nos. C25-C26 (2)	.40	.40

Nos. 273, 282, 286, 288, 300, 302, 305 Surcharged in Red or Black

#C29-C30, C32

#C31

#C33

#C34-C35

1930

Red or Black Surcharge

C29 A47 5c on 10c gray grn (R)	.20	.20
a. "AEREO" omitted	15.00	
C30 A47 5c on 70c ultra (R)	.20	.20
a. Vert. pair, imperf. between	20.00	
C31 A48 20c on 1p org red	.20	.20
a. "CORREO" double	3.00	3.00
b. "AEREO" double	3.00	3.00
C32 A47 40c on 50c org (R)	.20	.20
a. "AEREO" omitted	4.50	4.50
b. "CORREO" double	3.00	3.00
c. "AEREO" double	3.00	3.00
C33 A54 6p on 10p red	.75	.70
C34 A49 10p on 20p red	3.00	2.75
C35 A49 10p on 20p vio brn	3.00	2.75
Nos. C29-C35 (7)	7.55	7.00

Declaration of Independence AP11

1930, May 14 **Typo.**

C36 AP11 2.85p dark blue	.25	.25
C37 AP11 3.40p dark green	.25	.20
C38 AP11 4.75p deep lake	.25	.20
Nos. C36-C38 (3)	.75	.65

Natl. Independence Day, May 14, 1811.

Gunboat Type

Gunboat "Paraguay."

1931-39 *Perf. 11½, 12*

C39 A58 1p claret	.20	.20
C40 A58 1p dk blue ('36)	.20	.20
C41 A58 2p orange	.20	.20
C42 A58 2p dk brn ('36)	.20	.20
C43 A58 3p turq green	.25	.25
C44 A58 3p lt ultra ('36)	.25	.25
C45 A58 3p brt rose ('39)	.25	.20
C46 A58 6p dk green	.30	.30
C47 A58 6p violet ('36)	.35	.30
C48 A58 6p dull bl ('39)	.25	.25
C49 A58 10p vermilion	.70	.60
C50 A58 10p bluish grn ('35)	1.00	1.00
C51 A58 10p yel brn ('36)	.75	.75
C52 A58 10p dk blue ('36)	.50	.50
C53 A58 10p lt pink ('39)	.65	.65
Nos. C39-C53 (15)	6.00	5.85

1st constitution of Paraguay as a Republic and the arrival of the "Paraguay" and "Humaita."

Counterfeits of #C39-C53 are plentiful.

Regular Issue of 1924 Surcharged

1931, Aug. 22

C54 A44 3p on 4p lt bl	8.00	6.00

Overprinted

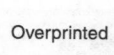

C55 A44 4p lt blue	7.00	5.00

On Nos. C54-C55 the Zeppelin is handstamped. The rest of the surcharge or overprint is typographed.

War Memorial AP13

Orange Tree and Yerba Mate — AP14

Yerba Mate — AP15

Palms — AP16

Eagle — AP17

1931-36 **Litho.**

C56 AP13 5c lt blue	.20	.20
a. Horiz. pair, imperf. btwn.	6.25	
C57 AP13 5c dp grn ('33)	.20	.20
C58 AP13 5c lt red ('33)	.20	.20
C59 AP13 5c violet ('35)	.20	.20
C60 AP14 10c dp violet	.20	.20
C61 AP14 10c brn lake ('33)	.20	.20
C62 AP14 10c yel brn ('33)	.20	.20
C63 AP14 10c ultra ('35)	.20	.20
a. Imperf., pair	5.50	
C64 AP15 20c red	.20	.20
C65 AP15 20c dl blue ('33)	.20	.20
C66 AP15 20c emer ('33)	.20	.20
C67 AP15 20c yel brn ('35)	.20	.20
a. Imperf., pair	3.75	
C68 AP16 40c dp green	.20	.20
C69 AP16 40c slate bl ('35)	.20	.20
C70 AP16 40c red ('36)	.20	.20
C71 AP17 80c dull blue	.20	.20

C72	AP17	80c dl grn ('33)	.20	.20
C73	AP17	80c scar ('33)	.20	.20
		Nos. C56-C73 (18)	3.60	3.60

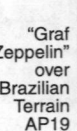

Airship "Graf Zeppelin" — AP18

1932, Apr. **Litho.**

C74	AP18	4p ultra	.85	.85
a.		Imperf., pair	5.00	
C75	AP18	8p red	1.40	1.00
C76	AP18	12p blue grn	1.10	.85
C77	AP18	16p dk violet	2.25	1.50
C78	AP18	20p orange brn	2.25	2.00
		Nos. C74-C78 (5)	7.85	6.20

For surcharges see Nos. 325-329.

"Graf Zeppelin" over Brazilian Terrain AP19

"Graf Zeppelin" over Atlantic — AP20

1933, May 5

C79	AP19	4.50p dp blue	2.00	1.25
C80	AP19	9p dp rose	3.00	2.25
a.		Horiz. pair, imperf. between	150.00	
C81	AP19	13.50p blue grn	4.00	3.00
C82	AP20	22.50p bis brn	8.00	6.00
C83	AP20	45p dull vio	10.00	10.00
		Nos. C79-C83 (5)	27.00	22.50

Excellent counterfeits are plentiful.
For overprints see Nos. C88-C97.

Posts and Telegraph Building, Asunción — AP21

1934-37 ***Perf. 11½***

C84	AP21	33.75p ultra	1.50	1.25
C85	AP21	33.75p car ('35)	1.50	1.25
a.		33.75p rose ('37)	1.25	1.25
C86	AP21	33.75p emerald ('36)	2.00	1.50
C87	AP21	33.75p bis brn ('36)	.50	.50
		Nos. C84-C87 (4)	5.50	4.50

For surcharge see No. C107.

Nos. C79-C83 Overprinted in Black

1934, May 26

C88	AP19	4.50p deep bl	2.00	1.50
C89	AP19	9p dp rose	2.50	2.00
C90	AP19	13.50p blue grn	7.00	5.00
C91	AP20	22.50p bis brn	6.00	4.00
C92	AP20	45p dull vio	9.00	7.00
		Nos. C88-C92 (5)	26.50	19.50

Types of 1933 Issue Overprinted in Black

1935

C93	AP19	4.50p rose red	3.00	2.00
C94	AP19	9p lt green	4.00	2.50
C95	AP19	13.50p brown	9.00	6.50
C96	AP20	22.50p violet	7.00	5.00
C97	AP20	45p blue	20.00	12.00
		Nos. C93-C97 (5)	43.00	28.00

Tobacco Plant — AP22

1935-39 **Typo.**

C98	AP22	17p lt brown	2.00	2.00
C99	AP22	17p carmine	3.75	3.75
C100	AP22	17p dark blue	2.50	2.50
C101	AP22	17p pale yel grn ('39)	1.50	1.50
		Nos. C98-C101 (4)	9.75	9.75

Excellent counterfeits are plentiful.

Church of Incarnation AP23

1935-38

C102	AP23	102p carmine	3.00	2.25
C103	AP23	102p blue	3.00	2.25
C103A	AP23	102p indigo ('36)	1.90	1.90
C104	AP23	102p yellow brn	2.00	2.00
a.		Imperf., pair	15.00	
C105	AP23	102p violet ('37)	.95	.95
C106	AP23	102p brn org ('38)	.85	.85
		Nos. C102-C106 (6)	11.70	10.20

Excellent counterfeits are plentiful.
For surcharges see Nos. C108-C109.

Types of 1934-35 Surcharged in Red

1937, Aug. 1

C107	AP21	24p on 33.75p sl bl	.50	.35
C108	AP23	65p on 102p ol bis	1.25	.90
C109	AP23	84p on 102p bl grn	1.25	.75
		Nos. C107-C109 (3)	3.00	2.00

Plane over Asunción AP24

1939, Aug. 3 **Typo.** ***Perf. 10½, 11½***

C110	AP24	3.40p yel green	.50	.50
C111	AP24	3.40p orange brn	.30	.25
C112	AP24	3.40p indigo	.30	.25
		Nos. C110-C112 (3)	1.10	1.00

Buenos Aires Peace Conference Type and

Map of Paraguay with New Chaco Boundary AP28

Designs: 1p, Flags of Paraguay and Bolivia. 5p, Pres. Ortiz of Argentina, flags of Paraguay, Argentina. 10p, Pres. Vargas, Brazil. 30p, Pres. Alessandri, Chile. 50p, US Eagle and Shield. 100p, Pres. Benavides, Peru. 200p, Pres. Baldomir, Uruguay.

Engr.; Flags Litho.

1939, Nov. ***Perf. 12½***

Flags in National Colors

C113	A69	1p	red brown	.20	.20
C114	A69	3p	dark blue	.20	.20
C115	A70	5p	olive blk	.20	.20
C116	A70	10p	violet	.20	.20
C117	A70	30p	orange	.20	.20
C118	A70	50p	black brn	.25	.20
C119	A70	100p	brt green	.35	.30
C120	A70	200p	green	1.90	1.25
C121	AP28	500p	black	8.00	6.00
			Nos. C113-C121 (9)	11.50	8.75

For overprints see Nos. 388-390.

University of Asuncion Type

Pres. Bernardino Caballero and Senator José S. Decoud.

1939, Sept. **Litho.** ***Perf. 12***

C122	A67	28p rose & blk	3.25	3.25
C123	A67	90p yel grn & blk	4.00	4.00

Map with Asunción to New York Air Route — AP35

1939, Nov. 30 **Engr.**

C124	AP35	30p brown	1.90	1.50
C125	AP35	80p orange	2.25	2.25
C126	AP35	90p purple	4.00	4.00
		Nos. C124-C126 (3)	8.15	7.75

New York World's Fair.

Pan American Union Type

1940, May ***Perf. 12***

C127	A85	20p rose car	.20	.20
C128	A85	70p violet bl	.45	.20
C129	A85	100p Prus grn	.50	.50
C130	A85	500p dk violet	2.25	1.75
		Nos. C127-C130 (4)	3.40	2.65

Asuncion 400th Anniv. Type

1942, Aug. 15

C131	A93	20p deep plum	.50	.40
C132	A94	70p fawn	1.50	1.10
C133	A95	500p olive gray	4.00	3.50
		Nos. C131-C133 (3)	6.00	5.00

Imperforates

Starting with No. C134, many Paraguayan air mail stamps exist imperforate.

Port of Asunción AP40

First Telegraph in South America AP41

Early Merchant Ship — AP42

Birthplace of Paraguay's Liberation AP43

Monument to Antequera AP44

Locomotive of First Paraguayan Railroad AP45

Monument to Heroes of Itororó — AP46

Primitive Postal Service among Indians — AP48

Government House AP47

Colonial Jesuit Altar — AP49

Ruins of Humaitá Church — AP50

Oratory of the Virgin — AP51

Marshal Francisco S. Lopez — AP52

1944-45 Unwmk. *Perf. 12½*

C134	AP40	1c blue	.20	.20
C135	AP41	2c green	.20	.20
C136	AP42	3c brown vio	.20	.20
C137	AP43	5c brt bl grn	.20	.20
C138	AP44	10c dk violet	.20	.20
C139	AP45	20c dk brown	.20	.20
C140	AP46	30c lt blue	.20	.20
C141	AP47	40c olive	.20	.20
C142	AP48	70c brown red	.30	.25
C143	AP49	1g orange yel	.70	.50
C144	AP50	2g copper brn	.85	.70
C145	AP51	5g black brn	2.00	2.00
C146	AP52	10g indigo	4.00	4.00
		Nos. C134-C146 (13)	9.45	9.05

See Nos. C158-C162. For surcharges see Nos. C154-C157.

Flags Type

20c, Ecuador. 40c, Bolivia. 70c, Mexico. 1g, Chile. 2g, Brazil. 5g, Argentina. 10g, US.

Engr.; Flags Litho. in Natl. Colors
1945, Aug. 15

C147	A106	20c orange	.20	.20
C148	A106	40c olive	.20	.20
C149	A106	70c lake	.20	.20
C150	A106	1g slate bl	.30	.30
C151	A106	2g blue vio	.40	.40
C152	A106	5g green	1.00	1.00
C153	A106	10g brown	3.00	3.00
		Nos. C147-C153 (7)	5.30	5.30

Sizes: Nos. C147-C151, 30x26mm; 5g, 32x28mm; 10g, 33x30mm.

Catalogue values for unused stamps in this section, from this point to the end of the section, are for Never Hinged items.

Nos. C139-C142 Surcharged "1946" and New Value in Black

1946 Engr. *Perf. 12½*

C154	AP45	5c on 20c dk brn	.40	.40
C155	AP46	5c on 30c lt blue	.40	.40
C156	AP47	5c on 40c olive	.40	.40
C157	AP48	5c on 70c brn red	.40	.40
		Nos. C154-C157 (4)	1.60	1.60

Types of 1944-45

1946, Sept. 21 Engr.

C158	AP50	10c dp car	.20	.20
C159	AP40	20c emerald	.20	.20
C160	AP47	1g brown org	.30	.30
C161	AP52	5g purple	.90	.90
C162	AP51	10g rose car	2.50	2.50
		Nos. C158-C162 (5)	4.10	4.10

Marshal Francisco Solano Lopez Type

1947, May. 15 *Perf. 12*

C163	A114	32c car lake	.20	.20
C164	A114	64c orange brn	.20	.20
C165	A114	1g Prus green	.25	.25
C166	A114	5g Prus grn & brn vio	.75	.75
C167	A114	10g dk car rose & dk yel grn	1.25	1.25
		Nos. C163-C167 (5)	2.65	2.65

Archbishopric of Asunción Types

1948, Jan. 6 Unwmk. *Perf. 12½*

Size: 25½x31mm

C168	A116	20c gray blk	.20	.20
C169	A117	30c dark blue	.20	.20
C170	A118	40c lilac	.20	.20
C171	A115	70c orange red	.20	.20
C172	A112	1g brown red	.20	.20
C173	A118	2g red	.50	.50

Size: 25½x34mm

C174	A115	5g brt car & dk bl	.90	.90
C175	A116	10g dk grn & brn	1.25	1.25
		Nos. C168-C175 (8)	3.65	3.65

For surcharges see Nos. B11, C178.

Type of Regular Issue of 1948 Inscribed "AEREO"

1948, Sept. 11 Engr. & Litho.

C176	A119	69c dk grn, red & bl	.50	.50
C177	A119	5g dk bl, red & bl	2.00	1.75

The Barefeet, a political group.

No. C171 Surcharged in Black

1949, June 29

C178	A115	5c on 70c org red	.20	.20

Archbishop Juan Sinforiano Bogarin (1863-1949).

Symbols of UPU — AP65

Franklin D. Roosevelt — AP66

1950, Sept. 4 Engr. *Perf. 13½x13*

C179	AP65	20c green & violet	.20	.20
C180	AP65	30c rose vio & brn	.20	.20
C181	AP65	50c gray & green	.25	.20
C182	AP65	1g blue & brown	.35	.20
C183	AP65	5g rose & black	1.00	.55
		Nos. C179-C183 (5)	2.00	1.35

UPU, 75th anniv. (in 1949).

Engr.; Flags Litho.
1950, Oct. 2 *Perf. 12½*
Flags in Carmine & Violet Blue.

C184	AP66	20c red	.20	.20
C185	AP66	30c black	.20	.20
C186	AP66	50c claret	.20	.20
C187	AP66	1g dk gray grn	.20	.20
C188	AP66	5g deep blue	.40	.40
		Nos. C184-C188 (5)	1.20	1.20

Franklin D. Roosevelt (1882-1945).

Urn Containing Remains of Columbus AP67

1952, Feb. 11 Litho. *Perf. 10*

C189	AP67	10c ultra	.20	.20
C190	AP67	20c green	.20	.20
C191	AP67	30c lilac	.20	.20
C192	AP67	40c rose	.20	.20
C193	AP67	50c bister brn	.20	.20
C194	AP67	1g blue	.20	.20
C195	AP67	2g orange	.20	.20
C196	AP67	5g red brown	.30	.30
		Nos. C189-C196 (8)	1.70	1.70

Queen Isabella I — AP68

1952, Oct. 12

C197	AP68	1g vio blue	.20	.20
C198	AP68	2g chocolate	.20	.20
C199	AP68	5g dull green	.25	.25
C200	AP68	10g lilac rose	.55	.55
		Nos. C197-C200 (4)	1.20	1.20

500th birth anniv. of Queen Isabella I of Spain (in 1951).

Pettirossi Type

1954, Mar.

C201	A122	40c brown	.20	.20
C202	A122	55c green	.20	.20
C203	A122	80c ultra	.20	.20
C204	A122	1.30g gray blue	.25	.25
		Nos. C201-C204 (4)	.85	.85

Church of San Roque AP70

1954, June 20 Engr. *Perf. 12x13*

C205	AP70	20c carmine	.20	.20
C206	AP70	30c brown vio	.20	.20
C207	AP70	50c ultra	.20	.20
C208	AP70	1g red brn & bl grn	.20	.20
C209	AP70	1g red brn & lil rose	.20	.20
C210	AP70	1g red brn & blk	.20	.20
C211	AP70	1g red brn & org	.20	.20
a.		Min. sheet of 4, #C208-C211, perf. 12x12½	.30	.30
C212	AP70	5g dk red brn & vio	.20	.20
C213	AP70	5g dk red brn & ol grn	.20	.20
C214	AP70	5g dk red brn & org yel	.20	.20
C215	AP70	5g dk red brn & yel org	.20	.20
a.		Min. sheet of 4, #C212-C215, perf. 12x12½	.65	.65
		Nos. C205-C215 (11)	2.20	2.20

Centenary (in 1953) of the establishment of the Church of San Roque, Asuncion.
Nos. C211a and C215a issued without gum.

Heroes Type

Unwmk.
1954, Aug. 15 Litho. *Perf. 10*

C216	A123	5g violet	.20	.20
C217	A123	10g olive green	.25	.25
C218	A123	20g gray brown	.45	.40
C219	A123	50g vermilion	1.00	1.00
C220	A123	100g blue	3.25	3.25
		Nos. C216-C220 (5)	5.15	5.10

Peron Visit Type

Photo. & Litho.
1955, Apr. Wmk. 90 *Perf. 13x13½*
Frames & Flags in Blue & Carmine

C221	A124	60c ol grn & cream	.20	.20
C222	A124	2g bl grn & cream	.20	.20
C223	A124	3g brn org & cream	.20	.20
C224	A124	4.10g brt rose pink & cr	.20	.20
		Nos. C221-C224 (4)	.80	.80

Monsignor Rodriguez Type

Jesuit Ruins: 3g, Corridor at Trinidad. 6g, Tower of Santa Rosa. 10g, San Cosme gate. 20g, Church of Jesus. 30g, Niche at Trinidad. 50g, Sacristy at Trinidad.

Perf. 12½x12, 12x12½
1955, June 19 Engr. Unwmk.

C225	A125	2g aqua	.20	.20
C226	A125	3g olive grn	.20	.20
C227	A126	4g lt blue grn	.20	.20
C228	A126	6g brown	.20	.20
C229	A125	10g rose	.20	.20
C230	A125	20g brown ol	.20	.20
C231	A126	30g dk green	.30	.25
C232	A126	50g dp aqua	.35	.30
		Nos. C225-C232 (8)	1.85	1.75

For surcharges see Nos. C252-C259.

Soldier and Flags — AP75

"Republic" and Soldier — AP76

1957, June 12 Photo. *Perf. 13½*
Granite Paper
Flags in Red and Blue

C233	AP75	10c ultra	.20	.20
C234	AP75	15c dp claret	.20	.20
C235	AP75	20c red	.20	.20
C236	AP75	25c light blue	.20	.20
C237	AP75	50c bluish grn	.20	.20
C238	AP75	1g rose car	.20	.20
C239	AP76	1.30g dp claret	.20	.20
C240	AP76	1.50p light blue	.20	.20
C241	AP76	2g emerald	.20	.20
C242	AP76	4.10g red	.20	.20
C243	AP76	5g gray black	.20	.20
C244	AP76	10g bluish grn	.20	.20
C245	AP76	25g ultra	.25	.20
		Nos. C233-C245 (13)	2.65	2.60

Heroes of the Chaco war.

Stroessner Type of Regular Issue

1958, Aug. 16 Litho. Wmk. 320
Center in Slate

C246	A130	12g rose lilac	.25	.25
C247	A130	18g orange	.30	.30
C248	A130	23g orange brn	.50	.50
C249	A130	36g emerald	.50	.50
C250	A130	50g citron	.65	.65
C251	A130	65g gray	1.00	1.00
		Nos. C246-C251 (6)	3.20	3.20

Re-election of Pres. General Alfredo Stroessner.

Nos. C225-C232 Surcharged like #545-551 in Red

Perf. 12½x12, 12x12½
1959, May 26 Unwmk.

C252	A125	4g on 2g aqua	.20	.20
C253	A125	12.45g on 3g ol grn	.20	.20
C254	A126	18.15g on 6g brown	.25	.25
C255	A125	23.40g on 10g rose	.35	.30
C256	A125	34.80g on 20g brn ol	.50	.40
C257	A126	36g on 4g lt bl grn	.55	.40
C258	A126	43.95g on 30g dk grn	.65	.45
C259	A126	100g on 50g deep aqua	1.50	1.00
		Nos. C252-C259 (8)	4.20	3.20

The surcharge is made to fit the stamps. Counterfeits of surcharge exist.

UN Emblem AP77

Unwmk.
1959, Aug. 27 Typo. *Perf. 11*

C260	AP77	5g ocher & ultra	.50	.40

Visit of Dag Hammarskjold, Secretary General of the UN, Aug. 27-29.

Map and UN Emblem AP78

Uprooted Oak Emblem AP79

1959, Oct. 24 Litho. *Perf. 10*

C261	AP78	12.45g blue & salmon	.20	.20

United Nations Day, Oct. 24, 1959.

Olympic Games Type of Regular Issue

Design: Basketball.

1960, Mar. 18 Photo. *Perf. 12½*

C262 A131 12.45g red & dk bl .20 .20
C263 A131 18.15g lilac & gray ol .20 .20
C264 A131 36g bl grn & rose car .40 .40
Nos. C262-C264 (3) .80 .80

The Paraguayan Philatelic Agency reported as spurious the imperf. souvenir sheet reproducing one of No. C264.

1960, Apr. 7 Litho. *Perf. 11*

C265 AP79 4g green & pink .70 .40
C266 AP79 12.45g bl & yel grn 1.25 .65
C267 AP79 18.15g car & ocher 1.75 .75
C268 AP79 23.40g red org & bl 2.10 1.50
Nos. C265-C268 (4) 5.80 3.30

World Refugee Year, July 1, 1959-June 30, 1960 (1st issue).

Human Rights Type of Regular Issue, 1960

Designs: 40g, UN Emblem. 60g, Hands holding scales. 100g, Flame.

1960, Apr. 21 *Perf. 12½x13*

C269 A133 40g dk ultra & red .25 .25
C270 A133 60g grnsh bl & org .30 .30
C271 A133 100g dk ultra & red .65 .65
Nos. C269-C271 (3) 1.20 1.20

An imperf. miniature sheet exists, containing one each of Nos. C269-C271, all printed in green and vermilion.

UN Type of Regular Issue

Perf. 13x13½

1960, Oct. 24 Photo. Unwmk.

C272 A134 3g orange, red & bl .20 .20
C273 A134 4g pale grn, red & bl .20 .20

International Bridge, Paraguay-Brazil AP80

1961, Jan. 26 Litho. *Perf. 14*

C274 AP80 3g carmine .20 .20
C275 AP80 12.45g brown lake .20 .20
C276 AP80 18.15g Prus grn .20 .20
C277 AP80 36g dk blue .40 .40
a. Souv. sheet of 4, #C274-C277, imperf. .75 .75
Nos. C274-C277 (4) 1.00 1.00

Inauguration of the International Bridge between Paraguay and Brazil.

"Paraguay en Marcha" Type of 1961

12.45g, Truck carrying logs. 18.15g, Logs on river barge. 22g, Radio tower. 36g, Jet plane.

1961, Apr. 10 Photo. *Perf. 13*

C278 A136 12.45g yel & vio bl .25 .20
C279 A136 18.15g pur & ocher .30 .25
C280 A136 22g ultra & ocher .40 .30
C281 A136 36g brt grn & yel .40 .40
Nos. C278-C281 (4) 1.35 1.15

Declaration of Independence — AP81

1961, May 16 Litho. *Perf. 14½*

C282 AP81 12.45g dl red brn .20 .20
C283 AP81 18.15g dk blue .20 .20
C284 AP81 23.40g green .25 .25
C285 AP81 30g lilac .30 .30
C286 AP81 36g rose .40 .40
C287 AP81 44g olive .50 .45
Nos. C282-C287 (6) 1.85 1.80

150th anniv. of Independence (1st issue).

"Paraguay" and Clasped Hands — AP82

South American Tapir — AP83

1961, June 12 *Perf. 14x14½*

C288 AP82 3g vio blue .20 .20
C289 AP82 4g rose claret .20 .20
C290 AP82 100g gray green .90 .80
Nos. C288-C290 (3) 1.30 1.20

Chaco Peace; 150th anniv. of Independence (2nd issue).

1961, Aug. 16 Unwmk. *Perf. 14*

C291 AP83 12.45g claret .65 .50
C292 AP83 18.15g ultra .65 .65
C293 AP83 34.80g red brown 1.25 1.25
Nos. C291-C293 (3) 2.55 2.40

150th anniv. of Independence (3rd issue).

Catholic University Type of 1961

1961, Sept. 18 *Perf. 14x14½*

C294 A140 3g bister brn .20 .20
C295 A140 12.45g lilac rose .20 .20
C296 A140 36g blue .40 .40
Nos. C294-C296 (3) .80 .80

Hotel Guarani Type of 1961

Design: Hotel Guarani, different view.

1961, Oct. 14 Litho. *Perf. 15*

C297 A141 3g dull red brn .20 .20
C298 A141 4g ultra .20 .20
C299 A141 18.15g orange .25 .25
C300 A141 36g rose car .35 .35
Nos. C297-C300 (4) 1.00 1.00

Tennis Type

1961, Oct. 16 Unwmk. *Perf. 11*

C301 A142 12.45g multi .25
C302 A142 20g multi .45
C303 A142 50g multi 1.00
Nos. C301-C303 (3) 1.70

Some specialists question the status of this issue.

Two imperf. souvenir sheets exist containing four 12.45g stamps each in a different color with simulated perforations and black marginal inscription.

WRY Type

Design: Oak emblem rooted in ground, wavy-lined frame.

1961, Dec. 30

C307 A145 18.15g brn & red .20
C308 A145 36g car & emer .45
C309 A145 50g emer & org .65
Nos. C307-C309 (3) 1.30

Imperforates in changed colors and souvenir sheets exist. Some specialists question the status of this issue.

Pres. Alfredo Stroessner and Prince Philip AP84

1962, Mar. 9 Litho.

Portraits in Ultramarine

C310 AP84 12.45g grn & buff .20 .20
C311 AP84 18.15g red & pink .20 .20
C312 AP84 36g brn & yel .30 .30
Nos. C310-C312 (3) .70 .70

Visit of Prince Philip, Duke of Edinburgh. perf. and imperf. souvenir sheets exist.

Illustrations AP85-AP89, AP92-AP94, AP96-AP97, AP99-AP105, AP107-AP110, AP113-AP115, AP117, AP123, AP127a, AP132-AP133, AP136, AP138, AP140, AP142, AP144-AP145, AP149-AP150, AP152-AP153, AP156, AP158-AP159, AP165, AP167, AP171, AP180, AP183-AP184, AP187, AP196, AP202, AP205, AP208, AP211, AP221-AP222, AP224-AP225, AP229, AP234-AP235, AP237 and AP240 are reduced.

Souvenir Sheet

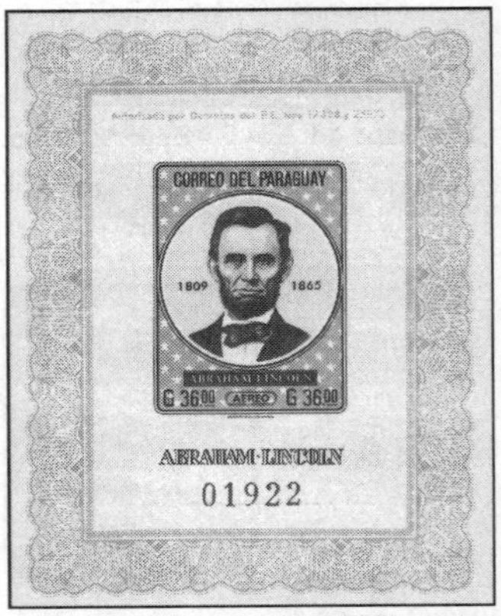

Abraham Lincoln (1809-1865), 16th President of US — AP85

1963, Aug. 21 Litho. *Imperf.*

C313 AP85 36g gray & vio brn

Limited Distribution Issues Beginning with No. C313, stamps with limited distribution are not valued.

Souvenir Sheet

1960 Summer Olympics, Rome — AP86

1963, Aug. 21 Litho. & Engr.

C314 AP86 50g lt bl, vio brn & sep

MUESTRA

Illustrations may show the word "MUESTRA." This means specimen and is not on the actual stamps.

Souvenir Sheet

Cattleya Cigas — AP87

1963, Aug. 21 Litho.

C315 AP87 66g multicolored

Souvenir Sheet

Pres. Alfredo Stroessner — AP88

1964, Nov. 3

C316 AP88 36g multicolored

Souvenir Sheet

Saturn V Rocket, Pres. John F. Kennedy — AP89

1968, Jan. 27 *Perf. 14*

C317 AP89 50g multicolored

Pres. Kennedy, 4th death anniv. (in 1967).

Torch, Book, Houses — AP90

1969, June 28 Wmk. 347 *Perf. 11*

C318 AP90 36g blue .50
C319 AP90 50g bister brn .65
C320 AP90 100g rose car 1.25
Nos. C318-C320 (3) 2.40

National drive for teachers' homes.

Souvenir Sheets

US Space Program — AP91

John F. Kennedy, Wernher von Braun, moon and: No. C321, Apollo 11 en route to moon. No. C322, Saturn V lift-off. No. C323, Apollo 9. No. C324, Apollo 10.

1969, July 9 *Perf. 14*

C321 AP91 23.40g multicolored
C322 AP91 23.40g multicolored

Imperf

C323 AP91 23.40g multicolored
C324 AP91 23.40g multicolored

Nos. C323-C324 each contain one 56x46mm stamp.

Souvenir Sheets

Events and Anniversaries — AP92

#C325, Apollo 14. #C326, Dwight D. Eisenhower, 1st death anniv. #C327, Napoleon Bonaparte, birth bicent. #C328, Brazil, winners of Jules Rimet World Cup Soccer Trophy.

1970, Dec. 16 *Perf. 13½*

C325 AP92 20g multicolored
C326 AP92 20g multicolored
C327 AP92 20g multicolored
C328 AP92 20g multicolored

Souvenir Sheets

Paraguayan Postage Stamps, Cent. — AP93

No. C329, Marshal Francisco Solano Lopez, Pres. Alfredo Stroessner, Paraguay #1. No. C330, #3, 1014, 1242. No. C331, #1243, C8, C74.

1971

C329 AP93 20g multicolored
C330 AP93 20g multicolored
C331 AP93 20g multicolored

Issued: #C329, 3/23; #C330-C331, 3/29.

Souvenir Sheets

Emblems of Apollo Space Missions — AP94

Designs: No. C332, Apollo 7, 8, 9, & 10. No. C333, Apollo 11, 12, 13, & 14.

1971, Mar. 26

C332 AP94 20g multicolored
C333 AP94 20g multicolored

Souvenir Sheet

Charles de Gaulle — AP95

1971, Dec. 24 *Perf. 14*

C334 AP95 20g multicolored

Souvenir Sheet

Taras Shevchenko (1814-1861), Ukrainian Poet — AP96

1971, Dec. 24 *Perf. 13½*

C335 AP96 20g multicolored

Souvenir Sheets

Johannes Kepler (1571-1630), German Astronomer — AP97

Kepler and: No. C336, Apollo lunar module over moon. No. C337, Astronaut walking in space.

1971, Dec. 24

C336 AP97 20g multicolored
C337 AP97 20g multicolored

Souvenir Sheet

10 years of US Space Program — AP98

1972, Jan. 61 *Perf. 13½*

C338 AP98 20g multicolored

Souvenir Sheet

Apollo 16 Moon Mission — AP99

1972, Mar. 29 Litho. *Perf. 13½*

C339 AP99 20g multicolored

Souvenir Sheets

History of the Olympics — AP100

Designs: No. C340, Pierre de Coubertin (1863-1937), founder of modern Olympics. No. C341, Skier, Garmisch-Partenkirchen, 1936. No. C342, Olympic flame, Sapporo, 1972. No. C343, French, Olympic flags. No. C344, Javelin thrower, Paris, 1924. No. C345, Equestrian event.

1972, Mar. 29 *Perf. 14½*

C340 AP100 20g multicolored
C341 AP100 20g multicolored
C342 AP100 20g multicolored
C343 AP100 20g multicolored
C344 AP100 20g multicolored
C345 AP100 20g multicolored

Souvenir Sheet

Medal Totals, 1972 Winter Olympics, Sapporo — AP101

1972, Nov. 18 *Perf. 13½*

C346 AP101 23.40g multicolored

Souvenir Sheets

French Contributions to Aviation and Space Exploration — AP102

Georges Pompidou, Charles de Gaulle and: No. C347, Concorde. No. C348, Satellite D2A, Mirage G 8 jets.

1972, Nov. 25

C347 AP102 23.40g multicolored
C348 AP102 23.40g multicolored

Souvenir Sheets

Summer Olympic Gold Medals, 1896-1972 — AP103

1972, Nov. 25

C349 AP103 23.40g 9 medals, 1896-1932, vert.
C350 AP103 23.40g 8 medals, 1936-1972

Souvenir Sheet

Adoration of the Shepherds by Murillo — AP104

1972, Nov. 25
C351 AP104 23.40g multicolored

Christmas.

Souvenir Sheet

Apollo 17 Moon Mission — AP105

1973, Mar. 13
C352 AP105 25g multicolored

Souvenir Sheet

Medal Totals, 1972 Summer Olympics, Munich — AP106

1973, Mar. 15 ***Perf. 13½***
C353 AP106 25g multicolored

Souvenir Sheets

The Holy Family by Peter Paul Rubens — AP107

Design: No. C355, In the Forest at Pierrefonds by Alfred de Dreux.

1973, Mar. 15
C354 AP107 25g multicolored
C355 AP107 25g multicolored

Souvenir Sheet

German Championship Soccer Team F.C. Bayern, Bavaria #2 — AP108

1973, June 29 ***Imperf.***
C356 AP108 25g multicolored

IBRA '73 Intl. Philatelic Exhibition, Munich,

Souvenir Sheet

Copernicus, 500th Birth Anniv. and Space Exploration — AP109

#C357, Lunar surface, Apollo 11. #C358, Copernicus, position of Earth at soltices and equinoxes, vert. #C359, Skylab space laboratory.

1973, June 29 ***Perf. 13½***
C357 AP109 25g multicolored
C358 AP109 25g multicolored
C359 AP109 25g multicolored

Souvenir Sheets

Exploration of Mars — AP110

1973, Oct. 8
C360 AP110 25g Mariner 9
C361 AP110 25g Viking probe, horiz.

Pres. Stroessner's Visit to Europe and Morocco — AP111

Designs: No. C362a, 5g, Arms of Paraguay, Spain, Canary Islands. b, 10g, Gen. Franco, Stroessner, vert. c, 25g, Arms of Paraguay, Germany. d, 50g, Stroessner, Giovanni Leone, Italy, vert. No. C363, Itaipu Dam between Paraguay and Brazil.

1973, Dec. 30 ***Perf. 14***
C362 AP111 Strip of 4, #a.-d.
C363 AP111 150g multicolored

Souvenir Sheet

Imperf

C364 AP111 100g Country flags

No. C364 contains one 60x50mm stamp.

1974 World Cup Soccer Championships, Munich — AP112

Abstract paintings of soccer players: No. C366a, 10g, Player seated on globe. b, 20g, Player as viewed from under foot. No. C367, Player kicking ball. No. C368, Goalie catching ball, horiz.

1974, Jan. 31 ***Perf. 14***
C365 AP112 5g shown
C366 AP112 Pair, #a.-b.

Souvenir Sheets

Perf. 13½

C367 AP112 25g multicolored
C368 AP112 25g multicolored

Nos. C367-C368 each contain one 50x60mm stamp.

Souvenir Sheets

Tourism Year — AP113

Design: No. C370, Painting, Birth of Christ by Louis le Nain (1593-1648), horiz.

1974, Feb. 4 ***Perf. 13½***
C369 AP113 25g multicolored
C370 AP113 25g multicolored

Christmas (No. C370).

Souvenir Sheets

Events and Anniversaries — AP114

1974, Mar. 20
C371 AP114 25g Rocket lift-off
C372 AP114 25g Solar system, horiz.
C373 AP114 25g Skylab 2 astronauts, horiz.
C374 AP114 25g Olympic Flame

UPU centennial (#C371-C372). 1976 Olympic Games (#C374).

President Stroessner Type of 1973

100g, Stroessner, Georges Pompidou. 200g, Stroessner and Pope Paul VI.

1974, Apr. 25 ***Perf. 14***
C375 AP111 100g multicolored

Souvenir Sheet

Perf. 13½

C376 AP111 200g multicolored

No. C376 contains one 60x50mm stamp.

Souvenir Sheet

Lufthansa Airlines Intercontinental Routes, 40th Anniv. — AP115

1974, July 13 ***Perf. 13½***
C377 AP115 15g multicolored

No. C377 face value was 15g plus 5g extra for a monument to Francisco Solano Lopez.

Souvenir Sheet

Hermann Oberth, 80th Anniv. of Birth — AP115a

1974, July 13 **Litho.** ***Perf. 13½***
C378 AP115a 15g multi

No. C378 face value was 15g plus 5g extra for a monument to Francisco Solano Lopez.

1974 World Cup Soccer Championships, West Germany — AP116

1974, July 13 ***Perf. 14***
C379 AP116 4g Goalie
C380 AP116 5g Soccer ball
C381 AP116 10g shown

Souvenir Sheet

Perf. 13½

C382 AP116 15g Soccer ball, diff.

No. C382 contains one 53x46mm stamp. No. C382 face value was 15g plus 5g extra for a monument for Francisco Solano Lopez.

Souvenir Sheet

First Balloon Flight over English Channel — AP117

1974, Sept. 13 ***Imperf.***
C383 AP117 15g multicolored

No. C383 face value was 15g plus 5g extra for a monument for Francisco Solano Lopez.

Anniversaries and Events — AP118

Designs: 4g, US #C76 on covers that went to Moon. No. C385a, 5g, Pres. Pinochet of Chile. No. C385b, 10g, Pres. Stroessner's visit to South Africa. No. C386, Mariner 10 over Mercury, horiz. No. C387, Paraguay permanent member of UPU. No. C388, UPU cent., Rousseau's "Zeppelins."

1974, Dec. 2 ***Perf. 14***
C384 AP118 4g multicolored
C385 AP118 Pair #a.-b.

Souvenir Sheets

Perf. 13½
C386 AP118 15g multicolored
C387 AP118 15g multicolored

Perf. 14½
C388 AP118 15g multicolored

Nos. C386-C387 contain one 60x50mm stamp, No. C388 one 50x35mm stamp. Face value was 15g plus 5g extra for a monument to Francisco Solano Lopez. Compare No. C386 with No. C392.

Anniversaries and Events — AP119

Designs: 4g, UPU, cent. 5g, 17th Congress, UPU, Lausanne. 10g, Intl. Philatelic Exposition, Montevideo, Uruguay. No. C392, Mariner 10 orbiting Mercury, horiz. No. C393, Figure skater, horiz. No. C394, Innsbruck Olympic emblem.

1974, Dec. 7 ***Perf. 14***
C389 AP119 4g multicolored
C390 AP119 5g multicolored
C391 AP119 10g multicolored

Souvenir Sheets

Perf. 13½
C392 AP119 15g bl & multi
C393 AP119 15g multicolored
C394 AP119 15g multicolored

UPU centennial (#C389). Nos. C392-C394 each contain one 60x50mm stamp and face value was 15g plus 5g extra for a monument to Francisco Solano Lopez.

German World Cup Soccer Champions — AP120

Design: No. C399, Hemispheres, emblems of 1974 and 1978 World Cup championships.

1974, Dec. 20 ***Perf. 14***
C395 AP120 4g Holding World Cup trophy, vert.
C396 AP120 5g Team on field
C397 AP120 10g Argentina '78 emblem, vert.

Souvenir Sheets

Perf. 13½
C398 AP120 15g Players holding trophy, vert.
C399 AP120 15g multicolored

No. C398 contains one 50x60mm stamp, and No. C399 contains one 60x50mm stamp. Face value of each sheet was 15g plus 5g extra for a monument to Francisco Solano Lopez.

Souvenir Sheet

Apollo-Soyuz — AP121

1974, Dec. 20 ***Perf. 13½***
C400 AP121 15g multicolored

Expo '75 — AP122

1975, Feb. 24 ***Perf. 14***
C401 AP122 4g Ryukyu-umurasaki, vert.
C402 AP122 5g Hibiscus
C403 AP122 10g Ancient sailing ship

Souvenir Sheet

Perf. 14½
C404 AP122 15g Expo emblem, vert.

No. C404 face value was 15g plus 5g extra for a monument to Francisco Solano Lopez.

Souvenir Sheets

Anniversaries and Events — AP123

Designs: No. C405, Dr. Kurt Debus, space scientist, 65th birth anniv. No. C406, 1976 Summer Olympics, Montreal, horiz.

1975, Feb. 24 ***Perf. 13½***
C405 AP123 15g multicolored
C406 AP123 15g multicolored

Nos. C405-C406 face value was 15g plus 5g extra for a monument to Francisco Solano Lopez.

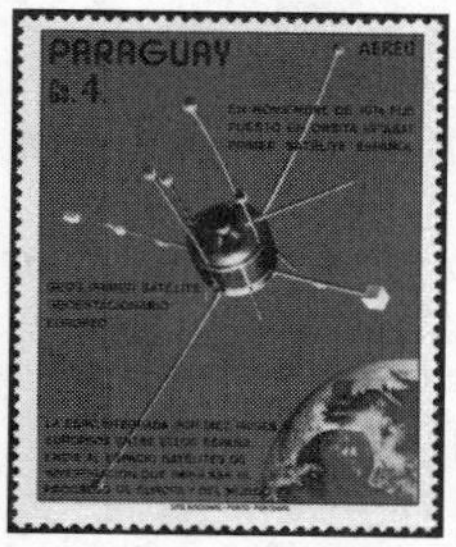

GEOS Satellite AP124

Designs: No. C408a, 5g, ESPANA 75. b, 10g, Mother and Child, Murillo.

1975, Aug. 21 ***Perf. 14***
C407 AP124 4g shown
C408 AP124 Pair, #1.-b.

Souvenir Sheet

Perf. 13½
C409 AP124 15g Spain #1139, 1838, C167, charity stamp
C410 AP124 15g Zeppelin, plane, satellites

Perf. 14½
C411 AP124 15g Jupiter

Nos. C409-C411 face value was 15g plus 5g extra for a monument to Francisco Solano Lopez.

Size of stamps: No. C409, 45x55mm; C410, 55x45mm; C411, 32x22mm.

Souvenir Sheets

Anniversaries and Events — AP125

#C413, UN emblem, Intl. Women's Year, vert. #C414, Helios space satellite.

1975, Aug. 26 ***Perf. 13½***
C413 AP125 15g multicolored
C414 AP125 15g multicolored

Nos. C413-C414 face value was 15g plus 5g extra for a monument to Francisco Solano Lopez.

Anniversaries and Events — AP125a

Designs: 4g, First Zeppelin flight, 75th anniv. 5g, Emblem of 1978 World Cup Soccer Championships, Argentina, vert. 10g, Emblem of Nordposta 75, statue.

1975, Oct. 13 **Litho.** ***Perf. 14***
C415-C417 AP125a Set of 3

Souvenir Sheets

Anniversaries and Events — AP126

No. C418, Zeppelin, boats. No. C419, Soccer, Intelsat IV, vert. No. C420, Viking Mars landing.

1975, Oct. 13 ***Perf. 13½***
C418 AP126 15g multicolored
C419 AP126 15g multicolored
C420 AP126 15g multicolored

Nos. C418-C420 face value was 15g plus 5g extra for a monument to Francisco Solano Lopez.

United States, Bicent. — AP127

#C421: a, 4g, Lunar rover. b, 5g, Ford Elite, 1975. c, 10g, Ford, 1896. No. C422, Airplanes and spacecraft. No. C423, Arms of Paraguay & US.

1975, Nov. 28 **Litho.** ***Perf. 14***
C421 AP127 Strip of 3, #a.-c.

Souvenir Sheets

Perf. 13½
C422 AP127 15g multicolored
C423 AP127 15g multicolored

Nos. C422-C423 each contain one 60x50mm stamp and face value was 15g plus 20g with 5g surtax for a monument to Francisco Solano Lopez.

Souvenir Sheet

La Musique by Francois Boucher — AP127a

1975, Nov. 28 ***Perf. 13½***

C424 AP127a 15g multicolored

No. C424 face value was 15g plus 5g extra for a monument to Francisco Solano Lopez.

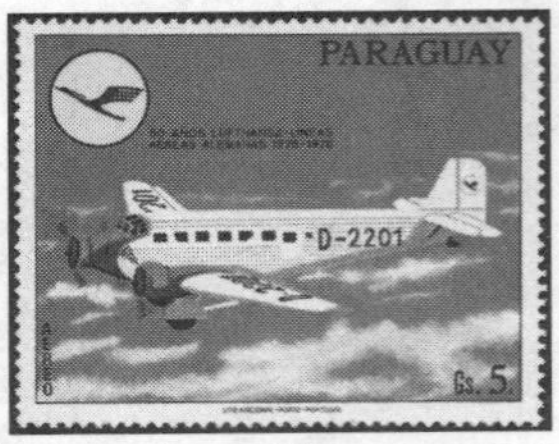

Anniversaries and Events — AP128

Designs: 4g, Flight of Concorde jet. 5g, JU 52/3M, Lufthansa Airlines, 50th anniv. 10g, EXFILMO '75 and ESPAMER '75. No. C428, Concorde, diff. No. C429, Dr. Albert Schweitzer, missionary and Konrad Adenauer, German statesman. No. C430, Ferdinand Porsche, auto designer, birth cent., vert.

1975, Dec. 20 ***Perf. 14***

C425 AP128 4g multicolored
C426 AP128 5g multicolored
C427 AP128 10g multicolored

Souvenir Sheets

Perf. 13½

C428 AP128 15g multicolored
C429 AP128 15g multicolored
C430 AP128 15g multicolored

Nos. C428-C430 face value was 15g plus 5g extra for a monument to Francisco Solano Lopez. No. C428 contains one 54x34mm stamp, No. C429 one 60x50mm stamp, No. C430 one 30x40mm stamp.

Anniversaries and Events — AP129

Details: 4g, The Transfiguration by Raphael, vert. 5g, Nativity by Del Mayno. 10g, Nativity by Vignon. No. C434, Detail from Adoration of the Shepherds by Ghirlandaio. No. C435, Austria, 1000th anniv., Leopold I, natl. arms, vert. No. C436, Sepp Herberger and Helmut Schon, coaches for German soccer team.

1976, Feb. 2 **Litho.** ***Perf. 14***

C431 AP129 4g multicolored
C432 AP129 5g multicolored
C433 AP129 10g multicolored

Souvenir Sheets

Perf. 13½

C434 AP129 15g multicolored
C435 AP129 15g multicolored

Perf. 13½x13

C436 AP129 15g multicolored

Nos. C434-C436 face value was 15g plus 5g extra for a monument to Francisco Solano Lopez. No. C434 contains one 40x30mm stamp, No. C435 one 30x40mm stamp, No. C436 one 54x34mm stamp.

Souvenir Sheet

Apollo-Soyuz — AP130

1976, Apr. 2 ***Perf. 13½x13***

C437 AP130 25g multicolored

Souvenir Sheet

Lufthansa, 50th Anniv. — AP131

1976, Apr. 7 ***Perf. 13½x13***

C438 AP131 25g multicolored

Souvenir Sheet

Interphil '76 — AP132

1976, May 12 ***Perf. 13½***

C439 AP132 15g multicolored

No. C439 face value was 15g plus 5g extra for a monument to Francisco Solano Lopez.

Souvenir Sheets

Anniversaries and Events — AP133

Designs: No. C440, Alexander Graham Bell, telephone cent. No. C441, Gold, silver, and bronze medals, 1976 Winter Olympics, Innsbruck. No. C442, Gold medalist Rosi Mittermaier, downhill and slalom, vert. No. C443, Viking probe on Mars. No. C444, UN Postal Administration, 25th anniv. and UPU, cent., vert. No. C445, Prof. Hermanm Oberth, Wernher von Braun. No. C446, Madonna and Child by Durer, vert.

1976 ***Perf. 13½***

C440 AP133 25g multicolored
C441 AP133 25g multicolored
C442 AP133 25g multicolored

Perf. 14½

C443 AP133 25g multicolored
C444 AP133 25g multicolored
C445 AP133 25g multicolored
C446 AP133 25g multicolored

No. C442 contains one 35x54mm stamp, No. C443 one 46x36mm stamp, No. C444 one 25x35mm stamp.

Issued: #C440-C441, 6/15; #C443, 7/8; #C442, C444, 7/15; #C445, 8/20; #C446, 9/9.

Souvenir Sheet

UN Offices in Geneva #22, UN #42 — AP136

1976, Dec. 18 ***Perf. 13½***

C447 AP136 25g multicolored

UN Postal Administration, 25th anniv. and telephone, cent.

Souvenir Sheet

Ludwig van Beethoven (1770-1827) — AP137

1977, Feb. 28 **Litho.** ***Perf. 14¼***

C448 AP137 25g multi

Souvenir Sheet

Alfred Nobel, 80th Death Anniv. and First Nobel Prize, 75th Anniv. — AP138

1977, June 7 ***Perf. 13½***

C449 AP138 25g multicolored

Souvenir Sheet

Coronation of Queen Elizabeth II, 25th Anniv. — AP139

1977, July 25 ***Perf. 14½***

C450 AP139 25g multicolored

Souvenir Sheet

Uruguay '77 Intl. Philatelic Exhibition — AP140

1977, Aug. 27 **Litho.** ***Perf. 13½***

C451 AP140 25g multicolored

Souvenir Sheets

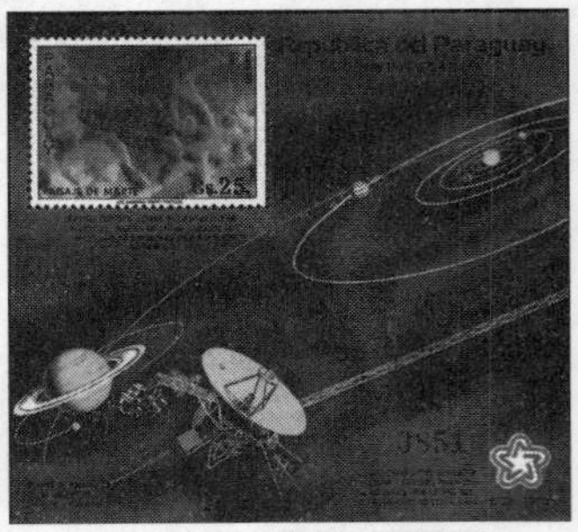

Exploration of Mars — AP141

1977, Sept. 5 ***Perf. 13½***

C452 AP141 25g Martian craters

Perf. 14¼x14½

1977, Nov. 28 **Litho.**

C453 AP141 25g Wernher von Braun

1977, Oct. 28 **Litho.** ***Perf. 13½***

C454 AP141 25g Projected Martian lander

Souvenir Sheet

Sepp Herberger, German Soccer Team Coach — AP142

1978, Jan. 23 Litho. *Perf. 13½*
C455 AP142 25g multicolored

Souvenir Sheet

Austria #B331, Canada #681, US #716, Russia #B66 — AP143

1978, Mar. 10 Litho. *Perf. 14½*
C456 AP143 25g multicolored

Inner perforations are simulated.

Souvenir Sheet

Alfred Nobel — AP144

1978, Mar. 15 Litho. *Perf. 13½*
C457 AP144 25g multicolored

Souvenir Sheets

Anniversaries and Events — AP145

Designs: No. C458, Queen Elizabeth II wearing St. Edward's Crown, holding orb and scepter. No. C459, Queen Elizabeth II presenting World Cup Trophy to English team captain. No. C460, Flags of nations participating in 1978 World Cup Soccer Championships. No. C461, Soccer action. No. C462, Argentina, 1978 World Cup Champions.

1978 *Perf. 14½, 13½ (#C461)*
C458 AP145 25g multicolored
C459 AP145 25g multicolored
C460 AP145 25g multicolored
C461 AP145 25g multicolored
C462 AP145 25g multicolored

Coronation of Queen Elizabeth II, 25th Anniv. (#C458-C459). 1978 World Cup Soccer Championships, Argentina (#C460-C462).

No. C460 contains one 70x50mm stamp, No. C461 one 39x57mm stamp.

Issued: #C458, 5/11; #C459-C460, 5/16; #C461, 6/30; #C462, 10/26.

Souvenir Sheet

Jean-Henri Dunant, 150th Birth Anniv. — AP146

1978, June 28 *Perf. 14½*
C463 AP146 25g multicolored

Souvenir Sheet

Capt. James Cook, 250th Birth Anniv. — AP147

1978, July 19 *Perf. 13½*
C464 AP147 25g multicolored

Discovery of Hawaii, Death of Capt. Cook, bicentennial; Hawaii Statehood, 20th anniv.

Souvenir Sheet

Adoration of the Magi by Albrecht Durer — AP149

1978, Oct. 31 *Perf. 13½*
C468 AP149 25g multicolored

Souvenir Sheet

Prof. Hermann Oberth, 85th Birth Anniv. — AP150

1979, Aug. 28 *Perf. 14½*
C469 AP150 25g multicolored

Souvenir Sheet

World Cup Soccer Championships — AP151

1979, Nov. 29
C470 AP151 25g multicolored

Souvenir Sheet

Helicopters — AP152

1979, Nov. 29 Litho. *Perf. 13½*
C471 AP152 25g multicolored

Souvenir Sheet

1980 Summer Olympics, Moscow — AP153

1979, Dec. 20 *Perf. 14½*
C472 AP153 25g Two-man canoe

Souvenir Sheet

1982 World Cup Soccer Championships, Spain — AP154

1979, Dec. 24 Litho. *Perf. 13x13½*
C473 AP154 25g Sheet of 1 + label

Souvenir Sheet

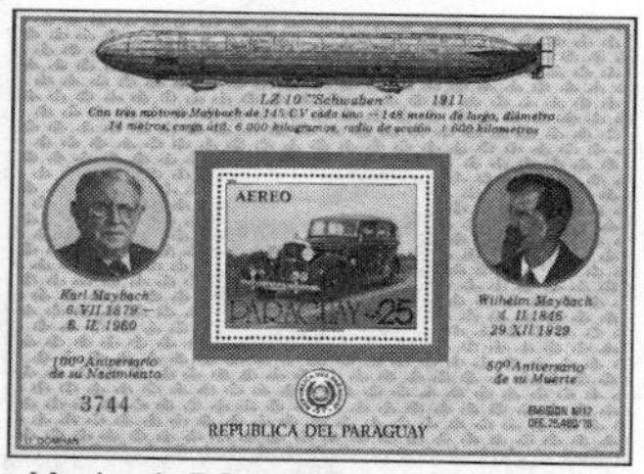

Maybach DS-8 "Zeppelin" — AP155

1980, Apr. 8 *Perf. 14½*
C474 AP155 25g multicolored

Wilhelm Maybach, 50th death anniv. Karl Maybach, 100th birth anniv.

Souvenir Sheet

Rotary Intl., 75th Anniv. — AP156

1980, July 1 Litho. *Perf. 14½*
C475 AP156 25g multicolored

Apollo 11 Type of 1970
Souvenir Sheet

Design: 1st steps on lunar surface.

1980, July 30 *Perf. 13½*
Size: 36x26mm
C476 A221 25g multicolored

Souvenir Sheet

Virgin Surrounded by Animals by Albrecht Durer — AP158

Photo. & Engr.
1980, Sept. 24 *Perf. 12*
C477 AP158 25g multicolored

Souvenir Sheet

1980 Olympic Games — AP159

1980, Dec. 15 Litho. *Perf. 14*
C478 AP159 25g multi

Metropolitan Seminary Centenary — AP160

1981, Mar. 26 Litho. Wmk. 347

C479	AP160	5g ultra	.20	.20
C480	AP160	10g red brn	.20	.20
C481	AP160	25g green	.20	.20
C482	AP160	50g gray	.40	.30
	Nos. C479-C482 (4)		1.00	.90

Anniversaries and Events — AP161

5g, George Washington, 250th birth anniv. (in 1982). 10g, Queen Mother Elizabeth, 80th birthday (in 1980). 30g, Phila Tokyo '81.

No. C486, Emperor Hirohito, 80th birthday. No. C487, Washington Crossing the Delaware.

1981, July 10 Unwmk. *Perf. 14*
C483 AP161 5g multicolored
C484 AP161 10g multicolored
C485 AP161 30g multicolored

Souvenir Sheets

Perf. 14½

C486 AP161 25g multicolored
C487 AP161 25g multicolored

No. C484 issued in sheets of 8 plus label. For overprints see Nos. 2126, C590-C591, C611.

First Space Shuttle Mission — AP162

Pres. Ronald Reagan and: 5g, Columbia in Earth orbit. 10g, Astronauts John Young and Robert Crippen. 30g, Columbia landing.

George Washington and: No. C491, Columbia re-entering atmosphere. No. C492, Columbia inverted above Earth.

1981, Oct. 9 *Perf. 14*
C488 AP162 5g multicolored
C489 AP162 10g multicolored
C490 AP162 30g multicolored

Souvenir Sheets

Perf. 13½

C491 AP162 25g multicolored
C492 AP162 25g multicolored

Nos. C491-C492 each contain one 60x50mm stamp. Inauguration of Pres. Reagan, George Washington, 250th birth anniv. (in 1982) (#C491-C492).

World Cup Soccer, Spain, 1982 AP163

1981, Oct. 15 *Perf. 14*

Color of Shirts

C493 AP163 5g yellow, green
C494 AP163 10g blue, white
C495 AP163 30g white & black, orange

Souvenir Sheet

Perf. 14½

C496 AP163 25g Goalie

No. C494 exists in sheets of 5 plus 4 labels.

Christmas AP164

Paintings: 5g, Virgin with the Child by Stefan Lochner. 10g, Our Lady of Caacupe. 25g, Altar of the Virgin by Albrecht Durer. 30g, Virgin and Child by Matthias Grunewald.

1981, Dec. 21 *Perf. 14*
C497 AP164 5g multicolored
C498 AP164 10g multicolored
C499 AP164 30g multicolored

Souvenir Sheet

Perf. 13½

C500 AP164 25g multicolored

No. C500 contains one 54x75mm stamp.

Souvenir Sheet

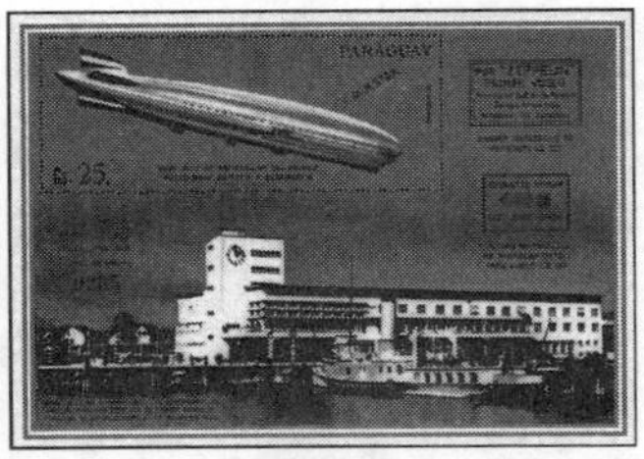

Graf Zeppelin's First Flight to South America, 50th Anniv. — AP165

1981, Dec. 28 *Perf. 14½*
C501 AP165 25g multicolored

Mother Maria Mazzarello (1837-1881), Co-Founder of Daughters of Mary AP166

Perf. 13x13½

1981, Dec. 30 Litho. Wmk. 347

C502	AP166	20g blk & grn	.20	.20
C503	AP166	25g blk & red brn	.20	.20
C504	AP166	50g blk & gray vio	.40	.30

Souvenir Sheet

The Magus (Dr. Faust) by Rembrandt — AP167

Litho. & Typo.

1982, Apr. 23 Unwmk. *Perf. 14½*
C505 AP167 25g blk, buff & gold

Johann Wolfgang von Goethe, 150th death anniv.

The following stamps were issued 4 each in sheets of 8 with 1 label: Nos. C590-C591, C669-C670, C677-C678, C682-C683, C690-C691, C699-C700, C718-C719, C747-C748.

The following stamps were issued in sheets of 4 with 5 labels: Nos. C765-C766, C774, C779-C780, C785, C803, C813, C818, C823.

The following stamps were issued in sheets of 3 with 6 labels: Nos. C739, C754.

The following stamps were issued in sheets of 5 with 4 labels: Nos. C507, C512, C515, C519, C524, C529, C535, C539, C542, C548, C550, C559, C569, C572, C579, C582, C585, C588, C596, C598, C615, C622, C626, C634, C642, C647, C650, C656, C705, C711, C731, C791, C798, C808.

The following stamp was issued in sheets of 7 with 2 labels: No. C660.

World Chess Championships Type of 1980

Illustrations from The Book of Chess: 5g, The Game of the Virgins. 10g, Two gothic ladies. 30g, Chess game at apothecary shop.

No. C509, Christians and Jews preparing to play in garden. No. C510, Indian prince introducing chess to Persia.

1982, June 10 Litho. *Perf. 14*
C506 A347 5g multicolored
C507 A347 10g multicolored
C508 A347 30g multicolored

Souvenir Sheets

Perf. 13½

C509 A347 25g multicolored

Perf. 14½

C510 A347 25g multicolored

No. C509 contains one 50x60mm stamp, No. C510 one 50x70mm stamp. For overprint see No. C665.

Italy, Winners of 1982 World Cup Soccer Championships — AP168

Players: 5g, Klaus Fischer, Germany. 10g, Altobelli holding World Cup Trophy. 25g, Forster, Altobelli, horiz. 30g, Fischer, Gordillo.

1982, Oct. 20 *Perf. 14*
C511 AP168 5g multicolored
C512 AP168 10g multicolored
C513 AP168 30g multicolored

Souvenir Sheet

C513A AP168 25g multicolored

Christmas — AP169

Paintings by Peter Paul Rubens: 5g, The Massacre of the Innocents. 10g, The Nativity, vert. 25g, The Madonna Adored by Four Penitents and Saints. 30g, The Flight to Egypt.

1982, Oct. 23
C514 AP169 5g multicolored
C515 AP169 10g multicolored
C516 AP169 30g multicolored

Souvenir Sheet

Perf. 14½

C517 AP169 25g multicolored

No. C517 contains one 50x70mm stamp.

The Sampling Officials of the Draper's Guild by Rembrandt — AP170

Details from Rembrandt Paintings: 10g, Self portrait, vert. 25g, Night Watch, vert. 30g, Self portrait, diff., vert.

1983, Jan. 21 *Perf. 14, 13 (10g)*
C518 AP170 5g multicolored
C519 AP170 10g multicolored
C520 AP170 30g multicolored

Souvenir Sheet

Perf. 13½

C521 AP170 25g multicolored

No. C521 contains one 50x60mm stamp.

Souvenir Sheet

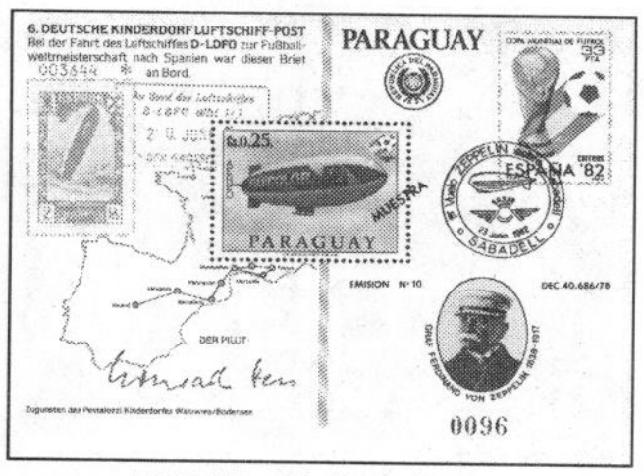

1982 World Cup Soccer Championships, Spain — AP171

1983, Jan. 21 ***Perf. 13½***

C522 AP171 25g Fuji blimp

German Rocket Scientists — AP172

Designs: 5g, Dr. Walter R. Dornberger, V2 rocket ascending. 10g, Nebel, Ritter, Oberth, Riedel, and Von Braun examining rocket mock-up. 30g, Dr. A. F. Staats, Cyrus B research rocket.

No. C526, Dr. Eugen Sanger, rocket design. No. C527, Fritz Von Opel, Opel-Sander rocket plane. No. C528, Friedrich Schmiedl, first rocket used for mail delivery.

1983 ***Perf. 14***

C523 AP172 5g multicolored
C524 AP172 10g multicolored
C525 AP172 30g multicolored

Souvenir Sheets

Perf. 14½

C526 AP172 25g multicolored
C527 AP172 25g multicolored
C528 AP172 25g multicolored

Issued: No. C528, Apr. 13; others, Jan. 24.

First Manned Flight, 200th Anniv. AP173

Balloons: 5g, Montgolfier brothers, 1783. 10g, Baron von Lutgendorf's, 1786. 30g, Adorne's, 1784.

No. C532, Montgolfier brothers, diff. No. C533, Profiles of Montgolfier Brothers. No. C534, Bicentennial emblem, nova.

1983 ***Perf. 14, 13 (10g)***

C529 AP173 5g multicolored
C530 AP173 10g multicolored
C531 AP173 30g multicolored

Souvenir Sheets

Perf. 13½

C532 AP173 25g multicolored
C533 AP173 25g multicolored
C534 AP173 25g multicolored

Nos. C532-C533 each contain one 50x60mm stamp, No. C534 one 30x40mm stamp.

Issued: #C529-C533, 2/25; #C534, 10/19.

1984 Summer Olympics, Los Angeles AP174

1932 Gold medalists: 5g, Wilson Charles, US, 100-meter dash. 10g, Ellen Preis, Austria, fencing. 25g, Rudolf Ismayr, Germany, weight lifting. 30g, John Anderson, US, discus.

1983, June 13 ***Perf. 14***

C535 AP174 5g multicolored
C536 AP174 10g multicolored
C537 AP174 30g multicolored

Souvenir Sheet

Perf. 14½

C538 AP174 25g Sheet of 1 + label

No. C535 incorrectly credits Charles with gold medal.

Flowers AP175

1983, Aug. 31 ***Perf. 14***

C539 AP175 5g Episcia reptans
C540 AP175 10g Lilium
C541 AP175 30g Heliconia

Intl. Maritime Organization, 25th Anniv. — AP176

5g, Brigantine Undine. 10g, Training ship Sofia, 1881, horiz. 30g, Training ship Stein, 1879.

No. C545, Santa Maria. No. C546, Santa Maria and Telstar communications satellite.

Perf. 14, 13½x13 (10g)

1983, Oct. 24 **Litho.**

C542 AP176 5g multicolored
C543 AP176 10g multicolored
C544 AP176 30g multicolored

Souvenir Sheets

Perf. 14½

C545 AP176 25g multicolored

Perf. 13½

C546 AP176 25g multicolored

No. C546 contains one 90x57mm stamp. Discovery of America, 490th Anniv. (in 1982) (#C545-C546). For overprint see No. 2198.

Space Achievements — AP177

Designs: 5g, Space shuttle Challenger. 10g, Pioneer 10, vert. 30g, Herschel's telescope, Cerro Tololo Obervatory, Chile, vert.

1984, Jan. 9 ***Perf. 14***

C547 AP177 5g multicolored
C548 AP177 10g multicolored
C549 AP177 30g multicolored

Summer Olympics, Los Angeles AP178

5g, 400-meter hurdles. 10g, Small bore rifle, horiz. 25g, Equestrian, Christine Stuckleberger. 30g, 100-meter dash.

1984, Jan. ***Perf. 14***

C550 AP178 5g multicolored
C551 AP178 10g multicolored
C552 AP178 30g multicolored

Souvenir Sheet

Perf. 14½

C553 AP178 25g multicolored

For overprint see No. 2130.

1984 Winter Olympics, Sarajevo AP179

Perf. 14, 13x13½ (10g)

1984, Mar. 24

C554 AP179 5g Steve Podborski, downhill
C555 AP179 10g Olympic Flag
C556 AP179 30g Gaetan Boucher, speed skating

No. C555 printed se-tenant with label.

Souvenir Sheets

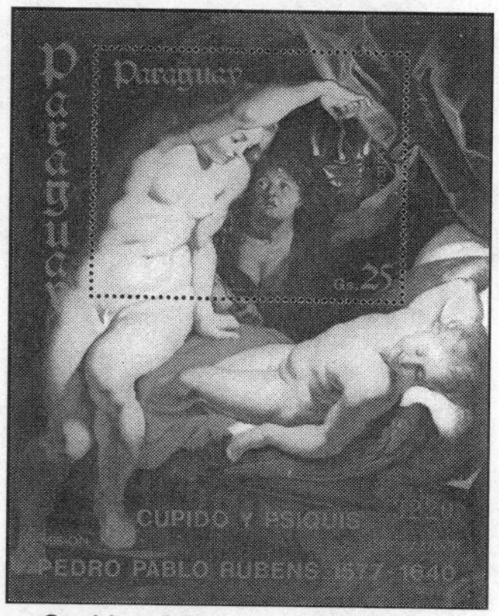

Cupid and Psyche by Peter Paul Rubens — AP180

Design: No. C558, Satyr and Maenad (copy of Rubens' Bacchanal) by Jean-Antoine Watteau (1684-1721).

1984, Mar. 26 ***Perf. 13½***

C557 AP180 25g multicolored
C558 AP180 25g multicolored

No. C558 contains one 78x57mm stamp.

1982, 1986 World Cup Soccer Championships, Spain, Mexico City — AP181

Soccer players: 5g, Tardelli, Breitner. 10g, Zamora, Stielke. 30g, Walter Schachner, player on ground.

No. C562, Player from Paraguay. No. C563, World Cup Trophy, Spanish, Mexican characters, horiz.

1984, Mar. 29 ***Perf. 14, 13 (10g)***

C559 AP181 5g multicolored
C560 AP181 10g multicolored
C561 AP181 30g multicolored

Souvenir Sheets

Perf. 14½

C562 AP181 25g multicolored
C563 AP181 25g multicolored

Souvenir Sheet

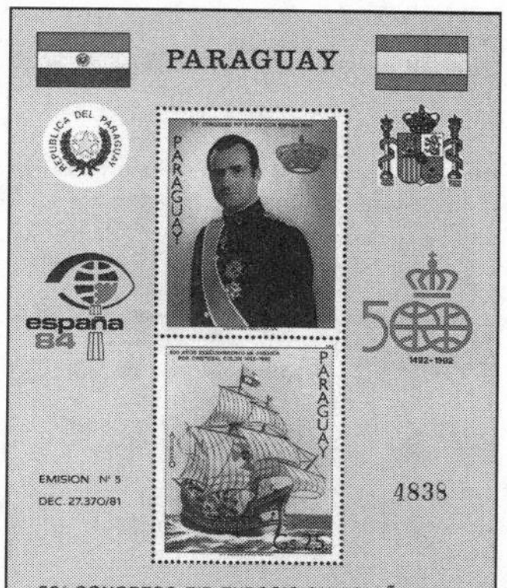

ESPANA '84 — AP182

1984, Mar. 31

C564 AP182 25g multicolored

No. C564 has one stamp and a label.

Souvenir Sheets

ESPANA '84 — AP183

No. C565, Holy Family of the Lamb by Raphael. No. C566, Adoration of the Magi by Rubens.

1984, Apr. 16 *Perf. 13½*

C565 AP183 25g multicolored
C566 AP183 25g multicolored

Souvenir Sheet

19th UPU Congress — AP184

1984, June 9

C567 AP184 25g multicolored

Intl. Chess Federation, 60th Anniv. AP185

Perf. 14, 13x13½ (10g)

1984, June 18

C568 AP185 5g shown
C569 AP185 10g Woman holding chess piece
C570 AP185 30g Bishop, knight

First Europe to South America Airmail Flight by Lufthansa, 50th Anniv. — AP186

Designs: 5g, Lockheed Superconstellation. 10g, Dornier Wal. 30g, Boeing 707.

Perf. 14, 13½x13 (10g)

1984, June 22

C571 AP186 5g multicolored
C572 AP186 10g multicolored
C573 AP186 30g multicolored

For overprint see No. C592.

Souvenir Sheets

First Moon Landing, 15th Anniv. — AP187

1984, June 23 *Perf. 14½*

C574 AP187 25g Apollo 11 lunar module
C575 AP187 25g Prof. Hermann Oberth

Hermann Oberth, 90th Birthday (#C575).

Souvenir Sheet

The Holy Family with John the Baptist — AP188

Photo. & Engr.

1984, Aug. 3 *Perf. 14*

C576 AP188 20g multicolored

Raphael, 500th birth anniv. (in 1983).

No. 2099 Overprinted in Red: ANIVERSARIO GOBIERNO CONSTRUCTIVO Y DE LA PAZ DEL PRESIDENTE CONSTITUCIONAL GRAL. DE EJERCITO ALFREDO STROESSNER 15 / 8 / 1964

1984, Aug. 15 *Perf. 13*

C577 A374 100g on No. 2099

1984 Winter Olympics, Sarajevo — AP189

Gold medalists: 5g, Max Julen, giant slalom, Switzerland. 10g, Hans Stanggassinger, Franz Wembacher, luge, West Germany. 30g, Peter Angerer, biathlon, Germany.

Perf. 14, 13½x13 (10g)

1984, Sept. 12

C578 AP189 5g multicolored
C579 AP189 10g multicolored
C580 AP189 30g multicolored

For overprint see No. C596.

Motorcycles, Cent. — AP190

1984, Nov. 9 *Perf. 14, 13½x13 (10g)*

C581 AP190 5g Reitwagen, Daimler-Maybach, 1885
C582 AP190 10g BMW, 1980
C583 AP190 30g Opel, 1930

Christmas AP191

1985, Jan. 18 *Perf. 13*

C584 AP191 5g shown
C585 AP191 10g Girl playing guitar
C586 AP191 30g Girl, candle, basket

1986 World Cup Soccer Championships, Mexico — AP192

Various soccer players.

1985, Jan. 21 *Perf. 13x13½, 13½x13*

Color of Shirt

C587 AP192 5g red & white
C588 AP192 10g white & black, horiz.
C589 AP192 30g blue

No. C484 Ovptd. in Silver

1985, Feb. 6 *Perf. 14*

C590 AP161 10g INTERPEX / 1985
C591 AP161 10g STAMPEX / 1985

No. C572 Ovptd. in Vermilion

STUTTGART 85

FISA

1985, Feb. 16 *Perf. 13½x13*

C592 AP186 10g on No. C572

No. 2053A Ovptd. "FINAL / ALEMANIA 1 : 3 ITALIA"

1985, Mar. 7 *Perf. 14½*

C593 A362 25g multicolored

Souvenir Sheets

Rotary Intl., 80th Anniv. — AP193

Designs: No. C594, Paul Harris, founder of Rotary Intl. No. C595, Rotary Intl. Headquarters, Evanston, IL, horiz.

1985, Mar. 11

C594 AP193 25g multicolored
C595 AP193 25g multicolored

No. C579 Ovptd. "OLYMPHILEX 85" in Black and Olympic Rings in Silver

1985, Mar. 18 *Perf. 13½x13*

C596 AP189 10g on No. C579

Music Year — AP194

Designs: 5g, Agustin Barrios (1885-1944), musician, vert. 10g, Johann Sebastian Bach, composer, score. 30g, Folk musicians.

Perf. 14, 13½x13 (10g)

1985, Apr. 16

C597 AP194 5g multicolored
C598 AP194 10g multicolored
C599 AP194 30g multicolored

1st Paraguayan Locomotive, 1861 — AP195

1985, Apr. 20 *Perf. 14*

C600 AP195 5g shown
C601 AP195 10g Transrapid 06, Germany
C602 AP195 30g TGV, France

Souvenir Sheet

Visit of Pope John Paul II to South America — AP196

1985, Apr. 22 **Litho.** ***Perf. 13½***
C603 AP196 25g silver & multi

No. C603 also exists with gold inscriptions.

Inter-American Development Bank, 25th Anniv. — AP197

1985, Apr. 25 **Litho.** **Wmk. 347**

C604	AP197	3g dl red brn, org & yel	.20	.20
C605	AP197	5g vio, org & yel	.20	.20
C606	AP197	10g rose vio, org & yel	.20	.20
C607	AP197	50g sep, org & yel	.20	.20
C608	AP197	65g bl, org & yel	.20	.20
C609	AP197	95g pale bl grn, org & yel	.20	.20
		Nos. C604-C609 (6)	1.20	1.20

No. 1875 Ovptd. in Black in Margin "V EXPOSICION MUNDIAL / ARGENTINA 85" and

1985, May 24 **Unwmk.** ***Perf. 13½***
C610 A326 25g on No. 1875

No. C485 Ovptd. in Dark Blue with Emblem and: "Expo '85/TSUKUBA"

1985, July 5 ***Perf. 14***
C611 AP161 30g on No. C485

No. 2149 Ovptd. in Dark Blue in Margin with UN emblem and "26.6.1985 - 40-ANIVERSARIO DE LA / FUNDACION DE LAS NACIONES UNIDAS"

1985, Aug. 5 ***Perf. 14½***
C612 A388 25g on No. 2149

Jean-Henri Dunant, Founder of Red Cross, 75th Death Anniv. — AP198

Dunant and: 5g, Enclosed ambulance. 10g, Nobel Peace Prize, Red Cross emblem. 30g, Open ambulance with passengers.

1985, Aug. 6 ***Perf. 13***
C614 AP198 5g multicolored
C615 AP198 10g multicolored
C616 AP198 30g multicolored

World Chess Congress, Austria — AP199

5g, The Turk, copper engraving, Book of Chess by Racknitz, 1789. 10g, King seated, playing chess, Book of Chess, 14th cent. 25g, Margrave Otto von Brandenburg playing chess with his wife, Great Manuscript of Heidelberg Songs, 13th cent. 30g, Three men playing chess, Book of Chess, 14th cent.

1985, Aug. 9 **Litho.** ***Perf. 13***
C617 AP199 5g multicolored
C618 AP199 10g multicolored
C619 AP199 30g multicolored

Souvenir Sheet

Perf. 13½

C620 AP199 25g multicolored

No. C620 contains one 60x50mm stamp.

Discovery of America 500th Anniv. AP200

Explorers, ships: 5g, Marco Polo and ship. 10g, Vicente Yanez Pinzon, Nina, horiz. 25g, Christopher Columbus, Santa Maria. 30g, James Cook, Endeavor.

Perf. 14, 13½x13 (10g)

1985, Oct. 19 **Litho.**
C621 AP200 5g multicolored
C622 AP200 10g multicolored
C623 AP200 30g multicolored

Souvenir Sheet

Perf. 14½

C624 AP200 25g multicolored

Year of Cook's death is incorrect on No. C623. For overprint see No. C756.

ITALIA '85 — AP201

Nudes (details): 5g, La Fortuna, by Guido Reni, vert. 10g, The Triumph of Galatea, by Raphael. 25g, The Birth of Venus, by Botticelli, vert. 30g, Sleeping Venus, by Il Giorgione.

1985, Dec. 3 ***Perf. 14***
C625 AP201 5g multicolored
C626 AP201 10g multicolored
C627 AP201 30g multicolored

Souvenir Sheet

Perf. 13½

C628 AP201 25g multicolored

No. C628 contains one 49x60mm stamp.

Souvenir Sheet

Maimonides, Philosopher, 850th Birth Anniv. — AP202

1985, Dec. 31 ***Perf. 13½***
C629 AP202 25g multicolored

UN, 40th Anniv. AP203

1986, Feb. 27 **Wmk. 392**

C630	AP203	5g bl & sepia	.20	.20
C631	AP203	10g bl & gray	.20	.20
C632	AP203	50g bl & grysh brn	.20	.20
		Nos. C630-C632 (3)	.60	.60

For overprint see No. C726.

AMERIPEX '86 AP204

Discovery of America 500th anniv. emblem and: 5g, Spain #424. 10g, US #233. 25g, Spain #426, horiz. 30g, Spain #421.

Perf. 14, 13½x13 (10g)

1986, Mar. 19 **Unwmk.**
C633 AP204 5g multicolored
C634 AP204 10g multicolored
C635 AP204 30g multicolored

Souvenir Sheet

Perf. 13½

C636 AP204 25g multicolored

No. C636 contains one 60x40mm stamp. For overprint see No. C755.

Souvenir Sheet

1984 Olympic Gold Medalist, Dr. Reiner Klimke on Ahlerich — AP205

1986, Mar. 20 ***Perf. 14½***
C637 AP205 25g multicolored

Tennis Players AP206

Designs: 5g, Martina Navratilova, US. 10g, Boris Becker, W. Germany. 30g, Victor Pecci, Paraguay.

1986, Mar. 26 ***Perf. 14, 13 (10g)***
C638 AP206 5g multicolored
C639 AP206 10g multicolored
C640 AP206 30g multicolored

Nos. C638-C640 exist with red inscriptions, perf. 13. For overprints see Nos. C672-C673.

Halley's Comet — AP207

5g, Bayeux Tapestry, c. 1066, showing comet. 10g, Edmond Halley, comet. 25g, Comet, Giotto probe. 30g, Rocket lifting off, Giotto probe, vert.

Perf. 14, 13½x13 (10g)

1986, Apr. 30
C641 AP207 5g multicolored
C642 AP207 10g multicolored
C643 AP207 30g multicolored

Souvenir Sheet

Perf. 14½

C644 AP207 25g multicolored

Souvenir Sheet

Madonna by Albrecht Durer — AP208

1986, June 4 Typo. ***Rough Perf. 11***
Self-Adhesive

C645 AP208 25g black & red

No. C645 was printed on cedar.

Locomotives — AP209

1986, June 23 Litho. ***Perf. 13***

C646 AP209 5g #3038
C647 AP209 10g Canadian Pacific A1E, 1887
C648 AP209 30g 1D1 #483, 1925

1986 World Cup Soccer Championships — AP210

Paraguay vs.: 5g, Colombia. 10g, Chile. 30g, Chile, diff.
25g, Paraguay Natl. team.

Perf. 13, 13½x13 (10g)

1986, June 24

C649 AP210 5g multicolored
C650 AP210 10g multicolored
C651 AP210 30g multicolored

Souvenir Sheet
Perf. 14½

C652 AP210 25g multicolored

No. C652 contains one 81x75mm stamp. For overprints see Nos. C693-C695.

No. 1289 Ovptd. in Silver on Dark Blue with Mercury Capsule and "MERCURY / 5-V-1961 / 25 Anos Primer / Astronauta / Americano / Alan B. Shepard / 1986"

1986, July 11 ***Perf. 13½***

C653 A226 23.40g on No. 1289

Souvenir Sheet

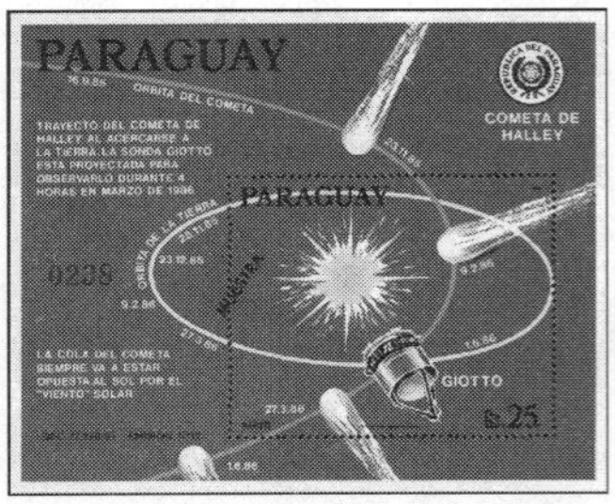

Trajectory Diagram of Halley's Comet, Giotto Probe — AP211

1986, July 28

C654 AP211 25g multicolored

German Railroads, 150th Anniv. — AP212

25g, Christening of the 1st German Train, 1835, by E. Shilling & B. Goldschmidt.

1986, Sept. 1 ***Perf. 13½x13***

C655 AP212 5g VT 10 501DB, 1954
C656 AP212 10g 1st Electric, 1879
C657 AP212 30g Hydraulic diesel, class 218

Souvenir Sheet
Perf. 13½

C658 AP212 25g multicolored

No. C658 contains one 54x75mm stamp.

Intl. Peace Year AP213

Details from The Consequences of War by Rubens: 5g, Two women. 10g, Woman nursing child. 30g, Two men.

1986, Oct. 27 ***Perf. 13***

C659 AP213 5g multicolored
C660 AP213 10g multicolored
C661 AP213 30g multicolored

Japanese Emigrants in Paraguay, 50th Anniv. — AP214

1986, Nov. 6 ***Perf. 13½x13, 13x13½***

C662	AP214	5g	La Colemna Vineyard	.20	.20
C663	AP214	10g	Cherry, lapacho flowers	.20	.20
C664	AP214	20g	Integration monument, vert.	.20	.20
	Nos. C662-C664 (3)			.60	.60

No. C507 Ovptd. in Silver "XXVII-DUBAI / Olimpiada de / Ajedrez - 1986"

1986, Dec. 30 Unwmk. ***Perf. 14***

C665 A347 10g on No. C507

1986 World Cup Soccer Championships, Mexico — AP214a

Match scenes.

1987, Feb. 19 ***Perf. 14***

C666 AP214a 5g England vs. Paraguay
C667 AP214a 10g Larios catching ball
C668 AP214a 20g Trejo, Ferreira

Perf. 13½x13

C669 AP214a 25g Torales, Flores, Romero
C670 AP214a 30g Mendonza

Souvenir Sheet
Perf. 14½

C671 AP214a 100g Romero

Nos. C669-C670 are horiz. No. C671 contains one 40x50mm stamp.

Nos. C639-C640 Ovptd. in Silver including Olympic Rings and "NUEVAMENTE EL / TENIS EN LAS / OLYMPIADAS 1988 / SEOUL COREA"

1987, Apr. 15 ***Perf. 13***

C672 AP206 10g on No. C639
C673 AP206 30g on No. C640

Automobiles — AP215

1987, May 29 Litho. ***Perf. 13½***

C674 AP215 5g Mercedes 300 SEL 6.3
C675 AP215 10g Jaguar Mk II 3.8
C676 AP215 20g BMW 635 CSI
C677 AP215 25g Alfa Romeo GTA
C678 AP215 30g BMW 1800 Tisa

1988 Winter Olympics, Calgary — AP216

Gold medalists or Olympic competitors: 5g, Michela Figini, Switzerland, downhill, 1984, vert. 10g, Hanni Wenzel, Liechtenstein, slalom and giant slalom, 1980. 20g, 4-Man bobsled, Switzerland, 1956, 1972. 25g, Markus Wasmeier, downhill. 30g, Ingemar Stenmark, Sweden, slalom and giant slalom, 1980. 100g, Pirmin Zurbriggen, Switzerland, vert. (downhill, 1988).

1987, Sept. 10 ***Perf. 14***

C679 AP216 5g multicolored
C680 AP216 10g multicolored
C681 AP216 20g multicolored

Perf. 13½x13

C682 AP216 25g multicolored
C683 AP216 30g multicolored

Souvenir Sheet
Perf. 13½

C684 AP216 100g multicolored

No. C684 contains one 45x57mm stamp.

Nos. 2211 and C467 Ovptd. in Red on Silver "11.IX.1887 - 1987 / Centenario de la fundacion de / la A.N.R. (Partido Colarado) / Bernardino Caballero Fundador / General de Ejercito / D. Alfredo Stroessner Continuador"

1987, Sept. 11 ***Perf. 13, 14***

C685 A401 200g on No. 2211
C686 AP148 1000g on No. C467

1988 Summer Olympics, Seoul — AP217

Medalists and competitors: 5g, Sabine Everts, West Germany, javelin. 10g, Carl Lewis, US, 100 and 200-meter run, 1984. 20g, Darrell Pace, US, archery, 1976, 1984. 25g, Juergen Hingsen, West Germany, decathalon, 1984. 30g, Claudia Losch, West Germany, shot put, 1984. 100g, Fredy Schmidtke, West Germany, cycling, 1984.

1987, Sept. 22 ***Perf. 14***

C687 AP217 5g multi
C688 AP217 10g multi, vert.
C689 AP217 20g multi

Perf. 13½x13

C690 AP217 25g multi, vert.
C691 AP217 30g multi, vert.

Souvenir Sheet
Perf. 14½

C692 AP217 100g multi, vert.

Nos. C650-C652 Ovptd. in Violet or Blue (#C694) with Soccer Ball and "ZURICH 10.VI.87 / Lanzamiento ITALIA '90 / Italia 3 - Argentina 1"

Perf. 13½x13, 13

1987, Oct. 19 Litho.

C693 AP210 10g on No. C650
C694 AP210 30g on No. C651

Souvenir Sheet
Perf. 14½

C695 AP210 25g on No. C652

Paintings by Rubens AP218

Details from: 5g, The Virtuous Hero Crowned. 10g, The Brazen Serpent, 1635. 20g, Judith with the Head of Holofernes, 1617. 25g, Assembly of the Gods of Olympus. 30g, Venus, Cupid, Bacchus and Ceres.

1987, Dec. 14 ***Perf. 13***

C696 AP218 5g multicolored
C697 AP218 10g multicolored
C698 AP218 20g multicolored

Perf. 13x13½

C699 AP218 25g multicolored
C700 AP218 30g multicolored

Christmas
AP219

Details from paintings: 5g, Virgin and Child with St. Joseph and St. John the Baptist, anonymous. 10g, Madonna and Child under the Veil with St. Joseph and St. John, by Marco da Siena. 20g, Sacred Conversation with the Donors, by Titian. 25g, The Brotherhood of the Rosary, by Durer. 30g, Madonna with Standing Child, by Rubens. 100g, Madonna and Child, engraving by Albrecht Durer.

1987 **Litho.** ***Perf. 14***
C701 AP219 5g multicolored
C702 AP219 10g multicolored
C703 AP219 20g multicolored
C704 AP219 25g multicolored

Perf. 13x13½
C705 AP219 30g multicolored

Souvenir Sheet
Perf. 14½
C706 AP219 100g multi

Issued: #C701-C705, 12/16; #C706, 12/17.

Austrian Railways,
Sesquicentennial — AP220

Locomotives: 5g, Steam #3669, 1899. 10g, Steam #GZ 44074. 20g, Steam, diff. 25g, Diesel-electric. 30g, Austria No. 1067. 100g, Steam, vert.

1988, Jan. 2 ***Perf. 14***
C707 AP220 5g multicolored
C708 AP220 10g multicolored
C709 AP220 20g multicolored
C710 AP220 25g multicolored

Perf. 13½x13
C711 AP220 30g multicolored

Souvenir Sheet
Perf. 13½
C712 AP220 100g multicolored

No. C712 contains one 50x60mm stamp.

Souvenir Sheet

Christmas — AP221

1988, Jan. 4 ***Perf. 13½***
C713 AP221 100g Madonna, by Rubens

Souvenir Sheet

1988 Summer Olympics,
Seoul — AP222

1988, Jan. 18 ***Perf. 14½***
C714 AP222 100g gold & multi

Exists with silver lettering and frame.

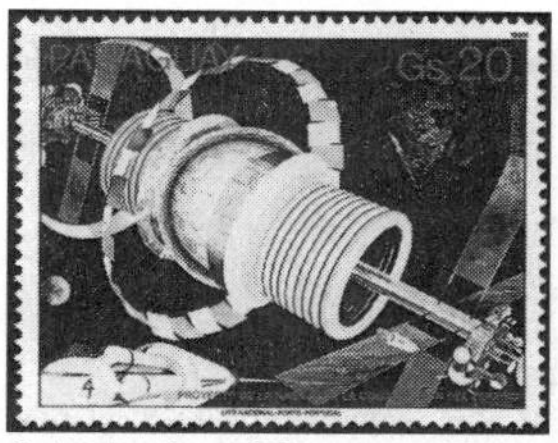

Colonization of Space — AP223

5g, NASA-ESA space station. 10g, Eurospace module Columbus docked at space station. 20g, NASA space sation. 25g, Ring section of space station, vert. 30g, Space station living quarters in central core, vert.

1988, Mar. 9 **Litho.** ***Perf. 13½x13***
C715 AP223 5g multicolored
C716 AP223 10g multicolored
C717 AP223 20g multicolored

Perf. 13x13½
C718 AP223 25g multicolored
C719 AP223 30g multicolored

Souvenir Sheet

Berlin, 750th Anniv. — AP224

1988, Mar. 10 **Litho.** ***Perf. 14½***
C720 AP224 100g multicolored

LUPOSTA '87.

Souvenir Sheet

Apollo 15 Launch, 1971 — AP225

1988, Apr. 12
C721 AP225 100g multicolored

No. 2210 Ovptd. in Metallic Red with

1988, Apr. 28 ***Perf. 13***
C722 A401 100g on No. 2210

Caacupe Basilica and Pope John Paul II — AP226

Perf. 13½x13
1988, May 5 **Litho.** **Wmk. 347**
C723 AP226 100g multi .45 .35
C724 AP226 120g multi .55 .40
C725 AP226 150g multi .70 .50
Nos. C723-C725 (3) 1.70 1.25

Visit of Pope John Paul II.

No. C631 Overprinted

Perf. 13x13½
1988, June 15 **Wmk. 392**
C726 AP203 10g blue & gray .20 .20

Paraguay Philatelic Center, 75th Anniv.

Berlin, 750th Anniv. Paintings Type of 1988

5g, Venus and Cupid, 1742, by Francois Boucher. 10g, Perseus Liberates Andromeda, 1662, by Rubens. 20g, Venus and the Organist by Titian. 25g, Leda and the Swan by Correggio. 30g, St. Cecilia by Rubens.

1988, June 15 **Unwmk.** ***Perf. 13***
C727 A409 5g multi, horiz.
C728 A409 10g multi, horiz.
C729 A409 20g multi, horiz.
C730 A409 25g multi, horiz.

Perf. 13x13½
C731 A409 30g multicolored

Founding of "New Germany" and 1st Cultivation of Herbal Tea, Cent. — AP227

Perf. 13x13½, 13½x13
1988, June 18 **Litho.** **Wmk. 347**
C732 AP227 90g Cauldron, vert. .40 .30
C733 AP227 105g Farm workers carrying crop .50 .35
C734 AP227 120g like 105g .55 .45
Nos. C732-C734 (3) 1.45 1.10

1990 World Cup Soccer Championships, Italy — AP228

5g, Machine slogan cancel from Montevideo, May 21, 1930. 10g, Italy #324, vert. 20g, France #349. 25g, Brazil #696, vert. 30g, Paraguayan commemorative cancel for ITALIA 1990.

1988, Aug. 1 **Unwmk.** ***Perf. 13***
C735 AP228 5g multicolored
C736 AP228 10g multicolored
C737 AP228 20g multicolored
C738 AP228 25g multicolored

Perf. 13½x13
C739 AP228 30g multicolored

For overprint see No. 2284.

Souvenir Sheet

Count Ferdinand von Zeppelin, Airship Designer, Birth Sesquicentennial — AP229

1988, Aug. 3 ***Perf. 14½***
C740 AP229 100g multicolored

Government Palace and Pres. Stroessner — AP230

Wmk. 347
1988, Aug. 5 **Litho.** ***Perf. 13½***
C741 AP230 200g multi .40 .30
C742 AP230 500g multi 1.00 1.00
C743 AP230 1000g multi 2.00 2.00
Nos. C741-C743 (3) 3.40 3.30

Pres. Stroessner's new term in office, 1988-1993. Size of letters in watermark on 200g, 1000g: 5mm. On 500g, 10mm.

1988 Winter Olympics, Calgary — AP231

Gold medalists: 5g, Hubert Strolz, Austria, Alpine combined. 10g, Alberto Tomba, Italy, giant slalom and slalom. 20g, Franck Piccard, France, super giant slalom. 25g, Thomas Muller, Hans-Peter Pohl and Hubert Schwarz, Federal Republic of Germany, Nordic combined team, vert. 30g, Vreni Schneider, Switzerland, giant slalom and slalom, vert. 100g, Marina Kiehl, Federal Republic of Germany, downhill, vert.

Perf. 13½x13

1988, Sept. 2 **Unwmk.**

C744 AP231 5g multicolored
C745 AP231 10g multicolored
C746 AP231 20g multicolored

Perf. 13x13½

C747 AP231 25g multicolored
C748 AP231 30g multicolored

Souvenir Sheet

Perf. 14½

C749 AP231 100g multicolored

1990 World Cup Soccer Championships, Italy — AP232

Designs: 5g, Mexico #C350. 10g, Germany #1146. 20g, Argentina #1147, vert. 25g, Spain #2211. 30g, Italy #1742.

1988, Oct. 4 ***Perf. 13***

C750 AP232 5g multicolored
C751 AP232 10g multicolored
C752 AP232 20g multicolored
C753 AP232 25g multicolored

Perf. 14

C754 AP232 30g multicolored

For overprint see No. 2285.

No. C635 Ovptd. in Metallic Red:

1988, Nov. 25 ***Perf. 14***

C755 AP204 30g on No. C635

No. C623 Ovptd. in Gold

1988, Nov. 25 ***Perf. 14***

C756 AP200 30g on No. C623

1988 Summer Olympics, Seoul — AP233

Gold medalists: No. C757, Nicole Uphoff, individual dressage. No. C758, Anja Fichtel, Sabine Bau, Zita Funkenhauser, Anette Kluge and Christine Weber, team foil. No. C759, Silvia Sperber, smallbore standard rifle. No. C760, Mathias Baumann, Claus Erhorn, Thies Kaspareit and Ralph Ehrenbrink, equestrian team 3-day event. No. C761, Anja Fichtel, individual foil, vert. No. C762, Franke Sloothaak, Ludger Beerbaum, Wolfgang Brinkmann and Dirk Hafemeister, equestrian team jumping. No. C763, Arnd Schmitt, individual epee, vert. No. C764, Jose Luis Doreste, Finn class yachting. No. C765, Steffi Graf, tennis. No. C766, Michael Gross, 200-meter butterfly, vert. No. C767, West Germany, coxed eights. No. C768, Nicole Uphoff, Monica Theodorescu, Ann Kathrin Linsenhoff and Reiner Klimke, team dressage.

1989 ***Perf. 13***

C757 AP233 5g multicolored
C758 AP233 5g multicolored
C759 AP233 10g multicolored
C760 AP233 10g multicolored
C761 AP233 20g multicolored
C762 AP233 20g multicolored
C763 AP233 25g multicolored
C764 AP233 25g multicolored

Perf. 13½x13

C765 AP233 30g multicolored
C766 AP233 30g multicolored

Souvenir Sheets

Perf. 14½

C767 AP233 100g multicolored
C768 AP233 100g multicolored

Nos. C767-C768 each contain one 80x50mm stamp.

Issue dates: Nos. C757, C759, C761, C763, C765, and C767, Mar. 3. Others, Mar. 20.

For overprints see Nos. 2292, 2359.

Souvenir Sheet

Intl. Red Cross, 125th Anniv. (in 1988) — AP234

1989, Apr. 17 **Litho.** ***Perf. 13½***

C769 AP234 100g #803 in changed colors

No. C769 has perforated label picturing Nobel medal.

Olympics Type of 1989

1988 Winter Olympic medalists or competitors: 5g, Pirmin Zurbriggen, Peter Mueller, Switzerland, and Franck Piccard, France, Alpine skiing. 10g, Sigrid Wolf, Austria, super giant slalom, vert. 20g, Czechoslovakia vs. West Germany, hockey, vert. 25g, Piccard, skiing, vert. 30g, Piccard, wearing medal, vert.

1989, Apr. 17 ***Perf. 13½x13***

C770 AP233 5g multicolored

Perf. 13x13½

C771 AP233 10g multicolored
C772 AP233 20g multicolored
C773 AP233 25g multicolored
C774 AP233 30g multicolored

Souvenir Sheet

1990 World Cup Soccer Championships, Italy — AP235

1989, Apr. 21 ***Perf. 14½***

C775 AP235 100g Sheet of 1 + label

1st Moon Landing, 20th Anniv. — AP236

Designs: 5g, Wernher von Braun, Apollo 11 launch, vert. 10g, Michael Collins, lunar module on moon. 20g, Neil Armstrong, astronaut on lunar module ladder, vert. 25g, Buzz Aldrin, solar wind experiment, vert. 30g, Kurt Debus, splashdown of Columbia command module, vert.

1989, May 24 ***Perf. 13***

C776 AP236 5g multicolored
C777 AP236 10g multicolored
C778 AP236 20g multicolored
C779 AP236 25g multicolored
C780 AP236 30g multicolored

Souvenir Sheet

Luis Alberto del Parana and the Paraguayans — AP237

1989, May 25 ***Perf. 14½***

C780A AP237 100g multicolored

A clear plastic phonograph record is affixed to the souvenir sheet.

Hamburg, 800th Anniv. — AP238

Hamburg anniv. emblem, SAIL '89 emblem, and: 5g, Galleon and Icarus, woodcut by Pieter Brueghel. 10g, Windjammer, vert. 20g, Bark in full sail. 25g, Old Hamburg by A.E. Schliecker, vert. 30g, Commemorative coin issued by Federal Republic of Germany. 100g, Hamburg, 13th cent. illuminated manuscript, vert.

1989, May 26 ***Perf. 13½x13, 13x13½***

C781 AP238 5g multicolored
C782 AP238 10g multicolored
C783 AP238 20g multicolored
C784 AP238 25g multicolored
C785 AP238 30g multicolored

Souvenir Sheet

Perf. 14½

C786 AP238 100g multicolored

No. C786 contains one 40x50mm stamp.

French Revolution, Bicent. — AP239

Details from paintings: 5g, Esther Adorns Herself for her Presentation to King Ahasuerus, by Theodore Chasseriau, vert. 10g, Olympia, by Manet, vert. 20g, The Drunker Erigone with a Panther, by Louis A. Reisener. 25g, Anniv. emblem and natl. coats of arms. 30g, Liberty Leading the People, by Delacroix, vert. 100g, The Education of Maria de Medici, by Rubens, vert.

1989, May 27 ***Perf. 13x13½, 13½x13***

C787 AP239 5g multicolored
C788 AP239 10g multicolored
C789 AP239 20g multicolored
C790 AP239 25g multicolored
C791 AP239 30g multicolored

Souvenir Sheet

Perf. 14½

C792 AP239 100g multicolored

Souvenir Sheet

Railway Zeppelin, 1931 — AP240

1989, May 27 **Litho.** ***Perf. 13½***

C793 AP240 100g multicolored

Jupiter and Calisto by Rubens AP241

Details from paintings by Rubens: 10g, Boreas Abducting Oreithyia (1619-20). 20g, Fortuna (1625). 25g, Mars with Venus and Cupid (1625). 30g, Virgin with Child (1620).

1989, Dec. 27 **Litho.** ***Perf. 14***

C794 AP241 5g multicolored
C795 AP241 10g multicolored
C796 AP241 20g multicolored
C797 AP241 25g multicolored

Perf. 13

C798 AP241 30g multicolored

Death of Rubens, 350th anniversary.

Penny Black, 150th Anniv. AP242

Penny Black, 500 years of postal services emblem, Stamp World '90 emblem and: 5g, Brazil #1. 10g, British Guiana #2. 20g, Chile #1. 25g, Uruguay #1. 30g, Paraguay #1.

1989, Dec. 30 ***Perf. 14***

C799 AP242 5g multicolored
C800 AP242 10g multicolored
C801 AP242 20g multicolored
C802 AP242 25g multicolored

Perf. 13

C803 AP242 30g multicolored

Animals AP243

Designs: 5g, Martucha. 10g, Mara. 20g, Lobo de crin. 25g, Rana cornuda tintorera, horiz. 30g, Jaguar, horiz. Inscribed 1989.

1990, Jan. 8 ***Perf. 13x13½, 13½x13***

C804 AP243 5g multicolored
C805 AP243 10g multicolored
C806 AP243 20g multicolored
C807 AP243 25g multicolored
C808 AP243 30g multicolored

Columbus' Fleet AP244

Discovery of America 500th anniversary emblem and: 10g, Olympic rings, stylized basketball player, horiz. 20g, Medieval nave, Expo '92 emblem. 25g, Four-masted barkentine, Expo '92 emblem, horiz. 30g, Similar to Spain Scott 2571, Expo '92 emblem.

1990, Jan. 27 ***Perf. 14***

C809 AP244 5g multicolored
C810 AP244 10g multicolored
C811 AP244 20g multicolored
C812 AP244 25g multicolored

Perf. 13½x13

C813 AP244 30g multicolored

Postal Transportation, 500th Anniv. — AP245

500th Anniv. Emblem and: 5g, 10g, 20g, 25g, Penny Black and various post coaches, 10g, vert. 30g, Post coach.

1990, Mar. 9 ***Perf. 13½x13, 13x13½***

C814 AP245 5g multicolored
C815 AP245 10g multicolored
C816 AP245 20g multicolored
C817 AP245 25g multicolored
C818 AP245 30g multicolored

Fort and City of Arco by Durer — AP246

Paintings by Albrecht Durer, postal transportation 500th anniversary emblem and: 10g, Trent Castle. 20g, North Innsbruck. 25g, Fort yard of Innsbruck, vert. 30g, Virgin of the Animals. No. C824, Madonna and Child, vert. No. C825, Postrider, vert.

1990, Mar. 14 ***Perf. 14***

C819 AP246 5g multicolored
C820 AP246 10g multicolored
C821 AP246 20g multicolored
C822 AP246 25g multicolored

Perf. 13

C823 AP246 30g multicolored

Souvenir Sheets

Perf. 14½

C824 AP246 100g multicolored
C825 AP246 100g multicolored

Nos. C824-C825 each contain one 40x50mm stamp.

For overprint see No. 2358.

AP247

1988? Photo. Wmk. 347 ***Perf. 11***

C826 AP247 40g red lilac 1.00 .85
C827 AP247 60g bright green 1.50 1.25

POSTAGE DUE STAMPS

D1

D2

1904 Unwmk. Litho. ***Perf. 11½***

J1 D1 2c green .20 .20
J2 D1 4c green .20 .20
J3 D1 10c green .20 .20
J4 D1 20c green .20 .20
Nos. J1-J4 (4) .80 .80

1913 **Engr.**

J5 D2 1c yellow brown .20 .20
J6 D2 2c yellow brown .20 .20
J7 D2 5c yellow brown .20 .20
J8 D2 10c yellow brown .20 .20
J9 D2 20c yellow brown .20 .20
J10 D2 40c yellow brown .20 .20
J11 D2 1p yellow brown .20 .20
J12 D2 1.50p yellow brown .20 .20
Nos. J5-J12 (8) 1.60 1.60

For overprints and surcharges see Nos. 220-224, 229, 232, 264, L5.

INTERIOR OFFICE ISSUES

The "C" signifies "Campana" (rural). These stamps were sold by Postal Agents in country districts, who received a commission on their sales. These stamps were available for postage in the interior but not in Asunción or abroad.

Nos. 243-244 Overprinted in Red

1922

L1 A42 50c car & dk bl .20 .20
L2 A42 1p dk bl & brn .20 .20

The overprint on No. L2 exists double or inverted. Counterfeits exist. Double or inverted overprints on No. L1 and all overprints in black are counterfeit.

Nos. 215, 218, J12 Surcharged

1924

L3 A40 50c on 75c deep bl .20 .20
L4 A40 1p on 1.25p pale bl .20 .20
L5 D2 1p on 1.50p yel brn .20 .20
Nos. L3-L5 (3) .60 .60

Nos. L3-L4 exist imperf.

Nos. 254, 257-260 Overprinted in Black or Red

C

1924-26

L6 A45 50c red ('25) .20 .20
L7 A44 1p dk blue (R) .20 .20
L8 A45 1p dk bl (R) ('25) .20 .20
L9 A46 1p blue (R) ('25) .20 .20
L10 A45 1p emerald ('26) .20 .20
Nos. L6-L10 (5) 1.00 1.00

Nos. L6, L8-L9 exist imperf. Value $2.50 each pair.

Same Overprint on Stamps and Type of 1927-36 in Red or Black

1927-39

L11 A47 50c ultra (R) .20 .20
L12 A47 50c dl red ('28) .20 .20
L13 A47 50c orange ('29) .20 .20
L14 A47 50c lt bl ('30) .20 .20
L15 A47 50c gray (R) ('31) .20 .20
L16 A47 50c bluish grn (R) ('33) .20 .20
L17 A47 50c vio (R) ('34) .20 .20
L18 A48 1p emerald .20 .20
L19 A48 1p org red ('29) .20 .20
L20 A48 1p lil brn ('31) .20 .20
L21 A48 1p dk bl (R) ('33) .20 .20
L22 A48 1p brt vio (R) ('35) .20 .20
L23 A49 1.50p brown .20 .20
a. Double overprint 1.50
L24 A49 1.50p lilac ('28) .20 .20
L25 A49 1.50p dull bl (R) .20 .20
L26 A50 2.50p bister ('28) .20 .20
L27 A50 2.50p vio (R) ('36) .20 .20
L28 A51 3p gray (R) .20 .20
L29 A51 3p rose red ('39) .20 .20
L30 A52 5p vio (R) ('36) .20 .20
L31 A57 10p gray brn (R) ('36) .30 .25
Nos. L11-L31 (21) 4.30 4.25

Types of 1931-35 and No. 305 Overprinted in Black or Red

1931-36

L32 A59 1p light red .20 .20
L33 A58 1.50p dp bl (R) .20 .20
L34 A60 1.50p bis brn ('32) .20 .20
L35 A60 1.50p grn (R) ('34) .20 .20
L36 A60 1.50p bl (R) ('36) .20 .20
L37 A54 10p vermilion 1.25 1.25
Nos. L32-L37 (6) 2.25 2.25

OFFICIAL STAMPS

O1

O2

O3

O4

O5

O6

O7

Unwmk.

1886, Aug. 20 **Litho.** ***Imperf.***

O1 O1 1c orange 3.00 3.00
O2 O2 2c violet 3.00 3.00
O3 O3 5c red 3.00 3.00
O4 O4 7c green 3.00 3.00
O5 O5 10c brown 3.00 3.00
O6 O6 15c slate blue 3.00 3.00
a. Wavy lines on face of stamp
b. "OFICIAL" omitted 1.25
O7 O7 20c claret 3.00 3.00
Nos. O1-O7 (7) 21.00 21.00

Nos. O1 to O7 have the date and various control marks and letters printed on the back of each stamp in blue and black.

The overprints exist inverted on all values.

Nos. O1 to O7 have been reprinted from new stones made from slightly retouched dies.

Types of 1886 With Overprint

1886 ***Perf. 11½***

O8 O1 1c dark green .50 .50
O9 O2 2c scarlet .50 .50
O10 O3 5c dull blue .50 .50
O11 O4 7c orange .50 .50
O12 O5 10c lake .50 .50
O13 O6 15c brown .50 .50
O14 O7 20c blue .50 .50
Nos. O8-O14 (7) 3.50 3.50

The overprint exists inverted on all values. Value, each $1.50.

No. 20 Overprinted

1886, Sept. 1

O15	A11	1c dark green	1.50	1.50

Types of 1889 Regular Issue Surcharged

Handstamped Surcharge in Black

1889 ***Imperf.***

O16	A13	3c on 15c violet	1.50	1.00
O17	A13	5c on 15c red brn	1.50	1.00

Perf. 11½

O18	A13	1c on 15c maroon	1.50	1.00
O19	A13	2c on 15c maroon	1.50	1.00
		Nos. O16-O19 (4)	6.00	4.00

Counterfeits of Nos. O16-O19 abound.

Regular Issue of 1887 Handstamp Overprinted in Violet

Perf. 11½-12½ & Compounds

1890 **Typo.**

O20	A12	1c green	.20	.20
O21	A12	2c rose red	.20	.20
O22	A12	5c blue	.20	.20
O23	A12	7c brown	3.75	2.50
O24	A12	10c lilac	.20	.20
O25	A12	15c orange	.45	.25
O26	A12	20c pink	.40	.30
		Nos. O20-O26 (7)	5.40	3.85

Nos. O20-O26 exist with double overprint and all but the 20c with inverted overprint.

Nos. O20-O22, O24-O26 exist with blue overprint. The status is questioned. Value, set $15.

Stamps and Type of 1887 Regular Issue Overprinted in Black

1892

O33	A12	1c green	.20	.20
O34	A12	2c rose red	.20	.20
O35	A12	5c blue	.20	.20
O36	A12	7c brown	1.75	1.00
O37	A12	10c lilac	.65	.25
O38	A12	15c orange	.20	.20
O39	A12	20c pink	.25	.20
O40	A12	50c gray	.20	.20
		Nos. O33-O40 (8)	3.65	2.45

No. 26 Overprinted

1893

O41	A12	7c brown	10.00	5.00

Counterfeits of No. O41 exist.

O16

1901, Feb. **Engr.** ***Perf. 11½, 12½***

O42	O16	1c dull blue	.20	.20
O43	O16	2c rose red	.20	.20
O44	O16	4c dark brown	.20	.20
O45	O16	5c dark green	.20	.20
O46	O16	8c orange brn	.20	.20
O47	O16	10c car rose	.20	.20
O48	O16	20c deep blue	.20	.20
		Nos. O42-O48 (7)	1.40	1.40

A 12c deep green, type O16, was prepared but not issued.

No. 45 Overprinted

1902 ***Perf. 12x12½***

O49	A12	1p olive grn	.20	.20
a.		Inverted overprint	10.00	

Counterfeits of No. O49a exist.

Regular Issue of 1903 Overprinted

1903 ***Perf. 11½***

O50	A32	1c gray	.20	.20
O51	A32	2c blue green	.20	.20
O52	A32	5c blue	.20	.20
O53	A32	10c orange brn	.20	.20
O54	A32	20c carmine	.20	.20
O55	A32	30c deep blue	.20	.20
O56	A32	60c purple	.20	.20
		Nos. O50-O56 (7)	1.40	1.40

O17

O18

1905-08 **Engr.** ***Perf. 11½, 12***

O57	O17	1c gray grn	.20	.20
O58	O17	1c ol grn ('05)	.20	.20
O59	O17	1c brn org ('06)	.45	.20
O60	O17	1c ver ('08)	.25	.20
O61	O17	2c brown org	.20	.20
O62	O17	2c gray grn ('05)	.20	.20
O63	O17	2c red ('06)	.75	.25
O64	O17	2c gray ('08)	.40	.20
O65	O17	5c deep bl ('06)	.20	.20
O66	O17	5c gray bl ('08)	1.50	1.00
O67	O17	5c grnsh bl ('08)	.75	.65
O68	O17	10c violet ('06)	.20	.20
O69	O17	20c violet ('08)	.70	.40
		Nos. O57-O69 (13)	6.00	4.10

1908

O70	O17	10c bister	3.50
O71	O17	10c emerald	3.50
O72	O17	10c red lilac	4.50
O73	O17	20c bister	3.00
O74	O17	20c salmon pink	3.50
O75	O17	20c green	3.50
O76	O17	30c turquoise bl	3.50
O77	O17	30c blue gray	3.50
O78	O17	30c yellow	1.50
O79	O17	60c chocolate	4.00
O80	O17	60c orange brn	5.00
O81	O17	60c deep ultra	4.00
O82	O18	1p brt rose & blk	24.00
O83	O18	1p lake & blk	24.00
O84	O18	1p brn org & blk	25.00
		Nos. O70-O84 (15)	116.00

Nos. O70-O84 were not issued, but were surcharged or overprinted for use as regular postage stamps. See Nos. 131-138, 141-145, 158-165, 171-173.

O19

1913 ***Perf. 11½***

O85	O19	1c gray	.20	.20
O86	O19	2c orange	.20	.20
O87	O19	5c lilac	.20	.20
O88	O19	10c green	.20	.20
O89	O19	20c dull red	.20	.20
O90	O19	50c rose	.20	.20
O91	O19	75c deep blue	.20	.20
O92	O19	1p dull blue	.20	.20
O93	O19	2p yellow	.20	.20
		Nos. O85-O93 (9)	1.80	1.80

For surcharges see Nos. 268, C1-C3.

Type of Regular Issue of 1927-38 Overprinted in Red **OFICIAL**

1935

O94	A47	10c light ultra	.20	.20
O95	A47	50c violet	.20	.20
O96	A48	1p orange	.20	.20
O97	A60	1.50p green	.20	.20
O98	A50	2.50p violet	.20	.20
		Nos. O94-O98 (5)	1.00	1.00

Overprint is diagonal on 1.50p.

University of Asunción Type

1940 **Litho.** ***Perf. 12***

O99	A67	50c red brn & blk	.20	.20
O100	A67	1p rose pink & blk	.20	.20
O101	A67	2p lt bl grn & blk	.20	.20
O102	A67	5p ultra & blk	.20	.20
O103	A67	10p lt vio & blk	.20	.20
O104	A67	50p dp org & blk	.30	.25
		Nos. O99-O104 (6)	1.30	1.25

PENRHYN ISLAND

pen-'rin 'ī-lənd

(Tongareva)

AREA — 3 sq. mi.
POP. — 395 (1926)

Stamps of Cook Islands were used in Penrhyn from 1932 until 1973.

12 Pence = 1 Shilling

Catalogue values for unused stamps in this country are for Never Hinged items, beginning with Scott 35 in the regular postage section, Scott B1 in the semi-postal section and Scott O1 in the officials section.

Watermarks

Wmk. 61- N Z and Star Close Together

Wmk. 63- Double-lined N Z and Star

On watermark 61 the margins of the sheets are watermarked "NEW ZEALAND POSTAGE" and parts of the double-lined letters of these words are frequently found on the stamps. It occasionally happens that a stamp shows no watermark whatever.

Stamps of New Zealand Surcharged in Carmine, Vermilion, Brown or Blue:

½ pence

1 pence

2½ pence

1902 **Wmk. 63** ***Perf. 14***

1	A18	½p green (C)	1.25	*2.50*
a.		No period after "ISLAND"	90.00	100.00
2	A35	1p carmine (Br)	3.25	*5.00*
a.		Perf. 11	*1,000.*	*1,000.*
b.		Perf. 11x14	*1,000.*	*1,000.*

Wmk. 61 ***Perf. 14***

5	A18	½p green (V)	1.00	*3.50*
a.		No period after "ISLAND"	60.00	65.00
6	A35	1p carmine (Bl)	1.00	*2.75*
a.		No period after "ISLAND"	40.00	40.00
b.		Perf. 11x14	*9,000.*	*8,500.*

Unwmk. ***Perf. 11***

8	A22	2½p blue (C)	2.50	*5.00*
a.		"½" and "PENI" 2mm apart	10.50	*16.00*
9	A22	2½p blue (V)	2.50	*5.00*
a.		"½" and "PENI" 2mm apart	10.50	*16.00*
		Nos. 1-9 (6)	11.50	*23.75*

Stamps with compound perfs. also exist perf. 11 or 14 on one or more sides.

d

e

f

1903 **Wmk. 61**

10	A23(d)	3p yel brn (Bl)	9.00	*19.00*
11	A26(e)	6p rose (Bl)	15.00	*32.50*
12	A29(f)	1sh org red (Bl)	45.00	*55.00*
a.		1sh bright red (Bl)	50.00	*50.00*
b.		1sh brown red (Bl)	55.00	*55.00*
		Nos. 10-12 (3)	69.00	*106.50*

1914-15 ***Perf. 14, 14x14½***

13	A41(a)	½p yel grn (C)	1.00	4.00
a.		No period after "ISLAND"	32.50	*55.00*
b.		No period after "PENI"	75.00	*125.00*
14	A41(a)	½p yel grn (V) ('15)	.90	5.00
a.		No period after "ISLAND"	13.00	25.00
b.		No period after "PENI"	37.50	*60.00*
15	A41(e)	6p car rose (Bl)	25.00	45.00
16	A41(f)	1sh ver (Bl)	40.00	*65.00*
		Nos. 13-16 (4)	66.90	*119.00*

New Zealand Stamps of 1915-19 Overprinted in Red or Dark Blue

Perf. 14x13½, 14x14½

1917-20 **Typo.**

17	A43	½p yel grn (R) ('20)	.75	1.60
18	A47	1½p gray black (R)	5.75	4.00
19	A47	1½p brn org (R) ('19)	.50	*4.00*
20	A43	3p choc (Bl) ('19)	3.00	4.50

Engr.

21	A44	2½p dull bl (R) ('20)	1.75	2.75
22	A45	3p vio brn (Bl) ('18)	8.25	*16.00*
23	A45	6p car rose (Bl) ('18)	4.50	*11.00*
24	A45	1sh vermilion (Bl)	10.50	*22.50*
		Nos. 17-24 (8)	35.00	*66.35*

Landing of Capt. Cook
A10

Avarua Waterfront
A11

Capt. James Cook — A12

Coconut Palm — A13

Arorangi Village, Rarotonga — A14

Avarua Harbor — A15

1920 Unwmk. Perf. 14

25 A10 ½p emerald & blk 1.00 *5.00*
a. Center inverted 625.00
26 A11 1p red & black 1.25 *5.00*
a. Center inverted 850.00
27 A12 1½p violet & blk 5.00 *10.00*
28 A13 3p red org & blk 3.75 *7.50*
29 A14 6p dk brn & red brn 4.50 *17.50*
30 A15 1sh dull bl & blk 10.00 *20.00*
Nos. 25-30 (6) 25.50 *65.00*

Rarotongan Chief (Te Po) — A16

1927 Engr. Wmk. 61

31 A16 2½p blue & red brn 2.00 *4.00*

Types of 1920 Issue

1928-29

33 A10 ½p yellow grn & blk 5.00 *4.00*
34 A11 1p carmine rose & blk 4.50 *5.25*

PENRHYN

Northern Cook Islands

POP. — 606 (1996).

The Northern Cook Islands include six besides Penrhyn that are inhabited: Nassau, Palmerston (Avarua), Manihiki (Humphrey), Rakahanga (Reirson), Pukapuka (Danger) and Suwarrow (Anchorage).

100 Cents = 1 Dollar

Catalogue values for unused stamps in this section are for Never Hinged items.

Cook Islands Nos. 200-201, 203, 205-208, 211-212, 215-217 Overprinted

1973 Photo. Unwmk. Perf. 14x13½

35 A34 1c gold & multi .20 .20
36 A34 2c gold & multi .20 .20
37 A34 3c gold & multi .20 .20
38 A34 4c gold & multi .20 .20
a. Overprinted on #204
39 A34 5c gold & multi .20 .20
40 A34 6c gold & multi .20 .20
41 A34 8c gold & multi .20 .20
42 A34 15c gold & multi .35 .35
43 A34 20c gold & multi 1.50 .45
44 A34 50c gold & multi 1.25 1.40
45 A35 $1 gold & multi 1.25 1.50
46 A35 $2 gold & multi 1.25 3.50
Nos. 35-46 (12) 7.00 8.60

Nos. 45-46 are overprinted "Penrhyn" only. Overprint exists with broken "E" or "O."

Issued with and without fluorescent security underprinting.

Issued: #35-45, Oct. 24; #46, Nov. 14.

Cook Islands Nos. 369-371 Overprinted in Silver: "PENRHYN / NORTHERN"

1973, Nov. 14 Photo. Perf. 14

47 A60 25c Princess Anne .50 .50
48 A60 30c Mark Phillips 1.00 .90
49 A60 50c Princess and Mark Phillips 1.00 .90
Nos. 47-49 (3) 2.50 2.30

Wedding of Princess Anne and Capt. Mark Phillips.

Fluorescence

Starting with No. 50, stamps carry a "fluorescent security underprinting" in a multiple pattern combining a sailing ship, "Penrhyn Northern Cook Islands" and stars.

Ostracion A17

Aerial View of Penrhyn Atoll — A18

Designs: ½c-$1, Various fish of Penrhyn. $5, Map showing Penrhyn's location.

1974-75 Photo. Perf. 13½x14

50 A17 ½c multicolored .20 .20
51 A17 1c multicolored .20 .20
52 A17 2c multicolored .20 .20
53 A17 3c multicolored .20 .20
54 A17 4c multicolored .20 .20
55 A17 5c multicolored .20 .20
56 A17 8c multicolored .20 .20
57 A17 10c multicolored .20 .20
58 A17 20c multicolored .45 .45
59 A17 25c multicolored .50 .50
60 A17 60c multicolored 1.25 1.25
61 A17 $1 multicolored 2.00 2.00
62 A18 $2 multicolored 4.00 4.00
63 A18 $5 multicolored 9.50 9.50
Nos. 50-63 (14) 19.30 19.30

Issued: $2, 2/12/75; $5, 3/12/75; others 8/15/74.

For surcharges and overprints see Nos. 72, 352-353, O1-O12.

Map of Penrhyn and Nos. 1-2 — A19

UPU, cent.: 50c, UPU emblem, map of Penrhyn and Nos. 27-28.

1974, Sept. 27 Perf. 13

64 A19 25c violet & multi .25 .25
65 A19 50c slate grn & multi .75 .75

Adoration of the Kings, by Memling — A20

Christmas: 10c, Adoration of the Shepherds, by Hugo van der Goes. 25c, Adoration of the Kings, by Rubens. 30c, Holy Family, by Orazio Borgianni.

1974, Oct. 30

66 A20 5c multicolored .20 .20
67 A20 10c multicolored .20 .20
68 A20 25c multicolored .50 .50
69 A20 30c multicolored .60 .60
Nos. 66-69 (4) 1.50 1.50

Churchill Giving "V" Sign — A21

1974, Nov. 30 Photo.

70 A21 30c shown .50 .60
71 A21 50c Portrait .75 .90

Winston Churchill (1874-1965).

No. 63 Overprinted

1975, July 24 Perf. 13½x13

72 A18 $5 multicolored 3.00 3.00

Safe splashdown of Apollo space capsule.

Madonna, by Dirk Bouts A22

Pietà, by Michelangelo A23

Madonna Paintings: 15c, by Leonardo da Vinci. 35c, by Raphael.

1975, Nov. 21 Photo. Perf. 14½x13

73 A22 7c gold & multi .40 .20
74 A22 15c gold & multi .75 .40
75 A22 35c gold & multi 1.10 .75
Nos. 73-75 (3) 2.25 1.35

Christmas 1975.

1976, Mar. 19 Photo. Perf. 14x13

76 A23 15c gold & dark brown .25 .25
77 A23 20c gold & deep purple .40 .40
78 A23 35c gold & dark green .60 .60
a. Souvenir sheet of 3, #76-78 1.50 1.50
Nos. 76-78 (3) 1.25 1.25

Easter and for the 500th birth anniv. of Michelangelo Buonarroti (1475-1564), Italian sculptor, painter and architect.

The Spirit of '76, by Archibald M. Willard — A24

No. 79, Washington Crossing the Delaware, by Emmanuel Leutze.

1976, May 20 Photo. Perf. 13½

79 A24 Strip of 3 1.10 1.10
a. 30c Boatsman .35 .35
b. 30c Washington .35 .35
c. 30c Men in boat .35 .35
80 A24 Strip of 3 2.00 2.00
a. 50c Drummer boy .55 .55
b. 50c Old drummer .55 .55
c. 50c Fifer .55 .55
d. Souvenir sheet, #79-80 3.50 3.50

American Bicentennial. Nos. 79-80 printed in sheets of 15, 5 strips of 3 and 3-part corner labels.

For overprint see No. O13.

Running A25

Montreal Olympic Games Emblem and: 30c, Long jump. 75c, Javelin.

1976, July 9 Photo. Perf. 13½

81 A25 25c multicolored .25 .25
82 A25 30c multicolored .30 .30
83 A25 75c multicolored .75 .75
a. Souvenir sheet of 3, #81-83, perf. 14½x13½ 1.60 1.60
Nos. 81-83 (3) 1.30 1.30

21st Olympic Games, Montreal, Canada, July 17-Aug. 1. Nos. 81-83 printed in sheets of 6 (2x3).

Flight into Egypt, by Dürer A26

Etchings by Albrecht Dürer: 15c, Adoration of the Shepherds. 35c, Adoration of the Kings.

1976, Oct. 20 Photo. Perf. 13x13½

84 A26 7c silver & dk brown .20 .20
85 A26 15c silver & slate grn .25 .25
86 A26 35c silver & purple .55 .45
Nos. 84-86 (3) 1.00 .90

Christmas. Nos. 84-86 printed in sheets of 8 (2x4) with decorative border.

Elizabeth II and Westminster Abbey — A27

$1, Elizabeth II & Prince Philip. $2, Elizabeth II.

1977, Mar. 24 Photo. Perf. 13½x13

87 A27 50c silver & multi .20 .20
88 A27 $1 silver & multi .40 .40
89 A27 $2 silver & multi .80 .80
a. Souvenir sheet of 3, #87-89 1.60 1.60
Nos. 87-89 (3) 1.40 1.40

25th anniversary of reign of Queen Elizabeth II. Nos. 87-89 issued in sheets of 4.

For overprints see Nos. O14-O15.

Annunciation A28

Designs: 15c, Announcement to Shepherds. 35c, Nativity. Designs from "The Bible in Images," by Julius Schnorr von Carolsfeld (1794-1872).

1977, Sept. 23 Photo. *Perf. 13½*

90	A28	7c multicolored	.25	.25
91	A28	15c multicolored	.50	.50
92	A28	35c multicolored	1.25	1.25
		Nos. 90-92 (3)	2.00	2.00

Christmas. Issued in sheets of 6.

A29

#93a, Red Sickle-bill (I'wii). #93b, Chief's Feather Cloak. #94a, Crimson creeper (apapane). #94b, Feathered head of Hawaiian god. #95a, Hawaiian gallinule (alae). #95b, Chief's regalia: feather cape, staff (kahili) and helmet. #96a, Yellow-tufted bee-eater (o'o). #96b, Scarlet feathered image (head).
Birds are extinct; their feathers were used for artifacts shown.

1978, Jan. 19 Photo. *Perf. 12½x13*

93	A29	20c Pair, #a.-b.	1.50	.80
94	A29	30c Pair, #a.-b.	1.60	.90
95	A29	35c Pair, #a.-b.	1.75	1.00
96	A29	75c Pair, #a.-b.	2.75	1.50
c.		Souv. sheet, #93a, 94a, 95a, 96a	4.00	4.00
d.		Souv. sheet, #93b, 94b, 95b, 96b	4.00	4.00
		Nos. 93-96 (4)	7.60	4.20

Bicentenary of Capt. Cook's arrival in Hawaii. Printed in sheets of 8 (4x2).

A31

A32

Rubens' Paintings: 10c, St. Veronica by Rubens. 15c, Crucifixion. 35c, Descent from the Cross.

1978, Mar. 10 Photo. *Perf. 13½x13*
Size: 25x36mm

101	A31	10c multicolored	.20	.20
102	A31	15c multicolored	.30	.30
103	A31	35c multicolored	.70	.70
a.		Souvenir sheet of 3	1.25	1.25
		Nos. 101-103 (3)	1.20	1.20

Easter and 400th birth anniv. of Peter Paul Rubens (1577-1640). Nos. 101-103 issued in sheets of 6. No. 103a contains one each of Nos. 101-103 (27x36mm).

Miniature Sheet

1978, May 24 Photo. *Perf. 13*

104		Sheet of 6	2.00	2.00
a.		A32 90c Arms of United Kingdom	.40	.30
b.		A32 90c shown	.40	.30
c.		A32 90c Arms of New Zealand	.40	.30
d.		Souvenir sheet of 3, #104a-104c	2.00	2.00

25th anniv. of coronation of Elizabeth II.
No. 104 contains 2 horizontal se-tenant strips of Nos. 104a-104c, separated by horizontal gutter showing coronation.

A33

Paintings by Dürer: 30c, Virgin and Child. 35c, Virgin and Child with St. Anne.

1978, Nov. 29 Photo. *Perf. 14x13½*

105	A33	30c multicolored	.60	.60
106	A33	35c multicolored	.75	.75
a.		Souvenir sheet of 2, #105-106	1.40	1.40

Christmas and 450th death anniv. of Albrecht Dürer (1471-1528), German painter. Nos. 105-106 issued in sheets of 6.

A34

#107a, Penrhyn #64-65. #107b, Rowland Hill, Penny Black. #108a, Penrhyn #104b. #108b, Hill portrait.

1979, Sept. 26 Photo. *Perf. 14*

107	A34	75c Pair, #a.-b.	1.25	1.25
108	A34	90c Pair, #a.-b.	1.50	1.50
c.		Souvenir sheet of 4, #107-108	3.25	3.25

Sir Rowland Hill (1795-1879), originator of penny postage. Issued in sheets of 8.

Max and Moritz, IYC Emblem — A35

IYC: Scenes from Max and Moritz, by Wilhelm Busch (1832-1908).

1979, Nov. 20 Photo. *Perf. 13x12½*

111		Sheet of 4	.75
a.		A35 12c shown	.20
b.		A35 12c Looking down chimney	.20
c.		A35 12c With stolen chickens	.20
d.		A35 12c Woman and dog, empty pan	.20
112		Sheet of 4	.90
a.		A35 15c Sawing bridge	.20
b.		A35 15c Man falling into water	.20
c.		A35 15c Broken bridge	.20
d.		A35 15c Running away	.20
113		Sheet of 4	1.25
a.		A35 20c Baker	.30
b.		A35 20c Sneaking into bakery	.30
c.		A35 20c Falling into dough	.30
d.		A35 20c Baked into breads	.30
		Nos. 111-113 (3)	2.90

Sheets come with full labels at top and bottom showing text from stories or trimmed with text removed.

A36

A37

Easter (15th Century Prayerbook Illustrations): 12c, Jesus Carrying the Cross. 20c, Crucifixion, by William Vreland. 35c, Descent from the Cross.

1980, Mar. 28 Photo. *Perf. 13x13½*

114	A36	12c multicolored	.20	.20
115	A36	20c multicolored	.35	.35
116	A36	35c multicolored	.60	.60
a.		Souvenir sheet of 3, #114-116	1.10	1.10
		Nos. 114-116 (3)	1.15	1.15

See Nos. B4-B6.

1980, Sept. 17 Photo. *Perf. 13*

117	A37	$1 multicolored	1.60	1.60

Souvenir Sheet

118	A37	$2.50 multicolored	3.00	3.00

Queen Mother Elizabeth, 80th birthday.

A38

Platform diving: #119a, Falk Hoffman, DDR. #119b, Martina Jaschke.
Archery: #120a, Tomi Polkolainen. #120b, Kete Losaberidse.
Soccer: #121a, Czechoslovakia, gold. #121b, DDR, silver.
Running: #122a, Barbel Wockel. #122b, Pietro Mennea.

1980, Nov. 14 Photo. *Perf. 13½*

119	A38	10c Pair, #a.-b.	.20	.20
120	A38	20c Pair, #a.-b.	.40	.40
121	A38	30c Pair, #a.-b.	.60	.60
122	A38	50c Pair, #a.-b.	1.00	1.00
		Nos. 119-122 (4)	2.20	2.20

Souvenir Sheet

123	A38	Sheet of 8	2.50	2.50

22nd Summer Olympic Games, Moscow, July 19-Aug. 3.
No. 123 contains #119-122 with gold borders and white lettering at top and bottom.

A39

Christmas (15th Century Virgin and Child Paintings by): 20c, Virgin and Child, by Luis Dalmau. 35c, Serra brothers. 50c, Master of the Porciuncula.

1980, Dec. 5 Photo. *Perf. 13*

127	A39	20c multicolored	.20	.20
128	A39	35c multicolored	.35	.35
129	A39	50c multicolored	.45	.45
a.		Souvenir sheet of 3, #127-129	1.75	1.75
		Nos. 127-129 (3)	1.00	1.00

See Nos. B7-B9.

A40

A41

Cutty Sark, 1869 A42

#160a, 165a, Amatasi. #160b, 165a, Ndrua. #160c, 165a, Waka. #160d, 165a, Tongiaki. #161a, 166a, Va'a teu'ua. #161b, 166b, Victoria, 1500. #161c, 166c, Golden Hinde, 1560. #161d, 166d, Boudeuse, 1760. #162a, 167a, Bounty, 1787. #162b, 167b, Astrolabe, 1811. #162c, 167c, Star of India, 1861. #162d, 167d, Great Rep., 1853. #163a, 168a, Balcutha, 1886. #163b, 168b, Coonatto, 1863. #163c, 168c, Antiope, 1866. #163d, 168d, Teaping, 1863. #164a, 169a, Preussen, 1902. #164b, 169b, Pamir, 1921. #164c, 169c, Cap Hornier, 1910. #164d, 169d, Patriarch, 1869.

1981 Photo. *Perf. 14*

160	A40	1c Block of 4, #a.-d.	.20	.20
161	A40	3c Block of 4, #a.-d.	.20	.20
162	A40	4c Block of 4, #a.-d.	.30	.30
163	A40	6c Block of 4, #a.-d.	.45	.45
164	A40	10c Block of 4, #a.-d.	.80	.80
		Perf. 13½x14½		
165	A41	15c Block of 4, #a.-d.	1.25	1.25
166	A41	20c Block of 4, #a.-d.	1.60	1.60
167	A41	30c Block of 4, #a.-d.	2.50	2.50
168	A41	50c Block of 4, #a.-d.	4.00	4.00
169	A41	$1 Block of 4, #a.-d.	8.00	8.00
		Perf. 13½		
170	A42	$2 shown	4.00	4.00
171	A42	$4 Mermerus, 1872	8.00	8.00
172	A42	$6 Resolution, Discovery, 1776	13.50	13.50
		Nos. 160-172 (13)	44.80	44.80

Issued: 1c-10c, Feb. 16; 15c-50c, Mar. 16; $1, May 15; $2, $4, June 26; $6, Sept. 21.
For surcharges and overprints see Nos. 241-243, 251, 254, 395, O35, O37, O39.

Christ with Crown of Thorns, by Titan — A44

Easter: 30c, Jesus at the Grove, by Paolo Veronese. 50c, Pieta, by Van Dyck.

1981, Apr. 5 *Perf. 14*

173	A44	30c multicolored	.50	.35
174	A44	40c multicolored	.65	.50
175	A44	50c multicolored	.85	.75
a.		Souv. sheet, #173-175, perf 13½	2.50	2.50
		Nos. 173-175 (3)	2.00	1.60

See Nos. B10-B12.

A45

A46

Designs: Portraits of Prince Charles.

1981, July 10 Photo. *Perf. 14*

176	A45	40c multicolored	.20	.20
177	A45	50c multicolored	.25	.25
178	A45	60c multicolored	.30	.30
179	A45	70c multicolored	.40	.40
180	A45	80c multicolored	.45	.45
a.		Souv. sheet of 5, #176-180+label	2.00	2.00
		Nos. 176-180 (5)	1.60	1.60

Royal wedding. Nos. 176-180 each issued in sheets of 5 plus label showing couple.
For overprints and surcharges see Nos. 195-199, 244-245, 248, 299-300, B13-B18.

1981, Dec. 7 Photo. *Perf. 13*

Shirts: #181: a, Red. b, Striped. c, Blue.

#182: a, Blue. b, Red. c, Striped.
#183: a, Orange. b, Purple. c, Black.

181	A46	15c Strip of 3, #a.-c.	.40	.40
182	A46	35c Strip of 3, #a.-c.	1.10	1.10
183	A46	50c Strip of 3, #a.-c.	1.50	1.25
		Nos. 181-183 (3)	3.00	2.75

1982 World Cup Soccer. See No. B19.

Christmas — A47

21st Birthday of Princess Diana — A48

Dürer Engravings: 30c, Virgin on a Crescent, 1508. 40c, Virgin at the Fence, 1503. 50c, Holy Virgin and Child, 1505.

1981, Dec. 15 Photo. *Perf. 13x13½*

184	A47	30c multicolored	.75	.75
185	A47	40c multicolored	1.00	1.00
186	A47	50c multicolored	1.25	1.25
a.		Souvenir sheet of 3	2.25	2.25
		Nos. 184-186 (3)	3.00	3.00

Souvenir Sheets

Perf. 14x13½

187	A47	70c + 5c like #184	1.50	1.50
188	A47	70c + 5c like #185	1.50	1.50
189	A47	70c + 5c like #186	1.50	1.50

No. 186a contains Nos. 184-186 each with 2c surcharge. Nos. 187-189 each contain one 25x40mm stamp. Surtaxes were for childrens' charities.

1982, July 1 Photo. *Perf. 14*

Designs: Portraits of Diana.

190	A48	30c multicolored	.60	.60
191	A48	50c multicolored	.75	.75
192	A48	70c multicolored	.90	.90
193	A48	80c multicolored	1.00	1.00
194	A48	$1.40 multicolored	2.00	2.00
a.		Souv. sheet, #190-194 + label	5.75	5.75
		Nos. 190-194 (5)	5.25	5.25

For new inscriptions, overprints and surcharges, see Nos. 200-204, 246-247, 249-250, 301-302.

Nos. 176-180a Overprinted: "BIRTH OF PRINCE WILLIAM OF WALES 21 JUNE 1982"

1982, July 30

195	A45	40c multicolored	.50	.50
196	A45	50c multicolored	.65	.65
197	A45	60c multicolored	.75	.75
198	A45	70c multicolored	1.00	1.00
199	A45	80c multicolored	1.10	1.10
a.		Souv. sheet, #195-199 + label	6.00	6.00
		Nos. 195-199 (5)	4.00	4.00

Nos. 190-194a Inscribed in Silver: 21 JUNE 1982 BIRTH OF/PRINCE WILLIAM OF WALES (a) or COMMEMORATING THE BIRTH OF/PRINCE WILLIAM OF WALES (b)

1982 Photo. *Perf. 14*

200	A48	30c Pair, #a.-b.	.50	.50
201	A48	50c Pair, #a.-b.	.75	.75
202	A48	70c Pair, #a.-b.	1.25	1.25
203	A48	80c Pair, #a.-b.	1.50	1.50
204	A48	$1.40 Pair, #a.-b.	2.75	2.75
c.		Souv. sheet, #200a, 201a, 202a, 203a, 204a + label	4.00	4.00
		Nos. 200-204 (5)	6.75	6.75

Miniature sheets of each denomination were issued containing 2 "21 JUNE 1982...," 3 "COMMEMORATING...," and a label.
Se-tenant pairs come with or without label.
For surcharges see Nos. 247, 250, 253.

A49

Christmas: Virgin and Child Paintings.

1982, Dec. 10 Photo. *Perf. 14*

205	A49	35c Joos Van Cleve (1485-1540)	.50	.50
206	A49	48c Filippino Lippi (1457-1504)	.65	.65
207	A49	60c Cima Da Conegliano (1459-1517)	.80	.80
a.		Souvenir sheet of 3	2.25	2.25
		Nos. 205-207 (3)	1.95	1.95

Souvenir Sheets

208	A49	70c + 5c like 35c	1.40	1.40
209	A49	70c + 5c like 48c	1.40	1.40
210	A49	70c + 5c like 60c	1.40	1.40

Nos. 205-207 were printed in sheets of five plus label. No. 207a contains Nos. 205-207 each with 2c surcharge. Nos. 208-210 each contain one stamp, perf. 13½. Surtaxes were for childrens' charities.

A50

#a, Red coral. #b, Aerial view. #c, Eleanor Roosevelt, grass skirt. #d, Map.

1983, Mar. 14 *Perf. 13½x13*

211	A50	60c Block of 4, #a.-d.	2.75	2.75

Commonwealth day.
For surcharges see No. O27.

Scouting Year A51

Emblem and various tropical flowers.

1983, Apr. 5 *Perf. 13½x14½*

215	A51	36c multicolored	1.25	.60
216	A51	48c multicolored	1.50	.80
217	A51	60c multicolored	2.00	1.00
		Nos. 215-217 (3)	4.75	2.40

Souvenir Sheet

218	A51	$2 multicolored	3.25	3.25

Nos. 215-218 Overprinted: "XV / WORLD JAMBOREE / CANADA / 1983"

1983, July 8 Photo. *Perf. 13½x14½*

219	A51	36c multicolored	1.25	.60
220	A51	48c multicolored	1.75	1.00
221	A51	60c multicolored	1.75	1.00
		Nos. 219-221 (3)	4.75	2.60

Souvenir Sheet

222	A51	$2 multicolored	3.25	3.25

15th World Boy Scout Jamboree.

Save the Whales Campaign A52

Various whale hunting scenes.

1983, July 29 Photo. *Perf. 13*

223	A52	8c multicolored	.40	.30
224	A52	15c multicolored	.60	.40
225	A52	35c multicolored	1.25	.75
226	A52	60c multicolored	2.00	1.50
227	A52	$1 multicolored	3.25	2.50
		Nos. 223-227 (5)	7.50	5.45

World Communications Year — A53

Designs: Cable laying Vessels.

1983, Sept. Photo. *Perf. 13*

228	A53	36c multicolored	.75	.60
229	A53	48c multicolored	1.00	.80
230	A53	60c multicolored	1.25	1.00
		Nos. 228-230 (3)	3.00	2.40

Souvenir Sheet

231		Sheet of 3	2.50	2.50
a.		A53 36c + 3c like No. 228	.65	.65
b.		A53 48c + 3c like No. 229	.85	.85
c.		A53 60c + 3c like No. 230	.95	.95

Surtax was for local charities.

Nos. 164, 166-167, 170, 172, 178-180, 192-194, 202-204 Surcharged

Perf. 14, 13½x14½, 13½

1983 Photo.

Blocks of 4, #a.-d. (#241-243)

Pairs, #a.-b. (#247, 250, 253)

241	A40	18c on 10c #164	1.40	1.40
242	A41	36c on 20c #166	2.75	2.75
243	A41	36c on 30c #167	2.75	2.75
244	A45	48c on 60c multi	.90	.90
245	A45	72c on 70c multi	1.50	1.50
246	A48	72c on 70c #192	1.50	1.50
247	A48	72c on 70c #202	3.00	3.00
248	A45	96c on 80c multi	1.75	1.75
249	A48	96c on 80c #193	1.75	1.75
250	A48	96c on 80c #203	3.50	3.50
251	A42	$1.20 on $2 multi	2.25	2.25
252	A48	$1.20 on $1.40 #194	2.25	2.25
253	A48	$1.20 on $1.40 #204	4.50	4.50
254	A42	$5.60 on $6 multi	10.50	10.50
		Nos. 241-254 (14)	40.30	40.30

Issued: #241-243, 245, 251, Sept. 26; #244, 246, 249, 252, 254, Oct. 28; others Dec. 1.

First Manned Balloon Flight, 200th Anniv. — A54

Designs: 36c, Airship, Sir George Cayley (1773-1857). 48c, Man-powered airship, Dupuy de Lome (1818-1885). 60c, Brazilian Aviation Pioneer, Alberto Santos Dumont (1873-1932). 96c, Practical Airship, Paul Lebaudy (1858-1937). $1.32, L-Z 127 Graf Zeppelin.

1983, Oct. 31 Litho. *Perf. 13*

255	A54	36c multicolored	.60	.60
256	A54	48c multicolored	.80	.80
257	A54	60c multicolored	.95	.95
258	A54	96c multicolored	1.50	1.50
259	A54	$1.32 multicolored	2.25	2.25
a.		Souvenir sheet of 5, #255-259	6.00	6.00
		Nos. 255-259 (5)	6.10	6.10

Nos. 255-259 se-tenant with labels. Sheets of 5 for each value exist.
Nos. 255-259 are misspelled "ISLANS." For correcting overprints see Nos. 287-291.

Christmas A55

Raphael Paintings: 36c, Madonna in the Meadow. 42c, Tempi Madonna. 48c, Small Cowper Madonna. 60c, Madonna Della Tenda.

1983, Nov. 30 Photo. *Perf. 13x13½*

260	A55	36c multicolored	.65	.55
261	A55	42c multicolored	.75	.65
262	A55	48c multicolored	1.00	.75
263	A55	60c multicolored	1.10	.95
a.		Souvenir sheet of 4	3.50	3.00
		Nos. 260-263 (4)	3.50	2.90

Souvenir Sheets

Perf. 13½

264	A55	75c + 5c like #260	1.25	1.25
265	A55	75c + 5c like #261	1.25	1.25
266	A55	75c + 5c like #262	1.25	1.25
267	A55	75c + 5c like #263	1.25	1.25

No. 263a contains Nos. 260-263 each with 3c surcharge. Nos. 264-267 each contain one 29x41mm stamp. Issued Dec. 28. Surtaxes were for children's charities.

Waka Canoe — A56

1984 Photo. *Perf. 14½*

268	A56	2c shown	.20	.20
269	A56	4c Amatasi fishing boat	.20	.20
270	A56	5c Ndrua canoe	.20	.20
271	A56	8c Tongiaki canoe	.20	.20
272	A56	10c Victoria, 1500	.20	.20
273	A56	18c Golden Hind, 1560	.25	.25
274	A56	20c Boudeuse, 1760	.30	.30
275	A56	30c Bounty, 1787	.40	.40
276	A56	36c Astrolabe, 1811	.50	.50
277	A56	48c Great Republic, 1853	.65	.65
278	A56	50c Star of India, 1861	.70	.70
279	A56	60c Coonatto, 1863	.80	.80
280	A56	72c Antiope, 1866	1.00	1.00
281	A56	80c Balcutha, 1886	1.10	1.10
282	A56	96c Cap Hornier, 1910	1.40	1.40
283	A56	$1.20 Pamir, 1921	1.60	1.60

Perf. 13

Size: 42x34mm

284	A56	$3 Mermerus, 1872	3.00	3.00
285	A56	$5 Cutty Sark, 1869	4.75	4.75
286	A56	$9.60 Resolution, Discovery	9.00	9.00
		Nos. 268-286 (19)	26.45	26.45

Issue dates: Nos. 268-277, Feb. 8. Nos. 278-283, Mar. 23. Nos. 284-286 June 15.
For overprints and surcharges see Nos. O16-O26, O31-O34, O36, O38, O40.

Nos. 255-259a Ovptd. with Silver Bar and "NORTHERN COOK ISLANDS" in Black

1984 Litho. *Perf. 13*

287	A54	36c multicolored	.85	.85
288	A54	48c multicolored	1.10	1.10
289	A54	60c multicolored	1.40	1.40
290	A54	96c multicolored	2.25	2.25
291	A54	$1.32 multicolored	3.00	3.00
a.		Souvenir sheet of 5, #287-291	7.50	*8.75*
		Nos. 287-291 (5)	8.60	8.60

1984 Los Angeles Summer Olympic Games A57

1984, July 20 Photo. *Perf. 13½x13*

292 A57 35c Olympic flag .40 .40
293 A57 60c Torch, flags .60 .60
294 A57 $1.80 Classic runners, Memorial Coliseum 1.90 1.90
Nos. 292-294 (3) 2.90 2.90

Souvenir Sheet

295 Sheet of 3 + label 2.75 2.75
a. A57 35c + 5c like #292 .30 .30
b. A57 60c + 5c like #293 .55 .55
c. A57 $1.80 + 5c like #294 1.90 1.90

Surtax for amateur sports.

AUSIPEX '84 — A57a

1984, Sept. 20

296 A57a 60c Nos. 136, 108, 180, 104b .60 .60
297 A57a $1.20 Map of South Pacific 1.25 1.25

Souvenir Sheet

298 Sheet of 2 2.00 2.00
a. A57a 96c like #296 1.00 1.00
b. A57a 96c like #297 1.00 1.00

For surcharge see No. 345.

Nos. 176-177, 190-191 Ovptd. "Birth of/Prince Henry/15 Sept. 1984" and Surcharged in Black or Gold

1984, Oct. 18 *Perf. 14*

299 A45 $2 on 40c 2.00 2.00
300 A45 $2 on 50c 2.00 2.00
301 A48 $2 on 30c 2.00 2.00
302 A48 $2 on 50c 2.00 2.00
Nos. 299-302 (4) 8.00 8.00

Nos. 209-302 printed in sheets of 5 plus one label each picturing a portrait of the royal couple or an heraldic griffin.

Christmas 1984 — A58

Paintings: 36c, Virgin and Child, by Giovanni Bellini. 48c, Virgin and Child, by Lorenzo di Credi. 60c, Virgin and Child, by Palma, the Older. 96c, Virgin and Child, by Raphael.

1984, Nov. 15 Photo. *Perf. 13x13½*

303 A58 36c multicolored .50 .50
304 A58 48c multicolored .75 .75
305 A58 60c multicolored .85 .85
306 A58 96c multicolored 1.40 1.40
a. Souvenir sheet of 4 3.50 3.50
Nos. 303-306 (4) 3.50 3.50

Souvenir Sheets

307 A58 96c + 10c like #303 1.25 1.25
308 A58 96c + 10c like #304 1.25 1.25
309 A58 96c + 10c like #305 1.25 1.25
310 A58 96c + 10c like #306 1.25 1.25

No. 306a contains Nos. 303-306, each with 5c surcharge. Nos. 307-310 issued Dec. 10. Surtax for children's charities.

Audubon Bicentenary — A59

1985, Apr. 9 Photo. *Perf. 13*

311 A59 20c Harlequin duck 1.00 1.00
312 A59 55c Sage grouse 2.50 2.50
313 A59 65c Solitary sandpiper 3.00 3.00
314 A59 75c Red-backed sandpiper 3.50 3.50
Nos. 311-314 (4) 10.00 10.00

Souvenir Sheets

Perf. 13½x13

315 A59 95c Like #311 2.00 1.50
316 A59 95c Like #312 2.00 1.50
317 A59 95c Like #313 2.00 1.50
318 A59 95c Like #314 2.00 1.50

For surcharges see Nos. 391-394.

Queen Mother, 85th Birthday — A60

1985, June 24 Photo. *Perf. 13x13½*

319 A60 75c Photograph, 1921 .50 *.65*
320 A60 95c New mother, 1926 .65 *.80*
321 A60 $1.20 Coronation day, 1937 .85 *1.00*
322 A60 $2.80 70th birthday 2.00 *2.50*
a. Souvenir sheet of 4, #319-322 14.00 14.00
Nos. 319-322 (4) 4.00 4.95

Souvenir Sheet

323 A60 $5 Portrait, c. 1980 3.75 *4.25*

No. 322a issued on 8/4/86, for 86th birthday.

Intl. Youth Year — A61

Grimm Brothers' fairy tales.

1985, Sept. 10 *Perf. 13x13½*

324 A61 75c House in the Wood 1.25 1.25
325 A61 95c Snow White and Rose Red 2.00 2.00
326 A61 $1.15 Goose Girl 2.75 2.75
Nos. 324-326 (3) 6.00 6.00

Christmas 1985 A62

Paintings (details) by Murillo: 75c, No. 330a, The Annunciation. $1.15, No. 330b, Adoration of the Shepherds. $1.80, No. 330c, The Holy Family.

1985, Nov. 25 Photo. *Perf. 14*

327 A62 75c multicolored 1.00 1.00
328 A62 $1.15 multicolored 1.50 1.50
329 A62 $1.80 multicolored 2.50 2.50
Nos. 327-329 (3) 5.00 5.00

Souvenir Sheets

Perf. 13½

330 Sheet of 3 3.50 3.50
a.-c. A62 95c any single 1.10 1.10
331 A62 $1.20 like #327 1.25 1.25
332 A62 $1.45 like #328 1.50 1.50
333 A62 $2.75 like #329 2.75 2.75

Halley's Comet — A63

Fire and Ice, by Camille Rendal. Nos. 334-335 se-tenant in continuous design.

1986, Feb. 4 *Perf. 13½x13*

334 A63 $1.50 Comet head 3.25 3.25
335 A63 $1.50 Comet tail 3.25 3.25
a. Pair, #334-335 6.50 6.50

Size: 109x43mm

Imperf

336 A63 $3 multicolored 3.50 3.50
Nos. 334-336 (3) 10.00 10.00

Elizabeth II, 60th Birthday A64

1986, Apr. 21 *Perf. 14*

337 A64 95c Age 3 1.25 1.25
338 A64 $1.45 Wearing crown 1.50 1.50

Size: 60x34mm

Perf. 13½x13

339 A64 $2.50 Both portraits 2.75 2.75
Nos. 337-339 (3) 5.50 5.50

A65

A66

Statue of Liberty, Cent.: 95c, Statue, scaffolding. $1.75 Removing copper facade. $3, Restored statue on Liberty Island.

1986, June 27 Photo. *Perf. 13½*

340 A65 95c multicolored .90 .90
341 A65 $1.75 multicolored 1.75 1.75
342 A65 $3 multicolored 3.00 3.00
Nos. 340-342 (3) 5.65 5.65

1986, July 23 *Perf. 13x13½*

343 A66 $2.50 Portraits 3.25 3.25
344 A66 $3.50 Profiles 4.00 4.00

Wedding of Prince Andrew and Sarah Ferguson. Nos. 343-344 each printed in sheets of 4 plus 2 center decorative labels.

No. 298 Surcharged with Gold Circle, Bar, New Value in Black and Exhibition Emblem in Gold and Black

1986, Aug. 4

345 Sheet of 2 8.00 8.00
a. A57a $2 on 96c #298a 4.00 4.00
b. A57a $2 on 96c #298b 4.00 4.00

STAMPEX '86, Adelaide, Aug. 4-10.

Christmas A67

Engravings by Rembrandt: 65c, No. 349a, Adoration of the Shepherds. $1.75, No. 349b, Virgin and Child. $2.50, No. 349c, The Holy Family.

1986, Nov. 20 Litho. *Perf. 13x13½*

346 A67 65c multicolored 2.00 2.00
347 A67 $1.75 multicolored 3.25 3.25
348 A67 $2.50 multicolored 4.75 4.75
Nos. 346-348 (3) 10.00 10.00

Souvenir Sheet

Perf. 13½x13

349 Sheet of 3 11.00 11.00
a.-c. A67 $1.50 any single 3.50 3.50

Corrected inscription is black on silver.
For surcharges see Nos. B20-B23.

Souvenir Sheets

Statue of Liberty, Cent. — A68

Photographs: No. 350a, Workmen, crown. No. 350b, Ellis Is., aerial view. No. 350c, Immigration building, Ellis Is. No. 350d, Buildings, opposite side of Ellis Is. No. 350e, Workmen inside torch structure. No. 351a, Liberty's head and torch. No. 351b, Torch. No. 351c, Workmen on scaffold. No. 351d, Statue, full figure. No. 351e, Workmen beside statue. Nos. 351a-351e vert.

1987, Apr. 15 Litho. *Perf. 14*

350 Sheet of 5 + label 5.50 5.50
a.-e. A68 65c any single 1.10 1.10
351 Sheet of 5 + label 5.50 5.50
a.-e. A68 65c any single 1.10 1.10

Nos. 62-63 Ovptd. "Fortieth Royal Wedding / Anniversary 1947-87" in Lilac Rose

1987, Nov. 20 Photo. *Perf. 13½x14*

352 A18 $2 multicolored 2.00 2.00
353 A18 $5 multicolored 5.25 5.25

Christmas A69

Paintings (details) by Raphael: 95c, No. 357a, The Garvagh Madonna, the National Gallery, London. $1.60, No. 357b, The Alba Madonna, the National Gallery of Art, Washington. $2.25, No. 357c, $4.80, The Madonna of the Fish, Prado Museum, Madrid.

1987, Dec. 11 Photo. *Perf. 13½*

354 A69 95c multicolored 2.00 2.00
355 A69 $1.60 multicolored 2.50 2.50
356 A69 $2.25 multicolored 4.00 4.00
Nos. 354-356 (3) 8.50 8.50

Souvenir Sheets

357 Sheet of 3 + label 13.50 13.50
a.-c. A69 $1.15 any single 4.50 4.50
358 A69 $4.80 multicolored 15.00 15.00

No. 358 contains one 31x39mm stamp.

1988 Summer Olympics, Seoul — A70

Events and: 55c, $1.25, Seoul Games emblem. 95c, Obverse of a $50 silver coin issued in 1987 to commemorate the participation of Cook Islands atheletes in the Olympics for the 1st time. $1.50, Coin reverse.

Perf. 13½x13, 13x13½

1988, July 29			Photo.	
359 A70	55c	Running	.75	.75
360 A70	95c	High jump, vert.	1.40	1.40
361 A70	$1.25	Shot put	1.60	1.60
362 A70	$1.50	Tennis, vert.	2.75	2.75
		Nos. 359-362 (4)	6.50	6.50

Souvenir Sheet

363	Sheet of 2	6.00	6.00
a.	A70 $2.50 like 95c	3.00	3.00
b.	A70 $2.50 like $1.50	3.00	3.00

Nos. 359-363 Ovptd. for Olympic Gold Medalists

a. "CARL LEWIS / UNITED STATES / 100 METERS"

b. "LOUISE RITTER / UNITED STATES / HIGH JUMP"

c. "ULF TIMMERMANN / EAST GERMANY / SHOT-PUT"

d. "STEFFI GRAF / WEST GERMANY / WOMEN'S TENNIS"

e. "JACKIE / JOYNER-KERSEE / United States / Heptathlon"

f. "STEFFI GRAF / West Germany / Women's Tennis / MILOSLAV MECIR / Czechoslovakia / Men's Tennis"

Perf. 13½x13, 13x13½

1988, Oct. 14			Photo.	
364 A70(a)	55c	on No. 359	.75	.75
365 A70(b)	95c	on No. 360	1.40	1.40
366 A70(c)	$1.25	on No. 361	1.60	1.60
367 A70(d)	$1.50	on No. 362	3.25	3.25
		Nos. 364-367 (4)	7.00	7.00

Souvenir Sheet

368	Sheet of 2	7.50	7.50
a.	A70(e) $2.50 on No. 363a	3.75	3.75
b.	A70(f) $2.50 on No. 363b	3.75	3.75

Christmas A71

Virgin and Child paintings by Titian.

1988, Nov. 9			*Perf. 13x13½*	
369 A71	70c	multicolored	1.25	1.25
370 A71	85c	multi, diff.	1.40	1.40
371 A71	95c	multi, diff.	1.75	1.75
372 A71	$1.25	multi, diff.	2.00	2.00
		Nos. 369-372 (4)	6.40	6.40

Souvenir Sheet

Perf. 13

373 A71	$6.40 multi, diff.	8.50	8.50

No. 373 contains one diamond-shaped stamp, size: 55x55mm.

1st Moon Landing, 20th Anniv. A72

Apollo 11 mission emblem, US flag and: 55c, First step on the Moon. 75c, Astronaut carrying equipment. 95c, Conducting experiment. $1.25, Crew members Armstrong, Collins and Aldrin. $1.75, Armstrong and Aldrin aboard lunar module.

1989, July 24	Photo.	*Perf. 14*	
374-378 A72	Set of 5	8.50	8.50

Christmas A73

Details from *The Nativity,* by Albrecht Durer, 1498, center panel of the Paumgartner altarpiece: 55c, Madonna. 70c, Christ child, cherubs. 85c, Joseph. $1.25, Attendants. $6.40, Entire painting.

1989, Nov. 17	Photo.	*Perf. 13x13½*	
379-382 A73	Set of 4	6.00	6.00

Souvenir Sheet

383 A73	$6.40 multicolored	9.00	9.00

No. 383 contains one 31x50mm stamp.

Queen Mother, 90th Birthday — A74

1990, July 24	Photo.	*Perf. 13½*	
384 A74	$2.25 multicolored	3.00	3.00

Souvenir Sheet

385 A74	$7.50 multicolored	13.50	13.50

Christmas — A75

Paintings: 55c, Adoration of the Magi by Veronese. 70c, Virgin and Child by Quentin Metsys. 85c, Virgin and Child Jesus by Van Der Goes. $1.50, Adoration of the Kings by Jan Gossaert. $6.40, Virgin and Child with Saints Francis, John the Baptist, Zenobius and Lucy by Domenico Veneziano.

1990, Nov. 26	Litho.	*Perf. 14*	
386-389 A75	Set of 4	7.50	7.50

Souvenir Sheet

390 A75	$6.40 multicolored	8.00	8.00

Nos. 311-314 Surcharged in Red or Black

1990, Dec. 5		Photo.	*Perf. 13*	
391 A59	$1.50	on 20c (R)	2.25	2.25
392 A59	$1.50	on 55c	2.25	2.25
393 A59	$1.50	on 65c	2.25	2.25
394 A59	$1.50	on 75c (R)	2.25	2.25
		Nos. 391-394 (4)	9.00	9.00

Birdpex '90, 20th Intl. Ornithological Cong., New Zealand. Surcharge appears in various locations.

No. 172 Overprinted "COMMEMORATING 65th BIRTHDAY OF H.M. QUEEN ELIZABETH II"

1991, Apr. 22	Photo.	*Perf. 13½*	
395 A42	$6 multicolored	10.00	10.00

Christmas — A76

Paintings: 55c, Virgin and Child with Saints, by Gerard David. 85c, The Nativity, by Tintoretto. $1.15, Mystic Nativity, by Botticelli. $1.85, Adoration of the Shepherds, by Murillo. $6.40, Madonna of the Chair, by Raphael.

1991, Nov. 11	Litho.	*Perf. 14*	
396-399 A76	Set of 4	8.50	8.50

Souvenir Sheet

400 A76	$6.40 multicolored	12.50	12.50

1992 Summer Olympics, Barcelona — A77

1992, July 27		Litho.	*Perf. 14*	
401 A77	75c	Runners	1.50	1.50
402 A77	95c	Boxing	1.75	1.75
403 A77	$1.15	Swimming	2.00	2.00
404 A77	$1.50	Wrestling	2.25	2.25
		Nos. 401-404 (4)	7.50	7.50

6th Festival of Pacific Arts, Rarotonga — A78

Festival poster and: $1.15, Marquesan canoe. $1.75, Statue of Tangaroa. $1.95, Manihiki canoe.

1992, Oct. 16	Litho.	*Perf. 14x15*	
405 A78	$1.15 multicolored	1.75	1.75
406 A78	$1.75 multicolored	2.00	2.00
407 A78	$1.95 multicolored	2.25	2.25
	Nos. 405-407 (3)	6.00	6.00

For overprints see Nos. 455-457.

Overprinted "ROYAL VISIT"

1992, Oct. 16			
408 A78	$1.15 on #405	2.00	2.00
409 A78	$1.75 on #406	2.75	2.75
410 A78	$1.95 on #407	3.25	3.25
	Nos. 408-410 (3)	8.00	8.00

Christmas A79

Paintings by Ambrogio Borgognone: 55c, $6.40, Virgin with Child and Saints. 85c, Virgin on Throne. $1.05, Virgin on Carpet. $1.85, Virgin of the Milk.

1992, Nov. 18	Litho.	*Perf. 13½*	
411-414 A79	Set of 4	6.75	6.75

Souvenir Sheet

415 A79	$6.40 multicolored	9.00	9.00

No. 415 contains one 38x48mm stamp.

Discovery of America, 500th Anniv. — A80

Designs: $1.15, Vicente Yanez Pinzon, Nina. $1.35, Martin Alonso Pinzon, Pinta. $1.75, Columbus, Santa Maria.

1992, Dec. 4		*Perf. 15x14*	
416 A80	$1.15 multicolored	2.40	2.40
417 A80	$1.35 multicolored	2.50	2.50
418 A80	$1.75 multicolored	3.50	3.50
	Nos. 416-418 (3)	8.40	8.40

Coronation of Queen Elizabeth II, 40th Anniv. — A81

1993, June 4	Litho.	*Perf. 14x14½*	
419 A81	$6 multicolored	8.00	8.00

Marine Life — A82

Marine Life — A82a

1993-98			Litho.	*Perf. 14*	
420	A82	5c	Helmet shell	.20	.20
421	A82	10c	Daisy coral	.20	.20
422	A82	15c	Hydroid coral	.20	.20
423	A82	20c	Feather star	.25	.25
424	A82	25c	Sea star	.30	.30
425	A82	30c	Nudibranch	.35	.35
426	A82	50c	Smooth sea star	.55	.55
427	A82	70c	Black pearl oyster	.80	.80
428	A82	80c	Pyjama nudibranch	.90	.90
429	A82	85c	Prickly sea cucumber	.95	.95
430	A82	90c	Organ pipe coral	1.00	1.00
431	A82	$1	Aeolid nudibranch	1.10	1.10
432	A82	$2	Textile cone shell	2.25	2.25
433	A82a	$3	pink & multi	3.25	3.25
434	A82a	$5	lilac & multi	5.50	5.50
			Perf. 14x13½		
435	A82a	$8	blue & multi	11.00	11.00
435A	A82a	$10	grn & multi	11.00	11.00
			Nos. 420-435A (17)	39.80	39.80

For overprints see #O41-O53.

Issued: 80c, 85c, 90c, $1, $2, 12/3/93; $3, $5, 11/21/94; $8, 11/17/97; $10, 10/1/98; others, 10/18/93.

This is an expanding set. Numbers will change if necessary.

Christmas — A83

Details from Virgin on Throne with Child, by Cosimo Tura: 55c, Madonna and Child. 85c, Musicians. $1.05, Musicians, diff. $1.95, Woman. $4.50, Entire painting.

1993, Nov. 2		Litho.	*Perf. 14*	
436 A83	55c	multicolored	1.00	1.00
437 A83	85c	multicolored	1.60	1.60
438 A83	$1.05	multicolored	1.75	1.75

439 A83 $1.95 multicolored 2.75 2.75

Size: 32x47mm

Perf. 13½

440 A83 $4.50 multicolored 6.25 6.25
Nos. 436-440 (5) 13.35 13.35

First Manned Moon Landing, 25th Anniv. A84

1994, July 20 Litho. *Perf. 14*
441 A84 $3.25 multicolored 9.00 9.00

Christmas — A85

Details or entire paintings: No. 442a, Virgin and Child with Saints Paul & Jerome, by Vivarini. b, The Virgin and Child with St. John, by B. Luini. c, The Virgin and Child with Saints Jerome & Dominic, by F. Lippi. d, Adoration of Shepherds, by Murillo.

No. 443a, Adoration of the Kings, by Reni. b, Madonna & Child with the Infant Baptist, by Raphael. c, Adoration of the Kings, by Reni, diff. d, Virgin and Child, by Bergognone.

1994, Nov. 30 Litho. *Perf. 14*
442 A85 90c Block of 4, #a.-d. 5.25 5.25
443 A85 $1 Block of 4, #a.-d. 5.75 5.75

End of World War II, 50th Anniv. — A86

Designs: a, Battleships on fire, Pearl Harbor, Dec. 7, 1941. b, B-29 bomber Enola Gay, A-bomb cloud, Aug. 1945.

1995, Sept. 4 Litho. *Perf. 13*
444 A86 $3.75 Pair, #a.-b. 10.00 10.00

Queen Mother, 95th Birthday A87

1995, Sept. 14 Litho. *Perf. 13½*
445 A87 $4.50 multicolored 6.00 6.00

No. 445 was issued in sheets of 4.

UN, 50th Anniv. — A88

1995, Oct. 20 Litho. *Perf. 13½*
446 A88 $4 multicolored 5.25 5.25

No. 446 was issued in sheets of 4.

1995, Year of the Sea Turtle — A89

No. 447: a, Loggerhead. b, Hawksbill.
No. 448: a, Olive ridley. b, Green.

1995, Dec. 7 Litho. *Perf. 13½*
447 A89 $1.15 Pair, #a.-b. 3.00 3.00
448 A89 $1.65 Pair, #a.-b. 4.50 4.50

Queen Elizabeth II, 70th Birthday A90

1996, June 20 Litho. *Perf. 14*
449 A90 $4.25 multicolored 6.00 6.00

No. 449 was issued in sheets of 4.

1996 Summer Olympic Games, Atlanta A91

1996, July 12 Litho. *Perf. 14*
450 A91 $5 multicolored 6.90 6.90

Queen Elizabeth II and Prince Philip, 50th Wedding Anniv. A92

1997, Nov. 20 Litho. *Perf. 14*
451 A92 $3 multicolored 4.25 4.25

Souvenir Sheet

452 A92 $4 multicolored 5.50 5.50

No. 452 is a continuous design.

Diana, Princess of Wales (1961-97) — A93

1998, May 7 Litho. *Perf. 14*
453 A93 $1.50 multicolored 1.75 1.75

Souvenir Sheet

454 A93 $3.75 like #453 4.50 4.50

No. 453 was issued in sheets of 5 + label. For surcharge see #B24.

Nos. 405-407 Ovptd. "KIA ORANA / THIRD MILLENNIUM"

Methods and Perfs as before

1999, Dec. 31
455 A77 $1.15 multi 1.10 1.10
456 A77 $1.75 multi 1.75 1.75
457 A77 $1.95 multi 2.00 2.00
Nos. 455-457 (3) 4.85 4.85

Queen Mother, 100th Birthday — A94

No. 458: a, With King George VI. b, With Princess Elizabeth. c, With King George VI, Princesses Elizabeth and Margaret. d, With Princesses.

2000, Oct. 20 Litho. *Perf. 14*
458 A94 $2.50 Sheet of 4, #a-d 8.25 8.25

Souvenir Sheet

459 A94 $10 Portrait 8.25 8.25

2000 Summer Olympics, Sydney — A95

No. 460, horiz.: a, Ancient javelin. b, Javelin. c, Ancient discus. d, Discus.

2000, Dec. 14
460 A95 $2.75 Sheet of 4, #a-d 10.00 10.00

Souvenir Sheet

461 A95 $3.50 Torch relay 3.25 3.25

SEMI-POSTAL STAMPS

Catalogue values for unused stamps in this section are for Never Hinged items.

Easter Type of 1978
Souvenir Sheets

Rubens Paintings: No. B1, like #101. No. B2, like #102. No. B3, like #103.

1978, Apr. 17 Photo. *Perf. 13½x13*
B1 A31 60c + 5c multi .60 .60
B2 A31 60c + 5c multi .60 .60
B3 A31 60c + 5c multi .60 .60
Nos. B1-B3 (3) 1.80 1.80

Surtax was for school children.

Easter Type of 1980
Souvenir Sheets

1980, Mar. 28 Photo. *Perf. 13x13½*
B4 A36 70c + 5c like #114 .60 .60
B5 A36 70c + 5c like #115 .60 .60
B6 A36 70c + 5c like #116 .60 .60
Nos. B4-B6 (3) 1.80 1.80

Surtax was for local charities.

Christmas Type of 1980
Souvenir Sheets

1980, Dec. 5 Photo. *Perf. 13*
B7 A39 70c + 5c like #127 1.00 1.00
B8 A39 70c + 5c like #128 1.00 1.00
B9 A39 70c + 5c like #129 1.00 1.00
Nos. B7-B9 (3) 3.00 3.00

Surtax was for local charities.

Easter Type of 1981
Souvenir Sheets

1981, Apr. 5 Photo. *Perf. 13½*
B10 A44 70c + 5c like #173 .90 .90
B11 A44 70c + 5c like #174 .90 .90
B12 A44 70c + 5c like #175 .90 .90
Nos. B10-B12 (3) 2.70 2.70

Surtax was for local charities.

Nos. 176-180a Surcharged

1981, Nov. 30 Photo. *Perf. 14*
B13 A45 40c + 5c like #176 .25 *.35*
B14 A45 50c + 5c like #177 .30 *.40*
B15 A45 60c + 5c like #178 .30 *.50*
B16 A45 70c + 5c like #179 .30 *.60*
B17 A45 80c + 5c like #180 .30 *.65*
Nos. B13-B17 (5) 1.45 *2.50*

Souvenir Sheet

B18 Sheet of 5 2.00 *2.50*
a. A45 40c + 10c like #176 .40 *.50*
b. A45 50c + 10c like #177 .40 *.50*
c. A45 60c + 10c like #178 .40 *.50*
d. A45 70c + 10c like #179 .40 *.50*
e. A45 80c + 10c like #180 .40 *.50*

Intl. Year of the Disabled. Surtax was for the disabled.

Soccer Type of 1981

1981, Dec. 7 *Perf. 13*
B19 A46 Sheet of 9 5.00 3.00

No. B19 contains Nos. 181-183. Surtax was for local sports.

Nos. 346-349 Surcharged ".SOUTH PACIFIC PAPAL VISIT . 21 TO 24 NOVEMBER 1986" in Metallic Blue

1986, Nov. 24 Litho. *Perf. 13x13½*
B20 A67 65c + 10c multi 2.75 2.00
B21 A67 $1.75 + 10c multi 4.75 4.00
B22 A67 $2.50 + 10c multi 5.50 4.25
Nos. B20-B22 (3) 13.00 10.25

Souvenir Sheet

Perf. 13½x13

B23 Sheet of 3 14.00 14.00
a.-c. A67 $1.50 + 10c on #349a-349c 4.50 4.50

No. B23 inscribed "COMMEMORATING FIRST PAPAL VISIT TO SOUTH PACIFIC / VISIT OF POPE JOHN PAUL II . NOVEMBER 1986."

No. 454 Surcharged "CHILDREN'S CHARITIES" in Silver
Souvenir Sheet

1998, Nov. 19 Litho. *Perf. 14*
B24 A93 $3.75 +$1 multi 5.00 5.00

OFFICIAL STAMPS

Catalogue values for unused stamps in this section are for Never Hinged items.

Nos. 51-60, 80, 88-89 Overprinted or Surcharged in Black, Silver or Gold

Perf. 13½x14, 13½, 13½x13

1978, Nov. 14 **Photo.**

O1	A17	1c multi	.20	.20
O2	A17	2c multi	.20	.20
O3	A17	3c multi	.25	.20
O4	A17	4c multi	.25	.20
O5	A17	5c multi	.30	.20
O6	A17	8c multi	.35	.20
O7	A17	10c multi	.40	.20
O8	A17	15c on 60c multi	.45	.30
O9	A17	18c on 60c multi	.50	.30
O10	A17	20c multi	.50	.30
O11	A17	25c multi (S)	.55	.35
O12	A17	30c on 60c multi	.60	.40
O13	A24	Strip of 3, multi	2.75	2.00
a.		50c, No. 80a (G)	.80	.65
b.		50c, No. 80b (G)	.80	.65
c.		50c, No. 80c (G)	.80	.65
O14	A27	$1 multi (S)	2.25	.55
O15	A27	$2 multi (G)	4.00	.60
		Nos. O1-O15 (15)	13.55	6.20

Overprint on No. O14 diagonal.

Nos. 268-276, 278, 277, 211-214, 280, 282, 281, 283, 170, 284, 171, 285, 172, 286 Surcharged with Bar and New Value or Ovptd. "O.H.M.S." in Silver or Metallic Red

1985-87 **Photo.** ***Perfs. as before***

O16	A56	2c multi	.20	.20
O17	A56	4c multi	.20	.20
O18	A56	5c multi	.20	.20
O19	A56	8c multi	.20	.20
O20	A56	10c multi	.20	.20
O21	A56	18c multi	.20	.20
O22	A56	20c multi	.20	.20
O23	A56	30c multi	.30	.30
O24	A56	40c on 36c	.40	.40
O25	A56	50c multi	.50	.50
O26	A56	55c on 48c	.55	.55
O27	A50	65c on 60c #211	.65	.65
O28	A50	65c on 60c #212	.65	.65
O29	A50	65c on 60c #213	.65	.65
O30	A50	65c on 60c #214	.65	.65
O31	A56	75c on 72c	.75	.75
O32	A56	75c on 96c	.75	.75
O33	A56	80c multi	.80	.80
O34	A56	$1.20 multi	1.10	1.00
O35	A42	$2 multi (R)	1.75	1.50
O36	A56	$3 multi	2.75	2.10
O37	A42	$4 multi (R)	3.50	2.50
O38	A56	$5 multi	4.50	3.50
O39	A42	$6 multi (R)	5.50	4.00
O40	A56	$9.60 multi	9.00	6.50
		Nos. O16-O40 (25)	36.15	29.15

Issued: #O16-O30, 8/15; #O31-O37, 4/29/86; #O38-O40, 11/2/87.

Nos. 420-432 Ovptd. "O.H.M.S." in Silver

1998 **Litho.** ***Perf. 14***

O41	A82	5c multicolored	.20	.20
O42	A82	10c multicolored	.20	.20
O43	A82	15c multicolored	.20	.20
O44	A82	20c multicolored	.20	.20
O45	A82	25c multicolored	.20	.20
O46	A82	30c multicolored	.30	.30
O47	A82	50c multicolored	.40	.40
O48	A82	70c multicolored	.55	.55
O49	A82	85c multicolored	.70	.70
O50	A82	70c multicolored	.70	.70
O51	A82	90c multicolored	.75	.75
O52	A82	$1 multicolored	.85	.85
O53	A82	$2 multicolored	1.75	1.75
		Nos. O41-O53 (13)	7.00	7.00

Nos. O41-O52 were not sold unused to local customers.
Issued: $2, 9/30; others, 7/20.

PERU

pə-'rü

LOCATION — West coast of South America
GOVT. — Republic
AREA — 496,093 sq. mi.
POP. — 24,800,768 (1998 est.)
CAPITAL — Lima

8 Reales = 1 Peso (1857)
100 Centimos = 8 Dineros = 4 Pesetas = 1 Peso (1858)
100 Centavos = 1 Sol (1874)
100 Centimos = 1 Inti (1985)
100 Centimos = 1 Sol (1991)

Catalogue values for unused stamps in this country are for Never Hinged items, beginning with Scott 426 in the regular postage section, Scott B1 in the semi-postal section, Scott C78 in the airpost section, Scott CB1 in the airpost semi-postal section, and Scott RA31 in the postal tax section.

Watermark

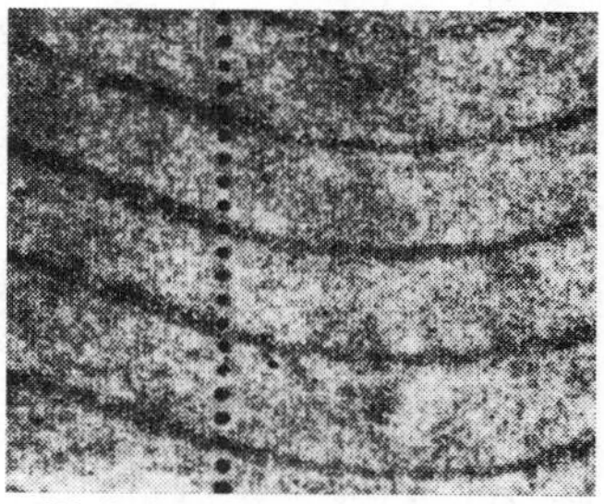

Wmk. 346- Parallel Curved Lines

Sail and Steamship — A1

Design: 2r, Ship sails eastward.

Unwmk.

1857, Dec. 1 **Engr.** ***Imperf.***

1	A1	1r blue, *blue*	1,250.	1,450.
2	A1	2r brn red, *blue*	1,350.	1,600.

The Pacific Steam Navigation Co. gave a quantity of these stamps to the Peruvian government so that a trial of prepayment of postage by stamps might be made.
Stamps of 1 and 2 reales, printed in various colors on white paper, laid and wove, were prepared for the Pacific Steam Navigation Co. but never put in use. Value $50 each on wove paper, $400 each on laid paper.

Coat of Arms
A2 A3

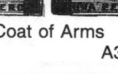

A4

Wavy Lines in Spandrels

1858, Mar. 1 **Litho.**

3	A2	1d deep blue	200.	27.50
4	A3	1p rose red	850.	125.
5	A4	½peso rose red	*3,750.*	*3,000.*
6	A4	½peso buff	*1,600.*	300.
a.		½peso orange yellow	*1,600.*	300.

A5 A6

Large Letters

1858, Dec.

Double-lined Frame

7	A5	1d slate blue	250.00	27.50
8	A6	1p red	250.00	37.50

A7 A8

1860-61

Zigzag Lines in Spandrels

9	A7	1d blue	100.00	6.50
a.		1d Prussian blue	100.00	12.00
b.		Cornucopia on white ground	225.00	47.50
c.		Zigzag lines broken at angles	125.00	14.00
10	A8	1p rose	250.00	25.00
a.		1p brick red	250.00	25.00
b.		Cornucopia on white ground	250.00	30.00

Retouched, 10 lines instead of 9 in left label

11	A8	1p rose	125.00	25.00
a.		Pelure paper	200.00	25.00
		Nos. 9-11 (3)	475.00	56.50

A9 A10

1862-63 **Embossed**

12	A9	1d red	13.00	2.75
a.		Arms embossed sideways	425.00	90.00
b.		Thick paper	27.50	8.00
c.		Diag. half used on cover		140.00
13	A10	1p brown ('63)	72.50	22.50
a.		Diag. half used on cover		1,000.

Counterfeits of Nos. 13 and 15 exist.

A11

1868-72

14	A11	1d green	11.00	2.25
a.		Arms embossed inverted	*1,200.*	*700.00*
b.		Diag. half used on cover		350.00
15	A10	1p orange ('72)	90.00	32.50
a.		Diag. half used on cover		—

Nos. 12-15, 19 and 20 were printed in horizontal strips. Stamps may be found printed on two strips of paper where the strips were joined by overlapping.

Llamas — A12 A13

A14

1866-67 **Engr.** ***Perf. 12***

16	A12	5c green	6.00	.60
17	A13	10c vermilion	6.00	1.40
18	A14	20c brown	20.00	4.00
a.		Diagonal half used on cover		375.00
		Nos. 16-18 (3)	32.00	6.00

See Nos. 109, 111, 113.

Locomotive and Arms — A15

Llama — A16

1871, Apr. **Embossed** ***Imperf.***

19	A15	5c scarlet	75.00	25.00
a.		5c pale red	75.00	25.00

20th anniv. of the first railway in South America, linking Lima and Callao.
The so-called varieties "ALLAO" and "CALLA" are due to over-inking.

1873, Mar. ***Rouletted Horiz.***

20	A16	2c dk ultra	30.00	*250.00*

Counterfeits are plentiful.

Sun God of the Incas — A17

Coat of Arms
A18 A19

A20 A21

A22 A23

Embossed with Grill

1874-84 **Engr.** ***Perf. 12***

21	A17	1c orange ('79)	.50	.40
22	A18	2c dk violet	.65	.50
23	A19	5c blue ('77)	.85	.25
24	A19	5c ultra ('79)	8.50	2.00
25	A20	10c green ('76)	.25	.20
a.		Imperf., pair	25.00	
26	A20	10c slate ('84)	2.00	.25
a.		Diag. half used as 5c on cover		—
27	A21	20c brown red	2.00	.65
28	A22	50c green	9.00	2.50
29	A23	1s rose	1.50	1.50
		Nos. 21-29 (9)	25.25	8.25

No. 25a lacks the grill.
No. 26 with overprint "DE OFICIO" is said to have been used to frank mail of Gen. A. A. Caceres during the civil war against Gen. Miguel Iglesias, provisional president. Experts question its status.

1880

30	A17	1c green	2.00	
31	A18	2c rose	2.00	

Nos. 30 and 31 were prepared for use but not issued without overprint.
See Nos. 104-108, 110, 112, 114-115.
For overprints see Nos. 32-103, 116-128, J32-J33, O2-O22, N11-N23, 1N1-1N9, 3N11-3N20, 5N1, 6N1-6N2, 7N1-7N2, 8N7, 8N10-8N11, 9N1-9N3, 10N3-10N8, 10N10-10N11, 11N1-11N5, 12N1-12N3, 13N1, 14N1-14N16, 15N5-15N8, 15N13-15N18, 16N1-16N22.

Stamps of 1874-80 Overprinted in Red, Blue or Black

Reduced illustration

1880, Jan. 5

32	A17	1c green (R)	.50	.40
a.		Inverted overprint	10.00	10.00
b.		Double overprint	13.50	13.50
33	A18	2c rose (Bl)	1.00	.65
a.		Inverted overprint	10.00	10.00
b.		Double overprint	14.00	12.00
34	A18	2c rose (Bk)	45.00	35.00
a.		Inverted overprint		
b.		Double overprint		
35	A19	5c ultra (R)	2.00	1.00
a.		Inverted overprint	10.00	10.00
b.		Double overprint	14.00	14.00
36	A22	50c green (R)	27.50	17.50
a.		Inverted overprint	45.00	45.00
b.		Double overprint	55.00	55.00
37	A23	1s rose (Bl)	70.00	45.00
a.		Inverted overprint	110.00	110.00
b.		Double overprint	110.00	110.00
		Nos. 32-37 (6)	146.00	99.55

Stamps of 1874-80 Overprinted in Red or Blue

Reduced illustration

1881, Jan. 28

38	A17	1c green (R)	.75	.60
a.		Inverted overprint	8.25	8.25
b.		Double overprint	14.00	14.00
39	A18	2c rose (Bl)	14.00	9.00
a.		Inverted overprint	17.50	15.00
b.		Double overprint	25.00	20.00
40	A19	5c ultra (R)	1.50	.75
a.		Inverted overprint	14.00	14.00
b.		Double overprint	20.00	20.00
41	A22	50c green (R)	450.00	250.00
a.		Inverted overprint	600.00	
42	A23	1s rose (Bl)	82.50	55.00
a.		Inverted overprint	150.00	

Reprints of Nos. 38 to 42 were made in 1884. In the overprint the word "PLATA" is 3mm high instead of 2½mm. The cross bars of the letters "A" of that word are set higher than on the original stamps. The 5c is printed in blue instead of ultramarine.

For stamps of 1874-80 overprinted with Chilean arms or small UPU "horseshoe," see Nos. N11-N23.

Stamps of 1874-79 Handstamped in Black or Blue

1883

65	A17	1c orange (Bk)	.85	.65
66	A17	1c orange (Bl)	45.00	
68	A19	5c ultra (Bk)	7.50	5.00
69	A20	10c green (Bk)	.75	.65
70	A20	10c green (Bl)	5.00	4.00
71	A22	50c green (Bk)	7.00	3.50
73	A23	1s rose (Bk)	10.00	6.00
		Nos. 65-73 (7)	76.10	
		Nos. 65,68-73 (6)	31.10	19.80

This overprint is found in 11 types.

The 1c green, 2c dark violet and 20c brown red, overprinted with triangle, are fancy varieties made for sale to collectors and never placed in regular use.

Overprinted Triangle and "Union Postal Universal Peru" in Oval

1883

77	A22	50c grn (R & Bk)	125.00	60.00
78	A23	1s rose (Bl & Bk)	140.00	90.00

The 1c green, 2c rose and 5c ultramarine, over printed with triangle and "U. P. U. Peru" oval, were never placed in regular use.

Overprinted Triangle and "Union Postal Universal Lima" in Oval

1883

79	A17	1c grn (R & Bl)	50.00	37.50
80	A17	1c grn (R & Bk)	4.00	4.00
a.		Oval overprint inverted		
b.		Double overprint of oval		
81	A18	2c rose (Bl & Bk)	4.00	4.00
82	A19	5c ultra (R & Bk)	6.50	6.00
83	A19	5c ultra (R & Bl)	6.50	6.00
84	A22	50c grn (R & Bk)	140.00	90.00
85	A23	1s rose (Bl & Bk)	150.00	125.00
		Nos. 79-85 (7)	361.00	272.50

Some authorities question the status of No. 79.

Nos. 80, 81, 84, and 85 were reprinted in 1884. They have the second type of oval overprint with "PLATA" 3mm high.

Overprinted Triangle and

86	A17	1c grn (Bk & Bk)	1.00	.80
a.		Horseshoe inverted	10.00	
87	A17	1c grn (Bl & Bk)	5.00	3.50
88	A18	2c ver (Bk & Bk)	1.00	.75
89	A19	5c bl (Bk & Bk)	1.25	1.00
90	A19	5c bl (Bl & Bk)	7.00	6.50
91	A19	5c bl (R & Bk)	*1,500.*	*1,100.*

Overprinted Horseshoe Alone

1883, Oct. 23

95	A17	1c green	1.25	1.25
96	A18	2c vermilion	1.25	*4.00*
a.		Double overprint		
97	A19	5c blue	2.00	2.00
98	A19	5c ultra	20.00	15.00
99	A22	50c rose	57.50	57.50
100	A23	1s ultra	30.00	22.50
		Nos. 95-100 (6)	112.00	102.25

The 2c violet overprinted with the above design in red and triangle in black also the 1c green overprinted with the same combination plus the horseshoe in black, are fancy varieties made for sale to collectors.

No. 23 Overprinted in Black

1884, Apr. 28

103	A19	5c blue	.65	.40
a.		Double overprint	5.00	5.00

Stamps of 1c and 2c with the above overprint, also with the above and "U. P. U. LIMA" oval in blue or "CORREOS LIMA" in a double-lined circle in red, were made to sell to collectors and were never placed in use.

Without Overprint or Grill

1886-95

104	A17	1c dull violet	.50	.20
105	A17	1c vermilion ('95)	.40	.20
106	A18	2c green	.75	.20
107	A18	2c dp ultra ('95)	.35	.20
108	A19	5c orange	.60	.30
109	A12	5c claret ('95)	1.25	.50
110	A20	10c slate	.40	.20
111	A13	10c orange ('95)	.60	.35
112	A21	20c blue	5.00	.65
113	A14	20c dp ultra ('95)	6.00	1.40
114	A22	50c red	1.50	.65
115	A23	1s brown	1.25	.50
		Nos. 104-115 (12)	18.60	5.35

Overprinted Horseshoe in Black and Triangle in Rose Red

1889

116	A17	1c green	.75	.50
a.		Horseshoe inverted	7.50	

Nos. 30 and 25 Overprinted "Union Postal Universal Lima" in Oval in Red

1889, Sept. 1

117	A17	1c green	1.50	1.25
117A	A20	10c green	1.50	1.50

The overprint on Nos. 117 and 117A is of the second type with "PLATA" 3mm high.

Stamps of 1874-80 Overprinted in Black

Pres. Remigio Morales Bermúdez

1894, Oct. 23

118	A17	1c orange	.60	.40
a.		Inverted overprint	7.00	7.00
b.		Double overprint	7.00	7.00
119	A17	1c green	.40	.35
a.		Inverted overprint	3.50	3.50
b.		Dbl. inverted ovpt.	5.00	5.00
120	A18	2c violet	.40	.35
a.		Diagonal half used as 1c		
b.		Inverted overprint	7.00	7.00
c.		Double overprint	7.00	
121	A18	2c rose	.40	.35
a.		Double overprint	7.00	7.00
b.		Inverted overprint	7.00	7.00
122	A19	5c blue	2.50	1.75
122A	A19	5c ultra	4.25	2.00
b.		Inverted overprint	10.00	10.00
123	A20	10c green	.40	.35
a.		Inverted overprint	7.00	7.00
124	A22	50c green	1.40	1.25
a.		Inverted overprint	10.00	10.00
		Nos. 118-124 (8)	10.35	6.80

Same, with Additional Overprint of Horseshoe

125	A18	2c vermilion	.35	.25
a.		Head inverted	2.50	2.50
b.		Head double	5.00	5.00
126	A19	5c blue	1.00	.50
a.		Head inverted	7.00	7.00
127	A22	50c rose	42.50	30.00
a.		Head double	55.00	45.00
b.		Head inverted		
128	A23	1s ultra	100.00	90.00
a.		Both overprints inverted	125.00	110.00
b.		Head double	125.00	110.00
		Nos. 125-128 (4)	143.85	120.75

A23a

1895 *Perf. 11½*

Vermilion Surcharge

129	A23a	5c on 5c grn	10.00	7.50
130	A23a	10c on 10c ver	8.00	6.00
131	A23a	20c on 20c brn	8.50	6.50
132	A23a	50c on 50c ultra	10.00	7.50
133	A23a	1s on 1s red brn	10.00	8.00
		Nos. 129-133 (5)	46.50	35.50

Nos 129-133 were used only in Tumbes. The basic stamps were prepared by revolutionaries in northern Peru.

A23b

"Liberty" A23c

1895, Sept. 8 **Engr.**

134	A23b	1c gray violet	1.40	.80
135	A23b	2c green	1.40	.80
136	A23b	5c yellow	1.40	.80
137	A23b	10c ultra	1.40	.80
138	A23c	20c orange	1.40	1.00
139	A23c	50c dark blue	7.25	5.50
140	A23c	1s car lake	40.00	27.50
		Nos. 134-140 (7)	54.25	37.20

Success of the revolution against the government of General Caceres and of the election of President Pierola.

Manco Capac, Founder of Inca Dynasty — A24

Francisco Pizarro Conqueror of the Inca Empire — A25

General José de La Mar — A26

1896-1900

141	A24	1c ultra	.50	.20
a.		1c blue (error)	40.00	35.00
142	A24	1c yel grn ('98)	.50	.20
143	A24	2c blue	.50	.20
144	A24	2c scar ('99)	.50	.20
145	A25	5c indigo	.75	.20
146	A25	5c green ('97)	.75	.20
147	A25	5c grnsh bl ('99)	.50	.20
148	A25	10c yellow	1.00	.25
149	A25	10c gray blk ('00)	1.00	.20
150	A25	20c orange	2.00	.25
151	A26	50c car rose	5.00	.80
152	A26	1s orange red	7.50	1.00
153	A26	2s claret	2.25	.80
		Nos. 141-153 (13)	22.75	4.70

The 5c in black is a chemical changeling.

For surcharges and overprints see Nos. 187-188, E1, O23-O26.

Paucartambo Bridge A27

Post and Telegraph Building, Lima — A28

Pres. Nicolás de Piérola — A29

1897, Dec. 31

154	A27	1c dp ultra	.65	.35
155	A28	2c brown	.65	.25
156	A29	5c bright rose	1.00	.25
		Nos. 154-156 (3)	2.30	.85

Opening of new P.O. in Lima.

A30

A31

1897, Nov. 8

157	A30	1c bister	.50	.45
a.		Inverted overprint	2.50	2.50
b.		Double overprint	10.00	10.00

1899

No.	Type	Description	Unused	Used
158	A31	5s orange red	1.60	1.60
159	A31	10s blue green	500.00	350.00

For surcharge see No. J36.

Pres. Eduardo de Romaña A32

Admiral Miguel L. Grau A33

1900 Frame Litho., Center Engr.

No.	Type	Description	Unused	Used
160	A32	22c yel grn & blk	8.00	.85

1901, Jan.

2c, Col. Francisco Bolognes. 5c, Pres. Romaña.

No.	Type	Description	Unused	Used
161	A33	1c green & blk	1.00	.25
162	A33	2c red & black	1.00	.25
163	A33	5c dull vio & blk	1.00	.25
		Nos. 161-163 (3)	3.00	.75

Advent of 20th century.

A34

Municipal Hygiene Institute Lima — A35

1902 Engr.

No.	Type	Description	Unused	Used
164	A34	22c green	.35	.20

1905

No.	Type	Description	Unused	Used
165	A35	12c dp blue & blk	1.00	.25

For surcharges see Nos. 166-167, 186, 189.

Same Surcharged in Red or Violet

1907

No.	Type	Description	Unused	Used
166	A35	1c on 12c (R)	.25	.20
a.		Inverted surcharge	8.00	8.00
b.		Double surcharge	8.00	8.00
167	A35	2c on 12c (V)	.50	.35
a.		Double surcharge	8.00	8.00
b.		Inverted surcharge	8.00	8.00

Monument of Bolognesi — A36

Admiral Grau — A37

Llama — A38

Statue of Bolivar — A39

City Hall, Lima, formerly an Exhibition Building — A40

School of Medicine, Lima — A41

Post and Telegraph Building, Lima — A42

Grandstand at Santa Beatrix Race Track — A43

Columbus Monument — A44

1907

No.	Type	Description	Unused	Used
168	A36	1c yel grn & blk	.35	.20
169	A37	2c red & violet	.35	.20
170	A38	4c olive green	5.50	.75
171	A39	5c blue & blk	.60	.20
172	A40	10c red brn & blk	1.00	.25
173	A41	20c dk grn & blk	22.50	.50
174	A42	50c black	22.50	1.00
175	A43	1s purple & grn	125.00	2.50
176	A44	2s dp bl & blk	125.00	100.00
		Nos. 168-176 (9)	302.80	105.60

For surcharges and overprint see #190-195, E2.

Manco Capac A45

Columbus A46

Pizarro A47

San Martin A48

Bolívar A49

La Mar A50

Ramón Castilla A51

Grau A52

Bolognesi — A53

1909

No.	Type	Description	Unused	Used
177	A45	1c gray	.20	.20
178	A46	2c green	.20	.20
179	A47	4c vermilion	.30	.20
180	A48	5c violet	.20	.20
181	A49	10c deep blue	.50	.20
182	A50	12c pale blue	1.00	.20
183	A51	20c brown red	1.10	.25
184	A52	50c yellow	5.00	.35
185	A53	1s brn red & blk	10.00	.35
		Nos. 177-185 (9)	18.50	2.15

See types A54, A78-A80, A81-A89.

For surcharges and overprint see Nos. 196-200, 208, E3.

No. 165 Surcharged in Red

1913, Jan.

No.	Type	Description	Unused	Used
186	A35	8c on 12c dp bl & blk	.65	.25

Stamps of 1899-1908 Surcharged in Magenta

a

b

c

1915

No.	Type	Description	Unused	Used
		On Nos. 142, 149		
187	A24(a)	1c on 1c	16.50	12.00
a.		Inverted surcharge	22.50	18.00
188	A25(a)	1c on 10c	.80	.75
		On No. 165		
189	A35(c)	2c on 12c	.25	.20
a.		Inverted surcharge		
		On Nos. 168-170, 172-174		
190	A36(a)	1c on 1c	.65	.65
191	A37(a)	1c on 2c	1.00	1.00
192	A38(b)	1c on 4c	1.60	1.60
a.		Inverted surcharge	6.00	6.00
193	A40(b)	1c on 10c	.35	.30
a.		Inverted surcharge	2.50	2.50
193C	A40(c)	2c on 10c	100.00	80.00
194	A41(c)	2c on 20c	14.00	12.00
195	A42(c)	2c on 50c	2.00	2.00
		Nos. 187-195 (10)	137.15	110.50

Nos. 182-184, 179, 185 Surcharged in Red, Green or Violet

d

e

f

1916

No.	Type	Description	Unused	Used
196	A50(d)	1c on 12c (R)	.20	.20
a.		Double surcharge	2.00	2.00
b.		Green surcharge	4.50	4.50
197	A51(d)	1c on 20c (G)	.20	.20
198	A52(d)	1c on 50c (G)	.20	.20
a.		Inverted surcharge	2.00	2.00
199	A47(e)	2c on 4c (V)	.20	.20
200	A53(f)	10c on 1s (G)	.50	.20
a.		"VALF"	3.50	3.50
		Nos. 196-200 (5)	1.30	1.00

Official Stamps of 1909-14 Overprinted or Surcharged in Green or Red:

g

h

1916

No.	Type	Description	Unused	Used
201	O1(g)	1c red (G)	.20	.20
202	O1(h)	2c on 50c ol grn (R)	.20	.20
203	O1(g)	10c bis brn (G)	.20	.20

Postage Due Stamps of 1909 Surcharged in Violet-Black

No.	Type	Description	Unused	Used
204	D7	2c on 1c brown	.40	.40
205	D7	2c on 5c brown	.20	.20
206	D7	2c on 10c brown	.20	.20
207	D7	2c on 50c brown	.20	.20
		Nos. 201-207 (7)	1.60	1.60

Many copies of Nos. 187 to 207 have a number of pin holes. It is stated that these holes were made at the time the surcharges were printed.

The varieties which we list of the 1915 and 1916 issues were sold to the public at post offices. Many other varieties which were previously listed are now known to have been delivered to one speculator or to have been privately printed by him from the surcharging plates which he had acquired.

No. 179 Surcharged in Black

1917

No.	Type	Description	Unused	Used
208	A47	1c on 4c ver	.25	.20
a.		Double surcharge	4.00	4.00
b.		Inverted surcharge	4.00	4.00

San Martín — A54

Columbus at Salamanca — A62

Funeral of Atahualpa A63

Battle of Arica, "Arica, the Last Cartridge" A64

Designs: 2c, Bolivar. 4c, José Gálvez. 5c, Manuel Pardo. 8c, Grau. 10c, Bolognesi. 12c, Castilla. 20c, General Cáceres.

1918 Engr.

Centers in Black

No.	Type	Description	Unused	Used
209	A54	1c orange	.20	.20
210	A54	2c green	.20	.20
211	A54	4c lake	.30	.20
212	A54	5c dp ultra	.25	.20
213	A54	8c red brn	.75	.25
214	A54	10c grnsh bl	.35	.20
215	A54	12c dl vio	1.00	.20
216	A54	20c ol grn	1.25	.20
217	A62	50c vio brn	5.00	.35
218	A63	1s greenish bl	12.00	.50
219	A64	2s deep ultra	21.00	.65
		Nos. 209-219 (11)	42.30	3.15

For surcharges see Nos. 232-233, 255-256.

Augusto B. Leguía — A65

1919, Dec. **Litho.**

220 A65 5c bl & blk	.20	.20
a. Imperf.	.35	.35
b. Center inverted	11.00	11.00
221 A65 5c brn & blk	.20	.20
a. Imperf.	.35	.35
b. Center inverted	11.00	11.00

Constitution of 1919.

San Martín — A66

Thomas Cochrane — A70

Oath of Independence — A69

Designs: 2c, Field Marshal Arenales. 4c, Field Marshal Las Heras. 10c, Martin Jean Guisse. 12c, Vidal. 20c, Leguia. 50c, San Martin monument. 1s, San Martin and Leguia.

1921, July 28 **Engr.; 7c Litho.**

222 A66 1c ol brn & red brn	.30	.20
a. Center inverted	350.00	325.00
223 A66 2c green	.30	.20
224 A66 4c car rose	.80	.60
225 A69 5c ol brn	.40	.20
226 A70 7c violet	.65	.25
227 A66 10c ultra	.80	.40
228 A66 12c blk & slate	2.50	.60
229 A66 20c car & gray blk	2.50	.80
230 A66 50c vio brn & dl vio	7.25	2.50
231 A69 1s car rose & yel grn	12.00	3.75
Nos. 222-231 (10)	27.50	9.50

Centenary of Independence.

Nos. 213, 212 Surcharged in Black or Red Brown

1923-24

232 A54 5c on 8c No. 213	.50	.25
233 A54 4c on 5c (RB) ('24)	.35	.20
a. Inverted surcharge	5.00	5.00
b. Double surcharge, one inverted	6.00	6.00

A78

A79

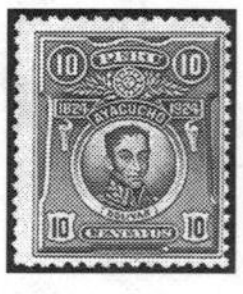

Simón Bolívar — A80

Perf. 14, 14x14½, 14½, 13½

1924 **Engr.; Photo. (4c, 5c)**

234 A78 2c olive grn	.30	.20
235 A79 4c yellow grn	.50	.20
236 A79 5c black	1.00	.20
237 A80 10c carmine	.60	.20
238 A78 20c ultra	1.25	.20
239 A78 50c dull violet	3.75	.80
240 A78 1s yellow brn	10.00	2.50
241 A78 2s dull blue	21.00	11.00
Nos. 234-241 (8)	38.40	15.30

Centenary of the Battle of Ayacucho which ended Spanish power in South America.
No. 237 exists imperf.

José Tejada Rivadeneyra A81

Mariano Melgar A82

Iturregui A83

Leguía A84

José de La Mar — A85

Monument of José Olaya — A86

Statue of María Bellido A87

De Saco A88

José Leguía — A89

1924-29 **Engr.** ***Perf. 12***
Size: 18½x23mm

242 A81 2c olive gray	.20	.20
243 A82 4c dk grn	.20	.20
244 A83 8c black	2.00	2.00
245 A84 10c org red	.20	.20
245A A85 15c dp bl ('28)	.60	.20
246 A86 20c blue	.80	.20
247 A86 20c yel ('29)	1.50	.20
248 A87 50c violet	5.00	.30
249 A88 1s bis brn	9.00	.80
250 A89 2s ultra	22.50	5.00
Nos. 242-250 (10)	42.00	9.30

See Nos. 258, 260, 276-282.
For surcharges and overprint see Nos. 251-253, 257-260, 262, 268-271, C1.

No. 246 Surcharged in Red:

DOS
Centavos

1925
a

b

1925

251 A86(a) 2c on 20c blue	350.00	
252 A86(b) 2c on 20c blue	.80	.50
a. Inverted surcharge	35.00	35.00
b. Double surch., one inverted	50.00	50.00

No. 245 Overprinted

1925

253 A84 10c org red	1.00	1.00
a. Inverted overprint	17.50	17.50

This stamp was for exclusive use on letters from the plebiscite provinces of Tacna and Arica, and posted on the Peruvian transport "Ucayali" anchored in the port of Africa.

No. 213 Surcharged

Habilitada
2 Cts.
1929
a

Habilitada
2 centavos
1929
b

1929

255 A54(a) 2c on 8c	.75	.75
256 A54(b) 2c on 8c	.75	.75

No. 247 Surcharged

257 A86 15c on 20c yellow	.75	.75
a. Inverted surcharge	7.50	7.50
Nos. 255-257 (3)	2.25	2.25

Stamps of 1924 Issue
Coil Stamps

1929 ***Perf. 14 Horizontally***

258 A81 2c olive gray	40.00	20.00
260 A84 10c orange red	45.00	17.50

Postal Tax Stamp of 1928 Overprinted

1930 ***Perf. 12***

261 PT6 2c dark violet	.35	.35
a. Inverted overprint	2.50	2.50

No. 247 Surcharged

262 A86 2c on 20c yellow	.25	.25

Air Post Stamp of 1928 Surcharged

Habilitada
Franqueo
2 Cts.
1930

263 AP1 2c on 50c dk grn	.20	.20
a. "Habitada"	1.00	1.00

Coat of Arms — A91

Lima Cathedral A92

10c, Children's Hospital. 50c, Madonna & Child.

Perf. 12x11½, 11½x12

1930, July 5 **Litho.**

264 A91 2c green	1.00	.75
265 A92 5c scarlet	1.75	1.25
266 A92 10c dark blue	1.25	1.00
267 A91 50c bister brown	21.00	12.00
Nos. 264-267 (4)	25.00	15.00

6th Pan American Congress for Child Welfare. By error the stamps are inscribed "Seventh Congress."

Type of 1924 Overprinted in Black, Green or Blue

1930, Dec. 22 **Photo.** ***Perf. 15x14***
Size: 18¼x22mm

268 A84 10c orange red (Bk)	.20	.20
a. Inverted overprint	10.00	10.00
b. Without overprint	6.50	6.50
c. Double surcharge	5.00	5.00

Same with Additional Surcharge of Numerals in Each Corner

269 A84 2c on 10c org red (G)	.20	.20
a. Inverted surcharge	12.00	
270 A84 4c on 10c org red (G)	.20	.20
a. Double surcharge	8.25	8.25

Engr.
Perf. 12
Size: 19x23½mm

271 A84 15c on 10c org red (Bl)	.30	.20
a. Inverted surcharge	10.00	10.00
b. Double surcharge	10.00	10.00
Nos. 268-271 (4)	.90	.80

Bolívar — A95

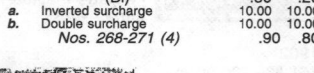

1930, Dec. 16 **Litho.**

272 A95 2c buff	.35	.35
273 A95 4c red	.65	.50
274 A95 10c blue green	.35	.25
275 A95 15c slate gray	.65	.65
Nos. 272-275 (4)	2.00	1.75

Death cent. of General Simón Bolivar.
For surcharges see Nos. RA14-RA16.

Types of 1924-29 Issues
Size: 18x22mm

1931 **Photo.** ***Perf. 15x14***

276 A81 2c olive green	.25	.20
277 A82 4c dark green	.25	.20
279 A85 15c deep blue	.75	.20
280 A86 20c yellow	1.25	.20
281 A87 50c violet	1.25	.25
282 A88 1s olive brown	2.00	.35
Nos. 276-282 (6)	5.75	1.40

Pizarro — A96

Old Stone Bridge, Lima — A97

1931, July 28 Litho. *Perf. 11*

283	A96	2c	slate blue	1.60	1.40
284	A96	4c	deep brown	1.60	1.40
285	A96	15c	dark green	1.60	1.40
286	A97	10c	rose red	1.60	1.40
287	A97	10c	mag & lt grn	1.60	1.40
288	A97	15c	yel & bl gray	1.60	1.40
289	A97	15c	dk slate & red	1.60	1.40
			Nos. 283-289 (7)	11.20	9.80

1st Peruvian Phil. Exhib., Lima, July, 1931.

Manco Capac A99

Sugar Cane Field A102

Oil Refinery A100

Guano Deposits A104

Picking Cotton A103

Mining A105

Llamas A106

Arms of Piura A107

1931-32 *Perf. 11, 11x11½*

292	A99	2c	olive black	.25	.20
293	A100	4c	dark green	.50	.20
295	A102	10c	red orange	1.00	.20
a.			Vertical pair, imperf. between	30.00	
296	A103	15c	turq blue	1.50	.20
297	A104	20c	yellow	5.00	.25
298	A105	50c	gray lilac	6.00	.25
299	A106	1s	brown olive	13.00	1.00
			Nos. 292-299 (7)	27.25	2.30

1932, July 28 *Perf. 11½x12*

300	A107	10c	dark blue	6.25	6.00
301	A107	15c	deep violet	6.25	6.00
			Nos. 300-301,C3 (3)	32.50	31.00

400th anniv. of the founding of the city of Piura. On sale one day. Counterfeits exist.

Parakas A108

Chimu A109

Inca — A110

1932, Oct. 15 *Perf. 11½, 12, 11½x12*

302	A108	10c	dk vio	.20	.20
303	A109	15c	brn red	.40	.20
304	A110	50c	dk brn	.90	.20
			Nos. 302-304 (3)	1.50	.60

4th cent. of the Spanish conquest of Peru.

Arequipa and El Misti — A111

President Luis M. Sánchez Cerro — A112

Monument to Simón Bolívar at Lima — A115

Statue of Liberty — A116

1932-34 Photo. *Perf. 13½*

305	A111	2c	black	.20	.20
306	A111	2c	blue blk	.20	.20
307	A111	2c	grn ('34)	.20	.20
308	A111	4c	dk brn	.20	.20
309	A111	4c	org ('34)	.20	.20
310	A112	10c	vermilion	13.00	10.00
311	A115	15c	ultra	.35	.20
312	A115	15c	mag ('34)	.35	.20
313	A115	20c	red brn	.75	.20
314	A115	20c	vio ('34)	.75	.20
315	A115	50c	dk grn ('33)	.75	.20
316	A115	1s	dp org	6.00	.20
317	A115	1s	org brn	7.50	.35
			Nos. 305-317 (13)	30.45	12.55

For overprint see No. RA24.

1934

318	A116	10c	rose	.50	.20

Pizarro — A117

The Inca — A119

Coronation of Huascar — A118

1934-35 *Perf. 13*

319	A117	10c	crimson	.25	.20
320	A117	15c	ultra	.75	.20
321	A118	20c	deep bl ('35)	1.25	.20
322	A118	50c	dp red brn	1.00	.20
323	A119	1s	dark vio	3.00	.35
			Nos. 319-323 (5)	6.25	1.15

For surcharges and overprint see Nos. 354-355, J54, O32.

Pizarro and the Thirteen A120

Belle of Lima — A122

Francisco Pizarro — A123

4c, Lima Cathedral. 1s, Veiled woman of Lima.

1935, Jan. 18 *Perf. 13½*

324	A120	2c	brown	.35	.20
325	A120	4c	violet	.50	.40
326	A122	10c	rose red	.50	.20
327	A123	15c	ultra	.80	.60
328	A120	20c	slate gray	1.40	.75
329	A122	50c	olive grn	2.00	1.50
330	A122	1s	Prus bl	4.50	3.00
331	A123	2s	org brn	10.50	8.00
			Nos. 324-331,C6-C12 (15)	66.10	46.15

Founding of Lima, 4th cent.

View of Ica — A125

Lake Huacachina, Health Resort — A126

Grapes — A127

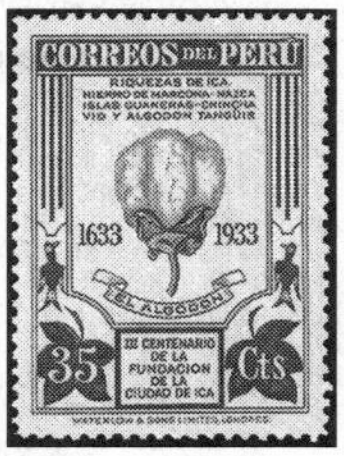

Cotton Boll — A128

Zuniga y Velazco and Philip IV — A129

Supreme God of the Nazcas — A130

Engr.; Photo. (10c)

1935, Jan. 17 *Perf. 12½*

332	A125	4c	gray blue	.80	.80
333	A126	5c	dark car	.30	.80
334	A127	10c	magenta	3.25	1.60
335	A126	20c	green	1.25	1.25
336	A128	35c	dark car	6.50	4.00
337	A129	50c	org & brn	4.50	4.00
338	A130	1s	pur & red	13.00	10.00
			Nos. 332-338 (7)	29.60	22.45

Founding of the City of Ica, 300th anniv.

Pizarro and the Thirteen — A131

1935-36 Photo. *Perf. 13½*

339	A131	2c	dp claret	.25	.20
340	A131	4c	bl grn ('36)	.25	.20

For surcharge and overprints see Nos. 353, J53, RA25-RA26.

"San Cristóbal," First Peruvian Warship — A132

Grand Marshal José de La Mar — A138

Naval College at Punta A133

Independence Square, Callao — A134

Aerial View of Callao A135

Plan of Walls of Callao in 1746 A137

Packetboat "Sacramento" — A139

Viceroy José Antonio Manso de Velasco — A140

Fort Maipú — A141

Plan of Fort Real Felipe A142

Design: 15c, Docks and Custom House.

1936, Aug. 27 Photo. *Perf. 12½*

341	A132	2c black	.55	.25
342	A133	4c bl grn	.55	.25
343	A134	5c yel brn	.55	.25
344	A135	10c bl gray	.55	.25
345	A135	15c green	.55	.25
346	A137	20c dk brn	.70	.25
347	A138	50c purple	1.40	.40
348	A139	1s olive grn	8.75	1.40

Engr.

349	A140	2s violet	15.00	6.75
350	A141	5s carmine	20.00	15.00
351	A142	10s red org & brn	50.00	40.00
		Nos. 341-351,C13 (12)	101.10	66.45

Province of Callao founding, cent.

Nos. 340, 321 and 323 Surcharged in Black

1936 *Perf. 13½, 13*

353	A131	2c on 4c bl grn	.20	.20
a.		"0.20" for "0.02"	3.50	3.50
354	A118	10c on 20c dp bl	.25	.20
a.		Double surcharge	3.50	
b.		Inverted surcharge	3.50	
355	A119	10c on 1s dk vio	.35	.35
		Nos. 353-355 (3)	.80	.75

Many varieties of the surcharge are found on these stamps: no period after "S," no period after "Cts," period after "2," "S" omitted, various broken letters, etc.

The surcharge on No. 355 is horizontal.

Peruvian Cormorants (Guano Deposits) — A143

Oil Well at Talara — A144

Avenue of the Republic, Lima A146

San Marcos University at Lima A148

Post Office, Lima — A149

Viceroy Manuel de Amat y Junyent — A150

Designs: 10c, "El Chasqui" (Inca Courier). 20c, Municipal Palace and Museum of Natural History. 5s, Joseph A. de Pando y Riva. 10s, Dr. José Dávila Condemarín.

1936-37 Photo. *Perf. 12½*

356	A143	2c lt brn	.60	.20
357	A143	2c grn ('37)	.75	.20
358	A144	4c blk brn	.60	.20
359	A144	4c int blk ('37)	.35	.20
360	A143	10c crimson	.35	.20
361	A143	10c ver ('37)	.20	.20
362	A146	15c ultra	.65	.20
363	A146	15c brt bl ('37)	.35	.20
364	A146	20c black	.65	.20
365	A146	20c blk brn ('37)	.25	.20
366	A148	50c org yel	2.50	.50
367	A148	50c dk gray vio ('37)	.75	.20
368	A149	1s brn vio	5.00	.65
369	A149	1s ultra ('37)	1.40	.20

Engr.

370	A150	2s ultra	10.00	2.00
371	A150	2s dk vio ('37)	3.25	.50
372	A150	5s slate bl	10.00	2.00
373	A150	10s dk vio & brn	55.00	22.50
		Nos. 356-373 (18)	92.65	30.55

No. 370 Surcharged in Black

1937

374	A150	1s on 2s ultra	2.50	2.50

Children's Holiday Center, Ancón — A153

Chavin Pottery — A154

Highway Map of Peru — A155

Archaeological Museum, Lima — A156

Industrial Bank of Peru — A157

Worker's Houses, Lima — A158

Toribio de Luzuriaga A159

Historic Fig Tree A160

Idol from Temple of Chavin — A161

Mt. Huascarán — A162

Imprint: "Waterlow & Sons Limited, Londres"

1938, July 1 Photo. *Perf. 12½, 13*

375	A153	2c emerald	.20	.20
376	A154	4c org brn	.20	.20
377	A155	10c scarlet	.20	.20
378	A156	15c ultra	.25	.20
379	A157	20c magenta	.20	.20
380	A158	50c greenish blue	.40	.20
381	A159	1s dp claret	1.00	.20
382	A160	2s green	3.00	.20

Engr.

383	A161	5s dl vio & brn	7.00	.40
384	A162	10s blk & ultra	12.00	.50
		Nos. 375-384 (10)	24.45	2.50

See Nos. 410-418, 426-433, 438-441.
For surcharges see Nos. 388, 406, 419, 445-446A, 456, 758.

Palace Square A163

Lima Coat of Arms A164

Government Palace — A165

1938, Dec. 9 Photo. *Perf. 12½*

385	A163	10c slate green	.50	.30

Engraved and Lithographed

386	A164	15c blk, gold, red & bl	.80	.40

Photo.

387	A165	1s olive	2.00	1.00
		Nos. 385-387,C62-C64 (6)	6.80	4.20

8th Pan-American Conf., Lima, Dec. 1938.

No. 377 Surcharged in Black

1940 *Perf. 13*

388	A155	5c on 10c scarlet	.20	.20
a.		Inverted surcharge		

National Radio Station A166

Overprint: "FRANQUEO POSTAL"

1941 Litho. *Perf. 12*

389	A166	50c dull yel	2.00	.20
390	A166	1s violet	2.00	.20
391	A166	2s dl gray grn	4.00	.60
392	A166	5s fawn	22.50	6.75
393	A166	10s rose vio	35.00	5.25
		Nos. 389-393 (5)	65.50	13.00

Gonzalo Pizarro and Orellana A167

Francisco de Orellana A168

Francisco Pizarro — A169

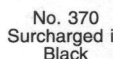

Map of South America with Amazon as Spaniards Knew It in 1542 — A170

Gonzalo Pizarro A171

Discovery of the Amazon River A172

1943, Feb. *Perf. 12½*

394 A167 2c crimson .20 .20
395 A168 4c slate .20 .20
396 A169 10c yel brn .20 .20
397 A170 15c vio blue .50 .20
398 A171 20c yel olive .20 .20
399 A172 25c dull org 1.60 .40
400 A168 30c dp magenta .40 .20
401 A170 50c blue grn .40 .30
402 A167 70c violet 2.25 .80
403 A171 80c lt bl 2.25 .80
404 A172 1s cocoa brn 4.00 .60
405 A169 5s intense blk 8.00 4.00
Nos. 394-405 (12) 20.20 8.10

400th anniv. of the discovery of the Amazon River by Francisco de Orellana in 1542.

No. 377 Surcharged in Black

1943 *Perf. 13*

406 A155 10c on 10c scar .20 .20

Samuel Finley Breese Morse — A173

1944 *Perf. 12½*

407 A173 15c light blue .20 .20
408 A173 30c olive gray .50 .20

Centenary of invention of the telegraph.

Types of 1938
Imprint: "Columbian Bank Note Co."

1945-47 Litho. *Perf. 12½*

410 A153 2c green .20 .20
411 A154 4c org brn ('46) .20 .20
412 A156 15c ultra .20 .20
413 A157 20c magenta 1.60 .20
414 A158 50c grnsh bl .20 .20
415 A159 1s vio brn .25 .20
416 A160 2s dl grn .65 .20
417 A161 5s dl vio & brn 4.00 .50
418 A162 10s blk & ultra ('47) 5.00 .75
Nos. 410-418 (9) 12.30 2.65

No. 415 Surcharged in Black

1946

419 A159 20c on 1s vio brn .30 .20
a. Surcharge reading down 8.25 8.25

A174

A175

A176

A177

A178

Overprinted in Black
Perf. 12½

1947, Apr. 15 Litho. Unwmk.

420 A174 15c blk & car .25 .20
421 A175 1s olive brn .40 .30
422 A176 1.35s yel grn .40 .35
423 A177 3s Prus blue .75 .60
424 A178 5s dull grn 1.60 1.25
Nos. 420-424 (5) 3.40 2.70

1st National Tourism Congress, Lima. The basic stamps were prepared, but not issued, for the 5th Pan American Highway Congress of 1944.

Catalogue values for unused stamps in this section, from this point to the end of the section, are for Never Hinged items.

Types of 1938
Imprint: "Waterlow & Sons Limited, Londres."

Perf. 13x13½, 13½x13

1949-51 Photo.

426 A154 4c chocolate .20 .20
427 A156 15c aquamarine .20 .20
428 A157 20c blue vio .20 .20
429 A158 50c red brn .25 .20
430 A159 1s blk brn .50 .20
431 A160 2s ultra 1.00 .20

Engr.
Perf. 12½

432 A161 5s ultra & red brn ('50) .90 .40
433 A162 10s dk bl grn & blk ('51) 3.00 .75
Nos. 426-433 (8) 6.25 2.35

Monument to Admiral Miguel L. Grau — A179

1949, June 6 *Perf. 12½*

434 A179 10c ultra & bl grn .20 .20

Types of 1938
Imprint: "Inst. de Grav. Paris."

1951 *Perf. 12½x12, 12x12½*

438 A156 15c peacock grn .20 .20
439 A157 20c violet .20 .20
440 A158 50c org brn .20 .20
441 A159 1s dark brn .30 .20
Nos. 438-441 (4) .90 .80

Nos. 375 and 438 Surcharged in Black

1951-52 *Perf. 12½, 12½x12*

445 A153 1c on 2c .20 .20
446 A156 10c on 15c .20 .20
446A A156 10c on 15c ('52) .20 .20
Nos. 445-446A (3) .60 .60

On No. 446A "Sl. 0.10" is in smaller type measuring 11½mm. See No. 456.

Nos. 445-446A exist with surcharge double.

Water Promenade A180

Post Boy — A181

Designs: 4c, 50c, 1s, 2s, Various buildings, Lima. 20c, Post Office Street, Lima. 5s, Lake Llangamuco, Ancachs. 10s, Ruins of Machu-Picchu.

Overprint: "V Congreso Panamericano de Carreteras 1951"

1951, Oct. 13 Unwmk. *Perf. 12*
Black Overprint

447 A180 2c dk grn .20 .20
448 A180 4c brt red .20 .20
449 A181 15c gray .20 .20
450 A181 20c ol brn .20 .20
451 A180 50c dp plum .25 .20
452 A180 1s blue .30 .20
453 A180 2s deep blue .45 .20
454 A180 5s brn lake 1.25 1.25
455 A181 10s chocolate 2.25 1.25
Nos. 447-455 (9) 5.30 3.90

5th Pan-American Congress of Highways, 1951.

No. 438 Surcharged in Black

1952 Unwmk. *Perf. 12½x12*

456 A156 5c on 15c pck grn .20 .20

Engineering School A182

Vicuña — A183

Contour Farming, Cuzco A184

Gen. Marcos Perez Jimenez — A185

Designs: 2c, Tourist Hotel, Tacna. 5c, Fishing boat and principal fish. 10c, Matarani. 15c, Locomotive No. 80 and coaches. 30c, Ministry of Public Health and Social Assistance. 1s, Paramonga fortress. 2s, Monument to Native Farmer.

Imprint: "Thomas De La Rue & Co. Ltd."

Perf. 13, 12 (A184)

1952-53 Litho. Unwmk.

457 A182 2c red lil ('53) .20 .20
458 A182 5c green .20 .20
459 A182 10c yel grn ('53) .20 .20
460 A182 15c gray ('53) .20 .20
461 A183 20c red brn ('53) .40 .20
462 A182 25c rose red .20 .20
463 A182 30c indigo ('53) .20 .20
464 A184 50c green ('53) .45 .20
465 A184 1s brown .30 .20
466 A184 2s Prus grn ('53) .35 .20
Nos. 457-466 (10) 2.70 2.00

See Nos. 468-478, 483-488, 497-501, C184-C185, C209.

For surcharges see Nos. C434, C437, C440-C441, C454, C494.

1956, July 25 Engr. *Perf. 13½x13*

467 A185 25c brown .20 .20

Visit of Gen. Marcos Perez Jimenez, Pres. of Venezuela, June 1955.

Types of 1952-53
Imprint: "Thomas De La Rue & Co. Ltd."

Designs as before.

1957-59 Litho. *Perf. 13, 12*

468 A182 15c brown ('59) .40 .20
469 A182 25c green ('59) .40 .20
470 A182 30c rose red .20 .20
471 A184 50c dull pur .30 .20
472 A184 1s lt vio bl .40 .20
473 A184 2s gray ('58) .50 .20
Nos. 468-473 (6) 2.20 1.20

Types of 1952-53
Imprint: "Joh. Enschedé en Zonen-Holland"

Designs as before.

Perf. 12½x13½, 13½x12½, 13x14

1960 Litho. Unwmk.

474 A183 20c lt red brn .20 .20
475 A182 30c lilac rose .20 .20
476 A184 50c rose vio .20 .20
477 A184 1s lt vio bl .20 .20
478 A184 2s gray .40 .20
Nos. 474-478 (5) 1.20 1.00

#475 measures 33x22mm, #470 32x22½mm.

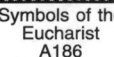

Symbols of the Eucharist
A186

Trumpeting Angels
A187

1960, Aug. 10 Photo. *Perf. 11½*

479 A186 50c Cross and "JHS" .20 .20
480 A186 1s shown .25 .25

Nos. 479-480 were intended for voluntary use to help finance the 6th National Eucharistic Congress at Piura, Aug. 25-28, 1960. Authorized for payment of postage on day of issue only, Aug. 10, but through misunderstanding within the Peruvian postal service they were accepted for payment of postage by some post offices until late in December. Reauthorized for postal use, they were again sold and used, starting in July, 1962. See Nos. RA37-RA38.

1961, Dec. 20 Litho. *Perf. 10½*

481 A187 20c bright blue .30 .20

Christmas. Valid for postage for one day, Dec. 20. Used thereafter as a voluntary seal to benefit a fund for postal employees.

Centenary Cedar, Main Square, Pomabamba — A188

Unwmk.

1962, Sept. 7 Engr. *Perf. 13*

482 A188 1s red & green .40 .20

Cent. (in 1961) of Pomabamba province.

Types of 1952-53

Designs: 20c, Vicuña. 30c, Port of Matarani. 40c, Gunboat. 50c, Contour farming. 60c, Tourist hotel, Tacna. 1s, Paramonga, Inca fortress.

Imprint: "Thomas De La Rue & Co. Ltd."

Perf. 13x13½, 13½x13, 12 (A184)

1962, Nov. 19 Litho. Wmk. 346

483 A183 20c rose claret .20 .20
484 A182 30c dark blue .20 .20
485 AP49 40c orange .20 .20
486 A184 50c lt bluish grn .20 .20
487 A182 60c grnsh blk .20 .20
488 A184 1s rose .25 .20
Nos. 483-488 (6) 1.25 1.20

Wheat Emblem and Symbol of Agriculture, Industry
A189

1963, July 23 Unwmk. *Perf. 12½*

489 A189 1s red org & ocher .20 .20

FAO "Freedom from Hunger" campaign. See No. C190.

Alliance for Progress Emblem — A190

Pacific Fair Emblem — A191

1964, June 22 Litho. *Perf. 12x12½*

490 A190 40c multi .20 .20
Nos. 490,C192-C193 (3) .65 .65

Alliance for Progress. See note after US No. 1234.

1965, Oct. 30 Litho. *Perf. 12x12½*

491 A191 1.50s multi .20 .20
492 A191 2.50s multi .20 .20
493 A191 3.50s multi .25 .20
Nos. 491-493 (3) .65 .60

4th Intl. Pacific Fair, Lima, Oct. 30-Nov. 14.

Santa Claus and Letter
A192

1965, Nov. 2 *Perf. 11*

494 A192 20c red & blk .20 .20
495 A192 50c grn & blk .20 .20
496 A192 1s bl & blk .35 .20
Nos. 494-496 (3) .75 .60

Christmas. Valid for postage for one day, Nov. 2. Used Nov. 3, 1965-Jan. 31, 1966, as voluntary seals for the benefit of a fund for postal employees. See #522-524. For surcharges see #641-643.

Types of 1952-62

20c, Vicuña. 30c, Port of Matarani. 40c, Gunboat. 50c, Contour farming. 1s, Paramonga, Inca fortress.

Imprint: "I.N.A."

Perf. 12, 13½x14 (A184)

1966, Aug. 8 Litho. Unwmk.

497 A183 20c brn red .20 .20
498 A182 30c dk bl .20 .20
499 AP49 40c orange .20 .20
500 A184 50c gray grn .20 .20
501 A184 1s rose .20 .20
Nos. 497-501 (5) 1.00 1.00

Postal Tax Stamps Nos. RA40, RA43 Surcharged

a

b

Perf. 14x14½, 12½x12

1966, May 9 Litho.

501A PT11 (a) 10c on 2c lt brn .20 .20
501B PT14 (b) 10c on 3c lt car .20 .20

Map of Peru, Cordillera Central and Pelton Wheel
A193

1966, Nov. 24 Photo. *Perf. 13½x14*

502 A193 70c bl, blk & vio bl .20 .20

Opening of the Huinco Hydroelectric Center. See No. C205.

Inca Wind Vane and Sun — A194

Perf. 13½x14

1967, Apr. 18 Photo. Unwmk.

503 A194 90c dp lil rose, blk & gold .20 .20

6-year building program. See No. C212.

Pacific Fair Emblem — A195

Indian and Wheat — A197

Gold Alligator, Mochica Culture
A196

1967, Oct. 9 Photo. *Perf. 12*

504 A195 1s gold, dk grn & blk .20 .20

5th Intl. Pacific Fair, Lima, Oct. 27-Nov. 12. See No. C216.

1968, Aug. 16 Photo. *Perf. 12*

Designs (gold sculptures of the pre-Inca Yunca tribes): 2.60s, Bird, vert. 3.60s, Lizard. 4.60s, Bird, vert. 5.60s, Jaguar.

Sculptures in Gold Yellow and Brown

505 A196 1.90s dp magenta .25 .20
506 A196 2.60s black .35 .20
507 A196 3.60s dp magenta .40 .30
508 A196 4.60s black .50 .35
509 A196 5.60s dp magenta .50 .35
Nos. 505-509 (5) 2.00 1.40

See Nos. B1-B5. For surcharge see No. 685.

1969, Mar. 3 Litho. *Perf. 11*

Designs: 3s, 4s, Farmer digging in field.

Black Surcharge

510 A197 2.50s on 90c brn & yel .20 .20
511 A197 3s on 90c lil & brn .20 .20
512 A197 4s on 90c rose & grn .25 .20
Nos. 510-512,C232-C233 (5) 1.25 1.00

Agrarian Reform Law.
#510-512 were not issued without surcharge.

Flag, Worker Holding Oil Rig and Map
A198

1969, Apr. 9 Litho. *Perf. 12*

513 A198 2.50s multi .20 .20
514 A198 3s gray & multi .20 .20
515 A198 4s lil & multi .20 .20
516 A198 5.50s lt bl & multi .25 .20
Nos. 513-516 (4) .85 .80

Nationalization of the Brea Parinas oilfields, Oct. 9, 1968.

Kon Tiki Raft, Globe and Jet — A199

1969, June 17 Litho. *Perf. 11*

517 A199 2.50s dp bl & multi .20 .20
Nos. 517,C238-C241 (5) 1.00 1.00

1st Peruvian Airlines (APSA) flight to Europe.

Capt. José A. Quiñones Gonzales (1914-41), Military Aviator — A200

1969, July 23 Litho. *Perf. 11*

518 A200 20s red & multi 1.25 .60

See No. C243.

Freed Andean Farmer
A201

1969, Aug. 28 Litho. *Perf. 11*

519 A201 2.50s dk bl, lt bl & red .20 .20
Nos. 519,C246-C247 (3) .60 .60

Enactment of the Agrarian Reform Law of June 24, 1969.

Adm. Miguel Grau
A202

1969, Oct. 8 Litho. *Perf. 11*

520 A202 50s dk bl & multi 3.00 2.25

Issued for Navy Day.

Flags and "6" — A203

1969, Nov. 14

521 A203 2.50s gray & multi .20 .20
Nos. 521,C251-C252 (3) .65 .60

6th Intl. Pacific Trade Fair, Lima, Nov. 14-30.

Santa Claus Type of 1965

Design: Santa Claus and letter inscribed "FELIZ NAVIDAD Y PROSPERO AÑO NUEVO."

1969, Dec. 1 Litho. *Perf. 11*

522 A192 20c red & blk .20 .20
523 A192 20c org & blk .20 .20
524 A192 20c brn & blk .20 .20
Nos. 522-524 (3) .60 .60

Christmas. Valid for postage for one day, Dec. 1, 1969. Used after that date as postal tax stamps.

Gen. Francisco Bolognesi and Soldier — A204

Puma-shaped Jug, Vicus Culture — A205

1969, Dec. 9
525 A204 1.20s lt ultra, blk & gold .20 .20

Army Day, Dec. 9. See No. C253.

1970, Feb. 23 Litho. *Perf. 11*
526 A205 2.50s buff, blk & brn .20 .20
Nos. 526,C281-C284 (5) 1.30 1.30

Ministry of Transport and Communications A206

1970, Apr. 1 Litho. *Perf. 11*
527 A206 40c org & gray .20 .20
528 A206 40c gray & lt gray .20 .20
529 A206 40c brick red & gray .20 .20
530 A206 40c brt pink & gray .20 .20
531 A206 40c org brn & gray .20 .20
Nos. 527-531 (5) 1.00 1.00

Ministry of Transport and Communications, 1st anniv.

Anchovy A207

Fish: No. 533, Pacific hake.

1970, Apr. 30 Litho. *Perf. 11*
532 A207 2.50s vio bl & multi .20 .20
533 A207 2.50s vio bl & multi .20 .20
a. Strip of 5, #532-533, C285-C287 1.10 1.10

Composite Head; Soldier and Farmer A208

1970, June 24 Litho. *Perf. 11*
534 A208 2.50s gold & multi .20 .20
Nos. 534,C290-C291 (3) .75 .60

"United people and army building a new Peru."

Cadets, Chorrillos College, and Arms — A209

Coat of Arms and: No. 536, Cadets of La Punta Naval College. No. 537, Cadets of Las Palmas Air Force College.

1970, July 27 Litho. *Perf. 11*
535 A209 2.50s blk & multi .40 .20
536 A209 2.50s blk & multi .40 .20
537 A209 2.50s blk & multi .40 .20
a. Strip of 3, #535-537 1.25 .75

Peru's military colleges.

Courtyard, Puruchuco Fortress, Lima — A210

1970, Aug. 6
538 A210 2.50s multi .20 .20
Nos. 538,C294-C297 (5) 1.40 1.40

Issued for tourist publicity.

Nativity, Cuzco School A211

Christmas paintings: 1.50s, Adoration of the Kings, Cuzco School. 1.80s, Adoration of the Shepherds, Peruvian School.

1970, Dec. 23 Litho. *Perf. 11*
539 A211 1.20s multi .20 .20
540 A211 1.50s multi .20 .20
541 A211 1.80s multi .20 .20
Nos. 539-541 (3) .60 .60

St. Rosa of Lima — A212

1971, Apr. 12 Litho. *Perf. 11*
542 A212 2.50s multi .20 .20

300th anniv. of the canonization of St. Rosa of Lima (1586-1617), first saint born in the Americas.

Tiahuanacoide Cloth — A213

Design: 2.50s, Chancay cloth.

1971, Apr. 19
543 A213 1.20s bl & multi .20 .20
544 A213 2.50s yel & multi .20 .20
Nos. 543-544,C306-C308 (5) 1.40 1.00

Nazca Sculpture, 5th Century, and Seriolella A214

1971, June 7 Litho. *Perf. 11*
545 A214 1.50s multi .20 .20
Nos. 545,C309-C312 (5) 2.10 1.00

Publicity for 200-mile zone of sovereignty of the high seas.

Mateo Garcia Pumacahua A215

#547, Mariano Melgar. #548, Micaela Bastidas. #549, Jose Faustino Sanchez Carrion. #550, Francisco Antonia de Zela. #551, Jose Baquijano y Carrillo. #552, Martin Jorge Guise.

1971
546 A215 1.20s ver & blk .20 .20
547 A215 1.20s gray & multi .20 .20
548 A215 1.50s dk bl & multi .20 .20
549 A215 2s dk bl & multi .20 .20
550 A215 2.50s ultra & multi .20 .20
551 A215 2.50s gray & multi .20 .20
552 A215 2.50s dk bl & multi .20 .20
Nos. 546-552,C313-C325 (20) 4.65 4.00

150th anniv. of independence, and to honor the heroes of the struggle for independence.

Issue dates: Nos. 546, 550, May 10; Nos. 547, 551, July 5; Nos. 548-549, 552, July 27.

Gongora Portentosa A216

Designs: Various Peruvian orchids.

1971, Sept. 27 *Perf. 13½x13*
553 A216 1.50s pink & multi .20 .20
554 A216 2s pink & multi .25 .20
555 A216 2.50s pink & multi .30 .20
556 A216 3s pink & multi .35 .20
557 A216 3.50s pink & multi .40 .20
Nos. 553-557 (5) 1.50 1.00

"Progress of Liberation," by Teodoro Nuñez Ureta A217

3.50s, Detail from painting by Nuñez Ureta.

1971, Nov. 4 *Perf. 13x13½*
558 A217 1.20s multi .20 .20
559 A217 3.50s multi .20 .20
Nos. 558-559,C331 (3) 3.40 1.40

2nd Ministerial meeting of the "Group of 77."

Plaza de Armas, Lima, 1843 A218

3.50s, Plaza de Armas, Lima, 1971.

1971, Nov. 6
560 A218 3s pale grn & blk .35 .20
561 A218 3.50s lt brick red & blk .40 .20

3rd Annual Intl. Stamp Exhibition, EXFILIMA '71, Lima, Nov. 6-14.

Army Coat of Arms — A219

1971, Dec. 9 Litho. *Perf. 13½x13*
562 A219 8.50s multi .75 .20

Sesquicentennial of Peruvian Army.

Flight into Egypt A220

Old Stone Sculptures of Huamanga: 2.50s, Three Kings. 3s, Nativity.

1971, Dec. 18 *Perf. 13x13½*
563 A220 1.80s multi .20 .20
564 A220 2.50s multi .25 .20
565 A220 3s gray & multi .35 .20
Nos. 563-565 (3) .80 .60

Christmas. See Nos. 597-599.

Fisherman, by J. M. Ugarte Elespuru — A221

Gold Statuette, Chimu, c. 1500 — A222

Paintings by Peruvian Workers: 4s, Threshing Grain in Cajamarca, by Camilo Blas. 6s, Huanca Highlanders, by José Sabogal.

1971, Dec. 30 *Perf. 13½x13*
566 A221 3.50s blk & multi .35 .20
567 A221 4s blk & multi .40 .20
568 A221 6s blk & multi .60 .20
Nos. 566-568 (3) 1.35 .60

To publicize the revolution and change of order.

1972, Jan. 31 Litho. *Perf. 13½x13*

Ancient Jewelry: 4s, Gold drummer, Chimu. 4.50s, Quartz figurine, Lambayeque culture,

5th century. 5.40s, Gold necklace and pendant, Mochiqua, 4th century. 6s, Gold insect, Lambayeque culture, 14th century.

569	A222	3.90s	red, blk & ocher	.40	.20
570	A222	4s	red, blk & ocher	.40	.20
571	A222	4.50s	brt bl, blk & ocher	.50	.20
572	A222	5.40s	red, blk & ocher	.60	.20
573	A222	6s	red, blk & ocher	.60	.20
			Nos. 569-573 (5)	2.50	1.00

Popeye Catalufa A223

Fish: 1.50s, Guadara. 2.50s, Jack mackerel.

1972, Mar. 20 ***Perf. 13x13½***

574	A223	1.20s	lt bl & multi	.25	.20
575	A223	1.50s	lt bl & multi	.25	.20
576	A223	2.50s	lt bl & multi	.25	.20
			Nos. 574-576,C333-C334 (5)	1.55	1.00

Seated Warrior, Mochica — A224

"Bringing in the Harvest" (July) — A225

Painted pottery jugs of Mochica culture, 5th cent.: 1.50s, Helmeted head. 2s, Kneeling deer. 2.50s, Helmeted head. 3s, Kneeling warrior.

1972, May 8 ***Perf. 13½x13***

Emerald Background

577	A224	1.20s	multi	.20	.20
578	A224	1.50s	multi	.25	.20
579	A224	2s	multi	.30	.20
580	A224	2.50s	multi	.35	.20
581	A224	3s	multi	.40	.20
			Nos. 577-581 (5)	1.50	1.00

1972-73 **Litho.** ***Perf. 13½x13***

Monthly woodcuts from Calendario Incaico.

Black Vignette & Inscriptions

582	A225	2.50s	red brn *(July)*	.35	.20
583	A225	3s	grn *(Aug.)*	.60	.20
584	A225	2.50s	rose *(Sept.)*	.35	.20
585	A225	3s	lt bl *(Oct.)*	.50	.20
586	A225	2.50s	org *(Nov.)*	.50	.20
587	A225	3s	lil *(Dec.)*	.50	.20
588	A225	2.50s	brn *(Jan.)* ('73)	.35	.20
589	A225	3s	pale grn *(Feb.)* ('73)	.50	.20
590	A225	2.50s	bl *(Mar.)* ('73)	.35	.20
591	A225	3s	org *(Apr.)* ('73)	.50	.20
592	A225	2.50s	lil rose *(May)* ('73)	.35	.20
593	A225	3s	yel & blk *(June)* ('73)	.50	.20
			Nos. 582-593 (12)	5.35	2.40

400th anniv. of publication of the Calendario Incaico by Felipe Guaman Poma de Ayala.

Family Tilling Field — A226

Oil Derricks — A228

Sovereignty of the Sea (Inca Frieze) — A227

Perf. 13½x13, 13x13½

1972, Oct. 31 **Litho.**

594	A226	2s	multi	.25	.20
595	A227	2.50s	multi	.25	.20
596	A228	3s	gray & multi	.25	.20
			Nos. 594-596 (3)	.75	.60

4th anniversaries of land reforms and the nationalization of the oil industry and 15th anniv. of the claim to a 200-mile zone of sovereignty of the sea.

Christmas Type of 1971

Sculptures from Huamanga, 17-18th cent.: 1.50s, Holy Family, wood, vert. 2s, Holy Family with lambs, stone. 2.50s, Holy Family in stable, stone, vert.

1972, Nov. 30

597	A220	1.50s	buff & multi	.20	.20
598	A220	2s	buff & multi	.20	.20
599	A220	2.50s	buff & multi	.20	.20
			Nos. 597-599 (3)	.60	.60

Morning Glory — A228a

Mayor on Horseback, by Fierro — A229

1972, Dec. 29 **Litho.** ***Perf. 13***

600	A228a	1.50s	shown	.20	.20
601	A228a	2.50s	Amaryllis	.25	.20
602	A228a	3s	Liabum excelsum	.30	.20
603	A228a	3.50s	Bletia (orchid)	.45	.20
604	A228a	5s	Cantua buxifolia	.35	.20
			Nos. 600-604 (5)	1.55	1.00

1973, Aug. 13 **Litho.** ***Perf. 13***

Paintings by Francisco Pancho Fierro (1803-1879): 2s, Man and Woman, 1830. 2.50s, Padre Abregu Riding Mule. 3.50s, Dancing Couple. 4.50s, Bullfighter Estevan Arredondo on Horseback.

605	A229	1.50s	salmon & multi	.20	.20
606	A229	2s	salmon & multi	.20	.20
607	A229	2.50s	salmon & multi	.25	.20
608	A229	3.50s	salmon & multi	.35	.20
609	A229	4.50s	salmon & multi	.55	.20
			Nos. 605-609 (5)	1.55	1.00

Presentation in the Temple — A230

Christmas Paintings of the Cuzqueña School: 2s, Holy Family, vert. 2.50s, Adoration of the Kings.

1973, Nov. 30 **Litho.** ***Perf. 13x13½***

610	A230	1.50s	multi	.20	.20
611	A230	2s	multi	.20	.20
612	A230	2.50s	multi	.20	.20
			Nos. 610-612 (3)	.60	.60

Peru No. 20 — A231

1974, Mar. 1 **Litho.** ***Perf. 13***

613	A231	6s	gray & dk bl	.45	.25

Peruvian Philatelic Assoc., 25th anniv.

Non-ferrous Smelting Plant, La Oroya A232

Colombia Bridge, San Martin A233

Designs: 8s, 10s, Different views, Santiago Antunez Dam, Tayacaja.

1974 **Litho.** ***Perf. 13x13½***

614	A232	1.50s	blue	.20	.20
615	A233	2s	multi	.20	.20
616	A232	3s	rose claret	.20	.20
617	A232	4.50s	green	.25	.20
618	A233	8s	multi	.35	.20
619	A233	10s	multi	.45	.20
			Nos. 614-619 (6)	1.65	1.20

"Peru Determines its Destiny."

Issued: 2s, 8s, 10s, 7/1; 1.50s, 3s, 4.50s, 12/6.

Battle of Junin, by Felix Yañez A234

2s, 3s, Battle of Ayacucho, by Felix Yañez.

1974 **Litho.** ***Perf. 13x13½***

620	A234	1.50s	multi	.20	.20
621	A234	2s	multi	.20	.20
622	A234	2.50s	multi	.25	.20
623	A234	3s	multi	.35	.20
			Nos. 620-623 (4)	1.00	.80

Sesquicentennial of the Battles of Junin and Ayacucho.

Issued: 1.50s, 2.50s, Aug. 6; 2s, 3s, Oct. 9.

See Nos. C400-C404.

Indian Madonna — A235

1974, Dec. 20 **Litho.** ***Perf. 13½x13***

624	A235	1.50s	multi	.20	.20

Christmas. See No. C417.

Maria Parado de Bellido A236

International Women's Year Emblem — A237

IWY Emblem, Peruvian Colors and: 2s, Micaela Bastidas. 2.50s, Juana Alarco de Dammert.

Perf. 13x13½, 13½x13

1975, Sept. 8 **Litho.**

625	A236	1.50s	bl grn, red & blk	.20	.20
626	A237	2s	blk & red	.20	.20
627	A236	2.50s	pink, blk & red	.20	.20
628	A237	3s	red, blk & ultra	.25	.20
			Nos. 625-628 (4)	.85	.80

International Women's Year.

St. Juan Macias — A238

1975, Nov. 14 ***Perf. 13½x13***

629	A238	5s	blk & multi	.25	.20

Canonization of Juan Macias in 1975.

Louis Braille A239

1976, Mar. 2 **Litho.** ***Perf. 13x13½***

630	A239	4.50s	gray, red & blk	.20	.20

Sesquicentennial of the invention of Braille system of writing for the blind by Louis Braille (1809-1852).

Peruvian Flag A240

1976, Aug. 29 Litho. ***Perf. 13x13½***
631 A240 5s gray, blk & red .20 .20

Revolutionary Government, phase II, 1st anniv.

St. Francis, by El Greco — A241

Indian Mother — A242

1976, Dec. 9 Litho. ***Perf. 13½x13***
632 A241 5s gold, buff & brn .25 .20

St. Francis of Assisi, 750th death anniv.

1976, Dec. 23
633 A242 4s multi .25 .20

Christmas.

Chasqui Messenger A243

"X" over Flags — A244

1977 Litho. ***Perf. 13½x13***
634 A243 6s grnsh bl & blk .25 .20
635 A243 8s red & blk .25 .20
636 A243 10s ultra & blk .40 .35
637 A243 12s lt grn & blk .40 .35
Nos. 634-637,C465-C467 (7) 4.05 2.40

For surcharge see No. C502.

1977, Nov. 25 Litho. ***Perf. 13½x13***
638 A244 10s multi .20 .20

10th Intl. Pacific Fair, Lima, Nov. 16-27.

Republican Guard Badge — A245

Indian Nativity — A246

1977, Dec. 1
639 A245 12s multi .25 .20

58th anniversary of Republican Guard.

1977, Dec. 23
640 A246 8s multi .20 .20

Christmas. See No. C484.

Nos. 495, 494, 496 Surcharged with New Value and Bar in Red, Dark Blue or Black: "FRANQUEO / 10.00 / RD-0161-77"

1977, Dec. ***Perf. 11***
641 A192 10s on 50c (R) .25 .20
642 A192 20s on 20c (DB) .50 .30
643 A192 30s on 1s (B) .65 .40
Nos. 641-643 (3) 1.40 .90

Inca Head — A247

1978 Litho. ***Perf. 13½x13***
644 A247 6s bright green .20 .20
645 A247 10s red .20 .20
646 A247 16s red brown .20 .20
Nos. 644-646,C486-C489 (7) 3.45 2.85

For surcharges see Nos. C498-C499, C501.

Flags of Germany, Argentina, Austria, Brazil A248

Argentina '78 Emblem and Flags of Participants: No. 648, 652, Hungary, Iran, Italy, Mexico. No. 649, 653, Scotland, Spain, France, Netherlands. No. 650, 654, Peru, Poland, Sweden and Tunisia. No. 651, like No. 647.

1978 Litho. ***Perf. 13x13½***
647 A248 10s blue & multi .30 .20
648 A248 10s blue & multi .30 .20
649 A248 10s blue & multi .30 .20
650 A248 10s blue & multi .30 .20
a. Block of 4, #647-650 1.25 1.00
651 A248 16s blue & multi .30 .20
652 A248 16s blue & multi .30 .20
653 A248 16s blue & multi .30 .20
654 A248 16s blue & multi .30 .20
a. Block of 4, #651-654 1.25 1.00
Nos. 647-654 (8) 2.40 1.60

11th World Soccer Cup Championship, Argentina, June 1-25.
Issued: #647-650, 6/28; #651-654, 12/4.

Thomas Faucett, Planes of 1928, 1978 A249

1978, Oct. 19 Litho. ***Perf. 13***
655 A249 40s multicolored .40 .25

Faucett Aviation, 50th anniversary.

Nazca Bowl, Huaco A250

1978-79 Litho. ***Perf. 13x13½***
656 A250 16s violet bl ('79) .20 .20
657 A250 20s green ('79) .20 .20
658 A250 25s lt green ('79) .25 .25
659 A250 35s rose red ('79) .40 .20
660 A250 45s dk brown .45 .25
661 A250 50s black .55 .30
662 A250 55s car rose ('79) .55 .30
663 A250 70s lilac rose ('79) .65 .55
664 A250 75s blue .75 .45
665 A250 80s salmon ('79) .75 .45
667 A250 200s brt vio ('79) 1.90 1.40
Nos. 656-667 (11) 6.65 4.55

For surcharges see Nos. 715, 731.

Peruvian Nativity — A252

Ministry of Education, Lima — A253

1978, Dec. 28 Litho. ***Perf. 13½x13***
672 A252 16s multicolored .20 .20

1979, Jan. 4
673 A253 16s multicolored .20 .20

National Education Program.

Nos. RA40, B1-B5 and 509 Surcharged in Various Colors. No. RA40 Surcharged also:

a

b

c

1978, July-Aug.
674 PT11(a) 2s on 2c (O) .20 .20
675 PT11(b) 3s on 2c (Bk) .20 .20
676 PT11(a) 4s on 2c (G) .20 .20
677 PT11(a) 5s on 2c (V) .20 .20
678 PT11(b) 6s on 2c (DBl) .20 .20
679 SP1 20s on 1.90s + 90c (G) .75 .75
680 SP1 30s on 2.60s + 1.30s (Bl) .75 .75
681 PT11(c) 35s on 2c (C) .25 .25
682 PT11(c) 50s on 2c (LtBl) 2.00 2.00
683 SP1 55s on 3.60s + 1.80s (VBl) 1.00 1.00
684 SP1 65s on 4.60s + 2.30s (Go) 1.00 1.00
685 A196 80s on 5.60s (VBl) .75 .75
686 SP1 85s on 20s + 10s (Bk) 1.50 1.50
Nos. 674-686 (13) 9.00 9.00

Surcharge on Nos. 679-680, 683-684, 686 includes heavy bar over old denomination.

Battle of Iquique A254

Heroes' Crypt — A255

Col. Francisco Bolognesi A256

War of the Pacific: No. 688, Col. Jose J. Inclan. No. 689, Corvette Union running Arica blockade. No. 690, Battle of Angamos, Aguirre, Miguel Grau (1838-1879), Perre. No. 690A, Lt. Col. Pedro Ruiz Gallo. 85s, Marshal Andres A. Caceres. No. 692, Naval Battle of Angamos. No. 693, Battle of Tarapaca. 115s, Adm. Miguel Grau. No. 697, Col. Bolognesi's Reply, by Angeles de la Cruz. No. 698, Col. Alfonso Ugarte on horseback.

Perf. 13½x13, 13x13½

1979-80 Litho.
687 A254 14s multicolored .20 .20
688 A256 25s multicolored .35 .20
689 A254 25s multicolored .20 .20
690 A254 25s multicolored .25 .20
690A A256 25s multicolored ('80) .20 .20
691 A256 85s multicolored .50 .50
692 A254 100s multicolored .65 .30
693 A254 100s multicolored .65 .30
694 A256 115s multicolored 1.25 .75
695 A255 200s multicolored 4.00 3.00
696 A256 200s multicolored 1.25 1.00
697 A254 200s multicolored 1.25 1.00
698 A254 200s multicolored 1.25 1.00
Nos. 687-698 (13) 12.00 8.85

For surcharges see Nos. 713, 732.

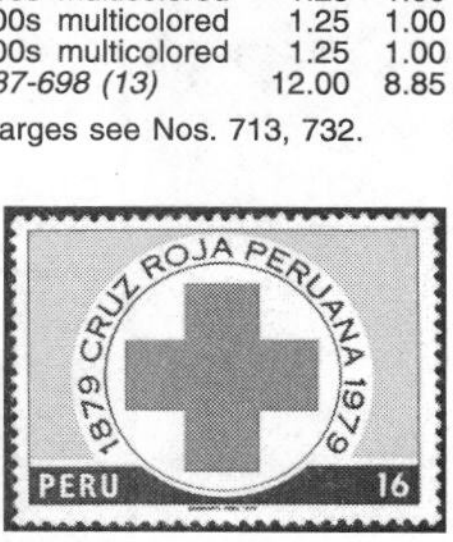

Peruvian Red Cross, Cent. A257

1979, May 4 ***Perf. 13x13½***
699 A257 16s multicolored .20 .20

Billiard Balls — A258

Arms of Cuzco — A259

1979, June 4 *Perf. 13½x13*
700 A258 34s multicolored .25 .25

For surcharge see No. 714.

1979, June 24
701 A259 50s multicolored .35 .20

Inca Sun Festival, Cuzco.

Peru Colors, Tacna Monument A260

Telecom 79 — A261

1979, Aug. 28 Litho. *Perf. 13½x13*
702 A260 16s multicolored .20 .20

Return of Tacna Province to Peru, 50th anniv.
For surcharge see No. 712.

1979, Sept. 20
703 A261 15s multicolored .20 .20

3rd World Telecommunications Exhibition, Geneva, Sept. 20-26.

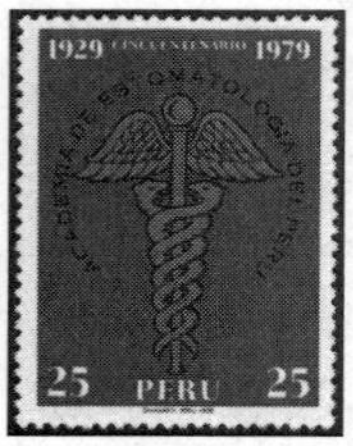

Caduceus A262

Gold Jewelry — A264

World Map, "11," Fair Emblem A263

1979, Nov. 13
704 A262 25s multicolored .20 .20

Stomatology Academy of Peru, 50th anniv.; 4th Intl. Congress.

1979, Nov. 24
705 A263 55s multicolored .40 .25

11th Pacific Intl. Trade Fair, Lima, 11/14-25.

1979, Dec. 19 *Perf. 13½x13*
706 A264 85s multicolored .55 .40

Larco Herrera Archaeological Museum.

Christmas A265

1979, Dec. 27 Litho. *Perf. 13x13½*
707 A265 25s multicolored .20 .20

Queen Sofia and King Juan Carlos I, Visit to Peru A266

1979 Litho. *Perf. 13x13½*
708 A266 75s multicolored .55 .25

No. RA40 Surcharged in Black, Green or Blue

1979, Oct. 8
709 PT11 7s on 2c brown .20 .20
710 PT11 9s on 2c brown (G) .20 .20
711 PT11 15s on 2c brown (B) .20 .20
Nos. 709-711 (3) .60 .60

Nos. 702, 687, 700, 663 Surcharged

Perf. 13½x13, 13x13½

1980, Apr. 14 **Litho.**
712 A260 20s on 16s multi .25 .20
713 A254 25s on 34s multi .30 .25
714 A258 65s on 34s multi .50 .40
715 A250 80s on 70s lilac rose .75 .30
Nos. 712-715,C501-C502 (6) 2.50 1.70

Liberty Holding Arms of Peru — A267

Chimu Cult Cup — A268

Civic duties: 15s, Respect the Constitution. 20s, Honor country. 25s, Vote. 30s, Military service. 35s, Pay taxes. 45s, Contribute to national progress. 50s, Respect rights.

1980 **Litho.**
716 A267 15s greenish blue .20 .20
717 A267 20s salmon pink .20 .20
718 A267 25s ultra .20 .20
719 A267 30s lilac rose .20 .20
720 A267 35s black .25 .20
721 A267 45s light blue green .30 .25
722 A267 50s brown .50 .25
Nos. 716-722 (7) 1.85 1.50

1980, July 9 **Litho.**
723 A268 35s multicolored .25 .20

Map of Peru and Liberty — A269

Return to Civilian Government — A270

Perf. 13½x13, 13x13½

1980, Sept. 9 **Litho.**
724 A269 25s multicolored .20 .20
725 A270 35s multicolored .25 .25

For surcharge see No. 730.

Machu Picchu A271

1980, Nov. 10 Litho. *Perf. 13x13½*
726 A271 25s multicolored .20 .20

World Tourism Conf., Manila, Sept. 27.

Tupac Amaru Rebellion Bicent. — A272

150th Death Anniv. of Simon Bolivar (in 1980) — A274

Christmas A273

1980, Dec. 22 Litho. *Perf. 13½x13*
727 A272 25s multicolored .20 .20

1980, Dec. 31 Litho. *Perf. 13*
728 A273 15s multicolored .20 .20

1981, Jan. 28 Litho. *Perf. 13½x13*
729 A274 40s multicolored .30 .25

Nos. 725, 667, 694 Surcharged

1981 Litho. *Perf. 13x13½*
730 A270 25s on 35s multi .20 .20
731 A250 85s on 200s brt violet .65 .50
732 A256 100s on 115s multi .75 .60
Nos. 730-732 (3) 1.60 1.30

Return to Constitutional Government, July 28, 1980 — A275

1981, Mar. 26 Litho. *Perf. 13½x13*
733 A275 25s multicolored .25 .20

For surcharges see Nos. 736-737, 737C.

Tupac Amaru and Micaela Bastidas, Bronze Sculptures, by Miguel Baca-Rossi A276

1981, May 18 Litho. *Perf. 13x13½*
734 A276 60s multicolored .45 .35

Rebellion of Tupac Amaru and Micaela Bastidas, bicentenary.

Nos. 733, RA41 and Voluntary Postal Tax Stamps of 1965 Surcharged in Black, Dull Brown or Lake

Cross, Unleavened Bread, Wheat A276a

Chalice, Host A276b

Perf. 13½x13, Rouletted 11 (#735, 737B), 11½ (#737A)

1981 Litho., Photo. (#737A-737B)
735 PT17 40s on 10c #RA41 .20 .20
736 A275 40s on 25s #733 .50 .25
737 A275 130s on 25s #733 (DB) .50 .25
737A A276a 140s on 50c brn, yel & red .30 .25
737B A276b 140s on 1s multi .30 .25
737C A275 140s on 25s #733 (L) .50 .25
Nos. 735-737C (6) 2.30 1.45

Issued: #735, Apr. 12; #736, 737, 737C, Apr. 6; #737A, Apr. 15; #737B, Apr. 28.

Carved Stone Head, Pallasca Tribe
A277

#739, 742, 749 Pottery vase, Inca, vert. #740, Head, diff., vert. #743, 749A-749B, Huaco idol (fish), Nazca. 100s, Pallasca, vert. 140s, Puma.

Perf. 13½x13, 13x13½

1981-82 **Litho.**

738	A277	30s	dp rose lilac	.25	.25
739	A277	40s	orange ('82)	.30	.20
740	A277	40s	ultra	.30	.20
742	A277	80s	brown ('82)	.75	.50
743	A277	80s	red ('82)	.75	.40
745	A277	100s	lilac rose	.75	.50
748	A277	140s	lt blue grn	1.00	.70
749	A277	180s	green ('82)	1.75	1.25
749A	A277	240s	grnsh blue ('82)	1.00	.70
749B	A277	280s	violet ('82)	1.40	1.00
			Nos. 738-749B (10)	8.25	5.70

For surcharges see #789, 798-799, 1026.

A278

A279

1981, May 31 ***Perf. 13½x13***

750 A278 130s multicolored .60 .60

Postal and Philatelic Museum, 50th anniv.

1981, Oct. 7 **Litho.** ***Perf. 13½x13***

751 A279 30s purple & gray .25 .25

1979 Constitution Assembly President Victor Raul Haya de la Torre.

Inca Messenger, by Guaman Poma (1526-1613)
A280

Intl. Year of the Disabled
A280a

1981 **Litho.** ***Perf. 12***

752	A280	30s	lilac & blk	.25	.20
753	A280	40s	vermilion & blk	.20	.40
754	A280	130s	brt yel grn & blk	.50	.40
755	A280	140s	brt blue & blk	.50	.50
756	A280	200s	yellow brn & blk	.75	.75
			Nos. 752-756 (5)	2.20	2.25

Christmas. Issue dates: 30s, 40s, 200s, Dec. 21; others, Dec. 31.

1981 **Litho.** ***Perf. 13½x13***

756A A280a 100s multicolored .60 .40

Nos. 377, C130, C143, J56, O33, RA36, RA39, RA40, RA42, RA43 Surcharged in Brown, Black, Orange, Red, Green or Blue

1982

757	PT11	10s on 2c (#RA40, Br)		.25	.25
758	A155	10s on 10c (#377)		.20	.20
758A	AP60	40s on 1.25s (#C143)		.20	.20
758B	PT15	70s on 5c (#RA36, R)		.20	.20
759	D7	80s on 10c (#J56)		.20	.20
760	O1	80s on 10c (#O33)		.20	.20
761	PT14	80s on 3c (#RA43, O)		.20	.20
762	PT17	100s on 10c (#RA42, R)		.25	.25
763	AP57	100s on 2.20s (#C130, R)		.25	.25
764	PT14	150s on 3c (#RA39, G)		.35	.35
765	PT14	180s on 3c (#RA43, R)		.40	.40
766	PT14	200s on 3c (#RA43, Bl)		.50	.50
767	AP60	240s on 1.25s (#C143, R)		.60	.60
768	PT15	280s on 5c (#RA36)		.70	.70
		Nos. 757-768 (14)		4.50	4.50

Nos. 758A, 763, 767 airmail. Nos. 759 and 760 surcharged "Habilitado / Franq. Postal / 80 Soles".

Jorge Basadre (1903-1908), Historian — A281

Julio C. Tello (1882-1947), Archaeologist — A282

Perf. 13½x13, 13x13½

1982, Oct. 13 **Litho.**

769	A281	100s	pale green & blk	.25	.20
770	A282	200s	lt green & dk bl	.50	.30

9th Women's World Volleyball Championship, Sept. 12-26 — A283

Rights of the Disabled — A284

1982, Oct. 18 ***Perf. 12***

771 A283 80s black & red .20 .20

For surcharge see No. 791.

1982, Oct. 22

772 A284 200s blue & red .35 .25

Brena Campaign Centenary
A285

1982, Oct. 26 ***Perf. 13x13½***

773 A285 70s Andres Caceres medallion .20 .20

For surcharge see No. 790.

1982 World Cup — A286

16th Intl. Congress of Latin Notaries, Lima, June — A287

1982, Nov. 2 ***Perf. 12***

774 A286 80s multicolored .20 .20

For surcharge see No. 800.

1982, Nov. 6

775 A287 500s Emblem .90 .60

Handicrafts Year
A288

1982, Nov. 24 ***Perf. 13x13½***

776 A288 200s Clay bull figurine .35 .25

Christmas
A289

Pedro Vilcapaza
A290

1982 ***Perf. 13½x13***

777 A289 280s Holy Family .50 .50

For surcharge see No. 797.

1982, Dec. 2 ***Perf. 13½x13***

778 A290 240s black & lt brn .45 .30

Death centenary of Indian leader against Spanish during Andes Rebellion.

For surcharges see Nos. 792.

Jose Davila Condemarin (1799-1882), Minister of Posts (1849-76) — A291

1982, Dec. 10 ***Perf. 13x13½***

779 A291 150s blue & blk .25 .25

10th Anniv. of Intl. Potato Study Center, Lima
A292

1982, Dec. 27 ***Perf. 13x13½***

780 A292 240s multicolored .45 .30

For surcharge see No. 793.

450th Anniv. of City of San Miguel de Piura
A293

1982, Dec. 31 ***Perf. 13x13½***

781 A293 280s Arms .50 .50

For surcharge see No. 795.

TB Bacillus Centenary
A294

1983, Jan. 18 ***Perf. 12***

782 A294 240s Microscope, slide .45 .45

For surcharge see No. 794.

St. Teresa of Jesus of Avila (1515-1582), by Jose Espinoza de los Monteros, 1682 — A295

1983, Mar. 1

783 A295 100s multicolored .20 .20

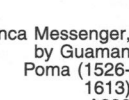

10th Anniv. of State Security Service
A296

1983, Mar. 8
784 A296 100s blue & orange .20 .20

Horseman's Ornamental Silver Shoe, 19th Cent.
A297

1983, Mar. 18
785 A297 250s multicolored .45 .30

30th Anniv. of Santiago Declaration
A298

75th Anniv. of Lima and Callao State Lotteries — A300

25th Anniv. of Lima-Bogota Airmail Service — A299

1983, Mar. 25
786 A298 280s Map .50 .50

For surcharge see No. 796.

1983, Apr. 8
787 A299 150s Jet .30 .20

1983, Apr. 26
788 A300 100s multicolored .20 .20

Nos. 739, 773, 771, 778, 780, 782, 781, 786, 777, 749, 774
Surcharged in Black or Green

1983 **Litho.**

789	A277	100s on 40s orange	.25	.20
790	A285	100s on 70s multi	.25	.20
791	A283	100s on 80s blk & red	.25	.20
792	A290	100s on 240s multi	.25	.20
793	A292	100s on 240s multi	.25	.25
794	A294	100s on 240s ol grn	.25	.25
795	A293	150s on 280s multi (G)	.30	.30
796	A298	150s on 280s multi	.30	.30
797	A289	200s on 280s multi	.45	.35
798	A277	300s on 180s green	.70	.45
799	A277	400s on 180s green	.90	.90
800	A286	500s on 80s multi	1.10	1.10
		Nos. 789-800 (12)	5.25	4.70

Military Ships
A301

1983, May 2 ***Perf. 12***
801 A301 150s Cruiser Almirante Grau, 1907 .25 .20
802 A301 350s Submarine Ferre, 1913 .65 .40

Simon Bolivar Birth Bicentenary
A302

Christmas
A303

1983, Dec. 13 **Litho.** ***Perf. 14***
803 A302 100s black & lt bl .20 .20

1983, Dec. 16
804 A303 100s Virgin and Child .20 .20

25th Anniv. of Intl. Pacific Fair — A304

Col. Leoncio Prado (1853-83)
A306

World Communications Year (in 1983) — A305

1983
805 A304 350s multicolored .65 .40

1984, Jan. 27 **Litho.** ***Perf. 14***
806 A305 700s multicolored 1.25 .90

1984, Feb. 3 **Litho.** ***Perf. 14***
807 A306 150s ol & ol brn .20 .20

Postal Building
A307

Pottery — A308

Arms of City of Callao — A310

Shipbuilding and Repair — A309

Peruvian Flora — A311

Peruvian Fauna — A312

1984 **Litho.** ***Perf. 14***

808	A307	50s	Ministry of Posts, Lima	.20	.20
809	A308	100s	Water jar	.20	.20
810	A308	150s	Llama	.20	.20
811	A308	200s	Painted vase	.20	.20
812	A309	250s	shown	.20	.20
813	A309	300s	Mixed cargo ship	.25	.20
814	A310	350s	shown	.30	.20
815	A310	400s	Arms of Cajamarca	.30	.20
816	A310	500s	Arms of Ayacucho	.40	.20
817	A311	700s	Canna edulis ker	.50	.30
818	A312	1000s	Lagothrix flavicauda	.75	.40
			Nos. 808-818 (11)	3.50	2.50

Issued: 50s, 8/29; 100s-200s, 5/9; 250s-300s, 2/22; 350s, 4/23; 400s, 6/21; 500s, 6/22; 700s, 9/12; 1000s, 7/3.
See Nos. 844-853, 880-885.

A313

A315

Designs: 50s, Hipolito Unanue (1758-1833). 200s, Ricardo Palma (1833-1919), Writer.

1984 **Litho.** ***Perf. 14***
819 A313 50s dull green .20 .20
820 A313 200s purple .20 .20

Issue dates: 50s, Nov. 14; 200s, Mar. 20.
See No. 828.

1984, Mar. 30
821 A315 500s Shooting .50 .25
822 A315 750s Hurdles 1.00 .35

1984 Summer Olympics.

Independence Declaration Act — A316

1984, July 18 **Litho.** ***Perf. 14***
823 A316 350s Signing document .20 .20

Admiral Grau — A317

Naval Battle — A318

1984, Oct. 8 **Litho.** ***Perf. 12½***
824 Block of 4 1.25 .75
a. A317 600s Knight of the Seas, by Pablo Muniz .30 .20
b. A318 600s Battle of Angamos .30 .20
c. A317 600s Congressional seat .30 .20
d. A318 600s Battle of Iquique .30 .20

Admiral Miguel Grau, 150th birth anniv.

Peruvian Naval Vessels
A319

1984, Dec. **Litho.** ***Perf. 14***
825 A319 250s Destroyer Almirante Guise, 1934 .20 .20
826 A319 400s Gunboat America, 1905 .20 .20

Christmas A320

1984, Dec. 11 Litho. ***Perf. 13x13½***
827 A320 1000s multi .45 .30

Famous Peruvians Type of 1984

1984, Dec. 14 Litho. ***Perf. 14***
828 A313 100s brown lake .20 .20

Victor Andres Belaunde (1883-1967), Pres. of UN General Assembly, 1959-60.

450th Anniv., Founding of Cuzco — A322

1984, Dec. 20 Litho. ***Perf. 13½x13***
829 A322 1000s Street scene .40 .30

15th Pacific Intl. Fair, Lima A323

1984, Dec. 28 Litho. ***Perf. 13x13½***
830 A323 1000s Llama .40 .30

450th Anniv., Lima — A324

Visit of Pope John Paul II — A325

1985, Jan. 17 Litho. ***Perf. 13½x13***
831 A324 1500s The Foundation of Lima, by Francisco Gamarra .50 .35

1985, Jan. 31 Litho. ***Perf. 13½x13***
832 A325 2000s Portrait .50 .35

Microwave Tower — A326

Jose Carlos Mariategui (1894-1924), Author — A327

1985, Feb. 28 Litho. ***Perf. 13½x13***
833 A326 1100s multi .50 .20

ENTEL Peru, Natl. Telecommunications Org., 15th anniv.

1985-86 Photo. ***Perf. 13½x13***

Designs: 500s, Francisco Garcia Calderon (1832-1905), president. No. 838, Oscar Miro Quesada (1884-1981), jurist. No. 839, Cesar Vallejo (1892-1938), author. No. 840, Jose Santos Chocano (1875-1934), poet.

836	A327	500s	lt olive grn	.20	.20
837	A327	800s	dull red	.20	.20
838	A327	800s	dk olive grn	.20	.20
839	A327	800s	Prus blue ('86)	.20	.20
840	A327	800s	dk red brn ('86)	.20	.20
			Nos. 836-840 (5)	1.00	1.00

See Nos. 901-905.

American Air Forces Cooperation System, 25th Anniv. — A328

1985, Apr. 16
842 A328 400s Member flags, emblem .20 .20

Jose A. Quinones Gonzales (1914-1941), Air Force Captain — A329

1985, Apr. 22 ***Perf. 13x13½***
843 A329 1000s Portrait, bomber .25 .20

Types of 1984

Design: 200s, Entrance arch and arcade, Central PO admin. building, vert. No. 845, Spotted Robles Moqo bisque vase, Pacheco, Ica. No. 846, Huaura bisque cat. No. 847, Robles Moqo bisque llama head. No. 848, Huancavelica city arms. No. 849, Huanuco city arms. No. 850, Puno city arms. No. 851, Llama wool industry. No. 852, Hymenocallis amancaes. No. 853, Penguins, Antarctic landscape.

1985-86 Litho. ***Perf. 13½x13***

844	A307	200s	slate blue	.20	.20
845	A308	500s	bister brn	.25	.20
846	A308	500s	dull yellow brn	.25	.20
847	A308	500s	black brn	.25	.20
848	A310	700s	brt org yel	.30	.20
849	A310	700s	brt bl ('86)	.30	.20
850	A310	900s	brown ('86)	.40	.20
851	A309	1100s	multicolored	.50	.20
852	A311	1100s	multicolored	.50	.20
853	A312	1500s	multicolored	.70	.20
			Nos. 844-853 (10)	3.65	2.00

Natl. Aerospace Institute Emblem, Globe A330

1985, May 24 ***Perf. 13x13½***
858 A330 900s ultra .20 .20

14th Inter-American Air Defense Day.

Founding of Constitution City — A333

1985, July Litho. ***Perf. 13½x13***
859 A333 300s Map, flag, crucifix .20 .20

Natl. Radio Society, 55th Anniv. A334

1985, July 24 ***Perf. 13x13½***
860 A334 1300s bl & brt org .20 .20

San Francisco Convent Church — A335

Doctrina Christiana Frontispiece, 1585, Lima — A336

1985, Oct. 12 ***Perf. 13½x13***
861 A335 1300s multicolored .20 .20

1985, Oct. 23
862 A336 300s pale buff & blk .20 .20

1st printed book in South America, 400th anniv.

Intl. Civil Aviation Org., 40th Anniv. A337

1985, Oct. 31 ***Perf. 13x13½***
863 A337 1100s 1920 Curtis Jenny .20 .20

Christmas A338

Postman, Child — A338a

1985, Dec. 30 Litho. ***Perf. 13½x13***
864 A338 2.50i Virgin and child, 17th cent. .40 .20

1985, Dec. 30 Litho. ***Perf. 13½x13***
864A A338a 2.50i multi .30 .25

Christmas charity for children's and postal workers' funds.

Founding of Trujillo, 450th Anniv. — A339

1986, Mar. 5 Litho. ***Perf. 13½x13***
865 A339 3i City arms .40 .25

Restoration of Chan Chan Ruins, Trujillo Province A340

1986, Apr. 5 Litho. ***Perf. 13x13½***
866 A340 50c Bas-relief .20 .20

Saint Rose of Lima, Birth Quadricent. A341

16th Intl. Pacific Fair — A342

1986, Apr. 30 Litho. ***Perf. 13½x13***
867 A341 7i multicolored .90 .60

1986, May 20
868 A342 1i Natl. products symbols .40 .20

Intl. Youth Year A343

1986, May 23 ***Perf. 13x13½***
869 A343 3.50i multicolored .40 .30

A344

A346

A345

1986, June 27 Litho. ***Perf. 13½x13***
870 A344 50c brown .20 .20

Pedro Vilcapaza (1740-81), independence hero.

1986, Aug. 8 Litho. ***Perf. 13x13½***
871 A345 3.50i multi .65 .30

UN, 40th anniv.

1986, Aug. 11 ***Perf. 13½x13***
872 A346 50c grysh brown .25 .20

Fernando and Justo Albujar Fayaque, Manuel Guarniz Lopez, natl. heroes.

Peruvian Navy A347

1986, Aug. 19 ***Perf. 13x13½***
873 A347 1.50i R-1, 1926 .20 .20
874 A347 2.50i Abtao, 1954 .30 .25

Flora Type of 1984

1986 Litho. ***Perf. 13½x13***
880 A311 80c Tropaeolum majus .20 .20
881 A311 80c Datura candida .20 .20
884 A312 2i Canis nudus .25 .20
885 A312 2i Penelope albipennis .35 .30
Nos. 880-885 (4) 1.00 .90

Canchis Province Folk Costumes A348

1986, Aug. 26 Litho. ***Perf. 13½x13***
890 A348 3i multicolored .35 .25

Tourism Day A349

1986, Aug. 29 ***Perf. 13x13½***
891 A349 4i Sacsayhuaman .50 .35

1986, Oct. 12 Litho. ***Perf. 13x13½***
891A A349 4i Intihuatana, Cuzco .50 .40

Interamerican Development Bank, 25th Anniv. — A350

1986, Sept. 4
892 A350 1i multicolored .25 .20

Beatification of Sr. Ana de Los Angeles — A351

1986, Sept. 15
893 A351 6i Sr. Ana, Pope John Paul II .70 .55

Jorge Chavez (1887-1910), Aviator, and Bleriot XI 1M — A352

VAN '86 — A353

1986, Sept. 23 ***Perf. 13½x13***
894 A352 5i multicolored .85 .45

Chavez's flight over the Alps, 75th anniv.

1986, Sept. 26
895 A353 50c light blue .20 .20

Ministry of Health vaccination campaign, Sept. 27-28, Oct. 25-26, Nov. 22-23.

Natl. Journalism Day — A354

1986, Oct. 1
896 A354 1.50i multi .20 .20

Peruvian Navy A355

1986, Oct. 7 Litho. ***Perf. 13x13½***
897 A355 1i Brigantine Gamarra, 1848 .20 .20
898 A355 1i Monitor Manco Capac, 1880 .20 .20

Institute of Higher Military Studies, 35th Anniv. A356

1986, Oct. 31 Litho. ***Perf. 13x13½***
899 A356 1i multicolored .20 .20

Boy, Girl — A357

1986, Nov. 3 ***Perf. 13½x13***
900 A357 2.50i red, brn & blk .40 .30

Christmas charity for children and postal workers' funds.

Famous Peruvians Type of 1985

1986-87
901 A327 50c Carrion .20 .20
902 A327 50c Barrenechea .20 .20
904 A327 80c Jose de la Riva Aguero .20 .20
905 A327 80c Barrenechea .20 .20
Nos. 901-905 (4) .80 .80

Issued: #904, 10/22/87; #905, 11/9/87.
This is an expanding set. Numbers will change if necessary.

Christmas A358

SENATI, 25th Anniv. — A359

1986, Dec. 3
908 A358 5i St. Joseph and Child .75 .60

1986, Dec. 19 ***Perf. 13½x13***
909 A359 4i multicolored .70 .45

Shipibo Tribal Costumes A360

World Food Day — A361

1987, Apr. 24 Litho. ***Perf. 13½x13***
910 A360 3i multicolored .45 .35

1987, May 26
911 A361 50c multicolored .20 .20

Preservation of the Nasca Lines — A362

Design: Nasca Lines and Dr. Maria Reiche (b. 1903), archaeologist.

1987, June 13 Litho. ***Perf. 13x13½***
912 A362 8i multicolored 1.25 .90

A363

A365

A364

1987, July 15 Litho. ***Perf. 13½x13***
913 A363 50c violet .20 .20

Mariano Santos (1850-1900), "The Hero of Tarapaca," 1879, Chilean war. Dated 1986.

1987, July 19 ***Perf. 13x13½***
914 A364 3i multicolored .45 .35

Natl. Horse Club, 50th anniv. Dated 1986.

1987, Aug 13 ***Perf. 13½x13***
915 A365 2i multicolored .30 .25

Gen. Felipe Santiago Salaverry (1806-1836), revolution leader. Dated 1986.

Colca's Canyon — A366

AMIFIL '87 — A367

1987, Sept. 8 Litho. ***Perf. 13½x13***
916 A366 6i multicolored .50 .40

10th Natl. Philatelic Exposition, Arequipa. Dated 1986.

1987, Sept. 10
917 A367 1i Nos. 1-2 .20 .20

Dated 1986.

Jose Maria Arguedas (b. 1911), Anthropologist, Author — A368

1987, Sept. 19
918 A368 50c brown .20 .20

Arequipa Chamber of Commerce & Industry A369

1987, Sept. 23 ***Perf. 13x13½***
919 A369 2i multicolored .25 .20

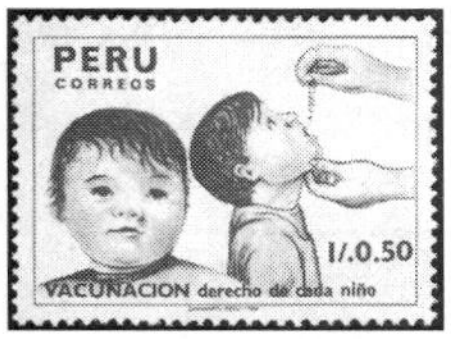

Vaccinate Every Child Campaign A370

1987, Sept. 30 Litho. ***Perf. 13x13½***
920 A370 50c orange brown .20 .20

Argentina, Winner of the 1986 World Cup Soccer Championships — A371

1987, Nov. 18
921 A371 4i multicolored .30 .25

Restoration of Chan Chan Ruins, Trujillo Province A372

Chimu culture (11th-15th cent.) bas-relief.

1987, Nov. 27
922 A372 50c multicolored .20 .20

See No. 936.

Halley's Comet A373

1987, Dec. 7
923 A373 4i Comet, Giotto satellite .30 .25

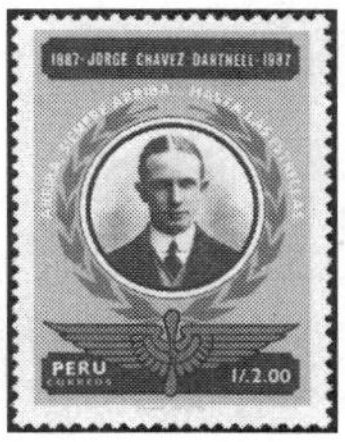

Jorge Chavez Dartnell (1887-1910), Aviator — A374

Founding of Lima, 450th Anniv. (in 1985) — A375

1987, Dec. 15 ***Perf. 13½x13***
924 A374 2i yel bis, claret brn & gold .30 .20

1987, Dec. 18 Litho. ***Perf. 13½x13***
925 A375 2.50i Osambela Palace .30 .20

Dated 1985.

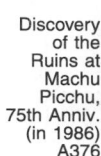

Discovery of the Ruins at Machu Picchu, 75th Anniv. (in 1986) A376

1987, Dec. ***Perf. 13x13½***
926 A376 9i multicolored .65 .50

Dated 1986.

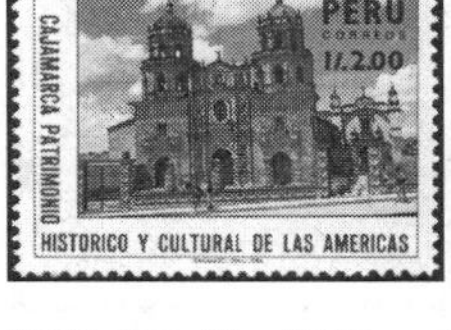

St. Francis's Church, Cajamarca A377

1988, Jan. 23 Litho. ***Perf. 13x13½***
927 A377 2i multicolored .30 .20

Cultural Heritage. Dated 1986.

Participation of Peruvian Athletes in the Olympics, 50th Anniv. — A378

Design: Athletes on parade, poster publicizing the 1936 Berlin Games.

1988, Mar. 1 Litho. ***Perf. 13½x13***
928 A378 1.50i multicolored .40 .20

Dated 1986.

Ministry of Education, 150th Anniv. A379

1988, Mar. 10 ***Perf. 13x13½***
929 A379 1i multicolored .20 .20

Coronation of the Virgin of the Evangelization by Pope John Paul II — A380

1988, Mar. 14 Litho. ***Perf. 13x13½***
930 A380 10i multicolored .50 .25

Dated 1986.

Rotary Intl. Involvement in Anti-Polio Campaign A381

1988, Mar. 16
931 A381 2i org, gold & dark blue .20 .20

Postman, Cathedral A382

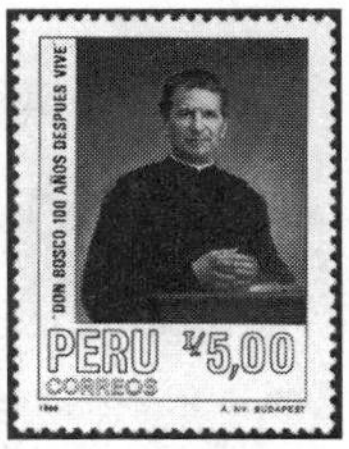

St. John Bosco (1815-1888), Educator — A384

Meeting of 8 Latin-American Presidents, Acapulco, 1st Anniv. — A383

1988, Apr. 29 Litho. ***Perf. 13½x13***
932 A382 9i brt blue .30 .20

Christmas charity for children and postal workers' funds.

1988, May 4 ***Perf. 13x13½***
933 A383 9i multicolored .30 .20

1988, June 1 ***Perf. 13½x13***
934 A384 5i multicolored .20 .20

1st Peruvian Scientific Expedition to the Antarctic A385

1988, June 2 ***Perf. 13x13½***
935 A385 7i Ship Humboldt, globe .20 .20

Restoration of Chan-Chan Ruins, Trujillo Province A386

1988, June 7
936 A386 4i Bas-relief .20 .20

Cesar Vallejo (1892-1938), Poet — A387

Journalists' Fund — A388

1988, June 15 ***Perf. 13½x13***
937 A387 25i buff, blk & brn .60 .30

1988, July 12 Litho. ***Perf. 13½x13***
938 A388 4i buff & deep ultra .20 .20

Type A44 — A389

1988, Sept. 1 Litho. ***Perf. 13½x13***
939 A389 20i blk, lt pink & ultra .20 .20

EXFILIMA '88, discovery of America 500th anniv.

17th Intl. Pacific Fair A390

1988, Sept. 6 *Perf. 13x13½*
940 A390 4i multicolored .20 .20

Painting by Jose Sabogal (1888-1956) — A391

1988, Sept. 7
941 A391 12i multicolored .20 .20

Peru Kennel Club Emblem, Dogs — A392

1988, Sept. 9 *Perf. 13½x13*
942 A392 20i multicolored .20 .20

CANINE '88 Intl. Dog Show, Lima.

Alfonso de Silva (1902-1934), Composer, and Score to Esplendido de Flores — A393

1988, Sept. 27 Litho. *Perf. 13x13½*
943 A393 20i multicolored .20 .20

2nd State Visit of Pope John Paul II — A394

1988, Oct. 10 *Perf. 13½x13*
944 A394 50i multicolored .40 .20

1988 Summer Olympics, Seoul — A395

1988, Nov. 10 Litho. *Perf. 13½x13*
945 A395 25i Women's volleyball .40 .20

Women's Volleyball Championships (1982) — A396

Chavin Culture Ceramic Vase — A397

1988, Nov. 16 *Perf. 12*
Surcharged in Red
946 A396 95i on 300s multi .80 .40

No. 946 not issued without overprint.
Christmas charity for children's and postal workers' funds.

1988 Litho. *Perf. 12*
Surcharged in Henna or Black
947 A397 40i on 100s red brn .20 .20
948 A397 80i on 10s blk .30 .20

Nos. 947-948 not issued without surcharge.
Issue dates: 40i, Dec. 15. 80i, Dec. 22.

Rain Forest Border Highway — A398

Codex of the Indian Kings, 1681 — A399

1989, Jan. 27 Litho. *Perf. 12*
Surcharged in Black
949 A398 70i on 80s multi .20 .20

Not issued without surcharge.

1989, Feb. 10
Surcharged in Olive Brown
950 A399 230i on 300s multi .50 .25

Not issued without surcharge.

Credit Bank of Peru, Cent. A400

1989, Apr. 9 Litho. *Perf. 13x13½*
951 A400 500i Huari Culture weaving .75 .35

Postal Services A401

1989, Apr. 20 *Perf. 13*
952 A401 50i SESPO, vert. .20 .20
953 A401 100i CAN .20 .20

El Comercio, 150th Anniv. — A402

1989, May 15
954 A402 600i multi .60 .30

Garcilaso de la Vega (1539-1616), Historian Called "The Inca" — A403

1989, July 11 Litho. *Perf. 12½*
955 A403 300i multi .30 .20

Express Mail Service A404

1989, July 12
956 A404 100i dark red, org & dark blue .20 .20

Federation Emblem and Roca — A405

1989, Aug. 29 Litho. *Perf. 13*
957 A405 100i multi .20 .20

Luis Loli Roca (1925-1988), founder of the Federation of Peruvian Newspaper Publishers.

Restoration of Chan Chan Ruins, Trujillo Province A406

Chimu culture (11th-15th cent.) bas-relief.

1989, Sept. 17 *Perf. 12½*
958 A406 400i multi .45 .25

Geographical Society of Lima, Cent. — A407

1989, Sept. 18 *Perf. 13*
959 A407 600i Early map of So. America .65 .30

Founders of Independence Soc. — A408

1989, Sept. 28 Litho. *Perf. 12½*
960 A408 300i multicolored .30 .20

3rd Meeting of the Presidential Consultation and Planning Board — A409

1989, Oct. 12 *Perf. 13*
961 A409 1300i Huacachina Lake 1.40 .70

For surcharge see No. 1017.

Children Mailing Letters — A410

1989, Nov. 29 Litho. *Perf. 12½*
962 A410 1200i multicolored .30

Christmas charity for children's and postal workers' funds.

Cacti A411

1989, Dec. 21 Litho. *Perf. 13*
963 A411 500i *Loxanthocereus acanthurus* .20
964 A411 500i *Corryocactus huincoensis* .20
965 A411 500i *Haageocereus clavispinus* .20
966 A411 500i *Trichocereus pervianus* .20
967 A411 500i *Matucana cereoides* .20
Nos. 963-967 (5) 1.00

Nos. 965-967 vert. For surcharges see Nos. 1028-1031

America Issue — A412

UPAE emblem and pre-Columbian medicine jars.

1989, Dec. 28 ***Perf. 12½***
968 A412 5000i shown 2.00
969 A412 5000i multi, diff. 2.00

Belen Church, Cajamarca A413

1990, Feb. 1 Litho. ***Perf. 12½***
970 A413 600i multicolored .20

Historic patrimony of Cajamarca and culture of the Americas.

Huascaran Natl. Park — A414

1990, Feb. 4 ***Perf. 13***
971 A414 900i Llanganuco Lagoons .20
972 A414 900i Mountain climber, Andes, vert. .20
973 A414 1000i Alpamayo mountain .20
974 A414 1000i *Puya raimondi,* vert. .20
975 A414 1100i Condor and Quenual .20
976 A414 1100i El Huascaran .20
Nos. 971-976 (6) 1.20

Pope and Icon of the Virgin — A415

1990, Feb. 6 ***Perf. 12½***
977 A415 1250i multicolored .50

Visit of Pope John Paul II. For surcharge see No. 1039.

Butterflies — A416

1990, Feb. 11 ***Perf. 13***
978 A416 1000i *Amydon* .20
979 A416 1000i *Agrias beata,* female .20
980 A416 1000i *Sardanapalus,* male .20
981 A416 1000i *Sardanapalus,* female .20
982 A416 1000i *Agrias beata,* male .20
Nos. 978-982 (5) 1.00

For surcharges see Nos. 1033-1037.

A417

A418

Victor Raul Haya de La Torre and Seat of Government.

1990, Feb. 24 ***Perf. 12½***
983 A417 2100i multicolored .55

Return to constitutional government, 10th anniv.

1990, May 24 Litho. ***Perf. 12½***
984 A418 300i multicolored .30

Peruvian Philatelic Assoc., 50th anniv. Dated 1989. For surcharge see No. 1038.

Prenfil '88 A419

1990, May 29
985 A419 300i multicolored .20

World Exposition of Stamp & Literature Printers, Buenos Aires. Dated 1989. For surcharge see No. 1032.

French Revolution, Bicentennial A420

#986, Liberty. #987, Storming the Bastille. #988, Lafayette celebrating the Republic. #989, Rousseau & symbols of the Revolution.

1990, June 5
986 A420 2000i multicolored .50
987 A420 2000i multicolored .50
988 A420 2000i multicolored .50
989 A420 2000i shown .50
a. Strip of 4, #986-989 + label 2.00

Dated 1989.

Arequipa, 450th Anniv. — A421

1990, Aug. 15 Litho. ***Perf. 13***
990 A421 50,000i multi .50

Lighthouse A422

Design: 230,000i, Hospital ship Morona.

1990, Sept. 19 ***Perf. 12½***
Surcharged in Black
991 A422 110,000i on 200i blue .85
992 A422 230,000i on 400i blue 1.75

Not issued without surcharge.

A423

A424

1990-91 Litho. ***Perf. 13***
993 A423 110,000i Torch bearer .55
994 A423 280,000i Shooting 1.40
995 A423 290,000i Running, horiz. 1.40
996 A423 300,000i Soccer 1.50
997 A423 560,000i Swimming, horiz. 2.25
998 A423 580,000i Equestrian 2.40
999 A423 600,000i Sailing 2.50
1000 A423 620,000i Tennis 2.50
Nos. 993-1000 (8) 14.50

4th South American Games, Lima. Issue dates: #993-996, Oct. 19. #997-1000, Feb. 5, 1991.

1990, Nov. 22 Litho. ***Die Cut***
Self-Adhesive
1001 A424 250,000i No. 1 1.50
1002 A424 350,000i No. 2 2.25

Pacific Steam Navigation Co., 150th anniv.

Postal Workers' Christmas Fund — A425

1990, Dec. 7 Litho. ***Perf. 12½***
1003 A425 310,000i multi 1.75

Maria Jesus Castaneda de Pardo, First Woman President of Peruvian Red Cross A426

1991, May 15 Litho. ***Perf. 12½***
1004 A426 .15im on 2500i red & blk .60

Dated 1990. Not issued without surcharge.

2nd Peruvian Scientific Expedition to Antarctica — A427

.40im, Penguins, man. .45im, Peruvian research station, skua. .50im, Whale, map, research station.

1991, June 20
1005 A427 .40im on 50,000i 1.60
1006 A427 .45im on 80,000i 1.75
1007 A427 .50im on 100,000i 2.00
Nos. 1005-1007 (3) 5.35

Not issued without surcharge.

A428

A429

St. Anthony Natl. Univ., Cuzco, 300th Anniv.: 10c, Siphoonandra ellipitica. 20c, Don Manuel de Mollinedo y Angulo, founder. 1s, University coat of arms.

1991, Sept. 26 Litho. ***Perf. 13½x13***
1008 A428 10c multicolored .25
1009 A428 20c multicolored .50
1010 A428 1s multicolored 2.40
Nos. 1008-1010 (3) 3.15

1991, Dec. 3 Litho. ***Perf. 13½x13***

Paintings: No. 1011, Madonna and child. No. 1012, Madonna with lambs and angels.

1011 A429 70c multicolored 1.50
1012 A429 70c multicolored 1.50

Postal Workers' Christmas fund.

America Issue A430

1991, Dec. 23 ***Perf. 13***
1013 A430 .50im Mangrove swamp 1.10
1014 A430 .50im Gera waterfall, vert. 1.10

Dated 1990.

Sir Rowland Hill and Penny Black
A431

1992, Jan. 15 Litho. *Perf. 13*

1015 A431 .40im gray, blk & bl .85

Penny Black, 150th anniv. (in 1990).

A432

A433

1992, Jan. 28

1016 A432 .30im multicolored .65

Our Lady of Guadalupe College, 150th anniv. (in 1990)

1992, Jan. 30 *Perf. 13½x13*

1017 A433 10c multicolored .20

Entre Nous Society, 80th anniv.

Peru-Bolivia Port Access Agreement — A434

1992, Feb. 25 Litho. *Perf. 12½*

1018 A434 20c multicolored .30

Restoration of Chan-Chan Ruins — A435

1992, Mar. 17

1019 A435 .15im multicolored .35

Dated 1990.

Antonio Raimondi, Naturalist and Publisher, Death Cent. — A436

1992, Mar. 31

1020 A436 .30im multicolored .75

Dated 1990.

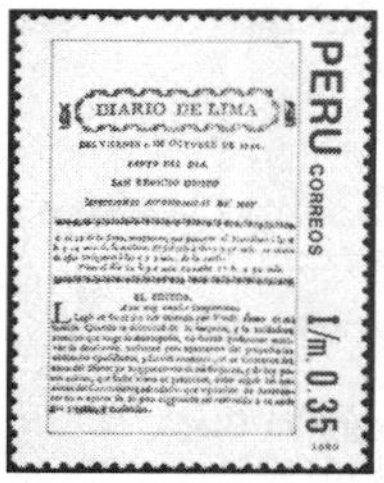

Newspaper "Diario de Lima", Bicent. (in 1990) — A437

1992, May 22 Litho. *Perf. 13*

1021 A437 .35im pale yel & black .65

Dated 1990.

Mariano Melgar (1790-1815), Poet — A438

1992, Aug. 5 Litho. *Perf. 12½x13*

1022 A438 60c multicolored .85

8 Reales, 1568, First Peruvian Coinage
A439

1992, Aug. 7 *Perf. 13x12½*

1023 A439 70c multicolored 1.00

Catholic Univeristy of Peru, 75th Anniv. — A440

1992, Aug. 18 *Perf. 12½*

1024 A440 90c black & tan 1.25

Pan-American Health Organization, 90th Anniv. — A441

1992, Dec. 2 Litho. *Die Cut*

Self-Adhesive

1025 A441 3s multicolored 3.75

Nos. 749, 961 Surcharged

Perf. 13½x13, 13

1992, Nov. 18 Litho.

1026 A277 50c on 180s #749 .65

1027 A409 1s on 1300i #961 1.25

Nos. 963, 965-967, 977-982, & 984-985 Surcharged

Perfs. as Before

1992, Dec. 24 Litho.

1028 A411 40c on 500i #963

1029 A411 40c on 500i #965

1030 A411 40c on 500i #966

1031 A411 40c on 500i #967

1032 A419 50c on 300i #985

1033 A416 50c on 1000i #978

1034 A416 50c on 1000i #979

1035 A416 50c on 1000i #980

1036 A416 50c on 1000i #981

1037 A416 50c on 1000i #982

1038 A418 1s on 300i #984

1039 A415 1s on 1250i #977

Virgin with a Spindle, by Urbina — A442

1993, Feb. 10 Litho. *Die Cut*

Self-Adhesive

1040 A442 80c multicolored .95

Sican Culture
A443

Various artifacts.

1993, Feb. 10

Self-Adhesive

1041 A443 2s multicolored 2.40

1042 A443 5s multi, vert. 6.00

Evangelization in Peru, 500th Anniv. — A444

1993, Feb. 12

Self-Adhesive

1043 A444 1s multicolored 1.25

Fruit Sellers, by Angel Chavez — A445

Dancers, by Monica Rojas — A446

1993, Feb. 12

Self-Adhesive

1044 A445 1.50s multicolored 1.75

1045 A446 1.50s multicolored 1.75

Statue of Madonna and Child — A447

1993, Feb. 24 Litho. *Die Cut*

Self-Adhesive

1046 A447 70c multicolored 1.10

Salesian Brothers in Peru, cent. (in 1991).

America Issue — A448

UPAEP: No. 1047a, 90c, Francisco Pizarro, sailing ship. b, 1s, Sailing ship, map of north-west coast of South America.

1993, Mar. 19 *Perf. 12½*

1047 A448 Pair, #a.-b. 2.40

Sipan Gold Head — A449

1993, Apr. 1

1048 A449 50c multicolored .70

Beatification of Josemaria Escriva, 1st Anniv. — A450

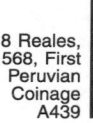

1993, July 7 Litho. *Die Cut*

Self-Adhesive

1049 A450 30c multicolored .50

Peru-Japan Treaty of Peace and Trade, 120th Anniv. — A451

Designs: 1.50s, Flowers. 1.70s, Peruvian, Japanese children, mountains.

1993, Aug. 21 Litho. *Perf. 11*

1050 A451 1.50s multicolored 2.00
1051 A451 1.70s multicolored 2.25

Sea Lions — A452

1993, Sept. 20 Litho. *Perf. 11*

1052 A452 90c shown 1.00
1053 A452 1s Parrot, vert. 1.10

Amifil '93 (#1052). Brasiliana '93 (#1053).

Based on available currency exchange rates, the face value of Nos. 1056-1057 is about $2.53. It appears that Peruvian stamps are appearing in the market at significantly higher prices. We have left some of Peru's new issues unvalued until we have more information on the relationship between face value and current retail prices.

A453

A454

1993, Nov. 9 Litho. *Die Cut*

Self-Adhesive

1054 A453 50c olive brown

Honorio Delgado, Physician and Author, Birth Cent. (in 1992).

1993, Nov. 12

Self-Adhesive

1055 A454 80c orange brown

Rosalia De LaValle De Morales Macedo, Social Reformer, Birth Cent.

A455

Intl. Pacific Fair, Lima — A456

Sculptures depicting Peruvian ethnic groups.

1993, Nov. 22

Self-Adhesive

1056 A455 2s Quechua
1057 A455 3.50s Orejon

1993, Nov. 25 Litho. *Perf. 11*

1058 A456 1.50s multicolored

Christmas — A457

Cultural Artifacts — A458

Design: 1s, Madonna of Loreto.

1993, Nov. 30 *Perf. 11*

1059 A457 1s multicolored

1993, Nov. 30 *Die Cut*

2.50s, Sican artifacts. 4s, Sican mask. 10s, Chancay ceramic statue, vert. 20s, Chancay textile.

Self-Adhesive

1060 A458 2.50s multicolored
1061 A458 4s multicolored
1062 A458 10s multicolored
1063 A458 20s multicolored

See Nos. 1079-1082.

Prevention of AIDS — A459

1993, Dec. 1 Litho. *Perf. 11*

1064 A459 1.50s multicolored

A460

A461

1994, Mar. 4 Litho. *Die Cut*

Self-Adhesive

1065 A460 1s multicolored 1.60

Natl. Council on Science and Technology (Concytec), 25th Anniv. Dated 1993.

1994

20c, 40c, 50c, Bridge of Huaman Poma de Ayala.

Self-Adhesive

1066 A461 20c blue .35
1067 A461 40c orange .65
1068 A461 50c purple .85
Nos. 1066-1068 (3) 1.85

Litho.

Perf. 12x11

1073 A461 30c brown .45
1074 A461 40c black .70
1075 A461 50c vermilion .85
Nos. 1073-1075 (3) 2.00

Issued: Nos. 1066-1068, 3/11/94; Nos. 1073-1075, 5/13/94.

This is an expanding set. Numbers may change.

Cultural Artifacts Type of 1993

No. 1079, Engraved silver container, vert. No. 1080, Engraved medallion. No. 1081, Carved bull, Pucara. No. 1082, Plate with fish designs.

1994, Mar. 25

Self-Adhesive

1079 A458 1.50s multicolored 2.50
1080 A458 1.50s multicolored 2.50
1081 A458 3s multicolored 4.75
1082 A458 3s multicolored 4.75
Nos. 1079-1082 (4) 14.50

Dated 1993.

Sipan Artifacts A464

1994, May 19 Litho. *Perf. 11*

1083 A464 3s Peanut-shaped beads 4.75
1084 A464 5s Mask, vert. 8.00

El Brujo Archaelogical Site, Trujillo — A465

1994, Nov. 3 Litho. *Perf. 14*

1085 A465 70c multicolored .65

Christmas A466

Ceramic figures: 1.80s, Christ child. 2s, Nativity scene. Dated 1994.

1995, Mar. 17 Litho. *Perf. 13x13½*

1086 A466 1.80s multicolored 1.60
1087 A466 2s multicolored 1.75

1994 World Cup Soccer Championships, US — A467

1995, Mar. 20 *Perf. 13½x13*

1088 A467 60c shown .50
1089 A467 4.80s Mascot, flags 4.25

Dated 1994.

Ministry of Transportation, 25th Anniv. — A468

1995, Mar. 22 *Perf. 13x13½*

1090 A468 20c multicolored .20

Dated 1994.

Cultural Artifacts A469

Mochican art: 40c, Pitcher with figures beneath blanket. 80c, Jeweled medallion. 90c, Figure holding severed head.

1995, Mar. 27 *Perf. 14*

1091 A469 40c multicolored .35
1092 A469 80c multicolored .70
1093 A469 90c multicolored .80
Nos. 1091-1093 (3) 1.85

Dated 1994.

Juan Parra del Riego, Birth Cent. — A470

No. 1095, Jose Carlos Mariategui, birth cent.

1995, Mar. 28 *Perf. 14*

1094 A470 90c multicolored .80

Perf. 13½x13

1095 A470 90c multicolored .80

Dated 1994.

Las Carmelitas Monastery, 350th Anniv. A471

1995, Mar. 31 Litho. *Perf. 13*

1096 A471 70c multicolored 1.10

Dated 1994.

Peru's Volunteer Fireman's Assoc. A472

Fire trucks: 50c, Early steam ladder. 90c, Modern aerial ladder.

1995, Apr. 12 *Perf. 14*

1097 A472 50c multicolored .85
1098 A472 90c multicolored 1.50

Dated 1994.

Musical Instruments A473

1995, Apr. 10 Litho. *Perf. 13½x13*

1099 A473 20c Cello .35
1100 A473 40c Drum .70

Union Club, Fountain, Plaza of Arms A474

Design: 1s, Santo Domingo Convent, Lima.

1995, Apr. 19 Litho. *Perf. 14*

1101 A474 90c multicolored 1.50
1102 A474 1s multicolored 1.75

Cultural history of Lima.

Ethnic Groups — A475

1995, Apr. 26 ***Perf. 13½x13***

1103 A475 1s Bora girl 1.75
1104 A475 1.80s Aguaruna man 3.00

World Food Program, 30th Anniv. A476

1995, May 3 ***Perf. 13x13½***

1105 A476 1.80s multicolored 3.00

Solanum Ambosinum A477

Reed Boat, Lake Titicaca — A478

Design: 2s, Mochica ceramic representation of papa flower.

1995, May 8 ***Perf. 13½x13***

1106 A477 1.80s multicolored 3.00
1107 A477 2s multicolored 3.50

1995, May 12

1108 A478 2s multicolored 3.50

Fauna A479

1995, May 18 ***Perf. 13½x13, 13x13½***

1109 A479 1s American owl, vert. 1.75
1110 A479 1.80s Jaguar 3.00

Andes Development Corporation, 25th Anniv. — A480

1995, Aug. 29 **Litho.** ***Perf. 14***

1111 A480 5s multicolored 8.00

World Tourism Day A481

1995, Sept. 27 ***Perf. 13x13½***

1112 A481 5.40s multicolored 8.50

Dated 1994.

World Post Day A482

1995, Oct. 9 ***Perf. 14***

1113 A482 1.80s Antique mail box 2.75

Dated 1994.

America Issue A483

Perf. 13½x14, 14x13½ (#1115)

1995, Oct. 12

1114 A483 1.50s Landing of Columbus 2.50
1115 A483 1.70s Guanaco, vert. 2.75
1116 A483 1.80s Early mail cart 2.75
1117 A483 2s Postal trucks 3.25
Nos. 1114-1117 (4) 11.25

No. 1116-1117 are dated 1994.

UN, 50th Anniv. A484

Design: 90c, Peruvian delegates, 1945.

1995, Oct. 28 ***Perf. 14***

1118 A484 90c multicolored 1.50

Entrys, Lima Cathedrals A485

Designs: 30c, St. Apolonia. 70c, St. Louis, side entry to St. Francis.

1995, Oct. 20

1119 A485 30c multicolored .55
1120 A485 70c multicolored 1.25

Dated 1994.

Artifacts from Art Museums A486

Carvings and sculptures: No. 1121, St. James on horseback, 19th cent. No. 1122, Church. 40c, Woman on pedestal. 50c, Archangel.

1995, Oct. 31 ***Perf. 14½x14***

1121 A486 20c multicolored .35
1122 A486 20c multicolored .35
1123 A486 40c multicolored .65
1124 A486 50c multicolored .80
Nos. 1121-1124 (4) 2.15

Dated 1994.

Scouting — A487

Designs: a, 80c, Lady Olave Baden-Powell. b, 1s, Lord Robert Baden-Powell.

1995, Nov. 9 **Litho.** ***Perf. 13½x13***

1125 A487 Pair, #a.-b. 2.75

Dated 1994.

A488

A489

Folk Dances: 1,80s, Festejo. 2s, Marinera limeña, horiz.

1995, Nov. 16 ***Perf. 14***

1126 A488 1.80s multicolored 2.75
1127 A488 2s multicolored 3.00

Dated 1994.

1995, Nov. 23

Biodiversity: 50c, Manu Natl. Park. 90c, Anolis punctatus, horiz.

1128 A489 50c multicolored .85
1129 A489 90c multicolored 1.50

Dated 1994.

A490

A491

Electricity for Development: 20c, Toma de Huinco. 40c, Antacoto Lake.

1995, Nov. 27

1130 A490 20c multicolored .30
1131 A490 40c multicolored .60

Dated 1994.

1995, Dec. 4

Peruvian Saints: 90c, St. Toribio de Mogrovejo. 1s, St. Francisco Solano.

1132 A491 90c multicolored 1.40
1133 A491 1s multicolored 1.50

Dated 1994.

FAO, 50th Anniv. A492

1996, Apr. 24 **Litho.** ***Perf. 14***

1134 A492 60c multicolored .90

Christmas 1995 A493

Local crafts: 30c, Nativity scene with folding panels, vert. 70c, Carved statues of three Magi.

1996, May 2

1135 A493 30c multicolored .45
1136 A493 70c multicolored 1.00

America Issue A494

Designs: 30c, Rock formations of Lachay. 70c, Coastal black crocodile.

1996, May 9

1137 A494 30c multicolored .45
1138 A494 70c multicolored 1.00

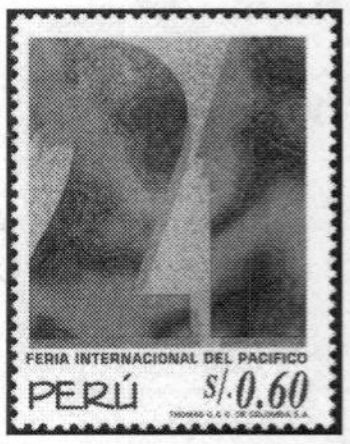

Intl. Pacific Fair — A495

1996, May 16

1139 A495 60c multicolored .90

1992 Summer Olympic Games, Barcelona A496

a, Shooting. b, Tennis. c, Swimming. d, Weight lifting.

1996, June 10 Litho. *Perf. 12½*
1140 A496 60c Block of 4, #a.-d. 3.00

Dated 1992.
For surcharges see #1220-1223.

Expo '92, Seville A497

1996, June 17
1141 A497 1.50s multicolored 2.25

Dated 1992.

Cesar Vallejo (1892-1938), Writer — A498

1996, June 25
1142 A498 50c black & gray .75

Dated 1992.

Lima, City of Culture — A499

1996, July 1
1143 A499 30c brown & tan .45

Dated 1992.
For surcharge see No. 1219.

Kon-Tiki Expedition, 50th Anniv. A500

1997, Apr. 28 Litho. *Perf. 12½*
1144 A500 3.30s multicolored 2.50

Beginning with No. 1145, most stamps have colored lines printed on the back creating a granite paper effect.

UNICEF, 50th Anniv. (in 1996) A501

Mochica Pottery — A502

1997, Aug. 7 Litho. *Perf. 13½x14*
1145 A501 1.80s multicolored 2.40

1997, Aug. 18 Litho. *Perf. 14½*

Designs: 20c, Owl. 30c, Ornamental container. 50c, Goose jar. 1s, Two monkeys on jar. 1.30s, Duck pitcher. 1.50s, Cat pitcher.

1146	A502	20c	green	.25
1147	A502	30c	lilac	.40
1148	A502	50c	black	.65
1149	A502	1s	red brown	1.25
1150	A502	1.30s	red	1.75
1151	A502	1.50s	brown	2.00
	Nos. 1146-1151 (6)			6.30

See Nos. 1179-1183, 1211-1214.

1996 Summer Olympics, Atlanta — A503

a, Shooting. b, Gymnastics. c, Boxing. d, Soccer.

1997, Aug. 25 *Perf. 14x13½*
1152 A503 2.70s Strip of 4, #a.-d. 8.25

College of Biology, 25th Anniv. — A504

1997, Aug. 26
1153 A504 5s multicolored 3.75

Scouting, 90th Anniv. — A505

1997, Aug. 29
1154 A505 6.80s multicolored 5.25

8th Intl. Conference Against Corruption, Lima A506

1997, Sept. 7 *Perf. 13½x14*
1155 A506 2.70s multicolored 2.00

Montreal Protocol on Substances that Deplete Ozone Layer, 10th Anniv. — A507

1997, Sept. 16 *Perf. 14x13½*
1156 A507 6.80s multicolored 5.25

Lord of Sipan Artifacts A508

Designs: 2.70s, Animal figure with large hands, feet. 3.30s, Medallion with warrior figure, vert.
10s, Tomb of Lord of Sipan, vert.

1997, Sept. 22 Litho. *Perf. 13½x14*
1157 A508 2.70s multicolored 3.50
1158 A508 3.30s multicolored 4.30

Souvenir Sheet

1159 A508 10s multicolored 13.00

Peruvian Indians — A509

1997, Oct. 12 Litho. *Perf. 14x13½*
1160 A509 2.70s Man 3.50
1161 A509 2.70s Woman 3.50

America Issue. Nos. 1160-1161 are dated 1996.

Heinrich von Stephan (1831-97) A510

1997, Oct. 9
1162 A510 10s multicolored 13.00

America Issue — A511

1997, Oct. 12
1163 A511 2.70s Early post carrier 3.50
1164 A511 2.70s Modern letter carrier 3.50

13th Bolivar Games — A512

a, Tennis. b, Soccer. c, Basketball. d, Shot put.

1997, Oct. 17 Litho. *Perf. 14x13½*
1165 A512 2.70s Block of 4, #a.-d. 14.00

Marshal Ramon Castilla (1797-1867) A513

1997, Oct. 17
1166 A513 1.80s multicolored 2.50

Treaty of Tlatelolco Banning Nuclear Weapons in Latin America, 30th Anniv. — A514

1997, Nov. 3
1167 A514 20s multicolored 26.00

Manu Natl. Park — A515

Birds: a, Kingfisher. b, Woodpecker. c, Crossbill. d, Eagle. e, Jabiru. f, Owl.

1997, Oct. 24

Sheet of 6

1168 A515 3.30s #a.-f. + label 25.00

8th Peruvian Antarctic Scientific Expedition A516

1997, Nov. 10
1169 A516 6s multicolored 7.75

Christmas A517

1997, Nov. 26
1170 A517 2.70s multicolored 3.50

Hipolito Unanue Agreement, 25th Anniv. — A518

1997, Dec. 18 Litho. ***Perf. 14x13½***
1171 A518 1s multicolored 1.25

Souvenir Sheet

Peruvian Gold Libra, Cent. — A519

1997, Dec. 18
1172 A519 10s multicolored 13.00

Dept. of Post and Telegraph, Cent. — A520

1997, Dec. 31
1173 A520 1s multicolored 1.25

Organization of American States (OAS), 50th Anniv. — A521

1998, Apr. 30 Litho. ***Perf. 14x13½***
1174 A521 2.70s multicolored 3.50

Chorrillos Military School, Cent. A522

1998, Apr. 29 ***Perf. 13½x14***
1175 A522 2.70s multicolored 3.50

Tourism — A523

1998, June 22 Litho. ***Perf. 14x13½***
1176 A523 5s multicolored 5.75

Peruvian Horse — A524

1998, June 5
1177 A524 2.70s pale violet & violet 3.25

1998 World Cup Soccer Championships, France — A525

a, 2.70s, Goalie. b, 3.30s, Two players. 10s, Player kicking ball.

1998, June 26
1178 A525 Pair, #a.-b. 7.00

Souvenir Sheet
Perf. 13½x14

1178C A525 10s multicolored 12.00 12.00

Mochica Pottery Type of 1997

1s, like #1149. 1.30s, like #1146. 1.50s, like #1151. 2.70s, like #1148. 3.30s, like #1150.

1998, June 19 Litho. ***Perf. 14½***
1179 A502 1s slate 1.25
1180 A502 1.30s violet 1.60
1181 A502 1.50s pale blue 1.90
1182 A502 2.70s bister 3.50
1183 A502 3.30s black brown 4.00
Nos. 1179-1183 (5) 12.25

Aero Peru, 25th Anniv. A526

1.50s, Cuzco Cathedral. 2.70s, Airplane.

1998, May 22 ***Perf. 13½x14***
1184 A526 1.50s multicolored 1.90
1185 A526 2.70s multicolored 3.50

Restoration of the Cathedral of Lima, Cent. — A527

1998, June 15 ***Perf. 14x13½***
1186 A527 2.70s multicolored 3.25

Inca Rulers — A528

1998, July 17 Litho. ***Perf. 14x13½***
1187 A528 2.70s Lloque Yupanqui 3.25 3.25
1188 A528 2.70s Sinchi Roca 3.25 3.25
1189 A528 9.70s Manco Capac 11.50 11.50
Nos. 1187-1189 (3) 18.00 18.00

See Nos. 1225-1228.

Intl. Year of the Ocean A529

1998, Aug. 8 ***Perf. 13½x14***
1190 A529 6.80s multicolored 8.00 8.00

Natl. Symphony Orchestra, 60th Anniv. — A530

1998, Aug. 11 ***Perf. 14x13½***
1191 A530 2.70s multicolored 3.25 3.25

Mother Teresa (1910-97) A531

1998, Sept. 5
1192 A531 2.70s multicolored 3.25 3.25

Peruvian Children's Foundation A532

1998, Sept. 17
1193 A532 8.80s multicolored 10.50 10.50

Souvenir Sheet

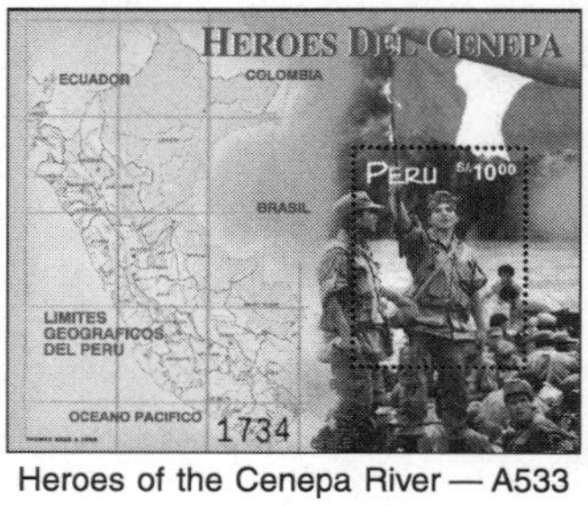

Heroes of the Cenepa River — A533

Illustration reduced.

1998, June 5
1194 A533 10s multicolored 12.00 12.00

Souvenir Sheet

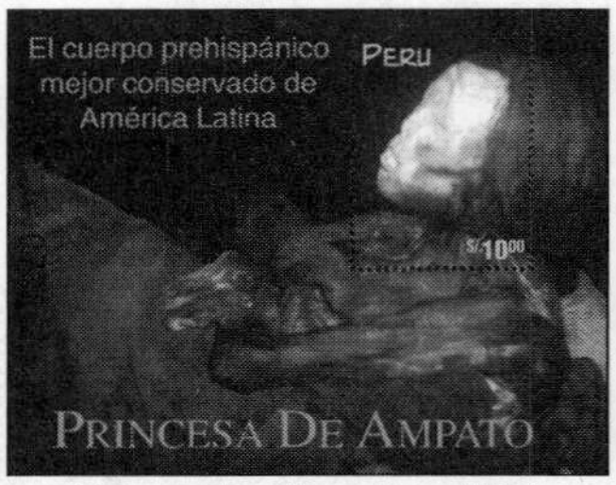

Princess De Ampato — A534

Illustration reduced.

1998, Sept. 8
1195 A534 10s multicolored 12.00 12.00

Fauna of Manu Natl. Park — A535

1998, Sept. 27 Litho. ***Perf. 14x13½***
1196 A535 1.50s multicolored 1.75 1.75

America Issue — A536

1998, Oct. 12
1197 A536 2.70s Chabuca 3.00 3.00

Stamp Day — A537

1998, Oct. 9
1198 A537 6.80s No. 3 7.75 7.75

Frogs — A538

No. 1199: a, Agalychnis craspedopus. b, Ceratophrys cornuta. c, Epipedobates macero. d, Phyllomedusa vaillanti. e, Dendrobates biolat. f, Hemiphractus proboscideus.

1998, Oct. 23 Litho. ***Perf. 14x13½***
1199 A538 3.30s Block of 6, #a.-f. + label *13.50 13.50*

Christmas A539

1998, Nov. 16 *Perf. 13½x14*
1200 A539 3.30s multicolored 2.25 2.25

Universal Declaration of Human Rights, 50th Anniv. A540

1998, Dec. 10 Litho. *Perf. 13½x14*
1201 A540 5s multicolored 3.50 3.50

Peru-Ecuador Peace Treaty — A541

1998, Nov. 26 Litho. *Perf. 13½x14*
1202 A541 2.70s multicolored 2.25 2.25

Brasilia '98.

19th World Scout Jamboree, Chile — A542

Designs: a, Scouting emblem, stylized tents. b, Emblem, tents, "SIEMPRE LISTO."

1999, Jan. 5 Litho. *Perf. 14x13½*
1203 A542 5s Pair, #a.-b. 6.50 6.50

Peruvian Philatelic Assoc., 50th Anniv. — A543

1999, Jan. 10
1204 A543 2.70s No. 19 1.75 1.75

Paintings by Pancho Fierro (1809-79) — A544

Designs: 2.70s, Once Upon Time in a Shaded Grove. 3.30s, Sound of the Devil.

1999, Jan. 16
1205 A544 2.70s multicolored 1.75 1.75
1206 A544 3.30s multicolored 2.25 2.25

Regional Dance — A545

1999, Feb. 10 Litho. *Perf. 14x13½*
1207 A545 3.30s multicolored 2.00 2.00

CENDAF, 25th Anniv. A546

1999, Mar. 1 *Perf. 13½x14*
1208 A546 1.80s multicolored 1.10 1.10

Ernest Malinowski (1818-99), Central Railroad A547

1999, Mar. 3
1209 A547 5s multicolored 3.00 3.00

Peruvian Foundation for Children's Heart Disease A548

1999, Mar. 6
1210 A548 2.70s multicolored 1.60 1.60

Mochica Pottery Type of 1997

Designs: 1s, like #1151. 1.50s, like #1148. 1.80s, like #1146. 2s, like #1150.

1999, Feb. 16 Litho. *Perf. 14½*
1211 A502 1s lake .65 .65
1212 A502 1.50s dark blue blk 1.00 1.00
1213 A502 1.80s brown 1.10 1.10
1214 A502 2s orange 1.25 1.25
Nos. 1211-1214 (4) 4.00 4.00

Fauna of the Peruvian Rain Forest — A549

1999, Apr. 23 *Perf. 14x13½*
1215 A549 5s multicolored 3.25 3.25

Souvenir Sheet

Fauna of Manu Natl. Park — A550

Illustration reduced.

1999, Apr. 23 *Perf. 13½x14*
1216 A550 10s multicolored 6.50 6.50

Milpo Mining Co., 50th Anniv. A551

1999, Apr. 6 *Perf. 13½x14*
1217 A551 1.50s multicolored 1.00 1.00

See note after No. 1145.

Japanese Immigration to Peru, Cent. — A552

1999, Apr. 3 *Perf. 14x13½*
1218 A552 6.80s multicolored 4.50 4.50

Nos. 1140, 1143 Surcharged in Black, Brown, Dark Blue, Red or Green

S/. 1.00

1999 Litho. *Perf. 12½*
1219 A499 2.40s on 30c (Br) multi 1.40 1.40

Blocks of 4

1220 A496 1s on 60c #a.-d. 2.40 2.40
1221 A496 1.50s on 60c (DB) #a.-d. 3.50 3.50
1222 A496 2.70s on 60c (R) #a.-d. 6.50 6.50
1223 A496 3.30s on 60c (G) #a.-d. 8.00 8.00

Size and location of surcharge varies.

Antarctic Treaty, 40th Anniv. A553

1999, May 24 *Perf. 13½x14*
1224 A553 6.80s multicolored 4.00 4.00

Inca Rulers Type of 1998

1999, June 24 Litho. *Perf. 14x13½*
1225 A528 3.30s Capac Yupanqui 2.00 2.00
1226 A528 3.30s Yahuar Huaca 2.00 2.00
1227 A528 3.30s Inca Roca 2.00 2.00
1228 A528 3.30s Maita Capac 2.00 2.00
Nos. 1225-1228 (4) 8.00 8.00

Souvenir Sheet

Nazca Lines — A554

Illustration reduced.

1999, June 8
1229 A554 10s multicolored 6.00 6.00

Margin shows Maria Reiche (1903-98), expert in Nazca Lines.

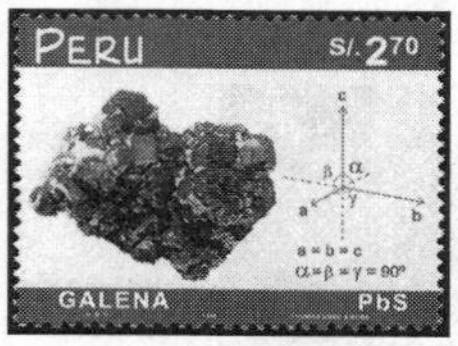

Minerals A555

Designs: 2.70s, Galena. 3.30s, Scheelite. 5s, Virgotrigonia peterseni.

1999, July 3 *Perf. 13½x14*
1230 A555 2.70s multicolored 1.60 1.60
1231 A555 3.30s multicolored 2.00 2.00
1232 A555 5s multicolored 3.00 3.00
Nos. 1230-1232 (3) 6.60 6.60

Virgin of Carmen — A556

1999, July 16 *Perf. 14x13½*
1233 A556 3.30s multicolored 2.00 2.00

Santa Catalina Monastery, Arequipa — A557

1999, Aug. 15 Litho. *Perf. 14x13½*
1234 A557 2.70s multicolored 1.75 1.75

Chinese Immigration to Peru, 150th Anniv. A558

1999 Litho. *Perf. 13½x14*
1235 A558 1.50s red & black .85 .85

Peruvian Medical Society, 25th Anniv. — A559

1999 Litho. *Perf. 14x13½*
1236 A559 1.50s multicolored .85 .85

UPU, 125th Anniv. A560

1999, Oct. 9 Litho. *Perf. 13½x14*
1237 A560 3.30s multicolored 1.90 1.90

America Issue, A New Millennium Without Arms A561

1999, Oct. 12 *Perf. 14x13½, 13½x14*
1238 A561 2.70s Earth, sunflower, vert. 1.60 1.60
1239 A561 3.30s shown 1.90 1.90

Señor de los Milagros Religious Procession A562

1999, Oct. 18 *Perf. 14x13½*
1240 A562 1s Incense burner .65 .65
1241 A562 1.50s Procession .95 .95

Inter-American Development Bank, 40th Anniv. — A563

1999, Oct. 22 *Perf. 13½x14*
1242 A563 1.50s multicolored .95 .95

Butterflies A564

Designs: a, Pterourus zagreus chrysomelus. b, Asterope buckleyi. c, Parides chabrias. d, Mimoides pausanias. e, Nessaea obrina. f, Pterourus zagreus zagreus.

1999, Oct. 23 *Perf. 14x13½*
Block of 6 + Label
1243 A564 3.30s #a.-f. 11.50 11.50

Border Disputes Settled by Brasilia Peace Accords A565

Maps of regions from: No. 1244, Cusumasa Bumbuiza to Yaupi Santiago. No. 1245, Lagatococha to Güeppi, vert. No. 1246, Cunhuime Sur to 20 de Noviembre, vert.

1999, Oct. 26 *Perf. 13½x14, 14x13½*
1244 A565 1s multicolored .65 .65
1245 A565 1s multicolored .65 .65
1246 A565 1s multicolored .65 .65
Nos. 1244-1246 (3) 1.95 1.95

Peruvian Postal Services, 5th Anniv. — A566

1999, Nov. 22 *Perf. 14x13½*
1247 A566 2.70s multicolored 1.60 1.60

Christmas A567

1999, Dec. 1 Litho. *Perf. 14x13½*
1248 A567 2.70s multicolored 1.60 1.60

Ricardo Bentín Mujica (1899-1979), Businessman — A568

1999, Dec. 29 Litho. *Perf. 13½x14*
1249 A568 2.70s multi 1.60 1.60

Souvenir Sheet

Millennium — A569

2000, Jan. 1
1250 A569 10s multi 5.75 5.75

Ricardo Cillóniz Oberti, Businessman A570

2000, Jan. 17 *Perf. 14x13½*
1251 A570 1.50s multi .90 .90

Printed se-tenant with label.

Alpaca Wool Industry — A571

a, Alpacas at right. b, Alpacas at left.

2000, Jan. 27 Litho. *Perf. 14x13½*
1252 A571 1.50s Pair, #a.-b. 1.75 1.75

Nuclear Energy Institute — A572

2000, Feb. 4
1253 A572 4s multi 2.40 2.40

Retamas S.A. Gold Mine — A573

Miner, mine and buildings: a, Text in white. b, Text in blue violet.

2000, Feb. 7
1254 A573 1s Pair, #a.-b. 1.25 1.25

Comptroller General, 70th Anniv. A574

2000, Feb. 28 *Perf. 13½x14*
1255 A574 3.30s multi 2.00 2.00

Emilio Guimoye, Field of Flowers A575

2000, Mar. 19 Litho. *Perf. 13½x14*
Granite Paper
1256 A575 1.50s multi 1.00 1.00

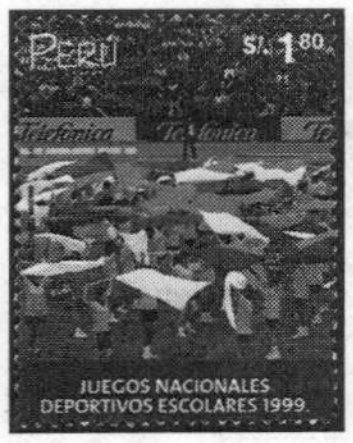

1999 Natl. Scholastic Games — A576

2000, May 3 *Perf. 14x13½*
Granite Paper
1257 A576 1.80s multi + label 1.10 1.10

Machu Picchu A577

2000, July 20 *Perf. 13½x14*
Granite Paper
1258 A577 1.30s multi .85 .85

Campaign Against Domestic Violence A578

2000, Aug. 22 Litho. *Perf. 13½x14*
Granite Paper
1259 A578 3.80s multi 2.25 2.25

Holy Year 2000 A579

2000, Aug. 23 Granite Paper
1260 A579 3.20s multi 1.90 1.90

Children's Drawing Contest Winners A580

Designs: No. 1261, 3.20s, Lake Yarinacocha, by Mari Trini Ramos Vargas. No. 1262, 3.20s, Ahuashiyacu Falls, by Susan Hidalgo Bacalla, vert. 3.80s, Arequipa Countryside, by Anibal Lajo Yañez.

Perf. 13½x14, 14x13½
2000, Aug. 25
Granite Paper
1261-1263 A580 Set of 3 6.00 6.00

"Millennium Assembly" of UN General Assembly A581

2000, Aug. 28 *Perf. 13½x14*
Granite Paper
1264 A581 3.20s multi 1.90 1.90

Gen. José de San Martín (1777-1850) — A582

2000, Sept. 1 **Granite Paper**

1265 A582 3.80s multi 2.25 2.25

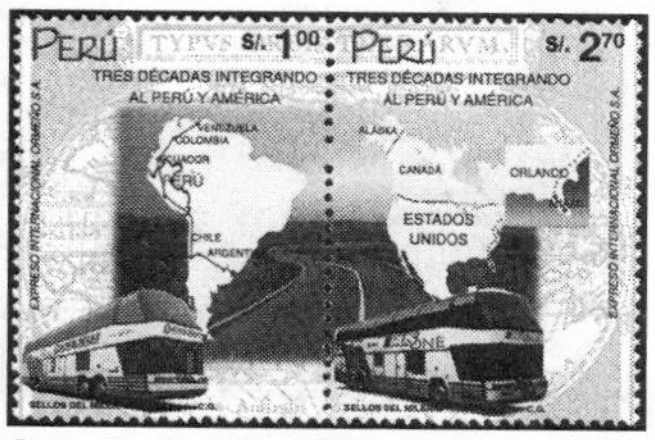

Ormeño Bus Co., 30th Anniv. — A583

No. 1266: a, 1s, Bus and map of South America. b, 2.70s, Bus and map of North America.
Illustration reduced.

2000, Sept. 3 ***Perf. 14x13½***
Granite Paper

1266 A583 Pair, #a-b 2.25 2.25

Intl. Cycling Union, Cent. A584

2000, Sept. 11 ***Perf. 13½x14***
Granite Paper

1267 A584 3.20s multi 1.90 1.90

World Meteorological Organization, 50th Anniv. — A585

2000, Sept. 13 **Granite Paper**

1268 A585 1.50s multi .90 .90

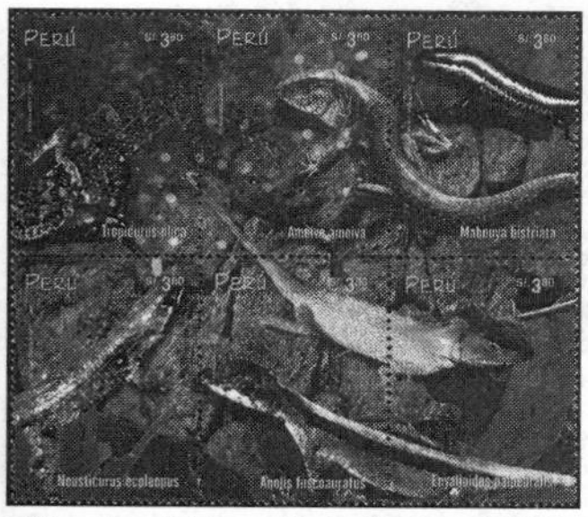

Lizards of Manu Natl. Park — A586

No. 1269: a, Tropidurus plica. b, Ameiva ameiva. c, Mabouya bistriata. d, Neusticurus ecpleopus. e, Anolis fuscoauratus. f, Enyalioides palpebralis.
Illustration reduced.

2000, Sept. 15 ***Perf. 14x13½***
Granite Paper

1269 A586 3.80s Block of 6, #a-f 13.50 13.50

Matucana Madisoniorum — A587

2000, Sept. 18 ***Perf. 13½x14***
Granite Paper

1270 A587 3.80s multi 2.25 2.25

Carlos Noriega, First Peruvian Astronaut A588

2000, Sept. 20 **Granite Paper**

1271 A588 3.80s multi 2.25 2.25

Toribio Rodríguez de Mendoza (1750-1825), Theologian A589

2000, Sept. 21 ***Perf. 14x13½***
Granite Paper

1272 A589 3.20s multi 1.90 1.90

Ucayali Province, Cent. A590

2000, Sept. 25 ***Perf. 13½x14***
Granite Paper

1273 A590 3.20s multi 1.90 1.90

Pisco Wine A591

2000, Sept. 27 **Granite Paper**

1274 A591 3.80s multi 2.25 2.25

Latin American Integration Association, 20th Anniv. — A592

2000, Sept. 29 ***Perf. 14x13½***
Granite Paper

1275 A592 10.20s multi 4.75 4.75

Peruvian Journalists Federation, 50th Anniv. — A593

2000, Sept. 30 **Granite Paper**

1276 A593 1.50s multi .90 .90

Sexi Petrified Forest A594

2000, Oct. 3 ***Perf. 13½x14***
Granite Paper

1277 A594 1.50s multi .90 .90

America Issue, Campaign Against Aids A595

2000, Oct. 12 **Granite Paper**

1278 A595 3.80s multi 2.25 2.25

Supreme Court A596

2000, Oct. 16 **Granite Paper**

1279 A596 1.50s multi .90 .90

Salvation Army in Peru, 90th Anniv. — A597

2000, Nov. 3 ***Perf. 14x13½***
Granite Paper

1280 A597 1.50s multi .90 .90

Peruvian Cancer League's Fight Against Cancer, 50th Anniv. A598

2000, Nov. 9 ***Perf. 13½x14***
Granite Paper

1281 A598 1.50s multi .90 .90

Border Map Type of 1999

Flags and maps of border separating Peru and: 1.10s, Chile, vert. 1.50s, Brazil, vert. 2.10s, Colombia. 3.20s, Ecuador. 3.80s, Bolivia, vert.

Perf. 14x13½, 13½x14
2000, Nov. 27
Granite Paper

1282-1286 A565 Set of 5 7.00 7.00

Railroads in Peru, 150th Anniv. A599

2000, Nov. 27 ***Perf. 13½x14***
Granite Paper

1287 A599 1.50s multi .90 .90

Luis Alberto Sanchez (1900-94), Politician — A600

2000, Nov. 27 ***Perf. 14x13½***
Granite Paper

1288 A600 3.20s multi 1.90 1.90

National Congress A601

2000, Dec. 7 ***Perf. 13½x14***
Granite Paper

1289 A601 3.80s multi 2.25 2.25

Caretas Magazine, 50th Anniv. A602

2000, Dec. 15 **Granite Paper**

1290 A602 3.20s multi 1.90 1.90

Cacti A603

Designs: 1.10s, Haageocereus acranthus, vert. 1.50s, Cleistocactus xylorhizus, vert. No. 1293, 2.10s, Mila caespitosa, vert. No. 1294, 2.10s, Haageocereus setosus, vert. 3.20s, Opuntia pachypus. 3.80s, Haageocereus tenuis.

Perf. 13½x13¾, 13¾x13½
2001, Aug. 24 **Litho.**

1291-1296 A603 Set of 6 8.00 8.00

San Marcos University, 450th Anniv. — A604

2001, Sept. 4 ***Perf. 13½x13¾***

1297 A604 1.50s multi .85 .85

Alianza Lima Soccer Team, Cent. — A605

No. 1298: a, Players. b, Players, ball.

2001, Sept. 6

1298	A605 3.20s Horiz. pair, #a-b		3.75	3.75

Anti-Drug Campaign — A606

2001, Sept. 7 ***Perf. 13¾x13½***

1299	A606 1.10s multi	.65	.65

Gen. Roque Sáenz Peña (1851-1914), Pres. of Argentina — A607

2001, Sept. 7

1300	A607 3.80s multi	2.25	2.25

Lurín River Valley A608

2001, Sept. 10

1301	A608 1.10s multi	.65	.65

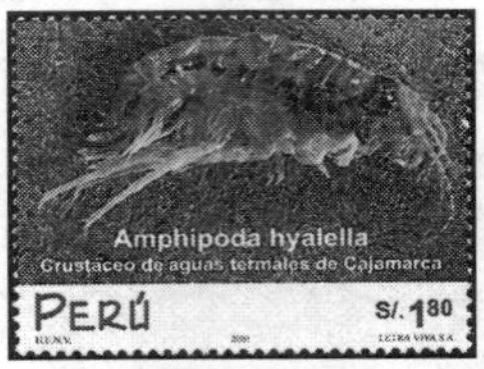

Amphipoda Hyalella — A609

2001, Sept. 10

1302	A609 1.80s multi	1.00	1.00

Postal and Philatelic Museum, 70th Anniv. — A610

2001, Oct. 9 ***Perf. 13½x13¾***

1303	A610 3.20s multi	1.90	1.90

SEMI-POSTAL STAMPS

Catalogue values for unused stamps in this section are for Never Hinged items.

Gold Funerary Mask SP1

Designs: 2.60s+1.30s, Ceremonial knife, vert. 3.60s+1.80s, Ceremonial vessel. 4.60s+2.30s, Goblet with precious stones, vert. 20s+10s, Earplug.

Perf. 12x12½, 12½x12

1966, Aug. 16 Photo. Unwmk.

B1	SP1 1.90s + 90c multi	.40	.40
B2	SP1 2.60s + 1.30s multi	.50	.50
B3	SP1 3.60s + 1.80s multi	.75	.75
B4	SP1 4.60s + 2.30s multi	1.00	1.00
B5	SP1 20s + 10s multi	4.00	4.00
	Nos. B1-B5 (5)	6.65	6.65

The designs show gold objects of the 12th-13th centuries Chimu culture. The surtax was for tourist publicity.

For surcharges see Nos. 679-680, 683-684, 686.

AIR POST STAMPS

No. 248 Overprinted in Black

1927, Dec. 10 Unwmk. *Perf. 12*

C1	A87 50c violet	37.50	20.00

Two types of overprint. Counterfeits exist.

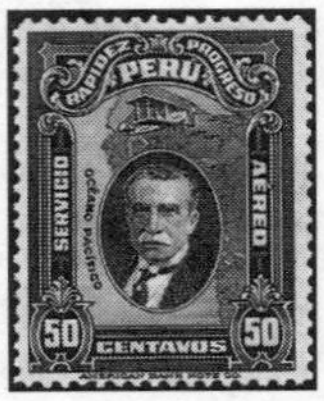

President Augusto Bernardino Leguía — AP1

1928, Jan. 12 Engr.

C2	AP1 50c dark green	.65	.35

For surcharge see No. 263.

Coat of Arms of Piura Type

1932, July 28 Litho.

C3	A107 50c scarlet	20.00	19.00

Counterfeits exist.

Airplane in Flight — AP3

1934, Feb. Engr. *Perf. 12½*

C4	AP3 2s blue	4.00	.35
C5	AP3 5s brown	8.00	.75

Funeral of Atahualpa AP4

Palace of Torre-Tagle AP7

Designs: 35c, Mt. San Cristobal. 50c, Avenue of Barefoot Friars. 10s, Pizarro and the Thirteen.

1935, Jan. 18 Photo. *Perf. 13½*

C6	AP4 5c emerald	.25	.20
C7	AP4 35c brown	.35	.30
C8	AP4 50c orange yel	.70	.60
C9	AP4 1s plum	1.25	.90
C10	AP7 2s red orange	2.00	1.75
C11	AP4 5s dp claret	8.50	5.25
C12	AP4 10s dk blue	32.50	22.50
	Nos. C6-C12 (7)	45.55	31.50

4th centenary of founding of Lima.

Nos. C6-C12 overprinted "Radio Nacional" are revenue stamps.

"La Callao," First Locomotive in South America AP9

1936, Aug. 27 *Perf. 12½*

C13	AP9 35c gray black	2.50	1.40

Founding of the Province of Callao, cent.

Nos. C4-C5 Surcharged "Habilitado" and New Value, like Nos. 353-355

1936, Nov. 4

C14	AP3 5c on 2s blue	.35	.20
C15	AP3 25c on 5s brown	.65	.35
a.	Double surcharge	13.50	13.50
b.	No period btwn. "O" & "25 Cts"	1.40	1.40
c.	Inverted surcharge	16.50	

There are many broken letters in this setting.

Mines of Peru AP10

Jorge Chávez AP14

Aerial View of Peruvian Coast AP16

View of the "Sierra" — AP17

St. Rosa of Lima — AP22

Designs: 5c, La Mar Park, Lima. 15c, Mail Steamer "Inca" on Lake Titicaca. 20c, Native Queña (flute) Player and Llama. 30c, Ram at Model Farm, Puno. 1s, Train in Mountains. 1.50s, Jorge Chavez Aviation School. 2s, Transport Plane. 5s, Aerial View of Virgin Forests.

1936-37 Photo. *Perf. 12½*

C16	AP10	5c brt green	.20	.20
C17	AP10	5c emer ('37)	.20	.20
C18	AP10	15c lt ultra	.40	.20
C19	AP10	15c blue ('37)	.25	.20
C20	AP10	20c gray blk	1.10	.20
C21	AP10	20c pale ol grn ('37)	.70	.25
C22	AP14	25c mag ('37)	.35	.20
C23	AP10	30c henna brn	3.50	.80
C24	AP10	30c dk ol brn ('37)	1.00	.20
C25	AP14	35c brown	2.00	1.75
C26	AP10	50c yellow	.35	.25
C27	AP10	50c brn vio ('37)	.50	.20
C28	AP16	70c Prus grn	4.25	3.75
C29	AP16	70c pck grn ('37)	.70	.55
C30	AP17	80c brn blk	5.00	3.75

C31	AP17	80c ol blk ('37)	1.00	.40
C32	AP10	1s ultra	3.50	.30
C33	AP10	1s red brn ('37)	1.75	.20
C34	AP14	1.50s red brn	5.50	4.25
C35	AP14	1.50s org yel ('37)	3.50	.30

Engr.

C36	AP10	2s deep blue	10.00	5.50
C37	AP10	2s yel grn ('37)	6.75	.60
C38	AP16	5s green	12.50	2.75
C39	AP22	10s car & brn	100.00	80.00
		Nos. C16-C39 (24)	165.00	107.00

Nos. C23, C25, C28, C30, C36 Surcharged in Black or Red

1936, June 26

C40	AP10	15c on 30c hn brn	.50	.30
C41	AP14	15c on 35c brown	.50	.20
C42	AP16	15c on 70c Prus grn	3.25	2.75
C43	AP17	25c on 80c brn blk (R)	3.25	2.75
C44	AP10	1s on 2s dp bl	5.25	3.75
		Nos. C40-C44 (5)	12.75	9.75

Surcharge on No. C43 is vertical, reading down.

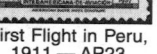

First Flight in Peru, 1911 — AP23

Jorge Chávez — AP24

Airport of Limatambo at Lima — AP25

Map of Aviation Lines from Peru — AP26

Designs: 10c, Juan Bielovucic (1889-?) flying over Lima race course, Jan. 14, 1911. 15c, Jorge Chavez-Dartnell (1887-1910), French-born Peruvian aviator who flew from Brixen to Domodossola in the Alps and died of plane-crash injuries.

1937, Sept. 15 Engr. *Perf. 12*

C45	AP23	10c violet	.35	.20
C46	AP24	15c dk green	.50	.20
C47	AP25	25c gray brn	.35	.20
C48	AP26	1s black	1.60	1.25
		Nos. C45-C48 (4)	2.80	1.85

Inter-American Technical Conference of Aviation, Sept. 1937.

Government Restaurant at Callao — AP27

Monument on the Plains of Junin — AP28

Rear Admiral Manuel Villar — AP29

View of Tarma — AP30

Dam, Ica River — AP31

View of Iquitos AP32

Highway and Railroad Passing AP33

Mountain Road — AP34

Plaza San Martín, Lima — AP35

National Radio of Peru AP36

Stele from Chavin Temple AP37

Ministry of Public Works, Lima — AP38

Crypt of the Heroes, Lima — AP39

Imprint: "Waterlow & Sons Limited, Londres."

1938, July 1 Photo. *Perf. 12½, 13*

C49	AP27	5c violet brn	.20	.20
C50	AP28	15c dk brown	.20	.20
C51	AP29	20c dp magenta	.30	.20
C52	AP30	25c dp green	.20	.20
C53	AP31	30c orange	.20	.20
C54	AP32	50c green	.25	.20
C55	AP33	70c slate bl	.40	.20
C56	AP34	80c olive	.70	.20
C57	AP35	1s slate grn	5.50	2.50
C58	AP36	1.50s purple	1.25	.20

Engr.

C59	AP37	2s ind & org brn	2.00	.50
C60	AP38	5s brown	10.00	1.00
C61	AP39	10s ol grn & ind	40.00	24.00
		Nos. C49-C61 (13)	61.20	29.80

See Nos. C73-C75, C89-C93, C103.
For surcharges see Nos. C65, C76-C77, C82-C88, C108C.

Torre-Tagle Palace — AP40

National Congress Building — AP41

Manuel Ferreyros, José Gregorio Paz Soldán and Antonio Arenas — AP42

1938, Dec. 9 Photo. *Perf. 12½*

C62	AP40	25c brt ultra	.65	.45
C63	AP41	1.50s brown vio	1.75	1.50
C64	AP42	2s black	1.10	.55
		Nos. C62-C64 (3)	3.50	2.50

8th Pan-American Conference at Lima.

No. C52 Surcharged in Black

1942 *Perf. 13*

C65	AP30	15c on 25c dp grn	1.00	.20

Types of 1938
Imprint: "Columbian Bank Note Co."

1945-46 Unwmk. Litho. *Perf. 12½*

C73	AP27	5c violet brown	.20	.20
C74	AP31	30c orange	.20	.20
C75	AP36	1.50s purple ('46)	.30	.25
		Nos. C73-C75 (3)	.70	.65

Nos. C73 and C54 Overprinted in Black

1947, Sept. 25 *Perf. 12½, 13*

C76	AP27	5c violet brown	.20	.20
C77	AP32	50c green	.20	.20

1st Peru Intl. Airways flight from Lima to New York City, Sept. 27-28, 1947.

Catalogue values for unused stamps in this section, from this point to the end of the section, are for Never Hinged items.

Peru-Great Britain Air Route — AP43

Basketball Players — AP44

Designs: 5s, Discus thrower. 10s, Rifleman.

1948, July 29 Photo. *Perf. 12½*

C78	AP43	1s blue	2.25	1.50

Carmine Overprint, "AEREO"

C79	AP44	2s red brown	3.00	2.00
C80	AP44	5s yellow green	5.00	3.25
C81	AP44	10s yellow	6.25	4.00
a.		Souv. sheet, #C78-C81, perf 13	27.50	27.50
		Nos. C78-C81 (4)	16.50	10.75

Peru's participation in the 1948 Olympic Games held at Wembley, England, during July and August. Postally valid for four days, July 29-Aug. 1, 1948. Proceeds went to the Olympic Committee.

A surtax of 2 soles on No. C81a was for the Children's Hospital.

Remainders of Nos. C78-C81 and C81a were overprinted "Melbourne 1956" and placed on sale Nov. 19, 1956, at all post offices as "voluntary stamps" with no postal validity. Clerks were permitted to postmark them to please collectors, and proceeds were to help pay the cost of sending Peruvian athletes to Australia. On April 14, 1957, postal authorities declared these stamps valid for one day, April 15, 1957. The overprint was applied to 10,000 sets and 21,000 souvenir sheets. Value, set, $20; sheet, $15.

No. C55 Surcharged in Red

1948, Dec. *Perf. 13*

C82	AP33	10c on 70c slate blue	.20	.20
C83	AP33	20c on 70c slate blue	.20	.20
C84	AP33	55c on 70c slate blue	.20	.20
		Nos. C82-C84 (3)	.60	.60

Nos. C52, C55 and C56 Surcharged in Black

1949, Mar. 25

C85	AP30	5c on 25c dp grn	.20	.20
C86	AP30	10c on 25c dp grn	.20	.20
C87	AP33	15c on 70c slate bl	.20	.20
C88	AP34	30c on 80c olive	.65	.20
		Nos. C85-C88 (4)	1.25	.80

The surcharge reads up, on No. C87.

Types of 1938
Imprint: "Waterlow & Sons Limited, Londres."
Perf. 13x13½, 13½x13

1949-50 Photo.

C89	AP27	5c olive bister	.20	.20
C90	AP31	30c red	.20	.20
C91	AP33	70c blue	.25	.20
C92	AP34	80c cerise	.40	.20
C93	AP36	1.50s vio brn ('50)	.50	.20
		Nos. C89-C93 (5)	1.55	1.00

Air View, Reserva Park, Lima — AP45

Flags of the Americas and Spain AP46

Designs: 30c, National flag. 55c, Huancayo Hotel. 95c, Blanca-Ancash Cordillera. 1.50s, Arequipa Hotel. 2s, Coal chute and dock, Chimbote. 5s, Town hall, Miraflores. 10s, Hall of National Congress, Lima.

Overprinted "U. P. U. 1874-1949" in Red or Black

1951, Apr. 2 Engr. *Perf. 12*

C94	AP45	5c	blue grn	.20	.20
C95	AP45	30c	black & car	.20	.20
a.			Inverted overprint		
C96	AP45	55c	yel grn (Bk)	.20	.20
C97	AP45	95c	dk green	.20	.20
C98	AP45	1.50s	dp car (Bk)	.20	.20
C99	AP45	2s	deep blue	.25	.20
C100	AP45	5s	rose car (Bk)	3.00	2.50
C101	AP45	10s	purple	4.00	3.50
C102	AP46	20s	dk brn & ultra	6.75	5.50
			Nos. C94-C102 (9)	15.00	12.70

UPU, 75th anniv. (in 1949).

Nos. C94-C102 exist without overprint, but were not regularly issued. Value, set, $200.

Type of 1938
Imprint: "Inst. de Grav. Paris."

1951, May Engr. *Perf. 12½x12*

C103	AP27	5c	olive bister	.20	.20

Type of 1938 Surcharged in Black

1951

C108	AP31	25c on 30c	rose red	.20	.20

Thomas de San Martin y Contreras and Jerónimo de Aliaga y Ramirez — AP47

San Marcos University — AP48

Designs: 50c, Church and convent of Santo Domingo. 1.20s, P. de Peralta Barnuevo, T. de San Martin y Contreras and J. Baquijano y Carrillo de Cordova. 2s, T. Rodriguez de Mendoza, J. Hipolito Unanue y Pavon and J. Cayetano Heredia y Garcia. 5s, Arms of the University, 1571 and 1735.

Perf. 11½x12½

1951, Dec. 10 Litho.

C109	AP47	30c	gray	.20	.20
C110	AP48	40c	ultra	.20	.20
C111	AP48	50c	car rose	.20	.20
C112	AP47	1.20s	emerald	.20	.20
C113	AP47	2s	slate	.25	.20
C114	AP47	5s	multicolored	1.10	.20
			Nos. C109-C114 (6)	2.15	1.20

400th anniv. of the founding of San Marcos University.

River Gunboat Marañon AP49

Peruvian Cormorants — AP50

National Airport, Lima AP51

Tobacco Plant AP52

Manco Capac Monument AP54

Garcilaso de la Vega AP53

Designs: 1.50s, Housing Unit No. 3. 2.20s, Inca Solar Observatory.

Imprint: "Thomas De La Rue & Co. Ltd."

1953-60 Unwmk. *Perf. 13, 12*

C115	AP49	40c	yellow grn	.20	.20
a.			40c blue green ('57)	.20	.20
C116	AP50	75c	dk brown	.75	.20
C116A	AP50	80c	pale brn red ('60)	.40	.20
C117	AP51	1.25s	blue	.20	.20
C118	AP49	1.50s	cerise	.20	.20
C119	AP51	2.20s	dk blue	.80	.25
C120	AP52	3s	brown	.95	.20
C121	AP53	5s	bister	.75	.20
C122	AP54	10s	dull vio brn	1.75	.35
			Nos. C115-C122 (9)	6.00	2.00

See #C158-C162, C182-C183, C186-C189, C210-C211.

For surcharges see #C420-C422, C429-C433, C435-C436, C438, C442-C443, C445-C450, C455, C471-C474, C476, C478-C479, C495.

Queen Isabella I — AP55

Fleet of Columbus — AP56

Perf. 12½x11½, 11½x12½

1953, June 18 Engr. Unwmk.

C123	AP55	40c	dp carmine	.20	.20
C124	AP56	1.25s	emerald	.20	.20
C125	AP55	2.15s	dp plum	.40	.30
C126	AP56	2.20s	black	.65	.30
			Nos. C123-C126 (4)	1.45	1.00

500th birth anniv. (in 1951) of Queen Isabella I of Spain.

For surcharge see No. C475.

Arms of Lima and Bordeaux AP57

Designs: 50c, Eiffel Tower and Cathedral of Lima. 1.25s, Admiral Dupetit-Thouars and frigate "La Victorieuse." 2.20s, Presidents Coty and Prado and exposition hall.

1957, Sept. 16 *Perf. 13*

C127	AP57	40c	claret, grn & ultra	.20	.20
C128	AP57	50c	grn, blk & hn brn	.20	.20
C129	AP57	1.25s	bl, ind & dk grn	.20	.20
C130	AP57	2.20s	bluish blk, bl & red brn	.40	.40
			Nos. C127-C130 (4)	1.00	1.00

French Exposition, Lima, Sept. 15-Oct. 1.

For surcharges see Nos. 763, C503-C505.

Pre-Stamp Postal Markings — AP58

10c, 1r Stamp of 1857. 15c, 2r Stamp of 1857. 25c, 1d Stamp of 1860. 30c, 1p Stamp of 1858. 40c, ½p Stamp of 1858. 1.25s, José Davila Condemarin. 2.20s, Ramon Castilla. 5s, Pres. Manuel Prado. 10s, Shield of Lima containing stamps.

Perf. 12½x13

1957, Dec. 1 Engr. Unwmk.

C131	AP58	5c	silver & blk	.20	.20
C132	AP58	10c	lil rose & bl	.20	.20
C133	AP58	15c	grn & red brn	.20	.20
C134	AP58	25c	org yel & bl	.20	.20
C135	AP58	30c	vio brn & org brn	.20	.20
C136	AP58	40c	black & bis	.20	.20
C137	AP58	1.25s	dk bl & dk brn	.30	.25
C138	AP58	2.20s	red & sl bl	.50	.50
C139	AP58	5s	lil rose & mar	1.25	1.00
C140	AP58	10s	ol grn & lil	2.00	1.75
			Nos. C131-C140 (10)	5.25	4.70

Centenary of Peruvian postage stamps. No. C140 issued to publicize the Peruvian Centenary Phil. Exhib. (PEREX).

Carlos Paz Soldan — AP59

Port of Callao and Pres. Manuel Prado AP60

Design: 1s, Ramon Castilla.

Perf. 14x13½, 13½x14

1958, Apr. 7 Litho. Wmk. 116

C141	AP59	40c	brn & pale rose	.20	.20
C142	AP59	1s	grn & lt grn	.20	.20
C143	AP60	1.25s	dull pur & ind	.20	.20
			Nos. C141-C143 (3)	.60	.60

Centenary of the telegraph connection between Lima and Callao and the centenary of the political province of Callao.

For surcharges see Nos. 758A, 767.

Flags of France and Peru — AP61

Cathedral of Lima and Lady AP62

1.50s, Horseback rider & mall in Lima. 2.50s, Map of Peru showing national products.

Perf. 12½x13, 13x12½

1958, May 20 Engr. Unwmk.

C144	AP61	50c	dl vio, bl & car	.20	.20
C145	AP62	65c	multi	.20	.20
C146	AP62	1.50s	bl, brn vio & ol	.20	.20
C147	AP61	2.50s	sl grn, grnsh bl & claret	.25	.20
			Nos. C144-C147 (4)	.85	.80

Peruvian Exhib. in Paris, May 20-July 10.

Bro. Martin de Porres Velasquez AP63

First Royal School of Medicine (Now Ministry of Government and Police) — AP64

Designs: 1.20s, Daniel Alcides Carrion Garcia. 1.50s, Jose Hipolito Unanue Pavon.

Perf. 13x13½, 13½x13

1958, July 24 Litho. Unwmk.

C148	AP63	60c	multi	.20	.20
C149	AP63	1.20s	multi	.20	.20
C150	AP63	1.50s	multi	.20	.20
C151	AP64	2.20s	black	.20	.20
			Nos. C148-C151 (4)	.80	.80

Daniel A. Carrion (1857-85), medical martyr.

Gen. Ignacio Alvarez Thomas AP65

1958, Nov. 13 ***Perf. 13x12½***

C152 AP65 1.10s brn lake, bis & ver .20 .20
C153 AP65 1.20s blk, bis & ver .20 .20

General Thomas (1787-1857), fighter for South American independence.

"Justice" and Emblem — AP66

1958, Nov. 13
Star in Blue and Olive Bister

C154 AP66 80c emerald .20 .20
C155 AP66 1.10s red orange .20 .20
C156 AP66 1.20s ultra .20 .20
C157 AP66 1.50s lilac rose .20 .20
Nos. C154-C157 (4) .80 .80

Lima Bar Assoc., 150th anniv.

Types of 1953-57

Designs: 80c, Peruvian cormorants. 3.80s, Inca Solar Observatory.

Imprint: "Joh. Enschedé en Zonen-Holland"

Perf. 12½x14, 14x13, 13x14
1959, Dec. 9 **Unwmk.**

C158 AP50 80c brown red .20 .20
C159 AP52 3s lt green .60 .25
C160 AP51 3.80s orange 1.00 .25
C161 AP53 5s brown .60 .25
C162 AP54 10s orange ver 1.25 .40
Nos. C158-C162 (5) 3.65 1.35

WRY Emblem, Dove, Rainbow and Farmer — AP67

Peruvian Cormorant Over Ocean — AP68

1960, Apr. 7 **Litho.** ***Perf. 14x13***

C163 AP67 80c multi .25 .25
C164 AP67 4.30s multi .55 .55
a. Souv. sheet of 2, #C163-C164, imperf. 7.00 6.00

World Refugee Year, 7/1/59-6/30/60. No. C164a sold for 15s.

1960, May 30 ***Perf. 14x13½***

C165 AP68 1s multi .35 .20

Intl. Pacific Fair, Lima, 1959.

Lima Coin of 1659 AP69

1961, Jan. 19 **Unwmk.** ***Perf. 13x14***

C166 AP69 1s org brn & gray .20 .20
C167 AP69 2s Prus bl & gray .20 .20

1st National Numismatic Exposition, Lima, 1959; 300th anniv. of the first dated coin (1659) minted at Lima.

The Earth AP70

1961, Mar. 8 **Litho.** ***Perf. 13½x14***

C168 AP70 1s multicolored .75 .20

International Geophysical Year.

Frigate Amazonas AP71

1961, Mar. 8 **Engr.** ***Perf. 13½***

C169 AP71 50c brown & grn .20 .20
C170 AP71 80c dl vio & red org .20 .20
C171 AP71 1s green & sepia .20 .20
Nos. C169-C171 (3) .60 .60

Centenary (in 1958) of the trip around the world by the Peruvian frigate Amazonas.

Machu Picchu Sheet

A souvenir sheet was issued Sept. 11, 1961, to commemorate the 50th anniversary of the discovery of the ruins of Machu Picchu, ancient Inca city in the Andes, by Hiram Bingham. It contains two bi-colored imperf. airmail stamps, 5s and 10s, lithographed in a single design picturing the mountaintop ruins. The sheet was valid for one day and was sold in a restricted manner. Value $7.50.

Olympic Torch, Laurel and Globe — AP72

Fair Emblem and Llama — AP73

1961, Dec. 13 **Unwmk.** ***Perf. 13***

C172 AP72 5s gray & ultra .40 .35
C173 AP72 10s gray & car .85 .60
a. Souv. sheet of 2, #C172-C173, imperf. 2.50 2.25

17th Olympic Games, Rome, 8/25-9/11/60.

1962, Jan. **Litho.** ***Perf. 10½x11***

C174 AP73 1s multi .20 .20

2nd International Pacific Fair, Lima, 1961.

Map Showing Disputed Border, Peru-Ecuador — AP74

1962, May 25 ***Perf. 10½***
Gray Background

C175 AP74 1.30s blk, red & car rose .20 .20
C176 AP74 1.50s blk, red & emer .20 .20
C177 AP74 2.50s blk, red & dk bl .25 .25
Nos. C175-C177 (3) .65 .65

Settlement of the border dispute with Ecuador by the Protocol of Rio de Janeiro, 20th anniv.

Cahuide and Cuauhtémoc — AP75

2s, Tupac Amaru (Jose G. Condorcanqui) & Miguel Hidalgo. 3s, Pres. Manuel Prado & Pres. Adolfo Lopez Mateos of Mexico.

1962, May 25 **Engr.** ***Perf. 13***

C178 AP75 1s dk car rose, red & brt grn .20 .20
C179 AP75 2s grn, red & brt grn .20 .20
C180 AP75 3s brn, red & brt grn .25 .20
Nos. C178-C180 (3) .65 .60

Exhibition of Peruvian art treasures in Mexico.

Agriculture, Industry and Archaeology AP76

1962, Sept. 7 **Litho.** ***Perf. 14x13½***

C181 AP76 1s black & gray .20 .20

Cent. (in 1961) of Pallasca Ancash province.

Types of 1953-60

1.30s, Guanayes. 1.50s, Housing Unit No. 3. 1.80s, Locomotive No. 80 (like #460). 2s, Monument to Native Farmer. 3s, Tobacco plant. 4.30s, Inca Solar Observatory. 5s, Garcilaso de la Vega. 10s, Inca Monument.

Imprint: "Thomas De La Rue & Co. Ltd."

1962-63 **Wmk. 346** **Litho.** ***Perf. 13***

C182 AP50 1.30s pale yellow .20 .20
C183 AP49 1.50s claret .25 .20
C184 A182 1.80s dark blue .25 .20

Perf. 12

C185 A184 2s emerald ('63) .25 .20
C186 AP52 3s lilac rose .35 .20
C187 AP51 4.30s orange .65 .25
C188 AP53 5s citron .65 .35

Perf. 13½x14

C189 AP54 10s vio bl ('63) 1.25 .50
Nos. C182-C189 (8) 3.85 2.10

Freedom from Hunger Type

1963, July 23 **Unwmk.** ***Perf. 12½***

C190 A189 4.30s lt grn & ocher .50 .50

Jorge Chávez and Wing — AP77

Fair Poster — AP78

1964, Feb. 20 **Engr.** ***Perf. 13***

C191 AP77 5s org brn, dk brn & bl .65 .35

1st crossing of the Alps by air (Sept. 23, 1910) by the Peruvian aviator Jorge Chávez, 50th anniv.

Alliance for Progress Type

Design: 1.30s, Same, horizontal.

Perf. 12½x12, 12x12½
1964, June 22 **Litho.**

C192 A190 1.30s multi .20 .20
C193 A190 3s multi .25 .25

1965, Jan. 15 **Unwmk.** ***Perf. 14½***

C194 AP78 1s multi .20 .20

3rd International Pacific Fair, Lima 1963.

Basket, Globe, Pennant — AP79

St. Martin de Porres — AP80

1965, Apr. 19 ***Perf. 12x12½***

C195 AP79 1.30s violet & red .25 .25
C196 AP79 4.30s bis brn & red .55 .55

4th Women's Intl. Basketball Championship.
For surcharge see No. C493.

1965, Oct. 29 **Litho.** ***Perf. 11***

Designs: 1.80s, St. Martin's miracle: dog, cat and mouse feeding from same dish. 4.30s, St. Martin with cherubim in Heaven.

C197 AP80 1.30s gray & multi .20 .20
C198 AP80 1.80s gray & multi .20 .20
C199 AP80 4.30s gray & multi .50 .50
Nos. C197-C199 (3) .90 .90

Canonization of St. Martin de Porres Velasquez (1579-1639), on May 6, 1962.
For surcharges see Nos. C439, C496.

Victory Monument, Lima, and Battle Scene — AP81

Designs: 3.60s, Monument and Callao Fortress. 4.60s, Monument and José Galvez.

1966, May 2 **Photo.** ***Perf. 14x13½***

C200 AP81 1.90s multicolored .25 .25
C201 AP81 3.60s brn, yel & bis .40 .40
C202 AP81 4.60s multicolored .60 .60
Nos. C200-C202 (3) 1.25 1.25

Centenary of Peru's naval victory over the Spanish Armada at Callao, May, 1866.

Civil Guard Emblem AP82

1.90s, Various activities of Civil Guard.

1966, Aug. 30 **Photo.** ***Perf. 13½x14***

C203 AP82 90c multicolored .20 .20
C204 AP82 1.90s dp lil rose, gold & blk .20 .20

Centenary of the Civil Guard.

Hydroelectric Center Type

1966, Nov. 24 **Photo.** ***Perf. 13½x14***

C205 A193 1.90s lil, blk & vio bl .20 .20

Sun Symbol, Ancient Carving — AP83

Designs: 3.60s, Map of Peru and spiral, horiz. 4.60s, Globe with map of Peru.

Perf. 14x13½, 13½x14

1967, Feb. 16 Litho.

C206 AP83 2.60s red org & blk .25 .20
C207 AP83 3.60s dp blue & blk .35 .25
C208 AP83 4.60s tan & multi .40 .30
Nos. C206-C208 (3) 1.00 .75

Photography exhibition "Peru Before the World" which opened simultaneously in Lima, Madrid, Santiago de Chile and Washington, Sept. 27, 1966.

For surcharges see #C444, C470, C492.

Types of 1953-60

2.60s, Monument to Native Farmer. 3.60s, Tobacco plant. 4.60s, Inca Solar Observatory.

Imprint: "I.N.A."

1967, Jan. *Perf. 13½x14, 14x13½*

C209 A184 2.60s brt green .25 .20
C210 AP52 3.60s lilac rose .35 .20
C211 AP51 4.60s orange .40 .25
Nos. C209-C211 (3) 1.00 .65

Wind Vane and Sun Type of Regular Issue

1967, Apr. 18 Photo. *Perf. 13½x14*

C212 A194 1.90s yel brn, blk & gold .25 .20

St. Rosa of Lima by Angelino Medoro — AP84

Lions Emblem — AP85

St. Rosa Painted by: 2.60s, Carlo Maratta. 3.60s, Cuzquena School, 17th century.

1967, Aug. 30 Photo. *Perf. 13½*
Black, Gold & Multi

C213 AP84 1.90s .25 .20
C214 AP84 2.60s .40 .20
C215 AP84 3.60s .60 .25
Nos. C213-C215 (3) 1.25 .65

350th death anniv. of St. Rosa of Lima.

For surcharge see No. C477.

Fair Type of Regular Issue

1967, Oct. 27 Photo. *Perf. 12*

C216 A195 1s gold, brt red lil & blk .20 .20

1967, Dec. 29 Litho. *Perf. 14x13½*

C217 AP85 1.60s brt bl & vio bl, *grysh* .25 .20

50th anniversary of Lions International.

Decorated Jug, Nazca Culture — AP86

Antarqui, Inca Messenger AP87

Painted pottery jugs of pre-Inca Nazca culture: 2.60s, Falcon. 3.60s, Round jug decorated with grain-eating bird. 4.60s, Two-headed snake. 5.60s, Marine bird.

1968, June 4 Photo. *Perf. 12*

C218 AP86 1.90s multi .25 .20
C219 AP86 2.60s multi .35 .20
C220 AP86 3.60s black & multi .35 .20
C221 AP86 4.60s brown & multi .45 .25
C222 AP86 5.60s gray & multi .90 .50
Nos. C218-C222 (5) 2.30 1.35

For surcharges see #C451-C453, C497, C500.

1968, Sept. 2 Litho. *Perf. 12*

Design: 5.60s, Alpaca and jet liner.

C223 AP87 3.60s multi .30 .30
C224 AP87 5.60s red, blk & brn .45 .45

12th anniv. of Peruvian Airlines (APSA).

For surcharges see Nos. C480-C482.

Human Rights Flame — AP88

1968, Sept. 5 Photo. *Perf. 14x13½*

C225 AP88 6.50s brn, red & grn .25 .20

International Human Rights Year.

Discobolus and Mexico Olympics Emblem AP89

1968, Oct. 19 Photo. *Perf. 13½*

C226 AP89 2.30s yel, brn & dk bl .20 .20
C227 AP89 3.50s yel grn, sl bl & red .20 .20
C228 AP89 5s brt pink, blk & ultra .25 .20
C229 AP89 6.50s lt bl, mag & brn .40 .30
C230 AP89 8s lil, ultra & car .40 .25
C231 AP89 9s org, vio & grn .40 .30
Nos. C226-C231 (6) 1.85 1.45

19th Olympic Games, Mexico City, 10/12-27.

Hand, Corn and Field AP90

1969, Mar. 3 Litho. *Perf. 11*

C232 AP90 5.50s on 1.90s grn & yel .25 .20
C233 AP90 6.50s on 1.90s bl, grn & yel .35 .20

Agrarian Reform Law. Not issued without surcharge.

Peruvian Silver 8-reales Coin, 1568 AP91

1969, Mar. 17 Litho. *Perf. 12*

C234 AP91 5s yellow, gray & blk .20 .20
C235 AP91 5s bl grn, gray & blk .20 .20

400th anniv. of the first Peruvian coinage.

Ramon Castilla Monument AP92

Design: 10s, Pres. Ramon Castilla.

1969, May 30 Photo. *Perf. 13½*
Size: 27x40mm

C236 AP92 5s emerald & indigo .35 .20

Perf. 12
Size: 21x37mm

C237 AP92 10s plum & brn .65 .30

Ramon Castilla (1797-1867), president of Peru (1845-1851 and 1855-1862), on the occasion of the unveiling of the monument in Lima.

Airline Type of Regular Issue

1969, June 17 Litho. *Perf. 11*

C238 A199 3s org & multi .20 .20
C239 A199 4s multi .20 .20
C240 A199 5.50s ver & multi .20 .20
C241 A199 6.50s vio & multi .20 .20
Nos. C238-C241 (4) .80 .80

First Peruvian Airlines (APSA) flight to Europe.

Radar Antenna, Satellite and Earth — AP93

1969, July 14 Litho. *Perf. 11*

C242 AP93 20s multi 1.25 .55
a. Souv. sheet 1.50 1.50

Opening of the Lurin satellite earth station near Lima.

No. C242a contains one imperf. stamp with simulated perforations similar to No. C242.

Gonzales Type of Regular Issue

1969, July 23 Litho. *Perf. 11*

C243 A200 20s red & multi 1.25 .55

WHO Emblem AP94

1969, Aug. 14 Photo. *Perf. 12*

C244 AP94 5s gray, red brn, gold & blk .20 .20
C245 AP94 6.50s dl org, gray bl, gold & blk .20 .20

WHO, 20th anniv.

Agrarian Reform Type of Regular Issue

1969, Aug. 28 Litho. *Perf. 11*

C246 A201 3s lil & blk .20 .20
C247 A201 4s brn & buff .20 .20

Garcilaso de la Vega — AP95

Designs: 2.40s, De la Vega's coat of arms. 3.50s, Title page of "Commemtarios Reales que tratan del origen de los Yncas," Lisbon, 1609.

1969, Sept. 18 Litho. *Perf. 12x12½*

C248 AP95 2.40s emer, sil & blk .20 .20
C249 AP95 3.50s ultra, buff & blk .20 .20
C250 AP95 5s sil, yel, blk & brn .20 .20
a. Souv. sheet of 3, #C248-C250, imperf. 1.10 1.10
Nos. C248-C250 (3) .60 .60

Garcilaso de la Vega, called "Inca" (1539-1616), historian of Peru.

Fair Type of Regular Issue, 1969

1969, Nov. 14 Litho. *Perf. 11*

C251 A203 3s bis & multi .20 .20
C252 A203 4s multi .25 .20

Bolognesi Type of Regular Issue

1969, Dec. 9 Litho. *Perf. 11*

C253 A204 50s lt brn, blk & gold 3.00 1.40

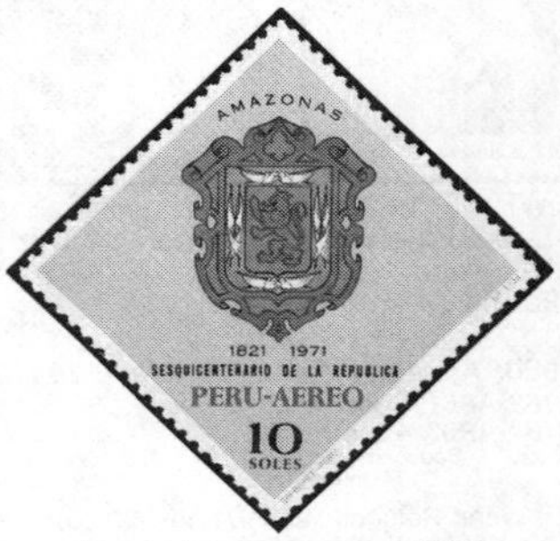

Arms of Amazonas — AP96

1970, Jan. 6 Litho. *Perf. 11*

C254 AP96 10s multi .50 .50

ILO Emblem AP97

1970, Jan. 16

C278 AP97 3s dk vio bl & lt ultra .25 .25

ILO, 50th anniv.

Motherhood and UNICEF Emblem AP98

1970, Jan. 16 Photo. *Perf. 13½x14*

C279 AP98 5s yel, gray & blk .25 .20
C280 AP98 6.50s brt pink, gray & blk .35 .20

Vicus Culture Type of Regular Issue

Ceramics of Vicus Culture, 6th-8th Centuries: 3s, Squatting warrior. 4s, Jug. 5.50s, Twin jugs. 6.50s, Woman and jug.

1970, Feb. 23 Litho. *Perf. 11*

C281 A205 3s buff, blk & brn .20 .20
C282 A205 4s buff, blk & brn .20 .20
C283 A205 5.50s buff, blk & brn .30 .30
C284 A205 6.50s buff, blk & brn .40 .40
Nos. C281-C284 (4) 1.10 1.10

Fish Type of Regular Issue

1970, Apr. 30 Litho. *Perf. 11*

C285 A207 3s Swordfish .20 .20
C286 A207 3s Yellowfin tuna .20 .20
C287 A207 5.50s Wolf fish .30 .30
Nos. C285-C287 (3) .70 .70

Telephone — AP99

1970, June 12 Litho. *Perf. 11*

C288 AP99 5s multi .25 .20
C289 AP99 10s multi .55 .25

Nationalization of the Peruvian telephone system, Mar. 25, 1970.

Soldier-Farmer Type of Regular Issue

1970, June 24 Litho. *Perf. 11*

C290 A208 3s gold & multi .20 .20
C291 A208 5.50s gold & multi .35 .20

UN Headquarters, NY — AP100

1970 June 26

C292 AP100 3s vio bl & lt bl .20 .20

25th anniversary of United Nations.

Rotary Club Emblem — AP101

1970, July 18

C293 AP101 10s blk, red & gold .70 .50

Rotary Club of Lima, 50th anniversary.

Tourist Type of Regular Issue

3s, Ruins of Sun Fortress, Trujillo. 4s, Sacsayhuaman Arch, Cuzco. 5.50s, Arch & Lake Titicaca, Puno. 10s, Machu Picchu, Cuzco.

1970, Aug. 6 Litho. *Perf. 11*

C294 A210 3s multi .20 .20
C295 A210 4s multi, vert. .20 .20
C296 A210 5.50s multi, vert. .30 .30
C297 A210 10s multi, vert. .50 .50
a. Souvenir sheet of 5 1.60 1.60
Nos. C294-C297 (4) 1.20 1.20

No. C297a contains 5 imperf. stamps similar to Nos. 538, C294-C297 with simulated perforations.

Procession, Lord of Miracles — AP102

4s, Cockfight, by T. Nuñez Ureta. 5.50s, Altar of Church of the Nazarene, vert. 6.50s, Procession, by J. Vinatea Reinoso. 8s, Procession, by José Sabogal, vert.

1970, Nov. 30 Litho. *Perf. 11*

C298 AP102 3s blk & multi .20 .20
C299 AP102 4s blk & multi .20 .20
C300 AP102 5.50s blk & multi .25 .20
C301 AP102 6.50s blk & multi .35 .20
C302 AP102 8s blk & multi .40 .20
Nos. C298-C302 (5) 1.40 1.00

October Festival in Lima.

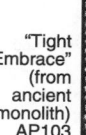

"Tight Embrace" (from ancient monolith) AP103

1971, Feb. 8 Litho. *Perf. 11*

C303 AP103 4s ol gray, yel & red .25 .20
C304 AP103 5.50s dk bl, pink & red .30 .20
C305 AP103 6.50s sl, buff & red .35 .20
Nos. C303-C305 (3) .90 .60

Issued to express Peru's gratitude to the world for aid after the Ancash earthquake, May 31, 1970.

Textile Type of Regular Issue

Designs: 3s, Chancay tapestry, vert. 4s, Chancay lace. 5.50s, Paracas cloth, vert.

1971, Apr. 19 Litho. *Perf. 11*

C306 A213 3s multi .25 .20
C307 A213 4s grn & multi .35 .20
C308 A213 5.50s multi .40 .20
Nos. C306-C308 (3) 1.00 .60

Fish Type of Regular Issue

Fish Sculptures and Fish: 3.50s, Chimu Inca culture, 14th century and Chilean sardine. 4s, Mochica culture, 5th century, and engraulis ringens. 5.50s, Chimu culture, 13th century, and merluccios peruanos. 8.50s, Nazca culture, 3rd century, and brevoortis maculatachilcae.

1971, June 7 Litho. *Perf. 11*

C309 A214 3.50s multi .30 .20
C310 A214 4s multi .40 .20
C311 A214 5.50s multi .50 .20
C312 A214 8.50s multi .70 .20
Nos. C309-C312 (4) 1.90 .80

Independence Type of 1971

Paintings: No. C313, Toribio Rodriguez de Mendoza. No. C314, José de la Riva Aguero. No. C315, Francisco Vidal. 3.50s, José de San Martin. No. C317, Juan P. Viscardo y Guzman. No. C318, Hipolito Unanue. 4.50s, Liberation Monument, Paracas. No. C320, José G. Condorcanqui-Tupac Amaru. No. C321, Francisco J. de Luna Pizarro. 6s, March of the Numancia Battalion, horiz. 7.50s, Peace Tower, monument for Alvarez de Arenales, horiz. 9s, Liberators' Monument, Lima, horiz. 10s, Independence Proclamation in Lima, horiz.

1971 Litho. *Perf. 11*

C313 A215 3s brt mag & blk .20 .20
C314 A215 3s gray & multi .20 .20
C315 A215 3s dk bl & multi .20 .20
C316 A215 3.50s dk bl & multi .20 .20
C317 A215 4s emer & blk .20 .20
C318 A215 4s gray & multi .20 .20
C319 A215 4.50s dk bl & multi .20 .20
C320 A215 5.50s brn & blk .25 .20
C321 A215 5.50s gray & multi .25 .20
C322 A215 6s dk bl & multi .25 .20
C323 A215 7.50s dk bl & multi .30 .20
C324 A215 9s dk bl & multi .40 .20
C325 A215 10s dk bl & multi .40 .20
Nos. C313-C325 (13) 3.25 2.60

150th anniversary of independence, and to honor the heroes of the struggle for independence. Sizes: 6s, 10s, 45x35mm, 7.50s, 9s, 41x39mm. Others 31x49mm.
Issued: #C313, C317, C320, 5/10; #C314, C318, C321, 7/5; others 7/27.

Ricardo Palma — AP104

Weight Lifter — AP105

1971, Aug. 27 *Perf. 13*

C326 AP104 7.50s ol bis & blk .60 .20

Sesquicentennial of National Library. Ricardo Palma (1884-1912) was a writer and director of the library.

1971, Sept. 15

C327 AP105 7.50s brt bl & blk .50 .20

25th World Weight Lifting Championships, Lima.

Flag, Family, Soldier's Head — AP106

1971, Oct. 4

C328 AP106 7.50s blk, lt bl & red .50 .20
a. Souv. sheet of 1, imperf. 1.25 1.00

3rd anniv. of the revolution of the armed forces.

"Sacramento" — AP107

1971, Oct. 8

C329 AP107 7.50s lt bl & dk bl .40 .20

Sesquicentennial of Peruvian Navy.

Peruvian Order of the Sun AP108

1971, Oct. 8

C330 AP108 7.50s multi .40 .40

Sequicentennial of the Peruvian Order of the Sun.

Liberation Type of Regular Issue

Design: 50s, Detail from painting "Progress of Liberation," by Teodoro Nuñez Ureta.

1971, Nov. 4 Litho. *Perf. 13x13½*

C331 A217 50s multi 3.00 1.00

2nd Ministerial meeting of the "Group of 77."

Fair Emblem AP109

1971, Nov. 12 *Perf. 13*

C332 AP109 4.50s multi .30 .20

7th Pacific International Trade Fair.

Fish Type of Regular Issue

3s, Pontinus furcirhinus dubius. 5.50s, Hogfish.

1972, Mar. 20 Litho. *Perf. 13x13½*

C333 A223 3s lt bl & multi .30 .20
C334 A223 5.50s lt bl & multi .50 .20

Teacher and Children, by Teodoro Nuñez Ureta AP110

1972, Apr. 10 Litho. *Perf. 13x13½*

C335 AP110 6.50s multi .50 .20

Enactment of Education Reform Law.

White-tailed Trogon — AP111

1972, June 19 Litho. *Perf. 13½x13*

C336 AP111 2s shown .20 .20
C337 AP111 2.50s Amazonian umbrella bird .20 .20
C338 AP111 3s Peruvian cock-of-the-rock .25 .20
C339 AP111 6.50s Cuvier's toucan .45 .20
C340 AP111 8.50s Blue-crowned motmot .65 .20
Nos. C336-C340 (5) 1.75 1.00

Quipu and Map of Americas AP112

Inca Runner, Olympic Rings — AP113

1972, Aug. 21

C341	AP112	5s blk & multi	.30	.20

4th Interamerican Philatelic Exhibition, EXFILBRA, Rio de Janeiro, Aug. 26-Sept. 2.

1972, Aug. 28

C342	AP113	8s buff & multi	.55	.35

20th Olympic Games, Munich, 8/26-9/11.

Woman of Catacaos, Piura — AP114

Funerary Tower, Sillustani, Puno — AP115

Regional Costumes: 2s, Tupe (Yauyos) woman of Lima. 4s, Indian with bow and arrow, from Conibo, Loreto. 4.50s, Man with calabash, Cajamarca. 5s, Moche woman, Trujillo. 6.50s, Man and woman of Ocongate, Cuzco. 8s, Chucupana woman, Ayacucho. 8.50s, Cotuncha woman, Junin. 10s, Woman of Puno dancing "Pandilla."

1972-73

C343	AP114	2s blk & multi	.20	.20
C344	AP114	3.50s blk & multi	.30	.30
C345	AP114	4s blk & multi	.35	.35
C346	AP114	4.50s blk & multi	.40	.40
C346A	AP114	5s blk & multi	.40	.40
C347	AP114	6.50s blk & multi	.50	.50
C347A	AP114	8s blk & multi	.60	.60
C347B	AP114	8.50s blk & multi	.65	.65
C348	AP114	10s blk & multi	.75	.75
		Nos. C343-C348 (9)	4.15	4.15

Issued: 3.50s, 4s, 6.50s, 9/29/72; 2s, 4.50s, 10s, 4/30/73; 5s, 8s, 8.50s, 10/15/73.

Perf. 13½x13, 13x13½

1972, Oct. 16 **Litho.**

Archaeological Monuments: 1.50s, Stone of the 12 angles, Cuzco. 3.50s, Ruins of Chavin, Ancash. 5s, Wall and gate, Chavin, Ancash. 8s, Ruins of Machu Picchu.

C349	AP115	1.50s multi	.20	.20
C350	AP115	3.50s multi, horiz.	.25	.20
C351	AP115	4s multi	.45	.20
C352	AP115	5s multi, horiz.	.55	.25
C353	AP115	8s multi, horiz.	.85	.35
		Nos. C349-C353 (5)	2.30	1.20

AP116

AP117

Inca ponchos, various textile designs.

1973, Jan. 29 **Litho.** ***Perf. 13½x13***

C354	AP116	2s multi	.20	.20
C355	AP116	3.50s multi	.20	.20
C356	AP116	4s multi	.20	.20
C357	AP116	5s multi	.25	.20
C358	AP116	8s multi	.50	.20
		Nos. C354-C358 (5)	1.35	1.00

1973, Mar. 19 **Litho.** ***Perf. 13½x13***

Antique Jewelry: 1.50s, Goblets and Ring, Mochica, 10th cent. 2.50s, Golden hands and arms, Lambayeque, 12th cent. 4s, Gold male statuette, Mochica, 8th ceny. 5s, Two gold brooches, Nazca, 8th cent. 8s, Flayed puma, Mochica, 8th cent.

C359	AP117	1.50s multi	.20	.20
C360	AP117	2.50s multi	.20	.20
C361	AP117	4s multi	.20	.20
C362	AP117	5s multi	.25	.25
C363	AP117	8s multi	.50	.20
		Nos. C359-C363 (5)	1.35	1.05

Andean Condor — AP118

Indian Guide, by José Sabogal — AP119

Protected Animals: 5s, Vicuña. 8s, Spectacled bear.

1973, Apr. 16 **Litho.** ***Perf. 13½x13***

C364	AP118	4s blk & multi	.25	.20
C365	AP118	5s blk & multi	.40	.20
C366	AP118	8s blk & multi	.75	.25
		Nos. C364-C366 (3)	1.40	.65

See Nos. C372-C376, C411-C412.

1973, May 7 **Litho.** ***Perf. 13½x13***

Peruvian Paintings: 8.50s, Portrait of a Lady, by Daniel Hernandez. 20s, Man Holding Figurine, by Francisco Laso.

C367	AP119	1.50s multi	.20	.20
C368	AP119	8.50s multi	.40	.30
C369	AP119	20s multi	.90	.50
		Nos. C367-C369 (3)	1.50	1.00

Basket and World Map AP120

1973, May 26 ***Perf. 13x13½***

C370	AP120	5s green	.25	.20
C371	AP120	20s lil rose	1.10	.50

1st International Basketball Festival.

Darwin's Rhea — AP121

Orchid — AP122

1973, Sept. 3 **Litho.** ***Perf. 13½x13***

C372	AP121	2.50s shown	.30	.20
C373	AP121	3.50s Giant otter	.45	.25
C374	AP121	6s Greater flamingo	.60	.25
C375	AP121	8.50s Bush dog, horiz.	.60	.35
C376	AP121	10s Chinchilla, horiz.	.75	.50
		Nos. C372-C376 (5)	2.70	1.55

Protected animals.

1973, Sept. 27

Designs: Various orchids.

C377	AP122	1.50s blk & multi	.20	.20
C378	AP122	2.50s blk & multi	.25	.20
C379	AP122	3s blk & multi	.30	.20
C380	AP122	3.50s blk & multi	.35	.20
C381	AP122	8s blk & multi	.75	.20
		Nos. C377-C381 (5)	1.85	1.00

Pacific Fair Emblem — AP123

1973, Nov. 14 **Litho.** ***Perf. 13½x13***

C382	AP123	8s blk, red & gray	.50	.30

8th International Pacific Fair, Lima.

Cargo Ship ILO AP124

Designs: 2.50s, Boats of Pescaperu fishing organization. 8s, Jet and seagull.

1973, Dec. 14 **Litho.** ***Perf. 13***

C383	AP124	1.50s multi	.20	.20
C384	AP124	2.50s multi	.30	.30
C385	AP124	8s multi	.60	.20
		Nos. C383-C385 (3)	1.10	.70

Issued to promote government enterprises.

Lima Monument AP125

1973, Nov. 27 ***Perf. 13***

C386	AP125	8.50s red & multi	.50	.20

50th anniversary of Air Force Academy. Monument honors Jorge Chavez, Peruvian aviator.

Bridge at Yananacu, by Enrique Camino Brant AP126

Paintings: 10c, Peruvian Birds, by Teodoro Nuñez Ureta, vert. 50s, Boats of Totora, by Jorge Vinatea Reinoso.

1973, Dec. 28 ***Perf. 13x13½, 13½x13***

C387	AP126	8s multi	.40	.20
C388	AP126	10s multi	.50	.25
C389	AP126	50s multi	2.25	1.25
		Nos. C387-C389 (3)	3.15	1.70

Moral House, Arequipa AP127

2.50s, El Misti Mountain, Arequipa. 5s, Puya Raymondi (cacti), vert. 6s, Huascaran Mountain. 8s, Lake Querococha. Views on 5s, 6s, 8s are views in White Cordilleras Range, Ancash Province.

1974, Feb. 11

C390	AP127	1.50s multi	.20	.20
C391	AP127	2.50s multi	.20	.20
C392	AP127	5s multi	.30	.20
C393	AP127	6s multi	.40	.20
C394	AP127	8s multi	.65	.20
		Nos. C390-C394 (5)	1.75	1.00

San Jeronimo's, Cuzco — AP128

Churches of Peru: 3.50s, Cajamarca Cathedral. 5s, San Pedro's, Zepita-Puno, horiz. 6s, Cuzco Cathedral. 8.50s, Santo Domingo, Cuzco.

1974, May 6

C395	AP128	1.50s multi	.20	.20
C396	AP128	3.50s multi	.20	.20
C397	AP128	5s multi	.30	.20
C398	AP128	6s multi	.35	.20
C399	AP128	8.50s multi	.50	.20
		Nos. C395-C399 (5)	1.55	1.00

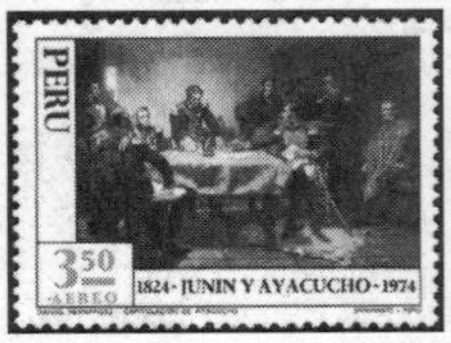

Surrender at Ayacucho, by Daniel Hernandez AP129

Designs: 6s, Battle of Junin, by Felix Yañex. 7.50s, Battle of Ayachucho, by Felix Yañez.

1974 **Litho.** ***Perf. 13x13½***

C400	AP129	3.50s multi	.25	.20
C401	AP129	6s multi	.25	.20
C402	AP129	7.50s multi	.45	.20
C403	AP129	8.50s multi	.50	.20
C404	AP129	10s multi	.65	.20
		Nos. C400-C404 (5)	2.10	1.00

Sesquicentennial of the Battles of Junin and Ayacucho and of the surrender at Ayacucho. Issued: 7.50s, 8/6; 6s, 10/9; others, 12/9.

Chavin Stone, Ancash AP130

Machu Picchu, Cuzco
AP131

#C407, C409, Different bas-reliefs from Chavin Stone. #C408, Baths of Tampumacchay, Cuzco. #C410, Ruins of Kencco, Cuzco.

1974, Mar. 25 ***Perf. 13½x13, 13x13½***

C405	AP130	3s multi		.20	.20
C406	AP131	3s multi		.20	.20
C407	AP130	5s multi		.30	.20
C408	AP131	5s multi		.30	.20
C409	AP130	10s multi		.60	.20
C410	AP131	10s multi		.60	.20
		Nos. C405-C410 (6)		2.20	1.20

Cacajao Rubicundus
AP132

1974, Oct. 21 ***Perf. 13½x13***

C411	AP132	8s multi	.50	.25
C412	AP132	20s multi	1.25	.40

Protected animals.

Inca Gold Mask
AP133

1974, Nov. 8 ***Perf. 13x13½***

C413 AP133 8s yel & multi .50 .20

8th World Mining Congress, Lima.

Chalan, Horseman's Cloak — AP134

1974, Nov. 11 Litho. ***Perf. 13½x13***

C414	AP134	5s multi	.25	.20
C415	AP134	8.50s multi	.50	.25

Pedro Paulet and Aerial Torpedo
AP135

1974, Nov. 28 Litho. ***Perf. 13x13½***

C416 AP135 8s bl & vio .50 .30

UPU, cent. Pedro Paulet, inventor of the mail-carrying aerial torpedo.

Christmas Type of 1974

Design: 6.50s, Indian Nativity scene.

1974, Dec. 20 ***Perf. 13½x13***

C417 A235 6.50s multi .25 .20

Andean Village, Map of South American West Coast
AP136

1974, Dec. 30

C418 AP136 6.50s multi .35 .25

Meeting of Communications Ministers of Andean Pact countries.

Map of Peru, Modern Buildings, UN Emblem — AP137

1975, Mar. 12 Litho. ***Perf. 13x13***

C419 AP137 6s blk, gray & red .20 .20

2nd United Nations Industrial Development Organization Conference, Lima.

Nos. C187, C211 and C160 Surcharged with New Value and Heavy Bar in Dark Blue

Wmk. 346

1975, April Litho. ***Perf. 12***

C420 AP51 2s on 4.30s org .20 .20

Perf. 13½x14, 13x14

Unwmk.

C421	AP51	2.50s on 4.60s org	.25	.20
C422	AP51	5s on 3.80s org	.25	.20
		Nos. C420-C422 (3)	.70	.60

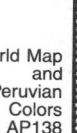

World Map and Peruvian Colors
AP138

1975, Aug. 25 Litho. ***Perf. 13x13½***

C423 AP138 6.50s lt bl, vio bl & red .25 .20

Conference of Foreign Ministers of Nonaligned Countries.

Map of Peru and Flight Route
AP139

1975, Oct. 23 Litho. ***Perf. 13x13½***

C424 AP139 8s red, pink & blk .35 .20

AeroPeru's first flights: Lima-Rio de Janeiro, Lima-Los Angeles.

Fair Poster — AP140

Col. Francisco Bolognesi
AP141

1975, Nov. 21 Litho. ***Perf. 13½x13***

C425 AP140 6s blk, bis & red .45 .25

9th International Pacific Fair, Lima, 1975.

1975, Dec. 23 Litho. ***Perf. 13½x13***

C426 AP141 20s multi .80 .50

160th birth anniv. of Col. Bolognesi.

Indian Mother and Child — AP142

Inca Messenger, UPAE Emblem — AP143

1976, Feb. 23 Litho. ***Perf. 13½x13***

C427 AP142 6s gray & multi .35 .25

Christmas 1975.

1976, Mar. 19 Litho. ***Perf. 13½x13***

C428 AP143 5s red, blk & tan .40 .25

11th Congress of the Postal Union of the Americas and Spain, UPAE.

Nos. C187, C211, C160, C209, C210 Surcharged in Dark Blue or Violet Blue (No Bar)

1976 **As Before**

C429	AP51	2s on 4.30s org	.20	.20
C430	AP51	3.50s on 4.60s org	.20	.20
C431	AP51	4.50s on 3.80s org	.20	.20
C432	AP51	5s on 4.30s org	.25	.20
C433	AP51	6s on 4.60s org	.35	.25
C434	A184	10s on 2.60s brt grn	.50	.20
C435	AP52	50s on 3.60s lil rose (VB)	2.00	1.75
		Nos. C429-C435 (7)	3.70	3.00

Stamps of 1962-67 Surcharged with New Value and Heavy Bar in Black, Red, Green, Dark Blue or Orange

1976-77 **As Before**

C436	AP52	1.50s on 3.60s (Bk) #C210	.20	.20
C437	A184	2s on 2.60s (R) #C209 ('77)	.20	.20
C438	AP52	2s on 3.60s (G) #C210	.20	.20
C439	AP80	2s on 4.30s (Bk) #C199	.20	.20
C440	A184	3s on 2.60s (Bk) #C209 ('77)	.20	.20
C441	A184	4s on 2.60s (DBl) #C209	.25	.20
C442	AP52	4s on 3.60s (DBl) #C210 ('77)	.25	.20
C443	AP51	5s on 4.30s (R) #C187	.30	.20
C444	AP83	6s on 4.60s (Bk) #C208 ('77)	.35	.20
C445	AP51	6s on 4.60s (DBl) #C211 ('77)	.35	.20
C446	AP51	7s on 4.30s (Bk) #C187 ('77)	.25	.20
C447	AP52	7.50s on 3.60s (DBl) #C210	.45	.25
C448	AP52	8s on 3.60s (O) #C210	.50	.20
C449	AP51	10s on 4.30s (Bk) #C187 ('77)	.30	.20
C450	AP51	10s on 4.60s (DBl) #C211	.60	.20
C451	AP86	24s on 3.60s (Bk) #C220 ('77)	1.75	.60
C452	AP86	28s on 4.60s (Bk) #C221 ('77)	1.00	.60
C453	AP86	32s on 5.60s (Bk) #C222 ('77)	1.00	.60
C454	A184	50s on 2.60s (O) #C209 ('77)	2.50	1.00
C455	AP52	50s on 3.60s (G) #C210	2.00	1.25
		Nos. C436-C455 (20)	12.85	7.10

AP144

AP145

Map of Tacna and Tarata Provinces.

1976, Aug. 28 Litho. ***Perf. 13½x13***

C456 AP144 10s multi .45 .25

Re-incorporation of Tacna Province into Peru, 47th anniversary.

1976, Sept. 15 Litho. ***Perf. 13½x13***

Investigative Police badge.

C457 AP145 20s multi .65 .35

Investigative Police of Peru, 54th anniv.

AP146

AP147

"Declaration of Bogota."

1976, Sept. 22

C458 AP146 10s multi .40 .20

Declaration of Bogota for cooperation and world peace, 10th anniversary.

1976, Nov. 2 Litho. ***Perf. 13½x13***

Pal Losonczi and map of Hungary.

C459 AP147 7s ultra & blk .40 .20

Visit of Pres. Pal Losonczi of Hungary, Oct. 1976.

Map of Amazon Basin, Colors of Peru and Brazil
AP148

1976, Dec. 16 Litho. *Perf. 13*
C460 AP148 10s bl & multi .35 .25

Visit of Gen. Ernesto Geisel, president of Brazil, Nov. 5, 1976.

Liberation Monument, Lima
AP149

1977, Mar. 9 Litho. *Perf. 13x13½*
C461 AP149 20s red buff & blk .75 .40

Army Day.

Map of Peru and Venezuela, South America
AP150

1977, Mar. 14
C462 AP150 12s buff & multi .50 .30

Meeting of Pres. Francisco Morales Bermudez Cerrutti of Peru and Pres. Carlos Andres Perez of Venezuela, Dec. 1976.

Electronic Tree — AP151

Map of Peru, Refinery, Tanker — AP152

1977, May 30 Litho. *Perf. 13½x13*
C463 AP151 20s gray, red & blk .65 .35

World Telecommunications Day.

1977, July 13 Litho. *Perf. 13½x13*
C464 AP152 14s multi .40 .30

Development of Bayovar oil complex.

Messenger Type of 1977

1977 Litho. *Perf. 13½x13*
C465 A243 24s mag & blk .75 .40
C466 A243 28s bl & blk 1.25 .40
C467 A243 32s rose brn & blk .75 .50
Nos. C465-C467 (3) 2.75 1.30

Arms of Arequipa
AP153

Gen. Jorge Rafael Videla — AP154

1977, Sept. 3 Litho. *Perf. 13½x13*
C468 AP153 10s multi .20 .20

Gold of Peru Exhibition, Arequipa 1977.

1977, Oct. 8 Litho. *Perf. 13½x13*
C469 AP154 36s multi .55 .25

Visit of Jorge Rafael Videla, president of Argentina.

Stamps of 1953-67 Surcharged with New Value and Heavy Bar in Black, Dark Blue or Green

1977 As Before
C470 AP83 2s on 3.60s #C207 .20 .20
C471 AP51 2s on 4.60s (DB) #C211 .20 .20
C472 AP51 4s on 4.60s (DB) #C211 .20 .20
C473 AP51 5s on 4.30s #C187 .35 .20
C474 AP52 5s on 3.60s #C210 .20 .20
C475 AP55 10s on 2.15s #C125 .40 .20
C476 AP52 10s on 3.60s (DB) #C210 .65 .20
C477 AP84 10s on 3.60s #C215 .50 .20
C478 AP52 20s on 3.60s (DB) #C210 .50 .25
C479 AP51 100s on 3.80s (G) #C160 2.00 1.75
Nos. C470-C479 (10) 5.20 3.60

Nos. C223-C224 Surcharged with New Value, Heavy Bars and: "FRANQUEO"

1977 Litho. *Perf. 12*
C480 AP87 6s on 3.60s multi .40 .25
C481 AP87 8s on 3.60s multi .50 .35
C482 AP87 10s on 5.60s multi .50 .40
Nos. C480-C482 (3) 1.40 1.00

Adm. Miguel Grau — AP155

1977, Dec. 15 Litho. *Perf. 13½x13*
C483 AP155 28s multi .40 .25

Navy Day. Miguel Grau (1838-1879), Peruvian naval commander.

Christmas Type of 1977

1977, Dec. 23
C484 A246 20s Indian Nativity .50 .20

Andrés Bello, Flag and Map of Participants
AP156

1978, Jan. 12 Litho. *Perf. 13*
C485 AP156 30s multi .40 .30

8th Meeting of Education Ministers honoring Andrés Bello, Lima.

Inca Type of 1978

1978 Litho. *Perf. 13½x13*
C486 A247 24s dp rose lil .30 .30
C487 A247 30s salmon .40 .30
C488 A247 65s brt bl .90 .65
C489 A247 95s dk bl 1.25 1.00
Nos. C486-C489 (4) 2.85 2.25

Antenna, ITU Emblem
AP157

1978, July 3 Litho. *Perf. 13x13½*
C490 AP157 50s gray & multi .65 .65

10th World Telecommunications Day.

San Martin, Flag Colors of Peru and Argentina
AP158

1978, Sept. 4 Litho. *Perf. 13½x13*
C491 AP158 30s multi .40 .40

Gen. José de San Martin (1778-1850), soldier and statesman, protector of Peru.

Stamps of 1965-67 Surcharged "Habilitado / R.D. No. O118" and New Value in Red, Green, Violet Blue or Black

1978 Litho.
C492 AP83 34s on 4.60s multi (R) #C208 .30 .25
C493 AP79 40s on 4.30s multi (G) #C196 .35 .30
C494 A184 70s on 2.60s brt grn (VB) #C209 .60 .50
C495 AP52 110s on 3.60s lil rose (Bk) #C210 .90 .75
C496 AP80 265s on 4.30s gray & multi (Bk) #C199 2.25 2.00
Nos. C492-C496 (5) 4.40 3.80

Stamps and Type of 1968-78 Surcharged in Violet Blue, Black or Red

1978 Litho.
C497 AP86 25s on 4.60s (VB) #C221 .25 .25
C498 A247 45s on 28s dk grn (Bk) .40 .25
C499 A247 75s on 28s dk grn (R) .65 .40
C500 AP86 105s on 5.60s (R) #C222 1.25 1.00
Nos. C497-C500 (4) 2.55 1.90

Nos. C498-C499 not issued without surcharge.

Nos. C486, C467 Surcharged

1980, Apr. 14 Litho. *Perf. 13½x13*
C501 A247 35s on 24s dp rose lil .30 .25
C502 A243 45s on 32s rose brn & blk .40 .30

No. C130 Surcharged in Black

1981, Nov. Engr. *Perf. 13*
C503 AP57 30s on 2.20s multi .30 .30
C504 AP57 40s on 2.20s multi .30 .25

No. C130 Surcharged and Overprinted in Green: "12 Feria / Internacional / del / Pacifico 1981"

1981, Nov. 30
C505 AP57 140s on 2.20s multi 1.10 .75

12th Intl. Pacific Fair.

AIR POST SEMI-POSTAL STAMPS

Catalogue values for unused stamps in this section are for Never Hinged items.

Chavin Griffin
SPAP1

1.50s+1s, Bird. 3s+2.50s, Cat. 4.30s+3s, Mythological figure, vert. 6s+ 4s, Chavin god, vert.

Perf. 12½x12, 12x12½
1963, Apr. 18 Litho. Wmk. 346
Design in Gray and Brown
CB1 SPAP1 1s + 50c sal pink .20 .20
CB2 SPAP1 1.50s + 1s blue .20 .20
CB3 SPAP1 3s + 2.50s lt grn .50 .50
CB4 SPAP1 4.30s + 3s green .80 .80
CB5 SPAP1 6s + 4s citron 1.00 1.00
Nos. CB1-CB5 (5) 2.70 2.70

The designs are from ceramics found by archaeological excavations of the 14th century Chavin culture. The surtax was for the excavations fund.

Henri Dunant and Centenary Emblem
SPAP2

Perf. 12½x12
1964, Jan. 29 Unwmk.
CB6 SPAP2 1.30s + 70c multi .20 .20
CB7 SPAP2 4.30s + 1.70s multi .40 .40

Centenary of International Red Cross.

SPECIAL DELIVERY STAMPS

No. 149 Overprinted in Black

EXPRESO

1908 Unwmk. *Perf. 12*
E1 A25 10c gray black 20.00 15.00

No. 172 Overprinted in Violet

EXPRESO

1909
E2 A40 10c red brn & blk 25.00 14.00

No. 1819 Handstamped in Violet

EXPRESO

1910
E3 A49 10c deep blue 14.00 12.00

Two handstamps were used to make No. E2. Impressions from them measure 22½x6½mm and 24x6½mm.

Counterfeits exist of Nos. E1-3.

POSTAGE DUE STAMPS

Coat of Arms — D1

Steamship and Llama
D2 D3

D4 D5

1874-79 Unwmk. Engr. *Perf. 12*

With Grill

J1	D1	1c bister ('79)	.25	.20
J2	D2	5c vermilion	.30	.20
J3	D3	10c orange	.35	.25
J4	D4	20c blue	.60	.35
J5	D5	50c brown	9.00	3.50
		Nos. J1-J5 (5)	10.50	4.50

A 2c green exists, but was not regularly issued.

For overprints and surcharges see Nos. 157, J6-J31, J37-J38, 8N14-8N15, 14N18.

1886

Without Grill

J1a	D1	1c bister	.20
J2a	D2	5c vermilion	.20
J3a	D3	10c orange	.20
J4a	D4	20c blue	.35
J5a	D5	50c brown	3.50
		Nos. J1a-J5a (5)	4.45

Nos. J1-J5 Overprinted in Blue or Red

1881

"PLATA" 2½mm High

J6	D1	1c bis (Bl)	3.50	2.50
J7	D2	5c ver (Bl)	6.50	6.00
a.		Double overprint		
b.		Inverted overprint	17.00	17.00
J8	D3	10c org (Bl)	6.50	6.50
a.		Inverted overprint	17.00	17.00
J9	D4	20c bl (R)	25.00	20.00
J10	D5	50c brn (Bl)	55.00	50.00
		Nos. J6-J10 (5)	96.50	85.00

In the reprints of this overprint "PLATA" is 3mm high instead of 2½mm. Besides being struck in the regular colors it was also applied to the 1, 5, 10 and 50c in red and the 20c in blue.

Overprinted in Red

1881

J11	D1	1c bister	5.00	5.00
J12	D2	5c vermilion	6.50	6.00
J13	D3	10c orange	8.00	6.50
J14	D4	20c blue	25.00	20.00
J15	D5	50c brown	80.00	65.00
		Nos. J11-J15 (5)	124.50	102.50

Originals of Nos. J11 to J15 are overprinted in brick-red, oily ink; reprints in thicker, bright red ink. The 5c exists with reprinted overprint in blue.

Overprinted "Union Postal Universal Lima Plata", in Oval in first named color and Triangle in second named color

1883

J16	D1	1c bis (Bl & Bk)	5.00	3.50
J17	D1	1c bis (Bk & Bl)	7.50	7.00
J18	D2	5c ver (Bl & Bk)	7.50	7.00
J19	D3	10c org (Bl & Bk)	7.50	6.00
J20	D4	20c bl (R & Bk)	*450.00*	*450.00*
J21	D5	50c brn (Bl & Bk)	55.00	42.50

Reprints of Nos. J16 to J21 have the oval overprint with "PLATA" 3mm. high. The 1c also exists with the oval overprint in red.

Overprinted in Black

1884

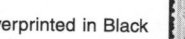

J22	D1	1c bister	.50	.50
J23	D2	5c vermilion	.50	.50
J24	D3	10c orange	.50	.50
J25	D4	20c blue	1.00	.50
J26	D5	50c brown	3.00	.90
		Nos. J22-J26 (5)	5.50	2.90

The triangular overprint is found in 11 types.

Overprinted "Lima Correos" in Circle in Red and Triangle in Black

1884

J27	D1	1c bister	12.50	11.00

Reprints of No. J27 have the overprint in bright red. At the time they were made the overprint was also printed on the 5, 10, 20 and 50c Postage Due stamps.

Postage Due stamps overprinted with Sun and "CORREOS LIMA" (as shown above No. 103), alone or in combination with the "U. P. U. LIMA" oval or "LIMA CORREOS" in double-lined circle, are fancy varieties made to sell to collectors and never placed in use.

Overprinted

1896-97

J28	D1	1c bister	.35	.30
a.		Double overprint		
J29	D2	5c vermilion	.45	.25
a.		Double overprint		
b.		Inverted overprint		
J30	D3	10c orange	.55	.35
a.		Inverted overprint		
J31	D4	20c blue	.65	.50
a.		Double overprint		
J32	A22	50c red ('97)	.75	.50
J33	A23	1s brown ('97)	1.00	.65
a.		Double overprint		
b.		Inverted overprint		
		Nos. J28-J33 (6)	3.75	2.55

Liberty — D6

1899 Engr.

J34	D6	5s yel grn	1.00	*5.00*
J35	D6	10s dl vio	900.00	900.00

For surcharge see No. J39.

1902

On No. 159

J36	A31	5c on 10s bl grn	1.00	.80
a.		Double surcharge	12.00	12.00

On No. J4

J37	D4	1c on 20c blue	.50	.40
a.		"DEFICIT" omitted	6.50	2.00
b.		"DEFICIT" double	6.50	2.00
c.		"UN CENTAVO" double	6.00	2.00
d.		"UN CENTAVO" omitted	8.25	6.00

Surcharged Vertically

J38	D4	5c on 20c blue	1.50	1.00

On No. J35

J39	D6	1c on 10s dull vio	.60	.50
		Nos. J36-J39 (4)	3.60	2.70

D7

1909 Engr. *Perf. 12*

J40	D7	1c red brown	.50	.20
J41	D7	5c red brown	.50	.20
J42	D7	10c red brown	.60	.20
J43	D7	50c red brown	.90	.20
		Nos. J40-J43 (4)	2.50	.80

1921

Size: 18¼x22mm

J44	D7	1c violet brown	.25	.20
J45	D7	2c violet brown	.25	.20
J46	D7	5c violet brown	.35	.20
J47	D7	10c violet brown	.50	.25
J48	D7	50c violet brown	1.60	.75
J49	D7	1s violet brown	7.50	3.00
J50	D7	2s violet brown	12.00	3.50
		Nos. J44-J50 (7)	22.45	8.10

Nos. J49 and J50 have the circle at the center replaced by a shield containing "S/.", in addition to the numeral.

In 1929 during a shortage of regular postage stamps, some of the Postage Due stamps of 1921 were used instead.

See Nos. J50A-J52, J55-J56. For surcharges see Nos. 204-207, 757.

Type of 1909-22

Size: 18¾x23mm

J50A	D7	2c violet brown	.75	.20
J50B	D7	10c violet brown	.75	.20

Type of 1909-22 Issues

1932 Photo. *Perf. 14½x14*

J51	D7	2c violet brown	.75	.25
J52	D7	10c violet brown	.75	.25

Regular Stamps of 1934-35 Overprinted in Black

1935 *Perf. 13*

J53	A131	2c deep claret	.75	.50
J54	A117	10c crimson	.75	.50

Type of 1909-32

Size: 19x23mm

Imprint: "Waterlow & Sons, Limited, Londres."

1936 Engr. *Perf. 12½*

J55	D7	2c light brown	.20	.20
J56	D7	10c gray green	.50	.50

OFFICIAL STAMPS

Regular Issue of 1886 Overprinted in Red

1890, Feb. 2

O2	A17	1c dl vio	1.40	1.40
a.		Double overprint	8.25	8.25
O3	A18	2c green	1.40	1.40
a.		Double overprint		
b.		Inverted overprint	8.25	8.25
O4	A19	5c orange	2.00	1.60
a.		Inverted overprint	8.25	8.25
b.		Double overprint	8.25	8.25
O5	A20	10c slate	1.00	.65
a.		Double overprint	8.25	8.25
b.		Inverted overprint	8.25	8.25
O6	A21	20c blue	3.00	2.00
a.		Double overprint	8.25	8.25
b.		Inverted overprint	8.25	8.25
O7	A22	50c red	4.00	2.00
a.		Inverted overprint	12.00	
b.		Double overprint		
O8	A23	1s brown	5.00	4.50
a.		Double overprint	17.00	17.00
b.		Inverted overprint	17.00	17.00
		Nos. O2-O8 (7)	17.80	13.55

Nos. 118-124 (Bermudez Ovpt.) Overprinted Type "a" in Red

1894, Oct.

O9	A17	1c green	1.40	1.40
a.		"Gobierno" and head invtd.	6.50	5.50
b.		Dbl. ovpt. of "Gobierno"		
O10	A17	1c orange	22.50	20.00
O11	A18	2c rose	1.40	1.40
a.		Overprinted head inverted	10.00	10.00
b.		Both overprints inverted		
O12	A18	2c violet	1.40	1.40
a.		"Gobierno" double		
O13	A19	5c ultra	22.50	20.00
a.		Both overprints inverted		
O14	A19	5c blue	10.00	9.00
O15	A20	10c green	3.50	3.50
O16	A22	50c green	5.00	5.00
		Nos. O9-O16 (8)	67.70	61.70

Nos. 125-126 ("Horseshoe" Ovpt.) Overprinted Type "a" in Red

O17	A18	2c vermilion	2.00	2.00
O18	A19	5c blue	2.00	2.00

Nos. 105, 107, 109, 113 Overprinted Type "a" in Red

1895, May

O19	A17	1c vermilion	8.25	8.25
O20	A18	2c dp ultra	8.25	8.25
O21	A12	5c claret	6.50	6.50
O22	A14	20c dp ultra	6.50	6.50
		Nos. O19-O22 (4)	29.50	29.50

Nos. O2-O22 have been extensively counterfeited.

Nos. 141, 148, 149, 151 Overprinted in Black

1896-1901

O23	A24	1c ultra	.20	.20
O24	A25	10c yellow	1.00	.50
a.		Double overprint		
O25	A25	10c gray blk ('01)	.20	.20
O26	A26	50c brt rose	.40	.25
		Nos. O23-O26 (4)	1.80	1.15

O1

1909-14 Engr. *Perf. 12*

Size: 18½x22mm

O27	O1	1c red	.20	.20
a.		1c brown red	.20	.20
O28	O1	1c orange ('14)	.50	.35
O29	O1	10c bis brn ('14)	.20	.20
a.		10c violet brown	.20	.20

O30 O1 50c ol grn ('14) .60 .35
a. 50c blue green 1.00 .35

Size: 18¾x23½mm

O30B O1 10c vio brn .50 .20
Nos. O27-O30B (5) 2.00 1.30

See Nos. O31, O33-O34. For overprints and surcharge see Nos. 201-203, 760.

1933 Photo. *Perf. 15x14*

O31 O1 10c violet brown .50 .20

No. 319 Overprinted in Black

1935 Unwmk. *Perf. 13*

O32 A117 10c crimson .20 .20

Type of 1909-33
Imprint: "Waterlow & Sons, Limited, Londres."

1936 Engr. *Perf. 12½*

Size: 19x23mm

O33 O1 10c light brown .20 .20
O34 O1 50c gray green .35 .35

PARCEL POST STAMPS

PP1

PP2

PP3

1897 Typeset Unwmk. *Perf. 12*

Q1	PP1	1c dull lilac	2.25	1.90
Q2	PP2	2c bister	2.50	2.25
a.		2c olive	2.50	2.25
b.		2c yellow	2.50	2.25
c.		Laid paper	65.00	65.00
Q3	PP2	5c dk bl	10.00	6.50
a.		Tête bêche pair	*375.00*	
Q4	PP3	10c vio brn	14.00	10.00
Q5	PP3	20c rose red	17.00	14.00
Q6	PP3	50c bl grn	45.00	37.50
		Nos. Q1-Q6 (6)	90.75	72.15

Surcharged in Black **UN CENTAVO**

1903-04

Q7	PP3	1c on 20c rose red	12.00	10.00
Q8	PP3	1c on 50c bl grn	12.00	10.00
Q9	PP3	5c on 10c vio brn	80.00	65.00
a.		Inverted surcharge	125.00	110.00
b.		Double surcharge		
		Nos. Q7-Q9 (3)	104.00	85.00

POSTAL TAX STAMPS

Plebiscite Issues

These stamps were not used in Tacna and Arica (which were under Chilean occupation) but were used in Peru to pay a supplementary tax on letters, etc.

It was intended that the money derived from the sale of these stamps should be used to help defray the expenses of the plebiscite.

Morro Arica — PT1

Adm. Grau and Col. Bolognesi Reviewing Troops — PT2

Bolognesi Monument PT3

1925-26 Unwmk. Litho. *Perf. 12*

RA1	PT1	5c dp bl	1.50	.35
RA2	PT1	5c rose red	.80	.25
RA3	PT1	5c yel grn	.70	.25
RA4	PT2	10c brown	3.00	.80
RA5	PT3	50c bl grn	19.00	9.00
		Nos. RA1-RA5 (5)	25.00	10.65

PT4

1926

RA6 PT4 2c orange .30 .20

PT5

1927-28

RA7	PT5	2c dp org	.60	.20
RA8	PT5	2c red brn	.60	.20
RA9	PT5	2c dk bl	.60	.20
RA10	PT5	2c gray vio	.40	.20
RA11	PT5	2c bl grn ('28)	.40	.20
RA12	PT5	20c red	2.50	1.00
		Nos. RA7-RA12 (6)	5.10	2.00

PT6

1928 Engr.

RA13 PT6 2c dk vio .20 .20

The use of the Plebiscite stamps was discontinued July 26, 1929, after the settlement of the Tacna-Arica controversy with Chile.

For overprint see No. 261.

Unemployment Fund Issues

These stamps were required in addition to the ordinary postage, on every letter or piece of postal matter. The money obtained by their sale was to assist the unemployed.

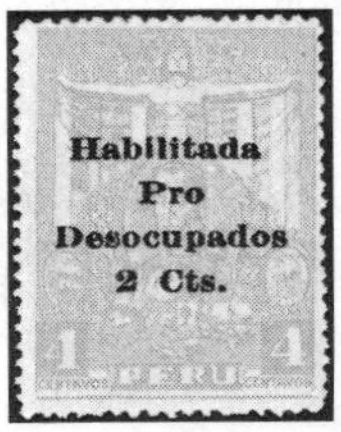

Nos. 273-275 Surcharged

1931

RA14	A95	2c on 4c red	.65	.50
a.		Inverted surcharge	3.50	3.50
RA15	A95	2c on 10c bl grn	.50	.50
a.		Inverted surcharge	3.50	3.50
RA16	A95	2c on 15c sl gray	.50	.50
a.		Inverted surcharge	3.50	3.50
		Nos. RA14-RA16 (3)	1.65	1.50

"Labor" PT7

Blacksmith PT8

Two types of Nos. RA17-RA18:
I - Imprint 15mm.
II - Imprint 13¾mm.

Perf. 12x11½, 11½x12

1931-32 Litho.

RA17	PT7	2c emer (I)	.20	.20
a.		Type II	.20	
RA18	PT7	2c rose car (I) ('32)	.20	.20
a.		Type II	.20	

1932-34

RA19 PT8 2c dp gray .20 .20
RA20 PT8 2c pur ('34) .20 .20

Monument of 2nd of May — PT9

Perf. 13, 13½, 13x13½

1933-35 Photo.

RA21	PT9	2c bl vio	.20	.20
RA22	PT9	2c org ('34)	.20	.20
RA23	PT9	2c brn vio ('35)	.20	.20
		Nos. RA21-RA23 (3)	.60	.60

For overprint see No. RA27.

No. 307 Overprinted in Black

1934 *Perf. 13½*

RA24 A111 2c green .20 .20
a. Inverted overprint 2.00 2.00

No. 339 Overprinted in Black

1935

RA25 A131 2c deep claret .20 .20

No. 339 Overprinted Type "a" in Black

1936 Unwmk. *Perf. 13½*

RA26 A131 2c deep claret .20 .20

No. RA23 Overprinted in Black

1936 *Perf. 13x13½*

RA27 PT9 2c brn vio .20 .20
a. Double overprint 1.40
b. Overprint reading down 1.40
c. Overprint double, reading down 1.40

St. Rosa of Lima — PT10

"Protection" by John Q. A. Ward — PT11

1937 Engr. *Perf. 12*

RA28 PT10 2c car rose .20 .20

Nos. RA27 and RA28 represented a tax to help erect a church.

Imprint: "American Bank Note Company"

1938 Litho.

RA29 PT11 2c brown .20 .20

The tax was to help the unemployed.

See Nos. RA30, RA34, RA40. For surcharges see Nos. 501A, 674-678, 681-682, 709-711, 757.

Type of 1938 Redrawn
Imprint: "Columbian Bank Note Company."

1943 *Perf. 12½*

RA30 PT11 2c dl claret brn .20 .20

See note above #RA14. See #RA34, RA40.

Catalogue values for unused stamps in this section, from this point to the end of the section, are for Never Hinged items.

PT12

PT13

1949 *Perf. 12½, 12*

Black Surcharge

RA31 PT12 3c on 4c vio bl .55 .20
RA32 PT13 3c on 10c blue .55 .20

The tax was for an education fund.

Symbolical of Education PT14

Emblem of Congress PT15

1950 Typo. *Perf. 14*

Size: 16½x21mm

RA33 PT14 3c dp car .20 .20

See Nos. RA35, RA39, RA43

For surcharges see Nos. 501B, 761, 764-766, RA45-RA48, RA58.

Type of 1938

Imprint: "Thomas De La Rue & Co. Ltd."

1951 **Litho.**

RA34 PT11 2c lt redsh brn .20 .20

Type of 1950

Imprint: "Thomas De La Rue & Company, Limited."

1952 **Unwmk.** ***Perf. 14, 13***

Size: 16½x21½mm

RA35 PT14 3c brn car .20 .20

1954 ***Rouletted 13***

RA36 PT15 5c bl & red .25 .20

The tax was to help finance the National Marian Eucharistic Congress.

For surcharges see Nos. 758B, 768.

Piura Arms and Congress Emblem — PT16

1960 **Litho.** ***Perf. 10½***

RA37 PT16 10c ultra, red, grn & yel .20 .20

a. Green ribbon inverted

RA38 PT16 10c ultra & red .25 .20

Nos. RA37-RA38 were used to help finance the 6th National Eucharistic Congress, Piura, Aug. 25-28. Obligatory on all domestic mail until Dec. 31, 1960. Both stamps exist imperf.

Type of 1950

Imprint: "Bundesdruckerei Berlin"

1961 ***Perf. 14***

Size: 17½x22½mm

RA39 PT14 3c dp car .20 .20

Type of 1938

Imprint: "Harrison and Sons Ltd"

1962, Apr. **Litho.** ***Perf. 14x14½***

RA40 PT11 2c lt brn .20 .20

Symbol of Eucharist — PT17

1962, May 8 ***Rouletted 11***

RA41 PT17 10c bl & org .20 .20

Issued to raise funds for the Seventh National Eucharistic Congress, Huancayo, 1964. Obligatory on all domestic mail.

See No. RA42. For surcharges and overprint see Nos. 735, 762, RA44.

1962

Imprint: "Iberia"

RA42 PT17 10c bl & org .20 .20

Type of 1950

1965, Apr. **Litho.** ***Perf. 12½x12***

Imprint: "Thomas de La Rue"

Size: 18x22mm

RA43 PT14 3c light carmine .20 .20

Type of 1962 Overprinted in Red with three "X," Bars and: "Periodista / Peruano / LEY / 16078"

1966, July 2 **Litho.** ***Pin Perf.***

Imprint: "Iberia"

RA44 PT17 10c vio & org .20 .20

No. RA43 Surcharged in Green or Black

HABILITADO
"Fondo del
Periodista
Peruano"
Ley 16078
S/o. 0.10

b

c

d

1966-67 ***Perf. 12x12½***

RA45 PT14 (b) 10c on 3c (G) .80 .20

RA46 PT14 (c) 10c on 3c (Bk) .80 .20

RA47 PT14 (c) 10c on 3c (G) .20 .20

RA48 PT14 (d) 10c on 3c (G) .20 .20

Nos. RA45-RA48 (4) 2.00 .80

The surtax of Nos. RA44-RA48 was for the Peruvian Journalists' Fund.

Pen Made of Newspaper PT18

Temple at Chan-Chan PT19

1967, Dec. **Litho.** ***Perf. 11***

RA49 PT18 10c dk red & blk .20 .20

The surtax was for the Peruvian Journalists' fund.

For surcharges see Nos. RA56-RA57.

1967, Dec. 27

Designs: No. RA51, Side view of temple. Nos. RA52-RA55, Various stone bas-reliefs from Chan-Chan.

RA50 PT19 20c bl & grn .20 .20

RA51 PT19 20c multi .20 .20

RA52 PT19 20c brt bl & blk .20 .20

RA53 PT19 20c emer & blk .20 .20

RA54 PT19 20c sep & blk .20 .20

RA55 PT19 20c lil rose & blk .20 .20

Nos. RA50-RA55 (6) 1.20 1.20

The surtax was for the excavations at Chan-Chan, northern coast of Peru. (Mochica-Chimu pre-Inca period).

Type of 1967 Surcharged in Red: "VEINTE / CENTAVOS / R.S. 16-8-68"

Designs: No. RA56, Handshake. No. RA57, Globe and pen.

1968, Oct. **Litho.** ***Perf. 11***

RA56 PT18 20c on 50c multi .50 .50

RA57 PT18 20c on 1s multi .50 .50

Nos. RA56-RA57 without surcharge were not obligatory tax stamps.

No. C199 surcharged "PRO NAVIDAD/ Veinte Centavos/R.S. 5-11-68" was not a compulsory postal tax stamp.

#RA43 Surchd. Similar to Type "c"

1968, Oct. ***Perf. 12½x12***

RA58 PT14 20c on 3c lt car .20 .20

Surcharge lacks quotation marks and 4th line reads: Ley 17050.

OCCUPATION STAMPS

Issued under Chilean Occupation

Stamps formerly listed as Nos. N1-N10 are regular issues of Chile canceled in Peru.

Stamps of Peru, 1874-80, Overprinted in Red, Blue or Black

1881-82 ***Perf. 12***

N11 A17 1c org (Bl) .50 1.00

a. Inverted overprint

N12 A18 2c dk vio (Bk) .50 4.00

a. Inverted overprint 16.50

b. Double overprint 22.50

N13 A18 2c rose (Bk) 1.60 *18.00*

a. Inverted overprint

N14 A19 5c bl (R) 55.00 62.50

a. Inverted overprint

N15 A19 5c ultra (R) 90.00 100.00

N16 A20 10c grn (R) .50 *1.60*

a. Inverted overprint 6.50 6.50

b. Double overprint 12.00 12.00

N17 A21 20c brn red (Bl) 80.00 125.00

Nos. N11-N17 (7) 228.10 312.10

Reprints of No. N17 have the overprint in bright blue; on the originals it is in dull ultramarine. Nos. N11 and N12 exist with reprinted overprint in red or yellow. There are numerous counterfeits with the overprint in both correct and fancy colors.

Same, with Additional Overprint in Black

1882

N19 A17 1c grn (R) .50 .80

a. Arms inverted 8.25 10.00

b. Arms double 5.50 6.50

c. Horseshoe inverted 12.00 13.50

N20 A19 5c bl (R) .80 .80

a. Arms inverted 13.50 15.00

b. Arms double 13.50 15.00

N21 A22 50c rose (Bk) 1.60 2.00

a. Arms inverted 10.00

N22 A22 50c rose (Bl) 1.60 2.75

N23 A23 1s ultra (R) 3.25 4.50

a. Arms inverted 13.50

b. Horseshoe inverted 16.50

c. Arms and horseshoe inverted 20.00

d. Arms double 13.50

Nos. N19-N23 (5) 7.75 10.85

PROVISIONAL ISSUES

Stamps Issued in Various Cities of Peru during the Chilean Occupation of Lima and Callao

During the Chilean-Peruvian War which took place in 1879 to 1882, the Chilean forces occupied the two largest cities in Peru, Lima & Callao. As these cities were the source of supply of postage stamps, Peruvians in other sections of the country were left without stamps and were forced to the expedient of making provisional issues from whatever material was at hand. Many of these were former canceling devices made over for this purpose. Counterfeits exist of many of the overprinted stamps.

ANCACHS

(See Note under "Provisional Issues")

Regular Issue of Peru, Overprinted in Manuscript in Black

1884 **Unwmk.** ***Perf. 12***

1N1 A19 5c blue 57.50 55.00

Regular Issues of Peru, Overprinted in Black

Overprinted **FRANCA**

1N2 A19 5c blue 18.00 16.50

Overprinted

1N3 A19 5c blue 90.00 82.50

1N4 A20 10c green 55.00 40.00

1N5 A20 10c slate 55.00 35.00

Same, with Additional Overprint "FRANCA"

1N6 A20 10c green 82.50 42.50

Overprinted

1N7 A19 5c blue 30.00 25.00

1N8 A20 10c green 30.00 25.00

Same, with Additional Overprint "FRANCA"

1N9 A20 10c green

A1

Revenue Stamp of Peru, 1878-79, Overprinted in Black "CORREO Y FISCAL" and "FRANCA"

1N10 A1 10c yellow 37.50 37.50

APURIMAC

(See Note under "Provisional Issues")

Provisional Issue of Arequipa Overprinted in Black

ADMON. PRAL. DE
CORREOS DEL DEPTO DE
APURIMAC
=ABANCAY=

Overprint Covers Two Stamps

1885 **Unwmk.** ***Imperf.***

2N1 A6 10c gray 100.00 90.00

Some experts question the status of No. 2N1.

AREQUIPA

(See Note under "Provisional Issues")

Coat of Arms

A1 A2

Overprint ("PROVISIONAL 1881-1882") in Black

1881, Jan. **Unwmk.** ***Imperf.***

3N1 A1 10c blue 2.50 3.50

a. 10c ultramarine 2.50 4.00

b. Double overprint 12.00 13.50

c. Overprinted on back of stamp 8.25 10.00

3N2 A2 25c rose 2.50 6.00

a. "2" in upper left corner invtd. 8.25

b. "Cevtavos" 8.25 10.00

c. Double overprint 12.00 13.50

The overprint also exists on 5s yellow.

The overprints "1883" in large figures or "Habilitado 1883" are fraudulent.

For overprints see Nos. 3N3, 4N1, 8N1, 10N1, 15N1-15N3.

With Additional Overprint Handstamped in Red

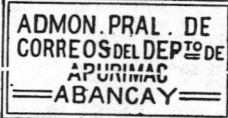

1881, Feb.

3N3 A1 10c blue 3.50 3.50
 a. 10c ultramarine 13.50 8.25

A4

1883 **Litho.**

3N7 A4 10c dull rose 3.50 5.00
 a. 10c vermilion 3.50 5.00

Overprinted in Blue like No. 3N3

3N9 A4 10c vermilion 5.00 4.00
 a. 10c dull rose 5.00 4.00

See No. 3N10. For overprints see Nos. 8N2, 8N9, 10N2, 15N4.

Reprints of No. 3N9 are in different colors from the originals, orange, bright red, etc. They are printed in sheets of 20 instead of 25.

Redrawn

3N10 A4 10c brick red (Bl) 160.00

The redrawn stamp has small triangles without arabesques in the lower spandrels. The palm branch at left of the shield and other parts of the design have been redrawn.

Same Overprint in Black, Violet or Magenta On Regular Issues of Peru

1884 Embossed with Grill ***Perf. 12***

3N11 A17 1c org (Bk, V or M) 6.50 6.50
3N12 A18 2c dk vio (Bk) 6.50 6.50
3N13 A19 5c bl (Bk, V or M) 2.00 1.40
 a. 5c ultramarine (Bk or M) 8.25 6.50
3N15 A20 10c sl (Bk) 3.50 2.50
3N16 A21 20c brn red (Bk, V or M) 25.00 25.00
3N18 A22 50c grn (Bk or V) 25.00 25.00
3N20 A23 1s rose (Bk or V) 35.00 35.00
 Nos. 3N11-3N20 (7) 103.50 101.90

A5

A6

Rear Admiral M. L. Grau
A7

Col. Francisco Bolognesi
A8

Same Overprint as on Previous Issues

1885 ***Imperf.***

3N22 A5 5c olive (Bk) 5.25 5.25
3N23 A6 10c gray (Bk) 5.25 4.75
3N25 A7 5c blue (Bk) 5.25 4.75
3N26 A8 10c olive (Bk) 5.25 3.25
 Nos. 3N22-3N26 (4) 21.00 18.00

For overprints see Nos. 2N1, 8N5-8N6, 8N12-8N13, 10N9, 10N12, 15N10-15N12.

These stamps have been reprinted without overprint; they exist however with forged overprint. Originals are on thicker paper with distinct mesh, reprints on paper without mesh.

Without Overprint

3N22a A5 5c olive 5.25 5.25
3N23a A6 10c gray 4.00 3.25
3N25a A7 5c blue 4.00 3.25
3N26a A8 10c olive 4.00 3.25
 Nos. 3N22a-3N26a (4) 17.25 15.00

AYACUCHO

(See Note under "Provisional Issues")

Provisional Issue of Arequipa Overprinted in Black

1881 **Unwmk.** ***Imperf.***

4N1 A1 10c blue 82.50 70.00
 a. 10c ultramarine 82.50 70.00

CHACHAPOYAS

(See Note under "Provisional Issues")

Regular Issue of Peru Overprinted in Black

1884 **Unwmk.** ***Perf. 12***

5N1 A19 5c ultra 100.00 90.00

CHALA

(See Note under "Provisional Issues")

Regular Issues of Peru Overprinted in Black

1884 **Unwmk.** ***Perf. 12***

6N1 A19 5c blue 8.25 6.50
6N2 A20 10c slate 10.00 8.25

CHICLAYO

(See Note under "Provisional Issues")

Regular Issue of Peru Overprinted in Black

1884 **Unwmk.** ***Perf. 12***

7N1 A19 5c blue 16.50 10.00

Same, Overprinted **FRANCA**

7N2 A19 5c blue 35.00 22.50

CUZCO

(See Note under "Provisional Issues")

Provisional Issues of Arequipa Overprinted in Black

1881-85 **Unwmk.** ***Imperf.***

8N1 A1 10c blue 70.00 60.00
8N2 A4 10c red 70.00 60.00

Overprinted "CUZCO" in an oval of dots

8N5 A5 5c olive 110.00 100.00
8N6 A6 10c gray 80.00 75.00

Regular Issue of Peru Overprinted in Black "CUZCO" in a Circle

Perf. 12

8N7 A19 5c blue 50.00 50.00

Provisional Issues of Arequipa Overprinted in Black

1883 ***Imperf.***

8N9 A4 10c red 10.00 10.00

Same Overprint in Black on Regular Issues of Peru

1884 ***Perf. 12***

8N10 A19 5c blue 16.50 10.00
8N11 A20 10c slate 16.50 10.00

Same Overprint in Black on Provisional Issues of Arequipa

Imperf

8N12 A5 5c olive 27.50 27.50
8N13 A6 10c gray 8.00 8.00

Postage Due Stamps of Peru Surcharged in Black

Perf. 12

8N14 D1 10c on 1c bis 110.00 100.00
8N15 D3 10c on 10c org 110.00 100.00

HUACHO

(See Note under "Provisional Issues")

Regular Issues of Peru Overprinted in Black

1884 **Unwmk.** ***Perf. 12***

9N1 A19 5c blue 8.00 8.00
9N2 A20 10c green 6.00 6.00
9N3 A20 10c slate 16.00 16.00
 Nos. 9N1-9N3 (3) 30.00 30.00

MOQUEGUA

(See Note under "Provisional Issues")

Provisional Issues of Arequipa Overprinted in Violet

Overprint 27mm wide (illustration reduced).

1881-83 **Unwmk.** ***Imperf.***

10N1 A1 10c blue 42.50 40.00
10N2 A4 10c red ('83) 42.50 40.00

Same Overprint on Regular Issues of Peru in Violet

1884 ***Perf. 12***

10N3 A17 1c orange 42.50 40.00
10N4 A19 5c blue 37.50 30.00

Red Overprint

10N5 A19 5c blue 30.00 20.00

Same Overprint in Violet on Provisional Issues of Peru of 1880

Perf. 12

10N6 A17 1c grn (R) 8.25 6.50
10N7 A18 2c rose (Bl) 10.00 10.00
10N8 A19 5c bl (R) 20.00 20.00

Same Overprint in Violet on Provisional Issue of Arequipa

1885 ***Imperf.***

10N9 A6 10c gray 57.50 50.00

Regular Issues of Peru Overprinted in Violet

Perf. 12

10N10 A19 5c blue 110.00 65.00
10N11 A20 10c slate 45.00 25.00

Same Overprint in Violet on Provisional Issue of Arequipa

Imperf

10N12 A6 10c gray 70.00 65.00

PAITA

(See Note under "Provisional Issues")

Regular Issues of Peru Overprinted

Black Overprint

1884 **Unwmk.** ***Perf. 12***

11N1 A19 5c blue 22.50 22.50
 a. 5c ultramarine
11N2 A20 10c green 15.00 15.00
11N3 A20 10c slate 22.50 22.50

Red Overprint

11N4 A19 5c blue 22.50 22.50

Overprint lacks ornaments on #11N4-11N5.

Violet Overprint. Letters 5½mm High

11N5 A19 5c ultra 22.50 22.50
 a. 5c blue

PASCO

(See Note under "Provisional Issues")

Regular Issues of Peru Overprinted in Magenta or Black

1884 **Unwmk.** ***Perf. 12***

12N1 A19 5c blue (M) 16.00 12.50
 a. 5c ultramarine (M) 22.50 22.50
12N2 A20 10c green (Bk) 35.00 30.00
12N3 A20 10c slate (Bk) 65.00 57.50
 Nos. 12N1-12N3 (3) 116.00 100.00

PISCO

(See Note under "Provisional Issues")

Regular Issue of Peru Overprinted in Black

1884 **Unwmk.** ***Perf. 12***

13N1 A19 5c blue 190.00 160.00

PIURA

(See Note under "Provisional Issues")

Regular Issues of Peru Overprinted in Black

1884 Unwmk. *Perf. 12*

14N1	A19	5c blue	20.00	10.00
a.		5c ultramarine	25.00	13.50
14N2	A21	20c brn red	82.50	82.50
14N3	A22	50c green	200.00	200.00

Same Overprint in Black on Provisional Issues of Peru of 1881

14N4	A17	1c grn (R)	22.50	22.50
14N5	A18	2c rose (Bl)	40.00	40.00
14N6	A19	5c ultra (R)	50.00	50.00

Regular Issues of Peru Overprinted in Violet, Black or Blue

14N7	A19	5c bl (V)	16.00	10.00
a.		5c ultramarine (V)	16.00	10.00
b.		5c ultramarine (Bk)	16.00	10.00
14N8	A21	20c brn red (Bk)	82.50	82.50
14N9	A21	20c brn red (Bl)	82.50	82.50

Same Overprint in Black on Provisional Issues of Peru of 1881

14N10	A17	1c grn (R)	20.00	20.00
14N11	A19	5c bl (R)	22.50	22.50
a.		5c ultramarine (R)	40.00	40.00

Regular Issues of Peru Overprinted in Black

14N13	A19	5c blue	4.00	3.50
14N14	A21	20c brn red	82.50	82.50

Regular Issues of Peru Overprinted in Black

14N15	A19	5c ultra	70.00	65.00
14N16	A21	20c brn red	140.00	125.00

Same Overprint on Postage Due Stamp of Peru

14N18	D3	10c orange	80.00	67.50

PUNO

(See Note under "Provisional Issues")

Provisional Issue of Arequipa Overprinted in Violet or Blue

Diameter of outer circle 20½mm, PUNO 11½mm wide, M 3½mm wide.

Other types of this overprint are fraudulent.

1882-83 Unwmk. *Imperf.*

15N1	A1	10c blue (V)	16.00	16.00
a.		10c ultramarine (V)	20.00	20.00
15N3	A2	25c red (V)	25.00	20.00
15N4	A4	10c dl rose (Bl)	25.00	25.00
a.		10c vermilion (Bl)	25.00	25.00

The overprint also exists on 5s yellow of Arequipa.

Same Overprint in Magenta on Regular Issues of Peru

1884 *Perf. 12*

15N5	A17	1c orange	12.00	12.00
15N6	A18	2c violet	35.00	35.00
15N7	A19	5c blue	8.25	8.25

Violet Overprint

15N8	A19	5c blue	8.25	8.25
a.		5c ultramarine	12.00	12.00

Same Overprint in Black on Provisional Issues of Arequipa

1885 *Imperf.*

15N10	A5	5c olive	16.00	13.50
15N11	A6	10c gray	5.50	5.50
15N12	A8	10c olive	10.00	10.00

Regular Issues of Peru Overprinted in Magenta

1884 *Perf. 12*

15N13	A17	1c orange	10.00	8.25
15N14	A18	2c violet	13.50	12.00
15N15	A19	5c blue	5.50	5.50
a.		5c ultramarine	11.00	11.00
15N16	A20	10c green		
15N17	A21	20c brn red	82.50	82.50
15N18	A22	50c green		

YCA

(See Note under "Provisional Issues")

Regular Issues of Peru Overprinted in Violet

1884 Unwmk. *Perf. 12*

16N1	A17	1c orange	40.00	40.00
16N3	A19	5c blue	12.00	6.75

Black Overprint

16N5	A19	5c blue	10.00	5.25

Magenta Overprint

16N6	A19	5c blue	10.00	5.25
16N7	A20	10c slate	30.00	30.00

Regular Issues of Peru Overprinted in Black

16N12	A19	5c blue	150.00	140.00
16N13	A21	20c brown	190.00	160.00

Regular Issues of Peru Overprinted in Carmine

16N14	A19	5c blue	150.00	140.00
16N15	A20	10c slate	190.00	160.00

Same, with Additional Overprint

16N21	A19	5c blue	160.00	150.00
16N22	A21	20c brn red	250.00	225.00

Various other stamps exist with the overprints "YCA" and "YCA VAPOR" but they are not known to have been issued. Some of them were made to fill a dealer's order and others are reprints or merely cancellations.

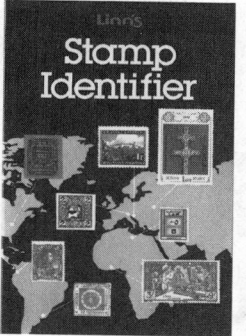

PHILIPPINES

ˌfi-lə-ˈpēnz

LOCATION — Group of about 7,100 islands and islets in the Malay Archipelago, north of Borneo, in the North Pacific Ocean
GOVT. — Republic
AREA — 115,830 sq. mi.
POP. — 68,614,536 (1995)
CAPITAL — Manila

The islands were ceded to the United States by Spain in 1898. On November 15, 1935, they were given their independence, subject to a transition period which ended July 4, 1946. On that date the Commonwealth became the Republic of the Philippines.

20 Cuartos = 1 Real
100 Centavos de Peso = 1 Peso (1864)
100 Centimos de Escudo = 1 Escudo (1871)
100 Centimos de Peseta = 1 Peseta (1872)
1000 Milesimas de Peso = 100 Centimos or Centavos = 1 Peso (1878)
100 Cents = 1 Dollar (1899)
100 Centavos = 1 Peso (1906)
100 Centavos (Sentimos) = 1 Peso (Piso) (1946)

Catalogue values for unused stamps in this country are for Never Hinged items, beginning with Scott 500 in the regular postage section, Scott B1 in the semi-postal section, Scott C64 in the air post section, Scott E11 in the special delivery section, Scott J23 in the postage due section, and Scott O50 in the officials section.

Watermarks

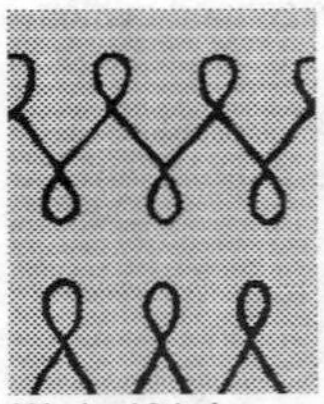
Wmk. 104- Loops

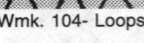

Wmk. 257- Curved Wavy Lines

Watermark 104: loops from different watermark rows may or may not be directly opposite each other.

Wmk. 190PI- Single-lined PIPS

Wmk. 191PI- Double-lined PIPS

Watermark 191 has double-lined USPS.

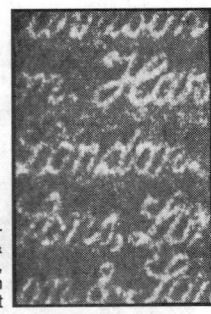

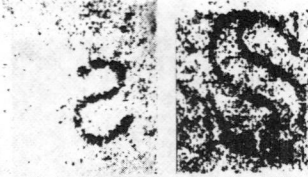
Wmk. 233- "Harrison & Sons, London." in Script

Wmk. 372- "K" and "P" Multiple

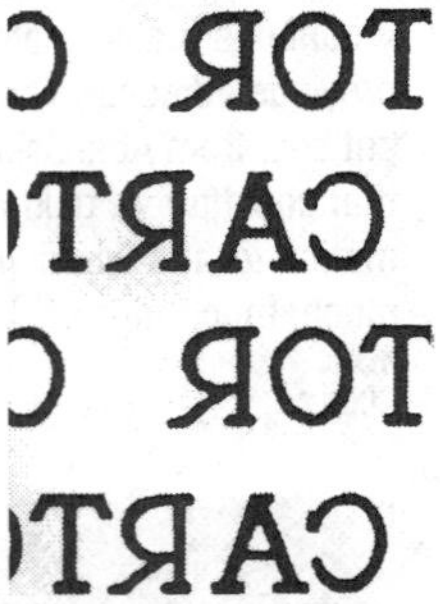
Wmk. 385

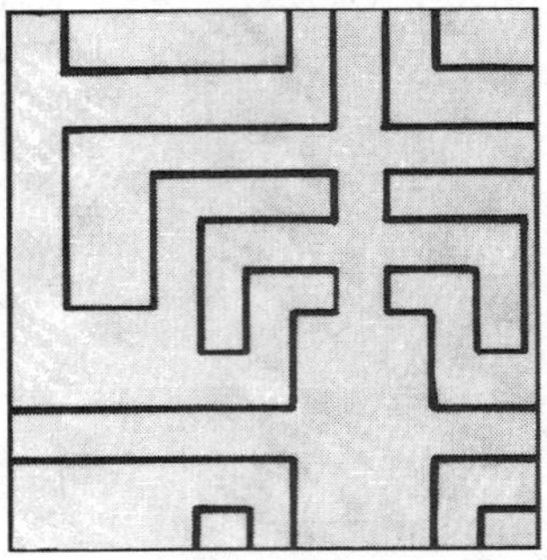
Wmk. 389

Wmk. 391- Natl. Crest, Rising Sun and Eagle, with inscr. "REPUBLIKA / NG / PILIPINAS," "KAWANIHAN / NG / KOREO"

Issued under Spanish Dominion

The stamps of Philippine Islands punched with a round hole were used on telegraph receipts or had been withdrawn from use and punched to indicate that they were no longer available for postage. In this condition they sell for less, as compared to postally used copies.

Queen Isabella II
A1 A2

1854 Unwmk. Engr. *Imperf.*

1	A1	5c orange	1,500.	225.
a.		5c brown orange	1,650.	275.
2	A1	10c carmine	400.	160.
a.		10c pale rose	625.	250.
4	A2	1r blue	450.	190.
a.		1r slate blue	600.	200.
b.		1r ultramarine	575.	200.
c.		"CORROS," (pos. 26)	*2,750.*	*1,000.*
5	A2	2r green	675.	125.
a.		2r yellow green	600.	300.

Forty varieties of each value.
The 10c black was never issued.
For overprints see Nos. 25-25A.

A3

1855 Litho.

6	A3	5c red	1,150.	325.

Four varieties.

Redrawn

7	A3	5c vermilion	*6,500.*	*750.*

In the redrawn stamp the inner circle is smaller and is not broken by the labels at top and bottom. Only one variety.
The 10c black was not issued. Value, $1,000.

Queen Isabella II — A4

1856 Typo. Wmk. 104

8	A4	1r gray green	40.00	75.00
9	A4	2r carmine	200.00	100.00

Nos. 8 and 9 can be distinguished from Cuba Nos. 2 and 3 only by the cancellations.
For overprints, see Nos. 26-27.

Queen Isabella II — A5

1859, Jan. 1 Litho. Unwmk.

10	A5	5c vermilion	10.00	5.00
a.		5c scarlet	14.00	7.00
b.		5c orange	21.00	10.00
11	A5	10c rose	10.00	*11.50*

Four varieties of each value.
For overprint see No. 28.

Dot after CORREOS
A6 A7

1861-62

12	A6	5c vermilion	25.00	8.50
13	A7	5c dull red ('62)	95.00	37.50

For overprint see No. 29.

Colon after CORREOS — A8

A8a

A9

A10

1863

14	A8	5c vermilion	8.50	6.50
15	A8	10c carmine	25.00	*27.50*
16	A8	1r violet	475.00	300.00
17	A8	2r blue	375.00	250.00
18	A8a	1r gray grn	200.00	95.00
20	A9	1r emerald	100.00	35.00
a.		1r green	110.00	37.50
		Nos. 14-20 (6)	1,183.	714.00

No. 18 has "CORREOS" 10½mm long, the point of the bust is rounded and is about 1mm from the circle which contains 94 pearls.
No. 20 has "CORREOS" 11mm long, and the bust ends in a sharp point which nearly touches the circle of 76 pearls.
For overprints see Nos. 30-34.

1864 Typo.

21	A10	3⅛c blk, *yel*	2.50	1.25
22	A10	6⅝c grn, *rose*	4.50	1.25
23	A10	12⅘c blue, *sal*	4.75	.75
24	A10	25c red, *buff*	6.50	2.50
		Nos. 21-24 (4)	18.25	5.75

For overprints see Nos. 35-38.

Cuba Nos. 2-3 and Preceding Issues Handstamped

HABILITADO
POR LA
NACION

1868-74

25	A2	1r sl bl ('74)	*1,700.*	*725.00*
b.		"CORROS," (pos. 26)		*2,750.*
25A	A2	2r grn ('74)	*3,250.*	*700.00*
26	A1	1r grn, *bl* ('73)	140.00	60.00
27	A1	2r car, *bl* ('73)	250.00	110.00
28	A5	10c rose ('74)	50.00	35.00
29	A7	5c dull red ('73)	100.00	65.00
30	A8	5c ver ('72)	85.00	25.00
31	A8	1r vio ('72)	400.00	325.00
32	A8	2r bl ('72)	400.00	225.00
33	A8a	1r gray grn ('71)	125.00	35.00
34	A9	1r emer ('71)	35.00	15.00
a.		1r green	40.00	20.00
35	A10	3⅛c blk, *yellow*	7.50	3.50
36	A10	6⅝c grn, *rose*	7.50	3.50
37	A10	12⅘c bl, *salmon*	25.00	12.50
38	A10	25c red, *buff*	22.50	8.00

Illustration for #26-27 (Cuba A1) follows #7.

Imperforates

Imperforates of designs A11-A14 probably are from proof or trial sheets.

"Spain"
A11

King Amadeo
A12

1871 Typo. *Perf. 14*

39	A11	5c blue	40.00	4.50
40	A11	10c deep green	5.50	3.75
41	A11	20c brown	47.50	25.00
42	A11	40c rose	60.00	30.00
		Nos. 39-42 (4)	153.00	63.25

1872

43	A12	12c rose	9.00	3.25
44	A12	16c blue	100.00	24.00
45	A12	25c gray lilac	7.00	3.25
46	A12	62c violet	21.00	6.00
47	A12	1p25c yellow brn	40.00	19.00
		Nos. 43-47 (5)	177.00	55.50

The 12c is known in dark blue, the 16c in ultramarine and the 16c in lilac. They were not regularly issued. Values, unused: $15, $110, $10, respectively.

"Peace"
A13

King Alfonso XII
A14

1874

48	A13	12c gray lilac	11.00	3.00
49	A13	25c ultra	3.75	1.50
50	A13	62c rose	32.50	3.00
51	A13	1p25c brown	160.00	47.50
		Nos. 48-51 (4)	207.25	55.00

1875-77

52	A14	2c rose	1.60	.45
53	A14	2c dk blue ('77)	150.00	62.50
54	A14	6c orange ('77)	7.75	*10.00*
55	A14	10c blue ('77)	2.75	.50
56	A14	12c lilac ('76	2.75	.50
57	A14	20c vio brn ('76	10.00	7.00
58	A14	25c dp green ('76	7.75	1.25
		Nos. 52-58 (7)	182.60	82.20

Nos. 52, 63 Handstamp Surcharged in Black or Blue

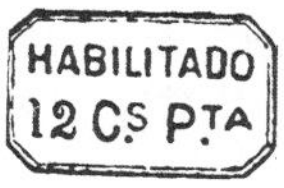

1877-79

59	A14	12c on 2c rose (Bk)	62.50	21.00
60	A16	12c on 25m blk (Bk) ('79)	62.50	21.00
61	A16	12c on 25m blk (Bl) ('79)	200.00	150.00
		Nos. 59-61 (3)	325.00	192.00

Surcharge exists inverted on Nos. 59-60, value for both, unused $1,200. Surcharge exists double on No. 59, value, unused $375.

A16

1878-79 **Typo.**

62	A16	0.0625 (62½m) gray	42.50	12.00
63	A16	25m black	2.10	.30
64	A16	25m green ('79)	45.00	*50.00*
65	A16	50m dull lilac	22.50	8.00
66	A16	100m car ('79)	72.50	30.00
67	A16	100m yel grn ('79)	6.75	2.00
68	A16	125m blue	3.75	.35
69	A16	200m rose ('79)	24.00	4.50
70	A16	200m vio rose ('79)	210.00	*500.00*
71	A16	250m bister ('79)	8.50	2.00
		Nos. 62-71 (10)	437.60	*609.15*

Imperforates of type A16 probably are from proof or trial sheets.

For surcharges see Nos. 60-61, 72-75.

Stamps of 1878-79 Surcharged:

a

b

1879

72	A16 (a)	2c on 25m grn	32.50	7.00
b.		Inverted surcharge	225.00	150.00
73	A16 (a)	8c on 100m car	27.50	5.50
a.		"COREROS"	82.50	50.00
74	A16 (b)	2c on 25m grn	125.00	35.00
75	A16 (b)	8c on 100m car	125.00	35.00
		Nos. 72-75 (4)	310.00	82.50

A19

Original state: The medallion is surrounded by a heavy line of color of nearly even thickness, touching the line below "Filipinas"; the opening in the hair above the temple is narrow and pointed.

1st retouch: The line around the medallion is thin, except at the upper right, and does not touch the horizontal line above it; the opening in the hair is slightly wider and rounded; the lock of hair above the forehead is shaped like a broad "V" and ends in a point; there is a faint white line below it, which is not found on the original. The shape of the hair and the width of the white line vary.

2nd retouch: The lock of hair is less pointed; the white line is much broader.

1880-88 **Typo.**

76	A19	2c carmine	.60	*.50*
77	A19	2½c brown	5.75	1.25
78	A19	2 4/8c ultra ('82)	.80	*1.50*
79	A19	2 4/8c ultra, 1st retouch ('83)	.60	*1.25*
80	A19	2 4/8c ultra, 2nd retouch ('86)	7.50	3.00
81	A19	5c gray ('82)	.60	1.25
a.		5c gray blue	1.00	*1.50*
82	A19	6 2/8c dp grn ('82)	4.75	*7.00*
83	A19	8c yellow brn	25.00	4.50
84	A19	10c green ('88)	250.00	250.00
85	A19	10c brn lil ('82)	2.50	*3.00*
a.		10c brown violet	10.00	5.00
86	A19	12 4/8c brt rose ('82)	1.25	1.25
87	A19	20c bis brn ('82)	2.50	1.25
88	A19	25c dk brn ('82)	3.25	1.25
		Nos. 76-83,85-88 (12)	55.10	27.00

See #137-139. For surcharges see #89-108, 110-111.

Surcharges exist double or inverted on many of Nos. 89-136.

Stamps and Type of 1880-86 Handstamp Surcharged in Black, Green, Yellow or Red:

c

d

e

f

1881-88

Design A19

Black Surcharge

89	(c)	2c on 2½c brn	3.00	1.75
91	(f)	10c on 2 4/8c ultra (#80) ('87)	4.50	1.40
92	(d)	20c on 8c brn ('83)	6.75	2.25
93	(d)	1r on 2c car ('83)	125.00	*200.00*
94	(d)	2r on 2 4/8c ultra (#78; '83)	4.50	1.50
a.		On No. 79	40.00	*50.00*
b.		On No. 80	15.00	*25.00*

Most used copies of No. 93 are hole puched. Postally used copies are rare.

Green or Yellow (#98A) Surcharge

95	(e)	8c on 2c car ('83)	5.00	1.60
95A	(d+e)	8c on 1r on 2c car ('83)	80.00	150.00
96	(d)	10c on 2c car ('83)	3.75	1.60
97	(d)	1r on 2c car ('83)	95.00	30.00
98	(d)	1r on 5c gray bl ('83)	4.50	2.25
98A	(d)	1r on 5c gray ('83)	80.00	150.00
99	(d)	1r on 8c brn ('83)	6.75	2.25

Red Surcharge

100	(f)	1c on 2 4/8c ultra (#79; '87)	.75	.60
101	(f)	1c on 2 4/8c ultra (#80; '87)	2.50	1.25
102	(d)	16c on 2 4/8c ultra (#78; '83)	6.75	2.25
103	(d)	1r on 2c car ('83)	4.50	2.25
104	(d)	1r on 5c bl gray ('83)	12.50	3.75

Handstamp Surcharged in Magenta

g

h

1887

105	A19 (g)	8c on 2 4/8c (#79)	.75	.45
106	A19 (g)	8c on 2 4/8c (#80)	3.00	2.00

1888

107	A19 (h)	2 4/8c on 1c gray grn	1.25	.75
108	A19 (h)	2 4/8c on 5c bl gray	1.50	.70
109	N1 (h)	2 4/8c on 1/8c grn	1.50	1.00
110	A19 (h)	2 4/8c on 50m bis	1.40	.65
111	A19 (h)	2 4/8c on 10c grn	1.25	.50
		Nos. 107-111 (5)	6.90	3.60

No. 109 is surcharged on a newspaper stamp of 1886-89 and has the inscriptions shown on cut N1.

On Revenue Stamps

Handstamp Surcharged or Overprinted in Black, Yellow, Green, Red, Blue or Magenta:

j

k

m

1881-88

Black Surcharge

112	R1 (c)	2c on 10c bis	35.00	9.00
113	R1 (j)	2 4/8c on 10c bis	2.25	.75
114	R1 (j)	2 4/8c on 2r bl	150.00	67.50
115	R1 (j)	8c on 10c bis	*300.00*	*200.00*
116	R1 (j)	8c on 2r bl	5.75	1.50
118	R1 (d)	1r on 12 4/8c gray bl ('83)	5.50	2.75
119	R1 (d)	1r on 10c bis ('82)	8.50	3.00

Yellow Surcharge

120	R2 (e)	2c on 200m grn ('82)	4.50	2.00
121	R1 (d)	16c on 2r bl ('83)	3.75	1.90

Green Surcharge

122	R1 (d)	1r on 10c bis ('83)	8.00	2.75

Red Surcharge

123	R1(d+e)	2r on 8c on 2r blue	30.00	15.00
a.		On 8c on 2r blue (d+d)	50.00	50.00
124	R1(d)	1r on 12 4/8c gray bl ('83)	11.00	10.00
125	R1(k)	6 2/8c on 12 4/8c gray bl ('85)	4.50	*10.00*
126	R3(d)	1r on 10p bis ('83)	70.00	19.00
127	R1(m)	1r green	225.00	*350.00*
127A	R1(m)	2r blue	425.00	*600.00*
127B	R1(d)	1r on 1r green	300.00	350.00
128	R2(d)	1r on 1p grn ('83)	25.00	12.00
129	R2(d)	1r on 200m grn ('83)	60.00	*70.00*
129A	R1(d)	2r on 2r blue	*200.00*	*400.00*

The surcharge on No. 129A is pale red.

Blue Surcharge

129B	R1(m)	10c bis ('81)	*250.00*	—

Magenta Surcharge

130	R2(h)	2 4/8c on 200m grn ('88)	3.00	1.25
131	R2(h)	2 4/8c on 20c brn ('88)	9.00	4.50

On Telegraph Stamps

T1

T2

Surcharged in Red, or Black

1883-88

132	T1 (d)	2r on 250m ultra (R)	6.00	3.00
133	T1 (d)	20c on 250m ultra	*55.00*	30.00
134	T1 (d)	2r on 250m ultra	7.50	3.75
135	T1 (d)	1r on 20c on 250m ultra (R & Bk)	6.75	3.75

Magenta Surcharge

136	T2 (h)	2 4/8c on 1c bis ('88)	.70	.50

Most, if not all, copies of No. 133 are hole-punched. Values are for examples with hole punches.

Type of 1880-86 Redrawn

1887-89

137	A19	50m bister	.50	*5.00*
138	A19	1c gray green ('88)	.50	*4.00*
a.		yellow green ('89)	.55	*5.00*
139	A19	6c yellow brn ('88)	8.00	*40.00*
		Nos. 137-139 (3)	9.00	*49.00*

King Alfonso XIII — A36

1890-97 **Typo.**

140	A36	1c violet ('92)	.50	*1.75*
141	A36	1c rose ('95)	12.50	10.00
142	A36	1c blue grn ('96)	1.75	*3.00*
143	A36	1c claret ('97)	10.00	*24.00*
144	A36	2c claret	.20	.20
145	A36	2c violet ('92)	.20	.20
146	A36	2c dk brown ('94)	.20	*1.75*
147	A36	2c ultra ('96)	.25	.25
148	A36	2c gray brn ('96)	.60	*1.75*
149	A36	2 4/8c dull blue	.35	.20
150	A36	2 4/8c ol gray ('92)	.20	*1.00*
151	A36	5c dark blue	.35	*1.00*
152	A36	5c dk ol gray	.60	*1.00*
152A	A36	5c violet black	—	—
153	A36	5c green ('92)	.50	.45
155	A36	5c violet brn ('96)	7.00	*10.00*
156	A36	5c blue grn ('96)	4.50	*6.00*
157	A36	6c brown vio ('92)	.20	*1.00*
158	A36	6c red orange ('94)	1.25	1.75
159	A36	6c car rose ('96)	4.50	*6.00*
160	A36	8c yellow grn	.20	.20
161	A36	8c ultra ('92)	.50	.20
162	A36	8c red brown ('94)	.60	.20
163	A36	10c blue grn	1.25	.20
164	A36	10c pale claret ('91)	1.00	.30
165	A36	10c claret ('92)	.50	.20
166	A36	10c yel brn ('96)	.60	.20
167	A36	12 4/8c yellow grn	.20	*1.00*
168	A36	12 4/8c org ('92)	.60	*1.00*
169	A36	15c red brn ('92)	.60	.20
170	A36	15c rose ('94)	1.50	.65
171	A36	15c bl grn ('96)	1.60	1.60
172	A36	20c rose	52.50	27.50
173	A36	20c sal ('91)	8.00	4.00
174	A36	20c gray brn ('92)	3.25	*8.75*
175	A36	20c dk vio ('94)	12.50	*15.00*
176	A36	20c org ('96)	3.50	1.75
177	A36	25c brown	7.00	1.40
178	A36	25c dull bl ('91)	1.60	*3.00*

179 A36 40c dk vio ('97) 17.50 *35.00*
180 A36 80c claret ('97) 25.00 *40.00*
Nos. 140-180 (40) 185.65 *213.65*

The 5c lilac is a perforated proof. Many of Nos. 140-180 exist imperf.
The existence of No. 152A has been questioned.

Stamps of Previous Issues Handstamp Surcharged in Blue, Red, Black or Violet

1897

Blue Surcharge

181 A36 5c on 5c green 3.00 2.00
182 A36 15c on 15c red brn 4.25 1.40
183 A36 20c on 20c gray brn 9.00 *10.00*

Red Surcharge

185 A36 5c on 5c green 3.50 4.00

Black Surcharge

187 A36 5c on 5c green 30.00 *150.00*
188 A36 15c on 15c rose 4.25 1.40
189 A36 20c on 20c dk vio 27.50 15.00
190 A36 20c on 25c brown 18.00 *20.00*

Violet Surcharge

191 A36 15c on 15c rose 8.00 5.75
Nos. 181-191 (9) 107.50 209.55

Inverted, double and other variations of this surcharge exist.
The 5c on 5c blue gray was released during US Administration. The surcharge is a mixture of red and black inks.
Impressions in violet black are believed to be reprints. The following varieties are known: 5c on 5c blue green, 15c on 15c rose, 15c on 15c red brown, 20c on 20c gray brown, 20c on 20c dark violet, 20c on 25c brown. These surcharges are to be found double, inverted, etc.

King Alfonso XIII — A39

1898 **Typo.**

192 A39 1m orange brown .20 .20
193 A39 2m orange brown .20 *1.00*
194 A39 3m orange brown .20 *1.00*
195 A39 4m orange brown 6.00 *25.00*
196 A39 5m orange brown .20 .20
197 A39 1c black violet .20 .20
198 A39 2c dk bl grn .20 .20
199 A39 3c dk brown .20 .20
200 A39 4c orange 11.50 *30.00*
201 A39 5c car rose .20 .20
202 A39 6c dk blue .75 *1.00*
203 A39 8c gray brown .35 .20
204 A39 10c vermilion 1.25 .75
205 A39 15c dull ol grn 1.25 .60
206 A39 20c maroon 1.40 .90
207 A39 40c violet .75 *1.00*
208 A39 60c black 3.00 2.25
209 A39 80c red brown 7.00 2.25
210 A39 1p yellow green 9.50 9.00
211 A39 2p slate blue 21.00 11.50
Nos. 192-211 (20) 65.35 *87.65*

Nos. 192-211 exist imperf. Value $650.

The Spanish surrendered in May 1898. Some Filipinos continued to fight until 1901. During this period provisional stamps were created in several areas. Some of these stamps may have been totally philatelic. See the Scott Specialized Catalogue of U. S. Stamps for stamps issued by Gen. Aguinaldo's Filipino Revolutionary Government.

Issued under US Administration

Regular Issues of the United States Overprinted in Black

On US No. 260

1899-1900 **Unwmk.** ***Perf. 12***

212 A96 50c orange 400.00 250.00

On US Nos. 279, 279d, 267, 268, 281, 282C, 283, 284, 275 and 275a

Wmk. 191

213 A87 1c yellow grn 3.00 .60
a. Inverted overprint *13,500.*
214 A88 2c red, IV 1.25 .60
a. 2c org red, type IV ('01) 1.25 .60
b. Booklet pane, 6 #214 ('00) 250.00 200.00
c. 2c reddish car, type IV 1.90 .90
d. 2c rose car, type IV 2.25 1.10
215 A89 3c purple 5.75 1.25
216 A91 5c blue 5.50 .90
a. Inverted overprint *3,750.*
217 A94 10c brown, I 17.50 4.00
217A A94 10c org brn, II 160.00 27.50
218 A95 15c olive grn 32.50 8.00
219 A96 50c orange 125.00 37.50
a. 50c red orange *260.00*
Nos. 213-219 (8) 350.50 80.35

No. 216a is valued in the grade of fine.

On US Nos. 280b, 282 and 272

1901

220 A90 4c orange brn 22.50 5.00
221 A92 6c lake 29.00 7.00
222 A93 8c violet brn 29.00 7.50
Nos. 220-222 (3) 80.50 19.50

On US Nos. 276, 276A, 277a and 278

Red Overprint

223 A97 $1 blk, type I 425. 275.
223A A97 $1 blk, type II 2,250. 750.
224 A98 $2 dk blue 450. 350.
225 A99 $5 dk green 800. *900.*

On US Nos. 300-313 and shades

1903-04

226 A115 1c blue green 4.00 .30
227 A116 2c carmine 7.50 1.10
228 A117 3c brt violet 67.50 12.50
229 A118 4c brown ('04) 75.00 22.50
a. 4c orange brown 75.00 20.00
230 A119 5c blue 11.00 1.00
231 A120 6c brnsh lake ('04) 80.00 22.50
232 A121 8c vio blk ('04) 45.00 15.00
233 A122 10c pale red brn ('04) 20.00 2.25
a. 10c red brown 25.00 3.00
b. Pair, one without ovpt. *1,500.*
234 A123 13c purple blk 32.50 17.50
a. 13c brown violet 32.50 17.50
235 A124 15c olive grn 60.00 15.00
236 A125 50c orange 125.00 35.00
Nos. 226-236 (11) 527.50 144.65

Red Overprint

237 A126 $1 black 450. 275.
238 A127 $2 dk blue ('04) 750. 850.
239 A128 $5 dk green ('04) 950. 1,000.

On US Nos. 319, 319c in Black

1904

240 A129 2c carmine 5.50 2.25
a. Booklet pane of 6 *1,100.*
b. 2c scarlet 6.25 2.75
c. As "b," booklet pane of 6

José Rizal A40

Arms of Manila A41

4c, McKinley. 6c, Magellan. 8c, Miguel Lopez de Legaspi. 10c, Gen. Henry W. Lawton. 12c, Lincoln. 16c, Adm. William T. Sampson. 20c, Washington. 26c, Francisco Carriedo. 30c, Franklin.

Each Inscribed "Philippine Islands / United States of America"

1906, Sept. 8 **Engr.** **Wmk. 191PI**

241 A40 2c dp green .25 .20
a. 2c yellow green ('10) .40 .20
b. Booklet pane of 6 475.00
242 A40 4c carmine .30 .20
a. 4c carmine lake ('10) .60 .20
b. Booklet pane of 6 650.00
243 A40 6c violet 1.25 .20
244 A40 8c brown 2.50 .70
245 A40 10c blue 1.75 .20
a. 10c dark blue 1.75 .20
246 A40 12c brown lake 5.00 2.00
247 A40 16c violet blk 3.75 .20
248 A40 20c orange brn 4.00 .30
249 A40 26c violet brn 6.00 2.25
250 A40 30c olive grn 4.75 1.50
251 A41 1p orange 27.50 7.00
252 A41 2p black 35.00 1.25
253 A41 4p dk blue 100.00 15.00
254 A41 10p dk green 225.00 70.00
Nos. 241-254 (14) 417.05 101.00

See Nos. 255-304, 326-353. For surcharges see Nos. 368-369, 450. For overprints see Nos. C1-C28, C36-C46, C54-C57, O5-O14.

Change of Colors

1909-13 ***Perf. 12***

255 A40 12c red orange 8.50 2.50
256 A40 16c olive green 3.50 .75
257 A40 20c yellow 7.50 1.25
258 A40 26c blue green 1.75 .75
259 A40 30c ultra 10.00 3.25
260 A41 1p pale violet 30.00 5.00
260A A41 2p vio brn ('13) 85.00 2.75
Nos. 255-260A (7) 146.25 16.25

1911 **Wmk. 190PI** ***Perf. 12***

261 A40 2c green .65 .20
a. Booklet pane of 6 550.00
262 A40 4c car lake 2.50 .20
a. 4c carmine — —
b. Booklet pane of 6 600.00
263 A40 6c dp violet 2.00 .20
264 A40 8c brown 8.50 .45
265 A40 10c blue 3.25 .20
266 A40 12c orange 2.50 .45
267 A40 16c olive grn 2.50 .20
a. 16c pale olive green 2.50 .20
268 A40 20c yellow 2.00 .20
a. 20c orange 2.00 .20
269 A40 26c blue green 3.00 .20
270 A40 30c ultra 3.50 .40
271 A41 1p pale violet 22.50 .55
272 A41 2p violet brn 27.50 .75
273 A41 4p dp blue 625.00 80.00
274 A41 10p dp green 225.00 25.00
Nos. 261-274 (14) 930.40 109.00

1914

275 A40 30c gray 10.00 .40

1914-23 ***Perf. 10***

276 A40 2c green 1.75 .20
a. Booklet pane of 6 *450.00*
277 A40 4c carmine 1.75 .20
a. Booklet pane of 6 *450.00*
278 A40 6c lt violet 37.50 9.00
a. 6c deep violet 42.50 6.00
279 A40 8c brown 40.00 10.00
280 A40 10c dk blue 25.00 .20
281 A40 16c olive grn 75.00 4.50
282 A40 20c orange 22.50 .85
283 A40 30c gray 55.00 2.75
284 A41 1p pale vio 110.00 3.00
Nos. 276-284 (9) 368.50 30.70

1918-26 ***Perf. 11***

285 A40 2c green 20.00 4.25
a. Booklet pane of 6 *750.00*
286 A40 4c carmine 25.00 2.50
a. Booklet pane of 6 *1,350.*
287 A40 6c dp violet 35.00 1.75
287A A40 8c lt brown 200.00 25.00
288 A40 10c dk blue 52.50 1.50
289 A40 16c olive grn 90.00 6.75
289A A40 20c orange 60.00 7.50
289C A40 30c gray 55.00 12.50
289D A41 1p pale violet 70.00 14.00
Nos. 285-289D (9) 607.50 75.75

1917-25 **Unwmk.** ***Perf. 11***

290 A40 2c yellow grn .20 .20
a. 2c dark green .20 .20
b. Vert. pair, imperf. horiz. *1,500.*
c. Horiz. pair, imperf. btwn. *1,500.* —
d. Vert. pair, imperf. btwn. *1,750.*
e. Booklet pane of 6 *27.50*
291 A40 4c carmine .20 .20
a. 4c light rose .20 .20
b. Booklet pane of 6 17.50 —
292 A40 6c deep violet .30 .20
a. 6c lilac .35 .20
b. 6c red violet .35 .20
c. Booklet pane of 6 *550.00* —
293 A40 8c yellow brown .20 .20
a. 8c orange brown .20 .20
294 A40 10c deep blue .20 .20
295 A40 12c red orange .30 .20
296 A40 16c lt ol grn 55.00 .25
a. 16c olive bister 55.00 .40
297 A40 20c orange yel .30 .20
298 A40 26c green .45 .45
a. 26c blue green .55 .25
299 A40 30c gray .55 .20
300 A41 1p pale violet 27.50 1.00
a. 1p red lilac 27.50 1.00
b. 1p pale rose lilac 27.50 1.10
301 A41 2p violet brn 25.00 .75
302 A41 4p blue 22.50 .45
a. 4p dark blue 22.50 .45
Nos. 290-302 (13) 132.70 4.50

1923-26

Design: 16c, Adm. George Dewey.

303 A40 16c olive bister .90 .20
a. 16c olive green 1.25 .20
304 A41 10p deep green ('26) 45.00 5.00

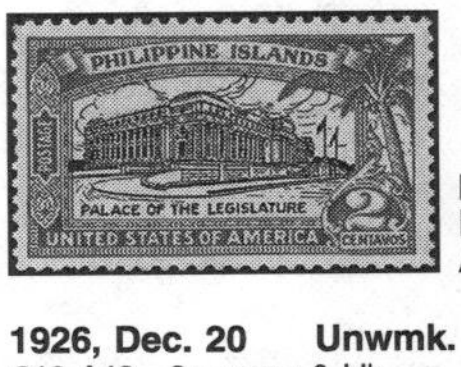

Legislative Palace A42

1926, Dec. 20 **Unwmk.** ***Perf. 12***

319 A42 2c green & blk .40 .25
a. Horiz. pair, imperf. btwn. *300.00*
b. Vert. pair, imperf. btwn. *550.00*
320 A42 4c carmine & blk .40 .35
a. Horiz. pair, imperf. btwn. *300.00*
b. Vert. pair, imperf. btwn. *575.00*
321 A42 16c ol grn & blk .75 .65
a. Horiz. pair, imperf. btwn. *350.00*
b. Vert. pair, imperf. btwn. *625.00*
c. Double impression of center *675.00*
322 A42 18c lt brown & blk .85 .50
a. Double impression of center *700.00*
b. Vert. pair, imperf. btwn. *675.00*
323 A42 20c orange & blk 1.25 .80
a. 20c orange & brown *600.00* —
b. Imperf., pair *575.00* *575.00*
c. As "a," imperf., pair *950.00*
d. Vert. pair, imperf. btwn. *675.00*
324 A42 24c gray & blk .85 .55
a. Vert. pair, imperf. btwn. *675.00*
325 A42 1p rose lil & blk 45.00 30.00
a. Vert. pair, imperf. btwn. *675.00*
Nos. 319-325 (7) 49.50 33.10

Opening of the Legislative Palace.
For overprints see Nos. O1-O4.

Coil Stamp

Rizal Type of 1906

1928 ***Perf. 11 Vertically***

326 A40 2c green 7.50 *15.00*

Types of 1906-23

1925-31 **Unwmk.** ***Imperf.***

340 A40 2c yel grn ('31) .20 .20
a. 2c green ('25) .25 .20
341 A40 4c car rose ('31) .20 .20
a. 4c carmine ('25) .40 .20
342 A40 6c violet ('31) 1.00 1.00
a. 6c deep violet('25) 8.00 4.00
343 A40 8c brown ('31) .90 .90
a. 8c yellow brown ('25) 6.00 3.00
344 A40 10c blue ('31) 1.75 1.40
a. deep blue ('25) 25.00 7.00
345 A40 12c dp org ('31) 2.50 2.10
a. red orange ('25) 25.00 7.00
346 A40 16c olive green (Dewey) ('31) 2.00 1.50
a. bister green ('25) 20.00 5.50
347 A40 20c org yel ('31) 2.00 1.50
a. yellow ('25) 20.00 5.50
348 A40 26c green ('31) 2.00 1.50
a. blue green ('25) 25.00 7.00
349 A40 30c light gray ('31) 2.25 1.75
a. gray ('25) 25.00 7.00
350 A41 1p lt violet ('31) 4.00 4.00
a. violet ('25) 90.00 35.00
351 A41 2p brn vio ('31) 10.00 10.00
a. violet brown ('25) 200.00 75.00
352 A41 4p blue ('31) 35.00 30.00
a. deep blue ('25) 1,000. 375.00
353 A41 10p green ('31) 100.00 100.00
a. deep green ('25) 2,000. 750.00
Nos. 340-353 (14) 163.80 156.05
Nos. 340a-353a (14) 4,569. 1,281.

Mount Mayon, Luzon A43

Post Office, Manila A44

Pier No. 7, Manila Bay — A45

(See footnote) — A46

Rice Planting A47

Rice Terraces A48

Baguio Zigzag A49

1932, May 3 *Perf. 11*

354	A43	2c yellow green	.40	.20
355	A44	4c rose carmine	.35	.25
356	A45	12c orange	.50	.50
357	A46	18c red orange	25.00	9.00
358	A47	20c yellow	.65	.55
359	A48	24c deep violet	1.00	.65
360	A49	32c olive brown	1.00	.70
		Nos. 354-360 (7)	28.90	11.85

The 18c vignette was intended to show Pagsanjan Falls in Laguna, central Luzon, and is so labeled. Through error the stamp pictures Vernal Falls in Yosemite National Park, California.

For overprints see #C29-C35, C47-C51, C63.

Nos. 302, 302a Surcharged in Orange or Red

1932

368	A41	1p on 4p blue (O)	2.00	.45
a.		1p on 4p dark blue (O)	2.75	1.25
369	A41	2p on 4p dk bl (R)	3.50	.75
a.		2p on 4p blue (R)	3.50	.75

Baseball Players A50

Tennis Player — A51

Basketball Players — A52

1934, Apr. 14 **Typo.** *Perf. 11½*

380	A50	2c yellow brn	1.50	.80
381	A51	6c ultra	.25	.20
a.		Vert. pair, imperf. btwn.	1,250.	
382	A52	16c violet brown	.50	.50
a.		Vert. pair, imperf. horiz.	1,250.	
		Nos. 380-382 (3)	2.25	1.50

Tenth Far Eastern Championship Games.

José Rizal — A53

Woman and Carabao A54

La Filipina — A55

Pearl Fishing A56

Fort Santiago A57

Salt Spring — A58

Magellan's Landing, 1521 — A59

"Juan de la Cruz" — A60

Rice Terraces A61

"Blood Compact," 1565 — A62

Barasoain Church, Malolos A63

Battle of Manila Bay, 1898 A64

Montalban Gorge A65

George Washington A66

1935, Feb. 15 **Engr.** *Perf. 11*

383	A53	2c rose	.20	.20
384	A54	4c yellow grn	.20	.20
385	A55	6c dk brown	.20	.20
386	A56	8c violet	.20	.20
387	A57	10c rose car	.20	.20
388	A58	12c black	.25	.20
389	A59	16c dark blue	.25	.20
390	A60	20c light olive green	.25	.20
391	A61	26c indigo	.30	.25
392	A62	30c orange red	.30	.25
393	A63	1p red orange & black	1.75	1.25
394	A64	2p bister brn & black	4.50	1.25
395	A65	4p blue & black	5.00	3.00
396	A66	5p green & black	10.00	3.00
		Nos. 383-396 (14)	23.60	10.60

For overprints see Nos. 411-424, 433-446, 463-466, 468, 472-474, 478-484, 485-494, C52-C53, O15-O36, O38, O40-O43, N2-N3, NO6. For surcharges see Nos. 449, N4-N9, N28, NO2-NO5.

Commonwealth Issues

The Temples of Human Progress — A67

1935, Nov. 15

397	A67	2c carmine rose	.20	.20
398	A67	6c dp violet	.20	.20
399	A67	16c blue	.20	.20
400	A67	36c yellow grn	.35	.30
401	A67	50c brown	.55	.55
		Nos. 397-401 (5)	1.50	1.45

Inauguration of the Philippine Commonwealth, Nov. 15, 1935.

Jose Rizal — A68

President Manuel L. Quezon — A69

1936, June 19 *Perf. 12*

402	A68	2c yellow brown	.20	.20
403	A68	6c slate blue	.20	.20
a.		Horiz. pair, imperf. vert.	1,350.	
404	A68	36c red brown	.50	.45
		Nos. 402-404 (3)	.90	.85

75th anniv. of the birth of José Rizal.

1936, Nov. 15 *Perf. 11*

408	A69	2c orange brown	.20	.20
409	A69	6c yellow green	.20	.20
410	A69	12c ultra	.20	.20
		Nos. 408-410 (3)	.60	.60

1st anniversary of the Commonwealth. For overprints see Nos. 467, 475.

Stamps of 1935 with Large Overprint in Black

COMMON-
WEALTH
a

COMMONWEALTH
b

1936-37 *Perf. 11*

411	A53 (a)	2c rose	.20	.20
a.		Booklet pane of 6	2.50	.65
412	A54 (b)	4c yel grn ('37)	.50	4.00
413	A55 (a)	6c dark brown	.20	.20
414	A56 (b)	8c violet ('37)	.25	.20
415	A57 (b)	10c rose carmine	.20	.20
a.		"Commonwealt"	—	
416	A58 (b)	12c black ('37)	.20	.20
417	A59 (b)	16c dk blue	.20	.20
418	A60 (a)	20c lt ol grn ('37)	.65	.40
419	A61 (b)	26c indigo ('37)	.45	.35
420	A62 (b)	30c orange red	.35	.20
421	A63 (b)	1p red org & blk	.65	.20
422	A64 (b)	2p bis brn & blk ('37)	5.00	2.75
423	A65 (b)	4p bl & blk ('37)	22.50	5.00
424	A66 (b)	5p grn & blk ('37)	3.00	1.50
		Nos. 411-424 (14)	34.35	
		Nos. 411,413-424 (13)		11.60

Map of Philippines A70

Arms of Manila A71

1937, Feb. 3

425	A70	2c yellow green	.20	.20
426	A70	6c lt brown	.20	.20
427	A70	12c sapphire	.20	.20
428	A70	20c dp orange	.25	.20
429	A70	36c dp violet	.50	.40
430	A70	50c carmine	.65	.35
		Nos. 425-430 (6)	2.00	1.55

33rd Eucharistic Congress.

1937, Aug. 27 *Perf. 11*

431	A71	10p gray	4.25	2.00
432	A71	20p henna brown	2.25	1.40

For overprints see Nos. 495-496. For surcharges see Nos. 451, C58.

Stamps of 1935 with Small Overprint in Black

COMMON-
WEALTH
a

COMMONWEALTH
b

1938-40 *Perf. 11*

433	A53 (a)	2c rose ('39)	.20	.20
a.		Booklet pane of 6	3.50	2.50
b.		"WEALTH COMMON-"	4,000.	—
c.		Hyphen omitted	—	—
434	A54 (b)	4c yel grn ('40)	1.25	30.00
435	A55 (a)	6c dk brn ('39)	.20	.20
a.		6c golden brown	.20	.20
436	A56 (b)	8c violet ('39)	.20	.20
a.		"Commonwealt"	90.00	
437	A57 (b)	10c rose car ('39)	.20	.20
a.		"Commonwealt"		—
438	A58 (b)	12c black ('40)	.20	.20
439	A59 (b)	16c dk blue	.20	.20
440	A60 (a)	20c lt ol grn ('39)	.20	.20
441	A61 (b)	26c indigo ('40)	.20	.20
442	A62 (b)	30c org red ('39)	1.40	.70
443	A63 (b)	1p red org & blk	.40	.20
444	A64 (b)	2p bis brn & blk	2.75	.75
445	A65 (b)	4p bl & blk ('40)	150.00	150.00
446	A66 (b)	5p grn & blk ('40)	6.00	3.25
		Nos. 433-446 (14)	163.40	
		Nos. 433,435-446 (13)		156.50

Overprint "b" measures 18½x1¾mm. No. 433b occurs in booklet pane, No. 433a, position 5; all copies are straight-edged, left and bottom.

Stamps of 1917-37 Surcharged in Red, Violet or Black

FIRST
FOREIGN
TRADE
WEEK
2
CENTAVOS
MAY 21-27,1939
a

FIRST FOREIGN TRADE WEEK
MAY 21-27, 1939
6 CENTAVOS 6
b

50 CENTAVOS 50
FIRST FOREIGN TRADE WEEK
MAY 21-27,1939
c

1939, July 5
449 A54 2c on 4c yel grn (R) .20 .20
450 A40 6c on 26c bl grn (V) .20 .20
a. 6c on 26c green .65 .30
451 A71 50c on 20p hn brn (Bk) 1.00 1.00
Nos. 449-451 (3) 1.40 1.40

Foreign Trade Week.

Triumphal Arch — A72

Malacañan Palace A73

1939, Nov. 15 ***Perf. 11***
452 A72 2c yellow green .20 .20
453 A72 6c carmine .20 .20
454 A72 12c bright blue .20 .20
Nos. 452-454 (3) .60 .60

For overprints see Nos. 469, 476.

1939, Nov. 15
455 A73 2c green .20 .20
456 A73 6c orange .20 .20
457 A73 12c carmine .20 .20
Nos. 455-457 (3) .60 .60

Nos. 452-457 commemorate the 4th anniv. of the Commonwealth.
For overprint see No. 470.

Pres. Quezon Taking Oath of Office — A74

1940, Feb. 8
458 A74 2c dk orange .20 .20
459 A74 6c dk green .20 .20
460 A74 12c purple .25 .20
Nos. 458-460 (3) .65 .60

4th anniversary of Commonwealth.
For overprints see Nos. 471, 477.

Jose´ Rizal — A75

Rotary Press Printing

1941, Apr. 14 ***Perf. 11x10½***
Size: 19x22½mm
461 A75 2c apple green .20 *.50*

Flat Plate Printing

1941-43 Size: 18¾x22mm ***Perf. 11***
462 A75 2c apple green ('43) .20 *.50*
a. 2c pale apple green .20 *.50*
b. Bklt. pane of 6 #462 ('43) 1.25 *5.00*
c. Bklt. pane of 6 #462a 2.50 *2.75*

No. 462 was issued only in booklet panes and all copies have straight edges.
Further printings were made in 1942 and 1943 in different shades from the first supply of stamps sent to the islands.
For type A75 overprinted see Nos. 464, O37, O39, N1, NO1.

Philippine Stamps of 1935-41, Handstamped in Violet **VICTORY**

1944 ***Perf. 11, 11x10½***
463 A53 2c (#411) *325.00* *160.00*
a. Booklet pane of 6 *3,250.*
463B A53 2c (#433) *1,400.* *1,350.*
464 A75 2c (#461) 3.75 3.00
465 A54 4c (#384) *42.50* *42.50*
466 A55 6c (#385) *1,900.* *1,650.*
467 A69 6c (#409) *150.00* *110.00*
468 A55 6c (#413) *875.00* *800.00*
469 A72 6c (#453) *150.00* *125.00*
470 A73 6c (#456) *850.00* *725.00*
471 A74 6c (#459) *225.00* *190.00*
472 A56 8c (#436) *17.50* *24.00*
473 A57 10c (#415) *125.00* *82.50*
474 A57 10c (#437) *150.00* *125.00*
475 A69 12c (#410) *750.00* *300.00*
476 A72 12c (#454) *4,000.* *2,250.*
477 A74 12c (#460) *275.00* *160.00*
478 A59 16c (#389) *800.00*
479 A59 16c (#417) *650.00* *450.00*
480 A59 16c (#439) *300.00* *190.00*
481 A60 20c (#440) 35.00 35.00
482 A62 30c (#420) *350.00* *225.00*
483 A62 30c (#442) *475.00* *350.00*
484 A63 1p (#443) *6,250.* *4,500.*

Nos. 463-484 are valued in the grade of fine to very fine.

Types of 1935-37 Overprinted

VICTORY
COMMON-WEALTH
a

VICTORY
COMMONWEALTH
b

1945 ***Perf. 11***
485 A53 (a) 2c rose .20 .20
486 A54 (b) 4c yellow grn .20 .20
487 A55 (a) 6c golden brn .20 .20
488 A56 (b) 8c violet .20 .20
489 A57 (b) 10c rose car .20 .20
490 A58 (b) 12c black .20 .20
491 A59 (b) 16c dk blue .25 .20
492 A60 (a) 20c lt olive grn .30 .20
493 A62 (b) 30c orange red .40 .35
494 A63 (b) 1p red org & blk 1.10 .25

Nos. 431-432 Overprinted in Black **VICTORY**

495 A71 10p gray 40.00 13.50
496 A71 20p henna brown 35.00 15.00
Nos. 485-496 (12) 78.25 30.70

Jose´ Rizal — A76

Rotary Press Printing

1946, May 28 ***Perf. 11x10½***
497 A76 2c sepia .20 .20

For overprints see Nos. 503, O44.

Catalogue values for unused stamps in this section, from this point to the end of the section, are for Never Hinged items.

Republic

Philippine Girl Holding Flag of the Republic — A77

Unwmk.
1946, July 4 Engr. ***Perf. 11***
500 A77 2c carmine .45 .25
501 A77 6c green .45 .25
502 A77 12c blue .90 .35
Nos. 500-502 (3) 1.80 .85

Philippine independence, July 4, 1946.

No. 497 Overprinted in Brown

PHILIPPINES
50TH ANNIVERSARY MARTYRDOM
OF RIZAL
1896 ~ 1946

1946, Dec. 30 ***Perf. 11x10½***
503 A76 2c sepia .40 .20

50th anniv. of the execution of Jose´ Rizal.

Rizal Monument A78

Bonifacio Monument A79

Jones Bridge — A80

Santa Lucia Gate — A81

Mayon Volcano — A82

Avenue of Palms — A83

1947 Engr. ***Perf. 12***
504 A78 4c black brown .30 .20
505 A79 10c red orange .30 .20
506 A80 12c deep blue .30 .20
507 A81 16c slate gray 2.00 .60
508 A82 20c red brown 2.00 .20
509 A83 50c dull green 1.60 .35
510 A83 1p violet 2.25 .35
Nos. 504-510 (7) 8.75 2.10

For surcharges see Nos. 613-614, 809. For overprints see Nos. 609, O50-O52, O54-O55.

Manuel L. Quezon — A84

1947, May 1 **Typo.**
511 A84 1c green .40 .20

See No. 515.

Pres. Manuel A. Roxas Taking Oath of Office A85

1947, July 4 Unwmk. ***Perf. 12½***
512 A85 4c carmine rose .40 .20
513 A85 6c dk green .60 .45
514 A85 16c purple 1.00 .85
Nos. 512-514 (3) 2.00 1.50

First anniversary of republic.

Quezon Type
Souvenir Sheet

1947, Nov. 28 ***Imperf.***
515 Sheet of 4 1.60 1.10
a. A84 1c bright green .20 .20

United Nations Emblem A87

1947, Nov. 24 ***Perf. 12½***
516 A87 4c dk car & pink 1.50 1.00
a. Imperf. 7.00 2.50
517 A87 6c pur & pale vio 1.50 1.00
a. Imperf. 6.00 2.50
518 A87 12c dp bl & pale bl 2.00 1.50
a. Imperf. 7.00 2.50
Nos. 516-518 (3) 5.00 3.50

Conference of the Economic Commission in Asia and the Far East, held at Baguio.

Gen. Douglas MacArthur — A88

1948, Feb. 3 Engr. ***Perf. 12***
519 A88 4c purple .75 .40
520 A88 6c rose car 1.00 .40
521 A88 16c brt ultra 1.25 .60
Nos. 519-521 (3) 3.00 1.40

Threshing Rice — A89

1948, Feb. 23 Typo. *Perf. 12½*

522 A89 2c grn & pale yel grn .75 .40
523 A89 6c brown & cream 1.00 .40
524 A89 18c dp bl & pale bl 2.00 1.25
Nos. 522-524 (3) 3.75 2.05

Conf. of the FAO held at Baguio. No. 524 exists imperf. See No. C67.

Manuel A. Roxas A90

José Rizal A91

1948, July 15 Engr. *Perf. 12*

525 A90 2c black .25 .20
526 A90 4c black .35 .20

Issued in tribute to President Manuel A. Roxas who died April 15, 1948.

1948, June 19 Unwmk.

527 A91 2c bright green .35 .20
a. Booklet pane of 6 3.00 2.10

For surcharges see Nos. 550, O56. For overprint see No. O53.

Scout Saluting — A92

Sampaguita, National Flower — A93

1948, Oct. 31 Typo. *Imperf.*

528 A92 2c chocolate & green .65 .30
a. Perf. 11½ 1.50 .75
529 A92 4c chocolate & pink .90 .40
a. Perf. 11½ 2.25 1.10

Boy Scouts of the Philippines, 25th anniv. No. 528 exists part perforate.

1948, Dec. 8 *Perf. 12½*

530 A93 3c blk, pale bl & grn .55 .30

UPU Monument, Bern A94

Unwmk.

1949, Oct. 9 Engr. *Perf. 12*

531 A94 4c green .70 .20
532 A94 6c dull violet .35 .20
533 A94 18c blue gray .35 .20
Nos. 531-533 (3) 1.40 .60

Souvenir Sheet

Imperf

534 Sheet of 3 2.50 1.50
a. A94 4c green .70 .35
b. A94 6c dull violet .70 .35
c. A94 18c blue .70 .35

75th anniv. of the UPU.

In 1960 an unofficial, 3-line overprint ("President D. D. Eisenhower /Visit to the Philippines/June 14-16, 1960") was privately applied to No. 534.

For surcharge & overprint see #806, 901.

Gen. Gregorio del Pilar at Tirad Pass — A95

1949, Dec. 2 *Perf. 12*

535 A95 2c red brown .25 .20
536 A95 4c green .40 .20

50th anniversary of the death of Gen. Gregorio P. del Pilar and fifty-two of his men at Tirad Pass.

Globe — A96

Red Lauan Tree — A97

1950, Mar. 1

537 A96 2c purple .25 .20
538 A96 6c dk green .30 .20
539 A96 18c dp blue .45 .25
Nos. 537-539,C68-C69 (5) 4.35 1.75

5th World Cong. of the Junior Chamber of Commerce, Manila, Mar. 1-8, 1950.

For surcharge see No. 825.

1950, Apr. 14

540 A97 2c green .45 .20
541 A97 4c purple .55 .20

50th anniversary of the Bureau of Forestry.

F. D. Roosevelt with his Stamps — A98

Lions Club Emblem — A99

1950, May 22

542 A98 4c dark brown .80 .20
543 A98 6c carmine rose .40 .25
544 A98 18c blue .40 .25
Nos. 542-544 (3) 1.60 .70

Honoring Franklin D. Roosevelt and for the 25th anniv. of the Philatelic Association of the Philippines. See No. C70.

1950, June 4 Engr.

545 A99 2c orange .90 .30
546 A99 4c violet .90 .35
Nos. 545-546,C71-C72 (4) 4.80 1.70

Convention of the Lions Club, Manila, June 1950.

Pres. Elpidio Quirino Taking Oath A100

1950, July 4 Unwmk. *Perf. 12*

547 A100 2c car rose .25 .20
548 A100 4c magenta .25 .20
549 A100 6c blue green .30 .25
Nos. 547-549 (3) .80 .65

Republic of the Philippines, 4th anniv.

No. 527 Surcharged in Black

1950, Sept. 20

550 A91 1c on 2c bright green .30 .20

Dove over Globe — A101

1950, Oct. 23

551 A101 5c green .60 .20
552 A101 6c rose carmine .45 .20
553 A101 18c ultra .45 .35
Nos. 551-553 (3) 1.50 .75

Baguio Conference of 1950.

For surcharge see No. 828.

Headman of Barangay Inspecting Harvest A102

1951, Mar. 31 Litho. *Perf. 12½*

554 A102 5c dull green .70 .20
555 A102 6c red brown .35 .25
556 A102 18c violet blue .35 .30
Nos. 554-556 (3) 1.40 .75

The government's Peace Fund campaign.

Imperf., Pairs

554a A102 5c dull green 3.00 2.00
555a A102 6c red brown 1.75 .90
556a A102 18c violet blue 1.25 .75
Nos. 554a-556a (3) 6.00 3.65

Arms of Manila A103

Arms of Cebu A104

Arms of Zamboanga A105

Arms of Iloilo A106

1951 Engr. *Perf. 12*

Various Frames

557 A103 5c purple 1.25 .25
558 A103 6c gray .95 .25
559 A103 18c bright ultra .60 .40

Various Frames

560 A104 5c crimson rose 1.25 .25
561 A104 6c bister brown .60 .25
562 A104 18c violet .95 .40

Various Frames

563 A105 5c blue green 1.60 .25
564 A105 6c red brown .95 .25
565 A105 18c light blue .95 .40

Various Frames

566 A106 5c bright green 1.60 .25
567 A106 6c violet .95 .25
568 A106 18c deep blue .95 .40
Nos. 557-568 (12) 12.60 3.60

Issued: A103, 2/3; A104, 4/27; A105, 6/19; A106, 8/26.

For surcharges see Nos. 634-636.

UN Emblem and Girl Holding Flag — A107

Liberty Holding Declaration of Human Rights — A108

1951, Oct. 24 Unwmk. *Perf. 11½*

569 A107 5c red 1.25 .25
570 A107 6c blue green .80 .25
571 A107 18c violet blue .80 .35
Nos. 569-571 (3) 2.85 .85

United Nations Day, Oct. 24, 1951.

1951, Dec. 10 *Perf. 12*

572 A108 5c green 1.25 .25
573 A108 6c red orange .80 .25
574 A108 18c ultra .80 .35
Nos. 572-574 (3) 2.85 .85

Universal Declaration of Human Rights.

Students and Department Seal — A109

1952, Jan. 31

575 A109 5c orange red .60 .30

50th anniversary (in 1951) of the Philippine Educational System.

Milkfish and Map A111

1952, Oct. 27 *Perf. 12½*

578 A111 5c orange brown 1.00 .30
579 A111 6c deep blue .50 .30

4th Indo-Pacific Fisheries Council Meeting, Quezon City, Oct. 23-Nov. 7, 1952.

Maria Clara — A112

1952, Nov. 16

580 A112 5c deep blue 1.00 .30
581 A112 6c brown .75 .30
Nos. 580-581,C73 (3) 3.35 1.30

1st Pan-Asian Philatelic Exhibition, PANAPEX, Manila, Nov. 16-22.

Wright Park, Baguio City — A113

Francisco Baltazar, Poet — A114

1952, Dec. 15 ***Perf. 12***

582 A113 5c red orange .90 .30
583 A113 6c dp blue green .60 .30

3rd Lions District Convention, Baguio City.

1953, Mar. 27

584 A114 5c citron .60 .30

National Language Week.

"Gateway to the East" — A115

Presidents Quirino and Sukarno — A116

1953, Apr. 30

585 A115 5c turq green .50 .25
586 A115 6c vermilion .40 .25

Philippines International Fair.

1953, Oct. 5 **Engr. & Litho.**

587 A116 5c multicolored .60 .35
588 A116 6c multicolored .30 .30

2nd anniversary of the visit of Indonesia's President Sukarno.

Marcelo H. del Pilar — A117

1c, Manuel L. Quezon. 2c, José Abad Santos (diff. frame). 3c, Apolinario Mabini (diff. frame). 10c, Father José Burgos. 20c, Lapu-Lapu. 25c, Gen. Antonio Luna. 50c, Cayetano Arellano. 60c, Andres Bonifacio. 2p, Graciano L. Jaena.

Perf. 12, 12½, 13, 14x13½

1952-60 **Engr.**

589 A117 1c red brn ('53) .30 .20
590 A117 2c gray ('60) .25 .20
591 A117 3c brick red ('59) .30 .20
592 A117 5c crim rose .30 .20
595 A117 10c ultra ('55) .50 .20
597 A117 20c car lake ('55) .80 .20
598 A117 25c yel grn ('58) 1.00 .20
599 A117 50c org ver ('59) 1.25 .20
600 A117 60c car rose ('58) 1.50 .50
601 A117 2p violet 4.00 1.00
Nos. 589-601 (10) 10.20 3.10

For overprints & surcharges see #608, 626, 641-642, 647, 830, 871, 875-877, O57-O61.

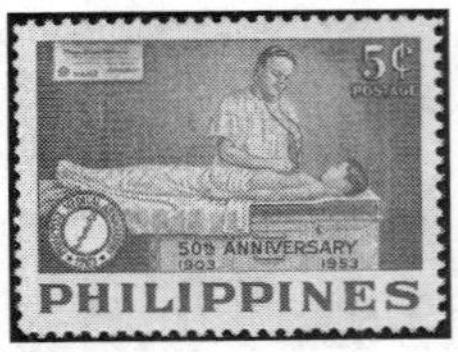

Doctor Examining Boy A118

1953, Dec. 16

603 A118 5c lilac rose .60 .25
604 A118 6c ultra .55 .25

50th anniversary of the founding of the Philippine Medical Association.

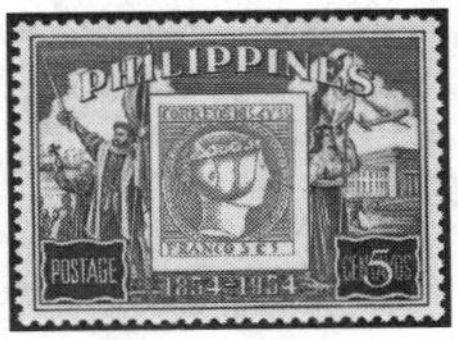

First Philippine Stamps, Magellan's Landing and Manila Scene A119

1954, Apr. 25 ***Perf. 13***

Stamp of 1854 in Orange

605 A119 5c purple .50 .30
606 A119 18c deep blue 1.25 .85
607 A119 30c green 3.00 2.00
Nos. 605-607,C74-C76 (6) 16.75 8.40

Centenary of Philippine postage stamps.
For surcharge see No. 829.

Nos. 592 and 509 Overprinted or Surcharged in Black

1954, Apr. 23 ***Perf. 12***

608 A117 5c crimson rose 1.50 .85
609 A83 18c on 50c dull grn 2.10 1.25

1st National Boy Scout Jamboree, Quezon City, April 23-30, 1954.
The surcharge on No. 609 is reduced to fit the size of the stamp.

Discus Thrower and Games Emblem A120

1954, May 31 ***Perf. 13***

610 A120 5c shown 2.75 .80
611 A120 18c Swimmer .90 .40
612 A120 30c Boxers 2.25 1.50
Nos. 610-612 (3) 5.90 2.70

2nd Asian Games, Manila, May 1-9.

Nos. 505 and 508 Surcharged in Blue

1954, Sept. 6 ***Perf. 12***

613 A79 5c on 10c red org .65 .45
614 A82 18c on 20c red brn .65 .45

Manila Conference, 1954.
The surcharge is arranged to obliterate the original denomination.

Allegory of Independence A121

"Immaculate Conception," by Murillo A122

1954, Nov. 30 ***Perf. 13***

615 A121 5c dark carmine .90 .20
616 A121 18c deep blue .60 .30

56th anniversary of the declaration of the first Philippine Independence.
For surcharge see No. 826.

1954, Dec. 30 ***Perf. 12***

617 A122 5c blue .55 .25

Issued to mark the end of the Marian Year.

Mayon Volcano, Moro Vinta and Rotary Emblem A123

1955, Feb. 23 **Engr.** ***Perf. 13***

618 A123 5c dull blue .30 .20
619 A123 18c dk car rose .65 .40
Nos. 618-619,C77 (3) 2.95 1.45

Rotary Intl., 50th anniv. For surcharge see #827.

Allegory of Labor — A124

Pres. Ramon Magsaysay A125

1955, May 26 ***Perf. 13x12½***

620 A124 5c brown .60 .25

Issued in connection with the Labor-Management Congress, Manila, May 26-28, 1955.

1955, July 4 ***Perf. 12½***

621 A125 5c blue .40 .20
622 A125 20c red 1.25 .50
623 A125 30c green 1.25 .50
Nos. 621-623 (3) 2.90 1.20

9th anniversary of the Republic.

Village Well A126

1956, Mar. 16 ***Perf. 12½x13½***

624 A126 5c violet .60 .25
625 A126 20c dull green .90 .40

Issued to publicize the drive for improved health conditions in rural areas.

No. 592 Overprinted

1956, Aug. 1 **Unwmk.** ***Perf. 12***

626 A117 5c crimson rose .55 .35

5th Annual Conf. of the World Confederation of Organizations of the Teaching Profession, Manila, Aug. 1-8, 1956.

Nurse and Disaster Victims A127

Engraved; Cross Lithographed in Red

1956, Aug. 30

627 A127 5c violet .40 .30
628 A127 20c gray brown 1.25 .60

50 years of Red Cross Service in the Philippines.

Monument to US Landing, Leyte — A128

1956, Oct. 20 **Litho.** ***Perf. 12½***

629 A128 5c carmine rose .50 .25
a. Imperf, pair ('57) 5.75 3.00

Landing of US forces under Gen. Douglas MacArthur on Leyte, Oct. 20, 1944.
Issue date: No. 629a, Feb. 16.

Santo Tomas University A129

1956, Nov. 13 **Photo.** ***Perf. 11½***

630 A129 5c brown car & choc .50 .35
631 A129 60c lilac & red brn 3.00 1.60

Statue of Christ by Rizal — A130

1956, Nov. 28 **Engr.** ***Perf. 12***

632 A130 5c gray olive .40 .25
633 A130 20c rose carmine 1.10 .60

2nd Natl. Eucharistic Cong., Manila, Nov. 28-Dec. 2, and for the centenary of the Feast of the Sacred Heart.

Nos. 561, 564 and 567 Surcharged with New Value in Blue or Black

1956 **Unwmk.** ***Perf. 12***

634 A104 5c on 6c bis brn (Bl) .50 .25
635 A105 5c on 6c red brn (Bl) .50 .25
636 A106 5c on 6c vio (Bk) .50 .25
Nos. 634-636 (3) 1.50 .75

Girl Scout, Emblem and Tents A131

1957, Jan. 19 Litho. *Perf. 12½*

637 A131 5c dark blue .60 .30
a. Imperf, pair 5.75 3.50

Centenary of the Scout movement and for the Girl Scout World Jamboree, Quezon City, Jan. 19-Feb. 2, 1957.

Copies of Nos. 637 and 637a (No. 48 in sheet) exist with heavy black rectangular handstamps obliterating erroneous date at left, denomination and cloverleaf emblem.

Pres. Ramon Magsaysay (1907-57) — A132

1957, Aug. 31 Engr. *Perf. 12*

638 A132 5c black .35 .20

"Spoliarium" by Juan Luna — A133

1957, Oct. 23 *Perf. 14x14½*

639 A133 5c rose carmine .35 .20

Centenary of the birth of Juan Luna, painter.

Sergio Osmena and First National Assembly — A134

1957, Oct. 16 *Perf. 12½x13½*

640 A134 5c blue green .35 .20

1st Philippine Assembly and honoring Sergio Osmeña, Speaker of the Assembly.

Nos. 595 and 597 Surcharged in Carmine or Black

1957, Dec. 30 *Perf. 14x13½*

641 A117 5c on 10c ultra (C) .60 .25
642 A117 10c on 20c car lake .60 .30

Inauguration of Carlos P. Garcia as president and Diosdado Macapagal as vice-president, Dec. 30.

University of the Philippines — A135

1958 Engr. *Perf. 13½x13*

643 A135 5c dk carmine rose .35 .20

50th anniversary of the founding of the University of the Philippines.

Pres. Carlos P. Garcia — A136

1958 Photo. *Perf. 11½*
Granite Paper

644 A136 5c multicolored .20 .20
645 A136 20c multicolored .40 .30

12th anniversary of Philippine Republic.

Manila Cathedral — A137

Perf. 13x13½, 12
1958, Dec. 8 Engr.

646 A137 5c multicolored .35 .20

Issued to commemorate the inauguration of the rebuilt Manila Cathedral, Dec. 8, 1958.

No. 592 Surcharged

1959 *Perf. 12*

647 A117 1c on 5c crim rose .35 .20

Nos. B4-B5 Surcharged with New Values and Bars

1959, Feb. 3 *Perf. 13*

648 SP4 1c on 2c + 2c red .25 .20
649 SP5 6c on 4c + 4c vio .25 .20

14th anniversary of the liberation of Manila from the Japanese forces.

Philippine Flag A138

1959, Feb. 8 Unwmk. *Perf. 13*

650 A138 6c dp ultra, yel & dp car .20 .20
651 A138 20c dp car, yel & dp ultra .45 .20

Seal of Bulacan Province A139

Seal of Bacolod City A140

1959 Engr. *Perf. 13*

652 A139 6c lt yellow grn .20 .20
653 A139 20c rose red .40 .20

60th anniversary of the Malolos constitution.
For surcharge see No. 848.

1959

Design: 6c, 25c, Seal of Capiz Province and portrait of Pres. Roxas.

654 A139 6c lt brown .25 .20
655 A139 25c purple .35 .25

Pres. Manuel A. Roxas, 11th death anniv.

1959

656 A140 6c blue green .20 .20
657 A140 10c rose lilac .40 .20

Nos. 658-803 were reserved for the rest of a projected series showing seals and coats of arms of provinces and cities.

Camp John Hay Amphitheater, Baguio — A141

Perf. 13½ (6c, 25c), 12 (6c)
1959, Sept. 1

804 A141 6c bright green .20 .20
805 A141 25c rose red .35 .20

50th anniversary of the city of Baguio.

No. 533 Surcharged in Red

1959, Oct. 24 *Perf. 12*

806 A94 6c on 18c blue .40 .20

Issued for United Nations Day, Oct. 24.

Maria Cristina Falls — A142

1959, Nov. 18 Photo. *Perf. 13½, 12*

807 A142 6c vio & dp yel grn .20 .20
808 A142 30c green & brown .50 .30

No. 504 Surcharged with New Value and Bars

1959 Engr. *Perf. 12*

809 A78 1c on 4c blk brn .35 .20

Manila Atheneum Emblem — A143

1959, Dec. 10 *Perf. 13½, 12*

810 A143 6c ultra .20 .20
811 A143 30c rose red .30 .25

Centenary of the Manila Atheneum (Ateneo de Manila), a school, and to mark a century of progress in education.

Manuel Quezon — A144

José Rizal — A145

1959-60 Engr. *Perf. 13*

812 A144 1c olive gray ('60) .30 .20

Perf. 14x12

813 A145 6c gray blue .40 .20

For overprint see No. O62.

A146

Perf. 12½x13½
1960 Unwmk. Photo.

814 A146 6c brown & gold .35 .20

25th anniversary of the Philippine Constitution. See No. C82.

Site of Manila Pact A147

1960 Engr. *Perf. 12½*

815 A147 6c emerald .20 .20
816 A147 25c orange .40 .20

5th anniversary (in 1959) of the Congress of the Philippines establishing the South-East Asia Treaty Organization (SEATO).
For overprints see Nos. 841-842.

Sunset at Manila Bay and Uprooted Oak Emblem — A148

1960, Apr. 7 Photo. *Perf. 13½*

817 A148 6c multicolored .25 .20
818 A148 25c multicolored .35 .20

World Refugee Year, 7/1/59-6/30/60.

A149

1960, July 29 ***Perf. 13½***

819 A149 5c lt grn, red & gold .30 .20
820 A149 6c bl, red & gold .30 .20

Philippine Tuberculosis Society, 50th anniv.

Basketball — A150

1960, Nov. 30 ***Perf. 13x13½***

821 A150 6c shown .35 .20
822 A150 10c Runner .50 .20
Nos. 821-822,C85-C86 (4) 2.35 1.45

17th Olympic Games, Rome, 8/25-9/11.

Presidents Eisenhower and Garcia and Presidential Seals — A151

1960, Dec. 30 ***Perf. 13½***

823 A151 6c multi .20 .20
824 A151 20c ultra, red & yel .30 .20

Visit of Pres. Dwight D. Eisenhower to the Philippines, June 14, 1960.

Nos. 539, 616, 619, 553, 606 and 598 Surcharged with New Values and Bars in Red or Black

1960-61 **Engr.** ***Perf. 12, 13, 12½***

825 A96 1c on 18c dp bl (R) .30 .20
826 A121 5c on 18c dp bl (R) .50 .25
827 A123 5c on 18c dp car rose .50 .20
828 A101 10c on 18c ultra (R) .50 .25
829 A119 10c on 18c dp bl & org (R) .50 .20
830 A117 20c on 25c yel grn ('61) .50 .25
Nos. 825-830 (6) 2.80 1.35

On No. 830, no bars are overprinted, the surcharge "20 20" serving to cancel the old denomination.

Mercury and Globe — A152

1961, Jan. 23 **Photo.** ***Perf. 13½***

831 A152 6c red brn, bl, blk & gold .50 .20

Manila Postal Conf., Jan. 10-23. See #C87.

Nos. B10, B11 and B11a Surcharged "2nd National Boy Scout Jamboree Pasonanca Park" and New Value in Black or Red

1961, May 2 **Engr.** ***Perf. 13***

Yellow Paper

832 SP8 10c on 6c + 4c car .25 .20
833 SP8 30c on 25c + 5c bl (R) .45 .35
a. Tete beche, *wht* (10c on 6c + 4c & 30c on 25c + 5c) (Bk) 1.00 .75

Second National Boy Scout Jamboree, Pasonanca Park, Zamboanga City.

De la Salle College, Manila A153

1961, June 16 **Photo.** ***Perf. 11½***

834 A153 6c multi .25 .20
835 A153 10c multi .25 .20

De la Salle College, Manila, 50th anniv.

José Rizal as Student A154

6c, Rizal & birthplace at Calamba, Laguna. 10c, Rizal & parents. 20c, Rizal with Juan Luna & F. R. Hidalgo in Madrid. 30c, Rizal's execution.

1961 **Unwmk.** ***Perf. 13½***

836 A154 5c multi .20 .20
837 A154 6c multi .20 .20
838 A154 10c grn & red brn .25 .20
839 A154 20c brn red & grnsh bl .30 .25
840 A154 30c vio, lil & org brn .50 .30
Nos. 836-840 (5) 1.45 1.15

Centenary of the birth of José Rizal.

Nos. 815-816 Overprinted

1961, July 4 **Engr.** ***Perf. 12½***

841 A147 6c emerald .20 .20
842 A147 25c orange .30 .25

15th anniversary of the Republic.

Colombo Plan Emblem and Globe Showing Member Countries — A155

1961, Oct. 8 **Photo.** ***Perf. 13x11½***

843 A155 5c multi .25 .20
844 A155 6c multi .25 .20

7th anniversary of the admission of the Philippines to the Colombo Plan.

Government Clerk — A156

1961, Dec. 9 **Unwmk.** ***Perf. 12½***

845 A156 6c vio, bl & red .25 .20
846 A156 10c gray bl & red .45 .20

Honoring Philippine government employees.

No. C83 Surcharged

1961, Nov. 30 **Engr.** ***Perf. 14x14½***

847 AP11 6c on 10c car .35 .20

Philippine Amateur Athletic Fed., 50th anniv.

No. 655 Surcharged with New Value and: "MACAPAGAL-PELAEZ INAUGURATION DEC. 30, 1961"

1961, Dec. 30 ***Perf. 12½***

848 A139 6c on 25c pur .35 .20

Inauguration of Pres. Diosdado Macapagal and Vice-Pres. Emanuel Pelaez.

No. B8 Surcharged

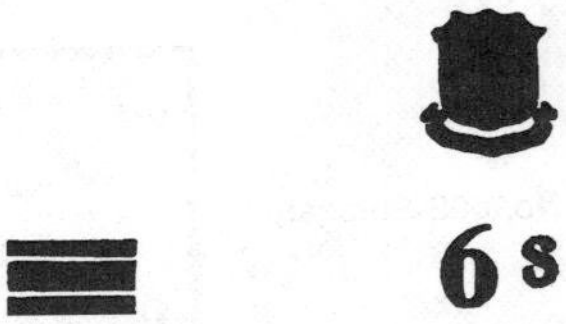

1962, Jan. 23 **Photo.** ***Perf. 13½x13***

849 SP7 6c on 5c grn & red .35 .20

Vanda Orchids A157

Apolinario Mabini A158

Orchids: 6c, White mariposa. 10c, Sander's dendrobe. 20c, Sanggumay.

1962, Mar. 9 **Photo.** ***Perf. 13½x14***

Dark Blue Background

850 A157 5c rose, grn & yel .50 .20
851 A157 6c grn & yel .50 .20
852 A157 10c grn, car & brn .50 .20
853 A157 20c lil, brn & grn .50 .20
a. Block of 4, #850-853 2.00 1.00
b. As "a," imperf. 2.75 1.50

Perf. 13½; 14 (1s); 13x12 (#857, 10s)

1962-69 **Engr.** **Unwmk.**

Portraits: 1s, Manuel L. Quezon. 5s, Marcelo H. del Pilar. No. 857, José Rizal. No. 857A, Rizal (wearing shirt). 10s, Father José Burgos. 20s, Lapu-Lapu. 30s, Rajah Soliman. 50s, Cayetano Arellano. 70s, Sergio Osmena. No. 863, Emilio Jacinto. No. 864, José M. Panganiban.

854 A158 1s org brn ('63) .20 .20
855 A158 3s rose red .20 .20
856 A158 5s car rose ('63) .20 .20
857 A158 6s dk red brn .25 .20
857A A158 6s pck bl ('64) .25 .20
858 A158 10s brt pur ('63) .25 .20
859 A158 20s Prus bl ('63) .30 .20
860 A158 30s vermilion .75 .20
861 A158 50s vio ('63) 1.00 .20
862 A158 70s brt bl ('63) 1.25 .20
863 A158 1p grn ('63) 2.40 .35
864 A158 1p dp org ('69) .80 .30
Nos. 854-864 (12) 7.85 2.65

For surcharges & overprints see #873-874, 946, 969, 1054, 1119, 1209, O63-O69.

Pres. Macapagal Taking Oath of Office — A159

1962 **Photo.** ***Perf. 13½***

Vignette Multicolored

865 A159 6s blue .20 .20
866 A159 10s green .20 .20
867 A159 30s violet .30 .20
Nos. 865-867 (3) .70 .60

Swearing in of President Diosdado Macapagal, Dec. 30, 1961.

Volcano in Lake Taal and Malaria Eradication Emblem A160

1962, Oct. 24 **Unwmk.** ***Perf. 11½***

Granite Paper

868 A160 6s multi .20 .20
869 A160 10s multi .20 .20
870 A160 70s multi .50 .50
Nos. 868-870 (3) .90 .90

Issued on UN Day for the WHO drive to eradicate malaria.

No. 598 Surcharged in Red

1962, Nov. 15 **Engr.** ***Perf. 12***

871 A117 20s on 25c yel grn .35 .20

Issued to commemorate the bicentennial of the Diego Silang revolt in Ilocos Province.

No. B6 Overprinted with Sideways Chevron Obliterating Surtax

1962, Dec. 23 ***Perf. 12***

872 SP6 5c on 5c + 1c dp bl .35 .20

Nos. 855, 857 Surcharged with New Value and Old Value Obliterated

1963 ***Perf. 13½***

873 A158 1s on 3s rose red .25 .20

Perf. 13x12

874 A158 5s on 6s dk red brn .25 .20

No. 601 Surcharged

1963, June 12 *Perf. 12*

875 A117 6s on 2p vio .20 .20
876 A117 20s on 2p vio .25 .20
877 A117 70s on 2p vio .45 .30
Nos. 875-877 (3) .90 .70

Diego Silang Bicentennial Art and Philatelic Exhibition, ARPHEX, Manila, May 28-June 30.

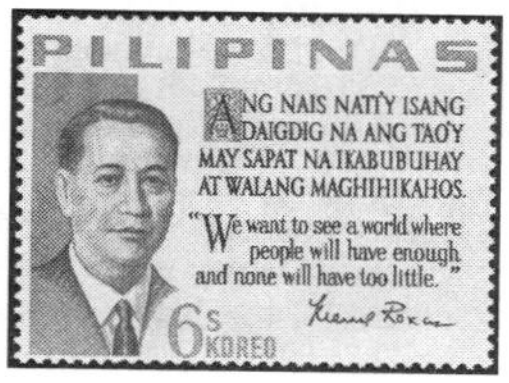

Pres. Manuel Roxas A161

1963-73 **Engr.** *Perf. 13½*

878 A161 6s brt bl & blk, *bluish* .30 .20
879 A161 30s brn & blk .70 .20

Pres. Ramon Magsaysay

880 A161 6s lil & blk .30 .20
881 A161 30s yel grn & blk .70 .20

Pres. Elpidio Quirino

882 A161 6s grn & blk ('65) .30 .20
883 A161 30s rose lil & blk ('65) .70 .20

Gen. (Pres.) Emilio Aguinaldo

883A A161 6s dp cl & blk ('66) .30 .20
883B A161 30s bl & blk ('66) .70 .20

Pres. José P. Laurel

883C A161 6s lt red brn & blk ('66) .30 .20
883D A161 30s bl & blk ('66) .50 .20

Pres. Manuel L. Quezon

883E A161 10s bl gray & blk ('67) .30 .20
883F A161 30s lt vio & blk ('67) .50 .20

Pres. Sergio Osmeña

883G A161 10s rose lil & blk ('70) .30 .20
883H A161 40s grn & blk ('70) .60 .20

Pres. Carlos P. Garcia

883I A161 10s multi ('73) .30 .20
883J A161 30s multi ('73) .70 .20
Nos. 878-883J (16) 7.50 3.20

Nos. 878-883J honor former presidents.
For surcharges see Nos. 984-985, 1120, 1146, 1160-1161.

Globe, Flags of Thailand, Korea, China, Philippines A162

Red Cross Centenary Emblem A163

1963, Aug. 26 **Photo.** *Perf. 13½x13*

884 A162 6s dk grn & multi .20 .20
885 A162 20s dk grn & multi .30 .20

Asian-Oceanic Postal Union, 1st anniv.
For surcharge see No. 1078.

1963, Sept. 1 *Perf. 11½*

886 A163 5s lt vio, gray & red .20 .20
887 A163 6s ultra, gray & red .20 .20
888 A163 20s grn, gray & red .20 .20
Nos. 886-888 (3) .60 .60

Centenary of the International Red Cross.

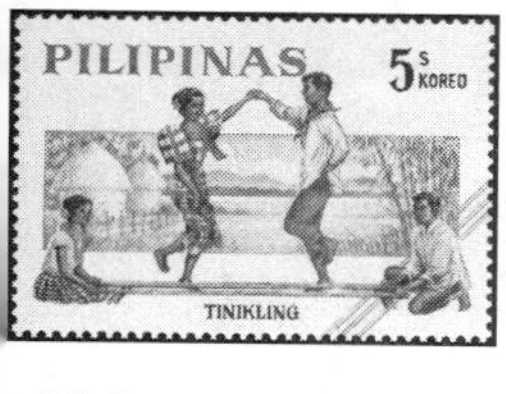

Bamboo Dance A164

Folk Dances: 6s, Dance with oil lamps. 10s, Duck dance. 20s, Princess Gandingan's rock dance.

1963, Sept. 15 **Unwmk.** *Perf. 14*

889 A164 5s multi .35 .20
890 A164 6s multi .35 .20
891 A164 10s multi .35 .20
892 A164 20s multi .35 .20
a. Block of 4, #889-892 1.40 1.00

For surcharges and overprints see #1043-1046.

Pres. Macapagal and Filipino Family — A165

1963, Sept. 28 *Perf. 14*

893 A165 5s bl & multi .20 .20
894 A165 6s yel & multi .20 .20
895 A165 20s lil & multi .30 .20
Nos. 893-895 (3) .70 .60

Issued to publicize Pres. Macapagal's 5-year Socioeconomic Program.
For surcharge see No. 1181.

Presidents Lopez Mateos and Macapagal — A166

1963, Sept. 28 **Photo.** *Perf. 13½*

896 A166 6s multi .20 .20
897 A166 30s multi .30 .20

Visit of Pres. Adolfo Lopez Mateos of Mexico to the Philippines.
For surcharge see No. 1166.

Andres Bonifacio — A167

1963, Nov. 30 **Unwmk.** *Perf. 12*

898 A167 5s gold, brn, gray & red .20 .20
899 A167 6s sil, brn, gray & red .25 .20
900 A167 25s brnz, brn, gray & red .30 .20
Nos. 898-900 (3) .75 .60

Centenary of the birth of Andres Bonifacio, national hero and poet.
For surcharges see Nos. 1147, 1162.

No. 534 Overprinted: "UN ADOPTION/DECLARATION OF HUMAN RIGHTS/15TH ANNIVERSARY DEC. 10, 1963"

1963, Dec. 10 **Engr.** *Imperf.*

Souvenir Sheet

901 A94 Sheet of 3 2.75 2.00

15th anniv. of the Universal Declaration of Human Rights.

Woman holding Sheaf of Rice — A168

1963, Dec. 20 **Photo.** *Perf. 13½x13*

902 A168 6s brn & multi .35 .20
Nos. 902,C88-C89 (3) 1.10 .70

FAO "Freedom from Hunger" campaign.

Bamboo Organ — A169

Apolinario Mabini — A170

1964, May 4 *Perf. 13½*

903 A169 5s multi .25 .20
904 A169 6s multi .25 .20
905 A169 20s multi .45 .25
Nos. 903-905 (3) .95 .65

The bamboo organ in the Church of Las Pinas, Rizal, was built by Father Diego Cera, 1816-1822.
For surcharge see No. 1055.

Wmk. 233

1964, July 23 **Photo.** *Perf. 14½*

906 A170 6s pur & gold .20 .20
907 A170 10s red brn & gold .25 .20
908 A170 30s brt grn & gold .30 .20
Nos. 906-908 (3) .75 .60

Apolinario Mabini (1864-1903), national hero and a leader of the 1898 revolution.
For surcharge see No. 1056.

Flags Surrounding SEATO Emblem A171

Pres. Macapagal Signing Code A172

Unwmk.

1964, Sept. 8 **Photo.** *Perf. 13*

Flags and Emblem Multicolored

909 A171 6s dk bl & yel .20 .20
910 A171 10s dp grn & yel .20 .20
911 A171 25s dk brn & yel .30 .20
Nos. 909-911 (3) .70 .60

10th anniversary of the South-East Asia Treaty Organization (SEATO).
For surcharge see No. 1121.

1964, Dec. 21 **Wmk. 233** *Perf. 14½*

912 A172 3s multi .25 .20
913 A172 6s multi .25 .20
Nos. 912-913,C90 (3) 1.00 .60

Signing of the Agricultural Land Reform Code. For surcharges see Nos. 970, 1234.

Basketball — A173

Sport: 10s, Women's relay race. 20s, Hurdling. 30s, Soccer.

1964, Dec. 28 *Perf. 14½x14*

915 A173 6s lt bl, dk brn & gold .20 .20
916 A173 10s gold, pink & dk brn .25 .20
b. Gold omitted
917 A173 20s gold, dk brn & yel .45 .20
918 A173 30s emer, dk brn & gold .60 .20
Nos. 915-918 (4) 1.50 .80

18th Olympic Games, Tokyo, Oct. 10-25.
For overprints and surcharge see Nos. 962-965, 1079.

Imperf., Pairs

915a A173 6s 1.25 .75
916a A173 10s 1.25 .75
917a A173 20s 2.75 1.75
918a A173 30s 2.75 1.75
Nos. 915a-918a (4) 8.00 5.00

Presidents Lubke and Macapagal and Coats of Arms — A174

1965, Apr. 19 **Unwmk.** *Perf. 13½*

919 A174 6s ol grn & multi .20 .20
920 A174 10s multi .25 .20
921 A174 25s dp bl & multi .30 .20
Nos. 919-921 (3) .75 .60

Visit of Pres. Heinrich Lubke of Germany, Nov. 18-23, 1964.
For surcharge see No. 1167.

Emblems of Manila Observatory and Weather Bureau — A175

1965, May 22 **Photo.** *Perf. 13½*

922 A175 6s lt ultra & multi .20 .20
923 A175 20s lt vio & multi .20 .20
924 A175 50s bl grn & multi .35 .25
Nos. 922-924 (3) .75 .65

Issued to commemorate the centenary of the Meteorological Service in the Philippines.
For surcharge see No. 1069.

Pres. John F. Kennedy (1917-63) — A176

Perf. 14½x14

1965, May 29 **Wmk. 233**

Center Multicolored

925 A176 6s gray .20 .20
926 A176 10s brt vio .20 .20
927 A176 30s ultra .35 .20
Nos. 925-927 (3) .75 .60

Nos. 925-927 exist with ultramarine of tie omitted.
The 6s and 30s exist imperf. Value, each $30.
For surcharges see Nos. 1148, 1210.

King and Queen of Thailand, Pres. and Mrs. Macapagal — A177

Perf. 12½x13

1965, June 12 **Unwmk.**

928 A177 2s brt bl & multi .20 .20
929 A177 6s bis & multi .20 .20
930 A177 30s red & multi .35 .20
Nos. 928-930 (3) .75 .60

Visit of King Bhumibol Adulyadej and Queen Sirikit of Thailand, July 1963.

For surcharge see No. 1122.

Princess Beatrix and Evangelina Macapagal A178

Perf. 13x12½

1965, July 4 Photo. Unwmk.

931 A178 2s bl & multi	.20	.20
932 A178 6s blk & multi	.20	.20
933 A178 10s multi	.35	.20
Nos. 931-933 (3)	.75	.60

Visit of Princess Beatrix of the Netherlands, Nov. 21-23, 1962.

For surcharge see No. 1188.

Cross and Rosary Held Before Map of Philippines — A179

Design: 6s, Map of Philippines, cross and Legaspi-Urdaneta monument.

1965, Oct. 4 Unwmk. *Perf. 13*

934 A179 3s multi	.25	.20
935 A179 6s multi	.25	.20
Nos. 934-935,C91-C92 (4)	2.00	.95

400th anniv. of the Christianization of the Philippines. See souvenir sheet No. C92a. For overprint see No. C108.

Presidents Sukarno and Macapagal and Prime Minister Tunku Abdul Rahman A180

1965, Nov. 25 *Perf. 13*

936 A180 6s multi	.20	.20
937 A180 10s multi	.20	.20
938 A180 25s multi	.35	.20
Nos. 936-938 (3)	.75	.60

Signing of the Manila Accord (Mapilindo) by Malaya, Philippines and Indonesia.

For surcharge see No. 1182.

Bicyclists and Globe A181

1965, Dec. 5 *Perf. 13½*

939 A181 6s multi	.20	.20
940 A181 10s multi	.20	.20
941 A181 25s multi	.35	.20
Nos. 939-941 (3)	.75	.60

Second Asian Cycling Championship, Philippines, Nov. 28-Dec. 5.

Nos. B21-B22 Surcharged

1965, Dec. 30 Engr. *Perf. 13*

942 SP12 10s on 6s + 4s	.20	.20
943 SP12 30s on 30s + 5s	.30	.25

Inauguration of President Ferdinand Marcos and Vice-President Fernando Lopez.

Antonio Regidor — A182

1966, Jan. 21 *Perf. 12x11*

944 A182 6s blue	.20	.20
945 A182 30s brown	.30	.20

Dr. Antonio Regidor, Sec. of the High Court of Manila and Pres. of Public Instruction.

For surcharges see Nos. 1110-1111.

No. 857A Overprinted in Red: "HELP ME STOP / SMUGGLING / Pres. MARCOS"

1966, May 1 Engr. *Perf. 13½*

946 A158 6s peacock blue	.35	.20

Anti-smuggling drive.

Exists with overprint inverted, double, double inverted and double with one inverted.

For surcharge see No. 1209.

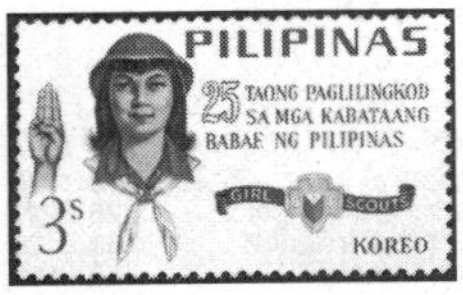

Girl Scout Giving Scout Sign A183

1966, May 26 Litho. *Perf. 13x12½*

947 A183 3s ultra & multi	.20	.20
948 A183 6s emer & multi	.20	.20
949 A183 20s brn & multi	.30	.20
Nos. 947-949 (3)	.70	.60

Philippine Girl Scouts, 25th anniversary.

For surcharge see No. 1019.

Pres. Marcos Taking Oath of Office — A184

1966, June 12 *Perf. 12½*

950 A184 6s bl & multi	.20	.20
951 A184 20s emer & multi	.20	.20
952 A184 30s yel & multi	.35	.20
Nos. 950-952 (3)	.75	.60

Inauguration of Pres. Ferdinand E. Marcos, 12/30/65.

For overprints & surcharge see #960-961, 1050.

Seal of Manila and Historical Scenes — A185

1966, June 24

953 A185 6s multi	.20	.20
954 A185 30s multi	.30	.20

Adoption of the new seal of Manila.

For surcharges see Nos. 1070, 1118, 1235.

Old and New Philippine National Bank Buildings — A186

Designs: 6s, Entrance to old bank building and 1p silver coin.

1966, July 22 Photo. *Perf. 14x13½*

955 A186 6s gold, ultra, sil & blk	.20	.20
956 A186 10s multi	.25	.20

50th anniv. of the Philippine Natl. Bank. See #C93. For surcharges see #1071, 1100, 1236.

Post Office, Annex Three A187

1966, Oct. 1 Wmk. 233 *Perf. 14½*

957 A187 6s lt vio, yel & grn	.20	.20
958 A187 10s rose cl, yel & grn	.25	.20
959 A187 20s ultra, yel & grn	.30	.20
Nos. 957-959 (3)	.75	.60

60th anniversary of Postal Savings Bank.

For surcharges see Nos. 1104, 1112, 1189.

Nos. 950 and 952 Overprinted in Emerald or Black

Perf. 12½

1966, Oct. 24 Litho. Unwmk.

960 A184 6s multi (E)	.20	.20
961 A184 30s multi	.30	.20

Manila Summit Conference, Oct. 23-27.

Nos. 915a-918a Overprinted

Wmk. 233

1967, Jan. 14 Photo. *Imperf.*

962 A173 6s lt bl, dk brn & gold	.35	.20
963 A173 10s gold, dk brn & pink	.35	.20
964 A173 20s gold, dk brn & yel	.45	.20
965 A173 30s emer, dk brn & gold	.60	.40
Nos. 962-965 (4)	1.75	1.00

Lions Intl., 50th anniv. The Lions emblem is in the lower left corner on the 6s, in the upper left corner on the 10s and in the upper right corner on the 30s.

"Succor" by Fernando Amorsolo — A188

Unwmk.

1967, May 15 Litho. *Perf. 14*

966 A188 5s sepia & multi	.25	.20
967 A188 20s blue & multi	.50	.20
968 A188 2p green & multi	1.25	.50
Nos. 966-968 (3)	2.00	.90

25th anniversary of the Battle of Bataan.

Nos. 857A and 913 Surcharged

1967, Aug. Engr. *Perf. 13½*

969 A158 4s on 6s pck bl	.25	.20

Wmk. 233

Photo. *Perf. 14½*

970 A172 5s on 6s multi	.35	.20

Issue dates: 4s, Aug. 10; 5s, Aug. 7.

Gen. Douglas MacArthur and Paratroopers Landing on Corregidor — A189

Unwmk.

1967, Aug. 31 Litho. *Perf. 14*

971 A189 6s multi	.35	.20
972 A189 5p multi	5.50	3.00

25th anniversary, Battle of Corregidor.

Bureau of Posts, Manila, Jones Bridge over Pasig River — A190

1967, Sept. 15 Litho. *Perf. 14x13½*

973 A190 4s multi & blk	.20	.20
974 A190 20s multi & red	.20	.20
975 A190 50s multi & vio	.30	.25
Nos. 973-975 (3)	.70	.65

65th anniversary of the Bureau of Posts.

For overprint see No. 1015.

Philippine Nativity Scene — A191

1967, Dec. 1 Photo. *Perf. 13½*

976 A191 10s multi	.20	.20
977 A191 40s multi	.30	.25

Christmas 1967.

Chinese Garden, Rizal Park, Presidents Marcos and Chiang Kai-shek — A192

Presidents' heads & scenes in Chinese Garden, Rizal Park, Manila: 10s, Gate. 20s, Landing pier.

1967-68 Photo. *Perf. 13½*

978 A192 5s multi	.20	.20
979 A192 10s multi ('68)	.35	.20
980 A192 20s multi	.70	.20
Nos. 978-980 (3)	1.25	.60

Sino-Philippine Friendship Year 1966-67.

Makati Center Post Office, Mrs. Marcos and Rotary Emblem — A193

1968, Jan. 9 Litho. *Perf. 14*

981 A193 10s bl & multi	.20	.20
982 A193 20s grn & multi	.25	.20
983 A193 40s multi	.45	.35
Nos. 981-983 (3)	.90	.75

1st anniv. of the Makati Center Post Office.

Nos. 882, 883C and B27 Surcharged with New Value and Two Bars

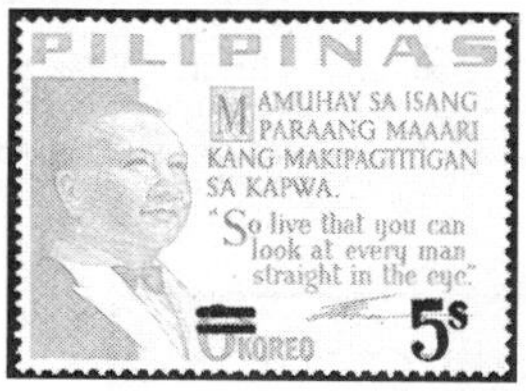

1968

984 A161 5s on 6s grn & blk	.40	.20
985 A161 5s on 6s lt red brn & blk	.40	.20
986 SP14 10s on 6s + 5s ultra & red	.45	.20
Nos. 984-986 (3)	1.25	.60

For similar surcharge see No. 1586.

Felipe G. Calderon, Barasoain Church and Malolos Constitution — A194

1968, Apr. 4 Litho. *Perf. 14*

987 A194 10s lt ultra & multi	.20	.20
988 A194 40s grn & multi	.30	.20
989 A194 75s multi	.60	.30
Nos. 987-989 (3)	1.10	.70

Calderon (1868-1909), lawyer and author of the Malolos Constitution.

Earth and Transmission from Philippine Station to Satellite — A195

1968, Oct. 21 Photo. *Perf. 13½*

990 A195 10s blk & multi	.30	.20
991 A195 40s multi	.55	.25
992 A195 75s multi	.90	.30
Nos. 990-992 (3)	1.75	.75

Issued to commemorate the inauguration of the Philcomsat Station in Tany, Luzon, May 2, 1968.

Tobacco Industry and Tobacco Board's Emblem — A196

1968, Nov. 15 Photo. *Perf. 13½*

993 A196 10s blk & multi	.20	.20
994 A196 40s bl & multi	.35	.30
995 A196 70s crim & multi	.60	.50
Nos. 993-995 (3)	1.15	1.00

Philippine tobacco industry.

Kudyapi A197

Philippine Musical Instruments: 20s, Ludag (drum). 30s, Kulintangan. 50s, Subing (bamboo flute).

1968, Nov. 22 Photo. *Perf. 13½*

996 A197 10s multi	.20	.20
997 A197 20s multi	.30	.20
998 A197 30s multi	.50	.25
999 A197 50s multi	.75	.45
Nos. 996-999 (4)	1.75	1.10

Concordia College A198

1968, Dec. 8 *Perf. 13x13½*

1000 A198 10s multi	.20	.20
1001 A198 20s multi	.25	.20
1002 A198 70s multi	.50	.30
Nos. 1000-1002 (3)	.95	.70

Centenary of the Colegio de la Concordia, Manila, a Catholic women's school. Issued Dec. 8 (Sunday), but entered the mail Dec. 9.

Singing Children — A199

1968, Dec. 16 *Perf. 13½*

1003 A199 10s multi	.20	.20
1004 A199 40s multi	.35	.35
1005 A199 75s multi	.70	.60
Nos. 1003-1005 (3)	1.25	1.15

Christmas 1968.

Animals A200

1969, Jan. 8 Photo. *Perf. 13½*

1006 A200 2s Tarsier	.20	.20
1007 A200 10s Tamarau	.25	.20
1008 A200 20s Carabao	.50	.20
1009 A200 75s Mouse deer	1.50	.75
Nos. 1006-1009 (4)	2.45	1.35

Opening of the hunting season.

Emilio Aguinaldo and Historical Building, Cavite — A201

1969, Jan. 23 Litho. *Perf. 14*

1010 A201 10s yel & multi	.20	.20
1011 A201 40s bl & multi	.40	.25
1012 A201 70s multi	.70	.55
Nos. 1010-1012 (3)	1.30	1.00

Emilio Aguinaldo (1869-1964), commander of Filipino forces in rebellion against Spain.

Guard Turret, San Andres Bastion, Manila, and Rotary Emblem — A202

1969, Jan. 29 Photo. *Perf. 12½*

1013 A202 10s ultra & multi	.35	.20
Nos. 1013,C96-C97 (3)	1.35	.80

50th anniv. of the Manila Rotary Club.

Senator Claro M. Recto (1890-1960), Lawyer and Supreme Court Judge — A203

1969, Feb. 10 Engr. *Perf. 13*

1014 A203 10s bright rose lilac	.35	.20

No. 973 Overprinted

1969, Feb. 14 Litho. *Perf. 14x13½*

1015 A190 4s multi & blk	.35	.20

Philatelic Week, Nov. 24-30, 1968.

José Rizal College, Mandaluyong — A204

1969, Feb. 19 Photo. *Perf. 13*

1016 A204 10s multicolored	.20	.20
1017 A204 40s multicolored	.30	.20
1018 A204 50s multicolored	.50	.25
Nos. 1016-1018 (3)	1.00	.65

Founding of Rizal College, 50th anniv.

No. 948 Surcharged in Red with New Value, 2 Bars and: "4th NATIONAL BOY / SCOUT JAMBOREE / PALAYAN CITY-MAY, 1969"

1969, May 12 Litho. *Perf. 13x12½*

1019 A183 5s on 6s multi	.35	.20

A205

A206

Map of Philippines, Red Crescent, Cross, Lion and Sun emblems.

1969, May 26 Photo. *Perf. 12½*

1020 A205 10s gray, ultra & red	.20	.20
1021 A205 40s lt ultra, dk bl & red	.30	.25
1022 A205 75s bister, brn & red	.50	.30
Nos. 1020-1022 (3)	1.00	.75

League of Red Cross Societies, 50th anniv.

1969, June 13 Photo. *Perf. 14*

Pres. and Mrs. Marcos harvesting miracle rice.

1023 A206 10s multicolored	.20	.20
1024 A206 40s multicolored	.25	.25
1025 A206 75s multicolored	.55	.30
Nos. 1023-1025 (3)	1.00	.75

Introduction of IR8 (miracle) rice, produced by the International Rice Research Institute.

Holy Child of Leyte and Map of Leyte — A207

1969, June 30 *Perf. 13½*

1026 A207 5s emerald & multi	.20	.20
1027 A207 10s crimson & multi	.25	.20

80th anniv. of the return of the image of the Holy Child of Leyte to Tacloban. See No. C98.

Philippine Development Bank — A208

1969, Sept. 12 Photo. *Perf. 13½*

1028 A208 10s dk bl, blk & grn	.20	.20
1029 A208 40s rose car, blk & grn	.40	.25
1030 A208 75s brown, blk & grn	.70	.30
Nos. 1028-1030 (3)	1.30	.75

Inauguration of the new building of the Philippine Development Bank in Makati, Rizal.

Common Birdwing A209

Butterflies: 20s, Tailed jay. 30s, Red Helen. 40s, Birdwing.

1969, Sept. 15 Photo. *Perf. 13½*

1031 A209 10s multicolored	.45	.20
1032 A209 20s multicolored	1.10	.20
1033 A209 30s multicolored	.90	.25
1034 A209 40s multicolored	.90	.35
Nos. 1031-1034 (4)	3.35	1.00

World's Children and UNICEF Emblem A210

1969, Oct. 6

1035 A210 10s blue & multi	.20	.20
1036 A210 20s multicolored	.25	.20
1037 A210 30s multicolored	.30	.20
Nos. 1035-1037 (3)	.75	.60

15th anniversary of Universal Children's Day.

Monument and Leyte Landing — A211

1969, Oct. 20 *Perf. 13½x14*

1038 A211 5s lt grn & multi	.20	.20
1039 A211 10s yellow & multi	.25	.20
1040 A211 40s pink & multi	.30	.20
Nos. 1038-1040 (3)	.75	.60

25th anniv. of the landing of the US forces under Gen. Douglas MacArthur on Leyte, Oct. 20, 1944.

Philippine Cultural Center, Manila — A212

1969, Nov. 4 Photo. *Perf. 13½*

1041 A212 10s ultra	.25	.20
1042 A212 30s brt rose lilac	.40	.20

Cultural Center of the Philippines, containing theaters, a museum and libraries.

Nos. 889-892 Surcharged or Overprinted: "1969 PHILATELIC WEEK"

1969, Nov. 24 Photo. *Perf. 14*

1043 A164 5s multicolored	.40	.20
1044 A164 5s on 6s multi	.40	.20
1045 A164 10s multicolored	.40	.25
1046 A164 10s on 20s multi	.40	.25
a. Block of 4, #1043-1046	1.75	1.25

Philatelic Week, Nov. 23-29.

Melchora Aquino — A213

1969, Nov. 30 *Perf. 12½*

1047 A213 10s multicolored	.20	.20
1048 A213 20s multicolored	.20	.20
1049 A213 30s dk bl & multi	.30	.20
Nos. 1047-1049 (3)	.70	.60

Melchora Aquino (Tandang Sora; 1812-1919), the Grand Old Woman of the Revolution.

No. 950 Surcharged with New Value, 2 Bars and: "PASINAYA, IKA -2 PANUNUNGKULAN / PANGULONG FERDINAND E. MARCOS / DISYEMBRE 30, 1969"

1969, Dec. 30 Litho. *Perf. 12½*

1050 A184 5s on 6s multi	.55	.20

Inauguration of Pres. Marcos and Vice Pres. Fernando Lopez for 2nd term, 12/30.

Pouring Ladle and Iligan Steel Mills — A214

1970, Jan. 20 Photo. *Perf. 13½*

1051 A214 10s ver & multi	.20	.20
1052 A214 20s multicolored	.20	.20
1053 A214 30s ultra & multi	.30	.20
Nos. 1051-1053 (3)	.70	.60

Iligan Integrated Steel Mills, Northern Mindanao, the first Philippine steel mills.

Nos. 857A, 904 and 906 Surcharged with New Value and Two Bars

1970, Apr. 30 As Before

1054 A158 4s on 6s peacock bl	.40	.20
1055 A169 5s on 6s multi	.55	.20
1056 A170 5s on 6s pur & gold	.55	.20
Nos. 1054-1056 (3)	1.50	.60

New UPU Headquarters and Monument, Bern — A215

Perf. 13½

1970, May 20 Unwmk. Photo.

1057 A215 10s bl, dk bl & yel	.20	.20
1058 A215 30s lt grn, dk bl & yel	.25	.20

Opening of the new UPU Headquarters in Bern.

Emblem, Mayon Volcano and Filipina — A216

1970, Sept. 6 Photo. *Perf. 13½x14*

1059 A216 10s brt blue & multi	.20	.20
1060 A216 20s multicolored	.25	.20
1061 A216 30s multicolored	.30	.20
Nos. 1059-1061 (3)	.75	.60

15th International Conference on Social Welfare, Manila, Sept. 6-12.

Crab, by Alexander Calder, and Map of Philippines A217

1970, Oct. 5 *Perf. 13x13½*

1062 A217 10s emerald & multi	.20	.20
1063 A217 40s multicolored	.30	.20
1064 A217 50s ultra & multi	.40	.30
Nos. 1062-1064 (3)	.90	.70

Campaign against cancer.

Scaled Tridacna A218

Sea Shells: 10s, Royal spiny oyster. 20s, Venus comb. 40s, Glory of the sea.

1970, Oct. 19 Photo. *Perf. 13½*

1065 A218 5s black & multi	.40	.20
1066 A218 10s dk grn & multi	.70	.20
1067 A218 20s multicolored	.70	.25
1068 A218 40s dk blue & multi	1.10	.30
Nos. 1065-1068 (4)	2.90	.95

Nos. 922, 953 and 955 Surcharged

Photogravure; Lithographed

1970, Oct. 26 *Perf. 13½, 12½*

1069 A175 4s on 6s multi	.70	.20
1070 A185 4s on 6s multi	1.10	.20
1071 A186 4s on 6s multi	1.10	.20
Nos. 1069-1071 (3)	2.90	.60

One line surcharge on No. 1071.

Map of Philippines and FAPA Emblem — A219

1970, Nov. 16 Photo. *Perf. 13½*

1072 A219 10s dp org & multi	.20	.20
1073 A219 50s lt violet & multi	.35	.20

Opening of the 4th General Assembly of the Federation of Asian Pharmaceutical Assoc. (FAPA) & the 3rd Asian Cong. of Pharmaceutical Sciences.

Hundred Islands of Pangasinan, Peddler's Cart — A220

20s, Tree house in Pasonanca Park, Zamboanga City. 30s, Sugar industry, Negros Island, Mt. Kanlaon, Woman & Carabao statue, symbolizing agriculture. 2p, Miagao Church, Iloilo, & horse-drawn calesa.

1970, Nov. 12 *Perf. 12½x13½*

1074 A220 10s multicolored	.20	.20
1075 A220 20s multicolored	.30	.20
1076 A220 30s multicolored	.75	.25
1077 A220 2p multicolored	2.40	1.00
Nos. 1074-1077 (4)	3.65	1.65

Tourist publicity. See Nos. 1086-1097.

No. 884 Surcharged: "UPU-AOPU / Regional Seminar / Nov. 23-Dec. 5, 1970 / TEN 10s"

1970, Nov. 22 Photo. *Perf. 13½x13*

1078 A162 10s on 6s multi	.35	.20

Universal Postal Union and Asian-Oceanic Postal Union Regional Seminar, 11/23-12/5.

No. 915 Surcharged Vertically: "1970 PHILATELIC WEEK"

Perf. 14½x14

1970, Nov. 22 Wmk. 233

1079 A173 10s on 6s multi	.35	.20

Philatelic Week, Nov. 22-28.

Pope Paul VI, Map of Far East and Australia — A221

Perf. 13½x14

1970, Nov. 27 Photo. Unwmk.

1080 A221 10s ultra & multi	.25	.20
1081 A221 30s multicolored	.45	.25
Nos. 1080-1081,C99 (3)	1.30	.70

Visit of Pope Paul VI, Nov. 27-29, 1970.

Mariano Ponce — A222

1970, Dec. 30 Engr. *Perf. 14½*

1082 A222 10s rose carmine	.35	.20

Mariano Ponce (1863-1918), editor and legislator. See #1136-1137. For surcharges & overprint see #1190, 1231, O70.

PATA Emblem A223

1971, Jan. 21 Photo. *Perf. 14½*

1083 A223 5s brt green & multi	.30	.20
1084 A223 10s blue & multi	.40	.20
1085 A223 70s brown & multi	.70	.30
Nos. 1083-1085 (3)	1.40	.70

Pacific Travel Association (PATA), 20th annual conference, Manila, Jan. 21-29.

Tourist Type of 1970

Designs: 10s, Filipina and Ang Nayong (7 village replicas around man-made lagoon). 20s, Woman and fisherman, Estancia. 30s, Pagsanjan Falls. 5p, Watch Tower, Punta Cruz, Boho.

Perf. 12½x13½

1971, Feb. 15 Photo.

1086 A220 10s multicolored	.35	.20
1087 A220 20s multicolored	.35	.20
1088 A220 30s multicolored	.85	.30
1089 A220 5p multicolored	3.50	1.75
Nos. 1086-1089 (4)	5.05	2.45

1971, Apr. 19

Designs: 10s, Cultured pearl farm, Davao. 20s, Coral divers, Davao, Mindanao. 40s, Moslem Mosque, Zamboanga. 1p, Rice terraces, Banaue.

1090 A220 10s multicolored	.30	.20
1091 A220 20s multicolored	.40	.20
1092 A220 40s multicolored	.90	.25
1093 A220 1p multicolored	1.75	.40
Nos. 1090-1093 (4)	3.35	1.05

1971, May 3

10s, Spanish cannon, Zamboanga. 30s, Magellan's cross, Cebu City. 50s, Big Jar monument in Calamba, Laguna. 70s, Mayon Volcano, Legaspi.

1094 A220 10s multicolored	.30	.20
1095 A220 30s multicolored	.40	.20
1096 A220 50s multicolored	.80	.25
1097 A220 70s multicolored	1.25	.35
Nos. 1094-1097 (4)	2.75	1.00

Family and Emblem A224

1971, Mar. 21 Photo. *Perf. 13½*

1098 A224 20s lt grn & multi	.20	.20
1099 A224 40s pink & multi	.25	.20

Regional Conf. of the Intl. Planned Parenthood Federation for SE Asia & Oceania, Baguio City, Mar. 21-27.

No. 955 Surcharged

1971, June 10 Photo. *Perf. 14x13½*
1100 A186 5s on 6s multi .35 .20

Allegory of Law
A225

1971, June 15 Photo. *Perf. 13*
1101 A225 15s orange & multi .35 .20

60th anniversary of the University of the Philippines Law College. See No. C100.

Manila Anniversary Emblem — A226

1971, June 24
1102 A226 10s multicolored .35 .20

Founding of Manila, 400th anniv. See #C101.

Santo Tomas University, Arms of Schools of Medicine and Pharmacology — A227

1971, July 8 Photo. *Perf. 13½*
1103 A227 5s yellow & multi .35 .20

Centenary of the founding of the Schools of Medicine and Surgery, and Pharmacology at the University of Santo Tomas, Manila. See No. C102.

No. 957 Surcharged

1971, July 11 Wmk. 233 *Perf. 14½*
1104 A187 5s on 6s multi .35 .20

World Congress of University Presidents, Manila.

Our Lady of Guia Appearing to Filipinos and Spanish Soldiers — A228

1971, July 8 Photo. *Perf. 13½*
1105 A228 10s multi .20 .20
1106 A228 75s multi .80 .35

4th centenary of appearance of the statue of Our Lady of Guia, Ermita, Manila.

Bank Building, Plane, Car and Workers — A229

1971, Sept. 14 *Perf. 12½*
1107 A229 10s blue & multi .25 .20
1108 A229 30s lt grn & multi .25 .20
1109 A229 1p multicolored .50 .30
Nos. 1107-1109 (3) 1.00 .70

1st Natl. City Bank in the Philippines, 70th anniv.

No. 944 Surcharged

Perf. 12x11
1971, Nov. 24 Engr. Unwmk.
1110 A182 4s on 6s blue .30 .20
1111 A182 5s on 6s blue .30 .20

No. 957 Surcharged

Wmk. 233
1971, Nov. 24 Photo. *Perf. 14½*
1112 A187 5s on 6s multi .35 .20

Philatelic Week, 1971.

Radar with Map of Far East and Oceania — A230

1972, Feb. 29 Photo. *Perf. 14x14½*
1113 A230 5s org yel & multi .20 .20
1114 A230 40s red org & multi .30 .20

Electronics Conferences, Manila, 12/1-7/71.

Fathers Gomez, Burgos and Zamora — A231

1972, Apr. 3 *Perf. 13x12½*
1115 A231 5s gold & multi .30 .20
1116 A231 60s gold & multi .45 .20

Centenary of the deaths of Fathers Mariano Gomez, José Burgos and Jacinto Zamora, martyrs for Philippine independence from Spain.

Digestive Tract — A232

1972, Apr. 11 Photo. *Perf. 12½x13*
1117 A232 20s ultra & multi .35 .20

4th Asian Pacific Congress of Gastroenterology, Manila, Feb. 5-12. See No. C103.

No. 953 Surcharged

1972, Apr. 20 *Perf. 12½*
1118 A185 5s on 6s multi .75 .20

No. O69 with Two Bars over "G." and "O."

1972, May 16 Engr. *Perf. 13½*
1119 A158 50s violet .60 .20

Nos. 883A, 909 and 929 Surcharged with New Value and 2 Bars

1972, May 29
1120 A161 10s on 6s dp cl & blk 1.00 .20
1121 A171 10s on 6s multi 1.00 .20
1122 A177 10s on 6s multi .90 .20
Nos. 1120-1122 (3) 2.90 .60

Independence Monument, Manila — A233

1972, May 31 Photo. *Perf. 13x12½*
1123 A233 5s brt blue & multi .20 .20
1124 A233 50s red & multi .45 .20
1125 A233 60s emerald & multi .60 .20
Nos. 1123-1125 (3) 1.25 .60

Visit ASEAN countries (Association of South East Asian Nations).

"K," Skull and Crossbones — A234

Development of Philippine Flag: No. 1126, 3 "K's" in a row ("K" stands for Katipunan). No. 1127, 3 "K's" as triangle. No. 1128, One "K." No. 1130, 3 "K's," sun over mountain on white triangle. No. 1131, Sun over 3 "K's." No. 1132, Tagalog "K" in sun. No. 1133, Sun with human face. No. 1134, Tricolor flag, forerunner of present flag. No. 1135, Present flag. Nos. 1126, 1128, 1130-1131, 1133, 1135 inscribed in Tagalog.

1972, June 12 Photo. *Perf. 13*
1126 A234 30s ultra & red 1.50 .30
1127 A234 30s ultra & red 1.50 .30
1128 A234 30s ultra & red 1.50 .30
1129 A234 30s ultra & blk 1.50 .30
1130 A234 30s ultra & red 1.50 .30
1131 A234 30s ultra & red 1.50 .30
1132 A234 30s ultra & red 1.50 .30
1133 A234 30s ultra & red 1.50 .30
1134 A234 30s ultra, red & blk 1.50 .30
1135 A234 30s ultra, yel & red 1.50 .30
a. Block of 10 17.50 10.00

Portrait Type of 1970

40s, Gen. Miguel Malvar. 1p, Julian Felipe.

1972 Engr. *Perf. 14*
1136 A222 40s rose red .25 .20
1137 A222 1p deep blue .55 .20

Honoring Gen. Miguel Malvar (1865-1911), revolutionary leader, and Julian Felipe (1861-1944), composer of Philippine national anthem.

Issue dates: 40s, July 10; 1p, June 26.

Parrotfish
A235

1972, Aug. 14 Photo. *Perf. 13*
1138 A235 5s shown .25 .20
1139 A235 10s Sunburst butterflyfish .85 .20
1140 A235 20s Moorish idol .80 .25
Nos. 1138-1140,C104 (4) 3.00 1.05

Tropical fish.

Development Bank of the Philippines
A236

1972, Sept. 12
1141 A236 10s gray blue & multi .20 .20
1142 A236 20s lilac & multi .20 .20
1143 A236 60s tan & multi .25 .20
Nos. 1141-1143 (3) .65 .60

Development Bank of the Philippines, 25th anniv.

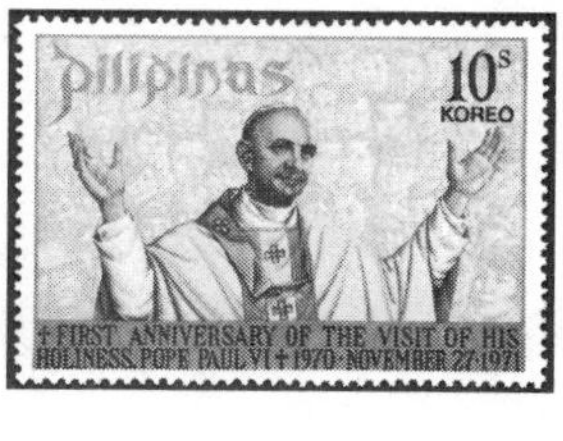

Pope Paul VI
A237

1972, Sept. 26 Unwmk. *Perf. 14*

1144 A237	10s lt green & multi	.25	.20
1145 A237	50s lt violet & multi	.50	.30
	Nos. 1144-1145,C105 (3)	1.35	.85

First anniversary (in 1971) of the visit of Pope Paul VI to the Philippines, and for his 75th birthday.

Nos. 880, 899 and 925 Surcharged with New Value and 2 Bars

1972, Sept. 29 As Before

1146 A161	10s on 6s lil & blk	1.00	.20
1147 A167	10s on 6s multi	1.00	.20
1148 A176	10s on 6s multi	.90	.20
	Nos. 1146-1148 (3)	2.90	.60

Charon's Bark, by Resurrección Hidalgo — A238

Paintings: 10s, Rice Workers' Meal, by F. Amorsolo. 30s, "Spain and the Philippines," by Juan Luna, vert. 70s, Song of Maria Clara, by F. Amorsolo.

Perf. 14x13

1972, Oct. 16 Unwmk. Photo.

Size: 38x40mm

1149 A238	5s silver & multi	.35	.20
1150 A238	10s silver & multi	.35	.20

Size: 24x56mm

1151 A238	30s silver & multi	.75	.20

Size: 38x40mm

1152 A238	70s silver & multi	.75	.30
	Nos. 1149-1152 (4)	2.20	.90

25th anniversary of the organization of the Stamp and Philatelic Division.

Lamp, Nurse, Emblem — A239

1972, Oct. 22 *Perf. 12½x13½*

1153 A239	5s violet & multi	.20	.20
1154 A239	10s blue & multi	.25	.20
1155 A239	70s orange & multi	.30	.25
	Nos. 1153-1155 (3)	.75	.65

Philippine Nursing Association, 50th anniv.

Heart, Map of Philippines A240

1972, Oct. 24 *Perf. 13*

1156 A240	5s purple, emer & red	.20	.20
1157 A240	10s blue, emer & red	.20	.20
1158 A240	30s emerald, bl & red	.35	.20
	Nos. 1156-1158 (3)	.75	.60

"Your heart is your health," World Health Month.

First Mass on Limasawa, by Carlos V. Francisco — A241

1972, Oct. 31 *Perf. 14*

1159 A241	10s brown & multi	.35	.20

450th anniversary of the first mass in the Philippines, celebrated by Father Valderama on Limasawa, Mar. 31, 1521. See No. C106.

Nos. 878, 882, 899 Surcharged: "ASIA PACIFIC SCOUT CONFERENCE NOV. 1972"

1972, Nov. 13 As Before

1160 A161	10s on 6s bl & blk	.55	.25
1161 A161	10s on 6s grn & blk	.75	.25
1162 A167	10s on 6s multi	.55	.25
	Nos. 1160-1162 (3)	1.85	.75

Asia Pacific Scout Conference, Nov. 1972.

Torch, Olympic Emblems — A242

Perf. 12½x13½

1972, Nov. 15 Photo.

1163 A242	5s blue & multi	.20	.20
1164 A242	10s multicolored	.50	.20
1165 A242	70s orange & multi	.90	.40
	Nos. 1163-1165 (3)	1.60	.80

20th Olympic Games, Munich, 8/26-9/11.
For surcharges see Nos. 1297, 1759-1760.

Nos. 896 and 919 Surcharged with New Value, Two Bars and: "1972 PHILATELIC WEEK"

1972, Nov. 23 Photo. *Perf. 13½*

1166 A166	10s on 6s multi	.45	.20
1167 A174	10s on 6s multi	.45	.20

Philatelic Week 1972.

Manunggul Burial Jar, 890-710 B.C. — A243

#1169, Ngipet Duldug Cave ritual earthenware vessel, 155 B.C. #1170, Metal age chalice, 200-600 A.D. #1171, Earthenware vessel, 15th cent.

1972, Nov. 29

1168 A243	10s green & multi	.30	.20
1169 A243	10s lilac & multi	.30	.20
1170 A243	10s blue & multi	.30	.20
1171 A243	10s yellow & multi	.30	.20
	Nos. 1168-1171 (4)	1.20	.80

College of Pharmacy and Univ. of the Philippines Emblems — A244

1972, Dec. 11 *Perf. 12½x13½*

1172 A244	5s lt vio & multi	.25	.20
1173 A244	10s yel grn & multi	.25	.20
1174 A244	30s ultra & multi	.40	.25
	Nos. 1172-1174 (3)	.90	.65

60th anniversary of the College of Pharmacy of the University of the Philippines.

Christmas Lantern Makers, by Jorgé Pineda — A245

1972, Dec. 14 Photo. *Perf. 12½*

1175 A245	10s dk bl & multi	.20	.20
1176 A245	30s brown & multi	.50	.20
1177 A245	50s green & multi	.75	.25
	Nos. 1175-1177 (3)	1.45	.65

Christmas 1972.

Red Cross Flags, Pres. Roxas and Mrs. Aurora Quezon A246

1972, Dec. 21

1178 A246	5s ultra & multi	.20	.20
1179 A246	20s multicolored	.25	.20
1180 A246	30s brown & multi	.30	.20
	Nos. 1178-1180 (3)	.75	.60

25th anniv. of the Philippine Red Cross.

Nos. 894 and 936 Surcharged with New Value and 2 Bars

1973, Jan. 22 Photo. *Perf. 14, 13*

1181 A165	10s on 6s multi	.55	.20
1182 A180	10s on 6s multi	.55	.20

San Luis University, Luzon — A247

1973, Mar. 1 Photo. *Perf. 13½x14*

1183 A247	5s multicolored	.25	.20
1184 A247	10s yellow & multi	.35	.20
1185 A247	75s multicolored	.40	.25
	Nos. 1183-1185 (3)	1.00	.65

60th anniversary of San Luis University, Baguio City, Luzon.
For surcharge see No. 1305.

Jesus Villamor and Fighter Planes — A248

1973, Apr. 9 Photo. *Perf. 13½x14*

1186 A248	10s multicolored	.25	.20
1187 A248	2p multicolored	1.25	.70

Col. Jesus Villamor (1914-1971), World War II aviator who fought for liberation of the Philippines.
For surcharge see No. 1230.

Nos. 932, 957, O70 Surcharged with New Values and 2 Bars

1973, Apr. 23 As Before

1188 A178	5s on 6s multi	1.10	.20
1189 A187	5s on 6s multi	1.00	.20
1190 A222	15s on 10s rose car	.75	.20
	Nos. 1188-1190 (3)	2.85	.60

Two additional bars through "G.O." on No. 1190.

ITI Emblem, Performance and Actor Vic Silayan — A249

1973, May 15 Photo. *Perf. 13x12½*

1191 A249	5s blue & multi	.20	.20
1192 A249	10s yel grn & multi	.25	.20
1193 A249	50s orange & multi	.45	.20
1194 A249	70s rose & multi	.60	.25
	Nos. 1191-1194 (4)	1.50	.85

1st Third World Theater Festival, sponsored by the UNESCO affiliated International Theater Institute, Manila, Nov. 19-30, 1971.
For surcharge see No. 1229.

Josefa Llanes Escoda — A250

#1196, Gabriela Silang. No. 1197, Rafael Palma. 30s, Jose Rizal. 60s, Marcela Agoncillo. 90s, Teodoro R. Yangco. 1.10p, Dr. Pio Venezuela. 1.20p, Gregoria de Jesus. #1204, Pedro A. Paterno. #1205, Teodora Alonso. 1.80p, Edilberto Evangelista. 5p, Fernando M. Guerrero.

1973-78 Engr. *Perf. 14½*

1195 A250	15s sepia	.20	.20

Litho. *Perf. 12½*

1196 A250	15s	violet ('74)	.20	.20
1197 A273	15s	emerald ('74)	.20	.20
1198 A250	30s	vio bl ('78)	.20	.20
1199 A250	60s	dl red brn	.55	.25
1200 A273	90s	brt bl ('74)	.75	.20
1202 A273	1.10p	brt bl ('74)	.90	.20
1203 A250	1.20p	dl red ('78)	.60	.20
1204 A250	1.50p	lil rose	1.25	.45
1205 A273	1.50p	brown ('74)	1.25	.20
1206 A250	1.80p	green	2.00	.55
1208 A250	5p	blue	4.25	1.75
		Nos. 1195-1208 (12)	12.35	4.60

1973-74 *Imperf.*

1196a	A250	15s	violet ('74)	.50	.40
1197a	A273	15s	emerald ('74)	.50	.40
1199a	A250	60s	dull red brown	2.50	1.00
1200a	A273	90s	bright blue ('74)	3.00	2.00
1202a	A273	1.10p	bright blue ('74)	4.00	2.50
1204a	A250	1.50p	lilac rose	4.50	3.00
1205a	A273	1.50p	brown ('74)	5.00	3.50

1206a A250 1.80p green 6.00 4.00
1208a A250 5p blue 15.00 8.00
Nos. 1196a-1208a (9) 41.00 24.80

Honoring: Escoda (1898-194?), leader of Girl Scouts and Federation of Women's Clubs. Silang (1731-63), "the Ilocana Joan of Arc". Palma (1874-1939), journalist, statesman, educator. Rizal (1861-96), natl. hero. Agoncillo (1859-1946), designer of 1st Philippine flag, 1898. Yangco (1861-1939), patriot and philanthropist. Valenzuela (1869-1956), physician and newspaperman.

Gregoria de Jesus, independence leader. Paterno (1857-1911), lawyer, writer, patriot. Alonso (1827-1911), mother of Rizal. Evangelista (1862-97), army engineer, patriot. Guerrero (1873-1929), journalist, political leader.

For overprint & surcharges see #1277, 1311, 1470, 1518.

No. 946 surcharged with New Value

1973, June 4 Engr. *Perf. 13½*
1209 A158 5s on 6s peacock bl .60 .20

Anti-smuggling campaign.

No. 925 Surcharged

1973, June 4 Wmk. 233
1210 A176 5s on 6s multi .60 .20

10th anniv. of death of John F. Kennedy.

Pres. Marcos, Farm Family, Unfurling of Philippine Flag — A251

Perf. 12½x13½

1973, Sept. 24 Photo. Unwmk.
1211 A251 15s ultra & multi .25 .20
1212 A251 45s red & multi .50 .20
1213 A251 90s multi .75 .25
Nos. 1211-1213 (3) 1.50 .65

75th anniversary of Philippine independence and 1st anniversary of proclamation of martial law.

Imelda Romualdez Marcos, First Lady of the Philippines A252

1973, Oct. 31 Photo. *Perf. 13*
1214 A252 15s dl bl & multi .20 .20
1215 A252 50s multicolored .40 .20
1216 A252 60s lil & multi .50 .25
Nos. 1214-1216 (3) 1.10 .65

Presidential Palace, Manila, Pres. and Mrs. Marcos — A253

1973, Nov. 15 Litho. *Perf. 14*
1217 A253 15s rose & multi .20 .20
1218 A253 50s ultra & multi .50 .20
Nos. 1217-1218,C107 (3) 1.35 .70

INTERPOL Emblem — A254

1973, Dec. 18 Photo. *Perf. 13*
1219 A254 15s ultra & multi .30 .20
1220 A254 65s lt grn & multi .40 .20

Intl. Criminal Police Organization, 50th anniv.

Cub and Boy Scouts — A255

15s, Various Scout activities; inscribed in Tagalog.

1973, Dec. 28 Litho. *Perf. 12½*
1221 A255 15s bister & emer .40 .20
a. Imperf, pair ('74) 2.50 1.50
1222 A255 65s bister & brt bl .75 .30
a. Imperf, pair ('74) 3.50 2.00

50th anniv. of Philippine Boy Scouts.
Nos. 1221a-1222a issued Feb. 4, although first day covers are dated Dec. 28, 1973.

Manila, Bank Emblem and Farmers — A256

Designs: 60s, Old bank building. 1.50p, Modern bank building.

1974, Jan. 3 Photo. *Perf. 12½x13½*
1223 A256 15s silver & multi .20 .20
1224 A256 60s silver & multi .35 .20
1225 A256 1.50p silver & multi 1.10 .40
Nos. 1223-1225 (3) 1.65 .80

Central Bank of the Philippines, 25th anniv.

UPU Emblem, Maria Clara Costume — A257

Filipino Costumes: 60s, Balintawak and UPU emblem. 80s, Malong costume and UPU emblem.

1974, Jan. 15 *Perf. 12½*
1226 A257 15s multicolored .20 .20
1227 A257 60s multicolored .45 .20
1228 A257 80s multicolored .80 .35
Nos. 1226-1228 (3) 1.45 .75

Centenary of Universal Postal Union.

No. 1192 Surcharged in Red with New Value, 2 Bars and: "1973 / PHILATELIC WEEK"

1974, Feb. 4 Photo. *Perf. 13x12½*
1229 A249 15s on 10s multi .60 .20

Philatelic Week, 1973. First day covers exist dated Nov. 26, 1973.

Nos. 1186 and 1136 Overprinted and Surcharged

1974, Mar. 25 Photo. *Perf. 13½x14*
1230 A248 15s on 10s multi .60 .20

Engr. *Perf. 14*
1231 A222 45s on 40s rose red .60 .20

Lions Intl. of the Philippines, 25th anniv. The overprint on #1230 arranged to fit shape of stamp.

Pediatrics Congress Emblem and Map of Participating Countries A258

1974, Apr. 30 Litho. *Perf. 12½*
1232 A258 30s brt bl & red .35 .20
a. Imperf, pair 2.50 1.50
1233 A258 1p dl grn & red .80 .30
a. Imperf, pair 5.00 3.50

Asian Congress of Pediatrics, Manila, Apr. 30-May 4.

Nos. 912, 954-955 Surcharged with New Value and Two Bars

1974, Aug. 1 As Before
1234 A172 5s on 3s multi .75 .25
1235 A185 5s on 6s multi 1.00 .25
1236 A186 5s on 6s multi 1.25 .25
Nos. 1234-1236 (3) 3.00 .75

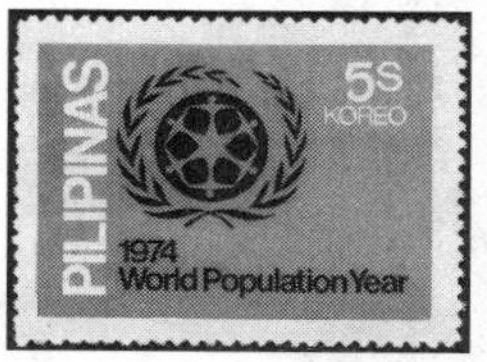

WPY Emblem A259

1974, Aug. 15 Litho. *Perf. 12½*
1237 A259 5s org & bl blk .35 .20
a. Imperf. 1.50 .75
1238 A259 2p lt grn & dk bl 1.50 .60
a. Imperf. 9.50 7.00

World Population Year, 1974.

Red Feather Community Chest Emblem A260

Wmk. 372

1974, Sept. 5 Litho. *Perf. 12½*
1239 A260 15s brt bl & red .20 .20
1240 A260 40s emer & red .45 .20
1241 A260 45s red brn & red .45 .20
Nos. 1239-1241 (3) 1.10 .60

Philippine Community Chest, 25th anniv.

Imperf. Pairs
1239a A260 15s 3.75 3.50
1240a A260 40s 1.75 1.25
1241a A260 45s 1.75 1.25
Nos. 1239a-1241a (3) 7.25 6.00

Sultan Kudarat, Flag, Order and Map of Philippines — A261

Perf. 13½x14

1975, Jan. 13 Photo. Unwmk.
1242 A261 15s multicolored .35 .20

Sultan Mohammad Dipatuan Kudarat, 16th-17th century ruler.

Mental Health Association Emblem A262

Wmk. 372

1975, Jan. 20 Litho. *Perf. 12½*
1243 A262 45s emer & org .35 .20
a. Imperf, pair 2.00 1.50
1244 A262 1p emer & pur .80 .30
a. Imperf, pair 4.00 3.00

Philippine Mental Health Assoc., 25th anniv.

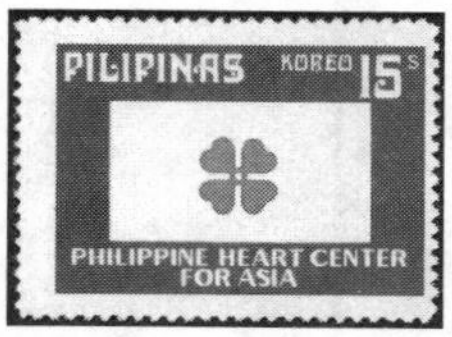

4-Leaf Clover A263

1975, Feb. 14
1245 A263 15s vio bl & red .35 .20
a. Imperf, pair 2.50 1.50
1246 A263 50s emer & red .80 .35
a. Imperf, pair 4.50 3.00

Philippine Heart Center for Asia, inauguration.

Military Academy, Cadet and Emblem — A264

Perf. 13½x14

1975, Feb. 17 Unwmk.
1247 A264 15s grn & multi .25 .20
1248 A264 45s plum & multi .45 .25

Philippine Military Academy, 70th anniv.

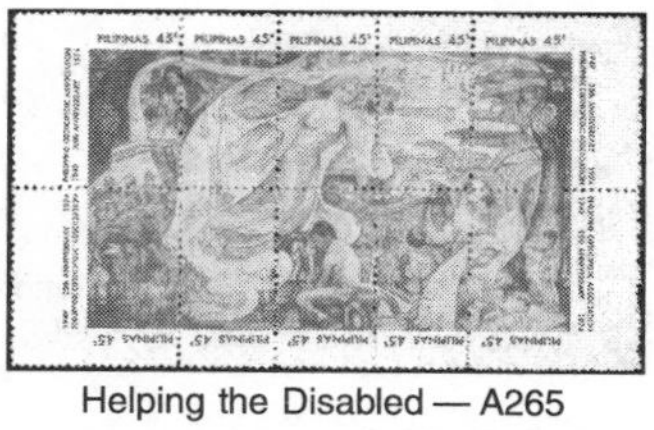

Helping the Disabled — A265

Perf. 12½, Imperf.

1975, Mar. 17 Wmk. 372
1249 A265 Block of 10 7.50 6.00
a.-j. 45s grn, any single .55 .35

25th anniversary (in 1974) of Philippine Orthopedic Association.
For surcharge see No. 1635.
No. 1249 exists imperf. Value unused, $10.

Nos. B43, B50-B51 Surcharged with New Value and Two Bars

1975, Apr. 15 **Unwmk.**

1250	SP18	5s on 15s + 5s	.60	.20
1251	SP16	60s on 70s + 5s	.90	.20
1252	SP18	1p on 1.10p + 5s	1.25	.35
		Nos. 1250-1252 (3)	2.75	.75

"Grow and Conserve Forests" — A266

1975, May 19 **Litho.** ***Perf. 14½***

1253		45s "Grow"	.30	.20
1254		45s "Conserve"	.30	.20
a.	A267	Pair, #1253-1254	.75	.50

Forest conservation.

Jade Vine — A268

1975, June 9 **Photo.** ***Perf. 14½***

1255	A268	15s multicolored	.35	.20

Imelda R. Marcos, IWY Emblem — A269

Civil Service Emblem — A270

Wmk. 372

1975, July 2 **Litho.** ***Perf. 12½***

1256	A269	15s bl & blk	.25	.20
a.		Imperf, pair	2.50	1.50
1257	A269	80s pink, bl & grn	.45	.25
a.		Imperf, pair	5.00	3.50

International Women's Year 1975.
For surcharges see Nos. 1500, 1505.

1975, Sept. 19 **Litho.** ***Perf. 12½***

1258	A270	15s multicolored	.25	.20
a.		Imperf, pair	2.00	1.50
1259	A270	50s multicolored	.45	.25
a.		Imperf, pair	3.25	2.00

Dam and Emblem A271

1975, Sept. 30

1260	A271	40s org & vio bl	.25	.20
a.		Imperf, pair	2.00	1.25
1261	A271	1.50p brt rose & vio bl	.90	.35
a.		Imperf, pair	5.50	4.50

For surcharges see Nos. 1517, 1520.

Manila Harbor, 1875 A272

1975, Nov. 4 **Unwmk.** ***Perf. 13x13½***

1262	A272	1.50p red & multi	1.25	.35

Hong Kong and Shanghai Banking Corporation, centenary of Philippines service.

Norberto Romualdez (1875-1941), Scholar and Legislator - A273

Jose Rizal Monument, Luneta Park — A273a

Noted Filipinos: No. 1264, Rafael Palma (1874-1939), journalist, statesman, educator. No. 1265, Rajah Kalantiaw, chief of Panay, author of ethical-penal code (1443). 65s, Emilio Jacinto (1875-1899), patriot. No. 1269, Gen. Gregorio del Pilar (1875-1899), military hero. No. 1270, Lope K. Santos (1879-1963), grammarian, writer. 1.60p, Felipe Agoncillo (1859-1941), lawyer, cabinet member.

Wmk. 372

1975-81 **Litho.** ***Perf. 12½***

1264	A273	30s brn ('77)	.20	.20
1265	A273	30s dp rose ('78)	.20	.20
1266	A273a	40s yel & blk ('81)	.40	.20
1267	A273	60s violet	.80	.20
a.		Imperf, pair	2.00	1.25
1268	A273	65s lilac rose	.75	.20
a.		Imperf, pair	2.00	1.25
1269	A273	90s lilac rose	1.25	.20
a.		Imperf, pair	3.00	2.25
1270	A273	90s grn ('78)	.50	.20
1272	A273	1.60p blk ('76)	1.75	.20
		Nos. 1264-1272 (8)	5.85	1.60

See #1195-1208. For overprint & surcharges see #1278, 1310, 1367, 1440, 1469, 1514, 1562, 1574, 1758-1760.

A274

1975, Nov. 22 **Litho.** ***Perf. 12½***

1275	A274	60s multicolored	.65	.20
1276	A274	1.50p multicolored	1.50	.50

1st landing of the Pan American World Airways China Clipper in the Philippines, 40th anniv.

Nos. 1199 and 1205 Overprinted

1975, Nov. 22 **Unwmk.**

1277	A250	60s dl red brn	.50	.25
1278	A273	1.50p brown	1.25	.30

Airmail Exhibition, Nov. 22-Dec. 9.

APO Emblem — A275

1975, Nov. 24 **Wmk. 372**

1279	A275	5s ultra & multi	.20	.20
a.		Imperf, pair	1.50	1.00
1280	A275	1p bl & multi	.50	.25
a.		Imperf, pair	6.00	4.50

Amateur Philatelists' Org., 25th anniv.
For surcharge see No. 1338.

A276

A277

Philippine Churches: 20s, San Agustin Church. 30s, Morong Church, horiz. 45s, Basilica of Taal, horiz. 60s, San Sebastian Church.

1975, Dec. 23 **Litho.** ***Perf. 12½***

1281	A276	20s bluish grn	.30	.20
1282	A276	30s yel org & blk	.30	.20
1283	A276	45s rose, brn & blk	.45	.20
1284	A276	60s yel, bis & blk	.75	.20
		Nos. 1281-1284 (4)	1.80	.80

Holy Year 1975.

Imperf. Pairs

1281a	A276	20s	2.00	1.40
1282a	A276	30s	2.00	1.40
1283a	A276	45s	3.50	2.00
1284a	A276	60s	5.00	3.50
		Nos. 1281a-1284a (4)	12.50	8.30

1976, Jan. 27

Conductor's hands.

1285	A277	5s org & multi	.25	.20
1286	A277	50s multicolored	.45	.20

Manila Symphony Orchestra, 50th anniv.

PAL Planes of 1946 and 1976 A278

1976, Feb. 14

1287	A278	60s bl & multi	.60	.25
1288	A278	1.50p red & multi	1.90	.60

Philippine Airlines, 30th anniversary.

National University A279

1976, Mar. 30

1289	A279	45s bl, vio bl & yel	.40	.20
1290	A279	60s lt bl, vio bl & pink	.75	.20

National University, 75th anniversary.

Eye Exam — A280

Book and Emblem — A281

1976, Apr. 7 **Litho.** ***Perf. 12½***

1291	A280	15s multicolored	.50	.20

World Health Day: "Foresight prevents blindness."

1976, May 24 **Unwmk.**

1292	A281	1.50p grn & multi	1.10	.30

National Archives, 75th anniversary.

Santo Tomas University, Emblems A282

1976, June 7 **Wmk. 372**

1293	A282	15s yel & multi	.20	.20
1294	A282	50s multicolored	.40	.20

Colleges of Education and Science, Santo Tomas University, 50th anniversary.

Maryknoll College — A283

Wmk. 372

1976, July 26 **Litho.** ***Perf. 12½***

1295	A283	15s lt bl & multi	.35	.20
1296	A283	1.50p bis & multi	.90	.25

Maryknoll College, Quezon City, 50th anniv.

No. 1164 Surcharged in Dark Violet

Perf. 12½x13½

1976, July 30 **Photo.**

1297 A242 15s on 10s multi .75 .25

21st Olympic Games, Montreal, Canada, July 17-Aug. 1.

Police College, Manila — A284

1976, Aug. 8 **Litho.** ***Perf. 12½***

1298 A284 15s multicolored .25 .20
a. Imperf, pair 1.75 1.25
1299 A284 60s multicolored .60 .25
a. Imperf, pair 5.75 4.25

Philippine Constabulary, 75th anniversary.

Surveyors — A285

1976, Sept. 2 **Wmk. 372**

1300 A285 80s multicolored 1.25 .30

Bureau of Lands, 75th anniversary.

Monetary Fund and World Bank Emblems — A286

Virgin of Antipollo A287

1976, Oct. 4 **Litho.** ***Perf. 12½***

1301 A286 60s multicolored .35 .20
1302 A286 1.50p multicolored .85 .35

Joint Annual Meeting of the Board of Governors of the International Monetary Fund and the World Bank, Manila, Oct. 4-8.
For surcharge see No. 1575.

1976, Nov. 26 ***Perf. 12½***

1303 A287 30s multicolored .30 .20
1304 A287 90s multicolored .90 .25

Virgin of Antipolo, Our Lady of Peace and Good Voyage, 350th anniv. of arrival of statue in the Philippines and 50th anniv. of the canonical coronation.

No. 1184 Surcharged with New Value and 2 Bars and Overprinted: "1976 PHILATELIC WEEK"

Perf. 13½x14

1976, Nov. 26 **Photo.** **Unwmk.**

1305 A247 30s on 10s multi .60 .20

Philatelic Week 1976.

People Going to Church A288

Wmk. 372

1976, Dec. 1 **Litho.** ***Perf. 12½***

1306 A288 15s bl & multi .30 .20
1307 A288 30s bl & multi .50 .20

Christmas 1976.

Symbolic Diamond and Book — A289

Galicano Apacible — A290

1976, Dec. 13

1308 A289 30s grn & multi .30 .20
1309 A289 75s grn & multi .40 .20

Philippine Educational System, 75th anniv.

No. 1202 and 1208 Surcharged with New Value and 2 Bars

1977, Jan. 17 **Unwmk.**

1310 A273 1.20p on 1.10p bl .90 .20
1311 A250 3p on 5p bl 2.50 .70

1977 **Litho.** **Wmk. 372** ***Perf. 12½***

Design: 30s, José Rizal.

1313 A290 30s multicolored .25 .20
1318 A290 2.30p multicolored 1.25 .25

Dr. José Rizal (1861-1896) physician, poet and national hero (30s). Dr. Galicano Apacible (1864-1949), physician, statesman (2.30p).
Issue dates: 30s, Feb. 16; 2.30p, Jan. 24.

Emblem, Flags, Map of AOPU A291

1977, Apr. 1 **Wmk. 372**

1322 A291 50s multicolored .40 .20
1323 A291 1.50p multicolored 1.00 .25

Asian-Oceanic Postal Union (AOPU), 15th anniv.

Cogwheels and Worker — A292

1977, Apr. 21 ***Perf. 12½***

1324 A292 90s blk & multi .50 .25
1325 A292 2.30p blk & multi 1.25 .45

Asian Development Bank, 10th anniversary.

Farmer at Work and Receiving Money A293

1977, May 14 **Litho.** **Wmk. 372**

1326 A293 30s org red & multi .35 .20

National Commission on Countryside Credit and Collection, campaign to strengthen the rural credit system.

Solicitor General's Emblem A294

1977, June 30 **Litho.** ***Perf. 12½***

1327 A294 1.65p multicolored 1.25 .25

Office of the Solicitor General, 75th anniv.
For surcharges see Nos. 1483, 1519.

Conference Emblem A295

1977, July 29 **Litho.** ***Perf. 12½***

1328 A295 2.20p bl & multi 1.25 .25

8th World Conference of the World Peace through Law Center, Manila, Aug. 21-26.
For surcharge see No. 1576.

ASEAN Emblem A296

1977, Aug. 8

1329 A296 1.50p grn & multi 1.25 .25

Association of South East Asian Nations (ASEAN), 10th anniversary.
For surcharge see No. 1559.

Cable-laying Ship, Map Showing Cable Route — A297

1977, Aug. 26 **Litho.** ***Perf. 12½***

1330 A297 1.30p multicolored .85 .25

Inauguration of underwater telephone cable linking Okinawa, Luzon and Hong Kong.

President Marcos — A298

1977, Sept. 11 **Wmk. 372**

1331 A298 30s multicolored .30 .20
1332 A298 2.30p multicolored 1.25 .35

Ferdinand E. Marcos, president of the Philippines, 60th birthday.

People Raising Flag — A299

1977, Sept. 21 **Litho.** ***Perf. 12½***

1333 A299 30s multicolored .35 .20
1334 A299 2.30p multicolored 1.10 .35

5th anniversary of "New Society."

Bishop Gregorio Aglipay — A300

1977, Oct. 1 **Litho.** ***Perf. 12½***

1335 A300 30s multicolored .25 .20
1336 A300 90s multicolored 1.00 .25

Philippine Independent Aglipayan Church, 75th anniversary.

Fairchild FC-2 over World Map — A301

1977, Oct. 28 **Wmk. 372**

1337 A301 2.30p multicolored 1.75 .50

First scheduled Pan American airmail service, Key West to Havana, 50th anniversary.

No. 1280 Surcharged with New Value, 2 Bars and Overprinted in Red: "1977 / PHILATELIC / WEEK"

1977, Nov. 22 **Litho.** ***Perf. 12½***

1338 A275 90s on 1p multi .90 .25

Philatelic Week.

Children Celebrating and Star from Lantern — A302

1977, Dec. 1 **Unwmk.**

1339	A302	30s multicolored	.25	.20
1340	A302	45s multicolored	.50	.20

Christmas 1977.

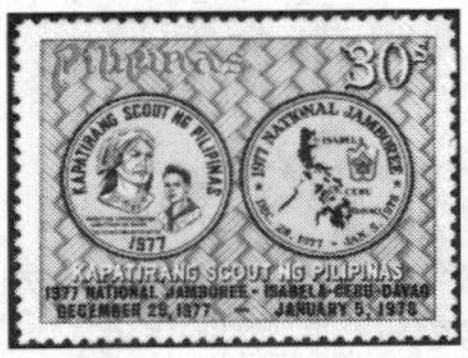

Scouts and Map showing Jamboree Locations A303

1977, Dec. 27

1341	A303	30s multicolored	.40	.20

National Boy Scout Jamboree, Tumauini, Isabela; Capitol Hills, Cebu City; Mariano Marcos, Davao, Dec. 27, 1977-Jan. 5, 1978.

Far Eastern University Arms — A304

1978, Jan. 26 **Litho.** **Wmk. 372**

1342	A304	30s gold & multi	.40	.20

Far Eastern University, 50th anniversary.

Sipa A305

Various positions of Sipa ball-game.

1978, Feb. 28 ***Perf. 12½***

1343	A305	5s bl & multi	.20	.20
1344	A305	10s bl & multi	.25	.20
1345	A305	40s bl & multi	.35	.20
1346	A305	75s bl & multi	.60	.25
a.		Block, #1343-1346	1.60	1.00

No. 1346a has continuous design.

Arms of Meycauayan A306

1978, Apr. 21 **Litho.** ***Perf. 12½***

1347	A306	1.05p multicolored	.70	.25

Meycauayan, founded 1578-1579.
For surcharge see No. 1560.

Moro Vinta and UPU Emblem — A307

2.50p, No. 1350b, Horse-drawn mail cart. No. 1350a, like 5p. No. 1350c, Steam locomotive. No. 1350d, Three-master.

1978, June 9 **Litho.** ***Perf. 13½***

1348	A307	2.50p multicolored	1.50	.40
1349	A307	5p multicolored	2.25	.80

Souvenir Sheet

Perf. 12½x13

1350		Sheet of 4	12.00	10.00
a.-d.		A307 7.50p, any single	2.50	2.50
e.		Sheet, imperf	14.50	12.50

CAPEX International Philatelic Exhibition, Toronto, Ont., June 9-18. No. 1350 contains 36½x25mm stamps.
No. 1350 exists imperf. in changed colors.

Andres Bonifacio Monument, by Guillermo Tolentino — A308

Wmk. 372

1978, July 10 **Litho.** ***Perf. 12½***

1351	A308	30s multicolored	.35	.20

Rook, Knight and Globe A309

1978, July 17

1352	A309	30s vio bl & red	.40	.20
1353	A309	2p vio bl & red	1.10	.25

World Chess Championship, Anatoly Karpov and Viktor Korchnoi, Baguio City, 1978.

Miners A310

1978, Aug. 12 **Litho.** ***Perf. 12½***

1354	A310	2.30p multicolored	1.25	.35

Benguet gold mining industry, 75th anniv.

Manuel Quezon and Quezon Memorial A311

1978, Aug. 19

1355	A311	30s multicolored	.25	.20
1356	A311	1p multicolored	1.00	.25

Manuel Quezon (1878-1944), first president of Commonwealth of the Philippines.

Law Association Emblem, Philippine Flag — A312

1978, Aug. 27 **Litho.** ***Perf. 12½***

1357	A312	2.30p multicolored	1.25	.35

58th Intl. Law Conf., Manila, 8/27-9/2.

Pres. Sergio Osmeña (1878-1961) A313

1978, Sept. 8

1358	A313	30s multicolored	.30	.20
1359	A313	1p multicolored	.90	.25

For surcharge see No. 1501.

Map Showing Cable Route, Cablelaying Ship — A314

1978, Sept. 30

1360	A314	1.40p multicolored	1.10	.25

ASEAN Submarine Cable Network, Philippines-Singapore cable system, inauguration.

Basketball, Games' Emblem A315

1978, Oct. 1

1361	A315	30s multicolored	.40	.20
1362	A315	2.30p multicolored	1.40	.40

8th Men's World Basketball Championship, Manila, Oct. 1-15.

San Lazaro Hospital and Dr. Catalino Gavino A316

1978, Oct. 13 **Litho.** ***Perf. 12½***

1363	A316	50s multicolored	.50	.20
1364	A316	90s multicolored	.75	.25

San Lazaro Hospital, 400th anniversary.
For surcharge see No. 1512.

Nurse Vaccinating Child — A317

1978, Oct. 24

1365	A317	30s multicolored	.40	.20
1366	A317	1.50p multicolored	1.40	.40

Eradication of smallpox.

No. 1268 Surcharged

1978, Nov. 23

1367	A273	60s on 65s lil rose	.75	.20

Philatelic Week.

"The Telephone Across Country and World" — A318

Wmk. 372

1978, Nov. 28 **Litho.** ***Perf. 12½***

1368	30s multicolored	.40	.20
1369	2p multicolored	1.40	.40
a.	A318 Pair, #1368-1369	1.90	1.10

Philippine Long Distance Telephone Company, 50th anniversary.

Traveling Family — A320

1978, Nov. 28

1370	A320	30s multicolored	.40	.20
1371	A320	1.35p multicolored	1.00	.25

Decade of Philippine children.
For surcharges see Nos. 1504, 1561.

Church and Arms of Agoo A321

1978, Dec. 7 **Litho.** ***Perf. 12½***

1372	A321	30s multicolored	.35	.20
1373	A321	45s multicolored	.35	.20

400th anniversary of the founding of Agoo.

Church and Arms of Balayan A322

1978, Dec. 8

1374	A322	30s multicolored	.30	.20
1375	A322	90s multicolored	.60	.20

400th anniv. of the founding of Balayan.

Dr. Honoria Acosta Sison (1888-1970), 1st Philippine Woman Physician — A323

1978, Dec. 15

1376	A323	30s multicolored	.40	.20

Family, Houses, UN Emblem A324

1978, Dec. Litho. *Perf. 12½*

1377	A324	30s multicolored	.40	.20
1378	A324	3p multicolored	1.75	.50

30th anniversary of Universal Declaration of Human Rights.

Chaetodon Trifasciatus — A325

Fish: 1.20p, Balistoides niger. 2.20p, Rhinecanthus aculeatus. 2.30p, Chelmon rostratus. No. 1383, Chaetodon mertensi. No. 1384, Euxiphipops xanthometapon.

1978, Dec. 29 *Perf. 14*

1379	A325	30s multi	.30	.20
1380	A325	1.20p multi	.85	.30
1381	A325	2.20p multi	1.40	.40
1382	A325	2.30p multi	1.40	.40
1383	A325	5p multi	3.00	.90
1384	A325	5p multi	3.00	.90
		Nos. 1379-1384 (6)	9.95	3.10

Carlos P. Romulo, UN Emblem A326

1979, Jan. 14 Litho. *Perf. 12½*

1385	A326	30s multi	.40	.20
1386	A326	2p multi	1.40	.40

Carlos P. Romulo (1899-1985), pres. of UN General Assembly and Security Council.

Rotary Emblem and "60" — A327

Rosa Sevilla de Alvero — A328

1979, Jan. 26 Wmk. 372

1387	A327	30s multi	.35	.20
1388	A327	2.30p multi	1.25	.40

Rotary Club of Manila, 60th anniversary.

1979, Mar. 4 Litho. *Perf. 12½*

1389	A328	30 rose	.40	.20

Rosa Sevilla de Alvero, educator and writer, birth centenary.

For surcharges see Nos. 1479-1482.

Oil Well and Map of Palawan A329

Wmk. 372

1979, Mar. 21 Litho. *Perf. 12½*

1390	A329	30s multi	.35	.20
1391	A329	45s multi	.50	.20

First Philippine oil production, Nido Oil Reef Complex, Palawan.

Merrill's Fruit Doves — A330

Birds: 1.20p, Brown tit babbler. 2.20p, Mindoro imperial pigeons. 2.30p, Steere's pittas. No. 1396, Koch's and red-breasted pittas. No. 1397, Philippine eared nightjar.

Perf. 14x13½

1979, Apr. 16 Unwmk.

1392	A330	30s multi	*.30*	.25
1393	A330	1.20p multi	*1.00*	.25
1394	A330	2.20p multi	*2.50*	.75
1395	A330	2.30p multi	*2.50*	.75
1396	A330	5p multi	*9.75*	1.75
1397	A330	5p multi	*9.75*	1.75
		Nos. 1392-1397 (6)	*25.80*	5.50

Association Emblem and Reader A331

Wmk. 372

1979, Apr. 3 Litho. *Perf. 12½*

1398	A331	30s multi	.25	.20
1399	A331	75s multi	.45	.20
1400	A331	1p multi	1.00	.30
		Nos. 1398-1400 (3)	1.70	.70

Association of Special Libraries of the Philippines, 25th anniversary.

UNCTAD Emblem A332

Wmk. 372

1979, May 3 Litho. *Perf. 12½*

1401	A332	1.20p multi	.70	.25
1402	A332	2.30p multi	1.40	.40

5th Session of UN Conference on Trade and Development, Manila, May 3-June 1.

Civet Cat A333

Philippine Animals: 1.20p, Macaque. 2.20p, Wild boar. 2.30p, Dwarf leopard. No. 1407, Asiatic dwarf otter. No. 1408, Anteater.

1979, May 14 *Perf. 14*

1403	A333	30s multi	.25	.20
1404	A333	1.20p multi	.75	.25
1405	A333	2.20p multi	1.25	.40
1406	A333	2.30p multi	1.25	.40
1407	A333	5p multi	2.75	.75
1408	A333	5p multi	2.75	.75
		Nos. 1403-1408 (6)	9.00	2.75

Dish Antenna — A334

1979, May 17 *Perf. 12½*

1409	A334	90s shown	1.10	.25
1410	A334	1.30p World map	1.10	.30

11th World Telecommunications Day, 5/17.

Mussaenda Donna Evangelina — A335

Philippine Mussaendas: 1.20p, Dona Esperanza. 2.20p, Dona Hilaria. 2.30p, Dona Aurora. No. 1415, Gining Imelda. No. 1416, Dona Trining.

1979, June 11 Litho. *Perf. 14*

1411	A335	30s multi	.25	.20
1412	A335	1.20p multi	.75	.25
1413	A335	2.20p multi	1.25	.40
1414	A335	2.30p multi	1.25	.40
1415	A335	5p multi	2.75	.75
1416	A335	5p multi	2.75	.75
		Nos. 1411-1416 (6)	9.00	2.75

Manila Cathedral, Coat of Arms — A336

1979, June 25 *Perf. 12½*

1417	A336	30s multi	.30	.20
1418	A336	75s multi	.60	.20
1419	A336	90s multi	.85	.25
		Nos. 1417-1419 (3)	1.75	.65

Archdiocese of Manila, 400th anniversary.

Patrol Boat, Naval Arms A337

1979, June 26

1420	A337	30s multi	.50	.20
1421	A337	45s multi	.65	.20

Philippine Navy Day.

Man Breaking Chains, Broken Syringe — A338

1979, July 23 Litho. *Perf. 12½*

1422	A338	30s multi	.25	.20
1423	A338	90s multi	.70	.20
1424	A338	1.05p multi	.85	.25
		Nos. 1422-1424 (3)	1.80	.65

Fight drug abuse.

For surcharge see Nos. 1480, 1513.

Afghan Hound A339

Designs: 90s, Striped tabbies. 1.20p, Dobermann pinscher. 2.20p, Siamese cats. 2.30p, German shepherd. 5p, Chinchilla cats.

1979, Aug. 6 *Perf. 14*

1425	A339	30s multi	.50	.20
1426	A339	90s multi	.90	.30
1427	A339	1.20p multi	1.10	.40
1428	A339	2.20p multi	1.75	.45
1429	A339	2.30p multi	1.75	.45
1430	A339	5p multi	3.75	.85
		Nos. 1425-1430 (6)	9.75	2.65

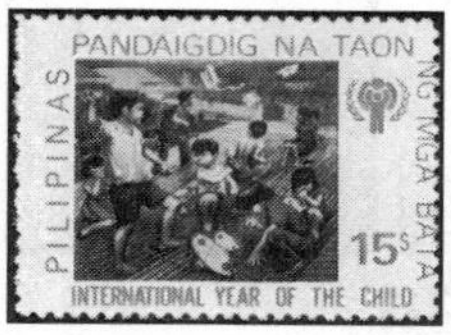

Children Playing IYC Emblem A340

Children playing and IYC emblem, diff.

1979, Aug. 31 Litho. *Perf. 12½*

1431	A340	15s multi	.25	.20
1432	A340	20s multi	.35	.20
1433	A340	25s multi	.35	.20
1434	A340	1.20p multi	.75	.20
		Nos. 1431-1434 (4)	1.70	.80

International Year of the Child.

Hands Holding Emblem — A341

1979, Sept. 27 Litho. *Perf. 12½*

1435	A341	30s multi	.25	.20
1436	A341	1.35p multi	1.00	.25

Methodism in the Philippines, 80th anniv.

Emblem and Coins A342

Wmk. 372

1979, Nov. 15 Litho. *Perf. 12½*

1437	A342	30s multi	.40	.20

Philippine Numismatic and Antiquarian Society, 50th anniversary.

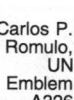

Concorde over Manila and Paris A343

Design: 2.20p, Concorde over Manila.

1979, Nov. 22

1438	A343	1.05p multi	1.00	.40
1439	A343	2.20p multi	2.50	.75

Air France service to Manila, 25th anniversary.

No. 1272 Surcharged in Red

1979, Nov. 23

1440	A273	90s on 1.60 blk	.75	.25

Philatelic Week. Surcharge similar to No. 1367.

Transport Association Emblem A344

1979, Nov. 27

1441	A344	75s multi	.60	.20
1442	A344	2.30p multi	1.60	.40

International Air Transport Association, 35th annual general meeting, Manila.

Local Government Year — A345

Mother and Children, Ornament — A346

1979, Dec. 14 Litho. *Perf. 12½*

1443	A345	30s multi	.20	.20
1444	A345	45s multi	.40	.20

For surcharge, see No. 1481.

1979, Dec. 17

1445	A346	30s shown	.30	.20
1446	A346	90s Stars	.95	.20

Christmas. For surcharge see No. 1515.

Rheumatic Pain Spots and Congress Emblem A347

Wmk. 372

1980, Jan. 20 Litho. *Perf. 12½*

1447	A347	30s multi	.40	.20
1448	A347	90s multi	1.40	.30

Southeast Asia and Pacific Area League Against Rheumatism, 4th Congress, Manila, Jan. 19-24.

Gen. Douglas MacArthur A348

30s, MacArthur's birthplace (Little Rock, AR) & burial place (Norfolk, VA). 2.30p, MacArthur's cap, Sunglasses & pipe. 5p, MacArthur & troops wading ashore at Leyte, Oct. 20, 1944.

1980, Jan. 26 Wmk. 372 *Perf. 12½*

1449	A348	30s multi	.30	.20
1450	A348	75s multi	.40	.20
1451	A348	2.30p multi	1.50	.60
		Nos. 1449-1451 (3)	2.20	1.00

Souvenir Sheet

Imperf

1452	A348	5p multi	3.00	2.50

Gen. Douglas MacArthur (1880-1964).
For overprint see No. 2198.

Knights of Columbus of Philippines, 75th Anniversary A349

1980, Feb. 14

1453	A349	30s multi	.25	.20
1454	A349	1.35p multi	1.00	.25

Philippine Military Academy, 75th Anniversary — A350

Wmk. 372

1980, Feb. 17 Litho. *Perf. 12½*

1455	A350	30s multi	.40	.20
1456	A350	1.20p multi	1.40	.40

Philippines Women's University, 75th Anniversary — A351

1980, Feb. 21

1457	A351	30s multi	.25	.20
1458	A351	1.05p multi	1.00	.25

Disaster Relief A352

Rotary International, 75th Anniversary (Paintings by Carlos Botong Francisco): Nos. 1459 and 1460 each in continuous design.

1980, Feb. 23 *Perf. 12½*

1459		Strip of 5	2.25	1.50
a.		A352 30s single stamp	.35	.20
1460		Strip of 5	9.25	7.50
a.		A352 2.30p single stamp	1.50	.75

A353

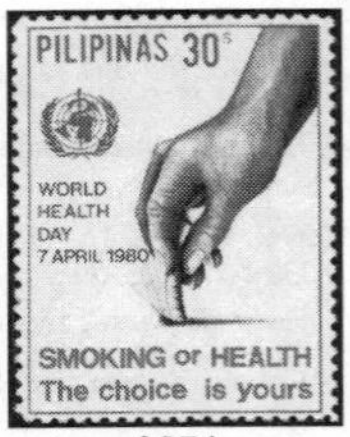

A354

Wmk. 372

1980, Mar. 28 Litho. *Perf. 12½*

1461	A353	30s multi	.60	.20
1462	A353	1.30p multi	1.75	.30

6th centenary of Islam in Philippines.

1980, Apr. 14

Hand crushing cigarette, WHO emblem.

1463	A354	30s multi	.50	.30
1464	A354	75s multi	2.50	.75

World Health Day (Apr. 17); anti-smoking campaign.

Philippine Girl Scouts, 40th Anniversary A355

Wmk. 372

1980, May 26 Litho. *Perf. 12½*

1465	A355	30s multi	.40	.20
1466	A355	2p multi	1.40	.35

Jeepney (Public Jeep) A356

1980, June 24 Litho. *Perf. 12½*

1467	A356	30s Jeepney, diff.	.40	.20
1468	A356	1.20p shown	1.25	.35

For surcharge see No. 1503.

Nos. 1272, 1206 Surcharged in Red

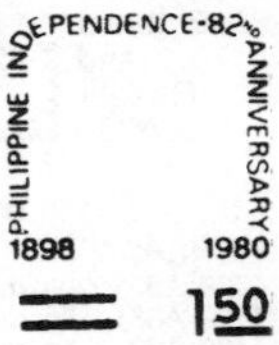

Wmk. 372 (1.35p)

1980, Aug. 1 Litho. *Perf. 12½*

1469	A273	1.35p on 1.60p blk	1.40	.35
1470	A250	1.50p on 1.80p grn	1.90	.60

Independence, 82nd Anniversary.

Association Emblem — A357

1980, Aug. 1 Wmk. 372

1471	A357	30s multi	.25	.20
1472	A357	2.30p multi	1.50	.40

International Association of Universities, 7th General Conference, Manila, Aug. 25-30.

Congress Emblem, Map of Philippines A358

Wmk. 372

1980, Aug. 18 Litho. *Perf. 12½*

1473	A358	30s lt grn & blk	.25	.20
1474	A358	75s lt bl & blk	.40	.20
1475	A358	2.30p sal & blk	1.10	.30
		Nos. 1473-1475 (3)	1.75	.70

Intl. Federation of Library Associations and Institutions, 46th Congress, Manila, 8/18-23.

Kabataang Barangay (New Society), 5th Anniversary — A359

1980, Sept. 19 Litho. *Perf. 12½*

1476	A359	30s multi	.25	.20
1477	A359	40s multi	.35	.20
1478	A359	1p multi	.80	.25
		Nos. 1476-1478 (3)	1.40	.65

Nos. 1389, 1422, 1443, 1445, 1327 Surcharged in Blue, Black or Red

Wmk. 372

1980, Sept. 26 Litho. *Perf. 12½*

1479	A328	40s on 30s rose (Bl)	.80	.20
1480	A338	40s on 30s multi	.80	.20
1481	A345	40s on 30s multi	.80	.20
1482	A346	40s on 30s multi (R)	1.50	.20
1483	A294	2p on 1.65p multi (R)	3.00	.30
		Nos. 1479-1483 (5)	6.90	1.10

Catamaran, Conference Emblem — A360

1980, Sept. 27

1484	A360	30s multi	.30	.20
1485	A360	2.30p multi	1.40	.50

World Tourism Conf., Manila, Sept. 27.

Stamp Day — A361

UN, 35th Anniv. — A362

1980, Oct. 9

1486	A361	40s multi	.40	.20
1487	A361	1p multi	.80	.25
1488	A361	2p multi	1.60	.50
		Nos. 1486-1488 (3)	2.80	.95

1980, Oct. 20

Designs: 40s, UN Headquarters and Emblem, Flag of Philippines. 3.20p, UN and Philippine flags, UN headquarters.

1489	A362	40s multi	.35	.20
1490	A362	3.20p multi	2.10	.65

Murex Alabaster A363

1980, Nov. 2

1491	A363	40s *shown*	.85	.20
1492	A363	60s *Bursa bubo*	.60	.20
1493	A363	1.20p *Homalocantha zamboi*	.85	.25
1494	A363	2p *Xenophora pallidula*	1.60	.35
		Nos. 1491-1494 (4)	3.90	1.00

INTERPOL Emblem on Globe — A364

1980, Nov. 5 Litho. Wmk. 372

1495	A364	40s multi	.30	.20
1496	A364	1p multi	.60	.20
1497	A364	3.20p multi	1.60	.55
		Nos. 1495-1497 (3)	2.50	.95

49th General Assembly Session of INTERPOL (Intl. Police Organization), Manila, Nov. 13-21.

Central Philippine University, 75th Anniversary A365

1980, Nov. 17 Unwmk.

1498	A365	40s multi	.75	.20
1499	A365	3.20p multi	2.25	.80

No. 1257 Surcharged

Wmk. 372

1980, Nov. 21 Litho. *Perf. 12½*

1500	A269	1.20p on 80s multi	1.25	.35

Philatelic Week. Surcharge similar to No. 1367.

No. 1358 Surcharged

1980, Nov. 30

1501	A313	40s on 30s multi	1.25	.35

APO Philatelic Society, 30th anniversary.

Christmas Tree, Present and Candy Cane — A366

Perf. 12½

1980, Dec. 15 Litho. Unwmk.

1502	A366	40s multi	.55	.20

Christmas 1980.

No. 1467 Surcharged

1981, Jan. 2

1503	A356	40c on 30s multi	1.50	.30

Nos. 1370, 1257 Surcharged in Red or Black

1981

1504	A320	10s on 30s (R) multi	1.10	.25
1505	A269	85s on 80s multi	2.25	.30

Issue dates: 10s, Jan. 12; 85s, Jan. 2.

Heinrich Von Stephan, UPU Emblem A367

1981, Jan. 30

1506	A367	3.20p multi	2.25	.75

Heinrich von Stephan (1831-1897), founder of UPU, birth sesquicentennial.

Pope John Paul II Greeting Crowd — A368

Designs: 90s, Pope, signature, vert. 1.20p, Pope, cardinals, vert. 3p, Pope giving blessing, Vatican arms, Manila Cathedral. 7.50p, Pope, light on map of Philippines, vert.

Perf. 13½x14

1981, Feb. 17 Unwmk.

1507	A368	90s multi	.75	.25
1508	A368	1.20p multi	.80	.25
1509	A368	2.30p multi	1.75	.50
1510	A368	3p multi	2.50	.65
		Nos. 1507-1510 (4)	5.80	1.65

Souvenir Sheet

1511	A368	7.50p multi	3.75	2.50

Visit of Pope John Paul, Feb. 17-22.

Nos. 1364, 1423, 1268, 1446, 1261, 1206, 1327 Surcharged

1981 Litho. *Perf. 12½*

1512	A316	40s on 90s multi	.90	.25
1513	A338	40s on 90s multi	.90	.20
1514	A273	40s on 65s lil rose	.90	.25
1515	A346	40s on 90s multi	1.50	.35
1517	A271	1p on 1.50p brt rose & vio bl	1.50	.25
1518	A250	1.20p on 1.80p grn	2.10	.40
1519	A294	1.20p on 1.65p multi	2.75	.40
1520	A271	2p on 1.50p brt rose & vio bl	3.50	.35
		Nos. 1512-1520 (8)	14.05	2.45

A369

A370

1981, Apr. 20 Wmk. 372

1521	A369	2p multi	1.25	.40
1522	A369	3.20p multi	1.75	.65

68th Spring Meeting of the Inter-Parliamentary Union, Manila, Apr. 20-25.

Unless otherwise stated, all issues on granite paper.

Wmk. 372

1981, May 22 Litho. *Perf. 12½*

1523	A370	40s Bubble coral	.60	.20
1524	A370	40s Branching coral	.60	.20
1525	A370	40s Brain coral	.60	.20
1526	A370	40s Table coral	.60	.20
a.		Block of 4, #1523-1526	2.50	2.00

Philippine Motor Assoc., 50th Anniv. — A371

Vintage cars.

1981, May 25

1527	A371	40s Presidents car	.55	.20
1528	A371	40s 1930	.55	.20
1529	A371	40s 1937	.55	.20
1530	A371	40s shown	.55	.20
a.		Block of 4, #1527-1530	2.25	1.60

Re-inauguration of Pres. Ferdinand E. Marcos — A372

1981, June 30

1531	A372	40s multi	.50	.20

Souvenir Sheet

Imperf

1532	A372	5p multi	4.00	2.50

No. 1531 exists imperf.

For overprint see No. 1753.

St. Ignatius Loyola, Founder of Jesuit Order A373

400th Anniv. of Jesuits in Philippines: No. 1534, Jose Rizal, Ateneo University. No. 1535, Father Federico Faura, Manila Observatory. No. 1536, Father Saturnino Urios, map of Philippines.

1981, July 31

1533	A373	40s multi	.45	.20
1534	A373	40s multi	.45	.20
1535	A373	40s multi	.45	.20
1536	A373	40s multi	.45	.20
a.		Block of 4, #1533-1536	1.80	1.00

Souvenir Sheet

Imperf

1537	A373	2p multi	3.50	2.50

#1537 contains vignettes of #1533-1536.

For surcharge see No. 1737.

A374

A375

Design: 40s, Isabelo de los Reyes (1867-1938), labor union founder. 1p, Gen. Gregorio del Pilar (1875-1899). No. 1540, Magsaysay. No. 1541, Francisco Dagohoy. No. 1543, Ambrosia R. Bautista, signer of Declaration of Independence, 1898, No. 1544, Juan Sumulong (1875-1942), statesman. 2.30p, Nicanor Abelardo (1893-1934), composer. 3.20p, Gen. Vicente Lim (1888-1945), first Philippine graduate of West Point.

Wmk. 372

1981-82 Litho. *Perf. 12½*

1538	A374	40s grnsh bl ('82)	.35	.20
1539	A374	1p blk & red brn	.60	.20
1540	A374	1.20p blk & lt red brn	.90	.25
1541	A374	1.20p brown ('82)	1.50	.35
1543	A374	2p blk & red brn	1.10	.35
1544	A374	2p rose lil ('82)	1.50	.35
1545	A374	2.30p lt red brn ('82)	1.75	.40
1546	A374	3.20p gray bl ('82)	2.00	.65
		Nos. 1538-1546 (8)	9.70	2.75

See Nos. 1672-1680, 1682-1683, 1685. For surcharges see Nos. 1668-1669.

1981, Sept. 2

1551	A375	40s multi	.50	.20

Chief Justice Fred Ruiz Castro, 67th birth anniv.

A376

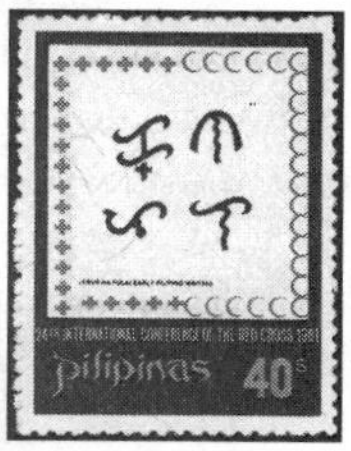

A376a

Wmk. 372

1981, Oct. 24 Litho. *Perf. 12½*

1552	A376	40s multi	.40	.20
1553	A376	3.20p multi	2.10	.65

Intl. Year of the Disabled.

1981, Nov. 7

1554	A376a	40s multi	.30	.20
1555	A376a	2p multi	1.40	.45
1556	A376a	3.20p multi	1.90	.60
		Nos. 1554-1556 (3)	3.60	1.25

24th Intl. Red Cross Conf., Manila, 11/7-14.

Intramuros Gate, Manila — A377

1981, Nov. 13

1557	A377	40s black	.50	.20

Manila Park Zoo Concert Series, Nov. 20-30 A378

1981, Nov. 20

1558	A378	40s multi	.50	.20

No. 1329 Overprinted "1981 Philatelic Week" and Surcharged

Wmk. 372

1981, Nov. 23 Litho. *Perf. 12½*

1559	A296	1.20p on 1.50p multi	1.75	.40

Nos. 1205, 1347, 1371 Surcharged

1981, Nov. 25 Litho. *Perf. 12½*

1560	A306	40s on 1.05p multi	1.25	.25
1561	A320	40s on 1.35p multi	1.25	.25
1562	A273	1.20p on 1.50p brn	3.50	.35
		Nos. 1560-1562 (3)	6.00	.85

11th Southeast Asian Games, Manila, Dec. 6-15
A379

1981, Dec. 3

1563 A379 40s Running .40 .20
1564 A379 1p Bicycling .75 .20
1565 A379 2p Pres. Marcos, Intl. Olympic Pres. Samaranch 1.60 .30
1566 A379 2.30p Soccer 2.00 .50
1567 A379 2.80p Shooting 2.50 .65
1568 A379 3.20p Bowling 2.75 .85
Nos. 1563-1568 (6) 10.00 2.70

Manila Intl. Film Festival, Jan. 18-29
A380

Wmk. 372

1982, Jan. 18 Litho. *Perf. 12½*

1569 A380 40s Film Center .40 .20
1570 A380 2p Golden trophy, vert. 1.50 .45
1571 A380 3.20p Trophy, diff., vert. 2.25 .75
Nos. 1569-1571 (3) 4.15 1.40

Manila Metropolitan Waterworks and Sewerage System Centenary — A381

1982, Jan. 22

1572 A381 40s blue .40 .20
1573 A381 1.20p brown 1.25 .30

Nos. 1268, 1302, 1328 Surcharged

1982, Jan. 28

1574 A273 1p on 65s lil rose 1.25 .40
1575 A286 1p on 1.50p multi 1.25 .40
1576 A295 3.20p on 2.20p multi 6.00 1.00
Nos. 1574-1576 (3) 8.50 1.80

Scouting Year — A382

1982, Feb. 22

1577 A382 40s Portrait .45 .20
1578 A382 2p Scout giving salute 1.75 .55

25th Anniv. of Children's Museum and Library Foundation
A383

1982, Feb. 25

1579 A383 40s Mural .30 .20
1580 A383 1.20p Children playing 1.10 .35

77th Anniv. of Philippine Military Academy
A384

Wmk. 372

1982, Mar. 25 Litho. *Perf. 12½*

1581 A384 40s multi .40 .20
1582 A384 1p multi .80 .25

40th Bataan Day
A385

1982, Apr. 9

1583 A385 40s Soldier .40 .20
1584 A385 2p "Reunion for Peace" 1.40 .30

Souvenir Sheet

Imperf

1585 A385 3.20p Cannon, flag 3.50 2.25

No. 1585 contains one 38x28mm stamp.
No. 1585 comes on two different papers, the second being thicker with cream gum.

For surcharge see No. 2114.

10s

No. B27 Surcharged

1982 Photo. *Perf. 13½*

1586 SP14 10s on 6 + 5s multi .70 .25

A386

A387

1982, Apr. 28 Litho. *Perf. 12½*

1587 A386 1p rose pink 1.50 .20

Aurora Aragon Quezon (1888-1949), former First Lady.

There are three types of No. 1587.

See Nos. 1684-1684A.

1982, May 1

1588 A387 40s Man holding award .40 .20
1589 A387 1.20p Award 1.25 .25

7th Towers Awards.

UN Conf. on Human Environment, 10th Anniv. — A388

1982, June 5

1590 A388 40s Turtle .65 .25
1591 A388 3.20p Philippine eagle 3.75 1.00

75th Anniv. of Univ. of Philippines College of Medicine
A389

1982, June 10

1592 A389 40s multi .30 .20
1593 A389 3.20p multi 1.90 .75

Natl. Livelihood Movement
A390

1982, June 12

1594 A390 40s multi .50 .20

See #1681-1681A. For overprint see #1634.

Adamson Univ., 50th Anniv. — A391

1982, June 21

1595 A391 40s bl & multi .35 .20
1596 A391 1.20p lt vio & multi 1.10 .25

Social Security, 25th Anniv. — A392

Pres. Marcos, 65th Birthday — A393

1982, Sept. 1 *Perf. 13½x13*

1597 A392 40s multi .30 .20
1598 A392 1.20p multi .90 .25

1982, Sept. 11 *Perf. 13½x13*

1599 A393 40s sil & multi .35 .20
1600 A393 3.20p sil & multi 1.75 .75
a. Souv. sheet of 2, #1599-1600, imperf. 3.75 3.00

For surcharge see No. 1666.

15th Anniv. of Assoc. of Southeast Asian Nations (ASEAN)
A394

1982, Sept. 22 Litho. *Perf. 12½*

1601 A394 40s Flags .55 .20

St. Teresa of Avila (1515-1582) — A395

1982, Oct. 15 *Perf. 13x13½*

1602 A395 40s Text .35 .20
1603 A395 1.20p Map .70 .25
1604 A395 2p like #1603 1.40 .25
Nos. 1602-1604 (3) 2.45 .70

10th Anniv. of Tenant Farmers' Emancipation Decree — A396

Perf. 13x13½

1982, Oct. 21 Litho. Wmk. 372

1605 A396 40s Pres. Marcos signing law 1.40 .25

See No. 1654.

350th Anniv. of St. Isabel College
A397

1982, Oct. 22

1606 A397 40s multi .30 .20
1607 A397 1p multi 1.25 .40

Reading Campaign
A398

1982, Nov. 4

1608 A398 40s yel & multi .30 .20
1609 A398 2.30p grn & multi 1.50 .60

For surcharge see No. 1713.

42nd Skal Club World Congress, Manila, Nov. 7-12
A399

1982, Nov. 7

1610 A399 40s Heads .35 .20
1611 A399 2p Chief 2.25 .60

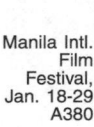

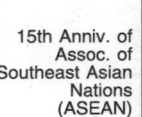

25th Anniv. of Bayanihan Folk Arts Center A400

Designs: Various folk dances.

1982, Nov. 10 Litho. *Perf. 13x13½*

1612 A400 40s multi		.35	.25
1613 A400 2.80p multi		2.50	.65

TB Bacillus Centenary A401

1982, Dec. 7 Wmk. 372

1614 A401 40s multi	.35	.20
1615 A401 2.80p multi	2.25	.75

Christmas 1982 A402

1982, Dec. 10

1616 A402 40s multi	1.00	.20
1617 A402 1p multi	2.75	.20

Philatelic Week, Nov. 22-28 A403

Perf. 13x13½

1982, Nov. 28 Litho. Wmk. 372

1618 A403 40s yel & multi	.30	.20
1619 A403 1p sil & multi	.90	.20

For surcharge see No. 1667.

Visit of Pres. Marcos to the US, Sept. A404

1982, Dec. 18

1620 A404 40s multi	.35	.20
1621 A404 3.20p multi	2.50	.75
a. Souv. sheet of 2, #1620-1621	4.00	3.00

UN World Assembly on Aging, July 26-Aug. 6 — A405

Senate Pres. Eulogio Rodriguez, Sr. (1883-1964) A406

1982, Dec. 24

1622 A405 1.20p Woman	1.00	.20
1623 A405 2p Man	1.50	.30

1983, Jan. 21

1624 A406 40s grn & multi	.30	.20
1625 A406 1.20p org & multi	.90	.20

1983 Manila Intl. Film Festival, Jan. 24-Feb. 4 A407

1983, Jan. 24

1626 A407 40s blk & multi	.35	.20
1627 A407 3.20p pink & multi	2.50	.75

Beatification of Lorenzo Ruiz (1981) — A408

Perf. 13x13½

1983, Feb. 18 Litho. Wmk. 372

1628 A408 40s multi	.35	.20
1629 A408 1.20p multi	1.10	.20

400th Anniv. of Local Printing Press A409

1983, Mar. 14

1630 A409 40s blk & grn	.50	.20

Safety at Sea — A410

1983, Mar. 17 *Perf. 13½x13*

1631 A410 40s multi	.50	.20

25th anniv. of Inter-Governmental Maritime Consultation Org. Convention.

Intl. Org. of Supreme Audit Institutions, 11th Congress, Manila, Apr. 19-27 A411

Perf. 13x13½

1983, Apr. 8 Litho. Wmk. 372

1632 A411 40s Symbols	.40	.20
1633 A411 2.80p Emblem	1.75	.60
a. Souv. sheet of 2, 1632-1633, imperf.	3.75	3.00

No. 1633a comes on two papers: cream gum, normal watermark; white gum, watermark made up of smaller letters.

Type of 1982 Overprinted in Red: "7th BSP NATIONAL JAMBOREE 1983"

1983, Apr. 13 *Perf. 12½*

1634 A390 40s multi	.50	.20

Boy Scouts of Philippines jamboree.

No. 1249 Surcharged

1983, Apr. 15

1635 Block of 10	10.00	7.50
a.-j. A265 40s on 45s, any single	.90	.25

A412

A413

Perf. 13½x13

1983, May 9 Litho. Wmk. 372

1636 A412 40s multi	.50	.20

75th anniv. of Dental Assoc.

Perf. 13½x13

1983, June 17 Litho. Wmk. 372

1637 A413 40s Statue	.30	.20
1638 A413 1.20p Statue, diff., diamond	.90	.25

75th anniv. of University of the Philippines.

Visit of Japanese Prime Minister Yasuhiro Nakasone, May 6-8 — A414

Perf. 13x13½

1983, June 20 Litho. Wmk. 372

1639 A414 40s multi	.50	.20

25th Anniv. of Natl. Science and Technology Authority A415

1983, July 11

1640 A415 40s Animals, produce	.45	.20
1641 A415 40s Heart, food, pill	.45	.20
1642 A415 40s Factories, windmill, car	.45	.20
1643 A415 40s Chemicals, house, book	.45	.20
a. Block of 4, #1640-1643	1.90	1.60

Science Week.

World Communications Year — A416

Wmk. 372

1983, Oct. 24 Litho. *Perf. 12½*

1644 A416 3.20p multi	2.10	.75

Philippine Postal System Bicentennial — A417

1983, Oct. 31

1645 A417 40s multi	.50	.20

Christmas — A418

Star of the East and Festival Scene in continuous design.

1983, Nov. 15 Litho. *Perf. 12½*

1646 Strip of 5	2.50	2.25
a.-e. A418 40s single stamp	.50	.20
f. Souvenir sheet	3.25	2.50

Xavier University, 50th Anniv. A419

1983, Dec. 1 Litho. *Perf. 14*

1647 A419 40s multi	.40	.20
1648 A419 60s multi	.80	.20

A420

A421

1983, Dec. 8 Litho. *Perf. 12½*

1649 A420 40s brt ultra & multi	.40	.20
1650 A420 60s gold & multi	.80	.20

Ministry of Labor and Employment, golden jubilee.

1983, Dec. 7

1651 A421 40s multi	.40	.20
1652 A421 60s multi	.80	.20

50th anniv. of Women's Suffrage Movement.

Philatelic Week A422

Stamp Collecting: a, Cutting. b, Sorting. c, Soaking. d, Affixing hinges. e, Mounting stamp.

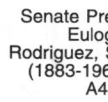

1983, Dec. 20
1653 Strip of 5 2.50 2.25
a.-e. A422 50s any single .35 .25

Emancipation Type of 1982
1983 Litho. *Perf. 13*
Size: 32x22mm
1654 A396 40s multi 1.50 .35

Philippine Cockatoo — A423

Princess Tarhata Kiram — A424

1984, Jan. 9 Unwmk. *Perf. 14*
1655 A423 40s shown .35 .25
1656 A423 2.30p Guaiabero *1.10* .45
1657 A423 2.80p Crimson-spotted racket-tailed parrots *1.40* .50
1658 A423 3.20p Large-billed parrot *1.75* .55
1659 A423 3.60p Tanygnathus sumatranus *1.75* .55
1660 A423 5p Hanging parakeets *2.50* .65
Nos. 1655-1660 (6) *8.85* 2.95

There were 500,000 of each value created cto with Jan 9 1984 cancel in the center of each block of 4. These were sold at a small fraction of face value. Used values are for ctos.

1984, Jan. 16 Wmk. 372 *Perf. 13*
1661 A424 3p grn & red 1.50 .30

Order of Virgin Mary, 300th Anniv. A425

Dona Concha Felix de Calderon A426

1984, Jan. 23 *Perf. 13½x13*
1662 A425 40s blk & multi .60 .20
1663 A425 60s red & multi 1.25 .20

1984, Feb. 9 *Perf. 13*
1664 A426 60s blk & bl grn .60 .20
1665 A426 3.60p red & bl grn 1.60 .25

Nos. 1546, 1599, 1618 Surcharged

1984, Feb. 20
1666 A393 60s on 40s (R) .35 .20
1667 A403 60s on 40s .40 .20
1668 A374 3.60p on 3.20p (R) 3.25 1.00
Nos. 1666-1668 (3) 4.00 1.40

No. 1685 Surcharged

1985, Oct. 21 Litho. *Perf. 12½*
1669 A374 3.60p on 4.20p rose lil 3.25 .75

Portrait Type of 1981

Designs: No. 1672, Gen. Artemio Ricarte. No. 1673, Teodoro M. Kalaw. No. 1674, Pres. Carlos P. Garcia. No. 1675, Senator Quintin Paredes. No. 1676, Dr. Deogracias V. Villadolid (1896-1976), 1st director, Bureau of Fisheries. No. 1677, Santiago Fonacier (1885-1940), archbishop. No. 1678, 2p, Vicente Orestes Romualdez (1885-1970), lawyer. 3p, Francisco Dagohoy.

Types of 3p:
Type I - Medium size "PILIPINAS," large, heavy denomination.
Type II - Large "PILIPINAS," medium denomination.

Perf. 13, 12½ (2p), 12½x13 (3p)
1984-85 Litho.
1672 A374 60s blk & lt brn 1.40 .20
1673 A374 60s blk & pur 1.75 .20
1674 A374 60s black 1.75 .25
1675 A374 60s dull blue .70 .20
1676 A374 60s brn blk ('85) .70 .20
1677 A374 60s dk red ('85) .50 .20
1678 A374 60s cobalt blue ('85) .85 .20
1679 A374 2p brt rose ('85) 3.50 .40
1680 A374 3p pale brn, type I 5.25 .30
1680A A374 3p pale brn, type II 6.00 .30
Nos. 1672-1680A (10) 22.40 2.45

Issued: #1672, 3/22; #1673, 3/31; #1674, 6/14; #1675, 9/12; #1676, 3/22; #1677, 5/21; #1678, 2p, 7/3; 3p, 9/7.

Types of 1982

Types of 3.60p:
Type I - Thick Frame line, large "P," "360" with line under "60."
Type II - Medium Frame line, small "p," "3.60."

1984-86
1681 A390 60s green & multi .25 .20
1681A A390 60s red & multi .25 .20
1682 A374 1.80p #1546 .95 .20
1683 A374 2.40p #1545 1.25 .20
1684 A386 3.60p Quezon, type I 1.40 .40
1684A A386 3.60p As #1684, type II 1.40 .40
1685 A374 4.20p #1544 1.75 .25
Nos. 1681-1685 (7) 7.25 1.85

Issued: #1681A, 10/19; #1684A, 2/14/86; others 3/26.

Ayala Corp. Sesquicentenary — A427

Night Views of Manila.

1984, Apr. 25 Litho. *Perf. 13x13½*
1686 A427 70s multi .50 .25
1687 A427 3.60p multi 2.00 .75

ESPANA '84 A428

Designs: 2.50p, No. 1690d, Our Lady of the Most Holy Rosary with St. Dominic, by C. Francisco. 5p, No. 1690a, Spoliarium, by Juan Luna. No. 1690b, Blessed Virgin of Manila as Patroness of Voyages, Galleon showing map of Panama-Manila. No. 1690c. Illustrations from The Monkey and the Turtle, by Rizal (first children's book published in Philippines, 1885.)

1984, Apr. 27 Unwmk. *Perf. 14*
1688 A428 2.50p multi .85 .50
1689 A428 5p multi 1.90 1.25
a. Pair, #1688-1689 3.50 2.75

Souvenir Sheet
Perf. 14½x15, Imperf.
1690 Sheet of 4 *19.00* 15.00
a.-d. A428 7.50p, any single 4.00 3.50

Maria Pax Mendoza Guazon — A429

1984, May 26 Wmk. 372 *Perf. 13*
1691 A429 60s brt blue & red 1.00 .25
1692 A429 65s brt blue, red & blk .80 .25

Butterflies — A430

Unwmk.
1984, Aug. 2 Litho. *Perf. 14*
1693 A430 60s Adolias amlana .50 .20
1694 A430 2.40p Papilio daedalus *1.00* .35
1695 A430 3p Prothoe frankii semperi *1.25* .50
1696 A430 3.60p Troides magellanus *1.25* .50
1697 A430 4.20p Yoma sabina vasuki *1.25* .60
1698 A430 5p Chilasa idaeoides *1.75* .60
Nos. 1693-1698 (6) *7.00* 2.75

There were 500,000 of each value created cto with Jul 5 1984 cancel in the center of each block of 4. These were sold at a small fraction of face value. Used values are for ctos.

Summer Olympics, Los Angeles, 1984 — A431

Designs: 60s, Running (man). 2.40p, Boxing. 6p, Swimming. 7.20p, Windsurfing. 8.40p, Cycling. 20p, Running (woman).

Unwmk.
1984, Aug. 9 Litho. *Perf. 14*
1699 A431 60s multi .25 .20
1700 A431 2.40p multi 1.00 .30
1701 A431 6p multi 2.50 .50
1702 A431 7.20p multi 3.00 .70
1703 A431 8.40p multi 3.25 .85
1704 A431 20p multi 8.00 1.00
Nos. 1698-1703 (6) 11.75 3.15

Souvenir Sheet
1705 Sheet of 4 15.00 12.50
a.-d. A431 6p, any single 2.50 2.50

There were 500,000 of each value created cto with Aug 8 1984 cancel in the center of each block of 4. These were sold at a small fraction of face value. Used value, set of 6 cto, $1.25.

Nos. 1699-1705 were also issued imperf, with blue, instead of red, stars at sides. Value, set of 6 stamps $75, souvenir sheet $25.

Baguio City, 75th Anniv. A432

Wmk. 372
1984, Aug. 24 Litho. *Perf. 12½*
1706 A432 1.20p The Mansion 1.25 .35

Light Rail Transit A433

1984, Sept. 10 *Perf. 13x13½*
1707 A433 1.20p multi 1.25 .35

A similar unlisted issue shows a streecar facing left on the 1.20p.

No. 1, Australia No. 59 and Koalas A434

Perf. 14½x15
1984, Sept. 21 Unwmk.
1708 A434 3p multi 2.00 1.00
1709 A434 3.60p multi 2.50 1.00

Souvenir Sheet
1710 Sheet of 3 *22.50* 17.50
a. A434 20p multi 6.00 5.00

AUSIPEX '84. No. 1710 exists imperf.

No. 1609 Surcharged with 2 Black Bars and Ovptd. "14-17 NOV. 84 / R.I. ASIA REGIONAL CONFERENCE"

Perf. 13x13½
1984, Nov. 11 Wmk. 372 Litho.
1713 A398 1.20p on 2.30p multi 1.40 .40

Philatelic Week — A435

1984, Nov. 22 *Perf. 13½x13*
1714 1.20p Gold medal .50 .35
1715 3p Winning stamp exhibit 1.50 .80
a. A435 Pair, #1714-1715 2.75 2.00

AUSIPEX '84 and Mario Que, 1st Philippine exhibitor to win FIP Gold Award.
For overprints see Nos. .

Ships A436

Perf. 13½x13
1984, Nov. Unwmk. Litho.
1718 A436 60s Caracao canoes .30 .25
1719 A436 1.20p Chinese junk .30 .30
1720 A436 6p Spanish galleon 1.40 .45
1721 A436 7.20p Casco 1.75 .60
1722 A436 8.40p Steamboat 2.00 .65
1723 A436 20p Cruise liner 4.25 1.00
Nos. 1718-1723 (6) *10.00* 3.25

There were 500,000 of each value created cto with Oct 5 1984 cancel in the center of each block of 4. These were sold at a small fraction of face value. Value, set of 6 cto, $1.25.

Ateneo de Manila University, 125th Anniv. A438

Perf. 13x13½
1984, Dec. 7 Wmk. 372 Litho.
1730 A438 60s ultra & gold .50 .20
1731 A438 1.20p dk ultra & sil 1.00 .30

A438a

60s, Manila-Dagupan, 1892. 1.20p, Light rail transit, 1984. 6p, Bicol Express, 1955. 7,20p, Tranvis (1905, electric street car). 8.40, Commuter train, 1984. 20p, Early street car pulled by horses, 1898.

Perf. 14x13¾

1984, Dec. 18 **Unwmk.**

1731A A438a 60s multi .40 .25
1731B A438a 1.20p multi .85 .30
1731C A438a 6p multi 2.50 .45
1731D A438a 7.20p multi 3.25 .60
1731E A438a 8.40p multi 3.50 .65
1731F A438a 20p multi 7.00 1.00
Nos. 1731A-1731F (6) 17.50 3.25

There were 500,000 of each value created cto with Dec 5 1984 cancel in the center of each block of 4. These were sold at a small fraction of face value. Value, set of 6 cto, $1.50.

For surcharges see #1772-1773.

Christmas
A439

Natl. Jaycees Awards, 25th anniv. — A440

Perf. 13½x13

1984, Dec. 8 **Wmk. 372**

1732 A439 60s Madonna and Child .75 .25
1733 A439 1.20p Holy family 1.25 .60
a. Pair, #1732-1733 2.25 1.75

1984, Dec. 19

Philippines Jaycees Commitment to Youth Development.

Abstract painting by Raoul G. Isidro.

1734 Strip of 10 *24.00* 17.50
a.-e. A440 60s any single .75 .50
f.-j. A440 3p any single 3.00 1.25

Dried Tobacco Leaf and Plant
A441

1985, Jan. 14 ***Perf. 13x13½***

1735 A441 60s multicolored .35 .25
1736 A441 3p multicolored 1.90 .85

Philippine-Virginia Tobacco Admin., 25th anniv.

No. 1537 Surcharged

1985, Jan. **Litho.** ***Imperf.***

1737 A373 3p on 2p multi 4.75 3.50

First printing had missing period ("p300").

Nos. 1714-1715 Overprinted "Philatelic Week 1984"

1985, Jan. ***Perf. 13½x13***

1737A A435 1.20p Gold medal .50 .35
1737B A435 3p Winning stamp exhibit 1.50 .85
c. Pair, #1737A-1737B 2.75 .20

Natl. Research Council Emblem
A442

1985, Feb. 3 **Litho.** ***Perf. 13x13½***

1738 A442 60s bl, dk bl & blk .30 .20
1739 A442 1.20p org, dk bl & blk .90 .25

Pacific Science Assoc., 5th intl. congress, Manila, Feb. 3-7.

Medicinal Plants
A443

1985, Mar. 15 ***Perf. 12½***

1740 A443 60s Carmona retusa .40 .20
1741 A443 1.20p Orthosiphon aristatus .80 .30
1742 A443 2.40p Vitex negundo 1.25 .45
1743 A443 3p Aloe barbadensis 1.25 .50
1744 A443 3.60p Quisqualis indica 1.60 .60
1745 A443 4.20p Blumea balsamifera 2.10 .75
Nos. 1740-1745 (6) 7.40 2.80

INTELSAT, 20th Anniv.
A444

1985, Apr. 6 ***Perf. 13x13½***

1746 A444 60s multicolored .35 .20
1747 A444 3p multicolored 2.25 .75

A444a

Philippine Horses: 60s, Pintos. 1.20p, Palomino. 6p, Bay. 7.20p, Brown. 8.40p, Gray. 20p, Chestnut.

#1747G: h, as 1.20p. i, as 7.20p. j, as 6p. k, as 20p.

Perf. 14x13¾

1984, Dec. 18 **Unwmk.**

1747A A444a 60s multi .40 .25
1747B A444a 1.20p multi .85 .35
1747C A444a 6p multi 2.00 .75
1747D A444a 7.20p multi 2.75 .90
1747E A444a 8.40p multi 3.25 1.00
1747F A444a 20p multi 6.75 1.25
Nos. 1747A-1747F (6) 16.00 4.50

Souvenir Sheet of 4

1747G A444a 8.40p h.-k. 15.00 12.50

There were 500,000 each of #1747A-1747F created cto with Apr 12 1985 cancel in the center of each block of 4. These were sold at a small fraction of face value. Value, set of 6 cto, $1.50.

Tax Research Institute, 25th Anniv. — A445

Perf. 13½x13

1985, Apr. 22 **Wmk. 372**

1748 A445 60s multicolored .60 .20

Intl. Rice Research Institute, 25th Anniv.
A446

1985, May 27 ***Perf. 13x13½***

1749 A446 60s Planting .40 .20
1750 A446 3p Paddies 2.10 .20

1st Spain-Philippines Peace Treaty, 420th Anniv. — A447

Designs: 1.20p, Blessed Infant of Cebu, statue, shrine and basilica. 3.60p, King Tupas of Cebu and Miguel Lopez de Legaspi signing treaty, 1565.

1985, June 4 ***Perf. 12½***

1751 A447 1.20p multi .35 .20
1752 A447 3.60p multi .90 .30
a. Pair, #1751-1752 + label 2.25 1.50

No. 1532 Ovptd. "10th Anniversary Philippines and People's Republic of China Diplomatic Relations 1975-1985"

1985, June 8 ***Imperf.***

1753 A372 5p multi 5.00 3.50

Arbor Week, June 9-15 — A448

1985, June 9 ***Perf. 13½x13***

1754 A448 1.20p multi 1.10 .35

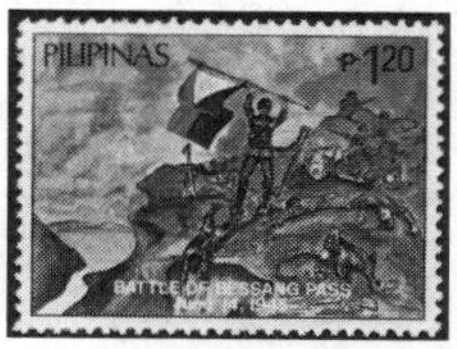

Battle of Bessang Pass, 40th Anniv.
A449

1985, June 14 ***Perf. 13x13½***

1755 A449 1.20p multi 1.10 .35

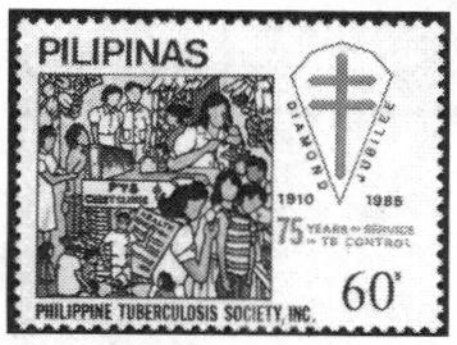

Natl. Tuberculosis Soc., 75th Anniv. — A450

1985, July 29

1756 A450 60s Immunization, research .35 .20
1757 A450 1.20p Charity seal .65 .25
a. Pair, #1756-1757 1.10 .85

No. 1297 Surcharged with Bars, New Value and Scout Emblem in Gold, Ovptd. "GSP" and "45th Anniversary Girl Scout Charter" in Black

Perf. 12½x13½

1985, Aug. 19 **Unwmk.** **Photo.**

1758 A242 2.40p on 15s on 10s 1.25 .45
1759 A242 4.20p on 15s on 10s 2.00 .65
1760 A242 7.20p on 15s on 10s 3.00 .90
Nos. 1758-1760 (3) 6.25 2.00

Virgin Mary Birth Bimillennium
A451

Statues and paintings.

Perf. 13½x13

1985, Sept. 8 **Wmk. 372** **Litho.**

1761 A451 1.20p Fatima .60 .20
1762 A451 2.40p Beaterio 1.40 .40
1763 A451 3p Penafrancia 1.90 .60
1764 A451 3.60p Guadalupe 2.40 1.00
Nos. 1761-1764 (4) 6.30 2.20

Intl. Youth Year
A452

Prize-winning children's drawings.

1985, Sept. 23 ***Perf. 13x13½***

1765 A452 2.40p Agriculture 1.00 .35
1766 A452 3.60p Education 1.75 .75

Girl and Rice Terraces
A453

1985, Sept. 26

1767 A453 2.40p multi 1.75 .65

World Tourism Organization, 6th general assembly, Sofia, Bulgaria, Sept. 17-26.

Export Year — A454

UN, 40th Anniv. — A455

1985, Oct. 8 ***Perf. 13½x13***

1768 A454 1.20p multi 1.10 .35

1985, Oct. 24

1769 A455 3.60p multi 2.25 .65

1st Transpacific Airmail Service, 50th Anniv. — A456

1985, Nov. 22 ***Perf. 13x13½***

1770 A456 3p China Clipper on water 2.10 .75
1771 A456 3.60p China Clipper, map 2.50 .75

Nos. 1731C-1731D Surcharged with Bars, New Value and "PHILATELIC WEEK 1985" in Black

Perf. 14x13¾

1985, Nov. 24 **Unwmk.**

1772 A438a 60s on 6p .75 .35
1773 A438a 3p on 7.20p 3.25 1.00

No. 1773 is airmail.

Natl. Bible Week A457

1985, Dec. 3 **Wmk. 372** ***Perf. 12½***

1774 A457 60s multicolored .40 .20
1775 A457 3p multicolored 2.25 .75

Christmas 1985 A458

1985, Dec. 8 ***Perf. 13x13½***

1776 A458 60s Panuluyan .50 .25
1777 A458 3p Pagdalaw 2.50 .75

Scales of Justice A459

1986, Jan. 12

1778 A459 60s lilac rose & blk .30 .25
1779 A459 3p brt grn, lil rose & blk 1.50 .60

University of the Philippines, College of Law, 75th anniv.
See No. 1838.

Flores de Heidelberg, by Jose Rizal — A460

Design: 60s, Noli Me Tangere.

1986 **Wmk. 391** **Litho.** ***Perf. 13***

1780 A460 60s violet .30 .20
1781 A460 1.20p bluish grn 1.25 .20
1782 A460 3.60p redsh brn 2.00 .35
Nos. 1780-1782 (3) 3.55 .75

Issued: 60s, 1.20p, Feb. 21; 3.60p, July 10.
For surcharges see Nos. 1834, 1913.

Philippine Airlines, 45th Anniv. — A461

Aircraft: No. 1783a, Douglas DC3, 1946. b, Douglas DC4 Skymaster, 1946. c, Douglas DC6, 1948. d, Vickers Viscount 784, 1957.

No. 1784a, Fokker Friendship F27 Mark 100, 1960. b, Douglas DC8 Series 50, 1962. c, Bac One Eleven Series 500, 1964. d, McDonnell Douglas DC10 Series 30, 1974.

No. 1785a, Beech Model 18, 1941. b, Boeing 747, 1980.

1986, Mar. 15

1783 Block of 4 *2.25* 2.00
a.-d. A461 60s, any single *.60* .25
1784 Block of 4 *7.25* 5.00
a.-d. A461 2.40p, any single *1.50* .75
1785 Pair *5.25* 4.00
a.-b. A461 3.60p, any single *2.25* 1.10
Nos. 1783-1785 (3) *14.75* 11.00

See No. 1842.

Bataan Oil Refining Corp., 25th Anniv. A462

Perf. 13½x13, 13x13½

1986, Apr. 12 **Wmk. 372**

1786 A462 60s Refinery, vert. .40 .20
1787 A462 3p shown 2.00 .75

EXPO '86, Vancouver A463

Perf. 13x13½

1986, May 2 **Wmk. 391**

1788 A463 60s multicolored .35 .20
1789 A463 3p multicolored 1.75 .55

Asian Productivity Organization, 25th Anniv. — A464

1986

1790 A464 60s multicolored .40 .20
1791 A464 3p multicolored 2.10 .75

Size: 30x22mm

1792 A464 3p pale brown 1.25 .30
Nos. 1790-1792 (3) 3.75 1.25

Issued: #1790-1791, 5/15; #1792, 7/10.

AMERIPEX '86 — A465

Election of Corazon Aquino, 7th Pres. — A466

1986, May 22 ***Perf. 13½x13***

1793 A465 60s No. 241 .40 .20
1794 A465 3p No. 390 2.00 .70

See No. 1835.

1986, May 25 **Wmk. 372**

Portrait of Aquino and: 60s, Salvador Laurel, vice-president, and hands in symbolic gestures of peace and freedom. 1.20p, Symbols of communication and transportation. 2.40p, Parade. 3p, Military. 7.20p, Vice-president, parade, horiz.

1795 A466 60s multi .25 .20
1796 A466 1.20p multi .40 .20
1797 A466 2.40p multi .95 .30
1798 A466 3p multi 1.00 .50
Nos. 1795-1798 (4) 2.60 1.20

Souvenir Sheet

Imperf

1799 A466 7.20p multi 3.75 3.00

For surcharge see No. 1939.

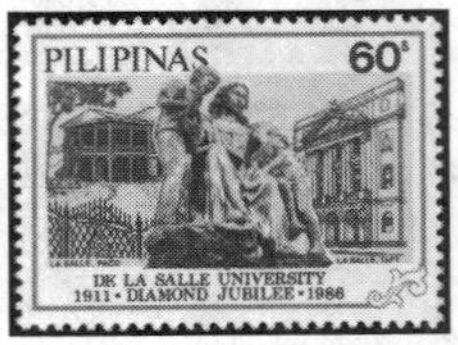

De La Salle University, 75th Anniv. A467

60s, Statue of St. John the Baptist de la Salle, Paco buildings, 1911, & university, 1986. 2.40p, St. Miguel Febres Cordero, buildings, 1911. 3p, St. Benilde, buildings, 1986. 7.20p, Founding fathers.

Perf. 13x13½

1986, June 16 **Wmk. 391**

1800 A467 60s grn, blk & pink .40 .20
1801 A467 2.40p grn, blk & bl 1.00 .35
1802 A467 3p grn, blk & yel 1.60 .60
Nos. 1800-1802 (3) 3.00 1.15

Souvenir Sheet

Imperf

1803 A467 7.20p grn & blk 4.75 3.50

For surcharge see No. 1940.

A468

Memorial to Benigno S. Aquino, Jr. (1932-83) A469

Perf. 13½x13, 13x13½

1986, Aug. 21 **Wmk. 389**

1804 A468 60s dl bluish grn .40 .20
1805 A469 2p shown 1.00 .35
1806 A469 3.60p The Filipino is worth dying for, horiz. 1.50 .45
Nos. 1804-1806 (3) 2.90 1.00

Souvenir Sheet

Imperf

1807 A469 10p Hindi ka nag-iisa, horiz. 4.50 3.50

See No. 1836. For surcharges see No. 1914 and 2706A.

Indigenous Orchids — A470

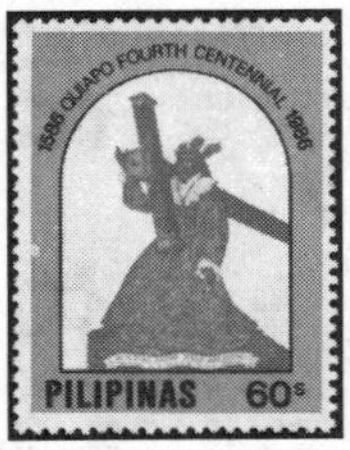

Quiapo District, 400th Anniv. — A471

1986, Aug. 28 ***Perf. 13½x13***

1808 A470 60s Vanda sanderiana *.50* .25
1809 A470 1.20p Epigeneium lyonii *1.50* .40
1810 A470 2.40p Paphiopedilum philippinense *2.75* .60
1811 A470 3p Amesiella philippinensis *3.25* .80
Nos. 1808-1811 (4) *8.00* 2.05

For surcharge see No. 1941.

Perf. 13½x13, 13x13½

1986, Aug. 29 **Wmk. 391**

60s, Our Lord Jesus the Nazarene, statue, Quiapo church. 3.60p, Quiapo church, 1930, horiz.

1812 A471 60s pink, blk & lake .35 .25
1813 A471 3.60p pale grn, blk & dk ultra 2.40 .75

For surcharge see No. 1915.

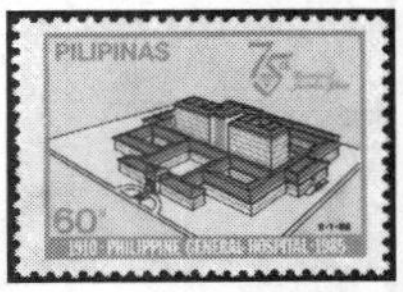

General Hospital, 75th Anniv. — A472

1986, Sept. 1 ***Perf. 13½x13***

1814 A472 60s bl & multi .30 .20
1815 A472 3p grn & multi 1.60 .40

See No. 1841. For surcharge see No. 1888.

Halley's Comet A473

Perf. 13x13½

1986, Sept. 25 **Wmk. 389**

1816 A473 60s Comet, Earth .45 .20
1817 A473 2.40p Comet, Earth, Moon 1.75 .50

For surcharge see No. 1942.

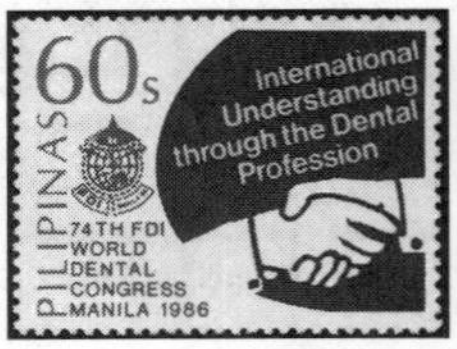

74th FDI World Dental Congress, Manila A474

1986, Nov. 10 **Litho.** ***Perf. 13x13½***

1818 A474 60s Handshake .75 .25
1819 A474 3p Jeepney bus *4.25* 1.00

See Nos. 1837, 1840.

Insects A475

Intl. Peace Year — A476

Manila YMCA, 75th Anniv. — A477

Perf. 13x13½, 13½x13

1986, Nov. 21

1820 A475 60s Butterfly, beetles *1.00* .30
1821 A476 1p blue & blk *2.00* .45
1822 A475 3p Dragonflies *3.00* .75
Nos. 1820-1822 (3) *6.00* 1.50

Philately Week.

Perf. 13x13½

1986, Nov. 28 Wmk. 391

1823 A477 2p blue *1.25* .40
1824 A477 3.60p red *2.75* .60

See No. 1839. For surcharge see No. 1916.

Philippine Normal College, 85th Anniv. A478

Various arrangements of college crest and buildings, 1901-1986.

1986, Dec. 12 Wmk. 389

1825 A478 60s multi *.75* .25
1826 A478 3.60p buff, ultra & gldn brn 2.50 .60

For surcharge see No. 1917.

Christmas A479

1986, Dec. 15 *Perf. 13½x13, 13x13½*

1827 A479 60s Holy family *.50* .20
1828 A479 60s Mother and child, doves *.50* .20
1829 A479 60s Child touching mother's face *.50* .20
1830 A479 1p Adoration of the shepherds *.65* .25
1831 A479 1p Mother, child signaling peace *.65* .25
1832 A479 1p Holy family, lamb *.65* .25
1833 A479 1p Mother, child blessing food *.65* .25
Nos. 1827-1833 (7) *4.10* 1.60

Nos. 1827-1829, vert.

No. 1780 Surcharged

Wmk. 391

1987, Jan. 6 Litho. Perf. 13

1834 A460 1p on 60s vio .90 .20

Types of 1986

Designs: 75s, No. 390, AMERIPEX '86. 1p, Benigno S. Aquino, Jr. 3.25p, Handshake, 74th World Dental Congress. 3.50p, Scales of Justice. 4p, Manila YMCA emblem. 4.75p, Jeepney bus. 5p, General Hospital. 5.50p, Boeing 747, 1980.

Types of 4p
Type I - "4" is taller than "0's."
Type II - "4" is same height as "0's."

1987 Litho. Perf. 13

Size: 22x31mm, 31x22mm

1835 A465 75s brt yel grn .35 .20
1836 A468 1p blue .40 .20
1837 A474 3.25p dull grn 1.10 .35
1838 A459 3.50p dark car 1.50 .35
1839 A477 4p blue, type I 1.50 .30
1839A A477 4p blue, type II 3.00 .40
1840 A474 4.75p dl yel grn 1.90 .40
1841 A472 5p olive bister 1.90 .45
1842 A461 5.50p dk bl gray 2.25 .45
Nos. 1835-1842 (9) *13.90* 3.10

All No. 1839 dated "1-1-87."
Issued: #1839A, 12/16; others, 1/16.

Manila Hotel, 75th Anniv. A480

Perf. 13x13½

1987, Jan. 30 Wmk. 389

1843 A480 1p Hotel, c. 1912 .50 .25
1844 A480 4p Hotel, 1987 2.10 .45
1845 A480 4.75p Lobby 2.50 .50
1846 A480 5.50p Foyer 3.75 .90
Nos. 1843-1846 (4) 8.85 2.10

Intl. Eucharistic Congress, Manila, 50th Anniv. A481

1987, Feb. 7 *Perf. 13½x13, 13x13½*

1847 A481 75s Emblem, vert. .50 .20
1848 A481 1p shown .70 .20

Pres. Aquino Taking Oath A482

Text — A483

1987, Mar. 4 *Perf. 13½x13, 13x13½*

1849 A482 1p multi .40 .25
1850 A483 5.50p bl & deep bis 2.25 .65

Ratification of the new constitution.
See No. 1905. For surcharge see No. 2005.

Lyceum College and Founder, Jose P. Laurel A484

1987, May 7 Litho. *Perf. 13x13½*

1851 A484 1p multi .50 .20
1852 A484 2p multi 1.25 .60

Lyceum of the Philippines, 35th anniv.

Government Service Insurance System — A485

1987, June 1 *Perf. 13½x13*

1853 A485 1p Salary and policy loans .45 .20
1854 A485 1.25p Disability, medicare .65 .20
1855 A485 2p Retirement benefits 1.10 .35
1856 A485 3.50p Life insurance 1.50 .55
Nos. 1853-1856 (4) 3.70 1.30

Davao City, 50th Anniv. A486

1987, Mar. 16 Litho. *Perf. 13x13½*

1857 A486 1p Falconer, woman planting, city seal .60 .20

Salvation Army in the Philippines, 50th Anniv. — A487

Natl. League of Women Voters, 50th Anniv. — A488

1987, June 5 Photo. *Perf. 13½x13*

1858 A487 1p multi 1.10 .35

1987, July 15

1859 A488 1p pink & blue .55 .20

A489

A490

#1851, Gen. Vicente Lukban (1860-1916). #1862, Wenceslao Q. Vinzons (1910-1942). #1863, Brig.-gen. Mateo M. Capinpin (1887-1958). #1864, Jesus Balmori (1882-1948).

Perf. 13x13½, 12½ (#1862)

1987 Litho. Wmk. 391

1861 A489 1p olive grn .40 .20
1862 A489 1p dull greenish blue .50 .20
1863 A489 1p dull red brn .50 .20
1864 A489 1p rose red & rose claret .40 .20
Nos. 1861-1864 (4) 1.80 .80

Issued: #1861, 7/31; #1862, 9/9; #1863, 10/15; #1864, 12/17.

Perf. 13½x13

1987, July 22 Litho. Wmk. 389

Nuns (1862-1987), children, Crucifix, Sacred Heart.

1881 A490 1p multi .75 .25

Daughters of Charity of St. Vincent de Paul in the Philippines, 125th anniv.

Map of Southeast Asia, Flags of ASEAN Members A491

1987, Aug. 7 *Perf. 13x13½*

1882 A491 1p multi .90 .25

ASEAN, 20th anniv.

Exports Campaign A492

1987, Aug. 11 Wmk. 391 *Perf. 13*

1883 A492 1p shown .40 .20
1884 A492 2p Worker, gearwheel .75 .20

See No. 1904.

Canonization of Lorenzo Ruiz by Pope John Paul II, Oct. 18 — A493

First Filipino saint: 1p, Ruiz, stained glass window showing Crucifixion. 5.50p, Ruiz at prayer, execution in 1637.

Perf. 13½x13

1987, Oct. 10 Litho. Wmk. 389

1885 A493 1p multi .65 .25
1886 A493 5.50p multi 3.00 .85

Size: 57x57mm

Imperf

1887 A493 8p like 5.50p 4.25 3.00
Nos. 1885-1887 (3) 7.90 4.10

No. 1887 has denomination at LL.

No. 1841 Surcharged **P4.75**

1987, Oct. 12 Wmk. 391 *Perf. 13*

1888 A472 4.75p on 5p olive bis 1.75 .55

Order of the Good Shepherd Sisters in Philippines, 65th Anniv. A494

Perf. 13x13½

1987, Oct. 27 Wmk. 389

1889 A494 1p multi 1.25 .35

Natl. Boy Scout Movement, 50th Anniv. A495

Founders: J. Vargas, M. Camus, J.E.H. Stevenot, A.N. Luz, V. Lim, C. Romulo and G.A. Daza.

1987, Oct. 28 Litho. *Perf. 13x13½*

1890 A495 1p multi .75 .25

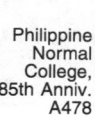

Philippine Philatelic Club, 50th Anniv. A496

1987, Nov. 7 ***Perf. 13x13½***
1891 A496 1p multi .75 .25

Order of the Dominicans in the Philippines, 400th Anniv. A497

Designs: 1p, First missionaries shipwrecked, church and image of the Virgin, vert. 4.75p, J.A. Jeronimo Guerrero, Br., Diego de St. Maria and Letran Dominican College. 5.50p, Pope with Dominican representatives.

Perf. 13½x13, 13x13½
1987, Nov. 11
1892 A497 1p multi .30 .20
1893 A497 4.75p multi 1.75 .40
1894 A497 5.50p multi 2.40 .60
Nos. 1892-1894 (3) 4.45 1.20

3rd ASEAN Summit Meeting, Dec. 14-15 A498

1987, Dec. 5 ***Perf. 13x13½***
1895 A498 4p multicolored 2.25 .70

Christmas 1987 — A499

1987, Dec. 8 ***Perf. 13½x13***
1896 A499 1p Postal service .40 .25
1897 A499 1p 5-Pointed stars .40 .25
1898 A499 4p Procession, church 2.00 .35
1899 A499 4.75p Gift exchange 2.00 .35
1900 A499 5.50p Bamboo cannons 2.75 .60
1901 A499 8p Pig, holiday foods 3.50 .75
1902 A499 9.50p Traditional foods 4.00 .85
1903 A499 11p Serving meal 4.75 1.00
Nos. 1896-1903 (8) 19.80 4.40

Exports Type of 1987

Design: Worker, gearwheel.

Wmk. 391
1987, Dec. 16 Litho. ***Perf. 13***
1904 A492 4.75p lt blue & blk 1.40 .25

Constitution Ratification Type of 1987

1987, Dec. 16 ***Perf. 13***
Size: 22x31½mm
1905 A483 5.50p brt yel grn & fawn 1.60 .45

Grand Masonic Lodge of the Philippines, 75th Anniv. A500

Perf. 13x13½
1987, Dec. 19 **Wmk. 389**
1906 A500 1p multi 1.10 .35

United Nations Projects A501

Designs: a, Intl. Fund for Agricultural Development (IFAD). b, Transport and Communications Decade for Asia and the Pacific. c, Intl. Year of Shelter for the Homeless (IYSH). d, World Health Day, 1987.

1987, Dec. 22 Litho. ***Perf. 13x13½***
1907 Strip of 4 + label *4.75* 4.00
a.-d. A501 1p, any single 1.10 .45

Label pictures UN emblem. Exists imperf.

7th Opening of Congress A502

Designs: 1p, Official seals of the Senate and Quezon City House of Representatives, gavel, vert. 5.50p, Congress in session.

1988, Jan. 25 ***Perf. 13½x13, 13x13½***
1908 A502 1p multi .65 .25
1909 A502 5.50p multi 3.00 .85

St. John Bosco (1815-1888), Educator — A503

1988, Jan. 31 ***Perf. 13x13½***
1910 A503 1p multi .30 .25
1911 A503 5.50p multi 2.25 .60

Buy Philippine Goods — A504

1988, Feb. 1 Litho. ***Perf. 13½x13***
1912 A504 1p buff, ultra, blk & scar .60 .20

Nos. 1782, 1806, 1813, 1824, 1826 Surcharged

Wmk. 389 (#1914, 1917), 391 (#1913, 1915, 1916)
Perf. 13 (#1782), 13x13½
1988, Feb. 14
1913 A460 3p on 3.60p redsh brn 2.50 .40
1914 A469 3p on 3.60p multi 2.50 .40
1915 A471 3p on 3.60p pale grn, blk & dark ultra 3.00 .40
1916 A477 3p on 3.60p red 3.50 .50
1917 A478 3p on 3.60p buff, ultra & golden brn 3.50 .50
Nos. 1913-1917 (5) 15.00 2.20

Use Zip Codes — A505

1988, Feb. 25 Wmk. 391 ***Perf. 13***
1918 A505 60s multi .30 .20
1919 A505 1p multi .45 .20

Insects That Prey on Other Insects — A506

1988, Mar. 11 ***Perf. 13***
1920 A506 1p Vesbius purpureus .40 .20
1921 A506 5.50p Campsomeris aurulenta 2.10 .65

Solar Eclipse 1988 A507

Perf. 13x13½
1988, Mar. 18 **Unwmk.**
1922 A507 1p multi .50 .20
1923 A507 5.50p multi 2.50 .50

Toribio M. Teodoro (1887-1965), Shoe Manufacturer A508

Wmk. 391
1988, Apr. 27 Litho. ***Perf. 13***
1924 A508 1p multicolored .60 .20
1925 A508 1.20p multicolored .90 .20

A509

A510

College of the Holy Spirit, 75th anniv.: 1p, Emblem and motto "Truth in Love." 4p, Arnold Janssen, founder, and Sr. Edelwina, director 1920-1947.

Perf. 13½x13
1988, May 22 **Unwmk.**
1926 A509 1p blk, mar & gold .35 .20
1927 A509 4p blk, ol grn & mar 1.75 .55

Perf. 13½x13
1988, June 4 Litho. Unwmk.
1928 A510 4p dark ultra, brt blue & blk 2.25 .65

Intl. Conf. of Newly Restored Democracies.

A511

A512

Juan Luna and Felix Hidalgo.

1988, June 15 Wmk. 391 ***Perf. 13***
1929 A511 1p multi .30 .20
1930 A511 5.50p multi 1.60 .55

First Natl. Juan Luna and Felix Resurreccion Hidalgo Commemorative Exhibition, June 15-Aug. 15. Artists Luna and Hidalgo won medals at the 1884 Madrid Fine Arts Exhibition.

Perf. 13½x13
1988, June 22 Litho. Wmk. 372
1931 A512 1p multi .40 .20
1932 A512 5.50p multi 2.10 .65

Natl. Irrigation Administration, 25th anniv.

Natl. Olympic Committee Emblem and Sporting Events A513

Designs: 1p, Scuba diving, Siquijor Is. 1.20p, Big game fishing, Aparri, Cagayan Province. 4p, Yachting, Manila Central. 5.50p, Climbing Mt. Apo. 8p, Golf, Cebu, Cebu Is. 11p, Cycling through Marawi, Mindanao Is.

1988, July 11 ***Perf. 13x13½***
1933 A513 1p multi .35 .25
1934 A513 1.20p multi .35 .25
1935 A513 4p multi 1.40 .40
1936 A513 5.50p multi 1.75 .40
1937 A513 8p multi 2.40 .60
1938 A513 11p multi 3.25 1.00
Nos. 1933-1938 (6) *9.50* 2.90

Exist imperf. 4p, 8p, 1p and 5.50p also exist in strips of 4 plus center label, perf and imperf, picturing torch and inscribed "Philippine Olympic Week, May 1-7, 1988."

Nos. 1797, 1801, 1810 and 1817 Surcharged with 2 Bars and New Value in Black or Gold (#1942)

1988, Aug. 1 **As Before**
1939 A466 1.90p on 2.40p #1797 1.10 .35
1940 A467 1.90p on 2.40p #1801 1.10 .60
1941 A470 1.90p on 2.40p #1810 1.10 .35
1942 A473 1.90p on 2.40p #1817 1.10 .35
Nos. 1939-1942 (4) 4.40 1.65

Land Bank of the Philippines, 25th Anniv. A514

Philippine Intl. Commercial Bank, 50th Anniv. A515

Perf. 13x13½
1988, Aug. 8 Litho. Wmk. 372
1943 A514 1p shown .40 .20
1944 A515 1p shown .40 .20
1945 A514 5.50p like No. 1943 2.50 .40
1946 A515 5.50p like No. 1944 2.50 .40
Nos. 1943-1946 (4) 5.80 1.20

Nos. 1943-1944 and 1945-1946 exist in se-tenant pairs from center rows of the sheet.

Profile of Francisco Balagtas Baltasar (b. 1788), Tagalog Language Poet, Author — A516

Wmk. 391

1988, Aug. 8 Litho. *Perf. 13*
1947 A516 1p Facing right .35 .20
1948 A516 1p Facing left .35 .20
a. Pair, #1947-1948 .75 .60

Quezon Institute, 50th Anniv. A517

Perf. 13x13½

1988, Aug. 18 Litho. Wmk. 372
1949 A517 1p multi .50 .25
1950 A517 5.50p multi 3.00 .65

Philippine Tuberculosis Soc.

Mushrooms A518

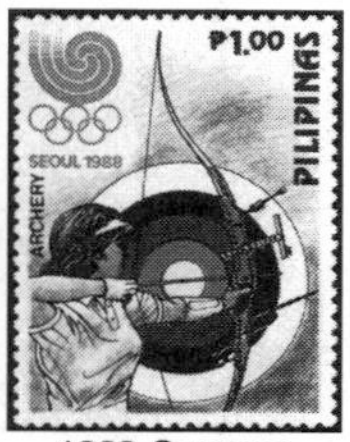

1988 Summer Olympics, Seoul A519

1988, Sept. 13 Wmk. 391 *Perf. 13*
1951 A518 60s Brown .25 .20
1952 A518 1p Rat's ear fungus .40 .20
1953 A518 2p Abalone 1.00 .25
1954 A518 4p Straw 1.25 .30
Nos. 1951-1954 (4) 2.90 .95

Perf. 13½x13

1988, Sept. 19 Wmk. 372
1955 A519 1p Women's archery .35 .20
1956 A519 1.20p Women's tennis .40 .20
1957 A519 4p Boxing 1.00 .35
1958 A519 5.50p Women's running 1.40 .45
1959 A519 8p Swimming 1.60 .55
1960 A519 11p Cycling 2.00 .65
Nos. 1955-1960 (6) 6.75 2.40

Souvenir Sheet

Imperf

1961 Sheet of 4 8.00 6.50
a. A519 5.50p Weight lifting 1.75 1.25
b. A519 5.50p Basketball, horiz. 1.75 1.25
c. A519 5.50p Judo 1.75 1.25
d. A519 5.50p Shooting, horiz. 1.75 1.25

Nos. 1955-1960 exist imperf.

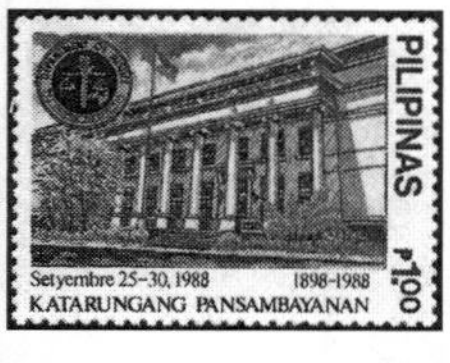

Department of Justice, Cent. A520

1988, Sept. 26 *Perf. 13x13½*
1962 A520 1p multi .60 .20

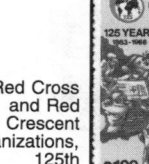

Intl. Red Cross and Red Crescent Organizations, 125th Annivs. — A521

Christian Children's Fund, 50th Anniv. — A522

1988, Sept. 30 *Perf. 13½x13*
1963 A521 1p multi .40 .20
1964 A521 5.50p multi 2.50 .70

1988, Oct. 6
1965 A522 1p multi .60 .20

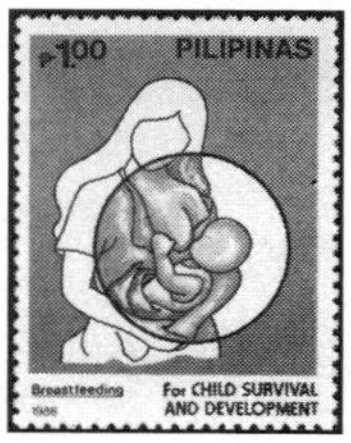

UN Campaigns A523

Designs: a, Breast-feeding. b, Growth monitoring. c, Immunization. d, Oral rehydration. e, Oral rehydration therapy. f, Youth on crutches.

1988, Oct. 24 Litho. *Perf. 13½x13*
1966 Strip of 5 *3.00* 2.50
a.-e. A523 1p any single .60 .25

Child Survival Campaign (Nos. 1966a-1966d); Decade for Disabled Persons (No. 1966e).

Bacolod City Charter, 50th Anniv. A524

1988, Oct. 19 Litho. *Perf. 13x13½*
1967 A524 1p multi .60 .20

UST Graduate School, 50th Anniv. — A525

Dona Aurora Aragon Quezon (b. 1888) — A526

1988, Dec. 20 Litho. *Perf. 13½x13*
1968 A525 1p multi .60 .20

1988, Nov. 7 Wmk. 391 *Perf. 13*
1969 A526 1p multi .30 .20
1970 A526 5.50p multi 1.90 .55

Malate Church, 400th Anniv. — A527

a, Church, 1776. b, Statue & anniv. emblem. c, Church, 1880. d, Church, 1988. Continuous design.

1988, Dec. 16 Wmk. 391
1971 Block of 4 1.50 1.25
a.-d. A527 1p any single .35 .20

UN Declaration of Human Rights, 40th Anniv. A528

Perf. 13½x13

1988, Dec. 9 Wmk. 372
1972 A528 1p shown .40 .20
1973 A528 1p Commission on human rights .40 .20
a. Pair, Nos. 1972-1973 .90 .75

Long Distance Telephone Company — A529

Philatelic Week, Nov. 24-30 — A530

1988, Nov. 28
1974 A529 1p Communications tower .50 .20

1988, Nov. 24 Wmk. 391 *Perf. 13*

Emblem and: a, Post Office, "1938." b, Stamp counter. c, Framed stamp exhibits, four people. d, Exhibits, 8 people. Has a continuous design.

1975 Block of 4 1.40 1.25
a.-d. A530 1p any single .35 .20

Christmas A531

Designs: 75s, Handshake, peave dove, vert. 1p, Children making ornaments. 2p, Boy carrying decoration. 3.50p, Tree, vert. 4.75p, Candle, vert. 5.50p, Man, star, heart.

1988, Dec. 2
1976 A531 75s multi .45 .20
1977 A531 1p multi .45 .20
1978 A531 2p multi .85 .25
1979 A531 3.50p multi 1.25 .35
1980 A531 4.75p multi 1.75 .35
1981 A531 5.50p multi 2.10 .50
Nos. 1976-1981 (6) 6.85 1.85

Gen. Santos City, 50th Anniv. A532

Perf. 13x13½

1989, Feb, 27 Litho. Wmk. 372
1982 A532 1p multi .60 .20

Guerrilla Fighters — A533

Emblem and: No. 1983, Miguel Z. Ver (1918-42). No. 1984, Eleuterio L. Adevoso (1922-75). Printed in continuous design.

1989, Feb. 18 Wmk. 391
1983 1p multi .30 .20
1984 1p multi .30 .20
a. A533 Pair, #1983-1984 .75 .65

Oblates of Mary Immaculate, 50th Anniv. — A534

Perf. 13½x13

1989, Feb. 17 Wmk. 372
1985 A534 1p multicolored .50 .20

Fiesta Islands '89 — A535

Perf. 13 (Nos. 1991, 1994, 1997), 13½x14

1989-90 Litho. Wmk. 391
1986 A535 60s Turumba .25 .20
1987 A535 75s Pahiyas .30 .20
1988 A535 1p Pagoda Sa Wawa .25 .20
1989 A535 1p Masskara .35 .20
1990 A535 3.50p Independence Day .95 .25
1990A A535 4p like #1995 2.25 .40
1991 A535 4.75p Sinulog 1.10 .25
1992 A535 4.75p Cagayan de Oro 1.10 .25
1993 A535 4.75p Grand Canao 1.10 .35
1994 A535 5.50p Lenten festival 1.10 .60
1995 A535 5.50p Penafrancia 1.40 .55
1996 A535 5.50p Fireworks 1.50 .45
1997 A535 6.25p Iloilo Paraw regatta 1.75 .40
Nos. 1986-1997 (13) 13.40 4.30

Issued: #1991, 1994, 6.25p, 3/1/89; 60s, 75s, 3.50p, 6/28/89; #1988, 1992, 1995, 9/1/89; #1989, 1993, 1996, 12/1/89; 4p, 8/6/90.

Great Filipinos — A536

Men and women: a, Don Tomas B. Mapua (1888-), educator. b, Camilo O. Osias (1889-), educator. c, Dr. Olivia D. Salamanca (1889-), physician. d, Dr. Francisco S. Santiago (1889-), composer. e, Leandro H. Fernandez (1889-), educator.

Perf. 14x13½

1989, May 18 Litho. Unwmk.
1998 Strip of 5 1.90 1.75
a.-e. A536 1p any single .35 .20

See Nos. 2022, 2089, 2151, 2240, 2307, 2360, 2414, 2486, 2536.

26th World Congress of the Intl. Federation of Landscape Architects A537

Designs: a, Adventure Pool. b, Paco Park. c, Beautification of Malacanang area streets. d, Erosion control at an upland farm.

1989, May 31 Wmk. 391
1999 Block of 4 1.40 1.25
a.-d. A537 1p any single .35 .20

Printed in continuous design.

French Revolution, Bicent. A538

1989, July 1 ***Perf. 14***
2000 A538 1p multi .30 .20
2001 A538 5.50p multi 1.90 .60

Supreme Court — A539

1989, June 11 **Wmk. 372**
2002 A539 1p multi .50 .20

Natl. Science and Technology Week — A540

1989, July 14
2003 1p GNP chart .30 .20
2004 1p Science High School emblem .30 .20
a. A540 Pair, #2003-2004 .75 .65

No. 1905 Surcharged

Wmk. 391
1989, Aug. 21 **Litho.** ***Perf. 13***
2005 A483 4.75p on 5.50p 1.10 .35

Philippine Environment Month — A542

1989, June 5 **Litho.** ***Perf. 14***
2006 1p Palawan peacock pheasant .50 .20
2007 1p Palawan bear cat .50 .20
a. A542 Pair, #2006-2007 1.10 .90

Asia-Pacific Telecommunity, 10th Anniv. — A544

Wmk. 372
1989, Oct. 30 **Litho.** ***Perf. 14***
2008 A544 1p multicolored .60 .20

Dept. of Natl. Defense, 50th Anniv. — A545

1989, Oct. 23
2009 A545 1p multicolored .60 .20

Intl. Maritime Organization — A546

1989, Nov. 13 ***Perf. 14***
2010 A546 1p multicolored .60 .20

World Stamp Expo '89 A546a

1989, Nov. 17 **Litho.** ***Perf. 14***
2010A A546a 1p #1, Y1 .60 .20
2010B A546a 4p #219, 398 1.90 .40
2010C A546a 5.50p #N1, 500 2.50 .60
Nos. 2010A-2010C (3) 5.00 1.20

Nos. 2010A-2010C withdrawn from sale week of release.

Teaching Philately in the Classroom, Close-up of Youth Collectors A547

1989, Nov. 20 ***Perf. 14x13½***
2011 A547 1p shown .45 .20
2012 A547 1p Class, diff. .45 .20

Christmas — A548

1989 ***Perf. 13½x14***
2013 A548 60s Annunciation .20 .20
2014 A548 75s Visitation .30 .20
2015 A548 1p Journey to Bethlehem .35 .20
2016 A548 2p Search for the inn .65 .25
2017 A548 4p Appearance of the star 1.00 .35
2018 A548 4.75p Birth of Jesus Christ 1.25 .40
Nos. 2013-2018 (6) 3.75 1.60

11th World Cardiology Congress A549

Wmk. 391
1990, Feb. 12 **Photo.** ***Perf. 14***
2019 A549 5.50p black, dark red & deep blue 1.25 .35

Beer Production, Cent. A550

1990, Apr. 16
2020 A550 1p multicolored .25 .20
2021 A550 5.50p multicolored 1.10 .35

Great Filipinos Type of 1989

Designs: a, Claro M. Recto (1890-1960), politician. b, Manuel H. Bernabe. c, Guillermo E. Tolentino. d, Elpidio R. Quirino (1890-1956), politician. e, Bienvenido Ma. Gonzalez.

Perf. 14x13½
1990, June 1 **Litho.** **Unwmk.**
2022 Strip of 5, #a.-e. 1.25 1.10

1990 Census — A551

Wmk. 391
1990, Apr. 30 **Photo.** ***Perf. 14***
Color of Buildings
2023 1p light blue .45 .20
2024 1p beige .45 .20
a. A551 Pair, #2023-2024 .90 .80

Legion of Mary, 50th Anniv. — A552

1990, July 21 **Photo.** ***Perf. 14***
2025 A552 1p multicolored .60 .20

Girl Scouts of the Philippines, 50th Anniv. A553

1990, May 21
2026 A553 1p yellow & multi .30 .20
2027 A553 1.20p lt lilac & multi .40 .20

Asian Pacific Postal Training Center, 20th Anniv. A554

Wmk. 391
1990, Sept. 10 **Photo.** ***Perf. 14***
2028 A554 1p red & multi .30 .20
2029 A554 4p blue & multi 1.10 .35

Natl. Catechetical Year — A555

1990, Sept. 28
2030 A555 1p blk & multi .25 .20
2031 A555 3.50p grn & multi 1.00 .30

Intl. Literacy Year A556

1990, Oct. 24 **Photo.** ***Perf. 14***
2032 A556 1p blk, org & grn .25 .20
2033 A556 5.50p blk, yel & grn 1.40 .40

UN Development Program, 40th Anniv. — A557

1990, Oct. 24
2034 A557 1p yel & multi .25 .20
2035 A557 5.50p orange & multi 1.40 .40

Flowers — A558

1990 **Photo.** **Wmk. 391** ***Perf. 14***
2036 A558 1p Waling waling .50 .20
2037 A558 4p Sampaguita 1.60 .50

29th Orient and Southeast Asian Lions forum.
Issued: 1p, Oct. 3; 4p, Oct. 18.

A559

Christmas A560

Drawings of the Christmas star: a, Yellow star, pink beading. b, Yellow star, white beading. c, Green, blue, yellow and orange star. d, Red star, white outlines.

1990, Dec. 3
2038 Strip of 4 1.25 1.00
a.-d. A559 1p any single .30 .20
2039 A560 5.50p multicolored 1.75 .50

Blind Safety Day A561

1990, Dec. 7 Photo. *Perf. 14*

2040 A561 1p bl, blk & yel .50 .20

Publication of Rizal's "Philippines After 100 Years," Cent. A562

1990, Dec.17

2041 A562 1p multicolored .50 .20

Philatelic Week A563

Paintings: 1p, Family by F. Amorsolo. 4.75p, The Builders by V. Edades. 5.50p, Laughter by A. Magsaysay-Ho.

1990, Nov. 16

2042 A563 1p multicolored .25 .20
2043 A563 4.75p multi, vert. 1.10 .40
2044 A563 5.50p multi, vert. 1.25 .50
Nos. 2042-2044 (3) 2.60 1.10

A564

A565

1991, Jan. 30

2045 A564 1p multicolored .50 .20

2nd Plenary Council of the Philippines.

1991, Mar. 15 Litho. *Perf. 14*

2046 A565 1p multicolored .20 .20
2047 A565 5.50p multicolored 1.25 .35

Philippine Airlines, 50th anniv. No. 2047 is airmail.

Flowers — A566

Flowers: 1p, 2p, Plumeria. 4p, 6p, Ixora. 4.75p, 7p, Bougainvillea. 5.50p, 8p, Hibiscus.

1991 Photo. *Perf. 14x13½*

2048 A566 60s Gardenia .30 .20
2049 A566 75s Allamanda *.30* .20
2050 A566 1p yellow *.35* .20
2051 A566 1p red *.35* .20
2052 A566 1p salmon *.35* .20
2053 A566 1p white *.35* .20
a. Block of 4, #2050-2053 *1.50* 1.25
2053B A566 1p like #2049 *.35* .20
2054 A566 1.20p Nerium *.45* .20
2055 A566 1.50p like #2048 *.60* .20
2056 A566 2p yellow *.75* .25
2057 A566 2p red *.75* .25
2058 A566 2p rose & yel *.75* .25
2059 A566 2p white *.75* .25
a. Block of 4, #2056-2059 *3.50* 3.00
2060 A566 3p like #2054 *1.10* .35
2061 A566 3.25p Cananga *1.25* .40
2062 A566 4p dull rose *1.40* .45
2063 A566 4p pale yellow *1.40* .45
2064 A566 4p orange yel *1.40* .45
2065 A566 4p scarlet *1.40* .45
a. Block of 4, #2062-2065 *6.75* 6.00
2066 A566 4.75p vermilion *1.75* .60
2067 A566 4.75p brt rose lil *1.75* .60
2068 A566 4.75p white *1.75* .60
2069 A566 4.75p lilac rose *1.75* .60
a. Block of 4, #2066-2069 *7.50* 6.50
2070 A566 5p Canna *2.10* .70
2071 A566 5p like #2061 *2.10* .70
2072 A566 5.50p red *2.25* .75
2073 A566 5.50p yellow *2.25* .75
2074 A566 5.50p white *2.25* .75
2075 A566 5.50p pink *2.25* .75
a. Block of 4, #2072-2075 *9.00* 8.00
2076 A566 6p dull rose *2.75* .90
2077 A566 6p pale yellow *2.75* .90
2078 A566 6p orange yel *2.75* .90
2079 A566 6p scarlet *2.75* .90
a. Block of 4, #2076-2079 *11.00* 10.00
2080 A566 7p vermilion *3.00* 1.00
2081 A566 7p brt rose lil *3.00* 1.00
2082 A566 7p white *3.00* 1.00
2083 A566 7p dp lil rose *3.00* 1.00
a. Block of 4, #2080-2083 *12.00* 11.00
2084 A566 8p red *3.25* 1.10
2085 A566 8p yellow *3.25* 1.10
2086 A566 8p white *3.25* 1.10
2087 A566 8p deep pink *3.25* 1.10
a. Block of 4, #2084-2087 *13.50* 12.50
2088 A566 10p like #2070 *4.25* 3.00
Nos. 2048-2088 (42) *74.80* 27.15

Issued: 60s, 75s, #2053a, 5.50p, 3/30; 1.20p, 4p, 4.75p, 5/17 (FDC, on sale 5/7), #2053B, 1/23/93.

Inscribed "1991" except for No. 2053B, which is inscribed "1992.".

Nos. 2048, 2053a, 2055, 2059a, 2060, 2070, 2079a, 2083a, 2087a, 2088 exist with "1992." Value for set, $150.

Great Filipinos Type of 1989

Designs: a, Jorge B. Vargas (1890-1980). b, Ricardo M. Paras (1891-1984). c, Jose P. Laurel (1891-1959), politician. d, Vincente Fabella (1891-1959). e, Maximo M. Kalaw (1891-1954).

1991, June 3 Litho. *Perf. 14x13½*

2089 A536 1p Strip of 5, #a.-e. 1.25 1.10

12th Asia-Pacific Boy Scout Jamboree A567

1991, Apr. 22 *Perf. 14x13½*

2090 A567 1p Square knot .30 .20
2091 A567 4p Sheepshank knot .90 .25
2092 A567 4.75p Figure 8 knot 1.00 .30
a. Souv. sheet of 3, #2090-2092, imperf. 4.50 4.00
Nos. 2090-2092 (3) 2.20 .75

No. 2092a sold for 16.50p and has simulated perfs.

Antipolo by Carlos V. Francisco A568

1991, June 23 Litho. *Perf. 14*
Granite Paper

2093 A568 1p multicolored .60 .20

Pithecophaga Jefferyi — A569

1991, July 31 Photo.

2094 A569 1p Head *.60* .20
2095 A569 4.75p Perched on limb *1.75* .25
2096 A569 5.50p In flight *3.00* .40
2097 A569 8p Feeding young *3.50* .60
Nos. 2094-2097 (4) *8.85* 1.45

World Wildlife Fund.

Philippine Bar Association, Cent. — A570

Wmk. 391

1991, Aug. 20 Photo. *Perf. 14*

2098 A570 1p multicolored .50 .20

A571

1991, Aug. 29

2099 A571 1p multicolored .60 .20

Size: 82x88mm

Imperf

2100 A571 16p like #2099 5.75 5.00

Induction of Filipinos into USAFFE (US Armed Forces in the Far East), 50th Anniv. For overprint see No. 2193.

A572

A573

Independence Movement, cent.: a, Basil at graveside. b, Simon carrying lantern. c, Father Florentino, treasure chest. d, Sister Juli with rosary.

1991, Sept. 18

2101 A572 1p Block of 4, #a.-d. 1.50 1.10

Wmk. 391

1991, Oct. 15 Photo. *Perf. 14*

2102 A573 1p multicolored .40 .20

Size: 60x60mm

Imperf

2103 A573 16p multicolored 3.75 3.00

St. John of the Cross, 400th death anniv.

United Nations Agencies A574

Designs: 1p, UNICEF, children. 4p, High Commissioner for Refugees, hands supporting boat people. 5.50p, Postal Administration, 40th anniv., UN #29, #C3.

1991, Oct. 24 *Perf. 14*

2104 A574 1p multicolored .20 .20
2105 A574 4p multicolored .80 .25
2106 A574 5.50p multicolored 1.25 .60
Nos. 2104-2106 (3) 2.25 1.05

Philatelic Week A575

Paintings: 2p, Bayanihan by Carlos Francisco. 7p, Sari-sari Vendor by Mauro Malang Santos. 8p, Give Us This Day by Vicente Manansala.

1991, Nov. 20

2107 A575 2p multicolored .35 .20
2108 A575 7p multicolored 1.50 .40
2109 A575 8p multicolored 1.90 .50
Nos. 2107-2109 (3) 3.75 1.10

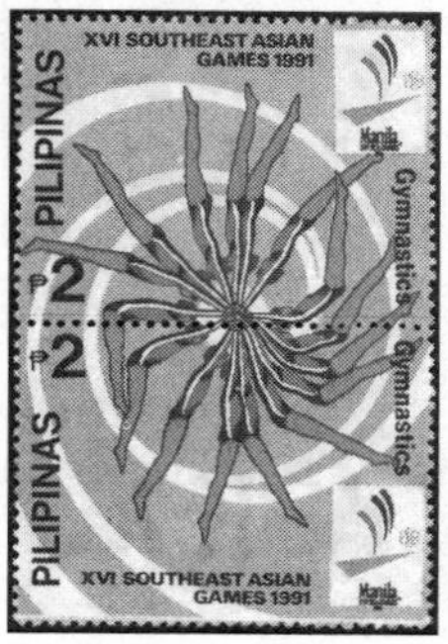

16th Southeast Asian Games, Manila A576

#2110, Gymnastics, games emblem at UR. #2111, Gymnastics, games emblem at LR. #2112, Martial arts, games emblem at LL, vert. #2113, Martial arts, games emblem at LR, vert.

Wmk. 391

1991, Nov. 22 Photo. *Perf. 14*

2110 2p multicolored .35 .20
2111 2p multicolored .35 .20
a. A576 Pair, #2110-2111 .75 .60
2112 6p multicolored 1.00 .35
2113 6p multicolored 1.00 .35
a. A576 Pair, #2112-2113 2.00 1.75
b. Souv. sheet of 2, #2112-2113, imperf. 3.00 2.50
c. Souv. sheet of 4, #2110-2113 4.00 3.50
Nos. 2110-2113 (4) 2.70 1.10

No. 2113b has simulated perforations.

No. 1585 Surcharged in Red
Souvenir Sheet

1991, Nov. 27 Wmk. 372 *Imperf.*

2114 A385 4p on 3.20p 2.50 2.00

First Philippine Philatelic Convention.

Children's Christmas Paintings — A577

1991, Dec. 4 Wmk. 391 *Perf. 14*

2115 A577 2p shown .40 .20
2116 A577 6p Wrapped gift 1.10 .35
2117 A577 7p Santa, tree 1.40 .40
2118 A577 8p Tree, star 1.50 .45
Nos. 2115-2118 (4) 4.40 1.40

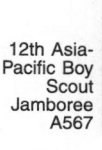

Insignias of Military Groups Inducted into USAFFE — A578

White background: No. 2119a, 1st Regular Div. b, 2nd Regular Div. c, 11th Div. d, 21st Div. e, 31st Div. f, 41st Div. g, 51st Div. h, 61st Div. i, 71st Div. j, 81st Div. k, 91st Div. l, 101st Div. m, Bataan Force. n, Philippine Div. o, Philippine Army Air Corps. p, Offshore Patrol.
Nos. 2120a-2120p, like #2119a-2119p with yellow background.

Perf. 14x13½

1991, Dec. 8 Photo. Wmk. 391

2119 A578 2p Block of 16, #a.-p. 6.00 4.50
2120 A578 2p Block of 16, #a.-p. 6.00 4.50
q. Block of 32, #2119-2120 *42.50* 40.00

Induction of Filipinos into USAFFE, 50th anniv.
Nos. 2119-2120 were printed in sheets of 200 containing 5 #2120q plus five blocks of 8.

Basketball, Cent. A579

Designs: 2p, PBA Games, vert. 6p, Map, player dribbling. 7p, Early players. 8p, Men shooting basketball, vert. 16p, Tip-off.

Wmk. 391

1991, Dec. 19 Litho. *Perf. 14*

2121 A579 2p multicolored .60 .20
2122 A579 6p multicolored 1.50 .50
2123 A579 7p multicolored 2.00 .65
2124 A579 8p multicolored 2.25 .75
a. Souv. sheet of 4, #2121-2124 7.25 6.00
Nos. 2121-2124 (4) 6.35 2.10

Souvenir Sheet

Imperf

2125 A579 16p multicolored 5.25 4.50

No. 2125 has simulated perforations.

New Year 1992, Year of the Monkey A580

Wmk. 391

1991, Dec. 27 Litho. *Perf. 14*

2126 A580 2p violet & multi *.90* .30
2127 A580 6p green & multi *2.60* .65

See Nos. 2459a, 2460a.

Services and Products A581

Wmk. 391

1992, Jan. 15 Litho. *Perf. 14*

2128 A581 2p Mailing center .40 .20
2129 A581 6p Housing project 1.10 .35
2130 A581 7p Livestock 1.40 .45
2131 A581 8p Handicraft 1.60 .55
Nos. 2128-2131 (4) 4.50 1.55

Medicinal Plants — A582

Wmk. 391

1992, Feb. 7 Litho. *Perf. 14*

2132 A582 2p Curcuma longa .75 .20
2133 A582 6p Centella asiatica 1.60 .40
2134 A582 7p Cassia alata 2.00 .50
2135 A582 8p Ervatamia pandacaqui 2.40 .60
Nos. 2132-2135 (4) 6.75 1.70

Love A583

"I Love You" in English on Nos. 2137a-2140a, in Filipino on Nos. 2137b-2140b with designs: No. 2137, Letters, map. No. 2138, Heart, doves. No. 2139, Bouquet of flowers. No. 2140, Map, Cupid with bow and arrow.

Wmk. 391

1992, Feb. 10 Photo. *Perf. 14*

2137 A583 2p Pair, #a.-b. 1.00 .45
2138 A583 6p Pair, #a.-b. 2.75 .90
2139 A583 7p Pair, #a.-b. 3.50 1.75
2140 A583 8p Pair, #a.-b. 7.50 3.75
Nos. 2137-2140 (4) 14.75 6.85

A584

A585

Wmk. 391

1992, Apr. 12 Litho. *Perf. 14*

2141 A584 2p blue & multi .40 .20
2142 A584 8p red vio & multi 1.75 .40

Our Lady of Sorrows of Porta Vaga, 400th anniv.

1992, Mar. 27

Expo '92, Seville: 2p, Man and woman celebrating. 8p, Philippine discovery scenes. 16p, Pavilion, horiz.

2143 A585 2p multicolored .40 .20
2144 A585 8p multicolored 1.75 .40

Souvenir Sheet

Imperf

2145 A585 16p multicolored 4.75 4.00

Department of Agriculture, 75th Anniv. A586

a, Man planting seed. b, Fish trap. c, Pigs.

1992, May 4

2146 A586 2p Strip of 3, #a.-c. 1.75 .75

Manila Jockey Club, 125th Anniv. A588

Wmk. 391

1992, May 14 Litho. *Perf. 14*

2149 A588 2p multicolored .75 .25

Souvenir Sheet

Imperf

2150 A588 8p multicolored 3.00 2.50

No. 2150 has simulated perfs.

Great Filipinos Type of 1989

Designs: a, Pres. Manuel A. Roxas (1892-1948). b, Justice Natividad Almeda-Lopez (1892-1977). c, Justice Roman A. Ozaeta (b. 1892). d, Engracia Cruz-Reyes (1892-1975). e, Fernando Amorsolo (1892-1972).

Perf. 14x13½

1992, June 1 Wmk. 391

2151 A536 2p Strip of 5, #a.-e. 1.75 1.40

30th Chess Olympiad, Manila A589

#2154: a, like #2152. b, like #2153.

1992, June 7 *Perf. 14*

2152 A589 2p No. 1352 .40 .20
2153 A589 6p No. B21 1.40 .35

Souvenir Sheet

Imperf

2154 A589 8p Sheet of 2, #a.-b. 4.50 4.00

No. 2154 has simulated perfs.

World War II, 50th Anniv. — A590

2p, Bataan, cross. 6p, Insignia of defenders of Bataan & Corregidor. 8p, Corregidor, Monument. #2158, Cross, map of Bataan. #2159, Monument, map of Corregidor.

Wmk. 391

1992, June 12 Photo. *Perf. 14*

2155 A590 2p multicolored .40 .20
2156 A590 6p multicolored 1.10 .35
2157 A590 8p multicolored 1.40 .45

Size: 63x76mm, 76x63mm

Imperf

2158 A590 16p multicolored 5.00 4.00
2159 A590 16p multicolored 5.00 4.00
Nos. 2155-2159 (5) 12.90 9.00

Nos. 2158-2159 have simulated perforations.

President Corazon C. Aquino and President-Elect Fidel V. Ramos — A591

1992, June 30 *Perf. 14*

2160 A591 2p multicolored .60 .20

Anniversary of Democracy.

Jose Rizal's Exile to Dapitan, Cent. A592

1992, June 17

2161 A592 2p Dapitan shrine .85 .25
2162 A592 2p Portrait, vert. .85 .25

ASEAN, 25th Anniv. A593

Contemporary paintings: Nos. 2163, 2165, Spirit of ASEAN. Nos. 2164, 2166, ASEAN Sea.

Wmk. 391

1992, July 18 Litho. *Perf. 14*

2163 A593 2p multicolored .40 .20
2164 A593 2p multicolored .40 .20
2165 A593 6p multicolored 1.25 .35
2166 A593 6p multicolored 1.25 .35
Nos. 2163-2166 (4) 3.30 1.10

Founding of Katipunan, Cent. A594

Details or entire paintings of revolutionaries, by Carlos "Botong" Francisco: No. 2167a, Preparing for battle, vert. No. 2167b, Attack leader (detail), vert. No. 2168a, Attack. No. 2168b, Signing papers.

Wmk. 391

1992, July 27 Photo. *Perf. 14*

2167 A594 2p Pair, #a.-b. 1.40 1.00
2168 A594 2p Pair, #a.-b. 1.40 1.00

Philippine League, Cent. A595

Wmk. 391

1992, July 31 Photo. *Perf. 14*

2169 A595 2p multicolored .75 .25

1992 Summer Olympics, Barcelona A596

Wmk. 391

1992, Aug. 4 Litho. *Perf. 14*

2170	A596 2p Swimming	.30	.20
2171	A596 7p Boxing	1.25	.45
2172	A596 8p Hurdling	1.60	.55
	Nos. 2170-2172 (3)	3.15	1.20

Souvenir Sheet

Imperf

2172A A596	Sheet of 3, #2171-2172, 2172Ab	4.25	3.50
b.	1p like #2170	.50	.25

No. 2172A has simulated perforations.

Religious of the Assumption in Philippines, Cent. — A597

Cathedral of San Sebastian, Cent. — A597a

Wmk. 391

1992, Aug. 15 Photo. *Perf. 14*

2173 A597	2p multicolored	.55	.20
2174 A597a	2p multicolored	.55	.20

Founding of Nilad Masonic Lodge, Cent. — A598

Various Masonic symbols and: 6p, A. Luna. 8p, M.H. Del Pilar.

Wmk. 391

1992, Aug. 15 Photo. *Perf. 14*

2175 A598	2p green & black	.35	.20
2176 A598	6p yellow, black & brown	1.50	.40
2177 A598	8p blue, black & violet	1.90	.55
	Nos. 2175-2177 (3)	3.75	1.15

Pres. Fidel V. Ramos Taking Oath of Office, June 30, 1992 A599

1992, July 30

2178 A599	2p Ceremony, people	.35	.20
2179 A599	8p Ceremony, flag	1.40	.60

Freshwater Aquarium Fish A600

Designs: No. 2180a, Red-tailed guppy, b, Tiger lacetail guppy. c, Flamingo guppy. d, Neon tuxedo guppy. e, King cobra guppy.

No. 2181a, Black moor. b, Bubble eye. c, Pearl scale goldfish. d, Red cap. e, Lionhead goldfish.

No. 2182, Golden arowana.

No. 2183a, Delta topsail variatus. b, Orange spotted hi-fin platy. c, Red lyretail swordtail. d, Bleeding heart hi-fin platy.

No. 2184a, 6p, Green discus. b, 6p, Brown discus. c, 7p, Red discus. d, 7p, Blue discus.

1992, Sept. 9 *Perf. 14*

2180 A600	1.50p Strip of 5, #a.-e.	3.00	2.25
2181 A600	2p Strip of 5, #a.-e.	3.50	3.00

Imperf

Size: 65x45mm

2182 A600	8p multicolored	3.00	2.50

Souvenir Sheets of 4

Perf. 14

2183 A600	4p #a.-d.	4.75	4.00
2184 A600	6p, 7p #a.-d.	8.25	7.00

Nos. 2182 and 2184 were overprinted "PHILIPPINE STAMP EXHIBITION 1992 - TAIPEI" in margins. Most of this overprinted issue was sold to the dealer to co-sponsored the exhibit.

See Nos. 2253-2257.

Birthday Greetings A601

1992, Sept 28 *Perf. 14*

2185 A601	2p Couple dancing	.35	.20
2186 A601	6p like #2185	1.25	.50
2187 A601	7p Cake, balloons	1.25	.50
2188 A601	8p like #2187	1.60	.75
	Nos. 2185-2188 (4)	4.45	1.95

Columbus' Discovery of America, 500th Anniv. A602

Various fruits and vegetables.

1992, Oct. 14

2189 A602	2p multicolored	.40	.20
2190 A602	6p multi, diff.	1.25	.35
2191 A602	8p multi, diff.	1.60	.45
	Nos. 2189-2191 (3)	3.25	1.00

Intl. Conference on Nutrition, Rome A603

1992, Oct. 27

2192 A603	2p multicolored	.60	.20

No. 2100 Ovptd. in Blue "Second / National Philatelic Convention / Cebu, Philippines, Oct. 22-24, 1992"

Wmk. 391

1992, Oct. 15 Photo. *Imperf.*

2193 A571	16p multicolored	5.75	5.00

Christmas A604

Various pictures of mother and child.

Wmk. 391

1992, Nov. 5 Litho. *Perf. 14*

2194 A604	2p multicolored	.35	.20
2195 A604	6p multicolored	1.25	.35
2196 A604	7p multicolored	1.25	.40
2197 A604	8p multicolored	1.60	.45
	Nos. 2194-2197 (4)	4.45	1.40

No. 1452 Ovptd. "INAUGURATION OF THE PHILIPPINE POSTAL MUSEUM / AND PHILATELIC LIBRARY, NOVEMBER 10, 1992" in Red

Wmk. 372

1992, Nov. 10 Litho. *Imperf.*

Souvenir Sheet

2198 A348	5p multicolored	2.50	2.00

A605

A606

Wmk. 391

1992, Nov. 15 Litho. *Perf. 14*

2199 A605	2p People, boat	.35	.20
2200 A605	8p People, boat, diff.	1.40	.45

Fight Against Drug Abuse.

1992, Nov. 24

Paintings: 2p, Family, by Cesar Legaspi. 6p, Pounding Rice, by Nena Saguil. 7p, Fish Vendors, by Romeo V. Tabuena.

2201 A606	2p multicolored	.35	.20
2202 A606	6p multicolored	1.25	.30
2203 A606	7p multicolored	1.25	.40
	Nos. 2201-2203 (3)	2.85	.90

Philatelic Week.

Birds A607

Designs: No. 2204a, Black shama. b, Philippine cockatoo. c, Sulu hornbill. d, Mindoro imperial pigeon. e, Blue-headed fantail.

No. 2205a, Philippine trogon, vert. b, Rufous hornbill, vert. c, White-bellied woodpecker, vert. d, Spotted wood kingfisher, vert.

No. 2206a, Brahminy kite. b, Philippine falconet. c, Pacific reef egret. d, Philippine mallard.

Wmk. 391

1992, Nov. 25 Litho. *Perf. 14*

2204 A607	2p Strip of 5, #a.-e.	2.50	2.00

Souvenir Sheets

2205 A607	2p Sheet of 4, #a.-d.	2.25	2.00
2206 A607	2p Sheet of 4, #a.-d.	2.25	2.00

No. 2204 printed in sheets of 10 with designs in each row shifted one space to the right from the preceding row. Two rows in each sheet are tete-beche.

The 1st printing of this set was rejected. The unissued stamps do not have the frame around the birds. The denominations on the sheet stamps and the 2nd souvenir sheet are larger. On the 1st souvenir sheet they are smaller.

For overprint see No. 2405.

New Year 1993, Year of the Rooster A608

1992

2207 A608	2p Native fighting cock	.40	.20
2208 A608	6p Legendary Maranao bird	1.40	.40
a.	Souvenir sheet of 2, #2207-2208 + 2 labels	2.50	2.25
b.	As "a," ovptd. in sheet margin	2.50	2.25

Nos. 2208a and 2208b exist imperf. Overprint on No. 2208b reads: "PHILIPPINE STAMP EXHIBIT / TAIPEI, DECEMBER 1-3, 1992" in English and Chinese.

Issued: #2207-2208, 2208a, 11/27; #2208b, 12/1.

See Nos. 2459b, 2460b.

Guerrilla Units of World War II — A609

Units: a, Bulacan Military Area, Anderson's Command, Luzon Guerrilla Army Forces. b, Marking's Fil-American Guerrillas, Hunters ROTC Guerrillas, President Quezon's Own Guerrillas. c, 61st Division, 71st Division, Cebu Area Command. d, 48th Chinese Guerrilla Squadron, 101st Division, Vinzons Guerrillas.

1992, Dec. 7

2209 A609	2p Block of 4, #a.-d.	3.50	3.00

National Symbols:

A610 Tree   A610c Fish

Flower

A610a   A610b

Flag

A610d   A610e

Animal

A610f   A610g

Bird

A610h A610i

Leaf

A610j A610k

Costume

A610l A610m

Fruit

A610n A610o

A610p A610q

Designs: #2219n, like #2213. #2215a, 2217a, 2219b, Natl. hero, Dr. Jose P. Rizal. #2215b, 2217b, 2219c, House. #2215c, 2217c, 2219d, Costume. #2215d, 2217d, 2219e, Natl. dance. #2215e, 2217e, 2219f, Natl. sport. #2215f, 2219g, Philippine eagle. #2217f, Maya bird. #2215g, 2219a, Flag, "Pilipinas" at top. #2215h, 2217h, 2219i, Animal. #2215i, 2217i, 2219j, Flower. #2215j, 2217j, 2219k, Tree. #2215k, 2217k, 2219 l, Fruit. #2215 l, 2217 l, 2219m, Leaf. #2215m, 2217m, 2219n, Fish. #2215n, 2219h, Flag, "Pilipinas" at bottom.

#2231: a, Flag. b, House. c, Costume. d, Tree. e, Flower (pink). f, Fruit. g, Leaf. h, Fish. i, Animal. j, Bird.

#2232: a, 2p, Aguinaldo. b, 3p, Rizal. c, 2p, Barasoain. d, 3p, Mabini.

Natl. flag and 1872 Cavite Mutiny: #2233; a, 2p, Cavite Arsenal. b, 3p, La Fuerza de San Felipe-Cavite. c, 2p, Commemorative marker. d, 3p, Cristanto de Los Reyes y Mendoza.

Nat'l Flag, 1896 Philippine Revolution: #2234: a, Cry of Pugadlawin. b, Battle of Pinaglabanan. c, Cry of Nueva Ecija. d, Battle of Binakayan.

Some positions from blocks of 14 or souvenir sheets may be identical or similar: #2215i (red "Pilipinas") and #2463A (blue "Pilipinas"), #2217n ("1993" level with top of "Pilipinas") and #2216A ("1993" level with bottom of "Pilipinas"), #2334e and #2211 (color of flower).

Philippine Independence Cent - #2235: a, Edilberto Evangelista. b, Vicente Alvarez. c, Francisco Del Castillo. d, Pantaleon Villegas.

Natl. flag and - #2236: a, Tres de Abril Uprising in Cebu, 1898. b, Negros uprising, 1898. c, Iligan uprinsing, 1898. d, Philippine centennial logo, Kalayaan.

1993-98 Litho. *Perf. 14x13½*

Wmk. 391, Unwmk.

(#2212A, 2214, 2215, 2216A, 2218A, 2219, 2220, 2222)

2210	A610	60s	multi	.25	.20
2211	A610b	1p	Red "Pilipinas"	.35	.20
2212	A610a	1p	multi	.25	.20
2212A	A610b	1p	Blue "Pilipinas"	.35	.20
2213	A610c	1.50p	Red "Pilipinas"	.50	.20
2214	A610c	1.50p	Blue "Pilipinas"	.25	.20
2215		2p	Block of 14, #a.-n.	8.75	7.50
2216	A610d	2p	multi	.50	.20
2216A	A610e	2p	multi	1.25	.40
2217		2p	Block of 14, #a.-l., #2216, 2216A	8.00	7.00
2218	A610f	3p	multi	1.00	.35
2218A	A610g	3p	multi	.50	.20
2219		4p	Block of 14, #a.-n.	14.00	12.50
2220	A610g	4p	like #2218A	1.00	.35
a.			Block of 14, #2219a-2219h, 2220, 2219j-2219n	13.00	11.50
2221	A610h	5p	multi	1.60	.55
2222	A610i	5p	multi	1.25	.40
2223	A610j	6p	multi	1.60	.55
2223A	A610k	6p	Blue "Pilipinas"	1.25	.40
2223B	A610k	6p	Red "Pilipinas"	2.40	.60
2224	A610l	7p	multi	1.75	.60
2224A	A610m	7p	Blue "Pilipinas"	1.40	.45
2224B	A610m	7p	Red "Pilipinas"	2.75	.90
2225	A610n	8p	multi	2.00	.65
2226	A610o	8p	Red "Pilipinas"	3.25	1.10
2227	A610o	8p	Blue "Pilipinas"	1.50	.50
2228	A610p	10p	Red "Pilipinas"	3.25	1.10
2229	A610p	10p	Blue "Pilipinas"	2.00	.65
			Nos. 2210-2229 (27)	62.95	38.15

Souvenir Sheets of 10 and 4

National Anthem

2231	1p #a.-j.+2 labels	3.50	3.00

Perf. 13½

Unwmk.

2232	A610q	2p, 3p #a.-d.	2.50	2.00
2233	A610q	2p, 3p #a.-d.	2.50	2.00
2234	A610q	4p #a.-d.	2.50	2.00
2235	A610q	4p #a.-d.	2.50	2.00
2236	A610q	4p #a.-d.	2.50	2.00

Nos. 2216, 2216A issued in sheets of 200 and with No. 2217.

No. 2215 has blue compressed security printing at top, smaller vignettes, "Pilipinas" in orange red, and is dated "1995." No. 2216 has "Pilipinas" in orange brown at UL. No. 2216A has "Pilipinas" in red at bottom of stamp and is dated "1993."

No. 2224B has larger design than No. 2224A.

Nos. 2212A, 2214, 2215, 2218A, 2219, 2220, 2222, 2223A, 2224A, 2227, 2229 have blue compressed security printing at top, smaller vignettes, "Pilipinas" in red (#2215) or dark blue.

Nos. 2236a-2236d have blue compressed security printing at right, "Pilipinas" in red.

No. 2219 is dated "1995;" No. 2220a, "1996."

Nos. 2218, 2221, 2228 exist dated "1994;" Nos. 2211, 2213, 2218, 2221, 2223B, 2224B, 2226, 2228, "1995." Nos. 2218A, 2222, 2223A, 2227, 2229, "1997."

No. 2220 was released because postal forgeries of No. 2219j were discovered.

Issued: #2212, 2216, 2223, 2224, 2225, 4/29/93; #2210, 2213, 2218, 2221, 2228, 2231, 6/12/93; #2217, 10/28/93; #2216A, 2/10/94: #2211, 53/94; #2232, 6/12/94; #2224B, 7/6/94; #2226, 10/4/94; #2223B, 12/1/94; #2233, 6/12/95; #2215, 11/2/95; #2219, 1/8/96; #2212A, 2214, 2218A, 2220, 2222, 2/12/96; #2224A, 2227, 2229, 4/19/96; #2234, 6/12/96; #2223A, 11/21/96; #2235, 6/12/97; #2236, 6/12/98.

See #2463-2469. For overprints see #2544-2545.

Butterflies A611

Designs: No. 2237a, Euploea mulciber. b, Cheritra orpheus. c, Delias henningia. d, Mycalesis ita. e, Delias diaphana.

No. 2238a, Papilio rumanzobia. b, Papilio palinurus. c, Trogonoptera trojana. d, Graphium agamemnon.

No. 2239, Papilio lowi, Valeria boebera, Delias themis.

1993 Litho. Wmk. 391 *Perf. 14*

2237	A611	2p Strip of 5, #a.-e.	3.00	2.25

Souvenir Sheets

2238	A611	2p Sheet of 4, #a.-d.	2.50	2.00
e.		Ovptd. in sheet margin	2.50	2.00
2239	A611	10p multicolored	3.50	3.00
a.		Ovptd. in sheet margin	3.50	3.00
b.		Ovptd. in blue in sheet margin	10.00	8.50

Issue dates: Nos. 2237-2239, May 28. Nos. 2238e, 2239a, May 29. No. 2239b, July 1.

Nos. 2238a-2238d are vert. No. 2239 contains one 116x28mm stamp.

Overprint on Nos. 2238e, 2239a reads "INDOPEX '93 / INDONESIA PHILATELIC EXHIBITION 1993" and "6th ASIAN INTERNATIONAL PHILATELIC EXHIBITION / 29th MAY-4th JUNE 1993 SURABAYA-INDONESIA."

Overprint on No. 2239b reads "Towards the Year 2000 / 46th PAF Anniversary 1 July 1993" and includes Philippine Air Force emblem and jet.

Great Filipinos Type of 1989

Designs: a, Nicanor Abelardo, composer. b, Pilar Hidalgo-Lim, mathematician, educator. c, Manuel Viola Gallego, lawyer, educator. d, Maria Ylagan Orosa (1893-1943), pharmacist, health advocate. e, Eulogio B. Rodriguez, historian.

1993, June 10 *Perf. 13½*

2240	A536	2p Strip of 5, #a.-e.	2.25	1.50

17th South East Asia Games, Singapore A612

No. 2241: a, Weight lifting, archery, fencing, shooting. b, Boxing, judo. c, Track, cycling, gymnastics, golf.

No. 2242: a, Table tennis, soccer, volleyball, badminton. b, Billiards, bowling. c, Swimming, water polo, yachting, diving.

No. 2243, Basketball, vert.

1993, June 18 *Perf. 13*

2241	A612	2p Strip of 3, #a.-c.	1.25	.75
2242	A612	6p Strip of 3, #a.-c.	3.75	2.25

Souvenir Sheet

2243	A612	10p multicolored	4.50	3.75

#2241a, 2241c, 2242a, 2242c are 80x30mm. No. 2243 contains one 30x40mm stamp. No. 2242a exists inscribed "June 13-20, 1993."

Orchids — A613

No. 2244: a, Spathoglottis chrysantha. b, Arachnis longicaulis. c, Phalaenopsis mariae. d, Coelogyne marmorata. e, Dendrobium sanderae.

No. 2245: a, Dendrobium serratilabium. b, Phalaenopsis equestris. c, Vanda merrillii. d, Vanda luzonica. e, Grammatophyllum martae.

No. 2246, Aerides quinquevulnera. No. 2247, Vanda lamellata.

1993, Aug. 14 Unwmk. *Perf. 14*

2244	A613	2p Block of 5, #a.-e.	2.25	1.50
2245	A613	3p Block of 5, #a.-e.	3.75	2.50

Souvenir Sheets

2246	A613	8p multicolored	2.50	2.00
a.		With additional inscription	2.50	2.00

Imperf

2247	A613	8p multicolored	2.50	2.00
a.		With additional inscription	2.50	2.00

No. 2246 contains one 27x78mm stamp.

Nos. 2246a, 2247a inscribed in sheet margin with Taipei '93 emblem in blue and yellow. Additional black inscription in English and Chinese reads: "ASIAN INTERNATIONAL INVITATION STAMP EXHIBITION / TAIPEI '93."

Greetings — A614

"Thinking of You" in English on Nos. 2248a-2251a, in Filipino on Nos. 2248b-2251b with designs: 2p, Flowers, dog at window. 6p, Dog looking at alarm clock. 7p, Dog looking at calendar. 8p, Dog with slippers.

Wmk. 391

1993, Aug. 20 Litho. *Perf. 14*

2248	A614	2p Pair, #a.-b.	1.00	.75
2249	A614	6p Pair, #a.-b.	3.25	2.25
2250	A614	7p Pair, #a.-b.	3.25	2.75
2251	A614	8p Pair, #a.-b.	4.25	3.50
		Nos. 2248-2251 (4)	11.75	9.25

A615

A616

1993, Aug. 24

2252	A615	2p multicolored	.60	.20

Natl. Coconut Week.

Fish Type of 1992

No. 2253: a, Paradise fish. b, Pearl gourami. c, Red-tailed black shark. d, Tiger barb. e, Cardinal tetra.

No. 2254: a, Albino ryukin goldfish. b, Black oranda goldfish. c, Lionhead goldfish. d, Celestial-eye goldfish. e, Pompon goldfish.

No. 2255: a, Pearl-scale angelfish. b, Zebra angelfish. c, Marble angelfish. d, Black angelfish.

No. 2256: a, Neon betta. b, Libby betta. c, Split-tailed betta. d, Butterfly betta.

No. 2257, Albino oscar.

1993 Unwmk. *Perf. 14*

2253	A600	2p Strip of 5, #a.-e.	2.50	2.00
2254	A600	2p Strip of 5, #a.-e.	2.50	2.00

Souvenir Sheets

Perf. 14

2255	A600	2p Sheet of 4, #a.-d.	2.00	1.75
2256	A600	3p Sheet of 4, #a.-d.	3.00	2.50
e.		Ovptd. in margin	3.25	2.75

Imperf

Stamp Size: 70x45mm

2257	A600	6p multicolored	1.50	1.00
a.		Ovptd. in margin	1.75	1.50

Nos. 2256e, 2257a overprinted in black "QUEEN SIRIKIT NATIONAL CONVENTION CENTER / 1-10 OCTOBER 1993," "BANGKOK WORLD PHILATELIC EXHIBITION 1993" with Bangkok '93 show emblem in purple in margin.

Nos. 2255a-2255d are vert.

Issued: #2256e, 2257a, 9/20; others, 9/9.

Wmk. 391

1993, Sept. 20 Photo. *Perf. 14*

2258	A616	2p multicolored	.50	.20

Basic Petroleum and Minerals, Inc., 25th anniv.

16th World Law Conference, Manila — A617

6p, Globe on scales, gavel, flag, vert. 7p, Justice holding scales, courthouse. 8p, Fisherman, vert.

Unwmk.

1993, Sept. 30 Litho. *Perf. 14*

2259 A617 2p multicolored .30 .20
2260 A617 6p multicolored 1.00 .30
2261 A617 7p multicolored 1.10 .35
2262 A617 8p multicolored 1.25 .40
Nos. 2259-2262 (4) 3.65 1.25

Our Lady of the Rosary of la Naval, 400th Anniv. A618

1993, Oct. 18 Wmk. 391

2263 A618 2p multicolored .50 .20

Intl. Year of Indigenous People — A619

People wearing traditional costumes.

1993, Oct. 24 Unwmk.

2264 A619 2p multicolored .40 .25
2265 A619 6p multicolored 1.40 .35
2266 A619 7p multicolored 1.40 .40
2267 A619 8p multicolored 1.75 .50
Nos. 2264-2267 (4) 4.95 1.50

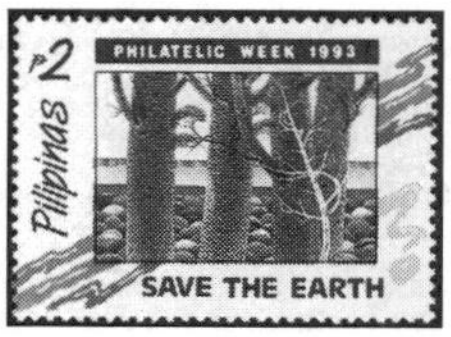

Environmental Protection — A620

Paintings: 2p, Trees. 6p, Marine life. 7p, Bird, trees. 8p, Man and nature.

1993, Nov. 22

2268 A620 2p multicolored .40 .25
2269 A620 6p multicolored 1.40 .35
2270 A620 7p multicolored 1.40 .40
2271 A620 8p multicolored 1.75 .50
Nos. 2268-2271 (4) 4.95 1.50

Philately Week.

A621

a, Lunar buggy. b, Floating power tiller.

Unwmk.

1993, Nov. 30 Litho. *Perf. 14*

2272 A621 2p Pair, #a.-b. .90 .65

Filipino Inventors Society, Inc., 50th Anniv.

1993, Nov. 30

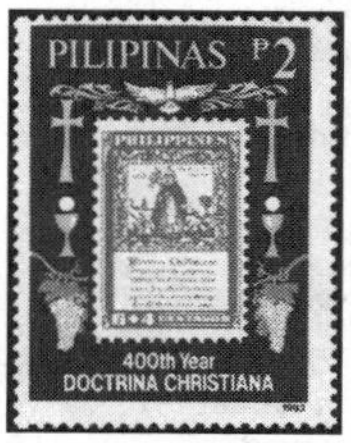

A622

2273 A622 2p multicolored .50 .20

Printing of Doctrina Christiana in Spanish and Tagalog, 400th anniv.

A623

A624

Christmas: 2p, Nativity scene. 6p, Church, people. 7p, Water buffalo carrying fruits, vegetables, sea food. 8p, Christmas lantern, carolers.

1993, Dec. 1

2274 A623 2p multicolored .35 .20
2275 A623 6p multicolored 1.00 .30
2276 A623 7p multicolored 1.10 .35
2277 A623 8p multicolored 1.25 .45
Nos. 2274-2277 (4) 3.70 1.30

1993, Dec. 10

Maps, Philippine guerrilla units of World War II: a, US Army Forces in the Philippines Northern Luzon. b, Bohol Area Command. c, Leyete Area Command. d, Palawan Special Battalion, Sulu Area Command.

2278 A624 2p Block or strip of 4, #a.-d. 2.40 1.60

Philippines 2000 A625

Designs: 2p, Peace and Order. 6p, Transportation, communications. 7p, Infrastructure, industry. No. 2282, People empowerment. No. 2283, Transportation, communications, buildings, people.

Unwmk.

1993, Dec. 14 Litho. *Perf. 14*

2279 A625 2p multicolored .25 .20
2280 A625 6p multicolored .90 .30
2281 A625 7p multicolored 1.10 .35
2282 A625 8p multicolored 1.25 .40

Imperf

Size: 110x85mm

2283 A625 8p multicolored 3.00 2.50
Nos. 2279-2282 (4) 3.50 1.25

New Year 1994 (Year of the Dog) A626

Unwmk.

1993, Dec. 15 Litho. *Perf. 14*

2284 A626 2p Manigong bagong taon .40 .20
2285 A626 6p Happy new year 1.40 .40
a. Souvenir sheet of 2, #2284-2285 + 2 labels 3.00 2.25

No. 2285a exists imperf.
See Nos. 2459c, 2460c.

First ASEAN Scout Jamboree, Mt. Makiling — A627

2p, Flags of ASEAN countries, Boy Scout emblem. 6p, Flags, Boy Scout, emblem.

1993, Dec. 28

2286 A627 2p multicolored .35 .25
2287 A627 6p multicolored 1.10 .35
a. Souv. sheet of 2, #2286-2287 3.50 3.25

Rotary Club of Manila, 75th Anniv. A628

Unwmk.

1994, Jan. 19 Litho. *Perf. 14*

2288 A628 2p multicolored .50 .20

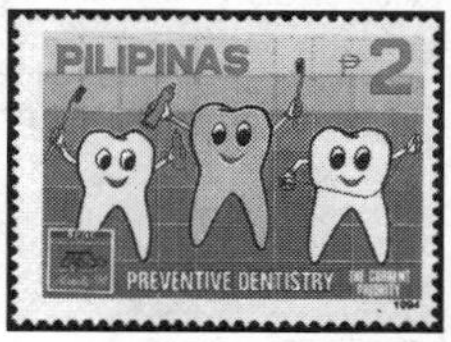

17th Asian Pacific Dental Congress, Manila A629

2p, Healthy teeth. 6p, Globe, flags, teeth.

1994, Feb. 3

2289 A629 2p multicolored .50 .25
2290 A629 6p multicolored 1.50 .35

Corals A630

#2291: a, Acropora micropthalma. b, Seriatopora hystrix. c, Acropora latistella. d, Millepora tenella. e, Millepora tenella, up close. f, Pachyseris valenciennesi. g, Pavona decussata. h, Galaxea fascicularis. i, Acropora formosa. j, Acropora humilis.

#2292: a, Isis. b, Plexaura. c, Dendronepthya. d, Heteroxenia.

#2293: a, Xenia puertogalerae. b, Plexaura, diff. c, Dendrophyllia gracilis. d, Plerogyra sinuosa.

1994, Feb. 15 Litho. *Perf. 14*

2291 A630 2p Block of 10, #a.-j. 4.50 4.00

Souvenir Sheets

2292 A630 2p Sheet of 4, #a.-d. 2.00 1.50
2293 A630 3p Sheet of 4, #a.-d. 3.00 2.50
e. With added inscription 6.25 5.00

No. 2293e is inscribed in sheet margin "NAPHILCON '94 / 1ST NATIONAL / PHILATELIC CONGRESS / 21 FEBRUARY - 5 MARCH 1994 / PHILATELY 2000."

Issued: No. 2293e, 2/21.

Hong Kong '94 — A631

2p, Nos. 2126, 2207. 6p, Nos. 2284, 2285.

1994, Feb. 18

2294 A631 2p multicolored .35 .25
2295 A631 6p multicolored 1.10 .35
a. Souv. sheet of 2, #2294-2295, blue 2.50 1.75
b. As "a," green 2.50 1.75

Backgrounds differ on Nos. 2295a, 2295b.

A632

A633

1994, Feb. 20

2296 A632 2p multicolored .50 .20

Philippine Military Academy Class of 1944, 50th Anniv.

1994, Mar. 1

2297 A633 2p multicolored .50 .20

Federation of Filipino-Chinese Chambers of Commerce and Industry, 40th Anniv.

A634

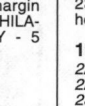

A635

"Congratulations" in English on Nos. 2298a-2301a, in Tagalog on Nos. 2293b-2301b with designs: No. 2298, Books, diploma, mortarboard. No. 2299, Baby carried by stork. No. 2300, Valentine bouquet with portraits in heart. No. 2301, Bouquet.

1994, Apr. 15

2298 A634 2p Pair, #a.-b. 1.00 .75
2299 A634 2p Pair, #a.-b. 1.00 .75
2300 A634 2p Pair, #a.-b. 1.00 .75
2301 A634 2p Pair, #a.-b. 1.00 .75
Nos. 2298-2301 (4) 4.00 3.00

1994, May 5 Litho. *Perf. 14*

1994 Miss Universe Pageant, Manila: Nos. 2302a (2p), 2304a, Gloria Diaz, 1969 winner. No. 2302b (6p), Crown, Philippine jeepney. Nos. 2303a (2p), 2304b, Margie Moran, 1973 winner. No. 2303b (7p), Pageant participant, Kalesa horse-drawn cart.

2302 A635 Pair, #a.-b. .90 .75
2303 A635 Pair, #a.-b. 1.10 1.00

Souvenir Sheet

2304 A635 8p Sheet of 2, #a.-b. 3.50 2.50

Great Filipinos Type of 1989

Designs: a, Antonio J. Molina, musician. b, Jose Yulo, politician. c, Josefa Jara-Martinez, social worker. d, Nicanor Reyes, Sr., accountant. e, Sabino B. Padilla, lawyer.

1994, June 10
2307 A536 2p Strip of 5, #a.-e. 2.10 1.60

Philippine Export Processing Zones A637

No. 2308: a, Baguio City. b, Bataan. c, Mactan. d, Cavite.
No. 2309a, 7p, Map of Philippines, export products. b, 8p, Export products flowing around world map.

Unwmk.

1994, July 4 Litho. *Perf. 14*
2308 A637 2p Block of 4, #a.-d. 1.60 1.00
2309 A637 Pair, #a.-b. 2.75 2.10

Fight Illegal Recruitment Year — A638

1994, July 15
2310 A638 2p multicolored .50 .20

Wildlife A639

a, Palawan bearcat. b, Philippine tarsier. c, Scaly anteater. d, Palawan porcupine.
12p, Visayan spotted deer.

1994, Aug. 12 Litho. *Perf. 14*
2311 A639 6p Block of 4, #a.-d. 4.50 3.00

Souvenir Sheet

2312 A639 12p multicolored 3.25 2.00
a. Ovptd. in margin 3.25 2.00

No. 2312a overprinted in white, black and red in sheet margin with "SINGPEX '94 / 31 August-3 September 1994" and show emblem.

PHILAKOREA '94 — A640

Shells: a, Conus gloriamaris. b, Conus striatus. c, Conus geographus. d, Conus textile.
No. 2314a, Conus marmoreus. No. 2314b, Conus geographus, diff. No. 2315a, Conus striatus, diff. No. 2315b, Conus marmoreus, diff.

1994, Aug. 16
2313 A640 2p Block of 4, #a.-d. 2.50 1.50

Souvenir Sheets

2314 A640 6p Sheet of 2, #a.-b. 3.00 2.25
2315 A640 6p Sheet of 2, #a.-b. 3.00 2.25

Landings at Leyte Gulf, 50th Anniv. A641

Designs: a, Pres. Sergio Osmena, Sr. b, Gen. MacArthur wading ashore. c, Dove of Peace. d, Carlos P. Romulo.

1994, Sept. 15
2316 A641 2p Block of 4, #a.-d. 1.90 1.75

See Nos. 2391a-2391d.

Intl. Anniversaries & Events — A642

Unwmk.

1994, Oct. 24 Litho. *Perf. 14*
2317 A642 2p Family .30 .25
2318 A642 6p Labor workers .90 .35
2319 A642 7p Feather, clouds 1.00 .45
Nos. 2317-2319 (3) 2.20 1.05

Intl. Year of the Family (#2317). ILO, 75th anniv. (#2318). ICAO, 50th anniv. (#2319).

Visit of US Pres. Bill Clinton A643

1994, Nov. 12
2320 A643 2p green & multi .40 .20
2321 A643 8p blue & multi 1.60 .45

East Asean Business Convention, Davao — A644

1994, Nov. 15
2322 A644 2p violet & multi .30 .20
2323 A644 6p brown & multi .90 .30

Nos. 2322-2323 not issued without overprint "Nov. 15-20, 1994" and obliterator covering original date at lower left.

Philatelic Week — A645

Christmas A646

Portraits by Philippine artists: 2p, Soteranna Puson Y Quintos de Ventenilla, by Dionisio de Castro. 6p, Quintina Castor de Sadie, by Simon Flores y de la Rosa. 7p, Artist's mother, by Felix Eduardo Resurreccion Hidalgo y Padilla. 8p, Una Bulaquena, by Juan Luna y Novicio.
12p, Cirilo and Severina Quiason Family, by Simon Flores y de la Rosa.

1994, Nov. 21
2324 A645 2p multicolored .25 .20
2325 A645 6p multicolored .80 .35
2326 A645 7p multicolored .90 .45
2327 A645 8p multicolored 1.00 .55
Nos. 2324-2327 (4) 2.95 1.55

Souvenir Sheet

2328 A645 12p multicolored 3.00 2.00

No. 2328 contains one 29x80mm stamp.

1994, Nov. 25
2329 A646 2p Wreath .20 .20
2330 A646 6p Angels .75 .25
2331 A646 7p Bells .85 .30
2332 A646 8p Basket 1.00 .35
Nos. 2329-2332 (4) 2.80 1.10

ASEANPEX '94 — A647

#2333: a, Blue-naped parrot. b, Bleeding heart pigeon. c, Palawan peacock pheasant. d, Koch's pitta.
No. 2334, Philippine eagle, vert.

1994
2333 A647 2p Block of 4, #a.-d. 2.00 1.50

Souvenir Sheet

2334 A647 12p multicolored 3.00 2.50

A648

Philippine Guerrilla Units in World War II — A649

No. 2335: a, Troops entering prison. b, Prisoners escaping.
Bombed building and - #2336: a, Emblem of East Central Luzon Guerrilla Area. b, Map, Mindoro Provincial Batallion, Marinduque Guerrilla Force. c, Map, Zambales Military District, Masbate Guerrilla Regiment. d, Map, Samar Area Command.

1994 Litho. Unwmk. *Perf. 14*
2335 A648 2p Pair, #a.-b. .75 .60
2336 A649 2p Block of 4, #a.-d. 2.00 1.50

No. 2335 is a continuous design.
See Nos. 2392a-2392b.

New Year 1995 (Year of the Boar) A650

1994
2337 A650 2p shown .40 .20
2338 A650 6p Boy, girl pigs 1.25 .35
a. Souvenir sheet of 2, #2337-2338 + 2 labels 3.00 2.00

No. 2338 exists imperf. Value, unused $3.
See Nos. 2459d, 2460d.

Kalayaan, Cent. (in 1998) — A651

a, Flag, 1898. b, Philippine flag. c, Cent. emblem.

1994
2339 A651 2p Strip of 3, #a.-c. 1.10 .35

AIDS Awareness A652

1994
2340 A652 2p multicolored 1.00 .30

Visit of Pope John Paul II A653

Pope John Paul II and: #2342, Papal arms, globe showing Philippines. 6p, Emblem, map of Asia. #2344, Children.
#2341, a, Archdiocese of Manila. b, Diocese of Cebu. c, Diocese of Caceres. d, Diocese of Nueva Segovia.
#2345, Pres. Fidel V. Ramos, Pope John Paul II.

1995, Jan. 2
2341 A653 2p Block of 4, #a.-d. .85 .70
2342 A653 2p multicolored .20 .20
2343 A653 6p multicolored .65 .25
2344 A653 8p multicolored .85 .35
Nos. 2341-2344 (4) 2.55 1.50

Souvenir Sheet

2345 A653 8p multicolored 3.00 2.25
a. Overprinted in margin 3.00 2.25

Federation of Asian Bishops' Conferences (#2343). 10th World Youth Day (#2344).
Overprint in margin of No. 2345a reads "CHRISTYPEX '95 / JANUARY 4-16, 1995 / University of Santo Tomas, Manila / PHILIPPINE PHILATELIC FEDERATION."

Lingayen Gulf Landings, 50th Anniv. — A654

a, Map of Lingayen Gulf, ships, troops. b, Map, emblems of 6th, 37th, 40th, 43rd Divisions.

1995, Jan. 9
2346 A654 2p Pair, #a.-b. 1.00 .75

No. 2346 is a continuous design.
See Nos. 2391e-2391f.

Liberation of Manila, 50th Anniv. — A655

Statue honoring victims and: 2p, 8p, Various destroyed buildings. Illustration reduced.

1995, Feb. 3
2347 A655 2p magenta & multi .45 .20
2348 A655 8p blue & multi 1.60 .60

See Nos. 2392m, 2392r.

Jose W. Diokno (1922-87), Politician — A656

1995, Feb. 26

2349 A656 2p multicolored .50 .20

Intl. School, Manila, 75th Anniv. A657

Unwmk. Litho. *Perf. 14*

1995, Mar. 4

2350 A657 2p shown .30 .20
2351 A657 8p Globe, cut out figures 1.25 .40

Wildlife A658

No. 2352: a, Mousedeer. b, Tamaraw. c, Visayan warty pig. d, Palm civet.
No. 2353, vert: a, Flying lemur. b, Philippine deer.

1995, Mar. 20

2352 A658 2p Block of 4, #a.-d. 1.75 1.50

Souvenir Sheet

2353 A658 8p Sheet of 2, #a.-b. 3.25 2.50

Battles of World War II, 50th Anniv. A659

Unit emblems and and maps showing: No. 2354, Battle of Nichols Airbase and Ft. Mckinley. No. 2355: a, Nasugbu landings. b, Tagaytay landings.

1995, Apr. 9

2354 A659 2p multicolored .65 .20
2355 A659 2p Pair, #a.-b. 1.25 .75

See Nos. 2391g-2391h, 2392c.

Liberation of Baguio, 50th Anniv. A660

1995, Apr. 27

2356 A660 2p multicolored .60 .25

See No. 2392d.

Liberation of Internment Camps, 50th Anniv. A661

1995, May 28

2357 A661 2p UST .60 .20
2358 A661 2p Cabanatuan .60 .20
2359 A661 2p Los Banos .60 .20
Nos. 2357-2359 (3) 1.80 .60

See Nos. 2392e-2392g.

Great Filipinos Type of 1989

Persons born in 1895: a, Victorio C. Edades. b, Jovita Fuentes. c, Candido M. Africa. d, Asuncion Arriola-Perez. e, Eduardo A. Quisumbing.

Perf. 14x13½

1995, June 1 Litho. Unwmk.

2360 A536 2p Strip of 5, #a.-e. 1.50 1.25

Catholic Bishops' Conference of the Philippines, 50th Anniv. A662

1995, July 22 *Perf. 14*

2361 A662 2p multicolored .50 .20

A663

A664

1995, Aug. 2

2362 A663 2p multicolored .50 .20

Jaime N. Ferrer (1916-87),

1995, Aug. 4

Jars - #2363: a, Manunggul. b, Non-anthropomorphic. c, Anthropomorphic. d, Leta-leta yawning jarlet.
12p, Double spouted and legged vessel, presentation tray.

2363 A664 2p Block of 4, #a.-d. 1.50 1.25

Souvenir Sheet

2364 A664 12p multi, no show emblem in margin 3.00 2.00
a. Show emblem in margin 3.00 2.00

Archaeological finds. No. 2364 contains one 80x30mm stamp.
No. 2364a has Jakarta '95 show emblem in margin. Issued 8/19/95.

ASEAN Environment Year 1995 — A665

Designs: Nos. 2365a, 2366a, Left hand holding turtle, wildlife scene. Nos. 2365b, 2366b, Right hand below fish, bird, wildlife scene.

1995, Aug. 10

2365 A665 2p Pair, #a.-b. .90 .75

Souvenir Sheet

2366 A665 6p Sheet of 2, #a.-b. 5.00 4.00

Nos. 2365-2366 are each continuous designs.

Souvenir Sheet

Philippine Eagle, New Natl. Bird — A666

Illustration reduced.

1995, Aug. 11

2367 A666 16p multicolored 3.50 2.75

Mercury Drug Co., 50th Anniv. A667

1995, Aug. 15

2368 A667 2p multicolored .50 .20

Parish of St. Louis Bishop, 400th Anniv. A668

1995, Aug. 18

2369 A668 2p multicolored .50 .20

Asian-Pacific Postal Training Center, 25th Anniv. — A669

Unwmk.

1995, Sept. 1 Litho. *Perf. 14*

2370 A669 6p multicolored .85 .40

UN, 50th Anniv. — A670

Filipinos serving in UN: No. 2371a, #2372, Carlos P. Romulo. b, Rafael M. Salas. c, Salvador P. Lopez. d, Jose D. Ingles.

1995, Sept. 25

2371 A670 2p Block of 4, #a.-d. 2.40 2.00
2371E A670 2p Cesar C. Bengzon
f. Block of 4, #2371b-2731d, 2371E *150.00*

Souvenir Sheet

2372 A670 16p multicolored 3.00 2.25

No. 2371E was issued with the wrong portrait and was withdrawn after two days.

FAO, 50th Anniv. A671

1995, Sept. 25

2373 A671 8p multicolored 1.50 .65

A671a

A672

Unwmk.

1995, Oct. 5 Litho. *Perf. 14*

2373A A671a 2p multicolored .50 .20

Manila Overseas Press Club, 50th anniv.

1995, Oct. 24

2374 A672 2p Total Eclipse of the Sun .75 .35

Natl. Stamp Collecting Month A673

Paintings: 2p, Two Igorot Women, by Victorio Edades. 6p, Serenade, by Carlos "Botong" Francisco. 7p, Tuba Drinkers, by Vincente Manansala. 8p, Genesis, by Hernando Ocampo.
12p, The Builders, by Edades.

1995, Nov. 6

2375 A673 2p multicolored .30 .20
2376 A673 6p multicolored .95 .40
2377 A673 7p multicolored 1.00 .50
2378 A673 8p multicolored 1.25 .60
Nos. 2375-2378 (4) 3.50 1.70

Souvenir Sheet

2379 A673 12p multicolored 3.00 2.25

No. 2379 contains one 76x26mm stamp.

Christmas A674

Musical instruments, Christmas carols.

1995, Nov. 22

2380 A674 2p Tambourine .30 .20
2381 A674 6p Maracas .95 .45
2382 A674 7p Guitar 1.00 .50
2383 A674 8p Drum 1.25 .65
Nos. 2380-2383 (4) 3.50 1.80

Sycip Gorres Velayo & Co. Accounting Firm, 50th Anniv. A675

1995, Nov. 27

2384 A675 2p Abacus .50 .20

Souvenir Sheet

Pres. Fidel V. Ramos Proclaiming November as Natl. Stamp Collecting Month — A676

1995, Nov. 29

2385 A676 8p multicolored 3.00 2.25

New Year 1996 (Year of the Rat) A677

1995, Dec. 1

2386 A677 2p shown .30 .20
2387 A677 6p Outline of rat .95 .45
a. Souv. sheet, #2386-2387+2 labels 3.00 2.25

No. 2387a exists imperf. Value, $3.
See Nos. 2459e, 2460e.

Philippine Guerrilla Units of World War II — A678

Designs: a, Emblem, FIL-American Irregular Troops (FAIT). b, Emblem, BICOL Brigade. c, Map, FIL-American Guerrilla Forces (Cavite), Hukbalahap Unit (Pampanga). d, Map, South Tarlac, Northwest Pampanga Military Districts.

1995, Dec. 8 Litho. *Perf. 14*

2388 A678 2p Block of 4, #a.-d. 2.50 1.50

Significant Events of World War II, 50th Anniv. A679

Designs: a, Map, liberation of Panay and Romblon, 61st Division. b, Map, Liberation of Cebu, Americal Division. c, Battle of Ipo Dam, 43rd Division, FIL-American Guerrillas. d, Map, Battle of Bessang Pass, 37th Division. e, Sculpture, surrender of Gen. Yamashita.

1995, Dec. 15

2389 A679 2p Strip of 5, #a.-e. 4.50 3.00

See Nos. 2392h-2392 l.

Revolutionary Heroes — A680

a, Jose P. Rizal (1861-96) b, Andres Bonifacio, (1863-97). c, Apolinario Mabini (1864-1903).

1995, Dec. 27

2390 A680 2p Set of 3, #a.-c. 1.50 1.00

Miniature Sheets

World War II Types of 1994-95 and

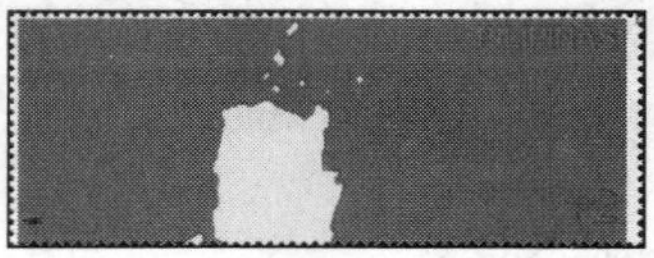

Map of Philippines — A681

Color of Pilipinas and denomination: Nos. 2391a-2391d, like #2316, red. Nos. 2391e-2391f, like #2346, red. Nos. 2391g-2391h, like #2355, red. Nos. 2391i-2391l, map of Philippines with blue background showing sites of Allied landings.

No. 2392: a-b, like #2335, white. c, like #2354, red. d, like #2356, white. e, like #2358, white. f, like #2357, white. g, like #2359, white. h.-l., like #2389a-2389e, purple. m, like #2347, red. n.-q., map of Philippines with green background showing location of prison camps. r, like #2348, red.

1995, Dec. 27 Litho. *Perf. 14*

2391 A681 2p Sheet of 12, #a.-l. 7.00 5.50
2392 A681 2p Sheet of 18, #a.-r. 11.00 8.50

23rd Intl. Congress of Internal Medicine — A682

1996, Jan. 10 Litho. *Perf. 14*

2393 A682 2p multicolored .50 .20

Sun Life Assurance Company of Canada in the Philippines, Cent. A683

1996, Jan. 26

2394 A683 2p shown .30 .20
2395 A683 8p Sun over horizon 1.25 .60

Valentine's Day A684

"I Love You" on Nos. 2396a-2399a, "Happy Valentine" on Nos. 2396b-2399b and: No. 2396, Pair of love birds. No. 2397, Cupid with bow and arrow. No. 2398, Box of chocolates. No. 2399, Bouquet of roses, butterfly.

1996, Feb. 9

2396 A684 2p Pair, #a.-b. .75 .30
2397 A684 6p Pair, #a.-b. 2.25 1.60
2398 A684 7p Pair, #a.-b. 2.50 1.75
2399 A684 8p Pair, #a.-b. 3.00 2.00
Nos. 2396-2399 (4) 8.50 5.65

St. Thomas University Hospital, 50th Anniv. A685

1996, Mar. 5

2400 A685 2p multicolored .50 .20

Gregorio Araneta University Foundation, 50th Anniv. — A686

1996, Mar. 5

2401 A686 2p multicolored .50 .20

Fish A687

No. 2402: a, Emperor fish. b, Mandarinfish. c, Regal angelfish. d, Clown triggerfish. e, Raccoon butterflyfish. g, Powder brown tang. h, Two-banded anemonefish. i, Moorish idol. j, Blue tang. k, Majestic angelfish.

No. 2403: a, like #2402d. b, like #2402k. c, like #2402c. d, like #2402h.

1996, Mar. 12

2402 A687 4p Strip of 5, #a.-e. 3.25 2.50
2402F A687 4p Strip of 5, #g.-k. 3.25 2.50

Miniature Sheet

2403 A687 4p Sheet of 4, #a.-d. 3.00 2.50
e. #2403 with new inscriptions 3.00 2.50

Souvenir Sheet

2404 A687 12p Lionfish 2.00 1.50
a. #2404 with new inscriptions 2.00 1.50

Nos. 2402, 2402F have blue compressed security printing at left, black denomination, white background, margin. Nos. 2403-2404 have blue background, violet denomination, continuous design.

ASEANPEX '96 (No. 2403-2404).

Nos. 2403e, 2404a inscribed in sheet margins with various INDONESIA '96 exhibition emblems. Issued: Nos. 2403e, 2404a, 3/21/96.

See Nos. 2410-2413.

No. 2206 Ovptd. in Green on all 4 Stamps

1996 Litho. Wmk. 391 *Perf. 14*

2405 A607 2p Sheet of 4, #a.-d. 2.50 2.00

Ovpt. in sheet margin reads: "THE YOUNG PHILATELISTS' SOCIETY 10TH ANNIVERSARY".

Souvenir Sheet

Basketball — A688

Illustration reduced.

1996, Apr. 14

2406 A688 10p multicolored *10.00* 7.50

PALARONG/PAMBANSA '96.

Francisco B. Ortigas, Sr. — A689

1996, Apr. 30 Unwmk.

2407 A689 4p multicolored .50 .20

Discovery of Radioactivity, Cent. — A690

1996, Apr. 30

2408 A690 4p multicolored .50 .20

Congregation of Dominican Sisters of St. Catherine of Siena, 300th Anniv. — A691

1996, Apr. 30

2409 A691 4p multicolored .50 .20

Fish Type of 1996

No. 2410: a, Long-horned cowfish. b, Queen angelfish. c, Long-nosed butterflyfish. d, Yellow tang. e, Blue-faced angelfish.

No. 2411: a, Saddleback butterflyfish. b, Sailfin tang. c, Harlequin tuskfish. d, Clown wrasse. e, Spotted boxfish.

No. 2412: a, like #2410e. b, like #2410c. c, like #2410b. d, like #2411c.

No. 2413, vert: a, Purple firefish. b, Pacific seahorse. c, Red-faced batfish. d, Long-nosed hawksfish.

1996

2410 A687 4p Strip of 5, #a.-e. 3.00 2.50
2411 A687 4p Strip of 5, #a.-e. 3.00 2.50
2412 A687 4p Sheet of 4, #a.-d. 2.50 2.00
e. With added inscription 2.50 2.00
2413 A687 4p Sheet of 4, #a.-d. 2.50 2.00
e. With added inscription 2.50 2.00

Nos. 2412-2413 have white background. Nos. 2410-2411 have blue background.

ASEANPEX '96 (#2412-2413). Added inscription in sheet margin of #2412e, 2413e includes CHINA '96 emblem and "CHINA '96 - 9th Asian International Exhibition" in red.

Issued: #2410-2413, 5/10; #2412e, 2413e, 5/16.

Great Filipinos Type of 1989

Designs: a, Carlos P. Garcia (1896-1971), politician. b, Casimiro del Rosario (1896-1962), physicist. c, Geronima T. Pecson (1896-1989), politician. d, Cesar C. Bengson (1896-1992), lawyer. e, Jose Corazon de Jesus (1896-1932), writer.

Perf. 13½

1996, June 1 Litho. Unwmk.

2414 A536 4p Strip of 5, #a.-e. 2.25 1.75

ABS CBN (Broadcasting Network), 50th Anniv. — A692

1996, June 13 ***Perf. 14***

2415 A692 4p shown .40 .20
2416 A692 8p Rooster, world map .95 .40

Manila, Convention City A693

1996, June 24

2417 A693 4p multicolored .50 .25

Jose Cojuangco, Sr. (1896-1976), Businessman, Public Official — A694

1996, July 3

2418 A694 4p multicolored .50 .25

Philippine-American Friendship Day — A695

Symbols of Philippines, US: 4p, Hats. 8p, National birds. 16p, Flags, vert.

1996, July 4

2419 A695 4p multicolored .50 .25
2420 A695 8p multicolored 1.00 .50

Souvenir Sheet

2421 A695 16p multicolored 3.25 2.25

Modern Olympic Games, Cent. A696

4p, No. 2426a, Boxing. 6p, No. 2426b, Athletics. 7p, No. 2426c, Swimming. 8p, No. 2426d, Equestrian.

Unwmk.

1996, July 19 Litho. ***Perf. 14***

2422 A696 4p multicolored .50 .25
2423 A696 6p multicolored .70 .40
2424 A696 7p multicolored .85 .45
2425 A696 8p multicolored .95 .50
Nos. 2422-2425 (4) 3.00 1.60

Miniature Sheet

2426 A696 4p Sheet of 4, #a.-d. 3.25 2.25

Nos. 2422-2425 have colored background, blue security code at right, denominations at LR. Nos. 2426a-2426d have colored circles on white background, blue security code at top, and denominations at UR, UL, LR, LL, respectively.

University of the East, 50th Anniv. A697

1996, Aug. 15

2427 A697 4p multicolored .50 .25

Orchids A698

No. 2428: a, Dendrobium anosmum. b, Phalaenopsis. equestris-alba. c, Aerides lawrenceae. d, Vanda javierii.
No. 2429: a, Renanthera philippinensis. b, Dendrobium schuetzei. c, Dendrobium taurinum. d, Vanda lamellata.
No. 2430: a, Coelogyne pandurata. b, Vanda merrilii. c, Cymbidium aliciae. d, Dendrobium topaziacum.

1996, Sept. 26

2428 A698 4p Block or strip of 4, #a.-d. 2.25 1.50
2429 A698 4p Block or strip of 4, #a.-d. 2.25 1.50

Miniature Sheet

2430 A698 4p Sheet of 4, #a.-d. 3.25 2.00

#2428-2429 were printed in sheets of 16 stamps.
ASEANPEX '96 (#2430). Complete sheets of Nos. 2428-2429 have ASEANPEX emblem in selvage.

6th Asia Pacific Intl. Trade Fair A699

1996, Sept. 30

2431 A699 4p multicolored .50 .25

UNICEF, 50th Anniv. — A700

TAIPEX '96 — A701

Children in montage of scenes studying, working, playing - #2432: a, Blue & multi. b, Purple & multi. c, Green & multi. d, Red & multi.
16p, Four children, horiz.

1996, Oct. 9

2432 A700 4p Block of 4, #a.-d. 2.00 1.50

Souvenir Sheet

2433 A700 16p multicolored 3.00 2.00

1996, Oct. 21 Litho. ***Perf. 14***

Orchids: No. 2434: a, Fran's Fantasy "Alea." b, Malvarosa Green Goddess "Nani." c, Ports of Paradise "Emerald Isle." d, Mem. Conrada Perez "Nani."
No. 2435: a, Pokai tangerine "Lea." b, Mem. Roselyn Reisman "Diana." c, C. Moscombe x Toshi Aoki. d, Mem. Benigno Aquino "Flying Aces."
12p, Pamela Hetherington "Coronation," Living Gold "Erin Treasure," Eleanor Spicer "White Bouquet."

2434 A701 4p Block of 4, #a.-d. 2.25 1.50
2435 A701 4p Block of 4, #a.-d. 2.25 1.50

Souvenir Sheet

2436 A701 12p multicolored 3.25 2.50

Nos. 2434-2435 were issued in sheets of 16 stamps. No. 2436 contains one 80x30mm stamp.

1996 Asia-Pacific Economic Cooperation — A702

Winning entries of stamp design competition: 4p, Sun behind mountains, airplane, skyscrapers, tower, ship, satellite dish, vert. 7p, Skyscrapers. 8p, Flags of nations beside path, globe, skyscrapers, sun, vert.

1996, Oct. 30

2437 A702 4p multicolored .55 .25
2438 A702 6p shown .85 .40
2439 A702 7p multicolored .95 .45
2440 A702 8p multicolored 1.10 .50
Nos. 2437-2440 (4) 3.45 1.60

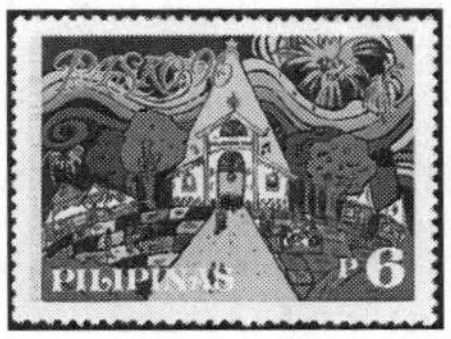

Christmas A703

Designs: 4p, Philippine Nativity scene, vert. 6p, Midnight Mass. 7p, Carolers. 8p, Carolers with Carabao, vert.

1996, Nov. 5

2441 A703 4p multicolored .55 .25
2442 A703 6p multicolored .85 .40
2443 A703 7p multicolored .95 .45
2444 A703 8p multicolored 1.10 .50
Nos. 2441-2444 (4) 3.45 1.60

Eugenio P. Perez (1896-1957), Politician — A704

1996, Nov. 11 Litho. ***Perf. 14***

2445 A704 4p multicolored .55 .25

New Year 1997 (Year of the Ox) A705

1996, Dec. 1

2446 A705 4p Carabao .60 .25
2447 A705 6p Tamaraw .90 .40
a. Souv. sheet, #2446-2447 + 2 labels 2.50 1.75

No. 2447a exists imperf. Value, $2.50.
See Nos. 2459f, 2460f.

ASEANPEX '96, Intl. Philatelic Exhibition, Manila — A706

Independence, Cent. (in 1998) — A707

Jose P. Rizal (1861-96): No. 2448: a, At 14 years. b, At 18. c, At 25. d, At 31.
No. 2449: a, "Noli Me Tangere." b, Gomburza to whom Rizal dedicated "El Filibusterismo." c, Oyang Dapitana, by Rizal. d, Ricardo Camicero, by Rizal.
No. 2450, horiz: a, Rizal's house, Calamba. b, University of St. Tomas, Manila, 1611. c, Orient Hotel, Manila. d, Dapitan during Rizal's time.
No. 2451, horiz: a, Central University, Madrid. b, British Museum, London. c, Botanical Garden, Madrid. d, Heidelberg, Germany.
No. 2452, Rizal at 14, horiz. No. 2453, Rizal at 18, horiz. No. 2454, Rizal at 25, horiz. No. 2455, Rizal at 31, horiz.

1996

2448 A706 4p Block of 4, #a.-d. 2.25 1.75
2449 A706 4p Block of 4, #a.-d. 2.25 1.75
2450 A706 4p Block of 4, #a.-d. 2.25 1.75
2451 A706 4p Block of 4, #a.-d. 2.25 1.75

Souvenir Sheets

2452 A706 12p multicolored 2.50 2.00
2453 A706 12p multicolored 2.50 2.00
2454 A706 12p multicolored 2.50 2.00
2455 A706 12p multicolored 2.50 2.00

Issued: #2448, 2452, 12/14; #2449, 2453, 12/15; #2450, 2454, 12/16; #2451, 2455, 12/17. Nos. 2448-2451 were issued in sheets of 16 stamps.

1996, Dec. 20

Revolutionary heroes: a, Fr. Mariano C. Gomez (1799-1872). b, Fr. Jose A. Burgos (1837-72). c, Fr. Jacinto Zamora (1835-72).

2456 A707 4p Strip of 3, #a.-c. 1.50 1.25

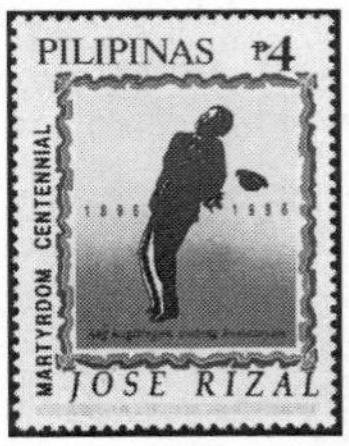

Jose Rizal — A709

1996, Dec. 30 Litho. ***Perf. 14***

2458 A709 4p multicolored .55 .25

New Year Types of 1991-96

Unwmk.

1997, Feb. 12 Litho. ***Perf. 14***

2459 Sheet of 6 3.75 2.50
a. A580 4p like #2126 .60 .25
b. A608 4p like #2208 .60 .25
c. A626 4p like #2284 .60 .25
d. A650 4p like #2337 .60 .25
e. A677 4p like #2386 .60 .25
f. A705 4p like #2446 .60 .25
2460 Sheet of 6 5.25 4.00
a. A580 6p like #2127 .85 .40
b. A608 6p like #2207 .85 .40
c. A626 6p like #2285 .85 .40
d. A650 6p like #2338 .85 .40
e. A677 6p like #2387 .85 .40
f. A705 6p like #2447 .85 .40

Hong Kong '97.

Nos. 2459a-2459b, 2460a-2460b have white margins, color differences. Nos. 2459c-2459d, 2459f, 2460c-2460d, 2460f have color differences. Nos. 2459e, 2460e, do not have blue security printing, and have color differences.

Nos. 2459a-2459f, 2460a-2460f are all dated "1997."

Holy Rosary Seminary, Bicent. A710

1997, Feb. 18

2461 A710 4p multicolored		.55	.25

Philippine Army, Cent. A711

1997, Feb. 18

2462 A711 4p multicolored		.55	.25

Natl. Symbols Type of 1993-96 and:

Gem — A711a

1997 Litho. Unwmk. *Perf. 14x13½*

2463	A610b	1p like #2212A	.25	.20
2463A	A610b	2p like #2212A	.50	.20
2464	A711a	4p multicolored	.70	.20
2465	A610i	5p like #2222	.65	.20
2466	A610k	6p like #2223A	.75	.20
2467	A610m	7p like #2224A	.90	.25
2468	A610o	8p like #2227	1.00	.30
2469	A610p	10p like #2229	1.25	.35
		Nos. 2463-2469 (8)	6.00	1.90

Nos. 2463, #2465-2469 do not have blue compressed security printing at top and are dated "1997."

Nos. 2463A, 2464 have blue compressed security printing at top and are dated "1997."

Issued: 5p, 2/26; 1p, 10p, 2/27; 8p, 3/6; 7p, 3/7; 6p, 3/10; 2p, 4/15; 4p, 6/10.

Dept. of Finance, Cent. A712

1997, Apr. 8 *Perf. 14*

2471 A712 4p multicolored		.55	.25

Philippine Red Cross, 50th Anniv. A713

1997, Apr. 8

2472 A713 4p multicolored		.55	.25

Philamlife Insurance Co., 50th Anniv. A714

1997, Apr. 8

2473 A714 4p multicolored		.55	.25

J. Walter Thompson Advertising, 50th Anniv. in Philippines A715

1997, Apr. 18

2474 A715 4p multicolored		.55	.25

Souvenir Sheet

Philippine-American Friendship Day, Republic Day, 50th Anniv. — A716

Illustration reduced.

1997, May 29

2475 A716 16p multicolored		3.75	2.50

PACIFIC 97.

Wild Animals A717

World Wildlife Fund: No. 2476, Visayan spotted deer. No. 2477, Visayan spotted deer (doe & fawn). No. 2478, Visayan warty pig. No. 2479, Visayan warty pig (adult, young).

1997, July 24

2476 A717 4p multicolored		.65	.30
a. Sheet of 8		5.50	5.50
2477 A717 4p multicolored		.65	.30
a. Sheet of 8		5.50	5.50
2478 A717 4p multicolored		.65	.30
a. Sheet of 8		5.50	5.50
2479 A717 4p multicolored		.65	.30
a. Sheet of 8		5.50	5.50
b. Block or strip of 4, #2476-2479		2.75	2.50

No. 2479b was issued in sheets of 16 stamps.

ASEAN, 30th Anniv. A718

Founding signatories: No. 2480, Adam Malik, Indonesia, Tun Abdul Razak, Malaysia, Narcisco Ramos, Philippines, S. Rajaratnam, Singapore, Thanat Khoman, Thailand. No. 2481, Natl. flags of founding signatories. No. 2482, Flags of current ASEAN countries. No. 2483, Flags of ASEAN countries surrounding globe.

1997, Aug. 7 *Perf. 14*

2480 A718 4p multicolored		.40	.25
2481 A718 4p multicolored		.40	.25
a. Pair, #2480-2481		.85	.70
2482 A718 6p multicolored		.70	.40
2483 A718 6p multicolored		.70	.40
a. Pair, #2482-2483		1.40	1.25
Nos. 2480-2483 (4)		2.20	1.30

World Scout Parliamentary Union, 2nd General Assembly A719

1997, Aug. 17

2484 A719 4p multicolored		.50	.25

Manuel L. Quezon University, 50th Anniv. A720

1997, Aug. 19

2485 A720 4p multicolored		.50	.25

Great Filipinos Type of 1989

Famous people: a, Justice Roberto Regala (1897-1979). b, Doroteo Espiritu, dental surgeon, inventor (b. 1897). c, Elisa R. Ochoa (1897-1978), nurse, tennis champion. d, Mariano Marcos (1897-1945), lawyer, educator. e, Jose F. Romero (1897-1978), editor.

Perf. 14x13½

1997, June 1 Litho. Unwmk.

2486 A536 4p Strip of 5, #a.-e.		1.75	1.50

Battle of Candon, 1898 A721

4p, Don Federico Isabelo Abaya, revolutionary leader against Spanish. 6p, Soldier on horseback.

1997, Sept. 24 *Perf. 14*

2487 A721 4p multi, vert.		.45	.25
2488 A721 6p multi		.75	.40

St. Therese of Lisieux (1873-97) A722

1997, Oct. 16

2489 A722 6p multicolored		.70	.40

Stamp and Philatelic Division, 50th Anniv. A723

Abstract art: 4p, Homage to the Heroes of Bessang Pass, by Hernando Ruiz Ocampo. 6p, Jardin III, by Fernando Zobel. 7p, Abstraction, by Nena Saguil, vert. 8p, House of Life, by Jose Joya, vert.

16p, Dimension of Fear, by Jose Joya.

1997, Oct. 16

2490 A723 4p multicolored		.40	.25
2491 A723 6p multicolored		.60	.40
2492 A723 7p multicolored		.70	.50
2493 A723 8p multicolored		.80	.55
Nos. 2490-2493 (4)		2.50	1.70

Souvenir Sheet

2494 A723 16p multicolored		3.25	2.50

No. 2494 contains one 80x30mm stamp.

Heinrich von Stephan (1831-97) A724

1997, Oct. 24 Litho. *Perf. 14*

2495 A724 4p multicolored		.50	.25

Asian and Pacific Decade of Disabled Persons A725

1997, Oct. 24 Litho. *Perf. 14*

2496 A725 6p multicolored		.70	.40

Intl. Year of the Reef — A726

Illustration reduced.

1997, Oct. 24 Litho. *Perf. 14*

2497 A726 8p multicolored		1.00	.50

Souvenir Sheet

2498 A726 16p multicolored		3.75	3.00

No. 2498 is a continuous design.

Natl. Stamp Collecting Month A726a

Paintings: 4p, Dalagang Bukid, by Fernando Amorsolo, vert. 6p, Bagong Taon, by Arturo Luz, vert. 7p, Jeepneys, by Vincente Manansala. 8p, encounter of the Nuestra Sra. de Cavadonga and the Centurion, by Alfredo Carmelo.

16p, Pista sa Nayon, by Carlos Francisco.

1997, Nov. 4 Litho. *Perf. 14*

2498A	A726a	4p multicolored	.40	.25
2498B	A726a	6p multicolored	.60	.40
2498C	A726a	7p multicolored	.70	.45
2498D	A726a	8p multicolored	.80	.50
		Nos. 2498A-2498D (4)	2.50	1.60

Souvenir Sheet

2498E	A726a	16p multicolored	3.25	2.50

No. 2498E contains one 80x30mm stamp.

Christmas A727

Independence, Cent. — A728

Various stained glass windows.

1997, Nov. 7

2499 A727 4p multicolored .40 .25
2500 A727 6p multicolored .60 .40
2501 A727 7p multicolored .70 .45
2502 A727 8p multicolored .80 .50
Nos. 2499-2502 (4) 2.50 1.60

1997, Nov. 30

Various monuments to Andres Bonifacio (1863-97), revolutionary, founder of the Katipunan: a, red & multi. b, yellow & multi. c, blue & multi.

2503 A728 4p Strip of 3, #a.-c. 1.50 1.25

New Year 1998 (Year of the Tiger) A729

1997, Dec. 1

2504 A729 4p shown .60 .25
2505 A729 6p Tigers, diff. .90 .40
a. Souvenir sheet, #2504-2505 + 2 labels 2.50 2.00

No. 2505a exists imperf. Value, $2.50.

Philippine Eagle A730

1997, Dec. 5

2506 A730 20p Looking right 2.00 1.25
2507 A730 30p Looking forward 3.00 1.75
2508 A730 50p On cliff 5.00 3.25
Nos. 2506-2508 (3) 10.00 6.25

Game Cocks A731

No. 2509: a, Hatch grey. b, Spangled roundhead. c, Racey mug. d, Silver grey.
No. 2510, vert: a, Grey. b, Kelso. c, Bruner roundhead. d, Democrat.
No. 2511, Cock fight, vert. No. 2512, Cocks facing each other ready to fight.

1997, Dec. 18

2509 A731 4p Block of 4, #a.-d. 2.00 1.40
2510 A731 4p Block of 4, #a.-d. 2.00 1.40

Souvenir Sheets

2511 A731 12p multicolored 1.75 1.25
2512 A731 16p multicolored 2.75 2.00

No. 2512 contains one 80x30mm stamp.

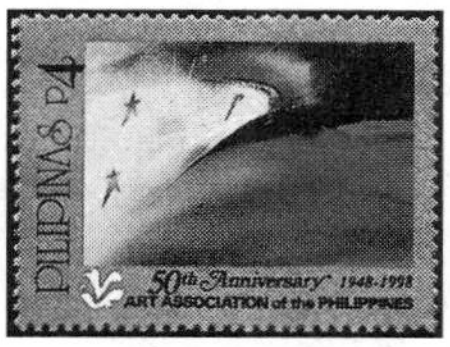

Art Association of the Philippines, 50th Anniv. A732

Stylized designs: No. 2513, Colors of flag, sunburst. No. 2514, Association's initials, clenched fist holding artist's implements.

Unwmk.

1998, Feb. 14 Litho. ***Perf. 14***

2513 A732 4p multicolored .60 .25
2514 A732 4p multicolored .60 .25
a. Pair, #2513-2514 1.25 1.00

Club Filipino Social Organization, Cent. — A733

Blessed Marie Eugenie (1817-98) A734

1998, Feb. 25

2515 A733 4p multicolored .50 .25

1998, Feb. 25

2516 A734 4p multicolored .50 .25

Fulbright Educational Exchange Program in the Philippines, 50th Anniv. — A735

1998, Feb. 25

2517 A735 4p multicolored .50 .25

Heroes of the Revolution — A736

National flag and: 4p, Melchora Aquino (1812-1919). 11p, Andres Bonifacio (1863-97). 13p, Apolinario Mabini (1864-1903). 15p, Emilio Aguinaldo (1869-1964).

1998 Litho. Unwmk. ***Perf. 13½***

2518 A736 4p multicolored .50 .30
2519 A736 11p multicolored 1.50 .65
2520 A736 13p multicolored 1.60 .80
2521 A736 15p multicolored 1.90 .90
Nos. 2518-2521 (4) 5.50 2.65

#2519-2521 exist dated "1999."
Issued: 4p, 3/3/98. 11p, 13p, 15p, 3/24/98.
See Nos. 2528, 2546-2550, 2578-2597, 2607.

Apo View Hotel, 50th Anniv. — A737

Philippine Cultural High School, 75th Anniv. — A738

1998, Mar. 20 ***Perf. 14***

2522 A737 4p multicolored .55 .30

1998, May 5

2523 A738 4p multicolored .55 .30

Victorino Mapa High School, 75th Anniv. A739

1998, May 5

2524 A739 4p multicolored .55 .30

Philippine Navy, Cent. A740

1998, May 5

2525 A740 4p multicolored .55 .30

University of Baguio, 50th Anniv. A741

1998, May 5

2526 A741 4p multicolored .55 .30

Philippine Maritime Institute, 50th Anniv. A742

1998, May 5

2527 A742 4p multicolored .55 .30

Heroes of the Revolution Type of 1998

Design: Gen. Antonio Luna (1866-99).

Perf. 13½

1998, Apr. 30 Litho. Unwmk.

2528 A736 5p multicolored .60 .30

Expo '98, Lisbon A743

4p, Boat on lake, vert. 15p, Vinta on water. 15p, Main lobby, Philippine Pavilion.

1998, May 22 ***Perf. 14***

2529 A743 4p multicolored .40 .25
2530 A743 15p multicolored 1.60 1.00

Souvenir Sheet

2531 A743 15p multicolored 3.25 2.50

No. 2531 contains one 80x30mm stamp.

Clark Special Economic Zone — A744

Illustration reduced.

1998, May 28

2532 A744 15p multicolored 1.60 1.00

Flowers A745

#2533: a, Artrabotrys hexapetalus. b, Hibiscus rosa-sinensis. c, Nerium oleander. d, Jasminum sambac.
#2534, vert: a, Gardenia jasminoides. b, Ixora coccinea. c, Erythrina indica. d, Abelmoschus moschatus.
#2535, Medinilla magnifica.

1998, May 29

2533 A745 4p Block of 4, #a.-d. 2.00 1.50
2534 A745 4p Block of 4, #a.-d. 2.00 1.50

Souvenir Sheet

2535 A745 15p multicolored 4.00 3.00

Great Filipinos Type of 1989

Designs: a, Andres R. Soriano (1898-1964). b, Tomas Fonacier (1898-1991). c, Josefa L. Escoda (1898-1945). d, Lorenzo M. Tañada (1898-1992). e, Lazaro Francisco (1898-1980).

1998, June 1 ***Perf. 14x13½***

2536 A536 4p Strip of 5, #a.-e. 2.00 1.60

Philippine Independence, Cent. — A746

No. 2537, Mexican flag, sailing ship. No. 2538, Woman holding Philippine flag, monument, sailing ship, map of Philippines. No. 2539, Spanish flag, Catholic Church, religious icon, Philippine flag.

1998, June 3 ***Perf. 14***

2537 A746 15p multicolored 1.40 .40
2538 A746 15p multicolored 1.40 .40
2539 A746 15p multicolored 1.40 .40
a. Strip of 3, #2537-2539 4.50 3.50
b. Souvenir sheet, #2537-2539 + 3 labels 5.00 4.00

See Mexico #2079-2080, Spain #2949. For overprint see #2629.

Philippine Independence, Cent. — A747

Patriots of the revolution: a, Melchora Aquino. b, Nazaria Lagos. c, Agueda Kahabagan.

Unwmk.

1998, June 9 Litho. ***Perf. 14***

2540 A747 4p Strip of 3, #a.-c. 1.00 .30

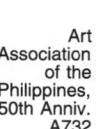

Pasig River Campaign for Waste Management — A748

1998, June 19

2541 A748 4p multicolored .50 .20

Marine Mammals A749

No. 2542: a, Bottlenose dolphin. b, Humpback whale. c, Fraser's dolphin. d, Melon-headed whale. e, Minke whale. f, Striped dolphin. g, Sperm whale. h, Pygmy killer whale. i, Cuvier's beaked whale. j, Killer whale. k, Bottlenose dolphin. l, Long-snouted pinner dolphin. m, Risso's dolphin. n, Finless porpoise. o, Pygmy sperm whale. p, Pantropical spotted dolphin. q, False killer whale. r, Blainville's beaked whale. s, Rough-toothed dolphin. t, Bryde's whale.
15p, Dugong.

1998, June 19

2542 A749 4p Sheet of 20, #a.-t. 7.50 6.50

Souvenir Sheet

2543 A749 15p multicolored 4.00 3.00

Nos. 2218, 2220a Ovptd. in Gold with Philippine Independence Centennial Emblem

1998 Litho. Unwmk. *Perf. 14x13½*

2544 A610f 3p multicolored .50 .25
2545 A610g 4p Block of 14, #a.-n. 8.50 7.50

Issued: 3p, 7/7/98; No. 2545, 6/12/98.

Heroes of the Revolution Type of 1998

2p, Emilio Jacinto. 4p, Jose P. Rizal. 8p, Marcelo H. del Pilar. 10p, Gregorio del Pilar. 18p, Juan Luna.

1998 *Perf. 13½*

2546 A736 2p multicolored .50 .25
2547 A736 4p multicolored .50 .30
2548 A736 8p multicolored 1.00 .50
2549 A736 10p multicolored 1.25 .70
2550 A736 18p multicolored 2.50 1.25
Nos. 2546-2550 (5) 5.75 3.00

#2548 and 2549 exist dated "1999."
Issued: 4p, 10p, 18p, 5/18/98. 2p, 8p, 7/20/98.

Philippine Centennial — A749a

No. 2550A: b, Spoliarium, by Juan Luna. c, 1st display of Philippine flag, 1898. d, Execution of Jose Rizal, 1896. e, Andres Bonifacio. f, Church, Malolos.

1998, July

2550A A749a Souv. booklet *32.50*
b. 4p multicolored .55
c. 8p multicolored 1.10
d.-e. 16p multicolored 2.25
f. 20p multicolored 2.75

No. 2550A contains panes of 4 each of Nos. 2550Ab-2550Ac and one pane of 1 each of Nos. 2550Ad-2550Af.

Philippine Coconut Industry, Cent. A750

1998, Oct. 9 *Perf. 14*

2551 A750 4p multicolored 1.00 .30

Holy Spirit Adoration Sisters in Philippines, 75th Anniv. A751

1998, Oct. 9

2552 A751 4p multicolored 1.25 .30

Universal Delclaration of Human Rights, 50th Anniv. — A752

1998, Oct. 24

2553 A752 4p multicolored .60 .30

Intl. Year of the Ocean — A753

Illustration reduced (#2554).

1998, Oct. 24

2554 A753 15p multicolored 2.40 1.10
a. Souvenir sheet, #2554 4.25 3.00

No. 2554a is a continuous design.

A754

A755

Philippine Postal Service, Cent. - #2555: a, Child placing envelope into mailbox, globe. b, Arms encircling globe, envelopes, Philippine flag as background. c, Airplane, globe, various stamps over building. d, Child holding up hands, natl. flag colors, envelopes.
15p, Child holding envelope as it crisscrosses globe.

1998, Nov. 4

2555 A754 6p Block of 4, #a.-d. 3.00 2.50

Souvenir Sheet

2556 A754 15p multicolored 4.00 3.25

No. 2556 contains one 76x30mm stamp.

1998, Nov. 5

Christmas: Various star lanterns.

2557 A755 6p multicolored .65 .35
2558 A755 11p multicolored 1.25 .70
2559 A755 13p multicolored 1.60 .85
2560 A755 15p multicolored 1.75 1.00
Nos. 2557-2560 (4) 5.25 2.90

Pasko '98.

Souvenir Sheets

Philippines '98, Philippine Cent. Invitational Intl. Philatelic Exhibition — A756

Revolutionary scenes, stamps of revolutionary govt.: No. 2561, Soldiers celebrating, #Y1-Y2. No. 2562, Signing treaty, telegraph stamps. No. 2563, Waving flag from balcony, #YF1, "Recibos" (Offical receipt) stamps. No. 2564, Procession, #Y3, perf. and imperf. examples of #YP1. No. 2565, New government convening, "Trans de Ganades" (cattle transfer) stamp, Libertad essay.
Illustration reduced.

1998

2561 A756 15p multicolored 5.50 4.50
2562 A756 15p multicolored 5.50 4.50
2563 A756 15p multicolored 5.50 4.50
2564 A756 15p multicolored 5.50 4.50
2565 A756 15p multicolored 5.50 4.50
Nos. 2561-2565 (5) 27.50 22.50

No. 2561 exists imperf. The first printing has varying amounts of black offset on the reverse. Value, $60. The second printing does not have the offset. Value, $12.50.
Nos. 2561-2565 were issued one each day from 11/5-11/9.

Pres. Joseph Ejercito Estrada A757

1998, Nov. 10

2566 A757 6p Taking oath .75 .40
2567 A757 15p Giving speech 1.75 1.00

Shells A758

No. 2568: a, Mitra papalis. b, Vexillum citrinum. c, Vexillum rugosum. d, Volema carinifera.
No. 2569: a, Teramachia dalli. b, Nassarius vitiensis. c, Cymbiola imperialis. d, Cymbiola aulica.
No. 2570: a, Nassarius papillosus. b, Fasciolaria trapezium.

Unwmk.

1998, Nov. 6 Litho. *Perf. 14*

2568 A758 4p Block of 4, #a.-d. 2.25 2.00
2569 A758 4p Block of 4, #a.-d. 2.25 2.00

Souvenir Sheet

2570 A758 8p Sheet of 2, #a.-b. 4.75 4.00
c. Souvenir sheet, Type II 10.00 7.50

Cloud in sheet margin touches "s" of Shells on #2570. On #2570c, cloud does not touch "s" of Shells. Colors are dark on #2570c, lighter on #2570.

Natl. Stamp Collecting Month — A759

Motion picture, director: 6p, "Dyesebel," Gerardo de Leon. 11p, "Ang Sawa Sa Lumang Simboryo," Gerardo de Leon. 13p, "Prinsipe Amante," Lamberto V. Avellana. No. 2574, "Anak Dalita," Lamberto V. Avellana.
No. 2575, "Siete Infantes de Lara," costume design by Carlos "Botong" Francisco.

1998, Nov. 25

2571 A759 6p black & blue .60 .40
2572 A759 11p black & brown 1.25 .70
2573 A759 13p black & lilac 1.40 .80
2574 A759 15p black & green 1.75 .95
Nos. 2571-2574 (4) 5.00 2.85

Souvenir Sheet

2575 A759 15p black 2.75 2.25

No. 2575 contains one 26x76mm stamp.

Philippine Centennial — A759a

Pride, various women and: No. 2575A, Eagle (Resources). No. 2575B, Costume (Heritage). No. 2575C, Flag (Filipino People). No. 2575D, Artifacts with text (Literature). No. 2575E, Rice terraces (Engineering). No. 2575F, "Noli Me Tangere" (Citizenry).

Unwmk.

1998, Nov. 20 Litho. *Imperf.*

2575A A759a 15p multi 2.50 2.00
2575B A759a 15p multi 2.50 2.00
2575C A759a 15p multi 2.50 2.00
2575D A759a 15p multi 2.50 2.00
2575E A759a 15p multi 2.50 2.00
2575F A759a 15p multi 2.50 2.00
Nos. 2575A-2575F (6) 15.00 12.00

Nos. 2575A-2575F have simulated perforations.

New Year 1999 (Year of the Rabbit) A760

1998, Dec. 1

2576 A760 4p shown .50 .25
2577 A760 11p Two rabbits 1.40 .70
a. Souvenir sheet, #2576-2577 3.00 2.50

No. 2577a exists imperf. Value, $3.

Heroes of the Revolution Type of 1998

1998, Dec. 15 Litho. *Perf. 13½*

Booklet Stamps

Yellow Background

2578 A736 6p like #2518 .60 .40
2579 A736 6p like #2519 .60 .40
2580 A736 6p like #2520 .60 .40
2581 A736 6p like #2521 .60 .40
2582 A736 6p like #2528 .60 .40
2583 A736 6p like #2547 .60 .40
2584 A736 6p like #2549 .60 .40
2585 A736 6p like #2550 .60 .40
2586 A736 6p like #2546 .60 .40
2587 A736 6p like #2548 .60 .40
a. Booklet pane, #2578-2587 6.25

Complete booklet, #2587a 6.50

Green Background

2588 A736 15p like #2546 1.90 .95
2589 A736 15p like #2518 1.90 .95
2590 A736 15p like #2547 1.90 .95
2591 A736 15p like #2528 1.90 .95
2592 A736 15p like #2548 1.90 .95
2593 A736 15p like #2549 1.90 .95
2594 A736 15p like #2519 1.90 .95
2595 A736 15p like #2520 1.90 .95
2596 A736 15p like #2521 1.90 .95
a. Booklet pane, 2c #2546, 8c #2548, 2 each 11c, 13c, #2519-2520, 6c #2583, #2596 10.50
Complete booklet, #2596a 11.00
2597 A736 15p like #2550 1.90 .95
a. Booklet pane, #2588-2597 16.00
Complete booklet, #2597a 16.00

Nos. 2587a, 2596a, 2597a were made available to collectors unattached to the booklet cover.

Philippine Central Bank, 50th Anniv. A761

1999, Jan. 3 Litho. *Perf. 14*
2598 A761 6p multicolored .60 .30

Philippine Centennial A762

Designs: a, Centennial emblem. b, Proclamation of Independence. c, Malolos Congress. d, Nov. 5th uprising. e, Cry of Santa Barbara Iloilo. f, Victory over colonial forces. g, Flag raising, Butuan City. h, Ratification of Malolos Constitution. i, Philippine Republic formed. j, Barasoain Church.

1999, Jan. 11
2599 A762 6p Sheet of 10, #a.-j. 8.00 8.00

Scouting — A762a

Designs: No. 2599K, Girl Scout, boys planting tree. No. 2599L, Boy Scout, Girl Scout, flag, people representing various professions.

Perf. 13½
1999, Jan. 16 Litho. Unwmk.
2599K A762a 5p multicolored 1.25 .30
2599L A762a 5p multicolored 1.25 .30

Nos. 2599K-2599L are dated 1995, are inscribed "THRIFT STAMP," and were valid for postage due to stamp shortage.

Dept. of Transportation and Communications, Cent. — A763

Emblem and: a, Ship. b, Jet. c, Control tower. d, Satellite dish, bus.
15p, Philpost Headquarters, truck, motorcycle on globe.

1999, Jan. 20
2600 A763 6p Block of 4, #a.-d. 3.25 3.25

Souvenir Sheet
2601 A763 15p multicolored 3.00 2.50

No. 2601 contains one 80x30mm stamp.

Filipino-American War, Cent. — A764

1999, Feb. 4
2602 A764 5p multicolored .55 .30

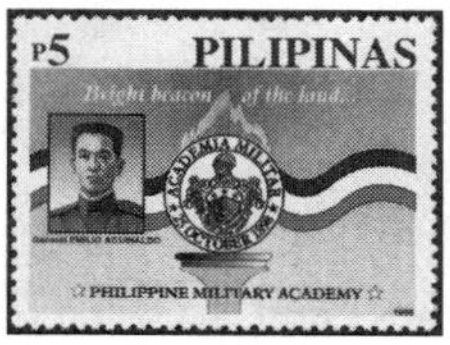

Philippine Military Academy, Cent. A765

1999, Feb. 4
2603 A765 5p multicolored .55 .30

Birds A766

#2604: a, Greater crested tern. b, Ruddy turnstone. c, Green-backed heron. d, Common tern.
#2605: a, Black-winged stilt. b, Asiatic dowitcher. c, Whimbrel. d, Reef heron.
#2606: a, Spotted greenshank. b, Tufted duck.

1999 Litho. *Perf. 14*
2604 A766 5p Block of 4, #a.-d. 2.25 1.75
2605 A766 5p Block of 4, #a.-d. 2.25 1.75

Souvenir Sheets
2606 A766 8p Sheet of 2, #a.-b. 4.25 3.50
a. As #2606, diff. sheet margin, inscription 3.25 2.50

Issued: #2604-2606, 2/22; #2606a, 3/19.
No. 2606a contains inscription, emblem for Australia '99 World Stamp Expo.

Heroes of the Revolution Type
Perf. 13½
1999, Mar. 12 Litho. Unwmk.
Pink Background
2607 A736 5p like #2547 .55 .30

Manila Lions Club, 50th Anniv. A767

Design: Emblem, Francisco "Paquito" Ortigas, Jr., first president.

1999, Mar. 20 *Perf. 14*
2608 A767 5p multicolored .55 .30

Philippine Orthopedic Assoc., 50th Anniv. — A768

1999, Mar. 20
2609 A768 5p multicolored .55 .30

La Union Botanical Garden, San Fernando A769

Designs: No. 2610, Entrance sign, birdhouse. No. 2611, Ticket booth at entrance.

1999, Mar. 20
2610 A769 5p multicolored .55 .30
2611 A769 5p multicolored .55 .30
a. Pair, #2610-2611 1.10 .75

Frogs — A770

#2612: a, Woodworth's frog. b, Giant Philippine frog. c, Gliding tree frog. d, Common forest frog.
#2613: a, Spiny tree frog. b, Truncate-toed chorus frog. c, Variable-backed frog.

1999, Apr. 5
2612 A770 5p Block of 4, #a.-d. 2.50 2.00

Sheet of 3
2613 A770 5p #a.-c. + label 3.75 3.00

Marine Life A771

No. 2614: a, Sea squirt. b, Banded sea snake. c, Manta ray. d, Painted rock lobster.
No. 2615: a, Sea grapes. b, Branching coral. c, Sea urchin.

1999, May 11 Litho. *Perf. 14*
2614 A771 5p Block of 4, #a.-d. 2.50 2.00

Sheet of 3
2615 A771 5p #a.-c. + label 3.50 3.00

Juan F. Nakpil, Architect, Birth Cent. A772

1999, May 25
2616 A772 5p multicolored .65 .30

UPU, 125th Anniv. A773

Designs: 5p, Globe, boy writing letter. 15p, Globe, girl looking at stamp collection.

1999, May 26 Litho. *Perf. 14*
2617 A773 5p multicolored .65 .30
2618 A773 15p multicolored 1.90 .95

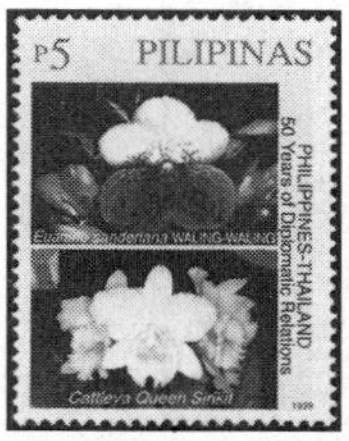

Philippines-Thailand Diplomatic Relations, 50th Anniv. — A774

Orchids: 5p, 11p, Euanthe sanderiana, cattleya Queen Sirikit.

1999, June 13 Litho. *Perf. 14*
2619 A774 5p multicolored .65 .30
2620 A774 11p multicolored 1.40 .70

Order of flowers from top is reversed on 11p value.
Issued in sheets of 20 (10 of each denomination in two rows of 5, separated by a central gutter). Most sheets of 20 were cut in half through the central gutter.
See #2623-2624, 2640-2641.

Masonic Charities for Crippled Children, Inc., 75th Anniv. A775

1999, July 5
2621 A775 5p multicolored .65 .30

Production of Eberhard Faber "Mongol" Pencils, 150th Anniv. — A776

1999, July 5
2622 A776 5p multicolored .65 .30

Diplomatic Relations Type of 1999

Philippines-Korea diplomatic relations, 50th anniv., flowers: 5p, 11p, Jasminum sambac, hibiscus synacus.

1999, Aug. 9 Litho. *Perf. 14*
2623 A774 5p multicolored .70 .35
2624 A774 11p multicolored 1.50 .75

Order of flowers from top is reversed on 11p value.
issued in sheets of 20 (10 of each denomination in two rows of 5, separated by a central gutter). Most sheets of 20 were cut in half through the central gutter.

Community Chest, 50th Anniv. A777

1999, Aug. 30
2625 A777 5p multicolored .60 .20

A778

A779

1999, Aug. 30

2626 A778 5p multicolored .60 .20

Philippine Bible Society, cent.

1999, Sept. 3

2627 A779 5p multicolored .60 .20

St. Francis of Assisi Parish, Sariaya, 400th anniv.

National Anthem, Cent. A780

1999, Sept. 3

2628 A780 5p multicolored .60 .20

Souvenir Sheet

No. 2539b Overprinted in Silver "25th ANNIVERSARY IPPS"

1999, Sept. 24 Litho. ***Perf. 14***

2629 A746 15p Sheet of 3, #a.-c., + 3 labels 4.00 3.00

Ovpt. in sheet margin has same inscription twice, "25th ANNIVERSARY INTERNATIONAL PHILIPPINE PHILATELIC SOCIETY 1974-99" and two society emblems.

Senate — A781

A782

1999, Oct. 15

2630 A781 5p multi .50 .20

1999, Oct. 20

2631 A782 5p multi .50 .20

New Building of Chiang Kai-shek College, Manila.

Issued in sheets of 10.

Tanza National Comprehensive High School, 50th Anniv. — A783

1999, Oct. 24

2632 A783 5p multi .50 .20

San Agustin Church, Paoay, World Heritage Site A784

Intl. Year of Older Persons A785

World Teachers' Day A786

1999, Oct. 24

2633 A784 5p multi .50 .20
2634 A785 11p multi 1.25 .45
2635 A786 15p multi 2.00 .65
Nos. 2633-2635 (3) 3.75 1.30

United Nations Day.

Christmas A787

1999, Oct. 27

Color of Angel's Gown

2636 A787 5p red violet .75 .20
2637 A787 11p yellow 1.50 .45
2638 A787 13p blue 1.75 .55
2639 A787 15p green 2.00 .65
a. Sheet of 4, #2636-2639 6.00 5.00
Nos. 2636-2639 (4) 6.00 1.85

Nos. 2636-2639 each issued in sheets of 10 stamps with two central labels.

Diplomatic Relations Type of 1999

Philippines-Canada diplomatic relations, 50th anniv., mammals: 5p, 15p, Tamaraw, polar bear.

1999, Nov. 15 ***Perf. 14***

2640 A774 5p multi .50 .25
2641 A774 15p multi 2.00 .65

Order of mammals from top is reversed on 15p value.

Issued in sheets of 20 (10 of each denomination in two rows of 5, separated by a central gutter). Most sheets of 20 were cut in half through central gutter.

Renovation of Araneta Coliseum A788

1999, Nov. 19 Litho.

2642 A788 5p multi .50 .20

A789

A790

1999, Nov. 19 **Color of Sky**

2643 A789 5p dark blue .50 .20
2644 A789 11p blue green 1.50 .45

3rd ASEAN Informal Summit.

1999, Nov. 29

Sculptures: No. 2645, Kristo, by Arturo Luz. 11p, Homage to Dodgie Laurel, by J. Elizalde Navarro. 13p, Hilojan, by Napoleon Abueva. No. 2648, Mother and Child, by Abueva.

No. 2649: a, 5p, Mother's Revenge, by José Rizal, horiz. b, 15p, El Ermitano, by Rizal, horiz.

2645 A790 5p multi .75 .20
2646 A790 11p multi 1.50 .45
2647 A790 13p multi 1.75 .55
2648 A790 15p multi 2.00 .65
Nos. 2645-2648 (4) 6.00 1.85

Souvenir Sheet

2649 A790 Sheet of 2, #a.-b. 2.75 2.00

Natl. Stamp Collecting Month.

New Year 2000 (Year of the Dragon) A791

1999, Dec. 1 ***Perf. 14***

2650 A791 5p Dragon in water .50 .20
2651 A791 11p Dragon in sky 1.75 .65
a. Sheet of 2, #2650-2651 1.75 1.25
b. As "a," imperf. 4.25 3.00

Battle of Tirad Pass, Cent. A792

1999, Dec. 2 ***Perf. 14***

2652 A792 5p multi .50 .20

Orchids — A793

No. 2653: a, Paphiopedilum urbanianum. b, Phalaenopsis schilleriana. c, Dendrobium amethystoglossum. d, Paphiopedilum barbatum.

No. 2654, horiz.: a, Paphiopedilum haynaldianum. b, Phalaenopsis stuartiana. c, Trichoglottis brachiata. d, Ceratostylis rubra.

1999, Dec. 3 Litho.

2653 A793 5p Block of 4, #a.-d. 3.00 2.00

Souvenir Sheet

2654 A793 5p Sheet of 4, #a.-d. 3.50 3.00

Battle of San Mateo, Cent. A794

1999, Dec. 19

2655 A794 5p multicolored .50 .20

People Power A795

People and: a, Tank. b, Tower. c, Crucifix.

1999, Dec. 31

2656 A795 5p Strip of 3, #a.-c. 2.50 2.00

Natl. Commission on the Role of Filipino Women — A796

2000, Jan. 7 Litho. ***Perf. 14***

2657 A796 5p multi .50 .20

Manila Bulletin, Cent. A797

2000, Feb. 2 Litho. ***Perf. 14***

2658 A797 5p multi .50 .20
a. Year at LR .50 .20

Issued: No. 2658a, 6/7.

La Union Province, 150th Anniv. A798

Arms of province and: a, Sailboat, golfer. b, Tractor, worker, building. c, Building, flagpole. d, Airplane, ship, telephone tower, people on telephone, computer.

2000, Mar. 2

2659 A798 5p Block of 4, #a.-d. 2.00 1.50

Civil Service Commission, Cent. — A799

2000, Mar. 20

2660 A799 5p multi .50 .20

Millennium A800

Designs: a, Golden Garuda of Palawan. b, First sunrise of the millennium, Pusan Point. c, Golden Tara of Agusan.

2000, Mar. 31

2661 A800 5p Strip of 3, #a.-c. 1.25 1.00

GMA Radio and Television Network, 50th Anniv. A802

2000, Mar. 1 Litho. *Perf. 14*

2662 A802 5p multi .50 .20

Philippine Presidents — A803

No. 2662A: b, Manuel Roxas. c, Elpidio Quirino. No. 2663: a, Presidential seal. b, Joseph Ejercito Estrada. c, Fidel V. Ramos. d, Corazon C. Aquino. e, Ferdinand E. Marcos. f, Diosdado Macapagal. g, Carlos P. Garcia. h, Ramon Magsaysay. i, Elpidio Quirino. j, Manuel Roxas.

2000 *Perf. 13½*

2662A Pair 1.00 .60
b.-c. A803 5p Any single .50 .20
2663 Block of 10 6.00 5.00
a.-j. A803 5p Any single .50 .20

Nos. 2662b-2662c have presidential seal but lack blue lines at bottom. No. 2663a has denomination at left. Nos. 2663b-2663j have small Presidential seal at bottom.

Issued: No. 2662A, 2/6. No. 2663, 3/16.

See Type A828 for stamps showing Presidential seal with colored background.

See Nos. 2672-2676.

Diplomatic Relations Type of 1999

5p, Sarimanok, Great Wall of China. 11p, Phoenix, Banaue rice terraces.

No. 2666: a, 5p, Great Wall, horiz. b, 11p, Rice terraces, horiz.

2000, May 8 *Perf. 14*

2664-2665 A774 Set of 2 1.25 .65

Souvenir Sheet

2666 A774 Sheet of 2, #a-b 2.25 1.50

Issued in sheets of 20 (10 of each denomination in two rows of 5, separated by a central gutter). Most sheets of 20 were cut in half through central gutter.

St. Thomas Aquinas Parish, Mangaldan, 400th Anniv. A805

2000, June 1

2667 A805 5p multi .50 .20

Battle Centenaries — A806

Battles in Philippine Insurrection: #2668, Mabitac. #2669, Paye, vert. #2670, Makahambus Hill, vert. #2671, Pulang Lupa.

2000, June 19

2668-2671 A806 5p Set of 4 2.00 .75

Presidents Type of 2000 Redrawn

No. 2672: a, Presidential seal. b, Joseph Ejercito Estrada. c, Fidel V. Ramos. d, Corazon C. Aquino. e, Ferdinand E. Marcos. f, Diosdado Macapagal. g, Carlos P. Garcia. h, Ramon Magsaysay. i, Elpidio Quirino. j, Manuel Roxas.

No. 2673: a, Magsaysay. b, Garcia.
No. 2674: a, Macapagal. b, Marcos.
No. 2675: a, Aquino. b, Ramos.
No. 2676: a, Estrada. b, Presidential seal.

2000 Litho. *Perf. 13½*

Blue Lines at Bottom

2672 Block of 10 6.75 5.50
a.-j. A803 5p Any single .50 .20
2673 Pair 2.75 2.00
a.-b. A803 10p Any single 1.00 .40
2674 Pair 3.00 2.25
a.-b. A803 11p Any single 1.10 .45
2675 Pair 3.50 2.50
a.-b. A803 13p Any single 1.25 .55
2676 Pair 4.00 3.00
a.-b. A803 15p Any single 1.50 .65
Nos. 2672-2676 (5) 20.00 15.25

Issued: No. 2672, 7/3; Nos. 2673-2674, 8/4. Nos. 2675-2676, 6/19.

No. 2672a has denomination at R, while No. 2663a has denomination at L. Nos. 2672b-2672j have no presidential seal, while Nos. 2662Ab-2662Ac, 2663b-2663j have seal.

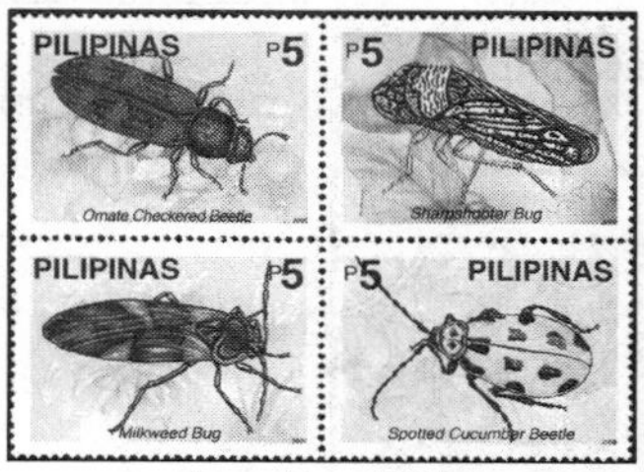

Insects — A807

No. 2677: a, Ornate checkered beetle. b, Sharpshooter bug. c, Milkweed bug. d, Spotted cucumber beetle.

No. 2678: a, Green June beetle. b, Convergent ladybird. c, Eastern Hercules beetle. d, Harlequin cabbage bug.

Illustration reduced.

2000, July 21 *Perf. 14*

2677 A807 5p Block of 4, #a-d 1.75 1.25
e. Souevnir sheet, #2677 2.50 1.60
2678 A807 5p Block of 4, #a-d 1.75 1.25
e. Souevnir sheet, #2678 2.50 1.60

Occupational Health Nurses Association, 50th Anniv. — A808

2000, Aug. 30

2679 A808 5p multi .50 .20

Diocese of Lucena, 50th Anniv. A809

2000. Aug. 30

2680 A809 5p multi .50 .20

Millennium A810

Boats: a, Balanghai. b, Vinta. c, Caracoa.

2000, Sept. 21

2681 Horiz. strip of 3 2.50 2.00
a.-c. A810 5p Any single .50 .20

Equitable PCI Bank, 50th Anniv. A811

2000, Sept. 26

2682 A811 5p multi .50 .20

Year of the Overseas Filipino Worker A812

2000, Sept. 29 Litho.

2683 A812 5p multi .50 .40

2000 Olympics, Sydney — A813

No. 2684: a, Running. b, Archery. c, Shooting. d, Diving.

No. 2685, horiz.: a, Boxing. b, Equestrian. c, Rowing. d, Taekwondo.

Illustration reduced.

2000, Sept. 30

2684 A813 5p Block of 4, #a-d 2.00 1.25

Souvenir Sheet

2685 A813 5p Sheet of 4, #a-d 3.50 1.25

Teresian Association in the Philippines, 50th Anniv. A814

2000, Oct. 10

2686 A814 5p multi .40 .20

House of Representatives A815

2000, Oct. 15 *Perf. 14*

2687 A815 5p multi .40 .20

Marine Corps, 50th Anniv. A816

2000, Oct. 18

2688 A816 5p multi .40 .20

Souvenir Sheet

Postal Service, Cent. (in 1998) — A817

2000, Nov. 6

2689 A817 15p multi 2.00 1.50

Clothing Exhibit at Metropolitan Museum of Manila — A818

No. 2690, 5p: a, Kalinga / Gaddang cotton loincloth. b, Portrait of Leticia Jimenez, by unknown artist.

No. 2691, 5p, horiz.: a, B'laan female upper garment. b, T'boli T'nalak abaca cloth.

No. 2692: a, 5p, Portrait of Teodora Devera Ygnacio, by Justiniano Asunción. b, 15p, Detail of Tawsug silk sash.

Illustration reduced.

2000, Nov. 15 Pairs, #a-b

2690-2691 A818 Set of 2 1.75 .50

Souvenir Sheet

2692 A818 Sheet of 2, #a-b 2.25 1.50

Natl. Stamp Collecting Month A819

Designs: 5p, Portrait of an Unkown Lady, by Juan Luna, vert. 11p, Nude, by José Joya. 13p, Lotus Odalisque, by Rodolfo Paras-Perez. No. 2696, 15p, Untitled Nude, by Fernando Amorsolo.

No. 2697, The Memorial, by Cesar Legaspi.

2000, Nov. 20 *Perf. 14*

2693-2696 A819 Set of 4 5.50 2.50

Souvenir Sheet

2697 A819 15p multi 3.00 2.00

No. 2697 contains one 80x29 stamp and label.

Christmas A820

Angels: No. 2698, 5p, In pink robe, with bouquet of flowers. No. 2699, 5p, As #2698, with Holy Year 2000 emblem and inscription.

11p, In green robe. 13p, In orange robe. 15p, In red robe, with garland of flowers.

2000, Nov. 22 **Litho.**
2698-2702 A820 Set of 5 4.50 1.25

APO Philatelic Society, 50th Anniv. — A821

Emblem and stamps: No. 2703, 5p, #620 (yellow background). No. 2704, 5p, #639 (light blue background), horiz. No. 2705, 5p, #850 (dull green background). No. 2706, 5p, #B21 (pink background), horiz.

2000, Nov. 23
2703-2706 A821 Set of 4 2.25 .80

No. 1806 Handstamp Surcharged in Red

Perf. 13x13½
2000, Nov. 24 **Litho.** **Wmk.**
2706A A469 5p on 3.60p multi — *5.00*

New Year 2001 (Year of the Snake) A822

Snakes with inscription in: 5p, Tagalog. 11p, English.

2000, Dec. 20 **Unwmk.** ***Perf. 14***
2707-2708 A822 Set of 2 2.00 .40
2708a Souvenir sheet, #2707-2708 + 2 labels 5.00 4.00

No. 2708a exists imperf.

Millennium A823

No. 2709: a, Trade and progress. b, Education and knowledge. c, Communication and information.

2000, Dec. 28
2709 Horiz. strip of 3 2.50 1.50
a.-c. A823 5p Any single .40 .20

Bank of the Philippine Islands, 150th Anniv. A824

2001, Jan. 30 **Litho.**
2710 A824 5p multi .40 .20

Hong Kong 2001 Stamp Exhibition A825

Designs: No. 2711a, 5p, No. 2712, 11p, Tamaraw. No. 2711b, 5p, No. 2713, 11p, Agila. No. 2711c, 5p, No. 2714, 11p, Tarsier. No. 2711d, 5p, No. 2715, 11p, Talisman Cove orchid. No. 2711e, 5p, No. 2716, 11p, Pawikan.

2001, Feb. 1
2711 Horiz. strip of 5 2.75 2.00
a.-e. A825 5p Any single .40 .20

Souvenir Sheets

2712-2716 A825 Set of 5 8.00 6.00
2713a Ovptd. in margin in red 2.00 2.00
2715a Ovptd. in margin in red 2.00 2.00

Nos. 2712-2716 have show emblem on sheet margin instead of on stamp.

Issued: Nos. 2713a, 2715a, 6/30/01. Overprint in margin on Nos. 2713a, 2715a has Chinese inscriptions and English text "PHILIPPINE-CHINESE PHILATELIC SOCIETY / 1951 GOLDEN JUBILEE 2001."

Gen. Paciano Rizal (1851-1930) A826

2001, Mar. 7 **Litho.** ***Perf. 14***
2717 A826 5p multi .35 .20

San Beda College, Cent. A827

2001, Mar. 9
2718 A827 5p multi .35 .20

Diplomatic Relations Type of 1999

Philippines-Vatican City diplomatic relations, 50th anniv., main altars at: 5p, St. Peter's Basilica, Vatican City. No. 2720, 15p, San Agustin Church, Manila.

No. 2721: a, Adam, from Creation of Adam, by Michelangelo. b, God, from Creation of Adam.

2001, Mar. 14
2719-2720 A774 Set of 2 1.25 .65

Souvenir Sheet

2721 A774 15p Sheet of 2, #a-b 3.25 1.60

Nos. 2719-2720 issued in sheets of 20 (10 of each denomination in two rows of 5, separated by a central gutter). Most sheets of 20 were cut in half through central gutter.

Presidential Seal With Colored Background — A828

2001, Apr. 5 ***Perf. 13¾***

Background Colors

2722 A828 5p yellow .30 .20
2723 A828 15p blue .90 .45

Stamps of the same denomination showing the Presidential seal with white backgrounds are listed as Nos. 2663a, 2672a and 2676b.

Tourist Spots A829

No. 2724: a, El Nido, Aklan Province. b, Vigan House, Ilocos Sur Province. c, Boracay, Aklan Province. d, Chocolate Hills, Bohol Province.

15p, Banaue Rice Terraces, Ifugao Province.

2001, Apr. 14 ***Perf. 14***
2724 Horiz. strip of 4 1.25 .65
a.-d. A829 5p Any single .30 .20

Souvenir Sheet

2725 A829 15p multi .90 .45

No. 2725 contains one 80x30mm stamp.

Canonical Coronation of Our Lady of Manaoag, 75th Anniv. — A830

2001, Apr. 22
2726 A830 5p multi .30 .20

Pres. Gloria Macapagal-Arroyo A831

Pres. Macapagal-Arroyo: No. 2727, 5p, Waving. No. 2728, 5p, Taking oath of office.

2001, Apr. 29
2727-2728 A831 Set of 2 .65 .30

Diplomatic Relations Type of 1999

Philippines-Australia diplomatic relations, landmarks: 5p, Nos. 2730-2731, 13p, Sydney Opera House, Cultural Center of the Philippines. No. 2731 is horiz.

2001, May 21
2729-2730 A774 Set of 2 1.10 .55

Souvenir Sheet

2731 A774 13p multi .80 .40

No. 2731 contains one 80x30mm stamp.

Supreme Court, Cent. A832

2001, May 31
2732 A832 5p multi .30 .20

Silliman University, Dumaguete City, Cent. A833

2001, June 1
2733 A833 5p multi .30 .20

Philippine Normal University, Cent. A834

2001, June 1
2734 A834 5p multi .30 .20

Joaquin J. Ortega (1870-1943), First Civil Governor of La Union Province — A835

2001, July 12
2735 A835 5p multi .30 .20

Eugenio Lopez (1901-75), Businessman A836

2001, July 12
2736 A836 5p multi .30 .20

Illustrations from Boxer Codex, c. 1590 — A837

No. 2737: a, Visayan couple. b, Tagalog couple. c, Moros of Luzon (multicolored frame). d, Moros of Luzon (blue frame).

No. 2738: a, Pintados (denomination at left). b, Pintados (denomination at right). c, Cagayan female. d, Zambal.

2001, Aug. 1
2737 A837 5p Block of 4, #a-d 1.25 .65

Souvenir Sheet

2738 A837 5p Sheet of 4, #a-d 1.25 .65
e. Sheet of 4, #a-d, with Phila Nippon '01 margin 1.25 .65

Arrival of American Educators (Thomasites), Cent. — A838

Designs: 5p, Thomasite teachers, US transport ship Thomas. 15p, Philippine students.

2001, Aug. 23
2739-2740 A838 Set of 2 1.25 .65

Technological University of the Philippines, Cent. — A839

2001, Aug. 20 Litho. *Perf. 14*

2741 A839 5p multi .30 .20

National Museum of the Philippines, Cent. A840

2001, Sept. 3

2742 A840 5p multi .30 .20

Lands Management Bureau, Cent. — A841

2001, Sept. 17

2743 A841 5p multi .30 .20

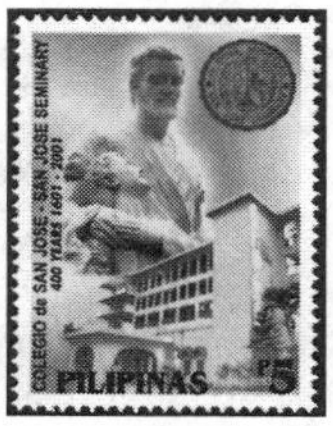

Colegio de San Jose and San Jose Seminary, 400th Anniv. — A842

2001, Oct. 1

2744 A842 5p multi .30 .20

Makati City Financial District A843

2001, Oct. 1

2745 A843 5p multi .30 .20

Presidential Seal With Colored Background Type of 2001

2001, Oct. 5 *Perf. 13¾*

Background Colors

2746 A828 10p green .60 .30
2747 A828 11p pink .65 .35
2748 A828 13p gray .80 .40
Nos. 2746-2748 (3) 2.05 1.05

Musical Instruments — A844

No. 2749: a, Trumpet. b, Tuba. c, French horn. d, Trombone.

No. 2750, vert.: a, Bass drum. b, Clarinet, oboe. c, Xylophone. d, Sousaphone.

Illustration reduced.

2001, Oct. 8 *Perf. 14*

2749 A844 5p Block of 4, #a-d 1.25 .60

Souvenir Sheet

2750 A844 5p Sheet of 4, #a-d 1.25 .60

Malampaya Deep Water Gas Power Project A845

Frame colors: 5p, Silver. 15p, Gold.

2001, Oct. 16

2751-2752 A845 Set of 2 1.25 .60

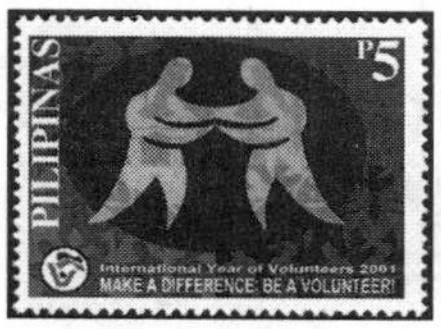

Intl. Volunteers Year A846

2001, Oct. 24

2753 A846 5p multi .30 .20

Year of Dialogue Among Civilizations A847

2001, Oct. 24

2754 A847 15p multi .90 .45

Christmas A848

Designs: 5p, Herald Angels. 11p, Kumukutikutitap. 13p, Pasko ni Bitoy. 15p, Pasko na naman.

2001, Oct. 30

2755-2758 A848 Set of 4 2.75 1.40

Philippines - Switzerland Relations, 150th Anniv. — A849

Monument statues by Richard Kissling: 5p, William Tell. No. 2760, 15p, Jose P. Rizal.

No. 2761, 15p, Mayon Volcano, Philippines, and Matterhorn, Switzerland.

2001, Nov. 26

2759-2760 A849 Set of 2 1.25 .60

Souvenir Sheet

2761 A849 15p multi .90 .45

No. 2761 contains one 79x29mm stamp. Nos. 2759-2760 issued in sheets of 20 (10 of each denomination in two rows of 5, separated by a central gutter). Most sheets of 20 were cut in half through central gutter.

Drawings of Manila Inhabitants, c. 1840 — A850

Designs: 17p, Woman with hat, man with green pants. 21p, Woman with veil, man with brown pants. 22p, Man, woman at mortar and pestle.

2001, Dec. 1 *Perf. 13¾*

2762 A850 17p multi 1.00 .50
2763 A850 21p multi 1.25 .60
2764 A850 22p multi 1.40 .70
Nos. 2762-2764 (3) 3.65 1.80

Solicitor General, Cent. — A851

2001, Dec. 7 *Perf. 14*

2765 A851 5p multi .30 .20

Natl. Stamp Collecting Month A852

Art: 5p, PUJ, by Antonio Austria. 17p, Hesus Nazareno, by Angelito Antonio. 21p, Three Women with Basket, by Anita Magsaysay-Ho, vert. No. 2769, 22p, Church with Yellow Background, by Mauro "Malang" Santos, vert.

No. 2770, 22p, Komedya ng Pakil, by Danilo Dalena.

2001, Dec. 7 Litho.

2766-2769 A852 Set of 4 4.00 2.00

Souvenir Sheet

2770 A852 22p multi 1.40 .70

No. 2770 contains one 79x29mm stamp.

New Year 2002 (Year of the Horse) A853

Horse color: 5p, Red. 17p, White.

2001, Dec. 14 *Perf. 14*

2771-2772 A853 Set of 2 1.40 .70
2772a Souvenir sheet, #2771-2772, + 2 labels 1.40 .70

No. 2772a exists imperf.

Josemaria Escrivá (1902-75), Founder of Opus Dei — A854

2002, Jan. 9

2773 A854 5p multi .30 .20

World Heritage Sites A855

Vigan City sites: 5p, St. Paul's Metropolitan Cathedral. 22p, Calle Crisologo.

2002, Jan. 22

2774-2775 A855 Set of 2 1.60 .80

Salvador Z. Araneta, Statesman, Birth Cent. — A856

2002, Jan. 31

2776 A856 5p multi .30 .20

Customs Service, Cent. A857

2002, Feb. 1

2777 A857 5p multi .30 .20

Valentine's Day — A858

No. 2778: a, Envelope. b, Man and woman. c, Cat and dog. d, Balloon.

2002, Feb. 7

2778 A858 5p Block of 4, #a-d 1.25 .60

SEMI-POSTAL STAMPS

Catalogue values for unused stamps in this section are for Never Hinged items.

Republic

Epifanio de los Santos, Trinidad H. Pardo and Teodoro M. Kalaw — SP1

Doctrina Christiana, Cover Page — SP2

"Noli Me Tangere," Cover Page — SP3

Unwmk.

1949, Apr. 1 Engr. *Perf. 12*

B1	SP1	4c + 2c sepia	1.50	.75
B2	SP2	6c + 4c violet	5.00	2.50
B3	SP3	18c + 7c blue	5.50	2.75
		Nos. B1-B3 (3)	12.00	6.00

The surtax was for restoration of war-damaged public libraries.

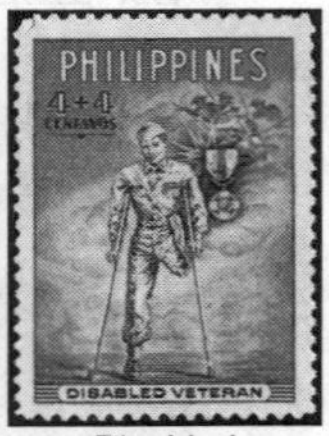

War Widow and Children — SP4

Disabled Veteran — SP5

1950, Nov. 30

B4	SP4	2c + 2c red	.25	.20
B5	SP5	4c + 4c violet	.35	.30

The surtax was for war widows and children and disabled veterans of World War II.
For surcharges see Nos. 648-649.

Mrs. Manuel L. Quezon SP6

1952, Aug. 19 *Perf. 12*

B6	SP6	5c + 1c dp bl	.25	.20
B7	SP6	6c + 2c car rose	.40	.30

The surtax was used to encourage planting and care of fruit trees among Philippine children. For surcharge see No. 872.

Quezon Institute SP7

1958, Aug. 19 Photo. *Perf. 13½, 12*
Cross in Red

B8	SP7	5c + 5c grn	.20	.20
B9	SP7	10c + 5c dp vio	.30	.30

These stamps were obligatory on all mail from Aug. 19-Sept. 30.
For surcharges see Nos. 849, B12-B13, B16.

The surtax on all semi-postals from Nos. B8-B9 onward was for the Philippine Tuberculosis Society unless otherwise stated.

Scout Cooking — SP8

1959 Engr. *Perf. 13*
Yellow Paper

B10	SP8	6c + 4c shown	.20	.20
B11	SP8	25c + 5c Archery	.55	.45
a.		Nos. B10-B11 tête bêche, *white*	1.00	.85
		Nos. B10-B11,CB1-CB3 (5)	2.75	2.50

10th Boy Scout World Jamboree, Makiling National Park, July 17-26. The surtax was to finance the Jamboree.
For souvenir sheet see No. CB3a. For surcharges see Nos. 832-833, C111.

Nos. B8-B9 Surcharged in Red

1959 Photo. *Perf. 13½, 12*

B12	SP7	3c + 5c on 5c + 5c	.25	.20
a.		"3 + 5" and bars omitted		
B13	SP7	6c + 5c on 10c + 5c	.35	.25

Bohol Sanatorium — SP9

1959, Aug. 19 Engr. *Perf. 12*
Cross in Red

B14	SP9	6c + 5c yel grn	.20	.20
B15	SP9	25c + 5c vio bl	.40	.30

No. B8 Surcharged "Help Prevent TB" and New Value

1960, Aug. 19 Photo. *Perf. 13½, 12*

B16	SP7	6c + 5c on 5c + 5c	.40	.20

Roxas Memorial T.B. Pavilion SP10

Perf. 11½

1961, Aug. 19 Unwmk. Photo.

B17	SP10	6c + 5c brn & red	.40	.20

Emiliano J. Valdes T.B. Pavilion SP11

1962, Aug. 19
Cross in Red

B18	SP11	6s + 5s dk vio	.20	.20
B19	SP11	30s + 5s ultra	.35	.20
B20	SP11	70s + 5s brt bl	.70	.50
		Nos. B18-B20 (3)	1.25	.90

José Rizal Playing Chess SP12

Design: 30s+5s, Rizal fencing.

1962, Dec. 30 Engr. *Perf. 13*

B21	SP12	6s + 4s grn & rose lil	.25	.20
B22	SP12	30s + 5s brt bl & cl	.75	.45

Surtax for Rizal Foundation.
For surcharges see Nos. 942-943.

Map of Philippines and Cross — SP13

1963, Aug. 19 Unwmk. *Perf. 13*

B23	SP13	6s + 5s vio & red	.20	.20
B24	SP13	10s + 5s grn & red	.30	.20
B25	SP13	50s + 5s brn & red	.75	.35
		Nos. B23-B25 (3)	1.25	.75

Negros Oriental T.B. Pavilion SP14

1964, Aug. 19 Photo. *Perf. 13½*
Cross in Red

B26	SP14	5s + 5s brt pur	.20	.20
B27	SP14	6s + 5s ultra	.20	.20
B28	SP14	30s + 5s brown	.30	.25
B29	SP14	70s + 5s green	.55	.50
		Nos. B26-B29 (4)	1.25	1.15

For surcharges see Nos. 986, 1586.

No. B27 Surcharged in Red with New Value and Two Bars

1965, Aug. 19
Cross in Red

B30	SP14	1s + 5s on 6s + 5s	.25	.20
B31	SP14	3s + 5s on 6s + 5s	.35	.20

Stork-billed Kingfisher — SP15

Birds: 5s+5s, Rufous hornbill. 10s+5s, Monkey-eating eagle. 30s+5s, Great-billed parrot.

1967, Aug. 19 Photo. *Perf. 13½*

B32	SP15	1s + 5s multi	.20	.20
B33	SP15	5s + 5s multi	.30	.20
B34	SP15	10s + 5s multi	.50	.25
B35	SP15	30s + 5s multi	2.00	.70
		Nos. B32-B35 (4)	3.00	1.35

1969, Aug. 15 Litho. *Perf. 13½*

Birds: 1s+5s, Three-toed woodpecker. 5s+5s, Philippine trogon. 10s+5s, Mt. Apo lorikeet. 40s+5s, Scarlet minivet.

B36	SP15	1s + 5s multi	.20	.20
B37	SP15	5s + 5s multi	.45	.20
B38	SP15	10s + 5s multi	.85	.30
B39	SP15	40s + 5s multi	1.75	.60
		Nos. B36-B39 (4)	3.25	1.30

Julia V. de Ortigas and Tuberculosis Society Building — SP16

1970, Aug. 3 Photo. *Perf. 13½*

B40	SP16	1s + 5s multi	.20	.20
B41	SP16	5s + 5s multi	.25	.20
B42	SP16	30s + 5s multi	.90	.45
B43	SP16	70s + 5s multi	1.00	.55
		Nos. B40-B43 (4)	2.35	1.40

Mrs. Julia V. de Ortigas was president of the Philippine Tuberculosis Soc., 1932-69.
For surcharge see No. 1251.

Mabolo, Santol, Chico, Papaya SP17

Philippine Fruits: 10s+5s, Balimbing, atis, mangosteen, macupa, bananas. 40s+5s, Susong-kalabao, avocado, duhat, watermelon, guava, mango. 1p+5s, Lanzones, oranges, sirhuelas, pineapple.

1972, Aug. 1 Litho. *Perf. 13*

B44	SP17	1s + 5s multi	.20	.20
B45	SP17	10s + 5s multi	.25	.20
B46	SP17	40s + 5s multi	.55	.25
B47	SP17	1p + 5s multi	1.40	.50
		Nos. B44-B47 (4)	2.40	1.15

Nos. B45-B46 Surcharged with New Value and 2 Bars

1973, June 15

B48	SP17	15s + 5s on 10s + 5s	.25	.20
B49	SP17	60s + 5s on 40s + 5s	.75	.35

Dr. Basilio J. Valdes and Veterans Memorial Hospital — SP18

1974, July 8 Litho. *Perf. 12½*
Cross in Red

B50	SP18	15s + 5s blue grn	.25	.20
a.		Imperf.	.60	.25
B51	SP18	1.10p + 5s vio blue	.75	.30
a.		Imperf.	2.40	.80

Dr. Valdes (1892-1970) was president of Philippine Tuberculosis Society.
For surcharges see Nos. 1250, 1252.

AIR POST STAMPS

Madrid-Manila Flight Issue

Regular Issue of 1917-26 Overprinted in Red or Violet

1926, May 13 Unwmk. *Perf. 11*

C1	A40	2c green (R)	8.75	8.75
C2	A40	4c carmine	11.50	11.50
a.		Inverted overprint	*2,500.*	—
C3	A40	6c lilac (R)	55.00	55.00
C4	A40	8c org brown	57.50	57.50
C5	A40	10c deep blue (R)	57.50	57.50
C6	A40	12c red orange	57.50	57.50
C7	A40	16c lt olive green *(Sampson)*	*2,000.*	*1,600.*
C8	A40	16c ol bister *(Sampson)* (R)	*3,750.*	*3,000.*
C9	A40	16c olive green *(Dewey)*	70.00	70.00
C10	A40	20c orange yellow	70.00	70.00
C11	A40	26c blue green	70.00	70.00
C12	A40	30c gray	70.00	70.00
C13	A41	2p vio brown (R)	550.00	300.00
C14	A41	4p dark blue (R)	750.00	500.00
C15	A41	10p deep green	1,350.	700.00

Same Overprint on No. 269

Perf. 12

Wmk. 190PI

C16 A40 26c blue green *3,000.*

Same Overprint on No. 284

Perf. 10

C17 A41 1p pale violet 200.00 175.00

Flight of Spanish aviators Gallarza and Loriga from Madrid to Manila.

London-Orient Flight Issue

Regular Issue of 1917-25 Overprinted in Red

1928, Nov. 9 Unwmk. *Perf. 11*

C18 A40 2c green .50 .30
C19 A40 4c carmine .60 .50
C20 A40 6c violet 2.10 1.75
C21 A40 8c orange brown 2.25 1.90
C22 A40 10c deep blue 2.25 1.90
C23 A40 12c red orange 3.25 2.75
C24 A40 16c ol green *(Dewey)* 2.40 1.90
C25 A40 20c orange yellow 3.25 2.75
C26 A40 26c blue green 9.50 6.50
C27 A40 30c gray 9.50 6.50

Same Overprint on No. 271

Perf. 12

Wmk. 190PI

C28 A41 1p pale violet 50.00 25.00
Nos. C18-C28 (11) 85.60 51.75

Commemorating an airplane flight from London to Manila.

Nos. 354-360 Overprinted

1932, Sept. 27 Unwmk. *Perf. 11*

C29 A43 2c yellow green .40 .30
C30 A44 4c rose carmine .40 .30
C31 A45 12c orange .60 .50
C32 A46 18c red orange 3.50 3.25
C33 A47 20c yellow 1.75 1.50
C34 A48 24c deep violet 1.75 1.50
C35 A49 32c olive brown 1.75 1.50
Nos. C29-C35 (7) 10.15 8.85

Visit of Capt. Wolfgang von Gronau on his round-the-world flight.

Regular Issue of 1917-25 Overprinted

1933, Apr. 11

C36 A40 2c green .40 .35
C37 A40 4c carmine .45 .35
C38 A40 6c deep violet .80 .75
C39 A40 8c orange brn 2.50 1.50
C40 A40 10c dk blue 2.25 1.00
C41 A40 12c orange 2.00 1.00
C42 A40 16c ol grn *(Dewey)* 2.00 1.00
C43 A40 20c yellow 2.00 1.00
C44 A40 26c green 2.25 1.50
a. 26c blue green 3.00 1.75
C45 A40 30c gray 3.00 1.75
Nos. C36-C45 (10) 17.65 10.20

Commemorating the flight from Madrid to Manila of aviator Fernando Rein y Loring.

No. 290a Overprinted

1933, May 26 Unwmk. *Perf. 11*

C46 A40 2c green .50 .40

Regular Issue of 1932 Overprinted

C47 A44 4c rose carmine .20 .20
C48 A45 12c orange .30 .20
C49 A47 20c yellow .30 .20
C50 A48 24c deep violet .40 .25
C51 A49 32c olive brown .50 .35
Nos. C46-C51 (6) 2.20 1.60

Nos. 387, 392 Overprinted in Gold

1935, Dec. 2

C52 A57 10c rose carmine .30 .20
C53 A62 30c orange red .50 .35

China Clipper flight from Manila to San Francisco, December 2-5, 1935.

Regular Issue of 1917-25 Surcharged in Various Colors

1936, Sept. 6 *Perf. 11*

C54 A40 2c on 4c car (Bl) .20 .20
C55 A40 6c on 12c red org (V) .20 .20
C56 A40 16c on 26c bl grn (Bk) .25 .20
a. 16c on 26c green 1.25 .70
Nos. C54-C56 (3) .65 .60

Manila-Madrid flight by aviators Antonio Arnaiz and Juan Calvo.

Regular Issue of 1917-37 Surcharged in Black or Red

1939, Feb. 17

C57 A40 8c on 26c bl grn (Bk) .75 .40
a. 8c on 26c green (Bk) 1.60 .55
C58 A71 1p on 10p gray (R) 3.00 2.25

1st Air Mail Exhibition, held Feb. 17-19, 1939.

Moro Vinta and Clipper AP1

1941, June 30

C59 AP1 8c carmine 1.00 .60
C60 AP1 20c ultra 1.25 .45
C61 AP1 60c blue green 1.75 1.00
C62 AP1 1p sepia .70 .50
Nos. C59-C62 (4) 4.70 2.55

For overprint see No. NO7. For surcharges see Nos. N10-N11, N35-N36.

No. C47 Handstamped in Violet **VICTORY**

1944, Dec. 3 Unwmk. *Perf. 11*

C63 A44 4c rose carmine *2,500. 2,500.*

Catalogue values for unused stamps in this section, from this point to the end of the section, are for Never Hinged items.

Republic

Manuel L. Quezon and Franklin D. Roosevelt AP2

Unwmk.

1947, Aug. 19 Engr. *Perf. 12*

C64 AP2 6c dark green .50 .50
C65 AP2 40c red orange 1.00 1.00
C66 AP2 80c deep blue 2.75 2.75
Nos. C64-C66 (3) 4.25 4.25

FAO Type

1948, Feb. 23 Typo. *Perf. 12½*

C67 A89 40c dk car & pink 10.00 6.50

Junior Chamber Type

1950, Mar. 1 Engr. *Perf. 12*

C68 A96 30c deep orange 1.25 .40
C69 A96 50c carmine rose 2.10 .70

F. D. Roosevelt Type

Souvenir Sheet

1950, May 22 *Imperf.*

C70 A98 80c deep green 2.50 2.00

Lions Club Type

1950, June 2 *Perf. 12*

C71 A99 30c emerald 1.40 .45
C72 A99 50c ultra 1.60 .60
a. Souvenir sheet of 2, #C71-C72 2.50 2.00

Maria Clara Type

1952, Nov. 16 *Perf. 12½*

C73 A112 30c rose carmine 1.60 .70

Postage Stamp Cent. Type

1954, Apr. 25 *Perf. 13*

1854 Stamp in Orange

C74 A119 10c dark brown 2.00 .85
C75 A119 20c dark green 3.25 1.40
C76 A119 50c carmine 6.75 3.00
Nos. C74-C76 (3) 12.00 5.25

Rotary Intl. Type

1955, Feb. 23

C77 A123 50c blue green 2.00 .85

Lt. José Gozar AP10

20c, 50c, Lt. Gozar. 30c, 70c, Lt. Basa.

1955 Engr. *Perf. 13*

C78 AP10 20c deep violet .45 .20
C79 AP10 30c red .50 .20
C80 AP10 50c bluish green .70 .20
C81 AP10 70c blue 1.10 .90
Nos. C78-C81 (4) 2.75 1.50

Lt. José Gozar and Lt. Cesar Fernando Basa, Filipino aviators in World War II.

Constitution Type of Regular Issue

1960, Feb. 8 Photo. *Perf. 12½x13½*

C82 A146 30c brt bl & silver .50 .25

Air Force Plane of 1935 and Saber Jet AP11

1960, May 2 Engr. *Perf. 14x14½*

C83 AP11 10c carmine .30 .20
C84 AP11 20c ultra .45 .25

25th anniversary of Philippine Air Force.
For surcharge see No. 847.

Olympic Type of Regular Issue

30c, Sharpshooter. 70c, Woman swimmer.

1960, Nov. 30 Photo. *Perf. 13x13½*

C85 A150 30c orange & brn .50 .35
C86 A150 70c grnsh bl & vio brn 1.00 .70

Postal Conference Type

1961, Feb. 23 *Perf. 13½x13*

C87 A152 30c multicolored .50 .25

Freedom from Hunger Type

1963, Dec. 20 Photo.

C88 A168 30s lt grn & multi .30 .20
C89 A168 50s multicolored .45 .30

Land Reform Type

1964, Dec. 21 Wmk. 233 *Perf. 14½*

C90 A172 30s multicolored .50 .20

Mass Baptism by Father Andres de Urdaneta, Cebu — AP12

70s, World map showing route of the Cross from Spain to Mexico to Cebu, and two galleons.

Unwmk.

1965, Oct. 4 Photo. *Perf. 13*

C91 AP12 30s multicolored .50 .20
C92 AP12 70s multicolored 1.00 .35
a. Souvenir sheet of 4 3.00 2.50

400th anniv. of the Christianization of the Philippines. No. C92a contains four imperf. stamps similar to Nos. 934-935 and C91-C92 with simulated perforation.
For surcharge see No. C108.

Souvenir Sheet

Family and Progress Symbols — AP13

1966, July 22 Photo. *Imperf.*

C93 AP13 70s multicolored 3.00 1.00

50th anniv. of the Philippine Natl. Bank. No. C93 contains one stamp with simulated perforation superimposed on a facsimile of a 50p banknote of 1916.

Eruption of Taal Volcano and Refugees — AP14

1967, Oct. 1 Photo. *Perf. 13½x13*

C94 AP14 70s multicolored .60 .45

Eruption of Taal Volcano, Sept. 28, 1965.

Eruption of Taal Volcano — AP15

1968, Oct. 1 Litho. *Perf. 13½*

C95 AP15 70s multicolored .60 .55

Eruption of Taal Volcano, Sept. 28, 1965.

Rotary Type of 1969

1969, Jan. 29 Photo. *Perf. 12½*

C96 A202 40s green & multi .35 .20
C97 A202 75s red & multi .65 .40

Holy Child Type of Regular Issue

1969, June 30 Photo. *Perf. 13½*

C98 A207 40s ultra & multi .60 .25

Pope Type of Regular Issue

1970, Nov. 27 Photo. *Perf. 13½x14*

C99 A221 40s violet & multi .60 .25

Law College Type of Regular Issue

1971, June 15 *Perf. 13*

C100 A225 1p green & multi .70 .45

Manila Type of Regular Issue

1971, June 24

C101 A226 1p multi & blue .70 .45

Santo Tomas Type of Regular Issue

1971, July 8 Photo. *Perf. 13½*

C102 A227 2p lt blue & multi 1.10 .80

Congress Type of Regular Issue

1972, Apr. 11 Photo. *Perf. 13½x13*

C103 A232 40s green & multi .50 .25

Tropical Fish Type of Regular Issue

1972, Aug. 14 Photo. *Perf. 13*

C104 A235 50s Dusky angelfish 1.10 .40

Pope Paul VI Type of Regular Issue

1972, Sept. 26 Photo. *Perf. 14*

C105 A237 60s lt blue & multi .60 .35

First Mass Type of Regular Issue

1972, Oct. 31 Photo. *Perf. 14*

C106 A241 60s multicolored .50 .25

Presidential Palace Type of Regular Issue

1973, Nov. 15 Litho. *Perf. 14*

C107 A253 60s multicolored .65 .30

No. C92a Surcharged and Overprinted with US Bicentennial Emblems and: "U.S.A. BICENTENNIAL / 1776-1976" in Black

Unwmk.

1976, Sept. 20 Photo. *Imperf.*

C108 Sheet of 4 1.50 1.25
- *a.* A179 5s on 3s multi .20 .20
- *b.* A179 5s on 6s multi .20 .20
- *c.* AP12 15s on 30s multi .30 .20
- *d.* AP12 50s on 70s multi .75 .35

American Bicentennial. Nos. C108a-C108d are overprinted with Bicentennial emblem and 2 bars over old denomination. Inscription and 2 Bicentennial emblems overprinted in margin. Overprint and surcharges exist in red.

Souvenir Sheet

Netherlands No. 1 and Philippines No. 1 and Windmill AP16

1977, May 26 Litho. *Perf. 14½*

C109 Sheet of 3 8.00 7.50
- *a.* AP16 7.50p multicolored 2.25 2.10

AMPHILEX '77, International Stamp Exhibition, Amsterdam, May 26-June 5.
Exists imperf. Value $17.50.

Souvenir Sheet

Philippines and Spain Nos. 1, Bull and Matador AP17

1977, Oct. 7 Litho. *Perf. 12½x13*

C110 Sheet of 3 8.00 8.00
- *a.* AP17 7.50p multicolored 2.00 2.00

ESPAMER '77 (Exposicion Filatelica de America y Europa), Barcelona, Spain, 10/7-13.
Exists imperf. Value $16.00.

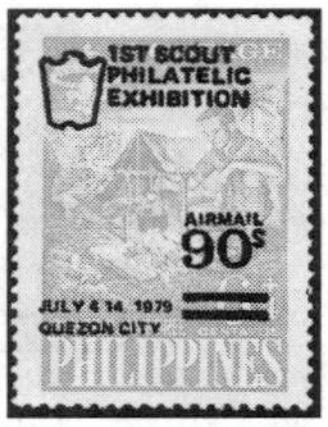

Nos. B10 and CB3a Surcharged

1979, July 5 Engr. *Perf. 13*

C111 SP8 90s on 6c + 4c car, *yel* 1.25 .45

Souvenir Sheet

White Paper

C112 Sheet of 5 3.00 2.50
- *a.* SP8 50s on 6c + 4c carmine .50 .35
- *b.* SP8 50s on 25c + 5c blue .50 .35
- *c.* SP8 50s on 30c + 10c green .50 .35
- *d.* SP8 50s on 70c + 20c red brown .50 .35
- *e.* SP8 50s on 80c + 20c violet .50 .35

First Scout Philatelic Exhibition, Quezon City, July 4-14, commemorating 25th anniversary of First National Jamboree.

Surcharge on No. C111 includes "AIR-MAIL." Violet marginal inscriptions on No. C112 overprinted with heavy bars; new commemorative inscriptions and Scout emblem added.

AIR POST SEMI-POSTAL STAMPS

Catalogue values for unused stamps in this section are for Never Hinged items.

Type of Semi-Postal Issue, 1959

Designs: 30c+10c, Bicycling. 70c+20c, Scout with plane model. 80c+20c, Pres. Carlos P. Garcia and scout shaking hands.

Unwmk.

1959, July 17 Engr. *Perf. 13*

CB1 SP8 30c + 10c green .30 .30
CB2 SP8 70c + 20c red brown .70 .65
CB3 SP8 80c + 20c violet 1.00 .90
- *a.* Souvenir sheet of 5 4.00 3.75

Nos. CB1-CB3 (3) 2.00 1.85

10th Boy Scout World Jamboree, Makiling Natl. Park, July 17-26. Surtax was for the Jamboree.

No. CB3a measures 171x89mm. and contains one each of Nos. CB1-CB3 and types of Nos. B10-B11 on white paper. Sold for 4p.

For surcharge see No. C112.

SPECIAL DELIVERY STAMPS

United States No. E5 Overprinted in Red

1901, Oct. 15 Wmk. 191 *Perf. 12*

E1 SD3 10c dark blue 125.00 100.00

Special Delivery Messenger SD2

1906 Engr. Wmk. 191PI

E2 SD2 20c ultra 30.00 7.50
- *b.* 20c pale ultra 30.00 7.50

See Nos. E3-E6. For overprints see Nos. E7-E10, EO1.

Special Printing

Overprinted in Red as No. E1 on United States No. E6

1907

E2A SD4 10c ultra *2,750.*

Type of 1906

1911 Wmk. 190PI

E3 SD2 20c dp ultra 20.00 1.75

1916 *Perf. 10*

E4 SD2 20c dp ultra 175.00 75.00

1919 Unwmk. *Perf. 11*

E5 SD2 20c ultra .60 .20
- *a.* 20c pale blue .75 .20
- *b.* 20c dull violet .60 .20

1925-31 *Imperf.*

E6 SD2 20c dull vio ('31) 20.00 *50.00*
- *a.* 20c violet blue ('25) 40.00 27.50

Type of 1919 Overprinted in Black

1939 *Perf. 11*

E7 SD2 20c blue violet .25 .20

Nos. E5b and E7, Handstamped in Violet

1944 *Perf. 11*

E8 SD2 20c dull vio (#E5b) *800.00 550.00*
E9 SD2 20c blue vio (#E7) *225.00 175.00*

Type SD2 Overprinted "VICTORY" As No. 486

1945

E10 SD2 20c blue violet .70 .55
- *a.* "IC" close together 3.25 2.75

Catalogue values for unused stamps in this section, from this point to the end of the section, are for Never Hinged items.

Republic

Manila Post Office and Messenger SD3

Unwmk.

1947, Dec. 22 Engr. *Perf. 12*

E11 SD3 20c rose lilac .50 .40

Post Office Building, Manila, and Hands with Letter — SD4

1962, Jan. 23 *Perf. 13½x13*

E12 SD4 20c lilac rose .60 .30

SPECIAL DELIVERY OFFICIAL STAMP

Type of 1906 Issue Overprinted

1931 Unwmk. *Perf. 11*

EO1 SD2 20c dull violet .65 *.75*
- *a.* No period after "B" 20.00 15.00
- *b.* Double overprint —

It is recommended that expert opinion be acquired for No. EO1 used.

POSTAGE DUE STAMPS

Postage Due Stamps of the United States Nos. J38 to J44 Overprinted in Black

1899, Aug. 16 Wmk. 191 *Perf. 12*

J1 D2 1c deep claret 6.50 1.50
J2 D2 2c deep claret 6.50 1.25
J3 D2 5c deep claret 15.00 2.50
J4 D2 10c deep claret 19.00 5.50
J5 D2 50c deep claret 200.00 100.00

1901, Aug. 31

J6 D2 3c deep claret 17.50 7.00
J7 D2 30c deep claret 225.00 110.00

Nos. J1-J7 (7) 489.50 227.75

No. J1 was used to pay regular postage September 5-19, 1902.

Post Office Clerk — D3

Unwmk.

1928, Aug. 21 Engr. *Perf. 11*

J8 D3 4c brown red .20 .20
J9 D3 6c brown red .20 .20
J10 D3 8c brown red .20 .20
J11 D3 10c brown red .20 .20
J12 D3 12c brown red .20 .20
J13 D3 16c brown red .20 .20
J14 D3 20c brown red .20 .20

Nos. J8-J14 (7) 1.40 1.40

For overprints see Nos. O16-O22, NJ1. For surcharge see No. J15.

No. J8 Surcharged in Blue

1937

J15 D3 3c on 4c brown red .20 .20

Nos. J8 to J14 Handstamped in Violet **VICTORY**

1944

J16 D3 4c brown red *140.00* —
J17 D3 6c brown red *90.00* —
J18 D3 8c brown red *95.00* —
J19 D3 10c brown red *90.00* —
J20 D3 12c brown red *90.00* —
J21 D3 16c brown red *95.00* —
J22 D3 20c brown red *95.00* —

Nos. J16-J22 (7) *695.00*

Catalogue values for unused stamps in this section, from this point to the end of the section, are for Never Hinged items.

Republic

D4

Unwmk.

1947, Oct. 20 Engr. *Perf. 12*

J23 D4 3c rose carmine .25 .20
J24 D4 4c brt violet blue .45 .25
J25 D4 6c olive green .60 .40
J26 D4 10c orange .70 .50

Nos. J23-J26 (4) 2.00 1.35

OFFICIAL STAMPS

Official Handstamped Overprints

"Officers purchasing stamps for government business may, if they so desire, overprint them with the letters 'O.B.' either in writing with black ink or by rubber stamps but in such a manner as not to obliterate the stamp that postmasters will be unable to determine whether the stamps have been previously used." C. M. Cotterman, Director of Posts, Dec. 26, 1905. Beginning with Jan. 1, 1906, all branches of the Insular Government used postage stamps to prepay postage instead of franking them as before. Some officials used manuscript, some utilized typewriters, some made press-printed overprints, but by far the larger number used rubber stamps. The majority of these read "O.B." but other forms were: "OFFICIAL BUSINESS" or "OFFICIAL MAIL" in two lines, with variations on many of these. These "O.B." overprints are known on US 1899-1901 stamps; on 1903-06 stamps in red and blue; on 1906 stamps in red, blue, black, yellow and green. "O.B." overprints were also made on the centavo and peso stamps of the Philippines, per order of May 25, 1907. Beginning in 1926 the stamps were overprinted and issued by the Post Office, but some government offices continued to handstamp "O.B."

Regular Issue of 1926 Overprinted in Red

1926, Dec. 20 Unwmk. *Perf. 12*

O1 A42 2c green & blk 2.25 1.00
O2 A42 4c carmine & blk 2.25 1.25
a. Vert. pair, imperf. btwn. *750.00*
O3 A42 18c lt brn & blk 7.00 4.00
O4 A42 20c orange & blk 18.25 1.75
Nos. O1-O4 (4) 18.25 8.00

Opening of the Legislative Palace.

Regular Issue of 1917-26 Overprinted

1931 *Perf. 11*

O5 A40 2c green .20 .20
a. No period after "B" 15.00 5.00
b. No period after "O" —
O6 A40 4c carmine .20 .20
a. No period after "B" 15.00 5.00
O7 A40 6c dp violet .20 .20
O8 A40 8c yellow brn .20 .20
O9 A40 10c deep blue .30 .20
O10 A40 12c red orange .25 .20
a. No period after "B" 32.50
O11 A40 16c lt ol grn *(Dewey)* .25 .20
a. 16c olive bister 1.25 .20
O12 A40 20c orange yel .25 .20
a. No period after "B" 22.50 15.00
O13 A40 26c green .40 .30
a. 26c blue green 1.00 .65
O14 A40 30c gray .30 .25
Nos. O5-O14 (10) 2.55 2.15

Same Overprint on Nos. 383-392

1935

O15 A53 2c rose .20 .20
a. No period after "B" 15.00 5.00
O16 A54 4c yellow green .20 .20
a. No period after "B" 15.00 8.50
O17 A55 6c dk brown .20 .20
a. No period after "B" 20.00 17.50
O18 A56 8c violet .20 .20
O19 A57 10c rose carmine .20 .20
O20 A58 12c black .20 .20
O21 A59 16c dark blue .20 .20
O22 A60 20c lt olive grn .20 .20
O23 A61 26c indigo .25 .20
O24 A62 30c orange red .30 .20
Nos. O15-O24 (10) 2.15 2.00

Same Overprint on Nos. 411, 418

1937-38 *Perf. 11*

O25 A53 2c rose .20 .20
a. No period after "B" 4.25 2.25
b. Period after "B" raised (UL4) —
O26 A60 20c lt ol grn ('38) .65 .50

Nos. 383-392 Overprinted in Black:

a

b

1938-40 *Perf. 11*

O27 A53(a) 2c rose .20 .20
a. Hyphen omitted 20.00 20.00
b. No period after "B" 25.00 25.00
O28 A54(b) 4c yellow grn .20 .20
O29 A55(a) 6c dk brown .20 .20
O30 A56(b) 8c violet .20 .20
O31 A57(b) 10c rose car .20 .20
a. No period after "O" 30.00 30.00
O32 A58(b) 12c black .20 .20
O33 A59(b) 16c dark blue .20 .20
O34 A60(a) 20c lt ol grn ('40) .25 .25
O35 A61(b) 26c indigo .30 .30
O36 A62(b) 30c orange red .25 .25
Nos. O27-O36 (10) 2.20 2.20

No. 461 Overprinted in Black

Perf. 11x10½

1941, Apr. 14 Unwmk.

O37 A75 2c apple green .20 .20

Official Stamps Handstamped in Violet

1944 *Perf. 11, 11x10½*

O38 A53 2c (#O27) 250.00 150.00
O39 A75 2c (#O37) 6.50 3.00
O40 A54 4c (#O16) 42.50 30.00
O40A A55 6c (#O29) 5,000. —
O41 A57 10c (#O31) 150.00
O42 A60 20c (#O22) 6,000.
O43 A60 20c (#O26) 1,550.

No. 497 Overprinted Type "c" in Black

Perf. 11x10½

1946, June 19 Unwmk.

O44 A76 2c sepia .20 .20

Catalogue values for unused stamps in this section, from this point to the end of the section, are for Never Hinged items.

Republic

Nos. 504, 505 and 507 Overprinted in Black — d

1948 Unwmk. *Perf. 12*

O50 A78 4c black brown .20 .20
a. Inverted overprint 25.00
b. Double overprint 25.00
O51 A79 10c red orange .20 .20
O52 A81 16c slate gray 1.40 .55
Nos. O50-O52 (3) 1.80 .95

The overprint on No. O51 comes in two sizes: 13mm, applied in Manila, and 12½mm, applied in New York.

Nos. 527, 508 and 509 Overprinted in Black — e

Overprint Measures 14mm

O53 A91 2c bright green .40 .20

1949

O54 A82 20c red brown .55 .20

Overprint Measures 12mm

O55 A83 50c dull green .90 .55

No. 550 Overprinted Type "e" in Black
Overprint Measures 14mm

1950

O56 A91 1c on 2c brt green .20 .20

Nos. 589, 592, 595 and 597 Overprinted in Black — f

Overprint Measures 15mm

1952-55

O57 A117 1c red brown ('53) .20 .20
O58 A117 5c crim rose .20 .20
O59 A117 10c ultra ('55) .20 .20
O60 A117 20c car lake ('55) .40 .20
Nos. O57-O60 (4) 1.00 .80

No. 647 Overprinted — g

1959 Engr. *Perf. 12*

O61 A117 1c on 5c crim rose .20 .20

No. 813 Overprinted Type "f"
Overprint measures 16½mm

1959

O62 A145 6c gray blue .20 .20

Nos. 856-861 Overprinted

h

j

k

l

1962-64 *Perf. 13½*

O63 A158(j) 5s car rose ('63) .20 .20

Perf. 13x12

O64 A158(h) 6s dk red brn .20 .20

Perf. 13½

O65 A158(k) 6s pck blue ('64) .20 .20
O66 A158(j) 10s brt purple ('63) .20 .20
O67 A158(j) 20s Prus blue ('63) .20 .20
O68 A158(j) 30s vermilion .30 .20
O69 A158(k) 50s violet ('63) .45 .20
Nos. O63-O69 (7) 1.75 1.40

"G.O." stands for "Gawaing Opisyal," Tagalog for "Official Business."

On 6s overprint "k" is 10mm wide.

For overprint see No. 1119.

No. 1082 Overprinted Type "l"

1970, Dec. 30 Engr. *Perf. 14*

O70 A222 10s rose carmine .20 .20

NEWSPAPER STAMPS

N1

N2

1886-89 Unwmk. Typo. *Perf. 14*

P1 N1 ⅛c yellow green .25 *3.00*
P2 N1 1m rose ('89) .25 *20.00*
P3 N1 2m blue ('89) .25 *20.00*
P4 N1 5m dk brown ('89) .25 *20.00*
Nos. P1-P4 (4) 1.00 *63.00*

1890-96

P5 N2 ⅛c dark violet .20 .20
P6 N2 ⅛c green ('92) 8.00 *10.00*
P7 N2 ⅛c orange brn ('94) .20 .20
P8 N2 ⅛c dull blue ('96) .75 .55
P9 N2 1m dark violet .20 .20
P10 N2 1m green ('92) 2.00 *5.00*
P11 N2 1m olive gray ('94) .20 .40
P12 N2 1m ultra ('96) .25 .20
P13 N2 2m dark violet .20 .40
P14 N2 2m green ('92) 2.25 *12.00*
P15 N2 2m olive gray ('94) .20 .40
P16 N2 2m brown ('96) .25 .20
P17 N2 5m dark violet .20 1.00
P18 N2 5m green ('92) 125.00 35.00
P19 N2 5m olive gray ('94) .20 .40
P20 N2 5m dp blue grn ('96) 2.25 1.25

Imperfs. exist of Nos. P8, P9, P11, P12, P16, P17 and P20.

POSTAL TAX STAMPS

Mt. Pinatubo Fund — PT1

25c, Lahar flow. #RA2, Erupting volcano. #RA3, Animals after eruption. #RA4, Village after eruption. #RA5, People clearing ash.

Wmk. 391

1992, Nov. 16 Litho. *Perf. 13¾*

RA1 PT1 25c multi .20 .20
RA2 PT1 1p multi .60 .60
RA3 PT1 1p multi .60 .60
RA4 PT1 1p multi .60 .60
RA5 PT1 1p multi .60 .60
a. Block of 4, #RA2-RA5 2.40 2.40
Nos. RA1-RA5 (5) 2.60 2.60

Use of Nos. RA1-RA5 as postal tax stamps was suspended on 2/1/93. These stamps subsequently became valid for postage.

OCCUPATION STAMPS

Issued under Japanese Occupation

Nos. 461, 438 and 439 Overprinted with Bars in Black

1942-43 Unwmk. *Perf. 11x10½, 11*

N1 A75 2c apple green .20 .20
a. Pair, one without overprint —
N2 A58 12c black ('43) .20 .20
N3 A59 16c dark blue 5.00 3.75
Nos. N1-N3 (3) 5.40 4.15

Nos. 435, 442, 443 and 423 Surcharged in Black

a

b

c

d

Perf. 11

N4	A55 5c on 6c gldn brn	.20	.20
a.	Top bar shorter, thinner	.20	.20
b.	5(c) on 6c dk brn	.20	.20
c.	As "b," top bar shorter and thinner	.20	.20
N5	A62 16c on 30c ('43)	.25	.25
N6	A63 50c on 1p ('43)	.60	.60
a.	Double surcharge		*300.00*
N7	A65 1p on 4p ('43)	125.00	200.00

On Nos. N4 and N4b, the top bar measures 1½x22½mm. On Nos. N4a and N4c, the top bar measures 1x21mm and the "5" is smaller and thinner.

No. 384 Surcharged in Black

1942, May 18

N8	A54 2c on 4c yel grn	6.00	6.00

Japan's capture of Bataan and Corregidor. The American-Filipino forces finally surrendered May 7, 1942.

No. 384 Surcharged in Black

1942, Dec. 8

N9	A54 5c on 4c yel grn	.50	.50

1st anniv. of the "Greater East Asia War."

Nos. C59 and C62 Surcharged in Black

1943, Jan. 23

N10	AP1 2c on 8c carmine	.25	.25
N11	AP1 5c on 1p sepia	.50	.50

Philippine Executive Commission, 1st anniv.

Nipa Hut
OS1

Rice Planting
OS2

Mt. Mayon and
Mt. Fuji — OS3

Moro
Vinta — OS4

Engr., Typo. (2c, 6c, 25c)

1943-44 Wmk. 257 *Perf. 13*

N12	OS1 1c deep orange	.20	.20
N13	OS2 2c bright green	.20	.20
N14	OS1 4c slate green	.20	.20
N15	OS3 5c orange brown	.20	.20
N16	OS2 6c red	.20	.20
N17	OS3 10c blue green	.20	.20
N18	OS4 12c steel blue	1.00	1.00
N19	OS4 16c dark brown	.20	.20
N20	OS1 20c rose violet	1.25	1.25
N21	OS3 21c violet	.20	.20
N22	OS2 25c pale brown	.20	.20
N23	OS3 1p deep carmine	.75	.75
N24	OS4 2p dull violet	5.50	5.50
N25	OS4 5p dark olive	14.00	9.00
	Nos. N12-N25 (14)	24.30	19.30

For surcharges see Nos. NB5-NB7.

Map of Manila Bay Showing Bataan and Corregidor
OS5

1943, May 7 Photo. Unwmk.

N26	OS5 2c carmine red	.20	.20
N27	OS5 5c bright green	.25	.25

Fall of Bataan & Corregidor, 1st anniv.

No. 440 Surcharged in Black

1943, June 20 Engr. *Perf. 11*

N28	A60 12c on 20c lt ol grn	.20	.20
a.	Double surcharge	—	

350th anniversary of the printing press in the Philippines. "Limbagan" is Tagalog for "printing press."

Rizal Monument, Filipina and Philippine Flag — OS6

1943, Oct. 14 Photo. *Perf. 12*

N29	OS6 5c light blue	.20	.20
a.	Imperf.	.20	.20
N30	OS6 12c orange	.20	.20
a.	Imperf.	.20	.20
N31	OS6 17c rose pink	.20	.20
a.	Imperf.	.20	.20
	Nos. N29-N31 (3)	.60	.60

"Independence of the Philippines." Japan granted "independence" Oct. 14, 1943, when the puppet republic was founded.

The imperforate stamps were issued without gum. See No. NB4.

José
Rizal — OS7

Rev. José
Burgos — OS8

Design: 17c, Apolinario Mabini.

1944, Feb. 17 Litho. *Perf. 12*

N32	OS7 5c blue	.20	.20
a.	Imperf.	.20	.20
N33	OS8 12c carmine	.20	.20
a.	Imperf.	.20	.20
N34	OS7 17c deep orange	.20	.20
a.	Imperf.	.20	.20
	Nos. N32-N34 (3)	.60	.60

See No. NB8.

Nos. C60 and C61 Surcharged in Black

1944, May 7 *Perf. 11*

N35	AP1 5c on 20c ultra	.50	.35
N36	AP1 12c on 60c blue grn	1.25	.85

Fall of Bataan & Corregidor, 2nd anniv.

José P.
Laurel — OS10

1945, Jan. 12 Litho. *Imperf.*

Without Gum

N37	OS10 5c dull violet brn	.20	.20
N38	OS10 7c blue green	.20	.20
N39	OS10 20c chalky blue	.20	.20
	Nos. N37-N39 (3)	.60	.60

Issued belatedly to commemorate the 1st anniv. of the puppet Philippine Republic, 10/14/44. "S" stands for "sentimos."

OCCUPATION SEMI-POSTAL STAMPS

Woman, Farming and Cannery — OSP1

Unwmk.

1942, Nov. 12 Litho. *Perf. 12*

NB1	OSP1 2c + 1c pale violet	.20	.20
NB2	OSP1 5c + 1c brt green	.25	.20
NB3	OSP1 16c + 2c orange	32.50	32.50

Campaign to produce and conserve food. The surtax aided the Red Cross.

"Independence of the Philippines" Type

Souvenir Sheet

1943, Oct. 14 *Imperf.*

Without Gum

NB4	Sheet of 3	50.00	*10.00*

No. NB4 contains one each of Nos. N29a-N31a. Lower inscription from Rizal's "Last Farewell." Size: 127x177mm. Sold for 2.50p.

Nos. N18, N20 and N21 Surcharged in Black

1943, Dec. 8 Wmk. 257 *Perf. 13*

NB5	OS4 12c + 21c steel blue	.20	.20
NB6	OS1 20c + 36c rose violet	.20	.20
NB7	OS3 21c + 40c violet	.20	.20
	Nos. NB5-NB7 (3)	.60	.60

The surtax was for the benefit of victims of a Luzon flood. "Baha" is Tagalog for "flood."

Type of 1944

Souvenir Sheet

Unwmk.

1944, Feb. 9 Litho. *Imperf.*

Without Gum

NB8	Sheet of 3	5.00	*3.00*

#NB8 contains 1 each of #N32a-N34a.

Sheet sold for 1p, surtax going to a fund for the care of heroes' monuments.

OCCUPATION POSTAGE DUE STAMP

No. J15 Overprinted with Bar in Blue

1942, Oct. 14 Unwmk. *Perf. 11*

NJ1	D3 3c on 4c brown red	35.00	20.00

On copies of No. J15, two lines were drawn in India ink with a ruling pen across "United States of America" by employees of the Short Paid Section of the Manila Post Office to make a provisional 3c postage due stamp which was used from Sept. 1, 1942, (when the letter rate was raised from 2c to 5c) until Oct. 14 when No. NJ1 went on sale.

OCCUPATION OFFICIAL STAMPS

Nos. 461, 413, 435, 435a and 442 Overprinted or Surcharged in Black with Bars and

1943-44 Unwmk. *Perf. 11x10½, 11*

NO1	A75 2c apple green	.20	.20
a.	Double overprint	*500.00*	
NO2	A55 5(c) on 6c dk brn (#413) ('44)	45.00	45.00
NO3	A55 5(c) on 6c gldn brn (#435a)	.20	.20
a.	Narrower spacing between bars	.20	.20
b.	5(c) on 6c dark brown (#435)	.20	.20
c.	As "b," narrower spacing between bars	.20	.20
d.	Double overprint	—	
NO4	A62 16c on 30c org red	.30	.30
a.	Wider spacing between bars	.30	.30

On Nos. NO3 and NO3b, the bar deleting "United States of America" is 9¾mm to 10mm above the bar deleting "Common-." On Nos. NO3a and NO3c, the spacing is 8mm to 8½mm.

On No. NO4 the center bar is 19mm long, 3½mm below the top bar and 6mm above the Japanese characters. On No. NO4a, the center bar is 20½mm long, 9mm below the top bar and 1mm above the Japanese characters.

"K. P." stands for Kagamitang Pampamahalaan, "Official Business" in Tagalog.

Nos. 435 and 435a Surcharged in Black

1944 *Perf. 11*

NO5	A55 5c on 6c golden brown	.20	.20
a.	5c on 6c dark brown	.20	.20

Nos. O34 and C62 Overprinted in Black

a

b

NO6	A60(a)	20c light olive green	.25	.25
NO7	AP1(b)	1p sepia	.65	.65
		Nos. NO5-NO7 (3)	1.10	1.10

PITCAIRN ISLANDS

'pit-ˌkarn 'ī-lənds

LOCATION — South Pacific Ocean, nearly equidistant from Australia and South America

GOVT. — British colony under the British High Commissioner in New Zealand

AREA — 18 sq. mi. (includes all islands)

POP. — 49 (1999 est.)

The district of Pitcairn also includes the uninhabited islands of Ducie, Henderson and Oeno.

Postal affairs are administered by New Zealand.

12 Pence = 1 Shilling
100 Cents = 1 Dollar (1967)

Catalogue values for all unused stamps in this country are for Never Hinged items.

Cluster of Oranges A1

Fletcher Christian with Crew and View of Pitcairn Island — A2

John Adams and His House A3

William Bligh and H. M. Armed Vessel "Bounty" A4

Map of Pitcairn and Pacific Ocean — A5

Bounty Bible — A6

H.M. Armed Vessel "Bounty" A7

Pitcairn School, 1949 — A8

Fletcher Christian and View of Pitcairn Island — A9

Fletcher Christian with Crew and Coast of Pitcairn A10

Perf. 12½, 11½x11

1940-51		**Engr.**		**Wmk. 4**
1	A1	½p blue grn & org	.30	*.45*
2	A2	1p red lil & rose vio	.45	*.55*
3	A3	1½p rose car & blk	.45	.40
4	A4	2p dk brn & brt grn	1.40	1.00
5	A5	3p dk blue & yel grn	1.00	*1.10*
5A	A6	4p dk blue grn & blk	12.00	8.00
6	A7	6p sl grn & dp brn	4.00	1.25
6A	A8	8p lil rose & grn	12.50	5.50
7	A9	1sh slate & vio	2.40	1.25
8	A10	2sh6p dk brn & brt grn	5.75	3.00
		Nos. 1-8 (10)	40.25	22.50

Nos. 1-5, 6 and 7-8 exist in a booklet of eight panes of one.

Issued: 4p, 8p, 9/1/51; others, 10/15/40.

Common Design Types pictured following the introduction.

Peace Issue
Common Design Type

1946, Dec. 2		***Perf. 13½x14***		
9	CD303	2p brown	.35	.35
10	CD303	3p deep blue	.65	.65

Silver Wedding Issue
Common Design Types

1949, Aug. 1		**Photo.** ***Perf. 14x14½***		
11	CD304	1½p scarlet	1.50	.75

Engraved; Name Typographed
Perf. 11½x11

12	CD305	10sh purple	60.00	*55.00*

UPU Issue
Common Design Types

Engr.; Name Typo. on 3p & 6p

1949, Oct. 10		***Perf. 13½, 11x11½***		
13	CD306	2½p red brown	5.00	2.00
14	CD307	3p indigo	5.00	2.00
15	CD308	6p green	10.00	4.00
16	CD309	1sh rose violet	17.50	8.00
		Nos. 13-16 (4)	37.50	16.00

Coronation Issue
Common Design Type

1953, June 2		***Perf. 13½x13***		
19	CD312	4p dk green & blk	2.50	1.75

Ti Plant — A11

Map — A12

Designs: 2p, John Adams and Bounty Bible. 2½p, Handicraft (Carving). 3p, Bounty Bay. 4p, School (actually Schoolteacher's House). 6p, Fiji-Pitcairn connection (Map). 8p, Inland scene. 1sh, Handicraft (Ship model). 2sh, Wheelbarrow. 2sh6p, Whaleboat.

Perf. 13x12½, 12½x13

1957, July 2		**Engr.**		**Wmk. 4**
20	A11	½p lilac & green	.60	.20
21	A12	1p olive grn & blk	2.50	.20
22	A12	2p blue & brown	.60	.25
23	A11	2½p orange & brn	.40	.30
24	A11	3p ultra & emer	.65	.40
25	A11	4p ultra & rose red *(Pitcairn School)*	.75	.50
26	A11	6p indigo & buff	1.00	.70
27	A11	8p magenta & grn	.50	*.80*
28	A11	1sh brown & blk	1.25	.75
29	A12	2sh dp org & grn	13.25	7.25
30	A11	2sh6p mag & ultra	18.50	6.00
		Nos. 20-30 (11)	40.00	17.35

See Nos. 31, 38.

Type of 1957 Corrected

1958, Nov. 5		***Perf. 13x12½***		
31	A11	4p ultra & rose red *(School-teacher's House)*	2.50	1.00

Simon Young and Pitcairn A13

Designs: 6p, Maps of Norfolk and Pitcairn Islands. 1sh, Schooner Mary Ann.

Perf. 14½x13½

1961, Nov. 15		**Photo.**		**Wmk. 314**
32	A13	3p yellow & black	.50	.50
33	A13	6p blue & red brown	1.25	1.00
34	A13	1sh brt green & dp org	1.25	1.00
		Nos. 32-34 (3)	3.00	2.50

Pitcairn Islanders return from Norfolk Island.

Freedom from Hunger Issue
Common Design Type

1963, June 4		***Perf. 14x14½***		
35	CD314	2sh6p ultra	15.00	7.50

Red Cross Centenary Issue
Common Design Type

1963, Dec. 9		**Litho.**		***Perf. 13***
36	CD315	2p black & red	.50	.25
37	CD315	2sh6p ultra & red	9.50	5.75

Type of 1957

Perf. 13x12½

1963, Dec. 4		**Engr.**		**Wmk. 314**
38	A11	½p lilac & green	1.00	1.00

Pitcairn Longboat A14

Queen Elizabeth II — A15

1p, H.M. Armed Vessel Bounty. 2p, Oarsmen rowing longboat. 3p, Great frigate bird. 4p, Fairy tern 6p, Pitcairn reed warbler. 8p, Red-footed booby. 10p, Red-tailed tropic birds. 1sh, Henderson Island flightless rail. 1sh6p, Henderson Island lory. 2sh6p, Murphy's petrel. 4sh, Henderson Island fruit pigeon.

1964-65		**Photo.**		***Perf. 14x14½***
39	A14	½p multicolored	.20	.20
40	A14	1p multicolored	.20	.20
41	A14	2p multicolored	.20	.20
42	A14	3p multicolored	.20	.20
43	A14	4p multicolored	.30	.20
44	A14	6p multicolored	.50	.30
45	A14	8p multicolored	.50	.35
	a.	Gray (beak) omitted	250.00	
46	A14	10p multicolored	.70	.45
47	A14	1sh multicolored	.70	.60
48	A14	1sh6p multicolored	4.50	.80
49	A14	2sh6p multicolored	4.25	1.50
50	A14	4sh multicolored	5.50	2.25
51	A15	8sh multicolored	2.25	2.25
		Nos. 39-51 (13)	20.00	9.50

Issued: ½p-4sh, 8/5/64; 8sh, 4/5/65.

For surcharges see Nos. 72-84.

ITU Issue
Common Design Type

1965, May 17		**Litho.**		***Perf. 11x11½***
52	CD317	1p red lilac & org brn	.40	.20
53	CD317	2sh6p grnsh blue & ultra	11.50	5.75

Intl. Cooperation Year Issue
Common Design Type

1965, Oct. 25 *Perf. 14½*

54	CD318	1p bl grn & cl	.35	.20
55	CD318	1sh6p lt vio & grn	14.00	6.00

Churchill Memorial Issue
Common Design Type

1966, Jan. 24 Photo. *Perf. 14*

Design in Black, Gold and Carmine Rose

56	CD319	2p brt blue	1.25	.75
57	CD319	3p green	3.75	1.00
58	CD319	6p brown	4.00	2.00
59	CD319	1sh violet	5.75	4.25
		Nos. 56-59 (4)	14.75	8.00

World Cup Soccer Issue
Common Design Type

1966, Aug. 1 Litho. *Perf. 14*

60	CD321	4p multi	1.00	.75
61	CD321	2sh6p multi	6.00	3.25

WHO Headquarters Issue
Common Design Type

1966, Sept. 20 Litho. *Perf. 14*

62	CD322	8p multi	3.50	1.50
63	CD322	1sh6p multi	7.50	5.50

UNESCO Anniversary Issue
Common Design Type

1966, Dec. 1 Litho. *Perf. 14*

64	CD323	½p "Education"	.20	.20
65	CD323	10p "Science"	4.00	2.00
66	CD323	2sh "Culture"	8.50	4.50
		Nos. 64-66 (3)	12.70	6.70

Mangarevan Canoe, c. 1325, and Pitcairn Island — A16

Designs: 1p, Pedro Fernandez de Quiros and galleon, 1606. 8p, "San Pedro," 17th century Spanish brigantine, 1606. 1sh, Capt. Philip Carteret and H.M.S. Swallow. 1sh6p, "Hercules," 1819.

Wmk. 314

1967, Mar. 1 Photo. *Perf. 14½*

67	A16	½p multicolored	.20	.20
68	A16	1p multicolored	.20	.20
69	A16	8p multicolored	.30	.25
70	A16	1sh multicolored	.50	.40
71	A16	1sh6p multicolored	.75	.70
		Nos. 67-71 (5)	1.95	1.75

Bicentenary of the discovery of Pitcairn Islands by Capt. Philip Carteret.

Nos. 39-51 Surcharged in Gold

1967, July 10 *Perf. 14x14½*

72	A14	½c on ½p	.20	.20
a.		Brown omitted	500.00	
73	A14	1c on 1p	.20	.20
74	A14	2c on 2p	.20	.20
75	A14	2½c on 3p	.20	.20
76	A14	3c on 4p	.25	.25
77	A14	5c on 6p	.35	.35
78	A14	10c on 8p	.75	.50
a.		"10c" omitted	750.00	
79	A14	15c on 10p	1.00	.75
80	A14	20c on 1sh	1.40	1.00
81	A14	25c on 1sh6p	1.50	1.25
82	A14	30c on 2sh6p	2.00	1.25
83	A14	40c on 4sh	3.00	2.50
84	A15	45c on 8sh	4.75	4.00
		Nos. 72-84 (13)	15.80	12.65

Size of gold rectangle and anchor varies. The anchor symbol is designed after the anchor of H.M.S. Bounty.

Admiral Bligh and Bounty's Launch — A17

Designs: 8c, Bligh and his followers adrift in a boat. 20c, Bligh's tomb, St. Mary's Cemetery, Lambeth, London.

Unwmk.

1967, Dec. 7 Litho. *Perf. 13*

85	A17	1c ultra, lt blue & blk	.20	.20
86	A17	8c brt rose, yel & blk	.25	.25
87	A17	20c brown, yel & blk	.60	.55
		Nos. 85-87 (3)	1.05	1.00

150th anniv. of the death of Admiral William Bligh (1754-1817), capt. of the Bounty.

Human Rights Flame A18

Perf. 13½x13

1968, Mar. 4 Litho. Wmk. 314

88	A18	1c rose & multi	.20	.20
89	A18	2c ocher & multi	.20	.20
90	A18	25c multicolored	.50	.40
		Nos. 88-90 (3)	.90	.80

International Human Rights Year.

Flower and Wood of Miro Tree A19

Pitcairn Handicraft: 10c, Carved flying fish. 15c, Two "hand" vases, vert. 20c, Old and new woven baskets, vert.

Perf. 14½x14, 14x14½

1968, Aug. 19 Photo. Wmk. 314

91	A19	5c chocolate & multi	.20	.20
92	A19	10c dp green & multi	.20	.20
93	A19	15c brt violet & multi	.30	.25
94	A19	20c black & multi	.40	.35
		Nos. 91-94 (4)	1.10	1.00

See Nos. 194-197.

Microscope, Cell, Germs and WHO Emblem — A20

20c, Hypodermic and jars containing pills.

1968, Nov. 25 Litho. *Perf. 14*

95	A20	2c vio blue, grnsh bl & blk	.20	.20
96	A20	20c black, magenta & org	.60	.50

20th anniv. of WHO.

Capt. Bligh and his Larcum-Kendall Chronometer — A21

1c, Pitcairn Island. 3c, Bounty's anchor, vert. 4c, Plan of the Bounty, drawn 1787. 5c, Breadfruit and method of transporting young plants. 6c, Bounty Bay. 8c, Pitcairn longboat. 10c, Ship Landing Point and palms. 15c, Fletcher Christian's Cave. 20c, Thursday October Christian's house. 25c, "Flying Fox" cable system (for hauling cargo), vert. 30c, Radio Station at Taro Ground. 40c, Bounty Bible.

Perf. 13x12½, 12½x13

1969, Sept. 17 Litho. Wmk. 314

97	A21	1c brn, yel & gold	.20	.20
98	A21	2c brn, blk & gold	.20	.20
99	A21	3c red, blk & gold	.20	.20
100	A21	4c buff, brn & gold	.25	.20
101	A21	5c gold & multi	.30	.20
102	A21	6c gold & multi	.35	.30
103	A21	8c gold & multi	.50	.40
104	A21	10c gold & multi	1.00	.75
105	A21	15c gold & multi	1.25	1.00
a.		Gold (Queen's head) omitted	600.00	
106	A21	20c gold & multi	1.50	1.40
107	A21	25c gold & multi	2.75	2.25
108	A21	30c gold & multi	3.50	3.25
109	A21	40c red lil, blk & gold	5.00	3.50
		Nos. 97-109 (13)	17.00	13.85

For overprint see No. 118.

Lantana — A22

Pitcairn Flowers: 2c, Indian shot (canna indica). 5c, Pulau (hibiscus tiliaceus). 25c, Wild gladioli.

1970, Mar. 23 Litho. *Perf. 14*

110	A22	1c black & multi	.20	.20
111	A22	2c black & multi	.20	.20
112	A22	5c black & multi	.45	.20
113	A22	25c black & multi	3.50	1.75
		Nos. 110-113 (4)	4.35	2.35

Rudderfish (Dream Fish) — A23

Fish: 5c, Groupers (Auntie and Ann). 15c, Wrasse (Elwyn's trousers). 20c, Wrasse (Whistling daughter).

Perf. 14½x14

1970, Oct. 12 Photo. Wmk. 314

114	A23	5c black & multi	1.00	.60
115	A23	10c grnsh bl & blk	1.75	1.00
116	A23	15c multicolored	2.75	1.50
117	A23	20c multicolored	4.00	1.75
		Nos. 114-117 (4)	9.50	4.85

No. 104 Overprinted in Silver: "ROYAL VISIT 1971"

1971, Feb. 22 Litho. *Perf. 13x12½*

118	A21	10c gold & multi	5.00	3.75

Polynesian Artifacts — A24

Polynesian Art on Pitcairn: 5c, Rock carvings, vert. 15c, Making of stone fishhook. 20c, Seated deity, vert.

1971, May 3 Litho. *Perf. 13½*

Queen's Head in Gold

119	A24	5c dk brown & bis	.75	.65
120	A24	10c ol green & blk	1.25	1.10
121	A24	15c black & lt vio	2.25	1.50
122	A24	20c black & rose red	2.75	1.75
		Nos. 119-122 (4)	7.00	5.00

Health Care A25

4c, South Pacific Commission flag & Southern Cross, vert. 18c, Education (elementary school). 20c, Economy (country store).

1972, Apr. 4 Litho. *Perf. 14x14½*

123	A25	4c vio bl, yel & ultra	.65	.50
124	A25	8c brown & multi	1.10	1.00
125	A25	18c yellow grn & multi	1.75	1.50
126	A25	20c orange & multi	2.00	1.75
		Nos. 123-126 (4)	5.50	4.75

So. Pacific Commission, 25th anniv.

Silver Wedding Issue, 1972
Common Design Type

Design: Queen Elizabeth II, Prince Philip, skuas and longboat.

1972, Nov. 20 Photo. Wmk. 314

127	CD324	4c slate grn & multi	.25	.20
128	CD324	20c ultra & multi	.85	.60

Pitcairn Coat of Arms A26

1973, Jan. 2 Litho. *Perf. 14½x14*

129	A26	50c multicolored	3.50	3.50

Rose Apple — A27

1973, June 25 *Perf. 14*

130	A27	4c shown	.75	.25
131	A27	8c Mountain apple	1.25	.50
132	A27	15c Lata (myrtle)	1.75	1.00
133	A27	20c Cassia	2.25	1.25
134	A27	35c Guava	4.00	2.00
		Nos. 130-134 (5)	10.00	5.00

Princess Anne's Wedding Issue
Common Design Type

1973, Nov. 14 Litho. *Perf. 14*

135	CD325	10c lilac & multi	.20	.20
136	CD325	25c gray grn & multi	.40	.35

Miter and Horn Shells A28

1974, Apr. 15

137	A28	4c shown	.40	.25
138	A28	10c Dove shells	1.00	.75
139	A28	18c Limpets and false limpet	1.60	1.25
140	A28	50c Lucine shells	4.50	3.75
a.		Souvenir sheet of 4, #137-140	9.50	6.00
		Nos. 137-140 (4)	7.50	6.00

Pitcairn Post Office, UPU Emblem A29

UPU, cent.: 20c, Stampless cover, "Posted at Pitcairn Island No Stamps Available." 35c, Longboat leaving Bounty Bay for ship offshore.

1974, July 22 Wmk. 314 *Perf. 14½*

141	A29	4c multicolored	.20	.20
142	A29	20c multicolored	.60	.50
143	A29	35c multicolored	1.25	1.00
		Nos. 141-143 (3)	2.05	1.70

Churchill: "Lift up your hearts . . ." — A30

Design: 35c, Churchill and "Give us the tools and we will finish the job."

1974, Nov. 30 Litho. Wmk. 373

144	A30	20c black & citron	.50	.40
145	A30	35c black & yellow	.75	.60

Sir Winston Churchill (1874-1965).

Queen Elizabeth II — A31

1975, Apr. 21 Wmk. 314 *Perf. 14½*

146	A31	$1 multicolored	9.50	9.50

Mailboats — A32

1975, July 22 Litho. *Perf. 14½*

147	A32	4c Seringapatam, 1830	.20	.20
148	A32	10c Pitcairn, 1890	.55	.55
149	A32	18c Athenic, 1901	1.00	1.00
150	A32	50c Gothic, 1948	2.75	2.75
a.		Souvenir sheet of 4, #147-150, perf. 14	12.50	12.50
		Nos. 147-150 (4)	4.50	4.50

Pitcairn Wasp A33

Insects: 6c, Grasshopper. 10c, Pitcairn moths. 15c, Dragonfly. 20c, Banana moth.

Wmk. 314

1975, Nov. 9 Litho. *Perf. 14½*

151	A33	4c blue grn & multi	.40	.25
152	A33	6c carmine & multi	.65	.50
153	A33	10c purple & multi	1.00	.75
154	A33	15c black & multi	1.50	1.00
155	A33	20c multicolored	1.75	1.50
		Nos. 151-155 (5)	5.30	4.00

Fletcher Christian — A34

H.M.S. Bounty — A35

American Bicentennial: 30c, George Washington. 50c, Mayflower.

1976, July 4 Wmk. 373 *Perf. 13½*

156	A34	5c multicolored	.20	.20
157	A35	10c multicolored	.40	.35
158	A34	30c multicolored	1.00	.90
a.		Pair, #156, 158	1.40	1.40
159	A35	50c multicolored	1.25	1.00
a.		Pair, #157, 159	1.65	1.65
		Nos. 156-159 (4)	2.85	2.45

Prince Philip's Arrival, 1971 Visit — A36

20c, Chair of homage. 50c, The enthronement.

1977, Feb. 6 *Perf. 13*

160	A36	8c silver & multi	.20	.20
161	A36	20c silver & multi	.30	.30
162	A36	50c silver & multi	.75	.75
		Nos. 160-162 (3)	1.25	1.25

25th anniv. of the reign of Elizabeth II.

Building Longboat — A37

Designs: 1c, Man ringing Island Bell, vert. 5c, Landing cargo. 6c, Sorting supplies. 9c, Cleaning wahoo (fish), vert. 10c, Farming. 15c, Sugar mill. 20c, Women grating coconuts and bananas. 35c, Island church. 50c, Gathering miro logs, Henderson Island. 70c, Burning obsolete stamps, vert. $1, Prince Philip and "Britannia." $2, Elizabeth II, vert.

1977-81 Litho. *Perf. 14½*

163	A37	1c multicolored	.25	.25
164	A37	2c multicolored	.25	.25
165	A37	5c multicolored	.25	.25
166	A37	6c multicolored	.25	.25
167	A37	9c multicolored	.25	.25
168	A37	10c multicolored	.25	.25
168A	A37	15c multicolored	.85	.85
169	A37	20c multicolored	.25	.25
170	A37	35c multicolored	.30	.30
171	A37	50c multicolored	.30	.30
171A	A37	70c multicolored	.85	.85
172	A37	$1 multicolored	.45	.45
173	A37	$2 multicolored	.50	.50
		Nos. 163-173 (13)	5.00	5.00

Issued: #168A, 171A, 10/1/81; others, 9/12/77.

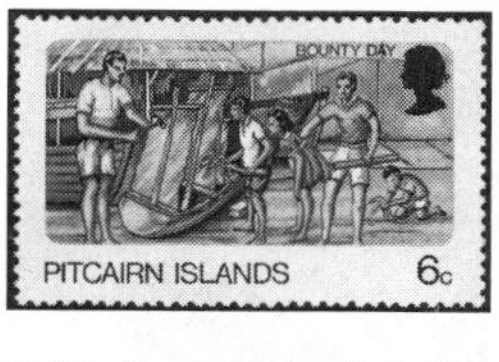

Building "Bounty" Model A38

Bounty Day: 20c, Bounty model afloat. 35c, Burning Bounty.

1978, Jan. 9 *Perf. 14½*

174	A38	6c yellow & multi	.20	.20
175	A38	20c yellow & multi	.85	.65
176	A38	35c yellow & multi	1.25	1.00
a.		Souvenir sheet of 3, #174-176	7.00	6.00
		Nos. 174-176 (3)	2.30	1.85

Souvenir Sheet

Elizabeth II in Coronation Regalia — A39

Wmk. 373

1978, Sept. Litho. *Perf. 12*

177	A39	$1.20 silver & multi	2.00	2.00

25th anniv. of coronation of Elizabeth II.

Unloading "Sir Geraint" A40

Designs: 15c, Harbor before development. 30c, Work on the jetty. 35c, Harbor after development.

Wmk. 373

1978, Dec. 18 Litho. *Perf. 13½*

178	A40	15c multicolored	.20	.20
179	A40	20c multicolored	.35	.35
180	A40	30c multicolored	.60	.60
181	A40	35c multicolored	.65	.65
		Nos. 178-181 (4)	1.80	1.80

Development of new harbor on Pitcairn.

John Adams A41

Design: 70c, John Adams' grave.

1979, Mar. 5 Litho. *Perf. 14½*

182	A41	35c multicolored	.30	*.50*
183	A41	70c multicolored	.60	*.75*

John Adams (1760-1829), founder of Pitcairn Colony, 150th death anniversary.

Pitcairn Island Seen from "Amphitrite" — A42

Engravings (c. 1850): 9c, Bounty Bay and Pitcairn Village, 20c, Lookout Ridge. 70c, Church and schoolhouse.

1979, Sept. 12 Litho. *Perf. 14*

184	A42	6c multicolored	.20	.20
185	A42	9c multicolored	.20	.20
186	A42	20c multicolored	.20	.20
187	A42	70c multicolored	.50	.50
		Nos. 184-187 (4)	1.10	1.10

Taking Presents to the Square, IYC Emblem — A43

IYC Emblem and Children's Drawings: 9c, Decorating trees with presents. 20c, Distributing presents. 35c, Carrying the presents home.

Wmk. 373

1979, Nov. 28 Litho. *Perf. 13½*

188	A43	6c multicolored	.20	.20
189	A43	9c multicolored	.20	.20
190	A43	20c multicolored	.30	.30
191	A43	35c multicolored	.50	.50
a.		Souvenir sheet of 4, #188-191	1.50	*2.00*
		Nos. 188-191 (4)	1.20	1.20

Christmas and IYC.

Souvenir Sheet

Mail Transport by Longboat A44

Wmk. 373

1980, May 6 Litho. *Perf. 14½*

192		Sheet of 4	1.25	1.25
a.	A44	35c shown	.25	.25
b.	A44	35c Mail crane lift	.25	.25
c.	A44	35c Tractor transport	.25	.25
d.	A44	35c Arrival at post office	.25	.25

London 80 Intl. Phil. Exhib., May 6-14.

Queen Mother Elizabeth Birthday Issue

Common Design Type

Wmk. 373

1980, Aug. 4 Litho. *Perf. 14*

193	CD330	50c multicolored	.50	.50

Handicraft Type of 1968

Perf. 14½x14, 14x14½

1980, Sept. 29 Litho. Wmk. 373

194	A19	9c Turtles	.20	.20
195	A19	20c Wheelbarrow	.20	.20
196	A19	35c Gannet, vert.	.25	.25
197	A19	40c Bonnet and fan, vert.	.35	.35
		Nos. 194-197 (4)	1.00	1.00

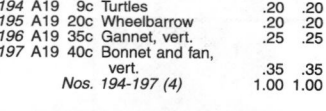

Big George — A45

Wmk. 373

1981, Jan. 22 Litho. *Perf. 14*

198	A45	6c View of Adamstown	.20	.20
199	A45	9c shown	.20	.20
200	A45	20c Christian's Cave, Gannet's Ridge	.20	.20
201	A45	35c Pawala Valley Ridge	.25	.25
202	A45	70c Tatrimoa	.40	.40
		Nos. 198-202 (5)	1.25	1.25

Citizens Departing for Norfolk Island — A46

1981, May 3 Photo. *Perf. 13x14½*

203	A46	9c shown	.20	.20
204	A46	35c Norfolk Isld. from Morayshire	.35	.35
205	A46	70c Morayshire	.70	.70
		Nos. 203-205 (3)	1.25	1.25

Migration to Norfolk Is., 125th anniv.

Royal Wedding Issue

Common Design Type

Wmk. 373

1981, July 22 Litho. *Perf. 14*

206	CD331	20c Bouquet	.20	.20
207	CD331	35c Charles	.20	.20
208	CD331	$1.20 Couple	.75	.75
		Nos. 206-208 (3)	1.15	1.15

Lemon A47

1982, Feb. 23 Litho. *Perf. 14½*

209 A47 9c shown .20 .20
210 A47 20c Pomegranate .30 .30
211 A47 35c Avocado .40 .40
212 A47 70c Pawpaw .85 .85
Nos. 209-212 (4) 1.75 1.75

Princess Diana Issue
Common Design Type

1982, July 1 Litho. *Perf. 14½x14*

213 CD333 6c Arms .20 .20
214 CD333 9c Diana .30 .30
215 CD333 70c Wedding .75 .75
216 CD333 $1.20 Portrait 1.25 1.25
Nos. 213-216 (4) 2.50 2.50

Christmas — A48

Designs: Various paintings of angels by Raphael. 50c, $1 vert.

1982, Oct. 19 Litho. *Perf. 14*

217 A48 15c multicolored .25 .25
218 A48 20c multicolored .25 .25
219 A48 50c multicolored .40 .40
220 A48 $1 multicolored .60 .60
Nos. 217-220 (4) 1.50 1.50

A48a

1983, Mar. 14

221 A48a 6c Radio operator .20 .20
222 A48a 9c Postal clerk .20 .20
223 A48a 70c Fisherman .50 .50
224 A48a $1.20 Artist .85 .85
Nos. 221-224 (4) 1.75 1.75

Commonwealth Day.

175th Anniv. of Capt. Folger's Discovery of the Settlers A49

Wmk. 373

1983, June 14 Litho. *Perf. 14*

225 A49 6c Topaz off Pitcairn Isld. .30 .30
226 A49 20c Topaz, islanders .45 .45
227 A49 70c John Adams welcoming Folger .75 .75
228 A49 $1.20 Presentation of Chronometer 1.25 1.25
Nos. 225-228 (4) 2.75 2.75

Local Trees A50

1983, Oct. 6 Litho. *Perf. 13½*

229 Pair .75 .75
a. A50 35c Hattie .40 .40
b. A50 35c Branch, wood painting .40 .40
230 Pair 1.25 1.25
a. A50 70c Pandanus .65 .65
b. A50 70c Branch, basket weaving .65 .65

See Nos. 289-290.

Pseudojuloides Atavai — A51

Wmk. 373

1984, Jan. 11 Litho. *Perf. 14½*

231 A51 1c shown .25 .20
232 A51 4c Halichoeres melasmapomus .35 .20
233 A51 6c Scarus longippinis .35 .20
234 A51 9c Variola louti .35 .20
235 A51 10c Centropyge hotumatua .35 .20
236 A51 15c Stegastes emeryi .35 .25
237 A51 20c Chaetodon smithi .45 .30
238 A51 35c Xanthichthys mento .60 .50
239 A51 50c Chrysiptera galba .60 *.70*
240 A51 70c Genicanthus spinus .80 *1.00*
241 A51 $1 Myripristis tiki .80 *1.25*
242 A51 $1.20 Anthias ventralis .85 *1.25*
243 A51 $2 Pseudocaranx dentex 1.40 *2.75*
Nos. 231-243 (13) 7.50 9.00

See Nos. 295-296.

Constellations — A52

1984, May 14 Wmk. 373

244 A52 15c Crux Australis .20 .20
245 A52 20c Piscis Australis .25 .25
246 A52 70c Canis Minor .65 .65
247 A52 $1 Virgo .90 .90
Nos. 244-247 (4) 2.00 2.00

Souvenir Sheet

AUSIPEX '84 — A53

Longboats.

1984, Sept. 21 Litho. Wmk. 373

248 Sheet of 2 2.50 2.50
a. A53 50c multicolored .50 .50
b. A53 $2 multicolored 2.00 2.00

HMS Portland off Bounty Bay, by J. Linton Palmer, 1853 — A54

Paintings by J. Linton Palmer, 1853, and William Smyth, 1825: 9c, Christian's Look Out at Pitcairn Island. 35c, The Golden Age. $2, View of Village, by Smyth.

Wmk. 373

1985, Jan. 16 Litho. *Perf. 14*

249 A54 6c multicolored .20 .20
250 A54 9c multicolored .20 .20
251 A54 35c multicolored .50 .50

Size: 48x32mm

252 A54 $2 multicolored 2.00 2.00
Nos. 249-252 (4) 2.90 2.90

Copies of No. 252 with "1835" date were not issued. Value, $110.

See Nos. 291-294.

Queen Mother 85th Birthday
Common Design Type
Perf. 14½x14

1985, June 7 Litho. Wmk. 384

253 CD336 6c In Dundee, 1964 .20 .20
254 CD336 35c At 80th birthday celebration .30 .30
255 CD336 70c Queen Mother .50 .50
256 CD336 $1.20 Holding Prince Henry 1.00 1.00
Nos. 253-256 (4) 2.00 2.00

Souvenir Sheet

257 CD336 $2 In coach at the Races, Ascot 2.25 2.25

Act 6 — A55

Essi Gina A56

1985, Aug. 28 *Perf. 14½x14*

258 A55 50c shown .90 .90
259 A55 50c Columbus Louisiana .90 .90

Perf. 14

260 A56 50c shown .90 .90
261 A56 50c Stolt Spirit .90 .90
Nos. 258-261 (4) 3.60 3.60

See Nos. 281-284.

Christmas A57

Madonna & child paintings: 6c, by Raphael. 9c, by Krause. 35c, by Andreas Mayer. $2, by an unknown Austrian master.

1985, Nov. 26 *Perf. 14*

262 A57 6c multicolored .20 .20
263 A57 9c multicolored .20 .20
264 A57 35c multicolored .45 .45
265 A57 $2 multicolored 2.50 2.50
Nos. 262-265 (4) 3.35 3.35

Turtles A58

Designs: 9c, 20c, Chelonia mydas. 70c, $1.20, Eretmochelys imbricata.

Wmk. 384

1986, Feb. 12 Litho. *Perf. 14½*

266 A58 9c multicolored .65 .65
267 A58 20c multi, diff. 1.10 1.10
268 A58 70c multicolored 2.00 2.00
269 A58 $1.20 multi, diff. 2.25 2.25
Nos. 266-269 (4) 6.00 6.00

Queen Elizabeth II 60th Birthday
Common Design Type

Designs: 6c, In Royal Lodge garden, Windsor, 1946. 9c, Wedding of Princess Anne and Capt. Mark Philips, 1973. 20c, Wearing mantle and robes of Order of St. Paul's Cathedral, 1961. $1.20, Concert, Royal Festival Hall, London, 1971. $2, Visting Crown Agents' offices, 1983.

1986, Apr. 21 Litho. *Perf. 14½*

270 CD337 6c multi .20 .20
271 CD337 9c multi .20 .20
272 CD337 20c multi .20 .20
273 CD337 $1.20 multi 1.00 1.00
274 CD337 $2 multi 1.75 1.75
Nos. 270-274 (5) 3.35 3.35

Royal Wedding Issue, 1986
Common Design Type

Designs: 20c, Informal portrait. $1.20, Andrew aboard royal navy vessel.

Wmk. 384

1986, July 23 Litho. *Perf. 14*

275 CD338 20c multi .30 .30
276 CD338 $1.20 multi 2.00 2.00

7th Day Adventist Church, Cent. — A59

Designs: 6c, First church, 1886, and John I. Tay, missionary. 20c, Second church, 1907, and mission ship Pitcairn, 1890. 35c, Third church, 1945, baptism and Down Isaac. $2, Church, 1954, and sailing ship.

1986, Oct. 18

277 A59 6c multicolored .20 .20
278 A59 20c multicolored .45 .45
279 A59 35c multicolored .75 .75
280 A59 $2 multicolored 4.25 4.25
Nos. 277-280 (4) 5.65 5.65

Ship Type of 1985

1987, Jan. 20 *Perf. 14x14½*

281 A55 50c Brussel 1.10 1.10
282 A55 50c Samoan Reefer 1.10 1.10

Perf. 14

283 A56 50c Australian Exporter 1.10 1.10
284 A56 50c Taupo 1.10 1.10
Nos. 281-284 (4) 4.40 4.40

Island Houses — A60

1987, May 21 Wmk. 373 *Perf. 14*

285 A60 70c It greenish blue, bluish grn & blk .60 .60
286 A60 70c cream, yel bister & blk .60 .60
287 A60 70c It blue, brt blue & blk .60 .60
288 A60 70c It lil, brt vio & blk .60 .60
Nos. 285-288 (4) 2.40 2.40

Tree Type of 1983

1987, Aug. 10 Wmk. 384 *Perf. 14½*

289 Pair 1.00 1.00
a. A50 40c Leaves, blossoms .50 .50
b. A50 40c Monkey puzzle tree .50 .50
290 Pair 3.50 3.50
a. A50 $1.80 Leaves, blossoms, nuts 1.75 1.75
b. A50 $1.80 Duduinut tree 1.75 1.75

Art Type of 1985

Paintings by Lt. Conway Shipley, 1848: 20c, House and Tomb of John Adams. 40c, Bounty Bay, with H.M.S. Calypso. 90c, School House and Chapel. $1.80, Pitcairn Island with H.M.S. Calypso.

1987, Dec. 7 Litho. *Perf. 14*

291 A54 20c multi .40 .40
292 A54 40c multi .65 .65
293 A54 90c multi 1.10 1.10

Size: 48x32mm

294 A54 $1.80 multi 1.75 1.75
Nos. 291-294 (4) 3.90 3.90

Fish Type of 1984
Wmk. 384

1988, Jan. 14 Litho. *Perf. 14½*
295 A51 90c Variola louti 2.75 2.75
296 A51 $3 Gymnothorax eurostus 4.75 4.75

Souvenir Sheet

Australia Bicentennial — A61

1988, May 9 Wmk. 384 *Perf. 14*
297 A61 $3 HMS *Bounty* replica under sail 4.00 4.00

Visiting Ships A62

Wmk. 373

1988, Aug. 14 Litho. *Perf. 13½*
298 A62 5c HMS *Swallow,* 1767 .20 .20
299 A62 10c HMS *Pandora,* 1791 .20 .20
300 A62 15c HMS *Briton* and HMS *Tagus,* 1814 .20 .20
301 A62 20c HMS *Blossom,* 1825 .20 .20
a. Wmk. 384 1.25 *1.50*
b. Booklet pane of 4, #301a 4.50
302 A62 30c S.V. *Lucy Anne,* 1831 .30 .30
303 A62 35c S.V. *Charles Doggett,* 1831 .35 .35
304 A62 40c HMS *Fly,* 1838 .40 .40
305 A62 60c LMS *Camden,* 1840 .60 .60
306 A62 90c HMS *Virago,* 1853 .85 .85
a. Wmk. 384 1.25 *1.50*
b. Booklet pane of 4, #306a 4.50
307 A62 $1.20 S.S. *Rakaia,* 1867 1.15 1.15
308 A62 $1.80 HMS *Sappho,* 1882 1.75 1.75
309 A62 $5 HMS *Champion,* 1893 4.50 4.50
Nos. 298-309 (12) 10.70 10.70

20c, 90c exist dated "1990."
Issued: #301a-301b, 306a-306b, 5/3/90.

Constitution, 150th Anniv. — A63

Text and: 20c, Raising the Union Jack. 40c, Signing of the constitution aboard the H.M.S. "Fly," 1838. $1.05, Suffrage. $1.80, Equal education.

1988, Nov. 30 Wmk. 373 *Perf. 14*
315 A63 20c multicolored .25 .25
316 A63 40c multicolored .40 .40
317 A63 $1.05 multicolored 1.00 1.00
318 A63 $1.80 multicolored 1.60 1.60
Nos. 315-318 (4) 3.25 3.25

Christmas A64

a, Angel, animals in stable. b, Holy Family. c, Two Magi. d, Magus and shepherd boy.

1988, Nov. 30 Wmk. 384 *Perf. 14*
319 Strip of 4 4.00 4.00
a.-d. A64 90c any single 1.00 1.00

Miniature Sheets

Pitcairn Isls., Bicent. A65

No. 320 (*Bounty* sets sail for the South Seas, Dec. 23, 1787): a, Fitting out the *Bounty* at Deptford. b, *Bounty* leaving Spithead. c, *Bounty* trying to round Cape Horn. d, Anchored in Adventure Bay, Tasmania. e, Ship's mates collecting breadfruit. f, Breadfruit in great cabin.

No. 321 (the mutiny, Apr. 28, 1789): a, *Bounty* leaving Matavai Bay. b, Mutineers waking Capt. Bligh. c, Confrontation between Fletcher Christian and Bligh. d, Bligh and crew members set adrift in an open boat. e, Castaways. f, Throwing breadfruit overboard.

No. 322: a, like No. 321e. b, Isle of Man #393. c, Norfolk Is. #453.

1989 Litho. Wmk. 373
320 Sheet of 6 4.50 4.50
a.-f. A65 20c any single .50 .50
321 Sheet of 6 12.00 12.00
a.-f. A65 90c any single 1.50 1.50

Souvenir Sheet
Wmk. 384
322 Sheet of 3 + label 4.50 4.50
a.-c. A65 90c any single 1.50 1.50

See #331, Isle of Man #389-394 and Norfolk Is. #452-456.
Issued: #320, Feb. 22; #321-322, Apr. 28.
Difference between #. 321e and 322a is inscription at bottom of #322a: "C. Abbott 1989 BOT."

Aircraft A66

Wmk. 384

1989, July 25 Litho. *Perf. 14½*
323 A66 20c RNZAF Orion .25 .25
324 A66 80c Beechcraft Queen Air 1.25 1.25
325 A66 $1.05 Navy helicopter, USS *Breton* 1.75 1.75
326 A66 $1.30 RNZAF Hercules 2.25 2.25
Nos. 323-326 (4) 5.50 5.50

Second mail drop on Pitcairn, Mar. 21, 1985 (20c); photo mission from Tahiti, Jan. 14, 1983 (80c); diesel fuel delivery by the navy, Feb. 12, 1969 ($1.05); and parachute delivery of a bulldozer, May 31, 1983 ($1.30).

The Islands A67

Wmk. 373

1989, Oct. 23 Litho. *Perf. 14*
327 A67 15c Ducie Is. .25 .25
328 A67 90c Henderson Is. 1.00 1.00
329 A67 $1.05 Oeno Is. 1.25 1.25
330 A67 $1.30 Pitcairn Is. 1.75 1.75
Nos. 327-330 (4) 4.25 4.25

Bicentennial Type of 1989
Miniature Sheet

Designs: a, Mutineers aboard *Bounty* anticipating landing on Pitcairn. b, Landing. c, Exploration of the island. d, Carrying goods ashore. e, Burning the *Bounty.* f, Settlement.

1990, Jan. 15 Wmk. 384 *Perf. 14*
331 Sheet of 6 + 3 labels 5.50 5.50
a.-f. A65 40c any single .70 .70

Stamp World London '90 — A68

Links with the UK: 80c, Peter Heywood and Ennerdale, Cumbria. 90c, John Adams and The Tower of St. Augustine, Hackney. $1.05, William Bligh and The Citadel Gateway, Plymouth. $1.30, Fletcher Christian and birthplace, Cockermouth.

1990, May 3 Wmk. 373 *Perf. 14*
332 A68 80c multicolored .80 .80
333 A68 90c multicolored .95 .95
334 A68 $1.05 multicolored 1.10 1.10
335 A68 $1.30 multicolored 1.40 1.40
Nos. 332-335 (4) 4.25 4.25

Queen Mother 90th Birthday
Common Design Types

1990, Aug. 4 Wmk. 384 *Perf. 14x15*
336 CD343 40c Portrait, 1937 .50 .50

Perf. 14½
337 CD344 $3 King, Queen in carriage 3.25 3.25

First Pitcairn Island Postage Stamps, 50th Anniv — A69

Historical items and Pitcairn Islands stamps.

Perf. 13½x14
1990, Oct. 15 Wmk. 373
338 A69 20c Chronometer, #2 .25 .25
339 A69 80c Bounty's Bible, #31 1.00 1.00
340 A69 90c Bounty's Bell, #108 1.25 1.25
341 A69 $1.05 Bounty, #172 1.50 1.50
342 A69 $1.30 Penny Black, #300 2.00 2.00
Nos. 338-342 (5) 6.00 6.00

Birds — A70

1990, Dec. 5 Wmk. 373 *Perf. 14*
343 A70 20c Redbreast .25 .25
344 A70 90c Wood pigeon 1.25 1.25
345 A70 $1.30 Sparrow 1.75 1.75
346 A70 $1.80 Flightless chicken 2.50 2.50
Nos. 343-346 (4) 5.75 5.75

Birdpex '90, 20th Intl. Ornithological Congress, New Zealand.

Miniature Sheet

Pitcairn Islands, Bicent. A71

Bicentennial celebrations: a, Re-enacting the landing. b, Commemorative plaque. c, Memorial church service. d, Cricket match. e, Bounty model burning. f, Fireworks.

Wmk. 384

1991, Mar. 24 Litho. *Perf. 14½*
347 A71 80c Sheet of 6, #a.-f. 10.00 10.00

Elizabeth & Philip, Birthdays
Common Design Types
Wmk. 384

1991, July 12 Litho. *Perf. 14½*
348 CD346 20c multicolored .25 .25
349 CD345 $1.30 multicolored 2.00 2.00
a. Pair, #348-349 + label 2.25 2.25

Cruise Ships A72

1991, June 17
350 A72 15c Europa .25 .25
351 A72 80c Royal Viking Star 1.25 1.25
352 A72 $1.30 World Discoverer 2.10 2.10
353 A72 $1.80 Sagafjord 3.00 3.00
Nos. 350-353 (4) 6.60 6.60

Island Vehicles A73

1991, Sept. 25 Wmk. 373 *Perf. 14*
354 A73 20c Bulldozer .40 .40
355 A73 80c Motorcycle 1.10 1.10
356 A73 $1.30 Tractor 1.10 1.10
357 A73 $1.80 All-terrain vehicle 1.90 1.90
Nos. 354-357 (4) 4.50 4.50

Christmas — A74

1991, Nov. 18 *Perf. 14x14½*
358 A74 20c The Annunciation .25 .25
359 A74 80c Shepherds .90 .90
360 A74 $1.30 Nativity scene 1.40 1.40
361 A74 $1.80 Three wise men 1.90 1.90
Nos. 358-361 (4) 4.45 4.45

Queen Elizabeth II's Accession to the Throne, 40th Anniv.
Common Design Type
Wmk. 384

1992, Feb. 6 Litho. *Perf. 14*
362 CD349 20c multicolored .25 .25
363 CD349 60c multicolored .75 .75
364 CD349 90c multicolored 1.00 1.00
365 CD349 $1 multicolored 1.00 1.00

Wmk. 373
366 CD349 $1.80 multicolored 1.75 1.75
Nos. 362-366 (5) 4.75 4.75

Sharks — A75

Designs: 20c, Carcharhinus galapagensis. $1, Eugomphodus taurus. $1.50, Carcharhinus melanopterus. $1.80, Carcharhinus amblyrhynchos.

Perf. 15x14½

1992, June 30 Litho. Wmk. 373

367	A75	20c multicolored	.25	.25
368	A75	$1 multicolored	1.25	1.25
369	A75	$1.50 multicolored	1.75	1.75
370	A75	$1.80 multicolored	2.50	2.50
		Nos. 367-370 (4)	5.75	5.75

Sir Peter Scott Commemorative Expedition to Pitcairn Islands, 1991-92 — A76

Designs: 20c, Montastrea, acropora coral sticks. $1, Henderson sandalwood. $1.50, Murphy's petrel. $1.80, Henderson hawkmoth.

Perf. 14x15

1992, Sept. 11 Litho. Wmk. 373

371	A76	20c multicolored	.25	.25
372	A76	$1 multicolored	1.25	1.25
373	A76	$1.50 multicolored	1.75	1.75
374	A76	$1.80 multicolored	2.50	2.50
		Nos. 371-374 (4)	5.75	5.75

Captain William Bligh, 175th Anniv. of Death A77

20c, Bligh's birthplace, St. Tudy, Cornwall, HMS Resolution. $1, On deck of HMAV Bounty, breadfruit plant. $1.50, Voyage in open boat, Bligh's answers at court martial. $1.80, Portrait by Rachel H. Combe, Battle of Camperdown, 1797.

Wmk. 373

1992, Dec. 7 Litho. *Perf. 14½*

375	A77	20c multicolored	.25	.25
376	A77	$1 multicolored	1.25	1.25
377	A77	$1.50 multicolored	1.75	1.75
378	A77	$1.80 multicolored	2.00	2.00
		Nos. 375-378 (4)	5.25	5.25

Royal Naval Vessels A78

Wmk. 384

1993, Mar. 10 Litho. *Perf. 14*

379	A78	15c HMS Chichester	.20	.20
380	A78	20c HMS Jaguar	.30	.30
381	A78	$1.80 HMS Andrew	2.75	2.75
382	A78	$3 HMS Warrior	4.50	4.50
		Nos. 379-382 (4)	7.75	7.75

Coronation of Queen Elizabeth II, 40th Anniv. A79

Wmk. 373

1993, June 17 Litho. *Perf. 13*

383	A79	$5 multicolored	7.00	7.00

Scenic Views A80

10c, Pawala Valley Ridge. 90c, St. Pauls. $1.20, Matt's Rocks from Water Valley. $1.50, Ridge Rope to St. Paul's Pool. $1.80, Ship Landing Point.

Wmk. 373

1993, Sept. 8 Litho. *Perf. 14*

384	A80	10c multicolored	.20	.20
385	A80	90c multicolored	.95	.95
386	A80	$1.20 multicolored	1.25	1.25
387	A80	$1.50 multicolored	1.50	1.50
388	A80	$1.80 multicolored	1.90	1.90
		Nos. 384-388 (5)	5.80	5.80

Lizards A81

Designs: 20c, Indopacific tree gecko. No. 390, Stump-toed gecko. No. 391, Mourning gecko. $1, Moth skink No. 393, Snake-eyed skink. No. 394, White-bellied skink.

Perf. 13x13½

1993, Dec. 14 Litho. Wmk. 373

389	A81	20c multicolored	.25	.25
390	A81	45c multicolored	.50	.50
391	A81	45c multicolored	.50	.50
	a.	Pair, #390-391	1.00	1.00
392	A81	$1 multicolored	1.10	1.10
393	A81	$1.50 multicolored	1.75	1.75
394	A81	$1.50 multicolored	1.75	1.75
	a.	Pair, #393-394	3.50	3.50
		Nos. 389-394 (6)	5.85	5.85

Nos. 390-391, 393-394 Ovptd. with Hong Kong '94 Emblem

Perf. 13x13½

1994, Feb. 18 Litho. Wmk. 373

395	A81	45c on #390	.75	.75
396	A81	45c on #391	.75	.75
	a.	Pair, #395-396	1.50	1.50
397	A81	$1.50 on #393	2.75	2.75
398	A81	$1.50 on #394	2.75	2.75
	a.	Pair, #397-398	5.50	5.50
		Nos. 395-398 (4)	7.00	7.00

Early Pitcairners — A82

Designs: 5c, Friday October Christian. 20c, Moses Young. $1.80, James Russell McCoy. $3, Rosalind Amelia Young.

1994, Mar. 7 *Perf. 14*

399	A82	5c multicolored	.20	.20
400	A82	20c multicolored	.25	.25
401	A82	$1.80 multicolored	2.00	2.00
402	A82	$3 multicolored	3.25	3.25
		Nos. 399-402 (4)	5.70	5.70

Shipwrecks A83

20c, Wildwave, Oeno Island, 1858. 90c, Cornwallis, Pitcairn Island, 1875. $1.80, Acadia, Ducie Island, 1881. $3, Oregon, Oeno Island, 1883.

Wmk. 373

1994, June 22 Litho. *Perf. 14*

403	A83	20c multicolored	.25	.25
404	A83	90c multicolored	1.00	1.00
405	A83	$1.80 multicolored	2.00	2.00
406	A83	$3 multicolored	3.50	3.50
		Nos. 403-406 (4)	6.75	6.75

Corals A84

Designs: 20c, Fire coral, vert. 90c, Cauliflower coral, arc-eye hawkfish. $1, Snubnose chub, lobe coral, vert.

$3, Coral garden, butterflyfish, vert.

Wmk. 373

1994, Sept. 15 Litho. *Perf. 14*

407	A84	20c multicolored	.25	.25
408	A84	90c multicolored	1.10	1.10
409	A84	$1 multicolored	1.25	1.25
		Nos. 407-409 (3)	2.60	2.60

Souvenir Sheet

410	A84	$3 multicolored	3.75	3.75

Christmas A85

Flowers: 20c, Morning glory. 90c, Hibiscus, vert. $1, Frangipani. $3, Ginsey, vert.

Wmk. 373

1994, Nov. 24 Litho. *Perf. 14*

411	A85	20c multicolored	.25	.25
412	A85	90c multicolored	1.10	1.10
413	A85	$1 multicolored	1.25	1.25
414	A85	$3 multicolored	3.75	3.75
		Nos. 411-414 (4)	6.35	6.35

Birds A86

Designs: 5c, Fairy tern. 10c, Red-tailed tropicbird chick, vert. 15c, Henderson rail. 20c, Red-footed booby, vert. 45c, Blue-gray noddy. 50c, Henderson reed warbler. 90c, Common noddy. $1, Masked booby, chick, vert. $1.80, Henderson fruit dove. $2, Murphy's petrel. $3, Christmas shearwater. $5, Red-tailed tropicbird juvenile.

1995, Mar. 8 *Perf. 13½*

415	A86	5c multicolored	.20	.20
416	A86	10c multicolored	.20	.20
417	A86	15c multicolored	.20	.20
418	A86	20c multicolored	.25	.25
419	A86	45c multicolored	.55	.55
420	A86	50c multicolored	.60	.60
421	A86	90c multicolored	1.10	1.10
422	A86	$1 multicolored	1.25	1.25
423	A86	$1.80 multicolored	2.25	2.25
424	A86	$2 multicolored	2.50	2.50
425	A86	$3 multicolored	3.75	3.75
426	A86	$5 multicolored	6.25	6.25
		Nos. 415-426 (12)	19.10	19.10

Oeno Island Vacation — A87

Designs: 20c, Boating. 90c, Volleyball on the beach. $1.80, Picnic. $3, Sing-a-long.

1995, June 26 *Perf. 14x15*

427	A87	20c multicolored	.25	.25
428	A87	90c multicolored	1.25	1.25
429	A87	$1.80 multicolored	2.50	2.50
430	A87	$3 multicolored	4.00	4.00
		Nos. 427-430 (4)	8.00	8.00

Souvenir Sheet

Queen Mother, 95th Birthday — A88

1995, Aug. 4 *Perf. 14½*

431	A88	$5 multicolored	6.75	6.75

Radio, Cent. — A89

Designs: 20c, Guglielmo Marconi, radio equipment, 1901. $1, Man, Pitcairn radio, 1938. $1.50, Woman, satellite earth station equipment, 1994. $3, Satellite in orbit, 1992.

1995, Sept. 5 *Perf. 13*

432	A89	20c multicolored	.25	.25
433	A89	$1 multicolored	1.25	1.25
434	A89	$1.50 multicolored	2.00	2.00
435	A89	$3 multicolored	4.00	4.00
		Nos. 432-435 (4)	7.50	7.50

UN, 50th Anniv.

Common Design Type

Designs: 20c, Lord Mayor's Show. $1, RFA Brambleleaf. $1.50, UN ambulance. $3, Royal Air Force Tristar.

Wmk. 373

1995, Oct. 24 Litho. *Perf. 14*

436	CD353	20c multicolored	.25	.25
437	CD353	$1 multicolored	1.25	1.25
438	CD353	$1.50 multicolored	2.00	2.00
439	CD353	$3 multicolored	4.00	4.00
		Nos. 436-439 (4)	7.50	7.50

Supply Ship Day — A90

1996, Jan. 30 ***Perf. 14x14½***

440 A90 20c Early morning .30 .30
441 A90 40c Meeting ship .55 .55
442 A90 90c Unloading supplies 1.20 1.20
443 A90 $1 Landing work 1.30 1.30
444 A90 $1.50 Supply sorting 2.00 2.00
445 A90 $1.80 Last load 2.40 2.40
Nos. 440-445 (6) 7.75 7.75

Queen Elizabeth II, 70th Birthday
Common Design Type

Various portraits of Queen, scenes from Pitcairn Islands: 20c, Bounty Bay. 90c, Jetty, Landing Point, Bounty Bay. $1.80, Matt's Rocks. $3, St. Paul's.

1996, Apr. 21 ***Perf. 13½x14***

446 CD354 20c multicolored .30 .30
447 CD354 90c multicolored 1.25 1.25
448 CD354 $1.80 multicolored 2.50 2.50
449 CD354 $3 multicolored 4.25 4.25
Nos. 446-449 (4) 8.30 8.30

CHINA '96, 9th Asian Intl. Philatelic Exhibition — A91

#450, Chinese junk. #451, HMAV Bounty. No. 452: a, Chinese rat. b, Polynesian rat.

1996, May 17 ***Perf. 14***

450 A91 $1.80 multicolored 2.50 2.50
451 A91 $1.80 multicolored 2.50 2.50

Souvenir Sheet

452 A91 90c Sheet of 2, #a.-b. 2.50 2.50

Amateur Radio — A92

Designs: 20c, Call signs of members in Amateur Radio Operator's Club, 1996. No. 454, VR6 1M calling for medical assistance. No. 455, Operator receiving transmission, physician standing by. $2.50, Andrew Young, Pitcairn's first operator, 1938.

1996, Sept. 4 **Wmk. 384** ***Perf. 14***

453 A92 20c multicolored .30 .30
454 A92 $1.50 multicolored 2.10 2.10
455 A92 $1.50 multicolored 2.10 2.10
a. Pair, #454-455 4.25 4.25
456 A92 $2.50 multicolored 3.50 3.50
Nos. 453-456 (4) 8.00 8.00

Birds A93

World Wildlife Fund: 5c, Henderson Island reed-warbler, vert. 10c, Stephen's lorikeet, vert. 20c, Henderson Island rail, vert. 90c, Henderson Island fruit-dove, vert. No. 461, Masked booby. No. 462, Common fairy-tern.

1996, Nov. 20 **Wmk. 373**

457 A93 5c multicolored .20 .20
458 A93 10c multicolored .20 .20
459 A93 20c multicolored .30 .30
460 A93 90c multicolored 1.25 1.25
461 A93 $2 multicolored 2.75 2.75
462 A93 $2 multicolored 2.75 2.75
Nos. 457-462 (6) 7.45 7.45

Souvenir Sheet

Coat of Arms — A94

Illustration reduced.

1997, Feb. 12 ***Perf. 14½x14***

463 A94 $5 multicolored 7.00 7.00

Hong Kong '97.

South Pacific Commission, 50th Anniv. — A95

a, MV David Baker. b, MV McLachlan.

Perf. 13½x14

1997, May 26 **Litho.** **Wmk. 373**

464 A95 $2.50 Sheet of 2, #a.-b. 7.00 7.00

Health Care A96

Designs: 20c, New Health Center. $1, Resident nurse treating patient. $1.70, Dental officer treating patient. $3, Patient being taken aboard ship.

Wmk. 373

1997, Sept. 12 **Litho.** ***Perf. 14***

465 A96 20c multicolored .25 .25
466 A96 $1 multicolored 1.25 1.25
467 A96 $1.70 multicolored 2.10 2.10
468 A96 $3 multicolored 3.75 3.75
Nos. 465-468 (4) 7.35 7.35

Queen Elizabeth II and Prince Philip, 50th Wedding Anniv. — A97

Designs: No. 469, Prince driving team of horses. No. 470, Queen wearing wide-brimmed hat. No. 471, Prince in formal riding attire. No. 472, Queen, horse. No. 473, Queen and Prince standing behind flowers. No. 474, Prince Charles riding horse.

Wmk. 373

1997, Nov. 20 **Litho.** ***Perf. 13***

469 20c multicolored .25 .25
470 20c multicolored .25 .25
a. A97 Pair, #469-470 .50 .50
471 $1 multicolored 1.25 1.25
472 $1 multicolored 1.25 1.25
a. A97 Pair, #471-472 2.50 2.50
473 $1.70 multicolored 2.10 2.10
474 $1.70 multicolored 2.10 2.10
a. A97 Pair, #473-474 4.25 4.25
Nos. 469-474 (6) 7.20 7.20

Christmas A98

Flower, picture: 20c, Gardenia taitensis, view of Island at night. 80c, Bauhinia variegata, ringing public bell. $1.20, Metrosideros collina, children's baskets hanging on line. $3, Hibiscus tiliaceus, Pitcairn Church, Square at Adamstown.

Wmk. 373

1997, Dec. 1 **Litho.** ***Perf. 13½***

475 A98 20c multicolored .25 .25
476 A98 80c multicolored .95 .95
477 A98 $1.20 multicolored 1.40 1.40
478 A98 $3 multicolored 3.50 3.50
Nos. 475-478 (4) 6.10 6.10

Views of Christian's Cave — A99

5c, Dorcas Apple, looking across Adamstown. 20c, Rocks near Betty's Edge looking past Tatinanny. 35c, Cave mouth. $5, Cave from road near where Fletcher Christian built home.

Wmk. 384

1998, Feb. 9 **Litho.** ***Perf. 13½***

479 A99 5c multi .20 .20
480 A99 20c multi .25 .25
481 A99 35c multi, vert. .40 .40
482 A99 $5 multi, vert. 5.75 5.75
Nos. 479-482 (4) 6.60 6.60

Sailing Ships A100

Designs: 20c, HMS Bounty, 1790. 90c, HMS Swallow, 1767. $1.80, HMS Briton & HMS Tagus, 1814. $3, HMS Fly, 1838.

Perf. 14½x14

1998, May 28 **Litho.** **Wmk. 373**

483 A100 20c multicolored .20 .20
484 A100 90c multicolored .95 .95
485 A100 $1.80 multicolored 1.90 1.90
486 A100 $3 multicolored 3.20 3.20
Nos. 483-486 (4) 6.25 6.25

Diana, Princess of Wales (1961-97)
Common Design Type of 1998

a, In evening dress. b, Wearing white hat, pearls. c, In houndstooth top. d, Wearing white hat, top.

Perf. 14½x14

1998, Aug. 31 **Litho.** **Wmk. 373**

487 CD355 90c Sheet of 4, #a.-d. 4.75 4.75

No. 487 sold for $3.60 + 40c with surtax being donated to the Princess Diana Memorial Fund.

Flowers A101

20c, Bidens mathewsii. 90c, Hibiscus. $1.80, Osteomeles anthyllidifolia. $3, Ipomoea littoralis.

Wmk. 373

1998, Oct. 20 **Litho.** ***Perf. 14***

488 A101 20c multicolored .20 .20
489 A101 90c multicolored .95 .95
490 A101 $1.80 multicolored 1.90 1.90
491 A101 $3 multicolored 3.25 3.25
Nos. 488-491 (4) 6.30 6.30

Flowers are below inscriptions on Nos. 489, 491.

Intl. Year of the Ocean A102

Designs: 20c, Fishing. 90c, Divers, vert. $1.80, Reef fish. $3, Murphy's petrel, vert.

Unwmk.

1998, Dec. 16 **Litho.** ***Perf. 14***

492 A102 20c multicolored .20 .20
493 A102 90c multicolored 1.00 1.00
494 A102 $1.80 multicolored 1.90 1.90
495 A102 $3 multicolored 3.25 3.25
a. Souv. sheet of 4, #492-495 + label 6.50 6.50
Nos. 492-495 (4) 6.35 6.35

Government Education on Pitcairn, 50th Anniv. — A103

Scenes on pages of books: 20c, Schoolmaster George Hunn Nobbs, students, 1828. 90c, Schoolmaster Simon Young, daughter Rosalind, teacher Hattie Andre, 1893. $1.80, Teacher Roy Clark, 1932. $3, Modern school at Palau, 1999.

Unwmk.

1999, Feb. 15 **Litho.** ***Perf. 14***

496 A103 20c multicolored .20 .20
497 A103 90c multicolored .95 .95
498 A103 $1.80 multicolored 1.90 1.90
499 A103 $3 multicolored 3.25 3.25
Nos. 496-499 (4) 6.30 6.30

Archaeological Expedition to Survey Wreck of the Bounty — A104

Scenes of ship during last voyage and: a, 50c, Anchor. b, $1, Cannon. c, $1.50, Chronometer. d, $2, Copper caldron.

1999, Mar. 19

500 A104 Sheet of 4, #a.-d. 5.25 5.25

19th Cent. Pitcairn Island A105

Designs: 20c, John Adams (d. 1829), Bounty Bay. 90c, Topaz, 1808. $1.80, George Hunn Nobbs, Norfolk Island. $3, HMS Champion, 1893.

Perf. 14½x14

1999, May 25 Litho. Wmk. 373

501 A105	20c multicolored	.20	.20
502 A105	90c multicolored	1.00	1.00
503 A105	$1.80 multicolored	2.00	2.00
504 A105	$3 multicolored	3.25	3.25
	Nos. 501-504 (4)	6.45	6.45

Wedding of Prince Edward and Sophie Rhys-Jones

Common Design Type

Perf. 13¾x14

1999, June 18 Litho. Wmk. 384

505 CD356	$2.50 Separate portraits	2.75	2.75
506 CD356	$2.50 Couple	2.75	2.75

Honey Bees A106

Designs: 20c, Beekeepers, hives. $1, Bee, white and purple flower. $1.80, Bees, honeycomb. $3, Bee on flower, honey jar.

Die Cut Perf. 9

1999, Sept. 12 Litho.

Self-Adhesive

507 A106	20c multicolored	.20	.20
508 A106	$1 multicolored	1.00	1.00
a.	Souvenir sheet of 1	1.00	1.00
509 A106	$1.80 multicolored	1.90	1.90
510 A106	$3 multicolored	3.00	3.00
	Nos. 507-510 (4)	6.10	6.10

China 1999 World Philatelic Exhibition, No. 508a. Issued 8/21.

Protection of Galapagos Tortoise "Mr. Turpen" A107

Designs: a, 5c, Arrival of the ship Yankee, 1937. b, 20c, Off-loading Mr. Turpen to a longboat. c, 35c, Mr. Turpen. d, $5, Close-up of tortoise's head.

Perf. 14¼

2000, Jan. 14 Litho. Unwmk.

511 A107	Strip of 4, #a.-d., + label	5.50	5.50

Flowers A108

Designs: 10c, Guettarda speciosa. 15c, Hibiscus tiliaceus. 20c, Selenicereus grandiflorus. 30c, Metrosideros collina. 50c, Alpinia zerumbet. $1, Syzygium jambos. $1.50, Commelina diffusa. $1.80, Canna indica. $2, Allamanda cathartica. $3, Calophyllum inophyllum. $5, Ipomea indica. $10, Bauhinia monandra (40x40mm).

Litho., Litho. with Foil Application ($10)

Perf. 13¾x13¼, 13¼x13¾ ($10)

2000, May 22 Unwmk.

512-523 A108	Set of 12	21.00	21.00
520a	Souvenir sheet, #518, 520	3.00	3.00

The Stamp Show 2000, London (No. 520a).

Millennium — A109

Old and modern pictures: 20c, Longboat at sea. 90c, Landing and longboat house. $1.80, Transportation of crops. $3, Communications.

Wmk. 373

2000, June 28 Litho. *Perf. 13¾*

524-527 A109	Set of 4	5.00	5.00

Souvenir Sheets

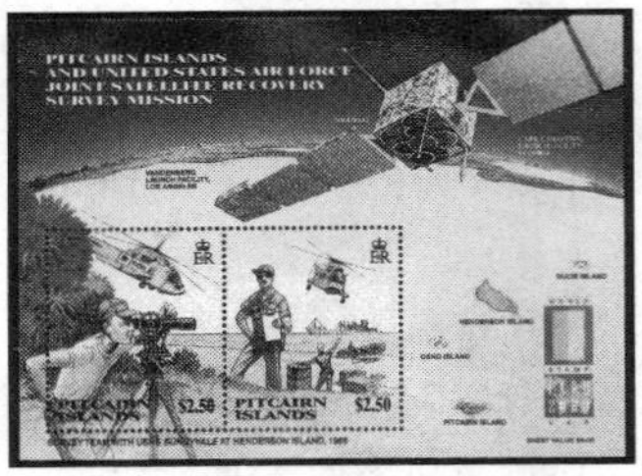

Satellite Recovery Mission — A110

No. 528: a, Surveryor, helicopter. b, Military personnel, boat, ship, helicopter.
Illustration reduced.

2000, July 7 Unwmk. *Perf. 14¼*

528 A110	$2.50 Sheet of 2, #a-b	4.25	4.25

World Stamp Expo 2000, Anaheim.
Illustration shows lower half of the entire sheet. The upper half, which has descriptive text, and is printed on the reverse, is the same size as the lower half. The entire sheet is folded where the halves meet.

Queen Mother, 100th Birthday — A111

No. 529: a, $2, Blue hat. b, $3, Maroon hat.
Illustration reduced.

2000, Aug. 4 *Perf. 14*

529 A111	Sheet of 2, #a-b	4.25	4.25

Christmas A112

Perf. 14½

2000, Nov. 22 Litho. Unwmk.

530	Strip of 4	5.00	5.00
a.	A112 20c Woman	.20	.20
b.	A112 80c Man, boy	.70	.70
c.	A112 $1.50 Woman, child	1.40	1.40
d.	A112 $3 Three children	2.75	2.75

Cruise Ships A113

Designs: No. 531, $1.50, Bremen. No. 532, $1.50, MV Europa. No. 533, $1.50, MS Rotterdam. No. 534, $1.50, Saga Rose.

Perf. 14¾

2001, Feb. 1 Litho. Unwmk.

531-534 A113	Set of 4	5.00	5.00

Values are for copies with surrounding selvage.

Tropical Fruit — A114

Designs: 20c, Cocos nucifera. 80c, Punica granatum. $1, Passiflora edulis. $3, Ananas comosus.

2001, Apr. 6 Litho. *Perf. 13½x13¼*

535-538 A114	Set of 4	4.00	4.00
538a	Souvenir sheet, #536, 538	3.00	3.00

Allocation of ".pn" Internet Domain Suffix — A115

CD and: 20c, Computer keyboard. 50c, Circuit board. $1, Integrated circuit. $5, Mouse.

2001, June 11 *Serpentine Die Cut*

Self-Adhesive

539-542 A115	Set of 4	5.50	5.50

Tropical Fish — A116

Designs: 20c, Chaetodon ornatissimus. 80c, Chaetodon reticulatus. $1.50, Chaetodon lunula. $2, Henochus chrysostomus.

Perf. 13x13¼

2001, Sept. 4 Litho. Unwmk.

543-546 A116	Set of 4	4.00	4.00
546a	Souvenir sheet, #543, 546	1.90	1.90

Wood Carving — A117

No. 547: a, 20c, Miro flower, man on beach carrying log. b, 50c, Toa flower, artisans carving fish. c, $1.50, Pulau flower, man using machine, woman looking at carved objects. d, $3, Ship, boat, carved objects.

2001, Oct. 11

547 A117	Horiz. strip of 4, #a-d, + central label	4.50	4.50

Cowrie Shells A118

Designs: 20c, Cypraea argus. 80c, Cypraea isabella. $1, Cypraea mappa. $3, Cypraea mauritana.

2001, Dec. 6 *Perf. 13¼x13*

548-551 A118	Set of 4	4.25	4.25

Reign Of Queen Elizabeth II, 50th Anniv. Issue

Common Design Type

Souvenir Sheet

No. 552: a, 50c, With Queen Mother and Princess Margaret. b, $1, Wearing tiara. c, $1.20, Without hat. d, $1.50, Wearing hat. e, $2, 1955 portrait by Annigoni (38x50mm).

Perf. 14¼x14½, 13¾ (#552e)

2002, Feb. 6 Litho. Wmk. 373

552 CD360	Sheet of 5, #a-e	5.25	5.25

POLAND

'pō-lənd

LOCATION — Europe between Russia and Germany
GOVT. — Republic
AREA — 120,628 sq. mi.
POP. — 38,608,929 (1999 est.)
CAPITAL — Warsaw

100 Kopecks = 1 Ruble
100 Fenigi = 1 Marka (1918)
100 Halerzy = 1 Korona (1918)
100 Groszy = 1 Zloty (1924)

Catalogue values for unused stamps in this country are for Never Hinged items, beginning with Scott 534 in the regular postage section, Scott B63 in the semi-postal section, Scott C28 in the airpost section, Scott CB1 in the airpost semi-postal section, and Scott J146 in the postage due section.

Watermarks

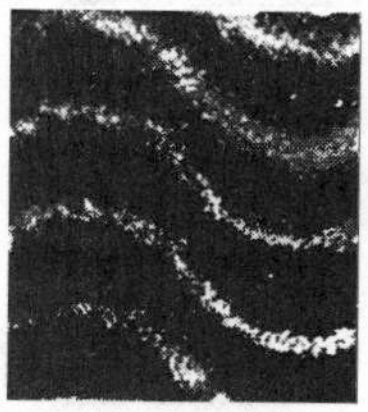

Wmk. 145- Wavy Lines

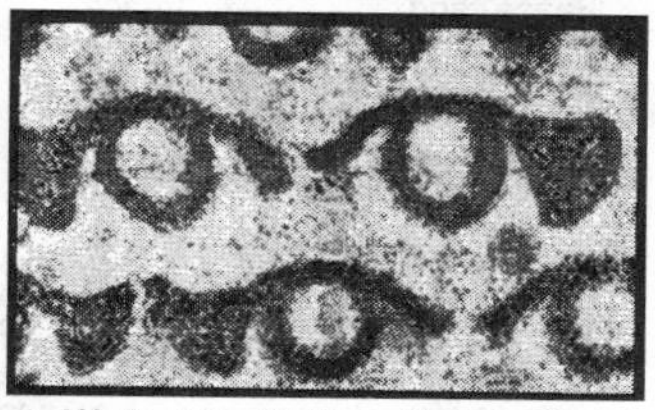

Wmk. 234- Multiple Post Horns

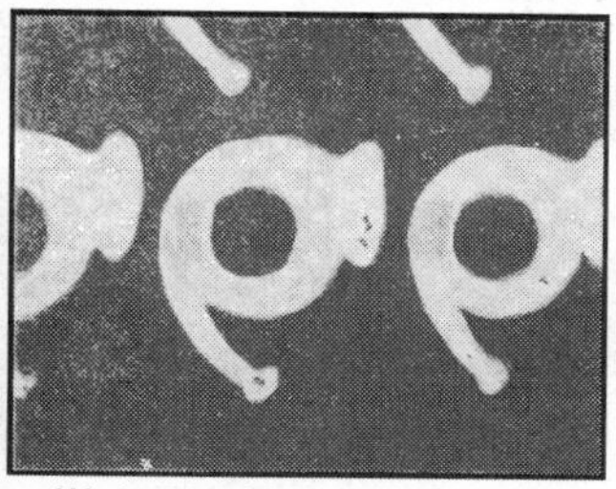

Wmk. 326- Multiple Post Horns

Issued under Russian Dominion

Coat of Arms — A1

Perf. 11½ to 12½

1860 Typo. Unwmk.

1	A1 10k blue & rose	800.	200.
a.	10k blue & carmine	950.	275.
b.	10k dark blue & rose	950.	275.
c.	Added blue frame for inner oval	1,400.	475.
d.	Imperf.		

Used for letters within the Polish territory and to Russia. Postage on all foreign letters was paid in cash.

These stamps were superseded by those of Russia in 1865.

Counterfeits exist.

Issues of the Republic

Local issues were made in various Polish cities during the German occupation.

In the early months of the Republic many issues were made by overprinting the German occupation stamps with the words "Poczta Polska" and an eagle or bars often with the name of the city.

These issues were not authorized by the Government but were made by the local authorities and restricted to local use. In 1914 two stamps were issued for the Polish Legion and in 1918 the Polish Expeditionary Force used surcharged Russian stamps. The regularity of these issues is questioned.

Numerous counterfeits of these issues abound.

Warsaw Issues

Statue of Sigismund III — A2

Coat of Arms of Warsaw — A3

Polish Eagle A4

Sobieski Monument A5

Stamps of the Warsaw Local Post Surcharged

1918, Nov. 17 Wmk. 145 *Perf. 11½*

11	A2 5f on 2gr brn & buff	1.25	.80
a.	Inverted surcharge	37.50	32.50
12	A3 10f on 6gr grn & buff	1.25	.75
a.	Inverted surcharge	4.50	4.00
13	A4 25f on 10gr rose & buff	2.75	1.60
a.	Inverted surcharge	9.00	8.00
14	A5 50f on 20gr bl & buff	7.75	4.75
a.	Inverted surcharge	130.00	100.00
	Nos. 11-14 (4)	13.00	7.90

Counterfeits exist.

Occupation Stamps Nos. N6-N16 Overprinted or Surcharged:

a

b

1918-19 Wmk. 125 *Perf. 14, 14½*

15	A16 3pf brown ('19)	19.00	12.00
16	A22 5pf on 2½pf gray	.30	.30
17	A16 5pf on 3pf brown	3.50	2.25
18	A16 5pf green	.65	.50
19	A16 10pf carmine	.20	.20
20	A22 15pf dark violet	.20	.20
21	A16 20pf blue	.20	.20
a.	20pf ultramarine	700.00	1,500.
23	A22 25pf on 7½pf org	.30	.20
24	A16 30pf org & blk, *buff*	.20	.20
25	A16 40pf lake & black	.45	.45
26	A16 60pf magenta	.65	.65
	Nos. 15-26 (11)	25.65	17.15

There are two settings of this overprint. The first printing, issued Dec. 5, 1918, has space of 3½mm between the middle two bars. The second printing, issued Jan. 15, 1919, has space of 4mm. No. 15 comes only in the second setting; all others in both. The German overprint on No. 21a is very glossy.

Varieties of this overprint and surcharge are numerous: double; inverted; misspellings (Pocata, Poczto, Pelska); letters omitted, inverted or wrong font; 3 bars instead of 4, etc.

No. 21a requires competent expertization. A number of shades of the blue No. 21 exist. Counterfeits exist.

Lublin Issue

Austrian Military Semi-Postal Stamps of 1918 Overprinted

1918, Dec. 5 Unwmk. *Perf. 12½x13*

27	MSP7 10h gray green	7.25	7.25
a.	Inverted overprint	19.00	19.00
28	MSP8 20h magenta	7.25	7.25
a.	Inverted overprint	19.00	19.00
29	MSP7 45h blue	7.25	7.25
a.	Inverted overprint	19.00	19.00
	Nos. 27-29 (3)	21.75	21.75

Austrian Military Stamps of 1917 Surcharged

1918-19 *Perf. 12½*

30	M3 3hal on 3h ol gray	32.50	19.00
a.	Inverted surcharge	225.00	225.00
b.	Perf. 11½	30.00	21.00
c.	Perf. 11½x12½	40.00	40.00
31	M3 3hal on 15h brt rose	4.75	2.00
a.	Inverted surcharge	20.00	20.00

Surcharged in Black

32	M3 10hal on 30h sl grn	4.75	1.75
a.	Inverted surcharge	20.00	20.00
b.	Brown surcharge (error)	60.00	50.00
34	M3 25hal on 40h ol bis	12.00	2.75
a.	Inverted surcharge	30.00	30.00
b.	Perf. 11½	15.00	9.00
35	M3 45hal on 60h rose	4.75	2.25
a.	Inverted surcharge	20.00	20.00
36	M3 45hal on 80h dl blue	7.25	4.25
a.	Inverted surcharge	30.00	30.00
37	M3 50hal on 60h rose	12.00	2.50
a.	Inverted surcharge	20.00	20.00

Similar surcharge with bars instead of stars over original value

38	M3 45hal on 80h dl blue	9.50	4.75
a.	Inverted surcharge	20.00	20.00

Overprinted

39	M3 50h deep green	27.50	17.00
a.	Inverted overprint	80.00	80.00
40	M3 90h dark violet	7.00	2.75
a.	Inverted overprint	20.00	20.00
	Nos. 30-40 (10)	122.00	59.00

Counterfeits

All Cracow issues, Nos. 41-60, J1-J12 and P1-P5, have been extensively counterfeited. Competent expertization is necessary. Prices apply only for authenticated stamps with identified plating position. Cost of certificate is not included in the catalogue value.

Cracow Issues

Austrian Stamps of 1916-18 Overprinted

1919, Jan. 17 Typo.

41	A37 3h brt violet	190.00	200.00
42	A37 5h lt green	190.00	210.00
43	A37 6h deep orange	25.00	19.50
a.	Inverted overprint	*6,000.*	
44	A37 10h magenta	190.00	190.00
45	A37 12h lt blue	35.00	35.00
46	A39 40h olive green	13.00	13.00
a.	Inverted overprint	100.00	100.00
b.	Double overprint	400.00	
47	A39 50h blue green	7.00	7.00
a.	Inverted overprint		*8,000.*
48	A39 60h deep blue	4.00	4.00
a.	Inverted overprint	100.00	75.00
49	A39 80h orange brown	4.00	4.50
a.	Inverted overprint.	100.00	100.00
b.	Double overprint	*125.00*	*125.00*
50	A39 90h red violet	625.00	725.00
51	A39 1k carmine, *yel*	7.00	6.00

Engr.

52	A40 2k blue	4.00	4.50
53	A40 3k carmine rose	75.00	60.00
54	A40 4k yellow green	125.00	100.00
55	A40 10k deep violet	*4,000.*	*5,000.*

The 3k is on granite paper.

The overprint on Nos. 52-55 is litho. and slightly larger than illustration with different ornament between lines of type.

Same Overprint on Nos. 168-171

1919 Typo.

56	A42 15h dull red	25.00	6.50
57	A42 20h dark green	125.00	125.00
58	A42 25h blue	1,250.	850.00
59	A42 30h dull violet	225.00	190.00

Austria No. 157 Surcharged

1919, Jan. 24

60 A39 25h on 80h org brn 2.75 2.75
a. Inverted surcharge 100.00 60.00

Excellent counterfeits of Nos. 27 to 60 exist.

Polish Eagle — A9

1919, Feb. 25 Litho. *Imperf.*

Without gum

Yellowish Paper

61 A9 2h gray .30 .35
62 A9 3h dull violet .30 .35
63 A9 5h green .20 .20
64 A9 6h orange 13.00 19.00
65 A9 10h lake .20 .20
66 A9 15h brown .20 .20
67 A9 20h olive green .30 .35

Bluish Paper

68 A9 25h carmine .20 .20
69 A9 50h indigo .20 .20
70 A9 70h deep blue .30 .35
71 A9 1k ol gray & car .55 .95
Nos. 61-71 (11) 15.75 22.35

Nos. 61-71 exist with privately applied perforations.
Counterfeits exist.
For surcharges see Nos. J35-J39.

Posen (Poznan) Issue

Germany Nos. 84-85, 87, 96, 98 Overprinted in Black

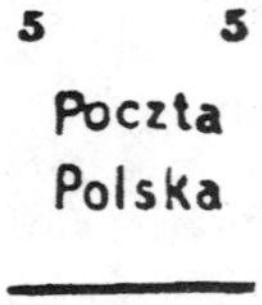

Perf. 14, 14½

1919, Aug. 5 Wmk. 125

72 A22 5pf on 2pf gray 18.00 15.00
73 A22 5pf on 7½pf org 1.90 1.25
a. Inverted surcharge 100.00
74 A16 5pf on 20pf bl vio 1.50 1.10
75 A16 10pf on 25pf org & blk, *yel* 3.75 3.00
76 A16 10pf on 40pf lake & blk 2.00 1.25
Nos. 72-76 (5) 27.15 21.60

Counterfeits exist.

Germany Nos. 96 and 98 Surcharged in Red or Green

a

b

1919, Sept. 15

77 A22 5pf on 2pf (R) 250.00 150.00
a. Inverted surcharge *4,250.*
78 A22 10pf on 7½pf (G) 150.00 110.00

Nos. 77-78 are a provisional issue for use in Gniezno. Counterfeit surcharges abound.

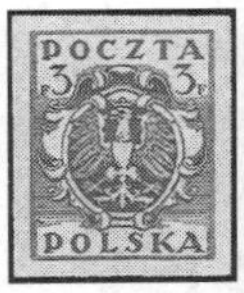

Eagle and Fasces, Symbolical of United Poland
A10 A11

"Agriculture" A12

"Peace" — A13

Polish Cavalryman A14

For Northern Poland

Denominations as "F" or "M"

1919, Jan. 27 *Imperf.*

Wove or Ribbed Paper

81 A10 3f bister brn .20 .20
82 A10 5f green .20 .20
83 A10 10f red violet .20 .20
84 A10 15f deep rose .20 .20
85 A11 20f deep blue .20 .20
86 A11 25f olive green .25 .20
87 A11 50f blue green .25 .20
88 A12 1m violet 2.50 2.00
89 A12 1.50m deep green 4.50 2.50
90 A12 2m dark brown 3.75 2.50
91 A13 2.50m orange brn 16.00 11.00
92 A14 5m red violet 20.00 11.00
Nos. 81-92 (12) 48.25 30.40

Perf. 10, 11, 11½, 10x11½, 11½x10

1919-20

93 A10 3f bister brn .20 .20
94 A10 5f green .20 .20
95 A10 10f red violet .20 .20
96 A10 10f brown ('20) .20 .20
97 A10 15f deep rose .20 .20
98 A10 15f vermilion ('20) .20 .20
99 A11 20f deep blue .20 .20
100 A11 25f olive green .20 .20
101 A11 40f brt violet ('20) .20 .20
102 A11 50f blue green .20 .20
103 A12 1m violet .45 .20
105 A12 1.50m deep green .75 .40
106 A12 2m dark brown .75 .40
107 A13 2.50m orange brn 1.25 1.00
108 A14 5m red violet 2.00 1.00
Nos. 93-108 (15) 7.20 5.00

Several denominations among Nos. 81-132 are found with double impression or in pairs imperf. between.
See #109-132, 140-152C, 170-175. For surcharges & overprints see #153, 199-200, B1-B14, 2K1-2K10, Eastern Silesia 41-50.

For Southern Poland

Denominations as "H" or "K"

1919, Jan. 27 *Imperf.*

109 A10 3h red brown .30 .20
110 A10 5h emerald .20 .20
111 A10 10h orange .20 .20
112 A10 15h vermilion .20 .20
113 A11 20h gray brown .20 .20
114 A11 25h light blue .20 .20
115 A11 50h orange brn .30 .20
116 A12 1k dark green .50 .20
117 A12 1.50k red brown 2.50 4.00
118 A12 2k dark blue 2.50 2.25
119 A13 2.50k dark violet 8.50 6.50
120 A14 5k slate blue 24.00 8.25
Nos. 109-120 (12) 39.60 22.60

Perf. 10, 11½, 10x11½, 11½x10

121 A10 3h red brown .20 .20
122 A10 5h emerald .20 .20
123 A10 10h orange .20 .20
124 A10 15h vermilion .20 .20
125 A11 20h gray brown .20 .20
126 A11 25h light blue .20 .20
127 A11 50h orange brn .20 .20
128 A12 1k dark green .50 .35
129 A12 1.50k red brown 1.10 .50
130 A12 2k dark blue 1.10 .50
131 A13 2.50k dark violet 1.25 .65
132 A14 5k slate blue 2.00 1.10
Nos. 121-132 (12) 7.35 4.50

National Assembly Issue

A20

Ignacy Jan Paderewski — A21

Adalbert Trampczynski — A22

Eagle Watching Ship — A24

25f, Gen. Josef Pilsudski. 1m, Griffin.

1919-20 *Perf. 11½*

Wove or Ribbed Paper

133 A20 10f red violet .20 .20
134 A21 15f brown red .40 .25
a. Imperf., pair 25.00
135 A22 20f dp brown (21x25mm) .30 .25
136 A22 20f dp brown (17x20mm) ('20) .60 .80
137 A21 25f olive green .20 .20
138 A24 50f Prus blue .25 .20
139 A24 1m purple .30 .25
Nos. 133-139 (7) 2.25 2.15

First National Assembly of Poland.

General Issue

1919 *Perf. 9 to 14½ and Compound*

Thin Laid Paper

140 A11 25f olive green .20 .20
141 A11 50f blue green .20 .20
142 A12 1m dark gray .35 .20
143 A12 2m bister brn 1.10 .20
144 A13 3m red brown .50 .20
a. Pair, imperf. vert. 5.00 5.75
145 A14 5m red violet .20 .20
146 A14 6m deep rose .20 .20
a. Pair, imperf. vert. 6.50 6.50
147 A14 10m brown red .35 .25
a. Horizontal pair, imperf. 6.50 6.50
148 A14 20m gray green .75 .40
Nos. 140-148 (9) 3.85 2.05

Type of 1919 Redrawn

Perf. 9 to 14½ and Compound

1920-22

Thin Laid or Wove Paper

149 A10 1m red .20 .20
150 A10 2m gray green .20 .20
151 A10 3m light blue .20 .20
152 A10 4m rose red .20 .20
152A A10 5m dark violet .20 .20
b. Horiz. pair, imperf. vert. 5.25 5.25
152C A10 8m gray brown ('22) .35 .25
Nos. 149-152C (6) 1.35 1.25

The word "POCZTA" is in smaller letters and the numerals have been enlarged.
The color of No. 152A varies from dark violet to red brown.

No. 101 Surcharged

Perf. 10, 11½, 10x11½, 11½x10

1921, Jan. 25

Thick Wove Paper

153 A11 3m on 40f brt vio .20 .20
a. Double surcharge 20.00 20.00
b. Inverted surcharge 20.00 20.00

Sower and Rainbow of Hope — A27

Perf. 9 to 14½ and Compound

1921 Litho.

Thin Laid or Wove Paper

Size: 28x22mm

154 A27 10m slate blue .20 .20
155 A27 15m light brown .40 .20
155A A27 20m red .20 .20
Nos. 154-155A (3) .80 .60

Signing of peace treaty with Russia.
See No. 191. For surcharges see Nos. 196-198.

Sun (Peace) Breaking into Darkness (Despair) — A28

"Peace" and "Agriculture" A29

"Peace" A30

Perf. 11, 11½, 12, 12½, 13 and Compound

1921, May 2

156 A28 2m green 1.40 .60
157 A28 3m blue 1.40 .60
158 A28 4m red .90 .60
a. 4m carmine rose (error) *300.00*
159 A29 6m carmine rose 1.40 .65
160 A29 10m slate blue 1.00 .80
161 A30 25m dk violet 2.50 1.90
162 A30 50m slate bl & buff 1.50 1.10
Nos. 156-162 (7) 10.10 6.25

Issued to commemorate the Constitution.

Polish Eagle — A31

Perf. 9 to 14½ and Compound

1921-23

163 A31 25m violet & buff .20 .20
164 A31 50m carmine & buff .20 .20
a. Vert. pair, imperf. horiz.
165 A31 100m blk brn & org .20 .20
166 A31 200m black & rose ('23) .35 .20
167 A31 300m olive grn ('23) .35 .20
168 A31 400m brown ('23) .35 .20
169 A31 500m brn vio ('23) .35 .20
169A A31 1000m orange ('23) .35 .20
169B A31 2000m dull blue ('23) .35 .20
Nos. 163-169B (9) 2.70 1.80

For surcharge see No. 195.

Type of 1919 and

Miner — A32

Perf. 9 to 14½ and Compound

1922-23

170 A10 5f blue .20 .25
171 A10 10f lt violet .20 .25
172 A11 20f pale red .20 .50
173 A11 40f violet brn .20 .25
174 A11 50f orange .20 1.00
175 A11 75f blue green .20 .50

176 A32 1m black .20 .25
177 A32 1.25m dark green .20 .25
178 A32 2m deep rose .20 .25
179 A32 3m emerald .20 .25
180 A32 4m deep ultra .20 .25
181 A32 5m yellow brn .20 .25
182 A32 6m red orange .20 .50
183 A32 10m lilac brn .20 .25
184 A32 20m deep violet .20 1.00
185 A32 50m olive green .20 1.00
187 A32 80m vermilion ('23) .40 3.00
188 A32 100m violet ('23) .40 3.50
189 A32 200m orange ('23) 1.50 4.50
190 A32 300m pale blue ('23) 4.50 5.00
Nos. 170-190 (20) 10.00 23.00

Union of Upper Silesia with Poland.
There were 2 printings of Nos. 176 to 190, the 1st being from flat plates, the 2nd from rotary press on thin paper, perf. 12½.
Nos. 173 and 175 are printed from new plates showing larger value numerals and a single "f."

Sower Type Redrawn
Size: 25x21mm

1922 **Thick or Thin Wove Paper**
191 A27 20m carmine .30 .20

In this stamp the design has been strengthened and made more distinct, especially the ground and the numerals in the upper corners.

Nicolaus Copernicus A33

Father Stanislaus Konarski — A34

1923 ***Perf. 10 to 12½***
192 A33 1000m indigo .80 .30
193 A34 3000m brown .45 .30
a. "Konapski" 15.00 15.00
194 A33 5000m rose .80 .30
Nos. 192-194 (3) 2.05 .90

Nicolaus Copernicus (1473-1543), astronomer (Nos. 192, 194); Stanislaus Konarski (1700-1773), educator, and the creation by the Polish Parliament of the Commission of Public Instruction (No. 193).

No. 163 Surcharged

1923 ***Perf. 9 to 14½ and Compound***
195 A31 10000m on 25m .30 .20
a. Double surcharge 5.00
b. Inverted surcharge 7.50

Stamps of 1921 Surcharged

196 A27 25000m on 20m red .60 .20
a. Double surcharge 5.00 5.00
b. Inverted surcharge 10.00
197 A27 50000m on 10m grnsh bl .30 .20
a. Double surcharge 5.00 5.00
b. Inverted surcharge 7.50 7.50

No. 191 Surcharged

198 A27 25000m on 20m car .50 .20
a. Double surcharge 5.00 5.00
b. Inverted surcharge 7.50

No. 150 Surcharged with New Value

1924
199 A10 20000m on 2m gray grn .70 .20
a. Inverted surcharge 7.50 7.50
b. Double surcharge 5.00 5.00

Type of 1919 Issue Surcharged with New Value
200 A10 100000m on 5m red brn .30 .20
a. Double surcharge 5.00 5.00
b. Inverted surcharge 7.50 7.50
Nos. 195-200 (6) 2.70 1.20

Arms of Poland — A35

Perf. 10 to 14½ and Compound
1924 **Litho.**

Thin Paper
205 A35 10,000m lilac brn .30 .25
206 A35 20,000m olive grn .30 .20
207 A35 30,000m scarlet 1.10 .35
208 A35 50,000m apple grn 2.25 .35
209 A35 100,000m brn org .60 .30
210 A35 200,000m lt blue .30 .20
211 A35 300,000m red vio .60 .35
212 A35 500,000m brown .60 .65
213 A35 1,000,000m pale rose .60 *2.75*
214 A35 2,000,000m dk green 1.10
Nos. 205-214 (10) 7.75
Set, never hinged 20.00

Arms of Poland A36

President Stanislaus Wojciechowski A37

Perf. 10 to 13½ and Compound
1924
215 A36 1g orange brown .35 .20
216 A36 2g dark brown .35 .20
217 A36 3g orange .40 .20
218 A36 5g olive green .90 .20
219 A36 10g blue green 1.10 .20
220 A36 15g red 1.10 .20
221 A36 20g blue 2.25 .20
222 A36 25g red brown 3.00 .35
a. 25g indigo *3,000.* *4,250.*
223 A36 30g deep violet 21.00 .25
a. 30g gray blue *250.00*
224 A36 40g indigo 4.00 .35
225 A36 50g magenta 3.75 .30

Perf. 11½, 12
226 A37 1z scarlet 22.50 1.25
Nos. 215-226 (12) 60.70 3.90
Set, never hinged 125.00

For overprints see Nos. 1K1-1K11.

Holy Gate of Wilno (Vilnius) — A38

Poznan Town Hall — A39

Sigismund Monument, Warsaw — A40

Wawel Castle at Cracow — A41

Sobieski Statue at Lwow — A42

Ship of State — A43

1925-27 ***Perf. 10 to 13***
227 A38 1g bister brown .40 .20
228 A42 2g brown olive .45 .25
229 A40 3g blue 1.75 .20
230 A39 5g yellow green 1.75 .20
231 A40 10g violet 1.75 .20
232 A41 15g rose red 1.65 .20
233 A43 20g dull red 1.90 .20
234 A38 24g gray blue 7.50 1.10
235 A42 30g dark blue 3.00 .20
236 A41 40g lt blue ('27) 3.50 .20
237 A43 45g dark violet 7.50 .20
Nos. 227-237 (11) 31.15 3.15
Set, never hinged 42.50

For overprints see Nos. 1K11A-1K17.

1926-27 **Redrawn**
238 A40 3g blue 2.75 .45
239 A39 5g yellow green 3.25 .20
240 A40 10g violet 4.75 .20
241 A41 15g rose red 4.75 .20
Nos. 238-241 (4) 15.50 1.05
Set, never hinged 22.50

On Nos. 229-232 the lines representing clouds touch the numerals. On the redrawn stamps the numerals have white outlines, separating them from the cloud lines.

Marshal Pilsudski — A44

Frederic Chopin — A45

1927 **Typo.** ***Perf. 12½, 11½***
242 A44 20g red brown 3.25 .50
243 A45 40g deep ultra 16.00 1.75
Set, never hinged 27.50

See No. 250. For overprint see No. 1K18.

President Ignacy Moscicki — A46

1927, May 4 ***Perf. 11½***
245 A46 20g red 5.50 .45
Never hinged 7.00

Dr. Karol Kaczkowski A47

Juliusz Slowacki A48

1927, May 27 ***Perf. 11½, 12½***
246 A47 10g gray green 2.75 2.25
247 A47 25g carmine 6.50 3.00
248 A47 40g dark blue 8.75 3.00
Nos. 246-248 (3) 18.00 8.25
Set, never hinged 40.00

4th Intl. Congress of Military Medicine and Pharmacy, Warsaw, May 30-June 4.

1927, June 28 ***Perf. 12½***
249 A48 20g rose 6.00 .50
Never hinged 8.00

Transfer from Paris to Cracow of the remains of Julius Slowacki, poet.

Pilsudski Type of 1927
Design Redrawn

1928 ***Perf. 11½, 12x11½, 12½x13***
250 A44 25g yellow brown 2.75 .25
Never hinged 6.00

Souvenir Sheet

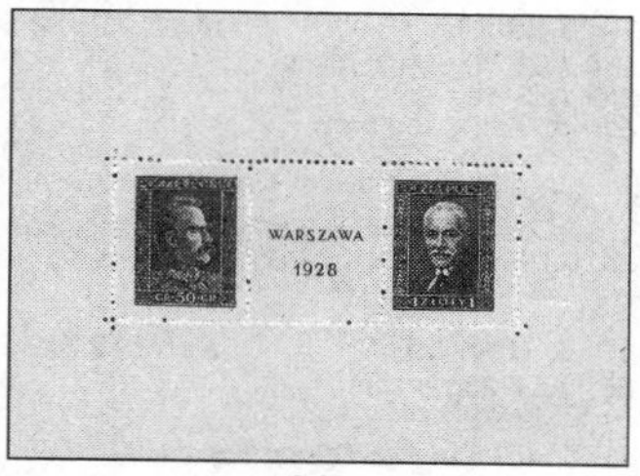
A49

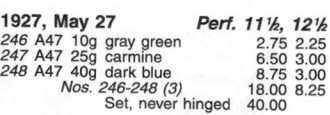

1928, May 3 **Engr.** ***Perf. 12½***
251 A49 Sheet of 2 250.00 325.00
Never hinged 375.00
a. 50g black brown 110.00 140.00
b. 1z black brown 110.00 140.00

1st Natl. Phil. Exhib., Warsaw, May 3-13.
Sold to each purchaser of a 1.50z ticket to the Warsaw Philatelic Exhibition.
Counterfeits exist.

Marshal Pilsudski A49a

Pres. Moscicki A50

Perf. 10½ to 14 and Compound
1928-31

Wove Paper
253 A49a 50g bluish slate 4.00 .20
254 A49a 50g blue grn ('31) 12.50 .20
Set, never hinged 22.50

See No. 315.

Perf. 12x12½, 11½ to 13½ and Compound
1928

Laid Paper
255 A50 1z black, *cream* 11.00 .20
Never hinged 17.00
a. Horizontally laid paper ('30) 70.00 2.50
Never hinged 90.00

See Nos. 305, 316. For surcharges and overprints see Nos. J92-J94, 1K19, 1K24.

General Josef Bem A51

Henryk Sienkiewicz A52

1928, May **Typo.** ***Perf. 12½***
Wove Paper
256 A51 25g rose red 4.00 .25
Never hinged 5.25

Return from Syria to Poland of the ashes of General Josef Bem.

1928, Oct.
257 A52 15g ultra 2.00 .20
Never hinged 3.25

For overprint see No. 1K23.

Eagle Arms — A53

"Swiatowid," Ancient Slav God — A54

1928-29 ***Perf. 12x12½***
258 A53 5g dark violet .35 .20
259 A53 10g green 1.00 .20
260 A53 25g red brown .55 .20
Nos. 258-260 (3) 1.90 .60
Set, never hinged 3.75

See design A58. For overprints see Nos. 1K20-1K22.

1928, Dec. 15 ***Perf. 12½x12***
261 A54 25g brown 2.50 .20
Never hinged 3.25

Poznan Agricultural Exhibition.

King John III Sobieski A55

Stylized Soldiers A56

1930, July ***Perf. 12x12½***
262 A55 75g claret 5.75 .25
Never hinged 7.50

1930, Nov. 1 ***Perf. 12½***
263 A56 5g violet brown .35 .20
264 A56 15g dark blue 2.25 .35
265 A56 25g red brown 1.25 .20
266 A56 30g dull red 6.25 3.75
Nos. 263-266 (4) 10.10 4.50
Set, never hinged 25.00

Centenary of insurrection of 1830.

Kosciuszko, Washington, Pulaski — A57

1932, May 3 ***Perf. 11½***
Laid Paper
267 A57 30g brown 2.75 .30
Never hinged 3.50

200th birth anniv. of George Washington.

A58

A59

Perf. 12x12½
1932-33 Typo. Wmk. 234
268 A58 5g dull vio ('33) .35 .20
269 A58 10g green .35 .20
270 A58 15g red brown ('33) .35 .20
271 A58 20g gray .75 .20
272 A58 25g buff .95 .20
273 A58 30g deep rose 3.25 .20
274 A58 60g blue 19.00 .35
Nos. 268-274 (7) 25.00 1.55
Set, never hinged 32.50

For overprints and surcharge see Nos. 280-281, 284, 292, 1K25-1K27.

1933, Jan. 2 Engr. ***Perf. 11½***
275 A59 60g Torun City Hall 37.50 .75
Never hinged 80.00

700th anniversary of the founding of the City of Torun by the Grand Master of the Knights of the Teutonic Order.
See No. B28.

Altar Panel of St. Mary's Church, Cracow — A60

Perf. 11½-12½ & Compound
1933, July 10 Unwmk.
Laid Paper
277 A60 80g red brown 15.00 1.50
Never hinged 21.00

400th death anniv. of Veit Stoss, sculptor and woodcarver.
For surcharge see No. 285.

John III Sobieski and Allies before Vienna, painted by Jan Matejko — A61

1933, Sept. 12 Laid Paper
278 A61 1.20z indigo 37.50 6.00
Never hinged 60.00

250th anniv. of the deliverance of Vienna by the Polish and allied forces under command of John III Sobieski, King of Poland, when besieged by the Turks in 1683.
For surcharge see No. 286.

Cross of Independence A62

Josef Pilsudski A63

Wmk. 234
1933, Nov. 11 Typo. ***Perf. 12½***
279 A62 30g scarlet 7.50 .40
Never hinged 8.75

15th anniversary of independence.

Type of 1932 Overprinted in Red or Black

1934, May 5 ***Perf. 12***
280 A58 20g gray (R) 30.00 24.00
281 A58 30g deep rose 30.00 24.00
Set, never hinged 100.00

Katowice Philatelic Exhibition. Counterfeits exist.

Perf. 11½ to 12½ and Compound
1934, Aug. 6 Engr. Unwmk.
282 A63 25g gray blue 1.25 .25
283 A63 30g black brown 3.00 .40
Set, never hinged 5.25

Polish Legion, 20th anniversary.
For overprint see No. 293.

Nos. 274, 277-278 Surcharged in Black or Red

1934 Wmk. 234 ***Perf. 12x12½***
284 A58 55g on 60g blue 6.00 .50

Perf. 11½-12½ & Compound
Unwmk.
285 A60 25g on 80g red brn 6.50 .65
286 A61 1z on 1.20z ind (R) 16.00 2.50
a. Figure "1" in surcharge 5mm high instead of 4½mm 18.00 2.50
Never hinged 21.00
Nos. 284-286 (3) 28.50 3.65
Set, never hinged 48.00

Surcharge of No. 286 includes bars.

Marshal Pilsudski — A64

1935 ***Perf. 11 to 13 and Compound***
287 A64 5g black .40 .20
288 A64 15g black .40 .20
289 A64 25g black 1.65 .20
290 A64 45g black 6.75 2.40
291 A64 1z black 10.75 5.00
Nos. 287-291 (5) 19.95 8.00
Set, never hinged 24.00

Pilsudski mourning issue.
Nos. 287-288 are typo., Nos. 290-291 litho. No. 289 exists both typo. and litho.
See No. B35b.

Nos. 270, 282 Overprinted in Blue or Red

1935 Wmk. 234 ***Perf. 12x12½***
292 A58 15g red brown 1.00 .45

Perf. 11½, 11½x12½
Unwmk.
293 A63 25g gray blue (R) 3.25 1.50
Set, never hinged 5.75

Issued in connection with the proposed memorial to Marshal Pilsudski, the stamps were sold at Cracow exclusively.

"The Dog Cliff" — A65

President Ignacy Moscicki — A75

Designs: 10g, "Eye of the Sea." 15g, M. S. "Pilsudski." 20g, View of Pieniny. 25g, Belvedere Palace. 30g, Castle in Mira. 45g, Castle at Podhorce. 50g, Cloth Hall, Cracow. 55g, Raczynski Library, Poznan. 1z, Cathedral, Wilno.

1935-36 Typo. ***Perf. 12½x13***
294 A65 5g violet blue .60 .20
295 A65 10g yellow green .60 .20
296 A65 15g Prus green 1.90 .20
297 A65 20g violet black .95 .20

Engr.
298 A65 25g myrtle green .80 .20
299 A65 30g rose red 2.00 .30
300 A65 45g plum ('36) 1.00 .30
301 A65 50g black ('36) 1.00 .30
302 A65 55g blue ('36) 9.50 .60
303 A65 1z brown ('36) 3.75 1.65
304 A75 3z black brown 2.25 2.50
Nos. 294-304 (11) 24.35 6.65
Set, never hinged 32.50

See Nos. 308-311. For overprints see Nos. 306-307, 1K28-1K32.

Type of 1928 inscribed "1926. 3. VI. 1936" on Bottom Margin

1936, June 3
305 A50 1z ultra 7.50 6.00
Never hinged 9.50

Presidency of Ignacy Moscicki, 10th anniv.

Nos. 299, 302 Overprinted in Blue or Red

1936, Aug. 15
306 A65 30g rose red 12.00 6.00
307 A65 55g blue (R) 12.00 6.00
Set, never hinged 30.00

Gordon-Bennett Intl. Balloon Race. Counterfeits exist.

Scenic Type of 1935-36

Designs: 5g, Church at Czestochowa. 10g, Maritime Terminal, Gdynia. 15g, University, Lwow. 20g, Municipal Building, Katowice.

1937 Engr. ***Perf. 12½***
308 A65 5g violet blue .20 .20
309 A65 10g green .55 .20
310 A65 15g red brown .40 .20
311 A65 20g orange brown .55 .20
Nos. 308-311 (4) 1.70 .80
Set, never hinged 3.00

For overprints see Nos. 1K31-1K32.

Marshal Smigly-Rydz A80

President Moscicki A81

1937 ***Perf. 12½x13***
312 A80 25g slate green .25 .20
313 A80 55g blue .60 .20
Set, never hinged 1.50

For surcharges see Nos. N30, N32.

Types of 1928-37
Souvenir Sheets

1937
314 Sheet of 4 25.00 25.00
a. A80 25g, dark brown 2.75 2.75
315 Sheet of 4 25.00 25.00
a. A49a 50g, deep blue 2.75 2.75
316 Sheet of 4 25.00 25.00
a. A50 1z, gray black 2.75 2.75
Set, never hinged 110.00

Visit of King Carol of Romania to Poland, June 26-July 1.
See No. B35c.

1938, Feb. 1 ***Perf. 12½***
317 A81 15g slate green .20 .20
318 A81 30g rose violet .60 .20
Set, never hinged 1.10

71st birthday of President Moscicki.
For surcharge see No. N31.

Kosciuszko, Paine and Washington and View of New York City — A82

1938, Mar. 17 *Perf. 12x12½*

319 A82 1z gray blue	1.25	1.75
Never hinged	2.00	

150th anniv. of the US Constitution.

Boleslaus I and Emperor Otto III at Gnesen — A83

Marshal Pilsudski — A95

Designs: 10g, King Casimir III. 15g, King Ladislas II Jagello and Queen Hedwig. 20g, King Casimir IV. 25g, Treaty of Lublin. 30g, King Stephen Bathory commending Wielock, the peasant. 45g, Stanislas Zolkiewski and Jan Chodkiewicz. 50g, John III Sobieski entering Vienna. 55g, Union of nobles, commoners and peasants. 75g, Dabrowski, Kosciuszko and Poniatowski. 1z, Polish soldiers. 2z, Romuald Traugutt.

1938, Nov. 11 **Engr.** *Perf. 12½*

320 A83 5g red orange	.20	.20
321 A83 10g green	.20	.20
322 A83 15g fawn	.30	.20
323 A83 20g peacock blue	.40	.20
324 A83 25g dull violet	.20	.20
325 A83 30g rose red	.65	.20
326 A83 45g black	.40	.20
327 A83 50g brt red vio	2.75	.20
328 A83 55g ultra	.85	.20
329 A83 75g dull green	2.00	1.50
330 A83 1z orange	1.60	1.40
331 A83 2z carmine rose	11.00	8.00
332 A95 3z gray black	9.00	14.00
Nos. 320-332 (13)	29.55	26.70
Set, never hinged	37.50	

20th anniv. of Poland's independence. See No. 339. For surcharges see Nos. N33-N47.

Souvenir Sheet

Marshal Pilsudski, Gabriel Narutowicz, President Moscicki, Marshal Smigly-Rydz — A96

1938, Nov. 11 *Perf. 12½*

333 A96 Sheet of 4	16.00	18.00
Never hinged	21.00	
a. 25g dull violet (Pilsudski)	1.60	1.75
b. 25g dull violet (Narutowicz)	1.60	1.75
c. 25g dull violet (Moscicki)	1.60	1.75
d. 25g dull violet (Smigly-Rydz)	1.60	1.75

20th anniv. of Poland's independence.

Poland Welcoming Teschen People — A97

Skier — A98

1938, Nov. 11

334 A97 25g dull violet	1.50	.45
Never hinged	2.00	

Restoration of the Teschen territory ceded by Czechoslovakia.

1939, Feb. 6

335 A98 15g orange brown	1.00	*1.10*
336 A98 25g dull violet	1.75	.50
337 A98 30g rose red	2.25	1.10
338 A98 55g brt ultra	10.00	4.00
Nos. 335-338 (4)	15.00	6.70
Set, never hinged	25.00	

Intl. Ski Meet, Zakopane, Feb. 11-19.

Type of 1938

15g, King Ladislas II Jagello, Queen Hedwig.

Re-engraved

1939, Mar. 2 *Perf. 12½*

339 A83 15g redsh brown	.25	.20
Never hinged	.55	

No. 322 with crossed swords and helmet at lower left. No. 339, swords and helmet have been removed.

Marshal Pilsudski Reviewing Troops — A99

1939, Aug. 1 **Engr.**

340 A99 25g dull rose violet	.60	.50
Never hinged	.80	

Polish Legion, 25th anniv. See No. B35a.

Polish Peoples Republic

Romuald Traugutt A100

Tadeusz Kosciuszko A101

Design: 1z, Jan Henryk Dabrowski.

Perf. 11½

1944, Sept. 7 **Litho.** **Unwmk.**

Without Gum

341 A100 25g crimson rose	37.50	40.00
342 A101 50g deep green	45.00	52.50
343 A101 1z deep ultra	40.00	52.50
Nos. 341-343 (3)	122.50	145.00

Counterfeits exist.
For surcharges see Nos. 362-363.

Polish Eagle — A103

Grunwald Monument, Cracow — A104

1944, Sept. 13 **Photo.** *Perf. 12½*

344 A103 25g deep red	.60	.35
a. 25g dull red, typo.	.85	
Never hinged	1.10	
345 A104 50g dk slate green	.45	.20
Set, never hinged	1.65	

No. 344a was not put on sale without surcharge. See Nos. 346, 349a. For surcharges see Nos. 345A-356, 364, B54, C19-C20.

No. 344 Surcharged in Black

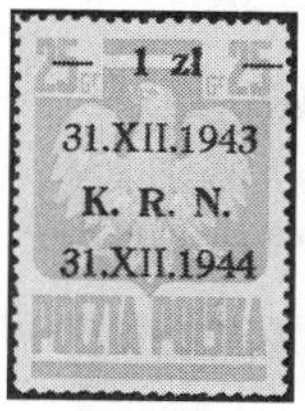

a

b

c

1944-45

345A A103 1z on 25g	1.90	2.00
345B A103 2z on 25g ('45)	1.90	2.00
345C A103 3z on 25g ('45)	1.90	2.00
Nos. 345A-345C (3)	5.70	6.00
Set, never hinged	7.00	

Issued to honor Polish government agencies. K. R. N. - Krajowa Rada Narodowa (Polish National Council), P. K. W. N. - Polski Komitet Wyzwolenia Narodu (Polish National Liberation Committee) and R. T. R. P. - Rzad Tymczasowy Rzeczypospolitej Polskiej (Temporary Administration of the Polish Republic).
Counterfeits exist.

No. 344a Surcharged in Brown

1945, Sept. 1

346 A103 1.50z on 25g dull red	.45	.20
Never hinged	.70	
a. 1.50z on 25g deep red, #344	350.00	250.00

Counterfeits of No. 346a exist.

No. 344 Surcharged in Blue

1945, Feb. 12

347 A103 3z on 25g	4.25	6.25
348 A103 3z on 25g *(Radom, 16. I. 1945)*	3.00	3.50
349 A103 3z on 25g *(Warszawa, 17. I. 1945)*	6.25	7.00
a. 3z on 25g dull red, #344a	110.00	125.00
350 A103 3z on 25g *(Czestochowa, 17. I. 1945)*	3.00	3.50
351 A103 3z on 25g *(Krakow, 19. I. 1945)*	3.00	3.50
352 A103 3z on 25g *(Lodz, 19. I. 1945)*	3.00	3.50
353 A103 3z on 25g *(Gniezno, 22. I. 1945)*	3.00	3.50
354 A103 3z on 25g *(Bydgoszcz, 23. I. 1945)*	3.00	3.50
355 A103 3z on 25g *(Kalisz, 24. I. 1945)*	3.00	3.50
356 A103 3z on 25g *(Zakopane, 29. I. 1945)*	3.00	3.50
Nos. 347-356 (10)	34.50	41.25
Set, never hinged	42.50	

Dates overprinted are those of liberation for each city.

Counterfeits exist.

Grunwald Monument, Cracow — A105

Kosciuszko Statue, Cracow — A106

Cloth Hall, Cracow A107

Copernicus Memorial — A108

Wawel Castle — A109

1945, Apr. 10 **Photo.** *Perf. 10½, 11*

357 A105 50g dk violet brn	.20	.20
a. 50g dark brown	.45	.35
Never hinged	1.00	
358 A106 1z henna brown	.30	.25
359 A107 2z sapphire	.45	.35
360 A108 3z dp red violet	1.25	.50
361 A109 5z blue green	2.75	3.25
Nos. 357-361 (5)	4.95	4.55
Set, never hinged	6.25	

Liberation of Cracow Jan. 19, 1945.
Nos. 357-361 exist imperforate.
No. 357a is a coarser printing from a new plate showing designer's name (J. Wilczyk) in lower left margin. No. 357 does not show his name.

Nos. 341-342 Surcharged in Black or Red:

d

e

1945 *Perf. 11½*

362 A100(d) 5z on 25g	27.50	32.50
363 A101(e) 5z on 50g (R)	6.00	9.00
Never hinged	7.00	

No. 362 was issued without gum.

No. 345 Surcharged in Brown

1945, Sept. 10 *Perf. 12½*

364 A104 1z on 50g dk sl grn	.40	.20
Never hinged	.60	

Lodz Skyline A110

Kosciuszko Monument, Lodz A111

Flag Bearer Carrying Wounded Comrade — A112

1945 Litho. *Perf. 11, 9 (3z)*

365 A110 1z deep ultra	.55	.20
366 A111 3z dull red violet	.60	.45
367 A112 5z deep carmine	2.00	1.90
Nos. 365-367 (3)	3.15	2.55
Set, never hinged	4.00	

Nos. 365 and 367 commemorate the liberation of Lodz and Warsaw.

Grunwald Battle Scene — A113

Eagle Breaking Fetters and Manifesto of Freedom — A114

1945, July 16

368 A113 5z deep blue	7.00	*9.00*
Never hinged	10.00	

Battle of Grunwald (Tannenberg), July 15, 1410.

1945, July 22

369 A114 3z rose carmine	10.00	*15.00*
Never hinged	15.00	

1st anniv. of the liberation of Poland.

Crane Tower, Gdansk — A115

Stock Tower, Gdansk — A116

Ancient High Gate, Gdansk A117

1945, Sept. 15 Photo. Unwmk.

370 A115 1z olive	.20	.20
371 A116 2z sapphire	.20	.20
372 A117 3c dark violet	.60	.25
Nos. 370-372 (3)	1.00	.65
Set, never hinged	1.50	

Recovery of Poland's access to the sea at Gdansk (Danzig).

Exist imperf. Value, set $25.

Civilian and Soldiers in Rebellion — A118

1945, Nov. 29

373 A118 10z black	7.75	*9.00*
Never hinged	9.00	

115th anniv. of the "November Uprising" against the Russians, Nov. 29, 1830.

Holy Cross Church — A119

Views of Warsaw, 1939 and 1945: 1.50z, Warsaw Castle, 1939 and 1945. 3z, Cathedral of St. John. 3.50z, City Hall. 6z, Post Office. 8z, Army General Staff Headquarters.

1945-46 Unwmk. *Imperf.*

374 A119 1.50z crimson	.20	.20
375 A119 3z dark blue	.40	.20
376 A119 3.50z lt blue grn	.95	.40
377 A119 6z gray black ('46)	.40	.25
378 A119 8z brown ('46)	1.90	.40
379 A119 10z dark violet ('46)	.80	.30
Nos. 374-379 (6)	4.65	1.75
Set, never hinged	6.00	

Nos. 374-379 Overprinted in Black

1946, Jan. 17

383 A119 1.50z crimson	1.25	2.25
384 A119 3z dark blue	1.25	2.25
385 A119 3.50z lt blue grn	1.25	2.25
386 A119 6z gray black	1.25	2.25
387 A119 8z brown	1.25	2.25
388 A119 10z dark violet	1.25	2.25
Nos. 383-388 (6)	7.50	13.50
Set, never hinged	10.00	

Liberation of Warsaw, 1/17/45, 1st anniv. Counterfeits exist.

Polish Revolutionist A125

Infantry Advancing A126

1946, Jan. 22 *Perf. 11*

389 A125 6z slate blue	6.00	*9.00*
Never hinged	7.50	

Revolt of Jan. 22, 1863.

1946, May 9

390 A126 3z brown	.30	.20
Never hinged	.50	

Polish freedom, first anniversary.

Premier Edward Osubka-Morawski Pres. Boleslaw Bierut and Marshal Michael Rola-Zymierski — A127

Perf. 11x10½

1946, July 22 Unwmk.

391 A127 3z purple	3.00	*4.00*
Never hinged	4.00	

For surcharge see No. B53.

Bedzin Castle — A128

Duke Henry IV of Silesia, from Tomb at Wroclaw — A129

Lanckrona Castle A130

1946, Sept. 1 Photo. *Imperf.*

392 A128 5z olive gray	.20	.20
393 A128 5z brown	.20	.20
Perf. 10½		
394 A129 6z gray black	.30	.20
Imperf		
395 A130 10z deep blue	.65	.20
Nos. 392-395 (4)	1.35	.80
Set, never hinged	2.00	

Perforated copies of Nos. 392, 393 and 395 have been privately made.

For surcharge see No. 404.

Jan Matejko, Jacek Malczewski, Josef Chelmonski — A131

Adam Chmielowski (Brother Albert) — A132

Designs: 3z, Chopin. 5z, Wojciech Boguslawski, Helena Modjeska and Stefan Jaracz. 6z, Alexander Swietockowski, Stephen Zeromski and Boleslaw Prus. 10z, Marie Sklodowska Curie. 15z, Stanislaw Wyspianski, Juliusz Slowacki and Jan Kasprowicz. 20z, Adam Mickiewicz.

1947 *Perf. 11*

396 A131 1z blue	.20	.20
397 A132 2z brown	.35	.20
398 A132 3z Prus green	.45	.20
399 A131 5z olive green	.65	.20
400 A131 6z gray green	1.00	.20
401 A132 10z gray brown	1.10	.40
402 A131 15z sepia	1.25	.50
403 A132 20z gray black	1.50	.70
Nos. 396-403 (8)	6.50	2.60
Set, never hinged	9.00	

Set exists imperf, value $12.

No. 394 Surcharged in Red

1947, Feb. 25 *Perf. 10½*

404 A129 5z on 6z gray blk	.40	.20
Never hinged	.70	

Types of 1947

1947 Photo. *Perf. 11, Imperf.*

405 A131 1z slate gray	.20	.20
406 A132 2z orange	.20	.20
407 A132 3z olive green	1.40	.35
408 A131 5z olive brown	.30	.20
409 A131 6z carmine rose	.50	.20
410 A132 10z blue	.90	.20
411 A131 15z chestnut brn	.75	.30
412 A132 20z dark violet	.50	.50
a. Souv. sheet of 8, #405-412	140.00	200.00
Never hinged	175.00	
Nos. 405-412 (8)	4.75	2.15
Set, never hinged	7.00	

No. 412a sold for 500z.

Laborer — A139

Farmer — A140

Fisherman A141

Miner A142

1947, Aug. 20 Engr. *Perf. 13*

413 A139 5z rose brown	.70	.20
414 A140 10z brt blue green	.20	.20
415 A141 15z dark blue	.75	.20
416 A142 20z brown black	.50	.20
Nos. 413-416 (4)	2.15	.80
Set, never hinged	3.00	

Allegory of the Revolution
A143

Insurgents
A144

1948, Mar. 15 Photo. *Perf. 11*

417 A143 15z brown .25 .20
Never hinged .50

Revolution of 1848. See Nos. 430-432.

1948, Apr. 19

418 A144 15z gray black 1.25 1.40
Never hinged 2.00

Ghetto uprising, Warsaw, 5th anniv.

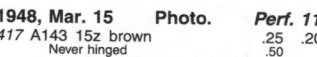

Decorated Bicycle Wheel
A145

1948, May 1

419 A145 15z brt rose & blue 2.00 1.10
Never hinged 3.00

1st Intl. Bicycle Peace Race, Warsaw-Prague-Warsaw.

Launching Ship — A146

Loading Freighter
A147

35z, Racing yacht "Gen. Mariusz Zaruski."

1948, June 22

420 A146 6z violet 1.10 *2.75*
421 A147 15z brown car 1.25 *3.50*
422 A147 35z slate gray 2.25 *3.75*
Nos. 420-422 (3) 4.60 10.00
Set, never hinged 6.00

Polish Merchant Marine.

Cyclists
A148

A149

1948, June 22

423 A148 3z gray 1.25 *3.00*
424 A148 6z brown 1.25 *3.75*
425 A148 15z green 2.00 *4.50*
Nos. 423-425 (3) 4.50 11.25
Set, never hinged 6.00

Poland Bicycle Race, 7th Circuit, 6/22-7/4.

1948, July 15

426 A149 6z blue .35 .30
427 A149 15z red .75 .30
428 A149 18z rose brown .65 .20
429 A149 35z dark brown .65 .30
Nos. 426-429 (4) 2.40 1.10
Set, never hinged 3.75

Exhibition to commemorate the recovery of Polish territories, Wroclaw, 1948.

Gen. Henryk Dembinski and Gen. Josef Bem — A150

Symbolical of United Youth — A151

Designs: 35z, S. Worcell, P. Sciegienny and E. Dembowski. 60z, Friedrich Engels and Karl Marx.

1948, July 15

430 A150 30z dark brown .50 .40
431 A150 35z olive green 2.25 .40
432 A150 60z bright rose .70 .55
Nos. 430-432 (3) 3.45 1.35
Set, never hinged 5.00

Revolution of 1848, cent. See No. 417.

1948, Aug. 8

433 A151 15z blue .45 .25
Never hinged .75

Intl. Congress of Democratic Youth, Warsaw, Aug.

Stagecoach Leaving Torun Gate — A152

1948, Sept. 4

434 A152 15z brown .45 .30
Never hinged .75

Philatelic Exhibition, Torun, Sept.

Clock Dial and Locomotive
A153

Pres. Boleslaw Bierut
A154

1948, Oct. 6 *Perf. 11½*

435 A153 18z blue 4.00 *10.00*
Never hinged 6.00

European Railroad Schedule Conference, Cracow.

1948-49 Unwmk. *Perf. 11, 11½*

436 A154 2z orange ('49) .20 .20
437 A154 3z blue grn ('49) .20 .20
438 A154 5z brown .20 .20
439 A154 6z slate .40 .20
440 A154 10z violet ('49) .20 .20
441 A154 15z dp carmine .20 .20
442 A154 18z gray green .45 .25
443 A154 30z blue .75 .20
444 A154 35z violet brown 2.00 .35
Nos. 436-444 (9) 4.60 2.00
Set, never hinged 8.00

Workers Carrying Flag
A155

Designs: 15z, Marx, Engels, Lenin and Stalin. 25z, Ludwig Warynski.

Inscribed: "Kongres Jednosci Klasy Robotniczej 8. XII. 1948."

1948, Dec. 8 *Perf. 11*

445 A155 5z crimson .50 .25
446 A155 15z dull violet .50 .65
447 A155 25z brown 1.25 .55
Nos. 445-447 (3) 2.25 1.45
Set, never hinged 3.50

Redrawn
Dated: "XII. 1948"

Designs as before.

1948, Dec. 15 *Perf. 11½*

448 A155 5z brown carmine 1.75 1.25
449 A155 15z bright blue 1.75 1.25
450 A155 25z dark green 2.50 2.50
Nos. 448-450 (3) 6.00 5.00
Set, never hinged 7.50

Congress of the Union of the Working Class, Warsaw, Dec. 1948.

"Socialism"
A156

Designs: 5z, "Labor." 15z, "Peace."

Perf. 11½

1949, May 31 Unwmk. Photo.

451 A156 3z carmine rose .75 *1.00*
452 A156 5z deep blue .90 *1.00*
453 A156 15z deep green 1.10 *1.40*
Nos. 451-453 (3) 2.75 3.40
Set, never hinged 3.75

8th Trade Union Congress, June 5, 1949.

Warsaw Scene — A157

Pres. Boleslaw Bierut — A158

Radio Station — A159

Perf. 13x12½, 12½x13

1949, July 22 Litho.

454 A157 10z gray black 2.00 2.00
455 A158 15z lilac rose 1.25 1.25
456 A159 35z gray blue 1.25 1.25
Nos. 454-456 (3) 4.50 4.50
Set, never hinged 6.00

5th anniv. of "People's Poland."

A160

A161

UPU, 75th Anniv.: 6z, Stagecoach and world map. 30z, Ship and map. 80z, Plane and map.

1949, Oct. 10 Engr. *Perf. 13x12½*

457 A160 6z gray purple .85 *1.50*
458 A160 30z blue 1.40 *1.75*
459 A160 80z dull green 3.75 *4.25*
Nos. 457-459 (3) 6.00 7.50
Set, never hinged 7.25

1949 *Perf. 13½x13*

Symbolical of United Poland.

460 A161 5z brown red .70 .20
461 A161 10z rose red .25 .20
462 A161 15z green .25 .20
463 A161 35z dark brown .70 .40
Nos. 460-463 (4) 1.90 1.00
Set, never hinged 2.75

Congress of the People's Movement for Unity.

Adam Mickiewicz
A162

Frederic Chopin
A163

Design: 35z, Juliusz Slowacki.

1949, Dec. 5 *Perf. 12½*

464 A162 10z brown violet 2.00 1.75
465 A163 15z brown rose 2.00 1.75
466 A162 35z deep blue 2.00 1.75
Nos. 464-466 (3) 6.00 5.25
Set, never hinged 8.75

Mail Delivery — A164

Adam Mickiewicz and Pushkin — A165

1950, Jan. 21

467 A164 15z red violet 2.00 *2.50*
Never hinged 3.00

3rd Congress of PTT Trade Unions, Jan. 21-23, 1950.

1949, Dec. 15

468 A165 15z lilac 2.00 *2.50*
Never hinged 3.50

Polish-Soviet friendship.

Pres. Boleslaw Bierut
A166

Julian Marchlewski
A167

1950, Feb. 25 Engr. *Perf. 12x12½*

469 A166 15z red .30 .20
Never hinged .90

See Nos. 478-484, 490-496. For surcharge see No. 522.

1950, Mar. 23 Photo. ***Perf. 11x10½***

470 A167 15z gray black .55 .30
Never hinged 1.00

25th death anniv. of Julian Marchlewski, author and political leader.

Reconstruction, Warsaw — A168

Perf. 11, 12 and Compounds of 13

1950, Apr. 15

471 A168 5z dark brown .20 .20
Never hinged .25

See No. 497.

Worker Holding Hammer, Flag and Olive Branch — A169

Workers of Three Races with Flag — A170

1950, Apr. 26 ***Perf. 11½***

472 A169 10z deep lilac rose 1.10 .20
473 A170 15z brown olive 1.10 .20
Set, never hinged 3.50

60th anniversary of Labor Day.

Freedom Monument, Poznan — A171

Dove on Globe — A172

1950, Apr. 27

474 A171 15z chocolate .25 .20
Never hinged .40

Poznan Fair, Apr. 29-May 14, 1950.

1950, May 15 **Unwmk.**

475 A172 10z dark green .65 .20
476 A172 15z dark brown .30 .20
Set, never hinged 1.50

Day of Intl. Action for World Peace.

Polish Workers — A173

Hibner, Kniewski and Rutkowski A174

1950, July 20 ***Perf. 12½x13***

477 A173 15z violet blue .20 .20
Never hinged .30

Poland's 6-year plan. See Nos. 507A-510, 539.

Bierut Type of 1950, No Frame

1950 Engr. ***Perf. 12x12½***

478 A166 5z dull green .20 .20
479 A166 10z dull red .20 .20
480 A166 15z deep blue .65 .20
481 A166 20z violet brown .20 .20
482 A166 25z yellow brown .30 .20
482A A166 30z rose brown .35 .20
483 A166 40z brown .25 .20
484 A166 50z olive 1.10 .25
Nos. 478-484 (8) 3.25 1.65
Set, never hinged 6.00

1950, Aug. 18 Photo. ***Perf. 11***

485 A174 15z gray black 1.75 .70
Never hinged 2.50

25th anniv. of the execution of three Polish revolutionists, Wladyslaw Hibner, Wladyslaw Kniewski and Henryk Rutkowski.

Worker and Dove — A175

Dove by Picasso — A176

1950, Aug. 31 Engr. ***Perf. 12½***

486 A175 15z gray green .30 .20
Never hinged .50

Polish Peace Congress, Warsaw, 1950.

"GROSZY"

To provide denominations needed as a result of the currency revaluation of Oct. 28, 1950, each post office was authorized to surcharge stamps of its current stock with the word "Groszy." Many types and sizes of this surcharge exist. The surcharge was applied to most of Poland's 1946-1950 issues. All stamps of that period could receive the surcharge upon request of anyone. Counterfeits exist.

1950, Nov. 13

487 A176 40g blue 1.25 .30
488 A176 45g brown red .40 .20
Set, never hinged 2.50

2nd World Peace Congress.

Josef Bem and Battle Scene — A177

1950, Dec. 10

489 A177 45g blue 2.00 1.50
Never hinged 3.00

Death centenary of Gen. Josef Bem.

Type of 1950 with Frame Omitted

Perf. 12x12½

1950, Dec. 16 Engr. Unwmk.

490 A166 5g brown violet .20 .20
491 A166 10g bluish green .20 .20
492 A166 15g dp yellow grn .20 .20
493 A166 25g dark red .20 .20
493A A166 30g red .25 .20
494 A166 40g vermilion .20 .20
495 A166 45g deep blue .95 .20
496 A166 75g brown .60 .20
Nos. 490-496 (8) 2.80 1.60
Set, never hinged 4.00

Reconstruction Type of 1950

Perf. 11, 11x11½, 13x11

1950 Photo.

497 A168 15g green .20 .20
Never hinged .25

Woman and Doves — A178

1951, Mar. 2 Engr. ***Perf. 12½***

498 A178 45g dark red .30 .20
Never hinged .50

Congress of Women, Mar. 3-4, 1951.

Gen. Jaroslaw Dabrowski — A179

1951, Mar. 24 ***Perf. 12x12½***

499 A179 45g dark green .20 .20
Never hinged .35

80th anniv. of the Insurrection of Paris and the death of Gen. Jaroslaw Dabrowski.

Dove Type of 1950 Surcharged

1951, Apr. 20 ***Perf. 12½***

500 A176 45g on 15z brn red .40 .20
Never hinged .60

Worker and Flag — A180

Steel Mill, Nowa Huta — A181

1951, Apr. 25 Photo. ***Perf. 14x11***

501 A180 45g scarlet .35 .20
Never hinged .55

Labor Day, May 1.

1951 Engr. ***Perf. 12½***

502 A181 40g dark blue .20 .20
503 A181 45g black .20 .20
504 A181 60g brown .20 .20
505 A181 90g dark carmine .40 .20
Nos. 502-505 (4) 1.00 .80
Set, never hinged 2.50

Pioneer Saluting A182

Boy and Girl Pioneers A183

1951, Apr. 1 **Photo.**

506 A182 30g olive brown .50 .50
507 A183 45g brt grnsh blue 6.00 .75
Set, never hinged 8.00

Issued to publicize Children's Day, June 1, 1951.

Workers Type of 1950

1951 Unwmk. Engr. ***Perf. 12½x13***

507A A173 45g violet blue .20 .20
508 A173 75g black brown .20 .20
509 A173 1.15z dark green .40 .20
510 A173 1.20z dark red .25 .20
Nos. 507A-510 (4) 1.05 .80
Set, never hinged 2.50

Issued to publicize Poland's 6-year plan.

Stanislaw Staszyk — A184

Congress Emblem — A186

Z. F. von Wroblewski and Karol S. Olszewski — A185

Portraits: 40g, Marie Sklodowska Curie. 60g, Marceli Nencki. 1.15z, Nicolaus Copernicus.

Perf. 12½, 14x11

1951, Apr. 25 **Photo.**

511 A184 25g carmine rose 1.90 1.50
512 A184 40g ultra .25 .20
513 A185 45g purple 7.00 1.50
514 A184 60g green .55 .20
515 A184 1.15z claret 1.90 .75
516 A186 1.20z gray 1.40 .60
Nos. 511-516 (6) 13.00 4.75
Set, never hinged 16.00

1st Congress of Polish Science.

Feliks E. Dzerzhinski — A187

1951, July 5 Engr. ***Perf. 12x12½***

517 A187 45g chestnut brown .20 .20
Never hinged .30

25th death anniv. of Feliks E. Dzerzhinski, Polish revolutionary, organizer of Russian secret police.

Pres. Boleslaw Bierut — A188

1951, July 22 ***Perf. 12½***

518 A188 45g dark carmine .50 .25
519 A188 60g deep green 12.00 6.75
520 A188 90g deep blue 1.00 .50
Nos. 518-520 (3) 13.50 7.50
Set, never hinged 19.00

7th anniv. of the formation of the Polish People's Republic.

Flag and Sports Emblem — A189

Youths Encircling Globe — A190

Perf. 12½, 14x11

1951, Sept. 8 **Photo.**

521 A189 45g green 1.00 .50
Never hinged 1.65

National Sports Festival, 1951.

Type of 1950 with Frame Omitted
Surcharged with New Value in Black

1951, Sept. 1 Engr. *Perf. 12½x11½*
522 A166 45g on 35z org red .20 .20
Never hinged .30

1951, Aug. 5 Photo. *Perf. 12½x11*
523 A190 40g deep ultra .60 .20
Never hinged .95

3rd World Youth Festival, Berlin, Aug. 5-19.

Joseph V. Stalin — A191

Frederic Chopin and Stanislaw Moniuszko — A192

1951, Oct. 30 Engr. *Perf. 12½*
524 A191 45g lake .20 .20
525 A191 90g gray black .40 .20
Set, never hinged 1.25

Month of Polish-Soviet friendship, Nov. 1951.

1951, Nov. 15 Unwmk.
526 A192 45g gray .20 .20
527 A192 90g brownish red .90 .25
Set, never hinged 1.75

Festival of Polish Music, 1951.

Apartment House Construction A193

Coal Mining A194

Design: #529-530, Electrical installation.

1951-52

Inscribed: "Plan 6," etc.

528 A193 30g dull green .20 .20
529 A193 30g gray black ('52) .20 .20
530 A193 45g red ('52) .25 .20
531 A194 90g chocolate .40 .20
532 A193 1.15z violet brn ('52) .40 .20
533 A194 1.20z deep blue ('52) .40 .20
Nos. 528-533,B68-B69A (9) 3.10 1.95
Set, never hinged 4.00

Poland's 6-year plan.

Catalogue values for unused stamps in this section, from this point to the end of the section, are for Never Hinged items.

Pawel Finder — A195

Flag, Workman, Mother and Child — A196

Portrait: 1.15z, Malgorzata Fornalska.

1952, Jan. 18
534 A195 90g chocolate .25 .20
535 A195 1.15z red orange .30 .20
Nos. 534-535,B63 (3) .75 .60

Polish Workers Party, 10th anniv.

See No. B63.

1952, Mar. 8 *Perf. 12½x12*
536 A196 1.20z deep carmine .40 .20

Intl. Women's Day. See No. B64.

Gen. Karol Swierczewski-Walter A197

Pres. Boleslaw Bierut A198

1952, Mar. 28 *Perf. 12½*
537 A197 90g blue gray .40 .20

Gen. Karol Swierczewski-Walter (1896-1947). See No. B65.

1952, Apr. 18
538 A198 90g dull green .70 .45
Nos. 538,B66-B67 (3) 1.70 .85

60th birth anniv. of Pres. Boleslaw Bierut.

Souvenir Sheet

A199

1951, Nov. 15
539 A199 Sheet of 4 20.00 12.50
a. 45g red brown (A173) 1.40 1.40
b. 75g red brown (A173) 1.40 1.40
c. 1.15z red brown (A173) 1.40 1.40
d. 1.20z red brown (A173) 1.40 1.40

Polish Philatelic Association Congress, Warsaw, 1951. Sold for 5 zloty.

Workers with Flag A200

J. I. Kraszewski A201

1952, May 1 Unwmk. *Perf. 12½*
540 A200 75g deep green .45 .20

Labor Day, May 1, 1952. See No. B70.

1952, May

1z, Hugo Kollontaj. 1.15z, Maria Konopnicka.

Various Frames

541 A201 25g brown violet .35 .20
542 A201 1z yellow green .40 .20
543 A201 1.15z red brown .75 .35
Nos. 541-543,B71-B72 (5) 2.25

Nikolai Gogol A202

Gymnast A203

1952, June 5
544 A202 25g deep green .75 .40

100th death anniv. of Nikolai V. Gogol, writer.

1952, June 21 Photo. *Perf. 13*
545 A203 1.15z Runners 1.40 .90
546 A203 1.20z shown .60 .50
Nos. 545-546,B75-B76 (4) 7.50 3.15

Racing Cyclists — A204

Shipyard Worker and Collier — A205

1952, Apr. 25 *Perf. 13½*
547 A204 40g blue 1.25 .40

5th Intl. Peace Bicycle Race, Warsaw-Berlin-Prague.

1952, June 28 Engr. *Perf. 12½*
548 A205 90g violet brown .95 .60
Nos. 548,B77-B78 (3) 4.40 1.75

Shipbuilders' Day, 1952.

Concrete Works, Wierzbica A206

Bugler A207

1952, June 17
549 A206 3z gray .95 .40
550 A206 10z brown red 1.50 .25

1952, July 17 *Perf. 12½x12*
551 A207 90g brown .45 .20

Youth Festival, 1952. See Nos. B79-B80.

Celebrating New Constitution A208

Power Plant, Jaworzno A209

1952, July 22 Photo. *Perf. 12½*
552 A208 3z vio & dk brn .40 .25

Proclamation of a new constitution. See No. B81.

1952, Aug. 7 Engr.
553 A209 1z black .65 .25
554 A209 1.50z deep green .65 .20
Nos. 553-554,B82 (3) 1.95 .65

Grywald — A210

Parachute Descent — A211

1952, Aug. 18
555 A210 60g dark green 1.60 .50
556 A210 1z red ("Niedzica") 2.50 .20
a. 1z red ("Niedziga") 6.00 1.00
Nos. 555-556,B85 (3) 5.00 .90

1952, Aug. 23
557 A211 90g deep blue .70 .45
Nos. 557,B86-B87 (3) 3.50 1.65

Aviation Day, Aug. 23.

Avicenna A212

Shipbuilding A213

Portrait: 90g, Victor Hugo.

1952, Sept. 1
558 A212 75g red brown .35 .20
559 A212 90g sepia .25 .20

Anniversaries of the births of Avicenna (1000th) and Victor Hugo (150th).

1952, Sept. 10
560 A213 5g deep green .20 .20
561 A213 15g red brown .20 .20

Reconstruction of Gdansk shipyards.

Assault on the Winter Palace, 1917 A214

1952, Nov. 7 *Perf. 12x12½*
562 A214 60g dark brown .55 .30

Russian Revolution, 35th anniv. See #B92. #562, B92 exist imperf. Value $30.

Auto Assembly Plant, Zeran — A215

Dove — A216

1952, Dec. 12 *Perf. 12½*
563 A215 1.15z brown .48 .20

See No. B99.

1952, Dec. 12 Photo.
564 A216 30g green .55 .20
565 A216 60g ultra 1.25 .50

Congress of Nations for Peace, Vienna, Dec. 12-19, 1952.

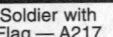

Soldier with Flag — A217

Karl Marx — A218

1953, Feb. 2 **Unwmk.** ***Perf. 11***

Flag in Carmine

566 A217 60g olive gray 4.50 1.60
567 A217 80g blue gray 1.00 .40

10th anniv. of the Battle of Stalingrad.

1953, Mar. 14 ***Perf. 12½***

568 A218 60g dull blue 19.00 10.00
569 A218 80g dark brown 1.00 .30

70th death anniv. of Karl Marx.

Cyclists and Arms of Warsaw — A219

Flag and Globe — A220

Arms: No. 571, Berlin. No. 572, Prague.

1953, Apr. 30

570 A219 80g dark brown 1.25 .50
571 A219 80g dark green 1.25 .50
572 A219 80g red 15.00 9.00
Nos. 570-572 (3) 17.50 10.00

6th Intl. Peace Bicycle Race, Warsaw-Berlin-Prague.

1953, Apr. 28

573 A220 60g vermilion 4.25 3.25
574 A220 80g carmine .70 .35

Labor Day, May 1, 1953.

Boxer — A221

Design: 95g, Boxing match.

1953, May 17

575 A221 40g red brown 1.00 .50
576 A221 80g orange 10.00 6.25
577 A221 95g violet brown 1.00 .50
Nos. 575-577 (3) 12.00 7.25

European Championship Boxing Matches, Warsaw, May 17-24, 1953.

Copernicus Watching Heavens, by Jan Matejko — A222

Nicolaus Copernicus — A223

Perf. 12x12½, 12½x12

1953, May 22 **Engr.**

578 A222 20g brown 1.50 .50
579 A223 80g deep blue 12.00 10.50

480th birth anniv. of Nicolaus Copernicus, astronomer.

Fishing Boat — A224

Old Part of Warsaw — A225

Design: 1.35z, Freighter "Czech."

1953, July 15 ***Perf. 12½***

580 A224 80g dark green 1.10 .45
581 A224 1.35z deep blue 2.00 1.50

Issued for Merchant Marine Day.

1953, July 15 **Photo.**

582 A225 20g red brown .40 .35
583 A225 2.35z blue 3.50 3.00

36th anniv. of the proclamation of "People's Poland."

Students of Two Races — A226

Schoolgirl and Dove — A227

1.35z, Congress badge (similar to AP7).

1953, Aug. 24

584 A226 40g dark brown .50 .20
585 A227 1.35z green 1.00 .20
586 A227 1.50z blue 2.50 *3.00*
Nos. 584-586,C32-C33 (5) 6.50 4.65

3rd World Congress of Students, Warsaw, 1953.

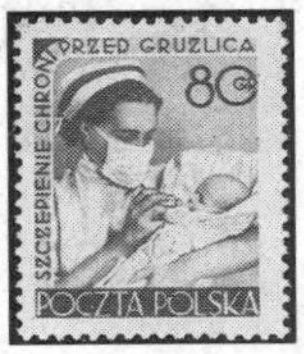

Nurse Feeding Baby — A228

Design: 1.75z, Nurse instructing mother.

1953, Nov. 21

587 A228 80g rose carmine 8.75 5.00
588 A228 1.75z deep green .25 .20

Poland's Social Health Service.

Mieczyslaw Kalinowski A229

Battle Scene, Polish and Soviet Flags A230

Portrait: 1.75z, Roman Pazinski.

1953, Oct. 10

589 A229 45g brown 3.50 2.25
590 A230 80g brown lake .55 .20
591 A229 1.75z olive gray .55 .20
Nos. 589-591 (3) 4.60 2.65

10th anniv. of Poland's People's Army.

Jan Kochanowski A231

Courtyard, Wawel Castle A232

Portrait: 1.35z, Mikolaj Rej.

1953, Nov. 10 **Engr.**

592 A231 20g red brown .20 .20
593 A232 80g deep plum .40 .20
594 A231 1.35z gray black 1.75 1.00
Nos. 592-594 (3) 2.35 1.40

Issued for the "Renaissance Year."
For surcharges see Nos. 733-736.

Palace of Culture, Warsaw A233

Designs: 1.75z, Constitution Square. 2z, Old Section, Warsaw.

1953, Nov. 30 ***Perf. 12x12½***

595 A233 80g vermilion 9.00 1.25
596 A233 1.75z deep blue .65 .40
597 A233 2z violet brown 5.50 2.50
Nos. 595-597 (3) 15.15 4.15

Issued for the reconstruction of Warsaw.

Ice Dancer — A236

Skier — A237

Design: 2.85z, Ice hockey player.

1953, Dec. 31 **Litho.** ***Perf. 12½***

602 A236 80g blue 1.25 .30
603 A237 95g blue green 1.75 .50
604 A236 2.85z dark red 4.75 2.00
Nos. 602-604 (3) 7.75 2.80

Canceled to Order

The government stamp agency began late in 1951 to sell canceled sets of new issues. Until 1990, at least, values in the second ("used") column are for these canceled-to-order stamps. Postally used copies are worth more.

Children at Play — A238

Designs: 80g, Girls on the way to school. 1.50z, Two students in class.

1953, Dec. 31 **Photo.**

605 A238 10g violet .20 .20
606 A238 80g red brown .80 .30
607 A238 1.50z dark green 6.00 2.00
Nos. 605-607 (3) 7.00 2.50

Krynica Spa A239

Dunajec Canyon, Pieniny Mountains A240

Designs: 80g, Morskie Oko, Tatra Mts. 2z, Windmill and framework, Ciechocinek.

1953, Dec. 16

608 A239 20g blue & rose brn .25 .20
609 A240 80g bl grn & dk vio 1.90 1.25
610 A240 1.75z ol bis & dk grn .75 .20
611 A239 2z brick red & blk 1.10 .20
Nos. 608-611 (4) 4.00 1.85

Electric Passenger Train — A241

Spinning Mill, Worker — A242

Design: 80g, Electric locomotive and cars.

1954, Jan. 26 **Engr.**

612 A241 60g deep blue 6.25 4.25
613 A241 80g red brown .75 .25

1954, Mar. 24 **Photo.**

Designs: 40g, Woman letter carrier. 80g, Woman tractor driver.

614 A242 20g deep green 1.50 .45
615 A242 40g deep blue .60 .20
616 A242 80g dark brown .40 .20
Nos. 614-616 (3) 2.50 .85

Flags and May Flowers — A243

"Peace" Uniting Three Capitals — A244

1954, Apr. 28

617 A243 40g chocolate .75 .30
618 A243 60g deep blue .75 .20
619 A243 80g carmine rose .75 .25
Nos. 617-619 (3) 2.25 .75

Labor Day, May 1, 1954.

1954, Apr. 29 ***Perf. 12½x12***

No. 621, Dove, olive branch and wheel.

620 A244 80g red brown .50 .20
621 A244 80g deep blue .50 .20

7th Intl. Bicycle Tour, May 2-17, 1954.

A245

Glider and Framed Clouds — A246

1954, Apr. 30 **Engr.** ***Perf. 11½***

622 A245 25g gray .95 .20
623 A245 80g brown carmine .30 .20

3rd Trade Union Congress, Warsaw 1954.

1954, May 31 Photo. *Perf. 12½*

60g, Glider, flags. 1.35z, Glider, large cloud.

624	A246	45g dark green	.20	.20
625	A246	60g purple	4.00	.80
626	A246	60g brown	.90	.20
627	A246	1.35z blue	.90	.30
		Nos. 624-627 (4)	6.00	1.50

Intl. Glider Championships, Leszno.

Fencing — A247

Handstand on Horizontal Bars — A248

Design: 1z, Relay racers.

1954, July 17

628	A247	25g violet brown	1.40	.35
629	A248	60g Prus blue	1.40	.25
630	A247	1z violet blue	2.75	.65
		Nos. 628-630 (3)	5.55	1.25

Javelin Throwers A249

Studzianki Battle Scene — A250

1954, July 17 *Perf. 12*

631	A249	60g rose brn & dk red brn	1.25	.25
632	A249	1.55z gray & black	1.10	.35

Nos. 628-632 were issued to publicize the second Summer Spartacist Games, 1954.

1954, Aug. 24 *Perf. 12½*

Design: 1z, Soldier and flag bearer.

633	A250	60g dark green	1.40	.25
634	A250	1z violet blue	6.00	2.75

10th anniversary, Battle of Studzianki.

Railway Signal — A251

Farmer Picking Fruit — A252

Design: 60g, Modern train.

1954, Sept. 9

635	A251	40g dull blue	4.00	1.00
636	A251	60g black	2.00	.50

Issued to publicize Railwaymen's Day.

1954, Sept. 15

637	A252	40g violet	1.40	.60
638	A252	60g black	.60	.20

Month of Polish-Soviet friendship.

View of Elblag A253

Chopin and Piano — A254

Cities: 45g, Gdansk. 60g, Torun. 1.40z, Malbork. 1.55z, Olsztyn.

1954, Oct. 16 Engr. *Perf. 12x12½*

639	A253	20g dk car, *bl*	2.75	.70
640	A253	45g brown, *yel*	.25	.20
641	A253	60g dk green, *cit*	.25	.20
642	A253	1.40z dk blue, *pink*	.50	.20
643	A253	1.55z dk vio brn, *cr*	1.25	.20
		Nos. 639-643 (5)	5.00	1.50

Pomerania's return to Poland, 500th anniv. For overprint see No. 866.

1954, Nov. 8 Photo. *Perf. 12½*

644	A254	45g dark brown	.50	.20
645	A254	60g dark green	.95	.20
646	A254	1z dark blue	2.25	.55
		Nos. 644-646 (3)	3.70	.95

5th Intl. Competition of Chopin's Music.

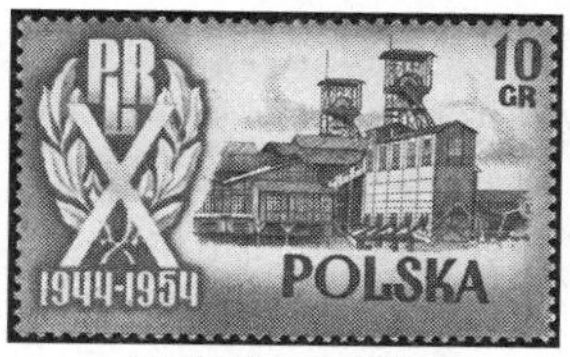

Coal Mine — A255

Designs: 20g, Soldier, flag and map. 25g, Steel mill. 40g, Relaxing worker in deck chair. 45g, Building construction. 60g, Tractor in field. 1.15z, Lublin Castle. 1.40z, Books and publications. 1.55z, Loading ship. 2.10z, Attacking tank.

Photo.; Center Engr.

1954-55 *Perf. 12½x12*

647	A255	10g red brn & choc	1.25	.20
648	A255	20g rose & grnsh blk	.65	.30
649	A255	25g bister & blk	1.50	.20
650	A255	40g yel org & choc	.50	.20
651	A255	45g claret & vio brn	.95	.20
652	A255	60g emerald & red brn	.95	.25
653	A255	1.15z brt bl grn & sep	.95	.50
654	A255	1.40z orange & choc	9.25	2.25
655	A255	1.55z blue & indigo	1.75	.65
656	A255	2.10z ultra & indigo	3.00	1.40
		Nos. 647-656 (10)	20.75	6.15

10th anniversary of "People's Poland." Issued: 25g, 60g, 1955; others, 12/23/54.

Photo.; Center Litho.

1954, Oct. 30

656A	A255	25g bister & blk	3.50	1.50
656B	A255	60g emer & red brn	1.75	1.00

Insurgents Attacking Russians — A256

60g, Gen. Tadeusz Kosciuszko and insurgents. 1.40z, Kosciuszko leading attack in Cracow.

1954, Nov. 30 Engr. *Perf. 12½*

657	A256	40g grnsh black	.40	.20
658	A256	60g violet brown	.60	.20
659	A256	1.40z dark gray	1.65	.70
		Nos. 657-659 (3)	2.65	1.10

160th anniv. of the Insurrection of 1794.

Bison — A257

60g, European elk. 1.90z, Chamois. 3z, Beaver.

Engr.; Background Photo.

1954, Dec. 22

660	A257	45g yel grn & blk brn	.40	.20
661	A257	60g emerald & dk brn	.40	.20
662	A257	1.90z blue & blk brn	.60	.20
663	A257	3z bl grn & dk brn	1.75	.50
		Nos. 660-663 (4)	3.15	1.10

Exist imperf. Value, set $4.50.

Liberators Entering Warsaw — A258

Frederic Chopin — A259

60g, Allegory of freedom (Warsaw Mermaid).

1955, Jan. 17 Photo.

664	A258	40g red brown	.85	.30
665	A258	60g dull blue	2.25	.65

Liberation of Warsaw, 10th anniversary.

1955, Feb. 22 Engr.

666	A259	40g dark brown	.35	.20
667	A259	60g indigo	.65	.20

5th Intl. Competition of Chopin's Music, Feb. 22-Mar. 21.

Brothers in Arms Monument A260

Sigismund III A261

Warsaw monuments: 5g, Mermaid. 10g, Feliks E. Dzerzhinski. 40g, Nicolaus Copernicus. 45g, Marie Sklodowska Curie. 60g, Adam Mickiewicz. 1.55z, Jan Kilinski.

1955, May 3 Unwmk. *Perf. 12½*

668	A260	5g dk grn, *grnsh*	.20	.20
669	A260	10g vio brn, *yel*	.20	.20
670	A261	15g blk brn, *bluish*	.20	.20
671	A260	20g dk bl, *pink*	.20	.20
672	A260	40g vio, *vio*	.60	.20
673	A261	45g vio brn, *cr*	.80	.25
674	A260	60g dk bl, *gray*	.60	.20
675	A261	1.55z sl bl, *grysh*	1.65	.30
		Nos. 668-675 (8)	4.45	1.75

See Nos. 737-739.

Palace of Culture and Flags of Poland and USSR — A262

Design: 60g, Monument.

Perf. 12½x12, 11

1955, Apr. 21 Photo.

676	A262	40g rose red	.20	.20
677	A262	40g lt brown	.60	.30
678	A262	60g Prus blue	.25	.20
679	A262	60g dk olive brn	.25	.20
		Nos. 676-679 (4)	1.30	.90

Polish-USSR treaty of friendship, 10th anniv.

Arms and Bicycle Wheels — A263

Poznan Town Hall and Fair Emblem — A264

Design: 60g, Three doves above road.

1955, Apr. 25 *Perf. 12*

680	A263	40g chocolate	.40	.20
681	A263	60g ultra	.25	.20

8th Intl. Peace Bicycle Race, Prague-Berlin-Warsaw.

1955, June 10 Photo. *Perf. 12½*

682	A264	40g brt ultra	.30	.20
683	A264	60g dull red	.20	.20

24th Intl. Fair at Poznan, July 3-24, 1955.

"Laikonik" Carnival Costume A265

A265a

1955, June 16 Typo. *Perf. 12*

Multicolored Centers

684	A265	20g emerald & henna	.30	.25
685	A265a	40g brt org & lil	.45	.20
686	A265	60g blue & carmine	1.25	.30
		Nos. 684-686 (3)	2.00	.75

Cracow Celebration Days.

Pansies — A266

40g, 60g, (#690), Dove & Tower of Palace of Science & Culture. 45g, Pansies. 60g, (#691), 1z, "Peace" (POKOJ) & Warsaw Mermaid.

1955, July 13 Litho. *Perf. 12*

687	A266	25g vio brn, org & car	.20	.20
688	A266	40g gray bl & gray blk	.20	.20
689	A266	45g brn lake, yel & car	.35	.20
690	A266	60g sepia & orange	.30	.20
691	A266	60g ultra & lt blue	.30	.20
692	A266	1z purple & lt blue	.90	.50
		Nos. 687-692 (6)	2.25	1.50

5th World Festival of Youth, Warsaw, July 31-Aug. 14, 1955.
Exist imperf. Value, set $3.

Motorcyclists A267

Stalin Palace of Culture and Science, Warsaw A268

1955, July 20 Photo. *Perf. 12½*

693 A267 40g chocolate .30 .20
694 A267 60g dark green .25 .20

13th Intl. Motorcycle Race in the Tatra Mountains, Aug. 7-9, 1955.

1955, July 21

695 A268 60g ultra .20 .20
696 A268 60g gray .20 .20
697 A268 75g blue green .45 .20
698 A268 75g brown .45 .20
Nos. 695-698 (4) 1.30 .80

Polish National Day, July 22, 1955. Sheets contain alternating copies of the 60g values or the 75g values respectively.

Athletes — A269

Stadium — A270

Designs: 40g, Hammer throwing. 1z, Basketball. 1.35z, Sculling. 1.55z, Swimming.

1955, July 27 Unwmk. *Perf. 12½*

699 A269 20g chocolate .20 .20
700 A269 40g plum .20 .20
701 A270 60g dull blue .30 .20
702 A269 1z orange ver .55 .20
703 A269 1.35z dull violet .70 .20
704 A269 1.55z peacock green 1.25 .50
Nos. 699-704 (6) 3.20 1.50

2nd International Youth Games, 1955. Exist imperf. Value, set $4.

Town Hall, Szczecin (Stettin) — A271

Rebels with Flag — A272

Designs: 40g, Cathedral, Wroclaw (Breslau) 60g, Town Hall, Zielona Gora (Grunberg). 95g, Town Hall, Opole (Oppeln).

1955, Sept. 22 Engr. *Perf. 11½*

705 A271 25g dull green .20 .20
706 A271 40g red brown .30 .20
707 A271 60g violet blue .60 .20
708 A271 95g dark gray .90 .30
Nos. 705-708 (4) 2.00 .90

10th anniv. of the acquisition of Western Polish Territories.

1955, Sept. 30 Photo. *Perf. 12x12½*

709 A272 40g dark brown .25 .20
710 A272 60g dk carmine rose .25 .20

Revolution of 1905, 50th anniversary.

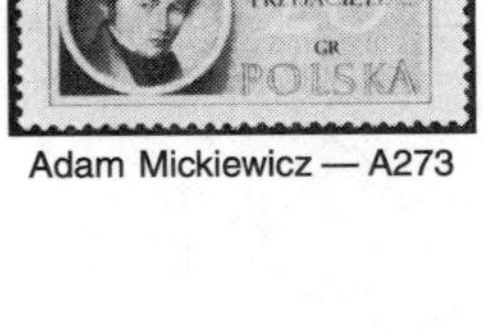

Adam Mickiewicz — A273

Mickiewicz Monument, Paris — A274

60g, Death mask. 95g, Statue, Warsaw.

1955, Oct. 10 *Perf. 12x12½, 12½*

711 A273 20g dark brown .20 .20
712 A274 40g brn org & dk brn .20 .20
713 A274 60g green & brown .25 .20
714 A274 95g brn red & blk 1.50 .50
Nos. 711-714 (4) 2.15 1.10

Death cent. of Adam Mickiewicz, poet, and to publicize the celebration of Mickiewicz year.

Teacher and Child — A275

Rook and Hands — A276

Design: 60g, Flame and open book.

Perf. 12½x13

1955, Oct. 21 Unwmk.

715 A275 40g brown 1.50 .25
716 A275 60g ultra 2.50 .85

Polish Teachers' Trade Union, 50th anniv.

1956, Feb. 9 *Perf. 12½*

Design: 60g, Chess knight and hands.

717 A276 40g dark red 1.90 .85
718 A276 60g blue 1.50 .20

First World Chess Championship of the Deaf and Dumb, Feb. 9-23.

Captain and S. S. Kilinski A277

10g, Sailor and barges. 20g, Dock worker and S. S. Pokoj. 45g, Shipyard and worker. 60g, Fisherman, S. S. Chopin and trawlers.

1956, Mar. 16 Engr. *Perf. 12x12½*

719 A277 5g green .20 .20
720 A277 10g carmine lake .20 .20
721 A277 20g deep ultra .20 .20
722 A277 45g rose brown .70 .20
723 A277 60g violet blue .55 .20
Nos. 719-723 (5) 1.85 1.00

Snowflake and Ice Skates — A278

Cyclist — A279

Designs: 40g, Snowflake and Ice Hockey sticks. 60g, Snowflake and Skis.

1956, Mar. 7 Photo. *Perf. 12½*

724 A278 20g brt ultra & blk 4.00 1.50
725 A278 40g brt grn & vio bl .55 .20
726 A278 60g lilac & lake .55 .20
Nos. 724-726 (3) 5.10 1.90

XI World Students Winter Sport Championship, Mar. 7-13.

1956, Apr. 25

727 A279 40g dark blue 1.25 .40
728 A279 60g dark green .20 .20

9th Intl. Peace Bicycle Race, Warsaw-Berlin-Prague, May 1-15.

Zakopane Mountains and Shelter — A280

40g, Map, compass & knapsack. 60g, Map of Poland & canoe. 1.15z, Skis & mountains.

1956, May 25

729 A280 30g dark green .30 .20
730 A280 40g lt red brown .30 .20
731 A280 60g blue 1.10 .50
732 A280 1.15z dull purple .55 .20
Nos. 729-732 (4) 2.25 1.10

Polish Tourist industry.

No. 593 Surcharged with New Values

1956, July 6 Engr. *Perf. 12½*

733 A232 10g on 80g dp plum .35 .20
734 A232 40g on 80g dp plum .30 .20
735 A232 60g on 80g dp plum .55 .20
736 A232 1.35z on 80g dp plum 1.25 .70
Nos. 733-736 (4) 2.45 1.30

The size and type of surcharge and obliteration of old value differ for each denomination.

Type of 1955

Warsaw Monuments: 30g, Ghetto Monument. 40g, John III Sobieski. 1.55z, Prince Joseph Poniatowski.

1956, July 10

737 A260 30g black .25 .20
738 A260 40g red brn, *grnsh* .50 .25
739 A260 1.55z vio brn, *pnksh* .70 .25
Nos. 737-739 (3) 1.45 .70

No. 737 measures 22½x28mm, instead of 21x27mm.

Polish and Russian Dancers A281

Design: 60g, Open book and cogwheels.

1956, Sept. 14 Litho. *Perf. 12*

740 A281 40g brn red & brn .35 .20
741 A281 60g bister & red .20 .20

Polish-Soviet Friendship month.

Ludwiga Warzynska and Children — A282

Bee on Clover and Beehive — A283

1956, Sept. 17 Photo. *Perf. 12½*

742 A282 40g dull red brown .70 .20
743 A282 60g blue .30 .20

Issued in honor of a heroic school teacher who saved three children from a burning house.

1956, Oct. 30 Litho. Unwmk.

Design: 60g, Father Jan Dzierzon.

744 A283 40g org yel & brn .95 .35
745 A283 60g yellow & brn .30 .20

50th death anniv. of Father Jan Dzierzon, the inventor of the modernized beehive.

"Lady with the Ermine" by Leonardo da Vinci A284

40g, Niobe. 60g, Madonna by Veit Stoss.

1956 Engr. *Perf. 11½x11*

746 A284 40g dark green 2.50 1.25
747 A284 60g dark violet .75 .20
748 A284 1.55z chocolate 1.75 .20
Nos. 746-748 (3) 5.00 1.65

Intl. Museum Week (UNESCO), Oct. 8-14.

Fencer A285

Designs: 20g, Boxer. 25g, Sculling. 40g, Steeplechase racer. 60g, Javelin thrower. No. 755, Woman gymnast. No. 756, Woman broad jumper.

1956 Engr. *Perf. 11½*

750 A285 10g slate & chnt .20 .20
751 A285 20g lt brn & dl vio .25 .20
a. Center inverted
752 A285 25g lt blue & blk .40 .20
753 A285 40g brt bl grn & redsh brn .30 .20
754 A285 60g rose car & ol brn .40 .20
755 A285 1.55z lt vio & sepia 1.50 1.00
756 A285 1.55z orange & chnt 1.00 .25
Nos. 750-756 (7) 4.05 2.25

16th Olympic Games, Melbourne, 11/22-12/8.

15th Century Mailman — A286

Lithographed and Engraved

1956, Nov. 30 Unwmk. *Perf. 12½*

757 A286 60g lt blue & blk 1.65 .80

Reopening of the Postal Museum in Wroclaw.

Skier and Snowflake A287

Ski Jumper and Snowflake — A288

Design: 1z, Skier in right corner.

1957, Jan. 18 Photo. *Perf. 12½*

758 A287 40g blue .25 .20
759 A288 60g dark green .25 .20
760 A287 1z purple .50 .30
Nos. 758-760 (3) 1.00 .70

50 years of skiing in Poland.

Globe and Tree A289

UN Emblem — A290

UN Building, NY — A291

1957, Feb. 26 Photo. *Perf. 12*

761 A289 5g mag & brt grnsh bl .35 .20
762 A290 15g blue & gray .40 .20
763 A291 40g brt bl grn & gray .75 .45
Nos. 761-763 (3) 1.50 .85

Issued in honor of the United Nations.
Exist imperf. Value, set $4.25.
An imperf. souvenir sheet exists, containing a 1.50z stamp in a redrawn design similar to A291. The stamp is blue and bright bluish green Value, $25 unused, $14 canceled.

Skier — A292

Sword, Foil and Saber on World Map — A293

1957, Mar. 22 *Perf. 12½*

764 A292 60g blue .60 .25
765 A292 60g brown .80 .30

12th anniv. of the death of the skiers Bronislaw Czech and Hanna Marusarzowna.

1957, Apr. 20 Unwmk. *Perf. 12½*

Designs: No. 767, Fencer facing right. No. 768, Fencer facing left.

766 A293 40g deep plum .55 .30
767 A293 60g carmine .40 .20
768 A293 60g ultra .40 .20
a. Pair, #767-768 1.25 .50

World Youth Fencing Championships, Warsaw.
No. 768a has continuous design.

Dr. Sebastian Petrycy A294

Bicycle Wheel and Carnation A295

Doctors' Portraits: 20g Wojciech Oczko. 40g, Jedrzej Sniadecki. 60g, Tytus Chalubinski. 1z, Wladyslaw Bieganski. 1.35z, Jozef Dietl. 2.50z, Benedykt Dybowski. 3z, Henryk Jordan.

Portraits Engr., Inscriptions Typo.

1957 *Perf. 11½*

769 A294 10g sepia & ultra .20 .20
770 A294 20g emerald & claret .20 .20
771 A294 40g gray & org red .20 .20
772 A294 60g blue & pale brn .50 .20
773 A294 1z org & dk blue .20 .20
774 A294 1.35z gray brn & grn .20 .20
775 A294 2.50z dull vio & lil rose .25 .20
776 A294 3z violet & ol brn .25 .20
Nos. 769-776 (8) 2.00 1.60

1957, May 4 Photo. *Perf. 12½*

777 A295 60g shown .55 .20
778 A295 1.50z Cyclist .20 .20

10th Intl. Peace Bicycle Race, Warsaw-Berlin-Prague.

Poznan Fair Emblem — A296

Turk's Cap — A297

1957, June 8 Litho. Unwmk.

779 A296 60g ultramarine .25 .20
780 A296 2.50z lt blue green .30 .20

Issued to publicize the 26th Fair at Poznan.

1957, Aug. 12 Photo. *Perf. 12*

Flowers: No. 782, Carline Thistle. No. 783, Sea Holly. No. 784, Edelweiss. No. 785, Lady's-slipper.

781 A297 60g bl grn & claret .25 .20
782 A297 60g gray, grn & yel .25 .20
783 A297 60g lt blue & grn .25 .20
784 A297 60g gray & yel grn .25 .20
785 A297 60g lt grn, mar & yel 1.00 .25
Nos. 781-785 (5) 2.00 1.05

Fire Fighter — A298

Town Hall, Leipzig and Congress Emblem — A299

60g, Child & flames. 2.50z, Grain & flames.

1957, Sept. 11 *Perf. 12*

786 A298 40g black & red .20 .20
787 A298 60g dk grn & org red .20 .20
788 A298 2.50z violet & red .50 .20
Nos. 786-788 (3) .90 .60

Intl. Fire Brigade Conf., Warsaw.

1957, Sept. 25 Photo. *Perf. 12½*

789 A299 60g violet .20 .20

4th Intl. Trade Union Cong., Leipzig, Oct. 4-15.

"Girl Writing Letter" by Fragonard A300

Karol Libelt — A301

1957, Oct. 9 *Perf. 12*

790 A300 2.50z dark blue green .50 .20

Issued for Stamp Day, Oct. 9.

1957, Nov. 15 Photo. *Perf. 12½*

791 A301 60g carmine lake .20 .20

Centenary of the Poznan Scientific Society and to honor Karol Libelt, politician and philosopher.

Broken Chain and Flag — A302

Jan A. Komensky (Comenius) A303

Design: 2.50z, Lenin Statue, Poronin.

1957, Nov. 7

792 A302 60g brt blue & red .20 .20
793 A302 2.50z black & red brn .25 .20

40th anniv. of the Russian Revolution.

1957, Dec. 11 *Perf. 12*

794 A303 2.50z brt carmine .25 .20

300th anniv. of the publication of "Didactica Opera Omnia."

Henri Wieniawski A304

Andrzej Strug A305

1957, Dec. 2 *Perf. 12½*

795 A304 2.50z blue .25 .20

3rd Wieniawski Violin Competition in Poznan.

1957, Dec. 16 Unwmk. *Perf. 12½*

796 A305 2.50z brown .20 .20

20th death anniv. of Andrzej Strug, novelist.

Joseph Conrad and "Torrens" A306

1957, Dec. 30 Engr. *Perf. 12x12½*

797 A306 60g brown, *grnsh* .20 .20
798 A306 2.50z dk blue, *pink* .45 .20

Birth cent. of Joseph Conrad, Polish-born English writer.

Postilion and Stylized Plane — A307

Town Hall at Biecz — A308

Designs: 40g, Tomb of Prosper Prowano, globe with plane and satellite. 60g, St. Mary's Church, Cracow, mail coach and plane. 95g, Mail coach and postal bus. 2.10z, Medieval postman and train. 3.40z, Medieval galleon and modern ships.

1958 Litho. *Perf. 12½*

799 A307 40g lt blue & vio brn .20 .20
800 A307 60g pale vio & blk .20 .20
801 A307 95g lemon & violet .20 .20
802 A307 2.10z gray & ultra .45 .35
803 A307 2.50z brt blue & blk .35 .20
804 A307 3.40z aqua & maroon .35 .25
Nos. 799-804 (6) 1.75 1.40

400th anniversary of the Polish posts.
Imperfs. exist of all but No. 803.

1958, Mar. 29 Engr. *Perf. 12½*

Town Halls: 40g, Wroclaw. 60g, Tarnow, horiz. 2.10z, Danzig. 2.50z, Zamosc.

805 A308 20g green .20 .20
806 A308 40g brown .20 .20
807 A308 60g dark blue .20 .20
808 A308 2.10z rose lake .30 .20
809 A308 2.50z violet .45 .20
Nos. 805-809 (5) 1.35 1.00

Giant Pike Perch A309

Fishes: 60g, Salmon, vert. 2.10z, Pike, vert. 2.50z, Trout, vert. 6.40z, Grayling.

1958, Apr. 22 Photo. *Perf. 12*

810 A309 40g bl, blk, grn & yel .20 .20
811 A309 60g yel grn, dk grn & bl .20 .20
812 A309 2.10z dk bl, grn & yel .40 .20
813 A309 2.50z pur, blk & yel grn 1.50 .30
814 A309 6.40z bl grn, brn & red .90 .35
Nos. 810-814 (5) 3.20 1.25

Casimir Palace, Warsaw University A310

Stylized Glider and Cloud A311

1958, May 14 Unwmk. *Perf. 12½*

815 A310 2.50z violet blue .20 .20

140th anniv. of the University of Warsaw.

1958, June 14 Litho.

Design: 2.50z, Design reversed.

816 A311 60g gray blue & blk .20 .20
817 A311 2.50z gray & blk .35 .20

7th Intl. Glider Competitions.

Fair Emblem — A312

Armed Postman and Mail Box — A313

1958, June 9

818 A312 2.50z black & rose .20 .20

27th Fair at Poznan.

1958, Sept. 1 Engr. *Perf. 11*

819 A313 60g dark blue .20 .20

19th anniv. of the defense of the Polish post office at Danzig (Gdansk). Inscribed: "You were the first."

Letter, Quill and Postmark A314

Polar Bear A315

1958, Oct. 9 Litho.

820 A314 60g blk, bl grn & ver .50 .25

Issued for Stamp Day. Exists imperf.

1958, Sept. 30 Photo. *Perf. 12½x12*

Design: 2.50z, Rocket and Sputnik.

821 A315 60g black .20 .20
822 A315 2.50z dark blue .55 .20

Intl. Geophysical Year.

Partisan's Cross — A316

Designs: 60g, Virtuti Militari Cross. 2.50z, Grunwald Cross.

1958, Oct. 10 *Perf. 11*

823 A316 40g black, grn & ocher .20 .20
824 A316 60g black, blue & yel .20 .20
825 A316 2.50z multicolored .60 .20
Nos. 823-825 (3) 1.00 .60

Polish People's Army, 15th anniv.

17th Century Ship — A317

UNESCO Building, Paris — A318

Design: 2.50z, Polish immigrants.

1958, Oct. 29 *Perf. 11*

826 A317 60g dk slate grn .20 .20
827 A317 2.50z dk carmine rose .25 .20

350th anniversary of the arrival of the first Polish immigrants in America.

1958, Nov. 3 Unwmk.

828 A318 2.50z yellow grn & blk .45 .20

UNESCO Headquarters in Paris, opening, Nov. 3.

Stagecoach — A319

Wmk. 326

1958, Oct. 26 Engr. *Perf. 12½*

829 A319 2.50z slate, *buff* 1.00 .50
a. Souvenir sheet of 6 7.50 7.50

Philatelic exhibition in honor of the 400th anniv. of the Polish post, Warsaw, Oct. 25-Nov. 10.

Souvenir Sheet

1958, Dec. 12 Unwmk. *Imperf.*

Printed on Silk

830 A319 50z dark blue 12.00 10.00

400th anniversary of the Polish posts.

Stanislaw Wyspianski A320

Kneeling Figure A321

Portrait: 2.50z, Stanislaw Moniuszko.

1958, Nov. 25 Engr. *Perf. 12½*

831 A320 60g dark violet .20 .20
832 A320 2.50z dk slate grn .35 .20

Stanislaw Wyspianski, painter and poet, and Stanislaw Moniuszko, composer.

1958, Dec. 10 Litho.

833 A321 2.50z lt brn & red brn .35 .20

Signing of the Universal Declaration of Human Rights, 10th anniv.

Red Flag — A322

Sailing — A323

1958, Dec. 16 Photo.

834 A322 60g plum & red .20 .20

Communist Party of Poland, 40th anniv.

1959, Jan. 3

Sports: 60g, Girl archer. 95g, Soccer. 2z, Horsemanship.

835 A323 40g lt bl & vio bl .20 .20
836 A323 60g salmon & brn vio .20 .20
837 A323 95g green & brn vio .30 .20
838 A323 2z dp bl & lt grn .30 .20
Nos. 835-838 (4) 1.00 .80

Hand at Wheel — A324

Wheat, Hammer and Flag — A325

1959, Mar. 10 Wmk. 326 *Perf. 12½*

839 A324 40gr shown .20 .20
840 A325 60gr shown .20 .20
841 A324 1.55z Factory .40 .20
Nos. 839-841 (3) .80 .60

3rd Workers Congress.

Amanita Phalloides — A326

Designs: Various mushrooms.

1959, May 8 Photo. *Perf. 11½*

842 A326 20g yel, grn & brn 1.40 .75
843 A326 30g multicolored .20 .20
844 A326 40g multicolored .60 .20
845 A326 60g yel grn, brn & ocher .60 .20
846 A326 1z multicolored .40 .20
847 A326 2.50z blue, grn & brn .80 .20
848 A326 3.40z multicolored 1.10 .40
849 A326 5.60z dl yel, brn & grn 3.00 1.50
Nos. 842-849 (8) 8.10 3.65

"Storks," by Jozef Chelmonski A327

Paintings by Polish Artists: 60g, Mother and Child, Stanislaw Wyspianski, vert. 1z, Mme. de Romanet, Henryk Rodakowski, vert. 1.50z, Old Man and Death, Jacek Malczewski, vert. 6.40z, River Scene, Aleksander Gierymski.

1959 Engr. *Perf. 12, 12½x12*

850 A327 40g gray green .20 .20
851 A327 60g dull purple .25 .20
852 A327 1z intense black .30 .20
853 A327 1.50z brown .50 .30
854 A327 6.40z blue 2.25 .70
Nos. 850-854 (5) 3.50 1.60

Nos. 850 and 854 measure 36x28mm; Nos. 851 and 853, 28x36mm; No. 852, 28x37mm.

Miner and Globe A328

Symbol of Industry A329

1959, July 1 Litho.

855 A328 2.50z multicolored .45 .20

3rd Miners' Conf., Katowice, July 1959.

Perf. 12x12½

1959, July 21 Wmk. 326

Map of Poland and: 40g, Map of Poland and Symbol of Agriculture. 1.50z, Symbol of art and science.

856 A329 40g black, bl & grn .20 .20
857 A329 60g black & ver .20 .20
858 A329 1.50z black & blue .20 .20
Nos. 856-858 (3) .60 .60

15 years of the Peoples' Republic of Poland.

Lazarus Ludwig Zamenhof A330

Map of Austria and Flower A331

Design: 1.50z, Star, globe and flag.

1959, July 24 *Perf. 12½*

859 A330 60g blk & grn, *ol* .20 .20
860 A330 1.50z ultra, grn & red, *gray* .40 .20

Centenary of the birth of Lazarus Ludwig Zamenhof, author of Esperanto, and in conjunction with the Esperanto Congress in Warsaw.

1959, July 27 Litho.

861 A331 60g sep, red & grn, *yel* .20 .20
862 A331 2.50z bl, red, & grn, *gray* .45 .20

7th World Youth Festival, Vienna, July 26-Aug. 14.

Symbolic Plane — A332

1959, Aug. 24 Wmk. 326 *Perf. 12½*

863 A332 60g vio bl, grnsh bl & blk .20 .20

30th anniv. of LOT, the Polish airline.

Sejm (Parliament) Building — A333

1959, Aug. 27 Photo. *Perf. 12x12½*

864 A333 60g lt grn, blk & red .20 .20
865 A333 2.50z vio gray, blk & red .40 .20

48th Interparliamentary Conf., Warsaw.

No. 640 Overprinted in Blue: "BALPEX I - GDANSK 1959"

1959, Aug. 30 Engr. Unwmk.

866 A253 45g brown, *yel* .65 .50

Intl. Phil. Exhib. of Baltic States at Gdansk.

Stylized Dove and Globe — A334

Red Cross Nurse — A335

Wmk. 326

1959, Sept. 1 Photo. *Perf. 12½*

867 A334 60g blue & gray .20 .20

World Peace Movement, 10th anniv.

1959, Sept. 21 Litho. *Perf. 12½*

Designs: 60g, Nurse. 2.50z, Henri Dunant.

Size: 21x26mm

868 A335 40g red, lt grn & blk .20 .20
869 A335 60g bis brn, brn & red .20 .20

Perf. 11

Size: 23x23mm

870 A335 2.50z red, pink & blk .65 .35
Nos. 868-870 (3) 1.05 .75

Polish Red Cross, 40th anniv.; Red Cross, cent.

Polish-Chinese Friendship Society Emblem — A336

Flower Made of Stamps — A337

Wmk. 326

1959, Sept. 28 Litho. *Perf. 11*

871 A336 60g multicolored .45 .20
872 A336 2.50z multicolored .30 .20

Polish-Chinese friendship.

1959, Oct. 9 *Perf. 12½*

873 A337 60g lt grnsh bl, grn & red .20 .20
874 A337 2.50z red, grn & vio .35 .20

Issued for Stamp Day, 1959.

Sputnik 3 — A338

60g, Luna I, sun. 2.50z, Earth, moon, Sputnik 2.

1959, Nov. 7 Photo. Wmk. 326

875 A338 40g Prus blue & gray .25 .20
876 A338 60g maroon & black .30 .20
877 A338 2.50z green & dk blue .90 .50
Nos. 875-877 (3) 1.45 .90

42nd anniv. of the Russian Revolution and the landing of the Soviet moon rocket.

Exist imperf. Value, set $3.

Child Doing Homework A339

Charles Darwin A340

Design: 60g, Three children leaving school.

Lithographed and Engraved

1959, Nov. 14 *Perf. 11½*

878 A339 40g green & dk brn .20 .20
879 A339 60g blue & red .20 .20

"1,000 Schools" campaign for the 1,000th anniversary of Poland.

1959, Dec. 10 Engr. *Perf. 11*

Scientists: 10g, Dmitri I. Mendeleev. 60g, Albert Einstein. 1.50z, Louis Pasteur. 1.55z, Isaac Newton. 2.50z, Nicolaus Copernicus.

880 A340 20g dark blue .20 .20
881 A340 40g olive gray .20 .20
882 A340 60g claret .20 .20
883 A340 1.50g dk violet brn .20 .20
884 A340 1.55z dark green .45 .20
885 A340 2.50z violet 1.00 .50
Nos. 880-885 (6) 2.25 1.50

Man from Rzeszow A341

Woman from Rzeszow A342

Regional Costumes: 40g, Cracow. 60g, Kurpiow. 1z, Silesia. 2z, Lowicz. 2.50z, Mountain people. 3.10z, Kujawy. 3.40z, Lublin. 5.60z, Szamotuli. 6.50z, Lubuski.

Engraved and Photogravure

1959-60 Wmk. 326 *Perf. 12, Imperf.*

886 A341 20g slate grn & blk .20 .20
887 A342 20g slate grn & blk .20 .20
a. Pair, #886-887 .20 .20
888 A341 40g lt bl & rose car ('60) .20 .20
889 A342 40g rose car & bl ('60) .20 .20
a. Pair, #888-889 .20 .20
890 A341 60g black & pink .20 .20
891 A342 60g black & pink .20 .20
a. Pair, #890-891 .20 .20
892 A341 1z grnsh red & dk red .20 .20
893 A342 1z grnsh bl & dk red .20 .20
a. Pair, #892-893 .20 .20
894 A341 2z yel & ultra ('60) .20 .20
895 A342 2z yel & ultra ('60) .20 .20
a. Pair, #894-895 .40 .25
896 A341 2.50z green & rose lil .30 .20
897 A342 2.50z green & rose lil .30 .20
a. Pair, #896-897 .60 .40
898 A341 3.10z yel grn & sl grn ('60) .40 .25
899 A342 3.10z yel grn & sl grn ('60) .40 .25
a. Pair, #898-899 .80 .50
900 A341 3.40z gray grn & brn ('60) .50 .30
901 A342 3.40z gray grn & brn ('60) .50 .30
a. Pair, #900-901 1.00 .60
902 A341 5.60z yel grn & gray bl .75 .50
903 A342 5.60z yel grn & gray bl .75 .50
a. Pair, #902-903 1.50 .75
904 A341 6.50z vio & gray grn ('60) 1.25 .50
905 A342 6.50z vio & gray grn ('60) 1.25 .50
a. Pair, #904-905 2.50 1.00
Nos. 886-905 (20) 8.40 5.50

Piano — A343

Frederic Chopin — A344

Design: 1.50z, Musical note and manuscript.

1960, Feb. 22 Litho. *Perf. 12*

906 A343 60g brt violet & blk .40 .35
907 A343 1.50z black, gray & red .60 .25

Perf. 12½x12

Engr.

908 A344 2.50z black 2.50 .90
Nos. 906-908 (3) 3.50 1.50

150th anniversary of the birth of Frederic Chopin and to publicize the Chopin music competition.

Stamp of 1860 A345

Designs: 60g, Ski meet stamp of 1939. 1.35z, Design from 1860 issue. 1.55z, 1945 liberation stamp. 2.50z, 1957 stamp day stamp.

Litho. (40g, 1.35z); Litho. and Photo.

Perf. 11½x11

1960, Mar. 21 Wmk. 326

909 A345 40g multicolored .20 .20
910 A345 60g violet, ultra & blk .30 .20
911 A345 1.35z gray, red & bl .75 .40
912 A345 1.55z green, car & blk .75 .25
913 A345 2.50z ap grn, dk grn & blk 1.00 .45
Nos. 909-913 (5) 3.00 1.50

Centenary of Polish stamps. Nos. 909-913 were also issued in sheets of 4. Value, $275.

For overprint see No. 934.

Discus Thrower, Amsterdam 1928 — A346

Polish Olympic Victories: No. 915, Runner. No. 916, Bicyclist. No. 917, Steeplechase. No. 918, Trumpeters. No. 919, Boxers. No. 920, Olympic flame. No. 921 Woman jumper.

Lithographed and Embossed

Perf. 12x12½

1960, June 15 Unwmk.

914 A346 60g blue & blk .20 .20
915 A346 60g car rose & blk .20 .20
916 A346 60g violet & blk .20 .20
917 A346 60g blue grn & blk .20 .20
a. Block of 4, #914-917 .80 .40
918 A346 2.50z ultra & blk .55 .25
919 A346 2.50z chestnut & blk .55 .25
920 A346 2.50z red & blk .55 .25
921 A346 2.50z emerald & blk .55 .25
a. Block of 4, #918-921 2.50 1.00
Nos. 914-921 (8) 3.00 1.80

17th Olympic Games, Rome, 8/25-9/11.

Nos. 917a and 921a have continuous design forming the stadium oval.

Nos. 914-921 exist imperf. Value, set $5.

Tomb of King Wladyslaw II Jagiello — A347

Battle of Grunwald by Jan Matejko — A348

90g, Detail from Grunwald monument.

Perf. 11x11½

1960 Wmk. 326 Engr.

922 A347 60g violet brown .35 .20
923 A347 90g olive gray .70 .35

Size: 78x37mm

924 A348 2.50z dark gray 2.00 1.10
Nos. 922-924 (3) 3.05 1.65

550th anniversary, Battle of Grunwald.

The Annunciation — A349

Carvings by Veit Stoss, St. Mary's Church, Cracow: 30g, Nativity. 40g, Adoration of the Kings. 60g, The Resurrection. 2.50z, The Ascension. 5.60z, Descent of the Holy Ghost. 10z, The Assumption of the Virgin, vert.

1960 Wmk. 326 Engr. *Perf. 12*

925 A349 20g Prus blue .25 .20
926 A349 30g lt red brown .20 .20
927 A349 40g violet .25 .20
928 A349 60g dull green .25 .20
929 A349 2.50z rose lake .80 .20
930 A349 5.60z dark brown 5.75 2.75
Nos. 925-930 (6) 7.50 3.75

Miniature Sheet

Imperf

931 A349 10z black 6.00 5.00

No. 931 contains one vertical stamp which measures 72x95mm.

A350

A351

1960, Sept. 26 *Perf. 12½*

932 A350 2.50z black .35 .20

Birth cent. of Ignacy Jan Paderewski, statesman and musician.

Engr. & Photo.

1960, Sept. 14 *Perf. 11*

Lukasiewicz and kerosene lamp.

933 A351 60g citron & black .20 .20

5th Pharmaceutical Congress; Ignacy Lukasiewicz, chemist-pharmacist.

No. 909 Overprinted: "DZIEN ZNACZKA 1960"

1960 Litho. *Perf. 11½x11*

934 A345 40g multicolored 1.25 .60

Issued for Stamp Day, 1960.

Great Bustard A352

Birds: 20g, Raven. 30g, Great cormorant. 40g, Black stork. 50g, Eagle owl. 60g, White-tailed sea eagle. 75g, Golden eagle. 90g, Short-toed eagle. 2.50z, Rock thrush. 4z, European kingfisher. 5.60z, Wall creeper. 6.50z, European roller.

1960 Unwmk. Photo. *Perf. 11½*
Birds in Natural Colors

935 A352 10g gray & blk .20 .20
936 A352 20g gray & blk .20 .20
937 A352 30g gray & blk .20 .20
938 A352 40g gray & blk .25 .20
939 A352 50g pale grn & blk .30 .20
940 A352 60g pale grn & blk .40 .20
941 A352 75g pale grn & blk .40 .20
942 A352 90g pale grn & blk .55 .20
943 A352 2.50z pale ol gray & blk 3.50 1.25
944 A352 4z pale ol gray & blk 2.50 .55
945 A352 5.60z pale ol gray & blk 4.25 .60
946 A352 6.50z pale ol gray & blk 6.00 2.00
Nos. 935-946 (12) 18.75 6.00

Gniezno — A353

Front Page of "Merkuriusz" A354

Historic Towns: 10g, Cracow. 20g, Warsaw. 40g, Poznan. 50g, Plock. 60g, Kalisz. No. 952A, Tczew. 80g, Frombork. 90g, Torun. 95g, Puck (ships). 1z, Slupsk. 1.15z, Gdansk (Danzig). 1.35z, Wroclaw. 1.50z, Szczecin. 1.55z, Opole. 2z, Kolobrzeg. 2.10z, Legnica. 2.50z, Katowice. 3.10z, Lodz. 5.60z, Walbrzych.

1960-61 Engr. *Perf. 11½, 13x12½*

947 A353 5g red brown .20 .20
948 A353 10g green .20 .20
949 A353 20g dark brown .20 .20
950 A353 40g vermilion .20 .20
951 A353 50g violet .20 .20
952 A353 60g rose claret .20 .20
952A A353 60g lt ultra ('61) .30 .20
953 A353 80g blue .20 .20
954 A353 90g brown ('61) .30 .20
955 A353 95g olive gray .20 .20

Engraved and Lithographed

956 A353 1z orange & gray .20 .20
957 A353 1.15z slate grn & sal .20 .20
958 A353 1.35z lil rose & lt grn .20 .20
959 A353 1.50z sep & pale grn .20 .20
960 A353 1.55z car lake & buff .20 .20
961 A353 2z dk blue & pink .30 .20
962 A353 2.10z sepia & yel .25 .20
963 A353 2.50z dl vio & pale grn .40 .20
964 A353 3.10z ver & gray .45 .20
965 A353 5.60z sl grn & lt grn 1.10 .20
Nos. 947-965 (20) 5.70 4.00

Lithographed and Embossed
1961 Wmk. 326 *Perf. 12*

Newspapers: 60g, "Proletaryat," first issue, Sept. 15, 1883. 2.50z, "Rzeczpospolita," first issue, July 23, 1944.

966 A354 40g black, ultra & emer .50 .20
967 A354 60g black, org brn & yel .50 .20
968 A354 2.50z black, violet & bl 3.00 2.50
Nos. 966-968 (3) 4.00 2.90

300th anniv. of the Polish newspaper Merkuriusz.

Ice Hockey A355

Part of Cogwheel A356

60g, Ski jump. 1z, Soldiers on skis. 1.50z, Slalom.

1961, Feb. 1 Litho. Wmk. 326

969 A355 40g lt violet, blk & yel .40 .20
970 A355 60g lt ultra, blk & car .40 .30
971 A355 1z lt blue, ol & red 6.00 2.00
972 A355 1.50z grnsh bl, blk & yel .45 .40
Nos. 969-972 (4) 7.25 2.90

1st Winter Spartacist Games of Friendly Armies.

1961, Feb. 11 *Perf. 12½*

973 A356 60g red & black .20 .20

Fourth Congress of Polish Engineers.

Maj. Yuri A. Gagarin A357

Design: 60g, Globe and path of rocket.

1961, Apr. 27 Photo. *Perf. 12*

974 A357 40g dark red & black .75 .35
975 A357 60g ultra, black & car .45 .20

1st man in space, Yuri A. Gagarin, Apr. 12, 1961.

Emblem of Poznan Fair — A358

1961, May 25 Litho. *Perf. 12½x12*

977 A358 40g brt bl, blk & red org .20 .20
978 A358 1.50z red org, blk & brt bl .20 .20
a. Souvenir sheet of 2 2.00 1.90

30th Intl. Fair at Poznan.
No. 978a contains two of No. 978 with simulated perforation and blue marginal inscriptions. Sold for 4.50z. Issued July 29, 1961.

Famous Poles A359

No. 979, Mieszko I. No. 980, Casimir Wielki. No. 981, Casimir Jagiello. No. 982, Nicolaus Copernicus. No. 983, Andrzej Frycz-Modrzewski. No. 984, Tadeusz Kosciuszko.

Photogravure and Engraved
1961, June 15 *Perf. 11x11½*
Black Inscriptions and Designs

979 A359 60g chalky blue .20 .20
980 A359 60g deep rose .20 .20
981 A359 60g slate .20 .20
982 A359 60g dull violet .65 .20
983 A359 60g lt brown .20 .20
984 A359 60g olive gray .20 .20
Nos. 979-984 (6) 1.65 1.20

See Nos. 1059-1064, 1152-1155.

Trawler — A360

Designs: Various Polish Cargo Ships.

Unwmk.
1961, June 24 Litho. *Perf. 11*

985 A360 60g multicolored .20 .20
986 A360 1.55z multicolored .35 .20
987 A360 2.50z multicolored .50 .20
988 A360 3.40z multicolored .80 .30
989 A360 4z multicolored 1.40 .60
990 A360 5.60z multicolored 3.75 1.50
Nos. 985-990 (6) 7.00 3.00

Polish ship industry. Sizes (width): 60g, 2.50z, 54mm; 1.55z, 3.40z, 4z, 80mm; 5.60z, 108mm.

Post Horn and Telephone Dial — A361

Post horn and: 60g, Radar screen. 2.50z, Conference emblem, globe.

1961, June 26

991 A361 40g sl, gray & red org .20 .20
992 A361 60g gray, yel & vio .20 .20
993 A361 2.50z ol bis, brt bl & vio bl .35 .25
a. Souvenir sheet of 3, #991-993 2.75 1.50
Nos. 991-993 (3) .75 .65

Conference of Communications Ministers of Communist Countries, Warsaw.
No. 993a sold for 5z.

Seal of Opole, 13th Century — A362

Cement Works, Opole A363

Designs: No. 996, Tombstone of Henry IV and seal, Wroclaw. No. 997, Apartment houses, Wroclaw. No. 998, Seal of Conrad II and Silesian eagle. No. 999, Steel works, Gorzow. No. 1000, Seal of Prince Barnim I. No. 1001, Seaport, Szczecin. No. 1002, Seal of Princess Elizabeth. No. 1003, Factory, Szczecinek. No. 1004, Seal of Unislaw. No. 1005, Shipyard, Gdansk. No. 1005A, Tower, Frombork Cathedral. No. 1005B, Chemical Laboratory, Kortowo.

1961-62 Wmk. 326 Engr. *Perf. 11*
Western Territories

994 A362 40g brown, *grysh* .20 .20
995 A363 40g brown, *grysh* .20 .20
a. "Block," #994-995 + label .20 .20
996 A362 60g violet, *pink* .20 .20
997 A363 60g violet, *pink* .20 .20
a. "Block," #996-997 + label .20 .20
998 A362 95g green, *bluish* .20 .20
999 A363 95g green, *bluish* .20 .20
a. "Block," #998-999 + label .30 .20
1000 A362 2.50z ol grn, *grnsh* .30 .20
1001 A363 2.50z ol grn, *grnsh* .30 .20
a. "Block," #1000-1001 + label .65 .40

Northern Territories

1002 A362 60g vio bl, *bluish* .20 .20
1003 A363 60g vio bl, *bluish* .20 .20
a. "Block," #1002-1003 + label .20 .20
1004 A362 1.55z brown, *buff* .20 .20
1005 A363 1.55z brown, *buff* .20 .20
c. "Block," #1004-1005 + label .50 .35
1005A A362 2.50z slate bl, *grysh* .30 .20
1005B A363 2.50z slate bl, *grysh* .30 .20
d. "Block," #1005A-1005B + label .65 .40
Nos. 994-1005B (14) 3.20 2.80

Issued: #994-997, 1000-1001, 7/21; 95g, 2/23/62; #1002-1005B, 7/21/62.

Kayak Race Start and "E" — A364

Designs: 60g, Four-man canoes and "E." 2.50z, Paddle, Polish flag and "E," vert.

Wmk. 326
1961, Aug. 18 Litho. *Perf. 12½*

1006 A364 40g bl grn, yel & red .20 .20
1007 A364 60g multicolored .20 .20
1008 A364 2.50z multicolored .90 .35
Nos. 1006-1008 (3) 1.30 .75

6th European Canoe Championships, Poznan, Aug. 18-20. Exist imperf. Value, set $2.

Maj. Gherman Titov, Star, Globe, Orbit A365

Dove and Earth A366

Perf. 12x12½
1961, Aug. 24 Photo. Unwmk.

1009 A365 40g pink, blk & red .30 .20
1010 A366 60g blue & black .30 .20

Manned space flight of Vostok 2, Aug. 6-7, in which Russian Maj. Gherman Titov orbited the earth 17 times.

Insurgents' Monument, St. Ann's Mountain A367

Design: 1.55z, Cross of Silesian Insurgents.

Wmk. 326
1961, Sept. 15 Litho. *Perf. 12*

1011 A367 60g gray & emerald .20 .20
1012 A367 1.55z gray & blue .20 .20

40th anniv. of the third Silesian uprising.

"PKO," Initials of Polish Savings Bank A368

Initials and: #1014, Bee and clover. #1015, Ant. #1016, Squirrel. 2.50z, Savings bankbook.

1961, Oct. 2 Wmk. 326 *Perf. 12*

1013 A368 40g ver, blk & org .20 .20
1014 A368 60g blue, blk & brt pink .20 .20
1015 A368 60g bis brn, blk & ocher .20 .20
1016 A368 60g brt grn, blk & dl red .20 .20
1017 A368 2.50z car rose, gray & blk 1.75 1.40
Nos. 1013-1017 (5) 2.55 2.20

Issued to publicize Savings Month.

Mail Cart, by Jan Chelminski — A369

1961, Oct. 9 Engr. *Perf. 12x12½*

1018	A369	60g deep green	.25	.20
1019	A369	60g violet brown	.25	.20

Polish Postal Museum, 40th anniv; Stamp Day.

Congress Emblem A370

1961, Nov. 20 Wmk. 326 *Perf. 12*

1020	A370	60g black	.20	.20

Issued to publicize the Fifth World Congress of Trade Unions, Moscow, Dec. 4-16.

Seal of Kopasyni Family, 1284 — A371

Child and Syringe — A372

60g, Seal of Bytom, 14th century. 2.50z, Emblem of International Miners Congress, 1958.

1961, Dec. 4 Litho. *Perf. 11x11½*

1021	A371	40g multicolored	.20	.20
1022	A371	60g bl, gray bl & vio bl	.20	.20
1023	A371	2.50z yel grn, grn & blk	.45	.25
		Nos. 1021-1023 (3)	.85	.65

1,000 years of the Polish mining industry.

1961, Dec. 11 *Perf. 12½x12, 12x12½*

Designs: 60g, Children of three races, horiz. 2.50z, Mother, child and milk bottle.

1024	A372	40g lt blue & blk	.20	.20
1025	A372	60g orange & blk	.20	.20
1026	A372	2.50z brt bl grn & blk	.50	.25
		Nos. 1024-1026 (3)	.90	.65

15th anniversary of UNICEF.

Emblem A373

Design: 60g, Map with oil pipe line from Siberia to Central Europe.

1961, Dec. 12 Wmk. 326 *Perf. 12*

1027	A373	40g dk red, yel & vio bl	.20	.20
1028	A373	60g vio bl, bl & red	.20	.20

15th session of the Council of Mutual Economic Assistance of the Communist States.

Ground Beetle — A374

Black Apollo Butterfly A375

Insects: 30g, Violet runner. 40g, Alpine longicorn beetle. 50g, Great oak capricorn beetle. 60g, Gold runner. 80g, Stag-horned beetle. 1.35z, Death's-head moth. 1.50z, Tiger-striped swallowtail butterfly. 1.55z, Apollo butterfly. 2.50z, Red ant. 5.60z, Bumble bee.

Perf. 12½x12

1961, Dec. 30 Photo. Unwmk.

Insects in Natural Colors

1029	A374	20g bister brown	.20	.20
1030	A374	30g pale gray grn	.20	.20
1031	A374	40g pale yellow grn	.20	.20
1032	A374	50g blue green	.20	.20
1033	A374	60g dull rose lilac	.20	.20
1034	A374	80g pale green	.25	.20
		Perf. 11½		
1035	A375	1.15z ultra	.30	.20
1036	A375	1.35z sapphire	.30	.20
1037	A375	1.50z bluish green	.55	.20
1038	A375	1.55z brt purple	.45	.20
1039	A375	2.50z brt green	1.40	.45
1040	A375	5.60z orange brown	7.25	2.75
		Nos. 1029-1040 (12)	11.50	5.20

Worker with Gun — A376

Women Skiers A377

#1042, Worker with trowel and gun. #1043, Worker with hammer. #1044, Worker at helm. #1045, Worker with dove and banner.

Perf. 12½x12

1962, Jan. 5 Litho. Unwmk.

1041	A376	60g red, blk & green	.20	.20
1042	A376	60g red, blk & slate	.20	.20
1043	A376	60g blk & vio bl, *red*	.20	.20
1044	A376	60g blk & bis, *red*	.20	.20
1045	A376	60g blk & gray, *red*	.20	.20
		Nos. 1041-1045 (5)	1.00	1.00

Polish Workers' Party, 20th anniversary.

Lithographed and Embossed

1962, Feb. 14 *Perf. 12*

Designs: 60g, Long distance skier. 1.50z, Ski jump, vert. 10z, FIS emblem, vert.

1046	A377	40g gray, red & gray bl	.20	.20
a.		40g sepia, red & dull blue	.45	.20
1047	A377	60g gray, red & gray bl	.20	.20
a.		60g sepia, red & dull blue	.55	.30
1048	A377	1.50z gray, red & gray bl	.30	.20
a.		1.50z gray, lilac & red	1.65	.80
		Nos. 1046-1048 (3)	.70	.60

Souvenir Sheet

Imperf

1049	A377	10z gray, red & gray bl	3.00	2.50

World Ski Championships at Zakopane (FIS).

No. 1049 contains one stamp with simulated perforation. The sheet sold for 15z.

Each of Nos. 1046-1048 exists in a souvenir sheet of four. Value, set of 3, $57.50.

Broken Flower and Prison Cloth (Auschwitz) — A378

Majdanek Concentration Camp — A379

Design: 1.50z, Proposed memorial, Treblinka concentration camp.

Wmk. 326

1962, Apr. 3 Engr. *Perf. 11½*

1050	A378	40g slate blue	.20	.20
1051	A379	60g dark gray	.30	.20
1052	A378	1.50z dark violet	.50	.25
		Nos. 1050-1052 (3)	1.00	.65

International Resistance Movement Month to commemorate the millions who died in concentration camps, 1940-45.

Bicyclist A380

2.50z, Cyclists in race. 3.40z, Wheel & arms of Berlin, Prague & Warsaw.

Unwmk.

1962, Apr. 27 Litho. *Perf. 12*

1053	A380	60g blue & blk	.20	.20
1054	A380	2.50z yellow & blk	.35	.20
1055	A380	3.40z lilac & blk	.50	.20
		Nos. 1053-1055 (3)	1.05	.60

15th Intl. Peace Bicycle Race, Warsaw-Berlin-Prague.

Size of #1053, 1055: 36x22mm, #1054: 74x22mm.

Lenin in Bialy Dunajec A381

Karol Swierczewski-Walter A382

Designs: 60g, Lenin. 2.50z, Lenin and Cracow fortifications.

Engraved and Photogravure

Perf. 11x11½

1962, May 25 Wmk. 326

1056	A381	40g pale grn & Prus grn	.50	.20
1057	A381	60g pink & dp claret	.20	.20
1058	A381	2.50z yellow & dk brn	.30	.20
		Nos. 1056-1058 (3)	1.00	.60

50th anniv. of Lenin's arrival in Poland.

Famous Poles Type of 1961

Famous Poles: No. 1059, Adam Mickiewicz. No. 1060, Juliusz Slowacki. No. 1061, Frederic Chopin. No. 1062, Romuald Traugutt. No. 1063, Jaroslaw Dabrowski. No. 1064, Maria Konopnicka.

1962, June 20 Engr. & Photo.

Black Inscriptions and Designs

1059	A359	60g dull green	.20	.20
1060	A359	60g brown orange	.20	.20
		Perf. 12x12½		
		Litho.		
1061	A359	60g dull blue	.20	.20
1062	A359	60g brown olive	.20	.20
1063	A359	60g rose lilac	.20	.20
1064	A359	60g blue green	.20	.20
		Nos. 1059-1064 (6)	1.20	1.20

Perf. 11x11½

1962, July 14 Engr. Unwmk.

1065	A382	60g black	.20	.20

15th death anniv. of General Karol Swierczewski-Walter, organizer of the new Polish army.

Crocus — A383

Flowers: No. 1067, Orchid. No. 1068, Monkshood. No. 1069, Gas plant. No. 1070, Water lily. No. 1071, Gentian. No. 1072, Daphne mezereum. No. 1073, Cowbell. No. 1074, Anemone. No. 1075, Globeflower. No. 1076, Snowdrop. No. 1077, Adonis vernalis.

Unwmk.

1962, Aug. 8 Photo. *Perf. 12*

Flowers in Natural Colors

1066	A383	60g dull yel & red	.20	.20
1067	A383	60g redsh brn & vio	.75	.45
1068	A383	60g pink & lilac	.20	.20
1069	A383	90g olive & green	.20	.20
1070	A383	90g yel grn & red	.20	.20
1071	A383	90g lt ol grn & red	.20	.20
1072	A383	1.50z gray bl & bl	.25	.20
1073	A383	1.50z yel grn & dk grn	.60	.20
1074	A383	1.50z Prus grn & dk bl	.30	.20
1075	A383	2.50z gray grn & dk bl	.80	.45
1076	A383	2.50z dk bl grn & dk bl	.80	.45
1077	A383	2.50z gray bl & grn	1.25	.55
		Nos. 1066-1077 (12)	5.75	3.50

The Poisoned Well by Jacek Malczewski — A384

1962, Aug. 15 Engr. Wmk. 326

1078	A384	60g black, *buff*	.30	.20

Issued in sheets of 40 with alternating label for FIP Day (Federation Internationale de Philatelie), Sept. 1. Also issued in miniature sheet of 4. Value, $40.

Pole Vault — A385

Designs: 60g, Relay race. 90g, Javelin. 1z, Hurdles. 1.50z, High jump. 1.55z, Discus. 2.50z, 100m. dash. 3.40z, Hammer throw.

Unwmk.

1962, Sept. 12 Litho. *Perf. 11*

1079	A385	40g multicolored	.20	.20
1080	A385	60g multicolored	.20	.20
1081	A385	90g multicolored	.20	.20
1082	A385	1z multicolored	.20	.20
1083	A385	1.50z multicolored	.20	.20
1084	A385	1.55z multicolored	.20	.20
1085	A385	2.50z multicolored	.35	.20
1086	A385	3.40z multicolored	.90	.25
		Nos. 1079-1086 (8)	2.45	1.65

7th European Athletic Championships, Belgrade, Sept. 12-16.

Exist imperf. Value, set $4.

Anopheles Mosquito A386

Pavel R. Popovich and Andrian G. Nikolayev A387

Designs: 1.50z, Malaria blood cells. 2.50z, Cinchona flowers. 3z, Anopheles mosquito.

1962, Oct. 1 Wmk. 326 *Perf. 13x12*

1087 A386 60g ol blk, dk brn & bl grn .20 .20
1088 A386 1.50z red, gray & brt vio .20 .20
1089 A386 2.50z multicolored .40 .20
Nos. 1087-1089 (3) .80 .60

Miniature Sheet

Imperf

1090 A386 3z multicolored 1.00 .60

WHO drive to eradicate malaria.

1962, Oct. 6 *Perf. 12½x12*

Design: 2.50z, Two stars in orbit around earth. 10z, Two stars in orbit.

1091 A387 60g violet, blk & citron .20 .20
1092 A387 2.50z Prus bl, blk & red .25 .20

Souvenir Sheet

Perf. 12x11

1093 A387 10z sl bl, blk & red 2.25 1.50

1st Russian group space flight, Vostoks III and IV, Aug. 11-15, 1962.

Woman Mailing Letter Warsaw — A388

1962, Oct. 9 Engr. *Perf. 12½x12*

1094 A388 60g black .20 .20
1095 A388 2.50z red brown .50 .20

Stamp Day. The design is from the painting "A Moment of Decision," by Anthony Kamienski.

Mazovian Princes' Mansion, A389

1962, Oct. 13 Litho.

1096 A389 60g red & black .20 .20

25th anniversary of the founding of the Polish Democratic Party.

Cruiser "Aurora" — A390

Photo. & Engr.

1962, Nov. 3 *Perf. 11*

1097 A390 60g red & dk blue .20 .20

Russian October revolution, 45th anniv.

Janusz Korczak by K. Dunikowski A391

King on Horseback A392

Illustrations from King Matthew books: 90g, King giving fruit to Island girl. 1z, King handcuffed and soldier with sword. 2.50z, King with dead bird. 5.60z, King ice skating in moonlight.

Perf. 13x12

1962, Nov. 12 Unwmk. Litho.

1098 A391 40g brn, bis & sep .20 .20
1099 A392 60g multicolored .20 .20
1100 A392 90g multicolored .35 .20
1101 A392 1z multicolored .35 .20
1102 A392 2.50z brn, yel & brt grn .55 .45
1103 A392 5.60z brn, dk bl & grn 1.60 .75
Nos. 1098-1103 (6) 3.25 2.00

20th anniversary of the death of Dr. Janusz Korczak (Henryk Goldszmit), physician, pedagogue and writer, in the Treblinka concentration camp, Aug. 5, 1942.

View of Old Warsaw — A393

1962, Nov. 26 Wmk. 326 *Perf. 11*

1104 A393 3.40z multicolored .40 .25
a. Sheet of 4 4.00 3.00

5th Trade Union Cong., Warsaw, 11/26-12/1.

Orphan Mary and the Dwarf — A394

Various Scenes from "Orphan Mary and the Dwarfs" by Maria Konopnicka.

Perf. 13x12

1962, Dec. 31 Unwmk. Litho.

1105 A394 40g multicolored .30 .20
1106 A394 60g multicolored 2.00 1.00
1107 A394 1.50z multicolored .45 .20
1108 A394 1.55z multicolored .45 .20
1109 A394 2.50z multicolored .55 .30
1110 A394 3.40z multicolored 2.00 1.10
Nos. 1105-1110 (6) 5.75 3.00

120th anniversary of the birth of Maria Konopnicka, poet and fairy tale writer.

Romuald Traugutt A395

Perf. 11½x11

1963, Jan. 31 Wmk. 326

1111 A395 60g aqua, blk & pale pink .20 .20

Centenary of the 1863 insurrection and to honor its leader, Romuald Traugutt.

Tractor and Wheat A396

Designs: 60g, Man reaping and millet. 2.50z, Combine and rice.

Perf. 12x12½

1963, Feb. 25 Litho. Wmk. 326

1112 A396 40g gray, bl, blk & ocher .20 .20
1113 A396 60g brn red, blk, brn & grn .50 .25
1114 A396 2.50z yel, buff, blk & grn .40 .20
Nos. 1112-1114 (3) 1.10 .65

FAO "Freedom from Hunger" campaign.

Cocker Spaniel — A397

30g, Polish sheep dog. 40g, Boxer. 50g, Airedale terrier, vert. 60g, French bulldog, vert. 1z, Poodle, vert. 2.50z, Hunting dog. 3.40z, Sheep dog, vert. 6.50z, Great Dane.

1963, Mar. 25 Unwmk. *Perf. 12½*

1115 A397 20g lil, blk & org brn .20 .20
1116 A397 30g rose car & blk .20 .20
1117 A397 40g lil, blk & yel grn .20 .20
1118 A397 50g multicolored .25 .20
1119 A397 60g lt blue & blk .40 .20
1120 A397 1z yel grn & blk .70 .35
1121 A397 2.50z org, blk & brn 1.00 .50
1122 A397 3.40z red org & blk 2.25 1.00
1123 A397 6.50z brt yel & blk 4.25 2.75
Nos. 1115-1123 (9) 9.45 5.60

Egyptian Ship — A398

Fighter and Ruins of Warsaw Ghetto — A399

Ancient Ships: 10g, Phoenician merchant ship. 20g, Greek trireme. 30g, 3rd century merchantman. 40g, Scandinavian "Gokstad." 60g, Frisian "Kogge." 1z. 14th century "Holk." 1.15z, 15th century "Caraca."

Photo. (Background) & Engr.

1963, Apr. 5 *Perf. 11½*

1124 A398 5g brown, *tan* .20 .20
1125 A398 10g green, *gray grn* .20 .20
1126 A398 20g ultra, *gray* .20 .20
1127 A398 30g black, *gray ol* .20 .20
1128 A398 40g lt bl, *bluish* .20 .20
1129 A398 60g claret, *gray* .20 .20
1130 A398 1z black, *bl* .20 .20
1131 A398 1.15z grn, *pale rose* .35 .20
Nos. 1124-1131 (8) 1.75 1.60

See Nos. 1206-1213, 1299-1306.

Perf. 11½x11

1963, Apr. 19 Wmk. 326

1132 A399 2.50z gray brn & gray .35 .20

Warsaw Ghetto Uprising, 20th anniv.

Centenary Emblem — A400

Perf. 12½x12

1963, May 8 Litho. Unwmk.

1133 A400 2.50z blue, yel & red .40 .20

Intl. Red Cross, cent. Every other stamp in sheet inverted.

Sand Lizard A401

40g, Smooth snake. 50g, European pond turtle. 60g, Grass snake. 90g, Slow worm. 1.15z, European tree frog. 1.35z, Alpine newt. 1.50z, Crested newt. 1.55z, Green toad. 2.50z, Firebellied toad. 3z, Fire salamander. 3.40z, Natterjack.

Perf. 11½

1963, June 1 Unwmk. Photo.

Reptiles and Amphibians in Natural Colors

1134 A401 30g grnsh gray & blk .20 .20
1135 A401 40g gray ol & blk .20 .20
1136 A401 50g bis brn & blk .20 .20
1137 A401 60g tan & blk .20 .20
1138 A401 90g gray grn & blk .20 .20
1139 A401 1.15z gray & blk .20 .20
1140 A401 1.35z gray bl & dk bl .35 .20
1141 A401 1.50z bluish grn & blk .40 .20
1142 A401 1.55z bluish gray & blk .35 .20
1143 A401 2.50z gray vio & blk .35 .20
1144 A401 3z gray grn & blk .75 .35
1145 A401 3.40z gray & blk 2.25 1.50
Nos. 1134-1145 (12) 5.65 3.85

Foil, Saber, Sword and Helmet A402

Designs: 40g, Fencers and knights in armor. 60g, Fencers and dragoons. 1.15z, Contemporary and 18th cent. fencers. 1.55z, Fencers and old houses, Gdansk. 6.50z, Arms of Gdansk, vert.

Perf. 12x12½, 12½x12

1963, June 29 Litho. Unwmk.

1146	A402	20g	brown & orange	.20	.20
1147	A402	40g	dk blue & blue	.20	.20
1148	A402	60g	red & dp org	.20	.20
1149	A402	1.15z	green & emer	.20	.20
1150	A402	1.55z	violet & lilac	.35	.20
1151	A402	6.50z	yel brn, mar & yel	1.25	.45
			Nos. 1146-1151 (6)	2.40	1.45

28th World Fencing Championships, Gdansk, July 15-28. A souvenir sheet exists containing one each of Nos. 1147-1150. Value, $40.

Famous Poles Type of 1961

No. 1152, Ludwik Warynski. No. 1153, Ludwik Krzywicki. No. 1154, Marie Sklodowska Curie. No. 1155, Karol Swierczewski-Walter.

Perf. 12x12½

1963, July 20 Wmk. 326

Black Inscriptions and Designs

1152	A359	60g	red brown	.20	.20
1153	A359	60g	gray brown	.20	.20
1154	A359	60g	blue	.30	.20
1155	A359	60g	green	.20	.20
			Nos. 1152-1155 (4)	.90	.80

Valeri Bykovski — A403

Designs: 60g, Valentina Tereshkova. 6.50z, Rockets "Falcon" and "Mew" and globe.

Unwmk.

1963, Aug. 26 Litho. Perf. 11

1156	A403	40g	ultra, emer & blk	.20	.20
1157	A403	60g	green, ultra & blk	.20	.20
1158	A403	6.50z	multicolored	1.25	.40
			Nos. 1156-1158 (3)	1.65	.80

Space flights of Valeri Bykovski June 14-19, and Valentina Tereshkova, first woman cosmonaut, June 16-19, 1963.

For overprints see Nos. 1175-1177.

Basketball A404

Designs: Various positions of ball, hands and players. 10z, Town Hall, People's Hall and Arms of Wroclaw.

1963, Sept. 16 Unwmk. Perf. 11½

1159	A404	40g	multicolored	.20	.20
1160	A404	50g	fawn, grn & blk	.20	.20
1161	A404	60g	red, lt grn & blk	.20	.20
1162	A404	90g	multicolored	.20	.20
1163	A404	2.50z	multicolored	.25	.20
1164	A404	5.60z	multicolored	1.25	.25
			Nos. 1159-1164 (6)	2.30	1.25

Souvenir Sheet

Imperf

1165	A404	10z	multicolored	2.50	1.25

13th European Men's Basketball Championship, Wroclaw, Oct. 4-13. No. 1165 contains one stamp; inscription on margin also commemorates the simultaneous European Sports Stamp Exhibition. Sheet sold for 15z.

Eagle and Ground-to-Air Missile — A405

Eagle and: 40g, Destroyer. 60g, Jet fighter plane. 1.15z, Radar. 1.35z, Tank. 1.55z, Self-propelled rocket launcher. 2.50z, Amphibious troop carrier. 3z, Swords and medieval and modern soldiers.

1963, Oct. 1 Perf. 12x12½

1166	A405	20g	multicolored	.20	.20
1167	A405	40g	violet, grn & red	.20	.20
1168	A405	60g	multicolored	.20	.20
1169	A405	1.15z	multicolored	.20	.20
1170	A405	1.35z	multicolored	.20	.20
1171	A405	1.55z	multicolored	.20	.20
1172	A405	2.50z	multicolored	.25	.20
1173	A405	3z	multicolored	.55	.20
			Nos. 1166-1173 (8)	2.00	1.60

Polish People's Army, 20th anniversary.

"Love Letter" by Wladyslaw Czachórski — A406

Perf. 11½

1963, Oct. 9 Unwmk. Engr.

1174	A406	60g	dark red brown	.20	.20

Issued for Stamp Day.

Nos. 1156-1158 Overprinted: "23-28 X. 1963" and name of astronaut

1963 Litho. Perf. 11

1175	A403	40g	multicolored	.25	.20
1176	A403	60g	multicolored	.30	.20
1177	A403	6.50z	multicolored	1.50	.80
			Nos. 1175-1177 (3)	2.05	1.20

Visit of Valentina Tereshkova and Valeri Bykovski to Poland, Oct. 23-28. The overprints are: 40g, W. F. Bykowski / w Polsce; 60g, W. W. Tiereszkowa / w Polsce; 6.50z, W. F. BYKOWSKI I W. W. TIERIESZKOWA W POLSCE.

Konstantin E. Tsiolkovsky's Rocket and Rocket Speed Formula — A407

American and Russian Spacecrafts: 40g, Sputnik 1. 50g, Explorer 1. 60g, Lunik 2. 1z, Lunik 3. 1.50z, Vostok 1. 1.55z, Friendship 7. 2.50z, Vostoks 3 & 4. 5.60z, Mariner 2. 6.50z, Mars 1.

Perf. 12½x12

1963, Nov. 11 Litho. Unwmk.

Black Inscriptions

1178	A407	30g	dull bl grn & gray	.20	.20
1179	A407	40g	lt ol grn & gray	.20	.20
1180	A407	50g	violet bl & gray	.20	.20
1181	A407	60g	brn org & gray	.20	.20
1182	A407	1z	brt grn & gray	.20	.20
1183	A407	1.50z	org red & gray	.20	.20
1184	A407	1.55z	blue & gray	.20	.20
1185	A407	2.50z	lilac & gray	.20	.20
1186	A407	5.60z	brt yel grn & gray	.50	.20
1187	A407	6.50z	grnsh bl & gray	.90	.20
			Nos. 1178-1187 (10)	3.00	2.00

Conquest of space. A souvenir sheet contains 2 each of Nos. 1186-1187. Value $40.

Arab Stallion "Comet" — A408

Horses from Mazury Region — A409

Horses: 30g, Tarpans (wild horses). 40g, Horse from Sokolka. 50g, Arab mares and foals, horiz. 90g, Steeplechasers, horiz. 1.55z, Arab stallion "Witez II." 2.50z, Head of Arab horse, facing right. 4z, Mixed breeds, horiz. 6.50z, Head of Arab horse, facing left.

Perf. 11½x11 (A408); 12½x12, 12

1963, Dec. 30 Photo.

1188	A408	20g	black, yel & car	.20	.20
1189	A408	30g	multicolored	.20	.20
1190	A408	40g	multicolored	.20	.20

Sizes: 75x26mm (50g, 90g, 4z); 28x38mm (60g, 1.55z, 2.50z, 6.50z)

1191	A409	50g	multicolored	.20	.20
1192	A409	60g	multicolored	.20	.20
1193	A409	90g	multicolored	.25	.20
1194	A409	1.55z	multicolored	.50	.20
1195	A409	2.50z	multicolored	.60	.20
1196	A409	4z	multicolored	1.40	.50
1197	A409	6.50z	yel, dl bl & blk	2.50	1.50
			Nos. 1188-1197 (10)	6.25	3.60

Issued to publicize Polish horse breeding.

Ice Hockey A410

Sports: 30g, Slalom. 40g, Skiing. 60g, Speed skating. 1z, Ski jump. 2.50z, Tobogganing. 5.60z, Cross-country skiing. 6.50z, Figure skating pair.

1964, Jan. 25 Litho. Perf. 12x12½

1198	A410	20g	multicolored	.20	.20
1199	A410	30g	multicolored	.20	.20
1200	A410	40g	multicolored	.20	.20
1201	A410	60g	multicolored	.20	.20
1202	A410	1z	multicolored	.25	.20
1203	A410	2.50z	multicolored	.45	.20
1204	A410	5.60z	multicolored	.75	.35
1205	A410	6.50z	multicolored	1.25	.70
			Nos. 1198-1205 (8)	3.50	2.25

9th Winter Olympic Games, Innsbruck, Jan. 29-Feb. 9. A souvenir sheet contains 2 each of Nos. 1203, 1205. Value $35.

Ship Type of 1963

Sailing Ships: 1.35z, Caravel of Columbus, vert. 1.50z, Galleon. 1.55z, Polish warship. 1627, vert. 2z, Dutch merchant ship, vert. 2.10z, Line ship. 2.50z, Frigate. 3z, 19th century merchantman. 3.40z, "Dar Pomorza," 20th century school ship, vert.

1964, Mar. 19 Engr. Perf. 12½

1206	A398	1.35z	ultra	.20	.20
1207	A398	1.50z	claret	.20	.20
1208	A398	1.55z	black	.20	.20
1209	A398	2z	violet	.20	.20
1210	A398	2.10z	green	.20	.20
1211	A398	2.50z	carmine rose	.25	.20
1212	A398	3z	olive green	.40	.20
1213	A398	3.40z	brown	.55	.20
			Nos. 1206-1213 (8)	2.20	1.60

European Cat — A411

40g, 60g, 1.55z, 2.50z, 6.50z, Various European cats. 50g, Siamese cat. 90g, 1.35z, 3.40z, Various Persian cats. 60g, 90g, 1.35z, 1.55z horiz.

1964, Apr. 30 Litho. Perf. 12½

Cats in Natural Colors; Black Inscriptions

1216	A411	30g	yellow	.20	.20
1217	A411	40g	orange	.20	.20
1218	A411	50g	yellow	.20	.20
1219	A411	60g	brt green	.40	.20
1220	A411	90g	lt brown	.20	.20
1221	A411	1.35z	emerald	.20	.20
1222	A411	1.55z	violet blue	.55	.20
1223	A411	2.50z	lilac	1.50	.60
1224	A411	3.40z	rose	1.90	1.00
1225	A411	6.50z	violet	3.50	1.65
			Nos. 1216-1225 (10)	8.85	4.65

King Casimir III, the Great — A412

Designs: No. 1227, Hugo Kollataj. No. 1228, Jan Dlugosz. No. 1229, Nicolaus Copernicus. 2.50z, King Wladyslaw II Jagiello and Queen Jadwiga.

1964, May 5 Engr. Perf. 11x11½

Size: 22x35mm

1226	A412	40g	dull claret	.20	.20
1227	A412	40g	green	.20	.20
1228	A412	60g	violet	.20	.20
1229	A412	60g	dark blue	.20	.20

Size: 35½x37mm

1230	A412	2.50z	gray brown	.35	.20
			Nos. 1226-1229 (4)	.80	.80

Jagiellonian University, Cracow, 600th anniv.

Lapwing A413

Waterfowl: 40g, White-spotted bluethroat. 50g, Black-tailed godwit. 60g, Osprey. 90g, Gray heron. 1.35z, Little gull. 1.55z, Shoveler. 5.60z, Arctic loon. 6.50z, Great crested grebe.

Perf. 11½

1964, June 5 Unwmk. Photo.

Birds in Natural Colors; Black Inscriptions

Size: 34x34mm

1231	A413	30g	chalky blue	.20	.20
1232	A413	40g	bister	.20	.20
1233	A413	50g	brt yellow grn	.20	.20

Perf. 11½x11

Size: 34x48mm

1234	A413	60g	blue	.20	.20
1235	A413	90g	lemon	.20	.20
1236	A413	1.35z	green	.30	.20

Perf. 11½

Size: 34x34mm

1237	A413	1.55z	olive	.30	.20
1238	A413	5.60z	blue green	.90	.40
1239	A413	6.50z	brt green	1.50	.60
			Nos. 1231-1239 (9)	4.00	2.40

Hands Holding Red Flag — A414

Designs: No. 1241, Red and white ribbon around hammer. No. 1242, Hammer and rye. No. 1243, Brick wall under construction and red flag.

1964, June 15 Litho. *Perf. 11*

1240 A414 60g ol bis, red, blk & pink .20 .20
1241 A414 60g red, gray & black .20 .20
1242 A414 60g magenta, blk & yel .20 .20
1243 A414 60g gray, red, sal & blk .20 .20
Nos. 1240-1243 (4) .80 .80

4th congress of the Polish United Workers Party.

Symbols of Peasant-Worker Alliance — A415

Atom Symbol and Book — A416

Shipyard, Gdansk — A417

Designs: No. 1245, Stylized oak. No. 1247, Factory and cogwheel. No. 1248, Tractor and grain. No. 1249, Pen, brush, mask and ornament. No. 1251, Lenin Metal Works, Nowa Huta. No. 1252, Cement factory, Chelm. No. 1253, Power Station, Turoszow. No. 1254, Oil refinery, Plock. No. 1255, Sulphur mine, Tarnobrzeg.

1964 Litho. *Perf. 12x12½*

1244 A415 60g red, org & blk .20 .20
1245 A415 60g grn, red, ocher, bl & blk .20 .20

Photo.

Perf. 11

1246 A416 60g gray & dp vio bl .20 .20
1247 A416 60g brt blue & blk .20 .20
1248 A416 60g emerald & blk .20 .20
1249 A416 60g orange & red .20 .20

Photogravure and Engraved

1250 A417 60g dl bl grn & ultra .20 .20
1251 A417 60g brt pink & pur .20 .20
1252 A417 60g gray & gray brn .20 .20
1253 A417 60g grn & slate grn .20 .20
1254 A417 60g salmon & claret .20 .20
1255 A417 60g citron & sepia .20 .20
Nos. 1246-1255 (10) 2.00 2.00

Polish People's Republic, 20 anniv.

Warsaw Fighters, 1944 — A418

1964, Aug. 1 Litho. *Perf. 12½x12*

1256 A418 60g multicolored .20 .20

20th anniv. of the Warsaw insurrection against German occupation.

Running — A419

Women's High Jump — A420

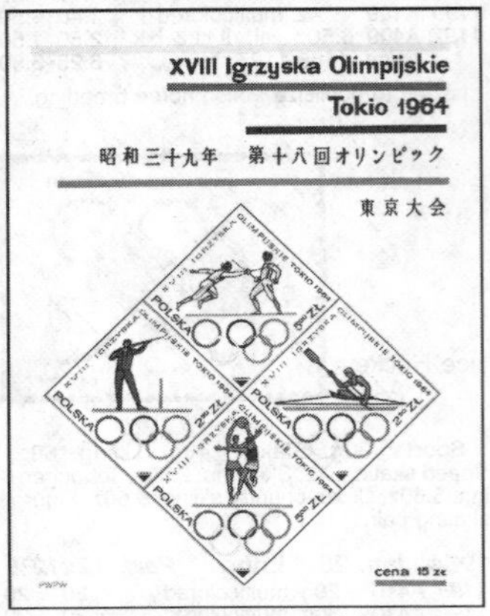

Olympic Sports — A421

Sport: 40g, Rowing (single). 60g, Weight lifting. 90g, Relay race (square). 1z, Boxing (square). 2.50z, Soccer (square). 6.50z, Diving.

Unwmk.

1964, Aug. 17 Litho. *Perf. 11*

1257 A419 20g multicolored .20 .20
1258 A419 40g grnsh bl, bl & yel .20 .20
1259 A419 60g vio bl, red & rose lil .20 .20
1260 A419 90g dk brown, red & yel .20 .20
1261 A419 1z dk violet, lil & gray .20 .20
1262 A419 2.50z multicolored .40 .20
1263 A420 5.60z multicolored .95 .50
1264 A420 6.50z multicolored 1.50 .80
Nos. 1257-1264 (8) 3.85 2.50

Souvenir Sheet

Imperf

1265 A421 Sheet of 4 3.50 1.65
a. 2.50z Sharpshooting .45 .25
b. 2.50z Canoeing .45 .25
c. 5z Fencing .45 .25
d. 5z Basketball .45 .25

18th Olympic Games, Tokyo, Oct. 10-25. Size of stamps in No. 1265: 24x24mm. A souvenir sheet containing 2 each of Nos. 1263-1264 with black marginal inscription exists. Value $45.

Warsaw Mermaid and Stars A422

Stefan Zeromski by Monika Zeromska A423

1964, Sept. 7 *Perf. 12½x12*

1266 A422 2.50z violet & black .40 .20

15th Astronautical Congress, Warsaw, Sept. 7-12.

1964, Sept. 21 Photo. *Perf. 12½*

1267 A423 60g olive gray .20 .20

Stefan Zeromski (1864-1925), writer.

Gun and Hand Holding Hammer — A424

Globe and Red Flag — A425

1964, Sept. 21 Litho. *Perf. 11*

1268 A424 60g brt grn, blk & red .20 .20

3rd Miners' Militia Cong., Warsaw, 9/24-26.

1964, Sept. 28 Photo. *Perf. 12½*

1269 A425 60g black & red orange .20 .20

First Socialist International, centenary.

Stagecoach by Jozef Brodowski — A426

1964, Oct. 9 Engr. *Perf. 11½*

1270 A426 60g green .20 .20
1271 A426 60g lt brown .20 .20

Issued for Stamp Day.

Eleanor Roosevelt (1884-1962) — A427

1964, Oct. 10 *Perf. 12½*

1272 A427 2.50z black .20 .20

Proposed Monument for Defenders of Westerplatte, 1939 — A428

Polish Soldiers Crossing Oder River, 1945 A429

Designs: No. 1274, Virtuti Military Cross. No. 1275, Nike, proposed monument for the martyrs of Bydgoszcz (woman with sword and torch). No. 1277, Battle of Studzianki, 1944.

Perf. 12x11, 11x12

1964, Nov. 16 Engr. Unwmk.

1273 A428 40g blue violet .20 .20
1274 A428 40g slate .20 .20
1275 A428 60g dark blue .20 .20
1276 A429 60g dark blue grn .20 .20
1277 A429 60g grnsh black .20 .20
Nos. 1273-1277 (5) 1.00 1.00

Struggle and martyrdom of the Polish people, 1939-45. The vertical stamps are printed in sheets of 56 stamps (8x7) with 7 labels in each outside vertical row. The horizontal stamps are printed in sheets of 50 stamps (5x10) with 10 labels in each outside vertical row. See Nos. 1366-1368.

Souvenir Sheet

Col. Vladimir M. Komarov, Boris B. Yegorov and Dr. Konstantin Feoktistov — A430

1964, Nov. 21 Litho. *Perf. 11½x11*

1278 A430 Sheet of 3 1.25 .70
a. 60g red & black (Komarov) .35 .20
b. 60g brt grn & blk (Feoktistov) .35 .20
c. 60g ultra & blk (Yegorov) .35 .20

Russian three-manned space flight in space ship Voskhod, Oct. 12-13, 1964. Size of stamps: 27x36mm.

Cyclamen A431

Garden Flowers: 30g, Freesia. 40g, Monique rose. 50g, Peony. 60g, Royal lily. 90g, Oriental poppy. 1.35z, Tulip. 1.50z, Narcissus. 1.55z, Begonia. 2.50z, Carnation. 3.40z, Iris. 5.60z, Camellia.

1964, Nov. 30 Photo. *Perf. 11*

Size: 35½x35½mm

Flowers in Natural Colors

1279 A431 20g violet .20 .20
1280 A431 30g deep lilac .20 .20
1281 A431 40g blue .20 .20
1282 A431 50g violet blue .20 .20
1283 A431 60g lilac .20 .20
1284 A431 90g deep green .20 .20

Size: 26x37½mm

1285 A431 1.35z dark blue .20 .20
1286 A431 1.50z deep carmine .40 .20
1287 A431 1.55z green .20 .20
1288 A431 2.50z ultra .35 .20
1289 A431 3.40z redsh brown .75 .25
1290 A431 5.60z olive gray 1.40 .50
Nos. 1279-1290 (12) 4.50 2.75

Future Interplanetary Spacecraft
A432

Designs: 30g, Launching of Russian rocket. 40g, Dog Laika and launching tower. 60g, Lunik 3 photographing far side of the Moon. 1.55z, Satellite exploring the ionosphere. 2.50z, Satellite "Elektron 2" exploring radiation belt. 5.60z, "Mars 1" between Mars and Earth.

Perf. 12½x12

1964, Dec. 30 Litho. Unwmk.

1291	A432	20g	multicolored	.20	.20
1292	A432	30g	multicolored	.20	.20
1293	A432	40g	ol grn, blk & bl	.20	.20
1294	A432	60g	dk bl, blk & dk red	.20	.20
1295	A432	1.55z	gray & multi	.25	.20
1296	A432	2.50z	multicolored	.55	.20
1297	A432	5.60z	multicolored	.90	.40
			Nos. 1291-1297,B108 (8)	4.00	2.25

Issued to publicize space research.

Warsaw Mermaid, Ruins and New Buildings
A433

1965, Jan. 15 Engr. *Perf. 11x11½*

1298	A433	60g	slate green	.20	.20

Liberation of Warsaw, 20th anniversary.

Ship Type of 1963

Designs as before.

1965, Jan. 25 Engr. *Perf. 12½*

1299	A398	5g	dark brown	.20	.20
1300	A398	10g	slate green	.20	.20
1301	A398	20g	slate blue	.20	.20
1302	A398	30g	gray olive	.20	.20
1303	A398	40g	dark blue	.20	.20
1304	A398	60g	claret	.20	.20
1305	A398	1z	red brown	.20	.20
1306	A398	1.15z	dk red brown	.20	.20
			Nos. 1299-1306 (8)	1.60	1.60

Edaphosaurus — A434

Dinosaurs: 30g, Cryptocleidus, vert. 40g, Brontosaurus. 60g, Mesosaurus, vert. 90g, Stegosaurus. 1.15z, Brachiosaurus, vert. 1.35z, Styracosaurus. 3.40z, Corythosaurus, vert. 5.60z, Rhamphorhynchus, vert. 6.50z, Tyrannosaurus.

1965, Mar. 5 Litho. *Perf. 12½*

1307	A434	20g	multicolored	.20	.20
1308	A434	30g	multicolored	.20	.20
1309	A434	40g	multicolored	.20	.20
1310	A434	60g	multicolored	.20	.20
1311	A434	90g	multicolored	.25	.20
1312	A434	1.15z	multicolored	.30	.20
1313	A434	1.35z	multicolored	.30	.20
1314	A434	3.40z	multicolored	.75	.20
1315	A434	5.60z	multicolored	1.50	.35
1316	A434	6.50z	multicolored	2.25	.90
			Nos. 1307-1316 (10)	6.15	2.85

See Nos. 1395-1403.

Symbolic Wax Seal — A435

Russian and Polish Flags, Oil Refinery-Chemical Plant, Plock — A436

1965, Apr. 21 *Perf. 12½x12, 12½*

1317	A435	60g	multicolored	.20	.20
1318	A436	60g	multicolored	.20	.20

20th anniversary of the signing of the Polish-Soviet treaty of friendship, mutual assistance and postwar cooperation.

Polish Eagle and Town Coats of Arms
A437

1965, May 8 Engr. *Perf. 11½*

1319	A437	60g	carmine rose	.20	.20

20th anniversary of regaining the Western and Northern Territories.

Dove
A438

1965, May 8 Litho. *Perf. 12x12½*

1320	A438	60g	red & black	.20	.20

Victory over Fascism, 20th anniversary.

ITU Emblem — A439

"The People's Friend" and Clover — A440

Factory and Rye
A441

Perf. 12½x12

1965, May 17 Litho. Unwmk.

1321	A439	2.50z	brt bl, lil, yel & blk	.45	.20

ITU, cent.

1965, June 5 *Perf. 11*

1322	A440	40g	multicolored	.20	.20
1323	A441	60g	multicolored	.20	.20

"Popular Movement" in Poland, 70th anniv.

Finn Class Yachts — A442

Yachts: 30g, Dragon class. 40g, 5.5-m. class. 50g, Group of Finn class. 60g, V-class. 1.35z, Group of Cadet class. 4z, Group of Star class. 5.60z, Two Flying Dutchmen. 6.50z, Two Amethyst class. 15z, Finn class race. (30g, 40g, 60g, 5.60z vertical.)

1965, June 14 Litho. *Perf. 12½*

1324	A442	30g	multicolored	.20	.20
1325	A442	40g	multicolored	.20	.20
1326	A442	50g	multicolored	.20	.20
1327	A442	60g	multicolored	.20	.20
1328	A442	1.35z	multicolored	.20	.20
1329	A442	4z	multicolored	.55	.25
1330	A442	5.60z	multicolored	1.00	.40
1331	A442	6.50z	multicolored	1.65	.70
			Nos. 1324-1331 (8)	4.20	2.35

Miniature Sheet

Perf. 11

1332	A442	15z	multicolored	2.00	1.25

World Championships of Finn Class Yachts, Gdynia, July 22-29. No. 1332 contains one stamp 48x22mm.

Marx and Lenin — A443

Photogravure and Engraved

1965, June 14 *Perf. 11½x11*

1333	A443	60g	black, *ver*	.20	.20

6th Conference of Ministers of Post of Communist Countries, Peking, June 21-July 15.

Warsaw's Coat of Arms, 17th Cent. — A444

Old Town Hall, 18th Cent. — A445

Designs: 10g, Artifacts, 13th century. 20g, Tombstone of last Duke of Mazovia. 60g, Barbican, Gothic-Renaissance castle. 1.50z, Arsenal, 19th century. 1.55z, National Theater. 2.50z, Staszic Palace. 3.40z, Woman with sword from Heroes' Memorial and Warsaw Mermaid seal.

Perf. 11x11½, 11½x11, 12x12½, 12½x12

1965, July 21 Engr. Unwmk.

1334	A444	5g	carmine rose	.20	.20
1335	A444	10g	green	.20	.20
1336	A445	20g	violet blue	.20	.20
1337	A445	40g	brown	.20	.20
1338	A445	60g	orange	.20	.20
1339	A445	1.50z	black	.20	.20
1340	A445	1.55z	gray blue	.20	.20
1341	A445	2.50z	lilac	.25	.20

Perf. 11½

Photogravure and Engraved

1342	A444	3.40z	citron & blk	.90	.60
			Nos. 1334-1342 (9)	2.55	2.20

700th anniversary of Warsaw.

No. 1342 is perforated all around, with lower right quarter perforated to form a 21x26mm stamp within a stamp. It was issued in sheets of 25 (5x5).

For surcharges see Nos. 1919-1926.

IQSY Emblem
A446

Designs: 2.50z, Radar screen, Torun. 3.40z, Solar system.

1965, Aug. 9 Litho.

1343	A446	60g	vio, ver, brt grn & blk	.20	.20
a.			60g ultra, org, yel, bl & blk	.20	.20
1344	A446	2.50z	red, yel, pur & blk	.25	.20
a.			2.50z red brn, yel, gray & blk	.25	.20
1345	A446	3.40z	orange & multi	.35	.20
a.			3.40z ol gray & multi	.35	.20
			Nos. 1343-1345 (3)	.80	.60
			Nos. 1343a-1345a (3)	.80	.60

International Quiet Sun Year, 1964-65.

Odontoglossum Grande — A447

Weight Lifting — A448

Orchids: 30g, Cypripedium hibridum. 40g, Lycaste skinneri. 50g, Cattleya. 60g, Vanda sanderiana. 1.35z, Cypripedium hibridum. 4z, Sobralia. 5.60z, Disa grandiflora. 6.50z, Cattleya labiata.

1965, Sept. 6 Photo. *Perf. 12½x12*

1346	A447	20g	multicolored	.20	.20
1347	A447	30g	multicolored	.20	.20
1348	A447	40g	multicolored	.20	.20
1349	A447	50g	multicolored	.20	.20
1350	A447	60g	multicolored	.20	.20
1351	A447	1.35z	multicolored	.25	.20
1352	A447	4z	multicolored	.60	.30
1353	A447	5.60z	multicolored	1.10	.40
1354	A447	6.50z	multicolored	1.75	.75
			Nos. 1346-1354 (9)	4.70	2.65

1965, Oct. 8 Photo. Unwmk.

Sport: 40g, Boxing. 50g, Relay race, men. 60g, Fencing. 90g, Women's 80-meter hurdles. 3.40z, Relay race, women. 6.50z, Hop, step and jump. 7.10z, Volleyball, women.

1355	A448	30g	gold & multi	.20	.20
1356	A448	40g	gold & multi	.20	.20
1357	A448	50g	silver & multi	.20	.20
1358	A448	60g	gold & multi	.20	.20
1359	A448	90g	silver & multi	.20	.20
1360	A448	3.40z	gold & multi	.50	.20
1361	A448	6.50z	gold & multi	.85	.40
1362	A448	7.10z	bronze & multi	1.00	.60
			Nos. 1355-1362 (8)	3.35	2.20

Victories won by the Polish team in 1964 Olympic Games. Each denomination printed in sheets of eight stamps and two center labels showing medals.

Mail Coach, by Piotr Michalowski — A449

Design: 2.50z, Departure of Coach, by Piotr Michalowski.

1965, Oct. 9 Engr. *Perf. 11x11½*

1363 A449 60g brown .20 .20
1364 A449 2.50z slate green .25 .20

Issued for Stamp Day, 1965. Sheets of 50 with labels se-tenant inscribed "Dzien Znaczka 1965 R."

UN Emblem — A450

Memorial, Plaszow — A451

1965, Oct. 24 Litho. *Perf. 12½x12*

1365 A450 2.50z ultra .35 .20

20th anniversary of United Nations.

Perf. 12x11, 11x12

1965, Nov. 29 Engr.

#1367, Kielce Memorial. #1368, Chelm Memorial.

1366 A451 60g grnsh gray .20 .20
1367 A451 60g chocolate .20 .20
1368 A451 60g black, horiz. .20 .20
Nos. 1366-1368 (3) .60 .60

Note after #1277 applies also to #1366-1368.

Wolf A452

1965, Nov. 30 Photo. *Perf. 11½*

1369 A452 20g shown .20 .20
1370 A452 30g Lynx .20 .20
1371 A452 40g Red fox .20 .20
1372 A452 50g Badger .20 .20
1373 A452 60g Brown bear .20 .20
1374 A452 1.50z Wild Boar .50 .20
1375 A452 2.50z Red deer .50 .20
1376 A452 5.60z European bison 1.00 .35
1377 A452 7.10z Moose 1.25 .75
Nos. 1369-1377 (9) 4.25 2.50

Gig — A453

Horse-drawn carriages, Lancut Museum: 40g, Coupé. 50g, Lady's basket. 60g, Vis-a-vis. 90g, Cab. 1.15z, Berlinka. 2.50z, Hunting break. 6.50z, Caleche à la Daumont. 7.10z, English break.

1965, Dec. 30 Litho. *Perf. 11*

Size: 50x23mm

1378 A453 20g multicolored .20 .20
1379 A453 40g lilac & multi .20 .20
1380 A453 50g orange & multi .20 .20
1381 A453 60g fawn & multi .20 .20
1382 A453 90g yellow & multi .20 .20

Size: 76x23mm

1383 A453 1.15z multicolored .20 .20
1384 A453 2.50z olive & multi .45 .20
1385 A453 6.50z multicolored 1.25 .45

Size: 103x23mm

1386 A453 7.10z blue & multi 1.75 .90
Nos. 1378-1386 (9) 4.65 2.75

Cargo Ship (No. 1389) — A454

#1387, Supervising Technical Organization (NOT) emblem, symbols of industry. #1388, Pit head & miners' badge, vert. #1390, Chemical plant, Plock. #1391, Combine. #1392, Railroad train. #1393, Building crane, vert. #1394, Pavilion & emblem of 35th Intl. Poznan Fair.

1966 Litho. *Perf. 11*

1387 A454 60g multicolored .20 .20
1388 A454 60g multicolored .20 .20
1389 A454 60g multicolored .20 .20
1390 A454 60g multicolored .20 .20
1391 A454 60g multicolored .20 .20
1392 A454 60g multicolored .20 .20
1393 A454 60g multicolored .20 .20
1394 A454 60g multicolored .20 .20
Nos. 1387-1394 (8) 1.60 1.60

20th anniversary of the nationalization of Polish industry. No. 1394 also commemorates the 35th International Poznan Fair. Nos. 1387-1388 issued in connection with the 5th Congress of Polish Technicians, Katowice. Printed in sheets of 20 stamps and 20 labels with commemorative inscription within cogwheel on each label.

Issued: #1387-1388, 2/10; others, 5/21.

Dinosaur Type of 1965

Prehistoric Vertebrates: 20g, Dinichthys. 30g, Eusthenopteron. 40g, Ichthyostega. 50g, Mastodonsaurus. 60g, Cynognathus. 2.50z, Archaeopteryx, vert. 3.40z, Brontotherium. 6.50z, Machairodus. 7.10z, Mammoth.

1966, Mar. 5 Litho. *Perf. 12½*

1395 A434 20g multicolored .20 .20
1396 A434 30g multicolored .20 .20
1397 A434 40g multicolored .20 .20
1398 A434 50g multicolored .20 .20
1399 A434 60g multicolored .30 .20
1400 A434 2.50z multicolored .35 .20
1401 A434 3.40z multicolored .55 .20
1402 A434 6.50z multicolored 1.25 .45
1403 A434 7.10z multicolored 2.00 .90
Nos. 1395-1403 (9) 5.25 2.75

Henryk Sienkiewicz A455

Photogravure and Engraved

1966, Mar. 30 *Perf. 11½*

1404 A455 60g black, *dl yel* .20 .20

Henryk Sienkiewicz (1846-1916), author and winner of 1905 Nobel Prize.

Soccer Game A456

Peace Dove and War Memorial A457

Designs: Various phases of soccer. Each stamp inscribed with the place and the result of final game in various preceding soccer championships.

1966, May 6 *Perf. 13x12*

1405 A456 20g multicolored .20 .20
1406 A456 40g multicolored .20 .20
1407 A456 60g multicolored .20 .20
1408 A456 90g multicolored .20 .20
1409 A456 1.50z multicolored .35 .20
1410 A456 3.40z multicolored .60 .25
1411 A456 6.50z multicolored 1.25 .60
1412 A456 7.10z multicolored 1.65 .95
Nos. 1405-1412 (8) 4.65 2.80

World Cup Soccer Championship, Wembley, England, July 11-30. Each denomination printed in sheets of 10 (5x2).

See No. B109.

Typo. & Engr.

1966, May 9 *Perf. 11½*

1413 A457 60g silver & multi .20 .20

21st anniversary of victory over Fascism.

Women's Relay Race A458

20g, Start of men's short distance race. 60g, Javelin. 90g, Women's 80-meter hurdles. 1.35z, Discus. 3.40z, Finish of men's medium distance race. 6.50z, Hammer throw. 7.10z, High jump.

Perf. 11½x11, 11x11½

1966, June 18 Litho.

1414 A458 20g multi, vert. .20 .20
1415 A458 40g multi .20 .20
1416 A458 60g multi, vert. .20 .20
1417 A458 90g multi .20 .20
1418 A458 1.35z multi, vert. .20 .20
1419 A458 3.40z multi .50 .20
1420 A458 6.50z multi, vert. .65 .30
1421 A458 7.10z multi .85 .50
Nos. 1414-1421 (8) 3.00 2.00

Souvenir Sheet

Design: 5z, Long distance race.

Imperf

1422 A458 5z multicolored 1.75 .90

European Athletic Championships, Budapest, August, 1966. No. 1422 contains one 57x27mm stamp.

Polish Eagle — A459

Flowers and Farm Produce — A460

Designs: Nos. 1424, 1426, Flag of Poland. No. 1425, Polish Eagle.

Photogravure and Embossed

Perf. 12½x12

1966, July 21 Unwmk.

1423 A459 60g gold, red & blk .20 .20
1424 A459 60g gold, red & blk .20 .20
1425 A459 2.50z gold, red & blk .25 .20
1426 A459 2.50z gold, red & blk .25 .20
Nos. 1423-1426 (4) .90 .80

1000th anniversary of Poland. Nos. 1423-1424 and 1425-1426 printed in 2 sheets of 10 (5x2); top row in each sheet in eagle design, bottom row in flag design.

1966, Aug. 15 Photo. *Perf. 11*

Designs: 60g, Woman holding loaf of bread. 3.40z, Farm girls holding harvest wreath.

Size: 22x50mm

1427 A460 40g gold & multi .25 .20
1428 A460 60g gold & multi .25 .20

Size: 48x50mm

1429 A460 3.40z violet bl & multi .55 .35
Nos. 1427-1429 (3) 1.05 .75

Issued to publicize the harvest festival.

Chrysanthemum — A461

Flowers: 20g, Poinsettia. 30g, Centaury. 40g, Rose. 60g, Zinnias. 90g, Nasturtium. 5.60z, Dahlia. 6.50z, Sunflower. 7.10z, Magnolia.

1966, Sept. 1 *Perf. 11½*

Flowers in Natural Colors

1430 A461 10g gold & black .20 .20
1431 A461 20g gold & black .20 .20
1432 A461 30g gold & black .20 .20
1433 A461 40g gold & black .20 .20
1434 A461 60g gold & black .20 .20
1435 A461 90g gold & black .60 .20
1436 A461 5.60z gold & black .75 .35
1437 A461 6.50z gold & black 1.10 .50
1438 A461 7.10z gold & black .85 .60
Nos. 1430-1438 (9) 4.30 2.65

Map Showing Tourist Attractions A462

Designs: 20g, Lighthouse, Hel. 40g, Amethyst yacht on Masurian Lake. No. 1442, Poniatowski Bridge, Warsaw, and sailboat. No. 1443, Mining Academy, Kielce. 1.15z, Dunajec Gorge. 1.35z, Old oaks, Rogalin. 1.55z, Planetarium, Katowice. 2z, M.S. Batory and globe.

Perf. 12½x12, 11½x12

1966, Sept. 15 Engr.

1439 A462 10g carmine rose .20 .20
1440 A462 20g olive gray .20 .20
1441 A462 40g grysh blue .20 .20
1442 A462 60g redsh brown .20 .20
1443 A462 60g black .20 .20
1444 A462 1.15z green .20 .20
1445 A462 1.35z vermilion .20 .20
1446 A462 1.55z violet .20 .20
1447 A462 2z dark gray .20 .20
Nos. 1439-1447 (9) 1.80 1.80

Stableman with Percherons, by Piotr Michalowski — A463

2.50z, "Horses and Dogs" by Michalowski.

1966, Sept. 8 *Perf. 11x11½*

1448 A463 60g gray brown .20 .20
1449 A463 2.50z green .20 .20

Issued for Stamp Day, 1966.

Capital of Romanesque Column from Tyniec and Polish Flag — A464

Engraved and Photogravure

1966, Oct. 7 ***Perf. 11½***

1450	A464	60g dark brn & rose	.20	.20

Polish Cultural Congress.

Soldier A465

1966, Oct. 20 **Litho.** ***Perf. 11x11½***

1451	A465	60g blk, ol grn, & dl red	.20	.20

Participation of the Polish Jaroslaw Dabrowski Brigade in the Spanish Civil War.

Green Woodpecker — A466

Forest Birds: 10g, The eight birds of the set combined. 30g, Eurasian jay. 40g, European golden oriole. 60g, Hoopoe. 2.50z, European redstart. 4z, Siskin (finch). 6.50z, Chaffinch. 7.10z, Great tit.

1966, Nov. 17 **Photo.** ***Perf. 11½***

Birds in Natural Colors; Black Inscription

1452	A466	10g	lt green	.20	.20
1453	A466	20g	dull violet bl	.20	.20
1454	A466	30g	dull green	.20	.20
1455	A466	40g	gray	.20	.20
1456	A466	60g	gray green	.20	.20
1457	A466	2.50z	lt olive grn	.40	.20
1458	A466	4z	dull violet	1.40	.40
1459	A466	6.50z	green	1.10	.45
1460	A466	7.10z	gray blue	2.00	.75
		Nos. 1452-1460 (9)		5.90	2.80

Ceramic Ram, c. 4000 B.C. — A467

Designs: No. 1462, Bronze weapons and ornaments, c. 3500 B.C., horiz. No. 1463, Biskupin, settlement plan, 2500 B.C.

1966, Dec. 10 **Engr.** ***Perf. 11x11½***

1461	A467	60g dull violet blue	.20	.20
1462	A467	60g brown	.20	.20
1463	A467	60g green	.20	.20
		Nos. 1461-1463 (3)	.60	.60

Polish Eagle, Hammer and Grain — A468

Designs: 60g, Eagle and map of Poland.

1966, Dec. 20 **Litho.** ***Perf. 11***

1464	A468	40g brn, red & bluish lil	.20	.20
1465	A468	60g brn, red & ol grn	.20	.20

Millenium of Poland.

Vostok (USSR) — A469

Spacecraft: 40g, Gemini, American Spacecraft. 60g, Ariel 2 (Great Britain). 1.35z, Proton 1 (USSR). 1.50z, FR 1 (France). 3.40z, Alouette (Canada). 6.50z, San Marco 1 (Italy). 7.10z, Luna 9 (USSR).

1966, Dec. 20 ***Perf. 11½x11***

1466	A469	20g	tan & multi	.20	.20
1467	A469	40g	brown & multi	.20	.20
1468	A469	60g	gray & multi	.20	.20
1469	A469	1.35z	multicolored	.20	.20
1470	A469	1.50z	multicolored	.20	.20
1471	A469	3.40z	multicolored	.50	.20
1472	A469	6.50z	multicolored	1.10	.25
1473	A469	7.10z	multicolored	1.40	.50
		Nos. 1466-1473 (8)		4.00	1.95

Dressage — A470

Horses: 20g, Horse race. 40g, Jump. 60g, Steeplechase. 90g, Trotting. 5.90z, Polo. 6.60z, Stallion "Ofir." 7z, Stallion "Skowronek."

1967, Feb. 25 **Photo.** ***Perf. 12½***

1474	A470	10g	ultra & multi	.20	.20
1475	A470	20g	orange & multi	.20	.20
1476	A470	40g	ver & multi	.20	.20
1477	A470	60g	multicolored	.20	.20
1478	A470	90g	green & multi	.25	.20
1479	A470	5.90z	multicolored	.95	.20
1480	A470	6.60z	multicolored	1.25	.45
1481	A470	7z	violet & multi	2.25	1.00
		Nos. 1474-1481 (8)		5.50	2.65

Janov Podlaski stud farm, 150th anniv.

Memorial at Auschwitz (Oswiecim) A471

Emblem of Memorials Administration A472

Memorials at: No. 1484, Oswiecim-Monowice. No. 1485, Westerplatte (Walcz). No. 1486, Lodz-Radugoszcz. No. 1487, Stutthof. No. 1488, Lambinowice-Jencom. No. 1489, Zagan.

1967 **Engr.** ***Perf. 11½x11, 11x11½***

1482	A471	40g brown olive	.20	.20
1483	A472	40g dull violet	.20	.20
1484	A472	40g black	.20	.20
1485	A472	40g green	.20	.20
1486	A472	40g black	.20	.20
1487	A471	40g ultra	.20	.20
1488	A471	40g brown	.20	.20
1489	A472	40g deep plum	.20	.20
		Nos. 1482-1489 (8)	1.60	1.60

Issued to commemorate the martyrdom and fight of the Polish people, 1939-45.

Issue dates: Nos. 1482-1484, Apr. 10. Nos. 1485-1487, Oct. 9. Nos. 1488-1489, Dec. 28.

See Nos. 1620-1624.

Striped Butterflyfish — A473

Tropical fish: 10g, Imperial angelfish. 40g, Barred butterflyfish. 60g, Spotted triggerfish. 90g, Undulate triggerfish. 1.50z, Striped triggerfish. 4.50z, Black-eye butterflyfish. 6.60z, Blue angelfish. 7z, Saddleback butterflyfish.

1967, Apr. 1 **Litho.** ***Perf. 11x11½***

1492	A473	5g	multicolored	.20	.20
1493	A473	10g	multicolored	.20	.20
1494	A473	40g	multicolored	.20	.20
1495	A473	60g	multicolored	.20	.20
1496	A473	90g	multicolored	.20	.20
1497	A473	1.50z	multicolored	.20	.20
1498	A473	4.50z	multicolored	.70	.20
1499	A473	6.60z	multicolored	.85	.80
1500	A473	7z	multicolored	1.50	.35
		Nos. 1492-1500 (9)		4.25	2.55

Bicyclists — A474

1967, May 5 **Litho.** ***Perf. 11***

1501	A474	60g multicolored	.20	.20

20th Warsaw-Berlin-Prague Bicycle Race.

Men's 100-meter Race — A475

Sports and Olympic Rings: 40g, Steeplechase. 60g, Women's relay race. 90g, Weight lifter. 1.35z, Hurdler. 3.40z, Gymnast on vaulting horse. 6.60z, High jump. 7z, Boxing.

1967, May 24 **Litho.** ***Perf. 11***

1502	A475	20g	multicolored	.20	.20
1503	A475	40g	multicolored	.20	.20
1504	A475	60g	multicolored	.20	.20
1505	A475	90g	multicolored	.20	.20
1506	A475	1.35z	multicolored	.20	.20
1507	A475	3.40z	multicolored	.35	.20
1508	A475	6.60z	multicolored	.75	.25
1509	A475	7z	multicolored	.90	.55
		Nos. 1502-1509 (8)		3.00	2.00

19th Olympic Games, Mexico City, 1968. Nos. 1502-1509 printed in sheets of 8, (2x4) with label showing emblem of Polish Olympic Committee between each two horizontal stamps. See No. B110.

Badge of Socialist Working Brigade A476

1967, June 2

1510	A476	60g multicolored	.20	.20

6th Congress of Polish Trade Unions. Printed in sheets of 20 stamps and 20 labels and in miniature sheets of 4 stamps and 4 labels.

Mountain Arnica — A477

Medicinal Plants: 60g, Columbine. 3.40z, Gentian. 4.50z, Ground pine. 5z, Iris sibirica. 10z, Azalea pontica.

1967, June 14 ***Perf. 11½x11***

Flowers in Natural Colors

1511	A477	40g	black & brn org	.20	.20
1512	A477	60g	black & lt blue	.20	.20
1513	A477	3.40z	black & dp org	.35	.20
1514	A477	4.50z	black & lt vio	.35	.20
1515	A477	5z	black & maroon	.40	.20
1516	A477	10z	black & bister	1.00	.40
		Nos. 1511-1516 (6)		2.50	1.40

Monument for Silesian Insurgents A478

1967, July 21 **Litho.** ***Perf. 11½***

1517	A478	60g multicolored	.20	.20

Unveiling of the monument for the Silesian Insurgents of 1919-21 at Katowice, July, 1967.

Marie Curie — A479

Designs: No. 1519, Curie statue, Warsaw. No. 1520, Nobel Prize diploma.

1967, Aug. 1 **Engr.** ***Perf. 11½x11***

1518	A479	60g dk carmine rose	.20	.20
1519	A479	60g violet	.20	.20
1520	A479	60g sepia	.20	.20
		Nos. 1518-1520 (3)	.60	.60

Marie Sklodowska Curie (1867-1934), discoverer of radium and polonium.

Sign Language and Emblem A480

1967, Aug. 1 **Litho.** ***Perf. 11x11½***

1521	A480	60g brt blue & blk	.20	.20

5th Congress of the World Federation of the Deaf, Warsaw, Aug. 10-17.

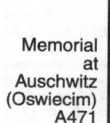

Flowers of the Meadows A481

Flowers: 40g, Poppy. 60g, Morning glory. 90g, Pansy. 1.15z, Common pansy. 2.50z, Corn cockle. 3.40z, Wild aster. 4.50z, Common pimpernel. 7.90z, Chicory.

1967, Sept. 5 Photo. *Perf. 11½*

1522	A481	20g	multicolored	.20	.20
1523	A481	40g	multicolored	.20	.20
1524	A481	60g	multicolored	.20	.20
1525	A481	90g	multicolored	.20	.20
1526	A481	1.15z	multicolored	.20	.20
1527	A481	2.50z	multicolored	.35	.20
1528	A481	3.40z	multicolored	.50	.20
1529	A481	4.50z	multicolored	1.00	.20
1530	A481	7.90z	multicolored	1.25	.30
			Nos. 1522-1530 (9)	4.10	1.90

Wilanow Palace, by Wincenty Kasprzycki — A482

Engraved and Photogravure

1967, Oct. 9 *Perf. 11½*

1531	A482	60g	olive blk & lt bl	.20	.20

Issued for Stamp Day, 1967.

Cruiser Aurora — A483

Designs: No. 1533, Lenin and library. No. 1534, Luna 10, earth and moon.

1967, Oct. 9 Litho. *Perf. 11*

1532	A483	60g	gray, red & blk	.20	.20
1533	A483	60g	gray, dull red & blk	.20	.20
1534	A483	60g	gray, red & blk	.20	.20
			Nos. 1532-1534 (3)	.60	.60

Russian Revolution, 50th anniv.

Tadeusz Kosciusko — A485

Engraved and Photogravure

1967, Oct. 14 *Perf. 12x11*

1540	A485	60g	choc & ocher	.20	.20
1541	A485	2.50z	sl grn & rose car	.20	.20

Tadeusz Kosciusko (1746-1817), Polish patriot and general in the American Revolution.

Vanessa Butterfly A486

Designs: Various Butterflies.

1967, Oct. 14 Litho. *Perf. 11½*

Butterflies in Natural Colors

1542	A486	10g	green	.20	.20
1543	A486	20g	lt violet bl	.20	.20
1544	A486	40g	yellow green	.20	.20
1545	A486	60g	gray	.20	.20
1546	A486	2z	lemon	.25	.20
1547	A486	2.50z	Prus green	.30	.20
1548	A486	3.40z	blue	.40	.20
1549	A486	4.50z	rose lilac	1.25	.60
1550	A486	7.90z	bister	2.00	.60
			Nos. 1542-1550 (9)	5.00	2.60

Polish Woman, by Antoine Watteau A487

Paintings from Polish Museums: 20g, Lady with the Ermine, by Leonardo da Vinci. 60g, Dog Fighting Heron, by Abraham Hondius. 2z, Guitarist after the Hunt, by J. Baptiste Greuze. 2.50z, Tax Collectors, by Marinus van Reymerswaele. 3.40z, Portrait of Daria Flodorowna, by Fiodor St. Rokotov. 4.50z, Still Life with Lobster, by Jean de Heem, horiz. 6.60z, Landscape (from the Good Samaritan), by Rembrandt, horiz.

Perf. 11½x11, 11x11½

1967, Nov. 15 Photo.

1551	A487	20g	gold & multi	.20	.20
1552	A487	40g	gold & multi	.20	.20
1553	A487	60g	gold & multi	.20	.20
1554	A487	2z	gold & multi	.20	.20
1555	A487	2.50z	gold & multi	.25	.20
1556	A487	3.40z	gold & multi	.40	.20
1557	A487	4.50z	gold & multi	.95	.45
1558	A487	6.60z	gold & multi	1.10	.70
			Nos. 1551-1558 (8)	3.50	2.35

Printed in sheets of 5 + label.

Ossolinski Medal, Book and Flags — A488

1967, Dec. 12 Litho. *Perf. 11*

1559	A488	60g	lt bl, red & lt brn	.20	.20

150th anniversary of the founding of the Ossolineum, a center for scientific and cultural activities, by Count Josef Maximilian Ossolinski.

Wladyslaw S. Reymont (1867-1924), Writer, Nobel Prize Winner — A489

1967, Dec. 12

1560	A489	60g	dk brn, ocher & red	.20	.20

Ice Hockey A490

Designs: 60g, Skiing. 90g, Slalom. 1.35z, Speed skating. 1.55z, Long-distance skiing. 2z, Sledding. 7z, Biathlon. 7.90z, Ski jump.

1968, Jan. 10

1561	A490	40g	multicolored	.20	.20
1562	A490	60g	multicolored	.20	.20
1563	A490	90g	multicolored	.20	.20
1564	A490	1.35z	multicolored	.20	.20
1565	A490	1.55z	multicolored	.20	.20
1566	A490	2z	multicolored	.20	.20
1567	A490	7z	multicolored	.45	.35
1568	A490	7.90z	multicolored	.85	.55
			Nos. 1561-1568 (8)	2.50	2.10

10th Winter Olympic Games, Grenoble, France, Feb. 6-18, 1968.

Puss in Boots — A491

Fairy Tales: 40g, The Fox and the Raven. 60g, Mr. Twardowski (man flying on a cock). 2z, The Fisherman and the Fish. 2.50z, Little Red Riding Hood. 3.40z, Cinderella. 5.50z, Thumbelina. 7z, Snow White.

1968, Mar. 15 Litho. *Perf. 12½*

1569	A491	20g	multicolored	.20	.20
1570	A491	40g	lt violet & multi	.20	.20
1571	A491	60g	multicolored	.20	.20
1572	A491	2z	olive & multi	.25	.20
1573	A491	2.50z	ver & multi	.35	.20
1574	A491	3.40z	multicolored	.65	.20
1575	A491	5.50z	multicolored	.90	.45
1576	A491	7z	multicolored	1.50	.60
			Nos. 1569-1576 (8)	4.25	2.25

Bird-of-Paradise Flower — A492

Exotic Flowers: 10g, Clianthus dampieri. 20g, Passiflora quadrangularis. 40g, Coryphanta vivipara. 60g, Odontonia. 90g, Protea cynaroides.

1968, May 15 Litho. *Perf. 11½*

1577	A492	10g	sepia & multi	.20	.20
1578	A492	20g	multicolored	.20	.20
1579	A492	30g	brown & multi	.20	.20
1580	A492	40g	ultra & multi	.20	.20
1581	A492	60g	multicolored	.20	.20
1582	A492	90g	multicolored	.20	.20
			Nos. 1577-1582,B111-B112 (8)	3.65	2.50

"Peace" by Henryk Tomaszewski A493

2.50z, Poster for Gounod's Faust, by Jan Lenica.

1968, May 29 Litho. *Perf. 11½x11*

1583	A493	60g	gray & multi	.20	.20
1584	A493	2.50z	gray & multi	.20	.20

2nd Intl. Poster Biennial Exhibition, Warsaw.

Zephyr Glider — A494

Polish Gliders: 90g, Storks. 1.50z, Swallow. 3.40z, Flies. 4z, Seal. 5.50z, Pirate.

1968, May 29 *Perf. 12½*

1585	A494	60g	multicolored	.20	.20
1586	A494	90g	multicolored	.20	.20
1587	A494	1.50z	multicolored	.20	.20
1588	A494	3.40z	multicolored	.55	.20
1589	A494	4z	multicolored	.80	.30
1590	A494	5.50z	multicolored	.95	.40
			Nos. 1585-1590 (6)	2.90	1.50

11th Intl. Glider Championships, Leszno.

Child Holding Symbolic Stamp — A495

Sosnowiec Memorial — A496

No. 1592, Balloon over Poznan Town Hall.

1968, July 2 Litho. *Perf. 11½x11*

1591	A495	60g	multicolored	.20	.20
1592	A495	60g	multicolored	.20	.20

75 years of Polish philately; "Tematica 1968" stamp exhibition in Poznan. Printed in sheets of 12 (4x3) se-tenant, arranged checkerwise.

Photogravure and Engraved

1968, July 20 *Perf. 11x11½*

1593	A496	60g	brt rose lilac & blk	.20	.20

The monument by Helena and Roman Husarski and Witold Ceckiewicz was unveiled Sept. 16, 1967, to honor the revolutionary deeds of Silesian workers and miners.

Relay Race and Sculptured Head A497

Sports and Sculptures: 40g, Boxing. 60g. Basketball. 90g, Long jump. 2.50z, Women's javelin. 3.40z, Athlete on parallel bars. 4z, Bicycling. 7.90z, Fencing.

1968, Sept. 2 Litho. *Perf. 11x11½*

Size: 35x26mm

1594	A497	30g	sepia & multi	.20	.20
1595	A497	40g	brn org, brn & blk	.20	.20
1596	A497	60g	gray & multi	.20	.20
1597	A497	90g	violet & multi	.20	.20
1598	A497	2.50z	multicolored	.20	.20
1599	A497	3.40z	brt grn, blk & lt ultra	.35	.20

1600 A497 4z multicolored .35 .35
1601 A497 7.90z multicolored .65 .40
Nos. 1594-1601,B113 (9) 4.25 2.75

19th Olympic Games, Mexico City, 10/12-27.

Jewish Woman with Lemons, by Aleksander Gierymski A498

Polish Paintings: 40g, Knight on Bay Horse, by Piotr Michalowski. 60g, Fisherman, by Leon Wyczolkowski. 1.35z, Eliza Parenska, by Stanislaw Wyspianski. 1.50z, "Manifest," by Wojciech Weiss. 4.50z, Stancyk (Jester), by Jan Matejko, horiz. 5z, Children's Band, by Tadeusz Makowski, horiz. 7z, Feast II, by Zygmunt Waliszewski, horiz.

Perf. 11½x11, 11x11½

1968, Oct. 10 **Litho.**

1602 A498 40g gray & multi .20 .20
1603 A498 60g gray & multi .20 .20
1604 A498 1.15z gray & multi .20 .20
1605 A498 1.35z gray & multi .35 .20
1606 A498 1.50z gray & multi .50 .30
1607 A498 4.50z gray & multi .50 .25
1608 A498 5z gray & multi .80 .60
1609 A498 7z gray & multi 1.25 .60
Nos. 1602-1609 (8) 4.00 2.55

Issued in sheets of 4 stamps and 2 labels inscribed with painter's name.

"September, 1939" by M. Bylina — A499

Paintings: No. 1611, Partisans, by L. Maciag. No. 1612, Tank in Battle, by M. Bylina. No. 1613, Monte Cassino, by A. Boratynski. No. 1614, Tanks Approaching Warsaw, by S. Garwatowski. No. 1615, Battle on the Neisse, by M. Bylina. No. 1616, On the Oder, by K. Mackiewicz. No. 1617, "In Berlin," by M. Bylina. No. 1618, Warship "Blyskawica" by M. Mokwa. No. 1619, "Pursuit" (fighter planes), by T. Kulisiewicz.

Litho., Typo. & Engr.

1968, Oct. 12 ***Perf. 11½***

1610 A499 40g pale yel, ol & vio .20 .20
1611 A499 40g lil, red lil & ind .20 .20
1612 A499 40g gray, dk bl & ol .20 .20
1613 A499 40g pale sal, org brn & blk .20 .20
1614 A499 40g pale grn, dk grn & plum .20 .20
1615 A499 60g gray, vio bl & blk .20 .20
1616 A499 60g pale grn, ol grn & vio brn .20 .20
1617 A499 60g pink, car & grnsh blk .20 .20
1618 A499 60g pink, brn & grn .20 .20
1619 A499 60g lt bl, grnsh bl & blk .20 .20
Nos. 1610-1619 (10) 2.00 2.00

Polish People's Army, 25th anniversary.

Memorial Types of 1967

Designs: No. 1620, Tomb of the Unknown Soldier, Warsaw. No. 1621, Nazi War Crimes Memorial, Zamosc. No. 1622, Guerrilla Memorial, Plichno. No. 1623, Guerrilla Memorial, Kartuzy. No. 1624, Polish Insurgents' Memorial, Poznan.

Perf. 11½x11, 11x11½

1968, Nov. 15 **Engr.**

1620 A471 40g slate .20 .20
1621 A472 40g dull red .20 .20
1622 A472 40g dark blue .20 .20
1623 A471 40g sepia .20 .20
1624 A472 40g sepia .20 .20
Nos. 1620-1624 (5) 1.00 1.00

Martyrdom & fight of the Polish people, 1939-45.

Strikers, S. Lentz A500

No. 1626, "Manifesto," by Wojciech Weiss. No. 1627, Party members, by F. Kowarski, horiz.

Perf. 11½x11, 11x11½

1968, Nov. 11 **Litho.**

1625 A500 60g dark red & multi .20 .20
1626 A500 60g dark red & multi .20 .20
1627 A500 60g dark red & multi .20 .20
Nos. 1625-1627 (3) .60 .60

5th Cong. of the Polish United Workers' Party.

Departure for the Hunt, by Wojciech Kossak — A501

Hunt Paintings: 40g, Hunting with Falcon, by Juliusz Kossak. 60g, Wolves' Raid, by A. Wierusz-Kowalski. 1.50z, Bear Hunt, by Julian Falat. 2.50z, Fox Hunt, by T. Sutherland. 3.40z, Boar Hunt, by Frans Snyders. 4.50z, Hunters' Rest, by W. G. Pierow. 8.50z, Lion Hunt in Morocco, by Delacroix.

1968, Nov. 20 ***Perf. 11***

1628 A501 20g multicolored .20 .20
1629 A501 40g multicolored .20 .20
1630 A501 60g multicolored .20 .20
1631 A501 1.50z multicolored .20 .20
1632 A501 2.50z multicolored .20 .20
1633 A501 3.40z multicolored .40 .20
1634 A501 4.50z multicolored .80 .40
1635 A501 8.50z multicolored 1.40 .80
Nos. 1628-1635 (8) 3.60 2.40

Afghan Greyhound A502

Dogs: 20g, Maltese. 40g, Rough-haired fox terrier, vert. 1.50z, Schnauzer. 2.50z, English setter. 3.40z, Pekinese. 4.50z, German shepherd. 8.50z, Pointer.

1969, Feb. 2 ***Perf. 11x11½, 11½x11***

Dogs in Natural Colors

1636 A502 20g gray & brt grn .20 .20
1637 A502 40g gray & orange .30 .20
1638 A502 60g gray & lilac .30 .20
1639 A502 1.50z gray & black .30 .20
1640 A502 2.50z gray & brt pink .45 .25
1641 A502 3.40z gray & dk grn .75 .30
1642 A502 4.50z gray & ver 1.40 .55
1643 A502 8.50z gray & violet 2.75 1.25
Nos. 1636-1643 (8) 6.45 3.15

General Assembly of the Intl. Kennel Federation, Warsaw, May 1969.

Eagle-on-Shield House Sign — A503

1969, Feb. 23 **Litho.** ***Perf. 11½x11***

1644 A503 60g gray, red & blk .20 .20

9th Congress of Democratic Movement.

Sheaf of Wheat A504

1969, Mar. 29 **Litho.** ***Perf. 11½x11***

1645 A504 60g multicolored .20 .20

5th Congress of the United Peasant Party, Warsaw, March 29-31.

Runner — A505

Olympic Rings and: 20g, Woman gymnast. 40g, Weight lifting. 60g, Women's javelin.

1969, Apr. 25 **Litho.** ***Perf. 11½x11***

1646 A505 10g orange & multi .20 .20
1647 A505 20g ultra & multi .20 .20
1648 A505 40g yellow & multi .20 .20
1649 A505 60g red & multi .20 .20
Nos. 1646-1649,B114-B117 (8) 3.10 1.65

50th anniv. of the Polish Olympic Committee, and the 75th anniv. of the Intl. Olympic Committee.

Sailboat and Lighthouse, Kolobrzeg Harbor — A506

40g, Tourist map of Swietokrzyski National Park. 60g, Ruins of 16th cent. castle, Niedzica, vert. 1.50z, Castle of the Dukes of Pomerania & ship, Szczecin. 2.50z, View of Torun & Vistula. 3.40z, View of Klodzko, vert. 4z, View of Sulejow. 4.50z, Market Place, Kazimierz Dolny, vert.

1969, May 20 **Litho.** ***Perf. 11***

1650 A506 40g multicolored .20 .20
1651 A506 60g multicolored .20 .20
1652 A506 1.35z multicolored .20 .20
1653 A506 1.50z multicolored .20 .20
1654 A506 2.50z multicolored .20 .20
1655 A506 3.40z multicolored .25 .20
1656 A506 4z multicolored .35 .20
1657 A506 4.50z multicolored .60 .25
Nos. 1650-1657 (8) 2.20 1.65

Issued for tourist publicity. Printed in sheets of 15 stamps and 15 labels. Domestic plants on labels of 40g, 60g and 1.35z, coats of arms on others.

See Nos. 1731-1735.

World Map and Sailboat Opty A507

1969, June 21 **Litho.** ***Perf. 11x11½***

1658 A507 60g multicolored .20 .20

Leonid Teliga's one-man voyage around the world, Casablanca, Jan. 21, 1967, to Las Palmas, Apr. 16, 1969.

Nicolaus Copernicus, Woodcut by Tobias Stimer — A508

Designs: 60g, Copernicus, by Jeremias Falck, 15th century globe and map of constellations. 2.50z, Copernicus, painting by Jan Matejko and map of heliocentric system.

Photo., Engr. & Litho.

1969, June 26 ***Perf. 11½***

1659 A508 40g dl yel, sep & dp car .20 .20
1660 A508 60g grnsh gray, blk & dp car .20 .20
1661 A508 2.50z lt vio brn, ol & dp car .40 .20
Nos. 1659-1661 (3) .80 .60

"Memory" Pathfinders' Cross and Protectors' Badge A509

Frontier Guard and Embossed Arms of Poland A510

Coal Miner — A511

#1663, "Defense," military eagle and Pathfinders' cross. #1664, "Labor," map of Poland and Pathfinders' cross.

Photo., Engr. & Litho.

1969, July 19 ***Perf. 11x11½***

1662 A509 60g ultra, blk & red .20 .20
1663 A509 60g green, blk & red .20 .20
1664 A509 60g carmine, blk & grn .20 .20
Nos. 1662-1664 (3) .60 .60

5th Natl. Alert of Polish Pathfinders' Union.

1969, July 21 **Litho. & Embossed**

Designs: No. 1666, Oil refinery-chemical plant, Plock. No. 1667, Combine harvester. No. 1668, Rebuilt Grand Theater, Warsaw. No. 1669, Marie Sklodowska-Curie Monument and University, Lublin. No. 1671, Chemical industry (sulphur) worker. No. 1672, Steelworker. No. 1673, Ship builder and ship.

1665 A510 60g red & multi .20 .20
1666 A510 60g red & multi .20 .20
1667 A510 60g red & multi .20 .20

1668 A510 60g red & multi .20 .20
1669 A510 60g red & multi .20 .20
a. Strip of 5, #1665-1669 .40 .40

Perf. 11½x11

Litho.

1670 A511 60g gray & multi .20 .20
1671 A511 60g gray & multi .20 .20
1672 A511 60g gray & multi .20 .20
1673 A511 60g gray & multi .20 .20
a. Strip of 4, #1670-1673 .35 .35
Nos. 1669a,1673a (2) .75 .75

25th anniv. of the Polish People's Republic.

Landing Module on Moon, and Earth — A512

1969, Aug. 21 Litho. *Perf. 12x12½*
1674 A512 2.50z multicolored .80 .40

Man's first landing on the moon, July 20, 1969. US astronauts Neil A. Armstrong and Col. Edwin E. Aldrin, Jr., with Lieut. Col. Michael Collins piloting Apollo 11. Issued in sheets of 8 stamps and 2 tabs with decorative border. One tab shows Apollo 11 with lunar landing module, the other shows module's take-off from moon. Value, sheet, $20.

"Hamlet," by Jacek Malczewski — A513

Polish Paintings: 20g, Motherhood, by Stanislaw Wyspianski. 60g, Indian Summer (sleeping woman), by Jozef Chelmonski. 2z, Two Girls, by Olga Boznanska, vert. 2.50z, "The Sun of May" (Breakfast on the Terrace), by Jozef Mehoffer, vert. 3.40z, Woman Combing her Hair, by Wladyslaw Slewinski. 5.50z, Still Life, by Jozef Pankiewicz. 7z, The Abduction of the King's Daughter, by Witold Wojtkiewicz.

Perf. 11x11½, 11½x11

1969, Sept. 4 Photo.
1675 A513 20g gold & multi .20 .20
1676 A513 40g gold & multi .20 .20
1677 A513 60g gold & multi .20 .20
1678 A513 2z gold & multi .20 .20
1679 A513 2.50z gold & multi .20 .20
1680 A513 3.40z gold & multi .30 .20
1681 A513 5.50z gold & multi .80 .30
1682 A513 7z gold & multi 1.25 .50
Nos. 1675-1682 (8) 3.35 2.00

Issued in sheets of 4 stamps and 2 labels inscribed with painter's name.

Nike — A514

1969, Sept. 19 Litho. *Perf. 11½x11*
1683 A514 60g gray, red & bister .20 .20

4th Congress of the Union of Fighters for Freedom and Democracy.

Details from Memorial, Majdanek Concentration Camp — A515

1969, Sept. 20 *Perf. 11*
1684 A515 40g brt lil, gray & blk .20 .20

Unveiling of a monument to the victims of the Majdanek concentration camp. The monument was designed by the sculptor Wiktor Tolkin.

Costumes from Krczonow, Lublin — A516

Regional Costumes: 60g, Lowicz, Lodz. 1.15z, Rozbark, Katowice. 1.35z, Lower Silesia, Wroclaw. 1.50z, Opoczno, Lodz. 4.50z, Sacz, Cracow. 5z, Highlanders, Cracow. 7z, Kurpiow, Warsaw.

1969, Sept. 30 Litho. *Perf. 11½x11*
1685 A516 40g multicolored .20 .20
1686 A516 60g multicolored .20 .20
1687 A516 1.15z multicolored .20 .20
1688 A516 1.35z multicolored .20 .20
1689 A516 1.50z multicolored .20 .20
1690 A516 4.50z multicolored .55 .25
1691 A516 5z multicolored .80 .45
1692 A516 7z multicolored .65 .30
Nos. 1685-1692 (8) 3.00 2.00

"Walk at Left" — A517

ILO Emblem and Welder's Mask — A518

Traffic safety: 60g, "Drive Carefully" (horses on road). 2.50z, "Lower your Lights" (automobile on road).

1969, Oct. 4 *Perf. 11*
1693 A517 40g multicolored .20 .20
1694 A517 60g multicolored .20 .20
1695 A517 2.50z multicolored .20 .20
Nos. 1693-1695 (3) .60 .60

1969, Oct. 20 *Perf. 11x11½*
1696 A518 2.50z violet bl & ol .20 .20

ILO, 50th anniversary.

Bell Foundry A519

Miniatures from Behem's Code, completed 1505: 60g, Painter's studio. 1.35z, Wood carvers. 1.55z, Shoemaker. 2.50z, Cooper. 3.40z, Bakery. 4.50z, Tailor. 7z, Bowyer's shop.

1969, Nov. 12 Litho. *Perf. 12½*
1697 A519 40g gray & multi .20 .20
1698 A519 60g gray & multi .20 .20
1699 A519 1.35z gray & multi .20 .20
1700 A519 1.55z gray & multi .20 .20
1701 A519 2.50z gray & multi .20 .20
1702 A519 3.40z gray & multi .25 .20
1703 A519 4.50z gray & multi .40 .25
1704 A519 7z gray & multi .85 .40
Nos. 1697-1704 (8) 2.50 1.85

Angel — A520

Folk Art (Sculptures): 40g, Sorrowful Christ (head). 60g, Sorrowful Christ (seated figure). 2z, Crying woman. 2.50z, Adam and Eve. 3.40z, Woman with birds.

1969, Dec. 19 Litho. *Perf. 12½*
Size: 21x36mm
1705 A520 20g lt blue & multi .20 .20
1706 A520 40g lilac & multi .20 .20
1707 A520 60g multicolored .20 .20
1708 A520 2z multicolored .20 .20
1709 A520 2.50z multicolored .20 .20
1710 A520 3.40z multicolored .30 .20
Nos. 1705-1710,B118-B119 (8) 2.50 1.75

Leopold Staff (1878-1957) A521

Polish Writers: 60g, Wladyslaw Broniewski (1897-1962). 1.35z, Leon Kruczkowski (1900-1962). 1.50z, Julian Tuwim (1894-1953). 1.55z, Konstanty Ildefons Galczynski (1905-1953). 2.50z, Maria Dabrowska (1889-1965). 3.40z, Zofia Nalkowska (1885-1954).

Litho., Typo. & Engr.
1969, Dec. 30 *Perf. 11x11½*
1711 A521 40g ol grn & blk, *grnsh* .20 .20
1712 A521 60g dp car & blk, *pink* .20 .20
1713 A521 1.35z vio bl & blk, *grysh* .20 .20
1714 A521 1.50z pur & blk, *pink* .20 .20
1715 A521 1.55z dp grn & blk, *grnsh* .20 .20
1716 A521 2.50z ultra & blk, *gray* .20 .20
1717 A521 3.40z red brn & blk, *pink* .30 .20
Nos. 1711-1717 (7) 1.50 1.40

Statue of Nike and Polish Colors A522

1970, Jan. 17 Photo. *Perf. 11½*
1718 A522 60g sil, gold, red & blk .20 .20

Warsaw liberation, 25th anniversary.

Medieval Print Shop and Modern Color Proofs — A523

1970, Jan. 20 Litho. *Perf. 11½x11*
1719 A523 60g multicolored .20 .20

Centenary of Polish printers' trade union.

Ringnecked Pheasant — A524

Game Birds: 40g, Mallard drake. 1.15z, Woodcock. 1.35z, Ruffs (males). 1.50z, Wood pigeon. 3.40z, Black grouse. 7z, Gray partridges (cock and hen). 8.50z, Capercaillie cock giving mating call.

1970, Feb. 28 Litho. *Perf. 11½*
1720 A524 40g multicolored .20 .20
1721 A524 60g multicolored 1.25 .20
1722 A524 1.15z multicolored .20 .20
1723 A524 1.35z multicolored .20 .20
1724 A524 1.50z multicolored .35 .20
1725 A524 3.40z multicolored .35 .20
1726 A524 7z multicolored 1.65 .65
1727 A524 8.50z multicolored 1.90 .65
Nos. 1720-1727 (8) 6.10 2.50

Lenin in his Kremlin Study, Oct. 1918, and Polish Lenin Steel Mill — A525

Designs: 60g, Lenin addressing 3rd International Congress in Leningrad, 1920, and Luna 13. 2.50z, Lenin with delegates to 10th Russian Communist Party Congress, Moscow, 1921, dove and globe.

Engr. & Typo.
1970, Apr. 22 *Perf. 11*
1728 A525 40g grnsh blk & dl red .20 .20
1729 A525 60g sep & dp lil rose .20 .20
a. Souvenir sheet of 4 1.25 .50
1730 A525 2.50z bluish blk & ver .20 .20
Nos. 1728-1730 (3) .60 .60

Lenin (1870-1924), Russian communist leader.

No. 1729a commemorates the Cracow Intl. Phil. Exhib.

Tourist Type of 1969

#1731, Townhall, Wroclaw, vert. #1732, Cathedral, Piast Castle tower and church towers, Opole. #1733, Castle, Legnica. #1734, Castle Tower, Bolkow. #1735, Town Hall, Brzeg.

1970, May 9 Litho. *Perf. 11*
1731 A506 60g Wroclaw .20 .20
1732 A506 60g Opole .20 .20
1733 A506 60g Legnica .20 .20
1734 A506 60g Bolkow .20 .20
1735 A506 60g Brzeg .20 .20
Nos. 1731-1735 (5) 1.00 1.00

Issued for tourist publicity. Printed in sheets of 15 stamps and 15 labels, showing coats of arms.

Polish and Russian Soldiers before Brandenburg Gate — A526

Flower, Eagle and Arms of 7 Cities — A527

Lithographed and Engraved

1970, May 9 ***Perf. 11***

1736 A526	60g tan & multi	.20	.20

Perf. 11½

1737 A527	60g sil, red & sl grn	.20	.20

25th anniv. of victory over Germany and of Polish administration of the Oder-Neisse border area.

Peasant Movement Flag A528

1970, May 15 **Litho.** ***Perf. 11½***

1738 A528	60g olive & multi	.20	.20

Polish peasant movement, 75th anniv.

A529 A530

1970, May 20

1739 A529	2.50z blue & vio bl	.20	.20

Inauguration of new UPU headquarters, Bern.

1970, May 30 ***Perf. 11½x11***

1740 A530	60g multicolored	.25	.20

European Soccer Cup Finals. Printed in sheets of 15 stamps and 15 se-tenant labels inscribed with the scores of the games.

Lamp of Learning A531

1970, June 3 ***Perf. 11½***

1741 A531	60g black, bis & red	.20	.20

Plock Scientific Society, 150th anniversary.

Cross-country Race — A532

#1743, Runners from ancient Greek vase. #1744, Archer, drawing by W. Skoczylas.

1970, June 16 **Photo.** ***Perf. 11x11½***

1742 A532	60g yellow & multi	.20	.20
1743 A532	60g black & multi	.20	.20
1744 A532	60g dark blue & multi	.20	.20
	Nos. 1742-1744 (3)	.60	.60

10th session of the Intl. Olympic Academy. See No. B120.

Copernicus, by Bacciarelli and View of Bologna — A533

Designs: 60g, Copernicus, by W. Lesseur and view of Padua. 2.50z, Copernicus, by Zinck Nora and view of Ferrara.

Photo., Engr. & Typo.

1970, June 26 ***Perf. 11½***

1745 A533	40g orange & multi	.20	.20
1746 A533	60g olive & multi	.20	.20
1747 A533	2.50z multicolored	.35	.20
	Nos. 1745-1747 (3)	.75	.60

Aleksander Orlowski (1777-1832), Self-portrait — A534

Miniatures: 40g, Jan Matejko (1838-1893), self-portrait. 60g, King Stefan Batory (1533-1586), anonymous painter. 2z, Maria Leszczynska (1703-1768), anonymous French painter. 2.50z, Maria Walewska (1789-1817), by Jacquotot Marie-Victoire. 3.40z, Tadeusz Kosciuszko (1746-1817), by Jan Rustem. 5.50z, Samuel Bogumil Linde (1771-1847), by G. Landolfi. 7z, Michal Oginski (1728-1800), by Windisch Nanette.

Litho. & Photo.

1970, Aug. 27 ***Perf. 11½***

1748 A534	20g gold & multi	.20	.20
1749 A534	40g gold & multi	.20	.20
1750 A534	60g gold & multi	.20	.20
1751 A534	2z gold & multi	.20	.20
1752 A534	2.50z gold & multi	.25	.20
1753 A534	3.40z gold & multi	.35	.25
1754 A534	5.50z gold & multi	.65	.35
1755 A534	7z gold & multi	1.10	.50
	Nos. 1748-1755 (8)	3.15	2.10

Nos. 1748-1755 printed in sheets of 4 stamps and 2 labels. The miniatures show famous Poles and are from collections in the National Museums in Warsaw and Cracow.

Poster for Chopin Competition A535

Photogravure and Engraved

1970, Sept. 8 ***Perf. 11x11½***

1756 A535	2.50z black & vio	.25	.20

8th Intl. Chopin Piano Competition, Warsaw, Oct. 7-25.

UN Emblem A536

1970, Sept. 8 **Photo.** ***Perf. 11½***

1757 A536	2.50z multicolored	.25	.20

United Nations, 25th anniversary.

Poles — A537

Design: 60g, Family, home and Polish flag.

1970, Sept. 15 **Litho.** ***Perf. 11½x11***

1758 A537	40g gray & multi	.20	.20
1759 A537	60g multicolored	.20	.20

National Census, Dec. 8, 1970.

Grunwald Cross and Warship Piorun (Thunderbolt) — A538

Grunwald Cross and Warship: 60g, Orzel (Eagle). 2.50z, Garland.

1970, Sept. 25 **Engr.** ***Perf. 11½x11***

1760 A538	40g sepia	.20	.20
1761 A538	60g black	.20	.20
1762 A538	2.50z deep brown	.45	.20
	Nos. 1760-1762 (3)	.85	.60

Polish Navy during World War II.

Cellist, by Jerzy Nowosielski A539

Paintings: 40g, View of Lodz, by Benon Liberski. 60g, Studio Concert, by Waclaw Taranczewski. 1.50z, Still Life, by Zbigniew Pronaszko. 2z, Woman Hanging up Laundry, by Andrzej Wroblewski. 3.40z, "Expressions," by Maria Jarema, horiz. 4z, Canal in the Forest, by Piotr Potworowski, horiz. 8.50z, "The Sun," by Wladyslaw Strzeminski, horiz.

1970, Oct. 9 **Photo.** ***Perf. 11½***

1763 A539	20g multicolored	.20	.20
1764 A539	40g multicolored	.20	.20
1765 A539	60g multicolored	.20	.20
1766 A539	1.50z multicolored	.20	.20
1767 A539	2z multicolored	.20	.20
1768 A539	3.40z multicolored	.30	.20
1769 A539	4z multicolored	.45	.20
1770 A539	8.50z multicolored	1.00	.35
	Nos. 1763-1770 (8)	2.75	1.75

Issued for Stamp Day.

Luna 16 Landing on Moon — A540

Stag — A541

1970, Nov. 20 **Litho.** ***Perf. 11½x11***

1771 A540	2.50z multicolored	.38	.20

Luna 16 Russian unmanned, automatic moon mission, Sept. 12-24. Issued in sheets of 8 stamps and 2 tabs. One tab shows rocket launching; the other, parachute landing of capsule. Value, sheet $16.

1970, Dec. 23 **Photo.** ***Perf. 11½x12***

16th Cent. Tapestries in Wawel Castle: 1.15z, Stork. 1.35z, Leopard fighting dragon. 2z, Man's head. 2.50z, Child holding bird. 4z, God, Adam & Eve. 4.50z, Panel with monogram of King Sigismund Augustus. 5.50z, Poland's coat of arms.

1772 A541	60g multicolored	.20	.20
1773 A541	1.15z purple & multi	.20	.20
1774 A541	1.35z multicolored	.20	.20
1775 A541	2z sepia & multi	.20	.20
1776 A541	2.50z dk blue & multi	.25	.20
1777 A541	4z green & multi	.60	.25
1778 A541	4.50z multicolored	.75	.35
	Nos. 1772-1778 (7)	2.40	1.60

Souvenir Sheet

Imperf

1779 A541	5.50z black & multi	1.00	.75

No. 1779 contains one 48x57mm stamp. See No. B121.

School Sailing Ship Dar Pomorza — A542

Polish Ships: 60g, Transatlantic Liner Stefan Batory. 1.15z, Ice breaker Perkun. 1.35z, Rescue ship R-1. 1.50z, Freighter Ziemia Szczecinska. 2.50z, Tanker Beskidy. 5z, Express freighter Hel. 8.50z, Ferry Gryf.

1971, Jan. 30 **Photo.** ***Perf. 11***

1780 A542	40g ver & multi	.20	.20
1781 A542	60g multicolored	.20	.20
1782 A542	1.15z blue & multi	.20	.20
1783 A542	1.35z yellow & multi	.20	.20
1784 A542	1.50z multicolored	.20	.20
1785 A542	2.50z violet & multi	.25	.20
1786 A542	5z multicolored	.50	.25
1787 A542	8.50z blue & multi	.85	.45
	Nos. 1780-1787 (8)	2.60	1.90

Checiny Castle A543

Polish Castles: 40g, Wisnicz. 60g, Bedzin. 2z, Ogrodzieniec. 2.50z, Niedzica. 3.40z, Kwidzyn. 4z, Pieskowa Skala. 8.50z, Lidzbark Warminski.

1971, Mar. 5 Litho. *Perf. 11*

1788	A543	20g multicolored	.20	.20
1789	A543	40g multicolored	.20	.20
1790	A543	60g multicolored	.20	.20
1791	A543	2z multicolored	.20	.20
1792	A543	2.50z multicolored	.20	.20
1793	A543	3.40z multicolored	.30	.20
1794	A543	4z multicolored	.35	.20
1795	A543	8.50z multicolored	.75	.40
		Nos. 1788-1795 (8)	2.40	1.80

Fighting in Pouilly Castle, Jaroslaw Dabrowski and Walery Wroblewski — A544

1971, Mar. 3 *Perf. 12½x12½*

1796 A544 60g vio bl, brn & red .20 .20

Centenary of the Paris Commune.

Seedlings A545

Bishop Marianos A546

1971, Mar. 30 Photo. *Perf. 11½x11*
Sizes: 26x34mm (40g, 1.50z); 26x47mm (60g)

1797	A545	40g shown	.20	.20
1798	A545	60g Forest	.20	.20
1799	A545	1.50z Clearing	.25	.20
		Nos. 1797-1799 (3)	.65	.60

Proper forest management.

1971, Apr. 20

Frescoes from Faras Cathedral, Nubia, 8th-12th centuries: 60g, St. Anne. 1.15z, 1.50z, 7z, Archangel Michael (diff. frescoes). 1.35z, Hermit Anamon of Tuna el Gabel. 4.50z, Cross with symbols of four Evangelists. 5z, Christ protecting Nubian dignitary.

1800	A546	40g gold & multi	.20	.20
1801	A546	60g gold & multi	.20	.20
1802	A546	1.15z gold & multi	.20	.20
1803	A546	1.35z gold & multi	.20	.20
1804	A546	1.50z gold & multi	.20	.20
1805	A546	4.50z gold & multi	.50	.20
1806	A546	5z gold & multi	.50	.25
1807	A546	7z gold & multi	.65	.30
		Nos. 1800-1807 (8)	2.65	1.75

Polish archaeological excavations in Nubia.

Silesian Insurrectionists — A547

1971, May 3 Photo. *Perf. 11*

1808 A547 60g dk red brn & gold .20 .20
a. Souv. sheet of 3+3 labels 1.65 .60

50th anniversary of the 3rd Silesian uprising. Printed in sheets of 15 stamps and 15 labels showing Silesian Insurrectionists monument in Katowice.

Peacock on the Lawn, by Dorota, 4 years old — A548

Children's Drawings and UNICEF Emblem: 40g, Our Army, horiz. 60g, Spring. 2z, Cat with Ball, horiz. 2.50z, Flowers in Vase. 3.40z, Friendship, horiz. 5.50z, Clown. 7z, The Unknown Planet, horiz.

1971, May 20 *Perf. 11½x11, 11x11½*

1809	A548	20g multicolored	.20	.20
1810	A548	40g multicolored	.20	.20
1811	A548	60g multicolored	.20	.20
1812	A548	2z multicolored	.20	.20
1813	A548	2.50z multicolored	.20	.20
1814	A548	3.40z multicolored	.30	.20
1815	A548	5.50z multicolored	.50	.25
1816	A548	7z multicolored	.80	.35
		Nos. 1809-1816 (8)	2.60	1.80

25th anniversary of UNICEF.

Fair Emblem — A549

1971, June 1 Photo. *Perf. 11½x11*

1817 A549 60g ultra, blk & dk car .20 .20

40th International Poznan Fair, June 13-22.

Collegium Maius, Cracow — A550

40g, Copernicus House, Torun, vert. 2.50z, Olsztyn Castle. 4z, Frombork Cathedral, vert.

1971, June Litho. *Perf. 11*

1818	A550	40g multicolored	.20	.20
1819	A550	60g blk, red brn & sep	.20	.20
1820	A550	2.50z multicolored	.25	.20
1821	A550	4z multicolored	.45	.20
		Nos. 1818-1821 (4)	1.10	.80

Nicolaus Copernicus (1473-1543), astronomer. Printed in sheets of 15 with labels showing portrait of Copernicus, page from "Euclid's Geometry," astrolabe or drawing of heliocentric system, respectively.

Paper Cut-out — A551

Worker, by Xawery Dunikowski — A552

Designs: Various paper cut-outs (folk art).

Photo., Engr. & Typo.

1971, July 12 *Perf. 12x11½*

1822	A551	20g blk & brt grn, *bluish*	.20	.20
1823	A551	40g sl grn & dk ol, *lt gray*	.20	.20
1824	A551	60g brn & bl, *gray*	.20	.20
1825	A551	1.15z plum & brn, *buff*	.20	.20
1826	A551	1.35z dk grn & ver, *yel grn*	.20	.20
		Nos. 1822-1826 (5)	1.00	1.00

1971, July 21 Photo. *Perf. 11½x12*

Sculptures: No. 1828, Founder, by Xawery Dunikowski. No. 1829, Miners, by Magdalena Wiecek. No. 1830, Woman harvester, by Stanislaw Horno-Poplawski.

1827	A552	40g silver & multi	.20	.20
1828	A552	40g silver & multi	.20	.20
1829	A552	60g silver & multi	.20	.20
1830	A552	60g silver & multi	.20	.20
a.		Souv. sheet of 4, #1827-1830	2.50	.85
		Nos. 1827-1830 (4)	.80	.80

Punched Tape and Cogwheel — A553

1971, Sept. 2 Litho. *Perf. 11x11½*

1831 A553 60g purple & red .20 .20

6th Congress of Polish Technicians, held at Poznan, February, 1971.

Angel, by Jozef Mehoffer, 1901 — A554

Water Lilies, by Wyspianski A555

Stained Glass Windows: 60g, Detail from "The Elements" by Stanislaw Wyspianski. 1.35z, Apollo, by Wyspianski, 1904. 1.55z, Two Kings, 14th century. 3.40z, Flight into Egypt, 14th century. 5.50z, St. Jacob the Elder, 14th century.

1971, Sept. 15 Photo. *Perf. 11½x11*

1832	A554	20g gold & multi	.20	.20
1833	A555	40g gold & multi	.20	.20
1834	A555	60g gold & multi	.20	.20
1835	A555	1.35z gold & multi	.20	.20
1836	A554	1.55z gold & multi	.20	.20
1837	A554	3.40z gold & multi	.30	.20
1838	A554	5.50z gold & multi	.50	.25
		Nos. 1832-1838,B122 (8)	2.70	1.90

Mrs. Fedorowicz, by Witold Pruszkowski (1846-1896) — A556

Paintings of Women: 50g, Woman with Book, by Tytus Czyzewski (1885-1945). 60g, Girl with Chrysanthemums, by Olga Boznanska (1865-1940). 2.50z, Girl in Red Dress, by Jozef Pankiewicz (1866-1940), horiz. 3.40z, Nude, by Leon Chwistek (1884-1944), horiz. 4.50z, Strange Garden (woman), by Jozef Mehoffer (1869-1946). 5z, Artist's Wife with White Hat, by Zbiginew Pronaszko (1885-1958).

Perf. 11½x11, 11x11½

1971, Oct. 9 Litho.

1839	A556	40g gray & multi	.20	.20
1840	A556	50g gray & multi	.20	.20
1841	A556	60g gray & multi	.20	.20
1842	A556	2.50z gray & multi	.20	.20
1843	A556	3.40z gray & multi	.30	.20
1844	A556	4.50z gray & multi	.40	.25
1845	A556	5z gray & multi	.55	.30
		Nos. 1839-1845,B123 (8)	2.75	1.90

Stamp Day, 1971. Printed in sheets of 4 stamps and 2 labels inscribed "Women in Polish Paintings."

Royal Castle, Warsaw A557

1971, Oct. 14 Photo. *Perf. 11x11½*

1846 A557 60g gold, blk & brt red .20 .20

P-11C Dive Bombers A558

Planes and Polish Air Force Emblem: 1.50z, PZL 23-A Karas fighters. 3.40z, PZL Los bomber.

1971, Oct. 14

1847	A558	90g multicolored	.20	.20
1848	A558	1.50z blue, red & blk	.20	.20
1849	A558	3.40z multicolored	.35	.20
		Nos. 1847-1849 (3)	.75	.60

Martyrs of the Polish Air Force, 1939.

Lunokhod 1 on Moon — A559

No. 1850, Lunar Rover and Astronauts.

Perf. 11x11½, 11½x11

1971, Nov. 17

1850	A559	2.50z multicolored	.50	.20
1851	A559	2.50z multicolored	.50	.20

Apollo 15 US moon exploration mission, July 26-Aug. 7 (No. 1850); Luna 17 unmanned automated USSR moon mission, Nov. 10-17 (No. 1851). Printed in sheets of 6 stamps and 2 labels, with marginal inscriptions.

Worker at Helm — A560

Shipbuilding A561

No. 1853, Worker. No. 1855, Apartment houses under construction. No. 1856, "Bison" combine harvester. No. 1857, Polish Fiat 125. No. 1858, Mining tower. No. 1859, Chemical plant.

1971, Dec. 8 ***Perf. 11½x11***

1852	A560 60g gray, ultra & red	.20	.20
1853	A560 60g red & gray	.20	.20
a.	Pair, #1852-1853 + label	.20	.20

Perf. 11x11½

1854	A561 60g red, gold & blk	.20	.20
1855	A561 60g red, gold & blk	.20	.20
1856	A561 60g red, gold & blk	.20	.20
1857	A561 60g red, gold & blk	.20	.20
1858	A561 60g red, gold & blk	.20	.20
1859	A561 60g red, gold & blk	.20	.20
a.	Souv. sheet of 6, #1854-1859	.90	.50
b.	Block of 6, #1854-1859	.60	.50
	Nos. 1853a,1859b (2)	.80	.70

6th Congress of the Polish United Worker's Party. No. 1859b has outline of map of Poland extending over the block.

Cherry Blossoms — A562

Blossoms: 20g, Niedzwiecki's apple. 40g, Pear. 60g, Peach. 1.15z, Japanese magnolia. 1.35z, Red hawthorne. 2.50z, Apple. 3.40z, Red chestnut. 5z, Acacia robinia. 8.50z, Cherry.

1971, Dec. 28 Litho. ***Perf. 12½***

Blossoms in Natural Colors

1860	A562	10g	dull blue & blk	.20	.20
1861	A562	20g	grnsh blue & blk	.20	.20
1862	A562	40g	lt violet & blk	.20	.20
1863	A562	60g	green & blk	.20	.20
1864	A562	1.15z	Prus bl & blk	.20	.20
1865	A562	1.35z	ocher & blk	.20	.20
1866	A562	2.50z	green & blk	.20	.20
1867	A562	3.40z	ocher & blk	.40	.20
1868	A562	5z	tan & blk	.55	.25
1869	A562	8.50z	bister & blk	1.10	.55
	Nos. 1860-1869 (10)			3.45	2.40

Fighting Worker, by J. Jarnuszkiewicz — A563

Photogravure and Engraved

1972, Jan. 5 ***Perf. 11½***

1870	A563 60g red & black	.20	.20

Polish Workers' Party, 30th anniversary.

Luge and Sapporo '72 Emblem — A564

Sapporo '72 Emblem and: 60g, Women's slalom, vert. 1.65z, Biathlon, vert. 2.50z, Ski jump.

1972, Jan. 12 Photo. ***Perf. 11***

1871	A564 40g silver & multi	.20	.20
1872	A564 60g silver & multi	.20	.20
1873	A564 1.65z silver & multi	.25	.20
1874	A564 2.50z silver & multi	.45	.25
	Nos. 1871-1874 (4)	1.10	.85

11th Winter Olympic Games, Sapporo, Japan, Feb. 3-13. See No. B124.

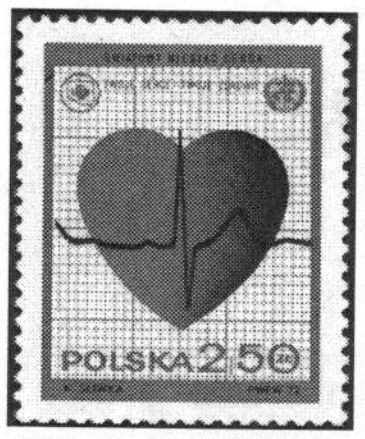

Heart and Electro-cardiogram — A565

Bicyclists Racing — A566

1972, Mar. 28 Photo. ***Perf. 11½x11***

1875	A565 2.50z blue, red & blk	.20	.20

"Your heart is your health," World Health Day.

1972, May 2 ***Perf. 11***

1876	A566 60g silver & multi	.20	.20

25th Warsaw-Berlin-Prague Bicycle Race.

Berlin Monument A567

Olympic Runner — A568

1972, May 9 Engr. ***Perf. 11½x11***

1877	A567 60g grnsh black	.20	.20

Unveiling of monument for Polish soldiers and German anti-Fascists in Berlin, May 14.

1972, May 20 ***Perf. 11½x11***

Olympic Rings and "Motion" Symbol and: 30g, Archery. 40g, Boxing. 60g, Fencing. 2.50z, Wrestling. 3.40z, Weight lifting. 5z, Bicycling. 8.50z, Sharpshooting.

1878	A568 20g multicolored	.20	.20
1879	A568 30g multicolored	.20	.20
1880	A568 40g multicolored	.20	.20
1881	A568 60g gray & multi	.20	.20
1882	A568 2.50z multicolored	.25	.20
1883	A568 3.40z multicolored	.40	.20
1884	A568 5z blue & multi	.50	.25
1885	A568 8.50z multicolored	.90	.50
	Nos. 1878-1885 (8)	2.85	1.95

20th Olympic Games, Munich, Aug. 26-Sept. 10. See No. B125.

Vistula and Cracow — A569

1972, May 28 Photo. ***Perf. 11½x11***

1886	A569 60g red, grn & ocher	.20	.20

50th anniversary of Polish Immigrants Society in Germany (Rodlo).

Knight of King Mieszko I — A570

1972, June 12

1887	A570 60g gold, red brn, yel & blk	.20	.20

Millennium of the Battle of Cedynia (Cidyny).

Zoo Animals — A571

1972, Aug. 20 Litho. ***Perf. 12½***

1888	A571	20g	Cheetah	.20	.20
1889	A571	40g	Giraffe, vert	.20	.20
1890	A571	60g	Toco toucan	.20	.20
1891	A571	1.35z	Chimpanzee	.25	.20
1892	A571	1.65z	Gibbon	.30	.20
1893	A571	3.40z	Crocodile	.35	.20
1894	A571	4z	Kangaroo	1.25	.55
1895	A571	4.50z	Tiger, vert	2.25	1.00
1896	A571	7z	Zebra	2.75	1.25
	Nos. 1888-1896 (9)			7.75	4.00

Ludwik Warynski — A572

1972, Sept. 1 Photo. ***Perf. 11***

1897	A572 60g multicolored	.20	.20

90th anniversary of Proletariat Party, founded by Ludwik Warynski. Printed in sheets of 25 stamps each se-tenant with label showing masthead of party newspaper "Proletariat."

Feliks Dzerzhinski A573

1972, Sept. 11 Litho. ***Perf. 11x11½***

1898	A573 60g red & black	.20	.20

Feliks Dzerzhinski (1877-1926), Russian politician of Polish descent.

Congress Emblem — A574

1972, Sept. 15 Photo. ***Perf. 11½x11***

1899	A574 60g multicolored	.20	.20

25th Congress of the International Cooperative Union, Warsaw, Sept. 1972.

"In the Barracks," by Moniuszko A575

Scenes from Operas or Ballets by Moniuszko: 20g, The Countess. 40g, The Frightful Castle. 60g, Halka. 1.15z, A New Don Quixote. 1.35z, Verbum Nobile. 1.55z, Ideal. 2.50z, Paria.

Photogravure and Engraved

1972, Sept. 15 ***Perf. 11½***

1900	A575	10g	gold & violet	.20	.20
1901	A575	20g	gold & dk brn	.20	.20
1902	A575	40g	gold & slate grn	.20	.20
1903	A575	60g	gold & indigo	.20	.20
1904	A575	1.15z	gold & dk blue	.20	.20
1905	A575	1.35z	gold & dk blue	.20	.20
1906	A575	1.55z	gold & grnsh blk	.20	.20
1907	A575	2.50z	gold & dk brown	.35	.20
	Nos. 1900-1907 (8)			1.75	1.60

Stanislaw Moniuszko (1819-72), composer.

"Amazon," by Piotr Michalowski — A576

Paintings: 40g, Ostafi Daszkiewicz, by Jan Matejko. 60g, "Summer Rain" (dancing woman), by Wojciech Gerson. 2z, Woman from Naples, by Aleksander Kotsis. 2.50z, Girl Taking Bath, by Pantaleon Szyndler. 3.40z, Count of Thun (child), by Artur Grottger. 4z, Rhapsodist (old man), by Stanislaw Wyspianski. 60g and 2.50z inscribed "DZIEN ZNACZKA 1972."

1972, Sept. 28 Photo. *Perf. 10½x11*

1908	A576	30g gold & multi	.20	.20
1909	A576	40g gold & multi	.20	.20
1910	A576	60g gold & multi	.20	.20
1911	A576	2z gold & multi	.20	.20
1912	A576	2.50z gold & multi	.20	.20
1913	A576	3.40z gold & multi	.35	.20
1914	A576	4z gold & multi	.75	.25
		Nos. 1908-1914,B126 (8)	3.60	2.00

Stamp Day.

Copernicus, by Jacob van Meurs, 1654, Heliocentric System — A577

Portraits of Copernicus: 60g, 16th century etching and Prussian coin, 1530. 2.50z, by Jeremiah Falck, 1645, and coat of arms of King of Prussia, 1520. 3.40z, Copernicus with lily of the valley, and page from Theophilactus Simocatta's "Letters on Customs."

1972, Sept. 28 Litho. *Perf. 11x11½*

1915	A577	40g brt blue & blk	.20	.20
1916	A577	60g ocher & blk	.20	.20
1917	A577	2.50z red & blk	.25	.20
1918	A577	3.40z yellow grn & blk	.55	.25
		Nos. 1915-1918 (4)	1.20	.85

See No. B127.

Nos. 1337-1338 Surcharged in Red or Black

a

b

1972 Engr. *Perf. 11½x11*

1919	A445(a)	50g on 40g (R)	.20	.20
1920	A445(a)	90g on 40g (R)	.20	.20
1921	A445(a)	1z on 40g (R)	.20	.20
1922	A445(b)	1.50z on 60g	.20	.20
1923	A445(a)	2.70z on 40g (R)	.20	.20
1924	A445(b)	4z on 60g	.30	.20
1925	A445(b)	4.50z on 60g	.35	.20
1926	A445(b)	4.90z on 60g	.45	.20
		Nos. 1919-1926 (8)	2.10	1.60

Issued: #1919-1920, 11/17; others, 10/2.

The Little Soldier, by E. Piwowarski A578

1972, Oct. 16 Litho. *Perf. 11½*

1927	A578	60g rose & black	.20	.20

Children's health center (Centrum Zdrowia Dzieck), to be built as memorial to children killed during Nazi regime.

Warsaw Royal Castle, 1656, by Erik J. Dahlbergh — A579

1972, Oct. 16 Photo. *Perf. 11x11½*

1928	A579	60g violet, bl & blk	.20	.20

Rebuilding of Warsaw Castle, destroyed during World War II.

Ribbons with Symbols of Trade Union Activities — A580

Mountain Lodge, Chocholowska Valley — A581

1972, Nov. 13 *Perf. 11½x11*

1929	A580	60g multicolored	.20	.20

7th and 13th Polish Trade Union congresses, Nov. 13-15.

1972, Nov. 13 *Perf. 11*

Mountain Lodges in Tatra National Park: 60g, Hala Ornak, West Tatra, horiz. 1.55z, Hala Gasienicowa. 1.65z, Pieciu Stawow Valley, horiz. 2.50z, Morskie Oko, Rybiego Potoku Valley

1930	A581	40g multicolored	.20	.20
1931	A581	60g multicolored	.20	.20
1932	A581	1.55z multicolored	.20	.20
1933	A581	1.65z multicolored	.20	.20
1934	A581	2.50z multicolored	.30	.20
		Nos. 1930-1934 (5)	1.10	1.00

Japanese Azalea — A582

Flowering Shrubs: 50g, Alpine rose. 60g, Pomeranian honeysuckle. 1.65z, Chinese quince. 2.50z, Viburnum. 3.40z, Rhododendron. 4z, Mock orange. 8.50z, Lilac.

1972, Dec. 15 Litho. *Perf. 12½*

1935	A582	40g gray & multi	.20	.20
1936	A582	50g blue & multi	.20	.20
1937	A582	60g multicolored	.20	.20
1938	A582	1.65z ultra & multi	.20	.20
1939	A582	2.50z ocher & multi	.25	.20
1940	A582	3.40z multicolored	.35	.20
1941	A582	4z multicolored	.60	.25
1942	A582	8.50z multicolored	1.25	.55
		Nos. 1935-1942 (8)	3.25	2.00

Emblem A583

Copernicus A584

1972, Dec. 15 Photo. *Perf. 11½*

1943	A583	60g red & multi	.20	.20

5th Congress of Socialist Youth Union.

Coil Stamps

1972, Dec. 28 Photo. *Perf. 14*

1944	A584	1z deep claret	.20	.20
1945	A584	1.50z yellow brown	.20	.20

Nicolaus Copernicus (1473-1543), astronomer. Black control number on back of every 5th stamp.

Piast Knight, 10th Century A585

Polish Cavalry: 40g, Knight, 13th century. 60g, Knight of Ladislas Jagello, 15th century, horiz. 1.35z, Hussar, 17th century. 4z, National Guard Uhlan, 18th century. 4.50z, Congress Kingdom Period, 1831. 5z, Light cavalry, 1939, horiz. 7z, Light cavalry, People's Army, 1945.

1972, Dec. 28 *Perf. 11*

1946	A585	20g violet & multi	.20	.20
1947	A585	40g multicolored	.20	.20
1948	A585	60g orange & multi	.20	.20
1949	A585	1.35z orange & multi	.20	.20
1950	A585	4z orange & multi	.35	.20
1951	A585	4.50z orange & multi	.45	.20
1952	A585	5z brown & multi	.80	.30
1953	A585	7z multicolored	1.10	.50
		Nos. 1946-1953 (8)	3.50	2.00

Man and Woman, Sculpture by Wiera Muchina — A586

Design: 60g, Globe with Red Star.

1972, Dec. 30

1954	A586	40g gray & multi	.20	.20
1955	A586	60g blk, red & vio bl	.20	.20

50th anniversary of the Soviet Union.

Nicolaus Copernicus, by M. Bacciarelli A587

Portraits of Copernicus: 1.50z, painted in Torun, 16th century. 2.70z, by Zinck Nor. 4z, from Strasbourg clock. 4.90z, Copernicus in his Observatory, by Jan Matejko, horiz.

Perf. 11½x11, 11x11½

1973, Feb. 18 Photo.

1956	A587	1z brown & multi	.20	.20
1957	A587	1.50z multicolored	.20	.20
1958	A587	2.70z multicolored	.20	.20
1959	A587	4z multicolored	.35	.20
1960	A587	4.90z multicolored	.50	.30
		Nos. 1956-1960 (5)	1.45	1.10

Piast Coronation Sword, 12th Century — A588

Lenin Monument, Nowa Huta — A589

Polish Art: No. 1962, Kruzlowa Madonna, c. 1410. No. 1963, Hussar's armor, 17th century. No. 1964, Wawel head, wood, 16th century. No. 1965, Cock, sign of Rifle Fraternity, 16th century. 2.70z, Cover of Queen Anna Jagiellonka's prayer book (eagle), 1582. 4.90z, Skarbimierz Madonna, wood, c. 1340. 8.50z, The Nobleman Tenczynski, portrait by unknown artist, 17th century.

1973, Mar. 28 Photo. *Perf. 11½x11*

1961	A588	50g violet & multi	.20	.20
1962	A588	1z lt blue & multi	.20	.20
1963	A588	1z ultra & multi	.20	.20
1964	A588	1.50z blue & multi	.20	.20
1965	A588	1.50z green & multi	.20	.20
1966	A588	2.70z multicolored	.20	.20
1967	A588	4.90z multicolored	.40	.20
1968	A588	8.50z black & multi	1.00	.35
		Nos. 1961-1968 (8)	2.60	1.75

1973, Apr. 28 Litho. *Perf. 11x11½*

1969	A589	1z multicolored	.20	.20

Unveiling of Lenin Monument at Nowa Huta.

Envelope Showing Postal Code A590

1973, May 5 *Perf. 11x11½*

1970	A590	1.50z multicolored	.20	.20

Introduction of postal code system in Poland.

Wolf — A591

1973, May 21 Photo. *Perf. 11*

1971	A591	50g shown	.20	.20
1972	A591	1z Mouflon	.20	.20
1973	A591	1.50z Moose	.20	.20
1974	A591	2.70z Capercaillie	.30	.20
1975	A591	3z Deer	.40	.20
1976	A591	4.50z Lynx	.55	.20
1977	A591	4.90z European hart	1.50	.40
1978	A591	5z Wild boar	1.65	.65
		Nos. 1971-1978 (8)	5.00	2.25

Intl. Hunting Committee Congress and 50th anniv. of Polish Hunting Assoc.

US Satellite "Copernicus" over Earth — A592

No. 1980, USSR satellite Salyut over earth.

1973, June 20

1979	A592	4.90z multicolored	.45	.25
1980	A592	4.90z multicolored	.45	.25

American and Russian astronomical observatories in space. No. 1979 and No. 1980 issued in sheets of 6 stamps and 2 labels.

Flame Rising from Book — A593

1973, June 26 **Litho.**

1981 A593 1.50z blue & multi .20 .20

2nd Polish Science Cong., Warsaw, June 26-29.

Arms of Poznan on 14th Century Seal — A594

Marceli Nowotko — A595

Polska '73 Emblem and: 1.50z, Tombstone of Nicolas Tomicki, 1524. 2.70z, Kalisz paten, 12th century. 4z, Lion knocker from bronze gate, Gniezno, 12th century, horiz.

Perf. 11½x11, 11x11½

1973, June 30

1982	A594	1z	pink & multi	.20	.20
1983	A594	1.50z	orange & multi	.20	.20
1984	A594	2.70z	buff & multi	.20	.20
1985	A594	4z	yellow & multi	.40	.20
			Nos. 1982-1985 (4)	1.00	.80

POLSKA '73 Intl. Phil. Exhib., Poznan, Aug. 19-Sept. 2. See No. B128.

1973, Aug. 8 **Litho.** ***Perf. 11½x11***

1986 A595 1.50z red & black .20 .20

Marceli Nowotko (1893-1942), labor leader, member of Central Committee of Communist Party of Poland.

Emblem and Orchard — A596

Human Environment Emblem and: 90g, Grazing cows. 1z, Stork's nest. 1.50z, Pond with fish and water lilies. 2.70z, Flowers on meadow. 4.90z, Underwater fauna and flora. 5z, Forest scene. 6.50z, Still life.

1973, Aug. 30 **Photo.** ***Perf. 11***

1987	A596	50g	black & multi	.20	.20
1988	A596	90g	black & multi	.20	.20
1989	A596	1z	black & multi	.20	.20
1990	A596	1.50z	black & multi	.20	.20
1991	A596	2.70z	black & multi	.20	.20
1992	A596	4.90z	black & multi	.60	.20
1993	A596	5z	black & multi	.90	.25
1994	A596	6.50z	black & multi	1.50	.40
			Nos. 1987-1994 (8)	4.00	1.85

Protection of the environment.

Motorcyclist — A597

1973, Sept. 2 ***Perf. 11½***

1995 A597 1.50z silver & multi .20 .20

Finals in individual world championship motorcycle race on cinder track, Chorzów, Sept. 2.

Tank — A598

1973, Oct. 12 **Litho.** ***Perf. 12½***

1996	A598	1z	shown	.20	.20
1997	A598	1z	Fighter plane	.20	.20
1998	A598	1.50z	Missile	.20	.20
1999	A598	1.50z	Warship	.20	.20
			Nos. 1996-1999 (4)	.80	.80

Polish People's Army, 30th anniversary.

Grzegorz Piramowicz — A599

Design: 1.50z, J. Sniadecki, Hugo Kollataj and Julian Ursyn Niemcewicz.

Photogravure and Engraved

1973, Oct. 13 ***Perf. 11½x11***

2000	A599	1z	buff & dk brn	.20	.20
2001	A599	1.50z	gray & sl grn	.20	.20

Natl. Education Commission, bicent.

Henryk Arctowski, and Penguins A600

Polish Scientists: No. 2003, Pawel Edmund Strzelecki and Kangaroo. No. 2004, Benedykt Tadeusz Dybowski and Lake Baikal. No. 2005, Stefan Rogozinski, sailing ship "Lucja-Malgorzata." 2z, Bronislaw Malinowski, Trobriand Island drummers. 2.70z, Stefan Drzewiecki and submarine. 3z, Edward Adolf Strasburger and plants. 8z, Ignacy Domeyko, geological strata.

1973, Nov. 30 **Photo.** ***Perf. 10½x11***

2002	A600	1z	gold & multi	.20	.20
2003	A600	1z	gold & multi	.20	.20
2004	A600	1.50z	gold & multi	.20	.20
2005	A600	1.50z	gold & multi	.20	.20
2006	A600	2z	gold & multi	.20	.20
2007	A600	2.70z	gold & multi	.20	.20
2008	A600	3z	gold & multi	.25	.20
2009	A600	8z	gold & multi	.80	.35
			Nos. 2002-2009 (8)	2.25	1.75

Polish Flag — A601

1973, Dec. 15 **Photo.** ***Perf. 11½x11***

2010 A601 1.50z dp ultra, red & gold .20 .20

Polish United Workers' Party, 25th anniv.

Jelcz-Berliet Bus — A602

Designs: Polish automotives.

1973, Dec. 28 **Photo.** ***Perf. 11x11½***

2011	A602	50g	shown	.20	.20
2012	A602	90g	Jelcz 316	.20	.20
2013	A602	1z	Polski Fiat 126p	.20	.20
2014	A602	1.50z	Polski Fiat 125p	.20	.20
2015	A602	4z	Nysa M-521 bus	.40	.20
2016	A602	4.50z	Star 660 truck	.50	.25
			Nos. 2011-2016 (6)	1.70	1.25

Iris — A603

Flowers: 1z, Dandelion. 1.50z, Rose. 3z, Thistle. 4z, Cornflowers. 4.50z, Clover. (Paintings by Stanislaw Wyspianski.)

1974, Jan. 22 **Engr.** ***Perf. 12x11½***

2017	A603	50g	lilac	.20	.20
2018	A603	1z	green	.20	.20
2019	A603	1.50z	red orange	.20	.20
2020	A603	3z	deep violet	.25	.20
2021	A603	4z	violet blue	.40	.20
2022	A603	4.50z	emerald	.45	.20
			Nos. 2017-2022 (6)	1.70	1.20

Cottage, Kurpie A604

Designs: 1.50z, Church, Sekowa. 4z, Town Hall, Sulmierzyce. 4.50z, Church, Lachowice. 4.90z, Windmill, Sobienie-Jeziory. 5z, Orthodox Church, Ulucz.

1974, Mar. 5 **Photo.** ***Perf. 11x11½***

2023	A604	1z	multicolored	.20	.20
2024	A604	1.50z	yellow & multi	.20	.20
2025	A604	4z	pink & multi	.30	.20
2026	A604	4.50z	lt blue & multi	.30	.20
2027	A604	4.90z	multicolored	.35	.20
2028	A604	5z	pink & multi	.45	.20
			Nos. 2023-2028 (6)	1.80	1.20

Mail Coach and UPU Emblem — A605

Embroidery from Cracow — A606

1974, Mar. 30 ***Perf. 11½x12***

2029 A605 1.50z multicolored .20 .20

Centenary of Universal Postal Union.

1974, May 7 **Photo.** ***Perf. 11½x11***

Embroideries from: 1.50z, Lowicz. 4z, Slask.

2030	A606	50g	multicolored	.20	.20
2031	A606	1.50z	multicolored	.20	.20
2032	A606	4z	multicolored	.40	.20
a.			Souvenir sheet of 3, #2030-2032, imperf.	1.75	1.25
b.			As "a," perf. 11½x11	6.00	4.50
			Nos. 2030-2032 (3)	.80	.60

SOCPHILEX IV International Philatelic Exhibition, Katowice, May 18-June 2.

No. 2032a sold for 17z.

No. 2032b sold for 17z plus 15z for 4 envelopes.

Association Emblem — A607

Soldier and Dove — A608

1974, May 8 **Litho.** ***Perf. 12x11½***

2033 A607 1.50z gray & red .20 .20

5th Congress of the Assoc. of Combatants for Liberty & Democracy, Warsaw, May 8-9.

1974, May 9 ***Perf. 11½x11***

2034 A608 1.50z org, lt bl & blk .20 .20

29th anniversary of victory over Fascism.

Comecon Building, Moscow A609

1974, May 15 ***Perf. 11x11½***

2035 A609 1.50z gray bl, bis & red .20 .20

25th anniv. of the Council of Mutual Economic Assistance.

Soccer Ball and Games' Emblem A610

Design: No. 2037, Soccer players, Olympic rings and 1972 medal.

1974, June 15 **Photo.** ***Perf. 11x11½***

2036	A610	4.90z	olive & multi	.50	.20
a.			Souv. sheet of 4 + 2 labels	4.50	2.00
2037	A610	4.90z	olive & multi	.50	.20
a.			Souv. sheet, 2 each #2036-2037	12.00	7.00

World Cup Soccer Championship, Munich, June 13-July 7.

No. 2036a issued to commemorate Poland's silver medal in 1974 Championship.

Sailing Ship, 16th Century — A611

Chess, by Jan Kochanowski A612

Polish Sailing Ships: 1.50z, "Dal," 1934. 2.70z, "Opty," sailed around the world, 1969. 4z, "Dar Pomorza," winner "Operation Sail," 1972. 4.90z, "Polonez," sailed around the world, 1973.

1974, June 29 Litho. *Perf. 11½x11*

2038	A611	1z	multicolored	.20	.20
2039	A611	1.50z	multicolored	.20	.20
2040	A611	2.70z	multicolored	.20	.20
2041	A611	4z	green & multi	.40	.25
2042	A611	4.90z	dp blue & multi	.60	.30
			Nos. 2038-2042 (5)	1.60	1.15

1974, July 15 Litho. *Perf. 11½x11*

Design: 1.50z, "Education," etching by Daniel Chodowiecki.

2043	A612	1z	multicolored	.20	.20
2044	A612	1.50z	multicolored	.22	.20

10th International Chess Festival, Lublin.

Man and Map of Poland — A613

Polish Eagle — A614

1974, July 21 Photo. *Perf. 11½x11*

2045	A613	1.50z	black, gold & red	.20	.20
2046	A614	1.50z	silver & multi	.20	.20
2047	A614	1.50z	red & multi	.20	.20
			Nos. 2045-2047 (3)	.60	.60

People's Republic of Poland, 30th anniv.

Lazienkowska Bridge Road — A615

1974, July 21 *Perf. 11x11½*

2048	A615	1.50z	multicolored	.20	.20

Opening of Lazienkowska Bridge over Vistula south of Warsaw.

Strawberries and Congress Emblem — A616

1974, Sept. 10 Photo. *Perf. 11½*

2049	A616	50g	shown	.20	.20
2050	A616	90g	Black currants	.20	.20
2051	A616	1z	Apples	.20	.20
2052	A616	1.50z	Cucumbers	.20	.20
2053	A616	2.70z	Tomatoes	.20	.20
2054	A616	4.50z	Peas	.40	.20
2055	A616	4.90z	Pansies	.60	.25
2056	A616	5z	Nasturtiums	1.25	.40
			Nos. 2049-2056 (8)	3.25	1.85

19th Intl. Horticultural Cong., Warsaw, Sept.

Civic Militia and Security Service Badge — A617

Polish Child, by Lukasz Orlowski — A618

1974, Oct. 3 Photo. *Perf. 11½x11*

2057	A617	1.50g	multicolored	.20	.20

30th anniv. of the Civic Militia and the Security Service.

1974, Oct. 9

Polish paintings of Children: 90g, Girl with Pigeon, Anonymous artist, 19th century. 1z, Girl, by Stanislaw Wyspianski. 1.50z, The Orphan from Poronin, by Wladyslaw Slewinski. 3z, Peasant Boy, by Kazimierz Sichulski. 4.50z, Florentine Page, by Aleksander Gierymski. 4.90z, The Artist's Son Tadeusz, by Piotr Michalowski. 6.50z, Boy with Doe, by Aleksander Kotsis.

2058	A618	50g	multicolored	.20	.20
2059	A618	90g	multicolored	.20	.20
2060	A618	1z	multicolored	.20	.20
2061	A618	1.50z	multicolored	.20	.20
2062	A618	3z	multicolored	.20	.20
2063	A618	4.50z	multicolored	.30	.20
2064	A618	4.90z	multicolored	.45	.25
2065	A618	6.50z	multicolored	.50	.30
			Nos. 2058-2065 (8)	2.25	1.75

Children's Day. The 1z and 1.50z are inscribed "Dzien Znaczka (Stamp Day) 1974."

Cracow Manger — A619

King Sigismund Vasa — A620

Masterpieces of Polish art: 1.50z, Flight into Egypt, 1465. 4z, King Jan Olbracht.

1974, Dec. 2 Litho. *Perf. 11½x11*

2066	A619	1z	multicolored	.20	.20
2067	A620	1.50z	multicolored	.20	.20
2068	A620	2z	multicolored	.25	.20
2069	A619	4z	multicolored	.60	.20
			Nos. 2066-2069 (4)	1.25	.80

Angler — A621

Designs: 1.50z, Hunter with bow and arrow. 4z, Boy snaring geese. 4.50z, Beekeeper. Designs from 16th century woodcuts.

1974-77 Engr. *Perf. 11½x11*

2070	A621	1z	black	.20	.20
2071	A621	1.50z	indigo	.20	.20
2071A	A621	4z	slate green	.25	.20
2071B	A621	4.50z	dark brown	.25	.20
			Nos. 2070-2071B (4)	.90	.80

Issued: 1z-1.50z, 12/30; 4z-4.50z, 12/12/77.

Pablo Neruda, by Osvaldo Guayasamin A622

1974, Dec. 31 Litho. *Perf. 11½x11*

2072	A622	1.50z	multicolored	.20	.20

Pablo Neruda (1904-1973), Chilean poet.

Nike Monument and Opera House, Warsaw — A623

1975, Jan. 17 Photo. *Perf. 11*

2073	A623	1.50z	multicolored	.20	.20

30th anniversary of the liberation of Warsaw.

Hobby Falcon — A624

"Auschwitz" A625

1975, Jan. 23 *Perf. 11½x12*

2074	A624	1z	Lesser kestrel, male	.20	.20
2075	A624	1z	same, female	.20	.20
a.			Pair, #2074-2075	.25	.20
2076	A624	1.50z	Red-footed falcon, male	.20	.20
2077	A624	1.50z	same, female	.20	.20
a.			Pair, #2076-2077	.35	.25
2078	A624	2z	shown	.40	.20
2079	A624	3z	Kestrel	.50	.25
2080	A624	4z	Merlin	1.50	.60
2081	A624	8z	Peregrine	2.25	1.10
			Nos. 2074-2081 (8)	5.45	2.95

Falcons.

Photogravure and Engraved

1975, Jan. 27 *Perf. 11½x11*

2082	A625	1.50z	red & black	.25	.20

30th anniversary of the liberation of Auschwitz (Oswiecim) concentration camp.

Women's Hurdle Race A626

Designs: 1.50z, Pole vault. 4z, Hop, step and jump. 4.90z, Sprinting.

1975, Mar. 8 Litho. *Perf. 11x11½*

2083	A626	1z	multicolored	.20	.20
2084	A626	1.50z	olive & multi	.20	.20
2085	A626	4z	multicolored	.35	.20
2086	A626	4.90z	green & multi	.40	.25
			Nos. 2083-2086 (4)	1.15	.85

6th European Indoor Athletic Championships, Katowice, Mar. 1975.

St. Anne, by Veit Stoss, Arphila Emblem A627

1975, Apr. 15 Photo. *Perf. 11x11½*

2087	A627	1.50z	multicolored	.20	.20

ARPHILA 75, International Philatelic Exhibition, Paris, June 6-10.

Amateur Radio Union Emblem, Globe A628

1975, Apr. 15 Litho. *Perf. 11½*

2088	A628	1.50z	multicolored	.20	.20

International Amateur Radio Union Conference, Warsaw, Apr. 1975.

Mountain Guides' Badge and Sudetic Mountains — A629

#2089, Pine, badge and Tatra Mountains, vert. #2090, Gentian and Tatra Mountains, vert. #2092, Yew branch with berries, and Sudetic Mountains. #2093, River, Beskids Mountains and badge, vert. #2094, Arnica and Beskids Mountains, vert.

1975, Apr. 30 — Photo. — *Perf. 11*

2089	A629	1z	multicolored	.20	.20
2090	A629	1z	multicolored	.20	.20
a.			Pair, #2089-2090	.20	.20
2091	A629	1.50z	multicolored	.20	.20
2092	A629	1.50z	multicolored	.20	.20
a.			Pair, #2091-2092	.30	.20
2093	A629	4z	multicolored	.40	.20
2094	A629	4z	multicolored	.40	.20
a.			Pair, #2093-2094	.80	.40
			Nos. 2090a,2092a,2094a (3)	1.30	.80

Centenary of Polish Mountain Guides Organizations. Pairs have continuous design.

Hands Holding Tulips and Rifle — A630

Warsaw Treaty Members' Flags — A631

1975, May 9 — *Perf. 11½x11*

2095 A630 1.50z blue & multi .20 .20

End of WWII, 30th anniv.; victory over Fascism.

1975, May 14

2096 A631 1.50z blue & multi .20 .20

20th anniversary of the signing of the Warsaw Treaty (Bulgaria, Czechoslovakia, German Democratic Rep., Hungary, Poland, Romania, USSR).

Cock and Hen, Congress Emblem — A632

1975, June 23 — Photo. — *Perf. 12x11½*

2097	A632	50g	shown	.20	.20
2098	A632	1z	Geese	.20	.20
2099	A632	1.50z	Cattle	.20	.20
2100	A632	2z	Cow	.30	.20
2101	A632	3z	Arabian stallion	.40	.20
2102	A632	4z	Wielkopolska horses	.50	.20
2103	A632	4.50z	Pigs	.85	.30
2104	A632	5z	Sheep	1.75	.50
			Nos. 2097-2104 (8)	4.40	2.00

20th Congress of the European Zootechnical Federation, Warsaw.

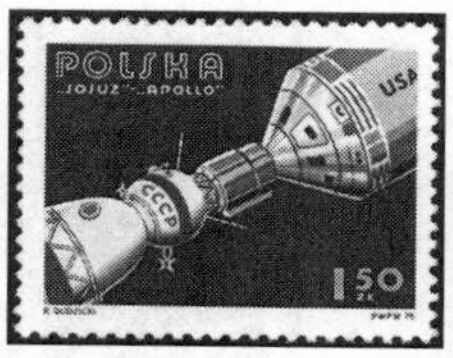

Apollo and Soyuz Linked in Space A633

1975, July 15 — *Perf. 11x11½*

2105	A633	1.50z	shown	.20	.20
2106	A633	4.90z	Apollo	.50	.25
2107	A633	4.90z	Soyuz	.50	.25
a.			Souv. sheet, 2 each #2106-2107 + 2 labels	7.50	3.50
b.			Pair, #2106-2107	1.00	.50
			Nos. 2105-2107 (3)	1.20	.70

Apollo Soyuz space test project (Russo-American cooperation), launching July 15; link-up, July 17.

Health Fund Emblem — A634

1975, July 12 — *Perf. 11½x11*

2108 A634 1.50z silver, blk & bl .20 .20

National Fund for Health Protection.

"E" and Polish Flag A635

1975, July 30 — Litho. — *Perf. 11x11½*

2109 A635 4z lt blue, red & blk .30 .20

European Security and Cooperation Conference, Helsinki, July 30-Aug. 1.

UN Emblem and Sunburst A636

1975, July 25

2110 A636 4z blue & multi .30 .20

30th anniversary of the United Nations.

Bolek and Lolek A637

Cartoon Characters and Children's Health Center Emblem: 1z, Jacek and Agatka. 1.50z, Reksio, the dog. 4z, Telesfor, the dragon.

1975, Aug. 30 — Photo. — *Perf. 11x11½*

2111	A637	50g	violet bl & multi	.20	.20
2112	A637	1z	multicolored	.20	.20
2113	A637	1.50z	multicolored	.20	.20
2114	A637	4z	multicolored	.45	.20
			Nos. 2111-2114 (4)	1.05	.80

Children's television programs.

Circular Bar Graph and Institute's Emblem — A638

IWY Emblem, White, Yellow and Brown Women — A639

1975, Sept. 1 — Litho. — *Perf. 11½x11*

2115 A638 1.50z multicolored .20 .20

International Institute of Statistics, 40th session, Warsaw, Sept. 1975.

1975, Sept. 8 — Photo.

2116 A639 1.50z multicolored .20 .20

International Women's Year.

First Poles Arriving on "Mary and Margaret" 1608 A640

George Washington A641

Designs: 1.50z, Polish glass blower and glass works, Jamestown, 1608. 2.70z, Helena Modrzejewska (1840-1909), Polish actress, came to US in 1877. 4z, Casimir Pulaski (1747-1779), and 6.40z, Tadeusz Kosciusko (1748-1817), heroes of American War of Independence.

1975, Sept. 24 — Litho. — *Perf. 11x11½*

2117	A640	1z	black & multi	.20	.20
2118	A640	1.50z	black & multi	.20	.20
2119	A640	2.70z	black & multi	.20	.20
2120	A640	4z	black & multi	.25	.20
2121	A640	6.40z	black & multi	.40	.30
			Nos. 2117-2121 (5)	1.25	1.10

Souvenir Sheet

Perf. 12

2122	Sheet of 3+3 labels	1.50	1.25
a.	A641 4.90z shown	.40	.25
b.	A641 4.90z Kosciusko	.40	.25
c.	A641 4.90z Pulaski	.40	.25

American Revolution, bicentenary.

Albatross Biplane, 1918-1925 A642

Design: 4.90z, IL 62 jet, 1975.

1975, Sept. 25 — *Perf. 11x11½*

2123 A642 2.40z buff & multi .20 .20
2124 A642 4.90z gray & multi .40 .20

50th anniversary of Polish air post stamps.

Frederic Chopin — A643

1975, Oct. 7 — Photo.

2125 A643 1.50z gold, lt vio & blk .20 .20

9th International Chopin Piano Competition, Warsaw, Oct. 7-28.

Printed in sheets of 50 stamps with alternating labels with commemorative inscription.

Dunikowski, Self-portrait A644

1975, Oct. 9 — *Perf. 11½x11*

Sculptures: 1z, "Breath." 1.50z, "Maternity."

2126	A644	50g	silver & multi	.20	.20
2127	A644	1z	silver & multi	.20	.20
2128	A644	1.50z	silver & multi	.20	.20
			Nos. 2126-2128 (3)	.60	.60

Stamp Day. Xawery Dunikowski (1875-1964), sculptor. See No. B131.

Town Hall, Zamosc — A645

Lodz, by Wladyslaw Strzeminski A646

1z, Arcades, Kazimierz Dolny, horiz.

Coil Stamps

1975, Nov. 11 — Photo. — *Perf. 14*

2129 A645 1z olive green .20 .20
2130 A645 1.50z rose brown .20 .20

European Architectural Heritage Year. Black control number on back of every fifth stamp of Nos. 2129-2130.

1975, Nov. 22 — Litho. — *Perf. 12½*

2131 A646 4.50z multicolored .45 .20
a. Souvenir sheet .90 .50

Lodz 75, 12th Polish Philatelic Exhibition, for 25th anniv. of Polish Philatelists Union.

Piast Family Eagle A647

1.50z, Seal of Prince Boleslaw of Legnica. 4z, Coin of Prince Jerzy Wilhelm (1660-1675).

1975, Nov. 29 Engr. ***Perf. 11x11½***

2132	A647	1z	green	.20	.20
2133	A647	1.50z	brown	.20	.20
2134	A647	4z	dull violet	.30	.20
			Nos. 2132-2134 (3)	.70	.60

Piast dynasty's influence on the development of Silesia.

"7" Inscribed "ZJAZD" and "PZPR" — A648

"VII ZJAZD PZPR" — A649

1975, Dec. 8 Photo. ***Perf. 11½x11***

2135	A648	1z	lt blue & multi	.20	.20
2136	A649	1.50z	silver, red & ultra	.20	.20

7th Cong. of Polish United Workers' Party.

Ski Jump A650

Designs (Winter Olympic Games Emblem and): 1z, Ice hockey. 1.50z, Slalom. 2z, Speed skating. 4z, Luge. 6.40z, Biathlon.

1976, Jan. 10 ***Perf. 11x11½***

2137	A650	50g	silver & multi	.20	.20
2138	A650	1z	silver & multi	.20	.20
2139	A650	1.50z	silver & multi	.20	.20
2140	A650	2z	silver & multi	.20	.20
2141	A650	4z	silver & multi	.40	.20
2142	A650	6.40z	silver & multi	.65	.25
			Nos. 2137-2142 (6)	1.85	1.25

12th Winter Olympic Games, Innsbruck, Austria, Feb. 4-15.

Engine by Richard Trevithick, 1803 — A651

Locomotives by: 1z, M. Murray and J. Blenkinsop, 1810. No. 2145, George Stephenson's Rocket, 1829. No. 2146, Polish electric locomotive, 1969. 2.70z, Stephenson, 1837. 3z, Joseph Harrison, 1840. 4.50z, Thomas Rogers, 1855. 4.90z, Chrzanow (Polish), 1922.

1976, Feb. 13 Photo. ***Perf. 11½x12***

2143	A651	50g	multicolored	.20	.20
2144	A651	1z	multicolored	.20	.20
2145	A651	1.50z	multicolored	.20	.20
2146	A651	1.50z	multicolored	.20	.20
2147	A651	2.70z	multicolored	.20	.20
2148	A651	3z	multicolored	.20	.20
2149	A651	4.50z	multicolored	.75	.20
2150	A651	4.90z	multicolored	.80	.20
			Nos. 2143-2150 (8)	2.75	1.60

History of the locomotive.

Telephone, Radar and Satellites, ITU Emblem — A652

1976, Mar. 10 ***Perf. 11***

2151	A652	1.50z	multicolored	.20	.20

Centenary of first telephone call by Alexander Graham Bell, Mar. 10, 1876.

Atom Symbol and Flags of Communist Countries A653

1976, Mar. 10 Litho. ***Perf. 11½***

2152	A653	1.50z	multicolored	.20	.20

Joint Institute of Nuclear Research, Dubna, USSR, 20th anniversary.

Ice Hockey — A654

Design: 1.50z, like 1z, reversed.

1976, Apr. 8 Photo. ***Perf. 11½x11***

2153	A654	1z	multicolored	.20	.20
2154	A654	1.50z	multicolored	.20	.20

Ice Hockey World Championship 1976, Katowice.

Soldier and Map of Sinai A655

1976, Apr. 30 Photo. ***Perf. 11x11½***

2155	A655	1.50z	multicolored	.20	.20

Polish specialist troops serving with UN Forces in Sinai Peninsula.

No. 2155 printed se-tenant with label with commemorative inscription.

Sappers' Monument, by Stanislaw Kulow, Warsaw — A656

Interphil 76, Philadelphia A657

Design: No. 2157, First Polish Army Monument, by Bronislaw Koniuszy, Warsaw.

1976, May 8 ***Perf. 11½***

2156	A656	1z	gold & multi	.20	.20
2157	A656	1z	silver & multi	.20	.20

Memorials unveiled on 30th anniv. of WWII victory.

1976, May 20 Litho. ***Perf. 11½x11***

2158	A657	8.40z	gray & multi	.70	.35

Interphil 76, Intl. Phil. Exhib., Philadelphia, May 29-June 6.

Wielkopolski Park and Owl — A658

National Parks: 1z, Wolinski Park and eagle. 1.50z, Slowinski Park and sea gull. 4.50z, Bieszczadzki Park and lynx. 5z, Ojcowski Park and bat. 6z, Kampinoski Park and elk.

1976, May 22 Photo. ***Perf. 12x11½***

2159	A658	90g	multicolored	.20	.20
2160	A658	1z	multicolored	.20	.20
2161	A658	1.50z	multicolored	.20	.20
2162	A658	4.50z	multicolored	.35	.20
2163	A658	5z	multicolored	.40	.20
2164	A658	6z	multicolored	.50	.25
			Nos. 2159-2164 (6)	1.85	1.25

UN Headquarters, Dove-shaped Globe — A659

1976, June 29 Litho. ***Perf. 11x11½***

2165	A659	8.40z	multicolored	.70	.35

UN postage stamps, 25th anniversary.

Fencing and Olympic Rings A660

1976, June 30 **Photo.**

2166	A660	50g	shown	.20	.20
2167	A660	1z	Bicycling	.20	.20
2168	A660	1.50z	Soccer	.20	.20
2169	A660	4.20z	Boxing	.35	.20
2170	A660	6.90z	Weight lifting	.55	.30
2171	A660	8.40z	Running	.65	.35
			Nos. 2166-2171 (6)	2.15	1.45

21st Olympic Games, Montreal, Canada, July 17-Aug. 1. See No. B132.

Polish Theater, Poznan — A662

1976, July 12 Litho. ***Perf. 11x11½***

2173	A662	1.50z	gray olive & org	.20	.20

Polish Theater in Poznan, centenary.

Czekanowski, Lake Baikal — A663

1976, Sept. 3 Photo. ***Perf. 11x11½***

2174	A663	1.50z	silver & multi	.20	.20

Aleksander Czekanowski (1833-1876), geologist, death centenary.

Siren A664

Designs: 1z, Sphinx, vert. 2z, Lion. 4.20z, Bull. 4.50z, Goat. Designs from Corinthian vases, 7th century B.C.

Perf. 11x11½, 11½x11

1976, Oct. 30 **Photo.**

2175	A664	1z	gold & multi	.20	.20
2176	A664	1.50z	gold & multi	.20	.20
2177	A664	2z	gold & multi	.20	.20
2178	A664	4.20z	gold & multi	.30	.20
2179	A664	4.50z	gold & multi	.30	.20
			Nos. 2175-2179,B133 (6)	2.30	1.50

Stamp Day.

Warszawa M20 — A665

Automobiles: 1.50z, Warszawa 223. 2z, Syrena 104. 4.90z, Polski Fiat 125.

1976, Nov. 6 Photo. ***Perf. 11***

2180	A665	1z	multicolored	.20	.20
2181	A665	1.50z	multicolored	.20	.20
2182	A665	2z	multicolored	.20	.20
2183	A665	4.90z	multicolored	.35	.20
a.			Souvenir sheet of 4, #2180-2183 + 2 labels	1.25	.55
			Nos. 2180-2183 (4)	.95	.80

Zeran Automobile Factory, Warsaw, 25th anniv.

Pouring Ladle — A666

Virgin and Child, Epitaph, 1425 — A667

1976, Nov. 26 Litho. *Perf. 11*

2184	A666	1.50z multicolored	.20	.20

First steel production at Katowice Foundry.

1976, Dec. 15

6z, The Beautiful Madonna, sculpture, c. 1410.

2185	A667	1z multicolored	.20	.20
2186	A667	6z multicolored	.40	.20

Polish Trade Union Emblem — A668

1976, Dec. 29

2187	A668	1.50z multicolored	.20	.20

8th Polish Trade Union Congress.

Tanker Zawrat Unloading, Gdansk — A669

Polish Ports: No. 2189, Ferry "Gryf" and cars at pier, Gdansk. No. 2190, Loading containers, Gdynia. No. 2191, "Stefan Batory" and "People of the Sea" monument, Gdynia. 2z, Barge and cargoship "Ziemia Szczecinska", Szczecin. 4.20z, Coal loading installations, Swinoujscie. 6.90z, Liner, hydrofoil and lighthouse, Kolobrzeg. 8.40z, Map of Polish Coast with ports, ships and emblem of Union of Polish Ports.

1976, Dec. 29 Photo. *Perf. 11*

2188	A669	1z multicolored	.20	.20
2189	A669	1z multicolored	.20	.20
2190	A669	1.50z multicolored	.20	.20
2191	A669	1.50z multicolored	.20	.20
2192	A669	2z multicolored	.20	.20
2193	A669	4.20z multicolored	.30	.20
2194	A669	6.90z multicolored	.55	.25
2195	A669	8.40z multicolored	.60	.30
		Nos. 2188-2195 (8)	2.45	1.75

Nurse Helping Old Woman — A670

Civilian Defense Medal — A671

1977, Jan. 24 Litho. *Perf. 11½x11*

2196	A670	1.50z multicolored	.20	.20

Polish Red Cross.

1977, Feb. 26 Litho. *Perf. 11*

2197	A671	1.50z multicolored	.20	.20

Civilian Defense.

Ball on the Road — A672

1977, Mar. 12 Photo.

2198	A672	1.50z olive & multi	.20	.20

Social Action Committee (founded 1966), "Stop, Child on the Road!"

Forest Fruits — A673

1977, Mar. 17 *Perf. 11½x11*

2199	A673	50g Dewberry	.20	.20
2200	A673	90g Cranberry	.20	.20
2201	A673	1z Wild strawberry	.20	.20
2202	A673	1.50z Bilberry	.20	.20
2203	A673	2z Raspberry	.20	.20
2204	A673	4.50z Blueberry	.40	.20
2205	A673	6z Dog rose	.40	.20
2206	A673	6.90z Hazelnut	.70	.25
		Nos. 2199-2206 (8)	2.50	1.65

Flags of USSR and Poland as Computer Tape — A674

Emblem and Graph — A675

1977, Apr. 4 Litho. *Perf. 11½x11*

2207	A674	1.50z red & multi	.20	.20

Scientific and technical cooperation between Poland and USSR, 30th anniversary.

1977, Apr. 22

2208	A675	1.50z red & multi	.20	.20

7th Congress of Polish Engineers.

Venus, by Rubens A676

Paintings by Flemish painter Peter Paul Rubens (1577-1640): 1.50z, Bathsheba. 5z, Helene Fourment. 6z, Self-portrait.

1977, Apr. 30 *Perf. 11½*

Frame in Gray Brown

2209	A676	1z multicolored	.20	.20
2210	A676	1.50z multicolored	.25	.20
2211	A676	5z multicolored	.75	.20
2212	A676	6z multicolored	.80	.25
		Nos. 2209-2212 (4)	2.00	.85

See No. B134.

Peace Dove A677

1977, May 6 *Perf. 11x11½*

2213	A677	1.50z black, ultra & yel	.20	.20

Congress of World Council of Peace, Warsaw, May 6-11.

Bicyclist A678

1977, May 6 Photo.

2214	A678	1.50z gray & multi	.20	.20

30th International Peace Bicycling Race, Warsaw-Berlin-Prague.

Wolf — A679

Violinist, by Jacob Toorenvliet A680

Wildlife Fund Emblem and: No. 2216, Great bustard. No. 2217, Kestrel. 6z, Otter.

1977, May 12 Photo. *Perf. 11½x11*

2215	A679	1z silver & multi	.20	.20
2216	A679	1.50z silver & multi	.20	.20
2217	A679	1.50z silver & multi	.20	.20
2218	A679	6z silver & multi	.50	.20
		Nos. 2215-2218 (4)	1.10	.80

Wildlife protection.

1977, May 16

2219	A680	6z gold & multi	.40	.25

AMPHILEX '77 Intl. Phil. Exhib., Amsterdam, May 26-June 5. No. 2219 issued in sheets of 6.

Midsummer Bonfire — A681

Folk Customs: 1z, Easter cock. 1.50z, Dousing the women on Easter Monday. 3z, Harvest festival. 6z, Christmas procession with crèche. 8.40z, Wedding dance. 1z, 1.50z, 3z, 6z vertical.

Perf. 11x11½, 11½x11

1977, June 13 Photo.

2220	A681	90g multicolored	.20	.20
2221	A681	1z multicolored	.20	.20
2222	A681	1.50z multicolored	.20	.20
2223	A681	3z multicolored	.25	.20
2224	A681	6z multicolored	.50	.20
2225	A681	8.40z multicolored	.65	.25
		Nos. 2220-2225 (6)	2.00	1.25

Henryk Wieniawski and Musical Symbol — A682

1977, June 30 Litho. *Perf. 11½x11*

2226	A682	1.50z gold, blk & red	.20	.20

Wieniawski Music Festivals, Poznan: 5th Intl. Lute Competition, June 30-July 10, and 7th Intl. Violin Competition, Nov. 13-27.

Parnassius Apollo — A683

Butterflies: No. 2228, Nymphalis polychloros. No. 2229, Papilio machaon. No. 2230, Nymphalis antiopa. 5z, Fabriciana adippe. 6.90z, Argynnis paphia.

1977, Aug. 22 Photo. *Perf. 11*

2227	A683	1z multicolored	.20	.20
2228	A683	1z multicolored	.20	.20
2229	A683	1.50z multicolored	.20	.20
2230	A683	1.50z multicolored	.20	.20
2231	A683	5z multicolored	.95	.25
2232	A683	6.90z multicolored	2.00	.85
		Nos. 2227-2232 (6)	3.75	1.90

Arms of Slupsk, Keyboard A684

Feliks Dzerzhinski A685

1977, Sept. 3 *Perf. 11½*

2233	A684	1.50z multicolored	.20	.20

Slupsk Piano Festival.

1977, Sept. 10 Litho. *Perf. 11½x11*

2234	A685	1.50z olive bis & sepia	.20	.20

Feliks E. Dzerzhinski (1877-1926), organizer and head of Russian Secret Police (Cheka).

Earth and Sputnik A686

1977, Oct. 1 Litho. *Perf. 11x11½*

2235	A686 1.50z ultra & car		.20	.20
a.	Souvenir sheet of 3+3 labels		.90	.60

60th anniv. of the Russian Revolution and 20th anniv. of Sputnik space flight. Printed in sheets of 15 stamps and 15 carmine labels showing Winter Palace, Leningrad.

Boleslaw Chrobry's Denarius, 11th Century — A687

Silver Coins: 1z, King Kazimierz Wielki's Cracow groszy, 14th century. 1.50z, Legniza-Brzeg-Wolow thaler, 17th century. 4.20z, King Augustus III guilder, Gdansk, 18th century. 4.50z, 5z (ship), 1936. 6z, 100z, Poland's millenium, 1966.

1977, Oct. 9 Photo. *Perf. 11½x11*

2236	A687	50g silver & multi	.20	.20
2237	A687	1z silver & multi	.20	.20
2238	A687	1.50z silver & multi	.20	.20
2239	A687	4.20z silver & multi	.30	.20
2240	A687	4.50z silver & multi	.40	.20
2241	A687	6z silver & multi	.70	.25
	Nos. 2236-2241 (6)		2.00	1.25

Stamp Day.

Monastery, Przasnysz — A688

Architectural landmarks: No. 2242, Wolin Gate, vert. No. 2243, Church, Debno, vert. No. 2245, Cathedral, Plock. 6z, Castle, Kornik. 6.90z, Palace and Garden, Wilanow.

Perf. 11½x11, 11x11½

1977, Nov. 21 Photo.

2242	A688	1z multicolored	.20	.20
2243	A688	1z multicolored	.20	.20
2244	A688	1.50z multicolored	.20	.20
2245	A688	1.50z multicolored	.20	.20
2246	A688	6z multicolored	.40	.20
2247	A688	6.90z multicolored	.55	.25
	Nos. 2242-2247 (6)		1.75	1.25

Vostok (USSR) and Mercury (USA) A689

1977, Dec. 28 Photo. *Perf. 11x11½*

2248	A689 6.90z ultra & multi		.50	.30
a.	Souvenir sheet of 6		4.25	3.00

20 years of space conquest. No. 2248a contains 6 No. 2248 (2 tete-beche pairs) and 2 labels, one showing Sputnik 1 and "4.X.1957," the other Explorer 1 and "31.1.1958."

DN Class Iceboats — A690

Design: No. 2250, One iceboat.

1978, Feb. 6 Litho. *Perf. 11*

2249	A690 1.50z lt ultra & blk		.20	.20
2250	A690 1.50z lt ultra & blk		.20	.20
a.	Pair, #2249-2250 + label		.30	.20

6th World Iceboating Championships, Feb. 6-11.

Electric Locomotive, Katowice Station, 1957 — A691

Locomotives in Poland: No. 2252, Narrow-gauge engine and Gothic Tower, Znin. No. 2253, Pm36 and Cegielski factory, Poznan, 1936. No. 2254, Electric train and Otwock Station, 1936. No. 2255, Marki Train and Warsaw Stalow Station, 1907. 4.50z, Ty51 coal train and Gdynia Station, 1933. 5z, Tr21 and Chrzanow factory, 1920. 6z, "Cockerill" and Vienna Station, 1848.

1978, Feb. 28 Photo. *Perf. 12x11½*

2251	A691	50g multicolored	.20	.20
2252	A691	1z multicolored	.20	.20
2253	A691	1z multicolored	.20	.20
2254	A691	1.50z multicolored	.20	.20
2255	A691	1.50z multicolored	.20	.20
2256	A691	4.50z multicolored	.40	.20
2257	A691	5z multicolored	.40	.20
2258	A691	6z multicolored	.50	.25
	Nos. 2251-2258 (8)		2.30	1.65

Pierwsze Wzloty, 1896, and Czeslaw Tanski A692

Polish Sport Planes: 1z, Zwyciezcy-Challenge, 1932, F. Zwirko and S. Wigura, vert. 1.50z, RWD-5 bis over South Atlantic, 1933, and S. Skarzynski, vert. 4.20z, MI-2 helicopter over mountains, Pezetel emblem, vert. 6.90z, PZL-104 Wilga 35, Pezetel emblem. 8.40z, Motoszybowiec SZD-45 Ogar.

1978, Apr. 15 *Perf. 11x11½, 11½x11*

2259	A692	50g multicolored	.20	.20
2260	A692	1z multicolored	.20	.20
2261	A692	1.50z multicolored	.20	.20
2262	A692	4.20z multicolored	.40	.20
2263	A692	6.90z multicolored	.75	.25
2264	A692	8.40z multicolored	.50	.25
	Nos. 2259-2264 (6)		2.25	1.30

Soccer — A693

Poster — A694

Design: 6.90z, Soccer ball, horiz.

Perf. 11½x11, 11x11½

1978, May 12 Litho.

2265	A693 1.50z multicolored		.20	.20
2266	A693 6.90z multicolored		.50	.25

11th World Cup Soccer Championships, Argentina, June 1-25.

1978, June 1 *Perf. 12x11½*

2267	A694 1.50z multicolored		.20	.20

7th International Poster Biennale, Warsaw.

Fair Emblem — A695

1978, June 10 *Perf. 11*

2268	A695 1.50z multicolored		.20	.20

50th International Poznan Fair.

Polonez Passenger Car — A696

1978, June 10 Photo. *Perf. 11*

2269	A696 1.50z multicolored		.20	.20

Maj. Miroslaw Hermaszewski A697

6.90z, Hermaszewski, globe & trajectory.

Perf. 11½x11, 11x11½

1978, June 27 Photo.

2270	A697 1.50z multi		.20	.20
a.	Without date		.30	.30
2271	A697 6.90z multi, horiz.		.50	.25
a.	Without date		1.00	1.00

1st Polish cosmonaut on Russian space mission. Nos. 2270a, 2271a printed in sheets of 6 stamps and 2 labels.

Stamps and sheets showing Zenon Jankowski were prepared but not issued.

Youth Festival Emblem A698

1978, July 12 Litho. *Perf. 11½*

2272	A698 1.50z multicolored		.20	.20

11th Youth Festival, Havana, July 28-Aug. 5.

Souvenir Sheet

Flowers — A699

Illustration reduced.

1978, July 20 *Perf. 11½x11*

2273	A699 1.50z gold & multi		.30	.20

30th anniv. of Polish Youth Movement.

Anopheles Mosquito and Blood Cells — A700

Design: 6z, Tsetse fly and blood cells.

1978, Aug. 19 Litho. *Perf. 11½x11*

2274	A700 1.50z multicolored		.20	.20
2275	A700 6z multicolored		.45	.20

4th International Parasitological Congress.

Norway Maple, Environment Emblem — A701

Human Environment Emblem and: 1z, English oak. 1.50z, White poplar. 4.20z, Scotch pine. 4.50z, White willow. 6z, Birch.

1978, Sept. 6 Photo. *Perf. 14*

2276	A701	50g gold & multi	.20	.20
2277	A701	1z gold & multi	.20	.20
2278	A701	1.50z gold & multi	.20	.20
2279	A701	4.20z gold & multi	.35	.20
2280	A701	4.50z gold & multi	.35	.20
2281	A701	6z gold & multi	.50	.20
	Nos. 2276-2281 (6)		1.80	1.20

Protection of the environment.

Souvenir Sheet

Jan Zizka, Battle of Grunwald, by Jan Matejko — A702

1978, Sept. 8 *Perf. 11½x11*

2282	A702 6z gold & multi		.90	.35

PRAGA '78 Intl. Phil. Exhib., Prague, Sept. 8-17.

Letter, Telephone and Satellite — A703

1978, Sept. 20 Litho. *Perf. 11*

2283	A703 1.50z multicolored		.20	.20

20th anniversary of the Organization of Ministers of Posts and Telecommunications of Warsaw Pact countries.

Peace, by Andre le Brun — A704

1978-79 Litho. ***Perf. 11½ (1z), 12½***

2284	A704	1z	violet	.20	.20
2285	A704	1.50z	steel blue ('79)	.20	.20
2286	A704	2z	brown ('79)	.20	.20
2287	A704	2.50z	ultra ('79)	.20	.20
			Nos. 2284-2287 (4)	.80	.80

Polish Unit, UN Middle East Emergency Force — A706

Designs: No. 2289, Color Guard, Kosziusko Division (4 soldiers). No. 2290, Color Guard, field training (3 soldiers).

1978, Oct. 6 Photo. ***Perf. 12x11½***

2289	A706	1.50z	multicolored	.20	.20
2290	A706	1.50z	multicolored	.20	.20
2291	A706	1.50z	multicolored	.20	.20
			Nos. 2289-2291 (3)	.60	.60

35th anniversary of People's Army.

Young Man, by Raphael A707

1978, Oct. 9 ***Perf. 11***

2292 A707 6z multicolored .40 .20

Stamp Day.

Dr. Korczak and Children — A708

1978, Oct. 11 Litho. ***Perf. 11½x11***

2293 A708 1.50z multicolored .20 .20

Dr. Janusz Korczak, physician, educator, writer, birth centenary.

Wojciech Boguslawski (1757-1829) — A709

Polish dramatists: 1z, Aleksander Fredro (1793-1878). 1.50z, Juliusz Slowacki (1809-1849). 2z, Adam Mickiewicz (1798-1855). 4.50z, Stanislaw Wyspianski (1869-1907). 6z, Gabriela Zapolska (1857-1921).

1978, Nov. 11 Litho. ***Perf. 11½***

2294	A709	50g	multicolored	.20	.20
2295	A709	1z	multicolored	.20	.20
2296	A709	1.50z	multicolored	.20	.20
2297	A709	2z	multicolored	.20	.20
2298	A709	4.50z	multicolored	.35	.20
2299	A709	6z	multicolored	.50	.20
			Nos. 2294-2299 (6)	1.65	1.20

Polish Combatants Monument, and Eiffel Tower, Paris — A710

1978, Nov. 2 Photo. ***Perf. 11x11½***

2300 A710 1.50z brown, red & bl .20 .20

Przewalski Mare and Colt — A711

Animals: 1z, Polar bears. 1.50z, Indian elephants. 2z, Jaguars. 4.20z, Gray seals. 4.50z, Hartebeests. 6z, Mandrills.

1978, Nov. 10

2301	A711	50g	multicolored	.20	.20
2302	A711	1z	multicolored	.20	.20
2303	A711	1.50z	multicolored	.20	.20
2304	A711	2z	multicolored	.20	.20
2305	A711	4.20z	multicolored	.30	.20
2306	A711	4.50z	multicolored	.40	.20
2307	A711	6z	multicolored	.50	.20
			Nos. 2301-2307 (7)	2.00	1.40

Warsaw Zoological Gardens, 50th anniv.

Adolf Warski (1868-1937) A712

Party Emblem A713

#2309, Julian Lenski (1889-1937). #2310, Aleksander Zawadzki (1899-1964). #2311, Stanislaw Dubois (1901-1942).

Perf. 11½x11, 11x11½

1978, Dec. 15 Photo.

2308	A712	1.50z	red & brown	.20	.20
2309	A712	1.50z	red & black	.20	.20
2310	A712	1.50z	red & dk vio	.20	.20
2311	A712	1.50z	red & dk blue	.20	.20
2312	A713	1.50z	black, red & gold	.20	.20
			Nos. 2308-2312 (5)	1.00	1.00

Polish United Workers' Party, 30th anniv.

LOT Planes, 1929 and 1979 A714

1979, Jan. 2 Photo. ***Perf. 11x11½***

2313 A714 6.90z gold & multi .45 .20

LOT, Polish airline, 50th anniversary.

Train and IYC Emblem — A715

Children's Paintings: 1z, Children with toys. 1.50z, Children in meadow. 6z, Family.

1979, Jan. 13 ***Perf. 11***

2314	A715	50g	multicolored	.20	.20
2315	A715	1z	multicolored	.20	.20
2316	A715	1.50z	multicolored	.20	.20
2317	A715	6z	multicolored	.50	.20
			Nos. 2314-2317 (4)	1.10	.80

International Year of the Child.

Artist's Wife, by Karol Mondral — A716

Modern Polish Graphic Arts: 50g, "Lightning," by Edmund Bartlomiejcyk, horiz. 1.50z, Musicians, by Tadeusz Kulisiewicz. 4.50z, Portrait of a Brave Man, by Wladyslaw Skoczylas.

Perf. 11½x12, 12x11½

1979, Mar. 5 Engr.

2318	A716	50g	brt violet	.20	.20
2319	A716	1z	slate green	.20	.20
2320	A716	1.50z	blue gray	.20	.20
2321	A716	4.50z	violet brown	.40	.20
			Nos. 2318-2321 (4)	1.00	.80

Andrzej Frycz-Modrzewski, Stefan Batory, Jan Zamoyski — A717

Photogravure and Engraved

1979, Mar. 12 ***Perf. 12x11½***

2322 A717 1.50z cream & sepia .20 .20

Royal Tribunal in Piotrkow Trybunalski, 400th anniversary.

Pole Vault and Olympic Emblem — A718

Olympic Emblem and: 1.50z, High jump. 6z, Cross-country skiing. 8.40z, Equestrian.

1979, Mar. 26 Photo. ***Perf. 12x11½***

2323	A718	1z	multicolored	.20	.20
2324	A718	1.50z	multicolored	.20	.20
2325	A718	6z	multicolored	.40	.20
2326	A718	8.40z	multicolored	.60	.20
			Nos. 2323-2326 (4)	1.40	.80

1980 Olympic Games.

Flounder — A720

Fish and Environmental Protection Emblem: 90g, Perch. 1z, Grayling. 1.50z, Salmon. 2z, Trout. 4.50z, Pike. 5z, Carp. 6z, Catfish and frog.

1979, Apr. 26 Photo. ***Perf. 11½x11***

2327	A720	50g	multicolored	.20	.20
2328	A720	90g	multicolored	.20	.20
2329	A720	1z	multicolored	.20	.20
2330	A720	1.50z	multicolored	.20	.20
2331	A720	2z	multicolored	.20	.20
2332	A720	4.50z	multicolored	.25	.20
2333	A720	5z	multicolored	.35	.20
2334	A720	6z	multicolored	.40	.20
			Nos. 2327-2334 (8)	2.00	1.60

Polish angling, centenary, and protection of the environment.

A721

1979, Apr. 30 Litho. ***Perf. 11x11½***

2335 A721 1.50z multicolored .20 .20

Council for Mutual Economic Aid of Socialist Countries, 30th anniversary.

Faces and Emblem — A722

1979, May 7 ***Perf. 11***

2336 A722 1.50z red & black .20 .20

6th Congress of Association of Fighters for Liberty and Democracy, Warsaw, May 7-8.

St. George's Church, Sofia A722a

1979, May 15 Photo. ***Perf. 11x11½***

2337 A722a 1.50z multicolored .20 .20

Philaserdica '79 Phil. Exhib., Sofia, Bulgaria, May 18-27.

Pope John Paul II, Cracow Cathedral A723

Designs: 8.40z, Pope John Paul II, Auschwitz-Birkenau Memorial. 50z, Pope John Paul II.

1979, June 2 Photo. ***Perf. 11x11½***

2338	A723	1.50z	multicolored	.20	.20
2339	A723	8.40z	multicolored	.80	.20

Souvenir Sheet

Perf. 11½x11

2340 A723 50z multicolored 6.00 3.00

Visit of Pope John Paul II to Poland, June 2-11. No. 2340 contains one 26x35mm stamp.

A variety of #2340 with silver margin exists.

Paddle Steamer Prince Ksawery and Old Warsaw — A724

Designs: 1.50z, Steamer Gen. Swierczewski and Gdansk, 1914. 4.50z, Tug Aurochs and Plock, 1960. 6z, Motor ship Mermaid and modern Warsaw, 1959.

1979, June 15 Litho. *Perf. 11*

2341 A724 1z multicolored .20 .20
2342 A724 1.50z multicolored .20 .20
2343 A724 4.50z multicolored .35 .20
2344 A724 6z multicolored .50 .20
Nos. 2341-2344 (4) 1.25 .80

Vistula River navigation, 150th anniversary.

Kosciuszko Monument, Philadelphia A725

1979, July 1 Photo. *Perf. 11½*

2345 A725 8.40z multicolored .60 .25

Gen. Tadeusz Kosziuszko (1746-1807), Polish soldier and statesman who served in American Revolution.

Mining Machinery A726

Eagle and People A727

Design: 1.50z, Salt crystals.

1979, July 14 Photo. *Perf. 14*

2346 A726 1z lt brown & blk .20 .20
2347 A726 1.50z blue grn & blk .20 .20

Wieliczka ancient rock-salt mines.

1979, July 21 *Perf. 11½x11*

No. 2349, Man with raised hand and flag.

2348 A727 1.50z red, blue & gray .20 .20
2349 A727 1.50z silver, red & blk .20 .20

35 years of Polish People's Republic.

Souvenir Sheet

1979, Sept. 2 Photo. *Perf. 11½x11*

2350 A727 Sheet of 2, #2348-2349 + label .50 .45

13th National Philatelic Exhibition.

Poland No. 1, Rowland Hill (1795-1879), Originator of Penny Postage — A728

1979, Aug. 16 Litho. *Perf. 11½x11*

2351 A728 6z multicolored .40 .20

Souvenir Sheet

The Rape of Europa, by Bernardo Strozzi — A729

1979, Aug. 20 Photo. *Perf. 11x11½*

2352 A729 10z multicolored .75 .50

Europhil '79, Intl. Phil. Exhib.

Wojciech Jastrzebowski A730

1979, Aug. 27 *Perf. 11½x11*

2353 A730 1.50z multicolored .20 .20

Economic Congress.

Postal Workers' Monument A731

1979, Sept. 1 *Perf. 11x11½*

2354 A731 1.50z multicolored .20 .20

40th anniversary of Polish postal workers' resistance to Nazi invaders. See No. B137.

ITU Emblem, Radio Antenna A732

1979, Sept. 24 *Perf. 11x11½*

2355 A732 1.50z multicolored .20 .20

Intl. Radio Consultative Committee (CCIR) of the ITU, 50th anniv.

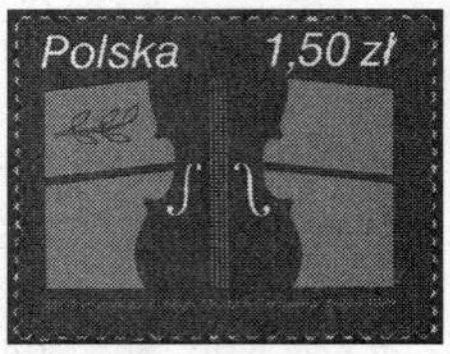

Violin A733

1979, Sept. 25 Litho.

2356 A733 1.50z dk blue, org, grn .20 .20

Henryk Wieniawski Young Violinists' Competition, Lublin.

Pulaski Monument, Buffalo — A734

Gen. Franciszek Jozwiak — A735

1979, Oct. 1 Photo. *Perf. 11½x12*

2357 A734 8.40z multicolored .50 .25

Gen. Casimir Pulaski (1748-1779), Polish nobleman who served in American Revolutionary War.

1979, Oct. 3 *Perf. 11½x11*

2358 A735 1.50z gray blue, dk blue & gold .20 .20

35th anniv. of Civil and Military Security Service, founded by Gen. Franciszek Jozwiak (1895-1966).

Drive-in Post Office — A736

Designs: 1.50z, Parcel sorting. 4.50z, Loading mail train. 6z, Mobile post office.

1979, Oct. 9 *Perf. 11½*

2359 A736 1z multicolored .20 .20
2360 A736 1.50z multicolored .20 .20
2361 A736 4.50z multicolored .35 .20
2362 A736 6z multicolored .50 .20
Nos. 2359-2362 (4) 1.25 .80

Stamp Day.

Holy Family — A737

Design: 6.90z, Nativity, horiz.

Perf. 11½x11, 11x11½

1979, Dec. 4 Photo.

2363 A737 2z multicolored .20 .20
2364 A737 6.90z multicolored .45 .20

A738

A739

Space Achievements: 1z, Soyuz 30 and Salyut 6. 1.50z, Kopernik 500 and Copernicus satellite. 2z, Lunik 2 and Ranger 7. 4.50z, Yuri Gagarin and Vostok. 6.90z, Neil Armstrong and Apollo 11.

1979, Dec. 28 Photo. *Perf. 11½x11*

2365 A738 1z multi .20 .20
2366 A738 1.50z multi .20 .20
2367 A738 2z multi .20 .20
2368 A738 4.50z multi .25 .20
2369 A738 6.90z multi .40 .20
a. Souvenir sheet of 5 1.60 1.25
Nos. 2365-2369 (5) 1.25 1.00

No. 2369a contains Nos. 2365-2369, tete beche plus label.

1980, Jan. 31 Photo. *Perf. 11½x12*

Designs: Horse Paintings.

2370 A739 1z Stagecoach .20 .20
2371 A739 2z Horse, trainer .20 .20
2372 A739 2.50z Trotters .20 .20
2373 A739 3z Fox hunt .25 .20
2374 A739 4z Sled .30 .20
2375 A739 6z Hay cart .50 .20
2376 A739 6.50z Pairs .55 .20
2377 A739 6.90z Hurdles .55 .20
Nos. 2370-2377 (8) 2.75 1.60

Sierakov horse stud farm, 150th anniv.

Party Slogan on Map of Poland — A740

Worker, by Janusz Stanny — A741

1980, Feb. 11 Photo. *Perf. 11½x11*

2378 A740 2.50z multi .20 .20
2379 A741 2.50z multi .20 .20

Polish United Workers' Party, 8th Congress.

Equestrian, Olympic Rings — A742

1980, Mar. 31 *Perf. 12x11½*

2380 A742 2z shown .20 .20
2381 A742 2.50z Archery .20 .20
2382 A742 6.50z Biathlon .50 .20
2383 A742 8.40z Volleyball .65 .25
Nos. 2381-2383 (3) 1.35 .65

13th Winter Olympic Games, Lake Placid, NY, Feb. 12-24 (6.50z); 22nd Summer Olympic Games, Moscow, July 19-Aug. 3. See No. B138.

Map and Old Town Hall, 1591, Zamosc A743

1980, Apr. 3 Litho. ***Perf. 11½***
2384 A743 2.50z multi .20 .20

Zamosc, 400th anniversary.

Arms of Poland and Russia A744

1980, Apr. 21 Litho. ***Perf. 11½***
2385 A744 2.50z multi .20 .20

Treaty of Friendship, Cooperation and Mutual Assistance between Poland and USSR, 35th anniversary.

Lenin, 110th Birth Anniversary — A745

1980, Apr. 22 Photo. ***Perf. 11***
2386 A745 2.50z multi .25 .20

Workers Marching A746

Dove Over Liberation Date — A747

1980, May 1 ***Perf. 11½x11***
2387 A746 2.50z multi .20 .20

Revolution of 1905, 75th anniversary.

1980, May 9 ***Perf. 11½x12***
2388 A747 2.50z multi .20 .20

Victory over fascism, 35th anniversary.

Arms of Treaty-signing Countries A748

1980, May 14 Litho. ***Perf. 11½x11***
2389 A748 2z red & blk .20 .20

Signing of Warsaw Pact (Bulgaria, Czechoslovakia, German Democratic Rep., Hungary, Poland, Romania, USSR), 25th anniversary.

Caverns, (1961 Expedition) Map of Cuba — A749

1980, May 22 Photo. ***Perf. 14***
2390 A749 2z shown .20 .20
2391 A749 2z Seals, Antarctica, 1959 .20 .20
2392 A749 2.50z Ethnology, Mongolia, 1963 .25 .20
2393 A749 2.50z Archaeology, Syria, 1959 .25 .20
2394 A749 6.50z Mountain climbing, Nepal, 1978 .50 .20
2395 A749 8.40z Paleontology, Mongolia, 1963 .65 .25
Nos. 2390-2395 (6) 2.05 1.25

Malachowski Lyceum, Arms of Polish Order of Labor — A750

Xerocomus Parasiticus — A751

1980, June 7 Photo. ***Perf. 11x12***
2396 A750 2z blk & dl grn .20 .20

Malachowski Lyceum (oldest school in Plock), 800th anniversary.

1980, June 30 ***Perf. 11½x11***
2397 A751 2z shown .20 .20
2398 A751 2z Clathrus ruber .20 .20
2399 A751 2.50z Phallus hadriani .25 .20
2400 A751 2.50z Strobilomyces floccopus .25 .20
2401 A751 8z Sparassis crispa .60 .25
2402 A751 10.50z Langermannia gigantea .80 .30
Nos. 2397-2402 (6) 2.30 1.35

Sandomierz Millenium — A752

1980, July 12 Photo. ***Perf. 11x11½***
2403 A752 2.50z dk brown .22 .20

"Lwow," T. Ziolkowski — A753

Ships and Teachers: 2.50z, Antoni Garnuszewski, A. Garnuszewski. 6z, Zenit, A. Ledochowski. 6.50z, Jan Turlejski, K. Porebski. 6.90z, Horyzon, G. Kanski. 8.40z, Dar Pomorza, K. Maciejewicz.

1980, July 21 Litho. ***Perf. 11***
2404 A753 2z multi .20 .20
2405 A753 2.50z multi .25 .20
2406 A753 6z multi .50 .20
2407 A753 6.50z multi .60 .25
2408 A753 6.90z multi .60 .25
2409 A753 8.40z multi .70 .30
Nos. 2404-2409 (6) 2.85 1.40

Marize Maritime High School.

A754

A755

Designs: Medicinal plants.

1980, Aug. 15 Litho. ***Perf. 11½x11***
2410 A754 2z Atropa belladonna .20 .20
2411 A754 2.50z Datura innoxia .25 .20
2412 A754 3.40z Valeriana .25 .20
2413 A754 5z Mentha piperita .45 .20
2414 A754 6.50z Calendula .55 .25
2415 A754 8z Salvia officinalis .60 .30
Nos. 2410-2415 (6) 2.30 1.35

1980, Aug. 20 ***Perf. 11***
2416 A755 2.50z multi .25 .20

Jan Kochanowski (1530-1584), poet.

United Nations, 35th Anniversary — A756

1980, Sept. 19 Photo. ***Perf. 11x11½***
2417 A756 8.40z multi .75 .30

Chopin Piano Competition — A757

1980, Oct. 2 Litho. ***Perf. 11½***
2418 A757 6.90z blk & tan .60 .30

Mail Pick-up — A758

1980, Oct. 9 Photo. ***Perf. 12x11½***
2419 A758 2z shown .20 .20
2420 A758 2.50z Letter sorting .20 .20
2421 A758 6z Loading mail plane .55 .25
2422 A758 6.50z Mail boxes .55 .25
a. Souvenir sheet of 4, #2419-2422 3.75 2.50
Nos. 2419-2422 (4) 1.50 .90

Stamp Day.

Girl Embracing Dove, UN Emblem A759

1980, Nov. 21 Litho. ***Perf. 11x11½***
2423 A759 8.40z multicolored .75 .35

UN Declaration on the Preparation of Societies for Life in Peace.

Battle of Olzynska Grochowska, by W. Kossak — A760

1980, Nov. 29 Photo. ***Perf. 11***
2424 A760 2.50z multicolored .25 .20

Battle of Olzynska Grochowska, 1830.

Horse-drawn Fire Engine — A761

Designs: Horse-drawn vehicles.

1980, Dec. 16
2425 A761 2z shown .20 .20
2426 A761 2.50z Passenger coach .25 .20
2427 A761 3z Beer wagon .25 .20
2428 A761 5z Sled .45 .20
2429 A761 6z Bus .50 .25
2430 A761 6.50z Two-seater .55 .25
Nos. 2425-2430 (6) 2.20 1.30

Honor to the Silesian Rebels, by Jan Borowczak — A762

1981, Jan. 22 Engr. *Perf. 11½*

2431 A762 2.50z gray grn .20 .20

Silesian uprising, 60th anniversary.

Pablo Picasso — A763

1981, Mar. 10 Photo. *Perf. 11½x11*

2432 A763 8.40z multi .55 .35
  a. Miniature sheet of 2 + 2 labels 2.50 1.25

Pablo Picasso (1881-1973), artist, birth centenary. No. 2432 se-tenant with label showing A Crying Woman. Sold for 20.80z.

Balloon Flown by Pilatre de Rozier, 1783 — A764

Gordon Bennett Cup (Balloons): No. 2434, J. Blanchard, J. Jeffries, 1875. 2.50z, F. Godard, 1850. 3z, F. Hynek, Z. Burzynski, 1933. 6z, Z. Burzynski, N. Wysocki, 1935. 6.50z, B. Abruzzo, M. Anderson, P. Newman, 1978. 10.50z, Winners' names, 1933-1935, 1938.

1981, Mar. 25 Photo. *Perf. 11½x12*

2433 A764 2z multi .20 .20
2434 A764 2z multi .20 .20
2435 A764 2.50z multi .25 .20
2436 A764 3z multi .25 .20
2437 A764 6z multi .55 .25
2438 A764 6.50z multi .60 .25
  Nos. 2433-2438 (6) 2.05 1.30

Souvenir Sheet

Imperf

2439 A764 10.50z multi .95 .70

Iphegenia, by Franz Anton Maulbertsch (1724-1796), WIPA '81 Emblem — A765

1981, May 11 Litho. *Perf. 11½*

2440 A765 10.50z multi 1.00 .48

WIPA '81 Intl. Phil. Exhib., Vienna, 5/22-31.

Wroclaw, 1493 — A766

Gen. Wladyslaw Sikorski (1881-1943) — A767

1981, May 15 Photo. *Perf. 14*

2441 A766 6.50z brown .50 .25

See #2456-2459. For surcharges see #2526, 2939.

1981, May 20 *Perf. 11½x11*

2442 A767 6.50z multi .40 .25

Kwan Vase, 18th Cent. — A768

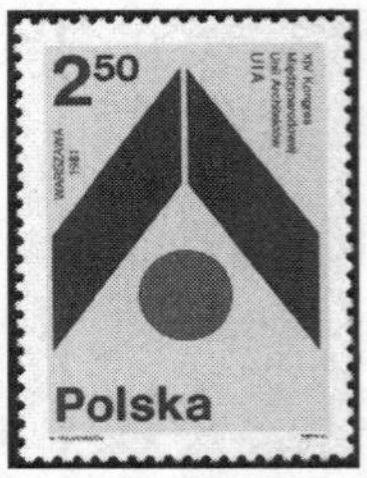

Intl. Architects Union, 14th Congress, Warsaw — A769

1981, June 15

2443 A768 1z shown .20 .20
2444 A768 2z Cup, saucer, 1820 .25 .20
2445 A768 2.50z Jug, 1820 .25 .20
2446 A768 5z Portrait plate, 1880 .50 .20
2447 A768 6.50z Vase, 1900 .65 .20
2448 A768 8.40z Basket, 1840 .75 .25
  Nos. 2443-2448 (6) 2.60 1.25

1981, July 15 Litho.

2449 A769 2.50z multi .20 .20

Moose, Rifle and Pouch — A770

A770a

1981, July 30

2450 A770 2z shown .20 .20
2451 A770 2z Boar .20 .20
2452 A770 2.50z Fox .25 .20
2453 A770 2.50z Elk .25 .20
2454 A770 6.50z Greylag goose, horiz. .65 .20
2455 A770 6.50z Fen duck .65 .20
  Nos. 2450-2455 (6) 2.20 1.20

City Type of 1981

Perf. 11x11½, 11½x13

1981, July 28 Photo.

2456 A766 4z Gdansk, 1652, vert. .30 .20
2457 A766 5z Krakow, 1493, vert. .40 .20
2458 A766 6z Legnica, 1744 .50 .25
2459 A766 8z Warsaw, 1618 .65 .30
  Nos. 2456-2459 (4) 1.85 .95

1982, Nov. 2 Photo. *Perf. 11½*

2461 A770a 12z Vistula River .25 .20
2463 A770a 17z Kasimierz Dolny .30 .20
2466 A770a 25z Gdansk .45 .25
  Nos. 2461-2466 (3) 1.00 .65

Wild Bison — A771

1981, Aug. 27 *Perf. 11½x11*

2471 Strip of 5 3.50 1.50
  a.-e. A771 6.50z, any single .65 .25

60th Anniv. of Polish Tennis Federation — A772

1981, Sept. 17 Photo. *Perf. 11x11½*

2472 A772 6.50z multi .60 .25

Model Airplane — A773

1981, Sept. 24 *Perf. 14*

2473 A773 1z shown .20 .20
2474 A773 2z Boats .30 .20
2475 A773 2.50z Racing cars .25 .20
2476 A773 4.20z Gliders .45 .20
2477 A773 6.50z Radio-controlled racing cars .65 .20
2478 A773 8z Yachts .70 .25
  Nos. 2473-2478 (6) 2.55 1.25

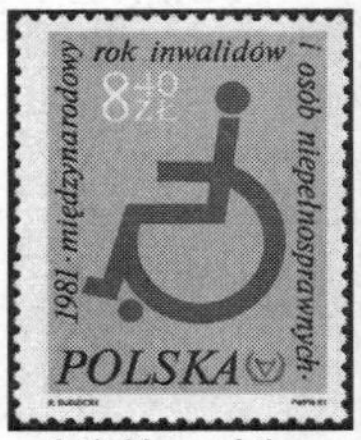

Intl. Year of the Disabled — A774

Stamp Day — A775

1981, Sept. 25 Litho. *Perf. 11½x11*

2479 A774 8.40z multi .75 .30

1981, Oct. 9 Photo. *Perf. 14*

2480 A775 2.50z Pistol, 18th cent., horiz. .25 .20
2481 A775 8.40z Sword, 18th cent. .75 .25

A776

A777

1981, Oct. 10 *Perf. 11½x12*

2482 A776 2.50z multi .25 .20

Henryk Wieniawski (1835-1880), violinist and composer.

1981, Oct. 15 Litho.

Working Movement Leaders: 50g, Bronislaw Wesolowski (1870-1919). 2z, Malgorzata Fornalska (1902-1944). 2.50z, Maria Koszutska (1876-1939). 6.50z, Marcin Kasprzak (1860-1905).

2483 A777 50g grn & blk .20 .20
2484 A777 2z bl & blk .20 .20
2485 A777 2.50z brn & blk .20 .20
2486 A777 6.50z lil rose & blk .45 .20
  Nos. 2483-2486 (4) 1.05 .80

World Food Day — A778

1981, Oct. 16 *Perf. 11½x11*

2487 A778 6.90z multi .65 .25

Old Theater, Cracow, 200th Anniv. — A779

Theater Emblem and: 2z, Helena Modrzejewska (1840-1909), actress. 2.50z, Stanislaw Kozmian (1836-1922), theater director, 1865-1885, founder of Cracow School. 6.50z, Konrad Swinarski (1929-1975), stage manager.

Photo. & Engr.

1981, Oct. 17 *Perf. 12x11½*

2488 A779 2z multi .25 .20
2489 A779 2.50z multi .30 .20
2490 A779 6.50z multi .60 .20
2491 A779 8z multi .75 .25
  Nos. 2488-2491 (4) 1.90 .85

Souvenir Sheet

Vistula River Project — A780

1981, Dec. 20 Litho. ***Perf. 11½x12***

2492 A780 10.50z multi 1.25 .75

Flowering Succulent Plants A781

1981, Dec. 22 Photo. ***Perf. 13***

2493 A781 90g Epiphyllopsis gaertneri .20 .20
2494 A781 1z Cereus tonduzii .20 .20
2495 A781 2z Cylindropuntia leptocaulis .20 .20
2496 A781 2.50z Cylindroppuntia fulgida .25 .20
2497 A781 2.50z Caralluma lugardi .25 .20
2498 A781 6.50z Nopalea cochenillifera .50 .20
2499 A781 6.50z Lithopsps helmutii .50 .25
2500 A781 10.50z Cylindropuntia spinosior .75 .35
Nos. 2493-2500 (8) 2.85 1.80

Polish Workers' Party, 40th Anniv. — A782

Stoneware Plate, 1890 — A783

1982, Jan. 5 Photo. ***Perf. 11½x11***

2501 A782 2.50z multi .25 .20

1982, Jan. 20

Porcelain or Stoneware: 2z, Plate, mug, 1790. 2.50z, Soup tureen, gravy dish, 1830. 6z, Salt and pepper dish, 1844, 8z, Stoneware jug, 1840. 10.50z, Stoneware figurine, 1740.

2502 A783 1z multi .20 .20
2503 A783 2z multi .20 .20
2504 A783 2.50z multi .25 .20
2505 A783 6z multi .60 .25
2506 A783 8z multi .80 .30
2507 A783 10.50z multi 1.00 .40
Nos. 2502-2507 (6) 3.05 1.55

Ignacy Lukasiewicz (1822-1882), Oil Lamp Inventor — A784

Designs: Various oil lamps.

1982, Mar. 22 Photo. ***Perf. 11½x11***

2508 A784 1z multi .20 .20
2509 A784 2z multi .20 .20
2510 A784 2.50z multi .25 .20
2511 A784 3.50z multi .30 .20
2512 A784 9z multi .85 .35
2513 A784 10z multi .90 .40
Nos. 2508-2513 (6) 2.70 1.55

Karol Szymanowski (1882-1937), Composer A785

1982, Apr. 8

2514 A785 2.50z dk brn & gold .25 .20

Victory in Challenge Trophy Flights A786

1982, May 5 Photo. ***Perf. 11x11½***

2515 A786 27z RWD-6 monoplane 1.25 .65
2516 A786 31z RWD-9 1.75 .85
a. Souv. sheet of 2, #2515-2516 3.00 1.75

Henryk Sienkiewicz (1846-1916), Writer — A787

1982 World Cup — A788

Polish Nobel Prize Winners: 15z, Wladyslaw Reymont (1867-1925), writer, 1924. 25z, Marie Curie (1867-1934), physicist 1903, 1911. 31z, Czeslaw Milosz (b. 1911), poet, 1980.

1982, May 10 Litho. ***Perf. 11½x11***

2517 A787 3z black & dk grn .20 .20
2518 A787 15z black & brown .65 .25
2519 A787 25z black 1.10 .40
2520 A787 31z black & gray 1.25 .50
Nos. 2517-2520 (4) 3.20 1.35

Perf. 11½x11, 11x11½

1982, May 28 Photo.

2521 A788 25z Ball 1.25 .60
2522 A788 27z Bull, ball, horiz. 1.50 .65

Souvenir Sheet

Maria Kaziera Sobieska — A789

1982, June 11 Photo. ***Perf. 11½x11***

2523 A789 65z multi 3.25 2.25

PHILEXFRANCE '82 Intl. Stamp Exhibition, Paris, June 11-21.

Assoc. Presidents Stanislaw Sierakowski and Boleslaw Domanski — A790

1982, July 20 Litho.

2524 A790 4.50z multi .45 .20

Assoc. of Poles in Germany, 60th anniv.

2nd UN Conference on Peaceful Uses of Outer Space, Vienna, Aug. 9-21 — A791

1982, Aug. 9 Photo.

2525 A791 31z Globe 1.25 .65

No. 2441 Surcharged

1982, Aug. 20

2526 A766 10z on 6.50z brn .40 .20

Black Madonna of Jasna Gora, 600th Anniv. A792

2.50z, Father Augustin Kordecki (1603-1673). 25z, Siege of Jasna Gora by Swedes, 1655, horiz.

1982, Aug. 26 ***Perf. 11***

2527 A792 2.50z multi .20 .20
2528 A792 25z multi .80 .25
2529 A792 65z multi 2.50 1.10
Nos. 2527-2529 (3) 3.50 1.55

A souvenir sheet of 2 No. 2529 exists.

Workers' Movement A793

1982, Sept. 3 ***Perf. 11½x11***

2530 A793 6z multicolored .35 .20

Norbert Barlicki (1880-1941) A794

Carved Head, Wawel Castle A795

Workers' Activists: 6z, Pawel Finder (1904-1944). 15z, Marian Buczek (1896-1939). 20z, Cezaryna Wojnarowska (1861-1911). 29z, Ignacy Daszynski (1866-1936).

1982, Sept. 10 ***Perf. 12x11½***

2531 A794 5z multi .30 .20
2532 A794 6z multi .30 .20
2533 A794 15z multi .75 .30
2534 A794 20z multi .95 .30
2535 A794 29z multi 1.10 .40
Nos. 2531-2535 (5) 3.40 1.40

1982, Sept. 25

2536 A795 60z Woman's head 2.25 1.00
2537 A795 100z Man's head 3.25 1.75

TB Bacillus Centenary A796

St. Maximilian Kolbe (1894-1941) A797

1982, Sept. 22 ***Perf. 11½x11***

2538 A796 10z Koch .40 .20
2539 A796 25z Oko Bujwid (1857-1942), bacteriologist 1.00 .40

1982, Oct.

2540 A797 27z multi 1.00 .45

50th Anniv. of Polar Research A798

1982, Oct. 25 Litho. ***Perf. 11½***

2541 A798 27z multi 1.00 .45

Stanislaw Zaremba (1863-1942), Mathematician — A799

Mathematicians: 6z, Waclaw Sierpinski (1882-1969). 12z, Zygmunt Janiszewski (1888-1920). 15z, Stefan Banach (1892-1945).

1982, Nov. 23 Photo. *Perf. 11x11½*

2542 A799 5z multicolored .20 .20
2543 A799 6z multicolored .25 .20
2544 A799 12z multicolored .50 .30
2545 A799 15z multicolored .60 .25
Nos. 2542-2545 (4) 1.55 .95

First Anniv. of Military Rule — A800

1982, Dec. 13 *Perf. 12x11½*

2546 A800 2.50z Medal obverse and reverse .20 .20

Cracow Monuments Restoration A801

1982, Dec. 20 Litho. *Perf. 11½x11*

2547 A801 15z Deanery portal .50 .25
2548 A801 25z Law College portal .80 .40

Souvenir Sheet
Lithographed and Engraved
Imperf

2549 A801 65z City map 1.25 1.00

No. 2549 contains one stamp 22x27mm.
See Nos. 2593-2594, 2656-2657, 2717-2718, 2809, 2847.

Map of Poland, by Bernard Wapowski, 1526 A802

Maps: 6z, Warsaw, Polish Kingdom Quartermaster, 1839. 8z, Poland, Romer's Atlas, 1908. 25z, Krakow, by A. Buchowiecki, 1703, astrolabe, 17th cent.

1982, Dec. 28 Litho. *Perf. 11½*

2550 A802 5z multicolored .20 .20
2551 A802 6z multicolored .20 .20
2552 A802 8z multicolored .30 .20
2553 A802 25z multicolored .85 .40
Nos. 2550-2553 (4) 1.55 1.00

120th Anniv. of 1863 Uprising — A803

1983, Jan. 22 Photo. *Perf. 12x11½*

2554 A803 6z The Battle, by Arthur Grottger (1837-67) .25 .20

Warsaw Theater Sesquicentennial — A804

1983, Feb. 24 Photo. *Perf. 11*

2555 A804 6z multicolored .25 .20

10th Anniv. of UN Conference on Human Environment, Stockholm — A805

1983, Mar. 24 Litho. *Perf. 11½*

2556 A805 5z Wild flowers .20 .20
2557 A805 6z Swan, carp, eel .25 .20
2558 A805 17z Hoopoe .55 .30
2559 A805 30z Fish 1.00 .50
2560 A805 31z Deer, fawn, buffalo 1.00 .50
2561 A805 38z Fruit 1.10 .60
Nos. 2556-2561 (6) 4.10 2.30

Karol Kurpinski (1785-1857), Composer A806

Famous People: 6z, Maria Jasnorzewska Pawlikowska (1891-1945), poet. 17z, Stanislaw Szober (1879-1938), linguist. 25z, Tadeusz Banachiewicz (1882-1954), astronomer. 27z, Jaroslaw Iwaszkiewicz (1894-1980), writer. 31z, Wladyslaw Tatarkiewicz (1886-1980), philosopher, art historian.

1983, Mar. 25 Photo. *Perf. 11½x11*

2562 A806 5z tan & brn .20 .20
2563 A806 6z pink & vio .25 .20
2564 A806 17z dk grn & lt grn .55 .30
2565 A806 25z bister & brn .85 .40
2566 A806 27z lt bl & dk bl .95 .45
2567 A806 31z violet & pur 1.10 .55
Nos. 2562-2567 (6) 3.90 2.10

Polish Medalists in 22nd Olympic Games, 1980 A807

1983, Apr. 5 *Perf. 11x11½*

2568 A807 5z Steeplechase .20 .20
2569 A807 6z Equestrian .20 .20
2570 A807 15z Soccer, 1982 World Cup .50 .25
2571 A807 27z + 5z Pole vault 1.00 .50
Nos. 2568-2571 (4) 1.90 1.15

Warsaw Ghetto Uprising, 40th Anniv. — A808

1983, Apr. 19 Photo. *Perf. 11½x11*

2572 A808 6z Heroes' Monument, by Natan Rappaport .25 .20

Se-tenant with label showing anniversary medal.

Customs Cooperation Council, 30th Anniv. — A809

1983, Apr. 28

2573 A809 5z multicolored .20 .20

Second Visit of Pope John Paul II — A810

Portraits of Pope. 31z vert.

1983, June 16 Photo. *Perf. 11*

2574 A810 31z multicolored 1.10 .50
2575 A810 65z multicolored 2.25 1.10
a. Souvenir sheet 2.25 1.75

Army of King John III Sobieski — A811

1983, July 5 *Perf. 11½x11*

2576 A811 5z Dragoons .20 .20
2577 A811 5z Knight in armor .20 .20
2578 A811 6z Non-commissioned infantry officers .20 .20
2579 A811 15z Light cavalryman .50 .25
2580 A811 27z Hussars .90 .45
Nos. 2576-2580 (5) 2.00 1.30

750th Anniv. of Torun Municipality — A812

1983, Aug. 25 Photo. *Perf. 11*

2581 A812 6z multicolored .25 .20
a. Souvenir sheet of 4 3.00 2.75

No. 2581a had limited distribution.

60th Anniv. of Polish Boxing Union A813

1983, Nov. 4 Litho. *Perf. 11½x11*

2582 A813 6z multicolored .25 .20

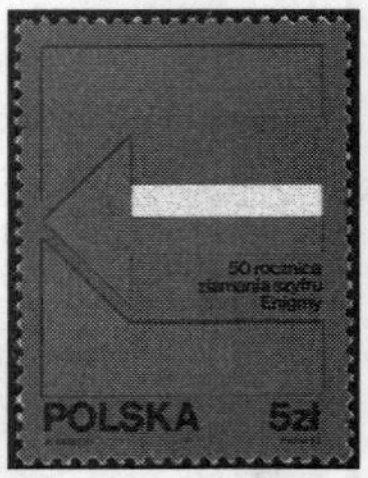

Enigma Decoding Machine, 50th Anniv. — A813a

Girl Near House — A813b

1983, Aug. 16 Litho. *Perf. 11½x11*

2582A A813a 5z multicolored .20 .20

1983 Photo. *Perf. 11½x12*

2582B A813b 6z multicolored .25 .20

Public courtesy campaign.

Portrait of King John III Sobieski A814

King's Portraits by: #2584, Unknown court painter. #2585, Sobieski on Horseback, by Francesco Trevisani (1656-1746). 25z, Jerzy Eleuter Szymonowicz-Siemiginowski (1660-1711). 65z+10z, Sobieski at Vienna, by Jan Matejko (1838-1893).

1983, Sept. 12 *Perf. 11*

2583 A814 5z multicolored .20 .20
2584 A814 6z multicolored .25 .20
2585 A814 6z multicolored .25 .20
2586 A814 25z multicolored .95 .40
Nos. 2583-2586 (4) 1.65 1.00

Souvenir Sheet
Imperf

2587 A814 65z + 10z multi 2.50 2.00

Victory over the Turks in Vienna, 300th anniv.

Polish Peoples' Army, 40th Anniv. — A815

#2588, General Zygmunt Berling (1896-1980). #2589, Wanda Wasilewska (1905-64). #2591, Troop formation.

1983, Oct. 12 Photo. *Perf. 11*

2588 A815 5z multicolored .20 .20
2589 A815 5z multicolored .20 .20
2590 A815 6z multicolored .20 .20
2591 A815 6z multi, horiz. .20 .20
Nos. 2588-2591 (4) .80 .80

World Communications Year — A816

1983, Oct. 18 Photo. *Perf. 11*

2592 A816 15z multicolored .50 .25

Cracow Restoration Type of 1982

1983, Nov. 25 Litho. *Perf. 11*

2593 A801 5z Cloth Hall, horiz. .20 .20
2594 A801 6z Town Hall Tower .30 .20

Traditional Hats — A818

Natl. People's Council, 40th Anniv. — A819

1983, Dec. 16 Photo. *Perf. 11½x11*

2595 A818 5z Biskupianski .20 .20
2596 A818 5z Rozbarski .20 .20
2597 A818 6z Warminsko-Mazurski .20 .20
2598 A818 6z Cieszynski .20 .20
2599 A818 25z Kurpiowski .75 .40
2600 A818 38z Lubuski 1.10 .55
Nos. 2595-2600 (6) 2.65 1.75

1983, Dec. 31

2601 A819 6z Hand holding sword (poster) .25 .20

People's Army, 40th Anniv. — A820

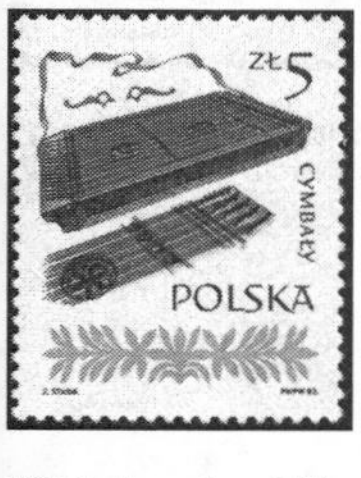

Musical Instruments A821

1984, Jan. 1 Litho. *Perf. 11½x11*

2602 A820 5z Gen. Bem Brigade badge .20 .20

1984, Feb. 10 Photo.

2603 A821 5z Dulcimer .20 .20
2604 A821 6z Drum, tambourine .20 .20
2605 A821 10z Accordion .35 .20
2606 A821 15z Double bass .40 .20
2607 A821 17z Bagpipes .60 .25
2608 A821 29z Figurines by Tadeusz Zak 1.10 .40
Nos. 2603-2608 (6) 2.85 1.45

Wincenty Witos (1874-1945), Prime Minister — A822

1984, Mar. 2 Litho. *Perf. 11½x11*

2609 A822 6z green & sepia .20 .20

Local Flowers (Clematis Varieties) A823

1984, Mar. 26 Photo. *Perf. 11x11½*

2610 A823 5z Lanuginosa .20 .20
2611 A823 6z Tangutica .25 .20
2612 A823 10z Texensis .30 .20
2613 A823 17z Alpina .65 .25
2614 A823 25z Vitalba .90 .35
2615 A823 27z Montana 1.00 .40
Nos. 2610-2615 (6) 3.30 1.60

The Ecstasy of St. Francis, by El Greco A824

1984, Apr. 21 *Perf. 11*

2616 A824 27z multicolored 1.00 .30

1984 Olympics A825

1984, Apr. 25 Litho. *Perf. 11x11½*

2617 A825 5z Handball .20 .20
2618 A825 6z Fencing .25 .20
2619 A825 15z Bicycling .55 .20
2620 A825 16z Running .60 .25
2621 A825 17z Running, diff. .65 .25
a. Souv. sheet of 2, #2620-2621 1.50 1.25
2622 A825 31z Skiing 1.00 .45
Nos. 2617-2622 (6) 3.25 1.55

No. 2621a sold for 43z.

Battle of Monte Cassino, 40th Anniv. — A826

1984, May 18 Photo. *Perf. 11½x11*

2623 A826 15z Memorial Cross .50 .20

View of Warsaw from the Praga Bank, by Bernardo Belotto Canaletto — A827

Paintings of Vistula River views: 6z, Trumpet Festivity, by Aleksander Gierymski. 25z, The Vistula near the Bielany District, by Jozef Rapacki. 27z, Steamship Harbor in the Powisle District, by Franciszek Kostrzewski.

1984, June 20 Photo. *Perf. 11*

2624 A827 5z multicolored .20 .20
2625 A827 6z multicolored .20 .20
2626 A827 25z multicolored .80 .35
2627 A827 27z multicolored .80 .40
Nos. 2624-2627 (4) 2.00 1.15

Warrior's Head, Wawel Castle — A828

Sculptures: 3.50z, Eastern ruler. No. 2628A, Woman wearing wreath. 10z, Man wearing hat.

1984-85 Photo. *Perf. 11½x12*

2628 A828 3.50z brown .20 .20
2628A A828 5z dark claret .20 .20
2628B A828 10z brt ultra .30 .20
Nos. 2628-2628B (3) .70 .60

Coil Stamp

Perf. 13½x14

2629 A828 5z dark blue green .20 .20

Issued: 3.50z, 1/24/85; #2628A, 10z, 7/8/85; #2629, 7/10/84.

No. 2629 has black control number on back of every fifth stamp.

See Nos. 2738-2744.

Order of Grunwald Cross — A829

Designs: 6z, Order of Revival of Poland. 10z, Order of the Banner of Labor, First Class. 16z, Order of Builders of People's Poland.

1984, July 21 Photo. *Perf. 11½*

2630 A829 5z multicolored .20 .20
2631 A829 6z multicolored .20 .20
2632 A829 10z multicolored .30 .20
2633 A829 16z multicolored .50 .25
a. Sheet of 4, #2630-2633, perf. 11½x12 3.25 3.00
Nos. 2630-2633 (4) 1.20 .85

40th anniversary of July Manifesto (Origin of Polish People's Republic).

Warsaw Uprising, 40th Anniv. A830

1984, Aug. 1

2634 A830 4z multicolored .20 .20
2635 A830 5z multicolored .20 .20
2636 A830 6z multicolored .20 .20
2637 A830 25z multicolored .75 .35
Nos. 2634-2637 (4) 1.35 .95

Broken Heart Monument, Lodz — A831

1984, Aug. 31

2638 A831 16z multicolored .50 .25

Defense of Oksywie Holm, Col. S. Dabek — A832

1984, Sept. 1

2639 A832 5z shown .20 .20
2640 A832 6z Bzura River battle, Gen. T. Kutrzeba .25 .20

Invasion of Poland, 45th anniversary.

See Nos. 2692-2693, 2757, 2824-2826, 2864-2866, 2922-2925.

Polish Militia, 40th Anniv. A833

1984, Sept. 29 Photo. *Perf. 11½*

2641 A833 5z shown .20 .20
2642 A833 6z Militiaman at Control Center .25 .20

Polish Aviation A834

1984, Nov. 6 Photo. *Perf. 11x11½*

2643 A834 5z Balloon ascent, 1784 .20 .20
2644 A834 5z Powered flight, 1911 .20 .20
2645 A834 6z Balloon Polonez, 1983 .20 .20
2646 A834 10z Modern gliders .30 .20
2647 A834 16z Wilga, 1983 .50 .25
2648 A834 27z Farman, 1914 .90 .40
2649 A834 31z Los and PZL P-7 .95 .40
Nos. 2643-2649 (7) 3.25 1.85

Protected Animals A835

1984, Dec. 4 Photo. *Perf. 11x11½*

2650 A835 4z Mustela nivalis .20 .20
2651 A835 5z Martes foina .20 .20
2652 A835 5z Mustela erminea .20 .20

Perf. 11½x11

2653 A835 10z Castor fiber, vert. .30 .20
2654 A835 10z Lutra lutra, vert. .30 .20
2655 A835 65z Marmota marmota, vert. 1.90 .70
Nos. 2650-2655 (6) 3.10 1.70

Cracow Restoration Type of 1982

Perf. 11½x11, 11x11½

1984, Dec. 10 Litho.

2656 A801 5z Royal Cathedral, Wawel .20 .20
2657 A801 15z Royal Castle, Wawel, horiz. .30 .20

Religious Buildings A837

Perf. 11½x12, 12x11½

1984, Dec. 28 Photo.

2658 A837 5z Protestant Church, Warsaw .20 .20
2659 A837 10z Saint Andrew Church, Cracow .30 .20
2660 A837 15z Greek Orthodox Church, Rychwald .45 .20
2661 A837 20z Orthodox Church, Warsaw .55 .20
2662 A837 25z Tykocin Synagogue, horiz. .70 .25
2663 A837 31z Tartar Mosque, Kruszyniany, horiz. .80 .30
Nos. 2658-2663 (6) 3.00 1.35

Classic and Contemporary Fire Engines — A838

Designs: 4z, Horse-drawn fire pump, 19th cent. 10z, Polski Fiat, c. 1930. 12z, Jelcz 315, 1970s. 15z, Horse-drawn hand pump, 1899. 20z, Jelcz engine, Magirus power ladder, 1970s. 30z, Hand pump, 18th cent.

1985, Feb. 25 Photo. *Perf. 11x11½*

2664 A838 4z multicolored .20 .20
2665 A838 10z multicolored .30 .20
2666 A838 12z multicolored .30 .20
2667 A838 15z multicolored .40 .20
2668 A838 20z multicolored .55 .25
2669 A838 30z multicolored .85 .35
Nos. 2664-2669 (6) 2.60 1.40

Battle of Raclawice, April, 1794, by Jan Styka, 1894 — A839

1985, Apr. 4 *Perf. 11*

2670 A839 27z multicolored .75 .30

Kosciuszko Insurrection cent.

A840

A841

1985, Apr. 11 Litho. *Perf. 11½*

2671 A840 10z sal rose & dk vio bl .25 .20

Wincenty Rzymowski (1883-1950),Democratic Party founder.

1985, Apr. 25 Photo. *Perf. 11½x11*

2672 A841 15z Blue jeans, badge .35 .20

Intl. Youth Year.

Prince Boleslaw Krzywousty (1085-1138) — A842

Regional maps and: 10z, Wladyslaw Gomulka (1905-82), sec.-gen. of the Polish Workers Party, prime minister 1945-49. 20z, Piotr Zaremba (b. 1910), president of Gdansk Province 1945-50.

1985, May 8 Litho. *Perf. 11½*

2673 A842 5z multicolored .20 .20
2674 A842 10z multicolored .25 .20
2675 A842 20z multicolored .55 .20
Nos. 2673-2675 (3) 1.00 .60

Restoration of the Western & Northern Territories to Polish control, 40th anniv.

Victory Berlin 1945, by Jozef Mlynarski (b. 1925) — A843

Painting: Polish and Soviet soldiers at Brandenburg Gate, May 9, 1945.

1985, May 9 Photo. *Perf. 12x11½*

2676 A843 5z multicolored .20 .20

Liberation from German occupation, 40th anniv.

Warsaw Treaty Org., 30th Anniv. — A844

1985, May 14 Litho. *Perf. 11½x11*

2677 A844 5z Emblem, member flags .20 .20

World Wildlife Fund A845

Endangered Wildlife: Canis lupus.

1985, May 25 Photo. *Perf. 11x11½*

2678 A845 5z Wolves, winter landscape .40 .20
2679 A845 10z Female, cubs .50 .35
2680 A845 10z Wolf .50 .35
2681 A845 20z Wolves, summer landscape 1.25 .75
Nos. 2678-2681 (4) 2.65 1.65

A846

A847

Folk instruments.

1985, June 25 *Perf. 11½x11*

2682 A846 5z Wooden rattle .20 .20
2683 A846 10z Jingle .25 .20
2684 A846 12z Clay whistles .35 .20
2685 A846 20z Wooden fiddles .60 .20
2686 A846 25z Tuned bells .70 .25
2687 A846 31z Shepherd's flutes, ram's horn, ocarina .90 .35
Nos. 2682-2687 (6) 3.00 1.40

Photogravure and Engraved

1985, June 29

Design: O.R.P. Iskra and emblem.

2688 A847 5z bluish blk & yel .20 .20

Polish Navy, 40th anniv.

Tomasz Nocznicki (1862-1944) — A848

Polish Labor Movement founders: 20z, Maciej Rataj (1884-1940).

1985, July 26 Engr. *Perf. 11x11½*

2689 A848 10z grnsh black .30 .20
2690 A848 20z brown black .50 .25

Natl. labor movement, 90th anniv.

Polish Field Hockey Assn., 50th Anniv. A849

1985, Aug. 22 Litho. *Perf. 11½x11*

2691 A849 5z multicolored .25 .20

World War II Battles Type of 1984

Designs: 5z, Defense of Wizny, Capt. Wladyslaw Raginis. 10z, Attack on Mlawa, Col. Wilhelm Andrzej Liszka-Lawicz.

1985, Sept. 1 Photo. *Perf. 12x11½*

2692 A832 5z multicolored .20 .20
2693 A832 10z multicolored .35 .20

Pafawag Railway Rolling Stock Co. A850

1985, Sept. 18 Litho. *Perf. 11½*

2694 A850 5z Box car .20 .20
2695 A850 10z 201 E locomotive .30 .20
2696 A850 17z Two-axle coal car .50 .25
2697 A850 20z Passenger car .60 .30
Nos. 2694-2697 (4) 1.60 .95

Wild Ducks A851

1985, Oct. 21 Photo. *Perf. 11x11½*

2698 A851 5z Anas crecca .20 .20
2699 A851 5z Anas querquedula .20 .20
2700 A851 10z Aythya fuligula .30 .20
2701 A851 15z Bucephala clangula .40 .20
2702 A851 25z Somateria mollissima .65 .30
2703 A851 29z Netta rufina .80 .35
Nos. 2698-2703 (6) 2.55 1.45

UN, 40th Anniv. A852

1985, Oct. 24 Litho. *Perf. 11½x11*

2704 A852 27z multicolored .75 .30

Polish Ballet, 200th Anniv. — A853

1985, Dec. 4

2705 A853 5z Prima ballerina .20 .20
2706 A853 15z Male dancer .40 .20

Paintings by Stanislaw Ignacy Witkiewicz (1885-1939) — A854

5z, Marysia and Burek in Ceylon. No. 2708, Woman with a Fox. No. 2709, Self-portrait, 1931. 20z, Compositions, 1917. 25z, Portrait of Nena Stachurska, 1929. Nos. 2707, 2709-2711 vert.

Perf. 11½x11, 11x11½

1985, Dec. 6 Photo.

2707 A854 5z multicolored .20 .20
2708 A854 10z multicolored .30 .20
2709 A854 10z multicolored .30 .20
2710 A854 20z multicolored .55 .25
2711 A854 25z multicolored .70 .30
Nos. 2707-2711 (5) 2.05 1.15

Souvenir Sheet

Johann Sebastian Bach — A855

1985, Dec. 30 ***Perf. 11½x11***

2712 A855 65z multicolored 1.75 1.00
a. With inscription 7.00 7.00

No. 2712a inscribed "300 Rocznica Urodzin Jana Sebastiana Bacha." Distribution was limited.

Profile, Emblem, Sigismund III Column, Royal Castle Tower — A856

Intl. Peace Year — A858

Halley's Comet A857

1986, Jan. 16 ***Perf. 11½x11***

2713 A856 10z lt ultra, brt ultra & ultra .25 .20

Congress of Intellectuals for World Peace, Warsaw.

1986, Feb. 7 Photo. ***Perf. 11½***

Designs: No. 2714, Michal Kamienski (1879-1973), astronomer, orbit diagram. No. 2715, Comet, Vega, Giotto, Planet-A, ICE-3 space probes.

2714 A857 25z multicolored .60 .30
2715 A857 25z multicolored .60 .30
a. Pair, #2714-2715 1.20 .60

1986, Mar. 20 Photo. ***Perf. 11½x11***

2716 A858 25z turq bl, yel & ultra .60 .40

Cracow Restoration Type of 1982

Designs: 5z, Collegium Maius, Jagiellonian Museum. 10z, Town Hall, Kazimierz.

1986, Mar. 20 Litho. ***Perf. 11½***

2717 A801 5z multicolored .20 .20
2718 A801 10z multicolored .25 .20

Wildlife A859

1986, Apr. 15 Photo. ***Perf. 11½x11***

2719 A859 5z Perdix perdix .20 .20
2720 A859 5z Oryctolagus cuniculus .20 .20
2721 A859 10z Dama dama .20 .20
2722 A859 10z Phasianus colchicus .20 .20
2723 A859 20z Lepus europaeus .40 .20
2724 A859 40z Ovis ammon .80 .35
Nos. 2719-2724 (6) 2.00 1.35

Nos. 2719-2720, 2723-2724 vert.

Stanislaw Kulczynski (1895-1975), Scientist, Party Leader — A860

Photogravure and Engraved

1986, May 3 ***Perf. 11½x11***

2725 A860 10z buff & choc .25 .20

Warsaw Fire Brigade, 150th Anniv. — A861

Painting detail: The Fire Brigade on the Cracow Outskirts on Their Way to a Fire, 1871, by Josef Brodowski (1828-1900).

1986, May 16 ***Perf. 11***

2726 A861 10z dl brn & dk brn .25 .20

Paderewski A862

1986, May 22 ***Perf. 11½x11***

2727 A862 65z multicolored 1.50 .70

AMERIPEX'86.

1986 World Cup Soccer Championships, Mexico — A863

1986, May 26 ***Perf. 11½***

2728 A863 25z multicolored .50 .25

Ferryboats — A864

1986, June 18 Photo. ***Perf. 11***

2729 A864 10z Wilanow .20 .20
2730 A864 10z Wawel .20 .20
a. Souv. sheet of 2, #2729-2730 1.65 1.65
2731 A864 15z Pomerania .30 .20
2732 A864 25z Rogalin .55 .25
a. Souv. sheet of 2, #2731-2732 3.25 3.25
Nos. 2729-2732 (4) 1.25 .85

Nos. 2729-2732 printed se-tenant with labels picturing historic sites from the names of cities serviced. No. 2730a sold for 30z; No. 2732a for 55z. Surtax for the Natl. Assoc. of Philatelists.

Antarctic Agreement, 25th Anniv. — A865

Map of Antarctica and: 5z, A. B. Dobrowolski, Kopernik research ship. 40z, H. Arctowski, Professor Siedlecki research ship.

1986, June 23 Litho. ***Perf. 11½x11***

2733 A865 5z ver, pale grn & blk .20 .20
2734 A865 40z org, pale vio & dk vio 1.10 .40

Polish United Workers' Party, 10th Congress A866

1986, July 29 Photo. ***Perf. 11x11½***

2735 A866 10z red & dk gray bl .25 .20

Wawel Heads Type of 1984-85

Designs: 15z, Woman wearing a wreath (like No. 2628A). No. 2739, Thinker. No. 2740, Eastern ruler. 40z, Youth wearing beret. 60z, Warrior. 200z, Man's head.

Perf. 11½x12, 14 (15z, No. 2740, 60z)

Engr., Photo. (15z, No. 2740, 60z)

1986-89

2738 A828 15z rose brown .20 .20
2739 A828 20z green .35 .20
2740 A828 20z peacock blue .20 .20
2742 A828 40z gray .75 .35
2743 A828 60z dark green .25 .20
2744 A828 200z dark gray 3.75 1.75
Nos. 2738-2744 (6) 5.50 2.90

Issued: 15z, 9/22/88; #2739, 2742, 7/30/86; #2740, 3/31/89; 60z, 12/15/89; #2744, 11/11/86.

No. 2740 and 60z are coil stamps, have black control number on back of every 5th stamp.

For surcharge see No. 2954.

This is an expanding set. Numbers will change if necessary.

Jasna Gora Monastery Collection A867

Designs: No. 2746, The Paulinite Church on Skalka in Cracow, oil painting detail, circa 1627. No. 2747, Jesse's Tree, oil on wood, 17th cent. No. 2748, Gilded chalice, 18th cent. No. 2749, Virgin Mary embroidery, 15th cent.

1986, Aug. 15 Photo. ***Perf. 11½x11***

2746 A867 5z multicolored .20 .20
2747 A867 5z multicolored .20 .20
2748 A867 20z multicolored .40 .20
2749 A867 40z multicolored .80 .40
Nos. 2746-2749 (4) 1.60 1.00

Victories of Polish Athletes at 1985 World Championships — A868

Designs: No. 2750, Precision Flying, Kissimmee, Florida, won by Waclaw Nycz. No. 2751, Wind Sailing. Tallinn, USSR, won by Malgorzata Palasz-Piasecka. No. 2752, Glider Acrobatics, Vienna, won by Jerzy Makula. No. 2753, Greco-Roman Wrestling (82kg), Kolboten, Norway, won by Bogdan Daras. No. 2754, Road Cycling, Giavera del Montello, Italy, won by Lech Piasecki. No. 2755, Women's Modern Pentathlon, Montreal, won by Barbara Kotowska.

1986, Aug. 21 ***Perf. 11½***

2750 A868 5z multicolored .20 .20
2751 A868 10z multicolored .25 .20
2752 A868 10z multicolored .25 .20
2753 A868 15z multicolored .35 .20
2754 A868 20z multicolored .55 .20
2755 A868 30z multicolored .70 .30
Nos. 2750-2755 (6) 2.30 1.30

STOCKHOLMIA '86 — A869

1986, Aug. 28 ***Perf. 11x11½***

2756 A869 65z multicolored 1.50 .75
a. Souvenir sheet 1.50 .75

World War II Battles Type of 1984

Design: Battle of Jordanow, Col. Stanislaw Maczek, motorized cavalry 10th brigade commander-in-chief.

1986, Sept. 1 ***Perf. 12x11½***

2757 A832 10z multicolored .25 .20

Albert Schweitzer A870

World Post Day A871

Photogravure and Engraved

1986, Sept. 26 *Perf. 12x11½*
2758 A870 5z pale bl vio, sep & buff .20 .20

1986, Oct. 9 Litho. *Perf. 11x11½*
2759 A871 40z org, ultra & sep .75 .35
a. Souvenir sheet of 2 10.00 10.00

No. 2759a sold for 120z.

Folk and Fairy Tale Legends A872

Designs: No. 2760, Basilisk. No. 2761, Duke Popiel, vert. No. 2762, Golden Duck. No. 2763, Boruta, the Devil, vert. No. 2764, Janosik the Thief, vert. No. 2765, Lajkonik, conqueror of the Tartars, 13th cent., vert.

1986, Oct. 28 Photo. *Perf. 11½x11*

2760	A872	5z	multicolored	.20	.20
2761	A872	5z	multicolored	.20	.20
2762	A872	10z	multicolored	.20	.20
2763	A872	10z	multicolored	.20	.20
2764	A872	20z	multicolored	.35	.20
2765	A872	50z	multicolored	.95	.50
			Nos. 2760-2765 (6)	2.10	1.50

Prof. Tadeusz Kotarbinski (1886-1981) — A873

1986, Nov. 19 Litho. *Perf. 11½*
2766 A873 10z sepia, buff & brn blk .30 .20

17th-20th Cent. Architecture — A874

Designs: No. 2767, Church, Baczal Dolny. No. 2768, Windmill, Zygmuntow. 10z, Oravian cottage, Zubrzyca Gorna. 15z, Kashubian Arcade cottage, Wazydze. 25z, Barn, Grzawa. 30z, Water mill, Molkowice Stare.

Perf. 11x11½, 11½x11

1986, Nov. 26 **Photo.**

2767	A874	5z	multicolored	.20	.20
2768	A874	5z	multi, vert.	.20	.20
2769	A874	10z	multicolored	.20	.20
2770	A874	15z	multicolored	.30	.20
2771	A874	25z	multicolored	.50	.25
2772	A874	30z	multicolored	.55	.30
			Nos. 2767-2772 (6)	1.95	1.35

Royalty A875

Photogravure and Engraved

1986, Dec. 4 *Perf. 11*
2773 A875 10z Mieszko I .20 .20
2774 A875 25z Dobrava .50 .25

See Nos. 2838-2839, 2884-2885, 2932-2933, 3033-3034, 3068-3069, 3141-3144, 3191-3192, 3222-3225, 3309-3312, 3366-3369, 3394-3397, 3479-3482. For surcharges see Nos. 3016-3017.

New Year 1987 A876

1986, Dec. 12 Photo. *Perf. 11x11½*
2775 A876 25z multicolored .50 .30

Warsaw Cyclists Soc., Cent. A877

#2776, First trip to Bielany, uniformed escort, 1887. #2777, Jan Stanislaw Skrodzki (1867-1957), 1895 record-holder. #2778, Dynasy Society building, 1892-1937. #2779, Mieczyslaw Baranski, champion, 1896. #2780, Karolina Kociecka (b. 1875), female competitor. #2781, Henryk Weiss (d. 1912), Dynasy champion, 1904-1908.

Perf. 13x12½, 12½x13

1986, Dec. 19 **Litho.**

2776	A877	5z	multi	.20	.20
2777	A877	5z	multi, vert.	.20	.20
2778	A877	10z	multi, vert.	.20	.20
2779	A877	10z	multi, vert.	.20	.20
2780	A877	30z	multi, vert.	.55	.30
2781	A877	50z	multi, vert.	.95	.45
			Nos. 2776-2781 (6)	2.30	1.55

Henryk Arctowski Antarctic Station, King George Island, 10th Anniv. A878

Wildlife and ships: No. 2782, Euphausia superba, training freighter Antoni Garnuszewski. No. 2783, Notothenia rossi, Dissostichus mawsoni, Zulawy transoceanic ship. No. 2784, Fulmarus glacialoides, yacht Pogoria. No. 2785, Pigoscelis adeliae, yacht Gedania. 30z, Arctocephalus, research boat Dziunia. 40z, Hydrurga leptonyx, ship Kapitan Ledochowski.

1987, Feb. 13 Litho. *Perf. 11½*

2782	A878	5z	multicolored	.20	.20
2783	A878	5z	multicolored	.20	.20
2784	A878	10z	multicolored	.20	.20
2785	A878	10z	multicolored	.20	.20
2786	A878	30z	multicolored	.60	.30
2787	A878	40z	multicolored	.85	.40
			Nos. 2782-2787 (6)	2.25	1.50

Paintings by Leon Wyczolkowski (1852-1936) — A879

1987, Mar. 20 Photo. *Perf. 11*

2788	A879	5z	Cineraria Flowers, 1924	.20	.20
2789	A879	10z	Portrait of a Woman, 1883	.20	.20
2790	A879	10z	Wood Church, 1910	.20	.20
2791	A879	25z	Harvesting Beetroot, 1910	.50	.25
2792	A879	30z	Wading Fishermen, 1891	.60	.30
2793	A879	40z	Self-portrait, 1912	.80	.40
			Nos. 2788-2793 (6)	2.50	1.55

Nos. 2789 and 2791 vert.

The Ravage, 1866, by Artur Grottger (1837-1867) — A880

1987, Mar. 26 Photo. *Perf. 11*
2794 A880 15z dk brown & buff .25 .20

Gen. Karol Swierczewski-Walter (1897-1947) — A881

1987, Mar. 27 Engr. *Perf. 11½x12*
2795 A881 15z olive green .25 .20

Pawel Edmund Strzelecki (1797-1873), Explorer — A882

1987, Apr. 23 Photo. *Perf. 11½x11*
2796 A882 65z olive black 1.10 .65

Colonization of Australia, bicentennial.

2nd PRON Congress A883

1987, May 8 Litho. *Perf. 11½*
2797 A883 10z pale gray, brn, red & brt ultra .20 .20

Patriotic Movement of the National Renaissance Congress.

Motor Vehicles — A884

1987, May 19 Photo. *Perf. 12x11½*

2798	A884	10z	1936 Saurer-Zawrat	.20	.20
2799	A884	10z	1928 CWS T-1	.20	.20
2800	A884	15z	1928 Ursus-A	.30	.20
2801	A884	15z	1936 Lux-Sport	.30	.20
2802	A884	25z	1939 Podkowa 100	.50	.25
2803	A884	45z	1935 Sokol 600 RT	.90	.45
			Nos. 2798-2803 (6)	2.40	1.50

Royal Castle, Warsaw — A885

1987, June 5
2804 A885 50z multicolored .90 .50

A souvenir sheet of 1 exists.

A886

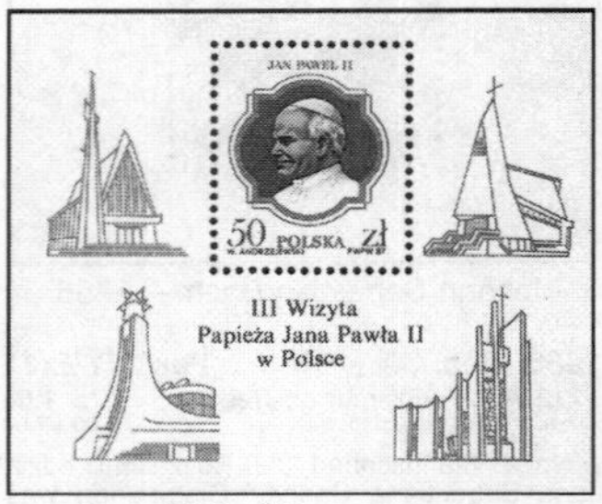

State Visit of Pope John Paul II — A887

1987, June 8 *Perf. 11*
2805 A886 15z shown .30 .20
2806 A886 45z Portrait, diff. .90 .45
a. Pair, #2805-2806 1.20 .60

Souvenir Sheet

Perf. 12x11½

2807 A887 50z shown 1.00 1.00

No. 2806a has continuous design.

Cracow Restoration Type of 1982

1987, July 6 Litho. *Perf. 11½*
2809 A801 10z Barbican Gate, Wawel, horiz. .20 .20

Esperanto Language, Cent. — A890

1987, July 25 Litho. *Perf. 11½*

2811 A890 45z Ludwig L. Zamenhof .80 .40

A891

A892

Poznan and Town Hall, by Stanislaw Wyspianski.

1987, Aug. 3

2812 A891 15z blk & pale salmon .25 .20

POZNAN '87, Aug. 8-16.

1987, Aug. 20 Photo. *Perf. 11½x11*

2813 A892 10z Queen .20 .20
2814 A892 10z Worker .20 .20
2815 A892 15z Drone .30 .20
2816 A892 15z Box hive, orchard .30 .20
2817 A892 40z Bee collecting pollen .75 .35
2818 A892 50z Beekeeper collecting honey .90 .45
Nos. 2813-2818 (6) 2.65 1.60

31st World Apiculture Congress, Warsaw.

Success of Polish Athletes at World Championship Events — A894

1987, Sept. 24 Litho. *Perf. 14*

2820 A894 10z Acrobatics, France .20 .20
2821 A894 15z Kayak, Canada .25 .20
2822 A894 20z Marksmanship, E. Germany .30 .20
2823 A894 25z Wrestling, Hungary .40 .20
Nos. 2820-2823 (4) 1.15 .80

World War II Battles Type of 1984

Designs: No. 2824, Battle of Mokra, Julian Filipowicz. No. 2825, Battle scene near Oleszycami, Brig.-Gen. Josef Rudolf Kustron. 15z, Air battles over Warsaw, pilot Stefan Pawlikowski.

1987, Sept. 1 Photo. *Perf. 12x11½*

2824 A832 10z multicolored .20 .20
2825 A832 10z multicolored .20 .20
2826 A832 15z multicolored .30 .20
Nos. 2824-2826 (3) .70 .60

Jan Hevelius (1611-1687), Astronomer, and Constellations — A895

1987, Sept. 15 Litho. *Perf. 11½*

2827 A895 15z Hevelius, sextant, vert. .25 .20
2828 A895 40z shown .65 .35

Souvenir Sheet

1st Artificial Satellite, Sputnik, 30th Anniv. — A896

1987, Oct. 2 Photo. *Perf. 11½x11*

2829 A896 40z Stacionar 4 satellite 1.00 1.00

World Post Day A897

Design: Ignacy Franciszek Przebendowski (1730-1791), postmaster general, and post office building, 19th cent., Krakowskie Przedmiescie, Warsaw.

1987, Oct. 9 Litho.

2830 A897 15z lt olive grn & rose claret .25 .20

Col. Stanislaw Wieckowski — A898

Photo. & Engr.

1987, Oct. 16 *Perf. 12x11½*

2831 A898 15z deep blue & blk .25 .20

Col. Wieckowski (1884-1942), physician and social reformer executed by the Nazis at Auschwitz.

HAFNIA '87 — A899

Fairy tales by Hans Christian Andersen (1805-1875): No. 2832, The Little Mermaid. No. 2833, The Nightingale. No. 2834, The Wild Swan. No. 2835, The Match Girl. 30z, The Snow Queen. 40z, The Brave Toy Soldier.

1987, Oct. 16 Photo. *Perf. 11x11½*

2832 A899 10z multicolored .20 .20
2833 A899 10z multicolored .20 .20
2834 A899 20z multicolored .40 .20
2835 A899 20z multicolored .40 .20
2836 A899 30z multicolored .60 .30
2837 A899 40z multicolored .80 .40
Nos. 2832-2837 (6) 2.60 1.50

Royalty Type of 1986

Photo. & Engr.

1987, Dec. 4 *Perf. 11*

2838 A875 10z Boleslaw I Chrobry .20 .20
2839 A875 15z Mieszko II .30 .20

No. 2838 exists with label.

New Year 1988 A900

1987, Dec. 14 Photo. *Perf. 11x11½*

2840 A900 15z multicolored .25 .20

Dragonflies — A901

Perf. 11x11½, 11½x11

1988, Feb. 23 Photo.

2841 A901 10z Anax imperator .20 .20
2842 A901 15z Libellula quadrimaculata, vert. .25 .20
2843 A901 15z Calopteryx splendens .25 .20
2844 A901 20z Cordulegaster annulatus, vert. .35 .20
2845 A901 30z Sympetrum pedemontanum .50 .25
2846 A901 50z Aeschna viridis, vert. .90 .45
Nos. 2841-2846 (6) 2.45 1.50

Cracow Restoration Type of 1982

1988, Mar. 8 Litho. *Perf. 11½x11*

2847 A801 15z Florianska Gate, 1300 .25 .20

Intl. Year of Graphic Design A903

1988, Apr. 28 Photo. *Perf. 11x11½*

2848 A903 40z multicolored .50 .25

Antique Clocks — A904

Clocks in the Museum of Artistic and Precision Handicrafts, Warsaw, and clockworks: No. 2849, Frisian wall clock, 17th cent., vert. No. 2850, Anniversary clock and rotary pendulum, 20th cent. No. 2851, Carriage clock, 18th cent., vert. No. 2852, Louis XV rococo bracket clock, 18th cent., vert. 20z, Pocket watch, 19th cent. 40z, Gdansk six-sided clock signed by Benjamin Zoll, 17th cent.

Perf. 11½x12, 12x11½

1988, May 19 Photo.

2849 A904 10z lt green & multi .20 .20
2850 A904 10z purple & multi .20 .20
2851 A904 15z dull org & multi .25 .20
2852 A904 15z brown & multi .25 .20
2853 A904 20z multicolored .30 .20
2854 A904 40z multicolored .65 .30
Nos. 2849-2854 (6) 1.85 1.30

1988 Summer Olympics, Seoul A905

1988, June 27 Photo. *Perf. 11x11½*

2855 A905 15z Triple jump .20 .20
2856 A905 20z Wrestling .25 .20
2857 A905 20z Two-man kayak .25 .20
2858 A905 25z Judo .35 .20
2859 A905 40z Shooting .50 .20
2860 A905 55z Swimming .75 .20
Nos. 2855-2860 (6) 2.30 1.20

See No. B148.

Natl. Industry A906

1988, Aug. 23 Photo. *Perf. 11x11½*

Size: 35x27mm

2861 A906 45z Los "Elk" aircraft .75 .40

State Aircraft Works, 60th anniv.

See Nos. 2867, 2871, 2881-2883.

16th European Regional FAO Conference, Cracow — A907

15z, Computers and agricultural growth. 40z, Balance between industry and nature.

1988, Aug. 22 *Perf. 11½x11*

2862 A907 15z multicolored .25 .20
2863 A907 40z multicolored .60 .30

World War II Battles Type of 1984

Battle scenes and commanders: 15z, Modlin, Brig.-Gen. Wiktor Thommee. No. 2865, Warsaw, Brig.-Gen. Walerian Czuma. No. 2866, Tomaszow Lubelski, Brig.-Gen. Antoni Szylling.

1988, Sept. 1 Photo. *Perf. 12x11½*

2864 A832 15z multicolored .25 .20
2865 A832 20z multicolored .30 .20
2866 A832 20z multicolored .30 .20
Nos. 2864-2866 (3) .85 .60

Natl. Industries Type of 1988

Design: Stalowa Wola Ironworks, 50th anniv.

1988, Sept. 5 *Perf. 11x11½*

Size: 35x27mm

2867 A906 15z multicolored .25 .20

World Post Day A909

Design: Postmaster Tomasz Arciszewski (1877-1955), Post and Telegraph Administration emblem used from 1919 to 1927.

1988, Oct. 9 Litho. *Perf. 11½x11*

2868 A909 20z multicolored .25 .20

Also printed in sheet of 12 plus 12 labels.

World War II Combat Medals — A910

1988, Oct. 12 **Photo.**

2869 A910 20z Battle of Lenino Cross .30 .20
2870 A910 20z shown .30 .20

See Nos. 2930-2931.

Natl. Industries Type of 1988

Air Force Medical Institute, 60th anniv.

1988, Oct. 12 ***Perf. 11x11½***
Size: 38x27mm

2871 A906 20z multicolored .25 .20

Stanislaw Malachowski, Kazimierz Nestor Sapieha — A912

1988, Oct. 16 ***Perf. 11***

2872 A912 20z multicolored .25 .20

Four Years' Sejm (Parliament) (1788-1792), bicent.

National Leaders — A913

1988, Nov. 11 ***Perf. 12x11½***

2873 A913 15z Wincenty Witos .25 .20
2874 A913 15z Ignacy Daszynski .25 .20
2875 A913 20z Wojciech Korfanty .25 .20
2876 A913 20z Stanislaw Wojciechowski .25 .20
2877 A913 20z Julian Marchlewski .25 .20
2878 A913 200z Ignacy Paderewski 2.25 1.00
2879 A913 200z Jozef Pilsudski 2.25 1.00
2880 A913 200z Gabriel Narutowicz 2.25 1.00
a. Souvenir sheet of 3, #2878-2880 17.50 17.50
Nos. 2873-2880 (8) 8.00 4.00

Natl. independence, 70th anniv.

Natl. Industry Types of 1988

15z, Wharf, Gdynia. 20z, Industrialist Hipolit Cegielski, 1883 steam locomotive. 40z, Poznan fair grounds, Upper Silesia Tower.

1988 **Photo.** ***Perf. 11x11½***
Size: 39x27mm

2881 A906 15z multicolored .30 .20
2882 A906 20z multicolored .40 .20

Size: 35x27mm

2883 A906 40z multicolored .80 .40
Nos. 2881-2883 (3) 1.50 .80

70th anniv. of Polish independence. Gdynia Port, 65th anniv (15z); Metal Works in Poznan, 142nd anniv. (20z); and Poznan Intl. Fair 60th anniv. (40z).
Issued: 15z, 12/12; 20z, 11/28; 40z, 12/21.

Royalty Type of 1986
Photo. & Engr.

1988, Dec. 4 ***Perf. 11***

2884 A875 10z Rycheza .20 .20
2885 A875 15z Kazimierz I Odnowiciel .30 .20

New Year 1989 A914

1988, Dec. 9 **Photo.** ***Perf. 11x11½***

2886 A914 20z multicolored .30 .20

Unification of Polish Workers' Unions, 40th Anniv. — A915

1988, Dec. 15 ***Perf. 11½x12***

2887 A915 20z black & ver .30 .20

Fire Boats — A916

1988, Dec. 29 **Litho.** ***Perf. 14***

2888 A916 10z Blysk .20 .20
2889 A916 15z Zar .25 .20
2890 A916 15z Plomien .25 .20
2891 A916 20z Strazak 4 .30 .20
2892 A916 20z Strazak 11 .30 .20
2893 A916 45z Strazak 25 .75 .40
Nos. 2888-2893 (6) 2.05 1.40

Horses — A917

1989, Mar. 6 **Photo.** ***Perf. 11***

2894 A917 15z Lippizaner .25 .20
2895 A917 15z Arden, vert. .25 .20
2896 A917 20z English .35 .20
2897 A917 20z Arabian, vert. .35 .20
2898 A917 30z Wielkopolski .55 .25
2899 A917 70z Polish, vert. 1.00 .25
Nos. 2894-2899 (6) 2.75 1.30

Dogs — A918

Battle of Monte Cassino, 45th Anniv. — A919

1989, May 3 **Photo.** ***Perf. 11½x11***

2900 A918 15z Wire-haired dachshund .20 .20
2901 A918 15z Cocker spaniel .20 .20
2902 A918 20z Czech fousek pointer .20 .20
2903 A918 20z Welsh terrier .20 .20
2904 A918 25z English setter .20 .20
2905 A918 45z Pointer .40 .20
Nos. 2900-2905 (6) 1.40 1.20

1989, May 18 ***Perf. 11½x12***

Design: 165z, Battle of Falaise, General Stanislaw Maczek, horiz. 210z, Battle of Arnhem, Gen. Stanislaw Sosabowski, vert.

2906 A919 80z Gen. W. Anders .45 .25
2907 A919 165z multicolored .85 .40
2907A A919 210z multicolored 1.20 .60
Nos. 2906-2907 (2) 1.30 .65

1st Armored Division at the Battle of Falaise, 45th anniv. Battle of Arnhem, 45th anniv.
See No. 2968.

A 50z stamp for Gen. Grzegorz Korczynski was prepared but not released.

Woman Wearing a Phrygian Cap — A920

1989, July 3 **Litho.** ***Perf. 11½x11***

2908 A920 100z blk, dark red & dark ultra .70 .30
a. Souv. sheet of 2+2 labels 2.00 2.00

French revolution bicent., PHILEXFRANCE '89. No. 2908 printed se-tenant with inscribed label picturing exhibition emblem. No. 2908a sold for 270z. Surcharge benefited the Polish Philatelic Union.

Polonia House, Pultusk — A921

1989, July 16 **Photo.** ***Perf. 11½***

2909 A921 100z multicolored .70 .30

First Moon Landing, 20th Anniv. A922

1989, July 21 ***Perf. 11x11½***

2910 A922 100z multicolored .70 .30
a. Souvenir sheet of 1 .70 .30

No. 2910a exists imperf.

Polish People's Republic, 45th Anniv. — A923

Winners of the Order of the Builders of People's Poland: No. 2911, Ksawery Dunikowski (1875-1964), artist. No. 2912, Stanislaw Mazur (1897-1964), agriculturist. No. 2913, Natalia Gasiorowska (1881-1964), historian. No. 2914, Wincenty Pstrowski (1904-1948), coal miner.

1989, July 21 ***Perf. 11½x11***

2911 A923 35z multicolored .25 .20
2912 A923 35z multicolored .25 .20
2913 A923 35z multicolored .25 .20
2914 A923 35z multicolored .25 .20
Nos. 2911-2914 (4) 1.00 .80

Security Service and Militia, 45th Anniv. A924

1989, July 21 ***Perf. 11x11½***

2915 A924 35z dull brn & slate blue .35 .20

World Fire Fighting Congress, July 25-30, Warsaw — A925

1989, July 25 ***Perf. 11½x11***

2916 A925 80z multicolored .55 .30

Daisy — A926

Designs: 60z, Juniper. 150z, Daisy. 500z, Wild rose. 1000z, Blue corn flower.

1989 **Photo.** ***Perf. 11x12***

2917 A926 40z slate green .20 .20
2918 A926 60z violet blue .20 .20
2919 A926 150z rose lake .20 .20
2920 A926 500z bright violet .55 .25
2921 A926 1000z bright blue 1.10 .50
Nos. 2917-2921 (5) 2.25 1.35

Issue dates: 40z, 60z, Aug. 25. 150z, Dec. 4; 500z, 1000z, Dec. 19.
See Nos. 2978-2979, 3026. For surcharge see No. 2970.

World War II Battles Type of 1984

Battle scenes and commanders: No. 2922, Westerplatte, Capt. Franciszek Dabrowski. No. 2923, Hel, Artillery Capt. B. Przybyszewski. No. 2924, Kock, Brig.-Gen. Franciszek Kleeberg. No. 2925, Lwow, Brig.-Gen. Wladyslaw Langner.

1989, Sept. 1 ***Perf. 12x11½***

2922 A832 25z multicolored .20 .20
2923 A832 25z multicolored .20 .20
2924 A832 35z multicolored .25 .20
2925 A832 35z multicolored .25 .20
Nos. 2922-2925 (4) .90 .80

Nazi invasion of Poland, 50th anniv.

Caricature Museum — A927

1989, Sept. 15 **Photo.** ***Perf. 11½x11***

2926 A927 40z multicolored .20 .20

Teaching Surgery at Polish Universities, Bicent., and Surgeon's Soc. Cent. — A928

Surgeons: 40z, Rafal Jozef Czerwiakowski (1743-1813), 1st professor of surgery and founder of the 1st surgical department, Jagellonian University, Cracow. 60z, Ludwik Rydygier (1850-1920), founder of the Polish Surgeons Society.

1989, Sept. 18 ***Perf. 11½x12***

2927 A928 40z black & brt ultra .20 .20
2928 A928 60z black & brt green .30 .20

World Post Day — A929

Design: Emil Kalinski (1890-1973), minister of the Post and Telegraph from 1933-1939.

1989, Oct. 9 ***Perf. 12x11½***

2929 A929 60z multicolored .30 .20

Printed se-tenant with label picturing postal emblem of the second republic.

WWII Decorations Type of 1988

Medals: No. 2930, Participation in the Struggle for Control of the Nation. No. 2931, Defense of Warsaw, 1939-45.

1989, Oct. 12 Photo. ***Perf. 11½x11***

2930 A910 60z multicolored .25 .20
2931 A910 60z multicolored .25 .20

Royalty Type of 1986

Photo. & Engr.

1989, Oct. 18 ***Perf. 11***

2932 A875 20z Boleslaw II Szczodry .20 .20
2933 A875 30z Wladyslaw I Herman .20 .20

World Stamp Expo '89, Washington, DC, Nov. 17-Dec.3 — A930

1989, Nov. 14 Photo. ***Perf. 11x11½***

2934 A930 500z multicolored 1.65 .80

Exists imperf.

Polish Red Cross Soc., 70th Anniv. — A931

1989, Nov. 17 ***Perf. 11½x11***

2935 A931 200z blk, brt yel grn & scar .75 .30

Treaty of Versailles, 70th Anniv. A932

Design: State arms and representatives of Poland who signed the treaty, including Ignacy Jan Paderewski (1860-1941), pianist, composer, statesman, and Roman Dmowski (1864-1939), statesman.

1989, Nov. 21 ***Perf. 11x11½***

2936 A932 350z multicolored 1.25 .50

Camera Shutter as the Iris of the Eye — A933

Designs: 40z, Photographer in silhouette, Maksymilian Strasz (1804-1870), pioneer of photography in Poland.

Perf. 11½x12, 12x11½

1989, Nov. 27

2937 A933 40z multicolored .20 .20
2938 A933 60z shown .20 .20

Photography, 150th anniv.

No. 2456 Surcharged

1989, Nov. 30 Photo. ***Perf. 11x11½***

2939 A766 500z on 4z dark violet 1.25 .50

Flowers, Still-life Paintings in the National Museum, Warsaw A934

1989, Dec. 18 ***Perf. 13***

2940 A934 25z Jan Ciaglinski .20 .20
2941 A934 30z Wojciech Weiss .20 .20
2942 A934 35z Antoni Kolasinski .20 .20
2943 A934 50z Stefan Nacht-Samborski .20 .20
2944 A934 60z Jozef Pankiewicz .20 .20
2945 A934 85z Henryka Beyer .25 .20
2946 A934 110z Wladyslaw Slewinski .30 .20
2947 A934 190z Czeslaw Wdowiszewski .50 .30
Nos. 2940-2947 (8) 2.05 1.70

Religious Art — A935

1989, Dec. 21 ***Perf. 11½x11***

2948 A935 50z Jesus, shroud .25 .20
2949 A935 60z Two saints .25 .20
2950 A935 90z Three saints .25 .20

Perf. 11x11½

2951 A935 150z Jesus, Mary, Joseph .45 .25
2952 A935 200z Madonna and Child Enthroned .60 .30
2953 A935 350z Holy Family with angels 1.25 .50
Nos. 2948-2953 (6) 3.05 1.65

Nos. 2951-2953 vert.

Republic of Poland

No. 2738 Surcharged

1990, Jan. 31 Photo. ***Perf. 11½x12***

2954 A828 350z on 15z rose brn .25 .20

Opera Singers — A936

Portraits: 100z, Krystyna Jamroz (1923-1986). 150z, Wanda Werminska (1900-1988). 350z, Ada Sari (1882-1968). 500z, Jan Kiepura (1902-1966).

1990, Feb. 9 ***Perf. 12x11½***

2955 A936 100z multicolored .20 .20
2956 A936 150z multicolored .20 .20
2957 A936 350z multicolored .20 .20
2958 A936 500z multicolored .30 .20
Nos. 2955-2958 (4) .90 .80

Yachting A937

1990, Mar. 29 ***Perf. 11x11½***

2959 A937 100z shown .20 .20
2960 A937 200z Rugby .20 .20
2961 A937 400z High jump .20 .20
2962 A937 500z Figure skating .25 .20
2963 A937 500z Diving .25 .20
2964 A937 1000z Rhythmic gymnastics .50 .25
Nos. 2959-2964 (6) 1.60 1.25

Roman Kozlowski (1889-1977), Paleontologist — A938

1990, Apr. 17 Photo. ***Perf. 11x11½***

2965 A938 500z red & olive bis .30 .20

Pope John Paul II, 70th Birthday A939

1990, May 18 ***Perf. 11***

2966 A939 1000z multicolored .55 .25

Souvenir Sheet

First Polish Postage Stamp, 130th Anniv. — A940

Design includes No. 1 separated by simulated perforations from 1000z commemorative version at right.

1990, May 25 ***Perf. 11½***

2967 A940 1000z multicolored .55 .25

Battle Type of 1989

Design: Battle of Narvik, 1940, General Z. Bohusz-Szyszko.

1990, May 28 ***Perf. 11½x12***

2968 A919 1500z multicolored .60 .25

World Cup Soccer Championships, Italy — A941

1990, June 8 ***Perf. 11½x11***

2969 A941 1000z multicolored .60 .30

No. 2918 Surcharged in Vermilion

1990, June 18 Photo. ***Perf. 11x12***

2970 A926 700z on 60z vio bl .40 .20

Memorial to Victims of June 1956 Uprising, Poznan — A942

1990, June 28 Photo. ***Perf. 12x11½***

2971 A942 1500z multicolored .70 .30

Social Insurance Institution, 70th Anniv. — A943

1990, July 5 ***Perf. 11x11½***

2972 A943 1500z multicolored .75 .35

Shells — A944

#2973, Mussel. #2974, Fresh water snail.

1990, July 16 ***Perf. 14***

2973 A944 B (500z) dk pur .20 .20
2974 A944 A (700z) olive grn .35 .20

Katyn Forest Massacre, 50th Anniv. — A945

1990, July 20

2975 A945 1500z gray, red & blk .75 .35

Polish Meteorological Service — A946

1990, July 27 ***Perf. 11x11½***

2976 A946 500z shown .25 .20
2977 A946 700z Water depth gauge .40 .20

Flower Type of 1989

2000z, Nuphar. 5000z, German iris.

1990, Aug. 13 ***Die Cut***

Self Adhesive

2978	A926	2000z	olive grn	.75	.55
2979	A926	5000z	violet	2.00	.95

World Kayaking Championships, Poznan — A947

Design: 1000z, One-man kayak.

1990, Aug. 22 Photo. ***Perf. 11x11½***

2980	A947	700z	multicolored	.40	.20
2981	A947	1000z	multicolored	.60	.30
a.			Souv. sheet of 1 + label	4.50	4.50

A948

A949

1990, Aug. 31 ***Perf. 11½x11***

2982	A948	1500z	blk, red & gray	.75	.35

Solidarity, 10th anniv.

1990, Sept. 24 Photo. ***Perf. 11½x11***

Flowers.

2983	A949	200z	Polemonium coeruleum	.20	.20
2984	A949	700z	Nymphoides peltata	.35	.20
2985	A949	700z	Dracocephalum ruyschiana	.35	.20
2986	A949	1000z	Helleborus purpurascens	.55	.25
2987	A949	1500z	Daphne cneorum	.80	.30
2988	A949	1700z	Dianthus superbus	.90	.40
			Nos. 2983-2988 (6)	3.15	1.55

Cmielow Porcelain Works, Bicentennial — A950

Designs: 700z, Platter, 1870-1887. 800z, Plate, 1887-1890, vert. No. 2991, Figurine, 1941-1944, vert. No. 2992, Cup, saucer, c. 1887. 1500z, Candy box, 1930-1990. 2000z, Vase, 1979, vert.

1990, Oct. 31 Photo. ***Perf. 11***

2989	A950	700z	multicolored	.20	.20
2990	A950	800z	multicolored	.20	.20
2991	A950	1000z	multicolored	.35	.20
2992	A950	1000z	multicolored	.35	.20
2993	A950	1500z	multicolored	.60	.30
2994	A950	2000z	multicolored	1.00	.40
			Nos. 2989-2994 (6)	2.70	1.50

Owls — A951

1990, Nov. 6 Litho. ***Perf. 14***

2995	A951	200z	Athene noctua	.20	.20
2996	A951	500z	shown	.30	.20
2997	A951	500z	Strix aluco, winter	.30	.20
2998	A951	1000z	Asio flammeus	.60	.25
2999	A951	1500z	Asio otus	.90	.40
3000	A951	2000z	Tyto alba	1.25	.50
			Nos. 2995-3000 (6)	3.55	1.75

Pres. Lech Walesa, 1983 Nobel Peace Prize Winner A952

1990, Dec. 12 Litho. ***Perf. 11x11½***

3001	A952	1700z	multicolored	1.00	.45

A953

A954

1990, Dec. 21 Photo. ***Perf. 11½x11***

3002	A953	1500z	multicolored	.75	.35

Polish participation in Battle of Britain, 50th anniv.

1990, Dec. 28 Litho. ***Perf. 11½***

Architecture: 700z, Collegiate Church, 12th cent., Leczyca. 800z, Castle, 14th cent., Reszel. 1500z, Town Hall, 16th cent., Chelmno. 1700z, Church of the Nuns of the Visitation, 18th cent., Warsaw.

3003	A954	700z	multicolored	.35	.20
3004	A954	800z	multicolored	.40	.20
3005	A954	1500z	multicolored	.80	.30
3006	A954	1700z	multicolored	.90	.35
			Nos. 3003-3006 (4)	2.45	1.05

No. 3006 printed with se-tenant label for World Philatelic Exhibition, Poland '93.

Art Treasures of the Natl. Gallery, Warsaw A955

Paintings: 500z, King Sigismund Augustus. 700z, The Adoration of the Magi, Pultusk Codex. 1000z, St. Matthew, Pultusk Codex. 1500z, Christ Removing the Moneychangers by Mikolaj Haberschrack. 1700z, The Annunciation. 2000z, The Three Marys by Haberschrack.

1991, Jan. 11 Photo. ***Perf. 11***

3007	A955	500z	multicolored	.20	.20
3008	A955	700z	multicolored	.30	.20
3009	A955	1000z	multicolored	.35	.20
3010	A955	1500z	multicolored	.50	.20
3011	A955	1700z	multicolored	.55	.25
3012	A955	2000z	multicolored	.65	.30
			Nos. 3007-3012 (6)	2.55	1.35

Pinecones — A956

1991, Feb. 22 ***Perf. 12x11½***

3013	A956	700z	Abies alba	.20	.20
3014	A956	1500z	Pinus strobus	.40	.20

See Nos. 3163-3164, 3231-3232.

Radziwill Palace A957

1991, Mar. 3 Photo. ***Perf. 11x12***

3015	A957	1500z	multicolored	.40	.20

Admission to CEPT.

Royalty Type of 1986 Surcharged in Red

Designs: 1000z, Boleslaw III Krzywousty. 1500z, Wladyslaw II Wygnaniec.

Photo. & Engr.

1991, Mar. 25 ***Perf. 11***

3016	A875	1000z	on 40z, grn & blk	.30	.20
3017	A875	1500z	on 50z, red vio & gray blk	.50	.25

Not issued without surcharge.

Brother Albert (Adam Chmielowski, 1845-1916) — A958

1991, Mar. 29 Photo. ***Perf. 12x11½***

3018	A958	2000z	multicolored	.50	.25

Battle of Legnica, 750th Anniv. A959

Photo. & Engr.

1991, Apr. 9 ***Perf. 14½x14***

3019	A959	1500z	multicolored	.45	.25

See Germany No. 1635.

Polish Icons A960

Designs: 500z, 1000z, 1500z, Various paintings of Madonna and Child. 700z, 2000z, 2200z, Various paintings of Jesus.

1991, Apr. 22 Photo. ***Perf. 11***

3020	A960	500z	multicolored	.20	.20
3021	A960	700z	multicolored	.25	.20
3022	A960	1000z	multicolored	.35	.20
3023	A960	1500z	multicolored	.50	.25
3024	A960	2000z	multicolored	.70	.30
3025	A960	2200z	multicolored	.75	.35
			Nos. 3020-3025 (6)	2.75	1.50

Flower Type of 1989

Design: 700z, Lily of the Valley.

1991, Apr. 26 Litho. ***Perf. 14***

3026	A926	700z	dk blue green	.25	.20

Royalty Type of 1986

Designs: 1000z, Boleslaw IV Kedzierzawy. 1500z, Mieszko III Stary.

Photo. & Engr.

1991, Apr. 30 ***Perf. 11x11½***

3033	A875	1000z	brn red & black	.35	.20
3034	A875	1500z	brt bl & bluish blk	.60	.20

A961

A962

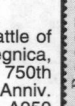

2000z, Title page of act. 2500z, Debate in the Sejm. 3000z, Adoption of Constitution, May 3, 1791, by Jan Matejko (1838-1893).

1991, May 2 Litho. *Perf. 11½*
3035 A961 2000z brown & ver .50 .20
3036 A961 2500z brown & ver .70 .40

Souvenir Sheet

3037 A961 3000z multicolored 1.25 .75

May 3, 1791 Polish constitution, bicent.

1991, May 6 Litho. *Perf. 11½x11*
3038 A962 1000z multicolored .50 .20

Europa.

European Conference for Protection of Cultural Heritage, Cracow — A963

1991, May 27 Litho. *Perf. 11½*
3039 A963 2000z blue & lake .75 .30

Sinking of the Bismarck, 50th Anniv. — A964

1991, May 27
3040 A964 2000z multicolored .75 .30

A965

A966

Designs: 1000z, Pope John Paul II. 2000z, Pope wearing white.

1991, June 1 Litho. *Perf. 11½x11*
3041 A965 1000z multicolored .30 .20
3042 A965 2000z multicolored .70 .30

1991, June 21 Litho. *Perf. 11½*
3043 A966 2000z multicolored .60 .25

Antarctic Treaty, 30th anniv.

Polish Paper Industry, 500th Anniv. A967

1991, July 8
3044 A967 2500z lake & gray .75 .30

Victims of Stalin — A968

1991, July 29 Litho. *Perf. 11½x12*
3045 A968 2500z black & red .75 .30

Souvenir Sheet

Pope John Paul II — A969

1991, Aug. 15 Photo. *Perf. 11½x11*
3046 A969 3500z multicolored 1.00 .50

Basketball, Cent. — A970

1991, Aug. 19 Litho. *Perf. 11x11½*
3047 A970 2500z multicolored .75 .30

Leon Wyczolkowski (1852-1936), painter — A971

1991, Sept. 7 Photo. *Perf. 11½x12*
3048 A971 3000z olive brown .80 .40
a. Sheet of 4 4.50 4.50

16th Polish Philatelic Exhibition, Bydgoszcz '91.

Kazimierz Twardowski (1866-1938) — A972

1991, Oct. 10 *Perf. 11x11½*
3049 A972 2500z sepia & blk .60 .30

Butterflies — A973

1991, Nov. 16 Litho. *Perf. 12½*
3050 A973 1000z Papilio machaon .20 .20
3051 A973 1000z Mormonia sponsa .20 .20
3052 A973 1500z Vanessa cardui .30 .20
3053 A973 1500z Iphiclides podalirius .30 .20
3054 A973 2500z Panaxia dominula .50 .30
3055 A973 2500z Nymphalis io .50 .30
a. Block of 6, #3050-3055 1.75 1.00

Souvenir Sheet

3056 A973 15,000z Aporia crataegi 4.00 4.00

No. 3056 has a holographic image on the stamp and comes se-tenant with a Phila Nippon '91 label. The image may be affected by soaking in water. Varieties such as missing hologram, double and shifted images, and imperfs exist.

On Jan. 15, 1994, the Polish postal administration demonetized No. 3056.

Nativity Scene, by Francesco Solimena A974

1991, Nov. 25 Photo. *Perf. 11*
3057 A974 1000z multicolored .30 .20

Polish Armed Forces at Tobruk, 50th Anniv. — A975

1991, Dec. 10 Photo. *Perf. 11½*
3058 A975 2000z Gen. Stanislaw Kopanski .60 .30

A976

A977

World War II Commanders: 2000z, Brig. Gen. Michal Tokarzewski-Karaszewicz (1893-1964). 2500z, Gen. Kazimierz Sosukowski (1885-1969). 3000z, Gen. Stefan Rowecki (1895-1944). 5000z, Gen. Tadeusz Komorowski (1895-1966). 6500z, Brig. Gen. Leopold Okulicki (1898-1946).

1991, Dec. 20 Litho.
3059 A976 2000z vermilion & blk .40 .20
3060 A976 2500z violet bl & lake .60 .30
3061 A976 3000z magenta & dk bl .75 .40
3062 A976 5000z olive & brn 1.25 .60
3063 A976 6500z brn org & brn 1.50 1.00
Nos. 3059-3063 (5) 4.50 2.50

1991, Dec. 30 Photo. *Perf. 12x11½*

Boy Scouts in Poland, 80th anniv.: 1500z, Lord Robert Baden-Powell, founder of Boy Scouts. 2000z, Andrzej Malkowski (1889-1919), founder of Boy Scouts in Poland. 2500z, Scout standing guard, 1920. 3500z, Soldier scout, 1944.

3064 A977 1500z multicolored .45 .20
3065 A977 2000z multicolored .55 .25
3066 A977 2500z multicolored .70 .35
3067 A977 3500z multicolored 1.00 .55
Nos. 3064-3067 (4) 2.70 1.35

Royalty Type of 1986

Designs: 1500z, Kazimierz II Sprawiedliwy. 2000z, Leszek Bialy.

Photo. & Engr.

1992, Jan. 15 *Perf. 11*
3068 A875 1500z olive green & brn .25 .20
3069 A875 2000z gray blue & blk .30 .20

Paintings A978

Paintings (self-portraits except for 2200z) by: 700z, Sebastien Bourdon. 1000z, Sir Joshua Reynolds. 1500z, Sir Gottfried Kneller. 2000z, Murillo. 2200z, Rubens. 3000z, Diego de Silva y Velazquez.

1992, Jan. 16 Photo.
3070 A978 700z multicolored .20 .20
3071 A978 1000z multicolored .20 .20
3072 A978 1500z multicolored .25 .20
3073 A978 2000z multicolored .30 .20
3074 A978 2200z multicolored .30 .20
3075 A978 3000z multicolored .45 .25
Nos. 3070-3075 (6) 1.70 1.25

1992 Winter Olympics, Albertville A979

1992, Feb. 8 Litho. *Perf. 11x11½*
3076 A979 1500z Skiing .25 .20
3077 A979 2500z Hockey .35 .20

See Nos. 3095-3098.

Tadeusz Manteuffel (1902-1970), Historian A980

1992, Mar. 5 Photo. *Perf. 11½x11*
3078 A980 2500z brown .95 .40

Famous Poles A981

Designs: 1500z, Nicolaus Copernicus, astronomer. 2000z, Frederic Chopin, composer. 2500z, Henryk Sienkiewicz, novelist. 3500z, Marie Sklodowska Curie, scientist. 5000z, Casimir Funk, biochemist.

1992, Mar. 5 Litho. *Perf. 11x11½*

3079	A981	1500z multicolored	.20	.20
3080	A981	2000z multicolored	.30	.25
3081	A981	2500z multicolored	.50	.40
3082	A981	3500z multicolored	1.00	.50
		Nos. 3079-3082 (4)	2.00	1.35

Souvenir Sheet

3083	A981	5000z multicolored	1.50	.60

Expo '92, Seville (#3083).

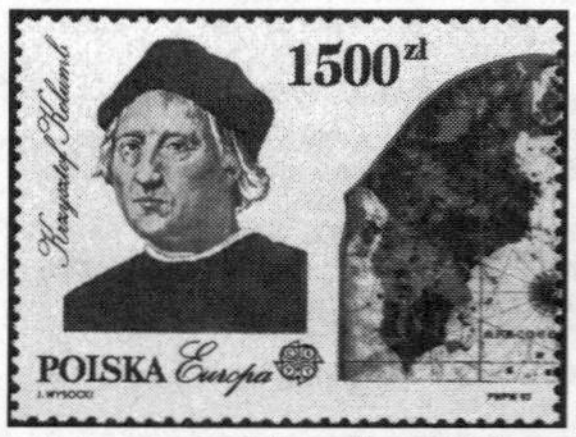

Discovery of America, 500th Anniv. — A982

1992, May 5

3084	A982	1500z Columbus, chart	.50	.25
3085	A982	3000z Chart, Santa Maria	1.00	.50
a.		Pair, #3084-3085	1.75	.75

Europa.

Waterfalls A983

1992, June 1 Litho. *Perf. 11½*

3086	A983	2000z Pstrag (trout)	.35	.20
3087	A983	2500z Zimorodek (kingfisher)	.45	.20
3088	A983	3000z Jelec (whiting)	.50	.25
3089	A983	3500z Pluszcz	.60	.25
		Nos. 3086-3089 (4)	1.90	.90

Order of Virtuti Militari, Bicent. A984

Designs: 1500z, Prince Jozef Poniatowski (1763-1813). 3000z, Marshal Jozef Pilsudski (1867-1935). No. 3092, Black Madonna of Czestochowa.

1992, June 18 *Perf. 11*

3090	A984	1500z multi	.25	.20
3091	A984	3000z multi	.50	.25

Souvenir Sheet

Imperf

3092	A984	20,000z multi	3.50

No. 3092 contains one 39x60mm stamp.

Children's Drawings of Love — A985

1500z, Heart between woman and man. 3000z, Butterfly, animals with sun and rain.

1992, June 26 Litho. *Perf. 11½x11*

3093	A985	1500z multicolored	.25	.20
3094	A985	3000z multicolored	.50	.25
a.		Pair, #3093-3094	.80	.35

Olympics Type of 1992

1992, July 25 Litho. *Perf. 11x11½*

3095	A979	1500z Fencing	.30	.20
3096	A979	2000z Boxing	.40	.20
3097	A979	2500z Sprinting	.45	.25
3098	A979	3000z Cycling	.75	.40
		Nos. 3095-3098 (4)	1.90	1.05

1992 Summer Olympics, Barcelona.

Souvenir Sheet

OLYMPHILEX '92, Barcelona — A986

1992, July 29

3099	A986	20,000z Runners	4.00	2.50

Exists imperf.

Janusz Korczak (1879-1942), Physician, Concentration Camp Victim — A987

1992, Aug. 5 Photo. *Perf. 11x11½*

3100	A987	1500z multicolored	.35	.20

Polish Emigrants Assoc. World Meeting — A988

1992, Aug. 19 *Perf. 12x11½*

3101	A988	3000z multicolored	.70	.35

World War II Combatants World Meeting — A989

1992, Aug. 14 *Perf. 11½x11*

3102	A989	3000z multicolored	.75	.40

Stefan Cardinal Wyszynski (1901-1981) — A990

3000z, Pope John Paul II embracing person.

1992, Aug. 15 Litho.

3103	A990	1500z multicolored	.40	.20
3104	A990	3000z multicolored	.85	.40
a.		Block of 2, #3103-3104 + 2 labels	1.25	

6th World Youth Cong., Czestochowa (#3104).

Adampol, Polish Village in Turkey, 150th Anniv. A991

1992, Sept. 15 Photo. *Perf. 11x11½*

3105	A991	3500z multicolored	.85	.40

World Post Day — A992

1992, Oct. 9 *Perf. 11½x11*

3106	A992	3500z multicolored	.85	.40

Bruno Schulz (1892-1942), Author — A993

1992, Oct. 26 Litho. *Perf. 11x11½*

3107	A993	3000z multicolored	.70	.35

Polish Sculptures, Natl. Museum, Warsaw A994

Designs: 2000z, Seated Girl, by Henryk Wicinski. 2500z, Portrait of Tytus Czyzewski, by Zbigniew Pronaszko. 3000z, Polish Nike, by Edward Wittig. 3500z, The Nude, by August Zamoyski.

1992, Oct. 29 *Perf. 11½*

3108	A994	2000z multicolored	.55	.30
3109	A994	2500z multicolored	.70	.35
3110	A994	3000z multicolored	.80	.40
3111	A994	3500z multicolored	.95	.50
a.		Souvenir sheet of 4, #3108-3111	3.00	1.50
		Nos. 3108-3111 (4)	3.00	1.55

Polska '93 (#3111a).

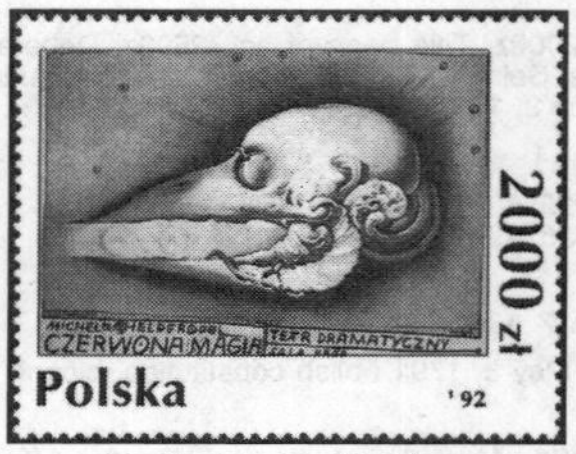

Posters — A995

Designs: 1500z, 10th Theatrical Summer in Zamosc, by Jan Mlodozeniec, vert. 2000z, Red Magic, by Franciszek Starowieyski. 2500z, Circus, by Waldemar Swierzy, vert. 3500z, Mannequins, by Henryk Tomaszewski.

1992, Oct. 30 *Perf. 13½*

3112	A995	1500z multicolored	.35	.20
3113	A995	2000z multicolored	.45	.25
3114	A995	2500z multicolored	.60	.30
3115	A995	3500z multicolored	.80	.40
		Nos. 3112-3115 (4)	2.20	1.15

Illustrations by Edward Lutczyn A996

Designs: 1500z, Girl using snake as jump rope. 2000z, Boy on rocking horse with rockers reversed. 2500z, Boy using bird as arrow. 3500z, Girl with ladder, wind-up giraffe with keys on back.

1992, Nov. 16 Photo. *Perf. 11*

3116	A996	1500z multicolored	.30	.20
3117	A996	2000z multicolored	.40	.20
3118	A996	2500z multicolored	.50	.25
3119	A996	3500z multicolored	.65	.30
		Nos. 3116-3119 (4)	1.85	.95

Polska '93.

Home Army A997

1992, Nov. 20 Litho. *Perf. 13½*

3120	A997	1500z shown	.30	.20
3121	A997	3500z Soldiers, diff.	.65	.30
a.		Pair, #3120-3121	.95	.50

Souvenir Sheet

3122	A997	20,000z +500z "WP AK," vert.	4.00	2.00

Christmas A998

1992, Nov. 25 Photo. *Perf. 11½*

3123	A998	1000z multicolored	.25	.20

A999

A1000

1992, Dec. 5 Photo. *Perf. 11½x11*
3124 A999 1500z Wheat stalks .40 .20
3125 A999 3500z Food products 1.00 .50

Intl. Conference on Nutrition, Rome.

1992, Dec. 10 Litho.
3126 A1000 3000z multicolored .70 .35

Postal Agreement with the Sovereign Military Order of Malta, Aug. 1, 1991.

Natl. Arms — A1001

1992, Dec. 14 Photo. *Perf. 12x11½*
3127 A1001 2000z 1295 .55 .30
3128 A1001 2500z 15th cent. .70 .35
3129 A1001 3000z 18th cent. .85 .40
3130 A1001 3500z 1919 1.00 .45
3131 A1001 5000z 1990 1.40 .65
Nos. 3127-3131 (5) 4.50 2.15

Polish Philatelic Society, Cent. A1002

1993, Jan. 6 Photo. *Perf. 11½*
3132 A1002 1500z multicolored .50 .25

A1003

A1004

1993, Feb. 5 *Perf. 11½x11*
3133 A1003 3000z multicolored 1.00 .50

1993 Winter University Games, Zakopane.

1993, Feb. 14

Design: I Love You.

3134 A1004 1500z shown .50 .25
3135 A1004 3000z Heart on envelope 1.00 .50

Amber — A1005

Various pieces of amber.

1993, Jan. 29 Litho. *Perf. 13½*
3136 A1005 1500z multicolored .40 .20
3137 A1005 2000z multicolored .55 .30
3138 A1005 2500z multicolored .70 .35
3139 A1005 3000z multicolored .85 .40
Nos. 3136-3139 (4) 2.50 1.25

Souvenir Sheet

3140 A1005 20,000z Necklace, map, horiz. 4.00 3.00

Polska '93 (#3140).

Royalty Type of 1986

Designs: 1500z, Wladyslaw Laskonogi. 2000z, Henryk I Brodaty (1201-38). 2500z, Konrad I Mazowiecki. 3000z, Boleslaw V Wstydliwy.

Photo. & Engr.

1993, Mar. 25 *Perf. 11*
3141 A875 1500z yel grn & brn .40 .20
3142 A875 2000z red vio & ind .55 .30
3143 A875 2500z gray & black .70 .35
3144 A875 3000z yel brn & brn .85 .40
Nos. 3141-3144 (4) 2.50 1.25

#3144 printed with se-tenant label for Polska '93.

Battle of the Arsenal, 50th Anniv. — A1006

1993, Mar. 26 Photo. *Perf. 11½*
3145 A1006 1500z multicolored .40 .20

Intl. Medieval Knights' Tournament, Golub-Dobrzyn — A1007

Various knights on horseback.

1993, Mar. 29 *Perf. 11x11½*
3146 A1007 1500z multicolored .40 .20
3147 A1007 2000z multicolored .55 .30
3148 A1007 2500z multicolored .70 .35
3149 A1007 3500z multicolored .90 45
Nos. 3146-3149 (4) 2.55 1.28

City of Szczecin, 750th Anniv. A1008

1993, Apr. 3 Litho. *Perf. 11½x11*
3150 A1008 1500z multicolored .40 .20

Warsaw Ghetto Uprising, 50th Anniv. — A1009

1993, Apr. 19 Litho. *Perf. 14*
3151 A1009 4000z gray, blk & yel 1.10 .60

See Israel No. 1163.

Europa — A1010

Contemporary art by: No. 3152, A. Szapocznikow and J. Lebenstein. No. 3153, S. Gierowski and B. Linke.

1993, Apr. 30 Photo. *Perf. 11x11½*
3152 A1010 1500z multicolored .30 .20
3153 A1010 4000z multicolored .70 .40
a. Pair, #3152-3153 1.00 .60

Polish Parliament (Sejm), 500th Anniv. — A1011

1993, May 2 Photo. *Perf. 11*
3154 A1011 2000z multicolored .55 .30

Death of Francesco Nullo, 130th Anniv. — A1012

1993, May 5 Litho. *Perf. 11x11½*
3155 A1012 2500z multicolored .70 .35

Souvenir Sheet

Legend of the White Eagle — A1013

1993, May 7 Engr. *Perf. 13½*
3156 A1013 50,000z dark brn 9.00 5.00

Polska '93.

Cadets of Second Polish Republic — A1014

1993, May 21 Litho. *Perf. 11x11½*
3157 A1014 2000z multicolored .55 .30

Nicolaus Copernicus (1473-1543) — A1015

1993, May 24
3158 A1015 2000z multicolored .55 .30

Kornel Makuszymski, 40th Death Anniv. — A1016

Illustrations: 1500z, Lion, monkey. 2000z, Goat walking. 3000z, Monkey. 5000z, Goat riding bird.

1993, June 1
3159 A1016 1500z multicolored .40 .20
3160 A1016 2000z multicolored .55 .30
3161 A1016 3000z multicolored .85 .40
3162 A1016 5000z multicolored 1.40 .70
Nos. 3159-3162 (4) 3.20 1.60

Pine Cone Type of 1991

1993, June 30 Photo. *Perf. 12x11½*
3163 A956 10,000z Pinus cembra 1.75 .75
3164 A956 20,000z Pinus sylvestris 2.75 1.75

Birds — A1017

1993, July 15 Litho. *Perf. 11½*
3165 A1017 1500z Passer montanus .25 .20
3166 A1017 2000z Motacilla alba .30 .20
3167 A1017 3000z Dendrocopos syriacus .50 .25
3168 A1017 4000z Carduelis carduelis .65 .30
3169 A1017 5000z Sturnus vulgaris .80 .40
3170 A1017 6000z Pyrrhula pyrrhula .95 .50
Nos. 3165-3170 (6) 3.45 1.85

Polish Natl. Anthem, Bicent. A1018

1993, July 20 Photo. *Perf. 11x11½*
3171 A1018 1500z multicolored .25 .20

See No. 3206.

Madonna and Child A1019

Designs: 1500z, Stone carving from Basilica, Lesna Podlaska. 2000z, Statue, Swieta Lipska.

Perf. 11x11½ Syncopated Type A

1993, Aug. 15

3172 A1019 1500z multicolored .20 .20
3173 A1019 2000z multicolored .25 .20

World Post Day — A1020

Photo. & Engr.

1993, Oct. 9 ***Perf. 11½x11***

3174 A1020 2500z multicolored .30 .20

Polish Parachute Brigade A1021

Perf. 11x11½, Syncopated Type A

1993, Sept. 25 **Photo.**

3175 A1021 1500z multicolored .25 .20

Death of St. Hedwig (Jadwiga), 750th Anniv. — A1022

1993, Oct. 14 **Litho.** ***Perf. 14***

3176 A1022 2500z multicolored .35 .20

See Germany No. 1816.

35th Intl. Jazz Jamboree — A1023

Perf. 11½ Syncopated Type A

1993, Sept. 27 **Litho.**

3177 A1023 2000z multicolored .25 .20

Souvenir Sheet

Election of Pope John Paul II, 15th Anniv. — A1024

1993, Oct. 16

3178 A1024 20,000z multicolored 3.00 2.00

A1025

A1026

1993, Nov. 11

3179 A1025 4000z Eagle, crown .50 .25

Souvenir Sheet

3180 A1025 20,000z Dove 2.75 1.40

Independence, 75th anniv. No. 3180 has a continuous design.

1993, Nov. 25

3181 A1026 1500z multicolored .25 .20

Christmas.

Posters A1027

Designs: 2000z, "Come and see Polish mountains." 5000z, Alban Berg Wozzeck.

1993, Dec. 10

3182 A1027 2000z multicolored .30 .20
3183 A1027 5000z multicolored .65 .30

See Nos. 3203-3204, 3259-3260.

"I Love You" — A1028

A1029

Perf. 11½x11 Syncopated Type A

1994, Jan. 14 **Litho.**

3184 A1028 1500z multicolored .25 .20

1994, Feb. 12 **Photo.** ***Perf. 11½x11***

3185 A1029 2500z Cross-country skiing .30 .20
3186 A1029 5000z Ski jumping .60 .30

Souvenir Sheet

3187 A1029 10,000z Downhill skiing 1.50 1.50

1994 Winter Olympics, Lillehammer. Intl. Olympic Committee, cent. (#2187).

Kosciuszko Insurrection, Bicent. — A1030

Perf. 11½x11 Syncopated Type A

1994, Mar. 24 **Photo.**

3188 A1030 2000z multicolored .30 .20

Zamosc Academy, 400th Anniv. — A1031

1994, Mar. 15

3189 A1031 5000z brn, blk & gray .65 .30

Gen. Jozef Bem (1794-1850) — A1032

Perf. 11½ Syncopated Type A

1994, Mar. 14

3190 A1032 5000z multicolored .65 .30

Royalty Type of 1986 with Denomination at Bottom

Photo. & Engr.

1994, Apr. 15 ***Perf. 11***

3191 A875 2500z Leszek Czarny .30 .20
3192 A875 5000z Przemysl II .60 .30

Inventions A1033

Europa: 2500z, Petroleum lamp, invented by I. Lukasiewicz (1822-82). 6000z, Astronomical sighting device, with profile of Copernicus (1473-1543).

Perf. 11½x11 Syncopated Type A

1994, Apr. 30 **Litho.**

3193 A1033 2500z multicolored .45 .25
3194 A1033 6000z multicolored .80 .50

St. Mary's Sanctuary A1034

4000z, Our Lady of Kalwaria Zebrzydowska.

Perf. 11½x11 Syncopated Type A

1994, May 16 **Litho.**

3195 A1034 4000z multicolored .55 .25

Battle of Monte Cassino, 50th Anniv. A1035

Perf. 11x11½ Syncopated Type A

1994, May 18

3196 A1035 6000z multicolored .80 .40

Traditional Dances A1036

Perf. 11½ Syncopated Type A

1994, May 25

3197 A1036 3000z Mazurka .35 .20
3198 A1036 4000z Goralski .50 .25
3199 A1036 9000z Krakowiak 1.25 .60
Nos. 3197-3199 (3) 2.10 1.05

ILO, 75th Anniv. A1037

Perf. 11½x11 Syncopated Type A

1994, June 7 **Litho.**

3200 A1037 6000z multicolored .75 .35

Polish Electricians Assoc., 75th Anniv. A1038

Perf. 11x11½ Syncopated Type A

1994, June 10

3201 A1038 4000z multicolored .55 .30

1994 World Soccer Cup Championships, US — A1039

Perf. 11½x11 Syncopated Type A

1994, June 17
3202 A1039 6000z multicolored .75 .40

Poster Art Type of 1993

4000z, Mr. Fabre, by Wiktor Gorka. 6000z, VIII OISTAT Congress, by Hubert Hilscher, horiz.

Perf. 11x11½, 11½x11 Syncopated Type A

1994, July 4 Litho.
3203 A1027 4000z multicolored .60 .30
3204 A1027 6000z multicolored .90 .45

Florian Znaniecki (1882-1958), Sociologist A1040

Perf. 11½ Syncopated Type A

1994, July 15 Litho.
3205 A1040 9000z multicolored 1.10 .55

Polish Natl. Anthem Type of 1993

Design: 2500z, Battle of Raclawice, 1794.

1994, July 20 Photo. *Perf. 11x11½*
3206 A1018 2500z multicolored .35 .20

A1042

A1043

Perf. 11½x11 Syncopated Type A

1994, Aug. 1 Litho.
3207 A1042 2500z Natl. arms .35 .20

Warsaw Uprising, 50th anniv.

1994, Aug. 16
3208 A1043 4000z PHILAKOREA '94 .50 .25

Stamp Day.

Basilica of St. Brigida, Gdansk A1044

1994, Aug. 28
3209 A1044 4000z multicolored .50 .25

Modern Olympic Games, Cent. A1045

Perf. 11x11½ Syncopated Type A

1994, Sept. 5
3210 A1045 4000z multicolored .70 .35

Krzysztof Komeda (1931-69), Jazz Muscian — A1046

Perf. 11½ Syncopated Type A

1994, Sept. 22 Litho.
3211 A1046 6000z multicolored .70 .35

Aquarium Fish — A1047

Designs: No. 3212a, Ancistrus dolichopterus. b, Pterophyllum scalare. c, Xiphophorus helleri, paracheirodon innesi. d, Poecilia reticulata.

Perf. 11½x11 Syncopated Type A

1994, Sept. 28 Litho.
3212 Strip of 4 2.00 1.50
a.-d. A1047 4000z any single .50 .40

World Post Day — A1048

1994, Oct. 9
3213 A1048 4000z Postal Arms, 1858 .50 .25

St. Maximilian Kolbe (1894-1941), Concentration Camp Victim — A1049

1994, Oct. 24 Photo. *Perf. 11x11½*
3214 A1049 2500z multicolored .35 .20

Pigeons A1050

a, Mewka polska. b, Krymka biatostacka. c, Srebrniak polski. d, Sokot gdanski. 10,000z, Polski golab pocztowy.

Perf. 11x11½ Syncopated Type A

1994, Oct. 28 Litho.
3215 Block of 4 2.25 1.10
a.-b. A1050 4000z any single .45 .20
c.-d. A1050 6000z any single .65 .30

Souvenir Sheet

3216 A1050 10,000z multicolored 1.25 .60

Christmas A1051

Perf. 11x11½ Syncopated Type A

1994, Nov. 25 Litho.
3217 A1051 2500z multicolored .35 .20

European Union A1052

1994, Dec. 15
3218 A1052 6000z multicolored .75 .35

Love Stamp — A1053

Perf. 11½x11 Syncopated Type A

1995, Jan. 31 Litho.
3219 A1053 35g dk bl & rose car .40 .20

Hydro-Meteorological Service, 75th Anniv. — A1054

Perf. 11x11½ Syncopated Type A

1995, Jan. 31
3220 A1054 60g multicolored .50 .25

Poland's Renewed Access to the Sea, 75th Anniv. A1055

1995, Feb. 10
3221 A1055 45g multicolored .50 .25

Polish Royalty Type of 1986 with Denomination at Bottom

Photo. & Engr.

1995, Feb. 28 *Perf. 11*
3222 A875 35g Waclaw II .40 .20
3223 A875 45g Wladyslaw I Lokietek .45 .25
3224 A875 60g Kazimierz III, the Great .65 .30
3225 A875 80g Ludwik Wegierski .80 .40
Nos. 3222-3225 (4) 2.30 1.15

St. John of God (1495-1550), Initiator of Order — A1056

Perf. 12x11½ Syncopated Type A

1995, Mar. 8 Litho.
3226 A1056 60g multicolored .70 .35

Easter Eggs A1057

Each stamp showing various designs on 3 eggs.

Perf. 11½ Syncopated Type A

1995, Mar. 16

Background Color

3227 A1057 35g dull red .35 .20
3228 A1057 35g violet .35 .20
3229 A1057 45g bright blue .45 .25
3230 A1057 45g blue green .45 .25
Nos. 3227-3230 (4) 1.60 .90

Pinecone Type of 1991

1995, Mar. 27 Photo. *Perf. 11½*
3231 A956 45g Larix decidua .45 .25
3232 A956 80g Pinus mugo .80 .40

Katyn Forest Massacre, 55th Anniv. A1058

Perf. 11½ Syncopated Type A

1995, Apr. 13 Litho.
3233 A1058 80g multicolored .85 .45

Europa A1060

Perf. 11x11½ Syncopated Type A

1995, Apr. 28 Litho.
3234 A1060 35g shown .35 .25
3235 A1060 80g Flowers in helmet .85 .50

Ruturn of Western Polish Territories, 50th Anniv. — A1061

Perf. 11½ Syncopated Type A

1995, May 6 Litho.
3236 A1061 45g multicolored .50 .25

Pope John Paul II, 75th Birthday
A1062

Perf. 11½ Syncopated Type A

1995, May 18 **Litho.**

3237 A1062 80g multicolored .85 .45

Groteska Theatre of Fairy Tales, 50th Anniv.
A1063

Designs: No. 3238, Two performing. No. 3239, Stage scene. No. 3240, Puppet leaning on barrel, vert. No. 3241, Character holding flower, vert.

1995, May 25

3238 A1063 35g multicolored .35 .20
3239 A1063 35g multicolored .35 .20
a. Pair, #3238-3239 .70 .35
3240 A1063 45g multicolored .50 .25
3241 A1063 45g multicolored .50 .25
a. Pair, #3240-3241 1.00 .50
Nos. 3238-3241 (4) 1.70 .90

Polish Railways, 150th Anniv.
A1064

Designs: 35g, Warsaw-Vienna steam train, 1945. 60g, Combustion fuel powered train, 1927. 80g, Electric train, 1936. 1z, Euro City Sobieski, Warsaw-Vienna, 1992.

1995, June 9

3242 A1064 35g multicolored .35 .20
3243 A1064 60g multicolored .65 .30
a. Pair, #3242-3243 1.00 .50
3244 A1064 80g multicolored .85 .45
3245 A1064 1z multicolored 1.10 .55
a. Pair, #3244-3245 2.00 1.00
Nos. 3242-3245 (4) 2.95 1.50

UN, 50th Anniv.
A1065

Perf. 11½ Syncopated Type A

1995, June 26 **Litho.**

3246 A1065 80g multicolored .90 .45

Handlowy Bank, Warsaw, 125th Anniv. — A1066

1995, June 30

3247 A1066 45g multicolored .50 .25

Polish Peasants' Movement, Cent.
A1067

Perf. 11½ Syncopated Type A

1995, July 13 **Litho.**

3248 A1067 45g multicolored .50 .25

Polish Natl. Anthem, Bicent.
A1068

1995, July 20 **Photo.** ***Perf. 11x11½***

3249 A1068 35g multicolored .40 .20

Deciduous Trees — A1069

1995, July 31 ***Perf. 12x11½***

3250 A1069 B Quercus petraea .40 .20
3251 A1069 A Sorbus aucuparia .50 .25

On day of issue #3250 was valued at 35g; #3551at 45g.

St. Mary of Consolation, Holy Trinity and All Saints Basilica, Lezajsk
A1070

Perf. 11½ Syncopated Type A

1995, Aug. 2 **Litho.**

3252 A1070 45g multicolored .45 .20

Battle of Warsaw, 75th Anniv.
A1071

Design: 45g, Jósef Pilsudski (1867-1935).

1995, Aug. 14

3253 A1071 45g multicolored .45 .20

Horse-Equipage Driving World Championships, Poznan — A1072

Designs: 60g, Horses pulling carriage, men in formal attire. 80g, Marathon race through water, around pylons.

Perf. 11½ Syncopated Type A

1995, Aug. 23 **Litho.**

3254 A1072 60g multicolored .65 .30
3255 A1072 80g multicolored .85 .45
a. Pair, #3254-3255 1.50 .75

18th All Polish Philatelic Exhibition, Warsaw
A1073

Designs: 35g, Warsaw Technical University, School of Architecture. 1z, Warsaw Castle Place, Old Town, horiz.

Perf. 11½ Syncopated Type A

1995, Aug. 30 **Litho.**

3256 A1073 35g multicolored .35 .20

Souvenir Sheet

3257 A1073 1z multicolored 1.10 .55

11th World Congress of Space Flight Participants, Warsaw
A1074

Perf. 11½ Syncopated Type A

1995, Sept. 10 **Litho.**

3258 A1074 80g multicolored .80 .40

Poster Art Type of 1993

35g, The Crazy Locomotive, by Jan Sawka. 45g, The Wedding, by Eugeniusz Get Stankiewicz.

Perf. 11½ Syncopated Type A

1995, Sept. 27 **Litho.**

3259 A1027 35g multicolored .35 .20
3260 A1027 45g multicolored .50 .25

13th Intl. Chopin Piano Festival
A1076

Perf. 11½ Syncopated Type A

1995, Oct. 1 **Litho.**

3261 A1076 80g Polonaise score .80 .40

A1077

A1078

World Post Day 45g, Postman in uniform, Polish Kingdom. 80g, Feather, wax seal of Stanislaw II Poniatowski.

1995, Oct. 9

3262 A1077 45g multicolored .45 .20
3263 A1077 80g multicolored .80 .40

1995, Oct. 26

3264 A1078 45g multicolored .45 .20

Acrobatic Sports World Championships, Wroclaw.

Janusz Groszkowski (1898-1984), Physicist — A1079

Perf. 11½ Syncopated Type A

1995, Nov. 10 **Litho.**

3265 A1079 45g multicolored .50 .25

Christmas — A1080

1995, Nov. 27

3266 35g Nativity .35 .20
3267 45g Magi, tree .50 .25
a. A1080 Pair, Nos. 3266-3267 .85 .45

No. 3267a is a continuous design.

Songbird Chicks
A1081

Designs: a, 35g, Parus caeruleus. b, 45g, Aegithalos caudatus. c, 60g, Lanius excubitor. d, 80g, Coccothraustes.

1995, Dec. 15

3268 A1081 Block of 4, #a.-d. 2.25 1.10

See No. 3377.

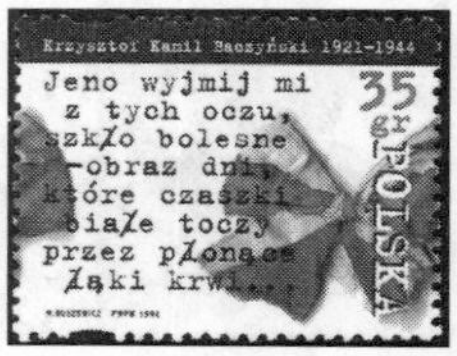

Krzysztof Kamil Baczynski (1921-44), Poet
A1082

Perf. 11½ Syncopated Type A

1996, Jan. 22 **Litho.**

3269 A1082 35g multicolored .35 .20

Love — A1083

1996, Jan. 31

3270 A1083 40g Cherries .40 .20

Architecture
A1084

40g, Romanesque style church, Inowlodz, 11-12th cent. 55g, Gothic syle, St. Virgin Mary's Church, Cracow, 14th cent. 70g, Renaissance period, St. Sigismundus Chapel of Cracow, Wawel Castle, 1519-33. 1z, Order of Holy Sacrament Nuns Baroque Church, Warsaw, 1688-92.

Perf. 11½ Syncopated Type A

1996, Feb. 27 **Litho.**

3271 A1084 40g multicolored .35 .20
3272 A1084 55g multicolored .50 .25
3273 A1084 70g multicolored .65 .30
3274 A1084 1z multicolored .90 .45
Nos. 3271-3274 (4) 2.40 1.20

Polish Sailing Ships A1085

Designs: a, 40g, Topmast schooner, "Oceania," 1985. b, 55c, Staysail schooner, "Zawisza Czarny," 1961. c, 70g, Schooner, "General Zaruski," 1939. d, 75g, Brig, "Fryderyk Chopin," 1992.

1996, Mar. 11

3275 A1085 Strip of 4, #a.-d. 2.20 1.10

Warsaw, Capital of Poland, 400th Anniv. A1086

1996, Mar. 18

3276 A1086 55g multicolored .55 .25

Signs of the Zodiac — A1087

1996 **Photo.** ***Perf. 12x11½***

3277 A1087 5g Aquarius .20 .20
3278 A1087 10g Pisces .20 .20
3279 A1087 20g Taurus .20 .20
3280 A1087 25g Gemini .25 .20
3281 A1087 30g Cancer .30 .20
3282 A1087 40g Virgo .40 .20
3283 A1087 50g Leo .50 .25
3284 A1087 55g Libra .55 .25
3285 A1087 70g Aries .65 .30
3286 A1087 1z Scorpio .95 .50
3287 A1087 2z Sagittarius 1.90 .95
3288 A1087 5z Capricorn 4.75 2.40
Nos. 3277-3288 (12) 10.85 5.85

Design will dissolve when soaked on at least three denominations, 5g, 20g and 25g, from the second printing which is on fluorescent paper.

Issued: 70g, 3/21; 20g, 4/21; 25g, 5/10; 30g, 5/20; 40g, 50g, 5/31; 55g, 6/10; 1z, 6/20; 2z, 6/28; 5z, 7/10; 5g, 7/19; 10g, 7/31.

Famous Women A1088

Europa: 40g, Hanka Ordonówa (1902-50), singer. 1z, Pola Negri (1896-1987), actress.

Perf. 11½ Syncopated Type A

1996, Apr. 30 **Litho.**

3289 A1088 40g multicolored .40 .25
3290 A1088 1z multicolored 1.00 .50

3rd Silesian Uprising, 75th Anniv. A1089

Perf. 11 ½ Syncopated Type A

1996, May 2 **Litho.**

3291 A1089 55g multicolored .50 .25

UNICEF, 50th Anniv. — A1090

Illustrations from tales of Jan Brzechwa: No. 3292, Cat and mouse. No. 3293. Man at table, waiters. No. 3294, People with "onion heads." No. 3295, Chef, duck, vegetables at table. No. 3296, Man talking to bird with human head. No. 3297, Fox standing in front of bears.

1996, May 31

3292 A1090 40g multicolored .35 .20
3293 A1090 40g multicolored .35 .20
3294 A1090 55g multicolored .50 .25
3295 A1090 55g multicolored .50 .25
3296 A1090 70g multicolored .65 .30
3297 A1090 70g multicolored .65 .30
Nos. 3292-3297 (6) 3.00 1.50

Drawings by Stanislaw Noakowski (1867-1928) A1091

Designs: 40g, Renaissance building. 55g, Renaissance bedroom. 70g, Gothic village church. 1z, Stanislaw August Library, 18th cent.

1996, June 28

3298 A1091 40g multicolored .35 .20
3299 A1091 55g multicolored .50 .25
3300 A1091 70g multicolored .65 .30
3301 A1091 1z multicolored .90 .45
Nos. 3298-3301 (4) 2.40 1.20

1996 Summer Olympic Games, Atlanta A1092

40g, Discus as medallion, vert. 55g, Tennis ball. 70g, Polish flag, Olympic rings. 1z, Tire & wheel of mountain bicycle, vert.

1996, July 5

3302 A1092 40g multicolored .35 .20
3303 A1092 55g multicolored .50 .25
3304 A1092 70g multicolored .65 .30
3305 A1092 1z multicolored .90 .45
Nos. 3302-3305 (4) 2.40 1.20

OLYMPHILEX '96, Atlanta — A1093

1996, July 5

3306 A1093 1z multicolored .90 .45

National Anthem, Bicent. A1094

1996, July 20 **Photo.** ***Perf. 11x11½***

3307 A1094 40g multicolored .35 .20

Madonna and Child, St. Mary's Ascension Church, Przeczyce A1095

Perf. 11½x11 Syncopated Type A

1996, Aug. 2 **Litho.**

3308 A1095 40g multicolored .40 .20

Royalty Type of 1986

Designs: 40g, Jadwiga. 55g, Wladyslaw II Jagiello. 70g, Wladyslaw II Warnenczyk. 1z, Kazimierz Jagiellonczyk.

1996, Aug. 29 **Engr.** ***Perf. 11***

3309 A875 40g olive brown & brown .40 .20
3310 A875 55g red violet & violet .55 .25
3311 A875 70g gray & black .65 .30
3312 A875 1z yellow green & green .95 .50
Nos. 3309-3312 (4) 2.55 1.25

Mountain Scenes, Tatra Natl. Park A1096

Perf. 11½ Syncopated Type A

1996, Sept. 5 **Litho.**

3313 A1096 40g Giewont .35 .20
3314 A1096 40g Krzesanica .35 .20
3315 A1096 55g Swinica .50 .25
3316 A1096 55g Koscielec .50 .25
3317 A1096 70g Rysy .65 .30
3318 A1096 70g Miguszowieckie Szczyty .65 .30
Nos. 3313-3318 (6) 3.00 1.50

Zbigniew Seifert (1946-79), Jazz Musician A1097

Perf. 11½ Syncopated Type A

1996, Sept. 25 **Litho.**

3319 A1097 70g multicolored .65 .30

Post and Telecommunications Museum, Wroclaw, 75th Anniv. — A1098

Paintings: 40g, Horse Exchange and Post Station, by M. Watorski. 1z+20g, Stagecoach in Jagniatkowo, by Prof. Täger.

1996, Oct. 9 **Photo.** ***Perf. 12x11½***

3320 A1098 40g multicolored .35 .20

Souvenir Sheet

Perf. 11x11½

3321 A1098 1z +20g multi 1.15 .60

Nos. 3321 contains one 43x31mm stamp.

Christmas A1099

Perf. 11½ Syncopated Type A

1996, Nov. 27 **Litho.**

3322 A1099 40g Santa in sleigh .40 .20
3323 A1099 55g Carolers .50 .25

Bison Bonasus A1100

1996, Dec. 4

3324 A1100 55g shown .50 .25
3325 A1100 55g Facing .50 .25
3326 A1100 55g Two animals .50 .25
3327 A1100 55g Adult male .50 .25
a. Strip of 4, #3324-3327 2.00 1.00

Wislawa Szymborska, 1996 Nobel Laureate in Literature A1101

1996, Dec. 10

3328 A1101 1z multicolored .95 .50

Queen of Hearts A1102

Perf. 11x11½ Syncopated Type A

1997, Jan. 14 **Litho.**

3329 A1102 B King of Hearts .40 .20
3330 A1102 A Queen of Hearts .50 .25
a. Pair, #3329-3330 .90 .45
Complete booklet, 4 #3330a 3.60

Nos. 3329-3330 sold for 40g and 55g, respectively, on day of issue.

Easter Traditions A1103

50g, Man, woman in traditional costumes holding palms. 60g, Decorating eggs. 80g, Blessing the Easter meal. 1.10z, Man pouring water on woman.

Perf. 11x11½ Syncopated Type A

1997, Mar. 14 **Litho.**

3331 A1103 50g multicolored .40 .20
3332 A1103 60g multicolored .50 .25
3333 A1103 80g multicolored .65 .30
3334 A1103 1.10z multicolored .90 .45
Nos. 3331-3334 (4) 2.45 1.20

A1104

St. Adalbert (955?-97) A1105

50g, St. Adalbert among heathen, horiz.

1997 Engr. *Perf. 11x11½x 11½x11*

3335 A1104	50g	brown	.50	.25
3336 A1104	60g	slate	.60	.30
3337 A1105	1.10z	purple	1.00	.50
Nos. 3335-3337 (3)			2.10	1.05

See Czech Republic No. 3012, Germany No. 1964, Hungary No. 3569, Vatican City No. 1040.

Issued: #3335-3336, 4/19; #3337, 4/23.

Stories and Legends A1106

Europa: 50g, shown. 1.10z, Mermaid.

Perf. 11½ Syncopated Type A

1997, May 5

3338 A1106	50g	multicolored	.50	.40
3339 A1106	1.10z	multicolored	1.00	.60

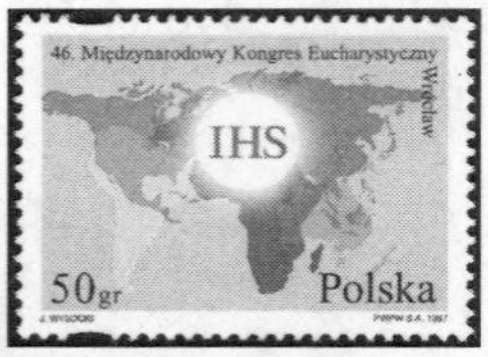

46th Eucharistic Congress — A1107

1997, May 6

3340 A1107	50g multicolored	.50	.25

Souvenir Sheet

Pope John Paul II — A1108

Perf. 11x11½ Syncopated Type A

1997, May 28

3341 A1108	1.10z multicolored	1.00	1.00

City of Gdansk, 1000th Anniv. — A1109

Design: 1.10z, View of city, horiz.

Perf. 11½x11, 11x11½

1997, Apr. 18 Engr.

3342 A1109	50g multicolored	.50	.25

Souvenir Sheet

3343 A1109	1.10z multicolored	1.10	.55

Polish Country Estates — A1110

1997 Photo. *Perf. 11½x12*

3344 A1110	50g	Lopusznej	.40	.30
3345 A1110	60g	Zyrzyna	.50	.40
3346 A1110	1.10z	Ozarowie	.75	.60
3347 A1110	1.70z	Tulowicach	1.10	1.00
3348 A1110	2.20z	Kuznocinie	1.40	1.25
3349 A1110	10z	Koszutach	6.50	5.00
Nos. 3344-3349 (6)			10.65	8.55

Issued: 50g, 60g, 4/26/97; 1.10z, 1.70z, 2.20z, 10z, 5/23/97.

See Nos. 3385-3390, 3463-3467, 3511-3514.

PACIFIC 97 — A1111

Design: San Francisco-Oakland Bay Bridge.

Perf. 11½ Syncopated Type A

1997, May 20 Litho.

3350 A1111	1.30z multicolored	1.00	.50

Bats A1113

50g, Plecotus auritus. 60g, Nyctalus noctula. 80g, Myotis myotis. 1.30z, Vespertilio murinus.

1997, May 30

3352 A1113	50g	multicolored	.45	.20
3353 A1113	60g	multicolored	.55	.25
3354 A1113	80g	multicolored	.70	.35
3355 A1113	1.30z	multicolored	1.15	.60
Nos. 3352-3355 (4)			2.85	1.40

Jagiellon University School of Theology, 600th Anniv. A1114

Painting by Jan Matejko.

1997, June 6 *Perf. 11*

3356 A1114	80g multicolored	.70	.35

Polish Settlement in Argentina, Cent. — A1115

Perf. 11½ Syncopated Type A

1997, June 6

3357 A1115	1.40z multicolored	1.25	.60

Paintings, by Juliusz Kossak (1824-99) — A1116

Designs: 50g, Man on horse, woman, child. 60g, Men on galloping horses, carriage. 80g, Feeding horses in stable. 1.10z, Man with horses.

1997, July 4 Photo. *Perf. 11*

3358 A1116	50g	multicolored	.45	.20
3359 A1116	60g	multicolored	.50	.25
3360 A1116	80g	multicolored	.70	.35
3361 A1116	1.10z	multicolored	.95	.50
Nos. 3358-3361 (4)			2.60	1.30

Polish Natl. Anthem, Bicent. A1117

Designs: 50g, People in city waving hats at Gen. Jan Henryk Dabrowski.

1.10z, Words to Natl. Anthem, Dabrowski.

1997, July 18 *Perf. 11x11½*

3362 A1117	50g multicolored	.45	.20

Souvenir Sheet

3363 A1117	1.10z multicolored	.95	.50

Pawel Edmund Strzelecki (1797-1873), Geographer — A1118

Perf. 11½ Syncopated Type A

1997, July 20 Litho.

3364 A1118	1.50z multicolored	1.30	.65

Virgin of Consolation, Church of the Virgin of Consolation and St. Michael Archangel, Gorka Duchowna A1119

Perf. 11½x11 Syncopated Type A

1997, Aug. 28

3365 A1119	50g multicolored	.45	.20

Royalty Type of 1986

Kings: 50g, Jan I Olbracht (1459-1501). 60g, Aleksander (1461-1506). 80g, Sigismundus I Stary (1467-48). 1.10z, Sigismundus II Augustus (1520-72).

1997, Sept. 22 Engr. *Perf. 11*

3366 A875	50g	brn & dk brn	.40	.20
3367 A875	60g	blue & dp brn	.50	.25
3368 A875	80g	grn & dk slate	.65	.35
3369 A875	1.10z	mag & dk mag	.90	.45
Nos. 3366-3369 (4)			2.45	1.25

Mieczyslaw Kosz (1944-73), Jazz Musician A1120

World Post Day A1121

Perf. 11½ Syncopated Type A

1997, Oct. 3 Litho.

3370 A1120	80g multicolored	.65	.35

1997, Oct. 9

3371 A1121	50g multicolored	.45	.20

Moscow '97 Intl. Philatelic Exhibition A1122

Perf. 11½ Syncopated Type B

1997, Oct. 13

3372 A1122	80g multicolored	.70	.35

Theater Poster Art — A1123

#3373, "Sam Pierze Radion," black cat becoming white cat, by T. Gronowski, 1926. #3374, "Szewcy" (Bootmakers), by R. Cieslewicz, 1971. #3375, "Goya," by W. Sadowski, 1983. #3376, "Maz i zona," by A. Pagowski, 1977.

Perf. 11x11½, 11½x11 Syncopated Type A

1997, Nov. 14 Litho.

3373 A1123	50g	multi	.55	.30
3374 A1123	50g	multi, vert.	.55	.30
3375 A1123	60g	multi, vert.	.65	.35
3376 A1123	60g	multi, vert.	.65	.35
Nos. 3373-3376 (4)			2.40	1.30

Chick Type of 1995

Designs: a, Tadorna tadorna. b, Mergus merganser. c, Gallinago gallinago. d, Gallinula chloropus.

Perf. 11½ Syncopated Type A

1997, Dec. 5

3377 A1081	50g Block of 4, #a.-d.	1.60	.80

Christmas A1124

50g, Nativity. 60g, Food, candles. 80g, Outdoor winter scene, star, church. 1.10z, Carolers.

Perf. 11½x11, 11x11½ Syncopated Type A

1997, Nov. 27

3378	A1124	50g multi, vert.	.35	.25
3379	A1124	60g multi	.50	.35
3380	A1124	80g multi	.75	.45
3381	A1124	1.10z multi, vert.	1.00	.60
		Nos. 3378-3381 (4)	2.60	1.65

A1125

A1126

Perf. 11½ Syncopated Type A

1998, Jan. 5 **Litho.**

3382	A1125	1.40z multicolored	.85	.50

1998 Winter Olympic Games, Nagano.

Perf. 12x11½ Syncopated Type A

1998, Jan. 14

Love Stamps: B, Face of dog, cat on shirt. A, Face of cat, dog on shirt.

3383	A1126	B multicolored	.35	.20
3384	A1126	A multicolored	.40	.20

Nos. 3383-3384 were valued at 55g and 65g, respectively, on day of issue.

Polish Country Estates Type of 1997

Designs: B, Gluchach. 55g, Oblegorku. A, Czarnolesie. 65g, Bronowicach. 90g, Oborach. 1.20z, Romanowie.

1998 **Photo.** ***Perf. 11½x12***

3385	A1110	B multicolored	.35	.20
3386	A1110	55g multicolored	.35	.20
3387	A1110	A multicolored	.40	.20
3388	A1110	65g multicolored	.40	.20
3389	A1110	90g multicolored	.55	.25
3390	A1110	1.20z multicolored	.70	.35
		Nos. 3385-3390 (6)	2.75	1.40

No. 3385 was valued at 55g, and No. 3387 was valued at 65g on day of issue.

Issued: B, A, 1/15; 55g, 65g, 90g, 1.20z, 3/3.

Easter — A1127

Perf. 11½ Syncopated Type A

1998, Mar. 12 **Litho.**

3391	A1127	55g shown	.35	.20
3392	A1127	65g Image of Christ	.40	.20

European Revolutionary Movements of 1848, 150th Anniv. — A1128

1998, Mar. 20 **Engr.** ***Perf. 11x11½***

3393	A1128	55g gray violet	.35	.20

Royalty Type of 1986

Designs: 55g, Henryk Walezy. 65g, Anna Jagiellonka. 80g, Stefan Batory. 90g, Zygmunt III.

1998, Mar. 31 ***Perf. 11***

3394	A875	55g multicolored	.35	.20
3395	A875	65g multicolored	.40	.20
3396	A875	80g multicolored	.45	.25
3397	A875	90g multicolored	.55	.25
		Nos. 3394-3397 (4)	1.75	.90

Protection of the Baltic Sea — A1129

Marine life: #3398, Halichoerus grypus. #3399, Pomatoschistus microps. #3400, Alosa fallax, syngnathus typhle. #3401, Acipenser sturio. #3402, Salmo salar. #3403, Phocoena phocoena.

1.20z, Halichoerus grypus.

Perf. 11½ Syncopated Type B

1998, Apr. 28 **Litho.**

3398	A1129	65g multicolored	.40	.20
3399	A1129	65g multicolored	.40	.20
3400	A1129	65g multicolored	.40	.20
3401	A1129	65g multicolored	.40	.20
3402	A1129	65g multicolored	.40	.20
3403	A1129	65g multicolored	.40	.20
a.		Strip of 6, #3398-3403	2.40	1.20

Souvenir Sheet

3404	A1129	1.20z multicolored	.70	.35

Israel '98 World Philatelic Exhibition, Tel Aviv — A1130

Perf. 11½ Syncopated Type A

1998, Apr. 30

3405	A1130	90g Israel No. 8, logo	.55	.25

Natl. Holidays and Festivals A1131

Europa: 55g, Logo of Warwaw Autumn, Intl. Festival of Contemporary Music. 1.20z, First bars of song, "Welcome the May Dawn," 3rd of May Constitution Day.

1998, May 5

3406	A1131	55g multicolored	.30	.30
3407	A1131	1.20z multicolored	.70	.70
a.		Pair, #3406-3407	1.00	1.00

Coronation of Longing Holy Mother — A1132

Perf. 11½x12 Syncopated Type A

1998, June 28 **Litho.**

3408	A1132	55g multicolored	.40	.20

Nikifor (Epifan Drowniak) (1895-1968), Artist — A1133

Paintings: 55g, "Triple Self-portrait." 65g, "Cracow Office." 1.20z, "Orthodox Church." 2.35z, "Ucrybów Station."

Perf. 11½ Syncopated Type A

1998, July 10 **Litho.**

3409	A1133	55g multicolored	.40	.30
3410	A1133	65g multicolored	.45	.35
3411	A1133	1.20z multicolored	.85	.60
3412	A1133	2.35z multicolored	1.60	1.25
		Nos. 3409-3412 (4)	3.30	2.50

Main Board of Statistics, 80th Anniv. A1134

Perf. 11x11½ Syncopated Type A

1998, July 13

3413	A1134	55g multicolored	.40	.20

15th Cent. Statue of Madonna and Child, Sejny Basilica A1135

Perf. 11½ Syncopated Type A

1998, Aug. 14

3414	A1135	55g multicolored	.40	.20

Warsaw Diocese, Bicent. A1136

1998, Aug. 28

3415	A1136	65g multicolored	.50	.25

Souvenir Sheet

17th Polish Philatelic Exhibition, Szczecin — A1137

View of city, 1624: a, People on raft, pier. b, Sailing ships, pier.

1998, Sept. 18 **Engr.** ***Perf. 11x11½***

3416	A1137	65g Sheet of 2, #a.-b.	.95	.45

Discovery of Radium and Polonium, Cent. A1138

Perf. 11½ Syncopated Type A

1998, Sept. 18 **Litho.**

3417	A1138	1.20z Pierre, Marie Curie	.90	.50

Mazowsze Song and Dance Ensemble, 50th Anniv. — A1139

Couple dancing, denomination at: No. 3418, LL. No. 3419, LR.

1998, Sept. 22

3418	65g multicolored	.45	.25
3419	65g multicolored	.45	.25
a.	A1139 Pair, #3418-3419	.90	.50

Mniszech Palace (Belgian Embassy), Warsaw, Bicent. A1140

Photo. & Engr.

1998, Sept. 28 ***Perf. 11½***

3420	A1140	1.20z multicolored	.90	.45

See Belgium No. 1706.

Sigismund III Vasa (1566-1632), King of Sweden and Poland — A1141

1998, Oct. 3 **Engr.** ***Perf. 11½x11***

3421	A1141	1.20z deep claret	.90	.45

See Sweden No. 2312.

World Stamp Day — A1142

Pontificate of John Paul II, 20th Anniv. — A1143

Perf. 11½x11 Syncopated Type A

1998, Oct. 9 **Litho.**

3422	A1142	65g multicolored	.45	.25

Perf. 11½x12 Syncopated Type A
1998, Oct. 16
3423 A1143 65g multicolored .45 .25

Independence, 80th Anniv. — A1144

Perf. 12x11½ Syncopated Type A
1998, Nov. 11
3424 A1144 65g multicolored .45 .25

Christmas
A1145

Paintings: 55g, Nativity scene. 65g, Adoration of the Magi.

1998, Nov. 27 Photo. ***Perf. 11½x11***
3425 A1145 55g multicolored .40 .20
3426 A1145 65g multicolored .45 .25

Universal Declaration of Human Rights, 50th Anniv.
A1146

Perf. 11x11½ Syncopated Type A
1998, Dec. 10 Litho.
3427 A1146 1.20z blue & dark blue .90 .45

Adam Mickiewicz (1798-1855), Poet — A1147

Scenes, quotations from poems: 55g, Maryla Wereszczakówna, flower, night landscape. 65g, Cranes flying over tomb of Maria Potocka. 90g, Burning candles, cross. 1.20z, Nobleman's house, flowers, uhlan's cap.
2.45z, Bust of Mickiewicz, by Jean David d'Angers.

Perf. 12x11½ Syncopated Type A
1998, Dec. 24
3428 A1147 55g multicolored .40 .20
3429 A1147 65g multicolored .45 .25
3430 A1147 90g multicolored .65 .35
3431 A1147 1.20z multicolored .90 .45
Nos. 3428-3431 (4) 2.40 1.25

Souvenir Sheet
3432 A1147 2.45z multicolored 1.75 .90

No. 3432 contains one 27x35mm stamp.

Polish Navy, 80th Anniv. (in 1998)
A1148

No. 3433, Destroyer ORP Piorun, 1942-46. No. 3434, Frigate ORP Piorun, 1994.

Perf. 11¼x11½ Syncopated Type A
1999, Jan. 4 Litho.
3433 A1148 55g multicolored .35 .20
3434 A1148 55g multicolored .35 .20
a. Pair, #3433-3434 .70 .40

Love Stamps
A1149

Perf. 11½x11¼ Syncopated Type A
1999, Feb. 5
3435 A1149 B Dominoes .40 .20
3436 A1149 A Dominoes, diff. .50 .25

Nos. 3535-3436 were valued at 55g and 65g, respectively, on day of issue.

Famous Polish Men
A1150

Designs: 1z, Ernest Malinowski (1818-99), constructor of Central Trans-Andean Railway, Peru. 1.60z, Rudolf Modrzejewski (Ralph Modjeski) (1861-1940), bridge builder.

Perf. 11½ Syncopated Type A
1999, Feb. 12
3437 A1150 1z multicolored .65 .35
3438 A1150 1.60z multicolored 1.10 .55

Easter — A1151

Scenes from Srudziadz Polyptych: 60g, Prayer in Ogrójec. 65g, Carrying cross. 1.40z, Resurrection.
1z, Tubadzin Pieta, 15th cent.

1999, Mar. 5 ***Perf. 11½x11¼***
3439 A1151 60g multicolored .40 .20
3440 A1151 65g multicolored .45 .20
3441 A1151 1z multicolored .65 .35
3442 A1151 1.40z multicolored .90 .45
Nos. 3439-3442 (4) 2.40 1.20

Souvenir Sheet

China 1999, World Philatelic Exhibition — A1152

Illustration reduced.

Perf. 11½x11¼ Syncopated Type A
1999, Mar. 31
3443 A1152 1.70z Ideogram, dragon 1.25 .65

Virgin Mary, Patron Saint of Soldiers
A1153

Perf. 11½x11¾ Syncopated Type A
1999, Apr. 2 Litho.
3444 A1153 60g shown .50 .25
3445 A1153 70g Katyn .60 .30

Characters from Works by Henryk Sienkiewicz — A1154

Perf. 11¾x11½ Syncopated Type B
1999, Apr. 6 Litho.
3446 A1154 70g Jan Skrzetuski .45 .25
3447 A1154 70g Onufry Zagloba .45 .25
3448 A1154 70g Longin Podbipieta .45 .25
3449 A1154 70g Bohun .45 .25
3450 A1154 70g Andrzej Kmicic .45 .25
3451 A1154 70g Michal Jerzy Wolodyjowski .45 .25
a. Block of 6, # 3446-3451 2.75 1.50

Poland's Admission to NATO — A1155

Perf. 11½ Syncopated Type B
1999, Apr. 22 Litho.
3452 A1155 70g multicolored .60 .30

Council of Europe, 50th Anniv. — A1156

Perf. 11½x11 Syncopated Type A
1999, May 5 Litho.
3453 A1156 1z multicolored .65 .35

Europa
A1157

Perf. 11½ Syncopated Type A
1999, May 5 Litho.
3454 A1157 1.40z multicolored .90 .75

Sports
A1158

Perf. 11½ Syncopated Type B
1999, June 1 Litho.
3455 A1158 60g Cycling .40 .20
3456 A1158 70g Snowboarding .45 .25
3457 A1158 1z Skateboarding .65 .35
3458 A1158 1.40z Roller blading .90 .45
Nos. 3455-3458 (4) 2.40 1.25

Visit of Pope John Paul II — A1159

Pope and: 60g, Church of the Virgin Mary, Cracow, crowd with Solidarity banners. 70g, Crowd with crosses. 1z, Crowd with flags. 1.40z, Eiffel Tower, Monument to Christ the Redeemer, Rio, Shrine of Our Lady of Fatima.

Perf. 11¾x11½ Syncopated Type A
1999, June 5 Litho.
3459 A1159 60g multicolored .40 .20
Complete booklet, 10 #3459 4.00
3460 A1159 70g multicolored .45 .25
Complete booklet, 10 #3460 4.50
3461 A1159 1z multicolored .65 .35
3462 A1159 1.40z multicolored .90 .45
Nos. 3459-3462 (4) 2.40 1.25

Country Estates Type of 1997
Perf. 11½x11¾
1999, June 15 Photo.
3463 A1110 70g Modlnicy .45 .35
3464 A1110 1z Krzeslawicach .65 .50
3465 A1110 1.40z Winnej Górze .90 .65
3466 A1110 1.60z Potoku Zlotym 1.10 .75
3467 A1110 1.85z Kasnej Dolnej 1.25 .90
Nos. 3463-3467 (5) 4.35 3.15

Versailles Treaty, 80th Anniv.
A1159a

Perf. 11¼x11½ Syncopated Type A
1999, June 29 Litho.
3467A A1159a 1.40z multi .90 .45

Depictions of the Virgin Mary — A1160

Designs: 60g, Painting from church in Rokitno. 70g, Crowned statue.

Perf. 11½x11¼ Syncopated Type A
1999, July 9 Litho.
3468 A1160 60g multi .40 .20
3469 A1160 70g multi .45 .25

Insects — A1161

Designs: No. 3470, Corixa punctata. No. 3471, Dytiscus marginalis. No. 3472, Perla marginata. No. 3473, Limnophilus. No. 3474, Anax imperator. No. 3475, Ephemera vulgata.

Perf. 11½x11¾ Syncopated Type B

1999, July 16 **Litho.**

3470	A1161	60g multi	.40	.30
3471	A1161	60g multi	.40	.30
3472	A1161	70g multi	.45	.30
3473	A1161	70g multi	.45	.30
3474	A1161	1.40z multi	.90	.60
3475	A1161	1.40z multi	.90	.60
		Nos. 3470-3475 (6)	3.50	2.40

Souvenir Sheet

Ksiaz Castle — A1162

Engr. (Margin Photo.)

1999, Aug. 14 ***Perf. 11¼x11***

3476	A1162	1z blue	.80	.40

Natl. Philatelic Exhibition, Walbrzych, Czeslaw Slania's 1001st stamp design

Polish-Ukrainian Cooperation in Nature Conservation — A1163

Designs: No. 3477, Cervus elaphus. No. 3478, Felis silvestris.

Perf. 11x11½ Syncopated Type A

1999, Sept. 22 **Litho.**

3477	A1163	1.40z multi	.90	.45
3478	A1163	1.40z multi	.90	.45
a.		Pair, #3477-3478	1.80	.90

See Ukraine No. 354.

Royalty Type of 1986 with Denomination at Bottom

Designs: 60g, Wladyslaw IV. 70g, Jan II Kazimierz. 1z, Michal Korybut Wisniowiecki. 1.40z, Jan III Sobieski.

Photo. & Engr.

1999, Sept. 25 ***Perf. 10¾x11***

3479	A875	60g olive & black	.40	.20
3480	A875	70g brn & dk brn	.45	.25
3481	A875	1z blue & black	.65	.30
3482	A875	1.40z lilac & claret	.90	.45
		Nos. 3479-3482 (4)	2.40	1.20

UPU, 125th Anniv., World Post Day A1164

Perf. 11¾x11½ Syncopated Type A

1999, Oct. 9 **Litho.**

3483	A1164	1.40z multi	.90	.45

Frédéric Chopin (1810-49), Composer — A1165

1999, Oct. 17 **Engr.** ***Perf. 11x11½***

3484	A1165	1.40z dark green	.90	.45

Jerzy Popieluszko (1947-84), Priest Murdered by Secret Police — A1166

Perf. 11½x11¼ Syncopated Type A

1999, Oct. 19 **Litho.**

3485	A1166	70g multi	.45	.20

Souvenir Sheet

Memorial to Heroes of World War II — A1167

Illustration reduced.

1999, Oct. 21

3486	A1167	1z multi	.60	.30

Christmas A1168

Various angels.

Perf. 11¼x11½ Syncopated Type A

1999, Nov. 26 **Litho.**

Panel Color

3487	A1168	60g orange	.40	.20
3488	A1168	70g blue	.45	.25
3489	A1168	1z red	.65	.30
3490	A1168	1.40z olive green	.90	.45
		Nos. 3487-3490 (4)	2.40	1.20

Polish Cultural Buildings in Foreign Countries A1169

Designs: 1z, Polish Museum, Rapperswil, Switzerland. 1.40z, Marian Fathers' Museum at Fawley Court Historic House, United Kingdom. 1.60z, Polish History and Literary Society Library, Paris. 1.80z, Polish Institute and Sikorski Museum, London.

Perf. 11½x11¾ Syncopated Type A

1999, Dec. 6 **Litho.**

3491	A1169	1z multi	.60	.30
3492	A1169	1.40z multi	.85	.40
3493	A1169	1.60z multi	.95	.50
3494	A1169	1.80z multi	1.10	.55
		Nos. 3491-3494 (4)	3.50	1.75

New Year 2000 — A1170

Perf. 11½x11¾ Syncopated Type A

2000, Jan. 2 **Litho.**

3495	A1170	A multi	.45	.25

No. 3495 sold for 70g on day of issue.

Famous Poles A1171

Designs: 1.55z, Bronislaw Malinowski (1884-1942), ethnologist. 1.95z, Józef Zwierzycki (1888-1961), geologist.

Perf. 11¼x11½ Syncopated Type A

2000, Feb. 22

3496	A1171	1.55z multi	.90	.45
3497	A1171	1.95z multi	1.10	.55

Gniezno Summit, 1000th Anniv. — A1172

Designs: 70g, Holy Roman Emperor Otto III granting crown to Boleslaw Chrobry. 80g, Four bishops.

1.55z, Sclaunia, Germania, Gallia, Roma and Otto III, horiz.

Perf. 11½x11¼

2000, Mar. 12 **Photo.**

3498	A1172	70g multi	.40	.20
3499	A1172	80g multi	.45	.25

Souvenir Sheet

Perf. 11¼x11½

3500	A1172	1.55z multi	.90	.45

Organization of Roman Catholic Church in Poland, 1000th anniv.

Easter A1173

Designs: 70g, Christ in tomb. 80g, Resurrected Christ.

Perf. 11¼x11½ Syncopated Type B

2000, Mar. 24 **Litho.**

3501	A1173	70g multi	.40	.20
3502	A1173	80g multi	.45	.25

Dinosaurs — A1174

#3503, Saurolophus. #3504, Gallimimus. #3505, Saichania. #3506, Protoceratops. #3507, Prenocephale. #3508, Velociraptor.

Perf. 11¾x11½ Syncopated Type A

2000, Mar. 24 **Litho.**

3503	A1174	70g multi	.40	.20
3504	A1174	70g multi	.40	.20
3505	A1174	80g multi	.45	.25
3506	A1174	80g multi	.45	.25
3507	A1174	1.55z multi	.90	.45
3508	A1174	1.55z multi	.90	.45
a.		Souvenir sheet, #3503-3508	*7.50*	*3.75*
		Nos. 3503-3508 (6)	3.50	1.80

Awarding of Honorary Academy Award to Director Andrzej Wajda A1175

2000, Mar. 26

3509	A1175	1.10z blk & gray	.60	.30
a.		Tete beche pair	1.25	.60

Holy Year 2000 — A1176

Perf. 11½x11¼ Syncopated Type B

2000, Apr. 7

3510	A1176	80g multi	.45	.25

Country Estates Type of 1997

Perf. 11½x11¾

2000, Apr. 14 **Photo.**

3511	A1110	80g Grabonóg	.45	.25
3512	A1110	1.55z Zelazowa Wola	.90	.45
3513	A1110	1.65z Sucha, Wegrów	.95	.50
3514	A1110	2.65z Liwia, Wegrów	1.60	.80
		Nos. 3511-3514 (4)	3.90	2.00

Cracow, 2000 European City of Culture — A1177

70g, Jan Matejko, Franciszek Joseph, Stanislaw Wyspianski, Konstanty Ildefons Galczynski, Stanislaw Lem, Slawomir Mrozek, Piotr Skrzynecki and Cloth Hall. 1.55z, Queen Jadwiga, Józef Dietl, Krzystof Penderecki, Casimir the Great, Pope John Paul II, Jerzy Turowicz, Brother Albert, Copernicus, Collegium Maius and St. Mary's Church.

1.75z, Panorama of Cracow from 1493 wood engraving.

Perf. 11½x11¼ Syncopated Type A

2000, Apr. 26 **Litho.**

3515	A1177	70g multi	.40	.20
3516	A1177	1.55z multi	.90	.45

Souvenir Sheet
Engr.

Perf. 11¼x11½ Syncopated Type A

3517 A1177 1.75z blue 1.00 .50

No. 3517 contains one 39x31mm stamp.
No. 3517 exists imperf.

Fight Against Drug Addiction A1178

Perf. 11¼x11½ Syncopated Type B

2000, Apr. 28 **Litho.**

3518 A1178 70g multi .40 .20

Europa, 2000
Common Design Type

Perf. 11½x11¾ Syncopated Type B

2000, May 9

3519 CD17 1.55z multi .90 .45

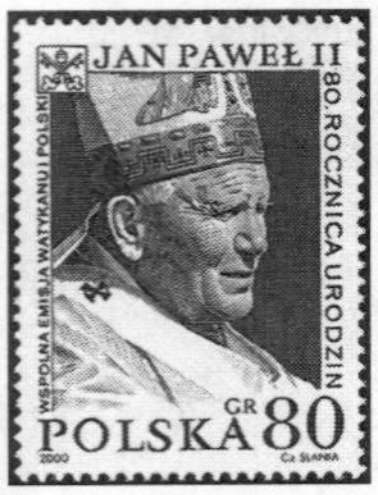

Pope John Paul II, 80th Birthday A1179

Designs: 80g, Pope. 1.10z, Black Madonna of Jasna Gora. 1.55z, Pope's silver cross.

Engr., Litho. & Engr. (1.10z)

2000, May 9 ***Perf. 12¾***

3520 A1179 80g purple .45 .25
3521 A1179 1.10z multi .65 .30
3522 A1179 1.55z green .90 .45
Nos. 3520-3522 (3) 2.00 1.00

See Vatican City Nos. 1153-1155.

España 2000 Intl. Philatelic Exhibition A1180

Perf. 11½x11¼ Syncopated Type A

2000, May 26 **Litho.**

3523 A1180 1.55z multi .85 .45

Parenthood A1181

Perf. 11½x11¼ Syncopated Type B

2000, May 31

3524 A1181 70g multi .40 .20

Souvenir Sheet

Wroclaw, 1000th Anniv. — A1182

Illustration reduced.

Perf. 11¼x11½ Syncopated Type A

2000, June 15

3525 A1182 1.55z multi .85 .45

Social Activists A1183

70g, Karol Marcinkowski (1800-46), philantropist. 80g, Blessed Josemaría Escrivá de Balaguer, (1902-75), founder of Opus Dei.

Perf. 11¼x11½ Suncopated Type B

2000, June 23

3526-3527 A1183 Set of 2 .80 .40

Illustrations of Characters from Pan Tadeusz, by Adam Mickiewicz A1184

#3528, 70g, Gerwazy & Count. #3529, 70g, Telimena & Judge. #3530, 80g, Father Robak, Judge &Gerwazy. #3531, 80g, Wojski. #3532, 1.10z, Jankiel. #3533, 1.10z, Zofia & Tadeusz.

2000, June 30 **Engr.** ***Perf. 11x11¼***

3528-3533 A1184 Set of 6 2.40 1.25

National Pilgrimage to Rome — A1185

Designs: 80g, Pope John Paul II, St. Peter's Basilica. 1.55z, Cross, Colosseum.

Perf. 11½x11¾ Syncopated Type B

2000, July 1 **Litho.**

3534-3535 A1185 Set of 2 1.10 .55

Piotr Michalowski (1800-55), Artist — A1186

70g, Self-portrait, vert. 80g, Portrait of Boy in a Hat, vert. 1.10z, Stableboy Bridling Percherons. 1.55z, Horses & a Horse Cart.

Perf. 11½x11¼ (no syncopation), 11¾x11½ Syncopated Type A

2000, July 2

3536-3539 A1186 Set of 4 2.25 1.10

Depictions of the Virgin Mary — A1187

Designs: 70g, Rózanostok. 1.55z, Lichen.

Perf. 11½x11¼ Syncopated Type A

2000, Aug. 14

3540-3541 A1187 Set of 2 1.25 .60

St. John Bosco and Adolescents A1188

Perf. 11¼x11½ Syncopated Type B

2000, Aug. 25

3542 A1188 80g multi .45 .20

Educational work of Salesian order.

Souvenir Sheet

Solidarity Labor Union, 20th Anniv. — A1189

Illustration reduced.

Perf. 11½x11¼ Syncopated Type B

2000, Aug. 31

3543 A1189 1.65z multi .90 .45

2000 Summer Olympics, Sydney A1190

Designs: 70g, Runners. 80g, Diving, sailing, rowing. 1.10z, High jump, weight lifting, fencing. 1.55z, Basketball, judo, runner.

Perf. 11¾x11½ Syncopated Type A

2000, Sept. 1

3544-3547 A1190 Set of 4 2.25 1.10

World Post Day — A1191

Children's art by: 70g, Tomasz Wistuba, vert. 80g, Katarzyna Chrzanowska. 1.10z, Joanna Żbik. 1.55z, Katarzyna Lonak.

Perf. 11½x11¼, 11¼x11½ All Sync. Type B

2000, Oct. 9 **Litho.**

3548-3551 A1191 Set of 4 2.60 1.25

Souvenir Sheet

Polish Philatelic Union, 50th Anniv. — A1192

Perf. 11¼x11½ Sync. Type B

2000, Oct. 12

3552 A1192 1.55z multi .95 .45

Royalty Type of 1986 With Denominations at Bottom

Designs: 70g, August II. 80g, Stanislaw Leszczynski. 1.10z, August III. 1.55z, Stanislaw August Poniatowski.

2000, Oct. 23 **Engr.** ***Perf. 10¾x11***

3553-3556 A875 Set of 4 2.60 1.25

Katyn Massacre, 60th Anniv. — A1193

Designs: 70g, Priest and cross. 80g, Pope John Paul II at monument in Warsaw.

Perf. 11½x11¾ Sync. Type A

2000, Nov. 15 **Litho.**

3557-3558 A1193 Set of 2 .90 .45

Christmas A1194

Scenes from the life of Jesus: 70g, Nativity. 80g, Wedding at Cana. 1.10g, Last Supper. 1.55z, Ascension.

Perf. 11½ Sync. Type A

2000, Nov. 27

3559-3562 A1194 Set of 4 2.60 1.25

Zacheta Art Museum, Warsaw, Cent. — A1195

Perf. 11½x11¼ Sync. Type B

2000, Dec. 4

3563 A1195 70g multi .45 .20

Underground Post During Martial Law — A1196

Illustration reduced.

Perf. 11½x11¼ Sync. Type A

2000, Dec. 13

3564 A1196 80g multi + label .50 .25
a. Tete beche block of 2 stamps + 2 labels 1.00 .50

End of Holy Year 2000 — A1197

Type C Syncopation (1st stamp #3565): Like Type A Syncopation but with oval hole on shorter sides rather than longer sides.

Perf. 11¾x11½ Sync. Type C

2001, Jan. 6 **Litho.**

3565 A1197 A multi .55 .25

Sold for 1z on day of issue.

20th Winter Universiade, Zakopane — A1198

Perf. 11¼x11½ Sync. Type B

2001, Feb. 7

3566 A1198 1z multi .55 .25

Internet A1199

Perf. 11¼x11½ Sync. Type A

2001, Feb. 22

3567 A1199 1z multi .55 .25

World Ski Championships, Lahti, Finland — A1200

Perf. 11½ Sync. Type A

2001, Feb. 23

3568 A1200 1z shown .55 .25

With Inscription "Adam Malysz" in Black

3569 A1200 1z multi .55 .25

As #3569, With Inscription "Mistrzem Swiata" in Red

3570 A1200 1z multi .55 .25
Nos. 3568-3570 (3) 1.65 .75

Country Estates Type of 1997

Perf. 11½x11¾

2001, Feb. 28 **Photo.**

3571 A1110 10g Lipków .20 .20
3572 A1110 1.50z Sulejówek .95 .50
3573 A1110 1.90z Petrykozy 1.10 .55
3574 A1110 3z Janowiec 1.75 .85

Issued: 1.90z, 3z, 2/28. 10g, 1.50z, 6/20.

Easter A1201

Designs: 1z, Women at empty tomb. 1.90z, Resurrected Christ with apostles.

Perf. 11½ Sync. Type A

2001, Mar. 16 **Litho.**

3575-3576 A1201 Set of 2 1.60 .80

12th Salesian Youth World Championships — A1202

Perf. 11¾x11½ Sync. Type C

2001, Apr. 28

3577 A1202 1z multi .55 .25

Europa — A1203

Perf. 11½x11¼ Sync. Type A

2001, May 5

3578 A1203 1.90z multi 1.10 .55

Greetings A1204

Designs: No. 3579, 1z, All the best (couple in field of flowers). No. 3580, 1z, Vacation greetings (merman and mermaid at beach).

Perf. 11½x11¾ Syncopated Type B

2001, May 10 **Litho.**

3579-3580 A1204 Set of 2 1.25 .65

Wrzesnia Children's Strike Against German Language, Cent. — A1205

Perf. 11½x11¾ Syncopated Type A

2001, May 20

3581 A1205 1z multi .65 .30

Polish Cultural Buildings in North America A1206

Designs: 1z, Poland Scientific Institute and Wanda Stachiewicz Polish Library, Montreal. 1.90z, Josef Pilsudski Institute, New York. 2.10z, Polonia Archives, Library and Museum, Orchard Lake, Mich. 2.20z, Polish Museum, Chicago.

Perf. 11½ Syncopated Type B

2001, June 29

3582 A1206 1z multi .65 .30
a. Tete beche pair 1.30 .60
3583 A1206 1.90z multi 1.25 .60
a. Tete beche pair 2.50 1.20
3584 A1206 2.10z multi 1.40 .70
a. Tete beche pair 2.80 1.40
3585 A1206 2.20z multi 1.40 .70
a. Tete beche pair 2.80 1.40
Nos. 3582-3585 (4) 4.70 2.30

Endangered Flora and Fauna — A1207

Convention on Intl. Trade in Endangered Species emblem and: No. 3586, 1z, Parnassius apollo, Orchis sambucina. No. 3587, 1z, Bubo bubo, Adonis vernalis. No. 3588, 1z, Galanthus nivalis, Lynx lynx. No. 3589, 1.90z, Orchis latifolia, Lutra lutra. No. 3590, 1.90z, Falco peregrinus, Orchis pallens. No. 3591, 1.90z, Cypripedium calceolus, Ursus arctos. 2z, World map.

Perf. 11½ Syncopated Type A

2001, July 10

3586-3591 A1207 Set of 6 5.50 2.75

Souvenir Sheet

Perf. 11¼x11½ Syncopated Type A

3592 A1207 2z multi 1.25 .65

No. 3592 contains one 39x30mm stamp.

Stefan Cardinal Wyszynski (1901-81) A1208

Perf. 11¾x11½ Syncopated Type A

2001, Aug. 3

3593 A1208 1z multi .65 .30

St. Maximilian Kolbe (1894-1941) — A1209

Perf. 11¾x11½ Syncopated Type B

2001, Aug. 14

3594 A1209 1z multi .65 .30

Depictions of the Virgin Mary — A1210

Designs: No. 3595, 1z, Pieknej Milosci, Bydgoszcz. No. 3596, 1z, Królowa Podhala, Ludzmierz. 1.90z, Mariampol, Wroclaw.

Perf. 11½x11¼ Syncopated Type A

2001, Aug. 14

3595-3597 A1210 Set of 3 2.50 1.25

Extension of God's Mercy Sanctuary, Cracow — A1211

2001, Aug. 31

3598 A1211 1z multi .65 .30

Euro Cuprum 2001 Philatelic Exhibition, Lubin — A1212

Designs: 1z, Copper smelter. 1.90z, Copper engravers at work. 2z, Copying with a copper engraving press.

3z, Engraver's burin, view of Lubin, 18th cent.

Perf. 11½x11¼ Syncopated Type A

2001, Sept. 1 **Litho. & Engr.**

3599-3601 A1212 Set of 3 3.25 1.60

Souvenir Sheet

Litho.

3602 A1212 3z multi 1.90 .95

No. 3602 exists imperf.

Premiere of Movie "Quo Vadis," Directed by Jerzy Kawalerowicz — A1213

No. 3603: a, Ligia, Vinicius, Petrinius (red and light yellow inscriptions). b, Nero singing (blue and red inscriptions). c, Apostle Peter in catacombs, baptism of Chilon Chilonides (orange and yellow inscriptions). d, Chilon Chilonides, fire in Rome (white and yellow inscriptions). e, Ligia tied to back of aurochs, Ursus holding Ligia (red and white inscriptions). f, Apostle Peter blessing Vinicius and Ligia, close-up of Peter (purple and pink inscriptions).

Perf. 11¾x11½ Syncopated Type A

2001, Sept. 1 **Litho.**

3603 A1213 1z Sheet of 6, #a-f 4.00 2.00

Exhibition on Christian Traditions in Military at Polish Army Museum A1214

Perf. 11¾x11½ Syncopated

2001, Sept. 10 **Litho.**

3604 A1214 1z multi .65 .30

Polish State Railways, 75th Anniv. — A1215

2001, Sept. 24

3605 A1215 1z multi .65 .30

Children's Stamp Design Contest Winners A1216

Art by: 1z, Marcin Kuron. 1.90z, Agata Grzyb, vert. 2z, Joanna Sadrakula.

Perf. 11½ Syncopated

2001, Sept. 28

3606-3608 A1216 Set of 3 3.25 1.60

Poland's Advancement to 2002 World Cup Soccer Championships A1217

Perf. 11½x11¾ Syncopated

2001, Oct. 6

3609 A1217 1z multi .65 .30

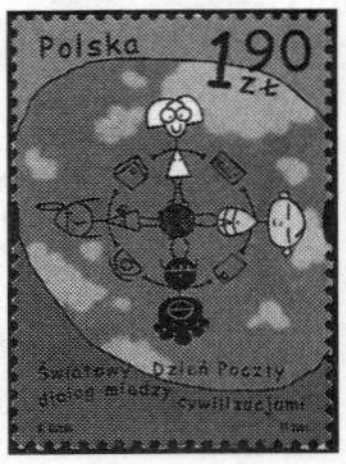

Year of Dialogue Among Civilizations A1218

2001, Oct. 9

3610 A1218 1.90z multi 1.25 .60
 a. Tete beche pair 2.50 1.20

12th Intl. Henryk Wieniawski Violin Competition — A1219

Perf. 11¾x11½ Syncopated

2001, Oct. 13

3611 A1219 1z multi .65 .30

Papal Day — A1220

Perf. 11½x11¾ Syncopated

2001, Oct. 14

3612 A1220 1z multi .65 .30

Warsaw Philharmonic, Cent. — A1221

Perf. 11½x11¼ Syncopated

2001, Nov. 5

3613 A1221 1z multi .65 .30
 a. Tete beche pair 1.30 .60

Millennium — A1222

No. 3614: a, Pope John Paul II, Gniezno Doors. b, Pres. Lech Walesa taking oath, cover of May 1791 Constitution. c, Covers of three magazines. d, Playwright Wojciech Boguslawski and Director Jerzy Grotowski, manuscript by Adam Mickiewicz. e, Marshal Józef Pilsudski, Solidarity posters. f, NATO emblem, Gen. Casimir Pulaski. g, Astronomers Nicolaus Copernicus and Aleksander Wolszczan, text from De Revolutionibus Orbium Coelestium, by Copernicus. h, Woodcut of mathematician Jan of Glogow, physicist Tadeusz Kotarbinski. i, Detail from 1920 poster and painting, Battle of Grunwald, by Jan Matejko. j, Four members of the Belvedere Group, masthead of Warszawa Walczy newspaper, soldiers at Warsaw Uprising of 1944, seal of Marian Langiewicz. k, Head of John the Apostle, by Veit Stoss, and self-sculpture, by Magdalena Abakanowicz. l, Composers Krzysztof Penderecki and Frederic Chopin, Mazurka No. 10, Opus 50, by Karol Szymanowski. m, Engraving of Cracow and Royal Castle, Warsaw. n, Portrait of Jan III Sobieski, flag of European Union. o, Writers Wislawa Szymborska and Mikolaj Rej. p, Runners Janusz Kusocinski and Robert Korzeniowski.

Perf. 11¼x11½ Syncopated

2001, Nov. 11

3614 A1222 1z Sheet of 16, #a-p 10.50 5.25

Christmas A1223

Creches from Lower Silesia: 1z, 1.90z.

2001, Nov. 27

3615-3616 A1223 Set of 2 1.90 .95

Radio Maryja, 10th Anniv. A1224

Designs: No. 3617, 1z, Head of Virgin Mary statue, building.

No. 3618: a, 1z, Statue of Virgin Mary praying, crowd with flag. b, 1z, Statue of crowned Virgin Mary, crowd with flag.

2001, Dec. 7

3617 A1224 1z multi .65 .30

Souvenir Sheet

3618 A1224 1z Sheet, #a-b, 3617 2.00 1.00

SEMI-POSTAL STAMPS

Regular Issue of 1919 Surcharged in Violet

a

b

1919, May 3 **Unwmk.** ***Imperf.***

B1	A10(a)	5f + 5f grn	.20	.20
B2	A10(a)	10f + 5f red vio	2.00	1.40
B3	A10(a)	15f + 5f dp red	.40	.20
B4	A11(b)	25f + 5f ol grn	.40	.20
B5	A11(b)	50f + 5f bl grn	.60	.30
		Perf. 11½		
B6	A10(a)	5f + 5f grn	.25	.20
B7	A10(a)	10f + 5f red vio	.50	.20
B8	A10(a)	15f + 5f dp red	.25	.20
B9	A11(b)	25f + 5f ol grn	.30	.20
B10	A11(b)	50f + 5f bl grn	1.00	.40
		Nos. B1-B10 (10)	5.90	3.50

First Polish Philatelic Exhibition. The surtax benefited the Polish White Cross Society.

Regular Issue of 1920 Surcharged in Carmine

1921, Mar. 5 ***Perf. 9***

Thin Laid Paper

B11	A14	5m + 30m red vio	5.00	7.00
B12	A14	6m + 30m dp rose	5.00	7.00
B13	A14	10m + 30m lt red	12.00	*19.00*
B14	A14	20m + 30m gray grn	37.50	*65.00*
		Nos. B11-B14 (4)	59.50	98.00

Counterfeits, differently perforated, exist of Nos. B11-B14.

SP1

Light of Knowledge — SP2

1925, Jan. 1 **Typo.** ***Perf. 12½***

B15	SP1	1g orange brn	12.00	14.00
B16	SP1	2g dk brown	12.00	14.00
B17	SP1	3g orange	12.00	14.00
B18	SP1	5g olive grn	12.00	14.00
B19	SP1	10g blue grn	12.00	14.00
B20	SP1	15g red	12.00	14.00
B21	SP1	20g blue	12.00	14.00
B22	SP1	25g red brown	12.00	14.00
B23	SP1	30g dp violet	12.00	14.00
B24	SP1	40g indigo	35.00	14.00
B25	SP1	50g magenta	12.00	14.00
		Nos. B15-B25 (11)	155.00	154.00
		Set, never hinged	200.00	

"Na Skarb" means "National Funds." These stamps were sold at a premium of 50 groszy each, for charity.

1927, May 3 ***Perf. 11½***

B26	SP2	10g + 5g choc & grn	7.00	4.50
B27	SP2	20g + 5g dk bl & buff	7.00	4.50
		Set, never hinged	24.00	

"NA OSWIATE" means "For Public Instruction." The surtax aided an Association of Educational Societies.

Torun Type of 1933

1933, May 21 **Engr.**

B28	A59	60g (+40g) red brn, *buff*	16.00	12.00
		Never hinged	21.00	

Philatelic Exhibition at Torun, May 21-28, 1933, and sold at a premium of 40g to aid the exhibition funds.

Souvenir Sheet

Stagecoach and Wayside Inn — SP3

1938, May 3 **Engr.** ***Perf. 12, Imperf.***

B29	SP3	Sheet of 4	72.50	65.00
		Never hinged	90.00	
a.		45g green	7.50	7.50
b.		55g blue	7.50	7.50

5th Phil. Exhib., Warsaw, May 3-8. The sheet contains two 45g and two 55g stamps. Sold for 3z.

Souvenir Sheet

Stratosphere Balloon over Mountains — SP4

1938, Sept. 15 ***Perf. 12½***

B31	SP4	75g dp vio, sheet	55.00	60.00
		Never hinged	75.00	

Issued in advance of a proposed Polish stratosphere flight. Sold for 2z.

Winterhelp Issue

SP5

1938-39

B32	SP5	5g + 5g red org	.55	.95
B33	SP5	25g + 10g dk vio ('39)	.90	1.40
B34	SP5	55g + 15g brt ultra ('39)	1.75	2.25
		Nos. B32-B34 (3)	3.20	4.60
		Set, never hinged	5.00	

For surcharges see Nos. N48-N50.

Souvenir Sheet

SP6

1939, Aug. 1

B35	SP6	Sheet of 3, dark blue gray	27.50	20.00
		Never hinged	32.50	
a.		25g Marshal Pilsudski Reviewing Troops	4.75	3.50
b.		25g Marshal Pilsudski	4.75	3.50
c.		25g Marshal Smigly-Rydz	4.75	3.50

25th anniv. of the founding of the Polish Legion. The sheets sold for 1.75z, the surtax going to the National Defense fund.

See types A64, A80, A99.

Polish People's Republic

Polish Warship SP7

Sailing Vessel — SP8

Polish Naval Ensign and Merchant Flag — SP9

Crane and Crane Tower, Gdansk SP10

1945, Apr. 24 **Typo.** ***Perf. 11***

B36	SP7	50g + 2z red	2.50	4.25
B37	SP8	1z + 3z dp bl	2.50	4.25
B38	SP9	2z + 4z dk car	2.50	4.25
B39	SP10	3z + 5z ol grn	2.50	4.25
		Nos. B36-B39 (4)	10.00	17.00
		Set, never hinged	13.00	

Polish Maritime League, 25th anniv.

City Hall, Poznan — SP11

1945, June 16 **Photo.**

B40	SP11	1z + 5z green	15.00	20.00
		Never hinged	20.00	

Postal Workers' Convention, Poznan, June 16, 1945. Exists imperf. Value, $35.

Last Stand at Westerplatte — SP12

1945, Sept. 1

B41	SP12	1z + 9z steel blue	12.00	20.00
		Never hinged	15.00	

Polish army's last stand at Westerplatte, Sept. 1, 1939. Exists imperf. Value, $21.

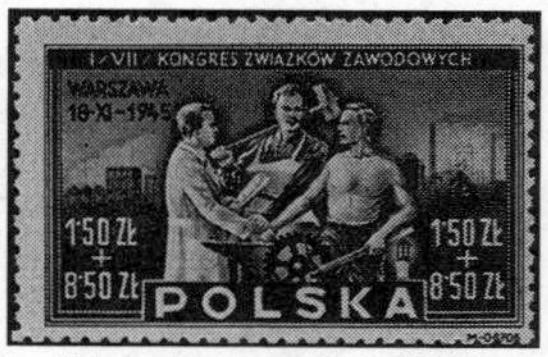

"United Industry" — SP13

1945, Nov. 18 **Unwmk.** ***Perf. 11***

B42	SP13	1.50z + 8.50z sl blk	5.00	7.50
		Never hinged	7.00	

Trade Unions Congress, Warsaw, Nov. 18.

Polish Volunteers in Spain — SP14

1946, Mar. 10

B43	SP14	3z + 5z red	3.00	4.25
		Never hinged	4.00	

Participation of the Jaroslaw Dabrowski Brigade in the Spanish Civil War.

14th Century Piast Eagle and Soldiers — SP15

"Death" Spreading Poison Gas over Majdanek Prison Camp — SP16

1946, May 2

B44	SP15	3z + 7z brn	.60	.50
		Never hinged	1.00	

Silesian uprisings of 1919-21, 1939-45.

1946, Apr. 29

B45	SP16	3z + 5z Prus grn	2.00	3.00
		Never hinged	3.00	

Issued to recall Majdanek, a concentration camp of World War II near Lublin.

Bydgoszcz (Bromberg) Canal — SP17

Map of Polish Coast and Baltic Sea — SP18

1946, Apr. 19 **Unwmk.** ***Perf. 11***

B46	SP17	3z + 2z ol blk	2.25	6.00
		Never hinged	3.75	

600th anniv. of Bydgoszcz (Bromberg).

1946, July 21

B47	SP18	3z + 7z dp bl	1.25	2.00
		Never hinged	2.00	

Maritime Holiday of 1946. The surtax was for the Polish Maritime League.

Salute to P.T.T. Casualty and Views of Gdansk — SP19

1946, Sept. 14

B48 SP19 3z + 12z slate 1.40 2.00
Never hinged 2.00

Polish postal employees killed in the German attack on Danzig (Gdansk), Sept. 1939.

School Children — SP20

Designs: 6z+24z, Courtyard of Jagiellon University, Cracow. 11z+19z, Gregor Piramowicz (1735-1801), founder of Education Commission.

1946, Oct. 10 Unwmk. *Perf. 11½*

B49 SP20 3z + 22z dk red 22.50 35.00
B49A SP20 6z + 24z dk bl 22.50 35.00
B49B SP20 11z + 19z dk grn 22.50 35.00
c. Souv. sheet of 3, #B49-B49B 315.00 375.00
Never hinged 400.00
Nos. B49-B49B (3) 67.50 105.00
Never hinged 77.50

Polish educational work. Surtax was for International Bureau of Education.
No. B49Bc sold for 100z.

Stanislaw Stojalowski, Jakob Bojko, Jan Stapinski and Wincenty Witos — SP21

1946, Dec. 1

B50 SP21 5z + 10z bl grn 1.00 1.40
B51 SP21 5z + 10z dull blue 1.00 1.40
B52 SP21 5z + 10z dk olive 1.00 1.40
Nos. B50-B52 (3) 3.00 4.20
Never hinged 4.00

50th anniv. of the Peasant Movement. The surtax was for education and cultural improvement among the Polish peasantry.

No. 391 Surcharged in Red

1947, Feb. 4 *Perf. 11x10½*

B53 A127 3z + 7z purple 5.50 8.00
Never hinged 6.75

Opening of the Polish Parliament, 1/19/47.

No. 344 Surcharged in Blue

1947, Feb. 21 *Perf. 12½*

B54 A103 5z + 15z on 25g 1.25 3.50
Never hinged 2.50

Ski Championship Meet, Zakopane. Counterfeits exist.

Emil Zegadlowicz — SP22

1947, Mar. 1 Photo. *Perf. 11*

B55 SP22 5z + 15z dl gray grn 1.25 1.50
Never hinged 1.50

Nurse and War Victims SP23

Adam Chmielowski SP24

1947, June 1 *Perf. 10½*

B56 SP23 5z + 5z ol blk & red 2.50 3.50
Never hinged 3.25

The surtax was for the Red Cross.

1947, Dec. 21 *Perf. 11*

B57 SP24 2z + 18z dk vio 1.25 2.25
Never hinged 1.65

Zamkowy Square and Proposed Highway SP25

1948, Nov. 1

B58 SP25 15z + 5z green .30 .25
Never hinged .50

The surtax was to aid in the reconstruction of Warsaw.

Infant and TB Crosses — SP26

Various Portraits of Children

1948, Dec. 16 *Perf. 11½*

B59 SP26 3z + 2z dl grn 2.00 2.50
B60 SP26 5z + 5z brn 2.00 2.50
B61 SP26 6z + 4z vio 1.65 2.50
B62 SP26 15z + 10z car lake 1.65 2.50
Nos. B59-B62 (4) 7.30 10.00
Set, never hinged 9.00

Alternate vertical rows of stamps was ten different labels. The surtax was for anti-tuberculosis work among children.

Catalogue values for unused stamps in this section, from this point to the end of the section, are for Never Hinged items.

Workers Party Type of 1952
Perf. 12½

1952, Jan. 18 Engr. Unwmk.

B63 A195 45g + 15g Marceli Nowotko .20 .20

Women's Day Type of 1952

1952, Mar. 8 *Perf. 12½x12*

B64 A196 45g + 15g chocolate .30 .20

Swierczewski-Walter Type of 1952

1952, Mar. 28 *Perf. 12½*

B65 A197 45g + 15g chocolate .40 .20

Bierut Type of 1952

1952, Apr. 18

B66 A198 45g + 15g red .50 .20
B67 A198 1.20z + 15g ultra .50 .20

Type of Regular Issue of 1951-52 Inscribed "Plan 6," etc.

Design: 45g+15g, Electrical installation.

1952

B68 A193 30g + 15g brn red .35 .20
B69 A193 45g + 15g chocolate .60 .30
B69A A194 1.20z + 15g red org .30 .25
Nos. B68-B69A (3) 1.25 .75

Labor Day Type of Regular Issue of 1952

1952, May 1

B70 A200 45g + 15g car rose .30 .20

Similar to Regular Issue of 1952

#B71, Maria Konopnicka. #B72, Hugo Kollataj.

1952, May
Different Frames

B71 A201 30g + 15g blue green .50 .20
B72 A201 45g + 15g brown .25 .20

Issued: No. B71, May 10. No. B72, May 20.

Leonardo da Vinci — SP28

1952, June 1

B73 SP28 30g + 15g ultra .85 .50

500th birth anniv. of Leonardo da Vinci.

Pres. Bierut and Children — SP29

1952, June 1 Photo. *Perf. 13½x14*

B74 SP29 45g + 15g blue 2.50 .60

Intl. Children's Day, June 1.

Sports Type

1952, June 21 *Perf. 13*

45g+15g, Soccer players and trophy.

B75 A203 30g + 15g blue 3.75 1.40
B76 A203 45g + 15g purple 1.75 .35

Yachts SP31 — "Dar Pomorza" SP32

1952, June 28 Engr. *Perf. 12½*

B77 SP31 30g + 15g dp bl grn 2.75 .90
B78 SP32 45g + 15g dp ultra .70 .25

Shipbuilders' Day, 1952.

Workers on Holiday — SP33

Students SP34

1952, July 17 *Perf. 12½x12, 12x12½*

B79 SP33 30g + 15g dp grn .30 .20
B80 SP34 45g + 15g red .70 .20

Issued to publicize the Youth Festival, 1952.

Constitution Type of Regular Issue

1952, July 22 Photo. *Perf. 11*

B81 A208 45g + 15g lt bl grn & dk brn 1.10 .25

Power Plant Type of Regular Issue

1952, Aug. 7 Engr. *Perf. 12½*

B82 A209 45g + 15g red .65 .20

Ludwik Warynski SP36 — Church of Frydman SP37

1952, July 31

B83 SP36 30g + 15g dk red .40 .20
B84 SP36 45g + 15g blk brn .40 .20

70th birth anniv. of Ludwik Warynski, political organizer.

1952, Aug. 18

B85 SP37 45g + 15g vio brn .90 .20

Aviator Watching Glider SP38 — Henryk Sienkiewicz SP39

Design: 45g+15g, Pilot entering plane.

1952, Aug. 23

B86 SP38 30g + 15g grn .55 .30
B87 SP38 45g + 15g brn red 2.25 .90

Aviation Day, Aug. 23.

1952, Oct. 25

B88 SP39 45g + 15g vio brn .35 .25

Henryk Sienkiewicz (1846-1916), author of "Quo Vadis" and other novels, Nobel prizewinner (literature, 1905).

Revolution Type of Regular Issue

1952, Nov. 7 ***Perf. 12x12½***

B92 A214 45g + 15g red brn .70 .20

Exists imperforate. See #562.

Lenin — SP42

Miner — SP43

1952, Nov. 7 ***Perf. 12½***

B93 SP42 30g + 15g vio brn .30 .20
B94 SP42 45g + 15g brn .70 .30
a. "LENIN" omitted 20.00

Month of Polish-Soviet friendship, Nov. 1952.

1952, Dec. 4

B95 SP43 45g + 15g blk brn .20 .20
B96 SP43 1.20z + 15g brn .50 .20

Miners' Day, Dec. 4.

Henryk Wieniawski and Violin — SP44

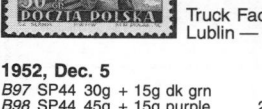

Truck Factory, Lublin — SP45

1952, Dec. 5 **Photo.**

B97 SP44 30g + 15g dk grn .55 .30
B98 SP44 45g + 15g purple 2.75 .60

Henryk Wieniawski; 2nd Intl. Violin Competition.

Type of Regular Issue of 1952

1952, Dec. 12 **Engr.**

B99 A215 45g + 15g dp grn .30 .20

1953, Feb. 20

B100 SP45 30g + 15g dp bl .20 .20
B101 SP45 60g + 20g vio brn .40 .20

Souvenir Sheet

Town Hall in Poznan — SP46

Photo. & Litho.

1955, July 7 ***Imperf.***

B102 SP46 2z pck grn & ol grn 3.50 2.00
B103 SP46 3z car rose & ol blk 19.00 10.50

6th Polish Philatelic Exhibition in Poznan. Sheets sold for 3z and 4.50z respectively.

Souvenir Sheet

"Peace" (POKOJ) and Warsaw Mermaid — SP47

Design: 1z, Pansies (A266) and inscription on map of Europe, Africa and Asia.

1955, Aug. 3

B104 SP47 1z bis, rose vio & yel 4.25 1.50
B105 SP47 2z ol gray, ultra & lt bl 20.00 7.50

Intl. Phil. Exhib., Warsaw, Aug. 1-14, 1955. Sheets sold for 2z and 3z respectively.

Souvenir Sheet

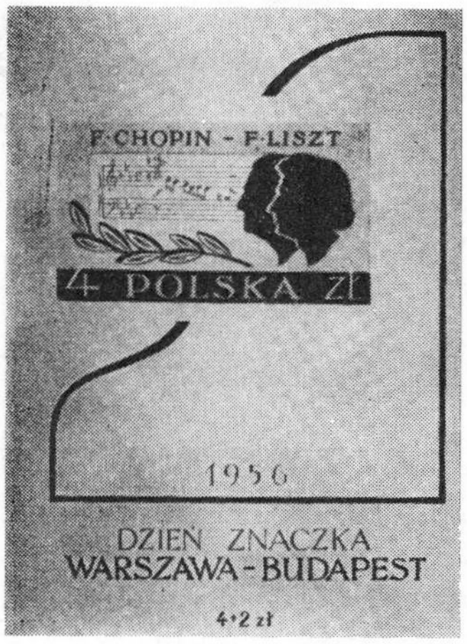

Chopin and Liszt — SP48

1956, Oct. 25 **Photo.** ***Imperf.***

B106 SP48 4z dk blue grn 30.00 16.00

Day of the Stamp; Polish-Hungarian friendship. The sheet sold for 6z.

Souvenir Sheet

Stamp of 1860 — SP49

Wmk. 326

1960, Sept. 4 **Litho.** ***Perf. 11***

B107 SP49 Sheet of 4 40.00 35.00
a. 10z + 10z blue, red & black 9.00 9.00

Intl. Phil. Exhib. "POLSKA 60," Warsaw, 9/3-11.

Sold only with 5z ticket to exhibition.

Type of Space Issue, 1964

Design: Yuri A. Gagarin in space capsule.

Perf. 12½x12

1964, Dec. 30 **Unwmk.**

B108 A432 6.50z + 2z Prus grn & multi 1.50 .65

Souvenir Sheet

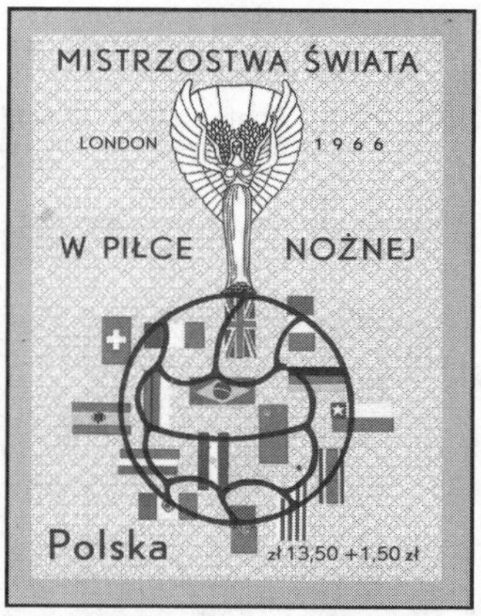

Jules Rimet Cup and Flags of Participating Countries — SP50

1966, May 9 **Litho.** ***Imperf.***

B109 SP50 13.50z + 1.50z multi 2.50 1.50

World Cup Soccer Championship, Wembley, England, July 11-30.

Souvenir Sheet

J. Kusocinski, Olympic Winner 10,000-Meter Race, 1932 — SP51

1967, May 24 **Litho.** ***Imperf.***

B110 SP51 10z + 5z multi 1.50 1.00

19th Olympic Games, Mexico City, 1968. Simulated perforations.

Flower Type of Regular Issue

Flowers: 4z+2z, Abutilon. 8z+4z, Rosa polyantha hybr.

1968, May 15 **Litho.** ***Perf. 11½***

B111 A492 4z + 2z vio & multi .80 .40
B112 A492 8z + 4z lt vio & multi 1.65 .90

Olympic Type of Regular Issue, 1968

Design: 10z+5z, Runner with Olympic torch and Chin cultic carved stone disc showing Mayan ball player and game's scoreboard.

1968, Sept. 2 **Litho.** ***Perf. 11½***

Size: 56x45mm

B113 A497 10z + 5z multi 1.90 .80

19th Olympic Games, Mexico City, Oct. 12-27. The surtax was for the Polish Olympic Committee.

Olympic Type of Regular Issue, 1969

Olympic Rings and: 2.50z+50g, Women's discus. 3.40z+1z, Running. 4z+1.50z, Boxing. 7z+2z, Fencing.

1969, Apr. 25 **Litho.** ***Perf. 11½x11***

B114 A505 2.50z + 50g multi .30 .20
B115 A505 3.40z + 1z multi .40 .20
B116 A505 4z + 1.50z multi .60 .20
B117 A505 7z + 2z multi 1.00 .25
Nos. B114-B117 (4) 2.30 .85

Folk Art Type of Regular Issue

5.50z+1.50z, Choir. 7z+1.50z, Organ grinder.

1969, Dec. 19 **Litho.** ***Perf. 11½x11***

Size: 24x36mm

B118 A520 5.50z + 1.50z multi .50 .25
B119 A520 7z + 1.50z multi .70 .30

Sports Type of Regular Issue

Souvenir Sheet

Design: "Horse of Glory," by Z. Kaminski.

1970, June 16 **Photo.** ***Imperf.***

B120 A532 10z + 5z multi 1.75 1.00

The surtax was for the Polish Olympic Committee. No. B120 contains one imperf. stamp with simulated perforations.

Tapestry Type of Regular Issue

Souvenir Sheet

Design: 7z+3z, Satyrs holding monogram of King Sigismund Augustus.

1970, Dec. 23 **Photo.** ***Imperf.***

B121 A541 7z + 3z multi 1.75 1.00

Type of Regular Issue

Design: 8.50z+4z, Virgin Mary, 15th century stained glass window.

1971, Sept. 15 ***Perf. 11½x11***

B122 A555 8.50z + 4z multi .90 .45

Painting Type of Regular Issue

7z+1z, Nude, by Wojciech Weiss (1875-1950).

1971, Oct. 9 **Litho.**
B123 A556 7z + 1z multi .70 .35

Winter Olympic Type of Regular Issue
Souvenir Sheet

Slalom and Sapporo '72 emblem, vert.

1972, Jan. 12 **Photo.** ***Imperf.***
B124 A564 10z + 5z multi 2.00 1.25

No. B124 contains one stamp with simulated perforations, 27x52mm.

Summer Olympic Type of Regular Issue
Souvenir Sheet

Design: 10z+5z, Archery (like 30g).

1972, May 20 **Photo.** ***Perf. 11½x11***
B125 A568 10z + 5z multi 1.75 1.00

Painting Type of Regular Issue, 1972

Design: 8.50z+4z, Portrait of a Young Lady, by Jacek Malczewski, horiz.

1972, Sept. 28 **Photo.** ***Perf. 11x10½***
B126 A576 8.50z + 4z multi 1.50 .55

Souvenir Sheet

Copernicus — SP52

Engraved and Photogravure

1972, Sept. 28 ***Perf. 11½***
B127 SP52 10z + 5z vio bl, gray & car 1.50 .85

Nicolaus Copernicus (1473-1543), astronomer. No. B127 shows the Ptolemaic and Copernican concepts of solar system from L'Harmonica Microcosmica, by Cellarius, 1660.

Souvenir Sheet

Poznan, 1740, by F. B. Werner — SP53

1973, Aug. 19 ***Imperf.***
B128 SP53 10z + 5z ol & dk brn 2.00 .90
a. 10z + 5z pale lilac & dk brn 6.00 4.00

POLSKA 73 Intl. Phil. Exhib., Poznan, Aug. 19-Sept. 2. No. B128 contains one stamp with simulated perforations.

No. B128a was sold only in combination with an entrance ticket.

Copernicus, by Marcello Baciarelli — SP54

1973, Sept. 27 **Photo.** ***Perf. 11x11½***
B129 SP54 4z + 2z multi .50 .30

Stamp Day. The surtax was for the reconstruction of the Royal Castle in Warsaw.

Souvenir Sheet

Montreal Olympic Games Emblem — SP55

Photo. & Engr.

1975, Mar. 8 ***Perf. 12***
B130 SP55 10z + 5z sil & grn 1.50 1.00

21st Olympic Games, Montreal, July 17-Aug. 8, 1976.

Outer edge of souvenir sheet is perforated.

Dunikowski Type of 1975

Design: 8z+4z, Mother and Child, from Silesian Insurrectionist Monument, by Dunikowski.

1975, Oct. 9 **Photo.** ***Perf. 11½x11***
B131 A644 8z + 4z multi 1.00 .45

Souvenir Sheet

Volleyball — SP56

Engraved and Photogravure

1976, June 30 ***Perf. 11½***
B132 SP56 10z + 5z blk & car 1.40 .70

21st Olympic Games, Montreal, Canada, July 17-Aug. 1. No. B132 contains one perf. 11½ stamp and is perf. 11½ all around.

Corinthian Art Type 1976

Design: 8z+4z, Winged Sphinx, vert.

1976, Oct. 30 **Photo.** ***Perf. 11½x11***
B133 A664 8z + 4z multi 1.10 .50

Souvenir Sheet

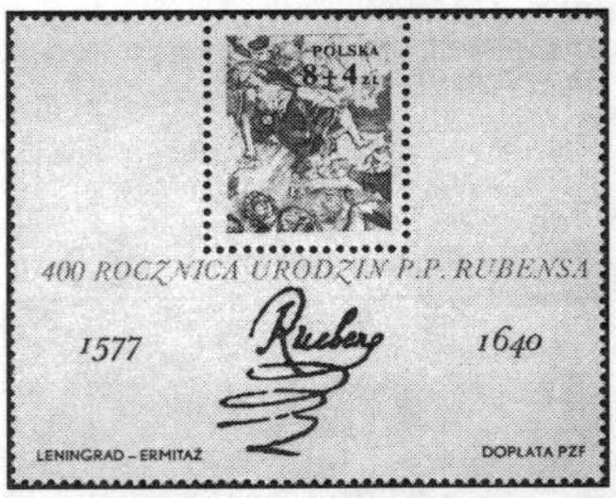

Stoning of St. Stephen, by Rubens — SP57

1977, Apr. 30 **Engr.** ***Perf. 12x11½***
B134 SP57 8z + 4z sepia 1.10 .65

Peter Paul Rubens (1577-1640), Flemish painter.

Outer edge of souvenir sheet is perforated.

Souvenir Sheet

Kazimierz Gzowski — SP58

1978, June 6 **Photo.** ***Perf. 11½x11***
B135 SP58 8.40z + 4z multi 1.10 .55

CAPEX, '78 Canadian Intl. Phil. Exhib., Toronto, June 9-18.

K. S. Gzowski (1813-1898), Polish engineer and lawyer living in Canada, built International Bridge over Niagara River.

Souvenir Sheet

Olympic Rings — SP59

1979, May 19 **Engr.** ***Imperf.***
B136 SP59 10z + 5z black 1.00 .75

1980 Olympic Games.

Monument Type of 1979
Souvenir Sheet

1979, Sept. 1 **Photo.** ***Imperf.***
B137 A731 10z + 5z multi 1.25 .75

Surtax was for monument.

Summer Olympic Type of 1980
Souvenir Sheet

1980, Mar. 31 **Photo.** ***Perf. 11x11½***
B138 A742 10.50z + 5z Kayak 1.00 .75

No. B138 contains one stamp 42x30mm.

Souvenir Sheet

Intercosmos Cooperative Space Program — SP60

1980, Apr. 12 ***Perf. 11½x11***
B139 SP60 6.90z + 3z multi .85 .75

SP61

1970 Uprising Memorial: 2.50z + 1z, Triple Crucifix, Gdansk (27x46mm). 6.50z + 1z, Monument, Gdynia.

1981, Dec. 16 **Photo.** ***Perf. 11½x12***
B140 SP61 2.50 + 1z blk & red .70 .30
B141 SP61 6.50 + 1z blk & lil 1.00 .70

SP62

1984, May 15 **Photo.** ***Perf. 11½x12***

Portrait of a German Princess, by Lucas Cranach

B142 SP62 27z + 10z multi 1.50 .80

1984 UPU Congress, Hamburg. No. B142 issued se-tenant with multicolored label showing UPU emblem and text.

Souvenir Sheet

Madonna with Child, St. John and the Angel, by Sandro Botticelli (1445-1510), Natl. Museum, Warsaw — SP63

1985, Sept. 25 Photo. *Perf. 11*

B143 SP63 65z + 15z multi 2.25 1.25
a. Inscribed: 35 LAT POLSKIEGO . . . 4.50 4.50

ITALIA '85. Surtax for Polish Association of Philatelists.
No. B143a was for the 35th anniv. of the Polish Philatelic Union. Distribution was limited.

Joachim Lelewel (1786-1861), Historian — SP64

1986, Dec. 22 Photo. *Perf. 11½x12*

B144 SP64 10z + 5z multi .30 .20

Surtax for the Natl. Committee for School Aid.

Polish Immigrant Settling in Kasubia, Ontario — SP65

1987, June 13 Photo. *Perf. 12x11½*

B145 SP65 50z + 20z multi 1.40 .70

CAPEX '87, Toronto, Canada. Surtaxed for the Polish Philatelists' Union.

Souvenir Sheet

OLYMPHILEX '87, Rome — SP66

1987, Aug. 28 Litho. *Perf. 14*

B146 SP66 45z + 10z like #2617 1.10 1.10

FINLANDIA '88 — SP67

1988, June 1 Photo. *Perf. 12x11½*

B147 SP67 45z +20z Salmon, reindeer 1.25 .65

Souvenir Sheet

Jerzy Kukuczka, Mountain Climber Awarded Medal by the Intl. Olympic Committee for Climbing the Himalayas — SP68

1988, Aug. 17 Photo. *Perf. 11x11½*

B148 SP68 70z +10z multi 1.50 .80

Surtax for the Polish Olympic Fund.

Aid for Victims of 1997 Oder River Flood — SP69

1997, Aug. 18 Photo. *Perf. 11½x12*

B149 SP69 60g +30g multi .80 .40

Souvenir Sheet

Museum of Posts and Telecommunications, 80th Anniv. — SP70

2001, Oct. 9 Photo. *Perf. 11¼x11½*

B150 SP70 3z +75g multi 2.40 1.25

AIR POST STAMPS

Biplane — AP1

Perf. 12½

1925, Sept. 10 Typo. Unwmk.

C1	AP1	1g lt blue	.65	2.25
C2	AP1	2g orange	.65	2.25
C3	AP1	3g yellow brn	.65	2.25
C4	AP1	5g dk brown	.65	.85
C5	AP1	10g dk green	1.65	.75
C6	AP1	15g red violet	2.50	.85
C7	AP1	20g olive grn	10.50	4.25
C8	AP1	30g dull rose	6.75	1.50
C9	AP1	45g dk violet	8.50	4.25
		Nos. C1-C9 (9)	32.50	19.20
		Set, never hinged	45.00	

Counterfeits exist.
For overprint see No. C11.

Capt. Franciszek Zwirko and Stanislaus Wigura — AP2

Perf. 11½ to 12½ and Compound

1933, Apr. 15 Engr. Wmk. 234

C10 AP2 30g gray green 14.00 1.00
Never hinged 20.00

Winning of the circuit of Europe flight by two Polish aviators in 1932. The stamp was available for both air mail and ordinary postage.
For overprint see No. C12.

Nos. C7 and C10 Overprinted in Red

1934, Aug. 28 Unwmk. *Perf. 12½*

C11 AP1 20g olive green 12.50 6.75

Wmk. 234

Perf. 11½

C12 AP2 30g gray green 7.00 2.25
Set, never hinged 26.00

Polish People's Republic

Douglas Plane over Ruins of Warsaw — AP3

Unwmk.

1946, Mar. 5 Photo. *Perf. 11*

C13	AP3	5z grnsh blk	.40	.20
a.		Without control number	4.00	.40
		Never hinged	6.00	
C14	AP3	10z dk violet	.40	.20
C15	AP3	15z blue	1.25	.25
C16	AP3	20z rose brn	.80	.20
C17	AP3	25z dk bl grn	1.65	.40
C18	AP3	30z red	2.50	.55
		Nos. C13-C18 (6)	7.00	1.80
		Set, never hinged	10.00	

The 10z, 20z and 30z were issued only with control number in lower right stamp margin. The 15z and 25z exist only without number. The 5z comes both ways.
Nos. C13-C18 exist imperforate.

Nos. 345, 344 and 344a Surcharged in Red or Black

a

b

1947, Sept. 10 *Perf. 12½*

C19	A104(a)	40z on 50g (R)	1.65	.90
C20	A103(b)	50z on 25g dl red	1.90	1.75
a.		50z on 25g deep red	2.75	2.50
		Never hinged, #C20a	3.50	
		Set, never hinged	5.50	

Counterfeits exist.

Centaur AP4

1948 *Perf. 11*

C21	AP4	15z dk violet	1.50	.25
C22	AP4	25z deep blue	.80	.20
C23	AP4	30z brown	.65	.45
C24	AP4	50z dk green	1.25	.45
C25	AP4	75z gray black	1.50	.55
C26	AP4	100z red orange	1.50	.45
		Nos. C21-C26 (6)	7.20	2.35
		Set, never hinged	9.50	

Pres. F. D. Roosevelt AP5

Airplane Mechanic and Propeller - AP5a

100z, Casimir Pulaski. 120z, Tadeusz Kosciusko.

1948, Dec. 30 Photo. *Perf. 11½*

Granite Paper

C26A	AP5	80z blue blk	13.00	*22.50*
C26B	AP5	100z purple	14.00	*19.00*
C26C	AP5	120z deep blue	14.00	*19.00*
d.		Souvenir sheet of 3	140.00	*190.00*
		Never hinged	200.00	
		Nos. C26A-C26C (3)	41.00	*60.50*
		Set, never hinged	50.00	

No. C26Cd contains stamps similar to Nos. C26A-C26C with colors changed: 80z ultramarine, 100z carmine rose, 120z dark green. Sold for 500z.

1950, Feb. 6 Engr. *Perf. 12½*

C27 AP5a 500z rose lake 3.25 3.50
Never hinged 5.00

Catalogue values for unused stamps in this section, from this point to the end of the section, are for Never Hinged items.

Seaport AP6

Designs: 90g, Mechanized farm. 1.40z, Warsaw. 5z, Steel mill.

1952, Apr. 10 *Perf. 12x12½*

C28	AP6	55g intense blue	.20	.20
C29	AP6	90g dull green	.30	.20
C30	AP6	1.40z violet brn	.45	.20
C31	AP6	5z gray black	1.65	.60
		Nos. C28-C31 (4)	2.60	1.20

Nos. C28-C31 exist imperf. Value $15.

Congress Badge — AP7

1953, Aug. 24 Photo. *Imperf.*

C32 AP7 55g brown lilac 1.00 .25
C33 AP7 75g brown org 1.50 1.00

3rd World Congress of Students, Warsaw 1953.

Souvenir Sheet

AP8

1954, May 23 Engr. *Perf. 12x12½*

C34 AP8 5z gray green	30.00	20.00

3rd congress of the Polish Phil. Assoc., Warsaw, 1954. Sold for 7.50 zlotys. A similar sheet, imperf. and in dark blue, was issued but had no postal validity.

Paczkow Castle, Luban
AP9

Plane over "Peace" Steelworks
AP10

80g, Kazimierz Dolny. 1.15z, Wawel castle, Cracow. 1.50z, City Hall, Wroclaw. 1.55z, Lazierski Square, Warsaw. 1.95z, Cracow gate, Lublin.

1954, July 9 *Perf. 12½*

C35 AP9 60g dk gray grn	.20	.20
C36 AP9 80g red	.20	.20
C37 AP9 1.15z black	1.00	.40
C38 AP9 1.50z rose lake	.40	.20
C39 AP9 1.55z dp gray bl	.40	.20
C40 AP9 1.95z chocolate	.80	.35
Nos. C35-C40 (6)	3.00	1.55

Wmk. 326 ('58 Values); Unwmkd.

1957-58 Engr. & Photo. *Perf. 12½*

Plane over: 1.50z, Castle Square, Warsaw. 3.40z, Old Market, Cracow. 3.90z, King Boleslaw Chrobry Wall, Szczecin. 4z, Karkonosze mountains. 5z, Gdansk. 10z, Ruins of Liwa Castle. 15z, Old City, Lublin. 20z, Kasprowy Wierch Peak and cable car. 30z, Porabka dam. 50z, M. S. Batory and Gdynia harbor.

C41 AP10 90g black & pink	.20	.20
C42 AP10 1.50z brn & salmon	.20	.20
C43 AP10 3.40z sep & buff	.35	.20
C44 AP10 3.90z dk brn & cit	.60	.45
C45 AP10 4z ind & lt grn	.30	.20
C46 AP10 5z maroon & gray	.55	.20
C47 AP10 10z sepia & grn	1.10	.25
C48 AP10 15z vio bl & pale bl	1.40	.45
C49 AP10 20z vio blk & lem	2.75	.60
C50 AP10 30z ol gray & bis	3.75	1.25
C51 AP10 50z dk bl & gray	6.00	1.65
Nos. C41-C51 (11)	17.20	5.65

Issue dates: 5z, 10z, 20z, 30z, 50z, Dec. 15, 1958. Others, Dec. 6, 1957.

1959, May 23 Litho. Wmk. 326

C52 AP10 10z sepia	1.75	1.50
a. With 5z label	2.00	2.00

65th anniv. of the Polish Philatelic Society. Sheet of 6 stamps and 2 each of 3 different labels. Each label carries an added charge of 5z for a fund to build a Society clubhouse in Warsaw.

Jantar Glider — AP11

Contemporary aviation: 10z, Mi6 transport helicopter. 20z, PZL-106 Kruk, crop spraying plane. 50z, Plane over Warsaw Castle.

1976-78 Unwmk. Engr. *Perf. 11½*

C53 AP11 5z dk blue grn	.40	.25
C54 AP11 10z dk brown	.80	.50
C55 AP11 20z grnsh black	1.50	.75
C56 AP11 50z claret	3.00	1.90
Nos. C53-C56 (4)	5.70	3.40

Issued: 5z, 10z, 3/27/76; 20z, 2/15/77; 50z, 2/2/78.

AIR POST SEMI-POSTAL STAMP

Catalogue values for unused stamps in this section are for Never Hinged items.

Polish People's Republic

Wing of Jet Plane and Letter — SPAP1

Perf. 11½

1957, Mar. 28 Unwmk. Photo.

CB1 SPAP1 4z + 2z blue	3.00	3.50
a. Souv. sheet of 1, ultra, imperf.	10.00	4.50

7th Polish National Philatelic Exhibition, Warsaw. Sheet of 12 with 4 diagonally arranged gray labels.

POSTAGE DUE STAMPS

Cracow Issues

Postage Due Stamps of Austria, 1916, Overprinted in Black or Red

1919, Jan. 10 Unwmk. *Perf. 12½*

J1 D4 5h rose red	7.00	6.00
J2 D4 10h rose red	*2,500.*	*1,750.*
J3 D4 15h rose red	3.75	*6.00*
a. Inverted overprint	150.00	
J4 D4 20h rose red	275.00	*350.00*
J5 D4 25h rose red	17.50	*25.00*
J6 D4 30h rose red	*800.00*	*750.00*
J7 D4 40h rose red	*700.00*	*600.00*
J8 D5 1k ultra (R)	*2,400.*	*2,400.*
J9 D5 5k ultra (R)	*2,400.*	*2,400.*
J10 D5 10k ultra (R)	*10,000.*	*9,000.*
a. Black overprint	*20,000.*	—

Overprint on Nos. J1-J7, J10a is type. Overprint on Nos. J8-J10 is slightly larger than illustration, has a different ornament between lines of type and is litho.

D6

Type of Austria, 1916-18, Surcharged in Black

1919, Jan. 10

J11 D6 15h on 36h vio	300.00	200.00
J12 D6 50h on 42h choc	30.00	*50.00*
a. Double surcharge	—	*8,000.*

See note above No. 41.
Counterfeits exist of Nos. J1-J12.

Regular Issues

Numerals of Value
D7 D8

1919 Typo. *Perf. 11½*

For Northern Poland

J13 D7 2f red orange	.40	.30
J14 D7 4f red orange	.20	.20
J15 D7 5f red orange	.20	.20
J16 D7 10f red orange	.20	.20
J17 D7 20f red orange	.20	.20
J18 D7 30f red orange	.20	.20
J19 D7 50f red orange	.20	.20
J20 D7 100f red orange	.75	.45
J21 D7 500f red orange	1.75	1.25

For Southern Poland

J22 D7 2h dark blue	.20	.20
J23 D7 4h dark blue	.20	.20
J24 D7 5h dark blue	.20	.20
J25 D7 10h dark blue	.20	.20
J26 D7 20h dark blue	.20	.20
J27 D7 30h dark blue	.20	.20
J28 D7 50h dark blue	.20	.20
J29 D7 100h dark blue	.30	.25
J30 D7 500h dark blue	1.40	1.10
Nos. J13-J30 (18)	7.20	5.95

Counterfeits exist.

1920 *Perf. 9, 10, 11½*

Thin Laid Paper

J31 D7 20f dark blue	.70	.50
J32 D7 100f dark blue	.35	.25
J33 D7 200f dark blue	.60	.50
J34 D7 500f dark blue	.35	.25
Nos. J31-J34 (4)	2.00	1.50

Regular Issue of 1919 Surcharged

1921, Jan. 25 *Imperf.*

Wove Paper

J35 A9 6m on 15h brown	.75	.40
J36 A9 6m on 25h car	.75	.40
J37 A9 20m on 10h lake	1.50	1.10
J38 A9 20m on 50h indigo	2.00	1.40
J39 A9 35m on 70h dp bl	12.00	12.00
Nos. J35-J39 (5)	17.00	15.30

Counterfeits exist.

Perf. 9 to 14½ and Compound

1921-22 Typo.

Thin Laid or Wove Paper

Size: 17x22mm

J40 D8 1m indigo	.30	.20
J41 D8 2m indigo	.30	.20
J42 D8 4m indigo	.30	.20
J43 D8 6m indigo	.30	.20
J44 D8 8m indigo	.30	.20
J45 D8 20m indigo	.30	.20
J46 D8 50m indigo	.30	.20
J47 D8 100m indigo	.60	.20
Nos. J40-J47 (8)	2.70	1.60

Nos. J44-J45, J41 Surcharged

Perf. 9 to 14½ and Compound

1923, Nov.

J48 D8 10,000(m) on 8m indigo	1.50	.20
J49 D8 20,000(m) on 20m indigo	1.50	.20
J50 D8 50,000(m) on 2m indigo	7.00	.70
Nos. J48-J50 (3)	10.00	1.10

Type of 1921-22 Issue

1923 Typo. *Perf. 12½*

Size: 19x24mm

J51 D8 50m indigo	.20	.20
J52 D8 100m indigo	.20	.20
J53 D8 200m indigo	.20	.20
J54 D8 500m indigo	.20	.20
J55 D8 1000m indigo	.20	.20
J56 D8 2000m indigo	.20	.20
J57 D8 10,000m indigo	.20	.20
J58 D8 20,000m indigo	.20	.20
J59 D8 30,000m indigo	.20	.20
J60 D8 50,000m indigo	.40	.20
J61 D8 100,000m indigo	.40	.20
J62 D8 200,000m indigo	.45	.20
J63 D8 300,000m indigo	.45	.30
J64 D8 500,000m indigo	.65	.20
J65 D8 1,000,000m indigo	1.50	.60
J66 D8 2,000,000m indigo	2.75	.60
J67 D8 3,000,000m indigo	3.00	.85
Nos. J51-J67 (17)	11.40	4.95

D9 D10

Perf. 10 to 13½ and Compound

1924

Size: 20x25½mm

J68 D9 1g brown	.30	.25
J69 D9 2g brown	.30	.25
J70 D9 4g brown	.30	.25
J71 D9 6g brown	.55	.25
J72 D9 10g brown	3.25	.25
J73 D9 15g brown	2.50	.40
J74 D9 20g brown	6.00	.40
J75 D9 25g brown	5.00	.40
J76 D9 30g brown	1.10	.40
J77 D9 40g brown	1.10	.40
J78 D9 50g brown	1.10	.40
J79 D9 1z brown	1.00	.55
J80 D9 2z brown	1.00	.55
J81 D9 3z brown	1.90	2.25
J82 D9 5z brown	1.90	.85
Nos. J68-J82 (15)	27.30	7.85

Nos. J68-J69 and J72-J75 exist measuring 19½x24½mm.

For surcharges see Nos. J84-J91.

1930, July *Perf. 12½*

J83 D10 5g olive brown	.70	.20
Never hinged	1.00	

Postage Due Stamps of 1924 Surcharged

Perf. 10 to 13½ and Compound

1934-38

J84 D9 10g on 2z brown ('38)	.40	.30
J85 D9 15g on 2z brown	.40	.30
J86 D9 20g on 1z brown	.40	.30
J87 D9 20g on 5z brown	2.00	.55
J88 D9 25g on 40g brown	1.25	.55
J89 D9 30g on 40g brown	.85	.55
J90 D9 50g on 40g brown	.85	.70
J91 D9 50g on 3z brown ('35)	1.75	1.00
Nos. J84-J91 (8)	7.90	4.25
Set, never hinged	18.00	

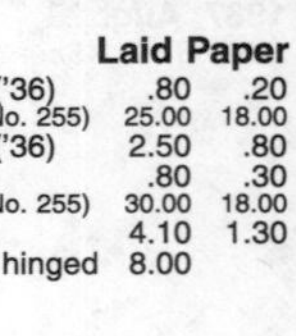

No. 255a Surcharged in Red or Indigo

1934-36 Laid Paper

J92 A50 10g on 1z (R) ('36)	.80	.20
a. Vertically laid paper (No. 255)	25.00	18.00
J93 A50 20g on 1z (R) ('36)	2.50	.80
J94 A50 25g on 1z (I)	.80	.30
a. Vertically laid paper (No. 255)	30.00	18.00
Nos. J92-J94 (3)	4.10	1.30
Set, never hinged	8.00	

D11

1938-39 Typo. *Perf. 12½x12*

J95 D11 5g dark blue green .20 .20
J96 D11 10g dark blue green .20 .20
J97 D11 15g dark blue green .20 .20
J98 D11 20g dark blue green .60 .20
J99 D11 25g dark blue green .20 .20
J100 D11 30g dark blue green .40 .20
J101 D11 50g dark blue green .80 1.25
J102 D11 1z dark blue green 2.50 1.65
Nos. J95-J102 (8) 5.10 4.10
Set, never hinged 12.00

For surcharges see Nos. N51-N55.

Polish People's Republic

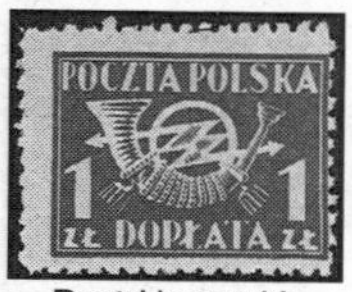

Post Horn with Thunderbolts
D12

Polish Eagle
D13

Perf. 11x10½

1945, May 20 Litho. Unwmk.
Size: 25½x19mm

J103 D12 1z orange brown .20 .20
J104 D12 2z orange brown .20 .20
J105 D12 3z orange brown .25 .20
J106 D12 5z orange brown .35 .30
Nos. J103-J106 (4) 1.00 .90
Set, never hinged 2.00

Type of 1945

Perf. 11, 11½ (P) or Imperf. (I)

1946-49 Photo.
Size: 29x21½mm

J106A D12 1z org brn (P) ('49) .20 .20
J107 D12 2z org brn (P,I) .20 .20
J108 D12 3z org brn (P,I) .20 .20
J109 D12 5z org brn (I) .20 .20
J110 D12 6z org brn (I) .20 .20
J111 D12 10z org brn (I) .20 .20
J112 D12 15z org brn (P,I) .55 .30
J113 D12 25z org brn (P,I) .75 .60
J114 D12 100z brn (P) ('49) 1.50 .90
J115 D12 150z brn (P) ('49) 2.00 1.00
Nos. J106A-J115 (10) 6.00 4.00
Set, never hinged 8.00

1950 Engr. *Perf. 12x12½*

J116 D13 5z red brown .20 .20
J117 D13 10z red brown .20 .20
J118 D13 15z red brown .25 .30
J119 D13 20z red brown .30 .35
J120 D13 25z red brown .45 .45
J121 D13 50z red brown .70 .60
J122 D13 100z red brown .90 .90
Nos. J116-J122 (7) 3.00 3.00
Set, never hinged 6.00

1951-52

J123 D13 5g red brown .20 .20
J124 D13 10g red brown .20 .20
J125 D13 15g red brown .20 .20
J126 D13 20g red brown .20 .20
J127 D13 25g red brown .20 .20
J128 D13 30g red brown .20 .20
J129 D13 50g red brown .30 .30
J130 D13 60g red brown .35 .30
J131 D13 90g red brown .50 .45
J132 D13 1z red brown .60 .55
J133 D13 2z red brown 1.25 .95
J134 D13 5z brown violet 2.75 2.25
Nos. J123-J134 (12) 6.95 6.00
Set, never hinged 9.00

1953, Apr. Photo.
Without imprint

J135 D13 5g red brown .25 .25
J136 D13 10g red brown .25 .25
J137 D13 15g red brown .25 .25
J138 D13 20g red brown .25 .25
J139 D13 25g red brown .25 .25
J140 D13 30g red brown .25 .25
J141 D13 50g red brown .50 .40
J142 D13 60g red brown .70 .60
J143 D13 90g red brown .95 .75
J144 D13 1z red brown 1.10 1.00
J145 D13 2z red brown 2.25 1.75
Nos. J135-J145 (11) 7.00 6.00
Set, never hinged 9.00

Catalogue values for unused stamps in this section, from this point to the end of the section, are for Never Hinged items.

1980, Sept. 2 Litho. *Perf. 12½*

J146 D13 1z lt red brown .20 .20
J147 D13 2z gray olive .20 .20
J148 D13 3z dull violet .30 .20
J149 D13 5z brown .45 .20
Nos. J146-J149 (4) 1.15 .80

D14

1998, June 18 Litho. *Perf. 14*

J150 D14 5g lilac, blk & yel .20 .20
J151 D14 10g green blue, blk & yel .20 .20
J152 D14 20g green, blk & yel .20 .20
J153 D14 50g yellow & black .35 .20
J154 D14 80g orange, blk & yel .60 .30
J155 D14 1z red, blk & yel .75 .40
Nos. J150-J155 (6) 2.30 1.50

OFFICIAL STAMPS

O1

Perf. 10, 11½, 10x11½, 11½x10

1920, Feb. 1 Litho. Unwmk.

O1 O1 3f vermilion .35 *.45*
O2 O1 5f vermilion .35 *.45*
O3 O1 10f vermilion .35 *.45*
O4 O1 15f vermilion .35 *.45*
O5 O1 25f vermilion .35 *.45*
O6 O1 50f vermilion .35 *.45*
O7 O1 100f vermilion .35 *.45*
O8 O1 150f vermilion .65 .45
O9 O1 200f vermilion .65 .45
O10 O1 300f vermilion .50 .45
O11 O1 600f vermilion .75 .45
Nos. O1-O11 (11) 5.00 4.95

Numerals Larger
Stars inclined outward

1920, Nov. 20 *Perf. 11½*
Thin Laid Paper

O12 O1 5f red .25 *.40*
O13 O1 10f red .75 .70
O14 O1 15f red .50 *.95*
O15 O1 25f red 1.10 .95
O16 O1 50f red 1.40 1.00
Nos. O12-O16 (5) 4.00 4.00

Polish Eagle
O3 O4

Perf. 12x12½

1933, Aug. 1 Typo. Wmk. 234

O17 O3 (30g) vio (Zwyczajna) .95 .20
O18 O3 (80g) red (Polecona) 2.25 .30
Set, never hinged 4.00

1935, Apr. 1

O19 O4 (25g) bl vio (Zwyczajna) .20 .20
O20 O4 (55g) car (Polecona) .30 .20
Set, never hinged .75

Stamps inscribed "Zwyczajna" or "Zwykla" were for ordinary official mail. Those with "Polecona" were for registered official mail.

Polish People's Republic

Polish Eagle — O5

Perf. 11, 14

1945, July 1 Photo. Unwmk.

O21 O5 (5z) bl vio (Zwykla) .35 .20
a. Imperf. 1.00 1.00
O22 O5 (10z) red (Polecona) .65 .20
a. Imperf. 1.65 1.25
Set, never hinged, #O21, O22 2.00
Set, never hinged, #O21a, O22a 4.00

Control number at bottom right: M-01705 on No. O21; M-01706 on No. O22.

Type of 1945 Redrawn

1946, July 31

O23 O5 (5z) dl bl vio (Zwykla) .30 .20
O24 O5 (10z) dl rose red (Polecona) .50 .25
Set, never hinged 1.50

The redrawn stamps appear blurred and the eagle contains fewer lines of shading.
Control number at bottom right: M-01709 on Nos. O23-O26.

Redrawn Type of 1946

1946, July 31 *Imperf.*

O25 O5 (60g) dl bl vio (Zwykla) .40 .20
O26 O5 (1.55z) dl rose red (Polecona) .40 .20
Set, never hinged 1.25

Type of 1945, 2nd Redrawing
No Control Number at Lower Right

Perf. 11, 11½, 11x12½

1950-53 Unwmk.

O27 O5 (60g) blue (Zwykla) .25 .20
O28 O5 (1.55z) red (Polecona) ('53) .40 .20
Set, never hinged .80

Redrawn Type of 1952

1954 *Perf. 13x11, 11½, 14*

O29 O5 (60g) slate gray (Zwykla) 3.00 1.00
Never hinged 5.00

O6

Perf. 11x11½, 12x12½

1954, Aug. 15 Engr.

O30 O6 (60g) dark blue (Zwykla) .25 .20
O31 O6 (1.55z) red (Polecona) .45 .25
Set, never hinged 1.00

Polish People's Republic, 10th anniversary.

NEWSPAPER STAMPS

Austrian Newspaper Stamps of 1916 Overprinted

1919, Jan. 10 Unwmk. *Imperf.*

P1 N9 2h brown 9.50 *15.75*
P2 N9 4h green 2.75 *5.25*
P3 N9 6h dark blue 2.75 *5.25*
P4 N9 10h orange 67.50 62.50
P5 N9 30h claret 7.50 11.25
Nos. P1-P5 (5) 90.00 100.00

See note above No. 41.
Counterfeits exist of Nos. P1-P5.

OCCUPATION STAMPS

Issued under German Occupation

German Stamps of 1905 Overprinted

Perf. 14, 14½

1915, May 12 Wmk. 125

N1 A16 3pf brown 1.25 .90
N2 A16 5pf green 2.00 .90
N3 A16 10pf carmine 2.00 .90
N4 A16 20pf ultra 4.00 1.25
N5 A16 40pf lake & blk 11.75 6.25
Nos. N1-N5 (5) 21.00 10.20

German Stamps of 1905-17 Overprinted

1916-17

N6 A22 2½pf gray 1.25 .90
N7 A16 3pf brown 1.25 .90
N8 A16 5pf green 1.25 .90
N9 A22 7½pf orange 1.25 .90
N10 A16 10pf carmine 1.25 .90
N11 A22 15pf yel brn 4.25 1.10
N12 A22 15pf dk vio ('17) 1.25 .90
N13 A16 20pf ultra 1.75 .90
N14 A16 30pf org & blk, *buff* 7.00 6.00
N15 A16 40pf lake & blk 1.00 .90
N16 A16 60pf magenta 3.50 1.25
Nos. N6-N16 (11) 25.00 15.55

For overprints and surcharges see #15-26.

German Stamps of 1934 Surcharged in Black

1939, Dec. 1 Wmk. 237 *Perf. 14*

N17 A64 6g on 3pf bister .25 .30
N18 A64 8g on 4pf dl bl .25 .35
N19 A64 12g on 6pf dk grn .25 .30
N20 A64 16g on 8pf vermilion .70 1.00
N21 A64 20g on 10pf choc .25 .30
N22 A64 24g on 12pf dp car .25 .30
N23 A64 30g on 15pf maroon .80 .90
N24 A64 40g on 20pf brt bl .70 .40
N25 A64 50g on 25pf ultra .70 .75
N26 A64 60g on 30pf ol grn .70 .45
N27 A64 80g on 40pf red vio .90 .90
N28 A64 1z on 50pf dk grn & blk 2.00 1.40
N29 A64 2z on 100(pf) org & blk 3.75 3.00
Nos. N17-N29 (13) 11.50 10.35
Set, never hinged 16.00

Stamps of Poland 1937, Surcharged in Black or Brown

1940 Unwmk. *Perf. 12½, 12½x13*

N30 A80 24g on 25g sl grn 1.10 1.75
N31 A81 40g on 30g rose vio .40 .65
N32 A80 50g on 55g blue .35 .50

Similar Surcharge on Stamps of 1938-39

N33 A83 2g on 5g red org .25 .35
N34 A83 4(g) on 5g red org .25 .35
N35 A83 6(g) on 10g grn .25 .35
N36 A83 8(g) on 10g grn (Br) .30 .45
N37 A83 10(g) on 10g grn .25 .35
N38 A83 12(g) on 15g redsh brn (#339) .25 .35
N39 A83 16(g) on 15g redsh brn (#339) .30 .45

N40	A83	24g on 25g dl vio		.25	.35
N41	A83	30(g) on 30g rose red		.30	.45
N42	A83	50(g) on 50g brt red vio		.35	.55
N43	A83	60(g) on 55g ultra		7.50	9.25
N44	A83	80(g) on 75g dl grn		7.50	9.25
N45	A83	1z on 1z org		7.50	9.25
N46	A83	2z on 2z car rose		5.00	5.75
N47	A95	3z on 3z gray blk		5.00	5.75

Similar Surcharge on Nos. B32-B34

N48	SP5	30g on 5g+5g	.35	.55
N49	SP5	40g on 25g+10g	.35	.55
N50	SP5	1z on 55g+15g	7.25	6.50

Similar Surcharge on Nos. J98-J102

Perf. 12½x12

N51	D11	50(g) on 20g	.65	1.25
N52	D11	50(g) on 25g	13.00	13.00
N53	D11	50(g) on 30g	40.00	35.00
N54	D11	50(g) on 50g	.65	1.00
N55	D11	50(g) on 1z	1.10	1.00
		Nos. N30-N55 (26)	100.45	105.00
		Set, never hinged	140.00	

The surcharge on Nos. N30 to N55 is arranged to fit the shape of the stamp and obliterate the original denomination. On some values, "General Gouvernement" appears at the bottom. Counterfeits exist.

St. Florian's Gate, Cracow — OS1

Palace, Warsaw — OS13

Designs: 8g, Watch Tower, Cracow. 10g, Cracow Gate, Lublin. 12g, Courtyard and statue of Copernicus. 20g, Dominican Church, Cracow. 24g, Wawel Castle, Cracow. 30g, Church, Lublin. 40g, Arcade, Cloth Hall, Cracow. 48g, City Hall, Sandomierz. 50g, Court House, Cracow. 60g, Courtyard, Cracow. 80g, St. Mary's Church, Cracow.

1940-41 Unwmk. Photo. *Perf. 14*

N56	OS1	6g	brown	.30	.55
N57	OS1	8g	brn org	.30	.55
N58	OS1	8g	bl blk ('41)	.30	.40
N59	OS1	10g	emerald	.20	.25
N60	OS1	12g	dk grn	3.00	.30
N61	OS1	12g	dp vio ('41)	.30	.20
N62	OS1	20g	dk ol brn	.20	.20
N63	OS1	24g	henna brn	.20	.20
N64	OS1	30g	purple	.20	.20
N65	OS1	30g	vio brn ('41)	.20	.30
N66	OS1	40g	slate blk	.20	.20
N67	OS1	48g	chnt brn ('41)	.60	.80
N68	OS1	50g	brt bl	.20	.20
N69	OS1	60g	slate grn	.20	.25
N70	OS1	80g	dull pur	.25	.30
N71	OS13	1z	rose lake	2.00	1.10
N72	OS13	1z	Prus grn ('41)	.55	.55
			Nos. N56-N72 (17)	9.20	6.55
			Set, never hinged	11.00	

For surcharges see Nos. NB1-NB4.

Cracow Castle and City, 15th Century OS14

1941, Apr. 20 Engr. *Perf. 14½*

N73	OS14	10z red & ol blk	2.00	2.00
		Never hinged	2.50	

Printed in sheets of 8.

Rondel and Florian's Gate, Cracow OS15

Design: 4z, Tyniec Monastery, Vistula River.

1941 Perf. 13½x14

N74	OS15	2z dk ultra	.35	.45
N75	OS15	4z slate grn	.50	.60
		Set, never hinged	1.25	

Adolf Hitler — OS17

1941-43 Unwmk. Photo. *Perf. 14*

N76	OS17	2g	gray blk	.20	.20
N77	OS17	6g	golden brn	.20	.20
N78	OS17	8g	slate blue	.20	.20
N79	OS17	10g	green	.20	.20
N80	OS17	12g	purple	.20	.20
N81	OS17	16g	org red	.50	.50
N82	OS17	20g	blk brn	.20	.20
N83	OS17	24g	henna	.20	.20
N84	OS17	30g	rose vio	.45	.20
N85	OS17	32g	dk bl grn	.50	.40
N86	OS17	40g	brt blue	.20	.20
N87	OS17	48g	chestnut	.55	.40
N88	OS17	50g	vio bl ('43)	.20	.20
N89	OS17	60g	dk olive ('43)	.20	.20
N90	OS17	80g	dk vio ('43)	.20	.20
			Nos. N76-N90 (15)		3.70
			Set, never hinged	4.50	

A 20g black brown exists with head of Hans Frank substituted for that of Hitler. It was printed and used by Resistance movements.

Nos. N76-N80, N82-N90 exist imperf.

1942-44 Engr. *Perf. 12½*

N91	OS17	50g	vio bl	.40	.50
N92	OS17	60g	dk ol	.40	.50
N93	OS17	80g	dk red vio	.40	.50
N94	OS17	1z	slate grn	.40	.50
a.			Perf. 14 ('44)	.50	.60
N95	OS17	1.20z	dk brn	.45	.55
a.			Perf. 14 ('44)	.60	.80
N96	OS17	1.60z	bl vio	.50	.60
a.			Perf. 14 ('44)	.75	1.10
			Nos. N91-N96 (6)	2.55	3.15
			Set, never hinged	3.50	
			Set, #N94a, N95a, N96a, never hinged	3.00	

Exist imperf.

Rondel and Florian's Gate, Cracow OS18

Designs: 4z, Tyniec Monastery, Vistula River. 6z, View of Lwow. 10z, Cracow Castle and City, 15th Century.

1943-44 Perf. 13½x14

N100	OS18	2z slate grn	.20	.20
N101	OS18	4z dk gray vio	.30	.35
N102	OS18	6z sepia ('44)	.50	.50
N103	OS18	10z org brn & gray blk	.50	.60
		Nos. N100-N103 (4)	1.50	1.65
		Set, never hinged	1.90	

OCCUPATION SEMI-POSTAL STAMPS

Issued under German Occupation

Types of 1940 Occupation Postage Stamps Surcharged in Red

Unwmk.

1940, Aug. 17 Photo. *Perf. 14*

NB1	OS1	12g + 8g olive gray	3.00	3.50
NB2	OS1	24g + 16g olive gray	3.00	3.50
NB3	OS1	50g + 50g olive gray	3.50	4.00
NB4	OS1	80g + 80g olive gray	3.50	4.00
		Nos. NB1-NB4 (4)	13.00	15.00
		Set, never hinged	15.00	

German Peasant Girl in Poland OSP1

Designs: 24g+26g, Woman wearing scarf. 30g+20g, Similar to type OSP4.

1940, Oct. 26 Engr. *Perf. 14½*

Thick Paper

NB5	OSP1	12g + 38g dk sl grn	2.25	2.75
NB6	OSP1	24g + 26g cop red	2.25	2.75
NB7	OSP1	30g + 20g dk pur	2.75	3.75
		Nos. NB5-NB7 (3)	7.25	9.25
		Set, never hinged	8.50	

1st anniversary of the General Government.

German Peasant OSP4

1940, Dec. 1 Perf. 12

NB8	OSP4	12g + 8g dk grn	1.00	.90
NB9	OSP4	24g + 16g rose red	1.65	1.65
NB10	OSP4	30g + 30g vio brn	2.00	2.00
NB11	OSP4	50g + 50g ultra	2.75	2.50
		Nos. NB8-NB11 (4)	7.40	7.05
		Set, never hinged	9.25	

The surtax was for war relief.

Adolf Hitler — OSP5

Unwmk.

1942, Apr. 20 Engr. *Perf. 11*

Thick Cream Paper

NB12	OSP5	30g + 1z brn car	.30	.35
NB13	OSP5	50g + 1z dk ultra	.30	.35
NB14	OSP5	1.20z + 1z brown	.30	.35
		Nos. NB12-NB14 (3)	.90	1.05
		Set, never hinged	1.40	

To commemorate Hitler's 53rd birthday. Printed in sheets of 25.

Ancient Lublin — OSP6

Designs: 24g+6g, 1z+1z, Modern Lublin.

1942, Aug. 15 Photo. *Perf. 12½*

NB15	OSP6	12g + 8g rose vio	.20	.20
NB16	OSP6	24g + 6g henna	.20	.20
NB17	OSP6	50g + 50g dp bl	.20	.25
NB18	OSP6	1z + 1z dp grn	.40	.55
		Nos. NB15-NB18 (4)	1.00	1.20
		Set, never hinged	1.40	

600th anniversary of Lublin.

Veit Stoss — OSP8

Adolf Hitler — OSP13

Designs: 24g+26g, Hans Durer. 30g+30g, Johann Schuch. 50g+50g, Joseph Elsner. 1z+1z, Nicolaus Copernicus.

1942, Nov. 20 Engr. *Perf. 13½x14*

NB19	OSP8	12g + 18g dl pur	.20	.20
NB20	OSP8	24g + 26g dl henna	.20	.20
NB21	OSP8	30g + 30g dl rose vio	.20	.20
NB22	OSP8	50g + 50g dl bl vio	.20	.25
NB23	OSP8	1z + 1z dl myr grn	.40	.45
		Nos. NB19-NB23 (5)		1.30
		Set, never hinged	1.40	

For overprint see No. NB27.

1943, Apr. 20

NB24	OSP13	12g + 1z purple	.20	.25
NB25	OSP13	24g + 1z rose car	.20	.25
NB26	OSP13	84g + 1z myrtle grn	.25	.40
		Nos. NB24-NB26 (3)	.65	.90
		Set, never hinged	1.20	

To commemorate Hitler's 54th birthday.

Type of 1942 Overprinted in Black

1943, May 24

NB27	OSP8	1z + 1z rose lake	.80	1.10
		Never hinged	1.10	

Nicolaus Copernicus. Printed in sheets of 10, with marginal inscription.

Cracow Gate, Lublin — OSP14

Adolf Hitler — OSP19

Designs: 24g+76g, Cloth Hall, Cracow. 30g+70g, New Government Building, Radom. 50g+1z, Bruhl Palace, Warsaw. 1z+2z, Town Hall, Lwow.

The center of the designs is embossed with the emblem of the National Socialist Party.

1943 Photogravure, Embossed

NB28	OSP14	12g + 38g dk grn	.20	.20
NB29	OSP14	24g + 76g red	.20	.20
NB30	OSP14	30g + 70g rose vio	.20	.20
NB31	OSP14	50g + 1z brt bl	.20	.20
NB32	OSP14	1z + 2z bl blk	.20	.35
		Nos. NB28-NB32 (5)		1.15
		Set, never hinged	.90	

3rd anniversary of the National Socialist Party in Poland.

1944, Apr. 20 Photo. *Perf. 14x13½*

NB33	OSP19	12g + 1z green	.20	.20
NB34	OSP19	24g + 1z brn red	.20	.20
NB35	OSP19	84g + 1z dk vio	.20	.20
		Nos. NB33-NB35 (3)		.60
		Set, never hinged	.55	

To commemorate Hitler's 55th birthday. Printed in sheets of 25.

Conrad Celtis — OSP20

Designs: 24g+26g, Andreas Schluter. 30g+30g, Hans Boner. 50g+50g, Augustus II. 1z+1z, Georg Gottlieb Pusch.

1944, July 15 Engr. *Perf. 13½x14*

NB36	OSP20	12g + 18g dk grn	.20	.20
NB37	OSP20	24g + 26g dk red	.20	.20
NB38	OSP20	30g + 30g rose vio	.20	.30
NB39	OSP20	50g + 50g ultra	.20	.30
NB40	OSP20	1z + 1z dl red brn	.20	.30
		Nos. NB36-NB40 (5)		1.20
		Set, never hinged	.85	

Cracow Castle OSP25

1944, Oct. 26 — *Perf. 14½*

NB41	OSP25 10z + 10z red & blk	7.50	12.00
	Never hinged	11.00	
a.	Imperf.	9.00	
	Never hinged	12.00	
b.	10z + 10z car & greenish blk	12.50	18.00

5th anniv. of the General Government, Oct. 26, 1944. Printed in sheets of 8.

OCCUPATION RURAL DELIVERY STAMPS

Issued under German Occupation

OSD1

Perf. 13½

1940, Dec. 1 — **Photo.** — **Unwmk.**

NL1	OSD1	10g red orange	.45	*.65*
NL2	OSD1	20g red orange	.45	*1.00*
NL3	OSD1	30g red orange	.45	*1.00*
NL4	OSD1	50g red orange	1.10	*2.00*
		Nos. NL1-NL4 (4)	2.45	*4.65*
		Set, never hinged	4.00	

OCCUPATION OFFICIAL STAMPS

Issued under German Occupation

Eagle and Swastika OOS1

Perf. 12, 13½x14

1940, Apr. — **Photo.** — **Unwmk.**

Size: 31x23mm

NO1	OOS1	6g lt brown	.95	1.50
NO2	OOS1	8g gray	.95	1.50
NO3	OOS1	10g green	.95	1.50
NO4	OOS1	12g dk green	1.10	1.90
NO5	OOS1	20g dk brown	1.10	3.25
NO6	OOS1	24g henna brn	17.50	.50
NO7	OOS1	30g rose lake	1.50	2.75
NO8	OOS1	40g dl violet	1.50	4.50
NO9	OOS1	48g dl olive	6.25	4.75
NO10	OOS1	50g royal bl	1.25	2.75
NO11	OOS1	60g dk ol grn	.95	1.90
NO12	OOS1	80g rose vio	.95	1.90

Size: 35x26mm

NO13	OOS1	1z gray blk & brn vio	3.00	4.75
NO14	OOS1	3z gray blk & chnt	3.00	4.50
NO15	OOS1	5z gray blk & org brn	4.25	6.25
		Nos. NO1-NO15 (15)	45.20	44.20
		Set, never hinged	65.00	

1940 — *Perf. 12*

Size: 21¼x16¼mm

NO16	OOS1	6g brown	.65	1.10
NO17	OOS1	8g slate	1.10	1.75
NO18	OOS1	10g dp grn	1.75	2.00
NO19	OOS1	12g slate grn	1.75	2.00
NO20	OOS1	20g blk brn	.90	1.10
NO21	OOS1	24g cop brn	.65	1.10
NO22	OOS1	30g rose lake	1.10	1.75
NO23	OOS1	40g dl pur	1.75	2.00
NO24	OOS1	50g royal blue	1.75	2.00
		Nos. NO16-NO24 (9)	11.40	14.80
		Set, never hinged	16.00	

Nazi Emblem and Cracow Castle — OOS2

1943 — **Photo.** — *Perf. 14*

NO25	OOS2	6g brown	.20	.20
NO26	OOS2	8g slate blue	.20	.20
NO27	OOS2	10g green	.20	.20
NO28	OOS2	12g dk vio	.35	.25
NO29	OOS2	16g red org	.20	.20
NO30	OOS2	20g dk brn	.20	.20
NO31	OOS2	24g dk red	.35	.20
NO32	OOS2	30g rose vio	.20	.20
NO33	OOS2	40g blue	.20	.20
NO34	OOS2	60g olive grn	.20	.20
NO35	OOS2	80g dull claret	.30	.20
NO36	OOS2	100g slate blk	.35	.60
		Nos. NO25-NO36 (12)	2.95	2.85
		Set, never hinged	3.50	

POLISH OFFICES ABROAD

OFFICES IN DANZIG

Poland Nos. 215-225 Overprinted

1925, Jan. 5 — **Unwmk.** — *Perf. 11½x12*

1K1	A36	1g orange brn	.45	1.10
1K2	A36	2g dk brown	.60	3.25
1K3	A36	3g orange	.60	1.10
1K4	A36	5g olive grn	15.00	7.50
1K5	A36	10g blue grn	5.00	2.25
1K6	A36	15g red	30.00	5.75
1K7	A36	20g blue	1.75	1.10
1K8	A36	25g red brown	1.75	1.10
1K9	A36	30g dp violet	2.00	1.10
1K10	A36	40g indigo	2.00	1.10
1K11	A36	50g magenta	5.50	1.65
		Nos. 1K1-1K11 (11)	64.65	27.00

Same Ovpt. on Poland Nos. 230-231

1926 — *Perf. 11½, 12*

1K11A	A39	5g yellow grn	52.50	37.50
1K12	A40	10g violet	12.50	15.00

Counterfeit overprints are known on Nos. 1K1-1K32.

No. 232 Overprinted

1926-27

1K13	A41	15g rose red	45.00	40.00

Same Overprint on Redrawn Stamps of 1926-27

Perf. 13

1K14	A39	5g yellow grn	2.00	1.75
1K15	A40	10g violet	2.00	1.75
1K16	A41	15g rose red	4.00	3.75
1K17	A43	20g dull red	3.25	2.25
		Nos. 1K14-1K17 (4)	11.25	9.50

Same Ovpt. on Poland Nos. 250, 255a

1928-30 — *Perf. 12½*

1K18	A44	25g yellow brn	4.75	1.50

Laid Paper

Perf. 11½x12, 12½x11½

1K19	A50	1z blk, *cr* ('30)	30.00	30.00
		Set, never hinged	47.50	

Poland Nos. 258-260 Overprinted — **PORT GDAŃSK**

1929-30 — *Perf. 12x12½*

1K20	A53	5g dk violet	1.65	1.40
1K21	A53	10g green ('30)	1.65	1.40
1K22	A53	25g red brown	2.75	1.40
		Nos. 1K20-1K22 (3)	6.05	4.20
		Set, never hinged	8.00	

Same Overprint on Poland No. 257

1931, Jan. 5 — *Perf. 12½*

1K23	A52	15g ultra	3.50	4.00
		Never hinged	5.00	

Poland No. 255 Overprinted in Dark Blue

1933, July 1 — *Perf. 11½*

Laid Paper

1K24	A50	1z black, *cream*	82.50	100.00
		Never hinged	110.00	

Poland Nos. 268-270 Overprinted in Black

1934-36 — **Wmk. 234** — *Perf. 12x12½*

1K25	A58	5g dl violet	3.25	3.75
1K26	A58	10g green ('36)	35.00	*72.50*
1K27	A58	15g red brown	3.25	3.75
		Nos. 1K25-1K27 (3)	41.50	*80.00*
		Set, never hinged	60.00	

Poland Nos. 294, 296, 298 Overprinted in Black in one or two lines

1935-36 — **Unwmk.** — *Perf. 12½x13*

1K28	A65	5g violet blue	3.50	3.00
1K29	A65	15g Prus green	3.50	4.75
1K30	A65	25g myrtle green	3.50	2.00
		Nos. 1K28-1K30 (3)	10.50	9.75
		Set, never hinged	14.00	

Same Overprint in Black on Poland Nos. 308, 310

1937, June 5

1K31	A65	5g violet blue	1.10	1.75
1K32	A65	15g red brown	1.10	1.75
		Set, never hinged	3.25	

Polish Merchants Selling Wheat in Danzig, 16th Century — A2

1938, Nov. 11 — **Engr.** — *Perf. 12½*

1K33	A2	5g red orange	.65	.95
1K34	A2	15g red brown	.65	.95
1K35	A2	25g dull violet	.65	1.65
1K36	A2	55g brt ultra	1.65	3.00
		Nos. 1K33-1K36 (4)	3.60	6.55
		Set, never hinged	5.25	

OFFICES IN THE TURKISH EMPIRE

Stamps of Poland 1919, Overprinted in Carmine

1919, May — **Unwmk.** — *Perf. 11½*

Wove Paper

2K1	A10	3f bister brn	42.50	75.00
2K2	A10	5f green	42.50	75.00
2K3	A10	10f red vio	42.50	75.00
2K4	A10	15f red	42.50	75.00
2K5	A11	20f dp blue	42.50	75.00
2K6	A11	25f olive grn	42.50	75.00
2K7	A11	50f blue grn	42.50	75.00

Overprinted

2K8	A12	1m violet	42.50	75.00
2K9	A12	1.50m dp green	42.50	75.00
2K10	A12	2m dk brown	42.50	75.00
2K11	A13	2.50m orange brn	42.50	75.00
2K12	A14	5m red violet	42.50	75.00
		Nos. 2K1-2K12 (12)	510.00	900.00

Counterfeit cancellations are plentiful.

Counterfeits exist of Nos. 2K1-2K12.

Reissues are lighter, shiny red. Value, set $17.50.

Polish stamps with "P.P.C." overprint (Poste Polonaise Constantinople) were used on consular mail for a time.

Seven stamps with these overprints were not issued. Value, set $20.

EXILE GOVERNMENT IN GREAT BRITAIN

These stamps were issued by the Polish government in exile for letters posted from Polish merchant ships and warships.

United States Embassy Ruins, Warsaw — A1

Polish Ministry of Finance Ruins, Warsaw — A2

Destruction of Mickiewicz Monument, Cracow — A3

Polish Submarine "Orzel" — A8

Ruins of Warsaw A4

Polish Machine Gunners A5

Armored Tank A6

Polish Planes in Great Britain A7

Perf. 12½, 11½x12

1941, Dec. 15		Engr.	Unwmk.	
3K1	A1	5g rose violet	.35	.50
3K2	A2	10g dk bl grn	.75	.70
3K3	A3	25g black	1.25	1.25
3K4	A4	55g dark blue	1.50	1.50
3K5	A5	75g olive grn	3.75	3.75
3K6	A6	80g dk car rose	3.75	3.75
3K7	A7	1z slate blue	3.75	3.75
3K8	A8	1.50z copper brn	3.75	4.25
		Nos. 3K1-3K8 (8)	18.85	19.45
		Set, never hinged	25.00	

These stamps were used for correspondence carried on Polish ships and, on certain days, in Polish Military camps in Great Britain.

For surcharges see Nos. 3K17-3K20.

Polish Air Force in Battle of the Atlantic — A9

Polish Army in France, 1939-40 — A11

Polish Merchant Navy A10

Polish Army in Narvik, Norway, 1940 — A12

The Homeland Fights On — A15

Polish Army in Libya, 1941-42 A13

General Sikorsky and Polish Soldiers in the Middle East, 1943 A14

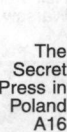

The Secret Press in Poland A16

1943, Nov. 1				
3K9	A9	5g rose lake	.30	.65
3K10	A10	10g dk bl grn	.65	1.00
3K11	A11	25g dk vio	.65	1.00
3K12	A12	55g sapphire	1.00	1.65
3K13	A13	75g brn car	1.65	2.25
3K14	A14	80g rose car	2.25	2.75
3K15	A15	1z olive blk	2.25	2.75
3K16	A16	1.50z black	3.00	3.25
		Nos. 3K9-3K16 (8)	11.75	15.30
		Set, never hinged	15.00	

Nos. 3K5 to 3K8 Surcharged in Blue

MONTE CASSINO
18. V. 1944

Gr55

Perf. 12½, 11½x12

1944, June 27			Unwmk.	
3K17	A5	45g on 75g	6.00	17.50
3K18	A6	55g on 80g	6.00	17.50
3K19	A7	80g on 1z	6.00	17.50
3K20	A8	1.20z on 1.50z	6.00	17.50
		Nos. 3K17-3K20 (4)	24.00	70.00
		Set, never hinged	35.00	

Capture of Monte Cassino by the Poles, May 18, 1944.

EXILE GOVERNMENT IN GREAT BRITAIN SEMI-POSTAL STAMP

Heroic Defenders of Warsaw — SP1

Perf. 11½

1945, Feb. 3		Unwmk.	Engr.	
3KB1	SP1	1z + 2z slate green	3.75	7.50
		Never hinged	6.00	

Warsaw uprising, Aug. 1-Oct. 3, 1944.

PONTA DELGADA

ˌpän-tə del-ˈgä-də

LOCATION — Administrative district of the Azores comprising the islands of Sao Miguel and Santa Maria
GOVT. — A district of Portugal
AREA — 342 sq. mi.
POP. — 124,000 (approx.)
CAPITAL — Ponta Delgada

1000 Reis = 1 Milreis

King Carlos
A1 A2

Perf. 12½, 11½ (25r), 13½ (75r, 150r)

1892-93		Typo.	Unwmk.	
1	A1	5r yellow	2.75	.75
c.		Diagonal half used as 2½r on piece		17.50
2	A1	10r reddish vio	2.75	1.50
3	A1	15r chocolate	4.00	2.00
4	A1	20r lavender	5.00	2.00
a.		Perf. 13½	7.50	1.50
5	A1	25r deep green	9.00	1.00
6	A1	50r ultra	7.50	2.25
7	A1	75r carmine	7.00	4.50
8	A1	80r yellow grn	11.00	6.50
9	A1	100r brn, *yel*	11.00	5.00
10	A1	150r car, *rose*	62.50	30.00
11	A1	200r dk bl, *bl*	62.50	40.00
12	A1	300r dk bl, *salmon*	62.50	42.50
		Nos. 1-12 (12)	247.50	138.00

The reprints are on paper slightly thinner than that of the originals, and unsurfaced. They have white gum and clean-cut perf. 13½ or 11½. Lowest valued, Nos. 1-9, $4 each, Nos. 10-12, $20 each.

See the *Scott Classic Specialized Catalogue* for listings by perforation.

1897-1905			Perf. 11½	
		Name and Value in Black except Nos. 25 and 34		
13	A2	2½r gray	.55	.30
14	A2	5r orange	.55	.30
15	A2	10r lt green	.55	.30
16	A2	15r brown	7.75	6.00
17	A2	15r gray grn ('99)	2.00	1.00
18	A2	20r dull violet	2.00	1.00
19	A2	25r sea green	2.75	1.00
20	A2	25r rose red ('99)	2.00	.35
21	A2	50r blue	2.75	1.10
22	A2	50r ultra ('05)	16.00	10.00
23	A2	65r slate blue ('98)	1.25	.35
24	A2	75r rose	6.25	1.10
25	A2	75r brn & car, *yel* ('05)	12.50	8.00
26	A2	80r violet	1.75	1.10
27	A2	100r dk bl, *bl*	3.75	1.10
28	A2	115r org brn, *rose* ('98)	3.00	1.50
29	A2	130r gray brn, *buff* ('98)	3.50	1.50
30	A2	150r lt brn, *buff*	3.50	2.00
31	A2	180r sl, *pnksh* ('98)	3.50	2.00
32	A2	200r red vio, *pnksh*	7.00	5.00
33	A2	300r blue, *rose*	7.50	5.00
a.		Perf. 12½	40.00	27.50
34	A2	500r blk & red, *bl*	14.00	9.00
a.		Perf. 12½	20.00	12.00
		Nos. 13-34 (22)	104.40	59.00

Imperfs are proofs.

The stamps of Ponta Delgada were superseded by those of the Azores, which in 1931 were replaced by those of Portugal.

PORTUGAL

ˈpōr-chi-gəl

LOCATION — Southern Europe, on the western coast of the Iberian Peninsula
GOVT. — Republic
AREA — 35,516 sq. mi.
POP. — 9,918,040 (1999 est.)
CAPITAL — Lisbon

Figures for area and population include the Azores and Madeira, which are integral parts of the republic. The republic was established in 1910. See Azores, Funchal, Madeira.

1000 Reis = 1 Milreis
10 Reis = 1 Centimo
100 Centavos = 1 Escudo (1912)
100 Cents = 1 Euro (2002)

Catalogue values for unused stamps in this country are for Never Hinged items, beginning with Scott 662 in the regular postage section, Scott C11 in the airpost section, Scott J65 in the postage due section, and Scott O2 in the officials section.

Queen Maria II
A1 A2

A3 A4

Typo. & Embossed

1853		Unwmk.	Imperf.	
1	A1	5r reddish brown	2,700.	525.00
2	A2	25r blue	850.00	11.00
3	A3	50r dp yellow grn	2,850.	525.00
a.		50r blue green	28,000.	925.00
4	A4	100r lilac	27,500.	1,200.

The stamps of the 1853 issue were reprinted in 1864, 1885, 1905 and 1953. Many stamps of subsequent issues were reprinted in 1885 and 1905. The reprints of 1864 are on thin white paper with white gum. The originals have brownish gum which often stains the paper. The reprints of 1885 are on a stout, very white paper. They are usually ungummed, but occasionally have a white gum with yellowish spots. The reprints of 1905 are on creamy white paper of ordinary quality with shiny white gum.

When perforated the reprints of 1885 have a rather rough perforation 13½ with small holes; those of 1905 have a clean-cut perforation 13½ with large holes making sharp pointed teeth.

The colors of the reprints usually differ from those of the originals, but actual comparison is necessary.

The reprints are often from new dies which differ slightly from those used for the originals.

5 reis: There is a defect in the neck which makes the Adam's apple appear very large in the first reprint. The later ones can be distinguished by the paper and the shades and by the absence of the pendant curl.

25 reis: The burelage of the ground work in the original is sharp and clear, while in the 1864 reprints it is blurred in several places; the upper and lower right hand corners are very thick and blurred. The central oval is less than ½mm from the frame at the sides in the originals and fully ¾mm in the 1885 and 1905 reprints.

50 reis: In the reprints of 1864 and 1885 there is a small break in the upper right hand diagonal line of the frame, and the initials of the engraver (F. B. F.), which in the originals are plainly discernible in the lower part of the bust, do not show. The reprints of 1905 have not the break in the frame and the initials are distinct.

100 reis: The small vertical lines at top and bottom at each side of the frame are heavier in the reprints of 1864 than in the originals. The reprints of 1885 and 1905 can be distinguished only by the paper, gum and shades.

Reprints of 1953 have thick paper, no gum and dates "1853/1953" on back.

Values of lowest-cost reprints (1885) of Nos. 1-3, $50 each; of No. 4, $100.

King Pedro V
A5 A6

A7 A8

1855			With Straight Hair	

TWENTY-FIVE REIS:
Type I - Pearls mostly touch each other and oval outer line.
Type II - Pearls are separate from each other and oval outer line.

5	A5	5r red brown	7,750.	575.00
6	A6	25r blue, type II	875.00	16.00
a.		25r blue, type I	1,000.	18.00
7	A7	50r green	450.00	45.00
8	A8	100r lilac	675.00	60.00

Several types of No. 5 exist, differing in number of pearls encircling head (74 to 89) and other details.

All values were reprinted in 1885 and 1905. Value for lowest-cost, $15 each.

See note after No. 4.

1856			With Curled Hair	

TWENTY-FIVE REIS:
Type I - The network is fine (single lines).
Type II - The network is coarse (double lines).

9	A5	5r brown (shades)	360.00	42.50
10	A6	25r blue, type II	350.00	9.00
a.		25r blue, type I	*8,250.*	35.00

1858				
11	A6	25r rose, type II	250.00	3.00

The 5r dark brown, formerly listed and sold at about $1, is now believed by the best authorities to be a reprint made before 1866. It is printed on thin yellowish white paper with yellowish white gum and is known only unused. The same remarks will apply to a 25r blue which is common unused but not known used. It is printed from a die which was not used for the issued stamps but the differences are slight and can only be told by expert comparison.

Nos. 9 and 10, also 10a in rose, were reprinted in 1885 and Nos. 9, 10, 10a and 11

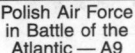

in 1905. Value of lowest-cost reprints, $15 each.
See note after No. 4.

King Luiz
A9 A10

A11

A12

A13

1862-64

FIVE REIS:
Type I - The distance between "5" and "reis" is 3mm.
Type II - The distance between "5" and "reis" is 2mm.

12	A9	5r brown, type I	125.00	10.00
a.		5r brown, type II	165.00	20.00
13	A10	10r orange	140.00	35.00
14	A11	25r rose	100.00	3.25
15	A12	50r yellow green	725.00	55.00
16	A13	100r lilac ('64)	775.00	65.00
		Nos. 12-16 (5)	1,865.	168.25

All values were reprinted in 1885 and all except the 25r in 1905. Value of lowest-cost reprints, $10 each.
See note after No. 4.

King Luiz
A14 A15

1866-67 *Imperf.*

17	A14	5r black	110.00	6.50
18	A14	10r yellow	200.00	100.00
19	A14	20r bister	175.00	40.00
20	A14	25r rose ('67)	200.00	5.25
21	A14	50r green	250.00	50.00
22	A14	80r orange	250.00	50.00
23	A14	100r dk lilac ('67)	275.00	75.00
24	A14	120r blue	300.00	45.00
		Nos. 17-24 (8)	1,760.	371.75

Some values with unofficial percé en croix (diamond) perforation were used in Madeira.
All values were reprinted in 1885 and 1905. Value $10 each.
See note after No. 4.

Typographed & Embossed

1867-70 *Perf. 12½*

25	A14	5r black	125.00	25.00
26	A14	10r yellow	250.00	75.00
27	A14	20r bister ('69)	300.00	75.00
28	A14	25r rose	65.00	4.50
29	A14	50r green ('68)	250.00	85.00
30	A14	80r orange ('69)	350.00	75.00
31	A14	100r lilac ('69)	250.00	85.00
32	A14	120r blue	300.00	40.00
33	A14	240r pale vio ('70)	1,000.	300.00
		Nos. 25-33 (9)	3,190.	764.50

Nos. 25-33 frequently were separated with scissors. Slightly blunted perfs on one or two sides are to be expected for stamps of this issue.
Two types each of 5r and 100r differ in the position of the "5" at upper right and the "100" at lower right in relation to the end of the label.
Nos. 25-33 were reprinted in 1885 and 1905. Some of the 1885 reprints were perforated 12½ as well as 13½. Value of the lowest-cost reprints, $10 each.
See note after No. 4.

1870-84 *Perf. 12½, 13½*

34	A15	5r black	45.00	4.00
a.		Imperf.	450.00	
b.		Perf. 11		500.00
c.		Perf. 14	200.00	77.50
35	A15	10r yellow ('71)	70.00	19.00
a.		Imperf.	450.00	
b.		Perf. 11		500.00
c.		Perf. 14	400.00	175.00
36	A15	10r bl grn ('79)	375.00	150.00
37	A15	10r yellow grn ('80)	125.00	18.00
38	A15	15r lilac brn ('75)	100.00	19.00
39	A15	20r bister	70.00	16.00
a.		Imperf.	450.00	
b.		Perf. 11		500.00
40	A15	20r rose ('84)	300.00	30.00
41	A15	25r rose	30.00	2.25
a.		Imperf.	450.00	
b.		Perf. 11		500.00
c.		Perf. 14	400.00	14.00
42	A15	50r pale green	140.00	14.00
b.		Perf. 11		500.00
43	A15	50r blue ('79)	325.00	35.00
44	A15	80r orange	100.00	12.00
a.		Perf. 14	1,000.	475.00
b.		Perf. 11		500.00
45	A15	100r pale lil ('71)	60.00	6.00
a.		Perf. 14	1,250.	475.00
46	A15	120r bl, perf. 12½ ('71)	275.00	40.00
a.		Perf. 13½		—
47	A15	150r pale bl ('76)	350.00	75.00
b.		Perf. 13½	750.00	200.00
48	A15	150r yellow ('80)	150.00	10.00
49	A15	240r pale vio ('73)	1,500.	800.00
b.		Perf. 11		—
50	A15	300r dull vio ('76)	125.00	19.00
51	A15	1000r black ('84)	250.00	50.00

Two types each of 15r, 20r and 80r differ in the distance between the figures of value.
Imperfs probably are proofs.
For overprints and surcharges see Nos. 86-87, 94-96.
All values of the issues of 1870-84 were reprinted in 1885 and 1905. Value of the lowest-cost reprints, $10 each.
See note after No. 4.

King Luiz
A16 A17

A18

A19

1880-81 Typo. *Perf. 12½, 13½*

52	A16	5r black	30.00	2.75
53	A17	25r bluish gray	325.00	19.00
54	A18	25r gray	35.00	2.50
55	A18	25r brown vio ('81)	45.00	2.50
56	A19	50r blue ('81)	325.00	9.50
		Nos. 52-56 (5)	760.00	36.25

All values were reprinted in 1885 and 1905. Value of the lowest-cost reprints, $5 each.
See note after No. 4.

A20

A21

King Luiz
A22 A23

A24

A24a

1882-87 *Perf. 11½, 12½, 13½*

57	A20	2r black ('84)	22.50	10.00
58	A21	5r black ('83)	14.00	.90
59	A22	10r green ('84)	35.00	2.75
60	A23	25r brown	30.00	1.60
61	A24	50r blue	45.00	2.00
62	A24a	500r black ('84)	600.00	200.00
63	A24a	500r vio, perf. 12½ ('87)	275.00	35.00
a.		Perf. 13½	750.00	250.00
		Nos. 57-63 (7)	1,021.	252.25

For overprints see Nos. 79-82, 85, 88-89, 93.
The stamps of the 1882-87 issues were reprinted in 1885, 1893 and 1905. Value of the lowest-cost reprints, $5 each.
See note after No. 4.

A25

A26

1887 *Perf. 11½*

64	A25	20r rose	45.00	12.00
65	A26	25r violet	30.00	2.00
66	A26	25r lilac rose	40.00	2.00
		Nos. 64-66 (3)	115.00	16.00

For overprints see Nos. 83-84, 90-92.
Nos. 64-66 were reprinted in 1905. Value $5 each. See note after No. 4.

King Carlos — A27

1892-93 *Perf. 11½, 12½, 13½*

67	A27	5r orange	12.00	1.25
68	A27	10r redsh violet	30.00	1.40
69	A27	15r chocolate	30.00	2.75
70	A27	20r lavender	35.00	6.50
71	A27	25r dk green	27.50	1.25
72	A27	50r blue	35.00	3.75
73	A27	75r carmine ('93)	67.50	5.25
a.		Perf. 11½	325.00	8.50
74	A27	80r yellow grn	90.00	25.00
75	A27	100r brn, *buff* ('93)	65.00	5.00
a.		Perf. 11½	375.00	10.50
76	A27	150r car, *rose* ('93)	165.00	25.00
77	A27	200r dk bl, *bl* ('93)	165.00	30.00
78	A27	300r dk bl, *sal* ('93)	175.00	45.00
		Nos. 67-78 (12)	897.00	152.15

Nos. 76-78 were reprinted in 1900 (perf. 11½), and all values in 1905 (perf. 13½). Values of the lowest-cost reprints of Nos. 67-75, $6 each; of Nos. 76-78, $12 each.
See note after No. 4.

Stamps and Types of Previous Issues Overprinted in Black or Red:

PROVISORIO
a

PROVISORIO
b

PROVISORIO
c

1892

79	A21 (a)	5r gray blk	15.00	6.00
a.		Double overprint	600.00	275.00
80	A22 (b)	10r green	15.00	6.00
a.		Inverted overprint	—	—
b.		Double overprint	600.00	275.00

1892-93

81	A21 (c)	5r gray blk (R)	7.25	5.00
82	A22 (c)	10r green (R)	8.25	6.50
a.		Inverted overprint	140.00	92.50
83	A25 (c)	20r rose	42.50	14.00
a.		Inverted overprint	200.00	175.00
84	A26 (c)	25r rose lilac	14.50	4.00
a.		Perf. 12½	450.00	47.50
85	A24 (c)	50r bl (R; '93)	77.50	40.00
		Nos. 81-85 (5)	150.00	69.50

1893

86	A15 (c)	15r bister brn (R)	16.00	8.00
87	A15 (c)	80r yellow	110.00	60.00

Nos. 86-87 are found in two types each. See note below No. 51.
Some of Nos. 79-87 were reprinted in 1900 and all values in 1905. Value of lowest-cost reprint, $10.
See note after No. 4.

Stamps and Types of Previous Issues Overprinted or Surcharged in Black or Red:

1893
PROVISORIO
d

1893
PROVISORIO
20 rs.
e

1893 *Perf. 11½, 12½*

88	A21 (d)	5r gray blk (R)	24.00	15.00
89	A22 (d)	10r green (R)	22.50	16.00
a.		"1938"	210.00	160.00
b.		"1863"	210.00	160.00
c.		"1838"	210.00	160.00
d.		Perf. 12½	1,500.	700.00
90	A25 (d)	20r rose	40.00	24.00
a.		Inverted overprint	100.00	65.00
b.		"1938"	240.00	160.00
91	A26 (e)	20r on 25r lil rose	47.50	32.50
92	A26 (d)	25r lilac rose	100.00	65.00
a.		Inverted overprint	240.00	160.00
93	A24 (d)	50r blue (R)	100.00	72.50

Perf. 12½

94	A15 (e)	50r on 80r yel	110.00	72.50
95	A15 (e)	75r on 80r yel	72.50	47.50
96	A15 (d)	80r yellow	100.00	60.00
		Nos. 88-96 (9)	616.50	405.00

Nos. 94-96 are found in two types each. See note below No. 51.

Some of Nos. 88-96 were reprinted in 1900 and all values in 1905. Value of lowest-cost reprint, $10 each.

See note after No. 4.

Prince Henry on his Ship — A46

Prince Henry Directing Fleet Maneuvers A47

Symbolic of Prince Henry's Studies — A48

1894 Litho. *Perf. 14*

97	A46	5r orange	2.50	.40
98	A46	10r magenta	2.50	.40
99	A46	15r red brown	7.75	2.10
100	A46	20r dull violet	7.75	2.50
101	A47	25r gray green	6.75	.80
102	A47	50r blue	19.00	4.00
103	A47	75r car rose	37.50	7.25
104	A47	80r yellow grn	37.50	9.25
105	A47	100r lt brn, *pale buff*	27.50	6.50

Engr.

106	A48	150r lt car, *pale rose*	82.50	19.00
107	A48	300r dk bl, *sal buff*	90.00	21.00
108	A48	500r dp vio, *pale lil*	200.00	45.00
109	A48	1000r gray blk, *grysh*	350.00	65.00
		Nos. 97-109 (13)	871.25	183.20

5th centenary of the birth of Prince Henry the Navigator.

King Carlos — A49

1895-1905 Typo. *Perf. 11½*
Value in Black or Red (#122, 500r)

110	A49	2½r gray	.20	.20
111	A49	5r orange	.20	.20
112	A49	10r lt green	.25	.20
113	A49	15r brown	60.00	2.25
114	A49	15r gray grn ('99)	30.00	1.50
115	A49	20r gray violet	.40	.25
116	A49	25r sea green	40.00	.20
117	A49	25r car rose ('99)	.25	.20
118	A49	50r blue	55.00	.25
119	A49	50r ultra ('05)	.35	.20
120	A49	65r slate bl ('98)	.35	.20
121	A49	75r rose	70.00	3.00
122	A49	75r brn, *yel* ('05)	1.00	.45
123	A49	80r violet	1.40	.70
124	A49	100r dk bl, *bl*	.55	.25
125	A49	115r org brn, *pink* ('98)	3.25	1.75
126	A49	130r gray brn, *straw* ('98)	2.50	.95
127	A49	150r lt brn, *straw*	97.50	15.00
128	A49	180r sl, *pnksh* ('98)	11.00	6.50
129	A49	200r red lil, *pnksh*	4.00	.70
130	A49	300r blue, *rose*	2.75	1.10
131	A49	500r blk, *bl* ('96)	6.50	2.75
a.		Perf. 12½	90.00	25.00
		Nos. 110-131 (22)	387.45	38.80

Several values of the above type exist without figures of value, also with figures inverted or otherwise misplaced but they were not regularly issued.

St. Anthony and his Vision — A50

St. Anthony Ascends to Heaven — A52

St. Anthony Preaching to Fishes — A51

St. Anthony, from Portrait — A53

Perf. 11½, 12½ and Compound

1895 Typo.

132	A50	2½r black	3.25	.80

Litho.

133	A51	5r brown org	3.25	.80
134	A51	10r red lilac	10.50	5.50
135	A51	15r chocolate	11.50	5.50
136	A51	20r gray violet	11.50	5.75
137	A51	25r green & vio	10.00	.80
138	A52	50r blue & brn	25.00	15.00
139	A52	75r rose & brn	37.50	27.50
140	A52	80r lt grn & brn	47.50	40.00
141	A52	100r choc & blk	42.50	20.00
142	A53	150r car & bis	125.00	70.00
143	A53	200r blue & bis	125.00	70.00
144	A53	300r slate & bis	160.00	80.00
145	A53	500r vio brn & grn	300.00	175.00
146	A53	1000r violet & grn	500.00	225.00
		Nos. 132-146 (15)	1,412.	741.65

7th centenary of the birth of Saint Anthony of Padua. Stamps have eulogy in Latin printed on the back.

Common Design Types pictured following the introduction.

Vasco da Gama Issue
Common Design Types

1898 Engr. *Perf. 12½ to 16*

147	CD20	2½r blue green	1.10	.25
148	CD21	5r red	1.10	.25
149	CD22	10r red violet	7.00	.95
150	CD23	25r yel grn	4.00	.30
151	CD24	50r dark blue	8.25	1.75
152	CD25	75r violet brown	35.00	7.00
153	CD26	100r bis brn	24.00	6.75
154	CD27	150r bister	55.00	18.00
		Nos. 147-154 (8)	135.45	35.25

For overprints and surcharges see Nos. 185-192, 199-206.

King Manuel II
A62 A63

1910 Typo. *Perf. 14½x15*

156	A62	2½r violet	.20	.20
157	A62	5r black	.20	.20
158	A62	10r gray green	.25	.20
159	A62	15r lilac brown	2.25	1.00
160	A62	20r carmine	.70	.50
161	A62	25r violet brn	.50	.20
162	A62	50r dark blue	1.25	.45
163	A62	75r bister brn	7.75	3.50
164	A62	80r slate	2.10	1.50
165	A62	100r brn, *lt grn*	8.50	2.00
166	A62	200r dk grn, *sal*	4.75	2.75
167	A62	300r blk, *azure*	5.75	3.25
168	A63	500r ol grn & vio brn	11.00	8.25
169	A63	1000r dk bl & blk	25.00	16.00
		Nos. 156-169 (14)	70.20	40.00

For overprint see No. RA1.

Preceding Issue Overprinted in Carmine or Green

REPUBLICA

1910

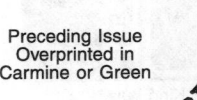

170	A62	2½r violet	.25	.20
171	A62	5r black	.25	.20
172	A62	10r gray green	3.00	.90
173	A62	15r lilac brn	.95	.70
174	A62	20r carmine (G)	3.75	1.25
175	A62	25r violet brn	.70	.20
176	A62	50r dk blue	5.25	1.75
177	A62	75r bister brn	7.75	3.00
178	A62	80r slate	2.75	1.90
179	A62	100r brn, *lt grn*	1.75	.60
180	A62	200r dk grn, *sal*	2.10	1.40
181	A62	300r blk, *azure*	3.25	2.40
182	A63	500r ol grn & vio brn	8.25	7.00
183	A63	1000r dk bl & blk	20.00	17.00
		Nos. 170-183 (14)	60.00	38.50

The numerous inverted and double overprints on this issue were unofficially and fraudulently made.

The 50r with blue overprint is a fraud.

Vasco da Gama Issue Overprinted or Surcharged:

REPUBLICA
a

REPUBLICA
REIS 15 REIS
b

REPUBLICA
1$000
c

1911 *Perf. 12½ to 16*

185	CD20(a)	2½r blue grn	.30	.20
a.		Inverted overprint	10.50	8.50
186	CD21(b)	15r on 5r red	.55	.25
a.		Inverted surcharge	8.00	7.00
187	CD23(a)	25r yel grn	.30	.20
188	CD24(a)	50r dark blue	2.25	1.00
a.		Inverted overprint		
189	CD25(a)	75r violet brn	30.00	20.00
190	CD27(b)	80r on 150r bis	4.50	3.00
191	CD26(a)	100r bister brn	4.50	1.75
a.		Inverted overprint	25.00	20.00
192	CD22(c)	1000r on 10r red vio	42.50	24.00
		Nos. 185-192 (8)	84.90	50.40

Postage Due Stamps of 1898 Overprinted or Surcharged for Regular Postage:

REPUBLICA
d

REPUBLICA
R$ 300 R$
e

1911 *Perf. 12*

193	D1(d)	5r black	.55	.20
a.		Double ovpt., one inverted	12.50	10.00
194	D1(d)	10r magenta	.80	.40
195	D1(d)	20r orange	3.50	2.40
196	D1(d)	200r brn, *buff*	80.00	55.00
197	D1(e)	300r on 50r slate	57.50	32.50
198	D1(e)	500r on 100r car, *pink*	29.00	20.00
a.		Inverted surcharge	90.00	60.00
		Nos. 193-198 (6)	171.35	110.50

Vasco da Gama Issue of Madeira Overprinted or Surcharged Types "a," "b" and "c"

1911 *Perf. 12½ to 16*

199	CD20(a)	2½r blue grn	8.75	5.75
a.		Double overprint		
200	CD21(b)	15r on 5r red	1.90	1.50
a.		Inverted surcharge	12.50	12.50
201	CD23(a)	25r yel grn	4.25	3.50
202	CD24(a)	50r dk blue	8.25	5.75
a.		Inverted overprint		
203	CD25(a)	75r violet brn	8.25	4.00
a.		Inverted overprint		
204	CD27(b)	80r on 150r bis	9.50	7.50
a.		Inverted surcharge		
205	CD26(a)	100r bister brn	27.50	6.00
a.		Inverted overprint	75.00	75.00
206	CD22(c)	1000r on 10r red vio	27.50	16.00
		Nos. 199-206 (8)	95.90	50.00

Ceres — A64

With Imprint

1912-31 Typo. *Perf. 15x14, 12x11½*

207	A64	¼c dark olive	.35	.25
208	A64	½c black	.35	.25
209	A64	1c deep green	.60	.20
210	A64	1c choc ('18)	.20	.20
211	A64	1½c chocolate	5.00	2.25
212	A64	1½c dp green ('18)	.20	.20
213	A64	2c carmine	5.00	2.25
214	A64	2c orange ('18)	.20	.20
215	A64	2c yellow ('24)	.50	.25
216	A64	2c choc ('26)	1.25	*1.25*
217	A64	2½c violet	.20	.20
218	A64	3c car rose ('17)	.20	.20
219	A64	3c ultra ('21)	.45	.25
220	A64	3½c lt grn ('18)	.20	.20
221	A64	4c lt grn ('19)	.20	.20
222	A64	4c orange ('26)	1.25	1.50
223	A64	5c deep blue	5.00	.50
224	A64	5c yel brn ('18)	.90	.35
225	A64	5c ol brn ('23)	.25	.25
226	A64	5c blk brn ('31)	.20	.20
227	A64	6c pale rose ('20)	.20	.20
228	A64	6c brown ('24)	.50	.25

229	A64	6c	red brn ('30)	.20	.20
230	A64	7½c	yellow brn	11.00	2.25
231	A64	7½c	dp bl ('18)	.20	.20
232	A64	8c	slate	.20	.20
233	A64	8c	bl grn ('22)	.40	.25
234	A64	8c	orange ('24)	.40	.40
235	A64	10c	orange brn	.40	.25
236	A64	10c	red ('31)	.40	.25
237	A64	12c	bl gray ('20)	1.10	.60
238	A64	12c	dp grn ('21)	.40	.35
239	A64	13½c	chlky bl ('20)	1.25	.40
240	A64	14c	dk bl, *yel* ('20)	3.00	1.10
241	A64	14c	brt vio ('21)	1.00	.50
242	A64	15c	plum	3.00	.75
243	A64	15c	black ('23)	.35	.25
244	A64	16c	brt ultra ('24)	.80	.60
245	A64	20c	vio brn, *grn*	12.00	1.40
246	A64	20c	brn, *buff* ('20)	14.00	3.25
247	A64	20c	dk brn ('21)	.45	.25
248	A64	20c	dp grn ('23)	.40	.25
249	A64	20c	gray ('24)	.20	.20
250	A64	24c	grnsh bl ('21)	.40	.25
251	A64	25c	sal pink ('23)	.40	.25
252	A64	25c	lt gray ('26)	.40	.25
253	A64	25c	bl grn ('30)	.80	.25
254	A64	30c	brn, *pink*	95.00	8.50
255	A64	30c	lt brn, *yel* ('17)	8.00	1.50
256	A64	30c	gray brn ('21)	.45	.25
257	A64	30c	dk brn ('24)	6.00	1.50
258	A64	32c	dp grn ('24)	1.00	.35
259	A64	36c	red ('21)	1.60	.40
260	A64	40c	dk bl ('23)	.80	.50
261	A64	40c	choc ('24)	.40	.40
262	A64	40c	green ('26)	.20	.20
263	A64	48c	rose ('24)	5.00	3.00
264	A64	50c	org, *sal*	11.00	1.00
265	A64	50c	yellow ('21)	1.75	.65
266	A64	50c	bister ('30)	2.00	1.25
267	A64	50c	red brn ('30)	2.00	1.25
268	A64	60c	blue ('21)	1.25	.55
269	A64	64c	pale ultra ('24)	6.00	4.00
270	A64	75c	dull rose ('23)	11.00	5.00
271	A64	75c	car rose ('30)	2.00	1.00
272	A64	80c	brn rose ('21)	1.25	1.00
273	A64	80c	violet ('24)	.90	.50
274	A64	80c	dk grn ('30)	2.00	1.00
275	A64	90c	chalky bl ('21)	1.50	.75
276	A64	96c	dp rose ('26)	25.00	22.50
277	A64	1e	dp grn, *bl*	6.00	1.00
278	A64	1e	violet ('21)	4.00	1.75
a.			Perf. 15x14	125.00	70.00
279	A64	1e	dk bl ('23)	4.50	2.00
280	A64	1e	gray vio ('24)	1.40	1.00
281	A64	1e	brn lake ('30)	6.00	1.00
282	A64	1.10e	yel brn ('21)	4.00	1.50
283	A64	1.20e	yel grn ('21)	2.25	1.25
284	A64	1.20e	buff ('24)	45.00	30.00
285	A64	1.20e	pur brn ('31)	4.00	1.00
286	A64	1.25e	dk bl ('31)	4.00	1.00
287	A64	1.50e	blk vio ('23)	12.00	3.00
288	A64	1.50e	lilac ('24)	27.50	4.50
289	A64	1.60e	dp bl ('24)	17.00	4.50
290	A64	2e	sl grn ('21)	35.00	5.00
291	A64	2e	red vio ('31)	17.00	6.00
292	A64	2.40e	ap grn ('26)	150.00	100.00
293	A64	3e	pink ('26)	150.00	90.00
294	A64	3.20e	gray grn ('24)	30.00	11.00
295	A64	4.50e	org ('31)	60.00	40.00
296	A64	5e	emer ('24)	32.50	8.00
297	A64	10e	pink ('24)	125.00	45.00
298	A64	20e	pale turq ('24)	250.00	150.00
			Nos. 207-298 (92)	1,249.	592.05

See design A85. For surcharges & overprints see #453-495, RA2.

Presidents of Portugal and Brazil and Aviators Cabral and Coutinho A65

1923 Litho. Perf. 14

299	A65	1c	brown	.20	.30
300	A65	2c	orange	.20	.30
301	A65	3c	ultra	.20	.30
302	A65	4c	yellow grn	.20	.30
303	A65	5c	bister brn	.20	.30
304	A65	10c	brown org	.20	.30
305	A65	15c	black	.20	.30
306	A65	20c	blue grn	.20	.30
307	A65	25c	rose	.20	.30
308	A65	30c	olive brn	.45	.80
309	A65	40c	chocolate	.20	.35
310	A65	50c	yellow	.20	.40
311	A65	75c	violet	.25	.80
312	A65	1e	dp blue	.30	1.00
313	A65	1.50e	olive grn	.45	2.50
314	A65	2e	myrtle grn	.45	2.00
			Nos. 299-314 (16)	4.10	10.55

Flight of Sacadura Cabral and Gago Coutinho from Portugal to Brazil.

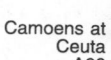

Camoens at Ceuta A66

Camoens Saving the Lusiads — A67

Luis de Camoens — A68

First Edition of the Lusiads — A69

Monument to Camoens — A72

Camoens Dying — A70

Tomb of Camoens A71

Engr.; Values Typo. in Black

1924, Nov. 11 Perf. 14, 14½

315	A66	2c	lt blue	.20	.20
316	A66	3c	orange	.20	.20
317	A66	4c	dk gray	.20	.20
318	A66	5c	yellow grn	.20	.20
319	A66	6c	lake	.20	.20
320	A67	8c	orange brn	.20	.20
321	A67	10c	gray vio	.20	.20
322	A67	15c	olive grn	.20	.20
323	A67	16c	violet brn	.20	.20
324	A67	20c	dp orange	.30	.20
325	A68	25c	lilac	.30	.20
326	A68	30c	dk brown	.30	.20
327	A68	32c	dk green	.80	.50
328	A68	40c	ultra	.30	.20
329	A68	48c	red brown	1.25	.80
330	A69	50c	red orange	1.40	.65
331	A69	64c	green	1.40	.65
332	A69	75c	dk violet	1.40	.65
333	A69	80c	bister	1.10	.65
334	A69	96c	lake	1.10	.60
335	A70	1e	slate	1.10	.55
336	A70	1.20e	lt brown	5.25	3.25
337	A70	1.50e	red	1.25	.55
338	A70	1.60e	dk blue	1.25	.55
339	A70	2e	apple grn	5.25	3.25
340	A71	2.40e	green, *grn*	3.75	1.75
341	A71	3e	dk bl, *bl*	1.60	.70
a.			Value double	75.00	75.00
b.			Value omitted		
342	A71	3.20e	blk, *green*	1.60	.65
343	A71	4.50e	blk, *orange*	4.00	1.90
344	A71	10e	dk brn, *pnksh*	9.75	5.00
345	A72	20e	dk vio, *lil*	9.50	4.75
			Nos. 315-345 (31)	55.75	30.00

Birth of Luis de Camoens, poet, 400th anniv.

For overprints see Nos. 1S6-1S71.

Castello-Branco's House at Sao Miguel de Seide — A73

Castello-Branco's Study — A74

Camillo Castello-Branco A75

Teresa de Albuquerque A76

Mariana and Joao de Cruz — A77

Simao de Botelho — A78

1925, Mar. 26 Perf. 12½

346	A73	2c	orange	.20	.20
347	A73	3c	green	.20	.20
348	A73	4c	ultra	.20	.20
349	A73	5c	scarlet	.20	.20
350	A73	6c	brown vio	.20	.20
a.			"6" and "C" omitted		
351	A73	8c	black brn	.20	.20
352	A74	10c	pale blue	.20	.20
353	A75	15c	olive grn	.20	.20
354	A74	16c	red orange	.25	.20
355	A74	20c	dk violet	.25	.20
356	A75	25c	car rose	.25	.20
357	A74	30c	bister brn	.25	.20
358	A74	32c	green	.90	.70
359	A75	40c	green & blk	.55	.45
360	A74	48c	red brn	2.40	1.90
361	A76	50c	blue green	.55	.45
362	A76	64c	orange brn	2.40	1.90
363	A76	75c	gray blk	.50	.40
364	A75	80c	brown	.50	.40
365	A76	96c	car rose	1.25	.95
366	A76	1e	gray vio	1.10	.90
367	A76	1.20e	yellow grn	1.25	.95
368	A77	1.50e	dk bl, *bl*	21.00	8.75
369	A75	1.60e	indigo	3.75	2.40
370	A77	2e	dk grn, *grn*	5.25	2.75
371	A77	2.40e	red, *org*	42.50	21.00
372	A77	3e	lake, *bl*	55.00	26.00
373	A77	3.20e	*green*	26.00	20.00
374	A75	4.50e	red & blk	10.00	2.40
375	A77	10e	brn, *yel*	10.50	2.50
376	A78	20e	*orange*	12.00	2.50
			Nos. 346-376 (31)	200.00	99.70

Centenary of the birth of Camillo Castello-Branco, novelist.

First Independence Issue

Alfonso the Conqueror, First King of Portugal — A79

Batalha Monastery and King John I — A80

Battle of Aljubarrota A81

Filipa de Vilhena Arming her Sons A82

King John IV (The Duke of Braganza) A83

Independence Monument, Lisbon — A84

1926, Aug. 13 Perf. 14, 14½

Center in Black

377	A79	2c	orange	.20	.20
378	A80	3c	ultra	.20	.20
379	A79	4c	yellow grn	.20	.20
380	A80	5c	black brn	.20	.20
381	A79	6c	ocher	.20	.20
382	A80	15c	dk green	.20	.20
383	A79	16c	dp blue	.70	.45
384	A81	20c	dull violet	.70	.45
385	A82	25c	scarlet	.70	.45
386	A81	32c	dp green	.90	.60
387	A82	40c	yellow brn	.55	.35
388	A80	46c	carmine	3.00	2.00
389	A82	50c	olive bis	3.00	2.00
390	A83	64c	blue green	4.25	2.75
391	A82	75c	red brown	4.25	2.75
392	A84	96c	dull red	6.50	4.25
393	A83	1e	black vio	6.50	4.25
394	A81	1.60e	myrtle grn	8.75	6.00
395	A84	3e	plum	26.00	17.50
396	A84	4.50e	olive grn	32.50	22.50
397	A81	10e	carmine	52.50	35.00
			Nos. 377-397 (21)	152.00	102.50

The use of these stamps instead of the regular issue was obligatory on Aug. 13th and 14th, Nov. 30th and Dec. 1st, 1926.

Surcharged with Bars and

2 C.

1926

Center in Black

397A	A80	2c on 5c	blk brn	1.00	.80
397B	A80	2c on 46c	car	1.00	.80
397C	A83	2c on 64c	bl grn	1.25	.90
397D	A82	3c on 75c	red brn	1.00	.80
397E	A84	3c on 96c	dull red	1.75	1.25
397F	A83	3c on 1e	blk vio	1.40	1.00
397G	A81	4c on 1.60e	myr grn	10.00	7.25
397H	A84	4c on 3e	plum	3.25	2.40
397J	A84	6c on 4.50e	ol grn	3.25	2.40
397K	A81	6c on 10e	carmine	3.25	2.40
			Nos. 397A-397K (10)	27.15	20.00

There are two styles of the ornaments in these surcharges.

Ceres — A85

Without Imprint

1926, Dec. 2 Typo. *Perf. 13½x14*

No.	Type	Description	Unused	Used
398	A85	2c chocolate	.20	.20
399	A85	3c brt blue	.20	.20
400	A85	4c dp orange	.20	.20
401	A85	5c dp brown	.20	.20
402	A85	6c orange brn	.20	.20
403	A85	10c orange red	.20	.20
404	A85	15c black	.25	.20
405	A85	16c ultra	.25	.20
406	A85	25c gray	.25	.20
407	A85	32c dp green	.40	.25
408	A85	40c blue green	.30	.20
409	A85	48c rose	.80	.55
410	A85	50c ocher	1.40	1.00
411	A85	64c deep blue	1.40	1.00
412	A85	80c violet	3.00	.35
413	A85	96c car rose	1.60	.70
414	A85	1e red brown	7.50	.65
415	A85	1.20e yellow brn	7.50	.65
416	A85	1.60e dark blue	1.60	.35
417	A85	2e green	11.00	.65
418	A85	3.20e olive grn	4.00	.65
419	A85	4.50e yellow	4.00	.65
420	A85	5e brown olive	57.50	2.10
421	A85	10e red	6.00	1.10
		Nos. 398-421 (24)	109.95	12.65

See design A64.

Second Independence Issue

Gonçalo Mendes da Maia — A86

Dr. Joao das Regras — A88

Guimaraes Castle — A87

Battle of Montijo — A89

Brites de Almeida — A90

Joao Pinto Ribeiro — A91

1927, Nov. 29 Engr. *Perf. 14*

Center in Black

No.	Type	Description	Unused	Used
422	A86	2c brown	.20	.20
423	A87	3c ultra	.20	.20
424	A86	4c orange	.20	.20
425	A88	5c olive brn	.20	.20
426	A89	6c orange brn	.20	.20
427	A87	15c black brn	.30	.25
428	A88	16c deep blue	.85	*.20*
429	A86	25c gray	.95	*.70*
430	A89	32c blue grn	2.00	*1.00*
431	A90	40c yellow grn	.40	*.30*
432	A86	48c brown red	9.00	*6.25*
433	A87	80c dk violet	6.50	*4.25*
434	A90	96c dull red	11.50	*8.25*
435	A88	1.60e myrtle grn	12.00	*9.25*
436	A91	4.50e bister	18.00	*13.50*
		Nos. 422-436 (15)	62.50	*44.95*

The use of these stamps instead of the regular issue was compulsory on Nov. 29-30, Dec. 1-2, 1927. The money derived from their sale was used for the purchase of a palace for a war museum, the organization of an international exposition in Lisbon, in 1940, and for fêtes to be held in that year in commemoration of the 8th cent. of the founding of Portugal and the 3rd cent. of its restoration.

Third Independence Issue

Gualdim Paes — A93

The Siege of Santarem — A94

Battle of Rolica — A95

Battle of Atoleiros A96

Joana de Gouveia A97

Matias de Albuquerque A98

1928, Nov. 28

Center in Black

No.	Type	Description	Unused	Used
437	A93	2c lt blue	.20	.20
438	A94	3c lt green	.20	.20
439	A95	4c lake	.20	.20
440	A96	5c olive grn	.20	.20
441	A97	6c orange brn	.20	.20
442	A94	15c slate	.55	*.45*
443	A95	16c dk violet	.55	*.45*
444	A93	25c ultra	.55	*.45*
445	A97	32c dk green	2.50	*2.10*
446	A96	40c olive brn	.55	*.45*
447	A95	50c red orange	6.50	*3.25*
448	A94	80c lt gray	6.75	*4.25*
449	A97	96c carmine	12.50	*9.00*
450	A96	1e claret	20.00	*16.00*
451	A93	1.60e dk blue	9.25	*6.75*
452	A98	4.50e yellow	9.75	*8.00*
		Nos. 437-452 (16)	70.45	*52.15*

Obligatory 11/27-30. See note after #436.

Type and Stamps of 1912-28 Surcharged in Black

1928-29 *Perf. 12x11½, 15x14*

No.	Type	Description	Unused	Used
453	A64	4c on 8c orange	.40	.25
454	A64	4c on 30c dk brn	.40	.25
455	A64	10c on ¼c dk ol	.40	.25
a.		Inverted surcharge	90.00	67.50
456	A64	10c on ½c blk (R)	.50	.40
a.		Perf. 15x14	15.00	10.00
457	A64	10c on 1c choc	.50	.40
a.		Perf. 15x14	*60.00*	*40.00*
458	A64	10c on 4c grn	.40	.30
a.		Perf. 15x14	*70.00*	*45.00*
459	A64	10c on 4c orange	.40	.30
460	A64	10c on 5c ol brn	.40	.30
461	A64	15c on 16c blue	1.00	.70
462	A64	15c on 16c ultra	1.00	.70
463	A64	15c on 20c brn	29.00	29.00
464	A64	15c on 20c gray	.40	.25
465	A64	15c on 24c grnsh bl	1.90	1.40
466	A64	15c on 25c gray	.40	.25
467	A64	15c on 25c sal pink	.40	.25
468	A64	16c on 32c dp grn	.80	.70
469	A64	40c on 2c orange	.40	.25
470	A64	40c on 2c yellow	4.00	*2.90*
471	A64	40c on 2c choc	.35	.25
472	A64	40c on 3c ultra	.40	.30
473	A64	40c on 50c yel	.35	.25
474	A64	40c on 60c dull bl	.80	.60
a.		Perf. 15x14	8.00	5.50
475	A64	40c on 64c pale ultra	.80	.70
476	A64	40c on 75c dl rose	.80	.75
477	A64	40c on 80c violet	.55	.45
478	A64	40c on 90c chlky bl	4.00	2.90
a.		Perf. 15x14	9.00	6.00
479	A64	40c on 1e gray vio	.75	.70
480	A64	40c on 1.10e yel brn	.80	.70
481	A64	80c on 6c pale rose	.75	.65
482	A64	80c on 6c choc	.75	.65
483	A64	80c on 48c rose	1.10	.95
484	A64	80c on 1.50e lil	1.75	1.10
485	A64	96c on 1.20e yel grn	3.25	2.10
486	A64	96c on 1.20e buff	3.25	2.40
487	A64	1.60e on 2e slate grn	32.50	24.50
488	A64	1.60e on 3.20e gray grn	9.00	6.25
489	A64	1.60e on 20e pale turq	12.50	8.25
		Nos. 453-489 (37)	117.15	93.30

Stamps of 1912-26 Overprinted in Black or Red

Revalidado

1929 *Perf. 12x11½*

No.	Type	Description	Unused	Used
490	A64	10c orange brn	.35	.20
a.		Perf. 15x14	175.00	175.00
491	A64	15c black (R)	.35	.20
492	A64	40c lt green	.40	.30
493	A64	40c chocolate	.50	.30
494	A64	96c dp rose	4.25	3.00
495	A64	1.60e brt blue	17.00	11.00
a.		Double overprint	95.00	67.50
		Nos. 490-495 (6)	22.85	15.00

Liberty A100

"Portugal" Holding Volume of "Lusiads" A101

1929, May *Perf. 12x11½*

No.	Type	Description	Unused	Used
496	A100	1.60e on 5c red brn	11.00	7.00

1931-38 Typo. *Perf. 14*

No.	Type	Description	Unused	Used
497	A101	4c bister brn	.20	.20
498	A101	5c olive gray	.20	.20
499	A101	6c lt gray	.20	.20
500	A101	10c dk violet	.20	.20
501	A101	15c gray blk	.20	.20
502	A101	16c brt blue	.95	.30
503	A101	25c deep green	2.40	.25
504	A101	25c brt bl ('33)	2.50	.25
505	A101	30c dk grn ('33)	1.40	.25
506	A101	40c orange red	4.75	.20
507	A101	48c fawn	.95	.55
508	A101	50c lt brown	.20	.20
509	A101	75c car rose	3.75	.60
510	A101	80c emerald	.30	.20
511	A101	95c car rose ('33)	11.00	4.00
512	A101	1e claret	22.50	.20
513	A101	1.20e olive grn	1.60	.50
514	A101	1.25e dk blue	1.50	.20
515	A101	1.60e dk blue ('33)	22.50	2.50
516	A101	1.75e dk blue ('38)	.60	.25
517	A101	2e dull violet	.40	.20
518	A101	4.50e orange	1.10	.20
519	A101	5e yellow grn	1.10	.20
		Nos. 497-519 (23)	80.50	12.05
		Set, never hinged	125.00	

Birthplace of St. Anthony A102

Font where St. Anthony was Baptized A103

Lisbon Cathedral A104

St. Anthony with Infant Jesus A105

Santa Cruz Cathedral A106

St. Anthony's Tomb at Padua A107

1931, June Typo. *Perf. 12*

No.	Type	Description	Unused	Used
528	A102	15c plum	.50	.20
		Litho.		
529	A103	25c gray & pale grn	.60	.20
530	A104	40c gray brn & buff	.40	.20
531	A105	75c dl rose & pale rose	17.50	8.75
532	A106	1.25e gray & pale bl	40.00	19.00
533	A107	4.50e gray vio & lil	20.00	2.00
		Nos. 528-533 (6)	79.00	30.35
		Set, never hinged	140.00	

7th centenary of the death of St. Anthony of Padua and Lisbon.

For surcharges see Nos. 543-548.

Nuno Alvares Pereira (1360-1431), Portuguese Warrior and Statesman — A108

1931, Nov. 1 Typo. *Perf. 12x11½*

No.	Type	Description	Unused	Used
534	A108	15c black	.85	.65
535	A108	25c gray grn & blk	8.50	.65
536	A108	40c orange	2.00	.30
a.		Value omitted	125.00	125.00
537	A108	75c car rose	17.50	13.00
538	A108	1.25e dk bl & pale bl	20.00	13.00
539	A108	4.50e choc & lt grn	100.00	32.50
a.		Value omitted	300.00	300.00
		Nos. 534-539 (6)	148.85	60.10
		Set, never hinged	225.00	

For surcharges see Nos. 549-554.

Nos. 528-533 Surcharged

40 C.

1933 *Perf. 12*

No.	Type	Description	Unused	Used
543	A104	15c on 40c	.65	.25
544	A102	40c on 15c	1.60	.75
545	A103	40c on 25c	1.25	.50
546	A105	40c on 75c	5.50	3.25
547	A106	40c on 1.25e	5.50	3.25
548	A107	40c on 4.50e	5.50	3.25
		Nos. 543-548 (6)	20.00	11.25
		Set, never hinged	32.50	

Nos. 534-539 Surcharged

15 C.

1933 *Perf. 12x11½*

549 A108 15c on 40c	.45	.30
550 A108 40c on 15c	2.50	1.75
551 A108 40c on 25c	.60	.60
552 A108 40c on 75c	5.50	2.75
553 A108 40c on 1.25e	5.50	2.75
554 A108 40c on 4.50e	5.50	2.75
Nos. 549-554 (6)	20.05	10.90
Set, never hinged	32.50	

President Carmona A109

Head of a Colonial A110

1934, May 28 **Typo.** *Perf. 11½*

556 A109 40c brt violet	12.50	.25
Never hinged	21.00	

1934, July *Perf. 11½x12*

558 A110 25c dk brown	2.10	.40
559 A110 40c scarlet	14.00	.25
560 A110 1.60e dk blue	21.00	5.00
Nos. 558-560 (3)	37.10	5.65
Set, never hinged	70.00	

Colonial Exposition.

Roman Temple, Evora A111

Prince Henry the Navigator A112

"All for the Nation" A113

Coimbra Cathedral A114

1935-41 *Perf. 11½x12*

561 A111 4c black	.30	.20
562 A111 5c blue	.35	.20
563 A111 6c choc ('36)	.60	.25

Perf. 11½, 12x11½ (1.75e)

564 A112 10c turq grn	.55	.20
565 A112 15c red brown	.20	.20
a. Booklet pane of 4		
566 A113 25c dp blue	4.50	.30
a. Booklet pane of 4		
567 A113 40c brown	1.50	.20
a. Booklet pane of 4		
568 A113 1e rose red	7.00	.35
568A A114 1.75e blue	57.50	.75
568B A113 10e gray blk ('41)	16.00	1.60
569 A113 20e turq grn ('41)	22.50	1.40
Nos. 561-569 (11)	111.00	5.65
Set, never hinged	175.00	

For overprint see No. O1.

Queen Maria A115

Rod and Bowl of Aesculapius A116

Typographed, Head Embossed

1935, June 1 *Perf. 11½*

570 A115 40c scarlet	1.00	.20
Never hinged	1.60	

First Portuguese Philatelic Exhibition.

1937, July 24 **Typo.** *Perf. 11½x12*

571 A116 25c blue	7.00	.60
Never hinged	11.00	

Centenary of the establishment of the School of Medicine in Lisbon and Oporto.

Gil Vicente A117

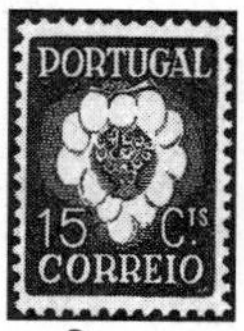

Grapes A118

1937

572 A117 40c dark brown	13.00	.20
573 A117 1e rose red	2.00	.20
Set, never hinged	22.50	

400th anniversary of the death of Gil Vicente (1465-1536), Portuguese playwright. Design shows him in cowherd role in his play, "Auto do Vaqueiro."

1938 *Perf. 11½*

575 A118 15c brt purple	.85	.35
576 A118 25c brown	1.90	.85
577 A118 40c dp red lilac	7.75	.25
578 A118 1.75e dp blue	22.50	14.50
Nos. 575-578 (4)	33.00	15.95
Set, never hinged	50.00	

International Vineyard and Wine Congress.

Emblem of Portuguese Legion — A119

1940, Jan. 27 **Unwmk.** *Perf. 11½*

579 A119 5c dull yellow	.25	.20
580 A119 10c violet	.25	.20
581 A119 15c brt blue	.25	.20
582 A119 25c brown	14.00	.70
583 A119 40c dk green	24.00	.25
584 A119 80c yellow grn	1.40	.30
585 A119 1e brt red	35.00	2.10
586 A119 1.75e dark blue	4.75	1.60
a. Souv. sheet of 8, #579-586	210.00	250.00
Never hinged	425.00	
Nos. 579-586 (8)	79.90	5.55
Set, never hinged	125.00	

Issued in honor of the Portuguese Legion.

No. 586a sold for 5.50e, the proceeds going to various charities.

Portuguese World Exhibition A120

King John IV — A121

Discoveries Monument, Belém — A122

King Alfonso I — A123

1940 **Engr.** *Perf. 12x11½, 11½x12*

587 A120 10c brown violet	.20	.20
588 A121 15c dk grnsh bl	.20	.20
589 A122 25c dk slate grn	.80	.20
590 A121 35c yellow green	.60	.20
591 A123 40c olive bister	1.60	.20
592 A120 80c dk violet	3.25	.20
593 A122 1e dark red	7.00	.85
594 A123 1.75e ultra	3.75	1.50
a. Souv. sheet of 8, #587-594 ('41)	85.00	75.00
Never hinged	150.00	
Nos. 587-594 (8)	17.40	3.55
Set, never hinged	26.00	

Portuguese Intl. Exhibition, Lisbon (10c, 80c); restoration of the monarchy, 300th anniv (15c, 35c); Portuguese independence, 800th anniv (40c, 1.75e).

No. 594a sold for 10e.

Sir Rowland Hill — A124

1940, Aug. 12 **Typo.** *Perf. 11½x12*

595 A124 15c dk violet brn	.20	.20
596 A124 25c dp org brn	.20	.20
597 A124 35c green	.20	.20
598 A124 40c brown violet	.30	.20
599 A124 50c turq green	11.00	2.50
600 A124 80c lt blue	1.25	.60
601 A124 1e crimson	13.00	2.00
602 A124 1.75e dk blue	4.00	2.00
a. Souv. sheet of 8, #595-602 ('41)	45.00	60.00
Never hinged	75.00	
Nos. 595-602 (8)	30.15	7.90
Set, never hinged	45.00	

Postage stamp centenary.

No. 602a sold for 10e.

Fisherwoman of Nazare A126

Native of Coimbra A127

Native of Saloio — A128

Fisherwoman of Lisbon — A129

Native of Olhao — A130

Native of Aveiro — A131

Native of Madeira A132

Native of Viana do Castelo A133

Rancher of Ribatejo A134

Peasant of Alentejo A135

1941, Apr. 4 **Typo.** *Perf. 11½*

605 A126 4c sage green	.20	.20
606 A127 5c orange brn	.20	.20
607 A128 10c red violet	2.10	.75
608 A129 15c lt yel grn	.20	.20
609 A130 25c rose violet	1.40	.40
610 A131 40c yellow grn	.20	.20
611 A132 80c lt blue	2.25	1.40
612 A133 1e rose red	6.25	.90
613 A134 1.75e dull blue	6.75	2.75
614 A135 2e red orange	25.00	14.00
a. Sheet of 10, #605-614	75.00	100.00
Never hinged	125.00	
Nos. 605-614 (10)	44.55	21.00
Set, never hinged	70.00	

No. 614a sold for 10e.

Ancient Sailing Vessel — A136

1943 *Perf. 14*

615 A136 5c black	.20	.20
616 A136 10c fawn	.20	.20
617 A136 15c lilac gray	.20	.20
618 A136 20c dull violet	.20	.20
619 A136 30c brown violet	.20	.20
620 A136 35c dk blue grn	.20	.20
621 A136 50c plum	.20	.20
622 A136 1e deep rose	5.00	.20
623 A136 1.75e indigo	15.00	.20
624 A136 2e dull claret	1.10	.20
625 A136 2.50e crim rose	1.75	.20
626 A136 3.50e grnsh blue	7.00	.35
627 A136 5e dp orange	.85	.20
628 A136 10e blue gray	2.00	.20
629 A136 15e blue green	19.00	.45
630 A136 20e olive gray	57.50	.20
631 A136 50e salmon	160.00	.50
Nos. 615-631 (17)	270.60	4.10
Set, never hinged	500.00	

See Nos. 702-710.

Farmer A137

Postrider A138

1943, Oct. *Perf. 11½*

632 A137 10c dull blue	.55	.20
633 A137 50c red	.85	.20
Set, never hinged	2.10	

Congress of Agricultural Science.

1944, May **Unwmk.**

No.	Type	Value	Color	Unused	Used
634	A138	10c	dk violet brn	.25	.20
635	A138	50c	purple	.25	.20
636	A138	1e	cerise	2.25	.30
637	A138	1.75e	brt blue	2.25	.80
a.			Sheet of 4, #634-637	20.00	30.00
			Never hinged	40.00	
			Nos. 634-637 (4)	5.00	1.50
			Set, never hinged	7.50	

3rd Philatelic Exhibition, Lisbon.
No. 637a sold for 7.50e.

Portrait of Avellar Brotero — A139

Statue of Brotero — A140

1944, Nov. 23 **Typo.** ***Perf. 11½x12***

No.	Type	Value	Color	Unused	Used
638	A139	10c	chocolate	.20	.20
639	A140	50c	dull green	1.40	.20
640	A140	1e	carmine	5.50	.85
641	A139	1.75e	dark blue	5.00	1.50
a.			Sheet of 4,#638-641 ('45)	24.00	30.00
			Never hinged	37.50	
			Nos. 638-641 (4)	12.10	2.75
			Set, never hinged	17.50	

Avellar Brotero, botanist, 200th birth anniv.
No. 641a sold for 7.50e.

Gil Eannes — A141

Designs: 30c, Joao Goncalves Zarco. 35c, Bartolomeu Dias. 50c, Vasco da Gama. 1e, Pedro Alvares Cabral. 1.75e, Fernando Magellan. 2e, Goncalo Velho. 3.50e, Diogo Cao.

1945, July 29 **Engr.** ***Perf. 13½***

No.	Type	Value	Color	Unused	Used
642	A141	10c	violet brn	.20	.20
643	A141	30c	yellow brn	.20	.20
644	A141	35c	blue green	.25	.20
645	A141	50c	dk olive grn	.80	.20
646	A141	1e	vermilion	2.00	.40
647	A141	1.75e	slate blue	2.50	1.25
648	A141	2e	black	2.75	1.50
649	A141	3.50e	carmine rose	6.00	2.50
a.			Sheet of 8, #642-649	17.50	30.00
			Never hinged	27.50	
			Nos. 642-649 (8)	14.70	6.45
			Set, never hinged	22.50	

Portuguese navigators of 15th and 16th centuries.
No. 649a sold for 15e.

Pres. Antonio Oscar de Fragoso Carmona A149

Astrolabe A150

Perf. 11½

1945, Nov. 12 **Photo.** **Unwmk.**

No.	Type	Value	Color	Unused	Used
650	A149	10c	bright violet	.20	.20
651	A149	30c	copper brown	.20	.20
652	A149	35c	dark green	.20	.20
653	A149	50c	dark olive	.25	.20
654	A149	1e	dark red	5.50	.75
655	A149	1.75e	dark blue	4.50	2.25
656	A149	2e	deep claret	25.00	2.75
657	A149	3.50e	slate black	17.00	4.50
a.			Sheet of 8, #650-657	70.00	85.00
			Never hinged	140.00	
			Nos. 650-657 (8)	52.85	11.05
			Set, never hinged	90.00	

No. 657a sold for 15e.

1945, Dec. 27 **Litho.**

No.	Type	Value	Color	Unused	Used
658	A150	10c	light brown	.25	.20
659	A150	50c	gray green	.25	.20
660	A150	1e	brown red	1.60	.45
661	A150	1.75e	dull chalky bl	1.90	1.40
a.			Sheet of 4, #658-661 ('46)	17.50	22.50
			Never hinged	27.50	
			Nos. 658-661 (4)	4.00	2.25
			Set, never hinged	6.00	

Centenary of the Portuguese Naval School.
No. 661a, issued Apr. 29, sold for 7.50e.

Catalogue values for unused stamps in this section, from this point to the end of the section, are for Never Hinged items.

Silves Castle A151

Almourol Castle A152

Castles: 30c, Leiria. 35c, Feira. 50c, Guimaraes. 1.75e, Lisbon. 2e, Braganca. 3.50e, Ourem.

1946, June 1 **Engr.**

No.	Type	Value	Color	Unused	Used
662	A151	10c	brown vio	.20	.20
663	A151	30c	brown red	.20	.20
664	A151	35c	olive grn	.20	.20
665	A151	50c	gray blk	.35	.20
666	A152	1e	brt carmine	20.00	.50
667	A152	1.75e	dk blue	11.50	1.25
a.			Sheet of 4	125.00	80.00
			Hinged	85.00	
668	A152	2e	dk gray grn	40.00	2.25
669	A152	3.50e	orange brn	17.50	2.75
			Nos. 662-669 (8)	89.95	7.55

No. 667a printed on buff granite paper, size 135x102mm, sold for 12.50e.

Figure with Tablet and Arms — A153

Madonna and Child — A154

1946, Nov. 19 ***Perf. 12x11½***

No.	Type	Value	Color	Unused	Used
670	A153	50c	dark blue	.75	.20
a.			Sheet of 4	100.00	70.00
			Hinged	65.00	

Establishment of the Bank of Portugal, cent.
No. 670a measures 155x143½mm and sold for 7.50e.

1946, Dec. 8 **Unwmk.** ***Perf. 13½***

No.	Type	Value	Color	Unused	Used
671	A154	30c	gray black	.20	.20
672	A154	50c	deep green	.20	.20
673	A154	1e	rose car	1.90	.60
674	A154	1.75e	brt blue	3.75	1.10
a.			Sheet of 4, #671-674 ('47)	45.00	42.50
			Nos. 671-674 (4)	6.05	2.10

300th anniv. of the proclamation making the Virgin Mary patroness of Portugal.
No. 674a sold for 7.50e.

Shepherdess, Caramullo — A155

Surrender of the Moors, 1147 — A163

30c, Timbrel player, Malpique. 35c, Flute player, Monsanto. 50c, Woman of Avintes. 1e, Field laborer, Maia. 1.75e, Woman of Algarve. 2e, Bastonet player, Miranda. 3.50e, Woman of the Azores.

1947, Mar. 1 **Photo.** ***Perf. 11½***

No.	Type	Value	Color	Unused	Used
675	A155	10c	rose violet	.20	.20
676	A155	30c	dark red	.20	.20
677	A155	35c	dk olive grn	.20	.20
678	A155	50c	dark brown	.35	.20
679	A155	1e	red	12.00	.20
680	A155	1.75e	slate blue	13.00	1.50
681	A155	2e	peacock bl	42.50	1.75
682	A155	3.50e	slate blk	32.50	2.75
a.			Sheet of 8, #675-682	190.00	190.00
			Hinged	110.00	
			Nos. 675-682 (8)	100.95	7.00

No. 682a sold for 15e.

1947, Oct. 13 **Engr.** ***Perf. 12½***

No.	Type	Value	Color	Unused	Used
683	A163	5c	blue green	.20	.20
684	A163	20c	dk carmine	.20	.20
685	A163	50c	violet	.25	.20
686	A163	1.75e	dark blue	5.00	2.50
687	A163	2.50e	chocolate	7.00	3.50
688	A163	3.50e	slate black	12.50	5.75
			Nos. 683-688 (6)	25.15	12.35

Conquest of Lisbon from the Moors, 800th anniv.

St. John de Britto
A164 A165

1948, May 28 ***Perf. 11½x12***

No.	Type	Value	Color	Unused	Used
689	A164	30c	green	.20	.20
690	A165	50c	dark brown	.20	.20
691	A164	1e	rose carmine	7.00	.75
692	A165	1.75e	blue	9.00	1.10
			Nos. 689-692 (4)	16.40	2.25

Birth of St. John de Britto, 300th anniv.

Architecture and Engineering A166

King John I — A167

1948, May 28 ***Perf. 13x12½***

No.	Type	Value	Color	Unused	Used
693	A166	50c	violet brn	.50	.20

Exposition of public Works and Natl. Congress of Engineering and Architecture, 1948.

Perf. 11½

1949, May 6 **Unwmk.** **Photo.**

Designs: 30c, Philippa of Lancaster. 35c, Prince Ferdinand. 50c, Prince Henry the Navigator. 1e, Nuno Alvarez Pereira. 1.75e, John das Regras. 2e, Fernao Lopes. 3.50e, Affonso Domingues.

No.	Type	Value	Color	Unused	Used
694	A167	10c	brn vio & cr	.25	.20
695	A167	30c	dk bl grn & cr	.25	.20
696	A167	35c	dk ol grn & cr	.40	.20
697	A167	50c	dp blue & cr	1.00	.20
698	A167	1e	dk red & cr	1.10	.20
699	A167	1.75e	dk gray & cr	21.00	5.00
700	A167	2e	dk gray bl & cr	11.00	1.00
701	A167	3.50e	dk brn & gray	40.00	13.00
a.			Sheet of 8, #694-701	65.00	60.00
			Nos. 694-701 (8)	75.00	20.00

No. 701a sold for 15e. Stamps from No. 701a differ from Nos. 694-701 in that they do not have "P. GUEDES" and "COURVOISIER S.A." below the design. Each stamp from the sheet of 8 has the same retail value.

Ship Type of 1942

1948-49 **Typo.** ***Perf. 14***

No.	Type	Value	Color	Unused	Used
702	A136	80c	dp green	3.50	.25
703	A136	1e	dp claret ('48)	2.25	.20
704	A136	1.20e	dp carmine	3.50	.20
705	A136	1.50e	olive	40.00	.25
706	A136	1.80e	yellow org	35.00	1.75
707	A136	2e	deep blue	5.25	.25
708	A136	4e	orange	55.00	1.50
709	A136	6e	yellow grn	100.00	2.10
710	A136	7.50e	grnsh gray	30.00	1.75
			Nos. 702-710 (9)	274.50	8.25
			Set, hinged	175.00	

Angel, Coimbra Museum A168

Symbols of the UPU A169

1949, Dec. 20 **Engr.** ***Perf. 13x14***

No.	Type	Value	Color	Unused	Used
711	A168	1e	red brown	8.25	.20
712	A168	5e	olive brown	1.75	.20

16th Intl. Congress of History and Art.

1949, Dec. 29

No.	Type	Value	Color	Unused	Used
713	A169	1e	brown violet	.25	.20
714	A169	2e	deep blue	.75	.20
715	A169	2.50e	deep green	3.25	.60
716	A169	4e	brown red	8.75	2.00
			Nos. 713-716 (4)	13.00	3.00

75th anniv. of the UPU.

Madonna of Fatima — A170

St. John of God Helping Ill Man — A171

1950, May 13 ***Perf. 11½x12***

No.	Type	Value	Color	Unused	Used
717	A170	50c	dark green	.50	.20
718	A170	1e	dark brown	2.25	.20
719	A170	2e	blue	5.25	1.10
720	A170	5e	lilac	70.00	16.00
			Nos. 717-720 (4)	78.00	17.50

Holy Year, 1950, and to honor "Our Lady of the Rosary" at Fatima.

1950, Oct. 30 **Engr.** **Unwmk.**

No.	Type	Value	Color	Unused	Used
721	A171	20c	gray violet	.25	.20
722	A171	50c	cerise	.35	.20
723	A171	1e	olive grn	1.40	.20
724	A171	1.50e	deep orange	11.00	1.40
725	A171	2e	blue	9.50	1.25
726	A171	4e	chocolate	37.50	4.25
			Nos. 721-726 (6)	60.00	7.50

400th anniv. of the death of St. John of God.

Guerra Junqueiro A172

Fisherman and Catch — A173

1951, Mar. 2 **Litho.** ***Perf. 13½***

727	A172	50c dark brown	3.50	.20
728	A172	1e dk slate gray	1.00	.20

Birth centenary of Guerra Junqueiro, poet.

1951, Mar. 9

729	A173	50c gray grn, *buff*	2.75	.25
730	A173	1e rose lake, *buff*	.75	.20

3rd National Congress of Fisheries.

Dove — A174

Pope Pius XII — A175

1951, Oct. 11

731	A174	20c dk brn & buff	.30	.20
732	A174	90c dk ol grn & cr	8.00	.85
733	A175	1e dp cl & pink	8.00	.20
734	A175	2.30e dk bl grn & bl	11.00	1.00
		Nos. 731-734 (4)	27.30	2.25

End of the Holy Year.

15th Century Colonists, Terceira A176

1951, Oct. 24 ***Perf. 13x13½***

735	A176	50c dk bl, *salmon*	1.50	.25
736	A176	1e dk brn, *cream*	1.00	.25

500th anniversary (in 1950) of the colonizing of the island of Terceira.

Student, Soldiers and Workers A177

1951, Nov. 22 ***Perf. 13½x13***

737	A177	1e violet brown	5.50	.20
738	A177	2.30e dark blue	3.50	.40

25th anniversary of the national revolution.

16th Century Coach A178

Designs: Various coaches.

Perf. 13x13½

1952, Jan. 8 **Engr.** **Unwmk.**

739	A178	10c purple	.20	.20
740	A178	20c olive gray	.20	.20
741	A178	50c steel blue	.45	.20
742	A178	90c green	2.10	.95
743	A178	1e red orange	.80	.20
744	A178	1.40e rose pink	4.75	2.75
745	A178	1.50e rose brown	4.75	1.40
746	A178	2.30e deep ultra	2.75	1.25
		Nos. 739-746 (8)	16.00	7.15

National Museum of Coaches.

Symbolical of NATO — A179

1952, Apr. 4 **Litho.** ***Perf. 12½***

747	A179	1e green & blk	9.00	.20
748	A179	3.50e gray & vio bl	225.00	13.00
		Set, hinged	110.00	

North Atlantic Treaty signing, 3rd anniv.

Hockey Players on Roller Skates A180

1952, June 28 ***Perf. 13x13½***

749	A180	1e dk blue & gray	3.25	.20
750	A180	3.50e dk red brown	4.25	1.25

Issued to publicize the 8th World Championship Hockey-on-Skates matches.

Francisco Gomes Teixeira — A181

St. Francis and Two Boys — A182

1952, Nov. 25 ***Perf. 14x14½***

751	A181	1e cerise	.60	.20
752	A181	2.30e deep blue	5.50	2.10

Centenary of the birth of Francisco Gomes Teixeira (1851-1932), mathematician.

1952, Dec. 23 ***Perf. 13½***

753	A182	1e dark green	.45	.20
754	A182	2e dp claret	1.40	.20
755	A182	3.50e chalky blue	18.00	6.00
756	A182	5e dark purple	32.50	1.75
		Nos. 753-756 (4)	52.35	8.15

400th anniv. of the death of St. Francis Xavier.

Marshal Carmona Bridge A183

Designs: 1.40e, "28th of May" Stadium. 2e, University City, Coimbra. 3.50e, Salazar Dam.

1952, Dec. 10 **Unwmk.** ***Perf. 12½***
Buff Paper

757	A183	1e red brown	.50	.25
758	A183	1.40e dull purple	10.50	3.00
759	A183	2e dark green	5.50	1.50
760	A183	3.50e dark blue	11.00	2.25
		Nos. 757-760 (4)	27.50	7.00

Centenary of the foundation of the Ministry of Public Works.

Equestrian Seal of King Diniz — A184

1953-56 **Litho.**

761	A184	5c green, *citron*	.20	.20
762	A184	10c ind, *salmon*	.20	.20
763	A184	20c org red, *citron*	.20	.20
763A	A184	30c rose lil, *cr* ('56)	.20	.20
764	A184	50c gray	.20	.20
765	A184	90c dk grn, *cit*	13.00	.40
766	A184	1e vio brn, *rose*	.35	.20
767	A184	1.40e rose red	13.50	.60
768	A184	1.50e red, *cream*	.55	.20
769	A184	2e gray	.60	.20
770	A184	2.30e blue	17.00	.55
771	A184	2.50e gray blk, *sal*	1.10	.20
772	A184	5e rose vio, *cr*	1.10	.20
773	A184	10e blue, *citron*	3.75	.20
774	A184	20e bis brn, *cit*	11.00	.20
775	A184	50e rose violet	4.25	.30
		Nos. 761-775 (16)	67.20	4.25

St. Martin of Braga A185

Guilherme Gomes Fernandes A186

Perf. 13x13½

1953, Feb. 26 **Unwmk.**

776	A185	1e gray blk & gray	1.25	.20
777	A185	3.50e dk brn & yel	8.75	3.50

14th centenary of the arrival of St. Martin of Dume on the Iberian peninsula.

1953, Mar. 28 ***Perf. 13***

778	A186	1e red violet	.75	.20
779	A186	2.30e deep blue	7.25	3.25

Birth of Guilherme Gomes Fernandes, General Inspector of the Firemen of Porto.

Emblems of Automobile Club — A187

1953, Apr. 15 ***Perf. 12½***

780	A187	1e dk grn & yel grn	.50	.20
781	A187	3.50e dk brn & buff	9.50	2.75

Portuguese Automobile Club, 50th anniv.

Princess St. Joanna — A188

Queen Maria II — A189

Perf. 14½x14

1953, May 14 **Litho.** **Unwmk.**

782	A188	1e blk & gray grn	1.50	.20
783	A188	3.50e dk blue & blue	10.00	3.50

Birth of Princess St. Joanna, 500th anniv.

1953, Oct. 3 **Photo.** ***Perf. 13½***
Background of Lower Panel in Gold

784	A189	50c red brown	.20	.20
785	A189	1e claret brn	.20	.20
786	A189	1.40e dk violet	1.50	.35
787	A189	2.30e dp blue	3.75	1.10
788	A189	3.50e violet blue	3.75	1.10
789	A189	4.50e dk blue grn	2.40	.80
790	A189	5e dk ol grn	5.75	.80
791	A189	20e red violet	52.50	4.50
		Nos. 784-791 (8)	70.05	9.05

Centenary of Portugal's first postage stamp.

Allegory A190

1954, Sept. 22 ***Perf. 13***

792	A190	1e bl & dk grnsh bl	.40	.20
793	A190	1.50e buff & dk brn	2.10	.25

150th anniversary of the founding of the State Secretariat for Financial Affairs.

Open Textbook A191

Cadet and College Arms — A192

1954, Oct. 15 **Litho.**

794	A191	50c blue	.25	.20
795	A191	1e red	.25	.20
796	A191	2e dk green	24.00	1.25
797	A191	2.50e orange brn	20.00	1.10
		Nos. 794-797 (4)	44.50	2.75

National literacy campaign.

1954, Nov. 17

798	A192	1e choc & lt grn	1.25	.20
799	A192	3.50e dk bl & gray grn	5.25	1.40

150th anniversary of the Military College.

Manuel da Nobrega and Crucifix — A193

King Alfonso I — A194

1954, Dec. 17 **Engr.** ***Perf. 14x13***

800	A193	1e brown	.45	.25
801	A193	2.30e deep blue	40.00	13.50
802	A193	3.50e gray green	11.00	1.50
803	A193	5e green	35.00	2.75
		Nos. 800-803 (4)	86.45	18.00

Founding of Sao Paulo, Brazil, 400th anniv.

1955, Mar. 17 ***Perf. 13½x13***

Kings: 20c, Sancho I. 50c, Alfonso II. 90c, Sancho II. 1e, Alfonso III. 1.40e, Diniz. 1.50e, Alfonso IV. 2e, Pedro I. 2.30e, Ferdinand I.

804	A194	10c rose violet	.20	.20
805	A194	20c dk olive grn	.20	.20
806	A194	50c dk blue grn	.35	.20
807	A194	90c green	2.75	.75
808	A194	1e red brown	1.25	.20
809	A194	1.40e carmine rose	7.50	1.75
810	A194	1.50e olive brn	3.00	.60
811	A194	2e deep orange	9.25	1.70
812	A194	2.30e violet blue	8.00	1.40
		Nos. 804-812 (9)	32.50	7.00

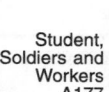

Telegraph Pole — A195

A. J. Ferreira da Silva — A196

1955, Sept. 16 Litho. *Perf. 13½*

813 A195 1e ocher & hn brn .50 .20
814 A195 2.30e gray grn & Prus bl 20.00 2.10
815 A195 3.50e lemon & dp grn 17.50 1.60
Nos. 813-815 (3) 38.00 3.90

Centenary of the telegraph system in Portugal.

1956, May 8 Photo. Unwmk.

816 A196 1e blue & dk blue .30 .20
817 A196 2.30e grn & dk grn 11.50 2.75

Centenary of the birth of Prof. Antonio Joaquim Ferreira da Silva, chemist.

Steam Locomotive, 1856 — A197

Madonna, 15th Century — A198

Design: 1.50e, 2e, Electric train, 1956.

1956, Oct. 28 Litho. *Perf. 13*

818 A197 1e lt & dk ol grn .45 .20
819 A197 1.50e Prus bl & lt grnsh bl 3.00 .20
820 A197 2e dk org brn & bis 25.00 .70
821 A197 2.50e choc & brn 35.00 .90
Nos. 818-821 (4) 63.45 2.00

Centenary of the Portuguese railways.

1956, Dec. 8 Photo.

822 A198 1e dp grn & lt ol grn .25 .20
823 A198 1.50e dk red brn & ol bis .75 .25

Mothers' Day, Dec. 8.

J. B. Almeida Garrett A199

1957, Mar. 7 Engr. *Perf. 13½x14*

824 A199 1e sepia .50 .20
825 A199 2.30e lt purple 32.50 6.00
826 A199 3.50e dull green 7.00 .70
827 A199 5e rose carmine 55.00 5.75
Nos. 824-827 (4) 95.00 12.65

Issued in honor of Joao Baptista da Silva Leitao de Almeida Garrett, poet.

Cesarío Verde A200

Exhibition Emblems A201

1957, Dec. 12 Litho. *Perf. 13½*

828 A200 1e citron & brown .35 .20
829 A200 3.30e gray grn, yel grn & dk ol 1.40 .55

Jose Joaquim de Cesario Verde (1855-86), poet.

1958, Apr. 7

830 A201 1e multicolored .25 .20
831 A201 3.30e multicolored 1.25 .55

Universal & Intl. Exposition at Brussels.

Queen St. Isabel — A202

Institute for Tropical Medicine A203

Design: 2e, 5e, St. Teotonio.

Perf. 14½x14

1958, July 10 Photo. Unwmk.

832 A202 1e rose brn & buff .20 .20
833 A202 2e dk green & buff .45 .25
834 A202 2.50e purple & buff 3.75 .35
835 A202 5e brown & buff 4.75 .45
Nos. 832-835 (4) 9.15 1.25

1958, Sept. 4 Litho. *Perf. 13*

836 A203 1e dk grn & lt gray 1.50 .20
837 A203 2.50e bl & pale bl 5.75 .55

6th Intl. Cong. for Tropical Medicine and Malaria, Lisbon, Sept. 1958, and opening of the new Tropical Medicine Institute.

Cargo Ship and Loading Crane — A204

1958, Nov. 27 Unwmk. *Perf. 13*

838 A204 1e brn & dk brn 4.75 .20
839 A204 4.50e vio bl & dk bl 3.25 1.00

2nd Natl. Cong. of the Merchant Marine, Porto.

Queen Leonor A205

1958, Dec. 17

840 A205 1e multi .20 .20
841 A205 1.50e bis, blk, bl & dk bis brn 3.00 .25
a. Dark bister brown omitted
842 A205 2.30e multi 2.75 .45
843 A205 4.10e multi 2.50 .60
Nos. 840-843 (4) 8.45 1.50

500th anniv. of the birth of Queen Leonor.

Arms of Aveiro — A206

Symbols of Hope and Peace — A207

1959, Aug. 30 Litho. *Perf. 13*

844 A206 1e ol bis, brn, gold & sil 1.00 .20
845 A206 5e grnsh gray, gold & sil 8.50 .90

Millennium of Aveiro.

1960, Mar. 2 *Perf. 12½*

846 A207 1e lt violet & blk .25 .20
847 A207 3.50e gray & dk grn 2.75 .90

10th anniversary (in 1959) of NATO.

Open Door to "Peace" and WRY Emblem — A208

Glider — A209

1960, Apr. 7 Unwmk. *Perf. 13*

848 A208 20c multi .20 .20
849 A208 1e multi .35 .20
850 A208 1.80e yel grn, org & blk .70 .25
Nos. 848-850 (3) 1.25 .65

World Refugee Year, 7/1/59-6/30/60.

1960, May 2

Designs: 1.50e, Plane. 2e, Plane and parachutes. 2.50e, Model plane.

851 A209 1e yel, gray & bl .20 .20
852 A209 1.50e multicolored .40 .20
853 A209 2e bl grn, yel & blk .90 .35
854 A209 2.50e grnsh bl, ocher & red 1.75 .50
Nos. 851-854 (4) 3.25 1.25

Aero Club of Portugal, 50th anniv. (in 1959).

Father Cruz — A210

University of Evora Seal — A211

1960, July 18 Unwmk. *Perf. 13*

855 A210 1e deep brown .25 .20
856 A210 4.30e Prus blue & blk 5.75 2.75

Father Cruz, "father of the poor."

1960, July 18 Litho.

857 A211 50c violet blue .20 .20
858 A211 1e red brn & yel .25 .20
859 A211 1.40e rose cl & rose 1.75 .60
Nos. 857-859 (3) 2.20 1.00

Founding of the University of Evora, 400th anniv.

Arms of Prince Henry — A212

Arms of Lisbon and Symbolic Ship — A213

Designs: 2.50e, Caravel. 3.50e, Prince Henry. 5e, Prince Henry's motto. 8e, Prince Henry's sloop. 10e, Old chart of Sagres region of Portugal.

1960, Aug. 4 Photo. *Perf. 12x12½*

860 A212 1e gold & multi .25 .20
861 A212 2.50e gold & multi 2.40 .20
862 A212 3.50e gold & multi 3.00 .80
863 A212 5e gold & multi 5.25 .40
864 A212 8e gold & multi 1.10 .40
865 A212 10e gold & multi 9.00 1.00
Nos. 860-865 (6) 21.00 3.00

500th anniversary of the death of Prince Henry the Navigator.

Europa Issue, 1960

Common Design Type

1960, Sept. 16 Litho. *Perf. 13*

Size: 31x21mm

866 CD3 1e ultra & gray blue .20 .20
867 CD3 3.50e brn red & rose red 2.75 .90

1960, Nov. 17 *Perf. 13*

868 A213 1e gray ol, blk & vio bl .25 .20
869 A213 3.30e bl, blk & ultra 3.75 1.75

5th Natl. Philatelic Exhibition, Lisbon, part of the Prince Henry the Navigator festivities. (The ship in the design is in honor of Prince Henry).

Flag and Laurel — A214

1960, Dec. 20 Litho. *Perf. 13*

870 A214 1e multicolored .20 .20

50th anniversary of the Republic.

King Pedro V A215

1961, Aug. 3 Engr. *Perf. 13*

871 A215 1e gray brn & dk grn .20 .20
872 A215 6.50e dk blue & blk 2.10 .35

Centenary of the founding of the Faculty of Letters, Lisbon University.

Setubal Sea Gate and Ships A216

1961, Aug. 24 Litho. *Perf. 12x11½*

873 A216 1e gold & multi .25 .20
874 A216 4.30e gold & multi 10.50 2.75

Centenary of the city of Setubal.

Clasped Hands and CEPT Emblem — A217

Tomar Castle and River Nabao — A218

Europa Issue, 1961

1961, Sept. 18 ***Perf. 13½x13***

875 A217 1e blue & lt blue .20 .20
876 A217 1.50e green & brt green .85 .60
877 A217 3.50e brown, pink & red .95 .80
Nos. 875-877 (3) 2.00 1.60

1962, Jan. 26 ***Perf. 11½x12***

878 A218 1e gold & multi .20 .20
879 A218 3.50e gold & multi .95 .55

800th anniversary of the city of Tomar.

National Guardsman A219

Archangel Gabriel A220

1962, Feb. 20 Unwmk. ***Perf. 13½***

880 A219 1e multi .20 .20
881 A219 2e multi 1.25 .40
882 A219 2.50e multi 1.25 .30
Nos. 880-882 (3) 2.70 .90

Republican National Guard, 50th anniv.

1962, Mar. 24 Litho. ***Perf. 13***

883 A220 1e ol, pink & red brn .50 .20
884 A220 3.50e ol, pink & dk grn .30 .25

Issued for St. Gabriel's Day. St. Gabriel is patron of telecommunications.

Tents and Scout Emblem A221

1962, June 11 Unwmk. ***Perf. 13***

885 A221 20c gray, bis, yel & blk .20 .20
a. Double impression of gray frame lettering
886 A221 50c multi .20 .20
887 A221 1e multi .40 .20
888 A221 2.50e multi 2.50 .25
889 A221 3.50e multi .55 .25
890 A221 6.50e multi .70 .30
Nos. 885-890 (6) 4.55 1.40

50th anniv. of the Portuguese Boy Scouts and the 18th Boy Scout World Conf., Sept. 19-24, 1961.

Children Reading A222

Designs: 1e, Vaccination. 2.80e, Children playing ball. 3.50e, Guarding sleeping infant.

1962, Sept. 10 Litho. ***Perf. 13½***

891 A222 50c bluish grn, yel & blk .20 .20
892 A222 1e pale bl, yel & blk .40 .20
893 A222 2.80e dp org yel & blk 1.40 .45
894 A222 3.50e dl rose, yel & blk 3.00 .75
Nos. 891-894 (4) 5.00 1.60

10th Intl. Cong. of Pediatrics, Lisbon, Sept. 9-15.

19-Cell Honeycomb A223

1962, Sept. 17

895 A223 1e bl, dk bl & gold .20 .20
896 A223 1.50e lt & dk grn & gold .90 .35
897 A223 3.50e dp rose, mar & gold 1.10 .65
Nos. 895-897 (3) 2.20 1.20

Europa. The 19 cells represent the 19 original members of the Conference of European Postal and Telecommunications Administrations, C.E.P.T.

St. Zenon, the Courier — A224

European Soccer Cup and Emblem — A225

1962, Dec. 1 Unwmk. ***Perf. 13½***

898 A224 1e multi .20 .20
899 A224 2e multi .60 .40
900 A224 2.80e multi 1.10 .90
Nos. 898-900 (3) 1.90 1.50

Issued for Stamp Day.

1963, Feb. 5 ***Perf. 13½***

901 A225 1e multi .45 .20
902 A225 4.30e multi .80 .60

Victories of the Benfica Club of Lisbon in the 1961 and 1962 European Soccer Championships.

Wheat Emblem A226

1963, Mar. 21 Litho.

903 A226 1e multi .20 .20
904 A226 3.30e multi .70 .55
905 A226 3.50e multi .70 .50
Nos. 903-905 (3) 1.60 1.25

FAO "Freedom from Hunger" campaign.

Stagecoach — A227

1963, May 7 ***Perf. 12x11½***

906 A227 1e gray, lt & dk bl .20 .20
907 A227 1.50e bis, dk brn & lil rose 1.10 .25
908 A227 5e org brn, dk brn & rose lil .30 .20
Nos. 906-908 (3) 1.60 .65

1st Intl. Postal Conference, Paris, 1863.

St. Vincent de Paul by Monsaraz — A228

1963, July 10 Photo. ***Perf. 13½x14***

Gold Inscription

909 A228 20c lt blue & ultra .20 .20
a. Gold inscription omitted 55.00
910 A228 1e gray & slate .20 .20
911 A228 2.80e green & slate 1.75 1.00
a. Gold inscription omitted 65.00
912 A228 5e dp rose car & sl 2.25 .35
Nos. 909-912 (4) 4.40 1.75

Tercentenary of the death of St. Vincent de Paul.

Emblem of Order and Knight A229

1963, Aug. 13 Litho. ***Perf. 11½***

913 A229 1e multi .20 .20
914 A229 1.50e multi .20 .20
915 A229 2.50e multi 1.00 .30
Nos. 913-915 (3) 1.40 .70

800th anniv. of the Military Order of Avis.

Europa Issue, 1963

Stylized Bird — A230

1963, Sept. 16 ***Perf. 13½***

916 A230 1e lt bl, gray & blk *.50* .20
917 A230 1.50e grn, gray & blk *3.25* .55
918 A230 3.50e red, gray & blk *5.50* 1.25
Nos. 916-918 (3) *9.25* 2.00

Jet Plane — A231

Apothecary Jar — A232

1963, Dec. 1 Unwmk. ***Perf. 13½***

919 A231 1e dk bl & lt bl .20 .20
920 A231 2.50e dk grn & yel grn .65 .25
921 A231 3.50e org brn & org .85 .55
Nos. 919-921 (3) 1.70 1.00

Transportes Aéreos Portugueses, TAP, 10th anniv.

1964, Apr. 9 Litho.

922 A232 50c brn ol, dk brn & blk .20 .20
923 A232 1e rose brn, dp cl & blk .20 .20
924 A232 4.30e dk gray, sl & blk 2.75 2.10
Nos. 922-924 (3) 3.15 2.50

4th centenary of the publication (in Goa, Apr. 10, 1563) of "Coloquios Dos Simples e Drogas" (Herbs and Drugs in India) by Garcia D'Orta.

Emblem of National Overseas Bank — A233

Mt. Sameiro Church — A234

1964, May 19 Unwmk. ***Perf. 13½***

925 A233 1e bister, yel & dk bl .20 .20
926 A233 2.50e ocher, yel & grn 1.25 .40
927 A233 3.50e bister, yel & brn 1.00 .50
Nos. 925-927 (3) 2.45 1.10

Centenary of National Overseas Bank.

1964, June 5 Litho.

928 A234 1e red brn, bis & dl brn .20 .20
929 A234 2e brn, bis & dl brn .95 .40
930 A234 5e dk vio bl, bis & gray 1.10 .50
Nos. 928-930 (3) 2.25 1.10

Centenary of the Shrine of Our Lady of Mt. Sameiro, Braga.

Europa Issue, 1964

Common Design Type

1964, Sept. 14 Unwmk. ***Perf. 13½***

Size: 19x32mm.

931 CD7 1e bl, lt bl & dk bl *1.00* *.20*
932 CD7 3.50e rose brn, buff & dk brn *7.00* *.55*
933 CD7 4.30e grn, yel grn & dk grn *12.00* *2.25*
Nos. 931-933 (3) *20.00* 3.00

Partial Eclipse of Sun — A235

Olympic Rings, Emblems of Portugal and Japan — A236

1964

934 A235 1e multicolored .20 .20
935 A235 8e multicolored .90 .55

International Quiet Sun Year, 1964-65.

1964, Dec. 1 Unwmk. ***Perf. 13½***

Black Inscriptions; Olympic Rings in Pale Yellow

936 A236 20c tan, red & vio bl .20 .20
937 A236 1e ultra, red & vio bl .20 .20
938 A236 1.50e yel grn, red & vio bl .70 .60
939 A236 6.50e rose lil, red & vio bl 1.40 1.00
Nos. 936-939 (4) 2.50 2.00

18th Olympic Games, Tokyo, Oct. 10-25.

Eduardo Coelho — A237

Traffic Signs and Signals A238

1964, Dec. 28 Litho. *Perf. 13½*

940 A237 1e multicolored .25 .20
941 A237 5e multicolored 3.75 .30

Centenary of the founding of Portugal's first newspaper, "Diario de Noticias," and to honor the founder, Eduardo Coelho, journalist.

1965, Feb. 15 Litho.

942 A238 1e yellow, red & emer .20 .20
943 A238 3.30e multicolored 4.00 2.10
944 A238 3.50e red, yellow & emer 2.40 .70
Nos. 942-944 (3) 6.60 3.00

1st National Traffic Cong., Lisbon, 2/15-19.

Ferdinand I, Duke of Braganza — A239

Coimbra Gate, Angel with Censer and Sword — A240

1965, Mar. 16 Unwmk. *Perf. 13½*

945 A239 1e rose brown & blk .20 .20
946 A239 10e Prus green & blk 1.25 .30

500th anniv. of the city of Braganza (in 1964).

1965, Apr. 27 *Perf. 11½x12*

947 A240 1e blue & multi .20 .20
948 A240 2.50e multi 1.40 .80
949 A240 5e multi 1.40 1.00
Nos. 947-949 (3) 3.00 2.00

9th centenary (in 1964) of the capture of the city of Coimbra from the Moors.

ITU Emblem — A241

1965, May 17 *Perf. 13½*

950 A241 1e bis brn, ol grn & ol .20 .20
951 A241 3.50e ol, rose cl & dp cl .85 .70
952 A241 6.50e yel grn, dl bl & sl bl .70 .60
Nos. 950-952 (3) 1.75 1.50

International Telecommunication Union, cent.

Calouste Gulbenkian A242

1965, July 20 Litho. *Perf. 13½*

953 A242 1e multicolored .35 .20
954 A242 8e multicolored .45 .25

Gulbenkian (1869-1955), oil industry pioneer and sponsor of the Gulbenkian Foundation.

Red Cross — A243

1965, Aug. 17 Unwmk. *Perf. 13½*

955 A243 1e grn, red & blk .20 .20
956 A243 4e ol, red & blk 1.25 .60
957 A243 4.30e lt rose brn, red & blk 6.50 4.50
Nos. 955-957 (3) 7.95 5.30

Centenary of the Portuguese Red Cross.

Europa Issue, 1965

Common Design Type

1965, Sept. 27 Litho. *Perf. 13*

Size: 31x24mm

958 CD8 1e saph, grnsh bl & dk bl *.50* .20
959 CD8 3.50e rose brn, sal & brn *11.50* .75
960 CD8 4.30e grn, yel grn & dk grn *27.50* *3.50*
Nos. 958-960 (3) 39.50 4.45

Military Plane — A244

1965, Oct. 20 *Perf. 13½*

961 A244 1e ol grn, red & dk grn .20 .20
962 A244 2e sepia, red & dk grn 1.00 .35
963 A244 5e chlky bl, red & dk grn 1.75 .85
Nos. 961-963 (3) 2.95 1.40

Portuguese Air Force founding, 50th anniv.

Woman — A245

Chrismon with Alpha and Omega A246

Designs: Characters from Gil Vicente Plays.

1965, Dec. 1 Litho. *Perf. 13½*

964 A245 20c ol, pale yel & blk .20 .20
965 A245 1e brn, pale yel & blk .25 .20
966 A245 2.50e dk red, buff & blk 1.60 .25
967 A245 6.50e blue, gray & blk .55 .25
Nos. 964-967 (4) 2.60 .90

Gil Vicente (1465?-1536?).

1966, Mar. 28 Litho. *Perf. 13½*

968 A246 1e ol bis, gold & blk .20 .20
969 A246 3.30e gray, gold & blk 3.50 2.25
970 A246 5e rose cl, gold & blk 2.25 .55
Nos. 968-970 (3) 5.95 3.00

Congress of the International Committee for the Defense of Christian Civilization, Lisbon.

Symbols of Peace and Labor — A247

1966, May 28 Litho. *Perf. 13½*

971 A247 1e dk bl, sl bl & lt sl bl .20 .20
972 A247 3.50e ol, ol brn, & lt ol 1.40 .65
973 A247 4e dk brn, brn car & dl rose 1.40 .55
Nos. 971-973 (3) 3.00 1.40

40th anniversary of National Revolution.

Knight Giraldo on Horseback A248

1966, June 8

974 A248 1e multicolored .20 .20
975 A248 8e multicolored .45 .35

Conquest of Evora from the Moors, 800th anniv.

Salazar Bridge — A249

Designs: 2.80e, 4.30e, View of bridge, vert.

1966, Aug. 6 Litho. *Perf. 13½*

976 A249 1e gold & red .20 .20
977 A249 2.50e gold & ultra .80 .40
978 A249 2.80e silver & dp ultra 1.40 .85
979 A249 4.30e silver & dk grn 1.50 .90
Nos. 976-979 (4) 3.90 2.35

Issued to commemorate the opening of the Salazar Bridge over the Tejo River, Lisbon.

Europa Issue, 1966

Common Design Type

1966, Sept. 26 Litho. *Perf. 11½x12*

Size: 26x32mm

980 CD9 1e blue & blk *.50* .20
981 CD9 3.50e red brn & blk *18.00* 1.25
982 CD9 4.30e yel grn & blk *19.00* 2.00
Nos. 980-982 (3) *37.50* 3.45

Pestana A250

Bocage A251

Portraits: 20c, Camara Pestana (1863-1899), bacteriologist. 50c, Egas Moniz (1874-1955), neurologist. 1e, Antonio Pereira Coutinho (1851-1939), botanist. 1.50e, José Corrêa da Serra (1750-1823), botanist. 2e, Ricardo Jórge (1858-1938), hygienist and anthropologist. 2.50e, J. Liete de Vasconcelos (1858-1941), ethnologist. 2.80e, Maximiano Lemos (1860-1923), medical historian. 4.30e, José Antonio Serrano, anatomist.

1966, Dec. 1 Litho. *Perf. 13½*

Portrait and Inscription in Dark Brown and Bister

983 A250 20c gray green .20 .20
984 A250 50c orange .20 .20
985 A250 1e lemon .20 .20
986 A250 1.50e bister brn .20 .20
987 A250 2e brown org .95 .20
988 A250 2.50e pale green 1.10 .25
989 A250 2.80e salmon 1.25 .80
990 A250 4.30e Prus blue 1.90 1.50
Nos. 983-990 (8) 6.00 3.55

Issued to honor Portuguese scientists.

1966, Dec. 28 Litho. *Perf. 11½x12*

991 A251 1e bis, grnsh gray & blk .20 .20
992 A251 2e brn org, grnsh gray & blk .45 .25
993 A251 6e gray, grnsh gray & blk .70 .35
Nos. 991-993 (3) 1.35 .80

200th anniversary of the birth of Manuel Maria Barbosa du Bocage (1765-1805), poet.

Europa Issue, 1967

Common Design Type

1967, May 2 Litho. *Perf. 13*

Size: 21½x31mm

994 CD10 1e lt bl, Prus bl & blk *.35* .20
995 CD10 3.50e sal, brn red & blk *14.00* .70
996 CD10 4.30e yel grn, ol grn & blk *21.00* 1.40
Nos. 994-996 (3) 35.35 2.30

Apparition of Our Lady of Fatima — A252

Statues of Roman Senators — A253

Designs: 2.80e, Church and Golden Rose. 3.50e, Statue of the Pilgrim Virgin, with lilies and doves. 4e, Doves holding crown over Chapel of the Apparition.

1967, May 13 *Perf. 11½x12*

997 A252 1e multicolored .20 .20
998 A252 2.80e multicolored .30 .35
999 A252 3.50e multicolored .25 .20
1000 A252 4e multicolored .25 .25
Nos. 997-1000 (4) 1.00 1.00

50th anniversary of the apparition of the Virgin Mary to 3 shepherd children at Fatima.

1967, June 1 Litho. *Perf. 13*

1001 A253 1e gold & rose claret .20 .20
1002 A253 2.50e gold & dull blue 1.25 .65
1003 A253 4.30e gold & gray green .55 .65
Nos. 1001-1003 (3) 2.00 1.50

Introduction of a new civil law code.

Shipyard, Margueira, Lisbon — A254

Design: 2.80e, 4.30e, Ship's hull and map showing location of harbor.

1967, June 23

1004 A254 1e aqua & multi .20 .20
1005 A254 2.80e multicolored 1.40 .65
1006 A254 3.50e multicolored .75 .50
1007 A254 4.30e multicolored 1.25 .65
Nos. 1004-1007 (4) 3.60 2.00

Issued to commemorate the inauguration of the Lisnave Shipyard at Margueira, Lisbon.

Symbols of Healing — A255

Flags of EFTA Nations — A256

1967, Oct. 8 Litho. *Perf. 13½*

1008 A255 1e multicolored .20 .20
1009 A255 2e multicolored .70 .30
1010 A255 5e multicolored 1.00 .60
Nos. 1008-1010 (3) 1.90 1.10

Issued to publicize the 6th European Congress of Rheumatology, Lisbon, Oct. 8-13.

1967, Oct. 24 Litho. *Perf. 13½*

1011 A256 1e bister & multi .20 .20
1012 A256 3.50e buff & multi .70 .50
1013 A256 4.30e gray & multi 2.10 1.50
Nos. 1011-1013 (3) 3.00 2.20

Issued to publicize the European Free Trade Association. See note after Norway No. 501.

Tables of the Law — A257

1967, Dec. 27 Litho. *Perf. 13½*

1014 A257 1e olive .20 .20
1015 A257 2e red brown .70 .35
1016 A257 5e green 1.10 .70
Nos. 1014-1016 (3) 2.00 1.25

Centenary of abolition of death penalty.

Bento de Goes — A258

1968, Feb. 14 Engr. *Perf. 12x11½*

1017 A258 1e olive, indigo & dk brn .35 .20
1018 A258 8e org brn, dl pur & ol grn .65 .25

360th anniversary (in 1967) of the death of Bento de Goes (1562-1607), Jesuit explorer of the route to China.

Europa Issue, 1968
Common Design Type

1968, Apr. 29 Litho. *Perf. 13*
Size: 31x21mm

1019 CD11 1e multicolored .60 .20
1020 CD11 3.50e multicolored *12.50* 1.25
1021 CD11 4.30e multicolored *24.00* 2.75
Nos. 1019-1021 (3) 37.10 4.20

Mother's and Child's Hands — A259

1968, May 26 Litho. *Perf. 13½*

1022 A259 1e lt gray, blk & red .20 .20
1023 A259 2e salmon, blk & red 1.00 .30
1024 A259 5e lt bl, blk & red 1.75 .70
Nos. 1022-1024 (3) 2.95 1.20

Mothers' Organization for Natl. Education. 30th anniv.

"Victory over Disease" and WHO Emblem A260

1968, July 10 Litho. *Perf. 12½*

1025 A260 1e multicolored .20 .20
1026 A260 3.50e multicolored .80 .40
1027 A260 4.30e tan & multi 4.00 3.00
Nos. 1025-1027 (3) 5.00 3.60

20th anniv. of WHO.

Madeira Grapes and Wine A261

Joao Fernandes Vieira — A262

Designs: 1e, Fireworks on New Year's Eve. 1.50e, Mountains and valley. 3.50e, Woman doing Madeira embroidery. 4.30e, Joao Gonçalves Zarco. 20e, Muschia aurea (flower.)

Perf. 12x11½, 11½x12

1968, Aug. 17 Litho.

1028 A261 50c multi .20 .20
1029 A261 1e multi .20 .20
1030 A261 1.50e multi .20 .20
1031 A262 2.80e multi 1.10 .75
1032 A262 3.50e multi .75 .50
1033 A262 4.30e multi 4.00 3.00
1034 A262 20e multi 1.90 .55
Nos. 1028-1034 (7) 8.35 5.40

Issued to publicize Madeira and the Lubrapex 1968 stamp exhibition.
Design descriptions in Portuguese, French and English printed on back of stamps.

Pedro Alvares Cabral A263

Cabral's Fleet A264

Design: 3.50e, Cabral's coat of arms, vert.

Perf. 12x12½, 12½x12

1969, Jan. 30 Engr.

1035 A263 1e vio bl, bl & gray bl .20 .20
1036 A263 3.50e deep claret 2.50 1.40

Litho.

1037 A264 6.50e green & multi 1.50 1.25
Nos. 1035-1037 (3) 4.20 2.85

5th cent. of the birth of Pedro Alvarez Cabral (1468-1520), navigator, discoverer of Brazil. Nos. 1035-1037 have description of the designs printed on the back in Portuguese, French and English.

Europa Issue, 1969
Common Design Type

1969, Apr. 28 Litho. *Perf. 13*
Size: 31x22½mm

1038 CD12 1e dp blue & multi .65 .20
1039 CD12 3.50e multicolored 16.00 .90
1040 CD12 4.30e green & multi 30.00 2.00
Nos. 1038-1040 (3) 46.65 3.10

King José I and Arms of National Press — A265

1969, May 14 Litho. *Perf. 11½x12*

1041 A265 1e multicolored .20 .20
1042 A265 2e multicolored .60 .25
1043 A265 8e multicolored .60 .40
Nos. 1041-1043 (3) 1.40 .85

Bicentenary of the National Press.

ILO Emblem A266

1969, May 28 *Perf. 13*

1044 A266 1e bluish grn, blk & sil .20 .20
1045 A266 3.50e red, blk & sil .80 .35
1046 A266 4.30e brt bl, blk & sil 1.25 .80
Nos. 1044-1046 (3) 2.25 1.35

50th anniversary of the ILO.

Juan Cabrillo Rodriguez A267

Vianna da Motta, by Columbano Bordalo Pinheiro — A268

1969, July 16 Litho. *Perf. 11½x12*

1047 A267 1e multi .20 .20
1048 A267 2.50e multi .80 .25
1049 A267 6.50e multi .90 .55
Nos. 1047-1049 (3) 1.90 1.00

Bicent. of San Diego, Calif., & honoring Juan Cabrillo Rodriguez, explorer of California coast.
Backs inscribed. See note below No. 1034.

1969, Sept. 24 Litho. *Perf. 12*

1050 A268 1e multicolored .45 .20
1051 A268 9e gray & multi .45 .30

Centenary of the birth of Vianna da Motta (1868-1948), pianist and composer.

Gago Coutinho and 1922 Seaplane A269

Design: 2.80e, 4.30e, Adm. Coutinho and Coutinho sextant.

1969, Oct. 22

1052 A269 1e grnsh gray, dk & lt brn .20 .20
1053 A269 2.80e yel bis, dk & lt brn .95 .75
1054 A269 3.30e gray bl, dk & lt brn 1.10 1.10
1055 A269 4.30e lt rose brn, dk & lt brn 1.25 1.10
Nos. 1052-1055 (4) 3.50 3.15

Admiral Carlos Viegas Gago Coutinho (1869-1959), explorer and aviation pioneer.

Vasco da Gama A270

Designs: 2.80e, Da Gama's coat of arms. 3.50e, Map showing route to India and compass rose, horiz. 4e, Da Gama's fleet, horiz.

Perf. 12x11½, 11½x12

1969, Dec. 30 Litho.

1056 A270 1e multi .25 .20
1057 A270 2.80e multi 1.75 1.60
1058 A270 3.50e multi 1.25 .65
1059 A270 4e multi 1.25 .55
Nos. 1056-1059 (4) 4.50 3.00

Vasco da Gama (1469-1525), navigator who found sea route to India.
Design descriptions in Portuguese, French and English printed on back of stamps.

Europa Issue, 1970
Common Design Type

1970, May 4 Litho. *Perf. 13½*
Size: 31x22mm

1060 CD13 1e multicolored *.60* .20
1061 CD13 3.50e multicolored *16.00* *.80*
1062 CD13 4.30e multicolored *29.00* *3.00*
Nos. 1060-1062 (3) 45.60 4.00

Distillation Plant — A271

Design: 2.80e, 6e, Catalytic cracking tower.

1970, June 5 Litho. *Perf. 13*

1063 A271 1e dk bl & dl bl .20 .20
1064 A271 2.80e sl grn & pale grn 1.40 .75
1065 A271 3.30e dk ol grn & ol .90 .55
1066 A271 6e dk brn & dl ocher .70 .35
Nos. 1063-1066 (4) 3.20 1.85

Opening of the Oporto Oil Refinery.

Marshal Carmona and Oak Leaves A272

Designs: 2.50e, Carmona, Portuguese coat of arms and laurel. 7e, Carmona and ferns.

Litho. & Engr.

1970, July 1 *Perf. 12x12½*

1067 A272 1e ol grn & blk .20 .20
1068 A272 2.50e red, ultra & blk .90 .30
1069 A272 7e slate bl & blk .80 .50
Nos. 1067-1069 (3) 1.90 1.00

Centenary of the birth of Marshal Antonio Oscar de Fragoso Carmona (1869-1951), President of Portugal, 1926-1951.

Emblem of Plant Research Station A273

1970, July 29 Litho.

1070 A273 1e multi .20 .20
1071 A273 2.50e multi .65 .20
1072 A273 5e multi .90 .35
Nos. 1070-1072 (3) 1.75 .75

25th anniv. of the Plant Research Station at Elvas.

Compass Rose and EXPO Emblem — A274

Designs: 5e, Monogram of Christ (IHS) and EXPO emblem. 6.50e, "Portugal and Japan" as written in old manuscripts, and EXPO emblem.

1970, Sept. 16 Litho. *Perf. 13*

1073 A274	1e	gold & multi	.20	.20
1074 A274	5e	silver & multi	.80	.45
1075 A274	6.50e	multicolored	2.00	1.10
		Nos. 1073-1075,C11 (4)	3.35	1.95

EXPO '70 International Exhibition, Osaka, Japan, Mar. 15-Sept. 13.

Castle (from Arms of Santarem) A275

#1077, Star & wheel, from Covilha coat of arms. 2.80e, Ram & Covilha coat of arms. 4e, Knights on horseback & Santarem coat of arms.

1970, Oct. 7 Litho. *Perf. 12x11½*

1076 A275	1e	multicolored	.20	.20
1077 A275	1e	ultra & multi	.20	.20
1078 A275	2.80e	red & multi	1.25	1.00
1079 A275	4e	gray & multi	.85	.45
		Nos. 1076-1079 (4)	2.50	1.85

City of Santarem, cent. (#1076, 1079); City of Covilha, cent. (#1077-1078).

Paddlesteamer Great Eastern Laying Cable — A276

Designs: 2.80e, 4e, Cross section of cable.

1970, Nov. 21 Litho. *Perf. 14*

1080 A276	1e	multi	.20	.20
1081 A276	2.50e	multi	.95	.30
1082 A276	2.80e	multi	1.90	1.50
1083 A276	4e	multi	.95	.45
		Nos. 1080-1083 (4)	4.00	2.45

Centenary of the Portugal-Great Britain submarine telegraph cable.

Grapes and Woman Filling Baskets A277

Designs: 1e, Worker carrying basket of grapes, and jug. 3.50e, Glass of wine, and barge with barrels on River Douro. 7e, Wine bottle and barrels.

1970, Dec. 20 Litho. *Perf. 12x11½*

1084 A277	50c	multi	.20	.20
1085 A277	1e	multi	.20	.20
1086 A277	3.50e	multi	.40	.20
1087 A277	7e	multi	.45	.30
		Nos. 1084-1087 (4)	1.25	.90

Publicity for port wine export.

Mountain Windmill, Bussaco Hills — A278

Francisco Franco (1885-1955) A279

Windmills: 50c, Beira Litoral Province. 1e, Estremadura Province. 2e, St. Miguel, Azores. 3.30e, Porto Santo, Madeira. 5e, Pico, Azores.

1971, Feb. 24 Litho. *Perf. 13*

1088 A278	20c	multicolored	.20	.20
1089 A278	50c	lt blue & multi	.20	.20
1090 A278	1e	gray & multi	.20	.20
1091 A278	2e	multicolored	.45	.20
1092 A278	3.30e	ocher & multi	1.25	.90
1093 A278	5e	multicolored	1.10	.30
		Nos. 1088-1093 (6)	3.40	2.00

Backs inscribed. See note below No. 1034.

Europa Issue, 1971

Common Design Type

1971, May 3 Photo. *Perf. 14*

Size: 32x22mm

1094 CD14	1e	dk bl, lt grn & blk	*.60*	.20
1095 CD14	3.50e	red brn, yel & blk	*12.00*	*.65*
1096 CD14	7.50e	olive, yel & blk	*22.50*	*1.75*
		Nos. 1094-1096 (3)	35.10	2.60

Perf. 11½x12½; 13½ (2.50e, 4e)

1971, July 7 Engr.

Portuguese Sculptors: 1e, Antonio Teixeira Lopes (1866-1942). 1.50e, Antonio Augusto da Costa Mota (1862-1930). 2.50e, Rui Roque Gameiro (1906-1935). 3.50e, José Simoes de Almedia (nephew; 1880-1950). 4e, Francisco dos Santos (1878-1930).

1097 A279	20c	black	.20	.20
a.		Perf. 13½	1.50	.30
1098 A279	1e	claret	.20	.20
1099 A279	1.50e	sepia	.30	.25
1100 A279	2.50e	dark blue	.55	.20
1101 A279	3.50e	carmine rose	.75	.30
1102 A279	4e	gray green	1.40	.55
		Nos. 1097-1102 (6)	3.40	1.70

Pres. Antonio Salazar — A280

1971, July 27 Engr. *Perf. 13½*

1103 A280	1e	multicolored	.20	.20
a.		Perf. 12½x12	*60.00*	2.00
1104 A280	5e	multicolored	.90	.20
1105 A280	10e	multicolored	1.50	.40
a.		Perf. 12½x12	*14.00*	1.00
		Nos. 1103-1105 (3)	2.60	.80

Wolframite Crystals A281

Minerals: 2.50e, Arsenopyrite (gold). 3.50e, Beryllium. 6.50e, Chalcopyrite (copper).

1971, Sept. 24 Litho. *Perf. 12*

1106 A281	1e	multicolored	.20	.20
1107 A281	2.50e	carmine & multi	1.90	.30
1108 A281	3.50e	green & multi	.65	.20
1109 A281	6.50e	blue & multi	1.25	.30
		Nos. 1106-1109 (4)	4.00	1.00

Spanish-Portuguese-American Economic Geology Congress.

Town Gate, Castelo Branco — A282

Weather Recording Station and Barograph Charts — A283

Designs: 3e, Memorial column. 12.50e, Arms of Castelo Branco, horiz.

1971, Oct. 7 *Perf. 14*

1110 A282	1e	multi	.20	.20
1111 A282	3e	multi	.70	.30
1112 A282	12.50e	multi	.65	.30
		Nos. 1110-1112 (3)	1.55	.80

Bicentenary of Castelo Branco as a town.

1971, Oct. 29 *Perf. 13½*

Designs: 4e, Stratospheric weather balloon and weather map of southwest Europe and North Africa. 6.50e, Satellite and aerial map of Atlantic Ocean off Portugal.

1113 A283	1e	buff & multi	.20	.20
1114 A283	4e	multicolored	1.25	.50
1115 A283	6.50e	blk, dl red brn & org	.80	.30
		Nos. 1113-1115 (3)	2.25	1.00

25 years of Portuguese meteorological service.

Missionaries and Ship — A284

1971, Nov. 24

1116 A284	1e	gray, ultra & blk	.20	.20
1117 A284	3.30e	dp bis, lil & blk	1.10	.70
1118 A284	4.80e	olive, grn & blk	1.10	.70
		Nos. 1116-1118 (3)	2.40	1.60

400th anniv. of the martyrdom of a group of Portuguese missionaries on the way to Brazil.

"Man" A285

Nature Conservation: 3.30e, "Earth" (animal, vegetable, mineral). 3.50e, "Air" (birds). 4.50e, "Water" (fish).

1971, Dec. 22 Litho. *Perf. 12*

1119 A285	1e	brown & multi	.20	.20
1120 A285	3.30e	lt bl, yel & grn	.35	.25
1121 A285	3.50e	lt bl, rose & vio	.35	.20
1122 A285	4.50e	lt bl, grn & ultra	1.50	.60
		Nos. 1119-1122 (4)	2.40	1.25

City Hall, Sintra — A286

Designs: 5c, Aqueduct, Lisbon. 50c, University, Coimbra. 1e, Torre dos Clerigos, Porto. 1.50e, Belem Tower, Lisbon. 2.50e, Castle, Vila da Feira. 3e, Misericordia House, Viana do Castelo. 3.50e, Window, Tomar Convent. 8e, Ducal Palace, Guimaraes. 10e, Cape Girao, Madeira. 20e, Episcopal Garden, Castelo Branco. 100e, Lakes of Seven Cities, Azores.

1972-73 Litho. *Perf. 12½*

Size: 22x17½mm

1123 A286	5c	gray, grn & blk	.20	.20
1124 A286	50c	gray bl, blk & org	.20	.20
1125 A286	1e	green, blk & brn	.20	.20
1126 A286	1.50e	blue, bis & blk	.20	.20
1127 A286	2.50e	brn, dk brn & gray	.20	.20
1128 A286	3e	yellow, blk & brn	.20	.20
1129 A286	3.50e	dp org, sl & brn	.20	.20
1130 A286	8e	blk, ol & grn	1.40	.30

Perf. 13½

Size: 31x22mm

1131 A286	10e	gray & multi	.50	.20
1132 A286	20e	green & multi	3.75	.20
1133 A286	50e	gray bl, ocher & blk	3.75	.35
1134 A286	100e	green & multi	5.25	.65
		Nos. 1123-1134 (12)	16.05	3.10

"CTT" and year date printed in minute gray multiple rows on back of stamps. Values are for most common dates.

Issue dates: 1e, 1.50e, 50e, 100e, Mar. 1; 50c, 3e, 10e, 20e, Dec. 6, 1972; 5c, 2.50e, 3.50e, 8e, Sept. 5, 1973.

See Nos. 1207-1214.

Tagging

Starting in 1975, phosphor (bar or L-shape) was applied to the face of most definitives and commemoratives.

Stamps issued both with and without tagging include Nos. 1124-1125, 1128, 1130-1131, 1209, 1213-1214, 1250, 1253, 1257, 1260, 1263.

Window, Pinhel Church — A287

Heart and Pendulum A288

1e, Arms of Pinhel, horiz. 7.50e, Stone lantern.

1972, Mar. 29 *Perf. 13½*

1135 A287	1e	blue & multi	.20	.20
a.		Perf. 11½x12½	55.00	2.50
1136 A287	2.50e	multicolored	.85	.25
1137 A287	7.50e	blue & multi	.70	.30
		Nos. 1135-1137 (3)	1.75	.75

Bicentenary of Pinhel as a town.

1972, Apr. 24

Designs: 4e, Heart and spiral pattern. 9e, Heart and continuing coil pattern.

1138 A288	1e	violet & red	.20	.20
1139 A288	4e	green & red	1.90	.80
1140 A288	9e	brown & red	.90	.50
		Nos. 1138-1140 (3)	3.00	1.50

"Your heart is your health," World Health Day.

Europa Issue 1972

Common Design Type

1972, May 1 *Perf. 13½*

Size: 21x31mm

1141 CD15	1e	gray & multi	*.75*	*.20*
1142 CD15	3.50e	salmon & multi	*6.75*	*.40*
1143 CD15	6e	green & multi	*25.00*	*1.40*
		Nos. 1141-1143 (3)	32.50	2.00

Trucks — A289

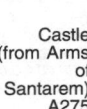

1972, May 17 Litho. *Perf. 13½*

1144 A289 1e shown .20 .20
1145 A289 4.50e Taxi 1.00 .50
1146 A289 8e Autobus .90 .40
Nos. 1144-1146 (3) 2.10 1.10

13th Congress of International Union of Road Transport (I.R.U.), Estoril, May 15-18.

Soccer, Olympic Rings A290

1972, July 26 Litho. *Perf. 14*

1147 A290 50c shown .20 .20
1148 A290 1e Running .20 .20
1149 A290 1.50e Equestrian .20 .20
1150 A290 3.50e Swimming, women's .50 .25
1151 A290 4.50e Yachting .65 .40
1152 A290 5e Gymnastics, women's 1.25 .45
Nos. 1147-1152 (6) 3.00 1.70

20th Olympic Games, Munich, 8/26-9/11.

Marquis of Pombal — A291

Tomé de Sousa — A292

1972, Aug. 28 *Perf. 13½*

1153 A291 1e shown .20 .20
1154 A291 2.50e Scientific apparatus .80 .30
1155 A291 8e Seal of Univ. of Coimbra .90 .50
Nos. 1153-1155 (3) 1.90 1.00

Bicentenary of the Pombaline reforms of University of Coimbra.

1972, Oct. 5 Litho. *Perf. 13½*

Designs: 2.50e, José Bonifacio. 3.50e, Dom Pedro IV. 6e, Allegory of Portuguese-Brazilian Community.

1156 A292 1e gray & multi .20 .20
1157 A292 2.50e green & multi .40 .20
1158 A292 3.50e multicolored .40 .20
1159 A292 6e blue & multi .80 .30
Nos. 1156-1159 (4) 1.80 .90

150th anniv. of Brazilian independence.

Sacadura Cabral, Gago Coutinho and Plane — A293

2.50e, 3.80e, Map of flight from Lisbon to Rio.

1972, Nov. 15 *Perf. 11½x12½*

1160 A293 1e blue & multi .20 .20
  a. Perf. 13½ 25.00 .85
1161 A293 2.50e multi .45 .20
1162 A293 2.80e multi .55 .45
1163 A293 3.80e multi .90 .65
  a. Perf. 13½ *75.00* *25.00*
Nos. 1160-1163 (4) 2.10 1.50

50th anniv. of the Lisbon to Rio flight by Commander Arturo de Sacadura Cabral and Adm. Carlos Viegas Gago Coutinho, Mar. 30-June 5, 1922.

Luiz Camoens A294

Designs: 3e, Hand saving manuscript from sea. 10e, Symbolic of man's questioning and discovering the unknown.

1972, Dec. 27 Litho. *Perf. 13*

1164 A294 1e org brn, buff & blk .20 .20
1165 A294 3e dull bl, lt grn & blk .75 .30
1166 A294 10e red brn, buff & yel .90 .35
Nos. 1164-1166 (3) 1.85 .85

4th centenary of the publication of The Lusiads by Luiz Camoens (1524-1580).

Graphs and Sequence Count — A295

1973, Apr. 11 Litho. *Perf. 14½*

1167 A295 1e shown .20 .20
1168 A295 4e Odometer .70 .30
1169 A295 9e Graphs .65 .25
Nos. 1167-1169 (3) 1.55 .75

Productivity Conference '72, 1/17-22/72.

Europa Issue 1973

Common Design Type

1973, Apr. 30 *Perf. 13*

Size: 31x29mm

1170 CD16 1e multicolored *1.40* *.20*
1171 CD16 4e brn red & multi *25.00* *.90*
1172 CD16 6e green & multi *29.00* *1.90*
Nos. 1170-1172 (3) 55.40 3.00

Gen. Medici, Arms of Brazil and Portugal A296

2.80e, 4.80e, Gen. Medici and world map.

Lithographed and Engraved

1973, May 16 *Perf. 12x11½*

1173 A296 1e dk grn, blk & sep .20 .20
1174 A296 2.80e olive & multi .50 .30
1175 A296 3.50e dk bl, blk & buff .50 .30
1176 A296 4.80e multicolored .50 .30
Nos. 1173-1176 (4) 1.70 1.10

Visit of Gen. Emilio Garrastazu Medici, President of Brazil, to Portugal.

Child and Birds — A297

4e, Child and flowers. 7.50e, Child.

1973, May 28 Litho. *Perf. 13*

1177 A297 1e ultra & multi .20 .20
1178 A297 4e multicolored .85 .30
1179 A297 7.50e bister & multi .95 .40
Nos. 1177-1179 (3) 2.00 .90

To pay renewed attention to children.

Transportation, Weather Map — A298

3.80e, Communications: telegraph, telephone, radio, satellite. 6e, Postal service: mailbox, truck, mail distribution diagram.

1973, June 25

1180 A298 1e multi .20 .20
1181 A298 3.80e multi .35 .20
1182 A298 6e multi .85 .30
Nos. 1180-1182 (3) 1.40 .70

Ministry of Communications, 25th anniv.

Pupil and Writing Exercise — A299

Designs: 4.50e, Illustrations from 18th century primer. 5.30e, School and children, by 9-year-old Marie de Luz, horiz. 8e, Symbolic chart of teacher-pupil link, horiz.

1973, Oct. 24 Litho. *Perf. 13*

1183 A299 1e blue & multi .20 .20
1184 A299 4.50e brown & multi .95 .25
1185 A299 5.30e lt blue & multi .85 .35
1186 A299 8e green & multi 2.40 .70
Nos. 1183-1186 (4) 4.40 1.50

Primary state school education, bicent.

Oporto Streetcar, 1910 A300

Designs: 1e, Horse-drawn streetcar, 1872. 3.50e, Double-decker Leyland bus, 1972.

1973, Nov. 7

Size: 31½x34mm

1187 A300 1e brn, yel & blk .20 .20
1188 A300 3.50e choc & multi 1.40 .60

Size: 37½x27mm

Perf. 12½

1189 A300 7.50e buff & multi 1.40 .55
Nos. 1187-1189 (3) 3.00 1.35

Cent. of public transportation in Oporto.

Servicemen's League Emblem A301

Death of Nuño Gonzalves A302

Designs: 2.50e, Sailor, soldier and aviator. 11e, Military medals.

1973, Nov. 28 Litho. *Perf. 13*

1190 A301 1e multi .20 .20
1191 A301 2.50e multi 1.25 .35
1192 A301 11e dk blue & multi .90 .30
Nos. 1190-1192 (3) 2.35 .85

50th anniv. of the Servicemen's League.

1973, Dec. 19

1193 A302 1e slate blue & org .20 .20
1194 A302 10e violet brn & org 1.10 .40

600th anniv. of the heroism of Nuno Gonzalves, alcaide of Faria Castle.

Damiao de Gois, by Dürer (?) — A303

"The Exile," by Soares dos Reis — A304

Designs: 4.50e, Title page of Cronica de Principe D. Joao. 7.50e, Lute and score of Dodecachordon.

1974, Apr. 5 Litho. *Perf. 12*

1195 A303 1e multi .20 .20
1196 A303 4.50e multi 1.40 .25
1197 A303 7.50e multi .80 .25
Nos. 1195-1197 (3) 2.40 .70

400th anniversary of the death of Damiao de Gois (1502-1574), humanist, writer, composer.

Europa Issue 1974

1974, Apr. 29 Litho. *Perf. 13*

1198 A304 1e multicolored 1.25 .20
1199 A304 4e dk red & multi 32.50 1.00
1200 A304 6e dk grn & multi 37.50 2.00
Nos. 1198-1200 (3) 71.25 3.20

Pattern of Light Emission A305

Designs: 4.50e, Spiral wave radiation pattern. 5.30e, Satellite and earth.

1974, June 26 Litho. *Perf. 14*

1201 A305 1.50e gray olive .20 .20
1202 A305 4.50e dark blue .80 .35
1203 A305 5.30e brt rose lilac 1.25 .55
Nos. 1201-1203 (3) 2.25 1.10

Establishment of satellite communications network via Intelsat among Portugal, Angola and Mozambique.

Diffusion of Hertzian Waves A306

Designs (Symbolic): 3.30e, Messages through space. 10e, Navigation help.

1974, Sept. 4 Litho. *Perf. 12*

1204 A306 1.50e multi .20 .20
1205 A306 3.30e multi 1.25 .50
1206 A306 10e multi .80 .30
Nos. 1204-1206 (3) 2.25 1.00

Guglielmo Marconi (1874-1937), Italian electrical engineer and inventor.

Buildings Type of 1972-73

Designs: 10c, Ponte do Lima (Roman bridge). 30c, Alcobaça Monastery, interior. 2e, City Hall, Bragança. 4e, New Gate, Braga. 4.50e, Dolmen of Carrazeda. 5e, Roman Temple, Evora. 6e, Leca do Balio Monastery. 7.50e, Almourol Castle.

1974, Sept. 18 Litho. *Perf. 12½*

Size: 22x17½mm

1207 A286 10c multi .20 .20
1208 A286 30c multi .20 .20
1209 A286 2e multi .20 .20
1210 A286 4e multi .40 .20
1211 A286 4.50e multi .60 .20
1212 A286 5e multi 4.00 .20
1213 A286 6e multi 1.50 .20
1214 A286 7.50e multi .80 .20
Nos. 1207-1214 (8) 7.90 1.60

"CTT" and year date printed in minute gray multiple rows on back of stamps. Values are for most common dates.

Postilion, Truck and Letter
A307

Designs: 2e, Hand holding letter. 3.30e, Packet and steamship. 4.50e, Pigeon and letters. 5.30e, Hand holding sealed letter. 20e, Old and new locomotives.

1974, Oct. 9 Litho. *Perf. 13*

1220	A307	1.50e	brown & multi	.20	.20
1221	A307	2e	multicolored	.40	.20
1222	A307	3.30e	olive & multi	.25	.20
1223	A307	4.50e	multicolored	.75	.25
1224	A307	5.30e	multicolored	.30	.20
1225	A307	20e	multicolored	1.40	.45
a.			Souvenir sheet of 6	5.00	5.00
			Nos. 1220-1225 (6)	3.30	1.50

Centenary of UPU. No. 1225a contains one each of Nos. 1220-1225, arranged to show a continuous design with a globe in center. Sold for 50e.

Luisa Todi, Singer (1753-1833)
A308

Marcos Portugal, Composer (1762-1838)
A309

Portuguese Musicians: 2e, Joao Domingos Bomtempo (1775-1842). 2.50e, Carlos Seixas (1704-1742). 3e, Duarte Lobo (1565-1646). 5.30e, Joao de Sousa Carvalho (1745-1798).

1974, Oct. 30 Litho. *Perf. 12*

1226	A308	1.50e	brt pink	.20	.20
1227	A308	2e	vermilion	.70	.20
1228	A308	2.50e	brown	.50	.20
1229	A308	3e	bluish black	.60	.20
1230	A308	5.30e	slate green	.50	.35
1231	A309	11e	rose lake	.50	.35
			Nos. 1226-1231 (6)	3.00	1.50

Coat of Arms of Beja
A310

2,000th Anniv. of Beja: 3.50e, Men of Beja in costumes from Roman times to date. 7e, Moorish Arches and view across plains.

1974, Nov. 13

1232	A310	1.50e	multi	.20	.20
1233	A310	3.50e	multi	1.40	.50
1234	A310	7e	multi	1.40	.55
			Nos. 1232-1234 (3)	3.00	1.25

Annunciation
A311

Rainbow and Dove — A312

Christmas: 4.50e, Adoration of the Shepherds. 10e, Flight into Egypt. Designs show Portuguese costumes from Nazare township.

1974, Dec. 4 Litho. *Perf. 13*

1235	A311	1.50e	red & multi	.20	.20
1236	A311	4.50e	multicolored	2.00	.30
1237	A311	10e	blue & multi	1.50	.40
			Nos. 1235-1237 (3)	3.70	.90

1974, Dec. 18 *Perf. 12*

1238	A312	1.50e	multi	.20	.20
1239	A312	3.50e	multi	1.75	.65
1240	A312	5e	multi	1.00	.25
			Nos. 1238-1240 (3)	2.95	1.10

Armed Forces Movement of Apr. 25, 1974.

Egas Moniz — A313

Soldier as Farmer, Farmer as Soldier — A314

3.30e, Lobotomy probe and Nobel Prize medal, 1949. 10e, Cerebral angiograph, 1927.

1974, Dec. 27 Engr. *Perf. 11½x12*

1241	A313	1.50e	yellow & multi	.20	.20
1242	A313	3.30e	brown & ocher	.70	.25
1243	A313	10e	gray & ultra	2.10	.35
			Nos. 1241-1243 (3)	3.00	.80

Egas Moniz (1874-1955), brain surgeon, birth centenary.

1975, Mar. 21 Litho. *Perf. 12*

1244	A314	1.50e	green & multi	.20	.20
1245	A314	3e	gray & multi	1.00	.30
1246	A314	4.50e	multicolored	1.50	.40
			Nos. 1244-1246 (3)	2.70	.90

Cultural progress and citizens' guidance campaign.

Hands and Dove — A315

4.50e, Brown hands reaching for dove. 10e, Dove with olive branch and arms of Portugal.

1975, Apr. 23 Litho. *Perf. 13½*

1247	A315	1.50e	red & multi	.20	.20
1248	A315	4.50e	brown & multi	1.50	.35
1249	A315	10e	green & multi	1.75	.55
			Nos. 1247-1249 (3)	3.45	1.10

Movement of April 25th, first anniversary. Slogans in Portuguese, French and English printed on back of stamps.

God's Hand Reaching Down — A316

Designs: 4.50e, Jesus' hand holding up cross. 10e, Dove (Holy Spirit) descending.

1975, May 13 Litho. *Perf. 13½*

1250	A316	1.50e	multicolored	.20	.20
1251	A316	4.50e	plum & multi	2.10	.60
1252	A316	10e	blue & multi	2.40	.60
			Nos. 1250-1252 (3)	4.70	1.40

Holy Year 1975.

Horseman of the Apocalypse, 12th Century
A317

Europa: 10e, The Poet Fernando Pessoa, by Almada Negreiros (1893-1970).

1975, May 26

1253	A317	1.50e	multi	*2.00*	*.20*
1254	A317	10e	multi	*60.00*	*.55*

Assembly Building
A318

1975, June 2 Litho. *Perf. 13½*

1255	A318	2e	red, blk & yel	.20	.20
1256	A318	20e	emer, blk & yel	3.50	.80

Opening of Constituent Assembly.

Hikers — A319

Designs: 4.50e, Campsite on lake. 5.30e, Mobile homes on the road.

1975, Aug. 4 Litho. *Perf. 13½*

1257	A319	2e	multicolored	.55	.20
1258	A319	4.50e	multicolored	1.75	.40
1259	A319	5.30e	multicolored	.95	.40
			Nos. 1257-1259 (3)	3.25	1.00

36th Rally of the International Federation of Camping and Caravanning, Santo Andre Lake.

People and Sapling
A320

Designs (UN Emblem and): 4.50e, People and dove. 20e, People and grain.

1975, Sept. 17 Litho. *Perf. 13½*

1260	A320	2e	green & multi	.25	.20
1261	A320	4.50e	vio & multi	.95	.25
1262	A320	20e	multicolored	2.00	.55
			Nos. 1260-1262 (3)	3.20	1.00

United Nations, 30th anniversary.

Icarus and Rocket — A321

Designs: 4.50e, Apollo and Soyuz in space. 5.30e, Robert H. Goddard, Robert Esnault-Pelterie, Hermann Oberth and Konstantin Tsiolkovski. 10e, Sputnik, man in space, moon landing module.

1975, Sept. 26 Litho. *Perf. 13½*

Size: 30½x26½mm

1263	A321	2e	green & multi	.30	.20
1264	A321	4.50e	brown & multi	1.25	.35
1265	A321	5.30e	lilac & multi	.60	.35

Size: 65x28mm

1266	A321	10e	blue & multi	2.50	.60
			Nos. 1263-1266 (4)	4.65	1.50

26th Congress of International Astronautical Federation, Lisbon, Sept. 1975.

Land Survey
A322

Designs: 8e, Ocean survey. 10e, People of many races and globe.

1975, Nov. 19 Litho. *Perf. 12x12½*

1267	A322	2e	ocher & multi	.20	.20
1268	A322	8e	blue & multi	.70	.30
1269	A322	10e	dk vio & multi	1.75	.50
			Nos. 1267-1269 (3)	2.65	1.00

Centenary of Lisbon Geographical Society.

Arch and Trees — A323

Designs: 8e, Plan, pencil and ruler. 10e, Hand, old building and brick tower.

1975, Nov. 28 *Perf. 13½*

1270	A323	2e	dk bl & gray	.20	.20
1271	A323	8e	dk car & gray	1.75	.65
1272	A323	10e	ocher & multi	1.75	.90
			Nos. 1270-1272 (3)	3.70	1.75

European Architectural Heritage Year 1975.

Nurse and Hospital Ward — A324

Designs (IWY Emblem and): 2e, Farm workers. 3.50e, Secretary. 8e, Factory worker.

1975, Dec. 30 Litho. *Perf. 13½*

1273	A324	50c	multicolored	.20	.20
1274	A324	2e	multicolored	.50	.20
1275	A324	3.50e	multicolored	.55	.30
1276	A324	8e	multicolored	.85	.55
a.			Souvenir sheet of 4	2.50	2.50
			Nos. 1273-1276 (4)	2.10	1.25

International Women's Year 1975. No. 1276a contains 4 stamps similar to Nos. 1273-1276 in slightly changed colors. Sold for 25e.

Pen Nib as Plowshare
A325

1976, Feb. 6 Litho. *Perf. 12*

1277 A325 3e dk bl & red org .25 .20
1278 A325 20e org, ultra & red 2.50 .60

Portuguese Soc. of Writers, 50th anniv.

Telephones, 1876, 1976 — A326

10.50e, Alexander Graham Bell & telephone.

1976, Mar. 10 Litho. *Perf. 12x12½*

1279 A326 3e yel grn, grn & blk .50 .20
1280 A326 10.50e rose, red & blk 1.75 .50

Centenary of first telephone call by Alexander Graham Bell, March 10, 1876.

Industry and Shipping — A327

1e, Garment, food and wine industries.

1976, Apr. 7 Litho. *Perf. 12½*

1281 A327 50c red brown .20 .20
1282 A327 1e slate .30 .20

Support of national production.

Carved Spoons, Olive Wood A328

Europa: 20e, Gold filigree pendant, silver box and CEPT emblem.

1976, May 3 Litho. *Perf. 12x12½*

1283 A328 3e olive & multi *5.00* .20
1284 A328 20e tan & multi *80.00 3.75*

Stamp Collectors A329

Designs: 7.50e, Stamp exhibition and hand canceler. 10e, Printing and designing stamps.

1976, May 29 Litho. *Perf. 14½*

1285 A329 3e multicolored .20 .20
1286 A329 7.50e multicolored .55 .30
1287 A329 10e multicolored .75 .30
Nos. 1285-1287 (3) 1.50 .80

Interphil 76, International Philatelic Exhibition, Philadelphia, Pa., May 29-June 6.

King Ferdinand I — A330

Designs: 5e, Plowshare, farmers chasing off hunters. 10e, Harvest.

1976, July 2 Litho. *Perf. 12*

1288 A330 3e lt bl & multi .20 .20
1289 A330 5e yel grn & multi .90 .25
1290 A330 10e multicolored 1.10 .35
a. Souv. sheet of 3, #1288-1290 2.75 2.50
Nos. 1288-1290 (3) 2.20 .80

Agricultural reform law (compulsory cultivation of uncultivated lands), 600th anniversary. No. 1290a sold for 30e.

Torch Bearer A331

7e, Women's relay race. 10.50e, Olympic flame.

1976, July 16 *Perf. 13½*

1291 A331 3e red & multi .20 .20
1292 A331 7e red & multi .85 .60
1293 A331 10.50e red & multi 1.10 .75
Nos. 1291-1293 (3) 2.15 1.55

21st Olympic Games, Montreal, Canada, July 17-Aug. 1.

Farm A332

1976, Sept. 15 Litho. *Perf. 12*

1294 A332 3e shown .50 .20
1295 A332 3e Ship .50 .20
1296 A332 3e City .50 .20
1297 A332 3e Factory .80 .20
b. Souv. sheet of 4, #1294-1297 11.00 11.00
Nos. 1294-1297 (4) 2.30 .80

Fight against illiteracy. #1297b sold for 25e.

Perf. 13½

1294a A332 3e *30.00 15.00*
1295a A332 3e 1.50 1.10
1296a A332 3e *35.00 18.00*
1297a A332 3e .60 .45
Nos. 1294a-1297a (4) 67.10 34.55

Azure-winged Magpie A333

Designs: 5e, Lynx. 7e, Portuguese laurel cherry. 10.50e, Little wild carnations.

1976, Sept. 30 Litho. *Perf. 12*

1298 A333 3e multi .25 .20
1299 A333 5e multi 1.00 .25
1300 A333 7e multi 1.00 .75
1301 A333 10.50e multi 1.50 1.00
Nos. 1298-1301 (4) 3.75 2.20

Portucale 77, 2nd International Thematic Exhibition, Oporto, Oct. 29-Nov. 6, 1977.

Exhibition Hall — A334

Design: 20e, Symbolic stamp and emblem.

1976, Oct. 9 Litho. *Perf. 13½*

1302 A334 3e bl & multi .25 .20
1303 A334 20e ocher & multi 1.75 1.10
a. Souv. sheet of 2, #1302-1303 3.00 3.00

6th Luso-Brazilian Phil. Exhib., LUBRAPEX 76, Oporto, Oct. 9. #1303a sold for 30e.

Bank Emblem and Family A335

7e, Grain. 15e, Cog wheels.

1976, Oct. 29 *Perf. 12*

1304 A335 3e org & multi .20 .20
1305 A335 7e grn & multi .95 .45
1306 A335 15e bl & multi 1.10 .55
Nos. 1304-1306 (3) 2.25 1.20

Trust Fund Bank centenary.

Sheep Grazing on Marsh A336

Designs: 3e, Drainage ditches. 5e, Fish in water. 10e, Ducks flying over marsh.

1976, Nov. 24 Litho. *Perf. 14*

1307 A336 1e multicolored .20 .20
1308 A336 3e multicolored .45 .20
1309 A336 5e multicolored .95 .30
1310 A336 10e multicolored 1.25 .45
Nos. 1307-1310 (4) 2.85 1.15

Protection of wetlands.

"Liberty" — A337

1976, Nov. 30 Litho. *Perf. 13½*

1311 A337 3e gray, grn & ver .45 .20

Constitution of 1976.

Mother Examining Child's Eyes A338

Designs: 5e, Welder with goggles. 10.50e, Blind woman reading Braille.

1976, Dec. 13

1312 A338 3e multicolored .20 .20
1313 A338 5e multicolored .75 .25
1314 A338 10.50e multicolored 1.10 .65
Nos. 1312-1314 (3) 2.05 1.10

World Health Day and campaign against blindness.

Hydroelectric Energy — A339

Abstract Designs: 4e, Fossil fuels. 5e, Geothermal energy. 10e, Wind power. 15e, Solar energy.

1976, Dec. 30

1315 A339 1e multicolored .20 .20
1316 A339 4e multicolored .30 .20
1317 A339 5e multicolored .40 .20
1318 A339 10e multicolored .75 .50
1319 A339 15e multicolored 1.25 1.00
Nos. 1315-1319 (5) 2.90 2.10

Sources of energy.

Map of Council of Europe Members A340

1977, Jan. 28 Litho. *Perf. 12*

1320 A340 8.50e multicolored .50 .50
1321 A340 10e multicolored .50 .50

Portugal's joining Council of Europe.

Alcoholic and Bottle — A341

Designs (Bottle and): 5e, Symbolic figure of broken life. 15e, Bars blotting out the sun.

1977, Feb. 4 *Perf. 13*

1322 A341 3e multicolored .20 .20
1323 A341 5e ocher & multi .50 .30
1324 A341 15e org & multi 1.25 .70
Nos. 1322-1324 (3) 1.95 1.20

Anti-alcoholism Day and 10th anniversary of Portuguese Anti-alcoholism Society.

Trees Tapped for Resin — A342

Designs: 4e, Trees stripped for cork. 7e, Trees and logs. 15e, Trees at seashore as windbreakers.

1977, Mar. 21 Litho. *Perf. 13½*

1325 A342 1e multicolored .20 .20
1326 A342 4e multicolored .25 .20
1327 A342 7e multicolored .90 .35
1328 A342 15e multicolored 1.00 .65
Nos. 1325-1328 (4) 2.35 1.40

Forests, a natural resource.

"Suffering" A343

6e, Man exercising. 10e, Group exercising. All designs include emblems of WHO & Portuguese Institute for Rheumatology.

1977, Apr. 13 Litho. *Perf. 12x12½*

1329 A343 4e blk, brn & ocher .20 .20
1330 A343 6e blk, bl & vio 1.25 .75
1331 A343 10e blk, pur & red 1.10 .50
Nos. 1329-1331 (3) 2.55 1.45

International Rheumatism Year.

Southern Plains Landscape A344

Europa: 8.50e, Northern mountain valley.

1977, May 2

1332 A344 4e multi .50 .20
1333 A344 8.50e multi 2.75 .80
a. Min. sheet, 2 each #1332-1333 50.00 45.00

Pope John XXI Enthroned A345

Petrus Hispanus, the Physician A346

1977, May 20 Litho. *Perf. 13½*

1334	A345	4e multicolored	.25	.20
1335	A346	15e multicolored	.60	.60

Pope John XXI (Petrus Hispanus), only Pope of Portuguese descent, 7th death centenary.

Compass Rose, Camoens Quotation A347

1977, June 8 *Perf. 12*

1336	A347	4e multi	.25	.20
1337	A347	8.50e multi	.55	.50

Camoens Day and to honor Portuguese overseas communities.

Student, Computer and Book — A348

Designs (Book and): No. 1339, Folk dancers, flutist and boat. No. 1340, Tractor drivers. No. 1341, Atom and people.

1977, July 20 Litho. *Perf. 12x12½*

1338	A348	4e multicolored	.25	.20
1339	A348	4e multicolored	.25	.20
1340	A348	4e multicolored	.25	.20
1341	A348	4e multicolored	.25	.20
a.		Souv. sheet of 4, #1338-1341	3.50	3.50
		Nos. 1338-1341 (4)	1.00	.80

Continual education. #1341a sold for 20e.

Pyrites, Copper, Chemical Industry A349

Designs: 5e, Marble, statue, public buildings. 10e, Iron ore, girders, crane. 20e, Uranium ore, atomic diagram.

1977, Oct. 4 Litho. *Perf. 12x11½*

1342	A349	4e multicolored	.25	.20
1343	A349	5e multicolored	.50	.20
1344	A349	10e multicolored	.75	.25
1345	A349	20e multicolored	2.00	.55
		Nos. 1342-1345 (4)	3.50	1.20

Natural resources from the subsoil.

Alexandre Herculano — A350

1977, Oct. 19 Engr. *Perf. 12x11½*

1346	A350	4e multicolored	.20	.20
1347	A350	15e multicolored	.55	.50

Alexandre Herculano de Carvalho Araujo (1810-1877), historian, novelist, death centenary.

Maria Pia Bridge A351

4e, Arrival of first train, ceramic panel by Jorge Colaco, St. Bento railroad station.

1977, Nov. 4 Litho. *Perf. 12x11½*

1348	A351	4e multicolored	.20	.20
1349	A351	10e multicolored	.80	.80

Centenary of extension of railroad across Douro River.

Poveiro Bark A352

Coastal Fishing Boats: 3e, Do Mar bark. 4e, Nazaré bark. 7e, Algarve skiff. 10e, Xavega bark. 15e, Bateira de Buarcos.

1977, Nov. 19 *Perf. 12*

1350	A352	2e multicolored	.30	.20
1351	A352	3e multicolored	.20	.20
1352	A352	4e multicolored	.20	.20
1353	A352	7e multicolored	.25	.20
1354	A352	10e multicolored	.40	.40
1355	A352	15e multicolored	.90	.65
a.		Souv. sheet of 6, #1350-1355	3.00	3.00
		Nos. 1350-1355 (6)	2.25	1.85

PORTUCALE 77, 2nd International Topical Exhibition. Oporto, Nov. 19-20. No. 1355a sold for 60e.

Nativity A353

Children's Drawings: 7e, Nativity. 10e, Holy Family, vert. 20e, Star and Christ Child, vert.

Perf. 12x11½, 11½x12

1977, Dec. 12 Litho.

1356	A353	4e multicolored	.20	.20
1357	A353	7e multicolored	.45	.30
1358	A353	10e multicolored	.45	.35
1359	A353	20e multicolored	1.65	.75
		Nos. 1356-1359 (4)	2.75	1.60

Christmas 1977.

Old Desk and Computer — A354

Designs: Work tools, old and new.

1978-83 Litho. *Perf. 12½*

Size: 22x17mm

1360	A354	50c	Medical	.20	.20
1361	A354	1e	Household	.20	.20
1362	A354	2e	Communications	.20	.20
1363	A354	3e	Garment making	.20	.20
1364	A354	4e	Office	.20	.20
1365	A354	5e	Fishing craft	.20	.20
1366	A354	5.50e	Weaving	.20	.20
1367	A354	6e	Plows	.20	.20
1368	A354	6.50e	Aviation	.20	.20
1369	A354	7e	Printing	.20	.20
1370	A354	8e	Carpentry	.20	.20
1371	A354	8.50e	Potter's wheel	.20	.20
1372	A354	9e	Photography	.20	.20
1373	A354	10e	Saws	.20	.20
1373A	A354	12.50e	Compasses ('83)	.40	.20
1373B	A354	16e	Mail processing ('83)	.50	.20

Perf. 13½

Size: 31x22mm

1374	A354	20e Construction	.55	.35
1375	A354	30e Steel industry	.65	.30
a.		Incomplete arch	.65	.30
1376	A354	40e Transportation	.75	.70
1377	A354	50e Chemistry	1.10	.55
1378	A354	100e Shipbuilding	2.00	.90
1379	A354	250e Telescopes	4.75	2.75
		Nos. 1360-1379 (22)	13.50	8.75

Red Mediterranean Soil — A355

Designs: 5e, Stone formation. 10e, Alluvial soil. 20e, Black soil.

1978, Mar. 6 Litho. *Perf. 12*

1380	A355	4e multicolored	.20	.20
1381	A355	5e multicolored	.20	.20
1382	A355	10e multicolored	.30	.30
1383	A355	20e multicolored	1.25	.55
		Nos. 1380-1383 (4)	1.95	1.25

Soil, a natural resource.

Street Crossing A356

Designs: 2e, Motorcyclist. 2.50e, Children in back seat of car. 5e, Hands holding steering wheel. 9e, Driving on country road. 12.50e, "Avoid drinking and driving."

1978, Apr. 19 Litho. *Perf. 12*

1384	A356	1e multi	.20	.20
1385	A356	2e multi	.20	.20
1386	A356	2.50e multi	.25	.20
1387	A356	5e multi	.40	.20
1388	A356	9e multi	.55	.30
1389	A356	12.50e multi	.65	.60
		Nos. 1384-1389 (6)	2.25	1.70

Road safety campaign.

Roman Tower, Belmonte A357

Europa: 40e, Belém Monastery of Hieronymite monks (inside).

1978, May 2

1390	A357	10e multicolored	*1.50*	.20
1391	A357	40e multicolored	*4.50*	.80
a.		Souv. sheet, 2 each #1390-1391	35.00	30.00

No. 1391a sold for 120e.

Trajan's Bridge — A358

Roman Tablet from Bridge — A359

1978, June 14 Litho. *Perf. 13½*

1392	A358	5e multicolored	.20	.20
1393	A359	20e multicolored	.95	.95

1900th anniv. of Chaves (Aquae Flaviae).

Running A360

1978, July 24 Litho. *Perf. 12*

1394	A360	5e shown	.20	.20
1395	A360	10e Bicycling	.30	.20
1396	A360	12.50e Watersport	.45	.45
1397	A360	15e Soccer	.45	.30
		Nos. 1394-1397 (4)	1.40	1.15

Sport for all the people.

Pedro Nunes A361

Design: 20e, "Nonio" navigational instrument and diagram from "Tratado da Rumaçao do Globo."

1978, Aug. 9 Litho. *Perf. 12x11½*

1398	A361	5e multicolored	.20	.20
1399	A361	20e multicolored	.75	.50

Nunes (1502-78), navigator and cosmographer.

Trawler, Frozen Fish Processing, Can of Sardines — A362

Fishing Industry: 9e, Deep-sea trawler, loading and unloading at dock. 12.50e, Trawler with radar and instruction in use of radar. 15e, Trawler with echo-sounding equipment, microscope and test tubes.

1978, Sept. 16 Litho. *Perf. 12x11½*

1400	A362	5e multi	.20	.20
1401	A362	9e multi	.20	.20
1402	A362	12.50e multi	.45	.40
1403	A362	15e multi	.55	.30
		Nos. 1400-1403 (4)	1.40	1.10

Natural resources.

Postrider A363

Designs: No. 1405, Carrier pigeon. No. 1406, Envelopes. No. 1407, Pen.

1978, Oct. 30 Litho. *Perf. 12*

1404	A363	5e yel & multi	.25	.20
1405	A363	5e bl gray & multi	.25	.20
1406	A363	5e grn & multi	.25	.20
1407	A363	5e red & multi	.25	.20
		Nos. 1404-1407 (4)	1.00	.80

Introduction of Postal Code.

Human Figure, Flame Emblem A364

Design: 40e, Human figure pointing the way and flame emblem.

1978, Dec. 7 Litho. *Perf. 12*

1408 A364 14e multicolored	.25	.25
1409 A364 40e multicolored	1.10	1.10
a. Souv. sheet, 2 ea #1408-1409	3.75	3.75

Universal Declaration of Human Rights, 30th anniv. and 25th anniv. of European Declaration.

Sebastiao Magalhaes Lima — A365

1978, Dec. 7

1410 A365 5e multicolored	.20	.20

Sebastiao Magalhaes Lima (1850-1928), lawyer, journalist, statesman.

Mail Boxes and Scale A366

Designs: 5e, Telegraph and condenser lens. 10e, Portugal Nos. 2-3 and postal card printing press, 1879. 14e, Book and bookcases, 1879, 1979.

1978, Dec. 20

1411 A366 4e multicolored	.20	.20
1412 A366 5e multicolored	.20	.20
1413 A366 10e multicolored	.30	.20
1414 A366 14e multicolored	.75	.65
a. Souv. sheet of 4, #1411-1414	1.65	1.65
Nos. 1411-1414 (4)	1.45	1.25

Centenary of Postal Museum and Postal Library; 125th anniversary of Portuguese stamps (10e). No. 1414a sold for 40e.

Emigrant at Railroad Station A367

Designs: 14e, Farewell at airport. 17e, Emigrant greeting child at railroad station.

1979, Feb. 21 Litho. *Perf. 12*

1415 A367 5e multicolored	.20	.20
1416 A367 14e multicolored	.30	.30
1417 A367 17e multicolored	.75	.65
Nos. 1415-1417 (3)	1.25	1.15

Portuguese emigration.

Automobile Traffic — A368

Combat noise pollution: 5e, Pneumatic drill. 14e, Man with bull horn.

1979, Mar. 14 *Perf. 13½*

1418 A368 4e multicolored	.20	.20
1419 A368 5e multicolored	.20	.20
1420 A368 14e multicolored	.35	.35
Nos. 1418-1420 (3)	.75	.75

NATO Emblem A369

1979, Apr. 4 Litho. *Perf. 12*

1421 A369 5e multicolored	.20	.20
1422 A369 50e multicolored	1.40	1.25
a. Souv. sheet, 2 ea #1421-1422	3.25	3.25

NATO, 30th anniv.

Mail Delivery, 16th Century A370

Europa: 40e, Mail delivery, 19th century.

1979, Apr. 30 Litho. *Perf. 12*

1423 A370 14e multicolored	*.50*	*.30*
1424 A370 40e multicolored	*1.25*	*.80*
a. Souv. sheet, 2 ea #1423-1424	17.50	16.00

Mother, Infant, Dove A371

Designs (IYC Emblem and): 5.50e, Children playing ball. 10e, Child in nursery school. 14e, Black and white boys.

1979, June 1 Litho. *Perf. 12x12½*

1425 A371 5.50e multi	.20	.20
1426 A371 6.50e multi	.20	.20
1427 A371 10e multi	.25	.20
1428 A371 14e multi	.45	.40
a. Souv. sheet of 4, #1425-1428	3.75	2.75
Nos. 1425-1428 (4)	1.10	1.00

Intl. Year of the Child. No. 1428a sold for 40e.

Salute to the Flag — A372

1979, June 8

1429 A372 6.50e multicolored	.25	.20
a. Souvenir sheet of 9	2.00	2.00

Portuguese Day.

Pregnant Woman A373

Designs: 17e, Boy sitting in a cage. 20e, Face, and hands using hammer.

1979, June 6 Litho. *Perf. 12x12½*

1430 A373 6.50e multi	.35	.20
1431 A373 17e multi	.80	.50
1432 A373 20e multi	1.10	.60
Nos. 1430-1432 (3)	2.25	1.30

Help for the mentally retarded.

Children Reading Book, UNESCO Emblem A374

17e, Teaching deaf child, and UNESCO emblem.

1979, June 25

1433 A374 6.50e multi	.20	.20
1434 A374 17e multi	.50	.50

Intl. Bureau of Education, 50th anniv.

Water Cart, Brasiliana '79 Emblem A375

Brasiliana '79 Philatelic Exhibition: 5.50e, Wine sledge. 6.50e, Wine cart. 16e, Covered cart. 19e, Mogadouro cart. 20e, Sand cart.

1979, Sept. 15 Litho. *Perf. 12*

1435 A375 2.50e multi	.20	.20
1436 A375 5.50e multi	.20	.20
1437 A375 6.50e multi	.20	.20
1438 A375 16e multi	.35	.35
1439 A375 19e multi	.40	.35
1440 A375 20e multi	.45	.30
Nos. 1435-1440 (6)	1.80	1.60

Antonio Jose de Almeida (1866-1929) A376

Republican Leaders: 6.50e, Afonso Costa (1871-1937). 10e, Teofilo Braga (1843-1924). 16e, Bernardino Machado (1851-1944). 19.50e, Joao Chagas (1863-1925). 20e, Elias Garcia (1830-1891).

1979, Oct. 4 *Perf. 12½x12*

1441 A376 5.50e multi	.20	.20
1442 A376 6.50e multi	.20	.20
1443 A376 10e multi	.20	.20
1444 A376 16e multi	.30	.30
1445 A376 19.50e multi	.35	.60
1446 A376 20e multi	.35	.30
Nos. 1441-1446 (6)	1.60	1.80

See Nos. 1454-1459.

Red Cross and Family A377

20e, Doctor examining elderly man.

1979, Oct. 26 *Perf. 12x12½*

1447 A377 6.50e multi	.20	.20
1448 A377 20e multi	.55	.55

National Health Service Campaign.

Holy Family, 17th Century Mosaic A378

Mosaics, Lisbon Tile Museum: 6.50e, Nativity, 16th century. 16e, Flight into Egypt, 18th century.

1979, Dec. 5 Litho. *Perf. 12x12½*

1449 A378 5.50e multi	.20	.20
1450 A378 6.50e multi	.20	.20
1451 A378 16e multi	.45	.45
Nos. 1449-1451 (3)	.85	.85

Christmas 1979.

Rotary International, 75th Anniversary — A379

1980, Feb. 22 *Perf. 12x11½*

1452 A379 16e shown	.40	.40
1453 A379 50e Emblem, torch	1.10	1.10

Portrait Type of 1979

Leaders of the Republican Movement: 3.50e, Alvaro de Castro (1878-1928). 5.50e, Antonio Sergio (1883-1969). 6.50e, Norton de Matos (1867-1955). 11e, Jaime Cortesao (1884-1960). 16e, Teixeira Gomes (1860-1941). 20e, Jose Domingues dos Santos (1885-1958). Nos. 1454-1459 horizontal.

1980, Mar. 19

1454 A376 3.50e multi	.20	.20
1455 A376 5.50e multi	.20	.20
1456 A376 6.50e multi	.20	.20
1457 A376 11e multi	.35	.35
1458 A376 16e multi	.50	.40
1459 A376 20e multi	.50	.30
Nos. 1454-1459 (6)	1.95	1.65

Europa Issue

Serpa Pinto (1864-1900), Explorer of Africa — A380

1980, Apr. 14

1460 A380 16e shown	.50	.45
1461 A380 60e Vasco da Gama	1.75	1.00
a. Souv. sheet, 2 each #1460-1461	10.00	9.00

Barn Owl A381

1980, May 6 Litho. *Perf. 12x11½*

1462 A381 6.50e shown	.25	.20
1463 A381 16e Red fox	.60	.50
1464 A381 19.50e Timber wolf	.75	.50
1465 A381 20e Golden eagle	1.00	.60
a. Souv. sheet of 4, #1462-1465	4.00	3.00
Nos. 1462-1465 (4)	2.60	1.80

European Campaign for the Protection of Species and their Habitat (Lisbon Zoo animals); London 1980 International Stamp Exhibition, May 6-14.

Luiz Camoens (1524-80) A382

Lithographed & Engraved

1980, June 9 *Perf. 11½x12*

1466 A382 6.50e multi + label	.20	.20
1467 A382 20e multi + label	.50	.50

Mendes Pinto and Chinese Men A383

1980, June 30 Litho. *Perf. 12x11½*

1468 A383 6.50e shown	.20	.20
1469 A383 10e Battle at sea	.30	.30

A Peregrinacao (The Peregrination,) by Fernao Mendes Pinto (1509-1583), written in 1580, published in 1614.

St. Vincent and Old Lisbon
A384

Designs: 8e, Lantern Tower, Evora Cathedral. 11e, Jesus with top hat, Miranda do Douro Cathedral, and mountain. 16e, Our Lady of the Milk, Braga Cathedral, and Canicada Dam. 19.50e, Pulpit, Santa Cruz Monastery, Coimbra, and Aveiro River. 20e, Algarve chimney, and Rocha Beach.

1980, Sept. 17 Litho. *Perf. 12x12½*

1470	A384	6.50e	multi	.20	.20
1471	A384	8e	multi	.20	.20
1472	A384	11e	multi	.25	.20
1473	A384	16e	multi	.35	.35
1474	A384	19.50e	multi	.40	.40
1475	A384	20e	multi	.40	.30
			Nos. 1470-1475 (6)	1.80	1.65

World Tourism Conf., Manila, Sept. 27.

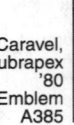

Caravel, Lubrapex '80 Emblem
A385

1980, Oct. 18 Litho. *Perf. 12x11½*

1476	A385	6.50e	shown	.20	.20
1477	A385	8e	Three-master Nau	.25	.20
1478	A385	16e	Galleon	.40	.40
1479	A385	19.50e	Paddle steam	.50	.30
a.			Souv. sheet of 4, #1476-1479	3.50	3.50
			Nos. 1476-1479 (4)	1.35	1.10

Lubrapex '80 Stamp Exhib., Lisbon, Oct. 18-26.

Car Emitting Gas Fumes
A386

1980, Oct. 31

1480	A386	6.50e	Light bulbs	.20	.20
1481	A386	16e	shown	.40	.40

Energy conservation.

Student, School and Sextant
A387

1980, Dec. 19 Litho. *Perf. 12x11½*

1482	A387	6.50e	Founder, book, emblem	.20	.20
1483	A387	19.50e	shown	.40	.40

Lisbon Academy of Science bicentennial.

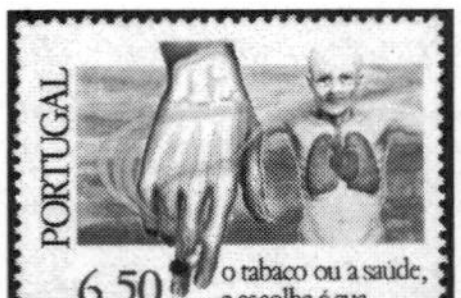

Man with Diseased Heart and Lungs, Hand Holding Cigarette
A388

1980, Dec. 19 *Perf. 13½*

1484	A388	6.50e	shown	.20	.20
1485	A388	19.50e	Healthy man rejecting cigarette	.50	.50

Anti-smoking campaign.

Census Form and Houses
A389

1981, Jan. 28 Litho. *Perf. 13½*

1486	A389	6.50e	Form, head	.20	.20
1487	A389	16e	shown	.40	.40

Fragata on Tejo River
A390

1981, Feb. 23 Litho. *Perf. 12x12½*

1488	A390	8e	shown	.20	.20
1489	A390	8.50e	Rabelo, Douro River	.20	.20
1490	A390	10e	Moliceiro, Aveiro River	.20	.20
1491	A390	16e	Barco, Lima River	.30	.30
1492	A390	19.50e	Carocho, Minho River	.35	.30
1493	A390	20e	Varino, Tejo River	.35	.25
			Nos. 1488-1493 (6)	1.60	1.45

Rajola Tile, Valencia, 15th Century
A391

Designs: No. 1495, Moresque tile, Coimbra 16th cent. No. 1496, Arms of Duke of Braganza, 1510. No. 1497, Pisanos design, 1595.

1981 Litho. *Perf. 11½x12*

1494	A391	8.50e	multi	.25	.20
a.			Miniature sheet of 6	2.50	2.00
1495	A391	8.50e	multi	.25	.20
a.			Miniature sheet of 6	2.50	2.00
1496	A391	8.50e	multi	.25	.20
a.			Miniature sheet of 6	2.50	2.00
1497	A391	8.50e	multi	.25	.20
a.			Miniature sheet of 6	2.50	2.00
b.			Souv. sheet of 4, #1494-1497	3.00	2.25
			Nos. 1494-1497 (4)	1.00	.80

Issued: #1494, 3/16; #1495, 6/13; #1496, 8/28; #1497, 12/16. See #1528-1531, 1563-1566, 1593-1596, 1617-1620.

Perdigueiro
A392

1981, Mar. 16 *Perf. 12*

1498	A392	7e	Cao de agua	2.00	1.50
1499	A392	8.50e	Serra de aires	.75	.25
1500	A392	15e	shown	.75	.25
1501	A392	22e	Podengo	1.50	1.00
1502	A392	25.50e	Castro laboreiro	1.50	1.00
1503	A392	33.50e	Serra da estrela	1.50	1.00
			Nos. 1498-1503 (6)	8.00	5.00

Portuguese Kennel Club, 50th anniversary.

Workers and Rainbow
A393

1981, Apr. 30 Litho. *Perf. 12x12½*

1504	A393	8.50e	shown	.25	.25
1505	A393	25.50e	Rainbow, demonstration	.50	.50

International Workers' Day.

Europa Issue

Dancer in National Costume — A394

1981, May 11 *Perf. 13½*

1506	A394	22e	shown	.75	.45
1507	A394	48e	Painted boat, horiz.	1.50	1.25
a.			Souv. sheet, 2 ea #1506-1507	15.00	12.50

St. Anthony Writing
A395

St. Anthony of Lisbon, 750th Anniversary of Death: 70e, Blessing people.

1981, June 13 *Perf. 12x11½*

1508	A395	8.50e	multi	.20	.20
1509	A395	70e	multi	1.40	1.40

500th Anniv. of King Joao II
A396

1981, Aug. 28 *Perf. 12x11½*

1510	A396	8.50e	shown	.30	.30
1511	A396	27e	Joao II leading army	.95	.95

125th Anniv. of Portuguese Railroads — A397

Designs: Locomotives.

1981, Oct. 28 Litho. *Perf. 12x11½*

1512	A397	8.50e	Dom Luis, 1862	.25	.20
1513	A397	19e	Pacific 500, 1925	.40	.35
1514	A397	27e	ALCO 1500, 1948	.55	.45
1515	A397	33.50e	BB 2600 ALSTHOM, '74	.75	.40
			Nos. 1512-1515 (4)	1.95	1.40

Pearier Pump Fire Engine, 1856 — A398

1981, Nov. 18 Litho. *Perf. 12x12½*

1516	A398	7e	shown	.35	.20
1517	A398	8.50e	Ford, 1927	.65	.20
1518	A398	27e	Renault, 1914	1.25	.40
1519	A398	33.50e	Snorkel, Ford 1978	1.75	.50
			Nos. 1516-1519 (4)	4.00	1.30

A399

A400

Christmas: Clay creches.

1981, Dec. 16 *Perf. 12½x12*

1520	A399	7e	multi	.20	.20
1521	A399	8.50e	multi	.25	.20
1522	A399	27e	multi	.70	.50
			Nos. 1520-1522 (3)	1.15	.90

1982, Jan. 20 Litho. *Perf. 12½x12*

1523	A400	8.50e	With animals	.25	.20
1524	A400	27e	Building church	.60	.45

800th birth anniv. of St. Francis of Assisi.

Centenary of Figueira da Foz
A401

1982, Feb. 24 Litho. *Perf. 13½*

1525	A401	10e	St. Catherine Fort	.25	.20
1526	A401	19e	Tagus Bridge, ships	.40	.30

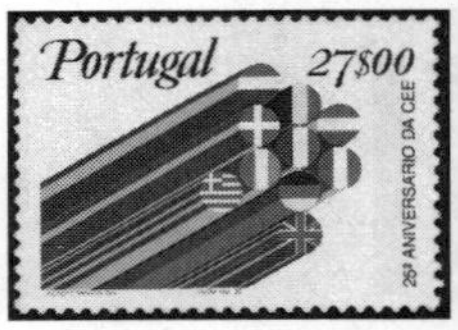

25th Anniv. of European Economic Community
A402

1982, Feb. 24 *Perf. 12x11½*

1527	A402	27e	multi	1.00	.50
a.			Souvenir sheet of 4	5.00	3.00

Tile Type of 1981

Designs: No. 1528, Italo-Flemish pattern, 17th cent. No. 1529, Oriental fabric pattern altar frontal, 17th cent. No. 1530, Greek cross, 1630-1640. No. 1531, Blue and white design, Mother of God Convent, Lisbon, 1670.

1982 Litho. *Perf. 12x11½*

1528	A391	10e	multi	.25	.20
a.			Miniature sheet of 6	2.50	2.00
1529	A391	10e	multi	.25	.20
a.			Miniature sheet of 6	2.50	2.00
1530	A391	10e	multi	.25	.20
a.			Miniature sheet of 6	2.50	2.00
1531	A391	10e	red & blue	.25	.20
a.			Miniature sheet of 6	2.50	2.00
b.			Souv. sheet of 4, #1528-1531	3.00	2.00
			Nos. 1528-1531 (4)	1.00	.80

Issued: No. 1528, Mar. 24; No. 1529, June 11; No. 1530, Sept. 22; No. 1531, Dec. 15.

A403

A404

Major Sporting Events of 1982: 27e, Lisbon Sail. 33.50e, 25th Roller-hockey Championships, Lisbon and Barcelos, May 1-16. 50e, Intl. 470 Class World Championships, Cascais Bay. 75e, Espana '82 World Cup Soccer.

1982, Mar. 24 ***Perf. 12x12½***

1532	A403	27e	multi	.60	.35
1533	A403	33.50e	multi	.70	.45
1534	A403	50e	multi	1.10	.65
1535	A403	75e	multi	1.60	1.00
			Nos. 1532-1535 (4)	4.00	2.45

1982, Apr. 14 Litho. ***Perf. 11½x12***

1536	A404	10e	Phone, 1882	.20	.20
1537	A404	27e	1887	.55	.40

Telephone centenary.

Europa 1982 A405

Embassy of King Manuel to Pope Leo X, 1514.

1982, May 3 ***Perf. 12x11½***

1538	A405	33.50e	multi	2.00	.75
a.			Miniature sheet of 4	16.00	15.00

Visit of Pope John Paul II — A406

Designs: Pope John Paul and cathedrals.

1982, May 13 ***Perf. 14***

1539	A406	10e	Fatima	.30	.20
1540	A406	27e	Sameiro	.85	.50
1541	A406	33.50e	Lisbon	1.00	.65
a.			Min. sheet, 2 each #1539-1541	4.75	4.75
			Nos. 1539-1541 (3)	2.15	1.35

Tejo Estuary Nature Reserve Birds — A407

1982, June 11 ***Perf. 11½x12***

1542	A407	10e	Dunlin	.25	.20
1543	A407	19e	Red-crested pochard	.45	.30
1544	A407	27e	Greater flamingo	.65	.40
1545	A407	33.50e	Black-winged stilt	.85	.50
			Nos. 1542-1545 (4)	2.20	1.40

PHILEXFRANCE '82 Stamp Exhibition, Paris, June 11-21.

TB Bacillus Centenary — A408

1982, July 27 ***Perf. 12x11½***

1546	A408	27e	Koch	.55	.30
1547	A408	33.50e	Virus, lungs	.70	.25

Don't Drink and Drive! — A409

1982, Sept. 22 ***Perf. 12***

1548	A409	10e	multicolored	.25	.20

Boeing 747 A410

Lubrapex '82 Stamp Exhibition (Historic Flights): 10e, South Atlantic crossing, 1922. 19e, South Atlantic night crossing, 1927. 33.50e, Lisbon-Rio de Janeiro discount fare flights, 1960-1967. 50e, Portugal-Brazil service, 10th anniv.

1982, Oct. 15 ***Perf. 12x11½***

1549	A410	10e	Fairey III D MK2	.25	.20
1550	A410	19e	Dornier DO	.40	.25
1551	A410	33.50e	DC-7C	.65	.40
1552	A410	50e	shown	1.00	.60
a.			Souv. sheet of 4, #1549-1552	3.50	3.00
			Nos. 1549-1552 (4)	2.30	1.45

Marques de Pombal, Statesman, 200th Anniv. of Death — A411

1982, Nov. 24 Litho. ***Perf. 12x11½***

1553	A411	10e	multicolored	.25	.20

75th Anniv. of Port Authority of Lisbon — A412

1983, Jan. 5 ***Perf. 12½***

1554	A412	10e	Ships	.25	.20

French Alliance Centenary A413

1983, Jan. 5 ***Perf. 12x11½***

1555	A413	27e	multicolored	.55	.35

Export Effort A414

1983, Jan. 28

1556	A414	10e	multicolored	.20	.20

World Communications Year — A415

1983, Feb. 23 Litho. ***Perf. 11½x12***

1557	A415	10e	blue & multi	.20	.20
1558	A415	33.50e	lt brown & multi	.65	.40

Naval Uniforms and Ships — A416

1983, Feb. 23 ***Perf. 13½***

1559	A416	12.50e	Midshipman, 1782, Vasco da Gama	.30	.20
1560	A416	25e	Sailor, 1845, Estefania	.45	.30
1561	A416	30e	Sergeant, 1900, Adamastor	.60	.35
1562	A416	37.50e	Midshipman, 1892, Comandante Joao Belo	.75	.45
a.			Bklt. pane of 4, #1559-1562	4.00	
			Nos. 1559-1562 (4)	2.10	1.30

See Nos. 1589-1592.

Tile Type of 1981

No. 1563, Hunting scene, 1680. No. 1564, Birds, 18th cent. No. 1565, Flowers and Birds, 18th cent. No. 1566, Figurative tile, 18th cent.

1983 ***Perf. 12x11½***

1563	A391	12.50e	multi	.25	.20
a.			Miniature sheet of 6	2.50	2.00
1564	A391	12.50e	multi	.30	.20
a.			Miniature sheet of 6	2.50	2.00
1565	A391	12.50e	multi	.25	.20
a.			Miniature sheet of 6	2.50	2.00
1566	A391	12.50e	multi	.25	.20
a.			Miniature sheet of 6	2.50	2.00
b.			Souv. sheet of 4, #1563-1566	3.00	2.00
			Nos. 1563-1566 (4)	1.05	.80

Issued: No. 1563, Mar. 16; No. 1563, June 16; No. 1563, Oct. 19; No. 1563, Nov. 23.

17th European Arts and Sciences Exhibition, Lisbon — A417

Portuguese Discoveries and Renaissance Europe: 11e, Helmet, 16th cent. 12.50e, Astrolabe. 25e, Ships, Flemish tapestry. 30e, Column capital, 12th cent. 37.50e, Hour glass. 40e, Chinese panel painting.

1983, Apr. 6

1567	A417	11e	multi	.25	.20
1568	A417	12.50e	multi	.30	.20
1569	A417	25e	multi	.55	.30
1570	A417	30e	multi	.65	.40
1571	A417	37.50e	multi	.85	.50
1572	A417	40e	multi	.90	.50
a.			Souv. sheet of 6, #1567-1572	4.50	3.75
			Nos. 1567-1572 (6)	3.50	2.10

Europa Issue

Antonio Egas Moniz (1874-1955), Cerebral Angiography and Pre-frontal Leucotomy Pioneer — A418

1983, May 5 Litho. ***Perf. 12½***

1573	A418	37.50e	multi	2.75	.60
a.			Souvenir sheet of 4	20.00	17.50

European Conference of Ministers of Transport — A419

1983, May 16

1574	A419	30e	multi	.85	.40

Endangered Sea Mammals — A420

1983, July 29 Litho. ***Perf. 12x11½***

1575	A420	12.50e	Sea wolf	.50	.20
1576	A420	30e	Dolphin	.75	.40
1577	A420	37.50e	Killer whale	1.00	.50
1578	A420	80e	Humpback whale	2.00	.75
a.			Souv. sheet of 4, #1575-1578	5.00	3.25
			Nos. 1575-1578 (4)	4.25	1.85

BRASILIANA '83 Intl. Stamp Exhibition, Rio de Janeiro, July 29-Aug. 7.

600th Anniv. of Revolution of 1383 — A421

1983, Sept. 14 ***Perf. 13½***

1579	A421	12.50e	Death of Joao Fernandes Andeiro	.25	.20
1580	A421	30e	Rebellion	.60	.30

First Manned Balloon Flight A422

Designs: 16e, Bartolomeu Lourenco de Gusmao, Passarola flying machine. 51e, Montgolfier Balloon, first flight.

1983, Nov. 9 Litho. ***Perf. 12x11½***

1581	A422	16e	multicolored	.30	.20
1582	A422	51e	multicolored	.85	.50

Christmas 1983 — A423

Stained Glass Windows, Monastery at Batalha: 12.50e, Adoration of the Magi. 30e, Flight to Egypt.

1983, Nov. 23 ***Perf. 12½***

1583	A423	12.50e	multi	.25	.20
1584	A423	30e	multi	.50	.30

Lisbon Zoo Centenary — A424

1984, Jan. 18 Litho. *Perf. 12x11½*

1585	A424	16e	Siberian tigers	.50	.30
1586	A424	16e	White rhinoceros	.50	.30
1587	A424	16e	Damalisco Albifronte	.50	.30
1588	A424	16e	Cheetahs	.50	.30
a.			Strip of 4, #1585-1588	2.00	1.25

Military Type of 1983

Air Force Dress Uniforms and Planes: 16e, 1954; Hawker Hurricane II, 1943. 35e, 1960; Republic F-84G Thunderjet. 40e, Paratrooper, 1966; 2502 Nord Noratlas, 1960. 51e, 1966; Corsair II, 1982.

1984, Feb. 5 Litho. *Perf. 13½*

1589	A416	16e	multi	.25	.20
1590	A416	35e	multi	.55	.35
1591	A416	40e	multi	.65	.40
1592	A416	51e	multi	.80	.50
a.			Bklt. pane of 4, #1589-1592	3.00	
			Nos. 1589-1592 (4)	2.25	1.45

Tile Type of 1981

Design: No. 1593, Royal arms, 19th cent. No. 1594, Pombal Palace wall tile, 19th cent. No. 1595, Facade covering, 19th cent. No. 1596, Grasshoppers, by Rafael Bordaro Pinhiero, 19th cent.

1984, Mar. 8 Litho. *Perf. 12x11½*

1593	A391	16e	multi	.25	.20
a.			Miniature sheet of 6	2.50	1.65
1594	A391	16e	multi	.25	.20
a.			Miniature sheet of 6	2.50	1.75
1595	A391	16e	multi	.25	.20
a.			Miniature sheet of 6	2.50	1.75
1596	A391	16e	multi	.25	.20
a.			Miniature sheet of 6	2.50	1.75
b.			Souv. sheet of 4, #1593-1596	2.00	1.50
			Nos. 1593-1596 (4)	1.00	.80

Issued: No. 1593, Mar. 8; No. 1594, July 18; No. 1595, Aug. 3; No. 1596, Oct. 17 .

25th Lisbon Intl. Fair, May 9-13 A425

Events: 40e, World Food Day. 51e, 15th Rehabilitation Intl. World Congress, Lisbon, June 4-8, vert.

1984, Apr. 3

1597	A425	35e	multicolored	.75	.35
1598	A425	40e	multicolored	.90	.40
1599	A425	51e	multicolored	1.10	.50
			Nos. 1597-1599 (3)	2.75	1.25

April 25th Revolution, 10th Anniv. — A426

1984, Apr. 25 *Perf. 13½*

1600	A426	16e	multicolored	.40	.20

Europa (1959-84) A427

1984, May 2 *Perf. 12x11½*

1601	A427	51e	multicolored	2.25	1.00
a.			Souvenir sheet of 4	16.00	15.00

LUBRAPEX '84 and Natl. Early Art Museum Centenary — A428

Paintings: 16e, Nun, 15th cent. 40e, St. John, by Master of the Retable of Santiago, 16th cent. 51e, View of Lisbon, 17th cent. 66e, Cabeca de Jovem, by Domingos Sesqueira, 19th cent.

1984, May 9 Litho. *Perf. 12x11½*

1602	A428	16e	multicolored	.30	.20
1603	A428	40e	multicolored	.70	.40
1604	A428	51e	multicolored	.95	.50
1605	A428	66e	multicolored	1.10	.60
a.			Souv. sheet of 4, #1602-1605	3.75	2.75
			Nos. 1602-1605 (4)	3.05	1.70

1984 Summer Olympics A429

1984, June 5

1606	A429	35e	Fencing	.50	.30
1607	A429	40e	Gymnastics	.60	.40
1608	A429	51e	Running	.75	.45
1609	A429	80e	Pole vault	1.25	.75
			Nos. 1606-1609 (4)	3.10	1.90

Souvenir Sheet

1610	A429	100e	Hurdles	3.00	2.00

Historical Events — A430

Designs: 16e, Gil Eanes, explorer who reached west coast of Africa, 1434. 51e, King Peter I of Brazil and IV of Portugal.

1984, Sept. 24 *Perf. 12x11½*

1611	A430	16e	multicolored	.30	.20
1612	A430	51e	multicolored	.85	.45

See Brazil No. 1954.

Infantry Grenadier, 1740 — A431

1985, Jan. 23 Litho. *Perf. 13½*

1613	A431	20e	shown	.30	.20
1614	A431	46e	5th Cavalry Regiment Officer, 1810	.70	.35
1615	A431	60e	Artillery Corporal, 1892	.90	.45
1616	A431	100e	Engineering Soldier, 1985	1.50	.75
a.			Bklt. pane of 4, #1613-1616	5.00	
			Nos. 1613-1616 (4)	3.40	1.75

Tile Type of 1981

Designs: No. 1617, Tile from entrance hall of Lisbon's Faculdade de Letras, by Jorge Barradas, 20th cent.; No. 1618, Explorer and sailing ship, detail from tile panel by Maria Keil, Avenida Infante Santo, Lisbon; No. 1619, Profile and key, detail from a 20th century tile mural by Querubim Lapa; No. 1620, Geometric designs and flowers, by Manuel Cargaleiro.

1985 Litho. *Perf. 12x11½*

1617	A391	20e	multicolored	.30	.20
a.			Miniature sheet of 6	1.90	1.90
1618	A391	20e	multicolored	.25	.20
a.			Miniature sheet of 6	1.60	1.60
1619	A391	20e	multicolored	.30	.20
a.			Miniature sheet of 6	1.90	1.90
1620	A391	20e	multicolored	.25	.20
a.			Miniature sheet of 6	1.60	1.60
b.			Souv. sheet of 4, #1617-1620	2.00	1.50
			Nos. 1617-1620 (4)	1.10	.80

Issued: No. 1617, Feb. 13; No. 1617, June 11; No. 1617, Aug. 20; No. 1617, Nov. 15.

Kiosks — A432

1985, Mar. 19 Litho. *Perf. 11½x12*

1621	A432	20e	Green kiosk	.50	.20
1622	A432	20e	Red kiosk	.50	.20
1623	A432	20e	Gray kiosk	.50	.20
1624	A432	20e	Blue kiosk	.50	.20
a.			Strip of 4, #1621-1624	2.00	

25th Anniv., European Free Trade Association — A433

1985, Apr. 10 Litho. *Perf. 12x11½*

1625	A433	46e	Flags of members	.80	.30

Intl. Youth Year A434

1985, Apr. 10 Litho.

1626	A434	60e	Heads of boy and girl	1.10	.40

Europa 1985-Music A435

1985, May 6 Litho. *Perf. 11½x12*

1627	A435	60e	Woman playing tambourine	2.25	1.00
a.			Souvenir sheet of 4	10.00	6.00

Historic Anniversaries — A436

20e, King John I at the Battle of Aljubarrota, 1385. 46e, Queen Leonor (1458-1525) founding the Caldas da Rainha Hospital. 60e, Cartographer Pedro Reinel, earliest Portuguese map, c. 1483.

1985, July 5 Litho. *Perf. 12x11½*

1628	A436	20e	multicolored	.30	.20
1629	A436	46e	multicolored	.60	.30
1630	A436	60e	multicolored	.80	.40
			Nos. 1628-1630 (3)	1.70	.90

See Nos. 1678-1680.

Traditional Architecture A437

1985-89 Litho. *Perf. 12*

1631	A437	50c	Saloia, Estremadura	.20	.20
1632	A437	1e	Beira interior	.20	.20
1633	A437	1.50e	Ribatejo	.20	.20
1634	A437	2.50e	Transmontanas	.20	.20
1635	A437	10e	Minho and Douro Litoral	.20	.20
1636	A437	20e	Farm house, Minho	.30	.20
1637	A437	22.50e	Alentejo	.30	.20
1638	A437	25e	African Sitio, Algarve	.35	.20
1639	A437	27e	Beira Interior	.45	.25
1640	A437	29e	Hill country	.45	.25
1641	A437	30e	Algarve	.50	.25
1642	A437	40e	Beira Interior	.60	.30
1643	A437	50e	Private home, Beira Litoral	.70	.35
1644	A437	55e	Tras-os-Montes	.90	.45
1645	A437	60e	Beira Litoral	.95	.50
1646	A437	70e	Estremadura Sul and Alentejo	1.10	.55
1647	A437	80e	Estremadura	1.10	.55
1648	A437	90e	Minho	1.25	.60
1649	A437	100e	Adobe Monte, Alentejo	1.30	.65
1650	A437	500e	Algarve	7.40	3.70
			Nos. 1631-1650 (20)	18.65	10.00

Issued: 20e, 25e, 50e, 100e, 8/20; 2.50e, 22.50e, 80e, 90e, 3/10/86; 10e, 40e, 60e, 70e, 3/6/87; 1.50e, 27e, 30e, 55e, 3/15/88; 50c, 1e, 29e, 500e, 3/8/89.

Aquilino Ribeiro (1885-1963), Author — A438

46e, Fernando Pessoa (1888-1935), poet.

1985, Oct. 2 Litho. *Perf. 12*

1651	A438	20e	multicolored	.25	.20
1652	A438	46e	multicolored	.60	.30

Natl. Parks and Reserves A439

1985, Oct. 25

1653	A439	20e	Berlenga Island	.25	.20
1654	A439	40e	Estrela Mountain Chain	.60	.30
1655	A439	46e	Boquilobo Marsh	.70	.35
1656	A439	80e	Formosa Lagoon	1.10	.55
			Nos. 1653-1656 (4)	2.65	1.40

Souvenir Sheet

1657	A439	100e	St. Jacinto Dunes	2.50	2.00

ITALIA '85.

Christmas 1985 — A440

Illuminated codices from The Prayer Times Book, Book of King Manuel, 1517-1538.

1985, Nov. 15 ***Perf. 11½x12***

1658 A440 20e The Nativity .25 .20
1659 A440 46e Adoration of the Magi .60 .30

Postrider A441

1985, Dec. 13 Litho. ***Perf. 13½***

1660 A441 A(22.50e) lt yel grn & dp yel grn .75 .20

See No. 1938 for another stamp with postrider inscribed "Serie A."

Flags of EEC Member Nations A442

Design: 57.50e, Map of EEC, flags.

1986, Jan. 7 Litho. ***Perf. 12***

1661 A442 20e multi .25 .20
1662 A442 57.50e multi .75 .40
a. Souv. sheet, 2 ea #1661-1662 4.00 3.00

Admission of Portugal and Spain to the European Economic Community, Jan. 1. See Spain Nos. 2463-2466.

No. 1662a contains 2 alternating pairs of Nos. 1661-1662.

Castles A443

1986, Feb. 18 Litho. ***Perf. 12***

1663 A443 22.50e Beja .30 .20
a. Booklet pane of 4 2.00
1664 A443 22.50e Feira .30 .20
a. Booklet pane of 4 2.00

1986, Apr. 10

1665 A443 22.50e Guimaraes .30 .20
a. Booklet pane of 4 2.00
1666 A443 22.50e Braganca .30 .20
a. Booklet pane of 4 2.00

1986, Sept. 18

1667 A443 22.50e Montemor-o-Velho .30 .20
a. Booklet pane of 4 2.00
1668 A443 22.50e Belmonte .30 .20
a. Booklet pane of 4 2.00
Nos. 1663-1668 (6) 1.80 1.20

See Nos. 1688-1695, 1723-1726.

Intl. Peace Year A445

1986, Feb. 18 Litho. ***Perf. 12***

1669 A445 75e multicolored 1.00 .50

Automobile Centenary A446

1986, Apr. 10 Litho. ***Perf. 12***

1670 A446 22.50e 1886 Benz .30 .20
1671 A446 22.50e 1886 Daimler .30 .20
a. Pair, #1670-1671 .65 .40

Europa 1986 A447

1986, May 5 Litho.

1672 A447 68.50e Shad 2.50 1.00
a. Souvenir sheet of 4 17.50 15.00

Horse Breeds A448

1986, May 22 Litho. ***Perf. 12***

1673 A448 22.50e Alter .60 .25
1674 A448 47.50e Lusitano 2.00 .40
1675 A448 52.50e Garrano 2.40 .60
1676 A448 68.50e Sorraia 3.00 .75
Nos. 1673-1676 (4) 8.00 2.00

Souvenir Sheet

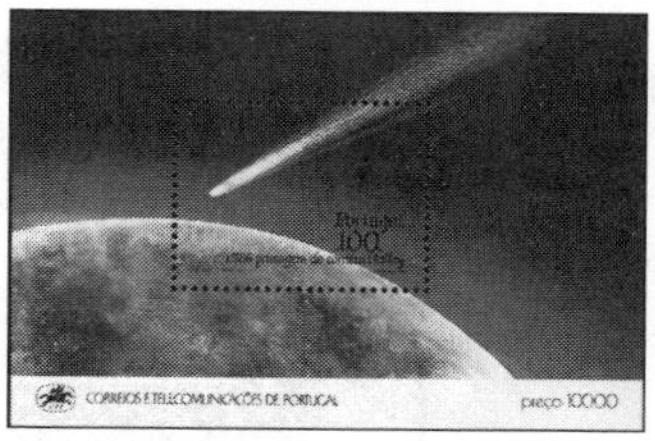

Halley's Comet — A449

1986, June 24

1677 A449 100e multi 12.00 8.00

Anniversaries Type of 1985

Designs: 22.50e, Diogo Cao, explorer, heraldic pillar erected at Cape Lobo, 1484, 1st expedition. No. 1679, Manuel Passos, Corinthian column. No. 1680, Joao Baptista Ribeiro, painter, Oporto Academy director, c. 1836, and musicians.

1986, Aug. 28 Litho.

1678 A436 22.50e multi .30 .20
1679 A436 52.50e multi .75 .40
1680 A436 52.50e multi .75 .40
Nos. 1678-1680 (3) 1.80 1.00

Diogo Cao's voyages, 500th anniv. Academies of Fine Art, 150th anniv.

Stamp Day — A450

Natl. Guard, 75th Anniv. — A451

Order of Engineers, 50th Anniv. — A452

No. 1681, Postal card, 100th anniv.

1986, Oct. 24 Litho.

1681 A450 22.50e multi .30 .20
1682 A451 47.50e multi .70 .35
1683 A452 52.50e multi .75 .40
Nos. 1681-1683 (3) 1.75 .95

Watermills A453

1986, Nov. 7

1684 A453 22.50e Duoro .30 .20
1685 A453 47.50e Coimbra .70 .35
1686 A453 52.50e Gerez .75 .40
1687 A453 90e Braga 1.25 .60
a. Souv. sheet of 4, #1684-1687 5.00 4.00
Nos. 1684-1687 (4) 3.00 1.55

LUBRAPEX '86. #1687a issued Nov. 21.

Castle Type of 1986

1987-88 Litho.

1688 A443 25e Silves .35 .20
a. Booklet pane of 4 2.50
1689 A443 25e Evora Monte .35 .20
a. Booklet pane of 4 2.50
1690 A443 25e Leiria .40 .20
a. Booklet pane of 4 2.50
1691 A443 25e Trancoso .40 .20
a. Booklet pane of 4 2.50
1692 A443 25e St. George .40 .20
a. Booklet pane of 4 2.50
1693 A443 25e Marvao .40 .20
a. Booklet pane of 4 2.50
1694 A443 27e Fernando's Walls of Oporto .45 .25
a. Booklet pane of 4 2.50
1695 A443 27e Almourol .45 .25
a. Booklet pane of 4 2.50
Nos. 1688-1695 (8) 3.20 1.70

Issued: #1688-1689, 1/16; #1690-1691, 4/10; #1692-1693, 9/15; #1694-1695, 1/19/88.

Natl. Tourism Organization, 75th Anniv. — A454

1987, Feb. 10 Litho. ***Perf. 12***

1696 A454 25e Beach houses, Tocha .40 .20
1697 A454 57e Boats, Espinho .90 .45
1698 A454 98e Chafariz Fountain, Arraioles 1.50 .75
Nos. 1696-1698 (3) 2.80 1.40

European Nature Conservation Year — A455

1987, Mar. 20 ***Perf. 12x12½***

1699 A455 25e shown .40 .20
1700 A455 57e Hands, flower, map .90 .45
1701 A455 74.50e Hands, star, rainbow 1.10 .60
Nos. 1699-1701 (3) 2.40 1.25

Europa 1987 A456

Modern architecture: Bank Borges and Irmao Agency, 1986, Vila do Conde.

1987, May 5 Litho. ***Perf. 12***

1702 A456 74.50e multi 2.25 1.00
a. Souvenir sheet of 4 17.50 15.00

A457

A458

Lighthouses

1987, June 12 ***Perf. 11½x12***

1703 A457 25e Aveiro .40 .20
1704 A457 25e Berlenga .40 .20
1705 A457 25e Cape Mondego .40 .20
1706 A457 25e Cape St. Vincente .40 .20
a. Strip of 4, #1703-1706 1.60 .80

1987, Aug. 27 Litho. ***Perf. 12***

1707 A458 74.50e multi 1.10 .55

Amadeo de Souza-Cardoso (1887-1919), painter.

Portguese Royal Library, Rio de Janeiro, 150th anniv. A459

1987, Aug. 27 ***Perf. 12x11½***

1708 A459 125e multicolored 2.00 1.00

Paper Currency of Portugal, 300th Anniv. A460

1987, Aug. 27 ***Perf. 12x11½***

1709 A460 100e multicolored 1.50 .75

Voyages of Bartolomeu Dias (d. 1499), 500th Anniv. — A461

1987, Aug. 27 ***Perf. 12x11½***

1710 25e Departing from Lisbon, 1487 .50 .20
1711 25e Discovering the African Coast, 1488 .50 .20
  a. A461 Pair, #1710-1711 2.00 .50

No. 1711a has continuous design. See Nos. 1721-1722.

Souvenir Sheet

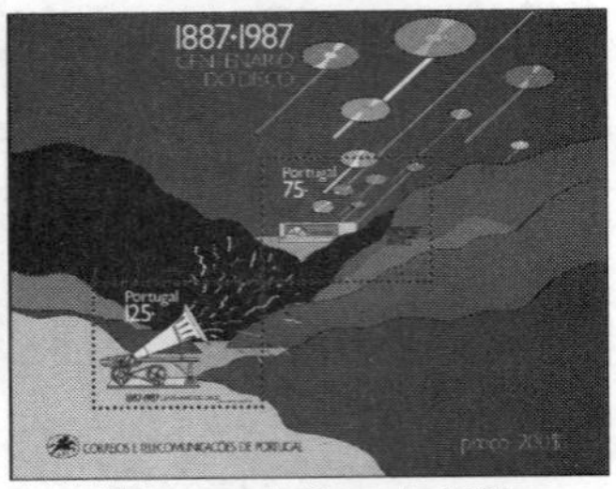

Phonograph Record, 100th Anniv. — A462

1987, Oct. 9 **Litho.** ***Perf. 12***

1712 A462 Sheet of 2 6.00 6.00
  a. 75e Compact-disc player 2.00 2.00
  b. 125e Gramophone 4.00 4.00

Christmas A463

Various children's drawings, Intl. Year of the Child emblem.

1987, Nov. 6

1713 A463 25e Angels, magi, tree .30 .20
1714 A463 57e Friendship circle .75 .45
1715 A463 74.50e Santa riding dove 1.00 .60
  a. Souv. sheet of 3, #1713-1715 5.00 4.00
  Nos. 1713-1715 (3) 2.05 1.25

World Wildlife Fund A464

Lynx, *Lynx pardina.*

1988, Feb. 3 **Litho.** ***Perf. 12***

1716 A464 27e Stalking 1.00 .20
1717 A464 27e Carrying prey 1.00 .20
1718 A464 27e Two adults 1.00 .20
1719 A464 27e Adult, young 1.00 .20
  a. Strip of 4, Nos. 1716-1719 6.00 1.80

Printed in a continuous design.

Journey of Pero da Covilha to the East, 500th Anniv. A465

1988, Feb. 3

1720 A465 105e multi 1.60 .80

Bartolomeu Dias Type of 1987

Discovery of the link between the Atlantic and Indian Oceans by Dias, 500th Anniv.: No. 1721, Tidal wave, ship. No. 1722, Henricus Martelus Germanus's map (1489), picturing the African coast and linking the two oceans.

1988, Feb. 3

1721 A461 27e multi .75 .25
1722 A461 27e multi .75 .25
  a. Bklt. pane of 4, Nos. 1710-1711, 1721-1722 6.00
  b. Pair, #1721-1722 2.00 .60

No. 1722b has continuous design.

Castle Type of 1986

1988, Mar. 15 **Litho.** ***Perf. 12***

1723 A443 27e Vila Nova de Cerveira .45 .25
  a. Bklt. pane of 4 2.00
1724 A443 27e Palmela .45 .25
  a. Bklt. pane of 4 2.00

1988, July 1

1725 A443 27e Chaves .45 .25
  a. Bklt. pane of 4 2.00
1726 A443 27e Penedono .45 .25
  a. Bklt. pane of 4 2.00
  Nos. 1723-1726 (4) 1.80 1.00

Europa 1988 A466

Transportation: Mail coach, Lisbon-Oporto route, 1855-1864.

1988, Apr. 21 **Litho.** ***Perf. 12***

1735 A466 80e multi 2.00 1.00
  a. Souv. sheet of 4 15.00 14.00

Jean Monnet (1888-1979), Economist — A467

1988, May 9 **Litho.**

1736 A467 60e multi 1.00 .50

Souvenir Sheet

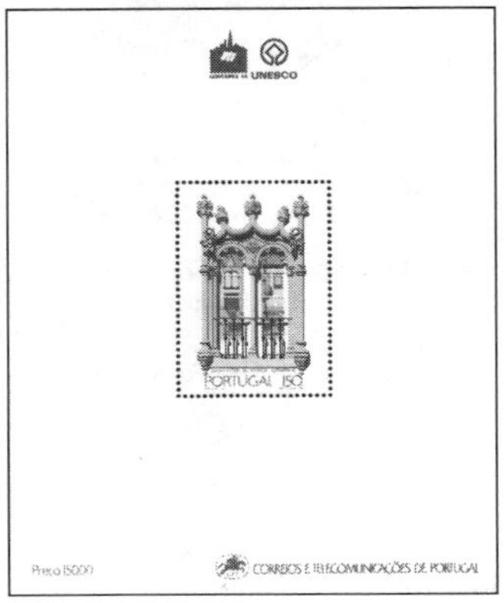

National Heritage (Patrimony) — A468

Design: 150e, Belvedere of Cordovil House and Fountain of Porta de Moura reflected in the Garcia de Resende balcony window, Evora, 16th cent.

1988, May 13 ***Perf. 13½x12½***

1737 A468 150e multi 2.50 2.50

No. 1737 has inscribed margin picturing LUBRAPEX '88 and UNESCO emblems.

20th Cent. Paintings by Portuguese Artists — A469

Designs: 27e, *Viola,* c. 1916, by Amadeo de Souza-Cardoso (1887-1918). 60e, *Jugglers and Tumblers Do Not Fall,* 1949, by Jose de Almada Negreiros (1893-1970). 80e, *Still-life with Guitar,* c. 1940, by Eduardo Viana (1881-1967).

1988, Aug. 23 **Litho.** ***Perf. 11½x12***

1738 A469 27e multi .40 .20
1739 A469 60e multi .90 .45
1740 A469 80e multi 1.25 .60
  a. Min. sheet of 3, #1738-1740 4.00 3.00
  Nos. 1738-1740 (3) 2.55 1.25

See Nos. 1748-1750, 1754-1765.

1988 Summer Olympics, Seoul A470

1988, Sept. 16 **Litho.** ***Perf. 12x11½***

1741 A470 27e Archery .40 .20
1742 A470 55e Weight lifting .80 .40
1743 A470 60e Judo .90 .45
1744 A470 80e Tennis 1.25 .60
  Nos. 1741-1744 (4) 3.35 1.65

Souvenir Sheet

1745 A470 200e Yachting 5.00 4.00

Remains of the Roman Civilization in Portugal A471

Mozaics: 27e, "Winter Image," detail of *Mosaic of the Four Seasons,* limestone and glass, 3rd cent., House of the Waterworks, Coimbra. 80e, *Fish in Marine Water,* limestone, 3rd-4th cent., cover of a tank wall, public baths, Faro.

1988, Oct. 18 **Litho.** ***Perf. 12***

1746 A471 27e multi .40 .20
1747 A471 80e multi 1.15 .60

20th Cent. Art Type of 1988

Paintings by Portuguese artists: 27e, *Burial,* 1938, by Mario Eloy. 60e, *Lisbon Roofs,* c. 1936, by Carlos Botelho. 80e, *Avejao Lirico,* 1939, by Antonio Pedro.

1988, Nov. 18 **Litho.** ***Perf. 11½x12***

1748 A469 27e multi .40 .20
1749 A469 60e multi .90 .45
1750 A469 80e multi 1.25 .60
  a. Souv. sheet of 3, #1748-1750 4.00 3.50
  b. Souv. sheet of 6, #1738-1740, 1748-1750 9.00 6.00
  Nos. 1748-1750 (3) 2.55 1.25

Braga Cathedral, 900th Anniv. A472

1989, Jan. 20 ***Perf. 12***

1751 A472 30e multi .45 .25

INDIA '89 — A473

55e, Caravel, Sao Jorge da Mina Fort, 1482. 60e, Navigator using astrolabe, 16th cent.

1989, Jan. 20

1752 A473 55e multi .85 .40
1753 A473 60e multi .90 .45

20th Cent. Art Type of 1988

Paintings by Portuguese artists: 29e, *Antithesis of Calm,* 1940, by Antonio Dacosta. 60c, *Lunch of the Unskilled Mason,* c. 1926, by Julio Pomar. 87e, *Simums,* 1949, by Vespeira.

1989, Feb. 15 **Litho.** ***Perf. 11½x12***

1754 A469 29e multi .40 .20
1755 A469 60e multi .80 .40
1756 A469 87e multi 1.25 .60
  a. Souv. sheet of 3, #1754-1756 4.00 3.00
  Nos. 1754-1756 (3) 2.45 1.20

1989, July 7

Paintings by Portuguese artists: 29e, *046-72,* 1972, by Fernando Lanhas. 60e, *Les Spirales,* 1954, by Nadir Afonso. 87e, *Sim,* 1987, by Carlos Calvet.

1757 A469 29e multi .35 .20
1758 A469 60e multi .75 .40
1759 A469 87e multi 1.10 .55
  a. Souv. sheet of 3, #1757-1759 4.00 3.00
  b. Souv. sheet of 6, #1754-1759 8.00 6.00
  Nos. 1757-1759 (3) 2.20 1.15

1990, Feb. 14

Paintings by Portuguese artists: 32e, *Aluenda-Tordesillas* by Joaquim Rodrigo. 60e, *Pintura* by Noronha da Costa. 95e, *Pintura* by Vasco Costa (1917-1985).

1760 A469 32e multicolored .40 .25
1761 A469 60e multicolored .80 .40
1762 A469 95e multicolored 1.25 .65
  a. Souv. sheet of 3, #1760-1762 4.00 3.00
  Nos. 1760-1762 (3) 2.45 1.30

1990, Sept. 21

Paintings by Portuguese artists: 32e, Costa Pinheiro. 60e, Paula Rego. 95e, Jose De Guimaraes.

1763 A469 32e multicolored .40 .25
1764 A469 60e multicolored .80 .40
1765 A469 95e multicolored 1.30 .65
  a. Min. sheet of 3, #1763-1765 4.00 2.50
  b. Min. sheet of 6, #1760-1765 8.00 5.00
  Nos. 1763-1765 (3) 2.50 1.30

A474

A475

1989, Feb. 15 **Litho.** ***Perf. 12***

1772 A474 29e multi .40 .20
  a. Bklt. pane of 8 3.25
1773 A474 60e With love .80 .40
  a. Bklt. pane of 8 6.50

Special occasions.

1989, Mar. 8 **Litho.** ***Perf. 11½x12***

1774 A475 60e multi .90 .45

European Parliament elections.

Europa 1989 A476

Children's toys.

1989, Apr. 26 Litho. *Perf. 12*

1775 A476 80e Top 1.75 1.00

Souvenir Sheet

1776 Sheet of 4, 2 each #1775, 1776a 24.00 22.50
a. A476 80e Tops 2.50 1.25

Surface Transportation, Lisbon — A477

29e, Carris Co. elevated railway, Bica Street. 65e, Carris electric tram. 87e, Carmo Elevator, Santa Justa Street. 100e, Carris doubledecker bus. 250e, Transtejo Co. riverboat *Cacilheiro,* horiz.

1989, May 22 Litho.

1777 A477 29e multi .45 .25
1778 A477 65e multi 1.00 .50
1779 A477 87e multi 1.25 .65
1780 A477 100e multi 1.50 .75
Nos. 1777-1780 (4) 4.20 2.15

Souvenir Sheet

1781 A477 250e multi 6.00 5.00

Windmills A478

1989, June 14 Litho.

1782 A478 29e Ansiao .45 .25
1783 A478 60e Santiago do Cacem 1.00 .50
1784 A478 87e Afife 1.25 .65
1785 A478 100e Caldas da Rainha 1.50 .75
a. Bklt. pane of 4, #1782-1785 7.00
Nos. 1782-1785 (4) 4.20 2.15

Souvenir Sheet

French Revolution, 200th Anniv. — A479

1989, July 7 Litho. *Perf. 11½x12*

1786 A479 250e Drummer 7.00 5.00

No. 1786 has multicolored inscribed margin picturing the PHILEXFRANCE '89 emblem and the storming of the Bastille.

Natl. Palaces A480

1989, Oct. 18 Litho. *Perf. 12*

1787 A480 29e Ajuda, Lisbon, and King Luiz I .35 .20
1788 A480 60e Queluz .75 .40

Death cent. of King Luiz.

Exhibition Emblem and Wildflowers A481

1989, Nov. 17 Litho.

1789 A481 29e *Armeria pseudarmeria* .40 .20
1790 A481 60e *Santolina impressa* .75 .40
1791 A481 87e *Linaria lamarckii* 1.10 .55
1792 A481 100e *Limonium multiforum* 1.25 .60
a. Bklt. pane of 4, #1789-1792 3.50
Nos. 1789-1792 (4) 3.50 1.75

World Stamp Expo '89, Washington, DC.

Portuguese Faience, 17th Cent. A482

1990, Jan. 24 Litho. *Perf. 12x11½*

1793 A482 33e shown .45 .25
1794 A482 33e Nobleman (plate) .45 .25
1795 A482 35e Urn .50 .25
1796 A482 60e Fish (pitcher) .80 .40
1797 A482 60e Crown, shield (plate) .80 .40
1798 A482 60e Lidded bowl .80 .40
Nos. 1793-1798 (6) 3.80 1.95

Souvenir Sheet

Perf. 12

1799 A482 250e Plate 6.00 5.00

No. 1799 contains one 52x45mm stamp. See Nos. 1829-1835, 1890-1896.

Score, Alfred Keil and Henrique Lopes de Mondonca A483

1990, Mar. 6 *Perf. 12x11½*

1804 A483 32e multicolored .40 .25

A Portuguesa, the Natl. Anthem, cent. (32e).

University Education in Portugal, 700th Anniv. — A484

1990, Mar. 6 *Perf. 11½x12*

1805 A484 70e multicolored .95 .50

Europa 1990 A485

1990, Apr. 11 *Perf. 12x11½*

1806 A485 80e Santo Tirso P.O. 1.25 1.00

Souvenir Sheet

1807 Sheet of 4, 2 each #1806, 1807a 17.50 15.00
a. A485 80e Mala Posta P.O. 1.75 1.25

Souvenir Sheet

Gentleman Using Postage Stamp, 1840 — A486

1990, May 3

1808 A486 250e multicolored 3.35 3.35

Stamp World London '90 and 150th anniv. of the Penny Black.

Greetings Issue A487

"FELICITACOES" and street scenes.

1990, June 5 Litho. *Perf. 12*

1809 A487 60e Stairway .80 .40
1810 A487 60e Automobile .80 .40
1811 A487 60e Man in street .80 .40
1812 A487 60e shown .80 .40
Nos. 1809-1812 (4) 3.20 1.60

Perf. 13 Vert.

1809a A487 60e .80 .40
1810a A487 60e .80 .40
1811a A487 60e .80 .40
1812a A487 60e .80 .40
b. Bklt. pane of 4, #1809a-1812a 3.25

Camilo Castelo Branco (1825-1890), Writer — A488

Designs: 70e, Friar Bartolomeu dos Martires (1514-1590), theologian.

1990, July 11 Litho. *Perf. 12x11½*

1813 A488 65e multicolored .90 .45
1814 A488 70e multicolored .95 .50

Ships A489

1990, Sept. 21 Litho. *Perf. 12*

1815 A489 32e Barca .40 .25
1816 A489 60e Caravela Pescareza .80 .40
1817 A489 70e Barinel .95 .50
1818 A489 95e Caravela 1.25 .65
Nos. 1815-1818 (4) 3.40 1.80

Perf. 13½ Vert.

1815a A489 32e .40 .25
1816a A489 60e .80 .40
1817a A489 70e .95 .50
1818a A489 95e 1.25 .65
b. Bklt. pane of 4, #1815a-1818a 4.50

National Palaces — A490

1990, Oct. 11 *Perf. 12*

1819 A490 32e Pena .45 .25
1820 A490 60e Vila .80 .40
1821 A490 70e Mafra .95 .50
1822 A490 120e Guimaraes 1.65 .80
Nos. 1819-1822 (4) 3.85 1.95

Francisco Sa Carneiro (1934-1980), Politician — A491

1990, Nov. 7

1823 A491 32e ol brn & blk .45 .25

Rossio Railway Station, Cent. A492

Various locomotives.

1990, Nov. 7

1824 A492 32e Steam, 1887 .45 .25
1825 A492 60e Steam, 1891 .80 .40
1826 A492 70e Steam, 1916 .95 .50
1827 A492 95e Electric, 1956 1.30 .65
Nos. 1824-1827 (4) 3.50 1.80

Souvenir Sheet

1828 A492 200e Railway station 6.00 5.00

Ceramics Type of 1990

1991, Feb. 7 Litho. *Perf. 12*

1829 A482 35e Lavabo .50 .25
1830 A482 35e Tureen and plate .50 .25
1831 A482 35e Flower vase .50 .25
1832 A482 60e Finger bowl .85 .45
1833 A482 60e Coffee pot .85 .45
1834 A482 60e Mug .85 .45
Nos. 1829-1834 (6) 4.05 2.10

Souvenir Sheet

1835 A482 250e Plate 6.00 5.00

No. 1835 contains one 52x44mm stamp.

European Tourism Year A494

1991, Mar. 6 Litho. *Perf. 12*

1836 A494 60e Flamingos .95 .50
1837 A494 110e Chameleon 1.70 .85

Souvenir Sheet

1838 A494 250e Deer 7.50 6.00

Portuguese Navigators A495

1990-94 Litho. *Perf. 12x11½*

1839 A495 2e Joao Goncalves Zarco .20 .20
1840 A495 3e Pedro Lopes de Sousa .20 .20
1841 A495 4e Duarte Pacheco Pereira .20 .20
1842 A495 5e Tristao Vaz Teixeira .20 .20
1843 A495 6e Pedro Alvares Cabral .20 .20
1844 A495 10e Joao de Castro .20 .20
1845 A495 32e Bartolomeu Perestrelo .40 .25
1846 A495 35e Gil Eanes .50 .25
1847 A495 38e Vasco da Gama .60 .30
1848 A495 42e Joao de Lisboa .60 .30
1849 A495 45e Joaoa Rodriques Cabrillo .65 .35
1850 A495 60e Nuno Tristao .85 .45
1851 A495 65e Joao da Nova 1.00 .50
1852 A495 70e Ferdinand Magellan 1.00 .50
1853 A495 75e Pedro Fernandes de Queiros 1.10 .55
1854 A495 80e Diogo Gomes 1.15 .60
1855 A495 100e Diogo de Silves 1.35 .70
1856 A495 200e Estevao Gomes 2.75 1.40
1857 A495 250e Diogo Cao 3.60 1.80
1858 A495 350e Bartolomeu Dias 5.30 2.65
Nos. 1839-1858 (20) 22.05 11.80

Issued: 2e, 5e, 32e, 100e, 3/6; 6e, 38e, 65e, 350e, 3/6/91; 35e, 60e, 80e, 250e, 3/6/92; 4e, 42e, 70e, 200e, 4/6/93; 3e, 10e, 45e, 75e, 4/29/94.

Europa A496

1991, Apr. 11 Litho. *Perf. 12*

1859 A496 80e Eutelsat II 1.50 1.00

Souvenir Sheet

1860 Sheet, 2 ea #1859, 1860a 17.50 15.00
a. A496 80e Olympus I 2.00 1.75

Souvenir Sheet

Princess Isabel & Philip le Bon — A497

1991, May 27 Litho. *Perf. 12½*

1861 A497 300e multicolored 4.00 4.00

Europalia '91. See Belgium No. 1402.

Discovery Ships A498

1991, May 27 Litho. *Perf. 12*

1862 A498 35e Caravel .50 .25
1863 A498 75e Nau 1.10 .55
1864 A498 80e Nau, stern 1.25 .60
1865 A498 110e Galleon 1.75 .85
Nos. 1862-1865 (4) 4.60 2.25

Perf. 13½ Vert.

1862a A498 35e .50 .25
1863a A498 75e 1.10 .55
1864a A498 80e 1.25 .60
1865a A498 110e 1.75 .85
b. Bklt. pane of 4, #1862a-1865a 5.00

Portuguese Crown Jewels — A499

Designs: 35e, Running knot, diamonds & emeralds, 18th cent. 60e, Royal scepter, 19th cent. 70e, Sash of the Grand Cross, ruby & diamonds, 18th cent. 80e, Court saber, gold & diamonds in hilt, 19th cent. 140e, Royal crown, 19th cent.

1991, July 8 Litho. *Perf. 12*

1866 A499 35e multicolored .50 .25
1867 A499 60e multicolored .90 .45
1868 A499 80e multicolored 1.15 .60
1869 A499 140e multicolored 2.00 1.00
Nos. 1866-1869 (4) 4.55 2.30

Perf. 13½ Vert.

1870 A499 70e multicolored 2.50 .50
a. Booklet pane of 5 8.00

See Nos. 1898-1902.

Antero de Quental (1842-1891), Poet — A500

First Missionaries to Congo, 500th Anniv. — A501

1991, Aug. 2 *Perf. 12*

1871 A500 35e multicolored .50 .25
1872 A501 110e multicolored 1.70 .85

Architectural Heritage — A502

Designs: 35e, School of Architecture, Oporto University, by Siza Vieira. 60e, Torre do Tombo, by Ateliers Associates of Arsenio Cordeiro. 80e, Railway Bridge over Douro River, by Edgar Cardoso. 110e, Setubal-Braga highway bridge.

1991, Sept. 4 Litho. *Perf. 12*

1873 A502 35e multicolored .50 .25
1874 A502 60e multicolored .80 .45
1875 A502 80e multicolored 1.15 .60
1876 A502 110e multicolored 1.70 .85
Nos. 1873-1876 (4) 4.15 2.15

1992 Summer Olympics, Barcelona A503

1991, Oct. 9 Litho. *Perf. 12*

1877 A503 35e Equestrian .55 .30
1878 A503 60e Fencing .90 .45
1879 A503 80e Shooting 1.15 .60
1880 A503 110e Sailing 1.70 .85
Nos. 1877-1880 (4) 4.30 2.20

History of Portuguese Communications — A504

Designs: 35e, King Manuel I appointing first Postmaster, 1520. 60e, Mailbox, telegraph, 1881. 80e, Automobile, telephone, 1911. 110e, Airplane, mail truck, 1991.

1991, Oct. 9

1881 A504 35e multicolored .55 .30
1882 A504 60e multicolored .90 .45
1883 A504 80e multicolored 1.15 .60
Nos. 1881-1883 (3) 2.60 1.35

Souvenir Sheet

1884 A504 110e multicolored 5.00 4.00

Automobile Museum, Caramulo A505

Designs: No. 1889a, Mercedes 380K, 1934. b, Hispano-Suiza, 1924.

1991, Nov. 15

1885 A505 35e Peugeot, 1899 .55 .30
1886 A505 60e Rolls Royce, 1911 .90 .45
1887 A505 80e Bugatti 35B, 1930 1.10 .60
1888 A505 110e Ferrari 195 Inter, 1950 1.75 .85
Nos. 1885-1888 (4) 4.30 2.20

Souvenir Sheet

1889 Sheet, 2 each #1889a-1889b 8.00 4.25
a.-b. A505 70e any single 1.50 1.00

Phila Nippon '91 (#1889). See #1903-1906A.

Ceramics Type of 1990

1992, Jan. 24 Litho. *Perf. 12*

1890 A482 40e Tureen with lid .60 .30
1891 A482 40e Plate .60 .30
1892 A482 40e Pitcher with lid .60 .30
1893 A482 65e Violin .95 .50
1894 A482 65e Bottle in form of woman .95 .50
1895 A482 65e Man seated on barrel .95 .50
Nos. 1890-1895 (6) 4.65 2.40

Souvenir Sheet

1896 A482 260e Political caricature 5.50 5.00

No. 1896 contains one 51x44mm stamp.

Portuguese Presidency of the European Community Council of Ministers A506

1992, Jan. 24

1897 A506 65e multicolored .95 .50

Crown Jewels Type of 1991

Designs: 38e, Coral flowers, 19th cent. 65e, Clock of gold, enamel, ivory and diamonds, 20th cent. 70e, Tobacco box encrusted with diamonds and emeralds, 1755. 85e, Royal scepter, 1828. 125e, Eighteen star necklace with diamonds, 1863.

1992, Feb. 7 Litho. *Perf. 11½x12*

1898 A499 38e multicolored .45 .20
1899 A499 70e multicolored .85 .40
1900 A499 85e multicolored 1.10 .65
1901 A499 125e multicolored 1.50 .80

Perf. 13½ Vert.

1902 A499 65e multicolored 1.10 .50
a. Booklet pane of 5 5.00
Nos. 1898-1902 (5) 5.00 2.55

Automobile Museum Type of 1991

Designs: 38e, Citroen Torpedo, 1922. 65e, Rochet Schneider, 1914. 85e, Austin Seven, 1933. 120e, Mercedes Benz 770, 1938. No. 1906b, Renault, 1911. c, Ford Model T, 1927.

1992, Mar. 6 Litho. *Perf. 12*

1903 A505 38e multicolored .60 .30
1904 A505 65e multicolored 1.00 .50
1905 A505 85e multicolored 1.25 .65
1906 A505 120e multicolored 1.75 .90
Nos. 1903-1906 (4) 4.60 2.35

Souvenir Sheet

1906A Sheet of 2 each, #b.-c. 8.00 4.25
b.-c. A505 70e any single 2.00 1.00

Automobile Museum, Oeiras.

Portuguese Arrival in Japan, 450th Anniv. A508

Granada '92: 120e, Three men with gifts, Japanese.

1992, Apr. 24 Litho. *Perf. 12*

1907 A508 38e shown .60 .30
1908 A508 120e multicolored 1.75 .90

Portuguese Pavilion, Expo '92, Seville — A509

1992, Apr. 24 Litho. *Perf. 11½x12*

1909 A509 65e multicolored 1.00 .50

Instruments of Navigation — A510

1992, May 9 Litho. *Perf. 12x11½*

1910 A510	60e Cross staff	.80	.25
1911 A510	70e Quadrant	.95	.50
1912 A510	100e Astrolabe	1.40	.55
1913 A510	120e Compass	1.50	.70
a.	Souv. sheet of 4, #1910-1913	9.00	6.00
	Nos. 1910-1913 (4)	4.65	2.00

Lubrapex '92 (#1913a).

Royal Hospital of All Saints, 500th Anniv. A511

1992, May 11

1914 A511 38e multicolored .60 .30

Apparitions of Fatima, 75th Anniv. A512

1992, May 11

1915 A512 70e multicolored 1.10 .55

Port of Leixoes, Cent. A513

1992, May 11

1916 A513 120e multicolored 1.90 .95

A514

Voyages of Columbus — A515

Designs: 85e, King John II with Columbus. No. 1918, Columbus in sight of land. No. 1919, Landing of Columbus. No. 1920, Columbus soliciting aid from Queen Isabella. No. 1921, Columbus welcomed at Barcelona. No. 1922, Columbus presenting natives. No. 1923, Columbus.

Nos. 1918-1923 are similar in design to US Nos. 230-231, 234-235, 237, 245.

1992, May 22 Litho. *Perf. 12x11½*

1917 A514 85e gold & multi 1.50 .75

Souvenir Sheets

Perf. 12

1918 A515	260e blue	5.00	4.50
1919 A515	260e brown violet	5.00	4.50
1920 A515	260e brown	5.00	4.50
1921 A515	260e violet black	5.00	4.50
1922 A515	260e black	5.00	4.50
1923 A515	260e black	5.00	4.50

Europa.

See US Nos. 2624-2629, Italy Nos. 1883-1888, and Spain Nos. 2677-2682.

UN Conference on Environmental Development — A516

70e, Bird flying over polluted water system. 120e, Clean water system, butterfly, bird, flowers.

1992, June 12 Litho. *Perf. 12x11½*

1924	70e multicolored	1.10	.55
1925	120e multicolored	2.00	1.00
a.	A516 Pair, #1924-1925	4.00	2.00

1992 Summer Olympics, Barcelona A517

1992, July 29 Litho. *Perf. 11½x12*

1926 A517	38e Women's running	.65	.30
1927 A517	70e Soccer	1.15	.60
1928 A517	85e Hurdles	1.40	.70
1929 A517	120e Roller hockey	2.00	1.00
	Nos. 1926-1929 (4)	5.20	2.60

Souvenir Sheet

Perf. 12

1930 A517 250e Basketball 9.00 6.00

Olymphilex '92 (#1930).

Campo Pequeno Bull Ring, Lisbon, Cent. A518

Various scenes of picadors.

1992, Aug. 18 *Perf. 12x11½*

1931 A518	38e multicolored	.65	.30
1932 A518	65e multicolored	1.10	.55
1933 A518	70e multicolored	1.25	.60
1934 A518	155e multicolored	2.50	1.25
	Nos. 1931-1934 (4)	5.50	2.70

Souvenir Sheet

Perf. 13½x12½

1935 A518 250e Bull ring, vert. 7.50 5.00

No. 1935 contains one 35x50mm stamp.

Single European Market A519

1992, Nov. 4 Litho. *Perf. 12x11½*

1936 A519 65e multicolored .95 .50

European Year for Security, Hygiene and Health at Work A520

1992, Nov. 4 *Perf. 12x11½*

1937 A520 120e multicolored 1.75 .90

Postrider A521

1993, Mar. 9 Litho. *Perf. 12x12½*

1938 A521 (A) henna brown, gray & black .65 .30

No. 1938 sold for 42e on date of issue.

See No. 2276A.

Almada Negreiros (1893-1970), Artist — A522

1993, Mar. 9 Litho. *Perf. 11½x12*

1939 A522	40e Portrait	.60	.30
1940 A522	65e Ships	.95	.50

Instruments of Navigation — A523

1993, Apr. 6 *Perf. 12x11½*

1941 A523	42e Hourglass	.60	.30
1942 A523	70e Nocturlabe	1.00	.50
1943 A523	90e Kamal	1.30	.65
1944 A523	130e Backstaff	1.90	.95
	Nos. 1941-1944 (4)	4.80	2.40

Contemporary Paintings by Jose Escada (1934-1980) — A524

Europa: No. 1945, Cathedral, 1979. No. 1946a, Abstract shapes, 1966.

1993, May 5 Litho. *Perf. 12x11½*

1945 A524 90e multicolored 1.25 .60

Souvenir Sheet

1946	Sheet, 2 each #1945, 1946a	7.00	5.00
a.	A524 90e multicolored	1.75	1.25

Assoc. of Volunteer Firemen of Lisbon, 125th Anniv. A525

1993, June 21 Litho. *Perf. 12x11½*

1947 A525 70e multicolored .90 .45

Sao Carlos Natl. Theatre, Bicent. A526

1993, June 21

1948 A526	42e Rossini	.50	.25
1949 A526	70e Verdi	.90	.45
1950 A526	90e Wagner	1.15	.55
1951 A526	130e Mozart	1.65	.80
	Nos. 1948-1951 (4)	4.20	2.05

Souvenir Sheet

1952 A526 300e Theatre 6.00 5.00

Union of Portuguese Speaking Capitals — A527

1993, July 30 Litho. *Perf. 11½x12*

1953 A527	130e multicolored	1.60	.80
a.	Miniature sheet of 4 + 2 labels	9.00	6.00

Brasiliana '93 (#1953a).

Sculpture — A528

Designs: 42e, Annunciation Angel, 12th cent. 70e, St. Mark, 16th cent., horiz. No. 1956, Virgin and Child, 17th cent. 90e, Archangel St. Michael, 18th cent. 130e, Conde de Ferreira, 19th cent. 170e, Modern sculpture, 20th cent.

No. 1960a, Head of Agrippina, the Elder, 1st cent. No. 1960b, Virgin of the Annunciation, 16th cent. No. 1960c, The Widow, 19th cent. No. 1960d, Love Ode, 20th cent.

Perf. 11½x12, 12x11½

1993, Aug. 18

1954 A528	42e multicolored	.55	.30
1955 A528	70e multicolored	.90	.45
1956 A528	75e multicolored	.95	.50
1957 A528	90e multicolored	1.10	.60
1958 A528	130e multicolored	1.60	.80
1959 A528	170e multicolored	2.25	1.10
	Nos. 1954-1959 (6)	7.35	3.75

Souvenir Sheet

1960	Sheet of 4	6.00	5.00
a.-d.	A528 75e any single	.95	.95

See Nos. 2001-2007, 2067-2073.

Railway World Congress A529

90e, Cars on railway overpass, train. 130e, Traffic jam, train. 300e, Train, track skirting tree.

1993, Sept. 6 *Perf. 12x11½*

1961 A529	90e multicolored	1.10	.55
1962 A529	130e multicolored	1.60	.80

Souvenir Sheet

1963 A529 300e multicolored 6.00 5.00

Portuguese Arrival in Japan, 450th Anniv. A530

Designs: 42e, Japanese using musket. 130e, Catholic priests. 350e, Exchanging items of trade.

1993, Sept. 22 Litho. *Perf. 12*

1964	A530	42e multicolored	.55	.30
1965	A530	130e multicolored	1.60	.85
1966	A530	350e multicolored	4.50	2.25
		Nos. 1964-1966 (3)	6.65	3.40

See Macao Nos. 704-706.

Trawlers A531

1993, Oct. 1 Litho. *Perf. 12x11½*

1967	A531	42e Twin-mast	.55	.30
1968	A531	70e Single-mast	.90	.45
1969	A531	90e SS Germano 3	1.10	.55
1970	A531	130e Steam-powered	1.75	.85
		Nos. 1967-1970 (4)	4.30	2.15

Perf. 11½

1967a	A531	42e	.55	.30
1968a	A531	70e	.90	.45
1969a	A531	90e	1.10	.55
1970a	A531	130e	1.75	.85
b.		Booklet pane of 4, #1967a-1970a	5.00	

A532

A533

Mailboxes: 42e, Rural mail bag, 1880. 70e, Railroad wall-mounted mailbox, 19th cent. 90e, Free-standing mailbox, 19th cent. 130e, Modern mailbox, 1992. 300e, Mailbox from horse-drawn postal vehicle, 19th cent.

1993, Oct. 9 Litho. *Perf. 12*

1971	A532	42e multicolored	.50	.25
1972	A532	70e multicolored	.80	.40
1973	A532	90e multicolored	1.00	.50
1974	A532	130e multicolored	1.50	.75
		Nos. 1971-1974 (4)	3.80	1.90

Souvenir Sheet

1975	A532	300e multicolored	6.00	5.00

No. 1975 has continuous design.

1993, Oct. 9

Endangered birds of prey.

1976	A533	42e Imperial eagle	.50	.25
1977	A533	70e Royal eagle owl	.80	.40
1978	A533	130e Peregrine falcon	1.50	.75
1979	A533	350e Hen harrier	4.00	2.00
		Nos. 1976-1979 (4)	6.80	3.40

Brazil-Portugal Treaty of Consultation and Friendship, 40th Anniv. — A534

1993, Nov. 3

1980	A534	130e multicolored	1.50	.75

See Brazil No. 2430.

Souvenir Sheet

Conference of Zamora, 850th Anniv. — A535

1993, Dec. 9

1981	A535	150e multicolored	3.00	2.00

West European Union, 40th Anniv. A536

1994, Jan. 27 Litho. *Perf. 12*

1982	A536	85e multicolored	1.10	.55

Intl. Olympic Committee, Cent. A537

Design: No. 1984, Olympic torch, rings.

1994, Jan. 27

1983	A537	100e multicolored	1.25	.65
1984	A537	100e multicolored	1.25	.65

Issued in sheets of 8, 4 each + label.

Oliveira Martins (1845-94), Historian A538

100e, Florbela Espanca (1894-1930), poet.

1994, Feb. 21

1985	A538	45e multicolored	.60	.30
1986	A538	100e multicolored	1.25	.65

Prince Henry the Navigator (1394-1460) — A539

Illustration reduced.

1994, Mar. 4

1987	A539	140e multicolored	1.75	.85

See Brazil No. 2463, Cape Verde No. 664, Macao No. 719.

Transfer of Power, 20th Anniv. A540

1994, Apr. 22 Litho. *Perf. 12x11½*

1988	A540	75e multicolored	.90	.45

Europa A541

1994, May 5 Litho. *Perf. 12x11½*

1989	A541	100e People of Ormuz	1.25	.65

Souvenir Sheet

1990		Sheet of 4, 2 each #1989, 1990a	6.00	4.50
a.		A541 100e Ears of corn	1.25	1.25

Intl. Year of the Family A542

1994, May 15 Litho. *Perf. 12x11½*

1991	A542	45e blk, red & brn	.55	.30
1992	A542	140e blk, red & grn	1.75	.85

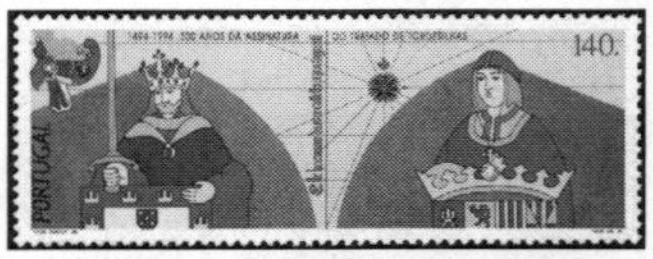

Treaty of Tordesillas, 500th Anniv. — A543

Illustration reduced.

1994, June 7 Litho. *Perf. 12x11½*

1993	A543	140e multicolored	1.75	.90

1994 World Cup Soccer Championships, US — A544

1994, June 7

1994	A544	100e shown	1.25	.60
1995	A544	140e Ball, 4 shoes	1.90	.95

Lisbon '94, European Capital of Culture A545

Birds and: 45e, Music. 75e, Photography. 100e, Theater and ballet. 145e, Art.

1994, July 1

1996	A545	45e multicolored	.55	.30
1997	A545	75e multicolored	.95	.50
1998	A545	100e multicolored	1.25	.60
1999	A545	140e multicolored	1.90	.95
a.		Souvenir sheet of 4, #1996-1999	11.00	10.00
		Nos. 1996-1999 (4)	4.65	2.35

Year of Road Safety — A545a

1994, Aug. 16 Litho. *Perf. 11½x12*

2000	A545a	45e blk, red & grn	.60	.30

Sculpture Type of 1993

Designs: 45e, Pedra Formosa, Castreja culture. No. 2002, Carved pilaster, 7th cent., vert. 80e, Capital carved with figures, 12th cent. 100e, Laying Christ in the Tomb, 16th cent. 140e, Reliquary chapel, 17th cent. 180e, Bas relief, 20th cent.

No. 2007: a, Sarcophagus of Queen Urraca, 13th cent. b, Sarcophagus of Dom Afonso. c, Tomb of Dom Joao de Noronha and Dona Isabel de Sousa, 16th cent. d, Mausoleum of Adm. Machado Santos, 20th cent.

Perf. 12x11½, 11½x12

1994, Aug. 16

2001	A528	45e multicolored	.60	.30
2002	A528	75e multicolored	.95	.50
2003	A528	80e multicolored	1.00	.50
2004	A528	100e multicolored	1.25	.60
2005	A528	140e multicolored	1.75	.85
2006	A528	180e multicolored	2.25	1.10
		Nos. 2001-2006 (6)	7.80	3.85

Souvenir Sheet

Perf. 12x11½

2007		Sheet of 4	6.00	5.00
a.-d.		A528 75e any single	.95	.95

Falconry A546

Designs: 45e, Falconer, hooded bird, dog. 75e, Falcon flying after prey. 100e, Falcon, prey on ground. 140e, Three falcons on perches. 250e, Hooded falcon.

1994, Sept. 16 Litho. *Perf. 12*

2008	A546	45e multicolored	.60	.30
2009	A546	75e multicolored	.95	.50
2010	A546	100e multicolored	1.25	.60
2011	A546	140e multicolored	1.75	.85
		Nos. 2008-2011 (4)	4.55	2.25

Souvenir Sheet

2012	A546	250e multicolored	6.00	5.00

Trawlers A547

1994, Sept. 16 *Perf. 12x11½*

2013	A547	45e Maria Arminda	.60	.30
2014	A547	75e Bom Pastor	.95	.50
2015	A547	100e With triplex haulers	1.25	.60
2016	A547	140e Sueste	1.75	.85
		Nos. 2013-2016 (4)	4.55	2.25

Perf. 11½ Vert.

2013a	A547	45e	.60	.30
2014a	A547	75e	.95	.50
2015a	A547	100e	1.25	.60
2016a	A547	140e	1.75	.85
b.		Booklet pane of 4, #2013a-2016a	6.00	

Modern Railway Transport — A548

45e, Sintra Railway, electric multiple car unit. 75e, 5600 series locomotives. 140e, Lisbon subway cars. Illustration reduced.

1994, Oct. 10 Litho. *Perf. 12*

2017 A548 45e multicolored .55 .30
2018 A548 75e multicolored .90 .45
2019 A548 140e multicolored 1.75 .90
Nos. 2017-2019 (3) 3.20 1.65

Vehicles of Postal Transportation — A549

45e, Horse-drawn mail coach, 19th cent. 75e, Railway postal ambulance, 1910. 100e, Mercedes station wagon, No. 222, 1950. 140e, Volkswagen van, 1952. 250e, DAF 2500 truck, 1983.

1994, Oct. 10

2020 A549 45e multicolored .55 .30
2021 A549 75e multicolored .90 .45
2022 A549 100e multicolored 1.25 .65
2023 A549 140e multicolored 1.75 .90
Nos. 2020-2023 (4) 4.45 2.30

Souvenir Sheet

2024 A549 250e multicolored 6.00 5.00

First Savings Bank in Portugal, 150th Anniv. A550

1994, Oct. 31

2025 A550 45e Pelican medallion .55 .30
2026 A550 100e Modern coins 1.25 .65

World Wide Savings Day (#2026).

American Society of Travel Agents, 64th Congress, Lisbon A551

1994, Nov. 7

2027 A551 140e multicolored 1.75 .90

Historical Inns A552

45e, S. Filipe Fort, Setubal. 75e, Obidos Castle. 100e, Dos Loios Convent, Evora. 140e, St. Marinha Guimaraes Monastery.

1994, Nov. 7

2028 A552 45e multicolored .55 .30
2029 A552 75e multicolored .90 .45
2030 A552 100e multicolored 1.25 .60
2031 A552 140e multicolored 1.75 .90
Nos. 2028-2031 (4) 4.45 2.25

Evangelization and Meeting of Cultures — A553

45e, Carving of missionary, Mozambique, 19th cent., vert. 75e, Sculpture, young Jesus ministering to the people, India, 17th cent., vert. 100e, Chalice, Macao, 17th cent., vert. 140e, Carving of native, Angola, 19th cent.

1994, Nov. 17 Litho. *Perf. 12*

2032 A553 45e multicolored .55 .30
2033 A553 75e multicolored .95 .45
2034 A553 100e multicolored 1.25 .60
2035 A553 140e multicolored 1.75 .90
Nos. 2032-2035 (4) 4.50 2.25

Arrival of Portuguese in Senegal, 550th Anniv. A554

1994, Nov. 17

2036 A554 140e multicolored 1.75 .90

See Senegal No. 1083.

Souvenir Sheet

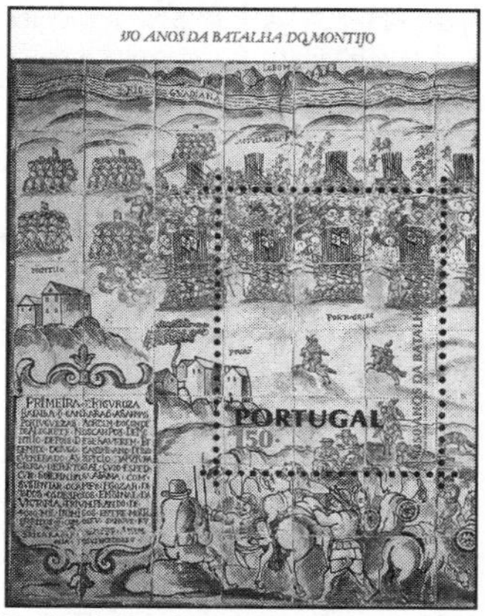

Battle of Montijo, 350th Anniv. — A555

Illustration reduced.

1994, Dec. 1

2037 A555 150e multicolored 4.00 3.00

Souvenir Sheet

Christmas — A556

1994, Dec. 8

2038 A556 150e Magi 1.90 .95

Nature Conservation in Europe — A557

Designs: 42e, Otis tarda. 90e, Pandion haliaetus. 130e, Lacerta schreiberi.

1995, Feb. 22 Litho. *Perf. 12*

2039 A557 42e multicolored .60 .30
2040 A557 90e multicolored 1.25 .60
2041 A557 130e multicolored 1.75 .85
a. Souvenir sheet of 3, #2039-2041 6.00 5.00
Nos. 2039-2041 (3) 3.60 1.75

St. Joao de Deus (1495-1550), Founder of Order of Hospitalers A558

1995, Mar. 8 Litho. *Perf. 12*

2042 A558 45e multicolored .60 .30

Trams & Automobiles in Portugal, Cent. — A559

Designs: 90e, 1895 Electric tram, 1895. 130e, 1895 Panhard & Levassor automobile.

1995, Mar. 8

2043 A559 90e multicolored 1.25 .60
2044 A559 130e multicolored 1.90 .95

19th Century Professions A560

Designs: 1e, Baker woman. 20e, Spinning wheel and spoon vendor. 45e, Junk dealer. 50e, Fruit vendor. 75e, Whitewasher.

1995, Apr. 20 Litho. *Perf. 12*

2045 A560 1e multicolored .20 .20
2046 A560 20e multicolored .30 .20
2047 A560 45e multicolored .60 .30
Complete booklet, 10 #2047 6.00
2048 A560 50e multicolored .70 .35
2049 A560 75e multicolored 1.00 .50
Complete booklet, 10 #2049 10.00
Nos. 2045-2049 (5) 2.80 1.55

See Nos. 2088-2092, 2147-2151, 2210-2214, 2277-2281B.

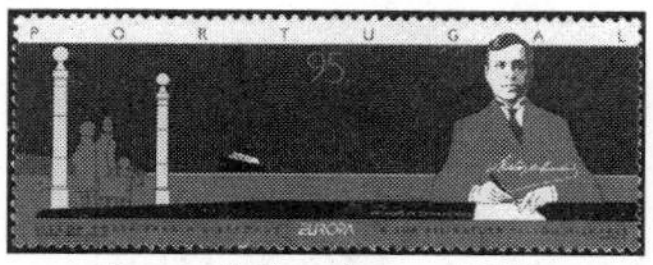

Peace & Freedom — A561

Europa: No. 2050, People awaiting ships for America, Aristides de Sousa Mendes signing entrance visas, 1940. No. 2051, Transportion of refugees from Gibraltar to Madeira, 1940. Illustration reduced.

1995, May 5 Litho. *Perf. 12*

2050 A561 95e multicolored 1.00 .50
2051 A561 95e multicolored 1.00 .50

UN, 50th Anniv. A562

135e, like #2052, clouds in background.

1995, May 5

2052 A562 75e multicolored 1.00 .50
2053 A562 135e multicolored 1.75 .90
a. Souv. sheet, 2 ea #2052-2053 8.00 6.00

A563

St. Anthony of Padua (1195-1231) A564

1995, June 13 Litho. *Perf. 12*

2054 A563 45e shown .60 .30
2055 A564 75e shown 1.00 .50
2056 A563 135e Statue holding Christ 1.90 .95
Nos. 2054-2056 (3) 3.50 1.75

Souvenir Sheet

2057 A563 250e Statue holding 7.00 5.00

See Italy Nos. 2040-2041, Brazil No. 2539.

Firemen in Portugal, 600th Anniv. A565

Designs: No. 2058, Carpenters with axes, women with pitchers, 1395. No. 2059, Dutch firemen, water pumper, 1701. 75e, Fireman of Lisbon, water wagon, 1780, firemen, 1782. 80e, Firemen pulling pumper, carrying water kegs, 1834. 95e, Fire chief directing firemen on Merryweather steam pumper, 1867. 135e, Firemen, hydrant, early fire truck, 1908.

1995, July 4 Litho. *Perf. 12*

2058 A565 45e multicolored .60 .30
2059 A565 45e multicolored 2.00 .30
a. Miniature sheet of 4 8.00 1.25
2060 A565 75e multicolored 2.50 .50
a. Miniature sheet of 4 10.00 2.00
2061 A565 80e multicolored 1.10 .55
2062 A565 95e multicolored 1.25 .65
2063 A565 135e multicolored 1.90 .90
Nos. 2058-2063 (6) 9.35 3.20

Dom Manuel I, 500th Anniv. of Acclamation — A566

1995, Aug. 4 Litho. *Perf. 12*

2064 A566 45e buff, brown & red .60 .30
a. Miniature sheet of 4 5.00 4.00

New Electric Railway Tram — A567

Illustration reduced.

1995, Sept. 1

2066	A567	80e multicolored	1.10	.55
a.		Booklet pane of 4	4.50	
		Complete booklet, No. 2066a	5.00	

Sculpture Type of 1993

Designs: 45e, Warrior, Castreja culture. 75e, Two-headed fountain. 80e, Statue, "The Truth," by Texeira Lopes. 95e, Monument to the war dead. 135e, Statue of Fernão Lopes, by Martins Correia. 190e, Monument to Fernando Pessoa, by Lagoa Henriques.

Equestrian statues: No. 2073: a, Medieval cavalryman. b, D. José I. c, D. João IV. d, Vímara Peres.

1995, Sept. 27 Litho. *Perf. 11½x12*

2067	A528	45e multicolored	.60	.30
2068	A528	75e multicolored	1.00	.50
2069	A528	80e multicolored	1.10	.55
2070	A528	95e multicolored	1.25	.65
2071	A528	135e multicolored	1.80	.90
2072	A528	190e multicolored	2.50	1.25
		Nos. 2067-2072 (6)	8.25	4.15

Souvenir Sheet

2073		Sheet of 4	7.00	5.00
a.-d.		A528 75e any single	1.00	1.00

Portuguese Expansion Period Art — A568

45e, Statue of the Guardian Angel of Portugal. 75e, Reliquary of Queen D. Leonor. 80e, Statue of Dom Manuel. 95e, Painting, St. Anthony, by Nuno Goncalves. 135e, Painting, Adoration of the Magi, by Vasco Fernandez. 190e, Painting, Christ on the Way to Mount Calvary, by Jorge Afonso.

200e, Altarpiece for Convent of St. Vincent, by Nuno Goncalves.

1995, Oct. 9 Litho. *Perf. 12*

2074	A568	45e multicolored	.60	.25
2075	A568	75e multicolored	1.00	.50
2076	A568	80e multicolored	1.00	.50
2077	A568	95e multicolored	1.25	.60
2078	A568	135e multicolored	1.75	.90
2079	A568	190e multicolored	2.50	1.25
		Nos. 2074-2079 (6)	8.10	4.00

Souvenir Sheet

2080	A568	200e multicolored	6.00	4.00

No. 2080 contains one 76x27mm stamp.

José Maria Eca de Queiroz (1845-1900), Writer — A569

1995, Oct. 27 Litho. *Perf. 12*

2081	A569	135e multicolored	1.75	.90

Christmas A570

1995, Nov. 14

2082	A570	80e Annunciation angel	1.00	.50
a.		"PORTUGAL" omitted	1.00	.50
b.		Miniature sheet, 4 #2082	4.00	4.00
c.		Miniature sheet, 4 #2082a	4.00	4.00

TAP Air Portugal, 50th Anniv. A571

1995, Nov. 14

2083	A571	135e Airbus A340/300	1.75	.90

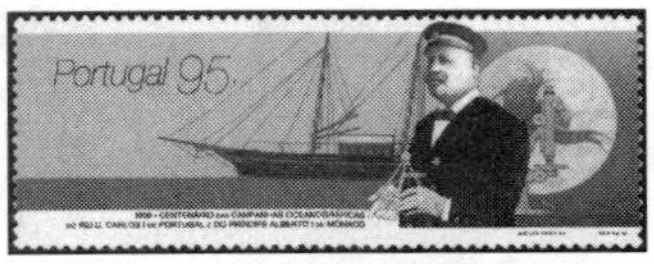

Oceanographic Voyages of King Charles I of Portugal and Prince Albert I of Monaco, Cent. — A572

95e, Ship, King Charles I holding sextant, microscope, sea life. 135e, Fish in sea, net, Prince Albert I holding binoculars, ship.

Illustration reduced.

1996, Feb. 1

2084	A572	95e multicolored	1.25	.60
2085	A572	135e multicolored	1.75	.90

See Monaco Nos. 1992-1993.

Natl. Library, Bicent. A573

1996, Feb. 29

2086	A573	80e multicolored	1.00	.50

Use of Portuguese as Official Language, 700th Anniv. — A574

1996, Feb. 29

2087	A574	200e multicolored	2.50	1.25

Type of 1995

Designs: 3e, Exchange broker. 47e, Woman selling chestnuts. 78e, Cloth seller. 100e, Black woman selling mussels. 250e, Water seller.

1996, Mar. 20 Litho. *Perf. 11½x12*

2088	A560	3e multicolored	.20	.20
2089	A560	47e multicolored	.60	.30
a.		Booklet pane, 10 #2089	6.00	
		Complete booklet, #2089a	6.00	
2090	A560	78e multicolored	1.00	.50
a.		Booklet pane, 10 #2090	10.00	
		Complete booklet, #2090a	10.00	
2091	A560	100e multicolored	1.25	.65
2092	A560	250e multicolored	3.20	1.60
		Nos. 2088-2092 (5)	6.25	3.25

Joao de Deus (1830-96), Founder of New Method to Teach Reading A576

1996, Apr. 12 *Perf. 12*

2093	A576	78e multicolored	1.00	.50

UNICEF, 50th Anniv. — A577

Illustration reduced.

1996, Apr. 12

2094	A577	78e shown	1.00	.50
2095	A577	140e Children	1.75	.90
a.		Bklt. pane, 2 ea #2094-2095	5.50	
		Complete booklet, #2095a	5.50	

Joao de Barros (1496-1570), Writer — A578

1996, Apr. 12

2096	A578	140e multicolored	1.75	.90

Helena Vieira da Silva (1908-92), Painter — A579

1996, May 3

2097	A579	98e multicolored	1.00	.60
a.		Souvenir sheet of 3	3.00	1.90

Europa.

Euro '96, European Soccer Championships, Great Britain — A580

1996, June 7 Litho. *Perf. 12*

2098	A580	78e Soccer players	1.00	.50
2099	A580	140e Soccer players, diff.	1.80	.90
a.		Souvenir sheet, #2098-2099	2.80	2.80

Joao Vaz Corte-Real, Explorer, 500th Death Anniv. — A581

Illustration reduced.

1996, June 7

2100	A581	140e multicolored	1.80	.90

Souvenir Sheet

2101	A581	315e like #2100	4.00	4.00

No. 2101 contains one 40x31 stamp with a continuous design.

1996 Summer Olympics, Atlanta A582

1996, June 24

2102	A582	47e Wrestling	.60	.30
2103	A582	78e Equestrian	1.00	.50
2104	A582	98e Boxing	1.30	.65
2105	A582	140e Running	1.80	.90
		Nos. 2102-2105 (4)	4.70	2.35

Souvenir Sheet

2106	A582	300e Early track event	4.00	4.00

Olymphilex '96 (#2106).

Augusto Hilário (1864-96), Singer A583

1996, July 1 Litho. *Perf. 12x11½*

2107	A583	80e multicolored	1.00	.50

Alphonsine Condification of Statutes, 550th Anniv. — A584

1996, Aug. 7

2108	A584	350e multicolored	4.50	2.25

Motion Pictures, Cent. A585

Directors, stars of motion pictures: 47e, António Silva. 78e, Vasco Santana. 80e, Laura Alves. 98e, Aurélio Pais dos Reis. 100e, Leitao de Barros. 140e, António Lopes Ribeiro.

1996, Aug. 7

2109	A585	47e multicolored	.60	.30
2110	A585	78e multicolored	1.00	.50
2111	A585	80e multicolored	1.00	.50
a.		Souvenir sheet, #2109-2111	2.60	2.60
2112	A585	98e multicolored	1.30	.65
2113	A585	100e multicolored	1.30	.65
2114	A585	140e multicolored	1.80	.90
a.		Souvenir sheet, #2112-2114	4.50	4.50
b.		Souvenir sheet, #2109-2114	7.00	7.00
		Nos. 2109-2114 (6)	7.00	3.50

Azeredo Perdigao (1896-1993), Lawyer, Chairman of Calouste Gulbenkian Foundation — A586

1996, Sept. 19 Litho. *Perf. 12*

2115	A586	47e multicolored	.60	.30

Arms of the Districts of Portugal A587

1996, Sept. 27

2116	A587	47e Aveiro	.60	.30
2117	A587	78e Beja	1.00	.50
2118	A587	80e Braga	1.00	.50
a.		Souvenir sheet, #2116-2118	2.60	2.60
2119	A587	98e Branganca	1.30	.65
2120	A587	100e Castelo Branco	1.30	.65
2121	A587	140e Coimbra	1.80	.90
a.		Souvenir sheet, #2119-2121	4.50	4.50
		Nos. 2116-2121 (6)	7.00	3.50

County of Portucale, 900th Anniv. A588

1996, Oct. 9
2122 A588 47e multicolored .60 .30

Home Mail Delivery, 175th Anniv. — A589

Designs: 47e, Mail carrier, 1821. 78e, Postman, 1854. 98e, Rural mail distrubutor, 1893. 100e, Postman, 1939. 140e, Postman, 1992.

1996, Oct. 9
2123 A589 47e multicolored .60 .30
2124 A589 78e multicolored 1.00 .50
2125 A589 98e multicolored 1.30 .65
2126 A589 100e multicolored 1.30 .65
2127 A589 140e multicolored 1.80 .90
Nos. 2123-2127 (5) 6.00 3.00

Traditional Food A590

47e, Minho-style pork. 78e, Trout, Boticas. 80e, Tripe, Oporto. 98e, Baked codfish, potatoes. 100e, Eel chowder, Aveiro. 140e, Lobster, Peniche.

1996, Oct. 9
2128 A590 47e multicolored .60 .30
2129 A590 78e multicolored 1.00 .50
2130 A590 80e multicolored 1.00 .50
2131 A590 98e multicolored 1.30 .65
2132 A590 100e multicolored 1.30 .65
2133 A590 140e multicolored 1.80 .90
Nos. 2128-2133 (6) 7.00 3.50

See Nos. 2170-2175.

Bank of Portugal, 150th Anniv. A591

1996, Nov. 12 **Litho.** ***Perf. 12***
2134 A591 78e multicolored 1.00 .50

Rights of the People of East Timor A592

1996, Nov. 12
2135 A592 140e black & red 1.75 .90

Discovery of Maritime Route to India, 500th Anniv. — A593

Voyage of Vasco da Gama: 47e, Visit of D. Manuel I to shipyards. 78e, Departure from Lisbon, July 8, 1497. 98e, Trip over Atlantic Ocean. 140e, Passing Cape of Good Hope. 315e, Dream of Manuel.

1996, Nov. 12 ***Perf. 13½***
2136 A593 47e multicolored .60 .30
2137 A593 78e multicolored 1.00 .50
2138 A593 98e multicolored 1.25 .60
2139 A593 140e multicolored 1.75 .85
Nos. 2136-2139 (4) 4.60 2.25

Souvenir Sheet

2140 A593 315e multicolored 4.00 4.00

See Nos. 2191-2195, 2265-2270.

Souvenir Sheet

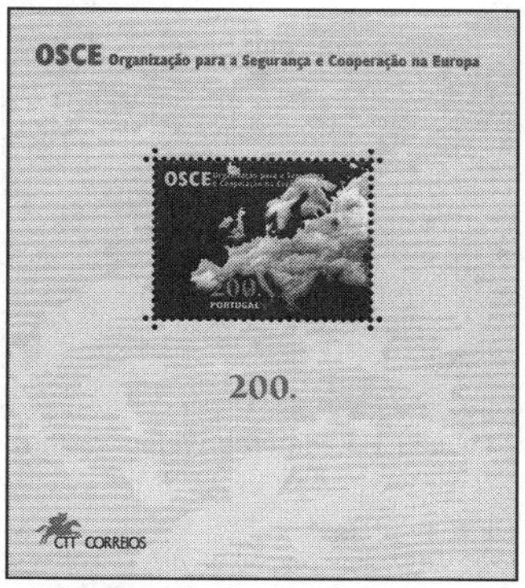
1996 Organization for Security and Cooperation in Europe Summit, Lisbon — A594

Illustration reduced.

1996, Dec. 2 ***Perf. 12***
2141 A594 200e multicolored 2.50 2.50

Ships of the Indian Shipping Line A595

Designs: 49e, Portuguese galleon, 16th cent. 80e, "Principe da Beira," 1780. 100e, Bow of Frigate "D. Fernando II e Gloria," 1843. 140e, Stern of "D. Fernando II e Gloria."

1997, Feb. 12 **Litho.** ***Perf. 12***
2142 A595 49e multicolored .60 .30
2143 A595 80e multicolored .95 .45
2144 A595 100e multicolored 1.15 .60
2145 A595 140e multicolored 1.65 .80
Nos. 2142-2145 (4) 4.35 2.15

Project Life — A596

1997, Feb. 20
2146 A596 80e multicolored .95 .45
a. Booklet pane of 5 4.75
Complete booklet, #2146a 4.75

19th Cent. Professions Type of 1995

Designs: 2e, Laundry woman. 5e, Broom seller. 30e, Olive oil seller. 49e, Woman with cape. 80e, Errand boy.

1997, Mar. 12 **Litho.** ***Perf. 11½x12***
2147 A560 2e multicolored .20 .20
2148 A560 5e multicolored .20 .20
2149 A560 30e multicolored .35 .20
2150 A560 49e multicolored .60 .30
a. Booklet pane of 10 6.00
Complete booklet, #2150a 6.00
2151 A560 80e multicolored .95 .50
a. Booklet pane of 10 9.50
Complete booklet, #2151a 9.50
Nos. 2147-2151 (5) 2.30 1.40

Managing Institute of Public Credit, Bicent. A597

1997, Mar. 12 **Litho.** ***Perf. 12***
2152 A597 49e multicolored .60 .30

World Wildlife Fund — A598

Galemys pyreanicus: No. 2153, Looking upward. No. 2154, Paws around nose. No. 2155, Eating earthworm. No. 2156, Heading downward.

1997, Mar. 12 ***Perf. 12***
2153 A598 49e multicolored .65 .30
2154 A598 49e multicolored .65 .30
2155 A598 49e multicolored .65 .30
2156 A598 49e multicolored .65 .30
a. Strip of 4, #2153-2156 2.75 1.50

Stories and Legends — A599

Europa: Moorish girl watching over treasures.

1997, May 5 **Litho.** ***Perf. 12***
2157 A599 100e multicolored 1.10 .55
a. Souvenir sheet of 3 4.50 3.25

Sports A600

#2162: a, BMX bike riding. b, Hang gliding.

1997, May 29 ***Perf. 12***
2158 A600 49e Surfing .50 .25
2159 A600 80e Skate boarding .90 .40
2160 A600 100e Roller blading 1.10 .60
2161 A600 140e Parasailing 1.50 .75
Nos. 2158-2161 (4) 4.00 2.00

Souvenir Sheet

2162 Sheet of 2 5.00 4.00
a.-b. A600 150e any single 1.60 1.60

Capture of Lisbon and Santarém from the Moors, 850th Anniv. — A601

Designs: No. 2163, Soldier on horse, front of fortress of Lisbon. No. 2164, Soldiers climbing ladders into Santareém at night.

1997, June 9 ***Perf. 12***
2163 80e multicolored .85 .40
2164 80e multicolored .85 .40
a. A601 Pair, #2163-2164 1.70 .80
b. Souvenir sheet, 2 #2164a 3.40 3.40

Fr. Luís Fróis (1532-97), Missionary, Historian — A602

Fr. José de Anchieta (1534-97), Missionary in Brazil — A603

80e, Fróis on mission in Orient. #2166, Fróis holding hands across chest. #2167, Fróis, church.

1997, June 9
2165 A602 80e multi, horiz. .85 .45
2166 A602 140e multi 1.50 .75
2167 A602 140e multi 1.50 .75
Nos. 2165-2167 (3) 3.85 1.95

1997, June 9

Design: No. 2169, Fr. António Vieira (1608-97), missionary in Brazil, diplomat.

2168 A603 140e multicolored 1.50 .75
2169 A603 350e multicolored 3.75 1.90

Traditional Food Type of 1996

10e, Roasted kid, Beira Baixa. 49e, Fried shad. 80e, Lamb stew. 100e, Fish chowder. 140e, Swordfish fillets with corn. 200e, Stewed octopus, Azores.

1997, July 5 **Litho.** ***Perf. 12***
2170 A590 10e multicolored .20 .20
2171 A590 49e multicolored .60 .30
2172 A590 80e multicolored 1.00 .50
2173 A590 100e multicolored 1.25 .65
2174 A590 140e multicolored 1.70 .85
2175 A590 200e multicolored 2.50 1.25
Nos. 2170-2175 (6) 7.25 3.75

Souvenir Sheet

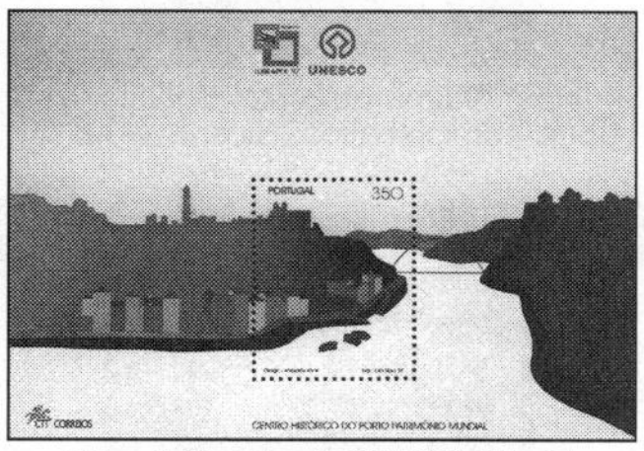
City of Oporto, UNESCO World Heritage Site — A605

Illustration reduced.

1997, July 5 **Litho.** ***Perf. 12***
2176 A605 350e multicolored 3.75 3.75

A606

A607

1997, July 19 Litho. *Perf. 12*
2177 A606 100e multicolored 1.25 .65

Brotherhood of the Yeoman of Beja, 700th anniv.

1997, Aug. 29 Litho. *Perf. 12*
2178 A607 50e multicolored .55 .30

Natl. Laboratory of Civil Engineering, 50th anniv.

Treaty of Alcanices, 700th Anniv. A608

1997, Sept. 12
2179 A608 80e multicolored .90 .45

Arms of the Districts of Portugal A609

1997, Sept. 17
2180 A609 10e Evora .20 .20
2181 A609 49e Faro .55 .30
2182 A609 80e Guarda .90 .45
2183 A609 100e Leiria 1.10 .55
2184 A609 140e Lisboa 1.60 .80
a. Souv. sheet, #2180, 2182, 2184 2.65 1.40
2185 A609 200e Portalegre 2.25 1.10
a. Souv. sheet, #2181, 2183, 2185 4.00 4.00
Nos. 2180-2185 (6) 6.60 3.40

See Nos. 2249-2254.

Incorporation of Postal Service in State Administration, Bicent. — A610

1997, Oct. 9
2186 A610 80e multicolored .90 .45

Portuguese Cartography — A611

Designs: 49e, Map from atlas of Lopo Homen-Reineis, 1519. 80e, Map from atlas of Joao Freire, 1546. 100e, Chart by Diogo Ribeiro, 1529. 140e, Anonymous map, 1630.

1997, Oct. 9
2187 A611 49e multicolored .55 .30
2188 A611 80e multicolored .90 .45
2189 A611 100e multicolored 1.15 .60
2190 A611 140e multicolored 1.60 .80
a. Souvenir sheet, #2187-2190 4.25 4.25
Nos. 2187-2190 (4) 4.20 2.15

Discovery of Maritime Route to India Type of 1996

Voyage of Vasco da Gama: 49e, St. Gabriel's cross, Quelimane. 80e, Stop at island off Mozambique. 100e, Arrival in Mombasa. 140e, Reception for king of Melinde. 315e, Trading with natives, Natal.

1997, Nov. 5 *Perf. 13½*
2191 A593 49e multicolored .55 .30
2192 A593 80e multicolored .90 .45
2193 A593 100e multicolored 1.15 .60
2194 A593 140e multicolored 1.60 .80
Nos. 2191-2194 (4) 4.20 2.15

Souvenir Sheet

2195 A593 315e multicolored 3.50 3.50

Expo '98 — A612

Plankton: 49e, Loligo vulgaris. 80e, Scyllarus arctus. 100e, Pontellina plumata. 140e, Solea senegalensis.

No. 2200: a, Calcidiscus leptoporus. b, Tabellaria.

1997, Nov. 5 *Perf. 12*
2196 A612 49e multicolored .55 .30
2197 A612 80e multicolored .90 .45
2198 A612 100e multicolored 1.10 .55
2199 A612 140e multicolored 1.60 .80
Nos. 2196-2199 (4) 4.15 2.10

Souvenir Sheet

Perf. 12½

2200 Sheet of 2 2.25 2.25
a.-b. A612 100e any single 1.10 1.10

See Nos. 2215-2219, 2226-2244.

Souvenir Sheet

Sintra, UNESCO World Heritage Site — A613

1997, Dec. 5 *Perf. 12*
2201 A613 350e multicolored 4.00 4.00

Portuguese Military Engineering, 350th Anniv. — A614

Engineering officer, map of fortress: 50e, Almeida. 80e, Miranda do Douro. 100e, Moncao. 140e, Elvas.

1998, Jan. 28 Litho. *Perf. 12*
2202 A614 50e multicolored .55 .30
2203 A614 80e multicolored .90 .45
2204 A614 100e multicolored 1.10 .55
2205 A614 140e multicolored 1.60 .80
a. Booklet pane, #2202-2205, perf. 12 vert. 4.25
Complete booklet, #2205a 4.25
Nos. 2202-2205 (4) 4.15 2.10

Roberto Ivens (1850-98), Naturalist A615

1998, Jan. 28
2206 A615 140e multicolored 1.60 .80

Misericórdias (Philanthropic Organizations), 500th Anniv. — A616

Sculptures: 80e, Madonna wearing crown surrounded by angels, people kneeling in praise, vert. 100e, People of antiquity gathered around another's bedside.

1998, Feb. 20
2207 A616 80e multicolored .90 .45
2208 A616 100e multicolored 1.10 .55

Souvenir Sheet

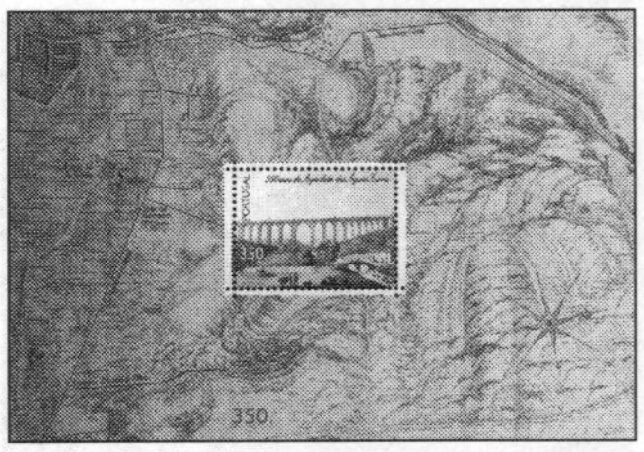

Aqueduct of the Free Waters, 250th Anniv. — A617

1998, Feb. 20
2209 A617 350e multicolored 3.90 1.90

19th Cent. Professions Type of 1995

10e, Fish seller. 40e, Collector of alms. 50e, Ceramics seller. 85e, Duck and eggs vendor. 250e, Queijadas (small cakes made of cheese) seller.

1998, Mar. 20 *Perf. 11½x12*
2210 A560 10e multicolored .20 .20
2211 A560 40e multicolored .45 .25
2212 A560 50e multicolored .55 .30
a. Booklet pane of 10 5.50
Complete booklet, #2212a 5.50
2213 A560 85e multicolored .95 .50
a. Booklet pane of 10 9.50
Complete booklet, #2213a 9.50
2214 A560 250e multicolored 2.75 1.40
Nos. 2210-2214 (5) 4.90 2.65

Expo '98 Type of 1997

Plankton: 50e, Pilumnus hirtellus. 85e, Lophius piscatorius. 100e, Sparus aurata. 140e, Cladonema radiatum.

No. 2219: a, Noctiluca miliaris. b, Dinophysis acuta.

1998, Mar. 20 *Perf. 12*
2215 A612 50e multicolored .55 .30
2216 A612 85e multicolored .95 .50
2217 A612 100e multicolored 1.10 .55
2218 A612 140e multicolored 1.60 .80
Nos. 2215-2218 (4) 4.20 2.15

Souvenir Sheet

2219 A612 100e Sheet of 2, #a.-b. 2.25 1.10
c. Sheet of 12, #2196-2199, 2200a-2200b, 2215-2218, 2219a-2219b 13.00 6.50

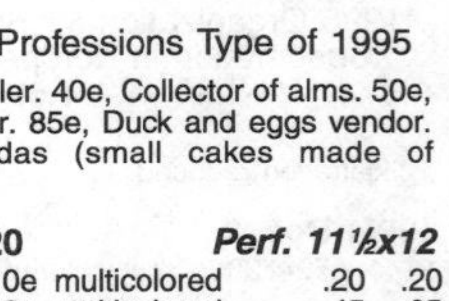

Opening of the Vasco Da Gama Bridge A618

1998, Mar. 29 Litho. *Perf. 12*
2220 A618 200e multicolored 2.25 1.10

Souvenir Sheet

2221 A618 200e like #2220 2.25 1.10

Stamp in No. 2221 is a continuous design and shows bridge cables overlapping at far left.

Oporto Industrial Assoc., 150th Anniv. A619

1998, Apr. 30
2222 A619 80e multicolored .90 .45

Vasco da Gama Aquarium, Cent. A620

1998, May 13
2223 A620 50e Seahorse .55 .30
2224 A620 80e Fish .90 .45

National Festivals A621

1998, May 21
2225 A621 100e People's Saints 1.00 .55
a. Souvenir sheet of 3 3.00 1.75

Europa.

Expo '98 Type of 1997

Designs: No. 2226, Portuguese sailing ship, face on stone cliff. No. 2227, Diver, astrolabe. No. 2228, Various fish. No. 2229, Research submersible, fish. No. 2230, Mermaid swimming. No. 2231, Children under water holding globe.

No. 2232: a, Portuguese Pavilion. b, Pavilion of the Future. c, Oceans Pavilion. d, Knowledge of the Seas Pavilion. e, Pavilion of Utopia. f, Mascot putting letter into mailbox.

No. 2233, like #2216. No. 2234, like #2219a. No. 2235, like #2215. No. 2236, like #2217. No. 2237, like #2219b. No. 2238, like #2218.

No. 2239, like #2227. No. 2240, like #2229. No. 2241, like #2231. No. 2242, like #2226. No. 2243, like #2228. No. 2244, like #2230.

1998, May 21
2226 A612 50e multicolored .55 .30
2227 A612 50e multicolored .55 .30
2228 A612 85e multicolored .95 .45
2229 A612 85e multicolored .95 .45
2230 A612 140e multicolored 1.50 .75
2231 A612 140e multicolored 1.50 .75
a. Sheet of 6, #2226-2231 6.00 3.00

Sheet of 6

2232 #a.-f. 6.50 3.25
a. A612 50e multicolored .55 .30
b.-c. A612 85e any single .95 .45
d.-e. A612 140e any single 1.50 .75
f. A612 80e multicolored .90 .45
g. Souvenir sheet, #2232a-2232e 5.50 2.75

Die Cut 11½

Self-Adhesive Coil Stamps

Size: 29x24mm

2233 A612 50e multicolored .55 .30
2234 A612 50e multicolored .55 .30
2235 A612 50e multicolored .55 .30
2236 A612 50e multicolored .55 .30
2237 A612 50e multicolored .55 .30
2238 A612 50e multicolored .55 .30
a. Strip of 6, #2233-2238 3.30
2239 A612 85e multicolored .95 .45
2240 A612 85e multicolored .95 .45
2241 A612 85e multicolored .95 .45
2242 A612 85e multicolored .95 .45
2243 A612 85e multicolored .95 .45
2244 A612 85e multicolored .95 .45
a. Strip of 6, #2239-2244 5.75

Nos. 2233-2238 are not inscribed with Latin names.

Discovery of Radium, Cent. — A622

1998, June 1 ***Perf. 12***
2245 A622 140e Marie Curie 1.60 .80

Ferreira de Castro (1898-1974), Writer — A623

1998, June 10
2246 A623 50e multicolored .55 .30

Bernardo Marques, Writer, Birth Cent. — A624

1998, June 10
2247 A624 85e multicolored .95 .45

Souvenir Sheet

Universal Declaration of Human Rights, 50th Anniv. — A625

Illustration reduced.

1998, June 18
2248 A625 315e multicolored 3.50 1.75

District Arms Type of 1997

1998, June 23
2249 A609 50e Vila Real .55 .30
2250 A609 85e Setubal .95 .45
2251 A609 85e Viana do Castelo .95 .45
2252 A609 100e Santarem 1.10 .55
2253 A609 100e Viseu 1.10 .55
a. Souvenir sheet of 3, #2250, 2252-2253 3.25 1.60
2254 A609 200e Porto 2.25 1.10
a. Souvenir sheet of 3, #2249, 2251, 2254 3.75 1.90
Nos. 2249-2254 (6) 6.90 3.40

Marinha Grande Glass Industry, 250th Anniv. A626

Designs: 50e, Blowing glass, furnace. 80e, Early worker heating glass, ornament. 100e, Factory, bottles. 140e, Modern worker heating glass, vases.

1998, July 7
2255 A626 50e multicolored .55 .30
2256 A626 80e multicolored .90 .45
2257 A626 100e multicolored 1.10 .55
2258 A626 140e multicolored 1.60 .80
Nos. 2255-2258 (4) 4.15 2.10

1998 Vasco da Gama Regatta A627

Sailing ship, country represented: 50e, Sagres, Portugal. No. 2260, Asgard II, Ireland. No. 2261, Rose, US. No. 2262, Kruzenshtern, Russia. No. 2263, Amerigo Vespucci, Italy. 140e, Creoula, Portugal.

1998, July 31
2259 A627 50e multicolored .55 .30
2260 A627 85e multicolored .95 .45
2261 A627 85e multicolored .95 .45
2262 A627 100e multicolored 1.10 .55
2263 A627 100e multicolored 1.10 .55
2264 A627 140e multicolored 1.60 .80
Nos. 2259-2264 (6) 6.25 3.10

Discovery of Maritime Route to India Type of 1996

Voyage of Vasco da Gama: No. 2265, Meeting with pilot, Ibn Madjid. 80e, Storm in the Indian Ocean. 100e, Arrival in Calicut. 140e, Meeting with the Samorin of Calicut.

No. 2269: a, like #2136. b, like #2137. c, like #2138. d, like #2139. e, like #2191. f, like #2192. g, like #2193. h, like #2194. i, like #2266. j, like #2267. k, like #2268.

315e, King of Melinde listening to narration of the history of Portugal.

1998, Sept. 4 ***Perf. 13½***
2265 A593 50e multicolored .55 .30
2266 A593 80e multicolored .90 .45
2267 A593 100e multicolored 1.10 .55
2268 A593 140e multicolored 1.60 .80
Nos. 2265-2268 (4) 4.15 2.10

Sheet of 12

2269 A593 50e #a.-k. + #2265 6.75 3.50

Souvenir Sheet

2270 A593 315e multicolored 3.75 1.90

Lisbon-Coimbra Mail Coach, Decree to Reorganize Maritime Mail to Brazil, Bicent. — A628

50e, Modern van delivering mail, postal emblm. 140e, Sailing ship, Postilhao da America, mail coach.

1998, Oct. 9 ***Perf. 12x11½***
2271 A628 50e multicolored .55 .30
2272 A628 140e multicolored 1.60 .80

See Brazil No. 2691.

Souvenir Sheet

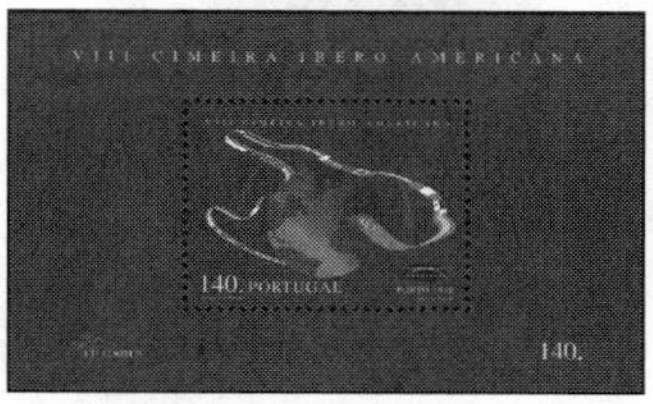

8th Iberian-American Summit, Oporto — A629

Illustration reduced.

1998, Oct. 18 ***Perf. 12½***
2273 A629 140e multicolored 1.60 .80

Souvenir Sheet

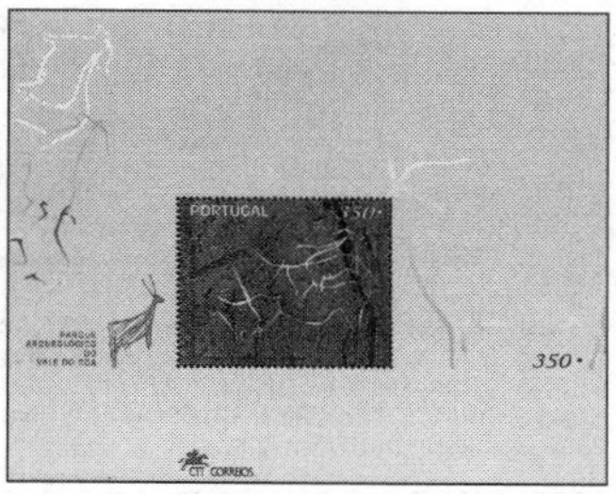

Coa Valley Archaeological Park — A630

1998, Oct. 23 ***Perf. 13½***
2274 A630 350e multicolored 4.00 2.00

Health in Portugal — A631

1998, Nov. 5 ***Perf. 12***
2275 A631 100e multicolored 1.10 .55

Souvenir Sheet

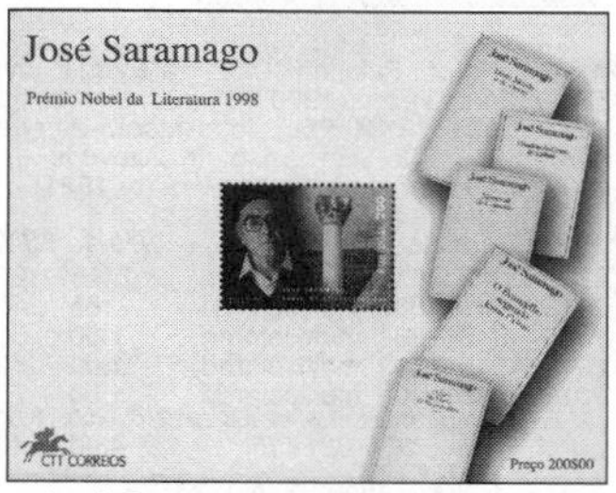

José Saramago, 1998 Nobel Prize Winner for Literature — A632

1998, Dec. 15 **Litho.** ***Perf. 12***
2276 A632 200e multicolored 2.25 1.10

Postrider Type of 1993

1999, Jan. 11 **Litho.** ***Perf. 13¼***
2276A A521 A brown, gray & black .60 .30

No. 2276A sold for 51e on date of issue. Inscription at LR reads "Imp : Lito Maia 99."

19th Cent. Professions Type

Designs: 51e, Knife grinder. 86e, Female bread seller. 95e, Coachman. 100e, Milkmaid. 210e, Basket seller.

1999, Feb. 26 **Litho.** ***Perf. 11½x12***
2277 A560 51e multicolored .55 .25
2278 A560 86e multicolored .90 .45
2279 A560 95e multicolored 1.00 .50
2280 A560 100e multicolored 1.10 .55
2281 A560 210e multicolored 2.25 1.10
Nos. 2277-2281 (5) 5.80 2.85

Booklet Stamps
Self-Adhesive
Serpentine Die Cut 11¼

2281A A560 51e like #2277 .55 .25
c. Booklet pane of 10 5.50
2281B A560 95e like #2279 1.00 .50
d. Booklet pane of 10 10.00

Nos. 2281Ac, 2281Bd are complete booklets. The peelable backing serves as a booklet cover.

Beginning with No. 2282 denominations are on the stamps in both escudos and euros. Listings show the value in escudos.

Introduction of the Euro — A633

1999, Mar. 15 ***Perf. 12***
2282 A633 95e multicolored 1.00 .50

Australia '99, World Stamp Expo — A634

Portuguese in Australia: No. 2283, Sailing ship offshore, kangaroos. No. 2284, Sailing ship, natives watching.

350e, like #2283-2284.

1999, Mar. 19
2283 140e multicolored 1.50 .75
2284 140e multicolored 1.50 .75
a. A634 Pair, #2283-2284 3.00 1.50

Souvenir Sheet

2285 A634 350e multicolored 3.75 1.90

No. 2285 contains one 80x30mm stamp and is a continuous design.

Presidential Campaign of José Norton de Matos, 50th Anniv. — A635

1999, Mar. 24
2286 A635 80e multicolored .85 .45

Joao Almeida Garrett (1799-1854), Writer — A636

1999, Mar. 24
2287 A636 95e multicolored 1.00 .50

Souvenir Sheet

2288 A636 210e like #2287 2.25 1.10

Flight Between Portugal and Macao, 75th Anniv. A637

Airplanes: No. 2289, Breguet 16 Bn2, "Patria." No. 2290, DH9.

1999, Apr. 19
2289 A637 140e multicolored 1.50 .75
2290 A637 140e multicolored 1.50 .75
a. Souvenir sheet, #2289-2290 3.00 1.50

A638

Revolution, 25th Anniv. — A639

Illustration reduced (#2292).

1999, Apr. 25

2291 A638 51e Carnation .55 .25
2292 A639 80e Assembly building .85 .45
a. Souvenir sheet, #2291-2292 1.40 .70

Council of Europe, 50th Anniv. A640

1999, May 5 Litho. *Perf. 12x11¾*

2293 A640 100e multicolored 1.00 .50

Europa A641

1999, May 5

2294 A641 100e Wolf, iris, Peneda-Gerês Natl. Park 1.00 .50
a. Souvenir sheet of 3 3.00 3.00

Marquis de Pombal (1699-1782), Statesman — A642

No. 2295: 80e, Portrait.
No. 2296: a, 80e, Portrait and portion of statue. b, 210e, Hand, quill pen.

1999, May 13

2295 A642 80e multicolored .85 .40

Souvenir Sheet

2296 A642 Sheet of 2, #a.-b. 3.00 3.00

Meeting of Portuguese and Chinese Cultures in Macao — A643

Designs: 51e, Ship, junk, bridge. 80e, Macao dancers in Portuguese outfits. 95e, Virgin Mary statue, dragon heads. 100e, Church, temple. 140e, Statues in park, horiz.

Perf. 11¾x12, 12x11¾

1999, June 24 Litho.

2297 A643 51e multicolored .55 .25
2298 A643 80e multicolored .85 .40
2299 A643 95e multicolored 1.00 .50
2300 A643 100e multicolored 1.00 .50
2301 A643 140e multicolored 1.50 .75
Nos. 2297-2301 (5) 4.90 2.40

Portuguese Air Force, 75th Anniv. A644

Designs: No. 2302, De Havilland DH 82A Tiger Moth. No. 2303, Supermarine Spitfire Vb. No. 2304, Breguet Bre XIV A2. No. 2305, Spad S. VII-C1. No. 2306, Caudron G.III. No. 2307, Junkers Ju-52/3m g3e.

1999, July 1 *Perf. 12x11¾*

2302 A644 51e multicolored .55 .25
2303 A644 51e multicolored .55 .25
2304 A644 85e multicolored .90 .45
2305 A644 85e multicolored .90 .45
2306 A644 95e multicolored 1.00 .50
2307 A644 95e multicolored 1.00 .50
a. Souv. sheet of 6, #2302-2307 5.00 5.00
Nos. 2302-2307 (6) 4.90 2.40

Surrealist Group of Lisbon, 50th Anniv. A645

Sections of Painting "Cadavre Exquis" by: 51e, António Pedro (1909-66). 80e, Marcellino Vespeira (b. 1926). 95e, Joao Moniz Pereira (1920-89). 100e, Fernando de Azevedo (b. 1923). 140e, António Domingues (b. 1921).

1999, July 2 Litho. *Perf. 13¼*

2308 A645 51e multicolored .55 .25
2309 A645 80e multicolored .85 .40
2310 A645 95e multicolored 1.00 .50
2311 A645 100e multicolored 1.00 .50
2312 A645 140e multicolored 1.50 .75
a. Souv. sheet of 5, #2308-2312 5.00 5.00
Nos. 2308-2312 (5) 4.90 2.40

PhilexFrance 99, No. 2312a.

Inauguration of Rail Link Over 25th of April Bridge — A646

51e, No. 2315, Train, tunnel entrance. 95e, No. 2316, Train, viaduct, Tagus River.

1999, July 29 Litho. *Perf. 12x11¾*

2313 A646 51e multicolored .55 .25
2314 A646 95e multicolored 1.00 .50

Souvenir Sheets

2315 A646 350e multicolored 3.75 3.75
2316 A646 350e multicolored 3.75 3.75

Nos. 2315-2316 each contain one 80x30mm stamp.

UPU, 125th Anniv. A647

Designs: 95e, Heinrich von Stephan, earth, letter. 140e, Computer, earth, letter. 315e, Von Stephan, computer, earth, letters.

1999, Aug. 21

2317 A647 95e multicolored 1.00 .50
2318 A647 140e multicolored 1.50 .75

Souvenir Sheet

2319 A647 315e multicolored 3.25 3.25

No. 2319 contains one 80x30mm stamp.

Desserts Originating in Convents A648

Designs: 51e, Trouxas de ovos. 80e, Pudim de ovos (egg pudding). 95e, Papos de anjo. 100e, Palha de Abrantes. 140e, Castanhas de Viseu. 210e, Bolo de mel (honey cake).

1999, Aug. 30

2320 A648 51e multicolored .55 .25
2321 A648 80e multicolored .85 .40
2322 A648 95e multicolored 1.00 .50
2323 A648 100e multicolored 1.00 .50
2324 A648 140e multicolored 1.50 .75
2325 A648 210e multicolored 2.25 1.10
Nos. 2320-2325 (6) 7.15 3.50

See Nos. 2366-2371.

Conquest of Algarve, 750th Anniv. A649

1999, Sept. 3 Litho. *Perf. 12x11¾*

2326 A649 100e multi .95 .50

Medical Pioneers A650

#2327, Ricardo Jorge (1858-1939), Natl. Health Inst. #2328, Camara Pestana (1863-99), microscope, Pestana Bacteriological Inst. #2329, Francisco Gentil (1878-1964), Portuguese Inst. of Oncology. #2330, Egas Moniz (1874-1955), cerebral angiogram. #2331, Reynaldo dos Santos (1880-1970), arteriogram. #2332, Joao Cid dos Santos (1907-76), performer of 1st endarterectomy.

1999, Sept. 20

2327 A650 51e multi .50 .25
2328 A650 51e multi .50 .25
2329 A650 80e multi .75 .40
2330 A650 80e multi .75 .40
2331 A650 95e multi .90 .45
2332 A650 95e multi .90 .45
Nos. 2327-2332 (6) 4.30 2.20

José Diogo de Mascarenhas Neto, First Superintendent of Posts — A651

1999, Oct. 9

2333 A651 80e multi .75 .40

Postal reorganization and provisional mail regulations, bicent.

Jaime Martins Barata (1899-1970), Painter, Philatelic Art Consultant — A652

1999, Oct. 9

2334 A652 80e multi .75 .40

Christmas A653

Art by handicapped persons: 51e, Maria F. Gonçalves (Magi). 95e, Marta Silva. 140e, Luis F. Farinha. 210e, Gonçalves (Nativity).

1999, Nov. 19

2335 A653 51e multi .50 .25
2336 A653 95e multi .90 .45
2337 A653 140e multi 1.40 .65
2338 A653 210e multi 2.00 1.00
Nos. 2335-2338 (4) 4.80 2.35

Souvenir Sheet

Meeting of Portuguese and Chinese Cultures — A654

1999, Nov. 19 *Perf. 11¾x12*

2339 A654 140e multi 1.40 .65

See Macao No. 1009.

Souvenir Sheet

Retrospective of Macao's Portuguese History — A655

1999, Dec. 19 Litho. *Perf. 12x11¾*

2340 A655 350e multi 3.50 1.75

See Macao No. 1011.

Birth of Jesus Christ, 2000th Anniv. — A656

2000, Feb. 15 Litho. *Perf. 11¾x12*

2341 A656 52e multi .50 .25

The 20th Century A657

Designs: 86e, Astronaut and spacecraft.

No. 2343: a, Human rights. b, Fashions (60x30mm). c, Ecology (60x30mm). d, Transportation (old). e, Transportation (modern). f, Like No. 2342. g, Space shuttle.

No. 2344: a, Authors Marcel Proust, Thomas Mann, James Joyce, Franz Kafka, Fernando Pessoa, Jorge Luis Borges, Samuel Beckett (50x30mm). b, Musicians and composers Claude Debussy, Igor Stravinsky, Arnold Schoenberg, Béla Bartók, George Gershwin, Charlie Parker, Bill Evans (50x30mm). c, Stage. d, Stage, diff. (60x30mm). e, Art (50x30mm). f, Art (30x30mm). g. Cinema (50x30mm). h, Cinema and television (30x30mm). i, Architecture (denomination at LL). j, Architecture (denomination at LR). k, Architecture (denomination at center).

No. 2345: a, Philosophers Edmund Husserl, Ludwig Wittgenstein, Martin Heidegger. b, Mathematicians Jules-Henri Poincaré, Kurt Gödel, Andrei Kolmogorov. c, Physicists Max Planck, Albert Einstein, Niels Bohr (50x30mm). d, Anthropologists Franz Boas, Claude Lévi-Strauss, Margaret Mead. e, Psychoanalyst Sigmund Freud and medical researcher Sir Alexander Fleming (30x30mm). f, Transplant pioneer Dr. Christiaan Barnard. g, Economists Joseph Schumpeter, John Maynard Keynes. h, Technology. i, Technology (30x30mm). j, Computer pioneers Alan Turing, John von Neumann. k, Radio pioneer Guglielmo Marconi. l, Information and communications (30x30mm).

2000, Feb. 18 ***Perf. 12x11¾***

2342 A657 86e multi	.80	.40

Souvenir Sheets of 7, 11, 12

2343 A657 52e #a.-g.	3.50	1.75
2344 A657 52e #a.-k.	5.50	2.75
2345 A657 52e #a.-l.	6.00	3.00

Birds — A658

Designs: 52e, Golden eagle. 85e, Great crested grebe. 90e, Flamingo. 100e, Gannet. 215e, Teal.

2000, Mar. 2 Litho. ***Perf. 11¾x11½***

2346 A658 52e multi	.50	.25
2347 A658 85e multi	.80	.40
2348 A658 90e multi	.85	.45
2349 A658 100e multi	.95	.50
2350 A658 215e multi	2.00	1.00
Nos. 2346-2350 (5)	5.10	2.60

Booklet Stamps

Serpentine Die Cut 11¼

Self-Adhesive

2351 A658 52e Like #2346	.50	.25
a. Booklet, 10 #2351	5.00	
2352 A658 100e Like #2349	.95	.50
a. Booklet, 10 #2352	9.50	

See Nos. 2401-2407.

Portuguese Presidency of Council of Europe A659

2000, Mar. 23 ***Perf. 12x11¾***

2353 A659 100e multi	.95	.50

Discovery of Brazil, 500th Anniv. A660

Designs: 52e, Two sailors, three natives, parrot. 85e, sailor, ships, four natives. 100e, Sailors, natives, sails. 140e, Sailor and natives inspecting tree.

2000, Apr. 11 Litho. ***Perf. 12x11¾***

2354 A660 52e multi	.50	.25
2355 A660 85e multi	.80	.40
2356 A660 100e multi	.95	.50
2357 A660 140e multi	1.25	.60
a. Souvenir sheet, #2354-2357	3.50	1.75
Nos. 2354-2357 (4)	3.50	1.75

Lubrapex 2000 (#2357a). See Brazil No. 2738.

Europa, 2000

Common Design Type

2000, May 9 ***Perf. 11¾x12***

2358 CD17 100e multi	.95	.50
a. Souvenir sheet of 3	3.00	1.50

Visit of Pope John Paul II A661

2000, May 12 ***Perf. 12x11¾***

2359 A661 52e multi	.50	.25

Intl. Cycling Union, Cent. and The Stamp Show 2000, London A662

Bicycles: 52e, Draisenne, 1817. 85e, Michaux, 1868. 100e, Ariel, 1871. 140e, Rover, 1888. 215e, BTX, 2000. 350e, GT, 2000.

2000, May 22

2360 A662 52e multi	.50	.25
2361 A662 85e multi	.80	.40
2362 A662 100e multi	.95	.50
2363 A662 140e multi	1.25	.60
2364 A662 215e multi	2.00	1.00
2365 A662 350e multi	3.25	1.60
a. Souvenir sheet, #2360-2365	8.75	4.50
Nos. 2360-2365 (6)	8.75	4.35

Desserts Type of 1999

Designs: 52e, Fatias de Tomar. 85e, Dom rodrigos. 100e, Sericaia. 140e, Pao-de-ló. 215e, Pao de rala. 350e, Bolo real paraíso.

2000, May 30

2366 A648 52e multi	.50	.25
2367 A648 85e multi	.80	.40
2368 A648 100e multi	.95	.50
2369 A648 140e multi	1.25	.60
2370 A648 215e multi	2.00	1.00
2371 A648 350e multi	3.25	1.60
Nos. 2366-2371 (6)	8.75	4.35

Fishermen's Day — A663

2000, May 31

2372 A663 52e multi	.50	.25

Expo 2000, Hanover — A664

Illustration reduced.

Designs: 100e, Portuguese landscapes. 350e, Portuguese pavilion.

2000, June 1

2373 A664 100e multi	.95	.50

Souvenir Sheet

2374 A664 350e multi	3.25	1.60

No. 2374 contains one 40x31mm stamp.

Constituent Assembly, 25th Anniv. A665

2000, June 2

2375 A665 85e multi	.80	.40

Cod Fishing A666

Cod, various fishermen and boats.

2000, June 24 ***Perf. 12x11¾***

Color of Denominations

2376 A666 52e rose	.50	.25
2377 A666 85e claret	.80	.40
2378 A666 100e green	.95	.50
2379 A666 100e red	.95	.50
2380 A666 140e yellow	1.25	.60
2381 A666 215e brown	2.00	1.00
a. Souvenir sheet, #2376-2381	6.50	3.25
Nos. 2376-2381 (6)	6.45	3.25

Eça de Queiroz (1845-1900), Writer — A667

2000, Aug. 16 Litho. ***Perf. 12x11¾***

2382 A667 85e multi	.80	.40

2000 Summer Olympics, Sydney A668

Designs: 52e, Runner. 85e, Show jumping. 100e, Yachting. 140e, Diving.

No. 2387: a, 85e, Fencing. b, 215e, Beach volleyball.

2000, Sept. 15

2383-2386 A668 Set of 4	3.50	1.75

Souvenir Sheet

2387 A668 Sheet of 2, #a-b	3.00	1.50

Olymphilex 2000, Sydney (No. 2387).

Snoopy A669

Snoopy: No. 2388, 52e, At computer on dog house. No. 2389, 52e, Mailing letter. 85e, Driving mail truck. 100e, At letter sorting machine. 140e, Delivering mail. 215e, Reading letter.

2000, Oct. 6

2388-2393 A669 Set of 6	6.00	3.00
2393a Souvenir sheet, #2393a	6.00	3.00

Lisbon Geographic Society, 125th Anniv. — A670

No. 2394: a, 85e, African native, geographer, theodolite, sextant. b, 100e, Sextant, society emblem, map, zebras.

Illustration reduced.

2000, Nov. 10

2394 A670 Horiz. pair, #a-b	1.75	.90

Famous People — A671

No. 2395: a, Carolina Michaelis de Vasconcellos (1851-1925), teacher. b, Miguel Bombarda (1851-1910), doctor, politician. c, Bernardino Machado (1851-1944), politician. d, Tomás Alcaide (1901-67), singer. e, José Régio (1901-69), writer. f, José Rodrigues Miguéis (1901-80), writer. g, Vitorino Nemésio (1901-78), writer. h, Bento de Jesus Caraça (1901-48), writer.

2001, Feb. 20 Litho. ***Perf. 12x11¾***

2395 Sheet of 8 + 4 labels	6.00	3.00
a.-h. A671 85e Any single	.75	.35

World Indoor Track and Field Championships — A672

Designs: 85e, Runners. 90e, Pole vault. 105e, Shot put. 250e, High jump.

2001, Mar. 1

2396-2399 A672 Set of 4	4.75	2.40

Souvenir Sheet

2400 A672 350e Hurdles	3.25	1.60

Bird Type of 2000 and

A672a

Designs: 53e, Sisao. No. 2402, Caimao. 105e, Perdiz-do-mar. 140e, Peneireiro cinzento. 225e, Abutre do Egipto.

2001, Mar. 6 Litho. ***Perf. 11¾x11½***

2401 A658 53e multi	.50	.25
2402 A658 85e multi	.80	.40
2403 A658 105e multi	.95	.45
2404 A658 140e multi	1.25	.65
2405 A658 225e multi	2.00	1.00
Nos. 2401-2405 (5)	5.50	2.75

Serpentine Die Cut 11½x12

Self-Adhesive

2406 A658 53e multi	.50	.25
a. Booklet of 10	5.00	
2406B A672a 85e shown	.80	.40
2407 A658 105e multi	.95	.45
a. Booklet of 10	9.50	

Arab Heritage in Portugal A673

Designs: 53e, Plate with ship design, 15th cent. 90e, Tiles, 16th cent. 105e, Tombstone, 14th cent. 140e, Gold dinar, 12th cent. 225e, container, 11th cent. 350e, Ceramic jug, 12th-13th cent.

2001, Mar. 28 Litho. ***Perf. 12x11¾***

2408-2413 A673 Set of 6	8.75	4.50

Stampin' the Future Children's Stamp Design Contest Winners A674

Art by: 85e, Angela M. Lopes. 90e, Maria G. Silva, vert. 105e, Joao A. Ferreira.

Perf. 12x11¾, 11¾x12

2001, Apr. 10 **Litho.**
2414-2416 A674 Set of 3 2.50 1.25

Natl. Fine Arts Society, Cent. A675

Designs: 85e, Sculpture, building, stained glass window. 105e, Artist, painting.
350p, Hen and Chicks, by Girao.

2001, Apr. 19 ***Perf. 12x11¾***
2417-2418 A675 Set of 2 1.75 .85

Souvenir Sheet

2419 A675 350e multi 3.25 3.25

Constitution, 25th Anniv. — A676

2001, Apr. 25
2420 A676 85e multi .75 .35

Europa A677

2001, May 9
2421 A677 105e multi .90 .45
a. Souvenir sheet of 3 2.75 2.75

Congratulations A678

Designs: No. 2422, 85e, Couple, hearts. No. 2423, 85e, Birthday cake. No. 2424, 85e, Drinks. No. 2425, 85e, Flowers.

2001, May 16 ***Perf. 11¾x12***
2422-2425 A678 Set of 4 3.00 1.50
2425a Souvenir sheet, #2422-2425 3.00 3.00

Porto, European City of Culture A679

Bridge and: 53e, Open book. 85e, Globe, binary code. 105e, Piano. 140e, Stage curtain. 225e, Picture frame. 350e, Fireworks.

2001, May 23 ***Perf. 12x11¾***
2426-2431 A679 Set of 6 8.25 4.25
2431a Souvenir sheet, #2426-2431 8.25 8.25

Military Museum, 150th Anniv. A680

Designs: 85e, Shell, 1773. 105e, Suit of armor, 16th cent.
No. 2434: a, 53e, Pistol of King Joseph I, 1757. b, 53e, Cannon, 1797. c, 140e, Cannon, 1533. d, 140e, Helmet, 14th-15th cent.

2001, June 7
2432-2433 A680 Set of 2 1.60 .80

Souvenir Sheet

2434 A680 Sheet of 4, #a-d 3.50 3.50

Animals at Lisbon Zoo A681

Designs: 53e, Bear. 85e, Monkey. 90e, Iguana. 105e, Penguin. 225e, Toucan. 350e, Giraffe.
No. 2441, vert.: a, 85e, Elephant. b, 85e, Zebra. c, 225e, Lion. d, 225e, Rhinoceros.

2001, June 11 ***Perf. 12x11¾***
2435-2440 A681 Set of 6 7.75 4.00

Souvenir Sheet

2441 A681 Sheet of 4, #a-d 5.50 5.50

Belgica 2001 Intl. Stamp Exhibition, Brussels (#2441).

2001 Lions Intl. European Forum A682

2001, Sept. 6 **Litho.** ***Perf. 12x11¾***
2442 A682 85e multi .80 .40

Pillars A683

No. 2443: a, Azinhoso. b, Soajo. c, Bragança. d, Linhares. e, Arcos de Valdevez. f, Vila de Rua. g, Sernancelhe. h, Frechas.

2001, Sept. 19
2443 Block of 8 4.00 2.00
a.-h. A683 53e Any single .50 .25

Year of Dialogue Among Civilizations A684

2001, Oct. 9
2444 A684 140e multi 1.25 .65

Walt Disney (1901-66) A685

Designs: No. 2445, Disney and sketches.
No. 2446 - Various tiles and: a, Huey, Dewey and Louie. b, Mickey Mouse. c, Minnie Mouse. d, Goofy. e, Pluto. f, Donald Duck. g, Scrooge McDuck. h, Daisy Duck.

2001, Oct. 18 **Litho.** ***Perf. 12x11¾***
2445 A685 53e multi .50 .25

Souvenir Sheet

2446 Sheet of 9, #a-h, 2445 4.50 4.50
a.-h. A685 53e Any single .50 .25

Security Services, 200th Anniv. A686

Designs: 53e, Royal police guards, Lisbon, 1801. 85e, Municipal guard, Lisbon, 1834. 90e, National infantry guard, 1911. 105e, National cavalry guard, 1911. 140e, Transit brigade guard, 1970. 350e, Fiscal brigade guard, 1993.
225e, National cavalry guard, 1911, diff.

2001, Oct. 22
2447-2452 A686 Set of 6 7.50 3.75

Souvenir sheet

2453 A686 225e multi 2.00 2.00

Sailing Ships — A687

No. 2454: a, Chinese junk, 13th cent. b, Portuguese caravel, 15th cent.
Illustration reduced.

2001, Nov. 8
2454 A687 53e Horiz. pair, #a-b .95 .45

See People's Republic of China No. 3146.

100 Cents = 1 Euro (€)

Introduction of the Euro A688

2002, Jan. 2 **Litho.** ***Perf. 12x11¾***

2455	A688	1c	1c coin	.20	.20
2456	A688	2c	2c coin	.20	.20
2457	A688	5c	5c coin	.20	.20
2458	A688	10c	10c coin	.20	.20
2459	A688	20c	20c coin	.35	.35
2460	A688	50c	50c coin	.85	.85
2461	A688	€1	€1 coin	1.75	1.75
2462	A688	€2	€2 coin	3.50	3.50
			Nos. 2455-2462 (8)	7.25	7.25

Postrider A689

2002, Jan. 2 ***Perf. 13¼***
2463 A689 A multi .50 .50

No. 2463 sold for 28c on day of issue.

Damiao de Góis (1502-74), Diplomat and Historian — A690

Illustration reduced.

2002, Feb. 26 ***Perf. 12x11¾***
2464 A690 45c multi .80 .80

Bird Type of 2000 With Euro Denominations Only

Designs: 2c, Abelharuco. 28c, Andorinha do mar ana. 43c, Bufo real. 54c, Cortiçol de barriga branca. 60c, Noitibó de nuca vermelha. 70c, Cuco rabilongo.

2002, Feb. 26 ***Perf. 11¾x11½***

2465	A658	2c	multi	.20	.20
2466	A658	28c	multi	.50	.50
2467	A658	43c	multi	.75	.75
2468	A658	54c	multi	.95	.95
2469	A658	60c	multi	1.00	1.00
2470	A658	70c	multi	1.25	1.25
			Nos. 2465-2470 (6)	4.65	4.65

Pedro Nunes (1502-78), Mathematician and Geographer — A691

Designs: No. 2474, 28c, Ship, Earth. No. 2475, 28c, Ship, sextant. €1.15, Nunes.

2002, Mar. 6 ***Perf. 12x11¾***
2474-2476 A691 Set of 3 3.00 3.00
2476a Souvenir sheet, #2474-2476 3.00 3.00

America Issue - Youth, Education and Literacy A692

Children and: No. 2477, 70c, Flower. No. 2478, 70c, Pencil. No. 2479, 70c, Book.

2002, Mar. 12
2477-2479 A692 Set of 3 3.75 3.75

AIR POST STAMPS

Symbol of Aviation AP1

Perf. 12x11½

1936-41 **Unwmk.** **Typo.**

C1	AP1	1.50e	dark blue	.75	.70
C2	AP1	1.75e	red orange	1.25	.70
C3	AP1	2.50e	rose red	1.50	.70
C4	AP1	3e	brt bl ('41)	8.50	10.00
C5	AP1	4e	dp yel grn ('41)	14.00	15.00
C6	AP1	5e	car lake	2.25	.75
C7	AP1	10e	brown lake	3.00	.65
C8	AP1	15e	orange ('41)	9.00	9.00
C9	AP1	20e	black brn	9.00	2.50
C10	AP1	50e	brn vio ('41)	100.00	60.00
			Nos. C1-C10 (10)	149.25	100.00
			Never hinged	300.00	

Nos. C1-C10 exist imperf.

Catalogue values for unused stamps in this section, from this point to the end of the section, are for Never Hinged items.

EXPO Type of Regular Issue

1970, Sept. 16 Litho. *Perf. 13*

C11	A274	3.50e silver & multi	.35	.20

TAP-Airline of Portugal 35th Anniversary AP2

Design: 19e, Jet flying past sun.

1979, Sept. 21 Litho. *Perf. 12x11½*

C12	AP2	16e multicolored	.35	.35
C13	AP2	19e multicolored	.45	.45

POSTAGE DUE STAMPS

Vasco da Gama Issue

The Zamorin of Calicut Receiving Vasco da Gama — D1

Unwmk.

1898, May 1 Typo. *Perf. 12*

Denomination in Black

J1	D1	5r black	3.00	1.50
a.		Value and "Continente" omitted	10.00	5.00
J2	D1	10r lilac & blk	4.00	1.75
J3	D1	20r orange & blk	6.50	2.25
J4	D1	50r slate & blk	52.50	9.00
J5	D1	100r car & blk, *pink*	87.50	32.50
J6	D1	200r brn & blk, *buff*	92.50	42.50
		Nos. J1-J6 (6)	246.00	89.50

For overprints and surcharges see Nos. 193-198.

D2

D3

1904 *Perf. 11½x12*

J7	D2	5r brown	.45	.50
J8	D2	10r orange	3.00	.70
a.		Imperf.	—	
J9	D2	20r lilac	8.75	2.75
J10	D2	30r gray green	5.75	2.25
J11	D2	40r gray violet	7.00	2.25
J12	D2	50r carmine	52.50	3.75
a.		Imperf.		
J13	D2	100r dull blue	8.75	4.50
a.		Imperf.		
		Nos. J7-J13 (7)	86.20	16.70

Preceding Issue Overprinted in Carmine or Green **REPUBLICA**

1910

J14	D2	5r brown	.50	.25
J15	D2	10r orange	.50	.25
J16	D2	20r lilac	1.50	.70
J17	D2	30r gray green	1.40	.25
J18	D2	40r gray violet	1.40	.25
J19	D2	50r carmine (G)	6.00	3.25
J20	D2	100r dull blue	6.50	3.75
		Nos. J14-J20 (7)	17.80	8.70

See note after No. 183.

1915, Mar. 18 Typo.

J21	D3	½c brown	.60	.60
J22	D3	1c orange	.60	.60
J23	D3	2c claret	.60	.60
J24	D3	3c green	.60	.60
J25	D3	4c gray violet	.60	.60
J26	D3	5c carmine	.60	.60
J27	D3	10c dark blue	.60	.60
		Nos. J21-J27 (7)	4.20	4.20

1921-27

J28	D3	½c gray green ('22)	.20	.20
J29	D3	4c gray green ('27)	.20	.20
J30	D3	8c gray green ('23)	.20	.20
J31	D3	10c gray green ('22)	.40	.40
J32	D3	12c gray green	.75	.40
J33	D3	16c gray green ('23)	.75	.40
J34	D3	20c gray green	.75	.40
J35	D3	24c gray green	.75	.40
J36	D3	32c gray green ('23)	.75	.40
J37	D3	36c gray green	2.00	.65
J38	D3	40c gray green ('23)	2.00	.65
J39	D3	48c gray green ('23)	1.00	.50
J40	D3	50c gray green	.60	.50
J41	D3	60c gray green	1.00	.50
J42	D3	72c gray green	1.00	.50
J43	D3	80c gray green ('23)	3.25	3.00
J44	D3	1.20e gray green	2.50	1.50
		Nos. J28-J44 (17)	18.10	10.80

D4

D5

1932-33

J45	D4	5c buff	.40	.40
J46	D4	10c lt blue	.40	.40
J47	D4	20c pink	.80	.60
J48	D4	30c blue green	1.00	.80
J49	D4	40c lt green	1.00	.80
J50	D4	50c gray	1.25	.80
J51	D4	60c rose	2.50	2.00
J52	D4	80c violet brn	5.00	4.00
J53	D4	1.20e gray ol ('33)	7.00	6.00
		Nos. J45-J53 (9)	19.35	15.80

1940, Feb. 1 Unwmk. *Perf. 12½*

J54	D5	5c bister, perf. 14	.20	.50
J55	D5	10c rose lilac	.20	.50
J56	D5	20c dk car rose	.20	.50
J57	D5	30c purple	.20	.50
J58	D5	40c cerise	.20	.50
J59	D5	50c brt blue	.20	.50
J60	D5	60c yellow grn	.20	.50
J61	D5	80c scarlet	.60	.55
J62	D5	1e brown	1.25	.55
J63	D5	2e dk rose vio	1.70	.55
J64	D5	5e org yel, perf. 14	9.50	7.50
a.		Perf. 12½		
		Nos. J54-J64 (11)	14.45	12.65

Nos. J54-J64 were first issued perf. 14. In 1955 all but the 5c were reissued in perf. 12½.

Catalogue values for unused stamps in this section, from this point to the end of the section, are for Never Hinged items.

D6

1967-84 Litho. *Perf. 11½*

J65	D6	10c dp org, red brn & yel	.20	.20
J66	D6	20c bis, dk brn & yel	.20	.20
J67	D6	30c org, red brn & yel	.20	.20
J68	D6	40c ol bis, dk brn & yel	.20	.20
J69	D6	50c ultra, dk bl & bl	.20	.20
J70	D6	60c grnsh bl, dk grn & lt bl	.20	.20
J71	D6	80c bl, dk bl & lt bl	.20	.20
J72	D6	1e vio bl, dk bl & lt bl	.20	.20
J73	D6	2e grn, dk grn & lt grn	.20	.20
J74	D6	3e lt grn, grn & yel ('75)	.20	.20
J75	D6	4e bl grn, dk grn & yel ('75)	.20	.20
J76	D6	5e cl, dp cl & pink	.20	.20
J77	D6	9e vio, dk vio & pink ('75)	.30	.30
J78	D6	10e lil, pur & pale vio ('75)	.30	.30
J79	D6	20e red, brn & pale vio ('75)	.50	.50
J80	D6	40e dp red lil, rose vio & bluish lil ('84)	1.05	1.05
J81	D6	50e lil, brn & pale gray ('84)	1.35	1.35
		Nos. J65-J81 (17)	5.90	5.90

D7

1992-93 Litho. *Perf. 12x11½*

J82	D7	1e multicolored	.20	.20
J83	D7	2e multicolored	.20	.20
J84	D7	5e multicolored	.20	.20
J85	D7	10e multicolored	.20	.20
J86	D7	20e multicolored	.25	.25
J87	D7	50e multicolored	.65	.65
J88	D7	100e multicolored	1.25	1.25
J89	D7	200e multicolored	2.50	2.50
		Nos. J82-J89 (8)	5.45	5.45

Issued: 1e, 2e, 5e, 200e, 10/7/92; 10e, 20e, 50e, 100e, 3/9/93.

Type D7 Inscribed "CTT CORREIOS"

1995

J90	D7	3e multicolored	.20	.20
J91	D7	4e multicolored	.20	.20
J92	D7	9e multicolored	.20	.20
J93	D7	40e multicolored	.55	.55

1995-96

J94	D7	5e multicolored	.20	.20
J95	D7	10e multicolored	.20	.20
J96	D7	20e multicolored	.25	.25
J97	D7	50e multicolored	.60	.60
J98	D7	100e multicolored	1.20	1.20
		Nos. J90-J98 (9)	3.60	3.60

Issued: 3e, 4e, 9e, 40e, 4/20/95; 50e, 5/22/95; 5e, 10e, 20e, 100e, 5/24/96.

This is an expanding set. Numbers will change when complete.

Numerals — D8

2002, Jan. 2 Litho. *Perf. 11¾x11½*

J99	D8	1c multi	.20	.20
J100	D8	2c multi	.20	.20
J101	D8	5c multi	.20	.20
J102	D8	10c multi	.20	.20
J103	D8	25c multi	.40	.40
J104	D8	50c multi	.85	.85
J105	D8	€1 multi	1.75	1.75
		Nos. J99-J105 (7)	3.80	3.80

OFFICIAL STAMPS

No. 567 Overprinted in Black **OFICIAL**

1938 Unwmk. *Perf. 11½*

O1	A113	40c brown	.20	.20

Catalogue values for unused stamps in this section, from this point to the end of the section, are for Never Hinged items.

O1

1952, Sept. Litho. *Perf. 12½*

O2	O1	black & cream	.20	.20

1975, June

O3	O1	black & yellow	1.00	.75

NEWSPAPER STAMPS

N1

Perf. 11½, 12½, 13½

1876 Typo. Unwmk.

P1	N1	2½r bister	14.00	.90
a.		2½r olive green	14.00	.90

Various shades.

PARCEL POST STAMPS

Mercury and Commerce PP1

1920-22 Unwmk. Typo. *Perf. 12*

Q1	PP1	1c lilac brown	.20	.20
Q2	PP1	2c orange	.20	.20
Q3	PP1	5c lt brown	.20	.20
Q4	PP1	10c red brown	.20	.20
Q5	PP1	20c gray blue	.25	.20
Q6	PP1	40c carmine rose	.25	.20
Q7	PP1	50c black	.35	.30
Q8	PP1	60c dk blue ('21)	.35	.30
Q9	PP1	70c gray brn ('21)	1.25	1.25
Q10	PP1	80c ultra ('21)	1.65	1.65
Q11	PP1	90c lt vio ('21)	1.50	1.50
Q12	PP1	1e lt green	1.50	.60
Q13	PP1	2e pale lilac ('22)	4.25	2.00
Q14	PP1	3e olive ('22)	5.00	3.00
Q15	PP1	4e ultra ('22)	14.00	6.00
Q16	PP1	5e gray ('22)	15.00	4.00
Q17	PP1	10e chocolate ('22)	32.50	8.00
		Nos. Q1-Q17 (17)	78.65	29.80

Parcel Post Package PP2

1936 *Perf. 11½*

Q18	PP2	50c olive brown	.20	.20
Q19	PP2	1e bister brown	.20	.20
Q20	PP2	1.50e purple	.25	.20
Q21	PP2	2e carmine lake	1.10	.20
Q22	PP2	2.50e olive green	1.10	.20
Q23	PP2	4.50e brown lake	1.40	.20
Q24	PP2	5e violet	3.50	.25
Q25	PP2	10e orange	4.25	.70
		Nos. Q18-Q25 (8)	12.00	2.15

POSTAL TAX STAMPS

These stamps represent a special fee for the delivery of postal matter on certain days in each year. The money derived from their sale is applied to works of public charity.

Regular Issues Overprinted in Carmine **ASSISTENCIA**

1911, Oct. 4 Unwmk. *Perf. 14½x15*

RA1	A62	10r gray green	7.00	2.00

The 20r carmine of this type was for use on telegrams.

1912, Oct. 4 *Perf. 15x14½*

RA2	A64	1c deep green	5.00	1.65

The 2c carmine of this type was for use on telegrams.

"Lisbon" — PT1

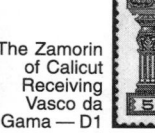

"Charity" — PT2

1913, June 8 Litho. *Perf. 12x11½*

RA3	PT1	1c dark green	.80	.80

The 2c dark brown of this type was for use on telegrams.

1915, Oct. 4 Typo.

RA4	PT2	1c carmine	.40	.30

The 2c plum of this type was for use on telegrams.
See No. RA6.

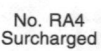

No. RA4 Surcharged

1924, Oct. 4

RA5	PT2	15c on 1c dull red	1.25	.70

The 30c on 2c claret of this type was for use on telegrams.

Charity Type of 1915 Issue

1925, Oct. 4 *Perf. 12½*

RA6	PT2	15c carmine	.25	.20

The 30c brown violet of this type was for use on telegrams.

Comrades of the Great War Issue

Muse of History with Tablet — PT3

1925, Apr. 8 Litho. *Perf. 11*

RA7	PT3	10c brown	.45	.40
RA8	PT3	10c green	.45	.40
RA9	PT3	10c rose	.45	.40
RA10	PT3	10c ultra	.45	.40
		Nos. RA7-RA10 (4)	1.80	1.60

The use of these stamps, in addition to the regular postage, was obligatory on certain days of the year. If the tax represented by these stamps was not prepaid, it was collected by means of Postal Tax Due Stamp No. RAJ1.

Pombal Issue

Common Design Types

Engraved; Value and "Continente" Typographed in Black

1925, May 8 *Perf. 12½*

RA11	CD28	15c ultra	.20	.20
RA12	CD29	15c ultra	.35	.45
RA13	CD30	15c ultra	.35	.45
		Nos. RA11-RA13 (3)	.90	1.10

Olympic Games Issue

Hurdler — PT7

1928 Litho. *Perf. 12*

RA14	PT7	15c dull red & blk	4.00	*6.00*

The use of this stamp, in addition to the regular postage, was obligatory on May 22-24, 1928. 10% of the money thus obtained was retained by the Postal Administration; the balance was given to a Committee in charge of Portuguese participation in the Olympic games at Amsterdam.

POSTAL TAX DUE STAMPS

PTD1

PTD2

Comrades of the Great War Issue

1925 Unwmk. Typo. *Perf. 11x11½*

RAJ1	PTD1	20c brown orange	.90	1.00

See Note after No. RA10.

Pombal Issue

Common Design Types

1925 *Perf. 12½*

RAJ2	CD28	30c ultra	1.00	1.10
RAJ3	CD29	30c ultra	1.00	1.10
RAJ4	CD30	30c ultra	1.00	1.10
		Nos. RAJ2-RAJ4 (3)	3.00	3.30

When the compulsory tax was not paid by the use of stamps #RA11-RA13, double the amount was collected by means of #RAJ2-RAJ4.

Olympic Games Issue

1928 Litho. *Perf. 11½*

RAJ5	PTD2	30c lt red & blk	1.65	*1.75*

FRANCHISE STAMPS

These stamps are supplied by the Government to various charitable, scientific and military organizations for franking their correspondence. This franking privilege was withdrawn in 1938.

FOR THE RED CROSS SOCIETY

F1

Perf. 11½

1889-1915 Unwmk. Typo.

1S1	F1	rose & blk ('15)	1.25	.45
a.		Vermilion & black ('08)	5.00	1.10
b.		Red & black, perf. 12½	67.50	5.00

No. 1S1 Overprinted in Green

COMISSAO PORTUGUESA DOS PRISIONEIROS DE GUERRA

1917

1S3	F1	rose & black	60.00	50.00
a.		Inverted overprint	150.00	150.00

"Charity" Extending Hope to Invalid — F1a

1926 Litho. *Perf. 14*

Inscribed "LISBOA"

1S4	F1a	black & red	6.00	6.00

Inscribed "DELEGACOES"

1S5	F1a	black & red	6.00	6.00

No. 1S4 was for use in Lisbon. No. 1S5 was for the Red Cross chapters outside Lisbon.
For overprints see Nos. 1S72-1S73.

Camoens Issue of 1924 Overprinted in Black or Red

CRUZ VERMELHA
Porte franco
1927

1927

1S6	A68	40c ultra	.90	*.90*
1S7	A68	48c red brown	.90	*.90*
1S8	A69	64c green	.90	*.90*
1S9	A69	75c dk violet	.90	*.90*
1S10	A71	4.50e blk, *org* (R)	.90	*.90*
1S11	A71	10e dk brn, *pnksh*	.90	*.90*
		Nos. 1S6-1S11 (6)	5.40	*5.40*

Camoens Issue of 1924 Overprinted in Red

1928

1S12	A67	15c olive grn	.90	*1.00*
1S13	A67	16c violet brn	.90	*1.00*
1S14	A68	25c lilac	.90	*1.00*
1S15	A68	40c ultra	.90	*1.00*
1S16	A70	1.20e lt brown	.90	*1.00*
1S17	A70	2e apple green	.90	*1.00*
		Nos. 1S12-1S17 (6)	5.40	*6.00*

Camoens Issue of 1924 Overprinted in Red

1929

1S18	A68	30c dk brown	.90	*.90*
1S19	A68	40c ultra	.90	*.90*
1S20	A69	80c bister	.90	*.90*
1S21	A70	1.50e red	.90	*.90*
1S22	A70	1.60e dark blue	.90	*.90*
1S23	A71	2.40e green, *grn*	.90	*.90*
		Nos. 1S18-1S23 (6)	5.40	*5.40*

Same Overprint Dated "1930"

1930

1S24	A68	40c ultra	.90	*.90*
1S25	A69	50c red orange	.90	*.90*
1S26	A69	96c lake	.90	*.90*
1S27	A70	1.60e dk blue	.90	*.90*
1S28	A71	3e dk blue, *bl*	.90	*.90*
1S29	A72	20e dk violet, *lil*	.90	*.90*
		Nos. 1S24-1S29 (6)	5.40	*5.40*

Camoens Issue of 1924 Overprinted in Red

1931

1S30	A68	25c lilac	1.00	*1.00*
1S31	A68	32c dk green	1.00	*1.00*
1S32	A68	40c ultra	1.00	*1.00*
1S33	A69	96c lake	1.00	*1.00*
1S34	A70	1.60e dark blue	1.00	*1.00*
1S35	A71	3.20e black, *green*	1.00	*1.00*
		Nos. 1S30-1S35 (6)	6.00	*6.00*

Same Overprint Dated "1932"

1931

1S36	A67	20c dp orange	1.25	*1.25*
1S37	A68	40c ultra	1.25	*1.25*
1S38	A68	48c red brown	1.25	*1.25*
1S39	A69	64c green	1.25	*1.25*
1S40	A70	1.60e dark blue	1.25	*1.25*
1S41	A71	10e dk brown, *pnksh*	1.25	*1.25*
		Nos. 1S36-1S41 (6)	7.50	*7.50*

Nos. 1S6-1S11 Overprinted in Red

1932

1S42	A68	40c ultra	1.25	*1.40*
1S43	A68	48c red brown	1.25	*1.40*
1S44	A69	64c green	1.25	*1.40*
1S45	A69	75c dk violet	1.25	*1.40*
1S46	A71	4.50e blk, *orange*	1.25	*1.40*
1S47	A71	10e dk brn, *pnksh*	1.25	*1.40*
		Nos. 1S42-1S47 (6)	7.50	*8.40*

Dated "1934"

1933

1S48	A68	40c ultra	1.75	*1.75*
1S49	A68	48c red brown	1.75	*1.75*
1S50	A69	64c green	1.75	*1.75*
1S51	A69	75c dark violet	1.75	*1.75*
1S52	A71	4.50e blk, *orange*	1.75	*1.75*
1S53	A71	10e dk brown, *pnksh*	1.75	*1.75*
		Nos. 1S48-1S53 (6)	10.50	*10.50*

Dated "1935"

1935

1S54	A68	40c ultra	2.25	*2.25*
1S55	A68	48c red brown	2.25	*2.25*
1S56	A69	64c green	2.25	*2.25*
1S57	A69	75c dk violet	2.25	*2.25*
1S58	A71	4.50e black, *orange*	2.25	*2.25*
1S59	A71	10e dk brn, *pnksh*	2.25	*2.25*
		Nos. 1S54-1S59 (6)	13.50	*13.50*

Camoens Issue of 1924 Overprinted in Black or Red

1935

1S60	A68	25c lilac	.90	*.90*
1S61	A68	40c ultra (R)	.90	*.90*
1S62	A69	50c red orange	.90	*.90*
1S63	A70	1e slate	.90	*.90*
1S64	A70	2e apple green	.90	*.90*
1S65	A72	20e dk violet, *lilac*	.90	*.90*
		Nos. 1S60-1S65 (6)	5.40	*5.40*

Camoens Issue of 1924 Overprinted in Red

1936

1S66	A68	30c dk brown	.90	*.90*
1S67	A68	32c dk green	.90	*.90*
1S68	A69	80c bister	.90	*.90*
1S69	A70	1.20e lt brown	.90	*.90*
1S70	A71	3e dk blue, *bl*	.90	*.90*
1S71	A71	4.50e black, *yel*	.90	*.90*
		Nos. 1S66-1S71 (6)	5.40	*5.40*

No. 1S4 Overprinted "1935"

1936 Unwmk. *Perf. 14*

1S72	F1a	black & red	7.00	7.00

Same Stamp with Additional Overprint "Delegacoes"

1S73	F1a	black & red	7.00	7.00

After the government withdrew the franking privilege in 1938, the Portuguese Red Cross Society distributed charity labels which lacked postal validity.

FOR CIVILIAN RIFLE CLUBS

Rifle Club Emblem — F2

Perf. 11½x12

1899-1910 Typo. Unwmk.

2S1	F2	bl grn & car ('99)	10.00	10.00
2S2	F2	brn & yel grn ('00)	10.00	10.00
2S3	F2	car & buff ('01)	1.50	1.50
2S4	F2	bl & org ('02)	1.50	1.50
2S5	F2	grn & org ('03)	1.50	1.50
2S6	F2	lt brn & car ('04)	1.50	1.50
2S7	F2	mar & ultra ('05)	1.50	1.50
2S8	F2	ultra & buff ('06)	1.50	1.50
2S9	F2	choc & yel ('07)	1.50	1.50
2S10	F2	car & ultra ('08)	1.50	1.50
2S11	F2	bl & yel grn ('09)	1.50	1.50
2S12	F2	bl grn & brn, *pink* ('10)	1.50	1.50
		Nos. 2S1-2S12 (12)	35.00	35.00

FOR THE GEOGRAPHICAL SOCIETY OF LISBON

Coat of Arms

F3 F4

1903-34 Unwmk. Litho. *Perf. 11½*

3S1	F3	blk, rose, bl & red	14.00	3.25
3S2	F3	bl, yel, red & grn ('09)	16.00	4.00
3S3	F4	blk, org, bl & red ('11)	2.00	.75
3S4	F4	blk & brn org ('22)	3.50	2.75
3S5	F4	blk & bl ('24)	8.50	4.50
3S6	F4	blk & rose ('26)	5.00	2.25
3S7	F4	blk & grn ('27)	5.00	2.25
3S8	F4	bl, yel & red ('29)	4.25	1.50
3S9	F4	bl, red & vio ('30)	4.25	1.50
3S10	F4	dp bl, lil & red ('31)	4.25	1.50
3S11	F4	bis brn & red ('32)	4.25	1.50
3S12	F4	lt grn & red ('33)	4.25	1.50
3S13	F4	blue & red ('34)	4.25	1.50
		Nos. 3S1-3S13 (13)	79.50	28.75

No. 3S12 with three-line overprint, "C.I.C.I. Portugal 1933," was not valid for postage and was sold only to collectors.

No. 3S2 was reprinted in 1933. Green vertical lines behind "Porte Franco" omitted. Value $7.50.

F5

1934 Litho. *Perf. 11½*

3S15	F5	blue & red	1.50	1.25

1935-38 *Perf. 11*

3S16	F5	blue	6.00	6.00
3S17	F5	dk bl & red ('36)	6.00	2.00
3S18	F5	lil & red ('37)	2.50	1.00
3S19	F5	blk, grn & car ('38)	2.50	1.00
		Nos. 3S16-3S19 (4)	17.00	10.00

The inscription in the inner circle is omitted on Nos. 3S16-3S17.

FOR THE NATIONAL AID SOCIETY FOR CONSUMPTIVES

F10

Perf. 11½x12

1904, July Typo. Unwmk.

4S1	F10	brown & green	4.75	4.00
4S2	F10	carmine & yellow	4.75	4.00

AZORES

Starting in 1980, stamps inscribed Azores and Madeira were valid and sold in Portugal. See Vols. 1 and 4 for prior issues.

Azores No. 2 — A33

Design: 19.50e, Azores No. 6.

1980, Jan. 2 Litho. *Perf. 12*

314	A33 6.50e	multi	.20	.20
315	A33 19.50e	multi	.50	.20
a.		Souvenir sheet of 2, #314-315	2.25	2.00

No. 315a exists overprinted for Capex 87.

Map of Azores A34

1980, Sept. 17 Litho. *Perf. 12x11½*

316	A34	50c shown	.20	.20
317	A34	1e Cathedral	.20	.20
318	A34	5e Windmill	.20	.20
319	A34	6.50e Local women	.20	.20
320	A34	8e Coastline	.20	.20
321	A34	30e Ponta Delgada	.60	.30
		Nos. 316-321 (6)	1.60	1.30

World Tourism Conf., Manila, Sept. 27.

Europa Issue 1981

St. Peter's Cavalcade, St. Miguel Island A35

1981, May 11 Litho. *Perf. 12*

322	A35	22e multicolored	.55	.25
a.		Souvenir sheet of 2	2.50	2.00

Bulls Attacking Spanish Soldiers A36

Battle of Salga Valley, 400th Anniv.: 33.50e, Friar Don Pedro leading citizens.

1981, July 24 Litho. *Perf. 12x11½*

323	A36	8.50e multi	.20	.20
324	A36	33.50e multi	.80	.45

Tolpis Azorica — A37

Designs: Local flora.

1981, Sept. 21 Litho. *Perf. 12½x12*

325	A37	7e shown	.20	.20
326	A37	8.50e Ranunculus azoricus	.20	.20
327	A37	20e Platanthera micranta	.40	.20
328	A37	50e Laurus azorica	1.00	.30
a.		Booklet pane of 4, #325-328	3.00	
		Nos. 325-328 (4)	1.80	.90

1982, Jan. 29

329	A37	4e Myosotis azorica	.20	.20
330	A37	10e Lactuca watsoniana	.25	.20
331	A37	27e Vicia dennesiana	.60	.25
332	A37	33.50e Azorina vidalii	.75	.25
a.		Booklet pane of 4	3.00	
		Nos. 329-332 (4)	1.80	.90

See Nos. 338-341.

Europa Type of Portugal

Heroes of Mindelo embarkation, 1832.

1982, May 3 Litho. *Perf. 12x11½*

333	A405	33.50e multi	.65	.30
a.		Souvenir sheet of 3	3.50	2.00

Chapel of the Holy Ghost — A39

Various Chapels of the Holy Ghost.

1982, Nov. 24 Litho. *Perf. 12½x12*

334	A39	27e multi	.75	.25
335	A39	33.50e multi	.95	.40

Europa 1983 A40

1983, May 5 Litho. *Perf. 12½*

336	A40	37.50e Geothermal energy	.70	.35
a.		Souvenir sheet of 3	2.50	2.50

Flag of the Autonomous Region — A41

1983, May 23 Litho. *Perf. 12x11½*

337	A41	12.50e multi	.30	.20

Flower Type of 1981

1983, June 16 *Perf. 12½x12*

338	A37	12.50e St. John's wort	.25	.20
339	A37	30e Prickless bramble	.60	.30
340	A37	37.50e Romania bush	.75	.40
341	A37	100e Common juniper	1.90	1.00
a.		Booklet pane of 4, #338-341	5.00	
		Nos. 338-341 (4)	3.50	1.90

Woman Wearing Terceira Cloaks — A42

1984, Mar. 8 Litho. *Perf. 13½*

342	A42	16e Jesters costumes, 18th cent.	.30	.20
343	A42	51e shown	.90	.45

Europa Type of Portugal

1984, May 2 *Perf. 12x11½*

344	A427	51e multicolored	.90	.40
a.		Souvenir sheet of 3	5.00	4.00

Megabombus Ruderatus — A44

1984, Sept. 3 Litho. *Perf. 12x11½*

345	A44	16e shown	.25	.20
346	A44	35e Pieris brassicae azorensis	.50	.25
347	A44	40e Chrysomela banksi	.60	.30
348	A44	51e Phlogophora interrupta	.75	.40
		Nos. 345-348 (4)	2.10	1.15

Perf. 12 Vert.

345a	A44	16e	.25	.20
346a	A44	35e	.50	.25
347a	A44	40e	.60	.30
348a	A44	51e	.75	.40
b.		Bklt. pane of 4, #345a-348a	6.00	

1985, Feb. 13 *Perf. 12x11½*

349	A44	20e Polyspilla polyspilla	.30	.20
350	A44	40e Sphaerophoria nigra	.65	.30
351	A44	46e Colias croceus	.75	.40
352	A44	60e Hipparchia azorina	1.00	.50
		Nos. 349-352 (4)	2.70	1.40

Perf. 12 Vert.

349a	A44	20e	.30	.20
350a	A44	40e	.65	.30
351a	A44	46e	.75	.40
352a	A44	60e	1.00	.50
b.		Bklt. pane of 4, #349a-352a	6.00	

Europa Type of Portugal

1985, May 6 Litho. *Perf. 11½x12*

353	A435	60e Man playing folia drum	1.00	.40
a.		Souvenir sheet of 3	6.00	3.00

Native Boats — A46

1985, June 19 Litho. *Perf. 12x12½*

354	A46	40e Jeque	.60	.25
355	A46	60e Bote	.90	.40

Europa Type of Portugal

1986, May Litho.

356	A447	68.50e Pyrrhula murina	1.00	.50
a.		Souvenir sheet of 3	6.00	3.25

Regional Architecture A48

19th Century fountains: 22.50e, Alto das Covas, Angra do Heroismo. 52.50e, Faja de Baixo, San Miguel. 68.50e, Gates of St. Peter, Terceira. 100e, Agua d'Alto, San Miguel.

1986, Sept. 18 Litho. *Perf. 12*

357 A48 22.50e multi .35 .20
358 A48 52.50e multi .80 .40
359 A48 68.50e multi 1.00 .50
360 A48 100e multi 1.50 .75
a. Booklet pane of 4, #357-360 5.00
Nos. 357-360 (4) 3.65 1.85

Traditional Modes of Transportation — A49

1986, Nov. 7 Litho.

361 A49 25e Isle of Santa Maria ox cart .35 .20
362 A49 75e Ram cart 1.00 .50

Europa Type of Portugal

Modern architecutre: Regional Assembly, Horta, designed by Manuel Correia Fernandes and Luis Miranda.

1987, May 5 Litho. *Perf. 12*

363 A456 74.50e multicolored 1.25 .60
a. Souvenir sheet of 4 6.00 5.00

Windows and Balconies A51

1987, July 1 *Perf. 12*

364 A51 51e Santa Cruz, Graciosa .80 .40
365 A51 74.50e Ribiera Grande, San Miguel 1.10 .55

Aviation History A52

Seaplanes.

1987, Oct. 9 *Perf. 12x11½*

366 A52 25e NC-4 Curtiss Flyer, 1919 .40 .20
367 A52 57e Dornier DO-X, 1932 .90 .45
368 A52 74.50e Savoia-Marchetti S 55-X, 1933 1.10 .60
369 A52 125e Lockheed Sirius, 1933 1.90 .95
Nos. 366-369 (4) 4.30 2.20

Perf. 12 Vert.

366a A52 25e .38 .20
367a A52 57e .88 .45
368a A52 74.50e 1.15 .60
369a A52 125e 1.90 .95
b. Bklt. pane of 4, #366a-369a 4.25

Europa Type of Portugal

1988, Apr. 21 Litho. *Perf. 12*

370 A466 80e multicolored 1.40 .70
a. Souvenir sheet of 4 7.00 5.50

Birds — A54

1988, Oct. 18 Litho.

371 A54 27e Columba palambus azorica .40 .20
372 A54 60e Scolopax rusticola .90 .45
373 A54 80e Sterna dougallii 1.15 .60
374 A54 100e Buteo buteo 1.45 .72
a. Booklet pane of 4, #371-374 5.00
Nos. 371-374 (4) 3.90 1.97

Coats of Arms A55

1988, Nov. 18 Litho.

375 A55 55e Dominion of Azores .85 .40
376 A55 80e Bettencourt family 1.20 .60

Wildlife Conservation A56

Various kinglets, *Regulus regulus.*

1989, Jan. 20 Litho.

377 A56 30e Adult on branch .45 .25
378 A56 30e Two adults .45 .25
379 A56 30e Adult, nest .45 .25
380 A56 30e Bird in flight .45 .25
a. Strip of 4, Nos. 377-380 1.80 1.00

See Nos. 385-388.

Europa Type of Portugal

Children's toys.

1989, Apr. 26 Litho.

381 A476 80e Tin boat 1.20 .60

Souvenir Sheet

382 Sheet, 2 each #381, 382a 8.00 6.00
a. A476 80e Tin boat, diff. 1.20 1.20

Settlement of the Azores, 550th Anniv. A58

1989, Sept. 20 Litho.

383 A58 29e Friar Goncalho Velho .40 .20
384 A58 87e Settlers farming 1.10 .55

Bird Type of 1989 With World Wildlife Fund Emblem

Various *Pyrrhula murina.*

1990, Feb. 14 Litho. *Perf. 12*

385 A56 32e Adult on branch .75 .50
386 A56 32e Two adults .75 .50
387 A56 32e Brooding .75 .50
388 A56 32e Bird in flight .75 .50
a. Strip of 4, #385-388 3.00 2.00

No. 388a has continuous design.

Europa Type of Portugal

1990, Apr. 11 Litho. *Perf. 12x11½*

389 A486 80e Vasco da Gama P.O. 1.10 .55

Souvenir Sheet

390 Sheet of 4, 2 each #389, 390a 7.00 5.00
a. A486 80e Maia P.O. 1.10 1.10

Professions A61

1990, July 11 Litho. *Perf. 12*

391 A61 5e Cart maker .20 .20
392 A61 32e Potter .45 .45
393 A61 60e Metal worker .80 .80
394 A61 100e Cooper 1.35 1.35
Nos. 391-394 (4) 2.80 2.80

Perf. 13½ Vert.

391a A61 5e .20 .20
392a A61 32e .45 .45
393a A61 60e .80 .80
394a A61 100e 1.35 1.35
b. Bklt. pane of 4, #391a-394a 4.00

See Nos. 397-400, 406-409.

Europa A62

1991, Apr. 11 Litho. *Perf. 12*

395 A62 80e Hermes space shuttle 1.10 .60

Souvenir Sheet

396 Sheet, 2 each #395, 396a 7.50 5.00
a. A62 80e Sanger 1.10 .60

Professions Type of 1990

1991, Aug. 2 Litho. *Perf. 12x11½*

397 A61 35e Tile makers .50 .25
398 A61 65e Mosaic artists .90 .45
399 A61 70e Quarrymen 1.00 .50
400 A61 110e Stonemasons 1.60 .80
Nos. 397-400 (4) 4.00 2.00

Perf. 13½ Vert.

397a A61 35e .50 .25
398a A61 65e .95 .45
399a A61 70e 1.00 .50
400a A61 110e 1.60 .80
b. Bklt. pane of 4, #397a-400a 5.00

Transportation in the Azores — A63

Ships and Planes: 35e, Schooner Helena, 1918. 60e, Beechcraft CS, 1947. 80e, Yacht, Cruzeiro do Canal, 1987. 110e, British Aerospace ATP, 1991.

1991, Nov. 15 Litho. *Perf. 12x11½*

401 A63 35e multicolored .50 .25
402 A63 60e multicolored .90 .45
403 A63 80e multicolored 1.20 .60
404 A63 110e multicolored 1.65 .80
Nos. 401-404 (4) 4.25 2.10

See Nos. 410-413.

Europa Type of Portugal

85e, Columbus aboard Santa Maria.

1992, May 22 Litho. *Perf. 12x11½*

405 A514 85e gold & multi 1.40 .70

Professions Type of 1990

1992, June 12 Litho. *Perf. 12x11½*

406 A61 10e Guitar maker .20 .20
407 A61 38e Carpenter .65 .30
408 A61 85e Basket maker 1.40 .70
409 A61 120e Boat builders 2.00 1.00
Nos. 406-409 (4) 4.25 2.20

Perf. 13½ Vert.

406a A61 10e .20 .20
407a A61 38e .65 .30
408a A61 85e 1.40 .70
409a A61 120e 2.00 1.00
b. Bklt. pane of 4, #406a-409a 6.00

Transportation Type of 1991

Ships.

1992, Oct. 7 Litho. *Perf. 12x11½*

410 A63 38e Insulano .60 .30
411 A63 65e Carvalho Araujo 1.00 .50
412 A63 85e Funchal 1.25 .65
413 A63 120e Terceirense 1.80 .90
Nos. 410-413 (4) 4.65 2.35

Contemporary Paintings by Antonio Dacosta (1914-90) — A64

Europa: No. 414, Two Mermaids at the Entrance to a Cave, 1980. No. 415a, Acoriana, 1986.

1993, May 5 Litho. *Perf. 12x11½*

414 A64 90e multicolored 1.25 .60

Souvenir Sheet

415 Sheet, 2 each #414, 415a 8.00 6.00
a. A64 90e multicolored 1.25 .60

Grinding Stones A64a

Designs: 42e, Animal-powered mill. 130e, Woman using hand-driven mill.

1993, May 5 Litho. *Perf. 12x11*

416 A64a 42e multicolored .50 .25
417 A64a 130e multicolored 1.50 .75

Architecture A65

Church of Praia da Vitoria: 42e, Main entry. 70e, South entry.
Church of Ponta Delgada: 90e, Main entry. 130e, South entry.

1993, Nov. 3 Litho. *Perf. 12*

418 A65 42e multicolored .50 .25
419 A65 70e multicolored .80 .40
420 A65 90e multicolored 1.00 .50
421 A65 130e multicolored 1.50 .75
Nos. 418-421 (4) 3.80 1.90

Tile Used in Religious Architecture A66

Designs: 40e, Blue and white pattern, Caloura church, Sao Miguel. 70e, Blue, white and yellow pattern, Caloura church, Sao Miguel. 100e, Drawing of Adoration of the Wise Men, by Bartolomeu Antunes, Esperanca monastery, Ponta Delgada. 150e, Drawing, frontal altar, Nossa Senhora dos Anjos chapel.

1994, Mar. 28 Litho. *Perf. 12*

422 A66 40e multicolored .50 .25
423 A66 70e multicolored .90 .45
424 A66 100e multicolored 1.25 .65
425 A66 150e multicolored 2.00 .50
Nos. 422-425 (4) 4.65 1.85

Perf. 11½ Vert.

422a A66 40e .50 .25
423a A66 70e .90 .45
424a A66 100e 1.25 .65
425a A66 150e 2.00 .50
b. Bklt. pane of 4, #422a-425a 6.00

Europa Type of Portugal

Wildlife, country: No. 426, Monkey, Brazil. No. 427a, Armadillo, Africa.

1994, May 5 Litho. *Perf. 12*
426 A541 100e multicolored 1.25 .60

Souvenir Sheet

427 Sheet, 2 each #426, 427a 8.00 6.00
a. A541 100e multicolored 1.25 .60

Architecture Type of 1993

45e, Church of Santa Barbara, Manueline Entry, Cedros. 140e, Railed window, Ribeira Grande.

1994, Sept. 16 Litho. *Perf. 12*
428 A65 45e multicolored .60 .30
429 A65 140e multicolored 1.75 .85

Advocates of Local Autonomy A67

42e, Aristides Moreira da Motta (1855-1942). 130e, Gil Mont'Alverne de Sequeira (1859-1931).

1995, Mar. 2 Litho. *Perf. 12*
430 A67 42e multicolored .60 .30
431 A67 130e multicolored 1.90 .95

19th Century Architecture A68

Designs: 45e, Santana Palace, Ponta Delgada. 80e, Our Lady of Victories Chapel, Furnas Lake. 95e, Hospital of the Santa Casa da Misericórdia, Ponta Delgada. 135e, Residence of Ernesto do Canto, Myrthes Park, Furnas Lake

1995, Sept. 1 Litho. *Perf. 12*
432 A68 45e multicolored .60 .30
433 A68 80e multicolored 1.00 .50
434 A68 95e multicolored 1.25 .60
435 A68 135e multicolored 1.75 .90
Nos. 432-435 (4) 4.60 2.30

Perf. 11½ Vert.
432a A68 45e .60 .60
433a A68 80e 1.00 1.00
434a A68 95e 1.25 .60
435a A68 135e 1.75 .90
b. Bklt. pane, #432a-435a 4.75
Complete booklet, No. 435b 6.00

Natália Correia (1923-93), Writer A69

1996, May 3 Litho. *Perf. 12*
436 A69 98e multicolored 1.50 .60
a. Souvenir sheet of 3 6.00 5.00

Europa.

Lighthouses — A70

Designs: 47e, Contendas, Terceira Island. 78e, Molhe, Port of Ponte Delgada, San Miguel Island. 98e, Arnel, San Miguel. 140e, Santa Clara, San Miguel. 200e, Ponta da Barca, Graciosa Island.
Illustration reduced.

1996, May 3
437 A70 47e multicolored .60 .30
438 A70 78e multicolored .90 .45
439 A70 98e multicolored 1.25 .60
440 A70 140e multicolored 1.75 .90
Nos. 437-440 (4) 4.50 2.25

Souvenir Sheet

441 A69 200e multicolored 4.00 3.00

Carved Work from Church Altar Pieces A71

49e, Leaves, berries, bird, St. Peter Church, Ponta Delgada, Sao Miguel. 80e, Cherub, Church of the Convent of St. Peter de Alcântara, Sao Roque, Pico. 100e, Cherub, All Saints Church, former Jesuits' College, Ponta Delgada. 140e, Figure holding scroll above head, St. Joseph Church, Ponta Delgada.

1997, Apr. 16 Litho. *Perf. 12*
442 A71 49e multicolored .55 .30
443 A71 80e multicolored .90 .45
444 A71 100e multicolored 1.15 .60
445 A71 140e multicolored 1.60 .80
Nos. 442-445 (4) 4.20 2.15

Perf. 11½ Vert.
442a A71 49e .55 .30
443a A71 80e .90 .45
444a A71 100e 1.15 .60
445a A71 140e 1.60 .80
b. Bklt. pane, #442a-445a 5.00
Complete booklet, #445b 5.25

Stories and Legends Type of Portugal

Europa: Man on ship from "Legend of the Island of Seven Cities," horiz.

1997, May 5 Litho. *Perf. 12*
446 A599 100e multicolored 1.10 .55
a. Souvenir sheet of 3 5.00 1.75

Natl. Festivals Type of Portugal

1998, May 21 Litho. *Perf. 12*
447 A621 100e Holy Spirit 1.10 .55
a. Souvenir sheet of 3 5.00 1.75

Europa.

Ocean Creatures A72

Designs: 50e, Stenella frontalis. 140e, Physeter macrocephalus.

1998, Aug. 4 Litho. *Perf. 12*
448 A72 50e multicolored .55 .30

Size: 80x30mm

449 A72 140e multicolored 1.60 .80

Perf. 11½ Vert.
448a A72 50e .55 .30
449a A72 140e 1.60 .80
b. Booklet pane, #448a-449a + label 3.00
Complete booklet, #449b 3.00

Europa Type of Portugal

1999, May 5 Litho. *Perf. 12x11¾*
450 A641 100e Flowers, Pico Mountain Natural Reserve 1.00 .50
a. Souvenir sheet of 3 3.00 3.00

Paintings of the Azores A73

51e, Emigrants, by Domingos Rebelo (1891-1975). 95e, Portrait of Vitorino Nemésino, by Antonio Dacosta (1914-90), vert. 100e, Espera de Gado no Alto das Covas, by José Van der Hagen. 140e, The Vila Franca Islanders, by Duarte Maia (1867-1922).

Perf. 12x11¾, 11¾x12

1999, Sept. 3 Litho.
451 A73 51e multi .50 .25
452 A73 95e multi .95 .45
453 A73 100e multi 1.00 .50
454 A73 140e multi 1.40 .70

Perf. 11¾ Vert., 11¾ Horiz. (#452a)
451a A73 51e multi .50 .25
452a A73 95e multi .95 .45
453a A73 100e multi 1.00 .50
454a A73 140e multi 1.40 .70
b. Bklt. pane of 4, #451a-454a 4.00
Complete booklet, #454b 4.00

Europa, 2000

Common Design Type

2000, May 9 *Perf. 11¾x12*
455 CD17 100e multi .95 .50
a. Souvenir sheet of 3 3.00 1.50

Mail Delivery Systems of the Past — A74

Designs: 85e, Buoy mail. 140e, Zeppelin mail, vert.

Perf. 12x11¾, 11¾x12

2000, Oct. 9 Litho.
456-457 A74 Set of 2 2.10 1.10

Europa Type of Portugal

2001, May 9 Litho. *Perf. 12x11¾*
458 A677 105e Marine life .90 .45
a. Souvenir sheet of 3 2.75 2.75

Angra do Heroismo World Heritage Site — A75

View of town, sea and: 53e, Archway. 85e, Monument. 140e, Window.

2001, June 4
459-461 A75 Set of 3 2.40 1.25

Souvenir Sheet

462 A75 350e Map 3.00 3.00

MADEIRA

Type of Azores, 1980

6.50e, Madeira #2. 19.50e, Madeira #5.

1980, Jan. 2 Litho. *Perf. 12*
66 A33 6.50e multi .20 .20
67 A33 19.50e multi .50 .20
a. Souvenir sheet of 2, #66-67 2.75 2.00

No. 67a exists overprinted for Capex 87.

Grapes and Wine — A7

1980, Sept. 17 Litho. *Perf. 12x11½*
68 A7 50c Bullock cart .20 .20
69 A7 1e shown .20 .20
70 A7 5e Produce map of Madeira .20 .20
71 A7 6.50e Basket and lace .20 .20
72 A7 8e Orchid .20 .20
73 A7 30e Madeira boat .55 .35
Nos. 68-73 (6) 1.55 1.35

World Tourism Conf., Manila, Sept. 27.

Europa Issue 1981

O Bailinho Folk Dance A8

1981, May 11 Litho. *Perf. 12*
74 A8 22e multi .40 .25
a. Souvenir sheet of 2 3.00 1.10

Explorer Ship — A9

1981, July 1 Litho. *Perf. 12x11½*
75 A9 8.50e shown .20 .20
76 A9 33.50e Map .60 .20

Discovery of Madeira anniv.

A10

A12

Designs: Local flora.

1981, Oct. 6 Litho. *Perf. 12½x12*
77 A10 7e Dactylorhiza foliosa .20 .20
78 A10 8.50e Echium candicans .20 .20
79 A10 20e Geranium maderense .40 .20
80 A10 50e Isoplexis sceptrum .95 .40
a. Booklet pane of 4, #77-80 3.00
Nos. 77-80 (4) 1.75 1.00

See Nos. 82-85, 90-93.

Europa Type of Portugal

1982, May 3 Litho. *Perf. 12x11½*
81 A405 33.50e Sugar mills, 15th cent. .60 .30
a. Souvenir sheet of 3 2.00 2.00

1982, Aug. 31 Litho. *Perf. 12½x12*
82 A10 9e Goodyera macrophylla .20 .20
83 A10 10e Armeria maderensis .20 .20
84 A10 27e Viola paradoxa .35 .20
85 A10 33.50e Scilla maderensis .90 .40
a. Booklet pane of 4, #82-85 3.00
Nos. 82-85 (4) 1.65 1.00

1982, Dec. 15 Litho. *Perf. 13½*
86 A12 27e Brinco dancing dolls .65 .40
87 A12 33.50e Dancers .85 .50

Europa 1983 A13

1983, May 5 Litho. *Perf. 12½*
88 A13 37.50e Levadas irrigation system .70 .30
a. Souvenir sheet of 3 6.00 4.00

Flag of the Autonomous Region — A14

1983, July 1 Litho. *Perf. 12x11½*
89 A14 12.50e multi .30 .30

Flower Type of 1981

1983, Oct. 19 Litho. *Perf. 12½x12*
90 A10 12.50e Matthiola maderensis .30 .30
91 A10 30e Erica maderensis .65 .30
92 A10 37.50e Cirsium latifolium .75 .30
93 A10 100e Clethra arborea 2.00 1.00
a. Booklet pane of 4, #90-93 5.00
Nos. 90-93 (4) 3.70 1.90

Europa Type of Portugal

1984, May 2 Litho. *Perf. 12x11½*
94 A427 51e multi .80 .40
a. Souvenir sheet of 3 3.00 3.00

Madeira Rally (Auto Race), 25th Anniv. — A16

Various cars.

1984, Aug. 3 Litho. *Perf. 11½x12*
95 A16 16e multicolored .40 .20
96 A16 51e multicolored 1.00 .50

Traditional Means of Transportation — A17

1984, Nov. 22 *Perf. 12*
97 A17 16e Mountain sledge .25 .20
98 A17 35e Hammock .50 .25
99 A17 40e Winebag carriers' procession .60 .30
100 A17 51e Carreira Boat .75 .40
a. Booklet pane of 4, Nos. 97-100 3.50
Nos. 97-100 (4) 2.10 1.15

See Nos. 104-107.

Europa Type of Portugal

1985, May 6 Litho. *Perf. 11½x12*
101 A435 60e Man playing guitar 1.00 .40
a. Souvenir sheet of 3 6.00 4.00

Marine Life — A19

1985, July 5 Litho. *Perf. 12*
102 A19 40e Aphanopus carbo .50 .30
103 A19 60e Lampris guttatus .80 .40

See Nos. 108-109.

Transportation type of 1984

1985, Sept. 11 Litho. *Perf. 12x11½*
104 A17 20e Ox-drawn sledge .35 .20
105 A17 40e Mountrain train .65 .30
106 A17 46e Fish vendors .75 .40
107 A17 60e Coastal steamer 1.00 .50
a. Booklet pane of 4, Nos. 104-107 4.00
Nos. 104-107 (4) 2.75 1.40

Marine Life Type of 1985

1986, Jan. 7 Litho.
108 A19 20e Thunnus obesus .25 .20
109 A19 75e Beryx decadactylus 1.00 .50

Europa Type of Portugal

1986, May 5 Litho.
110 A447 68.50e Great Shearwater 1.00 .50
a. Souvenir sheet of 3 6.00 3.25

Forts in Funchal and Machico A21

1986, July 1 Litho. *Perf. 12*
111 A21 22.50e Sao Lourenco, 1583 .30 .20
112 A21 52.50e Sao Joao do Pico, 1611 .75 .40
113 A21 68.50e Sao Tiago, 1614 1.00 .50
114 A21 100e Sao do Amparo, 1706 1.45 .75
a. Booklet pane of 4, #111-114 5.00
Nos. 111-114 (4) 3.50 1.85

A22

A24

Indigenous birds.

1987, Mar. 6 Litho.
115 A22 25e Regulus ignicapillus madeirensis .40 .20
116 A22 57e Columba trocaz .90 .45
117 A22 74.50e Tyto alba schmitzi 1.10 .60
118 A22 125e Pterodroma madeira 1.95 1.00
a. Booklet pane of 4, #115-118 6.00
Nos. 115-118 (4) 4.35 2.25

See Nos. 123-126.

Europa Type of Portugal

Modern Architecture: Social Services Center, Funchal, designed by Raul Chorao Ramalho.

1987, May 5 Litho. *Perf. 12*
119 A456 74.50e multicolored 1.20 .60
a. Souvenir sheet of 4 8.00 5.00

1987, July 1 *Perf. 12x12½*

Natl. monuments.

120 A24 51e Funchal Castle, 15th cent. .80 .40
121 A24 74.50e Old Town Hall, Santa Cruz, 16th cent. 1.15 .60

Europa Type of Portugal

Transportation Modern mail boat PS 13 TL.

1988, Apr. 21 Litho. *Perf. 12*
122 A466 80e multicolored 1.35 .70
a. Souvenir sheet of 4 8.00 5.40

Bird Type of 1987

1988, June 15 Litho.
123 A22 27e Erithacus rubecula .45 .25
124 A22 60e Petronia 1.00 .50
125 A22 80e Fringilla coelebs 1.25 .65
126 A22 100e Accipiter nisus 1.60 .80
a. Booklet pane of 4, #123-126 6.00
Nos. 123-126 (4) 4.30 2.20

Portraits of Christopher Columbus and Purported Residences on Madeira A27

1988, July 1 Litho.
127 A27 55e Funchal, 1480-1481, vert. .90 .45
128 A27 80e Porto Santo 1.25 .65

Europa Type of Portugal

Children's toys.

1989, Apr. 26 Litho.
129 A476 80e Kite 1.25 .60

Souvenir Sheet

130 Sheet, 2 each #129, 130a 8.00 6.00
a. A476 80e Kite, diff. 1.25 1.25

Monuments A29

Churches: 29e, Church of the Colegio (St. John the Evangelist Church). 87e, Santa Clara Church and convent.

1989, July 28 Litho.
131 A29 29e multi .35 .20
132 A29 87e multi 1.00 .50

Fish — A30

1989, Sept. 20 Litho.
133 A30 29e *Argyropelecus aculeatus* .40 .20
134 A30 60e *Pseudolepidaplois scrofa* .80 .40
135 A30 87e *Coris julis* 1.10 .55
136 A30 100e *Scorpaena maderensis* 1.25 .65
a. Booklet pane of 4, #133-136 5.00
Nos. 133-136 (4) 3.55 1.80

Europa Type of Portugal

1990, Apr. 11 Litho. *Perf. 12x11½*
137 A486 80e Zarco P.O. 1.10 .55

Souvenir Sheet

138 Sheet, 2 ea #137, 138a 7.50 5.00
a. A486 80e Porto da Cruz P.O. 1.10 1.10

Subtropical Fruits and Plants — A32

1990, June 5 Litho. *Perf. 12*
139 A32 5e Banana .20 .20
140 A32 32e Avocado .40 .20
141 A32 60e Sugar apple .80 .40
142 A32 100e Passion fruit 1.40 .70
Nos. 139-142 (4) 2.80 1.50

Perf. 13½ Vert.
139a A32 5e .20 .20
140a A32 32e .40 .40
141a A32 60e .80 .80
142a A32 100e 1.35 1.35
b. Bklt. pane of 4, #139a-142a 4.00

See Nos. 153-160.

Boats of Madeira A33

1990, Aug. 24 *Perf. 12*
143 A33 32e Tuna .40 .20
144 A33 60e Desert islands .80 .40
145 A33 70e Maneiro .95 .50
146 A33 95e Chavelha 1.25 .65
Nos. 143-146 (4) 3.40 1.75

See Nos. 162-165.

Columba Trocaz Heineken — A34

1991, Jan. 23 Litho. *Perf. 12*
147 A34 35e shown .50 .25
148 A34 35e On branch .50 .25
149 A34 35e In flight .50 .25
150 A34 35e On nest .50 .35
a. Strip of 4, #147-150 2.00 1.00

Europa A35

1991, Apr. 11 Litho. *Perf. 12*
151 A35 80e ERS-1 1.15 .60

Souvenir Sheet

152 Sheet, 2 each #151, 152a 7.50 5.00
a. A35 80e SPOT 1.10 .60

Subtropical Fruits Type of 1990

1991, June 7 Litho. *Perf. 12*
153 A32 35e Mango .50 .25
154 A32 65e Surinam cherry .90 .45
155 A32 70e Brazilian guava .95 .50
156 A32 110e Papaya 1.50 .75
Nos. 153-156 (4) 3.85 1.95

Perf. 13½ Vert.
153a A32 35e .50 .25
154a A32 65e .90 .45
155a A32 70e .95 .50
156a A32 110e 1.50 .75
b. Bklt. pane of 4, #153a-156a 5.00

1992, Feb. 21 Litho. *Perf. 11½x12*
157 A32 10e Prickly pear .20 .20
158 A32 38e Tree tomato .40 .20
159 A32 85e Ceriman 1.30 .65
160 A32 125e Guava 1.90 .95
Nos. 157-160 (4) 3.80 2.00

Perf. 13½ Vert.
157a A32 10e .20 .20
158a A32 38e .42 .25
159a A32 85e 1.30 .65
160a A32 125e 1.90 .95
b. Bklt. pane of 4, #157a-160a 5.00

Europa Type of Portugal

Europa: 85e, Columbus at Funchal.

1992, May 22 Litho. *Perf. 12x11½*
161 A514 85e gold & multi 1.40 .70

Ships Type of 1990

1992, Sept. 18 Litho. *Perf. 12x11½*
162 A33 38e Gaviao .65 .30
163 A33 65e Independencia 1.10 .55
164 A33 85e Madeirense 1.40 .70
165 A33 120e Funchalense 2.00 1.00
Nos. 162-165 (4) 5.15 2.55

Contemporary Paintings by Lourdes Castro — A36

Europa: No. 166, Shadow Projection of Christa Maar, 1968. No. 167a, Shadow Projection of a Dahlia, c. 1970.

1993, May 5 Litho. *Perf. 11½x12*

166 A36 90e multicolored 1.25 .60

Souvenir Sheet

167 Sheet, 2 each #166, 167a 8.00 5.00
a. A36 90e multicolored 1.25 .60

Nature Preservation — A37

Monachus monachus: No. 168, Adult on rock. No. 169, Swimming. No. 170, Mother nursing pup. No. 171, Two on rocks.

1993, June 30 Litho. *Perf. 12x11½*

168 A37 42e multicolored 1.00 .50
169 A37 42e multicolored 1.00 .50
170 A37 42e multicolored 1.00 .50
171 A37 42e multicolored 1.00 .50
a. Strip of 4, #168-171 4.50 2.00

Architecture A38

Designs: 42e, Window from Sao Francisco Convent, Funchal. 130e, Window of Mercy (Old Hospital), Funchal.

1993, July 30 *Perf. 11½x12*

172 A38 42e multicolored .50 .25
173 A38 130e multicolored 1.60 .80

Europa Type of Portugal

Discoveries: No. 174, Native with bow and arrows. No. 175a, Palm tree.

1994, May 5 Litho. *Perf. 12*

174 A541 100e multicolored 1.25 .60

Souvenir Sheet

175 Sheet, 2 each, #174-175a 7.50 5.00
a. A541 100e multicolored 1.25 .60

Native Handicrafts A39

1994, May 5 *Perf. 12x11½*

176 A39 45e Embroidery .55 .30
177 A39 75e Tapestry .90 .45
178 A39 100e Shoes 1.25 .60
179 A39 140e Wicker work 1.65 .85
Nos. 176-179 (4) 4.35 2.20

Perf. 11½ Vert.

176a A39 45e .55 .30
177a A39 75e .90 .45
178a A39 100e 1.25 .60
179a A39 140e 1.60 .85
b. Bklt. pane of 4, #176a-179a 6.00

Arms of Madeira Districts — A40

1994, July 1 Litho. *Perf. 11½x12*

180 A40 45e Funchal .55 .30
181 A40 140e Porto Santo 1.90 .95

Traditional Arts & Crafts — A41

Designs: 45e, Chicken puppets made of flour paste. 80e, Inlaid wood furniture piece. 95e, Wicker bird cage. 135e, Knitted wool bonnet.

1995, June 30 Litho. *Perf. 11½x12*

182 A41 45e multicolored .60 .30
183 A41 80e multicolored 1.10 .55
184 A41 95e multicolored 1.25 .65
185 A41 135e multicolored 1.90 .95
Nos. 182-185 (4) 4.85 2.45

Perf. 11½ Vert.

182a A41 45e .60 .30
183a A41 80e 1.10 .55
184a A41 95e 1.25 .65
185a A41 135e 1.90 .95
b. Booklet pane, #182a-185a 6.00
Complete booklet, #185b 6.00

Famous Woman Type of Azores, 1996

Europa: Guiomar Vilhena (1705-89), entrepeneur.

1996, May 3 Litho. *Perf. 12*

186 A69 98e multicolored 1.25 .60
a. Souvenir sheet of 3 3.75 1.90

Paintings from Flemish Group, Museum of Sacred Paintings of Funchal (Madeira) A42

Designs: 47e, The Adoration of the Magi, vert. 78e, St. Mary Magdalene, vert. 98e, Annunciation. 140e, St. Peter, St. Paul and St. Andrew.

Perf. 11½x12, 12x11½

1996, July 1 Litho.

187 A42 47e multicolored .60 .30
188 A42 78e multicolored 1.00 .50
189 A42 98e multicolored 1.30 .65
190 A42 140e multicolored 1.80 .90
Nos. 187-190 (4) 4.70 2.35

Perf. 11½ on 2 Sides

187a A42 47e .60 .30
188a A42 78e 1.00 .50
189a A42 98e 1.30 .65
190a A42 140e 1.80 .90
b. Booklet pane, #187a-190a 6.00
Complete booklet, #190b 6.00

Moths & Butterflies A43

Designs: 49e, Eumichtis albostigmata. 80e, Menophra maderae. 100e, Vanessa indica vulcania. 140e, Pieris brassicae wollastoni.

1997, Feb. 12 Litho. *Perf. 12*

191 A43 49e multicolored .60 .30
192 A43 80e multicolored .95 .45
193 A43 100e multicolored 1.15 .60
194 A43 140e multicolored 1.65 .80
Nos. 191-194 (4) 4.35 2.15

Perf. 11½ Vert.

191a A43 49e multicolored .60 .30
192a A43 80e multicolored .95 .45
193a A43 100e multicolored 1.10 .60
194a A43 140e multicolored 1.60 .80
b. Booklet pane, #191a-194a 6.00
Complete booklet, #194b 6.00

See Nos. 197-200.

Stories and Legends Type of Portugal

Europa: Man holding woman from "Legend of Machico," horiz.

1997, May 5 Litho. *Perf. 12*

195 A599 100e multicolored 1.10 .55
a. Souvenir sheet of 3 5.00 3.00

Natl. Festivals Type of Portugal

1998, May 21 Litho. *Perf. 12*

196 A621 100e New Year's Eve 1.25 .55
a. Souvenir sheet of 3 5.00 3.00

Europa.

Moths and Butterflies Type of 1997

Designs: 50e, Gonepteryx cleopatra. 85e, Xanthorhoe rupicola. 100e, Noctua teixeirai. 140e, Xenochlorodes nubigena.

1998, Sept. 6 Litho. *Perf. 12*

197 A43 50e multicolored .55 .30
198 A43 85e multicolored .95 .45
199 A43 100e multicolored 1.10 .55
200 A43 140e multicolored 1.60 .80
a. Booklet pane, #197-200, perf. 12 vert. 6.00
Complete booklet, #200a 6.00
Nos. 197-200 (4) 4.20 2.10

Europa Type of Portugal

1999, May 5 Litho. *Perf. 12x11¾*

201 A641 100e Flowers, Madeira Island Natural Park 1.00 .50
a. Souvenir sheet of 3 3.00 3.00

Glazed Tiles From Frederico de Freitas Museum, Funchal A44

Designs: 51e, Griffin, from Middle East, 13th-14th cent. 80e, Flower, from England, 19th-20th cent. 95e, Bird, from Persia, 14th cent. 100e, Geometric, from Moorish Spain, 13th cent. 140e, Ship, from Holland, 18th cent. 210e, Flowers from Syria, 13th-14th cent.

1999, July 1

202 A44 51e multicolored .55 .25
203 A44 80e multicolored .85 .40
204 A44 95e multicolored 1.00 .50
205 A44 100e multicolored 1.00 .50
206 A44 140e multicolored 1.50 .75
207 A44 210e multicolored 2.25 1.10
a. Souvenir sheet of 6, #202-207 7.25 7.25
Nos. 202-207 (6) 7.15 3.50

Europa, 2000

Common Design Type

2000, May 9 *Perf. 11¾x12*

208 CD17 100e multi .95 .50
a. Souvenir sheet of 3 3.00 1.50

Plants from Laurissilva Forest A45

52e, Purple orchid. 85e, White orchid. No. 211, 100e, Folhado. No. 212, 100e, Laurel tree. 140e, Barbusano. 350e, Visco.

2000, July 4 Litho. *Perf. 12x11¾*

209-214 A45 Set of 6 7.75 4.00
214a Souvenir sheet, #209-214 7.75 4.00

Expansion of Madeira Airport A46

2000, Sept. 15

215 A46 140e multi 1.40 .70
a. Souvenir sheet of 1 1.40 .70

Europa Type of Portugal

2001, May 9 Litho. *Perf. 12x11¾*

216 A677 105e Signals .90 .45
a. Souvenir sheet of 3 2.75 2.75

Scenes of Traditional Life — A47

Designs: 53e, People retruning home. 85e, On the road to the marketplace. 105e, Traditional clothes.
350e, Leisure time.

2001, July 19 Litho. *Perf. 12x11¾*

217-219 A47 Set of 3 2.25 1.10

Souvenir Sheet

220 A47 350e multi 3.25 1.60

PORTUGUESE AFRICA

'pōr-chə-,gēz 'a-fri-kə

For use in any of the Portuguese possessions in Africa.

1000 Reis = 1 Milreis
100 Centavos = 1 Escudo

Common Design Types pictured following the introduction.

Vasco da Gama Issue
Common Design Types
Inscribed "Africa - Correios"

Perf. 13½ to 15½

1898, Apr. 1 Engr. Unwmk.

1	CD20	2½r blue green	.90	.90
2	CD21	5r red	.90	.90
3	CD22	10r red violet	.90	.90
4	CD23	25r yellow green	.90	.90
5	CD24	50r dark blue	1.10	1.10
6	CD25	75r violet brown	6.25	6.25
7	CD26	100r bister brown	5.00	4.50
8	CD27	150r bister	7.50	6.25
		Nos. 1-8 (8)	23.45	21.70
		Set, never hinged	30.00	

Vasco da Gama's voyage to India.

POSTAGE DUE STAMPS

D1

1945 Unwmk. Typo. *Perf. 11½x12*
Denomination in Black

J1	D1	10c claret	.70	.70
J2	D1	20c purple	.70	.70
J3	D1	30c deep blue	.70	.70
J4	D1	40c chocolate	.70	.70
J5	D1	50c red violet	1.00	*1.25*
J6	D1	1e orange brown	2.00	*4.00*
J7	D1	2e yellow green	5.00	*7.00*
J8	D1	3e bright carmine	12.00	12.00
J9	D1	5e orange yellow	25.00	25.00
		Nos. J1-J9 (9)	47.80	52.05
		Set, never hinged	62.50	

WAR TAX STAMPS

Liberty
WT1

Perf. 12x11½, 15x14

1919 Typo. Unwmk.
Overprinted in Black, Orange or Carmine

MR1	WT1	1c green (Bk)	.75	.75
a.		Figures of value omitted	25.00	
MR2	WT1	4c green (O)	1.00	
MR3	WT1	5c green (C)	.75	.75
		Nos. MR1-MR3 (3)	2.50	

Some authorities consider No. MR2 a revenue stamp.

PORTUGUESE CONGO

'pōr-chi-gēz 'käŋ-,gō

LOCATION — The northernmost district of the Portuguese Angola Colony on the southwest coast of Africa
CAPITAL — Cabinda

Stamps of Angola replaced those of Portuguese Congo.

1000 Reis = 1 Milreis
100 Centavos = 1 Escudo (1913)

King Carlos
A1 A2

Perf. 12½

1894, Aug. 5 Typo. Unwmk.

1	A1	5r yellow	.85	.65
b.		5r orange yellow, perf. 13½	15.00	12.50
2	A1	10r redsh violet	1.60	.80
a.		Perf. 13½	17.50	14.00
3	A1	15r chocolate	2.75	2.00
4	A1	20r lavender	2.50	1.75
5	A1	25r green	1.50	.80
		Perf. 13½		
6	A1	50r light blue	2.75	2.00
		Perf. 11½		
7	A1	75r rose	4.50	3.75
a.		Perf. 12½	18.00	15.00
8	A1	80r yellow green	7.00	6.00
a.		Perf. 12½	17.50	12.50
9	A1	100r brown, *yel*	5.25	3.25
a.		Perf. 13½	30.00	15.00
		Perf. 12½		
10	A1	150r carmine, *rose*	11.00	9.00
11	A1	200r dk blue, *bl*	12.00	9.00
12	A1	300r dk blue, *salmon*	15.00	11.00
		Nos. 1-12 (12)	66.70	50.00

For surcharges and overprints see Nos. 36-47, 127-131.

1898-1903 *Perf. 11½*
Name & Value in Black except 500r

13	A2	2½r gray	.35	.25
14	A2	5r orange	.35	.25
15	A2	10r lt green	.55	.35
16	A2	15r brown	1.50	1.10
17	A2	15r gray grn ('03)	.90	.55
18	A2	20r gray violet	.90	.60
19	A2	25r sea green	1.40	.90
20	A2	25r car rose ('03)	.90	.45
21	A2	50r deep blue	1.65	1.25
22	A2	50r brown ('03)	2.75	1.75
23	A2	65r dull blue ('03)	7.50	6.50
24	A2	75r rose	4.00	2.25
25	A2	75r red lilac ('03)	2.75	2.25
26	A2	80r violet	3.00	2.50
27	A2	100r dk bl, *bl*	2.25	1.75
28	A2	115r org brn, *pink* ('03)	6.00	5.00
29	A2	130r brn, *straw* ('03)	15.00	11.00
30	A2	150r brown, *buff*	4.00	2.50
31	A2	200r red lilac, *pnksh*	5.00	3.00
32	A2	300r dk blue, *rose*	6.00	3.25
33	A2	400r dl bl, *straw* ('03)	11.00	9.50
34	A2	500r blk & red, *bl* ('01)	15.00	9.00
35	A2	700r vio, *yelsh* ('01)	25.00	17.50
		Nos. 13-35 (23)	117.75	83.45

For overprints and surcharges see Nos. 49-53, 60-74, 117-126, 136-138.

Surcharged in Black

1902 *Perf. 11½, 12½, 13½*
On Issue of 1894

36	A1	65r on 15r choc	3.50	3.00
a.		Perf. 11½	15.00	7.50
37	A1	65r on 20r lav	4.00	3.00
38	A1	65r on 25r green	4.00	3.00
a.		Perf. 11½	15.00	9.00
39	A1	65r on 300r bl, *sal*	4.50	4.50
40	A1	115r on 10r red vio	4.00	3.00
41	A1	115r on 50r lt bl	3.75	2.50
42	A1	130r on 5r yellow	4.00	2.75
a.		Inverted surcharge	27.50	27.50
43	A1	130r on 75r rose	3.50	3.00
a.		Perf. 12½	7.00	6.00
44	A1	130r on 100r brn, *yel*	5.00	3.75
a.		Inverted surcharge	40.00	35.00
b.		Perf. 11½	18.00	12.50
45	A1	400r on 80r yel grn	1.75	1.25
46	A1	400r on 150r car, *rose*	2.25	1.50
47	A1	400r on 200r bl, *bl*	2.25	1.50
		On Newspaper Stamp of 1894		
48	N1	115r on 2½r brn	3.75	2.50
a.		Inverted surcharge	25.00	25.00
		Nos. 36-48 (13)	46.25	35.25

Nos. 16, 19, 21 and 24 Overprinted in Black

1902 *Perf. 11½*

49	A2	15r brown	2.00	1.25
50	A2	25r sea green	2.00	1.40
51	A2	50r blue	2.00	1.40
52	A2	75r rose	4.00	2.75
		Nos. 49-52 (4)	10.00	6.80

No. 23 Surcharged

1905

53	A2	50r on 65r dull blue	3.50	2.25

Angola Stamps of 1898-1903 (Port. Congo type A2) Overprinted or Surcharged:

a

b

1911

54	(a)	2½r gray	1.00	.90
55	(a)	5r orange	1.40	1.25
56	(a)	10r lt green	1.40	1.25
a.		"REPUBLICA" inverted	17.50	17.50
57	(a)	15r gray green	1.40	1.25
a.		"REPUBLICA" inverted	17.50	17.50
58	(b)	25r on 200r red vio, *pnksh*	2.25	2.00
a.		"REPUBLICA" inverted	17.50	17.50
b.		"CONGO" double	17.50	17.50
		Thin Bar and "CONGO" as Type "b"		
59	(a)	2½r gray	1.10	.90
		Nos. 54-59 (6)	8.55	7.55

Issue of 1898-1903 Overprinted in Carmine or Green — c

1911

60	A2	2½r gray	.20	.20
61	A2	5r orange	.25	.20
62	A2	10r lt green	.25	.20
63	A2	15r gray grn	.25	.25
64	A2	20r gray vio	.40	.25
65	A2	25r car rose (G)	.50	.25
66	A2	50r brown	.60	.30
67	A2	75r red lilac	1.00	.50
68	A2	100r dk bl, *bl*	.80	.55
69	A2	115r org brn, *pink*	1.90	1.25
70	A2	130r brown, *straw*	1.90	1.25
71	A2	200r red vio, *pnksh*	2.75	1.75
72	A2	400r dull bl, *straw*	2.75	2.25
73	A2	500r blk & red, *bl*	3.75	2.00
74	A2	700r violet, *yelsh*	3.75	2.00
		Nos. 60-74 (15)	21.05	13.20

Numerous inverts and doubles exist. These are printer's waste or made to order.

Common Design Types pictured following the introduction.

Vasco da Gama Issue of Various Portuguese Colonies Surcharged

1913
On Stamps of Macao

75	CD20	¼c on ½a bl grn	1.10	1.10
76	CD21	½c on 1a red	1.10	1.10
77	CD22	1c on 2a red vio	1.10	1.10
78	CD23	2½c on 4a yel grn	1.10	1.10
79	CD24	5c on 8a dk blue	1.10	1.10
80	CD25	7½c on 12a vio brn	2.25	2.25
81	CD26	10c on 16a bis brn	1.60	1.60
82	CD27	15c on 24a bister	1.60	1.60
		Nos. 75-82 (8)	10.95	10.95
		On Stamps of Portuguese Africa		
83	CD20	¼c on 2½r bl grn	.75	.75
84	CD21	½c on 5r red	.75	.75
85	CD22	1c on 10r red vio	.75	.75
86	CD23	2½c on 25r yel grn	.75	.75
87	CD24	5c on 50r dk bl	1.00	1.00
88	CD25	7½c on 75r vio brn	1.75	1.75
89	CD26	10c on 100r bis brn	1.10	1.10
a.		Inverted surcharge	22.50	22.50
90	CD27	15c on 150r bister	1.40	1.40
		Nos. 83-90 (8)	8.25	8.25
		On Stamps of Timor		
91	CD20	¼c on ½a bl grn	1.10	1.10
92	CD21	½c on 1a red	1.10	1.10
93	CD22	1c on 2a red vio	1.10	1.10
94	CD23	2½c on 4a yel grn	1.10	1.10
95	CD24	5c on 8a dk blue	1.10	1.10
a.		Double surcharge	22.50	22.50
96	CD25	7½c on 12a vio brn	2.25	2.25
97	CD26	10c on 16a bis brn	2.00	2.00
98	CD27	15c on 24a bister	2.00	2.00
		Nos. 91-98 (8)	11.75	11.75
		Nos. 75-98 (24)	30.95	30.95

Ceres — A3

1914 Typo. *Perf. 15x14*
Name and Value in Black

99	A3	¼c olive brn	.30	*.45*
a.		Inscriptions inverted		
100	A3	½c black	.55	*.90*
101	A3	1c blue grn	2.75	*3.75*
102	A3	1½c lilac brn	1.10	*1.25*
103	A3	2c carmine	1.10	*1.25*
104	A3	2½c lt violet	.35	*.80*
105	A3	5c dp blue	.65	*1.25*
106	A3	7½c yellow brn	.90	*1.25*
107	A3	8c slate	1.50	*3.00*
108	A3	10c orange brn	1.50	*3.00*
109	A3	15c plum	1.75	*3.00*
110	A3	20c yellow grn	2.00	*3.00*
111	A3	30c brown, *grn*	2.50	*4.50*
112	A3	40c brown, *pink*	4.00	*6.00*
113	A3	50c orange, *salmon*	4.00	*6.00*
114	A3	1e green, *blue*	5.00	*8.00*
		Nos. 99-114 (16)	29.95	*47.40*

Issue of 1898-1903 Overprinted Locally in Green or Red

1914-18 *Perf. 11½*

117	A2	50r brown (G)	.85	.60
118	A2	75r rose (G)	*400.00*	
119	A2	75r red lilac (G)	2.00	1.40
120	A2	100r blue, *bl* (R)	.85	.70
121	A2	200r red vio, *pink* (G)	1.75	1.10
122	A2	400r dl bl, *straw* (R) ('18)	72.50	50.00
123	A2	500r blk & red, *bl* (R)	57.50	37.50
		Same on Nos. 51-52		
124	A2	50r blue (R)	.85	.65
125	A2	75r rose (G)	1.40	1.00
		Same on No. 53		
126	A2	50r on 65r dl bl (R)	1.10	1.00
		Nos. 117,119-126 (9)	138.80	93.95

No. 118 was not regularly issued.

Provisional Issue of 1902 Overprinted Type "c" in Red

1915 *Perf. 11½, 12½, 13½*

127	A1	115r on 10r red vio	.25	.20
a.		Perf. 13½	15.00	12.50
128	A1	115r on 50r lt bl	.25	.20
a.		Perf. 11½	1.75	.60
129	A1	130r on 5r yellow	.30	.25
130	A1	130r on 75r rose	1.40	.60
131	A1	130r on 100r brn, *buff*	.40	.35
135	N1	115r on 2½r brn	.40	.35
		Nos. 49, 51 Overprinted Type "c"		
136	A2	15r brown	.60	.50
137	A2	50r blue	.40	.35
		No. 53 Overprinted Type "c"		
138	A2	50r on 65r dull blue	.50	.35
		Nos. 127-138 (9)	4.50	3.15

NEWSPAPER STAMP

N1

Perf. 12½, 13½

1894, Aug. 5 Typo. Unwmk.

P1	N1	2½r brown	.90	.55

For surcharge and overprint see Nos. 48, 135.

PORTUGUESE GUINEA

'pōr-chi-gēz 'gi-nē

LOCATION — On the west coast of Africa between Senegal and Guinea
GOVT. — Portuguese Overseas Territory
AREA — 13,944 sq. mi.
POP. — 560,000 (est. 1970)
CAPITAL — Bissau

The territory, including the Bissagos Islands, became an independent republic on Sept. 10, 1974. See Guinea-Bissau in Vol. 3.

1000 Reis = 1 Milreis
100 Centavos = 1 Escudo (1913)

Catalogue values for unused stamps in this country are for Never Hinged items, beginning with Scott 273 in the regular postage section, Scott J40 in the postage due section, and Scott RA17 in the postal tax section.

Nos. 1-7 are valued with small faults such as short perfs or small thins. Completely fault-free examples of any of these stamps are very scarce and are worth more than the values given.

Stamps of Cape Verde, 1877-85 Overprinted in Black

1881 Unwmk. *Perf. 12½*

Without Gum (Nos. 1-7)

1	A1	5r black	*1,000.*	*800.*
1A	A1	10r yellow	*1,500.*	*800.*
2	A1	20r bister	*475.*	*250.*
3	A1	25r rose	*1,250.*	*750.*
4	A1	40r blue	*1,250.*	*800.*
a.		Cliché of Mozambique in Cape Verde plate	*15,000.*	*11,000.*
4B	A1	50r green	*2,000.*	*725.*
5	A1	100r lilac	275.	150.
6	A1	200r orange	*550.*	*375.*
7	A1	300r brown	*550.*	*400.*

Excellent forgies exist of Nos. 1-7.

Overprinted in Red or Black

1881-85 *Perf. 12½, 13½*

8	A1	5r black (R)	3.75	2.50
9	A1	10r yellow	150.00	110.00
10	A1	10r green ('85)	5.75	5.50
11	A1	20r bister	2.75	1.75
12	A1	20r rose ('85)	6.25	5.00
a.		Double overprint		
13	A1	25r carmine	2.25	1.25
a.		Perf. 13½	67.50	37.50
14	A1	25r violet ('85)	2.75	1.75
a.		Double overprint		
15	A1	40r blue	165.00	77.50
a.		Cliché of Mozambique in Cape Verde plate	*1,250.*	*800.00*
16	A1	40r yellow ('85)	1.75	1.25
a.		Cliché of Mozambique in Cape Verde plate	37.50	25.00
b.		Imperf.		
c.		As "a," imperf.		
d.		Double overprint		
17	A1	50r green	165.00	77.50
18	A1	50r blue ('85)	4.75	2.50
a.		Imperf.		
b.		Double overprint		
19	A1	100r lilac	7.50	4.50
a.		Inverted overprint		
20	A1	200r orange	11.00	6.50
21	A1	300r yellow brn	13.00	10.00
a.		300r lake brown	16.00	12.50

Varieties of this overprint may be found without accent on "E" of "GUINE," or with grave instead of acute accent.

Stamps of the 1879-85 issues were reprinted on a smooth white chalky paper, ungummed, and on thin white paper with shiny white gum and clean-cut perforation 13½.

See Scott Classic Catalogue for listings by perforation.

King Luiz — A3

1886 Typo. *Perf. 12½, 13½*

22	A3	5r gray black	5.00	3.25
a.		Imperf.		
23	A3	10r green	6.00	3.00
a.		Perf. 13½	7.00	4.25
b.		Imperf.		
24	A3	20r carmine	9.00	4.00
25	A3	25r red lilac	9.00	4.00
a.		Imperf.		
26	A3	40r chocolate	7.00	4.50
a.		Perf. 12½	67.50	40.00
27	A3	50r blue	14.50	3.75
a.		Imperf.		
28	A3	80r gray	13.00	10.00
a.		Perf. 12½	67.50	42.50
29	A3	100r brown	13.00	11.00
a.		Perf. 12½	30.00	18.00
30	A3	200r gray lilac	30.00	18.00
31	A3	300r orange	40.00	27.50
a.		Perf. 13½	180.00	150.00
		Nos. 22-31 (10)	146.50	89.00

For surcharges and overprints see Nos. 67-76, 180-183.

Reprinted in 1905 on thin white paper with shiny white gum and clean-cut perforation 13½.

King Carlos

A4 A5

1893-94 *Perf. 11½*

32	A4	5r yellow	1.60	.90
a.		Perf. 12½	2.00	1.25
33	A4	10r red violet	1.60	1.10
34	A4	15r chocolate	2.25	1.25
35	A4	20r lavender	2.25	1.25
36	A4	25r blue green	2.25	1.25
37	A4	50r lt blue	4.00	2.25
a.		Perf. 12½	15.00	8.50
38	A4	75r rose	10.50	7.50
39	A4	80r lt green	10.50	7.50
40	A4	100r brn, *buff*	11.00	7.50
41	A4	150r car, *rose*	12.00	8.00
42	A4	200r dk bl, *bl*	14.00	10.00
43	A4	300r dk bl, *sal*	16.00	10.00
		Nos. 32-43 (12)	87.95	58.50

Almost all of Nos. 32-43 were issued without gum.

For surcharges and overprints see #77-88, 184-188, 203-205.

1898-1903 *Perf. 11½*

Name & Value in Black except 500r

44	A5	2½r gray	.35	.30
45	A5	5r orange	.35	.30
46	A5	10r lt green	.35	.30
47	A5	15r brown	3.00	2.00
48	A5	15r gray grn ('03)	1.60	1.10
49	A5	20r gray violet	1.25	1.00
50	A5	25r sea green	1.65	.80
51	A5	25r carmine ('03)	.90	.50
52	A5	50r dark blue	2.50	1.25
53	A5	50r brown ('03)	3.00	2.00
54	A5	65r dl blue ('03)	10.00	8.00
55	A5	75r rose	15.00	7.25
56	A5	75r lilac ('03)	3.50	2.00
57	A5	80r brt violet	2.75	1.75
58	A5	100r dk bl, *bl*	2.50	1.75
a.		Perf. 12½	47.50	20.00
59	A5	115r org brn, *pink* ('03)	7.75	5.50
a.		115r orange brown, *yellowish*	7.50	4.50
60	A5	130r brn, *straw* ('03)	9.00	6.75
61	A5	150r lt brn, *buff*	10.00	3.00
62	A5	200r red lilac, *pnksh*	9.00	3.00
63	A5	300r blue, *rose*	10.00	3.75
64	A5	400r dl bl, *straw* ('03)	12.00	9.00
65	A5	500r blk & red, *bl* ('01)	13.00	7.00
66	A5	700r vio, *yelsh* ('01)	15.00	9.00
		Nos. 44-66 (23)	134.45	77.30

Stamps issued in 1903 were without gum.

For overprints and surcharges see Nos. 90-115, 190-194, 197.

Issue of 1886 Surcharged in Black or Red

1902, Oct. 20 *Perf. 12½, 13½*

67	A3	65r on 10r green	6.00	5.00
68	A3	65r on 20r car	6.00	4.50
69	A3	65r on 25r red lilac	6.00	4.50
70	A3	115r on 40r choc	5.25	4.00
a.		Perf. 13½	12.00	8.75
71	A3	115r on 50r blue	5.25	4.00
72	A3	115r on 300r orange	6.50	5.25
73	A3	130r on 80r gray	6.50	4.50
a.		Perf. 13½	12.50	5.25
74	A3	130r on 100r brown	7.00	5.25
a.		Perf. 13½	18.00	12.50
75	A3	400r on 200r gray lil	12.00	8.00
76	A3	400r on 5r gray blk (R)	30.00	21.00
		Nos. 67-76 (10)	90.50	66.00

Reprints of No. 76 are in black and have clean-cut perforation 13½.

Same Surcharge on Issue of 1893-94

Perf. 11½, 12½, 13½

77	A4	65r on 10r red vio	5.25	3.25
78	A4	65r on 15r choc	5.25	3.25
79	A4	65r on 20r lav	5.25	3.25
80	A4	65r on 50r lt bl	2.75	2.00
a.		Perf. 13½	3.00	2.25
81	A4	115r on 5r yel	5.00	2.75
a.		Inverted surcharge	40.00	40.00
b.		Perf. 12½	50.00	35.00
82	A4	115r on 25r bl grn	5.50	3.00
83	A4	130r on 150r car, *rose*	5.50	3.00
84	A4	130r on 200r dk bl, *bl*	6.00	4.00
85	A4	130r on 300r dk bl, *sal*	6.00	4.00
86	A4	400r on 75r rose	4.00	2.75
87	A4	400r on 80r lt grn	2.75	1.50
88	A4	400r on 100r brn, *buff*	3.50	1.50

Same Surcharge on No. P1

89	N1	115r on 2½r brn	4.00	3.00
a.		Perf. 13½	4.75	3.50
		Nos. 77-89 (13)	60.75	37.25

Issue of 1898 Overprinted in Black

1902, Oct. 20 *Perf. 11½*

90	A5	15r brown	2.25	1.10
91	A5	25r sea green	2.25	1.50
92	A5	50r dark blue	2.75	1.50
93	A5	75r rose	5.25	3.50
		Nos. 90-93 (4)	12.50	7.60

No. 54 Surcharged in Black

1905

94	A5	50r on 65r dull blue	4.00	2.25

Issue of 1898-1903 Overprinted in Carmine or Green

1911 *Perf. 11½*

95	A5	2½r gray	.35	.30
a.		Inverted overprint	17.50	17.50
96	A5	5r orange	.35	.30
97	A5	10r lt green	.65	.45
98	A5	15r gray green	.65	.45
99	A5	20r gray violet	.65	.45
100	A5	25r carmine (G)	.65	.45
a.		Double overprint	14.00	14.00
101	A5	50r brown	.40	.35
102	A5	75c lilac	.40	.35
103	A5	100r dk bl, *bl*	1.40	.70
104	A5	115r org brn, *pink*	1.40	.90
105	A5	130r brn, *straw*	1.40	.90
106	A5	200r red lil, *pink*	6.00	3.00
107	A5	400r dl bl, *straw*	2.25	1.40
108	A5	500r blk & red, *bl*	2.50	1.40
109	A5	700r vio, *yelsh*	3.75	2.00
		Nos. 95-109 (15)	22.80	13.40

Issued without gum: #101-102, 104-105, 107.

Issue of 1898-1903 Overprinted in Red

REPUBLICA

1913 *Perf. 11½*

Without Gum (Nos. 110-115)

110	A5	15r gray grn	9.00	6.00
111	A5	75r lilac	9.00	6.00
a.		Inverted overprint	30.00	30.00
112	A5	100r bl, *bl*	5.50	4.00
a.		Inverted overprint	30.00	30.00
113	A5	200r red lil, *pnksh*	27.50	22.50
a.		Inverted overprint	75.00	75.00

Same Overprint on Nos. 90, 93 in Red

114	A5	15r brown	9.00	6.50
a.		"REPUBLICA" double	*30.00*	*30.00*
b.		"REPUBLICA" inverted	*27.50*	*27.50*
115	A5	75r rose	9.00	6.50
a.		"REPUBLICA" inverted	30.00	30.00
		Nos. 110-115 (6)	69.00	51.50

Vasco da Gama Issue of Various Portuguese Colonies Surcharged

1913

On Stamps of Macao

116	CD20	¼c on ½a bl grn	1.50	1.50
117	CD21	½c on 1a red	1.50	1.50
118	CD22	1c on 2a red vio	1.50	1.50
119	CD23	2½c on 4a yel grn	1.50	1.50
120	CD24	5c on 8a dk bl	1.50	1.50
121	CD25	7½c on 12a vio brn	3.00	3.00
122	CD26	10c on 16a bis brn	1.50	1.50
a.		Inverted surcharge	27.50	27.50
123	CD27	15c on 24a bis	2.50	2.50
		Nos. 116-123 (8)	14.50	14.50

On Stamps of Portuguese Africa

124	CD20	¼c on 2½c bl grn	1.25	1.25
125	CD21	½c on 5r red	1.25	1.25
126	CD22	1c on 10r red vio	1.25	1.25
127	CD23	2½c on 25r yel grn	1.25	1.25
128	CD24	5c on 50r dk bl	1.25	1.25
129	CD25	7½c on 75r vio brn	2.75	2.75
130	CD26	10c on 100r bis brn	1.25	1.25
131	CD27	15c on 150r bis	3.50	3.50
		Nos. 124-131 (8)	13.75	13.75

On Stamps of Timor

132	CD20	¼c on ½a bl grn	1.50	1.50
133	CD21	½c on 1a red	1.50	1.50
134	CD22	1c on 2a red vio	1.50	1.50
135	CD23	2½c on 4a yel grn	1.50	1.50
136	CD24	5c on 8a dk blue	1.50	1.50
137	CD25	7½c on 12a vio brn	2.75	2.75
138	CD26	10c on 16a bis brn	1.50	1.50
139	CD27	15c on 24a bister	2.75	2.75
		Nos. 132-139 (8)	14.50	14.50
		Nos. 116-139 (24)	42.75	42.75

Ceres — A6

1914-26 *Perf. 15x14, 12x11½*

Name and Value in Black

140	A6	¼c olive brown	.20	.20
141	A6	½c black	.20	.20
142	A6	1c blue green	1.25	1.25
143	A6	1c yel grn ('22)	.20	.20
144	A6	1½c lilac brn	.20	.20

145	A6	2c carmine	.20	.20
146	A6	2c gray ('25)	.20	*1.50*
147	A6	2½c lt violet	.20	.20
148	A6	3c orange ('22)	.20	*1.50*
149	A6	4c deep red ('22)	.20	*1.50*
150	A6	4½c gray ('22)	.20	*1.50*
151	A6	5c deep blue	.60	.50
152	A6	5c brt blue ('22)	.20	.20
153	A6	6c lilac ('22)	.20	*1.50*
154	A6	7c ultra ('22)	.30	*1.50*
155	A6	7½c yellow brn	.20	.20
156	A6	8c slate	.20	.20
157	A6	10c orange brn	.20	.20
158	A6	12c blue grn ('22)	.60	.45
159	A6	15c plum	7.50	6.50
160	A6	15c brn rose ('22)	.45	.30
161	A6	20c yellow grn	.20	.20
162	A6	24c ultra ('25)	1.75	1.50
163	A6	25c brown ('25)	2.25	2.00
164	A6	30c brown, *grn*	6.25	5.50
165	A6	30c gray grn ('22)	.80	.25
166	A6	40c brown, *pink*	3.25	3.00
167	A6	40c turq bl ('22)	.80	.35
168	A6	50c orange, *salmon*	3.25	3.00
169	A6	50c violet ('25)	1.75	.80
170	A6	60c dk blue ('22)	1.75	.85
171	A6	60c dp rose ('26)	2.25	1.60
172	A6	80c brt rose ('22)	1.50	.90
173	A6	1e green, *blue*	3.50	3.25
174	A6	1e pale rose ('22)	2.50	1.40
175	A6	1e indigo ('26)	3.25	2.50
176	A6	2e dk violet ('22)	2.75	1.40
177	A6	5e buff ('25)	12.00	9.50
178	A6	10e pink ('25)	25.00	16.00
179	A6	20e pale turq ('25)	55.00	30.00
		Nos. 140-179 (40)	143.50	104.00

For surcharges see Nos. 195-196, 211-213.

Provisional Issue of 1902 Overprinted in Carmine

1915 ***Perf. 11½, 12½, 13½***

180	A3	115r on 40r choc	1.00	.60
a.		Perf. 13½	12.00	7.75
181	A3	115r on 50r blue	1.25	.70
182	A3	130r on 80r gray	4.00	1.75
a.		Perf. 12½	25.00	20.00
183	A3	130r on 100r brn	3.25	1.75
a.		Perf. 13½	13.00	10.00
184	A4	115r on 5r yellow	.75	.60
a.		Perf. 11½	4.50	4.00
185	A4	115r on 25r bl grn	.70	.60
186	A4	130r on 150r car, *rose*	1.10	.75
187	A4	130r on 200r bl, *bl*	.75	.65
188	A4	130r on 300r dk bl, *sal*	1.00	.75
189	N1	115r on 2½r brn	1.10	.80
a.		Perf. 13½	12.00	10.00
b.		Inverted overprint	20.00	20.00

On Nos. 90, 92, 94

Perf. 11½

190	A5	15r brown	.75	.65
191	A5	50r dark blue	.75	.65
192	A5	50r on 65r dl bl	.75	.65
		Nos. 180-192 (13)	17.15	10.90

Nos. 64, 66 Overprinted

1919 **Without Gum** ***Perf. 11½***

193	A5	400r dl bl, *straw*	30.00	19.00
194	A5	700r vio, *yelsh*	10.00	5.75

Nos. 140, 141 and 59 Surcharged:

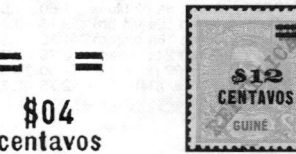

= =

$04

centavos

a

b

1920, Sept. ***Perf. 15x14, 11½***

Without Gum

195	A6(a)	4c on ¼c	3.00	2.50
196	A6(a)	6c on ½c	3.50	2.50
197	A5(b)	12c on 115r	5.00	4.00
		Nos. 195-197 (3)	11.50	9.00

Nos. 86-88 Surcharged

1925 ***Perf. 11½***

203	A4	40c on 400r on 75r	.85	.70
204	A4	40c on 400r on 80r	.65	.50
205	A4	40c on 400r on 100r	.65	.50
		Nos. 203-205 (3)	2.15	1.70

Nos. 171-172, 176 Surcharged

1931 ***Perf. 12x11½***

211	A6	50c on 60c dp rose	3.00	1.50
212	A6	70c on 80c pink	3.00	1.75
213	A6	1.40e on 2e dk vio	6.00	3.50
		Nos. 211-213 (3)	12.00	6.75

Ceres — A7

1933 **Wmk. 232** ***Perf. 12 x 11½***

214	A7	1c bister	.20	.20
215	A7	5c olive brn	.20	.20
216	A7	10c violet	.20	.20
217	A7	15c black	.20	.20
218	A7	20c gray	.20	.20
219	A7	30c dk green	.25	.20
220	A7	40c red orange	.40	.20
221	A7	45c lt blue	1.00	.75
222	A7	50c lt brown	1.00	.50
223	A7	60c olive grn	1.25	.50
224	A7	70c orange brn	2.50	.60
225	A7	80c emerald	1.40	.75
226	A7	85c deep rose	2.75	1.25
227	A7	1e red brown	1.25	.80
228	A7	1.40e dk blue	6.00	2.00
229	A7	2e red violet	4.00	1.75
230	A7	5e apple green	9.00	5.25
231	A7	10e olive bister	16.00	8.75
232	A7	20e orange	50.00	22.50
		Nos. 214-232 (19)	97.80	46.80

Common Design Types pictured following the introduction.

Common Design Types

Engr.; Name & Value Typo. in Black

1938 **Unwmk.** ***Perf. 13½x13***

233	CD34	1c gray grn	.20	.20
234	CD34	5c orange brn	.20	.20
235	CD34	10c dk carmine	.20	.20
236	CD34	15c dk vio brn	.20	.20
237	CD34	20c slate	.35	.20
238	CD35	30c rose violet	.55	.25
239	CD35	35c brt green	.60	.30
240	CD35	40c brown	1.00	.30
241	CD35	50c brt red vio	1.00	.30
242	CD36	60c gray black	1.50	.30
243	CD36	70c brown vio	1.50	.30
244	CD36	80c orange	1.75	.65
245	CD36	1e red	1.40	.45
246	CD37	1.75e blue	1.90	.90
247	CD37	2e brown car	4.50	1.25
248	CD37	5e olive grn	5.00	2.00
249	CD38	10e blue vio	6.75	2.50
250	CD38	20e red brown	20.00	4.00
		Nos. 233-250 (18)	48.60	14.50

Fort of Cacheu A8

Nuno Tristam — A9

Ulysses S. Grant — A10

Designs: 3.50e, Teixeira Pinto. 5e, Honorio Barreto. 20e, Bissau Church.

Unwmk.

1946, Jan. 12 **Litho.** ***Perf. 11***

251	A8	30c gray & lt gray	.75	.65
252	A9	50c black & pink	.75	.35
253	A9	50c gray grn & lt grn	.75	.35
254	A10	1.75e blue & lt blue	3.00	1.50
255	A10	3.50e red & pink	4.25	2.40
256	A10	5e lt brn & buff	9.25	5.00
257	A8	20e vio & lt vio	13.25	6.75
a.		Sheet of 7, #251-257 ('47)	65.00	65.00
		Nos. 251-257 (7)	32.00	17.00

Discovery of Guinea, 500th anniversary. No. 257a sold for 40 escudos.

Guinea Village — A11

UPU Symbols — A12

Designs: 10c, Crowned crane. 20c, 3.50e, Tribesman. 35c, 5e, Woman in ceremonial dress. 50c, Musician. 70c, Man. 80c, 20e, Girl. 1e, 2e, Drummer. 1.75e, Antelope.

1948, Apr. **Photo.** ***Perf. 11½***

258	A11	5c chocolate	.20	.20
259	A11	10c lt violet	.60	.60
260	A11	20c dull rose	.40	.25
261	A11	35c green	.35	.25
262	A11	50c dp orange	.35	.20
263	A11	70c dp gray bl	.40	.25
264	A11	80c dk ol grn	.85	.30
265	A11	1e rose red	.85	.40
266	A11	1.75e ultra	3.50	2.00
267	A11	2e blue	7.50	1.00
268	A11	3.50e orange brn	2.50	.80
269	A11	5e slate	4.50	1.25
270	A11	20e violet	10.00	3.00
a.		Sheet of 13, #258-270 + 2 labels	60.00	60.00
		Nos. 258-270 (13)	32.00	10.50

No. 270a sold for 40 escudos.

Lady of Fatima Issue

Common Design Type

1948, Oct. **Litho.** ***Perf. 14½***

271	CD40	50c deep green	3.00	2.75

1949, Oct. ***Perf. 14***

272	A12	2e dp org & cream	4.00	2.25

Universal Postal Union, 75th anniversary.

Catalogue values for unused stamps in this section, from this point to the end of the section, are for Never Hinged items.

Holy Year Issue

Common Design Types

1950, May ***Perf. 13x13½***

273	CD41	1e brown lake	1.25	1.00
274	CD42	3e blue green	1.90	1.40

Holy Year Extension Issue

Common Design Type

1951, Oct. ***Perf. 14***

275	CD43	1e choc & pale brn	.90	.60

Medical Congress Issue

Common Design Type

Design: Physical examination.

1952 ***Perf. 13½***

276	CD44	50c purple & choc + label	.40	.30

Stamps without label attached sell for less.

Exhibition Entrance — A13

Stamp of Portugal and Arms of Colonies — A14

1953, Jan. **Litho.** ***Perf. 13***

277	A13	10c brn lake & ol	.20	.20
278	A13	50c dk blue & bister	.75	.25
279	A13	3e blk, dk brn & sal	2.00	.90
		Nos. 277-279 (3)	2.95	1.35

Exhibition of Sacred Missionary Art held at Lisbon in 1951.

1953 **Photo.** **Unwmk.**

280	A14	50c multicolored	.60	.50

Centenary of Portugal's first postage stamps.

Analeptes Trifasciata — A15

1953 ***Perf. 11½***

Various Beetles in Natural Colors

281	A15	5c yellow	.20	.20
282	A15	10c blue	.20	.20
283	A15	30c org vermilion	.20	.20
284	A15	50c yellow grn	.20	.20
285	A15	70c gray brn	.40	.25
286	A15	1e orange	.40	.25
287	A15	2e pale ol grn	1.00	.25
288	A15	3e lilac rose	1.50	.65
289	A15	5e lt blue grn	2.50	.80
290	A15	10e lilac	4.00	1.00
		Nos. 281-290 (10)	10.60	4.00

Sao Paulo Issue

Common Design Type

1954 **Litho.** ***Perf. 13½***

291	CD46	1e lil rose, bl gray & blk	.30	.20

Belem Tower, Lisbon, and Colonial Arms — A16

1955, Apr. 14

292	A16	1e blue & multi	.20	.20
293	A16	2.50e gray & multi	.45	.20

Visit of Pres. Francisco H. C. Lopes.

Fair Emblem, Globe and Arms — A17

1958 **Unwmk.** ***Perf. 12x11½***

294	A17	2.50e multicolored	.60	.50

World's Fair at Brussels.

Tropical Medicine Congress Issue

Common Design Type

Design: Maytenus senegalensis.

1958 ***Perf. 13½***

295	CD47	5e multicolored	1.90	1.00

Honorio Barreto — A18

Nautical Astrolabe — A19

1959, Apr. 29 Litho. *Perf. 13½*

296 A18 2.50e multicolored	.35	.20

Centenary of the death of Honorio Barreto, governor of Portuguese Guinea.

1960, June 25 *Perf. 13½*

297 A19 2.50e multicolored	.35	.20

500th anniversary of the death of Prince Henry the Navigator.

Traveling Medical Unit — A20

1960 Unwmk. *Perf. 14½*

298 A20 1.50e multicolored	.35	.20

10th anniv. of the Commission for Technical Cooperation in Africa South of the Sahara (C.C.T.A.).

Sports Issue

Common Design Type

1962, Jan. 18 Litho. *Perf. 13½*

299	CD48	50c	Automobile race	.25	.20
300	CD48	1e	Tennis	.90	.25
301	CD48	1.50e	Shot put	.65	.20
302	CD48	2.50e	Wrestling	.65	.20
303	CD48	3.50e	Trapshooting	.65	.20
304	CD48	15e	Volleyball	1.50	.80
			Nos. 299-304 (6)	4.60	1.85

Anti-Malaria Issue

Common Design Type

Design: Anopheles gambiae.

1962 Unwmk. *Perf. 13½*

305 CD49 2.50e multicolored	.60	.30

African Spitting Cobra — A21

Snakes: 35c, African rock python. 70c, Boomslang. 80c, West African mamba. 1.50e, Smythe's water snake. 2e, Common night adder, horiz. 2.50e, Green swamp snake. 3.50e, Brown house snake. 4e, Spotted wolf snake. 5e, Common puff adder. 15e, Striped beauty snake. 20e, African egg-eating snake, horiz.

1963, Jan. 17 Litho. *Perf. 13½*

306	A21	20c	multicolored	.25	.20
307	A21	35c	multicolored	.25	.20
308	A21	70c	multicolored	.40	.30
309	A21	80c	multicolored	.50	.30
310	A21	1.50e	multicolored	.75	.30
311	A21	2e	multicolored	.60	.20
312	A21	2.50e	multicolored	2.00	.40
313	A21	3.50e	multicolored	.75	.40
314	A21	4e	multicolored	.75	.40
315	A21	5e	multicolored	.75	.65
316	A21	15e	multicolored	2.00	.75
317	A21	20e	multicolored	2.50	.75
			Nos. 306-317 (12)	11.50	4.85

For overprints see Guinea-Bissau Nos. 696-703.

Airline Anniversary Issue

Common Design Type

1963 Litho. *Perf. 14½*

318 CD50 2.50e lt brown & multi	.60	.30

National Overseas Bank Issue

Common Design Type

Design: 2.50e, Joao de Andrade Córvo.

1964, May 16 *Perf. 13½*

319 CD51 2.50e multicolored	.60	.35

ITU Issue

Common Design Type

1965, May 17 Unwmk. *Perf. 14½*

320 CD52 2.50e lt blue & multi	1.75	.70

Soldier, 1548 A22

Sacred Heart of Jesus Monument and Chapel of the Apparition A23

40c, Rifleman, 1578. 60c, Rifleman, 1640. 1e, Grenadier, 1721. 2.50e, Fusiliers captain, 1740. 4.50e, Infantryman, 1740. 7.50e, Sergeant major, 1762. 10e, Engineers' officer, 1806.

1966, Jan. 8 Litho. *Perf. 13½*

321	A22	25c	multicolored	.20	.20
322	A22	40c	multicolored	.20	.20
323	A22	60c	multicolored	.30	.20
324	A22	1e	multicolored	.40	.20
325	A22	2.50e	multicolored	1.10	.35
326	A22	4.50e	multicolored	1.90	1.00
327	A22	7.50e	multicolored	1.90	1.25
328	A22	10e	multicolored	2.50	1.50
			Nos. 321-328 (8)	8.50	4.90

National Revolution Issue

Common Design Type

2.50e, Berta Craveiro Lopes School and Central Pavilion of Bissau Hospital.

1966, May 28 Litho. *Perf. 11½*

329 CD53 2.50e multicolored	.50	.30

Navy Club Issue

Common Design Type

Designs: 50c, Capt. Oliveira Muzanty and cruiser Republica. 1e, Capt. Afonso de Cerqueira and torpedo boat Guadiana.

1967, Jan. 31 Litho. *Perf. 13*

330 CD54 50c multicolored	.35	.25
331 CD54 1e multicolored	.75	.60

1967, May 13 *Perf. 12½x13*

332 A23 50c multicolored	.30	.30

50th anniv. of the appearance of the Virgin Mary to three shepherd children at Fatima.

Pres. Rodrigues Thomas — A24

Cabral's Coat of Arms — A25

1968, Feb. 2 Litho. *Perf. 13½*

333 A24 1e multicolored	.20	.20

Issued to commemorate the 1968 visit of Pres. Americo de Deus Rodrigues Thomaz.

1968, Apr. 22 Litho. *Perf. 14*

334 A25 2.50e multicolored	.50	.20

Pedro Alvares Cabral, navigator who took possession of Brazil for Portugal, 500th birth anniv.

Admiral Coutinho Issue

Common Design Type

Design: 1e, Adm. Coutinho and astrolabe.

1969, Feb. 17 Litho. *Perf. 14*

335 CD55 1e multicolored	.30	.20

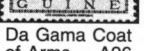

Da Gama Coat of Arms — A26

Arms of King Manuel I — A27

Vasco da Gama Issue

1969, Aug. 29 Litho. *Perf. 14*

336 A26 2.50e multicolored	.30	.20

Vasco da Gama (1469-1524), navigator.

Administration Reform Issue

Common Design Type

1969, Sept. 25 Litho. *Perf. 14*

337 CD56 50c multicolored	.20	.20

King Manuel I Issue

1969, Dec. 1 Litho. *Perf. 14*

338 A27 2e multicolored	.30	.20

Pres. Ulysses S. Grant and View of Bolama — A28

1970, Oct. 25 Litho. *Perf. 13½*

339 A28 2.50e multicolored	.40	.20

Centenary of Pres. Grant's arbitration in 1868 of Portuguese-English dispute concerning Bolama.

Marshal Carmona Issue

Common Design Type

Design: 1.50e, Antonio Oscar Carmona in general's uniform.

1970, Nov. 15 Litho. *Perf. 14*

340 CD57 1.50e multicolored	.30	.20

Luiz Camoens — A29

1972, May 25 Litho. *Perf. 13*

341 A29 50c brn org & multi	.20	.20

4th centenary of publication of The Lusiads by Luiz Camoens (1524-1580).

Olympic Games Issue

Common Design Type

Design: 2.50e, Weight lifting, hammer throw and Olympic emblem.

1972, June 20 *Perf. 14x13½*

342 CD59 2.50e multicolored	.40	.20

Lisbon-Rio de Janeiro Flight Issue

Common Design Type

1e, "Lusitania" taking off from Lisbon.

1972, Sept. 20 Litho. *Perf. 13½*

343 CD60 1e multicolored	.20	.20

WMO Centenary Issue

Common Design Type

1973, Dec. 15 Litho. *Perf. 13*

344 CD61 2e lt brown & multi	.40	.30

AIR POST STAMPS

Common Design Type

Perf. 13½x13

1938, Sept. 19 Engr. Unwmk.

Name and Value in Black

C1	CD39	10c	red orange	.40	.30
C2	CD39	20c	purple	.45	.30
C3	CD39	50c	orange	.45	.30
C4	CD39	1e	ultra	.55	.40
C5	CD39	2e	lilac brown	4.75	3.25
C6	CD39	3e	dark green	1.25	.85
C7	CD39	5e	red brown	3.50	.95
C8	CD39	9e	rose carmine	3.50	2.00
C9	CD39	10e	magenta	8.50	2.75
			Nos. C1-C9 (9)	23.35	11.10

No. C7 exists with overprint "Exposicao Internacional de Nova York, 1939-1940" and Trylon and Perisphere.

POSTAGE DUE STAMPS

D1

D2

1904 Unwmk. Typo. *Perf. 12*

Without Gum

J1	D1	5r	yellow green	.55	.40
J2	D1	10r	slate	.55	.40
J3	D1	20r	yellow brown	.60	.50
J4	D1	30r	red orange	1.75	1.50
J5	D1	50r	gray brown	1.75	1.50
J6	D1	60r	red brown	3.75	2.50
J7	D1	100r	lilac	3.75	2.50
J8	D1	130r	dull blue	3.00	1.90
J9	D1	200r	carmine	6.00	4.75
J10	D1	500r	violet	10.00	5.50
			Nos. J1-J10 (10)	31.70	21.45

Same Overprinted in Carmine or Green

1911

Without Gum

J11	D1	5r	yellow green	.25	.20
J12	D1	10r	slate	.25	.20
J13	D1	20r	yellow brown	.30	.30
J14	D1	30r	red orange	.30	.30
J15	D1	50r	gray brown	.30	.30
J16	D1	60r	red brown	.90	.75
J17	D1	100r	lilac	1.75	1.25
J18	D1	130r	dull blue	1.75	.90
J19	D1	200r	carmine (G)	1.75	1.40
J20	D1	500r	violet	1.00	.90
			Nos. J11-J20 (10)	8.55	6.50

Nos. J2-J10 Overprinted

1919

Without Gum

J21	D1	10r	slate	7.50	7.50
J22	D1	20r	yellow brown	8.25	8.25
J23	D1	30r	red orange	6.00	5.25
J24	D1	50r	gray brown	2.25	1.90
J25	D1	60r	red brown	500.00	400.00
J26	D1	100r	lilac	2.00	1.75
J27	D1	130r	dull blue	20.00	17.50
J28	D1	200r	carmine	2.50	2.25
J29	D1	500r	violet	21.00	18.00
			Nos. J21-J24,J26-J29 (8)	69.50	62.40

No. J25 was not regularly issued but exists on genuine covers.

1921

J30	D2	½c	yellow green	.20	.20
J31	D2	1c	slate	.20	.20
J32	D2	2c	orange brown	.20	.20
J33	D2	3c	orange	.20	.20
J34	D2	5c	gray brown	.20	.20
J35	D2	6c	light brown	.20	.20

J36	D2	10c	red violet	.25	.25
J37	D2	13c	dull blue	.25	.25
J38	D2	20c	carmine	.30	.30
J39	D2	50c	gray	.30	.30
			Nos. J30-J39 (10)	2.30	2.30

Catalogue values for unused stamps in this section, from this point to the end of the section, are for Never Hinged items.

Common Design Type

Photogravure and Typographed

1952 Unwmk. *Perf. 14*

Numeral in Red, Frame Multicolored

J40	CD45	10c	olive green	.20	.20
J41	CD45	30c	purple	.20	.20
J42	CD45	50c	dark green	.20	.20
J43	CD45	1e	violet blue	.30	.30
J44	CD45	2e	olive black	.45	.45
J45	CD45	5e	brown red	.90	.90
			Nos. J40-J45 (6)	2.25	2.25

WAR TAX STAMPS

WT1

Perf. 11½x12

1919, May 20 Typo. Unwmk.

MR1	WT1	10r	brn, buff & blk	40.00	25.00
MR2	WT1	40r	brn, buff & blk	35.00	20.00
MR3	WT1	50r	brn, buff & blk	37.50	22.50
			Nos. MR1-MR3 (3)	112.50	67.50

The 40r is not overprinted "REPUBLICA."

Some authorities consider Nos. MR2-MR3 to be revenue stamps.

NEWSPAPER STAMP

N1

Perf. 12½, 13½

1893 Typo. Unwmk.

P1	N1	2½r	brown	1.10	.70
a.			Perf. 13½	1.10	.80

For surcharge & overprint see #89, 189.

POSTAL TAX STAMPS

Pombal Issue

Common Design Types

1925 Unwmk. Engr. *Perf. 12½*

RA1	CD28	15c	red & black	.50	.40
RA2	CD29	15c	red & black	.50	.40
RA3	CD30	15c	red & black	.50	.40
			Nos. RA1-RA3 (3)	1.50	1.20

Coat of Arms — PT7

1934, Apr. 1 Typo. *Perf. 11½*

Without Gum

RA4	PT7	50c	red brn & grn	5.75	3.50
a.			Tête beche pair		400.00

Coat of Arms

PT8 PT9

1938-40

Without Gum

RA5	PT8	50c	ol bis & citron	5.50	3.00
RA6	PT8	50c	lt grn & ol brn ('40)	5.50	3.00

1942 *Perf. 11*

Without Gum

RA7	PT9	50c	black & yellow	1.50	.90

1959, July Unwmk.

Without Gum

RA8	PT9	30c	dark ocher & blk	.20	.20

See Nos. RA24-RA26.

Lusignian Cross

PT10 PT11

1967 Typo. *Perf. 11x11½*

Without Gum

RA9	PT10	50c	pink, red & blk	.75	.75
RA10	PT10	1e	grn, red & blk	.75	.75
RA11	PT10	5e	gray, red & blk	1.00	1.00
RA12	PT10	10e	lt bl, red & blk	2.00	2.00
			Nos. RA9-RA12 (4)	4.50	4.50

The tax was for national defense.

A 50e was used for revenue only.

1967, Aug. Typo. *Perf. 11*

Without Gum

RA13	PT11	50c	pink, blk & red	.50	.50
RA14	PT11	1e	pale grn, blk & red	.50	.50
RA15	PT11	5e	gray, blk & red	1.00	1.00
RA16	PT11	10e	lt bl, blk & red	2.00	2.00
			Nos. RA13-RA16 (4)	4.00	4.00

The tax was for national defense.

Catalogue values for unused stamps in this section, from this point to the end of the section, are for Never Hinged items.

Carved Figurine — PT12

Art from Bissau Museum: 1e, Tree of Life, with 2 birds, horiz. #RA19, Man wearing horned headgear ("Vaca Bruto"). #RA20, as #RA19, inscribed "Tocador de Bombolon." 2.50e, The Magistrate. 5e, Man bearing burden on head. 10e, Stylized pelican.

1968 Litho. *Perf. 13½*

RA17	PT12	50c	gray & multi	.20	.20
a.			Yellow paper	.75	
RA18	PT12	1e	multi	.20	.20
RA19	PT12	2e	*(Vaca Bruto)*	.20	.20
RA20	PT12	2e	*(Tocador de Bombolon)*	7.00	
RA21	PT12	2.50e	multi	.25	.25
RA22	PT12	5e	multi	.30	.30
RA23	PT12	10e	multi	.70	.70
			Nos. RA17-RA19,RA21-RA23 (6)	1.85	1.85

Obligatory on all inland mail Mar. 15-Apr. 15 and Dec. 15-Jan. 15, and all year on parcels.

A souvenir sheet embracing Nos. RA17-RA19 and RA21-RA23 exists. The stamps have simulated perforations. Value $3.50.

For surcharges see Nos. RA27-RA28.

Arms Type of 1942

1968 Typo. *Perf. 11*

Without Gum

RA24	PT9	2.50e	lt blue & blk	.40	.40
RA25	PT9	5e	green & blk	.75	.75
RA26	PT9	10e	dp blue & blk	1.50	1.50
			Nos. RA24-RA26 (3)	2.65	2.65

No. RA20 Surcharged

1968 Litho. *Perf. 13½*

RA27	PT12	50c	on 2e multi	.30	.30
RA28	PT12	1e	on 2e multi	.30	.30

Black and White Hands Holding Sword — PT13

Mother and Children — PT14

1968 Litho. *Perf. 13½*

RA29	PT13	50c	pink & multi	.20	.20
RA30	PT13	1e	multicolored	.20	.20
RA31	PT13	2e	yellow & multi	.20	.20
RA32	PT13	2.50e	buff & multi	.25	.25
RA33	PT13	3e	multicolored	.30	.30
RA34	PT13	4e	gray & multi	.35	.35
RA35	PT13	5e	multicolored	.40	.40
RA36	PT13	10e	multicolored	.80	.80
			Nos. RA29-RA36 (8)	2.70	2.70

The surtax was for national defense. Other denominations exist: 8e, 9e, 15e.

1971, June Litho. *Perf. 13½*

RA37	PT14	50c	multicolored	.20	.20
RA38	PT14	1e	multicolored	.20	.20
RA39	PT14	2e	multicolored	.20	.20
RA40	PT14	3e	multicolored	.25	.20
RA41	PT14	4e	multicolored	.30	.25
RA42	PT14	5e	multicolored	.40	.35
RA43	PT14	10e	multicolored	.80	.50
			Nos. RA37-RA43 (7)	2.35	1.90

A 20e exists.

POSTAL TAX DUE STAMPS

Pombal Issue

Common Design Types

1925 Unwmk. *Perf. 12½*

RAJ1	CD28	30c	red & black	.50	.40
RAJ2	CD29	30c	red & black	.50	.40
RAJ3	CD30	30c	red & black	.50	.40
			Nos. RAJ1-RAJ3 (3)	1.50	1.20

PORTUGUESE INDIA

'pōr-chi-gēz 'in-dē-ə

LOCATION — West coast of the Indian peninsula

GOVT. — Portuguese colony

AREA — 1,537 sq. mi.

POP. — 649,000 (1958)

CAPITAL — Panjim (Nova-Goa)

The colony was seized by India on Dec. 18, 1961, and annexed by that republic.

1000 Reis = 1 Milreis

12 Reis = 1 Tanga (1881-82)

(Real = singular of Reis)

16 Tangas = 1 Rupia

100 Centavos = 1 Escudo (1959)

Catalogue values for unused stamps in this country are for Never Hinged items, beginning with Scott 490 in the regular postage section, Scott J43 in the postage due section, and Scott RA6 in the postal tax section.

Expect Nos. 1-55, 70-112 to have rough perforations. Stamps frequently were cut apart because of the irregular and missing perforations. Scissor separations that do not remove perfs do not negatively affect value.

Numeral of Value

A1 A2

A1: Large figures of value.

"REIS" in Roman capitals. "S" and "R" of "SERVICO" smaller and "E" larger than the other letters. 33 lines in background. Side ornaments of four dashes.

A2: Large figures of value.

"REIS" in block capitals. "S," "E" and "R" same size as other letters of "SERVICO." 44 lines in background. Side ornaments of five dots.

Handstamped from a Single Die

Perf. 13 to 18 & Compound

1871, Oct. 1 Unwmk.

Thin Transparent Brittle Paper

1	A1	10r	black	625.00	320.00
2	A1	20r	dk carmine	1,350	250.00
a.			20r orange vermilion	1,350.	275.00
3	A1	40r	Prus blue	475.00	310.00
4	A1	100r	yellow grn	550.00	375.00
5	A1	200r	ocher yel	800.00	425.00

1872

Thick Soft Wove Paper

5A	A1	10r	black	*1,500.*	310.00
6	A1	20r	dk carmine	*1,625.*	310.00
7	A1	20r	orange ver	*1,800.*	300.00
7A	A1	100r	yellow grn		—
8	A1	200r	ocher yel	*1,700.*	600.00
9	A1	300r	dp red violet		*2,250.*

The 600r and 900r of type A1 are bogus.

See Nos. 24-28. For surcharges see Nos. 70-71, 73, 83, 94, 99, 104, 108.

Perf. 12½ to 14½ & Compound

1872

10	A2	10r	black	235.00	90.00
11	A2	20r	vermilion	225.00	80.00
a.			"20" omitted		*1,000.*
12	A2	40r	blue	65.00	60.00
a.			Tête bêche pair	*5,250.*	*5,000.*
b.			40r dark blue	80.00	60.00
13	A2	100r	deep green	65.00	60.00
14	A2	200r	yellow	275.00	250.00
15	A2	300r	red violet	275.00	200.00
a.			Imperf.		
16	A2	600r	red violet	160.00	110.00
a.			"600" double	*675.00*	
17	A2	900r	red violet	190.00	175.00
			Nos. 10-17 (8)	1,490.	1,025.

An unused 100r blue green exists with watermark of lozenges and gray burelage on back. Experts believe it to be a proof.

White Laid Paper

18	A2	10r	black	35.00	10.00
a.			Tête bêche pair	*13,250.*	*6,500.*
b.			10r brownish black	35.00	
19	A2	20r	vermilion	35.00	10.00
20	A2	40r	blue	65.00	25.00
a.			"40" double	*400.00*	
b.			Tête bêche pair	*1,800.*	*1,800.*
21	A2	100r	green	60.00	36.00
a.			"100" double	*400.00*	
22	A2	200r	yellow	180.00	170.00
			Nos. 18-22 (5)	375.00	251.00

See No. 23. For surcharges see Nos. 72, 82, 95-96, 100-101, 105-106, 109-110.

1873

Re-issues

Thin Bluish Toned Paper

23	A2	20r vermilion	185.00	160.00
24	A1	10r black	13.50	6.50
a.		"1" inverted	125.00	100.00
b.		"10" double	400.00	
25	A1	20r vermilion	16.00	8.00
a.		"20" double	400.00	
b.		"20" inverted		
26	A1	300r dp violet	110.00	65.00
a.		"300" double	450.00	
27	A1	600r dp violet	130.00	75.00
a.		"600" double	525.00	
b.		"600" inverted	625.00	
28	A1	900r dp violet	135.00	75.00
a.		"900" double	625.00	
b.		"900" triple	1,000.	
		Nos. 23-28 (6)	589.50	389.50

Nos. 23 to 26 are re-issues of Nos. 11, 5A, 7, and 9. The paper is thinner and harder than that of the 1871-72 stamps and slightly transparent. It was originally bluish white but is frequently stained yellow by the gum.

A3

A4

A3: Same as A1 with small figures.
A4: Same as A2 with small figures.

1874

Thin Bluish Toned Paper

29	A3	10r black	35.00	27.50
a.		"10" and "20" superimposed	450.00	*350.00*
30	A3	20r vermilion	550.00	275.00
a.		"20" double		*625.00*

For surcharge see No. 84.

1875

31	A4	10r black	36.00	22.50
a.		Value sideways		375.00
32	A4	15r rose	12.50	9.00
a.		"15" inverted	450.00	
b.		"15" double		
c.		Value omitted	1,100.	
33	A4	20r vermilion	65.00	30.00
a.		"0" missing	800.00	
b.		"20" sideways	*800.00*	
c.		"20" double		
		Nos. 31-33 (3)	113.50	61.50

For surcharges see Nos. 74, 78, 85.

A5

A6

A5: Re-cutting of A1.
Small figures. "REIS" in Roman capitals. Letters larger. "V" of "SERVICO" barred. 33 lines in background. Side ornaments of five dots.
A6: First re-cutting of A2.
Small figures. "REIS" in block capitals. Letters re-cut. "V" of "SERVICO" barred. 41 lines above and 43 below "REIS." Side ornaments of five dots.

Perf. 12½ to 13½ & Compound

1876

34	A5	10r black	20.00	12.50
35	A5	20r vermilion	15.00	11.00
a.		"20" double		
36	A6	10r black	6.25	3.50
a.		Double impression	500.00	
b.		"10" double	500.00	
37	A6	15r rose	400.00	300.00
a.		"15" omitted		*1,000.*
38	A6	20r vermilion	21.00	13.50
39	A6	40r blue	105.00	85.00
40	A6	100r green	150.00	125.00
a.		Imperf.		
41	A6	200r yellow	1,000.	625.00
42	A6	300r violet	550.00	450.00
a.		"300" omitted		
43	A6	600r violet	*800.00*	*675.00*
44	A6	900r violet	*1,000.*	*750.00*

For surcharges see Nos. 75-76, 78C-80, 86-87, 91-92, 98, 102, 107, 111.

A7

A8

A9

A7: Same as A5 with addition of a star above and a bar below the value.
A8: Second re-cutting of A2. Same as A6 but 41 lines both above and below "REIS." Star above and bar below value.
A9: Third re-cutting of A2. 41 lines above and 38 below "REIS." Star above and bar below value. White line around central oval.

1877

45	A7	10r black	30.00	25.00
46	A8	10r black	40.00	27.50
47	A9	10r black	27.50	25.00
a.		"10" omitted		
48	A9	15r rose	32.50	27.50
49	A9	20r vermilion	8.00	6.50
50	A9	40r blue	16.00	13.50
a.		"40" omitted	40.00	25.00
51	A9	100r green	65.00	60.00
a.		"100" omitted		
52	A9	200r yellow	70.00	67.50
53	A9	300r violet	95.00	67.50
54	A9	600r violet	95.00	72.50
55	A9	900r violet	95.00	75.00
		Nos. 45-55 (11)	574.00	467.50

No. 47, 20r, 40r and 200r exist imperf.
For surcharges see Nos. 77, 81, 88-90, 93, 112.

Portuguese Crown — A10

1877, July 15 Typo. *Perf. 12½, 13½*

56	A10	5r black	4.75	2.90
57	A10	10r yellow	9.00	7.25
a.		Imperf.		
58	A10	20r bister	9.50	6.00
59	A10	25r rose	10.00	8.00
60	A10	40r blue	13.50	11.00
a.		Perf. 12½	160.00	120.00
61	A10	50r yellow grn	32.50	20.00
62	A10	100r lilac	15.00	11.50
63	A10	200r orange	21.00	17.00
64	A10	300r yel brn	29.00	25.00
		Nos. 56-64 (9)	144.25	108.65

1880-81

65	A10	10r green	15.00	9.50
66	A10	25r slate	42.50	32.50
a.		Perf. 12½	67.50	37.50
67	A10	25r violet	35.00	17.50
68	A10	40r yellow	35.00	20.00
69	A10	50r dk blue	35.00	17.50
		Nos. 65-69 (5)	162.50	97.00

For surcharges see Nos. 113-161.

The stamps of the 1877-81 issues were reprinted in 1885, on stout very white paper, ungummed and with rough perforation 13½. They were again reprinted in 1905 on thin white paper with shiny white gum and clean-cut perforation 13½ with large holes. Value of the lowest-cost reprint, $1 each.

Stamps of 1871-77 Surcharged with New Values

Black Surcharge

1881

70	A1	1½r on 20r (#2)		*800.00*
71	A1	1½r on 20r (#7)		*700.00*
72	A2	1½r on 20r (#11)		*600.00*
73	A1	1½r on 20r (#25)	225.00	200.00
74	A4	1½r on 20r (#33)	135.00	125.00
a.		Inverted surcharge		
75	A5	1½r on 20r (#35)	110.00	80.00
76	A6	1½r on 20r (#38)	125.00	110.00
77	A9	1½r on 20r (#49)	200.00	140.00
78	A4	5r on 15r (#32)	2.50	2.50
a.		Double surcharge	10.00	
b.		Inverted surcharge	10.00	
78C	A6	5r on 15r (#37)	175.00	165.00
79	A5	5r on 20r (#35)	2.75	2.75
a.		Double surcharge	7.00	
b.		Inverted surcharge	7.00	
80	A6	5r on 20r (#38)	2.75	2.00
a.		Double surcharge	7.00	
b.		Inverted surcharge	7.00	
81	A9	5r on 20r (#49)	5.00	4.50
a.		Double surcharge	10.00	
b.		Invtd. surcharge	10.00	

Red Surcharge

82	A2	5r on 10r (#18)	*425.00*	*325.00*
83	A1	5r on 10r (#24)	*475.00*	*275.00*
84	A3	5r on 10r (#29)	*1,600.*	
85	A4	5r on 10r (#31)	*110.00*	*110.00*
86	A5	5r on 10r (#34)	5.50	5.50
a.		Double surcharge	15.00	
87	A6	5r on 10r (#36)	8.75	7.00
a.		Inverted surcharge		
88	A7	5r on 10r (#45)	80.00	45.00
a.		Inverted surcharge	150.00	
89	A8	5r on 10r (#46)	175.00	75.00
90	A9	5r on 10r (#47)	35.00	30.00
a.		Inverted surcharge	75.00	
b.		Double surcharge	75.00	

Similar Surcharge, Handstamped

Black Surcharge

1883

91	A5	1½r on 10r (#34)	1,500.	*750.00*
92	A6	1½r on 10r (#36)	1,000.	*750.00*
93	A9	1½r on 10r (#47)	*750.00*	*550.00*
94	A1	4½r on 40r (#3)	2,000.	*700.00*
95	A2	4½r on 40r (#12)	32.50	32.50
96	A2	4½r on 40r (#20)	32.50	32.50
98	A6	4½r on 40r (#39)	32.50	32.50
99	A1	4½r on 100r (#4)	2,000.	*700.00*
100	A2	4½r on 100r (#13)	40.00	37.50
101	A2	4½r on 100r (#21)	40.00	37.50
102	A6	4½r on 100r (#40)	35.00	37.50
104	A1	6r on 100r (#4)	2,000.	*1,100.*
105	A2	6r on 100r (#13)	*350.00*	*250.00*
106	A2	6r on 100r (#21)	*250.00*	*200.00*
107	A6	6r on 100r (#40)	*325.00*	*250.00*
108	A1	6r on 200r (#5)	*750.00*	*550.00*
109	A2	6r on 200r (#14)		*200.00*
110	A2	6r on 200r (#22)	*200.00*	*200.00*
111	A6	6r on 200r (#41)		*400.00*
112	A9	6r on 200r (#52)	*500.00*	*500.00*

1½

Stamps of 1877-81 Surcharged in Black

1881-82

113	A10	1½r on 5r blk	1.25	1.00
a.		With additional surcharge "4½" in blue	110.00	100.00
114	A10	1½r on 10r grn	1.25	1.00
a.		With additional surch. "6"	150.00	100.00
115	A10	1½r on 20r bis	10.50	8.00
a.		Inverted surcharge	25.00	
b.		Double surcharge	25.00	
c.		Pair, one without surcharge	—	
116	A10	1½r on 25r slate	35.00	30.00
117	A10	1½r on 100r lil	55.00	42.50
118	A10	4½r on 10r grn	165.00	150.00
119	A10	4½r on 20r bis	3.50	2.50
a.		Inverted surcharge	75.00	60.00
120	A10	4½r on 25r vio	10.50	10.00
121	A10	4½r on 100r lil	200.00	150.00
122	A10	6r on 10r yel	42.50	40.00
123	A10	6r on 10r grn	9.25	7.25
124	A10	6r on 20r bis	15.00	14.00
125	A10	6r on 25r slate	30.00	25.00
126	A10	6r on 25r vio	2.00	1.65
127	A10	6r on 40r blue	75.00	62.50
128	A10	6r on 40r yel	37.50	30.00
129	A10	6r on 50r grn	42.50	35.00
130	A10	6r on 50r blue	100.00	80.00
		Nos. 113-130 (18)	835.75	690.40

1
T

Surcharged in Black

131	A10	1t on 10r grn	400.00	300.00
a.		With additional surch. "6"	800.00	700.00
132	A10	1t on 20r bis	42.50	37.50
133	A10	1t on 25r slate	32.50	27.50
134	A10	1t on 25r vio	12.00	8.25
135	A10	1t on 40r blue	17.00	16.00
136	A10	1t on 50r grn	50.00	42.50
137	A10	1t on 50r blue	22.50	17.00
138	A10	1t on 100r lil	21.00	12.00
139	A10	1t on 200r org	42.50	37.50
140	A10	2t on 25r slate	32.50	30.00
a.		Small "T"	50.00	35.00
141	A10	2t on 25r vio	12.50	10.50
142	A10	2t on 40r blue	37.50	30.00
143	A10	2t on 40r yel	47.50	37.50
144	A10	2t on 50r grn	14.00	12.00
a.		Inverted surcharge	100.00	90.00
145	A10	2t on 50r blue	80.00	67.50
146	A10	2t on 100r lil	10.50	8.50
147	A10	2t on 200r org	35.00	30.00
148	A10	2t on 300r brn	30.00	27.50
149	A10	4t on 10r grn	12.50	10.50
a.		Inverted surcharge	40.00	40.00
150	A10	4t on 50r grn	12.00	9.25
a.		With additional surch. "2"	150.00	95.00
151	A10	4t on 200r org	35.00	30.00
152	A10	8t on 20r bis	30.00	21.00
153	A10	8t on 25r rose	165.00	150.00
154	A10	8t on 40r blue	42.50	35.00
155	A10	8t on 100r lil	35.00	30.00
156	A10	8t on 200r org	30.00	27.50
157	A10	8t on 300r brn	42.50	35.00
		Nos. 131-157 (27)	1,344.	1,100.

1882

Blue Surcharge

158	A10	4½r on 5r black	11.00	9.50

Similar Surcharge, Handstamped

1883

159	A10	1½r on 5r black	50.00	30.00
160	A10	1½r on 10r grn	75.00	40.00
161	A10	4½r on 100r lil	*350.00*	*300.00*

The "2" in "½" is 3mm high, instead of 2mm as on Nos. 113, 114 and 121.
The handstamp is known double on #159-161.

A12

1882-83 Typo.

With or Without Accent on "E" of "REIS"

162	A12	1½r black	.50	.40
a.		"½" for "1½"		
163	A12	4½r olive bister	.85	.40
164	A12	6r green	.75	.40
165	A12	1t rose	.75	.40
166	A12	2t blue	.75	.40
167	A12	4t lilac	3.00	2.50
168	A12	8t orange	3.00	2.50
		Nos. 162-168 (7)	9.60	7.00

There were three printings of the 1882-83 issue. The first had "REIS" in thick letters with acute accent on the "E." The second had "REIS" in thin letters with accent on the "E." The third had the "E" without accent. In the first printing the "E" sometimes had a grave or circumflex accent.

The third printing may be divided into two sets, with or without a small circle in the cross of the crown.

Stamps doubly printed or with value omitted, double, inverted or misplaced are printer's waste.

Nos. 162-168 were reprinted on thin white paper, with shiny white gum and clean-cut perforation 13½. Value of lowest-cost reprint, $1 each.

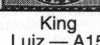

"REIS" no serifs — A13

"REIS" with serifs — A14

1883 Litho. *Imperf.*

169	A13	1½r black	1.25	1.00
a.		Tête bêche pair		
b.		"1½" double	*375.00*	*300.00*
170	A13	4½r olive grn	12.50	11.00
a.		"4½" omitted	325.00	250.00
171	A13	6r green	12.50	11.00
a.		Tête bêche pair	1,100.	
b.		"6" omitted	350.00	275.00
172	A14	1½r black	87.50	50.00
a.		"1½" omitted	325.00	300.00
173	A14	6r green	57.50	45.00
a.		"6" omitted	375.00	325.00
		Nos. 169-173 (5)	171.25	118.00

Nos. 169-171 exist with unofficial perf. 12.

King Luiz — A15

King Carlos — A16

Perf. 12½, 13½

1886, Apr. 29 Embossed

174	A15	1½r black	2.25	1.25
a.		Perf. 13½	100.00	62.50
175	A15	4½r bister	3.00	1.40
a.		Perf. 13½	27.50	12.50
176	A15	6r dp green	4.00	1.60
a.		Perf. 13½	30.00	14.00
177	A15	1t brt rose	6.00	2.75
178	A15	2t deep blue	8.00	4.00
179	A15	4t gray vio	10.00	4.00
180	A15	8t orange	9.00	4.25
		Nos. 174-180 (7)	42.25	19.25

For surcharges and overprints see Nos. 224-230, 277-278, 282, 317-323, 354, 397.

Nos. 178-179 were reprinted. Originals have yellow gum. Reprints have white gum and clean-cut perforation 13½. Value, $4 each.

1895-96 Typo. *Perf. 11½, 12½, 13½*

181	A16	1½r black	1.25	.60
182	A16	4½r pale orange	1.25	.60
a.		Perf. 13½	7.25	1.50
183	A16	6r green	1.25	.60
a.		Perf. 12½	2.75	1.00
184	A16	9r gray lilac	3.75	2.75
185	A16	1t lt blue	1.25	.50
a.		Perf. 12½	5.00	2.25
186	A16	2t rose	.90	.60
a.		Perf. 12½	3.75	2.00
187	A16	4t dk blue	1.50	.75
a.		Perf. 12½	4.75	3.00
188	A16	8t brt violet	3.00	2.50
		Nos. 181-188 (8)	14.15	8.90

For surcharges and overprints see Nos. 231-238,275-276, 279-281, 324-331, 352.

No. 184 was reprinted. Reprints have white gum, and clean-cut perforation 13½. Value $10.

Common Design Types pictured following the introduction.

Vasco da Gama Issue
Common Design Types

1898, May 1 Engr. *Perf. 14 to 15*

189	CD20	1½r blue green	.90	.80
190	CD21	4½r red	.90	.80
191	CD22	6r red violet	.90	.70
192	CD23	9r yellow green	.90	.90
193	CD24	1t dk blue	1.50	1.50
194	CD25	2t violet brn	2.00	1.75
195	CD26	4t bister brn	2.00	1.75
196	CD27	8t bister	4.00	3.50
		Nos. 189-196 (8)	13.10	11.70

For overprints and surcharges see Nos. 290-297, 384-389.

King Carlos — A17

1898-1903 Typo. *Perf. 11½*
Name and Value in Black except No. 219

197	A17	1r gray ('02)	.30	.20
198	A17	1½r orange	.30	.25
199	A17	1½r slate ('02)	.40	.25
200	A17	2r orange ('02)	.30	.25
201	A17	2½r yel brn ('02)	.40	.25
202	A17	3r dp blue ('02)	.40	.25
203	A17	4½r lt green	.65	.50
204	A17	6r brown	.65	.50
205	A17	6r gray grn ('02)	.40	.25
206	A17	9r dull vio	.75	.50
a.		9r gray lilac	1.60	1.60
208	A17	1t sea green	.75	.45
209	A17	1t car rose ('02)	.55	.25
210	A17	2t blue	1.25	.50
a.		Perf. 13½	27.50	7.00
211	A17	2t brown ('02)	3.00	1.90
212	A17	2½t dull bl ('02)	10.00	6.00
213	A17	4t blue, *blue*	3.00	2.00
214	A17	5t brn, *straw* ('02)	4.00	1.90
215	A17	8t red lil, *pnksh*	5.00	1.25
216	A17	8t red vio, *pink* ('02)	4.50	2.75
217	A17	12t blue, *pink*	6.00	2.00
218	A17	12t grn, *pink* ('02)	4.50	3.00
219	A17	1rp blk & red, *bl*	9.00	6.00
220	A17	1rp dl bl, *straw* ('02)	10.00	6.50
221	A17	2rp vio, *yelsh*	13.00	7.50
222	A17	2rp gray blk, *straw* ('03)	15.00	11.00
		Nos. 197-222 (25)	94.10	56.20

Several stamps of this issue exist without value or with value inverted but they are not known to have been issued in this condition. The 1r and 6r in carmine rose are believed to be color trials.

For surcharges and overprints see Nos. 223, 239-259, 260C-274, 283-289, 300-316, 334-350, 376-383, 390-396, 398-399.

No. 210 Surcharged in Black

1900

223	A17	1½r on 2t blue	4.00	1.00
a.		Inverted surcharge		
b.		Perf. 13½	32.50	20.00

Stamps of 1885-96 Surcharged in Black or Red

On Stamps of 1886

1902 *Perf. 12½, 13½*

224	A15	1r on 2t blue	1.00	.45
225	A15	2r on 4½r bis	.60	.45
a.		Inverted surcharge	20.00	20.00
b.		Double surcharge		
226	A15	2½r on 6r green	.50	.25
227	A15	3r on 1t rose	.50	.25
228	A15	2½t on 1½r blk (R)	2.00	1.25
229	A15	2½t on 4t gray vio	3.00	1.25
230	A15	5t on 8t orange	2.00	.60
a.		Perf. 12½	25.00	15.00

On Stamps of 1895-96
Perf. 11½, 12½, 13½

231	A16	1r on 6r green	.45	.25
232	A16	2r on 8t brt vio	.30	.25
233	A16	2½r on 9r gray vio	.30	.30
234	A16	3r on 4½r yel	1.60	.90
a.		Inverted surcharge	21.00	21.00
235	A16	3r on 1t lt bl	1.25	.80
236	A16	2½t on 1½r blk (R)	2.00	.75
237	A16	5t on 2t rose	2.00	.75
a.		Perf. 12½	32.50	20.00
238	A16	5t on 4t dk bl	2.00	.75
a.		Perf. 12½	32.50	20.00
		Nos. 224-238 (15)	19.50	9.25

Nos. 224, 229, 231, 233, 234, 235 and 238 were reprinted in 1905. They have whiter gum than the originals and very clean-cut perf. 13½. Value $2.50 each.

Nos. 204, 208, 210 Overprinted

1902 *Perf. 11½*

239	A17	6r brown	2.00	1.25
a.		Inverted overprint		
240	A17	1t sea green	3.00	1.25
241	A17	2t blue	2.50	1.25
a.		Perf. 13½	140.00	90.00
		Nos. 239-241 (3)	7.50	3.75

No. 212 Surcharged in Black

1905

243	A17	2t on 2½t dull blue	2.00	1.50

Stamps of 1898-1903 Overprinted in Lisbon in Carmine or Green

1911

244	A17	1r gray	.20	.20
a.		Inverted overprint	10.00	10.00
245	A17	1½r slate	.20	.20
a.		Double overprint	10.00	10.00
246	A17	2r orange	.25	.20
a.		Double overprint	14.00	14.00
b.		Inverted overprint	10.00	10.00
247	A17	2½r yellow brn	.25	.20
248	A17	3r deep blue	.25	.20
249	A17	4½r light green	.30	.20
250	A17	6r gray green	.20	.20
251	A17	9r gray lilac	.30	.20
252	A17	1t car rose (G)	.30	.20
253	A17	2t brown	.30	.20
254	A17	4t blue, *blue*	1.25	.95
255	A17	5t brn, *straw*	1.25	.95
256	A17	8t vio, *pink*	3.75	2.25
257	A17	12t grn, *pink*	4.00	2.25
258	A17	1rp dl bl, *straw*	5.25	4.25
259	A17	2rp gray blk, *straw*	8.00	6.75
		Nos. 244-259 (16)	26.05	19.40

A18

Values are for pairs, both halves.

1911 Perforated Diagonally

260	A18	1r on 2r orange	.75	.65
a.		Without diagonal perf.	4.00	3.50
b.		Cut diagonally instead of perf.	3.25	3.00

Stamps of Preceding Issues Perforated Vertically through the Middle and Each Half Surcharged with New Value:

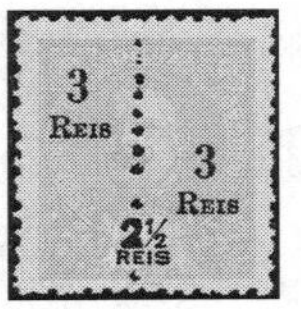

a

b

Values are for pairs, both halves of the stamp.

1912-13

On Issue of 1898-1903

260C	A17(a)	1r on 2r org	.25	.20
261	A17(a)	1r on 1t car	.25	.20
262	A17(a)	1r on 5t brn, *straw*	250.00	200.00
263	A17(b)	1r on 5t brn, *straw*	7.00	5.50
264	A17(a)	1½r on 2½r yel brn	.70	.60
264C	A17(a)	1½r on 4½r lt grn	11.00	7.00
265	A17(a)	1½r on 9r gray lil	.50	.40
266	A17(a)	1½r on 4t bl, *bl*	.50	.40
267	A17(a)	2r on 2½r yel brn	.65	.40
268	A17(a)	2r on 4t bl, *bl*	.90	.65
269	A17(a)	3r on 2½r yel brn	.65	.40
270	A17(a)	3r on 2t brown	.65	.45
271	A17(a)	6r on 4½r lt grn	.65	.55
272	A17(a)	6r on 9r gray lil	.65	.50
273	A17(a)	6r on 9r dull vio	4.00	3.25
274	A17(b)	6r on 8t red vio, *pink*	1.50	.90

On Nos. 237-238, 230, 226, 233

275	A16(b)	1r on 5t on 2t	18.00	15.00
276	A16(b)	1r on 5t on 4t	9.00	8.50
277	A15(b)	1r on 5t on 8t	4.50	3.00
278	A15(a)	2r on 2½r on 6r	3.75	3.00
279	A16(a)	2r on 2½r on 9r	22.50	21.00
280	A16(b)	3r on 5t on 2t	7.00	5.75
281	A16(b)	3r on 5t on 4t	7.00	5.75
282	A15(b)	3r on 5t on 8t	2.25	1.50

On Issue of 1911

283	A17(a)	1r on 1r gray	.25	.25
283B	A17(a)	1r on 2r org	.25	.25
284	A17(a)	1r on 1t car	.30	.25
285	A17(a)	1r on 5t brn, *straw*	.30	.25
285A	A17(b)	1r on 5t brn, *straw*	750.00	500.00
285B	A17(a)	1½r on 4½r lt grn	.60	.45
286	A17(a)	3r on 2t brn	10.50	7.75
289	A17(a)	6r on 9r gray lil	.50	.40

There are several settings of these surcharges and many minor varieties of the letters and figures, notably a small "6." Nos. 260-289 were issued mostly without gum.

More than half of Nos. 260C-289 exist with inverted or double surcharge, or with bisecting perforation omitted. The legitimacy of these varieties is questioned. Price of inverted surcharges, $3-$15; double surcharges, $1-$4; perf. omitted, $1.50-$15.

Similar surcharges made without official authorization on stamps of type A17 are: 2r on 2½r, 3r on 2½r, 3r on 5t, and 6r on 4½r.

Vasco da Gama Issue Overprinted **REPUBLICA**

1913

290	CD20	1½r blue green	.30	.25
291	CD21	4½r red	.30	.25
a.		Double overprint	20.00	
292	CD22	6r red violet	.40	.35
a.		Double overprint	20.00	
293	CD23	9r yellow grn	.40	.35
294	CD24	1t dark blue	.90	.50
295	CD25	2t violet brown	2.00	1.10
296	CD26	4t orange brn	1.10	.90
297	CD27	8t bister	2.00	1.25
		Nos. 290-297 (8)	7.40	4.95

Issues of 1898-1913 Overprinted Locally in Red

1913-15

On Issues of 1898-1903

300	A17	2r orange	9.00	9.00
301	A17	2½r yellow brn	.85	.75
302	A17	3r dp blue	17.00	15.00
303	A17	4½r lt green	1.75	1.50
304	A17	6r gray grn	22.50	18.00
305	A17	9r gray lilac	1.75	1.25
306	A17	1t sea green	40.00	30.00
307	A17	2t blue	45.00	30.00
309	A17	4t blue, *blue*	35.00	25.00
310	A17	5t brn, *straw*	50.00	30.00
311	A17	8t red vio, *pink*	60.00	40.00
312	A17	12t grn, *pink*	3.50	2.50
313	A17	1rp blk & red, *bl*	90.00	75.00
314	A17	1rp dl bl, *straw*	60.00	40.00
315	A17	2rp gray blk, *straw*	75.00	50.00
316	A17	2rp vio, *yelsh*	70.00	40.00
		Nos. 300-316 (16)	581.35	408.00

Inverted or double overprints exist on 2½r, 4½r, 9r, 1rp and 2rp.

Nos. 300-316 were issued without gum except 4½r and 9r.

Nos. 302, 304, 306, 307, 310, 311 and 313 were not regularly issued. Nor were the 1½r, 2t brown and 12t blue on pink with preceding overprint.

Same Overprint in Red or Green
On Provisional Issue of 1902

317	A15	1r on 2t blue	40.00	25.00
a.		"REPUBLICA" inverted	125.00	
318	A15	2r on 4½r bis	40.00	25.00
a.		"REPUBLICA" inverted	125.00	
319	A15	2½r on 6r grn	.70	.60
a.		"REPUBLICA" inverted	17.00	17.00
320	A15	3r on 1t rose (R)	10.00	8.00
321	A15	2½t on 4t gray vio	100.00	40.00
323	A15	5t on 8t org (G)	10.00	7.50
a.		Red overprint	25.00	20.00
324	A16	1r on 6r grn	30.00	20.00
325	A16	2r on 8t vio	30.00	20.00
a.		Inverted surcharge	100.00	
327	A16	3r on 4½r yel	75.00	50.00
328	A16	3r on 1t lt bl	75.00	50.00
329	A16	5t on 2t rose (G)	7.00	2.75
330	A16	5t on 4t bl (G)	7.00	2.75
331	A16	5t on 4t bl (R)	7.00	3.75
a.		"REPUBLICA" inverted	50.00	
b.		"REPUBLICA" double	50.00	
		Nos. 317-331 (13)	431.70	255.35

The 2½r on 1½r of types A15 and A16, the 3r on 1t (A15) and 2½r on 9r (A16) were clandestinely printed.

Some authorities question the status of No. 317-318, 320-321, 324, 327-328.

Same Overprint on Nos. 240-241

1913-15

334	A17	1t sea green	15.00	5.00
335	A17	2t blue	15.00	6.00

This overprint was applied to No. 239 without official authorization.

On Issue of 1912-13 Perforated through the Middle

Values are for pairs, both halves of the stamp.

336	A17(a)	1r on 2r org	15.00	10.00
340	A17(a)	1½r on 4½r lt grn	15.00	10.00
341	A17(a)	1½r on 9r gray lil	18.00	
342	A17(a)	1½r on 4t bl, *bl*	25.00	
343	A17(a)	2r on 2½r yel brn	18.00	
344	A17(a)	2r on 4t bl, *bl*	25.00	6.50
345	A17(a)	3r on 2½r yel brn	20.00	
346	A17(a)	3r on 2t brn	15.00	4.75
347	A17(a)	6r on 4½r lt grn	1.00	.80
348	A17(a)	6r on 9r gray lil	1.50	1.50
350	A17(b)	6r on 8t red vio, *pink*	1.50	1.50
352	A16(b)	1r on 5t on 4t bl	100.00	
354	A15(a)	2r on 2½r on 6r grn	12.00	
		Nos. 334-354 (15)	297.00	

The 1r on 5t (A15), 1r on 1t (A17), 1½r on 2½r (A17), 3r on 5t on 8t (A15), and 6r on 9r (A17) were clandestinely printed.

Nos. 336, 347 exist with inverted surcharge.

Some authorities question the status of Nos. 341-345, 352 and 354.

Ceres — A21

1913-21 Typo. *Perf. 12x11½, 15x14*

Name and Value in Black

357	A21	1r olive brn	.30	.25
358	A21	1½r yellow grn	.30	.25
a.		Imperf.		
359	A21	2r black	.35	.30
360	A21	2½r olive grn	.35	.40
361	A21	3r lilac	.35	.20
362	A21	4½r orange brn	.35	.20
363	A21	5r blue green	.65	.45
364	A21	6r lilac brown	.35	.20
365	A21	9r ultra	.55	.25
366	A21	10r carmine	.85	.50
367	A21	1t lt violet	.40	.25
368	A21	2t deep blue	.85	.30
369	A21	3t yellow brown	1.75	.85
370	A21	4t slate	2.00	1.10
371	A21	8t plum	4.00	3.50
372	A21	12t brown, *green*	3.50	3.00
373	A21	1rp brown, *pink*	21.00	16.00
374	A21	2rp org, *salmon*	14.00	11.00
375	A21	3rp green, *blue*	20.00	15.00
		Nos. 357-375 (19)	71.90	54.00

The 1, 2, 2½, 3, 4½r, 1, 2, and 4t exist with the black inscriptions inverted and the 2½r with them double, one inverted, but it is not known that any of these were regularly issued.

See Nos. 401-410. For surcharges see Nos. 400, 420, 423.

Nos. 249, 251-253, 256-259 Surcharged in Black

1½
REIS

1914

376	A17	1½r on 4½r grn	.30	.25
377	A17	1½r on 9r gray lil	.40	.30
378	A17	1½r on 12t grn, *pink*	.50	.45
379	A17	3r on 1t car rose	.40	.35
380	A17	3r on 2t brn	3.00	2.50
381	A17	3r on 8t red vio, *pink*	2.25	2.00
382	A17	3r on 1rp dl bl, *straw*	.95	.55
383	A17	3r on 2rp gray blk, *straw*	1.00	.80

There are 3 varieties of the "2" in "1½."
Nos. 376-377 exist with inverted surcharge.

Vasco da Gama Issue Surcharged in Black

384	CD21	1½r on 4½r red	.35	.30
385	CD23	1½r on 9r yel grn	.45	.30
386	CD24	3r on 1t dk bl	.35	.30
387	CD25	3r on 2t vio brn	.55	.45
388	CD26	3r on 4t org brn	.30	.25
389	CD27	3r on 8t bister	1.20	1.10
		Nos. 376-389 (14)	12.00	9.90

Double, inverted and other surcharge varieties exist on Nos. 384-386, 389.

Stamps of 1898-1903 Surcharged in Red

REPUBLICA

1½
REIS

1915

390	A17	1½r on 4½r grn	40.00	20.00
a.		"REPUBLICA" omitted	*70.00*	*42.50*
b.		"REPUBLICA" inverted	75.00	
391	A17	1½r on 9r gray lil	12.50	7.50
a.		"REPUBLICA" omitted	30.00	
392	A17	1½r on 12t grn, *pink*	1.25	1.00
396	A17	3r on 2rp gray blk, *straw*	50.00	20.00
		Nos. 390-396 (4)	103.75	48.50

Nos. 390, 390a, 390b, 391, and 391a were not regularly issued. The 3r on 2½r (A17) was surcharged without official authorization.

Preceding Issues Overprinted in Carmine

REPUBLICA

1915

On No. 230

397	A15	5t on 8t org	2.50	1.40

On Nos. 241, 243

398	A17	2t blue	2.00	1.25
399	A17	2t on 2½t dl bl	2.50	1.25
		Nos. 397-399 (3)	7.00	3.90

No. 359 Surcharged in Carmine

1½
REAL

1922

400	A21	1½r on 2r black	.50	.40

Ceres Type of 1913-21

1922-25 Typo. *Perf. 12x11½*

Name and Value in Black

401	A21	4r blue	1.25	1.10
402	A21	1½t gray green	1.25	.85
403	A21	2½t turq blue	1.40	1.10
404	A21	3t yellow brn 4r	5.00	4.00
405	A21	4t gray ('25)	2.00	1.10
406	A21	8t dull rose	7.00	5.00
407	A21	1rp gray brn	16.50	15.00
408	A21	2rp yellow	22.50	*40.00*
409	A21	3rp bluish grn	30.00	*60.00*
410	A21	5rp carmine rose	35.00	*100.00*
		Nos. 401-410 (10)	121.90	228.15

Vasco da Gama and Flagship A22

1925, Jan. 30 Litho.

Without Gum

411	A22	6r brown	4.50	3.00
412	A22	1t red violet	6.25	4.50

400th anniv. of the death of Vasco da Gama (1469?-1524), Portuguese navigator.

Monument to St. Francis — A23

Image of St. Francis — A25

Autograph of St. Francis A24

Image of St. Francis — A26

Tomb of St. Francis — A28

Church of Bom Jesus at Goa — A27

1931, Dec. 3 *Perf. 14*

414	A23	1r gray green	.50	.45
415	A24	2r brown	.50	.45
416	A25	6r red violet	1.50	.50
417	A26	1½t yellow brn	5.25	3.25
418	A27	2t deep blue	6.25	3.75
419	A28	2½t light red	10.50	3.75
		Nos. 414-419 (6)	24.50	12.15

Exposition of St. Francis Xavier at Goa, in December, 1931.

Nos. 371 and 404 Surcharged

2½ T.

1931-32 *Perf. 15x14, 12x11½*

420	A21	1½r on 8t plum ('32)	1.40	1.00
423	A21	2½t on 3t4r yel brn	60.00	45.00

"Portugal" and Vasco da Gama's Flagship "San Gabriel" — A29

Perf. 11½x12

1933 Typo. Wmk. 232

424	A29	1r bister	.20	.20
425	A29	2r olive brn	.20	.20
426	A29	4r violet	.20	.20
427	A29	6r dk green	.20	.20
428	A29	8r black	.20	.20
429	A29	1t gray	.25	.20
430	A29	1½t dp rose	.30	.20
431	A29	2t brown	.35	.20
432	A29	2½t dk blue	2.00	.40
433	A29	3t brt blue	2.25	.40
434	A29	5t red orange	2.25	.40
435	A29	1rp olive grn	10.00	3.00
436	A29	2rp maroon	25.00	6.75
437	A29	3rp orange	35.00	8.00
438	A29	5rp apple grn	50.00	22.50
		Nos. 424-438 (15)	128.40	43.05

For surcharges see Nos. 454-463, 472-474, J34-J36.

Common Design Types

Perf. 13½x13

1938, Sept. 1 Engr. Unwmk.

Name and Value in Black

439	CD34	1r gray grn	.20	.20
440	CD34	2r orange brn	.20	.20
441	CD34	3r dk vio brn	.20	.20
442	CD34	6r brt green	.20	.20
443	CD35	10r dk carmine	.30	.25
444	CD35	1t brt red vio	.50	.25
445	CD35	1½t red	.80	.25
446	CD37	2t orange	.80	.25
447	CD37	2½t blue	.80	.25
448	CD37	3t slate	1.60	.30
449	CD36	5t rose vio	2.40	.45
450	CD36	1rp brown car	4.00	.80
451	CD36	2rp olive grn	7.00	2.50
452	CD38	3rp blue vio	12.00	6.00
453	CD38	5rp red brown	20.00	3.25
		Nos. 439-453 (15)	51.00	15.35

For surcharges see Nos. 492-495, 504-505.

Stamps of 1933 Surcharged in Black

1941, June Wmk. 232 *Perf. 11½x12*

454	A29	1t on 1½t dp rose	2.00	1.40
455	A29	1t on 1rp olive grn	2.00	1.40
456	A29	1t on 2rp maroon	2.00	1.40
457	A29	1t on 5rp apple grn	2.00	1.40
		Nos. 454-457 (4)	8.00	5.60

Nos. 430-431 Surcharged

3
RÉIS

1943

458	A29	3r on 1½t dp rose	1.50	.75
459	A29	1t on 2t brown	2.50	2.00

Nos. 434, 428, 437 and 432 Surcharged in Dark Blue or Carmine

1
REAL

a

b

1945-46 Wmk. 232 *Perf. 11½x12*

460	A29(a)	1r on 5t red org (DB)	.65	.45
461	A29(b)	2r on 8r blk (C)	.50	.40
462	A29(b)	3r on 3rp org (DB) ('46)	1.40	1.25
463	A29(b)	6r on 2½t dk bl (C)	1.50	1.50
		Nos. 460-463 (4)	4.05	3.60

St. Francis Xavier A30

Luis de Camoens A31

Garcia de Orta — A32

St. John de Britto — A33

Arch of the Viceroy A34

Affonso de Albuquerque A35

Vasco da Gama — A36

Francisco de Almeida — A37

Perf. 11½

1946, May 28 Litho. Unwmk.

464	A30	1r black & gray blk	.45	.25
465	A31	2r rose brn & pale rose brn	.45	.25
466	A32	6r ocher & dl yel	.45	.25
467	A33	7r vio & pale vio	2.00	*6.00*
468	A34	9r sepia & buff	2.00	.50
469	A35	1t dk sl grn & sl grn	2.00	.50
470	A36	3½t ultra & pale ultra	2.25	1.10
471	A37	1rp choc & bis brn	5.00	1.40
a.		Miniature sheet of 8, #464-471	19.00	19.00
		Nos. 464-471 (8)	14.60	10.25

No. 471a sold for 1½ rupias.

See #476. For surcharges see #595, J43-J46.

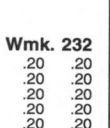

No. 428, 431 and 433 Surcharged in Carmine or Black

1 Real

1946 Wmk. 232 *Perf. 11½x12*

472 A29 (c)	1r on 8r blk (C)	.60	.50
473 A29 (b)	3r on 2t brn	.60	.55
474 A29 (b)	6r on 3t brt bl	2.00	1.75
	Nos. 472-474 (3)	3.20	2.80

Type of 1946 and

Joao de Castro — A38

José Vaz — A39

Luis de Ataide A40

Duarte Pacheco Pereira A41

1948 Unwmk. Litho. *Perf. 11½*

475 A38	3r brt ultra & lt bl	.90	.50
476 A30	1t dk grn & yel grn	1.25	.60
477 A39	1½t dk pur & dl vio	2.00	1.10
478 A40	2½t brt ver	2.25	1.65
479 A41	7½t dk brn & org brn	4.00	2.25
a.	Miniature sheet of 5	19.00	19.00
	Nos. 475-479 (5)	10.40	6.10

No. 476 measures 21x31mm.

No. 479a measures 106x146mm. and contains one each of Nos. 475-479. Marginal inscriptions in gray. The sheet sold for 16 tangas (1 rupia).

For surcharge see No. 591.

Lady of Fatima Issue
Common Design Type

1948 *Perf. 14½*

480 CD40	1t dk blue green	2.25	2.00

Our Lady of Fatima A42

UPU Symbols A42a

1949 Litho. *Perf. 14*

481 A42	1r blue	.75	.50
482 A42	3r orange yel	.75	.50
483 A42	9r dk car rose	1.25	.70
484 A42	2t green	3.25	1.75
485 A42	9t orange red	3.75	1.25
486 A42	2rp dk vio brn	6.25	2.75
487 A42	5rp olive grn	14.00	4.50
488 A42	8rp violet blue	30.00	12.00
	Nos. 481-488 (8)	60.00	23.95

Our Lady of the Rosary at Fatima, Portugal.

1949, Oct.

489 A42a	2½t scarlet & pink	2.25	1.50

UPU, 75th anniversary.

Catalogue values for unused stamps in this section, from this point to the end of the section, are for Never Hinged items.

Holy Year Issue
Common Design Types

1950, May *Perf. 13x13½*

490 CD41	1r olive bister	.60	.55
491 CD42	2t dk gray green	1.00	.55

See Nos. 496-503.

No. 443 Surcharged in Black

1950 *Perf. 13½x13*

492 CD35	1r on 10r dk car	.25	.25
493 CD35	2r on 10r dk car	.25	.25

Similar Surcharge on No. 447 in Black or Red

494 CD37	1r on 2½t blue	.25	.25
495 CD37	3r on 2½t blue (R)	.25	.25
	Nos. 492-495 (4)	1.00	1.00

Letters with serifs, small (lower case) "r" in "real" and "réis."

Holy Year Issue
Common Design Types

1951 Litho. *Perf. 13½*

496 CD41	1r dp car rose	.25	.25
497 CD41	2r emerald	.30	.25
498 CD42	3r red brown	.30	.25
499 CD41	6r gray	.35	.35
500 CD42	9r brt pink	.75	.65
501 CD41	1t blue violet	.50	.45
502 CD42	2t yellow	.85	.55
503 CD41	4t violet brown	.85	.55
	Nos. 496-503 (8)	4.15	3.30

No. 447 with Surcharge Similar to Nos. 492-493 in Red

1951 *Perf. 13½x13*

504 CD37	6r on 2½t blue	.30	.30
505 CD37	1t on 2½t blue	.25	.25

Letters with serifs, small (lower case) "r" in "réis."

Holy Year Extension Issue
Common Design Type

1951 Litho. *Perf. 14*

506 CD43	1rp bl vio & pale vio + label	1.50	.60

Stamp without label sells for less.

José Vaz — A43

Ruins of Sancoale Church — A44

Design: 12t, Altar.

1951 Litho. *Perf. 14½*

Dated: "1651-1951"

507 A43	1r Prus bl & pale bl	.25	.20
508 A44	2r ver & red brn	.25	.20
509 A43	3r gray blk & gray	.50	.25
510 A44	1t vio bl & ind	.25	.20
511 A43	2t dp cl & cl	.35	.20
512 A44	3t ol grn & blk	.50	.20
513 A43	9t indigo & ultra	.65	.40
514 A44	10t lilac & vio	1.00	.50
515 A44	12t blk brn & brn	1.75	.75
	Nos. 507-515 (9)	5.50	2.90

300th anniversary of the birth of José Vaz.

Medical Congress Issue
Common Design Type

Design: Medical School, Goa.

1952 Unwmk. *Perf. 13½*

516 CD44	4½t blk & lt blue	3.00	1.65

St. Francis Xavier Issue

Statue of Saint Francis Xavier — A44a

A45

St. Francis Xavier and his Tomb, Goa — A46

Designs: 2t, Miraculous Arm of St. Francis. 4t, 5t, Tomb of St. Francis.

1952, Oct. 25 Litho. *Perf. 14*

517 A44a	6r aqua & multi	.25	.20
518 A44a	2t cream & multi	2.00	.55
519 A44a	5t pink & silver	3.50	1.25
	Nos. 517-519 (3)	5.75	2.00

Souvenir Sheets

Perf. 13

520 A45	9t brn & dk brn	10.00	10.00
521 A46	12t Sheet of 2	10.00	10.00
a.	4t orange buff & black	3.00	3.00
b.	8t slate & black	3.00	3.00

400th anniv. of the death of St. Francis Xavier.

Numeral A47

St. Francis Xavier A48

1952, Dec. 4 Litho. *Perf. 13½*

522 A47	3t black	8.00	8.00
523 A48	5t dk violet & blk	8.00	8.00
a.	Strip of 2 + label	17.50	17.50

Issued to publicize Portuguese India's first stamp exhibition, Goa, 1952.

No. 523a consists of a tête bêche pair of Nos. 522-523 separated by a label publicizing the exhibition.

Statue of Virgin Mary — A49

Stamp of Portugal and Arms of Colonies — A49a

1953, Jan.

524 A49	6r dk & lt blue	.20	.20
525 A49	1t brown & buff	.75	.50
526 A49	3t dk pur & pale ol	2.50	1.25
	Nos. 524-526 (3)	3.45	1.95

Exhibition of Sacred Missionary Art held at Lisbon in 1951.

For surcharge see No. 594.

Stamp Centenary Issue

1953 **Typo.**

527 A49a	1t multicolored	.80	.65

Centenary of Portugal's first postage stamps.

C. A. da Gama Pinto, Ophthalmologist and Author, Birth Cent. — A50

1954, Apr. 10 Litho. *Perf. 11½*

528 A50	3r gray & ol grn	.25	.20
529 A50	2t black & gray blk	.20	.20

Sao Paulo Issue
Common Design Type

1954, Oct. 2 Unwmk. *Perf. 13½*

530 CD46	2t dk Prus bl, bl & blk	.25	.25

For surcharge see No. 593.

Affonso de Albuquerque School — A51

Msgr. Sebastiao Rodolfo Dalgado — A52

1955, Feb. 26

531 A51	9t multicolored	.85	.60

Centenary (in 1954) of the founding of the Affonso de Albuquerque National School.

1955, Nov. 15 Unwmk. *Perf. 13½*

532 A52	1r multicolored	.20	.20
533 A52	1t multicolored	.50	.25

Birth cent. of Msgr. Sebastiao Rodolfo Dalgado.

Francisco de Almeida — A53

Manuel Antonio de Susa — A54

Map of Bassein by Pedro Barreto de Resendo, 1635 — A55

Portraits: 9r, Affonso de Albuquerque. 1t, Vasco da Gama. 1½t, Filipe Nery Xavier. 3t, Nuno da Cunha. 4t, Agostino Vicente Lourenco. 8t, Jose Vaz. 9t, Manuel Godinho de Heredia. 10t, Joao de Castro. 2rp, Antonio Caetano Pacheco. 3rp, Constantino de Braganca.

Maps of ancient forts, drawn in 1635: 2½t, Mombaim (Bombay). 3½t, Damao (Daman). 5t, Diu. 12t, Cochin. 1rp, Goa.

Inscribed: "450 Aniversario da Fundacao do Estado da India 1505-1955."

Perf. 11½x12 (A53), 14½ (A54), 12½ (A55)

1956, Mar. 24 — Unwmk.

534	A53	3r multicolored	.20	.20
535	A54	6r multicolored	.20	.20
536	A53	9r multicolored	.30	.30
537	A53	1t multicolored	.30	.30
538	A54	1½t multicolored	.20	.20
539	A55	2t multicolored	1.90	1.40
540	A55	2½t multicolored	1.25	.90
541	A53	3t multicolored	.30	.20
542	A55	3½t multicolored	1.40	.90
543	A54	4t multicolored	.20	.20
544	A55	5t multicolored	.60	.40
545	A54	8t multicolored	.50	.40
546	A54	9t multicolored	.50	.40
547	A53	10t multicolored	.50	.35
548	A55	12t multicolored	1.10	.80
549	A55	1rp multicolored	2.00	1.40
550	A54	2rp multicolored	1.90	1.10
551	A53	3rp multicolored	2.50	1.50
		Nos. 534-551 (18)	15.85	11.15

Portuguese settlements in India, 450th anniv.

For surcharges see Nos. 575-577, 579-581, 592.

Map of Damao and Nagar Aveli — A56

Arms of Vasco da Gama — A57

1957 — Litho. — *Perf. 11½*

Map and Inscriptions in Black, Red, Ocher and Blue

552	A56	3r gray & buff	.20	.20
553	A56	6r bl grn & pale lem	.20	.20
554	A56	3t pink & lt gray	.20	.20
555	A56	6t blue	.35	.35
556	A56	11t ol bis & lt vio gray	.75	.55
557	A56	2rp lt vio & pale gray	1.75	1.10
558	A56	3rp citron & pink	2.00	1.50
559	A56	5rp magenta & pink	2.25	1.75
		Nos. 552-559 (8)	7.70	5.85

For surcharges see Nos. 571, 578, 584-585, 588-590.

1958, Apr. 3 — Unwmk. — *Perf. 13x13½*

Arms of: 6r, Lopo Soares de Albergaria. 9r, Francisco de Almeida. 1t, Garcia de Noronha. 4t, Alfonso de Albuquerque. 5t, Joao de Castro. 11t, Luis de Ataide. 1r, Nuno da Cunha.

Arms in Original Colors

Inscriptions in Black and Red

560	A57	2r buff & ocher	.20	.20
561	A57	6r gray & ocher	.20	.20
562	A57	9r pale blue & emer	.20	.20
563	A57	1t pale citron & brn	.35	.20
564	A57	4t pale bl grn & lil	.40	.20
565	A57	5t buff & blue	.50	.30
566	A57	11t pink & lt brn	.65	.40
567	A57	1rp pale grn & maroon	1.00	.60
		Nos. 560-567 (8)	3.50	2.30

For surcharges see Nos. 570, 572-574, 582-583, 586-587.

Exhibition Emblem and View — A58

1958, Dec. 15 — Litho. — *Perf. 14½*

568	A58	1rp multicolored	.50	.50

World's Fair, Brussels, Apr. 17-Oct. 19.

For surcharge see No. 597.

Tropical Medicine Congress Issue

Common Design Type

Design: Holarrhena antidysenterica.

1958, Dec. 15 — *Perf. 13½*

569	CD47	5t gray, brn, grn & red	1.00	.70

For surcharge see No. 596.

Stamps of 1955-58 Surcharged with New Values and Bars

1959, Jan. 1 — Litho. — Unwmk.

570	A57	5c on 2r (#560)	.20	.20
571	A56	10c on 3r (#552)	.20	.20
572	A57	15c on 6r (#561)	.20	.20
573	A57	20c on 9r (#562)	.20	.20
574	A57	30c on 1t (#563)	.20	.20
575	A55	40c on 2t (#539)	.20	.20
576	A55	40c on 2½t (#540)	.75	.30
577	A55	40c on 3½t (#542)	.30	.20
578	A56	50c on 3t (#554)	.20	.20
579	A53	80c on 3t (#541)	.20	.20
580	A53	80c on 10t (#547)	1.00	.75
581	A53	80c on 3rp (#551)	1.50	.85
582	A57	1e on 4t (#564)	.25	.20
583	A57	1.50e on 5t (#565)	.25	.20
584	A56	2e on 6t (#555)	.60	.30
585	A56	2.50e on 11t (#556)	.80	.25
586	A57	4e on 11t (#566)	1.00	.50
587	A57	4.50e on 1rp (#567)	1.00	.50
588	A56	5e on 2rp (#557)	1.00	.50
589	A56	10e on 3rp (#558)	2.00	1.50
590	A56	30e on 5rp (#559)	4.50	2.00
		Nos. 570-590 (21)	16.55	9.65

Types of 1946-1958 Surcharged with New Values, Old Values Obliterated

1959 — Litho. — Unwmk.

591	A39	40c on 1½t dl pur	.60	.20
592	A54	40c on 1½t multi	.60	.20
593	CD46	40c on 2t bl & gray	1.00	.75
594	A49	80c on 3t blk & pale cit	.60	.20
595	A36	80c on 3½t dk bl	.75	.20
596	CD47	80c on 5t gray, brn, grn & red	.75	.40
597	A58	80c on 1rp multi	2.00	.65
		Nos. 591-597 (7)	6.30	2.60

Coin, Manuel I — A59

Arms of Prince Henry — A60

Various Coins from the Reign of Manuel I (1495-1521) to the Republic.

Perf. 13½x13

1959, Dec. 1 — Litho. — Unwmk.

Inscriptions in Black and Red

598	A59	5c lt bl & gold	.20	.20
599	A59	10c pale brn & gold	.20	.20
600	A59	15c pale grn & gray	.20	.20
601	A59	30c salmon & gray	.20	.20
602	A59	40c pale yel & gray	.20	.20
603	A59	50c lilac & gray	.20	.20
604	A59	60c pale yel grn & gray	.20	.20
605	A59	80c lt bl & gray	.20	.20
606	A59	1e ocher & gray	.20	.20
607	A59	1.50e blue & gray	.20	.20
608	A59	2e pale bl & gold	.25	.20
609	A59	2.50e pale gray & gold	.30	.20
610	A59	3e citron & gray	.30	.20
611	A59	4e pink & gray	.45	.20
612	A59	4.40e pale bis & vio brn	.55	.30
613	A59	5e pale dl vio & gray	.70	.40
614	A59	10e brt yel & gray	1.00	.70
615	A59	20e beige & gray	2.25	1.60
616	A59	30e brt yel grn & lt cop brn	2.50	2.50
617	A59	50e lt gray & gray	4.00	4.00
		Nos. 598-617 (20)	14.30	12.30

1960, June 25 — *Perf. 13½*

618	A60	3e multicolored	.50	.50

500th anniversary of the death of Prince Henry the Navigator.

Portugal continued to print special-issue stamps for its lost colony after its annexation by India Dec. 18, 1961. Stamps of India were first used on Dec. 29. Stamps of Portuguese India remained valid until Jan. 5, 1962.

AIR POST STAMPS

Common Design Type

Perf. 13½x13

1938, Sept. 1 — Engr. — Unwmk.

Name and Value in Black

C1	CD39	1t red orange	.50	.25
C2	CD39	2½t purple	.60	.25
C3	CD39	3½t orange	.60	.25
C4	CD39	4½t ultra	1.50	.40
C5	CD39	7t lilac brown	1.60	.50
C6	CD39	7½t dark green	2.25	.75
C7	CD39	9t red brown	4.00	1.10
C8	CD39	11t magenta	4.50	1.10
		Nos. C1-C8 (8)	15.55	4.60

No. C4 exists with overprint "Exposicao Internacional de Nova York, 1939-1940" and Trylon and Perisphere.

POSTAGE DUE STAMPS

D1

1904 — Unwmk. — Typo. — *Perf. 11½*

Name and Value in Black

J1	D1	2r gray green	.45	.30
J2	D1	3r yellow grn	.45	.30
J3	D1	4r orange	.45	.40
J4	D1	5r slate	.45	.45
J5	D1	6r gray	.45	.45
J6	D1	9r yellow brn	.55	.55
J7	D1	1t red orange	2.00	.75
J8	D1	2t gray brown	3.00	1.50
J9	D1	5t dull blue	4.00	2.75
J10	D1	10t carmine	7.00	3.25
J11	D1	1rp dull vio	12.00	6.75
		Nos. J1-J11 (11)	30.80	17.45

Nos. J1-J11 Overprinted in Carmine or Green

1911

J12	D1	2r gray grn	.20	.20
J13	D1	3r yellow grn	.20	.20
J14	D1	4r orange	.20	.20
J15	D1	5r slate	.20	.20
J16	D1	6r gray	.40	.20
J17	D1	9r yellow brn	.50	.30
J18	D1	1t red org	.60	.30
J19	D1	2t gray brn	.80	.50
J20	D1	5t dull blue	2.00	1.25
J21	D1	10t carmine (G)	3.00	1.75
J22	D1	1rp dull violet	7.00	3.00
		Nos. J12-J22 (11)	15.10	8.10

Nos. J1-J11 Overprinted

1914

J23	D1	2r gray grn	1.00	1.00
J24	D1	3r yellow grn	1.00	1.00
J25	D1	4r orange	1.00	1.00
J26	D1	5r slate	1.00	1.00
J27	D1	6r gray	1.25	1.00
J28	D1	9r yellow brn	1.25	1.00
J29	D1	1t red org	3.00	1.00
J30	D1	2t gray brn	10.00	3.00
J31	D1	5t dull blue	15.00	4.00
J32	D1	10t carmine	20.00	6.00
J33	D1	1rp dull violet	30.00	8.00
		Nos. J23-J33 (11)	84.50	28.00

Nos. 432, 433 and 434 Surcharged In Red or Black

1943 — Wmk. 232 — *Perf. 11½x12*

J34	A29	3r on 2½t dk bl (R)	.60	.40
J35	A29	6r on 3t brt bl (R)	.80	.80
J36	A29	1t on 5t red org (Bk)	1.75	1.50
		Nos. J34-J36 (3)	3.15	2.70

D2

1945 — Typo. — Unwmk.

Country Name and Denomination in Black

J37	D2	2r brt carmine	1.75	1.75
J38	D2	3r blue	1.75	1.75
J39	D2	4r orange yel	1.75	1.75
J40	D2	6r yellow grn	1.75	1.75
J41	D2	1t bister brn	1.75	1.75
J42	D2	2t chocolate	1.75	1.75
		Nos. J37-J42 (6)	10.50	10.50

Catalogue values for unused stamps in this section, from this point to the end of the section, are for Never Hinged items.

Nos. 467 and 471 Surcharged in Carmine or Black

Porteado
2 Réis

1951, Jan. 1 — *Perf. 11½*

J43	A33	2r on 7r vio & pale vio (C)	.55	.55
J44	A33	3r on 7r vio & pale vio (C)	.55	.55
J45	A37	1t on 1rp choc & bis brn	.55	.55
J46	A37	2t on 1rp choc & bis brn	.55	.55
		Nos. J43-J46 (4)	2.20	2.20

Common Design Type

Photogravure and Typographed

1952 — *Perf. 14*

Numeral in Red; Frame Multicolored

J47	CD45	2r olive	.25	.25
J48	CD45	3r black	.35	.35
J49	CD45	6r dark blue	.50	.50
J50	CD45	1t dk carmine	.75	.75
J51	CD45	2t orange	1.00	1.00
J52	CD45	10t violet blue	2.75	2.75
		Nos. J47-J52 (6)	5.60	5.60

Nos. J47-J49 and J51-J52 Surcharged with New Value and Bars

1959, Jan.

Numeral in Red; Frame Multicolored

J53	CD45	5c on 2r olive	.20	.25
J54	CD45	10c on 3r black	.30	.40
J55	CD45	15c on 6r dk blue	.60	.75
J56	CD45	60c on 2t orange	.90	1.25
J57	CD45	60c on 10t vio blue	2.00	2.50
		Nos. J53-J57 (5)	4.00	5.15

WAR TAX STAMPS

WT1

Overprinted in Black or Carmine

Perf. 15x14

1919, Apr. 15 Typo. Unwmk.

Denomination in Black

MR1 WT1 0:00:05,48rp grn 1.40 1.10
MR2 WT1 0:01:09,94rp grn 4.00 2.75
MR3 WT1 0:02:03,43rp grn (C) 4.00 2.75
Nos. MR1-MR3 (3) 9.40 6.60

Some authorities consider No. MR2 a revenue stamp.

POSTAL TAX STAMPS

Pombal Issue

Common Design Types

1925 Unwmk. *Perf. 12½*

RA1 CD28 6r rose & black .45 .45
RA2 CD29 6r rose & black .45 .45
RA3 CD30 6r rose & black .45 .45
Nos. RA1-RA3 (3) 1.35 1.35

Mother and Child — PT1

1948 Litho. *Perf. 11*

RA4 PT1 6r yellow green 2.75 2.50
RA5 PT1 1t carmine 2.75 2.50

See Nos. RA7-RA7A, RA9, RA12. For surcharge and overprint see Nos. RA6, RA8.

Catalogue values for unused stamps in this section, from this point to the end of the section, are for Never Hinged items.

Type of 1948 Surcharged with New Value and Bar in Black

1951

RA6 PT1 1t on 6r carmine 3.00 2.00

Type of 1948

1952-53

RA7 PT1 1t gray 2.50 1.60
RA7A PT1 1t red orange ('53) 2.75 1.90

No. RA5 Overprinted in Black

«Revalidado»
P. A. P.

1953

RA8 PT1 1t carmine 7.25 6.00

Type of 1948

1954 Typo.

RA9 PT1 6r pale bister 4.00 3.75

Mother and Child
PT2 PT3

Surcharged in Black

1956 Typo. *Perf. 11*

RA10 PT2 1t on 4t lt blue 11.00 10.00

Litho. *Perf. 13*

RA11 PT3 1t blk, pale grn & red 1.25 .90

See No. RA14. For surcharges see Nos. RA13, RA15-RA16.

Type of 1948 Redrawn

1956 *Perf. 11*

Without Gum

RA12 PT1 1t bluish green 3.25 3.00

Denomination in white oval at left.

No. RA11 Surcharged with New Value and Bars in Red

1957 *Perf. 13½*

RA13 PT3 6r on 1t .90 .75

Type of 1956

1958 Unwmk. *Perf. 13*

RA14 PT3 1t dk bl, sal & grn .75 .60

No. RA14 Surcharged with New Values and Four Bars

1959, Jan. Litho. *Perf. 13*

RA15 PT3 20c on 1t .55 .55
RA16 PT3 40c on 1t .55 .55

Arms and People Seeking Help — PT4

1960 *Perf. 13½*

RA17 PT4 20c brown & red .25 .25

POSTAL TAX DUE STAMPS

Pombal Issue

Common Design Types

1925 Unwmk. *Perf. 12½*

RAJ1 CD28 1t rose & black .60 .60
RAJ2 CD29 1t rose & black .60 .60
RAJ3 CD30 1t rose & black .60 .60
Nos. RAJ1-RAJ3 (3) 1.80 1.80

See note after Portugal No. RAJ4.

PUERTO RICO

ˌpwer-tə-ˈrē-ˌkō

(Porto Rico)

LOCATION — A large island in the West Indies, east of Hispaniola
GOVT. — Former Spanish Colony
AREA — 3,435 sq. mi.
POP. — 953,243 (1899)
CAPITAL — San Juan

The island was ceded to the United States by the Treaty of 1898.

100 Centimes = 1 Peseta
1000 Milesimas = 100 Centavos = 1 Peso (1881)
100 Cents = 1 Dollar (1898)

Values for unused stamps are for examples with original gum as defined in the catalogue introduction. Very fine examples of Nos. 1-170, MR1-MR13 will have perforations clear of the design but will be noticeably poorly centered. Extremely fine examples will be well centered; these are scarce and command substantial premiums.

Issued under Spanish Dominion

Puerto Rican stamps of 1855-73, a part of the Spanish colonial period, were also used in Cuba. They are listed as Cuba Nos. 1-4, 9-14, 18-21, 31-34, 39-41, 47-49, 51-53, 55-57.

Stamps of Cuba Overprinted in Black:

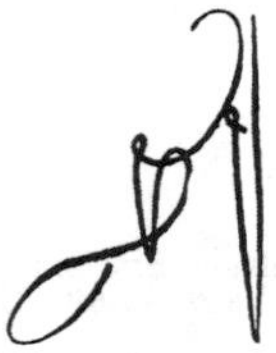

a

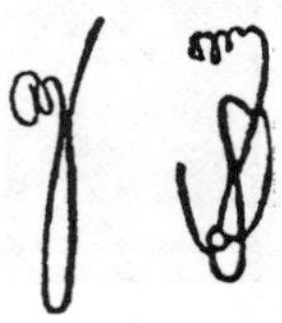

b

c

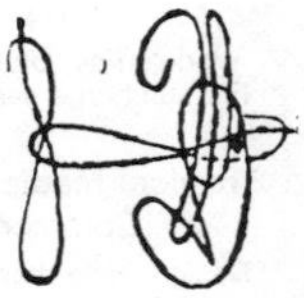

d

1873 Unwmk. *Perf. 14*

1 A10 (a) 25c gray 32.50 1.60
2 A10 (a) 50c brown 85.00 4.75
3 A10 (a) 1p red brown 200.00 16.00
Nos. 1-3 (3) 317.50 22.35

1874

4 A11 (b) 25c ultra 26.00 2.10
a. Double overprint 160.00
b. Inverted overprint 160.00

1875

5 A12 (b) 25c ultra 18.00 2.00
a. Inverted overprint 55.00 35.00
6 A12 (b) 50c green 25.00 2.25
a. Inverted overprint *125.00* *65.00*
7 A12 (b) 1p brown 100.00 11.00
Nos. 5-7 (3) 143.00 15.25

1876

8 A13 (c) 25c pale violet 3.50 1.60
9 A13 (c) 50c ultra 8.25 2.75
10 A13 (c) 1p black 35.00 10.00
11 A13 (d) 25c pale vio 27.50 1.10
12 A13 (d) 1p black 60.00 9.00
Nos. 8-12 (5) 134.25 24.45

Varieties of overprint on Nos. 8-11 include: inverted, double, partly omitted and sideways.
Counterfeit overprints exist.

King Alfonso XII
A5 A6

1877 Typo.

13 A5 5c yellow brown 5.50 2.00
a. 5c carmine (error) 210.00 —
14 A5 10c carmine 17.00 5.00
a. 10c brown (error) 210.00 —
15 A5 15c deep green 25.00 10.00
16 A5 25c ultra 10.50 1.75
17 A5 50c bister 17.00 4.25
Nos. 13-17 (5) 75.00 23.00

Dated "1878"

1878

18 A5 5c ol bister 12.50 12.50
19 A5 10c red brown 200.00 70.00
20 A5 25c deep green 1.60 .95
21 A5 50c ultra 5.75 2.10
22 A5 1p bister 10.50 4.75
Nos. 18-22 (5) 230.35 90.30

Dated "1879"

1879

23 A5 5c lake 10.00 4.50
24 A5 10c dark brown 10.00 4.50
25 A5 15c dk olive grn 10.00 4.50
26 A5 25c blue 3.50 1.50
27 A5 50c dark green 10.00 4.50
28 A5 1p gray 47.50 20.00
Nos. 23-28 (6) 91.00 39.50

Imperforates of type A5 are from proof or trial sheets.

1880

29 A6 ¼c deep green 22.50 17.00
30 A6 ½c brt rose 5.75 2.10
31 A6 1c brown lilac 10.00 8.50
32 A6 2c gray lilac 5.75 4.00
33 A6 3c buff 5.75 4.00
34 A6 4c black 5.75 4.00
35 A6 5c gray green 3.00 1.60
36 A6 10c rose 3.50 1.90
37 A6 15c yellow brn 5.75 3.00
38 A6 25c gray blue 3.00 1.40
39 A6 40c gray 11.50 1.50
40 A6 50c dark brown 24.00 13.00
41 A6 1p olive bister 80.00 17.00
Nos. 29-41 (13) 186.25 79.00

Dated "1881"

1881

42 A6 ½m lake .25 .25
43 A6 1m violet .25 .20
44 A6 2m pale rose .40 .25
45 A6 4m brt yellowish grn .70 .20
46 A6 6m brown lilac .70 .40
47 A6 8m ultra 1.75 1.00
48 A6 1c gray green 2.75 1.00
49 A6 2c lake 3.50 2.75
50 A6 3c dark brown 7.50 4.50
51 A6 5c grayish ultra 2.50 .30
52 A6 8c brown 2.50 1.25
53 A6 10c slate 22.50 7.00
54 A6 20c olive bister 27.50 12.50
Nos. 42-54 (13) 72.80 31.60

Alfonso XII
A7

Alfonso XIII
A8

1882-86

55 A7 ½m rose .25 .20
a. ½m salmon rose .50 .30
56 A7 ½m lake ('84) .50 .35
57 A7 1m pale lake .80 1.00
58 A7 1m brt rose ('84) .25 .20
59 A7 2m violet .25 .20
60 A7 4m brown lilac .25 .20
61 A7 6m brown .40 .20
62 A7 8m yellow green .40 .20
63 A7 1c gray green .25 .20
64 A7 2c rose 1.00 .20
65 A7 3c yellow 3.50 2.00
a. Cliché of 8c in plate of 3c 110.00
66 A7 3c yellow brn ('84) 3.50 .75
a. Cliché of 8c in plate of 3c 22.50
67 A7 5c gray blue 13.00 1.10
68 A7 5c gray bl, 1st retouch ('84) 13.00 2.50
69 A7 5c gray bl, 2nd retouch ('86) 100.00 5.00
70 A7 8c gray brown 3.25 .20
71 A7 10c dark green 3.25 .20
72 A7 20c gray lilac 4.75 .25
a. 20c olive brown (error) *100.00*
73 A7 40c blue 35.00 13.00
74 A7 80c olive bister 50.00 18.00
Nos. 55-74 (20) 233.60 46.00

For differences between the original and the retouched stamps see note on the 1883-86 issue of Cuba.

1890-97

75 A8 ½m black .25 .20
76 A8 ½m olive gray ('92) .20 .20
77 A8 ½m red brn ('94) .20 .20
78 A8 ½m dull vio ('96) .20 .20
79 A8 1m emerald .25 .20
80 A8 1m dk violet ('92) .20 .20
81 A8 1m ultra ('94) .20 .20
82 A8 1m dp brown ('96) .20 .20
83 A8 2m lilac rose .20 .20
84 A8 2m violet brn ('92) .20 .20
85 A8 2m red org ('94) .20 .20
86 A8 2m yel grn ('96) .20 .20
87 A8 4m dk olive grn 10.00 5.00
88 A8 4m ultra ('92) .20 .20
89 A8 4m yel brn ('94) .20 .20
90 A8 4m blue grn ('96) .90 .30
91 A8 6m dk brown 32.50 13.00
92 A8 6m pale rose ('92) .20 .20
93 A8 8m olive bister 25.00 19.00
94 A8 8m yel grn ('92) .20 .20
95 A8 1c yellow brown .25 .20
96 A8 1c blue grn ('91) .50 .20
97 A8 1c violet brn ('94) 5.25 .40
98 A8 1c claret ('96) .60 .20
99 A8 2c brownish violet .90 .75
100 A8 2c red brn ('92) .85 .20
101 A8 2c lilac ('94) 2.00 .40
102 A8 2c org brn ('96) .60 .20
103 A8 3c slate blue 6.50 .90
104 A8 3c orange ('92) .80 .20
105 A8 3c ol gray ('94) 5.25 .40
106 A8 3c blue ('96) 19.00 .30
107 A8 3c claret brn ('97) .25 .20
108 A8 4c slate bl ('94) 1.25 .40
109 A8 4c gray brn ('96) .65 .20
110 A8 5c brown violet 11.00 .40
111 A8 5c yel grn ('94) 5.00 1.00
112 A8 5c bl grn ('92) .80 .20
113 A8 5c blue ('96) .25 .20
114 A8 6c orange ('94) .40 .20
115 A8 6c violet ('96) .30 .20
116 A8 8c ultra 14.00 1.50
117 A8 8c gray brn ('92) .20 .20
118 A8 8c dull vio ('94) 11.00 4.25
119 A8 8c car rose ('96) 2.50 1.25
120 A8 10c rose 4.00 1.00
a. 10c salmon rose 10.00 2.25
121 A8 10c lilac rose ('92) 1.25 .30
122 A8 20c red orange 4.50 4.00
123 A8 20c lilac ('92) 2.00 .50

124	A8	20c car rose ('94)	1.40	.40
125	A8	20c olive gray ('96)	6.00	1.25
126	A8	40c orange	500.00	42.50
127	A8	40c slate blue ('92)	5.00	3.50
128	A8	40c claret ('94)	6.50	11.00
129	A8	40c salmon ('96)	6.00	1.40
130	A8	80c yellow green	475.00	160.00
131	A8	80c orange ('92)	12.50	10.00
132	A8	80c black ('97)	24.00	20.00

Imperforates of type A8 were not issued and are variously considered to be proofs or printer's waste.

Shades of No. 129 are often mistaken for No. 126. Value for No. 126 is for expertized copies.

For overprints see Nos. 154A-170, MR1-MR13.

Landing of Columbus on Puerto Rico — A9

Alfonso XIII — A10

1893, Nov. 19 Litho. *Perf. 12*

133	A9	3c dark green	190.00	40.00

400th anniversary, landing of Columbus on Puerto Rico.

This stamp was valid for postage for only one day and for internal use only..

Counterfeits exist.

1898 Typo.

135	A10	1m orange brown	.20	.20
136	A10	2m orange brown	.20	.20
137	A10	3m orange brown	.20	.20
138	A10	4m orange brown	1.25	.50
139	A10	5m orange brown	.20	.20
140	A10	1c black violet	.20	.20
a.		Tête bêche pair	850.00	
141	A10	2c dk blue green	.20	.20
142	A10	3c dk brown	.20	.20
143	A10	4c orange	1.25	1.00
144	A10	5c brt rose	.20	.20
145	A10	6c dark blue	.50	.20
146	A10	8c gray brown	.20	.20
147	A10	10c vermilion	.20	.20
148	A10	15c dull olive grn	.20	.20
149	A10	20c maroon	1.50	.45
150	A10	40c violet	1.10	1.25
151	A10	60c black	1.10	1.25
152	A10	80c red brown	4.00	4.50
153	A10	1p yellow green	9.00	9.00
154	A10	2p slate blue	21.00	12.50
		Nos. 135-154 (20)	42.90	32.85

Nos. 135-154 exist imperf. Value, set $900.

Stamps of 1890-97 Handstamped in Rose or Violet

1898

154A	A8	½m dull violet	14.00	8.00
155	A8	1m deep brown	1.25	1.25
156	A8	2m yellow green	.35	.35
157	A8	4m blue green	.35	.35
158	A8	1c claret	3.50	3.50
159	A8	2c orange brown	.50	.70
160	A8	3c blue	30.00	13.00
161	A8	3c claret brn	2.50	2.50
162	A8	4c gray brn	.60	.60
163	A8	4c slate blue	17.50	12.00
164	A8	5c yellow grn	8.00	6.25
165	A8	5c blue	.60	.60
166	A8	6c violet	.60	.40
167	A8	8c car rose (V)	1.00	.75
a.		Rose overprint	16.00	16.00
168	A8	20c olive gray	1.00	1.00
169	A8	40c salmon	2.50	2.50
170	A8	80c black	30.00	20.00
		Nos. 154A-170 (17)	114.25	73.75

As usual with handstamps there are many inverted, double and similar varieties. Counterfeits of Nos. 154A-170 abound.

Issued under US Administration

A11

A12

Ponce Issue

1898 Unwmk. *Imperf.*

200	A11	5c vio, *yelsh*	*7,000.*	

The only way No. 200 is known used is handstamped on envelopes. Both unused stamps and used envelopes have a violet control mark. Counterfeits exist of Nos. 200-201.

Coamo Issue

1898 Unwmk. *Imperf.*

201	A12	5c black	650.00	1,050.

There are ten varieties in the setting (See the Scott United States Specialized Catalogue). The stamps bear the control mark "F. Santiago" in violet.

United States Nos. 279, 279Bf, 281, 272 and 282C Overprinted in Black at 36 degree angle

1899 Wmk. 191 *Perf. 12*

210	A87	1c yellow green	5.00	1.40
a.		Ovpt. at 25 degree angle	7.50	2.25
211	A88	2c reddish car, type IV	4.25	1.25
a.		Ovpt. at 25 degree angle	5.50	2.25
212	A91	5c blue	9.00	2.50
213	A93	8c violet brown	27.50	17.50
a.		Ovpt. at 25 degree angle	32.50	19.00
c.		"PORTO RIC"	125.00	110.00
214	A94	10c brown, type I	17.50	6.00
		Nos. 210-214 (5)	63.25	28.65

Misspellings of the overprint, actually broken letters (PORTO RICU, PORTU RICO, FORTO RICO), are found on 1c, 2c, 8c and 10c.

United States Nos. 279 and 279B Overprinted Diagonally in Black

1900

215	A87	1c yellow green	6.50	1.40
216	A88	2c red, type IV	4.75	2.00
b.		Inverted overprint		*8,250.*

Stamps of Puerto Rico were replaced by those of the United States.

POSTAGE DUE STAMPS

United States Nos. J38, J39 and J42 Overprinted in Black at 36 degree angle

1899 Wmk. 191 *Perf. 12*

J1	D2	1c deep claret	22.50	5.50
a.		Overprint at 25 degree angle	22.50	7.50
J2	D2	2c deep claret	20.00	6.00
a.		Overprint at 25 degree angle	20.00	7.00
J3	D2	10c deep claret	160.00	60.00
a.		Overprint at 25 degree angle	175.00	85.00
		Nos. J1-J3 (3)	202.50	71.50

WAR TAX STAMPS

Stamps of 1890-94 Overprinted or Surcharged by Handstamp

1898 Unwmk. *Perf. 14*

Purple Overprint or Surcharge

MR1	A8	1c yellow brn	5.50	*4.00*
MR2	A8	2c on 2m orange	2.50	2.00
MR3	A8	2c on 5c blue grn	3.25	2.50
MR4	A8	2c dark violet	.65	.65
MR5	A8	2c lilac	.60	.60
MR6	A8	2c red brown	.30	.20
MR7	A8	5c blue green	1.25	1.25
MR8	A8	5c on 5c bl grn	6.00	4.00

Rose Surcharge

MR9	A8	2c on 2m orange	1.25	1.25
MR10	A8	5c on 1m dk vio	.20	.20
MR11	A8	5c on 1m dl bl	.55	.55

Magenta Surcharge

MR12	A8	5c on 1m dk vio	.30	.20
MR13	A8	5c on 1m dl bl	2.00	2.00
		Nos. MR1-MR13 (13)	24.35	19.40

Nos. MR2-MR13 were issued as War Tax Stamps (2c on letters or sealed mail; 5c on telegrams) but, during the early days of the American occupation, they were accepted for ordinary postage.

Double, inverted and similar varieties of overprints are numerous in this issue.

Counterfeit overprints exist.

QATAR

ˈkät-ər

LOCATION — A peninsula in eastern Arabia
GOVT. — Independent state
AREA — 4,575 sq. mi.
POP. — 580,000 (1998 est.)
CAPITAL — Doha

Qatar was a British protected sheikdom until Sept. 1, 1971, when it declared its independence. Stamps of Muscat were used until 1957.

100 Naye Paise = 1 Rupee
100 Dirhams = 1 Riyal (1967)

Catalogue values for all unused stamps in this country are for Never Hinged items.

Watermarks

Wmk. 368- JEZ Multiple

Great Britain Nos. 317-325, 328, 332-333 and 309-311 Surcharged "QATAR" and New Value in Black

Perf. 14½x14

1957, Apr. 1 Photo. Wmk. 308

1	A129	1np on 5p lt brn	.20	.20
2	A126	3np on ½p red org	.20	.20
3	A126	6np on 1p ultra	.20	.20
4	A126	9np on 1½p grn	.20	.20
5	A126	12np on 2p red brn	.20	.20
6	A127	15np on 2½p scarlet	.25	.50
7	A127	20np on 3p dk pur	.25	.20
8	A128	25np on 4p ultra	.40	.50
9	A129	40np on 6p lil rose	.30	.25
10	A130	50np on 9p dp ol grn	.55	.30
11	A132	75np on 1sh3p dk grn	1.00	.70
12	A131	1ru on 1sh6p dk bl	7.50	.50

Engr. *Perf. 11x12*

13	A133	2ru on 2sh6p dk brn	4.00	1.75
14	A133	5ru on 5sh crimson	5.50	3.50
15	A133	10ru on 10sh brt ultra	6.75	9.00
		Nos. 1-15 (15)	27.50	18.20

Both typeset and stereotyped overprints were used on Nos. 13-15. The typeset have bars close together and thick, bold letters. The stereotyped have bars wider apart and thinner letters.

Great Britain Nos. 334-336 Surcharged "QATAR," New Value and Square of Dots in Black

Perf. 14½x14

1957, Aug. 1 Photo. Wmk. 308

16	A138	15np on 2½p scarlet	.45	.35
17	A138	25np on 4p ultra	.90	.75
18	A138	75np on 1sh3p dk grn	1.40	1.25
		Nos. 16-18 (3)	2.75	2.35

50th anniv. of the Boy Scout movement and the World Scout Jubilee Jamboree, Aug. 1-12.

Great Britain Nos. 353-358, 362 Surcharged "QATAR" and New Value

1960 Wmk. 322 *Perf. 14½x14*

19	A126	3np on ½p red org	.85	1.90
20	A126	6np on 1p ultra	1.50	3.00
21	A126	9np on 1½p grn	.90	1.60
22	A126	12np on 2p red brn	4.50	7.25
23	A127	15np on 2½p scar	.45	.20
24	A127	20np on 3p dk pur	.45	.20
25	A129	40np on 6p lil rose	.75	.35
		Nos. 19-25 (7)	9.40	14.50

Sheik Ahmad bin Ali al Thani — A1

Dhow — A2

Oil Derrick — A3

Designs: 40np, Peregrine Falcon. 5r, 10r, Mosque.

Perf. 14½

1961, Sept. 2 Unwmk. Photo.

26	A1	5np rose carmine	.20	.20
27	A1	15np brown black	.20	.20
28	A1	20np claret	.20	.20
29	A1	30np deep green	.20	.20
30	A2	40np red	.25	.20
31	A2	50np sepia	.50	.25
32	A2	75np ultra	.25	1.00

Engr. *Perf. 13*

33	A3	1ru rose red	.30	.35
34	A3	2ru blue	.85	.75
35	A3	5ru green	5.50	2.75
36	A3	10ru black	14.50	5.00
		Nos. 26-36 (11)	22.95	11.10

Nos. 31-32, 34-36 Overprinted or Surcharged

1964, Oct. 25 Photo. *Perf. 14½*

37	A2	50np sepia	.65	*1.00*
38	A2	75np ultra	.90	*1.40*

Engr. *Perf. 13*

39	A3	1ru on 10r black	1.75	.85
40	A3	2ru blue	4.25	1.75
41	A3	5ru green	10.00	5.00
		Nos. 37-41 (5)	17.55	10.00

18th Olympic Games, Tokyo, Oct. 10-25.

For surcharges see Nos. 110-110D.

Nos. 31-32, 34-36 with Typographed Overprint or Surcharge

1964, Nov. 22 Photo. *Perf. 14½*

42	A2	50np sepia	.70	.50
43	A2	75np ultra	.90	.75

Engr. *Perf. 13*

44	A3	1ru on 10ru blk	1.75	1.50
45	A3	2ru blue	4.25	4.00
46	A3	5ru green	10.00	8.25
		Nos. 42-46 (5)	17.60	15.00

Pres. John F. Kennedy (1917-63).
For surcharges see Nos. 111-111D.

Column — A4

Designs: 2np, 1.50r, Isis Temple and Colonnade, Philae. 3np, 1r, Trajan's kiosk, Philae.

Perf. 14½x14

1965, Jan. 17 Photo. Unwmk.

47	A4	1np multicolored	.75	.20
48	A4	2np multicolored	.75	.20
49	A4	3np multicolored	.75	.20
50	A4	1ru multicolored	1.10	.25
51	A4	1.50ru multicolored	2.25	.40
52	A4	2ru multicolored	.75	.40
		Nos. 47-52 (6)	6.35	1.65

UNESCO world campaign to save historic monuments in Nubia.

Qatar Scout Emblem, Tents and Sheik Ahmad — A5

Scouts Saluting and Sheik Ahmad — A6

Designs: 1np, 4np, Qatar scout emblem.

Perf. 14 (A5), 14½x14 (A6)

1965, May 22 Photo. Unwmk.

53	A5	1np ol grn & dk red brn	.20	.20
54	A5	2np sal & dk vio bl	.20	.20
55	A5	3np dk vio bl & grn	.20	.20
56	A5	4np bl & dk red brn	.20	.20
57	A5	5np dk vio bl & grnsh bl	.20	.20
58	A6	30np multi	.70	.45
59	A6	40np multi	.80	.60
60	A6	1ru multi	3.00	1.25
		Nos. 53-60 (8)	5.50	3.30

Issued to honor the Qatar Boy Scouts. Perf. and imperf. souvenir sheets contain one each of Nos. 58-60 with red brown marginal inscription. Size: 108x76mm. Value, each $7.
For surcharges see Nos. 113-113G.

Eiffel Tower, Telstar, ITU Emblem and "Qatar" in Morse Code — A7

Designs: 2np, 1ru, Tokyo Olympic Games emblem and Syncom III. 3np, 40np, Radar tracking station and Relay satellite. 4np, 50np, Post Office Tower, London, and Echo II, Syncom III, Telstar and Relay satellites around globe.

Perf. 13½x14

1965, Oct. 16 Photo. Unwmk.

61	A7	1np dk bl & red brn	.25	.20
62	A7	2np bl & dk red brn	.25	.20
63	A7	3np dp yel grn & brt pur	.25	.20
64	A7	4np org brn & brt bl	.25	.20
65	A7	5np dl vio & dk ol bis	.25	.20
66	A7	40np dk car rose & blk	.65	.40
67	A7	50np sl grn & bis	.85	.50
68	A7	1ru emer & car	1.65	1.00
a.		Souvenir sheet of 2, #67-68	6.00	3.50
		Nos. 61-68 (8)	4.40	2.90

Cent. of the ITU. #68a also exists imperf.
For overprints and surcharges see Nos. 91-98, 114-114G, 117-117G.

Triggerfish — A8

Various Fish, including: 2np, 50np, Clown grunt. 2np, 10ru, Saddleback butterflyfish. 4np, 5ru, Butterflyfish. 15np, 3ru, Paradisefish. 20np, 1ru, Rio Grande perch. 75np, Triggerfish.

1965, Oct. 18 *Perf. 14x14½*

69	A8	1np multi & black	.20	.20
70	A8	2np multi & black	.20	.20
71	A8	3np multi & black	.20	.20
72	A8	4np multi & black	.20	.20
73	A8	5np multi & black	.20	.20
74	A8	15np multi & black	.50	.20
75	A8	20np multi & black	.55	.20
76	A8	30np multi & black	.65	.20
77	A8	40np multi & black	.90	.25
78	A8	50np multi & gold	1.25	.35
79	A8	75np multi & gold	2.00	.50
80	A8	1ru multi & gold	2.25	.65
81	A8	2ru multi & gold	5.25	1.25
82	A8	3ru multi & gold	7.75	1.90
83	A8	4ru multi & gold	10.00	2.50
84	A8	5ru multi & gold	14.00	3.50
85	A8	10ru multi & gold	30.00	6.50
		Nos. 69-85 (17)	76.10	19.00

Basketball — A9

No. 87, Horse jumping. No. 88, Running. No. 89, Soccer. No. 90, Weight lifting.

1966, Jan. 10 Photo. *Perf. 11½*

Granite Paper

86	A9	1ru gray, blk & dk red	1.00	.60
87	A9	1ru brn & dk ol grn	1.00	.60
88	A9	1ru dull rose & blue	1.00	.60
89	A9	1ru grn & blk	1.00	.60
90	A9	1ru bl & brn	1.00	.60
		Nos. 86-90 (5)	5.00	3.00

4th Pan Arab Games, Cairo, Sept. 2-11. Nos. 86-90 are printed in one sheet of 25 in horizontal rows of five.

Nos. 61-68 Overprinted in Black

1966, Feb. 9 Photo. *Perf. 13½x14*

91	A7	1np dk bl & red brn	.20	.20
92	A7	2np bl & dk red brn	.20	.20
93	A7	3np dp yel grn & brt pur	.20	.20
94	A7	4np org brn & brt bl	.20	.20
95	A7	5np dl vio & dk ol bis	.20	.20
96	A7	40np dk car rose & blk	.70	.25
97	A7	50np slate grn & bis	.80	.30
98	A7	1ru emer & car	1.75	.60
		Nos. 91-98 (8)	4.25	2.15

Issued to commemorate the rendezvous in space of Gemini 6 and 7, Dec. 15, 1965. Exist overprinted in blue.

For surcharges see Nos. 117-117G.

Sheik Ahmad - A9a

Designs: 3np, 5np, 40np, 80np, 2ru, 10ru, Reverse of coin with Arabic inscription.

Litho. & Embossed Gold or Silver Foil

1966, Feb. 24 *Imperf.*

99	A9a	1np ol & lil (S)	.20	.20
99A	A9a	3np blk & org (S)	.20	.20
99B	A9a	4np pur & red	.20	.20
99C	A9a	5np brt grn & red brn	.20	.20

Diameter: 55mm

99D	A9a	10np brn & brt vio (S)	.40	.20
99E	A9a	40np org red & bl (S)	.80	.35
99F	A9a	70np Prus bl & bl vio	1.25	.75
99G	A9a	80np car & grn	1.25	.75

Diameter: 65mm

99H	A9a	1ru red vio & blk (S)	2.25	.95
99J	A9a	2ru bl grn & cl (S)	4.25	1.90
99K	A9a	5ru red lil & ver	10.00	4.25
99L	A9a	10ru bl vio & brn car	19.00	10.00
		Nos. 99-99L (12)	40.00	19.95

John F. Kennedy, UN Headquarters, NY, and ICY Emblem — A10

Designs (ICY emblem and): #100, UN emblem. #100B, Dag Hammarskjold and UN General Assembly. #100C, Jawaharlal Nehru and dove.

1966, Mar. 8 *Perf. 11½*

Granite Paper

100	A10	40np brt bl, vio bl & red brn	1.50	1.00
100A	A10	40np brt grn, vio & brn	1.50	1.00
100B	A10	40np red brn, brt bl & blk	1.50	1.00
100C	A10	40np dk vio & brt grn	1.50	1.00
d.		Block of 4, #100-100C	6.00	4.00

UN Intl. Cooperation Year, 1965. Printed in sheets of 16 + 9 lables in shape of a cross.
An imperf. souvenir sheet of 4 contains one each of Nos. 100-100C.

Nos. 100-100C Overprinted in Black

U.N. 20th ANNIVERSARY

Telstar, Rocket - A10a

Designs: No. 101, John F. Kennedy, "In Memoriam / John F. Kennedy / 1917-1963." No. 101A, Olive branches, Churchill quote and "In Memoriam / 1874-1965." No. 101B, like #101 portrait facing left, no overprint. No. 101C, Eternal flame, Arabic inscription.

1966, Mar. 8

Granite Paper

101	A10a	5np bl grn, car & blk	
101A	A10a	5np bl grn, rose & blk	
101B	A10a	5np bl grn & blk	
101C	A10a	5np bl grn, rose & blk	
101D	A10a	5np bl brn, car & blk	
101E	A10	40np on No. 100	
101F	A10	40np on No. 100A	
101G	A10	40np on No. 100B	
101H	A10	40np on No. 100C	

Nos. 101-101H were made from the sheets of Nos. 100-100C. The 4 outer labels and the center label were surcharged to create Nos. 101-101D. The other 4 labels were overprinted but have no denomination. Exists with red overprints. The imperf. souvenir sheet exists with overprint in margin:"IN VICTORY, / MAGNAMIMITY. / IN PEACE / GOODWILL / WINSTON CHURCHILL." The margin overprint overlaps onto No. 101A on upper left quarter of stamp.
Nos. 101-101H exist imperf.
For surcharges see Nos. 118-118C.

John F. Kennedy (1917-1963) - A10b

Kennedy and: #102c, 10np, #102f, 70np, NYC. #102d, 30np, #102g, 80np, Rocket lifting off at Cape Kennedy. #102e, 60np, #102h, 1ru, Statue of Liberty. No. 102B, Statue of Liberty.

1966, July 18 *Perf. 13½*

102	A10b	Strip of 3, #c.-e.	2.50	1.50
102A	A10b	Strip of 3, #f.-h.	4.50	2.50

Souvenir Sheet

Imperf

102B	A10b	50np multicolored	5.50

Nos. 102-102A exist imperf. For surcharges see Nos. 119-119B.

1968 Summer Olympics, Mexico City - A10c

Designs: #103c, 1np, #103f, 70np, #103B, Equestrian. #103d, 4np, #103g, 80np, Running. #103e, 5np, #103h, 90np, Javelin.

1966, July 20 *Perf. 13½*

103	A10c	Strip of 3, #c.-e.	1.50	1.50
103A	A10c	Strip of 3, #f.-h.	6.00	4.00

Souvenir Sheet

Imperf

103B	A10c	50np multicolored	6.50

Nos. 103-103A exist imperf. For surcharges see Nos. 120-120B.

A10d

American Astronauts - A10e

Astronaut and space vehicle: No. 104c, 5np, James A. Lovell. d, 10np, Thomas P. Stafford. e, 15np, Alan B. Shepard.

No. 104f, 20np, John H. Glenn. g, 30np, M. Scott Carpenter. h, 40np, Walter M. Schirra. i, 50np, Virgil I. Grissom. j, 60np, L. Gordon Cooper, Jr.

No. 104B, Stafford, Schirra, Frank Borman, Lovell and diagram of space rendezvous.

1966, Aug. 20 ***Perf. 12***

104 A10d Strip of 3, #c.-e.
104A A10e Strip of 5, #f.-j.

Souvenir Sheet

Imperf

Size: 115x75mm

104B A10e 50np multicolored

The name of James A. Lovell is spelled "Lovel" on No. 104c. Nos. 104-104A exist imperf. For surcharges see Nos. 121-121B.

A10h

1966 World Cup Soccer Championships, London - A10i

Designs: 1np-4np, Jules Rimet Cup. 60np, #107H, Hands holding Cup, soccer ball. 70np, #107J, Cup, soccer ball. 80np, #107K, Soccer players, ball. 90np, #107L, Wembley Stadium.

1966, Nov. 27 **Photo.** ***Perf. 13½***

107 A10h 1np blue
107A A10h 2np blue
107B A10h 3np blue
107C A10h 4np blue
m. Block of 4, #107-107C
107D A10i 60np multicolored
107E A10i 70np multicolored
107F A10i 80np multicolored
107G A10i 90np multicolored
n. Block of 4, #107D-107G

Souvenir Sheets

Imperf

107H A10i 25np multicolored
107J A10i 25np multicolored
107K A10i 25np multicolored
107L A10i 25np multicolored

Nos. 107-107C are airmail. Issued in sheets of 36 containing 5 #107m and 4 #107n. Nos. 107-107G exist imperf.

Nos. 37-41 Surcharged with New Currency in Gray or Red

1966 **Photo.** ***Perf. 14½***

110 A2 50d on 50np #37 (G)
110A A2 75d on 75np #38

Engr.

Perf. 13

110B A3 1r on 1ru on 10ru #39
110C A3 2r on 2ru #40
110D A3 5r on 5ru #41

Nos. 42-46 Surcharged with New Currency in Gray or Red

1966 **Photo.** ***Perf. 14½***

111 A2 50d on 50np #42 (G)
111A A2 75d on 75np #43

Engr.

Perf. 13

111B A3 1r on 1ru on 10ru #44
111C A3 2r on 2ru #45
111D A3 5r on 5ru #46

Nos. 53-60 Surcharged with New Currency

Perf. 14 (A5), 14½x14 (A6)

1966 **Photo.**

113 A5 1d on 1np #53
113A A5 2d on 2np #54
113B A5 3d on 3np #55
113C A5 4d on 4np #56
113D A5 5d on 4np #57
113E A6 30d on 30np #58
113F A6 40d on 40np #59
113G A6 1r on 1ru #60

Exist imperf. Perf and imperf souvenir sheets contain one each of #113E-113G surcharged with new currency.

Nos. 61-68 Surcharged with New Currency in Black or Red

1966 ***Perf. 13½x14***

114 A7 1d on 1np #61
114A A7 2d on 2np #62
114B A7 3d on 3np #63
114C A7 4d on 4np #64
114D A7 5d on 5np #65
114E A7 40d on 40np #66
114F A7 50d on 50np #67
114G A7 1r on 1ru #68

Exist imperf.

Nos. 91-95 Surcharged with New Currency

1966 **Photo.** ***Perf. 13½x14***

117 A7 1d on 1np #91
117A A7 2d on 2np #92
117B A7 3d on 3np #93
117C A7 4d on 4np #94
117D A7 5d on 5np #95

Numbers have been reserved for additional values in this set.

Nos. 101E-101H with Red Overprint Surcharged with New Currency

1966 **Photo.** ***Perf. 11½***

Granite Paper

118 A10a 40d on 40np #101E
118A A10a 40d on 40np #101F
118B A10a 40d on 40np #101G
118C A10a 40d on 40np #101H
d. Block of 4, #118-118C

Exist imperf. Imperf. souvenir sheets mentioned after Nos. 100C, 101H exist surcharged with new currency.

Nos. 102-102B Surcharged with New Currency

1966 ***Perf. 13½***

119 Strip of 3
c. A10b 10d on 10np #102c
d. A10b 30d on 30np #102d
e. A10b 60d on 60np #102e
119A Strip of 3
f. A10b 70d on 70np #102f
g. A10b 80d on 80np #102g
h. A10b 1r on 1ru #102h

Souvenir Sheet

Imperf

119B A10b 50d on 50np #102B

Nos. 119-119A exist imperf.

Nos. 103-103B Surcharged with New Currency

1966 ***Perf. 13½***

120 Strip of 3
c. A10c 1d on 1np #103c
d. A10c 4d on 4np #103d
e. A10c 5d on 5np #103e
120A Strip of 3
f. A10c 70d on 70np #103f
g. A10c 80d on 80np #103g
h. A10c 90d on 90np #103h

Souvenir Sheet

Imperf

120B A10c 50d on 50np #103

Nos. 120-120 exist imperf.

Nos. 104-104B Surcharged with New Currency

1966 ***Perf. 12***

121 Strip of 3
c. A10d 5d on 5np #104c
d. A10d 10d on 10np #104d
e. A10d 15d on 15np #104e
121A Strip of 5
f. A10e 20d on 20np #104f
g. A10e 30d on 30np #104g
h. A10e 40d on 40np #104h
i. A10e 50d on 50np #104i
j. A10e 60d on 60np #104j

Souvenir Sheet

Imperf

121B A10e 50d on 50np #104B

Nos. 121-121A printed se-tenant with five labels showing Arabic inscription.

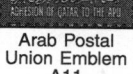

Arab Postal Union Emblem A11

Traffic Light and Intersection A12

Apollo Project - A11a

1967, Apr. 15 **Photo.** ***Perf. 11x11½***

122	A11	70d magenta & sepia	1.50	.50
122A	A11	80d dull blue & sepia	2.25	.60

Qatar's joining the Arab Postal Union.

1967, May 1 ***Perf. 12½***

Designs: 5d, 70d, Two astronauts on Moon. 10d, 80d, Command and lunar modules in lunar orbit. 20d, 1r, Lunar module on Moon. 30d, 1.20r, Lunar module ascending from Moon. 40d, 2r, Saturn 5 rocket.

123	A11a	5d multicolored	.20	.20
123A	A11a	10d multicolored	.20	.20
123B	A11a	20d multicolored	.20	.20
123C	A11a	30d multicolored	.25	.20
123D	A11a	40d multicolored	.35	.20
123E	A11a	70d multicolored	.70	.45
123F	A11a	80d multicolored	.85	.60
123G	A11a	1r multicolored	.90	.80
123H	A11a	1.20r multicolored	1.50	1.25
123J	A11a	2r multicolored	2.10	1.75

#123J exists in an imperf. souv. sheet of one.

1967, May 24 **Litho.** ***Perf. 13½***

124	A12	20d vio & multi	.35	.20
124A	A12	30d multi	.65	.35
124B	A12	50d multi	1.00	.45
124C	A12	1r ultra & multi	3.00	1.50
		Nos. 124-124C (4)	5.00	2.50

Issued for Traffic Day.

Boy Scouts and Sheik Ahmad A13

Designs: 1d, First Boy Scout camp, Brownsea Island, 1907, and tents, Idaho, US, 1967. 2d, Lord Baden-Powell. 5d, Boy Scout canoeing. 15d, Swimming. 75d, Mountain climbing. 2r, Boy Scout saluting flag and emblem of 12th World Jamboree. 1d and 2d lack head of Sheik Ahmad.

1967, Sept. 15 **Litho.** ***Perf. 11½x11***

125	A13	1d multicolored	.35	.20
125A	A13	2d buff & multi	.35	.20

Litho. and Engr.

125B	A13	3d rose & multi	.35	.20
125C	A13	5d lilac & multi	.35	.20
125D	A13	15d multicolored	.55	.25
125E	A13	75d green & multi	1.10	.80
125F	A13	2r sepia & multi	5.00	3.25
		Nos. 125-125F (7)	8.05	5.10

Nos. 125-125A for 60th anniv. of the Boy Scouts, Nos. 125B-125F for 12th Boy Scout World Jamboree, Farragut State Park, Idaho, Aug. 1-9.

Viking Ship (from Bayeux Tapestry) A14

Famous Ships: 2d, Santa Maria (Columbus). 3d, San Gabriel (Vasco da Gama). 75d, Victoria (Ferdinand Magellan). 1r, Golden Hind (Sir Francis Drake). 2r, Gipsy Moth IV (Sir Francis Chichester).

1967, Nov. 27 **Litho.** ***Perf. 13½***

126	A14	1d org & multi	.25	.20
126A	A14	2d lt bl, tan & blk	.25	.20
126B	A14	3d lt bl & multi	.25	.20
126C	A14	75d fawn & multi	.80	.60
126D	A14	1r gray, yel grn & red	1.50	1.25
126E	A14	2r multi	3.50	2.50
		Nos. 126-126E (6)	6.55	4.95

Professional Letter Writer — A15

Designs: 2d, Carrier pigeon and man releasing pigeon, vert. 3d, Postrider. 60d, Mail transport by rowboat, vert. 1.25r, Mailman riding camel, jet plane and modern buildings. 2r, Qatar No. 1, hand holding pen, paper, envelopes and inkwell.

1968, Feb. 14

127	A15	1d multicolored	.25	.20
127A	A15	2d multicolored	.25	.20
127B	A15	3d multicolored	.25	.20
127C	A15	60d multicolored	1.25	.70
127D	A15	1.25r multicolored	2.50	1.40
127E	A15	2r multicolored	4.25	2.25
		Nos. 127-127E (6)	8.75	4.95

Ten years of Qatar postal service.

Human Rights Flame and Barbed Wire A16

2d, Arab refugee family leaving concentration camp. 3d, Scales of Justice. 60d, Hands opening gates to the sun. 1.25r, Family and sun, vert. 2r, Stylized family groups.

1968, Apr. 10

128	A16	1d gray & multi	.20	.20
129	A16	2d multicolored	.20	.20
130	A16	3d brt grn, org & blk	.20	.20
131	A16	60d org, brn & blk	.90	.65
132	A16	1.25r brt grn, blk & yel	2.75	2.00
133	A16	2r multicolored	3.75	2.75
		Nos. 128-133 (6)	8.00	6.00

International Human Rights Year.

Nurse Attending Premature Baby — A17

Designs (WHO Emblem and): 2d, Operating room. 3d, Dentist. 60d, X-ray examination. 1.25r, Medical laboratory. 2r, State Hospital.

1968, June 20

134	A17	1d multi	.20	.20
135	A17	2d multi	.20	.20
136	A17	3d multi	.20	.20
137	A17	60d multi	1.00	.40

138	A17	1.25r multi	2.00	1.25
139	A17	2r multi	3.50	1.75
		Nos. 134-139 (6)	7.10	4.00

20th anniv. of the World Health Organization.

Olympic Rings and Gymnast
A18

Designs (Olympic Rings and): 1d, Discobolus and view of Mexico City. 2d, Runner and flaming torch. 60d, Weight lifting and torch. 1.25r, Olympic flame as a mosaic, vert. 2r, Mythological bird.

1968, Aug. 24

140	A18	1d multicolored	.20	.20
141	A18	2d multicolored	.20	.20
142	A18	3d multicolored	.20	.20
143	A18	60d multicolored	.70	.50
144	A18	1.25r multicolored	1.40	1.00
145	A18	2r multicolored	2.50	1.65
		Nos. 140-145 (6)	5.20	3.75

19th Olympic Games, Mexico City, 10/12-27.

Sheik Ahmad bin Ali al Thani
A19 A21

Dhow
A20

Designs: 40d, Desalination plant. 60d, Loading platform and oil tanker. 70d, Qatar Mosque. 1r, Clock Tower, Market Place, Doha. 1.25r, Doha Fort. 1.50r, Falcon.

1968 Litho. *Perf. 13½*

146	A19	5d blue & green	.20	.20
147	A19	10d brt bl & red brn	.20	.20
148	A19	20d blk & vermilion	.20	.20
149	A19	25d brt mag & brt grn	.35	.20

Lithographed and Engraved

Perf. 13

150	A20	35d grn & brt pink	.55	.20
151	A20	40d pur, lt bl & org	.75	.20
152	A20	60d lt bl, brn & lil	1.25	.35
153	A20	70d blk, lt bl & brt grn	1.50	.45
154	A20	1r vio bl, yel & brt grn	1.75	.60
155	A20	1.25r ind, brt bl & ocher	2.00	.75
156	A20	1.50r lt bl, dk grn & rose lil	3.50	.90

Perf. 11½

157	A21	2r brn, ocher & bl gray	3.50	1.25
158	A21	5r grn, lt grn & pur	8.75	3.00
159	A21	10r ultra, lt bl & sep	15.00	5.50
		Nos. 146-159 (14)	39.50	14.00

UN Headquarters, NY, and Flags — A22

1d, Flags. 4d, World map and dove. 60d, Classroom. 1.50r, Farmers, wheat and tractor. 2r, Sec. Gen. U Thant and General Assembly Hall.

1968, Oct. 24 Litho. *Perf. 13½x13*

160	A22	1d multi	.20	.20
161	A22	4d multi	.20	.20
162	A22	5d multi	.20	.20
163	A22	60d multi	1.00	.60
164	A22	1.50r multi	1.90	.90
165	A22	2r multi	2.75	1.50
		Nos. 160-165 (6)	6.25	3.60

United Nations Day, Oct. 24, 1968.

Fishing Vessel Ross Rayyan
A23

Progress in Qatar: 4d, Elementary School and children playing. 5d, Doha Intl. Airport. 60d, Cement factory and road building. 1.50r, Power station. 2r, Housing development.

1969, Jan. 13

166	A23	1d brt bl & multi	.20	.20
167	A23	4d green & multi	.20	.20
168	A23	5d dl org & multi	.20	.20
169	A23	60d lt brn & multi	1.10	.40
170	A23	1.50r brt lil & multi	2.50	.95
171	A23	2r buff & multi	3.00	1.40
		Nos. 166-171 (6)	7.20	3.35

Armored Cars
A24

Designs: 2d, Traffic police. 3d, Military helicopter. 60d, Military band. 1.25r, Field gun. 2r, Mounted police.

1969, May 6 Litho. *Perf. 13½*

172	A24	1d multicolored	.20	.20
173	A24	2d lt blue & multi	.20	.20
174	A24	3d gray & multi	.25	.20
175	A24	60d multicolored	1.00	.35
176	A24	1.25r multi	3.00	1.00
177	A24	2r blue & multi	4.50	1.50
		Nos. 172-177 (6)	9.15	3.45

Issued to honor the public security forces.

Oil Tanker
A25

2d, Research laboratory. 3d, Off-shore oil rig, helicopter. 60d, Oil rig, storage tanks. 1.50r, Oil refinery. 2r, Oil tankers, 1890-1968.

1969, July 4

178	A25	1d gray & multi	.20	.20
179	A25	2d olive & multi	.20	.20
180	A25	3d ultra & multi	.20	.20
181	A25	60d lilac & multi	1.65	.80
182	A25	1.50r red brn & multi	4.00	2.00
183	A25	2r brown & multi	5.25	2.50
		Nos. 178-183 (6)	11.50	5.90

Qatar oil industry.

Boy Scouts Building Boats
A26

Designs: 2d, Scouts at work and 10 symbolic candles. 3d, Parade. 60d, Gate to camp interior. 1.25r, Main camp gate. 2r, Hoisting Qatar flag, and Sheik Ahmad.

1969, Sept. 18 Litho. *Perf. 13½x13*

184	A26	1d multicolored	.20	.20
185	A26	2d multicolored	.20	.20
186	A26	3d multicolored	.20	.20
187	A26	60d multicolored	1.40	.70
a.		Souvenir sheet of 4, #184-187	5.50	3.25
188	A26	1.25r multicolored	3.00	1.40
189	A26	2r multicolored	4.50	2.25
		Nos. 184-189 (6)	9.50	4.95

10th Qatar Boy Scout Jamboree. No. 187a sold for 1r.

Neil A. Armstrong
A27

Designs: 2d, Col. Edwin E. Aldrin, Jr. 3d, Lt. Col. Michael Collins. 60d, Astronaut walking on moon. 1.25r, Blast-off from moon. 2r, Capsule and raft in Pacific, horiz.

1969, Dec. 6 *Perf. 13x13½, 13½x13*

190	A27	1d blue & multi	.20	.20
191	A27	2d multicolored	.20	.20
192	A27	3d grn & multi	.30	.20
193	A27	60d multicolored	1.10	.55
194	A27	1.25r pur & multi	2.50	1.25
195	A27	2r multicolored	3.25	1.75
		Nos. 190-195 (6)	7.55	4.15

See note after US No. C76.

UPU Emblem, Boeing Jet Loading in Qatar
A28

2d, Transatlantic ocean liner. 3d, Mail truck and mail bags. 60d, Qatar Post Office. 1.25r, UPU Headquarters, Bern. 2r, UPU emblem.

1970, Jan. 31 Litho. *Perf. 13½x13*

196	A28	1d multi	.20	.20
197	A28	2d multi	.20	.20
198	A28	3d multi	.25	.20
199	A28	60d multi	1.00	.60
200	A28	1.25r multi	2.00	1.25
201	A28	2r brt yel grn, blk & lt brn	3.25	2.25
		Nos. 196-201 (6)	6.90	4.70

Qatar's admission to the UPU.

Map of Arab League Countries, Flag and Emblem — A28a

1970, Mar. *Perf. 13x13½*

202	A28a	35d yellow & multi	.60	.45
203	A28a	60d blue & multi	.85	.55
204	A28a	1.25r multi	1.90	1.25
205	A28a	1.50r vio & multi	2.50	1.75
		Nos. 202-205 (4)	5.85	4.00

25th anniversary of the Arab League.

VC10 Touching down for Landing
A29

Designs: 2d, Hawk, and VC10 in flight. 3d, VC10 and airport. 60d, Map showing route Doha to London. 1.25r, VC10 over Gulftown. 2r, Tail of VC10 with emblem of Gulf Aviation.

1970, Apr. 5 *Perf. 13½x13*

206	A29	1d multi	.20	.20
207	A29	2d multi	.20	.20
208	A29	3d multi	.20	.20
209	A29	60d multi	1.00	.70
210	A29	1.25r multi	1.90	1.40
211	A29	2r multi	3.50	2.00
		Nos. 206-211 (6)	7.00	4.70

Issued to publicize the first flight to London from Doha by Gulf Aviation Company.

Education Year Emblem, Spaceship Trajectory, Koran Quotation — A30

1970, May 24 *Perf. 13x12½*

212	A30	35d blue & multi	.90	.35
213	A30	60d blue & multi	1.90	.75

Intl. Education Year. Translation of Koran quotation: "And say, O God, give me more knowledge."

Flowers — A31

1970, July 2 *Perf. 13x13½*

214	A31	1d Freesia	.25	.20
215	A31	2d Azalea	.25	.20
216	A31	3d Ixia	.30	.20
217	A31	60d Amaryllis	1.10	.70
218	A31	1.25r Cineraria	2.25	1.50
219	A31	2r Rose	3.75	2.00
		Nos. 214-219 (6)	7.90	4.80

For surcharges see Nos. 287-289.

EXPO Emblem and Fisherman on Shikoku Beach — A32

1d, Toyahama fishermen honoring ocean gods. 2d, Map of Japan. 60d, Mt. Fuji. 1.50r, Camphorwood torii. 2r, Tower of Motherhood, EXPO Tower and Mt. Fuji.

Perf. 13½x13, 13x13½

1970, Sept. 29

220	A32	1d multi, horiz.	.20	.20
221	A32	2d multi, horiz.	.20	.20
222	A32	3d multi	.20	.20
223	A32	60d multi	.70	.50
a.		Souvenir sheet of 4	5.00	4.00
224	A32	1.50r multi, horiz.	2.00	1.50
225	A32	2r multi	2.50	2.00
		Nos. 220-225 (6)	5.80	4.60

EXPO '70 Intl. Exhib., Osaka, Japan, Mar. 15-Sept. 13. No. 223a contains 4 imperf. stamps similar to Nos. 220-223 with simulated perforations. Sold for 1r.

Globe and UN Emblem — A33

UN, 25th anniv.: 2d, Cannon used as flower vase. 3d, Birthday cake and dove. 35d, Emblems of UN agencies forming wall. 1.50r, Trumpet and emblems of UN agencies. 2r, Two men, black and white, embracing, and globe.

1970, Dec. 7 Litho. *Perf. 14x13½*

226	A33	1d blue & multi	.20	.20
227	A33	2d multicolored	.20	.20
228	A33	3d brt pur & multi	.20	.20
229	A33	35d green & multi	.35	.20
230	A33	1.50r multi	1.90	1.00
231	A33	2r brn red & multi	2.25	1.25
		Nos. 226-231 (6)	5.10	3.05

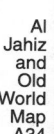

Al Jahiz and Old World Map A34

Designs: 2d, Sultan Saladin and palace. 3d, Al Farabi, sailboat and musical instruments. 35d, Iben al Haithum and palace. 1.50r, Al Motanabbi and camels. 2r, Avicenna and old world map.

1971, Feb. 20 *Perf. 13½x14*

232	A34	1d brt pink & multi	.20	.20
233	A34	2d pale bl & multi	.20	.20
234	A34	3d dl yel & multi	.20	.20
235	A34	35d lt bl & multi	.50	.30
236	A34	1.50r yel grn & multi	2.00	1.40
237	A34	2r pale grn & multi	3.00	2.00
		Nos. 232-237 (6)	6.10	4.30

Famous men of Islam.

Cormorant — A35

Designs: 2d, Lizard and prickly pear. 3d, Flamingos and palms. 60d, Oryx and yucca. 1.25r, Gazelle and desert dandelion. 2r, Camel, palm and bronzed chenopod.

1971, Apr. 14 Litho. *Perf. 11x12*

238	A35	1d multi	.20	.20
239	A35	2d multi	.20	.20
240	A35	3d multi	.20	.20
241	A35	60d multi	.90	.60
242	A35	1.25r multi	1.75	1.10
243	A35	2r multi	3.00	1.75
		Nos. 238-243 (6)	6.25	4.05

Goonhilly Satellite Tracking Station A36

Designs: 2d, Cable ship, and section of submarine cable. 3d, 35d, London Post Office Tower, and television control room. 4d, Various telephones. 5d, 75d, Video telephone. 3r, Telex machine and tape.

1971, May 17 *Perf. 13½x13*

244	A36	1d vio bl & multi	.20	.20
245	A36	2d multicolored	.20	.20
246	A36	3d rose red & multi	.20	.20
247	A36	4d magenta & multi	.20	.20
248	A36	5d rose red & multi	.20	.20
249	A36	35d multicolored	.65	.20
250	A36	75d magenta & multi	1.40	.35
251	A36	3r ocher & multi	5.75	1.50
		Nos. 244-251 (8)	8.80	3.05

3rd World Telecommunications Day.

State of Qatar

Arab Postal Union Emblem — A37

1971, Sept. 4 *Perf. 13*

252	A37	35d red & multi	.75	.20
253	A37	55d blue & multi	.90	.35
254	A37	75d brown & multi	1.50	.45
255	A37	1.25r violet & multi	2.50	.75
		Nos. 252-255 (4)	5.65	1.75

25th anniv. of the Conf. of Sofar, Lebanon, establishing the Arab Postal Union.

Boy Reading — A38

1971, Aug. 10 *Perf. 13x13½*

256	A38	35d brown & multi	.70	.25
257	A38	55d ultra & multi	1.00	.40
258	A38	75d green & multi	1.25	.50
		Nos. 256-258 (3)	2.95	1.15

International Literacy Day, Sept. 8.

Men Splitting Racism A39

2d, 3r, People fighting racism. 3d, Soldier helping war victim. 4d, Men of 4 races rebuilding. 5d, Children on swing. 35d, Wave of racism engulfing people. 75d, like 1d.

Perf. 13½x13, 13x13½

1971, Oct. 12 Litho.

259	A39	1d multi	.20	.20
260	A39	2d multi	.20	.20
261	A39	3d multi	.20	.20
262	A39	4d multi, vert.	.20	.20
263	A39	5d multi, vert.	.20	.20
264	A39	35d multi	.25	.20
265	A39	75d multi	.60	.50
266	A39	3r multi	2.75	2.50
		Nos. 259-266 (8)	4.60	4.20

Intl. Year Against Racial Discrimination.

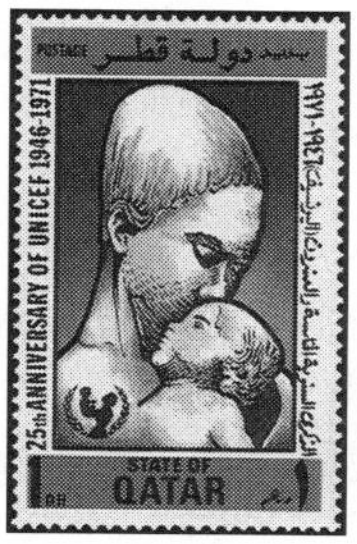

UNICEF Emblem, Mother and Child — A40

UNICEF, 25th anniv.: 2d, Child's head, horiz. 3d, 75d, Child with book. 4d, Nurse and child, horiz. 5d, Mother and child, horiz. 35d, Woman and daffodil. 3r, like 1d.

1971, Dec. 6 *Perf. 14x13½, 13½x14*

267	A40	1d blue & multi	.20	.20
268	A40	2d lil rose & multi	.20	.20
269	A40	3d blue & multi	.20	.20
270	A40	4d yellow & multi	.20	.20
271	A40	5d blue & multi	.20	.20
272	A40	35d lil rose & multi	.35	.25
273	A40	75d yellow & multi	.50	.40
274	A40	3r multicolored	2.50	1.75
		Nos. 267-274 (8)	4.35	3.40

Sheik Ahmad, Flags of Arab League and Qatar A41

"International Cooperation" A42

75d, Sheik Ahmad, flags of UN and Qatar. 1.25r, Sheik Ahmad bin Ali al Thani.

1972, Jan. 17 *Perf. 13½x13, 13x13½*

275	A41	35d black & multi	.50	.20
276	A41	75d black & multi	.90	.45
277	A42	1.25r lt brn & blk	1.25	.65
278	A42	3r multicolored	3.75	1.75
a.		Souvenir sheet	6.00	3.50
		Nos. 275-278 (4)	6.40	3.05

Independence 1971. No. 278a contains one stamp with simulated perforations.

European Roller — A43

Birds: 2d, European kingfisher. 3d, Rock thrush. 4d, Caspian tern. 5d, Hoopoe. 35d, European bee-eater. 75d, European golden oriole. 3r, Peregrine falcon.

1972, Mar. 1 Litho. *Perf. 12x11*

279	A43	1d sepia & multi	.20	.20
280	A43	2d emerald & multi	.20	.20
281	A43	3d bister & multi	.20	.20
282	A43	4d lt blue & multi	.20	.20
283	A43	5d yellow & multi	.20	.20
284	A43	35d vio bl & multi	.45	.20
285	A43	75d pink & multi	1.10	.50
286	A43	3r blue & multi	4.50	2.00
		Nos. 279-286 (8)	7.05	3.70

Nos. 217-219 Surcharged

1972, Mar. 7 *Perf. 13x13½*

287	A31	10d on 60d multi	.20	.20
288	A31	1r on 1.25r multi	2.25	.90
289	A31	5r on 2r multi	10.00	4.00
		Nos. 287-289 (3)	12.45	5.10

Sheik Khalifa bin Hamad al Thani
A44 A44a

1972 *Perf. 14*

Size: 23x27mm

290	A44	5d pur & ultra	.20	.20
291	A44	10d brn & rose red	.20	.20
291A	A44a	10d lt brown & lt red		
291B	A44a	25d violet & emerald		
292	A44	35d org & dl grn	.50	.25
293	A44	55d brt grn & lil	.75	.40
294	A44	75d vio & lil rose	.85	.50

Size: 26½x32mm

295	A44	1r bister & blk	1.50	.75
296	A44	1.25r olive & blk	1.75	.80
297	A44	5r blue & blk	8.00	3.50
298	A44	10r red & blk	15.00	7.00
		Nos. 290-298 (9)	28.75	13.60

Issued: Type A44, Mar. 7.

Book Year Emblem A45

1972, Apr. 23 *Perf. 13½x13*

299	A45	35d lt ultra & blk	.40	.30
300	A45	55d lt brown & blk	.65	.50
301	A45	75d green & blk	.90	.70
302	A45	1.25r violet & blk	1.25	1.00
		Nos. 299-302 (4)	3.20	2.50

International Book Year 1972.

Olympic Rings, Soccer A46

2d, 3r, Running. 3d, Bicycling. 4d, Gymnastics. 5d, Basketball. 35d, Discus. 75d, Like 1d.

1972, June 12 *Perf. 13½x13*

303	A46	1d green & multi	.20	.20
304	A46	2d yel grn & multi	.20	.20
305	A46	3d blue & multi	.20	.20
306	A46	4d lilac & multi	.20	.20
307	A46	5d blue & multi	.20	.20
308	A46	35d gray & multi	.40	.20
a.		Souvenir sheet of 6	3.25	1.50
309	A46	75d green & multi	.80	.40
310	A46	3r multicolored	3.25	1.40
		Nos. 303-310 (8)	5.45	3.00

20th Olympic Games, Munich, Aug. 26-Sept. 10. No. 308a contains stamps with simulated perforations similar to Nos. 303-308.

Installation of Underwater Pipe Line — A47

1972, Aug. 8 Litho. *Perf. 13x13½*

311	A47	1d Drilling for oil, vert.	.20	.20
312	A47	4d shown	.20	.20
313	A47	5d Drilling platform	.20	.20
314	A47	35d Ship searching for oil	.55	.30
315	A47	75d like 1d, vert.	1.25	.60
316	A47	3r like 5d	5.00	2.50
		Nos. 311-316 (6)	7.40	4.00

Oil from the sea.

Government Palace — A48

Designs: 35d, Clasped hands, Qatar flag. 75d, Clasped hands, UN flag. 1.25r, Sheik Khalifa bin Hamad al-Thani, vert.

1972, Sept. 3 ***Perf. 13½x13, 13x13½***

317	A48	10d yel & multi	.20	.20
318	A48	35d blk & multi	.60	.25
319	A48	75d blk & multi	1.25	.50
320	A48	1.25r gold & multi	2.00	.75
a.		Souvenir sheet of 1	4.00	3.00
		Nos. 317-320 (4)	4.05	1.70

Independence Day, 1st anniv. of independence.

No. 320a contains one stamp with simulated perforations similar to No. 320.

Qatar Flag, Council Emblem and Flag A49

1972, Dec. 4 **Litho.** ***Perf. 14x13½***

321	A49	25d blue & multi	1.10	.45
322	A49	30d vio bl & multi	1.40	.60

Civil Aviation Council of Arab States, 10th session.

Tracking Station, Satellite, Telephone, ITU and UN Emblems A50

Designs (Agency and UN Emblems): 2d, Surveyor, artist; UNESCO. 3d, Tractor, helicopter, fish, grain and fruit; FAO. 4d, Reading children, teacher; UNICEF. 5d, Weather satellite and map; WMO. 25d, Workers and crane; ILO. 55d, Health clinic; WHO. 1r, Mail plane and post office; UPU.

1972, Oct. 24 ***Perf. 13½x14***

323	A50	1d multicolored	.20	.20
324	A50	2d multicolored	.20	.20
325	A50	3d multicolored	.20	.20
326	A50	4d multicolored	.20	.20
327	A50	5d multicolored	.20	.20
328	A50	25d multicolored	.40	.20
329	A50	55d multicolored	.85	.45
330	A50	1r multicolored	1.40	.75
		Nos. 323-330 (8)	3.65	2.40

United Nations Day, Oct. 24, 1972. Each stamp dedicated to a different UN agency.

Road Building — A51

1973, Feb. 22 **Litho.** ***Perf. 13x13½***

331	A51	2d shown	.20	.20
332	A51	3d Housing development	.20	.20
333	A51	4d Operating room	.20	.20
334	A51	5d Telephone operators	.20	.20
335	A51	15d School, classroom	.20	.20
336	A51	20d Television studio	.25	.20
337	A51	35d Sheik Khalifa	.35	.25
338	A51	55d New Gulf Hotel	.60	.40
339	A51	1r Fertilizer plant	.90	.80
340	A51	1.35r Flour mill	1.65	1.10
		Nos. 331-340 (10)	4.75	3.75

1st anniv. of the accession of Sheik Khalifa bin Hamad al Thani as Emir of Qatar.

Aerial Pest Control — A52

WHO, 25th anniv.: 3d, Medicines. 4d, Poliomyelitis prevention. 5d, Malaria control. 55d, Mental health. 1r, Pollution control.

1973, May 14 **Litho.** ***Perf. 14***

341	A52	2d blue & multi	.20	.20
342	A52	3d blue & multi	.20	.20
343	A52	4d blue & multi	.20	.20
344	A52	5d blue & multi	.20	.20
345	A52	55d blue & multi	1.50	.70
346	A52	1r blue & multi	2.25	1.50
		Nos. 341-346 (6)	4.55	3.00

Weather Ship A53

Designs (WMO Emblem and): 3d, Launching of radiosonde balloon. 4d, Plane and meteorological data checking. 5d, Cup anemometers and meteorological station. 10d, Weather plane in flight. 1r, Nimbus I weather satellite. 1.55r, Launching of rocket carrying weather satellite.

1973, July **Litho.** ***Perf. 14x13***

347	A53	2d multicolored	.20	.20
348	A53	3d multicolored	.20	.20
349	A53	4d multicolored	.20	.20
350	A53	5d multicolored	.20	.20
351	A53	10d multicolored	.20	.20
352	A53	1r multicolored	1.50	.65
353	A53	1.55r multicolored	2.25	1.00
		Nos. 347-353 (7)	4.75	2.65

Cent. of intl. meteorological cooperation.

Sheik Khalifa — A54

Clock Tower, Doha — A55

1973-74 **Litho.** ***Perf. 14***

Size: 18x27mm

354	A54	5d green & multi	.20	.20
355	A54	10d lt bl & multi	.20	.20
356	A54	20d ver & multi	.20	.20
357	A54	25d orange & multi	.35	.20
358	A54	35d purple & multi	.50	.30
359	A54	55d dk gray & multi	.80	.40

Engr.

Perf. 13½

360	A55	75d lil, bl & yel grn	1.10	.60

Photo.

Perf. 13

Size: 27x32mm

360A	A54	1r multicolored	1.60	.85
360B	A54	5r multicolored	8.00	4.50
360C	A54	10r multicolored	16.00	11.00
		Nos. 354-360C (10)	28.95	18.45

Issue dates: 20d, 75d, July 3, 1973; 1r-10r, July 1974; others, Jan. 27, 1973.

Flag of Qatar, Handclasp, Sheik Khalifa — A56

Flag, Sheik and: 35d, Harvest. 55d, Government Building. 1.35r, Market and Clock Tower, Doha. 1.55r, Illuminated fountain.

1973, Oct. 4 **Litho.** ***Perf. 13***

361	A56	15d red & multi	.20	.20
362	A56	35d buff & multi	.30	.20
363	A56	55d multi	.60	.30
364	A56	1.35r vio & multi	1.50	.80
365	A56	1.55r multi	2.00	1.00
		Nos. 361-365 (5)	4.60	2.50

2nd anniversary of independence.

Planting Tree, Qatar and UN Flags, UNESCO Emblem — A57

Qatar and UN Flags and: 4d, UN Headquarters and flags. 5d, Pipe laying, cement mixer, helicopter and ILO emblem. 35d, Nurse, patient and UNICEF emblem. 1.35r, Telecommunications and ITU emblem. 3r, Cattle, wheat disease analysis and FAO emblem.

1973, Oct. 24

366	A57	2d multi	.20	.20
367	A57	4d multi	.20	.20
368	A57	5d multi	.25	.20
369	A57	35d multi	.50	.20
370	A57	1.35r multi	2.00	.90
371	A57	3r multi	5.00	2.50
		Nos. 366-371 (6)	8.15	4.20

United Nations Day.

Prison Gates Opening — A58

4d, Marchers with flags. 5d, Scales of Justice. 35d, Teacher and pupils. 1.35r, UN General Assembly. 3r, Human Rights flame, vert.

1973, Dec. **Litho.** ***Perf. 13x13½***

372	A58	2d yellow & multi	.20	.20
373	A58	4d pale lil & multi	.20	.20
374	A58	5d rose & multi	.20	.20
375	A58	35d ocher & multi	.40	.25
376	A58	1.35r lt bl & multi	1.75	1.00
377	A58	3r citron & multi	3.00	2.00
		Nos. 372-377 (6)	5.75	3.85

25th anniversary of the Universal Declaration of Human Rights.

Highway Overpass — A59

1974, Feb. 22 ***Perf. 14x13½***

378	A59	2s shown	.20	.20
379	A59	3d Symbol of learning	.20	.20
380	A59	5d Oil field	.20	.20
381	A59	35d Gulf Hotel, Doha	.35	.20
382	A59	1.55r Radar station	1.90	1.00
383	A59	2.25r Sheik Khalifa	2.50	1.50
		Nos. 378-383 (6)	5.35	3.30

Accession of Sheik Khalifa as Emir, 2nd, anniv.

Mail Truck, Camel Caravan and UPU Emblem — A60

UPU cent.: 3d, Old and new trains, Arab Postal Union emblem. 10d, Old and new ships and Qatar coat of arms. 35d, Old and new planes. 75d, Mail sorting by hand and computer, and Arab Postal Union emblem. 1.25r, Old and new post offices, and Qatar coat of arms.

1974, May 22 **Litho.** ***Perf. 13½***

384	A60	2d brt yel & multi	.20	.20
385	A60	3d lt bl & multi	.20	.20
386	A60	10d dp org & multi	.20	.20
387	A60	35d slate & multi	.45	.30
388	A60	75d yellow & multi	.90	.60
389	A60	1.25r lt bl & multi	1.75	1.00
		Nos. 384-389 (6)	3.70	2.50

Doha Hospital — A61

1974, July 13 **Litho.** ***Perf. 13½***

390	A61	5d shown	.20	.20
391	A61	10d WPY emblem and people	.20	.20
392	A61	15d WPY emblem	.20	.20
393	A61	35d World map	.30	.20
394	A61	1.75r Clock and infants	1.50	1.00
395	A61	2.25r Family	1.90	1.25
		Nos. 390-395 (6)	4.30	3.05

World Population Year 1974.

Television Station — A62

1974, Sept. 2 ***Perf. 13½x13***

399	A62	5d shown	.20	.20
400	A62	10d Palace of Doha	.20	.20
401	A62	15d Teachers'College	.20	.20
402	A62	75d Clock Tower and Mosque	.75	.50
403	A62	1.55r Traffic circle, Doha	1.25	.75
404	A62	2.25r Sheik Khalifa	1.90	1.25
		Nos. 399-404 (6)	4.50	3.10

3rd anniversary of independence.

Operating Room and WHO Emblem — A63

UN Day: 10d, Satellite earth station and ITU emblem. 20d, Tractor, UN and FAO emblems. 25d, School children, UN and UNESCO emblems. 1.75r, Open air court, UN Headquarters, emblems. 2r, UPU and UN emblems.

1974, Oct. 24 Litho. *Perf. 13x13½*

405	A63	5d multi	.20	.20
406	A63	10d multi	.20	.20
407	A63	20d multi	.20	.20
408	A63	25d multi	.25	.20
409	A63	1.75r multi	1.40	1.00
410	A63	2r multi	1.75	1.25
		Nos. 405-410 (6)	4.00	3.05

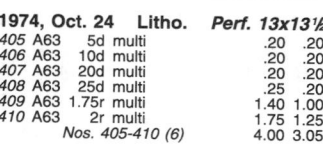

VC-10, Gulf Aviation Airliner — A64

Arab League and Qatar Flags, Civil Aviation Emblem — A65

Design: 25d, Doha Airport.

1974, Dec. 1 Litho. *Perf. 13½*

411	A64	20d multi	.25	.20
412	A64	25d yel & dk bl	.35	.25
413	A65	30d multi	.40	.30
414	A65	50d multi	.65	.50
		Nos. 411-414 (4)	1.65	1.25

Arab Civil Aviation Day.

Caspian Terns, Hoopoes and Shara'o Island — A66

Dhow by Moonlight — A67

5d, Clock Tower, Doha, vert. 15d, Zubara Fort. 35d, Gulf Hotel & sailboats. 75d, Arabian oryx. 1.25r, Khor Al-Udein. 1.75r, Ruins, Wakrah.

1974, Dec. 21 Litho. *Perf. 13½*

415	A66	5d multi	.20	.20
416	A66	10d multi	.20	.20
417	A66	15d multi	.20	.20
418	A66	35d multi	.25	.20
419	A67	55d multi	.45	.35
420	A66	75d multi	.70	.50
421	A67	1.25r multi	2.50	.90
422	A66	1.75r multi	3.50	1.25
		Nos. 415-422 (8)	8.00	3.80

Traffic Circle, Doha A68

Sheik Khalifa — A69

35d, Pipe line from offshore platform. 55d, Laying underwater pipe line. 1r, Refinery.

1975, Feb. 22 Litho. *Perf. 13½*

423	A68	10d multi	.20	.20
424	A68	35d multi	.55	.40
425	A68	55d multi	.80	.60
426	A68	1r multi	1.75	1.20
427	A69	1.35r sil & multi	2.00	1.50
428	A69	1.55r gold & multi	2.50	1.75
		Nos. 423-428 (6)	7.80	5.65

Accession of Sheik Khalifa, 3rd anniv.

Qatar Flag and Arab Labor Charter Emblem — A70

1975, May 28 Litho. *Perf. 13*

429	A70	10d bl, red brn & blk	.20	.20
430	A70	35d multicolored	.65	.35
431	A70	1r green & multi	1.75	1.00
		Nos. 429-431 (3)	2.60	1.55

Arab Labor Charter and Constitution, 10th anniversary.

Flintlock Pistol with Ornamental Grip — A71

Designs: 3d, Ornamental mosaic. 35d, View of museum. 75d, Arch and museum, vert. 1.25r, Flint arrowheads and tool. 3r, Gold necklace, vert.

1975, June 23 *Perf. 13*

432	A71	2d multi	.20	.20
433	A71	3d ver blk & gold	.20	.20
434	A71	35d bis & multi	.40	.25
435	A71	75d ver & multi	.90	.55
436	A71	1.25r vio & multi	1.50	.90
437	A71	3r fawn & multi	3.50	2.00
		Nos. 432-437 (6)	6.70	4.10

Opening of Qatar National Museum.

Traffic Signs, Policeman, Doha — A72

Designs: 15d, 55d, Cars, arrows, traffic lights, Doha Clock Tower. 35d, like 5d.

1975, June 24

438	A72	5d lt green & multi	.20	.20
439	A72	15d lt blue & multi	.50	.20
440	A72	35d lemon & multi	1.25	.45
441	A72	55d lt violet & multi	1.90	.75
		Nos. 438-441 (4)	3.85	1.60

Traffic Week.

Constitution, Arabic Text — A73

5d, Government buildings, horiz. 15d, Museum & Clock Tower, horiz. 55d, 1.25r, Sheik Khalifa & Qatar flag. 75d, Constitution, English text.

1975, Sept. 2

442	A73	5d multi	.20	.20
443	A73	15d multi	.40	.25
444	A73	35d multi	.45	.30
445	A73	55d multi	.70	.45
446	A73	75d multi	.95	.60
447	A73	1.25r multi	1.50	1.00
		Nos. 442-447 (6)	4.20	2.80

4th anniversary of independence.

Satellite over Globe, ITU Emblem — A74

UN, 30th anniv.: 15d, UN Headquarters, NY and UN emblem. 35d, UPU emblem over Eastern Arabia, UN emblem. 1r, Nurses and infant, WHO emblem. 1.25r, Road building equipment, ILO emblem. 2r, Students, UNESCO emblem.

1975, Oct. 25 Litho. *Perf. 13x13½*

448	A74	5d multi	.20	.20
449	A74	15d multi	.30	.20
450	A74	35d multi	.40	.20
451	A74	1r multi	1.10	.50
452	A74	1.25r multi	1.25	.60
453	A74	2r multi	2.25	1.00
		Nos. 448-453 (6)	5.50	2.70

Fertilizer Plant — A75

Designs: 10d, Flour mill, vert. 35d, Natural gas plant. 75d, Oil refinery. 1.25r, Cement works. 1.55r, Steel mill.

1975, Dec. 6

454	A75	5d salmon & multi	.20	.20
455	A75	10d yellow & multi	.25	.20
456	A75	35d multi	.55	.25
457	A75	75d multi	1.10	.60
458	A75	1.25r mag & multi	2.00	1.00
459	A75	1.55r multi	3.00	1.40
		Nos. 454-459 (6)	7.10	3.65

Modern Building, Doha — A76

10d, 35d, 1.55r, Various modern buildings. 55d, 75d, Sheik Khalifa & Qatar flag, diff.

1976, Feb. 22 Litho. *Perf. 13*

460	A76	5d multi	.20	.20
461	A76	10d multi	.20	.20
462	A76	35d multi	.35	.20
463	A76	55d multi	.55	.30
464	A76	75d multi	.80	.45
465	A76	1.55r multi	1.50	.90
		Nos. 460-465 (6)	3.60	2.25

Accession of Sheik Khalifa, 4th anniv.

Satellite Earth Station — A77

Designs: 55d, 1r, Satellite. 75d, Like 35d.

1976, Mar. 1

466	A77	35d multicolored	.65	.25
467	A77	55d dp bis & multi	.80	.30
468	A77	75d vermilion & multi	1.25	.45
469	A77	1r violet & multi	1.75	.60
		Nos. 466-469 (4)	4.45	1.60

Inauguration of satellite earth station in Qatar.

Telephones, 1876 and 1976 — A78

Arabian Soccer League Emblem — A79

1976, Mar. 10

470	A78	1r rose & multi	1.25	.75
471	A78	1.35r lt bl & multi	1.75	1.00

Centenary of first telephone call by Alexander Graham Bell, Mar. 10, 1876.

1976, Mar. 25 Litho. *Perf. 13½x13*

Designs: 10d, 1.25r, Stadium, Doha. 35d, Like 5d. 55d, Players. 75d, One player.

472	A79	5d lil & multi	.20	.20
473	A79	10d pink & multi	.20	.20
474	A79	35d bl grn & multi	.30	.25
475	A79	55d multi	.55	.40
476	A79	75d multi	.75	.60
477	A79	1.25r multi	1.25	1.00
		Nos. 472-477 (6)	3.25	2.65

4th Arabian Gulf Soccer Cup Tournament, Doha, Mar. 22-Apr.

Dhow A80

Designs: Various dhows.

1976, Apr. 19 *Perf. 13½x14*

478	A80	10d blue & multi	.20	.20
479	A80	35d blue & multi	.50	.20
480	A80	80d blue & multi	1.00	.45
481	A80	1.25r blue & multi	1.65	.75
482	A80	1.50r blue & multi	2.00	.90
483	A80	2r blue & multi	3.25	1.40
		Nos. 478-483 (6)	8.60	3.90

Soccer — A81

10d, Yachting. 35d, Steeplechase. 80d, Boxing. 1.25r, Weight lifting. 1.50r, Basketball.

1976, May 15 Litho. *Perf. 14x13½*

484 A81	5d	multicolored	.20	.20
485 A81	10d	blue & multi	.20	.20
486 A81	35d	orange & multi	.20	.20
487 A81	80d	bister & multi	.45	.40
488 A81	1.25r	lilac & multi	.85	.75
489 A81	1.50r	rose & multi	1.10	1.00
		Nos. 484-489 (6)	3.00	2.75

21st Olympic Games, Montreal, Canada, July 17-Aug. 1.

Village and Emblems — A82

35d, Emblems. 80d, Village. 1.25r, Sheik Khalifa.

1976, May 31 *Perf. 13½x14*

490 A82	10d	orange & multi	.20	.20
491 A82	35d	yellow & multi	.45	.20
492 A82	80d	citron & multi	.90	.45
493 A82	1.25r	dp blue & multi	1.50	.75
		Nos. 490-493 (4)	3.05	1.60

Habitat, UN Conf. on Human Settlements, Vancouver, Canada, May 31-June 11.

Snowy Plover A83

Birds: 10d, Great cormorant. 35d, Osprey. 80d, Flamingo. 1.25r, Rock thrush. 2r, Saker falcon. 35d, 80d, 1.25r, 2r, vertical.

Perf. 13½x14, 14x13½

1976, July 19 Litho.

494 A83	5d	multi	.45	.20
495 A83	10d	multi	1.00	.20
496 A83	35d	multi	2.75	.25
497 A83	80d	multi	5.25	.65
498 A83	1.25r	multi	9.00	1.10
499 A83	2r	multi	10.00	1.60
		Nos. 494-499 (6)	28.45	4.00

Sheik Khalifa and Qatar Flag — A84

Government Building — A85

Designs: 10d, like 5d. 80d, Government building. 1.25r, Offshore oil platform. 1.50r, UN emblem and Qatar coat of arms.

1976, Sept. 2 *Perf. 14x13½, 13½x14*

500 A84	5d	gold & multi	.20	.20
501 A84	10d	silver & multi	.20	.20
502 A85	40d	multicolored	.45	.25
503 A85	80d	multicolored	.80	.50
504 A85	1.25r	multicolored	1.25	.75
505 A85	1.50r	multicolored	1.65	.90
		Nos. 500-505 (6)	4.55	2.80

5th anniversary of independence.

Qatar Flag and UN Emblem — A86

1976, Oct. 24 Litho. *Perf. 13½x14*

506 A86	2r	multi	2.00	1.00
507 A86	3r	multi	2.75	1.50

United Nations Day 1976.

A87 Sheik Khalifa

A88 Sheik Khalifa

1977, Feb. 22 Litho. *Perf. 14x13½*

508 A87	20d	silver & multi	.25	.20
509 A87	1.80r	gold & multi	2.50	1.40

Accession of Sheik Khalifa, 5th anniv.

1977, Mar. 1 Litho. *Perf. 14x14½*

Size: 22x27mm

510 A88	5d	multicolored	.20	.20
511 A88	10d	aqua & multi	.20	.20
512 A88	35d	orange & multi	.45	.20
513 A88	80d	multicolored	1.00	.30

Perf. 13½

Size: 25x30mm

514 A88	1r	vio bl & multi	1.65	.45
515 A88	5r	yellow & multi	6.00	2.25
516 A88	10r	multicolored	15.00	4.50
		Nos. 510-516 (7)	24.50	8.10

Letter, APU Emblem, Flag — A89

1977, Apr. 12 *Perf. 14x13½*

517 A89	35d	blue & multi	.50	.25
518 A89	1.35r	blue & multi	1.75	1.00

Arab Postal Union, 25th anniversary.

Waves and Sheik Khalifa A90

1977, May 17 Litho. *Perf. 13½x14*

519 A90	35d	multi	.35	.25
520 A90	1.80r	multi	2.00	1.50

World Telecommunications Day.

Sheik Khalifa — A90a

Perf. 13½x13

1977, June 29 Litho. Wmk. 368

520A A90a	5d	multi		.20	.20
520B A90a	10d	multi		.20	.20
520C A90a	35d	multi		.20	.20
520D A90a	80d	multi		.45	.45
	e.	Bklt. pane, 4 5d, 3 10d, 2 35d, 80d		8.50	6.00
		Nos. 520A-520D (4)		1.05	1.05

Issued in booklets only.

Parliament, Clock Tower, Minaret — A91

Designs: No. 522, Main business district, Doha. No. 523, Highway crossings, Doha.

1977, Sept. 1 Litho. *Perf. 13x13½*

521 A91	80d	multicolored	1.00	.65
522 A91	80d	multicolored	1.00	.65
523 A91	80d	multicolored	1.00	.65
		Nos. 521-523 (3)	3.00	1.95

6th anniversary of independence.

UN Emblem, Flag — A92

1977, Oct. 24 Litho. *Perf. 13½x14*

524 A92	20d	green & multi	.25	.20
525 A92	1r	blue & multi	1.25	.75

United Nations Day.

Surgery — A93

20d, Steel mill. 1r, Classroom. 5r, Sheik Khalifa.

1978, Feb. 22 Litho. *Perf. 13½x14*

526 A93	20d	multicolored	.20	.20
527 A93	80d	multicolored	.50	.40
528 A93	1r	multicolored	.60	.50
529 A93	5r	multicolored	3.00	2.50
		Nos. 526-529 (4)	4.30	3.60

Accession of Sheik Khalifa, 6th anniv.

Oil Refinery — A94

80d, Office buildings, Doha. 1.35r, Traffic Circle, Doha. 1.80r, Sheik Khalifa and flag.

1978, Aug. 31 Litho. *Perf. 13½x14*

530 A94	35d	multi	.30	.20
531 A94	80d	multi	.75	.50
532 A94	1.35r	multi	1.25	.75
533 A94	1.80r	multi	1.75	1.00
		Nos. 530-533 (4)	4.05	2.45

7th anniversary of independence.

Man Learning to Read — A95

1978, Sept. 8 Litho. *Perf. 13½x14*

534 A95	35d	multicolored	.40	.20
535 A95	80d	multicolored	1.40	.65

International Literacy Day.

Flag and UN Emblem — A96

1978, Oct. 14 *Perf. 13x13½*

536 A96	35d	multi	.40	.20
537 A96	80d	multi	1.40	.65

United Nations Day.

Human Rights Emblem — A97

IYC Emblem — A98

Designs: 80d, like 35d. 1.25r, 1.80r, Scales and Human Rights emblem.

1978, Dec. 10 Litho. *Perf. 14x13½*

538 A97	35d	multi	.30	.20
539 A97	80d	multi	.70	.60
540 A97	1.25r	multi	.90	.80
541 A97	1.80r	multi	1.50	1.25
		Nos. 538-541 (4)	3.40	2.85

30th anniversary of Universal Declaration of Human Rights.

Wmk. JEZ Multiple (368)

1979, Jan. 1 Litho. *Perf. 13½x13*

542 A98	35d	multi	.40	.25
543 A98	1.80r	multi	1.50	1.25

International Year of the Child.

A99

Sheik Khalifa — A100

1979, Jan. 15 Unwmk. *Perf. 14*

544	A99	5d multi	.20	.20
545	A99	10d multi	.20	.20
546	A99	20d multi	.20	.20
547	A99	25d multi	.25	.20
548	A99	35d multi	.35	.20
549	A99	60d multi	.90	.30
550	A99	80d multi	1.00	.40

Size: 27x32mm

551	A99	1r multi	1.25	.50
552	A99	1.25r multi	1.40	.65
553	A99	1.35r multi	1.90	.75
554	A99	1.80r multi	2.00	.90
555	A99	5r multi	6.00	2.50
556	A99	10r multi	12.00	5.00
		Nos. 544-556 (13)	27.65	12.00

1979, Feb. 22 Wmk. 368

557	A100	35d multi	.30	.20
558	A100	80d multi	.65	.45
559	A100	1r multi	.80	.60
560	A100	1.25r multi	1.00	.75
		Nos. 557-560 (4)	2.75	2.00

7th anniv. of accession of Sheik Khalifa.

Cables and People — A101

1979, May 17 Litho. *Perf. 14x13½*

561	A101	2r multi	1.25	1.10
562	A101	2.80r multi	1.65	1.40

World Telecommunications Day.

Children Holding Globe, UNESCO Emblem — A102

Perf. 13x13½

1979, July 15 Litho. Unwmk.

563	A102	35d multicolored	.30	.20
564	A102	80d multicolored	1.40	.60

International Bureau of Education, Geneva, 50th anniversary.

Rolling Mill — A103

UN Day — A104

Wmk. 368

1979, Sept. 2 Litho. *Perf. 13½*

565	A103	5d shown	.20	.20
566	A103	10d Doha, aerial view	.20	.20
567	A103	1.25r Qatar flag	.85	.75
568	A103	2r Sheik Khalifa	1.40	1.00
		Nos. 565-568 (4)	2.65	2.15

Independence, 8th anniversary.

1979, Oct. 24 Litho. *Perf. 13½x13*

569	A104	1.25r multi	1.00	.75
570	A104	2r multi	1.75	1.25

Conference Emblem — A105

1979, Nov. 24 *Perf. 13x13½*

571	A105	35d multi	.55	.25
572	A105	1.80r multi	2.25	1.25

Hegira (Pilgrimage Year); 3rd World Conference on Prophets.

Sheik Khalifa, 8th Anniversary of Accession — A106

1980, Feb. 22 Litho. *Perf. 13x13½*

573	A106	20d multi	.20	.20
574	A106	60d multi	.45	.35
575	A106	1.25r multi	.85	.65
576	A106	2r multi	1.75	1.25
		Nos. 573-576 (4)	3.25	2.45

Map of Arab Countries — A107

1980, Mar. 1 Litho. *Perf. 13½x14*

577	A107	2.35r multi	1.75	.95
578	A107	2.80r multi	2.25	1.15

6th Congress of Arab Town Organization, Doha, Mar. 1-4.

Oil Refinery — A108

1980, Sept. 2 Litho. *Perf. 14½*

579	A108	10d shown	.20	.20
580	A108	35d View of Doha	.50	.25
581	A108	2r Oil rig	2.25	1.10
582	A108	2.35r Hospital	2.75	1.70
		Nos. 579-582 (4)	5.70	3.25

9th anniversary of independence.

Men Holding OPEC Emblem — A109

United Nations Day 1980 — A110

1980, Sept. 15 *Perf. 14x13½*

583	A109	1.35r multi	.90	.60
584	A109	2r multi	1.40	.90

OPEC, 20th anniversary.

1980, Oct. 24

585	A110	1.35r multi	1.10	.60
586	A110	1.80r multi	1.50	.80

Hegira (Pilgrimage Year) — A111

1980, Nov. 8 Litho. *Perf. 14½*

587	A111	10d multi	.20	.20
588	A111	35d multi	.25	.25
589	A111	1.25r multi	.80	.80
590	A111	2.80r multi	1.90	1.90
		Nos. 587-590 (4)	3.15	3.15

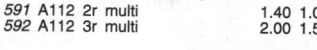

International Year of the Disabled — A112

1981, Jan. 5 Photo. *Perf. 11½*

Granite Paper

591	A112	2r multi	1.40	1.00
592	A112	3r multi	2.00	1.50

Education Day — A113

Sheik Khalifa, 9th Anniversary of Accession A114

Perf. 14x13½

1981, Feb. 22 Litho. Wmk. 368

593	A113	2r multi	1.75	.80
594	A113	3r multi	2.50	1.25

1981, Feb. 22

595	A114	10d multi	.20	.20
596	A114	35d multi	.20	.20
597	A114	80d multi	.50	.35
598	A114	5r multi	4.25	2.25
		Nos. 595-598 (4)	5.15	3.00

A115

A116

1981, May 17 Litho. *Perf. 13½x13*

599	A115	2r multi	1.50	.95
600	A115	2.80r multi	1.90	1.25

13th World Telecommunications Day.

1981, June 11 Litho. *Perf. 14x13½*

Championship emblem.

601	A116	1.25r multi	1.75	.55
602	A116	2.80r multi	3.75	1.25

30th Intl. Military Soccer Championship, Doha.

10th Anniv. of Independence — A117

Perf. 13½x14

1981, Sept. 2 Litho. Wmk. 368

603	A117	5d multicolored	.20	.20
604	A117	60d multicolored	.50	.30
605	A117	80d multicolored	.65	.40
606	A117	5r multicolored	3.75	2.75
		Nos. 603-606 (4)	5.10	3.65

World Food Day A118

1981, Oct. 16 Litho. *Perf. 13*

607 A118 2r multi 2.50 1.50
608 A118 2.80r multi 3.50 2.25

Red Crescent Society — A119

1982, Jan. 16 Litho. *Perf. 14x13½*

609 A119 20d multi .30 .20
610 A119 2.80r multi 4.00 2.00

10th Anniv. of Sheik Khalifa's Accession — A120

Perf. 13½x14

1982, Feb. 22 Litho. Wmk. 368

611 A120 10d multi .20 .20
612 A120 20d multi .25 .20
613 A120 1.25r multi 1.50 .65
614 A120 2.80r multi 3.00 1.40
Nos. 611-614 (4) 4.95 2.45

Sheik Khalifa — A121

Oil Refinery — A122

Designs: 5r, 10r, 15r, Hoda Clock Tower.

1982, Mar. 1 Photo. *Perf. 11½x12*
Granite Paper

615 A121 5d multi .20 .20
616 A121 10d multi .20 .20
617 A121 15d multi .20 .20
618 A121 20d multi .20 .20
619 A121 25d multi .20 .20
620 A121 35d multi .20 .20
621 A121 60d multi .35 .25
622 A121 80d multi .45 .35
623 A122 1r multi .60 .45
624 A122 1.25r multi .75 .60
625 A122 2r multi 1.20 .90
626 A122 5r multi 3.00 2.25
627 A122 10r multi 6.00 4.50
628 A122 15r multi 8.50 6.50
Nos. 615-628 (14) 22.05 17.00

Hamad General Hospital — A123

1982, Mar. Litho. *Perf. 13x13½*

629 A123 10d multi .20 .20
630 A123 2.35r multi 2.75 1.40

6th Anniv. of United Arab Shipping Co. — A124

1982, Mar. 6 Litho. *Perf. 13x13½*

631 A124 20d multi .25 .20
632 A124 2.35r multi 3.00 1.40

A125

A126

1982, Apr. 12 Litho. *Perf. 13½x13*

633 A125 35d yellow & multi .25 .20
634 A125 2.80r blue & multi 2.00 1.40

30th anniv. of Arab Postal Union.

1982, Sept. 2 Litho. *Perf. 13½x13*

635 A126 10d multi .25 .20
636 A126 80d multi .70 .40
637 A126 1.25r multi 1.25 .65
638 A126 2.80r multi 2.50 1.40
Nos. 635-638 (4) 4.70 2.65

11th anniv. of Independence.

World Communications Year — A127

1983, Jan. 10 Litho. *Perf. 13½x13*

639 A127 35d multi .45 .20
640 A127 2.80r multi 3.00 1.25

Gulf Postal Org., 2nd Conference, Doha, Apr. — A128

1983, Apr. 9 Litho. *Perf. 13½x14*

641 A128 1r multi 1.25 .50
642 A128 1.35r multi 1.50 .75

A129

A130

1983, Sept. 2 Litho. *Perf. 14*

643 A129 10d multi .20 .20
644 A129 35d multi .30 .20
645 A129 80d multi .70 .30
646 A129 2.80r multi 2.75 1.15
Nos. 643-646 (4) 3.95 1.85

12th anniv. of Independence.

1983, Nov. 7 Litho. *Perf. 13½x14*

647 A130 35d multi .30 .20
648 A130 2.80r multi 2.25 1.10

GCC Supreme Council, 4th regular session.

35th Anniv. of UN Declaration of Human Rights — A131

1983, Dec. 10 Litho. *Perf. 13½x14*

649 A131 1.25r Globe, emblem 1.75 .75
650 A131 2.80r Scale 3.00 1.50

A132

A133

1984, Mar. 1 Litho. *Perf. 13x13½*

651 A132 15d multi .20 .20
652 A132 40d multi .35 .25
653 A132 50d multi .45 .30

Perf. 14½x13½

654 A133 1r multi .75 .60
655 A133 1.50r multi 1.25 .90
656 A133 2.50r multi 2.00 1.50
657 A133 3r multi 2.50 1.75
658 A133 5r multi 4.25 3.00
659 A133 10r multi 8.25 6.00
Nos. 651-659 (9) 20.00 14.50

See Nos. 707-709, 792-801.

13th Anniv. of Independence — A134

1984, Sept. 2 Photo. *Perf. 12*

660 A134 15d multi .20 .20
661 A134 1r multi .90 .55
662 A134 2.50r multi 2.00 1.40
663 A134 3.50r multi 3.00 1.90
Nos. 660-663 (4) 6.10 4.05

Literacy Day, 1984 — A135

40th Anniv., ICAO — A136

1984, Sept. 8 Litho. *Perf. 14x13½*

664 A135 1r lilac & multi 1.00 .55
665 A135 1r orange & multi 1.00 .55

1984, Dec. 7 Litho. *Perf. 13½x13*

666 A136 20d multi .25 .20
667 A136 3.50r multi 3.75 1.90

League of Arab States, 40th Anniv. A137

1985, Mar. 22 Photo. *Perf. 11½*

668 A137 50d multi .50 .25
669 A137 4r multi 3.50 2.00

Intl. Youth Year — A138

Traffic Crossing — A139

1985, Mar. 4 *Perf. 11½x12*
Granite Paper

670 A138 50d multi 1.00 .25
671 A138 1r multi 2.00 .50

1985, Mar. 9 *Perf. 14x13½*

672 A139 1r lt bl & multi 1.25 .50
673 A139 1r pink & multi 1.25 .50

Gulf Cooperation Council Traffic Safety Week, Mar. 16-22.

Natl. Independence, 14th Anniv. — A140

1985, Sept. 2 *Perf. 11½x12*
Granite Paper

674 A140 40d Doha .35 .20
675 A140 50d Earth satellite station .40 .25
676 A140 1.50r Oil refinery 1.25 .75
677 A140 4r Storage facility 3.25 2.00
Nos. 674-677 (4) 5.25 3.20

Org. of Petroleum Exporting Countries, 25th Anniv. — A141

1985, Sept. 14 *Perf. 13½x14*

678 A141 1r brt yel grn & multi 1.00 .50
679 A141 1r salmon rose & multi 1.00 .50

UN, 40th Anniv. A142

1985, Oct. 24 **Litho.** *Perf. 13½x14*

680 A142 1r multi .85 .50
681 A142 3r multi 2.50 1.50

Population and Housing Census — A143

1986, Mar. 1 **Photo.** *Perf. 11½x12*

682 A143 1r multi .80 .55
683 A143 3r multi 2.25 1.65

United Arab Shipping Co., 10th Anniv. — A144

1986, May 30 **Litho.** *Perf. 13½x14*

684 A144 1.50r Qatari ibn al Fuja'a 1.25 .85
685 A144 4r Al Wajba 3.25 2.25

Natl. Independence, 15th Anniv. — A145

Perf. 13x13½
1986, Sept. 2 **Litho.** **Unwmk.**

686 A145 40d multi .35 .25
687 A145 50d multi .45 .30
688 A145 1r multi .90 .60
689 A145 4r multi 3.25 2.25
Nos. 686-689 (4) 4.95 3.40

Sheik Khalifa — A146

1987, Jan. 1 **Photo.** *Perf. 11½x12*
Granite Paper

690 A146 15r multi 8.00 7.00
691 A146 20r multi 11.00 9.00
692 A146 30r multi 17.00 14.00
Nos. 690-692 (3) 36.00 30.00

15th Anniv. of Sheik Khalifa's Accession A147

1987, Feb. 22 *Perf. 12x11½*
Granite Paper

693 A147 50d multi .35 .30
694 A147 1r multi .65 .60
695 A147 1.50r multi 1.00 .85
696 A147 4r multi 2.75 2.25
Nos. 693-696 (4) 4.75 4.00

Arab Postal Union, 35th Anniv. — A148

Perf. 14x13½
1987, Apr. 12 **Litho.** **Unwmk.**

697 A148 1r multi .60 .60
698 A148 1.50r multi .85 .85

Natl. Independence, 16th Anniv. — A149

1987, Sept. 2 **Litho.** *Perf. 13x13½*

699 A149 25d Housing complex .20 .20
700 A149 75d Water tower, city .55 .45
701 A149 2r Modern office building 1.40 1.25
702 A149 4r Oil refinery 3.00 2.25
Nos. 699-702 (4) 5.15 4.15

A150

A151

Perf. 13½x13
1987, Sept. 8 **Litho.** **Unwmk.**

703 A150 1.50r multi 1.25 .85
704 A150 4r multi 3.00 2.25

Intl. Literacy Day.

Perf. 14x13½
1987, Apr. 24 **Litho.** **Wmk. 368**

705 A151 1r multicolored 1.00 .60
706 A151 4r multicolored 3.75 2.25

Gulf Environment Day.

Sheik Type of 1984

1988, Jan. 1 *Perf. 13x13½*
Size of 25d, 75d: 22x27mm

707 A133 25d multicolored .20 .20
708 A133 75d multicolored .60 .45

Perf. 14½x13

709 A133 2r multicolored 1.50 1.15

This is an expanding set. Numbers will change if necessary.

WHO, 40th Anniv. — A152

1988, Apr. 7 *Perf. 14x13½*

714 A152 1.50r multicolored 1.25 .90
715 A152 2r multicolored 1.75 1.25

Independence, 17th Anniv. — A153

Perf. 11½x12
1988, Sept. 2 **Litho.** **Unwmk.**
Granite Paper

716 A153 50d multicolored .40 .30
717 A153 75d multicolored .60 .45
718 A153 1.50r multicolored 1.25 .90
719 A153 2r multicolored 1.50 1.25
Nos. 716-719 (4) 3.75 2.90

Opening of the Doha General P.O. — A154

1988, Sept. 3 *Perf. 13x13½*

720 A154 1.50r multicolored 1.25 .90
721 A154 4r multicolored 3.00 2.25

Arab Housing Day — A155

1988, Oct. 3 *Perf. 11½x12*
Granite Paper

722 A155 1.50r multicolored 1.25 .90
723 A155 4r multicolored 3.00 2.25

A156

A157

Perf. 14x13½
1988, Dec. 10 **Wmk. 368**

724 A156 1.50r multicolored 1.25 .90
725 A156 2r multicolored 1.50 1.25

Declaration of Human Rights, 40th anniv.

Perf. 12x11½
1989, May 17 **Unwmk.**
Granite Paper

726 A157 2r multicolored 1.50 1.25
727 A157 4r multicolored 3.00 2.25

World Telecommunications Day.

Qatar Red Crescent Soc., 10th Anniv. — A158

Perf. 13½x14
1989, Aug. 8 **Wmk. 368**

728 A158 4r multicolored 3.00 2.30

Natl. Independence, 18th Anniv. — A159

Perf. 13x13½
1989, Sept. 2 **Unwmk.**

729 A159 75d multicolored .60 .45
730 A159 1r multicolored .80 .60
731 A159 1.50r multicolored 1.25 .90
732 A159 2r multicolored 1.50 1.25
Nos. 729-732 (4) 4.15 3.20

Gulf Air, 40th Anniv.
A160

1990, Mar. 24 Litho. ***Perf. 13x13½***

733	A160	50d	multicolored	.30	.20
734	A160	75d	multicolored	.45	.30
735	A160	4r	multicolored	2.40	1.60
			Nos. 733-735 (3)	3.15	2.10

Independence, 19th Anniv. — A161

Designs: 75d, Map, sunburst. 1.50r, 2r, Swordsman, musicians.

1990, Sept. 2 ***Perf. 14x13½***

736	A161	50d	multicolored	.30	.20
737	A161	75d	multicolored	.45	.30
738	A161	1.50r	multicolored	.90	.60
739	A161	2r	multicolored	1.25	.80
			Nos. 736-739 (4)	2.90	1.90

Organization of Petroleum Exporting Countries (OPEC), 30th Anniv.
A162

1990, Sept. 14

740	A162	50d	shown	.30	.20
741	A162	1.50r	Flags	.90	.60

A163

A164

GCC Supreme Council, 11th Regular Session: 1r, Leaders of member nations. 1.50r, Flag, council emblem. 2r, State seal, emblem.

Perf. 14x13½

1990, Dec. 22 Litho. Wmk. 368

742	A163	50d	multicolored	.30	.20
743	A163	1r	multicolored	.55	.40
744	A163	1.50r	multicolored	.85	.60
745	A163	2r	multicolored	.55	.40
			Nos. 742-745 (4)	2.25	1.60

Perf. 12½x13½

1991, June 20 Litho. Wmk. 368

Plants.

747	A164	10d	Glossonema edule	.20	.20
750	A164	25d	Lycium shawii	.20	.20
752	A164	50d	Acacia tortilis	.45	.30
754	A164	75d	Acacia ehrenbergiana	.70	.45
756	A164	1r	Capparis spinosa	.90	.60
759	A164	4r	Cymhopogon parkeri	3.50	2.40
			Nos. 747-759 (6)	5.95	4.15

This is an expanding set. Numbers may change.

Independence, 20th Anniv. — A165

1991, Aug. 15 Litho. ***Perf. 14x14½***
Granite Paper

762	A165	25d	shown	.20	.20
763	A165	75d	red vio & multi	.60	.25

Perf. 14½x14

764	A165	1r	Doha skyline, horiz.	.85	.40
765	A165	1.50r	Palace, horiz.	1.25	.60
			Nos. 762-765 (4)	2.90	1.45

Fish
A166

Various species of fish.

1991, Dec. 1 ***Perf. 14x13½***

767	A166	10d	multicolored	.20	.20
768	A166	15d	multicolored	.20	.20
770	A166	25d	multicolored	.20	.20
772	A166	50d	multicolored	.30	.20
773	A166	75d	multicolored	.40	.25
774	A166	1r	multicolored	.60	.40
775	A166	1.50r	multicolored	.90	.60
776	A166	2r	multicolored	1.25	.80
			Nos. 767-776 (8)	4.05	2.85

This is an expanding set. Numbers may change.

A167

Sheik Khalifa, 20th Anniv. of Accession
A168

Perf. 14x13½

1992, Feb. 22 Litho. Wmk. 368

781	A167	25d	multicolored	.20	.20
782	A167	50d	multicolored	.30	.20
783	A168	75d	multicolored	.45	.25
784	A168	1.50r	multicolored	.90	.60
			Nos. 781-784 (4)	1.85	1.25

World Health Day
A169

1992, Apr. 7 ***Perf. 14x13½, 13½x14***

785	A169	50d	Heart with face, vert.	.30	.20
786	A169	1.50r	shown	.90	.60

Children's Paintings
A170

1992, June 15 Unwmk. ***Perf. 11½***

787	A170	25d	Girls dancing	.20	.20
788	A170	50d	Children playing	.30	.20
789	A170	75d	Ships	.45	.25
790	A170	1.50r	Fishing from boats	.90	.60
a.			Souvenir sheet of 4, #787-790		
			Nos. 787-790 (4)	1.85	1.25

Type of 1984 with Smaller Arabic Inscription and

A171

A172

Designs: 25d, 1.50r, Offshore oil field. 50d, 2r, 5r, Map. 75d, 3r, Storage tanks, horiz. 1r, 4r, 10r, Oil refinery, horiz.

1992 Litho. ***Perf. 13x13½***

791	A171	10d	multicolored	*.20*	*.20*
792	A132	25d	multicolored	*.20*	*.20*
793	A132	50d	multicolored	*.30*	*.25*

Perf. 13½x13

794	A132	75d	multicolored	*.45*	*.35*
795	A132	1r	multicolored	*.60*	*.50*

Size: 25x32mm

Perf. 14½x13, 13x14½

796	A132	1.50r	multicolored	*.90*	*.70*
797	A132	2r	multicolored	*1.25*	*1.00*
798	A132	3r	multicolored	*1.90*	*1.50*
799	A132	4r	multicolored	*2.50*	*2.00*
800	A132	5r	multicolored	*3.00*	*2.50*
801	A132	10r	multicolored	*6.25*	*5.00*
802	A172	15r	multicolored	*9.00*	*7.50*
803	A172	20r	multicolored	*12.50*	*10.00*
804	A172	30r	multicolored	*19.00*	*15.00*
			Nos. 791-804 (14)	*58.05*	*46.70*

Issued: 10-50d, 1.50, 2, 5, 15, 30r, 2/15; others, 5/14.

1992 Summer Olympics, Barcelona
A174

1992, July 25 Litho. ***Perf. 15***

805	A174	50d	Running	.30	.20
806	A174	1.50r	Soccer	.90	.60

11th Persian Gulf Soccer Cup
A175

1992, Nov. 27 Litho. ***Perf. 14½***

807	A175	50d	shown	.30	.20
808	A175	1r	Ball, net, vert.	.60	.20

A176

Independence, 21st Anniv. — A177

Sheik Khalifa and: No. 810, "21" in English and Arabic. No. 811, Tree, dhow in harbor. No. 812, Natural gas well, pen, dhow.

Unwmk.
1992, Sept. 2 Litho. ***Perf. 12***
Granite Paper

809	A176	50d	shown	.30	.20
810	A176	50d	multicolored	.30	.20
811	A177	1r	multicolored	.60	.40
812	A177	1r	multicolored	.60	.40
a.			Strip of 8, 2 each #809-812	5.50	4.00
			Nos. 809-812 (4)	1.80	1.20

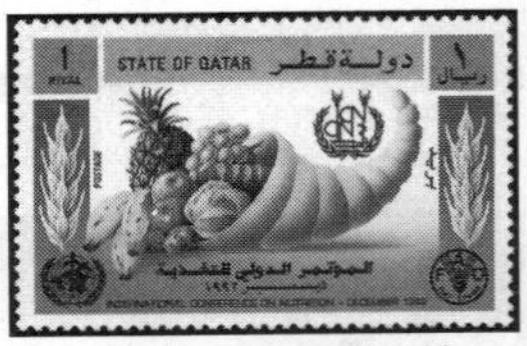

Intl. Conference on Nutrition, Rome — A178

1992, Dec. 12 ***Perf. 14½***

813	A178	50d	Globe, emblems, vert.	.30	.20
814	A178	1r	Cornucopia	.60	.40

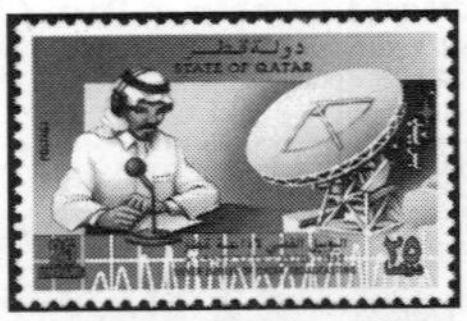

Qatar Broadcasting, Silver Jubilee — A179

Designs: 25d, Man at microphone, satellite dish. 50d, Rocket lift-off, satellite. 75d, Communications building. 1r, Technicians working on books.

1993, June 25 Photo. ***Perf. 12x11½***
Granite Paper

819	A179	25d	multicolored	.20	.20
820	A179	50d	multicolored	.30	.20
821	A179	75d	multicolored	.45	.30
822	A179	1r	multicolored	.60	.40
a.			Souvenir sheet of 4, #819-822		
			Nos. 819-822 (4)	1.55	1.10

Ruins
A180

Mosque with: a, Minaret (at left, shown). b, Minaret with side projections (at right). c, Minaret with catwalk, inside wall. d, Minaret at right, outside wall.

1993, May 10 Litho. *Perf. 12*
Granite Paper

823 A180 1r Strip of 4, #a.-d. 2.50 1.75

Independence, 22nd Anniv. — A181

Intl. Literacy Day — A182

Designs: 25c, Oil pumping station. 50d, Flag, clock tower. 75d, Coat of arms, "22." 1.50r, Flag, fortress tower.

1993, Sept. 2 Litho. *Perf. 11½*
Granite Paper

824	A181	25d multicolored	.20	.20
825	A181	50d multicolored	.30	.20
826	A181	75d multicolored	.45	.30
827	A181	1.50r multicolored	.90	.60
		Nos. 824-827 (4)	1.85	1.30

Perf. 14x13½

1993, Sept. 2 Litho. Wmk. 368

Designs: 25d, Quill, paper. 50d, Papers with English letters, pen. 75d, Papers with Arabic letters, pen. 1.50r, Scroll, Arabic letters, pen.

828	A182	25d multicolored	.20	.20
829	A182	50d multicolored	.30	.20
830	A182	75d multicolored	.45	.30
831	A182	1.50r multicolored	.90	.60
		Nos. 828-831 (4)	1.85	1.30

Children's Games A183

Designs: 25d, Girls with thread and spinners. 50d, Boys with stick and disk, vert. 75r, Children guiding wheels with sticks, vert. 1.50r, Girls with jump rope.

1993, Dec. 5 Litho. *Perf. 11½*
Granite Paper

832	A183	25d multicolored	.20	.20
833	A183	50d multicolored	.30	.20
834	A183	75d multicolored	.45	.30
a.		Souvenir sheet, 2 each #833, #834		
835	A183	1.50r multicolored	.90	.60
a.		Souvenir sheet, 2 each #832, #835		
		Nos. 832-835 (4)	1.85	1.30

Falcons — A184

A185

1993, Dec. 22
Granite Paper

836	A184	25d Lanner	.20	.20
837	A184	50d Saker	.35	.20
838	A184	75d Barbary	.55	.30
839	A184	1.50r Peregrine	1.10	.60
a.		Souvenir sheet, #836-839		
		Nos. 836-839 (4)	2.20	1.30

1994, May 6 Litho. *Perf. 14*

Society for Handicapped Welfare and Rehabilitation: 75d, Hands above and below handicapped symbol.

840	A185	25d shown	.20	.20
841	A185	75d multi	.45	.30

A186

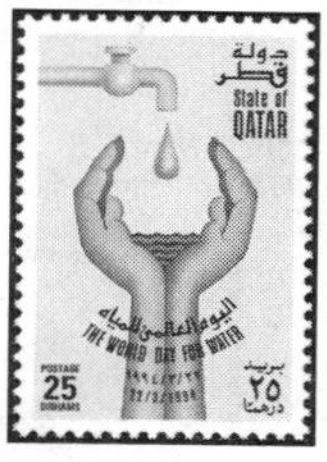

A187

Qatar Insurance Co., 30th Anniv.: 50d, Building. 1.50r, Co. arms, global tourist attractions.

Perf. 14½

1994, Mar. 11 Litho. Unwmk.

842	A186	50d gold & multi	.30	.20
843	A186	1.50r gold & multi	.90	.60

1994, Mar. 22 Litho. *Perf. 11½*

World Day for Water: 1r, UN emblem, hands catching water drop, tower, grain.

844	A187	25d shown	.20	.20
845	A187	1r multicolored	.55	.35

A188

A189

1994, Mar. 22 Litho. *Perf. 11½*

846	A188	75d shown	.40	.30
847	A188	2r Scales, gavel	1.10	.75

Intl. Law Conference.

Perf. 12x11½

1994, July 16 Litho. Unwmk.

848	A189	25d shown	.20	.20
849	A189	1r Family, UN emblem	.60	.40

Intl. Year of the Family.

Independence, 23rd Anniv. — A190

25d, 2r, Text. 75d, Island. 1r, Oil drilling plant.

1994, Sept. 2 Photo. *Perf. 12*
Granite Paper

850	A190	25d green & multi	.20	.20
851	A190	75d multicolored	.45	.30
852	A190	1r multicolored	.60	.40
853	A190	2r pink & multi	1.25	.80
		Nos. 850-853 (4)	2.50	1.70

ILO, 75th Anniv. — A191

1994, May 28 *Perf. 14*

854	A191	25d salmon & multi	.20	.20
855	A191	2r green & multi, diff.	1.10	.75

ICAO, 50th Anniv. A192

1994, Dec. 7 *Perf. 13½x14*

856	A192	25d shown	.20	.20
857	A192	75d Emblem, airplane	.40	.30

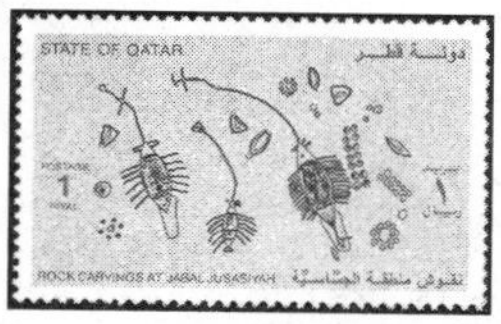

A193

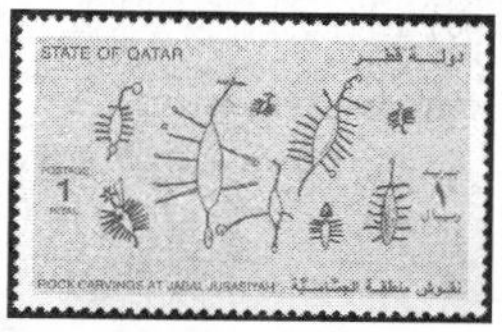

A194

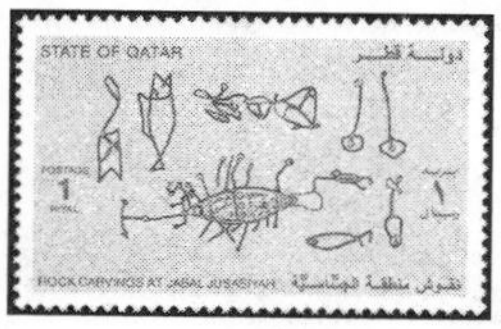

A195

A196

Rock Carvings at Jabal Jusasiyah — A197

1995, Mar. 18 Litho. *Perf. 14½x15*

858	A193	1r multicolored	.55	.35
859	A194	1r multicolored	.55	.35
860	A195	1r multicolored	.55	.35
861	A196	1r multicolored	.55	.35
862	A197	1r multicolored	.55	.35
863	A197	1r multi, diff.	.55	.35
a.		Vert. strip of 6, #858-863	3.25	2.25

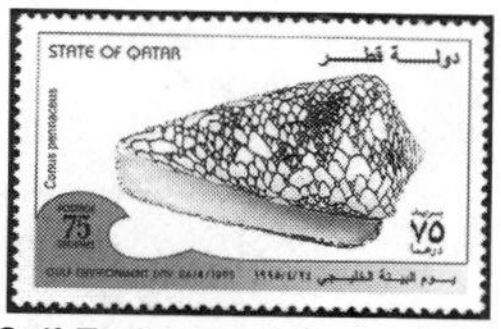

Gulf Environment Day — A198

Shells: No. 864a, Conus pennaceus. b, Cerithidea cingulata. c, Hexaplex kuesterianus. d, Epitonium scalare.

No. 865a, Murex scolopax. b, Thais mutabilis. c, Fusinus arabicus. d, Lambis truncata sebae.

1995, Apr. 24

864	A198	75d Strip of 4, #a.-d.	1.75	1.10
865	A198	1r Strip of 4, #a.-d.	2.25	1.50

Intl. Nursing Day — A199

Designs: 1r, Nurse adjusting IV for patient. 1.50r, Injecting shot into arm of infant.

1995, May 12

866	A199	1r multicolored	.55	.40
867	A199	1.50r multicolored	.85	.55

Independence, 24th Anniv. — A200

Designs: a, 1.50r, Shipping dock, city. b, 1r, Children in classroom. c, 1.50r, Aerial view of city. d, 1r, Palm trees.

1995, Sept. 2 Litho. *Perf. 13½x14*

868 A200 Block of 4, #a.-d. 2.75 1.40

UN, 50th Anniv. — A201

1995, Oct. 24 *Perf. 13½*

869 A201 1.50r multicolored .85 .55

Gazelles A202

No. 870; a, 75c, Gazella dorcas pelzelni. b, 50d, Dorcatragus megalotis. c, 25d, Gazella dama. d, 1.50r, Gazella spekei. e, 2r, Gazella soemmeringi. f, 1r, Gazella dorcas.

3r, Gazella spekei, gazella dorcas pelzelni, gazella soemmeringi.

1996, Jan. Litho. *Perf. 11½*

870 A202 Strip of 6, #a.-f. 5.00 3.00

Size: 121x81mm

Imperf

871 A202 3r multicolored 30.00 25.00

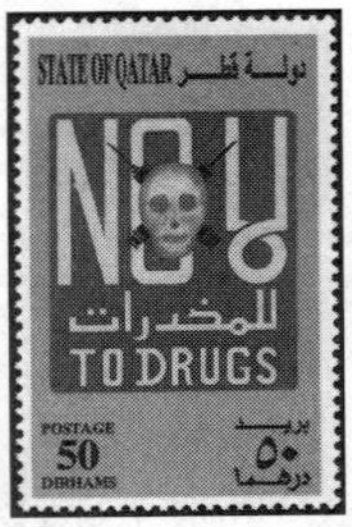

Fight Against Drug Abuse — A203

1996, June 26 Litho. *Perf. 14x13*

872 A203 50d shown .30 .20
873 A203 1r "NO," needles, hand .60 .40

1996 Summer Olympic Games, Atlanta — A204

a, 10d, Olympic emblem, map of Qatar. b, 15d, Shooting. c, 25d, Bowling. d, 50d, Table tennis. e, 1r, Athletics. f, 1.50r, Yachting.

1996, July 19 Litho. *Perf. 14x13½*

874 A204 Strip of 6, #a.-f. 2.00 1.30

Independence, 25th Anniv. - A204a

Litho. & Typo.

1996, Sept. 2 *Perf. 12*

Granite Paper

875 A204a 1.50r silver & multi .85 .55
876 A204a 2r gold & multi 1.10 .75

Forts A204b

25d, Al-Wajbah, vert. 75d, Al-Zubarah. 1r, Al-Kout. 3r, Umm Salal Mohammed.

1997, Jan. 15 Litho. *Perf. 14½*

877 A204b 25d multicolored .20 .20
878 A204b 75d multicolored .45 .30
879 A204b 1r multicolored .60 .35
880 A204b 3r multicolored 1.75 1.20
Nos. 877-880 (4) 3.00 2.05

Sheik Khalifa

A205 A206

1996, Nov. 16 Photo. *Perf. 11½x12*

Granite Paper

881 A205 25d pink & multi .20 .20
882 A205 50d green & multi .30 .20
883 A205 75d bl grn & multi .45 .30
884 A205 1r gray & multi .60 .40

Perf. 11½

885 A206 1.50r grn bl & multi .85 .50
886 A206 2r green & multi 1.25 .80
887 A206 4r ver & multi 2.40 1.60
888 A206 5r purple & multi 3.00 2.00
889 A206 10r brown & multi 6.00 4.00
890 A206 20r blue & multi 12.00 8.00
891 A206 30r orange & multi 18.00 12.00
Nos. 881-891 (11) 45.05 30.00

A207

A208

UNICEF, 50th Anniv.: No. 893, Children, open book emblem.

1996, Dec. 11 Litho. *Perf. 14½*

892 A207 75d blue & multi .45 .30
893 A207 75d violet & multi .45 .30

1996, Dec. 7

17th Session of GCC Supreme Council: 1.50r, Emblem, dove with olive branch, Sheik Khalifa.

894 A208 1r multicolored .60 .40
895 A208 1.50r multicolored .90 .60

Opening of Port of Ras Laffan — A209

Illustration reduced.

1997, Feb. 24 Litho. *Perf. 13½*

896 A209 3r multicolored 1.75 .85

Arabian Horses A210

1997, Mar. 19 Photo. *Perf. 12x11½*

897 A210 25d Red horse with tan mane .20 .20
898 A210 75d Black horse .45 .30
899 A210 1r White horse .55 .30
900 A210 1.50r Red brown horse .85 .45
Nos. 897-900 (4) 2.05 1.25

Size: 115x75mm

Imperf

901 A210 3r Mares, foals 25.00

Independence, 26th Anniv. — A211

1997, Sept. 2 Photo. *Perf. 11½x12*

Granite Paper

902 A211 1r shown .55 .30
903 A211 1.50r Oil refinery .85 .60

Doha '97, Doha-Mena Economic Conference — A212

1997, Nov. 16 Litho. *Perf. 11*

904 A212 2r multicolored 1.10 .75

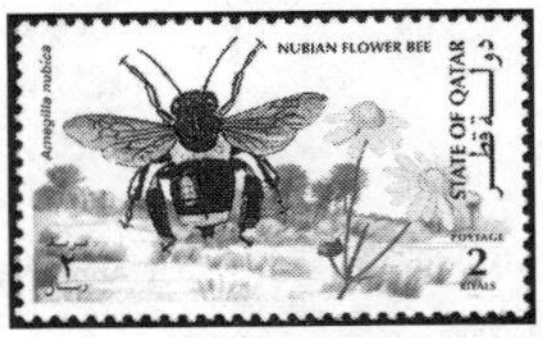

Insects — A213

a, Nubian flower bee. b, Domino beetle. c, Seven-spot ladybird. d, Desert giant ant. e, Eastern death's-head hawkmoth. f, Arabian darkling beetle. g, Yellow digger. h, Mole cricket. i, Migratory locust. j, Elegant rhinoceros beetle. k, Oleander hawkmoth. l, American cockroach. m. Girdled skimmer. n, Sabre-toothed beetle. o, Arabian cicada. p, Pinstriped ground weevil. q, Praying mantis. r, Rufous bombardier beetle. s, Diadem. t, Shore earwing.

1998, July 20 Litho. *Perf. 11½x12*

Granite Paper

905 A213 2r Sheet of 20, #a.-t. 22.50 15.00
u. Souvenir sheet, #905i *11.25 7.50*
v. Souvenir sheet, #905s *11.25 7.50*

Early Diving Equipment — A214

Perf. 11½x12, 12x11½

1998, Aug. 15 Photo.

Granite Paper

906 A214 25d Meflaja .20 .20
907 A214 75d Mahar .45 .35
908 A214 1r Dasta .55 .40
909 A214 1.50r Deyen, vert. .85 .65
Nos. 906-909 (4) 2.05 1.60

Souvenir Sheet

910 A214 2r Man seated in boat 1.10 .85

Qatar University, 25th Anniv. — A215

1998, Sept. 2 Litho. *Perf. 13½x13*

911 A215 1r blue & multi .55 .40
912 A215 1.50r gray & muti .85 .65

Independence, 27th Anniv. — A216

1998, Sept. 2 *Perf. 14*

913 A216 1r Sheik Khalifa, vert. .55 .40
914 A216 1.50r Sheik Khalifa .85 .65

Camels — A217

1999, Jan. 25 Litho. *Perf. 11½*

Granite Paper

915 A217 25d shown .20 .20
916 A217 75d One standing .45 .35
917 A217 1r Three standing .60 .45
918 A217 1.50r Four standing, group .85 .65
Nos. 915-918 (4) 2.10 1.65

Souvenir Sheet

919 A217 2r Adult, juvenile 1.10 .85

1999 FEI General Assembly Meeting, Doha — A218

1999 Litho. *Perf. 13¼x13*

920 A218 1.50r multicolored .85 .65

Ancient Coins — A219

Obverse, reverse of dirhams - #921: a, Umayyad (shown). b, Umayyad, diff. c, Abbasid (3 lines of text on obv.). d, Abbasid (6 lines of text obv.). e, Umayyad, diff. (small circles near edge at top of obv. & rev.).

Obv., rev. of dinars - #922: a, Abbasid (3 lines of text obv.). b, Umayyad. c, Abbasid (5 lines of text obv.). d, Marabitid. e, Fatimid.

Obverse and reverse of: No. 923, Arab Sasanian dirham. 3r, Umayyad dinar, diff.

1999 Litho. *Perf. 11½*

Granite Paper

921 A219 1r Strip of 5, #a.-e. 2.75 2.25
922 A219 2r Strip of 5, #a.-e. 5.75 4.75

Souvenir Sheets

923 A219 2r multicolored 1.10 1.10
924 A219 3r multicolored 1.60 1.60

Independence, 28th Anniv. — A220

Perf. 12¾x13¾

1999, Sept. 2 Litho. Wmk. 368

925 A220 1r violet & multi .55 .55
926 A220 1.50r yellow & multi .80 .80

A221

A222

UPU, 125th anniv.: 1r, Tree with letters. 1.50r, Building, horiz.

Perf. 11½

1999, Oct. 9 Litho. Unwmk.

Granite Paper

927	A221	1r multicolored	.55	.55
928	A221	1.50r multicolored	.80	.80

1999, Oct. 30 Granite Paper

Fifth Stamp Exhibition for the Arab Gulf Countries: 1r, Emblem, stamps. 1.50r, Emblem, horiz.

929	A222	1r multicolored	.55	.55
930	A222	1.50r multicolored	.80	.80

National Committee for Children with Special Needs — A223

Perf. 12¾x13¼

1999, Nov. 2 Litho. Wmk. 368

931	A223	1.50r multi	.80	.80

Millennium A224

Photo. & Embossed

2000, Jan. 1 Unwmk. ***Perf. 11¾***

Granite Paper

932	A224	1.50r red & gold	.80	.80
933	A224	2r blue & gold	1.10	1.10

Qatar Tennis Open — A225

Trophy and: 1r, Stadium. 1.50r, Racquet.

2000, Jan. 3 Litho. ***Perf. 13¼x13½***

934	A225	1r multi	.55	.55
935	A225	1.50r multi	.80	.80

GCC Water Week — A226

2000, Mar. 1 ***Perf. 13¾***

936	A226	1r Map, water drop	.55	.55
937	A226	1.50r Hands, water drop	.80	.80

15th Asian Table Tennis Championships, Doha — A227

2000, May 1 Photo. ***Perf. 11¾***

Granite Paper

938	A227	1.50r multi	.85	.85

Independence, 29th Anniv. — A228

Sheik Khalifa and: 1r, Fort. 1.50r, Oil derrick, city skyline.

Perf. 11½x11¾

2000, Sept. 2 Photo.

Granite Paper

939-940	A228	Set of 2	1.40	1.40

Post Office, 50th Anniv. A229

Monument, building and: 1.50r, Bird. 2r, Magnifying glass.

Photo. & Embossed

2000, Oct. 9 ***Perf. 11¾***

Granite Paper

941-942	A229	Set of 2	1.90	1.90

9th Islamic Summit Conference — A230

No. 943: a, 1r, Emblem (size: 21x28mm). b, 1.50r, Emblem, olive branch (size: 45x28mm).

2000, Nov. 12 Photo.

Granite Paper

943	A230	Pair, #a-b	1.40	1.40

Clean Environment Day — A231

Designs: 1r, Qatar Gas emblem, tanker ship, coral reef. 1.50r, RasGas emblem, refinery, antelopes. 2r, Ras Laffan Industrial City emblem, flamingos near industrial complex. 3r, Qatar Petroleum emblem, view of Earth from space.

2001, Feb. 26 Photo. ***Perf. 11½***

Granite Paper

944-947	A231	Set of 4	4.25	4.25

Independence, 30th Anniv. — A232

Background colors: 1r, Olive. 1.50r, Blue.

2001, Sept. 2 Litho. ***Perf. 14x14½***

948-949	A232	Set of 2	1.40	1.40

Year of Dialogue Among Civilizations A233

Designs: 1.50r, Shown. 2r, Branch with leaves of many colors.

2001, Oct. 9 ***Perf. 13¼***

950-951	A233	Set of 2	1.90	1.90

4th World Trade Organization Ministerial Conference — A234

Background colors: 1r, Yellow brown. 1.50r, Blue.

2001, Nov. 9

952-953	A234	Set of 2	1.40	1.40

Old Doors — A235

Various doors: 25d, 75d, 1.50r, 2r.

2001, Dec. 30 ***Perf. 14½***

954-957	A235	Set of 4	2.50	2.50

QUELIMANE

ˌkel-ə-ˈmän-ə

LOCATION — A district of the Mozambique Province in Portuguese East Africa
GOVT. — Part of the Portuguese East Africa Colony
AREA — 39,800 sq. mi.
POP. — 877,000 (approx.)
CAPITAL — Quelimane

This district was formerly a part of Zambezia. Quelimane stamps were replaced by those of Mozambique.

100 Centavos = 1 Escudo

Vasco da Gama Issue of Various Portuguese Colonies Surcharged as

1913 Unwmk. ***Perf. 12½ to 16***

On Stamps of Macao

1	CD20	¼c on ½a bl grn	6.00	6.00
2	CD21	½c on 1a red	3.00	3.00
3	CD22	1c on 2a red vio	3.00	3.00
4	CD23	2½c on 4a yel grn	3.00	3.00
5	CD24	5c on 8a dk bl	3.00	3.00
6	CD25	7½c on 12a vio brn	4.00	*5.00*
7	CD26	10c on 16a bis brn	3.00	3.00
a.		Inverted surcharge	45.00	
8	CD27	15c on 24a bister	3.00	3.00
		Nos. 1-8 (8)	28.00	29.00

On Stamps of Portuguese Africa

9	CD20	¼c on 2½r bl grn	2.00	*3.00*
10	CD21	½c on 5r red	2.00	*3.00*
11	CD22	1c on 10r red vio	2.00	*3.00*
12	CD23	2½c on 25r yel grn	2.00	*3.00*
13	CD24	5c on 50r dk bl	2.00	*3.25*
14	CD25	7½c on 75r vio brn	2.50	*4.50*
15	CD26	10c on 100r bister	2.00	*3.00*
16	CD27	15c on 150r bister	2.00	*3.00*
		Nos. 9-16 (8)	16.50	25.75

On Stamps of Timor

17	CD20	¼c on ½a bl grn	2.50	*3.00*
18	CD21	½c on 1a red	2.50	*3.00*
19	CD22	1c on 2a red vio	2.50	*3.00*
20	CD23	2½c on 4a yel grn	2.50	*3.00*
21	CD24	5c on 8a dk bl	2.50	*3.00*
22	CD25	7½c on 12a vio brn	4.00	*4.50*
23	CD26	10c on 16a bis brn	2.50	*3.00*
24	CD27	15c on 24a bister	2.50	*3.00*
		Nos. 17-24 (8)	21.50	25.50
		Nos. 1-24 (24)	66.00	80.25

Ceres — A1

1914 Typo. ***Perf. 15x14***

Name and Value in Black

25	A1	¼c olive brown	.80	*3.00*
26	A1	½c black	1.25	*3.00*
27	A1	1c blue green	1.10	*3.00*
a.		Imperf.		
28	A1	1½c lilac brown	1.60	*3.00*
29	A1	2c carmine	1.75	*3.00*
30	A1	2½c light violet	.50	*1.50*
31	A1	5c deep blue	1.25	*3.00*
32	A1	7½c yellow brown	1.25	*3.00*
33	A1	8c slate	2.00	*3.00*
34	A1	10c orange brown	1.75	*3.00*
35	A1	15c plum	3.00	*5.00*
36	A1	20c yellow green	2.50	*2.50*
37	A1	30c brown, *green*	5.00	*8.50*
38	A1	40c brown, *pink*	6.00	*8.50*
39	A1	50c orange, *salmon*	7.00	*9.50*
40	A1	1e green, *blue*	8.00	*11.00*
		Nos. 25-40 (16)	44.75	*73.50*

RAS AL KHAIMA

ˌräs al ˈkī-mə

LOCATION — Oman Peninsula, Arabia, on Persian Gulf
GOVT. — Sheikdom under British protection

Ras al Khaima was the 7th Persian Gulf sheikdom to join the United Arab Emirates, doing so in Feb. 1972.
See United Arab Emirates.

100 Naye Paise = 1 Rupee

Catalogue values for all unused stamps in this country are for Never Hinged items.

Sheik Saqr bin Mohammed al Qasimi — A1

Seven Palm Trees — A2

Dhow A3

Perf. 14½x14

1964, Dec. 21 Photo. Unwmk.

1	A1	5np	brown & black	.20	.20
2	A1	15np	deep blue & blk	.45	.25
3	A2	30np	ocher & black	.75	.45
4	A2	40np	blue & black	1.00	.60
5	A2	75np	brn red & blk	2.10	1.25
6	A3	1r	lt grn & sepia	3.00	1.75
7	A3	2r	brt vio & sepia	7.50	2.50
8	A3	5r	blue gray & sepia	20.00	8.00
			Nos. 1-8 (8)	35.00	15.00

RHODESIA

rō-ˈdē-zhˌē-ə

(British South Africa)

LOCATION — Southeastern Africa
GOVT. — Administered by the British South Africa Company
AREA — 440,653 sq. mi.
POP. — 1,738,000 (estimated 1921)
CAPITAL — Salisbury

In 1923 the area was divided and the portion south of the Zambezi River became the British Crown Colony of Southern Rhodesia. In the following year the remaining territory was formed into the Protectorate of Northern Rhodesia. The Federation of Rhodesia and Nyasaland (comprising Southern Rhodesia, Northern Rhodesia and Nyasaland) was established Sept. 3, 1953.

12 Pence = 1 Shilling
20 Shillings = 1 Pound

A1

A2

Coat of Arms — A3

Thin Paper

Engr. (A1, A3); Engr., Typo. (A2)

1890-94 Unwmk. *Perf. 14, 14½*

1	A2	½p	blue & ver ('91)	2.25	1.75
2	A1	1p	black	8.50	2.00
3	A2	2p	gray grn & ver ('91)	13.50	1.75
4	A2	3p	gray & grn ('91)	8.00	2.50
5	A2	4p	red brn & blk ('91)	13.50	1.90
6	A1	6p	ultra	47.50	17.00
7	A1	6p	deep blue	19.00	3.50
8	A2	8p	rose & bl ('91)	9.50	6.50
9	A1	1sh	gray brown	30.00	9.00
10	A1	2sh	vermilion	40.00	24.00
11	A1	2sh6p	dull lilac	25.00	26.00
			Revenue cancellation		.60
12	A2	3sh	brn & grn ('94)	110.00	65.00
			Revenue cancellation		2.00
13	A2	4sh	gray & ver ('93)	37.50	42.50
			Revenue cancellation		.90
14	A1	5sh	yellow	50.00	47.50
			Revenue cancellation		1.00
15	A1	10sh	deep green	65.00	*90.00*
			Revenue cancellation		1.00
16	A3	£1	dark blue	*160.00*	*125.00*
			Revenue cancellation		5.00
17	A3	£2	rose	*350.00*	*125.00*
			Revenue cancellation		12.00
18	A3	£5	yellow grn	*1,600.*	*450.00*
			Revenue cancellation		25.00
19	A3	£10	orange brn	*2,500.*	*800.00*
			Revenue cancellation		40.00
			Nos. 1-16 (16)	639.25	*465.90*

The paper of the 1891 issue has the trademark and initials of the makers in a monogram watermarked in each sheet. Some of the lower values were also printed on a slightly thicker paper without watermark.

Copies of #16-19 with cancellations removed are frequently offered as unused specimens.
See #24-25, 58.
For surcharges see #20-23, 40-42. For overprints see British Central Africa #1-20.

Nos. 6 and 9 Surcharged in Black **½d.**

1891, Mar.

20	A1	½p	on 6p ultra	85.00	*200.00*
21	A1	2p	on 6p ultra	85.00	*325.00*
22	A1	4p	on 6p ultra	100.00	*375.00*
23	A1	8p	on 1sh brown	110.00	*400.00*
			Nos. 20-23 (4)	380.00	*1,300.*

Beware of forged surcharges.

Thick Soft Paper

1895 *Perf. 12½*

24	A2	2p	green & red	20.00	6.75
25	A2	4p	ocher & black	22.50	*9.75*
a.			Imperf., pair	2,000.	

A4

1896 Engraved, Typo. *Perf. 14*

26	A4	½p	slate & violet	1.90	*2.50*
27	A4	1p	scar & emer	2.50	2.75
28	A4	2p	brn & rose lil	13.50	1.75
29	A4	3p	red brn & ultra	3.00	1.25
30	A4	4p	blue & red lil	7.00	.50
d.			Horiz. pair, imperf. btwn.		
31	A4	6p	vio & pale rose	6.00	.50
32	A4	8p	dp grn & vio, *buff*	4.50	.65
a.			Imperf. pair	2,750.	
b.			Horiz. pair, imperf. btwn.		
33	A4	1sh	brt grn & ultra	13.50	2.50
34	A4	2sh	dk bl & grn, *buff*	19.00	6.75
35	A4	2sh6p	brn & vio, *yel*	60.00	37.50
36	A4	3sh	grn & red vio, *bl*	50.00	28.00
a.			Imperf. pair	5,000.	
37	A4	4sh	red & bl, *grn*	40.00	3.00
38	A4	5sh	org red & grn	35.00	10.00
39	A4	10sh	sl & car, *rose*	90.00	55.00
			Nos. 26-39 (14)	345.90	152.65

The plates for this issue were made from two dies. Stamps of die I have a small dot at the right of the tail of the supporter at the right of the shield, and the body of the lion is not fully shaded. Stamps of die II have not the dot and the lion is heavily shaded.
See type A7.

Nos. 4, 13-14 Surcharged in Black

One Penny THREE PENCE.

1896, Apr. *Perf. 14*

40	A2	1p	on 3p	350.00	350.00
a.			"P" of "Penny" inverted	*21,000.*	
b.			"y" of "Penny" inverted	—	
c.			Double surcharge		
41	A2	1p	on 4sh	270.00	250.00
a.			"P" of "Penny" inverted	*17,000.*	
b.			Single bar in surch.	1,500.	1,600.
c.			"y" of "Penny" inverted	*17,000.*	
42	A1	3p	on 5s yellow	190.00	*225.00*
a.			"T" of "THREE" inverted	*21,000.*	
b.			"R" of "THREE" inverted	*17,500.*	
			Nos. 40-42 (3)	810.00	825.00

Cape of Good Hope Stamps Overprinted in Black

BRITISH SOUTH AFRICA COMPANY.

1896, May 22 Wmk. 16

43	A6	½p	slate	7.50	*12.50*
44	A15	1p	carmine	8.00	*12.50*
45	A6	2p	bister brown	9.00	7.50
46	A6	4p	deep blue	11.50	11.50
a.			"COMPANY" omitted	*9,000.*	
47	A3	6p	violet	40.00	*55.00*
48	A6	1sh	yellow buff	110.00	*120.00*

Wmk. 2

49	A6	3p	claret	40.00	*57.50*
			Nos. 43-49 (7)	226.00	*276.50*

Forgeries are plentiful.

Remainders

Rhodesian authorities made available remainders in large quantities of all stamps in 1897, 1898-1908, 1905, 1909 and 1910 issues, CTO. Some varieties exist only as remainders. See notes following Nos. 100 and 118.

A7

Type A7 differs from type A4 in having the ends of the scroll which is below the shield curved between the hind legs of the supporters instead of passing behind one leg of each. There are other minor differences.

Perf. 13½ to 16

1897 Unwmk. Engr.

50	A7	½p	slate & violet	2.25	*3.25*
51	A7	1p	ver & gray grn	2.75	*3.25*
52	A7	2p	brown & lil rose	3.60	.80
53	A7	3p	red brn & gray bl	2.25	.35
a.			Vert. pair, imperf. btwn.	*2,000.*	
54	A7	4p	ultra & red lilac	6.00	1.25
a.			Horiz. pair, imperf. btwn.	*6,000.*	*6,000.*
55	A7	6p	violet & salmon	5.50	3.25
56	A7	8p	dk grn & vio, *buff*	11.50	.45
a.			Vert. pair, imperf. btwn.	—	*2,000.*
57	A7	£1	black & red, *grn*	375.00	200.00
			Revenue cancellation		10.00
			Nos. 50-56 (7)	33.85	*12.60*

Thick Paper
Perf. 15

58 A3 £2 bright red 1,700. 400.00
Revenue cancellation 55.00

See note on remainders following No. 49.

A8

A9

A10

1898-1908 ***Perf. 13½ to 16***

59 A8 ½p yellow green 1.50 .20
a. Imperf. pair 675.00
b. Horiz. pair, imperf. vert. 625.00
60 A8 1p rose 1.75 .40
a. 1p red 3.00 .35
b. Horiz. or vert. pair, imperf. btwn. 500.00
d. Imperf. pair 550.00 550.00
61 A8 2p brown 1.75 .20
62 A8 2½p cobalt bl ('03) 3.75 .60
a. Horiz. pair, imperf. between 750.00 750.00
63 A8 3p claret ('08) 3.75 .70
a. Vert. pair, imperf. between 700.00
64 A8 4p olive green 4.00 .25
a. Vert. pair, imperf. between 700.00
65 A8 6p lilac 8.00 1.75
66 A9 1sh olive bister 10.00 1.50
a. Imperf., pair 2,800.
b. Horiz. or vert. pair, imperf. btwn. 2,800.
67 A9 2sh6p bluish gray ('06) 35.00 1.00
a. Vert. pair, imperf. between 1,000. 500.00
68 A9 3sh purple ('02) 10.50 1.10
69 A9 5sh orange ('01) 27.50 8.00
70 A9 7sh6p black ('01) 55.00 14.00
71 A9 10sh bluish grn ('08) 16.00 2.00
72 A10 £1 gray vio ('01) 140.00 60.00
Revenue cancellation 1.00
73 A10 £2 red brown ('08) 67.50 9.00
74 A10 £5 dk blue ('01) 2,500.
Revenue cancellation 6.00
75 A10 £10 blue lil ('01) 2,750.
Revenue cancellation 5.50
Nos. 59-73 (15) 386.00 100.70

For overprints and surcharges see #82-100.
See note on remainders following #49.

Victoria Falls — A11

1905, July 13 ***Perf. 13½ to 15***

76 A11 1p rose red 2.25 3.25
77 A11 2½p ultra 6.50 3.25
78 A11 5p magenta 15.00 35.00
79 A11 1sh blue green 16.00 20.00
a. Imperf., pair 12,500.
b. Horiz. pair, imperf. vert. 12,000.
c. Horiz. pair, imperf. btwn. 15,000.
d. Vert. pair, imperf. btn. 15,000.
80 A11 2sh6p black 85.00 125.00
81 A11 5sh violet 72.50 40.00
Nos. 76-81 (6) 197.25 226.50

Opening of the Victoria Falls bridge across the Zambezi River.
See note on remainders following No. 49.

Stamps of 1898-1908 Overprinted or Surcharged:

1909 ***Perf. 14, 15***

82 A8 ½p yellow green 1.25 1.00
83 A8 1p red 1.60 .75
a. Horiz. pair, imperf., vert. 400.00
84 A8 2p brown 1.25 3.25
85 A8 2½p cobalt blue .90 .70
86 A8 3p claret 1.25 .30
87 A8 4p olive green 2.25 1.00
88 A8 5p on 6p lilac 5.25 11.50
89 A8 6p lilac 4.00 3.50
90 A9 7½p on 2sh6p 2.75 3.50
91 A9 10p on 3sh pur 10.50 16.00
92 A9 1sh olive bis 14.00 .35
93 A9 2sh on 5sh org 9.50 7.75
94 A9 2sh6p bluish gray 12.50 8.25
95 A9 3sh purple 11.50 8.25
96 A9 5sh orange 20.00 27.50
97 A9 7sh6p black 60.00 14.50
98 A9 10sh bluish grn 22.50 10.00
99 A10 £1 gray violet 95.00 67.50
a. Pair, one without overprint 20,000.
b. Violet overprint 300.00 175.00
100 A10 £2 red brown 3,250. 300.00
Nos. 82-99 (18) 276.00 185.60

See note on remainders following No. 49. The remainders included inverted overprints of the 3p ($35), 4p ($15) and 2s6p ($27.50).
Nos. 82-87, 89, 92, 94, 96 and 98 exist without period after "Rhodesia."

Queen Mary and King George V
A12 A13

1910 Engr. ***Perf. 14, 15x14, 14x15***

101 A12 ½p green 7.50 1.00
a. ½p olive green 24.00 1.60
b. Perf. 15 250.00 13.00
c. Imperf., pair 8,500. 6,750.
d. Perf. 13½ 250.00 37.50
102 A12 1p rose car 11.00 1.00
a. Vertical pair, imperf. btwn. 18,500. 10,000.
b. Perf. 15 250.00 8.00
c. Perf. 13½ 1,750. 55.00
103 A12 2p gray & blk 32.50 6.00
a. Perf. 15 650.00 27.50
104 A12 2½p ultramarine 15.00 6.00
a. 2½p light blue 15.00 8.00
b. Perf. 15 75.00 37.50
c. Perf. 13½ 30.00 50.00
105 A12 3p ol yel & vio 22.50 20.00
a. Perf. 15 2,000. 55.00
106 A12 4p org & blk 25.00 10.00
a. 4p orange & violet black 55.00 45.00
b. Perf. 15x14 550.00
c. Perf. 15 35.00 67.50
107 A12 5p ol grn & brn 20.00 35.00
a. 5p olive yel & brn (error) 550.00 150.00
b. Perf. 15 675.00 115.00
108 A12 6p claret & brn 22.50 10.00
a. Perf. 15 1,000. 55.00
109 A12 8p brn vio & gray blk 100.00 75.00
a. Perf. 13½ 60.00 225.00
110 A12 10p plum & rose red 26.00 42.50
111 A12 1sh turq grn & black 32.50 10.00
b. Perf. 15 800.00 50.00
112 A12 2sh gray bl & black 60.00 50.00
a. Perf. 15 1,700 325.00
113 A12 2sh6p car rose & blk 325.00 275.00
114 A12 3sh vio & bl grn 140.00 125.00
115 A12 5sh yel grn & brn red 250.00 225.00
116 A12 7sh6p brt bl & car 600.00 450.00
117 A12 10sh red org & bl grn 375.00 250.00
a. 10sh red org & myrtle grn 525.00 250.00
118 A12 £1 bluish sl & car 900.00 375.00
a. £1 black & red 1,000. 325.00
c. Perf. 15 15,000. 4,750.
Nos. 101-118 (18) 2,964. 1,966.

See note on remainders following No. 49. The £1 in plum and red is from the remainders.

1913-19 ***Perf. 14***

119 A13 ½p green 3.50 .75
a. Horiz. pair, imperf. vert. 700.00 750.00
b. Perf. 15 8.00 9.00
c. Perf. 14x15 4,250. 200.00
d. Perf. 15x14 4,250. 300.00
120 A13 1p brown rose 2.75 .75
a. 1p bright rose 4.00 .75
b. As "a," horiz. pair, imperf btwn. 675.00 575.00
c. Perf. 15, brown rose 2.25 3.50
d. Perf. 15, rose red 500.00 20.00
e. As "d," horiz. pair, imperf btwn. 9,000.
121 A13 1½p bister 2.50 .50
a. Perf. 15 22.50 6.00
b. Perf. 15x14
c. Vert. pair, imperf. btwn. 1,400.
d. Horiz. pair, imperf. btwn. 525.00
122 A13 2p vio blk & blk 4.00 2.00
a. 2p gray & black 4.50 2.00
b. Perf. 15 3.50 3.50
c. Horiz. pair, imperf. btwn. 4,000.
123 A13 2½p ultra 3.25 16.00
a. Perf. 15 16.00 25.00
124 A13 3p org yel & blk 4.50 1.25
a. 3p yellow & black 5.00 3.00
b. Perf. 15 6.00 12.00
125 A13 4p org red & blk 7.00 20.00
a. Perf. 15 125.00 14.00
126 A13 5p yel grn & blk 3.75 7.50
127 A13 6p lilac & blk 4.00 3.00
a. Perf. 15 4.00 4.00
128 A13 8p gray grn & violet 10.00 40.00
a. Perf. 15 45.00 135.00
129 A13 10p car rose & bl, perf. 15 6.50 22.50
a. Perf. 14 9.00 45.00
130 A13 1sh turq bl & blk 5.50 6.00
a. Perf. 15 32.50 6.50
131 A13 1sh lt grn & blk ('19) 60.00 22.50
132 A13 2sh brn & blk, perf. 14 11.00 13.50
a. Perf. 15 11.00 22.50
133 A13 2sh6p ol gray & vio bl 35.00 60.00
a. 2sh6p gray & blue 37.50 22.50
b. Perf. 15 30.00 70.00
134 A13 3sh brt blue & red brown 60.00 85.00
a. Perf. 15 140.00 250.00
135 A13 5sh grn & bl 55.00 45.00
a. Perf. 15 90.00 100.00
136 A13 7sh6p black & vio, perf. 15 90.00 130.00
a. Perf. 14 165.00 200.00
137 A13 10sh yel grn & car 150.00 210.00
a. Perf. 15 140.00 225.00
138 A13 £1 violet & blk 400.00 550.00
a. £1 magenta & black 475.00 675.00
b. Perf. 15 650.00 1,200.
Nos. 119-138 (20) 918.25 1,236.

Three dies were used for the stamps of this issue: 1) Outline at top of cap absent or very faint and broken. Left ear not shaded or outlined and appears white; 2) Outline at top of cap faint and broken. Ear shaded all over, with no outline; 3) Outline at top of cap continuous. Ear shaded all over, with continuous outline.
The existence of #121b has been questioned.

No. 120 Surcharged in Dark Violet:

No. 139

No. 140

1917

139 A13 ½p on 1p 2.50 6.50
a. Inverted surcharge 1,500. 1,600.
140 A13 ½p on 1p 2.00 5.00

Nos. 141-190 are accorded to Rhodesia and Nyasaland.

RHODESIA AND NYASALAND

rō-ˈdē-zhˌē-ˌə ənˌdˌ nī-ˈa-sə-ˌland

LOCATION — Southern Africa
GOVT. — Federal State in British Commonwealth
AREA — 486,973 sq. mi.
POP. — 8,510,000 (est. 1961)
CAPITAL — Salisbury, Southern Rhodesia

The Federation of Southern Rhodesia, Northern Rhodesia and Nyasaland was created in 1953, dissolved at end of 1963.

12 Pence = 1 Shilling
20 Shillings = 1 Pound

Catalogue values for all unused stamps in this country are for Never Hinged items.

A14

A15

Queen Elizabeth II
A16

Perf. 13½ (A14), 13½x13 (A15), 14x13 (A16)

1954-56 Engr. Unwmk.

141 A14 ½p vermilion .20 .20
a. Booklet pane of 6 1.25
b. Perf. 12½x13½ .60 .40
142 A14 1p ultra .20 .20
a. Booklet pane of 6 1.25
b. Perf. 12½x13½ .80 .50
143 A14 2p emerald .20 .20
a. Booklet pane of 6 1.60
143B A14 2½p ocher ('56) 2.00 .20
144 A14 3p carmine .20 .20
145 A14 4p red brown .45 .20
146 A14 4½p blue green .20 .20
147 A14 6p red lilac 1.40 .20
148 A14 9p purple .65 .35
149 A14 1sh gray 1.25 .20
150 A15 1sh3p ultra & ver 2.25 .20
151 A15 2sh brn & dp bl 6.25 .70
152 A15 2sh6p car & blk 5.25 .55
153 A15 5sh ol & pur 12.00 1.40
154 A16 10sh red org & aqua 15.00 7.00
155 A16 £1 brn car & ol 22.50 21.00
Nos. 141-155 (16) 70.00 33.00

Issue dates: 2½p, Feb. 15, others, July 1.

Victoria Falls
A17 A18

1955, June 15 ***Perf. 13½***

156 A17 3p Plane .30 .20
157 A18 1sh David Livingstone .85 .55

Centenary of discovery of Victoria Falls.

Tea Picking — A19

Rhodes' Grave, Matopos — A20

Designs: 1p, V. H. F. Mast. 2p, Copper mining. 2½p, Kingsley Fairbridge Memorial. 4p, Boat on Lake Bangweulu. 6p, Victoria Falls. 9p, Railroad trains. 1sh, Tobacco. 1sh3p, Ship on Lake Nyasa. 2sh, Chirundu Bridge, Zambezi River. 2sh6p, Salisbury Airport. 5sh, Cecil Rhodes statue, Salisbury. 10sh, Mlanje mountain. £1, Coat of arms.

Perf. 13½x14, 14x13½

1959-63 Engr. Unwmk.

Size: 18½x22½mm, 22½x18½mm

158 A19 ½p emer & blk .55 .25
a. Perf. 12½x13½ 2.75 4.50
159 A19 1p blk & rose red .20 .20
a. Perf. 12½x13½ 2.75 4.50
b. Rose red (center) omitted 325.00
160 A19 2p ocher & vio .95 .40
161 A19 2½p slate & lil, perf. 14½ .35 .30
162 A20 3p blue & black .20 .20
a. Booklet pane of 4 ('63) 1.50
b. Black omitted 8,000.

Perf. 14½

Size: 24x27mm, 27x24mm

163 A19 4p olive & mag 1.10 .20
164 A19 6p grn & ultra .55 .20
164A A20 9p pur & ocher ('62) 6.50 2.10
165 A20 1sh ultra & yel grn .75 .20

166 A20 1sh3p sep & brt grn, perf. 14 2.50 .20
167 A20 2sh lake & grn 2.75 .50
168 A20 2sh6p ocher & bl 3.50 .25

Perf. 11½

Size: 32x27mm

169 A20 5sh yel grn & choc 6.50 2.00
170 A20 10sh brt rose & ol 22.50 10.50
171 A20 £1 violet & blk 40.00 32.50
Nos. 158-171 (15) 88.90 50.00

Nos. 158a and 159a are coils.
Issue dates: 9p, May 15, others, Aug. 12.

Kariba Gorge, 1955 A21

Designs: 6p, Power lines. 1sh, View of dam. 1sh3p, View of dam and lake. 2sh6p, Power station. 5sh, Dam and Queen Mother Elizabeth.

1960, May 17 Photo. *Perf. 14½x14*

172 A21 3p org & sl grn .40 .20
a. Orange omitted 1,200.
173 A21 6p yel brn & brn .50 .35
174 A21 1sh dull bl & emer 1.10 1.10
175 A21 1sh3p grnsh bl & ocher 2.25 1.75
176 A21 2sh6p org ver & blk 4.00 *6.00*
177 A21 5sh grnsh bl & lilac 7.75 *10.00*
Nos. 172-177 (6) 16.00 19.40

Miner with Drill — A22

Design: 1sh3p, Mining surface installations.

1961, May 8 Unwmk.

178 A22 6p chnt brn & ol grn .40 .35
179 A22 1sh3p lt blue & blk .70 .65

7th Commonwealth Mining and Metallurgical Cong., Apr. 10-May 20.

DH Hercules Biplane A23

Designs: 1sh3p, Flying boat over Zambezi River. 2sh6p, DH Comet, Salisbury Airport.

1962, Feb. 6

180 A23 6p ver & ol grn .50 .25
181 A23 1sh3p bl, blk, grn & yel 1.00 .50
182 A23 2sh6p dk pur & car rose 6.50 4.75
Nos. 180-182 (3) 8.00 5.50

30th anniv. of the inauguration of the Rhodesia-London airmail service.

Tobacco Plant — A24

Designs: 6p, Tobacco field. 1sh3p, Auction floor. 2sh6p, Cured tobacco.

1963, Feb. 18 Photo. *Perf. 14x14½*

184 A24 3p gray brown & grn .20 .20
185 A24 6p blue, grn & brn .20 .20
186 A24 1sh3p slate & red brn .35 .35
187 A24 2sh6p brown & org yel 1.50 2.75
Nos. 184-187 (4) 2.25 3.50

3rd World Tobacco Scientific Cong., Salisbury, Feb. 18-26 and the 1st Intl. Tobacco Trade Cong., Salisbury, March 6-16.

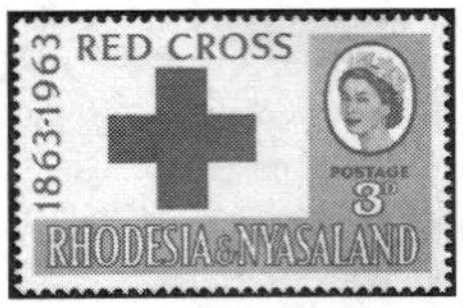

Red Cross A25

1963, Aug. 6 *Perf. 14½x14*

188 A25 3p red .80 .20

Centenary of the International Red Cross.

"Round Table" Emblem A26

1963, Sept. 11 Unwmk.

189 A26 6p multicolored .45 .45
190 A26 1sh3p multicolored .70 .70

World Council of Young Men's Service Clubs at University College of Rhodesia and Nyasaland, Sept. 8-15.

POSTAGE DUE STAMPS

D1

Perf. 12½

1961, Apr. 19 Unwmk. Typo.

J1 D1 1p vermilion 2.25 *3.00*
a. Horiz. pair, imperf. btwn. *350.00* 400.00
J2 D1 2p dark blue 2.25 *3.00*
J3 D1 4p emerald 2.25 *7.00*
J4 D1 6p dark purple 4.25 *7.00*
a. Horiz. pair, imperf. btwn. *550.00*
Nos. J1-J4 (4) 11.00 *20.00*

Nos. 142-143 exist with provisional "Poastage Due" handstamp.

RHODESIA

rō-ˈdē-zh̦ē-ə

Self-Governing State (formerly Southern Rhodesia)

LOCATION — Southeastern Africa, bordered by Zambia, Mozambique, South Africa and Botswana
GOVT. — Self-governing member of British Commonwealth
AREA — 150,333 sq. mi.
POP. — 4,670,000 (est. 1968)
CAPITAL — Salisbury

In Oct. 1964, Southern Rhodesia assumed the name Rhodesia. On Nov. 11, 1965, the white minority government declared Rhodesia independent. Rhodesia became Zimbabwe on Apr. 18, 1980. For earlier issues, see Southern Rhodesia and Rhodesia and Nyasaland.

12 Pence = 1 Shilling
20 Shillings = 1 Pound
100 Cents = 1 Dollar (1967)

Catalogue values for all unused stamps in this country are for Never Hinged items.

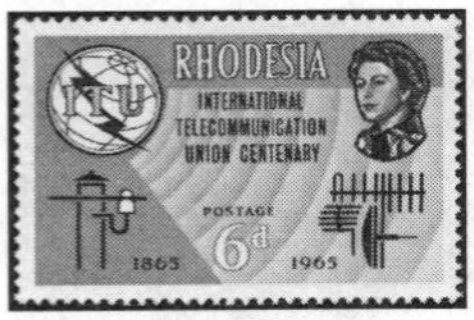

ITU Emblem, Old and New Communication Equipment — A27

Unwmk.

1965, May 17 Photo. *Perf. 14*

200 A27 6p apple grn & brt vio .80 .35
201 A27 1sh3p brt vio & dk vio 1.25 1.00
202 A27 2sh6p org brn & dk vio 4.25 4.25
Nos. 200-202 (3) 6.30 5.60

Cent. of the ITU.

Bangala Dam — A28

Designs: 4p, Irrigation canal through sugar plantation. 2sh6p, Worker cutting sugar cane.

1965, July 19 Photo. *Perf. 14*

203 A28 3p dull bl, grn & ocher .25 .20
204 A28 4p blue, grn & brn .75 .70
205 A28 2sh6p multicolored 4.00 3.25
Nos. 203-205 (3) 5.00 4.15

Issued to publicize Conservation Week of the Natural Resources Board.

Churchill, Parliament, Quill and Sword — A29

1965, Aug. 16

206 A29 1sh3p ultra & black .60 .35

Sir Winston Spencer Churchill (1874-1965), statesman and WWII leader.
For surcharge see No. 222.

Issues of Smith Government

Arms of Rhodesia A30

1965, Dec. 8 Photo. *Perf. 11*

207 A30 2sh6p violet & multi .30 .20
a. Imperf., pair 825.00

Declaration of independence by the government of Prime Minister Ian Smith.

Southern Rhodesia Nos. 95-108 Overprinted

Perf. 14½

1966, Jan. 17 Unwmk. Photo.

Size: 23x19mm

208 A30 ½p lt bl, yel & grn .20 .20
209 A30 1p ocher & pur .20 .20
210 A30 2p vio & org yel .20 .20
211 A30 3p lt blue & choc .20 .20
212 A30 4p sl grn & org .20 .20

Perf. 13½x13

Size: 27x23mm

213 A30 6p dull grn, red & yel .20 .20
a. Pair, one without overprint
214 A30 9p ol grn, yel & brn .25 .20
a. Double overprint 200.00
b. Inverted overprint
215 A30 1sh ocher & brt grn .30 .25
a. Double overprint 250.00
216 A30 1sh3p grn, vio & dk red .35 .30
217 A30 2sh dull bl & yel 1.00 2.00
218 A30 2sh6p ultra & red .65 .55
a. Red omitted

Perf. 14½x14

Size: 32x27mm

Overprint 26mm Wide

219 A30 5sh bl, grn, ocher & lt brn 8.00 9.25
a. Double overprint *425.00*
220 A30 10sh ocher, blk, red & bl 2.50 2.00
221 A30 £1 rose, sep, ocher & grn 2.00 2.50
Nos. 208-221 (14) 16.25 18.25

No. 206 Surcharged in Red

Perf. 14

222 A29 5sh on 1sh3p 20.00 *30.00*

Ansellia Orchid — A31

Designs: 1p, Cape Buffalo. 2p, Oranges. 3p, Kudu. 4p, Emeralds. 6p, Flame lily. 9p, Tobacco. 1sh, Corn. 1sh3p, Lake Kyle. 2sh, Aloe. 2sh6p, Tigerfish. 5sh, Cattle. 10sh, Gray-breasted helmet guinea fowl. £1, Arms of Rhodesia.

Printed by Harrison & Sons, London.

1966, Feb. 9 Photo. *Perf. 14½*

Size: 23x19mm

223 A31 1p ocher & pur .20 .20
224 A31 2p slate grn & org .20 .20
b. Orange omitted *1,000.*
225 A31 3p lt blue & choc .20 .20
b. Queen's head omitted
c. Booklet pane of 4 .85
d. Lt blue omitted *1,500.*
226 A31 4p gray & brt grn .50 .20

Perf. 13½x13

Size: 27x23mm

227 A31 6p dull grn, red & yel .20 .20
228 A31 9p purple & ocher .20 .20
229 A31 1sh lt bl, yel & grn .20 .20
230 A31 1sh3p dull blue & yel .25 .20
b. Yellow omitted *1,850.*
231 A31 1sh6p ol grn, yel & brn 1.25 .25
232 A31 2sh lt ol grn, vio & dk red .40 .70
233 A31 2sh6p brt grnsh bl, ultra & ver .50 .25

Perf. 14½x14

Size: 32x27mm

234 A31 5sh bl, grn, ocher & lt brn .55 .55
235 A31 10sh dl yel, blk, red & bl 3.25 3.25
236 A31 £1 sal pink, sep, ocher & grn 11.00 11.00
Nos. 223-236 (14) 18.90 17.60

See Nos. 245-248A.

Printed by Mardon Printers, Salisbury

1966-68 Litho. *Perf. 14½*

223a A31 1p ocher & pur .20 .20
224a A31 2p sl grn & org ('68) .20 .20
225a A31 3p lt bl & choc ('68) .20 .20
226a A31 4p sep & brt grn .30 .30
227a A31 6p gray grn, red & yel .45 .45
228a A31 9p pur & ocher ('68) .60 .60
230a A31 1sh3p dl bl & yel .80 .80
232a A31 2sh lt ol grn, vio & dk red 3.75 4.00

Perf. 14

234a	A31	5sh	brt bl, grn, ocher & brn	8.25	6.00
235a	A31	10sh	ocher, blk, red & bl	25.00	27.50
236a	A31	£1	sal pink, sep, ocher & grn	35.00	35.00
			Nos. 223a-236a (11)	74.75	75.25

Zeederberg Coach — A32

Designs: 9p, Sir Rowland Hill. 1sh6p, Penny Black. 2sh6p, Rhodesia No. 18, £5.

Perf. 14½

1966, May 2 Litho. Unwmk.

237	A32	3p	blue, org & blk	.20	.20
238	A32	9p	beige & brown	.20	.20
239	A32	1sh6p	blue & black	.40	.30
240	A32	2sh6p	rose, yel grn & blk	.70	.70
a.			Souvenir sheet of 4, #237-240	9.00	*15.00*
			Nos. 237-240 (4)	1.50	1.40

28th Cong. of the Southern Africa Phil. Fed. and the RHOPEX Exhib., Bulawayo, May 2-7.

No. 240a was printed in sheets of 12 and comes with perforations extending through the margins in four different versions. Many have holes in the top margin made when the sheet was cut into individual panes. Sizes of panes vary.

De Havilland Dragon Rapide A33

Planes: 1sh3p, Douglas DC-3. 2sh6p, Vickers Viscount. 5sh, Jet.

1966, June 1

241	A33	6p	multicolored	.80	.60
242	A33	1sh3p	multicolored	1.40	.70
243	A33	2sh6p	multicolored	3.50	2.75
244	A33	5sh	blue & black	6.00	4.25
			Nos. 241-244 (4)	11.70	8.30

20th anniv. of Central African Airways.

Dual Currency Issue

Type of 1966 with Denominations in Cents and Pence-Shillings

1967-68 Litho. *Perf. 14½*

245	A31	3p/2½c	lt blue & choc	.60	.20
246	A31	1sh/10c	multi	.75	.45
247	A31	1sh6p/15c	multi	4.00	.90
248	A31	2sh/20c	multi	6.50	*7.50*
248A	A31	2sh6p/25c	multi	32.50	*45.00*
			Nos. 245-248A (5)	44.35	*54.05*

These locally printed stamps were issued to acquaint Rhodesians with the decimal currency to be introduced in 1969-1970.

Issued: 3p, 3/15; 1sh, 11/1/67; 1sh6p, 2sh, 3/11/68; 2sh6p, 12/9/68.

Leander Starr Jameson, by Frank Moss Bennett A34

1967, May 17

249	A34	1sh6p	emerald & multi	.40	.40

Dr. Leander Starr Jameson (1853-1917), pioneer with Cecil Rhodes and Prime Minister of Cape Colony. See No. 262.

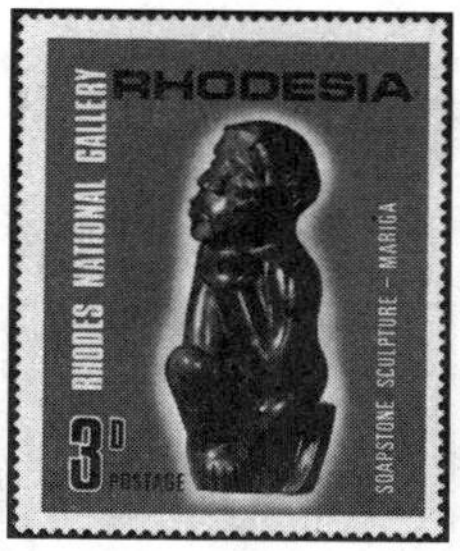

Soapstone Sculpture, by Joram Mariga A35

9p, Head of Burgher of Calais, by Auguste Rodin. 1sh3p, "Totem," by Roberto Crippa. 2sh6p, St. John the Baptist, by Michele Tosini.

1967, July 12 Litho. *Perf. 14*

250	A35	3p	brn, blk & ol grn	.20	.20
251	A35	9p	brt bl, blk & ol grn	.20	.20
a.			Perf. 13½	11.00	17.50
252	A35	1sh3p	multicolored	.20	.20
253	A35	2sh6p	multicolored	.50	.45
			Nos. 250-253 (4)	1.10	1.05

10th anniv. of the Rhodes Natl. Gallery, Salisbury.

White Rhinoceros — A36

#255, Parrot's beak gladioli, vert. #256, Baobab tree. #257, Elephants.

1967, Sept. 6 Unwmk. *Perf. 14½*

254	A36	4p	olive & black	.20	.20
255	A36	4p	dp orange & blk	.20	.20
256	A36	4p	brown & blk	.20	.20
257	A36	4p	gray & blk	.20	.20
			Nos. 254-257 (4)	.80	.80

Issued to publicize nature conservation.

Wooden Hand Plow, c. 1820 A37

Designs: 9p, Ox-drawn plow, c. 1860. 1sh6p, Steam tractor and plows, c. 1905. 2sh6p, Tractor and moldboard plow, 1968.

1968, Apr. 26 Litho. *Perf. 14½*

258	A37	3p	multicolored	.20	.20
259	A37	9p	multicolored	.20	.20
260	A37	1sh6p	multicolored	.25	.30
261	A37	2sh6p	multicolored	.35	.40
			Nos. 258-261 (4)	1.00	1.10

15th world plowing contest, Kent Estate, Norton.

Portrait Type of 1967

Design: 1sh6p, Alfred Beit (portrait at left).

1968, July 15 Unwmk. *Perf. 14½*

262	A34	1sh6p	orange, blk & red	.45	.45

Alfred Beit (1853-1906), philanthropist and friend of Cecil Rhodes.

Allan Wilson, Matopos Hills — A38

Matabeleland, 75th Anniversary: 3p, Flag raising, Bulawayo, 1893. 9p, Bulawayo arms, view of Bulawayo.

1968, Nov. 4 Litho. *Perf. 14½*

263	A38	3p	multicolored	.20	.20
264	A38	9p	multicolored	.25	.25
265	A38	1sh6p	multicolored	.35	.35
			Nos. 263-265 (3)	.80	.80

William Henry Milton (1854-1930), Adminstrator — A39

1969, Jan. 15

266	A39	1sh6p	multicolored	.50	.50

See Nos. 298-303.

Locomotive, 1890's — A40

Beira-Salisbury Railroad, 70th Anniversary: 9p, Steam locomotive, 1901. 1sh6p, Garratt articulated locomotive, 1950, 2sh6p, Diesel, 1955.

1969, May 22

267	A40	3p	multicolored	1.00	.20
268	A40	9p	multicolored	1.75	.55
269	A40	1sh6p	multicolored	5.00	3.00
270	A40	2sh6p	multicolored	6.25	6.25
			Nos. 267-270 (4)	14.00	10.00

Low Level Bridge A41

Bridges: 9p, Mpudzi River. 1sh6p, Umniati River. 2sh6p, Birchenough over Sabi River.

1969, Sept. 18

271	A41	3p	multicolored	.25	.20
272	A41	9p	multicolored	.90	.50
273	A41	1sh6p	multicolored	3.25	2.25
274	A41	2sh6p	multicolored	4.25	2.75
			Nos. 272-274 (3)	8.40	5.50

Blast Furnace — A42

Devil's Cataract, Victoria Falls — A43

1c, Wheat harvest. 2½c, Ruins, Zimbabwe. 3c, Trailer truck. 3½c, 4c, Cecil Rhodes statue. 5c, Mining. 6c, Hydrofoil, "Seaflight." 7½c, like 8c. 10c, Yachting, Lake McIlwaine. 12½c, Hippopotamus. 14c, 15c, Kariba Dam. 20c, Irrigation canal. 25c, Bateleur eagles. 50c, Radar antenna and Viscount plane. $1, "Air Rescue." $2, Rhodesian flag.

1970-73 Litho. *Perf. 14½*

Size: 22x18mm

275	A42	1c	multicolored	.20	.20
a.			Booklet pane of 4	.25	
b.			Min. sheet of 4, Rhophil	2.50	
276	A42	2c	multicolored	.20	.20
277	A42	2½c	multicolored	.20	.20
a.			Booklet pane of 4	.20	
b.			Min. sheet of 4, Rhophil	2.50	
278	A42	3c	multi ('73)	.75	.20
a.			Booklet pane of 4	3.75	
279	A42	3½c	multicolored	.20	.20
a.			Booklet pane of 4	.70	
b.			Min. sheet of 4, Rhophil	2.50	
280	A42	4c	multi ('73)	.85	.20
a.			Booklet pane of 4	4.00	
281	A42	5c	multicolored	.20	.20

Size: 27x23mm

282	A43	6c	multi ('73)	2.75	1.40
283	A43	7½c	multi ('73)	5.25	1.00
284	A43	8c	multicolored	1.25	.80
285	A43	10c	multicolored	.40	.20
286	A43	12½c	multicolored	.75	.20
287	A43	14c	multi ('73)	8.50	1.50
288	A43	15c	multi	2.00	.20
289	A43	20c	multicolored	1.50	.20

Size: 30x25mm

290	A43	25c	multicolored	2.00	.40
291	A43	50c	multicolored	2.00	.45
292	A43	$1	multicolored	6.25	5.00
293	A43	$2	multicolored	17.50	18.00
			Nos. 275-293 (19)	52.75	30.75

Booklet panes and miniature sheets were made by altering the plates used to print the stamps, eliminating every third horizontal and vertical row of stamps. The perforations extend through the margins in four different versions. In 1972 sheets of 4 overprinted in the margins were issued for Rhophil '72 Philatelic Exhibition.

Issue dates: Feb. 17, 1970, Jan. 1, 1973.

Despatch Rider, c. 1890 A44

Posts and Telecommunications Corporation, Inauguration: 3½c, Loading mail, Salisbury Airport. 15c, Telegraph line construction, c.1890. 25c, Telephone and telecommunications equipment.

1970, July 1

294	A44	2½c	multicolored	.25	.20
295	A44	3½c	multicolored	.60	.55
296	A44	15c	multicolored	1.40	1.75
297	A44	25c	multicolored	2.25	3.00
			Nos. 294-297 (4)	4.50	5.50

Famous Rhodesians Type of 1969

13c Dr. Robert Moffat (1795-1883), missionary. #299, Dr. David Livingstone (1813-73), explorer. #300, George Pauling (1854-1919), engineer. #301, Thomas Baines (1820-75), self-portrait. #302, Mother Patrick (1863-1900), Dominican nurse and teacher. #303, Frederick Courteney Selous (1851-1917), explorer, big game hunter.

1970-75 Litho. *Perf. 14½*

298	A39	13c	multi ('72)	1.25	1.25
299	A39	14c	multi ('73)	1.00	1.00
300	A39	14c	multi ('74)	1.25	1.25
301	A39	14c	multi ('75)	1.25	1.25
302	A39	15c	multi	.85	.85
303	A39	15c	multi ('71)	.70	.70
			Nos. 298-303 (6)	6.30	6.30

Issued: 2/14/72; 4/2/73; 5/15/74; 2/12/75; 11/16/70; 3/1/71.

African Hoopoe — A45

Porphyritic Granite — A46

Birds: 2½c, Half-collared kingfisher, horiz. 5c, Golden-breasted bunting. 7½c, Carmine bee-eater. 8c, Red-eyed bulbul. 25c, Wattled plover, horiz.

1971, June 1

304	A45	2c	multicolored	1.00	.20
305	A45	2½c	multicolored	1.00	.20
306	A45	5c	multicolored	2.50	.85
307	A45	7½c	multicolored	3.25	1.00
308	A45	8c	multicolored	3.25	1.25
309	A45	25c	multicolored	7.00	3.50
			Nos. 304-309 (6)	18.00	7.00

1971, Aug. 30

Granite '71, Geological Symposium, 8/30-9/19: 7½c, Muscovite mica, seen through microscope. 15c, Granite, seen through microscope. 25c, Geological map of Rhodesia.

310	A46	2½c	multicolored	.50	.50
311	A46	7½c	multicolored	1.75	1.75
312	A46	15c	multicolored	3.25	3.25
313	A46	25c	multicolored	4.00	4.00
			Nos. 310-313 (4)	9.50	9.50

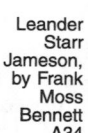

"Be Airwise" A47

Prevent Pollution: 3½c, Antelope (Be Country-wise). 7c, Fish (Be Waterwise). 13c, City (Be Citywise).

1972, July 17

314	A47	2½c multicolored	.20	.20
315	A47	3½c multicolored	.20	.20
316	A47	7c multicolored	.30	.30
317	A47	13c multicolored	.40	.40
		Nos. 314-317 (4)	1.10	1.10

The Three Kings — A48

W.M.O. Emblem — A49

1972, Oct. 18

318	A48	2c multicolored	.20	.20
319	A48	5c multicolored	.20	.20
320	A48	13c multicolored	.35	.35
		Nos. 318-320 (3)	.75	.75

Christmas.

1973, July 2

321	A49	3c multicolored	.20	.20
322	A49	14c multicolored	.60	.45
323	A49	25c multicolored	.95	1.60
		Nos. 321-323 (3)	1.75	2.25

Intl. Meteorological Cooperation, cent.

Arms of Rhodesia A50

1973, Oct. 10

324	A50	2½c multicolored	.20	.20
325	A50	4c multicolored	.20	.20
326	A50	7½c multicolored	.50	.50
327	A50	14c multicolored	.90	1.25
		Nos. 324-327 (4)	1.80	2.15

Responsible Government, 50th Anniversary.

Kudu A51

Thunbergia A52

Pearl Charaxes — A53

1974-76 Litho. Perf. 14½

328	A51	1c shown	.20	.20
329	A51	2½c Eland	.50	.20
330	A51	3c Roan antelope	.20	.20
331	A51	4c Reedbuck	.20	.20
332	A51	5c Bushbuck	.20	.20
333	A52	6c shown	.30	.20
334	A52	7½c Flame lily	3.25	1.75
335	A52	8c like 7½c ('76)	.25	.20
336	A52	10c Devil thorn	.25	.20
337	A52	12c Hibiscus ('76)	.40	.20
338	A52	12½c Pink sabi star	3.25	1.75
339	A52	14c Wild pimpernel	4.75	2.50
340	A52	15c like 12½c ('76)	.50	.25
341	A52	16c like 14c ('76)	.50	.25
342	A53	20c shown	.50	.25
343	A53	24c Yellow pansy ('76)	.95	.50
344	A53	25c like 24c	4.75	2.50
345	A53	50c Queen purple tip	1.25	.65
346	A53	$1 Striped sword-tail	2.50	1.25
347	A53	$2 Guinea fowl butterfly	4.75	2.50
		Nos. 328-347 (20)	29.45	15.95

Issue dates: Aug. 14, 1974, July 1, 1976.
For surcharges see Nos. 364-366.

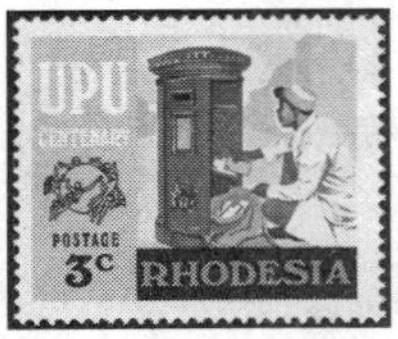
Mail Collection and UPU Emblem A54

1974, Nov. 20 Perf. 14½

348	A54	3c shown	.25	.20
349	A54	4c Mail sorting	.25	.20
350	A54	7½c Mail delivery	.50	.45
351	A54	14c Parcel post	.75	1.40
		Nos. 348-351 (4)	1.75	2.25

Universal Postal Union Centenary.

Euphorbia Confinalis — A55

1975, July 16

352	A55	2½c shown	.30	.30
353	A55	3c Aloe excelsa	.30	.30
354	A55	4c Hoodia lugardii	.30	.30
355	A55	7½c Aloe ortholopha	.40	.40
356	A55	14c Aloe musapana	.70	.70
357	A55	25c Aloe saponaria	1.25	1.25
		Nos. 352-357 (6)	3.25	3.25

Intl. Succulent Cong., Salisbury, July 1975.

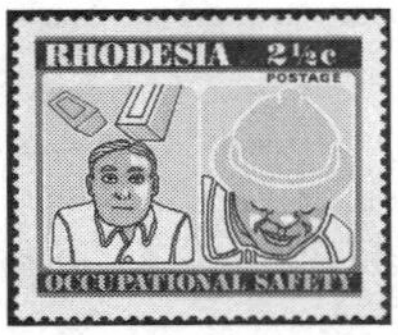
Head Injury and Safety Helmet — A56

Occupational Safety: 4c, Bandaged hand and safety glove. 7½c, Injured eye and safety eyeglass. 14c, Blind man and protective shield.

1975, Oct. 15

358	A56	2½c multicolored	.20	.20
359	A56	4c multicolored	.20	.20
360	A56	7½c multicolored	.30	.30
361	A56	14c multicolored	.35	.35
		Nos. 358-361 (4)	1.05	1.05

Telephones, 1876 and 1976 — A57

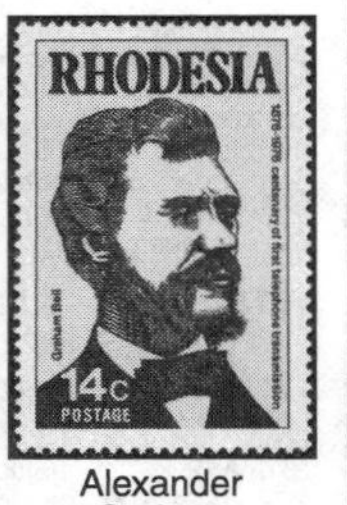
Alexander Graham Bell — A58

1976, Mar. 10

362	A57	3c light blue & blk	.20	.20
363	A58	14c buff & black	.20	.20

Centenary of first telephone call, by Alexander Graham Bell, Mar. 10, 1876.

Nos. 334, 339 and 344 Surcharged with New Value and Two Bars

1976, July 1

364	A52	8c on 7½c multi	.20	.20
365	A52	16c on 14c multi	.20	.20
366	A53	24c on 25c multi	.35	.35
		Nos. 364-366 (3)	.75	.75

Wildlife Protection A59

1976, July 21

367	A59	4c Roan Antelope	.20	.20
368	A59	6c Brown hyena	.20	.20
369	A59	8c Wild dog	.30	.30
370	A59	16c Cheetah	.40	.40
		Nos. 367-370 (4)	1.10	1.10

Brachystegia Spiciformis — A60

Black-eyed Bulbul — A61

1976, Nov. 17

371	A60	4c shown	.20	.20
372	A60	6c Red mahogany	.20	.20
373	A60	8c Pterocarpus angolensis	.20	.20
374	A60	16c Rhodesian teak	.25	.25
		Nos. 371-374 (4)	.85	.85

Flowering trees.

1977, Mar. 16

Birds: 4c, Yellow-mantled whydah. 6c, Orange-throated longclaw. 8c, Long-tailed shrike. 16c, Lesser blue-eared starling. 24c, Red-billed wood hoopoe.

375	A61	3c multicolored	.20	.20
376	A61	4c multicolored	.20	.20
377	A61	6c multicolored	.30	.30
378	A61	8c multicolored	.45	.35
379	A61	16c multicolored	.90	.90
380	A61	24c multicolored	1.10	1.10
		Nos. 375-380 (6)	3.15	3.15

Lake Kyle, by Joan Evans A62

Landscape Paintings: 4c, Chimanimani Mountains, by Evans. 6c, Rocks near Bonsor Reef, by Alice Balfour. 8c, Dwala (rock) near Devil's Pass, by Balfour. 16c, Zimbabwe, by Balfour. 24c, Victoria Falls, by Thomas Baines.

1977, July 20 Litho. Perf. 14½

381	A62	3c multicolored	.20	.20
382	A62	4c multicolored	.20	.20
383	A62	6c multicolored	.20	.20
384	A62	8c multicolored	.25	.25
385	A62	16c multicolored	.45	.45
386	A62	24c multicolored	.70	.70
		Nos. 381-386 (6)	2.00	2.00

Virgin and Child A63

Fair Spire and Fairgrounds A64

1977, Nov. 16

387	A63	3c multicolored	.20	.20
388	A63	6c multicolored	.20	.20
389	A63	8c multicolored	.20	.20
390	A63	16c multicolored	.40	.40
		Nos. 387-390 (4)	1.00	1.00

Christmas.

1978, Mar. 15

19th Rhodesian Trade Fair, Bulawayo: 8c, Fair spire.

391	A64	4c multicolored	.20	.20
392	A64	8c multicolored	.25	.25

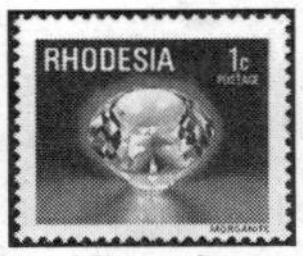
Morganite A65

Black Rhinoceros A66

Odzani Falls — A67

1978, Aug. 16 Litho. Perf. 14½

393	A65	1c shown	.20	.20
394	A65	3c Amethyst	.20	.20
395	A65	4c Garnet	.20	.20
396	A65	5c Citrine	.20	.20
397	A65	7c Blue topaz	.20	.20
398	A66	9c shown	.20	.20
399	A66	11c Lion	.20	.20
400	A66	13c Warthog	.20	.20
401	A66	15c Giraffe	.20	.20
402	A66	17c Zebra	.20	.20
403	A67	21c shown	.20	.20
404	A67	25c Goba Falls	.20	.20
405	A67	30c Inyangombe Falls	.20	.20
406	A67	$1 Bridal Veil Falls	.85	.85
407	A67	$2 Victoria Falls	1.75	1.25
		Nos. 393-407 (15)	5.20	4.70

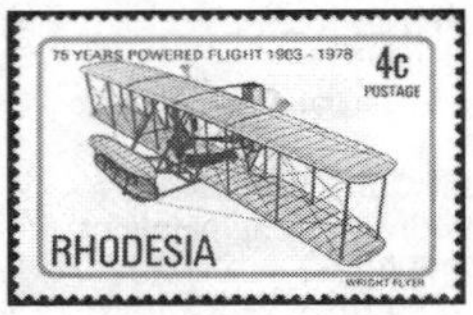
Wright's Flyer A A68

1978, Oct. 18

408	A68	4c shown	.20	.20
409	A68	5c Bleriot XI	.20	.20
410	A68	7c Vickers Vimy	.20	.20
411	A68	9c A.W. 15 Atalanta	.20	.20
412	A68	17c Vickers Viking 1B	.30	.30
413	A68	25c Boeing 720	.45	.45
		Nos. 408-413 (6)	1.55	1.55

75th anniversary of powered flight.

POSTAGE DUE STAMPS

Type of Rhodesia and Nyasaland, 1961, Inscribed "RHODESIA"

Hyphen Hole Perf. 5

1965, June 17 Typo. Unwmk.

J5	D1	1p vermilion	.90	2.00
a.		Rouletted 9½	3.00	12.00

Rouletted 9½

J6	D1	2p dark blue	.45	.90
J7	D1	4p emerald	.70	1.50
J8	D1	6p purple	1.50	3.00
		Nos. J5-J8 (4)	3.55	7.40

Soapstone Zimbabwe Bird — D2

1966, Dec. 15 Litho. Perf. 14½

J9	D2	1p crimson	.65	1.65
J10	D2	2p violet blue	.85	2.00
J11	D2	4p emerald	1.50	3.50

J12	D2	6p lilac	1.65	*4.00*
J13	D2	1sh dull red brown	2.25	*5.00*
J14	D2	2sh black	3.50	*8.00*
		Nos. J9-J14 (6)	10.40	*24.15*

1970-73 Litho. *Perf. 14½*
Size: 26x22½mm

J15	D2	1c bright green	.45	*.85*
J16	D2	2c ultramarine	.90	*1.65*
J17	D2	5c red violet	1.40	*2.50*
J18	D2	6c lemon	4.50	*8.00*
J19	D2	10c rose red	3.25	*6.00*
		Nos. J15-J19 (5)	10.50	*19.00*

Issued: 6c, 5/7/73; others, 2/1/70.

RIO DE ORO

ˌrē-ō dē ˈōr-ˌō

LOCATION — On the northwest coast of Africa, bordering on the Atlantic Ocean
GOVT. — Spanish Colony
AREA — 71,600 sq. mi.
POP. — 24,000
CAPITAL — Villa Cisneros

Rio de Oro became part of Spanish Sahara.

100 Centimos = 1 Peseta

King Alfonso XIII
A1 A2

Control Numbers on Back in Blue

1905 Unwmk. Typo. *Perf. 14*

1	A1	1c blue green	2.10	2.25
2	A1	2c claret	2.90	2.25
3	A1	3c bronze green	2.90	2.25
4	A1	4c dark brown	2.90	2.25
5	A1	5c orange red	2.90	2.25
6	A1	10c dk gray brown	2.90	2.25
7	A1	15c red brown	2.90	2.25
8	A1	25c dark blue	60.00	25.00
9	A1	50c dark green	27.50	10.00
10	A1	75c dark violet	27.50	14.50
11	A1	1p orange brown	17.50	6.00
12	A1	2p buff	60.00	37.50
13	A1	3p dull violet	40.00	14.00
14	A1	4p blue green	40.00	14.00
15	A1	5p dull blue	65.00	29.00
16	A1	10p pale red	160.00	95.00
		Nos. 1-16 (16)	517.00	260.75
		Set, never hinged	700.00	

For surcharges see Nos. 17, 34-36, 60-66.

No. 8 Handstamp Surcharged in Rose

a 

1907

17	A1	15c on 25c dk blue	150.00	52.50
		Never hinged	250.00	

The surcharge exists inverted, double and in violet, normally positioned. Value for each, $350.

Control Numbers on Back in Blue

1907 Typo.

18	A2	1c claret	1.75	1.75
19	A2	2c black	2.00	1.75
20	A2	3c dark brown	2.00	1.75
21	A2	4c red	2.00	1.75
22	A2	5c black brown	2.00	1.75
23	A2	10c chocolate	2.00	1.75
24	A2	15c dark blue	2.00	1.75
25	A2	25c deep green	5.25	1.75
26	A2	50c black violet	5.25	1.75
27	A2	75c orange brown	5.25	1.75
28	A2	1p orange	9.00	1.75
29	A2	2p dull violet	3.25	1.75
30	A2	3p blue green	3.25	1.75
a.		Cliché of 4p in plate of 3p	225.00	150.00
31	A2	4p dark blue	5.00	3.00
32	A2	5p red	5.00	3.25
33	A2	10p deep green	5.00	7.75
		Nos. 18-33 (16)	60.00	36.75
		Set, never hinged	95.00	

For surcharges see Nos. 38-43, 67-70.

Nos. 9-10 Handstamp Surcharged in Red

1907

34	A1	10c on 50c dk green	60.00	22.50
		Never hinged	110.00	
a.		"10" omitted	110.00	72.50
		Never hinged	160.00	
35	A1	10c on 75c dk violet	50.00	22.50
		Never hinged	75.00	

No. 12 Handstamp Surcharged in Violet

1908

36	A1	2c on 2p buff	37.50	22.50
		Never hinged	60.00	

No. 36 is found with "1908" measuring 11mm and 12mm.

Same Surcharge in Red on No. 26

38	A2	10c on 50c blk vio	15.00	3.50
		Never hinged	22.50	

A 5c on 10c (No. 23) was not officially issued.

Nos. 25, 27-28 Handstamp Surcharged Type "a" in Red, Violet or Green

1908

39	A2	15c on 25c dp grn (R)	19.00	3.50
40	A2	15c on 75c org brn (V)	42.50	17.00
a.		Green surcharge	25.00	6.50
		Never hinged	37.50	
41	A2	15c on 1p org (V)	35.00	14.50
42	A2	15c on 1p org (R)	35.00	14.50
43	A2	15c on 1p org (G)	25.00	6.50
		Nos. 39-43 (5)	156.50	56.00
		Set, never hinged	240.00	

As this surcharge is handstamped, it exists in several varieties: double, inverted, in pairs with one surcharge omitted, etc.

A3

Revenue stamps overprinted and surcharged

1908 *Imperf.*

44	A3	5c on 50c green (C)	57.50	24.00
		Never hinged	85.00	
45	A3	5c on 50c green (V)	80.00	40.00
		Never hinged	125.00	

The surcharge, which is handstamped, exists in many variations.

Nos. 44-45 are found with and without control numbers on back. Stamps with control numbers sell at about double the above values.

King Alfonso XIII — A4

Control Numbers on Back in Blue

1909 Typo. *Perf. 14½*

46	A4	1c red	.50	.40
47	A4	2c orange	.50	.40
48	A4	5c dark green	.50	.40
49	A4	10c orange red	.50	.40
50	A4	15c blue green	.50	.40
51	A4	20c dark violet	1.25	.60
52	A4	25c deep blue	1.25	.60
53	A4	30c claret	1.25	.60
54	A4	40c chocolate	1.25	.60
55	A4	50c red violet	2.25	.60
56	A4	1p dark brown	3.25	2.75
57	A4	4p carmine rose	3.75	4.00
58	A4	10p claret	8.25	6.75
		Nos. 46-58 (13)	25.00	18.50
		Set, never hinged	40.00	

Stamps of 1905 Handstamped in Black

1910
10
Céntimos

1910

60	A1	10c on 5p dull bl	10.00	6.00
a.		Red surcharge	65.00	37.50
		Never hinged	100.00	
62	A1	10c on 10p pale red	10.00	6.00
a.		Violet surcharge	100.00	45.00
		Never hinged	150.00	
b.		Green surcharge	100.00	45.00
		Never hinged	150.00	
65	A1	15c on 3p dull vio	10.00	6.00
a.		Imperf.	80.00	
		Never hinged	125.00	
66	A1	15c on 4p blue grn	10.00	6.00
a.		10c on 4p bl grn	600.00	200.00
		Never hinged	800.00	
		Nos. 60-66 (4)	40.00	24.00
		Set, never hinged	60.00	

See note after No. 43.

Nos. 31 and 33 Surcharged in Red or Violet

2
Cents

1911-13

67	A2	2c on 4p dk blue (R)	7.75	6.25
68	A2	5c on 10p dp grn (V)	20.00	6.25

Nos. 29-30 Surcharged in Black

10
Céntimos

69	A2	10c on 2p dull vio	10.50	6.25
69A	A2	10c on 3p bl grn ('13)	125.00	37.50

Nos. 30, 32 Handstamped Type "a"

69B	A2	15c on 3p bl grn ('13)	110.00	18.00
70	A2	15c on 5p red	7.75	7.00
		Nos. 67-70 (6)	281.00	81.25
		Set, never hinged	400.00	

King Alfonso XIII
A5 A6

Control Numbers on Back in Blue

1912 Typo. *Perf. 13½*

71	A5	1c carmine rose	.20	.20
72	A5	2c lilac	.20	.20
73	A5	5c deep green	.20	.20
74	A5	10c red	.20	.20
75	A5	15c brown orange	.20	.20
76	A5	20c brown	.20	.20
77	A5	25c dull blue	.20	.20
78	A5	30c dark violet	.20	.20
79	A5	40c blue green	.20	.20
80	A5	50c lake	.20	.20
81	A5	1p red	1.75	.50
82	A5	4p claret	4.00	2.40
83	A5	10p dark brown	5.75	3.75
		Nos. 71-83 (13)	13.50	8.65
		Set, never hinged	20.00	

For overprints see Nos. 97-109.

Control Numbers on Back in Blue

1914 *Perf. 13*

84	A6	1c olive black	.25	.20
85	A6	2c maroon	.25	.20
86	A6	5c deep green	.25	.20
87	A6	10c orange red	.25	.20
88	A6	15c orange red	.25	.20
89	A6	20c deep claret	.25	.20
90	A6	25c dark blue	.25	.20
91	A6	30c blue green	.25	.20
92	A6	40c brown orange	.25	.20
93	A6	50c dark brown	.25	.20
94	A6	1p dull lilac	1.75	1.50
95	A6	4p carmine rose	4.75	1.50
96	A6	10p dull violet	6.00	4.50
		Nos. 84-96 (13)	15.00	9.50
		Set, never hinged	21.00	

Nos. 71-83 Overprinted in Black

1917 *Perf. 13½*

97	A5	1c carmine rose	7.25	.65
98	A5	2c lilac	7.25	.65
99	A5	5c deep green	2.00	.65
100	A5	10c red	2.00	.65
101	A5	15c orange brn	2.00	.65
102	A5	20c brown	2.00	.65
103	A5	25c dull blue	2.00	.65
104	A5	30c dark violet	2.00	.65
105	A5	40c blue green	2.00	.65
106	A5	50c lake	2.00	.65
107	A5	1p red	10.00	3.00
108	A5	4p claret	17.00	4.50
109	A5	10p dark brown	27.50	6.75
		Nos. 97-109 (13)	85.00	20.75
		Set, never hinged	125.00	

Nos. 97-109 exist with overprint inverted or double (value 50 percent over normal) and in dark blue (value twice normal).

King Alfonso XIII — A7

Control Numbers on Back in Blue

1919 Typo. *Perf. 13*

114	A7	1c brown	.55	.35
115	A7	2c claret	.55	.35
116	A7	5c light green	.55	.35
117	A7	10c carmine	.55	.35
118	A7	15c orange	.55	.35
119	A7	20c orange	.55	.35
120	A7	25c blue	.55	.35
121	A7	30c green	.55	.35
122	A7	40c vermilion	.55	.35
123	A7	50c brown	.55	.35
124	A7	1p lilac	4.25	2.50
125	A7	4p rose	8.00	4.75
126	A7	10p violet	13.50	7.00
		Nos. 114-126 (13)	31.25	17.75
		Set, never hinged	42.50	

A8

A9

Control Numbers on Back in Blue

1920 *Perf. 13*

127	A8	1c gray lilac	.50	.35
128	A8	2c rose	.50	.35
129	A8	5c light red	.50	.35
130	A8	10c lilac	.50	.35
131	A8	15c light brown	.50	.35
132	A8	20c greenish blue	.50	.35
133	A8	25c yellow	.50	.40
134	A8	30c dull blue	3.00	3.00
135	A8	40c orange	1.75	1.25
136	A8	50c dull rose	1.75	1.25
137	A8	1p gray green	1.75	1.25
138	A8	4p lilac rose	3.25	2.75
139	A8	10p brown	8.00	7.00
		Nos. 127-139 (13)	23.00	19.00
		Set, never hinged	40.00	

Control Numbers on Back in Blue

1922

140	A9	1c yellow	.50	.50
141	A9	2c red brown	.50	.50
142	A9	5c blue green	.50	.50
143	A9	10c pale red	.50	.50
144	A9	15c myrtle green	.50	.50
145	A9	20c turq blue	.50	.50
146	A9	25c deep blue	.50	.50
147	A9	30c deep rose	.95	.90
148	A9	40c violet	.95	.90
149	A9	50c orange	.95	.90
150	A9	1p lilac	3.00	1.40
151	A9	4p claret	5.00	3.00
152	A9	10p dark brown	8.50	7.00
		Nos. 140-152 (13)	22.85	17.60
		Set, never hinged	47.50	

For subsequent issues see Spanish Sahara.

RIO MUNI

ˌrē-ō ˈmü-nē

LOCATION — West Africa, bordering on Cameroun and Gabon Republics
GOVT. — Province of Spain
AREA — 9,500 sq. mi.
POP. — 183,377 (1960)
CAPITAL — Bata

Rio Muni and the island of Fernando Po are the two provinces that constitute Spanish Guinea. Separate stamp issues for the two provinces were decreed in 1960.

Spanish Guinea Nos. 1-84 were used only in the territory now called Rio Muni.

Rio Muni united with Fernando Po on Oct. 12, 1968, to form the Republic of Equatorial Guinea.

100 Centimos = 1 Peseta

Catalogue values for all unused stamps in this country are for Never Hinged items.

Boy Reading and Missionary A1

Quina Plant A2

1960 Unwmk. Photo. *Perf. 13x12½*

1	A1	25c dull vio bl	.20	.20
2	A1	50c olive brown	.20	.20
3	A1	75c dull grysh pur	.20	.20
4	A1	1p orange ver	.20	.20
5	A1	1.50p brt blue grn	.20	.20
6	A1	2p red lilac	.20	.20
7	A1	3p sapphire	.25	.20
8	A1	5p red brown	.60	.20
9	A1	10p lt olive grn	1.00	.25
		Nos. 1-9 (9)	3.05	1.85

1960 *Perf. 13x12½*

10	A2	35c shown	.20	.20
11	A2	80c Croton plant	.20	.20

See Nos. B1-B2.

Map of Rio Muni — A3

Designs: 50c, 1p, Gen. Franco. 70c, Government Palace.

1961, Oct. 1 *Perf. 12½x13*

12	A3	25c gray violet	.20	.20
13	A3	50c olive brown	.20	.20
14	A3	70c brt green	.20	.20
15	A3	1p red orange	.20	.20
		Nos. 12-15 (4)	.80	.80

25th anniversary of the nomination of Gen. Francisco Franco as Chief of State.

Rio Muni Headdress — A4

Design: 50c, Rio Muni idol.

1962, July 10 *Perf. 13x12½*

16	A4	25c violet	.20	.20
17	A4	50c green	.20	.20
18	A4	1p orange brown	.20	.20
		Nos. 16-18 (3)	.60	.60

Issued for child welfare.

Cape Buffalo A5

Design: 35c, Gorilla, vert.

Perf. 13x12½, 12½x13
1962, Nov. 23 Photo. Unwmk.

19	A5	15c dark olive grn	.20	.20
20	A5	35c magenta	.20	.20
21	A5	1p brown orange	.20	.20
		Nos. 19-21 (3)	.60	.60

Issued for Stamp Day.

Mother and Child — A6

Father Joaquin Juanola — A7

1963, Jan. 29 *Perf. 13x12½*

22	A6	50c green	.20	.20
23	A6	1p brown orange	.20	.20

Issued to help the victims of the Seville flood.

1963, July 6 *Perf. 13x12½*

50c, Blessing hand, cross and palms.

24	A7	25c dull violet	.20	.20
25	A7	50c brown olive	.20	.20
26	A7	1p orange red	.20	.20
		Nos. 24-26 (3)	.60	.60

Issued for child welfare.

Praying Child and Arms — A8

Branch of Copal Tree — A9

1963, July 12

27	A8	50c dull green	.20	.20
28	A8	1p redsh brown	.20	.20

Issued for Barcelona flood relief.

Perf. 13x12½, 12½x13
1964, Mar. 6 Photo.

Design: 50c, Flowering quina, horiz.

29	A9	25c brt violet	.20	.20
30	A9	50c blue green	.20	.20
31	A9	1p dk carmine rose	.20	.20
		Nos. 29-31 (3)	.60	.60

Issued for Stamp Day 1963.

Tree Pangolin A10

Design: 50c, Chameleon.

1964, June 1 *Perf. 13x12½*

32	A10	25c violet blk	.20	.20
33	A10	50c olive gray	.20	.20
34	A10	1p fawn	.20	.20
		Nos. 32-34 (3)	.60	.60

Issued for child welfare.

Dwarf Crocodile A11

15c, 70c, 3p, Dwarf crocodile. 25c, 1p, 5p, Leopard. 50c, 1.50p, 10p, Black rhinoceros.

1964, July 1

35	A11	15c lt brown	.20	.20
36	A11	25c violet	.20	.20
37	A11	50c olive	.20	.20
38	A11	70c green	.20	.20
39	A11	1p brown car	.30	.20
40	A11	1.50p blue green	.30	.20
41	A11	3p dark blue	.40	.20
42	A11	5p brown	1.00	.40
43	A11	10p green	3.75	1.00
		Nos. 35-43 (9)	6.55	2.80

Greshoff's Tree Frog A12

Stamp Day: 1p, Helmet guinea fowl, vert.

Perf. 13x12½, 12½x13
1964, Nov. 23 Photo. Unwmk.

44	A12	50c green	.20	.20
45	A12	1p deep claret	.20	.20
46	A12	1.50p blue green	.20	.20
		Nos. 44-46 (3)	.60	.60

Issued for Stamp Day, 1964.

Woman's Head — A13

Woman Chemist — A14

1964 Photo. *Perf. 13x12½*

47	A13	50c shown	.20	.20
48	A14	1p shown	.20	.20
49	A14	1.50p Logger	.20	.20
		Nos. 47-49 (3)	.60	.60

Issued to commemorate 25 years of peace.

Goliath Beetle A15

Beetle: 1p, Acridoxena hewaniana.

1965, June 1 Photo. *Perf. 12½x13*

50	A15	50c Prus green	.20	.20
51	A15	1p sepia	.20	.20
52	A15	1.50p black	.20	.20
		Nos. 50-52 (3)	.60	.60

Issued for child welfare.

Ring-necked Pheasant — A16

Leopard and Arms of Rio Muni A17

Perf. 13x12½, 12½x13
1965, Nov. 23 Photo.

53	A16	50c grnsh gray	.20	.20
54	A17	1p sepia	.25	.20
55	A16	2.50p lilac	1.00	.35
		Nos. 53-55 (3)	1.45	.75

Issued for Stamp Day, 1965.

Elephant and Parrot A18

Design: 1.50p, Lion and boy.

Perf. 12½x13
1966, June 1 Photo. Unwmk.

56	A18	50c olive	.20	.20
57	A18	1p dk purple	.20	.20
58	A18	1.50p brt Prus blue	.20	.20
		Nos. 56-58 (3)	.60	.60

Issued for child welfare.

Water Chevrotain A19

Designs: 40c, 4p, Tree pangolin, vert.

1966, Nov. 23 Photo. *Perf. 13*

59	A19	10c brown & yel brn	.20	.20
60	A19	40c brown & yellow	.20	.20
61	A19	1.50p blue & rose lilac	.20	.20
62	A19	4p dk bl & emerald	.20	.20
		Nos. 59-62 (4)	.80	.80

Issued for Stamp Day, 1966.

A20

Potto — A21

Designs: 40c, 4p, Vine creeper.

1967, June 1 Photo. *Perf. 13*

63	A20	10c green & yellow	.20	.20
64	A20	40c blk, rose car & grn	.20	.20
65	A20	1.50p blue & orange	.20	.20
66	A20	4p black & green	.20	.20
		Nos. 63-66 (4)	.80	.80

Issued for child welfare.

1967, Nov. 23 Photo. *Perf. 13*

Designs: 1p, River hog, horiz. 3.50p, African golden cat, horiz.

67	A21	1p black & red brn	.20	.20
68	A21	1.50p brown & grn	.20	.20
69	A21	3.50p org brn & grn	.25	.20
		Nos. 67-69 (3)	.65	.60

Issued for Stamp Day 1967.

Zodiac Issue

Cancer — A22

1.50p, Taurus. 2.50p, Gemini.

1968, Apr. 25 Photo. *Perf. 13*

70	A22	1p brt mag, *lt yel*	.20	.20
71	A22	1.50p brown, *pink*	.20	.20
72	A22	2.50p dk vio, *yel*	.20	.20
		Nos. 70-72 (3)	.60	.60

Issued for child welfare.

SEMI-POSTAL STAMPS

Type of Regular Issue, 1960

Designs: 10c+5c, Croton plant. 15c+5c, Flower and leaves of croton.

1960 Unwmk. Photo. *Perf. 13x12½*

B1	A2	10c + 5c maroon	.20	.20
B2	A2	15c + 5c bister brown	.20	.20

The surtax was for child welfare.

Bishop Juan de Ribera — SP1

20c+5c, The clown Pablo de Valladolid by Velazquez. 30c+10c, Juan de Ribera statue.

1961 *Perf. 13x12½*

B3	SP1	10c + 5c rose brown	.20	.20
B4	SP1	20c + 5c dk slate grn	.20	.20
B5	SP1	30c + 10c olive brown	.20	.20
B6	SP1	50c + 20c brown	.20	.20
		Nos. B3-B6 (4)	.80	.80

Issued for Stamp Day, 1960.

Mandrill SP2

Design: 25c+10c, Elephant, vert.

Perf. 12½x13, 13x12½

1961, June 21 Unwmk.

B7	SP2	10c + 5c rose brown	.20	.20
B8	SP2	25c + 10c gray violet	.20	.20
B9	SP2	80c + 20c dark green	.20	.20
		Nos. B7-B9 (3)	.60	.60

The surtax was for child welfare.

Statuette — SP3

Design: 25c+10c, 1p+10c, Male figure.

1961, Nov. 23 *Perf. 13x12½*

B10	SP3	10c + 5c rose brown	.20	.20
B11	SP3	25c + 10c dark purple	.20	.20
B12	SP3	30c + 10c olive black	.20	.20
B13	SP3	1p + 10c red orange	.20	.20
		Nos. B10-B13 (4)	.80	.80

Issued for Stamp Day 1961.

ROMANIA

rō-ˈmā-nēə

(Rumania, Roumania)

LOCATION — Southeastern Europe, bordering on the Black Sea
GOVT. — Republic
AREA — 91,699 sq. mi.
POP. — 22,600,000 (est. 1984)
CAPITAL — Bucharest

Romania was formed in 1861 from the union of the principalities of Moldavia and Walachia in 1859. It became a kingdom in 1881. Following World War I, the original territory was considerably enlarged by the addition of Bessarabia, Bukovina, Transylvania, Crisana, Maramures and Banat. The republic was established in 1948.

40 Parale = 1 Piaster
100 Bani = 1 Leu (plural "Lei") (1868)

Catalogue values for unused stamps in this country are for Never Hinged items, beginning with Scott 475 in the regular postage section, Scott B82 in the semi-postal section, Scott C24 in the airpost section, Scott CB1 in the airpost semi-postal section, Scott J82 in the postage due section, Scott O1 in the official section, Scott RA16 in the postal tax section, and Scott RAJ1 in the postal tax postage due section.

Watermarks

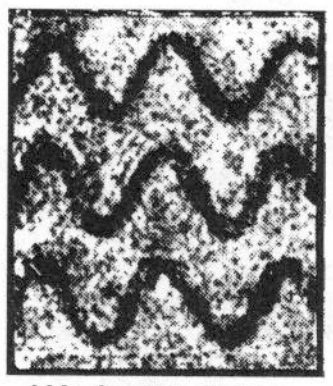

Wmk. 95- Wavy Lines

Wmk. 163- Coat of Arms

No. 163 is not a true watermark, having been impressed after the paper was manufactured.

Wmk. 164- PR

Wmk. 165- PR Interlaced

Wmk. 167- Coat of Arms Covering 25 Stamps

Reduced illustration.

Wmk. 200- PR

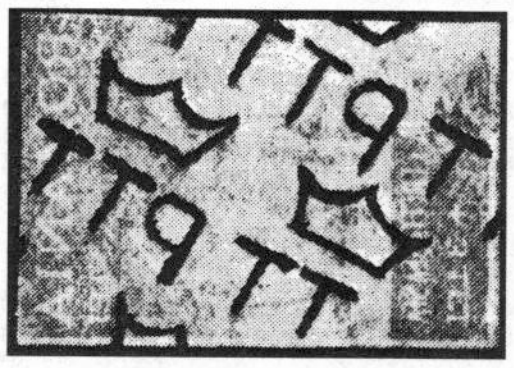

Wmk. 225 - Crown over PTT, Multiple

Wmk. 230- Crowns and Monograms

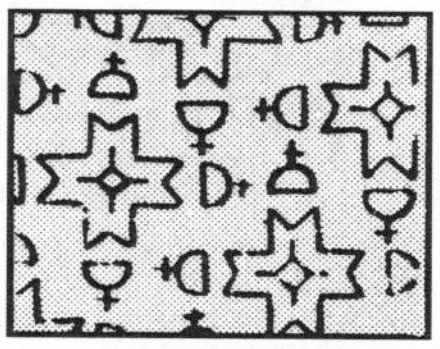

Wmk. 276- Cross and Crown Multiple

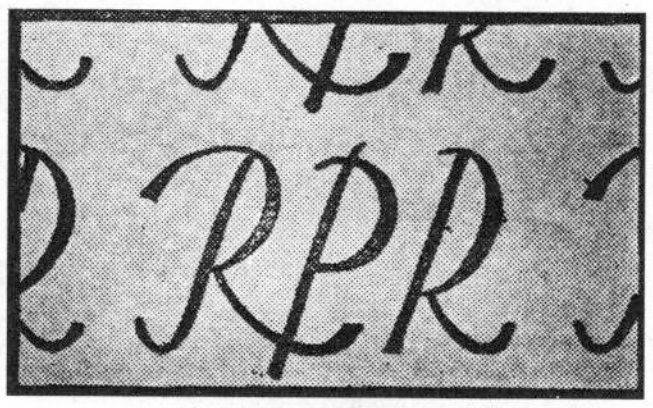

Wmk. 289- RPR Multiple

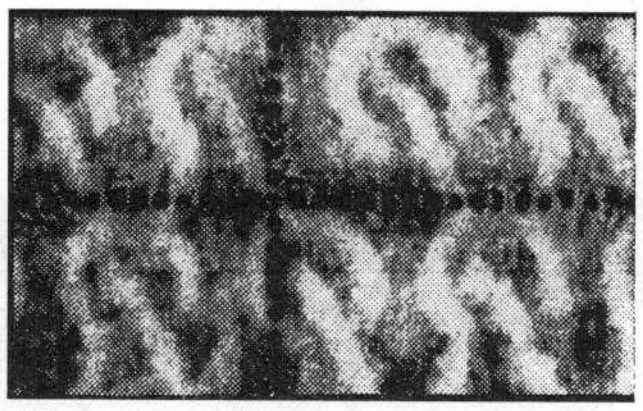

Wmk. 358- RPR Multiple in Endless Rows

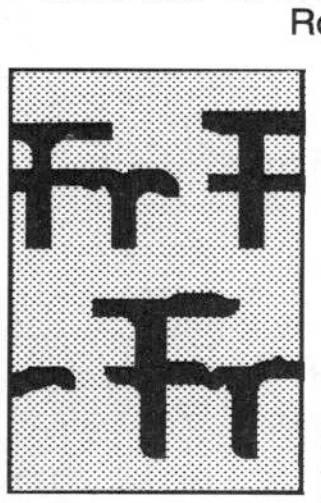

Wmk. 398- Fr Multiple

Values for unused stamps are for examples with original gum as defined in the catalogue introduction except for Nos. 1-4 which are valued without gum.

Moldavia

Coat of Arms
A1 A2

Handstamped

1858, July Unwmk. *Imperf.*

Laid Paper

1	A1	27pa blk, *rose*	*19,000*	*5,500.*
a.		Tête bêche pair		
2	A1	54pa blue, *grn*	*4,250.*	*2,250.*
3	A1	108pa blue, *rose*	*14,000.*	*5,250.*

Wove Paper

4	A1	81pa blue, *bl*	*21,000.*	*22,500.*

Cut to shape or octagonally, Nos. 1-4 sell for one-fourth to one-third of these prices.

1858

Bluish Wove Paper

5	A2	5pa black	*12,000.*	*4,750.*
a.		Tête bêche pair		
6	A2	40pa blue	175.	125.
a.		Tête bêche pair	*750.*	*2,000.*
7	A2	80pa red	*6,750.*	*400.*
a.		Tête bêche pair		

1859

White Wove Paper

8	A2	5pa black	*9,000.*	*5,000.*
a.		Tête bêche pair		
b.		Frame broken at bottom	100.	
c.		As "b," tête bêche pair	325.	
9	A2	40pa blue	110.	100.
b.		Tête bêche pair	375.	*1,150.*
10	A2	80pa red	300.	160.
b.		Tête bêche pair	*1,050.*	*3,100.*

No. 8b has a break in the frame at bottom below "A." It was never placed in use.

Moldavia-Walachia

Coat of Arms — A3

Printed by Hand from Single Dies

1862

White Laid Paper

11	A3	3pa orange	200.00	*2,250.*
a.		3pa yellow	210.00	*2,250.*
12	A3	6pa carmine	190.00	250.00
13	A3	6pa red	190.00	250.00
14	A3	30pa blue	55.00	75.00
		Nos. 11-14 (4)	635.00	

White Wove Paper

15	A3	3pa orange yel	55.00	*160.00*
a.		3pa lemon	60.00	*160.00*
16	A3	6pa carmine	55.00	*110.00*
17	A3	6pa vermilion	35.00	*90.00*
18	A3	30pa blue	50.00	30.00
		Nos. 15-18 (4)	195.00	

Tête bêche pairs

11b	A3	3pa orange	1,000.	
12a	A3	6pa carmine	1,000.	1,250.
14a	A3	30pa blue	150.00	1,000.
15b	A3	3pa orange yellow	140.00	*1,000.*
16a	A3	6pa carmine	150.00	1,000.
17a	A3	6pa vermilion	100.00	1,000.
18a	A3	30pa blue	140.00	1,000.

Nos. 11-18 were printed with a hand press, one at a time, from single dies. The impressions were very irregularly placed and occasionally overlapped. Sheets of 32 (4x8). The 3rd and 4th rows were printed inverted, making the second and third rows tête bêche. All values come in distinct shades, frequently even on the same sheet. The paper of this and the following issues through No. 52 often shows a bluish, grayish or yellowish tint.

1864 Typographed from Plates

White Wove Paper

19	A3	3pa yellow	32.50	*1,250.*
a.		Tête bêche pair	200.00	
b.		Pair, one sideways	100.00	
20	A3	6pa deep rose	4.50	
a.		Tête bêche pair	27.50	
b.		Pair, one sideways	11.00	
21	A3	30pa deep blue	5.25	*60.00*
a.		Tête bêche pair	32.50	
b.		Pair, one sideways	12.00	
c.		Bluish wove paper	*125.00*	
		Nos. 19-21 (3)	42.25	

Stamps of 1862 issue range from very clear to blurred impressions but rarely have broken or deformed characteristics. The 1864 issue, though rarely blurred, usually have various imperfections in the letters and numbers. These include breaks, malformations, occasional dots at left of the crown or above the "R" of "PAR," a doton the middle stroke of the "F," and many other bulges, breaks and spots of color.

The 1864 issue were printed in sheets of 40 (5x8). The first and second rows were inverted. Clichés in the third row were placed sideways, 4 with head to right and 4 with head to left, making one tête bêche pair. The fourth and fifth rows were normally placed.

No. 20 was never placed in use.

All values exist in shades, light to dark. Counterfeit cancellations exist on #11-21.

Three stamps in this design- 2pa, 5pa, 20pa- were printed on white wove paper in 1864, but never placed in use. Value, set $9.00.

Romania

Prince Alexandru Ioan Cuza — A4

TWENTY PARALES:
Type I - The central oval does not touch the inner frame. The "I" of "DECI" extends above and below the other letters.
Type II - The central oval touches the frame at the bottom. The "I" of the "DECI" is the same height as the other letters.

1865, Jan. Unwmk. Litho. *Imperf.*

22 A4 2pa orange 30.00 *125.00*
a. 2pa yellow 42.50 *150.00*
b. 2pa ocher 90.00 *175.00*
23 A4 5pa blue 20.00 *150.00*
24 A4 20pa red, type I 7.50 10.00
a. Bluish paper 175.00
25 A4 20pa red, type II 7.50 10.00
a. Bluish paper 175.00
Nos. 22-25 (4) 65.00

The 20pa types are found se-tenant.

White Laid Paper

26 A4 2pa orange 37.50 *125.00*
a. 2pa ocher 75.00
27 A4 5pa blue 60.00 *275.00*

Prince Carol — A5

Type I — A6

Type II — A7

TWENTY PARALES:
Type I - A6. The Greek border at the upper right goes from right to left.
Type II - A7. The Greek border at the upper right goes from left to right.

1866-67

Thin Wove Paper

29 A5 2pa blk, *yellow* 8.00 *45.00*
a. Thick paper 45.00 *200.00*
30 A5 5pa blk, *dk bl* 35.00 *275.00*
a. 5pa black, *indigo* 75.00 —
b. Thick paper 45.00 *275.00*
31 A6 20pa blk, *rose*, (I) 9.00 9.00
a. Dot in Greek border, thin paper 350.00 125.00
b. Thick paper 95.00 45.00
c. Dot in Greek border, thick paper 125.00 72.50
32 A7 20pa blk, *rose*, (II) 9.00 9.00
a. Thick paper 100.00 50.00
Nos. 29-32 (4) 61.00

The 20pa types are found se-tenant.
Faked cancellations are known on Nos. 22-27, 29-32.
The white dot of Nos. 31a and 31c occurs in extreme upper right border.
Thick paper was used in 1866, thin in 1867.

Prince Carol
A8 A9

1868-70

33 A8 2b orange 22.50 12.50
a. 2b yellow 30.00 27.50
34 A8 3b violet ('70) 22.50 20.00
35 A8 4b dk blue 45.00 25.00
36 A8 18b scarlet 175.00 9.00
a. 18b rose 175.00 9.00
Nos. 33-36 (4) 265.00 66.50

1869

37 A9 5b orange yel 52.50 20.00
a. 5b deep orange 55.00 *50.00*
38 A9 10b blue 25.00 12.50
a. 10b ultramarine 55.00 17.50
b. 10b indigo 65.00 27.50
40 A9 15b vermilion 25.00 12.50
41 A9 25b orange & blue 25.00 12.50
42 A9 50b blue & red 140.00 17.50
a. 50b indigo & red 150.00 20.00
Nos. 37-42 (5) 267.50 75.00

No. 40 on vertically laid paper was not issued. Value $1,250.

Prince Carol
A10 A11

1871-72 *Imperf.*

43 A10 5b rose 32.50 11.00
a. 5b vermilion 35.00 12.50
44 A10 10b orange yel 47.50 17.50
a. Vertically laid paper *450.00* *450.00*
45 A10 10b blue 125.00 30.00
46 A10 15b red 125.00 65.00
47 A10 25b olive brown 30.00 21.00
Nos. 43-47 (5) 360.00 144.50

1872

48 A10 10b ultra 20.00 26.00
a. Vertically laid paper 100.00 150.00
b. 10b greenish blue 110.00 125.00
49 A10 50b blue & red 150.00 165.00

No. 48 is a provisional issue printed from a new plate in which the head is placed further right.
Faked cancellations are found on No. 49.

1872 *Perf. 12½*

Wove Paper

50 A10 5b rose 40.00 20.00
a. 5b vermilion *1,000.* *500.00*
51 A10 10b blue 47.50 20.00
a. 10b ultramarine 50.00 25.00
52 A10 25b dark brown 22.50 22.50
Nos. 50-52 (3) 110.00 62.50

No. 43a with faked perforation is frequently offered as No. 50a.

Paris Print, Fine Impression

1872 Typo. *Perf. 14x13½*

Tinted Paper

53 A11 1½b brnz grn, *bluish* 7.50 .75
54 A11 3b green, *bluish* 12.50 1.25
55 A11 5b bis, *pale buff* 9.00 1.00
56 A11 10b blue 8.50 1.10
57 A11 15b red brn, *pale buff* 75.00 7.50
58 A11 25b org, *pale buff* 77.50 8.00
59 A11 50b rose, *pale rose* 100.00 12.50
Nos. 53-59 (7) 290.00 32.10

Nos. 53-59 exist imperf.

Bucharest Print, Rough Impression

Perf. 11, 11½, 13½, and Compound

1876-79

60 A11 1½b brnz grn, *bluish* 5.00 .50
61 A11 5b bis, *yelsh* 13.00 .55
b. Printed on both sides *75.00*
62 A11 10b bl, *yelsh* ('77) 14.00 .75
a. 10b pale bl, *yelsh* 12.00 .75
b. 10b dark blue, *yelsh* 22.50 1.25
d. Cliché of 5b in plate of 10b ('79) 190.00 80.00
63 A11 10b ultra, *yelsh* ('77) 25.00 1.25
64 A11 15b red brn, *yelsh* 27.50 1.25
a. Printed on both sides *100.00*
65 A11 30b org red, *yelsh* ('78) 125.00 10.00
a. Printed on both sides *210.00*
Nos. 60-65 (6) 209.50 14.30

#60-65 are valued in the grade of fine.
#62d has been reprinted in dark blue. The originals are in dull blue. Value of reprint, $35.

Perf. 11, 11½, 13½ and Compound

1879

66 A11 1½b blk, *yelsh* 2.50 .35
b. Imperf. 12.00
67 A11 3b ol grn, *bluish* 7.00 1.00
a. Diagonal half used as 1½b on cover
68 A11 5b green, *bluish* 2.50 .35
69 A11 10b rose, *yelsh* 9.00 .40
b. Cliché of 5b in plate of 10b 100.00 *475.00*
70 A11 15b rose red, *yelsh* 35.00 5.00
71 A11 25b blue, *yelsh* 75.00 4.50
72 A11 50b bister, *yelsh* 55.00 6.50
Nos. 66-72 (7) 186.00 18.10

#66-72 are valued in the grade of fine.
There are two varieties of the numerals on the 15b and 50b.
No. 69b has been reprinted in dark rose. Originals are in pale rose. Value of reprint, $40.

King Carol I
A12 A13

1880

White Paper

73 A12 15b brown 7.50 .40
74 A12 25b blue 14.00 .60

#73-74 are valued in the grade of fine.
No. 74 exists imperf.

Perf. 13½, 11½ & Compound

1885-89

75 A13 1½b black 2.00 .50
a. Printed on both sides
76 A13 3b violet 5.00 .60
a. Half used as 1½b on cover
77 A13 5b green 52.50 6.00
78 A13 15b red brown 10.00 .85
79 A13 25b blue 11.00 1.00
Nos. 75-79 (5) 80.50 8.95

Tinted Paper

80 A13 1½b blk, *bluish* 3.50 .65
81 A13 3b vio, *bluish* 3.50 .75
82 A13 3b ol grn, *bluish* 4.25 .65
83 A13 5b bl grn, *bluish* 4.25 .60
84 A13 10b rose, *pale buff* 4.25 .65
85 A13 15b red brn, *pale buff* 15.00 .75
86 A13 25b bl, *pale buff* 15.00 1.00
87 A13 50b bis, *pale buff* 55.00 6.00
Nos. 80-87 (8) 104.75 11.05

1889 Wmk. 163

Thin Pale Yellowish Paper

88 A13 1½b black 22.50 3.00
89 A13 3b violet 17.50 3.00
90 A13 5b green 17.50 3.00
91 A13 10b rose 17.50 3.25
92 A13 15b red brown 50.00 5.50
93 A13 25b dark blue 40.00 5.00
Nos. 88-93 (6) 165.00 22.75

King Carol I
A14 A15

1890 *Perf. 13½, 11½ & Compound*

94 A14 1½b maroon 4.25 .80
95 A14 3b violet 22.50 1.10
96 A14 5b emerald 9.50 1.10
97 A14 10b red 11.00 2.00
a. 10b rose 15.00 3.50
98 A14 15b dk brown 17.50 2.00
99 A14 25b gray blue 13.00 1.60
100 A14 50b orange 65.00 13.50
Nos. 94-100 (7) 142.75 22.10

1891 Unwmk.

101 A14 1½b lilac rose 1.40 .30
b. Printed on both sides *65.00*
102 A14 3b lilac 1.10 .40
a. 3b violet 2.00 .50
b. Printed on both sides
c. Impressions of 5b on back *100.00* *75.00*
103 A14 5b emerald 2.10 .50
104 A14 10b pale red 7.75 .60
a. Printed on both sides *140.00* *110.00*
105 A14 15b gray brown 9.50 .40
106 A14 25b gray blue 5.50 .70
107 A14 50b orange 57.50 6.00
Nos. 101-107 (7) 84.85 8.90

Nos. 101-107 exist imperf.

1891

108 A15 1½b claret 2.00 1.25
109 A15 3b lilac 2.00 1.25
110 A15 5b emerald 2.50 2.25
111 A15 10b red 2.75 2.25
112 A15 15b gray brown 2.25 2.00
Nos. 108-112 (5) 11.50 9.00

25th year of the reign of King Carol I.

1894 Wmk. 164

113 A14 3b lilac 6.50 2.50
114 A14 5b pale green 6.50 2.50
115 A14 25b gray blue 10.00 4.50
116 A14 50b orange 20.00 10.00
Nos. 113-116 (4) 43.00 19.50

King Carol I
A17 A18

A19

A20

A21

A23

1893-98 Wmk. 164 & 200

117 A17 1b pale brown .80 .20
118 A17 1½b black .60 .20
119 A18 3b chocolate .80 .20
120 A19 5b blue 1.10 .20
a. Cliché of the 25b in the plate of 5b 47.50 *60.00*
121 A19 5b yel grn ('98) 3.25 .35
a. 5b emerald 4.00 .35
122 A20 10b emerald 1.60 .20
123 A20 10b rose ('98) 3.25 .30
124 A21 15b rose 1.60 .20
125 A21 15b black ('98) 3.25 .30
126 A19 25b violet 2.50 .20
127 A19 25b indigo ('98) 5.75 .45
128 A19 40b gray grn 13.50 .90
129 A19 50b orange 6.50 .25
130 A23 1 l bis & rose 13.50 .35
131 A23 2 l orange & brn 17.00 .55
Nos. 117-131 (15) 75.00 4.45

This watermark may be found in four versions (Wmks. 164, 200 and variations). The paper also varies in thickness.
A 3b orange of type A18; 10b brown, type A20; 15b rose, type A21, and 25b bright green with similar but different border, all watermarked "P R," were prepared but never issued. Value, each $10.
See Nos. 132-157, 224-229. For overprints and surcharges see Romanian Post Offices in the Turkish Empire Nos. 1-6, 10-11.

King Carol I — A24

Perf. 11½, 13½ and Compound

1900-03 Unwmk.

Thin Paper, Tinted Rose on Back

132 A17 1b pale brown .70 .25
133 A24 1b brown ('01) .70 .25
134 A24 1b black ('03) .70 .25
135 A18 3b red brown .90 .20

136	A19	5b	emerald	1.25	.20
137	A20	10b	rose	1.50	.20
138	A21	15b	black	1.25	.20
139	A21	15b	lil gray ('01)	1.25	.20
140	A21	15b	dk vio ('03)	1.25	.25
141	A19	25b	blue	2.25	.25
142	A19	40b	gray grn	4.50	.30
143	A19	50b	orange	8.75	.35
144	A23	1 l	bis & rose ('01)	18.00	.60
145	A23	1 l	grn & blk ('03)	13.00	.80
146	A23	2 l	org & brn ('01)	13.00	.80
147	A23	2 l	red brn & blk ('03)	11.00	.90
			Nos. 132-147 (16)	80.00	6.00

#132 inscribed BANI; #133-134 BAN.

1900, July **Wmk. 167**

148	A17	1b	pale brown	5.00	1.90
149	A18	3b	red brown	4.25	1.90
150	A19	5b	emerald	5.00	1.90
151	A20	10b	rose	5.00	1.90
152	A21	15b	black	6.25	2.75
153	A19	25b	blue	7.00	3.25
154	A19	40b	gray grn	12.50	3.75
155	A19	50b	orange	12.50	3.75
156	A23	1 l	bis & rose	14.50	4.75
157	A23	2 l	orange & brn	19.00	5.75
			Nos. 148-157 (10)	91.00	31.60

Mail Coach Leaving P.O. — A25

King Carol I and Façade of New Post Office — A26

1903 **Unwmk.** ***Perf. 14x13½***

Thin Paper, Tinted Rose on Face

158	A25	1b	gray brown	*1.50*	.70
159	A25	3b	brown violet	*2.50*	1.00
160	A25	5b	pale green	*5.00*	1.40
161	A25	10b	rose	*4.00*	1.40
162	A25	15b	black	*4.00*	1.75
163	A25	25b	blue	*12.00*	6.25
164	A25	40b	dull green	*15.00*	6.75
165	A25	50b	orange	*27.50*	9.75
			Nos. 158-165 (8)	*71.50*	29.00

Counterfeits are plentiful. See note after No. 172. See No. 428.

1903 **Engr.** ***Perf. 13½x14***

Thick Toned Paper

166	A26	15b	black	2.00	1.25
167	A26	25b	blue	4.75	2.50
168	A26	40b	gray grn	6.75	3.25
169	A26	50b	orange	6.75	3.25
170	A26	1 l	dk brown	6.75	3.25
171	A26	2 l	dull red	55.00	24.00
a.			2 l orange (error)	85.00	70.00
172	A26	5 l	dull violet	67.50	37.50
			Nos. 166-172 (7)	149.50	75.00

Opening of the new PO in Bucharest (Nos. 158-172).
Counterfeits exist.

Prince Carol Taking Oath of Allegiance, 1866 — A27

Prince in Royal Carriage A28

Prince Carol at Calafat in 1877 — A29

Prince Carol Shaking Hands with His Captive, Osman Pasha — A30

Carol I as Prince in 1866 and King in 1906 — A31

Romanian Army Crossing Danube A32

Romanian Troops Return to Bucharest in 1878 — A33

Prince Carol at Head of His Command in 1877 — A34

King Carol I at the Cathedral in 1896 — A35

King Carol I at Shrine of St. Nicholas, 1904 — A36

1906 **Engr.** ***Perf. 12***

176	A27	1b	bister & blk	.20	.20
177	A28	3b	red brn & blk	.40	.20
178	A29	5b	dp grn & blk	.50	.20
179	A30	10b	carmine & blk	.30	.20
180	A31	15b	dull vio & blk	.30	.20
181	A32	25b	ultra & blk	2.50	1.40
a.			25b olive green & black	2.50	1.40
182	A33	40b	dk brn & blk	.65	.35
183	A34	50b	bis brn & blk	.75	.35
184	A35	1 l	vermilion & blk	.75	.45
185	A36	2 l	orange & blk	.90	.60
			Nos. 176-185 (10)	7.25	4.15

40 years' rule of Carol I as Prince & King.
No. 181a was never placed in use. Cancellations were by favor.

King Carol I — A37

1906

186	A37	1b	bister & blk	.40	.20
187	A37	3b	red brn & blk	1.00	.25
188	A37	5b	dp grn & blk	.60	.20
189	A37	10b	carmine & blk	.60	.20
190	A37	15b	dl vio & blk	.60	.20
191	A37	25b	ultra & blk	5.50	2.50
192	A37	40b	dk brn & blk	1.50	.40
193	A37	50b	bis brn & blk	1.50	.40
194	A37	1 l	red & blk	1.50	.40
195	A37	2 l	orange & blk	1.50	.40
			Nos. 186-195 (10)	14.70	5.15

25th anniversary of the Kingdom.

Plowman and Angel — A38

Exposition Building — A39

Exposition Buildings
A40 A41

King Carol I — A42

Queen Elizabeth (Carmen Sylva) — A43

1906 **Typo.** ***Perf. 11½, 13½***

196	A38	5b	yel grn & blk	1.50	.40
197	A38	10b	carmine & blk	1.50	.40
198	A39	15b	violet & blk	2.50	.70
199	A39	25b	blue & blk	2.50	.70
200	A40	30b	red & blk brn	3.00	.60
201	A40	40b	green & blk brn	3.50	.75
202	A41	50b	orange & blk	3.00	.95
203	A41	75b	lt brn & dk brn	3.00	.95
204	A42	1.50 l	red lil & blk brn	32.50	13.00
a.			Center inverted		
205	A42	2.50 l	yellow & brn	12.50	8.00
a.			Center inverted		
206	A43	3 l	brn org & brn	8.25	8.00
			Nos. 196-206 (11)	73.75	34.45

General Exposition. They were sold at post offices July 29-31, 1906, and were valid only for those three days. Those sold at the exposition are overprinted "S E" in black. Remainders were sold privately, both unused and canceled to order, by the Exposition promoters.

A44

A45

King Carol I — A46

Perf. 11½, 13½ & Compound

1908-18 **Engr.**

207	A44	5b	pale yel grn	1.50	.20
208	A44	10b	carmine	.50	.20
209	A45	15b	purple	8.25	1.90
210	A44	25b	deep blue	.95	.20
211	A44	40b	brt green	.60	.20
212	A44	40b	dk brn ('18)	3.75	1.90
213	A44	50b	orange	.45	.20
214	A44	50b	lt red ('18)	1.50	.60
215	A44	1 l	brown	1.25	.30
216	A44	2 l	red	7.50	1.90
			Nos. 207-216 (10)	26.25	7.60

Perf. 13½x14, 11½, 13½ & Compound

1909-18 **Typo.**

217	A46	1b	black	.45	.20
218	A46	3b	red brown	.90	.20
219	A46	5b	yellow grn	.45	.20
220	A46	10b	rose	.90	.20
221	A46	15b	dull violet	13.00	8.75
222	A46	15b	olive green	.90	.20
223	A46	15b	red brn ('18)	.80	.50
			Nos. 217-223 (7)	17.40	10.25

Nos. 217-219, 222 exist imperf.
No. 219 in black is a chemical changeling.
For surcharge and overprints see Nos. 240-242, 245-247, J50-J51, RA1-RA2, RA11-RA12, Romanian Post Offices in the Turkish Empire 7-9.

Types of 1893-99

1911-19 **White Paper** **Unwmk.**

224	A17	1½b	straw	1.25	.35
225	A19	25b	deep blue ('18)	.40	.20
226	A19	40b	gray brn ('19)	.75	.20
227	A19	50b	dull red ('19)	.75	.20
228	A23	1 l	gray grn ('18)	1.25	.20
229	A23	2 l	orange ('18)	1.40	.20
			Nos. 224-229 (6)	5.80	1.35

For overprints see Romanian Post Offices in the Turkish Empire Nos. 10-11.

Romania Holding Flag — A47

Romanian Crown and Old Fort on Danube — A48

Troops Crossing Danube — A49

View of Turtucaia — A50

Mircea the Great and Carol I — A51

View of Silistra — A52

Perf. 11½x13½, 13½x11½

1913, Dec. 25

230	A47	1b	black	.40	.20
231	A48	3b	ol gray & choc	1.00	.40
232	A49	5b	yel grn & blk brn	.80	.20
233	A50	10b	org & gray	.40	.20
234	A51	15b	bister & vio	1.00	.40
235	A52	25b	blue & choc	1.40	.55
236	A49	40b	bis & red vio	2.00	.90
237	A48	50b	yellow & bl	2.50	1.90
238	A48	1 l	bl & ol bis	7.00	4.75
239	A48	2 l	org red & rose	9.00	5.50
			Nos. 230-239 (10)	25.50	15.00

Romania's annexation of Silistra.

No. 217 Handstamped in Red

25
BANI

Perf. 13½x14, 11½, 13½ & Compound

1918, May 1

240	A46	25b on 1b black	.20	.20

This handstamp is found inverted.

No. 219 and 220 Overprinted in Black

1918

1918

241	A46	5b yellow green	.30	.20
a.		Inverted overprint	9.00	5.00
b.		Double overprint	9.00	
242	A46	10b rose	.30	.20
a.		Inverted overprint	9.00	5.00
b.		Double overprint	9.00	

Nos. 217, 219 and 220 Overprinted in Red or Black

1919, Nov. 8

245	A46	1b black (R)	.20	.20
a.		Inverted overprint	6.00	
b.		Double overprint	9.00	2.00
246	A46	5b yel grn (Bk)	.20	.20
a.		Double overprint	9.00	2.75
b.		Inverted overprint	6.00	1.75
247	A46	10b rose (Bk)	.20	.20
a.		Inverted overprint	6.00	1.75
b.		Double overprint	9.00	2.50
		Nos. 245-247 (3)	.60	.60

Recovery of Transylvania and the return of the King to Bucharest.

King Ferdinand
A53 A54

1920-22 **Typo.**

248	A53	1b black	.20	.20
249	A53	5b yellow grn	.20	.20
250	A53	10b rose	.20	.20
251	A53	15b red brown	.65	.25
252	A53	25b deep blue	1.25	.35
253	A53	25b brown	.65	.25
254	A53	40b gray brown	1.10	.30
255	A53	50b salmon	.30	.20
256	A53	1 l gray grn	1.10	.20
257	A53	1 l rose	.65	.25
258	A53	2 l orange	1.10	.25
259	A53	2 l dp blue	1.10	.25
260	A53	2 l rose ('22)	2.50	1.60
		Nos. 248-260 (13)	11.00	4.50

Nos. 248-260 are printed on two papers: coarse, grayish paper with bits of colored fiber, and thinner white paper of better quality.

Nos. 248-251, 253 exist imperf.

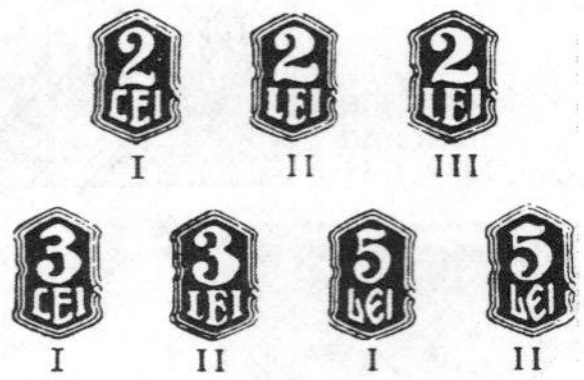

TWO LEI:

Type I - The "2" is thin, with tail 2½mm wide. Top of "2" forms a hook.

Type II - The "2" is thick, with tail 3mm wide. Top of "2" forms a ball.

Type III - The "2" is similar to type II. The "E" of "LEI" is larger and about 2mm wide.

THREE LEI:

Type I - Top of "3" begins in a point. Top and middle bars of "E" of "LEI" are without serifs.

Type II - Top of "3" begins in a ball. Top and middle bars of "E" of "LEI" have serifs.

FIVE LEI:

Type I - The "5" is 2½mm wide. The end of the final stroke of the "L" of "LEI" almost touches the vertical stroke.

Type II - The "5" is 3mm wide and the lines are broader than in type I. The end of the final stroke of the "L" of "LEI" is separated from the vertical by a narrow space.

Perf. 13½x14, 11½, 13½ & Compound

1920-26

261	A54	3b black	.20	.20
262	A54	5b black	.20	.20
263	A54	10b yel grn ('25)	.20	.20
a.		10b olive green ('25)	.35	
264	A54	25b bister brn	.20	.20
265	A54	25b salmon	.20	.20
266	A54	30b violet	.20	.20
267	A54	50b orange	.20	.20
268	A54	60b gray grn	.90	.40
269	A54	1 l violet	.20	.20
270	A54	2 l rose (I)	1.10	.25
a.		2 l claret (I)	25.00	
271	A54	2 l lt green (II)	.60	.20
a.		2 l light green (I)	.85	.20
b.		2 l light green (III)	.70	.20
272	A54	3 l blue (I)	2.25	.30
273	A54	3 l buff (I)	2.25	.25
a.		3 l buff (I)	10.00	.55
274	A54	3 l salmon (II)	.20	.20
a.		3 l salmon (I)	1.40	.90
275	A54	3 l car rose (II)	.55	.20
276	A54	5 l emer (I)	1.90	.25
277	A54	5 l lt brn (II)	.40	.20
a.		5 l light brown (I)	1.40	.50
278	A54	6 l blue	2.25	.75
279	A54	6 l carmine	5.25	1.25
280	A54	6 l ol grn ('26)	2.25	.40
281	A54	7½ l pale bl	1.90	.25
282	A54	10 l deep blue	1.90	.25
		Nos. 261-282 (22)	25.30	6.75

#273 and 273a, 274 and 274a, exist se-tenant. The 50b exists in three types.

For surcharge see No. Q7.

Alba Iulia Cathedral
A55

King Ferdinand
A56

Coat of Arms — A57

Queen Marie as Nurse — A58

Michael the Brave and King Ferdinand
A59

King Ferdinand
A60

Queen Marie — A61

Perf. 13½x14, 13½, 11½ & Compound

1922, Oct. 15 **Photo.** **Wmk. 95**

283	A55	5b black	.30	.25
a.		Engraver's name omitted	12.00	1.40
284	A56	25b chocolate	.75	.35
285	A57	50b dp green	.75	.50
286	A58	1 l olive grn	.90	.70
287	A59	2 l carmine	.90	.70
288	A60	3 l blue	1.75	1.10
289	A61	6 l violet	6.50	6.00
		Nos. 283-289 (7)	11.85	9.60

Coronation of King Ferdinand I and Queen Marie on Oct. 15, 1922, at Alba Iulia. All values exist imperforate.

King Ferdinand
A62 A63

1926, July 1 **Unwmk.** ***Perf. 11***

291	A62	10b yellow grn	.20	.20
292	A62	25b orange	.20	.20
293	A62	50b orange brn	.20	.20
294	A63	1 l dk violet	.20	.20
295	A63	2 l dk green	.20	.20
296	A63	3 l brown car	.20	.20
297	A63	5 l black brn	.20	.20
298	A63	6 l dk olive	.20	.20
a.		6 l bright blue (error)	70.00	70.00
300	A63	9 l slate	.20	.20
301	A63	10 l brt blue	.20	.20
b.		10 l brown carmine (error)	70.00	70.00
		Nos. 291-301 (10)	2.00	2.00

60th birthday of King Ferdinand.

Exist imperf. Imperf. examples with watermark 95 are proofs.

King Carol I and King Ferdinand
A69

King Ferdinand
A70

A71

1927, Aug. 1 ***Perf. 13½***

308	A69	25b brown vio	.20	.20
309	A70	30b gray blk	.20	.20
310	A71	50b dk green	.20	.20
311	A69	1 l bluish slate	.20	.20
312	A70	2 l dp green	.25	.25
313	A70	3 l violet	.35	.35
314	A71	4 l dk brown	.40	.40
315	A71	4.50 l henna brn	1.50	1.25
316	A70	5 l red brown	.40	.40
317	A71	6 l carmine	1.00	.85
318	A69	7.50 l grnsh bl	.60	.60
319	A69	10 l brt blue	1.00	.85
		Nos. 308-319 (12)	6.30	5.75

50th anniversary of Romania's independence from Turkish suzerainty.

Some values exist imperf. All exist imperf. and with value numerals omitted.

King Michael
A72 A73

Perf. 13½x14 (25b, 50b); 13½

1928-29 **Typo.** **Unwmk.**

Size: 19x25mm

320	A72	25b black	.20	.20
321	A72	30b fawn ('29)	.25	.20
322	A72	50b olive grn	.20	.20

Photo.

Size: 18½x24½mm

323	A73	1 l violet	.25	.20
324	A73	2 l dp green	.35	.20
325	A73	3 l brt rose	.40	.20
326	A73	5 l red brown	.70	.20
327	A73	7.50 l ultra	3.00	.40
328	A73	10 l blue	2.50	.20
		Nos. 320-328 (9)	7.85	2.00

See Nos. 343-345, 353-357. For overprints see Nos. 359-368A.

Parliament House, Bessarabia — A74

Designs: 1 l, 2 l, Parliament House, Bessarabia. 3 l, 5 l, 20 l, Hotin Fortress. 7.50 l, 10 l, Fortress Cetatea Alba.

1928, Apr. 29 **Wmk. 95** ***Perf. 13½***

329	A74	1 l deep green	.50	.35
330	A74	2 l deep brown	.50	.35
331	A74	3 l black brown	.50	.35
332	A74	5 l carmine lake	.65	.40
333	A74	7.50 l ultra	.65	.40
334	A74	10 l Prus blue	1.50	1.10
335	A74	20 l black vio	2.00	1.40
		Nos. 329-335 (7)	6.30	4.35

Reunion of Bessarabia with Romania, 10th anniv.

King Carol I and King Michael
A77

View of Constanta Harbor
A78

Trajan's Monument at Adam Clisi
A79

Cernavoda Bridge — A80

1928, Oct. 25

336	A77	1 l blue green	.45	.30
337	A78	2 l red brown	.45	.30
338	A77	3 l gray black	.60	.30
339	A79	5 l dull lilac	.75	.40
340	A79	7.50 l ultra	1.00	.45
341	A80	10 l blue	1.50	1.00
342	A80	20 l carmine rose	2.25	1.25
		Nos. 336-342 (7)	7.00	4.00

Union of Dobruja with Romania, 50th anniv.

Michael Types of 1928-29

Perf. 13½x14

1928, Sept. 1 **Typo.** **Wmk. 95**

343	A72	25b black	.50	.20

Photo.

344	A73	7.50 l ultra	1.50	.75
345	A73	10 l blue	3.00	.50
		Nos. 343-345 (3)	5.00	1.45

Ferdinand I; Stephen the Great; Michael the Brave; Corvin and Constantine Brancoveanu — A81

Union with Transylvania A82

Avram Jancu — A83

Prince Michael the Brave — A84

Castle Bran — A85

King Ferdinand I — A86

1929, May 10 Photo. Wmk. 95

347	A81	1 l dark violet	1.00	.60
348	A82	2 l olive green	1.10	.60
349	A83	3 l violet brown	1.50	.75
350	A84	4 l cerise	1.50	.90
351	A85	5 l orange	1.90	.90
352	A86	10 l brt blue	2.00	1.50
		Nos. 347-352 (6)	9.00	5.25

Union of Transylvania and Romania.

Michael Type of 1928

1930 Unwmk. *Perf. 14½x14*

Size: 18x23mm

353	A73	1 l deep violet	.45	.20
354	A73	2 l deep green	.70	.20
355	A73	3 l carmine rose	1.40	.20
356	A73	7.50 l ultra	2.75	.50
357	A73	10 l deep blue	9.50	3.50
		Nos. 353-357 (5)	14.80	4.60

Stamps of 1928-30 Overprinted **8 IUNIE 1930**

On Nos. 320-322, 326, 328

Perf. 13½x14, 13½

1930, June 8 Typo.

359	A72	25b black	.20	.20
360	A72	30b fawn	.25	.20
361	A72	50b olive green	.25	.20

Photo.

Size: 18½x24½mm

362	A73	5 l red brown	.50	.20
362A	A73	10 l brt blue	2.50	.55

On Nos. 353-357

Perf. 14½x14

Size: 18x23mm

363	A73	1 l deep violet	.30	.55
364	A73	2 l deep green	.25	.20
365	A73	3 l carmine rose	.50	.20
366	A73	7.50 l ultra	1.50	.35
367	A73	10 l deep blue	1.25	.20

On Nos. 343-344

Perf. 13½x14, 13½

Typo. Wmk. 95

368	A72	25b black	.50	.20

Photo.

Size: 18½x24½mm

368A	A73	7.50 l ultra	2.00	.50
		Nos. 359-368A (12)	10.00	3.55

Accession to the throne by King Carol II. This overprint exists on Nos. 323, 345.

A87

A88

King Carol II — A89

Perf. 13½, 14, 14x13½

1930 Wmk. 225

369	A87	25b black	.20	.20
370	A87	50b chocolate	.25	.20
371	A87	1 l dk violet	.20	.20
372	A87	2 l gray green	.20	.20
373	A88	3 l carmine rose	.35	.20
374	A88	4 l orange red	.35	.20
375	A88	6 l carmine brn	.45	.20
376	A88	7.50 l ultra	.50	.20
377	A89	10 l deep blue	1.25	.20
378	A89	16 l peacock grn	3.00	.20
379	A89	20 l orange	3.75	.25
		Nos. 369-379 (11)	10.50	2.25

Exist imperf. See Nos. 405-414.

A90

A91

1930, Dec. 24 Unwmk. *Perf. 13½*

380	A90	1 l dull violet	.50	.20
381	A91	2 l green	.80	.20
382	A91	4 l vermilion	1.00	.20
383	A91	6 l brown carmine	2.25	.20
		Nos. 380-383 (4)	4.55	.80

First census in Romania.

King Carol II — A92

King Carol I — A93

King Ferdinand — A96

King Carol II — A94

King Carol II, King Ferdinand and King Carol I — A95

1931, May 10 Photo. Wmk. 225

384	A92	1 l gray violet	3.00	1.75
385	A93	2 l green	3.50	1.75
386	A94	6 l red brown	5.00	2.75
387	A95	10 l blue	8.00	5.00
388	A96	20 l orange	9.00	6.75
		Nos. 384-388 (5)	28.50	18.00

50th anniversary of Romanian Kingdom.

Using Bayonet — A97

Romanian Infantryman 1870 — A98

Romanian Infantry 1830 — A99

King Carol I A100

Infantry Advance A101

King Ferdinand A102

King Carol II A103

1931, May 10

389	A97	25b gray black	.85	.50
390	A98	50b dk red brn	1.40	.65
391	A99	1 l gray violet	1.75	.80
392	A100	2 l deep green	3.00	1.00
393	A101	3 l carmine rose	5.50	3.00
394	A102	7.50 l ultra	7.50	6.50
395	A103	16 l blue green	10.00	3.00
		Nos. 389-395 (7)	30.00	15.45

Centenary of the Romanian Army.

Naval Cadet Ship "Mircea" A104

King Carol II — A108

10 l, Ironclad. 16 l, Light cruiser. 20 l, Destroyer.

1931, May 10

396	A104	6 l red brown	3.25	2.00
397	A104	10 l blue	4.50	2.25
398	A104	16 l blue green	17.00	2.75
399	A104	20 l orange	7.50	4.75
		Nos. 396-399 (4)	32.25	11.75

50th anniversary of the Romanian Navy.

1931 Unwmk. Engr. *Perf. 12*

400	A108	30 l ol bis & dk bl	.35	.20
401	A108	50 l red & dk bl	1.25	.35
402	A108	100 l dk grn & dk bl	1.50	.45
		Nos. 400-402 (3)	3.10	1.00

Exist imperf.

Carol II, Ferdinand, Carol I — A109

Wmk. 230

1931, Nov. 1 Photo. *Perf. 13½*

403	A109	16 l Prus green	7.50	.40

Exists imperf.

Carol II Types of 1930-31

Perf. 13½, 14, 14½ and Compound

1932 Wmk. 230

405	A87	25b black	.35	.20
406	A87	50b dark brown	.50	.20
407	A87	1 l dark violet	.85	.20
408	A87	2 l gray green	.85	.20
409	A88	3 l carmine rose	1.50	.20
410	A88	4 l orange red	2.50	.20
411	A88	6 l carmine brn	4.50	.20
412	A88	7.50 l ultra	6.50	.45
413	A89	10 l deep blue	75.00	.45
414	A89	20 l orange	75.00	5.00
		Nos. 405-414 (10)	167.55	7.30

Alexander the Good — A110

King Carol II — A111

1932, May *Perf. 13½*

415	A110	6 l carmine brown	8.50	5.75

500th death anniv. of Alexander the Good, Prince of Moldavia, 1400-1432.

1932, June

416	A111	10 l brt blue	9.00	.40

Exists imperf.

Cantacuzino and Gregory Ghika, Founders of Coltea and Pantelimon Hospitals — A112

Session of the Congress A113

Aesculapius and Hygeia — A114

1932, Sept. *Perf. 13½*

417	A112	1 l carmine rose	5.00	3.50
418	A113	6 l deep orange	12.50	5.50
419	A114	10 l brt blue	20.00	10.00
		Nos. 417-419 (3)	37.50	19.00

9th Intl. History of Medicine Congress, Bucharest.

Bull's Head and Post Horn A116

Lion Rampant and Bridge A117

Dolphins A118

Eagle and Castles A119

Coat of Arms — A120

Eagle and Post Horn — A121

Bull's Head and Post Horn — A122

1932, Nov. 20 Typo. *Imperf.*

421 A116	25b	black	.90	.25
422 A117	1 l	violet	1.40	.40
423 A118	2 l	green	1.90	.45
424 A119	3 l	car rose	2.00	.60
425 A120	6 l	red brown	2.75	.75
426 A121	7.50 l	lt blue	2.75	.75
427 A122	10 l	dk blue	3.50	1.10
		Nos. 421-427 (7)	15.20	4.30

75th anniv. of the first Moldavian stamps.

Mail Coach Type of 1903

1932, Nov. 20 *Perf. 13½*

428 A25	16 l	blue green	7.50	2.50

30th anniv. of the opening of the new post office, Bucharest, in 1903.

Arms of City of Turnu-Severin, Ruins of Tower of Emperor Severus — A123

Inauguration of Trajan's Bridge — A124

Prince Carol Landing at Turnu-Severin — A125

Bridge over the Danube A126

1933, June 2 Photo. *Perf. 14½x14*

429 A123	25b	gray green	.25	.20
430 A124	50b	dull blue	.45	.20
431 A125	1 l	black brn	.45	.25
432 A126	2 l	olive blk	1.10	.35
		Nos. 429-432 (4)	2.25	1.00

Centenary of the incorporation in Walachia of the old Roman City of Turnu-Severin. Exist imperf.

Queen Elizabeth and King Carol I — A127

Profiles of Kings Carol I, Ferdinand and Carol II — A128

Castle Peles, Sinaia A129

1933, Aug.

433 A127	1 l	dark violet	2.00	1.25
434 A128	3 l	olive brown	2.00	1.25
435 A129	6 l	vermilion	3.25	1.60
		Nos. 433-435 (3)	7.25	4.10

50th anniversary of the erection of Castle Peles, the royal summer residence at Sinaia. Exist imperf.

A130

A131

King Carol II — A132

1934, Aug. *Perf. 13½*

436 A130	50b	brown	.55	.20
437 A131	2 l	gray green	1.00	.25
438 A131	4 l	red	1.50	.35
439 A132	6 l	deep claret	4.50	.20
		Nos. 436-439 (4)	7.55	1.00

See Nos. 446-460 for stamps inscribed "Posta." Nos. 436, 439 exist imperf.

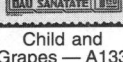

Child and Grapes — A133

Woman and Fruit — A134

1934, Sept. 14

440 A133	1 l	dull green	1.40	1.10
441 A134	2 l	violet brown	1.40	1.10

Natl. Fruit Week, Sept. 14-21. Exist imperf.

Crisan, Horia and Closca A135

1935, Feb. 28

442 A135	1 l	shown	.35	.25
443 A135	2 l	Crisan	.50	.40
444 A135	6 l	Closca	1.00	.50
445 A135	10 l	Horia	2.00	1.00
		Nos. 442-445 (4)	3.85	2.15

150th anniversary of the death of three Romanian martyrs. Exist imperf.

A139

A140

A141

A142

King Carol II — A143

1935-40 Wmk. 230 Photo. *Perf. 13½*

446	A139	25b	black brn	.20	.20
447	A142	50b	brown	.20	.20
448	A140	1 l	purple	.20	.20
449	A141	2 l	green	.20	.20
449A	A141	2 l	dk bl grn ('40)	.25	.25
450	A142	3 l	deep rose	.20	.20
450A	A142	3 l	grnsh bl ('40)	.30	.30
451	A141	4 l	vermilion	.40	.20
452	A140	5 l	rose car ('40)	.40	.40
453	A143	6 l	maroon	.35	.20
454	A140	7.50 l	ultra	.60	.20
454A	A142	8 l	magenta ('40)	.60	.60
455	A141	9 l	brt ultra ('40)	.90	.90
456	A142	10 l	brt blue	.35	.20
456A	A143	12 l	slate bl ('40)	.50	.50
457	A139	15 l	dk brn ('40)	.50	.50
458	A143	16 l	Prus blue	.60	.20
459	A143	20 l	orange	.40	.20
460	A143	24 l	dk car ('40)	.85	.85
			Nos. 446-460 (19)	8.00	6.50

Exist imperf.

Nos. 454, 456 Overprinted in Red

CEHOSLOVACIA YUGOSLAVIA

1920-1936

1936, Dec. 5

461 A140	7.50 l	ultra	2.25	1.75
462 A142	10 l	brt blue	2.25	1.75

16th anniversary of the Little Entente. Overprints in silver or gold are fraudulent.

Birthplace of Ion Creanga A144

Ion Creanga A145

1937, May 15

463 A144	2 l	green	.50	.35
464 A145	3 l	carmine rose	.50	.35
465 A144	4 l	dp violet	.75	.50
466 A145	6 l	red brown	.75	.65
		Nos. 463-466 (4)	2.50	1.85

Creanga (1837-89), writer. Exist imperf.

Cathedral at Curtea de Arges — A146

1937, July 1

467 A146	7.50 l	ultra	1.25	.40
468 A146	10 l	blue	2.25	.35

The Little Entente (Romania, Czechoslovakia, Yugoslavia). Exist imperf.

Souvenir Sheet

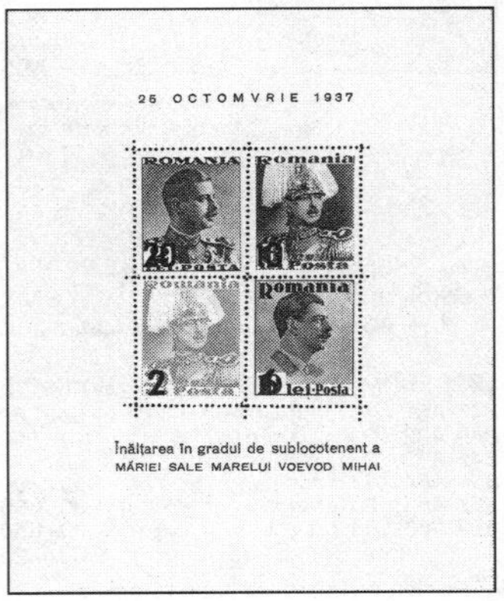

A146a

Surcharged in Black with New Values

1937, Oct. 25 Unwmk. *Perf. 13½*

469 A146a	Sheet of 4	3.00	3.00
a.	2 l on 20 l orange	.30	.30
b.	6 l on 10 l bright blue	.30	.30
c.	10 l on 6 l maroon	.30	.30
d.	20 l on 2 l green	.30	.30

Promotion of the Crown Prince Michael to the rank of Lieutenant on his 17th birthday.

Arms of Romania, Greece, Turkey and Yugoslavia A147

Perf. 13x13½

1938, Feb. 10 Wmk. 230

470 A147	7.50 l	ultra	.75	.50
471 A147	10 l	blue	1.25	.50

The Balkan Entente.

A148

King Carol II
A149 A150

1938, May 10 *Perf. 13½*

472 A148 3 l dk carmine .35 .20
473 A149 6 l violet brn .35 .20
474 A150 10 l blue .50 .20
Nos. 472-474 (3) 1.20 .60

New Constitution of Feb. 27, 1938.

Catalogue values for unused stamps in this section, from this point to the end of the section, are for Never Hinged items.

Prince Carol at Calatorie, 1866
A151

Examining Plans for a Monastery
A153

Prince Carol and Carmen Sylva (Queen Elizabeth)
A155

Sigmaringen and Peles Castles — A154

Prince Carol, Age 6 — A156

Equestrian Statue — A159

Battle of Plevna — A160

On Horseback
A161

Cathedral of Curtea de Arges
A164

King Carol I and Queen Elizabeth
A163

Designs: 50b, At Calafat. 4 l, In 1866. 5 l, In 1877. 12 l, in 1914.

Perf. 14, 13½

1939, Apr. 10 **Wmk. 230**

475 A151 25b olive blk .20 .20
476 A151 50b violet brn .20 .20
477 A153 1 l dk purple .20 .20
478 A154 1.50 l green .20 .20
479 A155 2 l myrtle grn .20 .20
480 A156 3 l red orange .20 .20
481 A156 4 l rose lake .20 .20
482 A156 5 l black .20 .20
483 A159 7 l olive blk .20 .20
484 A160 8 l dark blue .20 .20
485 A161 10 l deep mag .20 .20
486 A161 12 l dull blue .30 .20
487 A163 15 l ultra .40 .20
488 A164 16 l Prus green .90 .40
Nos. 475-488 (14) 3.80 3.00

Centenary of the birth of King Carol I.

Souvenir Sheets

1939 *Perf. 14x13½*

488A Sheet of 3, #475-476, 478 1.50 1.50
d. Imperf. ('40) 3.50 3.50

Perf. 14x15½

488B Sheet of 4, #480-482, 486 1.50 1.50
e. Imperf. ('40) 3.50 3.50
488C Sheet of 4, #479, 483-485 1.50 1.50
f. Imperf. ('40) 3.50 3.50

No. 488A sold for 20 l, Nos. 488B-488C for 50 l, the surtax for national defense.

Nos. 488A-488C and 488Ad-488Cf were overprinted "PRO-PATRIA 1940" to aid the armament fund. Value, set of 6, $100.

Nos. 488A-488C exist with overprint of "ROMA BERLIN 1940" and bars, but these are not recognized as having been officially issued.

Romanian Pavilion
A165

Romanian Pavilion
A166

1939, May 8 *Perf. 14x13½, 13½*

489 A165 6 l brown carmine .30 .30
490 A166 12 l brt blue .30 .30

New York World's Fair.

Mihail Eminescu
A167 A168

1939, May 22 *Perf. 13½*

491 A167 5 l olive gray .35 .35
492 A168 7 l brown carmine .35 .35

Mihail Eminescu, poet, 50th death anniv.

Three Types of Locomotives — A169

Modern Train
A170

Wood-burning Locomotive
A171

Streamlined Locomotive
A172

Railroad Terminal
A173

1939, June 10 **Typo.** *Perf. 14*

493 A169 1 l red violet .40 .30
494 A170 4 l deep rose .55 .30
495 A171 5 l gray lilac .60 .30
496 A171 7 l claret .70 .35
497 A172 12 l blue 1.00 1.00
498 A173 15 l green 2.00 1.25
Nos. 493-498 (6) 5.25 3.50

Romanian Railways, 70th anniversary.

Arms of Romania, Greece, Turkey and Yugoslavia — A174

Wmk. 230

1940, May 27 **Photo.** *Perf. 13½*

504 A174 12 l lt ultra .35 .35
505 A174 16 l dull blue .35 .35

The Balkan Entente.

King Michael — A175

1940-42 **Wmk. 230** *Perf. 14*

506 A175 25b Prus green .20 .20
506A A175 50b dk grn ('42) .20 .20
507 A175 1 l purple .20 .20
508 A175 2 l red orange .20 .20
508A A175 4 l slate ('42) .20 .20
509 A175 5 l rose pink .20 .20
509A A175 7 l dp blue ('42) .20 .20
510 A175 10 l dp magenta .25 .20
511 A175 12 l dull blue .20 .20
511A A175 13 l dk vio ('42) .20 .20
512 A175 16 l Prus blue .25 .20
513 A175 20 l brown 1.25 .20
514 A175 30 l yellow grn .20 .20
515 A175 50 l olive brn .20 .20
516 A175 100 l rose brown .30 .20
Nos. 506-516 (15) 4.25 3.00

See Nos. 535A-553.

Prince Duca — A176

1941, Oct. 6 *Perf. 13½*

517 A176 6 l lt brown .20 .20
518 A176 12 l dk violet .20 .20
519 A176 24 l brt blue .25 .25
Nos. 517-519 (3) .65 .65

Crossing of the Dniester River by Romanian forces invading Russia.

Nos. 517-519 each exist in an imperf., ungummed souvenir sheet of 4. These were prepared by the civil government of Trans-Dniestria to be sold for 300 lei apiece to aid the Red Cross, but were not recognized by the national government at Bucharest. The sheets reached philatelic channels in 1946.

See Nos. 554-557.

Hotin Chapel, Bessarabia
A177

Sucevita Monastery, Bucovina
A179

Inscribed "Basarabia" or "Bucovina" at bottom

Designs: 50b, 9.50 l, Hotin Fortress, Bessarabia. 1.50 l, Soroca Fortress, Bessarabia. 2 l, 5.50 l, Tighina Fortress, Bessarabia. 3 l, Dragomirna Monastery, Bucovina. 6.50 l, Cetatea Alba Fortress, Bessarabia. 10 l, 130 l, Putna Monastery, Bucovina. 13 l, Milisauti Monastery, Bucovina. 26 l, St. Nicholas Monastery, Suceava, Bucovina. 39 l, Rughi Monastery, Bessarabia.

1941, Dec. 1 *Perf. 13½*

520 A177 25b rose car .20 .20
521 A179 50b red brn .20 .20
522 A179 1 l dp vio .20 .20
523 A179 1.50 l green .20 .20
524 A179 2 l brn org .20 .20
525 A177 3 l dk ol grn .20 .20
526 A177 5 l olive blk .20 .20
527 A179 5.50 l brown .20 .20
528 A179 6.50 l magenta .30 .20
529 A179 9.50 l gray blk .30 .20
530 A179 10 l dk vio brn .20 .20
531 A177 13 l slate blue .25 .20
532 A179 17 l brn car .30 .20
533 A179 26 l gray grn .35 .25
534 A179 39 l bl grn .50 .40
535 A179 130 l yel org 2.00 1.50
Nos. 520-535,B179-B187 (25) 9.80 7.75

Type of 1940-42

1943-45 **Wmk. 276** *Perf. 14*

535A A175 25b Prus grn ('44) .20 .20
536 A175 50b dk grn ('44) .20 .20
537 A175 1 l dk vio ('43) .20 .20
538 A175 2 l red org ('43) .20 .20
539 A175 3 l red brn ('44) .20 .20
540 A175 3.50 l brn ('43) .20 .20
541 A175 4 l slate .20 .20
542 A175 4.50 l dk brn ('43) .20 .20
543 A175 5 l rose car .20 .20
544 A175 6.50 l dl vio .20 .20
545 A175 7 l dp bl .20 .20
546 A175 10 l dp mag .20 .20
547 A175 11 l brt ultra .20 .20

548	A175	12 l	dark blue	.20	.20
549	A175	15 l	royal blue	.20	.20
550	A175	16 l	dp blue	.20	.20
551	A175	20 l	brn ('43)	.20	.20
551A	A175	29 l	ultra ('45)	.50	.30
552	A175	30 l	yel grn	.20	.20
553	A175	50 l	olive blk	.20	.20
			Nos. 535A-553 (20)	4.30	4.10

Prince Duca Type of 1941

1943 ***Perf. 13½***

554	A176	3 l	red org	.20	.20
555	A176	6 l	dl brn	.20	.20
556	A176	12 l	dl vio	.20	.20
557	A176	24 l	brt bl	.20	.20
			Nos. 554-557 (4)	.80	.80

Andrei Saguna — A188

Andrei Muresanu A189

Transylvanians: 4.50 l, Samuel Micu. 11 l, Gheorghe Sincai. 15 l, Michael the Brave. 31 l, Gheorghe Lazar. 35 l, Avram Jancu. 41 l, Simeon Barnutiu. 55 l, Three Heroes. 61 l, Petru Maior.

1945 **Inscribed "1944"** ***Perf. 14***

558	A188	25b	rose red	.30	.30
559	A189	50b	orange	.20	.20
560	A189	4.50 l	brown	.20	.20
561	A188	11 l	lt ultra	.20	.20
562	A188	15 l	Prus grn	.20	.20
563	A189	31 l	dl vio	.20	.20
564	A188	35 l	bl blk	.20	.20
565	A188	41 l	olive gray	.20	.20
566	A189	55 l	red brown	.20	.20
567	A189	61 l	deep magenta	.20	.20
			Nos. 558-567,B251 (11)	2.60	2.60

Romania's liberation.

A198 A199

King Michael
A200 A201

1945 **Photo.**

568	A198	50b	gray blue	.20	.20
569	A199	1 l	dl brn	.20	.20
570	A199	2 l	violet	.20	.20
571	A198	2 l	sepia	.20	.20
572	A199	4 l	yel grn	.20	.20
573	A200	5 l	dp mag	.20	.20
574	A198	10 l	blue	.20	.20
575	A198	15 l	magenta	.20	.20
576	A198	20 l	dl blue	.20	.20
577	A200	25 l	red org	.20	.20
578	A200	35 l	brown	.20	.20
579	A200	40 l	car rose	.20	.20
580	A199	50 l	pale ultra	.20	.20
581	A199	55 l	red	.20	.20
582	A200	75 l	Prus grn	.20	.20
583	A201	80 l	orange	.20	.20
584	A201	100 l	dp red brn	.20	.20
585	A201	160 l	yel grn	.20	.20
586	A201	200 l	dk ol grn	.20	.20
587	A201	400 l	dl vio	.20	.20
			Nos. 568-587 (20)	4.00	4.00

Nos. 571, 573, 580, 581, 585 and 587 are printed on toned paper, Nos. 576, 577, 583, 584 and 586 on both toned and white papers, others on white paper only.

See Nos. 610-624, 651-660.

Mail Carrier A202

Telegraph Operator A203

Lineman A204

Post Office, Bucharest A205

1945, July 20 **Wmk. 276** ***Perf. 13***

588	A202	100 l	dk brn	.75	.75
589	A202	100 l	gray olive	.75	.75
590	A203	150 l	brown	1.25	1.25
591	A203	150 l	brt rose	1.25	1.25
592	A204	250 l	lt gray ol	1.50	1.50
593	A204	250 l	blue	1.50	1.50
594	A205	500 l	dp mag	10.50	10.50
			Nos. 588-594 (7)	17.50	17.50

Issued in sheets of 4.

I. Ionescu, G. Titeica, A. O. Idachimescu and V. Cristescu — A207

Allegory of Learning A208

1945, Sept. 5 ***Perf. 13½***

596	A207	2 l	sepia	.20	.20
597	A208	80 l	bl blk	.20	.20

50th anniversary of "Gazeta Matematica," mathematics journal.

Cernavoda Bridge, 50th Anniv. — A209

1945, Sept. 26 ***Perf. 14***

598	A209	80 l	bl blk	.20	.20

Blacksmith and Plowman — A210

1946, Mar. 6

599	A210	80 l	blue	.20	.20

Agrarian reform law of Mar. 23, 1945.

Atheneum, Bucharest A211 Numeral in Wreath A212

Georges Enescu — A213 Mechanic — A214

Wmk. 276

1946, Apr. 26 **Photo.** ***Perf. 13½***

600	A211	10 l	dk bl	.20	.20
601	A212	20 l	red brn	.20	.20
602	A212	55 l	peacock bl	.20	.20
603	A213	80 l	purple	.20	.20
a.			Tête bêche pair	.60	.60
604	A212	160 l	red org	.20	.20
			Nos. 600-604,B330-B331 (7)	2.50	2.50

Philharmonic Society, 25th anniv.

1946, May 1 ***Perf. 13½x13***

Labor Day: No. 606, Laborer. No. 607, Sower. No. 608, Reaper. 200 l, Students.

605	A214	10 l	Prus grn	*.40*	*.40*
606	A214	10 l	dk car rose	.20	.20
607	A214	20 l	dl bl	*.40*	*.40*
608	A214	20 l	dk red brn	.20	.20
609	A214	200 l	brt red	.20	.20
			Nos. 605-609 (5)	*1.40*	*1.40*

Michael Types of 1945

1946 **Wmk. 276** **Photo.** ***Perf. 14***

Toned Paper

610	A198	10 l	brt red brn	.20	.20
611	A198	20 l	vio brn	.20	.20
612	A201	80 l	blue	.20	.20
613	A198	137 l	yel grn	.20	.20
614	A201	160 l	chalky bl	.20	.20
615	A201	200 l	red org	.20	.20
616	A201	300 l	sapphire	.20	.20
617	A201	360 l	sepia	.20	.20
618	A199	400 l	red org	.20	.20
619	A201	480 l	brn red	.20	.20
620	A201	600 l	dk ol grn	.20	.20
621	A201	1000 l	Prus grn	.20	.20
622	A198	1500 l	Prus grn	.20	.20
623	A201	2400 l	magenta	.20	.20
624	A201	3700 l	dull bl	.20	.20
			Nos. 610-624,B338 (16)	3.50	3.25

See No. B339.

Demetrius Cantemir — A219 Soccer — A222

Designs: 100 l, "Cultural Ties." 300 l, "Economic Ties."

1946, Oct. 20 ***Perf. 13½***

625	A219	80 l	dk brn	.20	.20
626	A219	100 l	dp bl	.20	.20
627	A219	300 l	bl blk	.20	.20
			Nos. 625-627 (3)	.60	.60

Romania-Soviet friendship. See Nos. B338-B339.

1946, Sept. 1 ***Perf. 11½, Imperf.***

Designs: 20 l, Diving. 50 l, Running. 80 l, Mountain climbing.

628	A222	10 l	dp blue	.35	.35
629	A222	20 l	brt red	.35	.35
630	A222	50 l	dp violet	.35	.35
631	A222	80 l	chocolate	.35	.35
			Nos. 628-631,B340,C26,CB6 (7)	3.40	3.65

Issued in sheets of 16.

Weaving — A226 Child Receiving Bread — A227

Transporting Relief Supplies — A228

CGM Congress Emblem — A229

Wmk. 276

1946, Nov. 20 **Photo.** ***Perf. 14***

636	A226	80 l	dk ol brn	.20	.20
			Nos. 636,B342-B345 (5)	1.00	1.00

Democratic Women's Org. of Romania. See No. CB7.

1947, Jan. 15 ***Perf. 13½x14, 14x13½***

637	A227	300 l	dk ol brn	.20	.20
638	A228	600 l	magenta	.20	.20
			Nos. 637-638,B346-B347 (4)	.80	.80

Social relief fund. See #B348.

1947, Feb. 10 ***Perf. 13½***

639	A229	200 l	blue	.20	.20
640	A229	300 l	orange	.20	.20
a.			Pair, #639-640	.30	.30
b.			Pair, #640-641	.30	.30
641	A229	600 l	crimson	.20	.20
			Nos. 639-641 (3)	.60	.60

Congress of the United Labor Unions ("CGM").

Printed in sheets of 18 comprising 3 pairs of each denomination. Sheet yields 3 each of Nos. 640a and 640b.

Peace in Chariot A230

Peace — A231 Flags of US, Russia, GB & Romania — A232

Dove of Peace — A233

1947, Feb. 25 ***Perf. 14x13½, 13½x14***

642	A230	300 l	dl vio	.20	.20
643	A231	600 l	dk org brn	.20	.20
644	A232	3000 l	blue	.20	.20
645	A233	7200 l	sage grn	.20	.20
			Nos. 642-645 (4)	.80	.80

Signing of the peace treaty of Feb. 10, 1947.

King Michael — A234

1947 ***Perf. 13½***

Size: 25x30mm

646	A234	3000 l	blue	.20	.20
647	A234	7200 l	dl vio	.20	.20
648	A234	15,000 l	brt bl	.20	.20
649	A234	21,000 l	magenta	.20	.20
650	A234	36,000 l	violet	.25	.20
			Nos. 646-650 (5)	1.05	1.00

See Nos. 661-664.

Michael Types of 1945

1947 Wmk. 276 Photo. ***Perf. 14***

651	A199	10 l	red brn	.20	.20
652	A200	20 l	magenta	.20	.20
653	A198	80 l	blue	.20	.20
654	A199	200 l	brt red	.20	.20
655	A198	500 l	magenta	.20	.20
656	A200	860 l	vio brn	.20	.20
657	A199	2500 l	ultra	.20	.20
658	A198	5000 l	sl gray	.20	.20
659	A198	8000 l	Prus grn	.35	.20
660	A201	10,000 l	dk brn	.25	.20

Type of 1947

Size: 18x21½mm

661	A234	1000 l	gray bl	.20	.20
662	A234	5500 l	yel grn	.20	.20
663	A234	20,000 l	ol brn	.20	.20
664	A234	50,000 l	red org	.35	.20
			Nos. 651-664 (14)	3.15	2.80

For surcharge see No. B368.

Harvesting Wheat A235

Designs: 1 l, Log raft. 2 l, River steamer. 3 l, Resita. 5 l, Cathedral of Curtea de Arges. 10 l, View of Bucharest. 12 l, 36 l, Cernavoda Bridge. 15 l, 32 l, Port of Constantsa. 20 l, Petroleum field.

1947, Aug. 15 ***Perf. 14½x14***

666	A235	50b	red org	.20	.20
667	A235	1 l	red brn	.20	.20
668	A235	2 l	bl gray	.20	.20
669	A235	3 l	rose crim	.20	.20
670	A235	5 l	brt ultra	.20	.20
671	A235	10 l	brt blue	.25	.20
672	A235	12 l	violet	.35	.20
673	A235	15 l	dp ultra	.55	.20
674	A235	20 l	dk brown	1.00	.25
675	A235	32 l	violet brn	2.00	.50
676	A235	36 l	dk car rose	2.00	.25
			Nos. 666-676 (11)	7.15	2.60

For overprints & surcharge see #684-694, B369.

Beehive, Savings Emblem — A236

1947, Oct. 31 ***Perf. 13½***

677	A236	12 l	dk car rose	.30	.20

World Savings Day, Oct. 31, 1947.

People's Republic

Map, Workers and Children A237

1948, Jan. 25 ***Perf. 14½x14***

678	A237	12 l	brt ultra	.30	.20

1948 census. For surcharge see #819A.

Government Printing Plant and Press — A238

1948 ***Perf. 14½x14***

679	A238	6 l	magenta	.90	.50
680	A238	7.50 l	dk Prus grn	.50	.20
	b.		Tête bêche pair	1.25	.90

75th anniversary of Stamp Division of Romanian State Printing Works.
Issued: No. 680, Feb. 12; No. 679, May 20.

Romanian and Bulgarian Peasants Shaking Hands A239

1948, Mar. 25 **Wmk. 276**

680A	A239	32 l	red brown	.50	.20

Romanian-Bulgarian friendship.
For surcharge see No. 696.

Allegory of the People's Republic — A240

1948, Apr. 8 Photo. ***Perf. 14x14½***

681	A240	1 l	car rose	.35	.20
682	A240	2 l	dl org	.35	.20
683	A240	12 l	deep blue	.50	.30
			Nos. 681-683 (3)	1.20	.70

New constitution.
For surcharge see No. 820.

Nos. 666 to 676 Overprinted in Black

R·P·R

1948, Mar. ***Perf. 14½x14***

684	A235	50b	red org	.30	.20
685	A235	1 l	red brn	.30	.20
686	A235	2 l	bl gray	.55	.20
687	A235	3 l	rose crim	.55	.20
688	A235	5 l	brt ultra	.75	.20
689	A235	10 l	brt bl	1.10	.20
690	A235	12 l	violet	1.25	.25
691	A235	15 l	dp ultra	1.25	.30
692	A235	20 l	dk brn	1.50	.50
693	A235	32 l	vio brn	4.50	1.50
694	A235	36 l	dk car rose	4.50	1.50
			Nos. 684-694 (11)	16.55	5.25

Romanian Newspapers — A241

1948, Sept. 12

695	A241	10 l	red brn	.30	.20
			Nos. 695,B396-B398 (4)	2.55	2.45

Week of the Democratic Press, Sept. 12-19.

No. 680A Surcharged with New Value in Black

1948, Aug. 17

696	A239	31 l	on 32 l red brn	.55	.20

Monument to Soviet Soldier — A242

Proclamation of Islaz — A243

1948, Oct. 29 Photo. ***Perf. 14x14½***

697	A242	10 l	dk red	.45	.30
			Nos. 697,B399-B400,CB16 (4)	10.70	10.55

Sheets of 50 stamps and 50 labels.

1948, June 1 ***Perf. 14½x14***

698	A243	11 l	car rose	.35	.20
			Nos. 698,B409-B412 (5)	2.60	2.45

Centenary of Revolution of 1848.
For surcharge see No. 820A.

Arms of Romanian People's Republic — A243a

1948, July 8 **Wmk. 276**

698A	A243a	50b	red ("Lei 0.50")	.40	.30
698B	A243a	1 l	red brn	.25	.20
698C	A243a	2 l	dk grn	.25	.20
698D	A243a	3 l	grnsh blk	.35	.20
698E	A243a	4 l	chocolate	.35	.20
698F	A243a	5 l	ultra	.35	.20
698G	A243a	10 l	dp bl	1.10	.20

"Bani" instead of "Lei"

698H	A243a	50b	red ("Bani 0.50")	.50	.20
			Nos. 698A-698H (8)	3.55	1.70

See Nos. 712-717.

Nicolae Balcescu (1819-1852), Writer — A244

1948, Dec. 20 **Wmk. 289**

699	A244	20 l	scarlet	.35	.20

Release from Bondage — A245

1948, Dec. 30 ***Perf. 13½***

700	A245	5 l	brt rose	.30	.20

First anniversary of the Republic.

Lenin, 25th Death Anniv. — A246

Folk Dance — A247

1949, Jan. 21

701	A246	20 l	black	.35	.20

Exists imperf.

1949, Jan. 24 ***Perf. 13½***

702	A247	10 l	dp bl	.35	.20

90th anniv. of the union of the Danubian Principalities.

Ion C. Frimu and Revolutionary Scene — A248

1949, Mar. 22 ***Perf. 14½x14***

703	A248	20 l	red	.35	.20

Exists imperf.

Aleksander S. Pushkin, 150th Birth Anniv. — A249

1949, May 20 ***Perf. 14x14½***

704	A249	11 l	car rose	.50	.20
705	A249	30 l	Prus grn	.70	.30

For surcharges see Nos. 821-822.

Globe and Post Horn — A250

Evolution of Mail Transportation — A251

Perf. 13½, 14½x14

1949, June 30 Photo. Wmk. 289

706	A250	20 l	org brn	1.50	.90
707	A251	30 l	brt bl	1.10	.60

UPU, 75th anniv.
For surcharges see Nos. C43-C44.

Russian Army Entering Bucharest, August, 1944
A252

1949, Aug. 23 ***Perf. 14½x14, Imperf.***

708 A252 50 l choc, *bl grn* .60 .25

5th anniv. of the liberation of Romania by the Soviet army, Aug. 1944.

"Long Live Romanian-Soviet Amity" — A253

1949, Nov. 1 ***Perf. 13½x14½***

709 A253 20 l dp red .35 .20

Natl. week of Romanian-Soviet friendship celebration, 11/1-7/49. Exists imperf.

Symbols of Transportation
A254

Joseph V. Stalin
A256

1949, Dec. 10 ***Perf. 13½***

710	A254	11 l blue	.55	.20
711	A254	20 l crimson	.55	.20

Intl. Conference of Transportation Unions, Dec. 10, 1949.

Alternate vertical rows of stamps and labels in sheet. Exist imperf.

Arms Type of 1948

1949-50 **Wmk. 289** ***Perf. 14x13½***

712	A243a	50b red ("Lei 0.50")	.35	.20
713	A243a	1 l red brn	.35	.20
714	A243a	2 l dk grn	.35	.20
714A	A243a	3 l grnsh blk	.65	.20
715	A243a	5 l ultra	.50	.20
716	A243a	5 l rose vio ('50)	.70	.20
717	A243a	10 l dp blue	.90	.20
		Nos. 712-717 (7)	3.80	1.40

1949, Dec. 21 ***Perf. 13½***

718 A256 31 l olive black .50 .20

Stalin's 70th birthday. Exists imperf.

Mihail Eminescu — A257

Poem: "Life" — A258

#721, "Third Letter." #722, "Angel and Demon." #723, "Emperor and Proletariat."

1950, Jan. 15 **Photo.** **Wmk. 289**

719	A257	11 l blue	.45	.20
720	A258	11 l purple	.75	.20
721	A258	11 l dk grn	.45	.45
722	A258	11 l red brn	.45	.20
723	A258	11 l rose pink	.45	.20
		Nos. 719-723 (5)	2.55	1.25

Birth cent. of Mihail Eminescu, poet.

For surcharges see Nos. 823-827.

Fair at Dragaica
A259

Ion Andreescu (Self-portrait)
A260

Village Well
A261

1950, Mar. 25 ***Perf. 14½x14, 14x14½***

724	A259	5 l dk gray grn	.40	.20
725	A260	11 l ultra	.75	.20
726	A261	20 l brown	.85	.45
		Nos. 724-726 (3)	2.00	.85

Birth cent. of Ion Andreescu, painter. No. 725 also exists imperf.

For surcharges see Nos. 827A-827B.

Graph and Factories
A262

Design: 31 l, Tractor and Oil Derricks.

Inscribed: "Planul de Stat 1950."

Perf. 14½x14

1950, Apr. 23 **Wmk. 289**

727	A262	11 l red	.60	.20
728	A262	31 l violet	.85	.30

1950 plan for increased industrial production. No. 727 exists imperf.

For surcharges see Nos. 827C-827D.

Young Man Holding Flag
A263

Arms of Republic
A264

1950, May 1 ***Perf. 14x14½***

729 A263 31 l orange red .75 .20

Labor Day, May 1. Exists imperf.

For surcharge see No. 827E.

Canceled to Order

Canceled sets of new issues have long been sold by the government. Values in the second ("used") column are for these canceled-to-order stamps. Postally used copies are worth more.

1950 **Photo.** ***Perf. 12½***

730	A264	50b black	.20	.20
731	A264	1 l red	.20	.20
732	A264	2 l ol gray	.20	.20
733	A264	3 l violet	.20	.20
734	A264	4 l rose lilac	.20	.20
735	A264	5 l red brn	.20	.20
736	A264	6 l dp grn	.20	.20
737	A264	7 l vio brn	.20	.20
738	A264	7.50 l blue	.20	.20
739	A264	10 l dk brn	.45	.20
740	A264	11 l rose car	.45	.20
741	A264	15 l dp bl	.30	.20
742	A264	20 l Prus grn	.30	.20
743	A264	31 l dl grn	.45	.20
744	A264	36 l dk org brn	.75	.30
		Nos. 730-744 (15)	4.50	3.10

See Nos. 947-961 which have similar design with white denomination figures.

For overprint & surcharges see #758, 828-841.

Bugler and Drummer
A265

Designs: 11 l, Three school children. 31 l, Drummer, flag-bearer and bugler.

1950, May 25 ***Perf. 14½x14***

745	A265	8 l blue	.45	.30
746	A265	11 l rose vio	.75	.45
747	A265	31 l org ver	1.50	.90
		Nos. 745-747 (3)	2.70	1.65

Young Pioneers, 1st anniv.

For surcharges see Nos. 841A-841C.

Factory Worker — A266

Aurel Vlaicu and his First Plane — A267

1950, July 20 **Photo.** ***Perf. 14x14½***

748	A266	11 l red brn	.30	.20
749	A266	11 l red	.30	.20
750	A266	11 l blue	.30	.20
751	A266	11 l blk brn	.30	.20
		Nos. 748-751 (4)	1.20	.80

Nationalization of industry, 2nd anniv.

1950, July 22 **Wmk. 289** ***Perf. 12½***

752	A267	3 l dk grn	.35	.20
753	A267	6 l dk bl	.40	.20
754	A267	8 l ultra	.40	.20
		Nos. 752-754 (3)	1.15	.60

Aurel Vlaicu (1882-1913), pioneer of Romanian aviation.

For surcharges see Nos. 842-844.

Mother and Child — A268

Lathe and Operator — A269

1950, Sept. 9 ***Perf. 13½***

755	A268	11 l rose red	.30	.20
756	A269	20 l dk ol brn	.30	.20

Congress of the Committees for the Struggle for Peace.

For surcharge see No. 844A.

Statue of Soviet Soldier — A270

1950, Oct. 6 ***Perf. 14x14½***

757 A270 30 l red brn .45 .20

Celebration of Romanian-Soviet friendship, Oct. 7-Nov. 7, 1950.

No. 741 Overprinted in Carmine

TRĂIASCĂ
PRIETENIA
ROMÂNO-
MAGHIĂRAI

1950, Oct. 6 ***Perf. 12½***

758 A264 15 l deep blue .40 .20

Romanian-Hungarian friendship.

"Agriculture," "Manufacturing" and Sports Badge — A271

5 l, Student workers & badge. 11 l, Track team & badge. 31 l, Calisthenics & badge.

1950, Oct. 30 ***Perf. 14½x14***

759	A271	3 l rose car	.55	.45
760	A271	5 l red brn	.45	.30
761	A271	5 l brt bl	.45	.30
762	A271	11 l green	.45	.30
763	A271	31 l brn ol	1.10	.75
		Nos. 759-763 (5)	3.00	2.10

For surcharge see No. 845.

A272

"Industry" — A273

"Agriculture" — A274

1950, Nov. 2 ***Perf. 13½***

764	A272	11 l blue	.30	.20
765	A272	11 l red org	.30	.20

3rd Soviet-Romanian Friendship Congress.

Perf. 14x14½, 14½x14

1951, Feb. 9 **Photo.** **Wmk. 289**

766	A273	11 l red brn	.20	.20
767	A274	31 l deep bl	.40	.20

Industry and Agriculture Exposition. Exist imperf.

For surcharge see No. 846.

Ski Jump — A275

Ski Descent A276

5 l, Skating. 20 l, Hockey. 31 l, Bobsledding.

1951, Jan. 28 ***Perf. 13½***

768 A275 4 l blk brn .30 .20
769 A275 5 l vermilion .45 .20
770 A276 11 l dp bl .85 .20
771 A275 20 l org brn .90 .50
772 A275 31 l dk gray grn 2.00 1.00
Nos. 768-772 (5) 4.50 2.10

9th World University Winter Games.
For surcharges see Nos. 847-848.

Medal for Work — A277

Orders: 4 l, Star of the Republic, Classes III, IV & V. 11 l, Work. 35 l, As 4 l, Classes I & II.

1951, May 1 ***Perf. 13½***

773 A277 2 l ol gray .30 .20
774 A277 4 l blue .30 .20
775 A277 11 l crimson .30 .20
776 A277 35 l org brn .35 .20
Nos. 773-776 (4) 1.25 .80

Labor Day. Exist imperf.
For surcharges see Nos. 849-852.

Camp of Young Pioneers A278

Pioneers Greeting Stalin — A279

Admitting New Pioneers A280

1951, May 8 ***Perf. 14x14½, 14½x14***

777 A278 1 l gray grn .90 .40
778 A279 11 l blue .90 .20
779 A280 35 l red .75 .20
Nos. 777-779 (3) 2.55 .80

Romanian Young Pioneers Organization.
For surcharge see No. 853.

Woman Orator and Flags — A281

Ion Negulici — A282

1951, Mar. 8 ***Perf. 14x14½***

780 A281 11 l org brn .35 .20

Woman's Day, March 8. Exists imperf.

1951, June 20 ***Perf. 14x14½***

781 A282 35 l rose red .75 .45

Death cent. of Ion Negulici, painter.

Bicyclists A283

1951, July 9 ***Perf. 14½x14***

782 A283 11 l chnt brn 1.60 .50
a. Tête bêche pair 4.00 3.25

The 1951 Bicycle Tour of Romania.

Festival Badge — A284

Boy and Girl with Flag — A285

Youths Encircling Globe — A286

1951, Aug. 1 ***Perf. 13½***

783 A284 1 l scarlet .50 .20
784 A285 5 l deep blue .50 .20
785 A286 11 l deep plum .65 .50
Nos. 783-785 (3) 1.65 .90

3rd World Youth Festival, Berlin.

Filimon Sarbu — A287

"Romania Raising the Masses" — A288

"Revolutionary Romania" — A289

1951, July 23 ***Perf. 14x14½***

786 A287 11 l dk brn .30 .20

10th death anniv. of Filimon Sarbu, patriot.

1951, July 23 ***Perf. 14x14½, 14½x14***

787 A288 11 l yel brn 1.00 .25
788 A288 11 l rose vio 1.00 .25
789 A289 11 l dk grn 1.00 .25
790 A289 11 l org red 1.00 .25
Nos. 787-790 (4) 4.00 1.00

Death cent. of C. D. Rosenthal, painter.

Scanteia Building A290

1951, Aug. 16 ***Perf. 14½x14***

791 A290 11 l blue .35 .20

20th anniv. of the newspaper Scanteia.

Miner in Dress Uniform — A291

Order for National Defense — A293

Design: 11 l, Miner in work clothes.

1951, Aug. 12 ***Perf. 14x14½***

792 A291 5 l blue .25 .20
793 A291 11 l plum .25 .20

Miner's Day. For surcharge see #854.

1951, Aug. 12 ***Perf. 14x14½***

794 A293 10 l crimson .50 .20

For surcharge see No. 855.

Choir — A294

Music Week Emblem — A295

Design: No. 796, Orchestra and dancers.

Wmk. 358

1951, Sept. 22 **Photo.** ***Perf. 13½***

795 A294 11 l blue .35 .20
796 A294 11 l red brown .50 .30
797 A295 11 l purple .35 .20
Nos. 795-797 (3) 1.20 .70

Music Week, Sept. 22-30, 1951.

Soldier — A296

Oil Field — A297

1951, Oct. 2

798 A296 11 l blue .30 .20

Army Day, Oct. 2, 1951.

1951-52

Designs: 2 l, Coal mining. 3 l, Romanian soldier. 4 l, Smelting ore. 5 l, Agricultural machinery. 6 l, Canal construction. 7 l, Agriculture. 8 l, Self-education. 11 l, Hydroelectric production. 35 l, Manufacturing.

799 A297 1 l black brn .20 .20
800 A297 2 l chocolate .20 .20
801 A297 3 l scarlet .35 .20
802 A297 4 l yel brn ('52) .20 .20
803 A297 5 l green .35 .20
804 A297 6 l brt bl ('52) 1.25 .40
805 A297 7 l emerald .50 .40
806 A297 8 l brown ('52) .50 .40
807 A297 11 l blue .35 .20
808 A297 35 l purple 1.40 .80
Nos. 799-808,C35-C36 (12) 8.80 6.20

1951-55 Five Year Plan.
2 l and 11 l exist with wmk. 289.
For surcharges see Nos. 860-869.

Arms of Soviet Union and Romania — A298

1951, Oct. 7 **Wmk. 358**

809 A298 4 l chestnut brn, *cr* .35 .20
810 A298 35 l orange red .90 .45

Month of Romanian-Soviet friendship, Oct. 7-Nov. 7.
For surcharges see Nos. 870-871.

Pavel Tcacenco A299

Railroad Conductor A300

1951, Dec. 15 ***Perf. 14x14½***

811 A299 10 l ol brn & dk brn .35 .20

Revolutionary, 26th death anniv.
For surcharge see No. 872.

1952, Mar. 24 ***Perf. 13½***

812 A300 55b dark brown 1.50 .45

Railroad Workers' Day, Feb. 16.

Ion L. Caragiale — A301

Announcing Caragiale Celebration A302

Designs: No. 814, Book and painting "1907." No. 815, Bust and wreath.

1952, Apr. 1 ***Perf. 13½, 14½x14***

Inscribed: ". . . . I. L. Caragiale."

813 A301 55b chalky blue .85 .20
814 A302 55b scarlet .85 .20
815 A302 55b deep green .85 .20
816 A302 1 l brown 2.50 .25
Nos. 813-816 (4) 5.05 .85

Birth cent. of Ion L. Caragiale, dramatist.
For surcharges see Nos. 817-819.

Types of 1952 Surcharged with New Value in Black or Carmine

1952-53

817 A302 20b on 11 l scar (as #814) .60 .40
818 A302 55b on 11 l dp grn (as #815) (C) .75 .50
819 A301 75b on 11 l chlky bl (C) 1.25 .60

Various Issues Surcharged with New Values in Carmine or Black

On No. 678, Census

Perf. 14x13½

819A A237 50b on 12 l ultra 6.75 3.75

On No. 683, New Constitution

Perf. 14

820 A240 50b on 12 l dp bl 2.50 1.25

On No. 698, Revolution

820A A243 1.75 l on 11 l car rose (Bk) 25.00 12.00

On Nos. 704-705, Pushkin

1952 **Wmk. 358**

821 A249 10b on 11 l (Bk) 2.50 1.75
822 A249 10b on 30 l 2.50 1.75

On Nos. 719-723, Eminescu

Perf. 13½x13, 13x13½

823 A257 10b on 11 l blue 2.25 1.75
824 A258 10b on 11 l pur 2.25 1.75
825 A258 10b on 11 l dk grn 2.25 1.75
826 A258 10b on 11 l red brn (Bk) 2.25 1.75
827 A258 10b on 11 l rose pink (Bk) 3.50 1.75

On Nos. 724-725, Andreescu

Perf. 14

827A A259 55b on 5 l dk gray grn 7.50 2.75
827B A260 55b on 11 l ultra 5.00 2.75

On Nos. 727-728, Production Plan

Perf. 14½x14

827C A262 20b on 11 l red (Bk) 2.00 .75
827D A262 20b on 31 l vio 2.00 .75

On No. 729, Labor Day

Perf. 14

827E A263 55b on 31 l (Bk) 3.00 2.75

On Nos. 730-739 and 741-744, National Arms

Perf. 12½

828 A264 3b on 1 l red (Bk) .70 .45
829 A264 3b on 2 l ol gray (Bk) 1.10 .55
830 A264 3b on 4 l rose lil (Bk) .70 .30
831 A264 3b on 5 l red brn (Bk) 1.10 .55
832 A264 3b on 7.50 l bl (Bk) 3.25 1.40
833 A264 3b on 10 l dk brn (Bk) 1.10 .55
834 A264 55b on 50b blk brn 3.25 .45
835 A264 55b on 3 l vio 3.25 .45
836 A264 55b on 6 l dp grn 3.25 .45
837 A264 55b on 7 l vio brn 3.25 .45
838 A264 55b on 15 l dp bl 5.00 .45
839 A264 55b on 20 l Prus grn 3.25 .45
840 A264 55b on 31 l dl grn 3.25 .45
841 A264 55b on 36 l dk org brn 5.00 .45

On Nos. 745-747, Young Pioneers

Perf. 14

841A A265 55b on 8 l 10.00 5.75
841B A265 55b on 11 l 10.00 5.75
841C A265 55b on 31 l (Bk) 10.00 5.75

On Nos. 752-754, Vlaicu

Perf. 12½

842 A267 10b on 3 l dk grn 1.50 .75
843 A267 10b on 6 l dk bl 1.50 .75
844 A267 10b on 8 l ultra 1.50 .75

Original denomination canceled with an "X."

On No. 756, Peace Congress

Perf. 13½

844A A269 20b on 20 l 2.25 1.25

On No. 759, Sports

Perf. 14½x14

845 A271 55b on 3 l (Bk) 15.00 11.50

On No. 767, Exposition

846 A274 55b on 31 l dp bl 9.00 5.75

On Nos. 771-772, Winter Games

Perf. 13½

847 A275 55b on 20 l (Bk) 25.00 8.00
848 A275 55b on 31 l 25.00 8.00

On Nos. 773-776, Labor Medals

849 A277 20b on 2 l 3.75 2.25
850 A277 20b on 4 l 3.75 2.25
851 A277 20b on 11 l (Bk) 3.75 2.25
852 A277 20b on 35 l (Bk) 3.75 2.25

On Nov. 779, Young Pioneers

Perf. 14x14½

853 A280 55b on 35 l (Bk) 15.00 9.50

On No. 792, Miners' Day

854 A291 55b on 5 l bl 11.00 7.50

On No. 794, Defense Order

855 A293 55b on 10 l (Bk) 6.00 3.75

On Nos. B409-B412, 1848 Revolution

1952 **Wmk. 276** ***Perf. 13x13½***

856 SP280 1.75 l on 2 l + 2 l (Bk) 9.50 3.75
857 SP281 1.75 l on 5 l + 5 l 9.50 3.75
858 SP282 1.75 l on 10 l + 10 l 9.50 3.75
859 SP280 1.75 l on 36 l + 18 l 9.50 3.75

On Nos. 799-808, 5-Year Plan

Wmk. 358 ***Perf. 13½***

860 A297 35b on 1 l blk brn 1.90 .65
861 A297 35b on 2 l choc 6.00 .75
862 A297 35b on 3 l scar (Bk) 3.00 1.25
863 A297 35b on 4 l yel brn (Bk) 3.50 1.50
a. Red surcharge 15.00 8.00
864 A297 35b on 5 l grn 3.00 2.00
865 A297 1 l on 6 l brt bl 4.75 3.00
866 A297 1 l on 7 l emer 3.50 1.50
867 A297 1 l on 8 l brn 3.50 2.25
868 A297 1 l on 11 l bl 4.75 1.75
869 A297 1 l on 35 l pur 4.75 1.50

Nos. 861, 868 exist with wmk. 289.

On Nos. 809-810, Romanian-Soviet Friendship

870 A298 10b on 4 l (Bk) 1.50 .65
871 A298 10b on 35 l (Bk) 1.50 .65

On No. 811, Tcacenco

Perf. 13½x14

872 A299 10b on 10 l 1.90 .90
Nos. 817-872 (67) 350.60 165.00

A302a

A303

Perf. 13½x13

1952, Apr. 14 **Photo.** **Wmk. 358**

873 A302a 1 l Ivan P. Pavlov 1.60 .50

Meeting of Romanian-Soviet doctors in Bucharest.

1952, May 1

874 A303 55b Hammer & sickle medal .75 .20

Labor Day.

Medal for Motherhood A304

Leonardo da Vinci A305

Medals: 55b, Maternal glory. 1.75 l, Mother-Heroine.

1952, Apr. 7 ***Perf. 13x13½***

875 A304 20b plum & sl gray .30 .20
876 A304 55b henna brn .70 .20
877 A304 1.75 l rose red & brn buff 1.75 .40
Nos. 875-877 (3) 2.75 .80

International Women's Day.

1952, July 3

878 A305 55b purple 2.10 .50

500th birth anniv. of Leonardo da Vinci.

Gogol and Scene from Taras Bulba A306

Nikolai V. Gogol — A307

1952, Apr. 1 ***Perf. 13½x14, 14x13½***

879 A306 55b deep blue 1.00 .20
880 A307 1.75 l olive gray 1.50 .40

Gogol, Russian writer, death cent.

Pioneers Saluting — A308

Labor Day Paraders Returning A309

Design: 55b, Pioneers studying nature.

1952, May 21 ***Perf. 14***

881 A308 20b brown .45 .20
882 A308 55b dp green 1.25 .20
883 A309 1.75 l blue 2.10 .40
Nos. 881-883 (3) 3.80 .80

Third anniversary of Romanian Pioneers.

Infantry Attack, Painting by Grigorescu A310

Miner — A311

1.10 l, Romanian and Russian soldiers.

1952, June 7 ***Perf. 13x13½***

884 A310 50b rose brown .45 .20
885 A310 1.10 l blue .75 .25

Independence Proclamation of 1877, 75th anniv.

1952, Aug. 11 **Wmk. 358**

902 A311 20b rose red 1.25 .25
903 A311 55b purple 1.25 .20

Day of the Miner.

Book and Globe — A312

Students in Native Dress — A314

Chemistry Student A313

Design: 55b, Students playing soccer.

Perf. 13½x13, 13½x14, 13x13½

1952, Sept. 5

904 A312 10b deep blue .20 .20
905 A313 20b orange .70 .20
906 A312 55b deep green 2.00 .25
907 A314 1.75 l rose red 3.00 .50
Nos. 904-907 (4) 5.90 1.15

Intl. Student Union Congr., Bucharest, Sept.

Soldier, Sailor and Aviator — A316

1952, Oct. 2 ***Perf. 14***

909 A316 55b blue .50 .20

Armed Forces Day, Oct. 2, 1952.

"Russia" Leading Peace Crusade — A317

Allegory: Romanian-Soviet Friendship — A318

1952, Oct. 7 ***Perf. 13½x13, 13x13½***

910 A317 55b vermilion .65 .20
911 A318 1.75 l black brown 1.60 .65

Month of Romanian-Soviet friendship, Oct.

Rowing on Lake Snagov — A319

Nicolae Balcescu — A320

1.75 l, Athletes marching with flags.

1952, Oct. 20

912	A319	20b	deep blue	3.00	.50
913	A319	1.75 l	rose red	5.50	1.10

Values are for copies with poor perforations.

1952, Nov. 29

914	A320	55b	gray	2.00	.50
915	A320	1.75 l	lemon bister	4.00	1.25

Death cent. of Nicolae Balcescu, poet.

Arms of Republic — A321

1952, Dec. 6 **Wmk. 358**

916 A321 55b dull green .75 .25

5th anniversary of socialist constitution.

Arms and Industrial Symbols A322

1953, Jan. 8 ***Perf. 12½x13½***

917 A322 55b blue, yellow & red .90 .35

5th anniv. of the proclamation of the People's Republic.

Matei Millo, Costache Caragiale and Aristita Romanescu A323

1953, Feb. **Photo.** ***Perf. 13x13½***

918 A323 55b brt ultra 1.50 .35

National Theater of I. L. Caragiale, cent.

Iron Foundry Worker — A324

Worker — A325

Design: No. 921, Driving Tractor.

1953, Feb. ***Perf. 13½x13, 13x13½***

919	A324	55b	slate green	.30	.20
920	A325	55b	black brown	.30	.20
921	A325	55b	orange	.65	.25
			Nos. 919-921 (3)	1.25	.65

3rd Congress of the Syndicate of the Romanian People's Republic.

"Strike at Grivita," Painted by G. Miclossy A326

Arms of Romanian People's Republic A327

1953, Feb. 16 ***Perf. 13x13½***

922 A326 55b chestnut 1.25 .25

Oil industry strike, Feb. 16, 1933, 20th anniv.

1953 ***Perf. 12½***

923	A327	5b	crimson	.25	.20
924	A327	55b	purple	.75	.20

Flags of Romania and Russia, Farm Machinery A328

1953, Mar. 24 ***Perf. 14***

925 A328 55b dk brn, *bl* .95 .25

5th anniv. of the signing of a treaty of friendship and mutual assistance between Russia and Romania.

Map and Medal — A329

Rug — A330

Folk Dance - A330a

1953, Mar. 24

926	A329	55b	dk gray green	1.75	.40
927	A329	55b	chestnut	2.25	.40

20th World Championship Table Tennis Matches, Budapest, 1953.

1953

Designs: 10b, Ceramics. 20b, Costume of Campulung (Muscel). 55b, Apuseni Mts. costume.

Inscribed: "Arta Populara Romaneasca"

928	A330	10b	deep green	.75	.20
929	A330	20b	red brown	1.25	.20
929A	A330a	35b	purple	2.00	.20
930	A330	55b	violet blue	3.00	.20
931	A330	1 l	brt red violet	5.00	.25
			Nos. 928-931 (5)	12.00	1.05

Romanian Folk Arts.

Karl Marx — A331

Children Planting Tree — A332

Physics Class A333

1953, May 21 ***Perf. 13½x13***

932 A331 1.55 l olive brown 1.40 .45

70th death anniv. of Karl Marx.

1953, May 21 ***Perf. 14***

Design: 55b, Flying model planes.

933	A332	35b	deep green	1.00	.20
934	A332	55b	dull blue	1.40	.20
935	A333	1.75 l	brown	3.25	.45
			Nos. 933-935 (3)	5.65	.85

Women and Flags A334

Discus Thrower A335

Students Offering Teacher Flowers A336

1953, June 18 ***Perf. 13½x13***

936 A334 55b red brown 1.00 .20

3rd World Congress of Women, Copenhagen, 1953.

1953, Aug. 2 **Wmk. 358** ***Perf. 14***

Designs: 55b, Students reaching toward dove. 1.75 l, Dance in local costumes.

937	A335	20b	orange	.50	.20
938	A335	55b	deep blue	.90	.20
939	A336	65b	scarlet	1.25	.35
940	A336	1.75 l	red violet	3.50	.50
			Nos. 937-940 (4)	6.15	1.25

4th World Youth Festival, Bucharest, 8/2-16.

Waterfall — A337

Wheat Field — A338

Design: 55b, Forester holding seedling.

1953, July 29 **Photo.**

941	A337	20b	violet blue	.55	.20
942	A338	38b	dull green	1.40	.50
943	A337	55b	lt brown	1.50	.20
			Nos. 941-943 (3)	3.45	.90

Month of the Forest.

Vladimir V. Mayakovsky, 60th Birth Anniv. — A339

1953, Aug. 22

944 A339 55b brown .75 .20

Miner Using Drill A340

1953, Sept. 19

945 A340 1.55 l slate black 1.40 .40

Miners' Day.

Arms of Republic — A342

1952-53 ***Perf. 12½***

Size: 20x24mm

947	A342	3b	deep orange	.60	.20
948	A342	5b	crimson	.80	.20
949	A342	7b	dk blue grn	.80	.20
950	A342	10b	chocolate	1.00	.20
951	A342	20b	deep blue	1.25	.20
952	A342	35b	black brn	2.75	.20
953	A342	50b	dk gray grn	3.25	.20
954	A342	55b	purple	7.25	.20

Size: 24x29mm

955	A342	1.10 l	dk brown	6.50	.30
956	A342	1.75 l	violet	24.00	.40
957	A342	2 l	olive black	6.50	.50
958	A342	2.35 l	orange brn	8.00	.35
959	A342	2.55 l	dp orange	10.00	.40
960	A342	3 l	dk gray grn	10.00	.35
961	A342	5 l	deep crimson	12.00	.60
			Nos. 947-961 (15)	94.70	4.50

Stamps of similar design with value figures in color are Nos. 730-744.

Postal Administration Building and Telephone Employees — A343

Designs: 55b, Postal Adm. Bldg. and Letter carrier. 1 l, Map and communications symbols. 1.55 l, Postal Adm. Bldg. and Telegraph employees.

1953, Oct. 20 **Wmk. 358** ***Perf. 14***

964	A343	20b	dk red brn	.20	.20
965	A343	55b	olive green	.30	.20
966	A343	1 l	brt blue	.75	.20
967	A343	1.55 l	rose brown	1.10	.40
			Nos. 964-967 (4)	2.35	1.00

50th anniv. of the construction of the Postal Administration Building.

Liberation Medal — A344

Soldier and Flag — A345

1953, Oct. 20 ***Perf. 14x13½***
968 A344 55b dark brown .70 .20

9th anniv. of the liberation of Romania.

1953, Oct. 2 ***Perf. 13½***
969 A345 55b olive green .70 .25

Army Day, Oct. 2.

Girl with Model Plane A346

Civil Aviation: 20b, Parachute landing. 55b, Glider and pilot. 1.75 l, Plane in flight.

1953, Oct. 20 ***Perf. 14***

970	A346	10b org & dk gray grn	2.25	.30
971	A346	20b org brn & dk ol grn	4.50	.20
972	A346	55b dk scar & rose lil	7.25	.50
973	A346	1.75 l dk rose vio & brn	9.50	.75
		Nos. 970-973 (4)	23.50	1.75

Workers and Flags — A347

1.55 l, Spasski Tower, lock on Volga-Don Canal.

1953, Nov. 25 ***Perf. 13x13½***
974 A347 55b brown .50 .20
975 A347 1.55 l rose brown .70 .25

Month of Romanian-Soviet friendship, Oct. 7-Nov. 7.

Hemispheres and Clasped Hands — A348

Workers, Flags and Globe — A349

1953, Nov. 25 ***Perf. 14***
976 A348 55b dark olive .40 .20
977 A349 1.25 l crimson .90 .30

World Congress of Trade Unions.

Ciprian Porumbescu A350

Harvesting Machine A351

1953, Dec. 16
978 A350 55b purple 4.00 .45

Ciprian Porumbescu (1853-1883), composer.

Perf. 13x13½
1953, Dec. 16 **Wmk. 358**

Designs: 35b, Tractor in field. 2.55 l, Cattle.

979	A351	10b sepia	.30	.20
980	A351	35b dark green	.40	.20
981	A351	2.55 l orange brown	3.50	.75
		Nos. 979-981 (3)	4.20	1.15

Aurel Vlaicu — A352

Lenin — A353

1953, Dec. 26 ***Perf. 14***
982 A352 50b violet blue .75 .20

Vlaicu, aviation pioneer, 40th death anniv.

1954, Jan. 21 ***Perf. 13½***
983 A353 55b dk red brn, *buff* .75 .20

30th death anniv. of Lenin.

Red Deer — A354

Designs: 55b, Children planting trees. 1.75 l, Mountain scene.

1954, Apr. 1
Yellow Surface-colored Paper

984	A354	20b dark brown	1.50	.20
985	A354	55b violet	1.50	.20
986	A354	1.75 l dark blue	3.25	.45
		Nos. 984-986 (3)	6.25	.85

Month of the Forest.

Calimanesti Rest Home — A355

Workers' Rest Homes: 1.55 l, Sinaia. 2 l, Predeal. 2.35 l, Tusnad. 2.55 l, Govora.

1954, Apr. 15 ***Perf. 14***

987	A355	5b blk brn, *cream*	.30	.20
988	A355	1.55 l dk vio brn, *bl*	.90	.20
989	A355	2 l dk grn, *pink*	1.40	.20
990	A355	2.35 l ol blk, *grnsh*	1.40	.45
991	A355	2.55 l dk red brn, *cit*	2.00	.65
		Nos. 987-991 (5)	6.00	1.70

Octav Bancila — A356

Globe, Child, Dove and Flowers A357

1954, May 26 ***Perf. 13½***
992 A356 55b red brn & dk grn 2.75 1.00

10th death anniv. of Octav Bancila, painter.

1954, June 1 ***Perf. 13x13½***
993 A357 55b brown 1.25 .25

Children's Day, June 1.

Girl Feeding Calf A358

Designs: 55b, Girl holding sheaf of grain. 1.75 l, Young students.

1954, July 5 ***Perf. 14***

994	A358	20b grnsh blk	.25	.20
995	A358	55b blue	.60	.20
996	A358	1.75 l car rose	1.75	.30
		Nos. 994-996 (3)	2.60	.70

Stephen the Great — A359

Loading Coal on Conveyor Belt — A360

1954, July 10
997 A359 55b violet brown 1.50 .40

Stephen of Moldavia (1433?-1504).

1954, Aug. 8 ***Perf. 13x13½***
998 A360 1.75 l black 1.50 .40

Miners' Day.

Victor Babes — A361

Applicant Requesting Loan — A362

1954, Aug. 15 ***Perf. 14***
999 A361 55b rose red 1.50 .40

Birth cent. of Victor Babes, serologist.

1954, Aug. 20

Design: 55b, Mutual aid declaration.

1000 A362 20b deep violet .25 .20
1001 A362 55b dk redsh brn .45 .20

5th anniv. of the Mutual Aid Organization.

Sailor and Naval Scene — A363

Monument to Soviet Soldier — A364

1954, Aug. 19 ***Perf. 13x13½***
1002 A363 55b deep blue .90 .25

Navy Day.

1954, Aug. 23 ***Perf. 13½x13***
1003 A364 55b scarlet & purple .90 .25

10th anniv. of Romania's liberation.

House of Culture A365

Academy of Music, Bucharest — A366

Aviator — A367

55b, Scanteia building. 1.55 l, Radio station.

1954, Sept. 6 ***Perf. 14, 13½x13***

1004	A365	20b violet blue	.20	.20
1005	A366	38b violet	.40	.20
1006	A365	55b violet brown	.40	.20
1007	A366	1.55 l red brown	.75	.20
		Nos. 1004-1007 (4)	1.75	.80

Publicizing Romania's cultural progress during the decade following liberation.

Perf. 13½x13
1954, Sept. 13 **Wmk. 358**
1008 A367 55b blue .90 .40

Aviation Day.

Chemical Plant and Oil Derricks A368

Dragon Pillar, Peking — A369

1954, Sept. 21 ***Perf. 13x13½***

1009 A368 55b gray 1.25 .25

Intl. Conference of chemical and petroleum workers, Bucharest, Sept. 1954.

1954, Oct. 7 ***Perf. 14***

1010 A369 55b dk ol grn, *cream* 1.25 .25

Week of Chinese Culture.

Dumitri T. Neculuta — A370

ARLUS Emblem — A371

1954, Oct. 17 ***Perf. 13½x13***

1011 A370 55b purple 1.10 .25

Neculuta, poet, 50th death anniv.

1954, Oct. 22 ***Perf. 14***

65b, Romanian & Russian women embracing.

1012 A371 55b rose carmine .45 .20
1013 A371 65b dark purple .65 .20

Month of Romanian-Soviet Friendship.

Gheorghe Tattarescu A372

Barbu Iscovescu A373

1954, Oct. 24 ***Perf. 13½x13***

1014 A372 55b cerise 1.40 .40

Gheorghe Tattarescu (1820-1894), painter.

1954, Nov. 3 ***Perf. 14***

1015 A373 1.75 l red brown 2.50 .50

Death cent. of Barbu Iscovescu, painter.

Wild Boar — A374

Globe and Clasped Hands — A375

Month of the Forest: 65b, Couple planting tree. 1.20 l, Logging.

Perf. 13½x13

1955, Mar. 15 **Wmk. 358**

1016 A374 35b brown .50 .20
1017 A374 65b turq blue .90 .25
1018 A374 1.20 l dark red 1.75 .55
Nos. 1016-1018 (3) 3.15 1.00

1955, Apr. 5 **Photo.**

1019 A375 25b carmine rose .35 .20

Intl. Conference of Universal Trade Unions (Federation Syndicale Mondiale), Vienna, Apr. 1955.

Teletype — A376

Lenin — A377

1955, Dec. 20 ***Perf. 13½x13***

1020 A376 50b lilac .45 .20

Romanian telegraph system, cent.

1955, Apr. 22 ***Perf. 13½x14***

Various Portraits of Lenin.

1021 A377 20b ol bis & brn .20 .20
1022 A377 55b copper brown .40 .20
1023 A377 1 l vermilion .60 .20
Nos. 1021-1023 (3) 1.20 .60

85th anniversary of the birth of Lenin.

Chemist A378

Volleyball A379

Designs: 5b, Steelworker. 10b, Aviator. 20b, Miner. 30b, Tractor driver. 35b, Pioneer. 40b, Girl student. 55b, Mason. 1 l, Sailor. 1.55 l, Spinner. 2.35 l, Soldier. 2.55 l, Electrician.

1955-56 **Wmk. 358** ***Perf. 14***

1024 A378 3b blue .20 .20
1025 A378 5b violet .20 .20
1026 A378 10b chocolate .20 .20
1027 A378 20b lilac rose .25 .20
1027A A378 30b vio bl ('56) .40 .20
1028 A378 35b grnsh blue .30 .20
1028A A378 40b slate .70 .20
1029 A378 55b ol gray .40 .20
1030 A378 1 l purple .75 .20
1031 A378 1.55 l brown lake 1.40 .20
1032 A378 2.35 l bister brn 2.10 .35
1033 A378 2.55 l slate 2.25 .25
Nos. 1024-1033 (12) 9.15 2.60

1955, June 17

Design: 1.75 l, Woman volleyball player.

1034 A379 55b red vio, *pink* 1.40 .50
1035 A379 1.75 l lil rose, *cr* 3.50 .50

European Volleyball Championships, Bucharest.

Globe, Flag and Dove — A379a

Girls with Dove and Flag — A380

1955, May 7 **Photo.** ***Perf. 13½***

1035A A379a 55b ultra .75 .20

Peace Congress, Helsinki.

1955, June 1 ***Perf. 13½x14***

1036 A380 55b dark red brown .70 .20

International Children's Day, June 1.

Russian War Memorial, Berlin — A381

Theodor Aman Museum A382

1955, May 9

1037 A381 55b deep blue .60 .20

Victory over Germany, 10th anniversary.

1955, June 28 ***Perf. 13½, 14***

Bucharest Museums: 55b, Lenin and Stalin Museum. 1.20 l, Popular Arts Museum. 1.75 l, Arts Museum. 2.55 l, Simu Museum.

1038 A382 20b rose lilac .25 .20
1039 A382 55b brown .30 .20
1040 A382 1.20 l gray black .45 .30
1041 A382 1.75 l slate green .80 .30
1042 A382 2.55 l rose violet 1.50 .40
Nos. 1038-1042 (5) 3.30 1.40

#1038, 1040, 1042 measure 29x24½mm, #1039, 1041 32½x23mm.

Sharpshooter A383

1955, Sept. 11 ***Perf. 13½***

1043 A383 1 l pale brn & sepia 3.50 .45

European Sharpshooting Championship meeting, Bucharest, Sept. 11-18.

Fire Truck, Farm and Factory — A384

1955, Sept. 13 **Wmk. 358**

1044 A384 55b carmine .55 .25

Firemen's Day, Sept. 13.

Bishop Dosoftei A385

Mother and Child — A386

Romanian writers: #1046, Stolnicul Constantin Cantacuzino. #1047, Dimitrie Cantemir. #1048, Enachita Vacarescu. #1049, Anton Pann.

1955, Sept. 9 **Photo.**

1045 A385 55b bluish gray .75 .30
1046 A385 55b dp vio .75 .30
1047 A385 55b ultra .75 .30
1048 A385 55b rose vio .75 .30
1049 A385 55b ol gray .75 .30
Nos. 1045-1049 (5) 3.75 1.50

1955, July 7 ***Perf. 13½x14***

1050 A386 55b ultra .60 .20

World Congress of Mothers, Lausanne.

Pioneers and Train Set — A387

Rowing — A388

Designs: 20b, Pioneers studying nature. 55b, Home of the Pioneers.

1955 ***Perf. 12½***

1051 A387 10b brt ultra .20 .20
1052 A387 20b grnsh bl .45 .20
1053 A387 55b dp plum 1.25 .20
Nos. 1051-1053 (3) 1.90 .60

Fifth anniversary of the Pioneer headquarters, Bucharest.

1955, Aug. 22 ***Perf. 13x13½***

1054 A388 55b shown 3.25 .50
1055 A388 1 l Sculling 6.00 .70

European Women's Rowing Championship on Lake Snagov, Aug. 4-7.

Insect Pest Control A389

I. V. Michurin — A390

20b, Orchard. 55b, Vineyard. 1 l, Truck garden.

1955, Oct. 15 *Perf. 14x13½*

1056	A389	10b brt grn	.25	.20
1057	A389	20b lil rose	.30	.20
1058	A389	55b vio bl	.70	.20
1059	A389	1 l dp claret	1.25	.40
		Nos. 1056-1059 (4)	2.50	1.00

Quality products of Romanian agriculture. See Nos. 1068-1071.

1955, Oct. 25 *Perf. 13½x14*

1060	A390	55b Prus bl	.75	.20

Birth cent. of I. V. Michurin, Russian agricultural scientist.

Congress Emblem A391

Globes and Olive Branches — A392

1955, Oct. 20 *Perf. 13x13½*

1061	A391	20b cream & ultra	.30	.20

4th Soviet-Romanian Cong., Bucharest, Oct.

1955, Oct. 1 *Perf. 13½x13*

1 l, Three workers holding FSM banner.

1062	A392	55b dk ol grn	.30	.20
1063	A392	1 l ultra	.45	.20

Intl. Trade Union Org. (Federation Syndicale Mondiale), 10th anniv.

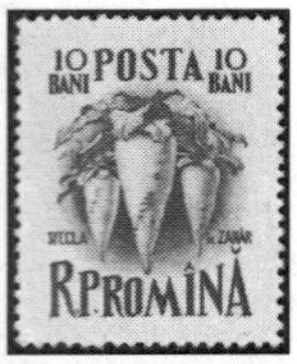

Sugar Beets — A393

Sheep and Shepherd A394

20b, Cotton. 55b, Flax. 1.55l, Sunflower.

1955, Nov. 10 *Perf. 13½*

1064	A393	10b plum	.30	.20
1065	A393	20b sl grn	.40	.20
1066	A393	55b brt ultra	1.25	.25
1067	A393	1.55 l dk red brn	2.75	.35
		Nos. 1064-1067 (4)	4.70	1.00

1955, Dec. 10 *Perf. 14x13½*

Stock Farming: 10b, Pigs. 35b, Cattle. 55b, Horses.

1068	A394	5b yel grn & brn	.30	.20
1069	A394	10b ol bis & dk vio	.60	.20
1070	A394	35b brick red & brn	1.25	.20
1071	A394	55b dk ol bis & brn	2.50	.40
		Nos. 1068-1071 (4)	4.65	1.00

Animal husbandry.

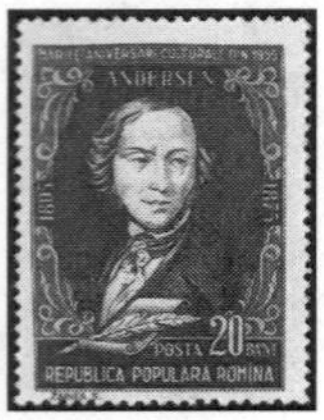

Hans Christian Andersen — A395

Portraits: 55b, Adam Mickiewicz. 1 l, Friedrich von Schiller. 1.55 l, Baron de Montesquieu. 1.75 l, Walt Whitman. 2 l, Miguel de Cervantes.

Perf. 13½x14

1955, Dec. 17 **Engr.** **Unwmk.**

1072	A395	20b sl bl	.30	.20
1073	A395	55b dp ultra	.50	.20
1074	A395	1 l grnsh blk	.65	.20
1075	A395	1.55 l vio brn	1.75	.35
1076	A395	1.75 l dl vio	2.00	.65
1077	A395	2 l rose lake	2.00	.65
		Nos. 1072-1077 (6)	7.20	2.25

Anniversaries of famous writers.

Bank Book and Savings Bank A396

Perf. 14x13½

1955, Dec. 29 **Photo.** **Wmk. 358**

1078	A396	55b dp vio	1.25	.50
1079	A396	55b blue	.60	.20

Advantages of systematic saving in a bank.

Census Date — A397

Design: 1.75 l, Family group.

Inscribed: "Recensamintul Populatiei"

1956, Feb. 3 *Perf. 13½*

1080	A397	55b dp org	.30	.20
1081	A397	1.75 l emer & red brn	.85	.25
a.		Center inverted	*200.00*	*200.00*

National Census, Feb. 21, 1956.

Ring-necked Pheasant A398

Great Bustard — A399

Street Fighting, Paris, 1871 — A400

Animals: No. 1082, Hare. No. 1083, Bustard. 35b, Trout. 50b, Boar. No. 1087, Brown bear. 1 l, Lynx. 1.55 l, Red squirrel. 2 l, Chamois. 3.25 l, Pintail (duck). 4.25 l, Fallow deer.

1956 **Wmk. 358** *Perf. 14*

1082	A398	20b grn & blk	1.40	.30
1083	A399	20b cit & gray blk	1.40	.30
1084	A399	35b brt bl & blk	1.40	.30
1085	A398	50b dp ultra & brn blk	1.40	.50
1086	A398	55b ol bis & ind	1.60	.50
1087	A398	55b dk bl grn & dk red brn	1.60	.50
1088	A398	1 l dk grn & red brn	3.00	.85
1089	A399	1.55 l lt ultra & red brn	3.25	1.25
1090	A399	1.75 l sl grn & dk brn	3.75	1.75
1091	A398	2 l ultra & brn blk	14.00	6.50
1092	A398	3.25 l lt grn & blk brn	14.00	3.25
1093	A399	4.25 l brn org & dk brn	14.00	4.00
		Nos. 1082-1093 (12)	60.80	20.00

Exist imperf. in changed colors. Value, set $25.

1956, May 29 *Perf. 13½*

1094	A400	55b vermilion	.70	.20

85th anniversary of Commune of Paris.

Globe and Child — A400a

Oak Tree — A401

1956, June 1 **Photo.** *Perf. 13½x14*

1095	A400a	55b dp vio	.90	.25

Intl. Children's Day. The sheet of 100 contains 10 labels, each with "Peace" printed on it in one of 10 languages.

1956, June 11 **Litho.** **Wmk. 358**

Design: 55b, Logging train in timberland.

1096	A401	20b dk bl grn, *pale grn*	.50	.20
1097	A401	55b brn blk, *pale grn*	1.50	.50

Month of the Forest.

Romanian Academy A402

1956, June 19 **Photo.** *Perf. 14*

1098	A402	55b dk grn & dl yel	.75	.20

90th anniversary of Romanian Academy.

Red Cross Worker — A403

Woman Speaker and Globe — A404

1956, June 7

1099	A403	55b olive & red	1.25	.40

Romanian Red Cross Congress, June 7-9.

1956, June 14

1100	A404	55b dk bl grn	.70	.20

Intl. Conference of Working Women, Budapest, June 14-17.

Traian Vuia and Planes — A405

1956, June 21 *Perf. 13x13½*

1101	A405	55b grnsh blk & brn	.70	.20

1st flight by Vuia, near Paris, 50th anniv.

Ion Georgescu A406

1956, June 25 *Perf. 14x13½*

1102	A406	55b dk red brn & dk grn	1.25	.25

Ion Georgescu (1856-1898), sculptor.

White Cabbage Butterfly A407

June Bug — A408

Design: 55b, Colorado potato beetle.

1956, July 30 *Perf. 14x13½, 13½x14*

1103	A407	10b dp vio, pale yel & blk	3.25	.25
1104	A407	55b ol blk & yel	5.00	.30
1105	A408	1.75 l lt ol & dp plum	6.00	5.75
1106	A408	1.75 l gray ol & dk vio brn	6.00	.70
		Nos. 1103-1106 (4)	20.25	7.00

Campaign against insect pests.

Girl Holding Sheaf of Wheat — A409

Dock Workers on Strike — A410

1956 *Perf. 13½x14*

1107	A409	55b "1949-1956"	1.40	.25
a.		"1951-1956" (error)	2.75	2.00

7th anniversary of collective farming.

1956, Aug. 6

1108	A410	55b dk red brn	.45	.20

Dock workers' strike at Galati, 50th anniv.

Title Page and Printer — A411

Maxim Gorki — A412

1956, Aug. 13 *Perf. 13½*

1109	A411	55b ultra	.45	.20

25th anniv. of the publication of "Scanteia" (The Spark).

1956, Aug. 29 *Perf. 13½x14*

1110	A412	55b brown	.45	.20

Maxim Gorki (1868-1936), Russian writer.

Theodor Aman
A413

Primrose and Snowdrops
A414

1956, Sept. 24 **Engr.**

1111	A413	55b gray blk	.70	.25

Aman, painter, 125th birth anniv.

1956, Sept. 26 Photo. *Perf. 14x14½*

55b, Daffodil and violets. 1.75 l, Snapdragon and bellflowers. 3 l, Poppies and lilies of the valley.

Flowers in Natural Colors

1112	A414	5b bl, yel & red	.50	.20
1113	A414	55b blk, yel & red	1.00	.25
1114	A414	1.75 l ind, pink & yel	3.00	.40
1115	A414	3 l bl grn, dk bl grn & yel	4.00	.55
		Nos. 1112-1115 (4)	8.50	1.40

Olympic Rings and Torch — A415

Janos Hunyadi — A416

Designs: 55b, Water polo. 1 l, Gymnastics. 1.55 l, Canoeing. 1.75 l, High jump.

1956, Oct. 25 ***Perf. 13½x14***

1116	A415	20b vermilion	.30	.20
1117	A415	55b ultra	.50	.20
1118	A415	1 l lil rose	.75	.20
1119	A415	1.55 l lt bl grn	1.25	.20
1120	A415	1.75 l dp pur	1.50	.40
		Nos. 1116-1120 (5)	4.30	1.20

16th Olympic Games, Melbourne, 11/22-12/8.

1956, Oct. **Wmk. 358**

1121	A416	55b dp vio	.60	.25

Janos Hunyadi (1387-1456), national hero of Hungary. No. 1121 is found se-tenant with label showing Hunyadi Castle.

Benjamin Franklin — A417

George Enescu as a Boy — A418

Portraits: 35b, Sesshu (Toyo Oda). 40b, G. B. Shaw. 50b, Ivan Franco. 55b, Pierre Curie. 1 l, Henrik Ibsen. 1.55 l, Fedor Dostoevski. 1.75 l, Heinrich Heine. 2.55 l, Mozart. 3.25 l, Rembrandt.

1956 **Unwmk.**

1122	A417	20b vio bl	.20	.20
1123	A417	35b rose lake	.25	.20
1124	A417	40b chocolate	.30	.20
1125	A417	50b brn blk	.35	.20
1126	A417	55b dk ol	.40	.20
1127	A417	1 l dk bl grn	.75	.20
1128	A417	1.55 l dp pur	1.00	.20
1129	A417	1.75 l brt bl	1.50	.20
1130	A417	2.55 l rose vio	2.00	.35
1131	A417	3.25 l dk bl	2.25	.90
		Nos. 1122-1131 (10)	9.00	2.85

Great personalities of the world.

1956, Dec. 29 **Engr.**

Portrait: 1.75 l, George Enescu as an adult.

1132	A418	55b ultramarine	.45	.20
1133	A418	1.75 l deep claret	1.25	.25

75th birth anniv. of George Enescu, musician and composer.

A419

A420

Fighting Peasants, by Octav Bancila.

1957, Feb. 28 Photo. Wmk. 358

1134	A419	55b dk bl gray	.75	.20

50th anniversary of Peasant Uprising.

1957, Apr. 24 ***Perf. 13½x14***

1147	A420	55b brown	.45	.20
1148	A420	55b olive black	.70	.20

Enthronement of Stephen the Great, Prince of Moldavia, 500th anniv.

Dr. George Marinescu, Marinescu Institute and Congress Emblem — A421

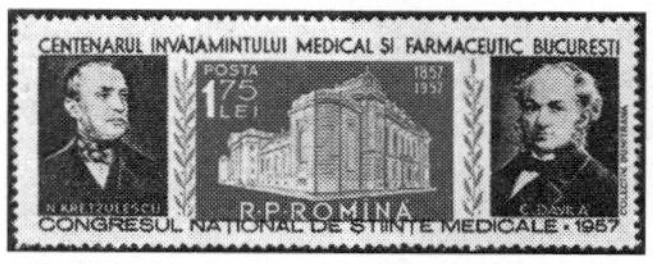

Dr. N. Kretzulescu, Medical School, Dr. C. Davila — A422

35b, Dr. I. Cantacuzino & Cantacuzino Hospital. 55b, Dr. V. Babes & Babes Institute.

1957, May 5 ***Perf. 14x13½***

1149	A421	20b dp grn	.20	.20
1150	A421	35b dp red brn	.30	.20
1151	A421	55b red lil	.50	.20
1152	A422	1.75 l brt ultra & dk red	1.40	.50
		Nos. 1149-1152 (4)	2.40	1.10

National Congress of Medical Science, Bucharest, May 5-6.

No. 1152 also for centenary of medical and pharmaceutical teaching in Bucharest. It measures 66x23mm.

Dove and Handle Bars — A423

1957, May 29 ***Perf. 13½x14***

1153	A423	20b shown	.20	.20
1154	A423	55b Cyclist	.50	.20

10th International Bicycle Peace Race.

Woman Watching Gymnast — A424

Woman Gymnast on Bar — A425

1957, May 21 ***Perf. 13½***

1155	A424	20b shown	.20	.20
1156	A425	35b shown	.35	.20
1157	A425	55b Vaulting horse	.70	.20
1158	A424	1.75 l Acrobat	1.75	.40
		Nos. 1155-1158 (4)	3.00	1.00

European Women's Gymnastic meet, Bucharest.

Slide Rule, Caliper & Atomic Symbol — A426

Rhododendron Hirsutum — A427

Wmk. 358

1957, May 29 Photo. *Perf. 14*

1159	A426	55b blue	.60	.20
1160	A426	55b brn red	1.00	.20

2nd Congress of the Society of Engineers and Technicians, Bucharest, May 29-31.

1957, June 22 Litho. Unwmk.

Carpathian Mountain Flowers: 10b, Daphne Blagayana. 20b, Lilium Bulbiferum L. 35b, Leontopodium Alpinum. 55b, Gentiana Acaulis L. 1 l, Dianthus Callizonus. 1.55 l, Primula Carpatica Griseb. 1.75 l, Anemone Montana Hoppe.

Light Gray Background

1161	A427	5b brt rose	.20	.20
1162	A427	10b dk grn	.30	.20
1163	A427	20b red org	.35	.20
1164	A427	35b olive	.50	.20
1165	A427	55b ultra	.65	.20
1166	A427	1 l red	1.00	.20
1167	A427	1.55 l yellow	2.00	.25
1168	A427	1.75 l dk pur	3.00	.40
		Nos. 1161-1168 (8)	8.00	1.85

Nos. 1161-1168 also come se-tenant with a decorative label.

"Oxcart" by Grigorescu
A428

Nicolae Grigorescu — A429

Painting: 1.75 l, Battle scene.

1957, June 29 Photo. Wmk. 358

1169	A428	20b dk bl grn	.40	.20
1170	A429	55b deep brown	.80	.20
1171	A428	1.75 l chalky blue	2.10	.60
		Nos. 1169-1171 (3)	3.30	1.00

Grigorescu, painter, 50th death anniv.

Warship
A430

1957, Aug. 3 ***Perf. 13x13½***

1172	A430	1.75 l Prus bl	1.10	.25

Navy Day.

Young Couple — A431

Festival Emblem — A432

Folk Dance — A433

Design: 55b, Girl with flags on hoop.

Perf. 14x14½, 14x14x12½ (A432), 13½x12½ (A433)

1957, July 28

1173	A431	20b red lilac	.20	.20
1174	A431	55b emerald	.30	.20
1175	A432	1 l red orange	.70	.25
1176	A433	1.75 l ultra	1.25	.20
		Nos. 1173-1176 (4)	2.45	.85

Moscow 1957 Youth Festival. No. 1173 measures 23x34mm, No. 1174 22x38mm.

No. 1175 was printed in sheets of 50, alternating with 40 labels inscribed "Peace and Friendship" in 20 languages.

Bugler — A434

Girl Holding Dove — A435

1957, Aug. 30 Wmk. 358 *Perf. 14*

1177	A434	20b brt pur	.65	.20

80th anniv. of the Russo-Turkish war.

1957, Sept. 3 ***Perf. 13½***

1178	A435	55b Prus grn & red	.65	.20

Honoring the Red Cross.

Battle Scene
A436

1957, Aug. 31

1179	A436	1.75 l brown	.65	.25

Battle of Marasesti, 40th anniv.

Jumper and Dove — A437

55b, Javelin thrower, bison. 1.75 l, Runner, stag.

1957, Sept. 14 Photo. *Perf. 13½*

1180 A437 20b brt bl & blk .30 .20
1181 A437 55b yel & blk .60 .20
1182 A437 1.75 l brick red & blk 2.00 .50
Nos. 1180-1182 (3) 2.90 .90

International Athletic Meet, Bucharest.

Statue of Ovid, Constanta A438

1957, Sept. 20 Photo. Wmk. 358

1183 A438 1.75 l vio bl 1.40 .35

2000th anniv. of the birth of the Roman poet Publius Ovidius Naso.

Oil Field — A439

Design: 55b, Horse pulling drill, 1857.

1957, Oct. 5

1184 A439 20b dl red brn .20 .20
1185 A439 20b indigo .20 .20
1186 A439 55b vio blk .50 .25
Nos. 1184-1186 (3) .90 .65

Centenary of Romanian oil industry.

Congress Emblem A440

1957, Sept. 28

1187 A440 55b ultra .40 .20

4th Intl. Trade Union Cong., Leipzig, 10/4-15.

Young Couple, Lenin Banner — A441

Endre Ady — A442

35b, Lenin & Flags. 55b, Lenin statue.

1957, Nov. 6 *Perf. 14x14½, 14½x14*

1188 A441 10b crimson .20 .20
1189 A441 35b plum, horiz. .25 .20
1190 A441 55b brown .35 .20
Nos. 1188-1190 (3) .80 .60

Russian Revolution, 40th anniversary.

1957, Dec. 5 *Perf. 14*

1191 A442 55b ol brn .55 .20

Ady, Hungarian poet, 80th birth anniv.

Oath of Bobilna A443

Bobilna Monument — A444

1957, Nov. 30

1192 A443 50b deep plum .30 .20
1193 A444 55b slate blue .40 .20

520th anniversary of the insurrection of the peasants of Bobilna in 1437.

Black-winged Stilt — A445

Animals: 10b, Great white egret. 20b, White spoonbill. 50b, Sturgeon. 55b, Ermine, horiz. 1.30 l, White pelican, horiz.

Perf. 13½x14, 14x13½

1957, Dec. 27 Photo. Wmk. 358

1194 A445 5b red brn & gray .20 .20
1195 A445 10b emer & ocher .20 .20
1196 A445 20b brt red & ocher .20 .20
1197 A445 50b bl grn & ocher .40 .20
1198 A445 55b dp cl & gray .45 .20
1199 A445 1.30 l pur & org 2.00 .30
Nos. 1194-1199,C53-C54 (8) 8.45 2.55

Sputnik 2 and Laika A446

1957, Dec. 20 *Perf. 14x13½*

1200 A446 1.20 l bl & dk brn 1.25 .35
1201 A446 1.20 l grnsh bl & choc 1.25 .35

Dog Laika, "first space traveler."

Romanian Arms, Flags — A447

Designs: 55b, Arms, "Industry and Agriculture." 1.20 l, Arms, "Art, Science and Sport (soccer)."

1957, Dec. 30 *Perf. 13½*

1202 A447 25b ultra, red & ocher .20 .20
1203 A447 55b dull yellow .35 .20
1204 A447 1.20 l crimson rose .55 .25
Nos. 1202-1204 (3) 1.10 .65

Proclamation of the Peoples' Republic, 10th anniv.

Flag and Wreath — A448

1958, Feb. 15 Unwmk. *Perf. 13½*

1205 A448 1 l dk bl & red, *buff* .40 .20
1206 A448 1 l brn & red, *buff* .40 .20

Grivita Strike, 25th anniversary.

Television, Radio Antennas A449

Design: 1.75 l, Telegraph pole and wires.

1958, Mar. 21 *Perf. 14x13½*

1207 A449 55b brt vio .30 .20
1208 A449 1.75 l dp mag .80 .25

Telecommunications Conference, Moscow, Dec. 3-17, 1957.

Nicolae Balcescu — A450

Romanian Writers: 10b, Ion Creanga. 35b, Alexandru Vlahuta. 55b, Mihail Eminescu. 1.75 l, Vasile Alecsandri. 2 l, Barbu S. Delavrancea.

1958 Wmk. 358 *Perf. 14x14½*

1209 A450 5b bluish blk .20 .20
1210 A450 10b int blk .20 .20
1211 A450 35b dk bl .20 .20
1212 A450 55b dk red brn .35 .20
1213 A450 1.75 l blk brn .70 .20
1214 A450 2 l dk sl grn 1.25 .20
Nos. 1209-1214 (6) 2.90 1.20

See Nos. 1309-1314.

Fencer in Global Mask A451

1958, Apr. 5 *Perf. 14½x14*

1215 A451 1.75 l brt pink 1.10 .25

Youth Fencing World Championships, Bucharest.

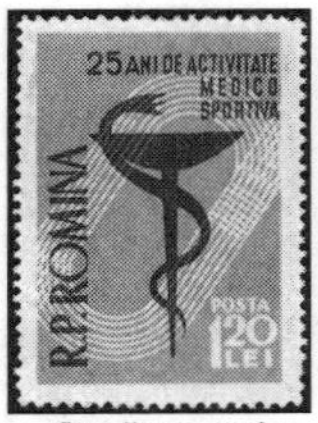

Stadium and Health Symbol — A452

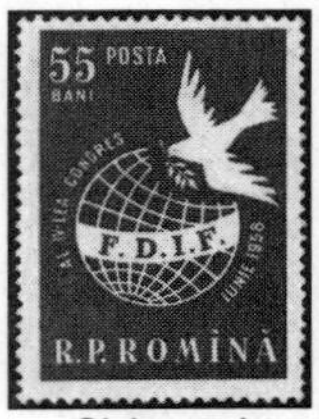

Globe and Dove — A453

1958, Apr. 16 *Perf. 14x14½*

1216 A452 1.20 l lt grn & red .85 .20

25 years of sports medicine.

1958, May 15 Photo.

1217 A453 55b brt bl .50 .20

4th Congress of the Intl. Democratic Women's Federation, June 1958.

Carl von Linné — A454

Clavaria Aurea — A456

Portraits: 20b, Auguste Comte. 40b, William Blake. 55b, Mikhail I. Glinka. 1 l, Henry W. Longfellow. 1.75 l, Carlo Goldoni. 2 l, Jan A. Komensky.

Perf. 14x14½

1958, May 31 Unwmk.

1218 A454 10b Prus grn .20 .20
1219 A454 20b brown .20 .20
1220 A454 40b dp lil .30 .20
1221 A454 55b dp bl .40 .20
1222 A454 1 l dp mag .60 .20
1223 A454 1.75 l dp vio bl .90 .20
1224 A454 2 l olive 1.60 .30
Nos. 1218-1224 (7) 4.20 1.50

Great personalities of the world.

1958, July Litho. Unwmk.

Mushrooms: 5b, Lepiota Procera. 20b, Amanita caesarea. 30b, Lactarius deliciosus. 35b, Armillaria mellea. 55b, Coprinus comatus. 1 l, Morchella conica. 1.55 l, Psalliota campestris. 1.75 l, Boletus edulis. 2 l, Cantharellus cibarius.

1225 A456 5b gray bl & brn .20 .20
1226 A456 10b ol, ocher & brn .20 .20
1227 A456 20b gray, red & yel .20 .20
1228 A456 30b grn & dp org .20 .20
1229 A456 35b lt bl & yel brn .20 .20
1230 A456 55b pale grn, fawn & brn .35 .20
1231 A456 1 l bl grn, ocher & brn .50 .20
1232 A456 1.55 l gray, lt gray & pink .85 .20
1233 A456 1.75 l emer, brn & buff 1.00 .20
1234 A456 2 l dl bl & org yel 1.90 .25
Nos. 1225-1234 (10) 5.60 2.05

Antarctic Map and Emil Racovita A457

Design: 1.20 l, Cave and Racovita.

1958, July 30 Photo. *Perf. 14½x14*

1235 A457 55b indigo & lt bl .50 .20
1236 A457 1.20 l ol bis & dk vio 1.00 .20

90th birth anniv. of Emil Racovita, explorer and naturalist.

Armed Forces Monument — A458

Designs: 75b, Soldier guarding industry. 1.75 l, Sailor raising flag and ship.

1958, Oct. 2 ***Perf. 13½x13***

1237 A458 55b orange brown .20 .20
1238 A458 75b deep magenta .20 .20
1239 A458 1.75 l bright blue .50 .25
Nos. 1237-1239,C55 (4) 2.00 1.05

Armed Forces Day.

Woman & Man from Oltenia — A459

Regional Costumes: 40b, Tara Oasului. 50b, Transylvania. 55b, Muntenia. 1 l, Banat. 1.75 l, Moldavia. Pairs: 'a' woman, 'b' man.

1958 Unwmk. Litho. ***Perf. 13½x14***

1240 A459 35b Pair, #a.-b. + label .40 .20
1241 A459 40b Pair, #a.-b. + label .40 .20
1242 A459 50b Pair, #a.-b. + label .50 .20
1243 A459 55b Pair, #a.-b. + label .80 .20
1244 A459 1 l Pair, #a.-b. + label 1.50 .40
1245 A459 1.75 l Pair, #a.-b. + label 2.00 .50
Nos. 1240-1245 (6) 5.60 1.70

Exist imperf. Value, set $16.

Printer and Hand Press A461

Moldavia Stamp of 1858 A462

55b, Scissors cutting strips of 1858 stamps. 1.20 l, Postilion, mail coach. 1.30 l, Postilion blowing horn, courier on horseback. 1.75 l, 2 l, 3.30 l, Various denominations of 1858 issue.

1958, Nov. 15 Engr. ***Perf. 14½x14***

1252 A461 35b vio bl .20 .20
1253 A461 55b dk red brn .35 .20
1254 A461 1.20 l dull bl .70 .20
1255 A461 1.30 l brown vio .90 .20
1256 A462 1.55 l gray brn 1.00 .20
1257 A462 1.75 l rose claret 1.10 .25
1258 A462 2 l dull vio 1.40 .45
1259 A462 3.30 l dull red brn 2.10 .55
Nos. 1252-1259 (8) 7.75 2.25

Cent. of Romanian stamps. See No. C57.
Exist imperf. Value, set $13.

Bugler — A463 Runner — A464

1958, Dec. 10 Photo. ***Perf. 13½x13***

1260 A463 55b crimson rose .50 .20

Decade of teaching reforms.

Perf. 13½x14

1958, Dec. 9 Wmk. 358

1261 A464 1 l deep brown .90 .25

Third Youth Spartacist Sports Meet.

Building and Flag — A465

Prince Alexandru Ioan Cuza A466

1958, Dec. 16

1262 A465 55b dk car rose .30 .20

Workers' Revolution, 40th anniversary.

Perf. 14x13½

1959, Jan. 27 Unwmk.

1263 A466 1.75 l dk blue .60 .25

Centenary of the Romanian Union.

Friedrich Handel — A467 Corn — A468

Sheep A469

Portraits: No. 1265, Robert Burns. No. 1266, Charles Darwin. No. 1267, Alexander Popov. No. 1268, Shalom Aleichem.

1959, Apr. 25 Photo. ***Perf. 13½x14***

1264 A467 55b brown .30 .20
1265 A467 55b indigo .30 .20
1266 A467 55b slate .30 .20
1267 A467 55b carmine .30 .20
1268 A467 55b purple .30 .20
Nos. 1264-1268 (5) 1.50 1.00

Various cultural anniversaries in 1959.

Perf. 13½x14, 14x13½

1959, June 1 Photo. Wmk. 358

No. 1270, Sunflower and bee. No. 1271, Sugar beet and refinery. No. 1273, Cattle. No. 1274, Rooster and hens. No. 1275, Tractor and grain. No. 276, Loaded farm wagon. No. 1277, Farm couple and "10."

1269 A468 55b brt green .30 .20
1270 A468 55b red org .30 .20
1271 A468 55b red lilac .30 .20
1272 A469 55b olive grn .30 .20
1273 A469 55b red brown .30 .20
1274 A469 55b yellow brn .30 .20
1275 A469 55b blue .30 .20
1276 A469 55b brown .30 .20

Unwmk.

1277 A469 5 l dp red lilac 3.00 .65
Nos. 1269-1277 (9) 5.40 2.25

10th anniv. of collective farming. Sizes: #1272-1276 33x23mm; #1277 38x27mm.

Young Couple — A470

Steel Worker and Farm Woman — A471

Design: 1.60 l, Dancer in folk costume.

Perf. 13½x14

1959, July 15 Unwmk.

1278 A470 1 l brt blue .35 .20
1279 A470 1.60 l car rose .70 .20

7th World Youth Festival, Vienna, 7/26-8/14.

1959, Aug. 23 Litho. ***Perf. 13½x14***

1280 A471 55b multicolored .50 .20
a. Souvenir sheet of 1 .70 .25

15th anniv. of Romania's liberation from the Germans.

No. 1280a is ungummed and imperf. The blue, yellow and red vignette shows large "XV" and Romanian flag. Brown 1.20 l denomination and inscription in margin.

Prince Vlad Tepes and Document — A472

Designs: 40b, Nicolae Balcescu Street. No. 1283, Atheneum. No. 1284, Printing Combine. 1.55 l, Opera House. 1.75 l, Stadium.

1959, Sept. 20 Photo.

Centers in Gray

1281 A472 20b blue .60 .20
1282 A472 40b brown .90 .20
1283 A472 55b bister brn 1.00 .20
1284 A472 55b rose lilac 1.25 .25
1285 A472 1.55 l pale violet 2.75 .50
1286 A472 1.75 l bluish grn 3.00 .75
Nos. 1281-1286 (6) 9.50 2.10

500th anniversary of the founding of Bucharest. See No. C71.

No. 1261 Overprinted with Shield in Silver, inscribed: "Jocurile Bucaresti Balcanice 1959"

1959, Sept. 12 Wmk. 358

1287 A464 1 l deep brown 3.25 3.25

Balkan Games.

Soccer — A473

Motorcycle Race — A474

1959 Unwmk. Litho. ***Perf. 13½***

1288 A473 20b shown .20 .20
1289 A474 35b shown .25 .20
1290 A474 40b Ice hockey .30 .20
1291 A473 55b Field ball .35 .20
1292 A473 1 l Horse race .50 .20
1293 A473 1.50 l Boxing .85 .20
1294 A474 1.55 l Rugby 1.00 .20
1295 A474 1.60 l Tennis 1.25 .25
Nos. 1288-1295,C72 (9) 6.45 2.05

Russian Icebreaker "Lenin" A475

Perf. 14½x13½

1959, Oct. 25 Photo.

1296 A475 1.75 l blue vio 1.10 .25

First atomic ice-breaker.

Stamp Album and Magnifying Glass — A476

1959, Nov. 15 Wmk. 358 ***Perf. 14***

1297 A476 1.60 l + 40b label 1.10 .40

Issued for Stamp Day.

Stamp and label were printed alternately in sheet. The 40b went to the Romanian Association of Philatelists.

Purple Foxglove — A477

1959, Dec. 15 Typo. Unwmk.

Medicinal Flowers in Natural Colors

1298 A477 20b shown .20 .20
1299 A477 40b Peppermint .20 .20
1300 A477 55b Cornflower .25 .20
1301 A477 55b Daisies .30 .20
1302 A477 1 l Autumn crocus .40 .20
1303 A477 1.20 l Monkshood .50 .20
1304 A477 1.55 l Poppies .70 .20
1305 A477 1.60 l Linden .80 .25
1306 A477 1.75 l Dog rose .90 .25
1307 A477 3.20 l Buttercup 1.75 .40
Nos. 1298-1307 (10) 6.00 2.30

Cuza University, Jassy, Centenary
A478

1960, Nov. 26 Photo. Wmk. 358
1308 A478 55b brown .40 .20

Romanian Writers Type of 1958

20b, Gheorghe Cosbuc. 40b, Ion Luca Caragiale. 50b, Grigore Alexandrescu. 55b, Alexandru Donici. 1 l, Costache Negruzzi. 1.55 l, Dimitrie Bolintineanu.

1960, Jan. 20 ***Perf. 14***
1309 A450 20b bluish blk .20 .20
1310 A450 40b dp lilac .25 .20
1311 A450 50b brown .30 .20
1312 A450 55b violet brn .35 .20
1313 A450 1 l violet .60 .20
1314 A450 1.55 l dk blue 1.10 .30
Nos. 1309-1314 (6) 2.80 1.30

Huchen (Salmon) — A480

Woman, Dove and Globe — A481

55b, Greek tortoise. 1.20 l, Shelduck.

1960, Feb. 1 Engr. Unwmk.
1315 A480 20b blue .20 .20
1316 A480 55b brown .30 .20
1317 A480 1.20 l dk purple .75 .20
Nos. 1315-1317,C76-C78 (6) 4.85 1.60

1960, Mar. 1 Photo. ***Perf. 14***
1318 A481 55b violet blue .50 .20

50 years of Intl. Women's Day, Mar. 8.

A482

A483

40b, Lenin. 55b, Lenin statue, Bucharest. 1.55 l, Head of Lenin.

1960, Apr. 22 Wmk. 358 ***Perf. 13½***
1319 A482 40b magenta .25 .20
1320 A482 55b violet blue .35 .20

Souvenir Sheet

1321 A482 1.55 l carmine 1.40 1.00

90th birth anniv. of Lenin.

1960, May 9 Wmk. 358 ***Perf. 14***
1322 A483 40b Heroes Monument .35 .20
1323 A483 55b Soviet war memorial .35 .25
a. Strip of 2, #1322-1323 + label 1.60 .65

15th anniversary of the liberation.

Nos. 1322-1323 exist imperf., printed in deep magenta. Value, set $3.25; label strip, $4.50.

Swimming
A484

Sports: 55b, Women's gymnastics. 1.20 l, High jump. 1.60 l, Boxing. 2.45 l, Canoeing.

1960, June Unwmk. Typo. ***Perf. 14***

Gray Background

1326 A484 40b blue & yel .35 .25
1327 A484 55b blk, yel & emer .40 .30
1328 A484 1.20 l emer & brick red .95 .70
a. Strip of 3, #1326-1328 1.75
1329 A484 1.60 l blue, yel & blk 1.75 1.25
1330 A484 2.45 l blk, emer & brick red 1.75 1.25
a. Pair, #1329-1330 + 2 labels 3.50
Nos. 1326-1330 (5) 5.20 3.75

17th Olympic Games, Rome, 8/25-9/11.

Nos. 1326-1330 were printed in one sheet, the top half containing No. 1328a, the bottom half No. 1330a, with gutter between. When the two strips are placed together, the Olympic rings join in a continuous design.

Exist imperf. (3.70 l replaced 2.45 l). Value, set $7.75.

Swimming — A485

Olympic Flame, Stadium — A486

40b, Women's gymnastics. 55b, High jump. 1 l, Boxing. 1.60 l, Canoeing. 2 l, Soccer.

1960 Photo. Wmk. 358
1331 A485 20b chalky blue .20 .20
1332 A485 40b dk brn red .30 .20
1333 A485 55b blue .45 .20
1334 A485 1 l rose red .60 .20
1335 A485 1.60 l rose lilac .75 .20
1336 A485 2 l dull violet 1.40 .30
Nos. 1331-1336 (6) 3.70 1.30

Souvenir Sheets

Perf. 11½

1337 A486 5 l ultra 4.50 2.25

Imperf

1338 A486 6 l dull red 7.25 3.75

17th Olympic Games.

A487

A488

Perf. 13½

1960, June 20 Unwmk. Litho.
1339 A487 55b red org & dk car .40 .20

Romanian Workers' Party, 3rd congress.

1960 Wmk. 358 Photo. ***Perf. 14***

Portraits: 10b, Leo Tolstoy. 20b, Mark Twain. 35b, Hokusai. 40b, Alfred de Musset. 55b, Daniel Defoe. 1 l, Janos Bolyai. 1.20 l, Anton Chekov. 1.55 l, Robert Koch. 1.75 l, Frederick Chopin.

1340 A488 10b dull pur .20 .20
1341 A488 20b olive .20 .20
1342 A488 35b blue .20 .20
1343 A488 40b slate green .20 .20
1344 A488 55b dull brn vio .40 .20
1345 A488 1 l Prus grn .70 .20
1346 A488 1.20 l dk car rose .90 .20
1347 A488 1.55 l gray blue 1.25 .20
1348 A488 1.75 l brown 1.40 .25
Nos. 1340-1348 (9) 5.45 1.85

Various cultural anniversaries.

Students
A489

Piano and Books
A490

Designs: 5b, Diesel locomotive. 10b, Dam. 20b, Miner with drill. 30b, Ambulance and doctor. 35b, Textile worker. 50b, Nursery. 55b, Timber industry. 60b, Harvester. 75b, Feeding cattle. 1 l, Atomic reactor. 1.20 l, Oil derricks. 1.50 l, Coal mine. 1.55 l, Loading ship. 1.60 l, Athlete. 1.75 l, Bricklayer. 2 l, Steam roller. 2.40 l, Chemist. 3 l, Radio and television.

1960 Wmk. 358 Photo. ***Perf. 14***
1349 A489 3b brt lil rose .20 .20
1350 A489 5b olive bis .20 .20
1351 A489 10b violet gray .20 .20
1352 A489 20b blue vio .20 .20
1353 A489 30b vermilion .20 .20
1354 A489 35b crimson .20 .20
1355 A490 40b ocher .20 .20
1356 A489 50b bluish vio .20 .20
1357 A489 55b blue .20 .20
1358 A490 60b green .20 .20
1359 A490 75b gray ol .30 .20
1360 A489 1 l car rose .50 .20
1361 A489 1.20 l black .40 .20
1362 A489 1.50 l plum .50 .20
1363 A490 1.55 l Prus grn .50 .20
1364 A490 1.60 l dp blue .55 .20
1365 A489 1.75 l red brown .65 .20
1366 A489 2 l dk ol gray .80 .20
1367 A489 2.40 l brt lilac 1.00 .20
1368 A489 3 l grysh blue 1.50 .20
Nos. 1349-1368,C86 (21) 9.95 4.20

Ovid Statue at Constanta
A491

Black Sea Resorts: 35b, Constanta harbor. 40b, Vasile Rosita beach and vase. 55b, Ionian column and Mangalia beach. 1 l, Eforie at night. 1.60 l, Eforie and sailboat.

1960, Aug. 2 Litho. Unwmk.
1369 A491 20b multicolored .20 .20
1370 A491 35b multicolored .20 .20
1371 A491 40b multicolored .20 .20
1372 A491 55b multicolored .25 .20
1373 A491 1 l multicolored .60 .20
1374 A491 1.60 l multicolored .90 .20
Nos. 1369-1374,C87 (7) 3.60 1.60

Emblem — A492

Petrushka, Russian Puppet — A493

Designs: Various Puppets.

1960, Aug. 20 Typo.
1375 A492 20b multi .20 .20
1376 A493 40b multi .20 .20
1377 A493 55b multi .20 .20
1378 A493 1 l multi .40 .20
1379 A493 1.20 l multi .40 .20
1380 A493 1.75 l multi .60 .20
Nos. 1375-1380 (6) 2.00 1.20

International Puppet Theater Festival.

Children on Sled — A494

Globe and Peace Banner — A495

Children's Sports: 35b, Boys playing ball, horiz. 55b, Ice skating, horiz. 1 l, Running. 1.75 l, Swimming, horiz.

Unwmk.

1960, Oct. 1 Litho. ***Perf. 14***
1381 A494 20b multi .20 .20
1382 A494 35b multi .20 .20
1383 A494 55b multi .25 .20
1384 A494 1 l multi .35 .20
1385 A494 1.75 l multi .75 .20
Nos. 1381-1385 (5) 1.75 1.00

Perf. 13½x14

1960, Nov. 26 Photo. Wmk. 358
1386 A495 55b brt bl & yel .25 .20

Intl. Youth Federation, 15th anniv.

Worker and Flags
A496

Perf. 14x13

1960, Nov. 26 Litho. Unwmk.
1387 A496 55b dk car & red org .30 .20

40th anniversary of the general strike.

Carp
A497

Fish: 20b, Pikeperch. 40b, Black Sea turbot. 55b, Allis shad. 1 l, Wels (catfish). 1.20 l, Sterlet. 1.60 l, Huchen (salmon).

1960, Dec. 5 Typo.
1388 A497 10b multi .20 .20
1389 A497 20b multi .20 .20
1390 A497 40b multi .25 .20
1391 A497 55b multi .30 .20
1392 A497 1 l multi .70 .20
1393 A497 1.20 l multi .70 .20
1394 A497 1.60 l multi 1.00 .25
Nos. 1388-1394 (7) 3.35 1.45

Kneeling Woman and Grapes — A498

Steelworker by I. Irimescu — A499

Designs: 30b, Farmers drinking, horiz. 40b, Loading grapes into basket, horiz. 55b, Woman cutting grapes. 75b, Vintner with basket. 1 l, Woman filling basket with grapes. 1.20 l, Vintner with jug. 5 l, Antique wine jug.

1960, Dec. 20 Litho. *Perf. 14*

1395	A498	20b brn & gray	.20	.20
1396	A498	30b red org & pale grn	.20	.20
1397	A498	40b dp ultra & gray ol	.25	.20
1398	A498	55b emer & buff	.35	.20
1399	A498	75b dk car rose & pale grn	.35	.20
1400	A498	1 l Prus grn & gray ol	.45	.20
1401	A498	1.20 l org brn & pale bl	.75	.25
		Nos. 1395-1401 (7)	2.55	1.45

Souvenir Sheet

Imperf

1402	A498	5 l dk car rose & bis	3.25	1.50

Each stamp represents a different wine-growing region: Dragasani, Dealul Mare, Odobesti, Cotnari, Tirnave, Minis, Murfatlar and Pietroasa.

Perf. 13½x14, 14x13½

1961, Feb. 16 Photo. Unwmk.

Modern Sculptures: 10b, G. Doja, I. Vlad. 20b, Meeting, B. Caragea. 40b, George Enescu, A. Angnel. 50b, Mihail Eminescu, C. Baraschi. 55b, Peasant Revolt, 1907, M. Constantinescu, horiz. 1 l, "Peace," I. Jalea. 1.55 l, Building Socialism, C. Medrea. 1.75 l, Birth of an Idea, A. Szobotka.

1403	A499	5b car rose	.20	.20
1404	A499	10b violet	.20	.20
1405	A499	20b ol blk	.20	.20
1406	A499	40b ol bis	.20	.20
1407	A499	50b blk brn	.20	.20
1408	A499	55b org ver	.20	.20
1409	A499	1 l dp plum	.40	.20
1410	A499	1.55 l brt ultra	.55	.20
1411	A499	1.75 l green	.85	.25
		Nos. 1403-1411 (9)	3.00	1.85

Peter Poni, and Chemical Apparatus — A500

Romanian Scientists: 20b, A. Saligny and Danube bridge, Cernavoda. 55b, C. Budeanu and electrical formula. 1.55 l, Gh. Titeica and geometrical symbol.

1961, Apr. 11 Litho. *Perf. 13½x13*

Portraits in Brown Black

1412	A500	10b pink & vio bl	.20	.20
1413	A500	20b citron & mar	.20	.20
1414	A500	55b blue & red	.20	.20
1415	A500	1.55 l ocher & lilac	.75	.20
		Nos. 1412-1415 (4)	1.35	.80

Freighter "Galati" A501

Ships: 40b, Passenger ship "Oltenita." 55b, Motorboat "Tomis." 1 l, Freighter "Arad." 1.55 l, Tugboat. 1.75 l, Freighter "Dobrogea."

1961, Apr. 25 Typo. *Perf. 14x13*

1416	A501	20b multi	.20	.20
1417	A501	40b multi	.20	.20
1418	A501	55b multi	.30	.20
1419	A501	1 l multi	.40	.20
1420	A501	1.55 l multi	.55	.20
1421	A501	1.75 l multi	.85	.25
		Nos. 1416-1421 (6)	2.50	1.25

Marx, Lenin and Engels on Red Flag — A502

Designs: 55b, Workers. 1 l, "Industry and Agriculture" and Workers Party Emblem.

1961, Apr. 29 Litho.

1422	A502	35b red, bl & ocher	.20	.20
1423	A502	55b mar, red & gray	.25	.20

Souvenir Sheet

Imperf

1424	A502	1 l multi	1.25	.50

40th anniv. of the Romanian Communist Party. #1424 contains one 55x33mm stamp.

Roe Deer and Bronze Age Hunting Scene — A503

Lynx and Prehistoric Hunter A504

35b, Boar, Roman hunter. 40b, Brown bear, Roman tombstone. 55b, Red deer, 16th cent. hunter. 75b, Red fox, feudal hunter. 1 l, Black goat, modern hunter. 1.55 l, Rabbit, hunter with dog. 1.75 l, Badger, hunter. 2 l, Roebuck, hunter.

1961, July *Perf. 13x14, 14x13*

1425	A503	10b multi	.20	.20
1426	A504	20b multi	.20	.20
1427	A504	35b multi	.25	.20
1428	A504	40b multi	.30	.20
1429	A503	55b multi	.40	.20
1430	A504	75b multi	.60	.20
1431	A503	1 l multi	.75	.20
1432	A503	1.55 l multi	.90	.20
1433	A503	1.75 l multi	1.40	.25
1434	A503	2 l multi	1.60	.35
		Nos. 1425-1434 (10)	6.60	2.20

Georges Enescu A505

1961, Sept. 7 Litho. *Perf. 14x13*

1435	A505	3 l pale vio & vio brn	1.40	.25

2nd Intl. George Enescu Festival, Bucharest.

Peasant Playing Panpipe — A506

Heraclitus — A507

Peasants playing musical instruments: 20b, Alpenhorn, horiz. 40b, Flute. 55b, Guitar. 60b, Bagpipe. 1 l, Zither.

Perf. 13x14, 14x13

1961 Unwmk. Typo.

Tinted Paper

1436	A506	10b multi	.20	.20
1437	A506	20b multi	.20	.20
1438	A506	40b multi	.20	.20
1439	A506	55b multi	.35	.20
1440	A506	60b multi	.35	.20
1441	A506	1 l multi	.55	.20
		Nos. 1436-1441 (6)	1.85	1.20

Perf. 13½x13

1961, Oct. 25 Photo. Wmk. 358

Portraits: 20b, Francis Bacon. 40b, Rabindranath Tagore. 55b, Domingo F. Sarmiento. 1.35 l, Heinrich von Kleist. 1.75 l, Mikhail V. Lomonosov.

1442	A507	10b maroon	.20	.20
1443	A507	20b brown	.20	.20
1444	A507	40b Prus grn	.20	.20
1445	A507	55b cerise	.20	.20
1446	A507	1.35 l brt bl	.50	.20
1447	A507	1.75 l purple	.70	.20
		Nos. 1442-1447 (6)	2.00	1.20

Swimming — A508

Gold Medal, Boxing A509

#1449, Olympic torch. #1450, Water polo, Melbourne. #1451, Women's high jump, Rome.

Perf. 14x14½

1961, Oct. 30 Photo. Unwmk.

1448	A508	20b bl gray	.20	.20
1449	A508	20b vermilion	.20	.20
1450	A508	55b ultra	.50	.20
1451	A508	55b blue	.50	.20
		Nos. 1448-1451 (4)	1.40	.80

Perf. 10½

Size: 33x33mm

Gold Medals: 35b, Pistol shooting, Melbourne. 40b, Sharpshooting, Rome. 55b, Wrestling. 1.35 l, Woman's high jump. 1.75 l, Three medals for canoeing.

Medals in Ocher

1452	A509	10b Prus grn	.20	.20
1453	A509	35b brown	.35	.20
1454	A509	40b plum	.40	.20
1455	A509	55b org red	.50	.20
1456	A509	1.35 l dp ultra	.80	.20

Size: 46x32mm

1457	A509	1.75 l dp car rose	1.50	.35
		Nos. 1452-1457 (6)	3.75	1.35
		Nos. 1448-1457 (10)	5.15	2.15

Romania's gold medals in 1956, 1960 Olympics.

#1452-1457 exist imperf. Value, set $3.75.

A souvenir sheet of one 4 l dark red & ocher was issued. Value unused $4.25, canceled $3.25.

Congress Emblem — A510

Primrose A511

1961, Dec. Litho. *Perf. 13½x14*

1458	A510	55b dk car rose	.50	.25

5th World Congress of Trade Unions, Moscow, Dec. 4-16.

Perf. 14x13½, 13½x14

1961, Sept. 15

Designs: 20b, Sweet William. 25b, Peony. 35b, Prickly pear. 40b, Iris. 55b, Buttercup. 1 l, Hepatica. 1.20 l, Poppy. 1.55 l, Gentian. 1.75 l, Carol Davilla and Dimitrie Brindza. 20b, 25b, 40b, 55b, 1.20 l, 1.55 l, are vertical.

1459	A511	10b multi	.20	.20
1460	A511	20b multi	.20	.20
1461	A511	25b multi	.20	.20
1462	A511	35b multi	.20	.20
1463	A511	40b multi	.20	.20
1464	A511	55b multi	.25	.20
1465	A511	1 l multi	.35	.20
1466	A511	1.20 l multi	.50	.20
1467	A511	1.55 l multi	.90	.25
		Nos. 1459-1467 (9)	3.00	1.85

Souvenir Sheet

Imperf

1468	A511	1.75 l car, blk & grn	3.00	2.00

Bucharest Botanical Garden, cent.

No. 1459-1467 exist imperf. Value, set $3.

United Nations Emblem — A512

Cock and Savings Book — A513

Designs: 20b, Map of Balkan peninsula and dove. 40b, Men of three races.

1961, Nov. 27 *Perf. 13½x14*

1469	A512	20b bl, yel & pink	.25	.20
1470	A512	40b multi	.50	.20
1471	A512	55b org, lil & yel	.65	.20
		Nos. 1469-1471 (3)	1.40	.60

UN, 15th anniv. Nos. 1469-1470 are each printed with alternating yellow labels.

Exist imperf. Value, set $2.75.

1962, Feb. 15 Typo. *Perf. 13½*

Savings Day: 55b, Honeycomb, bee and savings book.

1472	A513	40b multi	.25	.20
1473	A513	55b multi	.25	.20

Soccer Player and Map of Europe — A514

Wheat, Map and Tractor — A515

1962, Apr. 20 Litho. *Perf. 13x14*

1474	A514	55b emer & red brn	.50	.20

European Junior Soccer Championships, Bucharest. For surcharge see No. 1510.

1962, Apr. 27 *Perf. 13½x14*

Designs: 55b, Medal honoring agriculture. 1.55Nl, Sheaf of wheat, hammer & sickle.

1475	A515	40b org & dk car	.20	.20
1476	A515	55b yel, car & brn	.25	.20
1477	A515	1.55 l multi	.70	.20
		Nos. 1475-1477 (3)	1.15	.60

Collectivization of agriculture.

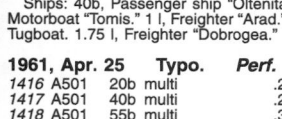

Canoe Race A516

20b, Kayak. 40b, 8-man shell. 55b, 2-man skiff. 1 l, Yachts. 1.20 l, Motorboats. 1.55 l, Sailboat. 3 l, Water slalom.

1962, May 15 Photo. *Perf. 14x13*
Vignette in Bright Blue

1478 A516 10b lil rose .20 .20
1479 A516 20b ol gray .20 .20
1480 A516 40b red brn .20 .20
1481 A516 55b ultra .20 .20
1482 A516 1 l red .25 .20
1483 A516 1.20 l dp plum .55 .20
1484 A516 1.55 l orange .75 .20
1485 A516 3 l violet 1.40 .20
Nos. 1478-1485 (8) 3.75 1.60

These stamps were also issued imperf. with color of denomination and inscription changed. Value, set unused $4.50, canceled $2.

Ion Luca Caragiale — A517

40b, Jean Jacques Rousseau. 1.75 l, Aleksander I. Herzen. 3.30 l, Ion Luca Caragiale (as a young man).

1962, June 9 *Perf. 13½x14*

1486 A517 40b dk sl grn .20 .20
1487 A517 55b magenta .20 .20
1488 A517 1.75 l dp bl .75 .25
Nos. 1486-1488 (3) 1.15 .65

Souvenir Sheet
Perf. 11½

1489 A517 3.30 l brown 3.00 1.75

Rousseau, French philosopher, 250th birth anniv.; Caragiale, Romanian author, 50th death anniv.; Herzen, Russian writer, 150th birth anniv. No. 1489 contains one 32x55mm stamp.

Globes Surrounded with Flags — A518

1962, July 6 Typo. *Perf. 11*

1490 A518 55b multi .40 .20

8th Youth Festival for Peace and Friendship, Helsinki, July 28-Aug. 6.

Traian Vuia — A519

Fieldball Player and Globe — A520

Portraits: 20b, Al. Davila. 35b, Vasile Pirvan. 40b, Ion Negulici. 55b, Grigore Cobilcescu. 1 l, Dr. Gheorghe Marinescu. 1.20 l, Ion Cantacuzino. 1.35 l, Victor Babes. 1.55 l, C. Levaditi.

Perf. 13½x14
1962, July 20 Photo. Wmk. 358

1491 A519 15b brown .20 .20
1492 A519 20b dl red brn .20 .20
1493 A519 35b brn mag .20 .20
1494 A519 40b bl vio .20 .20
1495 A519 55b brt bl .20 .20
1496 A519 1 l dp ultra .20 .20
1497 A519 1.20 l crimson .35 .20
1498 A519 1.35 l Prus grn .45 .20
1499 A519 1.55 l purple .90 .20
Nos. 1491-1499 (9) 2.90 1.80

Perf. 13x14
1962, May 12 Litho. Unwmk.

1500 A520 55b yel & vio .45 .20

2nd Intl. Women's Fieldball Championships, Bucharest.

Same Surcharged in Violet Blue: "Campionana Mondiala 5 lei"

1962, July 31

1501 A520 5 l on 55b yel & vio 4.25 2.10

Romanian victory in the 2nd Intl. Women's Fieldball Championships.

Rod Fishing A521

Various Fishing Scenes.

1962, July 25 *Perf. 14x13*

1502 A521 10b multi .20 .20
1503 A521 25b multi .20 .20
1504 A521 40b bl & brick red .20 .20
1505 A521 55b multi .20 .20
1506 A521 75b sl, gray & bl .30 .20
1507 A521 1 l multi .45 .20
1508 A521 1.75 l multi .75 .20
1509 A521 3.25 l multi 1.40 .20
Nos. 1502-1509 (8) 3.70 1.60

No. 1474 Surcharged in Dark Blue: "1962 Campioana Europeana 2 lei"

1962, July 31

1510 A514 2 l on 55b 1.60 1.00

Romania's victory in the European Junior Soccer Championships, Bucharest.

Child and Butterfly A522

Handicraft A523

Designs: 30b, Girl feeding bird. 40b, Boy and model sailboat. 55b, Children writing, horiz. 1.20 l, Girl at piano, and boy playing violin. 1.55 l, Pioneers camping, horiz.

Perf. 13x14, 14x13
1962, Aug. 25 Litho.

1511 A522 20b lt bl, red & brn .20 .20
1512 A522 30b org, bl & red brn .20 .20
1513 A522 40b chalky bl, dp org & Prus bl .20 .20
1514 A522 55b citron, bl & red .25 .20
1515 A522 1.20 l car, brn & dk vio .35 .20
1516 A522 1.55 l bis, red & vio .70 .20
Nos. 1511-1516 (6) 1.90 1.20

1962, Oct. 12 *Perf. 13x14*

Designs: 10b, Food and drink. 20b, Chemical industry. 40b, Chinaware. 55b, Leather industry. 75b, Textiles. 1 l, Furniture. 1.20 l, Electrical appliances. 1.55 l, Household goods (sewing machine and pots).

1517 A523 5b multi .20 .20
1518 A523 10b multi .20 .20
1519 A523 20b multi .20 .20
1520 A523 40b multi .20 .20
1521 A523 55b multi .20 .20
1522 A523 75b multi .20 .20
1523 A523 1 l multi .30 .20
1524 A523 1.20 l multi .55 .20
1525 A523 1.55 l multi .90 .25
Nos. 1517-1525,C126 (10) 4.20 2.05

4th Sample Fair, Bucharest.

Lenin — A524

Bull — A525

1962, Nov. 7 *Perf. 10½*

1526 A524 55b vio bl, red & bis .35 .20

Russian October Revolution, 45th anniv.

1962, Nov. 20 *Perf. 14x13, 13x14*

Designs: 20b, Sheep, horiz. 40b, Merino ram, horiz. 1 l, York pig. 1.35 l, Cow. 1.55 l, Heifer, horiz. 1.75 l, Pigs, horiz.

1527 A525 20b ultra & blk .20 .20
1528 A525 40b bl, yel & sep .20 .20
1529 A525 55b ocher, buff & sl grn .20 .20
1530 A525 1 l gray, yel & brn .25 .20
1531 A525 1.35 l dl grn, choc & blk .35 .20
1532 A525 1.55 l org red, dk brn & blk .60 .20
1533 A525 1.75 l dk vio bl, yel & org .75 .30
Nos. 1527-1533 (7) 2.55 1.50

Arms, Factory and Harvester A526

Perf. 14½x13½
1962, Dec. 30 Litho.

1534 A526 1.55 l multi .90 .20

Romanian People's Republic, 15th anniv.

Strikers at Grivita, 1933 A527

1963, Feb. 16 *Perf. 14x13½*

1535 A527 1.75 l red, vio & yel .70 .20

30th anniv. of the strike of railroad and oil industry workers at Grivita.

Tractor Driver and "FAO" Emblem A528

Tomatoes — A529

55b, Farm woman, cornfield & combine. 1.55 l, Child drinking milk & milking machine. 1.75 l, Woman with basket of grapes & vineyard.

1963, Mar. 21 Photo. *Perf. 14½x13*

1536 A528 40b vio bl .20 .20
1537 A528 55b bis brn .20 .20
1538 A528 1.55 l rose red .45 .20
1539 A528 1.75 l green .75 .25
Nos. 1536-1539 (4) 1.60 .85

FAO "Freedom from Hunger" campaign.

Perf. 13½x14, 14x13½
1963, Apr. 25 Litho. Unwmk.

40b, Hot peppers. 55b, Radishes. 75b, Eggplant. 1.20 l, Mild peppers. 3.25 l, Cucumbers, horiz.

1540 A529 35b multi .20 .20
1541 A529 40b multi .20 .20
1542 A529 55b multi .20 .20
1543 A529 75b multi .20 .20
1544 A529 1.20 l multi .60 .20
1545 A529 3.25 l multi 1.40 .30
Nos. 1540-1545 (6) 2.80 1.30

Woman Swimmer at Start — A530

Chicks — A531

Designs: 30b, Crawl, horiz. 55b, Butterfly stroke, horiz. 1 l, Backstroke, horiz. 1.35 l, Breaststroke, horiz. 1.55 l, Woman diver. 2 l, Water polo.

1963, June 15 *Perf. 13x14, 14x13*

1546 A530 25b yel brn, emer & gray .20 .20
1547 A530 30b ol grn, gray & yel .20 .20
1548 A530 55b bl, gray & red .20 .20
1549 A530 1 l grn, gray & red .25 .20
1550 A530 1.35 l ultra, car & gray .35 .20
1551 A530 1.55 l pur, gray & org .70 .20
1552 A530 2 l car rose, gray & org .75 .35
Nos. 1546-1552 (7) 2.65 1.55

1963, May 23 *Perf. 10½*

Domestic poultry: 30b, Hen. 40b, Goose. 55b, White cock. 70b, Duck. 1 l, Hen. 1.35 l, Tom turkey. 3.20 l, Hen.

Fowl in Natural Colors; Inscription in Dark Blue

1553 A531 20b ultra .20 .20
1554 A531 30b tan .20 .20
1555 A531 40b org brn .20 .20
1556 A531 55b brt grn .20 .20
1557 A531 70b lilac .25 .20
1558 A531 1 l blue .35 .20
1559 A531 1.35 l ocher .50 .20
1560 A531 3.20 l yel grn 1.10 .35
Nos. 1553-1560 (8) 3.00 1.75

Women and Globe A532

1963, June 15 Photo. *Perf. 14x13*

1561	A532	55b	dark blue	.30	.20

Intl. Women's Cong., Moscow, June 24-29.

William M. Thackeray, Writer A533

Portraits: 50b, Eugene Delacroix, painter. 55b, Gheorghe Marinescu, physician. 1.55 l, Giuseppe Verdi, composer. 1.75 l, Stanislavski, actor and producer.

1963, July Unwmk. *Perf. 14x13*

Portrait in Black

1562	A533	40b	pale vio	.20	.20
1563	A533	50b	bister brn	.20	.20
1564	A533	55b	olive	.25	.20
1565	A533	1.55 l	rose brn	.45	.20
1566	A533	1.75 l	pale vio bl	.75	.20
			Nos. 1562-1566 (5)	1.85	1.00

Walnuts A534

Designs: 20b, Plums. 40b, Peaches. 55b, Strawberries. 1 l, Grapes. 1.55 l, Apples. 1.60 l, Cherries. 1.75 l, Pears.

1963, Sept. 15 Litho. *Perf. 14x13½*

Fruits in Natural Colors

1567	A534	10b	pale yel & brn ol	.20	.20
1568	A534	20b	pale pink & red org	.20	.20
1569	A534	40b	lt bl & bl	.20	.20
1570	A534	55b	dl yel & rose car	.20	.20
1571	A534	1 l	pale vio & vio	.25	.20
1572	A534	1.55 l	yel grn & ultra	.45	.20
1573	A534	1.60 l	yel & bis	.75	.20
1574	A534	1.75 l	lt bl & grn	.75	.20
			Nos. 1567-1574 (8)	3.00	1.60

Women Playing Volleyball and Map of Europe — A535

40b, 3 men players. 55b, 3 women players. 1.75 l, 2 men players. 3.20 l, Europa Cup.

1963, Oct. 22 *Perf. 13½x14*

1575	A535	5b	gray & lil rose	.20	.20
1576	A535	40b	gray & vio bl	.20	.20
1577	A535	55b	gray & grnsh bl	.30	.20
1578	A535	1.75 l	gray & org brn	.55	.20
1579	A535	3.20 l	gray & vio	1.10	.35
			Nos. 1575-1579 (5)	2.35	1.15

European Volleyball Championships, Oct. 22-Nov. 4.

Pine Tree, Branch and Cone A536

Design: 1.75 l, Beech forest and branch.

Perf. 13½

1963, Dec. 5 Unwmk. Photo.

1580	A536	55b	dk grn	.20	.20
1581	A536	1.75 l	dk bl	.50	.20

Reforestation program.

Silkworm Moth — A537

18th Century House, Ploesti — A538

Designs: 20b, Chrysalis, moth and worm. 40b, Silkworm on leaf. 55b, Bee over mountains, horiz. 60b, 1.20 l, 1.35 l, 1.60 l, Bees pollinating various flowers, horiz.

1963, Dec. 12 Litho. *Perf. 13x14*

1582	A537	10b	multi	.20	.20
1583	A537	20b	multi	.20	.20
1584	A537	40b	multi	.20	.20
1585	A537	55b	multi	.25	.20
1586	A537	60b	multi	.35	.20
1587	A537	1.20 l	multi	.60	.20
1588	A537	1.35 l	multi	.75	.20
1589	A537	1.60 l	multi	1.10	.25
			Nos. 1582-1589 (8)	3.65	1.65

1963, Dec. 25 Engr. *Perf. 13*

Peasant Houses from Village Museum, Bucharest: 40b, Oltenia, 1875, horiz. 55b, Hunedoara, 19th Cent., horiz. 75b, Oltenia, 19th Cent. 1 l, Brasov, 1847. 1.20 l, Bacau, 19th Cent. 1.75 l, Arges, 19th Cent.

1590	A538	20b	claret	.20	.20
1591	A538	40b	blue	.20	.20
1592	A538	55b	dl vio	.20	.20
1593	A538	75b	green	.20	.20
1594	A538	1 l	brn & mar	.35	.20
1595	A538	1.20 l	gray ol	.45	.20
1596	A538	1.75 l	dk brn & ultra	.85	.20
			Nos. 1590-1596 (7)	2.45	1.40

Ski Jump A539

20b, Speed skating. 40b, Ice hockey. 55b, Women's figure skating. 60b, Slalom. 75b, Biathlon. 1 l, Bobsledding. 1.20 l, Cross-country skiing.

1963, Nov. 25 Litho. *Perf. 14*

1597	A539	10b	red & dk bl	.20	.20
1598	A539	20b	ultra & red brn	.20	.20
1599	A539	40b	emer & red brn	.20	.20
1600	A539	55b	vio & red brn	.30	.20
1601	A539	60b	org & vio bl	.40	.20
1602	A539	75b	lil rose & dk bl	.50	.20
1603	A539	1 l	bis & vio bl	.85	.25
1604	A539	1.20 l	grnsh bl & vio	.90	.35
			Nos. 1597-1604 (8)	3.55	1.80

9th Winter Olympic Games, Innsbruck, Jan. 29-Feb. 9, 1964.

Exist imperf. in changed colors. Value, set $5.50.

A souvenir sheet contains one imperf. 1.50 l ultramarine and red stamp showing the Olympic Ice Stadium at Innsbruck and the Winter Games emblem. Value $5.50.

Elena Teodorini as Carmen — A540

Munteanu Murgoci and Congress Emblem — A541

Designs: 10b, George Stephanescu, founder of Romanian opera. 35b, Ion Bajenaru as Petru Rares. 40b, D. Popovici as Alberich. 55b, Hariclea Darclée as Tosca. 75b, George Folescu as Boris Godunov. 1 l, Jean Athanasiu as Rigoletto. 1.35 l, Traian Grosavescu as Duke in Rigoletto. 1.55 l, N. Leonard as Hoffmann.

1964, Jan. 20 Photo. *Perf. 13*

Portrait in Dark Brown

1605	A540	10b	olive	.20	.20
1606	A540	20b	ultra	.20	.20
1607	A540	35b	green	.20	.20
1608	A540	40b	grnsh bl	.20	.20
1609	A540	55b	car rose	.20	.20
1610	A540	75b	lilac	.20	.20
1611	A540	1 l	blue	.55	.20
1612	A540	1.35 l	brt vio	.75	.20
1613	A540	1.55 l	red org	.85	.20
			Nos. 1605-1613 (9)	3.35	1.80

1964, Feb. 5 Unwmk. *Perf. 13*

1614	A541	1.60 l	brt bl, ind & bis	.70	.20

8th Intl. Soil Congress, Bucharest.

Asculaphid A542

Insects: 10b, Thread-waisted wasp. 35b, Wasp. 40b, Rhyparioides metelkana moth. 55b, Tussock moth. 1.20 l, Kanetisa circe butterfly. 1.55 l, Beetle. 1.75 l, Horned beetle.

1964, Feb. 20 Litho. *Perf. 14x13*

Insects in Natural Colors

1615	A542	5b	pale lilac	.20	.20
1616	A542	10b	lt bl & red	.20	.20
1617	A542	35b	pale grn	.20	.20
1618	A542	40b	olive green	.20	.20
1619	A542	55b	ultra	.20	.20
1620	A542	1.20 l	pale grn & red	.40	.20
1621	A542	1.55 l	yel & brn	.60	.20
1622	A542	1.75 l	orange & red	.65	.20
			Nos. 1615-1622 (8)	2.65	1.60

Tobacco Plant — A543

Jumping — A544

Garden flowers: 20b, Geranium. 40b, Fuchsia. 55b, Chrysanthemum. 75b, Dahlia. 1 l, Lily. 1.25 l, Day lily. 1.55 l, Marigold.

1964, Mar. 25 *Perf. 13x14*

1623	A543	10b	dk bl, grn & bis	.20	.20
1624	A543	20b	gray, grn & red	.20	.20
1625	A543	40b	pale grn, grn & red	.20	.20
1626	A543	55b	grn, lt grn & lil	.20	.20
1627	A543	75b	cit, red & grn	.25	.20
1628	A543	1 l	dp cl, rose cl, grn & org	.40	.20
1629	A543	1.25 l	sal, vio bl & grn	.45	.20
1630	A543	1.55 l	red brn, yel & grn	.55	.20
			Nos. 1623-1630 (8)	2.45	1.60

Unwmk.

1964, Apr. 25 Photo. *Perf. 13*

Horse Show Events: 40b, Dressage, horiz. 1.35 l, Jumping. 1.55 l, Galloping, horiz.

1631	A544	40b	lt bl, rose brn & blk	.20	.20
1632	A544	55b	lil, red & brn	.20	.20
1633	A544	1.35 l	brt grn, red & dk brn	.55	.20
1634	A544	1.55 l	pale yel, bl & dp claret	.80	.20
			Nos. 1631-1634 (4)	1.75	.80

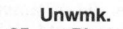

Hogfish A545

Mihail Eminescu — A546

Fish (Constanta Aquarium): 10b, Peacock blenny. 20b, Mediterranean scad. 40b, Sturgeon. 50b, Sea horses. 55b, Yellow gurnard. 1 l, Beluga. 3.20 l, Stingray.

1964, May 10 Litho. *Perf. 14*

1635	A545	5b	multi	.20	.20
1636	A545	10b	multi	.20	.20
1637	A545	20b	multi	.20	.20
1638	A545	40b	multi	.20	.20
1639	A545	50b	multi	.20	.20
1640	A545	55b	multi	.20	.20
1641	A545	1 l	multi	.45	.20
1642	A545	3.20 l	multi	1.10	.20
			Nos. 1635-1642 (8)	2.75	1.60

1964, June 20 Photo. *Perf. 13*

Portraits: 20b, Ion Creanga. 35b, Emil Girleanu. 55b, Michelangelo. 1.20 l, Galileo Galilei. 1.75 l, William Shakespeare.

Portraits in Dark Brown

1643	A546	5b	green	.20	.20
1644	A546	20b	magenta	.20	.20
1645	A546	35b	vermilion	.25	.20
1646	A546	55b	bister	.30	.20
1647	A546	1.20 l	ultra	.50	.20
1648	A546	1.75 l	violet	.90	.25
			Nos. 1643-1648 (6)	2.35	1.25

50th death anniv. of Emil Girleanu, writer; the 75th death anniversaries of Ion Creanga and Mihail Eminescu, writers; the 400th anniv. of the death of Michelangelo and the births of Galileo and Shakespeare.

Road through Gorge — A547

High Jump — A548

Tourist Publicity: 55b, Lake Bilea and cottage. 1 l, Ski lift, Polana Brasov. 1.35 l, Ceahlaul peak and Lake Bicaz, horiz. 1.75 l, Hotel Alpin.

1964, June 29 Engr.

1649	A547	40b	rose brn	.20	.20
1650	A547	55b	dk bl	.20	.20
1651	A547	1 l	dl pur	.30	.20
1652	A547	1.35 l	pale brn	.45	.20
1653	A547	1.75 l	green	.55	.20
			Nos. 1649-1653 (5)	1.70	1.00

1964, July 28 Photo.

1964 Balkan Games: 40b, Javelin throw. 55b, Running. 1 l, Discus throw. 1.20 l, Hurdling. 1.55 l, Map and flags of Balkan countries.

Size: 23x37½mm

1654 A548 30b ver, yel & yel grn .20 .20
1655 A548 40b grn, yel, brn & vio .20 .20
1656 A548 55b gldn brn, yel & bl grn .20 .20
1657 A548 1 l brt bl, yel, brn & red .45 .20
1658 A548 1.20 l pur, yel, brn & grn .55 .20

Litho.

Size: 23x45mm

1659 A548 1.55 l multi .90 .20
Nos. 1654-1659 (6) 2.50 1.20

Factory — A549

55b, Flag, Coat of Arms, vert. 75b, Combine. 1.20 l, Apartment buildings. 2 l, Flag, coat of arms, industrial & agricultural scenes. 55b, 2 l, Inscribed "A XX A aniversare a eliberarii patriei!"

1964, Aug. 23 Photo. *Perf. 13*

1660 A549 55b multi .20 .20
1661 A549 60b multi .25 .20
1662 A549 75b multi .25 .20
1663 A549 1.20 l multi .50 .20
Nos. 1660-1663 (4) 1.20 .80

Souvenir Sheet

Imperf

1664 A549 2 l multi 1.25 .55

20th anniv. of Romania's liberation. No. 1664 contains one stamp 110x70mm.

High Jump — A550

Sport: 30b, Wrestling. 35b, Volleyball. 40b, Canoeing. 55b, Fencing. 1.20 l, Women's gymnastics. 1.35 l, Soccer. 1.55 l, Sharpshooting.

1964, Sept. 1 Litho.

Olympic Rings in Blue, Yellow, Black, Green and Red

1665 A550 20b yel & blk .20 .20
1666 A550 30b lilac & blk .20 .20
1667 A550 35b grnsh bl & blk .20 .20
1668 A550 40b pink & blk .20 .20
1669 A550 55b lt yel grn & blk .35 .20
1670 A550 1.20 l org & blk .65 .20
1671 A550 1.35 l ocher & blk .80 .20
1672 A550 1.55 l bl & blk .90 .35
Nos. 1665-1672 (8) 3.50 1.75

18th Olympic Games, Tokyo, Oct. 10-25.
Nos. 1665-1669 exist imperf., in changed colors. Three other denominations exist, 1.60 l, 2 l and 2.40 l, imperf. Value, set of 8, unused $5.50, canceled $4.
An imperf. souvenir sheet contains a 3.25 l stamp showing a runner. Value unused $5.50 canceled $5.

George Enescu, Piano Keys and Neck of Violin — A551

Designs: 55b, Enescu at piano. 1.60 l, Enescu Festival medal. 1.75 l, Enescu bust by G. Anghel.

1964, Sept. 5 Engr.

1673 A551 10b bl grn .20 .20
1674 A551 55b vio blk .20 .20
1675 A551 1.60 l dk red brn .50 .20
1676 A551 1.75 l dk bl .85 .20
Nos. 1673-1676 (4) 1.75 .80

3rd Intl. George Enescu Festival, Bucharest, Sept., 1964.

Black Swans A552

5b, Indian python. 35b, Ostriches. 40b, Crowned cranes. 55b, Tigers. 1 l, Lions. 1.55 l, Grevy's zebras. 2 l, Bactrian camels.

Perf. 14x13

1964, Sept. 28 Litho. Unwmk.

1677 A552 5b multi .20 .20
1678 A552 10b multi .20 .20
1679 A552 35b multi .20 .20
1680 A552 40b multi .20 .20
1681 A552 55b multi .20 .20
1682 A552 1 l multi .35 .20
1683 A552 1.55 l multi .75 .20
1684 A552 2 l multi 1.00 .20
Nos. 1677-1684 (8) 3.10 1.60

Issued to publicize the Bucharest Zoo.
No. 1683 inscribed "BANI."

C. Brincoveanu, Stolnicul Cantacuzino, Gheorghe Lazar and Academy — A553

Designs: 40b, Alexandru Ioan Cuza, medal and University. 55b, Masks, curtain, harp, keyboard and palette, vert. 75b, Women students in laboratory and auditorium. 1 l, Savings Bank building.

Perf. 13x13½, 13½x13

1964, Oct. 14 Photo.

1685 A553 20b multi .20 .20
1686 A553 40b multi .20 .20
1687 A553 55b multi .20 .20
1688 A553 75b multi .25 .20
1689 A553 1 l dk brn, yel & org .40 .20
Nos. 1685-1689 (5) 1.25 1.00

No. 1685 for 250th anniv. of the Royal Academy; Nos. 1686, 1688 cent. of the University of Bucharest; No. 1687 cent. of the Academy of Art and No. 1689 cent. of the Savings Bank.

Soldier's Head and Laurel — A554

1964, Oct. 25 Litho. *Perf. 12x12½*

1690 A554 55b ultra & lt bl .30 .20

Army Day.

Canadian Kayak Singles Gold Medal, Melbourne, 1956 A555

Romanian Olympic Gold Medals: 30b, Boxing, Melbourne, 1956. 35b, Rapid Silhouette Pistol, Melbourne, 1956. 40b, Women's High Jump, Rome, 1960. 55b, Wrestling, Rome, 1960. 1.20 l, Clay Pigeon Shooting, Rome, 1960. 1.35 l, Women's High Jump, Tokyo, 1964. 1.55 l, Javelin, Tokyo, 1964.

1964, Nov. 30 Photo. *Perf. 13½*

Medals in Gold and Brown

1691 A555 20b pink & ultra .20 .20
1692 A555 30b yel grn & ultra .20 .20
1693 A555 35b bluish grn & ultra .25 .20
1694 A555 40b lil & ultra .40 .20
1695 A555 55b org & ultra .50 .20
1696 A555 1.20 l ol grn & ultra .70 .20
1697 A555 1.35 l gldn brn & ultra .90 .25
1698 A555 1.55 l rose lil & ultra 1.25 .35
Nos. 1691-1698 (8) 4.40 1.80

Romanian athletes who won gold medals in three Olympic Games.
Nos. 1691-1695 exist imperf., in changed colors. Three other denominations exist, 1.60 l, 2 l and 2.40 l, imperf. Value, set of 8, unused $5.75, canceled $4.
A 10 l souvenir sheet shows the 1964 Olympic gold medal and world map. Value unused $5.50, canceled $4.

Strawberries A556

Designs: 35b, Blackberries. 40b, Raspberries. 55b, Rose hips. 1.20 l, Blueberries. 1.35 l, Cornelian cherries. 1.55 l, Hazelnuts. 2.55 l, Cherries.

1964, Dec. 20 Litho. *Perf. 13½x14*

1703 A556 5b gray, red & grn .20 .20
1704 A556 35b ocher, grn & dk vio bl .20 .20
1705 A556 40b pale vio, car & grn .20 .20
1706 A556 55b yel grn, grn & red .20 .20
1707 A556 1.20 l sal pink, grn, brn & ind .35 .20
1708 A556 1.35 l lt bl, grn & red .40 .20
1709 A556 1.55 l gldn brn, grn & ocher .75 .20
1710 A556 2.55 l ultra, grn & red 1.50 .25
Nos. 1703-1710 (8) 3.80 1.65

Syncom 3 — A557

UN Headquarters, NY — A558

Space Satellites: 40b, Syncom 3 over TV antennas. 55b, Ranger 7 reaching moon, horiz. 1 l, Ranger 7 and moon close-up, horiz. 1.20 l, Voskhod. 5 l, Konstantin Feoktistov, Vladimir M. Komarov, Boris B. Yegorov and Voskhod.

Perf. 13x14, 14x13

1965, Jan. 5 Litho. Unwmk.

Size: 22x38mm, 38x22mm

1711 A557 30b multi .20 .20
1712 A557 40b multi .35 .20
1713 A557 55b multi .45 .20
1714 A557 1 l multi .50 .20
1715 A557 1.20 l multi, horiz. .85 .20

Perf. 13½x13

Size: 52x30mm

1716 A557 5 l multi 2.00 .50
Nos. 1711-1716 (6) 4.35 1.50

For surcharge see No. 1737.

1965, Jan. 25 *Perf. 12x12½*

1.60 l, Arms, flag of Romania, UN emblem.

1717 A558 55b ultra, red & gold .40 .20
1718 A558 1.60 l ultra, red, gold & yel .75 .20

20th anniv. of the UN and 10th anniv. of Romania's membership in the UN.

Greek Tortoise — A559

Reptiles: 10b, Bull lizard. 20b, Three-lined lizard. 40b, Sand lizard. 55b, Slow worm. 60b, Sand viper. 1 l, Desert lizard. 1.20 l, Orsini's viper. 1.35 l, Caspian whipsnake. 3.25 l, Four-lined snake.

1965, Feb. 25 Photo. *Perf. 13½*

1719 A559 5b multi .20 .20
1720 A559 10b multi .20 .20
1721 A559 20b multi .20 .20
1722 A559 40b multi .20 .20
1723 A559 55b multi .20 .20
1724 A559 60b multi .25 .20
1725 A559 1 l multi .35 .20
1726 A559 1.20 l multi .45 .20
1727 A559 1.35 l multi .60 .20
1728 A559 3.25 l multi 1.10 .25
Nos. 1719-1728 (10) 3.75 2.05

White Persian Cats — A560

Designs: 1.35 l, Siamese cat. Others; Various European cats. (5b, 10b, 3.25 l, horiz.)

1965, Mar. 20 Litho.

Size: 41x29mm, 29x41mm

Cats in Natural Colors

1729 A560 5b brn org & blk .20 .20
1730 A560 10b brt bl & blk .20 .20
1731 A560 40b yel grn, yel & blk .20 .20
1732 A560 55b rose red & blk .25 .20
1733 A560 60b yel & blk .40 .20
1734 A560 75b lt vio & blk .45 .20
1735 A560 1.35 l red org & blk .85 .20

Perf. 13x13½

Size: 62x29mm

1736 A560 3.25 l blue 1.60 .35
Nos. 1729-1736 (8) 4.15 1.75

No. 1714 Surcharged in Violet

1965, Apr. 25 *Perf. 14x13*

1737 A557 5 l on 1 l multi 12.50 12.50

Flight of the US rocket Ranger 9 to the moon, Mar. 24, 1965.

Dante Alighieri — A561

40b, Ion Bianu, philologist and historian. 55b, Anton Bacalbasa, writer. 60b, Vasile Conta, philosopher. 1 l, Jean Sibelius, Finnish composer. 1.35 l, Horace, Roman poet.

1965, May 10 Photo. *Perf. 13½*

Portrait in Black

1738	A561	40b	chalky blue	.20	.20
1739	A561	55b	bister	.20	.20
1740	A561	60b	light lilac	.20	.20
1741	A561	1 l	dl red brn	.45	.20
1742	A561	1.35 l	olive	.60	.20
1743	A561	1.75 l	orange red	1.10	.25
			Nos. 1738-1743 (6)	2.75	1.25

ITU Emblem, Old and New Communication Equipment — A562

1965, May 15 Engr.

1744	A562	1.75 l	ultra	.90	.40

ITU, centenary.

Iron Gate, Danube — A562a

Arms of Yugoslavia and Romania and Djerdap Dam — A562b

55b (50d), Iron Gate hydroelectric plant & dam.

Perf. 12½x12

1965, May 20 Litho. Unwmk.

1745	A562a	30b (25d)	lt bl & grn	.20	.20
1746	A562a	55b (50d)	lt bl & dk red	.25	.20

Miniature Sheet

Perf. 13½x13

1747	A562b		Sheet of 4	2.50	2.50
a.		80b multi		.20	.20
b.		1.20 l multi		.40	.20

Issued simultaneously by Romania and Yugoslavia for the start of construction of the Iron Gate hydroelectric plant and dam. Valid for postage in both countries.

No. 1747 contains one each of Nos. 1747a, 1747b and Yugoslavia Nos. 771a and 771b. Only Nos. 1747a and 1747b were valid in Romania. Sold for 4 l. See Yugoslavia Nos. 769-771.

Small-bore Rifle Shooting, Kneeling — A563

Designs: 40b, Rifle shooting, prone. 55b, Rapid-fire pistol and map of Europe. 1 l, Free pistol and map of Europe. 1.60 l, Small-bore rifle, standing, and map of Europe. 2 l, 5 l, Marksmen in various shooting positions (all horizontal).

Perf. 12x12½, 12½x12

1965, May 30 Litho. Unwmk.

Size: 23x43mm, 43x23mm

1748	A563	20b	multi	.20	.20
1749	A563	40b	dl grn, pink & blk	.20	.20
1750	A563	55b	multi	.20	.20
1751	A563	1 l	pale grn, blk & ocher	.35	.20
1752	A563	1.60 l	multi	.60	.20

Perf. 13½

Size: 51x28mm

1753	A563	2 l	multi	.75	.20
			Nos. 1748-1753 (6)	2.30	1.20

European Shooting Championships, Bucharest.

Nos. 1749-1752 were issued imperf. in changed colors. Two other denominations exist, 3.25 l and 5 l, imperf. Value, set of 6, unused $4.25, canceled $1.75.

Fat-Frumos and the Giant A564

Fairy Tales: 40b, Fat-Frumos on horseback and Ileana Cosinzeana. 55b, Harap Alb and the Bear. 1 l, "The Moralist Wolf." 1.35 l, "The Ox and the Calf." 2 l, Wolf and bear pulling sled.

1965, June 25 Photo. *Perf. 13*

1756	A564	20b	multi	.20	.20
1757	A564	40b	multi	.20	.20
1758	A564	55b	multi	.25	.20
1759	A564	1 l	multi	.40	.20
1760	A564	1.35 l	multi	.60	.20
1761	A564	2 l	multi	.85	.20
			Nos. 1756-1761 (6)	2.50	1.20

Bee and Blossoms A565

Space Achievements A566

Design: 1.60 l, Exhibition Hall, horiz.

Perf. 12x12½, 12½x12

1965, July 28 Litho. Unwmk.

1762	A565	55b	org, bl & pink	.25	.20
1763	A565	1.60 l	multi	.50	.20

20th Congress of the Intl Federation of Beekeeping Assocs. (Apimondia), Bucharest, Aug. 26-31.

1965, Aug. 25 Litho. *Perf. 12x12½*

Designs: 1.75 l, Col. Pavel Belyayev, Lt. Col. Alexei Leonov and Voskhod 2. 2.40 l, Early Bird over globe. 3.20 l, Lt. Col. Gordon Cooper and Lt. Com. Charles Conrad, Gemini 3 and globe.

1764	A566	1.75 l	dk bl, bl & ver	.80	.20
1765	A566	2.40 l	multi	1.10	.20
1766	A566	3.20 l	dk bl, lt bl & ver	2.25	.35
			Nos. 1764-1766 (3)	4.15	.75

European Quail — A567

Birds: 10b, Eurasian woodcock. 20b, Eurasian snipe. 40b, Turtle dove. 55b, Mallard. 60b, White-fronted goose. 1 l, Eurasian crane. 1.20 l, Glossy ibis. 1.35 l, Mute swan. 3.25 l, White pelican.

1965, Sept. 10 Photo. *Perf. 13½*

Size: 34x34mm

Birds in Natural Colors

1767	A567	5b	red brn & rose lil	.20	.20
1768	A567	10b	red brn & yel grn	.20	.20
1769	A567	20b	brn & bl grn	.20	.20
1770	A567	40b	lil & org brn	.20	.20
1771	A567	55b	brt grn & lt brn	.25	.20
1772	A567	60b	dl org & bl	.30	.20
1773	A567	1 l	red & lil	.40	.20
1774	A567	1.20 l	dk brn & grn	.60	.20
1775	A567	1.35 l	org & ultra	.80	.20

Size: 32x73mm

1776	A567	3.25 l	ultra & sep	2.10	.30
			Nos. 1779-1788 (10)	3.85	2.15

Marx and Lenin A568

Vasile Alecsandri A569

1965, Sept. 6 Photo.

1777	A568	55b	red, blk & yel	.40	.20

6th Conference of Postal Ministers of Communist Countries, Peking, June 21-July 15.

1965, Oct. 9 Unwmk. *Perf. 13½*

1778	A569	55b	red brn, dk brn & gold	.40	.20

Alecsandri (1821-1890), statesman and poet.

Bird-of-Paradise Flower — A570

Flowers from Cluj Botanical Gardens: 10b, Stanhope orchid. 20b, Paphiopedilum insigne. 30b, Zanzibar water lily, horiz. 40b, Ferocactus, horiz. 55b, Cotton blossom, horiz. 1 l, Hibiscus, horiz. 1.35 l, Gloxinia. 1.75 l, Victoria water lily, horiz. 2.30 l, Hibiscus, bird-of-paradise flower and greenhouse.

Perf. 12x12½, 12½x12

1965, Oct. 25 Litho.

Size: 23x43mm, 43x23mm

Flowers in Natural Colors

1779	A570	5b	brown	.20	.20
1780	A570	10b	green	.20	.20
1781	A570	20b	dk bl	.20	.20
1782	A570	30b	vio bl	.20	.20
1783	A570	40b	red brn	.20	.20
1784	A570	55b	dk red	.20	.20
1785	A570	1 l	ol grn	.30	.20
1786	A570	1.35 l	violet	.45	.20
1787	A570	1.75 l	dk grn	.80	.20

Perf. 13½

Size: 52x30mm

1788	A570	2.30 l	green	1.10	.35
			Nos. 1767-1776 (10)	5.25	2.10

The orchid on No. 1780 is attached to the bottom of the limb.

Running — A571

Pigeon and Post Horn — A572

1965, Nov. 10 Photo. *Perf. 13½*

1789	A571	55b	shown	.20	.20
1790	A571	1.55 l	Soccer	.45	.20
1791	A571	1.75 l	Woman diver	.55	.20
1792	A571	2 l	Mountaineering	.60	.20
1793	A571	5 l	Canoeing, horiz.	1.40	.30
			Nos. 1789-1793 (5)	3.20	1.10

Spartacist Games. No. 1793 commemorates the Romanian victory in the European Kayak Championships.

1965, Nov. 15 Engr.

Designs: 1 l, Pigeon on television antenna and post horn, horiz. 1.75 l, Flying pigeon and post horn, horiz.

1794	A572	55b	+ 45b label	.40	.20
1795	A572	1 l	green & brown	.40	.20
1796	A572	1.75 l	olive grn & sepia	.85	.20
			Nos. 1794-1796 (3)	1.65	.60

Issued for Stamp Day. No. 1794 is printed with alternating label showing post rider and emblem of Romanian Philatelists' Association and 45b additional charge. Stamp and label are imperf. between.

Chamois and Hunting Trophy A573

Hunting Trophy and: 1 l, Brown bear. 1.60 l, Red deer. 1.75 l, Wild boar. 3.20 l, Antlers of red deer.

1965, Dec. 10 Photo. *Perf. 13½*

Size: 37x22mm

1797	A573	55b	rose lil, yel & brn	.20	.20
1798	A573	1 l	brt grn, red & brn	.25	.20
1799	A573	1.60 l	lt vio bl, org & brn	.70	.20
1800	A573	1.75 l	rose, grn & blk	.90	.20

Size: 48x36½mm

1801	A573	3.20 l	gray, gold, blk & org	1.40	.30
			Nos. 1797-1801 (5)	3.45	1.10

Probe III Photographing Moon — A574

Designs: 5b, Proton I space station, vert. 15b, Molniya I telecommunication satellite, vert. 3.25 l, Mariner IV and Mars picture, vert. 5 l, Gemini 5.

Perf. 12x12½, 12½x12

1965, Dec. 25 **Litho.**

1802	A574	5b multi	.20	.20
1803	A574	10b vio bl, red & gray	.20	.20
1804	A574	15b pur, gray & org	.20	.20
1805	A574	3.25 l vio bl, blk & red	2.25	.20
1806	A574	5 l dk bl, gray & red org	3.50	.45
		Nos. 1802-1806 (5)	6.35	1.25

Achievements in space research.

Cocker Spaniel — A575

Hunting Dogs: 5b, Dachshund (triangle). 40b, Retriever. 55b, Terrier. 60b, Red setter. 75b, White setter. 1.55 l, Pointers (rectangle). 3.25 l, Duck hunter with retriever (rectangle).

1965, Dec. 28 **Photo.** ***Perf. 13½***

Size: 30x42mm

1807	A575	5b multi	.20	.20

Size: 33½x33½mm

1808	A575	10b multi	.20	.20
1809	A575	40b multi	.25	.20
1810	A575	55b multi	.35	.20
1811	A575	60b multi	.50	.20
1812	A575	75b multi	.70	.20

Size: 43x28mm

1813	A575	1.55 l multi	1.40	.20
1814	A575	3.25 l multi	2.75	.75
		Nos. 1807-1814 (8)	6.35	2.15

Chessboard, Queen and Jester — A576

Chessboard and: 20b, 1.60 l, Pawn and emblem. 55b, 1 l, Rook and knight on horseback.

1966, Feb. 25 **Litho.** ***Perf. 13***

1815	A576	20b multi	.20	.20
1816	A576	40b multi	.20	.20
1817	A576	55b multi	.25	.20
1818	A576	1 l multi	.55	.20
1819	A576	1.60 l multi	1.00	.20
1820	A576	3.25 l multi	2.50	.65
		Nos. 1815-1820 (6)	4.70	1.65

Chess Olympics in Cuba.

Tractor, Grain and Sun — A577

1966, Mar. 5

1821	A577	55b lt grn & ocher	.25	.20

Founding congress of the National Union of Cooperative Farms.

Gheorghe Gheorghiu-Dej A578

Congress Emblem A579

1966, Mar. **Photo.** ***Perf. 13½***

1822	A578	55b gold & blk	.30	.20
a.		5 l souvenir sheet	3.75	3.75

1st death anniv. of Pres. Gheorghe Gheorghiu-Dej (1901-65). No. 1822a contains design similar to No. 1822 with signature of Gheorghiu-Dej.

1966, Mar. 21 ***Perf. 13x14½***

1823	A579	55b yel & red	.30	.20

1966 Congress of Communist Youth.

Folk Dancers of Moldavia — A580

Folk Dances: 40b, Oltenia. 55b, Maramaros. 1 l, Muntenia. 1.60 l, Banat. 2 l, Transylvania.

1966, Apr. 4 **Engr.** ***Perf. 13½***

Center in Black

1824	A580	30b lilac	.20	.20
1825	A580	40b brick red	.20	.20
1826	A580	55b brt bl grn	.20	.20
1827	A580	1 l maroon	.40	.20
1828	A580	1.60 l dk bl	.75	.20
1829	A580	2 l yel grn	1.25	.30
		Nos. 1824-1829 (6)	3.00	1.30

Soccer Game — A581

Designs: 10b, 15b, 55b, 1.75 l, Scenes of soccer play. 4 l, Jules Rimet Cup.

1966, Apr. 25 **Litho.** **Unwmk.**

1830	A581	5b multi	.20	.20
1831	A581	10b multi	.20	.20
1832	A581	15b multi	.20	.20
1833	A581	55b multi	.45	.20
1834	A581	1.75 l multi	1.10	.20
1835	A581	4 l gold & multi	2.50	.60
a.		10 l souv. sheet	3.75	3.75
		Nos. 1830-1835 (6)	4.65	1.60

World Cup Soccer Championship, Wembley, England, July 11-30.

No. 1835a contains one imperf. 10 l multicolored stamp in design of 4 l, but larger (32x46mm). No gum. Issued June 20.

Symbols of Industry A582

Red-breasted Flycatcher A583

1966, May 14 **Photo.**

1836	A582	55b multi	.25	.20

Romanian Trade Union Congress.

1966, May 25 **Photo.** ***Perf. 13½***

Song Birds: 10b, Red crossbill. 15b, Great reed warbler. 20b, European redstart. 55b, European robin. 1.20 l, White-spotted bluethroat. 1.55 l, Yellow wagtail. 3.20 l, Common penduline tit.

1837	A583	5b gold & multi	.20	.20
1838	A583	10b sil & multi	.20	.20
1839	A583	15b gold & multi	.20	.20
1840	A583	20b sil & multi	.20	.20
1841	A583	55b sil & multi	.25	.20
1842	A583	1.20 l gold & multi	.35	.20
1843	A583	1.55 l sil & multi	1.00	.30
1844	A583	3.20 l gold & multi	1.60	.50
		Nos. 1837-1844 (8)	4.00	2.00

Venus 3 (USSR) — A584

Urechia Nestor — A585

Designs: 20b, FR-1 (France). 1.60 l, Luna 9 (USSR). 5 l, Gemini 6 and 7 (US).

1966, June 25

1845	A584	10b dp vio, gray & red	.20	.20
1846	A584	20b ultra, blk & red	.20	.20
1847	A584	1.60 l dk bl, blk & red	.55	.20
1848	A584	5 l bl, blk, brn & red	1.50	.40
		Nos. 1845-1848 (4)	2.45	1.00

International achievements in space.

1966, June 28

Portraits: 5b, George Cosbuc. 10b, Gheorghe Sincai. 40b, Aron Pumnul. 55b, Stefan Luchian. 1 l, Sun Yat-sen. 1.35 l, Gottfried Wilhelm Leibniz. 1.60 l, Romain Rolland. 1.75 l, Ion Ghica. 3.25 l, Constantin Cantacuzino.

1849	A585	5b grn, blk & dk bl	.20	.20
1850	A585	10b rose car, grn & blk	.20	.20
1851	A585	20b grn, plum & blk	.20	.20
1852	A585	40b vio bl, brn & blk	.20	.20
1853	A585	55b brn org, bl grn & blk	.20	.20
1854	A585	1 l ocher, vio & blk	.25	.20
1855	A585	1.35 l bl & blk	.35	.20
1856	A585	1.60 l brt grn, dl vio & blk	.55	.20
1857	A585	1.75 l org, dl vio & blk	.55	.20
1858	A585	3.25 l bl, dk car & blk	1.00	.25
		Nos. 1849-1858 (10)	3.70	2.05

Cultural anniversaries.

Country House, by Gheorghe Petrascu — A586

Paintings: 10b, Peasant Woman, by Nicolae Grigorescu, vert. 20b, Reapers at Rest, by Camil Ressu. 55b, Man with the Blue Cap, by Van Eyck, vert. 1.55 l, Train Compartment, by Daumier. 3.25 l, Betrothal of the Virgin, by El Greco, vert.

1966, July 25 **Unwmk.**

Gold Frame

1859	A586	5b Prus grn & brn org	.20	.20
1860	A586	10b red brn & crim	.20	.20
1861	A586	20b brn & brt grn	.20	.20
1862	A586	55b vio bl & lil	.25	.20
1863	A586	1.55 l dk sl grn & org	1.25	.35
1864	A586	3.25 l vio & ultra	2.75	1.00
		Nos. 1859-1864 (6)	4.85	2.15

See Nos. 1907-1912.

Hottonia Palustris A587

Marine Flora: 10b, Ceratophyllum submersum. 20b, Aldrovanda vesiculosa. 40b, Callitriche verna. 55b, Vallisneria spiralis. 1 l, Elodea Canadensis rich. 1.55 l, Hippuris vulgaris. 3.25 l, Myriophyllum spicatum.

1966, Aug. 25 **Litho.** ***Perf. 13½***

Size: 28x40mm

1865	A587	5b multi	.20	.20
1866	A587	10b multi	.20	.20
1867	A587	20b multi	.20	.20
1868	A587	40b multi	.20	.20
1869	A587	55b multi	.20	.20
1870	A587	1 l multi	.45	.20
1871	A587	1.55 l multi	.70	.25

Size: 28x50mm

1872	A587	3.25 l multi	1.40	.35
		Nos. 1865-1872 (8)	3.55	1.80

Derivation of the Meter — A588

Design: 1 l, Metric system symbols.

1966, Sept. 10 **Photo.** ***Perf. 13½***

1873	A588	55b salmon & ultra	.25	.20
1874	A588	1 l lt grn & vio	.35	.20

Introduction of metric system in Romania, centenary.

Statue of Ovid and Medical School Emblem — A589

Line Integral Denoting Work — A590

I. H. Radulescu, M. Kogalniceanu and T. Savulescu — A591

Design: 1 l, Academy centenary medal.

1966, Sept. 30

Size: 22x27mm

1875 A589 40b lil gray, ultra, sep & gold .20 .20
1876 A590 55b gray, brn, red & gold .20 .20

Size: 22x34mm

1877 A589 1 l ultra, brn & gold .35 .20

Size: 66x28mm

1878 A591 3 l org, dk brn & gold .95 .30
Nos. 1875-1878 (4) 1.70 .90

Centenary of the Romanian Academy.

Stone Crab A592

Molluscs and Crustaceans:5b, Crawfish. 10b, Nassa reticulata, vert. 40b, Campylaea trizona. 55b, Helix lucorum. 1.35 l, Mytilus galloprovincialis. 1.75 l, Lymnaea stagnalis. 3.25 l, Anodonta cygnaea. (10b, 40b, 55b, 1.75 l, are snails; 1.35 l, 3.25 l, are bivalves).

1966, Oct. 15

Animals in Natural Colors

1879 A592 5b dp org .20 .20
1880 A592 10b lt bl .20 .20
1881 A592 20b pale lil .20 .20
1882 A592 40b yel grn .20 .20
1883 A592 55b car rose .20 .20
1884 A592 1.35 l brt grn .45 .20
1885 A592 1.75 l ultra .55 .20
1886 A592 3.25 l brt org 1.40 .35
Nos. 1879-1886 (8) 3.40 1.75

Cave Bear A593

Prehistoric Animals: 10b, Mammoth. 15b, Bison. 55b, Cave elephant. 1.55 l, Stags. 4 l, Dinotherium.

1966, Nov. 25

Size: 36x22mm

1887 A593 5b ultra, bl grn & red brn .20 .20
1888 A593 10b vio, emer & brn .20 .20
1889 A593 15b ol, grn & dk brn .20 .20
1890 A593 55b lil, emer & brn .30 .20
1891 A593 1.55 l ultra, grn & brn .95 .20

Size: 43x27mm

1892 A593 4 l rose car, grn & brn 1.50 .50
Nos. 1887-1892 (6) 3.35 1.50

Putna Monastery, 500th Anniv. A594

1966 Photo. *Perf. 13½*

1893 A594 2 l multi .65 .20

Yuri A. Gagarin and Vostok 1 — A595

Russian Achievements in Space: 10b, Trajectory of Sputnik 1 around globe, horiz. 25b, Valentina Tereshkova and globe with trajectory of Vostok 6. 40b, Andrian G. Nikolayev, Pavel R. Popovich and globe with trajectory of Vostok 8. 55b, Alexei Leonov walking in space.

1967, Feb. 15 Photo. *Perf. 13½*

1894 A595 10b silver & multi .20 .20
1895 A595 20b silver & multi .20 .20
1896 A595 25b silver & multi .20 .20
1897 A595 40b silver & multi .20 .20
1898 A595 55b silver & multi .30 .20
Nos. 1894-1898,C163-C166 (9) 4.35 2.50

Ten years of space exploration.

Barn Owl A596

Birds of Prey: 20b, Eagle owl. 40b, Saker falcon. 55b, Egyptian vulture. 75b, Osprey. 1 l, Griffon vulture. 1.20 l, Lammergeier. 1.75 l, Cinereous vulture.

1967, Mar. 20 Photo. Unwmk.

Birds in Natural Colors

1899 A596 10b vio & olive .20 .20
1900 A596 20b bl & org .25 .20
1901 A596 40b emer & org .20 .20
1902 A596 55b yel grn & ocher .25 .20
1903 A596 75b rose lil & grn .25 .20
1904 A596 1 l yel org & blk .50 .20
1905 A596 1.20 l claret & yel .85 .20
1906 A596 1.75 l sal pink & gray 1.25 .50
Nos. 1899-1906 (8) 3.75 1.90

Painting Type of 1966

10b, Woman in Fancy Dress, by Ion Andreescu. 20b, Washwomen, by J. Al. Steriadi. 40b, Women weavers, by St. Dimitrescu, vert. 1.55 l, Venus and Amor, by Lucas Cranach, vert. 3.20 l, Hercules & the Lion of Numea, by Rubens. 5 l, Haman Asking Esther's Forgiveness, by Rembrandt, vert.

1967, Mar. 30 *Perf. 13½*

Gold Frame

1907 A586 10b dp bl & rose red .20 .20
1908 A586 20b dp grn & bis .20 .20
1909 A586 40b carmine & bl .20 .20
1910 A586 1.55 l dp plum & lt ultra .50 .20
1911 A586 3.20 l brown & grn .90 .20
1912 A586 5 l ol grn & org 2.00 .45
Nos. 1907-1912 (6) 4.00 1.45

Mlle. Pogany, by Brancusi A597

Sculptures: 5b, Girl's head. 10b, The Sleeping Muse, horiz. 20b, The Infinite Column. 40b, The Kiss, horiz. 55b, Earth Wisdom (seated woman). 3.25 l, Gate of the Kiss.

1967, Apr. 27 Photo. *Perf. 13½*

1913 A597 5b dl yel, blk brn & ver .20 .20
1914 A597 10b bl grn, blk & lil .20 .20
1915 A597 20b lt bl, blk & rose red .20 .20
1916 A597 40b pink, sep & brt grn .20 .20
1917 A597 55b yel grn, blk & ultra .25 .20
1918 A597 1.20 l bluish lil, ol blk & org .40 .20
1919 A597 3.25 l emer, blk & cer 1.10 .50
Nos. 1913-1919 (7) 2.55 1.70

Constantin Brancusi (1876-1957), sculptor.

Coins of 1867 A598

Design: 1.20 l, Coins of 1966.

1967, May 4

1920 A598 55b multicolored .25 .20
1921 A598 1.20 l multicolored 1.10 .25

Centenary of Romanian monetary system.

Infantry Soldier, by Nicolae Grigorescu A599

1967, May 9

1922 A599 55b multicolored .55 .20

90th anniv. of Romanian independence.

Peasants Marching, by Stefan Luchian — A600

Painting: 40b, Fighting Peasants, by Octav Bancila, vert.

1967, May 20 Unwmk. *Perf. 13½*

1923 A600 40b multicolored .25 .20
1924 A600 1.55 l multicolored 1.10 .70

60th anniversary of Peasant Uprising.

Centaury — A601

Carpathian Flora: 40b, Hedge mustard. 55b, Columbine. 1.20 l, Alpine violet. 1.75 l, Bell flower. 4 l, Dryas, horiz.

1967, June 10 Photo.

Flowers in Natural Colors

1925 A601 20b ocher .20 .20
1926 A601 40b violet .20 .20
1927 A601 55b bis & brn red .20 .20
1928 A601 1.20 l yel & red brn .30 .20
1929 A601 1.75 l bluish grn & car .45 .20
1930 A601 4 l lt ultra 1.25 .20
Nos. 1925-1930 (6) 2.60 1.20

Fortifications, Sibiu — A602

Map of Romania and ITY Emblem — A603

Designs: 40b, Cris Castle. 55b, Wooden Church, Plopis. 1.60 l, Ruins of Nuamtulua Fortress. 1.75 l, Mogosoaia Palace. 2.25 l, Voronet Church.

1967, June 29 Photo. *Perf. 13½*

Size: 33x33mm

1931 A602 20b ultra & multi .20 .20
1932 A602 40b vio & multi .20 .20
1933 A602 55b multi .20 .20
1934 A602 1.60 l multi .35 .20
1935 A602 1.75 l multi .45 .20

Size: 48x36mm

1936 A602 2.25 l bl & multi .75 .20
Nos. 1931-1936 (6) 2.15 1.20

Souvenir Sheet

Imperf

1937 A603 5 l lt bl, ultra & blk 2.50 1.40

International Tourist Year.

The Attack at Marasesti, by E. Stoica — A604

1967, July 24 Unwmk. *Perf. 13½*

1938 A604 55b gray, Prus bl & brn .35 .20

Battle of Marasesti & Oituz, 50th anniv.

Dinu Lipatti, Pianist — A605

Designs: 20b, Al. Orascu, architect. 40b, Gr. Antipa, zoologist. 55b, M. Kogalniceanu, statesman. 1.20 l, Jonathan Swift, writer. 1.75 l, Marie Curie, scientist.

1967, July 29 Photo. *Perf. 13½*

1939 A605 10b ultra, blk & pur .20 .20
1940 A605 20b org brn, blk & ultra .20 .20
1941 A605 40b bl grn, blk & org brn .20 .20
1942 A605 55b dp rose, blk & dk ol grn .20 .20
1943 A605 1.20 l ol, blk & brn .35 .20
1944 A605 1.75 l dl bl, blk & bl grn .70 .20
Nos. 1939-1944 (6) 1.85 1.20

Cultural anniversaries.

Wrestlers A606

Congress Emblem — A607

Designs: 20b, 55b, 1.20 l, 2 l, Various fight scenes and world map (20b, 2 l horizontal); on 2 l maps are large and wrestlers small.

1967, Aug. 28

1945	A606	10b	olive & multi	.20	.20
1946	A606	20b	citron & multi	.20	.20
1947	A606	55b	bister & multi	.20	.20
1948	A606	1.20 l	multi	.25	.20
1949	A606	2 l	ultra, gold & dp car	1.00	.30
			Nos. 1945-1949 (5)	1.85	1.10

World Greco-Roman Wrestling Championships, Bucharest.

1967, Aug. 28

1950	A607	1.60 l	lt bl, ultra & dp car	.50	.20

Intl. Linguists' Cong., Bucharest, 8/28-9/2.

Ice Skating — A608

Designs: 40b, Biathlon. 55b, 5 l, Bobsledding. 1 l, Skiing. 1.55 l, Ice Hockey. 2 l, Emblem of 10th Winter Olympic Games. 2.30 l, Ski jump.

1967, Sept. 28 Photo. *Perf. 13½x13*

1951	A608	20b	lt bl & multi	.20	.20
1952	A608	40b	multi	.20	.20
1953	A608	55b	bl & multi	.20	.20
1954	A608	1 l	lil & multi	.20	.20
1955	A608	1.55 l	multi	.30	.20
1956	A608	2 l	gray & multi	.50	.20
1957	A608	2.30 l	multi	.85	.35
			Nos. 1951-1957 (7)	2.45	1.55

Souvenir Sheet

Imperf

1958	A608	5 l	lt bl & multi	3.25	2.75

10th Winter Olympic Games, Grenoble, France, Feb. 6-18, 1968.

Nos. 1951-1957 issued in sheets of 10 (5x2) and 5 labels.

Curtea de Arges Monastery, 450th Anniv. — A609

1967, Nov. 1 Unwmk. *Perf. 13½*

1959	A609	55b	multicolored	.30	.20

Romanian Academy Library, Bucharest, Cent. — A610

1967, Sept. 25 Litho.

1960	A610	55b	ocher, gray & dk bl	.30	.20

Karl Marx and Title Page — A611

Lenin — A612

1967, Nov. 4 Photo.

1961	A611	40b	rose claret, blk & yel	.25	.20

Centenary of the publication of "Das Kapital" by Karl Marx.

1967, Nov. 3

1962	A612	1.20 l	red, blk & gold	.35	.20

Russian October Revolution, 50th anniv.

Monorail Leaving US EXPO Pavilion A613

Designs: 1 l, EXPO emblem and atom symbol. 1.60 l, Cup, world map and EXPO emblem. 2 l, EXPO emblem.

1967, Nov. 28 Photo.

1963	A613	55b	grnsh bl, vio & blk	.20	.20
1964	A613	1 l	red, blk & gray	.25	.20
1965	A613	1.60 l	multicolored	.40	.20
1966	A613	2 l	multicolored	.60	.20
			Nos. 1963-1966 (4)	1.45	.80

EXPO '67 Intl. Exhib., Montreal, Apr. 28-Oct. 27. No. 1965 also for Romania's victory in the World Fencing Championships in Montreal.

Truck — A614

Arms of the Republic — A615

Diesel Locomotive — A616

Map Showing Telephone Network A617

Designs: 10b, Communications emblem, vert. 20b, Train. 35b, Plane. 50b, Telephone, vert. 60b, Small loading truck. 1.20 l, Autobus. 1.35 l, Helicopter. 1.50 l, Trolley bus. 1.55 l, Radio station and tower. 1.75 l, Highway. 2 l, Mail truck. 2.40 l, Television tower. 3.20 l, Jet plane. 3.25 l, Steamship. 4 l, Electric train. 5 l, World map and teletype.

Photo.; Engr. (type A615)

1967-68 *Perf. 13½*

1967	A614	5b	lt ol grn ('68)	.20	.20
1968	A614	10b	henna brn ('68)	.20	.20
1969	A614	20b	gray ('68)	.20	.20
1970	A614	35b	bl blk ('68)	.20	.20
1971	A615	40b	violet blue	.20	.20
1972	A614	50b	orange ('68)	.20	.20
1973	A615	55b	dull orange	.20	.20
1974	A614	60b	orange brn ('68)	.20	.20

Size: 22½x28mm, 28x22½mm

1975	A616	1 l	emerald ('68)	.20	.20
1976	A617	1.20 l	red lil ('68)	.25	.20
1977	A617	1.35 l	brt blue ('68)	.30	.20
1978	A616	1.50 l	rose red ('68)	.35	.20
1979	A616	1.55 l	dk brown ('68)	.35	.20
1980	A615	1.60 l	rose red	.40	.20
1981	A617	1.75 l	dp green ('68)	.40	.20
1982	A617	2 l	citron ('68)	.60	.20
1983	A616	2.40 l	dk blue ('68)	.75	.20
1984	A617	3 l	grnsh blue	.75	.20
1985	A617	3.20 l	ocher ('68)	1.00	.20
1986	A616	3.25 l	ultra ('68)	1.00	.20
1987	A617	4 l	lil rose ('68)	1.25	.20
1988	A617	5 l	violet ('68)	1.40	.20
			Nos. 1967-1988 (22)	10.60	4.40

40th anniv. of the first automatic telephone exchange; introduction of automatic telephone service (No. 1984).

See Nos. 2078-2079, 2269-2284 and design A792.

Coat of Arms, Symbols of Agriculture and Industry A618

55b, Coat of arms. 1.60 l, Romanian flag. 1.75 l, Coat of arms, symbols of arts and education.

1967, Dec. 26 Photo. *Perf. 13½*

Size: 27x48mm

1989	A618	40b	multicolored	.20	.20
1990	A618	55b	multicolored	.20	.20

Size: 33½x48mm

1991	A618	1.60 l	multicolored	.30	.20

Size: 27x48mm

1992	A618	1.75 l	multicolored	.50	.25
			Nos. 1989-1992 (4)	1.20	.85

20th anniversary of the republic.

Souvenir Sheet

Anemones, by Stefan Luchian — A619

1968, Mar. 30 Litho. *Imperf.*

1993	A619	10 l	multi	4.75	4.75

Stefan Luchian, Romanian painter, birth cent.

Portrait of a Lady, by Misu Popp A620

Paintings: 10b, The Reveille of Romania, by Gheorghe Tattarescu. 20b, Composition, by Teodorescu Sionion, horiz. 35b, The Judgment of Paris, by Hendrick van Balen, horiz. 55b, Little Girl with Red Kerchief, by Nicolae Grigorescu. 60b, The Mystical Betrothal of St. Catherine, by Lamberto Sustris, horiz. 1 l, Old Nicolas, the Zither Player, by Stefan Luchian. 1.60 l, Man with a Skull, by Dierick Bouts (?). 1.75 l, Madonna and Child with Fruit Basket, by Jan van Bylert. 2.40 l, Medor and Angelica, by Sebastiano Ricci, horiz. 3 l, Summer, by Jacob Jordaens, horiz. 3.20 l, 5 l, Ecce Homo, by Titian.

1968 Photo. *Perf. 13½*

Gold Frame

Size: 28x49mm

1994	A620	10b	multi	.20	.20

Size: 48½x36½mm, 36x48½mm

1995	A620	20b	multi	.20	.20
1996	A620	35b	multi	.20	.20
1997	A620	40b	multi	.20	.20
1998	A620	55b	multi	.20	.20
1999	A620	60b	multi	.20	.20
2000	A620	1 l	multi	.25	.20
2001	A620	1.60 l	multi	.40	.20
2002	A620	1.75 l	multi	.40	.20
2003	A620	2.40 l	multi	.80	.30
2004	A620	3 l	multi	.90	.50
2005	A620	3.20 l	multi	1.40	.70
			Nos. 1994-2005 (12)	5.35	3.30

Miniature Sheet

Imperf

2006	A620	5 l	multi	4.50	4.50

Issued: 40, 55b, 1, 1.60, 2.40, 3.20, 5 l, 3/28; others, 9/9.

See Nos. 2088-2094, 2124-2130.

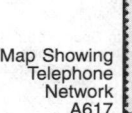

Human Rights Flame — A621

WHO Emblem — A622

1968, May 9 Unwmk. *Perf. 13½*

2007	A621	1 l	multicolored	.45	.20

Intl. Human Rights Year.

1968, May 14 Photo.

2008	A622	1.60 l	multi	.50	.20

WHO, 20th anniversary.

"Prince Dragos Hunting Bison," by Nicolae Grigorescu — A623

1968, May 17

2009	A623	1.60 l	multi	.60	.20

15th Hunting Cong., Mamaia, May 23-29.

Pioneers and Liberation Monument — A624

Pioneers: 40b, receiving scarfs. 55b, building model planes and boat. 1 l, as radio amateurs. 1.60 l, folk dancing. 2.40 l, Girl Pioneers in camp.

1968, June 9 Photo. *Perf. 13½*

2010	A624	5b	multi	.20	.20
2011	A624	40b	multi	.20	.20
2012	A624	55b	multi	.20	.20
2013	A624	1 l	multi	.30	.20
2014	A624	1.60 l	multi	.50	.20
2015	A624	2.40 l	multi	.70	.20
			Nos. 2010-2015 (6)	2.10	1.20

Ion Ionescu de la Brad — A625

Designs: 55b, Emil Racovita. 1.60 l, Prince Mircea of Walachia.

1968

Size: 28x43mm

2016	A625	40b	multicolored	.20	.20
2017	A625	55b	green & multi	.20	.20

Size: 28x48mm

2018	A625	1.60 l	gold & multi	.45	.20
			Nos. 2016-2018 (3)	.85	.60

Ion Ionescu de la Brad (1818-91); Emil Racovita (1868-1947), explorer and naturalist; 1.60 l, Prince Mircea (1386-1418). Issue dates: 40b, 55b, June 24; 1.60 l, June 22.

Geranium A626

Designs: Various geraniums.

1968, July 20 Photo. *Perf. 13½*

2019	A626	10b	multicolored	.20	.20
2020	A626	20b	multicolored	.20	.20
2021	A626	40b	multicolored	.20	.20
2022	A626	55b	multicolored	.20	.20
2023	A626	60b	multicolored	.20	.20
2024	A626	1.20 l	multicolored	.25	.20
2025	A626	1.35 l	multicolored	.35	.20
2026	A626	1.60 l	multicolored	.75	.20
			Nos. 2019-2026 (8)	2.35	1.60

Avram Iancu, by B. Iscovescu and Demonstrating Students — A627

Demonstrating Students and: 55b, Nicolae Balcescu, by Gheorghe Tattarescu. 1.60 l, Vasile Alecsandri, by N. Livaditti.

1968, July 25

2027	A627	55b	gold & multi	.20	.20
2028	A627	1.20 l	gold & multi	.45	.20
2029	A627	1.60 l	gold & multi	.70	.20
			Nos. 2027-2029 (3)	1.35	.60

120th anniversary of 1848 revolution.

Boxing — A628

Atheneum and Harp — A629

Aztec Calendar Stone and: 10b, Javelin, Women's. 20b, Woman diver. 40b, Volleyball. 60b, Wrestling. 1.20 l, Fencing. 1.35 l, Canoeing. 1.60 l, Soccer. 5 l, Running.

1968, Aug. 28

2030	A628	10b	multi	.20	.20
2031	A628	20b	multi	.20	.20
2032	A628	40b	multi	.20	.20
2033	A628	55b	multi	.20	.20
2034	A628	60b	multi	.20	.20
2035	A628	1.20 l	multi	.35	.20
2036	A628	1.35 l	multi	.40	.25
2037	A628	1.60 l	multi	.65	.25
			Nos. 2030-2037 (8)	2.40	1.70

Souvenir Sheet

Imperf

2038	A628	5 l	multi	2.25	1.75

19th Olympic Games, Mexico City, 10/12-17.

1968, Aug. 20 Litho. *Perf. 12x12½*

2039	A629	55b	multicolored	.25	.20

Centenary of the Philharmonic Orchestra.

Globe and Emblem — A630

1968, Oct. 4 Litho. *Perf. 13½*

2040	A630	1.60 l	ultra & gold	.50	.20

Intl. Fed. of Photograpic Art, 20th anniv.

Moldovita Monastery Church — A631

Historic Monuments: 10b, "The Triumph of Trajan," Roman metope, vert. 55b, Cozia monastery church. 1.20 l, Court of Tirgoviste Palace. 1.55 l, Palace of Culture, Jassy. 1.75 l, Corvinus Castle, Hunedoara.

1968, Nov. 25 Engr. *Perf. 13½*

2041	A631	10b	dk bl, ol & brn	.20	.20
2042	A631	40b	rose car, bl & brn	.20	.20
2043	A631	55b	ol, brn & vio	.20	.20
2044	A631	1.20 l	yel, mar & gray	.30	.20
2045	A631	1.55 l	vio brn, dk bl & lt grn	.50	.20
2046	A631	1.75 l	org, blk & ol	1.00	.20
			Nos. 2041-2046 (6)	2.40	1.20

Mute Swan — A632

Protected Birds and Animals: 20b, European stilts. 40b, Sheldrakes. 55b, Egret feeding young. 60b, Golden eagle. 1.20 l, Great bustards. 1.35 l, Chamois. 1.60 l, Bison.

1968, Dec. 20 Photo. *Perf. 13½*

2047	A632	10b	pink & multi	.20	.20
2048	A632	20b	multicolored	.20	.20
2049	A632	40b	lilac & multi	.20	.20
2050	A632	55b	olive & multi	.20	.20
2051	A632	60b	multicolored	.20	.20
2052	A632	1.20 l	multicolored	.45	.20
2053	A632	1.35 l	blue & multi	.50	.20
2054	A632	1.60 l	multicolored	.60	.20
			Nos. 2047-2054 (8)	2.55	1.60

Michael the Brave's Entry into Alba Iulia, by D. Stoica — A633

Designs: 1 l, "The Round Dance of Union," by Theodor Aman. 1.75 l, Assembly of Alba Iulia.

1968, Dec. 1 Litho. *Perf. 13½*

2055	A633	55b	gold & multi	.20	.20
2056	A633	1 l	gold & multi	.30	.20
2057	A633	1.75 l	gold & multi	.40	.35
	a.		Souv. sheet of 3, #2055-2057, imperf.	1.50	1.50
			Nos. 2055-2057 (3)	.90	.75

50th anniv. of the union of Transylvania and Romania. No. 2057a sold for 4 l.

Woman from Neamt — A634

Regional Costumes: 40b, Man from Neamt. 55b, Woman from Hunedoara. 1 l, Man from Hunedoara. 1.60 l, Woman from Brasov. 2.40 l, Man from Brasov.

1968, Dec. 28 *Perf. 12x12½*

2058	A634	5b	orange & multi	.20	.20
2059	A634	40b	blue & multi	.20	.20
2060	A634	55b	multi	.20	.20
2061	A634	1 l	brown & multi	.25	.20
2062	A634	1.60 l	brown & multi	.50	.20
2063	A634	2.40 l	multi	.95	.35
			Nos. 2058-2063 (6)	2.30	1.35

1969, Feb. 15

Regional Costumes: 5b, Woman from Dolj. 40b, Man from Dolj. 55b, Woman from Arges. 1 l, Man from Arges. 1.60 l, Woman from Timisoara. 2.40 l, Man from Timisoara.

2064	A634	5b	multi	.20	.20
2065	A634	40b	multi	.20	.20
2066	A634	55b	lil & multi	.20	.20
2067	A634	1 l	rose & multi	.25	.20
2068	A634	1.60 l	multi	.55	.20
2069	A634	2.40 l	brn & multi	1.00	.25
			Nos. 2064-2069 (6)	2.40	1.25

Fencing — A635

Sports: 20b, Women's javelin. 40b, Canoeing. 55b, Boxing. 1 l, Volleyball. 1.20 l, Swimming. 1.60 l, Wrestling. 2.40 l, Soccer.

1969, Mar. 10 Photo. *Perf. 13½*

Denominations Black, Athletes in Gray

2070	A635	10b	pale brown	.20	.20
2071	A635	20b	violet	.20	.20
2072	A635	40b	blue	.20	.20
2073	A635	55b	red	.20	.20
2074	A635	1 l	green	.25	.20
2075	A635	1.20 l	brt blue	.25	.20
2076	A635	1.60 l	cerise	.45	.20
2077	A635	2.40 l	dp green	.85	.20
			Nos. 2070-2077 (8)	2.60	1.60

Type of Regular Issue

1969, Jan. 10 Photo. *Perf. 13½*

2078	A614	40b	Power lines, vert.	.20	.20
2079	A614	55b	Dam, vert.	.20	.20

Painting Type of 1968

Paintings (Nudes): 10b, Woman Carrying Jug, by Gheorghe Tattarescu. 20b, Reclining Woman, by Theodor Pallady, horiz. 35b, Seated Woman, by Nicolae Tonitza. 60b, Venus and Amor, 17th century Flemish School. 1.75 l, 5 l, Diana and Endimion, by Marco Liberi. 3 l, The Three Graces, by Alessandro Varotari.

1969, Mar. 27 Photo. *Perf. 13½*

Gold Frame

Size: 37x49mm, 49x37mm

2088	A620	10b	multi	.20	.20
2089	A620	20b	multi	.20	.20
2090	A620	35b	multi	.20	.20
2091	A620	60b	multi	.30	.20
2092	A620	1.75 l	multi	.70	.25

Size: 27½x48½mm

2093 A620 3 l multi 1.50 .45
Nos. 2088-2093 (6) 3.10 1.50

Miniature Sheet

Imperf

2094 A620 5 l multi 3.00 3.00

No. 2094 contains one stamp 36½x48½mm. with simulated perforations.
No. 2093 is incorrectly inscribed Hans von Aachen.

ILO, 50th Anniv. — A636

Symbolic Head — A637

1969, Apr. 9 Photo. *Perf. 13½*

2095 A636 55b multicolored .40 .20

1969, Apr. 28

2096 A637 55b ultra & multi .35 .20
2097 A637 1.50 l red & multi .90 .35

Romania's cultural and economic cooperation with European countries.

Communications Symbol — A638

1969, May 12 Photo. *Perf. 13½*

2098 A638 55b vio bl & bluish gray .35 .20

7th Session of the Conference of Postal and Telecommunications Ministers, Bucharest.

Boxers, Referee and Map of Europe A639

Map of Europe and: 40b, Two boxers. 55b, Sparring. 1.75 l, Referee declaring winner.

1969, May 24

2099 A639 35b multicolored .20 .20
2100 A639 40b multicolored .20 .20
2101 A639 55b multicolored .25 .20
2102 A639 1.75 l blue & multi .60 .20
Nos. 2099-2102 (4) 1.25 .80

European Boxing Championships, Bucharest, May 31-June 8.

Apatura Ilia — A640

Designs: Various butterflies and moths.

1969, June 25 Photo. *Perf. 13½*

Insects in Natural Colors

2103 A640 5b yellow grn .20 .20
2104 A640 10b rose mag .20 .20
2105 A640 20b violet .20 .20
2106 A640 40b blue grn .20 .20
2107 A640 55b brt blue .20 .20
2108 A640 1 l blue .30 .20
2109 A640 1.20 l violet bl .40 .20
2110 A640 2.40 l yellow bis .80 .20
Nos. 2103-2110 (8) 2.50 1.60

Communist Party Flag — A641

1969, Aug. 6 Photo. *Perf. 13½*

2111 A641 55b multicolored .30 .20

10th Romanian Communist Party Congress.

Torch, Atom Diagram and Book — A642

Broken Chain — A643

Designs: 40b, Symbols of agriculture, science and industry. 1.75 l, Pylon, smokestack and cogwheel.

1969, Aug. 10

2112 A642 35b multicolored .20 .20
2113 A642 40b green & multi .20 .20
2114 A642 1.75 l multicolored .50 .20
Nos. 2112-2114 (3) .90 .60

Exhibition showing the achievements of Romanian economy during the last 25 years.

1969, Aug. 23

55b, Construction work. 60b, Flags.

2115 A643 10b multicolored .20 .20
2116 A643 55b yellow & multi .20 .20
2117 A643 60b multicolored .25 .20
Nos. 2115-2117 (3) .65 .60

25th anniversary of Romania's liberation from fascist rule.

Juggler on Unicycle — A644

Masks — A645

Circus Performers: 20b, Clown. 35b, Trapeze artists. 60b, Dressage and woman trainer. 1.75 l, Woman in high wire act. 3 l, Performing tiger and trainer.

1969, Sept. 29 Photo. *Perf. 13½*

2118 A644 10b lt blue & multi .20 .20
2119 A644 20b lemon & multi .20 .20
2120 A644 35b lilac & multi .20 .20
2121 A644 60b multicolored .20 .20
2122 A644 1.75 l multicolored .55 .20
2123 A644 3 l ultra & multi .90 .35
Nos. 2118-2123 (6) 2.25 1.35

Painting Type of 1968

10b, Venetian Senator, Tintoretto School. 20b, Sofia Kretzulescu, by Gheorghe Tattarescu. 35b, Phillip IV, by Velazquez. 60b, Man Reading and Child, by Hans Memling. 1.75 l, Doamnei d'Aguesseau, by Madame Vigée-Lebrun. 3 l, Portrait of a Woman, by Rembrandt. 5 l, The Return of the Prodigal Son, by Bernardino Licinio, horiz.

1969

Gold Frame

Size: 36½x49mm

2124 A620 10b multi .20 .20
2125 A620 20b multi .20 .20
2126 A620 35b multi .20 .20
2127 A620 60b multi .35 .20
2128 A620 1.75 l multi .70 .20
2129 A620 3 l multi 1.25 .35
Nos. 2124-2129 (6) 2.90 1.35

Miniature Sheet

Imperf

2130 A620 5 l gold & multi 2.00 1.50

No. 2130 contains one stamp with simulated perforations.
Issue dates: 5 l, July 31. Others, Oct. 1.

1969, Nov. 24 Photo. *Perf. 13½*

2131 A645 40b Branesti .20 .20
2132 A645 55b Tudora .20 .20
2133 A645 1.55 l Birsesti .50 .20
2134 A645 1.75 l Rudaria .60 .20
Nos. 2131-2134 (4) 1.50 .80

Armed Forces Memorial A646

1969, Oct. 25

2135 A646 55b red, blk & gold .20 .20

25th anniversary of the People's Army.

Locomotives of 1869 and 1969 — A647

1969, Oct. 31

2136 A647 55b silver & multi .25 .20

Bucharest-Filaret-Giurgevo railroad, cent.

A648

A649

Apollo 12 landing module.

1969, Nov. 24

2137 A648 1.50 l multi .55 .50

2nd landing on the moon, Nov. 19, 1969, astronauts Captains Alan Bean, Charles Conrad, Jr. and Richard Gordon.
Printed in sheets of 4 with 4 labels (one label with names of astronauts, one with Apollo 12 emblem and 2 silver labels with picture of landing module, Intrepid).

1969, Dec. 25 Photo. *Perf. 13½*

New Year: 40b, Mother Goose in Goat Disguise. 55b, Children singing and decorated tree, Sorcova. 1.50 l, Drummer, and singer, Buhaiul. 2.40 l, Singer and bell ringer, Plugusurol.

2138 A649 40b bister & multi .20 .20
2139 A649 55b lilac & multi .20 .20
2140 A649 1.50 l blue & multi .50 .20
2141 A649 2.40 l multicolored 1.00 .25
Nos. 2138-2141 (4) 1.90 .85

The Last Judgment (detail), Voronet Monastery — A650

North Moldavian Monastery Frescoes: 10b, Stephen the Great and family, Voronet. 20b, Three prophets, Sucevita. 60b, St. Nicholas (scene from his life), Sucevita, vert. 1.75 l, Siege of Constantinople, 7th century, Moldovita. 3 l, Plowman, Voronet, vert.

1969, Dec. 15

2142 A650 10b gold & multi .20 .20
2143 A650 20b gold & multi .20 .20
2144 A650 35b gold & multi .20 .20
2145 A650 60b gold & multi .20 .20
2146 A650 1.75 l gold & multi .30 .20
2147 A650 3 l gold & multi 1.00 .20
Nos. 2142-2147 (6) 2.10 1.20

Ice Hockey A651

Designs: 55b, Goalkeeper. 1.20 l, Two players with puck. 2.40 l, Player and goalkeeper.

1970, Jan. 20 *Perf. 13½*

2148 A651 20b yellow & multi .20 .20
2149 A651 55b multicolored .20 .20
2150 A651 1.20 l pink & multi .35 .20
2151 A651 2.40 l lt blue & multi 1.00 .30
Nos. 2148-2151 (4) 1.75 .90

World Ice Hockey Championships, Bucharest and Galati, Feb. 24-Mar. 5.

Pasqueflower A652

Flowers: 10b, Adonis vernalis. 20b, Thistle. 40b, Almond tree blossoms. 55b, Iris. 1 l, Flax. 1.20 l, Sage. 2.40 l, Peony.

1970, Feb. 25 Photo. *Perf. 13½*

2152 A652 5b yellow & multi .20 .20
2153 A652 10b green & multi .20 .20
2154 A652 20b lt bl & multi .20 .20
2155 A652 40b violet & multi .20 .20
2156 A652 55b ultra & multi .20 .20
2157 A652 1 l multicolored .20 .20
2158 A652 1.20 l red & multi .35 .20
2159 A652 2.40 l multicolored .70 .20
Nos. 2152-2159 (8) 2.25 1.60

Japanese Print and EXPO '70 Emblem A653

Design: 1 l, Pagoda, EXPO '70 emblem.

1970, Mar. 23

2160 A653 20b gold & multi .20 .20

Size: 29x92mm

2161 A653 1 l gold & multi .30 .20

EXPO '70 Intl. Exhib., Osaka, Japan, Mar. 15-Sept. 13.

A souvenir sheet exists with perforated label in pagoda design of 1 l. Issued Nov. 28, 1970. Value $1.65.

Camille, by Claude Monet (Maximum Card) — A654

1970, Apr. 19 Photo. *Perf. 13½*

2162 A654 1.50 l gold & multi .45 .20

Franco-Romanian Maximafil Phil. Exhib.

Cuza, by C. Popp de Szathmary — A655

Lenin (1870-1924) A656

1970, Apr. 20 *Perf. 13½*

2163 A655 55b gold & multi .20 .20

Alexandru Ioan Cuza (1820-1866), prince of Romania.

1970, Apr. 21 Photo. *Perf. 13½*

2164 A656 40b dk red & multi .20 .20

Map of Europe with Capital Cities A657

1970, Apr. 28

2165 A657 40b grn, brn org & blk .50 .35

2166 A657 1.50 l ultra, yel brn & blk 1.00 .70

Inter-European cultural and economic cooperation.

Victory Monument, Romanian and Russian Flags — A658

1970, May 9

2167 A658 55b red & multi .20 .20

25th anniv. of victory over the Germans.

Greek Silver Drachm, 5th Century B.C. — A659

Coins: 20b, Getic-Dacian silver didrachm, 2nd-1st centuries B.C. 35b, Emperor Trajan's copper sestertius, 106 A.D. 60b, Mircea ducat, 1400. 1.75 l, Stephen the Great's silver groschen, 1460. 3 l, Brasov klippe-taler, 1601, vert.

1970, May 15

2168 A659 10b ultra, blk & sil .20 .20

2169 A659 20b hn brn, blk & sil .20 .20

2170 A659 35b grn, dk brn & gold .20 .20

2171 A659 60b brn, blk & sil .20 .20

2172 A659 1.75 l brt bl, blk & sil .50 .20

2173 A659 3 l dk car, blk & sil 1.00 .25

Nos. 2168-2173 (6) 2.30 1.25

Soccer Players and Ball — A660

Soccer ball & various scenes from soccer game.

1970, May 26 *Perf. 13½*

2174 A660 40b multi .20 .20

2175 A660 55b multi .20 .20

2176 A660 1.75 l blue & multi .45 .20

2177 A660 3.30 l multi .85 .30

Nos. 2174-2177 (4) 1.70 .90

Souvenir Sheet

2178 Sheet of 4 2.00 1.50

a. A660 1.20 l multi .25 .20

b. A660 1.50 l multi .35 .20

c. A660 1.55 l multi .40 .20

d. A660 1.75 l multi .40 .20

9th World Soccer Championships for the Jules Rimet Cup, Mexico City, May 30-June 21. No. 2178 contains 4 stamps similar to Nos. 2174-2177, but with only one quarter of the soccer ball on each stamp, forming one large ball in the center of the block.

Moldovita Monastery — A661

Frescoes from North Moldavian Monasteries.

1970, June 29 *Perf. 13½*

Size: 36½x49mm

2179 A661 10b gold & multi .20 .20

Size: 27½x49mm

2180 A661 20b gold & multi .20 .20

Size: 36½x49mm, 48x37mm

2181 A661 40b gold & multi .20 .20

2182 A661 55b gold & multi .20 .20

2183 A661 1.75 l gold & multi .35 .20

2184 A661 3 l gold & multi 1.00 .35

Nos. 2179-2184 (6) 2.15 1.35

Miniature Sheet

2185 A661 5 l gold & multi 1.75 1.75

Friedrich Engels (1820-1895), German Socialist — A662

1970, July 10 Photo. *Perf. 13½*

2186 A662 1.50 l multi .45 .20

Aerial View of Iron Gate Power Station A663

1970, July 13

2187 A663 35b blue & multi .20 .20

Hydroelectric plant at the Iron Gate of the Danube.

Cargo Ship A664

1970, July 17

2188 A664 55b blue & multi .20 .20

Romanian merchant marine, 75th anniv.

Exhibition Hall and Oil Derrick A665

1970, July 20

2189 A665 1.50 l multi .45 .20

International Bucharest Fair, Oct. 13-24.

Opening of UPU Headquarters, Bern — A666

1970, Aug. 17 Photo. *Perf. 13½*

2190 A666 1.50 l ultra & slate green .45 .20

Education Year Emblem — A667

Iceberg Rose — A668

1970, Aug. 17

2191 A667 55b black, pur & red .20 .20

International Education Year.

1970, Aug. 21

Roses: 35b, Wiener charme. 55b, Pink luster. 1 l, Piccadilly. 1.50 l, Orange Delbard. 2.40 l, Sibelius.

2192 A668 20b dk red, grn & yel .20 .20

2193 A668 35b vio, yel & grn .20 .20

2194 A668 55b blue, rose & grn .20 .20

2195 A668 1 l grn, car rose & yel .30 .20

2196 A668 1.50 l dk bl, red & grn .45 .20

2197 A668 2.40 l brt bl, dp red & grn .85 .20

Nos. 2192-2197 (6) 2.20 1.20

Spaniel and Pheasant, by Jean B. Oudry A669

Paintings: 10b, The Hunt, by Domenico Brandi. 35b, The Hunt, by Jan Fyt. 60b, After the Chase, by Jacob Jordaens. 1.75 l, 5 l, Game Merchant, by Frans Snyders (horiz.). 3 l, The Hunt, by Adriaen de Gryeff. Sizes: 37x49mm (10b, 35b); 35x33mm (20b, 60b, 3 l); 49x37mm (1.75 l, 3 l).

1970, Sept. 20 Photo. *Perf. 13½*

2198 A669 10b gold & multi .20 .20

2199 A669 20b gold & multi .20 .20

2200 A669 35b gold & multi .20 .20

2201 A669 60b gold & multi .20 .20

2202 A669 1.75 l gold & multi .60 .30

2203 A669 3 l gold & multi 1.25 .45

Nos. 2198-2203 (6) 2.65 1.55

Miniature Sheet

2204 A669 5 l gold & multi 2.00 2.00

UN Emblem — A670

Mother and Child — A671

1970, Sept. 29

2205 A670 1.50 l lt bl, ultra & blk .45 .20

25th anniversary of the United Nations.

1970, Sept. 25

Designs: 1.50 l, Red Cross relief trucks and tents. 1.75 l, Rebuilding houses.

2206 A671 55b bl gray, blk & ol .20 .20

2207 A671 1.50 l ol, blk & car .45 .20

a. Strip of 3, #2206-2207, C179 1.40 .55

2208 A671 1.75 l blue & multi .70 .20

Nos. 2206-2208 (3) 1.35 .60

Plight of the Danube flood victims.

Arabian Thoroughbred — A672

Horses: 35b, American trotter. 55b, Ghidran (Anglo-American). 1 l, Northern Moravian. 1.50 l, Trotter thoroughbred. 2.40 l, Lippizaner.

1970, Oct. 10 Photo. *Perf. 13½*

2209	A672	20b	blk & multi	.20	.20
2210	A672	35b	blk & multi	.20	.20
2211	A672	55b	blk & multi	.20	.20
2212	A672	1 l	blk & multi	.25	.20
2213	A672	1.50 l	blk & multi	.40	.20
2214	A672	2.40 l	blk & multi	.95	.20
	Nos. 2209-2214 (6)			2.20	1.20

Ludwig van Beethoven (1770-1827), Composer — A673

1970, Nov. 2

2215 A673 55b multicolored .25 .20

Abstract, by Joan Miró — A674

1970, Dec. 10 Photo. *Perf. 13½*

2216 A674 3 l ultra & multi .85 .70

Souvenir Sheet

Imperf

2217 A674 5 l ultra & multi 1.90 1.90

Plight of the Danube flood victims. No. 2216 issued in sheets of 5 stamps and label with signature of Miró and date of flood. No. 2217 contains one stamp with simulated perforation.

The Sense of Sight, by Gonzales Coques A675

"The Senses," paintings by Gonzales Coques (1614-1684): 20b, Hearing. 35b, Smell. 60b, Taste. 1.75 l, Touch. 3 l, Bruckenthal Museum, Sibiu. 5 l, View of Sibiu, 1808, horiz.

1970, Dec. 15 Photo. *Perf. 13½*

2218	A675	10b	gold & multi	.20	.20
2219	A675	20b	gold & multi	.20	.20
2220	A675	35b	gold & multi	.20	.20
2221	A675	60b	gold & multi	.20	.20
2222	A675	1.75 l	gold & multi	.60	.25
2223	A675	3 l	gold & multi	1.00	.45
	Nos. 2218-2223 (6)			2.40	1.50

Miniature Sheet

Imperf

2224 A675 5 l gold & multi 2.00 2.00

Men of Three Races A676

1971, Feb. 23 Photo. *Perf. 13½*

2225 A676 1.50 l multi .45 .20

Intl. year against racial discrimination.

Tudor Vladimirescu, by Theodor Aman — A677

1971, Feb. 20

2226 A677 1.50 l gold & multi .45 .20

Vladimirescu, patriot, 150th death anniv.

German Shepherd A677a

Dogs: 35b, Bulldog. 55b, Fox terrier. 1 l, Setter. 1.50 l, Cocker spaniel. 2.40 l, Poodle.

1971, Feb. 22

2227	A677a	20b	blk & multi	.20	.20
2228	A677a	35b	blk & multi	.20	.20
2229	A677a	55b	blk & multi	.20	.20
2230	A677a	1 l	blk & multi	.25	.20
2231	A677a	1.50 l	blk & multi	.40	.20
2232	A677a	2.40 l	blk & multi	.85	.40
	Nos. 2227-2232 (6)			2.10	1.40

Paris Commune A678

Congress Emblem A679

1971, Mar. 15 Photo. *Perf. 13½*

2233 A678 40b multicolored .20 .20

Centenary of the Paris Commune.

1971, Mar. 23

2234 A679 55b multicolored .20 .20

Romanian Trade Unions Congress.

Rock Formation A680

Designs: 10b, Bicazului Gorge, vert. 55b, Winter resort. 1 l, Danube Delta view. 1.50 l, Lakeside resort. 2.40 l, Venus, Jupiter, Neptune Hotels on Black Sea.

1971, Apr. 15

Size: 23x38mm, 38x23mm

2235	A680	10b	multi	.20	.20
2236	A680	40b	multi	.20	.20
2237	A680	55b	multi	.20	.20
2238	A680	1 l	multi	.30	.20
2239	A680	1.50 l	multi	.50	.20

Size: 76½x28mm

2240	A680	2.40 l	multi	1.00	.35
	Nos. 2235-2240 (6)			2.40	1.35

Tourist publicity.

Arrow Pattern A681

Design: 1.75 l, Wave pattern.

1971, Apr. 28 Photo. *Perf. 13½*

2241	A681	55b	multi	.75	.60
2242	A681	1.75 l	multi	1.50	1.00

Inter-European Cultural and Economic Collaboration. Sheets of 10.

Historical Museum A682

Demonstration, by A. Anastasiu A684

Communist Party Emblem — A683

1971, May 7 Photo. *Perf. 13½*

2243 A682 55b blue & multi .20 .20

For Romania's Historical Museum.

1971, May 8

35b, Reading Proclamation, by Stefan Szonyi.

2244	A684	35b	multicolored	.20	.20
2245	A683	40b	multicolored	.20	.20
2246	A684	55b	multicolored	.20	.20
	Nos. 2244-2246 (3)			.60	.60

Romanian Communist Party, 50th anniv.

Souvenir Sheets

Motra Tone, by Kole Idromeno A685

Dancing the Hora, by Theodor Aman — A686

Designs: b, Maid by V. Dimitrov-Maystora. c, Rosa Botzaris, by Joseph Stieler. d, Woman in Costume, by Katarina Ivanovic. e, Argeseanca, by Carol Popp de Szathmary. f, Woman in Modern Dress, by Calli Ibrahim.

1971, May 25 Photo. *Perf. 13½*

2247 A685	Sheet of 6		3.50	3.00
a.-f.	1.20 l any single		.50	.35
2248 A686	5 l	multicolored	2.25	2.25

Balkanphila III Stamp Exhibition, Bucharest, June 27-July 2.

No. 2247 contains 6 stamps in 3 rows and 6 labels showing exhibition emblem and "60b."

Pomegranate Flower — A687

Flowers: 35b, Slipperwort. 55b, Lily. 1 l, Mimulus. 1.50 l, Morning-glory. 2.40 l, Leaf cactus, horiz.

1971, June 20

2249	A687	20b	ultra & multi	.20	.20
2250	A687	35b	red & multi	.20	.20
2251	A687	55b	ultra & multi	.20	.20
2252	A687	1 l	car & multi	.35	.20
2253	A687	1.50 l	car & multi	.60	.20
2254	A687	2.40 l	ultra & multi	.95	.25
	Nos. 2249-2254 (6)			2.50	1.25

Nude, by Iosif Iser A688

Paintings of Nudes: 20b, by Camil Ressu. 35b, by Nicolae Grigorescu. 60b, by Eugene Delacroix (odalisque). 1.75 l, by Auguste Renoir. 3 l, by Palma il Vecchio (Venus and Amor). 5 l, by Il Bronzino (Venus and Amor). 60b, 3 l, 5 l, horiz.

1971, July 25 Photo. *Perf. 13½*

Size: 38x50mm, 49x39mm, 29x50mm (20b)

2255	A688	10b	gold & multi	.20	.20
2256	A688	20b	gold & multi	.20	.20
2257	A688	35b	gold & multi	.20	.20
2258	A688	60b	gold & multi	.20	.20
2259	A688	1.75 l	gold & multi	.35	.20
2260	A688	3 l	gold & multi	1.40	.35
	Nos. 2255-2260 (6)			2.55	1.35

Miniature Sheet

Imperf

2261 A688 5 l gold & multi 2.00 2.00

Ships in Storm, by B. Peters — A689

Paintings of Ships by: 20b, Ludolf Backhuysen. 35b, Andries van Eertvelt. 60b, M. W. Arnold. 1.75 l, Ivan Konstantinovich Aivazovski. 3 l, Jean Steriadi. 5 l, N. Darascu, vert.

1971, Sept. 15 Photo. *Perf. 13½*

2262 A689 10b gold & multi .20 .20
2263 A689 20b gold & multi .20 .20
2264 A689 35b gold & multi .20 .20
2265 A689 60b gold & multi .20 .20
2266 A689 1.75 l gold & multi .45 .20
2267 A689 3 l gold & multi 1.00 .35
Nos. 2262-2267 (6) 2.25 1.35

Miniature Sheet

2268 A689 5 l gold & multi 2.00 2.00

Types of Regular Issue

Designs as Before and: 3.60 l, Mail collector. 4.80 l, Mailman. 6 l, Ministry of Posts.

1971 Photo. *Perf. 13½*
Size: 16½x23mm, 23x16½mm

2269 A616 1 l emerald .20 .20
2270 A617 1.20 l red lilac .25 .20
2271 A617 1.35 l brt blue .30 .20
2272 A616 1.50 l orange red .35 .20
2273 A616 1.55 l sepia .35 .20
2274 A617 1.75 l deep green .40 .20
2275 A617 2 l citron .45 .20
2276 A616 2.40 l dark blue .55 .20
2277 A617 3 l greenish bl .70 .20
2278 A617 3.20 l ocher .70 .20
2279 A616 3.25 l ultra .85 .20
2280 A616 3.60 l blue 1.00 .20
2281 A617 4 l lilac rose 1.25 .20
2282 A616 4.80 l grnsh blue 1.40 .20
2283 A617 5 l violet 1.40 .20
2284 A616 6 l dp magenta 1.50 .20
Nos. 2269-2284 (16) 11.65 3.20

Prince Neagoe Basarab A690

Theodor Pallady (Painter) — A691

1971, Sept. 20 *Perf. 13½*

2288 A690 60b gold & multi .20 .20

450th anniversary of the death of Prince Neagoe Basarab of Walachia.

1971, Oct. 12 Photo. *Perf. 13½*

Portraits of: 55b, Benvenuto Cellini (1500-1571), sculptor. 1.50 l, Antoine Watteau (1684-1721), painter. 2.40 l, Albrecht Dürer (1471-1528), painter.

2289 A691 40b gold & multi .20 .20
2290 A691 55b gold & multi .20 .20
2291 A691 1.50 l gold & multi .50 .20
2292 A691 2.40 l gold & multi 1.00 .25
Nos. 2289-2292 (4) 1.90 .85

Anniversaries of famous artists.

Proclamation of Cyrus the Great — A692

Figure Skating — A693

1971, Oct. 12

2293 A692 55b multicolored .20 .20

2500th anniversary of the founding of the Persian empire by Cyrus the Great.

1971, Oct. 25

Designs: 20b, Ice hockey. 40b, Biathlon (skier). 55b, Bobsledding. 1.75 l, Skiing. 3 l, Sapporo '72 emblem. 5 l, Olympic flame and emblem.

2294 A693 10b lt bl, blk & red .20 .20
2295 A693 20b multicolored .20 .20
2296 A693 40b multicolored .20 .20
2297 A693 55b lt bl, blk & red .20 .20
2298 A693 1.75 l lt bl, blk & red .50 .20
2299 A693 3 l lt bl, blk & red .80 .25
Nos. 2294-2299 (6) 2.10 1.25

Miniature Sheet
Imperf

2300 A693 5 l multicolored 2.00 2.00

11th Winter Olympic Games, Sapporo, Japan, Feb. 3-13, 1972. Nos. 2294-2296 printed se-tenant in sheets of 15 (5x3); Nos. 2297-2298 printed se-tenant in sheets of 10 (5x2). No. 2300 contains one stamp 37x50mm.

St. George and the Dragon A694

Frescoes from North Moldavian Monasteries: 10b, 20b, 40b, Moldovita. 55b, 1.75 l, 5 l, Voronet. 3 l, Arborea, horiz.

1971, Nov. 30 Photo. *Perf. 13½*

2301 A694 10b gold & multi .20 .20
2302 A694 20b gold & multi .20 .20
2303 A694 40b gold & multi .20 .20
2304 A694 55b gold & multi .20 .20
2305 A694 1.75 l gold & multi .60 .20
2306 A694 3 l gold & multi .90 .40
Nos. 2301-2306 (6) 2.30 1.40

Miniature Sheet
Imperf

2307 A694 5 l gold & multi 1.90 1.50

No. 2307 contains one stamp 44x56mm.

Ferdinand Magellan A695

Designs: 55b, Johannes Kepler and observation tower. 1 l, Yuri Gagarin and rocket orbiting earth. 1.50 l, Baron Ernest R. Rutherford, atom, nucleus and chemical apparatus.

1971, Dec. 20

2308 A695 40b grn, brt rose & dk bl .20 .20
2309 A695 55b lil, bl & gray grn .20 .20
2310 A695 1 l violet & multi .30 .20
2311 A695 1.50 l red brn, grn & bl .50 .20
Nos. 2308-2311 (4) 1.20 .80

Magellan (1480?-1521), navigator; Kepler (1571-1630), astronomer; Gagarin, 1st man in space, 10th anniv.; Ernest R. Rutherford (1871-1937), British physicist.

Matei Millo — A696

Young Communists Union Emblem — A697

Design: 1 l, Nicolae Iorga.

1971, Dec.

2312 A696 55b blue & multi .20 .20
2313 A696 1 l purple & multi .25 .20

Millo (1814-1896), playwright; Iorga (1871-1940), historian and politician.

1972, Feb.

2314 A697 55b dk bl, red & gold .20 .20

Young Communists Union, 50th anniv.

Young Animals — A698

1972, Mar. 10 Photo. *Perf. 13½*

2315 A698 20b Lynx .20 .20
2316 A698 35b Foxes .20 .20
2317 A698 55b Roe fawns .20 .20
2318 A698 1 l Wild pigs .25 .20
2319 A698 1.50 l Wolves .40 .20
2320 A698 2.40 l Bears .85 .25
Nos. 2315-2320 (6) 2.10 1.25

Wrestling — A699

Olympic Rings and: 20b, Canoeing. 55b, Soccer. 1.55 l, Women's high jump. 2.90 l, Boxing. 6.70 l, Field ball.

1972, Apr. 25 Photo. *Perf. 13½*

2321 A699 10b yel & multi .20 .20
2322 A699 20b multicolored .20 .20
2323 A699 55b gray & multi .20 .20
2324 A699 1.55 l grn & multi .35 .20
2325 A699 2.90 l multicolored .80 .25
2326 A699 6.70 l lil & multi 1.25 .50
Nos. 2321-2326 (6) 3.00 1.55

20th Olympic Games, Munich, Aug. 26-Sept. 10. See Nos. C186-C187.

Stylized Map of Europe and Links A700

Design: 2.90 l, Entwined arrows and links.

1972, Apr. 28

2327 A700 1.75 l dp car, gold & blk 1.10 .75
2328 A700 2.90 l grn, gold & blk 1.50 1.00
a. Pair, #2327-2328 2.60 2.00

Inter-European Cultural and Economic Collaboration.

UIC Emblem and Trains A701

1972, May 20 Photo. *Perf. 13½*

2329 A701 55b dp car rose, blk & gold .20 .20

50th anniv., Intl. Railroad Union (UIC).

Souvenir Sheet

"Summer," by Peter Brueghel, the Younger — A702

1972, May 20 *Perf. 13x13½*

2330 A702 6 l gold & multi 2.00 2.00

Belgica 72, Intl. Phil. Exhib., Brussels, June 24-July 9.

Peony — A703

Protected Flowers: 40b, Pink. 55b, Edelweiss. 60b, Nigritella rubra. 1.35 l, Narcissus. 2.90 l, Lady's slipper.

1972, June 5 Photo. *Perf. 13*
Flowers in Natural Colors

2331 A703 20b dk vio bl .20 .20
2332 A703 40b chocolate .20 .20
2333 A703 55b dp blue .20 .20
2334 A703 60b dk green .20 .20
2335 A703 1.35 l violet .50 .20
2336 A703 2.90 l dk Prus bl .90 .40
Nos. 2331-2336 (6) 2.20 1.40

Saligny Bridge, Cernavoda — A704

Danube Bridges: 1.75 l, Giurgeni Bridge, Vadul. 2.75 l, Friendship Bridge, Giurgiu-Ruse.

1972, June 25 Photo. *Perf. 13½*

2337	A704	1.35 l	multi	.35	.20
2338	A704	1.75 l	multi	.50	.20
2339	A704	2.75 l	multi	.85	.20
			Nos. 2337-2339 (3)	1.70	.60

North Railroad Station, Bucharest, Cent. A705

1972, July 4

2340	A705	55b	ultra & multi	.25	.20

Water Polo and Olympic Rings A706

Olympic Rings and: 20b, Pistol shoot. 55b, Discus. 1.55 l, Gymnastics, women's. 2.75 l, Canoeing. 6.40 l, Fencing.

1972, July 5 Photo. *Perf. 13½*

2341	A706	10b	ol, gold & lil	.20	.20
2342	A706	20b	red, gold & grn	.20	.20
2343	A706	55b	grn, gold & brn	.20	.20
2344	A706	1.55 l	vio, gold & ol	.25	.20
2345	A706	2.75 l	bl, gold & gray	.45	.20
2346	A706	6.40 l	pur, gold & gray	1.10	.35
			Nos. 2341-2346 (6)	2.40	1.35

20th Olympic Games, Munich, Aug. 26-Sept. 11. See No. C187.

Stamp Printing Press — A707

1972, July 25

2347	A707	55b	multicolored	.20	.20

Centenary of the stamp printing office.

Stefan Popescu, Self-portrait — A708

1972, Aug. 10

2348	A708	55b	shown	.20	.20
2349	A708	1.75 l	Octav Bancila	.25	.20
2350	A708	2.90 l	Gheorghe Petrascu	.50	.20
2351	A708	6.50 l	Ion Andreescu	1.25	.30
			Nos. 2348-2351 (4)	2.20	.90

Self-portraits by Romanian painters.

Runner with Torch, Olympic Rings — A709

City Hall Tower, Sibiu — A710

1972, Aug. 13

2352	A709	55b	sil, bl & claret	.20	.20

Olympic torch relay from Olympia, Greece, to Munich, Germany, passing through Romania.

1972 Photo. *Perf. 13*

Designs: 1.85 l, St. Michael's Cathedral, Cluj. 2.75 l, Sphinx Rock, Mt. Bucegi, horiz. 3.35 l, Heroes' Monument, Bucharest. 3.45 l, Sinaia Castle, horiz. 5.15 l, Hydroelectric Works, Arges, horiz. 5.60 l, Church of the Epiphany, Iasi. 6.20 l, Bran Castle. 6.40 l, Hunedoara Castle, horiz. 6.80 l, Polytechnic Institute, Bucharest, horiz. 7.05 l, Black Church, Brasov. 8.45 l, Atheneum, Bucharest. 9.05 l, Excavated Coliseum, Sarmizegetusa, horiz. 9.10 l, Hydroelectric Station, Iron Gate, horiz. 9.85 l, Monument, Cetatea. 11.90 l, Republic Palace, horiz. 12.75 l, Television Station. 13.30 l, Arch, Alba Iulia, horiz. 16.20 l, Clock Tower, Sighisoara.

Size: 23x18mm, 17x24mm

2353	A710	1.85 l	brt purple	.35	.20
2354	A710	2.75 l	gray	.50	.20
2355	A710	3.35 l	magenta	.60	.20
2356	A710	3.45 l	green	.55	.20
2357	A710	5.15 l	brt blue	.95	.20
2358	A710	5.60 l	blue	1.00	.20
2359	A710	6.20 l	cerise	1.10	.20
2360	A710	6.40 l	sepia	1.25	.20
2361	A710	6.80 l	rose red	1.25	.20
2362	A710	7.05 l	black	1.40	.20
2363	A710	8.45 l	rose red	1.50	.20
2364	A710	9.05 l	dull green	1.60	.20
2365	A710	9.10 l	ultra	1.60	.20
2366	A710	9.85 l	green	1.60	.20

Size: 19½x29mm, 29x21mm

2367	A710	10 l	dp brown	1.90	.20
2368	A710	11.90 l	bluish blk	2.25	.20
2369	A710	12.75 l	dk violet	2.50	.20
2370	A710	13.30 l	dull red	2.50	.20
2371	A710	16.20 l	olive grn	3.00	.25
			Nos. 2353-2371,C193 (20)	28.65	4.15

View of Satu-Mare — A711

1972, Oct. 5

2372	A711	55b	multicolored	.20	.20

Millennium of Satu-Mare.

Tennis Racket and Davis Cup A712

1972, Oct. 10 *Perf. 13½*

2373	A712	2.75 l	multi	.75	.25

Davis Cup finals between Romania and US, Bucharest, Oct. 13-15.

Venice, by Gheorge Petrascu — A713

Paintings of Venice by: 20b, N. Darascu. 55b, Petrascu. 1.55 l, Marius Bunescu. 2.75 l, N. Darascu, vert. 6 l, Petrascu. 6.40 l, Marius Bunescu.

1972, Oct. 20

2374	A713	10b	gray & multi	.20	.20
2375	A713	20b	gray & multi	.20	.20
2376	A713	55b	gray & multi	.20	.20
2377	A713	1.55 l	gray & multi	.25	.20
2378	A713	2.75 l	gray & multi	.55	.20
2379	A713	6.40 l	gray & multi	1.40	.35
			Nos. 2374-2379 (6)	2.80	1.35

Souvenir Sheet

2380	A713	6 l	gray & multi	2.00	2.00

Fencing, Bronze Medal — A714

Apollo 1, 2 and 3 — A715

20b, Team handball, bronze medal. 35b, Boxing, silver medal. 1.45 l, Hurdles, women's, silver medal. 2.75 l, Pistol shoot, silver medal. 6.20 l, Wrestling, gold medal.

1972, Oct. 28

2381	A714	10b	red org & multi	.20	.20
2382	A714	20b	lt grn & multi	.20	.20
2383	A714	35b	multicolored	.20	.20
2384	A714	1.45 l	multi	.25	.20
2385	A714	2.75 l	ocher & multi	.55	.25
2386	A714	6.20 l	bl & multi	1.40	.45
			Nos. 2381-2386 (6)	2.80	1.50

Romanian medalists at 20th Olympic Games. See No. C191. For surcharge see No. 2493.

Charity Labels

Stamp day issues frequently have an attached, fully perforated, label with a face value. These are Romanian Philatelic Association charity labels. They are inscribed "AFR." The stamps are valued with label attached. When the "label" is part of the stamp, the stamp is listed in the semi-postal section. See Nos. B426-B430.

Stamp Day Semi-Postal Type of 1968

Design: Traveling Gypsies, by Emil Volkers.

1972, Nov. 15 Photo. *Perf. 13½*

2386A	SP288	1.10 l + 90b	label	.55	.35

Stamp Day.

1972, Dec. 27 Photo. *Perf. 13½*

2387	A715	10b	shown	.20	.20
2388	A715	35b	Grissom, Chaffee and White, 1967	.20	.20
2389	A715	40b	Apollo 4, 5, 6	.20	.20
2390	A715	55b	Apollo 7, 8	.20	.20
2391	A715	1 l	Apollo 9, 10	.20	.20
2392	A715	1.20 l	Apollo 11, 12	.25	.20
2393	A715	1.85 l	Apollo 13, 14	.35	.20
2394	A715	2.75 l	Apollo 15, 16	.60	.20
2395	A715	3.60 l	Apollo 17	1.10	.30
			Nos. 2387-2395 (9)	3.30	1.90

Highlights of US Apollo space program. See No. C192.

"25" and Flags — A716

Designs: 1.20 l, "25" and national emblem. 1.75 l, "25" and factory.

1972, Dec. 25

2396	A716	55b	blue & multi	.20	.20
2397	A716	1.20 l	yel & multi	.35	.20
2398	A716	1.75 l	ver & multi	.60	.20
			Nos. 2396-2398 (3)	1.15	.60

25th anniversary of the Republic.

European Bee-eater A717

Globeflowers A718

Nature Protection: No. 2400, Red-breasted goose. No. 2401, Penduline tit. No. 2403, Garden Turk's-cap. No. 2404, Gentian.

1973, Feb. 5 Photo. *Perf. 13*

2399	A717	1.40 l	gray & multi	.25	.20
2400	A717	1.85 l	multi	.35	.20
2401	A717	2.75 l	blue & multi	.70	.20
a.			Strip of 3, #2399-2401	1.40	.60
2402	A718	1.40 l	multi	.25	.20
2403	A718	1.85 l	yellow & multi	.35	.20
2404	A718	2.75 l	multi	.70	.20
a.			Strip of 3, #2402-2404	1.40	.60

Nicolaus Copernicus — A719

1973, Feb. 19 Photo. *Perf. 13x13½*

2405	A719	2.75 l	multi	.70	.25

Nicolaus Copernicus (1473-1543), Polish astronomer. Printed with alternating label publicizing Intl. Phil. Exhib., Poznan, 8/19-9/2.

Suceava Woman A720

D. Paciurea (Sculptor) — A721

Regional Costumes: 40b, Suceava man. 55b, Harghita woman. 1.75 l, Harghita man. 2.75 l, Gorj woman. 6.40 l, Gorj man.

1973, Mar. 15

2406 A720	10b	lt bl & multi	.20	.20
2407 A720	40b	multicolored	.20	.20
2408 A720	55b	bis & multi	.20	.20
2409 A720	1.75 l	lil & multi	.30	.20
2410 A720	2.75 l	multi	.45	.20
2411 A720	6.40 l	multi	1.25	.35
		Nos. 2406-2411 (6)	2.60	1.35

1973, Mar. 26

Portraits: 40b, I. Slavici (1848-1925), writer. 55b, G. Lazar (1779-1823), writer. 6.40 l, A. Flechtenmacher (1823-1898), composer.

2412 A721	10b	multi	.20	.20
2413 A721	40b	multi	.20	.20
2414 A721	55b	multi	.20	.20
2415 A721	6.40 l	multi	1.10	.35
		Nos. 2412-2415 (4)	1.70	.95

Anniversaries of famous artists.

Map of Europe A722

Design: 3.60 l, Symbol of collaboration.

1973, Apr. 28 Photo. *Perf. 13½*

2416 A722	3.35 l	dp bl & gold	1.10	.70
2417 A722	3.60 l	brt mag & gold	1.25	1.00
a.		Pair, #2416-2417	2.40	2.00

Inter-European cultural and economic cooperation. Printed in sheets of 10 with blue marginal inscription.

Souvenir Sheet

The Rape of Proserpina, by Hans von Aachen — A723

1973, May 5

2418 A723	12 l	gold & multi	2.75	2.50

IBRA Munchen 1973, Intl. Stamp Exhib., Munich, May 11-20.

Prince Alexander I. Cuza — A724

Hand with Hammer and Sickle — A725

1973, May 5 Photo. *Perf. 13½*

2419 A724	1.75 l	multi	.50	.20

Alexander Ioan Cuza (1820-1873), prince of Romania, Moldavia and Walachia.

1973, May 5

2420 A725	40b	gold & multi	.20	.20

Workers and Peasants Party, 25th anniv.

Romanian Flag, Bayonets Stabbing Swastika — A726

WMO Emblem, Weather Satellite — A727

1973, May 5

2421 A726	55b	multicolored	.20	.20

Anti-fascist Front, 40th anniversary.

1973, June 15

2422 A727	2 l	ultra & multi	.50	.20

Intl. meteorological cooperation, cent.

Dimitrie Ralet Holding Letter — A728

Dimitrie Cantemir — A729

Portraits with letters. 60b, Enachita Vacarescu, by A. Chladek. 1.55 l, Serdarul Dimitrie Aman, by C. Lecca.

1973, June 20

2423 A728	40b	multi	.20	.20
2424 A728	60b	multi	.20	.20
2425 A728	1.55 l	multi	.50	.25
		Nos. 2423-2425,B432 (4)	2.15	1.15

"The Letter on Romanian Portraits." Socfilex III Philatelic Exhibition, Bucharest, July 20-29. See No. B433.

1973, June 25

6 l, Portrait of Cantemir in oval frame.

2426 A729	1.75 l	multi	.50	.20

Souvenir Sheet

2427 A729	6 l	multi	2.00	1.40

Dimitrie Cantemir (1673-1723), Prince of Moldavia, writer. No. 2427 contains one 38x50mm stamp.

Plate — A730

Designs: 10b, Fibulae, vert. 55b, Jug, vert. 1.55 l, Necklaces and fibula. 2.75 l, Plate, vert. 6.80 l, Octagonal bowl with animal handles. 12 l, Breastplate, vert.

1973, July 25 Photo. *Perf. 13½*

2428 A730	10b	vio bl & multi	.20	.20
2429 A730	20b	green & multi	.20	.20
2430 A730	55b	red & multi	.20	.20
2431 A730	1.55 l	multi	.35	.20
2432 A730	2.75 l	plum & multi	.55	.20
2433 A730	6.80 l	multi	1.50	.35
		Nos. 2428-2433 (6)	3.00	1.35

Souvenir Sheet

2434 A730	12 l	multi	2.75	2.50

Roman gold treasure of Pietroasa, 4th century.

Symbolic Flower, Map of Europe A731

Design: 5 l, Map of Europe, symbolic tree.

1973, Oct. 2 Photo. *Perf. 13½*

2435 A731	2.75 l	multi	1.10	.70
2436 A731	5 l	multi	1.75	1.00
a.		Sheet, 2 each + 2 labels	5.50	5.50

Conference for European Security and Cooperation, Helsinki, Finland, July 1973.

Jug and Cloth, Oboga — A732

Designs: 20b, Plate and Pitcher, Vama. 55b, Bowl, Marginea. 1.55 l, Pitcher and plate, Sibiu-Saschiz. 2.75 l, Bowl and jug, Pisc. 6.80 l, Figurine (fowl), Oboga.

1973, Oct. 15 *Perf. 13*

2437 A732	10b	multi	.20	.20
2438 A732	20b	multi	.20	.20
2439 A732	55b	multi	.20	.20
2440 A732	1.55 l	multi	.35	.20
2441 A732	2.75 l	multi	.55	.20
2442 A732	6.80 l	multi	1.50	.35
		Nos. 2437-2442 (6)	3.00	1.35

Pottery and cloths from various regions of Romania.

Postilion, by A. Verona — A732a

1973, Nov. 15 Photo. *Perf. 13½*

2442A A732a	1.10 l + 90b label		.40	.20

Stamp Day.

Women Workers, by G. Saru A733

Paintings of Workers: 20b, Construction Site, by M. Bunescu, horiz. 55b, Shipyard Workers, by H. Catargi, horiz. 1.55 l, Worker, by Catargi. 2.75 l, Miners, by A. Phoebus. 6.80 l, Spinner, by Nicolae Grigorescu. 12 l, Farmers at Rest, by Stefan Popescu, horiz.

1973, Nov. 26 Photo. *Perf. 13½*

2443 A733	10b	gold & multi	.20	.20
2444 A733	20b	gold & multi	.20	.20
2445 A733	55b	gold & multi	.20	.20
2446 A733	1.55 l	gold & multi	.35	.20
2447 A733	2.75 l	gold & multi	.55	.20
2448 A733	6.80 l	gold & multi	1.50	.35
		Nos. 2443-2448 (6)	3.00	1.35

Miniature Sheet

2449 A733	12 l	gold & multi	2.50	2.25

City Hall, Craiova — A734

Tugboat under Bridge — A735

Designs: 10b, Infinite Column, by Constantin Brancusi, vert. 20b, Heroes' Mausoleum, Marasesti. 35b, Risnov Citadel. 40b, Densus Church, vert. 50b, B j Church, vert. 55b, Maldaresti Fortress. 60b, National Theater, Iasi. 1 l, Curtea-de-Arges Monastery, vert. 1.20 l, Tirgu-Mures Citadel. 1.45 l, Cargoship Dimbovita. 1.50 l, Muntenia passenger ship. 1.55 l, Three-master Mircea. 1.75 l, Motorship Transilvania. 2.20 l, Ore carrier Oltul. 3.65 l, Trawler Mures. 4.70 l, Tanker Arges.

1973-74 Photo. *Perf. 13*

2450 A734	5b	lake	.20	.20
2451 A734	10b	brt blue	.20	.20
2452 A734	20b	orange	.20	.20
2453 A734	35b	green	.20	.20
2454 A734	40b	dk violet	.20	.20
2455 A734	50b	ultra	.20	.20
2456 A734	55b	orange brn	.20	.20
2457 A734	60b	carmine	.20	.20
2458 A734	1 l	dp ultra	.25	.20
2459 A734	1.20 l	olive grn	.30	.20
2460 A735	1.35 l	gray	.35	.20
2461 A735	1.45 l	dull blue	.35	.20
2462 A735	1.50 l	car rose	.35	.20
2463 A735	1.55 l	violet bl	.35	.20
2464 A735	1.75 l	slate grn	.45	.20
2465 A735	2.20 l	brt blue	.60	.20
2466 A735	3.65 l	dull lilac	1.00	.20
2467 A735	4.70 l	violet brn	1.40	.20
		Nos. 2450-2467 (18)	7.00	3.60

Issued: #2450-2459, 12/15/73; #2460-2467, 1/28/74.

Boats at Montfleur, by Claude Monet — A736

Impressionistic paintings: 40b, Church of Moret, by Alfred Sisley, vert. 55b, Orchard in Bloom, by Camille Pissarro. 1.75 l, Portrait of Jeanne, by Pissarro, vert. 2.75 l, Landscape, by Auguste Renoir. 3.60 l, Portrait of a Girl, by Paul Cezanne, vert. 10 l, Women Taking Bath, by Renoir, vert.

1974, Mar. 15 Photo. *Perf. 13½*

2468 A736	20b	blue & multi	.20	.20
2469 A736	40b	blue & multi	.20	.20
2470 A736	55b	blue & multi	.20	.20

2471	A736	1.75 l	blue & multi	.40	.20
2472	A736	2.75 l	blue & multi	.60	.20
2473	A736	3.60 l	blue & multi	.80	.25
			Nos. 2468-2473 (6)	2.40	1.25

Souvenir Sheet

2474	A736	10 l	blue & multi	2.25	2.00

Harness Racing A737

Designs: Various horse races.

1974, Apr. 5 Photo. *Perf. 13½*

2475	A737	40b	ver & multi	.20	.20
2476	A737	55b	bis & multi	.20	.20
2477	A737	60b	multi	.20	.20
2478	A737	1.55 l	multi	.35	.20
2479	A737	2.75 l	multi	.60	.20
2480	A737	3.45 l	multi	.80	.30
			Nos. 2475-2480 (6)	2.35	1.30

Centenary of horse racing in Romania.

Nicolae Titulescu (1883-1941) A738

1974, Apr. 16

2481	A738	1.75 l	multi	.50	.20

Interparliamentary Session, Bucharest, Apr. 1974. Titulescu was the first Romanian delegate to the League of Nations.

Souvenir Sheet

Roman Memorial with First Reference to Napoca (Cluj) — A739

1974, Apr. 18 Photo. *Perf. 13*

2482	A739	10 l	multi	2.00	2.00

1850th anniv. of the elevation of the Roman settlement of Napoca (Cluj) to a municipality.

Stylized Map of Europe A740

Design: 3.45 l, Satellite over earth.

1974, Apr. 25 Photo. *Perf. 13½x13*

2483	A740	2.20 l	multi	1.25	.70
2484	A740	3.45 l	multi	1.50	1.00
a.			Pair, #2483-2484	2.75	2.00

Inter-European Cultural Economic Cooperation.

Young Pioneers with Banners, by Pepene Cornelia — A741

1974, Apr. 25 Photo. *Perf. 13½*

2485	A741	55b	multicolored	.20	.20

25th anniv. of the Romanian Pioneers Org.

Mail Motorboat, UPU Emblem A742

UPU Emblem and: 40b, Mail train. 55b, Mailplane and truck. 1.75 l, Mail delivery by motorcycle. 2.75 l, Mailman delivering letter to little girl. 3.60 l, Young stamp collectors. 4 l, Mail collection. 6 l, Modern post office.

1974, May 11

2486	A742	20b	gray & multi	.20	.20
2487	A742	40b	multicolored	.20	.20
2488	A742	55b	ultra & multi	.20	.20
2489	A742	1.75 l	multi	.40	.20
2490	A742	2.75 l	brn & multi	.60	.20
2491	A742	3.60 l	org & multi	.85	.30
			Nos. 2486-2491 (6)	2.45	1.30

Souvenir Sheet

2492			Sheet of 2	3.25	2.50
a.	A742 4 l multi			.85	
b.	A742 6 l multi			1.40	

Centenary of Universal Postal Union.
Size of stamps of No. 2492, 28x24mm.
An imperf airmail UPU souvenir sheet of one (10 l) exists. The multicolored stamp is 49x38mm. This sheet is not known to have been sold to the public at post offices.

No. 2382 Surcharged with New Value and Overprinted: "ROMÂNIA / CAMPIOANA / MONDIALĂ / 1974"

1974, May 13

2493	A714	1.75 l	on 20b multi	2.50	1.75

Romania's victory in World Handball Championship, 1974.

Soccer and Games Emblem A743

"25" — A744

Designs: Games emblem and various scenes from soccer game.

1974, June 25 *Perf. 13½*

2494	A743	20b	purple & multi	.20	.20
2495	A743	40b	multi	.20	.20
2496	A743	55b	ultra & multi	.20	.20
2497	A743	1.75 l	brn & multi	.40	.20
2498	A743	2.75 l	multi	.60	.20
2499	A743	3.60 l	vio & multi	.85	.30
			Nos. 2494-2499 (6)	2.45	1.30

Souvenir Sheet

2500	A743	10 l	multi	2.50	2.00

World Cup Soccer Championship, Munich, June 13-July 7. No. 2500 contains one horizontal stamp 50x38mm.

An imperf. 10 l airmail souvenir sheet exists showing a globe as soccer ball and satellite. Gray blue margin showing Soccer Cup, radio tower and stadium; black control number.

1974, June 10

2501	A744	55b	blue & multi	.20	.20

25th anniv. of the Council for Mutual Economic Assistance (COMECON).

UN Emblem and People — A745

Hand Drawing Peace Dove — A746

1974, June 25 Photo. *Perf. 13½*

2502	A745	2 l	multicolored	.50	.20

World Population Year.

1974, June 28

2503	A746	2 l	ultra & multi	.50	.20

25 years of the National and Intl. Movement to Uphold the Cause of Peace.

Ioan, Prince of Wallachia — A747

Soldier, Industry and Agriculture A748

Hunedoara Iron and Steel Works — A749

Designs: 1.10 l, Avram Iancu (1824-1872). 1.30 l, Dr. C. I. Parhon (1874-1969). 1.40 l, Bishop Dosoftei (1624-1693).

1974 Photo. *Perf. 13*

2504	A747	20b	blue	.20	.20
2505	A748	55b	carmine rose	.20	.20
2506	A749	1 l	slate green	.25	.20
2507	A747	1.10 l	dk gray olive	.25	.20
2508	A747	1.30 l	deep magenta	.30	.20
2509	A747	1.40 l	dark violet	.35	.20
			Nos. 2504-2509 (6)	1.55	1.20

No. 2505 for Army Day, No. 2506 for 220th anniv. of Hunedoara Iron and Steel works; others for anniversaries of famous Romanians.
Issue dates: 1l, June 17; others June 25.

Romanians and Flags — A750

Design: 40b, Romanian and Communist flags forming "XXX," vert.

1974, Aug. 20

2510	A750	40b	gold, ultra & car	.20	.20
2511	A750	55b	yellow & multi	.20	.20

Romania's liberation from Fascist rule, 30th anniv.

Souvenir Sheet

View, Stockholm — A751

1974, Sept. 10 Photo. *Perf. 13*

2512	A751	10 l	multicolored	2.00	2.00

Stockholmia 74 International Philatelic Exhibition, Stockholm, Sept. 21-29.

Thistle — A752

Nature Protection: 40b, Checkered lily. 55b, Yew. 1.75 l, Azalea. 2.75 l, Forget-me-not. 3.60 l, Pinks.

1974, Sept. 15

2513	A752	20b	plum & multi	.20	.20
2514	A752	40b	multi	.20	.20
2515	A752	55b	multi	.20	.20
2516	A752	1.75 l	multi	.40	.20
2517	A752	2.75 l	brn & multi	.60	.20
2518	A752	3.60 l	multi	.85	.30
			Nos. 2513-2518 (6)	2.45	1.30

Isis, First Century A.D. A753

Archaeological art works excavated in Romania: 40b, Serpent, by Glycon. 55b, Emperor Trajan, bronze bust. 1.75 l, Roman woman, statue, 3rd century. 2.75 l, Mithraic bas-relief. 3.60 l, Roman man, statue, 3rd century.

1974, Oct. 20 Photo. *Perf. 13*

2519	A753	20b	multi	.20	.20
2520	A753	40b	ultra & multi	.20	.20
2521	A753	55b	multi	.20	.20
2522	A753	1.75 l	multi	.40	.20

2523 A753 2.75 l brn & multi .60 .20
2524 A753 3.60 l multi .85 .30
Nos. 2519-2524 (6) 2.45 1.30

Romanian Communist Party Emblem — A754

Design: 1 l, similar to 55b.

1974, Nov. 20

2525 A754 55b blk, red & gold .20 .20
2526 A754 1 l blk, red & gold .30 .20

9th Romanian Communist Party Congress.

Discobolus and Olympic Rings — A755

1974, Nov. 11

2527 A755 2 l ultra & multi .45 .20

Romanian Olympic Committee, 60th anniv.

Skylab A756

1974, Dec. 14 Photo. *Perf. 13*

2528 A756 2.50 l multi .60 .35

Skylab, manned US space laboratory. No. 2528 printed in sheets of 4 stamps and 4 labels. A 10 l imperf. souvenir sheet exists showing Skylab.

Field Ball and Games' Emblem A757

Designs: 1.75 l, 2.20 l, Various scenes from field ball; 1.75 l, vert.

1975, Jan. 3

2529 A757 55b ultra & multi .20 .20
2530 A757 1.75 l yellow & multi .40 .20
2531 A757 2.20 l multi .50 .20
Nos. 2529-2531 (3) 1.10 .60

World University Field Ball Championship.

Rocks and Birches, by Andreescu A758

Paintings by Ion Andreescu (1850-1882): 40b, Farm Woman with Green Kerchief. 55b, Winter in the Woods. 1.75 l, Winter in Barbizon, horiz. 2.75 l, Self-portrait. 3.60 l, Main Road, horiz.

1975, Jan. 24

2532 A758 20b multi .20 .20
2533 A758 40b multi .20 .20
2534 A758 55b multi .20 .20
2535 A758 1.75 l multi .40 .20
2536 A758 2.75 l multi .60 .20
2537 A758 3.60 l multi .85 .30
Nos. 2532-2537 (6) 2.45 1.30

Torch with Flame in Flag Colors and Coat of Arms — A759

1975, Feb. 1

2538 A759 40b multicolored .20 .20

Romanian Socialist Republic, 10th anniv.

Vaslui Battle, by O. Obedeanu A760

1975, Feb. 8 Photo. *Perf. 13½*

2539 A760 55b gold & multi .20 .20

Battle at the High Bridge, Stephan the Great's victory over the Turks, 500th anniv.

Woman Spinning, by Nicolae Grigorescu — A761

Michelangelo, Self-portrait A762

1975, Mar. 1

2540 A761 55b gold & multi .20 .20

International Women's Year.

1975, Mar. 10

2541 A762 5 l multicolored .85 .30

Michelangelo Buonarroti (1475-1564), Italian sculptor, painter and architect.

For overprint see No. 2581.

Souvenir Sheet

Escorial Palace and España 75 Emblem — A763

1975, Mar. 15 Photo. *Perf. 13*

2542 A763 10 l multi 2.00 1.75

Espana 75 Intl. Phil. Exhib., Madrid, 4/4-13.

Letter with Postal Code, Pigeon A764

1975, Mar. 26 Photo. *Perf. 13½*

2543 A764 55b blue & multi .20 .20

Introduction of postal code system.

Children's Science Pavilion — A765

1975, Apr. 10 Photo. *Perf. 13*

2544 A765 4 l multicolored .75 .20

Oceanexpo 75, International Exhibition, Okinawa, July 20, 1975-Jan. 1976.

Peonies, by N. Tonitza A766

3.45 l, Chrysanthemums, by St. Luchian.

1975, Apr. 28

2545 A766 2.20 l gold & multi .85 .50
2546 A766 3.45 l gold & multi 1.25 .95
a. Pair, #2545-2546 2.10 1.75

Inter-European Cultural and Economic Cooperation. Printed checkerwise in sheets of 10 (2x5).

1875 Meter Convention Emblem — A767

1975, May 10 Photo. *Perf. 13*

2547 A767 1.85 l bl, blk & gold .50 .20

Cent. of Intl. Meter Convention, Paris, 1875.

Mihail Eminescu and his Home — A768

1975, June 5

2548 A768 55b multicolored .20 .20

Milhail Eminescu (1850-1889), poet.

Marble Plaque and Dacian Coins 1st-2nd Centuries — A769

1975, May 26

2549 A769 55b multicolored .20 .20

2000th anniv. of the founding of Alba Iulia (Apulum).

Souvenir Sheet

"On the Bank of the Seine," by Th. Pallady — A770

1975, May 26

2550 A770 10 l multicolored 2.25 1.75

ARPHILA 75, Paris, June 6-16.

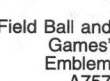

Dr. Albert Schweitzer (1875-1965), Medical Missionary — A771

1974, Dec. 20 Photo. *Perf. 13½*
2551 A771 40b black brown .20 .20

Ana Ipatescu A772

Policeman with Walkie-talkie A773

1975, June 2 Photo. *Perf. 13½*
2552 A772 55b lilac rose .20 .20

Ana Ipatescu, fighter in 1848 revolution.

1975, Sept. 1
2553 A773 55b brt blue .20 .20

Publicity for traffic rules.

Monument and Projected Reconstruction, Adam Clissi — A777

Roman Monuments: 55b, Emperor Trajan, bas-relief, vert. 1.20 l, Trajan's column, Rome, vert. 1.55 l, Governor Decibalus, bas-relief, vert. 2 l, Excavated Roman city, Turnu-Severin. 2.25 l, Trajan's Bridge, ruin and projected reconstruction. No. 2569, Roman fortifications, vert.

1975, June 26 Photo. *Perf. 13½*
2563 A777 55b red brn & blk .20 .20
2564 A777 1.20 l vio bl & blk .25 .20
2565 A777 1.55 l green & blk .25 .20
2566 A777 1.75 l dl rose & multi .35 .20
2567 A777 2 l dl yel & blk .40 .20
2568 A777 2.25 l brt bl & blk .55 .20
Nos. 2563-2568 (6) 2.00 1.20

Souvenir Sheet

2569 A777 10 l multicolored 2.75 2.00

European Architectural Heritage Year.
An imperf. 10 l gold and dark brown souvenir sheet exists showing the Roman wolf suckling Romulus and Remus.
A similar souvenir sheet exists with the Roman wolf 10 l imperf. It appeared in 1978, honoring the Intl. Stamp Fair, Essen, Germany.

Michael the Brave, by Sadeler A778

Michael the Brave Statue — A779

Designs: 1.20 l, Ottoman Messengers Offering Gifts to Michael the Brave, by Theodor Aman, horiz. 2.75 l, Michael the Brave in Battle of Calugareni, by Aman.

1975, July 7
2571 A778 55b gold & blk .20 .20
2572 A778 1.20 l gold & multi .25 .20
2573 A778 2.75 l gold & multi .55 .20
Nos. 2571-2573 (3) 1.00 .60

Souvenir Sheet
Imperf

2574 A779 10 l gold & multi 18.00 16.00

First political union of Romanian states under Michael the Brave, 375th anniv.
No. 2574 issued Sept. 20.

Larkspur — A780

1975, Aug. 15 Photo. *Perf. 13½*
2575 A780 20b shown .20 .20
2576 A780 40b Field poppies .20 .20
2577 A780 55b Xeranthemum annuum .20 .20
2578 A780 1.75 l Rockrose .40 .20
2579 A780 2.75 l Meadow sage .60 .20
2580 A780 3.60 l Wild chicory .85 .25
Nos. 2575-2580 (6) 2.45 1.25

No. 2541 Overprinted in Red:

1975, Aug. 23
2581 A762 5 l multicolored 1.75 .85

Intl. Phil. Exhib., Riccione, Italy, Aug. 23-25.

Map Showing Location of Craiova, 1750 — A781

Illustration reduced.

1975, Sept. 15 Photo. *Perf. 13½*
2582 A781 Strip of 3 .55 .30
a. 20b ocher, yellow, red & black .20 .20
b. 55b ocher, yellow, red & black .20 .20
c. 1 l ocher, yellow, red & black .25 .20

1750th anniv. of first documentation of Daco-Getian settlement of Pelendava and 500th anniversary of documentation of Craiova.
Size of Nos. 2582a, 2582c: 25x32mm; of No. 2582b: 80x32mm.

Muntenian Rug — A782

Romanian Peasant Rugs: 40b, Banat. 55b, Oltenia. 1.75 l, Moldavia. 2.75 l, Oltenia. 3.60 l, Maramures.

1975, Oct. 5 Photo. *Perf. 13½*
2583 A782 20b dk bl & multi .20 .20
2584 A782 40b black & multi .20 .20
2585 A782 55b multicolored .20 .20
2586 A782 1.75 l black & multi .40 .20
2587 A782 2.75 l multicolored .60 .20
2588 A782 3.60 l black & multi .80 .20
Nos. 2583-2588 (6) 2.40 1.20

Minibus A783

1975, Nov. 5 Photo. *Perf. 13½*
2589 A783 20b shown .20 .20
2590 A783 40b Gasoline truck .20 .20
2591 A783 55b Jeep .20 .20
2592 A783 1.75 l Flat-bed truck .40 .20
2593 A783 2.75 l Dacia automobile .60 .20
2594 A783 3.60 l Dump truck .85 .20
Nos. 2589-2594 (6) 2.45 1.20

Souvenir Sheet

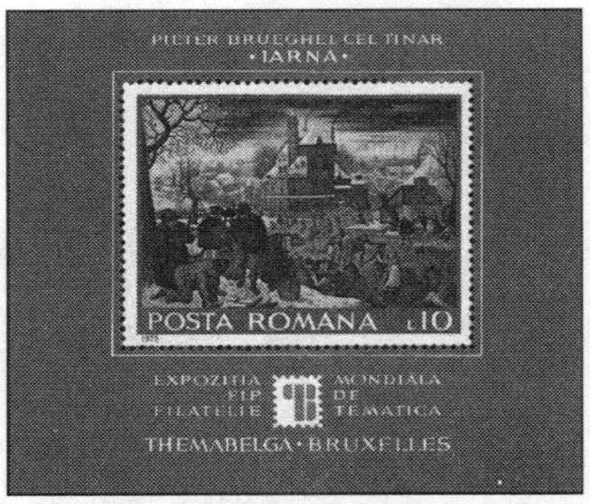

Winter, by Peter Brueghel, the Younger — A784

1975, Nov. 25 Photo. *Perf. 13½*
2595 A784 10 l multicolored 2.50 2.00

THEMABELGA Intl. Topical Phil. Exhib., Brussels, Dec. 13-21.

Luge and Olympic Games' Emblem — A785

Innsbruck Olympic Games' Emblem and: 40b, Biathlon, vert. 55b, Woman skier. 1.75 l, Ski jump. 2.75 l, Woman figure skater. 3.60 l, Ice hockey. 10 l, Two-man bobsled.

1976, Jan. 12 Photo. *Perf. 13½*
2596 A785 20b blue & multi .20 .20
2597 A785 40b multicolored .20 .20
2598 A785 55b multicolored .20 .20
2599 A785 1.75 l ol & multi .40 .20
2600 A785 2.75 l multi .60 .20
2601 A785 3.60 l multi .80 .35
Nos. 2596-2601 (6) 2.40 1.35

Souvenir Sheet

2602 A785 10 l multi 2.50 2.00

12th Winter Olympic Games, Innsbruck, Austria, Feb. 4-15. An imperf. 10 l souvenir sheet exists showing slalom; Romanian flag, Games' emblem.

Washington at Valley Forge, by W. T. Trego — A786

Paintings: 40b, Washington at Trenton, by John Trumbull, vert. 55b, Washington Crossing the Delaware, by Emanuel Leutze. 1.75 l, The Capture of the Hessians, by Trumbull. 2.75 l, Jefferson, by Thomas Sully, vert. 3.60 l, Surrender of Cornwallis at Yorktown, by Trumbull. 10 l, Signing of the Declaration of Independence, by Trumbull.

1976, Jan. 25 Photo. *Perf. 13½*
2603 A786 20b gold & multi .20 .20
2604 A786 40b gold & multi .20 .20
2605 A786 55b gold & multi .20 .20
2606 A786 1.75 l gold & multi .40 .20
2607 A786 2.75 l gold & multi .60 .25
2608 A786 3.60 l gold & multi .75 .35
Nos. 2603-2608 (6) 2.35 1.40

Souvenir Sheet

2609 A786 10 l gold & multi 2.50 2.00

American Bicentennial. No. 2609 also for Interphil 76 Intl. Phil. Exhib., Philadelphia, Pa., May 20-June 6. Printed in horizontal rows of 4 stamps with centered label showing Bicentennial emblem.

Prayer, by Brancusi A787

Designs: 1.75 l, Architectural Assembly, by Brancusi. 3.60 l, Constantin Brancusi.

1976, Feb. 15 Photo. *Perf. 13½*
2610 A787 55b purple & multi .20 .20
2611 A787 1.75 l blue & multi .40 .20
2612 A787 3.60 l multicolored .85 .35
Nos. 2610-2612 (3) 1.45 .75

Constantin Brancusi (1576-1957), sculptor.
For surcharge see No. B440.

Anton Davidoglu A788

Archives Museum A789

55b, Vlad Tepes. 1.20 l, Costache Negri.

1976, Feb. 25

2613	A788	40b	green & multi	.20	.20
2614	A788	55b	green & multi	.20	.20
2615	A788	1.20 l	green & multi	.30	.20
2616	A789	1.75 l	green & multi	.40	.20
			Nos. 2613-2616 (4)	1.10	.80

Anniversaries: Anton Davidoglu (1876-1958), mathematician; Prince Vlad Tepes, commander in war against the Turks (d. 1476); Costache Negri (1812-1876), Moldavian freedom fighter; Romanian National Archives Museum, founded 1926.

Dr. Carol Davila — A790

Vase with King Decebalus Portrait — A791

1.75 l, Nurse with patient. 2.20 l, First aid.

1976, Apr. 20

2617	A790	55b	multi	.20	.20
2618	A790	1.75 l	multi	.40	.20
2619	A790	2.20 l	yellow & multi	.50	.20
			Nos. 2617-2619,C199 (4)	1.70	.85

Romanian Red Cross cent.

1976, May 13

Design: 3.45 l, Vase with portrait of King Michael the Bold.

2620	A791	2.20 l	bl & multi	1.00	.50
2621	A791	3.45 l	multi	2.50	1.25

Inter-European Cultural Economic Cooperation. Nos. 2620-2621 each printed in sheets of 4 with marginal inscriptions.

Coat of Arms — A792

Spiru Haret — A793

1976, June 12

2622	A792	1.75 l	multi	.40	.20

See design A615.

1976, June 25

2628	A793	20b	multicolored	.20	.20

Spiru Haret (1851-1912), mathematician.

Woman Athlete — A794

Romanian Olympic Emblem and: 40b, Boxing. 55b, Team handball. 1.75 l, 2-man scull, horiz. 2.75 l, Gymnast on rings, horiz. 3.60 l, 2-man canoe, horiz. 10 l, Woman gymnast, horiz.

1976, June 25 Photo. *Perf. 13½*

2629	A794	20b	org & multi	.20	.20
2630	A794	40b	multi	.20	.20
2631	A794	55b	multi	.20	.20
2632	A794	1.75 l	multi	.40	.20
2633	A794	2.75 l	vio & multi	.60	.25
2634	A794	3.60 l	bl & multi	.85	.45
			Nos. 2629-2634 (6)	2.45	1.50

Souvenir Sheet

2635	A794	10 l	rose & multi	2.50	2.00

21st Olympic Games, Montreal, Canada, July 17-Aug. 1. No. 2635 contains one stamp 49x37mm.

An imperf. airmail 10 l souvenir sheet exists showing Olympic Stadium, Montreal.

Inscribed Stone Tablets, Banat — A795

Designs: 40b, Hekate, Bacchus, bas-relief. 55b, Ceramic fragment, bowl, coins. 1.75 l, Bowl, urn and cup. 2.75 l, Sword, lance and tombstone. 3.60 l, Lances, urn. 10 l, Clay vessel and silver coins.

1976, July 25

2636	A795	20b	multi	.20	.20
2637	A795	40b	multi	.20	.20
2638	A795	55b	org & multi	.20	.20
2639	A795	1.75 l	multi	.40	.20
2640	A795	2.75 l	fawn & multi	.60	.25
2641	A795	3.60 l	multi	.85	.35
			Nos. 2636-2641 (6)	2.45	1.40

Souvenir Sheet

2642	A795	10 l	yel & multi	2.50	2.00

Daco-Roman archaeological treasures. No. 2642 issued Mar. 25. An imperf. 10 l souvenir sheet exists showing a silver and gold vase and silver coins.

Wolf Statue, 4th Century Map A796

1976, Aug. 25

2643	A796	55b	multi	.20	.20

Founding of Buzau, 1600th anniv.

Game A797

1976, Sept. 20

2644	A797	20b	Red deer	.20	.20
2645	A797	40b	Brown bear	.20	.20
2646	A797	55b	Chamois	.20	.20
2647	A797	1.75 l	Boar	.40	.20
2648	A797	2.75 l	Red fox	.60	.20
2649	A797	3.60 l	Lynx	.85	.20
			Nos. 2644-2649 (6)	2.45	1.20

Dan Grecu, Bronze Medal — A798

Nadia Comaneci — A799

40b, Fencing, bronze medal. 55b Gheorge Megelea (Javelin), bronze medal. 1.75 l, Handball, silver medal. 2.75 l, Boxing, 1 bronze, 2 silver medals. 3.60 l, Wrestling, silver and bronze medals. 10 l, Vasile Daba (kayak), gold and silver medals, vert.

1976, Oct. 20 Photo. *Perf. 13½*

2650	A798	20b	multi	.20	.20
2651	A798	40b	car & multi	.20	.20
2652	A798	55b	grn & multi	.20	.20
2653	A798	1.75 l	red & multi	.40	.20
2654	A798	2.75 l	bl & multi	.60	.25
2655	A798	3.60 l	multi	.80	.40
2656	A799	5.70 l	multi	1.40	.45
			Nos. 2650-2656 (7)	3.80	1.90

Souvenir Sheet

2657	A798	10 l	multi	2.50	2.00

Romanian Olympic medalists. No. 2657 contains one 37x50mm stamp.

Milan Cathedral — A800

1976, Oct. 20 Photo. *Perf. 13½*

2658	A800	4.75 l	multi	1.10	.40

ITALIA 76 Intl. Phil. Exhib., Milan, 10/14-24.

Oranges and Carnations, by Luchian — A801

Paintings by Stefan Luchian (1868-1916): 40b, Flower arrangement. 55b, Vase with flowers. 1.75 l, Roses. 2.75 l, Cornflowers. 3.60 l, Carnations in vase.

1976, Nov. 5

2659	A801	20b	multi	.20	.20
2660	A801	40b	multi	.20	.20
2661	A801	55b	multi	.20	.20
2662	A801	1.75 l	multi	.40	.20
2663	A801	2.75 l	multi	.60	.25
2664	A801	3.60 l	multi	.85	.35
			Nos. 2659-2664 (6)	2.45	1.40

Arms of Alba — A802

Designs: Arms of Romanian counties.

1976-77 Photo. *Perf. 13½*

2665	A802	55b	shown	.25	.20
2666	A802	55b	Arad	.25	.20
2667	A802	55b	Arges	.25	.20
2668	A802	55b	Bacau	.25	.20
2669	A802	55b	Bihor	.25	.20
2670	A802	55b	Bistrita-Nasaud	.25	.20
2671	A802	55b	Botosani	.25	.20
2672	A802	55b	Brasov	.25	.20
2673	A802	55b	Braila	.25	.20
2674	A802	55b	Buzau	.25	.20
2675	A802	55b	Caras-Severin	.25	.20
2676	A802	55b	Cluj	.25	.20
2677	A802	55b	Constanta	.25	.20
2678	A802	55b	Covasna	.25	.20
2679	A802	55b	Dimbovita	.25	.20
2680	A802	55b	Dolj	.25	.20
2681	A802	55b	Galati	.25	.20
2682	A802	55b	Gorj	.25	.20
2683	A802	55b	Harghita	.25	.20
2684	A802	55b	Hunedoara	.25	.20
2685	A802	55b	Ialomita	.25	.20
2686	A802	55b	Iasi	.25	.20
2687	A802	55b	Ilfov	.25	.20
2688	A802	55b	Maramures	.25	.20
2689	A802	55b	Mehedinti	.25	.20
2690	A802	55b	Mures	.25	.20
2691	A802	55b	Neamt	.25	.20
2692	A802	55b	Olt	.25	.20
2693	A802	55b	Prahova	.25	.20
2694	A802	55b	Salaj	.25	.20
2695	A802	55b	Satu-Mare	.25	.20
2696	A802	55b	Sibiu	.25	.20
2697	A802	55b	Suceava	.25	.20
2698	A802	55b	Teleorman	.25	.20
2699	A802	55b	Timis	.25	.20
2700	A802	55b	Tulcea	.25	.20
2701	A802	55b	Vaslui	.25	.20
2702	A802	55b	Vilcea	.25	.20
2703	A802	55b	Vrancea	.25	.20
2704	A802	55b	Postal emblem	.25	.20
			Nos. 2665-2704 (40)	10.00	8.00

Sheets of 50 (10x5) contain 5 designs: Nos. 2665-2669; 2670-2674; 2675-2679; 2680-2684; 2685-2689; 2690-2694; 2695-2699; 2700-2704. Each row of 10 contains 5 pairs of each design.

Issued: #2665-2679, 12/20; #2680-2704, 9/5/77.

Oxcart, by Grigorescu — A803

Paintings by Nicolae Grigorescu (1838-1907): 1 l, Self-portrait, vert. 1.50 l, Shepherdess. 2.15 l, Woman Spinning with Distaff. 3.40 l, Shepherd, vert. 4.80 l, Rest at Well.

1977, Jan. 20 Photo. *Perf. 13½*

2705	A803	55b	gray & multi	.20	.20
2706	A803	1 l	gray & multi	.20	.20
2707	A803	1.50 l	gray & multi	.25	.20
2708	A803	2.15 l	gray & multi	.40	.20
2709	A803	3.40 l	gray & multi	.55	.30
2710	A803	4.80 l	gray & multi	.85	.35
			Nos. 2705-2710 (6)	2.45	1.45

Cheia Telecommunications Station — A804

1977, Feb. 1

2711	A804	55b multi	.20	.20

Red Deer A805

Protected Birds and Animals: 1 l, Mute swan. 1.50 l, Egyptian vulture. 2.15 l, Bison. 3.40 l, White-headed ruddy duck. 4.80 l, Kingfisher.

1977, Mar. 20 Photo. *Perf. 13½*

2712	A805	55b multi	.20	.20
2713	A805	1 l multi	.20	.20
2714	A805	1.50 l multi	.20	.20
2715	A805	2.15 l multi	.35	.20
2716	A805	3.40 l multi	.50	.20
2717	A805	4.80 l multi	.75	.20
		Nos. 2712-2717 (6)	2.20	1.20

Calafat Artillery Unit, by Sava Hentia — A806

Paintings: 55b, Attacking Infantryman, by Oscar Obedeanu, vert. 1.50 l, Infantry Attack in Winter, by Stefan Luchian, vert. 2.15 l, Battle of Plevna (after etching). 3.40 l, Artillery, by Nicolae Ion Grigorescu. 10 l, Battle of Grivita, 1877.

1977

2718	A806	55b gold & multi	.20	.20
2719	A806	1 l gold & multi	.20	.20
2720	A806	1.50 l gold & multi	.25	.20
2721	A806	2.15 l gold & multi	.60	.20
2722	A806	3.40 l gold & multi	.75	.20
		Nos. 2718-2722,B442 (6)	3.25	1.35

Souvenir Sheet

2723	A806	10 l gold & multi	2.75	2.00

Centenary of Romania's independence. A 10 l imperf. souvenir sheet exists showing victorious return of army, Dobruja, 1878.

Issued: #2718-2722, May 9; #2723, Apr. 25.

Sinaia, Carpathian Mountains — A807

Design: 2.40 l, Hotels, Aurora, Black Sea.

1977, May 17

2724	A807	2 l gold & multi	1.00	.85
2725	A807	2.40 l gold & multi	1.40	1.25

Inter-European Cultural and Economic Cooperation. Nos. 2724-2725 printed in sheets of 4 with marginal inscriptions.

Petru Rares — A808

Ion Luca Caragiale — A809

1977, June 10 Photo. *Perf. 13½*

2726	A808	40b multi	.20	.20

450th anniversary of the elevation of Petru Rares to Duke of Moldavia.

1977, June 10

2727	A809	55b multi	.20	.20

Ion Luca Caragiale (1852-1912), writer.

Red Cross Nurse, Children, Emblems A810

1977, June 10

2728	A810	1.50 l multi	.35	.20

23rd Intl. Red Cross Conf., Bucharest.

Arch of Triumph, Bucharest A811

1977, June 10

2729	A811	2.15 l multi	.50	.20

Battles of Marasesti and Oituz, 60th anniv.

Peaks of San Marino, Exhibition Emblem — A812

1977, Aug. 28 Photo. *Perf. 13½*

2730	A812	4 l brt bl & multi	1.00	.25

Centenary of San Marino stamps, and San Marino '77 Phil. Exhib., San Marino, 8/28-9/4.

Man on Pommel Horse — A813

Gymnasts: 40b, Woman dancer. 55b, Man on parallel bars. 1 l, Woman on balance beam. 2.15 l, Man on rings. 4.80 l, Woman on double bars.

1977, Sept. 25 Photo. *Perf. 13½*

2731	A813	20b multi	.20	.20
2732	A813	40b multi	.20	.20
2733	A813	55b multi	.20	.20
2734	A813	1 l multi	.20	.20
2735	A813	2.15 l multi	.35	.20
2736	A813	4.80 l multi	1.25	.20
		Nos. 2731-2736 (6)	2.40	1.20

"Carpati" near Cazane, Iron Gate — A814

Designs: 1 l, "Mircesti" at Orsova. 1.50 l, "Oltenita" at Calafat. 2.15 l, Water bus at Giurgiu. 3 l, "Herculane" at Tulcea. 3.40 l, "Muntenia" in Nature preserve, Sulina. 4.80 l, Map of Danube Delta with Sulina Canal. 10 l, Danubius, god of Danube, from Trajan's Column, Rome, vert.

1977, Dec. 28

2737	A814	55b multi	.20	.20
2738	A814	1 l multi	.20	.20
2739	A814	1.50 l multi	.25	.20
2740	A814	2.15 l multi	.40	.20
2741	A814	3 l multi	.60	.20
2742	A814	3.40 l multi	.65	.20
2743	A814	4.80 l multi	1.25	.30
		Nos. 2737-2743 (7)	3.55	1.50

Souvenir Sheet

2744	A814	10 l multi	2.75	2.00

European Danube Commission.

A 10 l imperf. souvenir sheet exists showing map of Danube from Regensburg to the Black Sea.

Flag and Arms of Romania A815

Designs: 1.20 l, Computer production in Romania. 1.75 l, National Theater, Craiova.

1977, Dec. 30

2745	A815	55b multi	.20	.20
2746	A815	1.20 l multi	.20	.20
2747	A815	1.75 l multi	.40	.20
		Nos. 2745-2747 (3)	.80	.60

Proclamation of Republic, 30th anniversary.

Dancers A816

Designs: Romanian male folk dancers.

1977, Nov. 28 Photo. *Perf. 13½*

2748	A816	20b multi	.20	.20
2749	A816	40b multi	.20	.20
2750	A816	55b multi	.20	.20
2751	A816	1 l multi	.20	.20
2752	A816	2.15 l multi	.35	.20
2753	A816	4.80 l multi	1.25	.20
		Nos. 2748-2753 (6)	2.40	1.20

Souvenir Sheet

2754	A816	10 l multi	2.00	2.00

Firiza Dam A817

Hydroelectric Stations and Dams: 40b, Negovanu. 55b, Piatra Neamt. 1 l, Izvorul Muntelui-Bicaz. 2.15 l, Vidraru. 4.80 l, Iron Gate.

1978, Mar. 10 Photo. *Perf. 13½*

2755	A817	20b multi	.20	.20
2756	A817	40b multi	.20	.20
2757	A817	55b multi	.20	.20
2758	A817	1 l multi	.20	.20
2759	A817	2.15 l multi	.35	.20
2760	A817	4.80 l multi	1.00	.20
		Nos. 2755-2760 (6)	2.15	1.20

Soccer and Argentina '78 Emblem A818

Various soccer scenes & Argentina '78 emblem.

1978, Apr. 15

2761	A818	55b bl & multi	.20	.20
2762	A818	1 l org & multi	.20	.20
2763	A818	1.50 l yel grn & multi	.20	.20
2764	A818	2.15 l ver & multi	.30	.20
2765	A818	3.40 l bl grn & multi	.50	.20
2766	A818	4.80 l lil rose & multi	1.00	.20
		Nos. 2761-2766 (6)	2.40	1.20

11th World Cup Soccer Championship, Argentina '78, June 1-25. See No. C222.

King Decebalus of Dacia Statue, Deva A819

Design: 3.40 l, King Mircea the Elder of Wallachia statue, Tulcea, and ship.

1978, May 22 Photo. *Perf. 13½*

2767	A819	1.30 l gold & multi	.90	.70
2768	A819	3.40 l gold & multi	1.60	1.25

Inter-European Cultural and Economic Cooperation. Each printed in sheet of 4.

Worker, Factory, Flag — A821

Spindle and Handle, Transylvania A822

1978, June 11 Photo. *Perf. 13½*
2770 A821 55b multi .20 .20

Nationalization of industry, 30th anniv.

1978, June 20

Wood Carvings: 40b, Cheese molds, Muntenia. 55b, Spoons, Oltenia. 1 l, Barrel, Moldavia. 2.15 l, Ladle and mug, Transylvania. 4.80 l, Water bucket, Oltenia.

2771 A822 20b multi .20 .20
2772 A822 40b multi .20 .20
2773 A822 55b multi .20 .20
2774 A822 1 l multi .20 .20
2775 A822 2.15 l multi .30 .20
2776 A822 4.80 l multi 1.00 .20
Nos. 2771-2776 (6) 2.10 1.20

Danube Delta — A823

Tourist Publicity: 1 l, Bran Castle, vert. 1.50 l, Monastery, Suceava, Moldavia. 2.15 l, Caves, Oltenia. 3.40 l, Ski lift, Brasov. 4.80 l, Mangalia, Black Sea. 10 l, Strehaia Fortress, vert.

1978, July 20 Photo. *Perf. 13½*
2777 A823 55b multi .20 .20
2778 A823 1 l multi .20 .20
2779 A823 1.50 l multi .20 .20
2780 A823 2.15 l multi .30 .20
2781 A823 3.40 l multi .50 .20
2782 A823 4.80 l multi 1.00 .35
Nos. 2777-2782 (6) 2.40 1.35

Miniature Sheet

2783 A823 10 l multi 2.50 2.00

No. 2783 contains one 37x51mm stamp. Issued July 30.

Electronic Microscope A824

Designs: 40b, Hydraulic excavator. 55b, Computer center. 1.50 l, Oil derricks. 3 l, Harvester combine. 3.40 l, Petrochemical plant.

1978, Aug. 15 Photo. *Perf. 13½*
2784 A824 20b multi .20 .20
2785 A824 40b multi .20 .20
2786 A824 55b multi .20 .20
2787 A824 1.50 l multi .25 .20
2788 A824 3 l multi, horiz. .55 .20
2789 A824 3.40 l multi .70 .20
Nos. 2784-2789 (6) 2.10 1.20

Industrial development.

Polovraci Cave, Carpathians A825

"Racial Equality" — A826

Caves: 1 l, Topolnita. 1.50 l, Ponoare. 2.15 l, Ratei, Mt. Bucegi. 3.40 l, Closani, Mt. Motrului. 4.80 l, Epuran. 1 l, 1.50 l, 4.80 l, Mt. Mehedinti.

1978, Aug. 25 Photo. *Perf. 13½*
2790 A825 55b multi .20 .20
2791 A825 1 l multi .20 .20
2792 A825 1.50 l multi .20 .20
2793 A825 2.15 l multi .30 .20
2794 A825 3.40 l multi .50 .20
2795 A825 4.80 l multi 1.00 .20
Nos. 2790-2795 (6) 2.40 1.20

1978, Sept. 28
2796 A826 3.40 l multi .50 .20

Anti-Apartheid Year.

Gold Bas-relief — A827

Designs: 40b, Gold armband. 55b, Gold cameo ring. 1 l, Silver bowl. 2.15 l, Eagle from Roman standard, vert. 4.80 l, Silver armband.

1978, Sept. 25
2797 A827 20b multi .20 .20
2798 A827 40b multi .20 .20
2799 A827 55b multi .20 .20
2800 A827 1 l multi .20 .20
2801 A827 2.15 l multi .30 .20
2802 A827 4.80 l multi 1.00 .35
Nos. 2797-2802 (6) 2.10 1.35

Daco-Roman archaeological treasures. An imperf. 10 l souvenir sheet exists showing gold helmet, vert.

Woman Gymnast, Games' Emblem A828

1 l, Running. 1.50 l, Skiing. 2.15 l, Equestrian. 3.40 l, Soccer. 4.80 l, Handball.

1978, Sept. 15
2803 A828 55b multi .20 .20
2804 A828 1 l multi .20 .20
2805 A828 1.50 l multi .20 .20
2806 A828 2.15 l multi .30 .20
2807 A828 3.40 l multi .50 .20
2808 A828 4.80 l multi 1.00 .25
Nos. 2803-2808 (6) 2.40 1.25

Ptolemaic Map of Dacia A829

Designs: 55b, Meeting House of Romanian National Council, Arad. 1.75 l, Pottery vases, 8th-9th centuries, found near Arad.

1978, Oct. 21 Photo. *Perf. 13½*
2809 A829 40b multi .20 .20
2810 A829 55b multi .20 .20
2811 A829 1.75 l multi .35 .20
b. Strip of 3, #2809-2811 .50 .30

2,000th anniversary of founding of Arad.

Dacian Warrior, from Trajan's Column, Rome — A829a

1978, Nov. 5 Photo. *Perf. 13x13½*
2811A A829a 6 l + 3 l label 1.60 .85

NATIONALA '78 Phil. Exhib., Bucharest. Stamp Day.

Assembly at Alba Iulia, 1919 — A830

Warrior, Bas-relief — A831

Design: 1 l, Open book and Romanian flag.

1978, Dec. 1
2812 A830 55b gold & multi .20 .20
2813 A830 1 l gold & multi .20 .20

60th anniversary of national unity.

1979 Photo. *Perf. 13½*

1.50 l, Warrior on horseback, bas-relief.

2814 A831 55b multi .20 .20
2815 A831 1.50 l multi .20 .20

2,050 years since establishment of first centralized and independent Dacian state.

"Heroes of Vaslui" — A832

Ice Hockey, Globe, Emblem — A833

Children's Drawings: 1 l, Building houses. 1.50 l, Folk music of Tica. 2.15 l, Industrial landscape, horiz. 3.40 l, winter customs, horiz. 4.80 l, Pioneer festival, horiz.

1979, Mar. 1
2816 A832 55b multi .20 .20
2817 A832 1 l multi .20 .20
2818 A832 1.50 l multi .20 .20
2819 A832 2.15 l multi .30 .20
2820 A832 3.40 l multi .50 .20
2821 A832 4.80 l multi 1.00 .25
Nos. 2816-2821 (6) 2.40 1.25

International Year of the Child.

1979, Mar. 16 Photo. *Perf. 13½*

3.40 l, Ice hockey players, globe & emblem.

2822 A833 1.30 l multi .30 .20
2823 A833 3.40 l multi .55 .20
a. Pair, #2822-2823 .85 .50

European Youth Ice Hockey Championship, Miercurea-Ciuc (1.30 l) and World Ice Hockey Championship, Galati (3.40 l).

Dog's-tooth Violet — A834

Protected Flowers: 1 l, Alpine violet. 1.50 l, Linum borzaeanum. 2.15 l, Persian bindweed. 3.40 l, Primula auricula. 4.80 l, Transylvanian columbine.

1979, Apr. 25 Photo. *Perf. 13½*
2824 A834 55b multi .20 .20
2825 A834 1 l multi .20 .20
2826 A834 1.50 l multi .20 .20
2827 A834 2.15 l multi .30 .20
2828 A834 3.40 l multi .50 .20
2829 A834 4.80 l multi 1.00 .25
Nos. 2824-2829 (6) 2.40 1.25

Mail Coach and Post Rider, 19th Century A835

1979, May 3 Photo. *Perf. 13*
2830 A835 1.30 l multi .40 .25

Inter-European Cultural and Economic Cooperation. Printed in sheets of 4.

See No. C231.

Oil Rig and Refinery — A836

Girl Pioneer — A837

1979, May 24 **Photo.** ***Perf. 13***

2832 A836 3.40 l multi	.50	.20

10th World Petroleum Congress, Bucharest.

1979, June 20

2833 A837 55b multi	.20	.20

30th anniversary of Romanian Pioneers.

Children with Flowers, IYC Emblem A838

IYC Emblem and: 1 l, Kindergarten. 2 l, Pioneers with rabbit. 4.60 l, Drummer, trumpeters, flags.

1979, July 18 **Photo.** ***Perf. 13½***

2834 A838 40b multi	.20	.20
2835 A838 1 l multi	.20	.20
2836 A838 2 l multi	.30	.20
2837 A838 4.60 l multi	.95	.20
Nos. 2834-2837 (4)	1.65	.80

International Year of the Child.

Lady in a Garden, by Tattarescu A839

Stefan Gheorghiu — A840

Paintings by Gheorghe Tattarescu: 40b, Mountain woman. 55b, Mountain man. 1 l, Portrait of Gh. Magheru. 2.15 l, The artist's daughter. 4.80 l, Self-portrait.

1979, June 16

2838 A839 20b multi	.20	.20
2839 A839 40b multi	.20	.20
2840 A839 55b multi	.20	.20
2841 A839 1 l multi	.20	.20
2842 A839 2.15 l multi	.30	.20
2843 A839 4.80 l multi	.90	.20
Nos. 2838-2843 (6)	2.00	1.20

1979, Aug.

Designs: 55b, Gheorghe Lazar monument. 2.15 l, Lupeni monument. 4.60 l, Women in front of Memorial Arch.

2844 A840 40b multi	.20	.20
2845 A840 55b multi	.20	.20
2846 A840 2.15 l multi	.30	.20
2847 A840 4.60 l multi	.95	.20
Nos. 2844-2847 (4)	1.65	.80

State Theater, Tirgu-Mures — A841

Modern Architecture: 40b, University, Brasov. 55b, Political Administration Buildings, Baia Mare. 1 l, Stefan Gheorghiu Academy, Bucharest. 2.15 l, Political Administration Building, Botosani. 4.80 l, House of Culture, Tirgoviste.

1979, June 25

2848 A841 20b multi	.20	.20
2849 A841 40b multi	.20	.20
2850 A841 55b multi	.20	.20
2851 A841 1 l multi	.20	.20
2852 A841 2.15 l multi	.25	.20
2853 A841 4.80 l multi	.85	.20
Nos. 2848-2853 (6)	1.90	1.20

Flags of Russia and Romania — A842

1 l, Workers' Militia, by L. Suhar, horiz.

1979, Aug. 20 **Photo.** ***Perf. 13½***

2854 A842 55b multi	.20	.20
2855 A842 1 l multi	.20	.20

Liberation from Fascism, 35th anniversary.

Cargo Ship Galati A843

Romanian Ships: 1 l, Cargo ship Bucuresti. 1.50 l, Ore carrier Resita. 2.15 l, Ore carrier Tomis. 3.40 l, Tanker Dacia. 4.80 l, Tanker Independenta.

1979, Aug. 27 **Photo.** ***Perf. 13½***

2856 A843 55b multi	.20	.20
2857 A843 1 l multi	.20	.20
2858 A843 1.50 l multi	.20	.20
2859 A843 2.15 l multi	.25	.20
2860 A843 3.40 l multi	.45	.20
2861 A843 4.80 l multi	.90	.25
Nos. 2856-2861 (6)	2.20	1.25

Olympic Stadium, Melbourne, 1956, Moscow '80 Emblem — A844

Moscow '80 Emblem and Olympic Stadiums: 1 l, Rome, 1960. 1.50 l, Tokyo, 1964. 2.15 l, Mexico City, 1968. 3.40 l, Munich, 1972. 4.80 l, Montreal, 1976. 10 l, Moscow, 1980.

1979, Oct. 23 **Photo.** ***Perf. 13½***

2862 A844 55b multi	.20	.20
2863 A844 1 l multi	.20	.20
2864 A844 1.50 l multi	.20	.20
2865 A844 2.15 l multi	.30	.20
2866 A844 3.40 l multi	.50	.20
2867 A844 4.80 l multi	1.00	.25
Nos. 2862-2867 (6)	2.40	1.25

Souvenir Sheet

2868 A844 10 l multi	2.50	2.00

22nd Summer Olympic Games, Moscow, July 19-Aug. 3, 1980. No. 2868 contains one 50x38mm stamp.

No. 2868 airmail.

Imperf 10 l souvenir sheets exist for the Eurpean Sports Conference and 1980 Olympics.

Arms of Alba Iulia — A845

Designs: Arms of Romanian cities.

1979, Oct. 25

2869 A845 1.20 l shown	.30	.20
2870 A845 1.20 l Arad	.30	.20
2871 A845 1.20 l Bacau	.30	.20
2872 A845 1.20 l Baia-Mare	.30	.20
2873 A845 1.20 l Birlad	.30	.20
2874 A845 1.20 l Botosani	.30	.20
2875 A845 1.20 l Braila	.30	.20
2876 A845 1.20 l Brasov	.30	.20
2877 A845 1.20 l Buzau	.30	.20
2878 A845 1.20 l Calarasi	.30	.20
2879 A845 1.20 l Cluj	.30	.20
2880 A845 1.20 l Constanta	.30	.20
2881 A845 1.20 l Craiova	.30	.20
2882 A845 1.20 l Dej	.30	.20
2883 A845 1.20 l Deva	.30	.20
2884 A845 1.20 l Turnu-Severin	.30	.20
2885 A845 1.20 l Focsani	.30	.20
2886 A845 1.20 l Galati	.30	.20
2887 A845 1.20 l Gheorghe Gheorghiu-Dej	.30	.20
2888 A845 1.20 l Giurgiu	.30	.20
2889 A845 1.20 l Hunedoara	.30	.20
2890 A845 1.20 l Iasi	.30	.20
2891 A845 1.20 l Lugoj	.30	.20
2892 A845 1.20 l Medias	.30	.20
2893 A845 1.20 l Odorheiu Seguiesc	.30	.20

1980, Jan. 5

2894 A845 1.20 l Oradea	.30	.20
2895 A845 1.20 l Petrosani	.30	.20
2896 A845 1.20 l Piatra-Neamt	.30	.20
2897 A845 1.20 l Pitesti	.30	.20
2898 A845 1.20 l Ploiesti	.30	.20
2899 A845 1.20 l Resita	.30	.20
2900 A845 1.20 l Rimnicu-Vilcea	.30	.20
2901 A845 1.20 l Roman	.30	.20
2902 A845 1.20 l Satu-Mare	.30	.20
2903 A845 1.20 l Sibiu	.30	.20
2904 A845 1.20 l Siget-Marmatiei	.30	.20
2905 A845 1.20 l Sighisoara	.30	.20
2906 A845 1.20 l Suceava	.30	.20
2907 A845 1.20 l Tecuci	.30	.20
2908 A845 1.20 l Timisoara	.30	.20
2909 A845 1.20 l Tirgoviste	.30	.20
2910 A845 1.20 l Tirgu-Jiu	.30	.20
2911 A845 1.20 l Tirgu-Mures	.30	.20
2912 A845 1.20 l Tulcea	.30	.20
2913 A845 1.20 l Turda	.30	.20
2914 A845 1.20 l Turnu Magurele	.30	.20
2915 A845 1.20 l Bucharest	.30	.20
Nos. 2869-2915 (47)	14.10	9.40

A846

A847

Regional Costumes: 20b, Maramures Woman. 40b, Maramures man. 55b, Vrancea woman. 1.50 l, Vrancea man. 3 l, Padureni woman. 3.40 l, Padureni man.

1979, Oct. 27

2916 A846 20b multi	.20	.20
2917 A846 40b multi	.20	.20
2918 A846 55b multi	.20	.20
2919 A846 1.50 l multi	.25	.20
2920 A846 3 l multi	.45	.20
2921 A846 3.40 l multi	.55	.20
Nos. 2916-2921 (6)	1.85	1.20

1979, July 27

Flower Paintings by Stefan Luchian: 40b, Snapdragons. 60b, Triple chrysanthemums. 1.55 l, Potted flowers on stairs.

2922 A847 40b multi	.20	.20
2923 A847 60b multi	.20	.20
2924 A847 1.55 l multi	.25	.20
Nos. 2922-2924,B445 (4)	1.40	1.35

Socfilex, International Philatelic Exhibition, Bucharest. See No. B446.

Souvenir Sheet

Romanian Communist Party, 12th Congress — A848

1979, Oct.

2925 A848 5 l multi	1.25	.50

Figure Skating, Lake Placid '80 Emblem, Olympic Rings — A849

1979, Dec. 27 **Photo.** ***Perf. 13½***

2926 A849 55b shown	.20	.20
2927 A849 1 l Downhill skiing	.20	.20
2928 A849 1.50 l Biathlon	.20	.20
2929 A849 2.15 l Two-man bobsledding	.25	.20
2930 A849 3.40 l Speed skating	.50	.20
2931 A849 4.80 l Ice hockey	1.00	.20
Nos. 2926-2931 (6)	2.35	1.20

Souvenir Sheet

2932 A849 10 l Ice hockey, diff.	2.25	1.75

13th Winter Olympic Games, Lake Placid, NY, Feb. 12-24, 1980. No. 2932 contains one 38x50mm stamp. An imperf. 10 l air post souvenir sheet exists showing four-man bobsledding.

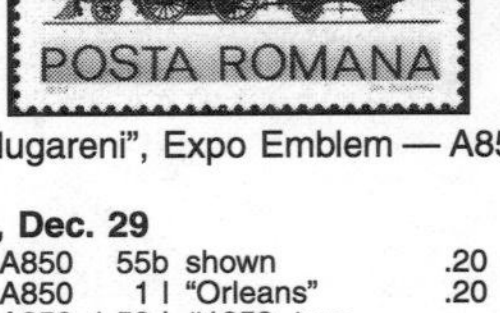

"Calugareni", Expo Emblem — A850

1979, Dec. 29

2933 A850 55b shown	.20	.20
2934 A850 1 l "Orleans"	.20	.20
2935 A850 1.50 l #1059, type fawn	.20	.20
2936 A850 2.15 l #15021, type 1E	.30	.20
2937 A850 3.40 l "Pacific"	.50	.20

2938 A850 4.80 l Electric engine 060-EA 1.00 .25
Nos. 2933-2938 (6) 2.40 1.25

Souvenir Sheet

2939 A850 10 l Diesel electric 2.50 2.00

Intl. Transport Expo., Hamburg, June 8-July 1. #2939 contains one 50x40mm stamp.

Dacian Warrior, Trajan's Column, Rome — A851

Design: 1.50 l, Two warriors.

1980, Feb. 9 Photo. *Perf. 13½*

2940 A851 55b multi .20 .20
2941 A851 1.50 l multi .30 .20

2,050 years since establishment of first centralized and independent Dacian state.

Kingfisher — A852

1980, Mar. 25 Photo. *Perf. 13½*

2942 A852 55b shown .20 .20
2943 A852 1 l Great white heron, vert. .20 .20
2944 A852 1.50 l Red-breasted goose .20 .20
2945 A852 2.15 l Red deer, vert. .25 .20
2946 A852 3.40 l Roe deer .45 .20
2947 A852 4.80 l European bison, vert. .90 .25
Nos. 2942-2947 (6) 2.20 1.25

European Nature Protection Year. A 10 l imperf. souvenir sheet exists showing bears; red control number. See No. C232.

Souvenir Sheets

George Enescu Playing Violin A853

1980, May 6

2948 Sheet of 4 1.50 1.50
a. A853 1.30 l shown .25 .20
b. A853 1.30 l Conducting .25 .20
c. A853 1.30 l Playing piano .25 .20
d. A853 1.30 l Composing .25 .20
2949 Sheet of 4 3.25 3.25
a. A853 3.40 l Beethoven in library .70 .25
b. A853 3.40 l Portrait .70 .25
c. A853 3.40 l At piano .70 .25
d. A853 3.40 l Composing .70 .25

Inter-European Cultural and Economic Cooperation.

Vallota Purpurea A854

Tudor Vladimirescu A855

1980, Apr. 10 Photo. *Perf. 13½*

2950 A854 55b shown .20 .20
2951 A854 1 l Eichhornia crasipes .20 .20
2952 A854 1.50 l Sprekelia formosissima .20 .20
2953 A854 2.15 l Hypericum calycinum .30 .20
2954 A854 3.40 l Camellia japonica .50 .20
2955 A854 4.80 l Nelumbo nucifera 1.00 .25
Nos. 2950-2955 (6) 2.40 1.25

1980, Apr. 24

55b, Mihail Sadoveanu. 1.50 l, Battle against Hungarians. 2.15 l, Tudor Arghezi. 3 l, Horea.

2956 A855 40b multi .20 .20
2957 A855 55b multi .20 .20
2958 A855 1.50 l multi .20 .20
2959 A855 2.15 l multi .30 .20
2960 A855 3 l multi .40 .20
Nos. 2956-2960 (5) 1.30 1.00

Anniversaries: 40b, Tudor Vladimirescu (1780-1821), leader of 1821 revolution; 55b, Mihail Sadoveanu (1880-1961), author; 1.50 l, Victory of Posada; 2.15 l, Tudor Arghezi (1880-1967), poet; 3 l, Horea (1730-1785), leader of 1784 uprising.

A856

A857

Dacian fruit bowl and cup.

1980, May 8

2961 A856 1 l multicolored .20 .20

Petrodava City, 2000th anniversary.

1980, June 20 Photo. *Perf. 13½*

2962 A857 55b Javelin .20 .20
2963 A857 1 l Fencing .20 .20
2964 A857 1.50 l Shooting .20 .20
2965 A857 2.15 l Kayak .30 .20
2966 A857 3.40 l Wrestling .50 .20
2967 A857 4.80 l Rowing 1.00 .25
Nos. 2962-2967 (6) 2.40 1.25

Souvenir Sheet

2968 A857 10 l Handball 2.25 1.75

22nd Summer Olympic Games, Moscow, July 19-Aug. 3. No. 2968 contains one 38x50mm stamp. An imperf. 10 l air post souvenir sheet exists showing gymnast.

Congress Emblem — A858

Fireman Rescuing Child — A859

1980, Aug. 10 Photo. *Perf. 13½*

2969 A858 55b multicolored .20 .20

15th Intl. Historical Sciences Congress, Bucharest.

1980, Aug. 25

2970 A859 55b multicolored .20 .20

Firemen's Day, Sept. 13.

Chinese and Romanian Young Pioneers at Stamp Show — A860

1980, Sept. 18

2971 A860 1 l multicolored .20 .20

Romanian-Chinese Phil. Exhib., Bucharest.

Souvenir Sheet

Parliament Building, Bucharest — A861

1980, Sept. 30

2972 A861 10 l multicolored 2.00 1.65

European Security Conference, Madrid. An imperf. 10 l air post souvenir sheet exists showing Plaza Mayor, Madrid.

Knights and Chessboard — A862

1980, Oct. 1 Photo. *Perf. 13½*

2973 A862 55b shown .20 .20
2974 A862 1 l Rooks .20 .20
2975 A862 2.15 l Man .30 .20
2976 A862 4.80 l Woman 1.00 .25
Nos. 2973-2976 (4) 1.70 .85

Chess Olympiad, Valletta, Malta, Nov. 20-Dec. 8.

Dacian Warrior — A863

Burebista Sculpture — A864

1980, Oct. 15

2977 A863 20b shown .20 .20
2978 A863 40b Moldavian soldier, 15th cent. .20 .20
2979 A863 55b Walachian horseman, 17th cent. .20 .20
2980 A863 1 l Flag bearer, 19th cent. .20 .20
2981 A863 1.50 l Infantryman, 19th cent. .20 .20
2982 A863 2.15 l Lancer, 19th cent. .30 .20
2983 A863 4.80 l Mounted Elite Corps Guard, 19th cent. 1.00 .35
Nos. 2977-2983 (7) 2.30 1.55

1980, Nov. 5 Photo. *Perf. 13½*

2984 A864 2 l multicolored .35 .20

2050 years since establishment of first centralized and independent Dacian state.

George Oprescu (1881-1969), Art Critic — A865

National Dog Show — A866

Famous Men: 2.15 l, Marius Bunescu (1881-1971), painter. 3.40 l, Ion Georgescu (1856-1898), sculptor.

1981, Feb. 20 Photo. *Perf. 13½*

2985 A865 1.50 l multi .20 .20
2986 A865 2.15 l multi .30 .20
2987 A865 3.40 l multi .50 .25
Nos. 2985-2987 (3) 1.00 .65

1981, Mar. 15

Designs: Dogs. 40b, 1 l, 1.50 l, 3.40 l horiz.

2988 A866 40b Mountain sheepdog .20 .20
2989 A866 55b Saint Bernard .20 .20
2990 A866 1 l Fox terrier .20 .20
2991 A866 1.50 l German shepherd .20 .20
2992 A866 2.15 l Boxer .30 .20
2993 A866 3.40 l Dalmatian .50 .20
2994 A866 4.80 l Poodle 1.00 .20
Nos. 2988-2994 (7) 2.60 1.40

River Steamer Stefan cel Mare — A867

1981, Mar. 25

2995 A867 55b shown .20 .20
2996 A867 1 l Vas de Supraveghere .20 .20
2997 A867 1.50 l Tudor Vladimirescu .25 .20
2998 A867 2.15 l Dredger Sulina .30 .20
2999 A867 3.40 l Republica Populara Romana .50 .25
3000 A867 4.80 l Sulina Canal 1.00 .35
Nos. 2995-3000 (6) 2.45 1.40

Souvenir Sheet

3001 A867 10 l Galati 2.50 2.00

European Danube Commission, 125th anniv. An imperf. 10 l souvenir sheet exists showing map of Danube.

Carrier Pigeon A868

Various carrier pigeons and doves.

1981, Apr. 15 Photo. *Perf. 13½*

3002 A868 40b multi .20 .20
3003 A868 55b multi .20 .20
3004 A868 1 l multi .20 .20
3005 A868 1.50 l multi .20 .20
3006 A868 2.15 l multi .30 .20
3007 A868 3.40 l multi .50 .25
Nos. 3002-3007 (6) 1.60 1.25

Romanian Communist Party, 60th Anniv. — A869

Singing Romania Festival — A871

Folkdance, Moldavia — A870

1981, Apr. 22 Photo. *Perf. 13½*

3008 A869 1 l multicolored .20 .20

1981, May 4 Photo. *Perf. 13½*

Designs: Regional folkdances.

3009 Sheet of 4 2.50 2.50
a. A870 2.50 l shown .45 .45
b. A870 2.50 l Transylvania .45 .45
c. A870 2.50 l Banat .45 .45
d. A870 2.50 l Muntenia .45 .45
3010 Sheet of 4 2.50 2.50
a. A870 2.50 l Maramures .45 .45
b. A870 2.50 l Dobruja .45 .45
c. A870 2.50 l Oltenia .45 .45
d. A870 2.50 l Crisana .45 .45

Inter-European Cultural and Economic Cooperation.

1981, July 15

3011 A871 55b Industry .20 .20
3012 A871 1.50 l Electronics .25 .20
3013 A871 2.15 l Agriculture .35 .20
3014 A871 3.40 l Culture .50 .30
Nos. 3011-3014 (4) 1.30 .90

University '81 Games, Bucharest — A872

Theodor Aman, Artist, Birth Sesquicentennial — A873

1981, July 17

3015 A872 1 l Book, flag .20 .20
3016 A872 2.15 l Emblem .35 .20
3017 A872 4.80 l Stadium, horiz. 1.00 .35
Nos. 3015-3017 (3) 1.55 .75

1981, July 28

Aman Paintings: 40b, Self-portrait. 55b, Battle of Giurgiu. 1 l, The Family Picnic. 1.50 l, The Painter's Studio. 2.15 l, Woman in Interior. 3.40 l, Aman Museum, Bucharest. 55b, 1 l, 1.50 l, 3.40 l horiz.

3018 A873 40b multi .20 .20
3019 A873 55b multi .20 .20
3020 A873 1 l multi .20 .20
3021 A873 1.50 l multi .25 .20
3022 A873 2.15 l multi .35 .20
3023 A873 3.40 l multi .60 .25
Nos. 3018-3023 (6) 1.80 1.25

Thinker of Cernavoda, 3rd Cent. BC — A874

1981, July 30

3024 A874 3.40 l multi .50 .25

16th Science History Congress.

Blood Donation Campaign A875

Romanian Musicians A877

Bucharest Central Military Hospital Sesquicentennial — A876

1981, Aug. 15 Photo. *Perf. 13½*

3025 A875 55b multicolored .20 .20

1981, Sept. 1

3026 A876 55b multicolored .20 .20

1981, Sept. 20

Designs: 40b, George Enescu (1881-1955). 55b, Paul Constantinescu (1909-1963). 1 l, Dinu Lipatti (1917-1950). 1.50 l, Ionel Periea (1900-1970). 2.15 l, Ciprian Porumbescu (1853-1883). 3.40 l, Mihail Jora (1891-1971).

3027 A877 40b multi .20 .20
3028 A877 55b multi .20 .20
3029 A877 1 l multi .20 .20
3030 A877 1.50 l multi .25 .20
3031 A877 2.15 l multi .35 .20
3032 A877 3.40 l multi .50 .25
Nos. 3027-3032 (6) 1.70 1.25

Stamp Day A879

1981, Nov. 5 Photo. *Perf. 13½*

3034 A879 2 l multicolored .35 .20

Children's Games — A880

Illustrations by Eugen Palade (40b, 55b, 1 l) and Norman Rockwell.

1981, Nov. 25

3035 A880 40b Hopscotch .20 .20
3036 A880 55b Soccer .20 .20
3037 A880 1 l Riding stick horse .20 .20
3038 A880 1.50 l Snagging the Big One .25 .20
3039 A880 2.15 l A Patient Friend .30 .20
3040 A880 3 l Doggone It .40 .20
3041 A880 4 l Puppy Love .45 .35
Nos. 3035-3041,C243 (8) 2.50 2.05

A881

A882

1981, Dec. 28

3042 A881 55b multi .20 .20
3043 A881 1 l multi .20 .20
3044 A881 1.50 l multi .25 .20
3045 A881 2.15 l multi .35 .20
3046 A881 3.40 l multi .50 .25
3047 A881 4.80 l multi 1.00 .35
Nos. 3042-3047 (6) 2.50 1.40

Souvenir Sheet

3048 A881 10 l multi 2.00 2.00

Espana '82 World Cup Soccer.

No. 3048 contains one 38x50mm stamp. An imperf. 10 l air post souvenir sheet exists showing game.

1982, Jan. 30 Photo. *Perf. 13½*

Designs: 1 l, Prince Alexander the Good of Moldavia (ruled 1400-1432). 1.50 l, Bogdan Petriceicu Hasdeu (1838-1907), scholar. 2.15 l, Nicolae Titulescu (1882-1941), diplomat.

3049 A882 1 l multi .20 .20
3050 A882 1.50 l multi .25 .20
3051 A882 2.15 l multi .40 .20
Nos. 3049-3051 (3) .85 .60

Bucharest Subway System A883

1982, Feb. 25

3052 A883 60b Union Square station entrance .20 .20
3053 A883 2.40 l Heroes' Station platform .40 .25

60th Anniv. of Communist Youth Union — A884

1982

3054 A884 1 l shown .20 .20
3055 A884 1.20 l Construction worker .20 .20
3056 A884 1.50 l Farm workers .25 .20
3057 A884 2 l Research .35 .20
3058 A884 2.50 l Workers .50 .25
3059 A884 3 l Musicians, dancers .60 .25
Nos. 3054-3059 (6) 2.10 1.30

Dog Sled A885

1 l, 3 l, 4 l, 4.80 l, 5 l, vertical.

1982, Mar. 28 Photo. *Perf. 13½*

3060 A885 55b Dog rescuing child .20 .20
3061 A885 1 l Shepherd, dog .20 .20
3062 A885 3 l Hunting dog .55 .35
3063 A885 3.40 l shown .60 .35
3064 A885 4 l Spitz, woman .70 .40
3065 A885 4.80 l Guide dog, woman .80 .45
3066 A885 5 l Dalmatian, girl .95 .50
3067 A885 6 l Saint Bernard 1.00 .40
Nos. 3060-3067 (8) 5.00 2.85

Bran Castle, Brasov, 1377 A886

1982, May 6

3068 Sheet of 4 2.50 2.50
a. A886 2.50 l shown .55 .55
b. A886 2.50 l Hunedoara, Corvinilor, 1409 .55 .55
c. A886 2.50 l Sinaia, 1873 .55 .55
d. A886 2.50 l Iasi, 1905 .55 .55
3069 Sheet of 4 2.50 2.50
a. A886 2.50 l Neuschwanstein .55 .55
b. A886 2.50 l Stolzenfels .55 .55
c. A886 2.50 l Katz-Loreley .55 .55
d. A886 2.50 l Linderhof .55 .55

Inter-European Cultural and Economic Cooperation.

Souvenir Sheet

Constantin Brancusi in Paris Studio — A887

1982, June 5

3070 A887 10 l multicolored 2.00 1.60

PHILEXFRANCE '82 Intl. Stamp Exhibition, Paris, June 11-21.

Gloria C-16 Combine Harvester — A888

1982, June 29

3071 A888 50b shown .20 .20
3072 A888 1 l Dairy farm .20 .20
3073 A888 1.50 l Apple orchard .25 .20
3074 A888 2.50 l Vineyard .40 .20
3075 A888 3 l Irrigation .50 .25
Nos. 3071-3075,C250 (6) 2.05 1.25

Souvenir Sheet

3076 A888 10 l Village 2.00 1.60

Agricultural modernization. No. 3076 contains one 50x38mm stamp.

A890

A891

Resort Hotels and Beaches. 1 l, 2.50 l, 3 l, 5 l horiz.

1982, Aug. 30 Photo. *Perf. 13½*

3078 A890 50b Baile Felix .20 .20
3079 A890 1 l Predeal .20 .20
3080 A890 1.50 l Baile Herculane .25 .20
3081 A890 2.50 l Eforie Nord .40 .20
3082 A890 3 l Olimp .60 .20
3083 A890 5 l Neptun .95 .30
Nos. 3078-3083 (6) 2.60 1.30

1982, Sept. 6

Designs: 1 l, Legend, horiz. 1.50 l, Contrasts, horiz. 3.50 l, Relay Runner, horiz. 4 l, Genesis of Romanian People, by Sabin Balasa.

3084 A891 1 l multicolored .20 .20
3085 A891 1.50 l multicolored .25 .20
3086 A891 3.50 l multicolored .60 .25
3087 A891 4 l multicolored .75 .35
Nos. 3084-3087 (4) 1.80 1.00

Souvenir Sheet

Merry Peasant Girl, by Nicolae Grigorescu (d. 1907) — A892

1982, Sept. 30 Photo. *Perf. 13½*

3088 A892 10 l multicolored 1.75 1.75

Bucharest Intl. Fair A893

1982, Oct. 2

3089 A893 2 l Exhibition Hall, flag .35 .20

Savings Week, Oct. 25-31 — A894

Stamp Day — A895

1982, Oct. 25

3090 A894 1 l Girl holding bank book .20 .20
3091 A894 2 l Poster .35 .20

1982, Nov. 10

3092 A895 1 l Woman letter carrier .20 .20
3093 A895 2 l Mailman .35 .20

Scene from Ileana Sinziana, by Petre Ispirescu A896

Arms, Colors, Book — A897

Fairytales: 50b, The Youngest Child and the Golden Apples, by Petre Ispirescu. 1 l, The Bear Hoaxed by the Fox, by Ion Creanga. 1.50 l, The Prince of Tear, by Mihai Eminescu. 2.50 l, The Little Bag with Two Coins Inside, by Ion Creanga. 5 l, Danila Prepeleac, by Ion Creanga.

1982, Nov. 30

3094 A896 50b multicolored .20 .20
3095 A896 1 l multicolored .20 .20
3096 A896 1.50 l multicolored .25 .20
3097 A896 2.50 l multicolored .40 .20
3098 A896 3 l multicolored .50 .20
3099 A896 5 l multicolored .95 .30
Nos. 3094-3099 (6) 2.50 1.30

1982, Dec. 16

3100 A897 1 l Closed book .20 .20
3101 A897 2 l Open book .35 .20

Natl. Communist Party Conference, Bucharest, Dec. 16-18.

A898

50b, Wooden flask, Suceava. 1 l, Ceramic plate, Radauti. 1.50 l, Wooden scoop, Valea Mare, horiz. 2 l, Plate, jug, Vama. 3 l, Butter churn, wooden bucket, Moldavia. 3.50 l, Ceramic plates, Leheceni, horiz. 4 l, Wooden spoon, platter, Cluj. 5 l, Bowl, pitcher, Marginea. 6 l, Jug, flask, Bihor. 7 l, Spindle, shuttle, Transylvania. 7.50 l, Water buckets, Suceava. 8 l, Jug, Oboga; plate, Horezu. 10 l, Water buckets, Hunedoara, Suceava, horiz. 20 l, Wooden flask, beakers, Horezu. 30 l, Wooden spoons, Alba, horiz. 50 l, Ceramic dishes, Horezu.

1982, Dec. 22 Photo. *Perf. 13½*

3102 A898 50b red orange .20 .20
3103 A898 1 l dark blue .20 .20
3104 A898 1.50 l orange brn .25 .20
3105 A898 2 l brt blue .30 .20
3106 A898 3 l olive green .40 .20
3107 A898 3.50 l dk green .55 .20
3108 A898 4 l lt brown .60 .20
3109 A898 5 l gray blue .75 .20

Size: 23x29mm, 29x23mm

3110 A898 6 l blue .90 .20
3111 A898 7 l lake 1.10 .20
3112 A898 7.50 l red violet 1.25 .20
3113 A898 8 l brt green 1.25 .20
3114 A898 10 l red 1.50 .20
3115 A898 20 l purple 3.25 .25
3116 A898 30 l Prus blue 4.50 .35
3117 A898 50 l dark brown 8.00 .65
Nos. 3102-3117 (16) 25.00 3.85

35th Anniv. of Republic — A899

Grigore Manolescu (1857-92), as Hamlet — A900

1982, Dec. 27

3118 A899 1 l Symbols of development .20 .20
3119 A899 2 l Flag .35 .20

1983, Feb. 28

Actors or Actresses in Famous Roles: 50b, Matei Millo (1814-1896) in The Discontented. 1 l, Mihail Pascaly (1829-1882) in Director Milo. 1.50 l, Aristizza Romanescu (1854-1918), in The Dogs. 2 l, C. I. Nottara (1859-1935) in Snowstorm. 3 l, Agatha Birsescu (1857-1939) in Medea. 4 l, Ion Brezeanu (1869-1940) in The Lost Letter. 5 l, Aristide Demetriad (1872-1930) in The Despotic Prince.

3120 A900 50b multi .20 .20
3121 A900 1 l multi .20 .20
3122 A900 1.50 l multi .25 .20
3123 A900 2 l multi .35 .20
3124 A900 2.50 l multi .40 .20
3125 A900 3 l multi .50 .20
3126 A900 4 l multi .70 .25
3127 A900 5 l multi .85 .30
Nos. 3120-3127 (8) 3.45 1.75

Hugo Grotius (1583-1645), Dutch Jurist — A901

1983, Apr. 30

3128 A901 2 l brown .35 .20

Romanian-Made Vehicles — A902

1983, May 3

3129 A902 50b ARO-10 .20 .20
3130 A902 1 l Dacia, 1300 station wagon .20 .20
3131 A902 1.50 l ARO-242 jeep .25 .20
3132 A902 2.50 l ARO-244 .40 .20
3133 A902 4 l Dacia 1310 .70 .35
3134 A902 5 l OLTCIT club passenger car .85 .40
Nos. 3129-3134 (6) 2.60 1.55

Johannes Kepler (1571-1630) — A903

Famous Men: No. 3135: b, Alexander von Humboldt (1769-1859), explorer. c, Goethe (1749-1832). d, Richard Wagner (1813-1883), composer.

No. 3136: a, Ioan Andreescu (1850-1882), painter. b, George Constantinescu (1881-1965), engineer. c, Tudor Arghezi (1880-1967), poet. d, C.I. Parhon (1874-1969), endocrinologist.

1983, May 16

3135 Sheet of 4 2.50 2.50
a.-d. A903 3 l multicolored .55 .55
3136 Sheet of 4 2.50 2.50
a.-d. A903 3 l multicolored .55 .55

Inter-European Cultural and Economic Cooperation.

Workers' Struggle, 50th Anniv. — A904

Birds — A905

1983, July 22 Photo. *Perf. 13½*

3137 A904 2 l silver & multi .35 .20

1983, Oct. 28 Photo. *Perf. 13½*

3138	A905	50b	Luscinia svecica	.20	.20
3139	A905	1 l	Sturnus roseus	.20	.20
3140	A905	1.50 l	Coracias garrulus	.20	.20
3141	A905	2.50 l	Merops apiaster	.35	.20
3142	A905	4 l	Emberiza schoeniclus	.65	.35
3143	A905	5 l	Lanius minor	.75	.40
			Nos. 3138-3143 (6)	2.35	1.55

Water Sports A906

1983, Sept. 16 Photo. *Perf. 13½*

3144	A906	50b	Kayak	.20	.20
3145	A906	1 l	Water polo	.20	.20
3146	A906	1.50 l	Canadian one-man canoes	.20	.20
3147	A906	2.50 l	Diving	.35	.20
3148	A906	4 l	Singles rowing	.60	.20
3149	A906	5 l	Swimming	.70	.25
			Nos. 3144-3149 (6)	2.25	1.25

Stamp Day A907

1983, Oct. 24

3150	A907	1 l	Mailman on bicycle	.20	.20
3151	A907	3.50 l	with 3 l label, flag	1.10	.55

Souvenir Sheet

3152	A907	10 l	Unloading mail plane	1.75	1.75

#3152 is airmail, contains one 38x51mm stamp.

Geum Reptans A908

Flora (No. 3154): b, Papaver dubium. c, Carlina acaulis. d, Paeonia peregrina. e, Gentiana excisa. Fauna (No. 3155): a, Sciurus vulgaria. b, Grammia quenselii. c, Dendrocopos medius. d, Lynx. e, Tichodroma muraria.

1983, Oct. 28 Photo. *Perf. 13½*

3154		Strip of 5	1.40	1.40
a.-e.	A908	1 l multicolored	.25	.25
3155		Strip of 5	1.40	1.40
a.-e.	A908	1 l multicolored	.25	.25

Issued in sheets of 15.

Lady with Feather, by Cornelius Baba — A909

1983, Nov. 3

3156	A909	1 l	shown	.20	.20
3157	A909	2 l	Citizens	.35	.20
3158	A909	3 l	Farmers, horiz.	.50	.20
3159	A909	4 l	Resting in the Field, horiz.	.70	.25
			Nos. 3156-3159 (4)	1.75	.85

A910

A911

1983, Nov. 30

3160	A910	1 l	Banner, emblem	.20	.20
3161	A910	2 l	Congress building, flags	.30	.20

Pact with Romania, 65th anniv.

1983, Dec. 17

Designs: 1 l, Flags of participating countries, post office, mailman. 2 l, Congress building, woman letter carrier. 10 l, Flags, Congress building.

3162	A911	1 l	multicolored	*.20*	*.20*
3163	A911	2 l	multicolored	*.30*	*.20*

Souvenir Sheet

3164	A911	10 l	multicolored	*1.60*	*1.60*

BALKANFILA '83 Stamp Exhibition, Bucharest. #3164 contains one 38x50mm stamp.

Souvenir Sheet

Orient Express Centenary (Paris-Istanbul) — A912

1983, Dec. 30

3165	A912	10 l	Leaving Gara de Nord, Bucharest, 1883	2.50	2.50

1984 Winter Olympics A913

1984, Jan. 14

3166	A913	50b	Cross-country skiing	.20	.20
3167	A913	1 l	Biathlon	.20	.20
3168	A913	1.50 l	Figure skating	.20	.20
3169	A913	2 l	Speed skating	.30	.20
3170	A913	3 l	Hockey	.40	.20
3171	A913	3.50 l	Bobsledding	.50	.20
3172	A913	4 l	Luge	.60	.25
3173	A913	5 l	Skiing	.75	.30
			Nos. 3166-3173 (8)	3.15	1.75

A 10 l imperf souvenir sheet exists showing ski jumping.

Souvenir Sheet

Prince Alexandru Ioan Cuza, Arms — A914

1984, Jan. 24 Photo. *Perf. 13½*

3174	A914	10 l	multi	1.75	1.75

Union of Moldavia and Walachia Provinces, 125th anniv.

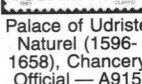

Palace of Udriste Naturel (1596-1658), Chancery Official — A915

Miron Costin (1633-91), Poet — A916

Famous Men: 1.50 l, Crisan (Marcu Giurgiu), (1733-85), peasant revolt leader. 2 l, Simion Barnutiu (1808-64), scientist. 3.50 l, Duiliu Zamfirescu (1858-1922), poet. 4 l, Nicolas Milescu (1636-1708), Court official.

1984, Feb. 8

3175	A915	50b	multi	.20	.20
3176	A916	1 l	multi	.20	.20
3177	A916	1.50 l	multi	.20	.20
3178	A916	2 l	multi	.20	.20
3179	A916	3.50 l	multi	.40	.20
3180	A916	4 l	multi	.45	.20
			Nos. 3175-3180 (6)	1.65	1.20

See Nos. 3210-3213.

Souvenir Sheet

15th Balkan Chess Match, Herculane A917

4 successive moves culminating in checkmate.

1984, Feb. 20 Photo. *Perf. 13½*

3181		Sheet of 4	2.25	2.25
a.-d.	A917	3 l, any single	.55	.55

Orsova Bridge A918

Bridges: No. 3182b, Arges. c, Basarabi. d, Ohaba.

No. 3183: a, Kohlbrand-Germany. b, Bosfor-Turcia. c, Europa-Austria. d, Turnului-Anglia.

1984, Apr. 24

3182		Sheet of 4	2.50	2.50
a.-d.	A918	3 l multi	.55	.55
3183		Sheet of 4	2.50	2.50
a.-d.	A918	3 l multi	.55	.55

Inter-European Cultural and Economic Cooperation.

Summer Olympics — A919

1984, May 25 Photo. *Perf. 13½*

3184	A919	50b	High jump	.20	.20
3185	A919	1 l	Swimming	.20	.20
3186	A919	1.50 l	Running	.25	.20
3187	A919	3 l	Handball	.50	.30
3188	A919	4 l	Rowing	.70	.40
3189	A919	5 l	2-man canoe	.85	.50
			Nos. 3184-3189 (6)	2.70	1.80

A 10 l imperf. airmail souvenir sheet containing a vert. stamp picturing a gymnast exists.

Environmental Protection — A920

1984, Apr. 26 Photo. *Perf. 13½*

3190	A920	1 l	Sunflower	.20	.20
3191	A920	2 l	Stag	.45	.20
3192	A920	3 l	Fish	.70	.20
3193	A920	4 l	Bird	.90	.30
			Nos. 3190-3193 (4)	2.25	.90

Danube Flowers — A921

45th Anniv., Youth Anti-Fascist Committee A922

1984, Apr. 30 Photo. *Perf. 13½*

3194	A921	50b	Sagittaria sagittifolia	.20	.20
3195	A921	1 l	Iris pseudacorus	.20	.20
3196	A921	1.50 l	Butomus umbellatus	.25	.20
3197	A921	3 l	Nymphaea alba, horiz.	.50	.25
3198	A921	4 l	Nymphoides peltata, horiz.	.70	.30
3199	A921	5 l	Nuphar luteum, horiz.	.85	.45
			Nos. 3194-3199 (6)	2.70	1.60

1984, Apr. 30 Photo. *Perf. 13½*

3200	A922	2 l	multicolored	.40	.20

25th Congress, Ear, Nose and Throat Medicine — A923

1984, May 30 Photo. *Perf. 13½*

3201	A923	2 l Congress seal	.40	.20

Souvenir Sheets

European Soccer Cup Championships - A923a

Soccer players and flags of: c, Romania. d, West Germany. e, Portugal. f, Spain. g, France. h, Belgium. i, Yugoslavia. j, Denmark.

1984, June 7 Photo. *Perf. 13½*

3201A		Sheet of 4	2.50	2.50
c.-f.		A923a 3 l, any single	.60	.60
3201B		Sheet of 4	2.50	2.50
g.-i.		A923a 3 l, any single	.60	.60

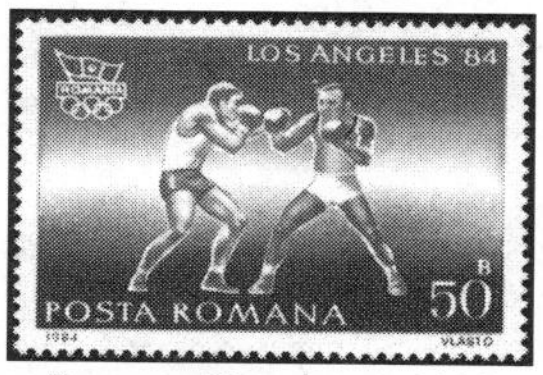

Summer Olympics — A924

1984, July 2 Photo. *Perf. 13½*

3202	A924	50b	Boxing	.20	.20
3203	A924	1 l	Rowing	.20	.20
3204	A924	1.50 l	Team handball	.20	.20
3205	A924	2 l	Judo	.25	.20
3206	A924	3 l	Wrestling	.40	.20
3207	A924	3.50 l	Fencing	.50	.20
3208	A924	4 l	Kayak	.55	.25
3209	A924	5 l	Swimming	.60	.30
	Nos. 3202-3209 (8)			2.90	1.75

Two imperf. 10 l airmail souvenir sheets, showing long jumping and gymnastics exist.

Famous Romanians Type

1984, July 28 Photo. *Perf. 13½*

3210	A916	1 l Micai Ciuca	.20	.20
3211	A916	2 l Petre Aurelian	.35	.20
3212	A916	3 l Alexandru Vlahuta	.50	.20
3213	A916	4 l Dimitrie Leonida	.70	.30
	Nos. 3210-3213 (4)		1.75	.90

40th Anniv., Romanian Revolution A925

1984, Aug. 17 Photo. *Perf. 13½*

3214	A925	2 l multicolored	.35	.20

Romanian Horses — A926

1984, Aug. 30 Photo. *Perf. 13½*

3215	A926	50b	Lippizaner	.20	.20
3216	A926	1 l	Hutul	.20	.20
3217	A926	1.50 l	Bucovina	.25	.20
3218	A926	2.50 l	Nonius	.40	.20
3219	A926	4 l	Arabian	.65	.30
3220	A926	5 l	Romanian Mixed-breed	.80	.40
	Nos. 3215-3220 (6)			2.50	1.50

1784 Uprisings, 200th Anniv. — A927

1984, Nov. 1 Photo. *Perf. 13½*

3221	A927	2 l Monument	.30	.20

Children A928

Paintings: 50b, Portrait of Child, by T. Aman. 1 l, Shepherd, by N. Grigorescu. 2 l, Girl with Orange, by S. Luchian. 3 l, Portrait of Child, by N. Tonitza. 4 l, Portrait of Boy, by S. Popp. 5 l, Portrait of Girl, by I. Tuculescu.

1984, Nov. 10 Photo. *Perf. 13½*

3222	A928	50b	multicolored	.20	.20
3223	A928	1 l	multicolored	.20	.20
3224	A928	2 l	multicolored	.35	.20
3225	A928	3 l	multicolored	.50	.20
3226	A928	4 l	multicolored	.70	.30
3227	A928	5 l	multicolored	.85	.35
	Nos. 3222-3227 (6)			2.80	1.45

Stamp Day A929

1984, Nov. 15 Photo. *Perf. 13½*

3228	A929	2 l + 1 l label	.50	.30

Souvenir Sheet

13th Party Congress — A930

1984, Nov. 17 Photo. *Perf. 13½*

3229	A930	10 l Party symbols	1.75	1.75

Souvenir Sheets

Romanian Medalists, 1984 Summer Olympic Games — A931

No. 3230: a, Ecaterina Szabo, gymnastic floor exercise. b, 500-meter four-women kayak. c, Anisoara Stanciu, long jump. d, Greco-Roman wrestling. e, Mircea Fratica, half middleweight judo. f, Corneliu Ion, rapid fire pistol.

No. 3231: a, 1000-meter two-man scull. b, Weight lifting. c, Women's relays. d, Canoeing, pair oars without coxswain. e, Fencing, team foil. f, Ecaterina Szabo, all-around gymnastics.

1984, Oct. 29 Photo. *Perf. 13½*

3230		Sheet of 6	3.25	3.25
a.-f.		A931 3 l, any single	.50	.50
3231		Sheet of 6	3.25	3.25
a.-f.		A931 3 l, any single	.50	.50

A932

A933

Pelicans of the Danube Delta.

1984, Dec. 15

3232	A932	50b	Flying	.40	.20
3233	A932	1 l	On ground	.75	.20
3234	A932	1 l	In water	.75	.20
3235	A932	2 l	Nesting	1.60	.20
	Nos. 3232-3235 (4)			3.50	.80

1984, Dec. 26

Famous Men: 50b, Dr. Petru Groza (1884-1958). 1 l, Alexandru Odobescu (1834-1895). 2 l, Dr. Carol Davila (1828-1884). 3 l, Dr. Nicolae G. Lupu (1884-1966). 4 l, Dr. Daniel Danielopolu (1884-1955). 5 l, Panait Istrati (1884-1935).

3236	A933	50b	multi	.20	.20
3237	A933	1 l	multi	.20	.20
3238	A933	2 l	multi	.35	.20
3239	A933	3 l	multi	.50	.20
3240	A933	4 l	multi	.70	.30
3241	A933	5 l	multi	.85	.35
	Nos. 3236-3241 (6)			2.80	1.45

Timisoara Power Station, Electric Street Lights, Cent. A934

1984, Dec. 29

3242	A934	1 l Generator, 1884	.20	.20
3243	A934	2 l Street arc lamp, Timisoara, 1884, vert.	.35	.20

Souvenir Sheets

European Music Year A935

Composers and opera houses, No. 3244a, Moscow Theater, Tchaichovsky (1840-1893). b, Bucharest Theater, George Enescu (1881-1955). c, Dresden Opera, Wagner (1813-1883). d, Warsaw Opera, Stanislaw Moniuszko (1819-1872).

No. 3245a, Paris Opera, Gounod (1818-1893). b, Munich Opera, Strauss (1864-1949). c, Vienna Opera, Mozart (1756-1791). d, La Scala, Milan, Verdi (1813-1901).

1985, Mar. 28

3244		Sheet of 4	2.50	2.50
a.-d.		A935 3 l, any single	.60	.60
3245		Sheet of 4	2.50	2.50
a.-d.		A935 3 l, any single	.60	.60

August T. Laurian (1810-1881), Linguist and Historian — A936

Intl. Youth Year — A937

Famous men: 1 l, Grigore Alexandrescu (1810-1885), author. 1.50 l, Gheorghe Pop de Basesti (1835-1919), politician. 2 l, Mateiu Caragiale (1885-1936), author. 3 l, Gheorghe Ionescu-Sisesti (1885-1967), scientist. 4 l, Liviu Rebreanu (1885-1944), author.

1985, Mar. 29

3246	A936	50b	multi	.20	.20
3247	A936	1 l	multi	.20	.20
3248	A936	1.50 l	multi	.30	.20
3249	A936	2 l	multi	.40	.20
3250	A936	3 l	multi	.60	.30
3251	A936	4 l	multi	.80	.40
	Nos. 3246-3251 (6)			2.50	1.50

1985, Apr. 15

3252	A937	1 l Scientific research	.20	.20
3253	A937	2 l Construction	.35	.20

Souvenir Sheet

3254	A937	10 l Intl. solidarity	1.75	1.75

No. 3254 contains one 54x42mm stamp.

Wildlife Conservation A938

End of World War II, 40th Anniv. — A939

1985, May 6

3255 A938 50b Nyctereutes procyonoides .20 .20
3256 A938 1 l Perdix perdix .20 .20
3257 A938 1.50 l Nyctea scandiaca .25 .20
3258 A938 2 l Martes martes .35 .20
3259 A938 3 l Meles meles .55 .20
3260 A938 3.50 l Lutra lutra .70 .25
3261 A938 4 l Tetrao urogallus .75 .30
3262 A938 5 l Otis tarda .90 .35
Nos. 3255-3262 (8) 3.90 1.90

1985, May 9

3263 A939 2 l War monument, natl. and party flags .35 .20

Union of Communist Youth, 12th Congress A940

1985, May 14

3264 A940 2 l Emblem .35 .20

Danube-Black Sea Canal Opening, May 26, 1984 — A942

1985, June 7 ***Perf. 13½***

3266 A942 1 l Canal, map .20 .20
3267 A942 2 l Bridge over lock, Cernavoda .35 .20
3268 A942 3 l Bridge over canal, Medgidea .50 .25
3269 A942 4 l Agigea lock, bridge .70 .35
Nos. 3266-3269 (4) 1.75 1.00

Souvenir Sheet

3270 A942 10 l Opening ceremony, Cernavoda, Ceaucescu 1.75 1.75

No. 3270 contains one 54x42mm stamp.

Audubon Birth Bicentenary — A943

No. American bird species. #3272-3275 vert.

1985, June 26

3271 A943 50b Turdus migratorius .20 .20
3272 A943 1 l Pelecanus occidentalis .20 .20
3273 A943 1.50 l Nyctanassa violarea .30 .20
3274 A943 2 l Icterus galbula .35 .20
3275 A943 3 l Podiceps grisegena .55 .25
3276 A943 4 l Anas platyrhynchos .70 .35
Nos. 3271-3276 (6) 2.30 1.40

20th Century Paintings by Ion Tuculescu — A944

1985, July 13

3277 A944 1 l Fire, vert. .20 .20
3278 A944 2 l Circuit, vert. .35 .20
3279 A944 3 l Interior .55 .25
3280 A944 4 l Sunset .70 .35
Nos. 3277-3280 (4) 1.80 1.00

Butterflies A945

1985, July 15

3281 A945 50b Inachis io .20 .20
3282 A945 1 l Papilio machaon .20 .20
3283 A945 2 l Vanessa atalanta .40 .20
3284 A945 3 l Saturnia pavonia .60 .30
3285 A945 4 l Ammobiota festiva .80 .40
3286 A945 5 l Smerinthus ocellatus 1.00 .50
Nos. 3281-3286 (6) 3.20 1.80

Natl. Communist Party Achievements — A946

Natl. and party flags, and: 1 l, Transfagarasan Mountain Road. 2 l, Danube-Black Sea Canal. 3 l, Bucharest Underground Railway. 4 l, Irrigation.

1985, July 29

3287 A946 1 l multicolored .20 .20
3288 A946 2 l multicolored .35 .20
3289 A946 3 l multicolored .55 .25
3290 A946 4 l multicolored .70 .35
Nos. 3287-3290 (4) 1.80 1.00

20th annivs.: Election of Gen.-Sec. Nicolae Ceausescu; Natl. Communist Congress.

Romanian Socialist Constitution, 20th Anniv. — A947

1985, Aug. 5

3291 A947 1 l Arms, wheat, dove .20 .20
3292 A947 2 l Arms, eternal flame .35 .20

1986 World Cup Soccer Preliminaries — A948

Flags of participants; Great Britain, Northern Ireland, Romania, Finland, Turkey and: 50b, Sliding tackle. 1 l, Trapping the ball. 1.50 l, Heading the ball. 2 l, Dribble. 3 l, Tackle. 4 l, Scissor kick. 10 l, Dribble, diff.

1985, Oct. 15

3293 A948 50b multi .20 .20
3294 A948 1 l multi .20 .20
3295 A948 1.50 l multi .30 .20
3296 A948 2 l multi .35 .20
3297 A948 3 l multi .55 .30
3298 A948 4 l multi .70 .35
Nos. 3293-3298 (6) 2.30 1.45

Souvenir Sheet

Motorcycle Centenary — A949

1985, Aug. 22 **Photo.** ***Perf. 13½***

3300 A949 10 l 1885 Daimler Einspur 1.90 .90

Retezat Natl. Park, 50th Anniv. — A950

1985, Aug. 29

3301 A950 50b Senecio glaberrimus .20 .20
3302 A950 1 l Rupicapra rupicapra .20 .20
3303 A950 2 l Centaurea retezatensis .35 .20
3304 A950 3 l Viola dacica .55 .25
3305 A950 4 l Marmota marmota .70 .35
3306 A950 5 l Aquila chrysaetos .90 .45
Nos. 3301-3306 (6) 2.90 1.65

Souvenir Sheet

3307 A950 10 l Lynx lynx 1.90 .90

No. 3307 contains one 42x54mm stamp.

Tractors Manufactured by Universal — A951

1985, Sept. 10

3308 A951 50b 530 DTC .20 .20
3309 A951 1 l 550 M HC .20 .20
3310 A951 1.50 l 650 Super .25 .20
3311 A951 2 l 850 .30 .20
3312 A951 3 l S 1801 IF .50 .25
3313 A951 4 l A 3602 IF .65 .30
Nos. 3308-3313 (6) 2.10 1.35

Folk Costumes — A952

Women's and men's costumes from same region printed in continuous design.

1985, Sept. 28

3314 50b Muscel woman .20 .20
3315 50b Muscel man .20 .20
a. A952 Pair, #3314-3315 .20 .20
3316 1.50 l Bistrita-Nasaud woman .25 .20
3317 1.50 l Bistrita-Nasaud man .25 .20
a. A952 Pair, #3316-3317 .50 .30
3318 2 l Vrancea woman .35 .20
3319 2 l Vrancea man .35 .20
a. A952 Pair, #3318-3319 .70 .30
3320 3 l Vilcea woman .50 .25
3321 3 l Vilcea man .50 .25
a. A952 Pair, #3320-3321 1.00 .50
Nos. 3314-3321 (8) 2.60 1.70

Admission to UN, 30th Anniv. — A953

1985, Oct. 21

3322 A953 2 l multicolored .35 .20

UN, 40th Anniv. — A954

Mineral Flowers — A955

1985, Oct. 21

3323 A954 2 l multicolored .35 .20

1985, Oct. 28

3324 A955 50b Quartz and calcite, Herja .20 .20
3325 A955 1 l Copper, Altin Tepe .20 .20
3326 A955 2 l Gypsum, Cavnic .30 .20
3327 A955 3 l Quartz, Ocna de Fier .60 .30
3328 A955 4 l Stibium, Baiut .80 .40
3329 A955 5 l Tetrahedrite, Cavnic 1.00 .50
Nos. 3324-3329 (6) 3.10 1.80

Stamp Day — A956

1985, Oct. 29

3330 A956 2 l + 1 l label .35 .20

A Connecticut Yankee in King Arthur's Court, by Mark Twain — A957

The Three Brothers, by Jacob and Wilhelm Grimm — A958

Disney characters in classic fairy tales.

1985, Nov. 28

3331	A957	50b	Hank Morgan awakes in Camelot	.30	.20
3332	A957	50b	Predicts eclipse of sun	.30	.20
3333	A957	50b	Mounting horse	.30	.20
3334	A957	50b	Sir Sagramor	.30	.20
3335	A958	1 l	Fencing with shadow	.65	.25
3336	A958	1 l	Fencing, father	.65	.25
3337	A958	1 l	Shoeing a horse	.65	.25
3338	A958	1 l	Barber, rabbit	.65	.25
3339	A958	1 l	Father, three sons	.65	.25
			Nos. 3331-3339 (9)	4.45	2.05

Souvenir Sheets

3340	A957	5 l	Tournament of knights	2.75	1.40
3341	A958	5 l	Cottage	2.75	1.40

Miniature Sheets

Intereuropa 1986 — A959

Fauna & flora: #3343: a, Felis silvestris. b, Mustela erminea. c, Tetrao urogallus. d, Urso arctos.

#3344: a, Dianthus callizonus. b, Pinus cembra. c, Salix sp. d, Rose pendulina.

1986, Mar. 25 Photo. *Perf. 13½*

3343		Sheet of 4	2.50	2.50
a.-d.	A959	3 l, any single	.60	.60
3344		Sheet of 4	2.50	2.50
a.-d.	A959	3 l, any single	.60	.60

Inventors and Adventurers — A960

Designs: 1 l, Orville and Wilbur Wright, Wright Flyer. 1.50 l, Jacques Cousteau, research vessel Calypso. 2 l, Amelia Earhart, Lockheed Electra. 3 l, Charles Lindbergh, Spirit of St. Louis. 3.50 l, Sir Edmund Hillary (1919-), first man to reach Mt. Everest summit. 4 l, Robert Edwin Peary, Arctic explorer. 5 l, Adm. Richard Byrd, explorer. 6 l, Neil Armstrong, first man on moon.

1985, Dec. 25 Photo. *Perf. 13½*

3345	A960	1 l	multi	.20	.20
3346	A960	1.50 l	multi	.30	.20
3347	A960	2 l	multi	.40	.30
3348	A960	3 l	multi	.60	.40
3349	A960	3.50 l	multi	.65	.50
3350	A960	4 l	multi	.75	.60
3351	A960	5 l	multi	1.00	.70
3352	A960	6 l	multi	1.25	.85
			Nos. 3345-3352 (8)	5.15	3.75

Paintings by Nicolae Tonitza — A961

1986, Mar. 12 Photo. *Perf. 13½*

3353	A961	1 l	Nina in Green	.25	.20
3354	A961	2 l	Irina	.60	.30
3355	A961	3 l	Woodman's Daughter	.90	.45
3356	A961	4 l	Woman on the Verandah	1.25	.60
			Nos. 3353-3356 (4)	3.00	1.55

Color Animated Films, 50th Anniv. — A962

Walt Disney characters in the Band Concert, 1935.

1986, Apr. 10 Photo. *Perf. 13½*

3357	A962	50b	Clarabelle	.25	.20
3358	A962	50b	Mickey Mouse	.25	.20
3359	A962	50b	Paddy and Peter	.25	.20
3360	A962	50b	Goofy	.25	.20
3361	A962	1 l	Donald Duck	.50	.20
3362	A962	1 l	Mickey Mouse, diff.	.50	.20
3363	A962	1 l	Mickey and Donald	.50	.20
3364	A962	1 l	Horace	.50	.20
3365	A962	1 l	Donald and trombonist	.50	.20
			Nos. 3357-3365 (9)	3.50	1.80

Souvenir Sheet

3366	A962	5 l	Finale	2.50	.85

1986 World Cup Soccer Championships, Mexico — A963

Various soccer plays and flags: 50b, Italy vs. Bulgaria. 1 l, Mexico vs. Belgium. 2 l, Canada vs. France. 3 l, Brazil vs. Spain. 4 l, Uruguay vs. Germany. 5 l, Morocco vs. Poland.

1986, May 9

3367	A963	50b	multi	.20	.20
3368	A963	1 l	multi	.30	.20
3369	A963	2 l	multi	.50	.25
3370	A963	3 l	multi	.75	.35
3371	A963	4 l	multi	1.00	.50
3372	A963	5 l	multi	1.25	.70
			Nos. 3367-3372 (6)	4.00	2.20

An imperf. 10 l airmail souvenir sheet exists picturing stadium, flags of previous winners, satellite and map.

Hotels — A964

1986, Apr. 23 Photo. *Perf. 13½*

3373	A964	50b	Diana, Herculane	.20	.20
3374	A964	1 l	Termal, Felix	.25	.20
3375	A964	2 l	Delfin, Meduza and Steaua de Mare, Eforie Nord	.45	.20
3376	A964	3 l	Caciulata, Calimanesti Caciulata	.65	.30
3377	A964	4 l	Palas, Slanic Moldova	.90	.45
3378	A964	5 l	Bradet, Sovata	1.10	.55
			Nos. 3373-3378 (6)	3.55	1.90

Nicolae Ceausescu, Party Flag — A965

1986, May 8 Photo. *Perf. 13½*

3379	A965	2 l	multicolored	.60	.30

Natl. Communist Party, 65th anniv.

Flowers — A966

1986, June 25 Photo. *Perf. 13½*

3380	A966	50b	Tulipa gesneriana	.20	.20
3381	A966	1 l	Iris hispanica	.25	.20
3382	A966	2 l	Rosa hybrida	.50	.25
3383	A966	3 l	Anemone coronaria	.70	.35
3384	A966	4 l	Freesia refracta	1.00	.50
3385	A966	5 l	Chrysanthemum indicum	1.25	.60
			Nos. 3380-3385 (6)	3.90	2.10

Mircea the Great, Ruler of Wallachia, 1386-1418 — A967

1986, July 17 Photo. *Perf. 13½*

3386	A967	2 l	multicolored	.60	.30

Ascent to the throne, 600th anniv.

Open Air Museum of Historic Dwellings, Bucharest, 50th Anniv. — A968

1986, July 21

3387	A968	50b	Alba	.20	.20
3388	A968	1 l	Arges	.25	.20
3389	A968	2 l	Constantia	.45	.20
3390	A968	3 l	Timis	.65	.30
3391	A968	4 l	Neamt	.90	.45
3392	A968	5 l	Gorj	1.10	.55
			Nos. 3387-3392 (6)	3.55	1.90

Polar Research — A969

Exploration: 50b, Julius Popper, exploration of Tierra del Fuego (1886-93). 1 l, Bazil G. Assan, exploration of Spitzbergen (1896). 2 l, Emil Racovita, Antarctic expedition (1897-99). 3 l, Constantin Dumbrava, exploration of Greenland (1927-8). 4 l, Romanians with the 17th Soviet Antarctic expedition (1971-72). 5 l, Research on krill fishing (1977-80).

1986, July 23 Photo. *Perf. 13½*

3393	A969	50b	multi	.20	.20
3394	A969	1 l	multi	.25	.20
3395	A969	2 l	multi	.45	.20
3396	A969	3 l	multi	.65	.30
3397	A969	4 l	multi	.90	.45
3398	A969	5 l	multi	1.10	.55
			Nos. 3393-3398 (6)	3.55	1.90

Natl. Cycling Championships A970

Various athletes.

1986, Aug. 29

3399	A970	1 l	multicolored	.25	.20
3400	A970	2 l	multicolored	.50	.25
3401	A970	3 l	multicolored	.70	.35
3402	A970	4 l	multicolored	1.00	.50
			Nos. 3399-3402 (4)	2.45	1.30

Souvenir Sheet

3403	A970	10 l	multicolored	2.50	1.25

No. 3403 contains one 42x54mm stamp.

Souvenir Sheet

Intl. Peace Year — A971

1986, July 25

3404	A971	5 l	multicolored	1.25	.60

Fungi — A972

A973

1986, Aug. 15

3405 A972 50b Amanita rubescens .20 .20
3406 A972 1 l Boletus luridus .25 .20
3407 A972 2 l Lactarius piperatus .50 .25
3408 A972 3 l Lepiota clypeolaria .70 .35
3409 A972 4 l Russula cyanoxantha 1.00 .50
3410 A972 5 l Tremiscus helvelloides 1.25 .60
Nos. 3405-3410 (6) 3.90 2.10

1986, Nov. 10 Photo. *Perf. 13½*

Famous Men: 50b, Petru Maior (c. 1761-1821), historian. 1 l, George Topirceanu (1886-1937), doctor. 2 l, Henri Coanda (1886-1972), engineer. 3 l, Constantin Budeanu (1886-1959), engineer.

3411 A973 50b dl cl, gold & dk bl grn .20 .20
3412 A973 1 l sl grn, gold & dk lil rose .25 .20
3413 A973 2 l rose cl, gold & brt bl .50 .25
3414 A973 3 l chlky bl, gold & choc .70 .35
Nos. 3411-3414 (4) 1.65 1.00

UNESCO, 40th Anniv. A974

1986, Nov. 10

3415 A974 4 l multicolored 1.00 .50

Stamp Day — A975

1986, Nov. 15

3416 A975 2 l + 1 l label .75 .35

Industry A976

1986, Nov. 28

3417 A976 50b F-300 oil rigs, vert. .20 .20
3418 A976 1 l Promex excavator .25 .20
3419 A976 2 l Pitesti refinery, vert. .45 .20
3420 A976 3 l 110-ton dump truck .65 .30
3421 A976 4 l Coral computer, vert. .90 .45
3422 A976 5 l 350-megawatt turbine 1.10 .55
Nos. 3417-3422 (6) 3.55 1.90

Folk Costumes — A977

1986, Dec. 26

3423 A977 50b Capra .20 .20
3424 A977 1 l Sorcova .25 .20
3425 A977 2 l Plugusorul .45 .20
3426 A977 3 l Buhaiul .65 .30
3427 A977 4 l Caiutii .90 .45
3428 A977 5 l Uratorii 1.10 .55
Nos. 3423-3428 (6) 3.55 1.90

Recycling Campaign — A978

1986, Dec. 30

3429 A978 1 l Metal .25 .20
3430 A978 2 l Trees .50 .25

Young Communists' League, 65th Anniv. — A979

1987, Mar. 18 Photo. *Perf. 13½*

3431 A979 1 l Flags, youth .25 .20
3432 A979 2 l Emblem .50 .25
3433 A979 3 l Flags, youth, diff. .75 .40
Nos. 3431-3433 (3) 1.50 .85

Miniature Sheets

Intereuropa — A980

Modern architecture: No. 3434a, Exposition Pavilion, Bucharest. b, Intercontinental Hotel, Bucharest. c, Europa Hotel, Black Sea coast. d, Polytechnic Institute, Bucharest.

No. 3435a, Administration Building, Satu Mare. b, House of Young Pioneers, Bucharest. c, Valahia Hotel, Tirgoviste. d, Caciulata Hotel, Caciulata.

1987, May 18 Photo. *Perf. 13½*

3434 Sheet of 4 2.50 2.50
a.-d. A980 3 l, any single .60 .60
3435 Sheet of 4 2.50 2.50
a.-d. A980 3 l, any single .60 .60

Collective Farming, 25th Anniv. — A981

1987, Apr. 25 Photo. *Perf. 13½*

3436 A981 2 l multicolored .50 .25

Birch Trees by the Lakeside, by I. Andreescu — A982

Paintings in Romanian museums: 1 l, Young Peasant Girls Spinning, by N. Grigorescu. 2 l, Washerwoman, by S. Luchian. 3 l, Inside the Peasant's Cottage, by S. Dimitrescu. 4 l, Winter Landscape, by A. Ciucurencu. 5 l, Winter in Bucharest, by N. Tonitza, vert.

1987, Apr. 28

3437 A982 50b multicolored .20 .20
3438 A982 1 l multicolored .20 .20
3439 A982 2 l multicolored .35 .20
3440 A982 3 l multicolored .50 .25
3441 A982 4 l multicolored .75 .35
3442 A982 5 l multicolored 1.00 .50
Nos. 3437-3442 (6) 3.00 1.70

Peasant Uprising of 1907, 80th Anniv. — A983

1987, May 30

3443 A983 2 l multicolored .50 .25

Men's World Handball Championships — A984

Various plays.

1987, July 15

3444 A984 50b multi, vert. .20 .20
3445 A984 1 l multi .20 .20
3446 A984 2 l multi, vert. .35 .20
3447 A984 3 l multi .50 .25
3448 A984 4 l multi, vert. .75 .35
3449 A984 5 l multi 1.00 .50
Nos. 3444-3449 (6) 3.00 1.70

A985

Natl. Currency — A986

A986 illustration reduced.

1987, July 15

3450 A985 1 l multicolored .20 .20

Souvenir Sheet

3451 A986 10 l multicolored 2.00 2.00

Landscapes — A987

1987, July 31 Photo. *Perf. 13½*

3452 A987 50b Pelicans over the Danube Delta .20 .20
3453 A987 1 l Transfagarasan Highway .20 .20
3454 A987 2 l Hairpin curve, Bicazului .35 .20
3455 A987 3 l Limestone peaks, Mt. Ceahlau .50 .25
3456 A987 4 l Lake Capra, Mt. Fagaras .70 .35
3457 A987 5 l Orchard, Borsa .90 .50
Nos. 3452-3457 (6) 2.85 1.70

A988

Scenes from Fairy Tale by Peter Ispirescu (b. 1887) — A988a

A988a illustration reduced.

1987, Sept. 25 Photo. Perf. 13½

3458 A988 50b shown .20 .20
3459 A988 1 l multi, diff. .20 .20
3460 A988 2 l multi, diff. .35 .20
3461 A988 3 l multi, diff. .50 .25
3462 A988 4 l multi, diff. .70 .35
3463 A988 5 l multi, diff. .85 .40
Nos. 3458-3463 (6) 2.80 1.60

Souvenir Sheet

3464 A988a 10 l shown 2.00 2.00

Miniature Sheets

Flora and Fauna A989

Flora: No. 3465a, Aquilegia alpina. b, Pulsatilla vernalis. c, Aster alpinus. d, Soldanella pusilla baumg. e, Lilium bulbiferum. f, Arctostaphylos uva-ursi. g, Crocus vernus. h, Crepis aurea. i, Cypripedium calceolus. j, Centaurea nervosa. k, Dryas octopetala. l, Gentiana excisa.

Fauna: No. 3466a, Martes martes. b, Felis lynx. c, Ursus maritimus. d, Lutra lutra. e, Bison bonasus. f, Branta ruficollis. g, Phoenicopterus ruber. h, Otis tarda. i, Lyrurus tetrix. j, Gypaetus barbatus. k, Vormela peregusna. l, Oxyura leucocephala.

1987, Oct. 16

Sheets of 12

3465 A989 1 l #a.-l. 3.25 1.50
3466 A989 1 l #a.-l. 3.25 1.50

Souvenir Sheet

PHILATELIA '87, Cologne — A990

1987, Oct. 19

3467 Sheet of 2 + 2 labels 3.75 3.75
a. A990 3 l Bucharest city seal 1.90 1.90
b. A990 3 l Cologne city arms 1.90 1.90

Locomotives — A991

1987, Oct. 15

3468 A991 50b L 45 H .20 .20
3469 A991 1 l LDE 125 .20 .20
3470 A991 2 l LDH 70 .40 .20
3471 A991 3 l LDE 2100 .65 .30
3472 A991 4 l LDE 3000 .90 .40
3473 A991 5 l LE 5100 1.00 .50
Nos. 3468-3473 (6) 3.35 1.80

Folk Costumes — A992

1987, Nov. 7

3474 1 l Tirnave (woman) .20 .20
3475 1 l Tirnave (man) .20 .20
a. A992 Pair, #3474-3475 .40 .20
3476 2 l Buzau (woman) .40 .20
3477 2 l Buzau (man) .40 .20
a. A992 Pair, #3476-3477 .80 .30
3478 3 l Dobrogea (woman) .60 .30
3479 3 l Dobrogea (man) .60 .30
a. A992 Pair, #3478-3479 1.25 .60
3480 4 l Ilfov (woman) .80 .40
3481 4 l Ilfov (man) .80 .40
a. A992 Pair, #3480-3481 1.60 .80
Nos. 3474-3481 (8) 4.00 2.20

Postwoman Delivering Mail — A993

1987, Nov. 15 Photo. Perf. 13½

3482 A993 2 l + 1 l label .75 .35

Stamp Day.

Apiculture — A994

1987, Nov. 16 Photo. Perf. 13½

3483 A994 1 l Apis mellifica carpatica .25 .20
3484 A994 2 l Bee pollinating sunflower .50 .25
3485 A994 3 l Hives, Danube Delta .75 .35
3486 A994 4 l Apiculture complex, Bucharest 1.00 .50
Nos. 3483-3486 (4) 2.50 1.30

1988 Winter Olympics, Calgary A995

1987, Dec. 28 Photo. Perf. 13½

3487 A995 50b Biathlon .20 .20
3488 A995 1 l Slalom .20 .20
3489 A995 1.50 l Ice hockey .30 .20
3490 A995 2 l Luge .40 .20
3491 A995 3 l Speed skating .60 .30
3492 A995 3.50 l Women's figure skating .65 .35
3493 A995 4 l Downhill skiing .80 .40
3494 A995 5 l Two-man bobsled 1.00 .50
Nos. 3487-3494 (8) 4.15 2.35

An imperf. 10 l souvenir sheet picturing ski jumping also exists.

Traffic Safety A996

Designs: 50b, Be aware of children riding bicycles in the road. 1 l, Young Pioneer girl as crossing guard. 2 l, Do not open car doors in path of moving traffic. 3 l, Be aware of pedestrian crossings. 4 l, Observe the speed limit; do not attempt curves at high speed. 5 l, Protect small children.

1987, Dec. 10 Photo. Perf. 13½

3495 A996 50b multicolored .20 .20
3496 A996 1 l multicolored .20 .20
3497 A996 2 l multicolored .40 .20
3498 A996 3 l multicolored .65 .30
3499 A996 4 l multicolored .85 .40
3500 A996 5 l multicolored 1.00 .45
Nos. 3495-3500 (6) 3.30 1.75

October Revolution, Russia, 70th Anniv. — A997

1987, Dec. 26

3501 A997 2 l multicolored .45 .20

40th Anniv. of the Romanian Republic — A998

1987, Dec. 30

3502 A998 2 l multicolored .45 .20

70th Birthday of President Nicolae Ceausescu — A999

1988, Jan. 26

3503 A999 2 l multicolored .45 .25

Pottery A1000

1988, Feb. 26 Photo. Perf. 13½

3504 A1000 50b Marginea .20 .20
3505 A1000 1 l Oboga .20 .20
3506 A1000 2 l Horezu .40 .20
3507 A1000 3 l Curtea De Arges .65 .25
3508 A1000 4 l Birsa .85 .35
3509 A1000 5 l Vama 1.00 .40
Nos. 3504-3509 (6) 3.30 1.60

Miniature Sheets

Intereuropa — A1001

Transportation and communication: No. 3510a, Mail coach. b, ECS telecommunications satellite. c, Oltcit automobile. d, ICE high-speed electric train.

No. 3511a, Santa Maria, 15th cent. b, Cheia Ground Station satellite dish receivers. c, Bucharest subway. d, Airbus-A320.

1988, Apr. 27 Photo. Perf. 13½

3510 Sheet of 4 2.50 2.50
a.-d. A1001 3 l any single .60 .60
3511 Sheet of 4 2.50 2.50
a.-d. A1001 3 l any single .60 .60

1988 Summer Olympics, Seoul — A1002

1988, Jun. 28

3512 A1002 50b Gymnastics .20 .20
3513 A1002 1.50 l Boxing .30 .20
3514 A1002 2 l Tennis .40 .20
3515 A1002 3 l Judo .60 .25
3516 A1002 4 l Running .80 .35
3517 A1002 5 l Rowing 1.00 .40
Nos. 3512-3517 (6) 3.30 1.60

An imperf. 10 l souvenir sheet exists.

19th-20th Cent. Clocks in the Ceasului Museum, Ploesti A1003

1988, May 20 Photo. Perf. 13½

3518 A1003 50b Arad Region porcelain .20 .20
3519 A1003 1.50 l French bronze .35 .20
3520 A1003 2 l French bronze, diff. .40 .20
3521 A1003 3 l Gothic bronze .65 .25
3522 A1003 4 l Saxony porcelain .85 .35
3523 A1003 5 l Bohemian porcelain 1.10 .45
Nos. 3518-3523 (6) 3.55 1.65

20th cent. timepiece (50b); others 19th cent.

Miniature Sheets

European Soccer Championships, Germany — A1003a

Soccer players and flags of: c, Federal Republic of Germany. d, Spain. e, Italy. f, Denmark. g, England. h, Netherlands. i, Ireland. j, Soviet Union.

1988, June 9 Litho. Perf. 13½

3523A Sheet of 4 3.25 3.25
c.-f. A1003a 3 l any single .80 .80
3523B Sheet of 4 3.25 3.25
g.-j. A1003a 3 l any single .80 .80

Accession of Constanin Brincoveanu as Prince Regent of Wallachia, 1688-1714, 300th Anniv. — A1004

1988, June 20

3524 A1004 2 l multicolored .50 .25

1988 Summer Olympics, Seoul — A1005

1988, Sept. 1 Photo. *Perf. 13½*

3525	A1005	50b	Women's running	.20	.20
3526	A1005	1 l	Canoeing	.20	.20
3527	A1005	1.50 l	Women's gymnastics	.25	.20
3528	A1005	2 l	Kayaking	.40	.20
3529	A1005	3 l	Weight lifting	.55	.25
3530	A1005	3.50 l	Women's swimming	.60	.25
3531	A1005	4 l	Fencing	.70	.30
3532	A1005	5 l	Women's rowing (double)	.95	.40
			Nos. 3525-3532 (8)	3.85	2.00

An imperf. 10 l souvenir sheet exists picturing women's gymnastics.

Romania-China Philatelic Exhibition — A1006

1988, Aug. 5 Photo. *Perf. 13½*

3533	A1006	2 l	multicolored	.50	.25

Souvenir Sheet

PRAGA '88 — A1007

1988, Aug. 26

3534	A1007	5 l	Carnations, by Stefan Luchian	2.00	2.00

Miniature Sheets

Orchids A1008

#3535: a, Oncidium lanceanum. b, Cattleya trianae. c, Sophronitis cernua. d, Bulbophyllum lobbii. e, Lycaste cruenta. f, Mormolyce ringens. g, Phragmipedium schlimii. h, Angraecum sesquipedale. i, Laelia crispa. j, Encyclia atropurpurea. k, Dendrobium nobile. l, Oncidium splendidum.

#3536: a, Brassavola perrinii. b, Paphiopedilum maudiae. c, Sophronitis coccinea. d, Vandopsis lissochiloides. e, Phalaenopsis lueddemanniana. f, Chysis bractescens. g, Cochleanthes discolor. h, Phalaenopsis amabilis. i, Pleione pricei. j, Sobralia macrantha. k, Aspasia lunata. l, Cattleya citrina.

1988, Oct. 24

3535	Sheet of 12		3.25	3.25
a.-l.	A1008 1 l any single		.25	.25
3536	Sheet of 12		3.25	3.25
a.-l.	A1008 1 l any single		.25	.25

Miniature Sheets

Events Won by Romanian Athletes at the 1988 Seoul Olympic Games A1009

Sporting event and medal: No. 3537a, Women's gymnastics. b, Free pistol shooting. c, Weight lifting (220 pounds). d, Featherweight boxing.

No. 3538a, Women's 1500 and 3000-meter relays. b, Women's 200 and 400-meter individual swimming medley. c, Wrestling (220 pounds). d, Rowing, coxless pairs and coxed fours.

1988, Dec. 7 Photo. *Perf. 13½*

3537	Sheet of 4		3.00	3.00
a.-d.	A1009 3 l any single		.75	.75
3538	Sheet of 4		3.00	3.00
a.-d.	A1009 3 l any single		.75	.75

Stamp Day — A1010

1988, Nov. 13 Photo. *Perf. 13½*

3539	A1010	2 l + 1 l	label	.75	.35

Unitary Natl. Romanian State, 70th Anniv. A1011

1988, Dec. 29

3540	A1011	2 l	multicolored	.50	.40

Anniversaries — A1012

Designs: 50b, Athenaeum, Bucharest. 1.50 l, Trajan's Bridge, Drobeta, on a Roman bronze sestertius used in Romania from 103 to 105 A.D. 2 l, Ruins, Suceava. 3 l, Pitesti municipal coat of arms, scroll, architecture. 4 l, Trajan's Column (detail), 113 A.D. 5 l, Gold helmet discovered in Prahova County.

1988, Dec. 30

3541	A1012	50b	shown	.20	.20
3542	A1012	1.50 l	multi	.30	.20
3543	A1012	2 l	multi	.45	.20
3544	A1012	3 l	multi	.65	.25
3545	A1012	4 l	multi	.85	.35
3546	A1012	5 l	multi	1.10	.45
			Nos. 3541-3546 (6)	3.55	1.65

Athenaeum, Bucharest, cent. (50b), Suceava, capital of Moldavia from 1401-1565, 600th anniv. (2 l), & Pitesti municipal charter, 600th anniv. (3 l).

Miniature Sheets

Grand Slam Tennis Championships — A1013

No. 3547: a, Men's singles, stadium in Melbourne. b, Men's singles, scoreboard. c, Mixed doubles, spectators. d, Mixed doubles, Roland Garros stadium.

No. 3548: a, Women's singles, stadium in Wimbledon. b, Women's singles, spectators. c, Men's doubles, spectators. d, Men's doubles, stadium in Flushing Meadows.

1988, Aug. 22 Photo. *Perf. 13½*

3547	Sheet of 4		3.00	3.00
a.-d.	A1013 3 l any single		.75	.75
3548	Sheet of 4		3.00	3.00
a.-d.	A1013 3 l any single		.75	.75

Australian Open (Nos. 3547a-3547b), French Open (Nos. 3547c-3547d), Wimbledon (Nos. 3548a-3548b) and US Open (Nos. 3548c-3548d).

Architecture — A1014

Designs: 50b, Zapodeni, Vaslui, 17th cent. 1.50 l, Berbesti, Maramures, 18th cent. 2 l, Voitinel, Suceava, 18th cent. 3 l, Chiojdu mic, Buzau, 18th cent. 4 l, Cimpanii de sus, Bihor, 19th cent. 5 l, Naruja, Vrancea, 19th cent.

1989, Feb. 8 Photo. *Perf. 13½*

3549	A1014	50b	multi	.20	.20
3550	A1014	1.50 l	multi	.30	.20
3551	A1014	2 l	multi	.45	.20
3552	A1014	3 l	multi	.65	.25
3553	A1014	4 l	multi	.85	.35
3554	A1014	5 l	multi	1.10	.45
			Nos. 3549-3554 (6)	3.55	1.65

Rescue and Relief Services — A1015

1989, Feb. 25

3555	A1015	50b	Relief worker	.20	.20
3556	A1015	1 l	shown	.20	.20
3557	A1015	1.50 l	Fireman, child	.25	.20
3558	A1015	2 l	Fireman's carry	.30	.20
3559	A1015	3 l	Rescue team on skis	.50	.20
3560	A1015	3.50 l	Mountain rescue	.60	.25
3561	A1015	4 l	Water rescue	.70	.30
3562	A1015	5 l	Water safety	.85	.35
			Nos. 3555-3562 (8)	3.60	1.90

Nos. 3555, 3557-3558, 3560-3561 vert.

Industries — A1016

Designs: 50b, Fasca Bicaz cement factory. 1.50 l, Bridge on the Danube near Cernavoda. 2 l, MS-2-2400/450-20 synchronous motor. 3 l, Bucharest subway. 4 l, Mangalia-Constanta ferry. 5 l, *Gloria* marine platform.

1989, Apr. 10 Photo. *Perf. 13½*

3563	A1016	50b	multi	.20	.20
3564	A1016	1.50 l	multi	.30	.20
3565	A1016	2 l	multi	.40	.20
3566	A1016	3 l	multi	.60	.25
3567	A1016	4 l	multi	.80	.35
3568	A1016	5 l	multi	1.00	.40
			Nos. 3563-3568 (6)	3.30	1.60

Anti-fascist March, 50th Anniv. — A1017

1989, May 1 Photo. *Perf. 13½*

3569	A1017	2 l	shown	.50	.25

Souvenir Sheet

3570	A1017	10 l	Patriots, flag	4.00	4.00

Souvenir Sheet

BULGARIA '89, Sofia, May 22-31 — A1018

Illustration reduced.

1989, May 20

3571	A1018	10 l	Roses	2.00	2.00

Miniature Sheets

Intereuropa 1989 — A1019

Children's activities and games: No. 3572a, Swimming. No. 3572b, Water slide. No. 3572c, Seesaw. No. 3572d, Flying kites. No. 3573a, Playing with dolls. No. 3573b, Playing ball. No. 3573c, Playing in the sand. No. 3573d, Playing with toy cars.

1989, June 15

3572	Sheet of 4		3.00	3.00
a.-d.	A1019 3 l any single		.75	.75
3573	Sheet of 4		3.00	3.00
a.-d.	A1019 3 l any single		.75	.75

Socialist Revolution in Romania, 45th Anniv. A1020

1989, Aug. 21 Photo. *Perf. 13½*

3574	A1020	2 l	multicolored	.50	.25

Cartoons — A1021

1989, Sept. 25

3575 A1021	50b	Pin-pin	.20	.20
3576 A1021	1 l	Maria	.25	.20
3577 A1021	1.50 l	Gore and Grigore	.30	.20
3578 A1021	2 l	Pisoiul, Balanel, Manole and Monk	.45	.20
3579 A1021	3 l	Gruia Lui Novac	.65	.25
3580 A1021	3.50 l	Mihaela	.80	.30
3581 A1021	4 l	Harap alb	.90	.35
3582 A1021	5 l	Homo sapiens	1.00	.40
		Nos. 3575-3582 (8)	4.55	2.10

Romanian Writers A1022

Portraits: 1 l, Ion Creanga (1837-1889). 2 l, Mihail Eminescu (1850-1889), poet. 3 l, Nicolae Teclu (1839-1916).

1989, Aug. 18 Photo. *Perf. 13½*

3583 A1022	1 l	multicolored	.30	.20
3584 A1022	2 l	multicolored	.60	.25
3585 A1022	3 l	multicolored	.90	.35
		Nos. 3583-3585 (3)	1.80	.80

Stamp Day — A1023

1989, Oct. 7

3586 A1023 2 l + 1 l label .75 .30

No. 3586 has a second label picturing posthorn.

Storming of the Bastille, 1789 A1024

Emblems of PHILEXFRANCE '89 and the Revolution — A1025

Designs: 1.50 l, Gavroche. 2 l, Robespierre. 3 l, *La Marseillaise,* by Rouget de Lisle. 4 l, Diderot. 5 l, 1848 Uprising, Romania.

1989, Oct. 14

3587 A1024	50b	shown	.20	.20
3588 A1024	1.50 l	multicolored	.30	.20
3589 A1024	2 l	multicolored	.40	.20
3590 A1024	3 l	multicolored	.60	.25
3591 A1024	4 l	multicolored	.80	.30
3592 A1024	5 l	multicolored	1.00	.40
		Nos. 3587-3592 (6)	3.30	1.55

Souvenir Sheet

3593 A1025 10 l shown 3.00 3.00

French revolution, bicent.

14th Romanian Communist Party Congress — A1025a

1989, Nov. 20 Photo. *Perf. 13½*

3593A A1025a 2 l multicolored .50 .25

Souvenir Sheet

3593B A1025a 10 l multicolored 4.00 4.00

Revolution of Dec. 22, 1989 — A1026

1990, Jan. 8 Photo. *Perf. 13½*

3594 A1026 2 l multicolored .40 .20

World Cup Soccer Preliminaries, Italy — A1027

Various soccer players in action.

1990, Mar. 19 Photo. *Perf. 13½*

3595 A1027	50b	multicolored	.20	.20
3596 A1027	1.50 l	multicolored	.30	.20
3597 A1027	2 l	multicolored	.40	.20
3598 A1027	3 l	multicolored	.60	.25
3599 A1027	4 l	multicolored	.80	.30
3600 A1027	5 l	multicolored	1.00	.40
		Nos. 3595-3600 (6)	3.30	1.55

An imperf. 10 l airmail souvenir sheet exists. Value, $8.50.

Souvenir Sheet

First Postage Stamp, 150th Anniv. — A1028

Illustration reduced.

1990, May 2 Litho. *Perf. 13½*

3601 A1028 10 l multicolored 2.00 2.00

Stamp World London '90.

World Cup Soccer Championships, Italy — A1029

Various soccer players in action.

1990, May 7 Photo. *Perf. 13½*

3602 A1029	50b	multicolored	.20	.20
3603 A1029	1 l	multicolored	.20	.20
3604 A1029	1.50 l	multicolored	.20	.20
3605 A1029	2 l	multicolored	.20	.20
3606 A1029	3 l	multicolored	.25	.20
3607 A1029	3.50 l	multicolored	.30	.20
3608 A1029	4 l	multicolored	.35	.20
3609 A1029	5 l	multicolored	.45	.20
		Nos. 3602-3609 (8)	2.15	1.60

An imperf. 10 l airmail souvenir sheet showing Olympic Stadium, Rome exists. Value, $7.50.

Intl. Dog Show, Brno, Czechoslovakia — A1030

1990, June 6

3610 A1030	50b	German shepherd	.20	.20
3611 A1030	1 l	English setter	.20	.20
3612 A1030	1.50 l	Boxer	.30	.20
3613 A1030	2 l	Beagle	.45	.20
3614 A1030	3 l	Doberman pinscher	.65	.25
3615 A1030	3.50 l	Great Dane	.75	.30
3616 A1030	4 l	Afghan hound	.90	.35
3617 A1030	5 l	Yorkshire terrier	1.10	.45
		Nos. 3610-3617 (8)	4.55	2.15

Riccione '90, Intl. Philatelic Exhibition A1031

1990, Aug. 24

3618 A1031 2 l multicolored .50 .20

See No. 3856.

Romanian-Chinese Philatelic Exhibition, Bucharest — A1032

1990, Sept. 8 Photo. *Perf. 13½*

3619 A1032 2 l multicolored .40 .20

For surcharge see No. 4186.

Paintings Damaged in 1989 Revolution — A1033

Designs: 50b, Old Nicolas, the Zither Player, by Stefan Luchian. 1.50 l, Woman in Blue by Ion Andreescu. 2 l, The Gardener by Luchian. 3 l, Vase of Flowers by Jan Brueghel, the Elder. 4 l, Springtime by Peter Brueghel, the Elder, horiz. 5 l, Madonna and Child by G. B. Paggi.

1990. Oct. 25 Photo. *Perf. 13½*

3620 A1033	50b	multicolored	.20	.20
3621 A1033	1.50 l	multicolored	.20	.20
3622 A1033	2 l	multicolored	.25	.20
3623 A1033	3 l	multicolored	.40	.20
3624 A1033	4 l	multicolored	.55	.25
3625 A1033	5 l	multicolored	.70	.30
		Nos. 3620-3625 (6)	2.30	1.35

For surcharges see #4365-4369.

Stamp Day — A1033a

1990, Nov. 10 Photo. *Perf. 13½*

3625A A1033a 2 l + 1 l label .25 .20

Famous Romanians A1034

Designs: 50b, Prince Constantin Cantacuzino (1640-1716). 1.50 l, Ienachita Vacarescu (c. 1740-1797), historian. 2 l, Titu Maiorescu (1840-1917), writer. 3 l, Nicolae Iorga (1871-1940), historian. 4 l, Martha Bibescu (1890-1973). 5 l, Stefan Procopiu (1890-1972), scientist.

1990, Nov. 27 Photo. *Perf. 13½*

3626 A1034	50b	sepia & dk bl	.20	.20
3627 A1034	1.50 l	grn & brt pur	.20	.20
3628 A1034	2 l	claret & dk bl	.20	.20
3629 A1034	3 l	dk bl & brn	.25	.20
3630 A1034	4 l	brn & dk bl	.30	.20
3631 A1034	5 l	brt pur & grn	.40	.20
		Nos. 3626-3631 (6)	1.55	1.20

For surcharges see #4356-4360.

National Day — A1035

1990, Dec. 1 Photo. *Perf. 13½*

3632 A1035 2 l multicolored .25 .20

No. 3594 Surcharged in Brown

1990, Dec. 22 Photo. *Perf. 13½*

3633	A1026	4 l on 2 l	.50	.20

Vincent Van Gogh, Death Cent. — A1036

Paintings: 50b, Field of Irises. 2 l, Artist's Room. 3 l, Night on the Coffee Terrace, vert. 3.50 l, Blossoming Fruit Trees. 5 l, Vase with Fourteen Sunflowers, vert.

1991, Mar. 29 Photo. *Perf. 13½*

3634	A1036	50b	multicolored	.20	.20
3635	A1036	2 l	multicolored	.20	.20
3636	A1036	3 l	multicolored	.35	.20
3637	A1036	3.50 l	multicolored	.40	.20
3638	A1036	5 l	multicolored	.60	.25
			Nos. 3634-3638 (5)	1.75	1.05

For surcharges see #4371-4372.

A1037

A1038

Birds: 50b, Larus marinus. 1 l, Sterna hirundo. 1.50 l, Recurvirostra avosetta. 2 l, Stercorarius pomarinus. 3 l, Vanellus vanellus. 3.50 l, Mergus serrator. 4 l, Egretta garzetta. 5 l, Calidris alpina. 6 l, Limosa limosa. 7 l, Childonias hybrida.

1991, Apr. 3 Photo. *Perf. 13½*

3639	A1037	50b	ultra	.20	.20
3640	A1037	1 l	blue green	.20	.20
3641	A1037	1.50 l	bister	.20	.20
3642	A1037	2 l	dark blue	.25	.20
3643	A1037	3 l	light green	.30	.20
3644	A1037	3.50 l	dark green	.30	.20
3645	A1037	4 l	purple	.40	.20
3646	A1037	5 l	brown	.50	.20
3647	A1037	6 l	yel brown	.50	.20
3648	A1037	7 l	light blue	.60	.25
			Nos. 3639-3648 (10)	3.45	2.05

1991, Apr. 5 Photo. *Perf. 13½*

3649	A1038	4 l multicolored	.35	.20

Easter.

Europa — A1039

1991, May 10 Photo. *Perf. 13½*

3650	A1039	4.50 l Eutelsat I	.50	.20

For surcharge see No. 4185.

Posthorn — A1040

1991, May 24 Photo. *Perf. 13½*

3651	A1040	4.50 l blue	.40	.20

Gymnastics A1041

1991, June 14

3652	A1041	1 l	Rings	.20	.20
3653	A1041	1 l	Parallel bars	.20	.20
3654	A1041	4.50 l	Vault	.40	.20
3655	A1041	4.50 l	Uneven parallel bars	.40	.20
3656	A1041	8 l	Floor exercise	.70	.30
3657	A1041	9 l	Balance beam	.80	.35
			Nos. 3652-3657 (6)	2.70	1.45

For surcharge on 5 l see No. 3735. For other surcharges see Nos. 3944, 3946, 4237-4238.

Monasteries — A1042

1991, July 4 Photo. *Perf. 13½*

3658	A1042	1 l	Curtea de Arges, vert.	.20	.20
3659	A1042	1 l	Putna, vert.	.20	.20
3660	A1042	4.50 l	Varatec, vert.	.40	.20
3661	A1042	4.50 l	Agapia	.40	.20
3662	A1042	8 l	Golia	.70	.30
3663	A1042	9 l	Sucevita	.80	.35
			Nos. 3658-3663 (6)	2.70	1.45

For surcharges see #4354-4355.

Hotels, Lodges, and Resorts
A1043 A1044

Designs: 1 l, Hotel Continental, Timisoara, vert. 2 l, Valea Caprei Lodge, Fagaras. 4 l, Hotel Intercontinental, Bucharest, vert. 5 l, Lebada Hotel, Crisan. 6 l, Muntele Rosu Lodge, Ciucas. 8 l, Transylvania Hotel, Cluj-Napoca. 9 l, Hotel Orizont, Predeal. 10 l, Hotel Roman, Herculane, vert. 18 l, Rarau Lodge, Rarau, vert. 20 l, Alpine Hotel, Poiana Brasov. 25 l, Constanta Casino. 30 l, Miorija Lodge, Bucegi. 45 l, Sura Dacilor Lodge, Poiana Brasov. 60 l, Valea Draganului, Tourist Complex,. 80 l, Hotel Florica, Venus Health Resort. 120 l, International Hotel, Baile Felix, vert. 160 l, Hotel Egreta, Tulcea, vert. 250 l, Motel Valea de Pesti, Valea Jiului. 400 l, Tourist Complex, Baisoara. 500 l, Hotel Bradul, Covasna. 800 l, Hotel Gorj, Tirgu Jiu.

1991 Photo. *Perf. 13½*

3664	A1043	1 l	blue	.20	.20
3665	A1043	2 l	dark green	.20	.20
3666	A1043	4 l	carmine	.20	.20
3667	A1043	5 l	violet	.30	.20
3668	A1043	6 l	olive brown	.20	.20
3669	A1043	8 l	brown	.20	.20
3670	A1043	9 l	red brown	.60	.20
3671	A1043	10 l	olive green	.65	.25
3672	A1043	18 l	bright red	.50	.20
3673	A1043	20 l	brown org	.40	.20
3674	A1043	25 l	bright blue	.30	.20
3675	A1043	30 l	magenta	.35	.20
3676	A1043	45 l	dark blue	.95	.30
3677	A1044	60 l	brown olive	1.25	.40
3678	A1044	80 l	purple	1.60	.55

Size: 27x41mm, 41x27mm

3679	A1044	120 l	gray bl & dk bl vio	1.80	.60
3680	A1044	160 l	lt ver & dk ver	2.25	.75
3681	A1044	250 l	lt bl & dk bl	2.90	1.00
3682	A1044	400 l	tan & dk brn	3.75	1.25
3683	A1044	500 l	lt bl grn & dk bl grn	4.25	1.50
3684	A1044	800 l	pink & dk lil rose	5.25	1.75
			Nos. 3664-3684 (21)	28.10	10.55

Issued: 1 l, 5 l, 9 l, 10 l, 8/27; 2 l, 4 l, 18 l, 25 l, 30 l, 10/8; 6 l, 8 l, 20 l, 45 l, 60 l, 80 l, 11/14; 120 l, 160 l, 250 l, 400 l, 500 l, 800 l, 12/5.

For surcharges see Nos. 4167-4174, 4204-4219.

Riccione '91, Intl. Philatelic Exhibition — A1045

1991, Aug. 27

3685	A1045	4 l multicolored	.40	.20

A1046

A1047

Vases: a, Decorated with birds. b, Decorated with flowers.

1991, Sept. 12

3686	A1046	5 l Pair, #a.-b.	.70	.35

Romanian-Chinese Philatelic Exhibition.

1991, Sept. 17

3687	A1047	1 l blue	.25	.20

Romanian Academy, 125th anniv.

A1048

A1049

Balkanfila '91 Philatelic Exhibition: 4 l, Flowers, by Nicu Enea. 5 l, Peasant Girl of Vlasca, by Georghe Tattarescu. 20 l, Sports Center, Bacau.

1991, Sept. 20

3688	A1048	4 l multicolored	.40	.20
3689	A1048	5 l multicolored	.45	.20

Souvenir Sheet

3690	A1048	20 l multicolored	1.75	1.75

No. 3689 printed se-tenant with 2 l Romanian Philatelic Assoc. label. No. 3690 contains one 54x42mm stamp.

Miniature Sheets

Birds: No. 3691a, Cissa erythrorhyncha. b, Malaconotus blanchoti. c, Sialia sialis. d, Sturnella neglecta. e, Harpactes fasciatus. f, Upupa epops. g, Malurus cyaneus. h, Brachypteracias squamigera. i, Leptopterus madagascariensis. j, Phoeniculus bollei. k, Melanerpes erythrocephalus. l, Pericrocotus flammeus.

No. 3692a, Melithreptus laetior. b, Rhynochetos jubatus. c, Turdus migratorius. d, Copsychus saularis. e, Monticola saxatilis. f, Xanthocephalus xanthocephalus. g, Scotopelia peli. h, Ptilogonys caudatus. i, Todus mexicanus. j, Copsychus malabaricus. k, Myzomela erythrocephala. l, Gymnostinops montezuma.

1991, Oct. 7 Sheets of 12

3691	A1049	2 l #a.-l.	2.50	2.50
3692	A1049	2 l #a.-l.	2.50	2.50

Natl. Census — A1050

1991, Oct. 15

3693	A1050	5 l multicolored	.30	.20

Phila Nippon '91 — A1051

1991, Nov. 13 Photo. *Perf. 13½*

3694	A1051	10 l Sailing ship	.75	.25
3695	A1051	10 l Bridge building	.75	.25

Miniature Sheets

Butterflies and Moths A1052

Designs: No. 3696a, Ornithoptera paradisea. b, Bhutanitis lidderdalii. c, Morpho helena. d, Ornithoptera croesus. e, Phoebis avellaneda. f, Ornithoptera victoriae. g, Teinopalpus imperialis. h, Hypolimnas dexithea. i, Dabasa payeni. j, Morpho achilleana. k, Heliconius melpomene. l, Agrias claudina sardanapalus.

No. 3697a, Graellsia isabellae. b, Antocharis cardamines. c, Ammobiota festiva. d, Polygonia c-album. e, Catocala promisa. f, Rhyparia purpurata. g, Arctia villica. h, Polyommatus daphnis. i, Zerynthia polyxena. j, Daphnis nerii. k, Licaena dispar rutila. l, Pararge roxelana.

1991, Nov. 30 Photo. *Perf. 13½*
Sheets of 12

3696	A1052	3 l #a.-l.	3.00	3.00
3697	A1052	3 l #a.-l.	3.00	3.00

For surcharges see #4266-4267.

A1053

A1054

1991, Nov. 21 Photo. *Perf. 13½*

3698 A1053 1 l Running .20 .20
3699 A1053 4 l Long jump .35 .20
3700 A1053 5 l High jump .45 .20
3701 A1053 5 l Runner in blocks .45 .20
3702 A1053 9 l Hurdles .80 .25
3703 A1053 10 l Javelin .90 .30
Nos. 3698-3703 (6) 3.15 1.35

World Track and Field Championships, Tokyo.

1991, Dec. 10 Photo. *Perf. 13½*

Famous People: 1 l, Mihail Kogalniceanu (1817-1891), politician. 4 l, Nicolae Titulescu (1882-1941), politician. No. 3706, Andrei Mureseanu (1816-1863), author. No. 3707, Aron Pumnul (1818-1866), author. 9 l, George Bacovia (1881-1957), author. 10 l, Perpessicius (1891-1971), writer.

3704 A1054 1 l multi .20 .20
3705 A1054 4 l multi .20 .20
3706 A1054 5 l multi .25 .20
3707 A1054 5 l multi .25 .20
3708 A1054 9 l multi .50 .20
3709 A1054 10 l multi .60 .20
Nos. 3704-3709 (6) 2.00 1.20

See Nos. 3759-3761, 3776-3781.
For surcharges see Nos. 4238A-4248.

Stamp Day — A1055

1991, Dec. 20

3710 A1055 8 l + 2 l label .50 .20

Central University Library, Bucharest, Cent. A1056

1991, Dec. 23

3711 A1056 8 l red brown .50 .20

Christmas A1057

1991, Dec. 25 Photo. *Perf. 13½*

3712 A1057 8 l multicolored .50 .20

See No. 3874.

1992 Winter Olympics, Albertville A1058

1992, Feb. 1 Photo. *Perf. 13½*

3713 A1058 4 l Biathlon .20 .20
3714 A1058 5 l Alpine skiing .20 .20
3715 A1058 8 l Cross-country skiing .20 .20
3716 A1058 10 l Two-man luge .20 .20
3717 A1058 20 l Speed skating .40 .20
3718 A1058 25 l Ski jumping .50 .20
3719 A1058 30 l Ice hockey .60 .25
3720 A1058 45 l Men's figure skating .90 .30
Nos. 3713-3720 (8) 3.20 1.75

Souvenir Sheets

3721 A1058 75 l Women's figure skating 2.25 2.25

Imperf

3722 A1058 125 l 4-Man bobsled *6.00 6.00*

No. 3721 is airmail and contains one 42x54mm stamp.

Porcelain — A1059

Designs: 4 l, Sugar and cream service. 5 l, Tea service. 8 l, Goblet and pitcher, vert. 30 l, Tea service, diff. 45 l, Vase, vert.

1992, Feb. 20 Photo. *Perf. 13½*

3723 A1059 4 l multicolored .20 .20
3724 A1059 5 l multicolored .20 .20
3725 A1059 8 l multicolored .20 .20
3726 A1059 30 l multicolored .70 .25
3727 A1059 45 l multicolored 1.00 .35
Nos. 3723-3727 (5) 2.30 1.20

Fish A1060

Designs: 4 l, Scomber scombrus. 5 l, Tinca tinca. 8 l, Salvelinus fontinalis. 10 l, Romanichthys valsanicola. 30 l, Chondrostoma nasus. 45 l, Mullus barbatus ponticus.

1992, Feb. 28 Photo. *Perf. 13½*

3728 A1060 4 l multicolored .20 .20
3729 A1060 5 l multicolored .20 .20
3730 A1060 8 l multicolored .30 .20
3731 A1060 10 l multicolored .40 .20
3732 A1060 30 l multicolored .65 .20
3733 A1060 45 l multicolored 1.00 .20
Nos. 3728-3733 (6) 2.75 1.20

A1060a

1992, Mar. 11 Photo. *Perf. 13½*

3734 A1060a 90 l on 5 l multi 1.75 .60

No. 3734 not issued without surcharge.

Olympics Type of 1991 Surcharged

1992, Mar. 11 Photo. *Perf. 13½*

3735 A1041 90 l on 5 l like #3657 1.75 .60

No. 3735 not issued without surcharge.

Horses A1061

Various stylized drawings of horses walking, running, or jumping.

1992, Mar. 17 Photo. *Perf. 13½*

3736 A1061 6 l multi, vert. .20 .20
3737 A1061 7 l multi .20 .20
3738 A1061 10 l multi, vert. .20 .20
3739 A1061 25 l multi, vert. .50 .20
3740 A1061 30 l multi .70 .20
3741 A1061 50 l multi, vert. 1.10 .20
Nos. 3736-3741 (6) 2.90 1.20

Miniature Sheet

Discovery of America, 500th Anniv. — A1062

Columbus and ships: a, Green background. b, Violet background. c, Blue background. d, Ship approaching island.

1992, Apr. 22 Photo. *Perf. 13½*

3742 A1062 35 l Sheet of 4, #a.-d. *6.50 6.50*

Europa.

Granada '92, Philatelic Exhibition — A1063

a, 25 l, Spain No. 1 and Romania No. 1. b, 10 l, Expo emblem. c, 30 l, Building and courtyard, Granada. Illustration reduced.

1992, Apr. 24 Photo. *Perf. 13½*

3743 A1063 Sheet of 3, #a.-c. 1.40 1.40

Icon of Christ's Descent into Hell, 1680 — A1064

1992, Apr. 24 Photo. *Perf. 13½*

3744 A1064 10 l multicolored .30 .20

Easter.

Fire Station, Bucharest, Cent. — A1065

1992, May 2

3745 A1065 10 l multicolored .30 .20

Chess Olympiad, Manila — A1066

1992, June 7 *Perf. 13½*

3746 A1066 10 l shown .30 .20
3747 A1066 10 l Building, chess board .30 .20

Souvenir Sheet

3748 A1066 75 l Shore, chess board 2.25 2.25

No. 3748 contains one 42x54mm stamp.

1992 Summer Olympics, Barcelona — A1067

1992, July 17 Photo. *Perf. 13½*

3749 A1067 6 l Shooting, vert. .20 .20
3750 A1067 7 l Weight lifting, vert. .20 .20
3751 A1067 9 l Two-man canoeing .20 .20
3752 A1067 10 l Handball, vert. .20 .20
3753 A1067 25 l Wrestling .30 .20
3754 A1067 30 l Fencing .35 .20
3755 A1067 50 l Running, vert. .65 .25
3756 A1067 55 l Boxing .75 .25
Nos. 3749-3756 (8) 2.85 1.70

Souvenir Sheets

3757 A1067 100 l Rowing 1.25 1.25

Imperf

3758 A1067 200 l Gymnastics 5.00 5.00

Nos. 3757-3758 are airmail. No. 3757 contains one 54x42mm stamp, No. 3758 one 40x53mm stamp.

Famous People Type of 1991

Designs: 10 l, Ion I. C. Bratianu (1864-1927), prime minister. 25 l, Ion Gh. Duca (1879-1933). 30 l, Grigore Gafencu (1892-1957), journalist and politician.

1992, July 27 Photo. *Perf. 13½*

3759	A1054	10 l	green & violet	.20	.20
3760	A1054	25 l	blue & lake	.20	.20
3761	A1054	30 l	lake & blue	.30	.20
			Nos. 3759-3761 (3)	.70	.60

Expo '92, Seville
A1068

Designs: 6 l, The Thinker, Cernavoda. 7 l, Trajan's bridge, Drobeta. 10 l, Mill. 25 l, Railroad bridge, Cernavoda. 30 l, Trajan Vuia's flying machine. 55 l, Herman Oberth's rocket. 100 l, Prayer sculpture, by C. Brancusi.

1992, Sept. 1

3762	A1068	6 l	multicolored	.20	.20
3763	A1068	7 l	multicolored	.20	.20
3764	A1068	10 l	multicolored	.20	.20
3765	A1068	25 l	multicolored	.25	.20
3766	A1068	30 l	multicolored	.30	.20
3767	A1068	55 l	multicolored	.50	.20
			Nos. 3762-3767 (6)	1.65	1.20

Souvenir Sheet

3768	A1068	100 l	multicolored	.75	.75

No. 3768 contains one 42x54mm stamp.

World Post Day — A1069

1992, Oct. 9

3769	A1069	10 l	multicolored	.20	.20

For surcharge see No. 3945.

Discovery of America, 500th Anniv. — A1070

Columbus and: 6 l, Santa Maria. 10 l, Nina. 25 l, Pinta. 55 l, Arrival in New World. 100 l, Sailing ship, vert.

1992, Oct. 30 Photo. *Perf. 13½*

3770	A1070	6 l	multicolored	.20	.20
3771	A1070	10 l	multicolored	.20	.20
3772	A1070	25 l	multicolored	.25	.20
3773	A1070	55 l	multicolored	.50	.20
			Nos. 3770-3773 (4)	1.15	.80

Souvenir Sheet

3774	A1070	100 l	multicolored	.90	.90

No. 3774 contains one 42x54mm stamp.

Romanian Postal Reorganization, 1st Anniv. — A1071

1992, Nov. 5 Photo. *Perf. 13½*

3775	A1071	10 l	multicolored	*.20*	*.20*

For surcharge see No. 4113.

Famous People Type of 1991

Designs: 6 l, Iacob Negruzzi (1842-1932), author. 7 l, Grigore Antipa (1867-1944), naturalist. 9 l, Alexe Mateevici (1888-1917), poet. 10 l, Cezar Petrescu (1892-1961), author. 25 l, Octav Onicescu (1892-1983), mathematician. 30 l, Ecaterina Teodoroiu (1894-1917), World War I soldier.

1992, Nov. 9 Photo. *Perf. 13½*

3776	A1054	6 l	green & violet	.20	.20
3777	A1054	7 l	lilac & green	.20	.20
3778	A1054	9 l	gray blue & purple	.20	.20
3779	A1054	10 l	brown & blue	.20	.20
3780	A1054	25 l	blue & brown	.20	.20
3781	A1054	30 l	slate & blue	.30	.20
			Nos. 3776-3781 (6)	1.30	1.20

Wild Animals — A1072

Designs: 6 l, Haliaeetus leucocephalus, vert. 7 l, Strix occidentalis, vert. 9 l, Ursus arctos, vert. 10 l, Haematopus bachmani. 25 l, Canis lupus. 30 l, Odocoileus virginianus. 55 l, Alces alces.

1992, Nov. 16 Litho. *Perf. 13½*

3782	A1072	6 l	multicolored	.20	.20
3783	A1072	7 l	multicolored	.20	.20
3784	A1072	9 l	multicolored	.20	.20
3785	A1072	10 l	multicolored	.20	.20
3786	A1072	25 l	multicolored	.25	.20
3787	A1072	30 l	multicolored	.30	.20
3788	A1072	55 l	multicolored	.60	.20
			Nos. 3782-3788 (7)	1.95	1.40

Souvenir Sheet

3789	A1072	100 l	Orcinus orca	.90	.90

Romanian Anniversaries and Events — A1073

7 l, Building, Galea Victoria St., 300th anniv. 9 l, Statue, School of Commerce, 600th anniv. 10 l, Curtea de Arges Monastery, 475th anniv. 25 l, School of Architecture, Bucharest, 80th anniv.

1992, Dec. 3 Photo. *Perf. 13½*

3790	A1073	7 l	multicolored	.20	.20
3791	A1073	9 l	multicolored	.20	.20
3792	A1073	10 l	multicolored	.20	.20
3793	A1073	25 l	multicolored	.25	.20
			Nos. 3790-3793 (4)	.85	.80

Natl. Arms — A1074

1992, Dec. 7

3794	A1074	15 l	multicolored	.20	.20

Christmas A1075

1992, Dec. 15

3795	A1075	15 l	multicolored	.20	.20

For surcharge see No. 4249.

New Telephone Numbering System A1076

1992, Dec. 28 Photo. *Perf. 13½*

3796	A1076	15 l	blue, black & red	*.20*	*.20*

For surcharges see #4268-4272.

Souvenir Sheets

1992 Summer Olympics, Barcelona A1077

No. 3797: a, Shooting. b, Wrestling. c, Weight lifting. d, Boxing.

No. 3798: a, Women's gymnastics. b, Four-man sculls. c, Fencing. d, High jump.

1992, Dec. 30 Photo. *Perf. 13½*

3797	A1077	35 l	Sheet of 4, #a.-d.	*1.10*	*1.10*
3798	A1077	35 l	Sheet of 4, #a.-d.	*1.10*	*1.10*

Historic Sites, Bucharest — A1078

Designs: 10 l, Mihai Voda Monastery. 15 l, Vacaresti Monastery. 25 l, Multi-purpose hall. 30 l, Mina Minovici Medical Institute.

1993, Feb. 11 Photo. *Perf. 13½*

3799	A1078	10 l	multicolored	.20	.20
3800	A1078	15 l	multicolored	.20	.20
3801	A1078	25 l	multicolored	.20	.20
3802	A1078	30 l	multicolored	.25	.20
			Nos. 3799-3802 (4)	.85	.80

Easter — A1079

1993, Mar. 25

3803	A1079	15 l	multicolored	.20	.20

Medicinal Plants — A1080

1993, Mar. 30

3804	A1080	10 l	Crataegus monogyna	.20	.20
3805	A1080	15 l	Gentiana phlogifolia	.20	.20
3806	A1080	25 l	Hippophae rhamnoides	.20	.20
3807	A1080	30 l	Vaccinium myrtillus	.25	.20
3808	A1080	50 l	Arnica montana	.35	.20
3809	A1080	90 l	Rosa canina	.65	.25
			Nos. 3804-3809 (6)	1.85	1.25

Nichita Stanescu (1933-1983), Poet — A1081

1993, Mar. 31

3810	A1081	15 l	brown and blue	.25	.20

Souvenir Sheet

Polska '93 — A1082

1993, Apr. 28 Photo. *Perf. 13½*

3811	A1082	200 l	multicolored	1.25	1.25

Birds A1083

Cats — A1084

1993, Apr. 30

3812	A1083	5 l	Pica pica	.20	.20
3813	A1083	10 l	Aquila chrysaetos	.20	.20
3814	A1083	15 l	Pyrrhula pyrrhula	.20	.20
3815	A1083	20 l	Upupa epops	.20	.20
3816	A1083	25 l	Dendrocopos major	.20	.20
3817	A1083	50 l	Oriolus oriolus	.25	.20

3818	A1083	65 l	Loxia leucoptera	.35	.20
3819	A1083	90 l	Hirundo rustica	.55	.20
3820	A1083	160 l	Parus cyanus	.90	.20
3821	A1083	250 l	Sturnus roseus	1.25	.20
			Nos. 3812-3821 (10)	4.30	2.00

Nos. 3812-3813 are horiz.

1993, May 24 Photo. *Perf. 13½*

Various cats.

3822	A1084	10 l	multicolored	.20	.20
3823	A1084	15 l	multicolored	.20	.20
3824	A1084	30 l	multicolored	.20	.20
3825	A1084	90 l	multicolored	.55	.20
3826	A1084	135 l	multicolored	.70	.20
3827	A1084	160 l	multicolored	.95	.20
			Nos. 3822-3827 (6)	2.80	1.20

Souvenir Sheet

Europa — A1085

Paintings and sculpture by: a, Pablo Picasso. b, Constantin Brancusi. c, Ion Irimescu. d, Alexandru Ciucurencu.

1993, May 31 Photo. *Perf. 13½*

3828	A1085	280 l	Sheet of 4, #a.-d.	2.75	2.75

A1086

A1087

1993, June 30 Photo. *Perf. 13½*

3829	A1086	10 l	Vipera berus	.20	.20
3830	A1086	15 l	Lynx lynx	.20	.20
3831	A1086	25 l	Tadorna tadorna	.20	.20
3832	A1086	75 l	Hucho hucho	.40	.20
3833	A1086	105 l	Limenitis populi	.50	.20
3834	A1086	280 l	Rosalia alpina	.75	.20
			Nos. 3829-3834 (6)	2.25	1.20

Nos. 3829, 3831-3834 are horiz.

1993, June 30

3835	A1087	10 l	Martes martes	.20	.20
3836	A1087	15 l	Oryctolagus cuniculus	.20	.20
3837	A1087	20 l	Sciurus vulgaris	.20	.20
3838	A1087	25 l	Rupicapra rupicapra	.20	.20
3839	A1087	30 l	Vulpes vulpes	.20	.20
3840	A1087	40 l	Ovis ammon	.20	.20
3841	A1087	75 l	Genetta genetta	.30	.20
3842	A1087	105 l	Eliomys quercinus	.45	.20
3843	A1087	150 l	Mustela erminea	.50	.20
3844	A1087	280 l	Herpestes ichneumon	1.25	.20
			Nos. 3835-3844 (10)	3.70	2.00

Nos. 3836, 3839, 3843-3844 are horiz.

Dinosaurs — A1088

1993, July 30 Photo. *Perf. 13½*

3845	A1088	29 l	Brontosaurus	.20	.20
3846	A1088	46 l	Plesiosaurus	.25	.20
3847	A1088	85 l	Triceratops	.35	.20
3848	A1088	171 l	Stegosaurus	.80	.20
3849	A1088	216 l	Tyrannosaurus	1.00	.20
3850	A1088	319 l	Archaeopteryx	1.40	.20
			Nos. 3845-3850 (6)	4.00	1.20

Souvenir Sheet

Telafila '93, Israel-Romanian Philatelic Exhibition — A1089

Woman with Eggs, by Marcel Lancu. Illustration reduced.

1993, Aug. 21

3851	A1089	535 l	multicolored	2.25	2.25

Icons — A1090

Designs: 75 l, St. Stephen. 171 l, Martyrs from Brancoveanu and Vacarescu families. 216 l, St. Anthony.

1993, Aug. 31

3852	A1090	75 l	multicolored	.20	.20
3853	A1090	171 l	multicolored	.50	.20
3854	A1090	216 l	multicolored	1.10	.35
			Nos. 3852-3854 (3)	1.80	.75

Rural Mounted Police, Cent. — A1091

1993, Sept. 1

3855	A1091	29 l	multicolored	.20	.20

No. 3618 Surcharged in Red

1993, Sept. 3

3856	A1031	171 l	on 2 l	.65	.25

Souvenir Sheet

Bangkok '93 — A1092

Illustration reduced.

1993, Sept. 20

3857	A1092	535 l	multicolored	2.25	2.25

Famous Men — A1093

Designs: 29 l, George Baritiu (1812-93), politician. 46 l, Horia Creanga (1892-1943), architect. 85 l, Armand Calinescu (1893-1939), politician. 171 l, Dumitru Bagdasar (1893-1946), physician. 216 l, Constantin Brailoiu (1893-1958), musician. 319 l, Iuliu Maniu (1873-1953), politician.

1993, Oct. 8

3858	A1093	29 l	multicolored	.20	.20
3859	A1093	46 l	multicolored	.20	.20
3860	A1093	85 l	multicolored	.25	.20
3861	A1093	171 l	multicolored	.55	.20
3862	A1093	216 l	multicolored	.65	.25
3863	A1093	319 l	multicolored	1.10	.35
			Nos. 3858-3863 (6)	2.95	1.40

Souvenir Sheet

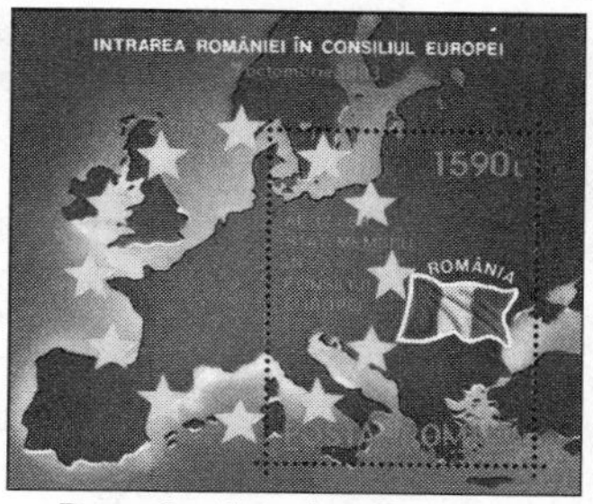

Romanian Entry into Council of Europe — A1094

1993, Nov. 26 Photo. *Perf. 13½*

3864	A1094	1590 l	multi	4.50	4.50

Expansion of Natl. Borders, 75th Anniv. — A1095

Government leaders: 115 l, Iancu Flondor (1865-1924). 245 l, Ion I. C. Bratianu (1864-1927). 255 l, Luliu Maniu (1873-1953). 325 l, Pantelimon Halippa (1883-1979). 1060 l, King Ferdinand I (1865-1927).

1993-94

3865	A1095	115 l	multi	.35	.20
3866	A1095	245 l	multi	.70	.25
3867	A1095	255 l	multi	.80	.25
3868	A1095	325 l	multi	1.00	.35
			Nos. 3865-3868 (4)	2.85	1.05

Souvenir Sheet

3869	A1095	1060 l	Romania in one color	3.25	3.25
a.			Romania in four colors	*10.00*	*10.00*

No. 3869a was redrawn because of an error in the map.

Issued: No. 3869, Feb. 1994; Nos. 3865-3868, 3869a, Dec. 1, 1993.

Anniversaries and Events A1096

Designs: 115 l, Emblem of the Diplomatic Alliance. 245 l, Statue of Johannes Honterus, founder of first Humanitarian School. 255 l, Arms, seal of Slatina, Olt River Bridge. 325 l, Map, arms of Braila.

1993, Dec. 15

3870	A1096	115 l	multicolored	.30	.20
3871	A1096	245 l	multicolored	.60	.20
3872	A1096	255 l	multicolored	.65	.25
3873	A1096	325 l	multicolored	.85	.30
			Nos. 3870-3873 (4)	2.40	.95

Diplomatic Alliance, 75th anniv. (#3870). Birth of Johannes Honterus, 450th anniv. (#3871). City of Slatina, 625th anniv. (#3872). County of Braila, 625th anniv. (#3873).

Christmas Type of 1991

1993, Dec. 20

3874	A1057	45 l	like #3712	.20	.20

Insects, Wildlife from Movile Cavern — A1097

Designs: 29 l, Clivina subterranea. 46 l, Nepa anophthalma. 85 l, Haemopis caeca. 171 l, Lascona cristiani. 216 l, Semisalsa dobrogica. 319 l, Armadilidium tabacarui. 535 l, Exploring cavern, vert.

1993, Dec. 27

3875	A1097	29 l	multicolored	.20	.20
3876	A1097	46 l	multicolored	.20	.20
3877	A1097	85 l	multicolored	.30	.20
3878	A1097	171 l	multicolored	.55	.20

3879 A1097 216 l multicolored .70 .25
3880 A1097 319 l multicolored 1.00 .35
Nos. 3875-3880 (6) 2.95 1.40

Souvenir Sheet

3881 A1097 535 l multicolored 1.75 1.75

Alexandru Ioan Cuza — A1098

1994, Jan. 24 Photo. *Perf. 13*

3882 A1098 45 l multicolored .20 .20

Historic Buildings, Bucharest — A1099

115 l, Opera House. 245 l, Vacaresti Monastery. 255 l, Church of St. Vineri. 325 l, Dominican House, Vacaresti Monastery.

1994, Feb. 7

3883 A1099 115 l multicolored .25 .20
3884 A1099 245 l multicolored .55 .20
3885 A1099 255 l multicolored .65 .25
3886 A1099 325 l multicolored .80 .25
Nos. 3883-3886 (4) 2.25 .90

1994 Winter Olympics, Lillehammer A1100

1994, Feb. 12 *Perf. 13½*

3887 A1100 70 l Speed skating .20 .20
3888 A1100 115 l Slalom skiing .25 .20
3889 A1100 125 l Bobsled .30 .20
3890 A1100 245 l Biathlon .55 .20
3891 A1100 255 l Ski jumping .60 .25
3892 A1100 325 l Figure skating .85 .30
Nos. 3887-3892 (6) 2.75 1.35

Souvenir Sheet

3893 A1100 1590 l Luge 4.00 4.00

No. 3893 contains one 43x54mm stamp.

Mills — A1101

1994, Mar. 31 *Perf. 13*

3894 A1101 70 l Sarichioi .20 .20
3895 A1101 115 l Valea Nucarilor .25 .20
3896 A1101 125 l Caraorman .30 .20
3897 A1101 245 l Romanii de Jos .60 .25
3898 A1101 255 l Enisala, horiz. .65 .25
3899 A1101 325 l Nistoresti .90 .30
Nos. 3894-3899 (6) 2.90 1.40

Dinosaurs — A1102

1994, Apr. 30 Photo. *Perf. 13½*

3900 A1102 90 l Struthiosaurs .20 .20
3901 A1102 130 l Megalosaurs .25 .20
3902 A1102 150 l Parasaurolophus .25 .20
3903 A1102 280 l Stenonychosaurus .55 .20
3904 A1102 500 l Camarasaurus .75 .25
3905 A1102 635 l Gallimimus .95 .30
Nos. 3900-3905 (6) 2.95 1.35

Romanian Legends A1103

Designs: 70 l, Calin the Madman. 115 l, Ileana Cosanzeana. 125 l, Ileana Cosanzeana, diff. 245 l, Ileana Cosanzeana, diff. 255 l, Agheran the Brave. 325 l, Wolf as Prince Charming, Ileana Cosanzeana.

1994, Apr. 8 Photo. *Perf. 13½*

3906 A1103 70 l multicolored .20 .20
3907 A1103 115 l multicolored .25 .20
3908 A1103 125 l multicolored .30 .20
3909 A1103 245 l multicolored .60 .20
3910 A1103 255 l multicolored .65 .25
3911 A1103 325 l multicolored .95 .30
Nos. 3906-3911 (6) 2.95 1.35

Easter A1104

Trees — A1105

1994, Apr. 21

3912 A1104 60 l multicolored .20 .20

Wmk. 398

1994, May 27 Photo. *Perf. 13¼*

3913 A1105 15 l Abies alba .20 .20
3914 A1105 35 l Pinus sylvestris .20 .20
3915 A1105 45 l Populus alba .20 .20
3916 A1105 60 l Quercus robur .20 .20
3917 A1105 70 l Larix decidua .20 .20
3918 A1105 125 l Fagus sylvatica .20 .20
3919 A1105 350 l Acer pseudoplatanus .40 .20
3920 A1105 940 l Fraxinus excelsior 1.00 .20
3921 A1105 1440 l Picea abies 1.60 .20
3922 A1105 3095 l Tilia platyphyllos 3.50 .40
Nos. 3913-3922 (10) 7.70 2.20

For surcharges see Nos. 4221-4224.

1994 World Cup Soccer Championships, US — A1106

1994, June 17 Unwmk.

3923 A1106 90 l Group A .20 .20
3924 A1106 130 l Group B .25 .20
3925 A1106 150 l Group C .25 .20
3926 A1106 280 l Group D .55 .20
3927 A1106 500 l Group E .75 .25
3928 A1106 635 l Group F .95 .30
Nos. 3923-3928 (6) 2.95 1.35

Souvenir Sheet

3929 A1106 2075 l Action scene 3.50 3.50

No. 3929 is airmail and contains one 54x42mm stamp.

Intl. Olympic Committee, Cent. — A1107

Ancient Olympians: 150 l, Torchbearer. 280 l, Discus thrower. 500 l, Wrestlers. 635 l, Arbitrator.

2075 l, Runners, emblem of Romanian Olympic Committee.

1994, June 23

3930 A1107 150 l multicolored .25 .20
3931 A1107 280 l multicolored .50 .20
3932 A1107 500 l multicolored .85 .30
3933 A1107 635 l multicolored 1.10 .35
Nos. 3930-3933 (4) 2.70 1.05

Souvenir Sheet

3934 A1107 2075 l multicolored 3.50 3.50

No. 3934 contains one 54x42mm stamp. Romanian Olympic Committee, 80th anniv. (#3934).

Miniature Sheets

Mushrooms A1108

Edible: No. 3935a, 30 l, Craterellus cornucopiodes. b, 60 l, Lepista nuda. c, 150 l, Boletus edulis. d, 940 l, Lycoperdon perlatum.

Poisonous: No. 3936a, 90 l, Boletus satanas. b, 280 l, Amanita phalloides. c, 350 l, Inocybe patonillardi. d, 500 l, Amanita muscaria.

1994, Aug. 8 Photo. *Perf. 13½*

3935 A1108 Sheet of 4, #a.-d. 2.25 2.00
3936 A1108 Sheet of 4, #a.-d. 2.25 2.00
Complete booklet, #3935-3936 4.75

PHILAKOREA '94 — A1109

1994, Aug. 16 *Perf. 13½*

3937 A1109 60 l Tuning fork .20 .20

Souvenir Sheet

3938 A1109 2075 l Korean drummer 3.25 3.25

No. 3938 contains one 42x54mm stamp.

Environmental Protection in Danube River Delta — A1110

Designs: 150 l, Huso huso. 280 l, Vipera ursini. 500 l, Haliaeetus albicilla. 635 l, Mustela lutreola.

2075 l, Periploca graeca.

1994, Aug. 31

3939 A1110 150 l multicolored .25 .20
3940 A1110 280 l multicolored .50 .20
3941 A1110 500 l multicolored .95 .30
3942 A1110 635 l multicolored 1.10 .35
Nos. 3939-3942 (4) 2.80 1.05

Souvenir Sheet

3943 A1110 2075 l multicolored 3.50 3.50

No. 3943 contains one 54x42mm stamp.

Nos. 3654-3655 Surcharged

No. 3769 Surcharged

1994 *Perfs., Etc. as Before*

3944 A1041 150 l on 4.50 l #3654 .25 .20
3945 A1069 150 l on 10 l #3769 .30 .20
3946 A1041 525 l on 4.50 l #3655 .90 .30
Nos. 3944-3946 (3) 1.45 .70

Issued: #3944, 3946 9/9/94; #3945, 10/7/94.

Circus Animal Acts — A1111

1994, Sept. 15 **Photo.** ***Perf. 13***

3947	A1111	90 l Elephant	.20	.20
3948	A1111	130 l Bear, vert.	.25	.20
3949	A1111	150 l Monkeys	.25	.20
3950	A1111	280 l Tiger	.50	.20
3951	A1111	500 l Lion	.95	.30
3952	A1111	635 l Horse	1.10	.35
		Nos. 3947-3952 (6)	3.25	1.45

20th Intl. Fair, Bucharest — A1112

1994, Oct. 10

3953	A1112	525 l multicolored	.90	.30

Fish A1113

World Wildlife Fund: 150 l, Acipenser ruthenus. 280 l, Acipenser guldenstaedti. 500 l, Acipenser stellatus. 635 l, Acipenser sturio.

1994, Oct. 29 **Photo.** ***Perf. 13½***

3954	A1113	150 l multicolored	.30	.20
3955	A1113	280 l multicolored	.60	.20
3956	A1113	500 l multicolored	1.00	.35
3957	A1113	635 l multicolored	1.25	.40
		Nos. 3954-3957 (4)	3.15	1.15

Chinese-Romanian Philatelic Exhibition — A1114

1994, Oct. 29 **Photo.** ***Perf. 13½***

3958	A1114	150 l Serpent	.25	.20
3959	A1114	1135 l Dragon	1.90	.60
a.		Pair, #3958-3959 + label	2.75	1.25

Romanian State Railway, 125th Anniv. A1115

1994, Oct. 31

3960	A1115	90 l multicolored	.20	.20

Famous People A1116

Designs: 30 l, Akex Drascu (1817-94). 60 l, Gh. Polizu (1819-86). 90 l, Gheorghe Tattarescu (1820-94), politician, prime minister. 150 l, Iulia Hasdeu (1869-88). 280 l, S. Mehedinti (1869-1962). 350 l, Camil Petrescu (1894-1957). 500 l, N. Paulescu (1869-1931). 940 l, L. Grigorescu (1894-1965).

1994 **Photo.** ***Perf. 13½***

3961	A1116	30 l multicolored	.20	.20
3962	A1116	60 l multicolored	.20	.20
3962A	A1116	90 l multicolored	.20	.20
3963	A1116	150 l multicolored	.25	.20
3964	A1116	280 l multicolored	.35	.20
3965	A1116	350 l multicolored	.55	.20
3966	A1116	500 l multicolored	.65	.25
3967	A1116	940 l multicolored	1.40	.45
		Nos. 3961-3967 (8)	3.80	1.90

Issued; 90 l, 12/28/94; others, 11/30/94.

Christmas — A1117

1994, Dec. 14 ***Perf. 13½***

3968	A1117	60 l multicolored	.20	.20

For surcharge see No. 4250.

St. Mary's Romanian Orthodox Church, Cleveland, Ohio, 90th Anniv. — A1118

1994, Dec. 21 **Photo.** ***Perf. 13½***

3969	A1118	610 l multicolored	.90	.30

World Tourism Organization, 20th Anniv. — A1119

1994, Dec. 22

3970	A1119	525 l multicolored	.90	.30

Miniature Sheet

Romanian Military Decorations A1120

Year of medal - #3971: a, 30 l, Distinguished Flying Cross, 1938. b, 60 l, Military Cross, 3rd class, 1916. c, 150 l, Distinguished Serivce Medal, 1st Class, 1880. d, 940 l, Order of the Romanian Star, 1877.

1994, Dec. 23

3971	A1120	Sheet of 4, #a.-d.	2.00	2.00

Baby Animals A1121

1994, Dec. 27 **Photo.** ***Perf. 13x½***

3972	A1121	90 l Kittens	.20	.20
3973	A1121	130 l Puppies	.20	.20
3974	A1121	150 l Kid goat	.20	.20
3975	A1121	280 l Foal	.35	.20
3976	A1121	500 l Bunnies	.80	.25
3977	A1121	635 l Lambs	1.00	.35
		Nos. 3972-3977 (6)	2.75	1.40

A1122

A1123

1995, Jan. 31 **Photo.** ***Perf. 13½***

3978	A1122	60 l dark blue	.20	.20

Save the Children organization.

1995, Feb. 25 **Photo.** ***Perf. 13½***

The Young Men of Brasov (Riders representing municipal districts of Brasov): 40 l, Tanar. 60 l, Batran. 150 l, Curcan. 280 l, Dorobant. 350 l, Brasovechean. 500 l, Rosior. 635 l, Albior.

3979	A1123	40 l multicolored	.20	.20
3980	A1123	60 l multicolored	.20	.20
3981	A1123	150 l multicolored	.20	.20
3982	A1123	280 l multicolored	.35	.20
3983	A1123	350 l multicolored	.55	.20
3984	A1123	500 l multicolored	.65	.25
3985	A1123	635 l multicolored	.90	.30
		Nos. 3979-3985 (7)	3.05	1.55

Liberation of Concentration Camps, 50th Anniv. — A1124

1995, Mar. 24 ***Perf. 13½***

3986	A1124	960 l black & red	.90	.30

FAO & UN, 50th Anniv. A1125

Designs: 675 l, FAO emblem, grain. 960 l, "50," UN emblem. 1615 l, Hand holding pen with flags of UN Charter countries.

1995, Apr. 12 ***Perf. 13½***

3987	A1125	675 l multicolored	.70	.25
3988	A1125	960 l multicolored	.95	.30
3989	A1125	1615 l multicolored	1.60	.55
		Nos. 3987-3989 (3)	3.25	1.10

Easter A1126

1995, Apr. 14

3990	A1126	60 l multicolored	.20	.20

Romanian Fairy Tales — A1127

Designs: 90 l, King riding horse across town. 130 l, Woman feeding animals, vert. 150 l, Man riding on winged horse. 280 l, Old man, young man. 500 l, Archer aiming at apple tree, vert. 635 l, Two people riding log pulled by galloping horses.

1995, Apr. 20 ***Perf. 13½***

3991	A1127	90 l multicolored	.20	.20
3992	A1127	130 l multicolored	.20	.20
3993	A1127	150 l multicolored	.20	.20
3994	A1127	280 l multicolored	.25	.20
3995	A1127	500 l multicolored	.50	.20
3996	A1127	635 l multicolored	.65	.25
		Nos. 3991-3996 (6)	2.00	1.25

Georges Enescu (1881-1955), Composer — A1128

1995, May 5 ***Perf. 13½***

3997	A1128	960 l black & dp yellow	.95	.30

Peace & Freedom A1129

Europa: 150 l, Dove carryng piece of rainbow. 4370 l, Dove under rainbow with wings forming "Europa."

1995, May 8

3998	A1129	150 l multicolored	.20	.20
3999	A1129	4370 l multicolored	9.00	9.00

Lucian Blaga (1895-1961), Poet — A1130

1995, May 9

4000	A1130	150 l	multicolored	.25	.20

See Nos. 4017-4021.

Methods of Transportation — A1131

Designs: 470 l, Bucharest Metro subway train, 1979. 675 l, Brasov aerial cable car, vert. 965 l, Sud Aviation SA 330 Puma helicopter. 2300 l, 1904 Trolleybus. 2550 l, Steam locomotive, 1869. 3410 l, Boeing 737-300.

1995, May 30 Photo. *Perf. 13½*

4001	A1131	470 l	blk, gray & yel	.60	.30
4002	A1131	675 l	blk, gray & red	.90	.45
4003	A1131	965 l	bl, blk & gray	1.25	.65
4004	A1131	2300 l	blk, gray & grn	3.00	1.50
4005	A1131	2550 l	blk, gray & red	3.25	1.60
4006	A1131	3410 l	bl, blk & gray	4.50	2.25
			Nos. 4001-4006 (6)	13.50	6.75

Nos. 4003, 4006 are airmail. No. 4006, 75th anniversary of Romanian air transportation.
See Nos. 4055-4060.

Romanian Maritime Service, Cent. — A1132

Ships: 90 l, Dacia, liner, vert. 130 l, Imparatul Traian, steamer. 150 l, Romania, steamer. 280 l, Costinesti, tanker. 960 l, Caransebes, container ship. 3410 l, Tutova, car ferry.

1995, May 31 Photo. *Perf. 13½*

4007	A1132	90 l	multicolored	.20	.20
4008	A1132	130 l	multicolored	.20	.20
4009	A1132	150 l	multicolored	.20	.20
4010	A1132	280 l	multicolored	.30	.20
4011	A1132	960 l	multicolored	1.00	.50
4012	A1132	3410 l	multicolored	3.75	1.90
			Nos. 4007-4012 (6)	5.65	3.20

A1133

A1134

European Nature Conservation Year: 150 l, Dama dama. 280 l, Otis tarda. 960 l, Cypripedium caiceolus. 1615 l, Ghetarul scarisoara (stalagmites).

1995, June 5

4013	A1133	150 l	multicolored	.20	.20
4014	A1133	280 l	multicolored	.30	.20
4015	A1133	960 l	multicolored	1.00	.50
4016	A1133	1615 l	multicolored	1.75	.90
			Nos. 4013-4016 (4)	3.25	1.80

Famous Romanians Type of 1995

Designs: 90 l, D.D. Rosca (1895-1980). 130 l, Vasile Conta (1845-1882). 280 l, Ion Barbu (1895-1961). 960 l, Iuliu Hatieganu (1885-1959). 1650 l, Dimitrie Brandza (1846-95).

1995, June 26 Photo. *Perf. 13½*

4017	A1130	90 l	multicolored	.20	.20
4018	A1130	130 l	multicolored	.20	.20
4019	A1130	280 l	multicolored	.30	.20
4020	A1130	960 l	multicolored	1.00	.50
4021	A1130	1650 l	multicolored	1.75	.90
			Nos. 4017-4021 (5)	3.45	2.00

1995, July 10 Photo. *Perf. 13½*

4022	A1134	1650 l	multicolored	1.75	.90

European Youth Olympic days.

Stamp Day — A1135

Illustration reduced.

1995, July 15

4023	A1135	960 l +715 l	label	1.75	.90

Cernavoda Bridge, Cent. — A1136

1995, July 27 Photo. *Perf. 13½*

4024	A1136	675 l	multicolored	.75	.40

A1137

A1138

Fowl: 90 l, Anas platyrhynchos. 130 l, Gallus gallus (hen). 150 l, Numida meleagris. 280 l, Meleagris gallopavo. 960 l, Anser anser. 1650 l, Gallus gallus (rooster).

1995, July 31 Photo. *Perf. 13½*

4025	A1137	90 l	multicolored	.20	.20
4026	A1137	130 l	multicolored	.20	.20
4027	A1137	150 l	multicolored	.20	.20
4028	A1137	280 l	multicolored	.30	.30
4029	A1137	960 l	multicolored	1.00	1.00
4030	A1137	1650 l	multicolored	1.75	1.75
			Nos. 4025-4030 (6)	3.65	3.65

1995, Aug. 5 Photo. *Perf. 13½*

Institute of Air Medicine, 75th Anniv.: Gen. Dr. Victor Anastasiu (1886-1972).

4031	A1138	960 l	multicolored	1.10	.55

Battle of Calugareni, 400th Anniv. — A1139

1995, Aug. 13

4032	A1139	100 l	multicolored	.20	.20

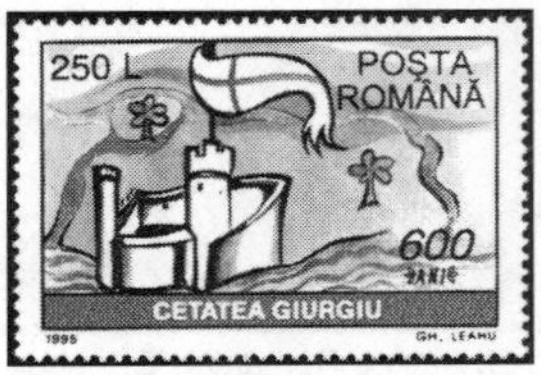

Romanian Buildings — A1140

Structure, year completed: 250 l, Giurgiu Castle, 1395. 500 l, Neamtului Castle, 1395, vert. 960 l, Sebes-Alba Mill, 1245. 1615 l, Dorohoi Church, 1495, vert. 1650 l, Military Observatory, Bucharest, 1895, vert.

1995, Aug. 28

4033	A1140	250 l	multicolored	.25	.20
4034	A1140	500 l	multicolored	.55	.25
4035	A1140	960 l	multicolored	1.10	.55
4036	A1140	1615 l	multicolored	1.75	.90
4037	A1140	1650 l	multicolored	1.75	.90
			Nos. 4033-4037 (5)	5.40	2.80

A1141

A1142

Buildings in Manastirea: 675 l, Moldovita Monastery. 960 l, Hurez Monastery. 1615 l, Biertan Castle, horiz.

1995, Aug. 31

4038	A1141	675 l	multicolored	.75	.35
4039	A1141	960 l	multicolored	1.00	.50
4040	A1141	1615 l	multicolored	1.75	.90
			Nos. 4038-4040 (3)	3.50	1.75

1995, Sept. 8

4041	A1142	1020 l	multicolored	1.10	.55

Intl. Open Tennis Tournament, Bucharest.

Magazine "Mathematics," Cent. — A1143

Design: Ion N. Ionescu, founder.

1995, Sept. 15

4042	A1143	100 l	multicolored	.20	.20

Plants from Bucharest Botantical Garden — A1144

Designs: 50 l, Albizia julibrissin. 100 l, Taxus baccata. 150 l, Paulownia tomentosa. 500 l, Strelitzia reginae. 960 l, Victoria amazonica. 2300 l, Rhododendron indicum.

1995, Sept. 29 Photo. *Perf. 13½*

4043	A1144	50 l	multicolored	.20	.20
4044	A1144	100 l	multicolored	.20	.20
4045	A1144	150 l	multicolored	.20	.20
4046	A1144	500 l	multicolored	.55	.30
4047	A1144	960 l	multicolored	1.00	.50
4048	A1144	2300 l	multicolored	2.50	1.25
			Nos. 4043-4048 (6)	4.65	2.65

A1145

A1146

1995, Oct. 1 Photo. *Perf. 13½*

4049	A1145	250 l	Church of St. John	.30	.20

City of Piatra Neamt, 600th anniv.

1995, Nov. 9

Emigres: 150 l, George Apostu (1934-86), sculptor. 250 l, Emil Cioran (1911-95), philosopher. 500 l, Eugen Ionescu (1909-94), writer. 960 l, Elena Vacarescu (1866-1947), writer. 1650 l, Mircea Eliade (1907-86), philosopher.

4050	A1146	150 l	grn, gray & blk	.20	.20
4051	A1146	250 l	bl, gray & blk	.30	.20
4052	A1146	500 l	tan, brn & blk	.55	.30
4053	A1146	960 l	lake, mag & blk	1.00	.50
4054	A1146	1650 l	tan, brn & blk	1.80	.90
			Nos. 4050-4054 (5)	3.85	2.10

Transportation Type of 1995

285 l, IAR 80 fighter planes. 630 l, Training ship, Mesagerul. 715 l, IAR-316 Red Cross helicopter. 755 l, Cargo ship, Razboieni. 1575 l, IAR-818H seaplane. 1615 l, First electric tram, Bucharest, 1896, vert.

1995, Nov. 16

4055	A1131	285 l	blk, gray & grn	.30	.20
4056	A1131	630 l	bl & red	.70	.35
4057	A1131	715 l	gray bl & red	.80	.40
4058	A1131	755 l	blk, bl & gray	.85	.40
4059	A1131	1575 l	blk, grn & gray	1.75	.85
4060	A1131	1615 l	blk, grn & gray	1.75	.90
			Nos. 4055-4060 (6)	6.15	3.10

Nos. 4055, 4057, 4059 are air mail.

1996 Summer Olympics, Atlanta — A1147

1995, Dec. 8

4061	A1147	50 l	Track	.20	.20
4062	A1147	100 l	Gymnastics	.20	.20
4063	A1147	150 l	Two-man canoe	.20	.20
4064	A1147	500 l	Fencing	.55	.25
4065	A1147	960 l	Rowing-eights	1.10	.55
4066	A1147	2300 l	Boxing	2.50	1.25
			Nos. 4061-4066 (6)	4.75	2.65

Souvenir Sheet

4067	A1147	2610 l	Gymnastics	2.75	1.40

No. 4067 contains one 42x54mm stamp.

Christmas A1148

1995, Dec. 15 Photo. *Perf. 13½*

4068	A1148	100 l	The Holy Family	.20	.20

Folk Masks & Costumes — A1149

1996, Jan. 31

4069	A1149	250 l	Maramures	.25	.20
4070	A1149	500 l	Moldova	.55	.30
4071	A1149	960 l	Moldova, vert.	1.00	.50
4072	A1149	1650 l	Moldova, diff., vert.	1.75	.90
			Nos. 4069-4072 (4)	3.55	1.90

Tristan Tzara (1896-1963), Writer — A1151

1500 l, Anton Pann (1796-1854), writer.

1996, Mar. 27 Photo. *Perf. 13½*

4078	A1151	150 l	multicolored	.25	.20
4079	A1151	1500 l	multicolored	1.60	.80

Easter A1152

1996, Mar. 29

4080	A1152	150 l	multicolored	.25	.20

Romfilex '96, Romanian-Israeli Philatelic Exhibition — A1153

Paintings from National History Museum: a, 370 l, On the Terrace at Sinaia, by Theodor Aman. b, 150 l, The Palace, by M. Stoican. c, 1500 l, Old Jerusalem, by Reuven Rubin.

1996, Apr. 5

4081	A1153		Sheet of 3, #a.-c.	2.25	1.10

For surcharges see No. 4202.

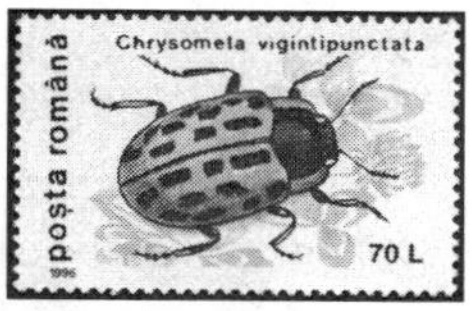

Insects A1154

Designs: 70 l, Chrysomela vigintipunctata. 220 l, Cerambyx cerdo. 370 l, Entomoscelis adonidis. 650 l, Coccinella bipunctata. 700 l, Calosoma sycophanta. 740 l, Hedobia imperialis. 960 l, Oryctes nasicornis. 1000 l, Trichius fasciatus. 1500 l, Purpuricenus kaehleri. 2500 l, Anthaxia salicis.

1996

4082	A1154	70 l	multicolored	.20	.20
4083	A1154	220 l	multicolored	.20	.20
4084	A1154	370 l	multicolored	.25	.20
4085	A1154	650 l	multicolored	.40	.20
4086	A1154	700 l	multicolored	.40	.20
4087	A1154	740 l	multicolored	.40	.20
4088	A1154	960 l	multicolored	.55	.20
4089	A1154	1000 l	multicolored	.55	.20
4090	A1154	1500 l	multicolored	.90	.20
4091	A1154	2500 l	multicolored	1.40	.45
			Nos. 4082-4091 (10)	5.25	2.25

Issued: 220, 740, 960, 1000, 1500 l, 4/16/96; 70, 370, 650, 700, 2500 l, 6/10/96.

For surcharges see Nos. 4283-4289.

Souvenir Sheet

Dumitru Prunariu, First Romanian Cosmonaut — A1155

Illustration reduced.

1996, Apr. 22

4092	A1155	2720 l	multicolored	3.00	1.50

ESPAMER '96, Aviation and Space Philatelic Exhibition, Seville, Spain.

1996 Summer Olympic Games, Atlanta — A1158

1996, July 12 Photo. *Perf. 13½*

4093	A1158	220 l	Boxing	.20	.20
4094	A1158	370 l	Athletics	.30	.20
4095	A1158	740 l	Rowing	.50	.30
4096	A1158	1500 l	Judo	1.10	.55
4097	A1158	2550 l	Gymnastics	1.90	.95
			Nos. 4093-4097 (5)	4.00	2.20

Souvenir Sheet

4098	A1158	4050 l	Gymnastics, diff.	3.00	1.50

No. 4098 is airmail and contains one 54x42mm stamp. Olymphilex '96 (#4098).

UNESCO World Heritage Sites — A1159

Designs: 150 l, Arbore Church. 1500 l, Voronet Monastery. 2550 l, Humor Monastery.

1996, Apr. 24 Photo. *Perf. 13½*

4099	A1159	150 l	multicolored	.20	.20
4100	A1159	1500 l	multicolored	1.60	.80
4101	A1159	2550 l	multicolored	2.75	1.25
			Nos. 4099-4101 (3)	4.55	2.25

Famous Women — A1160

Europa: 370 l, Ana Asian (1897-1988), physician. 4140 l, Lucia Bulandra (1873-1961), actress.

1996, May 6

4102	A1160	370 l	multicolored	.40	.20
4103	A1160	4140 l	multicolored	4.25	2.25
a.			Pair, #4102-4103 + 2 labels	4.75	2.50

UNICEF, 50th Anniv. — A1161

Children's paintings: 370 l, Mother and children. 740 l, Winter Scene. 1500 l, Children and Sun over House. 2550 l, House on Stilts.

1996, May 25

4104	A1161	370 l	multi	.40	.20
4105	A1161	740 l	multi	.80	.40
4106	A1161	1500 l	multi	1.60	.80
4107	A1161	2550 l	multi, vert.	2.75	1.25
			Nos. 4104-4107 (4)	5.55	2.65

Habitat II (#4107).

Euro '96, European Soccer Championships, Great Britain — A1162

Designs: a, 220 l, Goal keeper, ball. b, 370 l, Player with ball. c, Two players, ball. d, 1500 l, Three players, ball. e, 2550 l, Player dribbling ball.

4050 l, Two players, four balls.

1996, May 27

4108	A1162		Strip of 5, #a.-e.	5.50	2.75

Souvenir Sheet

4109	A1162	4050 l	multicolored	4.25	2.10

No. 4109 contains one 42x54mm stamp.

CAPEX '96 — A1163

Designs: 150 l, Toronto Convention Center. 4050 l, CN Tower, Skydome, Toronto skyline.

1996, May 29

4110	A1163	150 l	multicolored	.20	.20

Souvenir Sheet

4111	A1163	4050 l	multicolored	4.25	2.10

No. 4111 contains 42x54mm stamp.

Resita Factory, 225th Anniv. A1164

1996, June 20 Photo. *Perf. 13½*

4112	A1164	150 l	dark red brown	.20	.20

No. 3775 Surcharged

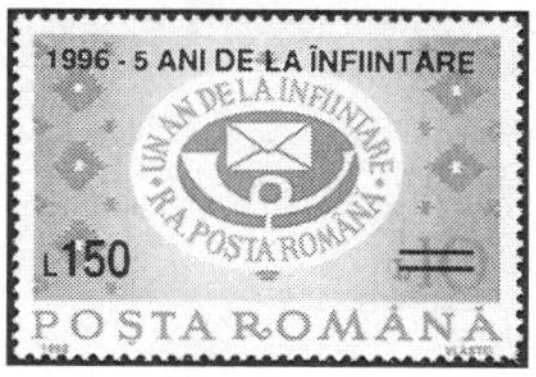

1996, June 22

4113	A1071	150 l	on 10 l multi	.20	.20

Stamp Day — A1165

Illustration reduced.

1996, July 15

4114	A1165	1500 l + 650 l label	1.60	.80

Conifers — A1166

1996, Aug. 1

4115	A1166	70 l	Picea glauca	.20	.20
4116	A1166	150 l	Picea omorica	.20	.20
4117	A1166	220 l	Picea pungeus	.20	.20
4118	A1166	740 l	Picea sitchensis	.30	.20
4119	A1166	1500 l	Pinus sylvestris	.65	.25
4120	A1166	3500 l	Pinus pinaster	1.60	.40
			Nos. 4115-4120 (6)	3.15	1.45

Wildlife — A1167

Designs: 70 l, Natrix natrix, vert. 150 l, Testudo hermanni, vert. 220 l, Alauda arvensis. 740 l, Vulpes vulpes. 1500 l, Phocaena phocaena, vert. 3500 l, Aquila chrysaetos, vert.

1996, Sept. 12 Photo. *Perf. 13½*

4121	A1167	70 l	multicolored	.20	.20
4122	A1167	150 l	multicolored	.20	.20
4123	A1167	220 l	multicolored	.20	.20
4124	A1167	740 l	multicolored	.30	.20
4125	A1167	1500 l	multicolored	.65	.25
4126	A1167	3500 l	multicolored	1.60	.40
			Nos. 4121-4126 (6)	3.15	1.45

For surcharge see No. 4348.

Famous Men — A1168

100 l, Stan Golestan (1875-1956). 150 l, Corneliu Coposu (1914-95). 370 l, Horia Vintila (1915-92). 1500 l, Alexandru Papana (1906-46).

1996, Nov. 29

4127	A1168	100 l	black & rose red	.20	.20
4128	A1168	150 l	black & lake	.20	.20
4129	A1168	370 l	blk & yel brn	.25	.20
4130	A1168	1500 l	black & ver	.95	.40
			Nos. 4127-4130 (4)	1.60	1.00

Madonna and Child — A1169

1996, Nov. 27

4131	A1169	150 l	multicolored	.20	.20

Antique Automobiles — A1170

No. 4132: a, 280 l, 1933 Mercedes Benz. b, 70 l, 1930 Ford Spider. c, 150 l, 1932 Citroen. d, 220 l, 1936 Rolls Royce.

No. 4133: a, 2550 l, 1936 Mercedes Benz 500k Roadster. b, 2500 l, 1934 Bugatti "Type 59." c. 2550 l, 1931 Alfa Romeo 8C. d, 120 l, 1937 Jaguar SS 100.

1996, Dec. 19 Photo. *Perf. 13½*

4132	A1170	Sheet of 4, #a.-d.	.60	.30
4133	A1170	Sheet of 4, #a.-d.	6.25	3.00

Souvenir Sheet

Deng Xiaoping, China, and Margaret Thatcher, Great Britain — A1171

1997, Jan. 20 Photo. *Perf. 13½*

4134	A1171	1500 l	multicolored	1.10	.55

Hong Kong '97.

Fur-Bearing Animals — A1172

Designs: 70 l, Mustela erminea. 150 l, Alopex lagopus. 220 l, Nyctereutes procyonoides. 740 l, Lutra lutra. 1500 l, Ondatra zibethica. 3500 l, Martes martes.

1997, Feb. 14

4135	A1172	70 l	multicolored	.20	.20
4136	A1172	150 l	multicolored	.20	.20
4137	A1172	220 l	multicolored	.20	.20
4138	A1172	740 l	multicolored	.25	.20
4139	A1172	1500 l	multicolored	.50	.25
4140	A1172	3500 l	multicolored	1.10	.55
			Nos. 4135-4140 (6)	2.45	1.60

For surcharge see No. 4349.

Greenpeace, 25th Anniv. — A1173

Various views of MV Greenpeace.

1997, Mar. 6

4141	A1173	150 l	multicolored	.20	.20
4142	A1173	370 l	multicolored	.20	.20
4143	A1173	1940 l	multicolored	.55	.25
4144	A1173	2500 l	multicolored	.75	.35
			Nos. 4141-4144 (4)	1.70	1.00

Souvenir Sheet

4145	A1173	4050 l	multicolored	1.50	.75

No. 4145 contains one 49x38mm stamp.

Famous People — A1174

Designs: 200 l, Thomas A. Edison. 400 l, Franz Schubert. 3600 l, Miguel de Cervantes Saavedra (1547-1616), Spanish writer.

1997, Mar. 27 Photo. *Perf. 13½*

4146	A1174	200 l	multicolored	.20	.20
4147	A1174	400 l	multicolored	.20	.20
4148	A1174	3600 l	multicolored	1.00	.50
			Nos. 4146-4148 (3)	1.40	.90

Inauguration of Mobile Telephone Network in Romania — A1175

1997, Apr. 7 Photo. *Perf. 13½*

4149	A1175	400 l	multicolored	.25	.20

Churches — A1176

A1177

1997, Apr. 21 Photo. *Perf. 13½*

4150	A1176	200 l	Surdesti	.20	.20
4151	A1176	400 l	Plopis	.20	.20
4152	A1176	450 l	Bogdan Voda	.20	.20
4153	A1176	850 l	Rogoz	.25	.20
4154	A1176	3600 l	Calinesti	1.00	.50
4155	A1176	6000 l	Birsana	1.75	.90
			Nos. 4150-4155 (6)	3.60	2.20

1997, Apr. 23 Photo. *Perf. 13½*

Shakespeare Festival, Craiova: a, 400 l, Constantin Serghe (1819-87) as Othello, 1855. b, 200 l, Al. Demetrescu Dan (1870-1948) as Hamlet, 1916. c, 3600 l, Ion Manolescu (1881-1959) as Hamlet, 1924. d, 2400 l, Gheorghe Cozorici (1933-93) as Hamlet, 1957.

4156	A1177	Sheet of 4, #a.-d. + 4 labels	2.50	1.25

A1178

A1179

Europa (Stories and Legends): 400 l, Vlad Tepes (Vlad the Impaler), prince upon which legend of Dracula said to be based. 4250 l, Dracula.

1997, May 5

4157	A1178	400 l	multicolored	.20	.20
4158	A1178	4250 l	multicolored	1.75	1.75
a.			Pair, #4157-4158 + label	1.40	.70

1997, June 27 Photo. *Perf. 13½*

Natl. Theater, Cathedral, Statue of Mihai Viteazul.

4159	A1179	450 l	multicolored	.20	.20

Balcanmax '97, Maximum Cards Exhibition, Cluj-Napoca.

Cacti A1180

Designs: 100 l, Dolichothele uberiformis. 250 l, Rebutia. 450 l, Echinofossulocactus lamellosus. 500 l, Ferocactus glaucescens. 650 l, Thelocactus. 6150 l, Echinofossulocactus albatus.

1997, June 27

4160	A1180	100 l	multicolored	.20	.20
4161	A1180	250 l	multicolored	.20	.20
4162	A1180	450 l	multicolored	.20	.20
4163	A1180	500 l	multicolored	.20	.20
4164	A1180	650 l	multicolored	.25	.20
4165	A1180	6150 l	multicolored	2.40	1.25
			Nos. 4160-4165 (6)	3.45	2.25

Stamp Day — A1181

Illustration reduced.

1997, July 15 Photo. *Perf. 13½*

4166	A1181	3600 l + 1500 l label	3.00	1.50

Nos. 3664-3670, 3672 Surcharged in Brownish Purple (#4167-4171, 4174) or Black (#4172-4173)

1997, July 17

4167	A1043	250 l on 1 l #3664	.20	.20
4168	A1043	250 l on 2 l #3665	.20	.20
4169	A1043	250 l on 4 l #3666	.20	.20
4170	A1043	450 l on 5 l #3667	.30	.20
4171	A1043	450 l on 6 l #3668	.30	.20
4172	A1043	450 l on 18 l #3672	.30	.20
4173	A1043	950 l on 9 l #3670	.60	.30
4174	A1043	3600 l on 8 l #3669	2.25	1.10
		Nos. 4167-4174 (8)	4.35	2.60

Castle Dracula, Sighisoara - A1181a

Designs: 650 l, Clocktower on Town Hall. 3700 l, Steps leading to castle and clocktower.

1997, July 31

4175	A1181a	250 l shown	.20	.20
4175A	A1181a	650 l multi	.40	.20
4175B	A1181a	3700 l multi	2.25	1.10
		Nos. 4175-4175B (3)	2.85	1.50

A1181b A1181c

Tourism Monument, Banat.

1997, Aug. 3

4175C	A1181b	950 l multi	.60	.30

1997, Aug. 13

4175D	A1181c	450 l multi	.30	.20

Stamp Printing Works, 125th anniv.

Belgian Antarctic Expedition, Cent. - A1181d

"Belgica" sailing ship and: 450 l, Emil Racovita, biologist. 650 l, Frederick A. Cook, anthropologist, photographer. 1600 l, Roald Amundsen. 3700 l, Adrien de Gerlache, expedition commander.

1997, Aug. 18

4175E	A1181d	450 l multi	.30	.20
4175F	A1181d	650 l multi	.45	.20
4175G	A1181d	1600 l multi	1.00	.50
4175H	A1181d	3700 l multi	2.25	1.10
		Nos. 4175E-4175H (4)	4.00	2.00

Sports A1182

1997, Nov. 21 Photo. *Perf. 13½*

4176	A1182	500 l Rugby	.20	.20
4177	A1182	700 l American football, vert.	.25	.20
4178	A1182	1750 l Baseball	.65	.35
4179	A1182	3700 l Mountain climbing, vert.	1.40	.70
		Nos. 4176-4179 (4)	2.50	1.45

Romanian Scouts A1183

300 l, Tents at campsite. 700 l, Scouting emblem. 1050 l, Hands reaching toward each other. 1750 l, Carvings. 3700 l, Scouts seated around campfire.

1997, Oct. 25 Photo. *Perf. 13½*

4180	A1183	300 l multicolored	.20	.20
4181	A1183	700 l multicolored	.45	.20
4182	A1183	1050 l multicolored	.60	.30
4183	A1183	1750 l multicolored	1.00	.50
4184	A1183	3700 l multicolored	2.25	1.10
a.		Strip of 5, #4180-4184	4.50	2.25

No. 3650 Surcharged in Red

1997, Sept. 27

4185	A1039	1050 l on 4.50 l	.45	.25

No. 3619 Surcharged in Red

1997, Oct. 28 Photo. *Perf. 13½*

4186	A1032	500 l on 2 l multi	.25	.20

Ion Mihalache (1882-1963), Politician — A1184

Design: 1050 l, King Carol I (1866-1914).

1997, Nov. 8

4187	A1184	500 l multicolored	.20	.20
4188	A1184	1050 l multicolored	.65	.30

Chamber of Commerce and Industry, Bucharest, 130th Anniv. — A1185

1998, Jan. 29 Photo. *Perf. 13½*

4189	A1185	700 l multicolored	.25	.20

No. 4189 is printed se-tenant with label.

1998 Winter Olympic Games, Nagano A1186

1998, Feb. 5

4190	A1186	900 l Skiing	.30	.20
4191	A1186	3900 l Figure skating	1.25	.65

Souvenir Sheet

Flag Day — A1187

Illustration reduced.

1998, Feb. 24 Photo. *Perf. 13½*

4192	A1187	900 l multicolored	.30	.20

National Festivals and Holidays — A1188

1998, Feb. 26 Photo. *Perf. 13x13½*

4193	A1188	900 l 4-Leaf clover	.50	.50
4194	A1188	3900 l Heart	3.50	3.50

Europa.

Famous People and Events of the 20th Century A1189

Designs: 700 l, Alfred Nobel, creation of Nobel Foundation, 1901. 900 l, Guglielmo Marconi, first radio transmission across Atlantic, 1901. 1500 l, Albert Einstein, theory of relativity, 1905. 3900 l, Trajan Vuia, flying machine, 1906.

1998, Mar. 31 Photo. *Perf. 13½*

4195	A1189	700 l multicolored	.20	.20
4196	A1189	900 l multicolored	.20	.20
4197	A1189	1500 l multicolored	.25	.20
4198	A1189	3900 l multicolored	.70	.40
		Nos. 4195-4198 (4)	1.35	1.00

See Nos. 4261-4265, 4312-4319, 4380-4383.

Roadside Shrines — A1190

1998, Apr. 17

4199	A1190	700 l Cluj	.20	.20
4200	A1190	900 l Prahova	.20	.20
4201	A1190	1500 l Arges	.25	.20
		Nos. 4199-4201 (3)	.65	.60

No. 4081 Surcharged in Red

Designs: a, 900 l on 370 l. b, 700 l on 150 l, c, 3900 l on 1500 l.

1998, May 12

4202	A1153	Sheet of 3, #a.-c.	1.00	.50

Surcharge on #4202a, 4202c does not include '98 show emblem. This appears in the selvage to the right and left of the stamps.

Romanian Surgical Society, Cent. — A1191

Thoma Ionescu (1860-1926), founder.

1998, May 18

4203	A1191	1050 l multicolored	.20	.20

Nos. 3665-3669, 3672, 3676 Surcharged in Black, Red, Bright Green, Violet, Red Violet, Orange Brown, Dark Green, Violet Brown or Deep Blue

1998 Photo. *Perf. 13½*

4204	A1043	50 l on 2 l #3665 (R)	.20	.20
4205	A1043	100 on 8 l #3669 (BG)	.20	.20
4206	A1043	200 on 4 l #3666	.20	.20
4207	A1043	250 on 45 l #3676 (Bl)	.20	.20
4208	A1043	350 on 45 l #3676	.40	.20
4209	A1043	400 on 6 l #3668 (V)	.45	.25
4210	A1043	400 on 45 l #3676 (BG)	.45	.25
4211	A1043	450 on 45l #3676 (RV)	.50	.25
4212	A1043	500 on 18 l #3672 (Bl)	.55	.25
4213	A1043	850 on 45 l #3676 (OB)	.90	.45
4214	A1043	900 on 45 l #3676 (V)	1.00	.50
4215	A1043	1000 on 45 l #3676 (DkG)	1.10	.55

4216	A1043	1000 on 9 l #3670		1.10	.55
4217	A1043	1500 on 5 l #3667 (R)		1.60	.75
4218	A1043	1600 on 45 l #3676 (VB)		1.60	.80
4219	A1043	2500 on 45 l #3676 (R)		2.75	1.40
	Nos. 4204-4219 (16)			13.20	7.00

Obliterator varies on Nos. 4204-4219.
Issued: Nos. 4204-4206, 4209, 4212, 5/21; Nos. 4216-4217, 7/6; others, 1998.

1998 World Cup Soccer Championships, France — A1192

Various soccer plays, stadium: a, 800 l. b, 1050 l. c, 1850 l. d, 4150 l.

1998, June 10 Photo. *Perf. 13½*

4220	A1192	Sheet of 4, #a.-d.	.90	.45

Nos. 3913-3915, 3918 Surcharged in Red Violet, Blue, Black, or Red

Wmk. 398
1998, June 30 Photo. *Perf. 13*
Design A1105

4221	700 l on 125 l #3918 (RV)	.25	.20
4222	800 l on 35 l #3914 (Bl)	.25	.20
4223	1050 l on 45 l #3915 (Blk)	.35	.20
4224	4150 l on 15 l #3913 (R)	1.25	.65
	Nos. 4221-4224 (4)	2.10	1.25

Night Birds A1193

Designs: 700 l, Apteryx australis, vert. 1500 l, Tyto alba, vert. 1850 l, Rallus aquaticus. 2450 l, Caprimulgus europaeus.

1998, Aug. 12 Unwmk.

4225	A1193	700 l multicolored	.25	.20
4226	A1193	1500 l multicolored	.50	.25
a.		Complete booklet, 4 each, #4225-4226	3.00	
4227	A1193	1850 l multicolored	.60	.30
4228	A1193	2450 l multicolored	.80	.40
a.		Complete booklet, 4 each, #4227-4228	5.75	
		Nos. 4225-4228 (4)	2.15	1.15

Stamp Day A1194

1998, July Litho. *Perf. 13½*

4229	A1194	700 l Romania #4	.25	.20
4230	A1194	1050 l Romania #1	.35	.20
a.		Complete booklet, #4225, 4 #4226	1.75	

Souvenir Sheet

4231	A1194	4150 l +850 l Romania #2-3	1.60	.80

No. 4231 contains one 54x42mm stamp.

Natl. Uprising, 150th Anniv. — A1195

1998, Sept. 28 Photo. *Perf. 13½*

4232	A1195	1050 l multicolored	.20	.20

A1196

A1197

German Personalities in Banat: 800 l, Nikolaus Lenau (1802-50). 1850 l, Stefan Jäger (1877-1962). 4150 l, Adam Müller-Guttenbrunn (1852-1923).

1998, Oct. 16

4233	A1196	800 l multicolored	.20	.20
4234	A1196	1850 l multicolored	.35	.20
4235	A1196	4150 l multicolored	.75	.40
		Nos. 4233-4235 (3)	1.30	.80

1998, Nov. 4 Photo. *Perf. 13½*

4236	A1197	1100 l multicolored	.40	.20

Intl. Year of the Ocean.

Nos. 3652-3653, 3704-3709, 3776-3779, 3781, 3795, 3968 Surcharged in Green, Black, Red, Red Violet or Deep Blue

1998 Photo. *Perf. 13½*

4237	A1041	50 l on #3652 (G)	.20	.20
4238	A1041	50 l on #3653 (Blk)	.20	.20
4238A	A1054	50 l on 1 l #3704 (Blk)	.20	.20
4239	A1054	50 l on #3705 (R)	.20	.20
4240	A1054	50 l on #3706 (R)	.20	.20
4241	A1054	50 l on #3707 (Blk)	.20	.20
4242	A1054	50 l on #3708 (Blk)	.20	.20
4243	A1054	50 l on #3709 (R)	.20	.20
4244	A1054	50 l on #3776 (RV)	.20	.20
4245	A1054	50 l on #3777 (DB)	.20	.20
4246	A1054	50 l on #3778 (Blk)	.20	.20
4247	A1054	50 l on #3779 (G)	.20	.20
4248	A1054	50 l on #3781 (R)	.20	.20
4249	A1075	2000 l on #3795 (G)	.60	.30
4250	A1117	2600 l on #3968 (R)	.80	.40
		Nos. 4237-4250 (15)	4.00	3.30

Obliterator varies on Nos. 4237-4250.
Issued: 4237-4238, 11/10; 4238A, 11/27; 4249-4250, 12/22.

A1198

A1199

Lighthouses.

1998, Dec. 28

4251	A1198	900 l Genovez	.25	.20
4252	A1198	1000 l Constanta	.30	.20
4253	A1198	1100 l Sfantu Gheorghe	.35	.20
4254	A1198	2600 l Sulina	.75	.40
		Nos. 4251-4254 (4)	1.65	1.00

1998, Nov. 25

Flowers: 350 l, Tulipa gesneriana. 850 l, Dahlia variabilis. 1100 l, Lillium martagon. 4450 l, Rosa centifolia.

4255	A1199	350 l multicolored	.20	.20
4256	A1199	850 l multicolored	.25	.20
4257	A1199	1100 l multicolored	.30	.20
4258	A1199	4450 l multicolored	1.25	.65
		Nos. 4255-4258 (4)	2.00	1.25

Universal Declaration of Human Rights, 50th Anniv. — A1200

1998, Dec. 10

4259	A1200	700 l multicolored	.25	.20

Dimitrie Paciurea (1873-1932), Sculptor - A1200a

1998, Dec. 11 Photo. *Perf. 13¼*

4259A	A1200a	850 l ocher & blk	.20	.20

Total Eclipse of the Sun, Aug. 11, 1999 — A1201

1998, Dec. 28

4260	A1201	1100 l multi + label	.35	.20

Events of the 20th Cent. Type

Designs: 350 l, Sinking of the Titanic, 1912. 1100 l, "Coanda 1910" aircraft with air-reactive (jet) engine, 1919, by Henri Coanda (1886-1972). 1600 l, Louis Blériot's (1872-1936) Calais-Dover flight, 1909. 2000 l, Opening of the Panama Canal, 1914. 2600 l, Russian Revolution, 1917.

1998, Dec. 22 Photo. *Perf. 13½*

4261	A1189	350 l multicolored	.20	.20
4262	A1189	1100 l multicolored	.30	.20
4263	A1189	1600 l multicolored	.45	.25
4264	A1189	2000 l multicolored	.60	.30
4265	A1189	2600 l multicolored	.75	.40
		Nos. 4261-4265 (5)	2.30	1.35

No. 3687 Surcharged in Red or Black

1999, Feb. 10 Photo. *Perf. 13½*

4266	A1047	100 l on 1 l (R)	.20	.20
4267	A1047	250 l on 1 l (Blk)	.20	.20

Obliterator is a guitar on #4266 and a saxophone on #4267.

No. 3796 Surcharged in Black, Red, Green, or Brown

1999, Jan. 22

4268	A1076	50 l on 15 l (Blk)	.20	.20
4269	A1076	50 l on 15 l (R)	.20	.20
4270	A1076	400 l on 15 l (Grn)	.20	.20
4271	A1076	2300 l on 15 l (Brn)	.70	.35
4272	A1076	3200 l on 15 l (Blk)	1.00	.50
		Nos. 4268-4272 (5)	2.30	1.45

Obliterator varies on Nos. 4268-4272.

Monasteries — A1203

1999, Jan. 17

4273	A1203	500 l Arnota	.20	.20
4274	A1203	700 l Bistrita	.20	.20
4275	A1203	1100 l Dintr'un Lemn	.30	.20
4276	A1203	2100 l Govora	.60	.30
4277	A1203	4850 l Tismana	1.40	.70
		Nos. 4273-4277 (5)	2.70	1.60

Shrub Flowers A1204

350 l, Magnolia x soulangiana. 1000 l, Stewartia malacodendron. 1100 l, Hibiscus rosa-sinensis. 5350 l, Clematis patens.

1999, Feb. 15

4278	A1204	350 l multicolored	.20	.20
4279	A1204	1000 l multicolored	.30	.20
4280	A1204	1100 l multicolored	.30	.20
4281	A1204	5350 l multicolored	1.50	.75
		Nos. 4278-4281 (4)	2.30	1.35

Easter A1205

1999, Mar. 15 Photo. *Perf. 13¼*

4282	A1205	1100 l multi	.25	.20

No. 4082 Surcharged in Bright Pink, Red, Violet, Black, Green or Blue

1999, Mar. 22 Litho. *Perf. 13½*

4283 A1154 100 l on 70 l (BP) .20 .20
4284 A1154 100 l on 70 l (R) .20 .20
4285 A1154 200 l on 70 l (V) .20 .20
4286 A1154 1500 l on 70 l .45 .20
4287 A1154 1600 l on 70 l (G) .45 .20
4288 A1154 3200 l on 70 l (Bl) .95 .45
4289 A1154 6000 l on 70 l (G) 1.75 .90
Nos. 4283-4289 (7) 4.20 2.35

Obliterators on Nos. 4283-4289 are various dinosaurs.

Jewelry — A1206

Birds — A1207

Designs: 1200 l, Keys on chain. 2100 l, Key holder. 2600 l, Necklace. 3200 l, Necklace, horiz.

1999, Mar. 29 Photo. *Perf. 13¼*

4290-4293 A1206 Set of 4 1.75 .90

Perf. 13½x13¼

1999, Apr. 26 Photo.

4294 A1207 1100 l Ara macao .25 .20
4295 A1207 2700 l Pavo albus .55 .30
4296 A1207 3700 l Pavo cristatus .75 .35
4297 A1207 5700 l Cacatua galerita 1.10 .55
Nos. 4294-4297 (4) 2.65 1.40

Council of Europe, 50th Anniv. — A1208

1999, May 5 Photo. *Perf. 13¼*

4298 A1208 2300 l multi + label .30 .20

A1209

A1210

Visit of Pope John Paul II to Romania: a, 6300 l, Pope John Paul II. b, 1300 l, St. Peter's Basilica. c, 1600 l, Patriarchal Cathedral, Bucharest. d, 2300 l, Patriarch Teoctist.

1999, May 7

4299 A1209 Sheet of 6 3.75 1.90

Issued in sheets containing one strip of #4299a-4299d, 1 ea #4299a, 4299d + 2 labels.

1999, May 17

Europa: 1100 l, Anas clypeata. 5700 l, Ciconia nigra.

4300 A1210 1100 l multicolored .20 .20
4301 A1210 5700 l multicolored .40 .40

Nos. 4300-4301 printed with se-tenant label.

Famous Personalities — A1211

Designs: 600 l, Gheorghe Cartan (1849-1911). 1100 l, George Calinescu (1899-1965), writer. 2600 l, Johann Wolfgang von Goethe (1749-1832), poet. 7300 l, Honoré de Balzac (1799-1850), novelist.

1999, May 31

4302 A1211 600 l multicolored .20 .20
4303 A1211 1100 l multicolored .25 .20
4304 A1211 2600 l multicolored .55 .25
4305 A1211 7300 l multicolored 1.50 .75
Nos. 4302-4305 (4) 2.50 1.40

Total Solar Eclipse, Aug. 11 — A1212

1999, June 21 Photo. *Perf. 13¼*

4306 A1212 1100 l multicolored .25 .20

No. 4306 printed se-tenant with label.

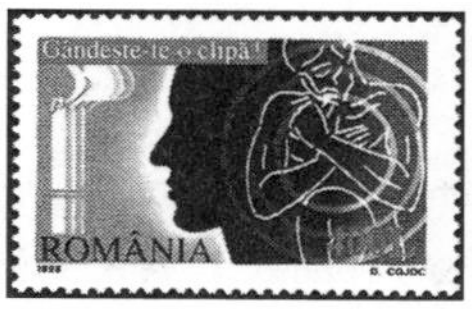

Health Dangers A1213

1999, July 29 Photo. *Perf. 13¼*

4307 A1213 400 l Smoking .20 .20
4308 A1213 800 l Alcohol .20 .20
4309 A1213 1300 l Drugs .25 .20
4310 A1213 2500 l AIDS .50 .25
Nos. 4307-4310 (4) 1.15 .85

Luciano Pavarotti Concert in Bucharest on Day of Solar Eclipse — A1214

1999, Aug. 9

4311 A1214 8100 l multi 1.60 .80

Events of the 20th Century Type

Designs: 800 l, Alexander Fleming discovers penicillin, 1928. 3000 l, League of Nations, 1920. 7300 l, Harold C. Urey discovers heavy water, 1931. 17,000 l, First marine oil drilling platform, off Beaumont, Texas, 1934.

1999, Aug. 30

4312 A1189 800 l multi .20 .20
4313 A1189 3000 l multi .60 .30
4314 A1189 7300 l multi 1.40 .75
4315 A1189 17,000 l multi 3.50 1.75
Nos. 4312-4315 (4) 5.70 3.00

1999, Sept. 24 Photo. *Perf. 13¼*

1500 l, Karl Landsteiner (1868-1943), discoverer of blood groups. 3000 l, Nicolae C. Paulescu (1869-1931), diabetes researcher. 7300 l, Otto Hahn (1879-1968), discoverer of nuclear fission. 17,000 l, Ernst Ruska (1906-88), inventor of electron microscope.

4316 A1189 1500 l multi .30 .20
4317 A1189 3000 l multi .55 .30
4318 A1189 7300 l multi 1.40 .70
4319 A1189 17,000 l multi 3.25 1.60
Nos. 4316-4319 (4) 5.50 2.80

UPU, 125th Anniv. — A1215

Comic Actors — A1216

1999, Oct. 9

4320 A1215 3100 l multi .60 .30

1999, Oct. 21

Designs: 900 l, Grigore Vasiliu Birlic. 1500 l, Toma Caragiu. 3100 l, Constantin Tanase. 7950 l, Charlie Chaplin. 8850 l, Oliver Hardy and Stan Laurel, horiz.

4321 A1216 900 l blk & brn red .20 .20
4322 A1216 1500 l blk & brn red .25 .20
4323 A1216 3100 l blk & brn red .55 .25
4324 A1216 7950 l blk & brn red 1.40 .70
4325 A1216 8850 l blk & brn red 1.50 .75
Nos. 4321-4325 (5) 3.90 2.10

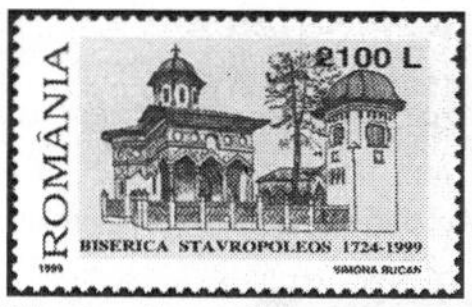

Stavropoleos Church, 275th Anniv. — A1217

1999, Oct. 29

4326 A1217 2100 l multi .40 .20

New Olympic Sports A1218

1999, Nov. 10

4327 A1218 1600 l Snowboarding .25 .20
4328 A1218 1700 l Softball .35 .20
4329 A1218 7950 l Taekwondo 1.40 .70
Nos. 4327-4329 (3) 2.00 1.10

Christmas — A1219

Designs: 1500 l, Christmas tree, bell. 3100 l, Santa Claus.

1999, Nov. 29 Photo. *Perf. 13¼*

4330-4331 A1219 Set of 2 .80 .40

UN Rights of the Child Convention, 10th Anniv. — A1220

Children's art by: 900 l, A. Vieriu. 3400 l, A. M. Bulete, vert. 8850 l, M. L. Rogojeanu.

1999, Nov. 30 Photo. *Perf. 13¼*

4332 A1220 900 l multi .20 .20
4333 A1220 3400 l multi .60 .30
4334 A1220 8850 l multi 1.50 .75
Nos. 4332-4334 (3) 2.30 1.25

Princess Diana — A1221

1999, Dec. 2

4335 A1221 6000 l multi .70 .35

Issued in sheets of 4.

Ferrari Automobiles — A1222

Designs: 1500 l, 1968 365 GTB/4. 1600 l, 1970 Dino 246 GT. 1700 l, 1973 365 GT/4 BB. 7950 l, Mondial 3.2. 8850 l, 1994 F 355. 14,500 l, 1998 456M GT.

1999, Dec. 17

4336 A1222 1500 l multi .25 .20
4337 A1222 1600 l multi .30 .20
4338 A1222 1700 l multi .30 .20
4339 A1222 7950 l multi 1.40 .70
4340 A1222 8850 l multi 1.50 .75
4341 A1222 14,500 l multi 2.50 1.25
Nos. 4336-4341 (6) 6.25 3.30

Romanian Revolution, 10th Anniv. — A1223

1999, Dec. 21 *Perf. 13¼*

4342 A1223 2100 l multi .35 .20

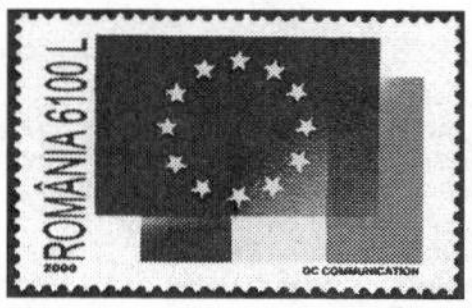

Start of Accession Negotiations With European Union — A1224

2000, Jan. 13 Photo. *Perf. 13¼*

4343 A1224 6100 l multi 1.00 .50

Souvenir Sheet

Mihail Eminescu (1850-89), Poet A1225

Scenes from poems and Eminescu: a, At R, clean-shaven. b, At R, with mustache. c, At L, with trimmed mustache. d, At L, with handlebar mustache.

2000, Jan. 15

4344	Sheet of 4	2.25	1.10
a.-d.	A1225 3400 l Any single	.55	.25

Valentine's Day — A1226

2000, Feb. 1 Photo. *Perf. 13¼*

4345	A1226	1500 l Cupid	.25	.20
4346	A1226	7950 l Couple kissing	1.25	.65

Easter — A1227

2000, Feb. 29

4347	A1227	1700 l multi	.30	.20

Nos. 4121, 4135 Surcharged in Red

Methods and Perfs. as Before

2000

4348	A1167	1700 l on 70 l multi	.30	.20
4349	A1172	1700 l on 70 l multi	.30	.20

Issued: No. 4348, 3/14; No. 4349, 3/13. Obliterator on No. 4349 is a crown.

Birds A1228

Designs: 1700 l, Paradisaea apoda. 2400 l, Diphyllodes magnificus. 9050 l, Lophorina superba. 10,050 l, Cicinnurus regius.

2000, Mar. 20 Photo. *Perf. 13¼*

4350	A1228	1700 l multi	.25	.20
4351	A1228	2400 l multi	.35	.20
4352	A1228	9050 l multi	1.40	.70
4353	A1228	10,050 l multi	1.50	.75
	Nos. 4350-4353 (4)		3.50	1.85

Nos. 3658-3659 Surcharged in Red

Methods & Perfs. as Before

2000, Mar. 31

4354	A1042	1900 l on 1 l (#3658)	.25	.20
4355	A1042	2000 l on 1 l (#3659)	.30	.20

Nos. 3626-3630 Surcharged

Methods & Perfs. as Before

2000, Apr. 12

4356	A1034	1700 l on 50b	.25	.20
4357	A1034	1700 l on 1.50 l	.25	.20
4358	A1034	1700 l on 2 l	.25	.20
4359	A1034	1700 l on 3 l	.25	.20
4360	A1034	1700 l on 4 l	.25	.20
	Nos. 4356-4360 (5)		1.25	1.00

Appearance of obliterator varies.

Flowers — A1229

Designs: 1700 l, Senecio cruentus. 3100 l, Clivia miniata. 5800 l, Plumeria rubra. 10,050 l, Fuchsia hybrida.

2000, Apr. 20 Photo. *Perf. 13¼*

4361	A1229	1700 l multi	.25	.20
4362	A1229	3100 l multi	.40	.20
4363	A1229	5800 l multi	.80	.40
4364	A1229	10,050 l multi	1.40	.70
	Nos. 4361-4364 (4)		2.85	1.50

Nos. 3620-3624 Surcharged

Methods & Perfs. as Before

2000, Apr. 24

4365	A1033	1700 l on 50b	.25	.20
4366	A1033	1700 l on 1.50 l	.25	.20
4367	A1033	1700 l on 2 l	.25	.20
4368	A1033	1700 l on 3 l	.25	.20
4369	A1033	1700 l on 4 l	.25	.20
	Nos. 4365-4369 (5)		1.25	1.00

Europa, 2000

Common Design Type

2000, May 9 Photo. *Perf. 13¼*

4370	CD17	10,150 l multi	1.40	.70

Nos. 3634, 3637 Surcharged in Red

Methods and Perfs as Before

2000, May 17

4371	A1036	1700 l on 50b	.40	.20
4372	A1036	1700 l on 3.50 l	.40	.20

Unification of Walachia, Transylvania and Moldavia by Michael the Brave, 400th Anniv. — A1230

2000, May 19 Photo. *Perf. 13¼*

4373	A1230	3800 l multi	.50	.25

Printing of Bible in Latin by Johann Gutenberg, 550th Anniv. — A1231

2000, May 19

4374	A1231	9050 l multi	1.25	.60

No. 4084 Surcharged in Red

2000, May 31 Photo. *Perf. 13¼*

4375	A1154	10,000 l on 370 l	1.40	.70
4376	A1154	19,000 l on 370 l	2.50	1.25
4377	A1154	34,000 l on 370 l	4.75	2.40
	Nos. 4375-4377 (3)		8.65	4.35

Souvenir Sheet

2000 European Soccer Championships — A1232

No. 4378: a, 3800 l, Romania vs. Portugal (red and green flag). b, 3800 l, England (red and white flag) vs. Romania. c, 10,150 l, Romania vs. Germany. d, 10,150 l, Goalie.

2000, June 20

4378	A1232	Sheet of 4, #a-d	3.75	1.90

First Zeppelin Flight, Cent. A1233

2000, July 12

4379	A1233	2100 l multi	.25	.20

Stamp Day.

20th Century Type of 1998

2100 l, Enrico Fermi, formula, 1st nuclear reactor, 1942. 2200 l, Signing of UN Charter, 1945. 2400 l, Edith Piaf sings "La Vie en Rose," 1947. 6000 l, 1st ascent of Mt. Everest, by Sir Edmund Hillary and Tenzing Norgay, 1953.

2000, July 12

4380-4383	A1189	Set of 4	1.60	.80

No. 3680 Surcharged in Green

Methods and Perfs as Before

2000, July 31

4384	A1044	1700 l on 160 l	.30	.20

20th Century Type of 1998

Designs: 1700 l, First artificial satellite, 1957. 3900 l, Yuri Gagarin, first man in space, 1961. 6400 l, First heart transplant perfromed by Christiaan Barnard, 1967. 11,300 l, Neil Armstrong, first man on the moon, 1969.

2000, Aug. 28 Photo. *Perf. 13¼*

4385-4388	A1189	Set of 4	2.75	1.40

2000 Summer Olympics, Sydney A1234

Designs: 1700 l, Boxing. 2200 l, High jump. 3900 l, Weight lifting. 6200 l, Gymnastics.

2000, Sept. 7
4389-4392 A1234 Set of 4 1.75 .85

Souvenir Sheet

4393 A1234 11,300 l Runner 1.40 .70

No. 4393 contains one 42x54mm stamp.

Souvenir Sheet

Olymphilex 2000, Sydney — A1235

2000, Sept. 7 *Imperf.*
4394 A1235 14,100 l Gabriela Szabo 1.75 .85

Bucharest Palaces A1236

Designs: 1700 l, Agricultural Ministry Palace, vert. 2200 l, Cantacuzino Palace. 2400 l, Grigore Ghica Palace. 3900 l, Stirbei Palace.

2000, Sept. 29 *Perf. 13¼*
4395-4398 A1236 Set of 4 1.25 .60

No. 4115 Surcharged in Brown

2000, Oct. 11 **Photo.** *Perf. 13½*
4403 A1166 300 l on 70 l multi .20 .20

No. 3664 Surcharged in Blue

2000, Oct. 26 *Perf. 13½*
4404 A1043 300 l on 1 l blue .20 .20

No. 3991 Surcharged in Red Violet

2000, Nov. 3 *Perf. 13½*
4405 A1127 2000 l on 90 l multi .20 .20

European Human Rights Convention, 50th Anniv. — A1237

2000, Nov. 3 *Perf. 13¼*
4406 A1237 11,300 l multi .90 .45

No. 3858 Surcharged

2000, Nov. 28 *Perf. 13½*
4407 A1093 2000 l on 29 l multi .20 .20

Endangered Wild Cats — A1238

Designs: 1200 l, Panthera pardus. 2000 l, Panthera uncia. 2200 l, Panthera leo. 2300 l, Lynx rufus. 4200 l, Puma concolor. 6500 l, Panthera tigris.
14,100 l, Panthera leo.

2000, Nov. 29 **Photo.** *Perf. 13½*
4408 A1238 1200 l multi .20 .20
4409 A1238 2000 l multi .20 .20
4410 A1238 2200 l multi .20 .20
4411 A1238 2300 l multi .20 .20
4412 A1238 4200 l multi .30 .20
4413 A1238 6500 l multi .50 .25
Nos. 4408-4413 (6) 1.60 1.25

Souvenir Sheet

4414 A1238 14,100 l multi 1.10 .55

No. 4414 contains one 54x42mm stamp.

Self-portraits A1239

Designs: 2000 l, Camil Ressu (1880-1962), 2400 l, Jean A. Steriadi (1880-1956). 4400 l, Nicolae Tonitza (1886-1940). 15,000 l, Nicolae Grigorescu (1838-1907).

2000 **Photo.** *Perf. 13½*
4415 A1239 2000 l multi .20 .20
4416 A1239 2400 l multi .20 .20
4417 A1239 4400 l multi .35 .20
4418 A1239 15,000 l multi 1.10 .55
Nos. 4415-4418 (4) 1.85 1.15

Issued: 2000 l, 12/8; others, 12/13.

Christmas — A1240

2000, Dec. 15 **Photo.** *Perf. 13½*
4419 A1240 4400 l multi .35 .20

Christianity, 2000th Anniv. — A1241

Stained glass windows: 2000 l, Resurrection of Jesus. 7000 l, Holy Trinity (22x38mm).

2000, Dec. 22 **Photo.** *Perf. 13¼*
4420-4421 A1241 Set of 2 .75 .40

No. 3922 Surcharged in Red Brown

Wmk. 398

2000, Dec. 28 **Photo.** *Perf. 13¼*
4422 A1105 7000 l on 3095 l multi .55 .25
4423 A1105 10,000 l on 3095 l multi .75 .40
4424 A1105 11,500 l on 3095 l multi .90 .45
Nos. 4422-4424 (3) 2.20 1.10

Obliterator on No. 4423 is a bear and on No. 4424 a bison.

Advent of the Third Millennium — A1242

Perf. 13½

2001, Jan. 19 **Photo.** **Unwmk.**
4425 A1242 11,500 l multi .90 .45

Sculptures by Constantin Brancusi (1876-1957) — A1243

No. 4426: a, 4600 l, b, 7200 l.

2001, Feb. 2
4426 A1243 Horiz. pair, #a-b .90 .45

No. 3844 Surcharged in Black or Red

Methods and Perfs as Before

2001, Feb. 9
4427 A1087 7400 l on 280 l multi .55 .25
4428 A1087 13,000 l on 280 l multi (R) .95 .45

Obliterator on No. 4428 is snake on branch.

Valentine's Day — A1244

Designs: 2200 l, Heart of rope. 11,500 l, Rope running through heart.

2001, Feb. 15 **Photo.** *Perf. 13½*
4429-4430 A1244 Set of 2 1.00 .50

Nos. 3894, 3895, 3897 Surcharged in Brown or Green

Methods and Perfs as Before

2001, Feb. 21
4431 A1101 1300 l on 245 l multi .20 .20
4432 A1101 2200 l on 115 l multi .20 .20
4433 A1101 5000 l on 115 l multi (G) .35 .20
4434 A1101 16,500 l on 70 l multi 1.25 .60
Nos. 4431-4434 (4) 2.00 1.20

Appearance of obliterators differ. Obliterators on Nos 4432-4433 are ears of corn.

Famous People A1245

Designs: 1300 l, Hortensia Papadat-Bengescu (1876-1955), writer. 2200 l, Eugen Lovinescu (1881-1943), writer. 2400 l, Ion Minulescu (1881-1944), writer. 4600 l, André Malraux (1901-76), writer. 7200 l, George H. Gallup (1901-84), pollster. 35,000 l, Walt Disney (1901-66), film producer.

2001 **Photo.** *Perf. 13¼*
4435-4440 A1245 Set of 6 4.00 2.00

Issued: 2200 l, 4600 l, 7200 l, 3/9; others 3/15.

Easter — A1246

Fruit — A1247

2001, Mar. 23
4441 A1246 2200 l multi .20 .20

2001, Apr. 12

Designs: 2200 l, Prunus spinosa. 4600 l, Ribes rubrum. 7400 l, Ribes uva-crispa. 11,500 l, Vaccinium vitis-idaea.

4442-4445 A1247 Set of 4 1.90 .95

Gheorge Hagi, Soccer Player — A1248

Designs: 2200 l, Wearing uniform. 35,000 l, Wearing team jacket.

2001, Apr. 23 *Perf. 13¼*
4446 A1248 2200 l multi .20 .20

Souvenir Sheet
Imperf
Without Gum

4447 A1248 35,000 l multi 2.75 1.40

No. 4447 is airmail and contains one 43x28mm stamp.

Europa — A1249

2001, May 4 *Perf. 13¼*
4448 A1249 13,000 l multi 1.00 .50

Dogs A1250

Designs: 1300 l, Collie. 5000 l, Basset hound. 8000 l, Siberian husky. 13,500 l, Sheepdog.

2001, June 16
4449-4452 A1250 Set of 4 2.25 1.10

Romanian Presidency of Organization for Security and Cooperation in Europe — A1251

2001, July 6
4453 A1251 11,500 l multi .90 .45

Millennium — A1252

Events of the 20th Century: 1300 l, Mariner 9, 1971. 1500 l, Telephone pioneer Augustin Maior and circuit diagram, 1906. 2400 l, Discovery of cave drawings in Ardeche, France, 1994. 5000 l, First Olympic perfect score of gymnast Nadia Comaneci, 1976. 5300 l, Pioneer 10, 1972. 8000 l, Fall of the Iron Curtain, 1989. 13,500 l, First microprocessor, 1971. 15,500 l, Hubble Space Telescope, 1990.

2001
4454-4461 A1252 Set of 8 3.50 1.75

Issued: 1300 l, 2400 l, 5000 l, 8000 l, 7/13; others, 9/25.

UN High Commissioner for Refugees, 50th Anniv. — A1253

2001, July 26
4462 A1253 13,500 l multi 1.00 .50

Nos. 3688, 3713, 3790, 3791, 3865, 3870, 3900, 3907, 3972, 4007, 4017, 4025, 4057, 4058, and 4060 Surcharged in Black, Red, Green or Blue

2001 **Photo.** *Perf. 13½*

4463 A1048 300 l on 4 l #3688		.20	.20
4464 A1058 300 l on 4 l #3713 (R)		.20	.20
4465 A1073 300 l on 7 l #3790 (R)		.20	.20
4466 A1073 300 l on 9 l #3791 (R)		.20	.20
4467 A1102 300 l on 90 l #3900		.20	.20
4468 A1121 300 l on 90 l #3972 (G)		.20	.20
4469 A1132 300 l on 90 l #4007		.20	.20
4470 A1130 300 l on 90 l #4017		.20	.20
4471 A1137 300 l on 90 l #4025 (G)		.20	.20
4472 A1095 300 l on 115 l #3865 (R)		.20	.20
4473 A1096 300 l on 115 l #3870 (R)		.20	.20
4474 A1103 300 l on 115 l #3907 (R)		.20	.20
4475 A1131 2500 on 715 l #4057 l (R)		.20	.20
4476 A1131 2500 on 755 l #4058 l (Bl)		.20	.20
4477 A1131 2500 on 1615 l l #4060		.20	.20
Nos. 4463-4477 (15)		3.00	3.00

Numbers have been reserved for additional surcharges. Design and location of obliterators and new value varies.

Issued: No. 4472, 8/20; No. 4473, 8/24; Nos. 4467, 4469, 8/28; No. 4470, 8/29; Nos. 4463, 4464, 4465, 4466, Nos. 4468, 4471, 4474-4477, 8/31.

Equestrian Sports A1254

Designs: 1500 l, Harness racing. 2500 l, Dressage. 5300 l, Steeplechase. 8300 l, Racing.

2001, Aug. 21 **Photo.** *Perf. 13¼*
4478-4481 A1254 Set of 4 1.25 .60

No. 3883 Surcharged

2001, Aug. 29 **Photo.** *Perf. 13½*
4482 A1099 300 l on 115 l multi .20 .20

Souvenir Sheets

Corals and Anemones — A1255

No. 4483: a, 2500 l, Porites porites. b, 8300 l, Condylactis gigantea. c, 13,500 l, Anemonia telia. 37,500 l, Gorgonia ventalina.
No. 4484: a, 9000 l, Corallium rubrum. b, 9000 l, Acropora palmata. c, 16,500 l, Actinia equina. d, 16,500 l, Metridium senile.

2001-02 **Sheets of 4, #a-d**
4483-4484 A1255 Set of 2 7.25 3.75

Issued: No. 4483, 9/27/01; No. 4484, 1/30/02.

Year of Dialogue Among Civilizations A1256

2001, Oct. 9
4485 A1256 8300 l multi .55 .25

Comic Strip A1257

No. 4486: a, Cat, bear, king. b, Fox with drum, cat. c, Fox plays drum for king. d, Cat gives drum to fox. e, Fox, exploding drum.

2001, Oct. 31
4486 Horiz. strip of 5 4.50 2.25
a.-e. A1257 13,500 l Any single .90 .45

Christmas A1258

No. 4487: a, Ribbon extending from wreath. b, No ribbon extending from wreath.

2001, Nov. 5
4487 A1258 2500 l Pair, #a-b .35 .20

Zodiac Signs A1259

Designs: No. 4488, 1500 l, Scorpio. No. 4489, 1500 l, Aries. No. 4490, 2500 l, Libra. No. 4491, 2500 l, Taurus. No. 4492, 5500 l, Capricorn. No. 4493, 5500 l, Gemini. 8700 l, Cancer. No. 4495, 9000 l, Pisces. No. 4496, 9000 l, Leo. 13,500 l, Aquarius. 16,500 l, Sagittarius. 23,500 l, Virgo.

2001-02

4488-4499	A1259	Set of 12	6.50	3.25

Issued: Nos. 4488, 4490, 4492, 4495, 4497, 4498, 11/23/01; others 1/4/02.

SEMI-POSTAL STAMPS

Queen Elizabeth Spinning — SP1

The Queen Weaving — SP2

Queen as War Nurse SP3

Perf. 11½, 11½x13½

1906, Jan. 14 Typo. Unwmk.

B1	SP1	3b (+ 7b) brown	3.00	2.00
B2	SP1	5b (+ 10b) lt grn	3.00	2.00
B3	SP1	10b (+ 10b) rose red	14.00	6.50
B4	SP1	15b (+ 10b) violet	10.00	4.50
		Nos. B1-B4 (4)	30.00	15.00

1906, Mar. 18

B5	SP2	3b (+ 7b) org brn	3.00	2.00
B6	SP2	5b (+ 10b) bl grn	3.00	2.00
B7	SP2	10b (+ 10b) car	16.50	6.50
B8	SP2	15b (+ 10b) red vio	10.00	4.55
		Nos. B5-B8 (4)	32.50	15.05

1906, Mar. 23 ***Perf. 11½, 13½x11½***

B9	SP3	3b (+ 7b) org brn	3.00	2.00
B10	SP3	5b (+ 10b) bl grn	3.00	2.00
B11	SP3	10b (+ 10b) car	16.50	6.50
B12	SP3	15b (+ 10b) red vio	10.00	4.55
		Nos. B9-B12 (4)	32.50	15.05
		Nos. B1-B12 (12)	95.00	45.10

Booklet panes of 4 exist of Nos. B1-B3, B5-B7, B9-B12.

Counterfeits of Nos. B1-B12 are plentiful. Copies of Nos. B1-B12 with smooth, even gum are counterfeits.

SP4

1906, Aug. 4 ***Perf. 12***

B13	SP4	3b (+ 7b) ol brn, buff & bl	1.50	1.00
B14	SP4	5b (+ 10b) grn, rose & buff	1.50	1.00
B15	SP4	10b (+ 10b) rose red, buff & bl	3.00	2.00
B16	SP4	15b (+ 10b) vio, buff & bl	6.50	3.00
		Nos. B13-B16 (4)	12.50	7.00

Guardian Angel Bringing Poor to Crown Princess Marie SP5

1907, Feb. Engr. ***Perf. 11***

Center in Brown

B17	SP5	3b (+ 7b) org brn	3.25	1.90
B18	SP5	5b (+ 10b) dk grn	2.25	1.00
B19	SP5	10b (+ 10b) dk car	2.25	1.00
B20	SP5	15b (+ 10b) dl vio	2.25	1.10
		Nos. B17-B20 (4)	10.00	5.00

Nos. B1-B20 were sold for more than face value. The surtax, shown in parenthesis, was for charitable purposes.

Map of Romania — SP9

Stephen the Great — SP10

Michael the Brave SP11

Kings Carol I and Ferdinand SP12

Adam Clisi Monument — SP13

1927, Mar. 15 Typo. ***Perf. 13½***

B21	SP9	1 l + 9 l lt vio	.70	.40
B22	SP10	2 l + 8 l Prus grn	.70	.40
B23	SP11	3 l + 7 l dp rose	.70	.40
B24	SP12	5 l + 5 l dp bl	.70	.40
B25	SP13	6 l + 4 l ol grn	1.90	.40
		Nos. B21-B25 (5)	4.70	2.00

50th anniv. of the Royal Geographical Society. The surtax was for the benefit of that society. The stamps were valid for postage only from 3/15-4/14.

Boy Scouts in Camp — SP15

The Rescue — SP16

Designs: 3 l+3 l, Swearing in a Tenderfoot. 4 l+4 l, Prince Nicholas Chief Scout. 6 l+6 l, King Carol II in Scout's Uniform.

1931, July 15 Photo. Wmk. 225

B26	SP15	1 l + 1 l car rose	1.25	1.00
B27	SP16	2 l + 2 l dp grn	1.60	1.25
B28	SP15	3 l + 3 l ultra	2.00	1.50
B29	SP16	4 l + 4 l ol gray	2.40	2.00
B30	SP16	6 l + 6 l red brn	3.25	2.00
		Nos. B26-B30 (5)	10.50	7.75

The surtax was for the benefit of the Boy Scout organization.

Boy Scout Jamboree Issue

Scouts in Camp SP20

Semaphore Signaling SP21

Trailing — SP22

Camp Fire — SP23

King Carol II — SP24

King Carol II and Prince Michael — SP25

1932, June 8 Wmk. 230

B31	SP20	25b + 25b pck grn	2.75	1.00
B32	SP21	50b + 50b brt bl	3.50	2.00
B33	SP22	1 l + 1 l ol grn	4.00	2.75
B34	SP23	2 l + 2 l org red	6.75	4.00
B35	SP24	3 l + 3 l Prus bl	12.00	8.00
B36	SP25	6 l + 6 l blk brn	14.00	10.00
		Nos. B31-B36 (6)	43.00	27.75

For overprints see Nos. B44-B49.

Tuberculosis Sanatorium — SP26

Memorial Tablet to Postal Employees Who Died in World War I — SP27

Carmen Sylva Convalescent Home — SP28

1932, Nov. 1

B37	SP26	4 l + 1 l dk grn	2.25	1.75
B38	SP27	6 l + 1 l chocolate	2.25	2.10
B39	SP28	10 l + 1 l dp bl	4.50	3.50
		Nos. B37-B39 (3)	9.00	7.35

The surtax was given to a fund for the employees of the postal and telegraph services.

Philatelic Exhibition Issue

Souvenir Sheet

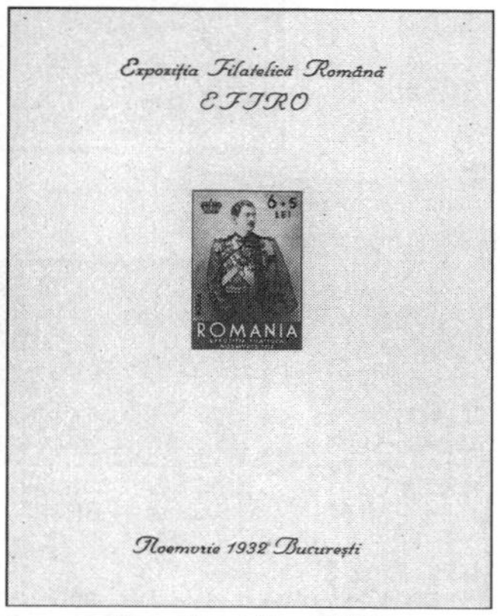
King Carol II — SP29

1932, Nov. 20 Unwmk. ***Imperf.***

B40	SP29	6 l + 5 l dk ol grn	12.00	12.00

Intl. Phil. Exhib. at Bucharest, Nov. 20-24, 1932. Each holder of a ticket of admission to the exhibition could buy a copy of the stamp. The ticket cost 20 lei.

Roadside Shrine — SP31

Woman Spinning — SP33

Woman Weaving SP32

1934, Apr. 16 Wmk. 230 ***Perf. 13½***

B41	SP31	1 l + 1 l dk brn	.75	.75
B42	SP32	2 l + 1 l blue	1.00	1.00
B43	SP33	3 l + 1 l slate grn	1.25	1.25
		Nos. B41-B43 (3)	3.00	3.00

Weaving Exposition.

Boy Scout Mamaia Jamboree Issue

Semi-Postal Stamps of 1932 Overprinted in Black or Gold

MAMAIA
1934

1934, July 8

B44	SP20	25b + 25b pck grn	1.75	1.75
B45	SP21	50b + 50b brt bl (G)	2.75	2.25
B46	SP22	1 l + 1 l ol grn	3.50	3.50
B47	SP23	2 l + 2 l org red	4.00	4.00
B48	SP24	3 l + 3 l Prus bl (G)	7.75	7.25
B49	SP25	6 l + 6 l blk brn (G)	12.00	9.50
		Nos. B44-B49 (6)	31.75	28.25

Sea Scout Saluting SP34

Scout Bugler SP35

Sea and Land Scouts SP36

King Carol II — SP37

Sea, Land and Girl Scouts — SP38

1935, June 8

B50	SP34	25b ol blk		.90	.70
B51	SP35	1 l violet		2.00	1.90
B52	SP36	2 l green		2.50	2.25
B53	SP37	6 l + 1 l red brn		3.75	3.25
B54	SP38	10 l + 2 l dk ultra		10.50	9.50
		Nos. B50-B54 (5)		19.65	17.60

Fifth anniversary of accession of King Carol II, and a national sports meeting held June 8. Surtax aided the Boy Scouts.
Nos. B50-B54 exist imperf.

King Carol II — SP39

1936, May

B55	SP39	6 l + 1 l rose car	.50	.35

Bucharest Exhibition and 70th anniversary of the dynasty. Exists imperf.

Girl of Oltenia — SP40

Girl of Saliste — SP42

Youth from Gorj — SP44

Designs: 1 l+1 l, Girl of Banat. 3 l+1 l, Girl of Hateg. 6 l+3 l, Girl of Neamt. 10 l+5 l, Youth and girl of Bucovina.

1936, June 8

B56	SP40	50b + 50b brown	.40	.25
B57	SP40	1 l + 1 l violet	.40	.25
B58	SP42	2 l + 1 l Prus grn	.40	.25
B59	SP42	3 l + 1 l car rose	.40	.25
B60	SP44	4 l + 2 l red org	.70	.55
B61	SP40	6 l + 3 l ol gray	.70	.60
B62	SP42	10 l + 5 l brt bl	1.40	1.10
		Nos. B56-B62 (7)	4.40	3.25

6th anniv. of accession of King Carol II. The surtax was for child welfare. Exist imperf.

Insignia of Boy Scouts
SP47 SP48

Jamboree Emblem — SP49

Submarine "Delfinul" SP50

1936, Aug. 20

B63	SP47	1 l + 1 l brt bl	1.90	1.75
B64	SP48	3 l + 3 l ol gray	2.75	2.50
B65	SP49	6 l + 6 l car rose	3.50	3.25
		Nos. B63-B65 (3)	8.15	7.50

Boy Scout Jamboree at Brasov (Kronstadt).

1936, Oct.

Designs: 3 l+2 l, Training ship "Mircea." 6 l+3 l, Steamship "S.M.R."

B66	SP50	1 l + 1 l pur	1.90	1.75
B67	SP50	3 l + 2 l ultra	1.75	1.50
B68	SP50	6 l + 3 l car rose	2.50	1.50
		Nos. B66-B68 (3)	6.15	4.75

Marine Exhibition at Bucharest. Exist imperf.

Soccer SP53

Swimming SP54

Throwing the Javelin — SP55

Skiing — SP56

King Carol II Hunting — SP57

Rowing SP58

Horsemanship SP59

Founding of the U.F.S.R. SP60

1937, June 8 Wmk. 230 *Perf. 13½*

B69	SP53	25b + 25b ol blk	.20	.20
B70	SP54	50b + 50b brown	.20	.20
B71	SP55	1 l + 50b violet	.20	.20
B72	SP56	2 l + 1 l slate grn	.25	.20
B73	SP57	3 l + 1 l rose lake	.45	.25
B74	SP58	4 l + 1 l red org	.70	.30
B75	SP59	6 l + 2 l dp claret	.90	.40
B76	SP60	10 l + 4 l brt blue	1.10	1.10
		Nos. B69-B76 (8)	4.00	2.85

25th anniversary of the Federation of Romanian Sports Clubs (U.F.S.R.); 7th anniversary of the accession of King Carol II.
Exist imperf.

Start of Race — SP61

Javelin Thrower — SP62

Designs: 4 l+1 l, Hurdling. 6 l+1 l, Finish of race. 10 l+1 l, High jump.

1937, Sept. 1 Wmk. 230 *Perf. 13½*

B77	SP61	1 l + 1 l purple	.35	.35
B78	SP62	2 l + 1 l green	.45	.40
B79	SP61	4 l + 1 l vermilion	.55	.55
B80	SP62	6 l + 1 l maroon	.85	.85
B81	SP61	10 l + 1 l brt bl	2.25	1.75
		Nos. B77-B81 (5)	4.45	3.90

8th Balkan Games, Bucharest. Exist imperf.

Catalogue values for unused stamps in this section, from this point to the end of the section, are for Never Hinged items.

King Carol II — SP66

1938, May 24

B82	SP66	6 l + 1 l deep magenta	.80	.20

Bucharest Exhibition (for local products), May 19-June 19, celebrating 20th anniversary of the union of Rumanian provinces.
Exists imperf.

Dimitrie Cantemir — SP67

Maria Doamna — SP68

Mircea the Great SP69

Constantine Brancoveanu SP70

Stephen the Great — SP71

Prince Cuza — SP72

Michael the Brave — SP73

Queen Elizabeth — SP74

King Carol II — SP75

King Ferdinand I — SP76

King Carol I — SP77

1938, June 8 *Perf. 13½*

B83	SP67	25b + 25b ol blk	.40	.25
B84	SP68	50b + 50b brn	.55	.25
B85	SP69	1 l + 1 l blk vio	.55	.25
B86	SP70	2 l + 2 l dk yel grn	.65	.25
B87	SP71	3 l + 2 l dp mag	.65	.25
B88	SP72	4 l + 2 l scarlet	.65	.25
B89	SP73	6 l + 2 l vio brn	.75	.75
B90	SP74	7.50 l gray bl	.95	.75
B91	SP75	10 l brt bl	1.10	.75
B92	SP76	16 l dk slate grn	1.75	1.25
B93	SP77	20 l vermilion	2.25	1.75
		Nos. B83-B93 (11)	10.25	6.75

8th anniv. of accession of King Carol II. Surtax was for Straja Tarii, a natl. org. for boys.
Exist imperf.

"The Spring" — SP78

"Escorting Prisoners" SP79

"Rodica, the Water Carrier" SP81

Nicolae Grigorescu SP82

Design: 4 l+1 l, "Returning from Market."

1938, June 23 **Perf. 13½**

B94	SP78	1 l + 1 l brt bl	.90	.40
B95	SP79	2 l + 1 l yel grn	1.00	.65
B96	SP79	4 l + 1 l vermilion	1.00	.70
B97	SP81	6 l + 1 l lake	1.50	1.00
B98	SP82	10 l + 1 l brt bl	2.10	1.25
		Nos. B94-B98 (5)	6.50	4.00

Birth centenary of Nicolae Grigorescu, Romanian painter. Exist imperf.

St. George and the Dragon — SP83

1939, June 8 **Photo.**

B99	SP83	25b + 25b ol gray	.40	.25
B100	SP83	50b + 50b brn	.40	.25
B101	SP83	1 l + 1 l pale vio	.40	.25
B102	SP83	2 l + 2 l lt grn	.40	.25
B103	SP83	3 l + 2 l red vio	.60	.25
B104	SP83	4 l + 2 l red org	.80	.30
B105	SP83	6 l + 2 l car rose	.90	.30
B106	SP83	8 l gray vio	1.00	.40
B107	SP83	10 l brt bl	1.25	.50
B108	SP83	12 l brt ultra	1.50	1.00
B109	SP83	16 l bl grn	1.75	1.25
		Nos. B99-B109 (11)	9.40	5.00

9th anniv. of accession of King Carol II. Exist imperf.

King Carol II
SP87 SP88

SP89

SP90

SP91

Wmk. 230

1940, June 8 **Photo.** **Perf. 13½**

B113	SP87	1 l + 50b dl pur	.60	.20
B114	SP88	4 l + 1 l fawn	.60	.30
B115	SP89	6 l + 1 l blue	.60	.40
B116	SP90	8 l rose brn	.80	.50
B117	SP89	16 l ultra	1.00	.60
B118	SP91	32 l dk vio brn	1.40	1.00
		Nos. B113-B118 (6)	5.00	3.00

10th anniv. of accession of King Carol II. Exist imperf.

King Carol II
SP92 SP93

1940, June 1

B119	SP92	1 l + 50b dk grn	.20	.20
B120	SP92	2.50 l + 50b Prus grn	.25	.20
B121	SP93	3 l + 1 l rose car	.35	.25
B122	SP92	3.50 l + 50b choc	.35	.30
B123	SP93	4 l + 1 l org brn	.45	.30
B124	SP93	6 l + 1 l sapphire	.65	.20
B125	SP93	9 l + 1 l brt bl	.75	.60
B126	SP93	14 l + 1 l dk bl grn	1.00	.80
		Nos. B119-B126 (8)	4.00	2.85

Surtax was for Romania's air force. Exist imperf.

View of Danube SP94

Greco-Roman Ruins — SP95

Designs: 3 l+1 l, Hotin Castle. 4 l+1 l, Hurez Monastery. 5 l+1 l, Church in Bucovina. 8 l+1 l, Tower. 12 l+2 l, Village church, Transylvania. 16 l+2 l, Arch in Bucharest.

1940, June 8 **Perf. 14½x14, 14x14½**
Inscribed: "Straja Tarii 8 Junie 1940"

B127	SP94	1 l + 1 l dp vio	.35	.20
B128	SP95	2 l + 1 l red brn	.40	.25
B129	SP94	3 l + 1 l yel grn	.45	.30
B130	SP94	4 l + 1 l grnsh blk	.50	.35
B131	SP95	5 l + 1 l org ver	.55	.40
B132	SP95	8 l + 1 l brn car	.75	.55
B133	SP95	12 l + 2 l ultra	.90	.80
B134	SP95	16 l + 2 l dk bl gray	1.60	1.25
		Nos. B127-B134 (8)	5.50	4.10

Issued to honor Straja Tarii, a national organization for boys. Exist imperf.

King Michael SP102

Corneliu Codreanu SP103

1940-42 **Photo.** **Wmk. 230**

B138	SP102	1 l + 50b yel grn	.20	.20
B138A	SP102	2 l + 50b yel grn	.20	.20
B139	SP102	2.50 l + 50b dk bl grn	.20	.20
B140	SP102	3 l + 1 l pur	.20	.20
B141	SP102	3.50 l + 50b rose pink	.20	.20
B141A	SP102	4 l + 50b org ver	.20	.20
B142	SP102	4 l + 1 l brn	.20	.20
B142A	SP102	5 l + 1 l dp plum	.40	.30
B143	SP102	6 l + 1 l lt ultra	.20	.20
B143A	SP102	7 l + 1 l sl grn	.25	.20
B143B	SP102	8 l + 1 l dp vio	.20	.20
B143C	SP102	12 l + 1 l brn vio	.25	.20
B144	SP102	14 l + 1 l brt bl	.25	.20
B144A	SP102	19 l + 1 l lil rose	.35	.30
		Nos. B138-B144A (14)	3.30	3.00

Issue years: #B138A, B141A, B142A, B143A, B143B, B143C, B144A, 1942; others, 1940.

1940, Nov. 8 **Unwmk.** **Perf. 13½**

B145	SP103	7 l + 30 l dk grn	3.75	3.00

13th anniv. of the founding of the Iron Guard by Corneliu Codreanu.

Vasile Marin — SP104

Design: 15 l+15 l, Ion Mota.

1941, Jan. 13

B146	SP104	7 l + 7 l rose brn	2.25	2.25
B147	SP104	15 l + 15 l slate bl	3.25	3.25

Souvenir Sheet
Imperf

B148	Sheet of 2	40.00	40.00
a.	SP104 7 l + 7 l Prus grn	8.00	*12.50*
b.	SP104 15 l + 15 l Prus green	8.00	*12.50*

Vasile Marin and Ion Mota, Iron Guardists who died in the Spanish Civil War.
No. B148 sold for 300 lei.

Crown, Leaves and Bible — SP107

Designs: 2 l+43 l, Library shelves. 7 l+38 l, Carol I Foundation, Bucharest. 10 l+35 l, King Carol I. 16 l+29 l, Kings Michael and Carol I.

Wmk. 230
1941, May 9 **Photo.** **Perf. 13½**
Inscribed: "1891 1941"

B149	SP107	1.50 l + 43.50 l pur	1.00	1.00
B150	SP107	2 l + 43 l rose brn	1.00	1.00
B151	SP107	7 l + 38 l rose	1.00	1.00
B152	SP107	10 l + 35 l ol blk	1.00	1.00
B153	SP107	16 l + 29 l brown	1.00	1.00
		Nos. B149-B153 (5)	5.00	5.00

50th anniv. of the Carol I Foundation, established to endow research and stimulate the arts.

Same Overprinted in Red or Black **CERNAUTI 5 Iulie 1941**

1941, Aug.

B154	SP107	1.50 l + 43.50 l (R)	1.40	*1.75*
B155	SP107	2 l + 43 l	1.40	*1.75*
B156	SP107	7 l + 38 l	1.40	*1.75*
B157	SP107	10 l + 35 l (R)	1.40	*1.75*
B158	SP107	16 l + 29 l	1.40	*1.75*

Occupation of Cernauti, Bucovina.

Same Overprinted in Red or Black **CHISINAU 16 Iulie 1941**

1941, Aug.

B159	SP107	1.50 l + 43.50 l (R)	1.40	*1.75*
B160	SP107	2 l + 43 l	1.40	*1.75*
B161	SP107	7 l + 38 l	1.40	*1.75*
B162	SP107	10 l + 35 l (R)	1.40	*1.75*
B163	SP107	16 l + 29 l	1.40	*1.75*
		Nos. B154-B163 (10)	14.00	17.50

Occupation of Chisinau, Bessarabia.

Romanian Red Cross — SP111

1941, Aug. **Perf. 13½**

B164	SP111	1.50 l + 38.50 l	.75	.45
B165	SP111	2 l + 38 l	.75	.45
B166	SP111	5 l + 35 l	.75	.45
B167	SP111	7 l + 33 l	.75	.45
B168	SP111	10 l + 30 l	1.00	1.00
		Nos. B164-B168 (5)	4.00	2.80

Souvenir Sheet
Imperf
Without Gum

B169	Sheet of 2	10.00	10.00
a.	SP111 7 l + 33 l brown & red	1.40	*1.75*
b.	SP111 10 l + 30 l brt blue & red	1.40	*1.75*

The surtax on Nos. B164-B169 was for the Romanian Red Cross.
No. B169 sold for 200 l.

King Michael and Stephen the Great SP113

Hotin and Akkerman Castles SP114

Romanian and German Soldiers SP115

Soldiers SP116

SP118

1941, Oct. 11 **Perf. 14½x13½**

B170	SP113	10 l + 30 l ultra	1.40	*2.00*
B171	SP114	12 l + 28 l dl org red	1.40	*2.00*
B172	SP115	16 l + 24 l lt brn	1.60	*2.00*
B173	SP116	20 l + 20 l dk vio	1.60	*2.00*
		Nos. B170-B173 (4)	6.00	8.00

Souvenir Sheet
Imperf
Without Gum

B174	SP118 Sheet of 2	6.75	*8.00*
a.	16 l blue gray	.75	*1.25*
b.	20 l brown carmine	.75	*1.25*

No. B174 sold for 200 l. The surtax aided the Anti-Bolshevism crusade.

Nos. B170-B174 Overprinted **ODESA 16 Oct.1941**

1941, Oct. **Perf. 14½x13½**

B175	SP113	10 l + 30 l ultra	1.40	*2.00*
B176	SP114	12 l + 28 l dl org red	1.40	*2.00*
B177	SP115	16 l + 24 l lt brn	1.60	*2.00*
B178	SP116	20 l + 20 l dk vio	1.60	*2.00*
		Nos. B175-B178 (4)	6.00	8.00

Souvenir Sheet
Imperf
Without Gum

B178A SP118 Sheet of 2 10.00 10.00

Occupation of Odessa, Russia.

Types of Regular Issue, 1941

Designs: 3 l+50b, Sucevita Monastery, Bucovina. 5.50 l+50b, Rughi Monastery, Soroca, Bessarabia. 5.50 l+1 l, Tighina Fortress, Bessarabia. 6.50 l+1 l, Soroca Fortress, Bessarabia. 8 l+1 l, St. Nicholas Monastery, Suceava, Bucovina. 9.50 l+1 l, Milisauti Monastery, Bucovina. 10.50 l+1 l, Putna Monastery, Bucovina. 16 l+1 l, Cetatea Alba Fortress, Bessarabia. 25 l+1 l, Hotin Fortress, Bessarabia.

1941, Dec. 1 Wmk. 230 ***Perf. 13½***

B179 A179 3 l + 50b rose brn .25 .20
B180 A179 5.50 l + 50b red org .40 .30
B181 A179 5.50 l + 1 l blk .40 .30
B182 A179 6.50 l + 1 l dk brn .45 .45
B183 A179 8 l + 1 l lt bl .40 .20
B184 A177 9.50 l + 1 l gray bl .45 .40
B185 A179 10.50 l + 1 l dk bl .50 .20
B186 A179 16 l + 1 l vio .55 .45
B187 A179 25 l + 1 l gray blk .60 .50
Nos. B179-B187 (9) 4.00 3.00

Titu Maiorescu — SP128

Statue of Miron Costin at Jassy — SP130

1942, Oct. 5

B188 SP128 9 l + 11 l dl vio .40 .40
B189 SP128 20 l + 20 l yel brn 1.10 1.10
B190 SP128 20 l + 30 l blue 1.25 1.25
Nos. B188-B190 (3) 2.75 2.75

Souvenir Sheet
Imperf
Without Gum

B191 SP128 Sheet of 3 4.75 4.75

The surtax aided war prisoners.
No. B191 contains one each of Nos. B188-B190, imperf. Sold for 200 l.

1942, Dec. ***Perf. 13½***

B192 SP130 6 l + 44 l sepia 1.10 *1.75*
B193 SP130 12 l + 38 l violet 1.10 *1.75*
B194 SP130 24 l + 26 l blue 1.10 *1.75*
Nos. B192-B194 (3) 3.30 5.25

Anniv. of the conquest of Transdniestria, and for use only in this territory which includes Odessa and land beyond the Duiester.

Michael, Antonescu, Hitler, Mussolini and Bessarabia Map SP131

Michael, Antonescu and (inset) Stephen of Moldavia SP132

Romanian Troops Crossing Pruth River to Retake Bessarabia — SP133

1942 Wmk. 230 Photo. ***Perf. 13½***

B195 SP131 9 l + 41 l red brn 1.75 *2.00*
B196 SP132 18 l + 32 l ol gray 1.75 *2.00*
B197 SP133 20 l + 30 l brt ultra 1.75 *2.00*
Nos. B195-B197 (3) 5.25 6.00

First anniversary of liberation of Bessarabia.

Bucovina Coats of Arms
SP134 SP135

Design: 20 l+30 l, Bucovina arms with triple-barred cross.

1942, Nov. 1

B198 SP134 9 l + 41 l brt ver 1.75 *2.00*
B199 SP135 18 l + 32 l blue 1.75 *2.00*
B200 SP135 20 l + 30 l car rose 1.75 *2.00*
Nos. B198-B200 (3) 5.25 6.00

First anniversary of liberation of Bucovina.

Andrei Muresanu SP137

1942, Dec. 30

B201 SP137 5 l + 5 l violet .60 .60

80th death anniv. of Andrei Muresanu, writer.

Avram Jancu, National Hero — SP138

1943, Feb. 15

B202 SP138 16 l + 4 l brown .70 .70

Nurse Aiding Wounded Soldier SP139

1943, Mar. 1 ***Perf. 14½x14***

B203 SP139 12 l + 88 l red brn & ultra .50 .50
B204 SP139 16 l + 84 l brt ultra & red .50 .50
B205 SP139 20 l + 80 l ol gray & red .50 .50
Nos. B203-B205 (3) 1.50 1.50

Souvenir Sheet
Imperf

B206 Sheet of 2 3.75 *4.50*
a. SP139 16 l + 84 l bright ultra & red 1.00 *1.25*
b. SP139 20 l + 80 l olive gray & red 1.00 *1.25*

Surtax on Nos. B203-B206 aided the Romanian Red Cross.
No. B206 sold for 500 l.

Sword Hilt — SP141

Sword Severing Chain — SP142

Soldier and Family, Guardian Angel — SP143

Perf. 14x14½

1943, June 22 Wmk. 276

B207 SP141 36 l + 164 l brn 1.50 1.50
B208 SP142 62 l + 138 l brt bl 1.50 1.50
B209 SP143 76 l + 124 l ver 1.50 1.50
Nos. B207-B209 (3) 4.50 4.50

Souvenir Sheet
Imperf

B210 Sheet of 2 11.00 11.00
a. SP143 62 l + 138 l deep blue 2.75 2.75
b. SP143 76 l + 124 l red org 2.75 2.75

2nd anniv. of Romania's entrance into WWII. No. B210 sold for 600 l.

Petru Maior — SP145

Horia, Closca and Crisan SP148

32 l+118 l, Gheorghe Sincai. 36 l+114 l, Timotei Cipariu. 91 l+109 l, Gheorghe Cosbuc.

Perf. 13½; 14½x14 (No. B214)

1943, Aug. 15 Photo. Wmk. 276

B211 SP145 16 l + 134 l red org .40 .40
B212 SP145 32 l + 118 l lt bl .40 .40
B213 SP145 36 l + 114 l vio .40 .40
B214 SP148 62 l + 138 l car rose .40 .40
B215 SP145 91 l + 109 l dk brn .40 .40
Nos. B211-B215 (5) 2.00 2.00

See Nos. B219-B223.

King Michael and Ion Antonescu SP150

1943, Sept. 6

B216 SP150 16 l + 24 l blue 1.50 1.50

3rd anniv. of the government of King Michael and Marshal Ion Antonescu.

Symbols of Sports — SP151

1943, Sept. 26 ***Perf. 13½***

B217 SP151 16 l + 24 l ultra .40 .30
B218 SP151 16 l + 24 l red brn .40 .30

Surtax for the benefit of Romanian sports.

Portrait Type of 1943

1943, Oct. 1

Designs: 16 l+134 l, Samuel Micu. 51 l+99 l, George Lazar. 56 l+144 l, Octavian Goga. 76 l+ 124 l, Simeon Barnutiu. 77 l+123 l, Andrei Saguna.

B219 SP145 16 l + 134 l red vio .25 .25
B220 SP145 51 l + 99 l orange .25 .25
B221 SP145 56 l + 144 l rose car .25 .25
B222 SP145 76 l + 124 l slate bl .25 .25
B223 SP145 77 l + 123 l brown .25 .25
Nos. B219-B223 (5) 1.25 1.25

The surtax aided refugees.

Calafat, 1877 — SP157

Designs: 2 l +2 l, World War I scene. 3.50 l+3.50 l, Stalingrad, 1943. 4 l+4 l, Tisza, 1919. 5 l+5 l, Odessa, 1941. 6.50 l+6.50 l, Caucasus, 1942. 7 l+7 l, Sevastopol, 1942. 20 l+20 l, Prince Ribescu and King Michael.

1943, Nov. 10 Photo. ***Perf. 13½***

B224 SP157 1 l + 1 l red brn .20 .20
B225 SP157 2 l + 2 l dl vio .20 .20
B226 SP157 3.50 l + 3.50 l lt ultra .20 .20
B227 SP157 4 l + 4 l mag .20 .20
B228 SP157 5 l + 5 l red org .25 .25
B229 SP157 6.50 l + 6.50 l bl .25 .25
B230 SP157 7 l + 7 l dp vio .35 .35
B231 SP157 20 l + 20 l crim .45 .45
Nos. B224-B231 (8) 2.10 2.10

Centenary of Romanian Artillery.

Emblem of Romanian Engineers' Association — SP165

1943, Dec. 19 ***Perf. 14***

B232 SP165 21 l + 29 l sepia .70 .50

Society of Romanian Engineers, 25th anniv.

Motorcycle, Truck and Post Horn — SP166

Post Wagon SP167

Roman Post Chariot SP168

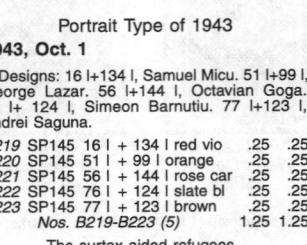

Post Rider — SP169

1944, Feb. 1 Wmk. 276 *Perf. 14*

B233 SP166 1 l + 49 l org red 1.25 1.25
B234 SP167 2 l + 48 l lil rose 1.25 1.25
B235 SP168 4 l + 46 l ultra 1.25 1.25
B236 SP169 10 l + 40 l dl vio 1.25 1.25
Nos. B233-B236 (4) 5.00 5.00

Souvenir Sheets

Perf. 14

B237 Sheet of 3 4.00 4.00
a. SP166 1 l + 49 l orange red .70 .70
b. SP167 2 l + 48 l orange red .70 .70
c. SP168 4 l + 46 l orange red .70 .70

Imperf

B238 Sheet of 3 4.00 4.00
a. SP166 1 l + 49 l dull violet .70 .70
b. SP167 2 l + 48 l dull violet .70 .70
c. SP168 4 l + 46 l dull violet .70 .70

The surtax aided communications employees.
No. B238 is imperf. between the stamps.
Nos. B237-B238 each sold for 200 l.

Nos. B233-B238 Overprinted

1744 1944

1944, Feb. 28

B239 SP166 1 l + 49 l org red 2.75 2.75
B240 SP167 2 l + 48 l lil rose 2.75 2.75
B241 SP168 4 l + 46 l ultra 2.75 2.75
B242 SP169 10 l + 40 l dl vio 2.75 2.75
Nos. B239-B242 (4) 11.00 11.00

Souvenir Sheets

Perf. 14

B243 Sheet of 3 8.25 *10.00*

Imperf

B244 Sheet of 3 8.25 *10.00*

Rugby Player SP171

Dr. N. Cretzulescu SP172

1944, Mar. 16 *Perf. 15*

B245 SP171 16 l + 184 l crimson 3.25 3.25

30th anniv. of the Romanian Rugby Assoc. The surtax was used to encourage the sport.

1944, Mar. 1 Photo. *Perf. 13½*

B246 SP172 35 l + 65 l brt ultra .70 .70

Centenary of medical teaching in Romania.

Queen Mother Helen — SP173

1945, Feb. 10

B247 SP173 4.50 l + 5.50 l multi .20 .20
B248 SP173 10 l + 40 l multi .25 .25
B249 SP173 15 l + 75 l multi .30 .30
B250 SP173 20 l + 80 l multi .50 .50
Nos. B247-B250 (4) 1.25 1.25

The surtax aided the Romanian Red Cross.

Kings Ferdinand and Michael and Map SP174

1945, Feb. *Perf. 14*

B251 SP174 75 l + 75 l dk ol brn .50 .50

Romania's liberation.

Stefan Tomsa Church, Radaseni SP175

Municipal Home SP176

Gathering Fruit — SP177

School SP178

1944 Wmk. 276 Photo. *Perf. 14*

B252 SP175 5 l + 145 l brt bl .50 .50
B253 SP176 12 l + 138 l car rose .50 .50
B254 SP177 15 l + 135 l red org .50 .50
B255 SP178 32 l + 118 l dk brn .50 .50
Nos. B252-B255 (4) 2.00 2.00

King Michael and Carol I Foundation, Bucharest — SP179

Design: 200 l, King Carol I and Foundation.

1945, Feb. 10 *Perf. 13*

B256 SP179 20 l + 180 l dp org .30 .30
B257 SP179 25 l + 175 l slate .30 .30
B258 SP179 35 l + 165 l cl brn .30 .30
B259 SP179 75 l + 125 l pale vio .30 .30
Nos. B256-B259 (4) 1.20 1.20

Souvenir Sheet

Imperf

Without Gum

B260 SP179 200 l blue 5.00 5.00

Surtax was to aid in rebuilding the Public Library, Bucharest.
#B256-B259 were printed in sheets of 4.
No. B260 sold for 1200 l.

Ion G. Duca SP181

16 l+184 l, Virgil Madgearu. 20 l+180 l, Nikolai Jorga. 32 l+168 l, Ilie Pintilie. 35 l+165 l, Bernath Andrei. 36 l+164 l, Filimon Sarbu.

1945, Apr. 30 *Perf. 13*

B261 SP181 12 l + 188 l dk bl .35 .35
B262 SP181 16 l + 184 l cl brn .35 .35
B263 SP181 20 l + 180 l blk brn .35 .35
B264 SP181 32 l + 168 l brt red .35 .35
B265 SP181 35 l + 165 l Prus bl .35 .35
B266 SP181 36 l + 164 l lt vio .35 .35
Nos. B261-B266 (6) 2.10 2.10

Souvenir Sheet

Imperf

B267 Sheet of 2 12.50 12.50
a. SP181 32 l + 168 l mag 2.50 2.75
b. SP181 35 l + 165 l mag 2.50 2.75

Honoring six victims of Nazi terrorism.
No. B267 sold for 1,000 l.

Books and Torch — SP188

Designs: #B269, Flags of Russia and Romania. #B270, Kremlin, Moscow. #B271, Tudor Vladimirescu and Alexander Nevsky.

1945, May 20 *Perf. 14*

B268 SP188 20 l + 80 l ol grn .20 .20
B269 SP188 35 l + 165 l brt rose .20 .20
B270 SP188 75 l + 225 l blue .20 .20
B271 SP188 80 l + 420 l cl brn .20 .20
Nos. B268-B271 (4) .80 .80

Souvenir Sheet

Imperf

Without Gum

B272 Sheet of 2 6.00 6.00
a. SP189 35 l + 165 l bright red 1.50 1.50
b. SP190 75 l + 225 l bright red 1.50 1.50

1st Soviet-Romanian Cong., May 20, 1945.
No. B272 sold for 900 l.

Karl Marx — SP193

120 l+380 l, Friedrich Engels. 155 l+445 l, Lenin.

1945, June 30 *Perf. 13½*

B273 SP193 75 l + 425 l car rose 1.75 1.75
B274 SP193 120 l + 380 l bl 1.75 1.75
B275 SP193 155 l + 445 l dk vio brn 1.75 1.75

Imperf

B276 SP193 75 l + 425 l bl 4.75 4.75
B277 SP193 120 l + 380 l dk vio brn 4.75 4.75
B278 SP193 155 l + 445 l car rose 4.75 4.75
Nos. B273-B278 (6) 19.50 19.50

Nos. B276-B278 were printed in sheets of 4.

Woman Throwing Discus — SP196

Designs: 16 l+184 l, Diving. 20 l+180 l, Skiing. 32 l+168 l, Volleyball. 35 l+165 l, Worker athlete.

Wmk. 276

1945, Aug. 5 Photo. *Perf. 13*

B279 SP196 12 l +188 l ol gray 1.00 1.00
B280 SP196 16 l +184 l lt ultra 1.00 1.00
B281 SP196 20 l +180 l dp grn 1.00 1.00
B282 SP196 32 l +168 l mag 1.00 1.00
B283 SP196 35 l +165 l brt bl 1.00 1.00

Imperf

B284 SP196 12 l +188 l org red 1.00 1.00
B285 SP196 16 l +184 l vio brn 1.00 1.00
B286 SP196 20 l +180 l dp vio 1.00 1.00
B287 SP196 32 l +168 l yel grn 1.00 1.00
B288 SP196 35 l +165 l dk ol grn 1.00 1.00
Nos. B279-B288 (10) 10.00 10.00

Printed in sheets of 9.

Mail Plane and Bird Carrying Letter SP201

1945, Aug. 5 *Perf. 13½*

B289 SP201 200 l + 1000 l bl & dk bl 3.00 3.00
a. With label 19.00 19.00

The surtax on Nos. B279-B289 was for the Office of Popular Sports.
Issued in sheets of 30 stamps and 10 labels, arranged 10x4 with second and fourth horizontal rows each having five alternating labels.

Agriculture and Industry United — SP202

King Michael SP203

1945, Aug. 23 *Perf. 14*

B290 SP202 100 l + 400 l red .40 .40
B291 SP203 200 l + 800 l blue .40 .40

The surtax was for the Farmers' Front.
For surcharges see Nos. B318-B325.

Political Amnesty SP204

Military Amnesty SP205

Agrarian Amnesty SP206

Tudor Vladimirescu SP207

Nicolae Horia SP208

Reconstruction — SP209

1945, Aug. ***Perf. 13***

B292 SP204 20 l + 580 l choc 8.00 8.00
B293 SP204 20 l + 580 l mag 8.00 8.00
B294 SP205 40 l + 560 l blue 8.00 8.00
B295 SP205 40 l + 560 l sl grn 8.00 8.00
B296 SP206 55 l + 545 l red 8.00 8.00
B297 SP206 55 l + 545 l dk vio brn 8.00 8.00
B298 SP207 60 l + 540 l ultra 8.00 8.00
B299 SP207 60 l + 540 l choc 8.00 8.00
B300 SP208 80 l + 520 l red 8.00 8.00
B301 SP208 80 l + 520 l mag 8.00 8.00
B302 SP209 100 l + 500 l sl grn 8.00 8.00
B303 SP209 100 l + 500 l red brn 8.00 8.00
Nos. B292-B303 (12) 96.00 96.00

1st anniv. of Romania's armistice with Russia. Issued in panes of four.

Nos. B292-B303 also exist on coarse grayish paper, ungummed (same value).

Electric Train SP210

Coats of Arms SP211

Truck on Mountain Road SP212

Oil Field SP213

"Agriculture" — SP214

1945, Oct. 1 ***Perf. 14***

B304 SP210 10 l + 490 l ol grn .25 .25
B305 SP211 20 l + 480 l red brn .25 .25
B306 SP212 25 l + 475 l brn vio .25 .25
B307 SP213 55 l + 445 l ultra .25 .25
B308 SP214 100 l + 400 l brn .25 .25

Imperf

B309 SP210 10 l + 490 l blue .25 .25
B310 SP211 20 l + 480 l violet .25 .25
B311 SP212 25 l + 475 l bl grn .25 .25
B312 SP213 55 l + 445 l gray .25 .25
B313 SP214 100 l + 400 l dp mag .25 .25
Nos. B304-B313 (10) 2.50 2.50

16th Congress of the General Assoc. of Romanian Engineers.

"Brotherhood" — SP215

160 l+1840 l, "Peace." 320 l+1680 l, Hammer crushing Nazism. 440 l+2560 l, "World Unity."

1945, Dec. 5 ***Perf. 14***

B314 SP215 80 l + 920 l mag 10.00 10.00
B315 SP215 160 l + 1840 l org brn 10.00 10.00
B316 SP215 320 l + 1680 l vio 10.00 10.00
B317 SP215 440 l + 2560 l yel grn 10.00 10.00
Nos. B314-B317 (4) 40.00 40.00

World Trade Union Congress at Paris, Sept. 25-Oct. 10, 1945.

Nos. B290 and B291 Surcharged in Various Colors

1946, Jan. 20

B318 SP202 10 l + 90 l (Bk) .50 .50
B319 SP203 10 l + 90 l (R) .50 .50
B320 SP202 20 l + 80 l (G) .50 .50
B321 SP203 20 l + 80 l (Bk) .50 .50
B322 SP202 80 l + 120 l (Bl) .50 .50
B323 SP203 80 l + 120 l (Bk) .50 .50
B324 SP202 100 l + 150 l (Bk) .50 .50
B325 SP203 100 l + 150 l (R) .50 .50
Nos. B318-B325 (8) 4.00 4.00

Re-distribution of Land — SP219

Sower SP220

Ox Team Drawing Hay SP221

Old and New Plowing Methods SP222

1946, Mar. 6

B326 SP219 50 l + 450 l red .25 .25
B327 SP220 100 l + 900 l red vio .25 .25
B328 SP221 200 l + 800 l orange .25 .25
B329 SP222 400 l + 1600 l dk grn .25 .25
Nos. B326-B329 (4) 1.00 1.00

Agrarian reform law of Mar. 23, 1945.

Philharmonic Types of Regular Issue

Perf. 13, 13½x13

1946, Apr. 26 Photo. Wmk. 276

B330 A211 200 l + 800 l brt red .70 .70
a. Sheet of 12 20.00 22.50
B331 A213 350 l + 1650 l dk bl .80 .80
a. Sheet of 12 20.00 22.50

Issued in sheets containing 12 stamps and 4 labels, with bars of music in the margins.

Agriculture SP223

Dove SP228

Designs: 10 l+200 l, Hurdling. 80 l+200 l, Research. 80 l+300 l, Industry. 200 l+400 l, Workers and flag.

Wmk. 276

1946, July 28 Photo. ***Perf. 11½***

B332 SP223 10 l + 100 l dk org brn & red .30 .30
B333 SP223 10 l + 200 l bl & red brn .30 .30
B334 SP223 80 l + 200 l brn vio & brn .30 .30
B335 SP223 80 l + 300 l dk org brn & rose lil .30 .30
B336 SP223 200 l + 400 l Prus bl & red .30 .30
Nos. B332-B336 (5) 1.50 1.50

Issued in panes of 4 stamps with marginal inscription.

1946, Oct. 20 ***Perf. 13½x13, Imperf.***

B338 SP228 300 l + 1200 l scar .50 .25

Souvenir Sheet

Perf. 14x14½

B339 SP228 1000 l scarlet 2.00 *2.25*

Romanian-Soviet friendship. No. B339 sold for 6000 lei.

Skiing — SP230

1946, Sept. 1 ***Perf. 11½, Imperf.***

B340 SP230 160 l + 1340 l dk grn .50 .50

Surtax for Office of Popular Sports.

Spinning SP231

Reaping SP232

Riding — SP233

Water Carrier — SP234

1946, Nov. 20 ***Perf. 14***

B342 SP231 80 l + 320 l brt red .20 .20
B343 SP232 140 l + 360 l dp org .20 .20
B344 SP233 300 l + 450 l brn ol .20 .20
B345 SP234 600 l + 900 l ultra .20 .20
Nos. B342-B345 (4) .80 .80

Democratic Women's Org. of Romania.

Angel with Food and Clothing SP235

Bread for Hungry Family SP236

Care for Needy — SP237

1947, Jan. 15 ***Perf. 13½x14***

B346 SP235 1500 l + 3500 l red org .20 .20
B347 SP236 3700 l + 5300 l dp vio .20 .20

Miniature Sheet

Imperf

Without Gum

B348 SP237 5000 l + 5000 l ultra 1.10 *1.25*

Surtax helped the social relief fund. No. B348 is miniature sheet of one.

Student Reciting SP238

Allegory of Education — SP242

SP243

#B350, Weaving class. #B351, Young machinist. #B352, Romanian school.

Perf. 14x13½

1947, Mar. 5 Photo. Wmk. 276

B349 SP238 200 l + 200 l vio bl .20 .20
B350 SP238 300 l + 300 l red brn .20 .20
B351 SP238 600 l + 600 l Prus grn .20 .20
B352 SP238 1200 l + 1200 l ultra .20 .20
B353 SP242 1500 l + 1500 l dp rose .20 .20
Nos. B349-B353 (5) 1.00 1.00

Souvenir Sheet

Imperf

B354 SP243 3700 l + 3700 l dl brn & dl bl 1.25 *1.50*

Romania's vocational schools, 50th anniv.

Victor Babes — SP244

#B356, Michael Eminescu. #B357, Nicolae Grigorescu. #B358, Peter Movila. #B359, Aleksander S. Pushkin. #B360, Mikhail V. Lomonosov. #B361, Peter I. Tchaikovsky. #B362, Ilya E. Repin.

1947, Apr. 18 ***Perf. 14***

B355 SP244 1500 l + 1500 l red org .20 .20
B356 SP244 1500 l + 1500 l dk ol grn .20 .20
B357 SP244 1500 l + 1500 l dk bl .20 .20
B358 SP244 1500 l + 1500 l dp plum .20 .20
B359 SP244 1500 l + 1500 l scar .20 .20
B360 SP244 1500 l + 1500 l rose brn .20 .20
B361 SP244 1500 l + 1500 l ultra .20 .20
B362 SP244 1500 l + 1500 l choc .20 .20
Nos. B355-B362 (8) 1.60 1.60

Transportation — SP252

Labor Day: No. B364, Farmer. No. B365, Farm woman. No. B366, Teacher and school. No. B367, Laborer and factory.

1947, May 1

B363 SP252 1000 l + 1000 l dk ol brn .20 .25
B364 SP252 1500 l + 1500 l red brn .20 .25
B365 SP252 2000 l + 2000 l blue .20 .25
B366 SP252 2500 l + 2500 l red vio .20 .25
B367 SP252 3000 l + 3000 l crim rose .20 .25
Nos. B363-B367 (5) 1.00 1.25

No. 650 Surcharged in Carmine

2+3 LEI
C.B.A.
1947

1947, Sept. 6 ***Perf. 13½***

B368 A234 2 l + 3 l on 36,000 l vio .60 .60

Balkan Games of 1947, Bucharest.

Type of 1947 Surcharged in Carmine

ARLUS +5
1-7.XI.
1947

Design: Cathedral of Curtea de Arges.

1947, Oct. 30 ***Imperf.***

B369 A235 5 l + 5 l brt ultra .35 .35

Soviet-Romanian Congress, Nov. 1-7.

Plowing — SP257

Perf. 14x14½

1947, Oct. 5 Photo. Wmk. 276

B370 SP257 1 l + 1 l shown .20 .20
B371 SP257 2 l + 2 l Sawmill .20 .20
B372 SP257 3 l + 3 l Refinery .20 .20
B373 SP257 4 l + 4 l Steel mill .20 .20
Nos. B370-B373,CB12 (5) 1.20 1.20

17th Congress of the General Assoc. of Romanian Engineers.

Allegory of Industry, Science and Agriculture — SP258

Winged Man Holding Hammer and Sickle SP259

1947, Nov. 10 ***Perf. 14½x14***

B374 SP258 2 l + 10 l rose lake .20 .20
B375 SP259 7 l + 10 l bluish blk .20 .20

2nd Trade Union Conf., Nov. 10.

SP260

SP264

Designs: 1 l+1 l, Convoy of Food for Moldavia. 2 l+2 l, "Everything for the Front-Everything for Victory." 3 l+3 l, Woman, child and hospital. 4 l+4 l, "Help the Famine-stricken Regions." 5 l+5 l, "Three Years of Action."

1947, Nov. 7 ***Perf. 14***

B376 SP260 1 l + 1 l dk gray bl .20 .20
B377 SP260 2 l + 2 l dk brn .20 .20
B378 SP260 3 l + 3 l rose lake .20 .20
B379 SP260 4 l + 4 l brt ultra .20 .20
B380 SP264 5 l + 5 l red .20 .20
Nos. B376-B380 (5) 1.00 1.00

Issued in sheets of four.

Discus Thrower — SP265

Labor — SP266

Youths Following Filimon Sarbu Banner — SP269

Balkan Games of 1947: 2 l+2 l, Runner. 5 l+5 l, Boy and girl athletes.

Wmk. 276

1948, Feb. Photo. ***Perf. 13½***

B381 SP265 1 l + 1 l dk brn .30 .30
B382 SP265 2 l + 2 l car lake .40 .40
B383 SP265 5 l + 5 l blue .65 .65
Nos. B381-B383,CB13-CB14 (5) 3.75 2.85

1948, Mar. 15

3 l+3 l, Agriculture. 5 l+5 l, Education.

B384 SP266 2 l + 2 l dk sl bl .25 .20
B385 SP266 3 l + 3 l gray grn .30 .20
B386 SP266 5 l + 5 l red brn .40 .20

Imperf

B387 SP269 8 l + 8 l dk car rose .60 .25
Nos. B384-B387,CB15 (5) 2.45 1.35

No. B387 issued in triangular sheets of 4.

Gliders — SP270

Sailboat Race SP271

Designs: No. B389, Early plane. No. B390, Plane over farm. No. B391, Transport plane. B393, Training ship, Mircea. B394, Danube ferry. B395, S.S. Transylvania.

1948, July 26 ***Perf. 14x14½***

B388 SP270 2 l + 2 l blue 1.25 1.25
B389 SP270 5 l + 5 l pur 1.25 1.25
B390 SP270 8 l + 8 l dk car rose 1.25 1.25
B391 SP270 10 l + 10 l choc 1.25 1.25
B392 SP271 2 l + 2 l dk grn 1.25 1.25
B393 SP271 5 l + 5 l slate 1.25 1.25
B394 SP271 8 l + 8 l brt bl 1.25 1.25
B395 SP271 10 l + 10 l ver 1.25 1.25
Nos. B388-B395 (8) 10.00 10.00

Air and Sea Communications Day.

Type of Regular Issue and

Torch, Pen, Ink and Flag SP272

Alexandru Sahia SP273

Romanian-Soviet Association Emblem SP274

Perf. 14x13½, 13½x14, Imperf.

1948, Sept. 12

B396 A241 5 l + 5 l crimson .50 .50
B397 SP272 10 l + 10 l violet .75 .75
B398 SP273 15 l + 15 l blue 1.00 1.00
Nos. B396-B398 (3) 2.25 2.25

Week of the Democratic Press, Sept. 12-19.

1948, Oct. 29 ***Perf. 14***

Design: 15 l+15 l, Spasski Tower, Kremlin.

B399 SP274 10 l + 10 l gray grn 1.25 1.25
B400 SP274 15 l + 15 l dp ultra 1.50 1.50

No. B399 was issued in sheets of 50 stamps and 50 labels.

Symbols of United Labor SP275

Agriculture SP276

Industry SP277

Automatic Riflemen SP278

Soldiers Cutting Barbed Wire SP279

1948, May 1 ***Perf. 14x13½, 13½x14***

B401 SP275 8 l + 8 l red 1.10 *1.75*
B402 SP276 10 l + 10 l ol grn 1.50 *2.50*
B403 SP277 12 l + 12 l red brn 2.00 *2.75*
Nos. B401-B403 (3) 4.60 7.00

Labor Day, May 1. See No. CB17.

1948, May 9

Flags and Dates: 23 Aug 1944-9 Mai 1945

B404 SP278 1.50 l + 1.50 l shown .25 .25
B405 SP279 2 l + 2 l shown .25 .25
B406 SP279 4 l + 4 l Field Artillery .50 .50
B407 SP279 7.50 l + 7.50 l Tank .85 .85
B408 SP279 8 l + 8 l War-ship .90 .90
Nos. B404-B408,CB18-CB19 (7) 13.25 13.25

Honoring the Romanian Army.

Nicolae Balcescu — SP280

Balcescu and Revolutionists SP281

Balcescu, Sandor Petöfi and Revolutionists — SP282

Revolution of 1848: #B412, Balcescu and revolutionists.

1948, June 1 ***Perf. 13x13½***

B409	SP280	2 l + 2 l car lake	.25	.25
B410	SP281	5 l + 5 l dk vio	.40	.40
B411	SP282	10 l + 10 l dk ol brn	.50	.50
B412	SP280	36 l + 18 l dp bl	1.10	1.10
		Nos. B409-B412 (4)	2.25	2.25

For surcharges see Nos. 856-859.

Loading Freighter SP283

Designs: 3 l+3 l, Lineman. 11 l+11 l, Transport plane. 15 l+15 l, Railroad train.

Wmk. 289

1948, Dec. 10 **Photo.** ***Perf. 14***

Center in Black

B413	SP283	1 l + 1 l dk grn	.45	.35
B414	SP283	3 l + 3 l redsh brn	.55	.50
B415	SP283	11 l + 11 l dp bl	2.25	1.75
B416	SP283	15 l + 15 l red	2.75	2.40
a.		Sheet of 4	15.00	15.00
		Nos. B413-B416 (4)	6.00	5.00

No. B416a contains four imperf. stamps similar to Nos. B413-B416 in changed colors, center in brown. No gum.

Runners — SP284

Parade of Athletes SP285

1948, Dec. 31 ***Perf. 13x13½, 13½x13***

B421	SP284	5 l + 5 l grn	2.00	2.00
B422	SP285	10 l + 10 l brn vio	3.25	3.25

Imperf

B423	SP284	5 l + 5 l grn	2.00	2.00
B424	SP285	10 l + 10 l red	3.25	3.25
		Nos. B421-B424,CB20-CB21 (6)	32.50	32.50

Nos. B421-B424 were issued in sheets of 4.

Souvenir Sheet

SP286

1950, Jan. 27

B425	SP286	10 l carmine	3.00	2.00

Philatelic exhib., Bucharest. Sold for 50 lei.

Crossing the Buzau, by Denis Auguste Marie Raffet — SP287

1967, Nov. 15 **Engr.** ***Perf. 13½***

B426	SP287	55b + 45b ocher & indigo	.40	.30

Stamp Day.

Old Bucharest, 18th Century Painting — SP288

1968, Nov. 15 **Photo.** ***Perf. 13½***

B427	SP288	55b + 45b label	.75	.40

Stamp Day. Label has printed perforations. See Nos. 2386A, B428-B429.

1969, Nov. 15

Design: Courtyard, by M. Bouquet.

B428	SP288	55b + 45b label	.65	.50

Stamp Day. Label at right of stamp has printed perforations.

1970, Nov. 15

Mail Coach in the Winter, by Emil Volkers.

B429	SP288	55b + 45b multi	.70	.55

Stamp Day.

Lady with Letter, by Sava Hentia SP289

1971, Nov. 15 **Photo.** ***Perf. 13½***

B430	SP289	1.10 l + 90b multi	.80	.50

Stamp Day. Label portion below stamp has printed perforations and shows Romania No. 12.

Portrait Type of Regular Issue

Designs: 4 l+2 l, Barbat at his Desk, by B. Iscovescu. 6 l+2 l, The Poet Alecsandri with his Family, by N. Livaditti.

1973, June 20 **Photo.** ***Perf. 13½***

B432	A728	4 l + 2 l multi	1.25	.50

Souvenir Sheet

B433	A728	6 l + 2 l multi	2.25	2.25

No. B433 contains one 38x50mm stamp.

Map of Europe with Emblem Marking Bucharest SP291

1974, June 25 **Photo.** ***Perf. 13½***

B435	SP291	4 l + 3 l multi	1.25	.40

EUROMAX, European Exhibition of Maximaphily, Bucharest, Oct. 6-13.

Marketplace, Sibiu — SP292

1974, Nov. 15 **Photo.** ***Perf. 13½***

B436	SP292	2.10 l + 1.90 l multi	.90	.30

Stamp Day.

No. B436 Overprinted in Red: "EXPOZITIA FILATELICA 'NATIONALA '74' / 15-24 noiembrie / Bucuresti"

1974, Nov. 15

B437	SP292	2.10 l + 1.90 l multi	1.75	1.75

NATIONALA '74 Philatelic Exhibition, Bucharest, Nov. 15-24.

Post Office, Bucharest SP293

Stamp Day: 2.10 l+1.90 l, like No. B438, side view.

1975, Nov. 15 **Photo.** ***Perf. 13½***

B438	SP293	1.50 l + 1.50 l multi	.75	.40
B439	SP293	2.10 l + 1.90 l multi	1.25	.60

No. 2612 Surcharged and Overprinted: "EXPOZITIA FILATELICA / BUCURESTI / 12-19.IX.1976"

1976, Sept. 12 **Photo.** ***Perf. 13½***

B440	A787	3.60 l + 1.80 l	3.00	2.50

Philatelic Exhibition, Bucharest, Sept. 12-19.

Elena Cuza, by Theodor Aman — SP294

Dispatch Rider Handing Letter to Officer — SP295

1976, Nov. 15 **Photo.** ***Perf. 13½***

B441	SP294	2.10 l + 1.90 l multi	.90	.60

Stamp Day.

Independence Type of 1977

Stamp Day: Battle of Rahova, after etching.

1977, May 9 **Photo.** ***Perf. 13½***

B442	A806	4.80 l + 2 l multi	1.25	.35

1977, Nov. **Photo.** ***Perf. 13½***

B443	SP295	2.10 l + 1.90 l multi	.90	.75

Socfilex Type of 1979

Flower Paintings by Luchian: 4 l+2 l, Field flowers. 10 l+5 l, Roses.

1979, July 27 **Photo.** ***Perf. 13½***

B445	A847	4 l + 2 l multi	.75	.75

Souvenir Sheet

B446	A847	10 l + 5 l multi	2.50	2.50

Socfilex Intl. Phil. Exhib., Bucharest, Oct. 26-Nov. 1. #B446 contains one 50x38mm stamp.

Stamp Day SP297

1979, Dec. 12 **Photo.** ***Perf. 13½***

B447	SP297	2.10 l + 1.90 l multi	.70	.25

Souvenir Sheet

Stamp Day — SP298

1980, July 1 **Photo.** ***Perf. 13½***

B448	SP298	5 l + 5 l multi	1.75	1.75

December 1989 Revolution — SP299

Designs: 50b+50b, Palace on fire, Bucharest. 1 l+ 1 l, Crowd, Timisoara. 1.50 l+1 l, Soldiers & crowd, Tirgu Mures. 2 l+1 l, Soldiers in Bucharest, vert. 3 l+1 l, Funeral, Timisoara. 3.50 l+1 l, Crowd celebrating, Brasov, vert. 4 l+1 l, Crowd with flags, Sibiu. No. B456, Cemetery, Bucharest. No. B457, Foreign aid.

1990, Oct. 1 **Photo.** ***Perf. 13½***

B449	SP299	50b +50b multi	.20	.20
B450	SP299	1 l +1 l multi	.20	.20
B451	SP299	1.50 l +1 l multi	.25	.20
B452	SP299	2 l +1 l multi	.30	.20
B453	SP299	3 l +1 l multi	.35	.20
B454	SP299	3.50 l +1 l multi	.40	.20
B455	SP299	4 l +1 l multi	.45	.20
B456	SP299	5 l +2 l multi	.60	.25
		Nos. B449-B456 (8)	2.75	1.65

Souvenir Sheet

B457	SP299	5 l +2 l multi	1.25	1.25

No. B457 contains one 54x42mm stamp.

Stamp Day — SP300

1992, July 15 **Photo.** ***Perf. 13½***

B458	SP300	10 l +4 l multi	.20	.20

For surcharge see No. B460.

Stamp Day — SP301

1993, Apr. 26 Photo. *Perf. 13½*

B459	SP301	15 l +10 l multi	.20	.20

No. B458 Surcharged in Red

35 ANI DE ACTIVITATE AFR-FFR
1958–1993

70L + 45

1993, Nov. 9 Photo. *Perf. 13½*

B460	SP300	70 l +45 l on 10 l+4 l	.40	.40

National History Museum, Bucharest SP302

1994, July 15 Photo. *Perf. 13½*

B461	SP302	90 l +60 l multi	.20	.20

Stamp Day.

AIR POST STAMPS

Capt. C. G. Craiu's Airplane AP1

Wmk. 95 Vertical

1928 Photo. *Perf. 13½*

C1	AP1	1 l red brown	2.00	2.00
C2	AP1	2 l brt blue	2.00	2.00
C3	AP1	5 l carmine rose	2.00	2.00

Wmk. 95 Horizontal

C4	AP1	1 l red brown	2.75	2.75
C5	AP1	2 l brt blue	2.75	2.75
C6	AP1	5 l carmine rose	2.75	2.75
		Nos. C1-C6 (6)	14.25	14.25

Nos. C4-C6 also come with white gum.

Nos. C4-C6 Overprinted **8 IUNIE 1930**

1930

C7	AP1	1 l red brown	4.50	4.50
C8	AP1	2 l brt blue	4.50	4.50
a.		Vert. pair, imperf. btwn.	*175.00*	
C9	AP1	5 l carmine rose	4.50	4.50
		Nos. C7-C9 (3)	13.50	13.50

Same Overprint on Nos. C1-C3

Wmk. 95 Vertical

C10	AP1	1 l red brown	32.50	32.50
C11	AP1	2 l brt blue	32.50	32.50
C12	AP1	5 l carmine rose	32.50	32.50
		Nos. C10-C12 (3)	97.50	97.50
		Nos. C7-C12 (6)	111.00	111.00

#C7-C12 for the accession of King Carol II.
Excellent connterfeits are known of #C10-C12.

King Carol II — AP2

1930, Oct. 4 Unwmk.

Bluish Paper

C13	AP2	1 l dk violet	.75	.75
C14	AP2	2 l gray green	.85	.85
C15	AP2	5 l red brown	1.90	1.10
C16	AP2	10 l brt blue	3.50	2.50
		Nos. C13-C16 (4)	7.00	5.20
		Never hinged	12.50	

Junkers Monoplane AP3

Monoplanes AP7

3 l, Monoplane with biplane behind. 5 l, Biplane. 10 l, Monoplane flying leftward.

1931, Nov. 4 Wmk. 230

C17	AP3	2 l dull green	.40	.30
C18	AP3	3 l carmine	.50	.40
C19	AP3	5 l red brown	.75	.50
C20	AP3	10 l blue	1.60	1.10
C21	AP7	20 l dk violet	3.25	1.60
		Nos. C17-C21 (5)	6.50	3.90
		Never hinged	14.00	

Exist imperforate.

Souvenir Sheets

Plane over Resita — AP8

Plane over Sinaia — AP9

Wmk. 276

1945, Oct. 1 Photo. *Perf. 13*

Without Gum

C22	AP8	80 l slate green	7.50	7.50

Imperf

C23	AP9	80 l magenta	5.00	5.00

16th Congress of the General Assoc. of Romanian Engineers.

Catalogue values for unused stamps in this section, from this point to the end of the section, are for Never Hinged items.

Plane AP10

Design: 500 l, Aviator and planes.

1946, Sept. 5 *Perf. 13½x13*

C24	AP10	200 l yel grn & bl	2.00	2.00
C25	AP10	500 l org red & dl bl	2.00	2.00

Sheets of four with marginal inscription.

Lockheed 12 Electra — AP12

CGM Congress Emblem — AP13

1946, Oct. *Perf. 11½*

C26	AP12	300 l crimson	.50	.50
a.		Pair, #C26, CB6	1.75	1.75

Sheet contains 8 each of Nos. C26 and CB6, arranged so se-tenant or normal pairs are available.

1947, Mar. Wmk. 276 *Perf. 13x14*

C27	AP13	1100 l blue	.35	.35

Congress of the United Labor Unions ("CGM"). Printed in sheets of 15.

"May 1" Supported by Parachutes AP14

Plane and Conference Banner AP17

Designs: No. C29, Air Force monument. No. C30, Plane over rural road.

1947, May 4 *Perf. 11½*

C28	AP14	3000 l vermilion	.20	.20
C29	AP14	3000 l grnsh gray	.20	.20
C30	AP14	3000 l blk brown	.20	.20
		Nos. C28-C30 (3)	.60	.60

Printed in sheets of four with marginal inscriptions.

1947, Nov. 10 *Perf. 14*

C31	AP17	11 l bl & dp car	.30	.30

2nd Trade Union Conference, Nov. 10.

Emblem of the Republic and Factories AP18

Industry and Agriculture — AP19

Transportation — AP20

Perf. 14x13½

1948, Nov. 22 Wmk. 289 Photo.

C32	AP18	30 l cerise	.30	.20
a.		30 l carmine ('50)	.40	.30
C33	AP19	50 l dk slate grn	.40	.20
C34	AP20	100 l ultra	1.10	.60
		Nos. C32-C34 (3)	1.80	1.00

No. C32a issued May 10. For surcharges see Nos. C37-C39.

Agriculture — AP21

Design: 50 l, Transportation.

1951-52 Wmk. 358 *Perf. 13½*

C35	AP21	30 l dk green ('52)	1.50	1.25
C36	AP21	50 l red brown	2.00	1.75

1951-55 Five Year Plan.
For surcharges see Nos. C40-C41.

Nos. C32-C36 Surcharged with New Values in Blue or Carmine

1952 Wmk. 289 *Perf. 14x13½*

C37	AP18	3b on 30 l car (Bl)	2.00	1.50
a.		3b on 30 l cerise (Bl)	*9.00*	*6.50*
C38	AP19	3b on 50 l dk sl grn	.50	.40
C39	AP20	3b on 100 l ultra	.50	.40

Perf. 13½

Wmk. 358

C40	AP21	1 l on 30 l dk grn	*6.75*	*1.25*
C41	AP21	1 l on 50 l red brn	*6.75*	*1.25*
		Nos. C37-C41 (5)	*16.50*	*4.80*

AERIANA

Nos. 706 and 707 Surcharged in Blue or Carmine

LEI3

1953 Wmk. 289 *Perf. 13½, 14*

C43	A250	3 l on 20 l org brn	*11.50*	*10.00*
C44	A251	5 l on 30 l brt bl (C)	*16.00*	*12.50*

Plane facing right and surcharge arranged to fit design on No. C44.

Plane over City — AP22

Sputnik 1 and Earth — AP23

Designs: 55b, Plane over Mountains. 1.75 l, over Harvest fields. 2.25 l, over Seashore.

Perf. 14½x14

1956, Dec. 15 Photo. Wmk. 358

C45	AP22	20b brt bl, org & grn	.35	.20
C46	AP22	55b brt bl, grn & ocher	.65	.20

C47 AP22 1.75 l brt bl & red org 1.75 .20
C48 AP22 2.55 l brt bl & red org 2.50 .40
Nos. C45-C48 (4) 5.25 1.00

1957, Nov. 6 ***Perf. 14***

3.75 l, Sputniks 1 and 2 circling globe.

C49 AP23 25b brt ultra .35 .20
C50 AP23 25b dk bl grn .35 .20
C51 AP23 3.75 l brt ultra 1.90 .60
a. Pair, #C49, C51 + label 2.25 .75
C52 AP23 3.75 l dk bl grn 1.90 .60
a. Pair, #C50, C52 + label 2.25 .75
Nos. C49-C52 (4) 4.50 1.60

Each sheet contains 27 triptychs with the center rows arranged tete-beche.
In 1958 Nos. C49-C52 were overprinted: 1.) "Expozitia Universal a Bruxelles 1958" and star. 2.) Large star. 3.) Small star.

Animal Type of Regular Issue, 1957

Birds: 3.30 l, Black-headed gull, horiz. 5 l, Sea eagle, horiz.

Perf. 14x13½
1957, Dec. 27 **Wmk. 358**
C53 A445 3.30 l ultra & gray 2.00 .50
C54 A445 5 l carmine & org 3.00 .75

Armed Forces Type of Regular Issue

Design: Flier and planes.

Perf. 13½x13
1958, Oct. 2 **Unwmk.** **Photo.**
C55 A458 3.30 l brt violet 1.10 .40

Day of the Armed Forces, Oct. 2.

Earth and Sputnik 3 Orbit AP24

1958, Sept. 20 ***Perf. 14x13½***
C56 AP24 3.25 l indigo & ocher 2.75 .75

Launching of Sputnik 3, May 15, 1958.

Type of Regular Issue, 1958
Souvenir Sheet

Design: Tête bêche pair of 27pa of 1858.

Perf. 11½
1958, Nov. 15 **Unwmk.** **Engr.**
C57 A462 10 l blue 27.50 27.50

A similar sheet, printed in dull red and imperf., exists.
No. C57 was overprinted in 1959 in vermilion to commemorate the 10th anniv. of the State Philatelic Trade.
Values, $25 and $50.

Lunik I Leaving Earth AP25

Frederic Joliot-Curie — AP26

1959, Feb. 4 **Photo.** ***Perf. 14***
C58 AP25 3.25 l vio bl, *pnksh* 7.50 .90

Launching of the "first artificial planet of the solar system."
For surcharge see No. C70.

1959, Apr. 25 ***Perf. 13½x14***
C59 AP26 3.25 l ultra 2.50 .50

Frederic Joliot-Curie; 10th anniv. of the World Peace Movement.

Rock Thrush AP27

Birds: 20b, European golden oriole. 35b, Lapwing. 40b, Barn swallow. No. C64, Goldfinch. No. C65, Great spotted woodpecker. No. C66, Great tit. 1 l, Bullfinch. 1.55 l, Long-tailed tit. 5 l, Wall creeper. Nos. C62-C67 vertical.

1959, June 25 **Litho.** ***Perf. 14***
Birds in Natural Colors

C60 AP27 10b gray, *cr* .20 .20
C61 AP27 20b gray, *grysh* .20 .20
C62 AP27 35b gray, *grysh* .20 .20
C63 AP27 40b gray & red, *pnksh* .20 .20
C64 AP27 55b gray, *buff* .25 .20
C65 AP27 55b gray, *grnsh* .25 .20
C66 AP27 55b gray & ol, *grysh* .25 .20
C67 AP27 1 l gray and red, *cr* .80 .20
C68 AP27 1.55 l gray & red, *pnksh* .90 .20
C69 AP27 5 l gray, *grnsh* 3.75 .70
Nos. C60-C69 (10) 7.00 2.50

No. C58 Surcharged in Red

1959, Sept. 14 **Photo.** **Unwmk.**
C70 AP25 5 l on 3.25 l 6.00 1.50

1st Russian rocket to reach the moon, 9/14/59.

Miniature Sheet

Prince Vlad Tepes and Document — AP28

1959, Sept. 15 **Engr.** ***Perf. 11½x11***
C71 AP28 20 l violet brn 50.00 50.00

500th anniv. of the founding of Bucharest.

Sport Type of Regular Issue, 1959
1959, Oct. 5 **Litho.** ***Perf. 13½***
C72 A474 2.80 l Boating 1.75 .40

Soviet Rocket, Globe, Dog and Rabbit — AP29

Photograph of Far Side of the Moon — AP30

Design: 1.75 l, Trajectory of Lunik 3, which hit the moon.

Perf. 14, 13½ (AP30)
1959, Dec. **Photo.** **Wmk. 358**
C73 AP29 1.55 l dk blue 2.00 .20
C74 AP30 1.60 l dk vio bl, *buff* 2.50 .40
C75 AP29 1.75 l dk blue 2.50 .40
Nos. C73-C75 (3) 7.00 1.00

Soviet conquest of space.

Animal Type of Regular Issue, 1960.

Designs: 1.30 l, Golden eagle. 1.75 l, Black grouse. 2 l, Lammergeier.

Unwmk.
1960, Mar. 3 **Engr.** ***Perf. 14***
C76 A480 1.30 l dk blue .85 .30
C77 A480 1.75 l olive grn 1.25 .30
C78 A480 2 l dk carmine 1.50 .40
Nos. C76-C78 (3) 3.60 1.00

Aurel Vlaicu and Plane of 1910 AP31

Bucharest Airport and Turbo-Jet — AP32

Designs: 20b, Plane and Aurel Vlaicu. 35b, Amphibian ambulance plane. 40b, Plane spraying crops. 55b, Pilot and planes, vert. 1.75 l, Parachutes at aviation sports meet.

1960, June 15 **Litho.** **Unwmk.**
C79 AP31 10b yellow & brn .20 .20
C80 AP31 20b red org & brn .20 .20

Photo. **Wmk. 358**
C81 AP31 35b crimson .20 .20
C82 AP31 40b violet .30 .20
C83 AP31 55b blue .40 .20

Litho. **Unwmk.**
C84 AP32 1.60 l vio bl, yel & emer .95 .20
C85 AP32 1.75 l bl, red, brn & pale grn 1.25 .35
Nos. C79-C85 (7) 3.50 1.55

50th anniv. of the first Romanian airplane flight by Aurel Vlaicu.
For surcharge see No. C145.

Bucharest Airport — AP33

Sputnik 4 Flying into Space AP34

1960 **Wmk. 358** **Photo.** ***Perf. 14***
C86 AP33 3.20 l brt ultra 1.25 .20

Type of Regular Issue, 1960

Black Sea Resort: 2 l, Beach at Mamaia.

1960, Aug. 2 **Litho.** **Unwmk.**
C87 A491 2 l grn, org & lt bl 1.25 .40

1960, June 8 **Photo.** **Wmk. 358**
C88 AP34 55b deep blue 1.25 .25

Launching of Sputnik 4, May 15, 1960.

Saturnia Pyri AP35

Papilio Machaon AP36

Limenitis Populi — AP37

Designs: 40b, Chrisophanus virgaureae. 1.60 l, Acherontia atropos. 1.75 l, Apatura iris.

Perf. 13, 14x12½, 14
1960, Oct. 10 **Typo.** **Unwmk.**
C89 AP35 10b multi .20 .20
C90 AP37 20b multi .20 .20
C91 AP37 40b multi .20 .20
C92 AP36 55b multi .45 .20
C93 AP36 1.60 l multi 1.40 .20
C94 AP36 1.75 l multi, horiz. 1.75 .20
Nos. C89-C94 (6) 4.20 1.20

Compass Rose and Jet — AP38

Perf. 13½x14
1960, Nov. 1 **Photo.** **Wmk. 358**
C95 AP38 55b brt bl + 45b label .35 .20

Stamp Day.

Skier AP39

Slalom — AP40

Maj. Yuri A. Gagarin — AP41

Designs: 25b, Skiers going up. 40b, Bobsled. 55b, Ski jump. 1 l, Mountain climber. 1.55 l, Long-distance skier.

Perf. 14x13½, 13½x14
1961, Mar. 18 **Litho.** **Unwmk.**
C96 AP39 10b olive & gray .20 .20
C97 AP40 20b gray & dk red .20 .20
C98 AP40 25b gray & bl grn .25 .20
C99 AP40 40b gray & pur .25 .20
C100 AP39 55b gray & ultra .30 .20

C101	AP40	1 l	gray & brn lake	.50	.20
C102	AP39	1.55 l	gray & brn	.80	.20
			Nos. C96-C102 (7)	2.50	1.40

Exist imperf. with changed colors. Value, set $4.00.

Perf. 14x14½, 14½x14

1961, Apr. 19 Photo. Unwmk.

Design: 3.20 l, Gagarin in space capsule and globe with orbit, horiz.

C103	AP41	1.35 l	brt blue	.75	.20
C104	AP41	3.20 l	ultra	1.75	.40

No. C104 exists imperf. in dark carmine rose. Value unused $4.50, canceled $2.

Eclipse over Republic Palace Place, Bucharest AP42

1.75 l, Total Eclipse, Scinteia House, telescope.

Perf. 14x13½

1961, June 13 Wmk. 358

C106	AP42	1.60 l	ultra	.90	.20
C107	AP42	1.75 l	dk blue	1.00	.20

Total solar eclipse of Feb. 15, 1961.

Maj. Gherman S. Titov — AP43

Globe and Stamps — AP44

55b, "Peace" and Vostok 2 rocket. 1.75 l, Yuri A. Gagarin and Gherman S. Titov, horiz.

Perf. 13½x14

1961, Sept. 11 Unwmk.

C108	AP43	55b	dp blue	.45	.20
C109	AP43	1.35 l	dp purple	.70	.20
C110	AP43	1.75 l	dk carmine	1.10	.20
			Nos. C108-C110 (3)	2.25	.60

Issued to honor the Russian space navigators Y. A. Gagarin and G. S. Titov.

1961, Nov. 15 Litho. *Perf. 13½x14*

C111	AP44	55b	multi + 45b label	.60	.20

Stamp Day.

Railroad Station, Constanta AP45

Buildings: 20b, Tower, RPR Palace place, vert. 55b, Congress hall, Bucharest. 75b, Mill, Hunedoara. 1 l, Apartment houses, Bucharest. 1.20 l, Circus, Bucharest. 1.75 l, Worker's Club, Mangalia.

Perf. 13½x14, 14x13½

1961, Nov. 20 Typo.

C112	AP45	20b	multi	.20	.20
C113	AP45	40b	multi	.20	.20
C114	AP45	55b	multi	.20	.20
C115	AP45	75b	multi	.25	.20
C116	AP45	1 l	multi	.30	.20
C117	AP45	1.20 l	multi	.65	.25
C118	AP45	1.75 l	multi	.95	.20
			Nos. C112-C118 (7)	2.75	1.45

Space Exploration Stamps and Dove AP46

Design: Each stamp shows a different group of Romanian space exploration stamps.

1962, July 27 *Perf. 14x13½*

C119	AP46	35b	yellow brn	.20	.20
C120	AP46	55b	green	.20	.20
C121	AP46	1.35 l	blue	.45	.20
C122	AP46	1.75 l	rose red	.90	.25
a.			Sheet of 4	2.50	1.25
			Nos. C119-C122 (4)	1.75	.85

Peaceful space exploration.

No. C122a contains four imperf. stamps similar to Nos. C119-C122 in changed colors and with one dove covering all four stamps. Stamps are printed together without space between.

Andrian G. Nikolayev — AP47

Designs: 1.60 l, Globe and trajectories of Vostoks 3 and 4. 1.75 l, Pavel R. Popovich.

Perf. 13½x14

1962, Aug. 20 Photo. Unwmk.

C123	AP47	55b	purple	.35	.20
C124	AP47	1.60 l	dark blue	1.00	.25
C125	AP47	1.75 l	rose claret	1.25	.30
			Nos. C123-C125 (3)	2.60	.75

1st Russian group space flight of Vostoks 3 and 4, Aug. 11-15, 1962.

Exhibition Hall — AP48

1962, Oct. 12 Litho. *Perf. 14x13*

C126	AP48	1.60 l	bl, vio bl & org	1.25	.20

4th Sample Fair, Bucharest.

The Coachmen by Szatmary — AP49

1962, Nov. 15 *Perf. 13½x14*

C127	AP49	55b	+ 45b label	.75	.25

Stamp Day. Alternating label shows No. 14 on cover.

No. C127 Overprinted in Violet

1963, Mar. 30

C128	AP49	55b	+ 45b label	2.25	1.25

Romanian Philatelists' Assoc. meeting at Bucharest, Mar. 30.

Sighisoara Glass and Crockery Factory AP50

Industrial Plants: 40b, Govora soda works. 55b, Tirgul-Jiu wood processing factory. 1 l, Savinesti chemical plant (synthetic fibers). 1.55 l, Hunedoara metal factory. 1.75 l, Brazi thermal power station.

Perf. 14x13

1963, Apr. 10 Unwmk. Photo.

C129	AP50	30b	dk bl & red	.20	.20
C130	AP50	40b	sl grn & pur	.20	.20
C131	AP50	55b	brn red & dp bl	.20	.20
C132	AP50	1 l	vio & brn	.20	.20
C133	AP50	1.551	ver & dk bl	.50	.20
C134	AP50	1.75 l	dk bl & magenta	.70	.20
			Nos. C129-C134 (6)	2.00	1.20

Industrial achievements.

Lunik 4 Approaching Moon — AP51

1963, Apr. 29 *Perf. 13½x14*

C135	AP51	55b	dk ultra & red	.45	.20

Imperf

C136	AP51	1.75 l	vio & red	.75	.20

Moon flight of Lunik 4, Apr. 2, 1963.

Steam Locomotive AP52

Designs: 55b, Diesel locomotive. 75b, Trolley bus. 1.35 l, Passenger ship. 1.75 l, Plane.

1963, July 10 Litho. *Perf. 14½x13*

C137	AP52	40b	multi	.25	.20
C138	AP52	55b	multi	.30	.20
C139	AP52	75b	multi	.40	.20
C140	AP52	1.35 l	multi	.70	.20
C141	AP52	1.75 l	multi	1.10	.20
			Nos. C137-C141 (5)	2.75	1.00

Valeri Bykovski AP53

Designs: 1.20 l, Bykovski, vert. 1.60 l, Tereshkova, vert. 1.75 l, Valentina Tereshkova.

1963 Photo.

C142	AP53	55b	blue	.25	.20
C143	AP53	1.75 l	rose red	1.00	.20

Souvenir Sheet

Perf. 13

C144			Sheet of 2	2.25	.75
a.	AP53	1.20 l	ultra	.60	.30
b.	AP53	1.60 l	ultra	.75	.40

Space flights of Valeri Bykovski, June 14-19, and Valentina Tereshkova, first woman cosmonaut, June 16-19, 1963.

No. C79 Surcharged and Overprinted: "1913-1963 50 ani de la moarte"

Unwmk.

1963, Sept. 15 Litho. *Perf. 14*

C145	AP31	1.75 l	on 10b	2.00	.75

50th death anniv. of Aurel Vlaicu, aviation pioneer.

Exists with "i" of "lei," missing.

Centenary Stamp of 1958 AP54

Stamps on Stamps: 40b, Sputnik 2 and Laika, #1200. 55b, Yurl A. Gagarin, #C104a. 1.20 l, Nikolayev and Popovich, #C123, C125. 1.55 l, Postal Administration Bldg. and letter carrier, #965.

1963, Nov. 15 Photo. *Perf. 14x13½*

Size: 38x26mm

C146	AP54	20b	lt bl & dk brn	.20	.20
C147	AP54	40b	brt pink & dk bl	.20	.20
C148	AP54	55b	lt ultra & dk car rose	.20	.20
C149	AP54	1.20 l	ocher & pur	.35	.20
C150	AP54	1.55 l	sal pink & ol gray	.50	.20
			Nos. C146-C150,CB22 (6)	2.45	1.50

15th UPU Congress, Vienna.

Pavel R. Popovich AP55

Astronauts and flag: 5b, Yuri A. Gagarin. 10b, Gherman S. Titov. 20b, John H. Glenn, Jr. 35b, M. Scott Carpenter. 40b, Andrian G. Nikolayev. 60b, Walter M. Schirra. 75b, Gordon L. Cooper. 1 l, Valeri Bykovski. 1.40 l, Valentina Tereshkova. (5b, 10b, 20b, 35b, 60b and 75b are diamond shaped).

Perf. 13½

1964, Jan. 15 Litho. Unwmk.

Light Blue Background

C151	AP55	5b	red, yel & vio bl	.20	.20
C152	AP55	10b	red, yel & pur	.20	.20
C153	AP55	20b	red, ultra & ol gray	.20	.20
C154	AP55	35b	red, ultra & sl bl	.20	.20
C155	AP55	40b	red, yel & ultra	.20	.20
C156	AP55	55b	red, yel & ultra	.40	.20
C157	AP55	60b	ultra, red & sep	.40	.20
C158	AP55	75b	red, ultra & dk bl	.45	.20
C159	AP55	1 l	red, yel & mar	.75	.20
C160	AP55	1.40 l	red, yel & mar	.90	.20
			Nos. C151-C160 (10)	3.90	2.00

Nos. C151-C160 exist imperf. in changed colors. Value, set $6.50.

A miniature sheet contains one imperf. horizontal 2 l ultramarine and yellow stamp. Size of stamp: 59½x43mm. Value unused $7.50, canceled $3.75.

Modern and 19th Century Post Office Buildings AP56

Engr. & Typo.

1964, Nov. 15 *Perf. 13½*

C161	AP56	1.60 l	ultra + 40b label	.75	.25

Stamp Day. Stamp and label are imperf. between.

Plane Approaching Airport and Coach Leaving Gate — AP57

Engr. & Typo.

1966, Oct. 20 ***Perf. 13½***

C162 AP57 55b + 45b label .60 .20

Stamp Day.

Space Exploration Type of Regular Issue

US Achievements in Space: 1.20 l, Early Bird satellite and globe. 1.55 l, Mariner 4 transmitting pictures of the moon. 3.25 l, Gemini 6 & 7, rendezvous in space. 5 l, Gemini 8 meeting Agena rocket, and globe.

1967, Feb. 15 Photo. ***Perf. 13½***

C163 A595 1.20 l silver & multi .50 .20
C164 A595 1.55 l silver & multi .65 .20
C165 A595 3.25 l silver & multi .85 .35
C166 A595 5 l silver & multi 1.25 .75
Nos. C163-C166 (4) 3.25 1.50

10 years of space exploration.

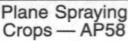

Plane Spraying Crops — AP58

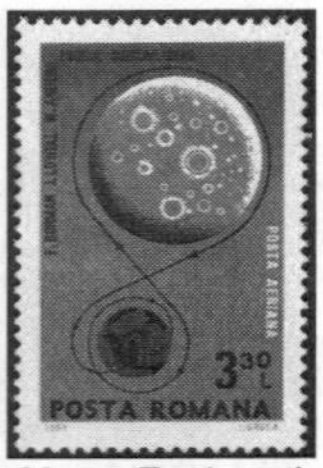

Moon, Earth and Path of Apollo 8 — AP59

Designs: 55b, Aerial ambulance over river, horiz. 1 l, Red Cross and plane. 2.40 l, Biplane and Mircea Zorileanu, aviation pioneer.

Perf. 12x12½, 12½x12

1968, Feb. 28 Litho. Unwmk.

C167 AP58 40b bl grn, blk & yel brn .20 .20
C168 AP58 55b multicolored .20 .20
C169 AP58 1 l ultra, pale grn & red org .20 .20
C170 AP58 2.40 l brt rose lil & multi .50 .30
Nos. C167-C170 (4) 1.10 .90

1969 Photo. ***Perf. 13½***

Design: No. C172, Soyuz 4 and 5 over globe with map of Russia.

C171 AP59 3.30 l multi 1.10 1.10
C172 AP59 3.30 l multi 1.10 1.10

1st manned flight around the Moon, Dec. 21-27, 1968, and the first team flights of the Russian spacecrafts Soyuz 4 and 5, Jan. 16, 1969. See note after Hungary No. C284.
Issued in sheets of 4.
Issued: #C171, Jan. 17, #C172, Mar. 28.

Apollo 9 and Lunar Landing Module over Earth AP60

Design: 2.40 l, Apollo 10 and lunar landing module over moon, vert.

1969, June 15 Photo. ***Perf. 13½***

C173 AP60 60b multi .20 .20
C174 AP60 2.40 l multi .70 .25

US space explorations, Apollo 9 and 10.

First Man on Moon — AP61

1969, July 24 Photo. ***Perf. 13½***

C175 AP61 3.30 l multi 1.10 .80

Man's first landing on the moon July 20, 1969, US astronauts Neil A. Armstrong and Col. Edwin E. Aldrin, Jr., with Lieut. Col. Michael Collins piloting Apollo 11. Printed in sheets of 4.

1970, June 29

1.50 l, Apollo 13 capsule splashing down in Pacific.

C176 AP61 1.50 l multi .50 .40

Flight and safe landing of Apollo 13, Apr. 11-17, 1970. Printed in sheets of 4.

BAC 1-11 Jet AP62

Design: 2 l, Fuselage BAC 1-11 and control tower, Bucharest airport.

1970, Apr. 6

C177 AP62 60b multi .20 .20
C178 AP62 2 l multi .55 .20

50th anniv. of Romanian civil aviation.

Flood Relief Type of Regular Issue

Design: 60b, Rescue by helicopter.

1970, Sept. 25 Photo. ***Perf. 13½***

C179 A671 60b bl gray, blk & olive .20 .20

Publicizing the plight of victims of the Danube flood. See No. 2207a.

Henri Coanda's Model Plane AP63

1970, Dec. 1

C180 AP63 60b multicolored .60 .20

Henri Coanda's first flight, 60th anniversary.

Luna 16 on Moon AP64

#C182, Lunokhod 1, unmanned vehicle on moon. #C183, US astronaut & vehicle on moon.

1971, Mar. 5 Photo. ***Perf. 13½***

C181 AP64 3.30 l silver & multi 1.00 1.00
C182 AP64 3.30 l silver & multi 1.00 1.00
a. Pair, #C181-C182 + 2 labels 2.00 2.00
C183 AP64 3.30 l silver & multi 1.00 1.00
Nos. C181-C183 (3) 3.00 3.00

No. C181 commemorates Luna 16 Russian unmanned, automatic moon mission, Sept. 12-24, 1970 (labels are incorrectly inscribed Oct. 12-24). No. C182 commemorates Lunokhod 1 (Luna 17), Nov. 10-17, 1970. Nos. C181-C182 printed in sheets of 4 stamps, arranged checkerwise, and 4 labels. No. C183 commemorates Apollo 14 moon landing, Jan. 31-Feb. 9. Printed in sheets of 4 with 4 labels showing portraits of US astronauts Alan B. Shepard, Edgar D. Mitchell, Stuart A. Roosa, and Apollo 14 emblem.

Souvenir Sheet

Cosmonauts Patsayev, Dobrovolsky and Volkov — AP65

1971, July 26 Litho. ***Perf. 13½***

C184 AP65 6 l black & ultra 4.50 4.50

In memory of Russian cosmonauts Viktor I. Patsayev, Georgi T. Dobrovolsky and Vladislav N. Volkov, who died during Soyuz 11 space mission, June 6-30, 1971.
No. C184 exists imperf. in black & blue green; Size: 130x90mm.

Lunar Rover on Moon AP66

1971, Aug. 26 Photo.

C185 AP66 1.50 l blue & multi 1.10 1.10

US Apollo 15 moon mission, July 26-Aug. 7, 1971. No. C185 printed in sheets of 4 stamps and 4 labels showing astronauts David Scott, James Irwin, Alfred Worden and Apollo 15 emblem with dates.
No. C185 exists imperf. in green & multicolored. The sheet has a control number.

Olympic Souvenir Sheets

Designs: No. C186, Torchbearer and map of Romania. No. C187, Soccer.

1972 Photo. ***Perf. 13½***

C186 A699 6 l pale grn & multi 6.00 6.00
C187 A699 6 l blue & multi 5.00 5.00

20th Olympic Games, Munich, Aug. 26-Sept. 11. No. C186 contains one stamp 50x38mm. No. C187 contains one stamp 48½x37mm.
Issued: #C186, Apr. 25; #C187, Sept. 29.
Two imperf. 6 l souvenir sheets exist, one showing equestrian, the other a satellite over globe.

Lunar Rover on Moon — AP67

1972, May 10 Photo. ***Perf. 13½***

C188 AP67 3 l vio bl, rose & gray grn .90 .75

Apollo 16 US moon mission, Apr. 15-27, 1972. No. C188 printed in sheets of 4 stamps and 4 gray green and black labels showing Capt. John W. Young, Lt. Comdr. Thomas K. Mattingly 2nd, Col. Charles M. Duke, Jr., and Apollo 16 badge.

Aurel Vlaicu and Monoplane — AP68

Romanian Aviation Pioneers: 3 l, Traian Vuia and his flying machine.

1972, Aug. 15

C189 AP68 60b multicolored .20 .20
C190 AP68 3 l multicolored .85 .30

Olympic Medals Type of Regular Issue Souvenir Sheet

Olympic silver and gold medals, horiz.

1972, Sept. 29 Litho. ***Perf. 13½***

C191 A714 6 l multicolored 6.50 6.50

Romanian medalists at 20th Olympic Games. An imperf. 6 l souvenir sheet exists showing gold medal.

Apollo Type of Regular Issue Souvenir Sheet

Design: 6 l, Lunar rover, landing module, rocket and astronauts on moon, horiz.

1972, Dec. 27 Photo. ***Perf. 13½***

C192 A715 6 l vio bl, bis & dl grn 7.00 7.00

No. C192 contains one stamp 48½x36mm.
An imperf. 6 l souvenir sheet exists showing surface of moon with landing sites of last 6 Apollo missions and landing capsule.

Type of Regular Issue, 1972

Design: Otopeni Airport, horiz.

1972, Dec. 20 Photo. ***Perf. 13***
Size: 29x21mm

C193 A710 14.60 l brt blue 1.25 .30

Apollo and Soyuz Spacecraft — AP69

3.25 l, Apollo and Soyuz after link-up.

1975, July 14 Photo. ***Perf. 13½***

C196 AP69 1.75 l vio bl, red & ol .45 .45
C197 AP69 3.25 l vio bl, red & ol .90 .90

Apollo Soyuz space test project (Russo-American cooperation), launching July 15; link-up, July 17. Nos. C196-C197 printed in sheets of 4 stamps, arranged checkerwise, and 4 rose lilac labels showing Apollo-Soyuz emblem.

European Security and Cooperation Conference — AP70

1975, July 30 Photo. ***Perf. 13½***

C198 AP70 Sheet of 4 2.50 2.50
a. 2.75 l Map of Europe .35 .35
b. 2.75 l Peace doves .35 .35
c. 5 l Open book .75 .75
d. 5 l Children playing .75 .75

European Security and Cooperation Conference, Helsinki, July 30-Aug. 1. No. C198b inscribed "posta aeriana."
An imperf. 10 l souvenir sheet exists showing Helsinki on map of Europe.

Red Cross Type of 1976

Design: Blood donors, Red Cross plane.

1976, Apr. 20 Photo. ***Perf. 13½***

C199 A790 3.35 l multi .60 .25

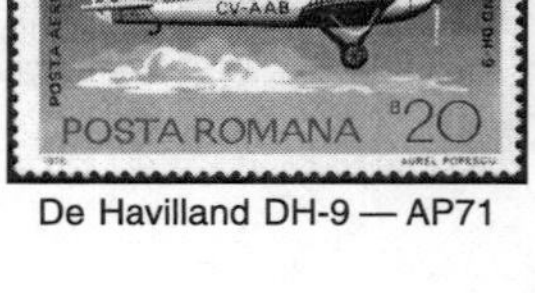

De Havilland DH-9 — AP71

Airplanes: 40b, I.C.A.R. Comercial. 60b, Douglas DC-3. 1.75 l, AN-24. 2.75 l, IL-62. 3.60 l, Boeing 707.

1976, June 24 Photo. *Perf. 13½*

C200 AP71 20b blue & multi .20 .20
C201 AP71 40b blue & multi .20 .20
C202 AP71 60b multi .20 .20
C203 AP71 1.75 l multi .40 .20
C204 AP71 2.75 l blue & multi .55 .20
C205 AP71 3.60 l multi .85 .30
Nos. C200-C205 (6) 2.40 1.30

Romanian Airline, 50th anniversary.

Glider I.C.A.R.-1 — AP72

Gliders: 40b, I.S.-3d. 55b, R.G.-5. 1.50 l, I.S.-11. 3 l, I.S.-29D. 3.40 l, I.S.-28B.

1977, Feb. 20 Photo. *Perf. 13*

C206 AP72 20b multi .20 .20
C207 AP72 40b multi .20 .20
C208 AP72 55b multi .20 .20
C209 AP72 1.50 l bl & multi .25 .20
C210 AP72 3 l multi .60 .20
C211 AP72 3.40 l multi .95 .25
Nos. C206-C211 (6) 2.40 1.25

Souvenir Sheet

Boeing 707 over Bucharest Airport and Pioneers — AP73

1977, June 28 Photo. *Perf. 13½*

C212 AP73 10 l multi 2.50 2.50

European Security and Cooperation Conference, Belgrade.

An imperf. 10 l souvenir sheet exists showing Boeing 707, map of Europe and buildings.

Woman Letter Carrier, Mailbox AP74

30 l, Plane, newspapers, letters, packages.

1977 Photo. *Perf. 13½*

C213 AP74 20 l multicolored 3.00 1.00
C214 AP74 30 l multicolored 4.50 1.50

Issue dates: 20 l, July 25, 30 l, Sept. 10.

LZ-1 over Friedrichshafen, 1900 — AP75

Airships: 1 l, Santos Dumont's dirigible over Paris, 1901. 1.50 l, British R-34 over New York and Statue of Liberty, 1919. 2.15 l, Italia over North Pole, 1928. 3.40 l, Zeppelin LZ-127 over Brasov, 1929. 4.80 l, Zeppelin over Sibiu, 1929. 10 l, Zeppelin over Bucharest, 1929.

1978, Mar. 20 Photo. *Perf. 13½*

C215 AP75 60b multi .20 .20
C216 AP75 1 l multi .20 .20
C217 AP75 1.50 l multi .25 .20
C218 AP75 2.15 l multi .30 .20
C219 AP75 3.40 l multi .55 .20
C220 AP75 4.80 l multi .90 .25
Nos. C215-C220 (6) 2.40 1.25

Souvenir Sheet

C221 AP75 10 l multi 2.25 2.25

History of airships. No. C221 contains one 50x37½mm stamp.

Soccer Type of 1978
Souvenir Sheet

10 l, 2 soccer players, Argentina '78 emblem.

1978, Apr. 15 Photo. *Perf. 13½*

C222 A818 10 l blue & multi 2.25 2.25

11th World Cup Soccer Championship, Argentina, June 1-25. No. C222 contains one stamp 37x50mm. A 10 l imperf souvenir sheet exists showing goalkeeper.

Wilbur and Orville Wright, Flyer A — AP76

Aviation History: 1 l, Louis Blériot and his plane over English Channel, 1909. 1.50 l, Anthony Fokker and Fokker F-VII trimotor, 1926. 2.15 l, Andrei N. Tupolev and ANT-25 monoplane, 1937. 3 l, Otto Lilienthal and glider, 1891-96. 3.40 l, Traian Vuia and his plane, Montesson, France, 1906. 4.80 l, Aurel Vlaicu and 1st Romanian plane, 1910. 10 l, Henri Coanda and his "jet," 1910.

1978, Dec. 18 Photo. *Perf. 13½*

C223 AP76 55b multi .20 .20
C224 AP76 1 l multi .20 .20
C225 AP76 1.50 l multi .20 .20
C226 AP76 2.15 l multi .35 .20
C227 AP76 3 l multi .35 .20
C228 AP76 3.40 l multi .40 .20
C229 AP76 4.80 l multi .45 .20
Nos. C223-C229 (7) 2.15 1.40

Souvenir Sheet

C230 AP76 10 l multi 2.25 2.25

No. C230 contains one stamp 50x38mm.

Inter-Europa Type of 1979

3.40 l, Jet, mail truck and motorcycle.

1979, May 3 Photo. *Perf. 13*

C231 A835 3.40 l multi .40 .40

Animal Type of 1980
Souvenir Sheet

1980, Mar. 25 Photo. *Perf. 13½*

C232 A852 10 l Pelicans 2.25 2.25

No. C232 contains one stamp 38x50mm.

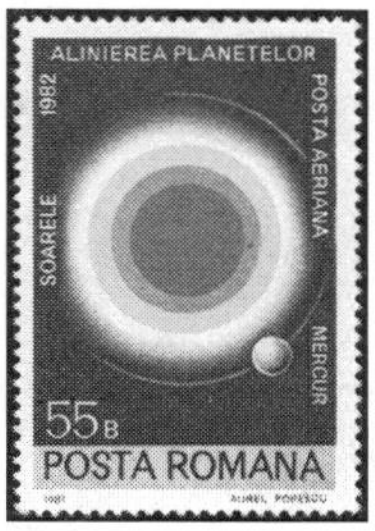

Mercury AP77

1981, June 30 Photo. *Perf. 13½*

C233 AP77 55b shown .20 .20
C234 AP77 1 l Venus, Earth, Mars .20 .20
C235 AP77 1.50 l Jupiter .20 .20
C236 AP77 2.15 l Saturn .20 .20
C237 AP77 3.40 l Uranus .40 .20
C238 AP77 4.80 l Neptune, Pluto .55 .30
Nos. C233-C238 (6) 1.75 1.30

Souvenir Sheet

C239 AP77 10 l Earth 1.75 1.75

No. C239 contains one stamp 37x50mm. An imperf. 10 l souvenir sheet exists showing planets in orbit.

Romanian-Russian Space Cooperation — AP78

1981 Photo. *Perf. 13½*

C240 AP78 55b Soyuz 40 .20 .20
C241 AP78 3.40 l Salyut 6, Soyuz 40 .30 .20

Souvenir Sheet

C242 AP78 10 l Cosmonauts, spacecraft 1.50 1.50

No. C242 contains one stamp 50x39mm.
Issued: 55b, 3.40 l, May 14; 10 l, June 30.

Children's Games Type of 1981

1981, Nov. 25

C243 A880 4.80 l Flying model planes .50 .50

Standard Glider — AP79

1982, June 20 Photo. *Perf. 13½*

C244 AP79 50b shown .20 .20
C245 AP79 1 l Excelsior D .20 .20
C246 AP79 1.50 l Dedal I .20 .20
C247 AP79 2.50 l Enthusiast .30 .20
C248 AP79 4 l AK-22 .40 .25
C249 AP79 5 l Grifrom .55 .30
Nos. C244-C249 (6) 1.85 1.35

Agriculture Type of 1982

1982, June 29

C250 A888 4 l Helicopter spraying insecticide .50 .20

Vlaicu's Glider, 1909 — AP80

Aurel Vlaicu (1882-19), Aviator: 1 l, Memorial, Banesti-Prahova, vert. 2.50 l, Hero Aviators Memorial, by Kotzebue and Fekete, vert. 3 l, Vlaicu-1 glider, 1910.

1982, Sept. 27 Photo. *Perf. 13½*

C251 AP80 50b multi .20 .20
C252 AP80 1 l multi .20 .20
C253 AP80 2.50 l multi .40 .20
C254 AP80 3 l multi .45 .20
Nos. C251-C254 (4) 1.25 .80

25th Anniv. of Space Flight AP81

Designs: 50b, H. Coanda, reaction motor, 1910. 1 l, H. Oberth, rocket, 1923. 1.50 l, Sputnik I, 1957. 2.50 l, Vostok I, 1961. 4 l, Apollo 11, 1969. 5 l, Columbia space shuttle, 1982. 10 l, Globe.

1983, Jan. 24

C255 AP81 50b multi .20 .20
C256 AP81 1 l multi .20 .20
C257 AP81 1.50 l multi .20 .20
C258 AP81 2.50 l multi .35 .20
C259 AP81 4 l multi .50 .20
C260 AP81 5 l multi .65 .25
Nos. C255-C260 (6) 2.10 1.25

Souvenir Sheet

C261 AP81 10 l multi 2.50 2.50

No. C261 contains one stamp 41x53mm.

First Romanian-built Jet Airliner — AP82

1983, Jan. 25 Photo. *Perf. 13½*

C262 AP82 11 l Rombac 1-11 1.50 .20

World Communications Year — AP83

1983, July 25 Photo. *Perf. 13½*

C263 AP83 2 l Boeing 707, Postal van .35 .20

40th Anniv., Intl. Civil Aviation Organization — AP84

1984, Aug. 15 Photo. *Perf. 13½*

C265 AP84 50b Lockheed L-14 .20 .20
C266 AP84 1.50 l BN-2 Islander .25 .20
C267 AP84 3 l Rombac .45 .20
C268 AP84 6 l Boeing 707 .90 .25
Nos. C265-C268 (4) 1.80 .85

Halley's Comet — AP85

1986, Jan. 27 Photo. *Perf. 13½*

C269 AP85 2 l shown .30 .20
C270 AP85 4 l Space probes .60 .30

An imperf. 10 l air post souvenir sheet exists showing comet and space probes, red control number.

Souvenir Sheet

Plane of Alexandru Papana, 1936 — AP86

1986, May 15 Photo. *Perf. 13½*

C271 AP86 10 l multi 2.00 2.00

AMERIPEX '86.

Aircraft
AP87

1987, Aug. 10

C272 AP87 50b Henri Auguste glider, 1909	.20	.20
C273 AP87 1 l Sky diver, IS-28 B2 glider	.20	.20
C274 AP87 2 l IS-29 D-2 glider	.25	.20
C275 AP87 3 l IS-32 glider	.35	.20
C276 AP87 4 l IAR-35 glider	.60	.20
C277 AP87 5 l IS-28 M2, route	.75	.30
Nos. C272-C277 (6)	2.35	1.30

1st Moon Landing, 20th Anniv. — AP88

Designs: 50b, C. Haas. 1.50 l, Konstantin Tsiolkovski (1857-1935), Soviet rocket science pioneer. 2 l, H. Oberth and equations. 3 l, Robert Goddard and diagram on blackboard. 4 l, Sergei Korolev (1906-66), Soviet aeronautical engineer. 5 l, Wernher von Braun (1912-77), lunar module.

1989, Oct. 25 Photo. *Perf. 13½*

C278 AP88 50b multicolored	.20	.20
C279 AP88 1.50 l multicolored	.30	.20
C280 AP88 2 l multicolored	.40	.20
C281 AP88 3 l multicolored	.55	.20
C282 AP88 4 l multicolored	.75	.20
C283 AP88 5 l multicolored	.95	.25
Nos. C278-C283 (6)	3.15	1.25

A 10 l souvenir sheet picturing Armstrong and *Eagle* lunar module was also issued.

Souvenir Sheet

World Stamp Expo '89, Washington, DC, Nov. 17-Dec. 3 — AP89

1989, Nov. 17 Photo. *Perf. 13½*

C284 AP89 5 l Postal coach	1.50	1.50

Captured Balloons — AP90

Balloons captured by Romanian army: 30 l, German balloon, Draken, 1903. 90 l, French balloon, Caquot, 1917.

1993, Feb. 26 Photo. *Perf. 13½*

C285 AP90 30 l multicolored	.20	.20
C286 AP90 90 l multicolored	.70	.20

Souvenir Sheet

European Inventions, Discoveries — AP91

Europa: a, 240 l, Hermann Oberth (1894-1989), rocket scientist. b, 2100 l, Henri Doanda (1886-1972), aeronautical engineer. Illustration reduced.

1994, May 25 Photo. *Perf. 13*

C287 AP91 Sheet of 2, #a.-b. + 2 labels	4.50	4.50

ICAO, 50th Anniv. AP92

Aircraft: 110 l, Traian Vuia, 1906. 350 l, Rombac 1-11. 500 l, Boeing 737-300. 635 l, Airbus A310.

1994. Aug. 12 Photo. *Perf. 13*

C288 AP92 110 l multicolored	.20	.20
C289 AP92 350 l multicolored	.55	.20
C290 AP92 500 l multicolored	.75	.20
C291 AP92 635 l multicolored	1.00	.20
Nos. C288-C291 (4)	2.50	.80

For surcharges see #C294-C297.

French-Romanian Aeronautical Agreement, 75th Anniv. — AP93

1995, Mar. 31 Photo. *Perf. 13x13¼*

C292 AP93 60 l shown	.20	.20
C293 AP93 960 l Biplane Potez IX	1.00	.20

No. C291 Surcharged in Red

Methods and Perfs as Before
2000, May 19

C294 AP92 1700 l on 635 l multi	.20	.20
C295 AP92 2000 l on 635 l multi	.30	.20
C296 AP92 3900 l on 635 l multi	.55	.25
C297 AP92 9050 l on 635 l multi	1.25	.60
Nos. C294-C297 (4)	2.30	1.25

No. C293 Surcharged in Red

2000, Oct. 27 Photo. *Perf. 13¼*

C298 AP93 2000 l on 960 l multi	.20	.20
C299 AP93 4200 l on 960 l multi	.35	.20
C300 AP93 4600 l on 960 l multi	.35	.20
C301 AP93 6500 l on 960 l multi	.55	.25
Nos. C298-C301 (4)	1.45	.85

AIR POST SEMI-POSTAL STAMPS

Catalogue values for unused stamps in this section are for Never Hinged items.

Corneliu Codreanu SPAP1

Unwmk.
1940, Dec. 1 Photo. *Perf. 14*

CB1 SPAP1 20 l + 5 l Prus grn	2.00	1.10

Propaganda for the Rome-Berlin Axis.
No. CB1 exists with overprint "1 Mai 1941 Jamboreea Nationala."

Plane over Sinaia — SPAP2

200 l+800 l, Plane over Mountains.

1945, Oct. 1 Wmk. 276 *Imperf.*

CB2 SPAP2 80 l + 420 l gray	1.00	1.00
CB3 SPAP2 200 l + 800 l ultra	1.00	1.00

16th Congress of the General Assoc. of Romanian Engineers.

Souvenir Sheet

Re-distribution of Land — SPAP4

1946, May 4 Photo. *Perf. 14*

CB4 SPAP4 80 l blue	4.00	*4.50*

Agrarian reform law of Mar. 23, 1945. The sheet sold for 100 lei.

Souvenir Sheet

Plane Skywriting — SPAP5

1946, May 1 *Perf. 13*

CB5 SPAP5 200 l bl & brt red	5.00	*5.50*

Labor Day. The sheet sold for 10,000 lei.

Lockheed 12 Electra — SPAP6

1946, Sept. 1 *Perf. 11½*

CB6 SPAP6 300 l + 1200 l dp bl	1.00	*1.25*

For se-tenant see No. C26a and note after No. C26.
The surtax was for the Office of Popular Sports.

Miniature Sheet

Women of Wallachia, Transylvania and Moldavia — SPAP7

1946, Dec. 20 Wmk. 276 *Imperf.*

CB7 SPAP7 500 l + 9500 l choc & red	1.90	2.25

Democratic Women's Org. of Romania.

SPAP8

1946, Oct. *Imperf.*

CB8 SPAP8 300 l deep plum	6.00	*7.00*

The surtax was for the Office of Popular Sports. Sheets of four. Stamp sold for 1300 l.

Laborer with Torch — SPAP9

1947, Mar. 1

CB9 SPAP9 3000 l + 7000 l choc	.50	.50

Sheets of four with marginal inscription.

Plane SPAP10

Plane above Shore Line SPAP11

1947, June 27 *Imperf.*

CB10	SPAP10	15,000 l + 15,000 l	.50	.50

Sheets of four with marginal inscription.

1947, May 1 *Perf. 14x13*

CB11	SPAP11	3000 l + 12,000 l bl	.30	.30

Planes over Mountains SPAP12

Plane over Athletic Field SPAP13

1947, Oct. 5 *Perf. 14x14½*

CB12	SPAP12	5 l + 5 l blue	.40	.40

17th Congress of the General Assoc. of Romanian Engineers.

Wmk. 276

1948, Feb. 20 **Photo.** *Perf. 13½*

CB13	SPAP13	7 l + 7 l vio	1.00	.60
		Imperf		
CB14	SPAP13	10 l + 10 l Prus grn	1.40	.90

Balkan Games. Sheets of four with marginal inscription.

Swallow and Plane SPAP14

1948, Mar. 15 *Perf. 14x13½*

CB15	SPAP14	12 l + 12 l blue	.90	.50

Bucharest-Moscow Passenger Plane, Douglas DC-3 Dakota — SPAP15

1948, Oct. 29 *Perf. 14*

CB16	SPAP15	20 l + 20 l dp bl	7.50	7.50

Printed in sheets of 8 stamps and 16 small, red brown labels. Sheet yields 8 triptychs, each comprising 1 stamp flanked by label with Bucharest view and label with Moscow view.

Douglas DC-4 — SPAP16

1948, May 1 *Perf. 13½x14*

CB17	SPAP16	20 l + 20 l blue	6.75	5.75

Issued to publicize Labor Day, May 1, 1948.

Pursuit Plane and Victim SPAP17

Launching Model Plane SPAP18

1948, May 9 *Perf. 13*

CB18	SPAP17	3 l + 3 l shown	4.25	4.25
CB19	SPAP17	5 l + 5 l Bomber	6.25	6.25

Issued to honor the Romanian army.

1948, Dec. 31 *Perf. 13x13½*

CB20	SPAP18	20 l + 20 l dp ultra	11.00	11.00
		Imperf		
CB21	SPAP18	20 l + 20 l Prus bl	11.00	11.00

Nos. CB20 and CB21 were issued in sheets of four stamps, with ornamental border and "1948" in contrasting color.

UPU Type of Air Post Issue, 1963

Design: 1.60 l+50b, Globe, map of Romania, planes and UPU monument.

Perf. 14x13½

1963, Nov. 15 **Litho.** **Unwmk.**

Size: 75x27mm

CB22	AP54	1.60 l + 50b multi	1.00	.50

Surtax for the Romanian Philatelic Federation.

POSTAGE DUE STAMPS

D1

Perf. 11, 11½, 13½ and Compound

1881 **Typo.** **Unwmk.**

J1	D1	2b brown	4.00	1.25
J2	D1	5b brown	22.50	2.00
a.		Tête bêche pair	*190.00*	*75.00*
J3	D1	10b brown	30.00	1.25
J4	D1	30b brown	32.50	1.25
J5	D1	50b brown	26.00	2.50
J6	D1	60b brown	21.00	3.00
		Nos. J1-J6 (6)	136.00	11.25

1885

J7	D1	10b pale red brown	8.00	.50
J8	D1	30b pale red brown	8.00	.50

1887-90

J9	D1	2b gray green	4.00	.75
J10	D1	5b gray green	8.00	3.00
J11	D1	10b gray green	8.00	3.00
J12	D1	30b gray green	8.00	.75
		Nos. J9-J12 (4)	28.00	7.50

1888

J14	D1	2b green, *yellowish*	.90	.75
J15	D1	5b green, *yellowish*	2.25	2.25
J16	D1	10b green, *yellowish*	32.50	2.75
J17	D1	30b green, *yellowish*	17.50	1.25
		Nos. J14-J17 (4)	53.15	7.00

1890-96 **Wmk. 163**

J18	D1	2b emerald	1.60	.45
J19	D1	5b emerald	.80	.45
J20	D1	10b emerald	1.25	.45
J21	D1	30b emerald	2.00	.45
J22	D1	50b emerald	6.50	.95
J23	D1	60b emerald	8.75	3.25
		Nos. J18-J23 (6)	20.90	6.00

1898 **Wmk. 200**

J24	D1	2b blue green	.70	.45
J25	D1	5b blue green	.90	.30
J26	D1	10b blue green	1.40	.30
J27	D1	30b blue green	1.90	.30
J28	D1	50b blue green	4.75	.90
J29	D1	60b blue green	5.50	1.75
		Nos. J24-J29 (6)	15.15	4.00

1902-10 **Unwmk.**

Thin Paper, Tinted Rose on Back

J30	D1	2b green	.85	.25
J31	D1	5b green	.50	.20
J32	D1	10b green	.40	.20
J33	D1	30b green	.50	.20
J34	D1	50b green	2.50	.90
J35	D1	60b green	5.25	2.25
		Nos. J30-J35 (6)	10.00	4.00

1908-11

White Paper

J36	D1	2b green	.80	.50
J37	D1	5b green	.60	.50
a.		Tête bêche pair	12.00	12.00
J38	D1	10b green	.40	.30
a.		Tête bêche pair	12.00	12.00
J39	D1	30b green	.50	.30
a.		Tête bêche pair	12.00	12.00
J40	D1	50b green	2.00	1.25
		Nos. J36-J40 (5)	4.30	2.85

D2

1911 **Wmk. 165**

J41	D2	2b dark blue, *green*	.20	.20
J42	D2	5b dark blue, *green*	.20	.20
J43	D2	10b dark blue, *green*	.20	.20
J44	D2	15b dark blue, *green*	.20	.20
J45	D2	20b dark blue, *green*	.20	.20
J46	D2	30b dark blue, *green*	.25	.25
J47	D2	50b dark blue, *green*	.30	.30
J48	D2	60b dark blue, *green*	.40	.40
J49	D2	2 l dark blue, *green*	.80	.80
		Nos. J41-J49 (9)	2.75	2.75

The letters "P.R." appear to be embossed instead of watermarked. They are often faint or entirely invisible.

The 20b, type D2, has two types, differing in the width of the head of the "2." This affects Nos. J45, J54, J58, and J63.

See Nos. J52-J77, J82, J87-J88. For overprints see Nos. J78-J81, RAJ1-RAJ2, RAJ20-RAJ21, 3NJ1-3NJ7.

Regular Issue of 1908 Overprinted

TAXA
DE PLATA

1918 **Unwmk.**

J50	A46	5b yellow green	.75	.25
a.		Inverted overprint	5.00	5.00
J51	A46	10b rose	.75	.25
a.		Inverted overprint	3.75	3.75

Postage Due Type of 1911

1920 **Wmk. 165**

J52	D2	5b black, *green*	.20	.20
J53	D2	10b black, *green*	.20	.20
J54	D2	20b black, *green*	4.00	.60
J55	D2	30b black, *green*	1.10	.40
J55A	D2	50b black, *green*	3.00	.90
		Nos. J52-J55A (5)	8.50	2.30

Perf. 11½, 13½ and Compound

1919 **Unwmk.**

J56	D2	5b black, *green*	.30	.20
J57	D2	10b black, *green*	.30	.20
J58	D2	20b black, *green*	1.00	.20
J59	D2	30b black, *green*	.90	.20
J60	D2	50b black, *green*	2.25	.40
		Nos. J56-J60 (5)	4.75	1.20

1920-26

White Paper

J61	D2	5b black	.20	.20
J62	D2	10b black	.20	.20
J63	D2	20b black	.20	.20
J64	D2	30b black	.25	.25
J65	D2	50b black	.40	.40
J66	D2	60b black	.20	.20
J67	D2	1 l black	.30	.30
J68	D2	2 l black	.20	.20
J69	D2	3 l black ('26)	.20	.20
J70	D2	6 l black ('26)	.30	.30
		Nos. J61-J70 (10)	2.45	2.45

1923-24

J74	D2	1 l black, *pale green*	.25	.20
J75	D2	2 l black, *pale green*	.45	.25
J76	D2	3 l black, *pale green* ('24)	1.10	.55
J77	D2	6 l blk, *pale green* ('24)	1.40	.55
		Nos. J74-J77 (4)	3.20	1.55

Postage Due Stamps of 1920-26 Overprinted

8 IUNIE 1930

1930 *Perf. 13½*

J78	D2	1 l black	.20	.20
J79	D2	2 l black	.20	.20
J80	D2	3 l black	.30	.20
J81	D2	6 l black	.45	.25
		Nos. J78-J81 (4)	1.15	.85

Accession of King Carol II.

Catalogue values for unused stamps in this section, from this point to the end of the section, are for Never Hinged items.

Type of 1911 Issue

1931 **Wmk. 225**

J82	D2	2 l black	.70	.35

D3

1932-37 **Wmk. 230**

J83	D3	1 l black	.20	.20
J84	D3	2 l black	.20	.20
J85	D3	3 l black ('37)	.20	.20
J86	D3	6 l black ('37)	.20	.20
		Nos. J83-J86 (4)	.80	.80

See Nos. J89-J98.

Type of 1911

1942 **Typo.** *Perf. 13½*

J87	D2	50 l black	.25	.20
J88	D2	100 l black	.40	.25

Type of 1932

1946-47 **Unwmk.** *Perf. 14*

J89	D3	20 l black	.60	.55
J90	D3	100 l black ('47)	.45	.25
J91	D3	200 l black	1.10	.55
		Nos. J89-J91 (3)	2.15	1.35

1946-47 **Wmk. 276**

J92	D3	20 l black	.20	.20
J93	D3	50 l black	.20	.20
J94	D3	80 l black	.20	.20
J95	D3	100 l black	.25	.20
J96	D3	200 l black	.45	.35
J97	D3	500 l black	.60	.50
J98	D3	5000 l black ('47)	2.50	1.25
		Nos. J92-J98 (7)	4.40	2.90

Crown and King Michael - D3a

Perf. 14½x13½

1947 **Typo.** **Wmk. 276**

J98A	D3a	2 l carmine	.40	.20
J98B	D3a	4 l gray blue	.75	.30
J98C	D3a	5 l black	1.10	.45
J98D	D3a	10 l violet brown	2.00	.75
		Nos. J98A-J98D (4)	4.25	1.70

Same Overprinted

R.P.R.

1948

J98E	D3a	2 l carmine	.30	.20
J98F	D3a	4 l gray blue	.60	.25
J98G	D3a	5 l black	.75	.30
J98H	D3a	10 l violet brown	1.50	.55
		Nos. J98E-J98H (4)	3.15	1.30

In use, Nos. J98A-J106 and following issues were torn apart, one half being affixed to the postage due item and the other half being pasted into the postman's record book. Values are for unused and canceled-to-order pairs.

Communications Badge and Postwoman — D4

1950 Unwmk. Photo. *Perf. 14½x14*
J99 D4 2 l orange vermilion .70 .70
J100 D4 4 l deep blue .70 .70
J101 D4 5 l dark gray green .90 .90
J102 D4 10 l orange brown 1.10 1.10

Wmk. 358
J103 D4 2 l orange vermilion 1.00 .70
J104 D4 4 l deep blue 1.00 .75
J105 D4 5 l dark gray green 1.50 .90
J106 D4 10 l orange brown 2.00 1.25
Nos. J99-J106 (8) 8.90 7.00

Postage Due Stamps of 1950 Surcharged with New Values in Black or Carmine

1952 Unwmk.
J107 D4 4b on 2 l .25 .25
J108 D4 10b on 4 l (C) .25 .25
J109 D4 20b on 5 l (C) .45 .45
J110 D4 50b on 10 l .75 .75
Nos. J107-J110 (4) 1.70 1.70

Wmk. 358
J111 D4 4b on 2 l
J112 D4 10b on 4 l (C)
J113 D4 20b on 5 l (C) *2.50 1.25*
J114 D4 50b on 10 l *3.00 1.25*

The existence of Nos. J111-J112 has been questioned.
See note after No. J98H.

General Post Office and Post Horn — D5

1957 Wmk. 358 *Perf. 14*
J115 D5 3b black .20 .20
J116 D5 5b red orange .20 .20
J117 D5 10b red lilac .20 .20
J118 D5 20b brt red .20 .20
J119 D5 40b lt bl grn .35 .20
J120 D5 1 l brt ultra 1.00 .20
Nos. J115-J120 (6) 2.15 1.20

See note after No. J98H.

General Post Office and Post Horn — D6

1967, Feb. 25 Photo. *Perf. 13*
J121 D6 3b brt grn .20 .20
J122 D6 5b brt bl .20 .20
J123 D6 10b lilac rose .20 .20
J124 D6 20b vermilion .20 .20
J125 D6 40b brown .20 .20
J126 D6 1 l violet .55 .20
Nos. J121-J126 (6) 1.55 1.20

See note after No. J98H.

1970, Mar. 10 Unwmk.
J127 D6 3b brt grn .20 .20
J128 D6 5b brt bl .20 .20
J129 D6 10b lilac rose .20 .20
J130 D6 20b vermilion .20 .20
J131 D6 40b brown .20 .20
J132 D6 1 l violet .35 .20
Nos. J127-J132 (6) 1.35 1.20

See note after No. J98H.

Symbols of Communications — D7

Designs: 10b, Like 5b. 20b, 40b, Pigeons, head of Mercury and post horn. 50b, 1 l, General Post Office, post horn and truck.

1974, Jan. 1 Photo. *Perf. 13*
J133 D7 5b brt bl .20 .20
J134 D7 10b olive .20 .20
J135 D7 20b lilac rose .20 .20
J136 D7 40b purple .20 .20
J137 D7 50b brown .20 .20
J138 D7 1 l orange .35 .20
Nos. J133-J138 (6) 1.35 1.20

See note after No. J98H.
See #J139-J144. For surcharges see #J147-J151.

1982, Dec. 23 Photo. *Perf. 13½*
J139 D7 25b like #J135 .20 .20
J140 D7 50b like #J133 .20 .20
J141 D7 1 l like #J135 .20 .20
J142 D7 2 l like #J137 .35 .20
J143 D7 3 l like #J133 .50 .20
J144 D7 4 l like #J137 .70 .20
Nos. J139-J144 (6) 2.15 1.20

See note after No. J98H.

Post Horn — D8

1992, Feb. 3 Photo. *Perf. 13½*
J145 D8 4 l red .25 .20
J146 D8 8 l blue .50 .20

See note after No. J98H.

L50

Nos. J140-J142, J144 Surcharged in Green, Deep Blue, or Black

1999, Mar. 12 Photo. *Perf. 13½*
J147 D7 50 l on 50b #J140 (G) .20 .20
J148 D7 50 l on 1 l #J141 (DBl) .20 .20
J149 D7 100 l on 2 l #J142 .20 .20
J150 D7 700 l on 1 l #J141 .30 .20
J151 D7 1100 l on 4 l #J144 .45 .25
Nos. J147-J151 (5) 1.35 1.05

OFFICIAL STAMPS

Catalogue values for unused stamps in this section are for Never Hinged items.

Eagle Carrying National Emblem O1

Coat of Arms O2

1929 Photo. Wmk. 95 *Perf. 13½*
O1 O1 25b red orange .25 .20
O2 O1 50b dk brown .25 .20
O3 O1 1 l dk violet .30 .20
O4 O1 2 l olive grn .30 .20
O5 O1 3 l rose car .45 .20
O6 O1 4 l dk olive .45 .20
O7 O1 6 l Prus blue 2.50 .20
O8 O1 10 l deep blue .80 .20
O9 O1 25 l carmine brn 1.60 1.25
O10 O1 50 l purple 4.75 3.50
Nos. O1-O10 (10) 11.65 6.35

Type of Official Stamps of 1929 Overprinted **8 IUNIE 1930**

1930 Unwmk.
O11 O1 25b red orange .20 .20
O12 O1 50b dk brown .20 .20
O13 O1 1 l dk violet .35 .20
O14 O1 3 l rose carmine .50 .20
Nos. O11-O14 (4) 1.25 .80

Nos. O11-O14 were not placed in use without overprint.

Same Overprint on Nos. O1-O10
Wmk. 95
O15 O1 25b red orange .25 .20
O16 O1 50b dk brown .25 .20
O17 O1 1 l dk violet .25 .20
O18 O1 2 l dp green .25 .20
O19 O1 3 l rose carmine .60 .20
O20 O1 4 l olive black .75 .20
O21 O1 6 l Prus blue 2.00 .20
O22 O1 10 l deep blue .80 .20
O23 O1 25 l carmine brown 3.00 2.50
O24 O1 50 l purple 4.00 3.50
Nos. O15-O24 (10) 12.15 7.60

Accession of King Carol II to the throne of Romania (Nos O11-O24).

Perf. 13½, 13½x14½

1931-32 Typo. Wmk. 225
O25 O2 25b black .30 .20
O26 O2 1 l lilac .30 .20
O27 O2 2 l emerald .60 .40
O28 O2 3 l rose 1.00 .70
Nos. O25-O28 (4) 2.20 1.50

1932 Wmk. 230 *Perf. 13½*
O29 O2 25b black .30 .25
O30 O2 1 l violet .40 .35
O31 O2 2 l emerald .65 .55
O32 O2 3 l rose .80 .65
O33 O2 6 l red brown 1.25 1.00
Nos. O29-O33 (5) 3.40 2.80

PARCEL POST STAMPS

PP1

Perf. 11½, 13½ and Compound
1895 Wmk. 163 Typo.
Q1 PP1 25b brown red 12.50 2.25

1896
Q2 PP1 25b vermilion 10.00 1.25

Perf. 13½ and 11½x13½
1898 Wmk. 200
Q3 PP1 25b brown red 7.00 1.25
a. Tête bêche pair
Q4 PP1 25b vermilion 7.00 .90

Thin Paper
Tinted Rose on Back

1905 Unwmk. *Perf. 11½*
Q5 PP1 25b vermilion 6.00 1.25

1911 White Paper
Q6 PP1 25b pale red 6.00 1.25

No. 263 Surcharged in Carmine

1928 *Perf. 13½*
Q7 A54 5 l on 10b yellow green .90 .20

POSTAL TAX STAMPS

Regular Issue of 1908 Overprinted **TIMBRU DE AJUTOR**

Perf. 11½, 13½, 11½x13½
1915 Unwmk.
RA1 A46 5b green .20 .20
RA2 A46 10b rose .30 .20

The "Timbru de Ajutor" stamps represent a tax on postal matter. The money obtained from their sale was turned into a fund for the assistance of soldiers' families.

Until 1923 the only "Timbru de Ajutor" stamps used for postal purposes were the 5b and 10b. Stamps of higher values with this inscription were used to pay the taxes on railway and theater tickets and other fiscal taxes. In 1923 the postal rate was advanced to 25b.

The Queen Weaving — PT1

1916-18 Typo.
RA3 PT1 5b gray blk .20 .20
RA4 PT1 5b green ('18) .45 .20
RA5 PT1 10b brown .30 .20
RA6 PT1 10b gray blk ('18) .45 .20
Nos. RA3-RA6 (4) 1.40 .80

For overprints see Nos. RA7-RA8, RAJ7-RAJ9, 3NRA1-3NRA8.

Stamps of 1916 Overprinted in Red or Black **1918**

1918 *Perf. 13½*
RA7 PT1 5b gray blk (R) .40 .25
a. Double overprint 5.00
c. Black overprint 5.00
RA8 PT1 10b brn (Bk) .45 .25
a. Double overprint 5.00
b. Double overprint, one inverted 5.00
c. Inverted overprint 5.00

Same Overprint on RA1 and RA2

1919
RA11 A46 5b yel grn (R) *19.00 12.50*
RA12 A46 10b rose (Bk) *19.00 12.50*

Charity — PT3

Perf. 13½, 11½, 13½x11½
1921-24 Typo. Unwmk.
RA13 PT3 10b green .20 .20
RA14 PT3 25b blk ('24) .20 .20

Type of 1921-24 Issue

1928 Wmk. 95
RA15 PT3 25b black .75 .25

Nos. RA13, RA14 and RA15 are the only stamps of type PT3 issued for postal purposes. Other denominations were used fiscally.

Catalogue values for unused stamps in this section, from this point to the end of the section, are for Never Hinged items.

Airplane PT4

Head of Aviator PT5

1931 Photo. Unwmk.
RA16 PT4 50b Prus bl .30 .20
a. Double impression 15.00
RA17 PT4 1 l dk red brn .30 .20
RA18 PT4 2 l ultra .60 .20
Nos. RA16-RA18 (3) 1.20 .60

The use of these stamps, in addition to the regular postage, was obligatory on all postal matter for the interior of the country. The money thus obtained was to augment the National Fund for Aviation. When the stamps were not used to prepay the special tax, it was collected by means of Postal Tax Due stamps Nos. RAJ20 and RAJ21.

Nos. RA17 and RA18 were also used for other than postal tax.

1932 Wmk. 230 *Perf. 14 x 13½*
RA19 PT5 50b Prus bl .20 .20
RA20 PT5 1 l red brn .35 .20
RA21 PT5 2 l ultra .45 .20
Nos. RA19-RA21 (3) 1.00 .60

See notes after No. RA18.
After 1937 use of Nos. RA20-RA21 was limited to other than postal matter.
Nos. RA19-RA21 exist imperf.
Two stamps similar to type PT5, but inscribed "Fondul Aviatiei," were issued in 1936: 10b sepia and 20b violet.

Aviator PT6

King Michael PT7

1937 *Perf. 13½*

RA22	PT6	50b Prus grn	.20	.20
RA23	PT6	1 l red brn	.35	.20
RA24	PT6	2 l ultra	.45	.20
		Nos. RA22-RA24 (3)	1.00	.60

Stamps overprinted or inscribed "Fondul Aviatiei" other than Nos. RA22, RA23 or RA24 were used to pay taxes on other than postal matters.

1943 Wmk. 276 Photo. *Perf. 14*

RA25	PT7	50b org ver	.20	.20
RA26	PT7	1 l lil rose	.20	.20
RA27	PT7	2 l brown	.20	.20
RA28	PT7	4 l lt ultra	.20	.20
RA29	PT7	5 l dull lilac	.20	.20
RA30	PT7	8 l yel grn	.20	.20
RA31	PT7	10 l blk brn	.20	.20
		Nos. RA25-RA31 (7)	1.40	1.40

The tax was obligatory on domestic mail.

Examples of these stamps with an overprint consisting of a red cross and text are unissued franchise stamps.

Protection of Homeless Children — PT8

1945

RA32	PT8	40 l Prus bl	.25	.20

PT9

"Hope" — PT10

1947 Unwmk. Typo. *Perf. 14x14½*

Black Surcharge

RA33	PT9	1 l on 2 l + 2 l pink	.30	.25
a.		Inverted surcharge	37.50	
RA34	PT9	5 l on 1 l + 1 l gray grn	*4.50*	*3.75*

1948 *Perf. 14*

RA35	PT10	1 l rose	*1.90*	.20
RA36	PT10	1 l rose violet	*2.10*	.20

A 2 lei blue and 5 lei ocher in type PT10 were issued primarily for revenue purposes.

POSTAL TAX DUE STAMPS

Catalogue values for unused stamps in this section are for Never Hinged items.

Postage Due Stamps of 1911 Overprinted — TIMBRU DE AJUTOR

Perf. 11½, 13½, 11½x13½

1915 **Unwmk.**

RAJ1	D2	5b dk bl, *grn*	.75	.20
RAJ2	D2	10b dk bl, *grn*	.75	.20
a.		Wmk. 165	10.00	1.00

PTD1

PTD2

1916 Typo. Unwmk.

RAJ3	PTD1	5b brn, *grn*	.40	.20
RAJ4	PTD1	10b red, *grn*	.40	.20

See Nos. RAJ5-RAJ6, RAJ10-RAJ11. For overprint see No. 3NRAJ1.

1918

RAJ5	PTD1	5b red, *grn*	.25	.20
a.		Wmk. 165	1.00	.25
RAJ6	PTD1	10b brn, *grn*	.25	.20
a.		Wmk. 165	1.75	.25

Postal Tax Stamps of 1916, Overprinted in Red, Black or Blue — TAXA DE PLATA

RAJ7	PT1	5b gray blk (R)	.40	.20
a.		Inverted overprint	7.50	
RAJ8	PT1	10b brn (Bk)	.80	.20
a.		Inverted overprint	7.50	
RAJ9	PT1	10b brn (Bl)	*5.00*	*5.00*
a.		Vertical overprint	*20.00*	*15.00*
		Nos. RAJ7-RAJ9 (3)	6.20	5.40

Type of 1916

1921

RAJ10	PTD1	5b red	.50	.20
RAJ11	PTD1	10b brown	.50	.20

1922-25 **Typo.**

Greenish Paper

RAJ12	PTD2	10b brown	.20	.20
RAJ13	PTD2	20b brown	.20	.20
RAJ14	PTD2	25b brown	.20	.20
RAJ15	PTD2	50b brown	.20	.20
		Nos. RAJ12-RAJ15 (4)	.80	.80

1923-26

RAJ16	PTD2	10b lt brn	.20	.20
RAJ17	PTD2	20b lt brn	.20	.20
RAJ18	PTD2	25b brown ('26)	.20	.20
RAJ19	PTD2	50b brown ('26)	.20	.20
		Nos. RAJ16-RAJ19 (4)	.80	.80

J82 and Type of 1911 Postage Due Stamps Overprinted in Red — TIMBRUL AVIATIEI

1931 Wmk. 225 *Perf. 13½*

RAJ20	D2	1 l black	.20	.20
RAJ21	D2	2 l black	.20	.20

When the Postal Tax stamps for the Aviation Fund issue (Nos. RA16 to RA18) were not used to prepay the obligatory tax on letters, etc., it was collected by affixing Nos. RAJ20 and RAJ21.

OCCUPATION STAMPS

ISSUED UNDER AUSTRIAN OCCUPATION

Emperor Karl of Austria
OS1 OS2

1917 Unwmk. Engr. *Perf. 12½*

1N1	OS1	3b ol gray	1.10	.75
1N2	OS1	5b ol grn	.80	.50
1N3	OS1	6b violet	.80	.50
1N4	OS1	10b org brn	.20	.20
1N5	OS1	12b dp bl	1.00	.60
1N6	OS1	15b brt rose	.80	.50
1N7	OS1	20b red brn	.20	.20
1N8	OS1	25b ultra	.20	.20
1N9	OS1	30b slate	.30	.25
1N10	OS1	40b olive bis	.30	.25
a.		Perf. 11½	40.00	19.00
b.		Perf. 11½x12½	45.00	20.00
1N11	OS1	50b dp grn	.30	.25
1N12	OS1	60b rose	.30	.25
1N13	OS1	80b dl bl	.20	.20
1N14	OS1	90b dk vio	.30	.25
1N15	OS2	2 l rose, *straw*	.45	.30
1N16	OS2	3 l grn, *bl*	.75	.40
1N17	OS2	4 l rose, *grn*	.75	.40
		Nos. 1N1-1N17 (17)	8.75	6.00

Nos. 1N1-1N14 have "BANI" surcharged in red.

Nos. 1N1-1N17 also exist imperforate. Value, set $20.

For overprints see Austria Nos. M51-M64 with "BANI" in red; Nos. M65-M67 for "LEI" in black.

OS3

OS4

1918

1N18	OS3	3b ol gray	.20	.20
1N19	OS3	5b ol grn	.20	.20
1N20	OS3	6b violet	.25	.25
1N21	OS3	10b org brn	.25	.25
1N22	OS3	12b dp bl	.20	.20
1N23	OS3	15b brt rose	.20	.20
1N24	OS3	20b red brn	.20	.20
1N25	OS3	25b ultra	.20	.20
1N26	OS3	30b slate	.20	.20
1N27	OS3	40b ol bis	.20	.20
1N28	OS3	50b dp grn	.25	.25
1N29	OS3	60b rose	.25	.25
1N30	OS3	80b dl bl	.20	.20
1N31	OS3	90b dk vio	.20	.20
1N32	OS4	2 l rose, *straw*	.25	.25
1N33	OS4	3 l grn, *bl*	.30	.30
1N34	OS4	4 l rose, *grn*	.30	.30
		Nos. 1N18-1N34 (17)	3.85	3.85

Exist. imperf. Value, set $17.50.

The complete series exists with "BANI" or "LEI" inverted, also with those words and the numerals of value inverted. Neither of these sets was regularly issued.

A set of 13 stamps similar to Austria Nos. M69-M81 was prepared for use in Romania in 1918, but not placed in use there. Denominations are in bani. It is reported that they were on sale after the armistice at the Vienna post office for a few days. Value $850.

ISSUED UNDER BULGARIAN OCCUPATION

Dobruja District

Bulgarian Stamps of 1915-16 Overprinted in Red or Blue — Пощавъ Ромѫния 1916—1917

1916 Unwmk. *Perf. 11½, 14*

2N1	A20	1s dk blue grn (R)	.20	.20
2N2	A23	5s grn & vio brn (R)	1.75	.40
2N3	A24	10s brn & brnsh blk (Bl)	.25	.20
2N4	A26	25s indigo & blk (Bl)	.25	.20
		Nos. 2N1-2N4 (4)	2.45	1.00

Many varieties of overprint exist.

ISSUED UNDER GERMAN OCCUPATION

German Stamps of 1905-17 Surcharged — M.V.i.R. (Red or Black) 15 Bani (Black)

1917 Wmk. 125 *Perf. 14*

3N1	A22	15b on 15pf dk vio (R)	1.00	1.00
3N2	A16	25b on 20pf ultra (Bk)	1.00	1.00
3N3	A16	40b on 30pf org & blk, *buff* (R)	17.50	17.50
		Nos. 3N1-3N3 (3)	19.50	19.50

"M.V.iR." are the initials of "Militär Verwaltung in Rumänien" (Military Administration of Romania).

German Stamps of 1905-17 Surcharged — M.V.i.R. 25 Bani

1917-18

3N4	A16	10b on 10pf car	.55	.55
3N5	A22	15b on 15pf dk vio	4.50	4.50
3N6	A16	25b on 20pf ultra	.75	.75
3N7	A16	40b on 30pf org & blk, *buff*	1.00	1.00
a.		"40" omitted	50.00	67.50
		Nos. 3N4-3N7 (4)	6.80	6.80

German Stamps of 1905-17 Surcharged — Rumänien 25 Bani

1918

3N8	A16	5b on 5pf grn	.20	.20
3N9	A16	10b on 10pf car	.20	.20
3N10	A22	15b on 15pf dk vio	.20	.20
3N11	A16	25b on 20pf bl vio	.20	.20
a.		25b on 20pf blue	1.50	1.50
3N12	A16	40b on 30pf org & blk, *buff*	.30	.30
		Nos. 3N8-3N12 (5)	1.10	1.10

German Stamps of 1905-17 Overprinted — Gültig 9. Armee

1918

3N13	A16	10pf carmine	7.50	*10.00*
3N14	A22	15pf dk vio	12.50	*15.00*
3N15	A16	20pf blue	1.25	*1.50*
3N16	A16	30pf org & blk, *buff*	10.00	*12.50*
		Nos. 3N13-3N16 (4)	31.25	*39.00*

POSTAGE DUE STAMPS ISSUED UNDER GERMAN OCCUPATION

Postage Due Stamps and Type of Romania Overprinted in Red — M.V.i.R.

Perf. 11½, 13½ and Compound

1918 **Wmk. 165**

3NJ1	D2	5b dk bl, *grn*	19.00	24.00
3NJ2	D2	10b dk bl, *grn*	26.00	30.00

The 20b, 30b and 50b with this overprint are fraudulent.

Unwmk.

3NJ3	D2	5b dk bl, *grn*	2.50	2.25
3NJ4	D2	10b dk bl, *grn*	2.50	2.25
3NJ5	D2	20b dk bl, *grn*	2.50	2.25
3NJ6	D2	30b dk bl, *grn*	2.50	2.25
3NJ7	D2	50b dk bl, *grn*	2.50	2.25
		Nos. 3NJ1-3NJ7 (7)	57.50	65.25

POSTAL TAX STAMPS ISSUED UNDER GERMAN OCCUPATION

Romanian Postal Tax Stamps and Type of 1916

Overprinted in Red or Black — M.V.i.R.

Perf. 11½, 13½ and Compound

1917 **Unwmk.**

3NRA1	PT1	5b gray blk (R)	.20	.20
3NRA2	PT1	10b brown (Bk)	.20	.20

Same, Overprinted — M.V.i.R.

1917-18

3NRA3	PT1	5b gray blk (R)	.40	.20
a.		Black overprint	5.00	5.00
3NRA4	PT1	10b brown (Bk)	.40	.20
3NRA5	PT1	10b violet (Bk)	.35	.20
		Nos. 3NRA3-3NRA5 (3)	1.15	.60

Same, Overprinted in Red or Black — M.V.i.R.

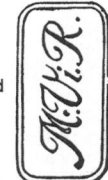

1918

3NRA6	PT1	5b gray blk (R)	*20.00*	
3NRA7	PT1	10b brown (Bk)	*20.00*	

Same, Overprinted **Gültig 9. Armee**

1918

3NRA8	PT1	10b violet (Bk)	.20	.20

POSTAL TAX DUE STAMP ISSUED UNDER GERMAN OCCUPATION

Type of Romanian Postal Tax Due Stamp of 1916 Overprinted **M.V.i.R.**

Perf. 11½, 13½, and Compound

1918 **Wmk. 165**

3NRAJ1	PTD1	10b red, *green*	2.00	2.50

ROMANIAN POST OFFICES IN THE TURKISH EMPIRE

40 Paras = 1 Piaster

King Carol I
A1 A2

Perf. 11½, 13½ and Compound

1896 **Wmk. 200**

Black Surcharge

1	A1	10pa on 5b blue	32.50	30.00
2	A2	20pa on 10b emer	24.00	22.50
3	A1	1pia on 25b violet	24.00	22.50
		Nos. 1-3 (3)	80.50	75.00

Violet Surcharge

4	A1	10pa on 5b blue	17.00	15.00
5	A2	20pa on 10b emer	17.00	15.00
6	A1	1pia on 25b violet	17.00	15.00
		Nos. 4-6 (3)	51.00	45.00

Romanian Stamps of 1908-18 Overprinted in Black or Red

1919 **Typo.** **Unwmk.**

7	A46	5b yellow grn	.40	.40
8	A46	10b rose	.55	.55
9	A46	15b red brown	.55	.55
10	A19	25b dp blue (R)	.70	.70
11	A19	40b gray brn (R)	1.40	1.40
		Nos. 7-11 (5)	3.60	3.60

All values exist with inverted overprint.

ROMANIAN POST OFFICES IN THE TURKISH EMPIRE POSTAL TAX STAMP

Romanian Postal Tax Stamp of 1918 Overprinted

1919 Unwmk. ***Perf. 11½, 11½x13½***

RA1	PT1	5b green	1.25	1.25

ROUAD, ILE

ēl-ru-ad

(Arwad)

LOCATION — An island in the Mediterranean, off the coast of Latakia, Syria
GOVT. — French Mandate

In 1916, while a French post office was maintained on Ile Rouad, stamps were issued by France.

25 Centimes = 1 Piaster

Stamps of French Offices in the Levant, 1902-06, Overprinted

ILE ROUAD

Perf. 14x13½

1916, Jan. 12 **Unwmk.**

1	A2	5c green	325.00	175.00
2	A3	10c rose red	325.00	175.00
3	A5	1pi on 25c blue	325.00	175.00

Dangerous counterfeits exist.

Stamps of French Offices in the Levant, 1902-06, Overprinted Horizontally **ILE ROUAD**

1916, Dec.

4	A2	1c gray	.70	.70
5	A2	2c violet brown	.70	.70
6	A2	3c red orange	.70	.70
a.		Double overprint	75.00	75.00
7	A2	5c green	1.00	1.00
8	A3	10c rose	1.10	1.10
9	A3	15c pale red	1.10	1.10
10	A3	20c brown violet	1.90	1.90
11	A5	1pi on 25c blue	1.40	1.40
12	A3	30c violet	1.40	1.40
13	A4	40c red & pale bl	2.75	2.75
14	A6	2pi on 50c bis brn & lavender	4.75	4.75
15	A6	4pi on 1fr cl & ol grn	7.50	7.50
16	A6	20pi on 5fr dk bl & buff	22.50	22.50
		Nos. 4-16 (13)	47.50	47.50

There is a wide space between the two words of the overprint on Nos. 13 to 16 inclusive. Nos. 4, 5 and 6 are on white and coarse, grayish (G. C.) papers.

(Note on G. C. paper follows France No. 184.)

RUANDA-URUNDI

rü-,än-də ü'rün-dē

(Belgian East Africa)

LOCATION — In central Africa, bounded by Congo, Uganda and Tanganyika
GOVT. — Former United Nations trusteeship administered by Belgium
AREA — 20,540 sq. mi.
POP. — 4,700,000 (est. 1958)
CAPITAL — Usumbura

See German East Africa in Vol. 3 for stamps issued under Belgian occupation.

In 1962 the two parts of the trusteeship became independent states, the Republic of Rwanda and the Kingdom of Burundi.

100 Centimes = 1 Franc

Catalogue values for unused stamps in this country are for Never Hinged items, beginning with Scott 151 in the regular postage section, Scott B26 in the semi-postal section, and Scott J8 in the postage due section.

Stamps of Belgian Congo, 1923-26, Overprinted **RUANDA URUNDI**

1924-26 ***Perf. 12***

6	A32	5c orange yel	.20	.20
7	A32	10c green	.20	.20
8	A32	15c olive brn	.20	.20
9	A32	20c olive grn	.20	.20
10	A44	20c green ('26)	.20	.20
11	A44	25c red brown	.20	.20
12	A44	30c rose red	.20	.20
13	A44	30c olive grn ('25)	.20	.20
14	A32	40c violet ('25)	.20	.20
15	A44	50c gray blue	.20	.20
16	A44	50c buff ('25)	.25	.20
17	A44	75c red org	.25	.25
18	A44	75c gray blue ('25)	.35	.20
19	A44	1fr bister brown	.40	.35
20	A44	1fr dull blue ('26)	.45	.20
21	A44	3fr gray brown	3.00	1.40
22	A44	5fr gray	5.50	4.00
23	A44	10fr gray black	11.50	10.00
		Nos. 6-23 (18)	23.70	18.60

Belgian Congo Nos. 112-113 Overprinted in Red or Black **RUANDA-URUNDI**

1925-27 ***Perf. 12½***

24	A44	45c dk vio (R) ('27)	.20	.20
25	A44	60c car rose (Bk)	.40	.30

Stamps of Belgian Congo, 1923-1927, Overprinted

1927-29

26	A32	10c green ('29)	.20	.20
27	A32	15c ol brn ('29)	.80	.60
28	A44	35c green	.20	.20
29	A44	75c salmon red	.25	.25
30	A44	1fr rose red	.40	.30
31	A32	1.25fr dull blue	.50	.35
32	A32	1.50fr dull blue	.45	.35
33	A32	1.75fr dull blue	.95	.65

No. 32 Surcharged

34	A32	1.75fr on 1.50fr dl bl	.45	.40
		Nos. 26-34 (9)	4.20	3.30

Nos. 30 and 33 Surcharged

1931

35	A44	1.25fr on 1fr rose red	2.25	1.25
36	A32	2fr on 1.75fr dl bl	3.00	1.75

Watusi Warriors — A1

Mountain Scene — A2

Designs: 5c, 60c, Porter. 15c, Warrior. 25c, Kraal. 40c, Cattle herders. 50c, Cape buffalo. 75c, Bahutu greeting. 1fr, Barundi women. 1.25fr, Bahutu mother. 1.50fr, 2fr, Making wooden vessel. 2.50fr, 3.25fr, Preparing hides. 4fr, Watuba potter. 5fr, Mututsi dancer. 20fr, Urundi prince.

1931-38 **Engr.** ***Perf. 11½***

37	A1	5c dp lil rose ('38)	.20	.20
38	A2	10c gray	.20	.20
39	A2	15c pale red	.20	.20
40	A2	25c brown vio	.20	.20
41	A1	40c green	.25	.25
42	A2	50c gray lilac	.20	.20
43	A1	60c lilac rose	.20	.20
44	A1	75c gray black	.20	.20
45	A2	1fr rose red	.20	.20
46	A1	1.25fr red brown	.20	.20
47	A2	1.50fr brown vio ('37)	.20	.20
48	A2	2fr deep blue	.25	.25
49	A2	2.50fr dp blue ('37)	.25	.25
50	A2	3.25fr brown vio	.25	.25
51	A2	4fr rose	.25	.25
52	A1	5fr gray	.30	.30
53	A1	10fr brown violet	.50	.40
54	A1	20fr brown	1.50	1.40
		Nos. 37-54 (18)	5.55	5.35
		Set, never hinged	12.00	

For surcharges see Nos. 56-59.

King Albert Memorial Issue

King Albert — A16

1934 **Photo.**

55	A16	1.50fr black	.35	.35
		Never hinged	1.25	

Stamps of 1931-38 Surcharged in Black

1941

56	A1	5c on 40c green	2.25	2.25
57	A2	60c on 50c gray lil	1.50	1.50
58	A2	2.50fr on 1.50fr brn vio	1.50	1.50
59	A2	3.25fr on 2fr dp bl	6.00	6.00
		Nos. 56-59 (4)	11.25	11.25
		Set, never hinged	27.50	

Belgian Congo No. 173 Overprinted in Black

1941 ***Perf. 11***

60	A70	10c light gray	4.50	4.50
		Never hinged	9.00	

Inverts exist.

Belgian Congo Nos. 179, 181 Overprinted in Black

1941

61	A70	1.75fr orange	3.00	3.00
62	A70	2.75fr vio bl	3.00	3.00
		Set, never hinged	14.00	

For surcharges see Nos. 64-65.

Belgian Congo No. 168 Surcharged in Black

1941 ***Perf. 11½***

63	A66	5c on 1.50fr dp red brn & blk	.20	.20
		Never hinged	.20	

Inverts exist.

Nos. 61-62 Surcharged with New Values and Bars in Black

1942

64	A70	75c on 1.75fr org	1.10	1.25
65	A70	2.50fr on 2.75fr vio bl	3.00	3.00
		Set, never hinged	8.25	

Inverts exist.

Belgian Congo Nos. 167, 183 Surcharged in Black:

1942 ***Perf. 11, 11½***

66	A65	75c on 90c car & brn	.70	.65
a.		Inverted surcharge	9.00	9.00
67	A70	2.50fr on 10fr rose red	1.10	.85
a.		Inverted surcharge	8.00	8.00
		Set, never hinged	3.00	
		Nos. 66a-67a, never hinged	35.00	

Oil Palms — A17

Oil Palms — A18

Watusi Chief — A19

Askari — A21

Leopard A20

Zebra — A22

Askari — A23

Design: 100fr, Watusi chief.

1942-43 **Engr.** ***Perf. 12½***

68	A17	5c red	.20	.20
69	A18	10c ol grn	.20	.20
70	A18	15c brn car	.20	.20
71	A18	20c dp ultra	.20	.20
72	A18	25c brn vio	.20	.20
73	A18	30c dull blue	.20	.20
74	A18	50c dp grn	.20	.20
75	A18	60c chestnut	.20	.20
76	A19	75c dl lil & blk	.20	.20
77	A19	1fr dk brn & blk	.25	.20
78	A19	1.25fr rose red & blk	.40	.20
79	A20	1.75fr dk gray brn	.80	.35
80	A20	2fr ocher	.80	.30
81	A20	2.50fr carmine	.80	.20
82	A21	3.50fr dk ol grn	.55	.20
83	A21	5fr orange	.80	.25
84	A21	6fr brt ultra	.80	.25
85	A21	7fr black	.80	.30
86	A21	10fr dp brn	.95	.35
87	A22	20fr org brn & blk	2.75	.90
88	A23	50fr red & blk ('43)	3.25	1.10
89	A23	100fr grn & blk ('43)	8.00	2.75
		Nos. 68-89 (22)	22.75	9.15

Nos. 68-89 exist imperforate, but have no franking value. Value, set never hinged $225, value set hinged $110.

Miniature sheets of Nos. 72, 76, 77 and 83 were printed in 1944 by the Belgian Government in London and given to the Belgian political review, "Message," which distributed them to its subscribers, one a month.

See note after Belgian Congo No. 225.

For surcharges see Nos. B17-B20.

Baluba Mask — A25

Carved Figures and Masks of Baluba Tribe: 10c, 50c, 2fr, 10fr, "Ndoha," figure of tribal king. 15c, 70c, 2.50fr, "Tshimanyi," an idol. 20c, 75c, 3.50fr, "Buangakokoma," statue of a kneeling beggar. 25c, 1fr, 5fr, "Mbuta," sacred double cup carved with two faces, Man and Woman. 40c, 1.25fr, 6fr, "Ngadimuashi," female mask. 1.50fr, 50fr, "Buadi-Muadi," mask with squared features (full face). 20fr, 100fr, "Mbowa," executioner's mask with buffalo horns.

1948-50 **Unwmk.** ***Perf. 12x12½***

90	A25	10c dp org	.20	.20
91	A25	15c ultra	.20	.20
92	A25	20c brt bl	.20	.20
93	A25	25c rose car	.25	.20
94	A25	40c violet	.20	.20
95	A25	50c ol brn	.20	.20
96	A25	70c yel grn	.20	.20
97	A25	75c magenta	.25	.20
98	A25	1fr yel org & dk vio	.30	.20
99	A25	1.25fr lt bl grn & mag	.30	.20
100	A25	1.50fr ol & mag ('50)	.85	.30
101	A25	2fr org & mag	.40	.20
102	A25	2.50fr brn red & bl grn	.40	.20
103	A25	3.50fr lt bl & blk	.50	.20
104	A25	5fr bis & mag	.80	.20
105	A25	6fr brn org & ind	.80	.20
106	A25	10fr pale vio & red brn	1.10	.20
107	A25	20fr red org & vio brn	1.75	.35
108	A25	50fr dp org & blk	3.25	.90
109	A25	100fr crim & blk brn	6.00	2.25
		Nos. 90-109 (20)	18.15	7.00

Nos. 102 and 105 Surcharged with New Value and Bars in Black

1949

110	A25	3fr on 2.50fr	.35	.20
111	A25	4fr on 6fr	.35	.20
112	A25	6.50fr on 6fr	.45	.25
		Nos. 110-112 (3)	1.15	.65

St. Francis Xavier — A26

Dissotis — A27

1953 ***Perf. 12½x13***

113	A26	1.50fr ultra & gray blk	.35	.30

Death of St. Francis Xavier, 400th anniv.

1953 **Unwmk.** **Photo.** ***Perf. 11½***

Flowers: 15c, Protea. 20c, Vellozia. 25c, Littonia. 40c, Ipomoea. 50c, Angraecum. 60c, Euphorbia. 75c, Ochna. 1fr, Hibiscus. 1.25fr, Protea. 1.50fr, Schizoglossum. 2fr, Ansellia. 3fr, Costus. 4fr, Nymphaea. 5fr, Thunbergia. 7fr, Gerbera. 8fr, Gloriosa. 10fr, Silene. 20fr, Aristolochia.

Flowers in Natural Colors

114	A27	10c plum & ocher	.20	.20
115	A27	15c red & yel grn	.20	.20
116	A27	20c green & gray	.20	.20
117	A27	25c dk grn & dl org	.20	.20
118	A27	40c grn & sal	.20	.20
119	A27	50c dk car & aqua	.20	.20
120	A27	60c bl grn & pink	.20	.20
121	A27	75c dp plum & gray	.20	.20
122	A27	1fr car & yel	.25	.20
123	A27	1.25fr dk grn & bl	.50	.40
124	A27	1.50fr vio & ap grn	.25	.20
125	A27	2fr ol grn & buff	1.90	.20
126	A27	3fr ol grn & pink	.55	.20
127	A27	4fr choc & lil	.55	.20
128	A27	5fr dp plum & lt bl grn	.85	.20
129	A27	7fr dk grn & fawn	1.00	.30
130	A27	8fr grn & lt yel	1.40	.30
131	A27	10fr dp plum & pale ol	2.50	.25
132	A27	20fr vio bl & dl sal	4.00	.80
		Nos. 114-132 (19)	15.35	4.85

King Baudouin and Tropical Scene A28

Designs: Various African Views.

1955 **Engr. & Photo.**

Portrait Photo. in Black

133	A28	1.50fr rose carmine	2.25	.35
134	A28	3fr green	2.00	.35
135	A28	4.50fr ultra	2.25	.50
136	A28	6.50fr deep claret	3.50	.80
		Nos. 133-136 (4)	10.00	2.00

Mountain Gorilla — A29

Cape Buffaloes A30

Animals: 40c, 2fr, Black-and-white colobus (monkey). 50c, 6.50fr, Impalas. 3fr, 8fr, Elephants. 5fr, 10fr, Eland and Zebras. 20fr, Leopard. 50fr, Lions.

1959-61 **Unwmk.** **Photo.** ***Perf. 11½***

Granite Paper

Size: 23x33mm, 33x23mm

137	A29	10c brn, crim, & blk brn	.20	.20
138	A30	20c blk, gray & ap grn	.20	.20
139	A29	40c mag, blk & gray grn	.20	.20
140	A30	50c grn, org yel & brn	.20	.20
141	A29	1fr brn, ultra & blk	.20	.20
142	A30	1.50fr blk, gray & org	.20	.20
143	A29	2fr grnsh bl, ind & brn	.20	.20
144	A30	3fr brn, dp car & blk	.20	.20
145	A30	5fr brn, dl yel, grn & blk	.20	.20
146	A30	6.50fr red, org yel & brn	.30	.20
147	A30	8fr bl, mag & blk	.45	.30
148	A30	10fr multi	.45	.20

Size: 45x26½mm

149	A30	20fr multi ('61)	.55	.50
150	A30	50fr multi ('61)	1.25	1.00
		Nos. 137-150 (14)	4.80	4.00

For surcharge see No. 153.

Catalogue values for unused stamps in this section, from this point to the end of the section, are for Never Hinged items.

Map of Africa and Symbolic Honeycomb A31

1960 **Unwmk.** ***Perf. 11½***

Inscription in French

151	A31	3fr ultra & red	.20	.20

Inscription in Flemish

152	A31	3fr ultra & red	.20	.20

10th anniversary of the Commission for Technical Co-operation in Africa South of the Sahara (C. C. T. A.)

No. 144 Surcharged with New Value and Bars

1960

153	A30	3.50fr on 3fr	.30	.20

SEMI-POSTAL STAMPS

Belgian Congo Nos. B10-B11 Overprinted

1925 **Unwmk.** ***Perf. 12½***

B1	SP1	25c + 25c car & blk	.20	.25
B2	SP1	25c + 25c car & blk	.20	.25

No. B2 inscribed "BELGISCH CONGO."

Commemorative of the Colonial Campaigns in 1914-1918. Nos. B1 and B2 alternate in the sheet.

Belgian Congo Nos. B12-B20 Overprinted in Blue or Red

1930 ***Perf. 11½***

B3	SP3	10c + 5c ver	.35	.35
B4	SP3	20c + 10c dk brn	.70	.70
B5	SP5	35c + 15c dp grn	1.40	1.40
B6	SP5	60c + 30c dl vio	1.60	1.60
B7	SP3	1fr + 50c dk car	2.50	2.50
B8	SP5	1.75fr + 75c dp bl (R)	2.75	2.75
B9	SP5	3.50fr + 1.50fr rose lake	5.75	5.75
B10	SP5	5fr + 2.50fr red brn	4.50	4.50
B11	SP5	10fr + 5fr gray blk	5.00	5.00
		Nos. B3-B11 (9)	24.55	24.55

On Nos. B3, B4 and B7 there is a space of 26mm between the two words of the overprint. The surtax was for native welfare.

Queen Astrid with Native Children — SP1

1936 **Photo.**

B12	SP1	1.25fr + 5c dk brn	.45	.45
B13	SP1	1.50fr + 10c dl rose	.45	.45
B14	SP1	2.50fr + 25c dk bl	.55	.55
		Nos. B12-B14 (3)	1.45	1.45
		Set, never hinged	2.75	

Issued in memory of Queen Astrid. The surtax was for the National League for Protection of Native Children.

Lion of Belgium and Inscription "Belgium Shall Rise Again" — SP2

1942 **Engr.** ***Perf. 12½***

B15	SP2	10fr + 40fr blue	1.75	*2.00*
B16	SP2	10fr + 40fr dark red	1.75	*2.00*

Nos. 74, 78, 79 and 82 Surcharged in Red

a

b

c

1945 **Unwmk.** ***Perf. 12½***

B17	A18 (a)	50c + 50fr	1.75	1.40
B18	A19 (b)	1.25fr + 100fr	2.00	1.60
B19	A20 (c)	1.75fr + 100fr	1.75	1.40
B20	A21 (b)	3.50fr + 100fr	2.00	1.60
		Nos. B17-B20 (4)	7.50	6.00

Mozart at Age 7 — SP3

Queen Elizabeth and Mozart Sonata — SP4

1956 **Engr.** ***Perf. 11½***

B21	SP3	4.50fr + 1.50fr bluish vio	1.00	*1.75*
B22	SP4	6.50fr + 2.50fr claret	2.50	*2.75*

200th anniv. of the birth of Wolfgang Amadeus Mozart.

Surtax for the Pro-Mozart Committee.

Nurse and Children — SP5

Designs: 4.50fr+50c, Patient receiving injection. 6.50fr+50c, Patient being bandaged.

1957 **Photo.** ***Perf. 13x10½***

Cross in Carmine

B23	SP5	3fr + 50c dk blue	.50	.45
B24	SP5	4.50fr + 50c dk grn	.65	.60
B25	SP5	6.50fr + 50c red brn	.85	.75
		Nos. B23-B25 (3)	2.00	1.80

The surtax was for the Red Cross.

Catalogue values for unused stamps in this section, from this point to the end of the section, are for Never Hinged items.

Soccer SP6

Sports: #B26, High Jumper. #B27, Hurdlers. #B29, Javelin thrower. #B30, Discus thrower.

1960 **Unwmk.** ***Perf. 13½***

B26	SP6	50c + 25c int bl & maroon	.20	.20
B27	SP6	1.50fr + 50c dk car & blk	.20	.20
B28	SP6	2fr + 1fr blk & dk car	.20	.20
B29	SP6	3fr + 1.25fr org ver & grn	1.00	*1.25*
B30	SP6	6.50fr + 3.50fr ol grn & red	1.00	*1.25*
		Nos. B26-B30 (5)	2.60	*3.10*

17th Olympic Games, Rome, Aug. 25-Sept. 11. The surtax was for the youth of Ruanda-Urundi.

Usumbura Cathedral — SP7

Designs: 1fr+50c, 5fr+2fr, Cathedral, sideview. 1.50fr+75c, 6.50fr+3fr, Stained glass window.

1961, Dec. 18 ***Perf. 11½***

B31	SP7	50c + 25c brn & buff	.20	.20
B32	SP7	1fr + 50c grn & pale grn	.20	.20
B33	SP7	1.50fr + 75c multi	.20	.20
B34	SP7	3.50fr + 1.50fr lt bl & brt bl	.20	.20
B35	SP7	5fr + 2fr car & sal	.30	.30
B36	SP7	6.50fr + 3fr multi	.40	.40
		Nos. B31-B36 (6)	1.50	1.50

The surtax went for the construction and completion of the Cathedral at Usumbura.

POSTAGE DUE STAMPS

Belgian Congo Nos. J1-J7 Overprinted

1924-27 **Unwmk.** ***Perf. 14***

J1	D1	5c black brn	.20	.20
J2	D1	10c deep rose	.20	.20
J3	D1	15c violet	.20	.20
J4	D1	30c green	.25	.25
J5	D1	50c ultra	.30	.30
J6	D1	50c brt blue ('27)	.30	.30
J7	D1	1fr gray	.40	.40
		Nos. J1-J7 (7)	1.85	1.85

Catalogue values for unused stamps in this section, from this point to the end of the section, are for Never Hinged items.

Belgian Congo Nos. J8-J12 Overprinted in Carmine

1943 ***Perf. 14x14½, 12½***

J8	D2	10c olive green	.20	.20
J9	D2	20c dk ultra	.20	.20
J10	D2	50c green	.20	.20
J11	D2	1fr dark brown	.20	.20
J12	D2	2fr yellow orange	.20	.20
		Nos. J8-J12 (5)	1.00	1.00

Nos. J8-J12 values are for stamps perf. 14x14½. Those perf. 12½ sell for about three times as much.

Belgian Congo Nos. J13-J19 Overprinted

1959 **Engr.** ***Perf. 11½***

J13	D3	10c olive brown	.20	.20
J14	D3	20c claret	.20	.20
J15	D3	50c green	.20	.20
J16	D3	1fr lt blue	.20	.20
J17	D3	2fr vermilion	.20	.20
J18	D3	4fr purple	.30	.30
J19	D3	6fr violet blue	.40	.40
		Nos. J13-J19 (7)	1.70	1.70

Both capital and lower-case U's are found in this overprint.

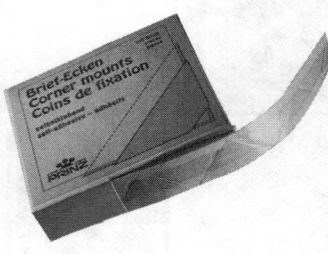

RUSSIA

ˈrəsh-ə

(Union of Soviet Socialist Republics)

LOCATION — Eastern Europe and Northern Asia
GOVT. — Republic
AREA — 6,592,691 sq. mi.
POP. — 147,100,000 (1999 est.)
CAPITAL — Moscow

An empire until 1917, the government was overthrown in that year and a socialist union of republics was formed under the name of the Union of Soviet Socialist Republics. The USSR includes the following autonomous republics which have issued their own stamps: Armenia, Azerbaijan, Georgia and Ukraine.

With the breakup of the Soviet Union on Dec. 26, 1991, eleven former Soviet republics established the Commonwealth of Independent States. Stamps inscribed "Rossija" are issued by the Russian Republic.

100 Kopecks = 1 Ruble

Catalogue values for unused stamps in this country are for Never Hinged items, beginning with Scott 1021 in the regular postage section, Scott B58 in the semi-postal section, and Scott C82 in the airpost section.

Watermarks

Wmk. 166- Colorless Numerals ("1" for Nos. 1-2, "2" for No. 3, "3" for No. 4)

Wmk. 168- Cyrillic EZGB & Wavy Lines

Initials are those of the State Printing Plant.

Wmk. 169- Lozenges

Wmk. 171- Diamonds

Wmk. 170- Greek Border and Rosettes

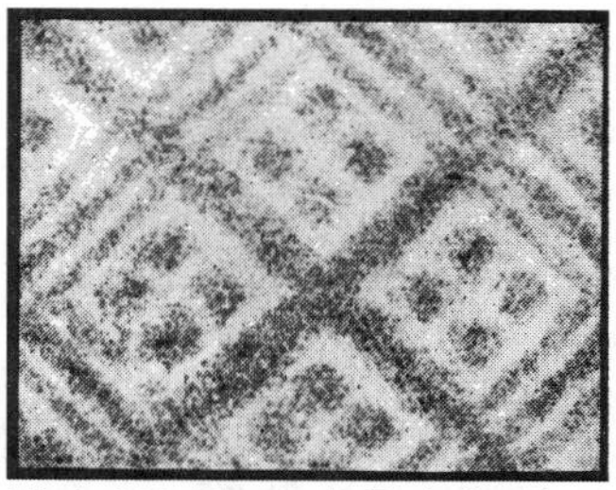

Wmk. 226- Diamonds Enclosing Four Dots

Wmk. 293- Hammer and Sickle, Multiple

Wmk. 383- Cyrillic Letters in Shield

Empire

Coat of Arms
A1 A2 A3

Wmk. 166

1857, Dec. 10 Typo. *Imperf.*

1	A1	10k brown & blue	*4,500.*	600.
		Pen cancellation		300.
		Penmark & postmark		425.

Genuine unused copies of No. 1 are exceedingly rare. Most of those offered are used with pen cancellation removed. The unused value is for a specimen without gum. The very few known stamps with original gum sell for much more.

See Poland for similar stamp inscribed "ZALOT KOP. 10."

1858, Jan. 10 *Perf. 14½, 15*

2	A1	10k brown & blue	1,750.	125.
3	A1	20k blue & orange	3,000.	700.
4	A1	30k carmine & green	4,500.	1,250.

1858-64 Unwmk. *Perf. 12½*

Wove Paper

5	A2	1k black & yel ('64)	50.00	35.00
a.		1k black & orange	60.00	35.00
6	A2	3k black & green ('64)	225.00	40.00
7	A2	5k black & lilac ('64)	175.00	47.50
8	A1	10k brown & blue	150.00	10.00
9	A1	20k blue & orange	350.00	85.00
a.		Half used as 10k on cover		—
10	A1	30k carmine & green	350.00	100.00
		Nos. 5-10 (6)	1,300.	317.50

1863

11	A3	5k black & blue	20.00	*150.00*

No. 11 was issued to pay local postage in St. Petersburg and Moscow. It is known to have been used in other cities. Copies canceled after July, 1864, are worth considerably less.

1865, June 2 *Perf. 14½, 15*

12	A2	1k black & yellow	42.50	15.00
a.		1k black & orange	50.00	20.00
13	A2	3k black & green	80.00	6.00
14	A2	5k black & lilac	100.00	8.50
15	A1	10k brown & blue	62.50	3.00
a.		Thick paper	115.00	7.50
17	A1	20k blue & orange	200.00	17.50
18	A1	30k carmine & green	225.00	30.00
		Nos. 12-18 (6)	710.00	80.00

1866-70 Wmk. 168

Horizontally Laid Paper

19	A2	1k black & yellow	3.00	.50
a.		1k black & orange	4.00	.75
b.		Imperf.		*1,000.*
c.		Vertically laid	175.00	25.00
d.		Groundwork inverted	*3,000.*	*1,500.*
e.		Thick paper	50.00	30.00
f.		As "c," imperf.	2,750.	2,250.
g.		As "b," "c" & "d"	*5,000.*	*5,000.*
h.		1k blk & org, vert. laid paper	175.00	25.00
20	A2	3k black & dp green	4.50	1.00
a.		3k black & yellow green	4.50	1.00
b.		Imperf.		*1,500.*
c.		Vertically laid	200.00	35.00
d.		V's in groundwork (error) ('70)	700.00	40.00
e.		3k black & blue green	4.50	.50
22	A2	5k black & lilac	6.00	.70
a.		5k black & gray	85.00	10.00
b.		Imperf.	2,500.	1,000.
c.		Vertically laid	1,050.	125.00
d.		As "c," imperf.		*4,000.*
23	A1	10k brown & blue	25.00	1.25
a.		Vertically laid	250.00	11.00
b.		Center inverted		*7,000.*
c.		Imperf.		*4,000.*
24	A1	20k blue & orange	75.00	6.00
a.		Vertically laid	1,100.	65.00
25	A1	30k carmine & green	75.00	25.00
a.		Vertically laid	500.00	40.00
		Nos. 19-25 (6)	188.50	34.45

Arms — A4

1875-79

Horizontally Laid Paper

26	A2	2k black & red	6.00	.50
a.		Vertically laid	1,250.	75.00
b.		Groundwork inverted		*7,500.*
27	A4	7k gray & rose ('79)	5.25	.25
a.		Imperf.		*4,250.*
b.		Vertically laid	450.00	55.00
c.		Wmkd. hexagons ('79)		*12,500.*
d.		Center inverted		*25,000.*
e.		Center omitted	*1,500.*	*1,500.*
f.		7k black & carmine ('80)	5.75	.35
		On cover		2.50
g.		7k pale gray & car ('82)	5.75	.35
28	A4	8k gray & rose	7.00	.75
a.		Vertically laid	900.00	70.00
b.		Imperf.		*1,500.*
c.		"C" instead of "B" in "Bocem"	200.00	75.00
29	A4	10k brown & blue	25.00	4.50
a.		Center inverted		*9,000.*
30	A4	20k blue & orange	37.50	7.50
a.		Cross-shaped "T" in bottom word	120.00	27.50
b.		Center inverted		*9,000.*
		Nos. 26-30 (5)	80.75	13.50

The hexagon watermark of No. 27c is that of revenue stamps. No. 27c exists with Perm and Riga postmarks.

See Finland for stamps similar to designs A4-A15, which have "dot in circle" devices or are inscribed "Markka," "Markkaa," "P en.," or "Pennia."

Imperial Eagle and Post Horns
A5 A6

Perf. 14 to 15 and Compound

1883-88 Wmk. 168

Horizontally Laid Paper

31	A5	1k orange	2.00	.20
a.		Imperf.	600.00	600.00
b.		Groundwork inverted	*4,000.*	*4,000.*
c.		1k yellow	2.00	.25
32	A5	2k dark green	3.00	.25
a.		2k yellow green ('88)	3.00	.25
b.		Imperf.	500.00	500.00
c.		Wove paper	500.00	325.00
d.		Groundwork inverted		*4,000.*
33	A5	3k carmine	4.00	.20
a.		Imperf.	450.00	450.00
b.		Groundwork inverted		*4,000.*
c.		Wove paper	500.00	410.00
34	A5	5k red violet	5.00	.20
a.		Groundwork inverted		*4,000.*
35	A5	7k blue	4.00	.20
a.		Imperf.	400.00	450.00
b.		Groundwork inverted	800.00	800.00
c.		Double impression of frame and center		*5,000.*
36	A6	14k blue & rose	5.00	.55
a.		Imperf.	800.00	800.00
b.		Center inverted	*7,000.*	*6,000.*
c.		Diagonal half surcharge "7" in red, on cover ('84)		*10,000.*
37	A6	35k violet & green	25.00	5.00
38	A6	70k brown & orange	30.00	5.00
		Nos. 31-38 (8)	78.00	11.60

Before 1882 the 1, 2, 3 and 5 kopecks had small numerals in the background; beginning with No. 31 these denominations have a background of network, like the higher values.

No. 36c is handstamped. It is known with cancellations of Tiflis and Kutais, both in Georgia. It is believed to be of philatelic origin.

A7

1884 ***Perf. 13½, 13½x11½***

Vertically Laid Paper

39	A7	3.50r black & gray	500.	400.
a.		Horiz. laid	10,000.	6,500.
40	A7	7r black & org	475.	400.

Forgeries exist, especially with forged postmarks.

Imperial Eagle and Post Horns with Thunderbolts
A8 A9

With Thunderbolts Across Post Horns

Perf. 14 to 15 and Compound

1889, May 14

Horizontally Laid Paper

41	A8	4k rose	.50	.25
a.		Groundwork inverted		3,000.
42	A8	10k dark blue	.50	.20
43	A8	20k blue & carmine	2.00	.30
44	A8	50k violet & green	2.25	.45

Perf. 13½

45	A9	1r lt brn, brn & org	17.50	2.50
a.		Pair, imperf. between	500.00	300.00
b.		Center omitted	500.00	500.00
		Nos. 41-45 (5)	22.75	3.70

See #57C, 60, 63, 66, 68, 82, 85, 87, 126, 129, 131. For surcharges see #216, 219, 223, 226.

A10

A11

A12

A13

With Thunderbolts Across Post Horns

1889-92 ***Perf. 14½x15***

Horizontally Laid Paper

46	A10	1k orange	.20	.20
a.		Imperf.	500.00	500.00
47	A10	2k green	.20	.20
a.		Imperf.	350.00	350.00
b.		Groundwork inverted		
48	A10	3k carmine	.25	.20
a.		Imperf.	350.00	350.00
49	A10	5k red violet	.50	.20
b.		Groundwork omitted	725.00	725.00
50	A10	7k dark blue	.25	.20
a.		Imperf.	500.00	500.00
b.		Groundwork inverted		2,000.
c.		Groundwork omitted	200.00	200.00
51	A11	14k blue & rose	3.00	.20
a.		Center inverted	4,500.	4,500.
52	A11	35k vio & green	5.75	.60

Perf. 13½

53	A12	3.50r black & gray	24.00	7.00
54	A12	7r black & yel	35.00	10.00
a.		Dbl. impression of black		275.00
		Nos. 46-54 (9)	69.15	18.80

Perf. 14 to 15 and Compound

1902-05

Vertically Laid Paper

55	A10	1k orange	.50	.35
a.		Imperf.	600.00	600.00
b.		Groundwork inverted	850.00	850.00
c.		Groundwork omitted	200.00	200.00
56	A10	2k yellow green	.50	.35
a.		2k deep green	7.50	.70
b.		Groundwork omitted	600.00	300.00
c.		Groundwork inverted	850.00	850.00
d.		Groundwork double	425.00	425.00
57	A10	3k rose red	.50	.35
a.		Groundwork omitted	350.00	175.00
b.		Double impression	200.00	165.00
d.		Imperf.	500.00	500.00
e.		Groundwork inverted	210.00	210.00
57C	A8	4k rose red ('04)	1.00	.50
f.		Double impression	200.00	200.00
g.		Groundwork inverted	4,000.	4,000.
58	A10	5k red violet	1.00	.50
a.		5k dull violet	4.25	2.00
b.		Groundwork inverted	750.00	750.00
c.		Imperf.	250.00	250.00
d.		Groundwork omitted	250.00	165.00
59	A10	7k dark blue	.50	.35
a.		Groundwork omitted	350.00	300.00
b.		Imperf.	375.00	375.00
c.		Groundwork inverted	800.00	800.00
60	A8	10k dk bl ('04)	.50	.35
a.		Groundwork inverted	12.50	5.00
b.		Groundwork omitted	165.00	35.00
c.		Groundwork double	165.00	35.00
61	A11	14k blue & rose	3.00	.35
a.		Center inverted	4,750.	3,500.
b.		Center omitted	1,100.	700.00
62	A11	15k brown vio & blue ('05)	3.00	1.00
a.		Center omitted		
b.		Center inverted	4,000.	3,500.
63	A8	20k blue & car ('04)	2.00	.75
64	A11	25k dull grn & lil ('05)	3.50	1.25
a.		Center inverted	4,000.	4,000.
b.		Center omitted	1,500.	1,500.
65	A11	35k dk vio & grn	5.00	1.00
a.		Center inverted		4,000.
b.		Center omitted	1,500.	
66	A8	50k vio & grn ('05)	10.00	1.00
67	A11	70k brown & org	10.00	1.25

Perf. 13½

68	A9	1r lt brown, brn & orange	10.00	1.00
a.		Perf. 11½	500.00	50.00
b.		Perf. 13½x11½, 11½x13½	675.00	575.00
c.		Imperf.	600.00	
d.		Center inverted	250.00	250.00
e.		Center omitted	250.00	150.00
f.		Pair, imperf. btwn.	500.00	165.00
69	A12	3.50r black & gray	9.00	3.00
a.		Center inverted	7,500.	7,500.
b.		Imperf., pair	2,000.	2,000.
70	A12	7r black & yel	9.00	4.00
a.		Center inverted	7,500.	7,500.
b.		Horiz. pair, imperf. btwn.	1,600.	1,600.
c.		Imperf., pair	2,000.	2,000.

1906 ***Perf. 13½***

71	A13	5r dk blue, grn & pale blue	25.00	4.50
a.		Perf. 11½	225.00	275.00
72	A13	10r car rose, yel & gray	100.00	10.00
		Nos. 55-72 (19)	194.00	31.85

The design of No. 72 differs in many details from the illustration. Nos. 71-72 were printed in sheets of 25.

See Nos. 80-81, 83-84, 86, 108-109, 125, 127-128, 130, 132-135, 137-138. For surcharges see Nos. 217-218, 220-222, 224-225, 227-229.

A14

A15

Vertical Lozenges of Varnish on Face

1909-12 **Unwmk.** ***Perf. 14x14½***

Wove Paper

73	A14	1k dull orange yellow	.20	.20
a.		1k orange yellow ('09)	.20	.20
c.		Double impression	100.00	100.00
74	A14	2k dull green	.20	.20
a.		2k green ('09)	.20	.20
b.		Double impression	100.00	100.00
75	A14	3k carmine	.20	.20
a.		3k rose red ('09)	.20	.20
76	A15	4k carmine	.20	.20
a.		4k carmine rose ('09)	.20	.20
77	A14	5k claret	.20	.20
a.		5k lilac ('12)	.65	.65
b.		Double impressions	100.00	100.00
78	A14	7k blue	.20	.20
a.		7k light blue ('09)	1.50	.65
b.		Imperf.	250.00	250.00
79	A15	10k dark blue	.20	.20
a.		10k light blue ('09)	500.00	85.00
b.		10k pale blue	6.00	1.00
80	A11	14k dk blue & car	.20	.20
a.		14k blue & rose ('09)	.20	.20
81	A11	15k red brown & dp blue	.20	.20
a.		15k dull violet & blue ('09)	.85	.40
c.		Center omitted	115.00	85.00
d.		Center double	50.00	50.00
82	A8	20k dull bl & dk car	.20	.20
a.		20k blue & carmine ('10)	.85	.55
b.		Groundwork omitted	20.00	13.00
c.		Center double	30.00	30.00
d.		Center and value omitted	85.00	85.00
83	A11	25k dl grn & dk vio	.20	.20
a.		25k green & violet ('09)	.30	.30
b.		Center omitted	115.00	115.00
c.		Center double	25.00	25.00
84	A11	35k red brn & grn	.20	.20
a.		35k brown vio & yel green	.50	.40
b.		35k violet & green ('09)	.50	.40
c.		Center double	25.00	25.00
85	A8	50k red brn & grn	.20	.20
a.		50k violet & green ('09)	.50	.40
b.		Groundwork omitted	20.00	20.00
c.		Center double	32.50	32.50
d.		Center and value omitted	115.00	115.00
86	A11	70k brn & red org	.20	.20
a.		70k lt brown & orange ('09)	.30	.25
b.		Center double	40.00	40.00
c.		Center omitted	115.00	115.00

Perf. 13½

87	A9	1r pale brown, dk brn & orange	.20	.25
a.		1r pale brn, brn & org ('10)	.25	.20
b.		Perf. 12½	.25	.20
c.		Groundwork inverted	20.00	20.00
d.		Pair, imperf. between	22.50	22.50
e.		Center inverted	25.00	25.00
f.		Center double	16.00	16.00
		Nos. 73-87 (15)	3.00	3.05

See Nos. 119-124. For surcharges see Nos. 117-118, B24-B29.

No. 87a was issued in sheets of 40 stamps, while Nos. 87 and 87b came in sheets of 50. Nos. 87g-87k are listed below No. 138a.

Nearly all values of this issue are known without the lines of varnish.

The 7k has two types:

I - The scroll bearing the top inscription ends at left with three short lines of shading beside the first letter. Four pearls extend at lower left between the leaves and denomination panel.

II - Inner lines of scroll at top left end in two curls; three pearls at lower left.

Three clichés of type II (an essay) were included by mistake in the plate used for the first printing. Value of pair, type I with type II, unused $2,500.

SURCHARGES

Russian stamps of types A6-A15 with various surcharges may be found listed under Armenia, Batum, Far Eastern Republic, Georgia, Latvia, Siberia, South Russia, Transcaucasian Federated Republics, Ukraine, Russian Offices in China, Russian Offices in the Turkish Empire and Army of the Northwest.

Peter I — A16

Alexander II — A17

Alexander III — A18

Peter I - A19

Nicholas II
A20 A21

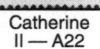

Catherine II — A22

Nicholas I — A23

Alexander I — A24

Alexis Mikhailovich A25

Paul I A26

Elizabeth Petrovna A27

Michael Feodorovich A28

The Kremlin — A29

Winter Palace — A30

Romanov Castle — A31

Nicholas II — A32

Without Lozenges of Varnish

1913, Jan. 2 **Typo.** ***Perf. 13½***

88	A16	1k brown orange	.30	.20
89	A17	2k yellow green	.30	.20
90	A18	3k rose red	.30	.20
b.		Double impression	700.00	
91	A19	4k dull red	.25	.20
92	A20	7k brown	.25	.20
b.		Double impression	350.00	350.00
93	A21	10k deep blue	.50	.20
94	A22	14k blue green	.45	.20
95	A23	15k yellow brown	.80	.20
96	A24	20k olive green	1.00	.20
97	A25	25k red violet	1.00	.35
98	A26	35k gray vio & dk grn	1.00	.35
99	A27	50k brown & slate	1.25	.45
100	A28	70k yel grn & brn	2.50	1.25

Engr.

101	A29	1r deep green	10.00	4.50
102	A30	2r red brown	9.00	4.50
103	A31	3r dark violet	24.00	13.50
104	A32	5r black brown	20.00	22.00
		Nos. 88-104 (17)	72.90	48.70

Imperf., Pairs

88a	A16	1k brown orange	1,500.
90a	A18	3k rose red	1,500.
92a	A20	7k brown	1,500.
93a	A21	10k deep blue	1,500.
102a	A30	2r red brown	1,500.
103b	A31	3r dark violet	1,500.

Tercentenary of the founding of the Romanov dynasty.

See #105-107, 112-116, 139-141. For surcharges see #110-111, Russian Offices in the Turkish Empire 213-227.

Arms & 5-line Inscription on Black

1915, Oct. Typo. *Perf. 13½*

Thin Cardboard

Without Gum

105	A21 10k blue	.75	*3.75*
106	A23 15k brown	.75	*3.75*
107	A24 20k olive green	.75	*3.75*
	Nos. 105-107 (3)	2.25	*11.25*

Imperf

105a	A21 10k	50.00	
106a	A23 15k	50.00	50.00
107a	A24 20k	50.00	

Nos. 105-107, 112-116 and 139-141 were issued for use as paper money, but contrary to regulations were often used for postal purposes. Back inscription means: "Having circulation on par with silver subsidiary coins."

Types of 1906 Issue

Vertical Lozenges of Varnish on Face

1915 *Perf. 13½, 13½x13*

108	A13 5r ind, grn & lt blue	.25	.20
a.	5r dk bl, grn & pale bl ('15)	2.50	.65
b.	Perf. 12½	3.25	1.00
c.	Center double	40.00	
d.	Pair, imperf. between	200.00	
109	A13 10r car lake, yel & gray	.25	.20
a.	10r carmine, yel & light gray	.40	.25
b.	10r rose red, yel & gray ('15)	.85	.50
c.	10r car, yel & gray blue (error)	1,250.	
d.	Groundwork inverted	400.00	
e.	Center double	50.00	50.00

Nos. 108a and 109b were issued in sheets of 25. Nos. 108, 108b, 109 and 109a came in sheets of 50. Chemical forgeries of No. 109c exist. Genuine copies usually are centered to upper right.

Nos. 92, 94 Surcharged

1916

110	A20 10k on 7k brown	.25	.25
a.	Inverted surcharge	70.00	70.00
111	A22 20k on 14k bl grn	.25	.25

Types of 1913 Issue

Arms, Value & 4-line inscription on Back

Surcharged Large Numerals on Nos. 112-113

1916-17

Thin Cardboard

Without Gum

112	A16 1 on 1k brn org ('17)	1.50	*4.50*
113	A17 2 on 2k yel green ('17)	1.50	*4.50*

Without Surcharge

114	A16 1k brown orange	18.00	*32.50*
115	A17 2k yellow green	35.00	*55.00*
116	A18 3k rose red	.75	*4.50*

See note after No. 107.

Nos. 78a, 80a Surcharged:

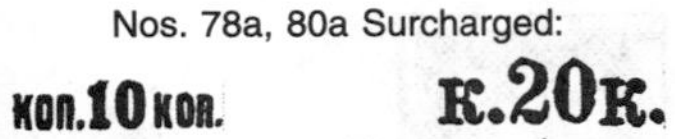

a b

1917 *Perf. 14x14½*

117	A14 10k on 7k lt blue	.20	.20
a.	Inverted surcharge	50.00	50.00
b.	Double surcharge	60.00	
118	A11 20k on 14k bl & rose	.20	.20
a.	Inverted surcharge	50.00	50.00

Provisional Government

Civil War

Type of 1889-1912 Issues

Vertical Lozenges of Varnish on Face

Two types of 7r:
Type I - Single outer frame line.
Type II - Double outer frame line.

1917 Typo. *Imperf.*

Wove Paper

119	A14 1k orange	.20	.20
120	A14 2k gray green	.20	.20
121	A14 3k red	.20	.20
122	A15 4k carmine	.20	.20
123	A14 5k claret	.20	.20
124	A15 10k dark blue	15.00	15.00
125	A11 15k red brn & dp blue	.20	.20
a.	Center omitted	65.00	
126	A8 20k blue & car	.20	.35
a.	Groundwork omitted	25.00	25.00
127	A11 25k grn & gray vio	.75	1.00
128	A11 35k red brn & grn	.20	.35
129	A8 50k brn vio & grn	.20	.25
a.	Groundwork omitted	25.00	25.00
130	A11 70k brn & orange	.20	.40
a.	Center omitted	115.00	
131	A9 1r pale brn, brn & red org	.20	.20
a.	Center inverted	20.00	20.00
b.	Center omitted	20.00	20.00
c.	Center double	20.00	20.00
d.	Groundwork double	14.00	14.00
e.	Groundwork inverted	20.00	20.00
f.	Groundwork omitted	22.50	22.50
g.	Frame double	16.00	16.00
132	A12 3.50r mar & lt green	.20	.25
133	A13 5r dk blue, grn & pale blue	.30	.35
a.	5r dk bl, grn & yel (error)	1,000.	
b.	Groundwork inverted	400.00	
134	A12 7r dk green & pink (I)	.75	1.00
a.	Center inverted		
135	A13 10r scarlet, yel & gray	35.00	30.00
a.	10r scarlet, green & gray (error)	1,250.	
	Nos. 119-135 (17)	54.20	50.35

Beware of trimmed copies of No. 109 offered as No. 135.

Vertical Lozenges of Varnish on Face

1917 *Perf. 13½, 13½x13*

137	A12 3.50r mar & lt grn	.20	.20
138	A12 7r dark green & pink (II)	.20	.20
d.	Type I	2.00	2.00

Perf. 12½

137a	A12 3.50r maroon & lt grn	.20	.20
138a	A12 7r dk grn & pink (II)	1.00	1.00

Horizontal Lozenges of Varnish on Face

Perf. 13½x13

87g	A9 1r pale brown, brn & red orange	.20	.20
h.	Imperf.	10.00	
i.	As "h," center omitted	22.50	
j.	As "h," center inverted	22.50	
k.	As "h," center double	22.50	
137b	A12 3.50r mar & lt green	.65	.20
d.	Imperf.	250.00	
138b	A12 7r dk grn & pink (II)	.65	.20
c.	Imperf.	250.00	

Nos. 87g, 137b and 138b often show the eagle with little or no embossing.

Types of 1913 Issue

Surcharge & 4-line Inscription on Back

Surcharged Large Numerals

1917

Thin Cardboard, Without Gum

139	A16 1 on 1k brown org	.75	*6.00*
a.	Imperf.	22.50	22.50
140	A17 2 on 2k yel green	.75	*6.00*
a.	Imperf.	22.50	22.50
b.	Surch. omitted, imperf.	45.00	45.00

Without Surcharge

141	A18 3k rose red	.75	*6.00*
a.	Imperf.		
	Nos. 139-141 (3)	2.25	*18.00*

See note after No. 107.

Stamps overprinted with a Liberty Cap on Crossed Swords or with reduced facsimiles of pages of newspapers were a private speculation and without official sanction.

RUSSIAN TURKESTAN

Russian stamps of 1917-18 surcharged as above are frauds.

Russian Soviet Federated Socialist Republic

Severing Chain of Bondage — A33

1918 Typo. *Perf. 13½*

149	A33 35k blue	.25	*5.00*
a.	Imperf., pair	225.00	
150	A33 70k brown	.25	*5.00*
a.	Imperf., pair	750.00	

In 1918-1922 various revenue stamps were permitted to be used for postal duty, sometimes surcharged with new values, more often not.

For surcharges see Nos. B18-B23, J1-J9 and note following No. B17.

Symbols of Agriculture — A40

Symbols of Industry — A41

Soviet Symbols of Agriculture and Industry — A42

Science and Arts — A43

1921 Unwmk. Litho. *Imperf.*

177	A40 1r orange	1.50	*1.75*
178	A40 2r lt brown	1.25	*1.25*
179	A41 5r dull ultra	1.50	.45
180	A42 20r blue	1.50	*3.00*
a.	Pelure paper	3.25	2.75
b.	Double impression	35.00	
181	A40 100r orange	.20	.20
a.	Pelure paper	.20	.20
182	A40 200r lt brown	.20	.25
a.	200r olive brown	15.00	15.00
183	A43 250r dull violet	.20	.20
a.	Pelure paper	.20	.20
b.	Chalk surfaced paper	.20	.20
c.	Tête bêche pair	15.00	15.00
d.	Double impression	35.00	
184	A40 300r green	.20	.25
a.	Pelure paper	15.00	20.00
185	A41 500r blue	.20	.35
186	A41 1000r carmine	.20	.30
a.	Chalk surfaced paper	.20	.20
b.	Thick paper	.20	.20
c.	Pelure paper	.20	.20
	Nos. 177-186 (10)	6.95	8.00

See #203, 205. For surcharges see #191-194, 196-199, 201, 210, B40, B43-B47, J10.

New Russia Triumphant A44

Type I - 37½mm by 23½mm.
Type II - 38½mm by 23¼mm.

1921, Aug. 10 Wmk. 169 Engr.

187	A44 40r slate, type II	.60	1.00
a.	Type I	1.00	1.10

The types are caused by paper shrinkage. One type has the watermark sideways in relation to the other.

For surcharges see Nos. 195, 200.

Initials Stand for Russian Soviet Federated Socialist Republic — A45

1921 Litho. Unwmk.

188	A45	100r orange	.20	.55
189	A45	250r violet	.20	.55
190	A45	1000r carmine rose	.75	1.40
		Nos. 188-190 (3)	1.15	2.50

4th anniversary of Soviet Government.
A 200r was not regularly issued. Value $45.

Nos. 177-179 Surcharged in Black **5000 руб.**

1922

191	A40	5000r on 1r orange	1.25	.80
a.		Inverted surcharge	100.00	22.50
b.		Double surch., red & blk	100.00	22.50
c.		Pair, one without surcharge	125.00	
192	A40	5000r on 2r lt brown	1.25	1.25
a.		Inverted surcharge	75.00	15.00
b.		Double surcharge	70.00	
193	A41	5000r on 5r ultra	2.00	2.00
a.		Inverted surcharge	75.00	30.00
b.		Double surcharge	75.00	

Beware of digitally created forgeries of the errors of Nos. 191-193 and 196-199.

No. 180 Surcharged

Р. С. Ф. С. Р.

5000 РУБЛЕЙ

194	A42	5000r on 20r blue	1.75	2.50
a.		Pelure paper	1.75	2.25
b.		Pair, one without surcharge	100.00	

Nos. 177-180, 187-187a Surcharged in Black or Red

РСФСР

10.000 Р.

Wmk. Lozenges (169)

195	A44	10,000r on 40r, type I	2.00	3.25
a.		Inverted surcharge	65.00	15.00
b.		Type II	2.50	2.50
c.		"1.0000" instead of "10.000"	200.00	
d.		Double surcharge	85.00	

Red Surcharge

Unwmk.

196	A40	5000r on 1r org	2.00	2.00
a.		Inverted surcharge	75.00	15.00
197	A40	5000r on 2r lt brn	2.00	2.00
a.		Inverted surcharge	100.00	100.00
198	A41	5000r on 5r ultra	2.00	2.00
199	A42	5000r on 20r blue	2.25	2.25
a.		Inverted surcharge	100.00	100.00
b.		Pelure paper	5.00	5.00

Wmk. Lozenges (169)

200	A44	10,000r on 40r, type I (R)	1.00	1.00
a.		Inverted surcharge	100.00	18.00
b.		Double surcharge	100.00	18.00
c.		With periods after Russian letters	300.00	35.00
d.		Type II	.75	.75
e.		As "a," type II	100.00	30.00
f.		As "c," type II	225.00	45.00

No. 183 Surcharged in Black or Blue Black

7500 РУБ.

1922, Mar. Unwmk.

201	A43	7500r on 250r (Bk)	.20	.20
a.		Pelure paper	.20	.20
b.		Chalk surfaced paper	.20	.25
c.		Blue black surcharge	.20	.20
		Nos. 191-201 (11)	17.70	19.25

Nos. 201, 201a and 201b exist with surcharge inverted (value about $15 each), and double (value about $25 each).
The horizontal surcharge was prepared but not issued.

Type of 1921 and

"Workers of the World Unite" A46

1922 Litho. Wmk. 171

202	A46	5000r dark violet	.75	3.25
203	A42	7500r blue	.25	.35
204	A46	10,000r blue	20.00	18.00

Unwmk.

205	A42	7500r blue, *buff*	.25	.40
a.		Double impression	100.00	
206	A46	22,500r dk violet, *buff*	.50	.60
		Nos. 202-206 (5)	21.75	22.60

For surcharges see Nos. B41-B42.

No. 183 Surcharged Diagonally

100,000 РУБ.

1922 Unwmk. *Imperf.*

210	A43	100,000r on 250r	.20	.20
a.		Inverted surcharge	60.00	60.00
b.		Pelure paper	.40	.50
c.		Chalk surfaced paper	.20	.20
d.		As "b," inverted surcharge	100.00	100.00

Marking 5th Anniversary of October Revolution — A48

1922 Typo.

211	A48	5r ocher & black	.20	.25
212	A48	10r brown & black	.20	.25
213	A48	25r violet & black	.50	.60
214	A48	27r rose & black	1.25	1.00
215	A48	45r blue & black	.90	.75
		Nos. 211-215 (5)	3.05	2.85

Pelure Paper

213a	A48	25r violet & black	60.00
214a	A48	27r rose & black	60.00
215a	A48	45r blue & black	65.00

5th anniv. of the October Revolution. Sold in the currency of 1922 which was valued at 10,000 times that of the preceding years.
For surcharges see Nos. B38-B39.

Nos. 81, 82a, 85-86, 125-126, 129-130 Surcharged

1922-23 *Perf. 14½x15*

216	A8	5r on 20k	.70	2.00
a.		Inverted surcharge	30.00	30.00
b.		Double surcharge	35.00	35.00
217	A11	20r on 15k	1.10	2.00
a.		Inverted surcharge	45.00	45.00
218	A11	20r on 70k	.70	.35
a.		Inverted surcharge	25.00	17.00
b.		Double surcharge	20.00	20.00
219	A8	30r on 50k	1.10	.50
a.		Inverted surcharge	25.00	25.00
c.		Groundwork omitted	30.00	30.00
d.		Double surcharge	16.00	16.00
220	A11	40r on 15k	.70	.35
a.		Inverted surcharge	25.00	25.00
b.		Double surcharge	30.00	30.00
221	A11	100r on 15k	.70	.35
a.		Inverted surcharge	22.50	22.50
b.		Double surcharge	30.00	30.00
222	A11	200r on 15k	.70	.35
a.		Inverted surcharge	30.00	30.00
b.		Double surcharge	20.00	20.00

Nos. 218-220, 222 exist in pairs, one without surcharge; Nos. 221-222 with triple surcharge; No. 221 with double surcharge, one inverted. Value, each $100.

Imperf

223	A8	5r on 20k	10.00	15.00
224	A11	20r on 15k	*1,500.*	
225	A11	20r on 70k	.80	1.00
a.		Inverted surcharge	17.50	17.50
226	A8	30r on 50k brn vio & green	5.00	4.50
227	A11	40r on 15k	.30	.30
a.		Inverted surcharge	35.00	35.00
b.		Double surcharge	27.50	27.50
228	A11	100r on 15k	2.25	1.10
a.		Inverted surcharge	50.00	50.00
229	A11	200r on 15k	2.25	1.00
a.		Inverted surcharge	50.00	50.00
b.		Double surcharge	35.00	35.00
		Nos. 216-223,225-229 (13)	26.30	28.80

Counterfeits of No. 223-229 exist.

Worker A49

Soldier A50

1922-23 Typo. *Imperf.*

230	A49	10r blue	.20	.25
231	A50	50r brown	.20	.25
232	A50	70r brown violet	.20	.25
233	A50	100r red	.20	.30
		Nos. 230-233 (4)	.80	1.05

1923 *Perf. 14x14½*

234	A49	10r dp bl, perf. 13½	.20	.25
a.		Perf. 14	15.00	16.00
b.		Perf. 12½	1.00	.85
235	A50	50r brown	.20	.25
a.		Perf. 12½	7.50	6.00
b.		Perf. 13½	1.50	2.00
236	A50	70r brown violet	.20	.25
a.		Perf. 12½	2.00	2.00
237	A50	100r red	.20	.40
a.		Cliché of 70r in plate of 100r	40.00	35.00
b.		Corrected cliché	125.00	175.00
		Nos. 234-237 (4)	.80	1.15

No. 237b has extra broken line at right.

Soldier- Worker- Peasant
A51 A52 A53

1923 *Perf. 14½x15*

238	A51	3r rose	.20	.25
239	A52	4r brown	.20	.25
240	A53	5r light blue	.20	.25
a.		Double impression	*50.00*	*50.00*
241	A51	10r gray	.20	.25
a.		Double impression	75.00	
241A	A51	20r brown violet	.20	.75
b.		Double impression	*75.00*	*75.00*
		Nos. 238-241A (5)	1.00	1.75

Imperf

238a	A51	3r rose	10.00	20.00
239a	A52	4r brown	10.00	25.00
b.		As "a," double impression	*75.00*	
240b	A53	5r light blue	5.50	10.00
241d	A51	10r gray	6.50	10.00
f.		As "d," double impression	75.00	
241c	A51	20r brown violet	150.00	75.00

Stamps of 1r buff, type A52, and 2r green, type A53, perf. 12 and imperf. were prepared but not put in use. Value $1 each.
The imperfs of Nos. 238-241A were sold only by the philatelic bureau in Moscow.
Stamps of 20r, type A51, printed in gray black or dull violet are essays. Value, $75 each.
The stamps of this and the following issues were sold for the currency of 1923, one ruble of which was equal to 100 rubles of 1922 and 1,000,000 rubles of 1921.

Union of Soviet Socialist Republics

Reaping — A54

Sowing — A55

Fordson Tractor A56

Symbolical of the Exhibition — A57

1923, Aug. 19 Litho. *Imperf.*

242	A54	1r brown & orange	1.25	2.00
243	A55	2r dp grn & pale grn	1.00	2.00
244	A56	5r dp bl & pale blue	1.25	2.75
245	A57	7r rose & pink	1.25	3.50

Perf. 12½, 13½

246	A54	1r brown & orange	3.00	3.50
a.		Perf. 12½	20.00	35.00
247	A55	2r dp grn & pale grn, perf. 12½	3.00	2.50
248	A56	5r dp bl & pale bl	3.00	4.25
a.		Perf. 13½	16.00	16.00
249	A57	7r rose & pink	4.00	5.00
a.		Perf. 12½	16.00	25.00
		Nos. 242-249 (8)	17.75	25.50

1st Agriculture and Craftsmanship Exhibition, Moscow.

Worker- Soldier- Peasant
A58 A59 A60

1923 Unwmk. Litho. *Imperf.*

250	A58	1k orange	.60	.25
251	A60	2k green	.90	.40
252	A59	3k red brown	.80	.40
253	A58	4k deep rose	.80	.65
254	A58	5k lilac	1.10	.65
255	A60	6k light blue	.60	.30
256	A59	10k dark blue	.60	.30
257	A58	20k yellow green	2.50	.55
258	A60	50k dark brown	3.50	1.90
259	A59	1r red & brown	4.50	2.25
		Nos. 250-259 (10)	15.90	7.65

1924 *Perf. 14½x15*

261	A58	4k deep rose	100.00	75.00
262	A59	10k dark blue	100.00	75.00
263	A60	30k violet	21.00	8.00
264	A59	40k slate gray	21.00	8.00
		Nos. 261-264 (4)	242.00	166.00

See Nos. 273-290, 304-321. For surcharges see Nos. 349-350.

Vladimir Ilyich Ulyanov (Lenin) A61

Worker A62

1924 *Imperf.*

265	A61	3k red & black	2.50	1.50
266	A61	6k red & black	2.50	1.50
267	A61	12k red & black	2.50	1.50
268	A61	20k red & black	2.50	1.50
		Nos. 265-268 (4)	10.00	6.00

Three printings of Nos. 265-268 differ in size of red frame.

Perf. 13½

269	A61	3k red & black	1.90	1.75
270	A61	6k red & black	1.90	1.75
271	A61	12k red & black	2.50	2.50
272	A61	20k red & black	3.75	3.00
		Nos. 269-272 (4)	10.05	9.00
		Nos. 265-272 (8)	20.05	15.00

Death of Lenin (1870-1924).
Forgeries of Nos. 265-272 exist.

Types of 1923

There are small differences between the lithographed stamps of 1923 and the typographed of 1924-25. On a few values this may be seen in the numerals.

Type A58: Lithographed. The two white lines forming the outline of the ear are continued across the cheek. Typographed. The outer lines of the ear are broken where they touch the cheek.

Type A59: Lithographed. At the top of the right shoulder a white line touches the frame at the left. Counting from the edge of the visor of the cap, lines 5, 6 and sometimes 7 touch at their upper ends. Typographed. The top line of the shoulder does not reach the frame. On the cap lines 5, 6 and 7 run together and form a white spot.

Type A60: In the angle above the first letter "C" there is a fan-shaped ornament enclosing four white dashes. On the lithographed stamps these dashes reach nearly to the point of the angle. On the typographed stamps the dashes are shorter and often only three are visible.

On unused copies of the typographed stamps the raised outlines of the designs can be seen on the backs of the stamps.

1924-25 Typo. *Imperf.*

273	A59	3k red brown	1.40	1.00
274	A58	4k deep rose	1.40	1.00
275	A59	10k dark blue	2.50	1.00
275A	A60	50k brown	700.00	25.00

Other typographed and imperf. values include: 2k green, 5k lilac, 6k light blue, 20k green and 1r red and brown. Value, unused: $150, $100, $37.50, $150, and $1,000, respectively.

Nos. 273-275A were regularly issued. The 7k, 8k, 9k, 30k, 40k, 2r, 3r, and 5r also exist imperf. Value, set of 8, $75.

Perf. 14½x15

Typo.

276	A58	1k orange	65.00	5.50
277	A60	2k green	1.00	.30
278	A59	3k red brown	1.25	.40
279	A58	4k deep rose	1.00	.40
280	A58	5k lilac	10.00	2.50
281	A60	6k lt blue	1.00	.50
282	A59	7k chocolate	1.00	.50
283	A58	8k brown olive	1.25	.70
284	A60	9k orange red	1.25	1.10
285	A59	10k dark blue	1.65	.55
286	A58	14k slate blue	35.00	4.00
287	A60	15k yellow	*6,000.*	*150.00*
288	A58	20k gray green	4.00	.80
288A	A60	30k violet	175.00	7.50
288B	A59	40k slate gray	175.00	7.50
289	A60	50k brown	50.00	8.00
290	A59	1r red & brown	10.00	2.00
291	A62	2r green & rose	15.00	3.50
		Nos. 276-286,288-291 (17)	548.40	45.75

See No. 323. Forgeries of No. 287 exist.

1925 *Perf. 12*

276a	A58	1k orange	.85	.20
277a	A60	2k green	8.00	.95
278a	A59	3k red brown	1.65	.70
279a	A58	4k deep rose	55.00	3.25
280a	A58	5k lilac	4.00	.80
282a	A59	7k chocolate	2.25	.20
283a	A58	8k brown olive	80.00	12.50
284a	A60	9k orange red	13.00	7.50
285a	A59	10k dark blue	3.00	.25
286a	A58	14k slate blue	3.50	.40
287a	A60	15k yellow	4.50	1.00
288c	A58	20k gray green	18.00	.45
288d	A60	30k violet	20.00	2.50
288e	A59	40k slate gray	20.00	2.75
289a	A60	50k brown	8.00	1.10
290a	A59	1r red & brown	750.00	150.00
		Nos. 276a-290a (16)	991.75	184.55

Soldier — A63

Worker — A64

1924-25 *Perf. 13½*

292	A63	3r blk brn & grn	11.00	4.75
a.		Perf. 10	400.00	50.00
b.		Perf. 13½x10	*1,000.*	325.00
293	A64	5r dk bl & gray brn	32.50	9.25
a.		Perf. 10½	50.00	62.50

See Nos. 324-325.

Lenin Mausoleum, Moscow — A65

Wmk. 170

1925, Jan. Photo. *Imperf.*

294	A65	7k deep blue	3.75	3.00
295	A65	14k dark green	3.75	3.00
296	A65	20k carmine rose	3.75	3.00
297	A65	40k red brown	3.75	3.50
		Nos. 294-297 (4)	15.00	12.50

Perf. 13½x14

298	A65	7k deep blue	4.50	2.75
299	A65	14k dark green	5.00	2.75
300	A65	20k carmine rose	5.00	2.75
301	A65	40k red brown	5.50	4.00
		Nos. 298-301 (4)	20.00	12.25
		Nos. 294-301 (8)	35.00	24.75

First anniversary of Lenin's death.

Nos. 294-301 are found on both ordinary and thick paper. Those on thick paper sell for twice as much, except for No. 301, which is scarcer on ordinary paper.

Lenin — A66

Wmk. 170

1925, July Engr. *Perf. 13½*

302	A66	5r red brown	27.50	6.00
a.		Perf. 12½	35.00	11.00
b.		Perf. 10½ ('26)	27.50	8.00
303	A66	10r indigo	27.50	11.00
a.		Perf. 12½	190.00	90.00
b.		Perf. 10½ ('26)	22.50	11.00

Imperfs. exist. Value, set $75.

See Nos. 407-408, 621-622

Types of 1923 Issue

1925-27 Wmk. 170 Typo. *Perf. 12*

304	A58	1k orange	.50	.35
305	A60	2k green	.45	.20
306	A59	3k red brown	.50	.35
307	A58	4k deep rose	.30	.25
308	A58	5k lilac	.40	.25
309	A60	6k lt blue	.60	.25
310	A59	7k chocolate	.45	.20
311	A58	8k brown olive	.95	.20
a.		Perf. 14½x15	100.00	50.00
312	A60	9k red	.70	.40
313	A59	10k dark blue	.70	.30
a.		10k pale blue ('27)	1.25	1.00
314	A58	14k slate blue	1.50	.35
315	A60	15k yellow	2.25	1.00
316	A59	18k violet	1.50	.25
317	A58	20k gray green	1.25	.25
318	A60	30k violet	1.50	.25
319	A59	40k slate gray	2.00	.35
320	A60	50k brown	3.25	.35
321	A59	1r red & brown	3.75	.35
a.		Perf. 14½x15	100.00	40.00
323	A62	2r green & rose red	22.50	5.50
a.		Perf. 14½x15	11.00	2.75

Perf. 13½

324	A63	3r blk brn & green	7.50	4.75
a.		Perf. 12½	40.00	14.00
325	A64	5r dark blue & gray brown	12.00	4.75
		Nos. 304-325 (21)	64.55	20.90

Nos. 304-315, 317-325 exist imperf. Value, set $60.

Mikhail V. Lomonosov and Academy of Sciences — A67

1925, Sept. Photo. *Perf. 12½, 13½*

326	A67	3k orange brown	4.75	3.00
a.		Perf. 12½x12	10.50	7.50
b.		Perf. 13½x12½	42.50	27.50
c.		Perf. 13½	17.50	10.00
327	A67	15k dk olive green	4.75	3.00
a.		Perf. 12½	17.50	7.50

Russian Academy of Sciences, 200th anniv. Exist unwatermarked, on thick paper with yellow gum, perf. 13½. These are essays, later perforated and gummed. Value, each $50.

Prof. Aleksandr S. Popov (1859-1905), Radio Pioneer — A68

1925, Oct. *Perf. 13½*

328	A68	7k deep blue	2.00	1.50
329	A68	14k green	3.25	1.90

For surcharge see No. 353.

Decembrist Exiles — A69

Street Rioting in St. Petersburg — A70

Revolutionist Leaders — A71

1925, Dec. 28 *Imperf.*

330	A69	3k olive green	2.25	3.00
331	A70	7k brown	2.25	2.50
332	A71	14k carmine lake	3.50	3.75

Perf. 13½

333	A69	3k olive green	2.50	2.25
a.		Perf. 12½	60.00	50.00
334	A70	7k brown	2.00	2.25
335	A71	14k carmine lake	3.00	2.50
		Nos. 330-335 (6)	15.50	16.25

Centenary of Decembrist revolution.

For surcharges see Nos. 354, 357.

Revolters Parading — A72

Speaker Haranguing Mob — A73

Street Barricade, Moscow — A74

1925, Dec. 20 *Imperf.*

336	A72	3k olive green	1.50	1.50
337	A73	7k brown	1.75	1.60
338	A74	14k carmine lake	2.25	2.00

Perf. 12½, 12x12½

339	A72	3k olive green	1.50	1.25
a.		Perf. 13½	4.50	4.25
340	A73	7k brown	3.50	3.00
a.		Perf. 13½	15.00	10.50
b.		Horiz. pair, imperf. btwn.	55.00	50.00
341	A74	14k carmine lake	2.50	2.00
a.		Perf. 13½	22.50	12.00
		Nos. 336-341 (6)	13.00	11.35

20th anniversary of Revolution of 1905.

For surcharges see Nos. 355, 358.

Lenin — A75

Liberty Monument, Moscow — A76

1926 Wmk. 170 Engr. *Perf. 10½*

342	A75	1r dark brown	4.50	2.50
343	A75	2r black violet	7.50	4.50
a.		Perf. 12½	75.00	30.00
344	A75	3r dark green	14.00	4.50
		Nos. 342-344 (3)	26.00	11.50

Nos. 342-343 exist imperf.

See Nos. 406, 620.

1926, July Litho. *Perf. 12x12½*

347	A76	7k blue green & red	2.00	1.50
348	A76	14k blue green & violet	2.50	1.50

6th International Esperanto Congress at Leningrad. Exist perf. 11½. Value, $500.

For surcharge see No. 356.

Nos. 282, 282a and 310 Surcharged in Black

8
КОП

1927, June Unwmk. *Perf. 14½x15*

349	A59	8k on 7k chocolate	3.00	1.25
a.		Perf. 12	8.50	7.50
b.		Inverted surcharge	125.00	105.00

Perf. 12

Wmk. 170

350	A59	8k on 7k chocolate	2.50	1.25
a.		Inverted surcharge	100.00	35.00

The surcharge on Nos. 349-350 comes in two types: With space of 2mm between lines, and with space of ¾mm. The latter is much scarcer.

Same Surcharge on Stamps of 1925-26 in Black or Red

Perf. 13½, 12½, 12x12½

353	A68	8k on 7k dp bl (R)	2.75	4.50
a.		Inverted "8"	75.00	100.00
354	A70	8k on 7k brown	8.00	9.25
355	A73	8k on 7k brown	10.50	12.25
356	A76	8k on 7k blue green & red	8.75	11.00

Imperf

357	A70	8k on 7k brown	3.50	5.25
358	A73	8k on 7k brown	3.50	5.25
		Nos. 349-350,353-358 (8)	42.50	50.00

Postage Due Stamps of 1925 Surcharged

ПОЧТОВАЯ
МАРКА
КОП. 8 КОП.

Two settings: A's aligned (shown), bottom A to left.

Lithographed or Typographed

1927, June Unwmk. *Perf. 12*

359	D1	8k on 1k red, typo.	2.75	1.10
a.		Litho.	*750.00*	100.00
360	D1	8k on 2k violet	3.75	1.75

Perf. 12, 14½x14

361	D1	8k on 3k lt blue	3.50	1.60
362	D1	8k on 7k orange	3.75	1.75
363	D1	8k on 8k green	2.75	1.10
364	D1	8k on 10k dk blue	3.50	1.60
365	D1	8k on 14k brown	2.75	1.10
		Nos. 359-365 (7)	22.75	10.00

Exist with inverted surcharge. Value each, $100.

Wmk. 170

1927, June Typo. *Perf. 12*

366	D1	8k on 1k red	1.25	1.90
367	D1	8k on 2k violet	1.25	1.90
368	D1	8k on 3k lt blue	2.50	2.25
369	D1	8k on 7k orange	2.50	2.25
370	D1	8k on 8k green	1.25	1.90
371	D1	8k on 10k dk blue	1.25	1.90
372	D1	8k on 14k brown	1.75	1.90
		Nos. 366-372 (7)	11.75	14.00

Nos. 366, 368-372 exist with inverted surcharge. Value each, $100.

Dr. L. L. Zamenhof A77

1927 Photo. *Perf. 10½*

373 A77 14k yel green & brown 2.00 2.00

Unwmk.

374 A77 14k yel green & brown 2.00 2.00

40th anniversary of creation of Esperanto.

No. 374 exists perf. 10, 10x10½ and imperf. Value, imperf. pair $500.

Worker, Soldier, Peasant — A78

Worker and Sailor — A81

Lenin in Car Guarded by Soldiers A79

Smolny Institute, Leningrad A80

Map of the USSR A82

Men of Various Soviet Republics — A83

Workers of Different Races; Kremlin in Background — A84

Typo. (3k, 8k, 18k), Engr. (7k), Litho. (14k), Photo. (5k, 28k)

Perf. 13½, 12½x12, 11

1927, Oct. Unwmk.

375 A78 3k bright rose .95 .80
  a. Imperf., pair 500.00
376 A79 5k deep brown 2.60 2.25
  a. Imperf. 500.00 175.00
  b. Perf. 12½ 20.00 27.50
  c. Perf. 12½x10½ 50.00 30.00
377 A80 7k myrtle green 3.00 2.75
  a. Perf. 11½ 50.00 30.00
  b. Imperf., pair 500.00
378 A81 8k brown & black 1.60 .95
  a. Perf. 10½x12½ *32.50* *27.50*
379 A82 14k dull blue & red 2.75 1.65
380 A83 18k blue 2.00 1.65
  a. Imperf. 1,000.
381 A84 28k olive brown 7.50 5.75
  a. Perf. 10 40.00 35.00
  Nos. 375-381 (7) 20.40 15.80

10th anniversary of October Revolution.

The paper of No. 375 has an overprint of pale yellow wavy lines.

No. 377b exists with watermark 170. Value, $1,000.

Worker — A85

Peasant — A86

Lenin — A87

1927-28 Typo. *Perf. 13½*

Chalk Surfaced Paper

382 A85 1k orange .30 .20
383 A86 2k apple green .30 .20
385 A85 4k bright blue .30 .20
386 A86 5k brown .30 .20
388 A86 7k dark red ('28) 1.75 .75
389 A85 8k green .90 .20
391 A85 10k light brown .90 .20
392 A87 14k dark green ('28) 1.25 .30
393 A87 18k olive green 1.25 .30
394 A87 18k dark blue ('28) 1.75 .45
395 A86 20k dark gray green 1.25 .30
396 A85 40k rose red 2.50 .45
397 A86 50k bright blue 3.00 .85
399 A85 70k gray green 3.50 .85
400 A86 80k orange 4.75 1.40
  Nos. 382-400 (15) 24.00 6.85

The 1k, 2k and 10k exist imperf. Value, each $250.

Soldier and Kremlin — A88

Sailor and Flag — A89

Cavalryman A90

Aviator A91

1928, Feb. 6

Chalk Surfaced Paper

402 A88 8k light brown .85 .35
  a. Imperf. 250.00 200.00
403 A89 14k deep blue 1.75 .90
404 A90 18k carmine rose 2.00 1.75
  a. Imperf. 550.00
405 A91 28k yellow green 2.40 2.00
  Nos. 402-405 (4) 7.00 5.00

10th anniversary of the Soviet Army.

Lenin Types of 1925-26

Perf. 10, 10½

1928-29 Engr. Wmk. 169

406 A75 3r dark green ('29) 5.75 2.00
407 A66 5r red brown 6.75 2.50
408 A66 10r indigo 11.50 4.50
  Nos. 406-408 (3) 24.00 9.00

No. 406 exists imperf. Value, $500.

Bugler Sounding Assembly
A92 A93

Perf. 12½x12

1929, Aug. 18 Photo. Wmk. 170

411 A92 10k olive brown 7.50 5.00
  a. Perf. 10½ 35.00 25.00
  b. Perf. 12½x12x10½x12 45.00 21.00
412 A93 14k slate 3.00 2.00
  a. Perf. 12½x12x10½x12 75.00 45.00

First All-Soviet Assembly of Pioneers.

Factory Worker A95

Peasant A96

Farm Worker A97

Soldier A98

Worker, Soldier, Peasant A100

Worker A103

Lenin A104

Peasant A107

Factory Worker A109

Farm Worker A111

Perf. 12x12½

1929-31 Typo. Wmk. 170

413 A103 1k orange .20 .20
  a. Perf. 10½ 25.00 13.00
  b. Perf. 14x14½ 50.00 35.00
414 A95 2k yellow green .20 .20
415 A96 3k blue .20 .20
  a. Perf. 14x14½ 50.00 35.00
416 A97 4k claret .30 .20
417 A98 5k orange brown .30 .20
  a. Perf. 10½ 75.00 75.00
418 A100 7k scarlet 1.10 .75
419 A103 10k olive green .50 .20
  a. Perf. 10½ 27.50 22.50

Unwmk.

420 A104 14k indigo 1.10 .75
  a. Perf. 10½ 4.25 3.25

Wmk. 170

421 A100 15k dk ol grn ('30) .85 .20
422 A107 20k green .85 .20
  a. Perf. 10½ 50.00 27.50
423 A109 30k dk violet 1.50 .60
424 A111 50k dp brown 2.00 1.40
425 A98 70k dk red ('30) 2.10 1.50
426 A107 80k red brown ('31) 2.00 1.50
  Nos. 413-426 (14) 13.20 8.10

Nos. 422, 423, 424 and 426 have a background of fine wavy lines in pale shades of the colors of the stamps.

See Nos. 456-466, 613A-619A. For surcharge see No. 743.

Symbolical of Industry A112

Tractors Issuing from Assembly Line — A113

Iron Furnace (Inscription reads, "More Metal More Machines") A114

Blast Furnace and Chart of Anticipated Iron Production A115

1929-30 *Perf. 12x12½*

427 A112 5k orange brown 1.25 1.00
428 A113 10k olive green 1.25 1.50

Perf. 12½x12

429 A114 20k dull green 3.50 3.00
430 A115 28k violet black 2.00 1.75
  Nos. 427-430 (4) 8.00 7.25

Publicity for greater industrial production. No. 429 exists perf. 10½. Value, $800.

Red Cavalry in Polish Town after Battle A116

Cavalry Charge A117

Staff Officers of 1st Cavalry Army A118

Plan of Action for 1st Cavalry Army — A119

1930, Feb. *Perf. 12x12½*

431 A116 2k yellow green 1.60 1.60
432 A117 5k light brown 1.60 1.60
433 A118 10k olive gray 3.50 2.50
434 A119 14k indigo & red 1.40 1.60
  Nos. 431-434 (4) 8.10 7.30

1st Red Cavalry Army, 10th anniversary.

Students Preparing a Poster Newspaper
A120

1930, Aug. 15
435 A120 10k olive green 2.00 1.50

Educational Exhibition, Leningrad, 7/1-8/15/30.

Telegraph Office, Moscow
A121

Lenin Hydroelectric Power Station on Volkhov River
A122

1930 Photo. Wmk. 169 *Perf. 10½*
436 A121 1r deep blue 6.00 4.00

Wmk. 170
437 A122 3r yel green & blk brn 7.50 6.00

See Nos. 467, 469.

Battleship Potemkin
A123

Inside Presnya Barricade
A124

Moscow Barricades in 1905 — A125

1930 Typo. *Perf. 12x12½, 12½x12*
438 A123 3k red 1.40 .55
439 A124 5k blue 1.40 .70
440 A125 10k dk green & red 2.50 1.00
Nos. 438-440 (3) 5.30 2.25

1931 *Imperf.*
452 A123 3k red 3.50 1.75
453 A124 5k deep blue 3.50 1.90
454 A125 10k dk green & red 5.00 2.25
Nos. 452-454 (3) 12.00 5.90
Nos. 438-454 (6) 17.30 8.15

Revolution of 1905, 25th anniversary.

Types of 1929-31 Regular Issue

1931-32 *Imperf.*
456 A103 1k orange 1.00 1.00
457 A95 2k yellow green 1.00 1.25
458 A96 3k blue 1.00 1.25
459 A97 4k claret 15.00 7.00
460 A98 5k orange brown 3.00 3.00
462 A103 10k olive green 40.00 20.00
464 A100 15k dk olive green 45.00 25.00
466 A109 30k dull violet 70.00 35.00
467 A121 1r dark blue 65.00 65.00
Nos. 456-467 (9) 241.00 158.50

Nos. 459, 462-467 were sold only by the philatelic bureau.

Type of 1930 Issue

1931 Wmk. 170 *Perf. 12x12½*
469 A121 1r dark blue 1.75 .75
Never hinged 2.75

Maxim Gorki — A133

1932-33 Photo.
470 A133 15k dark brown 4.00 3.50
a. Imperf. 120.00 120.00
471 A133 35k dp ultra ('33) 15.00 11.00
Set, never hinged 40.00

40th anniversary of Gorki's literary activity.

Lenin Addressing the People
A134

Revolution in Petrograd (Leningrad)
A135

Dnieper Hydroelectric Power Station
A136

Asiatics Saluting the Soviet Flag — A139

Breaking Prison Bars — A140

Designs (dated 1917 1932): 15k, Collective farm. 20k, Magnitogorsk metallurgical plant in Urals. 30k, Radio tower and heads of 4 men.

1932-33 *Perf. 12½x12; 12½ (30k)*
472 A134 3k dark violet 1.40 .75
473 A135 5k dark brown 1.40 .75
474 A136 10k ultra 3.25 1.40
475 A136 15k dark green 2.00 .85
476 A136 20k lake ('33) 2.50 1.10
477 A136 30k dark gray ('33) 9.50 2.25
478 A139 35k gray black 75.00 57.50
Nos. 472-478 (7) 95.05 64.60
Set, never hinged 150.00

October Revolution, 15th anniversary.

1932, Nov. Litho. *Perf. 12½x12*
479 A140 50k dark red 7.50 6.00
Never hinged 10.50

Intl. Revolutionaries' Aid Assoc., 10th anniv.

Trier, Birthplace of Marx — A141

Grave, Highgate Cemetery, London — A142

35k, Portrait & signature of Karl Marx (1818-83).

Perf. 12x12½, 12½x12

1933, Mar. Photo.
480 A141 3k dull green 3.50 1.00
481 A142 10k black brown 5.50 2.25
482 A142 35k brown violet 11.00 7.00
Nos. 480-482 (3) 20.00 10.25
Set, never hinged 50.00

Fine Arts Museum, Moscow — A145

1932, Dec. *Perf. 12½*
485 A145 15k black brown 15.00 13.00
486 A145 35k ultra 32.50 32.50
a. Perf. 10½ 60.00 35.00
Set, never hinged 100.00

Moscow Philatelic Exhibition, 1932.

Nos. 485 and 486 were also issued in imperf. sheets of 4 containing 2 of each value, on thick paper for presentation purposes. They were not valid for postage. Replicas of the sheet were made for Moscow 97 by the Canadian Society of Russian Philately.

Nos. 485 and 486a Surcharged

ЛЕНИНГРАД, 1933 г.

70
коп

1933, Mar. *Perf. 12½*
487 A145 30k on 15k black brn 35.00 25.00

Perf. 10½
488 A145 70k on 35k ultra 65.00 35.00
Set, never hinged 150.00

Leningrad Philatelic Exhibition, 1933.

Peoples of the Soviet Union

Kazaks
A146

Lezghians
A147

Tungus
A150

Crimean Tartars
A148

Jews, Birobidzhan
A149

Buryats — A151

Yakuts — A156

Chechens
A152

Abkhas
A153

Georgians
A154

Nientzians
A155

Great Russians — A157

Tadzhiks — A158

Transcaucasians — A159

Turkmen — A160

Ukrainians — A161

Uzbeks — A162

Byelorussians — A163

Koryaks A164

Bashkirs A165

Chuvashes A166

Perf. 12, 12x12½, 12½x12, 11x12, 12x11

1933, Apr.			**Photo.**	
489	A146	1k black brown	1.75	1.00
490	A147	2k ultra	1.75	1.00
491	A148	3k gray green	1.75	1.00
492	A149	4k gray black	1.75	1.00
493	A150	5k brown violet	1.75	1.00
494	A151	6k indigo	1.75	1.00
495	A152	7k black brown	1.75	1.00
496	A153	8k rose red	1.75	1.00
497	A154	9k ultra	3.25	1.25
498	A155	10k black brown	3.50	3.00
499	A156	14k olive green	3.00	1.25
500	A157	15k orange	3.50	1.25
501	A158	15k ultra	3.25	1.00
502	A159	15k dark brown	3.25	1.00
503	A160	15k rose red	4.75	2.75
504	A161	15k violet brown	4.25	1.25
505	A162	15k gray black	4.25	1.25
506	A163	15k dull green	3.75	1.25
507	A164	20k dull blue	11.50	3.00
508	A165	30k brown violet	11.50	3.00
509	A166	35k black	24.00	5.00
		Nos. 489-509 (21)	97.75	34.25
		Set, never hinged	150.00	

V. V. Vorovsky A169

3k, V. M. Volodarsky. 5k, M. S. Uritzky.

1933, Oct.			***Perf. 12x12½***	
514	A169	1k dull green	.75	.55
515	A169	3k blue black	1.10	.75
516	A169	5k olive brown	2.25	.90
		Nos. 514-516 (3)	4.10	2.20
		Set, never hinged	15.00	

10th anniv, of the murder of Soviet Representative Vorovsky; 15th anniv. of the murder of the Revolutionists Volodarsky and Uritzky.

See Nos. 531-532, 580-582.

Order of the Red Banner, 15th Anniv. — A173

1933, Nov. 17		**Unwmk.**	***Perf. 14***	
518	A173	20k black, red & yellow	1.50	1.25
		Never hinged	5.00	

No. 518, perf. 9½, is a proof.

Commissar Schaumyan A174

Commissar Prokofii A. Dzhaparidze A175

Commissars Awaiting Execution — A176

Designs: 35k, Monument to the 26 Commissars. 40k, Worker, peasant and soldier dipping flags in salute.

1933, Dec. 1				
519	A174	4k brown	9.50	1.65
520	A175	5k dark gray	9.50	1.65
521	A176	20k purple	6.50	1.65
522	A176	35k ultra	30.00	6.75
523	A176	40k carmine	18.00	8.25
		Nos. 519-523 (5)	73.50	19.95
		Set, never hinged	120.00	

15th anniv. of the execution of 26 commissars at Baku. No. 521 exists imperf.

Lenin's Mausoleum A179

1934, Feb. 7		**Engr.**	***Perf. 14***	
524	A179	5k brown	4.25	.55
	a.	Imperf.	150.00	125.00
525	A179	10k slate blue	7.25	2.00
	a.	Imperf.	150.00	125.00
526	A179	15k dk carmine	7.25	1.40
527	A179	20k green	7.25	1.40
528	A179	35k dark brown	11.50	2.25
		Nos. 524-528 (5)	37.50	7.60
		Set, never hinged	100.00	

10th anniversary of Lenin's death.

Ivan Fedorov A180

1934, Mar. 5				
529	A180	20k carmine rose	4.50	2.50
	a.	Imperf.	250.00	250.00
530	A180	40k indigo	10.00	3.50
	a.	Imperf.	250.00	250.00
		Set, never hinged	50.00	

350th anniv. of the death of Ivan Fedorov, founder of printing in Russia.

Portrait Type of 1933

Designs: 10k, Yakov M. Sverdlov. 15k, Victor Pavlovich Nogin.

1934, Mar.		**Photo.**	**Wmk. 170**	
531	A169	10k ultra	25.00	9.50
532	A169	15k red	30.00	15.00
		Set, never hinged	92.50	

Deaths of Yakov M. Sverdlov, chairman of the All-Russian Central Executive Committee of the Soviets, 15th anniv., Victor Pavlovich Nogin, chairman Russian State Textile Syndicate, 10th anniv.

A184

Dmitri Ivanovich Mendeleev A185

1934, Sept. 15		**Wmk. 170**	***Perf. 14***	
536	A184	5k emerald	7.50	1.75
537	A185	10k black brown	19.50	3.25
538	A185	15k vermilion	16.50	2.75
539	A184	20k ultra	12.50	2.75
		Nos. 536-539 (4)	56.00	10.50
		Set, never hinged	150.00	

Prof. D. I. Mendeleev (1834-1907), chemist who discovered the Periodic Law of Classification of the Elements.

Imperfs. exist of 5k (value $400) and 15k (value $400).

Lenin as Child and Youth
A186 A187

Demonstration before Lenin Mausoleum — A190

Designs: 5k, Lenin in middle age. 10k, Lenin the orator. 30k, Lenin and Stalin.

1934, Nov. 23		**Unwmk.**	***Perf. 14***	
540	A186	1k indigo & black	4.25	1.25
541	A187	3k indigo & black	4.25	1.50
542	A187	5k indigo & black	8.50	2.25
543	A187	10k indigo & black	6.50	2.25
544	A190	20k brn org & ultra	12.00	4.00
545	A190	30k brn org & car	40.00	9.00
		Nos. 540-545 (6)	75.50	20.25
		Set, never hinged	150.00	

First decade without Lenin.

See Nos. 931-935, 937.

Bombs Falling on City A192

"Before War and Afterwards" A194

Designs: 10k, Refugees from burning town. 20k, "Plowing with the sword." 35k, "Comradeship."

1935, Jan. 1		**Wmk. 170**	***Perf. 14***	
546	A192	5k violet black	6.00	4.00
547	A192	10k ultra	12.00	6.00
548	A194	15k green	14.00	6.00
549	A194	20k dark brown	12.00	6.00
550	A194	35k carmine	50.00	12.50
		Nos. 546-550 (5)	94.00	34.50
		Set, never hinged	150.00	

Ati-war propaganda, the designs symbolize the horrors of modern warfare.

Subway Tunnel A197

Subway Station Cross Section A198

Subway Station A199

Train in Station — A200

1935, Feb. 25		**Wmk. 170**	***Perf. 14***	
551	A197	5k orange	11.00	2.00
552	A198	10k dark ultra	14.00	3.25
553	A199	15k rose carmine	52.50	15.00
554	A200	20k emerald	22.50	12.00
		Nos. 551-554 (4)	100.00	32.25
		Set, never hinged	150.00	

Completion of Moscow subway.

Friedrich Engels (1820-1895), German Socialist and Collaborator of Marx — A201

1935, May		**Wmk. 170**	***Perf. 14***	
555	A201	5k carmine	7.50	1.25
556	A201	10k dark green	3.75	1.75
557	A201	15k dark blue	7.00	2.25
558	A201	20k brown black	5.00	3.50
		Nos. 555-558 (4)	23.25	8.75
		Set, never hinged	75.00	

Running — A202

Designs: 2k, Diving. 3k, Rowing. 4k, Soccer. 5k, Skiing. 10k, Bicycling. 15k, Tennis. 20k, Skating. 35k, Hurdling. 40k, Parade of athletes.

1935, Apr. 22 Unwmk. *Perf. 14*
559 A202 1k orange & ultra 1.75 .55
560 A202 2k black & ultra 2.25 .55
561 A202 3k grn & blk brn 4.50 1.25
562 A202 4k rose red & ultra 3.00 .85
563 A202 5k pur & blk brn 3.00 .85
564 A202 10k rose red & vio 11.50 3.00
565 A202 15k black & blk brn 22.50 6.00
566 A202 20k blk brn & ultra 19.00 5.00
567 A202 35k ultra & blk brn 27.50 9.00
568 A202 40k black brn & car 25.00 6.50
Nos. 559-568 (10) 120.00 33.55
Set, never hinged 150.00

International Spartacist Games, Moscow. The games never took place.

Silver Plate of Sassanian Dynasty A212

1935, Sept. 10 Wmk. 170
569 A212 5k orange red 5.75 1.75
570 A212 10k dk yellow green 5.75 1.75
571 A212 15k dark violet 6.50 3.00
572 A212 35k black brown 9.50 3.50
Nos. 569-572 (4) 27.50 10.00
Set, never hinged 100.00

3rd International Exposition of Persian Art, Leningrad, Sept. 12-18, 1935.

Kalinin, the Worker — A213

Mikhail Kalinin — A216

Kalinin as: 5k, farmer. 10k, orator.

1935, Nov. 20 Unwmk. *Perf. 14*
573 A213 3k rose lilac 1.25 .55
574 A213 5k green 1.25 .55
575 A213 10k blue slate 1.40 .85
576 A216 20k brown black 2.40 1.10
Nos. 573-576 (4) 6.30 3.05
Set, never hinged 15.00

60th birthday of Mikhail Kalinin, chairman of the Central Executive Committee of the USSR.
The 20k exists imperf. Value $110.

A217

Leo Tolstoy — A218

Design: 20k, Statue of Tolstoy.

1935, Dec. 4 *Perf. 14*
577 A217 3k ol black & vio 1.00 .75
578 A218 10k vio blk & blk brn 1.40 .95
579 A217 20k dk grn & blk brn 5.50 3.00
Nos. 577-579 (3) 7.90 4.70
Set, never hinged 15.00

Perf. 11
577a A217 3k 2.50 .75
578a A218 10k 4.50 1.75
579a A217 20k 10.00 2.50
Nos. 577a-579a (3) 17.00 5.00
Set, never hinged 25.00

25th anniv. of the death of Count Leo N. Tolstoy (1828-1910).

Portrait Type of 1933

Designs: 2k, Mikhail V. Frunze. 4k, N. E. Bauman. 40k, Sergei M. Kirov.

1935, Nov. Wmk. 170 *Perf. 11*
580 A169 2k purple 3.00 *2.75*
581 A169 4k brown violet 4.00 *4.50*
582 A169 40k black brown 8.00 *6.50*
Nos. 580-582 (3) 15.00 13.75
Set, never hinged 22.00

Perf. 14
580a A169 2k 7.25 .55
581a A169 4k 10.00 .55
582a A169 40k 24.00 1.65
Nos. 580a-582a (3) 41.25 2.75
Set, never hinged 60.00

Death of three revolutionary heroes.
Nos. 580-582 exist imperf. but were not regularly issued. Value, set $500.

Pioneers Preventing Theft from Mailbox A223

Designs: 3k, 5k, Pioneers preventing destruction of property. 10k, Helping recover kite. 15k, Girl Pioneer saluting.

1936, Apr. Unwmk. *Perf. 14*
583 A223 1k yellow green .65 .35
584 A223 2k copper red 2.00 .35
585 A223 3k slate blue 1.00 .90
586 A223 5k rose lake .85 .35
587 A223 10k gray blue 2.00 1.75
588 A223 15k brown olive 10.00 6.00
Nos. 583-588 (6) 16.50 9.70
Set, never hinged 35.00

Perf. 11
583a A223 1k 1.25 .55
584a A223 2k .65 .55
585a A223 3k 3.50 .75
586a A223 5k 6.00 1.50
587a A223 10k 15.00 1.75
588a A223 15k 3.00 2.00
Nos. 583a-588a (6) 29.40 7.10
Set, never hinged 60.00

Nikolai A. Dobrolyubov, Writer and Critic, Birth Cent. — A227

1936, Aug. 13 Typo. *Perf. 11½*
589 A227 10k rose lake 3.00 2.25
ever hinged 4.50
a. Perf. 14 4.00 2.50

Aleksander Sergeyevich Pushkin — A228

Statue of Pushkin, Moscow — A229

Perf. 11 to 14 and Compound
1937, Feb. 1
Chalky or Ordinary Paper
590 A228 10k yellow brown .35 .35
591 A228 20k Prus green .50 .40
592 A228 40k rose lake .65 .45
593 A229 50k blue 1.25 .55
594 A229 80k carmine rose 1.90 .75
595 A229 1r green 3.25 1.50
Nos. 590-595 (6) 7.90 4.00
Set, never hinged 12.00

Souvenir Sheet
Imperf
596 Sheet of 2 6.00 *10.00*
Never hinged 10.00
a. A228 10k brown .65 *2.25*
b. A229 50k brown .65 *2.25*

Pushkin (1799-1837), writer and poet.

Tchaikovsky Concert Hall — A230

Designs: 5k, 15k, Telegraph Agency House. 10k, Tchaikovsky Concert Hall. 20k, 50k, Red Army Theater. 30k, Hotel Moscow. 40k, Palace of the Soviets.

Unwmk.
1937, June Photo. *Perf. 12*
597 A230 3k brown violet .85 .40
598 A230 5k henna brown .85 .40
599 A230 10k dark brown 1.40 .40
600 A230 15k black 1.40 .40
601 A230 20k olive green .85 .90
602 A230 30k gray black .85 .90
a. Perf. 11 50.00 32.50
603 A230 40k violet 1.60 1.25
a. Souv. sheet of 4, imperf. 8.00 *17.00*
604 A230 50k dark brown 1.60 1.25
Nos. 597-604 (8) 9.40 5.90
Set, never hinged 50.00

First Congress of Soviet Architects. The 30k is watermarked Greek Border and Rosettes (170).
Nos. 597-601, 603-604 exist imperf. Value, each $250.

Feliks E. Dzerzhinski A235

Shota Rustaveli A236

1937, July 27 Typo. *Perf. 12*
606 A235 10k yellow brown .50 .25
607 A235 20k Prus green .75 .50
608 A235 40k rose lake 1.50 1.00
609 A235 80k carmine 2.00 1.25
Nos. 606-609 (4) 4.75 3.00
Set, never hinged 7.50

Dzerzhinski, organizer of Soviet secret police, 10th death anniv. Exist imperf. Value, each $350.

Unwmk.
1938, Feb. Photo. *Perf. 12*
610 A236 20k deep green 1.25 .50

750th anniversary of the publication of the poem "Knight in the Tiger Skin," by Shota Rustaveli, Georgian poet.
Exists imperf. Value $450.

Statue Surmounting Pavilion A237

Soviet Pavilion at Paris Exposition A238

1938 Typo.
611 A237 5k red .45 .20
a. Imperf. 100.00
612 A238 20k rose .80 .25
613 A237 50k dark blue 1.75 .55
Nos. 611-613 (3) 3.00 1.00
Set, never hinged 7.00

USSR participation in the 1937 International Exposition at Paris.

Types of 1929-32 and Lenin Types of 1925-26

1937-52 Unwmk. *Perf. 11½x12, 12*
613A A103 1k dull org ('40) 15.00 5.00
614 A95 2k yel grn ('39) 6.00 2.00
615 A97 4k claret ('40) 6.00 2.00
615A A98 5k org brn ('46) 100.00 15.00
616 A109 10k blue ('38) .50 .30
616A A103 10k olive ('40) 100.00 20.00
616B A109 10k black ('52) .50 .35
617 A97 20k dull green .50 .35
617A A107 20k green ('39) 100.00 12.50
618 A109 30k claret ('39) 15.00 4.50
619 A104 40k indigo ('38) 2.00 .90
619A A111 50k dp brn ('40) .85 .52

Engr.
620 A75 3r dk grn ('39) 1.50 .90
621 A66 5r red brn ('39) 2.00 1.25
622 A66 10r indigo ('39) 3.50 2.75
Nos. 613A-622 (15) 353.35 68.32
Set, never hinged 420.00

#615-619 exist imperf but were not regularly issued.
No. 616B was re-issued in 1954-56 in slightly smaller format, 14½x21mm, and in gray black. See note after No. 738.

Airplane Route from Moscow to North Pole — A239

Soviet Flag and Airplanes at North Pole — A240

1938, Feb. 25 Litho. *Perf. 12*
625 A239 10k drab & black 1.40 .45
626 A239 20k blue gray & blk 1.75 .65

Typo.
627 A240 40k dull green & car 5.00 3.00
a. Imperf. 200.00
628 A240 80k rose car & car 1.90 1.90
a. Imperf. 90.00
Nos. 625-628 (4) 10.05 6.00
Set, never hinged 16.50

Soviet flight to the North Pole.

Infantryman A241

Soldier A242

Stalin Reviewing Cavalry A246

Chapayev and Boy — A247

Designs: 30k, Sailor, 40k, Aviator. 50k, Antiaircraft soldier.

Unwmk.
1938, Mar. Photo. *Perf. 12*
629 A241 10k gray blk & dk red .50 .25
630 A242 20k gray blk & dk red .65 .40
631 A242 30k gray blk & dk red 1.25 .60
632 A242 40k gray blk & dk red 1.90 1.25
633 A242 50k gray blk & dk red 2.25 1.25

634	A246	80k gray blk & dk red	3.50	1.25

Typo.

Perf. 12x12½

635	A247	1r black & carmine	1.00	*1.25*
		Nos. 629-635 (7)	11.05	6.25
		Set, never hinged	30.00	

Workers' & Peasants' Red Army, 20th anniv. No. 635 exists imperf. Value $200.

Aviators Chkalov, Baidukov, Beliakov and Flight Route — A248

Aviators Gromov, Danilin, Yumashev and Flight Route — A249

1938, Apr. 10 **Photo.**

636	A248	10k black & red	1.00	.60
637	A248	20k brn blk & red	1.40	.90
638	A248	40k brown & red	2.10	2.00
639	A248	50k brown vio & red	3.50	2.00
		Nos. 636-639 (4)	8.00	5.50
		Set, never hinged	20.00	

First Trans-Polar flight, June 18-20, 1937, from Moscow to Vancouver, Wash. Nos. 636-639 exist imperf. Value $250 each.

1938, Apr. 13

640	A249	10k claret	1.75	.60
641	A249	20k brown black	2.00	1.25
642	A249	50k dull violet	2.25	1.50
		Nos. 640-642 (3)	6.00	3.35
		Set, never hinged	20.00	

First Trans-Polar flight, July 12-14, 1937, from Moscow to San Jacinto, Calif. Nos. 640-642 exist imperf. Value, each $250.

Arrival of the Rescuing Ice-breakers Taimyr and Murmansk A250

Ivan Papanin and His Men Aboard Ice-breaker Yermak — A251

1938, June 21 **Typo.** ***Perf. 12, 12½***

643	A250	10k violet brown	2.25	1.00
644	A250	20k dark blue	2.25	1.25

Photo.

645	A251	30k olive brown	6.00	1.65
646	A251	50k ultra	6.00	2.25
a.		Imperf.	150.00	
		Nos. 643-646 (4)	16.50	6.15
		Set, never hinged	40.00	

Rescue of Papanin's North Pole Expedition.

Arms of Uzbek — A252

Arms of USSR A253

#650

#651

#654

#655

#656

Designs: Different arms on each stamp.

Perf. 12, 12½

1937-38 **Unwmk.** **Typo.**

647	A252	20k dp bl (Armenia)	1.10	.70
648	A252	20k dull violet (Azerbaijan)	1.10	.70
649	A252	20k brown orange (Byelorussia)	*6.00*	*4.00*
650	A252	20k carmine rose (Georgia)	1.25	.95
651	A252	20k bl grn (Kazakh)	1.25	.95
652	A252	20k emer (Kirghiz)	1.25	.95
653	A252	20k yel org (Uzbek)	1.25	.95
654	A252	20k bl (R.S.F.S.R.)	1.25	.95
655	A252	20k claret (Tadzhik)	1.25	.95
656	A252	20k car (Turkmen)	1.25	.95
657	A252	20k red (Ukraine)	1.25	.95

Engr.

658	A253	40k brown red	3.00	2.40
		Nos. 647-658 (12)	21.20	15.40
		Set, never hinged	50.00	

Constitution of USSR. No. 649 has inscriptions in Yiddish, Polish, Byelorussian and Russian.

Issue dates: 40k, 1937. Others, 1938. See Nos. 841-842.

Nurse Weighing Child — A264

Children at Lenin's Statue — A265

Biology Lesson A266

Health Camp A267

Young Model Builders A268

1938, Sept. 15 **Unwmk.** ***Perf. 12***

659	A264	10k dk blue green	1.50	.35
660	A265	15k dk blue green	1.50	.55
661	A266	20k violet brown	1.90	.55
662	A267	30k claret	2.25	.95
663	A266	40k light brown	2.75	1.25
664	A268	50k deep blue	4.00	1.75
665	A268	80k light green	6.25	1.75
		Nos. 659-665 (7)	20.15	7.15
		Set, never hinged	45.00	

Child welfare.

View of Yalta A269

Crimean Shoreline — A272

Designs: No. 667, View along Crimean shore. No. 668, Georgian military highway. No, 670, View near Yalta. No. 671, "Swallows' Nest" Castle. 20k, Dzerzhinski Rest House for workers. 30k, Sunset in Crimea. 40k, Alupka. 50k, Gursuf. 80k, Crimean Gardens. 1r, "Swallows' Nest" Castle, horiz.

Unwmk.

1938, Sept. 21 **Photo.** ***Perf. 12***

666	A269	5k brown	1.00	1.40
667	A269	5k black brown	1.00	1.40
668	A269	10k slate green	1.50	1.40
669	A272	10k brown	1.50	1.40
670	A269	15k black brown	1.50	1.40
671	A272	15k black brown	1.50	1.40
672	A269	20k dark brown	2.25	1.40
673	A272	30k black brown	2.25	1.90
674	A269	40k brown	3.25	1.90
675	A272	50k slate green	3.25	4.00
676	A269	80k brown	5.00	4.00
677	A269	1r slate green	11.00	6.50
		Nos. 666-677 (12)	35.00	28.10
		Set, never hinged	85.00	

Children Flying Model Plane A281

Glider A282

Captive Balloon — A283

Dirigible over Kremlin — A284

Parachute Jumpers — A285

Hydroplane A286

Balloon in Flight — A287

Balloon Ascent — A288

Four-motor Plane A289

Unwmk.

1938, Oct. 7 **Typo.** ***Perf. 12***

678	A281	5k violet brown	.95	.55
679	A282	10k olive gray	.95	.55
680	A283	15k pink	1.75	.55
681	A284	20k deep blue	1.75	.55
682	A285	30k claret	2.60	.95
683	A286	40k deep blue	3.00	.95
684	A287	50k blue green	6.25	1.40
685	A288	80k brown	5.50	2.50
686	A289	1r blue green	7.25	2.00
		Nos. 678-686 (9)	30.00	10.00
		Set, never hinged	70.00	

For overprints see Nos. C76-C76D.

Mayakovsky Station, Moscow Subway — A290

Sokol Terminal — A291

Kiev Station — A292

Dynamo Station A293

Train in Tunnel A294

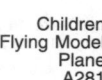

Revolution Square Station
A295

Unwmk.

1938, Nov. 7 Photo. *Perf. 12*

687	A290 10k deep red violet	4.25	.90
688	A291 15k dark brown	4.25	.90
689	A292 20k black brown	4.25	.90
690	A293 30k dark red violet	4.25	.90
691	A294 40k black brown	4.25	1.40
692	A295 50k dark brown	4.25	1.90
	Nos. 687-692 (6)	25.50	6.90
	Set, never hinged	40.00	

Second line of the Moscow subway opening.

Girl with Parachute
A296

Young Miner
A297

Harvesting
A298

Designs: 50k, Students returning from school. 80k, Aviator and sailor.

1938, Dec. 7 Typo. *Perf. 12*

693	A296 20k deep blue	.75	.60
694	A297 30k deep claret	.75	.60
695	A298 40k violet brown	.95	.60
696	A296 50k deep rose	1.25	1.10
697	A298 80k deep blue	3.75	1.60
	Nos. 693-697 (5)	7.45	4.50
	Set, never hinged	20.00	

20th anniv. of the Young Communist League (Komsomol).

Diving — A301

Discus Thrower — A302

Designs: 15k, Tennis. 20k, Acrobatic motorcyclists. 30k, Skier. 40k, Runners. 50k, Soccer. 80k, Physical culture.

Unwmk.

1938, Dec. 28 Photo. *Perf. 12*

698	A301 5k scarlet	1.75	.55
699	A302 10k black	1.75	.55
700	A302 15k brown	2.00	.55
701	A302 20k green	2.00	.90
702	A302 30k dull violet	5.25	1.10
703	A302 40k deep green	6.25	1.50
704	A302 50k blue	5.25	1.10
705	A302 80k deep blue	5.25	1.75
	Nos. 698-705 (8)	29.50	8.00
	Set, never hinged	55.00	

Gorki Street, Moscow — A309

Dynamo Subway Station
A315

Foundryman
A316

Moscow scenes: 20k, Council House & Hotel Moscow. 30k, Lenin Library. 40k, Crimea Bridge. 50k, Bridge over Moscow River. 80k, Khimki Station.

Paper with network as in parenthesis

1939, Mar. Typo. *Perf. 12*

706	A309 10k brn *(red brown)*	.95	.45
707	A309 20k dk sl grn *(lt blue)*	1.10	.45
708	A309 30k brn vio *(red brn)*	1.10	1.00
709	A309 40k blue *(lt blue)*	2.00	1.00
710	A309 50k rose lake *(red brn)*	3.25	1.25
711	A309 80k gray ol *(lt blue)*	3.50	1.25
712	A315 1r dk blue *(lt blue)*	6.00	2.00
	Nos. 706-712 (7)	17.90	7.40
	Set, never hinged	30.00	

"New Moscow." On 30k, denomination is at upper right.

1939, Mar.

713	A316 15k dark blue	1.00	.50
	Never hinged	1.25	
a.	Imperf.	250.00	
	Never hinged	100.00	

Statue on USSR Pavilion — A317

USSR Pavilion
A318

1939, May Photo.

714	A317 30k indigo & red	.45	.20
a.	Imperf. ('40)	.55	.35
715	A318 50k blue & bister brn	.55	.40
a.	Imperf. ('40)	.60	.45
	Set, never hinged	2.50	
	Set, imperf., never hinged	3.50	

Russia's participation in the NY World's Fair.

Paulina Osipenko
A318a

Marina Raskova
A318b

Design: 60k, Valentina Grizodubova.

1939, Mar.

718	A318a 15k green	1.25	.75
719	A318b 30k brown violet	1.25	.75
720	A318b 60k red	2.75	1.50
	Nos. 718-720 (3)	5.25	3.00
	Set, never hinged	10.00	

Non-stop record flight from Moscow to the Far East.

Exist imperf. Value, each $350.

Shevchenko, Early Portrait — A319

Monument at Kharkov — A321

30k, Shevchenko portrait in later years.

1939, Mar. 9

721	A319 15k black brn & blk	1.10	.55
722	A319 30k dark red & blk	1.10	.55
723	A321 60k green & dk brn	3.00	1.90
	Nos. 721-723 (3)	5.20	3.00
	Set, never hinged	10.00	

Taras G. Shevchenko (1814-1861), Ukrainian poet and painter.

Milkmaid with Prize Cow — A322

Tractor-plow at Work on Abundant Harvest
A323

Designs: 20k, Shepherd tending sheep. No. 727, Fair pavilion. No. 728, Fair emblem. 45k, Turkmen picking cotton. 50k, Drove of horses. 60k, Symbolizing agricultural wealth. 80k, Kolkhoz girl with sugar beets. 1r, Hunter with Polar foxes.

1939, Aug.

724	A322 10k rose pink	.50	.20
725	A323 15k red brown	.50	.20
726	A323 20k slate black	.50	.20
727	A323 30k purple	.50	.20
728	A322 30k red orange	.50	.20
729	A322 45k dark green	.60	.80
730	A322 50k copper red	.60	.80
731	A322 60k bright purple	1.10	1.10
732	A322 80k dark violet	1.10	1.10
733	A322 1r dark blue	2.25	1.40
	Nos. 724-733 (10)	8.15	6.20
	Set, never hinged	20.00	

Soviet Agricultural Fair.

A331

A332

Worker-Soldier-Aviator
A333

Arms of USSR
A334 A335

1939-43 Unwmk. Typo. *Perf. 12*

734	A331 5k red	.20	.20
735	A332 15k dark green	.25	.25
736	A333 30k deep blue	.25	.25
737	A334 60k fawn ('43)	.60	.25

Photo.

738	A335 60k rose carmine	.50	.35
	Nos. 734-738 (5)	1.80	1.30
	Set, never hinged	3.00	

No. 734 was re-issued in 1954-56 in slightly smaller format: 14x21½mm, instead of 14¾x22¼mm. Other values reissued in smaller format: 10k, 15k, 20k, 25k, 30k, 40k and 1r. (See notes following Nos. 622, 1260, 1347 and 1689.)

No. 416 Surcharged with New Value in Black

1939 Wmk. 170

743	A97 30k on 4k claret	10.00	8.00
	Never hinged	15.00	
a.	Unwmkd.	100.00	30.00

M.E. Saltykov (N. Shchedrin)
A336 A337

1939, Sept. Typo. Unwmk.

745	A336 15k claret	.30	.20
746	A337 30k dark green	.45	.35
747	A336 45k olive gray	.75	.35
748	A337 60k dark blue	.95	.55
	Nos. 745-748 (4)	2.45	1.45
	Set, never hinged	6.00	

Mikhail E. Saltykov (1826-89), writer & satirist who used pen name of N. Shchedrin.

Sanatorium of the State Bank — A338

Designs: 10k, 15k, Soviet Army sanatorium. 20k, Rest home, New Afyon. 30k, Clinical Institute. 50k, 80k, Sanatorium for workers in heavy industry. 60k, Rest home, Sukhumi.

1939, Nov. Photo. *Perf. 12*

749	A338 5k dull brown	.40	.20
750	A338 10k carmine	.40	.20
751	A338 15k yellow green	.40	.20
752	A338 20k dk slate green	.40	.20
753	A338 30k bluish black	.40	.20
754	A338 50k gray black	.85	.30
755	A338 60k brown violet	1.00	.45
756	A338 80k orange red	1.25	.60
	Nos. 749-756 (8)	5.10	2.35
	Set, never hinged	12.00	

Mikhail Y. Lermontov (1814-1841), Poet and Novelist, in 1837 — A346

Portrait in 1838 — A347

Portrait in 1841 — A348

1939, Dec.

757	A346 15k indigo & sepia	.75	.35
758	A347 30k dk grn & dull blk	1.75	.55
759	A348 45k brick red & indigo	3.00	2.10
	Nos. 757-759 (3)	5.50	3.00
	Set, never hinged	8.00	

Nikolai Chernyshevski A349

Anton Chekhov A350

1939, Dec. **Photo.**

760 A349 15k dark green	.90	.25
761 A349 30k dull violet	.90	.45
762 A349 60k Prus green	1.75	.45
Nos. 760-762 (3)	3.55	1.15
Set, never hinged	6.00	

50th anniversary of the death of Nikolai Chernyshevski, scientist and critic.

1940, Feb. **Unwmk.** ***Perf. 12***

Design: 20k, 30k, Portrait with hat.

763 A350 10k dark yellow green	.25	.25
764 A350 15k ultra	.25	.25
765 A350 20k violet	.50	.45
766 A350 30k copper brown	1.00	.55
Nos. 763-766 (4)	2.00	1.50
Set, never hinged	4.00	

Chekhov (1860-1904), playwright.

Welcome to Red Army by Western Ukraine and Western Byelorussia A352

Designs: 30k, Villagers welcoming tank crew. 50k, 60k, Soldier giving newspapers to crowd. 1r, Crowd waving to tank column.

1940, Apr.

767 A352 10k deep rose	.60	.20
768 A352 30k myrtle green	.60	.20
769 A352 50k gray black	1.10	.45
770 A352 60k indigo	1.10	.45
771 A352 1r red	1.75	.90
Nos. 767-771 (5)	5.15	2.20
Set, never hinged	15.00	

Liberation of the people of Western Ukraine and Western Byelorussia.

Ice-breaker "Josef Stalin," Captain Beloussov and Chief Ivan Papanin A356

Vadygin and Papanin A358

Map of the Drift of the Sedov and Crew Members — A359

Design: 30k, Icebreaker Georgi Sedov, Captain Vadygin and First Mate Trofimov.

1940, Apr.

772 A356 15k dull yel green	1.40	.55
773 A356 30k dull purple	2.75	.55
774 A358 50k copper brown	2.25	.55
775 A359 1r dark ultra	4.50	1.65
Nos. 772-775 (4)	10.90	3.30
Set, never hinged	15.00	

Heroism of the Sedov crew which drifted in the Polar Basin for 812 days.

A360

Vladimir V. Mayakovsky — A361

1940, June

776 A360 15k deep red	.30	.20
777 A360 30k copper brown	.55	.25
778 A361 60k dark gray blue	.60	.35
779 A361 80k bright ultra	.55	.35
Nos. 776-779 (4)	2.00	1.15
Set, never hinged	4.00	

Mayakovsky, poet (1893-1930).

K.A. Timiryazev and Academy of Agricultural Sciences A362

In the Laboratory of Moscow University A363

Last Portrait A364

Monument in Moscow — A365

1940, June

780 A362 10k indigo	.35	.25
781 A363 15k purple	.35	.35
782 A364 30k dk violet brown	.35	.35
783 A365 60k dark green	1.40	.60
Nos. 780-783 (4)	2.45	1.55
Set, never hinged	6.00	

20th anniversary of the death of K. A. Timiryasev, scientist and professor of agricultural and biological sciences.

Relay Race A366

Sportswomen Marching A367

Children's Sport Badge — A368

Skier A369

Throwing the Grenade A370

1940, July 21

784 A366 15k carmine rose	.75	.30
785 A367 30k sepia	1.50	.30
786 A368 50k dk violet blue	1.75	.60
787 A369 60k dk violet blue	2.25	.60
788 A370 1r grayish green	3.75	2.00
Nos. 784-788 (5)	10.00	3.80
Set, never hinged	25.00	

2nd All-Union Physical Culture Day.

Tchaikovsky Museum at Klin A371

Tchaikovsky & Passage from his Fourth Symphony A372

Peter Ilich Tchaikovsky and Excerpt from Eugene Onegin — A373

1940, Aug. **Unwmk.** **Typo.** ***Perf. 12***

789 A371 15k Prus green	1.50	.60
790 A372 20k brown	1.50	.60
791 A372 30k dark blue	1.50	.60
792 A371 50k rose lake	1.50	.80
793 A373 60k red	1.75	1.25
Nos. 789-793 (5)	7.75	3.85
Set, never hinged	15.00	

Tchaikovsky (1840-1893), composer.

Volga Provinces Pavilion A374

Northeast Provinces Pavilion — A376

#797 ПАВИЛЬОН МОСКОВСКОЙ, РЯЗАНСКОЙ И ТУЛЬСКОЙ ОБЛ.

ПАВИЛЬОН УКРАИНСКОЙ ССР #798

#799 ПАВИЛЬОН БЕЛОРУССКОЙ ССР

ПАВИЛЬОН АЗЕРБАЙДЖАНСКОЙ ССР #800

ПАВИЛЬОН ГРУЗИНСКОЙ ССР #801

#802 ПАВИЛЬОН АРМЯНСКОЙ ССР

„У ВХОДА В ПАВИЛЬОН УЗБЕКСКОЙ ССР" #803

ПАВИЛЬОН ТУРКМЕНСКОЙ ССР #804

#805 ПАВИЛЬОН ТАДЖИКСКОЙ ССР

ПАВИЛЬОН КИРГИЗСКОЙ ССР #806

#807 ПАВИЛЬОН КАЗАХСКОЙ ССР

ПАВИЛЬОН КАРЕЛО-ФИНСКОЙ ССР #808

1940, Oct. **Photo.**

794 A374 10k shown	1.25	.50
795 A374 15k Far East Provinces	1.25	.50
796 A376 30k shown	1.25	.70
797 A376 30k Central Regions	1.25	.70
798 A376 30k Ukrainian	1.25	.70
799 A376 30k Byelorussian	1.25	.70
800 A376 30k Azerbaijan	1.25	.70
801 A374 30k Georgian	1.25	.70
802 A376 30k Armenian	1.25	.70
803 A376 30k Uzbek	1.25	.70
804 A374 30k Turkmen	1.25	.70
805 A376 30k Tadzhik	1.25	.70
806 A376 30k Kirghiz	1.75	1.40
807 A376 30k Kazakh	1.75	1.40
808 A376 30k Karelian Finnish	1.75	1.40
809 A376 50k Main building	2.40	1.40
810 A376 60k Mechanizaton Pavilion, Stalin statue	2.75	1.40
Nos. 794-810 (17)	25.40	15.00
Set, never hinged	45.00	

All-Union Agricultural Fair.
Nos. 796-808 printed in three sheet formats with various vertical and horizontal se-tenant combinations.

Monument to Red Army Heroes — A391

Map of War Operations and M. V. Frunze — A393

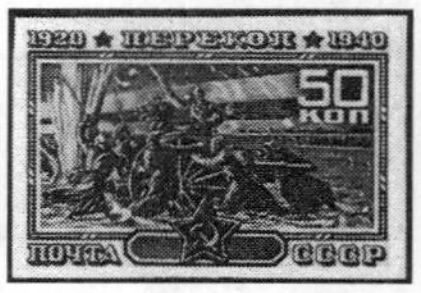

Heroic Crossing of the Sivash A394

Designs: 15k, Grenade thrower. 60k, Frunze's headquarters, Stroganovka. 1r, Victorious soldier.

1940 ***Imperf.***

811 A391 10k dark green	.50	.30
812 A391 15k orange ver	.50	.30
813 A393 30k dull brown & car	.50	.30
814 A394 50k violet brn	.50	.40
815 A394 60k indigo	.50	.60
816 A391 1r gray black	1.25	.60
Nos. 811-816 (6)	3.75	2.50
Set, never hinged	7.50	

20th anniversary of battle of Perekop.
Also issued perf. 12. Set price about 25% more.

Coal Miners — A397

Blast Furnace — A398

Bridge over Moscow-Volga Canal — A399

Three New Type Locomotives A400

Workers on a Collective Farm — A401

Automobiles and Planes A402

Oil Derricks — A403

1941, Jan. ***Perf. 12***

817	A397	10k deep blue	.65	.20
818	A398	15k dark violet	.65	.20
819	A399	20k deep blue	.65	.20
820	A400	30k dark brown	.85	.20
821	A401	50k olive brown	.85	.40
822	A402	60k olive brown	1.10	.55
823	A403	1r dark blue green	2.25	.80
		Nos. 817-823 (7)	7.00	2.55
		Set, never hinged	9.50	

Soviet industries.

Troops on Skis — A404

Sailor — A405

Soldiers with Cannon A406

20k, Cavalry. 30k, Machine gunners. 45k, Army horsemen. 50k, Aviator. 1r, 3r, Marshal's Star.

1941-43

824	A404	5k dark violet	.50	.20
825	A405	10k deep blue	.50	.20
826	A406	15k brt yellow green	.20	.20
827	A404	20k vermilion	.20	.20
828	A404	30k dull brown	.20	.20
829	A406	45k gray green	.60	.50
830	A404	50k dull blue	.35	.65
831	A404	1r dull blue green	.50	.90
831A	A404	3r myrtle grn ('43)	1.90	1.90
		Nos. 824-831A (9)	4.95	4.95
		Set, never hinged	10.00	

Army & Navy of the USSR, 23rd anniv.

Battle of Ismail — A412

Field Marshal Aleksandr Suvorov — A413

1941 **Unwmk.** ***Perf. 12***

832	A412	10k dark green	.40	.35
833	A412	15k carmine rose	.55	.55
834	A413	30k blue black	.80	.60
835	A413	1r olive brown	1.75	1.50
		Nos. 832-835 (4)	3.50	3.00
		Set, never hinged	5.00	

150th anniversary of the capture of the Turkish fortress, Ismail.

Kirghiz Horse Breeder A414

Kirghiz Miner A415

1941, Mar.

836	A414	15k dull brown	1.50	.45
837	A415	30k dull purple	2.00	.60
		Set, never hinged	4.75	

15th anniversary of the Kirghizian Soviet Socialist Republic.

Prof. N. E. Zhukovski A416

Zhukovski Lecturing A418

Military Air Academy A417

1941, Mar.

838	A416	15k deep blue	.55	.35
839	A417	30k carmine rose	.55	.50
840	A418	50k brown violet	.90	.65
		Nos. 838-840 (3)	2.00	1.50
		Set, never hinged	4.00	

Prof. Zhukovski, scientist (1847-1921).

Arms Type of 1938

Karelian-Finnish Soviet Socialist Republic.

1941, Mar.

841	A252	30k rose	.60	.40
842	A252	45k dark blue green	.90	.65
		Set, never hinged	2.50	

1st anniversary of the Karelian-Finnish Soviet Socialist Republic.

Spasski Tower, Kremlin — A420

Kremlin and Moscow River A421

1941, May **Typo.** **Unwmk.**

843	A420	1r dull red	.75	.50
844	A421	2r brown orange	1.25	1.00
		Set, never hinged	3.00	

"Suvorov's March through the Alps, 1799" A422

Vasili Ivanovich Surikov, Self-portrait A424

"Stepan Rasin on the Volga" A423

1941, June **Photo.** ***Perf. 12***

845	A422	20k black	1.25	.75
846	A423	30k scarlet	2.00	1.25
847	A422	50k dk violet brown	5.50	4.25
848	A423	1r gray green	6.75	5.25
849	A424	2r brown	12.00	6.00
		Nos. 845-849 (5)	27.50	17.50
		Set, never hinged	57.50	

Surikov (1848-1916), painter.

Mikhail Y. Lermontov, Poet, Death Centenary — A425

1941, July

850	A425	15k Prus green	5.50	2.25
851	A425	30k dark violet	6.50	3.50
		Set, never hinged	25.00	

Visitors in Lenin Museum A426

Lenin Museum A427

1941-42

852	A426	15k rose red	2.00	2.00
853	A427	30k dark violet ('42)	8.25	4.00
854	A426	45k Prus green	3.75	2.25
855	A427	1r orange brn ('42)	11.00	4.00
		Nos. 852-855 (4)	25.00	12.25
		Set, never hinged	50.00	

Fifth anniversary of Lenin Museum.

Mother's Farewell to a Soldier Son ("Be a Hero!") — A428

1941, Aug.

856	A428	30k carmine	15.00	15.00
		Never hinged	20.00	

Alisher Navoi — A429

People's Militia — A430

1942, Jan.

857	A429	30k brown	20.00	6.00
858	A429	1r dark violet	10.00	9.00
		Set, never hinged	50.00	

Alisher Navoi, Uzbekian poet, 500th birth anniv.

1941, Dec. **Typo.**

859	A430	30k dull blue	50.00	35.00
		Never hinged	75.00	

Junior Lieutenant Talalikhin Ramming German Plane in Midair A431

Captain Gastello and Burning Plane Diving into Enemy Gasoline Tanks A432

Major General Dovator and Cossack Cavalry in Action A433

Shura Chekalin Fighting Nazi Soldiers A434

Nazi Soldiers Leading Zoya Kosmodemjanskaja to her Death — A435

1942-44 Unwmk. Photo. *Perf. 12*

860 A431 20k bluish black .95 .45
860A A431 30k Prus grn ('44) .95 .45
861 A432 30k bluish black .95 .45
861A A432 30k dp ultra ('44) .95 .45
862 A433 30k black .95 .45
863 A434 30k black .95 .45
863A A434 30k brt yel green ('44) .95 .45
864 A435 30k black .95 .45
864A A435 30k rose vio ('44) .95 .45
865 A434 1r slate green 4.50 3.75
866 A435 2r slate green 7.00 5.50
Nos. 860-866 (11) 20.05 13.30
Set, never hinged 30.00

Issued to honor Soviet heroes.
For surcharges see Nos. C80-C81.

Anti-tank Artillery A436

Signal Corps in Action A437

Defense of Leningrad A440

Guerrilla Fighters A438

War Worker A439

Red Army Scouts — A441

1942-43

867 A436 20k black .40 .60
868 A437 30k sappire .70 .80
869 A438 30k Prus green ('43) .70 .80
870 A439 30k dull red brn ('43) .70 .80
871 A440 60k blue black 1.90 2.75
872 A441 1r black brown 3.25 4.25
Nos. 867-872 (6) 7.65 10.00
Set, never hinged 12.00

Women Workers and Soldiers A442

Flaming Tank A443

Women Preparing Food Shipments A444

Sewing Equipment for Red Army — A445

Anti-Aircraft Battery in Action — A446

1942-43 Typo. Unwmk.

873 A442 20k dark blue .65 .65
874 A443 20k dull rose violet .65 .65
875 A444 30k brown violet ('43) .70 .70
876 A445 45k dull rose red 1.50 1.50
877 A446 45k deep dull blue ('43) 1.50 1.50
Nos. 873-877 (5) 5.00 5.00
Set, never hinged 12.00

Manufacturing Explosives — A447

Designs: 10k, Agriculture. 15k, Group of Fighters. 20k, Storming the Palace. 30k, Lenin and Stalin. 60k, Tanks. 1r, Lenin. 2r, Revolution scene.

Inscribed: "1917 XXV 1942"

1943, Jan. Photo. *Perf. 12*

878 A447 5k black brown .40 .40
879 A447 10k black brown .40 .40
880 A447 15k blue black .40 .40
881 A447 20k blue black .55 .40
882 A447 30k black brown .60 .40
883 A447 60k black brown 1.25 .50
884 A447 1r dull red brown 1.90 1.00
885 A447 2r black 4.50 1.75
Nos. 878-885 (8) 10.00 5.25
Set, never hinged 20.00

25th anniversary of October Revolution.

Mount St. Elias, Alaska A455

Bering Sea and Bering's Ship — A456

1943, Apr.

886 A455 30k chalky blue .60 .35
887 A456 60k Prus green 1.00 .35
888 A455 1r yellow green 1.90 .35
889 A456 2r bister brown 3.50 .95
Nos. 886-889 (4) 7.00 2.00
Set, never hinged 12.00

200th anniv. of the death of Vitus Bering, explorer (1681-1741).

Medical Corpsmen and Wounded Soldier A457

Trench Mortar A458

Army Scouts A459

Repulsing Enemy Tanks A460

Snipers A461

1943

890 A457 30k myrtle green .65 .55
891 A458 30k brown bister .65 .55
892 A459 30k myrtle green .70 .55
893 A460 60k myrtle green 2.00 1.90
894 A461 60k chalky blue 2.00 1.90
Nos. 890-894 (5) 6.00 5.45
Set, never hinged 10.00

Maxim Gorki (1868-1936), Writer A462

1943, June

895 A462 30k green .35 .20
896 A462 60k slate black .45 .20
Set, never hinged 1.50

Patriotic War Medal A463

Order of Field Marshal Suvorov A464

1943, July Engr.

897 A463 1r black 1.00 1.00
898 A464 10r dk olive green 4.00 4.00
Set, never hinged 7.50

Sailors A465

Designs: 30k, Navy gunner and warship. 60k, Soldiers and tank.

1943, Oct. Photo.

899 A465 20k golden brown .20 .20
900 A465 30k dark myrtle green .20 .20
901 A465 60k brt yellow green .40 .20
902 A465 3r chalky blue 1.10 .50
Nos. 899-902 (4) 1.90 1.10
Set, never hinged 3.25

25th anniv. of the Red Army and Navy.

Karl Marx A468

Vladimir V. Mayakovsky A469

1943, Sept.

903 A468 30k blue black .40 .25
904 A468 60k dk slate green .60 .25
Set, never hinged 2.00

125th anniv. of the birth of Karl Marx.

1943, Oct.

905 A469 30k red orange .30 .25
906 A469 60k deep blue .40 .25
Set, never hinged 2.00

Mayakovsky, poet, 50th birth anniv.

Flags of US, Britain, and USSR A470

1943, Nov.

907 A470 30k blk, dp red & dk bl .40 .30
908 A470 3r sl blue, red & lt blue 2.60 .85
Set, never hinged 5.00

The Tehran conference.

Ivan Turgenev (1818-83), Poet — A471

1943, Oct.

909 A471 30k myrtle green 3.50 3.25
910 A471 60k dull purple 4.75 4.25
Set, never hinged 15.00

Map of Stalingrad A472

Harbor of Sevastopol and Statue of Lenin A473

Leningrad A474

Odessa A475

1944, Mar. *Perf. 12*

911	A472	30k dull brown & car	.30	.20
912	A473	30k dark blue	.30	.20
913	A474	30k dk slate green	.30	.20
914	A475	30k yel green	.30	.20
		Nos. 911-914 (4)	1.20	.80
		Set, never hinged	2.00	

Honoring the defenders of Stalingrad, Leningrad, Sevastopol and Odessa.
See No. 959.
No. 911 measures 33x22mm and also exists in smaller size: 32x21½mm.

USSR War Heroes A476

1944, Apr.

915	A476	30k deep ultra	.35	.25
		Never hinged	1.00	

Sailor Loading Gun — A477

Tanks — A478

Soldier Bayoneting a Nazi A479

Infantryman A480

Soldier Throwing Hand Grenade — A481

1943-44 **Photo.**

916	A477	15k deep ultra	.20	.20
917	A478	20k red orange ('44)	.20	.20
918	A479	30k dull brn & dk red ('44)	.25	.20
919	A480	1r brt yel green	.70	.40
920	A481	2r Prus green ('44)	1.25	1.00
		Nos. 916-920 (5)	2.60	2.00
		Set, never hinged	4.50	

25th anniversary of the Young Communist League (Komsomol).

Flags of US, USSR, Great Britain — A482

1944, May 30 **Unwmk.** *Perf. 12*

921	A482	60k black, red & blue	.50	.30
922	A482	3r dk bl, red & lt bl	2.75	1.10
		Set, never hinged	5.50	

Day of the Nations United Against Germany, June 14, 1944.

Patriotic War Order — A483

Order of Prince Alexander Nevsky — A484

Order of Field Marshal Suvorov — A485

Order of Field Marshal Kutuzov — A486

Paper with network as in parenthesis

1944 **Typo.** *Perf. 12, Imperf.*

923	A483	15k dull red *(rose)*	.20	.20
924	A484	20k blue *(lt blue)*	.20	.20
925	A485	30k green *(green)*	.45	.20
926	A486	60k dull red *(rose)*	.65	.35
		Set, never hinged	3.00	
		Nos. 923-926 (4)	1.50	.95

Beware of bogus perforation "errors" created from imperfs.

Order of Patriotic War — A487

Order of Prince, Alexander Nevski — A488

Order of Field Marshal Kutuzov A489

Order of Field Marshal Suvorov A490

1944, June **Unwmk.** **Engr.** *Perf. 12*

927	A487	1r black	.25	.20
928	A488	3r blue black	.55	.45
929	A489	5r dark olive green	.95	.60
930	A490	10r dark red	1.65	.70
		Nos. 927-930 (4)	3.40	1.95
		Set, never hinged	7.50	

Types of 1934, Inscribed 1924-1944 and

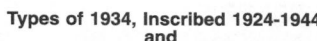

Lenin's Mausoleum — A491

30k (#931), 3r, Lenin & Stalin. 50k, Lenin in middle age. 60k, Lenin, the orator.

1944, June **Photo.**

931	A190	30k orange & car	.20	.20
932	A186	30k slate & black	.20	.20
933	A187	45k slate & black	.45	.30
934	A187	50k slate & black	.45	.30
935	A187	60k slate & black	.45	.30
936	A491	1r indigo & brn blk	1.10	.40
937	A190	3r bl blk & dull org	2.75	.85
		Nos. 931-937 (7)	5.60	2.55
		Set, never hinged	10.00	

20 years without Lenin.

Nikolai Rimski-Korsakov A492 A493

1944, June *Perf. 12, Imperf.*

938	A492	30k gray black	.20	.20
939	A493	60k slate green	.25	.20
940	A492	1r brt blue green	.55	.35
941	A493	3r purple	1.25	.50
		Nos. 938-941 (4)	2.25	1.25
		Set, never hinged	3.00	

Rimski-Korsakov (1844-1909), composer.

N.A. Schors A494

Sergei A. Chaplygin A497

Heroes of the 1918 Civil War: No. 943, V.I. Chapayev. No. 944, S.G. Lazho.

1944, Sept. *Perf. 12*

942	A494	30k gray black	.35	.20
943	A494	30k dark slate green	.35	.20
944	A494	30k brt yellow green	.35	.20
		Nos. 942-944 (3)	1.05	.60
		Set, never hinged	2.00	

See Nos. 1209-1211, 1403.

1944, Sept.

945	A497	30k gray	.25	.25
946	A497	1r lt brown	.85	.50
		Set, never hinged	2.50	

75th anniversary of the birth of Sergei A. Chaplygin, scientist and mathematician.

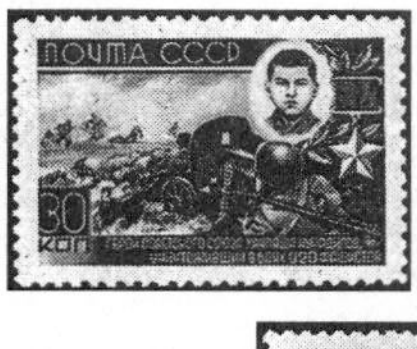
Khanpasha Nuradilov A498

A. Matrosov A499

F. Louzan A500

M. S. Polivanova and N. V. Kovshova A501

Pilot B. Safonov — A502

1944, July

947	A498	30k slate green	.20	.20
948	A499	60k dull purple	.40	.25
949	A500	60k dull blue	.40	.25
950	A501	60k bright green	.40	.25
951	A502	60k slate black	.60	.25
		Nos. 947-951 (5)	2.00	1.20
		Set, never hinged	4.50	

Soviet war heroes.

Ilya E. Repin — A503

Ivan A. Krylov — A505

"Cossacks' Reply to Sultan Mohammed IV" — A504

1944, Nov. *Perf. 12½, Imperf.*

952	A503	30k slate green	.25	.20
953	A504	50k dk blue green	.45	.20
954	A504	60k chalky blue	.45	.20
955	A503	1r dk orange brown	.60	.20
956	A504	2r dark purple	1.25	.30
		Nos. 952-956 (5)	3.00	1.10
		Set, never hinged	5.00	

I. E. Repin (1844-1930), painter.

1944, Nov. *Perf. 12*

957	A505	30k yellow brown	.20	.20
958	A505	1r dk violet blue	.25	.20
		Set, never hinged	.75	

Krylov, fable writer, death centenary.

Leningrad Type

Souvenir Sheet

1944, Dec. 6 *Imperf.*

959	Sheet of 4	5.00	4.75
	Never hinged	10.00	
a.	A474 30k dark slate green	.40	.40

Liberation of Leningrad, Jan. 27, 1944.

Partisan Medal — A507

Order for Bravery — A508

Order of Bogdan Chmielnicki
A509

Order of Victory
A510

Order of Ushakov
A511

Order of Nakhimov
A512

Paper with network as in parenthesis

Perf. 12½, Imperf.

1945, Jan. Typo. Unwmk.

960	A507	15k	black *(green)*	.20	.20
961	A508	30k	dp blue *(lt blue)*	.20	.20
962	A509	45k	dk blue	.20	.20
963	A510	60k	dl rose *(pale rose)*	.30	.20
964	A511	1r	dull blue *(green)*	.40	.20
965	A512	1r	yel green *(blue)*	.40	.20
			Nos. 960-965 (6)	1.70	1.20
			Set, never hinged	5.00	

Beware of bogus perforation "errors" created from imperfs.

Aleksandr S. Griboedov
A513

Red Army Soldier
A514

1945, Jan. Photo. *Perf. 12½*

966	A513	30k	dk slate green	.30	.20
967	A513	60k	gray brown	.55	.30
			Set, never hinged	1.25	

Griboedov (1795-1829), poet & statesman.

1945, Mar.

968	A514	60k	gray blk & henna	.50	.55
969	A514	3r	gray blk & henna	1.50	1.10
			Set, never hinged	4.50	

Souvenir Sheet

Imperf

970	Sheet of 4	30.00	30.00
	Never hinged	40.00	
a.	A514 3r gray brown & henna	7.50	7.50

Second anniv. of victory at Stalingrad.

Order for Bravery
A516

Order of Bogdan Chmielnicki
A517

Order of Victory — A518

1945 Engr. *Perf. 12*

971	A516	1r	indigo	.60	.45
972	A517	2r	black	2.00	1.10
973	A518	3r	henna	1.90	.95
			Nos. 971-973 (3)	4.50	2.50
			Set, never hinged	10.00	

See Nos. 1341-1342. For overprints see Nos. 992, 1709.

A519

A520

A521

A522

A523

Battle Scenes
A524

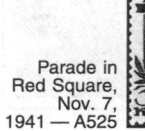

1945, Apr. Photo. *Perf. 12½*

974	A519	20k	sl grn, org red & black	.50	.40
975	A520	30k	bl blk & dull org	.50	.40
976	A521	30k	blue black	.50	.40
977	A522	60k	orange red	.85	.70
978	A523	1r	sl grn & org red	1.25	1.00
979	A524	1r	slate green	1.25	1.00
			Nos. 974-979 (6)	4.85	3.90
			Set, never hinged	7.00	

Red Army successes against Germany.

Parade in Red Square, Nov. 7, 1941 — A525

Designs: 60k, Soldiers and Moscow barricade, Dec. 1941. 1r, Air battle, 1941.

1945, June

980	A525	30k	dk blue violet	.25	.25
981	A525	60k	olive black	.40	.40
982	A525	1r	black brown	1.40	1.40
			Nos. 980-982 (3)	2.05	2.05
			Set, never hinged	4.00	

3rd anniversary of the victory over the Germans before Moscow.

Elite Guard Badge and Cannons
A528

Motherhood Medal
A529

Motherhood Glory Order — A530

Mother-Heroine Order — A531

1945, Apr. Typo.

983	A528	60k	red	1.00	.25
			Never hinged	1.50	

1945 *Perf. 12½, Imperf.*

Paper with network as in parenthesis

Size: 22x33¼mm

984	A529	20k	brown *(lt blue)*	.20	.20
985	A530	30k	yel brown *(green)*	.25	.20
986	A531	60k	dull rose *(pale rose)*	.40	.20

Perf. 12½

Engr.

Size: 20x38mm

986A	A529	1r	blk brn *(green)*	.40	.20
986B	A530	2r	dp bl *(lt blue)*	.90	.35
986C	A531	3r	brn red *(lt blue)*	1.00	.60
			Nos. 984-986C (6)	3.15	1.75
			Set, never hinged	4.00	

Academy Building, Moscow — A532

Academy at Leningrad and M. V. Lomonosov
A533

1945, June Photo. *Perf. 12½*

987	A532	30k	blue violet	.35	.20
a.			Horiz. pair, imperf. between	3.25	
988	A533	2r	grnsh black	1.25	.55
			Set, never hinged	2.00	

Academy of Sciences, 220th anniv.

Popov and his Invention
A534

Aleksandr S. Popov
A535

1945, July Unwmk.

989	A534	30k	dp blue violet	.40	.25
990	A534	60k	dark red	.85	.35
991	A535	1r	yellow brown	1.50	.50
			Nos. 989-991 (3)	2.75	1.10
			Set, never hinged	4.00	

"Invention of radio" by A. S. Popov, 50th anniv.

ПРАЗДНИК ПОБЕДЫ

9 мая 1945 года

No. 973 Overprinted in Blue

1945, Aug. *Perf. 12*

992	A518	3r	henna	1.00	.50
			Never hinged	1.50	

Victory of the Allied Nations in Europe.

Iakovlev Fighter — A536

Petliakov-2 Dive Bombers — A537

Ilyushin-2 Bombers
A538

#992A, 995, Iakovlev Fighter. #992B, 1000, Petliakov-2 dive bombers. #992C, 996, Ilyushin-2 bombers. #992D, 993, Petliakov-8 heavy bomber. #992E, 1001, Tupolev-2 bombers. #992F, 997, Ilyushin-4 bombers. #992G, 999, Polikarpov-2 biplane. #992H, 998, Lavochkin-7 fighters. #992I, 994, Iakovlev fighter in action.

1945-46 Unwmk. Photo. *Perf. 12*

992A	A536	5k	dk violet ('46)	.30	.20
992B	A537	10k	henna brn ('46)	.30	.20
992C	A538	15k	henna brn ('46)	.40	.20
992D	A536	15k	Prus grn ('46)	.40	.20
992E	A538	20k	gray brn ('46)	.45	.25
992F	A538	30k	violet ('46)	.45	.25
992G	A538	30k	brown ('46)	.45	.25
992H	A538	50k	blue vio ('46)	.95	.60
992I	A536	60k	dl bl vio ('46)	1.40	.60
993	A536	1r	gray black	2.50	1.50
994	A536	1r	henna brown	2.50	1.50
995	A536	1r	brown	2.50	1.50
996	A538	1r	deep brown	2.50	1.50
997	A538	1r	intense black	2.50	1.50
998	A538	1r	orange ver	2.50	1.50
999	A538	1r	bright green	2.50	1.50
1000	A537	1r	deep brown	2.50	1.50
1001	A538	1r	violet blue	2.50	1.50
			Nos. 992A-1001 (18)	27.60	16.25
			Set, never hinged	35.00	

Issued: #992A-992I, 3/26; #993-1001, 8/19.

A545

Lenin, 75th Birth Anniv. — A546

Various Lenin portraits.

Dated "1870-1945"

1945, Sept.				*Perf. 12½*	
1002	A545	30k	bluish black	.35	.25
1003	A546	50k	gray brown	.45	.25
1004	A546	60k	orange brown	.55	.25
1005	A546	1r	greenish black	.90	.35
1006	A546	3r	sepia	2.75	.80
			Nos. 1002-1006 (5)	5.00	1.90
			Set, never hinged	8.00	

Prince M. I. Kutuzov — A550

1945, Sept. 16					
1007	A550	30k	blue violet	.40	.30
1008	A550	60k	brown	.80	.45
			Set, never hinged	2.25	

Field Marshal Prince Mikhail Illarionovich Kutuzov (1745-1813).

Aleksandr Ivanovich Herzen A551

1945, Oct. 26					
1009	A551	30k	dark brown	.35	.25
1010	A551	2r	greenish black	1.10	.50
			Set, never hinged	3.25	

Herzen, author, revolutionist, 75th death anniv.

Ilya Mechnikov A552

Friedrich Engels A553

1945, Nov. 27					
1011	A552	30k	brown	.65	.25
1012	A552	1r	greenish black	1.25	.50
			Set, never hinged	3.75	

Ilya I. Mechnikov, zoologist and bacteriologist (1845-1916).

1945, Nov.			**Unwmk.**	*Perf. 12½*	
1013	A553	30k	dark brown	.45	.20
1014	A553	60k	Prussian green	.60	.30
			Set, never hinged	1.25	

125th anniversary of the birth of Friedrich Engels, collaborator of Karl Marx.

Tank Leaving Assembly Line — A554

Designs: 30k, Harvesting wheat. 60k, Airplane designing. 1r, Moscow fireworks.

1945, Dec. 25				**Photo.**	
1015	A554	20k	indigo & brown	.65	.25
1016	A554	30k	blk & org brn	.65	.60
1017	A554	60k	brown & green	1.10	.90
1018	A554	1r	dk blue & orange	1.60	1.25
			Nos. 1015-1018 (4)	4.00	3.00
			Set, never hinged	6.00	

Artillery Observer and Guns A558

Heavy Field Pieces A559

1945, Dec.					
1019	A558	30k	brown	.65	.50
1020	A559	60k	sepia	1.10	.75
			Set, never hinged	4.00	

Artillery Day, Nov. 19, 1945.

Catalogue values for unused stamps in this section, from this point to the end of the section, are for Never Hinged items.

Victory Medal — A560

Soldier with Victory Flag — A561

1946, Jan. 23					
1021	A560	30k	dk violet	.30	.20
1022	A560	30k	brown	.30	.20
1023	A560	60k	greenish black	.45	.20
1024	A560	60k	henna	.45	.20
1025	A561	60k	black & dull red	1.50	.70
			Nos. 1021-1025 (5)	3.00	1.50

Arms of USSR — A562

Red Square — A563

1946, Feb. 10					
1026	A562	30k	henna	.25	.20
1027	A563	45k	henna	.60	.45
1028	A562	60k	greenish black	2.40	.85
			Nos. 1026-1028 (3)	3.25	1.50

Elections to the Supreme Soviet of the USSR, Feb. 10, 1946.

Artillery in Victory Parade — A564

Victory Parade A565

1946, Feb. 23					
1029	A564	60k	dark brown	.75	.30
1030	A564	2r	dull violet	1.50	.60
1031	A565	3r	black & red	3.75	.85
			Nos. 1029-1031 (3)	6.00	1.75

Victory Parade, Moscow, June 24, 1945.

Order of Lenin — A566

Order of Red Star — A567

Medal of Hammer and Sickle A568

Order of Token of Veneration A569

Gold Star Medal — A570

Order of Red Banner — A571

Order of the Red Workers' Banner — A572

Paper with network as in parenthesis

1946		**Unwmk.**	**Typo.**	*Perf. 12½x12*	
1032	A566	60k	myrtle grn *(green)*	1.40	1.10
1033	A567	60k	dk vio brn *(brown)*	1.40	1.10
1034	A568	60k	plum *(pink)*	1.40	1.10
1035	A569	60k	dp blue *(green)*	1.40	1.10
1036	A570	60k	dk car *(salmon)*	1.40	1.10
1037	A571	60k	red *(salmon)*	1.40	1.10
1038	A572	60k	dk brn vio *(buff)*	1.40	1.10
			Nos. 1032-1038 (7)	9.80	7.70

See Nos. 1650-1654.

Workers' Achievement of Distinction A573

Workers' Gallantry A574

Marshal's Star — A575

Defense of Soviet Trans-Arctic Regions — A576

Meritorious Service in Battle A577

Defense of Caucasus A578

Defense of Moscow — A579

Bravery — A580

Paper with network as in parenthesis

1946					
1039	A573	60k	choc *(salmon)*	1.40	1.10
1040	A574	60k	brown *(salmon)*	1.40	1.10
1041	A575	60k	blue *(pale blue)*	1.40	1.10
1042	A576	60k	dk grn *(green)*	1.40	1.10
1043	A577	60k	dk blue *(green)*	1.40	1.10
1044	A578	60k	dk yel grn *(grn)*	1.40	1.10
1045	A579	60k	carmine *(pink)*	1.40	1.10
1046	A580	60k	dk violet *(blue)*	1.40	1.10
			Nos. 1039-1046 (8)	11.20	8.80

A581

Maxim Gorki A582

1946, June 18				**Photo.**	
1047	A581	30k	brown	.60	.25
1048	A582	60k	dark green	1.00	.25

10th anniversary of the death of Maxim Gorki (Alexei M. Peshkov).

Kalinin
A583

Chebyshev
A584

1946, June

1049	A583	20k sepia	2.00	.60

Mikhail Ivanovich Kalinin (1875-1946).

1946, May 25

1050	A584	30k brown	.65	.35
1051	A584	60k gray brown	.95	.65

Pafnuti Lvovich Chebyshev (1821-94), mathematician.

View of Sukhumi
A585

Sanatorium at Sochi — A587

Designs: #1053, Promenade at Gagri. 45k, New Afyon Sanatorium.

1946, June 18

1052	A585	15k dark brown	.40	.20
1053	A585	30k dk slate green	.50	.20
1054	A587	30k dark green	.50	.20
1055	A585	45k chestnut brown	.80	.20
		Nos. 1052-1055 (4)	2.20	.80

All-Union Parade of Physical Culturists — A589

1946, July 21

1056	A589	30k dark green	5.50	3.00

Tank Divisions in Red Square
A590

1946, Sept. 8

1057	A590	30k dark green	.75	.40
1058	A590	60k brown	1.25	.60

Honoring Soviet tankmen.

Belfry of Ivan the Great, Kremlin — A591

Bolshoi Theater, Moscow — A592

Hotel Moscow
A593

Red Square — A597

Spasski Tower and Statues of Minin and Pozharski — A598

Moscow scenes: 20k, Bolshoi Theater, Sverdlov Square. 45k, View of Kremlin. 50k, Lenin Museum.

1946, Sept. 5

1059	A591	5k brown	.35	.20
1060	A592	10k sepia	.35	.20
1061	A593	15k chestnut	.35	.20
1062	A593	20k light brown	.70	.20
1063	A593	45k dark green	1.00	.25
1064	A593	50k brown	1.50	.40
1065	A597	60k blue violet	1.75	.50
1066	A598	1r chestnut brown	2.50	.55
		Nos. 1059-1066 (8)	8.50	2.50

Workers' Achievement of Distinction
A599

Workers' Gallantry
A600

Partisan of the Patriotic War — A601

Defense of Soviet Trans-Arctic Regions — A602

Meritorious Service in Battle
A603

Defense of Caucasus
A604

Defense of Moscow — A605

Bravery — A606

1946, Sept. 5 **Engr.**

1067	A599	1r dark violet brown	1.65	.75
1068	A600	1r dark carmine	1.65	.75
1069	A601	1r carmine	1.65	.75
1070	A602	1r blue black	1.65	.75
1071	A603	1r black	1.65	.75
1072	A604	1r black brown	1.65	.75
1073	A605	1r olive black	1.65	.75
1074	A606	1r deep claret	1.65	.75
		Nos. 1067-1074 (8)	13.20	6.00

See Nos. 1650-1654.

Give the Country Each Year: 127 Million Tons of Grain
A607

60 Million Tons of Oil — A608

60 Million Tons of Steel — A610

500 Million Tons of Coal — A609

50 Million Tons of Cast Iron — A611

Perf. 12½x12

1946, Oct. 6 **Photo.** **Unwmk.**

1075	A607	5k olive brown	.20	.20
1076	A608	10k dk slate green	.20	.20
1077	A609	15k brown	.30	.20
1078	A610	20k dk blue violet	.50	.20
1079	A611	30k brown	.80	.20
		Nos. 1075-1079 (5)	2.00	1.00

Symbols of Transportation, Map and Stamps — A612

Early Soviet Stamp
A613

Stamps of Soviet Russia — A614

1946, Nov. 6 ***Perf. 12½***

1080	A612	15k black & dk red	.90	.55
a.		Sheet of 4, imperf.	50.00	45.00
1081	A613	30k dk green & brn	1.40	.60
a.		Sheet of 4, imperf.	50.00	45.00
1082	A614	60k dk green & blk	1.90	.85
a.		Sheet of 4, imperf.	50.00	45.00
		Nos. 1080-1082 (3)	4.20	2.00

1st Soviet postage stamp, 25th anniv.

Lenin and Stalin — A615

1946 **Photo.** ***Perf. 12½***

1083	A615	30k dp brown org	1.50	1.25
a.		Sheet of 4, imperf.	25.00	17.50
b.		Single, imperf	1.75	1.25
1084	A615	30k dk green	1.50	1.25
a.		Single, imperf	1.75	1.25

October Revolution, 29th anniv.

Issued: #1083b-1084a, 11/6; #1083-1084, 12/18; #1083a, 6/47.

Dnieprostroy Dam and Power Station — A616

1946, Dec. 23 ***Perf. 12½***

1085	A616	30k sepia	1.50	.60
1086	A616	60k chalky blue	2.50	.90

Aleksandr P. Karpinsky
A617

Nikolai A. Nekrasov
A618

1947, Jan. 17 **Unwmk.**

1087	A617	30k dark green	.75	.75
1088	A617	50k sepia	1.75	1.00

Karpinsky (1847-1936), geologist.

Canceled to Order

Canceled sets of new issues have long been sold by the government. Values in the second ("used") column are for these canceled-to-order stamps. Postally used copies are worth more.

1946, Dec. 4

1089	A618	30k sepia	.50	.25
1090	A618	60k brown	1.00	.75

Nikolai A. Nekrasov (1821-1878), poet.

Lenin's Mausoleum
A619

Lenin — A620

1947, Jan. 21

1091	A619	30k	slate blue	.65	.65
1092	A619	30k	dark green	.65	.65
1093	A620	50k	dark brown	2.50	1.25
			Nos. 1091-1093 (3)	3.80	2.55

23rd anniversary of the death of Lenin.
See Nos. 1197-1199.

F. P. Litke and Sailing Vessel A621

N. M. Przewalski, Mare and Foal — A622

1947, Jan. 27

1094	A621	20k	blue violet	1.40	.45
1095	A621	20k	sepia	1.40	.45
1096	A622	60k	olive brown	1.60	.55
1097	A622	60k	sepia	1.60	.55
			Nos. 1094-1097 (4)	6.00	2.00

Soviet Union Geographical Society, cent.

Nikolai E. Zhukovski (1847-1921), Scientist A623

1947, Jan. 17

1098	A623	30k	sepia	1.50	.40
1099	A623	60k	blue violet	2.25	.60

Stalin Prize Medal — A624

1946, Dec. 21 **Photo.**

1100	A624	30k	black brown	2.25	.75

Russian Soldier A625

Military Instruction A626

Aviator, Sailor and Soldier A627

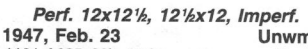

Perf. 12x12½, 12½x12, Imperf.

1947, Feb. 23 **Unwmk.**

1101	A625	20k	sepia	.45	.20
1102	A626	30k	slate blue	.45	.20
1103	A627	30k	brown	.45	.20
			Nos. 1101-1103 (3)	1.35	.60

29th anniversary of the Soviet Army.

Reprints

From here through 1953 many sets exist in two distinct printings from different plates.

Arms of:

Russian Socialist Federated Soviet Republic — A628

Armenian SSR — A629

Azerbaijan SSR — A630

Byelorussian SSR — A631

Estonian SSR — A632

Georgian SSR — A633

Karelo Finnish SSR — A634

Kazakh SSR — A635

Kirghiz SSR — A636

Latvian SSR — A637

Lithuanian SSR — A638

Moldavian SSR — A639

Tadzhkistan SSR — A640

Turkmen SSR — A641

Ukrainian SSR — A642

Uzbek SSR — A643

Soviet Union — A644

1947 **Unwmk.** **Photo.** ***Perf. 12½***

1104	A628	30k	henna brown	.90	.30
1105	A629	30k	chestnut	.90	.30
1106	A630	30k	olive brown	.90	.30
1107	A631	30k	olive green	.90	.30
1108	A632	30k	violet black	.90	.30
1109	A633	30k	dark vio brown	.90	.30
1110	A634	30k	dark violet	.90	.30
1111	A635	30k	deep orange	.90	.30
1112	A636	30k	dark violet	.90	.30
1113	A637	30k	yellow brown	.90	.30
1114	A638	30k	dark olive green	.90	.30
1115	A639	30k	dark vio brown	.90	.00
1116	A640	30k	dark green	.90	.30
1117	A641	30k	gray black	.90	.30
1118	A642	30k	blue violet	.90	.30
1119	A643	30k	brown	.90	.30

Litho.

1120	A644	1r	dk brn, bl, gold & red	3.00	1.00
			Nos. 1104-1120 (17)	17.40	5.50

Aleksander S. Pushkin (1799-1837), Poet — A645

1947, Feb. **Photo.** ***Perf. 12***

1121	A645	30k	sepia	.75	.35
1122	A645	50k	dk yellow green	1.25	.75

Classroom A646

Parade of Women — A647

1947, Mar. 11

1123	A646	15k	bright blue	1.00	.60
1124	A647	30k	red	1.25	.90

Intl. Day of Women, Mar. 8, 1947.

Moscow Council Building A648

1947 ***Perf. 12½***

1125	A648	30k	sep, gray blue & brick red	2.00	1.00

30th anniversary of the Moscow Soviet. Exists imperf. The imperf. exists also with gray blue omitted.

Both perf. and imperf. stamps exist in two sizes: 40x27mm and 41x27mm.

May Day Parade in Red Square — A649

1947, June 10 ***Perf. 12½***

1126	A649	30k	scarlet	.55	.35
1127	A649	1r	dk olive green	1.50	.55

Labor Day, May 1, 1947.

Nos. 1062, 1064-1066 Overprinted in Red

800 лет Москвы
1147 – 1947 гг.

1947, Sept. ***Perf. 12½x12***

1128	A593	20k	lt brown	.75	.20
1129	A593	50k	brown	1.00	.50
1130	A597	60k	blue violet	1.25	.60
1131	A598	1r	chestnut brown	2.00	.70
			Nos. 1128-1131 (4)	5.00	2.00

Overprint arranged in 4 lines on No. 1131.

Crimea Bridge, Moscow — A650

Gorki Street, Moscow A651

View of Kremlin, Moscow — A652

Designs: No. 1134, Central Telegraph Building. No. 1135, Kiev Railroad Station. No. 1136, Kazan Railroad Station. No. 1137, Kaluga St. No. 1138, Pushkin Square. 50k, View of Kremlin. No. 1141, Grand Kremlin Palace. No. 1142, "Old Moscow," by Vasnetsov. No. 1143, St. Basil Cathedral. 2r, View of Kremlin. 3r, View of Kremlin. 5r, Hotel Moscow and government building.

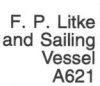

1947 Photo. *Perf. 12½*

Various Frames, Dated 1147-1947

1132	A650	5k	dk bl & dk brn	.35	.25
1133	A651	10k	red brown & brn black	.35	.25
1134	A650	30k	brown	.45	.25
1135	A650	30k	dk Prus blue	.45	.25
1136	A650	30k	ultra	.45	.25
1137	A650	30k	dp yel green	.45	.25
1138	A651	30k	yel green	.45	.25
1139	A650	50k	dp yel green	.65	.40
1140	A652	60k	red brown & brn blk	.70	.40
1141	A651	60k	gray blue	.70	.40
1142	A651	1r	dark violet	1.50	.95

Typo.

Colors: Blue, Yellow and Red

1143	A651	1r	multicolored	1.50	.95
1144	A651	2r	multicolored	2.75	1.90
1145	A650	3r	multicolored	5.25	1.90
a.			Souv. sheet of 4, imperf.	30.00	20.00
1146	A650	5r	multicolored	9.00	3.25
			Nos. 1132-1146 (15)	25.00	11.90

Nos. 1128-1146 for founding of Moscow, 800th anniv.

Nos. 1143-1146 were printed in a single sheet containing a row of each denomination plus a row of labels.

Karamyshevsky Dam — A653

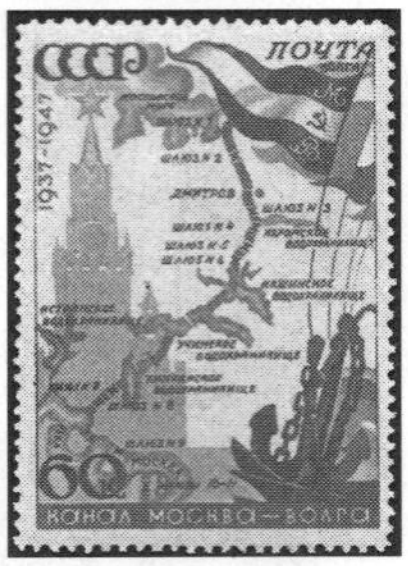

Map Showing Moscow-Volga Canal — A654

Designs: No. 1148, Direction towers, Yakromsky Lock. 45k, Yakromsky Pumping Station. 50k, Khimki Station. 1r, Lock #8.

1947, Sept. 7 Photo.

1147	A653	30k	sepia	.65	.20
1148	A653	30k	red brown	.65	.20
1149	A653	45k	henna brown	.65	.20
1150	A653	50k	bright ultra	.65	.20
1151	A654	60k	bright rose	.65	.20
1152	A653	1r	violet	.90	.20
			Nos. 1147-1152 (6)	4.15	1.20

Moscow-Volga Canal, 10th anniversary.

Elektrozavodskaya Station — A655

Mayakovsky Station — A656

Planes and Flag — A657

Moscow Subway scenes: No. 1154, Ismailovsky Station. No. 1155, Sokol Station. No. 1156, Stalinsky Station. No. 1158, Kiev Station.

1947, Sept.

1153	A655	30k	sepia	.65	.55
1154	A655	30k	blue black	.65	.55
1155	A655	45k	yellow brown	.90	.55
1156	A655	45k	deep violet	.90	.55
1157	A656	60k	henna brown	1.50	.65
1158	A655	60k	deep yel grn	1.50	.65
			Nos. 1153-1158 (6)	6.10	3.50

1947, Sept. 1

1159	A657	30k	deep violet	.35	.20
1160	A657	1r	bright ultra	.85	.30

Day of the Air Fleet. For overprints see Nos. 1246-1247.

Spasski Tower, Kremlin — A658

Perf. 12½

1947, Nov. Unwmk. Typo.

1161	A658	60k	dark red	10.00	4.00

See No. 1260.

Agave Plant at Sukhumi — A659

Gullripsh Sanatorium, Sukhumi A660

Peasants', Livadia A661

New Riviera A662

Russian sanatoria: No. 1166, Abkhasia, New Afyon. No. 1167, Kemeri, near Riga. No. 1168, Kirov Memorial, Kislovodsk. No. 1169, Voroshilov Memorial, Sochi. No. 1170, Riza, Gagri. No. 1171, Zapadugol, Sochi.

1947, Nov. Photo.

1162	A659	30k	dark green	.55	.20
1163	A660	30k	violet	.55	.20
1164	A661	30k	olive	.55	.20
1165	A662	30k	brown	.55	.20
1166	A660	30k	red brown	.55	.20
1167	A660	30k	black violet	.55	.20
1168	A660	30k	bright ultra	.55	.20
1169	A660	30k	dk brown violet	.55	.20
1170	A659	30k	dk yel green	.55	.20
1171	A660	30k	sepia	.55	.20
			Nos. 1162-1171 (10)	5.50	2.00

Blast Furnaces, Constantine A663

Tractor Plant, Kharkov A664

Tractor Plant, Stalingrad A665

Maxim Gorki Theater, Stalingrad A666

20k, #1180, Kirov foundry, Makeevka. #1175, 1179, Agricultural machine plant, Rostov.

1947, Nov. *Perf. 12½, Imperf.*

1172	A663	15k	yellow brown	.20	.20
1173	A663	20k	sepia	.35	.20
1174	A663	30k	violet brown	.55	.25
1175	A663	30k	dark green	.55	.25
1176	A664	30k	brown	.55	.25
1177	A665	30k	black brown	.55	.25
1178	A666	60k	violet brown	1.25	.70
1179	A663	60k	yellow brown	1.25	.70
1180	A663	1r	orange red	2.25	1.40
1181	A664	1r	red	2.25	1.40
1182	A665	1r	violet	2.25	1.40
			Nos. 1172-1182 (11)	12.00	7.00

Reconstruction of war-damaged cities and factories, and as Five-Year-Plan publicity.

Revolutionists — A667

Designs: 30k, No. 1185, Revolutionists. 50k, 1r, Industry. No. 1186, 2r, Agriculture.

1947, Nov. *Perf. 12½, Imperf.*

Frame in Dark Red

1183	A667	30k	greenish black	.50	.30
1184	A667	50k	blue black	.75	.40
1185	A667	60k	brown black	1.25	.55
1186	A667	60k	brown	1.25	.55
1187	A667	1r	black	2.00	.95
1188	A667	2r	greenish black	3.25	1.50
			Nos. 1183-1188 (6)	9.00	4.25

30th anniversary of October Revolution.

Palace of the Arts (Winter Palace) A668

Peter I Monument — A669

Designs (Leningrad in 1947): 60k, Sts. Peter and Paul Fortress. 1r, Smolny Institute.

1948, Jan. 10 *Perf. 12½*

1189	A668	30k	violet	.90	.40
1190	A669	50k	dk slate green	1.65	.45
1191	A668	60k	sepia	1.65	.75
1192	A669	1r	dk brown violet	2.75	1.10
			Nos. 1189-1192 (4)	6.95	2.70

5th anniversary of the liberation of Leningrad from the German blockade.

Government Building, Kiev — A670

50k, Dnieprostroy Dam. 60k, Wheat field, granary. 1r, Steel mill, coal mine.

1948, Jan. 25 *Perf. 12½*

1193	A670	30k	indigo	1.10	.40
1194	A670	50k	violet	1.65	.50
1195	A670	60k	golden brown	2.25	.85
1196	A670	1r	sepia	3.50	2.25
			Nos. 1193-1196 (4)	8.50	4.00

Ukrainian SSR, 30th anniv.

Lenin Types of 1947 Inscribed "1924-1948"

1948, Jan. 21 Unwmk.

1197	A619	30k	brown violet	1.00	.55
1198	A619	60k	dark gray blue	2.00	.70
1199	A620	60k	deep yellow green	2.00	.70
			Nos. 1197-1199 (3)	5.00	1.95

24th anniversary of the death of Lenin.

Vasili I. Surikov — A672

Soviet Soldier and Artillery — A675

Fliers and Planes A676

1948, Feb. 15 Photo. *Perf. 12*

1201	A672	30k	red brown	1.40	.75
1202	A672	60k	dark green	2.75	1.25

Vasili Ivanovich Surikov, artist, birth cent.

1948, Feb. 23

No. 1206, Soviet sailor. 60k, Military class.

1205	A675	30k	brown	1.10	.55
1206	A675	30k	gray	1.10	.55
1207	A676	30k	violet blue	1.10	.55
1208	A676	60k	red brown	1.75	.85
			Nos. 1205-1208 (4)	5.05	2.50

Hero Types of 1944

Designs: No. 1209, N.A. Schors. No. 1210, V.I. Chapayev. No. 1211, S.G. Lazho.

1948, Feb. 23

1209	A494	60k	deep green	1.60	1.00
1210	A494	60k	yellow brown	1.60	1.00
1211	A494	60k	violet blue	1.60	1.00
			Nos. 1209-1211 (3)	4.80	3.00

Nos. 1205-1211 for Soviet army, 30th anniv.

Karl Marx, Friedrich Engels and Communist Manifesto A677

1948, Apr.

1212	A677	30k	black	.60	.20
1213	A677	50k	henna brown	1.40	.30

Centenary of the Communist Manifesto.

Miner
A678

Marine
A679

Aviator
A680

Woman Farmer
A681

Arms of USSR
A682

Scientist
A683

Spasski Tower, Kremlin
A684

Soldier
A685

1948 **Photo.**

1214	A678	5k sepia	1.00	.45
1215	A679	10k violet	1.00	.45
1216	A680	15k bright blue	2.25	1.25
1217	A681	20k brown	2.50	1.10
1218	A682	30k henna brown	4.00	1.75
1219	A683	45k brown violet	4.50	2.75
1220	A684	50k bright blue	5.50	4.25
1221	A685	60k bright green	9.25	6.00
		Nos. 1214-1221 (8)	30.00	18.00

See Nos. 1306, 1343-1347, 1689.

May Day Parade in Red Square — A686

1948, June 5 ***Perf. 12***

1222	A686	30k deep car rose	1.00	.80
1223	A686	60k bright blue	2.00	1.25

Labor Day, May 1, 1948.

Vissarion G. Belinski (1811-48), Literary Critic — A687

1948, June 7 **Unwmk.** ***Perf. 12***

1224	A687	30k brown	.85	.85
1225	A687	50k dark green	1.40	.85
1226	A687	60k purple	1.75	.85
		Nos. 1224-1226 (3)	4.00	2.55

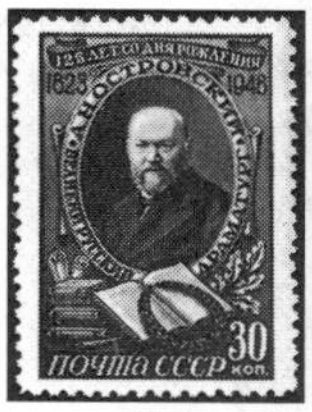

Aleksandr N. Ostrovski
A690 A691

1948, June 10 **Photo.** ***Perf. 12***

1227	A690	30k bright green	1.90	.85
1228	A691	60k brown	2.25	1.50
1229	A691	1r brown violet	3.75	2.50
		Nos. 1227-1229 (3)	7.90	4.85

Ostrovski (1823-1886), playwright.
Exist imperf. Value, set $250.

Ivan I. Shishkin (1832-1898), Painter — A692

"Field of Rye," by Shishkin
A693

60k, "Bears in a Forest," by Shishkin.

Photo. (30k, 1r), Typo. (50k, 60k)
1948, June 12

1230	A692	30k dk grn & vio brn	3.00	.55
1231	A693	50k multicolored	4.75	.60
1232	A693	60k multicolored	7.25	.75
1233	A692	1r brn & bl blk	9.00	1.10
		Nos. 1230-1233 (4)	24.00	3.00

Industrial Expansion
A694

Public Gathering at Leningrad — A695

Photo., Frames Litho. in Carmine
1948, June 25

1234	A694	15k red brown	2.00	1.00
1235	A695	30k slate	2.50	1.50
1236	A694	60k brown black	4.00	2.25
		Nos. 1234-1236 (3)	8.50	4.75

Industrial five-year plan.

Planting Crops
A696

#1238, 1r, Gathering vegetables. 45k, #1241, Baling cotton. #1242, Harvesting grain.

1948, July 12 **Photo.**

1237	A696	30k carmine rose	.40	.30
1238	A696	30k blue green	.40	.30
1239	A696	45k red brown	.80	.70
1240	A696	50k brown black	1.25	.70
1241	A696	60k dark green	.95	.80
1242	A696	60k dk blue green	.95	.80
1243	A696	1r purple	3.25	1.40
		Nos. 1237-1243 (7)	8.00	5.00

Agricultural five-year plan.

Arms and Citizens of USSR — A697

Soviet Miners — A698

Photo., Frames Litho. in Carmine
1948, July 25

1244	A697	30k slate	1.90	.90
1245	A697	60k greenish black	2.25	1.10

25th anniv. of the USSR.

ИЮЛЬ
1948
года

Nos. 1159 and 1160 Overprinted in Red

1948, Aug. 24 ***Perf. 12½***

1246	A657	30k deep violet	2.50	1.50
1247	A657	1r bright ultra	2.50	1.50

Air Fleet Day, 1948. On sale one day.

1948, Aug. **Photo.** ***Perf. 12½x12***

Miner's Day, Aug. 29: 60k, Scene in mine. 1r, Miner's badge.

1248	A698	30k blue	.75	.20
1249	A698	60k purple	1.50	.45
1250	A698	1r green	2.75	.85
		Nos. 1248-1250 (3)	5.00	1.50

A. A. Zhdanov — A699

Soviet Sailor — A700

1948, Sept. 3

1251	A699	40k slate	2.25	1.00

Andrei A. Zhdanov, statesman, 1896-1948.

1948, Sept. 12 ***Perf. 12***

1252	A700	30k blue green	1.65	1.25
1253	A700	60k bright blue	4.75	2.00

Navy Day, Sept. 12.

Slalom
A701

Motorcyclist — A702

Designs: No. 1254, Foot race. 30k, Soccer game. 45k, Motorboat race. 50k, Diving.

1948, Sept. 15 ***Perf. 12½x12***

1253A	A701	15k dark blue	1.00	.25
1254	A702	15k violet	1.00	.25
1254A	A702	20k dk slate blue	1.25	.25
1255	A701	30k brown	1.40	.25
1256	A701	45k sepia	1.65	.25
1257	A702	50k blue	2.50	.35
		Nos. 1253A-1257 (6)	8.80	1.60

Tankmen Group
A703

Design: 1r, Tank parade.

1948, Sept. 25

1258	A703	30k sepia	2.75	1.50
1259	A703	1r rose	6.75	3.50

Day of the Tankmen, Sept. 25.

Spasski Tower Type of 1947

1948 **Litho.** ***Perf. 12x12½***

1260	A658	1r brown red	.90	.25

No. 1260 was re-issued in 1954-56 in slightly smaller format: 14½x21½mm, instead of 14¾x22mm and in a paler shade. See note after No. 738.

Train — A704

Transportation 5-year plan: 60k, Auto and bus at intersection. 1r, Steamships at anchor.

1948, Sept. 30 **Photo.** ***Perf. 12½x12***

1261	A704	30k brown	3.50	1.75
1262	A704	50k dark green	5.00	2.00
1263	A704	60k blue	8.25	2.00
1264	A704	1r blue violet	10.50	3.50
		Nos. 1261-1264 (4)	27.25	9.25

Horses
A705

Livestock 5-year plan: 60k, Dairy farm.

1948, Sept. 30 ***Perf. 12***

1265	A705	30k slate gray	1.50	1.10
1266	A705	60k bright green	2.50	1.75
1267	A705	1r brown	3.50	2.25
		Nos. 1265-1267 (3)	7.50	5.10

Pouring Molten Metal
A706

Designs: 60k, 1r, Iron pipe manufacture.

1948, Oct. 14 ***Perf. 12½***

1268	A706	30k purple	1.25	.60
1269	A706	50k brown	1.50	.80
1270	A706	60k carmine	1.75	1.25
1271	A706	1r dull blue	3.50	2.00
		Nos. 1268-1271 (4)	8.00	4.65

Heavy Machinery Plant — A707

1948, Oct. 14

Design: 60k, Pump station interior.

1272	A707	30k purple	.90	.50
1273	A707	50k sepia	1.75	1.25
1274	A707	60k brown	2.50	1.40
		Nos. 1272-1274 (3)	5.15	3.15

Nos. 1268-1274 publicize the 5-year plan for steel, iron and machinery industries.

Khachatur Abovian (1809-1848), Armenian Writer and Poet — A708

1948, Oct. 16 *Perf. 12x12½*

1275	A708 40k purple		3.00	2.50
1276	A708 50k deep green		4.00	2.50

Farkhatz Hydroelectric Station A709

Design: 60k, Zouiev Hydroelectric Station.

1948, Oct. 24 *Perf. 12½*

1277	A709 30k green	2.50	1.50
1278	A709 60k red	5.25	2.75
1279	A709 1r carmine rose	4.75	2.75
	Nos. 1277-1279 (3)	12.50	7.00

Electrification five-year plan.

Coal Mine — A710

Designs: #1282, 1r, Oil field and tank cars.

1948, Oct. 24

1280	A710 30k sepia	1.90	.75
1281	A710 60k brown	2.00	1.10
1282	A710 60k red brown	2.00	1.10
1283	A710 1r blue green	4.00	2.50
	Nos. 1280-1283 (4)	9.90	5.45

Coal mining and oil production 5-year plan.

Flying Model Planes — A712

Pioneers Saluting — A714

Marching Pioneers A713

60k, Pioneer bugler. 1r, Pioneers at campfire.

1948, Oct. 26 *Perf. 12½*

1284	A712 30k dark bl grn	5.50	2.00
1285	A713 45k dark violet	7.25	2.25
1286	A714 45k deep carmine	7.25	2.25
1287	A714 60k deep ultra	9.00	3.25
1288	A713 1r deep blue	21.00	5.50
	Nos. 1284-1288 (5)	50.00	15.25

Young Pioneers, a Soviet youth organization, and governmental supervision of children's summer vacations.

Marching Youths A715

Farm Girl — A716

League Members and Flag — A717

Designs: 50k, Communist students. 1r, Flag and badges. 2r, Young worker.

1948, Oct. 29 *Perf. 12½*
Inscribed: "1918 1948 XXX"

1289	A715 20k violet brown	3.25	.80
1290	A716 25k rose red	2.00	1.00
1291	A717 40k brown & red	3.50	1.25
1292	A715 50k blue green	6.75	1.65
1293	A717 1r multicolored	22.50	3.50
1294	A716 2r purple	12.00	7.00
	Nos. 1289-1294 (6)	50.00	15.20

30th anniversary of the Young Communist League (Komsomol).

Stage of Moscow Art Theater A719

K. S. Stanislavski, V. I. Nemirovich Danchenko A720

1948, Nov. 1 *Perf. 12½*

1295	A719 40k gray blue	2.50	1.75
1296	A720 1r violet brown	3.50	3.25

Moscow Art Theater, 50th anniv.

Flag and Moscow Buildings — A721

1948, Nov. 7 *Perf. 12½*

1297	A721 40k red	1.50	1.25
1298	A721 1r green	2.25	1.75

31st anniversary of October Revolution.

House of Unions, Moscow A722

Player's Badge (Rook and Chessboard) A723

1948, Nov. 20 *Perf. 12½*

1299	A722 30k greenish blue	2.00	.35
1300	A723 40k violet	5.00	.50
1301	A722 50k orange brown	5.00	.90
	Nos. 1299-1301 (3)	12.00	1.75

16th Chess Championship.

Artillery Salute A724

1948, Nov. 19 *Perf. 12½*

1302	A724 30k blue	10.00	4.00
1303	A724 1r rose carmine	20.00	6.00

Artillery Day, Nov. 19, 1948.

Vasili Petrovich Stasov — A725

Stasov and Barracks of Paul's Regiment, Petrograd A726

1948, Nov. 27 **Unwmk.**

1304	A725 40k brown	1.40	.70
1305	A726 1r sepia	2.60	1.00

Stasov (1769-1848), architect.

Arms Type of 1948

1948 **Litho.** *Perf. 12x12½*

1306	A682 40k brown red	5.50	.20

Y. M. Sverdlov Monument A727

Design: 40k, Lenin Street, Sverdlovsk.

1948 **Photo.** *Perf. 12½*

1307	A727 30k blue	.25	.20
1308	A727 40k purple	.40	.20
1309	A727 1r bright green	.85	.20
	Nos. 1307-1309 (3)	1.50	.60

225th anniv. of the city of Sverdlovsk (before 1924, Ekaterinburg). Exist imperf. Value, set $10.

"Swallow's Nest," Crimea A729

Hot Spring, Piatigorsk A730

Shoreline, Sukhumi A731

Tree-lined Walk, Sochi A732

Formal Gardens, Sochi A733

Stalin Highway, Sochi — A734

Colonnade, Kislovodsk A735

Seascape, Gagri — A736

1948, Dec. 30 *Perf. 12½*

1310	A729 40k brown	.65	.20
1311	A730 40k bright red violet	.65	.20
1312	A731 40k dark green	.65	.20
1313	A732 40k violet	.65	.20
1314	A733 40k dark purple	.65	.20
1315	A734 40k dark blue green	.65	.20
1316	A735 40k bright blue	.65	.20
1317	A736 40k dark blue green	.65	.20
	Nos. 1310-1317 (8)	5.20	1.60

Byelorussian S.S.R. Arms — A737

1949, Jan. 4

1318	A737 40k henna brown	2.50	1.50
1319	A737 1r blue green	3.50	2.00

Byelorussian SSR, 30th anniv.

Mikhail V. Lomonosov — A738

Lomonosov Museum, Leningrad A739

1949, Jan. 10

1320 A738 40k red brown 1.10 *1.25*
1321 A738 50k green 1.50 1.25
1322 A739 1r deep blue 3.00 2.50
Nos. 1320-1322 (3) 5.60 5.00

Cape Dezhnev (East Cape) A740

Design: 1r, Map and Dezhnev's ship.

1949, Jan. 30

1323 A740 40k olive green 5.50 3.25
1324 A740 1r gray 9.50 6.50

300th anniv. of the discovery of the strait between Asia and America by S. I. Dezhnev.

Souvenir Sheet

A741

1949, Dec. ***Imperf.***

1325 A741 Sheet of 4 160.00 160.00
Hinged 100.00
a. 40k Stalin's birthplace, Gorki 12.00 18.00
b. 40k Lenin & Stalin, Leningrad, 1917 12.00 18.00
c. 40k Lenin & Stalin, Gorki 12.00 18.00
d. 40k Marshal Stalin 12.00 18.00

70th birthday of Joseph V. Stalin.

Lenin Mausoleum — A742

1949, Jan. 21 ***Perf. 12½***

1326 A742 40k ol green & org brown 4.00 3.00
1327 A742 1r gray black & org brown 8.00 5.00
a. Sheet of 4 225.00 200.00

25th anniversary of the death of Lenin. No. 1327a exists imperf. Value $700.

Admiral S. O. Makarov — A743

1949, Mar. 15

1328 A743 40k blue 1.75 1.10
1329 A743 1r red brown 2.40 1.75

Centenary of the birth of Admiral Stepan Osipovich Makarov, shipbuilder.

Kirov Military Medical Academy A744

Professors Botkin, Pirogov and Sechenov A745

1949, Mar. 24

1330 A744 40k red brown 1.75 1.00
1331 A745 50k blue 2.75 1.50
1332 A744 1r blue green 5.50 2.25
Nos. 1330-1332 (3) 10.00 4.75

150th anniversary of the foundation of Kirov Military Medical Academy, Leningrad.

Soviet Soldier A746

1949, Mar. 16 **Photo.**

1333 A746 40k rose red 10.50 6.00

31st anniversary of the Soviet army.

Textile Weaving A747

Political Leadership — A748

Designs: 25k, Preschool teaching. No. 1337, School teaching. No. 1338, Farm women. 1r, Women athletes.

1949, Mar. 8 ***Perf. 12½***

Inscribed: "8 МАРТА 1949г"

1334 A747 20k dark violet .35 .20
1335 A747 25k blue .40 .20
1336 A748 40k henna brown .55 .20
1337 A747 50k slate gray 1.00 .35
1338 A747 50k brown 1.00 .35
1339 A747 1r green 2.75 .50
1340 A748 2r copper red 4.00 1.50
Nos. 1334-1340 (7) 10.05 3.30

International Women's Day, Mar. 8.

Medal Types of 1945

1948-49 **Engr.**

1341 A517 2r green ('49) 2.25 1.00
1341A A517 2r violet brown 11.00 5.25
1342 A518 3r brown car ('49) 1.75 .75
Nos. 1341-1342 (3) 15.00 7.00

For overprint see No. 1709.

Types of 1948

1949 **Litho.** ***Perf. 12x12½***

1343 A678 15k black .55 .30
1344 A681 20k green .80 .30
1345 A680 25k dark blue 1.25 .30
1346 A683 30k brown 1.00 .30
1347 A684 50k deep blue 16.00 8.50
Nos. 1343-1347 (5) 19.60 9.70

The 20k, 25k and 30k were re-issued in 1954-56 in slightly smaller format. The 20k measures 14x21mm, instead of 15x22mm; 25k, 14½x21mm, instead of 14½x21¾mm, and 30k, 14½x21mm, instead of 15x22mm.

The smaller-format 20k is olive green, the 25k, slate blue. The 15k was reissued in 1959 (?) in smaller format: 14x21mm, instead of 14½x22mm. See note after No. 738.

See No. 1709.

Vasili R. Williams (1863-1939), Agricultural Scientist A749

1949, Apr. 18 **Photo.** ***Perf. 12½***

1348 A749 25k blue green 3.75 1.75
1349 A749 50k brown 5.25 2.50

Russian Citizens and Flag — A750

A. S. Popov and Radio — A751

Popov Demonstrating Radio to Admiral Makarov — A752

1949, Apr. 30 ***Perf. 12½***

1350 A750 40k scarlet 1.00 .65
1351 A750 1r blue green 2.00 1.25

Labor Day, May 1, 1949.

1949, May **Unwmk.**

1352 A751 40k purple 2.00 .75
1353 A752 50k brown 3.25 1.50
1354 A751 1r blue green 6.75 2.75
Nos. 1352-1354 (3) 12.00 5.00

54th anniversary of Popov's discovery of the principles of radio.

Soviet Publications A753

Reading Pravda A754

1949, May 4

1355 A753 40k crimson 3.00 2.25
1356 A754 1r dark violet 6.00 3.75

Soviet Press Day.

Ivan V. Michurin — A755

A. S. Pushkin, 1822 — A756

Pushkin Reading Poem A757

1949, July 28

1357 A755 40k blue gray 1.75 1.00
1358 A755 1r bright green 3.50 2.25

Michurin (1855-1925), agricultural scientist.

1949, June **Unwmk.**

No. 1360, Pushkin portrait by Kiprensky, 1827. 1r, Pushkin Museum, Boldino.

1359 A756 25k indigo & sepia 1.25 .55
1360 A756 40k org brn & sep 3.00 1.25
a. Souv. sheet of 4, 2 each #1361, 1363, imperf. 60.00 20.00
1361 A757 40k brn red & dk violet 3.00 1.40
1362 A757 1r choc & slate 6.75 3.00
1363 A757 2r brown & vio bl 11.00 5.00
Nos. 1359-1363 (5) 25.00 11.20

150th anniversary of the birth of Aleksander S. Pushkin.

Horizontal rows of Nos. 1361 and 1363 contain alternate stamps and labels.

No. 1360a issued July 20.

River Tugboat A758

1r, Freighter, motorship "Bolshaya Volga."

1949, July, 13

1364 A758 40k slate blue 5.00 2.75
1365 A758 1r red brown 10.00 4.00

Centenary of the establishment of the Sormovo Machine and Boat Works.

VCSPS No. 3, Kislovodsk A759

State Sanatoria for Workers: No. 1367, Communications, Khosta. No. 1368, Sanatorium No. 3, Khosta. No. 1369, Electric power, Khosta. No. 1370, Sanatorium No. 1, Kislovodsk. No. 1371, State Theater, Sochi. No. 1372, Frunze Sanatorium, Sochi. No. 1373, Sanatorium at Machindzhaury. No. 1374, Clinical, Chaltubo. No. 1375, Sanatorium No. 41, Zheleznovodsk.

1949, Sept. 10 **Photo.** ***Perf. 12½***

1366 A759 40k violet .60 .20
1367 A759 40k black .60 .20
1368 A759 40k carmine .60 .20
1369 A759 40k blue .60 .20
1370 A759 40k violet brown .60 .20
1371 A759 40k red orange .60 .20
1372 A759 40k dark brown .60 .20
1373 A759 40k green .60 .20
1374 A759 40k red brown .60 .20
1375 A759 40k blue green .60 .20
Nos. 1366-1375 (10) 6.00 2.00

Regatta A760

Sports, "1949": 25k, Kayak race. 30k, Swimming. 40k, Bicycling. No. 1380, Soccer. 50k, Mountain climbing. 1r, Parachuting. 2r, High jump.

1949, Aug. 7

1376 A760 20k bright blue .65 .20
1377 A760 25k blue green .65 .20
1378 A760 30k violet 1.10 .20
1379 A760 40k red brown 1.10 .20
1380 A760 40k green 1.10 .20
1381 A760 50k dk blue gray 1.40 .20
1382 A760 1r carmine rose 4.00 .40
1383 A760 2r gray black 8.00 .80
Nos. 1376-1383 (8) 18.00 2.40

V. V. Dokuchayev and Fields A761

1949, Aug. 8

1384	A761	40k	brown	1.00	.30
1385	A761	1r	green	1.50	.45

Vasili V. Dokuchayev (1846-1903), pioneer soil scientist.

Vasili Bazhenov and Lenin Library, Moscow A762

1949, Aug. 14 Photo. *Perf. 12½*

1386	A762	40k	violet	1.50	.35
1387	A762	1r	red brown	2.25	.45

Bazhenov, architect, 150th death anniv.

A. N. Radishchev — A763

Ivan P. Pavlov A764

1949, Aug. 31

1388	A763	40k	blue green	3.00	1.00
1389	A763	1r	gray	7.00	2.00

200th anniversary of the birth of Aleksandr N. Radishchev, writer.

1949, Sept. 30 Unwmk.

1390	A764	40k	deep brown	.50	.25
1391	A764	1r	gray black	1.25	.35

Pavlov (1849-1936), Russian physiologist.

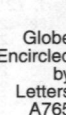

Globe Encircled by Letters A765

1949, Oct. *Perf. 12½*

1392	A765	40k	org brn & indigo	.30	.20
a.			Imperf.	7.50	2.50
1393	A765	50k	indigo & gray vio	.50	.30
a.			Imperf.	7.50	2.50

75th anniv. of the UPU.

Cultivators A766

Map of European Russia — A767

Designs: No. 1395, Peasants in grain field. 50k, Rural scene. 2r, Old man and children.

1949, Oct. 18 *Perf. 12½*

1394	A766	25k	green	10.25	4.25
1395	A766	40k	violet	2.50	1.00
1396	A767	40k	gray grn & blk	2.50	1.00
1397	A766	50k	deep blue	4.25	1.50
1398	A766	1r	gray black	6.75	3.00
1399	A766	2r	dark brown	8.75	4.25
			Nos. 1394-1399 (6)	35.00	15.00

Encouraging agricultural development.
Nos. 1394, 1398, 1399 measure 33x19mm. Nos. 1395, 1397 measure 33x22mm.

Maly (Little) Theater, Moscow A768

M. N. Ermolova, I. S. Mochalov, A. N. Ostrovski, M. S. Shchepkin and P. M. Sadovsky A769

1949, Oct. 27

1400	A768	40k	green	1.00	.25
1401	A768	50k	red orange	1.50	.40
1402	A769	1r	deep brown	3.50	.85
			Nos. 1400-1402 (3)	6.00	1.50

125th anniversary of the Maly Theater (State Academic Little Theater).

Chapayev Type of 1944

1949, Oct. 22 Photo.

1403	A494	40k	brown orange	5.00	3.00

30th anniversary of the death of V. I. Chapayev, a hero of the 1918 civil war.
Portrait and outer frame same as type A494. Dates "1919 1949" are in upper corners. Other details differ.

125th Anniv. of the Birth of Ivan Savvich Nikitin, Russian Poet (1824-1861) — A770

1949, Oct. 24 Unwmk.

1404	A770	40k	brown	1.10	.25
1405	A770	1r	slate blue	1.90	.35

Spasski Tower and Russian Citizens A771

1949, Oct. 29 *Perf. 12½*

1406	A771	40k	brown orange	2.75	1.50
1407	A771	1r	deep green	4.75	2.50

October Revolution, 32nd anniversary.

Sheep, Cattle and Farm Woman — A772

1949, Nov. 2

1408	A772	40k	chocolate	1.00	.25
1409	A772	1r	violet	1.50	.35

Encouraging better cattle breeding in Russia.

Arms and Flag of USSR — A773

1949, Nov. 30 Engr. *Perf. 12*

1410	A773	40k	carmine	10.00	6.00

Constitution Day.

Electric Trolley Car — A774

40k, 1r, Diesel train. 50k, Steam train.

1949, Nov. 19 Photo. *Perf. 12½*

1411	A774	25k	red	1.00	.20
1412	A774	40k	violet	1.25	.40
1413	A774	50k	brown	2.25	.40
1414	A774	1r	Prus green	4.50	1.00
			Nos. 1411-1414 (4)	9.00	2.00

Ski Jump — A775

Designs: 40k, Girl on rings. 50k, Ice hockey. 1r, Weight lifter. 2r, Wolf hunt.

1949, Nov. 12 Unwmk.

1415	A775	20k	dark green	.50	.20
1416	A775	40k	orange red	1.25	.20
1417	A775	50k	deep blue	1.50	.20
1418	A775	1r	red	4.50	.25
1419	A775	2r	violet	7.25	.80
			Nos. 1415-1419 (5)	15.00	1.65

Textile Mills — A776

Designs: 25k, Irrigation system. 40k, 1r, Government buildings, Stalinabad. 50k, University of Medicine.

1949, Dec. 7 Photo. *Perf. 12*

1420	A776	20k	blue	.50	.20
1421	A776	25k	green	.50	.20
1422	A776	40k	red orange	.75	.25
1423	A776	50k	violet	1.25	.25
1424	A776	1r	gray black	2.00	.85
			Nos. 1420-1424 (5)	5.00	1.75

Tadzhik Republic, 20th anniv.

"Russia" versus "War" — A777

Byelorussians and Flag — A778

1949, Dec. 25

1425	A777	40k	rose carmine	.75	.20
1426	A777	50k	blue	1.25	.30

Issued to portray Russia as the defender of world peace.

1949, Dec. 23 Unwmk.

Design: No. 1428, Ukrainians and flag.

Inscribed: "1939 1949"

1427	A778	40k	orange red	9.00	3.75
1428	A778	40k	deep orange	9.00	3.75

Return of western territories to the Byelorussian and Ukrainian Republics, 10th anniv.

Teachers College A779

25k, State Theater. #1431, Government House. #1432, Navol Street, Tashkent. 1r, Fergana Canal. 2r, Kuigonyarsk Dam.

1950, Jan. 3

1429	A779	20k	blue	.30	.20
1430	A779	25k	gray black	.30	.20
1431	A779	40k	red orange	.65	.25
1432	A779	40k	violet	.65	.25
1433	A779	1r	green	1.40	.40
1434	A779	2r	brown	3.00	.50
			Nos. 1429-1434 (6)	6.30	1.80

Uzbek Republic, 25th anniversary.

Lenin at Razliv — A780

Lenin's Office, Kremlin A781

Design: 1r, Lenin Museum.

1950, Jan. Unwmk. Litho. *Perf. 12*

1435	A780	40k	dk green & dk brn	.55	.20
1436	A781	50k	dk brn, red brn & green	.90	.20
1437	A781	1r	dk brn, dk grn & cream	1.65	.30
			Nos. 1435-1437 (3)	3.10	.70

26th anniversary of the death of Lenin.

Textile Factory, Ashkhabad A782

Designs: 40k, 1r, Power dam and Turkmenian arms. 50k, Rug making.

1950, Jan. 7 Photo.

1438	A782	25k	gray black	1.00	1.00
1439	A782	40k	brown	1.40	.75
1440	A782	50k	green	2.10	1.25
1441	A782	1r	purple	4.50	2.50
			Nos. 1438-1441 (4)	9.00	5.50

Turkmen Republic, 25th anniversary.

Motion Picture Projection A783

1950, Feb.

1442	A783	25k	brown	10.00	5.00

Soviet motion picture industry, 30th anniv.

Voter — A784

Kremlin — A785

1950, Mar. 8

1443	A784	40k	green, *yellow*	2.50	1.50
1444	A785	1r	rose carmine	3.50	2.50

Supreme Soviet elections, Mar. 12, 1950.

Morozov Monument, Moscow — A786

1950, Mar. 16 ***Perf. 12½***

1445	A786	40k	black brn & red	3.25	1.75
1446	A786	1r	dk green & red	6.75	3.00

Unveiling of a monument to Pavlik Morozov, Pioneer.

Globes and Communication Symbols — A787

1950, Apr. 1

1447	A787	40k	deep green	2.25	2.00
1448	A787	50k	deep blue	2.75	2.00

Meeting of the Post, Telegraph, Telephone and Radio Trade Unions.

State Polytechnic Museum A788

State Museum of Oriental Cultures A789

State University Museum — A790

Pushkin Museum A791

Museums: No. 1451, Tretiakov Gallery. No. 1452, Timiryazev Biology Museum. No. 1453, Lenin Museum. No. 1454, Museum of the Revolution. No. 1456, State History Museum.

Inscribed: "MOCKBA 1949" in Top Frame

1950, Mar. 28 Litho. ***Perf. 12½***

Multicolored Centers

1449	A788	40k	dark blue	1.10	.25
1450	A789	40k	dark blue	1.10	.25
1451	A789	40k	green	1.10	.25
1452	A789	40k	dark brown	1.10	.25
1453	A789	40k	olive brown	1.10	.25
1454	A789	40k	claret	1.10	.25
1455	A790	40k	red	1.10	.25
1456	A790	40k	chocolate	1.10	.25
1457	A791	40k	brown violet	1.10	.25
			Nos. 1449-1457 (9)	9.90	2.25

Soviets of Three Races A792

A. S. Shcherbakov A793

1r, 4 Russians and communist banner, horiz.

1950, May 1 Photo. ***Perf. 12½***

1458	A792	40k	org red & gray	2.50	1.75
1459	A792	1r	red & gray black	5.00	3.00

Labor Day, May 1, 1950.

1950, May Unwmk.

1460	A793	40k	black, *pale blue*	1.50	.75
1461	A793	1r	dk green, *buff*	2.50	1.75

Shcherbakov, political leader (1901-1945).

Monument A794

Victory Medal A795

Perf. 12x12½

1950 Photo. Wmk. 293

1462	A794	40k	dk brown & red	4.75	2.25

Unwmk.

1463	A795	1r	carmine rose	7.75	2.75

5th Intl. Victory Day, May 9, 1950.

A. V. Suvorov — A796

50k, Suvorov crossing Alps, 32½x47mm. 60k, Badge, flag and marchers, 24x39½mm. 2r, Suvorov facing left, 19x33½mm.

Various Designs and Sizes Dated "1800 1950"

1950 ***Perf. 12, 12½x12***

1464	A796	40k	blue,*pink*	2.50	1.75
1465	A796	50k	brown, *pink*	3.00	2.25
1466	A796	60k	gray black, *pale gray*	3.25	2.25
1467	A796	1r	dk brn, *lemon*	3.75	3.00
1468	A796	2r	greenish blue	7.50	5.75
			Nos. 1464-1468 (5)	20.00	15.00

Field Marshal Count Aleksandr V. Suvorov (1730-1800).

Farmers Studying Agronomic Techniques A797

No. 1470, 1r, Sowing on collective farm.

1950, June ***Perf. 12½***

1469	A797	40k	dk grn, *pale grn*	2.00	1.10
1470	A797	40k	gray black, *buff*	2.00	1.10
1471	A797	1r	blue, *lemon*	4.00	2.25
			Nos. 1469-1471 (3)	8.00	4.45

George M. Dimitrov — A798

1950, July 2

1472	A798	40k	gray black, *citron*	1.25	.90
1473	A798	1r	gray blk, *salmon*	2.75	2.10

Dimitrov (1882-1949), Bulgarian-born revolutionary leader and Comintern official.

Opera and Ballet Theater, Baku — A799

Designs: 40k, Azerbaijan Academy of Science. 1r, Stalin Avenue, Baku.

1950, July Photo. ***Perf. 12½***

1474	A799	25k	dp green, *citron*	.65	.55
1475	A799	40k	brown, *pink*	1.60	.95
1476	A799	1r	gray black, *buff*	4.75	3.50
			Nos. 1474-1476 (3)	7.00	5.00

Azerbaijan SSR, 30th anniversary.

Victory Theater — A800

Lenin Street A801

Designs: 50k, Gorky Theater. 1r, Monument marking Stalingrad defense line.

1950, June

1477	A800	20k	dark blue	.90	.40
1478	A801	40k	green	1.75	.80
1479	A801	50k	red orange	2.40	1.25
1480	A801	1r	gray	5.00	2.50
			Nos. 1477-1480 (4)	10.05	4.95

Restoration of Stalingrad.

Moscow Subway Stations: "Park of Culture" A802

#1482, Kaluzskaya station. #1483, Taganskaya. #1484, Kurskaya. #1485, Paveletskaya. #1486, Park of Culture. #1487, Taganskaya.

1950, July 30

Size: 33½x23mm

1481	A802	40k	deep carmine	.85	.30
1482	A802	40k	dark green, *buff*	.85	.30
1483	A802	40k	deep blue, *buff*	.85	.30
1484	A802	1r	dark brn, *citron*	1.90	1.00
1485	A802	1r	purple	1.90	1.00
1486	A802	1r	dark grn, *citron*	1.90	1.00

Size: 33x18½mm

1487	A802	1r	black, *pink*	1.75	.75
			Nos. 1481-1487 (7)	10.00	4.65

Socialist Peoples and Flags A803

1950, Aug. 4 Unwmk. ***Perf. 12½***

1488	A803	40k	multicolored	1.25	.20
1489	A803	50k	multicolored	2.25	.20
1490	A803	1r	multicolored	3.00	.30
			Nos. 1488-1490 (3)	6.50	.70

Trade Union Building, Riga — A804

Opera and Ballet Theater, Riga — A805

Designs: 40k, Latvian Cabinet building. 50k, Monument to Jan Rainis. 1r, Riga State Univ. 2r, Latvian Academy of Sciences.

1950 Photo. ***Perf. 12½***

1491	A804	25k	dark brown	1.25	.50
1492	A804	40k	scarlet	2.00	.80
1493	A804	50k	dark green	3.00	1.25
1494	A805	60k	deep blue	3.75	1.60
1495	A805	1r	lilac	5.50	2.10
1496	A804	2r	sepia	9.50	3.75
			Nos. 1491-1496 (6)	25.00	10.00

Latvian SSR, 10th anniv.

Lithuanian Academy of Sciences A806

Marite Melnik — A807

Design: 1r, Cabinet building.

1950

1497	A806	25k	deep bl, *bluish*	2.00	.50
1498	A807	40k	brown	4.00	1.00
1499	A806	1r	scarlet	14.00	2.50
			Nos. 1497-1499 (3)	20.00	4.00

Lithuanian SSR, 10th anniv.

Stalingrad Square, Tallinn A808

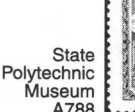

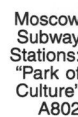

Victor Kingisepp — A809

Designs: 40k, Government building, Tallinn. 50k, Estonia Theater, Tallinn.

1950

1500	A808	25k	dark green	2.00	.80
1501	A808	40k	scarlet	2.40	.95
1502	A808	50k	blue, *yellow*	4.00	1.40
1503	A809	1r	brown, *blue*	12.00	3.00
			Nos. 1500-1503 (4)	20.40	6.15

Estonian SSR, 10th anniv.

Citizens Signing Appeal for Peace A810

Children and Governess — A811

Design: 50k, Peace Demonstration.

1950, Oct. 16 **Photo.**

1504	A810	40k	red, *salmon*	1.75	.90
1505	A811	40k	black	1.75	.90
1506	A811	50k	dark red	4.00	1.75
1507	A810	1r	brown, *salmon*	6.25	6.25
			Nos. 1504-1507 (4)	13.75	9.80

F. G. Bellingshausen, M. P. Lazarev and Globe — A812

Route of Antarctic Expedition — A813

1950, Oct. 25 **Unwmk.** ***Perf. 12½***
Blue Paper

1508	A812	40k	dark carmine	14.00	10.00
1509	A813	1r	purple	26.00	10.00

130th anniversary of the Bellingshausen-Lazarev expedition to the Antarctic.

M. V. Frunze — A814

M. I. Kalinin — A815

1950, Oct. 31

1510	A814	40k	blue, *buff*	2.50	1.75
1511	A814	1r	brown, *blue*	10.00	4.00

Frunze, military strategist, 25th death anniv.

1950, Nov. 20 **Engr.**

1512	A815	40k	deep green	1.25	.75
1513	A815	1r	reddish brown	2.75	1.25
1514	A815	5r	violet	6.00	2.25
			Nos. 1512-1514 (3)	10.00	4.25

75th anniversary of the birth of M. I. Kalinin, Soviet Russia's first president.

Gathering Grapes A816

Armenian Government Building A817

G. M. Sundukian — A818

1950, Nov. 29 **Photo.** ***Perf. 12½***

1515	A816	20k	dp blue, *buff*	1.75	1.00
1516	A817	40k	red org, *blue*	3.00	1.50
1517	A818	1r	ol gray, *yellow*	7.25	3.50
			Nos. 1515-1517 (3)	12.00	6.00

Armenian Republic, 30th anniv. 1r also for birth of Sundukian, playwright.

Apartment Building, Koteljnicheskaya Quay — A819

Hotel, Kalanchevkaya Square — A820

Various Buildings
Inscribed: "Mockba, 1950"

1950, Dec. 2 **Unwmk.**

1518	A819	1r	red brn, *buff*	24.00	17.50
1519	A819	1r	gray black	24.00	17.50
1520	A819	1r	brown, *blue*	24.00	17.50
1521	A819	1r	dk green, *blue*	24.00	17.50
1522	A820	1r	dp blue, *buff*	24.00	17.50
1523	A820	1r	black, *buff*	24.00	17.50
1524	A820	1r	red orange	24.00	17.50
1525	A819	1r	dk grn, *yellow*	24.00	17.50
			Nos. 1518-1525 (8)	192.00	140.00
			Set, hinged	125.00	

Skyscrapers planned for Moscow.

Spasski Tower, Kremlin — A821

1950, Dec. 4

1526	A821	1r	dk grn, red brn & yel brown	10.00	5.50

October Revolution, 33rd anniversary.

Golden Autumn by Levitan A822

I. I. Levitan (1861-90), Painter A823

1950, Dec. 6 **Litho.** ***Perf. 12½***

1527	A822	40k	multicolored	3.25	.55

Perf. 12
Photo.

1528	A823	50k	red brown	4.75	.55

Black Sea by Aivazovsky — A824

Ivan K. Aivazovsky (1817-1900) Painter A825

Design: 50k, "Ninth Surge."

1950, Dec. 6 **Litho.**
Multicolored Centers

1529	A824	40k	chocolate	1.75	.20
1530	A824	50k	chocolate	1.75	.40
1531	A825	1r	indigo	2.50	.90
			Nos. 1529-1531 (3)	6.00	1.50

Flags and Newspapers Iskra and Pravda — A826

1r, Flag and profiles of Lenin and Stalin.

1950, Dec. 23 **Photo.**

1532	A826	40k	gray blk & red	25.00	6.25
1533	A826	1r	dk brn & red	35.00	8.75

1st issue of the newspaper Iskra, 50th anniv.

Presidium of Supreme Soviet, Alma-Ata A827

Design: 1r, Opera and Ballet Theater.

1950, Dec. 27
Inscribed: "ALMA-ATA" in Cyrillic

1534	A827	40k	gray black, *blue*	7.25	3.00
1535	A827	1r	red brn, *yellow*	7.50	4.00

Kazakh Republic, 30th anniversary. Cyrillic charcters for "ALMA-ATA" are above building in vignette on 40k, immediately below building on right on 1r.

Decembrists and Senatskaya Square, Leningrad — A828

1950, Dec. 30 **Unwmk.**

1536	A828	1r	black brn, *yellow*	7.00	4.00

Decembrist revolution of 1825.

Lenin at Razliv A829

Design: 1r, Lenin and young communists.

1951, Jan. 21 **Litho.** ***Perf. 12½***
Multicolored Centers

1537	A829	40k	olive green	2.50	.30
1538	A829	1r	indigo	4.50	.70

27th anniversary of the death of Lenin.

Mountain Pasture A830

Government Building, Frunze A831

1951, Feb. 2 **Photo.** ***Perf. 12½***

1539	A830	25k	dk brown, *blue*	3.50	1.90
1540	A831	40k	dp green, *blue*	4.00	3.00

Kirghiz Republic, 25th anniv.

Government Building, Tirana A832

1951, Jan. 6 **Unwmk.** ***Perf. 12***

1541	A832	40k	green, *bluish*	10.00	8.00

Honoring the Albanian People's Republic.

Bulgarians Greeting Russian Troops A833

Lenin Square, Sofia — A834

Design: 60k, Monument to Soviet soldiers.

1951, Jan. 13

1542 A833	25k gray black, *bluish*		1.75	1.25
1543 A834	40k org red, *salmon*		3.25	2.50
1544 A834	60k blk brn, *salmon*		5.00	3.75
	Nos. 1542-1544 (3)		10.00	7.50

Honoring the Bulgarian People's Republic.

Choibalsan State University — A835

State Theater, Ulan Bator A836

Mongolian Republic Emblem and Flag — A837

1951, Mar. 12

1545 A835	25k purple, *salmon*	.55	.45
1546 A836	40k dp orange, *yellow*	1.10	.45
1547 A837	1r multicolored	2.75	1.50
	Nos. 1545-1547 (3)	4.40	2.40

Honoring the Mongolian People's Republic.

D. A. Furmanov (1891-1926) Writer — A838

Furmanov at Work A839

1951, Mar. 17 ***Perf. 12½***

1548 A838	40k brown	5.00	1.25
1549 A839	1r gray black, *buff*	6.00	2.00

Russian War Memorial, Berlin — A840

1951, Mar. 21 ***Perf. 12***

1550 A840	40k dk gray grn & dk red	10.00	3.00
1551 A840	1r brown blk & red	15.00	7.00

Stockholm Peace Conference.

Kirov Machine Works A841

1951, May 19 **Photo.** ***Perf. 12½***

1552 A841	40k brown, *cream*	4.00	2.50

Kirov Machine Works, 150th anniv.

Bolshoi Theater, Moscow — A842

Russian Composers A843

1951, May **Unwmk.**

1553 A842	40k multicolored	5.00	.55
1554 A843	1r multicolored	7.00	1.25

Bolshoi Theater, Moscow, 175th anniv.

Liberty Bridge, Budapest A844

Monument to Liberators — A845

Budapest Buildings: 40k, Parliament. 60k, National Museum.

1951, June 9 ***Perf. 12***

1555 A844	25k emerald	.65	.50
1556 A844	40k bright blue	1.10	.75
1557 A844	60k sepia	1.50	1.00
1558 A845	1r sepia, *salmon*	2.75	2.25
	Nos. 1555-1558 (4)	6.00	4.50

Honoring the Hungarian People's Republic.

Harvesting Wheat A846

Designs: 40k, Apiary. 1r, Gathering citrus fruits. 2r, Cotton picking.

1951, June 25

1559 A846	25k dark green	.50	.30
1560 A846	40k green, *bluish*	.95	.45
1561 A846	1r brown, *yellow*	1.75	1.25
1562 A846	2r dk green, *salmon*	3.00	2.50
	Nos. 1559-1562 (4)	6.20	4.50

Kalinin Museum, Moscow — A847

Mikhail I. Kalinin — A848

Design: 1r, Kalinin statue.

1951, Aug. 4 ***Perf. 12x12½, 12½x12***

1563 A847	20k org brn & black	.40	.20
1564 A848	40k dp green & choc	.75	.25
1565 A848	1r vio blue & gray	1.50	.55
	Nos. 1563-1565 (3)	2.65	1.00

5th anniv. of the death of Kalinin.

F. E. Dzerzhinski, 25th Death Anniv. — A849

Design: 1r, Profile of Dzerzhinski.

1951, Aug. 4 **Engr.** ***Perf. 12x12½***

1566 A849	40k brown red	3.75	1.75
1567 A849	1r gray black	5.25	3.25

Aleksandr M. Butlerov A850

A. Kovalevski A850a

P. K. Kozlov A850b

N. S. Kurnakov A850c

P. N. Lebedev A850d

N. I. Lobachevski A850e

A. N. Lodygin A850f

A. N. Svertzov A850g

K. E. Tsiolkovsky A850h

A. A. Aliabiev A851

Russian Scientists: No. 1570 Sonya Kovalevskaya. No. 1572, S. P. Krasheninnikov. No. 1577, D. I. Mendeleev. No. 1578, N. N. Miklukho-Maklai. No. 1580, A. G. Stoletov. No. 1581, K. A. Timiryasev. No. 1583, P. N. Yablochkov.

1951, Aug. 15 **Photo.** ***Perf. 12½***

1568	A850	40k org red, *bluish*	1.75	.80
1569	A850a	40k dk blue, *sal*	1.10	.30
1570	A850	40k pur, *salmon*	1.10	.30
1571	A850b	40k orange red	1.10	.30
1572	A850	40k purple	1.10	.30
1573	A850c	40k brown, *salmon*	1.10	.30
1574	A850d	40k blue	1.10	.30
1575	A850e	40k brown	1.10	.30
1576	A850f	40k green	1.10	.30
1577	A850	40k deep blue	1.10	.30
1578	A850	40k org red, *sal*	1.10	.30
1579	A850g	40k sepia, *salmon*	1.10	.30
1580	A850	40k green, *salmon*	1.10	.30
1581	A850	40k brown, *salmon*	1.10	.30
1582	A850h	40k gray blk, *blue*	1.75	.80
1583	A850	40k sepia	1.10	.30
		Nos. 1568-1583 (16)	18.90	5.80

Two printings exist in differing stamp sizes of most of this issue.

1951, Aug. 28

Design: No. 1585, V. S. Kalinnikov.

1584 A851	40k brown, *salmon*	10.00	5.00
1585 A851	40k gray, *salmon*	10.00	7.50

Russian composers.

Opera and Ballet Theater, Tbilisi — A852

Gathering Citrus Fruit — A853

40k, Principal street, Tbilisi. 1r, Picking tea.

1951 **Unwmk.** ***Perf. 12½***

1586 A852	20k dp green, *yellow*	1.40	.70
1587 A853	25k pur, org & brn	2.10	.70
1588 A853	40k dk brn, *blue*	3.25	1.50
1589 A853	1r red brn & dk grn	8.25	3.50
	Nos. 1586-1589 (4)	15.00	6.40

Georgian Republic, 30th anniversary.

Emblem of Aviation Society — A854

Planes and Emblem — A855

60k, Flying model planes. 1r, Parachutists.

1951, Sept. 19 Litho. *Perf. 12½*
Dated: "1951"

1590 A854 40k multicolored .75 .20
1591 A854 60k emer, lt bl & brn 1.40 .30
1592 A854 1r blue, sal & lilac 2.00 .45
1593 A855 2r multicolored 4.50 .80
Nos. 1590-1593 (4) 8.65 1.75

Promoting interest in aviation.

Victor M. Vasnetsov (1848-1926), Painter — A856

Three Heroes, by Vasnetsov — A857

1951, Oct. 15

1594 A856 40k dk bl, brn & buff 3.00 .25
1595 A857 1r multicolored 4.50 1.00

Hydroelectric Station, Lenin and Stalin — A858

Design: 1r, Spasski Tower, Kremlin.

1951, Nov. 6 Photo. *Perf. 12½*
Dated: "1917-1951"

1596 A858 40k blue vio & red 6.00 1.90
1597 A858 1r dk brown & red 9.00 3.25

34th anniversary of October Revolution.

Map, Dredge and Khakhovsky Hydroelectric Station — A859

Map, Volga Dam and Tugboat — A860

Designs (each showing map): 40k, Stalingrad Dam. 60k, Excavating Turkmenian canal. 1r, Kuibyshev dam.

1951, Nov. 28 *Perf. 12½*

1598 A859 20k multicolored 5.75 1.75
1599 A860 30k multicolored 6.75 2.25
1600 A860 40k multicolored 7.50 3.75
1601 A860 60k multicolored 12.00 4.25
1602 A860 1r multicolored 18.00 8.50
Nos. 1598-1602 (5) 50.00 20.50

Flag and Citizens Signing Peace Appeal — A861

1951, Nov. 30 *Perf. 12½*

1603 A861 40k gray & red 10.00 7.00

Third All-Union Peace Conference.

Mikhail V. Ostrogradski, Mathematician, 150th Birth Anniv. — A862

1951, Dec. 10 Unwmk.

1604 A862 40k black brn, *pink* 8.00 3.50

Monument to Jan Zizka, Prague — A863

Monument to Soviet Liberators A864

25k, Monument to Soviet Soldiers, Ostrava. 40k, Julius Fucik. 60k, Smetana Museum, Prague.

1951, Dec. 10 *Perf. 12½*

1605 A863 20k vio blue, *sal* 7.00 2.25
1606 A863 25k copper red, *yel* 14.00 4.75
1607 A863 40k red orange, *sal* 7.00 2.25
1608 A863 60k brnsh gray, *buff* 14.00 4.75
1609 A864 1r brnsh gray, *buff* 18.00 6.00
Nos. 1605-1609 (5) 60.00 20.00

Soviet-Czechoslovakian friendship.

Volkhovski Hydroelectric Station and Lenin Statue — A865

1951, Dec. 19

1610 A865 40k dk bl, gray & yel 2.50 .20
1611 A865 1r pur, gray & yel 5.50 .55

25th anniv. of the opening of the Lenin Volkhovski hydroelectric station.

Lenin as a Schoolboy A866

Horizontal Designs: 60k, Lenin among children. 1r, Lenin and peasants.

1952, Jan. 24 Photo. *Perf. 12½*
Multicolored Centers

1612 A866 40k dk blue green 1.75 .55
1613 A866 60k violet blue 2.25 .55
1614 A866 1r orange brown 3.50 .65
Nos. 1612-1614 (3) 7.50 1.75

28th anniversary of the death of Lenin.

Semenov A867

Kovalevski A868

1952, Feb. 1

1615 A867 1r sepia, *blue* 7.00 5.00

Petr Petrovich Semenov-Tianshanski (1827-1914), traveler and geographer who explored the Tian Shan mountains.

1952, Mar. 3 Unwmk.

1616 A868 40k sepia, *yellow* 12.50 10.00

V. O. Kovalevski (1843-1883), biologist and palaeontologist.

Skaters A869

1952, Mar. 3

1617 A869 40k shown 1.25 .25
1618 A869 60k Skiers 2.25 .35

N. V. Gogol and Characters from "Taras Bulba" — A870

Designs: 60k, Gogol and V. G. Belinski. 1r, Gogol and Ukrainian peasants.

1952, Mar. 4
Dated: "1852-1952"

1619 A870 40k sepia, *blue* .75 .20
1620 A870 60k multicolored 1.25 .20
1621 A870 1r multicolored 1.50 .25
Nos. 1619-1621 (3) 3.50 .65

Death centenary of N. V. Gogol, writer.

G. K. Ordzhonikidze A871

Workers and Soviet Flag A872

Workers' Rest Home A873

1952, Apr. 23 Photo. *Perf. 12½*

1622 A871 40k dp green, *pink* 3.75 3.50
1623 A871 1r sepia, *blue* 3.75 3.50

15th anniv. of the death of Grigori K. Ordzhonikidze, Georgian party worker.

1952, May 15 Unwmk.

#1626, Aged citizens. #1627, Schoolgirl.

1624 A872 40k red & blk, *cream* 4.50 3.75
1625 A873 40k red & dk grn, *pale gray* 4.50 3.75
1626 A873 40k red & brown, *pale gray* 4.50 3.75
1627 A872 40k red & black, *pale gray* 4.50 3.75
Nos. 1624-1627 (4) 18.00 15.00

Adoption of Stalin constitution., 15th anniv

A. S. Novikov-Priboy and Ship — A874

1952, June 5

1628 A874 40k blk, pale cit & bl grn .50 .30

Novikov-Priboy, writer, 75th birthanniv.

150th anniv. of Birth of Victor Hugo (1802-1855), French Writer — A875

1952, June 5 Unwmk. *Perf. 12½*
1629 A875 40k brn org, gray & black .50 .25

Julaev — A876

Sedov — A877

1952, June 28
1630 A876 40k rose red, *pink* .60 .20

200th anniversary of the birth of Salavat Julaev, Bashkir hero who took part in the insurrection of 1773-1775.

1952, July 4
1631 A877 40k dk bl, dk brn & blue green 12.00 5.00

Georgi J. Sedov, Arctic explorer (1877-1914).

Arms and Flag of Romania — A878

University Square, Bucharest A879

Design: 60k, Monument to Soviet soldiers.

1952, July 26
1632 A878 40k multicolored 2.75 .55
1633 A878 60k dk green, *pink* 4.50 1.25
1634 A879 1r bright ultra 5.75 2.50
Nos. 1632-1634 (3) 13.00 4.30

Zhukovski A880

Ogarev A881

Design: No. 1636, K. P. Bryulov.

1952, July 26 Pale Blue Paper
1635 A880 40k gray black .75 .30
1636 A880 40k brt blue green .75 .30

V. A. Zhukovski, poet, and Bryulov, painter (1799-1852).

1952, Aug. 29
1637 A881 40k deep green .50 .25

75th anniversary of the death of N. P. Ogarev, poet and revolutionary.

Uspenski — A882

Nakhimov — A883

1952, Sept. 4
1638 A882 40k indigo & dk brown 1.00 .50

Gleb Ivanovich Uspenski (1843-1902), writer.

1952, Sept. 9
1639 A883 40k multicolored 2.00 .75

Adm. Paul S. Nakhimov (1802-1855).

University Building, Tartu — A884

1952, Oct. 2
1640 A884 40k black brn, *salmon* 3.00 1.25

150th anniversary of the enlargement of the University of Tartu, Estonia.

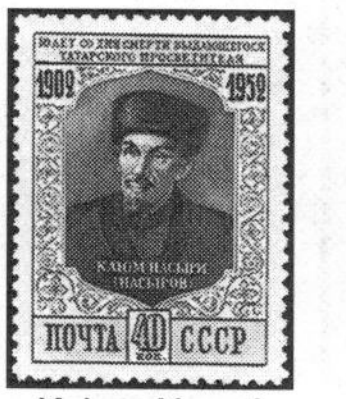
Kajum Nasyri A885

A. N. Radishchev A886

1952, Nov. 5
1641 A885 40k brown, *yellow* 3.00 1.25

Nasyri (1825-1902), Tartar educator.

1952, Oct. 23
1642 A886 40k blk, brn & dk red 2.00 1.00

Radishchev, writer, 150th death anniv.

M.S. Joseph Stalin at Entrance to Volga-Don Canal — A887

Design: 1r, Lenin, Stalin and red banners.

1952, Nov. 6 *Perf. 12½*
1643 A887 40k multicolored 3.00 1.50
1644 A887 1r brown, red & yel 5.00 3.00

35th anniversary of October Revolution.

Pavel Andreievitch Fedotov (1815-52), Artist — A888

1953, Nov. 26
1645 A888 40k red brn & black 1.00 .50

V. D. Polenov, Artist, 25th Death Anniv. — A889

"Moscow Courtyard" — A890

1952, Dec. 6
1646 A889 40k red brown & buff 1.25 .35
1647 A890 1r multicolored 2.25 .65

A. I. Odoyevski (1802-39) Poet — A891

1952, Dec. 8
1648 A891 40k gray blk & red org .80 .25

D. N. Mamin-Sibiryak — A892

1952, Dec. 15
1649 A892 40k dp green, *cream* 1.00 .25

Centenary of the birth of Dimitrii N. Mamin-Sibiryak (1852-1912), writer.

Composite Medal Types of 1946
Frames as A599-A606
Centers as Indicated

Medals: 1r, Token of Veneration. 2r, Red Star. 3r, Red Workers' Banner. 5r, Red Banner. 10r, Lenin.

1952-59 Engr. *Perf. 12½*
1650 A569 1r dark brown 7.00 7.00
1651 A567 2r red brown 1.10 .55
1652 A572 3r dp blue violet 1.50 .95
1653 A571 5r dk car ('53) 1.90 .95
1654 A566 10r bright rose 3.50 1.90
a. 10r dull red ('59) 3.00 2.00
Nos. 1650-1654 (5) 15.00 11.35

Vladimir M. Bekhterev (1857-1927), Neuropathologist A893

1952, Dec. 24 Photo.
1655 A893 40k vio bl, slate & blk .90 .30

Byelorusskaya Station — A894

Designs (Moscow Subway stations): 40k, Botanical Garden Station. 40k, Novoslobodskaya Station. 40k, Komsomolskaya Station.

1952, Dec. 30
Multicolored Centers
1656 A894 40k dull violet .60 .30
1657 A894 40k light ultra .60 .30
1658 A894 40k blue gray .60 .30
1659 A894 40k dull green .60 .30
a. Horiz. strip of 4, #1656-1659 2.50 2.00

USSR Emblem and Flags of 16 Union Republics — A895

1952, Dec. 30
1660 A895 1r grn, dk red & brn 2.50 1.75

30th anniversary of the USSR.

Lenin — A896

1953, Jan. 26
1661 A896 40k multicolored 5.00 4.00

29 years without Lenin.

Stalin Peace Medal — A897

Valerian V. Kuibyshev — A898

1953, Apr. 30 *Perf. 12½*
1662 A897 40k red brn, bl & dull yel 12.00 6.00

1953, June 6
1663 A898 40k red brn & black 1.00 .55

Kuibyshev (1888-1935), Bolshevik leader.

A899

A900

1953, July 21
1664 A899 40k buff & dk brown 2.00 1.25

Nikolai G. Chernyshevski (1828-1889), writer and radical leader; exiled to Siberia for 24 years.

1953, July 19
1665 A900 40k ver & gray brown 2.50 1.25

60th anniv. of the birth of Vladimir V. Mayakovsky, poet.

Tsymijanskaja Dam — A901

Volga-Don Canal: No. 1666, Lock No. 9, Volga-Don Canal. No. 1667, Lock 13. No. 1668, Lock 15. No. 1669, Volga River lighthouse. No. 1671, M. S. "Joseph Stalin" in canal.

1953, Aug. 29 **Litho.**
1666 A901 40k multicolored 1.00 .20
1667 A901 40k multicolored 1.00 .20
1668 A901 40k multicolored 1.00 .20
1669 A901 40k multicolored 1.00 .20
1670 A901 40k multicolored 1.00 .20
1671 A901 1r multicolored 2.25 .75
Nos. 1666-1671 (6) 7.25 1.75

V. G. Korolenko (1853-1921), Writer — A902

1953, Aug. 29 Photo. ***Perf. 12x12½***
1672 A902 40k brown 1.00 .25

Count Leo N. Tolstoy (1828-1910), Writer — A903

1953, Sept. ***Perf. 12***
1673 A903 1r dark brown 5.00 3.00

Moscow University and Two Youths — A904

1r, Komsomol badge and four orders.

1953, Oct. 29 ***Perf. 12½x12***
1674 A904 40k multicolored 2.50 1.40
1675 A904 1r multicolored 4.50 1.90

35th anniversary of the Young Communist League (Komsomol).

Nationalities of the Soviet Union — A905

60k, Lenin and Stalin at Smolny monastery.

1953, Nov. 6
1676 A905 40k multicolored 4.50 3.25
1677 A905 60k multicolored 10.00 6.75

36th anniversary of October Revolution.
No. 1676 measures 25½x38mm; No. 1677, 25½x42mm.

Lenin and His Writings — A906

1r, Lenin facing left and pages of "What to Do."

1953
1678 A906 40k multicolored 3.00 3.75
1679 A906 1r dk brn, org brn & red 6.50 4.75

Communist Party formation, 50th anniv. (40k). 2nd cong. of the Russian Socialist Party, 50th anniv. (1r).
Issued: 40k, 11/12; 1r, 12/14.

Lenin Statue — A907

Peter I Statue, Decembrists' Square — A908

Leningrad Views: Nos. 1681 & 1683, Admiralty building. Nos. 1685 & 1687, Smolny monastery.

1953, Nov. 23
1680 A907 40k brn blk, *yellow* 2.25 1.25
1681 A907 40k vio brn, *yellow* 2.25 1.25
1682 A907 40k dk brn, *pink* 2.25 1.25
1683 A907 40k brn blk, *cream* 2.25 1.25
1684 A908 1r dk brn, *blue* 5.00 3.00
1685 A908 1r dk green, *pink* 5.00 3.00
1686 A908 1r violet, *yellow* 5.00 3.00
1687 A908 1r blk brn, *blue* 5.00 3.00
Nos. 1680-1687 (8) 29.00 17.00

See Nos. 1944-1945, 1943a.

"Pioneers" and Model of Lomonosov Moscow University A909

Aleksandr S. Griboedov, Writer (1795-1829) A910

1953, Dec. 22 **Litho.** ***Perf. 12***
1688 A909 40k dk sl grn, dk brn & red 3.50 1.75

Arms Type of 1948

1954-57
1689 A682 40k scarlet 1.00 .50
a. 8 ribbon turns on wreath at left ('54) 4.25 1.65

No. 1689 was re-issued in 1954-56 typographed in slightly smaller format: 14½x21¾mm, instead of 14¾x21¾mm, and in a lighter shade. See note after No. 738.
No. 1689 has 7 ribbon turns on left side of wreath.

1954, Mar. 4 **Photo.**
1690 A910 40k dp claret, *cream* 1.40 .75
1691 A910 1r black, *green* 1.60 1.50

Kremlin View — A911

V. P. Chkalov — A912

1954, Mar. 7 Litho. ***Perf. 12½x12***
1692 A911 40k red & gray 6.00 3.00

1954 elections to the Supreme Soviet.

1954, Mar. 16 ***Perf. 12***
1693 A912 1r gray, vio bl & dk brown 6.00 1.25

50th anniversary of the birth of Valeri P. Chkalov (1904-1938), airplane pilot.

Lenin — A913

Lenin at Smolny A914

Designs: No. 1696, Lenin's home (later museum), Ulyanovsk. No. 1697, Lenin addressing workers. No. 1698, Lenin among students, University of Kazan.

1954, Apr. 16 **Photo.**
1694 A913 40k multicolored 4.00 2.00

Size: 38x27½mm
1695 A914 40k multicolored 4.00 2.00
1696 A914 40k multicolored 4.00 2.00

Size: 48x35mm
1697 A914 40k multicolored 4.00 2.00
1698 A914 40k multicolored 4.00 2.00
Nos. 1694-1698 (5) 20.00 10.00

30th anniversary of the death of Lenin.
For overprint see No. 2060.

Joseph V. Stalin — A915

1954, Apr. 30 **Unwmk.** ***Perf. 12***
1699 A915 40k dark brown 4.25 1.50

First anniversary of the death of Stalin.

Supreme Soviet Buildings in Kiev and Moscow A916

T. G. Shevchenko Statue, Kharkov — A917

Designs: No. 1701, University building, Kiev. No. 1702, Opera, Kiev. No. 1703, Ukranian Academy of Science. No. 1705, Bogdan Chmielnicki statue, Kiev. No. 1706 Flags of Soviet Russia and Ukraine. No. 1707, T. G. Shevchenko statue, Kanev. No. 1708, Chmielnicki proclaming reunion of Ukraine and Russia, 1654.

1954, May 10 **Litho.**

Size: 37½x26mm, 26x37½mm
1700 A916 40k red brn, sal, cream & black .95 .20
1701 A916 40k ultra, vio bl & brn .95 .20
1702 A916 40k red brn, buff, blue brown .95 .20
1703 A916 40k org brn, cream & grn .95 .20
1704 A917 40k rose red, blk, yel & brown 1.25 .20
1705 A917 60k multicolored 1.25 .30
1706 A917 1r multicolored 2.75 .50

Size: 42x28mm
1707 A916 1r multicolored 1.90 .50

Size: 45x29½mm
1708 A916 1r multicolored, *pink* 2.75 .50

No. 1341 Overprinted in Carmine

1709 A517 2r green 6.25 1.60
Nos. 1700-1709 (10) 19.95 4.40

300th anniversary of the union between the Ukraine and Russia.

Sailboat Race A918

Basketball A919

#1711, Hurdle race. #1712, Swimmers. #1713, Cyclists. #1714, Track. #1715, Skier. #1716, Mountain climbing.

1954, May 29

Frames in Orange Brown

1710 A918 40k blue & black 1.25 .20
1711 A918 40k vio gray & blk 1.25 .20
1712 A918 40k dk blue & black 1.25 .20
1713 A918 40k dk brn & buff 1.25 .20
1714 A918 40k black brn & buff 1.25 .20
1715 A918 1r blue & black 2.75 .25
1716 A918 1r blue & black 2.75 .25
1717 A919 1r dk brn & brn 2.75 .25
Nos. 1710-1717 (8) 14.50 1.75

For overprint see No. 2170.

Cattle A920

#1719, Potato planting and cultivation. #1720, Kolkhoz hydroelectric station.

1954, June 8

1718 A920 40k brn, cream, ind & blue gray 1.90 .85
1719 A920 40k gray grn, buff & brown 1.90 .85
1720 A920 40k blk, bl grn & vio bl 1.90 .85
Nos. 1718-1720 (3) 5.70 2.55

Anton P. Chekhov, Writer, 50th Death Anniv. — A921

1954, July 15

1721 A921 40k green & black brn .75 .25

F. A. Bredichin, V. J. Struve, A. A. Belopolski and Observatory — A922

1954, July 26

1722 A922 40k vio bl, blk & blue 6.00 1.00

Restoration of Pulkov Observatory.

Mikhail I. Glinka, Composer, 150th Birth Anniv. — A923

Pushkin and Zhukovsky Visiting Glinka A924

1954, July 26

1723 A923 40k dp cl, pink & blk brown 4.50 .75
1724 A924 60k multicolored 5.50 1.00

Nikolai A. Ostrovsky (1904-36), Blind Writer — A925

1954, Sept. 29 Photo. *Perf. 12½x12*

1725 A925 40k brn, dark red & yel 1.00 .40

Monument to Sunken Ships — A926

Defenders of Sevastopol — A927

Design: 1r, Admiral P. S. Nakhimov.

1954, Oct. 17 *Perf. 12½*

1726 A926 40k blue grn, blk & ol brown .60 .20
1727 A927 60k org brn, blk & brn .80 .25
1728 A926 1r brn, blk & ol green 1.60 .55
Nos. 1726-1728 (3) 3.00 1.00

Centenary of the defense of Sevastopol during the Crimean War.

Sculpture at Exhibition Entrance — A928

Agriculture Pavilion — A929

Cattle Pavilion A929a

Designs: No. 1732, Machinery pavilion. No. 1733, Main entrance. No. 1734, Main pavilion.

Perf. 12½, 12½x12, 12x12½

1954, Nov. 5 Litho.

Size: 26x37mm

1729 A928 40k multicolored .50 .25

Size: 40x29mm

1730 A929 40k multicolored .50 .25
1731 A929a 40k multicolored .50 .25
1732 A929 40k multicolored .50 .25

Size: 40½x33mm

1733 A929 1r multicolored 1.40 1.25

Size: 28½x40½mm

1734 A928 1r multicolored 1.40 1.25
Nos. 1729-1734 (6) 4.80 3.50

1954 Agricultural Exhibition.

Marx, Engels, Lenin and Stalin — A930

1954, Nov. 6 Photo. *Perf. 12½x12*

1735 A930 1r dk brn, pale org & red 6.00 2.25

37th anniversary of October Revolution.

Kazan University Building A931

1954, Nov. 11 *Perf. 12x12½*

1736 A931 40k deep blue .90 .50
1737 A931 60k claret 1.10 1.00

Founding of Kazan University, 150th anniv.

Salome Neris A932

1954, Nov. 17 *Perf. 12½x12*

1738 A932 40k red org & ol gray 2.00 .50

50th anniversary of the birth of Salome Neris (1904-1945), Lithuanian poet.

Vegetables and Garden A933

Cultivating Flax — A934

Designs: No. 1741, Tractor plowing field. No. 1742, Loading ensilage.

1954, Dec. 12 Litho. *Perf. 12x12½*

1739 A933 40k multicolored 1.00 .20
1740 A934 40k multicolored 1.00 .20
1741 A933 40k multicolored 1.00 .20
1742 A934 60k multicolored 1.25 .25
Nos. 1739-1742 (4) 4.25 .85

Joseph Stalin, 75th Birth Anniv. — A935

1954, Dec. 21 Engr. *Perf. 12½x12*

1743 A935 40k rose brown .60 .50
1744 A935 1r dark blue 1.40 .60

Anton G. Rubinstein (1829-94), Composer A936

1954, Dec. 30 Photo.

1745 A936 40k claret, gray & blk 4.00 .50

Vsevolod M. Garshin (1855-1888), Writer — A937

Lithographed and Photogravure

1955, Mar. 2 Unwmk. *Perf. 12*

1746 A937 40k buff, blk brn & green .50 .25

K. A. Savitsky and Painting A938

1955, Mar. 21 Photo.

1747 A938 40k multicolored 1.00 .30
a. Sheet of 4, black inscription 25.00 25.00
b. As "a," red brown inscription 35.00 25.00

K. A. Savitsky (1844-1905), painter. Size: Nos. 1747a, 1747b, 152x108mm.

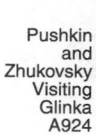

Globe and Clasped Hands — A939

1955, Apr. 9 **Litho.**

1748	A939	40k multicolored	.50	.25

International Conference of Public Service Unions, Vienna, April 1955.

Poets Pushkin and Mickiewicz — A940

Brothers in Arms Monument, Warsaw — A941

Palace of Culture and Science, Warsaw A942

Copernicus, Painting by Jan Matejko (in Medallion) — A943

Unwmk.

1955, Apr. 22 **Photo.** ***Perf. 12***

1749	A940	40k chalky blue, vio & black	1.25	.25
1750	A941	40k violet black	1.25	.25
1751	A942	1r brt red & gray black	2.75	.65
1752	A943	1r multicolored	2.75	.65
		Nos. 1749-1752 (4)	8.00	1.80

Polish-USSR treaty of friendship, 10th anniv.

Lenin at Shushinskoe — A944

Lenin at Secret Printing House — A945

Friedrich von Schiller — A946

Design: 1r, Lenin and Krupskaya with peasants at Gorki, 1921.

1955, Apr. 22
Frame and Inscription in Dark Red

1753	A944	60k multicolored	1.00	.35
1754	A944	1r multicolored	2.50	.45
1755	A945	1r multicolored	2.50	.45
		Nos. 1753-1755 (3)	6.00	1.25

85th anniversary of the birth of Lenin.

1955, May 10

1756	A946	40k chocolate	1.00	.50

150th anniversary of the death of Friedrich von Schiller, German poet.

A. G. Venezianov and "Spring on the Land" — A947

1955, June 21 **Photo.**

1757	A947	1r multicolored	1.50	.50
a.		Souvenir sheet of 4	22.50	15.00

Venezianov, painter, 175th birth anniv.

Anatoli K. Liadov (1855-1914), Composer — A948

1955, July 5 **Litho.**

1758	A948	40k red brn, blk & lt brn	1.50	.50

Aleksandr Popov — A949

1955, Nov. 5
Portraits Multicolored

1759	A949	40k light ultra	1.10	.20
1760	A949	1r gray brown	2.25	.35

60th anniv. of the construction of a coherer for detecting Hertzian electromagnetic waves by A. S. Popov, radio pioneer.

Lenin — A950

Storming the Winter Palace — A951

Design: 1r, Lenin addressing the people.

1955, Nov. 6

1761	A950	40k multicolored	1.25	.75
1762	A951	40k multicolored	1.25	.75
1763	A951	1r multicolored	3.00	1.00
		Nos. 1761-1763 (3)	5.50	2.50

38th anniversary of October Revolution.

Apartment Houses, Magnitogorsk — A952

1955, Nov. 29

1764	A952	40k multicolored	3.00	.25

25th anniversary of the founding of the industrial center, Magnitogorsk.

Arctic Observation Post — A953

Design: 1r, Scientist at observation post.

1955, Nov. 29 ***Perf. 12½x12***

1765	A953	40k multicolored	1.60	.20
1766	A953	60k multicolored	1.90	.30
1767	A953	1r multicolored	2.75	.45
a.		Souvenir sheet of 4 ('58)	35.00	25.00
		Nos. 1765-1767 (3)	6.25	.95

Publicizing the Soviet scientific drifting stations at the North Pole.

In 1962, No. 1767a was overprinted in red "1962" on each stamp and, in the lower sheet margin, a three-line Russian inscription meaning "25 years from the beginning of the work of "NP-1" station."

Sheet value, $40 unused, $35 canceled.

Fedor Ivanovich Shubin (1740-1805), Sculptor — A954

1955, Dec. 22 ***Perf. 12***

1768	A954	40k green & multi	.35	.20
1769	A954	1r brown & multi	.65	.25

Federal Socialist Republic Pavilion (R.S.F.S.R.) — A955

#1771

#1772

#1773

#1774

#1775

#1776

#1777

#1778

#1779

#1780

#1781

#1782

#1783

#1784

#1785

Designs: Pavilions.

1955 **Litho.** **Unwmk.**
Centers in Natural Colors; Frames in Blue Green and Olive

1770	A955	40k shown	.60	.20
a.		Sheet of 4	15.00	9.50
1771	A955	40k Tadzhik	.60	.20
1772	A955	40k Byelorussian	.60	.20
a.		Sheet of 4	15.00	9.50
1773	A955	40k Azerbaijan	.60	.20
1774	A955	40k Georgian	.60	.20
1775	A955	40k Armenian	.60	.20
1776	A955	40k Turkmen	.60	.20
1777	A955	40k Uzbek	.60	.20
1778	A955	40k Ukrainian	.60	.20
a.		Sheet of 4	15.00	9.50
1779	A955	40k Kazakh	.60	.20
1780	A955	40k Kirghiz	.60	.20
1781	A955	40k Karelo-Finnish	.60	.20
1782	A955	40k Moldavian	.60	.20
1783	A955	40k Estonian	.60	.20
1784	A955	40k Latvian	.60	.20
1785	A955	40k Lithuanian	.60	.20
		Nos. 1770-1785 (16)	9.60	3.20

All-Union Agricultural Fair.

Nos. 1773-1785 were printed in sheets containing various stamps, providing a variety of horizontal se-tenant pairs and strips. Value, $25 per sheet.

Lomonosov Moscow State University, 200th Anniv. — A956

Design: 1r, New University buildings.

1955, June 9 ***Perf. 12***

1786	A956	40k multicolored	.65	.25
a.		Sheet of 4 ('56)	6.00	*5.00*
1787	A956	1r multicolored	1.40	.30
a.		Sheet of 4 ('56)	12.00	*10.00*

Vladimir V. Mayakovsky — A957

1955, May 31

1788	A957	40k multicolored	1.00	.25

Mayakovsky, poet, 25th death anniv.

Race Horse — A958

Trotter A959

1956, Jan. 9

1789	A958	40k dark brown	.50	.20
1790	A958	60k Prus grn & blue green	.90	.25
1791	A959	1r dull pur & blue vio	1.60	.40
		Nos. 1789-1791 (3)	3.00	.85

International Horse Races, Moscow, Aug. 14-Sept. 4, 1955.

Alexei N. Krylov (1863-1945), Mathematician, Naval Architect — A960

1956, Jan. 9

1792	A960	40k gray, brown & black	.50	.20

Symbol of Spartacist Games, Stadium and Factories — A961

1956, Jan. 18

1793	A961	1r red vio & lt grn	.75	.25

5th All-Union Spartacist Games of Soviet Trade Union sport clubs, Moscow, Aug. 12-18, 1955.

Atomic Power Station A962

Design: 60k, Atomic Reactor.

1956, Jan. 31

1794	A962	25k multicolored	.70	.20
1795	A962	60k multicolored	1.10	.25
1796	A962	1r multicolored	1.60	.40
		Nos. 1794-1796 (3)	3.40	.85

Establishment of the first Atomic Power Station of the USSR Academy of Science. Inscribed in Russian: "Atomic Energy in the service of the people."

Statue of Lenin, Kremlin and Flags A963

1956, Feb.

1797	A963	40k multicolored	.90	.20
1798	A963	1r ol, buff & red org	1.10	.30

20th Congress of the Communist Party of the Soviet Union.

Khachatur Abovian, Armenian Writer, 150th Birth Anniv. — A964

1956, Feb. 25 **Unwmk.** ***Perf. 12***

1799	A964	40k black brn, *bluish*	5.00	.40

Workers with Red Flag — A965

Nikolai A. Kasatkin — A966

1956, Mar. 14

1800	A965	40k multicolored	2.00	.75

Revolution of 1905, 50th anniversary.

1956, Apr. 30

1801	A966	40k carmine lake	.50	.25

Kasatkin (1859-1930), painter.

"On the Oka River" A967

1956, Apr. 30
Center Multicolored

1802	A967	40k bister & black	1.50	.20
1803	A967	1r ultra & black	3.00	.30

A. E. Arkhipov, painter.

I. P. Kulibin, Inventor, 220th Birth Anniv. — A968

1956, May 12

1804	A968	40k multicolored	1.00	.25

Vassili Grigorievitch Perov (1833-82), Painter — A969

"Birdcatchers" — A970

Painting: No. 1807, "Hunters at Rest."

1956, May 12
Multicolored Centers

1805	A969	40k green	1.10	.20
1806	A970	1r brown	2.10	.35
1807	A970	1r orange brown	2.10	.45
		Nos. 1805-1807 (3)	5.30	1.00

Ural Pavilion A971

«ПАВИЛЬОН ТАТАРСКОЙ АССР»

#1809

ПАВИЛЬОН «ПОВОЛЖЬЕ»

#1810

ПАВИЛЬОН ЦЕНТРАЛЬНЫХ ЧЕРНОЗЕМНЫХ ОБЛАСТЕЙ

#1811

ПАВИЛЬОН СЕВЕРО-ВОСТОЧНЫХ ОБЛАСТЕЙ

#1812

ПАВИЛЬОН СЕВЕРНОГО КАВКАЗА

#1813

ПАВИЛЬОН БАШКИРСКОЙ АССР

#1814

ПАВИЛЬОН ДАЛЬНЕГО ВОСТОКА

#1815

ПАВИЛЬОН ЦЕНТРАЛЬНЫХ ОБЛАСТЕЙ

#1816

ПАВИЛЬОН ЮНЫХ НАТУРАЛИСТОВ

#1817

ПАВИЛЬОН «СИБИРЬ»

#1818

ПАВИЛЬОН «ЛЕНИНГРАД • СЕВЕРО-ЗАПАД»

#1819

ПАВИЛЬОН МОСКОВСКОЙ, ТУЛЬСКОЙ, КАЛУЖСКОЙ, РЯЗАНСКОЙ И БРЯНСКОЙ ОБЛАСТЕЙ

#1820

Pavilions: No. 1809, Tatar Republic. No. 1810, Volga District. No. 1811, Central Black Earth Area. No. 1812, Northeastern District. No. 1813, Northern Caucasus. No. 1814, Bashkir Republic. No. 1815, Far East. No. 1816, Central Asia. No. 1817, Young Naturalists. No. 1818, Siberia. No. 1819, Leningrad and Northwestern District. No. 1820, Moscow, Tula, Kaluga, Ryazan and Bryansk Districts.

1956, Apr. 25
Multicolored Centers

1808	A971	1r yel green & pale yel	1.10	.40
1809	A971	1r blue grn & pale yel	1.10	.40
1810	A971	1r dk blue grn & pale yel	1.10	.40
1811	A971	1r dk bl grn & yel grn	1.10	.40
1812	A971	1r dk blue grn & buff	1.10	.40
1813	A971	1r ol gray & pale yel	1.10	.40
1814	A971	1r olive & yellow	1.10	.40
1815	A971	1r olive grn & lemon	1.10	.40
1816	A971	1r olive brn & lemon	1.10	.40
1817	A971	1r olive brn & lemon	1.10	.40
1818	A971	1r brown & yellow	1.10	.40
1819	A971	1r redsh brown & yel	1.10	.40
1820	A971	1r dk red brn & yel	1.10	.40
		Nos. 1808-1820 (13)	14.30	5.20

All-Union Agricultural Fair, Moscow.

Six of the Pavilion set were printed se-tenant in one sheet of 30 (6x5), the strip containing Nos. 1809, 1816, 1817, 1813, 1818 and 1810 in that order. Two others, Nos. 1819-1820, were printed se-tenant in one sheet of 35. Value, $25 per sheet.

Lenin A972

Lobachevski A973

1956, May 25

1821	A972	40k lilac & multi	6.00	3.50

86th anniversary of the birth of Lenin.

1956, June 4

1822	A973	40k black brown	.50	.20

Nikolai Ivanovich Lobachevski (1793-1856), mathematician.

Nurse and Textile Factory A974

Design: 40k, First aid instruction.

1956, June 4 **Unwmk.**

1823	A974	40k lt ol grn, grnsh bl & red	.50	.20
1824	A974	40k red brn, lt bl & red	.50	.20

Red Cross and Red Crescent. No. 1823 measures 37x25mm; No. 1824, 40x28mm.

V. K. Arseniev (1872-1930), Explorer and Writer — A975

1956, June 15 Litho. *Perf. 12*

1825 A975 40k violet, black & rose 1.00 .25

I. M. Sechenov (1829-1905), Physiologist A976

1956, June 15

1826 A976 40k multicolored 1.00 .25

A. K. Savrasov, Painter — A977

1956, June 22

1827 A977 1r dull yel & brown 1.00 .20

I. V. Michurin, Scientist, Birth Centenary A978

Design: 60k, I. V. Michurin with Pioneers.

1956, June 22

Center Multicolored

1828 A978 25k dark brown .55 .20
1829 A978 60k green & lt blue 1.10 .40
1830 A978 1r light blue 2.25 .55
Nos. 1828-1830 (3) 3.90 1.15

Nos. 1828 and 1830 measure 32x25mm. No. 1829 measures 47x26mm.

Nadezhda K. Krupskaya A979

1956, June 28

1831 A979 40k brn, lt blue & pale brown 2.50 .75

Krupskaya (1869-1939), teacher and wife of Lenin.

See Nos. 1862, 1886, 1983, 2028.

S. M. Kirov (1886-1934), Revolutionary A980

1956, June 28

1832 A980 40k red, buff & brown .50 .25

Nikolai S. Leskov (1831-1895), Novelist — A981

1956, July 10

1833 A981 40k olive bister & brn .40 .20
1834 A981 1r green & dk brown .70 .40

Aleksandr A. Blok (1880-1921), Poet — A982

1956, July 10

1835 A982 40k olive & brn, *cream* .50 .40

Farm Machinery Factory A983

1956, July 23 *Perf. 12½x12*

1836 A983 40k multicolored .50 .25

Rostov Farm Machinery Works, 25th anniv.

A984

1956, July 23 Unwmk.

1837 A984 40k brown & rose vio 1.00 .25

G. N. Fedotova (1846-1925), actress. See No. 2026.

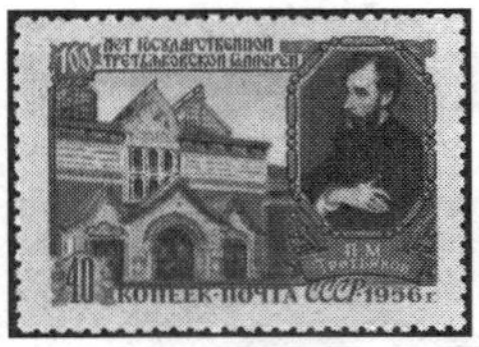

P. M. Tretiakov and Art Gallery A985

"The Rooks Have Arrived" by A. K. Savrasov A986

1956, July 31 *Perf. 12*

1838 A985 40k multicolored 4.00 .40
1839 A986 40k multicolored 4.00 .40

Tretiakov Art Gallery, Moscow, cent.

Relay Race A987

Volleyball — A988

#1842, Rowing. #1843, Swimming. #1844, Medal with heads of man and woman. #1845, Tennis. #1846, Soccer. #1847, Fencing. #1848, Bicycle race. #1849, Stadium and flag. #1850, Diving. #1851, Boxing. #1852, Gymnast. 1r, Basketball.

1956, Aug. 5

1840 A987 10k carmine rose .20 .20
1841 A988 25k dk orange brn .35 .20
1842 A988 25k brt grnsh blue .35 .20
1843 A988 25k grn, blue & lt brn .35 .20
1844 A988 40k org, pink, bis & yellow .50 .20
1845 A988 40k orange brown .50 .20
1846 A987 40k brt yel grn & dk brown .50 .20
1847 A987 40k grn, brt grn & dk brn, *grnsh* .50 .20
1848 A987 40k blue green .50 .20
1849 A988 40k brt yel grn & red .50 .20
1850 A988 40k greenish blue .50 .20
1851 A988 60k violet .80 .20
1852 A987 60k brt violet .80 .20
1853 A987 1r red brown 1.25 .40
Nos. 1840-1853 (14) 7.60 3.00

All-Union Spartacist Games, Moscow, Aug. 5-16.

Parachute Landing — A989

1956, Aug. 5 *Perf. 12x12½*

1854 A989 40k multicolored .50 .25

Third World Parachute Championships, Moscow, July 1956.

Building under Construction A990

Builders' Day: 60k, Building a factory. 1r, Building a dam.

1956 Photo. *Perf. 12*

1855 A990 40k deep orange .35 .20
1856 A990 60k brown carmine .65 .20
1857 A990 1r intense blue 1.00 .20
Nos. 1855-1857 (3) 2.00 .60

Ivan Franko — A991

Makhmud Aivazov — A992

1956, Aug. 27

1858 A991 40k deep claret .75 .25
1859 A991 1r bright blue 1.25 .30

Franko, writer (1856-1916).

1956, Aug. 27

Two types:
I - Three lines in panel with "148."
II - Two lines in panel with "148."

1860 A992 40k emerald (II) 7.50 4.00
a. Type I 21.00 18.00

148th birthday of Russia's oldest man, an Azerbaijan collective farmer.

Robert Burns, Scottish Poet, 160th Death Anniv. — A993

1956-57 Photo.

1861 A993 40k yellow brown 4.50 2.00

Engr.

1861A A993 40k lt ultra & brn ('57) 3.00 .85

For overprint see No. 2174.

Portrait Type of 1956

Lesya Ukrainka (1871-1913), Ukrainian writer.

1956, Aug. 27 Litho.

1862 A979 40k olive, blk & brown 2.00 .50

Statue of Nestor — A995

1956, Sept. 22 *Perf. 12x12½*

1863 A995 40k multicolored 1.25 .20
1864 A995 1r multicolored 1.75 .30

900th anniversary of the birth of Nestor, first Russian historian.

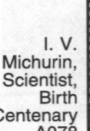

Aleksandr Andreevich Ivanov (1806-58), Painter — A996

1956, Sept. 22 **Unwmk.**

1865 A996 40k gray & brown .50 .25

I. E. Repin and "Volga River Boatmen" — A997

"Cossacks Writing a Letter to the Turkish Sultan" — A998

1956, Aug. 21

Multicolored Centers

1866 A997 40k org brn & black 5.00 .90
1867 A998 1r chalky blue & blk 10.00 1.10

Ilya E. Repin (1844-1930), painter.

Chicken Farm A999

Designs: No. 1869, Harvest. 25k, Harvesting corn. No. 1871, Women in corn field. No. 1872, Farm buildings. No. 1873, Cattle. No. 1874, Farm workers, inscriptions and silos.

1956, Oct. 7

1868 A999 10k multicolored .25 .25
1869 A999 10k multicolored .25 .25
1870 A999 25k multicolored .50 .25
1871 A999 40k multicolored 1.00 .25
1872 A999 40k multicolored 1.00 .25
1873 A999 40k multicolored 1.00 .25
1874 A999 40k multicolored 1.00 .25
Nos. 1868-1874 (7) 5.00 1.75

#1868, 1872, 1873 measure 37x25½mm; #1869-1871 37x27½mm; #1874 37x21mm.

Benjamin Franklin — A1000

G. B Shaw A1000a

Dostoevski A1000b

Portraits: #1876 Sesshu (Toyo Oda). #1877, Rembrandt. #1879, Mozart. #1880, Heinrich Heine. #1882, Ibsen. #1883, Pierre Curie.

1956, Oct. 17 **Photo.**

Size: 25x37mm

1875 A1000 40k copper brown 1.75 .60
1876 A1000 40k brt orange 1.75 .60
1877 A1000 40k black 1.75 .60
1878 A1000a 40k black 1.75 .60

Size: 21x32mm

1879 A1000 40k grnsh blue 1.75 .60
1880 A1000 40k violet 1.75 .60
1881 A1000b 40k green 1.75 .60
1882 A1000 40k brown 1.75 .60
1883 A1000 40k brt green 1.75 .60
Nos. 1875-1883 (9) 15.75 5.40

Great personalities of the world.

Antarctic Bases — A1001

1956, Oct. 22 **Litho.** ***Perf. 12x12½***

1884 A1001 40k slate, grnsh bl & red 1.00 .50

Soviet Scientific Antarctic Expedition.

G. I. Kotovsky (1881-1925), Military Commander A1002

1956, Oct. 30

1885 A1002 40k magenta 1.00 .20

Portrait Type of 1956

Portrait: Julia A. Zemaite (1845-1921), Lithuanian novelist.

1956, Oct. 30 ***Perf. 12***

1886 A979 40k lt ol green & brn .50 .25

Fedor A. Bredichin (1831-1904), Astronomer — A1004

1956, Oct. 30

1887 A1004 40k sepia & ultra 2.75 .75

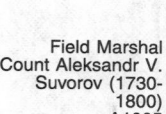

Field Marshal Count Aleksandr V. Suvorov (1730-1800) A1005

1956, Nov. 17 **Engr.**

1888 A1005 40k org & maroon .30 .20
1889 A1005 1r ol & dk red brn .85 .30
1890 A1005 3r lt red brn & black 2.10 .75
Nos. 1888-1890 (3) 3.25 1.25

Shatura Power Station A1006

1956 **Litho.** ***Perf. 12½x12***

1891 A1006 40k multicolored 1.00 .40

30th anniv. of the Shatura power station.

Kryakutni's Balloon, 1731 — A1007

1956, Nov. 17

1892 A1007 40k lt brn, sepia & yel 1.00 .40

225th anniv. of the 1st balloon ascension of the Russian inventor, Kryakutni.

A1008

1956, Dec. 3 **Unwmk.** ***Perf. 12***

1893 A1008 40k ultra & brown .75 .40

Yuli M. Shokalski (1856-1940), oceanographer and geodesist.

Apollinari M. Vasnetsov and "Winter Scene" A1009

1956, Dec. 30

1894 A1009 40k multicolored 1.00 .35

Vasnetsov (1856-1933), painter.

Indian Building and Books — A1010

1956, Dec. 26

1895 A1010 40k deep carmine .40 .25

Kalidasa, 5th century Indian poet.

Ivan Franko, Ukrainian Writer — A1011

1956, Dec. 26 **Engr.**

1896 A1011 40k dk slate green .50 .30

See Nos. 1858-1859.

Leo N. Tolstoy A1012

Portraits of Writers: No. 1898, Mikhail V. Lomonosov. No. 1899, Aleksander S. Pushkin. No. 1900, Maxim Gorki. No. 1901, Shota Rustaveli. No. 1902, Vissarion G. Belinski. No. 1903, Mikhail Y. Lermontov, poet, and Darjal Ravine in Caucasus.

1956-57 **Litho.** ***Perf. 12½x12***

Size: 37½x27½mm

1897 A1012 40k brt grnsh blue & brown .60 .20
1898 A1012 40k dk red, ol & brn olive .60 .20

Size: 35½x25½mm

1899 A1012 40k dk gray blue & brown .60 .20
1900 A1012 40k black & brn car .60 .20
1901 A1012 40k ol, brn & ol gray .60 .20
1902 A1012 40k bis, dl vio & brn ('57) .60 .20
1903 A1012 40k indigo & ol ('57) .60 .20
Nos. 1897-1903 (7) 4.20 1.40

Famous Russian writers.
See Nos. 1960-1962, 2031, 2112.

Fedor G. Volkov and Theater A1013

1956, Dec. 31 **Unwmk.**

1904 A1013 40k mag, gray & yel .60 .30

200th anniversary of the founding of the St. Petersburg State Theater.

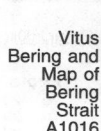

Vitus Bering and Map of Bering Strait A1016

1957, Feb. 6

1905 A1016 40k brown & blue 1.10 .50

275th anniversary of the birth of Vitus Bering, Danish navigator and explorer.

Dmitri I. Mendeleev A1017

1957, Feb. 6 *Perf. 12x12½*

1906 A1017 40k gray & gray brn 1.25 .60

D. I. Mendeleev (1834-1907), chemist.

Mikhail I. Glinka — A1018

1957, Feb. 23 *Perf. 12*

Design: 1r, Scene from opera Ivan Susanin.

1907 A1018 40k dk red, buff & sep .50 .30
1908 A1018 1r multicolored 1.00 .30

Mikhail I. Glinka (1804-1857), composer.

All-Union Festival of Soviet Youth, Moscow — A1019

1957, Feb. 23

1909 A1019 40k dk blue, red & ocher .50 .25

23rd Ice Hockey World Championship, Moscow — A1020

Designs: 25k, Emblem. 40k, Player. 60k, Goalkeeper.

1957, Feb. 24 **Photo.**

1910 A1020 25k deep violet .70 .20
1911 A1020 40k bright blue .70 .20
1912 A1020 60k emerald .70 .20
Nos. 1910-1912 (3) 2.10 .60

Dove and Festival Emblem — A1021

1957 **Litho.** *Perf. 12*

1913 A1021 40k multicolored .40 .20
1914 A1021 60k multicolored .60 .20

6th World Youth Festival, Moscow. Exist imperf. Value, each $30.

Assembly Line — A1022

1957, Mar. 15

1915 A1022 40k Prus grn & dp org .50 .40

Moscow Machine Works centenary.

Black Grouse A1023

Axis Deer — A1024

10k, Gray partridge. #1918, Polar bear. #1920, Bison. #1921, Mallard. #1922, European elk. #1923, Sable.

1957, Mar. 28
Center in Natural Colors

1916 A1024 10k yel brown .65 .20
1917 A1023 15k brown .65 .20
1918 A1023 15k slate blue .70 .20
1919 A1024 20k red orange .70 .20
1920 A1023 30k ultra .70 .20
1921 A1023 30k dk olive grn .70 .20
1922 A1023 40k dk olive grn 1.75 .30
1923 A1024 40k violet blue 1.75 .30
Nos. 1916-1923 (8) 7.60 1.80

See Nos. 2213-2219, 2429-2431.

Wooden Products, Hohloma A1025

National Handicrafts: No. 1925, Lace maker, Vologda. No. 1926, Bone carver, North Russia. No. 1927, Woodcarver, Moscow area. No. 1928,Rug weaver, Turkmenistan. No. 1929, Painting.

1957-58 **Unwmk.**

1924 A1025 40k red org, yel & black 1.50 .40
1925 A1025 40k brt car, yel & brown 1.50 .40
1926 A1025 40k ultra, buff & gray 1.50 .40
1927 A1025 40k brn, pale yel & hn brown 1.50 .40
1928 A1025 40k buff, brn, bl & org ('58) 1.00 .50
1929 A1025 40k multicolored ('58) 1.00 .50
Nos. 1924-1929 (6) 8.00 2.60

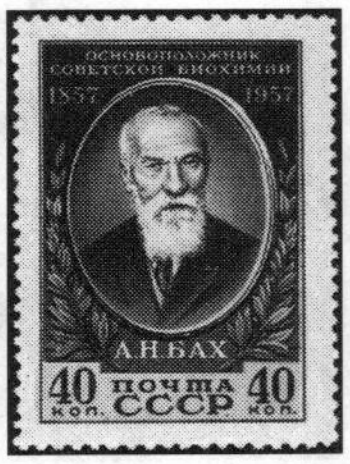

Aleksei Nikolaievitch Bach (1857-1946), Biochemist A1026

1957, Apr. 6 **Litho.** *Perf. 12*

1930 A1026 40k ultra, brn & buff .60 .30

Georgi Valentinovich Plekhanov (1856-1918), Political Philosopher A1027

1957, Apr. 6 **Engr.**

1931 A1027 40k dull purple .40 .25

Leonhard Euler A1028

1957, Apr. 17 **Litho.**

1932 A1028 40k lilac & gray .60 .25

Leonhard Euler (1707-1783), Swiss mathematician and physicist.

Lenin, 87th Birth Anniv. — A1029

Designs: No. 1934, Lenin talking to soldier and sailor. No. 1935, Lenin building barricades.

1957, Apr. 22
Multicolored Centers

1933 A1029 40k magenta & bis .60 .20
1934 A1029 40k magenta & bis .60 .20
1935 A1029 40k magenta & bis .60 .20
Nos. 1933-1935 (3) 1.80 .60

Youths of All Races Carrying Festival Banner — A1030

Design: 20k, Sculptor with motherhood statue. 40k, Young couples dancing. 1r, Festival banner and fireworks over Moscow University.

1957, May 27 *Perf. 12x12½*

1936 A1030 10k emer, pur & yel .20 .20
1937 A1030 20k multicolored .40 .20
1938 A1030 25k emer, pur & yel .45 .20
1939 A1030 40k rose, bl grn & bis brn .45 .20
1940 A1030 1r multicolored .50 .20
Nos. 1936-1940 (5) 2.00 1.00

6th World Youth Festival in Moscow. The 10k, 20k, and 1r exist imperf. Value each about $25.

Marine Museum Place and Neva — A1031

Henry Fielding — A1032

Designs: No. 1942, Lenin monument. No. 1943, Nevski Prospect and Admiralty.

1957, May 27 **Photo.** *Perf. 12*

1941 A1031 40k blue green .50 .20
1942 A1031 40k reddish brown .50 .20
1943 A1031 40k bluish violet .50 .20
a. Souv. sheet of 3, red border 7.50 6.00
Nos. 1941-1943 (3) 1.50 .60

250th anniversary of Leningrad.

No. 1943a contains imperf. stamps similar to #1941, 1680 (in reddish brown), 1943, and is for 40th anniv. of the October Revolution. Issued Nov. 7, 1957. A similar sheet is listed as No. 2002a.

Type of 1953 Overprinted in Red **250 лет Ленинграда**

Designs: No. 1944, Peter I Statue, Decembrists' Square. No. 1945, Smolny Institute.

1957, May 27 *Perf. 12½x12*

1944 A908 1r black brn, *greenish* .50 .20
1945 A908 1r green, *pink* .50 .20

250th anniversary of Leningrad.

The overprint is in one line on No. 1945.

1957, June 20 **Litho.**

1946 A1032 40k multicolored .50 .25

Fielding (1707-54), English playwright, novelist.

William Harvey — A1033

1957, May 20 **Photo.**

1947 A1033 40k brown .50 .25

300th anniversary of the death of the English physician William Harvey, discoverer of blood circulation.

M. A. Balakirev (1836-1910), Composer A1034

1957, May 20 **Engr.**

1948 A1034 40k bluish black .50 .25

A. I. Herzen and N. P. Ogarev A1035

1957, May 20 **Litho.**

1949 A1035 40k blk vio & dk ol gray .50 .25

Centenary of newspaper Kolokol (Bell).

Kazakhstan Workers' Medal — A1036

1957, May 20

1950 A1036 40k lt blue, blk & yel .50 .25

A1037 A1037a A1037b

Portraits: No. 1951, A. M. Liapunov. No. 1952, V. Mickevicius Kapsukas, writer. No. 1953, G. Bashindchagian, Armenian painter. No. 1954, Yakub Kolas, Byelorussian poet. No. 1955, Carl von Linné, Swedish botanist.

1957 **Photo.**

Various Frames

1951 A1037 40k dull red brown 3.00 2.25
1952 A1037a 40k sepia 1.75 1.75
1953 A1037 40k sepia 1.75 1.75
1954 A1037b 40k gray 1.75 1.75
1955 A1037 40k brown black 2.00 2.00
Nos. 1951-1955 (5) 10.25 9.50

See Nos. 2036-2038, 2059.

Bicyclist A1038

1957, June 20 **Litho.**

1956 A1038 40k claret & vio blue .50 .25

10th Peace Bicycle Race.

Telescope A1039

Designs: No. 1958, Comet and observatory. No. 1959, Rocket leaving earth.

1957, July 4

Size: 25½x37mm

1957 A1039 40k brn, ocher & blue .50 .35
1958 A1039 40k indigo, lt bl & yel 1.40 .35

Size: 14½x21mm

1959 A1039 40k blue violet 1.10 .55
Nos. 1957-1959 (3) 3.00 1.25

International Geophysical Year, 1957-58. See Nos. 2089-2091.

Folksinger A1040

1957, May 20

1960 A1040 40k multicolored .50 .25

"The Song of Igor's Army," Russia's oldest literary work.

Taras G. Shevchenko, Ukrainian Poet — A1041

Design: #1962, Nikolai G. Chernyshevski, writer and politician.

1957, July 20

1961 A1041 40k grn & dk red brn .40 .20
1962 A1041 40k orange brn & grn .40 .20

Woman Gymnast — A1043

25k, Wresting. No. 1965, Stadium. No. 1966, Youths of three races. 60k, Javelin thrower.

1957, July 15 **Litho.** ***Perf. 12***

1963 A1043 20k bluish vio & org brn .20 .20
1964 A1043 25k brt grn & claret .20 .20
1965 A1043 40k Prus bl, ol & red .35 .20
1966 A1043 40k crimson & violet .35 .20
1967 A1043 60k ultra & brown .40 .20
Nos. 1963-1967 (5) 1.50 1.00

Third International Youth Games, Moscow.

Javelin Thrower — A1044

Designs: No. 1969, Sprinter. 25k, Somersault. No. 1971, Boxers. No. 1972, Soccer players, horiz. 60k, Weight lifter.

1957, July 20 **Unwmk.**

1968 A1044 20k lt ultra & ol blk .35 .20
1969 A1044 20k brt grn, red vio & black .35 .20
1970 A1044 25k orange, ultra & blk .35 .20
1971 A1044 40k rose vio & blk .55 .20
1972 A1044 40k dp pink, bl, buff & black .55 .20
1973 A1044 60k lt violet & brn .85 .20
Nos. 1968-1973 (6) 3.00 1.20

Success of Soviet athletes at the 16th Olympic Games, Melbourne.

Kupala A1045 Kremlin A1046

1957, July 27 **Photo.**

1974 A1045 40k dark gray 2.00 1.50

Yanka Kupala (1882-1942), poet.

1957, July 27 **Litho.**

Moscow Views: No. 1976, Stadium. No. 1977, University. No. 1978, Bolshoi Theater.

Center in Black

1975 A1046 40k dull red brown .25 .20
1976 A1046 40k brown violet .25 .20
1977 A1046 1r red .50 .20
1978 A1046 1r brt violet blue .50 .20
Nos. 1975-1978 (4) 1.50 .80

Sixth World Youth Festival, Moscow.

Lenin Library A1047

1957, July 27 **Photo.**

1979 A1047 40k brt grnsh blue .50 .25
a. Souvenir sheet of 2, light blue, imperf. 10.00 *10.00*

Intl. Phil. Exhib., Moscow, July 29-Aug. 11. No. 1979 exists imperf. Value $10.

Pierre Jean de Beranger(1780-1857), French Song Writer — A1048

1957, Aug. 9

1980 A1048 40k brt blue green .50 .20

Globe, Dove and Olive Branch — A1049

1957, Aug. 8 **Litho.**

1981 A1049 40k bl, grn & bis brn 1.50 .60
1982 A1049 1r violet, grn & brn 3.50 1.25

Publicity for world peace.

Portrait Type of 1956

Portrait: 40k, Clara Zetkin (1857-1933), German communist.

1957, Aug. 9

1983 A979 40k gray blue, brn & blk 1.00 .20

Krenholm Factory, Narva A1050

1957, Sept. 8 **Photo.**

1984 A1050 40k black brown 1.00 .25

Centenary of Krenholm textile factory, Narva, Estonia.

Carrier Pigeon and Globes A1051

1957, Sept. 26 **Unwmk.** ***Perf. 12***

1985 A1051 40k blue .30 .20
1986 A1051 60k lilac .45 .20

Intl. Letter Writing Week, Oct. 6-12.

Vyborzhets Factory, Lenin Statue A1052

1957, Sept. 23 **Litho.**

1987 A1052 40k dark blue .80 .25

Krasny Vyborzhets factory, Leningrad, cent.

Vladimir Vasilievich Stasov (1824-1906), Art and Music Critic — A1053

1957, Sept. 23 **Engr.**

1988 A1053 40k brown .35 .20
1989 A1053 1r bluish black .65 .20

Congress Emblem A1054

1957, Oct. 7 **Litho.** ***Perf. 12***

1990 A1054 40k gray blue & blk, *bluish* .50 .25

4th International Trade Union Congress, Leipzig, Oct. 4-15.

Konstantin E. Tsiolkovsky and Rockets A1055

1957, Oct. 7

1991 A1055 40k dk blue & pale brown 1.75 .75

Tsiolkovsky (1857-1935), rocket and astronautics pioneer.
For overprint see No. 2021.

Sputnik 1 Circling Globe — A1056 Turbine Wheel, Kuibyshev Hydroelectric Station — A1057

1957 **Photo.**

1992 A1056 40k indigo, *bluish* 1.40 .50
1993 A1056 40k bright blue 1.40 .50

Launching of first artificial earth satellite, Oct. 4. Issue dates: No. 1992, Nov. 5; No. 1993, Dec. 28.

1957, Nov. 20 **Litho.**

1994 A1057 40k red brown .50 .20

All-Union Industrial Exhib. See #2030.

Meteor — A1058

Lenin — A1059

1957, Nov. 20
1995 A1058 40k multicolored 1.00 .40

Falling of Sihote Alinj meteor, 10th anniv.

1957, Oct. 30 **Engr.**

Design: 60k, Lenin reading Pravda, horiz.

1996 A1059 40k blue .75 .25
1997 A1059 60k rose red .75 .25

40th anniversary of October Revolution.

Students and Moscow University — A1060

Worker and Railroad A1061

#1999, Red flag, Lenin. #2000, Lenin addressing workers and peasants. 60k, Harvester.

Perf. 12½x12, 12x12½, 12½

1957, Oct. 15 **Litho.**
1998 A1060 10k buff, sepia & red .20 .20
1999 A1060 40k buff, red, sep & yel .25 .20
2000 A1060 40k red, black & yel .25 .20
2001 A1061 40k red, yel & green .25 .20
2002 A1061 60k red, ocher & vio brn .35 .20
a. Souvenir sheet of 3, #2000-2002, imperf. 7.50 5.00
Nos. 1998-2002 (5) 1.30 1.00

40th anniv. of the October Revolution. A similar sheet is listed as No. 1943a.
Nos. 1998-2002 exist imperf.

Federal Socialist Republic A1062

Uzbek Republic — A1063

Republic: #2005, Tadzhik (building, peasant girl). #2006, Byelorussia (truck). #2007, Azerbaijan (buildings). #2008, Georgia (valley, palm, couple). #2009, Armenia, (fruit, power line, mountains). #2010, Turkmen (couple, lambs). #2011, Ukraine (farmers). #2012, Kazakh (harvester, combine). #2013, Kirghiz (horseback rider, building). #2014, Moldavia (automatic sorting machine). #2015, Estonia (girl in national costume). #2016, Latvia (couple, sea, field). #2017, Lithuania (farm, farmer couple).

1957, Oct. 25
2003 A1062 40k multicolored .60 .30
2004 A1063 40k multicolored .60 .30
2005 A1062 40k multicolored .60 .30
2006 A1062 40k multicolored .60 .30
2007 A1062 40k multicolored .60 .30
2008 A1062 40k multicolored .60 .30
2009 A1062 40k multicolored .60 .30
2010 A1062 40k multicolored .60 .30
2011 A1063 40k multicolored .60 .30
2012 A1062 40k multicolored .60 .30
2013 A1062 40k multicolored .60 .30
2014 A1062 40k multicolored .60 .30
2015 A1063 40k multicolored .60 .30
2016 A1062 40k multicolored .60 .30
2017 A1062 40k multicolored .60 .30
Nos. 2003-2017 (15) 9.00 4.50

40th anniversary of the October Revolution.

Artists and Academy of Art — A1064

Red Army Monument, Berlin — A1065

1r, Worker and Peasant monument, Moscow.

1957, Dec. 16
2018 A1064 40k black, *pale salmon* .20 .20
2019 A1065 60k black .45 .20
2020 A1065 1r black, *pink* .85 .20
Nos. 2018-2020 (3) 1.50 .60

200th anniversary of the Academy of Arts, Leningrad. Artists on 40k are K. P. Bryulov, Ilya Repin and V. I. Surikov.

No. 1991 Overprinted in Black

1957, Nov. 28
2021 A1055 40k 12.50 5.00

Launching of Sputnik 1.

Ukrainian Arms, Symbolic Figures A1066

1957, Dec. 24
2022 A1066 40k yellow, red & blue .50 .25

Ukrainian Soviet Republic, 40th anniv.

Edvard Grieg A1067

Giuseppe Garibaldi A1068

1957, Dec. 24 **Photo.**
2023 A1067 40k black, *buff* 1.50 .20

Grieg, Norwegian composer, 50th death anniv.

1957, Dec. 24 **Litho.**
2024 A1068 40k plum, lt grn & blk .45 .20

Garibaldi, (1807-1882) Italian patriot.

Vladimir Lukich Borovikovsky (1757-1825), Painter — A1069

1957, Dec. 24 **Photo.**
2025 A1069 40k brown .50 .25

Portrait Type of 1956

Portrait: 40k, Mariya Nikolayevna Ermolova (1853-1928), actress.

1957, Dec. 28 **Litho.**
2026 A984 40k red brn & brt violet .75 .20

Kuibyshev Hydroelectric Station and Dam A1070

1957, Dec. 28
2027 A1070 40k dark blue, *buff* .70 .20

Type of 1956

Portrait: 40k, Rosa Luxemburg (1870-1919), German socialist.

1958, Jan. 8
2028 A979 40k blue & brown 1.00 .60

Chi Pai-shih A1070a

Flag and Symbols of Industry A1070b

1958, Jan. 8 **Photo.**
2029 A1070a 40k deep violet 1.00 .25

Chi Pai-shih (1860-1957), Chinese painter.

1958, Jan. 8 **Litho.**
2030 A1070b 60k gray vio, red & black .50 .25

All-Union Industrial Exhib. Exists imperf. Value, $150.

Aleksei N. Tolstoi, Novelist & Dramatist (1883-1945) A1071

1958, Jan. 28 **Photo.** ***Perf. 12***
2031 A1071 40k brown olive .50 .30

See Nos. 2112, 2175-2178C.

Symbolic Figure Greeting Sputnik 2 — A1072

1957-58 **Litho.**

Figure in Buff

2032 A1072 20k black & rose .45 .20
2033 A1072 40k black & grn ('58) .60 .25
2034 A1072 60k blk & lt brn ('58) .85 .25
2035 A1072 1r black & blue 1.10 .30
Nos. 2032-2035 (4) 3.00 1.00

Launching of Sputnik 2, Nov. 3, 1957.

Small Portrait Type of 1957

#2036, Henry W. Longfellow, American poet. #2037, William Blake, English artist, poet, mystic. #2038, E. Sharents, Armenian poet.

1958, Mar. **Unwmk.** ***Perf. 12***

Various Frames

2036 A1037 40k gray black 2.00 1.50
2037 A1037 40k gray black 2.00 1.50
2038 A1037 40k sepia 2.00 1.50
Nos. 2036-2038 (3) 6.00 4.50

Victory at Pskov A1073

Soldier and Civilian — A1074

Designs: No. 2040, Airman, sailor and soldier. No. 2042, Sailor and soldier. 60k, Storming of Berlin Reichstag building.

1958, Feb. 21
2039 A1073 25k multicolored .25 .20
2040 A1073 40k multicolored .50 .20
2041 A1074 40k multicolored .50 .20
2042 A1074 40k multicolored .50 .20
2043 A1073 60k multicolored .85 .20
Nos. 2039-2043 (5) 2.60 1.00

40th anniversary of Red Armed Forces.

Peter Ilich Tchaikovsky A1075

Swan Lake Ballet A1076

Design: 1r, Tchaikovsky, pianist and violinist.

1958, Mar. 18
2044 A1075 40k grn, bl, brn & red .45 .20
2045 A1076 40k grn, ultra, red & yel .45 .20
2046 A1075 1r lake & emerald 1.60 .35
Nos. 2044-2046 (3) 2.50 .75

Honoring Tchaikovsky and for the Tchaikovsky competitions for pianists and violinists. Exist imperf. Value, set $10.
Nos. 2044-2045 were printed in sheets of 30, including 15 stamps of each value and 5 se-tenant pairs.

V. F. Rudnev — A1077

Maxim Gorki — A1078

1958, Mar. 25 **Unwmk.**
2047 A1077 40k green, blk & ocher 1.00 .25

Rudnev, naval commander.

1958, Apr. 3 **Litho.** ***Perf. 12***
2048 A1078 40k multicolored .75 .25

Gorki, writer, 90th birth anniv.

Spasski Tower — A1079

1958, Apr. 9
2049 A1079 40k dp violet, *pinkish* .25 .20
2050 A1079 60k rose red .35 .20

13th Congress of the Young Communist League (Komsomol).

Russian Pavilion, Brussels A1080

1958, Apr.
2051 A1080 10k multicolored .25 .20
2052 A1080 40k multicolored .35 .20

Universal and International Exhibition at Brussels. Exist imperf. Value $2.

Lenin A1081

Jan A. Komensky (Comenius) A1082

1958, Apr. 22 **Engr.**
2053 A1081 40k dk blue gray .40 .20
2054 A1081 60k rose brown .50 .20
2055 A1081 1r brown .85 .20
Nos. 2053-2055 (3) 1.75 .60

88th anniversary of the birth of Lenin.

1958, May 5

Portrait: Nos. 2056-2058, Karl Marx.

2056 A1081 40k brown .40 .20
2057 A1081 60k dark blue .50 .20
2058 A1081 1r dark red 1.10 .20
Nos. 2056-2058 (3) 2.00 .60

140th anniversary of the birth of Marx.

1958, Apr. 17 **Photo.**
2059 A1082 40k green 1.90 1.25

No. 1695 Overprinted in Blue

1958, Apr. 22
2060 A914 40k multicolored 3.00 1.00

Academy of Arts, Moscow, 200th anniv.

Lenin Order — A1083

Carlo Goldoni — A1084

1958, Apr. 30 **Litho.**
2061 A1083 40k brown, yel & red .50 .30

1958, Apr. 28 **Photo.**
2062 A1084 40k blue & dk gray .50 .30

Carlo Goldoni, Italian dramatist.

Radio Tower, Ship and Planes A1085

1958, May 7
2063 A1085 40k blue green & red 2.50 .35

Issued for Radio Day, May 7.

Globe and Dove A1086

Ilya Chavchavadze A1087

1958, May 6 **Litho.**
2064 A1086 40k blue & black .30 .20
2065 A1086 60k ultra & black .45 .20

4th Congress of the Intl. Democratic Women's Federation, June, 1958, at Vienna.

1958, May 12 **Photo.**
2066 A1087 40k black & blue .50 .20

50th anniversary of the death of Ilya Chavchavadze, Georgian writer.

Flags and Communication Symbols — A1088

1958-59 **Litho.**
2067 A1088 40k blue, red, yel & blk 6.00 3.00
a. Red half of Czech flag at bottom 7.50 3.00

Communist ministers' meeting on social problems in Moscow, Dec. 1957.

On No. 2067, the Czech flag (center flag in vertical row of five) is incorrectly pictured with red stripe on top. This error is corrected on No. 2067a.

Bugler — A1089

Pioneers: 25k, Boy with model plane.

1958, May 29 **Unwmk.** ***Perf. 12***
2068 A1089 10k ultra, red & red brn .25 .20
2069 A1089 25k ultra, yel & red brn .25 .20

Children of Three Races — A1090

Design: No. 2071, Child and bomb.

1958, May 29
2070 A1090 40k car, ultra & brn .35 .20
2071 A1090 40k carmine & brown .35 .20

Intl. Day for the Protection of Children.

Soccer Players and Globe A1091

Rimski-Korsakov A1092

1958, June 5
2072 A1091 40k blue, red & buff .30 .20
2073 A1091 60k blue, red & buff .70 .30

6th World Soccer Championships, Stockholm, June 8-29. Exist imperf. Value $4.

1958, June 5 **Photo.**
2074 A1092 40k blue & brown 1.25 .20

Nikolai Andreevich Rimski-Korsakov (1844-1908), composer.

Girl Gymnast — A1093

No. 2076, Gymnast on rings and view.

1958, June 24 **Litho.**
2075 A1093 40k ultra, red & buff .50 .20
2076 A1093 40k blue, red buff & grn .50 .20

14th World Gymnastic Championships, Moscow, July 6-10.

Bomb, Globe, Atom, Sputniks, Ship A1094

1958, July 1
2077 A1094 60k dk blue, blk & org 1.75 .50

Conference for peaceful uses of atomic energy, held at Stockholm.

Street Fighters A1095

Congress Emblem A1097

Moscow State University A1096

1958, July 5
2078 A1095 40k red & violet blk .50 .25

Communist Party in the Ukraine, 40th anniv.

1958, July 8 ***Perf. 12***
2079 A1096 40k red & blue .25 .20
2080 A1097 60k lt grn, blue & red .35 .20
a. Souvenir sheet of 2 10.00 5.50

5th Congress of the International Architects' Organization, Moscow.

No. 2080a contains Nos. 2079-2080, imperf., with background design in yellow, brown, blue and red. Issued Sept. 8, 1958.

Young Couple A1098

1958, June 25
2081 A1098 40k blue & ocher .20 .20
2082 A1098 60k yel green & ocher .35 .20

Day of Soviet Youth.

Sputnik 3 Leaving Earth A1099

1958, June 16
2083 A1099 40k vio blue, grn & rose 1.00 .25

Launching of Sputnik 3, May 15. Printed in sheets with alternating labels, giving details of launching.

Sadriddin Aini — A1100

1958, July 15
2084 A1100 40k rose, black & buff .40 .20

80th birthday of Aini, Tadzhik writer.

Emblem
A1101

1958, July 21 Typo. *Perf. 12*

2085	A1101	40k lilac & blue	.50	.25

1st World Trade Union Conference of Working Youths, Prague, July 14-20.

Type of 1958-59 and

TU-104 and Globe
A1102

Design: 1r, Turbo-propeller liner AN-10.

1958, Aug. Litho.

2086	A1102	60k blue, red & bis	.35	.20
2087	A1123	1r yel, red & black	.75	.20

Soviet civil aviation. Exist imperf. Value, set $5.50. See Nos. 2147-2151.

L. A. Kulik
A1103

1958, Aug. 12

2088	A1103	40k sep, bl, yel & claret	1.00	.25

50th anniv. of the falling of the Tungus meteor and the 75th anniv. of the birth of L. A. Kulik, meteorist.

IGY Type of 1957

Designs: No. 2089, Aurora borealis and camera. No. 2090, Schooner "Zarja" exploringearth magnetism. No. 2091, Weather balloon and radar.

1958, July 29
Size: 25½x37mm

2089	A1039	40k blue & brt yel	.90	.25
2090	A1039	40k blue green	.90	.25
2091	A1039	40k bright ultra	.90	.25
		Nos. 2089-2091 (3)	2.70	.75

International Geophysical Year, 1957-58.

Crimea Observatory
A1104

Moscow University
A1105

Design: 1r, Telescope.

1958, Aug. Photo.

2092	A1104	40k brn & brt grnsh bl	.55	.20
2093	A1105	60k lt blue, vio & yel	.70	.20
2094	A1104	1r dp blue & org brn	1.00	.20
		Nos. 2092-2094 (3)	2.25	.60

10th Congress of the International Astronomical Union, Moscow.

Postilion, 16th Century
A1106

Designs: #2095, 15th cent. letter writer. #2097, A. L. Ordyn-Natshokin and sleigh mail coach, 17th cent. No. 2098, Mail coach and post office, 18th cent. #2099, Troika, 19th cent. #2100, Lenin stamp, ship and Moscow University. #2101, Jet plane and postilion. #2102, Leningrad Communications Museum, vert. #2103, V. N. Podbielski and letter carriers. #2104, Mail train. #2105, Loading mail on plane. #2106, Ship, plane, train and globe.

1958, Aug. Unwmk. Litho. *Perf. 12*

2095	A1106	10k red, blk, yel & lil	.20	.20
2096	A1106	10k multicolored	.20	.20
2097	A1106	25k ultra & slate	.25	.20
2098	A1106	25k black & ultra	.25	.20
2099	A1106	40k car lake & brn blk	.30	.20
2100	A1106	40k blk, mag & brn	.30	.20
2101	A1106	40k red, org & gray	.30	.20
2102	A1106	40k salmon & brown	.30	.20
2103	A1106	60k grnsh blue & red lil	.45	.20
2104	A1106	60k grnsh bl & lilac	.45	.20
2105	A1106	1r multicolored	.65	.25
2106	A1106	1r multicolored	.65	.25
		Nos. 2095-2106 (12)	4.30	2.50

Centenary of Russian postage stamps.

Two imperf. souvenir sheets exist, measuring 155x106mm. One contains one each of Nos. 2095-2099, with background design in red, ultramarine, yellow and brown. The other contains one each of Nos. 2100, 2103-2106, with background design in blue, gray, ocher, pink and brown. Value for both, $7.50 unused, $5 canceled.

Nos. 2096, 2100-2101 exist imperf. Value for both, $20 unused, $5 canceled.

M. I. Chigorin, Chess Player, 50th Death Anniv. — A1107

1958, Aug. 30 Photo.

2107	A1107	40k black & emerald	.50	.30

Golden Gate, Vladimir
A1108

60k, Gorki Street with trolley bus and truck.

1958, Aug. 23 Litho.

2108	A1108	40k multicolored	.30	.20
2109	A1108	60k lt violet, yel & blk	.45	.30

850th anniv. of the city of Vladimir.

Nurse Bandaging Man's Leg — A1109

2111, Hospital, & people of various races.

1958, Sept. 15

2110	A1109	40k multicolored	.30	.20
2111	A1109	40k olive, lemon & red	.30	.20

40 years of Red Cross-Red Crescent work.

Portrait Type of 1958

Mikhail E. Saltykov (Shchedrin), writer.

1958, Sept. 15

2112	A1071	40k brn black & mar	.75	.20

Rudagi — A1110

V. V. Kapnist — A1111

1958, Oct. 10 Litho. *Perf. 12*

2113	A1110	40k multicolored	.50	.20

1100th anniversary of the birth of Rudagi, Persian poet.

1958, Sept. 30

2114	A1111	40k blue & gray	.55	.25

200th anniversary of the birth of V. V. Kapnist, poet and dramatist.

Book, Torch, Lyre, Flower
A1112

1958, Oct. 4

2115	A1112	40k red org, ol & blk	.50	.25

Conf. of Asian & African Writers, Tashkent.

Chelyabinsk Tractor Factory
A1113

Designs: No. 2117, Zaporozstal foundry. No. 2118, Ural machine building plant.

1958, Oct. 20 Photo.

2116	A1113	40k green & yellow	.40	.20
2117	A1113	40k brown red & yel	.40	.20
2118	A1113	40k blue	.40	.20
		Nos. 2116-2118 (3)	1.20	.60

Pioneers of Russian Industry.

Ancient Georgian on Horseback
A1114

1958, Oct. 18 Litho.

2119	A1114	40k ocher, ultra & red	1.25	.20

1500th anniv. of Tbilisi, capital of Georgia.

Red Square, Moscow — A1115

АЛМА-АТА • ПЛОЩАДЬ им. В. И. ЛЕНИНА
#2121

ТБИЛИСИ • ПРОСПЕКТ РУСТАВЕЛИ
#2125

ФРУНЗЕ • УНИВЕРСИТЕТСКАЯ ПЛОЩАДЬ
#2127

ОБЩИЙ ВИД ГОРОДА ЕРЕВАН #2128

#2131 МИНСК • КРУГЛАЯ ПЛОЩАДЬ

Capitals of Soviet Republics: #2121, Lenin Square, Alma Ata. #2122, Lenin statue, Ashkhabad. #2123, Lenin statue, Tashkent. #2124, Lenin Square, Stalinabad. #2125, Rustaveli Ave., Tbilisi. #2126, View from Dvina River, Riga. #2127, University Square, Frunze. #2128, View, Yerevan. #2129, Communist Street, Baku. #2130, Lenin Prospect, Kishinev. #2131, Round Square, Minsk. #2132, Viru Gate, Tallinn. #2133, Main Street, Kiev. #2134, View, Vilnius.

1958 Engr.

2120	A1115	40k violet	.60	.30
2121	A1115	40k brt blue green	.60	.30
2122	A1115	40k greenish gray	.60	.30
2123	A1115	40k dark gray	.60	.30
2124	A1115	40k blue	.60	.30
2125	A1115	40k violet blue	.60	.30
2126	A1115	40k brown red	.60	.30
2127	A1115	40k dk blue gray	.60	.30
2128	A1115	40k brown	.60	.30
2129	A1115	40k purple	.60	.30
2130	A1115	40k olive	.60	.30
2131	A1115	40k gray brown	.60	.30
2132	A1115	40k emerald	.60	.30
2133	A1115	40k lilac rose	.60	.30
2134	A1115	40k orange ver	.60	.30
		Nos. 2120-2134 (15)	9.00	4.50

See No. 2836.

Young Civil War Soldier, 1919 — A1116

20k, Industrial brigade. 25k, Youth in World War II. 40k, Girl farm worker. 60k, Youth building new towns. 1r, Students, fighters for culture.

1958, Oct. 25 Litho.

2135	A1116	10k multicolored	.20	.20
2136	A1116	20k multicolored	.20	.20
2137	A1116	25k multicolored	.30	.20
2138	A1116	40k multicolored	.35	.20
2139	A1116	60k multicolored	.55	.20
2140	A1116	1r multicolored	1.25	.25
		Nos. 2135-2140 (6)	2.85	1.25

40th anniversary of the Young Communist League (Komsomol).

Marx and Lenin — A1117

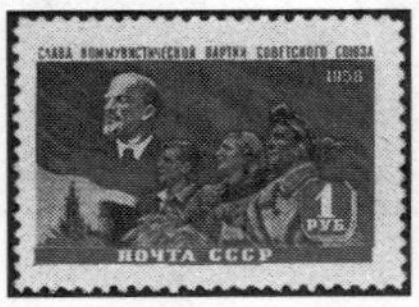

Lenin, Intellectual, Peasant and Miner
A1118

1958, Oct. 31

2141	A1117	40k multicolored	.40	.20
2142	A1118	1r multicolored	.60	.30

41st anniversary of Russian Revolution.

Torch, Wreath and Family
A1119

1958, Nov. 5

2143	A1119	60k blk, beige & dull bl	.50	.25

10th anniversary of the Universal Declaration of Human Rights.

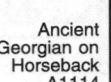

Sergei Esenin (1895-1925), Poet — A1120

1958, Nov. 29

2144 A1120 40k multicolored .50 .20

G. K. Ordzhonikidze A1121

Kuan Han-ching A1122

1958, Dec. 12 ***Perf. 12***

2145 A1121 40k multicolored .50 .20

G. K. Ordzhonikidze (1886-1937), Georgian party worker.

1958, Dec. 5

2146 A1122 40k dk blue & gray .50 .20

700th anniversary of the theater of Kuan Han-ching, Chinese dramatist.

Airliner IL-14 and Globe A1123

Soviet civil aviation: No. 2148, Jet liner TU-104. No. 2149, Turbo-propeller liner TU-114. 60k, Jet liner TU-110. 2r, Turbo-propeller liner IL-18.

1958-59

2147 A1123 20k ultra, blk & red .20 .20
2148 A1123 40k bl grn, blk & red .30 .20
2149 A1123 40k brt bl, blk & red .30 .20
2150 A1123 60k rose car & black .30 .20
2151 A1123 2r plum, red & black ('59) .90 .20
Nos. 2147-2151 (5) 2.00 1.00

Exist imperf.; value $10.
See Nos. 2086-2087.

Eleonora Duse — A1124

John Milton — A1125

1958, Dec. 26

2152 A1124 40k blue green & gray .50 .20

Duse, Italian actress, birth cent.

1958, Dec. 17

2153 A1125 40k brown .50 .20

John Milton (1608-1674), English poet.

K. F. Rulye — A1126

Fuzuli — A1127

1958, Dec. 26

2154 A1126 40k ultra & black .50 .25

Rulye, educator, death cent.

1958, Dec. 23 **Photo.**

2155 A1127 40k grnsh bl & brn .50 .25

400th anniv. of the death of Fuzuli (Mehmet Suleiman Oglou), Turkish poet.

Census Emblem and Family — A1128

Lunik and Sputniks over Kremlin — A1129

Design: No. 2157, Census emblem.

1958, Dec. **Litho.**

2156 A1128 40k multicolored .25 .20
2157 A1128 40k yel, gray, bl & red .25 .20

1959 Soviet census.

1959, Jan. **Unwmk.** ***Perf. 12***

Designs: 40k, Lenin and view of Kremlin. 60k, Workers and Lenin power plant on Volga.

2158 A1129 40k multicolored .30 .20
2159 A1129 60k multicolored .45 .30
2160 A1129 1r red, yel & vio bl 1.25 .75
Nos. 2158-2160 (3) 2.00 1.25

21st Cong. of the Communist Party and "the conquest of the cosmos by the Soviet people."

Lenin Statue, Minsk Buildings — A1130

1958, Dec. 20

2161 A1130 40k red, buff & brown .50 .20

Byelorussian Republic, 40th anniv.

Atomic Icebreaker "Lenin" A1131

Design: 60k, Diesel Locomotive "TE-3."

1958, Dec. 31

2162 A1131 40k multicolored .85 .50
2163 A1131 60k multicolored 1.40 .75

Shalom Aleichem A1132

Evangelista Torricelli A1133

1959, Feb. 10

2164 A1132 40k chocolate .40 .20

Aleichem, Yiddish writer, birth cent.

1959, Feb.

Scientists: #2166, Charles Darwin, English biologist. #2167, N. F. Gamaleya, microbiologist.

Various Frames

2165 A1133 40k blue green & blk .45 .20
2166 A1133 40k chalky blue & brn .55 .20
2167 A1133 40k dk red & black .50 .20
Nos. 2165-2167 (3) 1.50 .60

Woman Skater A1134

Frederic Joliot-Curie A1135

1959, Feb. 5

2168 A1134 25k ultra, black & ver .30 .20
2169 A1134 40k ultra & black .45 .20

Women's International Ice Skating Championships, Sverdlovsk.

No. 1717 Overprinted in Orange Brown

1959, Feb. 12

2170 A919 1r 6.50 5.00

"Victory of the USSR Basketball Team - Chile 1959." However, the 3rd World Basketball Championship honors went to Brazil when the Soviet team was disqualified for refusing to play Nationalist China.

1959, Mar. 3 **Litho.** ***Perf. 12***

2171 A1135 40k turq bl & gray brn, *beige* .50 .25

Joliot-Curie (1900-58), French scientist.

Selma Lagerlöf A1136

Peter Zwirka A1137

1959, Feb. 26

2172 A1136 40k red brown & black .50 .25

Lagerlöf (1858-1940), Swedish writer.

1959, Mar. 3

2173 A1137 40k hn brn & blk, *yel* .50 .25

Zwirka (1909-1947), Lithuanian writer.

No. 1861A Overprinted in Red: "1759 1959"

1959, Feb. 26 **Engr.**

2174 A993 40k lt ultra & brown 10.00 10.00

200th anniversary of the birth of Robert Burns, Scottish poet.

Type of 1958

Russian Writers: No. 2175, A. S. Griboedov. No. 2176, A. N. Ostrovski. No. 2177, Anton Chekhov. No. 2178, I. A. Krylov. No. 2178A, Nikolai V. Gogol. No. 2178B, S. T. Aksakov. No. 2178C, A. V. Koltzov. poet, and reaper.

1959 **Litho.**

2175 A1071 40k buff, cl, blk & vio .40 .40
2176 A1071 40k vio & brown .40 .40
2177 A1071 40k slate & hn brn .40 .40
2178 A1071 40k ol bister & brn .40 .40
2178A A1071 40k ol, gray & bis .40 .40
2178B A1071 40k brn, vio & bis .40 .40
2178C A1071 40k violet & black .40 .40
Nos. 2175-2178C (7) 2.80 2.80

No. 2178A for the 150th birth anniv. of Nikolai V. Gogol, writer, No. 2178B the centenary of the death of S. T. Aksakov, writer.

A. S. Popov and Rescue from Ice Float A1138

60k, Radio broadcasting "Peace" in 5 languages.

1959, Mar. 13

2179 A1138 40k brn, blk & dk blue .40 .25
2180 A1138 60k multicolored .60 .25

Centenary of the birth of A. S. Popov, pioneer in radio research.

M.S. Rossija at Odessa A1139

Ships: 10k, Steamer, Vladivostok-Petropavlovsk-Kamchatka line. 20k, M.S. Feliks Dzerzhinski, Odessa-Latakia line. No. 2184, Ship, Murmansk-Tyksi line. 60k, M.S. Mikhail Kalinin at Leningrad. 1r, M.S. Baltika, Leningrad-London line.

1959 **Litho.** **Unwmk.**

2181 A1139 10k multicolored .20 .20
2182 A1139 20k red, lt grn & dk bl .20 .20
2183 A1139 40k multicolored .20 .20
2184 A1139 40k blue, buff & red .20 .20
2185 A1139 60k bl grn, red & buff .35 .20
2186 A1139 1r ultra, red & yel .50 .20
Nos. 2181-2186 (6) 1.65 1.20

Honoring the Russian fleet.

Globe and Luna 1
A1140

Luna 1, launched Jan. 2, 1959: No. 2188, Globe and route of Luna 1.

1959, Apr. 13
2187 A1140 40k red brown & rose .55 .20
2188 A1140 40k ultra & blue .55 .20

Saadi and "Gulistan" A1141

1959, Mar. 20 **Photo.**
2189 A1141 40k dk blue & black .40 .25

Persian poet Saadi (Muslih-ud-Din) and 700th anniv. of his book, "Gulistan" (1258).

Suahan S. Orbeliani A1142

Drawing by Korin A1143

1959, Apr. 2
2190 A1142 40k dull rose & black .40 .20

Orbeliani (1658-1725), Georgian writer.

1959, Apr. 10 **Litho.**
2191 A1143 40k multicolored 1.00 .50

Ogata Korin (1653?-1716), Japanese artist.

Lenin — A1144

Cachin — A1146

1959, Apr. 17 **Engr.**
2192 A1144 40k sepia .50 .25

89th anniversary of the birth of Lenin.

1959, Apr. 27 **Photo.**
2194 A1146 60k dark brown .40 .20

Marcel Cachin (1869-1958), French Communist Party leader.

Joseph Haydn A1147

Alexander von Humboldt A1148

1959, May 8
2195 A1147 40k dk bl, gray & brn black .75 .20

Sesquicentennial of the death of Joseph Haydn, Austrian composer.

1959, May 6
2196 A1148 40k violet & brown .50 .25

Alexander von Humboldt, German naturalist and geographer, death centenary.

Three Races Carrying Flag of Peace — A1149

Mountain Climber — A1150

1959, Apr. 30 **Litho.**
2199 A1149 40k multicolored 1.00 .25

10th anniv. of World Peace Movement.

1959, May 15

Sports and Travel: No. 2201, Tourists reading map. No. 2202, Canoeing, horiz. No. 2203, Skiers.

2200 A1150 40k multicolored .30 .20
2201 A1150 40k multicolored .30 .20
2202 A1150 40k multicolored .30 .20
2203 A1150 40k multicolored .30 .20
Nos. 2200-2203 (4) 1.20 .80

I. E. Repin Statue, Moscow A1151

N. Y. Coliseum and Spasski Tower A1152

Statues: No. 2205, Lenin, Ulyanovsk. 20k, V. V. Mayakovsky, Moscow. 25k, Alexander Pushkin, Leningrad. 60k, Maxim Gorki, Moscow. 1r, Tchaikovsky, Moscow.

1959 **Photo.** **Unwmk.**
2204 A1151 10k ocher & sepia .20 .20
2205 A1151 10k red & black .20 .20
2206 A1151 20k violet & sepia .20 .20
2207 A1151 25k grnsh blue & blk .20 .20
2208 A1151 60k lt green & slate .20 .20
2209 A1151 1r lt ultra & gray .35 .20
Nos. 2204-2209 (6) 1.35 1.20

1959, June 25 **Litho.** ***Perf. 12***
2210 A1152 20k multicolored .20 .20
2211 A1152 40k multicolored .30 .20
a. Souv. sheet of 1, imperf. 2.50 1.25

Soviet Exhibition of Science, Technology and Culture, New York, June 20-Aug. 10.
No. 2211a issued July 20.

Animal Types of 1957

20k, Hare. #2214, Siberian horse. #2215, Tiger. #2216, Red squirrel. #2217, Pine marten. #2218, Hazel hen. #2219, Mute swan.

1959-60 **Litho.** ***Perf. 12***
Center in Natural Colors
2213 A1023 20k vio blue ('60) .30 .20
2214 A1023 25k blue black .30 .20
2215 A1023 25k brown .30 .20
2216 A1023 40k deep green .40 .20
2217 A1023 40k dark green .40 .20
2218 A1024 60k dark green .60 .40
2219 A1023 1r bright blue .95 .85
Nos. 2213-2219 (7) 3.25 2.25

Louis Braille — A1153

Musa Djalil — A1154

1959, July 16
2220 A1153 60k blue grn, bis & brn .50 .25

150th anniversary of the birth of Louis Braille, French educator of the blind.

1959, July 16 **Photo.**
2221 A1154 40k violet & black .50 .25

Musa Djalil, Tatar poet.

Sturgeon A1155

1959, July 16
2222 A1155 40k shown .40 .20
2223 A1155 60k Chum salmon .60 .20

See Nos. 2375-2377.

Gymnast A1156

Athletes Holding Trophy — A1157

Globe and Hands — A1158

Designs: 25k, Runner. 60k, Water polo.

1959, Aug. 7
2224 A1156 15k lilac rose & gray .20 .20
2225 A1156 25k yel green & red brn .20 .20
2226 A1157 30k brt red & gray .25 .20
2227 A1156 60k blue & org yel .35 .20
Nos. 2224-2227 (4) 1.00 .80

2nd National Spartacist Games.

1959, Aug. 12 **Litho.**
2228 A1158 40k yel, blue & red .40 .20

2nd Intl. Conf. of Public Employees Unions.

Cathedral and Modern Building A1159

1959, Aug. 21 **Unwmk.** ***Perf. 12***
2229 A1159 40k blue, ol, yel & red .40 .20

1100th anniv. of the city of Novgorod.

Schoolboys in Workshop — A1160

Design: 1r, Workers in night school.

1959, Aug. 27 **Photo.**
2230 A1160 40k dark purple .20 .20
2231 A1160 1r dark blue .50 .20

Strengthening the connection between school and life.

Glacier Survey — A1161

Rocket and Observatory A1162

Designs: 25k, Oceanographic ship "Vityaz" and map. 40k, Plane over Antarctica, camp and emperor penguin.

1959
2232 A1161 10k blue green .20 .20
2233 A1161 25k brt blue & red .30 .20
2234 A1161 40k ultra & red .50 .20
2235 A1162 1r ultra & buff 1.50 .30
Nos. 2232-2235 (4) 2.50 .90

Intl. Geophysical Year. 1st Russian rocket to reach the moon, Sept. 14, 1959 (#2235).

Workers and Farmers Holding Atom Symbol — A1163

1959, Sept. 23 **Litho.**
2236 A1163 40k red org & bister .40 .20

All-Union Economic Exhibition, Moscow.

Russian and Chinese Students A1164

40k, Russian miner and Chinese steel worker.

1959, Sept. 25 **Litho.** ***Perf. 12***
2237 A1164 20k multicolored .40 .25
2238 A1164 40k multicolored .60 .25

People's Republic of China, 10th anniv.

Letter Carrier A1165

1959, Sept.
2239 A1165 40k dk car rose & black .30 .20
2240 A1165 60k blue & black .60 .20

Intl. Letter Writing Week, Oct. 4-10.

Makhtumkuli A1166

1959, Sept. 30 Photo.
2241 A1166 40k brown .50 .20

225th anniversary of the birth of Makhtumkuli, Turkmen writer.

East German Emblem and Workers A1167

City Hall, East Berlin — A1168

1959, Oct. 6 Litho.
2242 A1167 40k multicolored .20 .20

Photo.
2243 A1168 60k dp claret & buff .35 .20

German Democratic Republic, 10th anniv.

Steel Production — A1169

7-Year Production Plan (Industries): #2244, Chemicals. #2245, Spasski Tower, hammer and sickle. #2246, Home building. #2247, Meat production, woman with farm animals. #2248, Machinery. #2249, Grain production, woman tractor driver. #2250, Oil. #2251, Textiles. #2252, Steel. #2253, Coal. #2254, Iron. #2255, Electric power.

1959-60 Litho.
2244 A1169 10k vio, grnsh blue & maroon .20 .20
2245 A1169 10k orange & dk car .20 .20
2246 A1169 15k brn, yel & red .20 .20
2247 A1169 15k brn, grn & mar .20 .20
2248 A1169 20k bl grn, yel & red .20 .20
2249 A1169 20k green, yel & red .20 .20
2250 A1169 30k lilac, sal & red .20 .20
2251 A1169 30k gldn brn, lil, red & green ('60) .20 .20
2252 A1169 40k vio bl, yel & org .20 .20
2253 A1169 40k dk blue, pink & dp rose .20 .20
2254 A1169 60k org red, yel, bl & maroon .30 .20
2255 A1169 60k ultra, buff & red .30 .20
Nos. 2244-2255 (12) 2.60 2.40

Arms of Tadzhikistan A1170

1959, Oct. 13
2258 A1170 40k red, emer, ocher & black .50 .20

Tadzhikistan statehood, 30th anniversary.

Path of Luna 3 and Electronics Laboratory A1171

1959, Oct. 12
2259 A1171 40k violet .75 .25

Flight of Luna 3 around the moon, Oct. 4, 1959.

Red Square, Moscow A1172

1959, Oct. 26 Engr.
2260 A1172 40k dark red .40 .20

42nd anniversary of October Revolution.

US Capitol, Globe and Kremlin — A1173

1959, Oct. 27 Photo.
2261 A1173 60k blue & yellow .50 .20

Visit of Premier Nikita Khrushchev to the US, Sept., 1959.

Helicopter — A1174

25k, Diver. 40k, Motorcyclist. 60k, Parachutist.

1959, Oct. 28
2262 A1174 10k vio blue & mar .20 .20
2263 A1174 25k blue & brown .20 .20
2264 A1174 40k red brn & indigo .20 .20
2265 A1174 60k blue & ol bister .30 .20
Nos. 2262-2265 (4) .90 .80

Honoring voluntary aides of the army.

Moon, Earth and Path of Rocket A1175

No. 2267, Kremlin and diagram showing rocket and positions of moon and earth.

1959, Nov. 1 Litho.
2266 A1175 40k bl, dk bl, red & bis .50 .20
2267 A1175 40k gray, pink & red .50 .20

Landing of the Soviet rocket on the moon, Sept. 14, 1959.

Sandor Petőfi A1176

Victory Statue and View of Budapest — A1177

1959, Nov. 9 *Perf. 12x12½, 12½x12*
2268 A1176 20k gray & ol bister .20 .20
2269 A1177 40k multicolored .30 .20

Soviet-Hungarian friendship.
For overprint see No. 2308.

Manolis Glezos and Acropolis A1178

1959, Nov. 12 Photo. *Perf. 12x12½*
2270 A1178 40k ultra & brown 7.50 5.00

Manolis Glezos, Greek communist.

A. A. Voskresensky, Chemist, 150th Birth Anniv. — A1179

1959, Dec. 7 *Perf. 12½x12*
2271 A1179 40k ultra & brown .40 .20

Chusovaya River, Ural — A1180

#2273, Lake Ritza, Caucasus. #2274, Lena River, Siberia. #2275, Seashore, Far East. #2276, Lake Iskander, Central Asia. #2277, Lake Baikal, Siberia. #2278, Belukha Mountain, Altai range. #2279, Gursuf region, Crimea. #2280, Crimea.

1959, Dec. Engr. *Perf. 12½*
2272 A1180 10k purple .20 .20
2273 A1180 10k rose carmine .20 .20
2274 A1180 25k dark blue .20 .20
2275 A1180 25k olive .20 .20
2276 A1180 25k dark red .20 .20
2277 A1180 40k claret .25 .20
2278 A1180 60k Prus blue .30 .20
2279 A1180 1r olive green .40 .20
2280 A1180 1r deep orange .40 .20
Nos. 2272-2280 (9) 2.35 1.80

"Trumpeters of 1st Cavalry" by M. Grekov — A1181

1959, Dec. 30 Litho. *Perf. 12½x12*
2283 A1181 40k multicolored .50 .35

40th anniversary of the 1st Cavalry.

Farm Woman — A1182

Designs: 25k, Architect. 60k, Steel worker.

1958-60 Engr. *Perf. 12½*
2286 A1182 20k slate grn ('59) 7.00 3.75
2287 A1182 25k sepia ('59) 3.25 1.60
2288 A1182 60k carmine 9.25 4.25

Perf. 12x12½
Litho.
2290 A1182 20k green ('60) .20 .20
2291 A1182 25k sepia ('60) .35 .20
2292 A1182 60k vermilion ('59) .25 .20
2293 A1182 60k blue ('60) .70 .20
Nos. 2286-2293 (7) 21.00 10.40

Mikhail V. Frunze (1885-1925), Revolutionary A1183

1960, Jan. 25 Photo. *Perf. 12½*
2295 A1183 40k dark red brown .40 .20

G.N. Gabrichevski, Microbiologist, Birth Cent. — A1184

Perf. 12½x12
1960, Jan. 30 Unwmk.
2296 A1184 40k brt violet & brown .50 .20

Anton Chekhov and Moscow Home A1185

40k, Chekhov in later years, Yalta home.

1960, Jan. 20 Litho. *Perf. 12x12½*
2297 A1185 20k red, gray & vio bl .20 .20
2298 A1185 40k dk blue, buff & brn .30 .20

Anton P. Chekhov (1860-1904), playwright.

Vera Komissarzhevskaya (1864-1910), Actress — A1186

1960, Feb. 5 Photo. *Perf. 12½x12*
2299 A1186 40k chocolate .40 .20

8th Olympic Winter Games, Squaw Valley, Calif., Feb. 18-29
A1187

Sports: 10k, Ice hockey. 25k, Speed skating. 40k, Skier. 60k, Woman figure skater. 1r, Ski jumper.

1960, Feb. 18 Litho. *Perf. 11½*

2300	A1187	10k	ocher & vio blue	.25	.20
2301	A1187	25k	multicolored	.30	.20
2302	A1187	40k	org, rose lil & vio blue	.35	.20
2303	A1187	60k	vio, grn & buff	.60	.20
2304	A1187	1r	bl, grn & brn	1.00	.20
			Nos. 2300-2304 (5)	2.50	1.00

Sword into Plowshare Statue, UN, NY — A1188

1960 *Perf. 12x12½*

2305	A1188	40k	grnsh bl, yel & brown	.40	.20
a.			Souvenir sheet	1.25	.50

No. 2305a for Premier Nikita Khrushchev's visit to the 15th General Assembly of the UN in NYC.

Women of Various Races
A1189

1960, Mar. 8

2306	A1189	40k	multicolored	.50	.20

50 years of Intl. Woman's Day, Mar. 8.

Planes in Combat and Timur Frunze
A1190

1960, Feb. 23 *Perf. 12½x12*

2307	A1190	40k	multicolored	1.75	1.00

Lieut. Timur Frunze, World War II hero.

No. 2269 Overprinted in Red

1960, Apr. 4

2308	A1177	40k	multicolored	3.00	2.00

15th anniversary of Hungary's liberation from the Nazis.

Lunik 3 Photographing Far Side of Moon — A1191

Design: 60k, Far side of the moon.

1960 Photo. *Perf. 12x12½*

2309	A1191	40k	pale bl, dk bl & yel	.60	.25

Litho.

2310	A1191	60k	lt bl, dk bl & citron	.60	.25

Photographing of the far side of the moon, Oct. 7, 1959.

Lenin as Child
A1192

Various Lenin Portraits and: 20k, Lenin with children and Christmas tree. 30k, Flag, workers and ship. 40k, Kremlin, banners and marchers. 60k, Map of Russia, buildings and ship. 1r, Peace proclamation and globe.

1960, Apr. 10 Litho. *Perf. 12½x12*

2311	A1192	10k	multicolored	.20	.20
2312	A1192	20k	red, green & blk	.20	.20
2313	A1192	30k	multicolored	.20	.20
2314	A1192	40k	multicolored	.25	.20
2315	A1192	60k	multicolored	.75	.20
2316	A1192	1r	red, vio bl & brn	.75	.20
			Nos. 2311-2316 (6)	2.35	1.20

90th anniversary of the birth of Lenin.

Steelworker
A1193

1960, Apr. 30 Photo.

2317	A1193	40k	brown & red	.40	.20

Industrial overproduction by 50,000,000r during the 1st year of the 7-year plan.

Government House, Baku
A1194

1960, Apr. Litho. *Perf. 12x12½*

2318	A1194	40k	bister & brown	.40	.20

Azerbaijan, 40th anniv.
For surcharge see #2898.

Brotherhood Monument, Prague — A1195

Design: 60k, Charles Bridge, Prague.

1960, Apr. 29 Photo. *Perf. 12½x12*

2319	A1195	40k	brt blue & black	.20	.20
2320	A1195	60k	black brn & yellow	.35	.20

Czechoslovak Republic, 15th anniv.

Radio Tower and Popov Central Museum of Communications, Leningrad — A1196

1960, May 6 Litho.

2321	A1196	40k	blue, ocher & brn	.50	.25

Radio Day.

Gen. I. D. Tcherniakovski and Soldiers — A1197

1960, May 4

2322	A1197	1r	multicolored	.60	.35

Gen. I. D. Tcherniakovski, World War II hero and his military school.

Robert Schumann (1810-56), German Composer
A1198

1960, May 20 Photo. *Perf. 12x12½*

2323	A1198	40k	ultra & black	.50	.25

Yakov M. Sverdlov (1885-1919), 1st USSR Pres. — A1199

1960, May 24 *Perf. 12½x12*

2324	A1199	40k	dk brn & org brn	.75	.35

Stamp of 1957 Under Magnifying Glass
A1200

1960, May 28 Litho. *Perf. 11½*

2325	A1200	60k	multicolored	.75	.35

Stamp Day.

Karl Marx Avenue, Petrozavodsk, Karelian Autonomous Republic — A1201

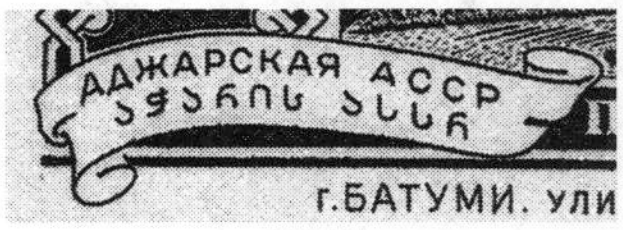

#2327

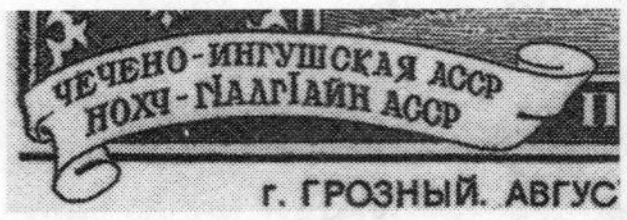

#2329

#2330

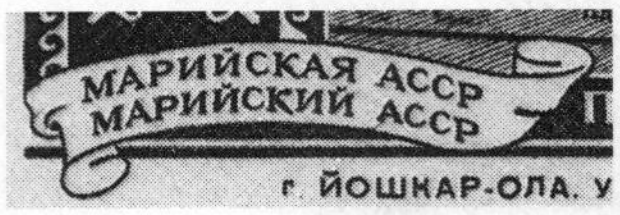

#2332

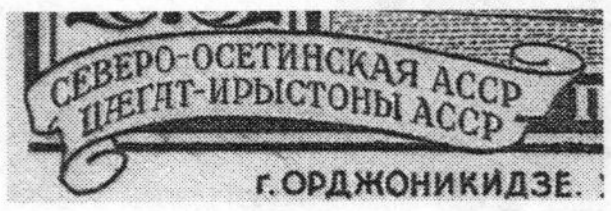

#2333

#2339

#2341

#2342

Capitals, Soviet Autonomous Republics: No. 2327, Lenin street, Batum, Adzhar. No. 2328, Cultural Palace, Izhevsk, Udmurt. No. 2329, August street, Grozny, Chechen-Ingush. No. 2330, Soviet House, Cheboksary, Chuvash. No. 2331, Buinak Street, Makhachkala, Dagestan. No. 2332, Soviet street, Ioshkar Ola, Mari. No. 2333, Chkalov street, Dzaudzhikau, North Ossetia. No. 2334, October street, Yakutsk, Yakut. No. 2335, House of Ministers, Nukus, Kara-Kalpak.

1960 Engr. *Perf. 12½*

2326	A1201	40k	Prus green	.40	.25
2327	A1201	40k	violet blue	.40	.25
2328	A1201	40k	green	.40	.25
2329	A1201	40k	maroon	.40	.25
2330	A1201	40k	dull red	.40	.25
2331	A1201	40k	carmine	.40	.25
2332	A1201	40k	dark brown	.40	.25
2333	A1201	40k	orange brown	.40	.25
2334	A1201	40k	dark blue	.40	.25
2335	A1201	40k	brown	.40	.25
			Nos. 2326-2335 (10)	4.00	2.50

See Nos. 2338-2344C. For overprints see Nos. 2336-2337.

No. 2326 Overprinted in Red

1960, June 4

2336	A1201	40k	Prus green	5.00	2.00

Karelian Autonomous Rep., 40th anniv.

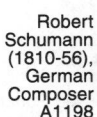

No. 2328 Overprinted in Red

1960, Nov. 4

2337 A1201 40k green 2.00 1.25

Udmurt Autonomous Rep., 40th anniv.

1961-62 ***Perf. 12½, 12½x12***

Capitals, Soviet Autonomous Republics: #2338, Rustaveli Street, Sukhumi, Abkhazia. #2339, House of Soviets, Nalchik, Kabardino-Balkar. #2340, Lenin Street, Ulan-Ude, Buriat. #2341, Soviet Street, Syktyvkar, Komi. #2342, Lenin Street, Nakhichevan, Nakhichevan. #2343, Elista, Kalmyk. #2344, Ufa, Bashkir. #2344A, Lobachevsky Square, Kazan, Tartar. #2344B, Kizil, Tuvinia. #2344C, Saransk, Mordovia.

2338	A1201	4k	orange ver	.25	.20
2339	A1201	4k	dark violet	.25	.20
2340	A1201	4k	dark blue	.25	.20
2341	A1201	4k	gray	.25	.20
2342	A1201	4k	dk car rose	.25	.20
2343	A1201	4k	olive green	.25	.20
2344	A1201	4k	dull purple	.25	.20
2344A	A1201	4k	grnsh blk ('62)	.25	.20
2344B	A1201	4k	claret ('62)	.25	.20
2344C	A1201	4k	deep grn ('62)	.25	.20
			Nos. 2338-2344C (10)	2.50	2.00

Denominations of Nos. 2338-2344C are in the revalued currency.

Children's Friendship A1202

Drawings by Children: 20k, Collective farm, vert. 25k, Winter joys. 40k, "In the Zoo."

Perf. 12x12½, 12½x12

1960, June 1 **Litho.**

2345	A1202	10k	multicolored	.20	.20
2346	A1202	20k	multicolored	.20	.20
2347	A1202	25k	multicolored	.20	.20
2348	A1202	40k	multicolored	.20	.20
			Nos. 2345-2348 (4)	.80	.80

Lomonosov University and Congress Emblem — A1203

1960, June 17 Photo. ***Perf. 12½x12***

2349 A1203 60k yellow & dk brown .70 .25

1st congress of the International Federation for Automation Control, Moscow.

Sputnik 4 and Globe — A1204

1960, June 17 ***Perf. 12x12½***

2350 A1204 40k vio blue & dp org 1.00 .50

Launching on May 15, 1960, of Sputnik 4, which orbited the earth with a dummy cosmonaut.

Kosta Hetagurov (1859-1906), Ossetian Poet — A1205

1960, June 20 Litho. ***Perf. 12½***

2351 A1205 40k gray blue & brown .40 .20

Flag and Tallinn, Estonia A1206

Soviet Republics, 20th Annivs.: No. 2353, Flag and Riga, Latvia. No. 2354, Flag and Vilnius, Lithuania.

Perf. 12x12½, 12½ (#2353)

1960 **Photo.**

2352 A1206 40k red & ultra .45 .20

Typo.

2353 A1206 40k blue, gray & red .45 .20

Litho.

2354 A1206 40k blue, red & grn .45 .20

Nos. 2352-2354 (3) 1.35 .60

Cement Factory, Belgorod A1207

Design: 40k, Factory, Novy Krivoi.

1960, June 28 ***Perf. 12½x12***

2355 A1207 25k ultra & black .25 .20

2356 A1207 40k rose brown & blk .25 .20

"New buildings of the 1st year of the 7-year plan."

Automatic Production Line and Roller Bearing A1208

#2358, Automatic production line and gear.

1960, June 13 ***Perf. 11½***

2357 A1208 40k rose violet .35 .20

2358 A1208 40k Prus green .35 .20

Publicizing mechanization and automation of factories.

Running A1209

Sports: 10k, Wrestling. 15k, Basketball. 20k, Weight lifting. 25k, Boxing. No. 2364, Fencing. No. 2365, Diving. No. 2366, Women's gymnastics. 60k, Canoeing. 1r, Steeplechase.

1960, Aug. 1 Litho. ***Perf. 11½***

2359	A1209	5k	multicolored	.20	.20
2360	A1209	10k	brn, blue & yel	.20	.20
2361	A1209	15k	multicolored	.20	.20
2362	A1209	20k	blk, crim & sal	.20	.20
2363	A1209	25k	lake, sl & rose	.20	.20
2364	A1209	40k	vio bl, bl & bis	.20	.20
2365	A1209	40k	vio, gray & pink	.20	.20
2366	A1209	40k	multicolored	.20	.20
2367	A1209	60k	multicolored	.30	.20
2368	A1209	1r	brown, lilac & pale green	.60	.40
			Nos. 2359-2368 (10)	2.50	2.20

17th Olympic Games, Rome, 8/25-9/11.

No. 2365 Overprinted in Red

1960, Aug. 23

2369 A1209 40k 7.50 5.00

12th San Marino-Riccione Stamp Fair.

Kishinev, Moldavian Republic A1210

1960, Aug. 2 ***Perf. 12x12½***

2370 A1210 40k multicolored .50 .20

20th anniversary of Moldavian Republic.

Tractor and Factory A1211

Book Museum, Hanoi — A1212

Perf. 12x12½, 12½x12

1960, Aug. 25

2371 A1211 40k green, ocher & blk .35 .20

2372 A1212 60k blue, lilac & brn .40 .20

15th anniversary of North Viet Nam.

Gregory N. Minkh, Microbiologist, 125th Birth Anniv. — A1213

1960, Aug. 25 Photo. ***Perf. 12½x12***

2373 A1213 60k bister brn & dk brn .50 .25

"March," by I. I. Levitan A1214

1960, Aug. 29

2374 A1214 40k ol bister & black .50 .30

I. I. Levitan, painter, birth cent.

Fish Type of 1959

Designs: 20k, Pikeperch. 25k, Fur seals. 40k, Ludogan whitefish.

1960, Sept. 3 ***Perf. 12½***

2375	A1155	20k	blue & black	.20	.20
2376	A1155	25k	vio gray & red brn	.20	.20
2377	A1155	40k	rose lilac & purple	.20	.20
			Nos. 2375-2377 (3)	.60	.60

Forest by I. I. Shishkin — A1215

1960, Aug. 29 **Engr.**

2378 A1215 1r red brown 1.50 .30

5th World Forestry Congress, Seattle, Wash., Aug. 29-Sept. 10.

Globe with USSR and Letter A1216

1960, Sept. 10 Litho. ***Perf. 12x12½***

2379 A1216 40k multicolored .25 .20

2380 A1216 60k multicolored .35 .20

Intl. Letter Writing Week, Oct. 3-9.

Farmer, Worker, Scientist A1217

1960, Oct. 4 Typo. ***Perf. 12½***

2381 A1217 40k multicolored .50 .20

Kazakh SSR, 40th anniv.

Globes and Olive Branch — A1218

1960, Sept. 29 Litho. ***Perf. 12½x12***

2382 A1218 60k pale vio, bl & gray .50 .20

World Federation of Trade Unions, 15th anniv.

Kremlin, Sputnik 5 and Dogs Belka and Strelka A1219

1960, Sept. 29 **Photo.**

2383 A1219 40k brt pur & yellow .55 .20

2384 A1219 1r blue & salmon .85 .25

Flight of Sputnik 5, Aug. 19-20, 1960.

Passenger Ship "Karl Marx" A1220

Ships: 40k, Turbo-electric ship "Lenin." 60k, Speedboat "Raketa" (Rocket).

1960, Oct. 24 Litho. ***Perf. 12x12½***

2385 A1220 25k bl, blk, red & yel .20 .20
2386 A1220 40k blue, black & red .35 .20
2387 A1220 60k blue, blk & rose .45 .20
Nos. 2385-2387 (3) 1.00 .60

A. N. Voronikhin and Kasansky Cathedral, Leningrad
A1221

1960, Oct. 24 Photo.

2388 A1221 40k gray & brn black .50 .25

Voronikhin, architect, 200th birth anniv.

J. S. Gogebashvili
A1222

1960, Oct. 29

2389 A1222 40k dk gray & mag .50 .25

120th anniversary of the birth of J. S. Gogebashvili, Georgian teacher and publicist.

Red Flag, Electric Power Station and Factory — A1223

1960, Oct. 29 Litho.

2390 A1223 40k red, yel & brown .50 .20

43rd anniversary of October Revolution.

Leo Tolstoy
A1224

Designs: 40k, Tolstoy in Yasnaya Polyana. 60k, Portrait, vert.

Perf. 12x12½, 12½x12

1960, Nov. 14

2391 A1224 20k violet & brown .25 .20
2392 A1224 40k blue & lt brown .35 .20
2393 A1224 60k dp claret & sepia .50 .20
Nos. 2391-2393 (3) 1.10 .60

50th anniversary of the death of Count Leo Tolstoy, writer.

Yerevan, Armenian Republic
A1225

1960, Nov. 14 ***Perf. 12x12½***

2394 A1225 40k bl, red, buff & brn .40 .20

Armenian Soviet Rep., 40th anniv.

Friedrich Engels, 140th Birth Anniv. — A1226

1960, Nov. 25 Engr. ***Perf. 12½***

2395 A1226 60k slate .60 .25

Badge of Youth Federation
A1227

1960, Nov. 2 Litho.

2396 A1227 60k brt pink, blk & yel .75 .25

Intl. Youth Federation, 15th anniv.

40-ton Truck MAL-530
A1228

Automotive Industry: 40k, "Volga" car. 60k, "Moskvitch 407" car. 1r, "Tourist LAS-697" Bus.

1960, Oct. 29 Photo. ***Perf. 12x12½***

2397 A1228 25k ultra & gray .20 .20
2398 A1228 40k ol bister & ultra .25 .20
2399 A1228 60k Prus green & dp car .40 .20

Litho.

2400 A1228 1r multicolored .90 .20
Nos. 2397-2400 (4) 1.75 .80

N. I. Pirogov — A1229

Friendship University and Students — A1230

1960, Dec. 13 Photo. ***Perf. 12½x12***

2401 A1229 40k green & brn black .40 .20

Pirogov, surgeon, 125th birth anniv.

1960, Nov. ***Perf. 12x12½***

2402 A1230 40k brown carmine .50 .20

Completion of Friendship of Nations University in Moscow.

For surcharge see No. 2462.

Mark Twain
A1231

1960, Nov. 30 ***Perf. 12½x12***

2403 A1231 40k dp org & brown .75 .40

Mark Twain, 125th birth anniv.

Dove and Globe
A1232

Akaki Zeretely
A1233

1960, Oct. 29 Photo.

2404 A1232 60k maroon & gray .50 .25

Intl. Democratic Women's Fed, 15th anniv.

1960, Dec. 27

2405 A1233 40k violet & black brn .60 .20

Zeretely, Georgian poet, 120th birth anniv.

Frederic Chopin, after Delacroix
A1234

1960, Dec. 24 ***Perf. 12x11½***

2406 A1234 40k bister & brown .50 .20

Chopin, Polish composer, 150th birth anniv.

North Korean Flag and Flying Horse — A1235

Crocus — A1236

1960, Dec. 24 Litho. ***Perf. 12½x12***

2407 A1235 40k multicolored .50 .20

15th anniversary of "the liberation of the Korean people by the Soviet army."

1960 ***Perf. 12x12½***

Asiatic Flowers: No. 2409, Tulip. No. 2410, Trollius. No. 2411, Tulip. No. 2412, Ginseng. No. 2413, Iris. No. 2414, Hypericum. 1r, Dog rose.

Flowers in Natural Colors

2408 A1236 20k green & violet .25 .20
2409 A1236 20k vio blue & black .25 .20
2410 A1236 25k gray .30 .20
2411 A1236 40k ol bister & black .35 .20
2412 A1236 40k grn & blk, wmkd. .35 .20
2413 A1236 60k yel, green & red .70 .20
2414 A1236 60k bluish grn & blk .70 .20
2415 A1236 1r slate grn & blk 1.10 .20
Nos. 2408-2415 (8) 4.00 1.60

The watermark on No. 2412 consists of vertical rows of chevrons.

Lithuanian Costumes
A1237

Regional Costumes: 60k, Uzbek.

Perf. 12½ (10k), 11½ (60k)

1960, Dec. 24 Typo. Unwmk.

2416 A1237 10k multicolored .25 .20
2417 A1237 60k multicolored .75 .20

Currency Revalued

1961-62 Litho. ***Perf. 11½***

Regional Costumes: No. 2418, Moldavia. No. 2419, Georgia. No. 2420, Ukrainia. No. 2421, White Russia. No. 2422, Kazakhstan. No. 2422A, Latvia. 4k, Koryak. 6k, Russia. 10k, Armenia. 12k, Estonia.

2418 A1237 2k buff, brn & ver .20 .20
2419 A1237 2k red, brn, ocher & black .20 .20
2420 A1237 3k ultra, buff, red & brown .25 .20
2421 A1237 3k red org, ocher & black .25 .20
2422 A1237 3k buff, brn, grn & red .25 .20
2422A A1237 3k org red, gray ol & blk ('62) .25 .20
2423 A1237 4k multicolored .45 .20
2424 A1237 6k multicolored .55 .25
2425 A1237 10k brn, ol bis & vermilion .80 .30
2426 A1237 12k red, ultra & black 1.10 .40
Nos. 2418-2426 (10) 4.30 2.35

See Nos. 2723-2726.

Lenin and Map Showing Electrification — A1238

1961 ***Perf. 12½x12***

2427 A1238 4k blue, buff & brown .20 .20
2428 A1238 10k red org & blue blk .40 .25

State Electrification Plan, 40th anniv. (in 1960).

Animal Types of 1957

1961, Jan. 7 ***Perf. 12½***

2429 A1024 1k Brown bear .20 .20
2430 A1023 6k Beaver .70 .35
2431 A1023 10k Roe deer .90 .55
Nos. 2429-2431 (3) 1.80 1.10

Georgian Flag and Views
A1239

1961, Feb. 15 ***Perf. 12½x12***

2432 A1239 4k multicolored .30 .20

40th anniv. of Georgian SSR.

Nikolai D. Zelinski, Chemist, Birth Cent.
A1240

1961, Feb. 6 Photo. ***Perf. 12x12½***

2433 A1240 4k rose violet .30 .20

Nikolai A. Dobrolyubov (1836-61), Journalist and Critic — A1241

1961, Feb. 5 ***Perf. 11½x12***

2434 A1241 4k brt blue & brown .50 .20

A1242

A1243

Designs: 3k, Cattle. 4k, Tractor in cornfield. 6k, Mechanization of Grain Harvest. 10k, Women picking apples.

1961 *Perf. 12x12½, 12x11½*

2435 A1242 3k blue & magenta .25 .20
2436 A1242 4k green & dk gray .25 .20
2437 A1242 6k vio blue & brn .60 .20
2438 A1242 10k maroon & ol grn .80 .20
Nos. 2435-2438 (4) 1.90 .80

Agricultural development.

Perf. 12x12½; 12x11½ (Nos. 2439A, 2442 & 12k)

1961-65 **Unwmk.**

Designs: 1k, "Labor" Holding Peace Flag. 2k, Harvester and silo. 3k, Space rockets. 4k, Arms and flag of USSR. 6k, Spasski tower. 10k, Workers' monument. 12k, Minin and Pozharsky Monument and Spasski tower. 16k, Plane over power station and dam.

Engr.

2439 A1243 1k olive bister 1.90 .20

Litho.

2439A A1243 1k olive bister .75 .20
2440 A1243 2k green .20 .20
2441 A1243 3k dk violet 2.50 .20

Engr.

2442 A1243 3k dk violet 4.25 .95

Litho.

2443 A1243 4k red .75 .20
2443A A1243 4k org brn ('65) 1.50 .35
2444 A1243 6k vermilion 10.00 .65
2445 A1243 6k dk car rose 1.90 .20
2446 A1243 10k orange 3.50 .20

Photo.

2447 A1243 12k brt magenta 3.50 .30

Litho.

2448 A1243 16k ultra 5.25 1.10
Nos. 2439-2448 (12) 36.00 4.75

V. P. Miroshnitchenko — A1244

1961, Feb. 23 **Photo.** *Perf. 12½x12*

2449 A1244 4k violet brn & slate .30 .20

Soldier hero of World War II.
See Nos. 2570-2571.

Taras G. Shevchenko and Birthplace — A1245

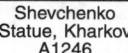

Shevchenko Statue, Kharkov A1246

Andrei Rubljov A1247

6k, Book, torch and Shevchenko with beard.

Perf. 12½, 11½x12

1961, Mar. **Litho.; Photo. (4k)**

2450 A1245 3k brown & violet .30 .20
2451 A1246 4k red orange & gray .60 .20
2452 A1245 6k black, grn & red brn .85 .25
Nos. 2450-2452 (3) 1.75 .65

Shevchenko, Ukrainian poet, death cent.
No. 2452 was printed with alternating green and black label, containing a quotation.
See No. 2852.

1961, Mar. 13 **Litho.** *Perf. 12½x12*

2453 A1247 4k ultra, bister & brn .30 .20

Rubljov, painter, 600th birth anniv.

N. V. Sklifosovsky A1248

Robert Koch A1249

1961, Mar. 26 **Photo.** *Perf. 11½x12*

2454 A1248 4k ultra & black .30 .20

Sklifosovsky, surgeon, 125th birth anniv.

1961, Mar. 26

2455 A1249 6k dark brown .30 .20

Koch, German microbiologist, 59th death anniv.

Globe and Sputnik 8 — A1250

10k, Space probe and its path to Venus.

1961, Apr. **Litho.** *Perf. 11½*

2456 A1250 6k dk & lt blue & org .60 .20

Photo.

2457 A1250 10k vio blue & yel .85 .30

Launching of the Venus space probe, 2/12/61.

Open Book and Globe A1251

1961, Apr. 7 **Litho.** *Perf. 12½x12*

2458 A1251 6k ultra & sepia .70 .20

Centenary of the children's magazine "Around the World."

Musician, Dancers and Singers A1252

1961, Apr. 7 **Unwmk.**

2459 A1252 4k yel, red & black .40 .20

Russian National Choir, 50th anniv.

African Breaking Chains and Map — A1253

6k, Globe, torch & black & white handshake.

1961, Apr. 15 *Perf. 12½*

2460 A1253 4k multicolored .35 .20
2461 A1253 6k blue, purple & org .35 .20

Africa Day and 3rd Conference of Independent African States, Cairo, Mar. 25-31.

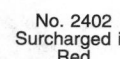

No. 2402 Surcharged in Red

1961, Apr. 15 **Photo.** *Perf. 12x12½*

2462 A1230 4k on 40k brown car .90 .20

Naming of Friendship University, Moscow, in memory of Patrice Lumumba, Premier of Congo.

Maj. Yuri A. Gagarin A1254

6k, Kremlin, rockets and radar equipment.
10k, Rocket, Gagarin with helmet and Kremlin.

1961, Apr. *Perf. 11½ (3k), 12½x12*

2463 A1254 3k Prus blue .25 .20

Litho.

2464 A1254 6k blue, violet & red .65 .20
2465 A1254 10k red, blue grn & brn 1.10 .35
Nos. 2463-2465 (3) 2.00 .75

1st man in space, Yuri A. Gagarin, Apr. 12, 1961. No. 2464 printed with alternating light blue and red label.
Nos. 2463-2465 exist imperf. Value $1.75.

Lenin — A1255

Rabindranath Tagore — A1256

1961, Apr. 22 **Litho.** *Perf. 12x12½*

2466 A1255 4k dp car, sal & blk .30 .20

91st anniversary of Lenin's birth.

1961, May 8 **Engr.** *Perf. 11½x12*

2467 A1256 6k bis, maroon & blk .60 .20

Tagore, Indian poet, birth cent.

The Hunchbacked Horse — A1257

Fairy Tales: 1k, The Geese and the Swans. 3k, Fox, Hare and Cock. 6k, The Peasant and the Bear. 10k, Ruslan and Ludmilla.

1961 **Litho.** *Perf. 12½*

2468 A1257 1k multicolored .20 .20
2469 A1257 3k multicolored .50 .30
2470 A1257 4k multicolored .20 .20
2471 A1257 6k multicolored .55 .35
2472 A1257 10k multicolored .65 .40
Nos. 2468-2472 (5) 2.10 1.45

"Man Conquering Space" A1258

Design: 6k, Giuseppe Garibaldi.

1961, May 24 **Photo.**

2481 A1258 4k orange brown .25 .20
2482 A1258 6k lilac & salmon .45 .20

International Labor Exposition, Turin.

Lenin A1259

Patrice Lumumba A1260

Various portraits of Lenin.

1961 **Photo.** *Perf. 12½x12*

Olive Bister Frame

2483 A1259 20k dark green 1.00 .85
2484 A1259 30k dark blue 2.25 1.90
2485 A1259 50k rose red 3.75 2.75
Nos. 2483-2485 (3) 7.00 5.50

1961, May 29 **Litho.**

2486 A1260 2k yellow & brown .35 .20

Lumumba (1925-61), premier of Congo.

Kindergarten — A1261

Children's Day: 3k, Young Pioneers in camp. 4k, Young Pioneers, vert.

Perf. 12½x12, 12x12½

1961, May 31 **Photo.**

2487 A1261 2k orange & ultra .20 .20
2488 A1261 3k ol bister & purple .20 .20
2489 A1261 4k red & gray .20 .20
Nos. 2487-2489 (3) .60 .60

Dog Zvezdochka and Sputnik 10 — A1263

Sputniks 9 and 10: 4k, Dog Chernushka and Sputnik 9, vert.

1961, June 8 Litho. *Perf. 12½, 11½*
2491 A1263 2k vio, Prus blue & blk .35 .20

Photo.
2492 A1263 4k Prus blue & brt grn .35 .20

Vissarion G. Belinski, Author, 150th Birth. Anniv. — A1265

Engraved and Photogravure
1961, June 13 *Perf. 11½x12*
2493 A1265 4k carmine & black .30 .20

Lt. Gen. D.M. Karbishev A1266

1961, June 22 Litho. *Perf. 12½*
2494 A1266 4k black, red & yel .30 .20

Karbishev was tortured to death in the Nazi prison camp at Mauthausen, Austria.

Hydro-meteorological Map and Instruments — A1267

1961, June 21 *Perf. 12x12½*
2495 A1267 6k ultra & green .50 .20

40th anniversary of hydro-meteorological service in Russia.

Gliders A1268

6k, Motorboat race. 10k, Motorcycle race.

1961, July 5 Photo. *Perf. 12½*
2497 A1268 4k dk slate grn & crim .30 .20

Litho.
2498 A1268 6k slate & vermilion .40 .20
2499 A1268 10k slate & vermilion 1.25 .20
Nos. 2497-2499 (3) 1.95 .60

USSR Technical Sports Spartakiad.

Javelin Thrower A1269

1961, Aug. 8 Photo. *Perf. 12½x12*
2500 A1269 6k dp carmine & pink .30 .20

7th Trade Union Spartacist Games.

S. I. Vavilov A1270

Vazha Pshavela A1271

1961, July 25
2501 A1270 4k lt green & sepia .30 .20

Vavilov, president of Academy of Science.

1961 Photo. *Perf. 11½x12*
2502 A1271 4k dk brown & cream .35 .20

Pshavela, Georgian poet, birth cent.

Scientists at Control Panel for Rocket — A1272

Globe and Youth Activities A1273

Design: 2k, Men pushing tank into river.

1961 Unwmk. *Perf. 11½*
2503 A1273 2k orange & sepia .20 .20
2504 A1272 4k lilac & dk green .35 .20
2505 A1273 6k ultra & citron .45 .20
Nos. 2503-2505 (3) 1.00 .60

International Youth Forum, Moscow.

Arms of Mongolian Republic and Sukhe Bator Statue A1274

1961, July 25 Litho. *Perf. 12½x12*
2506 A1274 4k multicolored .40 .20

Mongol national revolution, 40th anniv.

Knight Kalevipoeg A1275

Symbols of Biochemistry A1276

1961, July 31
2507 A1275 4k black, blue & yel .30 .20

1st publication of "Kalevipoeg," Estonian national saga, recorded by R. K. Kreutzwald, Estonian writer, cent.

1961, July 31
2508 A1276 6k multicolored .35 .20

5th Intl. Biochemistry Congress, Moscow.

Major Titov and Vostok 2 — A1277

4k, Globe with orbit and cosmonaut.

1961, Aug. Photo. *Perf. 11½*
2509 A1277 4k vio blue & dp plum .25 .20
2510 A1277 6k brown, grn & org .35 .20

1st manned space flight around the world, Maj. Gherman S. Titov, Aug. 6-7, 1961. Nos. 2509-2510 exist imperf. Value, set $2.50.

A. D. Zacharov and Admiralty Building, Leningrad A1278

1961, Aug. 8 *Perf. 12x11½*
2511 A1278 4k blue, dk brn & buff .30 .20

Zacharov (1761-1811), architect.

Defense of Brest, 1941 A1279

Designs: No. 2512, Defense of Moscow. No. 2514, Defense of Odessa. No. 2514A, Defense of Sevastopol. No. 2514B, Defense of Leningrad. No. 2514C, Defense of Kiev. No. 2514D, Battle of the Volga (Stalingrad).

1961-63 Photo. *Perf. 12½x12*
2512 A1279 4k blk & red brn (Moscow) .35 .20

Litho.
2513 A1279 4k (Brest) .35 .20
2514 A1279 4k (Odessa) .35 .20
2514A A1279 4k (Sevastopol; '62) .35 .20
2514B A1279 4k brn, dl bl & bis (Leningrad; '63) .35 .20
2514C A1279 4k blk & multi (Kiev; '63) .35 .20
2514D A1279 4k dl org & multi (Volga; '63) .35 .20
Nos. 2512-2514D (7) 2.45 1.40

"War of Liberation," 1941-1945.
See Nos. 2757-2758.

Students' Union Emblem A1280

1961, Aug. 8 Litho. *Perf. 12½*
2515 A1280 6k ultra & red .40 .20

15th anniversary of the founding of the International Students' Union.

Soviet Stamps A1281

Stamps and background different on each denomination.

1961, Aug. *Perf. 12½x12*
2516 A1281 2k multicolored .25 .20
2517 A1281 4k multicolored .45 .25
2518 A1281 6k multicolored .60 .30
2519 A1281 10k multicolored .85 .40
Nos. 2516-2519 (4) 2.15 1.15

40 years of Soviet postage stamps.

Nikolai A. Schors Statue, Kiev — A1282

Statue: 4k, Gregori I. Kotovski, Kishinev.

1961 Photo. *Perf. 11½x12*
2520 A1282 2k lt ultra & sepia .30 .20
2521 A1282 4k rose vio & sepia .30 .20

Letters and Means of Transportation — A1283

1961, Sept. 15 *Perf. 11½*
2522 A1283 4k dk car & black .30 .20

International Letter Writing Week.

Angara River Bridge, Irkutsk A1284

1961, Sept. 15 Litho. *Perf. 12½x12*
2523 A1284 4k ol bis, lilac & black .30 .20

300th anniversary of Irkutsk.

Lenin, Marx, Engels and Marchers — A1285

3k, Obelisk commemorating conquest of space and Moscow University. #2526, Harvester combine. #2527, Industrial control center. #2528, Worker pointing to globe.

1961 **Litho.**
2524 A1285 2k ver, yel & brown .55 .25
2525 A1285 3k org & deep blue .85 .25
2526 A1285 4k mar, bis & red brown .55 .25
2527 A1285 4k car rose, brn, org & blue .55 .25
2528 A1285 4k red & dk brown .55 .25
Nos. 2524-2528 (5) 3.05 1.25

22nd Congress of the Communist Party of the USSR, Oct. 17-31.

Soviet Soldier Monument, Berlin — A1286

1961, Sept. 28 Photo. *Perf. 12x12½*
2529 A1286 4k red & gray violet .40 .20

10th anniversary of the International Federation of Resistance, FIR.

Workers Studying Mathematics — A1287

Designs: 2k, Communist labor team. 4k, Workers around piano.

1961, Sept. 28 Litho. *Perf. 12½x12*
2530 A1287 2k plum & red, *cream* .20 .20
2531 A1287 3k brn & red, *yellow* .20 .20
2532 A1287 4k vio blue & red, *cr* .25 .20
Nos. 2530-2532 (3) .65 .60

Publicizing Communist labor teams in their efforts for labor, education and relaxation.

Rocket and Stars — A1288

Engraved on Aluminum Foil

1961, Oct. 17 ***Perf. 12½***
2533 A1288 1r black & red 13.00 6.00

Soviet scientific and technical achievements in exploring outer space.

Overprinted in Red XXII съезд КПСС

1961, Oct. 23
2534 A1288 1r black & red 13.00 6.00

Communist Party of the USSR, 22nd cong.

Amangaldi Imanov — A1289

1961, Oct. 25 Photo. *Perf. 11½x12*
2535 A1289 4k green, buff & brn .35 .20

Amangaldi Imanov (1873-1919), champion of Soviet power in Kazakhstan.

Franz Liszt (1811-86), Composer A1290

1961, Oct. 31 ***Perf. 12x11½***
2536 A1290 4k mar, dk brn & ocher .60 .20

Flags and Slogans A1291

1961, Nov. 4 ***Perf. 11½***
2537 A1291 4k red, yel & dark red .50 .20

44th anniversary of October Revolution.

Hand Holding Hammer — A1292

Congress Emblem A1293

Designs: Nos. 2538, 2542, Congress emblem. Nos. 2539, 2543, African breaking chains. No. 2541, Three hands holding globe.

1961, Nov. ***Perf. 12, 12½, 11½***
2538 A1293 2k scarlet & bister .20 .20
2539 A1293 2k dk purple & gray .20 .20
2540 A1292 4k plum, org & blue .35 .20
2541 A1293 4k blk, lt blue & pink .40 .20
2542 A1293 6k grn, bister & red .70 .20
2543 A1293 6k ind, dull yel & red .50 .20
Nos. 2538-2543 (6) 2.35 1.20

Fifth World Congress of Trade Unions, Moscow, Dec. 4-16.

Lomonosov Statue — A1294

Hands Holding Hammer and Sickle — A1295

Designs: 6k, Lomonosov at desk. 10k, Lomonosov, his birthplace and Leningrad Academy of Science, horiz.

Perf. 11½x12, 12x11½

1961, Nov. 19 Photo. & Engr.
2544 A1294 4k Prus blue, yel grn & brown .25 .20
2545 A1294 6k green, yel & black .40 .20
2546 A1294 10k maroon, slate & brn .95 .25
Nos. 2544-2546 (3) 1.60 .65

250th anniversary of the birth of M. V. Lomonosov, scientist and poet.

1961, Nov. 27 Litho. *Perf. 12x12½*
2547 A1295 4k red & yellow .30 .20

USSR constitution, 25th anniv.

Romeo and Juliet Ballet — A1296

Ballets: 2k, Red Flower. 3k, Paris Flame. 10k, Swan Lake.

1961-62 ***Perf. 12x12½***
2548 A1296 2k brn, car & lt green ('62) .20 .20
2549 A1296 3k multicolored ('62) .20 .20
2550 A1296 6k dk brn, bis & vio .40 .20
2551 A1296 10k blue, pink & dk brn .60 .20
Nos. 2548-2551 (4) 1.40 .80

Honoring the Russian Ballet.

Linemen A1297

1961 ***Perf. 12½***
2552 A1297 3k shown .20 .20
2553 A1297 4k Welders .25 .20
2554 A1297 6k Surveyor .35 .20
Nos. 2552-2554 (3) .80 .60

Honoring self-sacrificing work of youth in the 7-year plan.

Andrejs Pumpurs (1841-1902), Latvian Poet and Satirist A1298

1961, Dec. 20 ***Perf. 12x11½***
2555 A1298 4k gray & claret .30 .20

Bulgarian Couple, Flag, Emblem and Building A1299

1961, Dec. 28 ***Perf. 12½x12***
2556 A1299 4k multicolored .30 .20

Bulgarian People's Republic, 15th anniv.

Fridtjof Nansen A1300

1961, Dec. 30 Photo. *Perf. 11½*
2557 A1300 6k dk blue & brown 1.50 .55

Centenary of the birth of Fridtjof Nansen, Norwegian Polar explorer.

Mihael Ocipovich Dolivo-Dobrovolsky — A1301

1962, Jan. 25 ***Perf. 12x11½***
2558 A1301 4k bister & dark blue .30 .20

Dolivo-Dobrovolsky, scientist and electrical engineer, birth cent.

Woman and Various Activities A1302

1962, Jan. 26 ***Perf. 11½***
2559 A1302 4k bister, blk & dp org .30 .20

Honoring Soviet Women.

Aleksander S. Pushkin, 125th Death Anniv. — A1303

1962, Jan. 26 Litho. *Perf. 12½x12*
2560 A1303 4k buff, dk brown & ver .30 .20

Dancers A1304

1962, Feb. 6 ***Perf. 12x12½***
2561 A1304 4k bister & ver .30 .20

State ensemble of folk dancers, 25th anniv.

Speed Skating, Luzhniki Stadium A1305

Perf. 11½

1962, Feb. 17 Unwmk. Photo.
2562 A1305 4k orange & ultra .45 .20

Intl. Winter Sports Championships, Moscow.

No. 2562 Overprinted

1962, Mar. 3
2563 A1305 4k orange & ultra 1.50 .75

Victories of I. Voronina and V. Kosichkin, world speed skating champions, 1962.

Ski Jump A1305a

10k, Woman long distance skier, vert.

1962, May 31 ***Perf. 11½***
2564 A1305a 2k ultra, brn & red .25 .20
2565 A1305a 10k org, ultra & black .45 .20

Intl. Winter Sports Championships, Zakopane.

Hero Type of 1961

4k, V. S. Shalandin. 6k, Magomet Gadgiev.

1962, Feb. 22 ***Perf. 12½x12***
2570 A1244 4k dk blue & brown 1.50 .75
2571 A1244 6k brn & slate grn 1.50 .75

Soldier heroes of World War II.

Skier A1306

1962, Mar. 3 ***Perf. 11½***
2572 A1306 4k shown .30 .20
2573 A1306 6k Ice hockey .35 .20
2574 A1306 10k Ice skating .80 .20
Nos. 2572-2574 (3) 1.45 .60

First People's Winter Games, Sverdlovsk.
For overprints see Nos. 2717, 3612.

Aleksandr Ivanovich Herzen (1812-70), Political Writer A1307

1962, Mar. 28 Litho. ***Perf. 12x12½***
2575 A1307 4k ultra, black & buff .20 .20

Lenin — A1308

Design: 6k, Lenin, horiz.

1962, Mar. 28 ***Perf. 12x12½, 12½x12***
2576 A1308 4k brown, red & yel .30 .20
2577 A1308 6k blue, org & brn .30 .20

14th congress of the Young Communist League (Komsomol).

Vostok 1 — A1309

1962, Apr. Unwmk. ***Perf. 11x11½***
2578 A1309 10k multicolored 1.00 .50

1st anniv. of Yuri A. Gagarin's flight into space.

No. 2578 was printed in sheets of 20 stamps alternating with 20 labels.

No. 2578 was also issued imperf. Value $1.50.

Bust of Tchaikovsky A1310

1962, Apr. 19 Photo. ***Perf. 11½x12***
2579 A1310 4k blue, black & bister .45 .25

Second International Tchaikovsky Competition in Moscow.

Youths of 3 Races, Broken Chain, Globe A1311

1962, Apr. 19 ***Perf. 11½***
2580 A1311 6k black, brn & yel .30 .20

International Day of Solidarity of Youth against Colonialism.

Ulyanov (Lenin) Family Portrait A1312

Lenin A1313

1962, Apr. 21 ***Perf. 12x11½***
2581 A1312 4k gray, red & dk brn .35 .20

Typographed and Emboss

Perf. 12½

2582 A1313 10k dk red, gray & blk .65 .20
a. Souv. sheet of 2, perf. 12 5.00 3.00

92nd anniversary of the birth of Lenin.

No. 2582a for 94th anniv. of the birth of Lenin. Issued Nov. 6, 1964.

Cosmos 3 Satellite — A1314

1962, Apr. 26 Litho. ***Perf. 12½x12***
2586 A1314 6k blk, lt blue & vio .50 .20

Cosmos 3 earth satellite launching, Apr. 24.

Charles Dickens A1315

Karl Marx Monument, Moscow A1316

No. 2589, Jean Jacques Rousseau.

1962, Apr. 29
2588 A1315 6k blue, brn & pur .35 .20

Perf. 11½x12

Photo.

2589 A1315 6k gray, lilac & brn .35 .20

Charles Dickens, English writer, 150th birth anniv., and Jean Jacques Rousseau, French writer, 250th birth anniv.

1962, Apr. 29 ***Perf. 12x12½***
2590 A1316 4k deep ultra & gray .30 .20

Pravda, Lenin, Revolutionists A1317

Lenin Reading Pravda — A1318

No. 2592, Pravda, Lenin and rocket.

1962, May 4 **Litho.**
2591 A1317 4k black, bister & red .30 .20
2592 A1317 4k red, black & ocher .30 .20

Perf. 11½

Photo.

2593 A1318 4k ocher, dp claret & red .30 .20
Nos. 2591-2593 (3) .90 .60

50th anniversary of Pravda, Russian newspaper founded by Lenin.

Malaria Eradication Emblem and Mosquito A1319

1962
2594 A1319 4k Prus blue, red & blk .45 .20
2595 A1319 6k ol green, red & blk .45 .20

WHO drive to eradicate malaria.
Issue dates: 4k, May 6; 6k, June 23.
No. 2595 exists imperf. Value $1.

Pioneers Taking Oath before Lenin and Emblem A1320

Designs (Emblem and): 3k, Lenja Golikov and Valja Kotik. No. 2598, Pioneers building rocket model. No. 2599, Red Cross, Red Crescent and nurse giving health instruction. 6k, Pioneers of many races and globe.

1962, May 19 Litho. ***Perf. 12½x12***
2596 A1320 2k green, red & brn .20 .20
2597 A1320 3k multicolored .20 .20
2598 A1320 4k multicolored .25 .20
2599 A1320 4k multicolored .25 .20
2600 A1320 6k multicolored .45 .20
Nos. 2596-2600 (5) 1.35 1.00

All-Union Lenin Pioneers, 40th anniv.

Mesrob A1321

Ivan A. Goncharov A1322

1962, May 27 Photo. ***Perf. 12½x12***
2601 A1321 4k yellow & dk brown .75 .20

"1600th" anniversary of the birth of Bishop Mesrob (350?-439), credited as author of the Armenian and Georgian alphabets.

1962, June 18
2602 A1322 4k gray & brown .40 .20

Ivan Aleksandrovich Goncharov (1812-91), novelist, 150th birth anniv.

Volleyball A1323

Louis Pasteur A1324

2k, Bicyclists, horiz. 10k, Eight-man shell. 12k, Goalkeeper, soccer, horiz. 16k, Steeplechase.

1962, June 27 ***Perf. 11½***
2603 A1323 2k lt brn, blk & ver .20 .20
2604 A1323 4k brn org, black & buff .30 .20
2605 A1323 10k ultra, black & yel .70 .20
2606 A1323 12k lt blue, brn & yel .90 .20
2607 A1323 16k lt green, blk & red 1.10 .20
Nos. 2603-2607 (5) 3.20 1.00

Intl. Summer Sports Championships, 1962.

1962, June 30 ***Perf. 12½x12***
2608 A1324 6k black & brown org .30 .20

Invention of the sterilization process by Louis Pasteur, French chemist, cent.

Library, 1862
A1325

Design: No. 2610, New Lenin Library.

1962, June 30 **Photo.**

2609	A1325	4k slate & black	.20	.20
2610	A1325	4k slate & black	.20	.20
a.		Pair, #2609-2610	.30	.20

Centenary of the Lenin Library, Moscow.

Auction Building and Ermine — A1326

1962, June 30 **Litho.**

2611	A1326	6k multicolored	.50	.20

International Fur Auction, Leningrad.

Young Couple, Lenin, Kremlin — A1327

Workers of Three Races and Dove — A1328

1962, June 30 ***Perf. 12x12½***

2612	A1327	2k multicolored	.30	.20
2613	A1328	4k multicolored	.30	.20

Program of the Communist Party of the Soviet Union for Peace and Friendship among all people.

Hands Breaking Bomb
A1329

1962, July 7 ***Perf. 11½***

2614	A1329	6k blue, blk & olive	.30	.20

World Congress for Peace and Disarmament, Moscow, July 9-14.

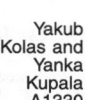

Yakub Kolas and Yanka Kupala
A1330

1962, July 7 **Photo.** ***Perf. 12½x12***

2615	A1330	4k henna brn & buff	.30	.20

Byelorussian poets. Kolas (1882-1956), and Kupala (1882-1942).

Alepker Sabir (1862-1911), Azerbaijani Poet, Satirist — A1331

1962, July 16 ***Perf. 11½***

2616	A1331	4k buff, dk brn & blue	.30	.20

Copies inscribed "Azerbajanyn" were withdrawn before release.

Cancer Congress Emblem
A1332

1962, July 16 **Litho.** ***Perf. 12½***

2617	A1332	6k grnsh blue, blk & red	.35	.20

8th Anti-Cancer Cong., Moscow, July 1962.

N. N. Zinin, Chemist, 150th Birth Anniv.
A1333

1962, July 16 **Photo.** ***Perf. 12x11½***

2618	A1333	4k violet & dk brown	.35	.20

I. M. Kramskoy, Painter — A1334

I. D. Shadr, Sculptor
A1335

M. V. Nesterov, Painter
A1336

1962, July 28 ***Perf. 11½x12, 12x12½***

2619	A1334	4k gray, mar & dk brn	.35	.20
2620	A1335	4k black & red brown	.35	.20
2621	A1336	4k multicolored	.35	.20
		Nos. 2619-2621 (3)	1.05	.60

Vostok 2 Going into Space — A1337

Perf. 11½

1962, Aug. 7 **Unwmk.** **Photo.**

2622	A1337	10k blk, lilac & blue	.60	.20
2623	A1337	10k blk, orange & blue	.60	.20

1st anniv. of Gherman Titov's space flight. Issued imperf. on Aug. 6. Value, set $4.50.

Friendship House, Moscow
A1338

1962, Aug. 15 ***Perf. 12x12½***

2624	A1338	6k ultra & gray	.30	.20

Kremlin and Atom Symbol — A1339

Design: 6k, Map of Russia, atom symbol and "Peace" in 10 languages.

1962, Aug. 15 **Litho.** ***Perf. 12½x12***

2625	A1339	4k multicolored	.35	.20
2626	A1339	6k multicolored	.35	.20

Use of atomic energy for peace.

Andrian G. Nikolayev
A1340

Cosmonauts in Space Helments — A1341

"To Space" Monument by G. Postnikov — A1342

Design: No. 2628, Pavel R. Popovich, with inscription at left and dated "12-15-VIII, 1962."

1962 **Photo.** ***Perf. 11½***

2627	A1340	4k blue, brn & red	.35	.20
2628	A1340	4k blue, brn & red	.35	.20

Perf. 12½x12

Litho.

2629	A1341	6k dk bl, lt bl, org & yellow	.95	.20

Perf. 11½

Photo.

2630	A1342	6k brt blue & multi	.90	.20
2631	A1342	10k violet & multi	.95	.20
		Nos. 2627-2631 (5)	3.50	1.00

Souvenir Sheet

Design: 1r, Monument and portraits of Gagarin, Titov, Nikolayev and Popovich.

1962, Nov. 27 **Litho.** ***Perf. 12½***

2631A	A1342	1r brt bl, blk & sil	7.50	3.50

Nos. 2627-2631A honor the four Russian "conquerors of space," with Nos. 2627-2629 for the 1st group space flight, by Vostoks 3 and 4, Aug. 11-15, 1962. Also issued imperf.

For overprint see No. 2662.

Carp and Bream — A1343

Design: 6k, Freshwater salmon.

1962, Aug. 28 **Photo.** ***Perf. 11½x12***

2632	A1343	4k blue & orange	.25	.20
2633	A1343	6k blue & orange	.55	.20

Fish preservation in USSR.

Feliks E. Dzerzhinski — A1344

1962, Sept. 6 **Litho.** ***Perf. 12½x12***

2634	A1344	4k ol green & dk blue	.30	.20

Dzerzhinski (1877-1926), organizer of Soviet secret police, 85th birth anniv.

O. Henry and New York Skyline
A1345

1962, Sept. 10 **Photo.** ***Perf. 12x11½***

2635	A1345	6k yel, red brn & black	.30	.20

O. Henry (William Sidney Porter, 1862-1910), American writer.

Barclay de Tolly, Mikhail I. Kutuzov, Petr I. Bagration
A1346

4k, Denis Davidov leading partisans. 6k, Battle of Borodino. 10k, Wasilisa Kozhina and partisans.

1962, Sept. 25 ***Perf. 12½x12***

2636	A1346	3k orange brown	.25	.20
2637	A1346	4k ultra	.25	.20
2638	A1346	6k blue gray	.60	.20
2639	A1346	10k violet	.70	.20
		Nos. 2636-2639 (4)	1.80	.80

War of 1812 against the French, 150th anniv.

Street in Vinnitsa
A1347

1962, Sept. 25 **Photo.**

2640	A1347	4k yel bister & black	.30	.20

Town of Vinnitsa, Ukraine, 600th anniv.

"Mail and Transportation" — A1348

1962, Sept. 25 *Perf. 11½*
2641 A1348 4k blue grn, blk & lilac .30 .20

Intl. Letter Writing Week, Oct. 7-13.

Cedar — A1349

4k, Canna. 6k, Arbutus. 10k, Chrysanthemum.

1962, Sept. 27 **Engr. & Photo.**
2642 A1349 3k ver, black & grn .25 .20
2643 A1349 4k multicolored .25 .20
2644 A1349 6k multicolored .25 .20
2645 A1349 10k multicolored .65 .20
Nos. 2642-2645 (4) 1.40 .80

Nikitsky Botanical Gardens, 150th anniv.

Construction Worker — A1350

Designs: No. 2647, Hiker. No. 2648, Surgeon. No. 2649, Worker and lathe. No. 2650, Farmer's wife. No. 2651, Textile worker. No. 2652, Teacher.

1962, Sept. 29 Litho. *Perf. 12x12½*
2646 A1350 4k org, gray & vio blue .20 .20
2647 A1350 4k yel, gray, grn & blue .20 .20
2648 A1350 4k grn, gray & lilac rose .20 .20
2649 A1350 4k ver, gray & lilac .20 .20
2650 A1350 4k bl, gray & emer .20 .20
2651 A1350 4k brt pink, gray & vio .20 .20
2652 A1350 4k yel, gray, dp vio, red & brown .20 .20
Nos. 2646-2652 (7) 1.40 1.40

Sputnik and Stars A1351

1962, Oct. 4 *Perf. 12½x12*
2653 A1351 10k multicolored .90 .25

5th anniversary, launching of Sputnik 1.

M. F. Ahundov, Azerbaijan Poet and Philosopher, 150th Birth Anniv. — A1352

1962, Oct. 2 **Photo.**
2654 A1352 4k lt green & dk brown .30 .20

Farm and Young Couple with Banner A1353

Designs: No. 2656, Tractors, map and surveyor. No. 2657, Farmer, harvester and map.

1962, Oct. 18 Litho. *Perf. 12½x12*
2655 A1353 4k multicolored .70 .40
2656 A1353 4k multicolored .70 .40
2657 A1353 4k brown, yel & red .70 .40
Nos. 2655-2657 (3) 2.10 1.20

Honoring pioneer developers of virgin soil.

N. N. Burdenko A1354

V. P. Filatov A1355

1962, Oct. 20 *Perf. 12½x12*
2658 A1354 4k red brn, lt brn & blk .30 .20
2659 A1355 4k multicolored .30 .20

Scientists and academicians.

Lenin Mausoleum, Red Square — A1356

1962, Oct. 26 **Litho.**
2660 A1356 4k multicolored .35 .20

92nd anniversary of Lenin's birth.

Worker, Flag and Factories A1357

1962, Oct. 29 *Perf. 12x12½*
2661 A1357 4k multicolored .35 .20

45th anniv. of the October Revolution.

No. 2631 Overprinted in Dark Violet

1962, Nov. 3 Photo. *Perf. 11½*
2662 A1342 10k violet & multi 2.50 1.00

Launching of a rocket to Mars.

Togolok Moldo (1860-1942), Kirghiz Poet A1358

Sajat Nova (1712-1795), Armenian Poet A1359

1962, Nov. 17 *Perf. 12x12½*
2663 A1358 4k brn red & black .20 .20
2664 A1359 4k ultra & black .20 .20

Arms, Hammer & Sickle and Map of USSR A1360

1962, Nov. 17 *Perf. 11½*
2665 A1360 4k red, org & dk red .30 .20

USSR founding, 40th anniv.

Space Rocket, Earth and Mars — A1361

1962, Nov. 17 *Perf. 12½x12*
Size: 73x27mm
2666 A1361 10k purple & org red .90 .25

Launching of a space rocket to Mars, Nov. 1, 1962.

Electric Power Industry — A1362

Designs: No. 2668, Machines. No. 2669, Chemicals and oil. No. 2670, Factory construction. No. 2671, Transportation. No. 2672, Telecommunications and space. No. 2673, Metals. No. 2674, Grain farming. No. 2675, Dairy, poultry and meat.

1962 Litho. *Perf. 12½x12*
2667 A1362 4k ultra, red, blk & gray .35 .20
2668 A1362 4k ultra, gray, yel & cl .35 .20
2669 A1362 4k yel, pink, blk, gray & brown .35 .20
2670 A1362 4k yel, blue, red brn & gray .35 .20
2671 A1362 4k mar, yel, red & blue .35 .20
2672 A1362 4k brt yel, blue & brn .35 .20
2673 A1362 4k lil, org, yel & dk brn .35 .20
2674 A1362 4k vio, bis, org red & dk brown .35 .20
2675 A1362 4k emer, dk brn, brn & gray .35 .20
Nos. 2667-2675 (9) 3.15 1.80

"Great decisions of the 22nd Communist Party Congress" and Russian people at work. Issued: #2667-2669, 11/19; others, 12/28.

Queen, Rook and Knight — A1363

Perf. 12½
1962, Nov. 24 Unwmk. Photo.
2676 A1363 4k orange yel & black .50 .25

30th Russian Chess Championships.

Gen. Vasili Blucher A1364

1962, Nov. 27 *Perf. 11½*
2677 A1364 4k multicolored .30 .20

General Vasili Konstantinovich Blucher (1889-1938).

V. N. Podbelski (1887-1920), Minister of Posts — A1365

1962, Nov. 27 *Perf. 12½x12*
2678 A1365 4k red brn, gray & blk .30 .20

Makharenko A1366

Gaidar A1367

1962, Nov. 30 *Perf. 11½x12*
2679 A1366 4k multicolored .25 .20
2680 A1367 4k multicolored .25 .20

A. S. Makharenko (1888-1939) and Arkadi Gaidar (1904-1941), writers.

Dove and Globe — A1368

1962, Dec. 22 Litho. *Perf. 12½x12*
2681 A1368 4k multicolored .30 .20

New Year 1963. Has alternating label inscribed "Happy New Year!" Issued imperf. on Dec. 20. Value $1.

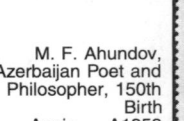

D. N. Prjanishnikov A1369

1962, Dec. 22 *Perf. 12x12½*

2682 A1369 4k multicolored .30 .20

Prjanishnikov, founder of Russian agricultural chemistry.

Rose-colored Starlings — A1370

4k, Red-breasted geese. 6k, Snow geese. 10k, White storks. 16k, Greater flamingos.

1962, Dec. 26 Photo. *Perf. 11½*

2683 A1370 3k grn, blk & pink .20 .20
2684 A1370 4k brn, blk & dp org .20 .20
2685 A1370 6k gray, blk & red .25 .20
2686 A1370 10k blue, blk & red .65 .20
2687 A1370 16k lt bl, rose & blk 1.10 .25
Nos. 2683-2687 (5) 2.40 1.05

FIR Emblem A1371

1962, Dec. 26 *Perf. 12x12½*

2688 A1371 4k violet & red .30 .20
2689 A1371 6k grnsh blue & red .30 .20

4th Cong. of the Intl. Federation of Resistance.

Map of Russia, Bank Book and Number of Savings Banks A1372

Design: 6k, as 4k, but with depositors.

1962, Dec. 30 Litho. *Perf. 12½x12*

2690 A1372 4k multicolored .30 .20
2691 A1372 6k multicolored .30 .20

40th anniv. of Russian savings banks.

Rustavsky Fertilizer Plant — A1373

Hydroelectric Power Stations: No. 2693, Bratskaya. No. 2964, Volzhskaya.

1962, Dec. 30 Photo. *Perf. 12½*

2692 A1373 4k ultra, lt blue & black .30 .20
2693 A1373 4k yel grn, bl grn & blk .30 .20
2694 A1373 4k gray bl, brt bl & blk .30 .20
Nos. 2692-2694 (3) .90 .60

Stanislavski A1374

Perf. 12½

1963, Jan. 15 Unwmk. Engr.

2695 A1374 4k slate green .30 .20

Stanislavski (professional name of Konstantin Sergeevich Alekseev, 1863-1938), actor, producer and founder of the Moscow Art Theater.

A. S. Serafimovich (1863-1949), Writer — A1375

1963, Jan. 19 Photo. *Perf. 11½*

2696 A1375 4k mag, dk brn & gray .30 .20

Children in Nursery A1376

Designs: No. 2698, Kindergarten. No. 2699, Pioneers marching and camping. No. 2700, Young people studying and working.

1963, Jan. 31

2697 A1376 4k brn org, org red & black .35 .20
2698 A1376 4k blue, mag & org .35 .20
2699 A1376 4k brt grn, red & brn .35 .20
2700 A1376 4k multicolored .35 .20
Nos. 2697-2700 (4) 1.40 .80

Wooden Dolls and Toys, Russia — A1377

National Handicrafts: 6k, Pottery, Ukraine. 10k, Bookbinding, Estonia. 12k, Metalware, Dagestan.

1963, Jan. 31 Litho. *Perf. 12x12½*

2701 A1377 4k multicolored .20 .20
2702 A1377 6k multicolored .20 .20
2703 A1377 10k multicolored .50 .20
2704 A1377 12k ultra, org & black .65 .20
Nos. 2701-2704 (4) 1.55 .80

Gen. Mikhail N. Tukhachevski — A1378

Designs: No. 2706, U. M. Avetisian. No. 2707, A. M. Matrosov. No. 2708, J. V. Panfilov. No. 2709, Y. F. Fabriscius.

Perf. 12½x12

1963, Feb. Photo. Unwmk.

2705 A1378 4k blue grn & slate grn .30 .20
2706 A1378 4k org brown & blk .30 .20
2707 A1378 4k ultra & dk brown .30 .20
2708 A1378 4k dp rose & black .30 .20
2709 A1378 4k rose lil & vio bl .30 .20
Nos. 2705-2709 (5) 1.50 1.00

45th anniv. of the Soviet Army and honoring its heroes. No. 2705 for Gen. Mikhail Nikolaevich Tukhachevski (1893-1937).

M. A. Pavlov — A1379

E. O. Paton and Dnieper Bridge, Kiev — A1379a

Portraits: #2711, I. V. Kurchatov. #2712, V. I. Vernadski. #2713, Aleksei N. Krylov. #2714, V. A. Obrutchev, geologist.

1963 *Perf. 11½x12*

Size: 21x32mm

2710 A1379 4k gray, buff & dk bl .30 .20
2711 A1379 4k slate & brown .30 .20

Perf. 12

2712 A1379 4k lilac gray & lt brn .30 .20

Perf. 11½

Size: 23x34½mm

2713 A1379 4k dk blue, sep & red .30 .20
2714 A1379 4k brn ol, gray & red .30 .20
2715 A1379a 4k grnsh bl, blk & red .30 .20
Nos. 2710-2715 (6) 1.80 1.20

Members of the Russian Academy of Science. No. 2715 for Eugene Oskarovich Paton (1870-1953), bridge building engineer.

Winter Sports A1380

1963, Feb. 28 *Perf. 11½*

2716 A1380 4k brt blue, org & blk .30 .20

5th Trade Union Spartacist Games. Printed in sheets of 50 (5x10) with every other row inverted.

No. 2573 Overprinted

1963, Mar. 20

2717 A1306 6k Prus blue & plum 1.25 .50

Victory of the Soviet ice hockey team in the World Championships, Stockholm. For overprint see No. 3612.

Victor Kingisepp A1381

1963, Mar. 24 *Perf. 12x12½*

2718 A1381 4k blue gray & choc .30 .20

75th anniversary of the birth of Victor Kingisepp, communist party leader. Exists imperf.

Rudolfs Blaumanis (1863-1908), Latvian Writer — A1382

1963, Mar. 24 *Perf. 12½x12*

2719 A1382 4k ultra & dk red brn .30 .20

Flower and Globe — A1383

Designs: 6k, Atom diagram and power line. 10k, Rocket in space.

1963, Mar. 26 *Perf. 11½*

2720 A1383 4k red, ultra & grn .25 .20
2721 A1383 6k red, grn & lilac .35 .20
2722 A1383 10k red, vio & lt blue .80 .20
Nos. 2720-2722 (3) 1.40 .60

"World without Arms and Wars."
The 10k exists imperf. Value $1.50.
For overprint see No. 2754.

Costume Type of 1960-62

Regional Costumes: 3k, Tadzhik. No. 2724, Kirghiz. No. 2725, Azerbaijan. No. 2726, Turkmen.

1963, Mar. 31 Litho. *Perf. 11½*

2723 A1237 3k blk, red, ocher & org .40 .20
2724 A1237 4k brown, ver, ocher & ultra .50 .20
2725 A1237 4k blk, ocher, red & grn .50 .20
2726 A1237 4k red, lil, ocher & blk .50 .20
Nos. 2723-2726 (4) 1.90 .80

Lenin A1384

1963, Mar. 30 Engr. *Perf. 12*

2727 A1384 4k red & brown 1.25 .60

93rd anniversary of the birth of Lenin.

Luna 4 Approaching Moon — A1385

1963, Apr. 2 Photo.

2728 A1385 6k black, lt blue & red .50 .20

Soviet rocket to the moon, Apr. 2, 1963. Exists imperforate. Value, $1.25.
For overprint see No. 3160.

Woman and Beach Scene A1386

Designs: 4k, Young man's head and factory. 10k, Child's head and kindergarden.

1963, Apr. 7 Litho. *Perf. 12½x12*

2729 A1386 2k multicolored .30 .25
2730 A1386 4k multicolored .30 .25
2731 A1386 10k multicolored .45 .25
Nos. 2729-2731 (3) 1.05 .75

15th anniversary of World Health Day.

A1387

#2732: a, d, Sputnik & Earth. b, e, Vostok 1, earth & moon. c, f, Rocket & Sun.

1963, Apr. 12

2732 Block of 6 7.50 2.10
a. A1387 10k "10k" blk, blue & lil rose 1.25 .35
b. A1387 10k "10k" lil rose, blue & blk 1.25 .35
c. A1387 10k "10k" black, red & yel 1.25 .35
d. A1387 10k "10k" blue 1.25 .35
e. A1387 10k "10k" lilac rose 1.25 .35
f. A1387 10k "10k" yellow 1.25 .35

Cosmonauts' Day.

Demian Bednii (1883-1945), Poet — A1388

Soldiers on Horseback and Cuban Flag — A1389

1963, Apr. 13 Photo.

2735 A1388 4k brown & black .30 .20

1963, Apr. 25 *Perf. 11½*

Soviet-Cuban friendship: 6k, Cuban flag, hands with gun and book. 10k, Cuban and USSR flags and crane lifting tractor.

2736 A1389 4k blk, red & ultra .25 .20
2737 A1389 6k blk, red & ultra .25 .20
2738 A1389 10k red, ultra & blk .50 .20
Nos. 2736-2738 (3) 1.00 .60

Karl Marx — A1390

Hasek — A1391

1963, May 9 *Perf. 12x12½*

2739 A1390 4k dk red brn & black .30 .20

145th anniversary of the birth of Marx.

1963, Apr. 29 *Perf. 11½x12*

2740 A1391 4k black .30 .20

Jaroslav Hasek (1883-1923), Czech writer.

Moscow P.O. for Foreign Mail A1392

1963, May 9 *Perf. 11½*

2741 A1392 6k brt violet & red brn .30 .20

5th Conference of Communications Ministers of Socialist countries, Budapest.

King and Pawn A1393

6k, Queen, bishop. 16k, Rook, knight.

1963, May 22 Photo.

2742 A1393 4k multicolored .25 .20
2743 A1393 6k ultra, brt pink & grnsh blue .35 .20
2744 A1393 16k brt plum, brt pink & black .90 .20
Nos. 2742-2744 (3) 1.50 .60

25th Championship Chess Match, Moscow. Exists imperf., issued May 18. Value $3.

Richard Wagner — A1394

Design: No. 2745A, Giuseppe Verdi.

1963 Unwmk. *Perf. 11½x12*

2745 A1394 4k black & red .75 .25
2745A A1394 4k red & violet brn .75 .25

150th annivs. of the births of Wagner and Verdi, German and Italian composers.

15th European Boxing Championships, Moscow A1395

4k, Boxers. 6k, Referee proclaiming victor.

1963, May 29 Litho. *Perf. 12½*

2746 A1395 4k multicolored .30 .20
2747 A1395 6k multicolored .30 .20

Valeri Bykovski — A1396

Valentina Tereshkova — A1397

Designs: No. 2749, Tereshkova. No. 2751, Bykovski. No. 2752, Symbolic man and woman fliers. No. 2753, Tereshkova, vert.

Litho. (A1396); Photo. (A1397)

1963 *Perf. 12½x12, 12x12½*

2748 A1396 4k multicolored .25 .20
2749 A1396 4k multicolored .25 .20
a. Pair #2748-2749 .50 .20
2750 A1397 6k grn & dk car rose .25 .20
2751 A1397 6k purple & brown .20 .20
2752 A1397 10k blue & red .85 .20
2753 A1396 10k multicolored 1.50 .35
Nos. 2748-2753 (6) 3.30 1.35

Space flights of Valeri Bykovski, June 14-19, and Valentina Tereshkova, 1st woman cosmonaut, June 16-19, 1963, in Vostoks 5 and 6.
No. 2749a has continuous design.
Nos. 2750-2753 exist imperf. Value $3.

No. 2720 Overprinted in Red

1963, June 24 Photo. *Perf. 11½*

2754 A1383 4k red, ultra & green .50 .25

Intl. Women's Cong., Moscow, June 24-29.

Globe, Camera and Film A1398

1963, July 7 Photo. *Perf. 11½*

2755 A1398 4k gray & ultra .40 .30

3rd International Film Festival, Moscow.

Vladimir V. Mayakovsky, Poet, 70th Birth Anniv. — A1399

1963, July 19 Engr. *Perf. 12½*

2756 A1399 4k red brown .30 .20

Tanks and Map A1400

Design: 6k, Soldier, tanks and flag.

1963, July Litho. *Perf. 12½x12*

2757 A1400 4k sepia & orange .40 .25
2758 A1400 6k org, slate green & blk .40 .25

20th anniversary of the Battle of Kursk in the "War of Liberation," 1941-1945.

Bicyclist — A1401

Sports: 4k, Long jump. 6k, Women divers, horiz. 12k, Basketball. 16k, Soccer.

1963, July 27 *Perf. 12½x12, 12x12½*

2759 A1401 3k multicolored .20 .20
2760 A1401 4k multicolored .20 .20
2761 A1401 6k multicolored .35 .20
2762 A1401 12k multicolored .60 .20
2763 A1401 16k multicolored .75 .20
a. Souvenir sheet of 4, imperf. 2.50 1.25
Nos. 2759-2763 (5) 2.10 1.00

3rd Spartacist Games.
Exist imperf. Value $2.
No. 2763a contains stamps similar to the 3k, 4k, 12k and 16k, with colors changed. Issued Dec. 22.

Ice Hockey — A1402

Lenin — A1403

1963, July 27 Photo.

2764 A1402 6k red & gray blue .50 .25

World Ice Hockey Championship, Stockholm.
For overprint see No. 3012.

1963, July 29

2765 A1403 4k red & black .30 .20

60th anniversary of the 2nd Congress of the Social Democratic Labor Party.

Freighter and Relief Shipment — A1404

Design: 12k, Centenary emblem.

1963, Aug. 8 *Perf. 12½*

2766 A1404 6k Prus green & red .35 .20
2767 A1404 12k dark blue & red .80 .20

Centenary of International Red Cross.

Lapp Reindeer Race A1405

Designs: 4k, Pamir polo, vert. 6k, Burjat archery. 10k, Armenian wrestling, vert.

1963, Aug. 8 *Perf. 11½*

2768 A1405 3k lt vio bl, brn & red .25 .20
2769 A1405 4k bis brn, red & blk .30 .20
2770 A1405 6k yel, black & red .30 .20
2771 A1405 10k sepia, blk & dk red .45 .20
Nos. 2768-2771 (4) 1.30 .80

A. F. Mozhaisky (1825-1890), Pioneer Airplane Builder — A1406

Aviation Pioneers: 10k, P. N. Nesterov (1887-1914), pioneer stunt flyer. 16k, N. E. Zhukovski (1847-1921), aerodynamics pioneer, and pressurized air tunnel.

1963, Aug. 18 **Engr. & Photo.**

2772 A1406 6k black & brt blue .25 .25
2773 A1406 10k black & brt blue .55 .25
2774 A1406 16k black & brt blue .90 .25
Nos. 2772-2774 (3) 1.70 .75

Alexander S. Dargomyzhski and Scene from "Rusalka" — A1408

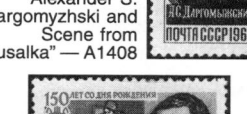

S. S. Gulak-Artemovsky and Scene from "Cossacks on the Danube" — A1409

No. 2777, Georgi O. Eristavi and theater.

Perf. 11½x12, 12x12½

1963, Sept. 10 **Photo.**

2776 A1408 4k violet & black .30 .20
2777 A1408 4k gray violet & brn .30 .20
2778 A1409 4k red & black .30 .20
Nos. 2776-2778 (3) .90 .60

Dargomyzhski, Ukrainian composer; Eristavi, Georgian writer, and Gulak-Artemovsky, Ukrainian composer, 150th birth annivs.

Map of Antarctica, Penguins, Research Ship and Southern Lights — A1410

Designs: 4k, Map, southern lights and snocats (trucks). 6k, Globe, camp and various planes. 12k, Whaler and whales.

1963, Sept. 16 **Litho.** ***Perf. 12½x12***

2779 A1410 3k multicolored .20 .20
2780 A1410 4k multicolored .30 .20
2781 A1410 6k vio, blue & red .45 .20
2782 A1410 12k multicolored 1.50 .20
Nos. 2779-2782 (4) 2.45 .80

"The Antarctic - Continent of Peace."

Letters, Globe, Plane, Train and Ship A1411

1963, Sept. 20 **Photo.** ***Perf. 11½***

2783 A1411 4k violet, black & org .30 .20

International Letter Writing Week.

Denis Diderot A1412

Gleb Uspenski A1414

1963, Oct. 10 **Unwmk.** ***Perf. 11½***

2784 A1412 4k dk blue, brn & yel bister .30 .20

Denis Diderot (1713-84), French philosopher and encyclopedist.

1963, Oct. 10

Portraits: No. 2787, N. P. Ogarev. No. 2788, V. Brusov. No. 2789, F. Gladkov.

2786 A1414 4k buff, red brn & dk brown .40 .20
2787 A1414 4k black & pale green .40 .20
2788 A1414 4k car, brown & gray .40 .20
2789 A1414 4k car, ol brn & gray .40 .20
Nos. 2786-2789 (4) 1.60 .80

Gleb Ivanovich Uspenski (1843-1902), historian and writer; Ogarev, politician, 150th birth anniv.; Brusov, poet, 90th birth anniv., Fyodor Gladkov (1883-1958), writer.

"Peace" Worker, Student, Astronaut and Lenin — A1415

Kirghiz Academy and Spasski Tower — A1416

Designs: No. 2794, "Labor," automatic controls. No. 2795, "Liberty," painter, lecturer, newspaper man. No. 2796, "Equality," elections, regional costumes. No. 2797, "Brotherhood," Recognition of achievement. No. 2798, "Happiness," Family.

1963, Oct. 15 **Litho.** ***Perf. 12½x12***

2793 A1415 4k dk red, red & blk .50 .35
2794 A1415 4k red, dk red & blk .50 .35
2795 A1415 4k dk red, red & blk .50 .35
2796 A1415 4k dk red, red & blk .50 .35
2797 A1415 4k dk red, red & blk .50 .35
2798 A1415 4k dk red, red & blk .50 .35
a. Strip of 6, #2793-2798 2.75 2.25

Proclaiming Peace, Labor, Liberty, Equality, Brotherhood and Happiness.

1963, Oct. 22 ***Perf. 12x12½***

2799 A1416 4k red, yel & vio blue .30 .20

Russia's annexation of Kirghizia, cent.

Lenin and Young Workers A1417

Design: No. 2801, Lenin and Palace of Congresses, the Kremlin.

1963, Oct. 24 **Photo.** ***Perf. 11½***

2800 A1417 4k crimson & black .20 .20
2801 A1417 4k carmine & black .20 .20

13th Congr. of Soviet Trade Unions, Moscow.

Olga Kobylyanskaya, Ukrainian Novelist, Birth Cent. — A1418

1963, Oct. 24 ***Perf. 11½x12***

2802 A1418 4k tan & dk car rose .50 .25

Ilya Mechnikov A1419

6k, Louis Pasteur. 12k, Albert Calmette.

1963, Oct. 28 ***Perf. 12***

2803 A1419 4k green & bister .20 .25
2804 A1419 6k purple & bister .30 .25
2805 A1419 12k blue & bister 1.00 .25
Nos. 2803-2805 (3) 1.50 .75

Pasteur Institute, Paris, 75th anniv; 12k for Albert Calmette (1863-1933), bacteriologist.

Cruiser Aurora and Rockets A1420

1963, Nov. 1

2806 A1420 4k mar, blk, gray & red orange .40 .20
2807 A1420 4k mar, blk, gray & brt rose red .40 .20

Development of the Armed Forces, and 46th anniv. of the October Revolution. The bright rose red ink of No. 2807 is fluorescent.

Mausoleum Gur Emi, Samarkand A1421

Architecture in Samarkand, Uzbekistan: #2809, Shahi-Zind Mosque. 6k, Registan Square.

1963, Nov. 14 **Litho.** ***Perf. 12***

Size: 27½x27½mm

2808 A1421 4k bl, yel & red brn .30 .20
2809 A1421 4k bl, yel & red brn .30 .20

Size: 55x27½mm

2810 A1421 6k bl, yel & red brn .70 .20
Nos. 2808-2810 (3) 1.30 .60

Proclamation, Spasski Tower and Globe A1422

1963, Nov. 15 **Photo.** ***Perf. 12x11½***

2811 A1422 6k purple & lt blue .50 .20

Signing of the Nuclear Test Ban Treaty between the US and the USSR.

Pushkin Monument, Kiev — A1423

M. S. Shchepkin A1424

Portrait: No. 2814, V. L. Durov (1863-1934), circus clown.

1963 **Engr.** ***Perf. 12x12½***

2812 A1423 4k dark brown .20 .20
2813 A1424 4k brown .20 .20
2814 A1424 4k brown black .20 .20
Nos. 2812-2814 (3) .60 .60

No. 2813 for M. S. Shchepkin, actor, 75th birth anniv.

Yuri M. Steklov, 1st Editor of Izvestia, 90th Birth Anniv. A1425

1963, Nov. 17 **Photo.** ***Perf. 11½***

2815 A1425 4k black & lilac rose .30 .20

Vladimir G. Shuhov and Moscow Radio Tower — A1426

1963, Nov. 17 ***Perf. 12½x12***

2816 A1426 4k green & black .30 .20

Shuhov, scientist, 110th birth anniv.

USSR and Czech Flags, Kremlin and Hradcany A1427

1963, Nov. 25 ***Perf. 11½***

2817 A1427 6k red, ultra & brown .40 .25

Russo-Czechoslovakian Treaty, 20th anniv.

Fyodor A. Poletaev — A1428

1963, Nov. 25 **Litho.** ***Perf. 12½x12***

2818 A1428 4k multicolored .40 .30

F. A. Poletaev, Hero of the Soviet Union, National Hero of Italy, and holder of the Order of Garibaldi.

Julian Grimau and Worker Holding Flag — A1429

1963, Nov. 29 **Photo.** ***Perf. 11½***

Flag and Name Panel Embossed

2819 A1429 6k vio black, red & buff .30 .20

Spanish anti-fascist fighter Julian Grimau.

Rockets, Sky and Tree — A1430

1963, Dec. 12 Litho. *Perf. 12x12½*
2820 A1430 6k multicolored .30 .20

"Happy New Year!" — A1431

Photogravure and Embossed
1963, Dec. 20 *Perf. 11½*
2821 A1431 4k grn, dk blue & red .30 .20
2822 A1431 6k grn, dk bl & fluor. rose red .30 .20

Nos. 2820-2822 issued for New Year 1964.

Mikas J. Petrauskas, Lithuanian Composer, 90th Birth Anniv. — A1432

1963, Dec. 20 Photo. *Perf. 11½x12*
2823 A1432 4k brt green & brown .75 .35

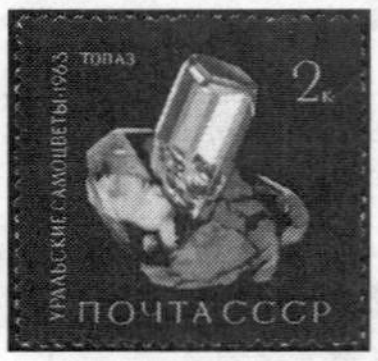

Topaz — A1433

Precious stones of the Urals: 4k, Jasper. 6k, Amethyst. 10k, Emerald. 12k, Rhodonite. 16k, Malachite.

1963, Dec. 26 Litho. *Perf. 12*
2824 A1433 2k brn, yel & blue .25 .20
2825 A1433 4k multicolored .70 .20
2826 A1433 6k red & purple .60 .20
2827 A1433 10k multicolored 1.00 .20
2828 A1433 12k multicolored 1.25 .20
2829 A1433 16k multicolored 1.40 .20
Nos. 2824-2829 (6) 5.20 1.20

Coat of Arms and Sputnik A1434

Rockets: No. 2831, Luna I. No. 2832, Rocket around the moon. No. 2833, Vostok I, first man in space. No. 2834, Vostok III & IV. No. 2835, Vostok VI, first woman astronaut.

1963, Dec. 27 Litho. & Embossed
2830 A1434 10k red, gold & gray .60 .20
2831 A1434 10k red, gold & gray .60 .20
2832 A1434 10k red, gold & gray .60 .20
2833 A1434 10k red, gold & gray .60 .20
2834 A1434 10k red, gold & gray .60 .20
2835 A1434 10k red, gold & gray .60 .20
a. Vert. strip of 6, #2830-2835 3.60 1.25

Soviet achievements in space.

Dyushambe, Tadzhikistan — A1435

1963, Dec. 30 Engr.
2836 A1435 4k dull blue .50 .30

No. 2836 was issued after Stalinabad was renamed Dyushambe.
For overprint see No. 2943.

Flame, Broken Chain and Rainbow A1436

1963, Dec. 30 Litho.
2837 A1436 6k multicolored .50 .25

15th anniversary of the Universal Declaration of Human Rights.

F. A. Sergeev A1437

1963, Dec. 30 Photo. *Perf. 12x12½*
2838 A1437 4k gray & red .35 .25

80th anniversary of the birth of the revolutionist Artjem (F. A. Sergeev).

Sun and Radar A1438

6k, Sun, Earth, vert. 10k, Earth, Sun.

1964, Jan. 1 Photo. *Perf. 11½*
2839 A1438 4k brt mag, org & blk .25 .25
2840 A1438 6k org yel, red & bl .40 .25
2841 A1438 10k blue, vio & org .45 .25
Nos. 2839-2841 (3) 1.10 .75

International Quiet Sun Year, 1964-65.

Christian Donalitius A1439

1964, Jan. 1 Unwmk. *Perf. 12*
2842 A1439 4k green & black .30 .20

Lithuanian poet Christian Donalitius (Donelaitis), 250th birth anniv.

Women's Speed Skating A1440

Designs: 4k, Women's cross country skiing. 6k, 1964 Olympic emblem and torch. 10k, Biathlon. 12k, Figure skating pair.

1964, Feb. 4 *Perf. 11½, Imperf.*
2843 A1440 2k ultra, blk & lilac rose .25 .20
2844 A1440 4k lilac rose, blk & ultra .25 .20
2845 A1440 6k dk bl, red & blk .30 .20
2846 A1440 10k grn, lil & blk .55 .25
2847 A1440 12k lil, blk & grn .75 .25
Nos. 2843-2847 (5) 2.10 1.10

9th Winter Olympic Games, Innsbruck Jan. 29-Feb. 9, 1964. See Nos. 2865, 2867-2870.

Anna S. Golubkina (1864-1927), Sculptor — A1441

1964, Feb. 4 Photo.
2848 A1441 4k gray, brown & buff .30 .20

No. 2450 Overprinted

and

Taras G. Shevchenko A1443

Designs: 4k, Shevchenko statue, Kiev. 10k, Shevchenko by Ilya Repin. (Portrait on 6k by I. Kramskoi.)

1964 Litho. *Perf. 12*
2852 A1245 3k brown & violet .30 .20

Engr.
2853 A1443 4k magenta .30 .20
2854 A1443 4k deep green .45 .20
2855 A1443 6k red brown .45 .20
2856 A1443 6k indigo .45 .20

Photo.
2857 A1443 10k bister & brown 1.10 .20
2858 A1443 10k buff & dull violet 1.10 .20
Nos. 2852-2858 (7) 4.15 1.40

Shevchenko, Ukrainian poet, 150th birth anniv.
Issued: #2852, 2857-2858, 2/22; Others, 3/1.

K. S. Zaslonov A1444

Soviet Heroes: No. 2860, N. A. Vilkov. No. 2861, J. V. Smirnov. No. 2862, V. S. Khorujaia (heroine). No. 2862A, I. M. Sivko. No. 2862B, I. S. Polbin.

1964-65 Photo.
2859 A1444 4k hn brn & brn blk .30 .20
2860 A1444 4k Prus bl & vio blk .30 .20
2861 A1444 4k brn red & ind .30 .20
2862 A1444 4k bluish gray & dk brown .30 .20
2862A A1444 4k lil & blk ('65) .30 .20
2862B A1444 4k blue & dk brn ('65) .30 .20
Nos. 2859-2862B (6) 1.80 1.20

Printer Inking Form, 16th Century A1445

6k, Statue of Ivan Fedorov, 1st Russian printer.

1964, Mar. 1 Litho. Unwmk.
2863 A1445 4k multicolored .35 .20
2864 A1445 6k multicolored .35 .20

400th anniv. of book printing in Russia.

Nos. 2843-2847 Overprinted

and

Ice Hockey A1446

Olympic Gold Medal, "11 Gold, 8 Silver, 6 Bronze" A1447

Design: 3k, Ice hockey.

1964, Mar. 9 Photo. *Perf. 11½*
2865 A1440 2k ultra, blk & lilac rose .20 .20
2866 A1446 3k blk, bl grn & red .25 .20
2867 A1440 4k lil rose, blk & ultra .30 .20
2868 A1440 6k dk bl, red & blk .70 .20
2869 A1440 10k grn, lil & blk .80 .20
2870 A1440 12k lilac, blk & grn .90 .20

Perf. 12
2871 A1447 16k org red & gldn brown 1.25 .25
Nos. 2865-2871 (7) 4.40 1.45

Soviet victories at the 9th Winter Olympic Games.
On Nos. 2865, 2867-2870 the black overprints commemorate victories in various events and are variously arranged in 3 to 6 lines, with "Innsbruck" in Russian added below "1964" on 2k, 4k, 10k and 12k.

Rubber Industry — A1448

Designs: No. 2873, Textile industry. No. 2874, Cotton, wheat, corn and helicopter spraying land.

1964 Litho. *Perf. 12x12½*
2872 A1448 4k org, lilac, ultra & blk .30 .20
2873 A1448 4k org, blk, grn & ultra .30 .20
2874 A1448 4k dull yel, ol, red & bl .30 .20
Nos. 2872-2874 (3) .90 .60

Importance of the chemical industry to the Soviet economy.
Issued: #2872, 2/10; #2873-2874, 3/27.

Regular and Volunteer Militiamen A1449

1964, Mar. 27 Photo. *Perf. 12*

2875 A1449 4k red & deep ultra .30 .30

Day of the Militia.

Sailor and Odessa Lighthouse — A1450

Liberation Monument, Minsk — A1451

No. 2877, Lenin statue and Leningrad.

1964 Litho. *Perf. 12½x12*

2876 A1450 4k red, lt grn, ultra & black .30 .20
2877 A1450 4k red, yel, grn, brn & black .30 .20
2878 A1451 4k bl, gray, red & emer .30 .20
Nos. 2876-2878 (3) .90 .60

Liberation of Odessa (#2876), Leningrad (#2877), Byelorussia (#2878), 20th anniv.
Issued: #2876, 4/10; #2877, 5/9; #2878, 6/30.

First Soviet Sputniks A1452

F. A. Tsander — A1453

Designs: 6k, Mars 1 spacecraft. No. 2886, Konstantin E. Tsiolkovsky. No. 2887, N. I. Kibaltchitch. No. 2888, Statue honoring 3 balloonists killed in 1934 accident. 12k, Gagarin and Kosmos 3.

Perf. 11½, Imperf.

1964, Apr. Photo.

2883 A1452 4k red org, blk & blue green .30 .20
2884 A1452 6k dk bl & org red .60 .20
2885 A1453 10k grn, blk & fluor. pink .75 .20
2886 A1453 10k dk bl grn, blk & fluor. pink .75 .20
2887 A1453 10k lilac, blk & lt grn .75 .20
2888 A1453 10k blue & black .75 .20
2889 A1452 12k blue grn, org brn & black .75 .25
Nos. 2883-2889 (7) 4.65 1.45

Leaders in rocket theory and technique.

Lenin, 94th Birth Anniv. A1454

Engraved and Photogravure

1964-65 *Perf. 12x11½*

2890 A1454 4k blk, buff & lilac rose 4.50 3.50
a. Re-engraved ('65) 3.50 2.00

On No. 2890a, the portrait shading is much heavier. Lines on collar are straight and unbroken, rather than dotted.
For souvenir sheet see No. 2582a.

William Shakespeare, 400th Birth Anniv. — A1455

1964, Apr. 23 *Perf. 11½*

2891 A1455 10k gray & red brown .60 .25

See Nos. 2985-2986.

"Irrigation" — A1456

1964, May 12 Litho. *Perf. 12x12½*

2892 A1456 4k multicolored .30 .20

A1457

Perf. 12½x11½

1964, May 12 Photo.

2893 A1457 4k blue & gray brown .30 .20

Y. B. Gamarnik, army commander, 70th birth anniv.

D. I. Gulia A1458

Portraits: No. 2895, Hamza Hakim-Zade Nijazi. No. 2896, Saken Seifullin. No. 2896A, M. M. Kotsyubinsky. No. 2896B, Stepanos Nazaryan. No. 2896C, Toktogil Satyiganov.

Engraved and Photogravure

1964 Unwmk. *Perf. 12x11½*

2894 A1458 4k grn, buff & blk .25 .20
2895 A1458 4k red, buff & blk .25 .20
2896 A1458 4k brn, ocher, buff & black .25 .20
2896A A1458 4k brn lake, blk & buff .25 .20
2896B A1458 4k blue, pale bl, blk & buff .25 .20
2896C A1458 4k red brn & blk .25 .20
Nos. 2894-2896C (6) 1.50 1.20

Abkhazian poet Gulia, 90th birth anniv.; Uzbekian writer and composer Nijazi, 75th birth anniv.; Kazakian poet Seifullin, 70th birth anniv.; Ukrainian writer Kotsyubinsky (1864-1913); Armenian writer Nazaryan (1814-1879); Kirghiz poet Satylganov (1864-1933).

Arkadi Gaidar (1904-41) A1459

Writers: No. 2897A, Nikolai Ostrovsky (1904-36) and battle scene (portrait at left).

1964 Photo. *Perf. 12*

2897 A1459 4k red orange & gray .30 .20

Engr.

2897A A1459 4k brn lake & blk .30 .20

No. 2318 Surcharged:

1964, May 27 Litho. *Perf. 12*

2898 A1194 4k on 40k bis & brn 3.00 .20

Azerbaijan's joining Russia, 150th anniv.

"Romania" A1460

No. 2900, "Poland," (map, Polish eagle, industrial and agricultural symbols). No. 2901, "Bulgaria" (flag, rose, industrial and agricultural symbols). No. 2902, Soviet and Yugoslav soldiers and embattled Belgrade. No. 2903, "Czechoslovakia" (view of Prague, arms, Russian soldier and woman). No. 2903A, Map and flag of Hungary, Liberty statue. No. 2903B, Statue of Russian Soldier and Belvedere Palace, Vienna. No. 2904, Buildings under construction, Warsaw; Polish flag and medal.

1964-65 Litho. *Perf. 12*

2899 A1460 6k gray & multi .25 .20
2900 A1460 6k ocher, red & brn .25 .20
2901 A1460 6k tan, grn & red .25 .20
2902 A1460 6k gray, blk, dl bl, ol & red .25 .20
2903 A1460 6k ultra, black & red ('65) .25 .20
2903A A1460 6k brn, red & green ('65) .25 .20
2903B A1460 6k dp org, gray bl & black ('65) .25 .20
2904 A1460 6k blue, red, yel & bister ('65) .25 .20
Nos. 2899-2904 (8) 2.00 1.60

20th anniversaries of liberation from German occupation of Romania, Poland, Bulgaria, Belgrade, Czechoslovakia, Hungary, Vienna and Warsaw.

Elephant A1461

Designs: 2k, Giant panda, horiz. 4k, Polar bear. 6k, European elk. 10k, Pelican. 12k, Tiger. 16k, Lammergeier.

Perf. 12x12½, 12½x12, Imperf.

1964 Photo.

Size: 25x36mm, 36x25mm

2905 A1461 1k red & black .20 .20
2906 A1461 2k tan & black .20 .20

Perf. 12

Size: 26x28mm

2907 A1461 4k grnsh gray, black & tan .25 .20

Perf. 12x12½

Size: 25x36mm

2908 A1461 6k ol, dk brn & tan .60 .25

Perf. 12

Size: 26x28mm

2909 A1461 10k ver, gray & blk .90 .40

Perf. 12½x12, 12x12½

Size: 36x25mm, 25x36mm

2910 A1461 12k brn, ocher & blk 1.25 .40
2911 A1461 16k ultra, blk, bis & yellow 1.60 .60
Nos. 2905-2911 (7) 5.00 2.25

100th anniv. of the Moscow zoo.
Issue dates: Perf., June 18. Imperf., May.

Leningrad Post Office A1462

1964, June 30 Litho. *Perf. 12*

2912 A1462 4k citron, black & red .30 .20

Leningrad postal service, 250th anniv.

Corn — A1463

Thorez — A1464

1964 Photo. *Perf. 11½, Imperf.*

2913 A1463 2k shown .20 .20
2914 A1463 3k Wheat .20 .20
2915 A1463 4k Potatoes .20 .20
2916 A1463 6k Beans .25 .20
2917 A1463 10k Beets .30 .20
2918 A1463 12k Cotton .60 .20
2919 A1463 16k Flax .90 .20
Nos. 2913-2919 (7) 2.65 1.40

Issue dates: Perf., July 10. Imperf., June 25.

1964, July 31

2920 A1464 4k black & red .75 .25

Maurice Thorez, chairman of the French Communist party.

Equestrian and Russian Olympic Emblem A1465

Designs: 4k, Weight lifter. 6k, High jump. 10k, Canoeing. 12k, Girl gymnast. 16k, Fencing.

1964, July *Perf. 11½, Imperf.*

2921 A1465 3k lt yel grn, red, brn & black .20 .20
2922 A1465 4k yel, black & red .20 .20
2923 A1465 6k lt blue, blk & red .25 .20
2924 A1465 10k bl grn, red & blk .50 .20
2925 A1465 12k gray, blk & red .60 .20
2926 A1465 16k lt ultra, blk & red .75 .20
Nos. 2921-2926 (6) 2.50 1.20

18th Olympic Games, Tokyo, 10/10-25/64.
Two 1r imperf. souvenir sheets exist, showing emblem, woman gymnast and stadium. Size: 91x71mm.
Value, red sheet, $4.75 unused, $1.75 canceled; green sheet, $165 unused, $225 canceled.

Three Races — A1466

1964, Aug. 8 **Photo.** ***Perf. 12***

2929	A1466	6k orange & black	.40	.35

International Congress of Anthropologists and Ethnographers, Moscow.

Indian Prime Minister Jawaharlal Nehru (1889-1964) A1467

1964, Aug. 20 ***Perf. 11½***

2930	A1467	4k brown & black	.40	.20

Conquest of Space

Souvenir Sheet

1964, Aug. 20 ***Perf. 11½x12***

2930A	sheet of 6	3.75	1.50
	On glossy paper	10.00	6.00

Marx and Engels A1468 — A. V. Vishnevsky A1469

Designs: No. 2932 Lenin and title page of "CPSS Program." No. 2933, Worker breaking chains around the globe. No. 2934, Title pages of "Communist Manifesto" in German and Russian. No. 2935, Globe and banner inscribed "Workers of the World Unite."

1964, Aug. 27 **Photo.** ***Perf. 11½x12***

2931	A1468	4k red, dk red & brown	.30	.20
2932	A1468	4k red, brn & slate	.30	.20
2933	A1468	4k blue, fluor. brt rose & black	.30	.20

Perf. 12½x12

Litho.

2934	A1468	4k ol blk, blk & red	.30	.20
2935	A1468	4k bl, red & ol bis	.30	.20
		Nos. 2931-2935 (5)	1.50	1.00

Centenary of First Socialist International.

1964 **Photo.** ***Perf. 11½***

Portraits: No. 2937, N. A. Semashko. No. 2938, D. Ivanovsky.

Size: 23½x35mm

2936	A1469	4k gray & brown	.30	.20
2937	A1469	4k buff, sepia & red	.30	.20

Litho.

Size: 22x32½mm

2938	A1469	4k tan, gray & brown	.30	.20
		Nos. 2936-2938 (3)	.90	.60

90th birth annivs. Vishnevsky, surgeon, and Semashko, founder of the Russian Public Health Service; Ivanovsky (1864-1920), physician.

Palmiro Togliatti (1893-1964), General Secretary of the Italian Communist Party — A1470

1964, Sept. 15 ***Perf. 12½x12***

2939	A1470	4k black & red	.30	.20

Letter, Aerogram and Globe A1471

1964, Sept. 20 **Litho.**

2940	A1471	4k tan, lilac rose & ultra	.30	.20

Intl. Letter Writing Week, Oct. 5-11.

Arms of German Democratic Republic, Factories, Ship and Train — A1472

1964, Oct. 7 ***Perf. 12***

2942	A1472	6k blk, yel, red & bister	.30	.20

German Democratic Republic, 15th anniv.

No. 2836 Overprinted in Red

1964, Oct. 7 **Engr.**

2943	A1435	4k dull blue	3.00	3.00

40th anniversary of Tadzhik Republic.

Woman Holding Bowl of Grain and Fruit A1473

Uzbek Farm Couple and Arms — A1474

Turkmen Woman Holding Arms — A1475

1964, Oct. **Litho.**

2944	A1473	4k red, green & brn	.40	.20
2945	A1474	4k red yel & claret	.40	.20
2946	A1475	4k red, black & red brn	.40	.20
		Nos. 2944-2946 (3)	1.20	.60

40th anniv. of the Moldavian, Uzbek and Turkmen Socialist Republics.

Issue dates: #2944, Oct. 7; others, Oct. 26.

Soldier and Flags A1476

1964, Oct. 14

2947	A1476	4k red, bis, dk brn & bl	.30	.20

Liberation of the Ukraine, 20th anniv.

Mikhail Y. Lermontov (1814-41), Poet — A1477

Designs: 4k, Birthplace of Tarchany. 10k, Lermontov and Vissarion G. Belinski.

1964, Oct. 14 **Engr.; Litho. (10k)**

2948	A1477	4k violet black	.20	.20
2949	A1477	6k black	.25	.20
2950	A1477	10k dk red brn & buff	.70	.20
		Nos. 2948-2950 (3)	1.15	.60

Hammer and Sickle A1478

1964, Oct. 14 **Litho.**

2951	A1478	4k dk blue, red, ocher & yellow	.30	.20

47th anniversary of October Revolution.

Col. Vladimir M. Komarov A1479

Komarov, Feoktistov and Yegorov — A1480

Designs: No. 2953, Boris B. Yegorov, M.D. No. 2954, Konstantin Feoktistov, scientist. 10k, Spacecraft Voskhod I and cosmonauts. 50k, Red flag with portraits of Komarov, Feoktistov and Yegorov, and trajectory around earth.

Perf. 11½ (A1479), 12½x12

1964 **Photo.**

2952	A1479	4k bl grn, blk & org	.20	.20
2953	A1479	4k bl grn, blk & org	.20	.20
2954	A1479	4k bl grn, blk & org	.20	.20

Size: 73x23mm

2955	A1480	6k vio & dk brn	.25	.20
2956	A1480	10k dp ultra & pur	.85	.20

Imperf

Litho.

Size: 90x45½mm

2957	A1480	50k vio, red & gray	5.00	1.40
		Nos. 2952-2957 (6)	6.70	2.40

3-men space flight of Komarov, Yegorov and Feoktistov, Oct. 12-13. Issued: #2952-2954, 10/19; #2955, 10/17; #2956, 10/13; #2957, 11/20.

A. I. Yelizarova-Ulyanova — A1482

Portrait: #2961, Nadezhda K. Krupskaya.

1964, Nov. 6 **Photo.** ***Perf. 11½***

2960	A1482	4k brn, org & indigo	.30	.20
2961	A1482	4k indigo, red & brn	.30	.20

Yelizarova-Ulyanova, Lenin's sister, birth cent. & Krupskaya, Lenin's wife, 95th birth anniv.

Farm Woman, Sheep, Flag of Mongolia A1483

1964, Nov. 20 **Litho.** ***Perf. 12***

2962	A1483	6k multicolored	.30	.20

Mongolian People's Republic, 40th anniv.

Mushrooms A1484

Designs: Various mushrooms.

1964, Nov. 25 **Litho.** ***Perf. 12***

2963	A1484	2k ol grn, red brn & yellow	.20	.20
2964	A1484	4k green & yellow	.20	.20
2965	A1484	6k bluish grn, brn & yellow	.50	.20
2966	A1484	10k grn, org red & brn	.65	.20
2967	A1484	12k ultra, yel & grn	1.25	.20
		Nos. 2963-2967 (5)	2.80	1.00

Nos. 2963-2967 exist varnished, printed in sheets of 25 with 10 labels in outside vertical rows. Issued Nov. 30. Value, set $5.

A. P. Dovzhenko — A1485

Design: 6k, Scene from "Tchapaev" (man and boy with guns).

1964, Nov. 30 **Photo.** ***Perf. 12***

2968	A1485	4k gray & dp ultra	.45	.25
2968A	A1485	6k pale olive & blk	.45	.25

Dovzhenko (1894-1956), film producer, and 30th anniv. of the production of the film "Tchapaev."

"Happy New Year" — A1486

V. J. Struve — A1487

Photogravure and Engraved

1964, Nov. 30 *Perf. 11½*

2969 A1486 4k multicolored .50 .30

New Year 1965. The bright rose ink is fluorescent.

1964-65 Photo. *Perf. 12½x11½*

Portraits: No. 2971, N. P. Kravkov. No. 2971A, P. K. Sternberg. No. 2971B, Ch. Valikhanov. No. 2971C, V. A. Kistjakovski.

2970 A1487 4k sl bl & dk brn .65 .20

Litho.

2971 A1487 4k brn, red & blk .35 .20

Photo.

Perf. 11½

2971A A1487 4k dk bl & dk brn .35 .20

Perf. 12

2971B A1487 4k rose vio & blk .35 .20

Litho.

2971C A1487 4k brn vio, blk & cit .35 .20

Nos. 2970-2971C (5) 2.05 1.00

Astronomer Struve (1793-1864), founder of Pulkov Observatory; Kravkov (1865-1924), pharmacologist; Sternberg (1865-1920), astronomer; Valikhanov (1835-1865), Kazakh scientist; Kistjakovski (1865-1952), chemist.
Issued: #2970, 11/30; #2971, 1/31/65; #2971A-2971B, 9/21/65; #2971C, 12/24.

S. V. Ivanov and Skiers A1488

1964, Dec. 22 Engr. *Perf. 12½*

2972 A1488 4k black & brown .50 .30

S. V. Ivanov (1864-1910), painter.

Chemical Industry: Fertilizers and Pest Control — A1489

Importance of the chemical industry for the national economy: 6k, Synthetics factory.

1964, Dec. 25 Photo. *Perf. 12*

2973 A1489 4k olive & lilac rose .30 .20

2974 A1489 6k dp ultra & black .30 .20

European Cranberries A1490

Wild Berries: 3k, Huckleberries. 4k, Mountain ash. 10k, Blackberries. 16k, Cranberries.

1964, Dec. 25 *Perf. 11½x12*

2975 A1490 1k pale grn & car .20 .20

2976 A1490 3k gray, vio bl & grn .20 .20

2977 A1490 4k gray, org red & brown .25 .20

2978 A1490 10k lt grn, dk vio blue & claret .40 .20

2979 A1490 16k gray, brt green & car rose .50 .20

Nos. 2975-2979 (5) 1.55 1.00

Academy of Science Library A1491

1964, Dec. 25 Typo. *Perf. 12x12½*

2980 A1491 4k blk, pale grn & red .30 .20

250th anniv. of the founding of the Academy of Science Library, Leningrad.

Congress Palace, Kremlin — A1492

Khan Tengri — A1493

1964, Dec. 25

2981 A1492 1r dark blue 4.50 1.00

1964, Dec. 29 Photo. *Perf. 11½*

Mountains: 6k, Kazbek, horiz. 12k, Twin peaks of Ushba.

2982 A1493 4k grnsh bl, vio bl & buff .30 .20

2983 A1493 6k yel, dk brn & ol .30 .20

2984 A1493 12k lt yel, grn & pur .40 .20

Nos. 2982-2984 (3) 1.00 .60

Development of mountaineering in Russia.

Portrait Type of 1964

Design: 6k, Michelangelo. 12k, Galileo.

Engraved and Photogravure

1964, Dec. 30 *Perf. 11½*

2985 A1455 6k sep, red brn & org .20 .20

2986 A1455 12k dk brn & green .80 .25

Michelangelo Buonarotti, artist, 400th death anniv. and Galileo Galilei, astronomer and physicist, 400th birth anniv.

Helmet A1494

Treasures from Kremlin Treasury: 6k, Saddle. 10k, Jeweled fur crown. 12k, Gold ladle. 16k, Bowl.

1964, Dec. 30 Litho.

2987 A1494 4k multicolored .20 .20

2988 A1494 6k multicolored .30 .20

2989 A1494 10k multicolored .45 .20

2990 A1494 12k multicolored 1.10 .20

2991 A1494 16k multicolored 1.25 .20

Nos. 2987-2991 (5) 3.30 1.00

Dante Alighieri (1265-1321), Italian Poet — A1495

1965, Jan. 29 Photo. *Perf. 11½*

2995 A1495 4k dk red brn & ol bis .35 .25

Blood Donor — A1496

Honoring blood donors: No. 2997, Hand holding carnation, and donors' emblem.

1965, Jan. 31 Litho. *Perf. 12*

2996 A1496 4k dk car, red, vio bl & bl .30 .20

2997 A1496 4k brt grn, red & dk grn .30 .20

Bandy — A1497

Police Dog — A1498

6k, Figure skaters and Moscow Sports Palace.

1965, Feb. Photo. *Perf. 11½x12*

2998 A1497 4k blue, red & yellow .30 .20

2999 A1497 6k green, blk & red .30 .20

4k issued Feb. 21, for the victory of the Soviet team in the World Bandy Championship, Moscow, Feb. 21-27; 6k issued Feb. 12, for the European Figure Skating Championship. For overprint see No. 3017.

Perf. 12x11½, 11½x12 (Photo. stamps); 12x12½, 12½x12 (Litho.)

Photo., Litho. (1k, 10k, 12k, 16k)

1965, Feb. 26

Dogs: 1k, Russian hound. 2k, Irish setter. No. 3003, Pointer. No. 3004, Fox terrier. No. 3005, Sheepdog. No. 3006, Borzoi. 10k, Collie. 12k, Husky. 16k, Caucasian sheepdog. (1k, 2k, 4k, 12k and No. 3006 horiz.)

3000 A1498 1k black, yel & mar .20 .20

3001 A1498 2k ultra, blk & red brown .25 .20

3002 A1498 3k blk, ocher & org red .25 .20

3003 A1498 4k org, yel grn & blk .40 .20

3004 A1498 4k brn, blk & lt grn .40 .20

3005 A1498 6k chalky blue, sep & red .50 .20

3006 A1498 6k chalky bl, org brn & black .50 .20

3007 A1498 10k yel green, ocher & red .90 .20

3008 A1498 12k gray, blk & ocher 1.10 .20

3009 A1498 16k multicolored 1.25 .25

Nos. 3000-3009 (10) 5.75 2.05

Richard Sorge (1895-1944), Soviet spy and Hero of the Soviet Union — A1499

1965, Mar. 6 Photo. *Perf. 12x12½*

3010 A1499 4k henna brn & black .75 .30

Communications Symbols — A1500

1965, Mar. 6 *Perf. 12½x12*

3011 A1500 6k grnsh blue, vio & brt purple .50 .30

Intl. Telecommunication Union, cent.

No. 2764 Overprinted

1965, Mar. 20 Photo. *Perf. 12*

3012 A1402 6k red & gray blue 1.00 .30

Soviet victory in the European and World Ice Hockey Championships.

Lt. Col. Alexei Leonov Taking Movies in Space — A1501

1r, Leonov walking in space and Voskhod 2.

1965, Mar. 23 Photo. *Perf. 12*

Size: 73x23mm

3015 A1501 10k brt ultra, org & gray .80 .35

First man walking in space, Lt. Col. Alexei Leonov, Mar. 17, 1965 ("18 March" on stamp).
Exists imperf. Value $1.

Souvenir Sheet

1965, Apr. 12 Litho.

3016 A1501 1r multicolored 5.50 2.00

Space flight of Voskhod 2. No. 3016 contains one 81x27mm stamp.

No. 2999 Overprinted

1965, Mar. 26 *Perf. 11½x12*

3017 A1497 6k green, black & red .80 .25

Soviet victory in the World Figure Skating Championships.

Flags of USSR and Poland A1502

1965, Apr. 12 Photo. *Perf. 12*

3018 A1502 6k bister & red .50 .20

20th anniversary of the signing of the Polish-Soviet treaty of friendship, mutual assistance and postwar cooperation.

Tsiolkovsky Monument, Kaluga; Globe and Rockets — A1503

Rockets, Radio Telescope, TV Antenna
A1504

Designs: 12k, Space monument, Moscow. 16k, Cosmonauts' monument, Moscow. No. 3023, Globe with trajectories, satellite and astronauts.

1965, Apr. 12 ***Perf. 11½***

3019 A1503 4k pale grn, black & brt rose .20 .20
3020 A1503 12k vio, pur & brt rose .50 .20
3021 A1503 16k multicolored .80 .20

Lithographed on Aluminum Foil

Perf. 12½x12

3022 A1504 20k black & red 5.00 3.00
3023 A1504 20k blk, blue & red 5.00 3.00
Nos. 3019-3023 (5) 11.50 6.60

National Cosmonauts' Day. On Nos. 3019-3021 the bright rose is fluorescent.

Lenin — A1505

1965, Apr. 16 **Engr.** ***Perf. 12***

3024 A1505 10k tan & indigo .50 .25

95th anniversary of the birth of Lenin.

Poppies — A1506

Flowers: 3k, Daisies. 4k, Peony. 6k, Carnation. 10k, Tulips.

1965, Apr. 23 **Photo.** ***Perf. 11***

3025 A1506 1k mar, red & grn .20 .20
3026 A1506 3k dk brn, yel & grn .20 .20
3027 A1506 4k blk, grn & lilac .45 .20
3028 A1506 6k dk sl grn, grn & red .65 .20
3029 A1506 10k dk plum, yel & grn 1.00 .20
Nos. 3025-3029 (5) 2.50 1.00

Soviet Flag, Broken Swastikas, Fighting in Berlin
A1507

Designs: 2k, "Fatherland Calling!" (woman with proclamation) by I. Toidze. 3k, "Attack on Moscow" by V. Bogatkin. No. 3033, "Rest after the Battle" by Y. Neprintsev. No. 3034, "Mother of Partisan" by S. Gerasimov. 6k, "Our Flag - Symbol of Victory" (soldiers with banner) by V. Ivanov. 10k, "Tribute to the Hero" (mourners at bier) by F. Bogorodsky. 12k, "Invincible Nation and Army" (worker and soldier holding shell) by V. Koretsky. 16k, "Victory celebration on Red Square" by K. Yuan. 20k, Soldier and symbols of war.

1965 ***Perf. 11½***

3030 A1507 1k red, blk & gold .25 .20
3031 A1507 2k crim, blk & gold .25 .20
3032 A1507 3k ultra & gold .30 .20
3033 A1507 4k green & gold .45 .20
3034 A1507 4k violet & gold .45 .20
3035 A1507 6k dp claret & gold .60 .20
3036 A1507 10k plum & gold 1.25 .20
3037 A1507 12k blk, red & gold 1.40 .20
3038 A1507 16k lilac rose & gold 1.50 .20
3039 A1507 20k red, blk & gold 2.50 .30
Nos. 3030-3039 (10) 8.95 2.10

20th anniv. of the end of World War II. Issued Apr. 25-May 1.

Souvenir Sheet

From Popov's Radio to Space Telecommunications — A1508

1965, May 7 **Litho.** ***Perf. 11½***

3040 A1508 1r blue & multi 5.50 3.00

70th anniv. of Aleksandr S. Popov's radio pioneer work. No. 3040 contains 6 labels without denominations or country name.

Marx, Lenin and Crowd with Flags — A1509

1965, May 9 **Photo.** ***Perf. 12x12½***

3041 A1509 6k red & black .30 .20

6th conference of Postal Ministers of Communist Countries, Peking, June 21-July 15.

Bolshoi Theater, Moscow — A1510

1965, May 20 ***Perf. 11x11½***

3042 A1510 6k grnsh blue, bis & blk .30 .20

International Theater Day.

Col. Pavel Belyayev
A1511

Design: No. 3044, Lt. Col. Alexei Leonov.

1965, May 23 ***Perf. 12x11½***

3043 A1511 6k magenta & silver .30 .20
3044 A1511 6k purple & silver .30 .20

Space flight of Voskhod 2, Mar. 18-19, 1965, and the 1st man walking in space, Lt. Col. Alexei Leonov.

Sverdlov
A1512

Grothewohl
A1513

Portrait: No. 3046, Juldash Akhunbabaev.

Photogravure and Engraved

1965, May 30 ***Perf. 11½x12***

3045 A1512 4k orange brn & blk .60 .30
3046 A1512 4k lt violet & blk .60 .30

Yakov M. Sverdlov, 1885-1919, 1st pres. of USSR, and J. Akhunbabaev, 1885-1943, pres. of Uzbek Republic.

1965, June 12 **Photo.** ***Perf. 12***

3051 A1513 4k black & magenta .30 .20

Otto Grotewohl, prime minister of the German Democratic Republic (1894-1964).

Maurice Thorez
A1514

Communica-tion by Satellite
A1515

1965, June 12

3052 A1514 6k brown & red .30 .20

Maurice Thorez (1900-1964), chairman of the French Communist party.

1965, June 15 **Litho.**

Designs: No. 3054, Pouring ladle, steel mill and map of India. No. 3055, Stars, satellites and names of international organizations.

3053 A1515 3k olive, blk & gold .25 .20
3054 A1515 6k emer, dk grn & gold .25 .20
3055 A1515 6k vio blue, gold & blk .25 .20
Nos. 3053-3055 (3) .75 .60

Emphasizing international cooperation through communication, economic cooperation and international organizations.

Symbols of Chemistry
A1516

1965, June 15 **Photo.** ***Perf. 11½***

3056 A1516 4k blk, brt rose & brt bl .30 .20

20th Cong. of the Intl. Union of Pure and Applied Chemistry (IUPAC), Moscow. The bright rose ink is fluorescent.

V. A. Serov
A1517

Design: 6k, Full-length portrait of Feodor Chaliapin, the singer, by Serov.

1965, June 25 **Typo.** ***Perf. 12½***

3057 A1517 4k red brn, buff & blk .30 .25
3058 A1517 6k olive bister & black .30 .25

Serov (1865-1911), historical painter.

Abay Kunanbaev, Kazakh Poet — A1518

Designs (writers and poets): No. 3060, Vsevolod Ivanov (1895-1963). No. 3060A, Eduard Vilde, Estonian writer. No. 3061, Mark Kropivnitsky, Ukrainian playwright. No. 3062, Manuk Apeghyan, Armenian writer and critic. No. 3063, Musa Djalil, Tartar poet. No. 3064, Hagop Hagopian, Armenian poet. No. 3064A, Djalil Mamedkulizade, Azerbaijan writer.

1965-66 **Photo.** ***Perf. 12½x12***

3059 A1518 4k lt violet & blk .55 .30
3060 A1518 4k rose lilac & blk .55 .30
3060A A1518 4k gray & black .55 .30
3061 A1518 4k black & org brn .55 .30

Perf. 12½

Typo.

3062 A1518 4k crim, blue grn & blk .55 .30

Perf. 11½

Photogravure and Engraved

3063 A1518 4k black & org brn ('66) .55 .30
3064 A1518 4k grn & blk ('66) .55 .30

Photo.

3064A A1518 4k Prus green & blk ('66) .55 .30
Nos. 3059-3064A (8) 4.40 2.40

Sizes: Nos. 3059-3062, 38x25mm. Nos. 3063-3064A, 35x23mm.

Jan Rainis
A1518a

1965, Sept. 8 **Photo.** ***Perf. 12½x12***

3064B A1518a 4k dull blue & black .35 .25

Rainis (1865-1929), Latvian playwright. "Rainis" was pseudonym of Jan Plieksans.

Film, Screen, Globe and Star
A1519

1965, July 5 **Litho.** ***Perf. 12***

3065 A1519 6k brt blue, gold & blk .35 .20

4th Intl. Film Festival, Moscow: "For Humanism in Cinema Art, for Peace and Friendship among Nations."

Concert Bowl, Tallinn
A1520

"Lithuania"
A1521

"Latvia"
A1522

1965, July *Perf. 12x11½, 11½x12*

3066 A1520 4k ultra, blk, red & ocher .30 .20
3067 A1521 4k red & brown .30 .20
3068 A1522 4k yel, red & blue .30 .20
Nos. 3066-3068 (3) .90 .60

25th anniversaries of Estonia, Lithuania and Latvia as Soviet Republics. Issued: #3066, 7/7; #3067, 7/14; #3068, 7/16.

"Keep Peace" — A1523

1965, July 10 **Photo.** *Perf. 11x11½*

3069 A1523 6k yellow, black & blue .40 .20

Protesting Women and Czarist Eagle
A1524

Designs: No. 3071, Soldier attacking distributor of handbills. No. 3072, Fighters on barricades with red flag. No. 3073, Monument for sailors of Battleship "Potemkin," Odessa.

1965, July 20 **Litho.** *Perf. 11½*

3070 A1524 4k black, red & ol grn .25 .20
3071 A1524 4k red, ol green & blk .25 .20
3072 A1524 4k red, black & brn .25 .20
3073 A1524 4k red & violet blue .25 .20
Nos. 3070-3073 (4) 1.00 .80

60th anniversary of the 1905 revolution.

Gheorghe Gheorghiu-Dej (1901-1965), President of Romanian State Council (1961-1965)
A1525

1965, July 26 **Photo.** *Perf. 12*

3074 A1525 4k black & red .30 .20

Relay Race
A1526

Sport: No. 3076, Bicycle race. No. 3077, Gymnast on vaulting horse.

1965, Aug. 5 **Litho.** *Perf. 12½x12*

3075 A1526 4k vio blue, bis brn & red brown .30 .20
3076 A1526 4k buff, red brn, gray & maroon .30 .20
3077 A1526 4k bl, mar, buff & lt brn .35 .20
Nos. 3075-3077 (3) .95 .60

8th Trade Union Spartacist Games.

Electric Power
A1527

Designs: 2k, Metals in modern industry. 3k, Modern chemistry serving the people. 4k, Mechanization, automation and electronics. 6k, New materials for building industry. 10k, Mechanization and electrification of agriculture. 12k, Technological progress in transportation. 16k, Application of scientific discoveries to industry.

1965, Aug. 5 **Photo.** *Perf. 12x11½*

3078 A1527 1k olive, bl & blk .20 .20
3079 A1527 2k org, blk & yel .20 .20
3080 A1527 3k yel, vio & bister .20 .20
3081 A1527 4k ultra, ind & red .25 .20
3082 A1527 6k ultra & bister .35 .20
3083 A1527 10k yel, org & red brn .70 .20
3084 A1527 12k Prus blue & red .80 .20
3085 A1527 16k rose lilac, blk & violet blue 1.25 .30
Nos. 3078-3085 (8) 3.95 1.70

Creation of the material and technical basis of communism.

Gymnast — A1528 Javelin and Running — A1529

Design: 6k, Bicycling.

1965, Aug. 12 *Perf. 11½*

3086 A1528 4k multi & red .25 .20
3087 A1528 6k grnsh bl, red & brn .25 .20

9th Spartacist Games for school children.

1965, Aug. 27

Designs: 6k, High jump and shot put. 10k, Hammer throwing and hurdling.

3088 A1529 4k brn, lilac & red .25 .20
3089 A1529 6k brn, yel green & red .25 .20
3090 A1529 10k brn, chlky bl & red .60 .20
Nos. 3088-3090 (3) 1.10 .60

US-Russian Track and Field Meet, Kiev.

Worker and Globe — A1530

Designs: No 3092, Heads of three races and torch. No. 3093, Woman with dove.

1965, Sept. 1

3091 A1530 6k dk purple & tan .30 .20
3092 A1530 6k brt bl, brn & red org .30 .20
3093 A1530 6k Prus green & tan .30 .20
Nos. 3091-3093 (3) .90 .60

Intl. Fed. of Trade Unions (#3091), Fed. of Democratic Youth (#3092), Democratic Women's Fed. (#3093), 20th annivs.

Flag of North Viet Nam, Factory and Palm — A1531

1965, Sept. 1 **Litho.** *Perf. 12*

3094 A1531 6k red, yel, brn & gray .50 .30

Republic of North Viet Nam, 20th anniv.

Scene from Film "Potemkin"
A1532

Film Scenes: 6k, "Young Guard." 12k, "Ballad of a Soldier."

1965, Sept. 29 **Litho.** *Perf. 12½x12*

3095 A1532 4k blue, blk & red .35 .25
3096 A1532 6k multicolored .35 .25
3097 A1532 12k multicolored .55 .25
Nos. 3095-3097 (3) 1.25 .75

Post Rider, 16th Century — A1533

History of the Post: No. 3099, Mail coach, 17th-18th centuries. 2k, Train, 19th century. 4k, Mail truck, 1920. 6k, Train, ship and plane. 12k, New Moscow post office, helicopter, automatic sorting and canceling machines. 16k, Lenin, airport and map of USSR.

1965 **Photo.** **Unwmk.** *Perf. 11½x12*

3098 A1533 1k org brn, dk gray & dk green .35 .30
3099 A1533 1k gray, ocher & dk brown .35 .30
3100 A1533 2k dl lil, brt bl & brn .20 .20
3101 A1533 4k bis, rose lake & blk .35 .20
3102 A1533 6k pale brn, Prus grn & black .55 .20
3103 A1533 12k lt ultra, lt brn & blk 1.10 .40
3104 A1533 16k gray, rose red & vio black 1.10 .55
Nos. 3098-3104 (7) 4.00 2.15

For overprint see No. 3175.

Atomic Icebreaker "Lenin"
A1534

#3106, Icebreakers "Taimir" and "Vaigitch." 6k, Dickson Settlement. 10k, Sailing ships "Vostok" and "Mirni," Bellinghausen-Lazarev expedition & icebergs. 16k, Vostok South Pole station.

1965, Oct. 23 **Litho.** *Perf. 12*

Size: 37x25mm

3106 A1534 4k bl, blk & org .25 .25
3107 A1534 4k bl, blk & org .25 .25
a. Pair #3106-3107 .60 .50
3108 A1534 6k sepia & dk vio .65 .25

Size: 33x33mm

3109 A1534 10k red, black & buff .80 .25

Size: 37x25mm

3110 A1534 16k vio blk & red brn 1.00 .25
Nos. 3106-3110 (5) 2.95 1.25

Scientific conquests of the Arctic and Antarctic. No. 3107a has continuous design.

Souvenir Sheet

Basketball, Map of Europe and Flags — A1535

1965, Oct. 29 **Litho.** *Imperf.*

3111 A1535 1r multicolored 4.00 1.00

14th European Basketball Championship, Moscow.

Timiryazev Agriculture Academy, Moscow — A1536

1965, Oct. 30 **Photo.** *Perf. 11*

3112 A1536 4k brt car, gray & vio bl .30 .20

Agriculture Academy, Moscow, cent.

Souvenir Sheet

Lenin — A1537

Lithographed and Engraved

1965, Oct. 30 *Imperf.*

3113 A1537 10k sil, blk & dp org 5.00 1.00

48th anniv. of the October Revolution.

Nicolas Poussin (1594-1665), French Painter — A1538

1965, Nov. 16 Photo. *Perf. 11½*

3114	A1538	4k gray blue, dk bl & dk brown	.30	.20

Kremlin A1539

1965, Nov. 16 *Perf. 12x11½*

3115	A1539	4k black, ver & silver	.30	.20

New Year 1966.

Mikhail Ivanovich Kalinin (1875-1946), USSR President (1923-1946) A1540

1965, Nov. 19 *Perf. 12½*

3116	A1540	4k dp claret & red	.30	.20

Klyuchevskaya Sopka — A1541

Kamchatka Volcanoes: 12k, Karumski erupting, vert. 16k, Koryakski snowcovered.

1965, Nov. 30 Litho. *Perf. 12*

3117	A1541	4k multicolored	.20	.20
3118	A1541	12k multicolored	.45	.20
3119	A1541	16k multicolored	.75	.20
		Nos. 3117-3119 (3)	1.40	.60

October Subway Station, Moscow — A1542

Subway Stations: No. 3121, Lenin Avenue, Moscow. No. 3122, Moscow Gate, Leningrad. No. 3123, Bolshevik Factory, Kiev.

1965, Nov. 30 Engr.

3120	A1542	6k indigo	.30	.25
3121	A1542	6k brown	.30	.25
3122	A1542	6k gray brown	.30	.25
3123	A1542	6k slate green	.30	.25
		Nos. 3120-3123 (4)	1.20	1.00

Buzzard — A1543

Birds: 2k, Kestrel. 3k, Tawny eagle. 4k, Red kite. 10k, Peregrine falcon. 12k, Golden eagle, horiz. 14k, Lammergeier, horiz. 16k, Gyrfalcon.

1965 Photo. *Perf. 11½x12*

3124	A1543	1k gray grn & black	.20	.20
3125	A1543	2k pale brn & blk	.25	.20
3126	A1543	3k lt ol grn & black	.25	.20
3127	A1543	4k lt gray brn & blk	.35	.20
3128	A1543	10k lt vio brn & blk	.75	.25
3129	A1543	12k blue & black	1.00	.35
3130	A1543	14k bluish gray & blk	1.10	.45
3131	A1543	16k dl red brn & blk	1.10	.50
		Nos. 3124-3131 (8)	5.00	2.35

Issued: 4k, 10k, Nov.; 1k, 2k, 12k, 14k, 12/24; 3k, 16k, 12/29.

Red Star Medal, War Scene and View of Kiev A1544

Red Star Medal, War Scene and view of: No. 3133, Leningrad. No. 3134, Odessa. No. 3135, Moscow. No. 3136, Brest Litovsk. No.3137, Volgograd (Stalingrad). No. 3138, Sevastopol.

1965, Dec. *Perf. 11½*

Red, Gold and:

3132	A1544	10k brown	.45	.20
3133	A1544	10k dark blue	.45	.20
3134	A1544	10k Prussian blue	.45	.20
3135	A1544	10k dark violet	.45	.20
3136	A1544	10k dark brown	.45	.20
3137	A1544	10k black	.45	.20
3138	A1544	10k gray	.45	.20
		Nos. 3132-3138 (7)	3.15	1.40

Honoring the heroism of various cities during World War II.
Issued: #3136-3138, 12/30; others, 12/20.

Map and Flag of Yugoslavia, and National Assembly Building A1545

1965, Dec. 30 Litho. *Perf. 12*

3139	A1545	6k vio blue, red & bis	.40	.20

Republic of Yugoslavia, 20th anniv.

Collective Farm Watchman by S.V. Gerasimov A1547

Painting: 16k, "Major's Courtship" by Pavel Andreievitch Fedotov, horiz.

1965, Dec. 31 Engr.

3145	A1547	12k red & sepia	1.10	.25
3146	A1547	16k red & dark blue	1.40	.50

Painters: Gerasimov, 80th birth anniv; Pavel A. Fedotov (1815-52).

Turkeys, Geese, Chicken and Globe A1548

Congress Emblems: No. 3147, Microscope and Moscow University. No. 3149, Crystals. No. 3150, Oceanographic instruments and ship. No. 3151, Mathematical symbols.

1966 Photo. *Perf. 11½*

3147	A1548	6k dull bl, blk & red	.25	.20
3148	A1548	6k gray, pur & black	.25	.20
3149	A1548	6k ol bis, blk & bl	.25	.20
3150	A1548	6k grnsh blue & blk	.25	.20
3151	A1548	6k dull yel, red brn & blk	.25	.20
		Nos. 3147-3151 (5)	1.25	1.00

Intl. congresses to be held in Moscow: 9th Cong. of Microbiology (#3147); 13th Cong. on Poultry Raising (#3148); 7th Cong. on Crystallography (#3149); 2nd Intl. Cong. of Oceanography (#3150); Intl. Cong. of Mathematicians (#3151).

See Nos. 3309-3310.

Mailman and Milkmaid, 19th Century Figurines — A1549

1966, Jan. 28 Litho.

3152	A1549	6k shown	.25	.25
3153	A1549	10k Tea set	.35	.25

Bicentenary of Dimitrov Porcelain Works.

Romain Rolland (1866-1944), French Writer — A1550

Portrait: No. 3155, Eugène Pottier (1816-1887), French poet and author of the "International."

1966 Photo. & Engr. *Perf. 11½*

3154	A1550	4k dk blue & brn org	.30	.20
3155	A1550	4k sl, red & dk red brn	.30	.20

Horseback Rider, and Flags of Mongolia and USSR — A1551

1966, Jan. 31 Litho. *Perf. 12½x12*

3159	A1551	4k red, ultra & vio brn	.35	.25

20th anniversary of the signing of the Mongolian-Soviet treaty of friendship and mutual assistance.

No. 2728 Overprinted in Silver

1966, Feb. 5 Photo. *Perf. 12*

3160	A1385	6k blk, lt blue & red	5.00	2.00

1st soft landing on the moon by Luna 9, Feb. 3, 1966.

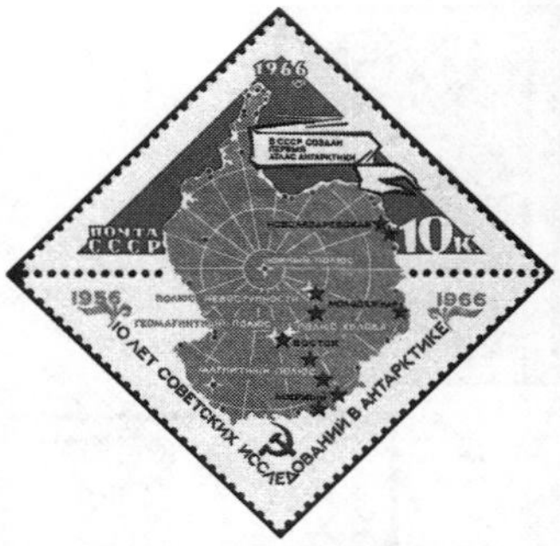

Map of Antarctica With Soviet Stations — A1552

Diesel Ship "Ob" and Emperor Penguins — A1553

#3164, Snocat tractors and aurora australis.

1966, Feb. 14 Photo. *Perf. 11*

3162	A1552	10k sky bl, sil & dk car	.70	.25
3163	A1553	10k silver & dk car	.70	.25
3164	A1553	10k dk car, sil & sky bl	.70	.25
a.		Strip of 3, #3162-3164	2.25	.75

10 years of Soviet explorations in Antarctica. No. 3162 has horizontal rows of perforation extending from either mid-side up to the map.

Lenin A1554

1966, Feb. 22 Photo. *Perf. 12x11½*

3165	A1554	10k grnsh black & gold	.65	.25
3166	A1554	10k dk red & silver	.65	.25

96th anniversary of the birth of Lenin.

N.Y. Iljin, Guardsman A1555

Soviet Heroes: #3168, Lt. Gen. G. P. Kravchenko. #3169, Pvt. Anatoli Uglovsky.

1966 *Perf. 11½x12*

3167	A1555	4k dp org & vio black	.30	.25
3168	A1555	4k grnsh bl & dk pur	.30	.25
3169	A1555	4k green & brown	.30	.25
		Nos. 3167-3169 (3)	.90	.75

Kremlin Congress Hall — A1556

1966, Feb. 28 Typo. *Perf. 12*
3172 A1556 4k gold, red & lt ultra .30 .20

23rd Communist Party Congress.

Hamlet and Queen from Film "Hamlet" A1557

Film Scene: 4k, Two soldiers from "The Quick and the Dead."

1966, Feb. 28 Litho.
3173 A1557 4k red, black & olive .35 .20
3174 A1557 10k ultra & black .35 .20

No. 3104 Overprinted

1966, Mar. 10 Photo. *Perf. 11½x12*
3175 A1533 16k multicolored 2.00 1.00

Constituent assembly of the All-Union Society of Philatelists, 1966.

Emblem and Skater — A1558

Designs: 6k, Emblem and ice hockey. 10k, Emblem and slalom skier.

1966, Mar. 11 *Perf. 11*
3176 A1558 4k ol, brt ultra & red .35 .20
3177 A1558 6k bluish lilac, red & dk brown .50 .20
3178 A1558 10k lt bl, red & dk brn .65 .20
Nos. 3176-3178 (3) 1.50 .60

Second Winter Spartacist Games, Sverdlovsk. The label-like upper halves of Nos. 3176-3178 are separated from the lower halves by a row of perforations.

Electric Locomotive — A1559

Designs: 6k, Map of the Lenin Volga-Baltic Waterway, Admiralty, Leningrad, and Kremlin. 10k, Ship passing through lock in waterway, vert. 12k, M.S. Aleksander Pushkin. 16k, Passenger liner and globe.

1966 Litho. *Perf. 12½x12, 12x12½*
3179 A1559 4k multicolored .20 .20
3180 A1559 6k gray, ultra, red & black .20 .20
3181 A1559 10k Prus bl, gray brn & black .45 .20
3182 A1559 12k blue, ver & blk .40 .20
3183 A1559 16k blue & multi .55 .20
Nos. 3179-3183 (5) 1.80 1.00

Modern transportation.
Issued: #3179-3181, 8/6; #3182-3183, 3/25.

Supreme Soviet Building, Frunze — A1560

Sergei M. Kirov — A1561

1966, Mar. 25 Photo. *Perf. 12*
3184 A1560 4k deep red .35 .25

40th anniv. of the Kirghiz Republic.

1966 Engr. *Perf. 12*

Portraits: No. 3186, Grigori Ordzhonikidze. No. 3187, Ion Yakir.

3185 A1561 4k dk red brown .50 .25
3186 A1561 4k slate green .50 .25
3187 A1561 4k dark gray violet .50 .25
Nos. 3185-3187 (3) 1.50 .75

Kirov (1886-1934), revolutionist and Secretary of the Communist Party Central Committee; Ordzhonikidze (1886-1937), a political leader of the Red Army and government official; Yakir, military leader in October Revolution, 70th birth anniv.
Issued: #3185, 3/27; #3186, 6/22; #3187, 7/30.

Souvenir Sheet

Lenin — A1563

Embossed and Typographed
1966, Mar. 29 *Imperf.*
3188 A1563 50k red & silver 3.00 1.00

23rd Communist Party Congress.

Aleksandr E. Fersman (1883-1945), Mineralogist A1564

Soviet Scientists: #3190, D. K. Zabolotny (1866-1929), microbiologist. #3191, M. A. Shatelen (1866-1957), physicist. #3191A, Otto Yulievich Schmidt (1891-1956), scientist and arctic explorer.

1966, Mar. 30 Litho. *Perf. 12½x12*
3189 A1564 4k vio blue & multi .50 .25
3190 A1564 4k red brn & multi .50 .25
3191 A1564 4k lilac & multi .50 .25
3191A A1564 4k Prus bl & brn .50 .25
Nos. 3189-3191A (4) 2.00 1.00

Luna 10 Automatic Moon Station — A1565

Overprinted in Red:

„Луна-10"—XXIII съезду КПСС

1966, Apr. 8 Typo. *Imperf.*
3192 A1565 10k gold, blk, brt bl & brt rose 1.75 .60

Launching of the 1st artificial moon satellite, Luna 10. The bright rose ink is fluorescent on Nos. 3192-3194.

Type A1565 Without Overprint

Design: 12k, Station on moon.

1966, Apr. 12 *Perf. 12*
3193 A1565 10k multicolored .40 .30
3194 A1565 12k multicolored .60 .30

Day of Space Research, Apr. 12, 1966.

Molniya 1 and Television Screens A1566

Ernst Thälmann A1567

1966, Apr. 12 Litho. *Perf. 12½*
3195 A1566 10k gold, blk, brt bl & red .50 .25

Launching of the communications satellite "Lightning 1," Apr. 23, 1965.

1966-67 Engr. *Perf. 12½x12*

Portraits: No. 3197, Wilhelm Pieck. No. 3198, Sun Yat-sen. No. 3199, Sen Katayama.

3196 A1567 6k rose claret .50 .25
3197 A1567 6k blue violet .50 .25
3198 A1567 6k reddish brown .50 .25

Photo.

3199 A1567 6k gray green ('67) .50 .25
Nos. 3196-3199 (4) 2.00 1.00

Thälmann (1886-1944), German Communist leader; Pieck (1876-1960), German Dem. Rep. Pres.; Sun Yat-sen (1866-1925), leader of the Chinese revolution; Katayama (1859-1933), founder of Social Democratic Party in Japan in 1901.
Issued: #3196, 4/16; #3197-3198, 6/22; #3199, 11/2/67.

Soldier, 1917, and Astronaut A1568

1966, Apr. 30 Litho. *Perf. 11½*
3200 A1568 4k brt rose & black .30 .20

15th Congress of the Young Communist League (Komsomol).

Ice Hockey Player — A1569

1966, Apr. 30
3201 A1569 10k red, ultra, gold & black .40 .25

Soviet victory in the World Ice Hockey Championships. For souvenir sheet see No. 3232. For overprint see No. 3315.

Nicolai Kuznetsov A1570

Heroes of Guerrilla Warfare during WWII (Gold Star of Hero of the Soviet Union and): No. 3203, Imant Sudmalis. No. 3204, Anya Morozova. No. 3205, Filipp Strelets. No. 3206, Tikhon Rumazhkov.

1966, May 9 Photo. *Perf. 12x12½*
3202 A1570 4k green & black .20 .20
3203 A1570 4k ocher & black .20 .20
3204 A1570 4k blue & black .20 .20
3205 A1570 4k brt rose & black .20 .20
3206 A1570 4k violet & black .20 .20
Nos. 3202-3206 (5) 1.00 1.00

Peter I. Tchaikovsky A1571

4k, Moscow State Conservatory, Tchaikovsky monument. 16k, Tchaikovsky House, Klin.

1966, May 26 Typo. *Perf. 12½*
3207 A1571 4k red, yel & black .25 .25
3208 A1571 6k yel, red & black .40 .30
3209 A1571 16k red, bluish gray & black .85 .35
Nos. 3207-3209 (3) 1.50 .90

Third International Tchaikovsky Contest, Moscow, May 30-June 29.

Runners — A1572

Designs: 6k, Weight lifters. 12k, Wrestlers.

1966, May 26 Photo. *Perf. 11x11½*
3210 A1572 4k emer, olive & brn .20 .20
3211 A1572 6k org, blk & lt brn .30 .20
3212 A1572 12k grnsh bl, brn ol & black .45 .20
Nos. 3210-3212 (3) .95 .60

No. 3210, Znamensky Brothers Intl. Track Competitions; No. 3211, Intl. Weightlifting Competitions; No. 3212, Intl. Wrestling Competitions for Ivan Poddubny Prize.

Jules Rimet World Soccer Cup, Ball and Laurel — A1573

Chessboard, Gold Medal, Pawn and King A1574

Designs: No. 3214, Soccer. 12k, Fencers. 16k, Fencer, mask, foil and laurel branch.

1966, May 31 Litho. *Perf. 11½*

3213	A1573	4k rose red, gold & black	.20	.20
3214	A1573	6k emer, tan, blk & red	.30	.20
3215	A1574	6k brn, gold, blk & white	.30	.20
3216	A1573	12k brt bl, ol & blk	.70	.20
3217	A1573	16k multicolored	.75	.20
		Nos. 3213-3217 (5)	2.25	1.00

Nos. 3213-3214 for World Cup Soccer Championship, Wembley, England, July 11-30; No. 3215 the World Chess Title Match between Tigran Petrosian and Boris Spassky; Nos. 3216-3217 the World Fencing Championships. For souvenir sheet see No. 3232.

Sable and Lake Baikal, Map of Barguzin Game Reserve — A1575

Design: 6k, Map of Lake Baikal region and Game Reserve, brown bear on lake shore.

1966, June 25 Photo. *Perf. 12*

3218	A1575	4k steel blue & black	.35	.25
3219	A1575	6k rose lake & black	.35	.25

Barguzin Game Reserve, 50th anniv.

Pink Lotus — A1576

6k, Palms and cypresses. 12k, Victoria cruziana.

1966, June 30 *Perf. 11½*

3220	A1576	3k grn, pink & yel	.20	.20
3221	A1576	6k grnsh bl, ol brn & dk brn	.30	.20
3222	A1576	12k multicolored	.50	.20
		Nos. 3220-3222 (3)	1.00	.60

Sukhum Botanical Garden, 125th anniv.

Dogs Ugolek and Veterok after Space Flight A1577

Designs: No. 3224, Diagram of Solar System, globe and medal of Venus 3 flight. No. 3225, Luna 10, earth and moon.

1966, July 15 *Perf. 12x11½*

3223	A1577	6k ocher, ind & org brn	.30	.20
3224	A1577	6k crim, blk & silver	.30	.20

Perf. 12x12½

3225	A1577	6k dk blue & bister brn	.30	.20
		Nos. 3223-3225 (3)	.90	.60

Soviet achievements in space.

Itkol Hotel, Mount Cheget and Map of USSR A1578

Arch of General Headquarters, Winter Palace and Alexander Column A1579

Resort Areas: 4k, Ship on Volga River and Zhigul Mountain. 10k, Castle, Kislovodsk. 12k, Ismail Samani Mausoleum, Bukhara, Uzbek. 16k, Hotel Caucasus, Sochi.

1966 Litho. *Perf. 12½x12, 12½ (6k)*

3226	A1578	1k multicolored	.20	.20
3227	A1578	4k multicolored	.20	.20
3228	A1579	6k multicolored	.20	.20
3229	A1578	10k multicolored	.25	.20
3230	A1578	12k multicolored	.40	.20
3231	A1578	16k multicolored	.55	.20
		Nos. 3226-3231 (6)	1.80	1.20

Issue dates: 10k, Sept. 14; others, July 20.

Souvenir Sheet

A1580

1966, July 26 Litho. *Perf. 11½*

3232	A1580	Sheet of 4	10.00	1.75
a.		10k Fencers	2.00	.40
b.		10k Chess	2.00	.40
c.		10k Soccer cup	2.00	.40
d.		10k Ice hockey	2.00	.40

World fencing, chess, soccer and ice hockey championships.

See Nos. 3201, 3213-3217.

Congress Emblem, Congress Palace and Kremlin Tower — A1581

1966, Aug. 6 Photo. *Perf. 11½x12*

3233	A1581	4k brown & yellow	.30	.20

Consumers' Cooperative Societies, 7th Cong.

Dove, Crane, Russian and Japanese Flags A1582

1966, Aug. 9 *Perf. 12½x11½*

3234	A1582	6k gray & red	.40	.25

Soviet-Japanese friendship, and 2nd meeting of Russian and Japanese delegates at Khabarovsk.

"Knight Fighting with Tiger" by Rustaveli A1583

Designs: 4k, Shota Rustaveli, bas-relief. 6k, "Avtandil at a Mountain Spring." 50k, Shota Rustaveli Monument and design of 3k stamp.

1966, Aug. 31 Engr. *Perf. 11½x12½*

3235	A1583	3k blk, *olive green*	.25	.20
3236	A1583	4k brown, *yellow*	.25	.20
3237	A1583	6k bluish black, *lt ultra*	.35	.20
		Nos. 3235-3237 (3)	.85	.60

Souvenir Sheet

Imperf

Engraved and Photogravure

3238	A1583	50k slate grn & bis	3.50	1.25

800th anniv. of the birth of Shota Rustaveli, Georgian poet, author of "The Knight in the Tiger's Skin." No. 3238 contains one 32x49mm stamp; dark green margin with design of 6k stamp.

Coat of Arms and Fireworks over Moscow A1584

Lithographed (Lacquered)

1966, Sept. 14 *Perf. 11½*

3239	A1584	4k multicolored	.30	.20

49th anniversary of October Revolution.

Grayling A1585

Designs (Fish and part of design of 6k stamp): 4k, Sturgeon. 6k, Trawler, net and map of Lake Baikal, vert. 10k, Two Baikal cisco. 12k, Two Baikal whitefish.

1966, Sept. 25 Photo. & Engr.

3240	A1585	2k multicolored	.20	.20
3241	A1585	4k multicolored	.20	.20
3242	A1585	6k multicolored	.30	.20
3243	A1585	10k multicolored	.60	.20
3244	A1585	12k gray, dk grn & red brown	.70	.20
		Nos. 3240-3244 (5)	2.00	1.00

Fish resources of Lake Baikal.

Map of USSR and Symbols of Transportation and Communication — A1586

Designs (map of USSR and): No. 3246, Technological education. No. 3247, Agriculture and mining. No. 3248, Increased productivity through five-year plan. No. 3249, Technology and inventions.

1966, Sept. 29 Photo. *Perf. 11½x12*

3245	A1586	4k ultra & silver	.40	.20
3246	A1586	4k car & silver	.40	.20
3247	A1586	4k red brn & silver	.40	.20
3248	A1586	4k red & silver	.40	.20
3249	A1586	4k dp green & silver	.40	.20
		Nos. 3245-3249 (5)	2.00	1.00

23rd Communist Party Congress decisions.

Government House, Kishinev, and Moldavian Flag — A1587

1966, Oct. 8 Litho. *Perf. 12½x12*

3250	A1587	4k multicolored	.50	.30

500th anniversary of Kishinev.

Symbolic Water Cycle A1588

1966, Oct. 12 *Perf. 11½*

3251	A1588	6k multicolored	.35	.20

Hydrological Decade (UNESCO), 1965-1974.

Nikitin Monument in Kalinin, Ship's Prow and Map — A1589

1966, Oct. 12 Photo.

3252	A1589	4k multicolored	.40	.25

Afanasii Nikitin's trip to India, 500th anniv.

Scene from Opera "Nargiz" by M. Magomayev — A1590

#3254, Scene from opera "Kerogli" by Y. Gadjubekov (knight on horseback and armed men).

1966, Oct. 12

3253	A1590	4k	black & ocher	.30	.20
3254	A1590	4k	blk & blue green	.30	.20
a.			Pair, #3253-3254	.60	.20

Azerbaijan opera. Printed in checkerboard arrangement.

Fighters A1591

1966, Oct. 26

3255	A1591	6k	red, blk & ol bister	.40	.20

30th anniversary of Spanish Civil War.

National Militia — A1592

Protest Rally — A1592a

1966, Oct. 26 Litho. ***Perf. 12x12½***

3256	A1592	4k	red & dark brown	.35	.20

25th anniv. of the National Militia.

1966, Oct. 26 ***Perf. 12***

3256A	A1592a	6k	yel, black & red	.40	.25

"Hands off Viet Nam!"

Soft Landing on Moon, Luna 9 — A1593

Symbols of Agriculture and Chemistry A1594

Designs: 1k, Congress Palace, Moscow, and map of Russia. 3k, Boy, girl and Lenin banner. 4k, Flag. 6k, Plane and Ostankino Television Tower. 10k, Soldier and Soviet star. 12k, Steel worker. 16k, "Peace," woman with dove. 20k, Demonstrators in Red Square, flags, carnation and globe. 50k, Newspaper, plane, train and Communications Ministry. 1r, Lenin and industrial symbols.

1966 Litho. ***Perf. 12***

Inscribed "1966"

3257	A1593	1k	dk red brown	.20	.20
3258	A1593	2k	violet	.20	.20
3259	A1593	3k	red lilac	.20	.20
3260	A1593	4k	bright red	.20	.20
3261	A1593	6k	ultra	.20	.20
3262	A1593	10k	olive	.35	.20
3263	A1593	12k	red brown	.65	.20
3264	A1593	16k	violet blue	.70	.20

Perf. 11½

Photo.

3265	A1594	20k	bis, red & dk bl	1.10	.20
3266	A1594	30k	dp grn & green	1.40	.30
3267	A1594	50k	blue & violet bl	3.00	.35
3268	A1594	1r	black & red	4.75	.55
			Nos. 3257-3268 (12)	12.95	3.00

No. 3260 was issued on fluorescent paper in 1969.

See Nos. 3470-3481.

Ostankino Television Tower, Molniya 1 Satellite and Kremlin A1595

1966, Nov. 19 Litho. ***Perf. 12***

3273	A1595	4k	multicolored	.35	.20

New Year, 1967, the 50th anniversary of the October Revolution.

Diagram of Luna 9 Flight — A1596

Arms of Russia and Pennant Sent to Moon — A1597

#3276, Luna 9 & photograph of moonscape.

1966, Nov. 25 Typo. ***Perf. 12***

3274	A1596	10k	black & silver	.50	.25
3275	A1597	10k	red & silver	.50	.25
3276	A1596	10k	black & silver	.50	.25
a.			Strip of 3, #3274-3276	2.00	2.00

Soft landing on the moon by Luna 9, Jan. 31, 1966, and the television program of moon pictures on Feb. 2.

Battle of Moscow, 1941 — A1598

Details from "Defense of Moscow" Medal and Golden Star Medal A1599

25th anniv. of Battle of Moscow: 10k, Sun rising over Kremlin. Ostankino Tower, chemical plant and rockets.

Perf. 12, 11½ (A1599)

1966, Dec. 1 Photo.

3277	A1598	4k	red brown	.20	.20
3278	A1599	6k	bister & brown	.45	.20
3279	A1598	10k	dp bister & yel	.60	.20
			Nos. 3277-3279 (3)	1.25	.60

Cervantes and Don Quixote A1600

1966, Dec. 15 Photo. ***Perf. 11½***

3280	A1600	6k	gray & brown	.30	.20

Miguel Cervantes Saavedra (1547-1616), Spanish writer.

Bering's Ship and Map of Voyage to Commander Islands — A1601

Far Eastern Territories: 2k, Medny Island and map. 4k, Petropavlosk-Kamchatski Harbor. 6k, Geyser, Kamchatka, vert. 10k, Avachinskaya Bay, Kamchatka. 12k, Fur seals, Bering Island. 16k, Guillemots in bird sanctuary, Kuril Islands.

1966, Dec. 25 Litho. ***Perf. 12***

3281	A1601	1k	bister & multi	.20	.20
3282	A1601	2k	bister & multi	.20	.20
3283	A1601	4k	dp blue & multi	.30	.20
3284	A1601	6k	multicolored	.40	.20
3285	A1601	10k	dp blue & multi	.60	.20
3286	A1601	12k	olive & multi	1.00	.20
3287	A1601	16k	lt blue & multi	1.75	.20
			Nos. 3281-3287 (7)	4.45	1.40

Communications Satellite, Molniya 1 — A1602

Design: No. 3289, Luna 11 moon probe, moon, earth and Soviet emblem.

1966, Dec. 29 Photo. ***Perf. 12x11½***

3288	A1602	6k	blk, vio bl & brt rose	.40	.20
3289	A1602	6k	black & brt rose	.40	.20

Space explorations. The bright rose is fluorescent.

Golden Stag, Scythia, 6th Century B.C. — A1603

Treasures from the Hermitage, Leningrad: 6k, Silver jug, Persia, 5th Century A.D. 10k, Statue of Voltaire by Jean Antoine Houdon. 12k, Malachite vase, Ural, 1840. 16k, "The Lute Player," by Michelangelo de Caravaggio. (6k, 10k, 12k are vertical).

1966, Dec. 29 Engr. ***Perf. 12***

3290	A1603	4k	yellow & black	.20	.20
3291	A1603	6k	gray & black	.30	.20
3292	A1603	10k	dull vio & black	.50	.20
3293	A1603	12k	emer & black	.75	.30
3294	A1603	16k	ocher & black	.85	.35
			Nos. 3290-3294 (5)	2.60	1.25

Sea Water Converter and Pavilion at EXPO '67 A1604

Pavilion and: 6k, Splitting atom, vert. 10k, "Proton" space station. 30k, Soviet pavilion.

1967, Jan. 25 Litho. ***Perf. 12***

3295	A1604	4k	multicolored	.25	.20
3296	A1604	6k	multicolored	.25	.20
3297	A1604	10k	multicolored	.30	.20
			Nos. 3295-3297 (3)	.80	.60

Souvenir Sheet

3298	A1604	30k	multicolored	3.00	1.25

EXPO '67, Intl. Exhib., Montreal, 4/28-10/27.

1st Lieut. B. I. Sizov A1605

Design: No. 3300, Sailor V. V. Khodyrev.

1967, Feb. 16 Photo. ***Perf. 12x11½***

3299	A1605	4k	dull yel & ocher	.25	.25
3300	A1605	4k	gray & dk gray	.25	.25

Heroes of World War II.

Woman's Head and Pavlov Shawl — A1606

1967, Feb. 16 ***Perf. 11***

3301	A1606	4k	violet, red & green	.30	.20

International Woman's Day, Mar. 8.

Movie Camera and Film — A1607

1967, Feb. 16 Photo. ***Perf. 11½***

3302	A1607	6k	multicolored	.40	.25

5th Intl. Film Festival, Moscow, July 5-20.

Trawler Fish Factory and Fish — A1608

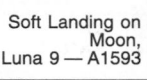

Designs: No. 3304, Refrigerationship. No. 3305, Crab canning ship. No. 3306, Fishing trawler. No. 3307, Black Sea seiner.

1967, Feb. 28 Litho. *Perf. 12x11½*
Ships in Black and Red

3303	A1608	6k blue & gray	.40	.25
3304	A1608	6k blue & gray	.40	.25
3305	A1608	6k blue & gray	.40	.25
3306	A1608	6k blue & gray	.40	.25
3307	A1608	6k blue & gray	.40	.25
a.		Vert. strip of 5, #3303-3307	2.00	1.25

Soviet fishing industry.

Newspaper Forming Hammer and Sickle, Red Flag — A1609

1967, Mar. 13 Litho. *Perf. 12x12½*

3308	A1609	4k cl brn, red, yel & brn	.30	.20

50th anniversary of newspaper Izvestia.

Congress Type of 1966

Congress Emblems and: No. 3309, Moscow State University, construction site and star. No. 3310, Pile driver, mining excavator, crossed hammers, globe and "V."

1967, Mar. 10 Photo. *Perf. 11½*

3309	A1548	6k ultra, brt blue & blk	.30	.20
3310	A1548	6k blk, org red & blue	.30	.20

Intl. congresses to be held in Moscow: 7th General Assembly Session of the Intl. Standards Association (#3309); 5th Intl. Mining Cong. (#3310).

International Tourist Year Emblem and Travel Symbols — A1610

1967, Mar. 10 *Perf. 11*

3314	A1610	4k blk, sky bl & silver	.30	.20

International Tourist Year, 1967.

No. 3201 Overprinted

1967, Mar. 29 Litho. *Perf. 11½*

3315	A1569	10k multicolored	1.50	.75

Victory of the Soviet team in the Ice Hockey Championships, Vienna, Mar. 18-29. Overprint reads: "Vienna-1967."

Space Walk — A1611

Designs: 10k, Rocket launching from satellite. 16k, Spaceship over moon, and earth.

1967, Mar. 30 Litho. *Perf. 12*

3316	A1611	4k bister & multi	.25	.20
3317	A1611	10k black & multi	.70	.20
3318	A1611	16k lilac & multi	1.00	.30
		Nos. 3316-3318 (3)	1.95	.70

National Cosmonauts' Day.

Lenin as Student, by V. Tsigal A1612

Sculptures of Lenin: 3k, Monument at Ulyanovsk by M. Manizer. 4k, Lenin in Razliv, by V. Pinchuk, horiz. 6k, Head, by G. Neroda. 10k, Lenin as Leader, statue, by N. Andreyev.

1967 Photo. *Perf. 12x11½, 11½x12*

3319	A1612	2k ol grn, sepia & buff	.20	.20
3320	A1612	3k maroon & brn	.20	.20
3321	A1612	4k ol black & gold	.30	.20
3322	A1612	6k dk bl, sil & blk	.40	.20
3323	A1612	10k sil, gray bl & blk	.75	.20
3323A	A1612	10k gold, gray & black	.75	.20
		Nos. 3319-3323A (6)	2.60	1.20

97th anniversary of the birth of Lenin.
Issued: #3323A, Oct. 25; others, Apr. 22.

Lt. M. S. Kharchenko and Battle Scenes — A1613

Designs: No. 3325, Maj. Gen. S. V. Rudnev. No. 3326, M. Shmyrev.

1967, Apr. 24 *Perf. 12x11½*

3324	A1613	4k brt purple & ol bis	.25	.20
3325	A1613	4k ultra & ol bister	.25	.20
3326	A1613	4k org brn & ol bister	.25	.20
		Nos. 3324-3326 (3)	.75	.60

Partisan heroes of WWII.

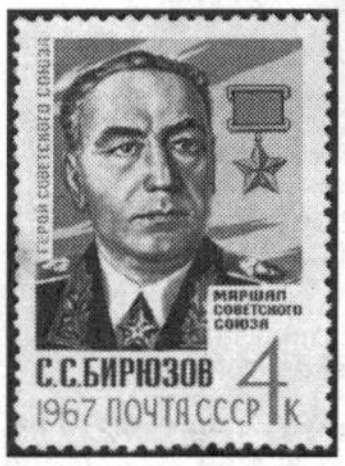

Marshal S. S. Biryuzov, Hero of the Soviet Union — A1614

1967, May 9 Photo. *Perf. 12*

3327	A1614	4k ocher & slate green	.40	.40

Driver Crossing Lake Ladoga A1615

1967, May 9 *Perf. 11½*

3328	A1615	4k plum & blue gray	.30	.20

25th anniversary of siege of Leningrad.

Views of Old and New Minsk A1616

1967, May 9

3329	A1616	4k slate green & black	.35	.20

900th anniversary of Minsk.

Red Cross and Tulip — A1617

1967, May 15 *Perf. 12*

3330	A1617	4k yel brown & red	.30	.20

Centenary of the Russian Red Cross.

Stamps of 1918 and 1967 — A1618

1967 Photo. *Perf. 11½*

3331	A1618	20k blue & black	.90	.30
a.		Souv. sheet of 2, imperf.	4.00	1.25

All-Union Philatelic Exhibition "50 Years of the Great October," Moscow, Oct. 1-10. Se-tenant with label showing exhibition emblem.
Issue dates: 20k, May 25. Sheet, Oct. 1.
No. 3331 was re-issued Oct. 3 with "Oct. 1-10" printed in blue on the label. Value $1.

Komsomolsk-on-Amur and Map of Amur River — A1619

1967, June 12 *Perf. 12x12½*

3332	A1619	4k red & brown	.40	.20

35th anniv. of the Soviet youth town, Komsomolsk-on-Amur. Printed with label showing boy and girl of Young Communist League and tents.

Souvenir Sheet

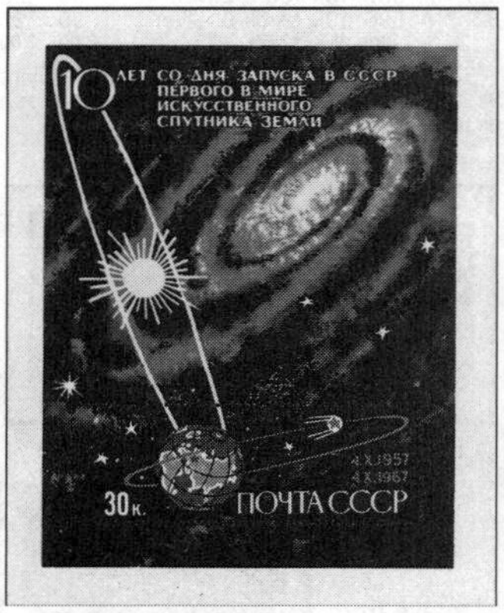

Sputnik Orbiting Earth — A1620

1967, June 24 Litho. *Perf. 13x12*

3333	A1620	30k black & multi	5.00	3.00

10th anniv. of the launching of Sputnik 1, the 1st artificial satellite, Oct. 4, 1957.

Motorcyclist A1621

Photogravure and Engraved
1967, June 24 *Perf. 12x11½*

3334	A1621	10k multicolored	.40	.20

Intl. Motor Rally, Moscow, July 19.

G. D. Gai (1887-1937), Corps Commander of the First Cavalry, 1920 — A1622

1967, June 30 Photo. *Perf. 12*

3335	A1622	4k red & black	.30	.20

Children's Games Emblem and Trophy A1623

1967, July 8 *Perf. 11½*

3336	A1623	4k silver, red & black	.30	.20

10th National Athletic Games of School Children, Leningrad, July, 1967.

Games Emblem and Trophy A1624

#3338, Cup and dancer. #3339, Cup and bicyclists. #3340, Cup and diver.

1967, July 20

3337	A1624	4k silver, red & black	.20	.20
3338	A1624	4k silver, red & black	.20	.20
a.		Pair, #3337-3338	.40	.20
3339	A1624	4k silver, red & black	.20	.20
3340	A1624	4k silver, red & black	.20	.20
a.		Pair, #3339-3340	.40	.20

4th Natl. Spartacist Games, & USSR 50th anniv.
Se-tenant in checkerboard arrangement.

V. G. Klochkov (1911-41), Hero of the Soviet Union — A1625

1967, July 20 *Perf. 12½x12*

3341	A1625	4k red & black	.40	.25

Alternating label shows citation.

Soviet Flag, Arms and Moscow Views A1626

Arms of USSR and Laurel — A1627

#3343

#3344

#3345

#3347

#3349

#3352

#3353

#3354

#3355

#3356

Flag, Crest and Capital of Republic.

1967, Aug. 4 Litho. *Perf. 12½x12*

3342	A1626	4k	shown	.40	.20
3343	A1626	4k	Armenia	.40	.20
3344	A1626	4k	Azerbaijan	.40	.20
3345	A1626	4k	Byelorussia	.40	.20
3346	A1626	4k	Estonia	.40	.20
3347	A1626	4k	Georgia	.40	.20
3348	A1626	4k	Kazakhstan	.40	.20
3349	A1626	4k	Kirghizia	.40	.20
3350	A1626	4k	Latvia	.40	.20
3351	A1626	4k	Lithuania	.40	.20
3352	A1626	4k	Moldavia	.40	.20
3353	A1626	4k	Tadzhikistan	.40	.20
3354	A1626	4k	Turkmenistan	.40	.20
3355	A1626	4k	Ukraine	.40	.20
3356	A1626	4k	Uzbekistan	.40	.20
3357	A1627	4k	red, gold & black	.40	.20
			Nos. 3342-3357 (16)	6.40	3.20

50th anniversary of October Revolution.

Communication Symbols — A1628

1967, Aug. 16 Photo. *Perf. 12*

3358	A1628	4k	crimson & silver	1.50	.30

Development of communications in USSR.

Flying Crane, Dove and Anniversary Emblem — A1629

1967, Aug. 20 *Perf. 12½x12*

3359	A1629	16k	silver, red & blk	.50	.30

Russo-Japanese Friendship Meeting, held at Khabarovsk. Emblem is for 50th anniv. of October Revolution.

Karl Marx and Title Page of "Das Kapital" — A1630

1967, Aug. 22 Engr. *Perf. 12½x12*

3360	A1630	4k	sepia & dk red	.40	.30

Centenary of the publication of "Das Kapital" by Karl Marx.

Russian Checkers Players A1631

Design: 6k, Woman gymnast.

Photogravure and Engraved

1967, Sept. 9 *Perf. 12x11½*

3361	A1631	1k	lt brn, dp brn & sl	.30	.20
3362	A1631	6k	ol bister & maroon	.30	.20

World Championship of Russian Checkers (Shashki) at Moscow, and World Championship of Rhythmic Gymnastics.

Javelin A1632

1967, Sept. 9 Engr. *Perf. 12x12½*

3363	A1632	2k	shown	.25	.20
3364	A1632	3k	Running	.25	.20
3365	A1632	4k	Jumping	.25	.20
			Nos. 3363-3365 (3)	.75	.60

Europa Cup Championships, Kiev, Sept. 15-17.

Ice Skating and Olympic Emblem A1633

Designs: 3k, Ski jump. 4k, Emblem of Winter Olympics, vert. 10k, Ice hockey. 12k, Long-distance skiing.

Photogravure and Engraved

1967, Sept. 20 *Perf. 11½*

3366	A1633	2k	gray, blk & bl	.20	.20
3367	A1633	3k	bis, ocher, blk & green	.20	.20
3368	A1633	4k	gray, bl, red & blk	.20	.20
3369	A1633	10k	bis, brn, bl & blk	.50	.20
3370	A1633	12k	gray, blk, lilac & green	.65	.20
			Nos. 3366-3370 (5)	1.75	1.00

10th Winter Olympic Games, Grenoble, France, Feb. 6-18, 1968.

Silver Fox A1634

Young Guards Memorial A1635

Fur-bearing Animals: 2k, Arctic blue fox, horiz. 6k, Red fox, horiz. 10k, Muskrat, horiz. 12k, Ermine. 16k, Sable. 20k, Mink, horiz.

1967, Sept. 20 Photo.

3371	A1634	2k	brn, blk & gray blue	.20	.20
3372	A1634	4k	tan, dk brn & gray blue	.30	.20
3373	A1634	6k	gray grn, ocher & black	.45	.20
3374	A1634	10k	yel grn, dk brn & ocher	.75	.20
3375	A1634	12k	lilac, blk & bis	.80	.20
3376	A1634	16k	org, brn & black	.90	.20
3377	A1634	20k	gray blue, blk & dk brown	1.10	.30
			Nos. 3371-3377 (7)	4.50	1.50

International Fur Auctions in Leningrad.

1967, Sept. 23

3378	A1635	4k	magenta, org & blk	.30	.20

25th anniv. of the fight of the Young Guards at Krasnodon against the Germans.

Map of Cedar Valley Reservation and Snow Leopard — A1636

1967, Oct. 14 *Perf. 12*

3379	A1636	10k	ol bister & black	.40	.20

Far Eastern Cedar Valley Reservation.

Planes and Emblem A1637

1967, Oct. 14 *Perf. 11½*

3380	A1637	6k	dp blue, red & gold	.30	.20

French Normandy-Neman aviators, who fought on the Russian Front, 25th anniv.

Militiaman and Soviet Emblem A1638

1967, Oct. 14 *Perf. 12½x12*

3381	A1638	4k	ver & ultra	.30	.20

50th anniversary of the Soviet Militia.

Space Station Orbiting Moon — A1639

Science Fiction: 6k, Explorers on the moon, horiz. 10k, Rocket flying to the stars. 12k, Landscape on Red Planet, horiz. 16k, Satellites from outer space.

1967 Litho. *Perf. 12x12½, 12½x12*

3382	A1639	4k	multicolored	.20	.20
3383	A1639	6k	multicolored	.35	.20
3384	A1639	10k	multicolored	.50	.20
3385	A1639	12k	multicolored	.65	.20
3386	A1639	16k	multicolored	.85	.20
			Nos. 3382-3386 (5)	2.55	1.00

Emblem of USSR and Red Star — A1640

Lenin Addressing 2nd Congress of Soviets, by V. A. Serov — A1641

Builders of Communism, by L. M. Merpert and Y. N. Skripkov — A1641a

Paintings: #3389, Lenin pointing to Map, by L. A. Schmatjko, 1957. #3390, The First Cavalry Army, by M. B. Grekov, 1924. #3391, Working Students on the March, by B. V. Yoganson, 1928. #3392, Russian Friendship for the World, by S. M. Karpov, 1924. #3393, Five-Year Plan Morning, by Y. D. Romas, 1934. #3394, Farmers' Holiday, by S. V. Gerasimov, 1937. #3395, Victory in the Great Patriotic War, by Y. K. Korolev, 1965.

Lithographed and Embossed

1967, Oct. 25 *Perf. 11½*

3387	A1640	4k	gold, yel, red & dk brown	.20	.20
3388	A1641	4k	gold & multi	.20	.20
3389	A1641	4k	gold & multi	.20	.20
3390	A1641	4k	gold & multi	.20	.20
3391	A1641	4k	gold & multi	.20	.20
3392	A1641	4k	gold & multi	.20	.20
3393	A1641	4k	gold & multi	.20	.20
3394	A1641	4k	gold & multi	.20	.20
3395	A1641	4k	gold & multi	.20	.20
3396	A1641a	4k	gold & multi	.20	.20
a.			Souvenir sheet of 2	3.00	1.00
			Nos. 3387-3396 (10)	2.00	2.00

50th anniversary of October Revolution. No. 3396a contains two 40k imperf. stamps similar to Nos. 3388 and 3396. Issued Nov. 5.

Souvenir Sheet

Hammer, Sickle and Sputnik — A1642

1967, Nov. 5 Engr. *Perf. 12½x12*

3397	A1642	1r	lake	5.00	2.00

50th anniv. of the October Revolution. Margin contains "50" as a watermark.

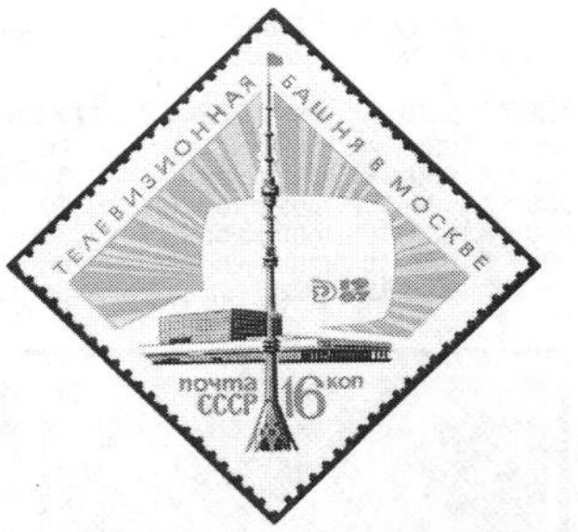

Ostankino Television Tower — A1643

1967, Nov. 5 Litho. *Perf. 11½*

3398 A1643 16k gray, org & black .60 .25

Jurmala Resort and Hepatica A1644

Health Resorts of the Baltic Region: 6k, Narva-Joesuu and Labrador tea. 10k, Druskininkai and cranberry blossoms. 12k, Zelenogradsk and Scotch heather, vert. 16k, Svetlogorsk and club moss, vert.

Perf. 12½x12, 12x12½

1967, Nov. 30 Litho.

Flowers in Natural Colors

3399 A1644 4k blue & black .20 .20
3400 A1644 6k ocher & black .45 .20
3401 A1644 10k green & black .50 .20
3402 A1644 12k gray olive & blk .55 .20
3403 A1644 16k brown & black .75 .20
Nos. 3399-3403 (5) 2.45 1.00

Emergency Commission Emblem — A1645

1967, Dec. 11 Photo. *Perf. 11½*

3404 A1645 4k ultra & red .40 .25

All-Russia Emergency Commission (later the State Security Commission), 50th anniv.

Hotel Russia and Kremlin A1646

1967, Dec. 14

3405 A1646 4k silver, dk brn & brt pink .30 .20

New Year 1968. The pink is fluorescent.

Soldiers, Sailors, Congress Building, Kharkov, and Monument to the Men of Arsenal — A1647

Designs: 6k, Hammer and sickle and scenes from industry and agriculture. 10k, Ukrainians offering bread and salt, monument of the Unknown Soldier, Kiev, and Lenin monument in Zaporozhye.

1967, Dec. 20 Litho. *Perf. 12½*

3406 A1647 4k multicolored .30 .20
3407 A1647 6k multicolored .30 .20
3408 A1647 10k multicolored .35 .20
Nos. 3406-3408 (3) .95 .60

50th anniv. of the Ukrainian SSR.

Three Kremlin Towers A1648

Kremlin: 6k, Cathedral of the Annunciation, horiz. 10k, Konstantin and Elena, Nabatnaya and Spasski towers. 12k, Ivan the Great bell tower. 16k, Kutafya and Troitskaya towers.

Engraved and Photogravure

1967, Dec. 25 *Perf. 12x11½, 11½x12*

3409 A1648 4k dk brn & claret .20 .20
3410 A1648 6k dk brn, yel & grn .20 .20
3411 A1648 10k maroon & slate .55 .20
3412 A1648 12k sl grn, yel & vio .60 .20
3413 A1648 16k brn, pink & red .80 .20
Nos. 3409-3413 (5) 2.35 1.00

Coat of Arms, Lenin's Tomb and Rockets A1649

Designs: No. 3415, Agricultural Progress: Wheat, reapers and silo. No. 3416, Industrial Progress: Computer tape, atom symbol, cogwheel and factories. No. 3417, Scientific Progress: Radar, microscope, university buildings. No. 3418, Communications progress: Ostankino TV tower, railroad bridge, steamer and Aeroflot emblem, vert.

1967, Dec. 25 Engr. *Perf. 12½*

3414 A1649 4k maroon .20 .20
3415 A1649 4k green .20 .20
3416 A1649 4k red brown .20 .20
3417 A1649 4k violet blue .20 .20
3418 A1649 4k dark blue .20 .20
Nos. 3414-3418 (5) 1.00 1.00

Material and technical basis of Russian Communism.

Monument to the Unknown Soldier, Moscow — A1650

1967, Dec. 25

3419 A1650 4k carmine .35 .25

Dedication of the Monument of the Unknown Soldier of WWII in the Kremlin Wall.

Seascape by Ivan Aivazovsky — A1651

Paintings: 3k, Interrogation of Communists by B. V. Yoganson, 1933. #3422, The Lacemaker, by V. A. Tropinin, 1823, vert. #3423, Bread-makers, by T. M. Yablonskaya, 1949. #3424, Alexander Nevsky, by P. D. Korin, 1942-43, vert. #3425, The Boyar Morozov Going into Exile by V. I. Surikov, 1887. #3426, The Swan Maiden, by M. A. Vrubel, 1900, vert. #3427, The Arrest of a Propagandist by Ilya E. Repin, 1878. 16k, Moscow Suburb in February by G. G. Nissky, 1957.

Perf. 12½x12, 12x12½, 12, 11½

1967, Dec. 29 Litho.

Size: 47x33mm, 33x47mm

3420 A1651 3k multicolored .20 .20
3421 A1651 4k multicolored .20 .20
3422 A1651 4k multicolored .20 .20

Size: 60x35mm, 35x60mm

3423 A1651 6k multicolored .20 .20
3424 A1651 6k multicolored .20 .20
3425 A1651 6k multicolored .20 .20

Size: 47x33mm, 33x47mm

3426 A1651 10k multicolored .35 .20
3427 A1651 10k multicolored .35 .20
3428 A1651 16k multicolored .45 .20
Nos. 3420-3428 (9) 2.35 1.80

Tretiakov Art Gallery, Moscow.

Globe, Wheel and Workers of the World — A1652

1968, Jan. 18 Photo. *Perf. 12*

3429 A1652 6k ver & green .35 .20

14th Trade Union Congress.

Lt. S. Baikov and Velikaya River Bridge A1653

Heroes of WWII (War Memorial and): #3431. Lt. A. Pokalchuk. #3432, P. Gutchenko.

1968, Jan. 20 *Perf. 12½x12*

3430 A1653 4k blue gray & black .30 .20
3431 A1653 4k rose & black .30 .20
3432 A1653 4k gray green & black .30 .20
Nos. 3430-3432 (3) .90 .60

Thoroughbred and Horse Race — A1654

Horses: 6k, Arab mare and dressage, vert. 10k, Orlovski trotters. 12k, Altekin horse performing, vert. 16k, Donskay race horse.

1968, Jan. 23 *Perf. 11½*

3433 A1654 4k ultra, blk & red lil .40 .20
3434 A1654 6k crim, blk & ultra .65 .20
3435 A1654 10k grnsh blue, blk & orange .95 .40
3436 A1654 12k org brn, black & apple green 1.25 .50
3437 A1654 16k ol grn, blk & red 1.75 .70
Nos. 3433-3437 (5) 5.00 2.00

Horse breeding.

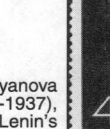

Maria I. Ulyanova (1878-1937), Lenin's Sister — A1655

1968, Jan. 30 *Perf. 12x12½*

3438 A1655 4k indigo & pale green .30 .20

Soviet Star and Flags of Army, Air Force and Navy A1656

Lenin Addressing Troops in 1919 — A1657

#3441, Dneprostroi Dam & sculpture "On Guard." #3442, 1918 poster & marching volunteers. #3443, Red Army entering Vladivostok, 1922, & soldiers' monument in Primorie. #3444, Poster "Red Army as Liberator," Western Ukraine. #3445, Poster "Westward," defeat of German army. #3446, "Battle of Stalingrad" monument & German prisoners of war. #3447, Victory parade on Red Square, May 24, 1945, & Russian War Memorial, Berlin. Nos. 3448-3449, Modern weapons and Russian flag.

1968, Feb. 20 Typo. *Perf. 12x12½*

3439 A1656 4k gold & multi .20 .20

Photo.

Perf. 11½x12

3440 A1657 4k blk, red, pink & silver .20 .20
3441 A1657 4k gold, black & red .20 .20

Litho.

Perf. 12½x12

3442 A1657 4k yel grn, blk, red & buff .20 .20
3443 A1657 4k grn, dk brn, red & bis .20 .20
3444 A1657 4k green & multi .20 .20
3445 A1657 4k yel green & multi .20 .20

Perf. 11½x12, 12x11½

Photo.

3446 A1657 4k blk, silver & red .20 .20
3447 A1657 4k gold, blk, pink & red .20 .20
3448 A1656 4k blk, red & silver .20 .20
Nos. 3439-3448 (10) 2.00 2.00

Souvenir Sheet

1968, Feb. 23 Litho. *Imperf.*

3449 A1656 1r blk, silver & red 3.50 1.50

50th anniv. of the Armed Forces of the USSR. No. 3449 contains one 25x37½mm stamp with simulated perforations.

Maxim Gorki (1868-1936), Writer — A1658

1968, Feb. 29 Photo. *Perf. 12*
3450 A1658 4k gray ol & dk brown .30 .20

Fireman, Fire Truck and Boat — A1659

1968, Mar. 30 Photo. *Perf. 12x12½*
3451 A1659 4k red & black .30 .20

50th anniversary of Soviet Fire Guards.

Link-up of Cosmos 186 and 188 Satellites — A1660

1968, Mar. 30 *Perf. 11½*
3452 A1660 6k blk, dp lilac rose & gold .30 .20

First link-up in space of two satellites, Cosmos 186 and Cosmos 188, Oct. 30, 1967.

N. N. Popudrenko — A1661

Design: No. 3453, P. P. Vershigora.

1968, Mar. 30 *Perf. 12½x12*
3453 A1661 4k gray green & black .30 .20
3454 A1661 4k lt purple & black .30 .20

Partisan heroes of World War II.

Globe and Hand Shielding from War A1662

1968, Apr. 11 *Perf. 11½*
3455 A1662 6k sil, mar, ver & black .50 .35

Emergency session of the World Federation of Trade Unions and expressing solidarity with the people of Vietnam.

Space Walk A1663

6k, Docking operation of Kosmos 186 & Kosmos 188. 10k, Exploration of Venus.

1968, Apr. 12 Litho.
3456 A1663 4k multicolored .20 .20
3457 A1663 6k multicolored .20 .20
3458 A1663 10k multicolored .35 .20
a. Block of 3, #3456-3458 + 3 labels .75 .50

National Astronauts' Day.

Lenin, 1919 A1664

Lenin Portraits: No. 3460, Addressing crowd on Red Square, Nov. 7, 1918. No. 3461, Full-face portrait, taken in Petrograd, Jan. 1918.

Engraved and Photogravure

1968, Apr. 16 *Perf. 12x11½*
3459 A1664 4k gold, brown & red .30 .20
3460 A1664 4k gold, red & black .30 .20
3461 A1664 4k gold, brn, buff & red .30 .20
Nos. 3459-3461 (3) .90 .60

98th anniversary of the birth of Lenin.

Alisher Navoi, Uzbek Poet, 525th Birth Anniv. — A1665

1968, Apr. 29 Photo. *Perf. 12x12½*
3462 A1665 4k deep brown .30 .20

Karl Marx (1818-83) A1666

1968, May 5 Engr. *Perf. 11½x12*
3463 A1666 4k black & red .30 .20

Frontier Guard — A1667 Jubilee Badge — A1668

1968, May 22 Photo. *Perf. 11½*
3464 A1667 4k sl green, ocher & red .30 .20
3465 A1668 6k sl grn, blk & red brn .30 .20

Russian Frontier Guards, 50th anniv.

Crystal and Congress Emblem A1669

Congress Emblems and: No. 3467, Power lines and factories. No. 3468, Ground beetle. No. 3469, Roses and carbon rings.

1968, May 30
3466 A1669 6k blue, dk blue & grn .25 .20
3467 A1669 6k org, gold & dk brn .25 .20
3468 A1669 6k red brn, gold & blk .25 .20
3469 A1669 6k lil rose, org & blk .25 .20
Nos. 3466-3469 (4) 1.00 .80

Intl. congresses, Leningrad: 8th Cong. for Mineral Research; 7th World Power Conf.; 13th Entomological Cong.; 4th Cong. for the Study of Volatile Oils.

Types of 1966

Designs as before.

1968, June 20 Engr. *Perf. 12*
3470 A1593 1k dk red brown .20 .20
3471 A1593 2k deep violet .20 .20
3472 A1593 3k plum .20 .20
3473 A1593 4k bright red .20 .20
3474 A1593 6k blue .40 .20
3475 A1593 10k olive .60 .20
3476 A1593 12k red brown .75 .20
3477 A1593 16k violet blue .90 .20

Perf. 12½
3478 A1594 20k red 1.00 .20
3479 A1594 30k bright green 1.65 .20
3480 A1594 50k violet blue 2.75 .30

Perf. 12x12½
3481 A1594 1r gray, red brn & black 6.00 .50
Nos. 3470-3481 (12) 14.85 2.80

Sadriddin Aini A1670

1968, June 30 Photo. *Perf. 12½x12*
3482 A1670 4k olive bister & mar .30 .20

Aini (1878-1954), Tadzhik poet.

Post Rider and C.C.E.P. Emblem A1671

#3484, Modern means of communications (train, ship, planes and C.C.E.P. emblem).

1968, June 30
3483 A1671 6k gray & red brown .30 .20
3484 A1671 6k orange brn & bister .30 .20

Annual session of the Council of the Consultative Commission on Postal Investigation of the UPU (C.C.E.P.), Moscow, 9/20-10/5.

Bolshevik Uprising, Kiev — A1672

1968, July 5 *Perf. 11½*
3485 A1672 4k gold, red & plum .30 .20

Ukrainian Communist Party, 50th anniv.

Athletes A1673

1968, July 9
3486 A1673 4k yel, dp car & bister .30 .20

1st Youth Summer Sports Games for 50th anniv. of the Leninist Young Communists League.

Field Ball — A1674

Table Tennis A1675

Designs: 6k, 20th Baltic Regatta. 10k, Soccer player and cup. 12k, Scuba divers.

Perf. 12x12½, 12½x12

1968, July 18 Litho.
3487 A1674 2k red & multi .20 .20
3488 A1675 4k purple & multi .20 .20
3489 A1674 6k blue & multi .25 .20
3490 A1674 10k multicolored .35 .20
3491 A1675 12k green & multi .45 .20
Nos. 3487-3491 (5) 1.45 1.00

European youth sports competitions.

Rhythmic Gymnast A1676

6k, Weight lifting. 10k, Rowing. 12k, Women's hurdling. 16k, Fencing. 40k, Running.

1968, July 31 Photo. *Perf. 11½*

Gold Background

3492 A1676 4k blue & green .20 .20
3493 A1676 6k dp rose & pur .30 .20
3494 A1676 10k yel grn & grn .55 .20
3495 A1676 12k org & red brn .60 .20
3496 A1676 16k ultra & pink .70 .20
Nos. 3492-3496 (5) 2.35 1.00

Souvenir Sheet

Perf. 12½x12

Lithographed and Photogravure

3497 A1676 40k gold, grn, org & gray 1.75 1.00

19th Olympic Games, Mexico City, 10/12-27.

Gediminas Tower, Vilnius — A1677

1968, Aug. 14 Photo. *Perf. 11½*
3498 A1677 4k magenta, tan & red .30 .20

Soviet power in Lithuania, 50th anniv.

Tbilisi State University A1678

1968, Aug. 14 ***Perf. 12***
3499 A1678 4k slate grn & lt brn .30 .20

Tbilisi State University, Georgia, 50th anniv.

Laocoon — A1679

1968, Aug. 16 ***Perf. 11½***
3500 A1679 6k sepia, blk & mar 2.75 2.00

"Promote solidarity with Greek democrats."

Red Army Man, Cavalry Charge and Order of the Red Banner of Battle — A1680

Designs: 3k, Young man and woman, Dneprostroi Dam and Order of the Red Banner of Labor. 4k, Soldier, storming of the Reichstag, Berlin, and Order of Lenin. 6k, "Restoration of National Economy" (workers), and Order of Lenin. 10k, Young man and woman cultivating virgin land and Order of Lenin. 50k, like 2k.

1968, Aug. 25 **Litho.** ***Perf. 12½x12***
3501 A1680 2k gray, red & ocher .20 .20
3502 A1680 3k multicolored .20 .20
3503 A1680 4k org, ocher & rose car .20 .20
3504 A1680 6k multicolored .20 .20
3505 A1680 10k olive & multi .20 .20
Nos. 3501-3505 (5) 1.00 1.00

Souvenir Sheet

Imperf

3506 A1680 50k ultra, red & bister 2.50 1.00

50th anniv. of the Lenin Young Communist League, Komsomol.

Chemistry Institute and Dimeric Molecule A1681

1968, Sept. 3 **Photo.** ***Perf. 11½***
3507 A1681 4k vio bl, dp lil rose & black .30 .20

50th anniversary of Kurnakov Institute for General and Inorganic Chemistry.

Letter, Compass Rose, Ship and Plane A1682

Compass Rose and Stamps of 1921 and 1965 A1683

1968, Sept. 16 **Photo.** ***Perf. 11½***
3508 A1682 4k dk car rose, brn & brt red .30 .20
3509 A1683 4k dk blue, blk & bister .30 .20

No. 3508 for Letter Writing Week, Oct. 7-13, and No. 3509 for Stamp Day and the Day of the Collector.

The 26 Baku Commissars, Sculpture by Merkurov — A1684

1968, Sept. 20
3510 A1684 4k multicolored .40 .20

50th anniversary of the shooting of the 26 Commissars, Baku, Sept. 20, 1918.

Toyvo Antikaynen (1898-1941), Finnish Workers' Organizer — A1685

1968, Sept. 30 ***Perf. 12***
3511 A1685 6k gray & sepia .60 .20

Russian Merchant Marine Emblem A1686

1968, Sept. 30 ***Perf. 12x11½***
3512 A1686 6k blue, red & indigo .40 .20

Russian Merchant Marine.

Order of the October Revolution — A1687

Typographed and Embossed

1968, Sept. 30 ***Perf. 12x12½***
3513 A1687 4k gold & multi .35 .25

51st anniv. of the October Revolution. Printed with alternating label.

Pavel P. Postyshev — A1688

1968-70 **Engr.** ***Perf. 12½x12***

Designs: No. 3515, Stepan G. Shaumyan (1878-1918). No. 3516, Amkal Ikramov. (1898-1938). No. 3516A, N. G. Markin (1893-1918). No. 3516B, P. E. Dybenko (1889-1938). No. 3516C, S. V. Kosior (1889-1939). No. 3516D, Vasili Kikvidze (1895-1919).

Size: 21½x32½mm

3514 A1688 4k bluish black .55 .20
3515 A1688 4k bluish black .55 .20
3516 A1688 4k gray black .55 .20
3516A A1688 4k black .55 .20
3516B A1688 4k dark car ('69) .55 .20
3516C A1688 4k indigo ('69) .55 .20
3516D A1688 4k dk brown ('70) .55 .20
Nos. 3514-3516D (7) 3.85 1.40

Honoring outstanding workers for the Communist Party and the Soviet State.
Issued: #3514-3516, 9/30/68; #3516A, 12/31/68; #3516D, 9/24/70; others, 5/15/69.
See #3782.

American Bison and Zebra A1689

Designs: No. 3518, Purple gallinule and lotus. No. 3519, Great white egrets, vert. No. 3520, Ostrich and golden pheasant, vert. No. 3521, Eland and guanaco. No. 3522, European spoonbill and glossy ibis.

Perf. 12½x12, 12x12½

1968, Oct. 16 **Litho.**
3517 A1689 4k ocher, brn & blk .65 .30
3518 A1689 4k ocher & multi .65 .30
3519 A1689 6k olive & black .75 .30
3520 A1689 6k gray & multi .75 .30
3521 A1689 10k dp grn & multi 1.10 .40
3522 A1689 10k emerald & multi 1.10 .40
Nos. 3517-3522 (6) 5.00 2.00

Askania Nova and Astrakhan state reservations.

Ivan S. Turgenev (1818-83), Writer — A1690

1968, Oct. 10 **Engr.** ***Perf. 12x12½***
3523 A1690 4k green 4.50 .50

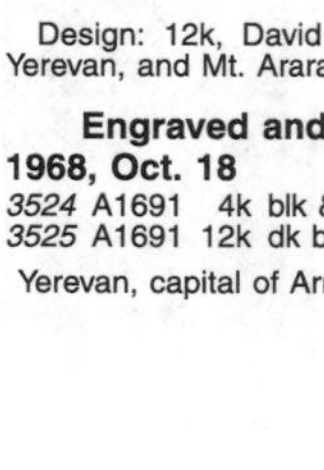

Warrior, 1880 B.C. and Mt. Ararat — A1691

Design: 12k, David Sasountsi monument, Yerevan, and Mt. Ararat.

Engraved and Photogravure

1968, Oct. 18 ***Perf. 11½***
3524 A1691 4k blk & dk blue, *gray* .25 .20
3525 A1691 12k dk brn & choc, *bis* .35 .20

Yerevan, capital of Armenia, 2,750th anniv.

First Radio Tube Generator and Laboratory A1692

1968, Oct. 26 **Photo.** ***Perf. 11½***
3526 A1692 4k dk bl, dp bis & blk .30 .20

50th anniversary of Russia's first radio laboratory at Gorki (Nizhni Novgorod).

Prospecting Geologist and Crystals A1693

6k, Prospecting for metals: seismographic test apparatus with shock wave diagram, plane, truck. 10k, Oil derrick in the desert.

1968, Oct. 31 **Litho.** ***Perf. 11½***
3527 A1693 4k blue & multi .40 .20
3528 A1693 6k multicolored .20 .20
3529 A1693 10k multicolored .55 .20
Nos. 3527-3529 (3) 1.15 .60

Geology Day. Printed with alternating label.

Borovoe, Kazakhstan — A1694

Landscapes: #3531, Djety-Oguz, Kirghizia, vert. #3532, Issyk-kul Lake, Kirghizia. #3533, Borovoe, Kazakhstan, vert.

Perf. 12½x12, 12x12½

1968, Nov. 20 **Typo.**
3530 A1694 4k dk red brn & multi .20 .20
3531 A1694 4k gray & multi .20 .20
3532 A1694 6k dk red brn & multi .20 .20
3533 A1694 6k black & multi .20 .20
Nos. 3530-3533 (4) .80 .80

Recreational areas in the Kazakh and Kirghiz Republics.

Medals and Cup, Riccione, 1952, 1961 and 1965 — A1695

4k, Medals, Eiffel Tower and Arc de Triomphe, Paris, 1964. 6k, Porcelain plaque, gold medal and Brandenburg Gate, Debria, Berlin, 1950, 1959. 12k, Medal and prize-winning stamp #2888, Buenos Aires. 16k, Cups and medals, Rome, 1952, 1954. 20k, Medals, awards and views, Vienna, 1961, 1965. 30k, Trophies, Prague, 1950, 1955, 1962.

1968, Nov. 27 **Photo.** ***Perf. 11½x12***
3534 A1695 4k dp cl, sil & blk .20 .20
3535 A1695 6k dl bl, gold & blk .25 .20
3536 A1695 10k light ultra, gold & black .40 .20
3537 A1695 12k blue, silver & blk .50 .20
3538 A1695 16k red, gold & blk .55 .20
3539 A1695 20k bright blue, gold & black .70 .20
3540 A1695 30k orange brown, gold & black 1.00 .30
Nos. 3534-3540 (7) 3.60 1.50

Awards to Soviet post office at foreign stamp exhibitions.

Worker with Banner — A1696

V. K. Lebedinsky and Radio Tower — A1697

1968, Nov. 29 ***Perf. 12x12½***

3541 A1696 4k red & black .50 .35

Estonian Workers' Commune, 50th anniv.

1968, Nov. 29 ***Perf. 11½x12***

3542 A1697 4k gray grn, blk & gray .50 .25

V. K. Lebedinsky (1868-1937), scientist.

Souvenir Sheet

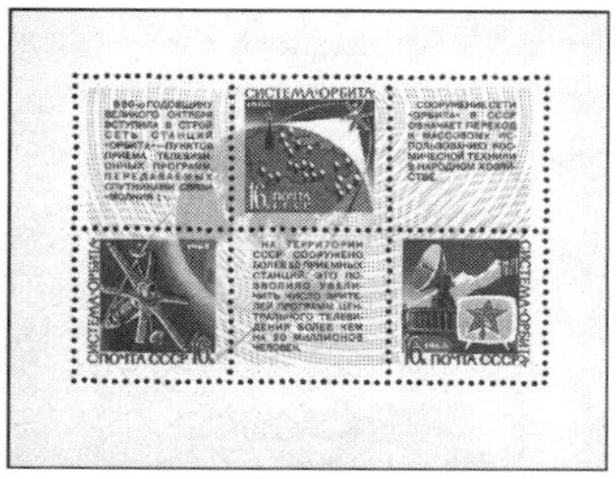

Communication via Satellite — A1698

1968, Nov. 29 **Litho.** ***Perf. 12***

3543 A1698 Sheet of 3 3.00 .70
- *a.* 16k Molniya I .70 .20
- *b.* 16k Map of Russia .70 .20
- *c.* 16k Ground Station "Orbite" .70 .20

Television transmission throughout USSR with the aid of the earth satellite Molniya I.

Sprig, Spasski Tower, Lenin Univ. and Library A1699

1968, Dec. 1 ***Perf. 11½***

3544 A1699 4k ultra, sil, grn & red .60 .30

New Year 1969.

Maj. Gen. Georgy Beregovoi A1700

1968, Dec. 14 **Photo.** ***Perf. 11½***

3545 A1700 10k Prus blue, blk & red .40 .25

Flight of Soyuz 3, Oct. 26-30.

Rail-laying and Casting Machines A1701

Soviet railroad transportation: 4k, Railroad map of the Soviet Union and Train.

1968, Dec. 14 ***Perf. 12½x12***

3546 A1701 4k rose mag & org .25 .20

3547 A1701 10k brown & emerald .25 .20

Newspaper Banner and Monument A1702

1968, Dec. 23 ***Perf. 11½***

3548 A1702 4k tan, red & dk brn .40 .25

Byelorussian communist party, 50th anniv.

The Reapers, by A. Venetzianov A1703

Knight at the Crossroads, by Viktor M. Vasnetsov — A1704

Paintings: 2k, The Last Day of Pompeii, by Karl P. Bryullov. 4k, Capture of a Town in Winter, by Vasili I. Surikov. 6k, On the Lake, by I.I. Levitan. 10k, Alarm, 1919 (family), by K. Petrov-Vodkin. 16k, Defense of Sevastopol, 1942, by A. Deineka. 20k, Sculptor with a Bust of Homer, by G. Korzhev. 30k, Celebration on Uristsky Square, 1920, by G. Koustodiev. 50k, Duel between Peresvet and Chelubey, by Avilov.

Perf. 12x12½, 12½

1968, Dec. 25 **Litho.**

3549	A1703	1k	multicolored	.20	.20
3550	A1704	2k	multicolored	.20	.20
3551	A1704	3k	multicolored	.20	.20
3552	A1704	4k	multicolored	.25	.20
3553	A1704	6k	multicolored	.35	.20
3554	A1703	10k	multicolored	.55	.20
3555	A1704	16k	multicolored	.60	.20
3556	A1703	20k	multicolored	.65	.20
3557	A1704	30k	multicolored	.85	.30
3558	A1704	50k	multicolored	1.65	.40
			Nos. 3549-3558 (10)	5.50	2.30

Russian State Museum, Leningrad.

House, Zaoneje, 1876 — A1705

Russian Architecture: 4k, Carved doors, Gorki Oblast, 1848. 6k, Castle, Kizhi, 1714. 10k, Fortress wall, Rostov-Yaroslav, 16th-17th centuries. 12k, Gate, Tsaritsino, 1785. 16k, Architect Rossi Street, Leningrad.

1968, Dec. 27 **Engr.** ***Perf. 12x12½***

3559	A1705	3k	dp brown, *ocher*	.25	.20
3560	A1705	4k	green, *yellow*	.25	.20
3561	A1705	6k	vio, *gray violet*	.35	.20
3562	A1705	10k	dl bl, *grnsh gray*	.45	.20
3563	A1705	12k	car, *gray*	.55	.20
3564	A1705	16k	black, *yellowish*	.70	.20
			Nos. 3559-3564 (6)	2.55	1.20

Banners of Young Communist League, October Revolution Medal — A1707

1968, Dec. 31 **Litho.** ***Perf. 12***

3566 A1707 12k red, yel & black .40 .30

Award of Order of October Revolution to the Young Communist League on its 50th anniversary.

Soldiers on Guard — A1708

1969, Jan. 1 ***Perf. 12x12½***

3567 A1708 4k orange & claret .40 .20

Latvian Soviet Republic, 50th anniv.

Revolutionaries and Monument — A1709

Designs: 4k, Partisans and sword. 6k, Workers and Lenin Medals.

1969, Jan. **Photo.** ***Perf. 11½***

3568	A1709	2k	ocher & rose claret	.25	.20
3569	A1709	4k	ocher & red	.25	.20
3570	A1709	6k	dk olive, mag & red	.25	.20
			Nos. 3568-3570 (3)	.75	.60

Byelorussian Soviet Republic, 50th anniv.

Souvenir Sheet

Vladimir Shatalov, Boris Volynov, Alexei S. Elisseyev, Evgeny Khrunov — A1710

1969, Jan. 22 ***Imperf.***

3571 A1710 50k dp bis & dk brn 4.00 1.25

1st team flights of Soyuz 4 and 5, 1/16/69.

Leningrad University A1711

1969, Jan. 23 **Photo.** ***Perf. 12½x12***

3572 A1711 10k black & maroon .40 .20

University of Leningrad, 150th anniv.

Ivan A. Krylov (1769?-1844), Fable Writer — A1712

1969, Feb. 13 **Litho.** ***Perf. 12x12½***

3573 A1712 4k black & multi .50 .30

Nikolai Filchenkov A1713

Designs: No. 3575, Alexander Kosmodemiansky. No. 3575A, Otakar Yarosh, member of Czechoslovak Svoboda Battalion.

1969 **Photo.**

3574	A1713	4k	dull rose & black	.20	.20
3575	A1713	4k	emerald & dk brn	.20	.20
3575A	A1713	4k	blue & black	.20	.20
			Nos. 3574-3575A (3)	.60	.60

Heroes of World War II. Issued: #3575A, May 9; others, Feb. 23.

"Shoulder to the Wheel," Parliament, Budapest A1714

Design: "Shoulder to the Wheel" is a sculpture by Zigmond Kisfaludi-Strobl.

1969, Mar. 21 **Typo.** ***Perf. 11½***

3576 A1714 6k black, ver & lt grn .30 .20

Hungarian Soviet Republic, 50th anniv.

Oil Refinery and Salavat Tualeyev Monument — A1715

1969, Mar. 22 **Litho.** ***Perf. 12***

3577 A1715 4k multicolored .30 .20

50th anniv. of the Bashkir Autonomous Socialist Republic.

Sergei P. Korolev, Sputnik 1, Space Monument, Moscow — A1716

Vostok on Launching Pad — A1717

Natl. Cosmonauts' Day: No. 3579, Zond 2 orbiting moon, and photograph of earth made by Zond 5. 80k, Spaceship Soyuz 3.

Perf. 12½x12, 12x12½

1969, Apr. 12 **Litho.**

3578 A1716 10k black, vio & grn .25 .20
3579 A1716 10k dk brn, yel & brn red .25 .20
3580 A1717 10k multicolored .25 .20
Nos. 3578-3580 (3) .75 .60

Souvenir Sheet

Perf. 12

3581 A1716 80k vio, green & red 3.00 1.25

No. 3581 contains one 37x24mm stamp.

Lenin University, Kazan, and Kremlin A1718

Lenin House, Kuibyshev A1718a

Lenin House, Pskov A1718b

Lenin House, Shushensko — A1718c

Smolny Institute, Leningrad A1718d

Places Connected with Lenin: #3586, Straw Hut, Razliv. #3587, Lenin Museum, Gorki. #3589, Lenin's room, Kremlin. #3590, Lenin Museum, Ulyanovsk. #3591, Lenin House, Ulyanovsk.

1969 **Photo.** ***Perf. 11½***

3582 A1718 4k pale rose & multi .20 .20
3583 A1718a 4k beige & multi .20 .20
3584 A1718b 4k bis brn & multi .20 .20
3585 A1718c 4k gray vio & multi .20 .20
3586 A1718 4k violet & multi .20 .20
3587 A1718 4k blue & multi .20 .20
3588 A1718d 4k brick red & multi .20 .20
3589 A1718 4k rose red & multi .20 .20
3590 A1718 4k lt red brn & multi .20 .20
3591 A1718 4k dull grn & multi .20 .20
Nos. 3582-3591 (10) 2.00 2.00

99th anniv. of the birth of Lenin.

Telephone, Transistor Radio and Trademark — A1719

1969, Apr. 25 ***Perf. 12½x12***

3592 A1719 10k sepia & dp org .40 .20

50th anniversary of VEF Electrical Co.

ILO Emblem and Globe — A1720

1969, May 9 ***Perf. 11***

3593 A1720 6k car rose & gold .35 .20

50th anniversary of the ILO.

Suleiman Stalsky A1721

1969, May 15 **Photo.** ***Perf. 12½x12***

3595 A1721 4k tan & ol green .40 .25

Stalsky (1869-1937), Dagestan poet.

Yasnaya Polyana Rose A1722

4k, "Stroynaya" lily. 10k, Cattleya orchid. 12k, "Listopad" dahlia. 14k, "Ural Girl" gladioli.

1969, May 15 **Litho.** ***Perf. 11½***

3596 A1722 2k multicolored .20 .20
3597 A1722 4k multicolored .20 .20
3598 A1722 10k multicolored .25 .20
3599 A1722 12k multicolored .40 .20
3600 A1722 14k multicolored .40 .20
Nos. 3596-3600 (5) 1.45 1.00

Work of the Botanical Gardens of the Academy of Sciences.

Ukrainian Academy of Sciences A1723

1969, May 22 **Photo.** ***Perf. 12½x12***

3601 A1723 4k brown & yellow .50 .25

Ukrainian Academy of Sciences, 50th anniv.

Film, Camera and Medal A1724

Ballet Dancers A1725

1969, June 3 **Litho.** ***Perf. 12x12½***

3602 A1724 6k rose car, blk & gold .30 .20
3603 A1725 6k dk brown & multi .30 .20

Intl. Film Festival in Moscow, and 1st Intl. Young Ballet Artists' Competitions.

Congress Emblem and Cell Division — A1726

1969, June 10 **Photo.** ***Perf. 11½***

3605 A1726 6k dp claret, lt bl & yel .50 .30

Protozoologists, 3rd Intl. Cong., Leningrad.

Estonian Singer and Festival Emblem — A1727

1969, June 14 ***Perf. 12x12½***

3606 A1727 4k ver & bister .50 .25

Centenary of the Estonian Song Festival.

Mendeleev and Formula with Author's Corrections — A1728

30k, Dmitri Ivanovich Mendeleev, vert.

Engraved and Lithographed

1969, June 20 ***Perf. 12***

3607 A1728 6k brown & rose .50 .30

Souvenir Sheet

3608 A1728 30k carmine rose 3.00 1.25

Cent. of the Periodic Law (classification of elements), formulated by Dimitri I. Mendeleev (1834-1907). No. 3608 contains one engraved 29x37mm stamp.

Hand Holding Peace Banner and World Landmarks A1729

1969, June 20 **Photo.** ***Perf. 11½***

3609 A1729 10k bl, dk brn & gold .40 .25

20th anniversary of the Peace Movement.

Laser Beam Guiding Moon Rocket — A1730

1969, June 20

3610 A1730 4k silver, black & red .50 .25

Soviet scientific inventions, 50th anniv.

Ivan Kotlyarevski (1769-1838), Ukrainian Writer — A1731

Typographed and Photogravure

1969, June 25 ***Perf. 12½x12***

3611 A1731 4k blk, olive & lt brn .50 .25

No. 2717 Overprinted in Vermilion

1969, June 25 **Photo.** ***Perf. 11½***

3612 A1306 6k Prus blue & plum 2.50 1.50

Soviet victory in the Ice Hockey World Championships, Stockholm, 1969.

"Hill of Glory" Monument and Minsk Battle Map A1732

1969, July 3 **Litho.** ***Perf. 12x12½***

3613 A1732 4k red & olive .30 .20

25th anniv. of the liberation of Byelorussia from the Germans.

Eagle, Flag and Map of Poland A1733

#3615, Hands holding torch, flags of Bulgaria, USSR, Bulgarian coat of arms.

1969, July 10 Photo. *Perf. 12*
3614 A1733 6k red & bister .60 .20

Litho.
3615 A1733 6k bis, red, grn & blk .60 .20

25th anniv. of the Polish Republic; liberation of Bulgaria from the Germans.

Monument to 68 Heroes — A1734

1969, July 15 Photo. *Perf. 12*
3616 A1734 4k red & maroon .50 .30

25th anniversary of the liberation of Nikolayev from the Germans.

Old Samarkand A1735

Design: 6k, Intourist Hotel, Samarkand.

1969, July 15 Typo.
3617 A1735 4k multicolored .30 .20
3618 A1735 6k multicolored .30 .20

2500th anniversary of Samarkand.

Volleyball A1736

Munkascy & "Woman Churning Butter" A1737

Design: 6k, Kayak race.

Photogravure and Engraved

1969, July 20 *Perf. 11½*
3619 A1736 4k dp org & red brn .35 .20
3620 A1736 6k multicolored .35 .20

Championships: European Junior Volleyball; European Rowing.

1969, July 20 Photo.
3621 A1737 6k dk brn, blk & org .40 .25

Mihaly von Munkascy (1844-1900), Hungarian painter.

Miners' Monument A1738

1969, July 30
3622 A1738 4k silver & magenta .40 .20

Centenary of the founding of the city of Donetsk, in the Donets coal basin.

Machine Gun Cart, by Mitrofan Grekov — A1739

1969, July 30 Engr. *Perf. 12½x12*
3623 A1739 4k red brn & brn red .40 .25

First Mounted Army, 50th anniv.

Barge Pullers Along the Volga, by Repin — A1740

Ilya E. Repin (1844-1930), Self-portrait A1741

Repin Paintings: 6k, "Not Expected." 12k, Confession. 16k, Dnieper Cossacks.

Perf. 12½x12, 12x12½

1969, Aug. 5 Litho.
3624 A1740 4k multicolored .25 .20
3625 A1740 6k multicolored .25 .20
3626 A1741 10k bis, red brn & blk .35 .20
3627 A1740 12k multicolored .50 .20
3628 A1740 16k multicolored .65 .20
Nos. 3624-3628 (5) 2.00 1.00

Runner A1742

Komarov A1743

Design: 10k, Athlete on rings.

1969, Aug. 9 *Perf. 12x12½*
3629 A1742 4k red, green & blk .25 .25
3630 A1742 10k grn, lt bl & blk .25 .25

Souvenir Sheet

Imperf
3631 A1742 20k red, bister & blk 1.75 .60

9th Trade Union Spartakiad, Moscow.

1969, Aug. 22 Photo. *Perf. 12x11½*
3632 A1743 4k olive & brown .30 .20

V. L. Komarov (1869-1945), botanist.

Hovannes Tumanian, Armenian Landscape — A1744

1969, Sept. 1 Typo. *Perf. 12½x12*
3633 A1744 10k blk & peacock blue .40 .25

Tumanian (1869-1923), Armenian poet.

Turkmenian Wine Horn, 2nd Century — A1745

Designs: 6k, Persian Simurg vessel (giant anthropomorphic bird), 13th century. 12k, Head of goddess Kannon, Korea, 8th century. 16k, Bodhisattva, Tibet, 7th century. 20k, Statue of Ebisu and fish (tai), Japan, 17th century.

1969, Sept. 3 Litho. *Perf. 12x12½*
3634 A1745 4k blue & multi .25 .20
3635 A1745 6k lilac & multi .35 .20
3636 A1745 12k red & multi .60 .20
3637 A1745 16k blue vio & multi .70 .20
3638 A1745 20k pale grn & multi .95 .30
Nos. 3634-3638 (5) 2.85 1.10

Treasures from the State Museum of Oriental Art.

Mahatma Gandhi (1869-1948) A1746

1969, Sept. 10 Engr.
3639 A1746 6k deep brown .40 .35

Black Stork Feeding Young A1747

Belovezhskaya Forest reservation: 6k, Doe and fawn (red deer). 10k, Fighting bison. 12k, Lynx and cubs. 16k, Wild pig and piglets.

1969, Sept. 10 Photo. *Perf. 12*
Size: 75x23mm, 10k; 35x23mm, others
3640 A1747 4k blk, yel grn & red .20 .20
3641 A1747 6k blue grn, dk brn & ocher .25 .20
3642 A1747 10k dk brn, dull org & dp org .55 .20
3643 A1747 12k dk & yel green, brn & gray .55 .20
3644 A1747 16k gray, yel grn & dk brown .65 .20
Nos. 3640-3644 (5) 2.20 1.00

Komitas A1748

1969, Sept. 18 Typo. *Perf. 12½x12*
3645 A1748 6k blk, gray & salmon .50 .30

Komitas (S. N. Sogomonian, 1869-1935), Armenian composer.

Lisa Chaikina A1749

A. Cheponis, J. Aleksonis and G. Borisa A1750

#3647, Major S. I. Gritsevets & fighter planes.

1969, Sept. 20 Photo. *Perf. 12½x12*
3646 A1749 4k olive & brt green .30 .20
3647 A1749 4k gray & black .30 .20

Perf. 11½
3648 A1750 4k hn brn, brn & buff .30 .20
Nos. 3646-3648 (3) .90 .60

Heroes of the Soviet Union.

Ivan Petrovich Pavlov(1849-1936), Physiologist — A1751

1969, Sept. 26
3649 A1751 4k multicolored .40 .25

East German Arms, TV Tower and Brandenburg Gate — A1752

1969, Oct. 7 Litho.
3650 A1752 6k red, black & yel .35 .25

German Democratic Republic, 20th anniv.

Aleksei Vasilievich Koltsov (1809-42), Poet — A1753

1969, Oct. 14 Photo. *Perf. 12x12½*
3652 A1753 4k lt blue & brown .40 .25

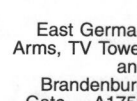

National Emblem A1754

1969, Oct. 14 ***Perf. 12x11½***
3653 A1754 4k gold & red .50 .30

25th anniversary of the liberation of the Ukraine from the Nazis.

Stars, Hammer and Sickle A1755

1969, Oct. 21 Typo. ***Perf. 11½***
3654 A1755 4k vio blue, gold, yel & red .40 .25

52nd anniversary of October Revolution.

Georgy Shonin and Valery Kubasov A1756

Designs: No. 3656, Anatoly Filipchenko, Vladislav Volkov and Viktor Gorbatko. No. 3657, Vladimir Shatalov and Alexey Elisyev.

1969, Oct. 22 Photo. ***Perf. 12½x12***
3655 A1756 10k black & gold .30 .20
3656 A1756 10k black & gold .30 .20
3657 A1756 10k black & gold .30 .20
a. Strip of 3, #3655-3657 1.25 .30

Group flight of the space ships Soyuz 6, Soyuz 7 and Soyuz 8, Oct. 11-13.

Lenin as a Youth A1757

1969, Oct. 25 Engr. ***Perf. 11½***
3658 A1757 4k dark red, *pink* .40 .25

1st Soviet Youth Philatelic Exhibition, Kiev, dedicated to Lenin's 100th birthday.

Emblem of Communications Unit of Army — A1758

1969, Oct. 30 Photo.
3659 A1758 4k dk red, red & bister .40 .25

50th anniversary of the Communications Troops of Soviet Army.

Souvenir Sheet

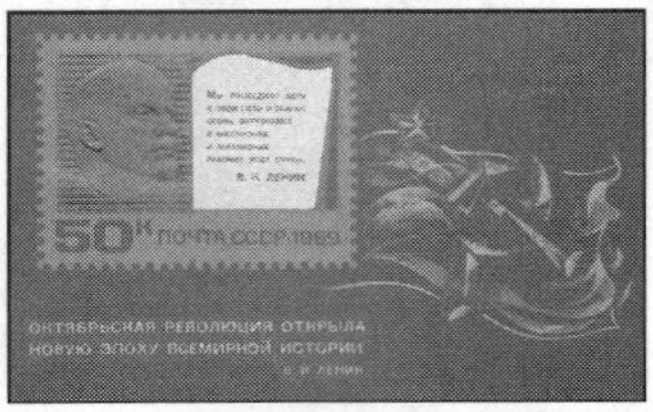

Lenin and Quotation — A1759

Lithographed and Embossed

1969, Nov. 6 ***Imperf.***
3660 A1759 50k red, gold & pink 2.25 1.00

52nd anniv. of the October Revolution.

Cover of "Rules of the Kolkhoz" and Farm Woman's Monument — A1760

1969, Nov. 18 Photo. ***Perf. 12½x12***
3661 A1760 4k brown & gold .40 .25

3rd All Union Collective Farmers' Congress, Moscow, Nov.-Dec.

Vasilissa, the Beauty, by Ivan Y. Bilibin A1761

Designs (Book Illustrations by Ivan Y. Bilibin): 10k, Marya Morevna. 16k, Finist, the Fine Fellow, horiz. 20k, The Golden Cock. 50k, The Sultan and the Czar. The inscriptions on the 16k and 20k are transposed. 4k, 10k, 16k are fairy tales; 20k and 50k are tales by Pushkin.

1969, Nov. 20 Litho. ***Perf. 12***
3662 A1761 4k gray & multi .25 .20
3663 A1761 10k gray & multi .60 .50
3664 A1761 16k gray & multi .75 .75
3665 A1761 20k gray & multi .85 .85
3666 A1761 50k gray & multi 3.00 1.40
a. Strip of 5, #3662-3666 5.50 4.50

Illustrator and artist Ivan Y. Bilibin.

USSR Emblems Dropped on Venus, Radar Installation and Orbits A1762

6k, Interplanetary station, space capsule, orbits.

1969, Nov. 25 Photo. ***Perf. 12x11½***
3667 A1762 4k bister, black & red .25 .20
3668 A1762 6k gray, lilac rose & blk .25 .20

Completion of the fights of the space stations Venera 5 and Venera 6.

Flags of USSR and Afghanistan — A1763

1969, Nov. 30 Photo. ***Perf. 11½***
3669 A1763 6k red, black & green .35 .25

50th anniversary of diplomatic relations between Russia and Afghanistan.

Coil Stamp

Russian State Emblem and Star — A1764

1969, Nov. 13 ***Perf. 11x11½***
3670 A1764 4k red .60 .30

MiG Jet and First MiG Fighter Plane — A1765

1969, Dec. 12 ***Perf. 11½x12***
3671 A1765 6k red, black & gray .40 .25

Soviet aircraft builders.

Lenin and Flag A1766

Typographed and Lithographed

1969, Dec. 25 ***Perf. 11½***
3672 A1766 4k gold, blue, red & blk .40 .25

Happy New Year 1970, birth cent. of Lenin.

Antonov 2 — A1767

Aircraft: 3k, PO-2. 4k, ANT-9. 6k, TsAGI 1-EA. 10k, ANT-20 "Maxim Gorki." 12k, Tupolev-104. 16k, MiG-10 helicopter. 20k, Ilyushin-62. 50k, Tupolev-144.

Photogravure and Engraved

1969 ***Perf. 11½x12***
3673 A1767 2k bister & multi .20 .20
3674 A1767 3k multicolored .20 .20
3675 A1767 4k multicolored .20 .20
3676 A1767 6k multicolored .25 .20
3677 A1767 10k lt vio & multi .40 .20
3678 A1767 12k multicolored .55 .20
3679 A1767 16k multicolored .65 .20
3680 A1767 20k multicolored .70 .20
Nos. 3673-3680 (8) 3.15 1.60

Souvenir Sheet

Imperf

3681 A1767 50k blue & multi 2.50 1.00

History of national aeronautics and aviation. No. 3681 margin contains signs of the zodiac, partly overlapping the stamp.

Issued: #3679, 3681, 12/31; others 12/25.

Photograph of Earth by Zond 7 — A1768

Designs: No. 3683a, same as 10k. No. 3683b, Photograph of moon.

1969, Dec. 26 Photo. ***Perf. 12x11½***
3682 A1768 10k black & multi .40 .30

Souvenir Sheet

Imperf

Litho.

3683 Sheet of 2 4.00 2.00
a. A1768 50k indigo & multi 1.65 .90
b. A1768 50k dark brown & multi 1.65 .90

Space explorations of the automatic stations Zond 6, Nov. 10-17, 1968, and Zond 7, Aug. 8-14, 1969. No. 3683 contains 27x40mm stamps with simulated perforations.

Model Aircraft — A1769

Technical Sports: 4k, Motorboats. 6k, Parachute jumping.

1969, Dec. 26 Engr. ***Perf. 12½x12***
3684 A1769 3k bright magenta .30 .20
3685 A1769 4k dull blue green .30 .20
3686 A1769 6k red orange .30 .20
Nos. 3684-3686 (3) .90 .60

Romanian Arms and Soviet War Memorial, Bucharest A1770

1969, Dec. 31 Photo. ***Perf. 11½***
3687 A1770 6k rose red & brown .60 .35

25th anniversary of Romania's liberation from fascist rule.

Ostankino Television Tower, Moscow A1771

1969, Dec. 31 Typo. *Perf. 12*
3688 A1771 10k multicolored .60 .35

Conversation with Lenin, by A. Shirokov (in front of red table) — A1772

Paintings: No. 3689, No. 3690, Lenin, by N. Andreyev. Lenin at Marxist Meeting, St. Petersburg, by A. Moravov (behind table). No. 3691, Lenin at Second Party Day, by Y. Vinogradov (next to table). No. 3692, First Day of Soviet Power, by F. Modorov (leading crowd). No. 3694, Farmers' Delegation Meeting Lenin, by Modorov (seated at desk). No. 3695, With Lenin, by V. A. Serov (with cap, in background). No. 3696, Lenin on May 1, 1920, by I. Brodsky (with cap, in foreground). No. 3697, Builder of Communism, by a group of painters (in red). No. 3698, Mastery of Space, by A. Deyneka (rockets).

1970, Jan. 1 Litho. *Perf. 12*
3689 A1772 4k multicolored .20 .20
3690 A1772 4k multicolored .20 .20
3691 A1772 4k multicolored .20 .20
3692 A1772 4k multicolored .20 .20
3693 A1772 4k multicolored .20 .20
3694 A1772 4k multicolored .20 .20
3695 A1772 4k multicolored .20 .20
3696 A1772 4k multicolored .20 .20
3697 A1772 4k multicolored .20 .20
3698 A1772 4k multicolored .20 .20
Nos. 3689-3698 (10) 2.00 2.00

Centenary of birth of Lenin (1870-1924).

Map of Antarctic, "Mirny" and "Vostok" A1773

Design: 16k, Camp and map of the Antarctic with Soviet Antarctic bases.

1970, Jan. 27 Photo. *Perf. 11½*
3699 A1773 4k multicolored .25 .25
3700 A1773 16k multicolored .70 .25

150th anniversary of the Bellingshausen-Lazarev Antarctic expedition.

F. W. Sychkov and "Tobogganing" — A1774

1970, Jan. 27 *Perf. 12½x12*
3701 A1774 4k sepia & vio blue .40 .25

F. W. Sychkov (1870-1958), painter.

Col. V. B. Borsoyev A1775

Design: No. 3703, Sgt. V. Peshekhonov.

1970, Feb. 10 *Perf. 12x12½*
3702 A1775 4k brown olive & brn .30 .20
3703 A1775 4k dark gray & plum .30 .20

Heroes of the Soviet Union.

Geographical Society Emblem and Globes — A1776

1970, Feb. 26 Photo. *Perf. 11½*
3704 A1776 6k bis, Prus bl & dk brn .40 .30

Russian Geographical Society, 125th anniv.

Torch of Peace — A1777

1970, Mar. 3 Litho. *Perf. 12*
3705 A1777 6k blue green & tan .30 .20

Intl. Women's Solidarity Day, Mar. 8.

Symbols of Russian Arts and Crafts — A1778

Lenin — A1780

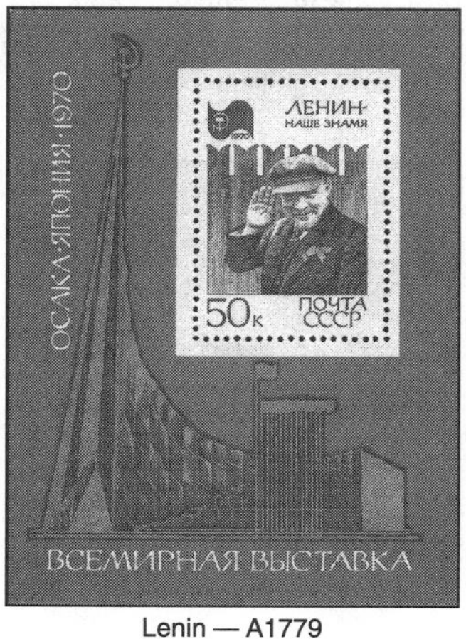

Lenin — A1779

Designs: 6k, Russian EXPO '70 pavilion. 10k, Boy holding model ship.

1970, Mar. 10 Photo. *Perf. 11½*
3706 A1778 4k dk blue grn, red & black .25 .20
3707 A1778 6k blk, silver & red .25 .20
3708 A1778 10k vio bl, sil & red .25 .20
Nos. 3706-3708 (3) .75 .60

Souvenir Sheet

Engr. & Litho.

Perf. 12x12½
3709 A1779 50k dark red 2.00 1.00

EXPO '70 Intl. Exhibition, Osaka, Japan, 3/15-4/13.

1970, Mar. 14 Photo. *Perf. 11½*
3710 A1780 4k red, blk & gold .40 .30

Souvenir Sheet

Photogravure and Embossed

Imperf
3711 A1780 20k red, blk & gold 2.00 1.00

USSR Philatelic Exhibition dedicated to the centenary of the birth of Lenin.

Friendship Tree, Sochi — A1781

1970, Mar. 18 Litho. *Perf. 11½*
3712 A1781 10k multicolored .50 .30

Friendship among people. Printed with alternating label.

National Emblem, Hammer and Sickle, Oil Derricks A1782

1970, Mar. 18 Photo. *Perf. 11½*
3713 A1782 4k dk car rose & gold .35 .25

Azerbaijan Republic, 50th anniversary.

Ice Hockey Players A1783

1970, Mar. 18
3714 A1783 6k blue & slate green .35 .20

World Ice Hockey Championships, Sweden.

Overprinted Inscription

1970, Apr. 1 Photo. *Perf. 11½*
3715 A1783 6k blue & slate green .40 .25

Soviet hockey players as the tenfold world champions.

D. N. Medvedev A1784

Portrait: No. 3717, K. P. Orlovsky.

1970, Mar. 26 Engr. *Perf. 12x12½*
3716 A1784 4k chocolate .25 .20
3717 A1784 4k dk redsh brown .25 .20

Heroes of the Soviet Union.

Worker, Books, Globes and UNESCO Symbol A1785

1970, Mar. 26 Photo. *Perf. 12½x12*
3718 A1785 6k car lake & ocher .30 .20

UNESCO-sponsored Lenin Symposium, Tampere, Finland, Apr. 6-10.

Hungarian Arms, Budapest Landmarks A1786

1970, Apr. 4 Typo. *Perf. 11½*
3719 A1786 6k multicolored .30 .20

Liberation of Hungary, 25th anniv.
See No. 3738.

Cosmonauts' Emblem A1787

1970, Apr. 12 Litho. *Perf. 11½*
3720 A1787 6k buff & multi .30 .20

Cosmonauts' Day.

Lenin, 1891 — A1788

Designs: Various portraits of Lenin.

Lithographed and Typographed

1970, Apr. 15 *Perf. 12x12½*
3721 A1788 2k green & gold .20 .20
3722 A1788 2k ol gray & gold .20 .20
3723 A1788 4k vio blue & gold .20 .20
3724 A1788 4k lake & gold .20 .20
3725 A1788 6k red brn & gold .20 .20
3726 A1788 6k lake & gold .20 .20
3727 A1788 10k dk brn & gold .25 .20
3728 A1788 10k dark rose brown & gold .35 .20
3729 A1788 12k blk, sil & gold .45 .20

Photo.
3730 A1788 12k red & gold .45 .20
Nos. 3721-3730 (10) 2.70 2.00

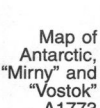

Souvenir Sheet

& 1970, Apr. 22 Litho. Typo.

3731 A1788 20k blk, silver & gold 2.00 .70

Cent. of the birth of Lenin. Issued in sheets of 8 stamps surrounded by 16 labels showing Lenin-connected buildings, books, coats of arms and medals. No. 3731 contains one stamp in same design as No. 3729.

Order of Victory — A1789

Designs: 2k, Monument to the Unknown Soldier, Moscow. 3k, Victory Monument, Berlin-Treptow. 4k, Order of the Great Patriotic War. 10k, Gold Star of the Order of Hero of the Soviet Union and Medal of Socialist Labor. 30k, Like 1k.

1970, May 8 Photo. *Perf. 11½*

3732 A1789 1k red lilac, gold & gray .20 .20
3733 A1789 2k dark brn, gold & red .20 .20
3734 A1789 3k dark brn, gold & red .20 .20
3735 A1789 4k dark brn, gold & red .20 .20
3736 A1789 10k red lil, gold & red .35 .20
Nos. 3732-3736 (5) 1.15 1.00

Souvenir Sheet

Imperf

3737 A1789 30k dark red, gold & gray 1.75 .60

25th anniv. of victory in WWII. No. 3737 has simulated perforations.

Arms-Landmark Type of 1970

Czechoslovakia arms and view of Prague.

1970, May 8 Typo. *Perf. 12½*

3738 A1786 6k dk brown & multi .35 .20

25th anniversary of the liberation of Czechoslovakia from the Germans.

Young Fighters, and Youth Federation Emblem A1791

1970, May 20 Litho. *Perf. 12*

3739 A1791 6k blue & black .30 .20

25th anniversary of the World Federation of Democratic Youth.

Lenin A1792

1970, May 20 Photo. *Perf. 11½*

3740 A1792 6k red .30 .20

Intl. Youth Meeting dedicated to the cent. of the birth of Lenin, UN, NY, June 1970.

Komsomol Emblem with Lenin — A1793

1970, May 20 Litho. *Perf. 12*

3741 A1793 4k red, yel & purple .30 .20

16th Congress of the Young Communist League, May 26-30.

Hammer and Sickle Emblem and Building of Supreme Soviet in Kazan A1794

#3744

#3744B

#3744C

Designs (Hammer-Sickle Emblem and Supreme Soviet Building in): No. 3743, Petrozavodsk. No. 3744, Cheboksary. No. 3744A, Elista. No. 3744B, Izhevsk. No. 3744C, Yoshkar-Ola.

1970 Engr. *Perf. 12x12½*

3742 A1794 4k violet blue .50 .20
3743 A1794 4k green .50 .20
3744 A1794 4k dark carmine .50 .20
3744A A1794 4k red .50 .20
3744B A1794 4k dark green .50 .20
3744C A1794 4k dark carmine .50 .20
Nos. 3742-3744C (6) 3.00 1.20

50th annivs. of the Tatar (#3742), Karelian (#3743), Chuvash (#3744), Kalmyk (#3744A), Udmurt (#3744B) and Mari (#3744C) autonomous SSRs.

Issued: #3742, 5/27; #3743, 6/5; #3744, 6/24; #3744A-3744B, 10/22; #3744C, 11/4.

See Nos. 3814-3823, 4286, 4806.

9th World Soccer Championships for the Jules Rimet Cup, Mexico City, May 29-June 21 — A1795

10k, Woman athlete on balancing bar.

1970, May 31 Photo. *Perf. 11½*

3745 A1795 10k lt gray & brt rose .40 .20
3746 A1795 16k dk grn & org brn .65 .20

17th World Gymnastics Championships, Ljubljana, Oct. 22-27 (#3745).

Sword into Plowshare Statue, UN, NY — A1796

1970, June 1 Litho. *Perf. 12x12½*

3747 A1796 12k gray & lake .50 .25

25th anniversary of the United Nations.

Soyuz 9, Andrian Nikolayev, Vitaly Sevastyanov A1797

1970, June 7 Photo. *Perf. 12x11½*

3748 A1797 10k multicolored .40 .20

424 hour space flight of Soyuz 9, June 1-19.

Friedrich Engels A1798

1970, June 16 Engr. *Perf. 12x12½*

3749 A1798 4k chocolate & ver .35 .20

Friedrich Engels (1820-1895), German socialist, collaborator with Karl Marx.

Armenian Woman and Symbols of Agriculture and Industry A1799

Design: No. 3751, Kazakh woman and symbols of agriculture and industry.

1970, June 16 Photo. *Perf. 11½*

3750 A1799 4k red brn & silver .30 .30
3751 A1799 4k brt rose lilac & gold .30 .30

50th anniv. of the Armenian & Kazakh Soviet Socialist Republics.

Missile Cruiser "Grozny" — A1800

Soviet Warships: 3k, Cruiser "Aurora." 10k, Cruiser "October Revolution." 12k, Missile cruiser "Varyag." 20k, Atomic submarine "Leninsky Komsomol."

1970, July 26 Photo. *Perf. 11½x12*

3752 A1800 3k lilac, pink & blk .20 .20
3753 A1800 4k yellow & black .25 .20
3754 A1800 10k rose & black .45 .20
3755 A1800 12k buff & dk brown .45 .20
3756 A1800 20k blue grn, dk brn & vio blue .90 .20
Nos. 3752-3756 (5) 2.25 1.00

Navy Day.

Soviet and Polish Workers and Flags — A1801

"History," Petroglyphs, Sputnik and Emblem — A1802

1970, July 26 *Perf. 12*

3757 A1801 6k red & slate .30 .20

25th anniversary of the Treaty of Friendship, Collaboration and Mutual Assistance between USSR and Poland.

1970, Aug. 16 *Perf. 11½*

3758 A1802 4k red brn, buff & blue .40 .25

13th International Congress of Historical Sciences in Moscow.

Mandarin Ducks A1803

Animals from the Sikhote-Alin Reserve: 6k, Pine marten. 10k, Asiatic black bear, vert. 16k, Red deer. 20k, Ussurian tiger.

Perf. 12½x12, 12x12½

1970, Aug. 19 Litho.

3759 A1803 4k multicolored .20 .20
3760 A1803 6k multicolored .25 .20
3761 A1803 10k multicolored .30 .20
3762 A1803 16k ultra & multi .45 .20
3763 A1803 20k gray & multi .60 .20
Nos. 3759-3763 (5) 1.80 1.00

Magnifying Glass over Stamp, and Covers — A1804

1970, Aug. 31 Photo. *Perf. 12x12½*

3764 A1804 4k red & silver .50 .25

2nd All-Union Philatelists' Cong., Moscow.

Pioneers' Badge — A1805

Soviet general education: 2k, Lenin and Children, monument. 4k, Star and scenes from play "Zarnitsa."

1970, Sept. 24 Photo. *Perf. 11½*

3765 A1805 1k gray, red & gold .25 .20
3766 A1805 2k brn red & slate grn .25 .20
3767 A1805 4k lt ol, car & gold .25 .20
Nos. 3765-3767 (3) .75 .60

Yerevan University A1806

1970, Sept. 24 Photo. ***Perf. 12½x12***

3768 A1806 4k ultra & salmon pink .30 .20

Yerevan State University, 50th anniv.

Library Bookplate, Vilnius University A1807

1970, Oct. Typo. ***Perf. 12x12½***

3772 A1807 4k silver, gray & blk .50 .25

Vilnius University Library, 400th anniv.

Woman Holding Flowers — A1808

1970, Oct. 30 **Photo.**

3773 A1808 6k blue & lt brown .30 .20

25th anniversary of the International Democratic Federation of Women.

Farm Woman, Cattle Farm — A1809

Designs: No. 3775, Farmer and mechanical farm equipment. No. 3776, Farmer, fertilization equipment and plane.

1970, Oct. 30 ***Perf. 11½x12***

3774 A1809 4k olive, yellow & red .20 .20
3775 A1809 4k ocher, yellow & red .20 .20
3776 A1809 4k lt vio, yellow & red .20 .20
Nos. 3774-3776 (3) .60 .60

Aims of the new agricultural 5-year plan.

Lenin — A1810

Lithographed and Embossed

1970, Nov. 3 ***Perf. 12½x12***

3777 A1810 4k red & gold .30 .20

Souvenir Sheet

3778 A1810 30k red & gold 1.75 .75

53rd anniv. of the October Revolution.

No. 3389 Overprinted in Gold

1970, Nov. 3 ***Perf. 11½***

3779 A1641 4k gold & multi .80 .75

50th anniversary of the GOELRO Plan for the electrification of Russia.

Spasski Tower and Fir Branch — A1811

A. A. Baykov — A1812

1970, Nov. 23 Litho. ***Perf. 12x12½***

3780 A1811 6k multicolored .30 .20

New Year, 1971.

1970, Nov. 25 Photo. ***Perf. 12½x12***

3781 A1812 4k sepia & golden brn .30 .20

Baykov (1870-1946), metallurgist and academician.

Portrait Type of 1968

Portrait: No. 3782, A. D. Tsyurupa.

1970, Nov. 25 Photo. ***Perf. 12x12½***

3782 A1688 4k brown & salmon .35 .25

Tsyurupa (1870-1928), First Vice Chairman of the Soviet of People's Commissars.

Vasily Blazhenny Church, Red Square A1813

Tourist publicity: 6k, Performance of Swan Lake. 10k, Two deer. 12k, Folk art. 14k, Sword into Plowshare statue, by E. Vouchetich, and museums. 16k, Automobiles and woman photographer.

Photogravure and Engraved

1970, Nov. 29 ***Perf. 12x11½***

Frame in Brown Orange

3783 A1813 4k multicolored .20 .20
3784 A1813 6k multicolored .20 .20
3785 A1813 10k brn org & sl green .35 .20
3786 A1813 12k multicolored .45 .20
3787 A1813 14k multicolored .50 .20
3788 A1813 16k multicolored .65 .20
Nos. 3783-3788 (6) 2.35 1.20

Daisy — A1814

1970, Nov. 29 Litho. ***Perf. 11½***

3789 A1814 4k shown .20 .20
3790 A1814 6k Dahlia .20 .20
3791 A1814 10k Phlox .40 .20
3792 A1814 12k Aster .50 .20
3793 A1814 16k Clementis .85 .20
Nos. 3789-3793 (5) 2.15 1.00

UN Emblem, African Mother and Child, Broken Chain — A1815

1970, Dec. 10 Photo. ***Perf. 12x12½***

3794 A1815 10k blue & dk brown .50 .20

United Nations Declaration on Colonial Independence, 10th anniversary.

Ludwig van Beethoven (1770-1827), Composer — A1816

1970, Dec. 16 Engr. ***Perf. 12½x12***

3795 A1816 10k deep claret, *pink* .50 .30

Skating — A1817

Luna 16 — A1818

Design: 10k, Skiing.

1970, Dec. 18 Photo. ***Perf. 11½***

3796 A1817 4k light gray, ultra & dark red .20 .20
3797 A1817 10k light gray, brt green & brown .30 .20

1971 Trade Union Winter Games.

1970, Dec. Photo. ***Perf. 11½***

Designs: No. 3799, 3801b, Luna 16 leaving moon. No. 3800, 3801c, Capsule landing on earth. No. 3801a, like No. 3798.

3798 A1818 10k gray blue .35 .20
3799 A1818 10k dk purple .35 .20
3800 A1818 10k gray blue .35 .20
Nos. 3798-3800 (3) 1.05 .60

Souvenir Sheet

3801 Sheet of 3 2.10 1.00
a. A1818 20k blue .70 .25
b. A1818 20k dark purple .70 .25
c. A1818 20k blue .70 .25

Luna 16 unmanned, automatic moon mission, Sept. 12-24, 1970.

Nos. 3801a-3801c have attached labels (no perf. between vignette and label). Issue dates: No. 3801. Dec. 18; Nos. 3798-3800, Dec. 28.

The Conestabile Madonna, by Raphael A1819

Paintings: 4k, Apostles Peter and Paul, by El Greco. 10k, Perseus and Andromeda, by Rubens, horiz. 12k, The Prodigal Son, by Rembrandt. 16k, Family Portrait, by van Dyck. 20k, The Actress Jeanne Samary, by Renoir. 30k, Woman with Fruit, by Gauguin. 50k, The Litte Madonna, by da Vinci. All paintings from the Hermitage in Leningrad, except 20k from Pushkin Museum, Moscow.

Perf. 12x12½, 12½x12

1970, Dec. 23 **Litho.**

3802 A1819 3k gray & multi .20 .20
3803 A1819 4k gray & multi .20 .20
3804 A1819 10k gray & multi .50 .20
3805 A1819 12k gray & multi .50 .20
3806 A1819 16k gray & multi .60 .20
3807 A1819 20k gray & multi .85 .20
3808 A1819 30k gray & multi 1.75 .25
Nos. 3802-3808 (7) 4.60 1.45

Souvenir Sheet

Imperf

3809 A1819 50k gold & multi 3.00 .90

Harry Pollyt and Shipyard A1820

1970, Dec. 31 Photo. ***Perf. 12***

3810 A1820 10k maroon & brown .40 .30

Pollyt (1890-1960), British labor leader.

International Cooperative Alliance A1821

1970, Dec. 31 ***Perf. 11½x12***

3811 A1821 12k yel green & red .40 .30

Intl. Cooperative Alliance, 75th anniv.

Lenin — A1822

1971, Jan. 1 ***Perf. 12***

3812 A1822 4k red & gold .25 .20

Year of the 24th Congress of the Communist Party of the Soviet Union.

Georgian Republic Flag A1823

1971, Jan. 12 Litho. *Perf. 11½*

3813	A1823	4k ol bister & multi	.25	.20

Georgian SSR, 50th anniversary.

Republic Anniversaries Type of 1970

#3816

#3818

Designs (Hammer-Sickle Emblem and): No. 3814, Supreme Soviet Building, Makhachkala. No. 3815, Fruit, ship, mountain, conveyor. No. 3816, Grapes, refinery, ship. No. 3817, Supreme Soviet Building, Nalchik. No. 3818, Supreme Soviet Building, Syktyvkar, and lumber industry. No. 3819, Natural resources, dam, mining. No. 3820, Industrial installations and natural products. No. 3821, Ship, "industry." No. 3822, Grapes, pylons and mountains. No. 3823, Kazbek Mountain, industrial installations, produce.

1971-74 Engr. *Perf. 12x12½*

3814	A1794	4k dk blue green	.20	.20
3815	A1794	4k rose red	.20	.20
3816	A1794	4k red	.20	.20
3817	A1794	4k blue	.20	.20
3818	A1794	4k green	.20	.20
3819	A1794	4k brt bl ('72)	.20	.20
3820	A1794	4k car rose ('72)	.20	.20
3821	A1794	4k brt ultra ('73)	.20	.20
3822	A1794	4k golden brn ('74)	.20	.20
		Litho.		
3823	A1794	4k dark red ('74)	.20	.20
		Nos. 3814-3823 (10)	2.00	2.00

50th annivers. of Dagestan (#3814), Abkazian (#3815), Adzhar (#3816), Kabardino-Balkarian (#3817), Komi (#3818), Yakut (#3819), Checheno-Ingush (#3820), Buryat (#3821), Nakhichevan (#3822), and North Ossetian (#3823) autonomous SSRs.

No. 3823 also for bicentenary of Ossetia's union with Russia.

Issued: #3814, 1/20; #3815, 3/3; #3816, 6/16; #3817-3818, 8/17; #3819, 4/20; #3820, 11/22; #3821, 5/24; #3822, 2/6; #3823, 7/7.

Tower of Genoa, Cranes, Hammer and Sickle A1824

1971, Jan. 28 Typo. *Perf. 12*

3824	A1824	10k dk red, gray & yel	.30	.20

Founding of Feodosiya, Crimea, 2500th anniv.

Palace of Culture, Kiev — A1825

1971, Feb. 16 Photo. *Perf. 11½*

3825	A1825	4k red, bister & blue	.25	.20

Ukrainian Communist Party, 24th cong.

N. Gubin, I. Chernykh, S. Kosinov A1826

1971, Feb. 16 *Perf. 12½x12*

3826	A1826	4k slate grn & vio brn	.25	.20

Heroes of the Soviet Union.

"Industry and Agriculture" A1827

1971, Feb. 16 *Perf. 12x12½*

3827	A1827	6k olive bister & red	.25	.20

State Planning Organization, 50th anniv.

Lesya Ukrayinka (1871-1913), Ukrainian Poet — A1828

1971, Feb. 25

3828	A1828	4k orange red & bister	.25	.20

"Summer" Dance — A1829

Dancers of Russian Folk Dance Ensemble: No. 3830, "On the Skating Rink." No. 3831, Ukrainian dance "Hopak." No. 3832, Adzharian dance. No. 3833, Gypsy dance.

1971, Feb. 25 Litho. *Perf. 12½x12*

3829	A1829	10k bister & multi	.40	.20
3830	A1829	10k olive & multi	.40	.20
3831	A1829	10k olive bis & multi	.40	.20
3832	A1829	10k gray & multi	.40	.20
3833	A1829	10k grnsh gray & multi	.40	.20
		Nos. 3829-3833 (5)	2.00	1.00

Luna 17 on Moon A1830

Designs: No. 3835, Ground control. No. 3836, Separation of Lunokhod 1 and carrier. 16k, Lunokhod 1 in operation.

1971, Mar. 16 Photo. *Perf. 11½*

3834	A1830	10k dp vio & sepia	.35	.20
3835	A1830	12k dk blue & sepia	.50	.20
3836	A1830	12k dk blue & sepia	.50	.20
3837	A1830	16k dp vio & sepia	.65	.20
a.		Souv. sheet of 4	2.50	1.00
		Nos. 3834-3837 (4)	2.00	.80

Luna 17 unmanned, automated moon mission, Nov. 10-17, 1970.

No. 3837a contains Nos. 3834-3837, size 32x21mm each.

Paris Commune, Cent. — A1831

1971, Mar. 18 Litho. *Perf. 12*

3838	A1831	6k red & black	.30	.20

Industry, Science, Culture A1832

1971, Mar. 29 *Perf. 11½*

3839	A1832	6k bister, brn & red	.25	.20

24th Communist Party Cong., 3/30-4/3.

Yuri Gagarin Medal A1833

1971, Mar. 30 Photo. *Perf. 11½*

3840	A1833	10k brown & lemon	.40	.20

10th anniv. of man's first flight into space.

Space Research A1834

1971, Mar. 30

3841	A1834	12k slate bl & vio brn	.40	.20

Cosmonauts' Day, Apr. 12.

E. Birznieks-Upitis (1871-1960), Latvian Writer — A1835

1971, Apr. 1 *Perf. 12x12½*

3842	A1835	4k red brown & gray	.25	.20

Bee and Blossom — A1836

1971, Apr. 1 *Perf. 11½*

3843	A1836	6k olive & multi	.25	.20

23rd International Beekeeping Congress, Moscow, Aug. 22-Sept. 2.

Souvenir Sheet

Cosmonauts and Spacecraft — A1837

Designs: 10k, Vostok. No. 3844b, Yuri Gagarin. No. 3844c, First man walking in space. 16k, First orbital station.

1971, Apr. 12 Litho. *Perf. 12*

3844	A1837	Sheet of 4	3.00	1.00
a.		10k violet brown	.45	.20
b.-c.		12k Prussian green	.45	.20
d.		16k violet brown	.50	.20

10th anniv. of man's 1st flight into space. Size of stamps: 26x19mm.

Lenin Memorial, Ulyanovsk — A1838

1971, Apr. 16 Photo. *Perf. 12*

3845	A1838	4k cop red & ol bister	.25	.20

Lenin's birthday. Memorial was built for centenary celebration of his birth.

Lt. Col. Nikolai I. Vlasov — A1839

1971, May 9 Photo. *Perf. 12x12½*

3846	A1839	4k gray olive & brn	.30	.20

Hero of the Soviet Union.

Khafiz Shirazi, Tadzhik-Persian Poet, 650th Birth Anniv. — A1840

1971, May 9 **Litho.**

3847 A1840 4k olive, brn & black .25 .20

GAZ-66 — A1841

Soviet Cars: 3k, BelAZ-540 truck. No. 3850, Moskvich-412. No. 3851, ZAZ-968. 10k, Volga.

1971, May 12 **Photo.** ***Perf. 11x11½***

3848 A1841 2k yellow & multi .20 .20
3849 A1841 3k lt blue & multi .20 .20
3850 A1841 4k lt lilac & multi .20 .20
3851 A1841 4k lt gray & multi .20 .20
3852 A1841 10k lt lilac & multi .20 .20
Nos. 3848-3852 (5) 1.00 1.00

Bogomolets A1842

Satellite A1843

1971, May 24 **Photo.** ***Perf. 12***

3853 A1842 4k orange & black .25 .20

A. A. Bogomolets, physician, 90th birth anniv.

1971, June 9 ***Perf. 11½***

3854 A1843 6k blue & multi .25 .20

15th General Assembly of the International Union of Geodesics and Geophysics.

Symbols of Science and History A1844

1971, June 9 ***Perf. 12***

3855 A1844 6k green & gray .25 .20

13th Congress of Science History.

Oil Derrick & Symbols A1845

1971, June 9 ***Perf. 11½***

3856 A1845 6k multicolored .20 .20

8th World Oil Congress.

Sukhe Bator Monument — A1846

1971, June 16 **Typo.** ***Perf. 12***

3857 A1846 6k red, gold & black .25 .20

50th anniversary of Mongolian revolution.

Monument of Defenders of Liepaja A1847

1971, June 21 **Photo.**

3858 A1847 4k gray, black & brn .30 .25

30th anniversary of the defense of Liepaja (Libau) against invading Germans.

Map of Antarctica and Station — A1848

Weather Map, Plane, Ship and Satellite — A1849

Engraved and Photogravure

1971, June 21 ***Perf. 11½***

3859 A1848 6k black, grn & ultra .50 .30

Antarctic Treaty pledging peaceful uses of & scientific co-operation in Antarctica, 10th anniv.

1971, June 21

3860 A1849 10k black, red & ultra .50 .30

50th anniversary of Soviet Hydrometeorological service.

FIR Emblem, "Homeland" by E. Vouchetich A1850

1971, June 21 **Photo.** ***Perf. 12x12½***

3861 A1850 6k dk red & slate .25 .20

International Federation of Resistance Fighters (FIR), 20th anniversary.

Discus and Running A1851

Designs: 4k, Archery (women). 6k, Dressage. 10k, Basketball. 12k, Wrestling.

Lithographed and Engraved

1971, June 24 ***Perf. 11½***

3862 A1851 3k violet blue, *rose* .20 .20
3863 A1851 4k slate grn, *pale pink* .20 .20
3864 A1851 6k red brn, *apple grn* .30 .20
3865 A1851 10k dk pur, *gray blue* .40 .20
3866 A1851 12k red brn, *yellow* .50 .20
Nos. 3862-3866 (5) 1.60 1.00

5th Summer Spartakiad.

Benois Madonna, by da Vinci A1852

Paintings: 4k, Mary Magdalene, by Titian. 10k, The Washerwoman, by Jean Simeon Chardin, horiz. 12k, Portrait of a Young Man, by Frans Hals. 14k, Tancred and Arminia, by Nicolas Poussin, horiz. 16k, Girl with Fruit, by Murillo. 20k, Girl with Ball, by Picasso.

Perf. 12x12½, 12½x12

1971, July 7 **Litho.**

3867 A1852 2k bister & multi .20 .20
3868 A1852 4k bister & multi .20 .20
3869 A1852 10k bister & multi .40 .20
3870 A1852 12k bister & multi .45 .20
3871 A1852 14k bister & multi .55 .20
3872 A1852 16k bister & multi .65 .20
3873 A1852 20k bister & multi .75 .20
Nos. 3867-3873 (7) 3.20 1.40

Foreign master works in Russian museums.

Kazakhstan Flag, Lenin Badge — A1853

1971, July 7 **Photo.** ***Perf. 11½***

3874 A1853 4k blue, red & brown .25 .20

50th anniversary of the Kazakh Communist Youth League.

Star Emblem and Letters A1854

1971, July 14

3875 A1854 4k oliver, blue & black .25 .20

International Letter Writing Week.

Nikolai A. Nekrasov, by Ivan N. Kramskoi A1855

Portraits: No. 3877, Aleksandr Spendiarov, by M. S. Saryan. 10k, Fedor M. Dostoevski, by Vassili G. Perov.

1971, July 14 **Litho.** ***Perf. 12x12½***

3876 A1855 4k citron & multi .25 .20
3877 A1855 4k gray blue & multi .25 .20
3878 A1855 10k multicolored .30 .20
Nos. 3876-3878 (3) .80 .60

Nikolai Alekseevitch Nekrasov (1821-1877), poet, Fedor Mikhailovich Dostoevski (1821-1881), novelist, Spendiarov (1871-1928), Armenian composer.

See Nos. 4056-4057.

Zachary Paliashvili (1871-1933), Georgian Composer and Score — A1856

1971, Aug. 3 **Photo.** ***Perf. 12x12½***

3879 A1856 4k brown .25 .20

Gorki Kremlin, Stag and Hydrofoil A1857

1971, Aug. 3 **Litho.** ***Perf. 12***

3880 A1857 16k multicolored .60 .25

Gorki (formerly Nizhni Novgorod), 750th anniv. See Nos. 3889, 3910-3914.

Federation Emblem and Students A1858

1971, Aug. 3 **Photo.** ***Perf. 11½***

3881 A1858 6k ultra & multi .25 .20

Intl. Students Federation, 25th anniv.

Common Dolphins A1859

Sea Mammals: 6k, Sea otter. 10k, Narwhals. 12k, Walrus. 14k, Ribbon seals.

Photogravure and Engraved

1971, Aug. 12 ***Perf. 11½***

3882 A1859 4k silver & multi .20 .20
3883 A1859 6k silver & multi .20 .20
3884 A1859 10k silver & multi .30 .20
3885 A1859 12k silver & multi .35 .20
3886 A1859 14k silver & multi .45 .20
Nos. 3882-3886 (5) 1.50 1.00

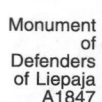

Miner's Star of Valor — A1860

1971, Aug. 17 **Photo.** ***Perf. 11½***

3887 A1860 4k bister, black & red .25 .20

250th anniversary of the discovery of coal in the Donets Basin.

Ernest Rutherford and Diagram of Movement of Atomic Particles A1861

1971, Aug. 24 **Photo.** ***Perf. 12***

3888 A1861 6k magenta & dk ol .25 .20

Rutherford (1871-1937), British physicist.

Gorki and Gorki Statue — A1862

1971, Sept. 14 ***Perf. 11½***

3889 A1862 4k steel blue & multi .25 .20

Gorki (see #3880).

Troika and Spasski Tower A1863

1971, Sept. 14

3890 A1863 10k black, red & gold .30 .20

New Year 1972.

Automatic Production Center — A1864

#3892, Agricultural development. #3893, Family in shopping center. #3894, Hydro-generators, thermoelectric station. #3895, Marchers, flags, books inscribed Marx and Lenin.

1971, Sept. 29 **Photo.** ***Perf. 12x11½***

3891	A1864 4k purple, red & blk	.20	.20
3892	A1864 4k ocher, red & brn	.20	.20
3893	A1864 4k yel, olive & red	.20	.20
3894	A1864 4k bister, red & brn	.20	.20
3895	A1864 4k ultra, red & slate	.20	.20
	Nos. 3891-3895 (5)	1.00	1.00

Resolutions of 24th Soviet Union Communist Party Congress.

The Meeting, by Vladimir Y. Makovsky A1865

Ivan N. Kramskoi, Self-portrait — A1866

Paintings: 4k, Woman Student, by Nikolai A. Yaroshenko. 6k, Woman Miner, by Nikolai A. Kasatkin. 10k, Harvest, by G. G. Myasoyedov, horiz. 16k, Country Road, by A. K. Savrasov. 20k, Pine Forest, by I. I. Shishkin, horiz.

Perf. 12x12½, 12½x12

1971, Oct. 14 **Litho.**

Frame in Light Gray

3896	A1865 2k multicolored	.20	.20
3897	A1865 4k multicolored	.20	.20
3898	A1865 6k multicolored	.25	.20
3899	A1865 10k multicolored	.50	.20
3900	A1865 16k multicolored	.55	.20
3901	A1865 20k multicolored	1.10	.20
	Nos. 3896-3901 (6)	2.80	1.20

Souvenir Sheet

Lithographed and Gold Embossed

3902 A1866 50k dk green & multi 2.00 .60

History of Russian painting.

V. V. Vorovsky, Bolshevik Party Leader and Diplomat, Birth Cent. — A1867

1971, Oct. 14 **Engr.** ***Perf. 12***

3903 A1867 4k red brown .25 .20

Cosmonauts Dobrovolsky, Volkov and Patsayev — A1868

1971, Oct. 20 **Photo.** ***Perf. 11½x12***

3904 A1868 4k black, lilac & org .25 .20

In memory of cosmonauts Lt. Col. Georgi T. Dobrovolsky, Vladislav N. Volkov and Viktor I. Patsayev, who died during the Soyuz 11 space mission, June 6-30, 1971.

Order of October Revolution — A1869

1971, Oct. 20 **Litho.** ***Perf. 12***

3905 A1869 4k red, yel & black .25 .20

54th anniversary of October Revolution.

E. Vakhtangov and "Princess Turandot" A1870

Designs: No. 3907, Boris Shchukin and scene from "Man with Rifle (Lenin)," horiz. No. 3908, Ruben Simonov and scene from "Cyrano de Bergerac," horiz.

Perf. 12x12½, 12½x12

1971, Oct. 26 **Photo.**

3906	A1870 10k mar & red brn	.35	.20
3907	A1870 10k brown & dull yel	.35	.20
3908	A1870 10k red brn & ocher	.35	.20
	Nos. 3906-3908 (3)	1.05	.60

Vakhtangov Theater, Moscow, 50th anniv.

Dzhambul Dzhabayev(1846-1945), Kazakh Poet — A1871

1971, Nov. 16 ***Perf. 12x12½***

3909 A1871 4k orange & brown .30 .25

Gorki Kremlin Type, 1971

Designs: 3k, Pskov Kremlin and Velikaya River. 4k, Novgorod Kremlin and eternal flame memorial. 6k, Smolensk Fortress and liberation monument. 10k,Kolomna Kremlin and buses. 50k, Moscow Kremlin.

1971, Nov. 16 **Litho.** ***Perf. 12***

3910	A1857 3k multicolored	.25	.20
3911	A1857 4k multicolored	.25	.20
3912	A1857 6k gray & multi	.25	.20
3913	A1857 10k olive & multi	.25	.20
	Nos. 3910-3913 (4)	1.00	.80

Souvenir Sheet

Engraved and Lithographed

Perf. 11½

3914 A1857 50k yellow & multi 1.75 1.00

Historic buildings. No. 3914 contains one 21½x32mm stamp.

William Foster, View of New York A1872

1971 **Litho.** ***Perf. 12***

3915 A1872 10k brn & blk ("-1961") .50 .25

a. "-1964" 10.00 7.25

William Foster (1881-1961), chairman of Communist Party of US.

No. 3915a was issued Nov. 16 with incorrect death date (1964). No. 3915, with corrected date (1961), was issued Dec. 8.

Aleksandr Fadeyev and Cavalrymen — A1873

1971, Nov. 25 **Photo.** ***Perf. 12½x12***

3916 A1873 4k slate & orange .30 .25

Aleksandr Fadeyev (1901-1956), writer.

Amethyst and Diamond Brooch A1874

Precious Jewels: #3918, Engraved Shakh diamond, India, 16th cent. #3919, Diamond daffodils, 18th cent. #3920, Amethyst & diamond pendant. #3921, Diamond rose made for centenary of Lenin's birth. 30k, Diamond & pearl pendant.

1971, Dec. 8 **Litho.** ***Perf. 11½***

3917	A1874 10k brt blue & multi	.20	.20
3918	A1874 10k dk red & multi	.20	.20
3919	A1874 10k grnsh black & multi	.20	.20
3920	A1874 20k grnsh black & multi	.40	.25
3921	A1874 20k rose red & multi	.40	.25
3922	A1874 30k black & multi	.60	.40
	Nos. 3917-3922 (6)	2.00	1.50

Souvenir Sheet

Workers with Banners, Congress Hall and Spasski Tower — A1875

1971, Dec. 15 **Photo.** ***Perf. 11x11½***

3923 A1875 20k red, pale green & brown 2.00 1.00

See note after No. 3895. No. 3923 contains one partially perforated stamp.

Vanda Orchid — A1876

Flowers: 1k, #3929b, shown. 2k, Anthurium. 4k, #3929c, Flowering crab cactus. 12k, #3929a, Amaryllis. 14k, #3929d, Medinilla magnifica.

1971, Dec. 15 **Litho.** ***Perf. 12x12½***

3924	A1876 1k olive & multi	.20	.20
3925	A1876 2k green & multi	.25	.20
3926	A1876 4k blue & multi	.40	.20
3927	A1876 12k multicolored	.50	.20
3928	A1876 14k multicolored	.65	.20
	Nos. 3924-3928 (5)	2.00	1.00

Miniature Sheet

Perf. 12

3929	Sheet of 4	2.00	.90
a.-d.	A1876 10k any single	.40	.25

Nos. 3929a-3929d have white background, black frame line and inscription. Size of stamps 19x57mm.

Issued: #3924-3928, 12/15; #3929, 12/30.

Peter I Reviewing Fleet, 1723 — A1877

History of Russian Fleet: 4k, Oriol, first ship built in Eddinovo, 1668, vert. 10k, Battleship Poltava, 1712, vert. 12k, Armed ship Ingermanland, 1715, vert. 16k, Frigate Vladimir, 1848.

Perf. 11½x12, 12x11½

1971, Dec. 15 Engr. & Photo.

3930	A1877	1k multicolored	.30	.25
3931	A1877	4k brown & multi	.35	.25
3932	A1877	10k multicolored	.75	.35
3933	A1877	12k multicolored	.75	.35
3934	A1877	16k lt green & multi	1.50	.40
		Nos. 3930-3934 (5)	3.65	1.60

Ice Hockey A1878

1971, Dec. 15 Litho. *Perf. 12½*

3935 A1878 6k multicolored .30 .25

25th anniversary of Soviet ice hockey.

A1879

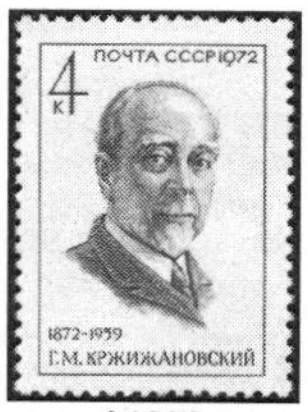

A1880

Oil rigs and causeway in Caspian Sea.

1971, Dec. 30 *Perf. 11½*

3936 A1879 4k dp blue, org & blk .25 .20

Baku oil industry.

1972, Jan. 5 Engr. *Perf. 12*

3937 A1880 4k yellow brown .25 .20

G. M. Krzhizhanovsky (1872-1959), scientist and co-worker with Lenin.

Alexander Scriabin (1872-1915), Composer A1881

1972, Jan. 6 Photo. *Perf. 12x12½*

3938 A1881 4k indigo & olive .30 .25

Bering's Cormorant A1882

Birds: 6k, Ross' gull, horiz. 10k, Barnacle geese. 12k, Spectacled eiders, horiz. 16k, Mediterranean gull.

1972, Jan. 12 *Perf. 11½*

3939	A1882	4k dk grn, blk & yel	.20	.20
3940	A1882	6k ind, pink & blk	.30	.20
3941	A1882	10k grnsh blue, blk & brown	.55	.20
3942	A1882	12k multicolored	.60	.20
3943	A1882	16k ultra, gray & red	.65	.20
		Nos. 3939-3943 (5)	2.30	1.00

Waterfowl of the USSR.

11th Winter Olympic Games, Sapporo, Japan, Feb. 3-13 — A1883

Designs (Olympic Rings and): 4k, Speed skating. 6k, Women's figure skating. 10k, Ice hockey. 12k, Ski jump. 16k, Long-distance skiing. 50k, Sapporo '72 emblem.

1972, Jan. 20 Litho. *Perf. 12x12½*

3944	A1883	4k bl grn, red & brn	.20	.20
3945	A1883	6k yel grn, blue & dp orange	.20	.20
3946	A1883	10k vio, bl & dp org	.35	.20
3947	A1883	12k light blue, blue & brick red	.40	.20
3948	A1883	16k gray, bl & brt rose	.70	.20
		Nos. 3944-3948 (5)	1.85	1.00

Souvenir Sheet

3949 A1883 50k multicolored 1.50 .75

For overprint see No. 3961.

Heart, Globe and Exercising Family — A1884

1972, Feb. 9 Photo.

3950 A1884 4k brt grn & rose red .25 .20

Heart Month sponsored by the WHO.

Leipzig Fair Emblem and Soviet Pavilion — A1885

1972, Feb. 22 *Perf. 11½*

3951 A1885 16k red & gold .60 .25

50th anniversary of the participation of the USSR in the Leipzig Trade Fair.

Hammer, Sickle and Cogwheel Emblem — A1886

1972, Feb. 29 *Perf. 12x12½*

3952 A1886 4k rose red & lt brown .25 .20

15th USSR Trade Union Congress, Moscow, March 1972.

Aloe A1887

Aleksandra Kollontai A1888

Medicinal Plants: 2k, Horn poppy. 4k, Groundsel. 6k, Orthosiphon stamineus. 10k, Nightshade.

1972, Mar. 14 Litho. *Perf. 12x12½*

Flowers in Natural Colors

3953	A1887	1k olive bister	.20	.20
3954	A1887	2k slate green	.20	.20
3955	A1887	4k brt purple	.20	.20
3956	A1887	6k violet blue	.20	.20
3957	A1887	10k dk brown	.35	.25
		Nos. 3953-3957 (5)	1.15	1.05

1972, Mar. 20 Engr. *Perf. 12½x12*

#3959, Georgy Chicherin. #3960, Kamo (pseudonym of S.A. Ter-Petrosyan).

3958	A1888	4k red brown	.20	.20
3959	A1888	4k claret	.20	.20
3960	A1888	4k olive bister	.20	.20
		Nos. 3958-3960 (3)	.60	.60

Outstanding workers of the Communist Party of the Soviet Union and for the State.

No. 3949 Overprinted in Margin Souvenir Sheet

1972, Mar. 20 Litho. *Perf. 12x12½*

3961 A1883 50k multicolored 4.00 2.00

Victories of Soviet athletes in the 11th Winter Olympic Games (8 gold, 5 silver, 3 bronze medals).

For similar overprints see Nos. 4028, 4416.

Orbital Station Salyut and Spaceship Soyuz Docking Above Earth — A1889

Designs: No. 3963, Mars 2 approaching Mars, and emblem dropped on Mars. 16k, Mars 3, which landed on Mars, Dec. 2, 1971.

1971, Apr. 5 Photo. *Perf. 11½x12*

3962	A1889	6k vio, blue & silver	.20	.20
3963	A1889	6k pur, ocher & sil	.20	.20
3964	A1889	16k pur, blue & silver	1.00	.20
		Nos. 3962-3964 (3)	1.40	.60

Cosmonauts' Day.

Shield and Products of Izhory Factory A1890

1972, Apr. 20 *Perf. 12½x12*

3965 A1890 4k purple & silver .25 .20

250th anniversary of Izhory Factory, founded by Peter the Great.

Leonid Sobinov in "Eugene Onegin," by Tchaikovsky — A1891

1972, Apr. 20

3966 A1891 10k dp brown & buff .30 .20

Sobinov (1872-1934), opera singer.

Book, Torch, Children and Globe A1892

1972, May 5 *Perf. 11½*

3967 A1892 6k brn, grnsh bl & buff .25 .20

International Book Year 1972.

Girl in Laboratory and Pioneers A1893

Designs: 1k, Pavlik Morosov (Pioneer hero), Pioneers saluting and banner. 3k, Pioneers with wheelbarrow, Chukchi boy, and Chukotka Pioneer House. 4k, Pioneer Honor Guard and Parade. 30k, Pioneer Honor Guard, vert.

1972, May 10

3968	A1893	1k red & multi	.20	.20
3969	A1893	2k multicolored	.20	.20
3970	A1893	3k multicolored	.20	.20
3971	A1893	4k gray & multi	.20	.20
		Nos. 3968-3971 (4)	.80	.80

Souvenir Sheet

Perf. 12x12½

3972 A1893 30k multicolored 2.00 .75

50th anniversary of the Lenin Pioneer Organization of the USSR.

Pioneer Bugler A1894

1972, May 27 Photo. *Perf. 11½*

3973 A1894 4k red, ocher & plum .25 .20

2nd Youth Philatelic Exhibition, Minsk, and 50th anniv. of Lenin Pioneer Org.

M. S. Ordubady (1872-1950), Azerbaijan Writer and Social Worker — A1895

1972, May 25 ***Perf. 12x12½***
3974 A1895 4k orange & rose brn .30 .20

Globe A1896

1972, May 25 ***Perf. 11½***
3975 A1896 6k multicolored .60 .30

European Safety and Cooperation Conference, Brussels.

Cossack Leader, by Ivan Nikitin A1897

Paintings: 4k, Fedor G. Volkov (actor), by Anton Losenko. 6k, V. Majkov (poet), by Fedor Rokotov. 10k, Nikolai I. Novikov (writer), by Dimitri Levitsky. 12k, Gavriil R. Derzhavin (poet, civil servant), by Vladimir Borovikovsky. 16k, Peasants' Supper, by Mikhail Shibanov, horiz. 20k, View of Moscow, by Fedor Alexeyev, horiz.

Perf. 12x12½, 12½x12
1972, June 7 **Litho.**
3976 A1897 2k gray & multi .20 .20
3977 A1897 4k gray & multi .20 .20
3978 A1897 6k gray & multi .20 .20
3979 A1897 10k gray & multi .30 .20
3980 A1897 12k gray & multi .30 .20
3981 A1897 16k gray & multi .45 .20
3982 A1897 20k gray & multi .60 .25
Nos. 3976-3982 (7) 2.25 1.45

History of Russian painting. See Nos. 4036-4042, 4074-4080, 4103-4109.

George Dimitrov (1882-1949), Bulgarian Communist Party Leader — A1898

1972, June 15 **Photo.** ***Perf. 12½x12***
3983 A1898 6k brown & ol bister .30 .20

20th Olympic Games, Munich, 8/26-9/11 A1899

Olympic Rings and: 4k, Fencing. 6k, Women's gymnastics. 10k, Canoeing. 14k, Boxing. 16k, Running. 50k, Weight lifting.

1972, July 1 ***Perf. 12x11½***
3984 A1899 4k brt mag & gold .20 .20
3985 A1899 6k dp green & gold .20 .20
3986 A1899 10k brt blue & gold .55 .20
3987 A1899 14k Prus bl & gold .60 .20
3988 A1899 16k red & gold .85 .20
Nos. 3984-3988 (5) 2.40 1.00

Souvenir Sheet

Perf. 11½

3989 A1899 50k gold & multi 2.00 .80

#3989 contains one 25x35mm stamp.
For overprint see No. 4028.

Congress Palace, Kiev A1900

1972, July 1 **Photo. & Engr.**
3990 A1900 6k Prus blue & bister .25 .20

9th World Gerontology Cong., Kiev, 7/2-7.

Roald Amundsen, "Norway," Northern Lights A1901

1972, July 13 **Photo.** ***Perf. 11½***
3991 A1901 6k vio blue & dp bister .40 .25

Roald Amundsen (1872-1928), Norwegian polar explorer.

17th Century House, Chernigov A1902

Designs: 4k, Market Square, Lvov, vert. 10k, Kovnirov Building, Kiev. 16k, Fortress, Kamenets-Podolski, vert.

Perf. 12x12½, 12½x12
1972, July 18 **Litho.**
3992 A1902 4k citron & multi .20 .20
3993 A1902 6k gray & multi .20 .20
3994 A1902 10k ocher & multi .40 .20
3995 A1902 16k salmon & multi .60 .20
Nos. 3992-3995 (4) 1.40 .80

Historic and architectural treasures of the Ukraine.

Asoka Pillar, Indian Flag, Red Fort, New Delhi A1903

1972, July 27 **Photo.** ***Perf. 11½***
3996 A1903 6k dk blue, emer & red .25 .20

25th anniversary of India's independence.

Miners' Emblem A1904

1972, Aug. 10
3997 A1904 4k violet gray & red .25 .20

25th Miners' Day.

Far East Fighters' Monument A1905

Designs: 4k, Monument for Far East Civil War heroes, industrial view. 6k, Vladivostok rostral column, Pacific fleet ships.

1972, Aug. 10
3998 A1905 3k red org, car & black .20 .20
3999 A1905 4k yel, sepia & blk .20 .20
4000 A1905 6k pink, dk car & black .20 .20
Nos. 3998-4000 (3) .60 .60

50th anniversary of the liberation of the Far Eastern provinces.

Boy with Dog, by Murillo A1906

Paintings from the Hermitage, Leningrad: 4k, Breakfast, Velazquez. 6k, Milkmaid's Family, Louis Le Nain. 16k, Sad Woman, Watteau. 20k, Moroccan Saddling Steed, Delacroix. 50k, Self-portrait, Van Dyck. 4k, 6k horiz.

Perf. 12½x12, 12x12½
1972, Aug. 15 **Litho.**
4001 A1906 4k multicolored .20 .20
4002 A1906 6k multicolored .25 .20
4003 A1906 10k multicolored .35 .20
4004 A1906 16k multicolored .50 .20
4005 A1906 20k multicolored .75 .20
Nos. 4001-4005 (5) 2.05 1.00

Souvenir Sheet

Perf. 12

4006 A1906 50k multicolored 2.50 1.00

Sputnik 1 — A1907

1972, Sept. 14 **Litho.** ***Perf. 12x11½***
4007 A1907 6k shown .20 .20
4008 A1907 6k Launching of Vostok 2 .20 .20
4009 A1907 6k Lenov floating in space .20 .20
4010 A1907 6k Lunokhod on moon .20 .20
4011 A1907 6k Venera 7 descending to Venus .20 .20
4012 A1907 6k Mars & descending to Mars .20 .20
Nos. 4007-4012 (6) 1.20 1.20

15 years of space era. Sheets of 6.

Konstantin Aleksandrovich Mardzhanishvili (1872-1933), Theatrical Producer A1908

1972, Sept. 20 **Engr.** ***Perf. 12x12½***
4013 A1908 4k slate green .30 .25

Museum Emblem, Communications Symbols — A1909

1972, Sept. 20 **Photo.** ***Perf. 11½***
4014 A1909 4k slate green & multi .25 .20

Centenary of the A. S. Popov Central Museum of Communications.

"Stamp" and Topical Collecting Symbols A1910

Engraved and Lithographed
1972, Oct. 4 ***Perf. 12***
4015 A1910 4k yel, black & red .25 .20

Philatelic Exhibition in honor of 50th anniversary of the USSR.

Lenin A1911

1972, Oct. 12 **Photo.** ***Perf. 11½***
4016 A1911 4k gold & red .25 .20

55th anniversary of October Revolution.

Militia Badge — A1912

1972, Oct. 12
4017 A1912 4k gold, red & dk brn .25 .20

55th anniv. of the Militia of the USSR.

Arms of USSR A1913

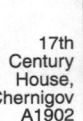

USSR, 50th anniv.: #4019, Arms and industrial scene. #4020, Arms, Supreme Soviet, Kremlin. #4021, Lenin. #4022, Arms, worker, book (Constitution). 30k, Coat of arms and Spasski Tower, horiz.

1972, Oct. 28 ***Perf. 12x11½***

4018 A1913 4k multicolored .20 .20
4019 A1913 4k multicolored .20 .20
4020 A1913 4k multicolored .20 .20
4021 A1913 4k multicolored .20 .20
4022 A1913 4k multicolored .20 .20
Nos. 4018-4022 (5) 1.00 1.00

Souvenir Sheet

Lithographed; Embossed

Perf. 12

4023 A1913 30k red & gold 1.50 .40

Kremlin and Snowflake A1914

Engraved and Photogravure

1972, Nov. 15 ***Perf. 11½***

4024 A1914 6k multicolored .25 .20

New Year 1973.

Savings Bank Book — A1915

1972, Nov. 15 Photo. ***Perf. 12x12½***

4025 A1915 4k lilac & slate .25 .20

50th anniv. of savings banks in the USSR.

Soviet Olympic Emblem and Laurel A1916

Design: 30k, Soviet Olympic emblem and obverse of gold, silver and bronze medals.

1972, Nov. 15 ***Perf. 11½***

4026 A1916 20k brn ol, red & gold .50 .40
4027 A1916 30k dp car, gold & brn 1.00 .60

No. 3989 Overprinted in Red

Souvenir Sheet

4028 A1899 50k gold & multi 2.00 1.25

Soviet medalists at 20th Olympic Games.

Battleship Peter the Great, 1872 — A1917

History of Russian Fleet: 3k, Cruiser Varyag, 1899. 4k, Battleship Potemkin, 1900. 6k, Cruiser Ochakov, 1902. 10k, Mine layer Amur, 1907.

Engraved and Photogravure

1972, Nov. 22 ***Perf. 11½x12***

4029 A1917 2k multicolored .35 .20
4030 A1917 3k multicolored .35 .20
4031 A1917 4k multicolored .45 .20
4032 A1917 6k multicolored .70 .20
4033 A1917 10k multicolored 1.10 .20
Nos. 4029-4033 (5) 2.95 1.00

Grigory S. Skovoroda (1722-1794), Ukrainian Philosopher and Humanist A1918

1972, Dec. 7 Engr. ***Perf. 12***

4034 A1918 4k dk violet blue .30 .20

Child Reading Traffic Rules — A1919

1972, Dec. 7 Photo. ***Perf. 11½***

4035 A1919 4k Prus blue, blk & red .25 .20

Traffic safety campaign.

Russian Painting Type of 1972

2k, Meeting of Village Party Members, by E. M. Cheptsov, horiz. 4k, Pioneer Girl, by Nicolai A. Kasatkin. 6k, Woman Delegate, by G. G. Ryazhsky. 10k, Winter's End, by K. F. Yuon, horiz. 16k, The Partisan A. G. Lunev, by N. I. Strunnikov. 20k, Igor E. Grabar, self-portrait. 50k, Blue Space (seascape with flying geese), by Arcadi A. Rylov, horiz.

Perf. 12x12½, 12½x12

1972, Dec. 7 **Litho.**

4036 A1897 2k olive & multi .20 .20
4037 A1897 4k olive & multi .20 .20
4038 A1897 6k olive & multi .20 .20
4039 A1897 10k olive & multi .40 .20
4040 A1897 16k olive & multi .55 .20
4041 A1897 20k olive & multi .80 .25
Nos. 4036-4041 (6) 2.35 1.25

Souvenir Sheet

Perf. 12

4042 A1897 50k multicolored 1.75 1.25

History of Russian painting.

Symbolic of Theory and Practice — A1920

Engraved and Photogravure

1972, Dec. 7 ***Perf. 11½***

4043 A1920 4k sl grn, yel & red brn .30 .20

Centenary of Polytechnic Museum, Moscow.

Venera 8 and Parachute A1921

1972, Dec. 28 Photo. ***Perf. 11½***

4044 A1921 6k dl claret, bl & blk .30 .20

Souvenir Sheet

Imperf

4045 Sheet of 2 9.00 3.00
a. A1921 50k Venera 8 2.50 .90
b. A1921 50k Mars 3 2.50 .90

Soviet space research. No. 4045 contains 2 40x20mm stamps with simulated perforations.

Globe, Torch and Palm — A1922

1973, Jan. 5 ***Perf. 11x11½***

4046 A1922 10k tan, vio blue & red .35 .30

15th anniversary of Afro-Asian Peoples' Solidarity Organization (AAPSO).

I. V. Babushkin A1923

"30," Map and Admiralty Tower, Leningrad A1924

1973, Jan. 10 Engr. ***Perf. 12***

4047 A1923 4k greenish black .25 .20

Babushkin (1873-1906), revolutionary.

1973, Jan. 10 Photo. ***Perf. 11½***

4048 A1924 4k pale brown, ocher & black .25 .20

30th anniversary of the breaking of the Nazi blockade of Leningrad.

TU-154 Turbojet Passenger Plane — A1925

1973, Jan. 10 Litho. ***Perf. 12***

4049 A1925 6k multicolored .25 .20

50th anniversary of Soviet Civil Aviation.

Gediminas Tower, Flag, Modern Vilnius A1926

1973, Jan. 10 Photo. ***Perf. 11½***

4050 A1926 10k gray, red & green .40 .30

650th anniversary of Vilnius.

Heroes' Memorial, Stalingrad — A1927

Designs (Details from Monument): 3k, Man with rifle and "Mother Russia," vert. 10k, Mourning mother and child. 12k, Arm with torch, vert. No. 4055a, Red star, hammer and sickle emblem and statuary like 3k. No. 4055b, "Mother Russia," vert.

1973, Feb. 1 Litho. ***Perf. 11½***

4051 A1927 3k dp org & blk .25 .20
4052 A1927 4k dp yel & blk .25 .20
4053 A1927 10k olive & multi .25 .20
4054 A1927 12k dp car & black .25 .20
Nos. 4051-4054 (4) 1.00 .80

Souvenir Sheet

Perf. 12x12½, 12½x12

4055 Sheet of 2 1.50 .75
a.-b. A1927 20k any single .45 .20

30th anniv, of the victory over the Germans at Stalingrad. #4055 contains 2 40x18mm stamps.

Large Portrait Type of 1971

Designs: 4k, Mikhail Prishvin (1873-1954), author. 10k, Fedor Chaliapin (1873-1938), opera singer, by K. Korovin.

1973 Litho. ***Perf. 11½x12***

4056 A1855 4k pink & multi .20 .20
4057 A1855 10k lt blue & multi .20 .20

Issue dates: 4k, Feb. 1; 10k, Feb. 8.

"Mayakovsky Theater" — A1928

"Mossovet Theater" — A1929

1973, Feb. 1 Photo. ***Perf. 11½***

4058 A1928 10k red, gray & indigo .30 .20
4059 A1929 10k red, mag & gray .30 .20

50th anniversary of the Mayakovsky and Mossovet Theaters in Moscow.

Copernicus and Solar System A1930

1973, Feb. 8 Engr. & Photo.

4060 A1930 10k ultra & sepia .40 .25

500th anniversary of the birth of Nicolaus Copernicus (1473-1543), Polish astronomer.

Ice Hockey A1931

Design: 50k, Two players, vert.

1973, Mar. 14 Photo. *Perf. 11½*

4061 A1931 10k gold, blue & sep .40 .25

Souvenir Sheet

4062 A1931 50k bl grn, gold & sep 1.75 1.00

European and World Ice Hockey Championships, Moscow.

See No. 4082.

Athletes and Banners of Air, Land and Naval Forces — A1932

Tank, Red Star and Map of Battle of Kursk — A1933

1973, Mar. 14

4063 A1932 4k bright blue & multi .30 .20

Sports Society of Soviet Army, 50th anniv.

1973, Mar. 14

4064 A1933 4k gray, black & red .30 .20

30th anniversary of Soviet victory in the Battle of Kursk during World War II.

Nikolai E. Bauman (1873-1905), Bolshevist Revolutionary A1934

1973, Mar. 20 Engr. *Perf. 12½x12*

4065 A1934 4k brown .30 .20

Red Cross and Red Crescent — A1935

6k, Theater curtain & mask. 16k, Youth Festival emblem & young people.

1973, Mar. 20 Photo. *Perf. 11*

4066 A1935 4k gray grn & red .20 .20

4067 A1935 6k violet blue & red .25 .20

4068 A1935 16k multicolored .80 .20

Nos. 4066-4068 (3) 1.25 .60

Union of Red Cross and Red Crescent Societies of the USSR, 50th annivs.; 15th Cong. of the Intl. Theater Institute; 10th World Festival of Youth and Students, Berlin.

Aleksandr N. Ostrovsky, by V. Perov A1936

1973, Apr. 5 Litho. *Perf. 12x12½*

4069 A1936 4k tan & multi .30 .20

Ostrovsky (1823-1886), dramatist.

Earth Satellite "Interkosmos" A1937

Lunokhod 2 on Moon and Lenin Moon Plaque A1938

1973, Apr. 12 Photo. *Perf. 11½*

4070 A1937 6k brn ol & dull cl .25 .20

4071 A1938 6k vio blue & multi .25 .20

Souvenir Sheets

Perf. 12x11½

4072 Sheet of 3, purple & multi 2.50 1.00

a. A1938 20k Lenin plaque .55 .30

b. A1938 20k Lunokhod 2 .55 .30

c. A1938 20k Telecommunications .55 .35

4073 Sheet of 3, slate grn & multi 2.50 1.00

a. A1938 20k Lenin plaque .55 .30

b. A1938 20k Lunokhod 2 .55 .30

c. A1938 20k Telecommunications .55 .30

Cosmonauts' Day. No. 4070 for cooperation in space research by European communist countries.

Souvenir sheets contain 3 50x21mm stamps.

Russian Painting Type of 1972

Paintings: 2k, Guitarist, V. A. Tropinin. 4k, Young Widow, by P. A. Fedotov. 6k, Self-portrait, by O. A. Kiprensky. 10k, Woman with Grapes ("An Afternoon in Italy") by K. P. Bryullov. 12k, Boy with Dog ("That was my Father's Dinner"), by A. Venetsianov. 16k, "Lower Gallery of Albano," by A. A. Ivanov. 20k, Soldiers ("Conquest of Siberia"), by V. I. Surikov, horiz.

Perf. 12x12½, 12½x12

1973, Apr. 18 Litho.

4074 A1897 2k gray & multi .20 .20

4075 A1897 4k gray & multi .20 .20

4076 A1897 6k gray & multi .25 .20

4077 A1897 10k gray & multi .45 .25

4078 A1897 12k gray & multi .60 .25

4079 A1897 16k gray & multi .65 .25

4080 A1897 20k gray & multi .80 .35

Nos. 4074-4080 (7) 3.15 1.70

Athlete, Ribbon of Lenin Order — A1939

1973, Apr. 18 Photo. *Perf. 11½*

4081 A1939 4k blue, red & ocher .25 .20

50th anniversary of Dynamo Sports Society.

No. 4062 with Blue Green Inscription and Ornaments Added in Margin

Souvenir Sheet

1973, Apr. 26 Photo. *Perf. 11½*

4082 A1931 50k multicolored 4.00 2.00

Soviet victory in European and World Ice Hockey Championships, Moscow.

"Mikhail Lermontov," Route Leningrad to New York — A1940

1973, May 20 Photo. *Perf. 11½*

4083 A1940 16k multicolored .60 .25

Inauguration of transatlantic service Leningrad to New York.

Ernest E. T. Krenkel, Polar Stations and Ship Chelyuskin A1941

1973, May 20 Litho. & Engr.

4084 A1941 4k dull blue & olive .40 .30

Krenkel (1903-1971), polar explorer.

Emblem and Sports — A1942

1973, May 20 Litho. *Perf. 12x12½*

4085 A1942 4k multicolored .25 .20

Sports Association for Labor and Defense.

Latvian Song Festival, Cent. — A1943

1973, May 24

4086 A1943 10k Singers .35 .25

Throwing the Hammer — A1944

Designs: 3k, Athlete on rings. 4k, Woman diver. 16k, Fencing. 50k, Javelin.

1973, June 14 Litho. *Perf. 11½*

4087 A1944 2k lemon & multi .20 .20

4088 A1944 3k blue & multi .20 .20

4089 A1944 4k citron & multi .20 .20

4090 A1944 16k lilac & multi .35 .20

Nos. 4087-4090 (4) .95 .80

Souvenir Sheet

4091 A1944 50k gold & multi 1.75 1.25

Universiad, Moscow, 1973.

Souvenir Sheet

Valentina Nikolayeva-Tereshkova — A1945

1973, June 14 Photo. *Perf. 12x11½*

4092 A1945 Sheet of 3 + label 3.00 1.25

a. 20k as cosmonaut .55 .25

b. 20k with Indian and African women .55 .25

c. 20k with daughter .55 .25

Flight of the 1st woman cosmonaut, 10th anniv.

European Bison — A1946

1973, July 26 Photo. *Perf. 11x11½*

4093 A1946 1k shown .20 .20

4094 A1946 3k Ibex .20 .20

4095 A1946 4k Caucasian snowcock .20 .20

4096 A1946 6k Beaver .35 .20

4097 A1946 10k Deer and fawns .50 .20

Nos. 4093-4097 (5) 1.45 1.00

Caucasus and Voronezh wildlife reserves.

Party Membership Card with Lenin Portrait — A1947

1973, July 26 Litho. *Perf. 11½*

4098 A1947 4k multicolored .25 .20

70th anniversary of 2nd Congress of the Russian Social Democratic Workers' Party.

Abu-al-Rayhan al-Biruni (973-1048), Arabian (Persian) Scholar and Writer — A1948

1973, Aug. 9 Engr. *Perf. 12x12½*

4099 A1948 6k red brown .25 .20

White House, Spasski Tower, Hemispheres — A1949

#4101, Eiffel Tower, Spasski Tower, globe. #4102, Schaumburg Palace, Bonn, Spasski Tower, globe. Stamps show representative buildings of Moscow, Washington, New York, Paris & Bonn.

1973, Aug. 10 Photo. *Perf. 11½x12*

4100	A1949	10k magenta & multi	.50	.50
4101	A1949	10k brown & multi	.50	.50
4102	A1949	10k dp car & multi	.50	.50
a.		Souv. sheet of 3 + 3 labels	2.50	2.50
		Nos. 4100-4102 (3)	1.50	1.50

Visit of General Secretary Leonid I. Brezhnev to Washington, Paris and Bonn. Nos. 4100-4102 each printed with se-tenant label with different statements by Brezhnev in Russian and English, French and German, respectively.

No. 4102a contains 4k stamps similar to Nos. 4100-4102 in changed colors. Issued Nov. 26.

See Nos. 4161-4162.

Russian Painting Type of 1972

2k, S. T. Konenkov, sculptor, by P. D. Korin. 4k, Tractor Operators at Supper, by A. A. Plastov. 6k, Letter from the Front, by A. I. Laktionov. 10k, Mountains, by M. S. Saryan. 16k, Wedding on a Future Street, by Y. I. Pimenov. 20k, Ice Hockey, mosaic by A. A. Deineka. 50k, Lenin at 3rd Congress of Young Communist League, by B. V. Yoganson.

1973, Aug. 22 Litho. *Perf. 12x12½*

Frame in Light Gray

4103	A1897	2k multicolored	.20	.20
4104	A1897	4k multicolored	.20	.20
4105	A1897	6k multicolored	.20	.20
4106	A1897	10k multicolored	.35	.20
4107	A1897	16k multicolored	.60	.20
4108	A1897	20k multicolored	.70	.20
		Nos. 4103-4108 (6)	2.25	1.20

Souvenir Sheet

Perf. 12

4109	A1897	50k multicolored	2.00	1.25

History of Russian Painting.

Museum, Tashkent — A1950

Y. M. Steklov — A1951

1973, Aug. 23 Photo. *Perf. 12x12½*

4110	A1950	4k multicolored	.25	.20

Lenin Central Museum, Tashkent branch.

1973, Aug. 27 Photo. *Perf. 11½x12*

4111	A1951	4k multicolored	.25	.20

Steklov (1873-1941), party worker, historian, writer.

Book, Pen and Torch — A1952

1973, Aug. 31 *Perf. 11½*

4112	A1952	6k multicolored	.25	.20

Conf. of Writers of Asia & Africa, Alma-Ata.

Echinopanax Elatum — A1953

Medicinal Plants: 2k, Ginseng. 4k, Orchis maculatus. 10k, Arnica montana. 12k, Lily of the valley.

1973, Sept. 5 Litho. *Perf. 12x12½*

4113	A1953	1k yellow & multi	.20	.20
4114	A1953	2k lt blue & multi	.20	.20
4115	A1953	4k gray & multi	.20	.20
4116	A1953	10k sepia & multi	.30	.20
4117	A1953	12k green & multi	.55	.20
		Nos. 4113-4117 (5)	1.45	1.00

Imadeddin Nasimi, Azerbaijani Poet, 600th Birth Anniv. — A1954

1973, Sept. 5 Engr.

4118	A1954	4k sepia	.30	.20

Cruiser Kirov — A1955

Soviet Warships: 4k, Battleship October Revolution. 6k, Submarine Krasnogvardeyets. 10k, Torpedo boat Soobrazitelny. 16k, Cruiser Red Caucasus.

Engraved and Photogravure

1973, Sept. 12 *Perf. 11½x12*

4119	A1955	3k violet & multi	.20	.20
4120	A1955	4k green & multi	.20	.20
4121	A1955	6k multicolored	.20	.20
4122	A1955	10k blue grn & multi	.30	.20
4123	A1955	16k multicolored	.50	.20
		Nos. 4119-4123 (5)	1.40	1.00

Globe and Red Flag Emblem — A1956

1973, Sept. 25 Photo. *Perf. 11½*

4124	A1956	6k gold, buff & red	.25	.20

15th anniversary of the international communist review "Problems of Peace and Socialism," published in Prague.

Emelyan I. Pugachev and Peasant Army — A1957

Engraved and Photogravure

1973, Sept. 25 *Perf. 11½x12*

4125	A1957	4k brn, bister & red	.25	.20

Bicentenary of peasant revolt of 1773-75 led by Emelyn Ivanovich Pugachev.

Crystal, Institute Emblem and Building A1958

1973, Oct. 5 *Perf. 11½*

4126	A1958	4k black & multi	.25	.20

Leningrad Mining Institute, 150th anniv.

Palm, Globe, Flower A1959

Elena Stasova A1960

1973, Oct. 5 Photo.

4127	A1959	6k red, gray & dk blue	.25	.20

World Cong. of Peace-loving Forces, Moscow.

1973, Oct. 5 *Perf. 11½x12*

4128	A1960	4k deep claret	.25	.20

Elena Dmitriyevna Stasova (1873-1966), communist party worker.

See Nos. 4228-4229.

Order of Friendship — A1961

1973, Oct. 5 Litho. *Perf. 12*

4129	A1961	4k red & multi	.25	.20

56th anniv. of the October Revolution. Printed se-tenant with coupon showing Arms of USSR and proclamation establishing Order of Friendship of People, in 1972, on the 50th anniv. of the USSR.

Marshal Malinovsky A1962

Ural Man, Red Guard, Worker A1963

1973, Oct. 5 Engr.

4130	A1962	4k slate	.25	.20

Rodion Y. Malinovsky (1898-1967).

See Nos. 4203-4205.

1973, Oct. 17 Photo. *Perf. 11½*

4131	A1963	4k red, gold & black	.25	.20

250th anniversary of the city of Sverdlovsk.

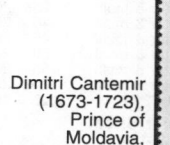

Dimitri Cantemir (1673-1723), Prince of Moldavia, Writer — A1964

1973, Oct. 17 Engr. *Perf. 12x12½*

4132	A1964	4k rose claret	.25	.20

Salvador Allende (1908-73), Pres. of Chile A1965

1973, Nov. 26 Photo. *Perf. 11½*

4133	A1965	6k rose brn & black	.25	.20

Spasski Tower, Kremlin A1966

Nariman Narimanov A1967

1973, Nov. 30 Litho. *Perf. 12x12½*

4134	A1966	6k brt blue & multi	.25	.20

New Year 1974.

1973, Nov. 30 Engr. *Perf. 12*

4135	A1967	4k slate green	.25	.20

Nariman Narimanov (1870-1925), Chairman of Executive Committee of USSR.

Russo-Balt, 1909 — A1968

Designs: 3k, AMO-F15 truck, 1924. 4k, Spartak, NAMI-1 car, 1927. 12k, Ya-6 autobus, 1929. 16k, GAZ-A car, 1932.

1973, Nov. 30 Photo. *Perf. 12x11½*

4136	A1968	2k purple & multi	.20	.20
4137	A1968	3k olive & multi	.20	.20
4138	A1968	4k ocher & multi	.20	.20
4139	A1968	12k vio blue & multi	.45	.20
4140	A1968	16k red & multi	.75	.20
		Nos. 4136-4140 (5)	1.80	1.00

Development of Russian automotive industry. See Nos. 4216-4220, 4325-4329, 4440-4444.

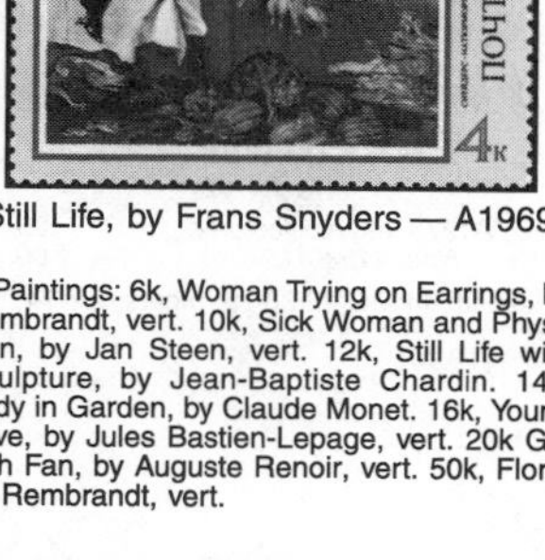

Still Life, by Frans Snyders — A1969

Paintings: 6k, Woman Trying on Earrings, by Rembrandt, vert. 10k, Sick Woman and Physician, by Jan Steen, vert. 12k, Still Life with Sculpture, by Jean-Baptiste Chardin. 14k, Lady in Garden, by Claude Monet. 16k, Young Love, by Jules Bastien-Lepage, vert. 20k Girl with Fan, by Auguste Renoir, vert. 50k, Flora, by Rembrandt, vert.

Perf. 12x11½, 11½x12

1973, Dec. 12 **Litho.**

4141 A1969 4k bister & multi .20 .20
4142 A1969 6k bister & multi .25 .20
4143 A1969 10k bister & multi .40 .20
4144 A1969 12k bister & multi .45 .20
4145 A1969 14k bister & multi .50 .20
4146 A1969 16k bister & multi .55 .20
4147 A1969 20k bister & multi .70 .20
Nos. 4141-4147 (7) 3.05 1.40

Souvenir Sheet

Perf. 12

4148 A1969 50k multicolored 2.00 1.00

Foreign paintings in Russian museums.

Pablo Picasso (1881-1973), Painter A1970

1973, Dec. 20 **Photo.** ***Perf. 12x11½***

4149 A1970 6k gold, slate grn & red .25 .20

Organ Pipes and Dome, Riga — A1971

#4151, Small Trakai Castle, Lithuania. #4152, Great Sea Gate, Tallinn, Estonia. 10k, Town Hall and "Old Thomas" weather vane, Tallinn.

1973, Dec. 20 **Engr.** ***Perf. 12x12½***

4150 A1971 4k blk, red & slate grn .20 .20
4151 A1971 4k gray, red & buff .20 .20
4152 A1971 4k black, red & grn .20 .20
4153 A1971 10k sep, grn, red & blk .25 .20
Nos. 4150-4153 (4) .85 .80

Architecture of the Baltic area.

I. G. Petrovsky A1972 — L. A. Artsimovich A1973

#4154, I. G. Petrovsky (1901-73), mathematician, rector of Moscow State University. #4155, L. A. Artsimovich (1909-73), physician, academician. #4156, K. D. Ushinsky (1824-71), teacher. #4157, M. D. Millionschikov (1913-73), vice president of Academy of Sciences.

1973-74 **Photo.** ***Perf. 11½***

4154 A1972 4k orange & multi .25 .20
4155 A1973 4k blk brn & olive .25 .20

Engr.

Perf. 12½x12

4156 A1973 4k multicolored .25 .20

Litho.

Perf. 12

4157 A1973 4k multicolored .25 .20
Nos. 4154-4157 (4) 1.00 .80

Issued: #4154, 12/28/73; others, 2/6/74.

Flags of India and USSR, Red Fort, Taj Mahal and Kremlin — A1974

Design: No. 4162, Flags of Cuba and USSR, José Marti Monument, Moncada Barracks and Kremlin.

1973-74 **Litho.** ***Perf. 12***

4161 A1974 4k lt ultra & multi .25 .20
4162 A1974 4k lt green & multi ('74) .25 .20

Visit of General Secretary Leonid I. Brezhnev to India and Cuba. Nos. 4161-4162 each printed with se-tenant label with different statements by Brezhnev in Russian and Hindi, and Russian and Spanish respectively.

Red Star, Soldier, Newspaper A1975

1974, Jan. 1 **Photo.** ***Perf. 11x11½***

4166 A1975 4k gold, red & black .25 .20

50th anniversary of the Red Star newspaper.

Victory Monument, Peter-Paul Fortress, Statue of Peter I — A1976

1974, Jan. 16 **Litho.** ***Perf. 11½***

4167 A1976 4k multicolored .25 .20

30th anniversary of the victory over the Germans near Leningrad.

Oil Workers, Refinery — A1977 — Comecon Building — A1978

1974, Jan. 16 **Photo.** ***Perf. 11½***

4168 A1977 4k dull blue, red & blk .25 .20

10th anniversary of the Tyumen oilfields.

1974, Jan. 16 **Photo.** ***Perf. 11½***

4169 A1978 16k red brn, ol & red .35 .25

25th anniversary of the Council for Mutual Economic Assistance.

Skaters and Rink, Medeo A1979

1974, Jan. 28

4170 A1979 6k slate, brn red & bl .25 .20

European Women's Skating Championships, Medeo, Alma-Ata.

Art Palace, Leningrad, Academy, Moscow A1980

1974, Jan. 30 **Photo. & Engr.**

4171 A1980 10k multicolored .35 .25

25th anniversary of the Academy of Sciences of the USSR.

3rd Winter Spartiakad Emblem — A1981 — Young People and Emblem — A1982

1974, Mar. 20 **Photo.** ***Perf. 11½***

4172 A1981 10k gold & multi .35 .25

Third Winter Spartiakad.

1974, Mar. 20 **Photo. & Engr.**

4173 A1982 4k multicolored .25 .20

Youth scientific-technical work.

Azerbaijan Theater — A1983

1974, Mar. 20 **Photo.** ***Perf. 11½***

4174 A1983 6k org, red brn & brn .30 .25

Centenary of Azerbaijan Theater.

Meteorological Satellite "Meteor" — A1984

Cosmonauts V. G. Lazarev and O. G. Makarov and Soyuz 12 — A1985

Design: No. 4177, Cosmonauts P. I. Klimuk and V. V. Lebedev, and Soyuz 13.

1974, Mar. 27 ***Perf. 11½***

4175 A1984 6k violet & multi .30 .20

Perf. 12x11½

4176 A1985 10k grnsh blue & multi .35 .20
4177 A1985 10k dull yel & multi .35 .20
Nos. 4175-4177 (3) 1.00 .60

Cosmonauts' Day.

Odessa by Moonlight, by Aivazovski — A1986

Seascapes by Aivazovski: 4k, Battle of Chesma, 1848, vert. 6k, St. George's Monastery. 10k, Stormy Sea. 12k, Rainbow (shipwreck). 16k, Shipwreck. 50k, Portrait of Aivazovski, by Kramskoy, vert.

Perf. 12x11½, 11½x12

1974, Mar. 30 **Litho.**

4178 A1986 2k gray & multi .20 .20
4179 A1986 4k gray & multi .20 .20
4180 A1986 6k gray & multi .35 .20
4181 A1986 10k gray & multi .50 .20
4182 A1986 12k gray & multi .55 .20
4183 A1986 16k gray & multi .85 .25
Nos. 4178-4183 (6) 2.65 1.25

Souvenir Sheet

4184 A1986 50k gray & multi 1.25 .90

Ivan Konstantinovich Aivazovski (1817-1900), marine painter. Sheets of Nos. 4178-4183 each contain 2 labels with commemorative inscriptions.

See Nos. 4230-4234.

Young Man and Woman, Banner A1987

1974, Mar. 30 **Litho.** ***Perf. 12½x12***

4185 A1987 4k red, yel & brown .25 .20

17th Cong. of the Young Communist League.

Lenin, by V. E. Tsigal A1988

1974, Mar. 30

4186 A1988 4k yel, red & brown .25 .20

50th anniversary of naming the Komsomol (Young Communist League) after Lenin.

Souvenir Sheet

Lenin at the Telegraph, by Igor E. Grabar — A1989

1974, Apr. 16 **Litho.** ***Perf. 12***

4187 A1989 50k multicolored 1.40 .90

104th anniv. of the birth of Lenin.

Rainbow, Swallow over Clouds — A1990

Congress Emblem and Clover — A1991

6k, Fish in water. 10k, Crystal. 16k, Rose. 20k, Fawn. 50k, Infant.

1974, Apr. 24 **Photo.** ***Perf. 11½***

4188	A1990	4k lilac & multi	.20	.20
4189	A1990	6k multicolored	.20	.20
4190	A1990	10k multicolored	.35	.20
4191	A1990	16k blue & multi	.50	.20
4192	A1990	20k citron & multi	.55	.20
		Nos. 4188-4192 (5)	1.80	1.00

Souvenir Sheet

Litho.

Perf. 12x12½

4193	A1990	50k blue & multi	1.50	.80

EXPO '74 World's Fair, theme "Preserve the Environment," Spokane, WA, May 4-Nov. 4.

1974, May 7 **Photo.** ***Perf. 11½***

4194	A1991	4k green & multi	.25	.20

12th International Congress on Meadow Cultivation, Moscow, 1974.

"Cobblestones, Weapons of the Proletariat," by I. D. Shadra — A1992

1974, May 7

4195	A1992	4k gold, red & olive	.25	.20

50th anniversary of the Lenin Central Revolutionary Museum of the USSR.

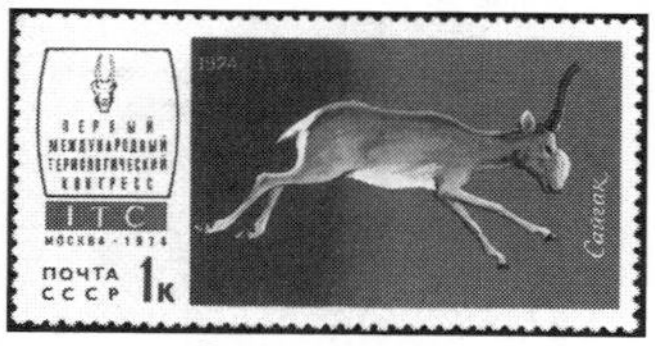

Saiga — A1993

Fauna of USSR: 3k, Koulan (wild ass). 4k, Desman. 6k, Sea lion. 10k, Greenland whale.

1974, May 22 **Litho.** ***Perf. 11½***

4196	A1993	1k olive & multi	.40	.20
4197	A1993	3k green & multi	.80	.35
4198	A1993	4k multicolored	.80	.35
4199	A1993	6k multicolored	1.10	.50
4200	A1993	10k multicolored	1.90	.60
		Nos. 4196-4200 (5)	5.00	2.00

Peter Ilich Tchaikovsky — A1994

1974, May 22 **Photo.** ***Perf. 11½***

4201	A1994	6k multicolored	.25	.20

5th International Tchaikovsky Competition, Moscow.

Souvenir Sheet

Aleksander S. Pushkin, by O. A. Kiprensky — A1995

1974, June 4 **Litho.** ***Imperf.***

4202	A1995	50k multicolored	1.75	.80

Aleksander S. Pushkin (1799-1837).

Marshal Type of 1973

Designs: #4203, Marshal F. I. Tolbukhin (1894-1949); #4204, Admiral I. S. Isakov (1894-1967); #4205, Marshal S. M. Budenny (1883-1973).

1974 **Engr.** ***Perf. 12***

4203	A1962	4k olive green	.20	.20
4204	A1962	4k indigo	.20	.20
4205	A1962	4k slate green	.20	.20
		Nos. 4203-4205 (3)	.60	.60

Issued: #4203, 6/5; #4204, 7/18; #4205, 8/20.

Stanislavski and Nemirovich-Danchenko — A1996

1974, June 12 **Litho.** ***Perf. 12***

4211	A1996	10k yel, black & dk red	.35	.20

75th anniv. of the Moscow Arts Theater.

Runner, Track, Open Book A1997

1974, June 12 **Photo.** ***Perf. 11½***

4212	A1997	4k multicolored	.25	.20

13th Natl. School Spartakiad, Alma-Ata.

Railroad Car A1998

1974, June 12

4213	A1998	4k multicolored	.30	.25

Egorov Railroad Car Factory, cent.

Victory Monument, Minsk — A1999

Liberation Monument, Poltava — A2000

#4215, Monument & Government House, Kiev.

1974, June 20

4214	A1999	4k violet, black & yel	.25	.20
4215	A1999	4k blue, black & yel	.25	.20

30th anniversary of liberation of Byelorussia (No. 4214), and of Ukraine (No. 4215).

Issued: #4214, June 20; #4215, July 18.

Automotive Type of 1973

Designs: 2k, GAZ AA truck, 1932. 3k, GAZ 03-30 bus, 1933. 4k, Zis 5 truck, 1933. 14k, Zis 8 bus, 1934. 16k, Zis 101 car, 1936.

1974, June 20 ***Perf. 12x11½***

4216	A1968	2k brown & multi	.20	.20
4217	A1968	3k multicolored	.20	.20
4218	A1968	4k orange & multi	.20	.20
4219	A1968	14k multicolored	.50	.20
4220	A1968	16k multicolored	.60	.20
		Nos. 4216-4220 (5)	1.70	1.00

Soviet automotive industry.

1974, July 7 ***Perf. 11½***

4221	A2000	4k dull red & sepia	.25	.20

800th anniversary of city of Poltava.

Nike Monument, Warsaw and Polish Flag — A2001

1974, July 7 **Litho.** ***Perf. 12½x12***

4222	A2001	6k olive & red	.25	.20

Polish People's Republic, 30th anniversary.

Mine Layer — A2002

Soviet Warships: 4k, Landing craft. 6k, Antisubmarine destroyer and helicopter. 16k, Antisubmarine cruiser.

Engraved and Photogravure

1974, July 25 ***Perf. 11½x12***

4223	A2002	3k multicolored	.20	.20
4224	A2002	4k multicolored	.20	.20
4225	A2002	6k multicolored	.40	.20
4226	A2002	16k multicolored	.75	.20
		Nos. 4223-4226 (4)	1.55	.80

Pentathlon A2003

1974, Aug. 7 **Photo.** ***Perf. 11½***

4227	A2003	16k gold, blue & brown	.50	.25

World Pentathlon Championships, Moscow.

Portrait Type of 1973

No. 4228, Dimitri Ulyanov (1874-1943). Soviet official and Lenin's brother. No. 4229, V. Menzhinsky (1874-1934), Soviet official.

1974, Aug. 7 **Engr.** ***Perf. 12½x12***

4228	A1960	4k slate green	.25	.20

Litho.

Perf. 12x11½

4229	A1960	4k rose lake	.25	.20

Painting Type of 1974

Russian paintings: 4k, Lilac, by W. Kontchalovski. 6k, "Towards the Wind" (sailboats), by E. Kalnins. 10k, "Spring" (girl and landscape), by O. Zardarjan. 16k, Northern Harbor, G. Nissky. 20k, Kirghiz Girl, by S. Chuikov, vert.

Perf. 12x11½, 11½x12

1974, Aug. 20 **Litho.**

4230	A1986	4k gray & multi	.20	.20
4231	A1986	6k gray & multi	.20	.20
4232	A1986	10k gray & multi	.35	.20
4233	A1986	16k gray & multi	.55	.20
4234	A1986	20k gray & multi	.75	.20
		Nos. 4230-4234 (5)	2.05	1.00

Printed in sheets of 18 stamps and 2 labels.

Page of First Russian Primer — A2004

Monument, Russian and Romanian Flags — A2005

1974, Aug. 20 **Photo.** ***Perf. 11½***

4235	A2004	4k black, red & gold	.25	.20

1st printed Russian primer, 400th anniv.

1974, Aug. 23

4236	A2005	6k dk blue, red & yel	.25	.20

Romania's liberation from Fascist rule, 30th anniversary.

Vitebsk A2006

1974, Sept. 4 **Litho.** ***Perf. 12***

4237	A2006	4k dk car & olive	.25	.20

Millennium of city of Vitebsk.

Kirghiz Republic A2007

50th Anniv. of Founding of Republics (Flags, industrial and agricultural themes): No. 4239, Moldavia. No. 4240, Turkmen. No. 4241, Uzbek. No. 4242, Tadzhik.

1974, Sept. 4 ***Perf. 11½x11***

4238	A2007	4k vio blue & multi	.20	.20
4239	A2007	4k maroon & multi	.20	.20
4240	A2007	4k yellow & multi	.20	.20
4241	A2007	4k green & multi	.20	.20
4242	A2007	4k lt blue & multi	.20	.20
		Nos. 4238-4242 (5)	1.00	1.00

Arms and Flag of Bulgaria — A2008

Photogravure and Engraved

1974, Sept. 4 ***Perf. 11½***

4243	A2008	6k gold & multi	.25	.20

30th anniv. of the Bulgarian revolution.

Arms of DDR and Soviet War Memorial, Treptow
A2009

1974, Sept. 4 **Photo.**

4244	A2009	6k multicolored	.25	.20

German Democratic Republic, 25th anniv.

Souvenir Sheet

Soviet Stamps and Exhibition Poster — A2010

1974, Sept. 4 **Litho.** ***Perf. 12x12½***

4245	A2010	50k multicolored	*7.50*	*3.00*

3rd Cong. of the Phil. Soc. of the USSR.

Maly State Theater — A2011

1974, Oct. 3 **Photo.** ***Perf. 11x11½***

4246	A2011	4k red, black & gold	.25	.20

150th anniversary of the Lenin Academic Maly State Theater, Moscow.

"Guests from Overseas," by N. K. Roerich — A2012

1974, Oct. 3 **Litho.** ***Perf. 12***

4247	A2012	6k multicolored	.25	.20

Nicholas Konstantin Roerich (1874-1947), painter and sponsor of Roerich Pact and Banner of Peace.

UPU Monument, Bern, and Arms of USSR
A2013

Development of Postal Service — A2014

UPU Cent.: No. 4248, Ukrainian coat of arms, letters, UPU emblem and headquarters, Bern. No. 4249, Arms of Byelorussia, UPU emblem, letters, stagecoach and rocket.

Photogravure and Engraved

1974, Oct. 9 ***Perf. 12x11½***

4248	A2013	10k red & multi	.35	.20
4249	A2013	10k red & multi	.35	.20
4250	A2013	10k red & multi	.35	.20
		Nos. 4248-4250 (3)	1.05	.60

Souvenir Sheet

Typo.

Perf. 11½x12

4251	A2014	Sheet of 3	7.50	3.00
a.		30k Jet and UPU emblem	2.00	.80
b.		30k Mail coach, UPU emblem	2.00	.80
c.		40k UPU emblem	2.00	.80

Order of Labor, 1st, 2nd and 3rd Grade
A2015

KAMAZ Truck Leaving Kama Plant — A2016

Design: #4254, Nurek Hydroelectric Plant.

1974, Oct. 16 **Litho.** ***Perf. 12½x12***

4252	A2015	4k multicolored	.25	.20
4253	A2016	4k multicolored	.25	.20
4254	A2016	4k multicolored	.25	.20
		Nos. 4252-4254 (3)	.75	.60

Space Stations Mars 4-7 over Mars
A2017

P. R. Popovitch, Y. P. Artyukhin and Soyuz 14 — A2018

Design: No. 4257, Cosmonauts G. V. Sarafanov and L. S. Demin, Soyuz 15, horiz.

Perf. 12x11½, 11½

1974, Oct. 28 **Photo.**

4255	A2017	6k multicolored	.25	.20
4256	A2018	10k multicolored	.40	.20
4257	A2018	10k multicolored	.40	.20
		Nos. 4255-4257 (3)	1.05	.60

Russian explorations of Mars (6k); flight of Soyuz 14 (No. 4256) and of Soyuz 15, Aug. 26-28 (No. 4257).

Mongolian Flag and Arms
A2019

1974, Nov. 14 **Photo.** ***Perf. 11½***

4258	A2019	6k gold & multi	.25	.20

Mongolian People's Republic, 50th anniv.

Guards' Ribbon, Estonian Government Building, Tower — A2020

1974, Nov. 14

4259	A2020	4k multicolored	.25	.20

Liberation of Estonia, 30th anniversary.

Tanker, Passenger and Cargo Ships — A2021

1974, Nov. 14 **Typo.** ***Perf. 12½x12***

4260	A2021	4k multicolored	.25	.20

USSR Merchant Marine, 50th anniversary.

Spasski Tower Clock — A2022

1974, Nov. 14 **Litho.** ***Perf. 12***

4261	A2022	4k multicolored	.30	.20

New Year 1975.

The Fishmonger, by Pieters
A2023

Paintings: 4k, The Marketplace, by Beukelaer, 1564, horiz. 10k, A Drink of Lemonade, by Gerard Terborch. 14k, Girl at Work, by Gabriel Metsu. 16k, Saying Grace, by Jean Chardin. 20k, The Spoiled Child, by Jean Greuze. 50k, Self-portrait, by Jacques Louis David.

Perf. 12x12½, 12½x12

1974, Nov. 20 **Litho.**

4262	A2023	4k bister & multi	.20	.20
4263	A2023	6k bister & multi	.25	.20
4264	A2023	10k bister & multi	.35	.20
4265	A2023	14k bister & multi	.50	.20
4266	A2023	16k bister & multi	.55	.20
4267	A2023	20k bister & multi	.75	.30
		Nos. 4262-4267 (6)	2.60	1.30

Souvenir Sheet

Perf. 12

4268	A2023	50k multicolored	1.50	.75

Foreign paintings in Russian museums. Printed in sheets of 16 stamps and 4 labels.

Morning Glory — A2024

Designs: Flora of the USSR.

1974, Nov. 20 ***Perf. 12x12½***

4269	A2024	1k red brn & multi	.20	.20
4270	A2024	2k green & multi	.20	.20
4271	A2024	4k multicolored	.20	.20
4272	A2024	10k brown & multi	.50	.20
4273	A2024	12k dk blue & multi	.55	.20
		Nos. 4269-4273 (5)	1.65	1.00

Ivan S. Nikitin (1824-1861), Poet — A2025

1974, Dec. 11 **Photo.** ***Perf. 11½***

4274	A2025	4k gray grn, grn & blk	.30	.25

Leningrad Mint — A2026

Photogravure and Engraved

1974, Dec. 11 ***Perf. 11***

4275	A2026	6k silver & multi	.25	.20

250th anniversary of the Leningrad Mint.

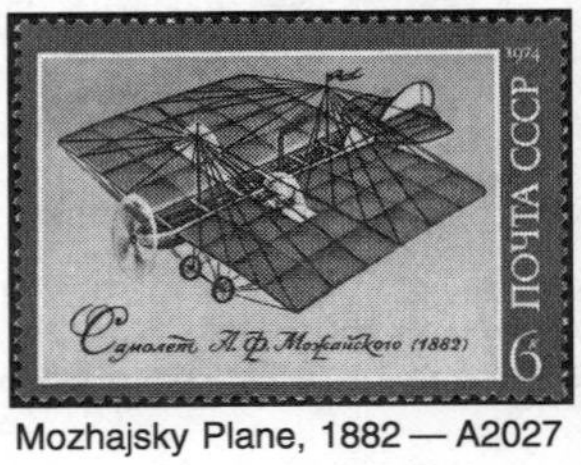

Mozhajsky Plane, 1882 — A2027

Early Russian Aircraft: No. 4277, Grizidubov-N biplane, 1910. No. 4278, Russia-A, 1910. No. 4279, Russian Vityaz (Sikorsky), 1913. No. 4280, Grigorovich flying boat, 1914.

1974, Dec. 25 Photo. *Perf. 11½x12*

4276 A2027 6k olive & multi .25 .20
4277 A2027 6k ultra & multi .25 .20
4278 A2027 6k magenta & multi .25 .20
4279 A2027 6k red & multi .25 .20
4280 A2027 6k brown & multi .25 .20
Nos. 4276-4280 (5) 1.25 1.00

Russian aircraft history, 1882-1914.

Souvenir Sheet

Sports and Sport Buildings, Moscow — A2028

1974, Dec. 25 *Perf. 11½*

4281 A2028 Sheet of 4 1.60 .50
a. 10k Woman gymnast .30 .20
b. 10k Running .30 .20
c. 10k Soccer .30 .20
d. 10k Canoeing .30 .20

Moscow preparing for Summer Olympic Games, 1980.

Rotary Press, Masthead A2029

1975, Jan. 20

4282 A2029 4k multicolored .25 .20

Komsomolskaya Pravda newspaper, 50th anniv.

Masthead and Pioneer Emblems A2030

Spartakiad Emblem and Skiers A2031

1975, Jan. 20

4283 A2030 4k red, blk & silver .25 .20

Pioneers' Pravda newspaper, 50th anniv.

1975, Jan. 20

4284 A2031 4k blue & multi .25 .20

8th Winter Spartakiad of USSR Trade Unions.

Games' Emblem, Hockey Player and Skier A2032

1975, Jan. 20

4285 A2032 16k multicolored .50 .25

5th Winter Spartakiad of Friendly Armies, Feb. 23-Mar. 1.

Republic Anniversaries Type of 1970

Design (Hammer-Sickle Emblem and): No. 4286, Landscape and produce.

1975, Jan. 24 Engr. *Perf. 12x12½*

4286 A1794 4k green .30 .20

50th anniversary of Karakalpak Autonomous Soviet Socialist Republic.

David, by Michelangelo — A2033

Michelangelo, Self-portrait — A2034

Works by Michelangelo: 6k, Squatting Boy. 10k, Rebellious Slave. 14k, The Creation of Adam. 20k, Staircase, Laurentian Library, Florence. 30k, The Last Judgment.

Lithographed and Engraved

1975, Feb. 27 *Perf. 12½x12*

4296 A2033 4k slate grn & grn .20 .20
4297 A2033 6k red brn & bister .20 .20
4298 A2033 10k slate grn & grn .35 .20
a. Min. sheet, 2 ea #4296-4298 5.00 5.00
4299 A2033 14k red brn & bister .50 .20
4300 A2033 20k slate grn & grn .70 .40
4301 A2033 30k red brn & bister .85 .60
a. Min. sheet, 2 ea #4299-4301 4.25 2.00
Nos. 4296-4301 (6) 2.80 1.80

Souvenir Sheet

Perf. 12x11½

4302 A2034 50k gold & multi 3.00 .80

Michelangelo Buonarroti (1475-1564), Italian sculptor, painter and architect. Issued only in the min. sheets of 6.

Mozhajski, Early Plane and Supersonic Jet TU-144 — A2035

1975, Feb. 27 Photo. *Perf. 12x11½*

4303 A2035 6k violet blue & ocher .25 .20

A. F. Mozhajski (1825-1890), pioneer aircraft designer, birth sesquicentennial.

"Metric System" A2036

1975, Mar. 14 *Perf. 11½*

4304 A2036 6k blk, vio blue & org .25 .20

Intl. Meter Convention, Paris, 1875, cent.

Spartakiad Emblem and Sports A2037

1975, Mar. 14

4305 A2037 6k red, silver & black .25 .20

6th Summer Spartakiad.

Liberation Monument, Parliament, Arms — A2038

Charles Bridge Towers, Arms and Flags — A2039

1975, Mar. 14

4306 A2038 6k gold & multi .25 .20
4307 A2039 6k gold & multi .25 .20

30th anniv. of liberation from fascism, Hungary (#4306) & Czechoslovakia (#4307).

Flags of France and USSR — A2040

Yuri A. Gagarin, by L. Kerbel — A2041

A. V. Filipchenko, N.N. Rukavishnikov, Russo-American Space Emblem, Soyuz 16 — A2042

1975, Mar. 25 Litho. *Perf. 12*

4308 A2040 6k lilac & multi .25 .20

50th anniv. of the establishment of diplomatic relations between France and USSR, 1st foreign recognition of Soviet State.

Perf. 11½x12, 12x11½

1975, Mar. 28 Photo.

Cosmonauts' Day: 10k, A. A. Gubarev, G. M. Grechko aboard Soyuz 17 & orbital station Salyut 4.

4309 A2041 6k blue, sil & red .20 .20
4310 A2042 10k blk, blue & red .40 .20
4311 A2042 16k multicolored .50 .20
Nos. 4309-4311 (3) 1.10 .60

Warsaw Treaty Members' Flags — A2043

1975, Apr. 16 Litho. *Perf. 12*

4312 A2043 6k multicolored .30 .20

Signing of the Warsaw Treaty (Bulgaria, Czechoslovakia, German Democratic Rep., Hungary, Poland, Romania, USSR), 20th anniv.

Lenin on Steps of Winter Palace, by V. G. Zyplakow A2044

1975, Apr. 22 *Perf. 12x12½*

4313 A2044 4k multicolored .30 .20

105th anniversary of the birth of Lenin.

Communications Emblem and Exhibition Pavilion — A2045

1975, Apr. 22 *Perf. 11½*

4314 A2045 6k ultra, red & silver .25 .20

International Communications Exhibition, Sokolniki Park, Moscow, May 1975.

Lenin and Red Flag — A2046

War Memorial, Berlin-Treptow A2048

Order of Victory — A2047

1975, Apr. 22 Typo. *Perf. 12*

4315 A2046 4k shown .25 .20
4316 A2046 4k Eternal Flame and guard .25 .20
4317 A2046 4k Woman munitions worker .25 .20
4318 A2046 4k Partisans .25 .20
4319 A2046 4k Soldier destroying swastika .25 .20
4320 A2046 4k Soldier with gun and banner .25 .20
Nos. 4315-4320 (6) 1.50 1.20

Souvenir Sheet

Litho., Typo. & Photo.

Imperf

4321 A2047 50k multicolored 5.00 3.00

World War II victory, 30th anniversary.

1975, Apr. 25 Litho. ***Perf. 12x12½***
4322 A2048 6k buff & multi .25 .20

Souvenir Sheet

4323 A2048 50k dull blue & multi 3.00 .60

Socfilex 75 Intl. Phil. Exhib. honoring 30th anniv. of WWII victory, Moscow, May 8-18.

Soyuz-Apollo Docking Emblem and Painting by Cosmonaut A. A. Leonov — A2049

1975, May 8 Photo. ***Perf. 12x11½***
4324 A2049 20k multicolored .60 .35

Russo-American space cooperation.

Automobile Type of 1973

2k, GAZ-M-I car, 1936. 3k, 5-ton truck, YAG-6, 1936. 4k, ZIZ-16, autobus, 1938. 12k, KIM-10 car, 1940. 16k, GAZ-67B jeep, 1943.

1975, May 23 Photo. ***Perf. 12x11½***
4325 A1968 2k dp org & multi .20 .20
4326 A1968 3k green & multi .20 .20
4327 A1968 4k dk green & multi .20 .20
4328 A1968 12k maroon & multi .30 .20
4329 A1968 16k olive & multi .45 .20
Nos. 4325-4329 (5) 1.35 1.00

Canal, Emblem, Produce — A2050

1975, May 23 ***Perf. 11½***
4330 A2050 6k multicolored .25 .20

9th Intl. Congress on Irrigation and Drainage, Moscow, and International Commission on Irrigation and Drainage, 25th anniv..

Flags and Arms of Poland and USSR, Factories A2051

1975, May 23
4331 A2051 6k multicolored .25 .20

Treaty of Friendship, Cooperation and Mutual Assistance between Poland & USSR, 30th anniv.

Man in Space and Earth A2052

1975, May 23
4332 A2052 6k multicolored .25 .20

First man walking in space, Lt. Col. Alexei Leonov, 10th anniversary.

Yakov M. Sverdlov (1885-1919), Organizer and Early Member of Communist Party — A2053

1975, June 4
4333 A2053 4k multicolored .30 .20

Congress, Emblem, Forest and Field A2054

1975, June 4
4334 A2054 6k multicolored .25 .20

8th International Congress for Conservation of Plants, Moscow.

Symbolic Flower with Plants and Emblem A2055

1975, June 20 Litho. ***Perf. 11½***
4335 A2055 6k multicolored .25 .20

12th International Botanical Congress.

Souvenir Sheet

UN Emblem — A2056

1975, June 20 Photo. ***Perf. 11½x12***
4336 A2056 50k gold & blue 2.50 1.00

30th anniversary of United Nations.

Globe and Film A2057

1975, June 20 Photo. ***Perf. 11½***
4337 A2057 6k multicolored .25 .20

9th Intl. Film Festival, Moscow, 1975.

Soviet and American Astronauts and Flags — A2058

Apollo and Soyuz After Link-up and Earth — A2059

Soyuz Launch A2060

Designs: No. 4340, Spacecraft before link-up, earth and project emblem. 50k, Soviet Mission Control Center.

1975, July 15 Litho. ***Perf. 11½***
4338 A2058 10k multicolored .55 .20
4339 A2059 12k multicolored .80 .20
4340 A2059 12k multicolored .80 .20
a. Vert. pair, #4339-4340 2.00 1.00
4341 A2060 16k multicolored .90 .40
Nos. 4338-4341 (4) 3.05 1.00

Souvenir Sheet

Photo.

Perf. 12x11½

4342 A2058 50k multicolored 2.00 1.25

Apollo-Soyuz space test project (Russo-American space cooperation), launching, July 15; link-up July 17.

No. 4342 contains one 50x21mm stamp.

See US Nos. 1569-1570.

Sturgeon, Caspian Sea, Oceanexpo 75 Emblem — A2061

Designs (Oceanexpo 75 Emblem and): 4k, Salt-water shell, Black Sea. 6k, Eel, Baltic Sea. 10k, Sea duck, Arctic Sea. 16k, Crab, Far Eastern waters. 20k, Chrisipther (fish), Pacific Ocean.

1975, July 22 Photo. ***Perf. 11***
4343 A2061 3k multicolored .20 .20
4344 A2061 4k multicolored .20 .20
4345 A2061 6k green & multi .25 .20
4346 A2061 10k dk blue & multi .40 .30
4347 A2061 16k purple & multi .60 .30
4348 A2061 20k multicolored .70 .65
Nos. 4343-4348 (6) 2.35 1.85

Souvenir Sheet

Perf. 12x11½

4349 Sheet of 2 2.00 .90
a. A2061 30k Dolphin rising .80 .30
b. A2061 30k Dolphin diving .80 .30

Oceanexpo 75, 1st Intl. Oceanographic Exhib., Okinawa, July 20, 1975-Jan. 1976. No. 4349 contains 55x25mm stamps.

Parade, Red Square, 1941, by K. F. Yuon — A2062

Paintings: 2k, Morning of Industrial Moscow, by Yuon. 6k, Soldiers Inspecting Captured Artillery, by Lansere. 10k, Excavating Metro Tunnel, by Lansere. 16k, Pushkin and His Wife at Court Ball, by Ulyanov, vert. 20k, De Lauriston at Kutuzov's Headquarters, by Ulyanov.

1975, July 22 Litho. ***Perf. 12½x11½***
4350 A2062 1k gray & multi .20 .20
4351 A2062 2k gray & multi .20 .20
4352 A2062 6k gray & multi .25 .20
4353 A2062 10k gray & multi .40 .20
4354 A2062 16k gray & multi .80 .25
4355 A2062 20k gray & multi .90 .30
Nos. 4350-4355 (6) 2.75 1.35

Konstantin F. Yuon (1875-1958), Yevgeni Y. Lansere (1875-1946), Nikolai P. Ulyanov (1875-1949).

Nos. 4350-4355 issued in sheets of 16 plus 4 labels.

Finlandia Hall, Map of Europe, Laurel — A2063

1975, Aug. 18 Photo. ***Perf. 11½***
4356 A2063 6k brt blue, gold & blk .25 .20

European Security and Cooperation Conference, Helsinki, July 30-Aug. 1. Printed se-tenant with label with quotation by Leonid I. Brezhnev, first secretary of Communist party.

Chuyrlenis, Waves and Lighthouse A2064

1975, Aug. 20 Photo. & Engr.
4357 A2064 4k grn, indigo & gold .50 .20

M. K. Chuyrlenis, Lithuanian composer, birth centenary.

Avetik Isaakyan, by Martiros Saryan A2065

1975, Aug. 20 Litho. ***Perf. 12x12½***

4358 A2065 4k multicolored .20 .20

Isaakyan (1875-1957), Armenian poet.

Jacques Duclos — A2066

al-Farabi — A2067

1975, Aug. 20 Photo. ***Perf. 11½x12***

4359 A2066 6k maroon & silver .25 .20

Duclos (1896-1975), French labor leader.

1975, Aug. 20 ***Perf. 11½***

4360 A2067 6k grnsh blue, brn & bis .25 .20

Nasr al-Farabi (870?-950), Arab philosopher.

Male Ruffs A2068

1975, Aug. 25 Litho. ***Perf. 12½x12***

4361 A2068 1k shown .20 .20
4362 A2068 4k Altai roebuck .20 .20
4363 A2068 6k Siberian marten .20 .20
4364 A2068 10k Old squaw (duck) .40 .20
4365 A2068 16k Badger .55 .20
Nos. 4361-4365 (5) 1.55 1.00

Berezina River and Stolby wildlife reservations, 50th anniversary.

A2069

A2070

Designs: #4366, Flags of USSR, North Korea, arms of N. K., Liberation monument, Pyongyang. #4367, Flags of USSR, North Viet Nam, arms of N.V., industrial development.

1975, Aug. 28 ***Perf. 12***

4366 A2069 6k multicolored .30 .20
4367 A2070 6k multicolored .30 .20

Liberation of North Korea from Japanese occupation (#4366); and establishment of Democratic Republic of Viet Nam (#4367), 30th annivs.

P. Klimuk and V. Sevastyanov, Soyuz 18 and Salyut 4 Docking — A2071

1975, Sept. 12 Photo. ***Perf. 12x11½***

4368 A2071 10k ultra, blk & dp org .30 .20

Docking of space ship Soyuz 18 and space station Salyut 4.

S. A. Esenin and Birches A2072

Photogravure and Engraved

1975, Sept. 12 ***Perf. 11½***

4369 A2072 6k brown & ocher .25 .20

Sergei A. Esenin (1895-1925), poet.

Standardization Symbols — A2073

1975, Sept. 12 Photo. ***Perf. 11½***

4370 A2073 4k red & multi .25 .20

USSR Committee for Standardization of Communications Ministry, 50th anniversary.

Karakul Lamb A2074

1975, Sept. 22 Photo. ***Perf. 11½***

4371 A2074 6k black, yel & grn .25 .20

3rd International Symposium on astrakhan production, Samarkand, Sept. 22-27.

Dr. M. P. Konchalovsky A2075

Exhibition Emblem A2076

1975, Sept. 30 ***Perf. 11½x12***

4372 A2075 4k brown & red .25 .20

Konchalovsky (1875-1942), physician.

1975, Sept. 30 ***Perf. 11½***

4373 A2076 4k deep blue & red .25 .20

3rd All-Union Youth Phil. Exhib., Erevan.

IWY Emblem and Rose — A2077

1975, Sept. 30 Litho. ***Perf. 12x11½***

4374 A2077 6k multicolored .25 .20

International Women's Year 1975.

Yugoslavian Flag and Parliament A2078

1975, Sept. 30 Photo. ***Perf. 11½***

4375 A2078 6k gold, red & blue .25 .20

Republic of Yugoslavia, 30th anniv.

Illustration from 1938 Edition, by V. A. Favorsky — A2079

Mikhail Ivanovich Kalinin — A2080

1975, Oct. 20 Typo. ***Perf. 12***

4376 A2079 4k buff, red & black .30 .20

175th anniversary of the 1st edition of the old Russian saga "Slovo o polku Igoreve."

1975, Oct. 20 Engr. ***Perf. 12***

#4378, Anatoli Vasilievich Lunacharski.

4377 A2080 4k sepia .25 .20
4378 A2080 4k sepia .25 .20

Kalinin (1875-1946), chairman of Central Executive Committee and Presidium of Supreme Soviet; Lunacharski (1875-1933), writer, commissar for education.

Hand Holding Torch and Lenin Quotation — A2081

1975, Oct. 20 Engr.

4379 A2081 4k red & olive .25 .20

First Russian Revolution (1905), 70th anniv.

Building Baikal-Amur Railroad — A2082

Novolipetsk Metallurgical Plant — A2083

Nevynomyssk Chemical Plant, Fertilizer Formula — A2084

1975, Oct. 30 Photo. ***Perf. 11½***

4380 A2082 4k gold & multi .20 .20
4381 A2083 4k red, gray & sl green .20 .20
4382 A2084 4k red, blue & silver .20 .20
Nos. 4380-4382 (3) .60 .60

58th anniversary of October Revolution.

Bas-relief of Decembrists and "Decembrists at the Senate Square," by D. N. Kardovsky — A2085

1975, Nov. 12 Litho. & Engr.

4383 A2085 4k gray & multi .25 .20

Sesquicentennial of Decembrist rising.

Star and "1976" — A2086

1975, Nov. 12 Litho. ***Perf. 12x12½***

4384 A2086 4k green & multi .35 .20

New Year 1976.

Village Street, by F. A. Vasilev A2087

Paintings by Vasilev: 4k, Road in Birch Forest. 6k, After the Thunderstorm. 10k, Swamp, horiz. 12k, In the Crimean Mountains. 16k, Meadow, horiz. 50k, Portrait, by Kramskoi.

Perf. 12x12½, 12½x12

1975, Nov. 25

4385 A2087 2k gray & multi .20 .20
4386 A2087 4k gray & multi .20 .20
4387 A2087 6k gray & multi .30 .20
4388 A2087 10k gray & multi .45 .20
4389 A2087 12k gray & multi .55 .20
4390 A2087 16k gray & multi .70 .25
Nos. 4385-4390 (6) 2.40 1.25

Souvenir Sheet

Perf. 12

4391 A2087 50k gray & multi 2.00 .90

Fedor Aleksandrovich Vasilev (1850-1873), landscape painter. Nos. 4385-4390 printed in sheets of 7 stamps and one label.

Landing Capsule, Venus Surface, Lenin Banner A2088

1975, Dec. 8 **Photo.** ***Perf. 11½***

4392 A2088 10k multicolored .35 .25

Flights of Soviet interplanetary stations Venera 9 and Venera 10.

Gabriel Sundoukian — A2089

1975, Dec. 8 **Litho.** ***Perf. 12***

4393 A2089 4k multicolored .50 .30

Sundoukian (1825-1912), Armenian playright.

Polar Poppies, Taiga A2090

Regional Flowers: 6k, Globeflowers, tundra. 10k, Buttercups, oak forest. 12k, Wood anemones, steppe. 16k, Eminium Lehmannii, desert.

Photogravure and Engraved

1975, Dec. 25 ***Perf. 12x11½***

4394 A2090 4k black & multi .20 .20
4395 A2090 6k black & multi .25 .20
4396 A2090 10k black & multi .35 .20
4397 A2090 12k black & multi .40 .20
4398 A2090 16k black & multi .50 .25
Nos. 4394-4398 (5) 1.70 1.05

A. L. Mints (1895-1974), Academician A2091

1975, Dec. 31 **Photo.** ***Perf. 11½x12***

4399 A2091 4k dp brown & gold .25 .20

Demon, by A. Kochupalov A2092

Paintings: 6k, Vasilisa the Beautiful, by I. Vakurov. 10k, Snow Maiden, by T. Zubkova. 16k, Summer, by K. Kukulieva. 20k, The Fisherman and the Goldfish, by I. Vakurov, horiz.

1975, Dec. 31 **Litho.** ***Perf. 12***

4400 A2092 4k bister & multi .20 .20
4401 A2092 6k bister & multi .30 .20
4402 A2092 10k bister & multi .50 .20
4403 A2092 16k bister & multi .60 .20
4404 A2092 20k bister & multi .80 .25
a. Strip of 5, #4400-4404 2.40 .60

Palekh Art State Museum, Ivanov Region.

Wilhelm Pieck (1876-1960), Pres. of German Democratic Republic — A2093

1976, Jan. 3 **Engr.** ***Perf. 12½x12***

4405 A2093 6k bluish black .20 .20

M. E. Saltykov-Shchedrin, by I.N. Kramskoi — A2094

1976, Jan. 14 **Litho.** ***Perf. 12x12½***

4406 A2094 4k multicolored .25 .20

Mikhail Evgrafovich Saltykov-Shchedrin (1826-1889), writer and revolutionist.

Congress Emblem — A2095 Lenin Statue, Kiev — A2096

1976, Feb. 2 **Photo.** ***Perf. 11½***

4407 A2095 4k red, gold & mar .25 .20

Souvenir Sheet

Perf. 11½x12

4408 A2095 50k red, gold & mar 1.75 .65

25th Congress of the Communist Party of the Soviet Union.

1976, Feb. 2 ***Perf. 11½***

4409 A2096 4k red, black & blue .25 .20

Ukrainian Communist Party, 25th Congress.

Ice Hockey, Games' Emblem A2097

Designs (Winter Olympic Games' Emblem and): 4k, Cross-country skiing. 6k, Figure skating, pairs. 10k, Speed skating. 20k, Luge. 50k, Winter Olympic Games' emblem, vert.

1976, Feb. 4 **Litho.** ***Perf. 12½x12***

4410 A2097 2k multicolored .20 .20
4411 A2097 4k multicolored .20 .20
4412 A2097 6k multicolored .30 .20
4413 A2097 10k multicolored .45 .20
4414 A2097 20k multicolored .95 .30
Nos. 4410-4414 (5) 2.10 1.10

Souvenir Sheet

Perf. 12x12½

4415 A2097 50k vio bl, org & red 2.00 1.00

12th Winter Olympic Games, Innsbruck, Austria, Feb. 4-15. No. 4415 contains one stamp; silver and violet blue margin showing designs of Nos. 4410-4414. Size: 90x80mm.

No. 4415 Overprinted in Red Souvenir Sheet

1976, Mar. 24

4416 A2097 50k multicolored 6.00 4.00

Success of Soviet athletes in 12th Winter Olympic Games. Translation of overprint: "Glory to Soviet Sport! The athletes of the USSR have won 13 gold, 6 silver and 8 bronze medals."

K.E. Voroshilov A2098

1976, Feb. 4 **Engr.** ***Perf. 12***

4417 A2098 4k slate green .40 .20

Kliment Efremovich Voroshilov (1881-1969), pres. of revolutionary military council, commander of Leningrad front, USSR pres. 1953-60. See Nos. 4487-4488, 4545-4548.

Flag over Kremlin Palace of Congresses, Troitskaya Tower A2099

Photogravure on Gold Foil

1976, Feb. 24 ***Perf. 12x11½***

4418 A2099 20k gold, grn & red 4.00 2.00

25th Congress of the Communist Party of the Soviet Union (CPSU).

Lenin on Red Square, by P. Vasiliev — A2100

1976, Mar. 10 **Litho.** ***Perf. 12½x12***

4419 A2100 4k yellow & multi .25 .20

106th anniversary of the birth of Lenin.

Atom Symbol and Dubna Institute — A2101

1976, Mar. 10 **Photo.** ***Perf. 11½***

4420 A2101 6k vio bl, red & silver .25 .20

Joint Institute of Nuclear Research, Dubna, 20th anniversary.

Bolshoi Theater — A2102

1976, Mar. 24 **Litho.** ***Perf. 11x11½***

4421 A2102 10k yel, blue & dk brn .30 .20

Bicentenary of Bolshoi Theater.

Back from the Fair, by Konchalovsky — A2103

Paintings by P. P. Konchalovsky: 2k, The Green Glass. 6k, Peaches. 16k, Meat, Game and Vegetables. 20k, Self-portrait, 1943, vert.

1976, Apr. 6 ***Perf. 12½x12, 12x12½***

4422 A2103 1k yellow & multi .20 .20
4423 A2103 2k yellow & multi .20 .20
4424 A2103 6k yellow & multi .30 .20
4425 A2103 16k yellow & multi .70 .20
4426 A2103 20k yellow & multi .85 .30
Nos. 4422-4426 (5) 2.25 1.10

Birth centenary of P. P. Konchalovsky.

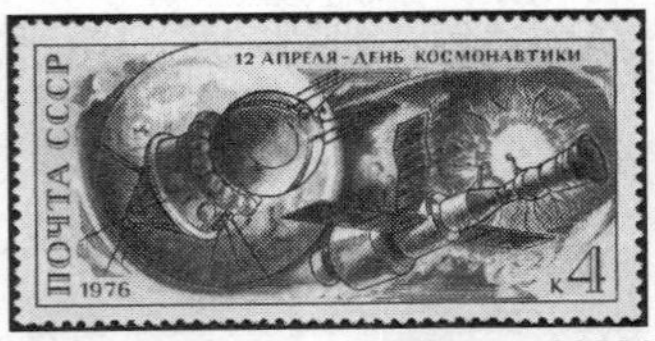

Vostok, Salyut-Soyuz Link-up — A2104

Yuri A. Gagarin — A2105

Designs: 6k, Meteor and Molniya Satellites, Orbita Ground Communications Center. 10k, Cosmonauts on board Salyut space station and Mars planetary station. 12k, Interkosmos station and Apollo-Soyuz linking.

Lithographed and Engraved

1976, Apr. 12 ***Perf. 11½***

4427 A2104 4k multicolored .20 .20
4428 A2104 6k multicolored .25 .20
4429 A2104 10k multicolored .35 .20
4430 A2104 12k multicolored .55 .20
Nos. 4427-4430 (4) 1.35 .80

Souvenir Sheet

Engr. ***Perf. 12***

4431 A2105 50k black 10.00 2.00

1st manned flight in space, 15th anniv.

I. A. Dzhavakhishvili A2106

Samed Vurgun and Derrick A2107

1976, Apr. 20 Photo. ***Perf. 11½x12***

4432 A2106 4k multicolored .25 .20

Dzhavakhishvili (1876-1940), scientist.

1976, Apr. 20 ***Perf. 11½***

4433 A2107 4k multicolored .25 .20

Vurgun (1906-56), natl. poet of Azerbaijan.

1st All-Union Festival of Amateur Artists — A2108

USSR Flag, Worker and Farmer Monument.

1976, May 12 Litho. ***Perf. 11½x12***

4434 A2108 4k multicolored .25 .20

Intl. Federation of Philately, 50th Anniv. — A2109

1976, May 12 Photo. ***Perf. 11½***

4435 A2109 6k FIP Emblem .25 .20

Souvenir Sheet

V. A. Tropinin, Self-portrait — A2110

1976, May 12 Litho. ***Perf. 12***

4436 A2110 50k multicolored 1.75 1.00

Vasily Andreevich Tropinin (1776-1857), painter.

Emblem, Dnieper Bridge A2111

Dr. N. N. Burdenko A2112

1976, May 20 Photo. ***Perf. 11½***

4437 A2111 4k Prus blue, gold & blk .25 .20

Bicentenary of Dnepropetrovsk.

1976, May 20 ***Perf. 11½x12***

4438 A2112 4k deep brown & red .25 .20

Burdenko (1876-1946), neurosurgeon.

K. A. Trenev (1876-1945), Playwright A2113

1976, May 20 ***Perf. 11½***

4439 A2113 4k black & multi .25 .20

Automobile Type of 1973

2k, ZIS-110 passenger car. 3k, GAZ-51 Gorky truck. 4k, GAZ-M-20 Pobeda passenger car. 12k, ZIS-150 Moscow Motor Works truck. 16k, ZIS-154 Moscow Motor Works bus.

1976, June 15 Photo. ***Perf. 12x11½***

4440 A1968 2k grnsh bl & multi .20 .20
4441 A1968 3k bister & multi .20 .20
4442 A1968 4k dk blue & multi .20 .20
4443 A1968 12k brown & multi .60 .20
4444 A1968 16k deep car & multi .80 .20
Nos. 4440-4444 (5) 2.00 1.00

Canoeing A2114

USSR National Olympic Committee Emblem and: 6k, Basketball, vert. 10k, Greco-Roman wrestling. 14k, Women's discus, vert. 16k, Target shooting. 50k, Olympic medal, obverse and reverse.

Perf. 12½x12, 12x12½

1976, June 23 Litho.

4445 A2114 4k red & multi .20 .20
4446 A2114 6k red & multi .20 .20
4447 A2114 10k red & multi .45 .20
4448 A2114 14k red & multi .60 .20
4449 A2114 16k red & multi .65 .25
Nos. 4445-4449 (5) 2.10 1.05

Souvenir Sheet

4450 A2114 50k red & multi 3.00 .75

21st Olympic Games, Montreal, Canada, July 17-Aug. 1.

For overprint see No. 4472.

Electric Trains, Overpass A2115

1976, June 23 Photo. ***Perf. 11½***

4451 A2115 4k multicolored 1.00 .20

Electrification of USSR railroads, 50th anniversary.

L. Emilio Rekabarren — A2116

1976, July 6

4452 A2116 6k gold, red & blk .25 .20

Luis Emilio Rekabarren (1876-1924), founder of Chilean Communist Party.

Ljudmilla Mikhajlovna Pavlichenko (1916-1974), WWII Heroine — A2117

1976, July 6

4453 A2117 4k dp brn, silver & yel .25 .20

Pavel Andreevich Fedotov (1815-1852), Painter A2118

Paintings: 2k, New Partner, by P. A. Fedotov. 4k, The Fastidious Fiancée, horiz. 6k, Aristocrat's Breakfast. 10k, Gamblers, horiz. 16k, The Outing. 50k, Self-portrait.

Perf. 12x12½, 12½x12

1976, July 15 Litho.

4454 A2118 2k black & multi .20 .20
4455 A2118 4k black & multi .20 .20
4456 A2118 6k black & multi .20 .20
4457 A2118 10k black & multi .45 .20
4458 A2118 16k black & multi .65 .25
Nos. 4454-4458 (5) 1.70 1.05

Souvenir Sheet

Perf. 12

4459 A2118 50k multicolored 2.50 .75

Nos. 4454-4458 each printed in sheets of 20 stamps and center label with black commemorative inscription.

S. S. Nametkin A2119

Squacco Heron A2120

1976, July 20 Photo. ***Perf. 11½x12***

4460 A2119 4k blue, black & buff .25 .20

Sergei Semenovich Nametkin (1876-1950), organic chemist.

1976, Aug. 18 Litho. ***Perf. 12x12½***

Waterfowl: 3k, Arctic loon. 4k, European coot. 6k, Atlantic puffin. 10k, Slender-billed gull.

4465 A2120 1k dk green & multi .20 .20
4466 A2120 3k ol green & multi .50 .50
4467 A2120 4k orange & multi .80 .80
4468 A2120 6k purple & multi 1.10 1.10
4469 A2120 10k brt blue & multi 2.40 2.40
Nos. 4465-4469 (5) 5.00 5.00

Nature protection.

Peace Dove A2121

1976, Aug. 25 Photo. ***Perf. 11½***

4470 A2121 4k salmon, gold & blue .25 .20

2nd Stockholm appeal and movement to stop arms race.

Resistance Movement Emblem A2122

1976, Aug. 25

4471 A2122 6k dk bl, blk & gold .25 .20

Intl. Resistance Movement Fed., 25th anniv.

No. 4450 Overprinted in Gold in Margin Souvenir Sheet

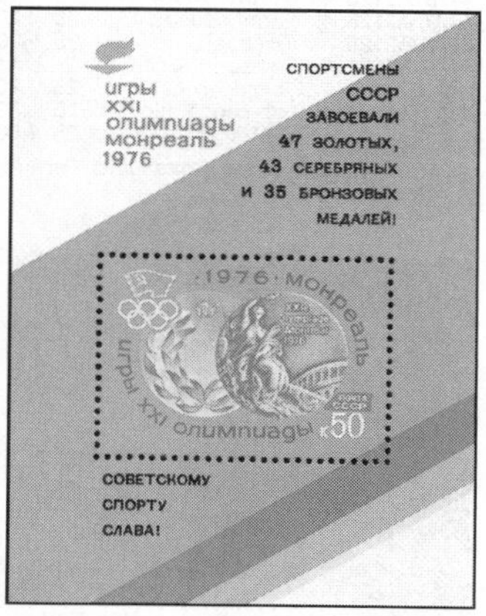

The two parts of the overprint have been moved closer together to fit the column.

1976, Aug. 25 Litho. ***Perf. 12½x12***

4472 A2114 50k red & multi 4.50 .75

Victories of Soviet athletes in 21st Olympic Games (47 gold, 43 silver and 35 bronze medals).

Flags of India and USSR — A2123

1976, Sept. 8 ***Perf. 12***

4473	A2123	4k multicolored	.25	.20

Friendship and cooperation between USSR and India.

UN, UNESCO Emblems, Open Book — A2124

1976, Sept. 8 Engr. ***Perf. 12x12½***

4474	A2124	16k multicolored	.40	.30

UNESCO, 30th anniv.

B. V. Volynov, V. M. Zholobov, Star Circling Globe — A2125

1976, Sept. 8 Photo. ***Perf. 12x11½***

4475	A2125	10k brn, blue & black	.50	.35

Exploits of Soyuz 21 and Salyut space station.

"Industry" — A2126

1976, Sept. 17

4476	A2126	4k shown	.25	.20
4477	A2126	4k Farm industry	.25	.20
4478	A2126	4k Science	.25	.20
4479	A2126	4k Transport & communications	.25	.20
4480	A2126	4k Intl. cooperation	.25	.20
		Nos. 4476-4480 (5)	1.25	1.00

25th Congress of the Communist Party of the Soviet Union.

Victory, by I. I. Vakurov A2127

Paintings: 2k, Plower, by I. I. Golikov, horiz. 4k, Au (woman), by I. V. Markichev. 12k, Firebird, by A. V. Kotuhin, horiz. 14k, Festival, by A. I. Vatagin. 20k, .

Perf. 12½x12, 12x12½

1976, Sept. 22 **Litho.**

4481	A2127	2k black & multi	.20	.20
4482	A2127	4k black & multi	.25	.20
4483	A2127	12k black & multi	1.10	.20
4484	A2127	14k black & multi	1.25	.20
4485	A2127	20k black & multi	1.65	.35
		Nos. 4481-4485 (5)	4.45	1.15

Palekh Art State Museum, Ivanov Region.

Shostakovich, Score from 7th Symphony, Leningrad — A2128

1976, Sept. 25 Engr. ***Perf. 12½x12***

4486	A2128	6k dk vio blue	.25	.20

Dimitri Dimitrievich Shostakovich (1906-1975), composer.

Voroshilov Type of 1976

#4487, Zhukov. #4488, Rokossovsky.

1976, Oct. 7 Engr. ***Perf. 12***

4487	A2098	4k slate green	.20	.20
4488	A2098	4k brown	.20	.20

Marshal Georgi Konstantinovich Zhukov (1896-1974), commander at Stalingrad and Leningrad and Deputy of Supreme Soviet; Marshal Konstantin K. Rokossovsky (1896-1968), commander at Stalingrad.

Intercosmos-14 A2129

10k, India's satellite Arryabata. 12k, Soyuz-19 and Apollo before docking. 16k, French satellite Aureole and Northern Lights. 20k, Docking of Soyuz-Apollo, Intercosmos-14 and Aureole.

1976, Oct. 15 Photo. ***Perf. 11½***

4489	A2129	6k black & multi	.20	.20
4490	A2129	10k black & multi	.30	.20
4491	A2129	12k black & multi	.45	.20
4492	A2129	16k black & multi	.50	.20
4493	A2129	20k black & multi	.65	.20
		Nos. 4489-4493 (5)	2.10	1.00

Interkosmos Program for Scientific and Experimental Research.

Vladimir I. Dahl A2130

Photogravure and Engraved

1976, Oct. 15 ***Perf. 11½***

4494	A2130	4k green & dk grn	.25	.20

Vladimir I. Dahl (1801-1872), physician, writer, compiled Russian Dictionary.

Electric Power Industry A2131

#4496, Balashovo textile mill. #4497, Laying of drainage pipes and grain elevator.

1976, Oct. 20 Photo. ***Perf. 11½***

4495	A2131	4k dk blue & multi	.20	.20
4496	A2131	4k rose brn & multi	.20	.20
4497	A2131	4k slate grn & multi	.20	.20
		Nos. 4495-4497 (3)	.60	.60

59th anniversary of the October Revolution.

Petrov Tumor Research Institute A2132

M. A. Novinski — A2133

1976, Oct. 28

4498	A2132	4k vio blue & gold	.50	.20
		Perf. 11½x12		
4499	A2133	4k dk brn, buff & blue	.40	.20

Petrov Tumor Research Institute, 50th anniversary, and 135th birth anniversary of M. A. Novinski, cancer research pioneer.

Aviation Emblem, Gakkel VII, 1911 A2134

Russian Aircraft (Russian Aviation Emblem and): 6k, Gakkel IX, 1912. 12k, I. Steglau No. 2, 1912. 14k, Dybovski's Dolphin, 1913. 16k, Iliya Muromets, 1914.

Lithographed and Engraved

1976, Nov. 4 ***Perf. 12x12½***

4500	A2134	3k multicolored	.20	.20
4501	A2134	6k multicolored	.20	.20
4502	A2134	12k multicolored	.50	.35
4503	A2134	14k multicolored	.55	.35
4504	A2134	16k multicolored	.60	.50
		Nos. 4500-4504 (5)	2.05	1.60

See Nos. C109-C120.

Saffron A2135

Flowers of the Caucasus: 2k, Pasqueflowers. 3k, Gentian. 4k, Columbine. 6k, Checkered lily.

1976, Nov. 17 ***Perf. 12x11½***

4505	A2135	1k multicolored	.40	.40
4506	A2135	2k multicolored	.40	.40
4507	A2135	3k multicolored	.40	.40
4508	A2135	4k multicolored	.40	.40
4509	A2135	6k multicolored	.40	.40
		Nos. 4505-4509 (5)	2.00	2.00

Spasski Tower Clock, Greeting Card A2136

1976, Nov. 25 Litho. ***Perf. 12½x12***

4510	A2136	4k multicolored	.25	.20

New Year 1977.

Parable of the Workers in the Vineyard, by Rembrandt — A2137

Rembrandt Paintings in Hermitage: 6k, birth anniversary. 10k, 14k, Holy Family, vert. 20k, Rembrandt's brother Adrian, 1654, vert. 50k, Artaxerxes, Esther and Haman.

Perf. 12½x12, 12x12½

1976, Nov. 25 **Photo.**

4511	A2137	4k multicolored	.20	.20
4512	A2137	6k multicolored	.20	.20
4513	A2137	10k multicolored	.50	.20
4514	A2137	14k multicolored	.65	.20
4515	A2137	20k multicolored	.90	.30
		Nos. 4511-4515 (5)	2.45	1.10

Souvenir Sheet

4516	A2137	50k multicolored	6.50	2.00

Rembrandt van Rijn (1606-69). Nos. 4511 and 4515 printed in sheets of 7 stamps and decorative label.

Armed Forces Order A2138

Worker and Farmer, by V. I. Muhina A2139

Marx and Lenin, by Fridman and Belostotsky A2140

Council for Mutual Economic Aid Building A2141

Lenin, 1920 Photograph A2142

Globe and Sputnik Orbits A2143

Designs: 2k, Golden Star and Hammer and Sickle medals. 4k, Coat of arms and "CCCP." 6k, TU-154 plane, globe and airmail envelope. 10k, Order of Labor. 12k, Space exploration medal with Gagarin portrait. 16k, Lenin Prize medal.

1976 Engr. ***Perf. 12x12½***

4517	A2138	1k greenish black	.20	.20
4518	A2138	2k brt magenta	.20	.20
4519	A2139	3k red	.20	.20

4520	A2138	4k	brick red	.20	.20
4521	A2139	6k	Prus blue	.25	.20
4522	A2138	10k	olive green	.45	.20
4523	A2139	12k	violet blue	.50	.20
4524	A2139	16k	deep green	.60	.20

Perf. 12½x12

4525	A2140	20k	brown red	.80	.20
4526	A2141	30k	brick red	1.10	.20
4527	A2142	50k	brown	1.90	.20
4528	A2143	1r	dark blue	4.00	.20
			Nos. 4517-4528 (12)	10.40	2.40

Issued: #4517-4524, 12/17; #4525-4528, 8/10.

See #4596-4607. For overprint see #5720.

Luna 24 Emblem and Moon Landing A2144

1976, Dec. 17 Photo. *Perf. 11½*

4531 A2144 10k multicolored .30 .20

Moon exploration of automatic station Luna 24.

Icebreaker "Pilot" — A2145

Icebreakers: 6k, Ermak, vert. 10k, Fedor Litke. 16k, Vladimir Ilich, vert. 20k, Krassin.

Perf. 12x11½, 11½x12

1976, Dec. 22 Litho. & Engr.

4532	A2145	4k	multicolored	.20	.20
4533	A2145	6k	multicolored	.20	.20
4534	A2145	10k	multicolored	.45	.20
4535	A2145	16k	multicolored	.55	.25
4536	A2145	20k	multicolored	.70	.30
			Nos. 4532-4536 (5)	2.10	1.15

See Nos. 4579-4585.

Soyuz 22 Emblem, Cosmonauts V. F. Bykofsky and V. V. Aksenov — A2146

1976, Dec. 28 Photo. *Perf. 12x11½*

4537 A2146 10k multicolored .30 .25

Soyuz 22 space flight, Sept. 15-23.

Society Emblem — A2147

1977, Jan. 1 *Perf. 11½*

4538 A2147 4k multicolored .25 .20

Red Banner Voluntary Soc., supporting Red Army, Navy & Air Force, 50th anniv.

S. P. Korolev, Vostok Rocket and Satellite A2148

1977, Jan. 12

4539 A2148 4k multicolored .25 .20

Sergei Pavlovich Korolev (1907-1966), creator of first Soviet rocket space system.

Globe and Palm A2149

1977, Jan. 12

4540 A2149 4k multicolored .25 .20

World Congress of Peace Loving Forces, Moscow, Jan. 1977.

Sedov and "St. Foka" A2150

1977, Jan. 25 Photo. *Perf. 11½*

4541 A2150 4k multicolored .25 .20

G.Y. Sedov (1877-1914), polar explorer and hydrographer.

Worker and Farmer Monument and Izvestia Front Page — A2151

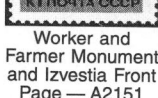

Ship Sailing Across the Oceans — A2152

1977, Jan. 25

4542 A2151 4k silver, black & red .25 .20

60th anniversary of newspaper Izvestia.

1977, Jan. 25

4543 A2152 6k deep blue & gold .30 .20

24th Intl. Navigation Cong., Leningrad.

Congress Hall and Troitskaya Tower, Kremlin — A2153

1977, Feb. 9 Photo. *Perf. 11½*

4544 A2153 4k red, gold & black .25 .20

16th Congress of USSR Trade Unions.

Voroshilov Type of 1976

Marshals of the Soviet Union: #4545, Leonid A. Govorov (1897-1955). #4546, Ivan S. Koniev. #4547, K. A. Merezhkov. #4548, W. D. Sokolovsky.

1977 Engr. *Perf. 12*

4545	A2154	4k	brown	.20	.20
4546	A2154	4k	slate green	.20	.20
4547	A2154	4k	brown	.20	.20
4548	A2154	4k	black	.20	.20
			Nos. 4545-4548 (4)	.80	.80

Issue dates: #4545, Feb. 9; others, June 7.

Academy, Crest, Anchor and Ribbons A2155

Photogravure and Engraved

1977, Feb. 9 *Perf. 11½*

4549 A2155 6k multicolored .25 .20

A. A. Grechko Naval Academy, Leningrad, sesquicentennial.

Jeanne Labourbe A2156

Queen and Knights A2157

1977, Feb. 25 Photo. *Perf. 11½*

4550 A2156 4k multicolored .25 .20

Jeanne Labourbe (1877-1919), leader of French communists in Moscow.

1977, Feb. 25

4551 A2157 6k multicolored .30 .20

4th European Chess Championships.

Cosmonauts V. D. Zudov and V. I. Rozhdestvensky — A2158

1977, Feb. 25 *Perf. 12x11½*

4552 A2158 10k multicolored .25 .20

Soyuz 23 space flight, Oct. 14-16, 1976.

A. S. Novikov-Priboy (1877-1944), Writer — A2159

1977, Mar. 16 Photo. *Perf. 11½*

4553 A2159 4k multicolored .25 .20

Welcome, by M. N. Soloninkin A2160

Folk Tale Paintings from Fedoskino Artists' Colony: 6k, Along the Street, by V. D. Antonov, horiz. 10k, Northern Song, by J. V. Karapaev. 12k, Tale of Czar Saltan, by A. I. Kozlov. 14k, Summer Troika, by V. A. Nalimov, horiz. 16k, Red Flower, by V. D. Lipitsky.

Perf. 12x12½, 12½x12

1977, Mar. 16 Litho.

4554	A2160	4k	black & multi	.20	.20
4555	A2160	6k	black & multi	.25	.20
4556	A2160	10k	black & multi	.50	.20
4557	A2160	12k	black & multi	.60	.20
4558	A2160	14k	black & multi	.70	.20
4559	A2160	16k	black & multi	.75	.20
			Nos. 4554-4559 (6)	3.00	1.20

Lenin on Red Square, by K.V. Filatov — A2161

1977, Apr. 12 *Perf. 12½x11½*

4560 A2161 4k multicolored .25 .20

107th anniversary of the birth of Lenin.

Electricity Congress Emblem A2162

1977, Apr. 12 Photo. *Perf. 11½*

4561 A2162 6k blue, red & gray .25 .20

World Electricity Congress, Moscow 1977.

Yuri Gagarin, Sputnik, Soyuz and Salyut — A2163

1977, Apr. 12 *Perf. 12x11½*

4562 A2163 6k multicolored .25 .20

Cosmonauts' Day.

N. I. Vavilov A2164

Feliks E. Dzerzhinski A2165

1977, Apr. 26 Photo. *Perf. 11½*

4563 A2164 4k multicolored .25 .20

Vavilov (1887-1943), agricultural geneticist.

1977, May 12 Engr. *Perf. 12½x12*

4564 A2165 4k black .30 .20

Feliks E. Dzerzhinski (1877-1926), organizer and head of secret police (OGPU).

Saxifraga Sibirica — A2166

Siberian Flowers: 3k, Dianthus repena. 4k, Novosieversia glactalis. 6k, Cerasticum maxinicem. 16k, Golden rhododendron.

1977, May 12 Litho. *Perf. 12x12½*

4565	A2166	2k multicolored	.20	.20
4566	A2166	3k multicolored	.20	.20
4567	A2166	4k multicolored	.20	.20
4568	A2166	6k multicolored	.30	.20
4569	A2166	16k multicolored	.80	.20
		Nos. 4565-4569 (5)	1.70	1.00

V. V. Gorbatko, Y. N. Glazkov, Soyuz 24 Rocket A2167

1977, May 16 Photo. *Perf. 12x11½*

4570	A2167	10k multicolored	.40	.25

Space explorations of cosmonauts on Salyut 5 orbital station, launched with Soyuz 24 rocket.

Film and Globe — A2168

1977, June 21 Photo. *Perf. 11½*

4571	A2168	6k multicolored	.25	.20

10th Intl. Film Festival, Moscow 1977.

Lion Hunt, by Rubens — A2169

Rubens Paintings, Hermitage, Leningrad: 4k, Lady in Waiting, vert. 10k, Workers in Quarry. 12k, Alliance of Water and Earth, vert. 20k, Landscape with Rainbow. 50k, Self-portrait.

Perf. 12x12½, 12½x12

1977, June 24 Litho.

4572	A2169	4k yellow & multi	.20	.20
4573	A2169	6k yellow & multi	.20	.20
4574	A2169	10k yellow & multi	.40	.20
4575	A2169	12k yellow & multi	.50	.20
4576	A2169	20k yellow & multi	.75	.30
		Nos. 4572-4576 (5)	2.05	1.10

Souvenir Sheet

4577	A2169	50k yellow & multi	2.50	.80

Peter Paul Rubens (1577-1640), painter. Sheets of No. 4575 contain 2 labels with commemorative inscriptions and Atlas statue from Hermitage entrance.

Souvenir Sheet

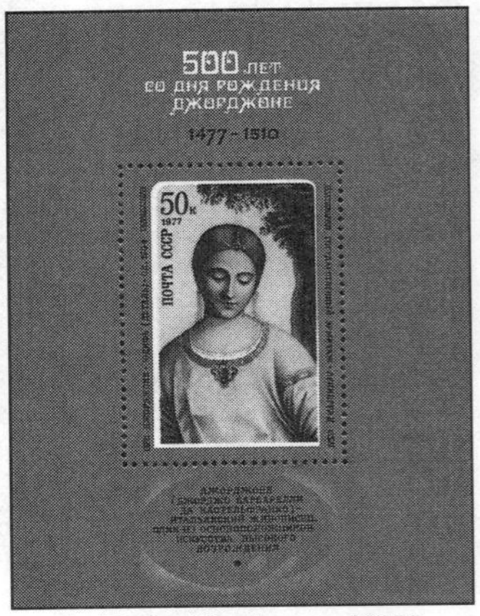

Judith, by Giorgione — A2170

1977, July 15 Litho. *Perf. 12x12½*

4578	A2170	50k multicolored	2.00	1.00

Il Giorgione (1478-1511), Venetian painter.

Icebreaker Type of 1976

Icebreakers: 4k, Aleksandr Sibiryakov. 6k, Georgi Sedov. 10k, Sadko. 12k, Dezhnev. 14k, Siberia. 16k, Lena. 20k, Amguyema.

Lithographed and Engraved

1977, July 27 *Perf. 12x11½*

4579	A2145	4k multicolored	.20	.20
4580	A2145	6k multicolored	.20	.20
4581	A2145	10k multicolored	.35	.20
4582	A2145	12k multicolored	.40	.20
4583	A2145	14k multicolored	.45	.25
4584	A2145	16k multicolored	.50	.35
4585	A2145	20k multicolored	.65	.45
		Nos. 4579-4585 (7)	2.75	1.85

Souvenir Sheet

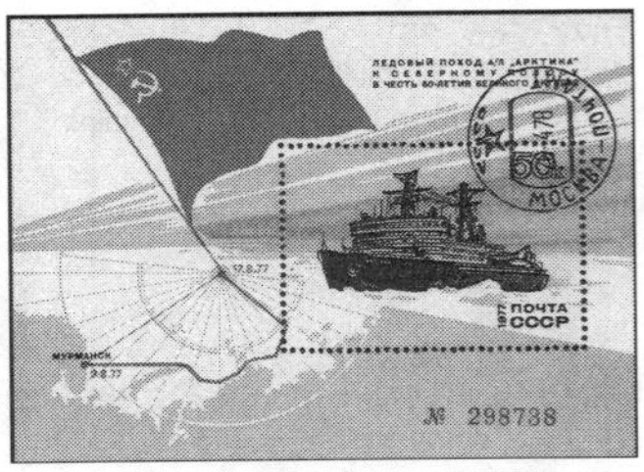

Icebreaker Arctica — A2171

Lithographed and Engraved

1977, Sept. 15 *Perf. 12½x12*

4586	A2171	50k multicolored	6.00	5.00

Arctica, first ship to travel from Murmansk to North Pole, Aug. 9-17.

View and Arms of Stavropol A2172

Stamps and Exhibition Emblem A2173

1977, Aug. 16 Photo. *Perf. 11½*

4587	A2172	6k multicolored	.25	.20

200th anniversary of Stavropol.

1977, Aug. 16

4588	A2173	4k multicolored	.25	.20

October Revolution Anniversary Philatelic Exhibition, Moscow.

Yuri A. Gagarin and Spacecraft — A2174

No. 4590, Alexei Leonov floating in space. No. 4591, Orbiting space station, cosmonauts at control panel.

Nos. 4592-4594, Various spacecraft: No. 4592, International cooperation for space research; No. 4593, Interplanetary flights; No. 4594, Exploring earth's atmosphere. 50k, "XX," laurel, symbolic Sputnik with Red Star.

1977, Oct. 4 Photo. *Perf. 11½x12*

4589	A2174	10k sepia & multi	.25	.20
4590	A2174	10k gray & multi	.25	.20
4591	A2174	10k gray green & multi	.25	.20
4592	A2174	20k green & multi	.60	.35
4593	A2174	20k vio bl & multi	.60	.35
4594	A2174	20k bister & multi	.60	.35
		Nos. 4589-4594 (6)	2.55	1.65

Souvenir Sheet

4595	A2174	50k claret & gold	*7.50*	*7.50*

20th anniv. of space research. No. 4595 contains one stamp, size: 22x32mm.

Types of 1976

Designs: 15k, Communications emblem and globes; others as before.

1977-78 Litho. *Perf. 12x12½*

4596	A2138	1k olive green	.20	.20
4597	A2138	2k lilac rose	.20	.20
4598	A2139	3k brick red	.20	.20
4599	A2138	4k vermilion	.20	.20
4600	A2139	6k Prus blue	.20	.20
4601	A2138	10k gray green	.40	.20
4602	A2139	12k vio blue	.45	.20
4602A	A2139	15k blue ('78)	.55	.20
4603	A2139	16k slate green	.60	.20

Perf. 12½x12

4604	A2140	20k brown red	.75	.20
4605	A2141	30k dull brick red	1.00	.20
4606	A2142	50k brown	2.00	.20
4607	A2143	1r dark blue	3.75	.20
		Nos. 4596-4607 (13)	10.50	2.60

Nos. 4596-4602A, 4604-4607 were printed on dull and shiny paper.

For overprint see #5720. For surcharges see Uzbekistan #16-17, 23, 27-29, 61A.

Souvenir Sheet

Bas-relief, 12th Century, Cathedral of St. Dimitri, Vladimir — A2175

6k, Necklace, Ryazan excavations, 12th cent. 10k, Mask, Cathedral of the Nativity, Suzdal, 13th cent. 12k, Archangel Michael, 15th cent. icon. 16k, Chalice by Ivan Fomin, 1449. 20k, St. Basil's Cathedral, Moscow, 16th cent.

1977, Oct. 12 Litho. *Perf. 12*

4608		Sheet of 6	2.50	1.25
a.	A2175	4k gold & black	.20	
b.	A2175	6k gold & multi	.20	
c.	A2175	10k gold & multi	.35	
d.	A2175	12k gold & multi	.45	
e.	A2175	16k gold & multi	.50	
f.	A2175	20k gold & multi	.60	

Masterpieces of old Russian culture.

Fir, Snowflake, Molniya Satellite — A2176

1977, Oct. 12 *Perf. 12x12½*

4609	A2176	4k multicolored	.30	.20

New Year 1978.

Cruiser Aurora and Torch A2177

60th Anniversary of Revolution Medal — A2178

60th Anniv. of October Revolution: #4611, Lenin speaking at Finland Station (monument), 1917. #4612, 1917 Peace Decree, Brezhnev's book about Lenin. #4613, Kremlin tower with star and fireworks.

1977, Oct. 26 Photo. *Perf. 12x11½*

4610	A2177	4k gold, red & black	.20	.20
4611	A2177	4k gold, red & black	.20	.20
4612	A2177	4k gold, red & black	.20	.20
4613	A2177	4k gold, red & black	.20	.20
		Nos. 4610-4613 (4)	.80	.80

Souvenir Sheet

Perf. 11½

4614	A2178	30k gold, red & black	1.50	.70

Flag of USSR, Constitution (Book) with Coat of Arms — A2179

Designs: No. 4616, Red banner, people and cover of constitution. 50k, Constitution, Kremlin and olive branch.

1977, Oct. 31 Litho. *Perf. 12½x12*

4615	A2179	4k red, black & yel	.20	.20
4616	A2179	4k red, black & yel	.20	.20

Souvenir Sheet

Perf. 11½x12½

Lithographed and Embossed

4617	A2179	50k red, gold & yel	1.75	1.00

Adoption of new constitution. No. 4617 contains one 70x50mm stamp.

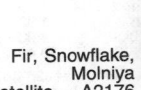

Souvenir Sheet

Leonid Brezhnev — A2180

Lithographed and Embossed

1977, Nov. 2 *Perf. 11½x12*

4618	A2180	50k gold & multi	1.75	1.00

Adoption of new constitution, General Secretary Brezhnev, chairman of Constitution Commission.

Postal Official and Postal Code — A2181

Mail Processing (Woman Postal Official and): No. 4620, Mail collection and Moskvich 430 car. No. 4621, Automatic letter sorting machine. No. 4622, Mail transport by truck, train, ship and planes. No. 4623, Mail delivery in city and country.

Lithographed and Engraved

1977, Nov. 16 *Perf. 12½x12*

4619	A2181 4k multicolored		.20	.20
4620	A2181 4k multicolored		.20	.20
4621	A2181 4k multicolored		.20	.20
4622	A2181 4k multicolored		.20	.20
4623	A2181 4k multicolored		.20	.20
	Nos. 4619-4623 (5)		1.00	1.00

Capital, Asoka Pillar, Red Fort — A2182

1977, Dec. 14 **Photo.** *Perf. 11½*

4624	A2182	6k maroon, gold & red	.25	.20

30th anniversary of India's independence.

Proclamation Monument, Charkov A2183

1977, Dec. 14 **Litho.** *Perf. 12x12½*

4625	A2183	6k multicolored	.25	.20

60th anniv. of Soviet power in the Ukraine.

Lebetina Viper — A2184

Protected Fauna: 1k to 12k, Venomous snakes, useful for medicinal purposes. 16k, Polar bear and cub. 20k, Walrus and calf. 30k, Tiger and cub.

Photogravure and Engraved

1977, Dec. 16 *Perf. 11½x12*

4626	A2184	1k black & multi	.20	.20
4627	A2184	4k black & multi	.20	.20
4628	A2184	6k black & multi	.20	.20
4629	A2184	10k black & multi	.35	.20
4630	A2184	12k black & multi	.45	.20
4631	A2184	16k black & multi	.55	.20
4632	A2184	20k black & multi	.75	.25
4633	A2184	30k black & multi	1.00	.35
		Nos. 4626-4633 (8)	3.70	1.80

Wheat, Combine, Silos — A2185

1978, Jan. 27 **Photo.** *Perf. 11½*

4634	A2185	4k multicolored	.25	.20

Gigant collective grain farm, Rostov Region, 50th anniversary.

Congress Palace, Spasski Tower — A2186

1978, Jan. 27 **Litho.** *Perf. 12x12½*

4635	A2186	4k multicolored	.25	.20

Young Communist League, Lenin's Komsomol, 60th anniv. and its 25th Cong.

Liberation Obelisk, Emblem, Dove — A2187

1978, Jan. 27 **Photo.** *Perf. 11½*

4636	A2187	6k multicolored	.25	.20

8th Congress of International Federation of Resistance Fighters, Minsk, Belorussia.

Soldiers Leaving for the Front — A2188

Designs: No. 4638, Defenders of Moscow Monument, Lenin banner. No. 4639, Soldier as defender of the people.

1978, Feb. 21 **Litho.** *Perf. 12½x12*

4637	A2188	4k red & multi	.20	.20
4638	A2188	4k red & multi	.20	.20
4639	A2188	4k red & multi	.20	.20
		Nos. 4637-4639 (3)	.60	.60

60th anniversary of USSR Military forces.

Celebration in Village — A2189

Kustodiev Paintings: 6k, Shrovetide (winter landscape). 10k, Morning, by Kustodiev. 12k, Merchant's Wife Drinking Tea. 20k, Bolshevik. 50k, Self-portrait, vert.

1978, Mar. 3 *Perf. 11½*

Size: 70x33mm

4640	A2189	4k lilac & multi	.20	.20
4641	A2189	6k lilac & multi	.20	.20

Size: 47x32mm

Perf. 12½x12

4642	A2189	10k lilac & multi	.40	.20
4643	A2189	12k lilac & multi	.50	.20
4644	A2189	20k lilac & multi	.70	.25
		Nos. 4640-4644 (5)	2.00	1.05

Souvenir Sheet

Perf. 11½x12½

4644A	A2189	50k lilac & multi	1.75	.75

Boris Mikhailovich Kustodiev (1878-1927), painter. Nos. 4640-4643 have se-tenant label showing museum where painting is kept. No. 4644A has label giving short biography.

Docking in Space, Intercosmos Emblem A2190

Designs: 6k, Rocket, Soviet Cosmonaut Aleksei Gubarev and Czechoslovak Capt. Vladimir Remek on launching pad. 32k, Weather balloon, helicopter, Intercosmos emblem, USSR and Czechoslovakian flags.

1978, Mar. 10 **Litho.** *Perf. 12x12½*

4645	A2190	6k multicolored	.20	.20
4646	A2190	15k multicolored	.40	.20
4647	A2190	32k multicolored	.85	.40
		Nos. 4645-4647 (3)	1.45	.80

Intercosmos, Soviet-Czechoslovak cooperative space program.

Festival Emblem — A2191

1978, Mar. 17 **Litho.** *Perf. 12x12½*

4648	A2191	4k blue & multi	.25	.20

11th Youth & Students' Cong., Havana.

Tulip, Bolshoi Theater A2192

Moscow Flowers: 2k, Rose "Moscow morning" and Lomonosov University. 4k, Dahlia "Red Star" and Spasski Tower. 10k, Gladiolus "Moscovite" and VDNH Building. 12k, Ilich anniversary iris and Lenin Central Museum.

1978, Mar. 17 *Perf. 12½x12*

4649	A2192	1k multicolored	.20	.20
4650	A2192	2k multicolored	.20	.20
4651	A2192	4k multicolored	.20	.20
4652	A2192	10k multicolored	.20	.20
4653	A2192	12k multicolored	.25	.20
		Nos. 4649-4653 (5)	1.05	1.00

IMCO Emblem and Waves — A2193

1978, Mar. 17 **Litho.** *Perf. 12x12½*

4654	A2193	6k multicolored	.25	.20

Intergovernmental Maritime Consultative Org., 20th anniv., and World Maritime Day.

Spaceship, Orbits of Salyut 5, Soyuz 26 and 27 — A2194

World Federation of Trade Unions Emblem — A2195

1978, Apr. 12 **Photo.** *Perf. 12*

4655	A2194	6k blue, dk blue & gold	.25	.20

Cosmonauts' Day, Apr. 12.

1978, Apr. 16 *Perf. 12*

4656	A2195	6k multicolored	.25	.20

9th World Trade Union Congress, Prague.

2-2-0 Locomotive, 1845, Petersburg and Moscow Stations — A2196

Locomotives: 1k, 1st Russian model by E. A. and M. W. Cherepanov, vert. 2k, 1-3-0 freight, 1845. 16k, Aleksandrov 0-3-0, 1863. 20k, 2-2-0 passenger and Sergievsk Pustyn platform, 1863.

1978, Apr. 20 **Litho.** *Perf. 11½*

4657	A2196	1k orange & multi	.20	.20
4658	A2196	2k ultra & multi	.20	.20
4659	A2196	3k yellow & multi	.20	.20
4660	A2196	16k green & multi	.60	.20
4661	A2196	20k rose & multi	.70	.25
		Nos. 4657-4661 (5)	1.90	1.05

Souvenir Sheet

Lenin, by V. A. Serov — A2197

1978, Apr. 22 *Perf. 12x12½*

4662 A2197 50k multicolored 1.50 .75

108th anniversary of the birth of Lenin.

A2198

No. 4663, Soyuz and Salyut 6 docking in space. No. 4664, Y. V. Romanenko and G. M. Grechko.

1978, June 15 *Perf. 12*

4663 15k multicolored .40 .20
4664 15k multicolored .40 .20
a. A2198 Pair, #4663-4664 .80 .40

Photographic survey and telescopic observations of stars by crews of Soyuz 26, Soyuz 27 and Soyuz 28, Dec. 10, 1977-Mar. 16, 1978. Nos. 4663-4664 printed se-tenant with label showing schematic pictures of various experiments.

Space Meteorology, Rockets, Spaceship, Earth — A2200

No. 4665, Natural resources of earth and Soyuz. No. 4667, Space communications, "Orbita" Station and Molnyia satellite. No. 4668, Man, earth and Vostok. 50k, Study of magnetosphere, Prognoz over earth.

1978, June 23 *Perf. 12x12½*

4665 A2200 10k green & multi .25 .20
4666 A2200 10k blue & multi .25 .20
4667 A2200 10k violet & multi .25 .20
4668 A2200 10k rose lil & multi .25 .20
Nos. 4665-4668 (4) 1.00 .80

Souvenir Sheet

Perf. 11½x12½

4669 A2200 50k multicolored 1.50 .75

Space explorations of the Intercosmos program. #4669 contains one 36x51mm stamp.

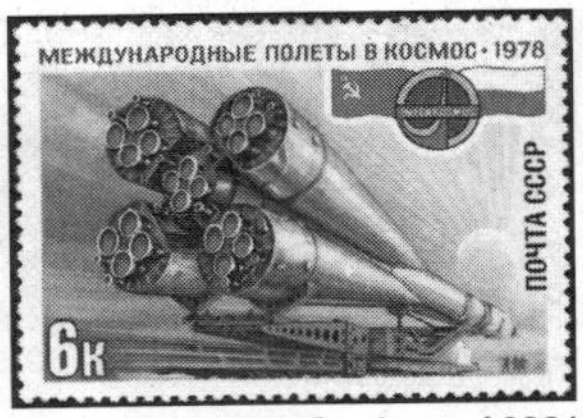

Soyuz Rocket on Carrier — A2201

Designs (Flags of USSR and Poland, Intercosmos Emblem): 15k, Crystal, spaceship (Sirena, experimental crystallogenesis in space). 32k, Research ship "Cosmonaut Vladimir Komarov," spaceship, world map and paths of Salyut 6, Soyuz 29-30.

1978, Litho. *Perf. 12½x12*

4670 A2201 6k multicolored .20 .20
4671 A2201 15k multicolored .40 .20
4672 A2201 32k multicolored .80 .40
Nos. 4670-4672 (3) 1.40 .80

Intercosmos, Soviet-Polish cooperative space program. Issued: 6k, 6/28; 15k, 6/30; 32k, 7/5.

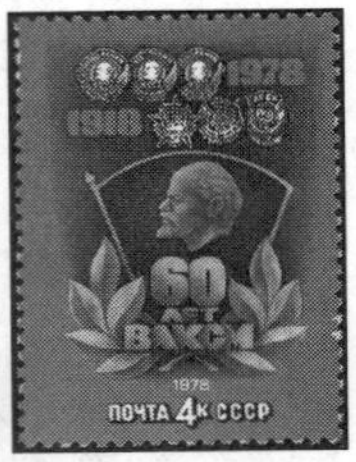

Lenin, Awards Received by Komsomol A2202

Kamaz Car, Train, Bridge, Hammer and Sickle — A2203

1978, July 5 *Perf. 12x12½*

4673 A2202 4k multicolored .20 .20
4674 A2203 4k multicolored .20 .20

Leninist Young Communist League (Komsomol), 60th anniv. (#4673); Komsomol's participation in 5-year plan (#4674).

For overprint see No. 4703.

M. V. Zaharov (1898-1972), Marshal of the Soviet Union — A2204

1978, July 5 Engr. *Perf. 12*

4675 A2204 4k sepia .25 .20

Torch, Flags of Participants A2205

1978, July 25 Litho. *Perf. 12x12½*

4676 A2205 4k multicolored .25 .20

Construction of Soyuz gas-pipeline (Friendship Line), Orenburg. Flags of participating countries shown: Bulgaria, Hungary, German Democratic Republic, Poland, Romania, USSR, Czechoslovakia.

Dr. William Harvey (1578-1657), Discoverer of Blood Circulation — A2206

1978, July 25 *Perf. 12*

4677 A2206 6k blue, black & dp grn .25 .20

Nikolai Gavilovich Chernyshevsky (1828-1889), Revolutionary — A2207

1978, July 30 Engr. *Perf. 12x12½*

4678 A2207 4k brown, *yellow* .25 .20

Whitewinged Petrel A2208

Antarctic Fauna: 1k, Crested penguin, horiz. 4k, Emperor penguin and chick. 6k, White-blooded pikes. 10k, Sea elephant, horiz.

Perf. 12x11½, 11½x12

1978, July 30 Litho.

4679 A2208 1k multicolored .25 .20
4680 A2208 3k multicolored .30 .20
4681 A2208 4k multicolored .60 .20
4682 A2208 6k multicolored .60 .20
4683 A2208 10k multicolored 1.25 .20
Nos. 4679-4683 (5) 3.00 1.00

The Red Horse, by Petrov-Votkin — A2209

Paintings by Petrov-Votkin: 6k, Mother and Child, Petrograd, 1918. 10k, Death of the Commissar. 12k, Still-life with Fruit. 16k, Still-life with Teapot and Flowers. 50k, Self-portrait, 1918, vert.

1978, Aug. 16 Litho. *Perf. 12½x12*

4684 A2209 4k silver & multi .20 .20
4685 A2209 6k silver & multi .20 .20
4686 A2209 10k silver & multi .45 .20
4687 A2209 12k silver & multi .55 .20
4688 A2209 16k silver & multi .65 .20
Nos. 4684-4688 (5) 2.05 1.00

Souvenir Sheet

Perf. 11½x12

4689 A2209 50k silver & multi 1.50 1.00

Kozma Sergeevich Petrov-Votkin (1878-1939), painter. Nos. 4684-4688 have se-tenant labels. No. 4689 has label the size of stamp.

Soyuz 31 in Shop, Intercosmos Emblem, USSR and DDR Flags A2210

Designs (Intercosmos Emblem, USSR and German Democratic Republic Flags and): 15k, Pamir Mountains photographed from space; Salyut 6, Soyuz 29 and 31 complex and spectrum. 32k, Soyuz 31 docking, photographed from Salyut 6.

1978 Litho. *Perf. 12x12½*

4690 A2210 6k multicolored .20 .20
4691 A2210 15k multicolored .85 .20
4692 A2210 32k multicolored 1.65 .45
Nos. 4690-4692 (3) 2.70 .85

Intercosmos, Soviet-East German cooperative space program.

Issued: 6k, 8/27; 15k, 8/31; 32k, 9/3.

PRAGA '78 Emblem, Plane, Radar, Spaceship A2211

Photogravure and Engraved

1978, Aug. 29 *Perf. 11½*

4693 A2211 6k multicolored .25 .20

PRAGA '78 International Philatelic Exhibition, Prague, Sept. 8-17.

Leo Tolstoi (1828-1910), Novelist and Philosopher A2212

1978, Sept. 7 Engr. *Perf. 12x12½*

4694 A2212 4k slate green 1.25 .90

Stag, Conference Emblem — A2213

1978 Photo. *Perf. 11½*

4695 A2213 4k multicolored .25 .20

14th General Assembly of the Society for Wildlife Preservation, Ashkhabad.

Bronze Figure, Erebuni, 8th Century A2214

Armenian Architecture: 6k, Etchmiadzin Cathedral, 4th century. 10k, Stone crosses, Dzaghkatzor, 13th century. 12k, Library, Erevan, horiz. 16k, Lenin statue, Lenin Square, Erevan, horiz.

1978 Litho. ***Perf. 12x12½, 12½x12***

4696	A2214	4k multicolored	.20	.20
4697	A2214	6k multicolored	.20	.20
4698	A2214	10k multicolored	.30	.20
4699	A2214	12k multicolored	.40	.20
4700	A2214	16k multicolored	.50	.20
		Nos. 4696-4700 (5)	1.60	1.00

Issued: 4k, 10k, 16k, 9/12; others, 10/14.

Memorial, Messina, Russian Warships A2215

1978, Sept. 12 Photo. ***Perf. 11½***

4701	A2215	6k multicolored	.25	.20

70th anniversary of aid given by Russian sailors during Messina earthquake.

Communications Emblem, Ostankino TV Tower — A2216

1978, Sept. 20 Photo. ***Perf. 11½***

4702	A2216	4k multicolored	.25	.20

Organization for Communication Cooperation of Socialist Countries, 20th anniv.

No. 4673 Overprinted

1978, Sept. 20 Litho. ***Perf. 12x12½***

4703	A2202	4k multicolored	1.25	.70

Philatelic Exhibition for the Leninist Young Communist League.

Souvenir Sheet

Diana, by Paolo Veronese — A2217

1978, Sept. 28 Litho. ***Perf. 12x11½***

4704	A2217	50k multicolored	1.50	1.00

Veronese (1528-88), Italian painter.

Kremlin, Moscow A2218

Souvenir Sheet

Lithographed and Embossed

1978, Oct. 7 ***Perf. 11½x12***

4705	A2218	30k gold & multi	1.50	.65

Russian Constitution, 1st anniversary.

Stepan Georgevich Shaumyan (1878-1918), Communist Party Functionary A2219

1978, Oct. 11 Engr. ***Perf. 12½x12***

4706	A2219	4k slate green	.25	.20

Ferry, Russian and Bulgarian Colors — A2220

Hammer and Sickle, Flags — A2221

1978, Oct. 14 Photo. ***Perf. 11½***

4707	A2220	6k multicolored	.25	.20

Opening of Ilychovsk-Varna Ferry.

1978, Oct. 26 Photo. ***Perf. 11½***

4708	A2221	4k gold & multi	.25	.20

61st anniversary of October Revolution.

Silver Gilt Cup, Novgorod, 12th Century — A2222

Old Russian Art: 10k, Pokrowna Nerli Church, 12th century, vert. 12k, St. George Slaying the Dragon, icon, Novgorod, 15th century, vert. 16k, The Czar, cannon, 1586.

Perf. 12½x12, 12x12½

1978, Nov. 28 Litho.

4709	A2222	6k multicolored	.20	.20
4710	A2222	10k multicolored	.40	.20
4711	A2222	12k multicolored	.50	.20
4712	A2222	16k multicolored	.60	.20
		Nos. 4709-4712 (4)	1.70	.80

Oncology Institute, Emblem — A2223

1978, Dec. 1 Photo. ***Perf. 11½***

4713	A2223	4k multicolored	.25	.20

P.A. Herzen Tumor Institute, 75th anniv.

Savior Tower, Kremlin — A2224

1978, Dec. 20 Litho. ***Perf. 12x12½***

4714	A2224	4k silver, blue & red	.25	.20

New Year 1979.

Nestor Pechersky, Chronicler, c. 885 — A2225

History of Postal Service: 6k, Birch bark letter and stylus. 10k, Messenger with trumpet and staff, from 14th century Psalm book. 12k, Winter traffic, from 16th century book by Sigizmund Gerberstein. 16k, Prikaz post office, from 17th century icon.

Lithographed and Engraved

1978, Dec. 20 ***Perf. 12½x12***

4715	A2225	4k multicolored	.20	.20
4716	A2225	6k multicolored	.20	.20
4717	A2225	10k multicolored	.50	.20
4718	A2225	12k multicolored	.55	.20
4719	A2225	16k multicolored	.65	.20
		Nos. 4715-4719 (5)	2.10	1.00

Kovalenok and Ivanchenkov, Salyut 6-Soyuz — A2226

1978, Dec. 20 Photo. ***Perf. 11½x12***

4720	A2226	10k multicolored	.30	.20

Cosmonauts V. V. Kovalenok and A. S. Ivanchenkov spent 140 days in space, June 15-Nov. 2, 1978.

Vasilii Pronchishchev — A2227

Icebreakers: 6k, Captain Belousov, 1954, vert. 10k, Moscow. 12k, Admiral Makarov, 1974. 16k, Lenin, 1959, vert. 20k, Nuclear-powered Arctica.

Perf. 11½x12, 12x11½

1978, Dec. 20 Photo. & Engr.

4721	A2227	4k multicolored	.20	.20
4722	A2227	6k multicolored	.20	.20
4723	A2227	10k multicolored	.25	.20
4724	A2227	12k multicolored	.25	.20
4725	A2227	16k multicolored	.35	.20
4726	A2227	20k multicolored	.40	.25
		Nos. 4721-4726 (6)	1.65	1.25

Souvenir Sheet

Mastheads and Globe with Russia — A2228

1978, Dec. 28 Litho. ***Perf. 12***

4727	A2228	30k multicolored	1.00	.35

Distribution of periodicals through the Post and Telegraph Department, 60th anniversary.

Cuban Flags Forming Star — A2229

1979, Jan. 1 Photo. ***Perf. 11½***

4728	A2229	6k multicolored	.25	.20

Cuban Revolution, 20th anniversary.

Russian and Byelorussian Flags, Government Building, Minsk — A2230

1979, Jan. 1

4729	A2230	4k multicolored	.25	.20

Byelorussian SSR and Byelorussian Communist Party, 60th annivs.

Ukrainian and Russian Flags, Reunion Monument A2231

1979, Jan. 16

4730	A2231	4k multicolored	.30	.20

Reunion of Ukraine & Russia, 325th anniv.

Old and New Vilnius University Buildings A2232

1979, Jan. 16 **Photo. & Engr.**
4731 A2232 4k black & salmon .25 .20

400th anniversary of University of Vilnius.

Bulgaria No. 1 and Exhibition Hall A2233

1979, Jan. 25 **Litho.** ***Perf. 12½x12***
4732 A2233 15k multicolored .35 .20

Filaserdica '79 Philatelic Exhibition, Sofia, for centenary of Bulgarian postal service.

Sputniks, Soviet Radio Hams Emblem — A2234

1979, Feb. 23 **Photo.** ***Perf. 11½***
4733 A2234 4k multicolored .25 .20

Sputnik satellites Radio 1 and Radio 2, launched, Oct. 1978.

1-3-0 Locomotive, 1878 — A2235

Locomotives: 3k, 1-4-0, 1912. 4k, 2-3-1, 1915. 6k, 1-3-1, 1925. 15k, 1-5-0, 1947.

1979, Feb. 23 **Litho.** ***Perf. 11½***

4734	A2235	2k multicolored	.20	.20
4735	A2235	3k multicolored	.20	.20
4736	A2235	4k multicolored	.20	.20
4737	A2235	6k multicolored	.25	.20
4738	A2235	15k multicolored	.65	.20
		Nos. 4734-4738 (5)	1.50	1.00

Souvenir Sheet

Medal for Land Development — A2236

1979, Mar. 14 ***Perf. 11½x12½***
4739 A2236 50k multicolored 1.50 .75

25th anniv. of drive to develop virgin lands.

Venera 11 and 12 over Venus — A2237

1979, Mar. 16 **Photo.** ***Perf. 11½***
4740 A2237 10k multicolored .30 .20

Interplanetary flights of Venera 11 and Venera 12, December 1978.

Albert Einstein, Equation and Signature A2238

1979, Mar. 16
4741 A2238 6k multicolored .30 .20

Einstein (1879-1955), theoretical physicist.

Congress Emblem A2239

1979, Mar. 16
4742 A2239 6k multicolored .25 .20

21st World Veterinary Congress, Moscow.

"To Arms," by R. Berens A2240

1979, Mar. 21
4743 A2240 4k multicolored .25 .20

Soviet Republic of Hungary, 60th anniv.

Salyut 6, Soyuz, Research Ship, Letters — A2241

1979, Apr. 12 **Litho.** ***Perf. 11½x12***
4744 A2241 15k multicolored .50 .20

Cosmonauts' Day.

Souvenir Sheet

Ice Hockey — A2242

1979, Apr. 14 **Photo.** ***Perf. 12x11½***
4745 A2242 50k multicolored 1.50 .75

World and European Ice Hockey Championships, Moscow, Apr. 14-27.
For overprint see No. 4751.

Souvenir Sheet

Lenin — A2243

1979, Apr. 18
4746 A2243 50k red, gold & brn 1.50 .75

109th anniversary of the birth of Lenin.

Astronauts' Training Center A2244

Design: 32k, Astronauts, landing capsule, radar, helicopter and emblem.

1979, Apr. 12 **Litho.** ***Perf. 11½***

4747	A2244	6k multicolored	.20	.20
4748	A2244	32k multicolored	.90	.40

Joint Soviet-Bulgarian space flight.

Exhibition Emblem — A2245

1979, Apr. 18 **Photo.** ***Perf. 11½***
4749 A2245 15k sil, red & vio blue .60 .20

National USSR Exhibition in the United Kingdom. Se-tenant label with commemorative inscription.

Blast Furance, Pushkin Theater, "Tent" Sculpture — A2246

1979, May 24 **Photo.** ***Perf. 11½***
4750 A2246 4k multicolored .25 .20

50th anniversary of Magnitogorsk City.

Souvenir Sheet

No. 4745 Overprinted in Margin in Red

1979, May 24 ***Perf. 12x11½***
4751 A2242 50k multicolored 3.00 .80

Victory of Soviet team in World and European Ice Hockey Championships.

Infant, Flowers, IYC Emblem — A2247

1979, June **Litho.** ***Perf. 12x12½***
4752 A2247 4k multicolored .25 .20

International Year of the Child.

Horn Player and Bears Playing Balalaika, Bogorodsk Wood Carvings — A2248

Folk Art: 3k, Decorated wooden bowls, Khokhloma. 4k, Tray decorated with flowers, Zhestovo. 6k, Carved bone boxes, Kholmogory. 15k, Lace, Vologda.

1979, June 14 **Litho.** ***Perf. 12½x12***

4753	A2248	2k multicolored	.20	.20
4754	A2248	3k multicolored	.20	.20
4755	A2248	4k multicolored	.20	.20
4756	A2248	6k multicolored	.20	.20
4757	A2248	15k multicolored	.50	.25
		Nos. 4753-4757 (5)	1.30	1.05

Nos. 4753-4757 printed in sheets of 7 stamps and decorative label.

V. A. Djanibekov, O. G. Makarov, Spacecraft A2249

1979, June ***Perf. 12x11½***
4758 A2249 4k multicolored .35 .20

Flights of Soyuz 26-27 and work on board of orbital complex Salyut 26-27.

COMECON Building, Members' Flags — A2250

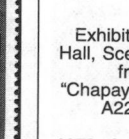

Scene from "Potemkin" and Festival Emblem — A2251

1979, June 26 ***Perf. 12***
4759 A2250 16k multicolored .50 .20

Council for Mutual Economic Aid of Socialist Countries, 30th anniversary.

Photogravure and Engraved

1979, July ***Perf. 11½***
4760 A2251 15k multicolored .50 .20

11th International Film Festival, Moscow, and 60th anniversary of Soviet film industry.

Lenin Square Station, Tashkent A2252

1979, July **Litho.** ***Perf. 12***
4761 A2252 4k multicolored .25 .20

Tashkent subway.

Souvenir Sheets

Atom Symbol, Factories, Dam — A2253

1979, July 23 **Photo.** ***Perf. 11½x12***
4762 A2253 30k multicolored 1.00 .45

50th anniversary of 1st Five-Year Plan.

USSR Philatelic Society Emblem — A2254

1979, July 25 **Litho.** ***Perf. 12x12½***
4763 A2254 50k gray grn & red 1.50 .70

4th Cong. of USSR Phil. Soc., Moscow.

Exhibition Hall, Scene from "Chapayev" A2255

1979, Aug. 8 **Photo.** ***Perf. 11½***
4764 A2255 4k multicolored .25 .20

60th anniversary of Soviet Film and Exhibition of History of Soviet Film.

Roses, by P. P. Konchalovsky, 1955 — A2256

Russian Flower Paintings: 1k, Flowers and Fruit, by I. F. Khrutsky, 1830. 2k, Phlox, by I. N. Kramskoi, 1884. 3k, Lilac, by K. A. Korovin, 1915. 15k, Bluebells, by S. V. Gerasimov, 1944. 2k, 3k, 15k, vert.

Perf. 12½x12, 12x12½

1979, Aug. 16 **Litho.**
4765 A2256 1k multicolored .20 .20
4766 A2256 2k multicolored .20 .20
4767 A2256 3k multicolored .20 .20
4768 A2256 15k multicolored .40 .30
4769 A2256 32k multicolored .75 .55
Nos. 4765-4769 (5) 1.75 1.45

John McClean — A2257

Soviet Circus Emblem — A2258

1979, Aug. 29 **Litho.** ***Perf. 11½***
4770 A2257 4k red & black .25 .20

John McClean (1879-1923), British Communist labor leader.

1979, Sept.
4771 A2258 4k multicolored .25 .20

Soviet Circus, 60th anniversary.

Friendship — A2259

Children's Drawings: 3k, Children and Horses. 4k, Dances. 15k, The Excursion.

1979, Sept. 10 ***Perf. 12½x12***
4772 A2259 2k multicolored .20 .20
4773 A2259 3k multicolored .20 .20
4774 A2259 4k multicolored .20 .20
4775 A2259 15k multicolored .30 .20
Nos. 4772-4775 (4) .90 .80

International Year of the Child. Exist imperf. Value, $50 each.

Oriolus oriolus — A2260

Birds: 3k, Dendrocopus minor. 4k, Parus cristatus. 10k, Tyto alba. 15k, Caprimulgus europaeus.

1979, Sept. 18
4776 A2260 2k multicolored .20 .20
4777 A2260 3k multicolored .20 .20
4778 A2260 4k multicolored .20 .20
4779 A2260 10k multicolored .35 .20
4780 A2260 15k multicolored .50 .20
Nos. 4776-4780 (5) 1.45 1.00

German Arms, Marx, Engels, Lenin, Berlin A2261

1979, Oct. 7 **Photo.** ***Perf. 11½***
4781 A2261 6k multicolored .25 .20

German Democratic Republic, 30th anniv.

Valery Ryumin, Vladimir Lyakhov, Salyut 6 — A2262

Design: No. 4783, Spacecraft.

1979, Oct. 10 ***Perf. 12x11½***
4782 A2262 15k multicolored .40 .25
4783 A2262 15k multicolored .40 .25
a. Pair, #4782-4783 .80 .50

175 days in space, Feb. 25-Aug. 19. No. 4783a has continuous design.

Star — A2264

Hammer and Sickle — A2265

1979, Oct. 18 ***Perf. 11½***
4784 A2264 4k multicolored .25 .20

USSR Armed Forces, 60th anniversary.

1979, Oct. 18
4785 A2265 4k multicolored .25 .20

October Revolution, 62nd anniversary.

Katherina, by T. G. Shevchenko A2266

Ukrainian Paintings: 3k, Working Girl, by K.K. Kostandi. 4k, Lenin's Return to Petrograd, by A.M. Lopuhov. 10k, Soldier's Return, by N.V. Kostesky. 15k, Going to Work, by M.G. Belsky.

1979, Nov. 18 **Litho.** ***Perf. 12x12½***
4786 A2266 2k multicolored .20 .20
4787 A2266 3k multicolored .20 .20
4788 A2266 4k multicolored .20 .20
4789 A2266 10k multicolored .20 .20
4790 A2266 15k multicolored .30 .20
Nos. 4786-4790 (5) 1.10 1.00

Shabolovka Radio Tower, Moscow — A2267

1979, Nov. 28 **Photo.** ***Perf. 12***
4791 A2267 32k multicolored 1.00 .50

Radio Moscow, 50th anniversary.

Mischa Holding Stamp — A2268

1979, Nov. 28 ***Perf. 12x12½***
4792 A2268 4k multicolored .50 .20

New Year 1980.

Hand Holding Peace Message A2269

Peace Program in Action: No. 4794, Hands holding cultural symbols. No. 4795, Hammer and sickle, flag.

1979, Dec. 5 **Litho.** ***Perf. 12***
4793 A2269 4k multicolored .20 .20
4794 A2269 4k multicolored .20 .20
4795 A2269 4k multicolored .20 .20
Nos. 4793-4795 (3) .60 .60

Policeman, Patrol Car, Helicopter A2270

Traffic Safety: 4k, Car, girl and ball. 6k, Speeding cars.

1979, Dec. 20 ***Perf. 12x12½***
4796 A2270 3k multicolored .20 .20
4797 A2270 4k multicolored .20 .20
4798 A2270 6k multicolored .20 .20
Nos. 4796-4798 (3) .60 .60

Vulkanolog — A2271

Research Ships and Portraits: 2k, Professor Bogorov. 4k, Ernst Krenkel. 6k, Vladislav Volkov. 10k, Cosmonaut Yuri Gagarin. 15k, Academician E.B. Kurchatov.

Lithographed and Engraved

1979, Dec. 25 *Perf. 12x11½*

4799 A2271 1k multicolored .20 .20
4800 A2271 2k multicolored .20 .20
4801 A2271 4k multicolored .20 .20
4802 A2271 6k multicolored .20 .20
4803 A2271 10k multicolored .30 .20
4804 A2271 15k multicolored .45 .20
Nos. 4799-4804 (6) 1.55 1.20

See Nos. 4881-4886.

Souvenir Sheet

Explorers Raising Red Flag at North Pole — A2272

1979, Dec. 25 Photo. *Perf. 11½x12*

4805 A2272 50k multicolored 1.50 .75

Komsomolskaya Pravda North Pole expedition.

Type of 1970

4k, Coat of arms, power line, factories.

1980, Jan. 10 Litho. *Perf. 12x12½*

4806 A1794 4k carmine .25 .20

Mordovian Autonomous SSR, 50th anniv.

Freestyle Skating A2273

1980, Jan. 22 *Perf. 12x12½, 12½x12*

4807 A2273 4k Speed skating .20 .20
4808 A2273 6k shown .20 .20
4809 A2273 10k Ice hockey .25 .20
4810 A2273 15k Downhill skiing .35 .25
4811 A2273 20k Luge, vert. .50 .35
Nos. 4807-4811 (5) 1.50 1.20

Souvenir Sheet

4812 A2273 50k Cross-country skiing, vert. 1.50 1.00

13th Winter Olympic Games, Lake Placid, NY, Feb. 12-24.

Nos. 4808, 4809 exist imperf. Value, $50 for both.

Nikolai Ilyitch Podvoiski (1880-1948), Revolutionary A2274

1980, Feb. 16 Engr. *Perf. 12½x12*

4813 A2274 4k claret brown .25 .20

Rainbow, by A.K. Savrasov — A2275

#4815, Summer Harvest, by A.G. Venetsianov, vert. #4816, Old Erevan, by M.S. Saryan.

1980, Mar. 4 Litho. *Perf. 11½*

4814 A2275 6k multicolored .25 .20
4815 A2275 6k multicolored .25 .20
4816 A2275 6k multicolored .25 .20
Nos. 4814-4816 (3) .75 .60

Souvenir Sheet

Cosmonaut Alexei Leonov — A2276

1980, Mar. 18 Litho. *Perf. 12½x12*

4817 A2276 50k multicolored 1.50 .75

Man's first walk in space (Voskhod 2, Mar. 18-19, 1965).

Georg Ots, Estonian Artist A2277

Lenin Order, 50th Anniversary A2278

1980, Mar. 21 **Engr.**

4818 A2277 4k slate blue .25 .20

1980, Apr. 6 Photo. *Perf. 11½*

4819 A2278 4k multicolored .25 .20

Souvenir Sheet

Cosmonauts, Salyut 6 and Soyuz — A2279

1980, Apr. 12 Litho. *Perf. 12*

4820 A2279 50k multicolored 1.50 1.00

Intercosmos cooperative space program.

Flags and Arms of Azerbaijan, Government House — A2280

"Mother Russia," Fireworks over Moscow — A2282

Lenin, 110th Birth Anniversary — A2281

1980, Apr. 22 **Photo.**

4821 A2280 4k multicolored .25 .20

Azerbaijan Soviet Socialist Republic, Communist Party of Azerbaijan, 60th anniv.

Souvenir Sheet

1980, Apr. 22 *Perf. 12x11½*

4822 A2281 30k multicolored 1.25 .75

1980, Apr. 25 **Litho.**

#4824, Soviet War Memorial, Berlin, raising of Red flag. #4825, Parade, Red Square, Moscow.

4823 A2282 4k multicolored .20 .20
4824 A2282 4k multicolored .20 .20
4825 A2282 4k multicolored .20 .20
Nos. 4823-4825 (3) .60 .60

35th anniv. of victory in World War II. Nos. 4824, 4825 exist imperf.

Workers' Monument A2283

"XXV" A2284

1980, May 12 Litho. *Perf. 12*

4826 A2283 4k multicolored .25 .20

Workers' Delegates in Ivanovo-Voznesensk, 75th anniversary.

1980, May 14 Photo. *Perf. 11½*

4827 A2284 32k multicolored 1.25 .75

Signing of Warsaw Pact (Bulgaria, Czechoslovakia, German Democratic Rep., Hungary, Poland, Romania, USSR), 25th anniv.

YaK-24 Helicopter, 1953 — A2285

1980, May 15 Litho. *Perf. 12½x12*

4828 A2285 1k shown .20 .20
4829 A2285 2k MI-8, 1962 .20 .20
4830 A2285 3k KA-26, 1965 .20 .20
4831 A2285 6k MI-6, 1957 .20 .20
4832 A2285 15k MI-10 .25 .20
4833 A2285 32k V-12 .55 .40
Nos. 4828-4833 (6) 1.60 1.40

Nos 4832-4833 exist imperf. Value, $50 for both.

David Anacht, Illuminated Manuscript A2286

1980, May 16 *Perf. 12*

4834 A2286 4k multicolored .25 .20

David Anacht, Armenian philosopher, 1500th birth anniversary.

Emblem, Training Lab — A2287

1980, June 4

4835 A2287 6k shown .20 .20
4836 A2287 15k Cosmonauts meeting .40 .25
4837 A2287 32k Press conference .80 .55
Nos. 4835-4837 (3) 1.40 1.00

Intercosmos cooperative space program (USSR-Hungary).

Polar Fox A2288

1980, June 25 Litho. *Perf. 12x12½*

4838 A2288 2k Dark silver fox, vert. .20 .20
4839 A2288 4k shown .20 .20
4840 A2288 6k Mink .20 .20
4841 A2288 10k Azerbaijan nutria, vert. .20 .20
4842 A2288 15k Black sable .30 .20
Nos. 4838-4842 (5) 1.10 1.00

Factory, Buildings, Arms of Tatar A.S.S.R. A2289

1980, June 25 *Perf. 12*

4843 A2289 4k multicolored .25 .20

Tatar Autonomous SSR, 60th anniv.

College — A2290

Ho Chi Minh — A2291

1980, July 1 Photo. *Perf. 11½*

4844	A2290	4k multicolored	.25	.20

Bauman Technological College, Moscow, 150th anniversary.

1980, July 7

4845	A2291	6k multicolored	.25	.20

Red Flag, Lithuanian Arms, Flag, Red Guards Monument A2292

1980, July 12 Litho. *Perf. 12*

4846	A2292	4k multicolored	.25	.20

Lithuanian SSR, 40th anniv.

Russian Flag and Arms, Latvian Flag, Monument, Buildings A2293

Design: No. 4848, Russian flag and arms, Estonian flag, monument, buildings.

1980, July 21 Litho. *Perf. 12*

4847	A2293	4k multicolored	.20	.20
4848	A2293	4k multicolored	.20	.20

Restoration of Soviet power.

Cosmonauts Boarding Soyuz A2294

1980, July 24 *Perf. 12x12½*

4849	A2294	6k shown	.20	.20
4850	A2294	15k Working aboard spacecraft	.45	.25
4851	A2294	32k Return flight	.80	.55
		Nos. 4849-4851 (3)	1.45	1.00

Center for Cosmonaut Training, 20th anniv.

Avicenna (980-1037), Philosopher and Physician — A2295

Photogravure and Engraved

1980, Aug. 16 *Perf. 11½*

4852	A2295	4k multicolored	.25	.20

Soviet Racing Car KHADI-7 — A2296

1980, Aug. 25 Litho. *Perf. 12*

4853	A2296	2k shown	.20	.20
4854	A2296	6k KHADI-10	.20	.20
4855	A2296	15k KHADI-113	.35	.25
4856	A2296	32k KHADI-133	.65	.45
		Nos. 4853-4856 (4)	1.40	1.10

No. 4856 exists imperf. Value, $50.

Kazakhstan Republic, 60th Anniversary A2297

1980, Aug. 26

4857	A2297	4k multicolored	.50	.20

Ingres, Self-portrait, and Nymph A2298

1980, Aug. 29 *Perf. 12x12½*

4858	A2298	32k multicolored	1.00	.50

Jean Auguste Dominique Ingres (1780-1867), French painter. Exists imperf.

Morning on the Field of Kulikovo, by A. Bubnov — A2299

1980, Sept. 6 Litho. *Perf. 12*

4859	A2299	4k multicolored	.25	.20

Battle of Kulikovo, 600th anniversary.

Town Hall, Tartu — A2300

1980, Sept. 15 Photo. *Perf. 11½*

4860	A2300	4k multicolored	.25	.20

Tartu, 950th anniversary.

Y.V. Malyshev, V.V. Aksenov A2301

1980, Sept. 15 Litho. *Perf. 12x12½*

4861	A2301	10k multicolored	.30	.25

Soyuz T-2 space flight.

Flight Training, Yuri Gagarin — A2302

1980, Sept. 15 Photo. *Perf. 11½x12*

4862	A2302	6k shown	.20	.20
4863	A2302	15k Space walk	.40	.25
4864	A2302	32k Endurance test	.80	.45
		Nos. 4862-4864 (3)	1.40	.90

Gagarin Cosmonaut Training Center, 20th anniversary.

Intercosmos A2303

6k, Intercosmos Emblem, Flags of USSR and Cuba, and Cosmonauts training. 15k, Inside weightless cabin. 32k, Landing.

1980, Sept. 15 Litho. *Perf. 12x12½*

4865	A2303	6k multicolored	.20	.20
4866	A2303	15k multicolored	.40	.25
4867	A2303	32k multicolored	.80	.45
		Nos. 4865-4867 (3)	1.40	.90

Intercosmos cooperative space program (USSR-Cuba).

October Revolution, 63rd Anniversary A2304

1980, Sept. 20 Photo. *Perf. 11½*

4868	A2304	6k multicolored	.25	.20

David Gurumishvily (1705-1792), Poet — A2305

1980, Sept. 20

4869	A2305	6k multicolored	.25	.20

Family with Serfs, by N.V. Nevrev (1830-1904) — A2305a

Design: No. 4869B, Countess Tarakanova, by K.D. Flavitsky (1830-1866), vert.

1980, Sept. 25 Litho. *Perf. 11½*

4869A	A2305a	6k multicolored	.25	.25
4869B	A2305a	6k multicolored	.25	.25

A.F. Joffe (1880-1960), Physicist — A2306

1980, Sept. 29

4870	A2306	4k multicolored	.25	.20

Siberian Pine A2307

1980, Sept. 29 Litho. *Perf. 12½x12*

4871	A2307	2k shown	.20	.20
4872	A2307	4k Oak	.20	.20
4873	A2307	6k Lime tree, vert.	.20	.20
4874	A2307	10k Sea bucthorn	.20	.20
4875	A2307	15k European ash	.30	.20
		Nos. 4871-4875 (5)	1.10	1.00

A.M. Vasilevsky (1895-1977), Soviet Marshal — A2308

1980, Sept. 30 Engr. *Perf. 12*

4876	A2308	4k dark green	.25	.20

Souvenir Sheet

Mischa Holding Olympic Torch — A2309

1980, Nov. 24 ***Perf. 12x12½***
4877 A2309 1r multicolored 7.50 1.75

Completion of 22nd Summer Olympic Games, Moscow, July 19-Aug. 3.

A.V. Suvorov (1730-1800), General and Military Theorist A2310

1980, Nov. 24 **Engr.**
4878 A2310 4k slate .25 .20

A2311

1980, Nov. 24 **Litho.** ***Perf. 12***
4879 A2311 4k multicolored .50 .20

Armenian SSR & Armenian Communist Party, 60th annivs.

Aleksandr Blok (1880-1921), Poet — A2312

1980, Nov. 24
4880 A2312 4k multicolored .25 .20

Research Ship Type of 1979

Lithographed and Engraved

1980, Nov. 24 ***Perf. 12x11½***
4881 A2271 2k Aju Dag, Fleet arms .20 .20
4882 A2271 3k Valerian Urywaev .20 .20
4883 A2271 4k Mikhail Somov .20 .20
4884 A2271 6k Sergei Korolev .20 .20
4885 A2271 10k Otto Schmidt .20 .20
4886 A2271 15k Ustislav Kelgysh .30 .20
Nos. 4881-4886 (6) 1.30 1.20

For overprint see No. 5499.

Russian Flag — A2313

Soviet Medical College, 50th Anniversary A2314

1980, Dec. 1 **Engr.** ***Perf. 12x12½***
4887 A2313 3k orange red .25 .20

1980, Dec. 1 **Photo.** ***Perf. 11½***
4888 A2314 4k multicolored .25 .20

New Year 1981 A2315

1980, Dec. 1 **Litho.** ***Perf. 12***
4889 A2315 4k multicolored .25 .20

Lenin, Electrical Plant A2316

1980, Dec. 18
4890 A2316 4k multicolored .25 .20

60th anniversary of GOELRO (Lenin's electro-economic plan).

A.N. Nesmeyanov (1899-1980), Chemist — A2317

1980, Dec. 19 ***Perf. 12½x12***
4891 A2317 4k multicolored .25 .20

Nagatinski Bridge, Moscow — A2318

Photogravure and Engraved

1980, Dec. 23 ***Perf. 11½x12***
4892 A2318 4k shown .20 .20
4893 A2318 6k Luzhniki Bridge .20 .20
4894 A2318 15k Kalininski Bridge .30 .20
Nos. 4892-4894 (3) .70 .60

S.K. Timoshenko (1895-1970), Soviet Marshal — A2319

1980, Dec. 25 **Engr.** ***Perf. 12***
4895 A2319 4k rose lake .25 .20

Flags of India and USSR, Government House, New Delhi A2320

1980, Dec. 30 **Litho.** ***Perf. 12x12½***
4896 A2320 4k multicolored .50 .35

Visit of Pres. Brezhnev to India. Printed se-tenant with inscribed label.

Mirny Base — A2321

1981, Jan. 5 ***Perf. 12***
4897 A2321 4k shown .20 .20
4898 A2321 6k Earth station, rocket .20 .20
4899 A2321 15k Map, supply ship .30 .20
Nos. 4897-4899 (3) .70 .60

Soviet Antarctic research, 25th anniv.

Dagestan Soviet Socialist Republic, 60th Anniversary A2322

1981, Jan. 20
4900 A2322 4k multicolored .25 .20

Bandy World Championship, Cheborovsk — A2323

1981, Jan. 20
4901 A2323 6k multicolored .25 .20

26th Congress of Ukrainian Communist Party. A2324

1981, Jan. 23 **Photo.** ***Perf. 11½***
4902 A2324 4k multicolored .25 .20

Lenin, "XXVI" A2325

Lenin and Congress Building — A2326

Banner and Kremlin — A2327

1981 **Photo.** ***Perf. 11½***
4903 A2325 4k multicolored .25 .20

Photogravure and Embossed

1982 ***Perf. 11½x12***
4904 A2326 20k multicolored 1.50 .75

Souvenir Sheet

Litho.

Perf. 12x12½
4905 A2327 50k multicolored 1.50 .75

26th Communist Party Congress. Issue dates: 4k, 20k, Jan. 22; 50k, Feb. 16.

Mstislav V. Keldysh A2328

Freighter, Flags of USSR and India A2329

1981, Feb. 10 **Photo.** ***Perf. 11½x12***
4906 A2328 4k multicolored .25 .20

Mstislav Vsevolodovich Keldysh (1911-1978), mathematician.

1981, Feb. 10 **Litho.** ***Perf. 12***
4907 A2329 15k multicolored .50 .30

Soviet-Indian Shipping Line, 25th anniv.

Baikal-Amur Railroad and Map — A2330

10th Five-Year Plan Projects (1976-1980): No. 4909, Gas plant, Urengoi (spherical tanks). No. 4910, Enisei River power station (dam). No. 4911, Atomic power plant. No. 4912, Paper mill. No. 4913, Coal mining, Ekibstyi.

1981, Feb. 18 ***Perf. 12½x12***
4908 A2330 4k multicolored .25 .20
4909 A2330 4k multicolored .25 .20
4910 A2330 4k multicolored .25 .20
4911 A2330 4k multicolored .25 .20
4912 A2330 4k multicolored .25 .20
4913 A2330 4k multicolored .25 .20
Nos. 4908-4913 (6) 1.50 1.20

Georgian Soviet Socialist Republic, 60th Anniv. A2331

1981, Feb. 25 *Perf. 12*

4914 A2331 4k multicolored .25 .20

Abkhazian Autonomous Soviet Socialist Republic, 60th Anniv. — A2332

1981, Mar. 4

4915 A2332 4k multicolored .25 .20

Exists imperf.

Communica-tions Institute A2333

Satellite, Radio Operator A2334

1981, Mar. 12 Photo. *Perf. 11½*

4916 A2333 4k multicolored .25 .20

Moscow Electrotechnical Institute of Communications, 60th anniv.

1981, Mar. 12

4917 A2334 4k multicolored .35 .25

30th All-Union Amateur Radio Designers Exhibition.

Cosmonauts L.I. Popov and V.V. Rumin A2335

1981, Mar. 20 Litho. *Perf. 12*

4918 A2335 15k shown .40 .25

4919 A2335 15k Spacecraft complex .60 .25

a. Pair, #4918-4919 + label 1.00 .50

185-day flight of Cosmos 35-Salyut 6-Cosmos 37 complex, Apr. 9-Oct. 11, 1980. No. 4919a has a continuous design.

Cosmonauts O. Makarov, L. Kizim and G. Strekalov — A2336

1981, Mar. 20 *Perf. 12½x12*

4920 A2336 10k multicolored .25 .20

Soyuz T-3 flight, Nov. 27-Dec. 10, 1980.

Lift-Off, Baikonur Base — A2337

1981, Mar. 23

4921 A2337 6k shown .20 .20

4922 A2337 15k Mongolians watching flight on TV .40 .25

4923 A2337 32k Re-entry .80 .50

Nos. 4921-4923 (3) 1.40 .95

Intercosmos cooperative space program (USSR-Mongolia).

Vitus Bering A2338

1981, Mar. 25 Engr. *Perf. 12x12½*

4924 A2338 4k dark blue .25 .20

Bering (1680-1741), Danish navigator.

Yuri Gagarin and Earth — A2339

Yuri Gagarin — A2340

1981, Apr. 12 Photo. *Perf. 11½x12*

4925 A2339 6k shown .20 .20

4926 A2339 15k S.P. Korolev (craft designer) .40 .25

4927 A2339 32k Monument .80 .50

Nos. 4925-4927 (3) 1.40 .95

Souvenir Sheet

4928 A2340 50k shown 5.00 1.00

Soviet space flights, 20th anniv. Nos. 4925-4927 each se-tenant with label.

Salyut Orbital Station, 10th Anniv. of Flight A2341

1981, Apr. 19 Litho. *Perf. 12x12½*

4929 A2341 32k multicolored 1.00 .50

Souvenir Sheet

111th Birth Anniv. of Lenin — A2342

1981, Apr. 22 *Perf. 11½x12½*

4930 A2342 50k multicolored 1.50 .60

Sergei Prokofiev (1891-1953), Composer A2343

New Hofburg Palace, Vienna A2344

1981, Apr. 23 Engr. *Perf. 12*

4931 A2343 4k dark purple .40 .25

1981, May 5 Litho.

4932 A2344 15k multicolored .50 .20

WIPA 1981 Phil. Exhib., Vienna, May 22-31.

Adzhar Autonomous Soviet Socialist Republic, 60th Anniv. — A2345

1981, May 7

4933 A2345 4k multicolored .25 .20

Centenary of Welding (Invented by N.N. Benardos) A2346

Lithographed and Engraved

1981, May 12 *Perf. 11½*

4934 A2346 6k multicolored .25 .20

Intl. Architects Union, 14th Congress, Warsaw — A2347

1981, May 12 Photo.

4935 A2347 15k multicolored .50 .25

Albanian Girl, by A.A. Ivanov A2348

#4937, Horseman, by F.A. Roubeau. #4938, The Demon, by M.A. Wrubel, horiz. #4939, Sunset over the Sea, by N.N. Ge, horiz.

1981, May 15 Litho. *Perf. 12x12½*

4936 A2348 10k multicolored .25 .20

4937 A2348 10k multicolored .25 .20

4938 A2348 10k multicolored .25 .20

4939 A2348 10k multicolored .25 .20

Nos. 4936-4939 (4) 1.00 .80

Cosmonauts in Training A2349

1981, May 15

4940 A2349 6k shown .20 .20

4941 A2349 15k In space .40 .25

4942 A2349 32k Return .80 .50

Nos. 4940-4942 (3) 1.40 .95

Intercosmos cooperative space program (USSR-Romania).

Dwarf Primrose — A2350

Flowers of the Carpathian Mountains: 6k, Great carline thistle. 10k, Mountain parageum. 15k, Alpine bluebell. 32k, Rhododendron kotschyi.

1981, May 20 *Perf. 12*

4943 A2350 4k multicolored .20 .20

4944 A2350 6k multicolored .20 .20

4945 A2350 10k multicolored .25 .20

4946 A2350 15k multicolored .40 .25

4947 A2350 32k multicolored .80 .50

Nos. 4943-4947 (5) 1.85 1.35

Luigi Longo, Italian Labor Leader, 1st Death Anniv. — A2351

1981, May 24 Photo. *Perf. 11½*

4948	A2351	6k	multicolored	.25	.20

Nizami Gjanshevi (1141-1209), Azerbaijan Poet — A2352

1981, May 25 Photo. & Engr.

4949	A2352	4k	multicolored	.25	.20

A2353

Mongolian Revolution, 60th anniv. — A2354

1981, June 18 Litho. *Perf. 12*

4950	A2353	4k	Running	.20	.20
4951	A2353	6k	Soccer	.20	.20
4952	A2353	10k	Discus throwing	.20	.20
4953	A2353	15k	Boxing	.30	.25
4954	A2353	32k	Diving	.60	.35
			Nos. 4950-4954 (5)	1.50	1.20

1981, July 6

4955	A2354	6k	multicolored	.25	.20

12th Intl. Film Festival, Moscow — A2355

1981, July 6 Photo. *Perf. 11½*

4956	A2355	15k	multicolored	.50	.25

River Tour Boat Lenin A2356

1981, July 9 Litho. *Perf. 12½*

4957	A2356	4k	shown	.20	.20
4958	A2356	6k	Cosmonaut Gagarin	.20	.20
4959	A2356	15k	Valerian Kuibyshev	.35	.20
4960	A2356	32k	Freighter Baltijski	.75	.40
			Nos. 4957-4960 (4)	1.50	1.00

Icebreaker Maligin — A2357

Photogravure and Engraved

1981, July 9 *Perf. 11½x12*

4961	A2357	15k	multicolored	.50	.25

26th Party Congress Resolutions (Intl. Cooperation) — A2358

1981, July 15 Photo. *Perf. 12x11½*

4962	A2358	4k	shown	.20	.20
4963	A2358	4k	Industry	.20	.20
4964	A2358	4k	Energy	.20	.20
4965	A2358	4k	Agriculture	.20	.20
4966	A2358	4k	Communications	.20	.20
4967	A2358	4k	Arts	.20	.20
			Nos. 4962-4967 (6)	1.20	1.20

I.N. Ulyanov (Lenin's Father), 150th Anniv. of Birth — A2359

1981, July 25 Engr. *Perf. 11½*

4968	A2359	4k	multicolored	.25	.20

Leningrad Theater, Sesquicentennial — A2360

1981, Aug. 12 Photo. *Perf. 11½*

4969	A2360	6k	multicolored	.25	.20

A.M. Gerasimov, Artist, Birth Centenary A2361

1981, Aug. 12 Litho. *Perf. 12*

4970	A2361	4k	multicolored	.25	.20

Physical Chemistry Institute, Moscow Academy of Science, 50th Anniv. A2362

1981, Aug. 12 Photo. *Perf. 11½*

4971	A2362	4k	multicolored	.25	.20

Siberian Tit A2363

Designs: Song birds.

Perf. 12½x12, 12x12½

1981, Aug. 20 Litho.

4972	A2363	6k	shown	.20	.20
4973	A2363	10k	Tersiphone paradisi, vert.	.35	.20
4974	A2363	15k	Emberiza jankovski	.45	.25
4975	A2363	20k	Sutora webbiana, vert.	.55	.30
4976	A2363	32k	Saxicola torquata, vert.	.90	.45
			Nos. 4972-4976 (5)	2.45	1.40

60th Anniv. of Komi Autonomous Soviet Socialist Republic — A2364

1981, Aug. 22 *Perf. 12*

4977	A2364	4k	multicolored	.35	.20

Svyaz-'81 Intl. Communications Exhibition — A2365

Photogravure and Engraved

1981, Aug. 22 *Perf. 11½*

4978	A2365	4k	multicolored	.25	.20

60th Anniv. of Kabardino-Balkar Autonomous Soviet Socialist Republic — A2366

1981, Sept. 1 Litho. *Perf. 12*

4979	A2366	4k	multicolored	.25	.20

War Veterans' Committee, 25th Anniv. — A2367

1981, Sept. 1 Photo. *Perf. 11½*

4980	A2367	4k	multicolored	.25	.20

Schooner Kodor — A2368

Training ships. 4k, 6k, 15k, 20k, horiz.

Perf. 12½x12, 12x12½

1981, Sept. 18 Litho.

4981	A2368	4k	4-masted bark Tovarich I	.20	.20
4982	A2368	6k	Barkentine Vega I	.20	.20
4983	A2368	10k	shown	.20	.20
4984	A2368	15k	3-masted bark Tovarich	.25	.20
4985	A2368	20k	4-masted bark Kruzenstern	.30	.25
4986	A2368	32k	4-masted bark Sedov	.50	.30
			Nos. 4981-4986 (6)	1.65	1.35

A2369

A2370

1981, Oct. 10 *Perf. 12*

4987	A2369	4k	multicolored	.25	.20

Kazakhstan's Union with Russia, 250th Anniv.

1981, Oct. 10 Photo. *Perf. 11½*

4988	A2370	4k	multicolored	.75	.50

Mikhail Alekseevich Lavrentiev (1900-80), mathematician. Exists imperf.

64th Anniv. of October Revolution — A2371

1981, Oct. 15 Litho.

4989	A2371	4k	multicolored	.25	.20

Ekran Satellite TV Broadcasting System — A2372

1981, Oct. 15 *Perf. 12*

4990	A2372	4k	multicolored	.25	.20

Salyut 6-Soyuz flight of V.V. Kovalionok and V.P. Savinykh A2373

1981, Oct. 15

4991	10k	Text	.30	.20
4992	10k	Cosmonauts	.30	.20
a.		A2373 Pair, #4991-4992	.60	.30

Birth Centenary of Pablo Picasso — A2375

Souvenir Sheet

1981, Oct. 25 *Perf. 12x12½*

4993 A2375 50k multicolored 2.75 .90

A2376

Photogravure and Engraved

1981, Nov. 5 *Perf. 11½*

4994 A2376 4k multicolored .25 .20

Sergei Dmitrievich Merkurov (1881-1952), artist.

Autumn, by Nino Pirosmanas, 1913 A2377

Paintings: 6k, Guriyka, by M.G. Kokodze, 1921. 10k, Fellow Travelers, by U.M. Dzhaparidze, 1936, horiz. 15k, Shota Rustaveli, by S.S. Kobuladze, 1938. 32k, Collecting Tea, by V.D. Gudiashvili, 1964, horiz.

Perf. 12x12½, 12½x12

1981, Nov. 5 **Litho.**

4995 A2377	4k	multicolored	.20	.20
4996 A2377	6k	multicolored	.20	.20
4997 A2377	10k	multicolored	.50	.20
4998 A2377	15k	multicolored	.65	.25
4999 A2377	32k	multicolored	1.40	.50
Nos. 4995-4999 (5)			2.95	1.35

New Year 1982 — A2378

1981, Dec. 2 **Litho.** *Perf. 12*

5000 A2378 4k multicolored .25 .20

Public Transportation 19th-20th Cent. — A2379

Photogravure and Engraved

1981, Dec. 10 *Perf. 11½x12*

5001 A2379	4k	Sled	.20	.20
5002 A2379	6k	Horse-drawn trolley	.20	.20
5003 A2379	10k	Coach	.30	.20
5004 A2379	15k	Taxi, 1926	.40	.25
5005 A2379	20k	Bus, 1926	.50	.30
5006 A2379	32k	Trolley, 1912	.80	.50
Nos. 5001-5006 (6)			2.40	1.65

Souvenir Sheet

Kremlin and New Delhi Parliament — A2380

1981, Dec. 17 **Photo.**

5007 A2380 50k multicolored 1.50 .75

1st direct telephone link with India.

A2381

A2382

1982, Jan. 11 **Litho.** *Perf. 12*

5008 A2381 4k multicolored .20 .20

5009 A2382 4k multicolored .20 .20

60th anniv. of Checheno-Ingush Autonomous SSR and of Yakutsk Autonomous SSR.

1500th Anniv. of Kiev — A2383

1982, Jan. 12 **Photo.** *Perf. 11½x12*

5010 A2383 10k multicolored .30 25

S.P. Korolev (1907-66), Rocket Designer — A2384

Nazym Khikmet (1902-1963), Turkish Poet — A2385

1982, Jan. 12 *Perf. 11½*

5011 A2384 4k multicolored .25 .20

1982, Jan. 20 **Litho.** *Perf. 12*

5012 A2385 6k multicolored .25 .20

10th World Trade Union Congress, Havana — A2386

1982, Feb. 1 **Photo.** *Perf. 11½*

5013 A2386 15k multicolored .50 .25

17th Soviet Trade Union Congress A2387

1982, Feb. 10 **Litho.**

5014 A2387 4k multicolored .25 .20

Edouard Manet (1832-1883) A2388

1982, Feb. 10 *Perf. 12x12½*

5015 A2388 32k multicolored 1.00 .45

Equestrian Sports A2389

1982, Feb. 16 **Photo.** *Perf. 11½*

5016 A2389	4k	Hurdles	.20	.20
5017 A2389	6k	Riding	.20	.20
5018 A2389	15k	Racing	.30	.20
Nos. 5016-5018 (3)			.70	.60

No. 5016 exists imperf.

2nd Death Anniv. of Marshal Tito of Yugoslavia A2390

1982, Feb. 25 **Litho.** *Perf. 12*

5019 A2390 6k olive black .25 .20

350th Anniv. of State University of Tartu A2392

1982, Mar. 4 **Photo.** *Perf. 11½*

5020 A2392 4k multicolored .25 .20

9th Intl. Cardiologists Congress, Moscow — A2393

1982, Mar. 4

5021 A2393 15k multicolored .50 .20

Souvenir Sheet

Biathlon, Speed Skating — A2394

1982, Mar. 6 **Litho.** *Perf. 12½x12*

5022 A2394 50k multicolored 1.50 .70

5th Natl. Athletic Meet.

Blueberry Bush — A2395

1982, Mar. 10 **Litho.** *Perf. 12x12½*

5023 A2395	4k	Blackberries	.20	.20
5024 A2395	6k	shown	.20	.20
5025 A2395	10k	Cranberries	.25	.20
5026 A2395	15k	Cherries	.30	.20
5027 A2395	32k	Strawberries	.70	.30
Nos. 5023-5027 (5)			1.65	1.10

Venera 13 and Venera 14 Flights — A2396

1982, Mar. 10 **Photo.** *Perf. 11½*

5028 A2396 10k multicolored .30 .25

Marriage Ceremony, by W.W. Pukirev (1832-1890) A2397

Paintings: No. 5030, M.I. Lopuchino, by Vladimir Borowikowsky (1757-1825). No. 5031, E.W. Davidov, by O.A. Kiprensky (1782-1836). No. 5032, Landscape.

1982, Mar. 18 *Perf. 12*

5029 A2397 6k multicolored .20 .20
5030 A2397 6k multicolored .20 .20
5031 A2397 6k multicolored .20 .20
5032 A2397 6k multicolored .20 .20
Nos. 5029-5032 (4) .80 .80

K.I. Tchukovsky (1882-1969), Writer — A2398

1982, Mar. 31 **Engr.**

5033 A2398 4k black .25 .20

Cosmonauts' Day — A2399

1982, Apr. 12 Photo. *Perf. 12x11½*

5034 A2399 6k multicolored .25 .20

Souvenir Sheet

112th Birth Anniv. of Lenin — A2400

1982, Apr. 22 Photo. *Perf. 11½x12*

5035 A2400 50k multicolored 1.50 .70

V.P. Soloviev-Sedoi (1907-79), Composer A2401

G. Dimitrov (1882-1949), 1st Bulgarian Prime Minister A2402

1982, Apr. 25 Engr. *Perf. 12*

5036 A2401 4k brown .25 .20

1982, Apr. 25

5037 A2402 6k green .25 .20

Kremlin Tower, Moscow — A2403

1982 Litho. *Perf. 12½x12*

5038 A2403 45k brown 1.10 .70
a. Engraved 1.10 .70

Issued: #5038, Apr. 25. #5038a, Oct. 12.

70th Anniv. of Pravda Newspaper A2404

1982, May 5 Photo. *Perf. 12x11½*

5039 A2404 4k multicolored .25 .20

UN Conf. on Human Environment, 10th anniv. — A2405

Pioneers' Org., 60th anniv. — A2406

1982, May 10 *Perf. 11½*

5040 A2405 6k multicolored .25 .20

1982, May 19

5041 A2406 4k multicolored .25 .20

Communist Youth Org., 19th Cong. — A2407

ITU Delegates Conf., Nairobi — A2408

1982, May 19

5042 A2407 4k multicolored .25 .20

1982, May 19

5043 A2408 15k multicolored .50 .25

TUL-80 Electric Locomotive — A2409

1982, May 20 *Perf. 12x11½*

5044 A2409 4k shown .20 .20
5045 A2409 6k TEP-75 diesel .20 .20
5046 A2409 10k TEP-7 diesel .25 .20
5047 A2409 15k WL-82m electric .40 .20
5048 A2409 32k EP-200 electric .85 .35
Nos. 5044-5048 (5) 1.90 1.15

1982 World Cup — A2410

1982, June 4 *Perf. 11½x12*

5049 A2410 20k olive & purple .50 .30

Rare Birds — A2411

18th Ornithological Cong., Moscow.

1982, June 10 Litho. *Perf. 12x12½*

5050 A2411 2k Grus Monacha .20 .20
5051 A2411 4k Haliaeetus pelagicus .20 .20
5052 A2411 6k Eurynorhynchus .20 .20
5053 A2411 10k Eulabeia indica .20 .20
5054 A2411 15k Chettusia gregaria .25 .20
5055 A2411 32k Ciconia boyciana .55 .35
Nos. 5050-5055 (6) 1.60 1.35

Komomolsk-on-Amur City, 50th Anniv. — A2412

Photogravure and Engraved

1982, June 10 *Perf. 11½*

5056 A2412 4k multicolored .25 .20

Tatchanka, by M.B. Grekov (1882-1934) — A2413

1982, June 15 Litho. *Perf. 12½x12*

5057 A2413 6k multicolored .25 .20

2nd UN Conference on Peaceful Uses of Outer Space, Vienna, Aug. 9-21 — A2414

1982, June 15 Photo. *Perf. 11½*

5058 A2414 15k multicolored .50 .20

Intercosmos Cooperative Space Program (USSR-France) — A2415

1982 Litho. *Perf. 12½x12*

5059 A2415 6k Cosmonauts .20 .20
5060 A2415 20k Rocket, globe .35 .20
5061 A2415 45k Satellites .80 .40
a. Miniature sheet of 8 50.00
Nos. 5059-5061 (3) 1.35 .80

Souvenir Sheet

5062 A2415 50k Emblem, satellite 1.50 .75

#5062 contains one 41x29mm stamp. Issue dates: 6k, 50k, June 24. 20k, 45k, July 2.

The Legend of the Goldfish, by P. Sosin, 1968 — A2416

Lacquerware Paintings, Ustera: 10k, Minin's Appeal to Count Posharski, by J. Phomitchev, 1953. 15k, Two Peasants, by A. Kotjagin, 1933. 20k, The Fisherman, by N. Klykov, 1933, 32k, The Arrest of the Propagandists, by N. Shishakov, 1968.

1982, July 6 Litho. *Perf. 12½x12*

5063 A2416 6k multicolored .20 .20
5064 A2416 10k multicolored .25 .20
5065 A2416 15k multicolored .30 .20
5066 A2416 20k multicolored .45 .20
5067 A2416 32k multicolored .65 .30
Nos. 5063-5067 (5) 1.85 1.10

Telephone Centenary A2417

1982, July 13 *Perf. 12*

5068 A2417 4k Phone, 1882 .20 .20

P. Schilling's Electro-magnetic Telegraph Sesquicentennial — A2418

Photogravure and Engraved

1982, July 16 *Perf. 11½*

5069 A2418 6k Voltaic cells .25 .20

Intervision Gymnastics Contest A2419

1982, Aug. 10 **Photo.**

5070 A2419 15k multicolored .50 .30

Gliders A2420

1982, Aug. 20 Litho. *Perf. 12½x12*

5071 A2420 4k Mastjahart Glider, 1923 .20 .20
5072 A2420 6k Red Star, 1930 .20 .20
5073 A2420 10k ZAGI-1, 1934 .20 .20

Size: 60x28mm

Perf. 11½x12

5074 A2420 20k Stakhanovets, 1939 .35 .20
5075 A2420 32k Troop carrier GR-29, 1941 .55 .35
Nos. 5071-5075 (5) 1.50 1.15

See Nos. 5118-5122.

Garibaldi (1807-1882) A2421

Intl. Atomic Energy Authority, 25th Anniv. A2422

1982, Aug. 25 Photo. *Perf. 11½*

5076 A2421 6k multicolored .25 .20

Exists imperf.

1982, Aug. 30

5077 A2422 20k multicolored .75 .30

Marshal B.M. Shaposhnikov (1882-1945) A2423

World Chess Championship A2424

1982, Sept. 10 Engr. *Perf. 12*

5078 A2423 4k red brown .25 .20

1982, Sept. 10 Photo. *Perf. 11½*

5079 A2424 6k King .25 .20
5080 A2424 6k Queen .25 .20

See #5084.

African Natl. Congress, 70th Anniv. A2425

S.P. Botkin (1832-89), Physician A2426

1982, Sept. 10

5081 A2425 6k multicolored .25 .20

1982, Sept. 17 Engr. *Perf. 12½x12*

5082 A2426 4k green .25 .20

Souvenir Sheet

25th Anniv. of Sputnik — A2427

1982, Sept. 17 Litho. *Perf. 12x12½*

5083 A2427 50k multicolored 5.00 .85

No. 5079 Overprinted in Gold for Karpov's Victory

1982, Sept. 22 Photo. *Perf. 11½*

5084 A2424 6k multicolored .60 .30

World War II Warships — A2428

Photogravure and Engraved

1982, Sept. 22 *Perf. 11½x12*

5085 A2428 4k Submarine S-56 .20 .20
5086 A2428 6k Minelayer Gremjashtsky .20 .20
5087 A2428 15k Mine sweeper T-205 .35 .20
5088 A2428 20k Cruiser Red Crimea .40 .25
5089 A2428 45k Sebastopol .90 .45
Nos. 5085-5089 (5) 2.05 1.30

65th Anniv. of October Revolution A2429

1982, Oct. 12 Litho. *Perf. 12*

5090 A2429 4k multicolored .25 .20

House of the Soviets, Moscow — A2430

60th Anniv. of USSR: No. 5092, Dnieper Dam, Komosomol Monument, Statue of worker. No. 5093, Soviet War Memorial, resistance poster. No. 5094, Worker at podium, decree text. No. 5095, Workers' Monument, Moscow, Rocket, jet. No. 5096, Arms, Kremlin.

1982, Oct. 25 Photo. *Perf. 11½x12*

5091 A2430 10k multicolored .25 .20
5092 A2430 10k multicolored .25 .20
5093 A2430 10k multicolored .25 .20
5094 A2430 10k multicolored .25 .20
5095 A2430 10k multicolored .25 .20
5096 A2430 10k multicolored .65 .20
Nos. 5091-5096 (6) 1.90 1.20

No. 5095 Overprinted in Red for All-Union Philatelic Exhibition, 1984

1982, Nov. 10

5097 A2430 10k multicolored .75 .20

Portrait of an Actor, by Domenico Fetti A2431

Paintings from the Hermitage: 10k, St. Sebastian, by Perugino. 20k, The Danae, by Titian, horiz. 45k, Portrait of a Woman, by Correggio. No. 5102, Portrait of a Young Man, by Capriola. No. 5103a, Portrait of a Young Woman, by Melzi.

Perf. 12x12½

1982, Nov. 25 Litho. Wmk. 383

5098 A2431 4k multicolored .20 .20
5099 A2431 10k multicolored .25 .20
5100 A2431 20k multicolored .40 .20
5101 A2431 45k multicolored .75 .40
5102 A2431 50k multicolored .75 .45
Nos. 5098-5102 (5) 2.35 1.45

Souvenir Sheet

5103 Sheet of 2 4.00 1.65
a. A2431 50k multicolored 1.00 .65

Printed in sheets of 24 stamps + label and 15 stamps + label.

See Nos. 5129-5134, 5199-5204, 5233-5238, 5310-5315, 5335-5340.

New Year 1983 — A2432

1982, Dec. 1 Unwmk.

5104 A2432 4k multicolored .25 .20

Exists imperf. Value, $50.

Souvenir Sheet

60th Anniv. of USSR — A2433

1982, Dec. 3 *Perf. 12½x12*

5105 A2433 50k multicolored 1.50 .90

Souvenir Sheet

Mountain Climbers Scaling Mt. Everest — A2434

1982, Dec. 20 Photo. *Perf. 11½x12*

5106 A2434 50k multicolored 2.00 .90

Lighthouses A2435

Mail Transport A2436

1982, Dec. 29 Litho. *Perf. 12*

5107 A2435 6k green & multi .20 .20
5108 A2435 6k lilac & multi .20 .20
5109 A2435 6k salmon & multi .20 .20
5110 A2435 6k lt gldn brn & multi .20 .20
5111 A2435 6k lt brown & multi .20 .20
Nos. 5107-5111 (5) 1.00 1.00

No. 5111 exists imperf.

See Nos. 5179-5183, 5265-5269.

1982, Dec. 22 *Perf. 12*

5112 A2436 5k greenish blue .50 .20

1983, May 20 Litho. *Perf. 12*

5113 A2436 5k blue 1.00 .20

For surcharge see Uzbekistan #61E.

Iskra Newspaper Masthead A2438

1983, Jan. 5 Litho. *Perf. 12x12½*

5114 A2438 4k multicolored .25 .20

80th anniv. of 2nd Social-Democratic Workers' Party.

Fedor P. Tolstoi (1783-1873), Painter — A2439

1983, Jan. 5 Photo. *Perf. 11½*
5115 A2439 4k multicolored .25 .20

65th Anniv. of Armed Forces — A2440

1983, Jan. 25 Litho. *Perf. 12*
5116 A2440 4k multicolored .25 .20

Exists imperf.

Souvenir Sheet

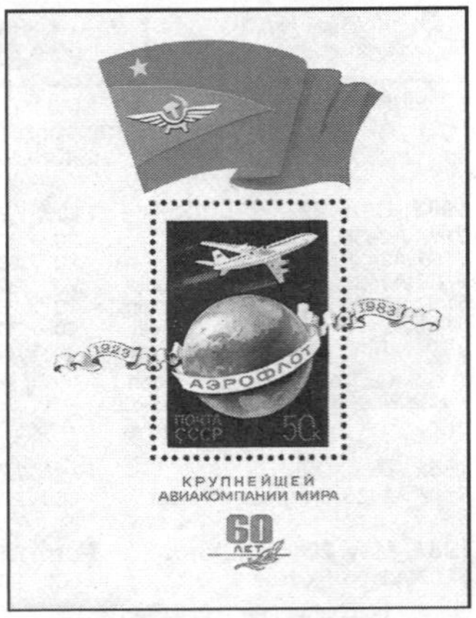

60th Anniv. of Aeroflot Airlines — A2441

1983, Feb. 9 *Perf. 12x12½*
5117 A2441 50k multicolored 1.50 1.00

Glider Type of 1982

1983, Feb. 10 *Perf. 12½x12*
5118 A2420 2k A-9, 1948 .20 .20
5119 A2420 4k KAJ-12, 1957 .20 .20
5120 A2420 6k A-15, 1960 .20 .20
5121 A2420 20k SA-7, 1970 .40 .25
5122 A2420 45k LAJ-12, 1979 .85 .55
Nos. 5118-5122 (5) 1.85 1.40

Tashkent Bimillenium — A2442

1983, Feb. 17 *Perf. 12½x12*
5123 A2442 4k View .25 .20

B.N. Petrov (1913-1980), Scientist — A2443

1983, Feb. 17
5124 A2443 4k multicolored .25 .20

Holy Family, by Raphael A2444

1983, Feb. 17 *Perf. 12x12½*
5125 A2444 50k multicolored 1.50 1.00

Soyuz T-7-Salyut 7-Soyuz T-5 Flight A2445

1983, Mar. 10 *Perf. 12x12½*
5126 A2445 10k L. Popov, A. Serebrav, S. Savitskaya .30 .20

Souvenir Sheet

World Communications Year — A2446

1983, Mar. 10 Photo. *Perf. 11½*
5127 A2446 50k multicolored 1.50 1.25

A.W. Aleksandrov, Natl. Anthem Composer — A2447

1983, Mar. 22 Litho. *Perf. 12*
5128 A2447 4k multicolored .50 .25

Exists imperf. Value, $50.

Hermitage Type of 1982

Rembrandt Paintings, Hermitage, Leningrad: 4k, Portrait of an Old Woman. 10k, Portrait of a Learned Man. 20k, Old Warrior. 45k, Portrait of Mrs. B. Martens Doomer. No. 5133, Sacrifice of Abraham. No. 5134a, Portrait of an Old Man in a Red Garment.

Perf. 12x12½

1983, Mar. 25 Wmk. 383
5129 A2431 4k multicolored .20 .20
5130 A2431 10k multicolored .30 .20
5131 A2431 20k multicolored .60 .35
5132 A2431 45k multicolored 1.40 .90
5133 A2431 50k multicolored 1.50 .95
Nos. 5129-5133 (5) 4.00 2.60

Souvenir Sheet

Lithographed and Embossed

5134 Sheet of 2 + label 4.00 3.00
a. A2431 50k multicolored 1.65 .70

Souvenir Sheet

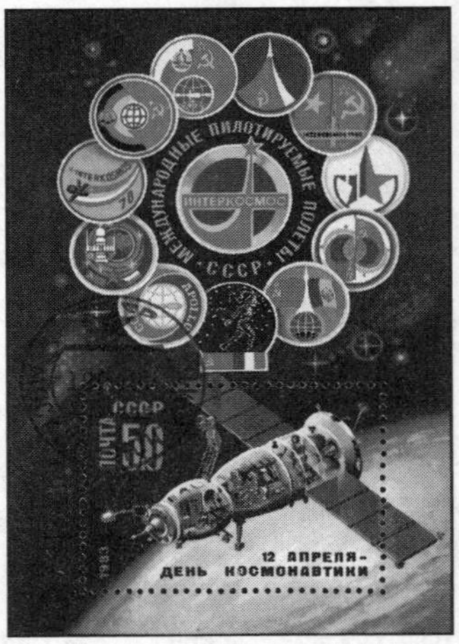

Cosmonauts' Day — A2449

Perf. 12½x12

1983, Apr. 12 Litho. Unwmk.
5135 A2449 50k Soyuz T *5.00* 3.50

Souvenir Sheet

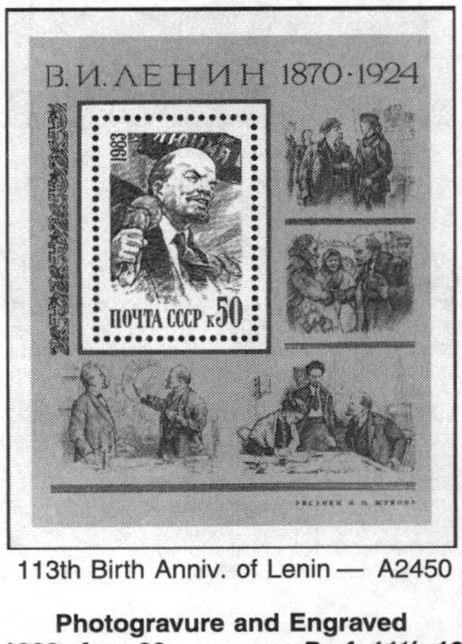

113th Birth Anniv. of Lenin — A2450

Photogravure and Engraved

1983, Apr. 22 *Perf. 11½x12*
5136 A2450 50k multicolored 1.50 .80

A. Berezovoy, V. Lebedev — A2451

Salyut 7-Soyuz 7 Spacecraft — A2452

1983, Apr. 25 Litho. *Perf. 12½x12*
5137 A2451 10k multicolored .30 .25
5138 A2452 10k multicolored .30 .25
a. Pair, #5137-5138 .60 .50

Salyut 7-Soyuz 7 211-Day Flight. Exists se-tenant with label.

Karl Marx (1818-1883) A2453

1983, May 5 *Perf. 12x12½*
5139 A2453 4k multicolored .25 .20

View of Rostov-on-Don — A2454

1983, May 5 Photo. *Perf. 11½*
5140 A2454 4k multicolored .25 .20

Exists imperf. Value, $50.

Buriat Autonomous Soviet Socialist Republic, 60th Anniv. — A2455

1983, May 12 Litho. *Perf. 12*
5141 A2455 4k multicolored .25 .20

Kirov Opera and Ballet Theater, Leningrad, 200th Anniv. — A2456

Photogravure and Engraved

1983, May 12 ***Perf. 11½x12***
5142 A2456 4k multicolored .20 .20

Emblem of Motorcycling, Auto Racing, Shooting, Motorboating, Parachuting Organization — A2457

1983, May 20 **Litho.** ***Perf. 11½***
5143 A2457 6k multicolored .25 .20

A.I. Khachaturian (1903-1978), Composer — A2458

1983, May 25 **Engr.** ***Perf. 12½x12***
5144 A2458 4k violet brown .50 .30

Chelyabinsk Tractor Plant, 50th Anniv. — A2459

1983, June 1 **Photo.** ***Perf. 11½***
5145 A2459 4k multicolored .25 .20

Simon Bolivar Bicentenary A2460

Photogravure and Engraved

1983, June 10 ***Perf. 12***
5146 A2460 6k brown & dk brown .25 .20

City of Sevastopol, 200th Anniv. — A2461

1983, June 14 **Photo.** ***Perf. 11½x12***
5147 A2461 5k multicolored .25 .20

Spring Flowers — A2462

1983, June 14 **Litho.** ***Perf. 12x12½***

5148	A2462	4k	multicolored	.20	.20
5149	A2462	6k	multicolored	.20	.20
5150	A2462	10k	multicolored	.25	.20
5151	A2462	15k	multicolored	.35	.30
5152	A2462	20k	multicolored	.45	.35
			Nos. 5148-5152 (5)	1.45	1.25

Valentina Tereshkova's Spaceflight, 20th Anniv. — A2463

1983, June 16 **Litho.** ***Perf. 12***
5153 A2463 10k multicolored .35 .20
a. Miniature sheet of 8 50.00

P.N. Pospelov (1898-1979), Academician A2464

10th European Cong. of Rheumatologists A2465

Photogravure and Engraved

1983, June 20 ***Perf. 11½***
5154 A2464 4k multicolored .25 .20

1983, June 21 **Photo.** ***Perf. 11½***
5155 A2465 4k multicolored .20 .20

13th International Film Festival, Moscow — A2466

1983, July 7 **Litho.** ***Perf. 12***
5156 A2466 20k multicolored .50 .25

Ships of the Soviet Fishing Fleet — A2467

Photogravure and Engraved

1983, July 20 ***Perf. 12x11½***

5157	A2467	4k	Two trawlers	.20	.20
5158	A2467	6k	Refrigerated trawler	.20	.20
5159	A2467	10k	Large trawler	.35	.20
5160	A2467	15k	Large refrigerated ship	.40	.20
5161	A2467	20k	Base ship	.50	.25
			Nos. 5157-5161 (5)	1.65	1.05

E.B. Vakhtangov (1883-1922), Actor and Producer — A2468

1983, July 20 **Photo.** ***Perf. 11½***
5162 A2468 5k multicolored .25 .20

"USSR-1" Stratospheric Flight, 50th Anniv. — A2469

1983, July 25 **Photo.** ***Perf. 12***
5163 A2469 20k multicolored .50 .40
a. Miniature sheet of 8 50.00

Food Fish A2470

4k, Oncorhynchus nerka. 6k, Perciformes. 15k, Anarhichas minor. 20k, Neogobius fluviatilis, 45k, Platichthys stellatus.

1983, Aug. 5 **Litho.** ***Perf. 12½x12***

5164	A2470	4k	multicolored	.20	.20
5165	A2470	6k	multicolored	.20	.20
5166	A2470	15k	multicolored	.35	.25
5167	A2470	20k	multicolored	.40	.30
5168	A2470	45k	multicolored	.90	.55
			Nos. 5164-5168 (5)	2.05	1.50

A2471

SOZPHILEX '83 Philatelic Exhibition — A2472

1983, Aug. 18 **Photo.** ***Perf. 11½***
5169 A2471 6k multicolored .25 .20

Souvenir Sheet

5170 A2472 50k Moscow Skyline 1.50 .80

Miniature Sheet

First Russian Postage Stamp, 125th Anniv. — A2473

Photogravure and Engraved

1983, Aug. 25 ***Perf. 11½x12***
5171 A2473 50k pale yel & black 1.50 .70

No. 5171 Ovptd. on Margin in Red for the 5th Philatelic Society Congress

1984, Oct. 1
5171A A2473 50k pale yel & blk 5.00 4.50

Namibia Day A2474

Palestinian Solidarity A2475

1983, Aug. 26 **Photo.** ***Perf. 11½***
5172 A2474 5k multicolored .25 .20

1983, Aug. 29 **Photo.** ***Perf. 11½***
5173 A2475 5k multicolored .25 .20

1st European Championship of Radio-Telegraphy, Moscow — A2476

1983, Sept. 1 **Photo.** ***Perf. 11½***
5174 A2476 6k multicolored .25 .20

Exists imperf. Value, $50.

4th UNESCO Council on Communications Development — A2477

1983, Sept. 2 Photo. *Perf. 12x11½*
5175 A2477 10k multicolored .30 .20

Muhammad Al-Khorezmi, Uzbek Mathematician, 1200th Birth Anniv. — A2478

Photogravure and Engraved

1983, Sept. 6 *Perf. 11½*
5176 A2478 4k multicolored .25 .20

Marshal A.I. Egorov (1883-1939) A2479

Union of Georgia and Russia, 200th Anniv. A2480

1983, Sept. 8 Engr. *Perf. 12*
5177 A2479 4k brown violet .25 .20

1983, Sept. 8 Photo. *Perf. 11½*
5178 A2480 6k multicolored .25 .20

Lighthouse Type of 1982

Baltic Sea lighthouses.

1983, Sept. 19 Litho. *Perf. 12*

5179	A2435	1k	Kipu	.20	.20
5180	A2435	5k	Keri	.20	.20
5181	A2435	10k	Stirsudden	.25	.20
5182	A2435	12k	Tahkun	.30	.20
5183	A2435	20k	Tallinn	.50	.25
			Nos. 5179-5183 (5)	1.45	1.05

Early Spring, by V.K. Bjalynitzky-Birulja, 1912 — A2481

Paintings by White Russians: 4k, Portrait of the Artist's Wife with Fruit and Flowers, by J.F. Krutzky, 1838. 15k, Young Partisan, by E.A. Zaitsev, 1943. 20k, Partisan Madonna, by M.A. Savitsky, 1967. 45k, Harvest, by V.K. Tsvirko, 1972. 15k, 20k, vert.

Perf. 12½x12, 12x12½

1983, Sept. 28

5184	A2481	4k	multicolored	.20	.20
5185	A2481	6k	multicolored	.20	.20
5186	A2481	15k	multicolored	.25	.20
5187	A2481	20k	multicolored	.30	.20
5188	A2481	45k	multicolored	.70	.45
			Nos. 5184-5188 (5)	1.65	1.25

Hammer and Sickle Steel Mill, Moscow, Centenary A2482

1983, Oct. 1 Photo. *Perf. 11½*
5189 A2482 4k multicolored .25 .20

Natl. Food Program A2483

1983, Oct. 10

5190	A2483	5k	Wheat production	.20	.20
5191	A2483	5k	Cattle, dairy products	.20	.20
5192	A2483	5k	Produce	.20	.20
			Nos. 5190-5192 (3)	.60	.60

October Revolution, 66th anniv. — A2484

1983, Oct. 12 Litho. *Perf. 12*
5193 A2484 4k multicolored .25 .20

Ivan Fedorov — A2485

1983, Oct. 12 Engr. *Perf. 12x12½*
5194 A2485 4k dark brown .25 .20

Ivan Fedorov, first Russian printer (Book of the Apostles), 400th death anniv.

Urengoy-Uzgorod Transcontinental Gas Pipeline Completion — A2486

1983, Oct. 12 Photo. *Perf. 12x11½*
5195 A2486 5k multicolored .25 .20

A.W. Sidorenko (1917-82), Geologist A2487

Campaign Against Nuclear Weapons A2488

1983, Oct. 19 Litho. *Perf. 12*
5196 A2487 4k multicolored .25 .20

1983, Oct. 19 Photo. *Perf. 11½*
5197 A2488 5k Demonstration .25 .20

Exists imperf.

Machtumkuli, Turkmenistan Poet, 250th Birth Anniv. — A2489

1983, Oct. 27
5198 A2489 5k multicolored .25 .20

Hermitage Painting Type of 1982

Paintings by Germans: 4k, Madonna and Child with Apple Tree, by Lucas Cranach the Elder. 10k, Self-portrait, by Anton R. Mengs. 20k, Self-portrait, by Jurgen Owen. 45k, Sailboat, by Caspar David Friedrich. No. 5203, Rape of the Sabines, by Johann Schoenfeld, horiz. No. 5204a, Portrait of a Young Man, by Ambrosius Holbein.

Perf. 12x12½, 12½x12

1983, Nov. 10 Litho. Wmk. 383

5199	A2431	4k	multicolored	.20	.20
5200	A2431	10k	multicolored	.40	.20
5201	A2431	20k	multicolored	.60	.35
5202	A2431	45k	multicolored	1.25	.70
5203	A2431	50k	multicolored	1.50	.75
			Nos. 5199-5203 (5)	3.95	2.20

Souvenir Sheet

5204		Sheet of 2	4.00	2.50
a.	A2431	50k multicolored	1.65	.65

Physicians Against Nuclear War Movement A2490

Perf. 11½

1983, Nov. 17 Photo. Unwmk.
5205 A2490 5k Baby, dove, sun .20 .20

Sukhe Bator (1893-1923), Mongolian People's Rep. Founder — A2491

1983, Nov. 17
5206 A2491 5k Portrait .25 .20

New Year 1984 A2492

1983, Dec. 1
5207 A2492 5k Star, snowflakes .25 .20

Printed in sheets of 16. No. 5207 exists imperf; Value, $25.

Newly Completed Buildings, Moscow — A2493

Perf. 12½x12, 12x12½

1983, Dec. 15 Engr.

5208	A2493	3k	Children's Musical Theater	.20	.20
5209	A2493	4k	Tourist Hotel, vert.	.20	.20
5210	A2493	6k	Council of Ministers	.20	.20
5211	A2493	20k	Ismaelovo Hotel	.70	.35
5212	A2493	45k	Novosti Press Agency	1.50	.70
			Nos. 5208-5212 (5)	2.80	1.65

Souvenir Sheet

Environmental Protection Campaign — A2494

1983, Dec. 20 Photo. *Perf. 11½*
5213 A2494 50k multicolored 5.00 5.00

Moscow Local Broadcasting Network, 50th anniv. — A2495

1984, Jan. 1
5214 A2495 4k multicolored .25 .20

European Women's Skating Championships — A2496

1984, Jan. 1 *Perf. 12x11½*
5215 A2496 5k multicolored .25 .20

Exists imperf. Value, $50.

Cuban Revolution, 25th Anniv. A2497

1984, Jan. 1 *Perf. 11½*

5216 A2497 5k Flag, "25" .25 .20

Exists imperf. Value, $50.

World War II Tanks — A2498

1984, Jan. 25 **Litho.** *Perf. 12½x12*

5217 A2498 10k KW .25 .20
5218 A2498 10k IS-2 .25 .20
5219 A2498 10k T-34 .25 .20
5220 A2498 10k ISU-152 .25 .20
5221 A2498 10k SU-100 .25 .20
Nos. 5217-5221 (5) 1.25 1.00

No. 5220 exists imperf. Value, $25.

1984 Winter Olympics — A2499

1984, Feb. 8 **Photo.** *Perf. 11½x12*

5222 A2499 5k Biathlon .20 .20
a. Miniature sheet of 8 20.00
5223 A2499 10k Speed skating .25 .20
a. Miniature sheet of 8 20.00
5224 A2499 20k Hockey .50 .25
a. Miniature sheet of 8 20.00
5225 A2499 45k Figure skating .90 .45
a. Miniature sheet of 8 20.00
Nos. 5222-5225 (4) 1.85 1.10

Exist imperf. Value, set $50.

Moscow Zoo, 120th Anniv. — A2500

1984, Feb. 16 **Litho.** *Perf. 12½x12*

5226 A2500 2k Mandrill .20 .20
5227 A2500 3k Gazelle .20 .20
5228 A2500 4k Snow leopard .20 .20
5229 A2500 5k Crowned crane .20 .20
5230 A2500 20k Macaw .40 .25
Nos. 5226-5230 (5) 1.20 1.05

Yuri Gagarin (1934-68) — A2501

1984, Mar. 9 **Engr.** *Perf. 12½x12*

5231 A2501 15k Portrait, Vostok .35 .25
a. Miniature sheet of 8 50.00

Souvenir Sheet

Mass Development of Virgin and Unused Land, 30th Anniv. — A2502

1984, Mar. 14 **Photo.** *Perf. 11½x12*

5232 A2502 50k multicolored 1.50 .75

Hermitage Painting Type of 1982

Paintings by English Artists: 4k, E.K. Vorontsova, by George Hayter. 10k, Portrait of Mrs. Greer, by George Romney. 20k, Approaching Storm, by George Morland, horiz. 45k, Portrait of an Unknown Man, by Marcus Gheeraerts Jr. No. 5237, Cupid and Venus, by Joshua Reynolds. No. 5238a, Portrait of a Lady in Blue, by Thomas Gainsborough.

Perf. 12x12½, 12½x12

1984, Mar. 20 **Litho.** **Wmk. 383**

5233 A2431 4k multicolored .20 .20
5234 A2431 10k multicolored .40 .20
5235 A2431 20k multicolored .60 .35
5236 A2431 45k multicolored 1.40 .70
5237 A2431 50k multicolored 1.65 .75
Nos. 5233-5237 (5) 4.25 2.20

Souvenir Sheet

5238 Sheet of 2 5.00 1.70
a. A2431 50k multicolored 2.00 .65

Nos. 5233-5237 each se-tenant with label showing text and embossed emblem.

S.V. Ilyushin A2503

Andrei S. Bubnov A2504

Perf. 11½

1984, Mar. 23 **Photo.** **Unwmk.**

5239 A2503 5k Aircraft designer, (1894-1977) .30 .20

1984, Apr. 3 *Perf. 11½x12*

5240 A2504 5k Statesman, (1884-1940) .25 .20

Intercosmos Cooperative Space Program (USSR-India) A2505

Designs: 5k, Weather Station M-100 launch. 20k, Geodesy (satellites, observatory). 45k, Rocket, satellites, dish antenna. 50k, Flags, cosmonauts.

1984 *Perf. 12x11½*

5241 A2505 5k multicolored .20 .20
5242 A2505 20k multicolored .45 .20
5243 A2505 45k multicolored 1.00 .45
Nos. 5241-5243 (3) 1.65 .85

Souvenir Sheet

5244 A2505 50k multicolored 1.50 .75

No. 5244 contains one 25x36mm stamp. Issue dates: 50k, Apr. 5; others, Apr. 3.

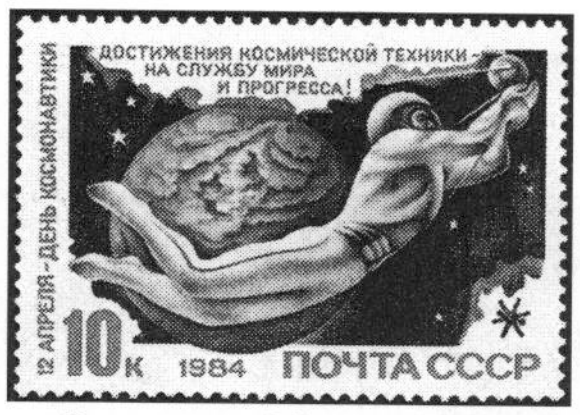

Cosmonauts' Day — A2506

1984, Apr. 12 *Perf. 11½x12*

5245 A2506 10k Futuristic spaceman .50 .30

Tchelyuskin Arctic Expedition, 50th Anniv. — A2507

Photogravure and Engraved

1984, Apr. 13 *Perf. 11½x12*

5246 A2507 6k Ship .20 .20
a. Miniature sheet of 8 16.00
5247 A2507 15k Shipwreck .50 .25
a. Miniature sheet of 8 16.00
5248 A2507 45k Rescue 1.50 .70
a. Miniature sheet of 8 16.00
Nos. 5246-5248 (3) 2.20 1.15

Souvenir Sheet

Photo.

5249 A2507 50k Hero of Soviet Union medal 1.50 .70

First HSU medal awarded to rescue crew. No. 5249 contains one 27x39mm stamp.

Souvenir Sheet

114th Birth Anniv. of Lenin — A2508

1984, Apr. 22 **Litho.** *Perf. 11½x12½*

5250 A2508 50k Portrait 1.50 .70

Aquatic Plants — A2509

1984, May 5 *Perf. 12x12½, 12½x12*

5251 A2509 1k Lotus .20 .20
5252 A2509 2k Euriola .20 .20
5253 A2509 3k Water lilies, horiz. .20 .20
5254 A2509 10k White nymphaea, horiz. .20 .20
a. Miniature sheet of 8 15.00
5255 A2509 20k Marshflowers, horiz. .40 .25
Nos. 5251-5255 (5) 1.20 1.05

Soviet Peace Policy — A2510

1984, May 8 **Photo.** *Perf. 11½*

5256 A2510 5k Marchers, banners (at left) .20 .20
5257 A2510 5k Text .20 .20
5258 A2510 5k Marchers, banners (at right) .20 .20
a. Strip of 3, #5256-5258 .45 .30

A2511

A2512

1984, May 15 **Photo.** *Perf. 11½*

5259 A2511 10k multicolored .30 .25

E.O. Paton Institute of Electric Welding, 50th anniv.

1984, May 21

5260 A2512 10k multicolored .30 .30

25th Conf. for Electric and Postal Communications Cooperation.

A2513

A2514

1984, May 29

5261 A2513 5k violet brown .25 .20

Maurice Bishop, Grenada Prime Minister (1944-83).

1984, May 31

5262 A2514 5k multicolored .25 .20

V.I. Lenin Central Museum, 60th anniv.

City of Archangelsk, 400th Anniv. — A2515

1984, June 1 **Photo. & Engr.**

5263 A2515 5k multicolored .25 .20

European Youth Soccer Championship — A2516

1984, June 1 Photo. *Perf. 12x11½*

5264 A2516 15k multicolored .50 .30

Lighthouse Type of 1982

Far Eastern seas lighthouses.

1984, June 14 Litho. *Perf. 12*

5265 A2435 1k Petropavlovsk .20 .20
5266 A2435 2k Tokarev .20 .20
5267 A2435 4k Basargin .20 .20
5268 A2435 5k Kronitsky .20 .20
5269 A2435 10k Marekan .20 .20
Nos. 5265-5269 (5) 1.00 1.00

Salyut 7-Soyuz T-9 150-Day Flight — A2517

1984, June 27 Litho. *Perf. 12*

5270 A2517 15k multicolored .35 .20

A2518

Photogravure and Engraved

1984, July 1 *Perf. 11½*

5271 A2518 10k multicolored .30 .25

Morflot, Merchant & Transport Fleet, 60th anniv.

60th Anniv. of Awarding V.I. Lenin Name to Youth Communist League — A2519

1984, July 1 Photo. *Perf. 11½x12*

5272 A2519 5k multicolored .25 .20

Liberation of Byelorussia, 40th Anniv. A2520

1984, July 3 Photo. *Perf. 12x11½*

5273 A2520 5k multicolored .25 .20

CMEA Conference, Moscow — A2521

1984, June 12 Photo. *Perf. 11½*

5274 A2521 5k CMEA Building & Kremlin .25 .20

A2522

A2523

1984, July 20 Photo. *Perf. 11½*

5275 A2522 5k Convention seal .25 .20

27th Intl. Geological Cong., Moscow.

1984, July 22 Photo. *Perf. 11½*

5276 A2523 5k Arms, draped flag .25 .20

People's Republic of Poland, 40th anniv.

B. V. Asafiev (1884-1949), Composer — A2524

1984, July 25 Engr. *Perf. 12½x12*

5277 A2524 5k greenish black .25 .20

Relations with Mexico, 60th Anniv. A2525

1984, Aug. 4 Litho. *Perf. 12*

5278 A2525 5k USSR, Mexican flags .25 .20

Miniature Sheet

Russian Folk Tales A2526

Designs: a, 3 archers. b, Prince and frog. c, Old man and prince. d, Crowd and swans. e, Wolf and men. f, Bird and youth. g, Youth on white horse. h, Couple with Tsar. i, Village scene. j, Man on black horse. k, Old man. l, Young woman.

1984, Aug. 10 Litho. *Perf. 12x12½*

5279 Sheet of 12 6.00 2.50
a.-l. A2526 5k, any single .30 .20

Friendship '84 Games A2527

1984, Aug. 15 Photo. *Perf. 11½*

5280 A2527 1k Basketball .20 .20
5281 A2527 5k Gymnastics, vert. .20 .20
5282 A2527 10k Weightlifting .25 .20
5283 A2527 15k Wrestling .40 .20
5284 A2527 20k High jump .50 .25
Nos. 5280-5284 (5) 1.55 1.05

A2528

A2529

1984, Aug. 23 Litho. *Perf. 12*

5285 A2528 5k Flag, monument .25 .20

Liberation of Romania, 40th anniv.

1984, Sept. 5 Litho. *Perf. 12½x12*

Subjects: 35k, 3r, Environmental protection. 2r, Arctic development. 5r, World peace.

5286 A2529 35k Sable .65 .20
5287 A2529 2r Ship, arctic map 3.50 .85

Engr.

5288 A2529 3r Child and globe 5.75 1.10
5289 A2529 5r Palm frond and globe 9.00 1.90
Nos. 5286-5289 (4) 18.90 4.05

See Nos. 6016B-6017A.

World Chess Championships A2530

Bulgarian Revolution, 40th Anniv. A2531

1984, Sept. 7 Photo. *Perf. 11½*

5290 A2530 15k Motherland statue, Volgograd .50 .30
5291 A2530 15k Spasski Tower, Moscow .50 .30

1984, Sept. 9 Photo. *Perf. 11½*

5292 A2531 5k Bulgarian arms .25 .20

Ethiopian Revolution, 10th Anniv. A2532

1984, Sept. 12 Litho. *Perf. 12*

5293 A2532 5k Ethiopian flag, seal .25 .20

Novokramatorsk Machinery Plant, 50th Anniv. — A2533

Photogravure and Engraved

1984, Sept. 20 *Perf. 11½*

5294 A2533 5k Excavator .25 .20

Nakhichevan ASSR, 60th Anniv. — A2534

1984, Sept. 20 Litho. *Perf. 12*

5295 A2534 5k Arms .25 .20

Television from Space, 25th Anniv. A2535

1984, Oct. 4 Photo. *Perf. 11½*

5296 A2535 5k Luna 3 .20 .20
5297 A2535 20k Venera 9 .35 .25
5298 A2535 45k Meteor satellite .80 .55
Nos. 5296-5298 (3) 1.35 1.00

Souvenir Sheet

Perf. 11½x12

5299 A2535 50k Camera, space walker, vert. 1.50 .75

No. 5299 contains one 26x37mm stamp.

German Democratic Republic, 35th Anniv. A2536

1984, Oct. 7 Photo. *Perf. 11½*

5300 A2536 5k Flag, arms .25 .20

Ukrainian Liberation, 40th Anniv. A2537

1984, Oct. 8 Photo. *Perf. 12x11½*

5301 A2537 5k Motherland statue, Kiev .25 .20

Soviet Republics and Parties, 60th Anniv. A2538

SSR Flags & Arms: #5302, Moldavian. #5303, Kirgiz. #5304, Tadzhik. #5305, Uzbek. #5306, Turkmen.

1984 Litho. *Perf. 12*

5302 A2538 5k multicolored .20 .20
5303 A2538 5k multicolored .20 .20
5304 A2538 5k multicolored .20 .20
5305 A2538 5k multicolored .20 .20
5306 A2538 5k multicolored .20 .20
Nos. 5302-5306 (5) 1.00 1.00

Issued: #5302, 10/12; #5303-5304, 10/14; #5305-5306, 10/27.

A2539

A2540

1984, Oct. 23 Photo. *Perf. 11½*

5307 A2539 5k Kremlin, 1917 flag		.25	.20

October Revolution, 67th anniv.

1984, Nov. 6 Photo. *Perf. 11½*

5308 A2540 5k Aircraft, spacecraft		.25	.20

M. Frunze Inst. of Aviation & Cosmonautics.

Baikal - Amur Railway Completion A2541

1984, Nov. 7 Photo. *Perf. 11½*

5309 A2541 5k Workers, map, engine		.30	.20

Hermitage Type of 1982

Paintings by French Artists: 4k, Girl in a Hat, by Jean Louis Voille. 10k, A Stolen Kiss, by Jean-Honore Fragonard. 20k, Woman Combing her Hair, by Edgar Degas. 45k, Pigmalion and Galatea, by Francois Boucher. 50k, Landscape with Polyphenus, by Nicholas Poussin. No. 5315a, Child with a Whip, by Pierre-Auguste Renoir.

Perf. 12x12½, 12½x12

1984, Nov. 20 Litho. Wmk. 383

5310 A2431 4k multicolored		.20	.20
5311 A2431 10k multi, horiz.		.35	.20
5312 A2431 20k multicolored		.55	.45
5313 A2431 45k multi, horiz.		1.25	.75
5314 A2431 50k multi, horiz.		1.40	.90
Nos. 5310-5314 (5)		3.75	2.50

Souvenir Sheet

5315 Sheet of 2		2.50	2.00
a. A2431 50k multicolored		1.00	.60

Mongolian Peoples' Republic, 60th Anniv. — A2542

Perf. 11½

1984, Nov. 26 Photo. Unwmk.

5316 A2542 5k Mongolian flag, arms		.30	.20

New Year 1985 — A2543

1984, Dec. 4 Litho. *Perf. 11½*

5317 A2543 5k Kremlin, snowflakes		.25	.20
a. Miniature sheet of 8		15.00	

Souvenir Sheet

Environmental Protection — A2544

1984, Dec. 4 Litho. *Perf. 12½x12*

5318 A2544 50k Leaf, pollution sources		1.50	.75

Russian Fire Vehicles — A2545

Photogravure and Engraved

1984, Dec. 12 *Perf. 12x11½*

5319 A2545 3k Crew wagon, 19th cent.		.20	.20
5320 A2545 5k Pumper, 19th cent.		.20	.20
5321 A2545 10k Ladder truck, 1904		.25	.20
5322 A2545 15k Pumper, 1904		.35	.20
5323 A2545 20k Ladder truck, 1913		.40	.20
Nos. 5319-5323 (5)		1.40	1.00

See Nos. 5410-5414.

Intl. Venus-Halley's Comet Project — A2546

1984, Dec. 15 Photo. *Perf. 12x11½*

5324 A2546 15k Satellite, flight path		.50	.25
a. Miniature sheet of 8		15.00	

Indira Gandhi (1917-1984), Indian Prime Minister — A2547

1984, Dec. 28 Litho. *Perf. 12*

5325 A2547 5k Portrait		1.00	.75

1905 Revolution A2548

1985, Jan. 22 Photo. *Perf. 11½*

5326 A2548 5k Flag, Moscow memorial		.25	.20

A2549

A2550

1985, Jan. 24

5327 A2549 5k multicolored		.25	.20

Patrice Lumumba Peoples' Friendship University, 25th Anniv.

1985, Feb. 2

5328 A2550 5k bluish, blk & ocher		.25	.20

Mikhail Vasilievich Frunze (1885-1925), party leader.

Karakalpak ASSR, 60th Anniv. A2551

1985, Feb. 16 *Perf. 12*

5329 A2551 5k Republic arms		.25	.20

10th Winter Spartakiad of Friendly Armies — A2552

1985, Feb. 23 *Perf. 11½*

5330 A2552 5k Hockey player, emblem		.25	.20

Kalevala, 150th Anniv. A2553

1985, Feb. 25 Litho. *Perf. 12*

5331 A2553 5k Rune singer, frontispiece		.25	.20

Finnish Kalevala, collection of Karelian epic poetry compiled by Elias Lonrot.

A2554

A2555

1985, Mar. 3 Engr. *Perf. 12½x12*

5332 A2554 5k rose lake		.25	.20

Yakov M. Sverdlov (1885-1919), party leader.

1985, Mar. 6 Photo. *Perf. 11½*

5333 A2555 5k Pioneer badge, awards		.25	.20

Pionerskaya Pravda, All-Union children's newspaper, 60th Anniv.

Maria Alexandrovna Ulyanova (1835-1916), Lenin's Mother — A2556

1985, Mar. 6 Engr. *Perf. 12½x12*

5334 A2556 5k black		.30	.20

Hermitage Type of 1982

Paintings by Spanish artists: 4k, The Young Virgin Praying, vert., by Francisco de Zurbaran (1598-1664). 10k, Still-life, by Antonio Pereda (c. 1608-1678). 20k, The Immaculate Conception, vert., by Murillo (1617-1682). 45k, The Grinder, by Antonio Puga. No. 5339, Count Olivares, vert., by Diego Velazques (1599-1660). No. 5340a, Portrait of the actress Antonia Zarate, vert., by Goya (1746-1828).

Perf. 12x12½, 12½x12

1985, Mar. 14 Litho. Wmk. 383

5335 A2431 4k multicolored		.20	.20
5336 A2431 10k multicolored		.30	.20
5337 A2431 20k multicolored		.50	.40
5338 A2431 45k multicolored		1.25	.90
5339 A2431 50k multicolored		1.40	.95
Nos. 5335-5339 (5)		3.65	2.65

Souvenir Sheet

Lithographed and Embossed

5340 Sheet of 2 + label		3.00	2.00
a. A2431 50k multicolored		1.10	.75

EXPO '85, Tsukuba, Japan A2557

Soviet exhibition, Expo '85 emblems and: 5k, Cosmonauts in space. 10k, Communications satellite. 20k, Alternative energy sources development. 45k, Future housing systems.

Perf. 12x11½

1985, Mar. 17 Photo. Unwmk.

5341 A2557 5k multicolored		.20	.20
5342 A2557 10k multicolored		.20	.20
5343 A2557 20k multicolored		.40	.35
5344 A2557 45k multicolored		.95	.70
Nos. 5341-5344 (4)		1.75	1.45

Souvenir Sheet

5345 A2557 50k Soviet exhibition emblem, globe		1.50	.90

Nos. 5341-5344 issued in sheets of 8.

Souvenir Sheet

Johann Sebastian Bach (1685-1750), Composer — A2558

Photogravure and Engraved

1985, Mar. 21 ***Perf. 12x11½***

5346 A2558 50k black 1.50 1.00

A2559

A2560

1985, Apr. 4 Litho. ***Perf. 12***

5347 A2559 5k Natl. crest, Budapest memorial .25 .20

Hungary liberated from German occupation, 40th Anniv.

1985, Apr. 5 Photo. ***Perf. 11½***

5348 A2560 15k Emblem .40 .30

Society for Cultural Relations with Foreign Countries, 60th anniv.

Victory over Fascism, 40th Anniv. A2561

#5349, Battle of Moscow, soldier, Kremlin, portrait of Lenin. #5350, Soldier, armed forces. #5351, Armaments production, worker. #5352, Partisan movement, cavalry. #5353, Berlin-Treptow war memorial, German Democratic Republic. #5354, Order of the Patriotic War, second class.

1985, Apr. 20 ***Perf. 12x11½***

5349	A2561	5k	multicolored	.25	.20
5350	A2561	5k	multicolored	.25	.20
5351	A2561	5k	multicolored	.25	.20
5352	A2561	5k	multicolored	.25	.20
5353	A2561	5k	multicolored	.25	.20
			Nos. 5349-5353 (5)	1.25	1.00

Souvenir Sheet

Perf. 11½

5354 A2561 50k multicolored 1.50 .50

No. 5354 contains one 28x40mm stamp. Issued in sheets of 8.

No. 5353 Ovptd. in Red for 40th Year Since World War II Victory All-Union Philatelic Exhibition

1985, Apr. 29 Photo. ***Perf. 12x11½***

5354A A2561 5k brn lake, gold & vermilion .50 .50

Yuri Gagarin Center for Training Cosmonauts, 25th Anniv. — A2562

Cosmonauts day: Portrait, cosmonauts, Soyuz-T spaceship.

1985, Apr. 12 Photo. ***Perf. 11½x12***

5355 A2562 15k multicolored .50 .25
 a. Miniature sheet of 8 *20.00*

12th World Youth Festival, Moscow A2563

1985, Apr. 15 Litho. ***Perf. 12x12½***

5356	A2563	1k	Three youths	.20	.20
5357	A2563	3k	African girl	.20	.20
5358	A2563	5k	Girl, rainbow	.20	.20
5359	A2563	20k	Asian youth, camera	.95	.35
5360	A2563	45k	Emblem	2.25	.75
			Nos. 5356-5360 (5)	3.80	1.70

No. 5358 issued in sheets of 8.

Souvenir Sheet

1985, July 4

5361 A2563 30k Emblem 1.50 1.00

115th Birth Anniv. of Lenin — A2564

Portrait and: No. 5362, Lenin Museum, Tampere, Finland. No. 5363, Memorial apartment, Paris, France.

1985, Apr. 22 Photo. ***Perf. 11½x12***

5362 A2564 5k multicolored .20 .20

5363 A2564 5k multicolored .20 .20

Souvenir Sheet

Litho.

Perf. 12x12½

5364 A2564 30k Portrait 1.50 1.00

No. 5364 contains one 30x42mm stamp.

Order of Victory — A2565

Photogravure and Engraved

1985, May 9 ***Perf. 11½***

5365 A2565 20k sil, royal bl, dk red & gold .60 .35

Allied World War II victory over Germany and Japan, 40th anniv.

A2566

A2567

1985, May 9 Litho. ***Perf. 12½x12***

5366 A2566 5k Arms .25 .20

Liberation of Czechoslovakia from German occupation, 40th Anniv.

1985, May 14 Photo. ***Perf. 11½***

5367 A2567 5k Flags of member nations .25 .20

Warsaw Treaty Org., 30th anniv.

Mikhail Alexandrovich Sholokhov (1905-1984), Novelist & Nobel Laureate — A2568

Portraits and book covers: No. 5368, Tales from the Don, Quiet Flows the Don, A Human Tragedy. No. 5369, The Quiet Don, Virgin Lands Under the Plow, Thus They Have Fought for Their Homeland. No. 5370, Portrait.

1985, May 24 Litho. ***Perf. 12½x12***

5368 A2568 5k Portrait at left .20 .20

5369 A2568 5k Portrait at right .20 .20

Photo.

Perf. 12x11½

Size: 37x52mm

5370 A2568 5k brn, gold & black .20 .20
 Nos. 5368-5370 (3) .60 .60

INTERCOSMOS Project Halley-Venus — A2570

1985, June 11 Litho. ***Perf. 12***

5372 A2570 15k Spacecraft, satellites, Venus .35 .20
 a. Miniature sheet of 8 25.00

Artek Pioneer Camp, 60th Anniv. A2571

1985, June 14 Photo. ***Perf. 11½***

5373 A2571 4k Camp, badges, Lenin Pioneers emblem .50 .20

Mutiny on the Battleship Potemkin, 80th Anniv. — A2572

Photogravure and Engraved

1985, June 16 ***Perf. 11½x12***

5374 A2572 5k dk red, gold & black .30 .20

Miniature Sheet

Soviet Railways Rolling Stock — A2573

Designs: a, Electric locomotive WL 80-R (grn). b, Tanker car (bl). c, Refrigerator car (bl). d, Sleeper car (brn). e, Tipper car (brn). f, Box car (brn). g, Shunting diesel locomotive (bl). h, Mail car (grn).

1985, June 15 Engr. ***Perf. 12½x12***

5375 Sheet of 8 2.50 1.65
 a.-h. A2573 10k any single .25 .20

Cosmonauts L. Kizim, V. Soloviov, O. Atkov and Salyut-7 Spacecraft — A2574

1985, June 25 **Litho.**

5376 A2574 15k multicolored .50 .25
 a. Miniature sheet of 8 *15.00*

Soyuz T-10, Salyut-7 and Soyuz T-11 flights, Feb. 8-Oct. 2, 1984.

Beating Sword into Plowshares, Sculpture Donated to UN Hdqtrs. by USSR — A2575

Photogravure and Engraved

1985, June 26 ***Perf. 11½***

5377 A2575 45k multicolored 1.50 .75

UN 40th anniv.

Intl. Youth Year A2576

1985, June 26 Photo. ***Perf. 12***

5378 A2576 10k multicolored .30 .25

Medicinal Plants from Siberia — A2577

1985, July 10 Litho. ***Perf. 12½x12***

5379	A2577	2k	O. dictiocarpum	.20	.20
5380	A2577	3k	Thermopsis lanceolata	.20	.20
5381	A2577	5k	Rosa acicularis lindi	.20	.20
5382	A2577	20k	Rhaponticum carthamoides	.70	.35
a.			Miniature sheet of 8	*15.00*	
5383	A2577	45k	Bergenia crassifolia fritsch	1.50	.70
			Nos. 5379-5383 (5)	2.80	1.65

Cosmonauts V. A. Dzhanibekov, S. E. Savistskaya, and I. P. Volk, Soyuz T-12 Mission, July 17-29, 1984 — A2578

1985, July 17
5384 A2578 10k multicolored .40 .20
a. Miniature sheet of 8 *15.00*

1st woman's free flight in space.

A2579

A2580

Caecilienhof Palace, Potsdam, Flags of UK, USSR, & US.

1985, July 17
5385 A2579 15k multicolored .50 .25

Potsdam Conference, 40th anniv.

1985, July 25 Photo. *Perf. 11½*
5386 A2580 20k Finlandia Hall, Helsinki .50 .30
a. Miniature sheet of 8 20.00

Helsinki Conference on European security and cooperation, 10th anniv.

Flags of USSR, North Korea, Liberation Monument in Pyongyang A2581

1985, Aug. 1
5387 A2581 5k multicolored .25 .20

Socialist Rep. of North Korea, 40th anniv.

Endangered Wildlife — A2582

Designs: 2k, Sorex bucharensis, vert. 3k, Cardiocranius paradoxus. 5k, Selevinia betpakdalensis, vert. 20k, Felis caracal. 45k, Gazella subgutturosa. 50k, Panthera pardus.

Perf. 12x12½, 12½x12

1985, Aug. 15 Litho.
5388 A2582 2k multicolored .20 .20
5389 A2582 3k multicolored .20 .20
5390 A2582 5k multicolored .20 .20

Size: 47x32mm

5391 A2582 20k multicolored .60 .30
a. Miniature sheet of 8 25.00
5392 A2582 45k multicolored 1.40 .60
Nos. 5388-5392 (5) 2.60 1.50

Souvenir Sheet

5393 A2582 50k multicolored 2.50 .75

Youth World Soccer Cup Championships, Moscow — A2583

1985, Aug. 24 *Perf. 12*
5394 A2583 5k multicolored .30 .25

Alexander G. Stakhanov, Coal Miner & Labor Leader A2584

1985, Aug. 30 Photo. *Perf. 11½*
5395 A2584 5k multicolored .25 .20

Stakhanovite Movement for high labor productivity, 50th anniv.

Bryansk Victory Memorial, Buildings, Arms A2585

1985, Sept. 1
5396 A2585 5k multicolored .30 .25

Millennium of Bryansk.

Socialist Republic of Vietnam, 40th Anniv. — A2586

1985, Sept. 2 Litho. *Perf. 12½x12*
5397 A2586 5k Arms .25 .20

A2587

1985, Sept. 2 Photo. *Perf. 11½*
5398 A2587 10k multicolored .50 .20

1985 World Chess Championship match, A. Karpov Vs. G. Kasparov, Moscow.

Lutsk City, Ukrainian SSR, 900th Anniv. — A2588

1985, Sept. 14
5399 A2588 5k Lutsk Castle .25 .20

Open Book, the Weeping Jaroslavna and Prince Igor's Army — A2589

Photogravure and Engraved

1985, Sept. 14 *Perf. 11½x12*
5400 A2589 10k multicolored .30 .20

The Song of Igor's Campaign, epic poem, 800th anniv.

Sergei Vasilievich Gerasimov (1885-1964), Painter A2590

1985, Sept. 26 *Perf. 12x11½*
5401 A2590 5k Portrait .25 .20

October Revolution, 68th Anniv. — A2591

UN 40th Anniv. — A2592

1985, Oct. 10 Photo. *Perf. 11½*
5402 A2591 5k multicolored .25 .20

1985, Oct. 24
5403 A2592 15k multicolored .50 .25

Krushjanis Baron (1835-1923), Latvian Folklorist — A2593

Lithographed and Engraved

1985, Oct. 31
5404 A2593 5k beige & black .30 .20

Lenin, Laborer Breaking Chains A2594

1985, Nov. 20 Photo.
5405 A2594 5k multicolored .25 .20

Petersburg Union struggle for liberation of the working classes, founded by Lenin, 90th anniv.

Largest Soviet Telescope, 10th Anniv. — A2595

1985, Nov. 20 Engr. *Perf. 12½x12*
5406 A2595 10k dark blue .50 .25

Soviet Observatory inauguration.

A2596

A2597

1985, Nov. 25 Photo.
5407 A2596 5k multicolored .25 .20

Angolan Independence, 10th anniv.

1985, Nov. 29 *Perf. 11½*
5408 A2597 5k multicolored .25 .20

Socialist Federal Republic of Yugoslavia, 40th anniv.

New Year — A2598

Samantha Smith — A2599

1985, Dec. 3 Litho. *Perf. 12*
5409 A2598 5k multicolored .25 .20
a. Miniature sheet of 8 *11.00*

Vehicle Type of 1984

1985, Dec. 18 Photo. *Perf. 12x11½*
5410 A2545 3k AMO-F15, 1926 .20 .20
5411 A2545 5k PMZ-1, 1933 .20 .20
5412 A2545 10k AC-40, 1977 .35 .20
5413 A2545 20k AL-30, 1970 .60 .35
5414 A2545 45k AA-60, 1978 1.25 .70
Nos. 5410-5414 (5) 2.60 1.65

1985, Dec. 25 *Perf. 12*
5415 A2599 5k vio blue, choc & ver .50 .20

American student invited to meet with Soviet leaders in 1984.

A2600

A2601

1985, Dec. 30 Litho.
5416 A2600 5k multicolored .25 .20

N.M. Emanuel (1915-1984), chemist.

1985, Dec. 30
5417 A2601 5k Sightseeing .20 .20
5418 A2601 5k Sports .20 .20

Family leisure activities.

Intl. Peace Year — A2602

1986, Jan. 2 Photo. *Perf. 11½*
5419 A2602 20k brt blue, bluish grn & silver .50 .30

Flags, Congress Palace, Carnation A2603

Lenin, Troitskaya Tower, Congress Palace A2604

Lenin — A2605

1986, Jan. 3
5420 A2603 5k multicolored .20 .20

Photogravure and Engraved
Perf. 12x11½
5421 A2604 20k multicolored .70 .30

Souvenir Sheet
Photo.
Perf. 11½
5422 A2605 50k multicolored 1.75 .70

27th Communist Party Congress.

A2606

A2607

1986, Jan. 10 *Perf. 11½x12*
5423 A2606 15k multicolored .50 .25

Modern Olympic Games, 90th anniv.

Perf. 12½x12, 12x12½
1986, Jan. 15 Litho.

Flora of Russian Steppes, different.

5424 A2607 4k multicolored .20 .20
5425 A2607 5k multi, horiz. .20 .20
5426 A2607 10k multicolored .30 .20
5427 A2607 15k multicolored .40 .30
5428 A2607 20k multicolored .50 .35
a. Miniature sheet of 8 15.00
Nos. 5424-5428 (5) 1.60 1.25

A2608

A2609

Vodovzvodnaya Tower, Grand Kremlin Palace.

1986, Jan. 20 *Perf. 12½x12*
5429 A2608 50k grayish green 1.50 .70

1986, Feb. 20 *Perf. 11½*
5430 A2609 5k multicolored .30 .20

Voronezh City, 400th anniv.

A2610 A2611

1986, Feb. 20 Engr. *Perf. 12*
5431 A2610 10k bluish black .35 .20

Bela Kun (1886-1939), Hungarian party leader.

1986, Feb. 28 *Perf. 12½x12*
5432 A2611 5k grayish black .25 .20

Karolis Pozhela (1896-1926), Lithuanian party founder.

Intercosmos Project Halley, Final Stage — A2612

1986, Mar. 6 Litho. *Perf. 12*
5433 A2612 15k Vega probe, comet .50 .25
a. Miniature sheet of 8

Souvenir Sheet
Perf. 12½x12
5434 A2612 50k Vega I, comet 1.75 .75

No. 5434 contains one 42x30mm stamp.

Butterflies A2613

1986, Mar. 18 *Perf. 12x12½*
5435 A2613 4k Utetheisa pulchella .20 .20
5436 A2613 5k Allancastria caucasica .20 .20
5437 A2613 10k Zegris eupheme .40 .20
5438 A2613 15k Catocala sponsa .50 .50
5439 A2613 20k Satyrus bischoffi .65 .55
a. Miniature sheet of 8 *20.00*
Nos. 5435-5439 (5) 1.95 1.65

EXPO '86, Vancouver A2614

1986, Mar. 25 Photo. *Perf. 12x11½*
5440 A2614 20k Globe, space station .75 .30
a. Miniature sheet of 8 6.00

S.M. Kirov (1886-1934), Party Leader — A2615

1986, Mar. 27 Engr. *Perf. 12½x12*
5441 A2615 5k black .30 .20

Cosmonauts' Day — A2616

Designs: 5k, Konstantin E. Tsiolkovsky (1857-1935), aerodynamics innovator, and futuristic space station. 10k, Sergei P. Korolev (1906-1966), rocket scientist, and Vostok spaceship, vert. 15k, Yuri Gagarin, 1st cosmonaut, Sputnik I and Vega probe.

Perf. 12½x12, 12x12½
1986, Apr. 12 Litho.
5442 A2616 5k multicolored .20 .20
a. Miniature sheet of 8 25.00
5443 A2616 10k multicolored .25 .20
a. Miniature sheet of 8 25.00
5444 A2616 15k multicolored .35 .25
a. Miniature sheet of 7 + label 25.00
Nos. 5441-5444 (4) 1.10 .85

No. 5444 printed se-tenant with label picturing Vostok and inscribed for the 25th anniv. of first space flight.

1986 World Ice Hockey Championships, Moscow — A2617

1986, Apr. 12 Photo. *Perf. 11½*
5445 A2617 15k multicolored .50 .25

Ernst Thalmann (1886-1944), German Communist Leader — A2618

1986, Apr. 16 Engr. *Perf. 12½x12*
5446 A2618 10k dark brown .30 .20
5447 A2618 10k reddish brown .30 .20

Lenin, 116th Birth Anniv. — A2619

Portraits and architecture: No. 5448, Social-ist-Democratic People's House, Prague. No. 5449, Lenin Museum, Leipzig. No. 5450, Lenin Museum, Poronino, Poland.

1986, Apr. 22 Photo. *Perf. 11½x12*
5448 A2619 5k multicolored .20 .20
5449 A2619 5k multicolored .20 .20
5450 A2619 5k multicolored .20 .20
Nos. 5448-5450 (3) .60 .60

Tambov City, 350th Anniv. A2620

1986, Apr. 27 *Perf. 11½*
5451 A2620 5k Buildings, city arms .25 .20

Soviet Peace Fund, 25th Anniv. A2621

1986, Apr. 27
5452 A2621 10k lt chalky bl, gold & brt ultra .40 .20

29th World Cycle Race, May 6-22 A2622

Toadstools A2623

1986, May 6
5453 A2622 10k multicolored .40 .20

1986, May 15 Litho. *Perf. 12*
5454 A2623 4k Amanita phalloides .20 .20
5455 A2623 5k Amanita muscaria .20 .20
5456 A2623 10k Amanita pantherina .45 .20
5457 A2623 15k Tylopilus felleus .50 .30
5458 A2623 20k Hypholoma fasciculare .65 .35
Nos. 5454-5458 (5) 2.00 1.25

A2624 A2625

1986, May 19 Photo. *Perf. 11½*

5459 A2624 10k multicolored	.35	.20

UNESCO Campaign, Man and Biosphere,

1986, May 20

5460 A2625 10k multicolored	.35	.20

9th Soviet Spartakiad.

A2626 A2627

Design: Lenin's House, Eternal Glory and V. I. Chapaiev monuments, Gorky State Academic Drama Theater.

1986, May 24

5461 A2626 5k multicolored	.25	.20

City of Kuibyshev, 400th anniv.

1986, May 25

5462 A2627 5k multicolored	.25	.20

"COMMUNICATION '86, Moscow."

1986 World Cup Soccer Championships, Mexico — A2628

5k, 10k, Various soccer plays. 15k, World Cup on FIFA commemorative gold medal.

1986, May 31

5463 A2628 5k multicolored	.20	.20
a. Miniature sheet of 8	10.00	
5464 A2628 10k multicolored	.25	.20
a. Miniature sheet of 8	10.00	
5465 A2628 15k multicolored	.40	.25
a. Miniature sheet of 8	10.00	
Nos. 5463-5465 (3)	.85	.65

Paintings in the Tretyakov Gallery, Moscow — A2629

Designs: 4k, Lane in Albano. 1837, by M.I. Lebedev, vert. 5k, View of the Kremlin in Foul Weather, 1851, by A.K. Savrasov. 10k, Sunlit Pine Trees, 1896, by I.I. Shishkin, vert. 15k, Return, 1896, by A.E. Arkhipov. 45k, Wedding Procession in Moscow, the 17th Century, 1901, by A.P. Ryabushkin.

Perf. 12x12½, 12½x12

1986, June 11 Litho.

5466 A2629 4k multicolored	.20	.20
5467 A2629 5k multicolored	.20	.20
5468 A2629 10k multicolored	.35	.20

Size: 74x37mm

Perf. 11½

5469 A2629 15k multicolored	.40	.30
5470 A2629 45k multicolored	1.10	.75
Nos. 5466-5470 (5)	2.25	1.65

Issued in sheets of 8.

Irkutsk City, 300th Anniv. — A2630

UNESCO Projects in Russia — A2632

Goodwill Games, Moscow, July 5-20 A2631

1986, June 28 Photo. *Perf. 11½*

5471 A2630 5k multicolored	.25	.20

1986, July 4 Photo. *Perf. 11½*

5472 A2631 10k Prus bl, gold & blk	.35	.20
5473 A2631 10k brt blue, gold & blk	.35	.20

1986, July 15

Designs: 5k, Information sciences. 10k, Geological correlation. 15k, Inter-governmental oceanographic commission. 35k, Intl. hydrologic program.

5474 A2632 5k multicolored	.20	.20
5475 A2632 10k multicolored	.40	.20
5476 A2632 15k multicolored	.50	.30
5477 A2632 35k multicolored	.95	.55
Nos. 5474-5477 (4)	2.05	1.25

Tyumen, 400th Anniv. A2633

1986, July 27

5478 A2633 5k multicolored	.25	.20

A2634 A2635

1986, Aug. 1 Photo. *Perf. 11½*

5479 A2634 10k multicolored	.35	.20

Olof Palme (1927-86), Prime Minister of Sweden.

1986, Aug. 8

5480 A2635 15k multicolored	.50	.25

10th World Women's Basketball Championships, Moscow, Aug. 15-17.

Natl. Sports Committee Intl. Alpinist Camps — A2636

1986, Sept. 5 Litho. *Perf. 12*

5481 A2636 4k Mt. Lenin	.20	.20
5482 A2636 5k Mt. E. Korzhenevskaya	.20	.20
a. Miniature sheet of 8	10.00	
5483 A2636 10k Mt. Belukha	.30	.20
5484 A2636 15k Mt. Communism	.35	.20
5485 A2636 30k Mt. Elbrus	.65	.30
Nos. 5481-5485 (5)	1.70	1.10

See Nos. 5532-5535.

Souvenir Sheet

Red Book, Rainbow, Earth — A2637

1986, Sept. 10 *Perf. 11½*

5486 A2637 50k multicolored	1.75	.75

Nature preservation.

A2638 A2640

A2639

1986, Sept. 13 Photo.

5487 A2638 5k multicolored	.25	.20

Chelyabinsk, 250th anniv.

1986, Sept. 23

5488 A2639 15k multicolored	.40	.25

Mukran, DDR to Klaipeda, Lithuania, Train Ferry, inauguration.

1986, Sept. 26

5489 A2640 5k multicolored	.25	.20

Siauliai, Lithuanian SSR, 750th anniv.

Trucks — A2641

1986, Oct. 15 *Perf. 11½x12*

5490 A2641 4k Ural-375D, 1964	.20	.20
5491 A2641 5k GAZ-53A, 1965	.20	.20
5492 A2641 10k KrAZ-256B, 1966	.35	.20
a. Miniature sheet of 8	15.00	
5493 A2641 15k MAZ-515B, 1974	.50	.30
5494 A2641 20k ZIL-133GY, 1979	.60	.35
Nos. 5490-5494 (5)	1.85	1.25

October Revolution, 69th anniv. — A2642

Design: Lenin Monument in October Square, Kremlin, Moscow.

1986, Oct. 1 Litho. *Perf. 12*

5495 A2642 5k multicolored	.25	.20

A2643

1986, Oct. 10 Photo. *Perf. 11½*

5496 5k Icebreaker, helicopters	.20	.20
5497 10k Mikhail Somov port side	.20	.20
a. A2643 Pair, #5496-5497	.30	.20
b. Miniature sheet of 8, 4 each	15.00	

Souvenir Sheet

Perf. 12½x11½

5498 A2643 50k Trapped in ice	2.25	.65

Mikhail Somov trapped in the Antarctic.

No. 5497a has a continuous design. No. 5498 contains one 51½x36½mm stamp.

No. 4883 Ovptd. in Black for Rescue of the Mikhail Somov

Lithographed & Engraved

1986, Oct. 10 *Perf. 12x11½*

5499 A2271 4k multicolored	.75	.20

Locomotives — A2644

1986, Oct. 15 Litho. *Perf. 12*

5500 A2644 4k EU 684-37, 1929	.20	.20
5501 A2644 5k FD 21-3000, 1941	.20	.20
5502 A2644 10k OV-5109, 1907	.55	.20
a. Miniature sheet of 8	15.00	
5503 A2644 20k C017-1613, 1944	.95	.40
5504 A2644 30k FDP 20-578, 1941	1.25	.65
Nos. 5500-5504 (5)	3.15	1.65

Grigori Konstantinovich Ordzhonikidze (1886-1937), Communist Party Leader — A2645

1986, Oct. 18 Engr. *Perf. 12½x12*
5505 A2645 5k dark blue green .25 .20

A.G. Novikov (1896-1984), Composer — A2646

1986, Oct. 30
5506 A2646 5k brown black .25 .20

A2647 A2648

1986, Nov. 4 Photo. *Perf. 11½*
5507 A2647 10k blue & silver .35 .20

UNESCO, 40th anniv.

1986, Nov. 12
5508 A2648 5k lt grnsh gray & blk .25 .20

Sun Yat-sen (1866-1925), Chinese statesman.

Mikhail Vasilyevich Lomonosov, Scientist A2649

1986, Nov. 19 Engr. *Perf. 12x12½*
5509 A2649 5k dk violet brown .25 .20

Aircraft by A.S. Yakovlev — A2650

1986, Nov. 25 Photo. *Perf. 11½x12*

5510	A2650	4k 1927	.20	.20
5511	A2650	5k 1935	.20	.20
a.		Miniature sheet of 8	*15.00*	
5512	A2650	10k 1946	.40	.20
5513	A2650	20k 1972	.65	.35
5514	A2650	30k 1981	.95	.50
		Nos. 5510-5514 (5)	2.40	1.45

New Year 1987 A2651

1986, Dec. 4 Litho. *Perf. 11½*
5515 A2651 5k Kremlin towers .25 .20
a. Miniature sheet of 8 *15.00*

27th Communist Party Cong., 2/25-3/6 — A2652

Red banner and: No. 5516, Computers. No. 5517, Engineer, computer, dish receivers. No. 5518, Aerial view of city. No. 5519, Council for Mutual Economic Assistance building, workers. No. 5520, Spasski Tower, Kremlin Palace.

1986, Dec. 12 Photo. *Perf. 11½x12*

5516	A2652	5k multicolored	.20	.20
5517	A2652	5k multicolored	.20	.20
5518	A2652	5k multicolored	.20	.20
5519	A2652	5k multicolored	.20	.20
5520	A2652	5k multicolored	.20	.20
		Nos. 5516-5520 (5)	1.00	1.00

A2653 A2654

1986, Dec. 24 Engr. *Perf. 12½x12*
5521 A2653 5k black .25 .20

Alexander Yakovlevich Parkhomenko (1886-1921), revolution hero.

1986, Dec. 25 Photo. *Perf. 11½*
5522 A2654 5k brown & buff .25 .20

Samora Moises Machel (1933-1986) Pres. of Mozambique.

Miniature Sheet

Palace Museums in Leningrad — A2655

1986, Dec. 25 Engr. *Perf. 12*

5523		Sheet of 5 + label	3.00	1.40
a.	A2655	5k State Museum, 1898	.20	.20
b.	A2655	10k The Hermitage, 1764	.35	.20
c.	A2655	15k Petrodvorets, 1728	.45	.30
d.	A2655	20k Yekaterininsky, 1757	.55	.35
e.	A2655	50k Pavlovsk, restored c. 1945	1.25	.75

18th Soviet Trade Unions Congress, Feb. 24-28 — A2656

1987, Jan. 7 Photo. *Perf. 11½*
5524 A2656 5k multicolored .25 .20

Butterflies A2657

1987, Jan. 15 Litho. *Perf. 12x12½*

5525	A2657	4k Atrophaneura alcinous	.20	.20
5526	A2657	5k Papilio machaon	.20	.20
5527	A2657	10k Papilio alexanor	.30	.20
5528	A2657	15k Papilio maackii	.35	.30
5529	A2657	30k Iphiclides podalirius	.70	.50
		Nos. 5525-5529 (5)	1.75	1.40

A2658 A2659

1987, Jan. 31 *Perf. 12½x12*
5530 A2658 5k multicolored .25 .20

Karlis Miyesniyek (1887-1977), Artist.

1987, Feb. 4 *Perf. 12*
5531 A2659 5k buff & lake .25 .20

Stasis Shimkus (1887-1943), composer.

Alpinist Camps Type of 1986

1987, Feb. 4

5532	A2636	4k Chimbulak Gorge	.20	.20
5533	A2636	10k Shavla Gorge	.30	.20
5534	A2636	20k Mts. Donguz-orun, Nakra-tau	.50	.35
5535	A2636	35k Mt. Kazbek	.75	.55
		Nos. 5532-5535 (4)	1.75	1.30

Vasily Ivanovich Chapayev (1887-1919), Revolution Hero — A2660

1987, Feb. 9 Engr.
5536 A2660 5k dark red brown .25 .20

Heino Eller (1887-1970), Estonian Composer — A2661

1987, Mar. 7 Litho. *Perf. 12*
5537 A2661 5k buff & brown .25 .20

A2662 A2663

1987, Mar. 8 Photo. *Perf. 11½*
5538 A2662 5k multicolored .25 .20

Souvenir Sheet

Perf. 11½x12

5539 A2662 50k "XX," and colored bands 1.75 .75

All-Union Leninist Young Communist League 20th Congress, Moscow. No. 5539 contains one 26x37mm stamp.

Photogravure and Engraved

1987, Mar. 20 *Perf. 11½*
5540 A2663 5k buff & sepia .25 .20

Iosif Abgarovich rbeli (1887-1961), first president of the Armenian Academy of Sciences.

World Wildlife Fund — A2664

Polar bears.

1987, Mar. 25 Photo. *Perf. 11½x12*

5541	A2664	5k multicolored	.20	.20
a.		Miniature sheet of 8	100.00	
5542	A2664	10k multicolored	.30	.20
a.		Miniature sheet of 8	100.00	
5543	A2664	20k multicolored	.70	.40
a.		Miniature sheet of 8	100.00	
5544	A2664	35k multicolored	1.00	.75
a.		Miniature sheet of 8	100.00	
		Nos. 5541-5544 (4)	2.20	1.55

Cosmonauts' Day — A2665

UN Emblem, ESCAP Headquarters, Bangkok — A2666

1987, Apr. 12 *Perf. 11½*

5545	A2665	10k Sputnik, 1957	.35	.20
5546	A2665	10k Vostok 3 and 4, 1962	.35	.20
5547	A2665	10k Mars 1, 1962	.35	.20
a.		Miniature sheet of 8	25.00	
		Nos. 5545-5547 (3)	1.05	.60

1987, Apr. 21
5548 A2666 10k multicolored .30 .20

UN Economic and Social Commission for Asia and the Pacific, 40th anniv.

Lenin, 117th Birth Anniv. — A2667

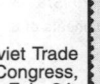

Paintings: No. 5549, Lenin's Birthday, by N.A. Sysoyev. No. 5550, Lenin with Delegates at the 3rd Congress of the Soviet Young Communist League, by P.O. Belousov. No. 5551a, Lenin's Underground Activity (Lenin, lamp), by D.A. Nalbandyan. No. 5551b, Before the Assault (Lenin standing at table), by S.P. Viktorov. No. 5551c, We'll Show the Earth the New Way (Lenin, soldiers, flags), by A.G. Lysenko. No. 5551d, Lenin in Smolny, October 1917 (Lenin seated), by M.G. Sokolov. No. 5551e, Lenin, by N.A. Andreyev.

1987, Apr. 22 Litho. *Perf. 12½x12*

5549 A2667 5k multicolored .20 .20
5550 A2667 5k multicolored .20 .20

Souvenir Sheet

Perf. 12

5551 Sheet of 5 1.75 .75
a.-e. A2667 10k any single .30 .20

Sizes: Nos. 5551a-5551d, 40x28mm; No. 5551e, 40x56mm.

A2668

1987, May 5 Photo. *Perf. 11½*

5552 A2668 10k multicolored .30 .20

European Gymnastics Championships, Moscow, May 18-26.

Bicycle Race — A2669 Fauna — A2670

1987, May 6

5553 A2669 10k multicolored .30 .20

40th Peace Bicycle Race, Poland-Czechoslovakia-German Democratic Republic, May.

Perf. 12½x12 (#5554), 12x12½

1987, May 15 Litho.

5554 A2670 5k Menzbira marmot .20 .20
a. Miniature sheet of 8 15.00
5555 A2670 10k Bald badger, horiz. .30 .20

Size: 32x47mm

5556 A2670 15k Snow leopard .40 .25
Nos. 5554-5556 (3) .90 .65

Passenger Ships — A2671

1987, May 20 Photo. *Perf. 12x11½*

5557 A2671 5k Maxim Gorki .20 .20
5558 A2671 10k Alexander Pushkin .35 .20
a. Miniature sheet of 8 15.00
5559 A2671 30k The Soviet Union 1.10 .45
Nos. 5557-5559 (3) 1.65 .85

Paintings by Foreign Artists in the Hermitage Museum A2672

4k, Portrait of a Woman, by Lucas Cranach Sr. (1472-1553). 5k, St. Sebastian, by Titian. 10k, Justice, by Durer. 30k, Adoration of the Magi, by Pieter Brueghel the Younger (c. 1564-1638). 50k, Ceres, by Rubens.

Perf. 12x12½, 12½x12

1987, June 5 Litho.

5560 A2672 4k multicolored .20 .20
5561 A2672 5k multicolored .20 .20
a. Miniature sheet of 8 10.00
5562 A2672 10k multicolored .30 .20
a. Miniature sheet of 8 20.00
5563 A2672 30k multicolored .70 .50
5564 A2672 50k multicolored 1.25 .75
Nos. 5560-5564 (5) 2.65 1.85

Tolyatti City, 250th Anniv. — A2673

Design: Zhiguli car, Volga Motors factory, Lenin Hydroelectric plant.

1987, June 6 Photo. *Perf. 11½*

5565 A2673 5k multicolored .25 .20

Aleksander Pushkin (1799-1837), Poet — A2674

1987, June 6 Litho.

5566 A2674 5k buff, yel brn & deep brown .25 .20

Printed se-tenant with label.

A2675 A2676

1987, June 7 Engr. *Perf. 12½x12*

5567 A2675 5k black .25 .20

Maj.-Gen. Sidor A. Kovpak (1887-1967), Vice-Chairman of the Ukranian SSR.

1987, June 23 Photo. *Perf. 11½*

5568 A2676 10k multicolored .30 .20

Women's World Congress on Nuclear Disarmament, Moscow, June 23-27.

Tobolsk City, 400th Anniv. — A2677

Design: Tobolsk kremlin, port, theater and Ermak Monument.

1987, June 25

5569 A2677 5k multicolored .25 .20

Mozambique-USSR Peace Treaty, 10th anniv. — A2678

1987, June 25

5570 A2678 5k Flag of Congo, man .20 .20
5571 A2678 5k Flags of Frelimo, USSR .20 .20
a. Pair, #5570-5571 .30 .30

Ferns — A2679 A2680

1987, July 2 Litho. *Perf. 12*

5572 A2679 4k Scolopendrium vulgare .20 .20
5573 A2679 5k Ceterach officinarum .20 .20
5574 A2679 10k Salvinia natans, horiz. .30 .20
5575 A2679 15k Matteuccia struthiopteris .40 .30
5576 A2679 50k Adiantum pedatum 1.10 .75
Nos. 5572-5576 (5) 2.20 1.65

1987, July 3

Designs: #5577, Kremlin and 2000 Year-old Coin of India. #5578, Red Fort, Delhi, Soviet hammer & sickle.

5577 A2680 5k shown .20 .20
5578 A2680 5k muticolored .20 .20
a. Pair, #5577-5578 .30 .30

Festivals 1987-88: India in the USSR (No. 5577) and the USSR in India (No. 5578).

15th Intl. Film Festival, July 16-17, Moscow — A2681

1987, July 6 Photo. *Perf. 11½*

5579 2681 10k multicolored .35 .20

Joint Soviet-Syrian Space Flight A2682

Mir Space Station — A2683

Flags, Intercosmos emblem and: 5k, Cosmonaut training and launch. 10k, Mir space station, Syrian parliament and cosmonauts. 15k, Gagarin Memorial, satellite dishes and cosmonauts wearing space suits.

1987 Litho. *Perf. 12x12½*

5580 A2682 5k multicolored .20 .20
5581 A2682 10k multicolored .25 .20
5582 A2682 15k multicolored .40 .25
Nos. 5580-5582 (3) .85 .65

Souvenir Sheet

5583 A2683 50k multicolored 1.75 .75

Issued: 5k, 7/22; 10k, 7/24; 15k, 50k 7/30.

Intl. Atomic Energy Agency, 30th Anniv. A2684

1987, July 29 Photo. *Perf. 11½*

5584 A2684 20k multicolored .60 .30

14th-16th Century Postrider — A2685

Designs: 5k, 17th cent. postman and 17th cent. kibitka (sled). 10k, 16th-17th cent. ship and 18th cent. packet. 30k, Railway station and 19th cent. mailcars. 35k, AMO-F-15 bus and car, 1905. 50k, Postal headquarters, Moscow, and modern postal delivery trucks.

Photo. & Engr.

1987, Aug. 25 *Perf. 11½x12*

5585 A2685 4k buff & black .20 .20
5586 A2685 5k buff & black .20 .20
5587 A2685 10k buff & black .30 .20
5588 A2685 30k buff & black .90 .50
5589 A2685 35k buff & black 1.00 .55
Nos. 5585-5589 (5) 2.60 1.65

Souvenir Sheet

5590 A2685 50k pale yel, dull gray grn & blk 1.75 .90

A2686

October Revolution, 70th Anniv. — A2687

Paintings by Russian artists: No. 5591, Long Live the Socialist Revolution! by V.V. Kuznetsov. No. 5592, V.I. Lenin Proclaims the Soviet Power (Lenin pointing), by V.A. Serov. No. 5593, V.I. Lenin (with pencil), by P.V. Vasiliev. No. 5594, On the Eve of the Storm (Lenin, Trotsky, Dzerzhinski), by V.V. Pimenov. No. 5595, Taking the Winter Palace by Storm, by V.A. Serov.

1987, Aug. 25 Litho. *Perf. 12½x12*

5591 A2686 5k shown .20 .20
5592 A2686 5k multicolored .20 .20
5593 A2686 5k multicolored .20 .20

Size: 70x33mm

Perf. 11½

5594 A2686 5k multicolored .20 .20
5595 A2686 5k multicolored .20 .20
Nos. 5591-5595 (5) 1.00 1.00

Souvenir Sheet

Photo. & Engr.

Perf. 12x11½

5596 A2687 30k gold & black 1.50 .45

For overprint see No. 5604.

Souvenir Sheet

Battle of Borodino, 175th Anniv. — A2688

1987, Sept. 7 Litho. *Perf. 12½x12*

5597 A2688 1r black, yel brn & blue gray 3.00 1.50

A2689

A2690

1987, Sept. 18 Engr.

5598 A2689 5k intense blue .25 .20

Pavel Petrovich Postyshev (1887-1939), party leader.

1987, Sept. 19 Photo. *Perf. 11½*

Design: 5k, Monument to founder Yuri Dolgoruki, by sculptor S. Orlov, A. Antropov, N. Stamm and architect V. Andreyev, in Sovetskaya Square, and buildings in Moscow.

5599 A2690 5k dk red brn, cr & dk org .25 .20

Moscow, 840th anniv.

Scientists — A2691

Designs: No. 5600, Muhammed Taragai Ulugh Begh (1394-1449), Uzbek astronomer and mathematician. No. 5601, Sir Isaac Newton (1642-1727), English physicist and mathematician. No. 5602, Marie Curie (1867-1934), physicist, chemist, Nobel laureate.

1987, Oct. 3 Photo. & Engr.

5600 A2691 5k dk bl, org brn & blk .20 .20
5601 A2691 5k dull grn, blk & dk ultra .20 .20
5602 A2691 5k brown & deep blue .20 .20
Nos. 5600-5602 (3) .60 .60

Nos. 5600-5602 each printed se-tenant with inscribed label.

Souvenir Sheet

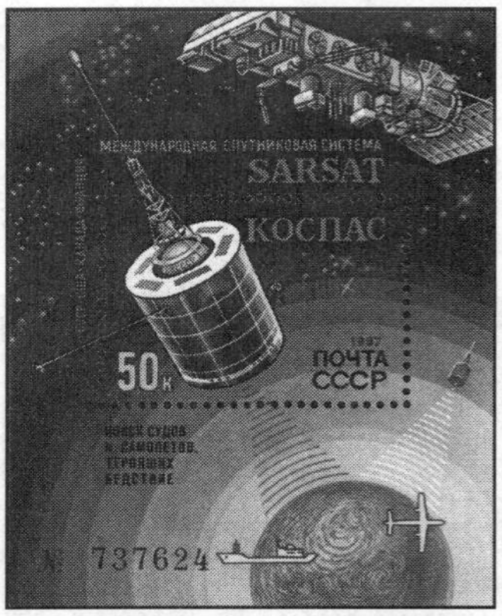

COSPAS-SARSAT Intl. Satellite System for Tracking Disabled Planes and Ships — A2692

1987, Oct. 15 Photo.

5603 A2692 50k multicolored 2.25 .75

No. 5595 Overprinted in Gold

1987, Oct. 17 Litho.

5604 A2686 5k multicolored 1.00 .20

All-Union Philatelic Exhibition and the 70th Anniv. of the October Revolution.

Sheet of 8 No. 5595 has the overprint in the margin.

My Quiet Homeland, by V.M. Sidorov — A2693

The Sun Above Red Square, by P.P. Ossovsky — A2694

Paintings by Soviet artists exhibited at the 7th Republican Art Exhibition, Moscow, 1985: 4k, There Will be Cities in the Taiga, by A.A. Yakovlev. 5k, Mother, by V.V. Shcherbakov. 30k, On Jakutian Soil, by A.N. Osipov. 35k, Ivan's Return, by V.I. Yerofeyev.

1987, Oct. 20 *Perf. 12x12½, 12½x12*

5605 A2693 4k multi, vert. .20 .20
5606 A2693 5k multi, vert. .20 .20
5607 A2693 10k multicolored .35 .20
5608 A2693 30k multicolored .75 .45
5609 A2693 35k multicolored .85 .50
Nos. 5605-5609 (5) 2.35 1.55

Souvenir Sheet

Perf. 11½x12½

5610 A2694 50k multicolored 2.50 1.00

John Reed (1887-1920), American Journalist — A2695

1987, Oct. 22 *Perf. 11½*

5611 A2695 10k buff & dark brown .35 .20

Samuil Yakovlevich Marshak (1887-1964), Author — A2696

1987, Nov. 3 Engr. *Perf. 12½x12*

5612 A2696 5k deep claret .25 .20

A2697

1987, Nov. 8

5613 A2697 5k slate blue .50 .20

Ilja Grigorjevich Chavchavadze (1837-1907), Georgian author.

A2698

A2699

1987, Nov. 19 Photo. *Perf. 11½*

5614 A2698 5k black & brown .25 .20

Indira Gandhi (1917-1984).

1987, Nov. 25 *Perf. 12½x12*

5615 A2699 5k black .25 .20

Vadim Nikolaevich Podbelsky (1887-1920), revolution leader.

A2700

A2701

1987, Nov. 25

5616 A2700 5k dark blue gray .25 .20

Nikolai Ivanovich Vavilov (1887-1943), botanist.

Photo. & Engr.

1987, Nov. 25 *Perf. 11½*

Modern Science: 5k, TOKAMAK, a controlled thermonuclear reactor. 10k, Kola Project (Earth strata study). 20k, RATAN-600 radiotelescope.

5617 A2701 5k grnsh gray & brn .20 .20
5618 A2701 10k dull grn, lt blue gray & dark blue .35 .20
5619 A2701 20k gray olive, blk & buff .70 .30
Nos. 5617-5619 (3) 1.25 .70

US and Soviet Flags, Spasski Tower and US Capitol — A2702

1987, Dec. 17 Photo.

5620 A2702 10k multicolored .50 .20

INF Treaty (eliminating intermediate-range nuclear missiles) signed by Gen.-Sec. Gorbachev and Pres. Reagan, Dec. 8.

New Year 1988 A2703

1987, Dec. 2 Litho. *Perf. 12x12½*

5621 A2703 5k Kremlin .25 .20
a. Miniature sheet of 8

Marshal Ivan Khristoforovich Bagramyan (1897-1982)
A2704

1987, Dec. 2 Engr. *Perf. 12½x12*
5622 A2704 5k black .25 .20

Miniature Sheet

18th-19th Cent. Naval Commanders and War Ships — A2705

Designs: 4k, Adm. Grigori Andreyevich Spiridov (1713-1790), Battle of Chesmen. 5k, Fedor Fedorovich Ushakov (1745-1817), Storming of Corfu. 10k, Adm. Dimitiri Nikolayevich Senyavin (1763-1831) and flagship at the Battle of Afon off Mt. Athos. 25k, Mikhail Petrovich Lazarev (1788-1851), Battle of Navarin. 30k, Adm. Pavel Stepanovich Nakhimov (1802-1855), Battle of Sinop.

1987, Dec. 22
5623 Sheet of 5 + label 2.50 1.25
a. A2705 4k dark blue & indigo .20 .20
b. A2705 5k maroon & indigo .20 .20
c. A2705 10k maroon & indigo .35 .20
d. A2705 25k dark blue & indigo .80 .40
e. A2705 30k dark blue & indigo 1.00 .50

No. 5623 contains corner label (LR) picturing ensign of period Russian Navy vessels and anchor.
See No. 5850.

Asia-Africa Peoples Solidarity Organization, 30th Anniv. — A2706

1987, Dec. 26 Photo. *Perf. 11½*
5624 A2706 10k multicolored .35 .20

1st Soviet Postage Stamp, 70th Anniv. — A2707

1988, Jan. 4 Photo. *Perf. 11½*
5625 A2707 10k #149, #150 UR .50 .20
5626 A2707 10k #150, #149 UR .50 .20
a. Pair, #5625-5626 1.00 .30

Lettering in brown on No. 5625, in blue on No. 5626.

A2708

A2709

1988, Jan. 4
5627 A2708 5k Biathlon .20 .20
a. Miniature sheet of 8 75.00
5628 A2708 10k Cross-country skiing .30 .20
a. Miniature sheet of 8 75.00
5629 A2708 15k Slalom .40 .30
a. Miniature sheet of 8 75.00
5630 A2708 20k Pairs figure skating .50 .35
a. Miniature sheet of 8 75.00
5631 A2708 30k Ski jumping .70 .50
a. Miniature sheet of 8 75.00
Nos. 5627-5631 (5) 2.10 1.55

Souvenir Sheet

5632 A2708 50k Ice hockey, horiz. 1.50 1.00

1988 Winter Olympics, Calgary.
For overprint see No. 5665.

1988, Jan. 7
5633 A2709 35k blue & gold 1.00 .65

World Health Org., 40th anniv.

Lord Byron (1788-1824), English Poet
A2710

Photo. & Engr.

1988, Jan. 22 *Perf. 12x11½*
5634 A2710 15k Prus blue, blk & grn black .50 .30

A2711

A2712

1988, Jan. 27 Photo. *Perf. 11½*
5635 A2711 20k multicolored .60 .40

Cultural, Technical and Educational Agreement with the US, 30th anniv.

1988, Feb. 5
5636 A2712 5k black & tan .25 .20

G.I. Lomov-Oppokov (1888-1938), party leader. See Nos. 5649, 5660, 5666, 5673, 5700, 5704, 5721, 5812.

Animated Soviet Cartoons — A2713

1988, Feb. 18 Litho. *Perf. 12½x12*
5637 A2713 1k Little Humpback Horse, 1947 .20 .20
5638 A2713 3k Winnie-the-Pooh, 1969 .20 .20
5639 A2713 4k Gena, the Crocodile, 1969 .20 .20
5640 A2713 5k Just you Wait! 1969 .20 .20
5641 A2713 10k Hedgehog in the Mist, 1975 .30 .20
Nos. 5637-5641 (5) 1.10 1.00

Souvenir Sheet

5642 A2713 30k Post, 1929 1.00 .60

A2714

A2715

1988, Feb. 21 Photo. *Perf. 11½*
5643 A2714 10k buff & black .30 .20

Mikhail Alexandrovich Bonch-Bruevich (1888-1940), broadcast engineer.

1988, Feb. 25
5644 A2715 15k blk, brt bl & dk red .50 .30
a. Miniature sheet of 8 *15.00*

Intl. Red Cross and Red Crescent Organizations, 125th annivs.

World Speed Skating Championships, Mar. 5-6, Alma-Ata — A2716

1988, Mar. 13 Photo. *Perf. 11½*
5645 A2716 15k blk, vio & brt blue .45 .30

No. 5645 printed se-tenant with label picturing Alma-Ata skating rink, Medeo.

A2717

1988, Mar. 13 Litho. *Perf. 12½x12*
5646 A2717 10k dark olive green .30 .20

Anton Semenovich Makarenko (1888-1939), teacher, youth development expert.

Franzisk Skorina (b. 1488), 1st Printer in Byelorussia
A2718

1988, Mar. 17 Engr. *Perf. 12x12½*
5647 A2718 5k gray black .25 .20

Labor Day — A2719

1988, Mar. 22 Photo. *Perf. 11½*
5648 A2719 5k multicolored .25 .20

Party Leader Type of 1988

1988, Mar. 24 Engr. *Perf. 12*
5649 A2712 5k dark green .25 .20

Victor Eduardovich Kingisepp (1888-1922).

Organized Track and Field Events in Russia, Cent.
A2721

1988, Mar. 24 Photo. *Perf. 11½*
5650 A2721 15k multicolored .50 .30

Marietta Sergeyevna Shaginyan (1888-1982), Author — A2722

1988, Apr. 2 Litho. *Perf. 12½x12*
5651 A2722 10k brown .30 .20

Soviet-Finnish Peace Treaty, 40th Anniv. — A2723

1988, Apr. 6 Photo. *Perf. 11½*
5652 A2723 15k multicolored .50 .30

Cosmonaut's Day — A2724

MIR space station, Soyuz TM transport ship, automated cargo ship *Progress* & *Quant* module.

1988, Apr. 12 *Perf. 11½x12*
5653 A2724 15k multicolored .50 .30
a. Miniature sheet of 8 *15.00*

Victory, 1948, Painted by P.A. Krivonogov
A2725

1988, Apr. 20 Litho. *Perf. 12x12½*
5654 A2725 5k multicolored .25 .20

Victory Day (May 9).

Sochi City, 150th Anniv.
A2726

1988, Apr. 20 Photo. *Perf. 11½*
5655 A2726 5k multicolored .25 .20

Branches of the Lenin Museum — A2727

Portrait of Lenin and: No. 5656, Central museum, Moscow, opened May 15, 1926. No. 5657, Branch, Leningrad, opened in 1937. No. 5658, Branch, Kiev, opened in 1938. No. 5659, Branch, Krasnoyarsk, opened in 1987.

1988, Apr. 22 Litho. *Perf. 12*

5656 A2727 5k vio brown & gold .20 .20
5657 A2727 5k brn vio, vio brown & gold .20 .20
5658 A2727 5k dp brn ol & gold .20 .20
5659 A2727 5k dark green & gold .20 .20
a. Block of 4, Nos. 5656-5659 .80 .40

See Nos. 5765-5767, 5885-5887.

Party Leader Type of 1988

1988, Apr. 24 Photo. *Perf. 11½*

5660 A2712 5k blue black .25 .20

Ivan Alexeyevich Akulov (1888-1939).

A2729

Karl Marx — A2730

1988, Apr. 30

5661 A2729 20k multicolored .55 .35

EXPO '88, Brisbane, Australia.

1988, May 5 Engr. *Perf. 12*

5662 A2730 5k chocolate .25 .20

Social and Economic Reforms — A2731

Designs: No. 5663, Cruiser *Aurora,* revolutionary soldiers, workers and slogans Speeding Up, Democratization, and Glasnost against Kremlin Palace. No. 5664, Worker, agriculture and industries.

1988, May 5 Photo. *Perf. 12x11½*

5663 A2731 5k multicolored .20 .20
5664 A2731 5k multicolored .20 .20

No. 5632 Ovptd. in Dark Red

Спортсмены СССР завоевали 11 золотых, 9 серебряных и 9 бронзовых медалей!

Souvenir Sheet

1988, May 12 Photo. *Perf. 11½*

5665 A2708 50k multicolored 2.00 1.25

Victory of Soviet athletes at the 1988 Winter Olympics, Calgary. No. 5665 overprinted below stamp on souvenir sheet margin. Soviet sportsmen won 11 gold, 9 silver and 9 bronze medals.

Party Leader Type of 1988

1988, May 19 Engr. *Perf. 12*

5666 A2712 5k black .25 .20

Nikolai Mikhailovich Shvernik (1888-1970).

Hunting Dogs — A2733

Designs: 5k, Russian borzoi, fox hunt. 10k, Kirghiz greyhound, falconry. 15k, Russian retrievers. 20k, Russian spaniel, duck hunt. 35k, East Siberian husky, bear hunt.

1988, May 20 Litho.

5667 A2733 5k multicolored .20 .20
5668 A2733 10k multicolored .35 .25
5669 A2733 15k multicolored .50 .35
5670 A2733 20k multicolored .75 .50
5671 A2733 35k multicolored 1.10 .80
Nos. 5667-5671 (5) 2.90 2.10

A2734

A2736

1988, May 29 Photo. *Perf. 11½*

5672 A2734 5k multicolored .30 .20

Soviet-US Summit Conf., May 29-June 2, Moscow.

Party Leader Type of 1988

1988, June 6 Engr. *Perf. 12*

5673 A2712 5k brown black .25 .20

Valerian Vladimirovich Kuibyshev (1888-1935).

1988, June 7 Photo. *Perf. 11½*

Design: Flags, Mir space station and Soyuz TM spacecraft.

5674 A2736 15k multicolored .50 .35

Shipka '88, USSR-Bulgarian joint space flight, June 7.

A2737

A2738

Design: Natl. & Canadian flags, skis & obe.

1988, June 16

5675 A2737 35k multicolored 1.00 .80

Soviet-Canada transarctic ski expedition, May-Aug.

1988, June 16

5676 A2738 5k multicolored .25 .20

For a world without nuclear weapons.

A2739

A2740

19th All-union Communist Party Conference, Moscow — A2741

1988, June 16 Litho. *Perf. 12*

5677 A2739 5k multicolored .20 .20

Photo.

Perf. 11½

5678 A2740 5k multicolored .20 .20

Souvenir Sheet

Perf. 11½x12

5679 A2741 50k multicolored 1.75 1.00

1988 Summer Olympics, Seoul A2742

1988, June 29 Litho. *Perf. 12*

5680 A2742 5k Hurdling .20 .20
a. Miniature sheet of 8 5.00
5681 A2742 10k Long jump .25 .20
a. Miniature sheet of 8 5.00
5682 A2742 15k Basketball .40 .30
a. Miniature sheet of 8 5.00
5683 A2742 20k Rhythmic gymnastics .50 .35
a. Miniature sheet of 8 5.00
5684 A2742 30k Swimming .70 .50
a. Miniature sheet of 8 5.00
Nos. 5680-5684 (5) 2.05 1.55

Souvenir Sheet

5685 A2742 50k Soccer 1.75 1.10

For overprint see No. 5722.

Phobos Intl. Space Project — A2743

Flowers Populating Deciduous Forests — A2744

1988, July 7 Photo. *Perf. 11½x12*

5686 A2743 10k Satellite, space probe .30 .20

For the study of Phobos, a satellite of Mars.

1988, July 7 Litho. *Perf. 12*

5687 A2744 5k Campanula latifolia .20 .20
5688 A2744 10k Orobus vernus, horiz. .35 .25
5689 A2744 15k Pulmonaria obscura .50 .35
5690 A2744 20k Lilium martagon .65 .45
5691 A2744 35k Ficaria verna 1.10 .75
Nos. 5687-5691 (5) 2.80 2.00

A2745

A2746

1988, July 14 Photo. *Perf. 11½*

5692 A2745 5k multicolored .25 .20

Leninist Young Communist League (Komsomol), 70th anniv. For overprint see No. 5699.

1988, July 18

5693 A2746 10k multicolored .30 .20

Nelson Mandela (b. 1918), South African anti-apartheid leader

Paintings in the Timiriazev Equestrian Museum of the Moscow Agricultural Academy — A2747

Paintings: 5k, *Light Gray Arabian Stallion,* by N.E. Sverchkov, 1860. 10k, *Konvoets, a Kabardian,* by M.A. Vrubel, 1882, vert. 15k, *Horsewoman Riding an Orlov-Rastopchinsky,* by N.E. Sverchkov. 20k, *Letuchya, a Gray Orlov Trotter,* by V.A. Serov, 1886, vert. 30k, *Sardar, an Akhaltekinsky Stallion,* by A.B. Villevalde, 1882.

1988, July 20 Litho. *Perf. 12½x12*

5694 A2747 5k multicolored .20 .20
5695 A2747 10k multicolored .25 .20
5696 A2747 15k multicolored .40 .25
5697 A2747 20k multicolored .55 .35
5698 A2747 30k multicolored .90 .65
Nos. 5694-5698 (5) 2.30 1.65

No. 5692 Ovptd. for the All-Union Philatelic Exhibition, Moscow, Aug. 10-17

1988, Aug. 10 Photo. *Perf. 11½*

5699 A2745 5k multicolored .40 .30

Party Leader Type of 1988

1988, Aug. 13 Engr. *Perf. 12½x12*

5700 A2712 5k black .25 .20

Petr Lazarevich Voykov (1888-1927), economic and trade union plenipotentiary.

Intl. Letter-Writing Week — A2749

1988, Aug. 25 Photo. *Perf. 11½*

5701 A2749 5k blue grn & dark blue green .25 .20

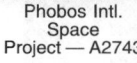

A2750

A2751

1988, Aug. 29

5702 A2750 15k Earth, Mir space station and Soyuz-TM .50 .30

Soviet-Afghan joint space flight.

1988, Sept. 1 Photo. *Perf. 11½*

5703 A2751 10k multicolored .30 .20

Problems of Peace and Socialism magazine, 30th anniv.

Party Leader Type of 1988

1988, Sept. 13 Engr. *Perf. 12*

5704 A2712 5k black .25 .20

Emmanuil Ionovich Kviring (1888-1937).

A2753

A2753a

A2753c

A2753b

A2753d

Designs: No. 5705, *Ilya Muromets,* Russian lore. No. 5706, *Ballad of the Cossack Golota,* Ukrainian lore. No. 5707, *Musician-Magician,* a Byelorussian fairy tale. No. 5708, *Koblandy-batyr,* a poem from Kazakh. No. 5709, *Alpamysh,* a fairy tale from Uzbek.

Perf. 12x12½, 12½x12

1988, Sept. 22 Litho.

5705 A2753 10k multicolored .30 .20
5706 A2753a 10k multicolored .30 .20
5707 A2753b 10k multicolored .30 .20
5708 A2753c 10k multicolored .30 .20
5709 A2753d 10k multicolored .30 .20
Nos. 5705-5709 (5) 1.50 1.00

Nos. 5705-5709 each printed se-tenant with inscribed labels. See design A2795.

Appeal of the Leader, 1947, by I.M. Toidze A2754

1988, Oct. 5 *Perf. 12x12½*

5710 A2754 5k multicolored .25 .20

October Revolution, 71st anniv.

A2755

A2756

1988, Oct. 18 Engr. *Perf. 12*

5711 A2755 10k black .30 .20

Andrei Timofeyevich Bolotov (1738-1833), agricultural scientist, publisher.

1988, Oct. 18

5712 A2756 10k steel blue .30 .20

Andrei Nikolayevich Tupolev (1888-1972), aeronautical engineer.

A2757

A2758

20k, Map of expedition route, atomic ice-breaker *Sibirj* & expedition members.

1988, Oct. 25 Litho.

5713 A2757 20k multicolored .60 .40

North Pole expedition (in 1987). Exists imperf.

1988, Oct. 30 Engr.

5714 A2758 5k brown black .25 .20

Dmitry F. Ustinov (1908-84), minister of defense.

Soviet-Vietnamese Treaty, 10th Anniv. — A2759

1988, Nov. 3 Photo. *Perf. 11½*

5715 A2759 10k multicolored .30 .20

State Broadcasting and Sound Recording Institute, 50th Anniv. — A2760

1988, Nov. 3

5716 A2760 10k multicolored .30 .20

UN Declaration of Human Rights, 40th Anniv. A2761

1988, Nov. 21

5717 A2761 10k multicolored .30 .20

New Year 1989 — A2762

Design: Preobrazhensky Regiment body-guard riding to announce Peter the Great's decree to celebrate new year's eve as of January 1, 1700.

1988, Nov. 24 Litho. *Perf. 12x11½*

5718 A2762 5k multicolored .25 .20

Soviet-French Joint Space Flight — A2763

1988, Nov. 26 Photo. *Perf. 11½*

5719 A2763 15k Space walkers .45 .30

No. 4607 Overprinted in Red

1988, Dec. 16 Litho. *Perf. 12½x12*

5720 A2143 1r dark blue 3.50 2.25

Space mail.

Party Leader Type of 1988

1988, Dec. 16 Engr.

5721 A2712 5k slate green .25 .20

Martyn Ivanovich Latsis (1888-1938).

Souvenir Sheet

No. 5685 Overprinted in Bright Blue

1988, Dec. 20 Litho. *Perf. 12*

5722 A2742 50k multicolored 1.75 1.00

Victory of Soviet athletes at the 1988 Summer Olympics, Seoul. Overprint on margin of No. 5722 specifies that Soviet athletes won 55 gold, 31 silver and 46 bronze medals.

Post Rider A2765

Fountains of Petrodvorets A2766

Designs: 3k, Cruiser *Aurora.* 4k, Spasski Tower, Lenin Mausoleum. 5k, Natl. flag, crest. 10k, *The Worker and the Collective Farmer,* 1935, sculpture by V.I. Mukhina. 15k, Satellite dish. 20k, Lyre, art tools, quill pen, parchment (arts and literature). 25k, *Discobolus,* 5th cent. sculpture by Myron (c. 480-440 B.C.). 30k, Map of the Antarctic, penguins. 35k, *Mercury,* sculpture by Giambologna (1529-1608). 50k, White cranes (nature conservation). 1r, UPU emblem.

1988, Dec. 22 Engr. *Perf. 12x11½*

5723 A2765 1k dark brown .20 .20
5724 A2765 3k dark blue green .20 .20
5725 A2765 4k indigo .20 .20
5726 A2765 5k red .20 .20
5727 A2765 10k claret .30 .20
5728 A2765 15k deep blue .45 .30
5729 A2765 20k olive gray .60 .40
5730 A2765 25k dark green .75 .50
5731 A2765 30k dark blue .90 .60
5732 A2765 35k dark red brown 1.00 .70
5733 A2765 50k sapphire 1.50 1.00

Perf. 12x12½

5734 A2765 1r blue gray 3.00 2.00
Nos. 5723-5734 (12) 9.30 6.50

See Nos. 5838-5849, 5984-5987. For surcharges see Uzbekistan #15, 22, 25-26, 61B, 61D, 61F.

1988, Dec. 25 Engr. *Perf. 11½x12*

Designs: 5k, Samson Fountain, 1723, and Great Cascade. 10k, Adam Fountain, 1722, and sculptures, 1718, by D. Bonazza. 15k, Golden Mountain Cascade, by N. Miketti (1721-1723) and M.G. Zemtsov. 30k, Roman Fountains, 1763. 50k, Oak Tree Fountain, 1735.

5735 A2766 5k myrtle green .20 .20
5736 A2766 10k myrtle green .20 .20
5737 A2766 15k myrtle green .30 .20
5738 A2766 30k myrtle green .60 .40
5739 A2766 50k myrtle green 1.00 .70
a. Pane of 5, #5735-5739 2.25 1.50

Panes have photogravure margin. Panes are printed bilaterally and separated in the center by perforations so that stamps in the 2nd pane are arranged in reverse order from the 1st pane.

19th Communist Party Congress — A2767

1988, Dec. 30 Photo. *Perf. 12x11½*
Multicolored and:

5740 A2767 5k deep car (power) .20 .20
5741 A2767 5k deep blue vio (industry) .20 .20
5742 A2767 5k green (land) .20 .20
Nos. 5740-5742 (3) .60 .60

Souvenir Sheet

Inaugural Flight of the *Buran* Space Shuttle, Nov. 15 — A2768

1988, Dec. 30 *Perf. 11½x12*
5743 A2768 50k multicolored 1.50 1.00

Luna 1, 30th Anniv. — A2769

1989, Jan. 2 Photo. *Perf. 11½*
5744 A2769 15k multicolored .50 .30

Jalmari Virtanen (1889-1939), Karelian Poet — A2770

1989, Jan. 8
5745 A2770 5k olive brown .25 .20

Council for Mutual Economic Assistance, 40th Anniv. A2771

1989, Jan. 8
5746 A2771 10k multicolored .30 .20

Environmental Protection — A2772

1989, Jan. 18 Litho. *Perf. 12½x12*
5747 A2772 5k Forest .20 .20
5748 A2772 10k Arctic deer .30 .20
5749 A2772 15k Stop desert encroachment .45 .30
Nos. 5747-5749 (3) .95 .70

Nos. 5747-5749 printed se-tenant with inscribed labels picturing maps.

Samovars A2773

Samovars in the State Museum, Leningrad: 5k, Pear-shaped urn, late 18th cent. 10k, Barrel-shaped urn by Ivan Listisin, early 19th cent. 20k, "Kabachok" urn by the Sokolov Bros., Tula, c. 1830. 30k, Vase-shaped urn by the Nikolari Malikov Studio, Tula, c. 1840.

1989, Feb. 8 Photo. *Perf. 11½*
5750 A2773 5k multicolored .20 .20
5751 A2773 10k multicolored .25 .20
5752 A2773 20k multicolored .45 .30
5753 A2773 30k multicolored .65 .45
Nos. 5750-5753 (4) 1.55 1.15

Modest Petrovich Mussorgsky (1839-1881), Composer — A2774

1989, Feb. 15 Litho. *Perf. 12½x12*
5754 A2774 10k dull vio & vio brn .30 .20

P.E. Dybenko (1889-1938), Military Commander A2775

1989, Feb. 28 Engr. *Perf. 12*
5755 A2775 5k black .25 .20

T.G. Shevchenko (1814-1861), Poet A2776

1989, Mar. 6 Litho. *Perf. 11½*
5756 A2776 5k pale grn, blk & brn .25 .20

Exists imperf. Value, $25.

Cultivated Lilies — A2777

1989, Mar. 15 *Perf. 12½x12*
5757 A2777 5k Lilium speciosum .20 .20
5758 A2777 10k African queen .25 .20
5759 A2777 15k Eclat du soir .40 .25
5760 A2777 30k White tiger .80 .55
Nos. 5757-5760 (4) 1.65 1.20

Souvenir Sheet

Labor Day, Cent. — A2778

1989, Mar. 25 *Perf. 11½x12*
5761 A2778 30k multicolored 1.00 .60

Victory Banner, by P. Loginov and V. Pamfilov A2779

1989, Apr. 5 Litho. *Perf. 12x12½*
5762 A2779 5k multicolored .25 .20

World War II Victory Day.

Cosmonauts' Day — A2780

Illustration reduced.

1989, Apr. 12 Photo. *Perf. 11x11½*
5763 A2780 15k Mir space station .45 .30

A2781

1989, Apr. 14 *Perf. 11½*
5764 A2781 10k multicolored .30 .20

Bering Bridge Soviet-American Expedition, Anadyr and Kotzebue.

Type of 1988

Portraits and branches of the Lenin Central Museum: No. 5765, Kazan. No. 5766, Kuibyshev. No. 5767, Frunze.

1989, Apr. 14 Litho. *Perf. 12*
5765 A2727 5k rose brown & multi .20 .20
5766 A2727 5k olive gray & multi .20 .20
5767 A2727 5k deep brown & multi .20 .20
Nos. 5765-5767 (3) .60 .60

Lenin's 119th Birth Anniv.

Souvenir Sheet

Launch of Interplanetary Probe *Phobos* — A2783

1989, Apr. 24 *Perf. 11½x12*
5768 A2783 50k multicolored 1.75 1.00

A2784

A2785

1989, May 5 Photo. *Perf. 11½*
5769 A2784 5k multicolored .25 .20

Hungarian Soviet Republic, 70th anniv.

1989, May 5 Photo. & Engr.
5770 A2785 5k multicolored .25 .20

Volgograd, 400th anniv.

Honeybees A2786

1989, May 18 Litho. *Perf. 12*
5771 A2786 5k Drone .20 .20
5772 A2786 10k Workers, flowers, man-made hive .20 .20
5773 A2786 20k Worker collecting pollen .45 .25
5774 A2786 35k Queen, drones, honeycomb .75 .50
Nos. 5771-5774 (4) 1.60 1.15

No. 5771 exists imperf.

Photography, 150th Anniv. — A2787

1989, May 24 Photo. *Perf. 11½*
5775 A2787 5k multicolored .25 .20

I.A. Kuratov (1839-1875), Author — A2788

1989, June 26 Litho. *Perf. 12½x12*
5776 A2788 5k dark golden brown .25 .20

Jean Racine (1639-1699), French Dramatist A2789

Photo. & Engr.

1989, June 16 ***Perf. 12x11½***
5777 A2789 15k multicolored .35 .25

Europe, Our Common Home — A2790

Designs: 5k, Map of Europe, stylized bird. 10k, Crane, two men completing a bridge, globe. 15k, Stork's nest, globe.

1989, June 20 **Photo.** ***Perf. 11½***
5778 A2790 5k multicolored .20 .20
5779 A2790 10k multicolored .35 .20
5780 A2790 15k multicolored .50 .35
Nos. 5778-5780 (3) 1.05 .75

Mukhina, by Nesterov A2791

1989, June 25 **Litho.** ***Perf. 12x12½***
5781 A2791 5k chalky blue .20 .20

Vera I. Mukhina (1889-1953), sculptor.

13th World Youth and Student Festival, Pyongyang A2792

1989, July 1 **Litho.** ***Perf. 12***
5782 A2792 10k multicolored .35 .20

Ducks A2793

1989, July 1
5783 A2793 5k *Tadorna tadorna* .20 .20
5784 A2793 15k *Anas crecca* .40 .25
5785 A2793 20k *Tadorna ferruginea* .50 .40
a. Min. sheet, 2 5k, 4 15k, 3 20k 4.25 3.00
Nos. 5783-5785 (3) 1.10 .85

French Revolution, Bicent. A2794

Designs: 5k, PHILEXFRANCE '89 emblem and Storming of the Bastille. 15k, Marat, Danton, Robespierre. 20k, "La Marseillaise," from the Arc de Triomphe carved by Francois Rude (1784-1855).

Photo. & Engr., Photo. (15k)

1989, July 7 ***Perf. 11½***
5786 A2794 5k multicolored .20 .20
5787 A2794 15k multicolored .40 .25
5788 A2794 20k multicolored .50 .40
a. Miniature sheet of 8 5.25
Nos. 5786-5788 (3) 1.10 .85

A2795

A2795a

A2795b

A2795c

Folklore and Legends A2795d

Designs: No. 5789, *Amiraniani,* Georgian lore. No. 5790, *Koroglu,* Azerbaijan lore. No. 5791, *Fir, Queen of the Grass-snakes,* Lithuanian lore. No. 5792, *Mioritsa,* Moldavian lore. No. 5793, *Lachplesis,* Latvian lore.

1989, July 12 **Litho.** ***Perf. 12x12½***
5789 A2795 10k multicolored .35 .20
5790 A2795a 10k multicolored .35 .20
5791 A2795b 10k multicolored .35 .20
5792 A2795c 10k multicolored .35 .20
5793 A2795d 10k multicolored .35 .20
Nos. 5789-5793 (5) 1.75 1.00

Each printed with a se-tenant label. See types A2753-A2753d & #5890-5894.

Tallinn Zoo, 50th Anniv. — A2796

Intl. Letter Writing Week — A2797

1989, July 20 **Photo.** ***Perf. 11½***
5794 A2796 10k Lynx .35 .20

1989, July 20 **Litho.** ***Perf. 12***
5795 A2797 5k multicolored .25 .20

Exists imperf.

Pulkovskaya Observatory, 150th Anniv. — A2798

Photo. & Engr.

1989, July 20 ***Perf. 11½***
5796 A2798 10k multicolored .35 .20

Souvenir Sheet

Peter the Great and Battle Scene — A2799

1989, July 27 **Photo.** ***Perf. 11½x12***
5797 A2799 50k dk bl & dk brn 1.75 1.10

Battle of Hango, 275th anniv.

City of Nikolaev, Bicent. A2800

1989, Aug. 3 **Photo.** ***Perf. 11½***
5798 A2800 5k multicolored .25 .20

80th Birth Anniv. of Kwame Nkrumah, 1st Pres. of Ghana — A2801

1989, Aug. 9
5799 A2801 10k multicolored .35 .20

6th Congress of the All-Union Philatelic Soc., Moscow A2802

1989, Aug. 9 ***Perf. 12***
5800 A2802 10k bl, blk & pink .35 .20

Printed se-tenant with label picturing simulated stamps and congress emblem.

James Fenimore Cooper (1789-1851), American Novelist A2803

Photo. & Engr.

1989, Aug. 19 ***Perf. 12x11½***
5801 A2803 15k multicolored .50 .35

A2804

Soviet Circus Performers — A2805

Performers and scenes from their acts: 1k, V.L. Durov, clown and trainer. 3k, M.N. Rumyantsev, clown. 4k, V.I. Filatov, bear trainer. 5k, E.T. Kio, magician. 10k, V.E. Lazarenko, acrobat and clown. 30k, Moscow Circus, Tsvetnoi Boulevard.

1989, Aug. 22 **Litho.** ***Perf. 12***
5802 A2804 1k multicolored .20 .20
5803 A2804 3k multicolored .20 .20
5804 A2804 4k multicolored .20 .20
5805 A2804 5k multicolored .20 .20
5806 A2804 10k multicolored .20 .20
Nos. 5802-5806 (5) 1.00 1.00

Souvenir Sheet

Perf. 12x12½
5807 A2805 30k multicolored 1.00 .70

Nos. 5802-5806 exist imperf. Value, $25 each.

5th World Boxing Championships, Moscow — A2806

1989, Aug. 25 **Photo.** ***Perf. 11½***
5808 A2806 15k multicolored .50 .35

Aleksandr Popov (1859-1905), Inventor of Radio in Russia — A2807

Design: *Demonstration of the First Radio Receiver,* 1895, by N. Sysoev.

1989, Oct. 5 Litho. *Perf. 12x12½*
5809 A2807 10k multicolored .35 .20

A2808

A2811

Polish People's Republic, 45th Anniv. A2809

1989, Oct. 7 Photo. *Perf. 11½*
5810 A2808 5k multicolored .20 .20

German Democratic Republic, 40th anniv.

1989, Oct. 7
5811 A2809 5k multicolored .25 .20

Party Leader Type of 1988

1989, Oct. 10 Engr. *Perf. 12*
5812 A2712 5k black .25 .20

S.V. Kosior (1889-1939).

1989, Oct. 10
5813 A2811 15k dark red brown .25 .25

Jawaharlal Nehru, 1st prime minister of independent India.

Guardsmen of October, by M.M. Chepik — A2812

1989, Oct. 14 Litho. *Perf. 12½x12*
5814 A2812 5k multicolored .25 .20

October Revolution, 72nd anniv.
Exists imperf. Value, $25.

Kosta Khetagurov (1859-1906), Ossetic Poet — A2813

1989, Oct. 14
5815 A2813 5k dark red brown .25 .20

Exists imperf.

A2814

A2815

1989, Oct. 14 Photo. *Perf. 11½*
5816 A2814 5k buff, sepia & black .25 .20

Li Dazhao (1889-1927), communist party leader of China.

1989, Oct. 20 Engr. *Perf. 12*
5817 A2815 5k black .25 .20

Jan Karlovich Berzin (1889-1938), army intelligence leader.

Russian — A2816

Musical Instruments: No. 5819, Byelorussian. No. 5820, Ukrainian. No. 5821, Uzbek.

Photo. & Engr.

1989, Oct. 20 *Perf. 12x11½*

Denomination Color

5818 A2816 10k blue .30 .20
5819 A2816 10k brown .30 .20
5820 A2816 10k lemon .30 .20
5821 A2816 10k blue green .30 .20
Nos. 5818-5821 (4) 1.20 .80

See Nos. 5929-5932, 6047-6049.

Scenes from Novels by James Fenimore Cooper A2817

Designs: No. 5822, *The Hunter,* (settlers, canoe). No. 5823, *Last of the Mohicans* (Indians, settlers). No. 5824, *The Pathfinder,* (couple near cliff). No. 5825, *The Pioneers* (women, wild animals). No. 5826, *The Prairie* (injured Indians, horse).

1989, Nov. 17 Litho. *Perf. 12x12½*
5822 A2817 20k multicolored .60 .40
5823 A2817 20k multicolored .60 .40
5824 A2817 20k multicolored .60 .40
5825 A2817 20k multicolored .60 .40
5826 A2817 20k multicolored .60 .40
a. Strip of 5, #5822-5826 3.00 2.00

Printed in a continuous design.

Monuments A2818

#5827, Pokrovsky Cathedral, St. Basil's, statue of K. Minin and D. Pozharsky, Moscow. #5828, Petropavlovsky Cathedral, statue of Peter the Great, Leningrad. #5829, Sofiisky Cathedral, Bogdan Chmielnicki monument, Kiev. #5830, Khodzha Akhmed Yasavi Mausoleum, Turkestan. #5831, Khazret-Khyzr Mosque, Samarkand.

1989, Nov. 20 *Perf. 11½*

Color of "Sky"

5827 A2818 15k tan .50 .30
5828 A2818 15k gray green .50 .30
5829 A2818 15k blue green .50 .30
5830 A2818 15k violet blue .50 .30
5831 A2818 15k bright blue .50 .30
Nos. 5827-5831 (5) 2.50 1.50

New Year 1990 A2819

1989, Nov. 22 *Perf. 12*
5832 A2819 5k multicolored .25 .20

Space Achievements A2820

Designs: Nos. 5833, 5837a, Unmanned Soviet probe on the Moon. Nos. 5834, 5837b, American astronaut on Moon, 1969. Nos. 5835, 5837c, Soviet cosmonaut and American astronaut on Mars. Nos. 5836, 5837d, Mars, planetary body, diff.

1989, Nov. 24
5833 A2820 25k multicolored .75 .55
5834 A2820 25k multicolored .75 .55
5835 A2820 25k multicolored .75 .55
5836 A2820 25k multicolored .75 .55
a. Block of 4, #5833-5836 3.00 2.20

Souvenir Sheet

Imperf

5837 Sheet of 4 3.00 2.20
a.-d. A2820 25k any single .75 .55

World Stamp Expo '89, Washington DC, Nov. 17-Dec. 3; 20th UPU Cong.
See US No. C126.

Type of 1988

Dated 1988

1989, Dec. 25 Litho. *Perf. 12x12½*
5838 A2765 1k dark brown .20 .20
5839 A2765 3k dark blue green .20 .20
5840 A2765 4k indigo .20 .20
5841 A2765 5k red .20 .20
5842 A2765 10k claret .30 .20
5843 A2765 15k deep blue .45 .30
5844 A2765 20k olive gray .60 .40
5845 A2765 25k dark green .75 .50
5846 A2765 30k dark blue .90 .60
5847 A2765 35k dark red brown 1.00 .70
5848 A2765 50k sapphire 1.50 1.00
5849 A2765 1r blue gray 3.00 2.00
Nos. 5838-5849 (12) 9.30 6.50

For surcharges see Uzbekistan #15, 22, 25-26, 61B, 61D, 61F.

Admirals Type of 1987

Miniature Sheet

Admirals & battle scenes: 5k, V.A. Kornilov (1806-54). 10k, V.I. Istomin (1809-55). 15k, G.I. Nevelskoi (1813-76). 20k, G.I. Butakov (1820-82). 30k, A.A. Popov (1821-98). 35k, Stepan O. Makarov (1849-1904).

1989, Dec. 28 Engr. *Perf. 12½x12*
5850 Sheet of 6 3.00 2.00
a. A2705 5k brown & Prus blue .20 .20
b. A2705 10k brown & Prus blue .25 .20
c. A2705 15k dark blue & Prus blue .40 .25
d. A2705 20k dark blue & Prus blue .50 .35
e. A2705 30k brown & Prus blue .75 .50
f. A2705 35k brown & Prus blue .85 .60

Global Ecology — A2821

10k, Flower dying, industrial waste entering the environment. 15k, Bird caught in industrial waste, Earth. 20k, Sea of chopped trees.

1990, Jan. 5 Photo. *Perf. 11½*
5851 A2821 10k multicolored .35 .20
5852 A2821 15k multicolored .50 .35
5853 A2821 20k multicolored .65 .45
Nos. 5851-5853 (3) 1.50 1.00

Capitals of the Republics

A2822

A2822a

A2822b

A2822c

A2822d

A2822e

A2822f

A2822g

A2822h

A2822i

A2822j

A2822k

A2822l

A2822m

A2822n

1990, Jan. 18 Litho. *Perf. 12x12½*

5854 A2822 5k Moscow .20 .20
5855 A2822a 5k Tallinn .20 .20
5856 A2822b 5k Riga .20 .20
5857 A2822c 5k Vilnius .20 .20
5858 A2822d 5k Minsk .20 .20
5859 A2822e 5k Kiev .20 .20
5860 A2822f 5k Kishinev .20 .20
5861 A2822g 5k Tbilisi .20 .20
5862 A2822h 5k Yerevan .20 .20
5863 A2822i 5k Baku .20 .20
5864 A2822j 5k Alma-Ata .20 .20
5865 A2822k 5k Tashkent .20 .20
5866 A2822l 5k Frunze .20 .20
5867 A2822m 5k Ashkhabad .20 .20
5868 A2822n 5k Dushanbe .20 .20
Nos. 5854-5868 (15) 3.00 3.00

A2823

A2824

1990, Feb. 3 *Perf. 11½*

5869 A2823 10k black & brown .35 .25

Ho Chi Minh (1890-1969).

1990, Feb. 3 Photo.

5870 A2824 5k multicolored .20 .20

Vietnamese Communist Party, 60th anniv.

Owls A2825

Perf. 12x12½, 12½x12

1990, Feb. 8 Litho.

5871 A2825 10k *Nyctea scandiaca* .30 .20
5872 A2825 20k *Bubo bubo,* vert. .60 .40
5873 A2825 55k *Asio otus* 1.60 1.00
Nos. 5871-5873 (3) 2.50 1.60

Penny Black, 150th Anniv. A2826

Emblems and various Penny Blacks: No. 5875, Position TP. No. 5876, Position TF. No. 5877, Position AH. No. 5878, Position VK. No. 5879, Position AE.

1990, Feb. 15 Photo. *Perf. 11½*

5874 A2826 10k shown .35 .20
5875 A2826 20k gold & black .65 .45
5876 A2826 20k gold & black .65 .45
5877 A2826 35k multicolored 1.10 .75
5878 A2826 35k multicolored 1.10 .75
Nos. 5874-5878 (5) 3.85 2.60

Souvenir Sheet

Perf. 12x11½

5879 A2826 1r dk green & blk 3.25 2.25

Stamp World London '90 (35k).
No. 5879 contains one 37x26mm stamp.

ITU, 125th Anniv. A2827

1990, Feb. 20 Photo. *Perf. 11½*

5880 A2827 20k multicolored .70 .45

Labor Day A2828

1990, Mar. 28 Photo. *Perf. 11½*

5881 A2828 5k multicolored .20 .20

Victory, 1945, by A. Lysenko A2829

1990, Mar. 28 Litho. *Perf. 12x12½*

5882 A2829 5k multicolored .20 .20

End of World War II, 45th anniv.

Mir Space Station, Cosmonaut A2830

1990, Apr. 12

5883 A2830 20k multicolored .60 .45

Cosmonauts' Day.

Lenin, 120th Birth Anniv. — A2831

1990, Apr. 14 Engr. *Perf. 11½*

5884 A2831 5k red brown .20 .20

LENINIANA '90 all-union philatelic exhibition.

Lenin Birthday Type of 1988

Portrait of Lenin and: No. 5885, Lenin Memorial (birthplace), Ulyanovsk. No. 5886, Branch of the Central Lenin Museum, Baku. No. 5887, Branch of the Central Lenin Museum, Tashkent.

1990, Apr. 14 Litho. *Perf. 12*

5885 A2727 5k dark car & multi .20 .20
5886 A2727 5k rose vio & multi .20 .20
5887 A2727 5k dark grn & multi .20 .20
Nos. 5885-5887 (3) .60 .60

Lenin, 120th Birth Anniv.

Tchaikovsky, Scene from *Iolanta* — A2832

1990, Apr. 25 Engr. *Perf. 12½x12*

5888 A2832 15k black .45 .30

Tchaikovsky (1840-1893), composer.

Kalmyk Legend *Dzhangar,* 550th Anniv. — A2833

1990, May 22 Litho. *Perf. 12x12½*

5889 A2833 10k blk & blk brn .30 .25

Folklore Type of 1989

Designs: No. 5890, *Manas,* Kirghiz legend (Warrior with saber leading battle). No. 5891, *Guraguli,* Tadzhik legend (Armored warriors and elephant). No. 5892, *David Sasunsky,* Armenian legend (Men, arches), vert. No. 5893, *Gerogly,* Turkmen legend (Sleeping woman, man with lute), vert. No. 5894, *Kalevipoeg,* Estonian legend (Man with boards), vert. Nos. 5890-5894 printed se-tenant with descriptive label.

1990, May 22 *Perf. 12½x12, 12x12½*

5890 A2795 10k multicolored .30 .20
5891 A2795 10k multicolored .30 .20
5892 A2795 10k multicolored .30 .20
5893 A2795 10k multicolored .30 .20
5894 A2795 10k multicolored .30 .20
Nos. 5890-5894 (5) 1.50 1.00

World Cup Soccer Championships, Italy 1990 — A2834

Various soccer players.

1990, May 25 *Perf. 12x12½*

5895 A2834 5k multicolored .20 .20
5896 A2834 10k multicolored .35 .25
5897 A2834 15k multicolored .45 .30
5898 A2834 25k multicolored .80 .55
5899 A2834 35k multicolored 1.10 .75
a. Strip of 5, #5895-5899 3.00 2.00

A2835

1990, June 5 Litho. *Perf. 11½*

5900 A2835 15k multicolored .45 .30

Final agreement, European Conference on Security and Cooperation, 15th anniv.

45th World Shooting Championships, Moscow — A2836

1990, June 5 Photo.

5901 A2836 15k multicolored .45 .30

Cooperation in Antarctic Research A2837

1990, June 13 Litho. *Perf. 12x12½*

5902 A2837 5k Scientists on ice .20 .20
5903 A2837 50k Krill 1.50 1.00
a. Souv. sheet of 2, #5902-5903 1.75

See Australia Nos. 1182-1183.

Goodwill Games A2838

1990, June 14 Litho. *Perf. 11½*

5904 A2838 10k multicolored .35 .25

Souvenir Sheet

Battle of the Neva River, 750th Anniv. — A2839

1990, June 20 Litho. *Perf. 12½x12*

5905 A2839 50k multicolored 1.75 1.25

Duck Conservation — A2840

1990, July 1 Litho. *Perf. 12*

5906 A2840 5k Anas platyrhychos .20 .20
5907 A2840 15k Bucephala clangula .55 .35
5908 A2840 20k Netta rufina .75 .50
Nos. 5906-5908 (3) 1.50 1.05

Poultry A2841

1990, July 1 *Perf. 12x12½*

5909 A2841 5k Obroshinsky geese .20 .20
5910 A2841 10k Adler rooster & hen .35 .25
5911 A2841 15k North Caucasian turkeys .55 .35
Nos. 5909-5911 (3) 1.10 .80

Spaso-Efrosinievsky Monastery, Polotsk — A2842

Statue of Nicholas Baratashvili and Pantheon, Mtasminda A2843

Palace of Shirvanshahs, Baku A2844

Statue of Stefan III the Great, Kishinev — A2845

St. Nshan's Church, Akhpat — A2846

Historic Architecture: No. 5915, Cathedral, Vilnius. No. 5917, St. Peter's Church, Riga. No. 5919, Niguliste Church, Tallinn.

1990, Aug. 1 Litho. *Perf. 11½*

5912	A2842	15k	multicolored	.40	.25
5913	A2843	15k	multicolored	.40	.25
5914	A2844	15k	multicolored	.40	.25
5915	A2842	15k	multicolored	.40	.25
5916	A2845	15k	multicolored	.40	.25
5917	A2842	15k	multicolored	.40	.25
5918	A2846	15k	multicolored	.40	.25
5919	A2842	15k	multicolored	.40	.25
			Nos. 5912-5919 (8)	3.20	2.00

See Nos. 5968-5970.

Prehistoric Animals — A2847

1990, Aug. 15

5920	A2847	1k	Sordes	.20	.20
5921	A2847	3k	Chalicotherium	.20	.20
5922	A2847	5k	Indricotherium	.20	.20
5923	A2847	10k	Saurolophus	.30	.20
5924	A2847	20k	Thyestes	.60	.45
			Nos. 5920-5924 (5)	1.50	1.25

Nos. 5921-5923 vert.

Indian Child's Drawing of the Kremlin A2848

No. 5926, Russian child's drawing of India.

1990, Aug. 15 *Perf. 12*

5925	A2848	10k	multicolored	.35	.25
5926	A2848	10k	multicolored	.35	.25
a.			Pair, #5925-5926	.70	.50

See India Nos. 1318-1319.

A2849 A2850

1990, Sept. 12 Engr. *Perf. 12x11½*

5927 A2849 5k blue .20 .20

Letter Writing Week.

1990, Sept. 12 *Perf. 11½*

5928 A2850 5k multicolored .20 .20

Traffic safety.

Musical Instruments Type of 1989

#5929, Kazakh. #5930, Georgian. #5931, Azerbaijanian. #5932, Lithuanian.

Photo. & Engr.

1990, Sept. 20 *Perf. 12x11½*

Denomination Color

5929	A2816	10k	brown	.35	.25
5930	A2816	10k	green	.35	.25
5931	A2816	10k	orange	.35	.25
5932	A2816	10k	blue	.35	.25
			Nos. 5929-5932 (4)	1.40	1.00

Killer Whales A2855

Northern Sea Lions A2856

Sea Otter A2857

Common Dolphin A2858

1990, Oct. 3 Litho. *Perf. 12x11½*

5933	A2855	25k	multicolored	.80	.55
5934	A2856	25k	multicolored	.80	.55
5935	A2857	25k	multicolored	.80	.55
5936	A2858	25k	multicolored	.80	.55
a.			Block of 4, #5933-5936	3.25	2.25

See US Nos. 2508-2511.

October Revolution, 73rd Anniv. — A2859

Design: Lenin Among the Delegates to the 2nd Congress of Soviets, by S.V. Gerasimov.

1990, Oct. 10 Litho. *Perf. 12x12½*

5937 A2859 5k multicolored .20 .20

Nobel Laureates in Literature — A2860

1990, Oct. 22 *Perf. 12*

#5938, Ivan A. Bunin (1870-1953). #5939, Boris Pasternak (1890-1960). #5940, Mikhail A. Sholokov (1905-1984).

5938	A2860	15k	brown olive	.40	.25
5939	A2860	15k	bluish black	.40	.25
5940	A2860	15k	black	.40	.25
			Nos. 5938-5940 (3)	1.20	.75

Submarines — A2861

1990, Nov. 14 Litho. *Perf. 12*

5941	A2861	5k	Sever-2	.20	.20
5942	A2861	10k	Tinro-2	.30	.20
5943	A2861	15k	Argus	.50	.30
5944	A2861	25k	Paisis	.80	.55
5945	A2861	35k	Mir	1.10	.75
			Nos. 5941-5945 (5)	2.90	2.00

A2862 A2863

Armenia-Mother Monument by E. Kochar.

1990, Nov. 27 Litho. *Perf. 11½*

5946 A2862 10k multicolored .35 .25

Armenia '90 Philatelic Exhibition.

1990, Nov. 29 Photo. *Perf. 11½*

Soviet Agents: #5947, Rudolf I. Abel (1903-71). #5948, Kim Philby (1912-88). #5949, Konon T. Molody (1922-70). #5950, S.A. Vaupshasov (1899-1976). #5951, I.D. Kudrya (1912-42).

5947	A2863	5k	black & brown	.20	.20
5948	A2863	5k	black & bluish blk	.20	.20
5949	A2863	5k	black & yel brown	.20	.20
5950	A2863	5k	black & yel green	.20	.20
5951	A2863	5k	black & brown	.20	.20
			Nos. 5947-5951 (5)	1.00	1.00

Joint Soviet-Japanese Space Flight — A2864

1990, Dec. 2 Litho. *Perf. 12*

5952 A2864 20k multicolored .70 .50

Happy New Year — A2865

Illustration reduced.

1990, Dec. 3 *Perf. 11½*

5953 A2865 5k multicolored .20 .20
b. Miniature sheet of 8

Charter for a New Europe — A2865a

1990, Dec. 31 Litho. *Perf. 11½*

5953A A2865a 30k Globe, Eiffel Tower 1.10 .80

Marine Life A2866

1991, Jan. 4 Litho. *Perf. 12*

5954	A2866	4k	Rhizostoma pulmo	.20	.20
5955	A2866	5k	Anemonia sulcata	.20	.20
5956	A2866	10k	Squalus acanthias	.30	.20
5957	A2866	15k	Engraulis encrasicolus	.50	.35
5958	A2866	20k	Tursiops truncatus	.65	.45
			Nos. 5954-5958 (5)	1.85	1.40

Chernobyl Nuclear Disaster, 5th Anniv. A2867

1991, Jan. 22 *Perf. 11½*

5959 A2867 15k multicolored .55 .40

Sorrento Coast with View of Capri, 1826, by S.F. Shchedrin (1791-1830) — A2868

Evening in the Ukraine, 1878, by A.I. Kuindzhi (1841-1910) — A2869

Paintings: No. 5961, New Rome, St. Angel's Castle, 1823, by Shchedrin. No. 5963, Birch Grove, 1879, by Kuindzhi.

1991, Jan. 25 *Perf. 12½x12*

5960	A2868	10k	multicolored	.35	.25
5961	A2868	10k	multicolored	.35	.25
a.			Pair, #5960-5961+label	.70	.50
5962	A2869	10k	multicolored	.35	.25
5963	A2869	10k	multicolored	.35	.25
a.			Pair, #5962-5963+label	.70	.50
			Nos. 5960-5963 (4)	1.40	1.00

Paul Keres (1916-1975), Chess Grandmaster — A2870

1991, Jan. 7 Litho. *Perf. 11½*

5964 A2870 15k dark brown .55 .40

Environmental Protection — A2871

Designs: 10k, Bell tower near Kaliazin, Volga River region. 15k, Lake Baikal. 20k, Desert zone of former Aral Sea.

1991, Feb. 5 Litho. *Perf. 11½*

5965	A2871	10k	multicolored	.30	.25
5966	A2871	15k	multicolored	.50	.35
5967	A2871	20k	multicolored	.65	.45
			Nos. 5965-5967 (3)	1.45	1.05

Moslem Tower, Uzgen, Kirghizia A2872

Mukhammed Bashar Mausoleum, Tadzhikstan A2873

Talkhatan-baba Mosque, Turkmenistan A2874

1991, Mar. 5

5968	A2872	15k	multicolored	.20	.20
5969	A2873	15k	multicolored	.20	.20
5970	A2874	15k	multicolored	.20	.20
			Nos. 5968-5970 (3)	.60	.60

See Nos. 5912-5919.

Russian Settlements in America — A2875

Designs: 20k, G. I. Shelekhov (1747-1795), Alaska colonizer. 30k, A. A. Baranov, (1746-1819), first governor of Russian America. 50k, I. A. Kuskov, founder of Fort Ross, California.

1991, Mar. 14 *Perf. 12x11½*

5971	A2875	20k	brt blue & black	.45	.35
5972	A2875	30k	olive brn & blk	.75	.55
5973	A2875	50k	red brn & black	1.25	.80
			Nos. 5971-5973 (3)	2.45	1.70

Yuri A. Gagarin A2876

МЕЖДУНАРОДНАЯ ВЫСТАВКА
«К ЗВЕЗДАМ-91»
КОСМОС НА СЛУЖБЕ МИРА И ПРОГРЕССА

No. 5977c Inscription

1991, Apr. 6 *Perf. 11½x12*

5974	A2876	25k	Pilot	.90	.70
5975	A2876	25k	Cosmonaut	.90	.70
5976	A2876	25k	Pilot, wearing hat	.90	.70
5977	A2876	25k	As civilian	.90	.70
a.			Block of 4, #5974-5977	3.60	2.80
b.			Sheet of 4, #5974-5977, imperf.	3.60	2.80
c.			As "b," inscribed	3.60	2.80
d.			Sheet, 2 each, #5974-5977, Perf. 12x11½	7.20	5.50

#5977b-5977c have simulated perforations.

May 1945 by A. and S. Tkachev A2877

1991, Apr. 10 *Perf. 12*

5978	A2877	5k	multicolored	.25	.20

World War II Victory Day.

Asia and Pacific Transport Network, 10th Anniv. — A2878

1991, Apr. 15 *Perf. 11½*

5979	A2878	10k	multicolored	.25	.20

Type of 1988 Dated 1991

Designs: 2k, Early ship, train, and carriage. 7k, Airplane, helicopter, ocean liner, cable car, van. 12k, Space shuttle. 13k, Space station.

1991, Apr. 15 Litho. *Perf. 12x12½*

5984	A2765	2k	orange brown	.20	.20
5985	A2765	7k	bright blue	.25	.20
a.			Perf. 12x11½, photo.	.25	.20
5986	A2765	12k	dk lilac rose	.45	.30
5987	A2765	13k	deep violet	.50	.35
			Nos. 5984-5987 (4)	1.40	1.05

For surcharges see Tadjikistan #10-11, Uzbekistan #18, 61C.

Lenin, 121st Birth Anniv. A2879

Painting: Lenin working on "Materialism and Empirical Criticism" by P.P. Belousov.

1991, Apr. 22 Litho. *Perf. 12*

5992	A2879	5k	multicolored	.20	.20

Sergei Prokofiev (1891-1953), Composer — A2880

1991, Apr. 23 *Perf. 12½x12*

5993	A2880	15k	brown	.50	.40

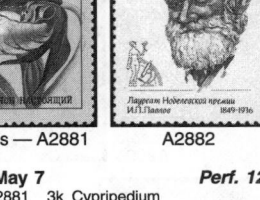

Orchids — A2881

A2882

1991, May 7 *Perf. 12*

5994	A2881	3k	Cypripedium calceolus	.20	.20
5995	A2881	5k	Orchis purpurea	.20	.20
5996	A2881	10k	Ophrys apifera	.25	.20
5997	A2881	20k	Calypso bulbosa	.45	.35
5998	A2881	25k	Epipactis palustris	.60	.40
			Nos. 5994-5998 (5)	1.70	1.35

1991, May 14

Nobel Prize Winners: #5999, Ivan P. Pavlov (1849-1936), 1904, Physiology. #6000, Elie Metchnikoff (1845-1916), 1908, Physiology. #6001, Andrei D. Sakharov, (1921-89), 1975, Peace.

5999	A2882	15k	black	.40	.30
6000	A2882	15k	black	.40	.30
6001	A2882	15k	blue black	.40	.30
			Nos. 5999-6001 (3)	1.20	.90

William Saroyan (1908-1981), American Writer — A2883

1991, May 22 *Perf. 11½*

6002	A2883	1r	multicolored	3.00	2.25

See US No. 2538.

Russia-Great Britain Joint Space Mission — A2884

1991, May 18 Litho. *Perf. 12*

6003	A2884	20k	multicolored	.70	.50

Cultural Heritage A2885

Designs: 10k, Miniature from "Ostomirov Gospel," by Sts. Cyril & Methodius, 1056-1057. 15k, "Russian Truth," manuscript, 11th-13th century by Jaroslav Mudrin. 20k, Sergei Radonezhski by Troitse Sergeiev Lavra, 1424. 25k, Trinity, icon by Andrei Rublev, c. 1411. 30k, Illustration from "Book of the Apostles," by Ivan Feodorov and Petr Mstislavetz, 1564.

1991, June 20 Litho. *Perf. 12x12½*

6004	A2885	10k	multicolored	.30	.25
6005	A2885	15k	multicolored	.50	.35
6006	A2885	20k	multicolored	.65	.50
6007	A2885	25k	multicolored	.80	.60
6008	A2885	30k	multicolored	1.00	.80
a.			Strip of #6004-6008	3.25	2.50

Ducks A2886

Designs: 5k, Anas acuta. 15k, Aythya marila. 20k, Oxyura leucocephala.

1991, July 1 *Perf. 12*

6009	A2886	5k	multicolored	.20	.20
6010	A2886	15k	multicolored	.45	.35
6011	A2886	20k	multicolored	.60	.45
a.			Min. sheet of 9, 2 #6009, 4 #6010, 3 #6011	4.75	3.25
			Nos. 6009-6011 (3)	1.25	1.00

Airships A2887

Designs: 1k, Albatross, 1910, vert. 3k, GA-42, 1987, vert. 4k, Norge, 1923. 5k, Victory, 1944. 20k, Graf Zeppelin, 1928.

1991, July 18

6012	A2887	1k	multicolored	.20	.20
6013	A2887	3k	multicolored	.20	.20
6014	A2887	4k	multicolored	.20	.20
6015	A2887	5k	multicolored	.20	.20
6016	A2887	20k	multicolored	.20	.20
a.			Miniature sheet of 8		
			Nos. 6012-6016 (5)	1.00	1.00

Types of 1984

1991-92 Litho. *Imperf.*

6016B	A2529	2r	Ship, Arctic map	.40	.20

Perf. 12½x12

6017	A2529	3r	Child & globe	.70	.45
6017A	A2529	5r	Palm frond and globe	3.25	2.25
			Nos. 6016B-6017A (3)	4.35	2.90

Issued: 3r, 6/25; 5r, 11/10; 2r, 4/20/92.

Conf. on Security and Cooperation in Europe — A2888

1991, July 1 Photo. *Perf. 11½*

6018	A2888	10k	multicolored	.25	.20

Bering & Chirikov's Voyage to Alaska, 250th Anniv. — A2889

Design: No. 6020, Sailing ship, map.

1991, July 27 *Perf. 12x11½*

6019	A2889	30k	multicolored	.40	.25
6020	A2889	30k	multicolored	.40	.25

A2890

A2891

1991, Aug. 1 *Perf. 12*
6021 A2890 30k multicolored .40 .25

Ukrainian declaration of sovereignty.

1991, Aug. 1 *Perf. 12x11½*
6022 A2891 7k brown .25 .20

Letter Writing Week.

1992 Summer Olympic Games, Barcelona A2892

1991, Sept. 4 Litho. *Perf. 12x12½*
6023 A2892 10k Canoeing .20 .20
a. Miniature sheet of 8
6024 A2892 20k Running .25 .20
a. Miniature sheet of 8
6025 A2892 30k Soccer .40 .25
a. Miniature sheet of 8
Nos. 6023-6025 (3) .85 .65

Victims of Aug. 1991 Failed Coup — A2893

Citizens Protecting Russian "White House" — A2893a

1991, Oct. 11 Litho. *Perf. 11½*
6026 A2893 7k Vladimir Usov, b. 1954 .20 .20
6027 A2893 7k Illya Krichevsky, b. 1963 .20 .20
6028 A2893 7k Dmitry Komar, b. 1968 .20 .20
Nos. 6026-6028 (3) .60 .60

Souvenir Sheet

6029 A2893a 50k multicolored .75 .35

USSR-Austria Joint Space Mission — A2894

1991, Oct. 2 Litho. *Perf. 11½*
6030 A2894 20k multicolored .25 .20

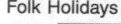

Folk Holidays

Ascension, Armenia A2895

New Year, Azerbaijan A2895a

Ivan Kupala Day, Byelorussia A2895b

Berikaoba, Georgia A2895d

New Year, Estonia A2895c

Kazakhstan — A2895e

Kys Kumai, Kirgizia A2895f

Ivan Kupala Day, Latvia A2895g

Palm Sunday, Lithuania A2895h

Plugushorul, Moldavia A2895i

Shrovetide, Russia — A2895j

New Year, Tadzhikistan A2895k

Spring Tulips, Uzbekistan A2895n

Harvest, Turkmenistan — A2895l

Christmas, Ukraine — A2895m

Perf. 12x12½, 12½x12

1991, Oct. 4 **Litho.**
6031 A2895 15k multicolored .20 .20
6032 A2895a 15k multicolored .20 .20
6033 A2895b 15k multicolored .20 .20
6034 A2895c 15k multicolored .20 .20
6035 A2895d 15k multicolored .20 .20
6036 A2895e 15k multicolored .20 .20
6037 A2895f 15k multicolored .20 .20
6038 A2895g 15k multicolored .20 .20
6039 A2895h 15k multicolored .20 .20
6040 A2895i 15k multicolored .20 .20
6041 A2895j 15k multicolored .20 .20
6042 A2895k 15k multicolored .20 .20
6043 A2895l 15k multicolored .20 .20
6044 A2895m 15k multicolored .20 .20
6045 A2895n 15k multicolored .20 .20
a. Min. sheet, 2 each #6031-6045 *11.25*
Nos. 6031-6045 (15) 3.00 3.00

A2896

1991, Oct. 29 Litho. *Perf. 11½*
6046 A2896 7k multicolored .25 .20

Election of Boris Yeltsin, 1st president of Russian Republic, June 12, 1991.

Musical Instruments Type of 1989

Musical Instruments: No. 6048, Moldavia. No. 6049, Latvia. No. 6050, Kirgiz.

Photo. & Engr.
1991, Nov. 19 *Perf. 12x11½*
Denomination Color
6047 A2816 10k red .20 .20
6048 A2816 10k brt greenish bl .20 .20
6049 A2816 10k red lilac .20 .20
Nos. 6047-6049 (3) .60 .60

New Year 1992 A2897

1991, Dec. 8 Litho. *Perf. 12x12½*
6050 A2897 7k multicolored .25 .20

A2899

A2900

Russian Historians: #6052, V. N. Tatischev (1686-1750). #6053, N. M. Karamzin (1766-1826). #6054, S. M. Soloviev (1820-79). #6055, Vasili O. Klyuchevsky (1841-1911).

1991, Dec. 12 Photo. & Engr.
6052 A2899 10k multicolored .20 .20
6053 A2899 10k multicolored .20 .20
6054 A2899 10k multicolored .20 .20
6055 A2899 10k multicolored .20 .20
Nos. 6052-6055 (4) .80 .80

With the breakup of the Soviet Union on Dec. 26, 1991, eleven former Soviet republics established the Commonwealth of Independent States. Stamps inscribed "Rossija" are issued by the Russian Republic.

1992, Jan. 10 Litho. *Perf. 11½x12*
6056 A2900 14k Cross-country skiing, ski jumping .20 .20
a. Miniature sheet of 8
6057 A2900 1r Freestyle skiing .25 .20
a. Miniature sheet of 8
6058 A2900 2r Bobsleds .55 .25
a. Miniature sheet of 8
Nos. 6056-6058 (3) 1.00 .65

1992 Winter Olympics, Albertville.

Souvenir Sheet

Battle on the Ice, 750th Anniv. — A2901

1992, Feb. 20 Litho. ***Perf. 12½x12***
6059 A2901 50k multicolored .75 .75

A2902

Designs: 10k, Golden Portal, Vladimir. 15k, Kremlin, Pskov. 20k, Georgy the Victor. 25k, 55k, Triumph Gate, Moscow. 30k, "Millennium of Russia," by M.O. Mikeshin, Novgorod. 50k, St. George Slaying the Dragon. 60k, Minin-Posharsky Monument, Moscow. 80k, "Millennium of Russia," by M.O. Mikeshin, Novgorod. 1r, Church, Kizki. 1.50r, Monument to Peter the Great, St. Petersburg. 2r, St. Basil's Cathedral, Moscow. 3r, Tretyakov Gallery, Moscow. 5r, Morosov House, Moscow. 10r, St. Isaac's Cathedral, St. Petersburg. 25r, Monument to Yuri Dolgoruky, Moscow. 100r, Kremlin, Moscow.

Perf. 12½x12, 11½x12 (15k, 25k, 3r)

1992 Litho.

6060	A2902	10k	salmon	.20	.20
6060A	A2902	15k	dark brn	.20	.20
6061	A2902	20k	red	.20	.20
6062	A2902	25k	red brown	.20	.20
6063	A2902	30k	black	.20	.20
6064	A2902	50k	dark blue	.20	.20
6065	A2902	55k	dark bl grn	.20	.20
6066	A2902	60k	blue green	.20	.20
6066A	A2902	80k	lake	.20	.20
6067	A2902	1r	yel brown	.20	.20
6067A	A2902	1.50r	olive	.25	.20
6068	A2902	2r	blue	.20	.20
6068A	A2902	3r	red	.20	.20
6069	A2902	5r	dark brn	.30	.25
6070	A2902	10r	bright blue	.35	.25
6071	A2902	25r	dark red	1.00	.50
6071A	A2902	100r	brt olive	2.00	1.00
	Nos. 6060-6071A (17)			6.30	4.60

Issued: 20k, 30k, 2/26; 10k, 60k, 2r, 4/20; 25r, 5/25; 10r, 100r, May; 1r, 1.50r, 5r, 6/25; 55k, 8/11; 50k, 80k, 8/18; 15k, 25k, 3r, 9/10.

See Nos. 6109-6125A.

Victory by N. N. Baskakov A2903

1992, Mar. 5 ***Perf. 12x12½***
6072 A2903 5k multicolored .20 .20

End of World War II, 47th anniv.

Prioksko-Terrasny Nature Reserve — A2904

1992, Mar. 12 ***Perf. 12***
6073 A2904 50k multicolored .20 .20

Russia-Germany Joint Space Mission — A2905

1992, Mar. 17
6074 A2905 5r multicolored .40 .30

Souvenir Sheet

Discovery of America, 500th Anniv. — A2906

1992, Mar. 18 ***Perf. 12x11½***
6075 A2906 3r Ship, Columbus .90 .90

Characters from Children's Books A2907

1992, Apr. 22 Litho. ***Perf. 12***
6076 A2907 25k Pinocchio .20 .20
6077 A2907 30k Cipollino .20 .20
6078 A2907 35k Dunno .20 .20
6079 A2907 50k Karlson .20 .20
Nos. 6076-6079 (4) .80 .80

Space Accomplishments — A2908

Designs: No. 6081, Astronaut, Russian space station and space shuttle. No. 6082, Sputnik, Vostok, Apollo Command and Lunar modules. No. 6083, Soyuz, Mercury and Gemini spacecraft.

1992, May 29 Litho. ***Perf. 11½x12***
6080 A2908 25r multicolored .50 .35
6081 A2908 25r multicolored .50 .35
6082 A2908 25r multicolored .50 .35
6083 A2908 25r multicolored .50 .35
a. Block of 4, #6080-6083 2.00 1.50

See US Nos. 2631-2634.

1992 Summer Olympics, Barcelona A2909

Perf. 11½x12, 12x11½
1992, June 5 Photo.
6084 A2909 1r Team handball, vert. .20 .20
a. Miniature sheet of 8 .85 .65
6085 A2909 2r Fencing .25 .20
a. Miniature sheet of 8 1.75 1.40
6086 A2909 3r Judo .40 .25
a. Miniature sheet of 8 2.50 2.00
Nos. 6084-6086 (3) .85 .65

Explorers — A2910

Designs: 55r, L. A. Zagoskin, Alaska-Yukon. 70r, N. N. Miklucho-Maklai, New Guinea. 1r, G. I. Langsdorf, Brazil.

1992, June 23 Litho. ***Perf. 12x11½***
6087 A2910 55k multicolored .20 .20
6088 A2910 70k multicolored .20 .20
6089 A2910 1r multicolored .20 .20
Nos. 6087-6089 (3) .60 .60

Ducks A2911

1992, July 1 ***Perf. 12***
6090 A2911 1r Anas querquedula .20 .20
6091 A2911 2r Aythya ferina .20 .20
6092 A2911 3r Anas falcata .20 .20
a. Min. sheet of 9, 3 #6090, 4 #6091, 2 #6092 1.90 1.75
Nos. 6090-6092 (3) .60 .60

The Saviour, by Andrei Rublev A2912

1992, July 3 ***Perf. 12x12½***
6093 A2912 1r multicolored .20 .20
a. Miniature sheet of 8 *1.40* 1.25

The Taj Mahal Mausoleum in Agra, by Vasili Vereshchagin (1842-1904) — A2913

Design: No. 6095, Let Me Approach (detail), by Vereshchagin.

1992, July 3 ***Perf. 12½x12***
6094 A2913 1.50r multicolored .25 .20
6095 A2913 1.50r multicolored .25 .20
a. Pair, #6094-6095 + label .50 .25

Cathedral of the Assumption, Moscow A2914

Cathedral of the Annunciation, Moscow A2915

No. 6098, Archangel Cathedral, Moscow.

1992, Sept. 3 Litho. ***Perf. 11½***
6096 A2914 1r multicolored .20 .20
a. Miniature sheet of 9 1.10
6097 A2915 1r multicolored .20 .20
a. Miniature sheet of 9 1.10
6098 A2915 1r multicolored .20 .20
a. Miniature sheet of 9 1.10
Nos. 6096-6098 (3) .60 .60

The Nutcracker, by Tchaikovsky, Cent. — A2916

Designs: No. 6099, Nutcrackers, one holding rifle. No. 6100, Nutcrackers, diff. No. 6101, Pas de deux before Christmas tree. No. 6102, Ballet scene.

1992, Nov. 4 Litho. ***Perf. 12½x12***
6099 A2916 10r multicolored .35 .25
6100 A2916 10r multicolored .35 .25
6101 A2916 25r multicolored .70 .50
6102 A2916 25r multicolored .70 .50
a. Block of 4, #6099-6102 2.10 1.75

A2917

A2918

A2919

Icons — A2920

Christmas: No. 6103, Joachim and Anna, 16th cent. No. 6104, Madonna and Child, 14th cent. No. 6105, Archangel Gabriel, 12th cent. No. 6106, St. Nicholas, 16th cent.

1992, Nov. 27 ***Perf. 11½***
6103 A2917 10r multicolored .45 .35
6104 A2918 10r multicolored .45 .35
6105 A2919 10r multicolored .45 .35
6106 A2920 10r multicolored .45 .35
a. Block of 4, #6103-6106 1.90 1.75

See Sweden Nos. 1979-1982.

New Year 1993 A2921

1992, Dec. 2 Litho. ***Perf. 12x12½***
6107 A2921 50k multicolored .20 .20
a. Miniature sheet of 9 1.50

Discovery of America, 500th Anniv. — A2922

1992, Dec. 29 ***Perf. 11½x12***
6108 A2922 15r Flags, sculpture .60 .40

Monuments Type of 1992

Designs: 4r, Church, Kizki. 6r, Monument to Peter the Great, St. Petersburg. 15r, 45r, The Horsebreaker, St. Petersburg. 50r, Kremlin, Rostov. 75r, Monument to Yuri Dolgoruky, Moscow. 150r, Golden Gate of Vladimir. 250r, Church, Bogolubova. 300r, Monument of Minin and Pozharsky. 500r, Lomonosov University, Moscow. 750r, State Library, Moscow. 1000r, Fortress of St. Peter and St. Paul, St. Petersburg. 1500r, Pushkin Museum, Moscow. 2500r, Admiralty, St. Petersburg. 5000r, Bolshoi Theater, Moscow.

Litho., Photo. (50r, 250r, 500r)
Perf. 12½x12, 12x11½ (1000r)

1992-95

6109	A2902	4r red brown	.20	.20
6110	A2902	6r gray blue	.20	.20
6111	A2902	15r brown	.25	.20
a.		Photo.	.25	.20
6113	A2902	45r slate	.90	.45
6114	A2902	50r purple	.25	.20
6115	A2902	75r red brown	1.75	.70
6118	A2902	150r blue	.30	.25
6119	A2902	250r green	.45	.30
6120	A2902	300r red brown	.60	.45
6121	A2902	500r violet	.90	.60
6122	A2902	750r olive grn	.45	.35
6123	A2902	1000r slate	.70	.50
6124	A2902	1500r green	.90	.60
6125	A2902	2500r olive brn	1.50	1.00
6125A	A2902	5000r blue grn	3.00	2.00
		Nos. 6109-6125A (15)	12.35	8.00

Values are as of date issued. Denominations still available may be sold at much lower prices.

Issued: #6111a, 6114, 6119, 6121, 12/25/92; #6109-6110, 6/4/93; #6113, 6115, 1/25/93; 150r, 300r, 12/30/93; 1000r, 1/27/95; 750r, 1500r, 2500r, 5000r, 2/21/95.

For surcharge see #6529.

This is an expanding set. Numbers may change.

Marius Petipa (1818-1910), Choreographer — A2923

Ballets: No. 6126, Paquita (1847). No. 6127, Sleeping Beauty (1890). No. 6128, Swan Lake (1895). No. 6129, Raymonda (1898).

1993, Jan. 14 Litho. *Perf. 12½x12*

6126	A2923	25r multicolored	.35	.25
6127	A2923	25r multicolored	.35	.25
6128	A2923	25r multicolored	.35	.25
6129	A2923	25r multicolored	.35	.25
a.		Block of 4, #6126-6129	1.75	1.50

A2924

A2925

Characters from Children's Books: a, 2r, Scrub and Rub. b, 3r, Big Cockroach. c, 10r, The Buzzer Fly. d, 15r, Doctor Doolittle. e, 25r, Barmalei.

1993, Feb. 25 Litho. *Perf. 12½x12*

6130	A2924	Strip of 5, #a.-e.	1.25	1.00

No. 6130 printed in continuous design.

1993, Mar. 18 Photo. *Perf. 11½x12*

6131	A2925	10r Vyborg Castle	.25	.20

City of Vyborg, 700th anniv.

Battle of Kursk, 50th Anniv. A2926

1993, Mar. 25 *Perf. 12x12½*

6132	A2926	10r multicolored	.25	.20

Victory Day.

Flowers A2927

Communications Satellites A2928

1993, Mar. 25 *Perf. 12½x12*

6133	A2927	10r Saintpaulia ionantha	.20	.20
6134	A2927	15r Hibiscus rosa-sinensis	.20	.20
6135	A2927	25r Cyclamen persicum	.25	.20
6136	A2927	50r Fuchsia hybrida	.45	.30
6137	A2927	100r Begonia semperflorens	.90	.60
		Nos. 6133-6137 (5)	2.00	1.50

See Nos. 6196-6200.

1993, Apr. 12 Photo. *Perf. 11½*

6138	A2928	25r Molniya-3	.20	.20
6139	A2928	45r Ekran-M	.30	.25
6140	A2928	50r Gorizont	.35	.30
6141	A2928	75r Luch	.55	.40
6142	A2928	100r Express	.70	.55
		Nos. 6138-6142 (5)	2.10	1.70

Souvenir Sheet
Perf. 12x11½

6143	A2928	250r Ground station, horiz.	2.00	1.40

No. 6143 contains one 37x26mm stamp.

Antique Silver A2929

15r, Snuff box, 1820, mug, 1849. 25r, Tea pot, 1896-1908. 45r, Vase, 1896-1908. 75r, Tray, candlestick holder, 1896-1908. 100r, Coffee pot, cream and sugar set, 1852. 250r, Sweet dish, 1896-1908, biscuit dish, 1844.

1993, May 5 Litho. *Perf. 11½*

6144	A2929	15r multicolored	.20	.20
6145	A2929	25r multicolored	.20	.20
6146	A2929	45r multicolored	.30	.20
6147	A2929	75r multicolored	.50	.35
6148	A2929	100r multicolored	.70	.50
		Nos. 6144-6148 (5)	1.90	1.45

Souvenir Sheet
Perf. 12½x12

6149	A2929	250r multicolored	1.75	1.25

No. 6149 contains one 52x37mm stamp.

A2930

Novgorod Kremlin A2931

Designs: No. 6150, Kremlin towers, 14th-17th cent. No. 6151, St. Sofia's Temple, 11th cent. No. 6152, Belfry of St. Sophia's, 15th-18th cent. 250r, Icon, "Sign of the Virgin," 12th cent.

1993, June 4 Litho. *Perf. 12*

6150	A2930	25r multicolored	.20	.20
6151	A2931	25r multicolored	.20	.20
6152	A2931	25r multicolored	.20	.20
		Nos. 6150-6152 (3)	.60	.60

Souvenir Sheet
Perf. 12½x12

6153	A2930	250r multicolored	1.40	1.25

No. 6153 contains one 42x30mm stamp.

Russian-Danish Relations, 500th Anniv. — A2932

1993, June 17 *Perf. 11½*

6154	A2932	90r grn & light grn	.35	.25

See Denmark No. 985.

Ducks A2933

90r, Somateria stelleri. 100r, Somateria mollissima. 250r, Somateria spectabilis.

1993, July 1 Litho. *Perf. 12*

6155	A2933	90r multicolored	.20	.20
6156	A2933	100r multicolored	.20	.20
6157	A2933	250r multicolored	.45	.30
a.		Min. sheet, 4 each #6155-6156, 1 #6157	3.00	
		Nos. 6155-6157 (3)	.85	.70

Sea Life A2934

1993, July 6

6158	A2934	50r Pusa hispida	.20	.20
6159	A2934	60r Paralithodes brevipes	.20	.20
6160	A2934	90r Todarodes pacificus	.35	.25
6161	A2934	100r Oncorhynchus masu	.35	.25
6162	A2934	250r Fulmarus glacialis	1.00	.75
		Nos. 6158-6162 (5)	2.10	1.65

Natl. Museum of Applied Arts and Folk Crafts, Moscow — A2935

Designs: No. 6163, Skopino earthenware candlestick. No. 6164, Painted tray, horiz. No. 6165, Painted box, distaff. No. 6166, Enamel icon of St. Dmitry of Solun. 250r, Fedoskino lacquer miniature Easter egg depicting the Resurrection.

Perf. 12x12½, 12½x12

1993, Aug. 11 Litho.

6163	A2935	50r multicolored	.20	.20
6164	A2935	50r multicolored	.20	.20
6165	A2935	100r multicolored	.35	.25
6166	A2935	100r multicolored	.35	.25
6167	A2935	250r multicolored	.80	.55
		Nos. 6163-6167 (5)	1.90	1.45

Goznak (Bank Note Printer and Mint), 175th Anniv. A2936

1993, Sept. 2 Litho. *Perf. 12*

6168	A2936	100r multicolored	.35	.25

Shipbuilders — A2937

#6169, Peter the Great (1672-1725), Goto Predestinatsia. #6170, K.A. Shilder (1786-1854), first all-metal submarine. #6171, I.A. Amosov (1800-78), screw steamship Archimedes. #6172, I.G. Bubnov (1872-1919), submarine Bars. #6173, B.M. Malinin (1889-1949), submarine Dekabrist. #6174, A.I. Maslov (1894-1968), cruiser Kirov.

1993, Sept. 7

6169	A2937	100r multicolored	.20	.20
6170	A2937	100r multicolored	.20	.20
6171	A2937	100r multicolored	.20	.20
6172	A2937	100r multicolored	.20	.20
6173	A2937	100r multicolored	.20	.20
6174	A2937	100r multicolored	.20	.20
a.		Block of 6, #6169-6174	1.25	1.00

A2938

Moscow Kremlin A2939

#6175, Granovitaya Chamber (1487-91). #6176, Church of Rizpolozheniye (1484-88). #6177, Teremnoi Palace (1635-36).

1993, Oct. 28 Litho. *Perf. 12*

6175	A2938	100r multicolored	.20	.20
6176	A2939	100r multicolored	.20	.20
6177	A2939	100r multicolored	.20	.20
		Nos. 6175-6177 (3)	.60	.60

Panthera Tigris A2940

Designs: 100r, Adult in woods. 250r, Two cubs. 500r, Adult in snow.

1993, Nov. 25 Litho. *Perf. 12½x12*

6178	A2940	50r	multicolored	.20	.20
6179	A2940	100r	multicolored	.20	.20
6180	A2940	250r	multicolored	.35	.25
6181	A2940	500r	multicolored	.90	.60
a.			Block of 4, #6178-6181	1.75	1.50
b.			Miniature sheet, 2 #6181a	4.00	

World Wildlife Fund.

New Year 1994 — A2941

1993, Dec. 2 Photo. *Perf. 11½*

6182	A2941	25r	multicolored	.20	.20
a.			Sheet of 8	.90	

A2942 Wildlife — A2943

1993, Nov. 25 Photo. *Perf. 11½x12*

6183	A2942	90r	gray, blk & red	.20	.20

Prevention of AIDS.

1993, Dec. 30 Litho. *Perf. 12½x12*

6184	A2943	250r	Phascolarctos cinereus	.35	.25
6185	A2943	250r	Monachus schauinslandi	.35	.25
6186	A2943	250r	Haliaeetus leucocephalus	.35	.25
6187	A2943	250r	Elephas maximus	.35	.25
6188	A2943	250r	Grus vipio	.35	.25
6189	A2943	250r	Ailuropoda melanoleuca	.35	.25
6190	A2943	250r	Phocoenoides dalli	.35	.25
6191	A2943	250r	Eschrichtius robustus	.35	.25
a.			Min. sheet of 8, #6184-6191	3.50	
			Nos. 6184-6191 (8)	2.80	2.00

Nikolai Rimsky-Korsakov (1844-1908), Scene from "Sadko" — A2944

Scenes from operas: No. 6193, "Golden Cockerel," 1907. No. 6194, "The Czar's Bride," 1898. No. 6195, "The Snow Maiden," 1881.

1994, Jan. 20 Litho. *Perf. 12½x12*

6192	A2944	250r	multicolored	.35	.25
6193	A2944	250r	multicolored	.35	.25
6194	A2944	250r	multicolored	.35	.25
6195	A2944	250r	multicolored	.35	.25
a.			Block of 4, #6192-6195	1.40	1.25

Flower Type of 1993

Designs: 50r, Epiphyllum peacockii. No. 6197, Mammillaria swinglei. No. 6198, Lophophora williamsii. No. 6199, Opuntia basilaris. No. 6200, Selenicereus grandiflorus.

1994, Feb. 25 Litho. *Perf. 12½x12*

6196	A2927	50r	multicolored	.20	.20
6197	A2927	100r	multicolored	.25	.20
6198	A2927	100r	multicolored	.25	.20
6199	A2927	250r	multicolored	.35	.25
6200	A2927	250r	multicolored	.35	.25
			Nos. 6196-6200 (5)	1.40	1.10

Cathedral of St. Peter, York, Great Britain — A2945

Metropolis Church, Athens — A2946

Gothic Church, Roskilde, Denmark A2947

Notre Dame Cathedral, Paris — A2948

St. Peter's Basilica, Vatican City — A2949

Cologne Cathedral, Germany A2950

St. Basil's Cathedral, Moscow — A2951

Seville Cathedral, Spain — A2952

#6207, St. Patrick's Cathedral, NYC, US.

1994, Mar. 24 Litho. *Perf. 12x12½*

6201	A2945	150r	multicolored	.25	.20
6202	A2946	150r	multicolored	.25	.20
6203	A2947	150r	multicolored	.25	.20
6204	A2948	150r	multicolored	.25	.20
6205	A2949	150r	multicolored	.25	.20
6206	A2950	150r	multicolored	.25	.20
6207	A2950	150r	multicolored	.25	.20
6208	A2951	150r	multicolored	.25	.20
6209	A2952	150r	multicolored	.25	.20
a.			Min. sheet of 9, #6201-6209	*2.75*	

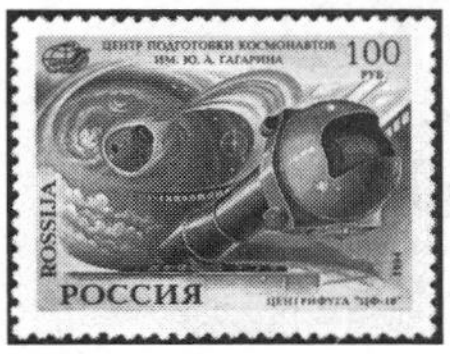

Space Research A2953

Designs: 100r, TS-18 Centrifuge, Soyuz landing module during re-entry. 250r, Soyuz spacecraft docked at Mir space station. 500r, Training in hydrolaboratory, cosmonaut during space walk.

1994, Apr. 12 Litho. *Perf. 12x11½*

6210	A2953	100r	multicolored	.20	.20
6211	A2953	250r	multicolored	.35	.25
6212	A2953	500r	multicolored	.70	.45
			Nos. 6210-6212 (3)	*1.25*	*.90*

Liberation of Soviet Areas, 50th Anniv. A2954

Battle maps and: a, Katyusha rockets, liberation of Russia. b, Fighter planes, liberation of Ukraine. c, Combined offensive, liberation of Belarus.

1994, Apr. 26 *Perf. 12*

6213	A2954	100r	Block of 3 + label	.55	.45

See Belarus No. 78, Ukraine No. 195.

Russian Architecture A2955

Structure, architect: 50r, Krasniye Vorota, Moscow, Prince D.V. Ukhtomsky (1719-74). 100r, Academy of Science, St. Petersburg, Giacomo Quarenghi (1744-1817). 150r, Trinity Cathedral, St. Petersburg, V.P. Stasov (1769-1848). 300r, Church of Christ the Saviour, Moscow, K.A. Ton (1794-1881).

1994, May 25 Litho. *Perf. 12½x12*

6214	A2955	50r	lt brown & blk	.20	.20
6215	A2955	100r	red brn & blk	.20	.20
6216	A2955	150r	olive grn & blk	.20	.20
6217	A2955	300r	gray vio & blk	.30	.25
			Nos. 6214-6217 (4)	.90	.85

Painting Type of 1992

Paintings by V. D. Polenov (1844-1927): No. 6218, Christ and the Adultress, 1886-87. No. 6219, Golden Autumn, 1893.

1994, June 1 Litho. *Perf. 12½x12*

6218	A2913	150r	multicolored	.20	.20
6219	A2913	150r	multicolored	.20	.20
a.			Pair, #6218-6219 + label	.45	.35

Ducks A2956

1994, July 1 *Perf. 12*

6220	A2956	150r	Anas penelope	.20	.20
6221	A2956	250r	Aythya fuligula	.25	.20
6222	A2956	300r	Anas formosa	.35	.25
a.			Min. sheet, 3 #6220, 4 #6221, 2 #6222	2.10	2.00
b.			As "a," overprinted	2.10	2.00
			Nos. 6220-6222 (3)	.80	.65

No. 6222b is overprinted in sheet margin: "World Philatelic Exhibition Moscow-97" in Cyrillic and Latin with four exhibition emblems.

A2957 A2958

1994, July 5 Photo. *Perf. 11½x12*

6223	A2957	100r	multicolored	.20	.20

1994 Goodwill Games, St. Petersburg.

1994, July 5 Litho. *Perf. 12*

Nobel Prize Winners in Physics: No. 6224, P.L. Kapitsa (1894-1984). No. 6225, P.A. Cherenkov (1904-90).

6224	A2958	150r	sepia	.20	.20
6225	A2958	150r	sepia	.20	.20

Intl. Olympic Committee, Cent. A2959

1994, July 5

6226	A2959	250r	multicolored	.30	.20

Russian Postal Day — A2960

1994, July 8 *Perf. 11½x12*

6227	A2960	125r	multicolored	.20	.20

Porcelain A2961

Designs: 50r, Snuff box, 1752. 100r, Candlestick, 1750-1760. 150r, Statue of watercarrier, 1818. 250r, Vase, 19th cent. 300r, Statue of lady with mask, 1910. 500r, Monogrammed dinner service, 1848.

1994, Aug. 10 Litho. *Perf. 11½*

6228	A2961	50r	multicolored	.20	.20
a.			Min. sheet of 9	.70	.65
b.			As "a," overprinted	.70	.65
6229	A2961	100r	multicolored	.20	.20
6230	A2961	150r	multicolored	.25	.20

6231 A2961 250r multicolored .25 .20
6232 A2961 300r multicolored .35 .25
Nos. 6228-6232 (5) 1.25 1.05

Souvenir Sheet

6233 A2961 500r multicolored .65 .65

No. 6228b is overprinted in sheet margin: "World Philatelic Exhibition Moscow 97" in Cyrillic and Latin with four exhibition logos.

Integration of Tuva into Russia, 50th Anniv. — A2962

1994, Oct. 13 Photo. *Perf. 11½x12*
6234 A2962 125r multicolored .20 .20

Russian Voyages of Exploration — A2963

Sailing ships and: No. 6235, V.M. Golovnin, Kurile Islands expedition, 1811. No. 6236, I.F. Kruzenstern, trans-global expedition, 1803-06. No. 6237, F.P. Wrangel, North American expedition, 1829-35. No. 6238, F.P. Litke, Novaya Zemlya expedition, 1821-24.

Photo. & Engr.

1994, Nov. 22 *Perf. 12x11½*
6235 A2963 250r multicolored .20 .20
6236 A2963 250r multicolored .20 .20
a. Miniature sheet of 8 1.25 1.10
6237 A2963 250r multicolored .20 .20
6238 A2963 250r multicolored .20 .20
Nos. 6235-6238 (4) .80 .80

Russian Fleet, 300th anniv. (#6236a).

New Year 1995 — A2964

1994, Dec. 6 Photo. *Perf. 12x11½*
6239 A2964 125r multicolored .20 .20
a. Min. sheet of 8 1.10 .80

Alexander Griboedov (1795-1829), Poet, Diplomat A2965

1995, Jan. 5 Litho. *Perf. 11½*
6240 A2965 250r sepia & black .25 .20

No. 6240 printed se-tenant with label.

A2966

Mikhail Fokine (1880-1942), Choreographer — A2967

Scenes from ballets: No. 6241, Scheherazade. No. 6242, The Fire Bird. No. 6243, Petrouchka.

1995, Jan. 18 Litho. *Perf. 12½x12*
6241 A2966 500r multicolored .30 .20
6242 A2967 500r multicolored .30 .20
6243 A2967 500r multicolored .30 .20
a. Block of 3 + label 1.05 .75

Mikhail Kutuzov (1745-1813), Field Marshal — A2968

1995, Jan. 20
6244 A2968 300r multicolored .20 .20
a. Miniature sheet of 8 1.50 1.25

16th-17th Cent. Architecture, Moscow A2969

Designs: 125r, English Yard, Varvarka St. 250r, Averki Kirillov's house, Bersenevskaya Embankment. 300r, Volkov's house, Kharitonievsky Lane.

1995, Feb. 15 Litho. *Perf. 12x12½*
6245 A2969 125r multicolored .20 .20
6246 A2969 250r multicolored .20 .20
6247 A2969 300r multicolored .20 .20
a. Min. sheet, 2 #6245, 4 #6246, 3 #6247 1.75 1.10
b. Min. sheet, as "a," diff. margin 1.75 1.10
Nos. 6245-6247 (3) .60 .60

Sheet margin on No. 6247b has emblems and inscriptions in Cyrillic and Latin for "World Philatelic Exhibition Moscow '97."

UN Fight Against Drug Abuse — A2970

1995, Mar. 1 *Perf. 12½x12*
6248 A2970 150r multicolored .20 .20

Endangered Species — A2971

a, Lake. b, Pusa hispida. c, Lynx. d, River, trees.

1995, Mar. 1 *Perf. 12x12½*
6249 A2971 250r Block of 4, #a.-d. .75 .65

Nos. 6249a-6249b, 6249c-6249d are continuous designs. See Finland No. 960.

End of World War II, 50th Anniv. A2972

#6250, Churchill, Roosevelt, Stalin at Yalta. #6251, Ruins of Reichstag, Berlin. #6252, Monument to concentration camp victims. #6253, Tomb of the Unknown Soldier, Moscow, vert. #6254, Potsdam Conference, map of divided Germany, vert. #6255, Russian planes over Manchuria. #6256, Victory parade, Moscow, vert.

1995, Apr. 7 *Perf. 12x12½, 12½x12*
6250 A2972 250r multicolored .20 .20
6251 A2972 250r multicolored .20 .20
6252 A2972 250r multicolored .20 .20
6253 A2972 250r multicolored .20 .20
6254 A2972 250r multicolored .22 .20
6255 A2972 250r multicolored .20 .20

Size: 37x52mm

6256 A2972 500r multicolored .25 .20
a. Souv. sheet of 1, perf 11½x12 .40 .40
Nos. 6250-6256 (7) 1.47 1.40

MIR-Space Shuttle Docking, Apollo-Soyuz Link-Up — A2973

a, Space shuttle Atlantis. b, MIR space station. c, Apollo command module. d, Soyuz spacecraft.

1995, June 29 Litho. *Perf. 12x12½*
6257 A2973 1500r Block of 4, #a.-d. 3.00 2.50

No. 6257 is a continuous design.

Radio, Cent. A2974

Design: 250r, Alexander Popov (1859-1905), radio-telegraph.

1995, May 3 Litho. *Perf. 11½*
6258 A2974 250r multicolored .20 .20

Flowers A2975

Songbirds A2976

#6259, Campanula patula. #6260, Leucanthemum vulgare. #6261, Trifolium pratense. #6262, Centaurea jacea. 500r, Geranium pratense.

1995, May 18 Litho. *Perf. 12½x12*
6259 A2975 250r multicolored .20 .20
6260 A2975 250r multicolored .20 .20
6261 A2975 300r multicolored .20 .20
a. Min. sheet of 8 1.50
b. As "a," different margin 1.50
6262 A2975 300r multicolored .20 .20
6263 A2975 500r multicolored .30 .20
Nos. 6259-6263 (5) 1.10 1.00

No. 6261b has emblems and inscriptions in Cyrillic and Latin for "World Philatelic Exhibition Moscow '97."

1995, June 15 Litho. *Perf. 12½x12*
6264 A2976 250r Alauda arvensis .20 .20
6265 A2976 250r Turdus philomelos .20 .20
6266 A2976 500r Carduelis carduelis .25 .20
6267 A2976 500r Cyanosylvia svecica .25 .20
6268 A2976 750r Luscinia luscinia .35 .25
a. Min. sheet, 2 each #6264-6265, 1 #6268 + label 1.25 1.10
b. Min. sheet, 2 each #6266-6267, 1 #6268 + label 1.75 1.50
Nos. 6264-6268 (5) 1.25 1.05

St. Trinity, Jerusalem A2977

Sts. Peter & Paul, Karlovy Vary — A2978

St. Nicholas, Vienna — A2979

St. Nicholas, New York — A2980

Russian Orthodox Churches abroad: 750r, St. Alexei, Leipzig.

1995, July 5 Litho. *Perf. 12x12½*
6269 A2977 300r multicolored .20 .20
6270 A2978 300r multicolored .20 .20
6271 A2979 500r multicolored .30 .20
6272 A2980 500r multicolored .30 .20
6273 A2980 750r multicolored .35 .25
a. Min. sheet, 2 ea #6269-6273 2.50 2.25
Nos. 6269-6273 (5) 1.35 1.05

Principality of Ryazan, 900th Anniv. — A2981

1995, July 20 Photo. *Perf. 11½*
6274 A2981 250r Kremlin Cathedral .20 .20

FabergéJewelry in Kremlin Museums — A2982

Designs: 150r, Easter egg, 1909, St. Petersburg. 250r, Goblet, 1899-1908, Moscow. 300r, Cross, 1899-1908, St. Petersburg. 600r, Ladle, 1890, Moscow. 750r, Easter egg, 1910, St. Petersburg.
1500r, Easter egg, 1904-06, St. Petersburg.

1995, Aug. 15 Litho. *Perf. 11½*

6275	A2982	150r multicolored	.20	.20
6276	A2982	250r multicolored	.20	.20
6277	A2982	300r multicolored	.20	.20
6278	A2982	500r multicolored	.25	.20
6279	A2982	750r multicolored	.35	.30
		Nos. 6275-6279 (5)	1.20	1.10

Souvenir Sheet

6280	A2982	1500r multicolored	.75	.65

No. 6280 contains one 37x51mm stamp.

Souvenir Sheet

Singapore '95 — A2983

Illustration reduced.

1995, Sept. 1 *Perf. 12½x12*

6281	A2983	2500r multicolored	1.10	1.00

Ducks A2984

Designs: 500r, Histrionicus histrionicus. 750r, Aythya baeri. 1000r, Mergus merganser.

1995, Sept. 1 *Perf. 12*

6284	A2984	500r multicolored	.25	.20
6285	A2984	750r multicolored	.35	.25
6286	A2984	1000r multicolored	.50	.40
a.		Miniature sheet, 2 #6284, 4 #6285, 3 #6286	3.75	3.50
		Nos. 6284-6286 (3)	1.10	.85

Russian Fleet, 300th Anniv. — A2985

Paintings: 250r, Battle of Grengam, 1720. 300r, Bay of Cesme, 1770. 500r, Battle of Revel Roadstead, 1790. 750r, Kronstadt Roadstead, 1840.

1995, Sept. 14 Litho. *Perf. 12*

6287	A2985	250r multicolored	.20	.20
6288	A2985	300r multicolored	.20	.20
6289	A2985	500r multicolored	.25	.20
6290	A2985	750r multicolored	.35	.25
		Nos. 6287-6290 (4)	1.00	.85

Arms & Flag of the Russian Federation — A2986

1995, Oct. 4 Litho. *Perf. 12x12½*

6291	A2986	500r multicolored	.30	.25

No. 6291 is printed with se-tenant label.

UN, 50th Anniv. — A2987

1995, Oct. 4

6292	A2987	500r multicolored	.30	.25

Peace and Freedom — A2988

Europa: No. 6293, Storks in nest, countryside. No. 6294, Stork in flight.

1995, Nov. 15 Litho. *Perf. 12x12½*

6293		1500r multicolored	.75	.70
6294		1500r multicolored	.75	.70
a.		A2988 Pair, Nos. 6293-6294	1.50	1.40

No. 6294a is a continuous design.

Christmas A2989

1995, Dec. 1 *Perf. 12*

6295	A2989	500r multicolored	.25	.20

A2990

A2990a

A2990b

Early Russian Dukes — A2990c

Designs: No. 6296, Yuri Dolgorouki (1090-1157), Duke of Souzdal, Grand Duke of Kiev, founder of Moscow. No. 6297, Alexander Nevski (1220-63), Duke of Novgorod, Grand Duke of Vladimir. No. 6298, Michael Alexandrovitsch (1333-39), Prince of Tver. No. 6299, Dimitri Donskoi (1350-89), Duke of Moscow, Vladimir. No. 6300, Ivan III (1440-1505), Grand Duke of Moscow.
Illustrations reduced.

Litho. & Engr.

1995, Dec. 21 *Perf. 12*

6296	A2990	1000r multicolored	.50	.35
6297	A2990a	1000r multicolored	.50	.35
6298	A2990b	1000r multicolored	.50	.35
6299	A2990c	1000r multicolored	.50	.35
6300	A2990c	1000r multicolored	.50	.35
		Nos. 6296-6300 (5)	2.50	1.75

See #6359-6362.

A2991

A2992

1996, Jan. 31 Litho. *Perf. 12*

6301	A2991	750r dull olive black	.30	.25

Nikolai N. Semenov (1896-1986), chemist.

1996, Feb. 22 Litho. *Perf. 12*

Flowers: 500r, Viola wittrockiana. No. 6303, Dianthus barbatus. No. 6304, Lathyrus odoratus. No. 6305, Fritillaria imperialis. No. 6306, Antirrhinum majus.

6302	A2992	500r multicolored	.20	.20
6303	A2992	750r multicolored	.30	.20
6304	A2992	750r multicolored	.30	.20
6305	A2992	1000r multicolored	.40	.30
6306	A2992	1000r multicolored	.40	.30
a.		Min. sheet of 20, 4 each #6302-6306 + 4 labels	6.25	5.50
		Nos. 6302-6306 (5)	1.60	1.20

Domestic Cats A2993

Designs: No. 6307, European tiger. No. 6308, Russian blue. No. 6309, Persian white. No. 6310, Siamese. No. 6311, Siberian.

1996, Mar. 21

Color of Background

6307	A2993	1000r orange	.40	.30
6308	A2993	1000r brown	.40	.30
6309	A2993	1000r red	.40	.30
6310	A2993	1000r blue violet	.40	.30
6311	A2993	1000r green	.40	.30
a.		Sheet, 2 each #6307-6311	4.00	
		Nos. 6307-6311 (5)	2.00	1.50

Souvenir Sheet

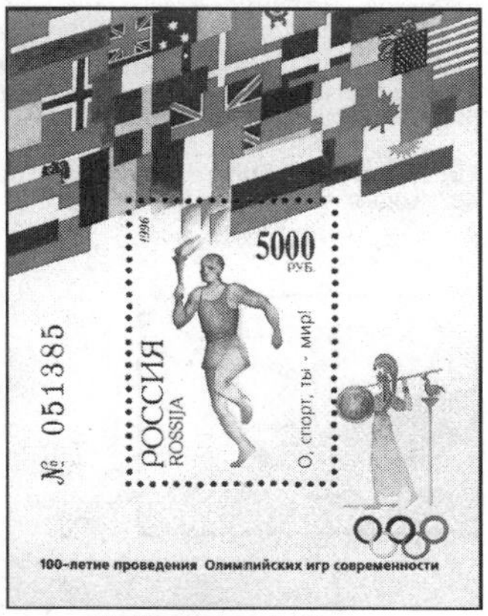

Modern Olympic Games, Cent. — A2994

Illustration reduced.

1996, Mar. 27

6312	A2994	5000r multicolored	1.90	1.75

Victory Day — A2995

Design: Painting, "Plunged Down Banners," by A. S. Mikhailov. Illustration reduced.

1996, Apr. 19 Litho. *Perf. 12*

6313	A2995	1000r multicolored	.40	.30
a.		Sheet of 8 + label	3.00	

Tula, 850th Anniv. A2996

1996, May 14 *Perf. 12½x12*

6314	A2996	1500r Tula Kremlin	.60	.40

Russian Trams A2997

Designs: 500r, Putilovsky plant. No. 6316, Sormovo, 1912. No. 6317, "X" series, 1928. No. 6318, "KM" series, 1931. No. 6319, LM-57, 1957. 2500r, Model 71-608 K, 1993.

1996, May 16 Photo. *Perf. 11½*

6315	A2997	500r multicolored	.20	.20
6316	A2997	750r multicolored	.30	.20
6317	A2997	750r multicolored	.30	.20
6318	A2997	1000r multicolored	.40	.30
6319	A2997	1000r multicolored	.40	.30
6320	A2997	2500r multicolored	1.25	.90
a.		Souvenir sheet	1.25	1.10
b.		Sheet of 6	7.25	
		Nos. 6315-6320 (6)	2.85	2.10

A2998

A2999

Europa (Famous Women): No. 6321, E.R. Daschkova (1744-1810), scientist. No. 6322, S.V. Kovalevskaya (1850-91), mathematician.

1996, May 20 Litho. *Perf. 12x12½*
6321 A2998 1500r green & black .60 .30
6322 A2998 1500r lilac & black .60 .30

1996, June 1 Litho. *Perf. 12½x12*
6323 A2999 1000r multicolored .50 .35

UNICEF, 50th anniv.

Summer, by P.P. Sokolov A3000

Post Troika, by P.N. Gruzinsky A3001

Design: No. 6326, Winter, by Sokolov.

1996, June 14
6324 A3000 1500r multicolored .75 .60
6325 A3001 1500r multicolored .75 .60
6326 A3000 1500r multicolored .75 .60
Nos. 6324-6326 (3) 2.25 1.80

Moscow, 850th Anniv. — A3002

Paintings of urban views: No. 6327, Yauza River, 1790's. No. 6328, Kremlin Palace, 1797. No. 6329, Kamenny Bridge, 1811. No. 6330, Volkhonka Steet, 1830's. No. 6331, Vorvarka St. 1830-40's. No. 6332, Petrovsky Park, troikas.

1996, June 20 Litho. *Perf. 12*
6327 A3002 500r multicolored .20 .20
6328 A3002 500r multicolored .20 .20
6329 A3002 750r multicolored .35 .25
6330 A3002 750r multicolored .35 .25
6331 A3002 1000r multicolored .40 .20
a. Sheet, 2 ea #6327, 6330-6331 2.50
6332 A3002 1000r multicolored .40 .20
a. Sheet, 2 ea #6328-6329, 6332 2.50
b. Sheet of 6, #6327-6332 2.50
Nos. 6327-6332 (6) 1.90 1.30

Traffic Police, 60th Anniv. A3003

a, Pedestrian crossing guard. b, Children receiving traffic safety education. c, Officer writing citation.

1996, July 3 Litho. *Perf. 12x12½*
6333 A3003 1500r Sheet of 3, #a.-c. 1.10 .55

1996 Summer Olympic Games, Atlanta — A3004

1996, July 10 *Perf. 12*
6334 A3004 500r Basketball .20 .20
6335 A3004 1000r Boxing .40 .20
6336 A3004 1000r Swimming .40 .20
6337 A3004 1500r Women's gymnastics .60 .30
6338 A3004 1500r Hurdles .60 .30
a. Sheet of 8 4.75
Nos. 6334-6338 (5) 2.20 1.20

A3005

Russian Navy, 300th Anniv. A3006

Ships: 750r, Yevstafy, 1762. No. 6340, Petropavlovsk, 1894. No. 6341, Novik, 1913. Nos. 6342, 6346a, Galera, 1696. Nos. 6343, 6346d, Aircraft carrier Admiral Kuznetzov, 1935. No. 6344, Tashkent, 1937. No. 6345, Submarine C-13, 1939.

No. 6346: b, Atomic submarine, 1981. c, Sailing ship Azov, 1826.

Litho. & Engr.

1996, July 26 *Perf. 12*
6339 A3005 750r multicolored .25 .20
6340 A3005 1000r multicolored .35 .20
6341 A3005 1000r multicolored .35 .20
6342 A3006 1000r multicolored .35 .20
6343 A3006 1000r multicolored .35 .20
a. Sheet, 3 each #6342-6343 2.25 1.20
6344 A3005 1500r multicolored .50 .25
6345 A3005 1500r multicolored .50 .25
Nos. 6339-6345 (7) 2.65 1.50

Souvenir Sheet

6346 A3006 1000r Sheet of 4, #a.-d. + label 1.75 .90

No. 6346 has blue background.

Aleksandr Gorsky (1871-1924), Choreographer — A3006a

a, 750r, Portrait, scenes from "The Daughter of Gudule," "Salambo." b, 1500r, Don Quixote. c, 1500r, Giselle. d, 750r, La Bayadere.

1996, Aug. 7 Litho. *Perf. 12½x12*
6347 A3006a Block of 4, #a.-d. 1.90 .95
e. Sheet of 6, #6347b 3.50 1.75

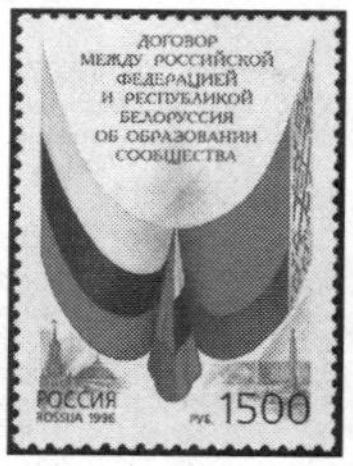

Treaty Between Russia and Belarus A3006b

1996, Aug. 27 *Perf. 12x12½*
6348 A3006b 1500r Natl. flags .60 .30

17th-20th Cent. Enamelwork — A3007

Designs: No. 6349, Chalice, 1679. No. 6350, Aromatic bottle, 17th cent. No. 6351, Ink pot, ink set, 17th-18th cent. No. 6352, Coffee pot, 1750-1760. No. 6353, Perfume bottle, 19th-20th cent.

5000r, Icon, Our Lady of Kazan, 1894.

1996, Sept. 10 *Perf. 11½*
6349 A3007 1000r multicolored .40 .20
6350 A3007 1000r multicolored .40 .20
a. Sheet of 9 3.60
6351 A3007 1000r multicolored .40 .20
6352 A3007 1500r multicolored .60 .30
6353 A3007 1500r multicolored .60 .30
a. Sheet of 9 5.50
Nos. 6349-6353 (5) 2.40 1.20

Souvenir Sheet

6354 A3007 5000r multicolored 2.00 1.00

No. 6353a inscribed in sheet margin for Moscow '97.

No. 6354 contains one 35x50mm stamp.

UNESCO, 50th Anniv. A3008

1996, Oct. 15 *Perf. 12x12½*
6355 A3008 1000r multicolored .40 .20

No. 6355 issued in sheets of 8.

Icons, Religious Landmarks A3009

Designs: a, Icon of Our Lady of Iverone, Moscow. b, Holy Monastery of Stavrovouni, Cyprus. c, Icon of St. Nicholas, Cyprus. d, Resurrection (Iverone), Gate, Moscow.

1996, Nov. 13 *Perf. 11½*
6356 A3009 1500r Block of 4, #a.-d. 2.40 1.20

See Cyprus Nos. 893-896.

New Year 1997 — A3010

Design: Chiming Clock of Moscow, Kremlin.

1996, Dec. 5
6357 A3010 1000r multicolored .40 .20
a. Sheet of 8 3.25 1.60

Natl. Ice Hockey Team, 50th Anniv. A3011

Action scenes: a, Two players. b, Three players. c, Three players, referee.

1996, Dec. 5 *Perf. 12*
6358 A3011 1500r Strip of 3, #a.-c. 1.75 .90

Basil III — A3012

Ivan IV (the Terrible) — A3013

Feodor Ivanovich — A3014

Boris Godunov — A3015

Litho. & Engr.

1996, Dec. 20 *Perf. 12*
6359 A3012 1500r multicolored .60 .30
6360 A3013 1500r multicolored .60 .30
6361 A3014 1500r multicolored .60 .30
6362 A3015 1500r multicolored .60 .30
Nos. 6359-6362 (4) 2.40 1.20

See #6296-6300.

Flowers — A3016

Designs: No. 6363, Chaenomeles japonica. No. 6364, Amygdalus triloba. No. 6365, Cytisus scoparius. No. 6366, Rosa pimpinellifolia. No. 6367, Philadelphus coronarius.

1997, Jan. 21 Litho. *Perf. 12½x12*
6363 A3016 500r multicolored .25 .20
6364 A3016 500r multicolored .25 .20
6365 A3016 1000r multicolored .45 .25
6366 A3016 1000r multicolored .45 .25
6367 A3016 1000r multicolored .45 .25
Nos. 6363-6367 (5) 1.85 1.15

Souvenir Sheet

Moscow, 850th Anniv. — A3017

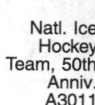

Illustration reduced.

1997, Feb. 20 *Perf. 12x12½*

6368 A3017 3000r Coat of arms 1.40 .70

Shostakovich Intl. Music Festival — A3018

Dmitri D. Shostakovich (1906-75), composer.

1997, Feb. 26 *Perf. 12*

6369 A3018 1000r multicolored .45 .25

Souvenir Sheet

Coat of Arms of Russia, 500th Anniv. — A3019

Illustration reduced.

1997, Mar. 20

6370 A3019 3000r multicolored 1.40 .70

Post Emblem — A3020

Designs: 100r, Agriculture. 150r, Oil rig. 250r, Cranes (birds). 300r, Radio/TV tower. 500r, Russian Post emblem. 750r, St. George slaying dragon. 1000r, Natl. flag, arms. 1500r, Electric power. 2000r, Train. 2500r, Moscow Kremlin. 3000r, Satellite. 5000r, Fine arts.

1997 *Perf. 12x12½*

6371 A3020 100r blk & yel brn .20 .20
6372 A3020 150r blk & red lilac .20 .20
6373 A3020 250r blk & olive .20 .20
6374 A3020 300r blk & dk grn .20 .20
6375 A3020 500r blk & dk bl .20 .20
6376 A3020 750r blk & brown .30 .20
6377 A3020 1000r blue & red .40 .20
6378 A3020 1500r blk & grn bl .60 .30
6379 A3020 2000r blk & green .80 .40
6380 A3020 2500r blk & red .90 .45
6381 A3020 3000r blk & purple 1.25 .60
6382 A3020 5000r blk & brown 2.00 1.00
Nos. 6371-6382 (12) 7.25 4.15

Issued: 500r, 750r, 1000r, 1500r, 2500r, 3/31; 100r, 150r, 250r, 300r, 2000r, 3000r, 5000r, 4/30.

See Nos. 6423-6433, 6550-6560.

A3021

A3022

1997, Mar. 31 **Litho.** *Perf. 12*

6383 A3021 1000r multicolored .40 .20

City of Vologda, 850th anniv.

1997, May 5 **Litho.** *Perf. 12x12½*

Europa (Stories and Legends): Legend of Volga.

6384 A3022 1500r multicolored .60 .30

Moscow, 850th Anniv. — A3023

Historic buildings: a, Cathedral of Christ the Savior. b, Turrets and roofs of the Kremlin. c, Grand Palace of the Kremlin, cathedral plaza. d, St. Basil's Cathedral. e, Icon, St. George slaying the Dragon. f, Text of first chronicled record of Moscow, 1147. g, Prince Aleksandr Nevski, Danilov Monastery. h, 16th cent. miniature of Moscow Kremlin. i, Miniature of coronation of Czar Ivan IV. j, 16th cent. map of Moscow.

1997, May 22

6385 A3023 1000r Sheet of 10, #a.-j. 3.75 1.90

Nos. 6385c, 6385h are 42x42mm.

Helicopters — A3024

1997, May 28 **Litho.** *Perf. 12½x12*

6386 A3024 500r Mi-14 .20 .20
6387 A3024 1000r Mi-24 .40 .20
6388 A3024 1500r Mi-26 .55 .55
6389 A3024 2000r Mi-28 .75 .40
a. Sheet of 6 4.50
6390 A3024 2500r Mi-34 .95 .45
Nos. 6386-6389 (4) 1.90 1.35

Fairy Tales — A3025

Designs: 500r, Man holding rope beside lake, devil running, from "Priest and Worker." 1000r, Two women, two men, from "Czar Sultan." 1500r, Man fishing in lake, fish, man, castle, from "Fisherman/Golden Fish." 2000r, Princess on steps, old woman holding apple, from "Dead Princess/Seven Knights." 3000r, Woman, King bowing while holding septor, rooster up in air, from "Golden Cockerel."

Photo. & Engr.

1997, June 6 *Perf. 12x12½*

6391 A3025 500r multicolored .20 .20
6392 A3025 1000r multicolored .40 .20
6393 A3025 1500r multicolored .60 .30
6394 A3025 2000r multicolored .80 .40
6395 A3025 3000r multicolored 1.25 .60
a. Strip of 5, #6391-6395 3.25 1.65
b. Sheet of 2 #6395a 6.40

Diplomatic Relations Between Russia and Thailand A3026

Design: St. Petersburg, Russian flag, Bangkok, Thailand flag.

1997, June 20 **Litho.** *Perf. 12½x12*

6396 A3026 1500r multicolored .60 .30

Wildlife A3027

Designs: a, 500r, Pteromys volans. b, 750r, Felix lynx. c, 1000r, Tetrao urogallus. d, 2000r, Lutra lutra. e, 3000r, Numenius arguata.

1997, July 10 *Perf. 12*

6397 A3027 Block of 5 + label 2.60 1.30

Russian Regions A3028

#6398, Winter scene, Archangel Oblast. #6399, Ocean, beach, Kaliningrad Oblast, vert. #6400, Ship, Krasnodarsky Krai. #6401, Mountains, Yakutia, vert. #6402, Mountain, sailing ship monument, Kamchatka Oblast.

1997, July 15 *Perf. 12½x12, 12x12½*

6398 A3028 1500r multicolored .55 .30
6399 A3028 1500r multicolored .55 .30
6400 A3028 1500r multicolored .55 .30
6401 A3028 1500r multicolored .55 .30
6402 A3028 1500r multicolored .55 .30
Nos. 6398-6402 (5) 2.75 1.50

Kljopa Puppets A3029

Designs: 500r, Rainbow, balloons. 1000r, Hang glider. 1500r, Troika.

1997, July 25 *Perf. 11½*

6403 A3029 500r multicolored .20 .20
6404 A3029 1000r multicolored .35 .20

Size: 45x33mm

Perf. 12

6405 A3029 1500r multicolored .55 .30
Nos. 6403-6405 (3) 1.10 .70

World Philatelic Exhibition, Moscow 97 — A3030

Designs: a, #1, #35. b, #6061.

1997, Aug. 5 *Perf. 11½*

6406 A3030 1500r Pair, #a.-b. 1.10 .55
c. Sheet of 6 stamps 4.25

A3031

History of Russia, Peter I: No. 6407, Planning new capital. No. 6408, Reforming the military. No. 6409, In Baltic Sea naval battle. No. 6410, Ordering administrative reform. No. 6411, Advocating cultural education.

5000r, Peter I (1672-1725).

1997, Aug. 15 *Perf. 12x12½*

6407 A3031 2000r multicolored .75 .35
6408 A3031 2000r multicolored .75 .35
6409 A3031 2000r multicolored .75 .35
6410 A3031 2000r multicolored .75 .35
6411 A3031 2000r multicolored .75 .35
Nos. 6407-6411 (5) 3.75 1.75

Souvenir Sheet

Litho. & Engr.

6411A A3031 5000r multicolored *3.25 1.60*

Indian Independence, 50th Anniv. — A3032

1997, Aug. 15 *Perf. 12*

6412 A3032 500r multicolored .20 .20

Russian Pentathlon, 50th Anniv. — A3033

1997, Sept. 1 *Perf. 12½x12*

6413 A3033 1000r multicolored .35 .20

Russian Soccer, Cent. A3034

1997, Sept. 4

6414 A3034 2000r multicolored .75 .35

World Ozone Layer Day A3035

1997, Sept. 16 *Perf. 12x12½*

6415 A3035 1000r multioclored .35 .20

A3036

1997, Oct. 1

6416 A3036 1000r multicolored .35 .20

Russia's admission to European Council. No. 6416 printed with se-tenant label.

Souvenir Sheet

Pushkin's "Eugene Onegin," Translated by Abraham Shlonsky — A3038

Illustration reduced.

1997, Nov. 19 Litho. *Perf. 12*

6418	A3038	3000r multicolored	1.25	.60

See Israel No. 1319.

Russian State Museum, St. Petersburg, Cent. — A3039

500r, Boris and Gleb, 14th cent. icon. 1000r, "The Volga Boatmen," by I. Repin. 1500r, "A Promenade," by Marc Chagall. 2000r, "A Merchant's Wife Having Tea," by Kustodiyev.

1997, Nov. 12 Litho. *Perf. 12*

6419	A3039	500r multi, vert.	.20	.20
6420	A3039	1000r multi, vert.	.40	.20
6421	A3039	1500r multi	.60	.30
6422	A3039	2000r multi, vert.	.80	.40
		Nos. 6419-6422 (4)	2.00	1.10

Nos. 6419-6422 were each issued in sheets of 8 + label.
See Nos. 6446-6450.

Post Emblem Type of 1997

1998, Jan. 1 Litho. *Perf. 12x12½*

6423	A3020	10k like #6371	.20	.20
6424	A3020	15k like #6372	.20	.20
6425	A3020	25k like #6373	.20	.20
6426	A3020	30k like #6374	.20	.20
6427	A3020	50k like #6375	.30	.20
6428	A3020	1r like #6377	.60	.30
6429	A3020	1.50r like #6378	.90	.45
6430	A3020	2r like #6379	1.25	.60
6431	A3020	2.50r like #6380	1.40	.70
6432	A3020	3r like #6381	1.75	.90
6433	A3020	5r like #6382	2.90	1.40
		Nos. 6423-6433 (11)	9.90	5.35

Vasily Surikov (1848-1916), V. Vasnetsov (1848-1926), Painters — A3040

Entire paintings or details by Surikov: No. 6434, Menchikov and Beresov, 1887. No. 6435, Russian Women of Morozov, 1887.
By Vasnetsov, vert.: No. 6436, The Struggle of Slavs with the Nomads, 1881. No. 6437, Ivan Tsarevitch on a Wolf, 1889.

1998, Jan. 24 *Perf. 12*

6434	A3040	1.50r multicolored	.90	.45
6435	A3040	1.50r multicolored	.90	.45
a.		Pair, #6434-6435 + label	1.80	.90
6436	A3040	1.50r multicolored	.90	.45
6437	A3040	1.50r multicolored	.90	.45
a.		Pair, #6436-6437 + label	1.80	.90

1998 Winter Olympic Games, Nagano — A3041

1998, Jan. 27 Litho. *Perf. 12*

6438	A3041	50k Cross country skiing	.30	.20
6439	A3041	1r Pairs figure skating	.60	.30
6440	A3041	1.50r Biathlon	.90	.45
a.		Sheet, 2 each #6438-6440	3.60	1.80
		Nos. 6438-6440 (3)	1.80	.95

Aquarium Fish A3042

Designs: No. 6441, Hyphessobrycon callistus. No. 6442, Epalzeorhynchus bicolor. 1r, Synodontis galinae. No. 6444, Botia kristinae. No. 6445, Cichlasoma labiatum.

1998, Feb. 25 Litho. *Perf. 12½x12*

6441	A3042	50k multicolored	.20	.20
6442	A3042	50k multicolored	.20	.20
6443	A3042	1r multicolored	.40	.20
a.		Sheet of 6	2.40	1.20
6444	A3042	1.50r multicolored	.60	.30
6445	A3042	1.50r multicolored	.60	.30
		Nos. 6441-6445 (5)	2.00	1.20

Russian State Museum, St. Petersburg, Cent., Type of 1997

#6446, The Last Day of Pompeii, by K.P. Bryulov, 1833. #6447, Our Lady of Malevolent Hearts Tenderness, by K.S. Petrov-Vodkin, 1914-15. #6448, Mast Pine Grove, by I.I. Shishkin, 1898. #6449, The Ninth Wave, by I.K. Aivazovsky, 1850.
3r, The Mihailovksy Palace (detail), by K.P. Beggrov, 1832.

1998, Mar. 17 *Perf. 12x12½*

6446	A3039	1.50r multicolored	.60	.30
6447	A3039	1.50r multicolored	.60	.30
6448	A3039	1.50r multicolored	.60	.30
6449	A3039	1.50r multicolored	.60	.30
a.		Sheet, 2 each #6446-6449 + label	4.80	2.40
		Nos. 6446-6449 (4)	2.40	1.20

Souvenir Sheet

6450	A3039	3r multicolored	1.20	.60

Souvenir Sheet

Expo '98, Lisbon — A3043

Illustration reduced.

1998, Apr. 15 *Perf. 12½x12*

6451	A3043	3r Emblem, dolphins	1.10	.55

Theater of Arts, Moscow, Cent. — A3044

1998, Apr. 24 *Perf. 12*

6452	A3044	1.50r multicolored	.55	.30

No. 6452 was printed se-tenant with label.

Shrove-tide Natl. Festival — A3045

1998, May 5 Litho. *Perf. 12½x12*

6453	A3045	1.50r multicolored	.55	.30

Europa.

A3046

A3046a

A3046b

Aleksander S. Pushkin (1799-1837), Poet — A3046c

Pushkin's drawings: No. 6454, Lyceum where Puskin studied 1811-17. No. 6455, A. N. Wolf, contemporary of Pushkin's. No. 6456, Tatyana, heroine of novel, "Eugene Onegin." No. 6457, Cover of 1830 manuscript. No. 6458, Self-portrait.

Litho. & Engr.

1998, May 28 *Perf. 12x12½*

6454	A3046	1.50r multicolored	.55	.30
6455	A3046a	1.50r multicolored	.55	.30
6456	A3046b	1.50r multicolored	.55	.30
6457	A3046c	1.50r multicolored	.55	.30
6458	A3046c	1.50r multicolored	.55	.30
a.		Sheet, 2 each #6454-6458	5.50	3.00
		Nos. 6454-6458 (5)	2.75	1.50

City of Ulyanovsk (Simbirsk), 350th Anniv. — A3047

1998, May 28 Litho. *Perf. 12½x12*

6459	A3047	1r multicolored	.40	.20

Czar Nicholas II (1868-1918) — A3048

1998, June 30 Litho. *Perf. 11½*

6460	A3048	3r multicolored	1.10	.55

Printed se-tenant with label.

City of Taganrog, 300th Anniv. — A3049

1998, June 10 Litho. *Perf. 12½x12*

6461	A3049	1r multicolored	.35	.20

Souvenir Sheet

1998 World Youth Games, Moscow — A3049a

1998, June 25 Litho. *Perf. 12½x12*

6461A	A3049a	3r multicolored	1.25	.65

A3050

A3051

Wild Berries: 50k, Vitis amurensis. 75k, Rubus idaeus. 1r, Schisandra chinensis. 1.50r, Vaccinium vitis-idaea. 2r, Rubus arcticus.

1998, July 10

6462	A3050	50k multicolored	.20	.20
6463	A3050	75k multicolored	.30	.20
6464	A3050	1r multicolored	.35	.20
6465	A3050	1.50r multicolored	.55	.30
6466	A3050	2r multicolored	.75	.35
		Nos. 6462-6466 (5)	2.15	1.25

1998, July 15

6467	A3051	1r multicolored	.35	.20

Ekaterinburg, 275th anniv.

Heroes of the Russian Federation A3052

#6468, L. R. Kvasnikov (1905-93). #6469, Morris Cohen (1910-95). #6470, Leontina Cohen (1913-92). #6471, A.A. Yatskov (1913-93).

1998, Aug. 10 Litho. *Perf. 12*

6468 A3052 1r green & black .35 .20
6469 A3052 1r brn, bister & blk .35 .20
6470 A3052 1r slate & black .35 .20
6471 A3052 1r claret & black .35 .20
Nos. 6468-6471 (4) 1.40 .80

Orders of Russia — A3053

1r, St. Andrey Pervozvanny. 1.50r St. Catherine. 2r, St. Alexander Nevsky. 2.50r, St. George.

1998, Aug. 20 Litho. *Perf. 12x12½*

6472 A3053 1r multi .35 .20
6472A A3053 1.50r multi .55 .25
6472B A3053 2r multi .70 .35
6472C A3053 2.50r multi .90 .45
d. Block of 4, #6472-6472C 2.50 1.25
e. Souvenir sheet of 4, #6472-6472C + label 2.50 1.25

See #6496-6500.

Murmansk Oblast A3054

Khabarovsk Krai — A3055

Karelia Republic — A3056 Buryat Republic — A3057

1998, Sept. 15 Litho. *Perf. 12*

6473 A3054 1.50r multicolored .55 .25
6474 A3055 1.50r multicolored .55 .25
6475 A3056 1.50r multicolored .55 .25
6476 A3057 1.50r multicolored .55 .25
6477 A3054 1.50r Primorski Krai .55 .25
Nos. 6473-6477 (5) 2.75 1.25

World Stamp Day A3058

1998, Oct. 9 Litho. *Perf. 12*

6478 A3058 1r multicolored .35 .20

Universal Declaration of Human Rights, 50th Anniv. — A3059

1998, Oct. 15

6479 A3059 1.50r multicolored .55 .25

No. 6479 released with se-tenant label.

Menatep Bank, 10th Anniv. — A3060

1998, Oct. 29

6480 A3060 2r multicolored .70 .35

20th Cent. Achievements — A3061

1998, Nov. 12

6481 A3061 1r Aviation .35 .20
6482 A3061 1r Space .35 .20
6483 A3061 1r Television .35 .20
6484 A3061 1r Genetics .35 .20
6485 A3061 1r Nuclear power .35 .20
6486 A3061 1r Computers .35 .20
Nos. 6481-6486 (6) 2.10 1.20

M.I. Koshkin (1898-1940), Tank Designer — A3062

1998, Nov. 20

6487 A3062 1r multicolored .35 .20

New Year — A3063

1998, Dec. 1 Litho. *Perf. 11½*

6488 A3063 1r multicolored .25 .20
a. Sheet of 9 2.25 1.10

Moscow-St. Petersburg Telephone Line, Cent. — A3064

1999, Jan. 13

6489 A3064 1r multicolored .25 .20

Hunting A3065

1999, Jan. 29 Litho. *Perf. 11¼*

6490 A3065 1r Wild turkey .25 .20
6491 A3065 1.50r Ducks .35 .20
6492 A3065 2r Releasing raptor .45 .20
6493 A3065 2.50r Wolves .60 .30
6494 A3065 3r Bear .70 .35
Nos. 6490-6494 (5) 2.35 1.25

Souvenir Sheet

Mediterranean Cruise of Feodor F. Ushakov, Bicent. — A3066

Illustration reduced.

1999, Feb. 19 *Perf. 12½x12*

6495 A3066 5r multicolored 1.25 .60

Order of Russia Type of 1998

1r, St. Vladimir, 1782. 1.50r, St. Anne, 1797. 2r, St. John of Jerusalem, 1798. 2.50r, White Eagles, 1815. 3r, St. Stanislas, 1815.

1999, Feb. 25 Litho. *Perf. 12x12¼*

6496 A3053 1r multicolored .20 .20
6497 A3053 1.50r multicolored .25 .20
6498 A3053 2r multicolored .30 .20
6499 A3053 2.50r multicolored .40 .20
6500 A3053 3r multicolored .50 .25
a. Sheet of 5, #6496-6500 1.60 .80

Children's Paintings — A3067

Designs: No. 6501, Family picnic. No. 6502, City, bridge, boats on water, helicopter. No. 6503, Stylized city, vert.

1999, Mar. 24 Litho. *Perf. 12¼x12*

6501 A3067 1.20r multicolored .20 .20
6502 A3067 1.20r multicolored .20 .20
6503 A3067 1.20r multicolored .20 .20
Nos. 6501-6503 (3) .60 .60

Souvenir Sheet

Russian Navy's Use of Flag with St. Andrew's Cross, 300th Anniv. — A3068

Illustration reduced.

1999, Mar. 24 Litho. *Perf. 12½x12*

6504 A3068 7r multicolored 1.10 .55

Souvenir Sheet

Intl. Space Station — A3069

Illustration reduced.

1999, Apr. 12 *Perf. 11½x12½*

6505 A3069 7r multicolored 1.00 .50

IBRA '99 World Philatelic Exhibition, Nuremberg — A3070

1999, Apr. 27 *Perf. 12½x12*

6506 A3070 3r multicolored .45 .25

Fishermen and Fishing Gear — A3071

1999, Apr. 30 *Perf. 11¾*

6507 A3071 1r Raft .20 .20
6508 A3071 2r Three fishermen .30 .20
6509 A3071 2r Fisherman, boat .30 .20
6510 A3071 3r Spear fishing .45 .25
6511 A3071 3r Ice fishermen .45 .25
Nos. 6507-6511 (5) 1.70 1.10

Council of Europe, 50th Anniv. A3072

1999, May 5 *Perf. 12x12¼*

6512 A3072 3r multicolored .45 .25

Europa A3073

1999, May 5 *Perf. 12½x12*

6513 A3073 5r Bison, Oka Natl. Nature Reserve .75 .35

Red Deer — A3074

Designs: a, Bucks. b, Does.

1999, May 18 *Perf. 12½x12*

6514	A3074 2.50r Pair, #a.-b.		.75	.35
	Complete booklet #6514		.75	

See People's Republic of China #2958-2959.

Aleksander Pushkin (1799-1837), Poet A3075

Paintings of Pushkin by: 1r, S. G. Chirikov, 1815. 3r, J. E. Vivien, 1826. 5r, Karl P. Bryulov, 1836.
7r, Vasily A. Tropinin, 1827

Litho. & Engr.

1999, May 27 *Perf. 12*

6515	A3075 1r multicolored	.20	.20
6516	A3075 3r multicolored	.45	.25
6517	A3075 5r multicolored	.75	.35
a.	Min. sheet, 2 ea #6515-6517	2.75	1.40
	Nos. 6515-6517 (3)	1.40	.80

Souvenir Sheet

Perf. 12x12½

6518	A3075 7r multicolored	1.00	.50

No. 6518 contains one 30x41mm stamp.

North Ossetia Republic A3076

Stavropol Kray A3077

Evenki Autonomous Okrug — A3078

Bashkir Republic — A3079

1999, June 2 **Litho.** *Perf. 12*

6519	A3076 2r multicolored	.30	.20
6520	A3077 2r multicolored	.30	.20
6521	A3078 2r multicolored	.30	.20
6522	A3079 2r multicolored	.30	.20
6523	A3076 2r Kirov Oblast	.30	.20
	Nos. 6519-6523 (5)	1.50	1.00

Roses — A3080

1999, June 10 *Perf. 12¼x11¾*

Color of Rose

6524	A3080 1.20r pink	.20	.20
6525	A3080 1.20r yellow	.20	.20
6526	A3080 2r red & yellow	.30	.20
6527	A3080 3r white	.45	.25
6528	A3080 4r red	.60	.30
a.	Min. sheet of 5, #6524-6528	1.75	1.10
b.	Strip of 5, #6524-6528	1.75	1.10
	Nos. 6524-6528 (5)	1.75	1.15

No. 6125A Surcharged

1999, June 22 **Litho.** *Perf. 12½x12*

6529	A2902 1.20r on 5000r	.20	.20

Rostov-on-Don, 250th Anniv. — A3081

1999, July 8 **Litho.** *Perf. 11¾x12¼*

6530	A3081 1.20r multi	.20	.20

UPU, 125th Anniv. — A3082

1999, Aug. 23 *Perf. 11¾*

6531	A3082 3r multi	.45	.25

Paintings of Karl P. Bryulov (1799-1852) — A3083

Paintings: a, Horsewoman, 1832. b, Portrait of Y. P. Samoilova and Amacillia Paccini.
Illustration reduced.

1999, Aug. 25 **Litho.** *Perf. 11¾x12*

6532	A3083 2.50r Pair, #a-b, + central label	.70	.35

Motorcycles — A3084

Designs: a, 1r, IZ-1, 1929. b, 1.50r, L-300, 1930. c, 2r, M-72, 1941. d, 2.50r, M-1A, 1945. e, 5r, IZ Planet 5, 1987.

1999, Sept. 9 **Litho.** *Perf. 11¾*

6533	A3084 Block of 5, #a.-e., + label	1.75	.85
	Booklet #6533	4.25	

The booklet also contains an unfranked cacheted envelope with First Day Cancel.

Field Marshal Aleksandr Suvorov's Alpine Campaign, Bicent. A3085

Designs: No. 6534, Suvorov and soldiers, monument at Schöllenen Gorge. No. 6535, Suvorov's vanguard at Lake Klöntal.

1999, Sept. 24 **Litho.** *Perf. 12x11½*

6534	A3085 2.50r multi	.35	.20
6535	A3085 2.50r multi	.35	.20

See Switzerland Nos. 1056-1057.

Native Sports — A3086

#6536, Kalmyk wrestling. #6537, Horse racing. #6538, Stick tossing. #6539, Reindeer racing. #6540, Weight lifting.

Perf. 11¾x11½, 11½x11¾

1999, Sept. 30 **Litho.**

6536	A3086 2r multi	.30	.20
6537	A3086 2r multi	.30	.20
6538	A3086 2r multi	.30	.20
6539	A3086 2r multi	.30	.20
6540	A3086 2r multi, vert.	.30	.20
	Nos. 6536-6540 (5)	1.50	1.00

Popular Singers A3087

Designs: No. 6542, Leonid Utesov (1895-1982). No. 6543, Mark Bernes (1911-69). No. 6544, Claudia Shulzhenko (1906-84). No. 6545, Lidia Ruslanova (1900-73). No. 6546, Bulat Okudzhava (1924-97). No. 6547, Vladimir Visotsky (1938-80). No. 6548, Viktor Tsoi (1962-90). No. 6549, Igor Talkov (1956-91).

1999, Oct. 6 **Litho.** *Perf. 12x12¼*

6542	A3087 2r multi	.30	.20
6543	A3087 2r multi	.30	.20
6544	A3087 2r multi	.30	.20
6545	A3087 2r multi	.30	.20
6546	A3087 2r multi	.30	.20
6547	A3087 2r multi	.30	.20
6548	A3087 2r multi	.30	.20
6549	A3087 2r multi	.30	.20
a.	Miniature sheet, #6542-6549	2.40	
	Nos. 6542-6549 (8)	2.40	1.60

Types of 1997 Redrawn with Microprinting Replacing Vertical Lines

1999, Oct. 26 **Litho.** *Perf. 12x12¼*

Granite Paper

6550	A3020	10k Like #6371	.20	.20
6551	A3020	15k Like #6372	.20	.20
6552	A3020	25k Like #6373	.20	.20
6553	A3020	30k Like #6374	.20	.20
6554	A3020	50k Like #6375	.20	.20
6555	A3020	1r Like #6377	.20	.20
6556	A3020	1.50r Like #6378	.20	.20
6557	A3020	2r Like #6379	.30	.20
6558	A3020	2.50r Like #6380	.30	.20
6559	A3020	3r Like #6381	.40	.20
6560	A3020	5r Like #6382	.65	.30
	Nos. 6550-6560 (11)		3.05	2.30

Dated 1998.

Spartak, Russian Soccer Champions A3088

1999, Nov. 27 *Perf. 12x12¼*

6561	A3088 2r multi	.30	.20

New Year 2000 — A3089

Designs: a, Grandfather Frost, planets. b, Tree, earth in shell.
Illustration reduced.

1999, Dec. 1 *Perf. 11½x11¾*

6562	A3089 1.20r Pair, #a-b	.35	.20
c.	Sheet of 6 #6562a	.95	
d.	Sheet of 6 #6562b	.95	

No. 6562 printed in sheets of 30 stamps.

Christianity, 2000th Anniv. — A3090

Paintings: No. 6563, The Raising of the Daughter of Jairus, by Vassili D. Polenov, 1871. No. 6564, Christ in the Wilderness, by Ivan N. Kramskoy, 1872. No. 6565, Christ in the House of Mary and Martha, by G. I. Semiradsky, 1886. No. 6566, What is Truth?, by Nikolai N. Gay, 1890, vert.
7r, Appearance of the Risen Christ, by Alexander A. Ivanov, 1837-57.

2000, Jan. 1 **Litho.** *Perf. 12*

6563	A3090 3r multi	.40	.20
6564	A3090 3r multi	.40	.20
6565	A3090 3r multi	.40	.20
6566	A3090 3r multi	.40	.20
	Nos. 6563-6566 (4)	1.60	.80

Souvenir Sheet

Perf. 12¼x12

6567	A3090 7r multi	.90	.45

No. 6567 contains one 52x37mm stamp.

Souvenir Sheet

Christianity, 2000th Anniv. — A3091

a, Mother of God mosaic, St. Sofia Cathedral, Kiev, 11th cent. b, Christ Pantocrator fresco, Church of the Savior's Transfiguration, Polotsk, Belarus, 12th cent. c, Volodymyr Madonna, Tretiakov Gallery, Moscow, 12th cent.
Illustration reduced.

2000, Jan. 5 *Perf. 12x12¼*

6568	A3091 3r Sheet of 3, #a-c	.90	.45

See Belarus No. 330, Ukraine No. 370.

Nikolai D. Psurtsev (1900-80), Communications Minister — A3092

Litho. & Engr.

2000, Feb. 1 *Perf. 12x12¼*

6569	A3092 2.50r multi	.35	.20

Souvenir Sheet

Christianity, 2000th Anniv. — A3093

Illustration reduced.

2000, Feb. 10 Litho. *Perf. 12¼*
6570 A3093 10r Kremlin Cathedrals 1.40 .70

No. 6570 contains two 37x52mm labels.

Polar Explorers — A3094

Designs: No. 6571, R. L. Samoilovich (1881-1940). No. 6572, V. Y. Vize (1886-1954). No. 6573, Mikhail M. Somov (1908-73). No. 6574, P. A. Gordienko (1913-82). No. 6575, A. F. Treshnikov (1914-91).
Illustration reduced.

2000, Feb. 24 *Perf. 11¾*

6571	A3094 2r multi	.30	.20
6572	A3094 2r multi	.30	.20
6573	A3094 2r multi	.30	.20
6574	A3094 2r multi	.30	.20
6575	A3094 2r multi	.30	.20
a.	Miniature sheet of 5, #6571-6575, + label	1.50	.75

National Sporting Milestones of the 20th Century — A3095

a, 25k, N. A. Panin-Kolomenkin, 1st Olympic champion, 1908. b, 30k, Stockholm Olympics, 1912. c, 50k, All-Russian Olympiad, 1913-14. d, 1r, All-Union Spartacist Games, 1928. e, 1.35r, Sports Association for Labor & Defense, 1931. f, 1.50r, Honored Master of Sport award, 1934. g, 2r, Helsinki Olympics, 1952. h, 2.50r, Vladimir P. Kuts, gold medalist at Melbourne Olympics, 1956. i, 3r, Gold medalist soccer team at Melbourne, 1956. j, 4r Mikhail M. Botvinnik, chess champion. k, 5r, Hockey series between Canada and Soviet Union, 1972. l, 6r, Moscow Olympics, 1980.

2000, Mar. 15 *Perf. 12¼x12*
6576 A3095 Sheet of 12, #a-l 3.75 1.90

Souvenir Sheet

World Meteorological Organization, 50th Anniv. — A3096

2000, Mar. 20
6577 A3096 7r multi .90 .45

A3097

A3098

End of World War II, 55th Anniv. — A3099

War effort posters: No. 6581, Soldier holding child.
5r, Soldier and medal.

2000, Apr. 10

6578	A3097 1.50r multi	.20	.20
6579	A3098 1.50r multi	.20	.20
6580	A3099 1.50r multi	.20	.20
6581	A3099 1.50r multi	.20	.20
	Nos. 6578-6581 (4)	.80	.80

Souvenir Sheet

6582	A3099 5r multi	.65	.30
a.	Miniature sheet, #6578-6581, 2 #6582	2.10	1.10

International Space Cooperation A3100

2r, Apollo-Soyuz mission. 3r, Intl. Space Station. 5r, Sea-based launching station.

2000, Apr. 12 *Perf. 12*

6583	A3100 2r multi, vert.	.25	.20
a.	Miniature sheet of 6	1.50	.75
6584	A3100 3r multi	.30	.20
6585	A3100 5r multi, vert.	.50	.25
	Nos. 6583-6585 (3)	1.05	.65

Traffic Safety Week — A3101

2000, Apr. 20 Litho. *Perf. 12x12½*
6586 A3101 1.75r multi .25 .20

Holocaust A3102

2000, May 5 *Perf. 12*
6587 A3102 2r multi .25 .20

Election of Vladimir V. Putin as President — A3103

2000, May 7 Litho. *Perf. 12*
6588 A3103 1.75r multi .25 .20

Europa, 2000
Common Design Type

2000, May 9 Litho. *Perf. 12½x12*
6589 CD17 7r multi .90 .45
ooklet, #6589 .90

Souvenir Sheet

Expo 2000, Hanover — A3104

2000, May 17 Litho. *Perf. 12½x12*
6590 A3104 10r multi 1.25 .60

Yamalo-Nenets Autonomous Okrug — A3105

Kalmykia Republic — A3106

Mari El Republic — A3107

Tatarstan Republic — A3108

2000, May 25 *Perf. 12*

6591	A3105 3r shown	.35	.20
6592	A3105 3r Chuvash Republic	.35	.20
6593	A3106 3r shown	.35	.20
6594	A3107 3r shown	.35	.20
6595	A3108 3r shown	.35	.20
6596	A3108 3r Udmurtia Republic	.35	.20
	Nos. 6591-6596 (6)	2.10	1.20

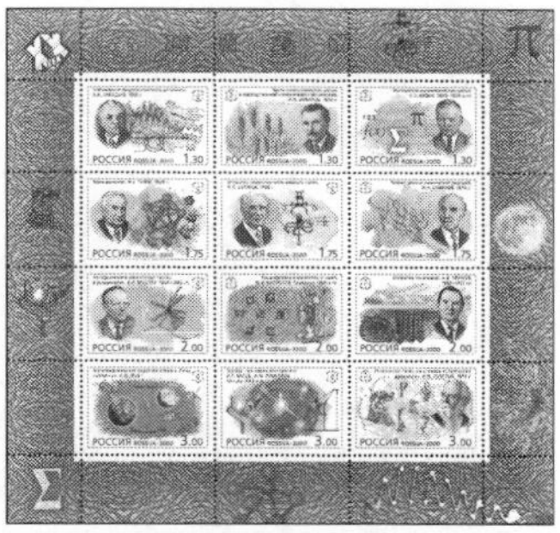

National Scientific Milestones in the 20th Century — A3109

No. 6597: a, 1.30r, Observation of ferromagnetic resonance by V. K. Arkadjev, 1913. b, 1.30r, Botanical diversity studies by N. I. Vavilov, 1920. c, 1.30r, Moscow Mathematical School, N. N. Luzin, 1920-30. d, 1.75r, Theories on light wave emissions by I. Y. Tamm, 1929. e, 1.75r, Discovery of superfluidity of liquid helium, by P. L. Kapitsa, 1938. f, 1.75r, Research in chemical chain reactions by N. N. Semenov, 1934. g, 2r, Phase stability in particle accelerators, by V. I. Veksler, 1944-45. h, 2r, Translation of Mayan texts by Y. V. Knorozov, 1950s. i, 2r, Research into pogonophorans by A. V. Ivanov. j, 3r, Photographing of the dark side of the moon by Luna 3, 1959. k, 3r, Research in quantum electronics by N. G. Basov and A. M. Prokhorov, 1960s. l, 3r, Slavic ethnolinguistic dictionary by N. I. Tolstoi, 1995.

2000, June 20 *Perf. 12½x12*
6597 A3109 Sheet of 12, #a-l 3.00 1.50

Dogs — A3110

2000, July 20 *Perf. 12x11¾*

6598 Horiz. strip of 5 1.10 .55
- *a.* A3110 1r Chihuahua .20 .20
- *b.* A3110 1.50r Toy terrier .20 .20
- *c.* A3110 2r Miniature poodle .20 .20
- *d.* A3110 2.50r French bulldog .30 .20
- *e.* A3110 3r Japanese chin .30 .20
- Booklet, #6598 1.10
- *f.* Souvenir sheet, #6598e, 2 each #6598a-6598d, perf. 11¾ 2.00 1.00

2000 Summer Olympics, Sydney — A3111

Designs: 2r, Fencing. 3r, Synchronized swimming. 5r, Volleyball.

2000, Aug. 15 **Litho.** *Perf. 12*

6599-6601 A3111 Set of 3 1.25 .65

Geological Service, 300th Anniv. — A3112

Minerals: 1r, Charoite. 2r, Hematite. 3r, Rock crystals. 4r, Gold.

2000, Aug. 22 *Perf. 11¾*

6602-6605 A3112 Set of 4 1.25 .60

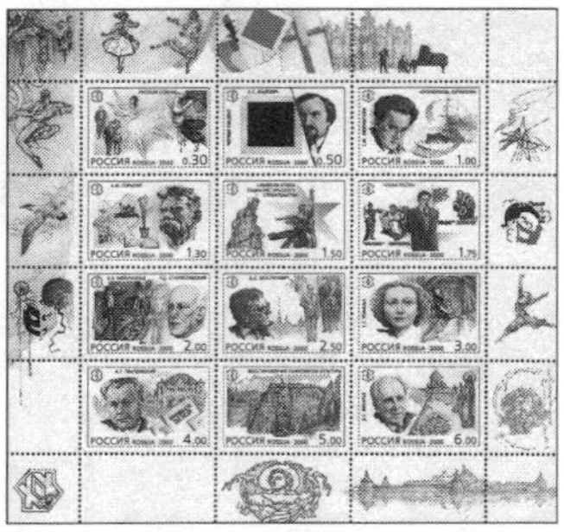

National Cultural Milestones in the 20th Century — A3113

No. 6606: a, 30k, Tours of Russian ballet and opera companies, 1908-14. b, 50k, Black Square on White, by Kazimir S. Malevich, 1913. c, 1r, Battleship Potemkin, movie by Sergein Eisenstein, 1925. d, 1.30r, Maxim Gorki, writer. e, 1.50r, Symbols of socialism. f, 1.75r, Vladimir V. Mayakovsky, poet, and propaganda posters. g, 2r, Vsevolod V. Meyerhold, Konstantin S. Stanislavsky, actors. h, 2.50r, Dmitry D. Shostakovich, composer. i, 3r, Galina S. Ulanova, ballet dancer. j, 4r, A. T. Tvardovsky, poet. k, 5r, Restoration of historical monuments and buildings. l, 6r, D. S. Likhachev, literary critic.

2000, Sept. 20 **Litho.** *Perf. 12½x12*

6606 A3113 Sheet of 12, #a-l 2.25 1.10

Fish in Lake Peipus A3114

No. 6607: a, Stizostedion lucioperka, Coregonus lauaretus manaenoides. b, Osmerus eperlanus spirinchus, Coregonus albula.

2000, Oct. 25 *Perf. 12x12¼*

6607 Horiz. pair + central label .40 .20
- *a.-b.* A3114 2.50r Any single .20 .20
- Booklet, #6607 .40

See Estonia No. 403.

National Technological Milestones in the 20th Century — A3115

No. 6608: a, 1.50r, Medicine. b, 1.50r, Construction. c, 1.50r, Motor transport. d, 2r, Power generation. e, 2r, Communications. f, 2r, Space technology. g, 3r, Aviation. h, 3r, Rail transport. i, 3r, Sea transport. j, 4r, Metallurgy. k, 4r, Oil refining. l, 4r, Mineral extraction.

2000, Nov. 28 *Perf. 12½x12*

6608 A3115 Sheet of 12, #a-l 2.50 1.25

Happy New Millennium — A3116

2000, Dec. 1 *Perf. 12*

6609 A3116 2r multi .20 .20
- *a.* Sheet of 6 1.00 .50

Foreign Intelligence Service, 80th Anniv. — A3117

2000, Dec. 14 **Litho.** *Perf. 12x12½*

6610 A3117 2.50r multi .25 .20

Kabardino-Balkaria Republic — A3118

Dagestan Republic A3119

Samara Oblast A3120

2001, Jan. 10 *Perf. 12*

6611 A3118 3r shown .25 .20
6612 A3119 3r shown .25 .20
6613 A3120 3r shown .25 .20
6614 A3118 3r Chita Oblast .25 .20
6615 A3118 3r Komi Republic, vert. .25 .20
Nos. 6611-6615 (5) 1.25 1.00

Souvenir Sheet

Naval Education in Russia, 300th Anniv. — A3121

No. 6616: a, 1.50r, Mathematics and Navigation School, Moscow. b, 2r, Geographical expeditions. c, 8r, St. Petersburg Naval Institute.

2001, Jan. 10 *Perf. 12x12¼*

6616 A3121 Sheet of 3, #a-c .95 .50

A3122

A3123

A3124

A3124a

Tulips — A3125

2001, Feb. 2 **Litho.** *Perf. 12¼x12*

6625 Horiz. strip of 5 .80 .40
- *a.* A3122 2r Happy Birthday .20 .20
- *b.* A3123 2r Be Happy .20 .20
- *c.* A3124 2r Congratulations .20 .20
- *d.* A3124a 2r Good luck .20 .20
- *e.* A3125 2r With Love .20 .20
- *f.* Sheet, #6625a-6625e + label .80 .40

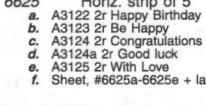

Paintings — A3126

No. 6626, 3r (brown background): a, Portrait of P. A. Bulakhov, by Vasily Andreevich Tropinin, 1823. b, Portrait of E. I. Karzinkina, by Tropinin, 1838.

No. 6627, 3r (tan and white background): a, Portrait of I. A. Galitsin, by A. M. Matveev, 1728 . b, Portrait of A. P. Galitsina, by Matveev, 1728.

Illustration reduced.

2001, Feb. 15 **Litho.** *Perf. 12*

Pairs, #a-b, + Central Label

6626-6627 A3126 Set of 2 1.00 .50

St. Petersburg, 300th Anniv. — A3127

Paintings: 1r, Senate Square and Peter the Great Monumnet, by B. Patersen, 1799. 2r, English Embankment Near senate, by Patersen, 1801. 3r, View of Mikhailovsky Castle From Fontanka Embankment, by Patersen, 1801. 4r, View of the River Moika Near the Stable Department Building, by A. E. Martynov, 1809. 5r, View of the Neva River From the Peter and Paul Fortress, by K. P. Beggrov, 19th cent.

2001, Mar. 15 *Perf. 12x11¾*

6628-6632	A3127	Set of 5	1.25	.60
6632a		Sheet, #6628-6632, + label	1.25	.60

Dragonflies — A3128

No. 6633: a, 1r, Pyrrhosoma nymphula. b, 1.50r, Epitheca bimaculata. c, 2r, Aeschna grandis. d, 3r, Libellula depressa. e, 5r, Coenagrion hastulatum.
Illustration reduced.

2001, Apr. 5 *Perf. 12x12¼*

6633	A3128	Block of 5, #a-e, + label	1.00	.50

First Manned Space Flight, 40th Anniv. — A3129

No. 6634: a, Cosmonaut Yuri Gagarin and rocket designer Sergei Korolev. b, Gagarin saluting.
Illustration reduced.

2001, Apr. 12 Litho. *Perf. 12½x12*

6634	A3129	3r Horiz. pair, #a-b	.50	.25
c.		Sheet, 3 #6634	1.50	.75

Europa — A3130

2001, May 9 Litho. *Perf. 11¾*

6635	A3130	8r multi	.65	.30
a.		Sheet of 6	4.00	2.00

Intl. Federation of Philately, 75th Anniv. — A3131

2001, May 17 *Perf. 11½*

6636	A3131	2.50r multi	.20	.20

Declaration of State Sovereignty Day — A3132

Litho. & Embossed

2001, June 5 *Perf. 13¼*

6637	A3132	5r multi	.40	.20

A3134

Houses of Worship — A3135

Designs: No. 6640, Cathedral, Vladimir, 1189. No. 6641, Cathedral, Zvenigorod, 1405. No. 6642, Cathedral, Moscow, 1792. No. 6643, Cathedral, Rostov-on-Don, 1792. No. 6644, Mosque, Ufa, 1830. No. 6645, Church, St, Petersburg, 1838. No. 6646, Mosque, Kazan, 1849. No. 6647, Synagogue, Moscow, 1891. No. 6648, Synagogue, St. Petersburg, 1893. No. 6649, Cathedral, Moscow, 1911. No. 6650, Temple, Ulan-Ude, 1976. No. 6651, Church, Bryansk, 1996. No. 6652, Church, Ryazan, 1996. No. 6653, Church, Lesosibirsk, 1999.

2001, July 12 Litho. *Perf. 11½*

6640	A3134	2.50r multi	.20	.20
6641	A3134	2.50r multi	.20	.20
6642	A3134	2.50r shown	.20	.20
6643	A3134	2.50r multi	.20	.20
6644	A3134	2.50r multi	.20	.20
6645	A3134	2.50r multi	.20	.20
6646	A3134	2.50r multi	.20	.20
6647	A3134	2.50r multi	.20	.20
6648	A3134	2.50r multi	.20	.20
6649	A3134	2.50r multi	.20	.20
6650	A3134	2.50r multi	.20	.20
6651	A3135	2.50r shown	.20	.20
6652	A3135	2.50r multi	.20	.20
6653	A3134	2.50r multi	.20	.20
		Nos. 6640-6653 (14)	2.80	2.80

Souvenir Sheet

First Russian Railroad, 150th Anniv. — A3136

2001, July 25 *Perf. 12*

6654	A3136	12r multi	.95	.50

SEMI-POSTAL STAMPS

Empire

Admiral Kornilov Monument, Sevastopol
SP1

Pozharski and Minin Monument, Moscow
SP2

Statue of Peter the Great, Leningrad
SP3

Alexander II Memorial and Kremlin, Moscow
SP4

Perf. 11½ to 13½ and Compound

1905 Typo. Unwmk.

B1	SP1	3k red, brn & grn	3.00	2.25
a.		Perf. 13½x 11½	190.00	150.00
b.		Perf. 13½	27.50	27.50
c.		Perf. 11½x13½	200.00	160.00
B2	SP2	5k lilac, vio & straw	2.25	1.75
B3	SP3	7k lt bl, dk bl & pink	3.50	2.25
a.		Perf. 13½	45.00	45.00
B4	SP4	10k lt blue, dk bl & yel	6.00	3.25
		Nos. B1-B4 (4)	14.75	9.50

These stamps were sold for 3 kopecks over face value. The surtax was donated to a fund for the orphans of soldiers killed in the Russo-Japanese war.

Ilya Muromets Legendary Russian Hero — SP5

Designs: 3k, Don Cossack Bidding Farewell to His Sweetheart. 7k, Symbolical of Charity. 10k, St. George Slaying the Dragon.

1914 *Perf. 11½, 12½*

B5	SP5	1k red brn & dk grn, *straw*	.40	.45
B6	SP5	3k mar & gray grn, *pink*	.40	.45
B7	SP5	7k dk brn & dk grn, *buff*	.40	.45
B8	SP5	10k dk blue & brn, *blue*	1.90	2.25
		Nos. B5-B8 (4)	3.10	3.60

Perf. 13½

B5a	SP5	1k	.30	.45
B6a	SP5	3k	35.00	32.50
B7a	SP5	7k	.25	.45
B8a	SP5	10k	5.75	7.25
		Nos. B5a-B8a (4)	41.30	40.65

Perf. 11½, 12½, 13½

1915 White Paper

B9	SP5	1k orange brn & gray	.25	.35
B10	SP5	3k car & gray black	.35	.45
a.		Horiz. pair, imperf btwn.	125.00	
B12	SP5	7k dk brn & dk grn	6.00	
B13	SP5	10k dk blue & brown	.20	.35
		Nos. B9-B13 (4)	6.80	

These stamps were sold for 1 kopeck over face value. The surtax was donated to charities connected with the war of 1914-17.

No. B12 not regularly issued. It exists only perf 11½ (with Specimen overprint) and 12½.

Nos. B5-B13 exist imperf. Value each, $150 unused, $250 canceled.

Russian Soviet Federated Socialist Republic
Volga Famine Relief Issue

Relief Work on Volga River — SP9

Administering Aid to Famine Victim — SP10

1921 Litho. *Imperf.*

B14	SP9	2250r green	3.00	6.50
a.		Pelure paper	100.00	55.00
B15	SP9	2250r deep red	2.50	4.50
a.		Pelure paper	15.00	12.50
B16	SP9	2250r brown	2.50	11.00
B17	SP10	2250r dark blue	6.00	14.00
		Nos. B14-B17 (4)	14.00	36.00

Forged cancels and counterfeits of Nos. B14-B17 are plentiful.

Stamps of type A33 with this overprint were not charity stamps nor did they pay postage in any form.

They represent taxes paid on stamps exported from or imported into Russia. In 1925 the semi-postal stamps of 1914-15 were surcharged for the same purpose. Stamps of the regular issues 1918 and 1921 have also been surcharged with inscriptions and new values, to pay the importation and exportation taxes.

Nos. 149-150 Surcharged in Black, Red, Blue or Orange

Р. С. Ф. С. Р.
ГОЛОДАЮЩИМ
250 р.+250 р

1922, Feb. *Perf. 13½*

B18 A33 100r + 100r on 70k .60 1.65
a. "100 p. + p. 100" 60.00 65.00
B19 A33 100r + 100r on 70k (R) .60 1.65
B20 A33 100r + 100r on 70k (Bl) .30 .85
B21 A33 250r + 250r on 35k .30 .85
B22 A33 250r + 250r on 35k (R) .60 1.65
B23 A33 250r + 250r on 35k (O) 1.10 3.25
Nos. B18-B23 (6) 3.50 9.90

Issued to raise funds for Volga famine relief.
Nos. B18-B22 exist with surcharge inverted. Values $20 to $40.

Regular Issues of 1909-18 Overprinted

РСФСР
Филателия
—детям
19—8—22

1922, Aug. 19 *Perf. 14*

B24 A14 1k orange 200.00 200.00
B25 A14 2k green 15.00 *25.00*
B26 A14 3k red 12.00 *25.00*
B27 A14 5k claret 15.00 *25.00*
B28 A15 10k dark blue 15.00 *25.00*

Imperf

B29 A14 1k orange 175.00 200.00
Nos. B24-B29 (6) 432.00 500.00

The overprint means "Philately for the Children". The stamps were sold at five million times their face values and 80% of the amount was devoted to child welfare. The stamps were sold only at Moscow and for one day.
Exist with overprint reading up. Counterfeits exist including those with overprint reading up. Reprints exist.

Worker and Peasant (Industry and Agriculture) — SP11

Allegory: Agriculture Will Help End Distress SP12

Star of Hope, Wheat and Worker-Peasant Handclasp — SP13

Sower — SP14

1922 **Litho.** *Imperf.*
Without Gum

B30 SP11 2t (2000r) green 8.50 *20.00*
B31 SP12 2t (2000r) rose 14.00 *35.00*
B32 SP13 4t (4000r) rose 14.00 *35.00*
B33 SP14 6t (6000r) green 14.00 *35.00*
Nos. B30-B33 (4) 50.50 125.00

Nos. B30-B33 exist with double impression. Value, each $150.
Counterfeits of Nos. B30-B33 exist; beware also of forged cancellations.
Miniature copies of Nos. B30-B33 exist, taken from the 1933 Soviet catalogue.

Automobile SP15

Steamship SP16

Railroad Train SP17

Airplane SP18

1922 *Imperf.*

B34 SP15 light violet .20 .20
B35 SP16 violet .20 .20
B36 SP17 gray blue .20 .20
B37 SP18 blue gray 2.00 *4.00*
Nos. B34-B37 (4) 2.60 *4.60*

Inscribed "For the Hungry." Each stamp was sold for 200,000r postage and 50,000r charity.
Counterfeits of Nos. B34-B37 exist.

Nos. 212, 183, 202 Surcharged in Bronze, Gold or Silver

1 мая 1923 г.
Филателия—
трудящимся.
2 р.+2 р.

1923 *Imperf.*

B38 A48 1r +1r on 10r 125.00 125.00
a. Inverted surcharge 250.00 250.00
B39 A48 1r +1r on 10r (G) 20.00 30.00
a. Inverted surcharge 250.00 250.00
B40 A43 2r +2r on 250r 16.00 25.00
a. Pelure paper 20.00 22.50
b. Inverted surcharge 200.00 200.00
c. Double surcharge

Wmk. 171

B41 A46 4r +4r on 5000r 17.50 22.50
a. Date spaced "1 923" 160.00 160.00
b. Inverted surcharge 275.00 275.00
B42 A46 4r +4r on 5000r (S) 450.00 400.00
a. Inverted surcharge 1,000. 850.00
b. Date spaced "1 923" 1,000. 850.00
c. As "b," inverted surch. *3,500.*
Nos. B38-B42 (5) 628.50 602.50

The inscriptions mean "Philately's Contribution to Labor." The stamps were on sale only at Moscow and for one day. The surtax was for charitable purposes.
Counterfeits of No. B42 exist.

Leningrad Flood Issue

Nos. 181-182, 184-186 Surcharged

С.С.С.Р.
пострадавшему
от наводнения
Ленинграду.
7 к. + 20 к.

1924 **Unwmk.** *Imperf.*

B43 A40 3k + 10k on 100r .80 1.25
a. Pelure paper 3.00 4.00
b. Inverted surcharge 175.00 125.00
B44 A40 7k + 20k on 200r .80 1.25
a. Inverted surcharge 175.00 125.00
B45 A40 14k + 30k on 300r .90 2.50
a. Pelure paper 250.00 210.00

Similar Surcharge in Red or Black

B46 A41 12k + 40k on 500r (R) 1.65 2.50
a. Double surcharge 110.00 110.00
b. Inverted surcharge 110.00 110.00
B47 A41 20k + 50k on 1000r 1.10 2.50
a. Thick paper 11.50 18.00
b. Pelure paper 20.00 25.00
c. Chalk surface paper 10.00 12.50
Nos. B43-B47 (5) 5.25 10.00

The surcharge on Nos. B43 to B45 reads: "S.S.S.R. For the sufferers by the inundation at Leningrad." That on Nos. B46 and B47 reads: "S.S.S.R. For the Leningrad Proletariat, 23, IX, 1924."
No. B46 is surcharged vertically, reading down, with the value as the top line.

Orphans SP19

Lenin as a Child SP20

1926 **Typo.** *Perf. 13½*

B48 SP19 10k brown *3.25* *3.00*
B49 SP20 20k deep blue *4.00* *4.25*

Wmk. 170

B50 SP19 10k brown 1.00 .90
B51 SP20 20k deep blue 1.50 1.65
Nos. B48-B51 (4) *9.75* *9.80*

Two kopecks of the price of each of these stamps was donated to organizations for the care of indigent children.

Types of 1926 Issue

1927

B52 SP19 8k + 2k yel green 1.25 .35
B53 SP20 18k + 2k deep rose 3.50 1.00

Surtax was for child welfare.

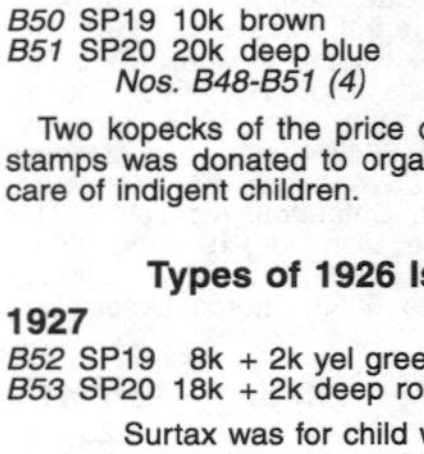

Industrial Training SP21

Agricultural Training SP22

Perf. 10, 10½, 12½

1929-30 **Photo.** **Unwmk.**

B54 SP21 10k +2k ol brn & org brn 2.50 2.50
a. Perf. 10½ 75.00 75.00
B55 SP21 10k +2k ol grn ('30) 1.50 1.25
B56 SP22 20k +2k blk brn & bl, perf. 10½ 2.00 3.50
a. Perf. 12½ 35.00 35.00
b. Perf. 10 10.00 10.00
B57 SP22 20k +2k bl grn ('30) 2.00 3.50
Nos. B54-B57 (4) 8.00 10.75

Surtax was for child welfare.

Catalogue values for unused stamps in this section, from this point to the end of the section, are for Never Hinged items.

"Montreal Passing Torch to Moscow" — SP23

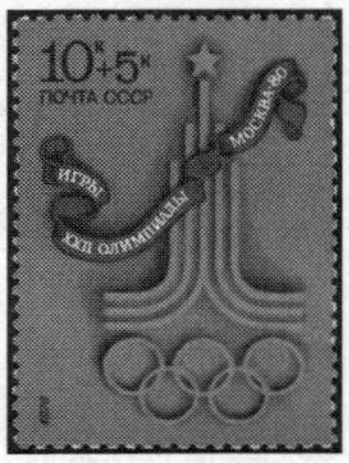

Moscow '80 Olympic Games Emblem — SP24

22nd Olympic Games, Moscow, 1980: 16k+6k, like 10k+5k. 60k+30k, Aerial view of Kremlin and Moscow '80 emblem.

1976, Dec. 28 **Litho.** *Perf. 12x12½*

B58 SP23 4k + 2k multi .25 .20
B59 SP24 10k + 5k multi .45 .35
B60 SP24 16k + 6k multi .85 .40
Nos. B58-B60 (3) 1.55 .95

Souvenir Sheet
Photo.
Perf. 11½

B61 SP23 60k + 30k multi 2.25 1.65

Greco-Roman Wrestling — SP25

Moscow '80 Emblem and: 6k+3k, Free-style wrestling. 10k+5k, Judo. 16k+6k, Boxing. 20k+10k, Weight lifting.

1977, June 21 **Litho.** *Perf. 12½x12*

B62 SP25 4k + 2k multi .20 .20
B63 SP25 6k + 3k multi .30 .20
B64 SP25 10k + 5k multi .40 .30
B65 SP25 16k + 6k multi .60 .35
B66 SP25 20k + 10k multi .80 .45
Nos. B62-B66 (5) 2.30 1.50

Perf. 12½x12, 12x12½

1977, Sept. 22

Designs: 4k+2k, Bicyclist. 6k+3k, Woman archer, vert. 10k+5k, Sharpshooting. 16k+6k, Equestrian. 20k+10k, Fencer. 50k+25k, Equestrian and fencer.

B67 SP25 4k + 2k multi .20 .20
B68 SP25 6k + 3k multi .25 .20
B69 SP25 10k + 5k multi .40 .30
B70 SP25 16k + 6k multi .55 .35
B71 SP25 20k + 10k multi .70 .45
Nos. B67-B71 (5) 2.10 1.50

Souvenir Sheet
Perf. 12½x12

B72 SP25 50k + 25k multi 3.00 1.65

1978, Mar. 24 *Perf. 12½x12*

Designs: 4k+2k, Swimmer at start. 6k+3k, Woman diver, vert. 10k+5k, Water polo.

16k+6k, Canoeing. 20k+10k, Canadian single. 50k+25k, Start of double scull race.

B73	SP25	4k + 2k multi	.20	.20
B74	SP25	6k + 3k multi	.25	.20
B75	SP25	10k + 5k multi	.40	.25
B76	SP25	16k + 6k multi	.55	.30
B77	SP25	20k + 10k multi	.70	.45
		Nos. B73-B77 (5)	2.10	1.40

Souvenir Sheet

B78	SP25	50k + 25k grn & blk	2.50	2.50

Star-class Yacht — SP26

Keel Yachts and Moscow '80 Emblem: 6k+3k, Soling class. 10k+5k, Centerboarder 470. 16k+6k, Finn class. 20k+10k, Flying Dutchman class. 50k+25k, Catamaran Tornado, horiz.

1978, Oct. 26 Litho. ***Perf. 12x12½***

B79	SP26	4k + 2k multi	.20	.20
B80	SP26	6k + 3k multi	.25	.20
B81	SP26	10k + 5k multi	.40	.20
B82	SP26	16k + 6k multi	.55	.30
B83	SP26	20k + 10k multi	.70	.40
		Nos. B79-B83 (5)	2.10	1.30

Souvenir Sheet

Perf. 12½x12

B84	SP26	50k + 25k multi	2.50	1.40

Women's Gymnastics SP27

Designs: 6k+3k, Man on parallel bars. 10k+5k, Man on horizontal bar. 16k+6k, Woman on balance beam. 20k+10k, Woman on uneven bars. 50k+25k, Man on rings.

1979, Mar. 21 Litho. ***Perf. 12x12½***

B85	SP27	4k + 2k multi	.20	.20
B86	SP27	6k + 3k multi	.25	.20
B87	SP27	10k + 5k multi	.40	.20
B88	SP27	16k + 6k multi	.55	.30
B89	SP27	20k + 10k multi	.70	.40
		Nos. B85-B89 (5)	2.10	1.30

Souvenir Sheet

Perf. 12½x12

B90	SP25	50k + 25k multi	2.00	1.40

1979, June ***Perf. 12½x12, 12x12½***

Designs: 4k+2k, Soccer. 6k+3k, Basketball. 10k+5k, Women's volleyball. 16k+6k, Handball. 20k+10k, Field hockey.

B91	SP25	4k + 2k multi	.20	.20
B92	SP27	6k + 3k multi	.25	.20
B93	SP27	10k + 5k multi	.40	.20
B94	SP25	16k + 6k multi	.55	.30
B95	SP25	20k + 10k multi	.70	.40
		Nos. B91-B95 (5)	2.10	1.30

22nd Olympic Games, Moscow, July 19-Aug. 3, 1980.

Running, Moscow '80 Emblem SP27a

1980 Litho. ***Perf. 12½x12, 12x12½***

B96	SP27a	4k + 2k shown	.20	.20
B97	SP27a	4k + 2k Pole vault	.20	.20
B98	SP27a	6k + 3k Discus	.25	.20
B99	SP27a	6k + 3k Hurdles	.25	.20
B100	SP27a	10k + 5k Javelin	.40	.20
B101	SP27a	10k + 5k Walking, vert.	.40	.20
B102	SP27a	16k + 6k Hammer throw	.70	.30
B103	SP27a	16k + 6k High jump	.70	.30
B104	SP27a	20k + 10k Shot put	.90	.40
B105	SP27a	20k + 10k Long jump	.90	.40
		Nos. B96-B105 (10)	4.90	2.60

Souvenir Sheet

B106	SP27a	50k + 25k Relay race	2.00	1.00

22nd Olympic Games, Moscow, July 19-Aug. 3. Issued: Nos. B96, B99, B101, B103, B105, Feb. 6; others, Mar. 12.

Moscow '80 Emblem, Relief from St. Dimitri's Cathedral, Arms of Vladimir — SP28

Moscow '80 Emblem and: No. B108, Bridge over Klyazma River and Vladimir Hotel. No. B109, Relief from Nativity Cathedral and coat of arms (falcon), Suzdal. No. B110, Tourist complex and Pozharski Monument, Suzdal. No. B111, Frunze Monument, Ivanovo, torch and spindle. No. B112, Museum of First Soviets, Fighters of the Revolution Monument, Ivanovo.

Photogravure and Engraved

1977, Dec. 30 ***Perf. 11½x12***

B107	SP28	1r + 50k multi	1.75	.90
B108	SP28	1r + 50k multi	1.75	.90
B109	SP28	1r + 50k multi	1.75	.90
B110	SP28	1r + 50k multi	1.75	.90
B111	SP28	1r + 50k multi	1.75	.90
B112	SP28	1r + 50k multi	1.75	.90
		Nos. B107-B112 (6)	10.50	5.40

"Tourism around the Golden Ring."

Fortifications and Arms of Zagorsk SP29

Moscow '80 Emblem and (Coat of Arms design): No. B114, Gagarin Palace of Culture and new arms of Zagorsk (building & horse). No. B115, Rostov Kremlin with St. John the Divine Church and No. B116, View of Rostov from Nero Lake (deer). No. B117, Alexander Nevski and WWII soldiers' monuments, Pereyaslav and No. B118, Peter the Great monument, Pereyaslav (lion & fish). No. B119, Tower and wall of Monastery of the Transfiguration, Jaroslaw and No. B120, Dock and monument for Soviet heroes, Jaroslaw (bear).

1978 ***Perf. 12x11½***

Multicolored and:

B113	SP29	1r + 50k gold	2.00	.80
B114	SP29	1r + 50k silver	2.00	.80
B115	SP29	1r + 50k silver	2.00	.80
B116	SP29	1r + 50k gold	2.00	.80
B117	SP29	1r + 50k gold	2.00	.80
B118	SP29	1r + 50k silver	2.00	.80
B119	SP29	1r + 50k gold	2.00	.80
B120	SP29	1r + 50k silver	2.00	.80
		Nos. B113-B120 (8)	16.00	6.40

Issued: #B113-B116, 10/16; #B117-B120, 12/25.

1979 ***Perf. 12x11½***

Moscow '80 Emblem and: No. B121, Narikaly Fortress, Tbilisi, 4th century. No. B122, Georgia Philharmonic Concert Hall, "Muse" sculpture, Tbilisi. No. B123, Chir-Dor Mosque, 17th century, Samarkand. No. B124, Peoples Friendship Museum, "Courage" monument, Tashkent. No. B125, Landscape, Erevan. B126, Armenian State Opera and Ballet Theater, Erevan.

Multicolored and:

B121	SP29	1r+50k sil, bl circle	2.25	1.40
B122	SP29	1r+50k gold, yel circle	2.25	1.40
B123	SP29	1r+50k sil, bl 8-point star	2.25	1.40
B124	SP29	1r+50k gold, red 8-point star	2.25	1.40
B125	SP29	1r+50k sil, bl diamond	2.25	1.40
B126	SP29	1r+50k gold, red diamond	2.25	1.40
		Nos. B121-B126 (6)	13.50	8.40

Issued: #B121-B124, 9/5; #B125-B126, Oct.

Kremlin SP29a

Kalinin Prospect, Moscow SP29b

Admiralteistvo, St. Isaak Cathedral, Leningrad — SP29c

World War II Defense Monument, Leningrad SP29d

Bogdan Khmelnitsky Monument, St. Sophia's Monastery Kiev SP29e

Metro Bridge, Dnieper River, Kiev — SP29f

Palace of Sports, Obelisk, Minsk SP29g

Republican House of Cinematography, Minsk — SP29h

Vyshgorodsky Castle, Town Hall, Tallinn SP29i

Viru Hotel, Tallinn SP29j

1980 ***Perf. 12x11½***

Moscow '80 Emblem, Coat of Arms,

B127	SP29a	1r + 50k multi	1.90	.75
B128	SP29b	1r + 50k multi	1.90	.75
B129	SP29c	1r + 50k multi	2.25	.90
B130	SP29d	1r + 50k multi	2.25	.90
B131	SP29e	1r + 50k multi	2.25	.90
B132	SP29f	1r + 50k multi	2.25	.90
B133	SP29g	1r + 50k multi	2.25	.90
B134	SP29h	1r + 50k multi	2.25	.90
B135	SP29i	1r + 50k multi	2.25	.90
B136	SP29j	1r + 50k multi	2.25	.90
		Nos. B127-B136 (10)	21.80	8.70

Tourism. Issue dates: #B127-B128, Feb. 29. #B129-B130, Mar. 25; #B131-B136, Apr. 30.

Soviet Culture Fund — SP30

Art treasures: No. B137, *Z.E. Serebriakova,* 1910, by O.K. Lansere, vert. No. B138, *Boyar's Wife Examining an Embroidery Design,* 1905, by K.V. Lebedev. No. B139, *Talent,* 1910, by N.P. Bogdanov-Belsky, vert. No. B140, *Trinity,* 15th-16th cent., Novgorod School, vert.

Perf. 12x12½, 12½x12

1988, Aug. 22 Litho.

B137	SP30	10k +5k multi	.40	.25
B138	SP30	15k +7k multi	.55	.35
B139	SP30	30k +15k multi	1.10	.75
		Nos. B137-B139 (3)	2.05	1.35

Souvenir Sheet

B140	SP30	1r +50k multi	4.50	3.00

SP31 SP33

Lenin Children's Fund SP32

1988, Oct. 20 Litho. *Perf. 12*

B141	SP31	10k +5k Bear	.25	.20
B142	SP31	10k +5k Wolf	.25	.20
B143	SP31	20k +10k Fox	.50	.35
B144	SP31	20k +10k Boar	.50	.35
B145	SP31	20k +10k Lynx	.50	.35
a.		Block of 5+label, #B141-B145	2.00	1.40

Zoo Relief Fund. See #B152-B156, B166-B168.

1988, Dec. 12 Litho. *Perf. 12*

Children's drawings and fund emblem: No. B146, Skating Rink. No. B147, Rooster. No. B148, May (girl and flowers).

B146	SP32	5k +2k multi	.25	.20
B147	SP32	5k +2k multi	.25	.20
B148	SP32	5k +2k multi	.25	.20
a.		Block of 3+label, #B146-B148	.75	.45

See Nos. B169-B171.

1988, Dec. 27 *Perf. 12½x12*

#B149, Tigranes I (c. 140-55 B.C.), king of Armenia, gold coin. #B150, St. Ripsime Temple, c. 618. #B151, *Virgin and Child,* fresco (detail) by Ovnat Ovnatanyan, 18th cent., Echmiadzin Cathedral.

B149	SP33	20k +10k multi	.60	.40
B150	SP33	30k +15k multi	.90	.60
B151	SP33	50k +25k multi	1.50	1.00
a.		Block of 3+label, #B149-B151	3.00	2.00

Armenian earthquake relief. For surcharges see Nos. B173-B175.

Zoo Relief Type of 1988

1989, Mar. 20 Litho. *Perf. 12*

B152	SP31	10k+5k Marten	.45	.30
B153	SP31	10k+5k Squirrel	.45	.30
B154	SP31	20k+10k Hare	.90	.60
B155	SP31	20k+10k Hedgehog	.90	.60
B156	SP31	20k+10k Badger	.90	.60
a.		Block of 5+label, #B152-B156	3.60	2.50

Lenin Children's Fund Type of 1988

Fund emblem and children's drawings: No. B157, Rabbit. No. B158, Cat. No. B159, Doctor. Nos. B157-B159 vert.

1989, June 14 Litho. *Perf. 12*

B157	SP32	5k +2k multi	.25	.20
B158	SP32	5k +2k multi	.25	.20
B159	SP32	5k +2k multi	.25	.20
a.		Block of 3+label, #B157-B159	.75	.45

Surtax for the fund.

Soviet Culture Fund SP34

Paintings and porcelain: No. B160, *Village Market,* by A. Makovsky. No. B161, *Lady Wearing a Hat,* by E. Zelenin. No. B162, *Portrait of the Actress Bazhenova,* by A. Sofronova. No. B163, *Two Women,* by H. Shaiber. No. B164, Popov porcelain coffee pot and plates, 19th cent.

1989 Litho. *Perf. 12x12½*

B160	SP34	4k +2k multi	.20	.20
B161	SP34	5k +2k multi	.25	.20
B162	SP34	10k +5k multi	.60	.35
B163	SP34	20k +10k multi	1.10	.65
B164	SP34	30k +15k multi	1.75	.95
		Nos. B160-B164 (5)	3.90	2.35

Souvenir Sheet

Nature Conservation — SP35

1989, Dec. 14 Photo. *Perf. 11½*

B165	SP35	20k + 10k Swallow	1.25	1.25

Surtax for the Soviet Union of Philatelists.

Zoo Relief Type of 1988

1990, May 4 Litho. *Perf. 12*

B166	SP31	10k +5k *Aquila chrysaetos*	.45	.30
B167	SP31	20k +10k *Falco cherrug*	1.00	.65
B168	SP31	20k +10k *Corvus corax*	1.00	.65
a.		Block of 3 + label, #B166-B168	2.50	1.65

Nos. B166-B168 horiz.

Lenin's Children Fund Type of 1988

#B169, Clown. #B170, Group of women. #B171, Group of children. #B169-B171, vert.

1990, July 3 Litho. *Perf. 12*

B169	SP32	5k +2k multi	.25	.20
B170	SP32	5k +2k multi	.25	.20
B171	SP32	5k +2k multi	.25	.20
a.		Block of 3, #B169-B171 + label	.75	.45

Nature Conservation — SP36

1990, Sept. 12 Litho. *Perf. 12*

B172	SP36	20k +10k multi	1.10	1.10

Surtax for Soviet Union of Philatelists.

Nos. B149-B151 Overprinted

#B173 #B174-B175

1990, Nov. 24 Litho. *Perf. 12x12½*

B173	SP33	20k +10k multi	1.10	.75
B174	SP33	30k +15k multi	1.65	1.10
B175	SP33	50k +25k multi	2.75	1.80
a.		Block of 3+label, #B173-B175	5.50	3.75

Armenia '90 Philatelic Exhibition.

Soviet Culture Fund — SP37

Paintings by N. K. Roerich: 10k+5k, Unkrada, 1909. 20k+10k, Pskovo-Pechorsky Monastery, 1907.

1990, Dec. 20 Litho. *Perf. 12½x12*

B176	SP37	10k +5k multi	.55	.35
B177	SP37	20k +10k multi	1.10	.75

Souvenir Sheet

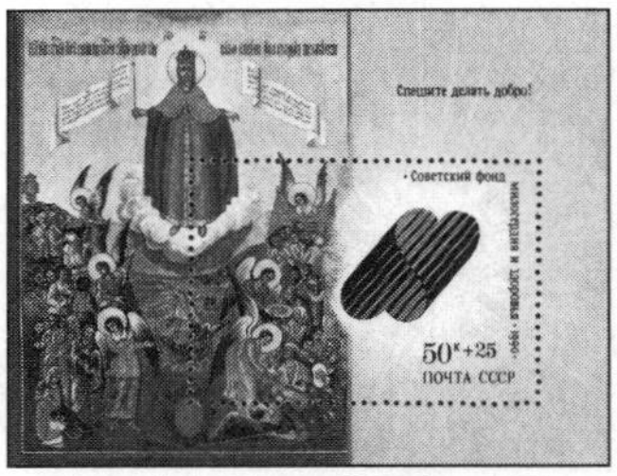

Joys of All Those Grieving, 18th Cent. — SP38

1990, Dec. 23 *Perf. 12½x12*

B178	SP38	50k +25k multi	2.75	2.75

Surtax for Charity and Health Fund.

Ciconia Ciconia SP39

1991, Feb. 4 Litho. *Perf. 12*

B179	SP39	10k +5k multi	.55	.35

Surtax for the Zoo Relief Fund.

Souvenir Sheet

USSR Philatelic Society, 25th Anniv. — SP40

1991, Feb. 15 *Perf. 12x12½*

B180	SP40	20k +10k multi	1.10	1.10

The Universe by V. Lukianets SP41

No. B182, Another Planet by V. Lukianets.

1991, June 1 Litho. *Perf. 12½x12*

B181	SP41	10k +5k multi	.20	.20
B182	SP41	10k +5k multi	.20	.20

SP42

1991, July 10 *Perf. 12x12½*

B183	SP42	20k +10k multi	.35	.25

Surtax for Soviet Culture Fund.

SP43

1991, July 10 *Perf. 12*

B184	SP43	20k +10k multi	.35	.25

Surtax for Soviet Charity & Health Fund

Souvenir Sheet

SP44

1992, Jan. 22 Litho. *Perf. 12½x12*

B185	SP44	3r +50k multi	.70	.70

Surtax for Nature Preservation.

AIR POST STAMPS

AP1

Fokker F-111 — AP2

Plane Overprint in Red

1922 Unwmk. *Imperf.*

C1	AP1	45r green & black	7.50	10.00

5th anniversary of October Revolution.
No. C1 was on sale only at the Moscow General Post Office. Counterfeits exist.

1923 Photo.

C2	AP2	1r red brown	2.75
C3	AP2	3r deep blue	3.75
C4	AP2	5r green	3.50
a.		Wide "5"	*5,000.*
C5	AP2	10r carmine	2.50
		Nos. C2-C5 (4)	12.50

Nos. C2-C5 were not placed in use.

Nos. C2-C5 Surcharged **10 коп. зол.**

1924

C6	AP2	5k on 3r dp blue	1.00	1.00
C7	AP2	10k on 5r green	1.00	1.00
a.		Wide "5"	250.00	250.00
b.		Inverted surcharge	900.00	450.00
C8	AP2	15k on 1r red brown	1.00	1.00
a.		Inverted surcharge	1,000.	500.00
C9	AP2	20k on 10r car	1.00	1.00
a.		Inverted surcharge	1,000.	500.00
		Nos. C6-C9 (4)	4.00	4.00

Airplane over Map of World AP3

1927, Septz. 1 Litho. *Perf. 13x12*

C10	AP3	10k dk bl & yel brn	6.00	4.00
C11	AP3	15k dp red & ol grn	7.00	7.00

1st Intl. Air Post Cong. at The Hague, initiated by the USSR.

Graf Zeppelin and "Call to Complete 5-Year Plan in 4 Years" — AP4

1930 Photo. Wmk. 226 *Perf. 12½*

C12	AP4	40k dk & dl blue	18.00	10.00
a.		Perf. 10½	18.00	19.00
b.		Imperf.	*1,000.*	*700.00*
C13	AP4	80k dk car & rose	22.50	15.00
a.		Perf. 10½	22.50	10.00
b.		Imperf.	*1,000.*	*700.00*

Flight of the Graf Zeppelin from Friedrichshafen to Moscow and return.

Symbolical of Airship Communication from the Tundra to the Steppes — AP5

Airship over Dneprostroi Dam — AP6

Airship over Lenin Mausoleum — AP7

Airship Exploring Arctic Regions — AP8

Constructing an Airship AP9

1931-32 Wmk. 170 Photo. *Imperf.*

C15	AP5	10k dark violet	20.00	16.00
		Litho.		
C16	AP6	15k gray blue	20.00	22.50
		Typo.		
C17	AP7	20k dk carmine	20.00	22.50
		Photo.		
C18	AP8	50k black brown	20.00	22.50
C19	AP9	1r dark green	20.00	22.50
		Nos. C15-C19 (5)	100.00	106.00

Perf. 10½, 12, 12½ and Compound

C20	AP5	10k dark violet	4.75	2.50
		Litho.		
C21	AP6	15k gray blue	9.00	3.75
		Typo.		
C22	AP7	20k dk carmine	6.50	2.00
a.		20k light red	7.50	3.00
		Photo.		
C23	AP8	50k black brown	4.75	2.00
a.		50k gray blue (error)	200.00	200.00
C24	AP9	1r dark green	5.50	2.00

Perf. 12½

Unwmk.

Engr.

C25	AP6	15k gray blk ('32)	1.00	.50
a.		Perf. 10½	*475.00*	125.00
b.		Perf. 14	57.50	37.50
c.		Imperf.	325.00	
		Nos. C20-C25 (6)	31.50	12.75

The 11½ perforation on Nos. C20-C25 is of private origin; beware also of bogus perforation "errors."

North Pole Issue

Graf Zeppelin and Icebreaker "Malygin" Transferring Mail — AP10

1931 Wmk. 170 *Imperf.*

C26	AP10	30k dark violet	12.50	12.50
C27	AP10	35k dark green	12.50	12.50
C28	AP10	1r gray black	15.00	12.50
C29	AP10	2r deep ultra	18.00	12.50
		Nos. C26-C29 (4)	58.00	50.00

Perf. 12x12½

C30	AP10	30k dark violet	25.00	25.00
C31	AP10	35k dark green	25.00	25.00
C32	AP10	1r gray black	25.00	25.00
C33	AP10	2r deep ultra	25.00	25.00
		Nos. C30-C33 (4)	100.00	100.00

Map of Polar Region, Airplane and Icebreaker "Sibiryakov" — AP11

1932 Wmk. 170 *Perf. 12, 10½*

C34	AP11	50k carmine rose	24.00	15.00
a.		Perf. 10½	*2,750.*	*2,750.*
b.		Perf. 10½x12		*3,000.*
C35	AP11	1r green	24.00	15.00
a.		Perf. 12	125.00	40.00

2nd International Polar Year in connection with flight to Franz-Josef Land.

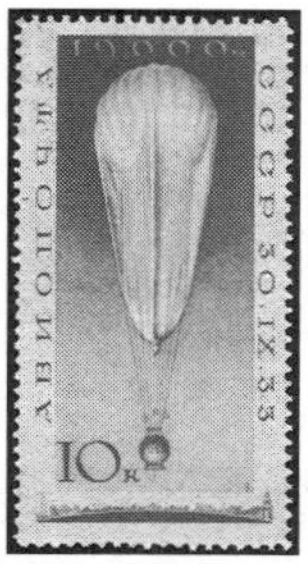

Stratostat "U.S.S.R." — AP12

1933 Photo. *Perf. 14*

C37	AP12	5k ultra	42.50	8.50
a.		Vert. pair, imperf. btwn.		*1,100.*
C38	AP12	10k carmine	42.50	8.50
a.		Horiz. pair, imperf. btwn.		*1,700.*
C39	AP12	20k violet	25.00	8.50
		Nos. C37-C39 (3)	110.00	25.50

Ascent into the stratosphere by Soviet aeronauts, Sept. 30th, 1933.

Furnaces of Kuznetsk AP13

Designs: 10k, Oil wells. 20k, Collective farm. 50k, Map of Moscow-Volga Canal project. 80k, Arctic cargo ship.

1933 Wmk. 170 *Perf. 14*

C40	AP13	5k ultra	11.00	4.75
C41	AP13	10k green	11.00	4.75
C42	AP13	20k carmine	24.00	9.00
C43	AP13	50k dull blue	30.00	9.00
C44	AP13	80k purple	24.00	9.00
		Nos. C40-C44 (5)	100.00	36.50

Unwmk.

C45	AP13	5k ultra	12.50	3.25
C46	AP13	10k green	12.50	3.25
a.		Horiz. pair, imperf. btwn.	450.00	350.00
C47	AP13	20k carmine	18.00	5.50
C48	AP13	50k dull blue	32.50	11.00
C49	AP13	80k purple	24.00	5.50
		Nos. C45-C49 (5)	99.50	28.50

10th anniversary of Soviet civil aviation and airmail service. Counterfeits exist, perf 11½.

I. D. Usyskin AP18

10k, A. B. Vasenko. 20k, P. F. Fedoseinko.

1934 Wmk. 170 *Perf. 11*

C50	AP18	5k vio brown	11.50	3.25
C51	AP18	10k brown	32.50	3.25
C52	AP18	20k ultra	32.50	3.25
		Nos. C50-C52 (3)	76.50	9.75

Perf. 14

C50a	AP18	5k	110.00	95.00
C51a	AP18	10k	185.00	185.00
C52a	AP18	20k	225.00	225.00
		Nos. C50a-C52a (3)	520.00	505.00

Honoring victims of the stratosphere disaster. See Nos. C77-C79.
Beware of copies of Nos. C50-C52 reperforated to resemble Nos. C50a-C52a.

Airship "Pravda" — AP19

Airship Landing — AP20

Airship "Voroshilov" — AP21

Sideview of Airship — AP22

Airship "Lenin" — AP23

1934 *Perf. 14*

C53	AP19	5k red orange	12.50	2.75
C54	AP20	10k claret	12.50	4.25
C55	AP21	15k brown	12.50	5.75
C56	AP22	20k black	27.50	8.75
C57	AP23	30k ultra	50.00	8.75
		Nos. C53-C57 (5)	115.00	30.25

Capt. V. Voronin and "Chelyuskin" — AP24

Prof. Otto Y. Schmidt — AP25

A. V. Lapidevsky AP26

S. A. Levanevsky AP27

"Schmidt Camp" — AP28

Designs: 15k, M. G. Slepnev. 20k, I. V. Doronin. 25k, M. V. Vodopianov. 30k, V. S. Molokov. 40k, N. P. Kamanin.

1935 ***Perf. 14***

C58 AP24	1k	red orange	5.50	2.50
C59 AP25	3k	rose carmine	6.50	2.50
C60 AP26	5k	emerald	5.50	2.50
C61 AP27	10k	dark brown	6.50	2.50
C62 AP27	15k	black	8.00	2.50
C63 AP27	20k	deep claret	11.00	4.75
C64 AP27	25k	indigo	27.50	9.25
C65 AP27	30k	dull green	40.00	11.00
C66 AP27	40k	purple	27.50	7.00
C67 AP28	50k	dark ultra	27.50	9.25
		Nos. C58-C67 (10)	165.50	53.75

Aerial rescue of ice-breaker Chelyuskin crew and scientific expedition.

No. C61 Surcharged in Red

Перелет Москва— Сан-Франциско через Сев. полюс 1935 1Р.

1935, Aug.

C68 AP27 1r on 10k dk brn		200.00	250.00
a.	Inverted surcharge	*5,000.*	*5,000.*
b.	Small Cyrillic "f"	300.00	300.00
c.	As "b," inverted surcharge	*20,000.*	

Moscow-San Francisco flight. Counterfeits exist.

Single-Engined Monoplane — AP34

Five-Engined Transport — AP35

20k, Twin-engined cabin plane. 30k, 4r-motored transport. 40k, Single-engined amphibian. 50k, Twin-motored transport. 80k, 8-motored transport.

1937 **Unwmk.** ***Perf. 12***

C69 AP34 10k yel brn & blk	1.10	.75
a. Imperf.		175.00
C70 AP34 20k gray grn & blk	1.10	.75
C71 AP34 30k red brn & blk	1.40	.75
C72 AP34 40k vio brn & blk	2.00	.95
C73 AP34 50k dk vio & blk	3.25	1.50
C74 AP35 80k bl vio & brn	3.00	1.50
C75 AP35 1r black, brown & buff	8.25	3.00
a. Sheet of 4, imperf.	90.00	100.00
Nos. C69-C75 (7)	20.10	9.20
Set, never hinged	120.00	

Jubilee Aviation Exhib., Moscow, Nov. 15-20.
Vertical pairs, imperf. between, exist for No. C71, value $100; No. C73, value $90.

Types of 1938 Regular Issue Overprinted in Various Colors

18 АВГУСТА ДЕНЬ АВИАЦИИ СССР

1939 **Typo.**

C76 A282 10k red (C)	1.40	.40
C76A A285 30k blue (R)	1.40	.40
C76B A286 40k dull green (Br)	1.40	.40
C76C A287 50k dull violet (R)	2.25	.55
C76D A289 1r brown (Bl)	3.00	1.75
Nos. C76-C76D (5)	9.45	3.50
Set, never hinged	15.00	

Soviet Aviation Day, Aug. 18, 1939.

Types of 1934 with "30.1.1944" Added at Lower Left

Designs: No. C77, P. F. Fedoseinko. No. C78, I. D. Usyskin. No. C79, A. B. Vasenko.

1944 **Photo.** ***Perf. 12***

C77 AP18 1r deep blue	1.75	.60
C78 AP18 1r slate green	1.75	.60
C79 AP18 1r brt yellow green	1.75	.75
Nos. C77-C79 (3)	5.25	1.95
Set, never hinged	6.50	

1934 stratosphere disaster, 10th anniv.

Nos. 860A and 861A Surcharged in Red

АВИАПОЧТА 1944 г. 1 РУБЛЬ

1944, May 25

C80 A431 1r on 30k Prus green	.50	.20
C81 A432 1r on 30k deep ultra	.50	.20
Set, never hinged	1.25	

Catalogue values for unused stamps in this section, from this point to the end of the section, are for Never Hinged items.

Planes and Soviet Air Force Flag — AP42

1948, Dec. 10 **Litho.** ***Perf. 12½***

C82 AP42 1r dark blue	4.00	1.00

Air Force Day.

Plane over Zages, Caucasus — AP43

Plane over Farm Scene AP44

Map of Russian Air Routes and Transport Planes — AP45

#C85, Sochi, Crimea. #C86, Far East. #C87, Leningrad. 2r, Moscow. 3r, Arctic.

Perf. 12x12½

1949, Nov. 9 **Photo.** **Unwmk.**

C83 AP43 50k red brn, *lemon*	1.65	.65
C84 AP44 60k sepia, *pale buff*	3.25	.80
C85 AP44 1r org brn, *yelsh*	3.25	1.10
C86 AP43 1r blue, *bluish*	3.25	1.10
C87 AP43 1r red brn, *pale fawn*	3.25	1.10
C88 AP45 1r blk, ultra & red, *gray*	7.00	3.25
C89 AP43 2r org brn, *bluish*	10.00	8.75
C90 AP43 3r dk green, *bluish*	16.00	3.25
Nos. C83-C90 (8)	47.65	20.00

Plane and Mountain Stream AP46

Globe and Plane AP47

Design: 1r, Plane over river.

1955 **Litho.** ***Perf. 12½x12***

C91 AP46 1r multicolored	1.75	.55
C92 AP46 2r black & yel grn	3.50	.75

For overprints see Nos. C95-C96.

1955, May 31 **Photo.**

C93 AP47 2r chocolate	1.40	.50
C94 AP47 2r deep blue	1.40	.50

Nos. C91 and C92 Overprinted in Red

Perf. 12x12½

1955, Nov. 22 **Litho.** **Unwmk.**

C95 AP46 1r multicolored	2.75	2.00
C96 AP46 2r black & yel grn	4.75	3.00

Issued for use at the scientific drifting stations North Pole-4 and North Pole-5. The inscription reads "North Pole-Moscow, 1955." Counterfeits exist.

Arctic Camp AP48

1956, June 8 ***Perf. 12½x12***

C97 AP48 1r blue, grn, brn, yel & red	1.50	.65

Opening of scientific drifting station North Pole-6.

Helicopter over Kremlin AP49

Air Force Emblem and Arms of Normandy AP50

1960, Mar. 5 **Photo.** ***Perf. 12***

C98 AP49 60k ultra	1.00	.30

Surcharged with New Value, Bars and "1961"

1961, Dec. 20

C99 AP49 6k on 60k ultra	.80	.30

1962, Dec. 30 **Unwmk.** ***Perf. 11½***

C100 AP50 6k blue grn, ocher & car	.60	.20

French Normandy-Neman Escadrille, which fought on the Russian front, 20th anniv.

Jet over Map Showing Airlines in USSR AP51

Designs: 12k, Aeroflot emblem and globe. 16k, Jet over map showing Russian international airlines.

1963, Feb.

C101 AP51 10k red, blk & tan	.60	.20
C102 AP51 12k blue, red, tan & blk	.85	.25
C103 AP51 16k blue, blk & red	1.00	.35
Nos. C101-C103 (3)	2.45	.80

Aeroflot, the civil air fleet, 40th anniv.

Tupolev 134 at Sheremetyevo Airport, Moscow — AP52

Civil Aviation: 10k, An-24 (Antonov) and Vnukovo Airport, Moscow. 12k, Mi-10 (Mil helicopter) and Central Airport, Moscow. 16k, Be-10 (Beriev) and Chinki Riverport, Moscow. 20k, Antei airliner and Domodedovo Airport, Moscow.

1965, Dec. 31

C104	AP52 6k org, red & vio	.30	.20
C105	AP52 10k lt green, org red & gray	.45	.20
C106	AP52 12k lilac, dk sep & lt grn	.45	.20
C107	AP52 16k lilac, lt brn, red & grn	.70	.20
C108	AP52 20k org red, pur & gray	.85	.25
	Nos. C104-C108 (5)	2.75	1.05

Aviation Type of 1976

Aviation 1917-1930 (Aviation Emblem and): 4k, P-4 BIS biplane, 1917. 6k, AK-1 monoplane, 1924. 10k, R-3 (ANT-3) biplane, 1925. 12k, TB-1 (ANT-4) monoplane, 1925. 16k, R-5 biplane, 1929. 20k, Shcha-2 amphibian, 1930.

Lithographed and Engraved

1977, Aug. 16 ***Perf. 12x11½***

C109	A2134 4k multicolored	.20	.20
C110	A2134 6k multicolored	.20	.20
C111	A2134 10k multicolored	.30	.20
C112	A2134 12k multicolored	.30	.20
C113	A2134 16k multicolored	.45	.30
C114	A2134 20k multicolored	.65	.35
	Nos. C109-C114 (6)	2.10	1.45

1978, Aug. 10

4k, PO-2 biplane, 1928. 6k, K-5 passenger plane, 1929. 10k, TB-3, cantilever monoplane, 1930. 12k, Stal-2, 1931. 16k, MBR-2 hydroplane, 1932. 20k, I-16 fighter plane, 1934.

C115	A2134 4k multicolored	.20	.20
C116	A2134 6k multicolored	.20	.20
C117	A2134 10k multicolored	.30	.20
C118	A2134 12k multicolored	.35	.20
C119	A2134 16k multicolored	.45	.20
C120	A2134 20k multicolored	.60	.25
	Nos. C115-C120 (6)	2.10	1.25

Aviation 1928-1934.

Jet and Compass Rose — AP53

1978, Aug. 4 **Litho.** ***Perf. 12***

C121	AP53 32k dark blue	.80	.30

Aeroflot Plane AH-28 — AP54

Designs: Various Aeroflot planes.

Photogravure and Engraved

1979 ***Perf. 11½x12***

C122	AP54 2k shown	.20	.20
C123	AP54 3k YAK-42	.20	.20
C124	AP54 10k T4-154	.30	.20
C125	AP54 15k IL76 transport	.45	.20
C126	AP54 32k IL86 jet liner	.85	.45
	Nos. C122-C126 (5)	2.00	1.25

AIR POST OFFICIAL STAMPS

Used on mail from Russian embassy in Berlin to Moscow. Surcharged on Consular Fee stamps. Currency: the German mark.

OA1

Surcharge in Carmine

1922, July **Litho.** ***Perf. 13½***

Bicolored Burelage

CO1	OA1	12m on 2.25r	67.50
CO2	OA1	24m on 3r	67.50
CO3	OA1	120m on 2.25r	77.50
CO4	OA1	600m on 3r	97.50
CO5	OA1	1200m on 10k	135.00
CO6	OA1	1200m on 50k	*15,000.*
CO7	OA1	1200m on 2.25r	850.00
CO8	OA1	1200m on 3r	1,000.

Three types of each denomination, distinguished by shape of "C" in surcharge and length of second line of surcharge. Used copies have pen or crayon cancel. Forgeries exist.

SPECIAL DELIVERY STAMPS

Motorcycle Courier — SD1

Express Truck — SD2

Design: 80k, Locomotive.

Perf. 12½x12, 12x12½

1932 **Photo.** **Wmk. 170**

E1	SD1	5k dull brown	7.50	6.25
E2	SD2	10k violet brown	9.75	6.25
E3	SD2	80k dull green	30.00	12.50
		Nos. E1-E3 (3)	47.25	25.00

Used values are for c-t-o.

POSTAGE DUE STAMPS

Regular Issue of 1918 Surcharged in Red or Carmine

Доплата
3 коп.
золотом

1924-25 **Unwmk.** ***Perf. 13½***

J1	A33	1k on 35k blue	.20	*.90*
J2	A33	3k on 35k blue	.20	*.90*
J3	A33	5k on 35k blue	.20	*.90*
a.		Imperf.	60.00	
J4	A33	8k on 35k blue ('25)	.25	*.90*
a.		Imperf.	40.00	
J5	A33	10k on 35k blue	.20	*1.10*
a.		Pair, one without surcharge	30.00	
J6	A33	12k on 70k brown	.20	*.90*
J7	A33	14k on 35k blue ('25)	.20	*.90*
a.		Imperf.	65.00	
J8	A33	32k on 35k blue	.20	*1.10*
J9	A33	40k on 35k blue	.20	*1.10*
a.		Imperf.	60.00	
		Nos. J1-J9 (9)	1.85	*8.70*

Surcharge is found inverted on Nos. J1-J2, J4, J6-J9, value $25-$50. Double on Nos. J2, J4-J6; value, $40-$50.

Regular Issue of 1921 Surcharged in Violet

ДОПЛАТА
1 коп.

1924 ***Imperf.***

J10	A40	1k on 100r orange	3.00	*6.00*
a.		1k on 100r yellow	4.00	*12.50*
b.		Pelure paper	4.00	*12.50*
c.		Inverted surcharge	*100.00*	

D1

Lithographed or Typographed

1925 ***Perf. 12***

J11	D1	1k red	2.00	1.50
J12	D1	2k violet	1.00	2.25
J13	D1	3k light blue	1.00	2.25
J14	D1	7k orange	1.00	2.25
J15	D1	8k green	1.00	3.00
J16	D1	10k dark blue	1.65	4.50
J17	D1	14k brown	2.00	4.50
		Nos. J11-J17 (7)	9.65	20.25

Perf. 14½x14

J13a	D1	3k	4.00	6.00
J14a	D1	7k	8.25	12.50
J16a	D1	10k	32.50	40.00
J17a	D1	14k	2.25	3.50
		Nos. J13a-J17a (4)	47.00	62.00

1925 **Wmk. 170** **Typo.** ***Perf. 12***

J18	D1	1k red	.45	.85
J19	D1	2k violet	.45	.85
J20	D1	3k light blue	.60	1.10
J21	D1	7k orange	.60	1.10
J22	D1	8k green	.60	1.10
J23	D1	10k dark blue	.75	1.65
J24	D1	14k brown	1.10	2.25
		Nos. J18-J24 (7)	4.55	8.90

For surcharges see Nos. 359-372.

WENDEN (LIVONIA)

A former district of Livonia, a province of the Russian Empire, which became part of Latvia, under the name of Vidzeme.

Used values for Nos. L2-L12 are for pen-canceled copies. Postmarked specimens sell for considerably more.

A1

1862 **Unwmk.** ***Imperf.***

L1	A1 (2k) blue	17.50	
a.	Tête bêche pair	*250.00*	

No. L1 may have been used for a short period of time but withdrawn because of small size. Some consider it an essay.

A2

A3

1863

L2	A2 (2k) rose & black	150.00	150.00
a.	Background inverted	275.00	275.00
L3	A3 (4k) blue grn & blk	70.00	70.00
a.	(4k) yellow green & black	150.00	150.00
b.	Half used as 2k on cover		*1,800.*
c.	Background inverted	150.00	150.00
d.	As "a," background inverted	210.00	210.00

The official imitations of Nos. L2 and L3 have a single instead of a double hyphen after "WENDEN."

Coat of Arms
A4 A5 A6

1863-71

L4	A4 (2k) rose & green	30.00	20.00
a.	Yellowish paper		
b.	Green frame around central oval	37.50	21.00
c.	Tête bêche pair	*1,800.*	
L5	A5 (2k) rose & grn ('64)	70.00	57.50
L6	A6 (2k) rose & green	21.00	21.00
	Nos. L4-L6 (3)	121.00	98.50

Official imitations of Nos. L4b and L5 have a rose instead of a green line around the central oval. The first official imitation of No. L6 has the central oval 5½mm instead of 6¼mm wide; the second imitation is less clearly printed than the original and the top of the "f" of "Briefmarke" is too much hooked.

Coat of Arms
A7 A8

1872-75 ***Perf. 12½***

L7	A7 (2k) red & green	40.00	21.00
L8	A8 2k yel grn & red ('75)	7.00	8.00
a.	Numeral in upper right corner resembles an inverted "3"	27.50	27.50

Reprints of No. L8 have no horizontal lines in the background. Those of No. L8a have the impression blurred and only traces of the horizontal lines.

A9

Wenden Castle — A10

1878-80

L9	A9 2k green & red	7.00	8.00
a.	Imperf.		
L10	A9 2k blk, grn & red ('80)	7.00	8.00
a.	Imperf., pair	15.00	

No. L9 has been reprinted in blue green and yellow green with perforation 11½ and in gray green with perforation 12½ or imperforate.

1884 ***Perf. 11½***

L11	A9 2k black, green & red	10.00	2.50
a.	Green arm omitted	21.00	
b.	Arm inverted	21.00	
c.	Arm double	27.50	
d.	Imperf., pair	21.00	

1901 **Litho.**

L12	A10 2k dk green & brown	6.00	6.00
a.	Tête bêche pair	30.00	
b.	Imperf., pair	30.00	

OCCUPATION STAMPS

Issued under Finnish Occupation

Finnish Stamps of 1917-18 Overprinted

Aunus

1919 **Unwmk.** ***Perf. 14***

N1	A19	5p green	12.50	12.50
N2	A19	10p rose	12.50	12.50
N3	A19	20p buff	12.50	12.50
N4	A19	40p red violet	12.50	12.50
N5	A19	50p orange brn	100.00	100.00
N6	A19	1m dl rose & blk	105.00	105.00
N7	A19	5m violet & blk	325.00	325.00
N8	A19	10m brown & blk	575.00	575.00
		Nos. N1-N8 (8)	1,155.	1,155.

"Aunus" is the Finnish name for Olonets, a town of Russia.

Counterfeits overprints exist.

Issued under German Occupation

Germany Nos. 506 to 523 Overprinted in Black

OSTLAND

1941-43 Unwmk. Typo. *Perf. 14*

N9	A115	1pf gray black	.20	.20
N10	A115	3pf light brown	.20	.20
N11	A115	4pf slate	.20	.20
N12	A115	5pf dp yellow green	.20	.20
N13	A115	6pf purple	.20	.20
N14	A115	8pf red	.20	.20
N15	A115	10pf dk brown ('43)	.20	*1.75*
N16	A115	12pf carmine ('43)	.20	*1.75*

Engr.

N17	A115	10pf dark brown	.20	.40
N18	A115	12pf brt carmine	.20	.40
N19	A115	15pf brown lake	.20	.20
N20	A115	16pf peacock grn	.20	.20
N21	A115	20pf blue	.20	.20
N22	A115	24pf orange brown	.20	.20
N23	A115	25pf brt ultra	.20	.20
N24	A115	30pf olive green	.20	.20
N25	A115	40pf brt red violet	.20	.20
N26	A115	50pf myrtle green	.20	.20
N27	A115	60pf dk red brown	.20	.20
N28	A115	80pf indigo	.20	.20
		Nos. N9-N28 (20)	4.00	*7.50*

Issued for use in Estonia, Latvia and Lithuania.

Same Overprinted in Black **UKRAINE**

Typo.

N29	A115	1pf gray black	.20	.20
N30	A115	3pf lt brown	.20	.20
N31	A115	4pf slate	.20	.20
N32	A115	5pf dp yel green	.20	.20
N33	A115	6pf purple	.20	.20
N34	A115	8pf red	.20	.20
N35	A115	10pf dk brown ('43)	.20	*1.60*
N36	A115	12pf carmine ('43)	.20	*1.60*

Engr.

N37	A115	10pf dk brown	.45	.55
N38	A115	12pf brt carmine	.45	.55
N39	A115	15pf brown lake	.20	.20
N40	A115	16pf peacock green	.20	.20
N41	A115	20pf blue	.20	.20
N42	A115	24pf orange brown	.20	.20
N43	A115	25pf bright ultra	.20	.20
N44	A115	30pf olive green	.20	.20
N45	A115	40pf brt red violet	.20	.20
N46	A115	50pf myrtle green	.20	.20
N47	A115	60pf dk red brown	.20	.20
N48	A115	80pf indigo	.20	.20
		Nos. N29-N48 (20)	4.50	*7.50*

ARMY OF THE NORTHWEST

(Gen. Nicolai N. Yudenich)

Russian Stamps of 1909-18 Overprinted in Black or Red **Сѣв.Зап. армія**

On Stamps of 1909-12

Perf. 14 to 15 and Compound

1919, Aug. 1

1	A14	2k green	2.50	4.25
2	A14	5k claret	2.50	4.25
3	A15	10k dk blue (R)	2.75	5.00
4	A11	15k red brn & bl	2.75	5.00
5	A8	20k blue & car	5.00	7.50
6	A11	25k grn & gray violet	8.50	12.00
7	A8	50k brn vio & grn	5.00	6.25

Perf. 13½

8	A9	1r pale brn, dk brn & org	10.50	14.00
9	A13	10r scar, yel & gray	30.00	52.50

On Stamps of 1917

Imperf

10	A14	3k red	1.40	3.50
11	A12	3.50r mar & lt grn	17.50	27.50
12	A13	5r dk blue, grn & pale bl	14.00	25.00
13	A12	7r dk green & pink	77.50	125.00

No. 2 Surcharged

Perf. 14, 14½x15

14	A14	10k on 5k claret	1.75	3.75
		Nos. 1-14 (14)	181.65	295.50

Nos. 1-14 exist with inverted overprint or surcharge. The 1, 3½, 5, 7 and 10 rubles with red overprint are trial printings (value $40 each). The 20k on 14k, perforated, and the 1, 2, 5, 15, 70k and 1r imperforate were overprinted but never placed in use. Value: $80, $30, $40, $40, $40, $40 and $60.

These stamps were in use from Aug. 1 to Oct. 15, 1919.

Counterfeits of Nos. 1-14 abound.

ARMY OF THE NORTH

A1

A2

A3

A4

A5

1919, Sept. Typo. *Imperf.*

1	A1	5k brown violet	.40	.70
2	A2	10k blue	.40	.70
3	A3	15k yellow	.40	.70
4	A4	20k rose	.40	.70
5	A5	50k green	.40	.70
		Nos. 1-5 (5)	2.00	3.50

The letters OKCA are the initials of Russian words meaning "Special Corps, Army of the North." The stamps were in use from about the end of September to the end of December, 1919.

Used values are for c-t-o stamps.

(General Miller)

A set of seven stamps of this design was prepared in 1919, but not issued. Value, set $25. Counterfeits exist.

RUSSIAN OFFICES ABROAD

For various reasons the Russian Empire maintained Post Offices to handle its correspondence in several foreign countries. These were similar to the Post Offices in foreign countries maintained by other world powers.

OFFICES IN CHINA

100 Kopecks = 1 Ruble
100 Cents = 1 Dollar (1917)

Russian Stamps Overprinted in Blue or Red **КИТАЙ**

On Issues of 1889-92
Horizontally Laid Paper

1899-1904 Wmk. 168 *Perf. 14½x15*

1	A10	1k orange (Bl)	.75	1.00
2	A10	2k yel green (R)	.75	1.00
3	A10	3k carmine (Bl)	.75	1.00
4	A10	5k red violet (Bl)	.75	1.00
5	A10	7k dk blue (R)	1.50	2.50
a.		Inverted overprint	*500.00*	
6	A8	10k dk blue (R)	1.50	2.50
7	A8	50k vio & grn (Bl) ('04)	4.50	5.00

Perf. 13½

8	A9	1r lt brn, brn & org (Bl) ('04)	50.00	50.00
		Nos. 1-8 (8)	60.50	64.00

On Issues of 1902-05
Vertically Laid Paper

Perf. 14½ to 15 and Compound

1904-08

Overprinted in Black, Red or Blue

9	A8	4k rose red (Bl)	2.00	2.50
10	A10	7k dk blue (R)	10.00	12.50
11	A8	10k dk blue (R)	1,200.	1,200.
a.		Groundwork inverted	*3,250.*	
12	A11	14k bl & rose (R)	5.00	3.50
13	A11	15k brn vio & blue (Bl) ('08)	5.00	4.50
14	A8	20k blue & car (Bl)	1.50	2.50
15	A11	25k dull grn & lil (R) ('08)	10.00	6.50
16	A11	35k dk vio & grn (R)	2.50	3.25
17	A8	50k vio & grn (Bl)	75.00	55.00
18	A11	70k brn & org (Bl)	20.00	12.50

Perf. 13½

19	A9	1r lt brn, brn & org (Bl)	15.00	11.50
20	A12	3.50r blk & gray (R)	10.00	13.00
21	A13	5r dk bl, grn & pale bl (R) ('07)	8.00	10.00
a.		Inverted overprint	*375.00*	
22	A12	7r blk & yel (Bl)	12.50	10.00
23	A13	10r scar, yel & gray (Bl) ('07)	40.00	50.00
		Nos. 9-10,12-23 (14)	216.50	197.25

On Issues of 1909-12
Wove Paper
Lozenges of Varnish on Face

1910-16 Unwmk. *Perf. 14x14½*

24	A14	1k orange yel (Bl)	.40	.50
25	A14	1k org yel (Bl Bk)	4.50	5.00
26	A14	2k green (Bk)	.40	.50
27	A14	2k green (Bl)	5.50	6.25
a.		Double ovpt. (Bk and Bl)		
28	A14	3k rose red (Bl)	.30	.50
29	A14	3k rose red (Bk)	10.00	10.00
30	A15	4k carmine (Bl)	.40	.35
31	A15	4k carmine (Bk)	7.00	7.25
32	A14	7k lt blue (Bk)	.40	.50
33	A15	10k blue (Bk)	.40	.35
34	A11	14k blue & rose (Bk)	.65	.65
35	A11	14k blue & rose (Bl)		
36	A11	15k dl vio & bl (Bk)	.45	1.00
37	A8	20k blue & car (Bk)	.40	.65
38	A11	25k green & vio (Bl)	3.00	5.00
39	A11	25k grn & vio (Bk)	.60	1.65
40	A11	35k vio & grn (Bk)	.50	.35
42	A8	50k vio & grn (Bl)	.25	.35
43	A8	50k brn vio & grn (Bk)	15.00	16.00
44	A11	70k lt brn & org (Bl)	.25	.50

Perf. 13½

45	A9	1r pale brn, brn & org (Bl)	1.00	1.75
47	A13	5r dk bl, grn & pale bl (R)	12.50	10.00

The existence of #35 is questioned.

Russian Stamps of 1902-12 Surcharged:

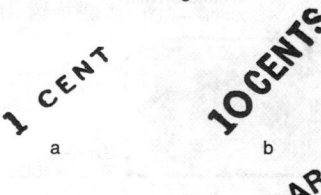

1 CENT
a

10 CENTS
b

1 DOLLAR
c

On Stamps of 1909-12

1917 *Perf. 11½, 13½, 14, 14½x15*

50	A14(a)	1c on 1k dl org yel	.60	*5.50*
51	A14(a)	2c on 2k dull grn	.60	*5.50*
52	A14(a)	3c on 3k car	.60	*5.50*
a.		Inverted surcharge	65.00	
b.		Double surcharge	150.00	
53	A15(a)	4c on 4k car	1.25	*4.25*
54	A14(a)	5c on 5k claret	1.25	*15.00*
55	A15(b)	10c on 10k dk bl	1.25	*15.00*
a.		Inverted surcharge	85.00	85.00
b.		Double surcharge	115.00	
56	A11(b)	14c on 14k dk bl & car	1.25	*10.00*
a.		Imperf.	6.00	
b.		Inverted surcharge	100.00	
57	A11(a)	15c on 15k brn lil & dp bl	1.25	*15.00*
58	A8(b)	20c on 20k bl & car	1.25	*15.00*
59	A11(a)	25c on 25k grn & violet	1.25	*15.00*
60	A11(a)	35c on 35k brn vio & green	1.50	*15.00*
a.		Inverted surcharge	27.50	
61	A8(a)	50c on 50k brn vio & green	1.25	*15.00*
62	A11(a)	70c on 70k brn & red orange	1.25	*15.00*
63	A9(c)	$1 on 1r pale brn, brn & org	1.25	*15.00*
		Nos. 50-63 (14)	15.80	*165.75*

On Stamps of 1902-05
Vertically Laid Paper

Perf. 11½, 13, 13½, 13½x11½

Wmk. Wavy Lines (168)

64	A12	$3.50 on 3.50r blk & gray	9.00	*32.50*
65	A13	$5 on 5r dk bl, grn & pale blue	9.00	*32.50*
66	A12	$7 on 7r blk & yel	8.50	*32.50*

On Stamps of 1915

Unwmk. *Perf. 13½*

Wove Paper

68	A13	$5 on 5r ind, grn & lt blue	13.00	*42.50*
a.		Inverted surcharge	250.00	
70	A13	$10 on 10r car lake, yel & gray	12.50	*100.00*
		Nos. 64-70 (5)	52.00	*240.00*

The surcharge on Nos. 64-70 is in larger type than on the $1.

Russian Stamps of 1909-18 Surcharged in Black or Red

2 Cent.

On Stamps of 1909-12

1920 *Perf. 14, 14½x15*

72	A14	1c on 1k dull org yellow	32.50	*37.50*
73	A14	2c on 2k dull grn (R)	16.00	*15.00*
74	A14	3c on 3k car	16.00	*15.00*
75	A15	4c on 4k car	16.00	*15.00*
a.		Inverted surcharge	130.00	
76	A14	5c on 5k claret	16.00	*15.00*
77	A15	10c on 10k dk bl (R)	100.00	*57.50*
78	A14	10c on 10k on 7k blue (R)	95.00	*57.50*

On Stamps of 1917-18

Imperf

79	A14	1c on 1k orange	22.50	*15.00*
a.		Inverted surcharge	45.00	*75.00*
80	A14	5c on 5k claret	30.00	*30.00*
a.		Inverted surcharge	140.00	
b.		Double surcharge	200.00	
c.		Surcharged "Cent" only	95.00	
		Nos. 72-80 (9)	344.00	*257.50*

OFFICES IN THE TURKISH EMPIRE

Various powers maintained post offices in the Turkish Empire before World War I by authority of treaties which ended with the signing of the Treaty of Lausanne in 1923. The foreign post offices were closed Oct. 27, 1923.

100 Kopecks = 1 Ruble
40 Paras = 1 Piaster (1900)

Coat of Arms A1

1863 Unwmk. Typo. *Imperf.*

1	A1	6k blue	275.00	*1,000.*
a.		6k light blue, thin paper	350.00	*1,350.*
b.		6k light blue, medium paper	325.00	*1,350.*
c.		6k dark blue, chalky paper	150.00	

Forgeries exist.

A2

A3

1865 Litho.

2	A2	(2k) brown & blue	700.00	625.00
3	A3	(20k) blue & red	900.00	850.00

Twenty-eight varieties of each.

A4 A5 A6

1866 Horizontal Network

4 A4 (2k) rose & pale bl 35.00 52.50
5 A5 (20k) dp blue & rose 55.00 57.50

1867 Vertical Network

6 A4 (2k) rose & pale bl 70.00 87.50
7 A5 (20k) dp blue & rose 100.00 150.00

The initials inscribed on Nos. 2 to 7 are those of the Russian Company of Navigation and Trade. Stamps of Russian Offices in the Turkish Empire overprinted with these initials were used in the Ukraine and are listed under that country.

The official imitations of Nos. 2 to 7 are on yellowish white paper. The colors are usually paler than those of the originals and there are minor differences in the designs.

Horizontally Laid Paper

1868 Typo. Wmk. 168 *Perf. 11½*

8 A6 1k brown 35.00 19.00
9 A6 3k green 35.00 19.00
10 A6 5k blue 35.00 19.00
11 A6 10k car & green 35.00 19.00
Nos. 8-11 (4) 140.00 76.00

Colors of Nos. 8-11 dissolve in water.

1872-90 *Perf. 14½x15*

12 A6 1k brown 6.25 3.00
13 A6 3k green 20.00 2.00
14 A6 5k blue 3.75 1.00
15 A6 10k pale red & grn ('90) 1.00 .50
b. 10k carmine & green 11.00 3.75
Nos. 12-15 (4) 31.00 6.50

Vertically Laid Paper

12a A6 1k 37.50 12.50
13a A6 3k 37.50 12.50
14a A6 5k 37.50 12.50
15a A6 10k 87.50 30.00
Nos. 12a-15a (4) 200.00 67.50

Nos. 12-15 exist imperf.

No. 15 Surcharged in Black or Blue:

8 7 7
a b c

1876

16 A6(a) 8k on 10k (Bk) 60.00 45.00
a. Vertically laid
b. Inverted surcharge 375.00
17 A6(a) 8k on 10k (Bl) 85.00 65.00
a. Vertically laid
b. Inverted surcharge

1879

18 A6(b) 7k on 10k (Bk) 85.00 65.00
a. Vertically laid 750.00 750.00
b. Inverted surcharge
19 A6(b) 7k on 10k (Bl) 100.00 85.00
a. Vertically laid
b. Inverted surcharge
19C A6(c) 7k on 10k (Bl) 700.00 550.00
19D A6(c) 7k on 10k (Bk) 550.00 500.00

Nos. 16-19D have been extensively counterfeited.

1879 *Perf. 14½x15*

20 A6 1k black & yellow 3.00 1.50
a. Vertically laid 9.00 7.50
21 A6 2k black & rose 4.50 4.25
a. Vertically laid 10.00 6.00
22 A6 7k carmine & gray 6.50 1.75
a. Vertically laid 27.50 12.50
Nos. 20-22 (3) 14.00 7.50

1884

23 A6 1k orange .45 .30
24 A6 2k green .70 .40
25 A6 5k pale red violet 2.75 .95
26 A6 7k blue 1.40 .40
Nos. 23-26 (4) 5.30 2.05

Nos. 23-26 imperforate are believed to be proofs.

No. 23 surcharged "40 PARAS" is bogus, though some copies were postally used.

Russian Company of Navigation and Trade

Р.О.П.и Т.

This overprint, in two sizes, was privately applied in various colors to Russian Offices in the Turkish Empire stamps of 1900-1910.

A7 A8 A9

A10 A11

Surcharged in Blue, Black or Red

1900

Horizontally Laid Paper

27 A7 4pa on 1k orange (Bl) .20 .20
a. Inverted surcharge 30.00 30.00
28 A7 4pa on 1k orange (Bk) .20 .20
a. Inverted surcharge 30.00 30.00
29 A7 10pa on 2k green .25 .25
a. Inverted surcharge
30 A8 1pi on 10k dk blue .50 .60
a. Inverted surcharge
Nos. 27-30 (4) 1.15 1.25

1903-05

Vertically Laid Paper

31 A7 10pa on 2k yel green .30 .50
a. Inverted surcharge 70.00
32 A8 20pa on 4k rose red (Bl) .30 .50
a. Inverted surcharge 25.00
33 A8 1pi on 10k dk blue .30 .50
a. Groundwork inverted 55.00 17.50
34 A8 2pi on 20k blue & car (Bk) .70 1.00
35 A8 5pi on 50k brn vio & grn 1.75 2.00
36 A9 7pi on 70k brn & org (Bl) 2.00 3.00

Perf. 13½

37 A10 10pi on 1r lt brn, brn & org (Bl) 3.25 4.75
38 A11 35pi on 3.50r blk & gray 9.75 13.00
39 A11 70pi on 7r blk & yel 11.20 15.00
Nos. 31-39 (9) 29.55 40.25

A12

A13 A14

Wove Paper
Lozenges of Varnish on Face

1909 Unwmk. *Perf. 14½x15*

40 A12 5pa on 1k orange .25 .35
41 A12 10pa on 2k green .30 .55
a. Inverted surcharge 7.25 8.50
42 A12 20pa on 4k carmine .60 .90
43 A12 1pi on 10k blue .65 1.00
44 A12 5pi on 50k vio & grn 1.40 1.75
45 A12 7pi on 70k brn & org 2.00 2.75

Perf. 13½

46 A13 10pi on 1r brn & org 3.00 5.00
47 A14 35pi on 3.50r mar & lt grn 10.50 14.00
48 A14 70pi on 7r dk grn & pink 18.00 25.00
Nos. 40-48 (9) 36.70 51.30

50th anniv. of the establishing of the Russian Post Offices in the Levant.

Nos. 40-48 Overprinted with Names of Various Cities

Overprinted "Constantinople"

Black Overprint

1909-10 *Perf. 14½x15*

61 A12 5pa on 1k .20 .30
62 A12 10pa on 2k .20 .30
63 A12 20pa on 4k .30 .45
64 A12 1pi on 10k .30 .55
65 A12 5pi on 50k .60 .90
66 A12 7pi on 70k 1.40 2.00

Perf. 13½

67 A13 10pi on 1r 5.50 8.75
a. "Constanttnople" 14.00
68 A14 35pi on 3.50r 16.00 27.50
69 A14 70pi on 7r 30.00 42.50

Blue Overprint

Perf. 14½x15

70 A12 5pa on 1k 2.50 3.50
Nos. 61-70 (10) 57.00 86.75

"Consnantinople"

61a A12 5pa on 1k 1.65
62a A12 10pa on 2k 1.25
63a A12 20pa on 4k 2.00
64a A12 1pi on 10k 2.75
65a A12 5pi on 50k 2.75
66a A12 7pi on 70k 5.00
68a A14 35pi on 3.50r 32.50
69a A14 70pi on 7r 60.00
70a A12 5pa on 1k 8.00
Nos. 61a-70a (9) 115.90

"Constantinopie"

61b A12 5pa on 1k 10.00
62b A12 10pa on 2k 10.00
63b A12 20pa on 4k 10.00
64b A12 1pi on 10k 10.00
65b A12 5pi on 50k 10.00
66b A12 7pi on 70k 10.00
68b A14 35pi on 3.50r 32.50
69b A14 70pi on 7r 60.00
Nos. 61b-69b (8) 152.50

Overprinted "Jaffa"

Black Overprint

71 A12 5pa on 1k 1.40 2.50
a. Inverted overprint 11.50
72 A12 10pa on 2k 1.75 2.75
a. Inverted overprint 11.50
73 A12 20pa on 4k 2.00 3.50
a. Inverted overprint 27.50
74 A12 1pi on 10k 2.50 3.50
a. Double overprint 32.50
75 A12 5pi on 50k 6.00 7.00
76 A12 7pi on 70k 7.25 9.75

Perf. 13½

77 A13 10pi on 1r 24.00 37.50
78 A14 35pi on 3.50r 60.00 87.50
79 A14 70pi on 7r 80.00 125.00

Blue Overprint

Perf. 14½x15

80 A12 5pa on 1k 4.00 6.25
Nos. 71-80 (10) 188.90 285.25

Overprinted "Ierusalem"

Black Overprint

81 A12 5pa on 1k 1.50 2.00
a. Inverted overprint 25.00
b. "erusalem" 8.25
82 A12 10pa on 2k 2.00 3.00
a. Inverted overprint 13.00
b. "erusalem" 8.25
83 A12 20pa on 4k 3.00 4.00
a. Inverted overprint 13.00
b. "erusalem" 8.25
84 A12 1pi on 10k 3.00 4.00
a. "erusalem" 11.50
85 A12 5pi on 50k 5.00 8.00
a. "erusalem" 22.50
86 A12 7pi on 70k 10.00 13.00
a. "erusalem" 22.50

Perf. 13½

87 A13 10pi on 1r 32.50 42.50
88 A14 35pi on 3.50r 75.00 90.00
89 A14 70pi on 7r 90.00 125.00

Blue Overprint

Perf. 14½x15

90 A12 5pa on 1k 4.50 6.50
Nos. 81-90 (10) 226.50 298.00

Overprinted "Kerassunde"

Black Overprint

91 A12 5pa on 1k .30 .45
a. Inverted overprint 8.75
92 A12 10pa on 2k .30 .45
a. Inverted overprint 8.75
93 A12 20pa on 4k .45 .60
a. Inverted overprint 10.50
94 A12 1pi on 10k .55 .70
95 A12 5pi on 50k 1.00 1.25
96 A12 7pi on 70k 1.40 2.00

Perf. 13½

97 A13 10pi on 1r 5.50 7.75
98 A14 35pi on 3.50r 17.50 21.00
99 A14 70pi on 7r 25.00 30.00

Blue Overprint

Perf. 14½x15

100 A12 5pa on 1k 3.75 5.50
Nos. 91-100 (10) 55.75 69.70

Overprinted "Mont Athos"

Black Overprint

101 A12 5pa on 1k .30 .60
b. Inverted overprint 14.00
102 A12 10pa on 2k .30 .60
b. Inverted overprint 14.00
103 A12 20pa on 4k .35 .65
b. Inverted overprint 15.00
104 A12 1pi on 10k .60 .85
b. Double overprint 22.50
105 A12 5pi on 50k 2.00 2.50
106 A12 7pi on 70k 3.00 4.25
b. Pair, one without "Mont Athos" 16.00

Perf. 13½

107 A13 10pi on 1r 10.00 12.50
108 A14 35pi on 3.50r 22.50 27.50
109 A14 70pi on 7r 40.00 55.00

Blue Overprint

Perf. 14½x15

110 A12 5pa on 1k 3.50 6.25
Nos. 101-110 (10) 82.55 110.70

"Mont Atho"

101a A12 5pa on 1k 13.00
102a A12 10pa on 2k 13.00
103a A12 20pa on 4k 13.00
104a A12 1pi on 10k 20.00
c. As "a," double overprint 85.00
105a A12 5pi on 50k 27.50
106a A12 7pi on 70k 40.00
110a A12 5pa on 1k 11.50

Overprinted **С. Афонъ**

111 A12 5pa on 1k .35 .55
112 A12 10pa on 2k .35 .55
113 A12 20pa on 4k .45 .90
114 A12 1pi on 10k .90 1.75
115 A12 5pi on 50k 1.75 2.75
116 A12 7pi on 70k 3.00 5.00

Perf. 13½

117 A13 10pi on 1r 18.00 25.00
Nos. 111-117 (7) 24.80 36.50

The overprint is larger on No. 117.

Overprinted "Salonique"

Black Overprint

Perf. 14½x15

131 A12 5pa on 1k .30 .60
a. Inverted overprint 6.50
b. Pair, one without overprint
132 A12 10pa on 2k .45 .90
a. Inverted overprint 10.00
133 A12 20pa on 4k .60 .90
a. Inverted overprint 13.00
134 A12 1pi on 10k .60 .90
135 A12 5pi on 50k 1.25 1.75
136 A12 7pi on 70k 2.50 3.00

Perf. 13½

137 A13 10pi on 1r 15.00 15.00
138 A14 35pi on 3.50r 27.50 32.50
139 A14 70pi on 7r 50.00 50.00

Blue Overprint

Perf. 14½x15

140 A12 5pa on 1k 7.00 8.00
Nos. 131-140 (10) 105.20 113.55

Overprinted "Smyrne"

Black Overprint

141 A12 5pa on 1k .35 .60
a. Double overprint
b. Inverted overprint 5.00
142 A12 10pa on 2k .35 .60
a. Inverted overprint 8.25
143 A12 20pa on 4k .70 .80
a. Inverted overprint 10.00
144 A12 1pi on 10k .70 .90
145 A12 5pi on 50k 1.50 1.50
146 A12 7pi on 70k 2.25 3.00

Perf. 13½

147 A13 10pi on 1r 9.00 10.50
148 A14 35pi on 3.50r 18.00 21.00
149 A14 70pi on 7r 27.00 32.50

Blue Overprint

Perf. 14½x15

150 A12 5pa on 1k 3.25 4.75
Nos. 141-150 (10) 63.10 76.15

"Smyrn"

141c A12 5pa on 1k 3.50 4.00
142b A12 10pa on 2k 3.25 4.00
143b A12 20pa on 4k 3.25 4.00
144a A12 1pi on 10k 4.50 5.75
145a A12 5pi on 50k 4.50 5.25
146a A12 7pi on 70k 6.50 6.50
Nos. 141c-146a (6) 25.50 29.50

Overprinted "Trebizonde"

Black Overprint

151 A12 5pa on 1k .35 .60
a. Inverted overprint 4.50
152 A12 10pa on 2k .35 .60
a. Inverted overprint 6.50
b. Pair, one without "Trebizonde"
153 A12 20pa on 4k .45 .40
a. Inverted overprint 10.00
154 A12 1pi on 10k .45 .75
a. Pair, one without "Trebizonde" 27.50
155 A12 5pi on 50k 1.00 1.50

156 A12 7pi on 70k 1.75 3.00

Perf. 13½

157 A13 10pi on 1r 9.00 10.50
158 A14 35pi on 3.50r 18.00 21.00
159 A14 70pi on 7r 27.50 32.50

Blue Overprint

Perf. 14½x15

160 A12 5pa on 1k 3.25 4.75
Nos. 151-160 (10) 62.10 75.60

On Nos. 158 and 159 the overprint is spelled "Trebisonde."

Overprinted "Beyrouth"

Black Overprint

1910
161 A12 5pa on 1k .25 .45
162 A12 10pa on 2k .25 .45
a. Inverted overprint 20.00
163 A12 20pa on 4k .40 .60
164 A12 1pi on 10k .40 .75
165 A12 5pi on 50k .80 1.50
166 A12 7pi on 70k 1.65 3.00

Perf. 13½

167 A13 10pi on 1r 8.25 10.50
168 A14 35pi on 3.50r 16.00 21.00
169 A14 70pi on 7r 25.00 32.50
Nos. 161-169 (9) 53.00 70.75

Overprinted "Dardanelles"

Perf. 14½x15

171 A12 5pa on 1k .30 .60
172 A12 10pa on 2k .30 .60
a. Pair, one without overprint
173 A12 20pa on 4k .60 .75
a. Inverted overprint 10.00
174 A12 1pi on 10k .60 .90
175 A12 5pi on 50k 1.25 1.75
176 A12 7pi on 70k 2.50 3.00

Perf. 13½

177 A13 10pi on 1r 8.25 10.25
178 A14 35pi on 3.50r 16.00 21.00
a. Center and ovpt. inverted
179 A14 70pi on 7r 25.00 32.50
Nos. 171-179 (9) 54.80 71.35

Overprinted "Metelin"

Perf. 14½x15

181 A12 5pa on 1k .40 .75
a. Inverted overprint 10.00
182 A12 10pa on 2k .40 .75
a. Inverted overprint 13.00
183 A12 20pa on 4k .70 1.25
a. Inverted overprint 13.00
184 A12 1pi on 10k .70 1.25
185 A12 5pi on 50k 1.75 2.50
186 A12 7pi on 70k 2.25 3.50

Perf. 13½

187 A13 10pi on 1r 11.00 15.00
188 A14 35pi on 3.50r 25.00 32.50
189 A14 70pi on 7r 35.00 45.00
Nos. 181-189 (9) 77.20 102.50

Overprinted "Rizeh"

Perf. 14½x15

191 A12 5pa on 1k .35 .60
a. Inverted overprint 6.50
192 A12 10pa on 2k .35 .60
a. Inverted overprint 10.00
193 A12 20pa on 4k .60 .75
a. Inverted overprint 10.00
194 A12 1pi on 10k .60 .75
195 A12 5pi on 50k 1.00 2.00
196 A12 7pi on 70k 1.90 3.50

Perf. 13½

197 A13 10pi on 1r 10.00 12.50
198 A14 35pi on 3.50r 16.00 21.00
199 A14 70pi on 7r 25.00 32.50
Nos. 191-199 (9) 55.80 74.20

Nos. 61-199 for the establishing of Russian Post Offices in the Levant, 50th anniv.

A15 A16 A17

Vertically Laid Paper

1910 Wmk. 168 *Perf. 14½x15*
200 A15 20pa on 5k red violet (Bl) .60 .60

Wove Paper

Vertical Lozenges of Varnish on Face

1910 Unwmk. *Perf. 14x14½*
201 A16 5pa on 1k org yel (Bl) .20 .25
202 A16 10pa on 2k green (R) .20 .25
203 A17 20pa on 4k car rose (Bl) .20 .25
204 A17 1pi on 10k blue (R) .20 .25
205 A8 5pi on 50k vio & grn (Bl) .40 .60
206 A9 7pi on 70k lt brn & org (Bl) .40 .65

Perf. 13½

207 A10 10pi on 1r pale brn, brn & org (Bl) .50 .75
Nos. 201-207 (7) 2.10 3.00

Russian Stamps of 1909-12 Surcharged in Black:

20 PARA No. 208 — **1½ PIASTRE** Nos. 209-212

1912 *Perf. 14x14½*
208 A14 20pa on 5k claret .20 .20
209 A11 1½pi on 15k dl vio & blue .20 .25
210 A8 2pi on 20k bl & car .20 .30
211 A11 2½pi on 25k grn & vio .25 .45
a. Double surcharge 50.00 50.00
212 A11 3½pi on 35k vio & grn .40 .55
Nos. 208-212 (5) 1.25 1.75

Russia Nos. 88-91, 93, 95-104 Surcharged:

PARA 5 PARA c — **10 PARA 10** d

1 PIASTRE 1 e — **PIAS 1½ TRE** f

g — **30 PIASTRES**

1913 *Perf. 13½*
213 A16(c) 5pa on 1k .20 .20
214 A17(d) 10pa on 2k .20 .20
215 A18(c) 15pa on 3k .20 .20
216 A19(c) 20pa on 4k .20 .20
217 A21(e) 1pi on 10k .20 .20
218 A23(f) 1½pi on 15k .45 .50
219 A24(f) 2pi on 20k .45 .50
220 A25(f) 2½pi on 25k .60 .70
221 A26(f) 3½pi on 35k 1.50 1.40
222 A27(e) 5pi on 50k 1.75 1.75
223 A28(f) 7pi on 70k 7.00 7.00
224 A29(e) 10pi on 1r 7.00 7.00
225 A30(e) 20pi on 2r 1.50 1.40
226 A31(g) 30pi on 3r 2.25 2.00
227 A32(e) 50pi on 5r 62.50 62.50
Nos. 213-227 (15) 86.00 85.75

Romanov dynasty tercentenary.
Forgeries exist of overprint on No. 227.

Russia Nos. 75, 71, 72 Surcharged:

15 PARA h — **PIAS 50 TRES** i

Perf. 14x14½

Wove Paper

228 A14(h) 15pa on 3k .20 .20

Perf. 13, 13½

230 A13(i) 50pi on 5r 5.00 10.00

Vertically Laid Paper

Wmk. Wavy Lines (168)

231 A13(i) 100pi on 10r 10.00 20.00
a. Double surcharge 24.00 40.00
Nos. 228-231 (3) 15.20 30.20

No. 228 has lozenges of varnish on face but No. 230 has not.

Wrangel Issues

For the Posts of Gen. Peter Wrangel's army and civilian refugees from South Russia, interned in Turkey, Serbia, etc.

Very few of the Wrangel overprints were actually sold to the public, and many of the covers were made up later with the original cancels. Reprints abound. Values probably are based on sales of reprints in most cases.

Russian Stamps of 1902-18 Surcharged in Blue, Red or Black

ПОЧТА
РУССКОИ
АРМІИ
1.000
РУБЛЕЙ

On Russia Nos. 69-70

Vertically Laid Paper

1921 Wmk. 168 *Perf. 13½*
232 A12 10,000r on 3.50r 25.00 25.00
233 A12 10,000r on 7r 25.00 25.00
234 A12 20,000r on 3.50r 25.00 25.00
235 A12 20,000r on 7r 25.00 25.00
Nos. 232-235 (4) 100.00 100.00

On Russia Nos. 71-86, 87a, 117-118, 137-138

Wove Paper

Perf. 14x14½, 13½

Unwmk.

236 A14 1000r on 1k .60 .60
237 A14 1000r on 2k (R) .60 .60
237A A14 1000r on 2k (Bk) 9.00 9.00
238 A14 1000r on 3k .20 .20
a. Inverted surcharge 1.25 1.25
239 A15 1000r on 4k .20 .20
a. Inverted surcharge 1.25 1.25
240 A14 1000r on 5k .20 .20
a. Inverted surcharge 1.25 1.25
241 A14 1000r on 7k .20 .20
a. Inverted surcharge 1.25 1.25
242 A15 1000r on 10k .20 .20
a. Inverted surcharge 1.25 1.25
243 A14 1000r on 10k on 7k .20 .20
244 A14 5000r on 3k .20 .20
245 A11 5000r on 14k 2.00 2.00
246 A11 5000r on 15k .20 .20
a. "PYCCKIN" 3.50 3.50
247 A8 5000r on 20k .65 .65
a. "PYCCKIN" 3.50 3.50
248 A11 5000r on 20k on 14k .65 .65
249 A11 5000r on 25k .20 .20
250 A11 5000r on 35k .20 .20
a. Inverted surcharge 1.25 1.25
b. New value omitted
251 A8 5000r on 50k .20 .20
a. Inverted surcharge
252 A11 5000r on 70k .20 .20
a. Inverted surcharge 2.00 2.00
253 A9 10,000r on 1r (Bl) .20 .20
254 A9 10,000r on 1r (Bk) 1.50 1.50
255 A12 10,000r on 3.50r .60 .60
256 A13 10,000r on 5r 9.00 9.00
257 A13 10,000r on 10r .75 .75
258 A9 20,000r on 1r .45 .45
259 A12 20,000r on 3.50r .45 .45
a. Inverted surcharge 6.50 6.50
b. New value omitted 55.00 55.00
260 A12 20,000r on 7r 18.00 18.00
261 A13 20,000r on 10r .40 .40
Nos. 236-261 (27) 47.25 47.25

On Russia No. 104

261A A32 20,000r on 5r

On Russia Nos. 119-123, 125-135

Imperf

262 A14 1000r on 1k .20 .25
263 A14 1000r on 2k (R) .20 .25
263A A14 1000r on 2k (Bk) .25 .30
264 A14 1000r on 3k .20 .25
265 A15 1000r on 4k 6.50 6.50
266 A14 1000r on 5k .25 .30
267 A14 5000r on 3k .20 .25
268 A11 5000r on 15k .25 .30
268A A8 5000r on 20k 10.00
268B A11 5000r on 25k 10.00
269 A11 5000r on 35k .50 .50
270 A8 5000r on 50k .50 .50
271 A11 5000r on 70k .20 .20
272 A9 10,000r on 1r (Bl) .20 .20
a. Inverted surcharge 1.00 .65
273 A9 10,000r on 1r (Bk) .20 .25
274 A12 10,000r on 3.50r .20 .25
275 A13 10,000r on 5r .85 1.00
276 A12 10,000r on 7r 5.25 5.25
276A A13 10,000r on 10r 32.50
277 A9 20,000r on 1r (Bl) .20 .20
a. Inverted surcharge 1.00 1.00
278 A9 20,000r on 1r (Bk) .20 .25
279 A12 20,000r on 3.50r .85 1.00
280 A13 20,000r on 5r .20 .20
281 A12 20,000r on 7r 4.00 4.00
281A A13 20,000r on 10r 32.50
Nos. 262-268,269-276,277-281 (21) 21.40 22.20

A18

A19

On Postal Savings Stamps

Perf. 14½x15

Wmk. 171

282 A18 10,000r on 1k red, *buff* .20 .20
283 A19 10,000r on 5k grn, *buff* .20 .20
a. Inverted surcharge 2.75
284 A19 10,000r on 10k brn, *buff* .20 .20
a. Inverted surcharge 2.75
Nos. 282-284 (3) .60 .60

On Stamps of Russian Offices in Turkey

On No. 38-39

Vertically Laid Paper

Wmk. Wavy Lines (168)

284B A11 20,000r on 35pi on 3.50r 150.00
284C A11 20,000r on 70pi on 7r 150.00

On Nos. 200-207

Vertically Laid Paper

284D A15 1000r on 20pa on 5k 1.10 1.10

Wove Paper

Unwmk.

285 A16 1000r on 5pa on 1k .35 .35
286 A16 1000r on 10pa on 2k .35 .35
287 A17 1000r on 20pa on 4k .30 .30
288 A17 1000r on 1pi on 10k .35 .35
289 A8 5000r on 5pi on 50k .40 .40
290 A9 5000r on 7pi on 70k .40 .40
291 A10 10,000r on 10pi on 1r 1.50 1.50
a. Inverted surcharge 4.75 4.75
b. Pair, one without surcharge 4.75 4.75
292 A10 20,000r on 10pi on 1r .30 .30
a. Inverted surcharge 4.75 4.75
b. Pair, one without surcharge 4.75 4.75
Nos. 284D-292 (9) 5.05 5.05

On Nos. 208-212

293 A14 1000r on 20pa on 5k .40 .40
294 A11 5000r on 1½pi on 15k .40 .40
295 A8 5000r on 2pi on 20k .40 .40
296 A11 5000r on 2½pi on 25k .40 .40
297 A11 5000r on 3½pi on 35k .50 .50
Nos. 293-297 (5) 2.10 2.10

On Nos. 228, 230-231

298 A14 1000r on 15pa on 3k .30 .30
299 A13 10,000r on 50pi on 5r 8.50 8.50
300 A13 10,000r on 100pi on 10r 10.50 10.50
301 A13 20,000r on 50pi on 5r .30 .30
302 A13 20,000r on 100pi on 10r 10.50 10.50
Nos. 298-302 (5) 30.10 30.10

On Stamps of South Russia

Denikin Issue

Imperf

303 A5 5000r on 5k org .20 .20
a. Inverted surcharge
304 A5 5000r on 10k grn .20 .20
305 A5 5000r on 15k red .20 .20
306 A5 5000r on 35k lt bl .20 .20
307 A5 5000r on 70k dk bl .20 .20
307A A5 10,000r on 70k dk bl 5.25 5.25
308 A6 10,000r on 1r brn & red .20 .20
309 A6 10,000r on 2r gray vio & yel .25 .30
a. Inverted surcharge 1.25 1.25
310 A6 10,000r on 3r dull rose & grn .45 .50
311 A6 10,000r on 5r slate & vio .50 .55
312 A6 10,000r on 7r gray grn & rose 10.00 10.00
313 A6 10,000r on 10r red & gray .45 .50
314 A6 20,000r on 1r brn & red .20 .20
315 A6 20,000r on 2r gray vio & yel (Bl) 3.25 3.25
a. Inverted surcharge 5.00 5.00
315B A6 20,000r on 2r gray vio & yel (Bk) .20 .25
316 A6 20,000r on 3r dull rose & grn (Bl) 5.25 5.25
316A A6 20,000r on 3r dull rose & grn (Bk) 2.75 2.75
317 A6 20,000r on 5r slate & vio .20 .25
318 A6 20,000r on 7r gray grn & rose 6.50 6.50
319 A6 20,000r on 10r red & gray .20 .25
Nos. 303-319 (20) 36.65 37.00

Trident Stamps of Ukraine Surcharged in Blue, Red, Black or Brown

1921 *Perf. 14, 14½x15*
320 A14 10,000r on 1k org .20 .20
321 A14 10,000r on 2k grn .65 .85
322 A14 10,000r on 3k red .20 .20
a. Inverted surcharge 1.25 1.25
323 A15 10,000r on 4k car .20 .20
324 A14 10,000r on 5k cl .20 .25

325 A14 10,000r on 7k lt bl .20 .20
a. Inverted surcharge 1.25 1.25
326 A15 10,000r on 10k dk bl .20 .20
a. Inverted surcharge 1.25 1.25
327 A14 10,000r on 10k on 7k lt bl .20 .20
a. Inverted surcharge 1.25 1.25
328 A8 20,000r on 20k bl & car (Br) .20 .20
a. Inverted surcharge 1.25 1.25
329 A8 20,000r on 20k bl & car (Bk) .20 .20
a. Inverted surcharge 1.25 1.25
330 A11 20,000r on 20k on 14k bl & rose .20 .20
331 A11 20,000r on 35k red brn & grn 10.00 10.00
332 A8 20,000r on 50k brn vio & grn .20 .20
a. Inverted surcharge 1.25 1.25
Nos. 320-332 (13) 12.85 13.10

Imperf

333 A14 10,000r on 1k org .20 .20
a. Inverted surcharge 1.65
334 A14 10,000r on 2k grn .35 .35
335 A14 10,000r on 3k red .20 .20
336 A8 20,000r on 20k bl & car .20 .20
337 A11 20,000r on 35k red brn & grn 4.00 4.00
338 A8 20,000r on 50k brn vio & grn .35 .35
Nos. 333-338 (6) 5.30 5.30

There are several varieties of the trident surcharge on Nos. 320 to 338.

Same Surcharge on Russian Stamps

On Stamps of 1909-18

Perf. 14x14½

338A A14 10,000r on 1k dl org yel .45 .25
339 A14 10,000r on 2k dl grn .45 .25
340 A14 10,000r on 3k car .20 .20
341 A15 10,000r on 4k car .20 .20
342 A14 10,000r on 5k dk cl .20 .20
343 A14 10,000r on 7k blue .20 .20
344 A15 10,000r on 10k dk bl .45 .30
344A A14 10,000r on 10k on 7k bl .90 .55
344B A11 20,000r on 14k dk bl & car 5.00 2.75
345 A11 20,000r on 15k red brn & dp bl .20 .20
346 A8 20,000r on 20k dl bl & dk car .20 .20
347 A11 20,000r on 20k on 14k dk bl & car .90 .55
348 A11 20,000r on 35k red brn & grn .35 .25
349 A8 20,000r on 50k brn vio & grn .20 .20
349A A11 20,000r on 70k brn & red org .45 .35
Nos. 338A-349A (15) 10.35 6.65

On Stamps of 1917-18

Imperf

350 A14 10,000r on 1k org .25 .20
351 A14 10,000r on 2k gray grn .25 .20
352 A14 10,000r on 3k red .25 .20
353 A15 10,000r on 4k car 7.75 5.25
354 A14 10,000r on 5k claret .25 .20
355 A11 20,000r on 15k red brn & dp bl .25 .20
356 A8 20,000r on 50k brn vio & grn .70 .55
357 A11 20,000r on 70k brn & org .35 .35
Nos. 350-357 (8) 10.05 7.15

Same Surcharge on Stamps of Russian Offices in Turkey

On Nos. 40-45

Perf. 14½x15

358 A12 10,000r on 5pa on 1k 2.50 1.65
359 A12 10,000r on 10pa on 2k 2.50 1.65
360 A12 10,000r on 20pa on 4k 2.50 1.65
361 A12 10,000r on 1pi on 10k 2.50 1.65
362 A12 20,000r on 5pi on 50k 2.50 1.65
363 A12 20,000r on 7pi on 70k 2.50 1.65
Nos. 358-363 (6) 15.00 9.90

On Nos. 201-206

364 A16 10,000r on 5pa on 1k .35 .35
365 A16 10,000r on 10pa on 2k .35 .35
366 A17 10,000r on 20pa on 4k .35 .35
367 A17 10,000r on 1pi on 10k .35 .35
368 A8 20,000r on 5pi on 50k .35 .35
369 A9 20,000r on 7pi on 70k .35 .35
Nos. 364-369 (6) 2.10 2.10

On Nos. 228, 208-212, Stamps of 1912-13

370 A14 10,000r on 15pa on 3k .20 .20
371 A14 10,000r on 20pa on 5k .35 .35
372 A11 20,000r on 1½pi on 15k .35 .35
373 A8 20,000r on 2pi on 20k .40
374 A11 20,000r on 2½pi on 25k .40
375 A11 20,000r on 3½pi on 35k .40

Same Surcharge on Stamp of South Russia, Crimea Issue

376 A8 20,000r on 5r on 20k bl & car 16.00
Nos. 370-376 (7) 18.10

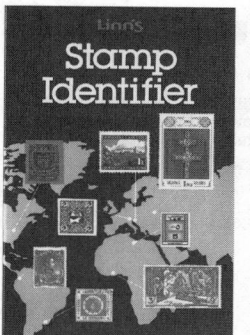

RWANDA

ru-'än-də

(Rwandaise Republic)

LOCATION — Central Africa, adjoining the ex-Belgian Congo, Tanganyika, Uganda and Burundi
GOVT. — Republic
AREA — 10,169 sq. mi.
POP. — 8,154,933(?) (1999 est.)
CAPITAL — Kigali

Rwanda was established as an independent republic on July 1, 1962. With Burundi, it had been a UN trusteeship territory administered by Belgium.
See Ruanda-Urundi.

100 Centimes = 1 Franc

Catalogue values for all unused stamps in this country are for Never Hinged items.

Watermark

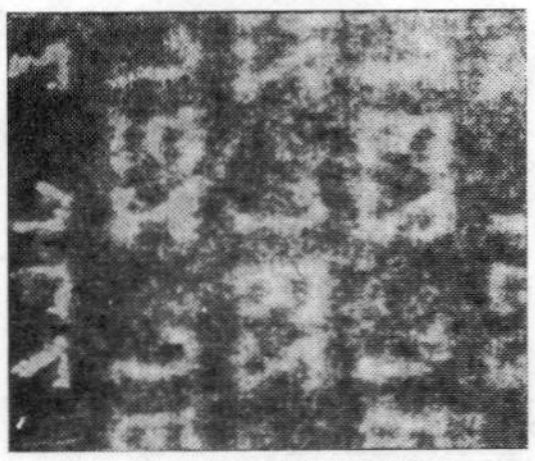

Wmk. 368- JEZ Multiple

Gregoire Kayibanda and Map of Africa — A1

Design: 40c, 1.50fr, 6.50fr, 20fr, Rwanda map spotlighted, "R" omitted.

Perf. 11½

1962, July 1 Unwmk. Photo.

1	A1	10c	brown & gray grn	.20	.20
2	A1	40c	brown & rose lil	.20	.20
3	A1	1fr	brown & blue	.60	.30
4	A1	1.50fr	brown & lt brn	.20	.20
5	A1	3.50fr	brown & dp org	.20	.20
6	A1	6.50fr	brown & lt vio bl	.20	.20
7	A1	10fr	brown & citron	.20	.20
8	A1	20fr	brown & rose	.40	.20
			Nos. 1-8 (8)	2.20	1.70

Map of Africa and Symbolic Honeycomb A2

Ruanda-Urundi Nos. 151-152 Overprinted with Metallic Frame Obliterating Previous Inscription and Denomination. Black Commemorative Inscription and "REPUBLIQUE RWANDAISE." Surcharged with New Value.

1963, Jan. 28 Unwmk. *Perf. 11½*

9	A2	3.50fr	sil, blk, ultra & red	.20	.20
10	A2	6.50fr	brnz, blk, ultra & red	.75	.60
11	A2	10fr	stl bl, blk, ultra & red	.25	.20
12	A2	20fr	sil, blk, ultra & red	.40	.35
			Nos. 9-12 (4)	1.60	1.35

Rwanda's admission to UN, Sept. 18, 1962.

Stamps of Ruanda-Urundi, 1953, Overprinted

Littonia — A3

Designs as before.

1963, Mar. 21 Unwmk. *Perf. 11½*
Flowers in Natural Colors; Metallic and Black Overprint

13	A3	25c	dk grn & dl org	.20	.20
14	A3	40c	green & salmon	.20	.20
15	A3	60c	bl grn & pink	.20	.20
16	A3	1.25fr	dk green & apple grn	.70	.60
17	A3	1.50fr	violet & apple grn	.55	.45
18	A3	2fr	on 1.50fr vio & ap grn	.85	.70
19	A3	4fr	on 1.50fr vio & ap grn	.85	.70
20	A3	5fr	dp plum & lt bl grn	.85	.70
21	A3	7fr	dk green & fawn	.85	.70
22	A3	10fr	dp plum & pale ol	.85	.70
			Nos. 13-22 (10)	6.10	5.15

The overprint consists of silver panels with black lettering. The panels on No. 19 are bluish gray.

Imperforates exist of practically every issue, starting with Nos. 23-26, except Nos. 36, 55-69, 164-169.

Wheat Emblem, Bow, Arrow, Hoe and Billhook — A4

1963, July 1 Photo. *Perf. 13½*

23	A4	2fr	brown & green	.20	.20
24	A4	4fr	magenta & ultra	.20	.20
25	A4	7fr	red & gray	.20	.20
26	A4	10fr	olive grn & yel	.55	.40
			Nos. 23-26 (4)	1.15	1.00

FAO "Freedom from Hunger" campaign.
The 20fr leopard and 50fr lion stamps of Ruanda-Urundi, Nos. 149-150, overprinted "Republique Rwandaise" at top and "Contre la Faim" at bottom, were intended to be issued Mar. 21, 1963, but were not placed in use.

Coffee A5

Designs: 10c, 40c, 4fr, Coffee. 20c, 1fr, 7fr, Bananas. 30c, 2fr, 10fr, Tea.

1963, July 1 *Perf. 11½*

27	A5	10c	violet bl & brn	.20	.20
28	A5	20c	slate & yellow	.20	.20
29	A5	30c	vermilion & grn	.20	.20
30	A5	40c	dp green & brown	.20	.20
31	A5	1fr	maroon & yellow	.20	.20
32	A5	2fr	dk blue & green	.65	.40
33	A5	4fr	red & brown	.20	.20
34	A5	7fr	yellow grn & yellow	.20	.20
35	A5	10fr	violet & green	.25	.20
			Nos. 27-35 (9)	2.30	2.00

First anniversary of independence.

Common Design Types pictured following the introduction.

African Postal Union Issue
Common Design Type

1963, Sept. 8 Unwmk. *Perf. 12½*

36	CD114	14fr	black, ocher & red	.60	.50

Post Horn and Pigeon — A6

1963, Oct. 25 Photo. *Perf. 11½*

37	A6	50c	ultra & rose	.20	.20
38	A6	1.50fr	brown & blue	.50	.40
39	A6	3fr	dp plum & gray	.20	.20
40	A6	20fr	green & yellow	.35	.20
			Nos. 37-40 (4)	1.25	1.00

Rwanda's admission to the UPU, Apr. 6.

Scales, UN Emblem and Flame A7

1963, Dec. 10 Unwmk. *Perf. 11½*

41	A7	5fr	crimson	.20	.20
42	A7	6fr	brt purple	.40	.30
43	A7	10fr	brt blue	.20	.20
			Nos. 41-43 (3)	.80	.70

15th anniversary of the Universal Declaration of Human Rights.

Children's Clinic — A8

Designs: 20c, 7fr, Laboratory examination, horiz. 30c, 10fr, Physician examining infant. 40c, 20fr, Litter bearers, horiz.

1963, Dec. Photo.

44	A8	10c	yel org, red & brn blk	.20	.20
45	A8	20c	grn, red & brn blk	.20	.20
46	A8	30c	bl, red & brn blk	.20	.20
47	A8	40c	red lil, red & brn	.20	.20
48	A8	2fr	bl grn, red brn & blk	.50	.40
49	A8	7fr	ultra, red & blk	.20	.20
50	A8	10fr	red brn, red & brn blk	.20	.20
51	A8	20fr	dp org, red & brn	.40	.20
			Nos. 44-51 (8)	2.10	1.80

Centenary of the International Red Cross.

Map of Rwanda and Woman at Water Pump — A9

1964, May 4 Unwmk. *Perf. 11½*

52	A9	3fr	lt grn, dk brn & ultra	.20	.20
53	A9	7fr	pink, dk brn & ultra	.30	.20
54	A9	10fr	yel, dk brn & ultra	.40	.30
			Nos. 52-54 (3)	.90	.70

Souvenir Sheet
Imperf

54A	A9	25fr	lilac, bl, brn & blk	3.25	3.25

UN 4th World Meteorological Day, Mar. 23.

Ruanda-Urundi Nos. 138-150, 153 Overprinted "REPUBLIQUE RWANDAISE", Some Surcharged, in Silver and Black

Buffaloes A10

Designs: 10c, 20c, 30c, Buffaloes. 40c, 2fr, Black-and-white colobus (monkey). 50c, 7.50fr, Impalas. 1fr, Mountain gorilla. 3fr, 4fr, 8fr, African elephants. 5fr, 10fr, Eland and zebras. 20fr, Leopard. 50fr, Lions. 40c, 1fr and 2fr are vertical.

1964, June 29 Photo. *Perf. 11½*
Size: 33x23mm, 23x33mm

55	A10	10c	on 20c gray, ap grn & blk	.20	.20
56	A10	20c	blk, gray & ap grn	.20	.20
57	A10	30c	on 1.50fr blk, gray & org	.20	.20
58	A10	40c	mag, blk & gray grn	.20	.20
59	A10	50c	grn, org yel & brn	.20	.20
60	A10	1fr	ultra, blk & brn	.20	.20
61	A10	2fr	grnsh bl, ind & brn	.20	.20
62	A10	3fr	brn, dp car & blk	.20	.20
63	A10	4fr	on 3.50fr on 3fr brn, dp car & blk	.25	.20
64	A10	5fr	brn, dl yel, grn & blk	.20	.20
65	A10	7.50fr	on 6.50fr red, org yel & brn	.45	.20
66	A10	8fr	blue, mag & blk	3.00	2.00
67	A10	10fr	brn, dl yel, brt pink & blk	.60	.20

Size: 45x26½mm

68	A10	20fr	hn brn, ocher & blk	1.00	.50
69	A10	50fr	dp blue & brown	1.60	1.25
			Nos. 55-69 (15)	8.70	6.15

Boy with Crutch and Gatagara Home — A11

Basketball — A12

Designs: 40c, 8fr, Girls with sewing machines, horiz. 4fr, 10fr, Girl on crutches, map of Rwanda and Gatagara Home.

1964, Nov. 10 Photo. *Perf. 11½*

70	A11	10c	lilac blk brn	.20	.20
71	A11	40c	blue & blk brn	.20	.20
72	A11	4fr	org red & blk brn	.20	.20
73	A11	7.50fr	yel grn & blk brn	.25	.20
74	A11	8fr	bister & blk brn	1.00	.60
75	A11	10fr	magenta & blk brn	.30	.20
			Nos. 70-75 (6)	2.15	1.60

Gatagara Home for handicapped children.

1964, Dec. 8 Litho. *Perf. 13½*

Sport: 10c, 4fr, Runner, horiz. 30c, 20fr, High jump, horiz. 40c, 50fr, Soccer.

Size: 26x38mm

76	A12	10c	gray, sl & dk grn	.20	.20
77	A12	20c	pink, sl & rose red	.20	.20
78	A12	30c	lt grn, sl & grn	.20	.20
79	A12	40c	buff, sl & brn	.20	.20
80	A12	4fr	vio gray, sl & vio	.20	.20
81	A12	5fr	pale grn, sl & yel grn	1.25	1.10
82	A12	20fr	pale lil, sl & red lil	.40	.30
83	A12	50fr	gray, sl & dk gray	.70	.60
a.			Souvenir sheet of 4	4.50	4.50
			Nos. 76-83 (8)	3.35	3.00

18th Olympic Games, Tokyo, Oct. 10-25. No. 83a contains 4 stamps (10fr, soccer; 20fr, basketball; 30fr, high jump; 40fr, runner). Size of stamps: 28x38mm.

Quill, Books, Radical and Retort — A13

Medical School and Student with Microscope — A14

30c, 10fr, Scales, hand, staff of Mercury and globe. 40c, 12fr, View of University.

1965, Feb. 22 Engr. *Perf. 11½*

84	A13	10c multicolored	.20	.20
85	A14	20c multicolored	.20	.20
86	A13	30c multicolored	.20	.20
87	A14	40c multicolored	.20	.20
88	A13	5fr multicolored	.20	.20
89	A14	7fr multicolored	.20	.20
90	A13	10fr multicolored	.75	.60
91	A14	12fr multicolored	.25	.20
		Nos. 84-91 (8)	2.20	2.00

National University of Rwanda at Butare.

Abraham Lincoln, Death Cent. A15

1965, Apr. 15 Photo. *Perf. 13½*

92	A15	10c emerald & dk red	.20	.20
93	A15	20c red brn & dk bl	.20	.20
94	A15	30c brt violet & red	.20	.20
95	A15	40c brt grnsh bl & red	.20	.20
96	A15	9fr orange brn & pur	.20	.20
97	A15	40fr black & brt grn	1.60	.60
		Nos. 92-97 (6)	2.60	1.60

Souvenir Sheet

98	A15	50fr red lilac & red	2.10	2.00

Marabous — A16

Zebras A17

30c, Impalas. 40c, Crowned cranes, hippopotami & cattle egrets. 1fr, Cape buffalos. 3fr, Cape hunting dogs. 5fr, Yellow baboons. 10fr, Elephant & map of Rwanda with location of park. 40fr, Anhinga, great & reed cormorants. 100fr, Lions.

1965, Apr. 28 Photo. *Perf. 11½*

Size: 32x23mm

99	A16	10c multicolored	.20	.20
100	A17	20c multicolored	.20	.20
101	A16	30c multicolored	.20	.20
102	A17	40c multicolored	.20	.20
103	A16	1fr multicolored	.20	.20
104	A17	3fr multicolored	.20	.20
105	A16	5fr multicolored	2.50	.90
106	A17	10fr multicolored	.20	.20

Size: 45x26mm

107	A17	40fr multicolored	.65	.25
108	A17	100fr multicolored	1.60	.20
		Nos. 99-108 (10)	6.15	2.75

Kagera National Park publicity.

Telstar and ITU Emblem A18

Designs: 40c, 50fr, Syncom satellite. 60fr, old and new communications equipment.

1965 Unwmk. *Perf. 13½*

109	A18	10c red brn, ultra & car	.20	.20
110	A18	40c violet, emer & yel	.20	.20
111	A18	4.50fr blk, car & dk bl	.75	.40
112	A18	50fr dk brn, yel grn & brt grn	.75	.20
		Nos. 109-112 (4)	1.90	1.00

Souvenir Sheet

113	A18	60fr blk brn, org brn & bl	2.25	2.25

ITU, cent. Issued: #113, 7/19; others, 5/17.

Papilio Bromius Chrapkowskii Suffert — A19

Cattle, ICY Emblem and Map of Africa — A20

Various butterflies and moths in natural colors.

1965-66 Photo. *Perf. 12½*

114	A19	10c black & yellow	.20	.20
115	A19	15c black & dp org ('66)	.20	.20
116	A19	20c black & lilac	.20	.20
117	A19	30c black & red lil	.20	.20
118	A19	35c dk brn & dk bl ('66)	.20	.20
119	A19	40c black & Prus bl	.20	.20
120	A19	1.50fr black & grn ('66)	.20	.20
121	A19	3fr dk brn & ol grn ('66)	2.25	.90
122	A19	4fr black & red brn	1.50	1.00
123	A19	10fr black & pur ('66)	.20	.20
124	A19	50fr black & brown	1.40	.90
125	A19	100fr dk brn & bl ('66)	2.50	.85
		Nos. 114-125 (12)	9.25	5.25

The 15c, 20c, 40c, 1.50fr, 10fr and 50fr are horizontal.

1965, Oct. 25 Unwmk. *Perf. 12*

Map of Africa and: 40c, Tree & lake. 4.50fr, Gazelle under tree. 45fr, Mount Ruwenzori.

126	A20	10c olive bis & bl grn	.20	.20
127	A20	40c lt ultra, red brn & grn	.20	.20
128	A20	4.50fr brt grn, yel & brn	.80	.35
129	A20	45fr rose claret	.70	.25
		Nos. 126-129 (4)	1.90	1.00

John F. Kennedy (1917-1963) — A21

1965, Nov. 22 Photo. *Perf. 11½*

130	A21	10c brt grn & dk brn	.20	.20
131	A21	40c brt pink & dk brn	.20	.20
132	A21	50c dk blue & dk brn	.20	.20
133	A21	1fr gray ol & dk brn	.20	.20
134	A21	8fr violet & dk brn	1.40	1.00
135	A21	50fr gray & dk brn	1.00	.80
		Nos. 130-135 (6)	3.20	2.60

Souvenir Sheet

136		Sheet of 2	6.75	6.75
a.	A21	40fr org & dark brown	3.25	3.25
b.	A21	60fr ultra & dark brown	3.50	3.50

Madonna — A22

1965, Dec. 20

137	A22	10c gold & dk green	.20	.20
138	A22	40c gold & dk brn red	.20	.20
139	A22	50c gold & dk blue	.20	.20
140	A22	4fr gold & slate	.50	.45
141	A22	6fr gold & violet	.20	.20
142	A22	30fr gold & dk brown	.40	.40
		Nos. 137-142 (6)	1.70	1.65

Christmas.

Father Joseph Damien and Lepers — A23

Designs: 40c, 45fr, Dr. Albert Schweitzer and Hospital, Lambarene.

1966, Jan. 31 *Perf. 11½*

143	A23	10c ultra & red brn	.20	.20
144	A23	40c dk red & vio bl	.20	.20
145	A23	4.50fr slate & brt grn	.20	.20
146	A23	45fr brn & hn brn	1.50	.80
		Nos. 143-146 (4)	2.10	1.40

Issued for World Leprosy Day.

Pope Paul VI, St. Peter's, UN Headquarters and Statue of Liberty — A24

Design: 40c, 50fr, Pope Paul VI, Papal arms and UN emblem.

1966, Feb. 28 Photo. *Perf. 12*

147	A24	10c henna brn & slate	.20	.20
148	A24	40c brt blue & slate	.20	.20
149	A24	4.50fr lilac & slate	1.00	.65
150	A24	50fr brt green & slate	.85	.30
		Nos. 147-150 (4)	2.25	1.35

Visit of Pope Paul VI to the UN, New York City, Oct. 4, 1965.

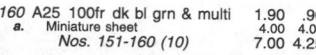

Globe Thistle — A25

Flowers: 20c, Blood lily. 30c, Everlasting. 40c, Natal plum. 1fr, Tulip tree. 3fr, Rendle orchid. 5fr, Aloe. 10fr, Ammocharis tinneana. 40fr, Coral tree. 100fr, Caper. (20c, 40c, 1fr, 3fr, 5fr, 10fr are vertical).

1966, Mar. 14 *Perf. 11½*

Granite Paper

151	A25	10c lt blue & multi	.20	.20
152	A25	20c orange & multi	.20	.20
153	A25	30c car rose & multi	.20	.20
154	A25	40c green & multi	.20	.20
155	A25	1fr multicolored	.20	.20
156	A25	3fr indigo & multi	.20	.20
157	A25	5fr multicolored	3.00	1.60
158	A25	10fr blue grn & multi	.20	.20
159	A25	40fr brown & multi	.70	.35
160	A25	100fr dk bl grn & multi	1.90	.90
a.		Miniature sheet	4.00	4.00
		Nos. 151-160 (10)	7.00	4.25

No. 160a contains one 100fr stamp in changed color, bright blue and multicolored.

Opening of WHO Headquarters, Geneva — A26

1966, May 1 Litho. *Perf. 12½x12*

161	A26	2fr lt olive green	.20	.20
162	A26	3fr vermilion	.20	.20
163	A26	5fr violet blue	.20	.20
		Nos. 161-163 (3)	.60	.60

Soccer — A27

Mother and Child, Planes Dropping Bombs — A28

20c, 9fr, Basketball. 30c, 50fr, Volleyball.

1966, May 30 Photo. *Perf. 15x14*

164	A27	10c dl grn, ultra & blk	.20	.20
165	A27	20c crimson, grn & blk	.20	.20
166	A27	30c bl, brt rose lil & blk	.20	.20
167	A27	40c yel bis, grn & blk	.20	.20
168	A27	9fr gray, red lil & blk	.25	.20
169	A27	50fr rose lil, Prus bl & blk	.75	.60
		Nos. 164-169 (6)	1.80	1.60

National Youth Sports Program.

1966, June 29 *Perf. 13½*

Design and Inscription Black and Red

170	A28	20c rose lilac	.20	.20
171	A28	30c yellow green	.20	.20
172	A28	50c lt ultra	.20	.20
173	A28	6fr yellow	.20	.20
174	A28	15fr blue green	.40	.20
175	A28	18fr lilac	.40	.30
		Nos. 170-175 (6)	1.60	1.30

Campaign against nuclear weapons.

A29

A30

Global soccer ball.

1966, July ***Perf. 11½***

176 A29	20c	org & indigo	.20	.20
177 A29	30c	lilac & indigo	.20	.20
178 A29	50c	brt grn & indigo	.20	.20
179 A29	6fr	brt rose & indigo	.20	.20
180 A29	12fr	lt vio brn & ind	.65	.25
181 A29	25fr	ultra & indigo	.80	.50
		Nos. 176-181 (6)	2.25	1.55

World Soccer Cup Championship, Wembley, England, July 11-30.

1966, Oct. 24 **Engr.** ***Perf. 14***

Designs: 10c, Mikeno Volcano and crested shrike, horiz. 40c, Nyamilanga Falls. 4.50fr, Gahinga and Muhabura volcanoes and lobelias, horiz. 55fr, Rusumu Falls.

182 A30	10c	green	.20	.20
183 A30	40c	brown carmine	.20	.20
184 A30	4.50fr	violet blue	.35	.30
185 A30	55fr	red lilac	.40	.30
		Nos. 182-185 (4)	1.15	1.00

UNESCO Emblem, African Artifacts and Musical Clef — A31

UNESCO 20th Anniv.: 30c, 10fr, Hands holding primer showing giraffe and zebra. 50c, 15fr, Atom symbol and power drill. 1fr, 50fr, Submerged sphinexes and sailboat.

1966, Nov. 4 **Photo.** ***Perf. 12***

186 A31	20c	brt rose & dk bl	.20	.20
187 A31	30c	grnsh blue & blk	.20	.20
188 A31	50c	ocher & blk	.20	.20
189 A31	1fr	violet & blk	.20	.20
190 A31	5fr	yellow grn & blk	.20	.20
191 A31	10fr	brown & blk	.25	.20
192 A31	15fr	red lilac & dk bl	.40	.30
193 A31	50fr	dull bl & blk	.45	.35
		Nos. 186-193 (8)	2.10	1.85

Rock Python — A32

Snakes: 20c, 20fr, Jameson's mamba. 30c, 3fr, Rock python. 50c, Gabon viper. 1fr, Black-lipped spitting cobra. 5fr, African sand snake. 70fr, Egg-eating snake. (20c, 50c, 3fr and 20fr are horizontal.)

1967, Jan. 30 **Photo.** ***Perf. 11½***

194 A32	20c	red & black	.20	.20
195 A32	30c	bl, dk brn & yel	.20	.20
196 A32	50c	yel grn & multi	.20	.20
197 A32	1fr	lt lil, blk & bis	.20	.20
198 A32	3fr	lt vio, dk brn & yel	.20	.20
199 A32	5fr	yellow & multi	.20	.20
200 A32	20fr	pale pink & multi	.80	.60
201 A32	70fr	pale vio, brn & blk	1.25	.65
		Nos. 194-201 (8)	3.25	2.45

Ntaruka Hydroelectric Station and Tea Flowers — A33

Designs: 30c, 25fr, Transformer and chrysanthemums (pyrethrum). 50c, 50fr, Sluice and coffee.

1967, Mar. 6 **Photo.** ***Perf. 13½***

202 A33	20c	maroon & dp bl	.20	.20
203 A33	30c	black & red brn	.20	.20
204 A33	50c	brown & violet	.20	.20
205 A33	4fr	dk grn & dp plum	.20	.20
206 A33	25fr	violet & sl grn	.30	.30
207 A33	50fr	dk blue & brn	.75	.50
		Nos. 202-207 (6)	1.85	1.60

Ntaruka Hydroelectric Station.

Souvenir Sheets

Cogwheels — A34

1967, Apr. 15 **Engr.** ***Perf. 11½***

208 A34	100fr	dk red brown	2.00	2.00
209 A34	100fr	brt rose lilac	2.00	2.00

7th "Europa" Phil. Exhib. and the Philatelic Salon of African States, Naples, Apr. 8-16.

Souvenir Sheet

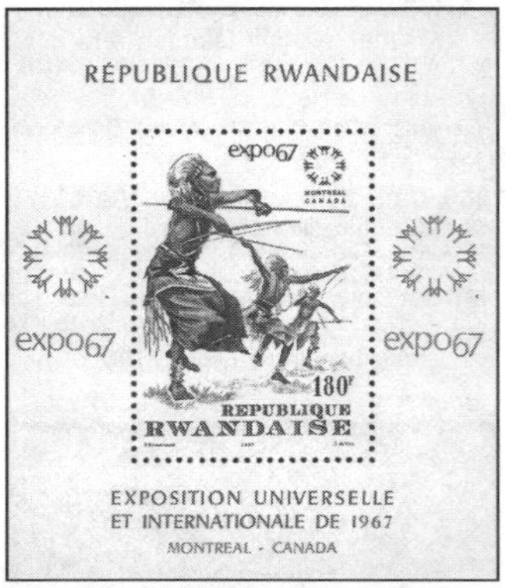

African Dancers and EXPO '67 Emblem — A35

1967, Apr. 28 ***Perf. 11½***

210 A35	180fr	dark purple	2.75	2.75

EXPO '67, Intl. Exhib., Montreal, Apr. 28-Oct. 27.

A similar imperf. sheet has the stamp in violet brown.

St. Martin, by Van Dyck and Caritas Emblem A36

Paintings: 40c, 15fr, Rebecca at the Well, by Murillo, horiz. 60c, 18fr, St. Christopher, by Dierick Bouts. 80c, 26fr, Job and his Friends, by Il Calabrese (Mattia Preti), horiz.

Perf. 13x11, 11x13

1967, May 8 **Photo.**

Black Inscription on Gold Panel

211 A36	20c	dark purple	.20	.20
212 A36	40c	blue green	.20	.20
213 A36	60c	rose carmine	.20	.20
214 A36	80c	deep blue	.20	.20
215 A36	9fr	redsh brown	.60	.35
216 A36	15fr	orange ver	.20	.20
217 A36	18fr	dk olive grn	.25	.20
218 A36	26fr	dk carmine rose	.35	.30
		Nos. 211-218 (8)	2.20	1.85

Issued to publicize the work of Caritas-Rwanda, Catholic welfare organization.

Round Table Emblem and Zebra — A37

Round Table Emblem and: 40c, Elephant. 60c, Cape buffalo. 80c, Antelope. 18fr, Wheat. 100fr, Palm tree.

1967, July 31 **Photo.** ***Perf. 14***

219 A37	20c	gold & multi	.20	.20
220 A37	40c	gold & multi	.20	.20
221 A37	60c	gold & multi	.20	.20
222 A37	80c	gold & multi	.20	.20
223 A37	18fr	gold & multi	.30	.20
224 A37	100fr	gold & multi	1.40	.65
		Nos. 219-224 (6)	2.50	1.65

Rwanda Table No. 9 of Kigali, a member of the Intl. Round Tables Assoc.

EXPO '67 Emblem, Africa Place and Dancers and Drummers — A38

EXPO '67 Emblem, Africa Place and: 30c, 3fr, Drum and vessels. 50c, 40fr, Two dancers. 1fr, 34fr, Spears, shields and bow.

1967, Aug. 10 **Photo.** ***Perf. 12***

225 A38	20c	brt blue & sepia	.20	.20
226 A38	30c	brt rose lil & sepia	.20	.20
227 A38	50c	orange & sepia	.20	.20
228 A38	1fr	green & sepia	.20	.20
229 A38	3fr	violet & sepia	.20	.20
230 A38	15fr	emerald & sepia	.20	.20
231 A38	34fr	rose red & sepia	.40	.30
232 A38	40fr	grnsh bl & sepia	.55	.40
		Nos. 225-232 (8)	2.15	1.90

Lions Emblem, Globe and Zebra — A39

1967, Oct. 16 **Photo.** ***Perf. 13½***

233 A39	20c	lilac, bl & blk	.20	.20
234 A39	80c	lt grn, bl & blk	.20	.20
235 A39	1fr	rose car, bl & blk	.20	.20
236 A39	8fr	bister, bl & blk	.20	.20
237 A39	10fr	ultra, bl & blk	.20	.20
238 A39	50fr	yel grn, bl & blk	.90	.65
		Nos. 233-238 (6)	1.90	1.65

50th anniversary of Lions International.

Woodland Kingfisher — A40

Birds: 20c, Red bishop, vert. 60c, Red-billed quelea, vert. 80c, Double-toothed barbet. 2fr, Pin-tailed whydah, vert. 3fr, Solitary cuckoo. 18fr, Green wood hoopoe, vert. 25fr, Blue-collared bee-eater. 80fr, Regal sunbird, vert. 100fr, Red-shouldered widowbird.

1967, Dec. 18 ***Perf. 11½***

239 A40	20c	multicolored	.20	.20
240 A40	40c	multicolored	.20	.20
241 A40	60c	multicolored	.20	.20
242 A40	80c	multicolored	.20	.20
243 A40	2fr	multicolored	.20	.20
244 A40	3fr	multicolored	.20	.20
245 A40	18fr	multicolored	.35	.20
246 A40	25fr	multicolored	.45	.20
247 A40	80fr	multicolored	1.25	.60
248 A40	100fr	multicolored	1.75	.70
		Nos. 239-248 (10)	5.00	2.90

Souvenir Sheet

Ski Jump, Speed Skating — A41

1968, Feb. 12 **Photo.** ***Perf. 11½***

249		Sheet of 2	3.00	3.00
a.	A41	50fr bl, blk & grn (skier)	1.50	1.50
b.	A41	50fr grn, blk & bl (skater)	1.50	1.50
c.		Souv. sheet of 2, #249a at right	3.00	3.00

10th Winter Olympic Games, Grenoble, France, Feb. 6-18.

Runner, Mexican Sculpture and Architecture — A42

Sport and Mexican Art: 40c, Hammer throw, pyramid and animal head. 60c, Hurdler and sculptures. 80c, Javelin and sculptures.

1968, May 27 **Photo.** ***Perf. 11½***

250 A42	20c	ultra & multi	.20	.20
251 A42	40c	multicolored	.20	.20
252 A42	60c	lilac & multi	.20	.20
253 A42	80c	orange & multi	.20	.20
		Nos. 250-253 (4)	.80	.80

19th Olympic Games, Mexico City, 10/12-27.

Souvenir Sheet

19th Olympic Games, Mexico City — A43

a, 8fr, Soccer. b, 10fr, Mexican horseman, cactus. c, 12fr, Field hockey. d, 18fr, Cathedral, Mexico City. e, 20fr, Boxing. f, 30fr, Modern buildings, musical instruments, vase.

1967, May 27 **Photo.** ***Perf. 11½***

Granite Paper

254 A43	Sheet of 6, #a.-f.	4.50	2.75

Three sets of circular gold "medal" overprints with black inscriptions were applied to the six stamps of No. 254 to honor 18 Olympic winners. Issued Dec. 12, 1968. Value $10.

Souvenir Sheet

Martin Luther King, Jr. — A44

1968, July 29 Engr. *Perf. 13½*

255	A44	100fr sepia	2.00	1.50

Rev. Dr. Martin Luther King, Jr. (1929-68), American civil rights leader. See No. 406.

Diaphant Orchid — A45

Flowers: 40c, Pharaoh's scepter. 60c, Flower of traveler's-tree. 80c, Costus afer. 2fr, Banana tree flower. 3fr, Flower and fruit of papaw tree. 18fr, Clerodendron. 25fr, Sweet potato flowers. 80fr, Baobab tree flower. 100fr, Passion flower.

1968, Sept. 9 Litho. *Perf. 13*

256	A45	20c lilac & multi	.20	.20
257	A45	40c multicolored	.20	.20
258	A45	60c bl grn & multi	.20	.20
259	A45	80c multicolored	.20	.20
260	A45	2fr brt yellow & multi	.20	.20
261	A45	3fr multicolored	.20	.20
262	A45	18fr multicolored	.25	.20
263	A45	25fr gray & multi	.35	.20
264	A45	80fr multicolored	1.40	.55
265	A45	100fr multicolored	1.60	.70
		Nos. 256-265 (10)	4.80	2.85

Equestrian and "Mexico 1968" A46

Designs: 40c, Judo and "Tokyo 1964." 60c, Fencing and "Rome 1960." 80c, High jump and "Berlin 1936." 38fr, Women's diving and "London 1908 and 1948." 60fr, Weight lifting and "Paris 1900 and 1924."

1968, Oct. 24 Litho. *Perf. 14x13*

266	A46	20c orange & sepia	.20	.20
267	A46	40c grnsh bl & sepia	.20	.20
268	A46	60c car rose & sepia	.20	.20
269	A46	80c ultra & sepia	.20	.20
270	A46	38fr red & sepia	.55	.25
271	A46	60fr emerald & sepia	1.00	.50
		Nos. 266-271 (6)	2.35	1.55

19th Olympic Games, Mexico City, 10/12-27.

Tuareg, Algeria — A47

African National Costumes: 40c, Musicians, Upper Volta. 60c, Senegalese women. 70c, Girls of Rwanda going to market. 8fr, Young married couple from Morocco. 20fr, Nigerian officials in state dress. 40fr, Man and women from Zambia. 50fr, Man and woman from Kenya.

1968, Nov. 4 Litho. *Perf. 13*

272	A47	30c multicolored	.20	.20
273	A47	40c multicolored	.20	.20
274	A47	60c multicolored	.20	.20
275	A47	70c multicolored	.20	.20
276	A47	8fr multicolored	.20	.20
277	A47	20fr multicolored	.30	.20
278	A47	40fr multicolored	.60	.30
279	A47	50fr multicolored	.70	.50
		Nos. 272-279 (8)	2.60	2.00

Souvenir Sheet

Nativity, by Giorgione — A48

1968, Dec. 16 Engr. *Perf. 11½*

280	A48	100fr green	2.50	2.50

Christmas.

See Nos. 309, 389, 422, 494, 564, 611, 713, 787, 848, 894.

Singing Boy, by Frans Hals — A49

Paintings and Music: 20c, Angels' Concert, by van Eyck. 40c, Angels' Concert, by Mathias Grunewald. 60c, No. 283a, Singing Boy, by Frans Hals. 80c, Lute Player, by Gerard Terborch. 2fr, The Fifer, by Manet. 6fr, No. 286a, Young Girls at the Piano, by Renoir.

1969, Mar. 31 Photo. *Perf. 13*

281	A49	20c gold & multi	.20	.20
282	A49	40c gold & multi	.20	.20
283	A49	60c gold & multi	.20	.20
a.		Souvenir sheet, 75fr	1.40	1.40
284	A49	80c gold & multi	.20	.20
285	A49	2fr gold & multi	.20	.20
286	A49	6fr gold & multi	.20	.20
a.		Souvenir sheet, 75fr	1.40	1.40
		Nos. 281-286,C6-C7 (8)	3.90	3.20

Tuareg Men — A50

African Headdresses: 40c, Ovambo woman, South West Africa. 60c, Guinean man and Congolese woman. 80c, Dagger dancer, Guinean forest area. 8fr, Mohammedan Nigerians. 20fr, Luba dancer, Kabondo, Congo. 40fr, Senegalese and Gambian women. 80fr, Rwanda dancer.

1969, May 29 Litho. *Perf. 13*

287	A50	20c multicolored	.20	.20
288	A50	40c multicolored	.20	.20
289	A50	60c multicolored	.20	.20
290	A50	80c multicolored	.20	.20
291	A50	8fr multicolored	.20	.20
292	A50	20fr multicolored	.30	.20
293	A50	40fr multicolored	.70	.35
294	A50	80fr multicolored	1.50	.60
		Nos. 287-294 (8)	3.50	2.15

See #398-405. For overprints see #550-557.

The Moneylender and his Wife, by Quentin Massys — A51

Design: 70fr, The Moneylender and his Wife, by Marinus van Reymerswaele.

71969, Sept. 10 Photo. *Perf. 13*

295	A51	30fr silver & multi	.60	.40
296	A51	70fr gold & multi	1.40	1.00

5th anniv. of the African Development Bank. Printed in sheets of 20 stamps and 20 labels with commemorative inscription.

For overprints see Nos. 612-613.

Souvenir Sheet

First Man on the Moon — A52

1969, Oct. 9 Engr. *Perf. 11½*

297	A52	100fr blue gray	2.25	2.25

See note after Mali No. C80. See No. 407.

Camomile and Health Emblem — A53

Worker with Pickaxe and Flag — A54

Medicinal Plants and Health Emblem: 40c, Aloe. 60c, Cola. 80c, Coca. 3fr, Hagenia abyssinica. 75fr, Cassia. 80fr, Cinchona. 100fr, Tephrosia.

1969, Nov. 24 Photo. *Perf. 13*

Flowers in Natural Colors

298	A53	20c gold, blue & blk	.20	.20
299	A53	40c gold, yel grn & blk	.20	.20
300	A53	60c gold, pink & blk	.20	.20
301	A53	80c gold, green & blk	.20	.20
302	A53	3fr gold, orange & blk	.20	.20
303	A53	75fr gold, yel & blk	1.25	.55
304	A53	80fr gold, lilac & blk	1.50	.65
305	A53	100fr gold, dl yel & blk	1.75	.80
		Nos. 298-305 (8)	5.50	3.00

For overprints & surcharge see #534-539, B1.

1969, Nov. Photo. *Perf. 11½*

306	A54	6fr brt pink & multi	.25	.20
307	A54	18fr ultra & multi	.50	.30
308	A54	40fr brown & multi	.85	.50
		Nos. 306-308 (3)	1.60	1.00

10th anniversary of independence.

For overprints see Nos. 608-610.

Christmas Type of 1968
Souvenir Sheet

Design: "Holy Night" (detail), by Correggio.

1969, Dec. 15 Engr. *Perf. 11½*

309	A48	100fr ultra	2.75	2.75

The Cook, by Pierre Aertsen — A55

Paintings: 20c, Quarry Worker, by Oscar Bonnevalle, horiz. 40c, The Plower, by Peter Brueghel, horiz 60c, Fisherman, by Constantin Meunier. 80c, Slipway, Ostende, by Jean van Noten, horiz. 10fr, The Forge of Vulcan, by Velasquez, horiz. 50fr, "Hiercheuse" (woman shoveling coal), by Meunier. 70fr, Miner, by Pierre Paulus.

1969, Dec. 22 Photo. *Perf. 13½*

310	A55	20c gold & multi	.20	.20
311	A55	40c gold & multi	.20	.20
312	A55	60c gold & multi	.20	.20
313	A55	80c gold & multi	.20	.20
314	A55	8fr gold & multi	.20	.20
315	A55	10fr gold & multi	.20	.20
316	A55	50fr gold & multi	.90	.40
317	A55	70fr gold & multi	1.25	.50
		Nos. 310-317 (8)	3.35	2.10

ILO, 50th anniversary.

Napoleon Crossing St. Bernard, by Jacques L. David — A56

Paintings of Napoleon Bonaparte (1769-1821): 40c, Decorating Soldier before Tilsit, by Jean Baptiste Debret. 60c, Addressing Troops at Augsburg, by Claude Gautherot. 80c, First Consul, by Jean Auguste Ingres. 8fr, Battle of Marengo, by Jacques Auguste Pajou. 20fr, Napoleon Meeting Emperor Francis II, by Antoine Jean Gros. 40fr, Gen. Bonaparte at Arcole, by Gros. 80fr Coronation, by David.

1969, Dec. 29

318	A56	20c gold & multi	.20	.20
319	A56	40c gold & multi	.20	.20
320	A56	60c gold & multi	.20	.20
321	A56	80c gold & multi	.20	.20
322	A56	8fr gold & multi	.20	.20
323	A56	20fr gold & multi	.50	.30
324	A56	40fr gold & multi	1.00	.50
325	A56	80fr gold & multi	1.75	1.00
		Nos. 318-325 (8)	4.25	2.80

Epsom Derby, by Gericault — A57

Paintings of Horses: 40c, Horses Emerging from the Sea, by Delacroix. 60c, Charles V at Muhlberg, by Titian, vert. 80c, Amateur Jockeys, by Edgar Degas, 8fr, Horsemen at Rest, by Philips Wouwerman. 20fr, Imperial Guards Officer, by Géricault, vert. 40fr, Friends of the Desert, by Oscar Bonnevalle. 80fr, Two Horses (detail from the Prodigal Son), by Rubens.

1970, Mar. 31 Photo. *Perf. 13½*

326	A57	20c gold & multi	.20	.20
327	A57	40c gold & multi	.20	.20
328	A57	60c gold & multi	.20	.20
329	A57	80c gold & multi	.20	.20
330	A57	8fr gold & multi	.20	.20
331	A57	20fr gold & multi	.40	.20
332	A57	40fr gold & multi	.70	.35
333	A57	80fr gold & multi	1.40	.65
		Nos. 326-333 (8)	3.50	2.20

Souvenir Sheet

Fleet in Bay of Naples, by Peter Brueghel, the Elder — A58

1970, May 2 Engr. *Perf. 11½*

334	A58	100fr brt rose lilac	2.00	2.00

10th Europa Phil. Exhib., Naples, Italy, May 2-10.

Copies of No. 334 were trimmed to 68x58mm and overprinted in silver or gold "NAPLES 1973" on the stamp, and "Salon Philatelique des Etats Africains / Exposition du Timbre-Poste Europa" in October, 1973.

Soccer and Mexican Decorations A59

Tharaka Meru Woman, East Africa — A60

Designs: Various scenes from soccer game and pre-Columbian decorations.

1970, June 15 Photo. *Perf. 13*

335	A59	20c gold & multi	.20	.20
336	A59	30c gold & multi	.20	.20
337	A59	50c gold & multi	.20	.20
338	A59	1fr gold & multi	.20	.20
339	A59	6fr gold & multi	.20	.20
340	A59	18fr gold & multi	.40	.20
341	A59	30fr gold & multi	.60	.40
342	A59	90fr gold & multi	1.75	.70
		Nos. 335-342 (8)	3.75	2.30

9th World Soccer Championships for the Jules Rimet Cup, Mexico City, 5/30-6/21.

1970, June 1 Litho.

African National Costumes: 30c, Musician with wooden flute, Niger. 50c, Woman water carrier, Tunisia. 1fr, Ceremonial costumes, North Nigeria. 3fr, Strolling troubadour "Griot," Mali. 5fr, Quipongos women, Angola. 50fr, Man at prayer, Mauritania. 90fr, Sinehatiali dance costumes, Ivory Coast.

343	A60	20c multi	.20	.20
344	A60	30c multi	.20	.20
345	A60	50c multi	.20	.20
346	A60	1fr multi	.20	.20
347	A60	3fr multi	.20	.20
348	A60	5fr multi	.20	.20
349	A60	50fr multi	.90	.40
350	A60	90fr multi	1.60	.70
		Nos. 343-350 (8)	3.70	2.30

For overprints and surcharges see Nos. 693-698, B2-B3.

Flower Arrangement, Peacock, EXPO '70 Emblem — A61

EXPO Emblem and: 30c, Torii and Camellias, by Yukihiko Yasuda. 50c, Kabuki character and Woman Playing Samisen, by Nampu Katayama. 1fr, Tower of the Sun, and Warrior Riding into Water. 3fr, Pavilion and Buddhist deity. 5fr, Pagoda and modern painting by Shuho Yamakawa. 20fr, Japanese inscription "Omatsuri" and Osaka Castle. 70fr, EXPO '70 emblem and Warrior on Horseback.

1970, Aug. 24 Photo. *Perf. 13*

351	A61	20c gold & multi	.20	.20
352	A61	30c gold & multi	.20	.20
353	A61	50c gold & multi	.20	.20
354	A61	1fr gold & multi	.20	.20
355	A61	3fr gold & multi	.20	.20
356	A61	5fr gold & multi	.20	.20
357	A61	20fr gold & multi	.30	.30
358	A61	70fr gold & multi	1.00	.50
		Nos. 351-358 (8)	2.50	2.00

EXPO '70 International Exhibition, Osaka, Japan, Mar. 15-Sept. 13.

Young Mountain Gorillas — A62

Various Gorillas. 40c, 80c, 2fr, 100fr are vert.

1970, Sept. 7

359	A62	20c olive & blk	.20	.20
360	A62	40c brt rose lil & blk	.20	.20
361	A62	60c blue, brn & blk	.20	.20
362	A62	80c org brn & blk	.20	.20
363	A62	1fr dp car & blk	.20	.20
364	A62	2fr black & multi	.20	.20
365	A62	15fr sepia & blk	.40	.20
366	A62	100fr brt bl & blk	2.50	1.50
		Nos. 359-366 (8)	4.10	2.90

Pierre J. Pelletier and Joseph B. Caventou A63

Designs: 20c, Cinchona flower and bark. 80c, Quinine powder and pharmacological vessels. 1fr, Anopheles mosquito. 3fr, Malaria patient and nurse. 25fr, "Malaria" (mosquito).

1970, Oct. 27 Photo. *Perf. 13*

367	A63	20c silver & multi	.20	.20
368	A63	80c silver & multi	.20	.20
369	A63	1fr silver & multi	.20	.20
370	A63	3fr silver & multi	.20	.20
371	A63	25fr silver & multi	.50	.25
372	A63	70fr silver & multi	1.40	.60
		Nos. 367-372 (6)	2.70	1.65

150th anniv. of the discovery of quinine by Pierre Joseph Pelletier (1788-1842) and Joseph Bienaimé Caventou (1795-1877), French pharmacologists.

Apollo Spaceship A64

Apollo Spaceship: 30c, Second stage separation. 50c, Spaceship over moon surface. 1fr, Landing module and astronauts on moon. 3fr, Take-off from moon. 5fr, Return to earth. 10fr, Final separation of nose cone. 80fr, Splashdown.

1970, Nov. 23 Photo. *Perf. 13*

373	A64	20c silver & multi	.20	.20
374	A64	30c silver & multi	.20	.20
375	A64	50c silver & multi	.20	.20
376	A64	1fr silver & multi	.20	.20
377	A64	3fr silver & multi	.20	.20
378	A64	5fr silver & multi	.20	.20
379	A64	10fr silver & multi	.20	.20
380	A64	80fr silver & multi	1.25	.90
		Nos. 373-380 (8)	2.65	2.30

Conquest of space.

Franklin D. Roosevelt and Brassocattleya Olympia Alba — A65

Portraits of Roosevelt and various orchids.

1970, Dec. 21 Photo. *Perf. 13*

381	A65	20c blue, blk & brn	.20	.20
382	A65	30c car rose, blk & brn	.20	.20
383	A65	50c dp org, blk & brn	.20	.20
384	A65	1fr green, blk & brn	.20	.20
385	A65	2fr maroon, blk & grn	.20	.20
386	A65	6fr lilac & multi	.20	.20
387	A65	30fr bl, blk & sl grn	.55	.30
388	A65	60fr lil rose, blk & sl grn	1.25	.50
		Nos. 381-388 (8)	3.00	2.00

Pres. Roosevelt, 25th death anniv.

Christmas Type of 1968
Souvenir Sheet

Design: 100fr, Adoration of the Shepherds, by José de Ribera, vert.

1970, Dec. 24 Engr. *Perf. 11½*

389	A48	100fr Prus blue	2.00	2.00

Pope Paul VI — A66

Popes: 20c, John XXIII, 1958-1963. 30c, Pius XII, 1939-1958. 40c, Pius XI, 1922-39. 1fr, Benedict XV, 1914-22. 18fr, St. Pius X, 1903-14. 20fr, Leo XIII, 1878-1903. 60fr, Pius IX, 1846-78.

1970, Dec. 31 Photo. *Perf. 13*

390	A66	10c gold & dk brn	.20	.20
391	A66	20c gold & dk grn	.20	.20
392	A66	30c gold & dp claret	.20	.20
393	A66	40c gold & indigo	.20	.20
394	A66	1fr gold & dk pur	.20	.20
395	A66	18fr gold & purple	.35	.20
396	A66	20fr gold & org brn	.40	.25
397	A66	60fr gold & blk brn	1.10	.55
		Nos. 390-397 (8)	2.85	2.00

Centenary of Vatican I, Ecumenical Council of the Roman Catholic Church, 1869-70.

Headdress Type of 1969

African Headdresses: 20c, Rendille woman. 30c, Young Toubou woman, Chad. 50c, Peul man, Niger. 1fr, Young Masai man, Kenya. 5fr, Young Peul girl, Niger. 18fr, Rwanda woman. 25fr, Man, Mauritania. 50fr, Rwanda women with pearl necklaces.

1971, Feb. 15 Litho. *Perf. 13*

398	A50	20c multi	.20	.20
399	A50	30c multi	.20	.20
400	A50	50c multi	.20	.20
401	A50	1fr multi	.20	.20
402	A50	5fr multi	.20	.20
403	A50	18fr multi	.30	.20
404	A50	25fr multi	.45	.30
405	A50	50fr multi	1.00	.50
		Nos. 398-405 (8)	2.75	2.00

M. L. King Type of 1968
Souvenir Sheet

Design: 100fr, Charles de Gaulle (1890-1970), President of France.

1971, Mar. 15 Engr. *Perf. 13½*

406	A44	100fr ultra	2.00	1.50

Astronaut Type of 1969 Inscribed in Dark Violet with Emblem and: "APOLLO / 14 / SHEPARD / ROOSA / MITCHELL"

1971, Apr. 15 Engr. *Perf. 11½*
Souvenir Sheet

407	A52	100fr brown orange	4.00	3.50

Apollo 14 US moon landing, Jan. 31-Feb. 9.

Beethoven, by Christian Horneman A67

Beethoven Portraits: 30c, Joseph Stieler. 50c, by Ferdinand Schimon. 3fr, by H. Best. 6fr, by W. Fassbender. 90fr, Beethoven's Funeral Procession, by Leopold Stöber.

1971, July 5 Photo. *Perf. 13*

408	A67	20c gold & multi	.20	.20
409	A67	30c gold & multi	.20	.20
410	A67	50c gold & multi	.20	.20
411	A67	3fr gold & multi	.20	.20
412	A67	6fr gold & multi	.20	.20
413	A67	90fr gold & multi	1.90	1.00
		Nos. 408-413 (6)	2.90	2.00

Ludwig van Beethoven (1770-1827), composer.

Equestrian — A68

Olympic Sports: 30c, Runner at start. 50c, Basketball. 1fr, High jump. 8fr, Boxing. 10fr, Pole vault. 20fr, Wrestling. 60fr, Gymnastics (rings).

1971, Oct. 25 Photo. *Perf. 13*

414	A68	20c gold & black	.20	.20
415	A68	30c gold & dp rose lil	.20	.20
416	A68	50c gold & vio bl	.20	.20
417	A68	1fr gold & dp grn	.20	.20
418	A68	8fr gold & henna brn	.20	.20
419	A68	10fr gold & purple	.20	.20
420	A68	20fr gold & dp brn	.40	.20
421	A68	60fr gold & Prus bl	1.25	.50
		Nos. 414-421 (8)	2.85	1.90

20th Summer Olympic Games, Munich, Aug. 26-Sept. 10, 1972.

Christmas Type of 1968
Souvenir Sheet

100fr, Nativity, by Anthony van Dyck, vert.

1971, Dec. 20 Engr. *Perf. 11½*

422	A48	100fr indigo	2.00	2.00

Adam by Dürer — A69

Paintings by Albrecht Dürer (1471-1528), German painter and engraver: 30c, Eve. 50c, Hieronymus Holzschuher, Portrait. 1fr, Lamentation of Christ. 3fr, Madonna with the Pear. 5fr, St. Eustace. 20fr, Sts. Paul and Mark. 70fr, Self-portrait, 1500.

1971, Dec. 31 Photo. *Perf. 13*

423 A69 20c gold & multi .20 .20
424 A69 30c gold & multi .20 .20
425 A69 50c gold & multi .20 .20
426 A69 1fr gold & multi .20 .20
427 A69 3fr gold & multi .20 .20
428 A69 5fr gold & multi .20 .20
429 A69 20fr gold & multi .40 .20
430 A69 70fr gold & multi 1.40 .90
Nos. 423-430 (8) 3.00 2.30

A 600fr on gold foil honoring Apollo 15 was issued Jan. 15, 1972.

Guardsmen Exercising — A70

National Guard Emblem and: 6fr, Loading supplies. 15fr, Helicopter ambulance. 25fr, Health Service for civilians. 50fr, Guardsman and map of Rwanda, vert.

1972, Feb. 7 *Perf. 13½x14, 14x13½*

431 A70 4fr dp org & multi .20 .20
432 A70 6fr yellow & multi .20 .20
433 A70 15fr lt blue & multi .20 .20
434 A70 25fr red & multi .50 .25
435 A70 50fr multicolored .90 .60
Nos. 431-435 (5) 2.00 1.45

"The National Guard serving the nation."
For overprints see Nos. 559-563.

Ice Hockey, Sapporo Olympics Emblem A71

1972, Feb. 12 *Perf. 13x13½*

436 A71 20c shown .20 .20
437 A71 30c Speed skating .20 .20
438 A71 50c Ski jump .20 .20
439 A71 1fr Men's figure skating .20 .20
440 A71 6fr Cross-country skiing .20 .20
441 A71 12fr Slalom .25 .20
442 A71 20fr Bobsledding .45 .25
443 A71 60fr Downhill skiing 1.40 .90
Nos. 436-443 (8) 3.10 2.35

11th Winter Olympic Games, Sapporo, Japan, Feb. 3-13.

Antelopes and Cercopithecus — A72

1972, Mar. 20 Photo. *Perf. 13*

444 A72 20c shown .20 .20
445 A72 30c Buffaloes .20 .20
446 A72 50c Zebras .20 .20
447 A72 1fr Rhinoceroses .20 .20
448 A72 2fr Wart hogs .20 .20
449 A72 6fr Hippopotami .20 .20
450 A72 18fr Hyenas .35 .20
451 A72 32fr Guinea fowl .60 .40
452 A72 60fr Antelopes 1.25 .70
453 A72 80fr Lions 1.60 1.00
Nos. 444-453 (10) 5.00 3.50

Akagera National Park.

A73

A74

Family raising flag of Rwanda.

1972, Apr. 4 *Perf. 13x12½*

454 A73 6fr dk red & multi .20 .20
455 A73 18fr green & multi .35 .20
456 A73 60fr brown & multi 1.10 .70
Nos. 454-456 (3) 1.65 1.10

10th anniversary of the Referendum establishing Republic of Rwanda.

1972, May 17 Photo. *Perf. 13*

Birds: 20c, Common Waxbills and Hibiscus. 30c, Collared sunbird. 50c, Variable sunbird. 1fr, Greater double-collared sunbird. 4fr, Ruwenzori puff-back flycatcher. 6fr, Red-billed fire finch. 10fr, Scarlet-chested sunbird. 18fr, Red-headed quelea. 60fr, Black-headed gonolek. 100fr, African golden oriole.

457 A74 20c dl grn & multi .20 .20
458 A74 30c buff & multi .20 .20
459 A74 50c yellow & multi .20 .20
460 A74 1fr lt blue & multi .20 .20
461 A74 4fr dl rose & multi .20 .20
462 A74 6fr lilac rose & multi .20 .20
463 A74 10fr pink & multi .20 .20
464 A74 18fr gray & multi .35 .20
465 A74 60fr multicolored 1.25 .70
466 A74 100fr violet & multi 1.75 1.25
Nos. 457-466 (10) 4.75 3.55

Belgica '72 Emblem, King Baudouin, Queen Fabiola, Pres. and Mrs. Kayibanda — A75

1972, June 24 Photo. *Perf. 13*

Size: 37x34mm

467 A75 18fr Rwanda landscape .40 .20
468 A75 22fr Old houses, Bruges .45 .20

Size: 50x34mm

469 A75 40fr shown .75 .40
a. Strip of 3, #467-469 1.60 1.00

Belgica '72 Intl. Phil. Exhib., Brussels, June 24-July 9.

Pres. Kayibanda Addressing Meeting — A76

Pres. Grégoire Kayibanda: 30c, promoting officers of National Guard. 50c, with wife and children. 6fr, casting vote. 10fr, with wife and dignitaries at Feast of Justice. 15fr, with Cabinet and members of Assembly. 18fr, taking oath of office. 50fr, Portrait, vert.

1972, July 4

470 A76 20c gold & slate grn .20 .20
471 A76 30c gold & dk pur .20 .20
472 A76 50c gold & choc .20 .20
473 A76 6fr gold & Prus bl .20 .20
474 A76 10fr gold & dk pur .20 .20
475 A76 15fr gold & dk bl .30 .20
476 A76 18fr gold & brn .40 .20
477 A76 50fr gold & Prus bl 1.00 .60
Nos. 470-477 (8) 2.70 2.00

10th anniversary of independence.

Equestrian, Olympic Emblems A77

Stadium, TV Tower and: 30c, Hockey. 50c, Soccer. 1fr, Broad jump. 6fr, Bicycling. 18fr, Yachting. 30fr, Hurdles. 44fr, Gymnastics, women's.

1972, Aug. 16 Photo. *Perf. 14*

478 A77 20c dk brn & gold .20 .20
479 A77 30c vio bl & gold .20 .20
480 A77 50c dk green & gold .20 .20
481 A77 1fr dp claret & gold .20 .20
482 A77 6fr black & gold .20 .20
483 A77 18fr brown & gold .30 .20
484 A77 30fr dk vio & gold .60 .30
485 A77 44fr Prus bl & gold .80 .40
Nos. 478-485 (8) 2.70 1.90

20th Olympic Games, Munich, 8/26-9/11.

Relay (Sport) and UN Emblem A78

1972, Oct. 23 Photo. *Perf. 13*

486 A78 20c shown .20 .20
487 A78 30c Musicians .20 .20
488 A78 50c Dancers .20 .20
489 A78 1fr Operating room .20 .20
490 A78 6fr Weaver & painter .20 .20
491 A78 18fr Classroom .20 .20
492 A78 24fr Laboratory .55 .25
493 A78 50fr Hands of 4 races reaching for equality 1.00 .55
Nos. 486-493 (8) 2.75 2.00

Fight against racism.

Christmas Type of 1968 Souvenir Sheet

Design: 100fr, Adoration of the Shepherds, by Jacob Jordaens, vert.

1972, Dec. 11 *Perf. 11½*

494 A48 100fr red brown 2.00 2.00

Phymateus Brunneri — A79

Various insects. 30c, 1fr, 6fr, 22fr, 100fr, vert.

1973, Jan. 31 Photo. *Perf. 13*

495 A79 20c multi .20 .20
496 A79 30c multi .20 .20
497 A79 50c multi .20 .20
498 A79 1fr multi .20 .20
499 A79 2fr multi .20 .20
500 A79 6fr multi .20 .20
501 A79 18fr multi .35 .20
502 A79 22fr multi .40 .20
503 A79 70fr multi 1.40 .80
504 A79 100fr multi 2.00 1.25
Nos. 495-504 (10) 5.35 3.65

Souvenir Sheet

Perf. 14

505 A79 80fr like 20c 1.75 1.75

No. 505 contains one stamp 43½x33½mm.

Emile Zola, by Edouard Manet — A80

Paintings Connected with Reading, and Book Year Emblem: 30c, Rembrandt's Mother. 50c, St. Jerome Removing Thorn from Lion's Paw, by Colantonio. 1fr, Apostles Peter and Paul, by El Greco. 2fr, Virgin and Child with Book, by Roger van der Weyden. 6fr, St. Jerome in his Cell, by Antonella de Messina. 40fr, St. Barbara, by Master of Flemalle. No. 513, Don Quixote, by Otto Bonevalle. No. 514, Pres. Kayibanda reading book.

1973, Mar. 12 Photo. *Perf. 13*

506 A80 20c gold & multi .20 .20
507 A80 30c gold & multi .20 .20
508 A80 50c gold & multi .20 .20
509 A80 1fr gold & multi .20 .20
510 A80 2fr gold & multi .20 .20
511 A80 6fr gold & multi .20 .20
512 A80 40fr gold & multi .65 .30
513 A80 100fr gold & multi 1.60 .75
Nos. 506-513 (8) 3.45 2.25

Souvenir Sheet

Perf. 14

514 A80 100fr gold, bl & ind 1.60 1.25

International Book Year.

Longombe A81

Rubens and Isabella Brandt, by Rubens — A82

Musical instruments of Central & West Africa.

1973, Apr. 9 Photo. *Perf. 13½*

515	A81	20c shown	.20	.20
516	A81	30c Horn	.20	.20
517	A81	50c Xylophone	.20	.20
518	A81	1fr Harp	.20	.20
519	A81	4fr Alur horns	.20	.20
520	A81	6fr Drum, bells and horn	.20	.20
521	A81	18fr Large drums (Ngoma)	.30	.20
522	A81	90fr Toba	1.60	.80
		Nos. 515-522 (8)	3.10	2.20

1973, May 11

Paintings from Old Pinakothek, Munich (IBRA Emblem and): 30c, Young Man, by Cranach. 50c, Woman Peeling Turnips, by Chardin. 1fr, The Abduction of Leucippa's Daughters, by Rubens. 2fr, Virgin and Child, by Filippo Lippi. 6fr, Boys Eating Fruit, by Murillo. 40fr, The Lovesick Woman, by Jan Steen. No. 530, Jesus Stripped of His Garments, by El Greco. No. 531, Oswalt Krehl, by Dürer.

523	A82	20c gold & multi	.20	.20
524	A82	30c gold & multi	.20	.20
525	A82	50c gold & multi	.20	.20
526	A82	1fr gold & multi	.20	.20
527	A82	2fr gold & multi	.20	.20
528	A82	6fr gold & multi	.20	.20
529	A82	40fr gold & multi	.70	.35
530	A82	100fr gold & multi	1.90	.80
		Nos. 523-530 (8)	3.80	2.35

Souvenir Sheet

531	A82	100fr gold & multi	2.00	1.60

IBRA München 1973 Intl. Phil. Exhib., Munich, May 11-20. #531 contains one 40x56mm stamp.

Map of Africa and Peace Doves A83

Design: 94fr, Map of Africa and hands.

1973, July 23 Photo. *Perf. 13½*

532	A83	6fr gold & multi	.20	.20
533	A83	94fr gold & multi	1.90	1.50

Org. for African Unity, 10th anniv.
For overprints see Nos. 895-896.

Nos. 298-303 Overprinted in Blue, Black, Green or Brown: "SECHERESSE / SOLIDARITE AFRICAINE"

1973, Aug. 23 Photo. *Perf. 13*

534	A53	20c multi (Bl)	.20	.20
535	A53	40c multi (Bk)	.20	.20
536	A53	60c multi (Bl)	.20	.20
537	A53	80c multi (G)	.20	.20
538	A53	3fr multi (G)	.20	.20
539	A53	75fr multi (Br)	1.50	.90
		Nos. 534-539,B1 (7)	5.00	4.15

African solidarity in drought emergency.

African Postal Union Issue
Common Design Type

1973, Sept. 12 Engr. *Perf. 13*

540	CD137	100fr dp brn, bl & brn	2.00	1.60

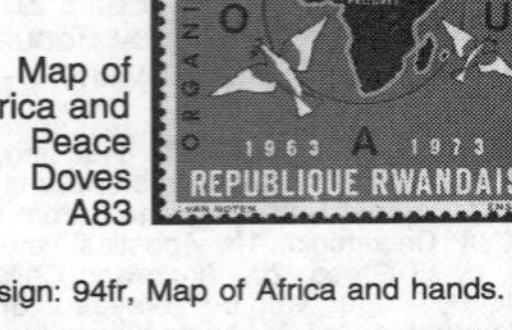

Six-lined Distichodus — A84

African Fish: 30c, Little triggerfish. 50c, Spotted upside-down catfish. 1fr, Nile mouthbreeder. 2fr, African lungfish. 6fr, Pareutropius mandevillei. 40fr, Congo characin. 100fr, Like 20c. 150fr, Julidochromis ornatus.

1973, Sept. 3 Photo. *Perf. 13*

541	A84	20c gold & multi	.20	.20
542	A84	30c gold & multi	.20	.20
543	A84	50c gold & multi	.20	.20
544	A84	1fr gold & multi	.20	.20
545	A84	2fr gold & multi	.20	.20
546	A84	6fr gold & multi	.20	.20
547	A84	40fr gold & multi	.70	.40
548	A84	150fr gold & multi	3.00	1.50
		Nos. 541-548 (8)	4.90	3.10

Souvenir Sheet

549	A84	100fr gold & multi	2.00	2.00

No. 549 contains one stamp 48x29mm.

Nos. 398-405 Overprinted in Black, Silver, Green or Blue

1973, Sept. 15 Litho.

550	A50	20c multi (Bk)	.20	.20
551	A50	30c multi (S)	.20	.20
552	A50	50c multi (Bk)	.20	.20
553	A50	1fr multi (G)	.20	.20
554	A50	5fr multi (S)	.20	.20
555	A50	18fr multi (Bk)	.35	.20
556	A50	25fr multi (Bk)	.50	.25
557	A50	50fr multi (Bl)	1.25	.55
		Nos. 550-557 (8)	3.10	2.00

Africa Weeks, Brussels, Sept. 15-30, 1973. On the 30c, 1fr and 25fr the text of the overprint is horizontal.

Nos. 431-435 Overprinted in Gold

Perf. 13½x14, 14x13½

1973, Oct. 31 Photo.

559	A70	4fr dp org & multi	.20	.20
560	A70	6fr yellow & multi	.20	.20
561	A70	15fr lt blue & multi	.40	.30
562	A70	25fr red & multi	.70	.40
563	A70	50fr multicolored	1.50	.80
		Nos. 559-563 (5)	3.00	1.90

25th anniv. of the Universal Declaration of Human Rights.

Christmas Type of 1968
Souvenir Sheet

Adoration of the Shepherds, by Guido Reni.

1973, Dec. 15 Engr. *Perf. 11½*

564	A48	100fr brt violet	2.00	2.00

Copernicus and Astrolabe A85

Pres. Juvénal Habyarimana — A86

Designs: 30c, 18fr, 100fr, Portrait. 50c, 80fr, Copernicus and heliocentric system. 1fr, like 20c.

1973, Dec. 26 Photo. *Perf. 13*

565	A85	20c silver & multi	.20	.20
566	A85	30c silver & multi	.20	.20
567	A85	50c silver & multi	.20	.20
568	A85	1fr gold & multi	.20	.20
569	A85	18fr gold & multi	.20	.20
570	A85	80fr gold & multi	1.25	.80
		Nos. 565-570 (6)	2.25	1.80

Souvenir Sheet

571	A85	100fr gold & multi	2.00	2.00

Nicolaus Copernicus (1473-1543).

1974, Apr. 8 Photo. *Perf. 11½*
Black Inscriptions

572	A86	1fr bister & sepia	.20	.20
573	A86	2fr ultra & sepia	.20	.20
574	A86	5fr rose red & sep	.20	.20
575	A86	6fr grnsh bl & sep	.20	.20
576	A86	26fr lilac & sepia	.45	.30
577	A86	60fr ol grn & sepia	1.25	.65
		Nos. 572-577 (6)	2.50	1.75

Souvenir Sheet

Christ Between the Thieves (Detail), by Rubens — A87

1974, Apr. 12 Engr. *Perf. 11½*

578	A87	100fr sepia	4.00	4.00

Easter.

Yugoslavia-Zaire Soccer Game — A88

Games' emblem and soccer games.

1974, July 6 Photo. *Perf. 13½*

579	A88	20c shown	.20	.20
580	A88	40c Netherlands-Sweden	.20	.20
581	A88	60c Germany (Fed.)-Australia	.20	.20
582	A88	80c Haiti-Argentina	.20	.20
583	A88	2fr Brazil-Scotland	.20	.20
584	A88	6fr Bulgaria-Uruguay	.20	.20
585	A88	40fr Italy-Poland	.70	.40
586	A88	50fr Chile-Germany (DDR)	1.00	.65
		Nos. 579-586 (8)	2.90	2.25

World Cup Soccer Championship, Munich, June 13-July 7.

Marconi's Laboratory Yacht "Elletra" — A89

Designs: 30c, Marconi and steamer "Carlo Alberto." 50c, Marconi's wireless apparatus and telecommunications satellites. 4fr, Marconi and globes connected by communications waves. 35fr, Marconi's radio, and radar. 60fr, Marconi and transmitter at Poldhu, Cornwall. 50fr, like 20c.

1974, Aug. 19 Photo. *Perf. 13½*

587	A89	20c violet, blk & grn	.20	.20
588	A89	30c green, blk & vio	.20	.20
589	A89	50c yellow, blk & lil	.20	.20
590	A89	4fr salmon, blk & bl	.20	.20
591	A89	35fr lilac, blk & yel	.60	.40
592	A89	60fr blue, blk & brnz	1.25	.70
		Nos. 587-592 (6)	2.65	1.90

Souvenir Sheet

593	A89	50fr gold, blk & lt bl	1.25	1.25

Guglielmo Marconi (1874-1937), Italian electrical engineer and inventor.

The Flute Player, by J. Leyster — A90

Messenger Monk — A91

Paintings: 20c, Diane de Poitiers, Fontainebleau School. 50c, Virgin and Child, by David. 1fr, Triumph of Venus, by Boucher. 10fr, Seated Harlequin, by Picasso. 18fr, Virgin and Child, 15th century. 20fr, Beheading of St. John, by Hans Fries. 50fr, Daughter of Andersdotter, by J. F. Höckert.

1974, Sept. 23 Photo. *Perf. 14x13*

594	A90	20c gold & multi	.20	.20
595	A90	30c gold & multi	.20	.20
596	A90	50c gold & multi	.20	.20
597	A90	1fr gold & multi	.20	.20
598	A90	10fr gold & multi	.20	.20
599	A90	18fr gold & multi	.30	.20
600	A90	20fr gold & multi	.35	.20
601	A90	50fr gold & multi	1.00	.60
		Nos. 594-601 (8)	2.65	2.00

INTERNABA 74 Intl. Phil. Exhib., Basel, June 7-10, and Stockholmia 74, Intl. Phil. Exhib., Stockholm, Sept. 21-29.

Six multicolored souvenir sheets exist containing two 15fr stamps each in various combinations of designs of Nos. 594-601. One souvenir sheet of four 25fr stamps exists with designs of Nos. 595, 597, 599 and 601.

1974, Oct. 9 *Perf. 14*

UPU Emblem and Messengers: 30c, Inca. 50c, Morocco. 1fr, India. 18fr, Polynesia. 80fr, Rwanda.

602	A91	20c gold & multi	.20	.20
603	A91	30c gold & multi	.20	.20
604	A91	50c gold & multi	.20	.20
605	A91	1fr gold & multi	.20	.20
606	A91	18fr gold & multi	.40	.35
607	A91	80fr gold & multi	1.60	1.60
		Nos. 602-607 (6)	2.80	2.75

Centenary of Universal Postal Union.

Nos. 306-308 Overprinted

1974, Dec. 16 Photo. *Perf. 11½*

608	A54	6fr brt pink & multi	3.50	3.50
609	A54	18fr ultra & multi	3.50	3.50
610	A54	40fr brn & multi	3.75	3.75
		Nos. 608-610 (3)	10.75	10.75

15th anniversary of independence.

Christmas Type of 1968
Souvenir Sheet

Adoration of the Kings, by Joos van Cleve.

1974, Dec. 23 Engr. *Perf. 11½*

611	A48	100fr slate green	4.00	4.00

Nos. 295-296 Overprinted: "1974 / 10e Anniversaire"

1974, Dec. 30 Photo. *Perf. 13*

612	A51	30fr sil & multi	.55	.55
613	A51	70fr gold & multi	1.10	1.10

African Development Bank, 10th anniversary.

Uganda Kob — A92

Antelopes: 30c, Bongos, horiz. 50c, Rwanda antelopes. 1fr, Young sitatungas, horiz. 4fr, Greater kudus. 10fr, Impalas, horiz. 34fr, Waterbuck. 40fr, Impalas. 60fr, Greater kudu. 100fr, Derby's elands, horiz.

1975, Mar. 17 Photo. *Perf. 13*

614	A92	20c multi	.20	.20
615	A92	30c multi	.20	.20
616	A92	50c multi	.20	.20
617	A92	1fr multi	.20	.20
618	A92	4fr multi	.20	.20
619	A92	10fr multi	.20	.20
620	A92	34fr multi	.50	.25
621	A92	100fr multi	1.60	.75
		Nos. 614-621 (8)	3.30	2.20

Miniature Sheets

622	A92	40fr multi	2.75	2.75
623	A92	60fr multi	2.75	2.75

Miniature Sheets

The Burial of Jesus, by Raphael — A93

1975, Apr. 1 Photo. *Perf. 13x14*

624	A93	20fr shown	1.00	1.00
625	A93	30fr Pietá, by Cranach the Elder	1.25	1.25
626	A93	50fr by van der Weyden	1.25	1.25
627	A93	100fr by Bellini	1.25	1.25
		Nos. 624-627 (4)	4.75	4.75

Easter. Size of stamps: 40x52mm.
See Nos. 681-684.

Souvenir Sheets

Prince Balthazar Charles, by Velazquez — A94

Paintings: 30fr, Infanta Margaret of Austria, by Velazquez. 50fr, The Divine Shepherd, by Murillo. 100fr, Francisco Goya, by V. Lopez y Portana.

1975, Apr. 4 Photo. *Perf. 13*

628	A94	20fr multi	1.00	1.00
629	A94	30fr multi	1.25	1.25
630	A94	50fr multi	1.25	1.25
631	A94	100fr multi	1.25	1.25
		Nos. 628-631 (4)	4.75	4.75

Espana 75 Intl. Phil. Exhib., Madrid, Apr. 4-13. Size of stamps: 38x48mm. See Nos. 642-643. For overprints see Nos. 844-847.

Pyrethrum (Insect Powder) — A95

1975, Apr. 14 *Perf. 13*

632	A95	20c shown	.20	.20
633	A95	30c Tea	.20	.20
634	A95	50c Coffee (beans and pan)	.20	.20
635	A95	4fr Bananas	.20	.20
636	A95	10fr Corn	.20	.20
637	A95	12fr Sorghum	.20	.20
638	A95	26fr Rice	.45	.25
639	A95	47fr Coffee (workers and beans)	1.10	.45
		Nos. 632-639 (8)	2.75	1.90

Souvenir Sheets

Perf. 13½

640	A95	25fr like 50c	.65	.65
641	A95	75fr like 47fr	1.60	1.60

Year of Agriculture and 10th anniversary of Office for Industrialized Cultivation.

Painting Type of 1975
Souvenir Sheets

75fr, Louis XIV, by Hyacinthe Rigaud. 125fr, Cavalry Officer, by Jean Gericault.

1975, June 6 Photo. *Perf. 13*

642	A94	75fr multi	1.60	1.60
643	A94	125fr multi	3.00	3.00

ARPHILA 75, Intl. Philatelic Exhibition, Paris, June 6-16. Size of stamps: 38x48mm.

Nos. 390-397 Overprinted: "1975 / ANNEE / SAINTE"

1975, June 23 Photo. *Perf. 13*

644	A66	10c gold & dk brn	.20	.20
645	A66	20c gold & dk grn	.20	.20
646	A66	30c gold & dp claret	.20	.20
647	A66	40c gold & indigo	.20	.20
648	A66	1fr gold & dk pur	.20	.20
649	A66	18fr gold & purple	.30	.20
650	A66	20fr gold & org brn	.40	.20
651	A66	60fr gold & blk brn	1.50	.80
		Nos. 644-651 (8)	3.20	2.20

Holy Year 1975.

White Pelicans — A96

Designs: African birds.

1975, June 20

652	A96	20c shown	.20	.20
653	A96	30c Malachite kingfisher	.20	.20
654	A96	50c Goliath herons	.20	.20
655	A96	1fr Saddle-billed storks	.20	.20
656	A96	4fr African jacana	.20	.20
657	A96	10fr African anhingas	.20	.20
658	A96	34fr Sacred ibis	.60	.35
659	A96	80fr Hartlaub ducks	1.60	.80
		Nos. 652-659 (8)	3.40	2.35

Miniature Sheets

660	A96	40fr Flamingoes	1.25	1.25
661	A96	60fr Crowned cranes	1.60	1.60

Globe Representing Races and WPY Emblem — A97

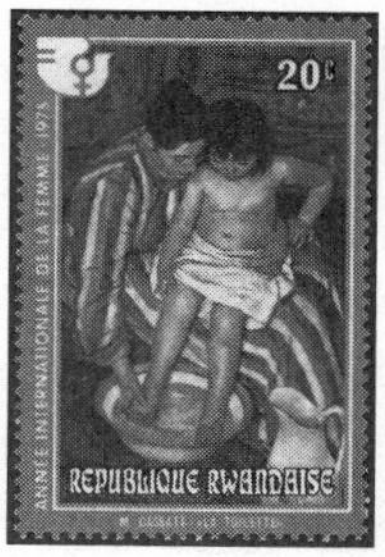

The Bath, by Mary Cassatt and IWY Emblem — A98

World Population Year: 26fr, Population graph and emblem. 34fr, Globe with open door and emblem.

1975, Sept. 1 Photo. *Perf. 13½x13*

662	A97	20fr dp bl & multi	.40	.20
663	A97	26fr dl red brn & multi	.50	.25
664	A97	34fr yel & multi	.70	.35
		Nos. 662-664 (3)	1.60	.80

1975, Sept. 15 *Perf. 13*

IWY Emblem and: 30c, Mother and Infant Son, by Julius Gari Melchers. 50c, Woman with Milk Jug, by Jan Vermeer. 1fr, Water Carrier, by Goya. 8fr, Rwanda woman cotton picker. 12fr, Scientist with microscope. 18fr, Mother and child. 25fr, Empress Josephine, by Pierre-Paul Prud'hon. 40fr, Madame Vigee-Lebrun and Daughter, self-portrait. 60fr, Woman carrying child on back and water jug on head.

665	A98	20c gold & multi	.20	.20
666	A98	30c gold & multi	.20	.20
667	A98	50c gold & multi	.20	.20
668	A98	1fr gold & multi	.20	.20
669	A98	8fr gold & multi	.20	.20
670	A98	12fr gold & multi	.20	.20
671	A98	18fr gold & multi	.30	.20
672	A98	60fr gold & multi	1.25	.60
		Nos. 665-672 (8)	2.75	2.00

Souvenir Sheets

Perf. 13½

673	A98	25fr multi	6.50	6.50
674	A98	40fr multi	6.50	6.50

International Women's Year. Nos. 673-674 each contain one stamp 37x49mm.

Owl, Quill and Book — A99

30c, Hygiene emblem. 1.50fr, Kneeling woman holding scales of Justice. 18fr, Chemist in laboratory. 26fr, Symbol of commerce & chart. 34fr, University Building.

1975, Sept. 29 *Perf. 13*

675	A99	20c pur & multi	.20	.20
676	A99	30c ultra & multi	.20	.20
677	A99	1.50fr lilac & multi	.20	.20
678	A99	18fr blue & multi	.30	.20
679	A99	26fr olive & multi	.40	.25
680	A99	34fr blue & multi	.70	.35
		Nos. 675-680 (6)	2.00	1.40

National Univ. of Rwanda, 10th anniv.

Painting Type of 1975
Souvenir Sheets

Paintings by Jan Vermeer (1632-1675): 20fr, Man and Woman Drinking Wine. 30fr, Young Woman Reading Letter. 50fr, Painter in his Studio. 100fr, Young Woman Playing Virginal.

1975, Oct. 13 Photo. *Perf. 13x14*

681	A93	20fr multi	.40	.40
682	A93	30fr multi	.60	.60
683	A93	50fr multi	1.00	1.00
684	A93	100fr multi	2.00	2.00
		Nos. 681-684 (4)	4.00	4.00

Size of stamps: 40x52mm.

Waterhole and Impatiens Stuhlmannii — A100

Designs: 30c, Antelopes, zebras, candelabra cactus. 50c, Brush fire, and tapinanthus prunifolius. 5fr, Bulera Lake and Egyptian white lotus. 8fr, Erosion prevention and protea madiensis. 10fr, Marsh and melanthera brownei. 26fr, Landscape, lobelias and senecons. 100fr, Sabyinyo Volcano and polystachya kermesina.

1975, Oct. 25 *Perf. 13*

685	A100	20c blk & multi	.20	.20
686	A100	30c blk & multi	.20	.20
687	A100	50c blk & multi	.20	.20
688	A100	5fr blk & multi	.20	.20
689	A100	8fr blk & multi	.20	.20
690	A100	10fr blk & multi	.20	.20
691	A100	26fr blk & multi	.50	.25
692	A100	100fr blk & multi	1.90	1.00
		Nos. 685-692 (8)	3.60	2.45

Nature protection.
For overprints see Nos. 801-808.

Nos. 343-348 Overprinted

SECHERESSE
SOLIDARITE
1975

1975, Nov. 10 Litho. *Perf. 13*

693	A60	20c multi	.20	.20
694	A60	30c multi	.20	.20
695	A60	50c multi	.20	.20
696	A60	1fr multi	.20	.20
697	A60	3fr multi	.20	.20
698	A60	5fr multi	.20	.20
		Nos. 693-698,B2-B3 (8)	4.70	3.70

African solidarity in drought emergency.

Fork-lift Truck on Airfield A101

Designs: 30c, Coffee packing plant. 50c, Engineering plant. 10fr, Farmer with hoe, vert. 35fr, Coffee pickers, vert. 54fr, Mechanized harvester.

Wmk. JEZ Multiple (368)

1975, Dec. 1 Photo. *Perf. 14x13½*

699	A101	20c gold & multi	.20	.20
700	A101	30c gold & multi	.20	.20
701	A101	50c gold & multi	.20	.20
702	A101	10fr gold & multi	.20	.20
703	A101	35fr gold & multi	.60	.35
704	A101	54fr gold & multi	1.00	.55
		Nos. 699-704 (6)	2.40	1.70

Basket Carrier and Themabelga Emblem — A102

Themabelga Emblem and: 30c, Warrior with shield and spear. 50c, Woman with beads. 1fr, Indian woman. 5fr, Male dancer with painted body. 7fr, Woman carrying child on back. 35fr, Male dancer with spear. 51fr, Female dancers.

1975, Dec. 8 Unwmk. *Perf. 13½*

705	A102	20c blk & multi	.20	.20
706	A102	30c blk & multi	.20	.20
707	A102	50c blk & multi	.20	.20
708	A102	1fr blk & multi	.20	.20
709	A102	5fr blk & multi	.20	.20
710	A102	7fr blk & multi	.20	.20
711	A102	35fr blk & multi	.60	.30
712	A102	51fr blk & multi	.90	.50
		Nos. 705-712 (8)	2.70	2.00

THEMABELGA Intl. Topical Philatelic Exhibition, Brussels, Dec. 13-21.

Christmas Type of 1968

Adoration of the Kings, by Peter Paul Rubens.

1975, Dec. 22 Engr. *Perf. 11½*

713	A48	100fr brt rose lil	3.50	3.50

Dr. Schweitzer, Keyboard, Score — A103

Albert Schweitzer and: 30c, 5fr, Lambaréné Hospital. 50c, 10fr, Organ pipes from Strassbourg organ, and score. 1fr, 80fr, Dr. Schweitzer's house, Lambaréné. 3fr, like 20c.

1976, Jan. 30 Photo. *Perf. 13½*

714	A103	20c maroon & pur	.20	.20
715	A103	30c grn & pur	.20	.20
716	A103	50c brn org & pur	.20	.20
717	A103	1fr red lil & pur	.20	.20
718	A103	3fr vio bl & pur	.20	.20
719	A103	5fr brn & pur	.20	.20
720	A103	10fr bl & pur	.20	.20
721	A103	80fr ver & pur	1.40	.80
		Nos. 714-721 (8)	2.80	2.20

World Leprosy Day.

For overprints see Nos. 788-795.

Surrender at Yorktown A104

American Bicentennial (Paintings): 30c, Instruction at Valley Forge. 50c, Presentation of Captured Colors at Yorktown. 1fr, Washington at Fort Lee. 18fr, Washington Boarding British Warship. 26fr, Washington Studying Battle Plans at Night. 34fr, Washington Firing Cannon. 40fr, Washington Crossing the Delaware. 100fr, Sailing Ship "Bonhomme Richard," vert.

1976, Mar. 22 Photo. *Perf. 13x13½*

722	A104	20c gold & multi	.20	.20
723	A104	30c gold & multi	.20	.20
724	A104	50c gold & multi	.20	.20
725	A104	1fr gold & multi	.20	.20
726	A104	18fr gold & multi	.35	.20
727	A104	26fr gold & multi	.40	.20
728	A104	34fr gold & multi	.60	.35
729	A104	40fr gold & multi	.65	.45
		Nos. 722-729 (8)	2.80	2.00

Souvenir Sheet

Perf. 13½

730	A104	100fr gold & multi	2.50	2.50

Sister Yohana, First Nun — A105

Yachting — A106

30c, Abdon Sabakati, one of first converts. 50c, Father Alphonse Brard, first Superior of Save Mission. 4fr, Abbot Balthazar Gafuku, one of first priests. 10fr, Msgr. Bigirumwami, first bishop. 25fr, Save Church, horiz. 60fr, Kabgayi Cathedral, horiz.

Perf. 13x13½, 13½x13

1976, Apr. 26 Photo.

731	A105	20c multi	.20	.20
732	A105	30c multi	.20	.20
733	A105	50c multi	.20	.20
734	A105	4fr multi	.20	.20
735	A105	10fr multi	.20	.20
736	A105	25fr multi	.45	.25
737	A105	60fr multi	1.00	.60
		Nos. 731-737 (7)	2.45	1.85

50th anniv. of the Roman Catholic Church of Rwanda.

1976, May 24 Photo. *Perf. 13x13½*

Montreal Games Emblem and: 30c, Steeplechase. 50c, Long jump. 1fr, Hockey. 10fr, Swimming. 18fr, Soccer. 29fr, Boxing. 51fr, Vaulting.

738	A106	20c gray & dk car	.20	.20
739	A106	30c gray & Prus bl	.20	.20
740	A106	50c gray & blk	.20	.20
741	A106	1fr gray & pur	.20	.20
742	A106	10fr gray & ultra	.25	.20
743	A106	18fr gray & dk brn	.35	.20
744	A106	29fr gray & blk	.60	.30
745	A106	51fr gray & slate grn	.90	.50
		Nos. 738-745 (8)	2.90	2.00

21st Olympic Games, Montreal, Canada, July 17-Aug. 1.

First Message, Manual Switchboard — A107

Designs: 30c, Telephone, 1876 and interested crowd. 50c, Telephone c. 1900, and woman making a call. 1fr, Business telephone exchange, c. 1905. 4fr, "Candlestick" phone, globe and A. G. Bell. 8fr, Dial phone and Rwandan man making call. 26fr, Telephone, 1976, satellite and radar. 60fr, Push-button telephone, Rwandan international switchboard operator.

1976, June 21 Photo. *Perf. 14*

746	A107	20c dl red & indigo	.20	.20
747	A107	30c grnsh bl & indigo	.20	.20
748	A107	50c brn & indigo	.20	.20
749	A107	1fr org & indigo	.20	.20
750	A107	4fr lilac & indigo	.20	.20
751	A107	8fr grn & indigo	.20	.20
752	A107	26fr dl red & indigo	.50	.25
753	A107	60fr vio & indigo	1.10	.55
		Nos. 746-753 (8)	2.80	2.00

Centenary of first telephone call by Alexander Graham Bell, Mar. 10, 1876.

Type of 1976 Overprinted in Silver with Bicentennial Emblem and "Independence Day"

Designs as before.

1976, July 4 *Perf. 13x13½*

754	A104	20c silver & multi	.20	.20
755	A104	30c silver & multi	.20	.20
756	A104	50c silver & multi	.20	.20
757	A104	1fr silver & multi	.20	.20
758	A104	18fr silver & multi	.35	.25
759	A104	26fr silver & multi	.50	.25
760	A104	34fr silver & multi	.60	.30
761	A104	40fr silver & multi	.65	.40
		Nos. 754-761 (8)	2.90	2.00

Independence Day.

Soccer, Montreal Olympic Emblem — A108

30c, Shooting. 50c, Woman canoeing. 1fr, Gymnast. 10fr, Weight lifting. 12fr, Diving. 26fr, Equestrian. 50fr, Shot put.

1976, Aug. 1 Photo. *Perf. 13½x13*

762	A108	20c multi	.20	.20
763	A108	30c multi	.20	.20
764	A108	50c multi	.20	.20
765	A108	1fr multi	.20	.20
766	A108	10fr multi	.20	.20
767	A108	12fr multi	.20	.20
768	A108	26fr multi	.40	.30
769	A108	50fr multi	1.00	.50
		Nos. 762-769 (8)	2.60	2.00

Souvenir Sheet

Various phases of hurdles race, horiz.

770		Sheet of 4	3.00	3.00
a.	A108	20fr Start	.35	.35
b.	A108	30fr Sprint	.55	.55
c.	A108	40fr Hurdle	.70	.70
d.	A108	60fr Finish	1.00	1.00

21st Olympic Games, Montreal, Canada, July 17-Aug. 1.

Apollo and Soyuz Take-offs, Project Emblem A109

Designs: 30c, Soyuz in space. 50c, Apollo in space. 1fr, Apollo. 2fr, Spacecraft before docking. 12fr, Spacecraft after docking. 30fr, Astronauts visiting in docked spacecraft. 54fr, Apollo splashdown.

1976, Oct. 29 Photo. *Perf. 13½x14*

771	A109	20c multi	.20	.20
772	A109	30c multi	.20	.20
773	A109	50c multi	.20	.20
774	A109	1fr multi	.20	.20
775	A109	2fr multi	.20	.20
776	A109	12fr multi	.25	.20
777	A109	30fr multi	.60	.30
778	A109	54fr multi	.90	.50
		Nos. 771-778 (8)	2.75	2.00

Apollo Soyuz space test program (Russo-American cooperation), July 1975.

For overprints see Nos. 836-843.

Eulophia Cucullata — A110

Hands and Symbols of Learning — A111

Orchids: 30c, Eulophia streptopetala. 50c, Disa Stairsii. 1fr, Aerangis kotschyana. 10fr, Eulophia abyssinica. 12fr, Bonatea steudneri. 26fr, Ansellia gigantea. 50fr, Eulophia angolensis.

1976, Nov. 22 Photo. *Perf. 14x13½*

779	A110	20c multi	.20	.20
780	A110	30c multi	.20	.20
781	A110	50c multi	.20	.20
782	A110	1fr multi	.20	.20
783	A110	10fr multi	.20	.20
784	A110	12fr multi	.25	.20
785	A110	26fr multi	.50	.30
786	A110	50fr multi	1.00	.50
		Nos. 779-786 (8)	2.75	2.00

Christmas Type of 1968

Souvenir Sheet

Design: Nativity, by Francois Boucher.

1976, Dec. 20 Engr. *Perf. 11½*

787	A48	100fr brt ultra	3.00	3.00

Nos. 714-721 Overprinted: "JOURNEE / MONDIALE / 1977"

1977, Jan. 29 Photo. *Perf. 13½*

788	A103	20c mar & pur	.20	.20
789	A103	30c grn & pur	.20	.20
790	A103	50c brn org & pur	.20	.20
791	A103	1fr red lil & pur	.20	.20
792	A103	3fr vio bl & pur	.20	.20
793	A103	5fr brn & pur	.20	.20
794	A103	10fr bl & pur	.25	.20
795	A103	80fr ver & pur	1.40	.80
		Nos. 788-795 (8)	2.85	2.20

World Leprosy Day.

1977, Feb. 7 Litho. *Perf. 12½*

Designs: 26fr, Hands and symbols of science. 64fr, Hands and symbols of industry.

796	A111	10fr multi	.20	.20
797	A111	26fr multi	.50	.40
798	A111	64fr multi	.90	.75
		Nos. 796-798 (3)	1.60	1.35

10th Summit Conference of the African and Malagasy Union, Kigali, 1976.

Souvenir Sheets

Descent from the Cross, by Rubens — A112

Easter: 25fr, Crucifixion, by Rubens.

1977, Apr. 27 Photo. *Perf. 13*

799	A112	25fr multi	.60	.60
800	A112	75fr multi	1.50	1.50

Size of stamp: 40x40mm.

Nos. 685-692 Overprinted

CONFERENCE MONDIALE DE L'EAU

1977, May 2

801	A100	20c blk & multi	.20	.20
802	A100	30c blk & multi	.20	.20
803	A100	50c blk & multi	.20	.20
804	A100	5fr blk & multi	.20	.20
805	A100	8fr blk & multi	.30	.20
806	A100	10fr blk & multi	.30	.20
807	A100	26fr blk & multi	.90	.45
808	A100	100fr blk & multi	3.00	1.90
		Nos. 801-808 (8)	5.30	3.55

World Water Conference.

Roman Fire Tower, African Tom-tom
A113

ITU Emblem and: 30c, Chappe's optical telegraph and postilion. 50c, Morse telegraph and code. 1fr, Tug Goliath laying cable in English Channel. 4fr, Telephone, radio, television. 18fr, Kingsport (US space exploration ship) and Marots communications satellite. 26fr, Satellite tracking station and O.T.S. satellite. 50fr, Mariner II, Venus probe.

1977, May 23 Litho. *Perf. 12½*

809	A113	20c multi	.20	.20
810	A113	30c multi	.20	.20
811	A113	50c multi	.20	.20
812	A113	1fr multi	.20	.20
813	A113	4fr multi	.20	.20
814	A113	18fr multi	.45	.20
815	A113	26fr multi	.60	.30
816	A113	50fr multi	1.25	.60
		Nos. 809-816 (8)	3.30	2.10

World Telecommunications Day.

Souvenir Sheets

Amsterdam Harbor, by Willem van de Velde, the Younger
A114

40fr, The Night Watch, by Rembrandt.

1977, May 26 Photo. *Perf. 13½*

817	A114	40fr multi	.80	.80
818	A114	60fr multi	1.25	1.25

AMPHILEX '277 Intl. Philatelic Exhibition, Amsterdam, May 27-June 5. Size of stamp: 38x49mm.

Road to Calvary, by Rubens — A115

Paintings by Peter Paul Rubens (1577-1640): 30c, Judgment of Paris, horiz. 50c, Marie de Medicis. 1fr, Heads of Black Men, horiz. 4fr, 26fr, Details from St. Ildefonso triptych. 8fr, Helene Fourment and her Children, horiz. 60fr, Helene Fourment.

1977, June 13 *Perf. 14*

819	A115	20c gold & multi	.20	.20
820	A115	30c gold & multi	.20	.20
821	A115	50c gold & multi	.20	.20
822	A115	1fr gold & multi	.20	.20
823	A115	4fr gold & multi	.20	.20
824	A115	8fr gold & multi	.20	.20
825	A115	26fr gold & multi	.50	.25
826	A115	60fr gold & multi	1.25	.55
		Nos. 819-826 (8)	2.95	2.00

Souvenir Sheet

Viking on Mars
A116

1977, June 27 Photo. *Perf. 13*

827	A116	100fr multi	5.00	5.00

US Viking landing on Mars, first anniv.

Crested Eagle — A117

Birds of Prey: 30c, Snake eagle. 50c, Fish eagle. 1fr, Monk vulture. 3fr, Red-tailed buzzard. 5fr, Yellow-beaked kite. 20fr, Swallow-tailed kite. 100fr, Bateleur.

1977, Sept. 12 Litho. *Perf. 14*

828	A117	20c multi	.20	.20
829	A117	30c multi	.20	.20
830	A117	50c multi	.20	.20
831	A117	1fr multi	.20	.20
832	A117	3fr multi	.20	.20
833	A117	5fr multi	.20	.20
834	A117	20fr multi	.40	.20
835	A117	100fr multi	2.00	1.00
		Nos. 828-835 (8)	3.60	2.40

Nos. 771-778 Overprinted: "in memoriam / WERNHER VON BRAUN / 1912-1977"

1977, Sept. 19 Photo. *Perf. 13½x14*

836	A109	20c multi	.20	.20
837	A109	30c multi	.20	.20
838	A109	50c multi	.20	.20
839	A109	1fr multi	.20	.20
840	A109	2fr multi	.20	.20
841	A109	12fr multi	.20	.20
842	A109	30fr multi	.55	.30
843	A109	54fr multi	1.25	.60
		Nos. 836-843 (8)	3.00	2.10

Wernher von Braun (1912-1977), space and rocket expert.

Nos. 628-631 Gold Embossed "ESPAMER '77" and ESPAMER Emblem
Souvenir Sheets

1977, Oct. 3 Photo. *Perf. 13*

844	A94	20fr multi	.50	.50
845	A94	30fr multi	.75	.75
846	A94	50fr multi	1.25	1.25
847	A94	100fr multi	2.50	2.50
		Nos. 844-847 (4)	5.00	5.00

ESPAMER '77, International Philatelic Exhibition, Barcelona, Oct. 7-13.

Christmas Type of 1968
Souvenir Sheet

100fr, Nativity, by Peter Paul Rubens.

1977, Dec. 12 Engr. *Perf. 13½*

848	A48	100fr violet blue	3.00	3.00

Marginal inscription typographed in red.

Boy Scout Playing Flute — A118

Chimpanzees
A119

Designs: 30c, Campfire. 50c, Bridge building. 1fr, Scouts with unit flag. 10fr, Map reading. 18fr, Boating. 26fr, Cooking. 44fr, Lord Baden-Powell.

1978, Feb. 20 Litho. *Perf. 12½*

849	A118	20c yel grn & multi	.20	.20
850	A118	30c blue & multi	.20	.20
851	A118	50c lilac & multi	.20	.20
852	A118	1fr blue & multi	.20	.20
853	A118	10fr pink & multi	.20	.20
854	A118	18fr lt grn & multi	.40	.20
855	A118	26fr orange & multi	.55	.25
856	A118	44fr salmon & multi	.90	.45
		Nos. 849-856 (8)	2.85	1.90

10th anniversary of Rwanda Boy Scouts.

1978, Mar. 20 Photo. *Perf. 13½x13*

Designs: 30c, Gorilla. 50c, Colobus monkey. 3fr, Galago. 10fr, Cercopithecus monkey (mone). 26fr, Potto. 60fr, Cercopithecus monkey (griuet). 150fr, Baboon.

857	A119	20c multi	.20	.20
858	A119	30c multi	.20	.20
859	A119	50c multi	.20	.20
860	A119	3fr multi	.20	.20
861	A119	10fr multi	.20	.20
862	A119	26fr multi	.55	.25
863	A119	60fr multi	1.25	.55
864	A119	150fr multi	3.00	1.50
		Nos. 857-864 (8)	5.80	3.30

Euporus Strangulatus — A120

Coleoptera: 30c, Rhina afzelii, vert. 50c, Pentalobus palini. 3fr, Corynodes dejeani, vert. 10fr, Mecynorhina torquata. 15fr, Mecocerus rhombeus, vert. 20fr, Macrotoma serripes. 25fr, Neptunides stanleyi, vert. 26fr, Petrognatha gigas. 100fr, Eudicella gralli, vert.

1978, May 22 Litho. *Perf. 14*

865	A120	20c multi	.20	.20
866	A120	30c multi	.20	.20
867	A120	50c multi	.20	.20
868	A120	3fr multi	.20	.20
869	A120	10fr multi	.20	.20
870	A120	15fr multi	.30	.20
871	A120	20fr multi	.40	.25
872	A120	25fr multi	.50	.30
873	A120	26fr multi	.50	.30
874	A120	100fr multi	2.00	1.40
		Nos. 865-874 (10)	4.70	3.45

Crossing "River of Poverty"
A121

Emblem and: 10fr, 60fr, Men poling boat, facing right. 26fr, like 4fr.

1978, May 29 *Perf. 12½*

875	A121	4fr multi	.20	.20
876	A121	10fr multi	.20	.20
877	A121	26fr multi	.50	.30
878	A121	60fr multi	1.25	.80
		Nos. 875-878 (4)	2.15	1.50

Natl. Revolutionary Development Movement (M.R.N.D.).

Soccer, Rimet Cup, Flags of Netherlands and Peru — A122

11th World cup, Argentina, June 1-25, (Various Soccer Scenes and Flags of): 30c, Sweden & Spain. 50c, Scotland & Iran. 2fr, Germany & Tunisia. 3fr, Italy & Hungary. 10fr, Brazil and Austria. 34fr, Poland & Mexico. 100fr, Argentina & France.

1978, June 19 *Perf. 13*

879	A122	20c multi	.20	.20
879A	A122	30c multi	.20	.20
879B	A122	50c multi	.20	.20
880	A122	2fr multi	.20	.20
881	A122	3fr multi	.20	.20
882	A122	10fr multi	.20	.20
883	A122	34fr multi	.50	.30
884	A122	100fr multi	1.50	1.00
		Nos. 879-884 (8)	3.20	2.50

Wright Brothers, Flyer I — A123

History of Aviation: 30c, Santos Dumont and Canard 14, 1906. 50c, Henry Farman and Voisin No. 1, 1908. 1fr, Jan Olieslaegers and Bleriot, 1910. 3fr, Marshal Balbo and Savoia S-17, 1919. 10fr, Charles Lindbergh and Spirit of St. Louis, 1927. 55fr, Hugo Junkers and Junkers JU52/3, 1932. 60fr, Igor Sikorsky and Sikorsky VS 300, 1939. 130fr, Concorde over New York.

1978, Oct. 30 Litho. *Perf. 13½x14*

885	A123	20c multi	.20	.20
886	A123	30c multi	.20	.20
887	A123	50c multi	.20	.20
888	A123	1fr multi	.20	.20
889	A123	3fr multi	.20	.20
890	A123	10fr multi	.20	.20
891	A123	55fr multi	1.10	.70
892	A123	60fr multi	1.25	.80
		Nos. 885-892 (8)	3.55	2.70

Souvenir Sheet

Perf. 13x13½

893	A123	130fr multi	2.25	2.25

No. 893 contains one stamp 47x35mm.

Christmas Type of 1968
Souvenir Sheet

Design: 200fr, Adoration of the Kings, by Albrecht Dürer, vert.

1978, Dec. 11 Engr. *Perf. 11½*

894	A48	200fr brown	4.00	4.00

Nos. 532-533, Overprinted "1963 1978" in Black or Blue

1978, Dec. 18 Photo. *Perf. 13½*

895	A83	6fr multi (Bk)	.20	.20
896	A83	94fr multi (Bl)	1.90	1.25

Org. for African Unity, 15th anniv.

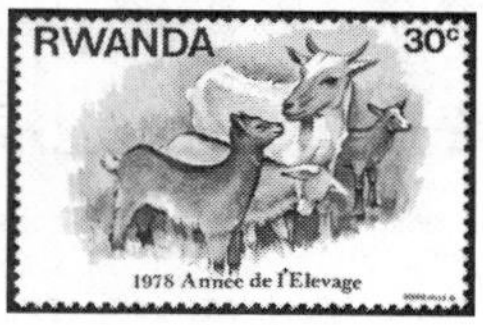

Goats
A124

20c, Ducks, vert. 50c, Cock and chickens, vert. 4fr, Rabbits. 5fr, Pigs, vert. 15fr, Turkey. 50fr, Sheep and cattle, vert. 75fr, Bull.

1978, Dec. 28 Litho. *Perf. 14*

897	A124	20c multi	.20	.20
898	A124	30c multi	.20	.20
899	A124	50c multi	.20	.20
900	A124	4fr multi	.20	.20
901	A124	5fr multi	.20	.20
902	A124	15fr multi	.30	.20
903	A124	50fr multi	1.00	.65
904	A124	75fr multi	1.50	1.00
		Nos. 897-904 (8)	3.80	2.85

Husbandry Year.

Papilio Demodocus
A125

Butterflies: 30c, Precis octavia. 50c, Charaxes smaragdalis. 4fr, Charaxes guderiana. 15fr, Colotis evippe. 30fr, Danaus limniace. 50fr, Byblia acheloia. 150fr, Utetheisa pulchella.

1979, Feb. 19 Photo. *Perf. 14½*

905	A125	20c multi	.20	.20
906	A125	30c multi	.20	.20
907	A125	50c multi	.20	.20
908	A125	4fr multi	.20	.20
909	A125	15fr multi	.30	.20
910	A125	30fr multi	.60	.35
911	A125	50fr multi	1.00	.65
912	A125	150fr multi	3.00	2.00
		Nos. 905-912 (8)	5.70	4.00

Euphorbia Grantii, Weavers A126

Design: 60fr, Drummers and Intelsat IV-A.

1979, June 8 Photo. *Perf. 13*

913 A126 40fr multi	.80	.55
914 A126 60fr multi	1.25	.80

Philexafrique II, Libreville, Gabon, June 8-17.

Entandrophragma Excelsum — A127

Trees and Shrubs: 20c, Polyscias fulva. 50c, Ilex mitis. 4fr, Kigelia Africana. 15fr, Ficus thonningi. 20fr, Acacia Senegal. 50fr, Symphonia globulifera. 110fr, Acacia sieberana. 20c, 50c, 15fr, 50fr, vertical.

1979, Aug. 27 *Perf. 14*

915 A127 20c multi	.20	.20
916 A127 30c multi	.20	.20
917 A127 50c multi	.20	.20
918 A127 4 fr multi	.20	.20
919 A127 15fr multi	.20	.20
920 A127 20fr multi	.30	.20
921 A127 50fr multi	.75	.50
922 A127 110fr multi	1.60	1.10
Nos. 915-922 (8)	3.65	2.80

Black and White Boys, IYC Emblem A128

26fr, 100fr, Children of various races, diff., vert.

Perf. 13½x13, 13x13½

1979, Nov. 19 Photo.

923 A128 Block of 8	4.50	3.00
a. 26fr, any single	.55	.35
924 A128 42fr multi	.80	.55

Souvenir Sheet

925 A128 100fr multi	2.00	1.50

Intl. Year of the Child. No. 923 printed in sheets of 16 (4x4).

Basket Weaving A129

Perf. 12½x13, 13x12½

1979, Dec. 3 Litho.

926 A129 50c shown	.20	.20
927 A129 1.50fr Wood carving, vert.	.20	.20
928 A129 2fr Metal working	.20	.20
929 A129 10fr Jewelry, vert.	.20	.20
930 A129 20fr Straw plaiting	.40	.20
931 A129 26fr Wall painting, vert.	.55	.25
932 A129 40fr Pottery	.80	.40
933 A129 100fr Smelting, vert.	2.00	1.00
Nos. 926-933 (8)	4.55	2.65

Souvenir Sheet

Children of Different Races, Christmas Tree — A130

1979, Dec. 24 Engr. *Perf. 12*

934 A130 200fr ultra & dp mag	6.00	3.00

Christmas; Intl. Year of the Child.

German East Africa #N5, Hill A131

Sir Rowland Hill (1795-1879), originator of penny postage, and Stamps of Ruanda-Urundi or: 30c, German East Africa #N23. 50c, German East Africa #NB9. 3fr, #25. 10fr, #42. 26fr, #123. 100fr, #B28.

1979, Dec. 31 Litho. *Perf. 14*

935 A131 20c multi	.20	.20
936 A131 30c multi	.20	.20
937 A131 50c multi	.20	.20
938 A131 3fr multi	.20	.20
939 A131 10fr multi	.20	.20
940 A131 26fr multi	.65	.25
941 A131 60fr multi	1.50	.60
942 A131 100fr multi	2.50	1.00
Nos. 935-942 (8)	5.65	2.85

Sarothrura Pulchra A132

Birds of the Nyungwe Forest: 20c Ploceus alienus, vert. 30c, Regal sunbird, vert. 3fr, Tockus alboterminatus. 10fr, Pygmy owl, vert. 26fr, Emerald cuckoo. 60fr, Finch, vert. 100fr, Stepanoaetus coronatus, vert.

Perf. 13½x13, 13x13½

1980, Jan. 7 Photo.

943 A132 20c multi	.20	.20
944 A132 30c multi	.20	.20
945 A132 50c multi	.20	.20
946 A132 3fr multi	.20	.20
947 A132 10fr multi	.20	.20
948 A132 26fr multi	.65	.25
949 A132 60fr multi	1.50	.60
950 A132 100fr multi	2.50	1.00
Nos. 943-950 (8)	5.65	2.85

First Footstep on Moon, Spacecraft A133

Spacecraft and Moon Exploration: 1.50fr, Descent onto lunar surface. 8fr, American flag. 30fr, Solar panels. 50fr, Gathering soil samples. 60fr, Adjusting sun screen. 200fr, Landing craft.

1980, Jan. 31 Photo. *Perf. 13x13½*

951 A133 50c multi	.20	.20
952 A133 1.50fr multi	.20	.20
953 A133 8fr multi	.20	.20
954 A133 30fr multi	.70	.30
955 A133 50fr multi	1.40	.50
956 A133 60fr multi	1.50	.60
Nos. 951-956 (6)	4.20	2.00

Souvenir Sheet

957 A133 200fr multi	5.00	2.00

Apollo 11 moon landing, 10th anniv. (1979).

Globe, Butare and 1905 Chicago Club Emblems A134

Rotary Intl., 75th Anniv. (Globe, Emblems of Butare or Kigali Clubs and): 30c, San Francisco, 1908. 50c, Chicago, 1910. 4fr, Buffalo, 1911. 15fr, London, 1911. 20fr, Glasgow, 1912. 50fr, Bristol, 1917. 60fr, Rotary Intl., 1980.

1980, Feb. 23 Litho. *Perf. 13*

958 A134 20c multi	.20	.20
959 A134 30c multi	.20	.20
960 A134 50c multi	.20	.20
961 A134 4fr multi	.20	.20
962 A134 15fr multi	.30	.20
963 A134 20fr multi	.40	.20
964 A134 50fr multi	1.00	.50
965 A134 60fr multi	1.25	.60
Nos. 958-965 (8)	3.75	2.30

Gymnast, Moscow '80 Emblem A135

1980, Mar. 10 *Perf. 12½*

966 A135 20c shown	.20	.20
967 A135 30c Basketball	.20	.20
968 A135 50c Bicycling	.20	.20
969 A135 3fr Boxing	.20	.20
970 A135 20fr Archery	.50	.20
971 A135 26fr Weight lifting	.65	.25
972 A135 50fr Javelin	1.25	.50
973 A135 100fr Fencing	2.50	1.00
Nos. 966-973 (8)	5.70	2.75

22nd Summer Olympic Games, Moscow, July 19-Aug. 3.

Souvenir Sheet

Amalfi Coast, by Giacinto Gigante — A136

1980, Apr. 28 Photo. *Perf. 13½*

974 A136 200fr multi	5.75	2.50

20th Intl. Philatelic Exhibition, Europa '80, Naples, Apr. 26-May 4.

Geaster Mushroom A137

1980, July 21 Photo. *Perf. 13½*

975 A137 20c shown	.20	.20
976 A137 30c Lentinus atrobrunneus	.20	.20
977 A137 50c Gomphus stereoides	.20	.20
978 A137 4fr Cantharellus cibarius	.20	.20
979 A137 10fr Stilbothamnium dybowskii	.20	.20
980 A137 15fr Xeromphalina tenuipes	.40	.20
981 A137 70fr Podoscypha elegans	1.60	.70
982 A137 100fr Mycena	2.25	1.00
Nos. 975-982 (8)	5.25	2.90

Still Life, by Renoir — A138

Impressionist Painters: 30c, 26fr, At the Theater, by Toulouse-Lautrec, vert. 50c, 10fr, Seaside Garden, by Monet. 4fr, Mother and Child, by Mary Cassatt, vert. 5fr, Starry Night, by Van Gogh. 10fr, Dancers at their Toilet, by Degas, vert. 50fr, The Card Players, by Cezanne. 70fr, Tahitian Women, by Gauguin, vert. 75fr, like 20c. 100fr, In the Park, by Seurat.

1980, Aug. 4 Litho. *Perf. 14*

983 A138 20c multi	.20	.20
984 A138 30c multi	.20	.20
985 A138 50c multi	.20	.20
986 A138 4fr multi	.20	.20
a. Sheet of 2, 4fr, 26fr	.70	.70
987 A138 5fr multi	.20	.20
a. Sheet of 2, 5fr, 75fr	2.00	2.00
988 A138 10fr multi	.20	.20
a. Sheet of 2, 10fr, 70fr	2.00	2.00
989 A138 50fr multi	1.40	.50
a. Sheet of 2, 50fr, 10fr	1.50	1.50
990 A138 70fr multi	1.60	.70
991 A138 100fr multi	2.25	1.00
Nos. 983-991 (9)	6.45	3.40

Souvenir Sheet

Virgin of the Harpies, by Andrea Del Sarto — A139

Photogravure and Engraved

1980, Dec. 22 *Perf. 11½*

992 A139 200fr multi	5.00	3.00

Christmas.

Belgian War of Independence, Engraving — A140

Belgian Independence Sesquicentennial: Engravings of War of Independence.

1980, Dec. 29 Litho. *Perf. 12½*

993 A140 20c pale grn & brn	.20	.20
994 A140 30c brn org & brn	.20	.20
995 A140 50c lt bl & brn	.20	.20
996 A140 9fr yel & brn	.20	.20
997 A140 10fr brt lil & brn	.20	.20
998 A140 20fr ap grn & brn	.40	.20
999 A140 70fr pink & brn	1.40	.70
1000 A140 90fr lem & brn	1.75	.90
Nos. 993-1000 (8)	4.55	2.80

Swamp Drainage A141

1980, Dec. 31 Photo. *Perf. 13½*

1001	A141	20c	shown	.20	.20
1002	A141	30c	Fertilizer shed	.20	.20
1003	A141	1.50fr	Rice fields	.20	.20
1004	A141	8fr	Tree planting	.20	.20
1005	A141	10fr	Terrace planting	.30	.20
1006	A141	40fr	Farm buildings	1.10	.55
1007	A141	90fr	Bean cultivation	2.50	1.25
1008	A141	100fr	Tea cultivation	2.75	1.40
			Nos. 1001-1008 (8)	7.45	4.20

Soil Conservation Year.

Pavetta Rwandensis — A142

1981, Apr. 6 Photo. *Perf. 13x13½*

1009	A142	20c	shown	.20	.20
1010	A142	30c	Cyrtorchis praetermissa	.20	.20
1011	A142	50c	Pavonia urens	.20	.20
1012	A142	4fr	Cynorkis kassnerana	.20	.20
1013	A142	5fr	Gardenia ternifolia	.20	.20
1014	A142	10fr	Leptactina platyphylla	.25	.20
1015	A142	20fr	Lobelia petiolata	.50	.25
1016	A142	40fr	Tapinanthus brunneus	1.00	.50
1017	A142	70fr	Impatiens niamniamensis	1.75	.90
1018	A142	150fr	Dissotis rwandensis	3.75	1.90
			Nos. 1009-1018 (10)	8.25	4.75

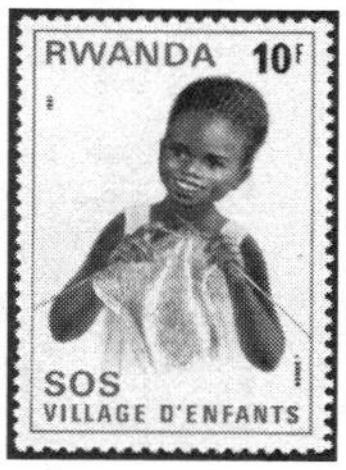

Girl Knitting — A143

SOS Children's Village: Various children.

1981, Apr. 27 *Perf. 13*

1019	A143	20c	multi	.20	.20
1020	A143	30c	multi	.20	.20
1021	A143	50c	multi	.20	.20
1022	A143	1fr	multi	.20	.20
1023	A143	8fr	multi	.20	.20
1024	A143	10fr	multi	.25	.20
1025	A143	70fr	multi	1.50	.70
1026	A143	150fr	multi	3.25	1.50
			Nos. 1019-1026 (8)	6.00	3.40

Carolers, by Norman Rockwell A144

Designs: Saturday Evening Post covers by Norman Rockwell.

1981, May 11 Litho. *Perf. 13½x14*

1027	A144	20c	multi	.20	.20
1028	A144	30c	multi	.20	.20
1029	A144	50c	multi	.20	.20
1030	A144	1fr	multi	.20	.20
1031	A144	8fr	multi	.20	.20
1032	A144	20fr	multi	.40	.20
1033	A144	50fr	multi	1.00	.50
1034	A144	70fr	multi	1.40	.70
			Nos. 1027-1034 (8)	3.80	2.40

Cerval A145

Designs: Meat-eating animals.

1981, June 29 Photo. *Perf. 13½x14*

1035	A145	20c	shown	.20	.20
1036	A145	30c	Jackals	.20	.20
1037	A145	2fr	Genet	.20	.20
1038	A145	2.50fr	Banded mongoose	.20	.20
1039	A145	10fr	Zorille	.20	.20
1040	A145	15fr	White-cheeked otter	.30	.20
1041	A145	70fr	Golden wild cat	1.40	.70
1042	A145	200fr	Hunting dog, vert.	4.00	2.00
			Nos. 1035-1042 (8)	6.70	3.90

Drummer Sending Message — A146

1981, Sept. 1 Litho. *Perf. 13*

1043	A146	20c	shown	.20	.20
1044	A146	30c	Map, communication waves	.20	.20
1045	A146	2fr	Jet, radar screen	.20	.20
1046	A146	2.50fr	Satellite, teletape	.20	.20
1047	A146	10fr	Dish antenna	.25	.20
1048	A146	15fr	Ship, navigation devices	.40	.20
1049	A146	70fr	Helicopter	1.75	.90
1050	A146	200fr	Satellite with solar panels	5.00	2.50
			Nos. 1043-1050 (8)	8.20	4.60

1500th Birth Anniv. of St. Benedict A147

Paintings and Frescoes of St. Benedict: 20c, Leaving his Parents, Mt. Oliveto Monastery, Maggiore. 30c, Oldest portrait, 10th cent., St. Chrisogone Church, Rome, vert. 50c, Portrait, Virgin of the Misericord polyptich, Borgo San Sepolcro. 4fr, Giving the Rules of the order to his Monks, Mt. Oliveto Monastery. 5fr, Monks at their Meal, Mt. Oliveto Monastery. 20fr, Portrait, 13th cent., Lower Chruch of the Holy Spirit, Subiaco, vert. 70fr, Our Lady in Glory with Sts. Gregory and Benedict, San Gimigniao, vert. 100fr, Priest Carrying Easter Meal to St. Benedict, by Jan van Coninxloo, 16th cent.

Perf. 13½x13, 13x13½

1981, Nov. 30 Photo.

1051	A147	20c	multi	.20	.20
1052	A147	30c	multi	.20	.20
1053	A147	50c	multi	.20	.20
1054	A147	4fr	multi	.20	.20
1055	A147	5fr	multi	.20	.20
1056	A147	20fr	multi	.40	.20
1057	A147	70fr	multi	1.40	.65
1058	A147	100fr	multi	2.00	2.00
			Nos. 1051-1058 (8)	4.80	3.85

Intl. Year of the Disabled A148

1981, Dec. 7 Litho. *Perf. 13*

1059	A148	20c	Painting	.20	.20
1060	A148	30c	Soccer	.20	.20
1061	A148	4.50fr	Crocheting	.20	.20
1062	A148	5fr	Painting vase	.20	.20
1063	A148	10fr	Sawing	.20	.20
1064	A148	60fr	Sign language	1.25	.65
1065	A148	70fr	Doing puzzle	1.40	.80
1066	A148	100fr	Juggling	2.00	1.10
			Nos. 1059-1066 (8)	5.65	3.55

Souvenir Sheet

Christmas — A149

Photo. & Engr.

1981, Dec. 21 *Perf. 13½*

1067	A149	200fr	Adoration of the Kings, by van der Goes	4.00	2.00

Natl. Rural Water Supply Year A150

1981, Dec. 28 Litho. *Perf. 12½*

1068	A150	20c	Deer drinking	.20	.20
1069	A150	30c	Women carrying water, vert.	.20	.20
1070	A150	50c	Pipeline	.20	.20
1071	A150	10fr	Filing pan, vert.	.20	.20
1072	A150	19fr	Drinking	.40	.20
1073	A150	70fr	Mother, child, vert.	1.40	.65
1074	A150	100fr	Lake pumping station, vert.	2.00	1.00
			Nos. 1068-1074 (7)	4.60	2.65

World Food Day, Oct. 16, 1981 A151

1982, Jan. 25 Litho. *Perf. 13*

1075	A151	20c	Cattle	.20	.20
1076	A151	30c	Bee	.20	.20
1077	A151	50c	Fish	.20	.20
1078	A151	1fr	Avocados	.20	.20
1079	A151	8fr	Boy eating banana	.20	.20
1080	A151	20fr	Sorghum	.40	.20
1081	A151	70fr	Vegetables	1.40	.65
1082	A151	100fr	Balanced diet	2.00	1.00
			Nos. 1075-1082 (8)	4.80	2.85

Hibiscus Berberidifolius — A152

1982, June 14 Litho. *Perf. 13*

1083	A152	20c	shown	.20	.20
1084	A152	30c	Hypericum lanceolatum, vert.	.20	.20
1085	A152	50c	Canarina eminii	.20	.20
1086	A152	4fr	Polygala ruwenxoriensis	.20	.20
1087	A152	10fr	Kniphofia grantii, vert.	.20	.20
1088	A152	35fr	Euphorbia candelabrum, vert.	.70	.35
1089	A152	70fr	Disa erubescens, vert.	1.40	.65
1090	A152	80fr	Gloriosa simplex	1.60	1.00
			Nos. 1083-1090 (8)	4.70	3.00

20th Anniv. of Independence — A153

1982, June 28

1091	A153	10fr	Flags	.20	.20
1092	A153	20fr	Hands releasing doves	.40	.20
1093	A153	30fr	Flag, handshake	.60	.30
1094	A153	50fr	Govt. buildings	1.00	.50
			Nos. 1091-1094 (4)	2.20	1.20

1982 World Cup — A154

Designs: Various soccer players.

1982, July 6 *Perf. 14x14½*

1095	A154	20c	multi	.20	.20
1096	A154	30c	multi	.20	.20
1097	A154	1.50fr	multi	.20	.20
1098	A154	8fr	multi	.20	.20
1099	A154	10fr	multi	.20	.20
1100	A154	20fr	multi	.40	.20
1101	A154	70fr	multi	1.40	.65
1102	A154	90fr	multi	1.90	.90
			Nos. 1095-1102 (8)	4.70	2.75

TB Bacillus Centenary — A155

1982, Nov. 22 Litho. *Perf. 14½*

1103	A155	10fr	Microscope, slide	.20	.20
1104	A155	20fr	Serum, slide	.40	.20
1105	A155	70fr	Lungs, slide	1.40	.60
1106	A155	100fr	Koch	2.00	1.00
			Nos. 1103-1106 (4)	4.00	2.00

Souvenir Sheets

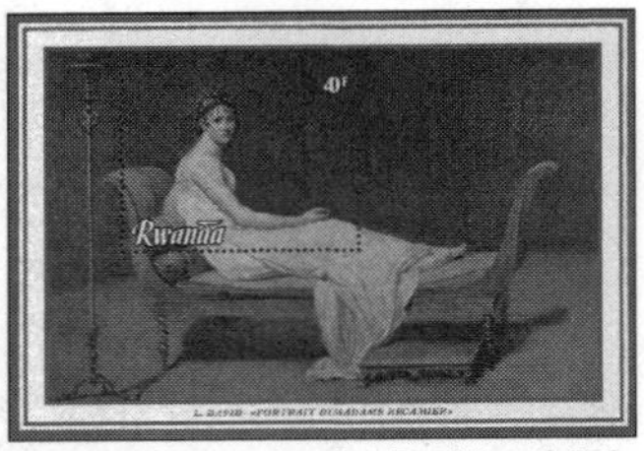

Madam Recamier, by David — A156

PHILEXFRANCE '82 Intl. Stamp Exhibition, Paris, June 11-21: No. 1108, St. Anne and Virgin and Child with Franciscan Monk, by H. van der Goes. No. 1109, Liberty Guiding the People, by Delacroix. No. 1110, Pygmalion, by P. Delvaux.

1982, Dec. 11 ***Perf. 13½***

1107	A156	40fr multi	.80	.40
1108	A156	40fr multi	.80	.40
1109	A156	60fr multi	1.25	.55
1110	A156	60fr multi	1.25	.55
		Nos. 1107-1110 (4)	4.10	1.90

Souvenir Sheet

Rest During the Flight to Egypt, by Murillo — A157

1982, Dec. 20 **Photo. & Engr.**

1111	A157	200fr carmine rose	4.00	2.00

Christmas.

10th Anniv. of UN Conference on Human Environment — A158

1982, Dec. 27 **Litho.** ***Perf. 14***

1112	A158	20c Elephants	.20	.20
1113	A158	30c Lion	.20	.20
1114	A158	50c Flower	.20	.20
1115	A158	4fr Bull	.20	.20
1116	A158	5fr Deer	.20	.20
1117	A158	10fr Flower, diff.	.20	.20
1118	A158	20fr Zebras	.40	.20
1119	A158	40fr Crowned cranes	.80	.40
1120	A158	50fr Bird	1.00	.50
1121	A158	70fr Woman pouring coffee beans	1.40	.70
		Nos. 1112-1121 (10)	4.80	3.00

Scouting Year A159

Perf. 13½x14½

1983, Jan. 17 **Photo.**

1122	A159	20c Animal first aid	.20	.20
1123	A159	30c Camp	.20	.20
1124	A159	1.50fr Campfire	.20	.20
1125	A159	8fr Scout giving sign	.20	.20
1126	A159	10fr Knot	.20	.20
1127	A159	20fr Camp, diff.	.40	.20
1128	A159	70fr Chopping wood	1.40	.65
1129	A159	90fr Sign, map	1.75	.90
		Nos. 1122-1129 (8)	4.55	2.75

For overprints see Nos. 1234-1241.

Nectar-sucking Birds — A160

Perf. 14x14½, 14½x14

1983, Jan. 31 **Litho.**

1130	A160	20c Angola nectar bird	.20	.20
1131	A160	30c Royal nectar birds	.20	.20
1132	A160	50c Johnston's nectar bird	.20	.20
1133	A160	4fr Bronze nectar birds	.20	.20
1134	A160	5fr Collared souimangas	.20	.20
1135	A160	10fr Blue-headed nectar bird	.30	.20
1136	A160	20fr Purple-bellied nectar bird	.40	.20
1137	A160	40fr Copper nectar birds	.80	.40
1138	A160	50fr Olive-bellied nectar birds	1.00	.50
1139	A160	70fr Red-breasted nectar bird	1.40	.70
		Nos. 1130-1139 (10)	4.90	3.00

30c, 4fr, 10fr, 40fr, 70fr horiz. Inscribed 1982.

Soil Erosion Prevention A161

1983, Feb. 14 ***Perf. 14½***

1140	A161	20c Driving cattle	.20	.20
1141	A161	30c Pineapple field	.20	.20
1142	A161	50c Interrupted ditching	.20	.20
1143	A161	9fr Hedges, ditches	.20	.20
1144	A161	10fr Reafforestation	.20	.20
1145	A161	20fr Anti-erosion barriers	.40	.20
1146	A161	30fr Contour planting	.60	.30
1147	A161	50fr Terracing	1.00	.50
1148	A161	60fr Protection of river banks	1.25	.60
1149	A161	70fr Fallow, planted strips	1.40	.65
		Nos. 1140-1149 (10)	5.65	3.25

For overprints & surcharges see #1247-1255.

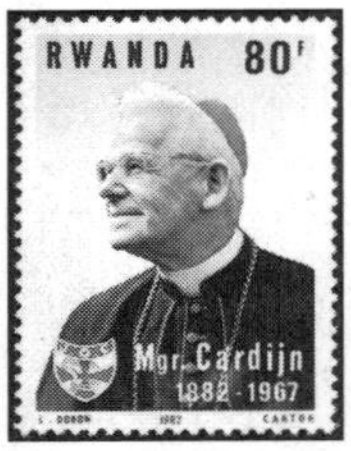

Cardinal Cardijn (1882-1967) A162

Gorilla — A163

Young Catholic Workers Movement Activities. Inscribed 1982.

1983, Feb. 22 ***Perf. 12½x13***

1150	A162	20c Feeding ducks	.20	.20
1151	A162	30c Harvesting bananas	.20	.20
1152	A162	50c Carrying melons	.20	.20
1153	A162	10fr Teacher	.25	.20
1154	A162	19fr Shoemakers	.50	.20
1155	A162	20fr Growing millet	.50	.25
1156	A162	70fr Embroidering	1.75	.75
1157	A162	80fr shown	2.00	1.00
		Nos. 1150-1157 (8)	5.60	3.00

1983, Mar. 14 ***Perf. 14***

Various gorillas. Nos. 1158-1163 horiz.

1158	A163	20c multi	.20	.20
1159	A163	30c multi	.20	.20
1160	A163	9.50fr multi	.20	.20
1161	A163	10fr multi	.20	.20
1162	A163	20fr multi	.40	.20
1163	A163	30fr multi	.60	.30
1164	A163	60fr multi	1.25	.60
1165	A163	70fr multi	1.40	.65
		Nos. 1158-1165 (8)	4.45	2.55

Souvenir Sheet

The Granduca Madonna, by Raphael — A164

Typo. & Engr.

1983, Dec. 19 ***Perf. 11½***

1166	A164	200fr multi	2.50	1.40

Christmas.

Local Trees — A165

1984, Jan. 15 **Litho.** ***Perf. 13½x13***

1167	A165	20c Hagenia abyssinica	.20	.20
1168	A165	30c Dracaena steudneri	.20	.20
1169	A165	50c Phoenix reclinata	.20	.20
1170	A165	10fr Podocarpus milanjianus	.20	.20
1171	A165	19fr Entada abyssinica	.25	.20
1172	A165	70fr Parinari excelsa	.90	.45
1173	A165	100fr Newtonia buchananii	1.40	.65
1174	A165	200fr Acacia gerrardi, vert.	2.50	1.40
		Nos. 1167-1174 (8)	5.85	3.50

World Communications Year — A166

1984, May 21 **Litho.** ***Perf. 12½***

1175	A166	20c Train	.20	.20
1176	A166	30c Ship	.20	.20
1177	A166	4.50fr Radio	.20	.20
1178	A166	10fr Telephone	.20	.20
1179	A166	15fr Mail	.20	.20
1180	A166	50fr Jet	.70	.35
1181	A166	70fr Satellite, TV screen	.90	.45
1182	A166	100fr Satellite	1.40	.65
		Nos. 1175-1182 (8)	4.00	2.45

1st Manned Flight Bicent. — A167

Historic flights: 20c, Le Martial, Sept. 19, 1783. 30c, La Montgolfiere, Nov. 21, 1783. 50c, Charles and Robert, Dec. 1, 1783, and Blanchard, Mar. 2, 1784. 9fr, Jean-Pierre Blanchard and wife in balloon. 10fr, Blanchard and Jeffries, 1785. 50fr, E. Demuyter, 1937. 80fr, Propane gas balloons. 200fr, Abruzzo, Anderson and Newman, 1978.

1984, June 4 **Litho.** ***Perf. 13***

1183	A167	20c multi	.20	.20
1184	A167	30c multi	.20	.20
1185	A167	50c multi	.20	.20
1186	A167	9fr multi	.20	.20
1187	A167	10fr multi	.20	.20
1188	A167	50fr multi	.65	.35
1189	A167	80fr multi	1.00	.50
1190	A167	200fr multi	2.50	1.40
		Nos. 1183-1190 (8)	5.15	3.25

1984 Summer Olympics — A168

1984, July 16 ***Perf. 14***

1191	A168	20c Equestrian	.20	.20
1192	A168	30c Wind surfing	.20	.20
1193	A168	50c Soccer	.20	.20
1194	A168	9fr Swimming	.20	.20
1195	A168	10fr Field hockey	.20	.20
1196	A168	40fr Fencing	.55	.25
1197	A168	80fr Running	1.10	.55
1198	A168	200fr Boxing	2.50	1.40
		Nos. 1191-1198 (8)	5.15	3.20

Zebras and Buffaloes — A169

1984, Nov. 26 **Litho.** ***Perf. 13***

1199	A169	20c Zebra with colt	.20	.20
1200	A169	30c Buffalo with calf, vert.	.20	.20
1201	A169	50c Two zebras, vert.	.20	.20
1202	A169	9fr Zebras fighting	.20	.20
1203	A169	10fr Buffalo, vert.	.20	.20
1204	A169	80fr Zebra herd	1.00	.55
1205	A169	100fr Zebra, vert.	1.25	.60
1206	A169	200fr Buffalo	2.50	1.25
		Nos. 1199-1206 (8)	5.75	3.40

Souvenir Sheet

Christmas 1984 — A170

1984, Dec. 24 **Typo. & Engr.**

1207	A170	200fr Virgin and Child, by Correggio	3.50	2.25

Gorilla Gorilla Beringei — A171

1985, Mar. 25 Litho. *Perf. 13*

1208 A171 10fr Adults and young *1.50* .75
1209 A171 15fr Adults *2.25* 1.10
1210 A171 25fr Female holding young *3.75* 1.90
1211 A171 30fr Three adults *5.00* 2.50
Nos. 1208-1211 (4) *12.50* 6.25

Souvenir Sheet

Perf. 11½x12

1212 A171 200fr Baby climbing branch, vert. *10.00* —

No. 1212 contains one 37x52mm stamp.

Self-Sufficiency in Food Production — A172

Designs: 20c, Raising chickens and turkeys. 30c, Pineapple harvest. 50c, Animal husbandry. 9fr, Grain products. 10fr, Education. 50fr, Sowing grain. 80fr, Food reserves. 100fr, Banana harvest.

1985, Mar. 30

1213 A172 20c multi .20 .20
1214 A172 30c multi .20 .20
1215 A172 50c multi .20 .20
1216 A172 9fr multi .20 .20
1217 A172 10fr multi .20 .20
1218 A172 50fr multi .60 .35
1219 A172 80fr multi 1.00 .50
1220 A172 100fr multi 1.40 .65
Nos. 1213-1220 (8) 4.00 2.50

Natl. Redevelopment Movement, 10th Anniv. — A173

1985, July 5

1221 A173 10fr multi .20 .20
1222 A173 30fr multi .40 .20
1223 A173 70fr multi .90 .45
Nos. 1221-1223 (3) 1.50 .85

UN, 40th Anniv. A174

1985, July 25

1224 A174 50fr multi .65 .35
1225 A174 100fr multi 1.40 .65

Audubon Birth Bicent. — A175

Illustrations of North American bird species by John J. Audubon.

1985, Sept. 18

1226 A175 10fr Barn owl .20 .20
1227 A175 20fr White-faced owl .25 .20
1228 A175 40fr Red-breasted hummingbird .55 .25
1229 A175 80fr Warbler 1.00 .50
Nos. 1226-1229 (4) 2.00 1.15

Intl. Youth Year A176

1985, Oct. 14

1230 A176 7fr Education and agriculture .20 .20
1231 A176 9fr Bicycling .20 .20
1232 A176 44fr Construction .60 .30
1233 A176 80fr Schoolroom 1.00 .50
Nos. 1230-1233 (4) 2.00 1.20

Nos. 1122-1129 Ovptd. in Green or Rose Violet with the Girl Scout Trefoil and "1910/1985"

1985, Nov. 25 *Perf. 13½x14½*

1234 A159 20c multi .20 .20
1235 A159 30c multi (RV) .20 .20
1236 A159 1.50fr multi .20 .20
1237 A159 8fr multi (RV) .20 .20
1238 A159 10fr multi .20 .20
1239 A159 20fr multi .25 .20
1240 A159 70fr multi (RV) .90 .45
1241 A159 90fr multi 1.10 .60
Nos. 1234-1241 (8) 3.25 2.25

Natl. Girl Scout Movement, 75th anniv.

Souvenir Sheet

Adoration of the Magi, by Titian — A177

Photo. & Engr.

1985, Dec. 24 *Perf. 11½*

1242 A177 200fr violet 3.00 2.00

Christmas.

Transportation and Communication — A178

1986, Jan. 27 Litho. *Perf. 13*

1243 A178 10fr Articulated truck .20 .20
1244 A178 30fr Hand-canceling letters .40 .20
1245 A178 40fr Kigali Satellite Station .55 .25

Size: 52x34mm

1246 A178 80fr Kayibanda Airport, Kigali 1.00 .50
Nos. 1243-1246 (4) 2.15 1.15

Nos. 1141-1149 Surcharged or Ovptd. with Silver Bar and "ANNEE 1986 / INTENSIFICATION AGRICOLE"

1986, May 5 Litho. *Perf. 14½*

1247 A161 9fr #1143 .20 .20
1248 A161 10fr on 30c #1141 .20 .20
1249 A161 10fr on 50c #1142 .20 .20
1250 A161 10fr #1144 .20 .20
1251 A161 20fr #1145 .40 .20
1252 A161 30fr #1146 .60 .30
1253 A161 50fr #1147 1.00 .50
1254 A161 60fr #1148 1.25 .60
1255 A161 70fr #1149 1.40 .70
Nos. 1247-1255 (9) 5.45 3.10

1986 World Cup Soccer Championships, Mexico — A179

Various soccer plays, natl. flags.

1986, June 16 *Perf. 13*

1256 A179 2fr Morocco, England .20 .20
1257 A179 4fr Paraguay, Iraq .20 .20
1258 A179 5fr Brazil, Spain .20 .20
1259 A179 10fr Italy, Argentina .20 .20
1260 A179 40fr Mexico, Belgium .80 .40
1261 A179 45fr France, USSR .90 .45
Nos. 1256-1261 (6) 2.50 1.65

For overprints see Nos. 1360-1365.

Akagera Natl. Park — A180

1986, Dec. 15 Litho. *Perf. 13*

1262 A180 4fr Antelopes .20 .20
1263 A180 7fr Shoebills .20 .20
1264 A180 9fr Cape elands .20 .20
1265 A180 10fr Giraffe .20 .20
1266 A180 80fr Elephants 1.60 .80
1267 A180 90fr Crocodiles 1.75 .90

Size: 48x34mm

1268 A180 100fr Weaver birds 2.00 1.00
1269 A180 100fr Pelican, zebras 2.00 1.00
a. Pair, #1268-1269 + label 4.00 2.00
Nos. 1262-1269 (8) 8.15 4.50

No. 1269a has continuous design.

Christmas, Intl. Peace Year — A181

1986, Dec. 24 Litho. *Perf. 13*

1270 A181 10fr shown .20 .20
1271 A181 15fr Dove, Earth .30 .20
1272 A181 30fr like 10fr .60 .30
1273 A181 70fr like 15fr 1.40 .70
Nos. 1270-1273 (4) 2.50 1.40

UN Child Survival Campaign A182

1987, Feb. 13

1274 A182 4fr Breast feeding .20 .20
1275 A182 6fr Rehydration therapy .20 .20
1276 A182 10fr Immunization .20 .20
1277 A182 70fr Growth monitoring 1.40 .70
Nos. 1274-1277 (4) 2.00 1.30

Year of Natl. Self-sufficiency in Food Production — A183

1987, June 15 Litho. *Perf. 13*

1278 A183 5fr Farm .20 .20
1279 A183 7fr Storing produce .20 .20
1280 A183 40fr Boy carrying basket of fish, produce .80 .40
1281 A183 60fr Tropical fruit 1.25 .60
Nos. 1278-1281 (4) 2.45 1.40

Nos. 1279-1281 vert.

Natl. Independence, 25th Anniv. — A184

10fr, Pres. Habyarimana, soldiers, farmers. 40fr, Pres. officiating government session. 70fr, Pres., Pope John Paul II. 100fr, Pres.

1987, July 1

1283 A184 10fr multi .20 .20
1284 A184 40fr multi .80 .40
1285 A184 70fr multi 1.40 .70
1286 A184 100fr multi, vert. 2.00 1.00
Nos. 1283-1286 (4) 4.40 2.30

Fruit A185

1987, Sept. 28

1287 A185 10fr Bananas, vert. .20 .20
1288 A185 40fr Pineapples .80 .40
1289 A185 80fr Papayas 1.60 .80
1290 A185 90fr Avocados 1.75 .90
1291 A185 100fr Strawberries, vert. 2.00 1.00
Nos. 1287-1291 (5) 6.35 3.30

Leopards — A186

1987, Nov. 18 Litho. *Perf. 13*

1292 A186	50fr	Female, cub	1.00	.50
1293 A186	50fr	Three cubs playing	1.00	.50
1294 A186	50fr	Adult attaching gazelle	1.00	.50
1295 A186	50fr	In tree	1.00	.50
1296 A186	50fr	Leaping from tree	1.00	.50
a.		Strip of 5, Nos. 1292-1296	5.00	2.50

Intl. Year of the Volunteer — A187

1987, Dec. 12

1297 A187	5fr	Constructing village water system	.20	.20
1298 A187	12fr	Education, vert.	.25	.20
1299 A187	20fr	Modern housing, vert.	.40	.20
1300 A187	60fr	Animal husbandry, vert.	1.25	.60
		Nos. 1298-1300 (3)	1.90	1.00

Souvenir Sheet

Virgin and Child, by Fra Angelico (c. 1387-1455) — A188

1987, Dec. 24 Engr. *Perf. 11½*

1301 A188	200fr	deep mag & dull blue	4.00	2.00

Christmas.

Maintenance of the Rural Economy Year — A189

1988, June 13 Litho. *Perf. 13*

1302 A189	10fr	Furniture store	.30	.20
1303 A189	40fr	Dairy farm	1.00	.50
1304 A189	60fr	Produce market	1.60	.80
1305 A189	80fr	Fruit market	2.10	1.00
		Nos. 1302-1305 (4)	5.00	2.50

Primates, Nyungwe Forest — A190

1988, Sept. 15 Litho. *Perf. 13*

1306 A190	2fr	Chimpanzee	.20	.20
1307 A190	3fr	Black and white colobus	.20	.20
1308 A190	10fr	Pygmy galago	.25	.20
1309 A190	90fr	Cercopithecidae ascagne	2.25	1.25
		Nos. 1306-1309 (4)	2.90	1.85

1988 Summer Olympics, Seoul — A191

1988, Sept. 19

1310 A191	5fr	Boxing	.20	.20
1311 A191	7fr	Relay	.20	.20
1312 A191	8fr	Table tennis	.20	.20
1313 A191	10fr	Women's running	.30	.20
1314 A191	90fr	Hurdles	2.25	1.10
		Nos. 1310-1314 (5)	3.15	1.90

Organization of African Unity, 25th Anniv. — A192

1988, Nov. 30 Litho. *Perf. 13*

1315 A192	5fr	shown	.20	.20
1316 A192	7fr	Handskake, map	.20	.20
1317 A192	8fr	"OAU" in brick, map	.20	.20
1318 A192	90fr	Slogan	2.25	1.25
		Nos. 1315-1318 (4)	2.85	1.85

Souvenir Sheet

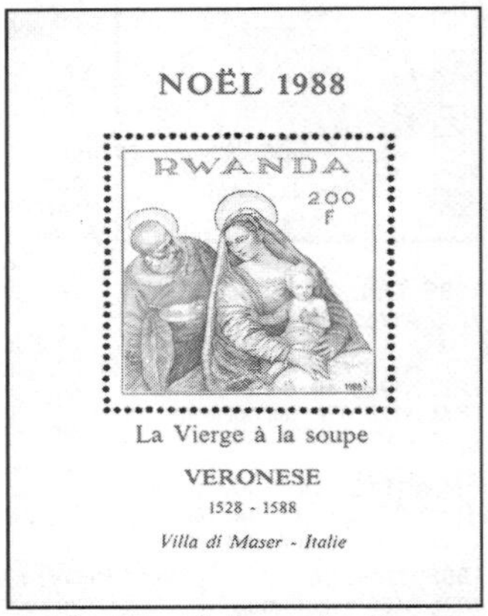

Detail of The Virgin and the Soup, by Paolo Veronese — A193

1988, Dec. 23 Engr. *Perf. 13½*

1319 A193	200fr	multicolored	5.25	5.25

Christmas. Margin is typographed.

Intl. Red Cross and Red Crescent Organizations, 125th Annivs. — A194

1988, Dec. 30 Litho. *Perf. 13*

1320 A194	10fr	Refugees	.25	.20
1321 A194	30fr	First aid	.80	.40
1322 A194	40fr	Elderly	1.00	.50
1323 A194	100fr	Travelling doctor	2.60	1.25
		Nos. 1320-1323 (4)	4.65	2.35

Nos. 1322-1323 vert.

Medicinal Plants — A195

1989, Feb. 15 Litho. *Perf. 13*

1324 A195	5fr	Plectranthus barbatus	.20	.20
1325 A195	10fr	Tetradenia riparia	.30	.20
1326 A195	20fr	Hygrophila auriculata	.55	.30
1327 A195	40fr	Datura stramonium	1.10	.55
1328 A195	50fr	Pavetta ternifolia	1.40	.75
		Nos. 1324-1328 (5)	3.55	2.00

Interparliamentary Union, Cent. — A196

1989, Oct. 20 Litho. *Perf. 13*

1329 A196	10fr	shown	.30	.20
1330 A196	30fr	Hills, lake	.85	.50
1331 A196	70fr	Hills, stream	2.10	1.10
1332 A196	90fr	Sun rays, hills	2.75	1.50
		Nos. 1329-1332 (4)	6.00	3.30

Souvenir Sheet

Christmas — A197

Adoration of the Magi by Rubens.

1989, Dec. 29 Engr. *Perf. 11½*

1333 A197	100fr	blk, red & grn	3.25	3.25

Rural Organization Year — A198

Designs: 10fr, Making pottery. 70fr, Carrying produce to market. 90fr, Firing clay pots. 100fr, Clearing land.

1989, Dec. 29 Litho. *Perf. 13½x13*

1334 A198	10fr	multi	.35	.20
1335 A198	70fr	multi, vert.	2.25	1.25
1336 A198	90fr	multi	3.00	1.60
1337 A198	200fr	multi	6.75	3.75
		Nos. 1334-1337 (4)	12.35	6.80

Revolution, 30th Anniv. (in 1989) — A199

Designs: 10fr, Improved living conditions. 60fr, Couple, farm tools. 70fr, Modernization. 100fr, Flag, map, native.

1990, Jan. 22 *Perf. 13*

1338 A199	10fr	multi	.35	.20
1339 A199	60fr	multi, vert.	2.00	1.10
1340 A199	70fr	multi	2.25	1.25
1341 A199	100fr	multi	3.25	1.85
		Nos. 1338-1341 (4)	7.85	4.40

Inscribed 1989.

French Revolution, Bicent. (in 1989) — A200

Paintings of the Revolution: 10fr, Triumph of Marat by Boilly. 60fr, Rouget de Lisle singing La Marseillaise by Pils. 70fr, Oath of the Tennis Court by David. 100fr, Trial of Louis XVI by Court.

1990, Jan. 22

1342 A200 10fr multicolored .35 .20
1343 A200 60fr multicolored 2.00 1.10
1344 A200 70fr multicolored 2.25 1.25
1345 A200 100fr multicolored 3.25 1.90
Nos. 1342-1345 (4) 7.85 4.45

Inscribed 1989.

African Development Bank, 25th Anniv. (in 1989) — A201

1990, Feb. 22 ***Perf. 13½x13***

1346 A201 10fr Building construction .35 .20
1347 A201 20fr Harvesting .70 .45
1348 A201 40fr Cultivation 1.40 .75
1349 A201 90fr Building, truck, harvesters 3.00 1.60
Nos. 1346-1349 (4) 5.45 3.00

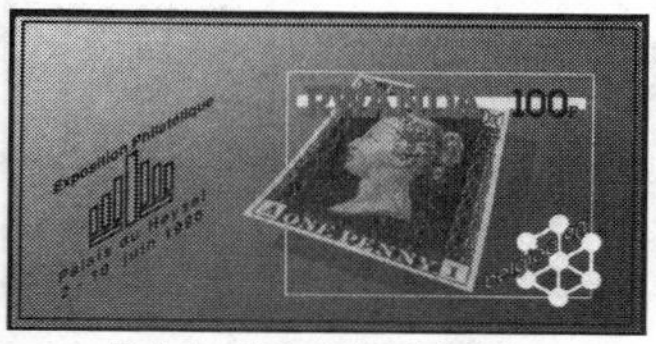

Belgica '90, Intl. Philatelic Exhibition — A202

Illustration reduced.

1990, May 21 **Litho.** ***Imperf.***

1350 A202 100fr Great Britain #1 3.50 1.75
1351 A202 100fr Belgium #B1011 3.50 1.75
1352 A202 100fr Rwanda #516 3.50 1.75
Nos. 1350-1352 (3) 10.50 5.25

Visit of Pope John Paul II A203

1990, Aug. 27 **Litho.** ***Perf. 13½x13***

1353 A203 10fr shown .35 .20
1354 A203 70fr Holding crucifix 2.25 1.25

Souvenir Sheet

Perf. 11½

1355 A203 100fr Hands together 3.25 1.75

No. 1355 contains one 36x51mm stamp.

Intl. Literacy Year A204

Designs: 10fr, Teacher at blackboard. 20fr, Teacher seated at desk. 50fr, Small outdoor class. 90fr, Large outdoor class.

1991, Jan. 25 **Litho.** ***Perf. 13½x13***

1356 A204 10fr multicolored .20 .20
1357 A204 20fr multicolored .40 .25
1358 A204 50fr multicolored .95 .55
1359 A204 90fr multicolored 1.75 1.00
Nos. 1356-1359 (4) 3.30 2.00

Nos. 1256-1261 Ovptd. in Black on Silver

1990, May 25 **Litho.** ***Perf. 13***

1360 A179 2fr on No. 1256 .20 .20
1361 A179 4fr on No. 1257 .20 .20
1362 A179 5fr on No. 1258 .20 .20
1363 A179 10fr on No. 1259 .30 .20
1364 A179 40fr on No. 1260 1.10 .55
1365 A179 45fr on No. 1261 1.25 .65
Nos. 1360-1365 (6) 3.25 2.00

Self-help Organizations — A205

1991, Jan. 25 **Litho.** ***Perf. 13½x13***

1366 A205 10fr Tool making .30 .20
1367 A205 20fr Animal husbandry .60 .30
1368 A205 50fr Textile manufacturing 1.40 .70
1369 A205 90fr Road construction 2.50 1.25
Nos. 1366-1369 (4) 4.80 2.45

Dated 1990.

Cardinal Lavigerie, Founder of the Order of White Fathers and Sisters, Death Cent. A206

5fr, Statue of Madonna. 15fr, One of the Order's nuns. 70fr, Group photo. 110fr, Cardinal Lavigerie.

1992, Oct. 1 **Litho.** ***Perf. 14***

1370 A206 5fr multi, vert. .20 .20
1371 A206 15fr multi .20 .20
1372 A206 70fr multi, vert. .45 .25
1373 A206 110fr multi, vert. .70 .35
Nos. 1370-1373 (4) 1.55 1.00

1992 Summer Olympic Games, Barcelona A207

Designs: a, 20fr, Runners. b, 30fr, Swimmer. c, 90fr, Soccer players.

1993, Feb. 1

1374 A207 Sheet of 3, #a.-c. .90 .45

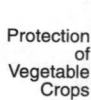

Protection of Vegetable Crops A208

Designs: 10fr, Removing parasites and weeds. 15fr, Spraying pesticides. 70fr, Zonocerus elegans on plants. 110fr, Phenacoccus manihoti.

1993, June 15 **Litho.** ***Perf. 14***

1375 A208 10fr multicolored .20 .20
1376 A208 15fr multicolored .20 .20
1377 A208 70fr multicolored .45 .25
1378 A208 110fr multicolored .70 .35
Nos. 1375-1378 (4) 1.55 1.00

World Conference on Nutrition, Rome — A209

Designs: 15fr, Man fishing. 50fr, People at fruit market. 100fr, Man milking cow. 500fr, Mother breastfeeding.

1992, Dec. **Litho.** ***Perf. 14***

1381 A209 15fr multicolored *.20 .20*
1382 A209 50fr multicolored *.70 .35*
1383 A209 100fr multicolored *1.25 .65*
1384 A209 500fr multicolored *6.75 3.50*
Nos. 1381-1384 (4) *8.90 4.70*

Wildlife A210

1998 **Litho.** ***Perf. 14***

1385 A210 15fr Toad
1386 A210 100fr Snail
1387 A210 150fr Porcupine
1388 A210 300fr Chameleon
a. Souvenir sheet, #1385-1388, imperf.

Plants A211

15fr, Opuntia. 100fr, Gloriosa superba. 150fr, Markhamia lutea. 300fr, Hagenia abyssinica.

1998 **Litho.** ***Perf. 14***

1389 A211 15fr multi, vert. .20 .20
1390 A211 100fr multi, vert. 1.00 .50
1391 A211 150fr multi, vert. 1.60 .80
1392 A211 300fr multi 3.25 1.60
a. Souvenir sheet, #1389-1392, imperf. 6.00 3.00
Nos. 1389-1392 (4) 6.05 3.10

Remembrance of Genocide Victims — A212

1999 (?) **Litho.** ***Perf. 14***

1392B A212 20fr Map, coffins, horiz.
1392C A212 30fr Orphans, horiz.
1393 A212 200fr multicolored

The editors suspect that more stamps were issued in this set, and would like to examine any examples.

Rwandan postal officials have declared "illegal" sets depicting: Millennium (eleven sheets of 9 with various subjects), Pornography (two sheets of 9), Chess (sheet of 9 unoverprinted, and also overprinted in Russian), Double-decker buses (sheet of 9), Butterflies (sheet of 9), Hot air balloons (sheet of 9), Old automobiles (sheet of 9), Motorcycle racing (sheet of 9), Trains (sheet of 9), Fungi (sheet of 6), Cats (sheet of 6), Roses (sheet of 6).

Genocide Type of 1999

1999 **Litho.** ***Perf. 14***

1394 A212 400fr People protesting

SEMI-POSTAL STAMPS

No. 305 Surcharged in Black and Overprinted in Brown: "SECHERESSE/SOLIDARITE AFRICAINE"

1973, Aug. 23 **Photo.** ***Perf. 13***

B1 A53 100fr + 50fr multi 2.50 2.25

African solidarity in drought emergency.

Nos. 349-350 Surcharged and Overprinted Like Nos. 693-698

1975, Nov. 10 **Litho.** ***Perf. 13***

B2 A60 50fr + 25fr multi 1.50 1.00
B3 A60 90fr + 25fr multi 2.00 1.50

African solidarity in drought emergency.

AIR POST STAMPS

African Postal Union Issue, 1967

Common Design Type

1967, Sept. 18 **Engr.** ***Perf. 13***

C1 CD124 6fr brown, rose cl & gray .20 .20
C2 CD124 18fr brt lil, ol brn & plum .40 .30
C3 CD124 30fr green, dp bl & red .65 .50
Nos. C1-C3 (3) 1.25 1.00

PHILEXAFRIQUE Issue

Alexandre Lenoir, by Jacques L. David AP1

1968, Dec. 30 **Photo.** ***Perf. 12½***

C4 AP1 100fr emerald & multi 1.90 .80

Issued to publicize PHILEXAFRIQUE, Philatelic exhibition in Abidjan, Feb. 14-23, 1969. Printed with alternating emerald label.

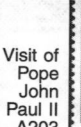

2nd PHILEXAFRIQUE Issue

Ruanda-Urundi No. 123, Cowherd and Lake Victoria — AP2

1969, Feb. 14 Litho. *Perf. 14*

C5	AP2	50fr multicolored	.90	.80

Opening of PHILEXAFRIQUE, Abidjan, 2/14.

Painting Type of Regular Issue

Paintings and Music: 50fr, The Music Lesson, by Fragonard. 100fr, Angels' Concert, by Memling, horiz.

1969, Mar. 31 Photo. *Perf. 13*

C6	A49	50fr gold & multi	.80	.40
C7	A49	100fr gold & multi	1.90	1.60

African Postal Union Issue, 1971

Common Design Type

Design: Woman and child of Rwanda and UAMPT Building, Brazzaville, Congo.

1971, Nov. 13 *Perf. 13x13½*

C8	CD135	100fr blue & multi	1.75	1.75

No. C8 Overprinted in Red

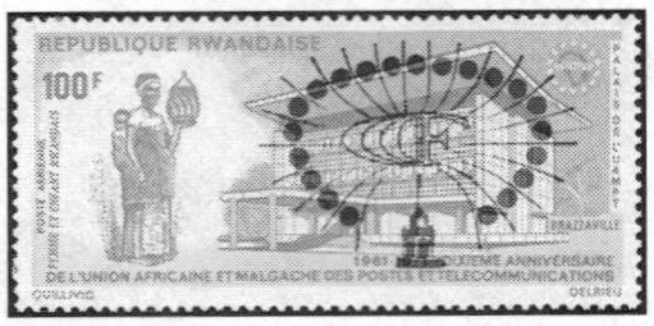

a

b

1973, Sept. 17 Photo. *Perf. 13x13½*

C9	CD135(a)	100fr multi	2.00	2.00
C10	CD135(b)	100fr multi	2.00	2.00
a.		Pair, #C9-C10	4.00	4.00

3rd Conference of French-speaking countries, Liège, Sept. 15-Oct. 14. Overprints alternate checkerwise in same sheet.

Sassenage Castle, Grenoble — AP3

1977, June 20 Litho. *Perf. 12½*

C11	AP3	50fr multi	1.25	1.00

Intl. French Language Council, 10th anniv.

Philexafrique II-Essen Issue

Common Design Types

Designs: No. C12, Okapi, Rwanda #239. No. C13, Woodpecker, Oldenburg #4.

1978, Nov. 1 Litho. *Perf. 12½*

C12	CD138	30fr multi	.60	.50
C13	CD139	30fr multi	.60	.50
a.		Pair, #C12-C13	1.25	1.00

SAAR

'sär

LOCATION — On the Franco-German border southeast of Luxembourg
POP. — 1,400,000 (1959)
AREA — 991 sq. mi.
CAPITAL — Saarbrücken

A former German territory, the Saar was administered by the League of Nations 1920-35. After a January 12, 1935, plebiscite, it returned to Germany, and the use of German stamps was resumed. After World War II, France occupied the Saar and later established a protectorate. The provisional semi-independent State of Saar was established Jan. 1, 1951. France returned the Saar to the German Federal Republic Jan. 1, 1957.

Saar stamps were discontinued in 1959 and replaced by stamps of the German Federal Republic.

100 Pfennig = 1 Mark
100 Centimes = 1 Franc (1921)

Catalogue values for unused stamps in this country are for Never Hinged items, beginning with Scott 221 in the regular postage section, and Scott B85 in the semi-postal section.

Watermark

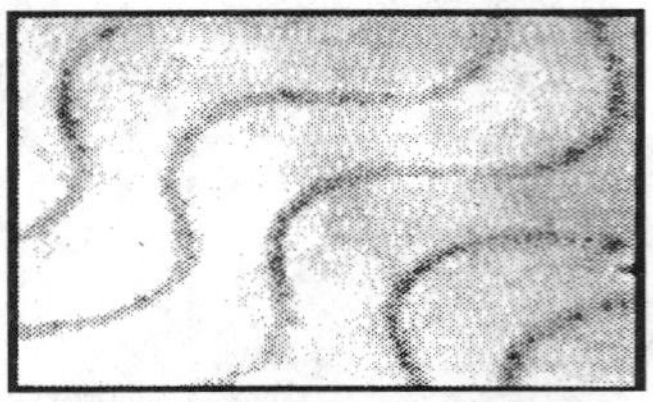

Wmk. 285- Marbleized Pattern

German Stamps of 1906-19 Overprinted **Sarre**

Perf. 14, 14½

1920, Jan. 30 Wmk. 125

1	A22	2pf	gray	.80	*2.50*
d.			Double overprint	*1,350.*	*1,800.*
2	A22	2½pf	gray	1.00	*3.50*
3	A16	3pf	brown	.50	*1.25*
4	A16	5pf	green	.30	*.50*
f.			Double overprint	575.00	*950.00*
5	A22	7½pf	orange	.40	*.80*
6	A16	10pf	carmine	.30	*.50*
d.			Double overprint	475.00	*775.00*
7	A22	15pf	dk violet	.30	.50
c.			Double overprint	475.00	*775.00*
8	A16	20pf	blue violet	.30	*.50*
c.			Double overprint	400.00	*625.00*
9	A16	25pf	org & blk, *yel*	7.25	13.00
10	A16	30pf	org & blk, *buff*	12.00	20.00
11	A22	35pf	red brown	.30	.50
12	A16	40pf	lake & blk	.35	.50
13	A16	50pf	pur & blk, *buff*	.30	*.50*
14	A16	60pf	red violet	.30	*.60*
15	A16	75pf	green & blk	.30	.50
16	A16	80pf	lake & blk, *rose*	140.00	175.00

Overprinted **Sarre**

17	A17	1m	carmine rose	20.00	*26.00*
b.			Double overprint	475.00	*775.00*
			Nos. 1-17 (17)	184.70	246.65

Three types of overprint exist on Nos. 1-5, 12, 13; two types on Nos. 6-11, 14-16.

The 3m type A19 exists overprinted like No. 17, but was not issued.

Overprint forgeries exist.

Inverted Overprint

1c	A22	2pf	gray	210.00	*325.00*
2c	A22	2½pf	gray	250.00	*375.00*
3c	A16	3pf	brown	210.00	*325.00*
4c	A16	5pf	green	400.00	*650.00*
5c	A22	7½pf	orange		*525.00*
6c	A16	10pf	carmine	375.00	*625.00*
9c	A16	25pf	org & blk, *yel*	550.00	1,500.
11c	A22	35pf	red brown	275.00	525.00
12c	A16	40pf	lake & blk	275.00	525.00
13c	A16	50pf	pur & blk, *buff*	275.00	*475.00*
15c	A16	75pf	green & blk	150.00	275.00
17a	A17	1m	carmine rose	450.00	725.00

Bavarian Stamps of 1914-16 Overprinted **Sarre**

Perf. 14x14½

1920, Mar. 1 Wmk. 95

19	A10	2pf	gray	*900.00*	*3,750.*
20	A10	3pf	brown	75.00	*425.00*
21	A10	5pf	yellow grn	.40	*1.00*
a.			Double overprint	525.00	
22	A10	7½pf	green	30.00	*175.00*
23	A10	10pf	carmine rose	.50	*1.25*
a.			Double overprint	210.00	*400.00*
24	A10	15pf	vermilion	.65	*1.25*
a.			Double overprint	250.00	*525.00*
25	A10	15pf	carmine	4.75	*11.00*
26	A10	20pf	blue	.40	*1.00*
a.			Double overprint	210.00	*425.00*
27	A10	25pf	gray	6.25	*11.50*
28	A10	30pf	orange	4.25	*7.25*
30	A10	40pf	olive green	7.00	*10.50*
31	A10	50pf	red brown	1.00	*1.50*
a.			Double overprint	210.00	*425.00*
32	A10	60pf	dark green	2.10	*6.25*

Overprinted **Sarre**

Perf. 11½

35	A11	1m	brown	12.50	*27.50*
a.			1m dark brown	12.50	*25.00*
36	A11	2m	violet	42.50	*100.00*
37	A11	3m	scarlet	80.00	*110.00*
			Nos. 35-37 (3)	135.00	*237.50*

Overprinted **SARRE**

38	A12	5m	deep blue	550.00	700.00
39	A12	10m	yellow green	90.00	*175.00*
a.			Double overprint	*2,100.*	*5,250.*

Nos. 19, 20 and 22 were not officially issued, but were available for postage. Examples are known legitimately used on cover. The 20m type A12 was also overprinted in small quantity.

Overprint forgeries exist.

German Stamps of 1906-20 Overprinted

Perf. 14, 14½

1920, Mar. 26 Wmk. 125

41	A16	5pf	green	.20	*.25*
42	A16	5pf	red brown	.30	.25
43	A16	10pf	carmine	.20	*.25*
44	A16	10pf	orange	.25	.25
45	A22	15pf	dk violet	.20	*.25*
46	A16	20pf	blue violet	.20	*.25*
47	A16	20pf	green	.30	.30
a.			Double overprint		
48	A16	30pf	org & blk, *buff*	.20	*.25*
a.			Double overprint	50.00	
49	A16	30pf	dull blue	.35	*.40*
50	A16	40pf	lake & blk	.20	*.25*
51	A16	40pf	carmine rose	.60	.40
52	A16	50pf	pur & blk, *buff*	.20	*.25*
a.			Double overprint	50.00	*250.00*
53	A16	60pf	red violet	.30	.25
54	A16	75pf	green & blk	.40	.25
a.			Double overprint	80.00	*250.00*
55	A17	1.25m	green	.80	.80
56	A17	1.50m	yellow brn	.80	.80
57	A21	2.50m	lilac rose	2.50	*7.75*
58	A16	4m	black & rose	5.25	*15.00*
a.			Double overprint		
			Nos. 41-58 (18)	13.25	*28.20*

On No. 57 the overprint is placed vertically at each side of the stamp.

Counterfeit overprints exist.

Inverted Overprint

41a	A16	5pf	green	11.50	*110.00*
43a	A16	10pf	carmine	32.50	*225.00*
44a	A16	10pf	orange	10.50	
45a	A22	15pf	dark violet	19.00	*160.00*
46a	A16	20pf	blue violet	19.00	—
48b	A16	30pf	org & blk, *buff*	—	
50a	A16	40pf	lake & blk	—	
52b	A16	50pf	pur & blk, *buff*	—	
53a	A16	60pf	red violet	52.50	*175.00*
54b	A16	75pf	green & black	82.50	
55a	A17	1.25m	green	67.50	
56a	A17	1.50m	yellow brown	67.50	

Germany No. 90 Surcharged in Black **20 SAARGEBIET**

1921, Feb.

65	A16	20pf on 75pf grn & blk	.25	*.75*
a.		Inverted surcharge	16.00	*32.50*
b.		Double surcharge	37.50	*72.50*

Germany No. 120 Surcharged **Mark 5 Mark**

66	A22	5m on 15pf vio brn	3.25	*10.00*
67	A22	10m on 15pf vio brn	4.25	*12.50*
		Nos. 65-67 (3)	7.75	*23.25*

Forgeries exist of Nos. 66-67.

Old Mill near Mettlach — A3

Miner at Work — A4

Entrance to Reden Mine — A5

Saar River Traffic — A6

Saar River near Mettlach — A7

Slag Pile at Völklingen — A8

Signal Bridge, Saarbrücken — A9

Church at Mettlach — A10

"Old Bridge," Saarbrücken A11

Cable Railway at Ferne — A12

Colliery Shafthead — A13

Saarbrücken City Hall — A14

Pottery at Mettlach — A15

St. Ludwig's Cathedral — A16

Presidential Residence, Saarbrücken A17

Burbach Steelworks, Dillingen A18

1921 Unwmk. Typo. *Perf. 12½*

68	A3	5pf ol grn & vio	.20	.25
a.		Tête bêche pair	4.00	12.50
c.		Center inverted	40.00	150.00
69	A4	10pf org & ultra	.20	.25
70	A5	20pf grn & slate	.20	.55
a.		Tête bêche pair	7.00	26.00
c.		Perf. 10½	14.50	125.00
d.		As "c," tête bêche pair	110.00	400.00
71	A6	25pf brn & dk bl	.25	.50
a.		Tête bêche pair	8.00	26.00
72	A7	30pf gray grn & brn	.25	.40
a.		Tête bêche pair	13.00	37.50
c.		30pf ol grn & blk	1.60	13.00
d.		As "c," tête bêche pair	10.50	50.00
e.		As "c," imperf., pair	72.50	
73	A8	40pf vermilion	.25	.25
a.		Tête bêche pair	20.00	52.50
74	A9	50pf gray & blk	.65	2.00
75	A10	60pf red & dk brn	1.00	2.00
76	A11	80pf deep blue	.40	.65
a.		Tête bêche pair	24.00	72.50
77	A12	1m lt red & blk	.50	1.00
a.		1m grn & blk	475.00	
78	A13	1.25m lt brn & dk grn	.65	1.25
79	A14	2m red & black	1.60	2.75
80	A15	3m brn & dk ol	2.00	5.75
a.		Center inverted	70.00	
81	A16	5m yellow & vio	6.25	15.00
82	A17	10m grn & red brn	7.75	16.00
83	A18	25m ultra, red & blk	22.50	47.50
		Nos. 68-83 (16)	44.65	96.10

Values for tête bêche are for vertical pair. Horizontal pairs sell for about twice as much.

The ultramarine ink on No. 69 appears to be brown where it overlays the orange.

Exist imperf. but were not regularly issued.

Nos. 70-83 Surcharged in Red, Blue or Black

5 cent. a

1 Fr. b

5 FRANKEN c

1921, May 1

85	A5(a)	3c on 20pf (R)	.25	.30
a.		Tête bêche pair	4.00	20.00
b.		Inverted surcharge	77.50	
d.		Perf. 10½	4.00	75.00
e.		As "d," tête bêche pair	17.50	
86	A6(a)	5c on 25pf (R)	.25	.25
a.		Tête bêche pair	72.50	250.00
87	A7(a)	10c on 30pf (Bl)	.25	.25
a.		Tête bêche pair	3.75	17.00
b.		Inverted surcharge	82.50	300.00
c.		Double surcharge	77.50	310.00
88	A8(a)	15c on 40pf (Bk)	.30	.25
a.		Tête bêche pair	72.50	250.00
b.		Inverted surcharge	82.50	300.00
89	A9(a)	20c on 50pf (R)	.25	.20
90	A10(a)	25c on 60pf (Bl)	.30	.20
91	A11(a)	30c on 80pf (Bk)	1.00	.60
a.		Tête bêche pair	10.00	40.00
c.		Inverted surcharge	100.00	400.00
d.		Double surcharge	110.00	400.00
92	A12(a)	40c on 1m (Bl)	1.25	.30
a.		Inverted surcharge	100.00	300.00
b.		Double surcharge	110.00	400.00
93	A13(a)	50c on 1.25m (Bk)	2.00	.60
a.		Double surcharge	200.00	625.00
b.		Perf. 10½	55.00	95.00
94	A14(a)	75c on 2m (Bl)	2.00	.90
a.		Inverted surcharge	87.50	
95	A15(b)	1fr on 3m (Bl)	2.50	1.50
96	A16(b)	2fr on 5m (Bl)	9.50	4.00
97	A17(b)	3fr on 10m (Bk)	11.50	16.00
b.		Double surcharge	140.00	525.00
98	A18(c)	5fr on 25m (Bl)	12.50	24.00
		Nos. 85-98 (14)	43.85	49.35

In these surcharges the period is occasionally missing and there are various wrong font and defective letters.

Values for tête bêche are for vertical pairs. Horizontal pairs sell for about twice as much.

Nos. 85-89, 91, 93, 97-98 exist imperf. but were not regularly issued.

Cable Railway, Ferne — A19

Miner at Work — A20

"Old Bridge," Saarbrücken A21

Saarbrücken City Hall — A22

Slag Pile at Völklingen A23

Pottery at Mettlach — A24

Saar River Traffic — A25

St. Ludwig's Cathedral A26

Colliery Shafthead A27

Mettlach Church — A28

Burbach Steelworks, Dillingen A29

Perf. 12½x13½, 13½x12½

1922-23 Typo.

99	A19	3c ol grn & straw	.25	.35
100	A20	5c orange & blk	.25	.20
101	A21	10c blue green	.25	.20
102	A19	15c deep brown	.80	.20
103	A19	15c orange ('23)	1.60	.25
104	A22	20c dk bl & lem	2.00	.20
105	A22	20c brt bl & straw ('23)	2.50	.25
106	A22	25c red & yellow	2.50	1.25
107	A22	25c mag & straw ('23)	1.60	.20
108	A23	30c carmine & yel	1.25	1.25
109	A24	40c brown & yel	.65	.20
110	A25	50c dk bl & straw	.65	.20
111	A24	75c dp grn & straw	6.25	12.50
112	A24	75c blk & straw ('23)	17.50	2.00
113	A26	1fr brown red	1.60	.55
114	A27	2fr deep violet	2.40	1.75
115	A28	3fr org & dk grn	11.00	4.00
116	A29	5fr brn & red brn	11.00	25.00
		Nos. 99-116 (18)	64.05	50.55

Nos. 99-116 exist imperforate but were not regularly issued.

For overprints see Nos. O1-O15.

Madonna of Blieskastel — A30

1925, Apr. 9 Photo. *Perf. 13½x12½*

Size: 23x27mm

118	A30	45c lake brown	1.75	2.50

Size: 31½x36mm

Perf. 12

119	A30	10fr black brown	11.00	16.00

Nos. 118-119 exist imperf. but were not regularly issued.

For overprint see No. 154.

Market Fountain, St. Johann — A31

View of Saar Valley A32

Colliery Shafthead A35

Burbach Steelworks A36

Designs: 15c, 75c, View of Saar Valley. 20c, 40c, 90c, Scene from Saarlouis fortifications. 25c, 50c, Tholey Abbey.

1927-32 *Perf. 13½*

120	A31	10c deep brown	.40	.20
121	A32	15c olive black	.25	.60
122	A32	20c brown orange	.25	.20
123	A32	25c bluish slate	.40	.25
124	A31	30c olive green	.60	.20
125	A32	40c olive brown	.40	.20
126	A32	50c magenta	.60	.20
127	A35	60c red org ('30)	2.25	.25
128	A32	75c brown violet	.40	.20
129	A35	80c red orange	2.00	6.25
130	A32	90c deep red ('32)	5.50	12.00
131	A35	1fr violet	1.75	.20
132	A36	1.50fr sapphire	3.00	.20
133	A36	2fr brown red	3.50	.20
134	A36	3fr dk olive grn	7.75	.80
135	A36	5fr deep brown	7.75	4.75
		Nos. 120-135 (16)	36.80	26.70

For surcharges and overprints see Nos. 136-153, O16-O26.

60 cent.

Nos. 126 and 129 Surcharged

1930-34

136	A32	40c on 50c mag ('34)	.75	.80
137	A35	60c on 80c red orange	1.25	1.60

Plebiscite Issue

Stamps of 1925-32 Overprinted in Various Colors

VOLKSABSTIMMUNG 1935

Perf. 13½, 13½x13, 13x13½

1934, Nov. 1

139	A31	10c brown (Br)	.25	.30
140	A32	15c black grn (G)	.25	.30
141	A32	20c brown org (O)	.35	.80
142	A32	25c bluish sl (Bl)	.35	.80
143	A31	30c olive grn (G)	.25	.25
144	A32	40c olive brn (Br)	.25	.40
145	A32	50c magenta (R)	.40	.80
146	A35	60c red orge (O)	.25	.30
147	A32	75c brown vio (V)	.40	.80
148	A32	90c deep red (R)	.40	.80
149	A35	1fr violet (V)	.40	.90

150 A36 1.50fr sapphire (Bl) .80 2.00
151 A36 2fr brown red (R) 1.00 2.75
152 A36 3fr dk ol grn (G) 1.75 4.75
153 A36 5fr dp brown (Br) 10.50 20.00

Size: 31½x36mm

Perf. 12

154 A30 10fr black brn (Br) 15.00 35.00
Nos. 139-154 (16) 32.60 70.95

French Administration

Miner A37

Steel Workers A38

Harvesting Sugar Beets — A39

Mettlach Abbey — A40

Marshal Ney — A41

Saar River near Mettlach A42

1947 Unwmk. Photo. *Perf. 14*

155 A37 2pf gray .20 .20
156 A37 3pf orange .20 .30
157 A37 6pf dk Prus grn .20 .20
158 A37 8pf scarlet .20 .20
159 A37 10pf rose violet .20 .20
160 A38 15pf brown .20 2.25
161 A38 16pf ultra .20 .20
162 A38 20pf brown rose .20 .20
163 A38 24pf dp brown org .20 .20
164 A39 25pf cerise .30 10.00
165 A39 30pf lt olive grn .20 .40
166 A39 40pf orange brn .20 .40
167 A39 50pf blue violet .30 10.00
168 A40 60pf violet .30 10.00
169 A40 80pf dp orange .20 .20
170 A41 84pf brown .20 .25
171 A42 1m gray green .20 .30
Nos. 155-171 (17) 35.50
Set, never hinged 3.00

Nos. 155-162, 164-171 exist imperf.

Types of 1947

1947 Wmk. 285

172 A37 12pf olive green .20 .20
173 A39 45pf crimson .20 8.50
174 A40 75pf brt blue .20 .25
Nos. 172-174 (3) 8.95
Set, never hinged .50

Nos. 172-174 exist imperf.

Types of 1947 Surcharged with New Value, Bars and Ornament in Black or Red

1947, Nov. 27 Unwmk.

Printing II

175 A37 10c on 2pf gray .20 .25
176 A37 60c on 3pf org .20 .25
177 A37 1fr on 10pf rose vio .20 .25
178 A37 2fr on 12pf ol grn .20 .75
179 A38 3fr on 15pf brn .20 .25
180 A38 4fr on 16pf ultra .20 2.00
181 A38 5fr on 20pf brn rose .20 .50
182 A38 6fr on 24pf dp brn org .20 .25
183 A39 9fr on 30pf lt ol grn .20 3.00
184 A39 10fr on 50pf bl vio (R) .30 5.00
185 A40 14fr on 60pf violet .35 2.50
186 A41 20fr on 84pf brn .25 3.75
187 A42 50fr on 1m gray grn .95 6.25
Nos. 175-187 (13) 25.00
Set, never hinged 3.50

Printing I

175a A37 10c on 2pf gray 75.00 200.00
176a A37 60c on 3pf orange 60.00 525.00
177a A37 1fr on 10pf rose vio 5.00 8.75
178a A37 2fr on 12pf ol grn, wmk. 285 .25 .50
179a A38 3fr on 15pf brown 400.00 1,200.
180a A38 4fr on 16pf ultra 9.00 65.00
181a A38 5fr on 20pf brn rose 35.00 2,000.
182a A38 6fr on 24pf dp brn org .25 1.00
183a A39 9fr on 30pf lt ol grn 37.50 475.00
184a A39 10fr on 50pf bl vio (R) 380.00 4,000.
185a A40 14fr on 60pf violet 90.00 575.00
186a A41 20fr on 84pf brown 2.00 3.75
187a A42 50fr on 1m gray grn 35.00 275.00
Nos. 175a-187a (13) 1,129.

Printing I was surcharged on Nos. 155-171. The crossbar of the A's in SAAR is high on the 10c, 60c, 1fr, 2fr, 9fr and 10fr; numeral "1" has no base serif on the 3fr and 4fr; wide space between vignette and SAAR panel; 1m inscribed "1M."

Printing II was surcharged on a special printing of the basic stamps, with details of design that differ on each denomination. The "A" crossbar is low on 10c, 60c, 1fr, 2fr, 9fr, 10fr; numeral "1" has base serif on 3fr and 4fr; narrow space between vignette and SAAR panel; 1m inscribed "1SM."

Inverted surcharges exist on Nos. 175-187 and 175a-187a.

French Protectorate

Clasped Hands — A43

Colliery Shafthead — A44

2fr, 3fr, Worker. 4fr, 5fr, Girl gathering wheat. 6fr, 9fr, Miner. 14fr, Smelting. 20fr, Reconstruction. 50fr, Mettlach Abbey portal.

Perf. 14x13, 13

1948, Apr. 1 Engr. Unwmk.

188 A43 10c henna brn .25 1.40
189 A43 60c dk Prus grn .25 1.40
190 A43 1fr brown blk .20 .20
191 A43 2fr rose car .20 .20
192 A43 3fr black brn .20 .20
193 A43 4fr red .20 .20
194 A43 5fr red violet .20 .20
195 A43 6fr henna brown .25 .20
196 A43 9fr dk Prus grn 1.65 .20
197 A44 10fr dark blue .90 .20
198 A44 14fr dk vio brn 1.25 .65
199 A44 20fr henna brn 2.25 .65
200 A44 50fr blue blk 5.00 2.00
Nos. 188-200 (13) 12.80 7.70
Set, never hinged 26.00

Map of the Saar A45

1948, Dec. 15 Photo. *Perf. 13½x13*

201 A45 10fr dark red .45 1.75
202 A45 25fr deep blue .75 2.50
Set, never hinged 3.00

French Protectorate establishment, ist anniv.

Caduceus, Microscope, Bunsen Burner and Book — A46

1949, Apr. 2 *Perf. 13x13½*

203 A46 15fr carmine 2.25 .30
Never hinged 5.25

Issued to honor Saar University.

Ludwig van Beethoven A47

Laborer Using Spade A51

Saarbrücken — A52

Designs: 10c, Building trades. 1fr, 3fr, Gears, factories. 5fr, Dumping mine waste. 6fr, 15fr, Coal mine interior. 8fr, Communications symbols. 10fr, Emblem of printing. 12fr, 18fr, Pottery. 25fr, Blast furnace worker. 45fr, Rock formation "Great Boot." 60fr, Reden Colliery, Landsweiler. 100fr, View of Weibelskirchen.

1949-51 Unwmk. *Perf. 13x13½*

204 A47 10c violet brn .20 .85
205 A47 60c gray ('51) .20 .85
206 A47 1fr carmine lake .60 .20
207 A47 3fr brown ('51) 2.75 .20
208 A47 5fr dp violet ('50) .80 .20
209 A47 6fr Prus grn ('51) 4.25 .20
210 A47 8fr olive grn ('51) .30 .20
211 A47 10fr orange ('50) 1.50 .20
212 A47 12fr dk green 5.25 .20
213 A47 15fr red ('50) 2.75 .20
214 A47 18fr brn car ('51) 1.00 2.50

Perf. 13½

215 A51 20fr gray ('50) .65 .20
216 A51 25fr violet blue 6.50 .20
217 A52 30fr red brown ('51) 5.50 .30
218 A52 45fr rose lake ('51) 1.90 .30
219 A51 60fr deep grn ('51) 1.90 .75
220 A51 100fr brown 2.75 1.00
Nos. 204-220 (17) 38.80 8.55
Set, never hinged 95.00

Catalogue values for unused stamps in this section, from this point to the end of the section, are for Never Hinged items.

Peter Wust — A54

St. Peter — A55

1950, Apr. 3

221 A54 15fr carmine rose 12.50 4.00

Wust (1884-1940), Catholic philosopher.

1950, June 29 Engr. *Perf. 13*

222 A55 12fr deep green 3.25 6.50
223 A55 15fr red brown 4.25 6.50
224 A55 25fr blue 7.50 15.00
Nos. 222-224 (3) 15.00 28.00

Holy Year, 1950.

Street in Ottweiler — A56

Symbols of the Council of Europe A57

1950, July 10 Photo. *Perf. 13x13½*

225 A56 10fr orange brown 4.00 5.00

Founding of Ottweiler, 400th anniv.

1950, Aug. 8 *Perf. 13½*

226 A57 25fr deep blue 35.00 9.00

Issued to commemorate the Saar's admission to the Council of Europe. See No. C12.

Post Rider and Guard — A62

1951, Apr. 29 Engr. *Perf. 13*

227 A62 15fr dk violet brn 6.50 15.00

Issued to publicize Stamp Day, 1951.

"Agriculture and Industry" and Fair Emblem — A63

Tower of Mittelbexbach and Flowers — A67

1951, May 12 Photo. *Perf. 13x13½*

228 A63 15fr dk gray grn 2.25 3.50

1951 Fair at Saarbrücken.

1951, June 9 Engr. *Perf. 13*

229 A67 15fr dark green 2.50 1.00

Exhibition of Gardens & Flowers, Bexbach, 1951.

Refugees — A68

Globe & Stylized Fair Building — A69

1952, May 2 Unwmk. *Perf. 13*

230 A68 15fr bright red 3.00 1.00

Issued to honor the Red Cross.

1952, Apr. 26

231 A69 15fr red brown 2.00 1.00

1952 Fair at Saarbrücken.

Mine Shafts A70

Ludwig's Gymnasium A71

General Post Office A72

Reconstruction of St. Ludwig's Cathedral A73

"SM" Monogram A74

3fr, 18fr, Bridge building. 6fr, Transporter bridge, Mettlach. 30fr, Saar University Library.

1952-55 Engr.

232	A70	1fr	dk bl grn ('53)	.20	.20
233	A71	2fr	purple ('53)	.20	.20
234	A72	3fr	dk car rose ('53)	.20	.20
235	A72	5fr	dk grn (no inscription)	5.00	.20
236	A72	5fr	dk grn ("Hauptpostamt Saarbrücken") ('54)	.20	.20
237	A72	6fr	vio brn ('53)	.25	.20
238	A71	10fr	brn ol ('53)	.40	.20
239	A72	12fr	green ('53)	.55	.20
240	A70	15fr	blk brn (no inscription)	7.50	.20
241	A70	15fr	blk brn ("Industrie-Landschaft") ('53)	3.25	.20
242	A70	15fr	dp car ('55)	.20	.20
243	A72	18fr	dk rose brn ('55)	2.50	*3.50*
244	A72	30fr	ultra ('53)	.75	*.65*
245	A73	500fr	brn car ('53)	15.00	*45.00*
			Nos. 232-245 (14)	36.20	*51.35*

For overprints see Nos. 257-259.

1953, Mar. 23

246 A74 15fr dark ultra 1.75 1.10

1953 Fair at Saarbrücken.

Bavarian and Prussian Postilions A75

1953, May 3

247 A75 15fr deep blue 3.00 *9.50*

Stamp Day.

Fountain and Fair Buildings — A76

1954, Apr. 10

248 A76 15fr deep green 1.75 .65

1954 International Fair at Saarbrücken.

Post Coach and Post Bus of 1920 — A77

1954, May 9 Engr.

249 A77 15fr red 3.25 *7.50*

Stamp Day, May 9, 1954.

Madonna and Child, Holbein A78

Designs: 10fr, Sistine Madonna, Raphael. 15fr, Madonna and Child with pear, Durer.

1954, Aug. 14

250	A78	5fr	deep carmine	.75	*1.00*
251	A78	10fr	dark green	.90	*1.25*
252	A78	15fr	dp violet bl	1.25	*2.50*
			Nos. 250-252 (3)	2.90	*4.75*

Centenary of the promulgation of the Dogma of the Immaculate Conception.

Cyclist and Flag — A79

Symbols of Industry and Rotary Emblem — A80

1955, Feb. 28 Photo. *Perf. 13x13½*

253 A79 15fr multicolored .30 *.50*

World championship cross country bicycle race.

1955, Feb. 28

254 A80 15fr orange brown .30 *.50*

Rotary International, 50th anniversary.

Flags of Participating Nations — A81

1955, Apr. 18 Photo. *Perf. 13x13½*

255 A81 15fr multicolored .30 *.50*

1955 International Fair at Saarbrücken.

Postman at Illingen A82

Unwmk.

1955, May 8 Engr. *Perf. 13*

256 A82 15fr deep claret .65 *1.25*

Issued to publicize Stamp Day, 1955.

Nos. 242-244 Overprinted "VOLKSBEFRAGUNG 1955"

1955, Oct. 22

257	A70	15fr	deep carmine	.20	*.25*
258	A72	18fr	dk rose brn	.25	*.30*
259	A72	30fr	ultra	.35	*.60*
			Nos. 257-259 (3)	.80	*1.15*

Plebiscite, Oct. 23, 1955.

Symbols of Industry and the Fair A83

Radio Tower, Saarbrücken A84

1956, Apr. 14 Photo. *Perf. 11½*

260 A83 15fr dk brn red & yel grn .20 *.50*

Intl. Fair at Saarbrücken, Apr. 14-29, 1956.

1956, May 6

Granite Paper

261 A84 15fr grn & grnsh bl .20 *.50*

Stamp Day.

German Administration

Arms of Saar — A85

Pres. Theodor Heuss — A86

Perf. 13x13½

1957, Jan. 1 Litho. Wmk. 304

262 A85 15fr brick red & blue .20 *.30*

Return of the Saar to Germany.

1957 Typo. *Perf. 14*

Size: 18x22mm

263	A86	1(fr)	brt green	.20	.20
264	A86	2(fr)	brt violet	.20	.20
265	A86	3(fr)	bister brown	.20	.20
266	A86	4(fr)	red violet	.25	*.50*
267	A86	5(fr)	lt olive green	.20	.20
268	A86	6(fr)	vermilion	.20	*.40*
269	A86	10(fr)	gray	.20	*.20*
270	A86	12(fr)	deep orange	.20	.20
271	A86	15(fr)	lt blue green	.20	.20
272	A86	18(fr)	carmine rose	.60	*1.50*
273	A86	25(fr)	brt lilac	.40	*.70*

Engr.

274	A86	30(fr)	pale purple	.30	*.60*
275	A86	45(fr)	gray olive	1.00	*2.00*
276	A86	50(fr)	violet brn	1.00	*1.00*
277	A86	60(fr)	dull rose	1.50	*2.50*
278	A86	70(fr)	red orange	2.75	*4.00*
279	A86	80(fr)	olive green	.85	*2.25*
280	A86	90(fr)	dark gray	2.50	*4.50*

Size: 24x29mm

281	A86	100(fr)	dk carmine	2.25	*6.50*
282	A86	200(fr)	violet	5.00	*17.50*
			Nos. 263-282 (20)	20.00	*45.35*

See Nos. 289-308.

Steel Industry — A87

Merzig Arms and St. Peter's Church — A88

Perf. 13x13½

1957, Apr. 20 Litho. Wmk. 304

284 A87 15fr gray & magenta .20 *.30*

The 1957 Fair at Saarbrücken.

1957, May 25 *Perf. 14*

285 A88 15fr blue .20 *.30*

Centenary of the town of Merzig.

"United Europe" — A89

Lithographed; Tree Embossed

Perf. 14x13½

1957, Sept. 16 Unwmk.

286 A89 20fr orange & yel .30 *.75*

287 A89 35fr violet & pink .70 *.90*

Europa, publicizing a united Europe for peace and prosperity.

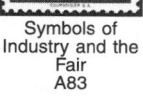

Carrier Pigeons — A90

Wmk. 304

1957, Oct. 5 Litho. *Perf. 14*

288 A90 15fr dp carmine & blk .20 *.30*

Intl. Letter Writing Week, Oct. 6-12.

Redrawn Type of 1957; "F" added after denomination

1957 Wmk. 304 Litho. *Perf. 14*

Size: 18x22mm

289	A86	1fr gray green	.20	*.20*
290	A86	3fr blue	.20	*.20*
291	A86	5fr olive	.20	*.20*
292	A86	6fr lt brown	.20	*.35*
293	A86	10fr violet	.20	*.20*
294	A86	12fr brown org	.20	*.20*
295	A86	15fr dull green	.30	*.20*
296	A86	18fr gray	1.75	*4.00*
297	A86	20fr lt olive grn	1.00	*2.25*
298	A86	25fr orange brn	.40	*.30*
299	A86	30fr rose lilac	.80	*.30*
300	A86	35fr brown	2.00	*2.50*
301	A86	45fr lt blue grn	1.75	*3.00*
302	A86	50fr dk red brown	.80	*1.50*
303	A86	70fr brt green	4.25	*4.00*
304	A86	80fr chalky blue	2.00	*4.00*
305	A86	90fr rose carmine	5.25	*5.00*

Engr.

Size: 24x29mm

306	A86	100fr orange	4.00	*6.00*
307	A86	200fr brt green	7.50	*17.50*
308	A86	300fr blue	9.00	*22.50*
		Nos. 289-308 (20)	42.00	*74.40*

"Max and Moritz" — A91

Design: 15fr, Wilhelm Busch.

Perf. 13½x13

1958, Jan. 9 Litho. Wmk. 304

309 A91 12fr lt ol grn & blk .20 *.20*
310 A91 15fr red & black .20 *.30*

Death of Wilhelm Busch, humorist, 50th anniv.

"Prevent Forest Fires" — A92

1958, Mar. 5 *Perf. 14*

311 A92 15fr brt red & blk .20 *.30*

Issued to aid in the prevention of forest fires.

Rudolf Diesel A93

1958, Mar. 18 Engr.

312 A93 12fr dk blue grn .20 *.25*

Centenary of the birth of Rudolf Diesel, inventor.

Fair Emblem and City Hall, Saarbrücken A94

View of Homburg A95

1958, Apr. 10 Litho. *Perf. 14*

313 A94 15fr dull rose .20 *.25*

1958 Fair at Saarbrücken.

1958, June 14 Engr. Wmk. 304

314 A95 15fr gray green .20 *.25*

400th anniversary of Homburg.

Turner Emblem A96

Herman Schulze-Delitzsch A97

1958, July 21 Litho. *Perf. 13½x14*

315 A96 12fr gray, blk & dl grn .20 *.25*

150 years of German Turners and the 1958 Turner Festival.

1958, Aug. 29 Engr. Wmk. 304

316 A97 12fr yellow green .20 *.25*

150th anniv. of the birth of Schultze-Delitzsch, founder of German trade organizations.

Common Design Types pictured following the introduction.

Europa Issue, 1958

Common Design Type

1958, Sept. 13 Litho.

Size: 24½x30mm

317 CD1 12fr yellow grn & bl .50 *.80*
318 CD1 30fr lt blue & red .65 *1.25*

Issued to show the European Postal Union at the service of European integration.

Jakob Fugger — A98

Old and New City Hall and Burbach Mill — A99

Perf. 13x13½

1959, Mar. 6 Wmk. 304

319 A98 15fr dk red & blk .20 *.25*

500th anniv. of the birth of Jakob Fugger the Rich, businessman and banker.

1959, Apr. 1 Engr. *Perf. 14x13½*

320 A99 15fr light blue .20 *.25*

Greater Saarbrucken, 50th anniversary.

Hands Holding Merchandise A100

Alexander von Humboldt — A101

1959, Apr. 1 Litho.

321 A100 15fr deep rose .20 *.25*

1959 Fair at Saarbrucken.

1959, May 6 Engr. *Perf. 13½x14*

322 A101 15fr blue .20 *.30*

Cent. of the death of Alexander von Humboldt, naturalist and geographer.

SEMI-POSTAL STAMPS

Red Cross Dog Leading Blind Man — SP1

Maternity Nurse with Child — SP4

Designs: #B2, Nurse and invalid. #B3, Children getting drink at spring.

Perf. 13½

1926, Oct. 25 Photo. Unwmk.

B1	SP1	20c + 20c dk ol grn	5.25	*11.50*
B2	SP1	40c + 40c dk brn	5.25	*11.50*
B3	SP1	50c + 50c red org	5.25	*10.50*
B4	SP4	1.50fr + 1.50fr brt bl	12.50	*32.50*
		Nos. B1-B4 (4)	28.25	*66.00*

Nos. B1-B4 Overprinted **1927-28**

1927, Oct. 1

B5	SP1	20c + 20c dk ol grn	7.75	*18.00*
B6	SP1	40c + 40c dk brn	7.75	*18.00*
B7	SP1	50c + 50c red org	6.25	*12.50*
B8	SP4	1.50fr + 1.50fr brt bl	10.50	*37.50*
		Nos. B5-B8 (4)	32.25	*86.00*

"The Blind Beggar" by Dyckmans SP5

"Almsgiving" by Schiestl SP6

"Charity" by Raphael — SP7

1928, Dec. 23 Photo.

B9	SP5	40c (+40c) blk brn	7.75	*47.50*
B10	SP5	50c (+50c) brn rose	7.75	*47.50*
B11	SP5	1fr (+1fr) dl vio	7.75	*47.50*
B12	SP6	1.50fr (+1.50fr) cob bl	7.75	*47.50*
B13	SP6	2fr (+2fr) red brn	10.00	*70.00*
B14	SP6	3fr (+3fr) dk ol grn	10.00	*95.00*
B15	SP7	10fr (+10fr) dk brn	250.00	*2,750.*
		Nos. B9-B15 (7)	301.00	

"Orphaned" by Kaulbach SP8

"St. Ottilia" by Feuerstein SP9

"Madonna" by Ferruzzio — SP10

1929, Dec. 22

B16	SP8	40c (+15c) ol grn	1.40	*3.75*
B17	SP8	50c (+20c) cop red	3.00	*6.25*
B18	SP8	1fr (+50c) vio brn	3.00	*7.25*
B19	SP9	1.50fr (+75c) Prus bl	3.00	*7.25*
B20	SP9	2fr (+1fr) brn car	3.00	*7.75*
B21	SP9	3fr (+2fr) sl grn	5.25	*16.00*
B22	SP10	10fr (+8fr) blk brn	30.00	*87.50*
		Nos. B16-B22 (7)	48.65	*135.75*

"The Safety-Man" SP11

"The Good Samaritan" SP12

"In the Window" — SP13

1931, Jan. 20

B23	SP11	40c (+15c)	5.25	*17.50*
B24	SP11	60c (+20c)	5.25	*17.50*
B25	SP12	1fr (+50c)	5.25	*30.00*
B26	SP11	1.50fr (+75c)	7.75	*30.00*
B27	SP12	2fr (+1fr)	7.75	*30.00*
B28	SP12	3fr (+2fr)	12.50	*30.00*
B29	SP13	10fr (+10fr)	62.50	*190.00*
		Nos. B23-B29 (7)	106.25	*345.00*

St. Martin of Tours — SP14

#B33-B35, Charity. #B36, The Widow's Mite.

1931, Dec. 23

B30	SP14	40c (+15c)	8.25	*24.00*
B31	SP14	60c (+20c)	8.25	*24.00*
B32	SP14	1fr (+50c)	10.50	*35.00*
B33	SP14	1.50fr (+75c)	12.50	*35.00*
B34	SP14	2fr (+1fr)	14.50	*35.00*
B35	SP14	3fr (+2fr)	18.00	*65.00*
B36	SP14	5fr (+5fr)	62.50	*210.00*
		Nos. B30-B36 (7)	134.50	*428.00*

Ruins at Kirkel — SP17

Illingen Castle, Kerpen SP23

Designs: 60c, Church at Blie. 1fr, Castle Ottweiler. 1.50fr, Church of St. Michael, Saarbrucken. 2fr, Statue of St. Wendel. 3fr, Church of St. John, Saarbrucken.

1932, Dec. 20

B37	SP17	40c (+15c)	6.25	*22.50*
B38	SP17	60c (+20c)	6.25	*22.50*
B39	SP17	1fr (+50c)	9.25	*35.00*
B40	SP17	1.50fr (+75c)	12.50	*30.00*
B41	SP17	2fr (+1fr)	12.50	*35.00*
B42	SP17	3fr (+2fr)	35.00	*110.00*
B43	SP23	5fr (+5fr)	75.00	*190.00*
		Nos. B37-B43 (7)	156.75	*445.00*

Scene of Neunkirchen Disaster — SP24

1933, June 1

B44	SP24	60c (+ 60c) org red	10.50	12.50
B45	SP24	3fr (+ 3fr) ol grn	22.50	*47.50*
B46	SP24	5fr (+ 5fr) org brn	22.50	*47.50*
		Nos. B44-B46 (3)	55.50	*107.50*

The surtax was for the aid of victims of the explosion at Neunkirchen, Feb. 10.

"Love" — SP25

Designs: 60c, "Anxiety." 1fr, "Peace." 1.50fr, "Solace." 2fr, "Welfare." 3fr, "Truth." 5fr, Figure on Tomb of Duchess Elizabeth of Lorraine

1934, Mar. 15 **Photo.**

B47	SP25	40c (+15c) blk brn	3.25	*10.00*
B48	SP25	60c (+20c) red org	3.25	*10.00*
B49	SP25	1fr (+50c) dl vio	4.75	*12.50*
B50	SP25	1.50fr (+75c) blue	8.25	*24.00*
B51	SP25	2fr (+1fr) car rose	7.25	*24.00*
B52	SP25	3fr (+2fr) ol grn	8.25	*24.00*
B53	SP25	5fr (+5fr) red brn	20.00	*55.00*
		Nos. B47-B53 (7)	55.00	*159.50*

Nos. B47-B53 Overprinted like Nos. 139-154 in Various Colors Reading up

1934, Dec. 1 ***Perf. 13x13½***

B54	SP25	40c (+15c) (Br)	2.50	*10.00*
B55	SP25	60c (+20c) (R)	2.50	*10.50*
B56	SP25	1fr (+50c) (V)	5.75	*19.00*
B57	SP25	1.50fr (+75c) (Bl)	4.75	*19.00*
B58	SP25	2fr (+1fr) (R)	6.75	*27.50*
B59	SP25	3fr (+2fr) (G)	5.75	*22.50*
B60	SP25	5fr (+5fr) (Br)	10.00	*30.00*
		Nos. B54-B60 (7)	38.00	*138.50*

French Protectorate

SP32

Various Flood Scenes — SP33

Perf. 13½x13, 13x13½

1948, Oct. 12 **Photo.**

Inscribed "Hochwasser-Hilfe 1947-48"

B61	SP32	5fr + 5fr dl grn	1.25	*22.50*
B62	SP33	6fr + 4fr dk vio	1.25	*22.50*
B63	SP32	12fr + 8fr red	1.75	*29.00*
B64	SP33	18fr + 12fr bl	2.10	*35.00*
a.		Souv. sheet of 4, #B61-B64, imperf.	175.00	*2,000.*
		Never hinged	400.00	
		Nos. B61-B64,CB1 (5)	15.35	*269.00*
		Set, never hinged	32.50	

The surtax was for flood relief.

Hikers and Ludweiler Hostel SP34

#B66, Hikers approaching Weisskirchen Hostel.

1949, Jan. 11 ***Perf. 13½x13***

B65	SP34	8fr + 5fr dk brn	1.25	*3.50*
B66	SP34	10fr + 7fr dk grn	1.25	*2.75*
		Set, never hinged	4.50	

The surtax aided youth hostels.

Mare and Foal SP35

Design: No. B68, Jumpers.

1949, Sept. 25 ***Perf. 13½***

B67	SP35	15fr + 5fr brn red	5.75	*20.00*
B68	SP35	25fr + 15fr blue	7.25	*21.00*
		Set, never hinged	26.00	

Day of the Horse, Sept. 25, 1949.

Detail from "Moses Striking the Rock" — SP36

#B70, "Christ at the Pool of Bethesda." #B71, "The Sick Child." #B72, "St. Thomas of Villeneuve." #B73, Madonna of Blieskastel.

1949, Dec. 20 **Engr.** ***Perf. 13***

B69	SP36	8fr + 2fr indigo	2.50	*30.00*
B70	SP36	12fr + 3fr dk grn	3.25	*35.00*
B71	SP36	15fr + 5fr brn lake	5.00	*57.50*
B72	SP36	25fr + 10fr dp ultra	7.00	*92.50*
B73	SP36	50fr + 20fr choc	12.50	*160.00*
		Nos. B69-B73 (5)	30.25	*375.00*
		Set, never hinged	67.50	

Adolph Kolping — SP37

Relief for the Hungry — SP38

1950, Apr. 3 **Photo.** ***Perf. 13x13½***

B74	SP37	15fr + 5fr car rose	13.00	*50.00*
		Never hinged	24.00	

Engraved and Typographed

1950, Apr. 28 ***Perf. 13***

B75	SP38	25fr + 10fr dk brn car & red	13.00	*42.50*
		Never hinged	24.00	

Stagecoach — SP39

1950, Apr. 22 **Engr.**

B76	SP39	15fr + 15fr brn red & dk brn	25.00	*85.00*
		Never hinged	52.50	

Stamp Day, Apr. 27, 1950. Sold at the exhibition and to advance subscribers.

Lutwinus Seeking Admission to Abbey SP40

Designs: 12fr+3fr, Lutwinus Building Mettlach Abbey. 15fr+5fr, Lutwinus as Abbot. 25fr+10fr, Bishop Lutwinus at Rheims. 50fr+20fr, Aid to the poor and sick.

1950, Nov. 10 **Unwmk.** ***Perf. 13***

B77	SP40	8fr + 2fr dk brn	3.25	*17.00*
B78	SP40	12fr + 3fr dk grn	3.25	*17.00*
B79	SP40	15fr + 5fr red brn	4.00	*24.00*
B80	SP40	25fr + 10fr blue	6.00	*40.00*
B81	SP40	50fr + 20fr brn car	8.25	*60.00*
		Nos. B77-B81 (5)	24.75	*158.00*
		Set, never hinged	40.00	

The surtax was for public assistance.

Mother and Child — SP41

John Calvin and Martin Luther — SP42

1951, Apr. 28

B82	SP41	25fr + 10fr dk grn & car	12.00	*35.00*
		Never hinged	21.00	

The surtax was for the Red Cross.

1951, Apr. 28

B83	SP42	15fr + 5fr blk brn	.90	*3.50*
		Never hinged	1.40	

Reformation in Saar, 375th anniv.

"Mother" — SP43

Runner with Torch — SP44

15fr+5fr, "Before the Theater." 18fr+7fr, "Sisters of Charity." 30fr+10fr, "The Good Samaritan." 50fr+ 20fr, "St. Martin and Beggar."

1951, Nov. 3

B84	SP43	12fr + 3fr dk grn	2.75	*10.00*
B85	SP43	15fr + 5fr pur	2.75	*10.00*
B86	SP43	18fr + 7fr dk red	3.25	*13.00*
B87	SP43	30fr + 10fr dp bl	5.25	*20.00*
B88	SP43	50fr + 20fr blk brn	12.50	*42.50*
		Nos. B84-B88 (5)	26.50	*95.50*
		Set, never hinged	47.50	

Catalogue values for unused stamps in this section, from this point to the end of the section, are for Never Hinged items.

1952, Mar. 29 **Unwmk.** ***Perf. 13***

30fr+5fr, Hand with olive branch, and globe.

B89	SP44	15fr + 5fr dp grn	5.00	*8.00*
B90	SP44	30fr + 5fr dp bl	5.00	*9.50*

XV Olympic Games, Helsinki, 1952.

Postrider Delivering Mail SP45

1952, Mar. 30

B91	SP45	30fr + 10fr dark blue	8.00	*20.00*

Stamp Day, Mar. 29, 1952.

Count Stroganoff as a Boy — SP46

Henri Dunant — SP47

Portraits: 18fr+7fr, The Holy Shepherd by Murillo. 30fr+10fr, Portrait of a Boy by Georg Melchior Kraus.

1952, Nov. 3

B92	SP46	15fr + 5fr dk brn	3.25	*7.50*
B93	SP46	18fr + 7fr brn lake	4.25	*10.00*
B94	SP46	30fr + 10fr dp bl	5.50	*11.50*
		Nos. B92-B94 (3)	13.00	*29.00*

The surtax was for child welfare.

1953, May 3 **Cross in Red**

B95	SP47	15fr + 5fr blk brn	1.75	*4.50*

Clarice Strozzi by Titian — SP48

Children of Rubens SP49

Portrait: 30fr+10fr, Rubens' son.

1953, Nov. 16

B96 SP48	15fr + 5fr purple	1.75	*4.00*
B97 SP49	18fr + 7fr dp claret	1.75	*4.25*
B98 SP48	30fr + 10fr dp ol grn	4.00	*7.50*
	Nos. B96-B98 (3)	7.50	*15.75*

The surtax was for child welfare.

St. Benedict Blessing St. Maurus — SP50

Child and Cross — SP51

1953, Dec. 18 **Litho.**

B99 SP50	30fr + 10fr black	1.75	*5.00*

The surtax was for the abbey at Tholey.

1954, May 10 **Engr.**

B100 SP51	15fr + 5fr chocolate	2.00	*4.50*

The surtax was for the Red Cross.

Street Urchin with Melon, Murillo — SP52

Nurse Holding Baby — SP53

Paintings: 10fr+5fr, Maria de Medici, Bronzino. 15fr+7fr, Baron Emil von Maucler, Dietrich.

1954, Nov. 15

B101 SP52	5fr + 3fr red	.65	*.75*
B102 SP52	10fr + 5fr dk grn	.65	*.85*
B103 SP52	15fr + 7fr purple	.70	*1.25*
	Nos. B101-B103 (3)	2.00	*2.85*

The surtax was for child welfare.

Perf. 13x13½

1955, May 5 **Photo.** **Unwmk.**

B104 SP53	15fr + 5fr blk & red	.40	*.75*

The surtax was for the Red Cross.

Dürer's Mother, Age 63 — SP54

Etchings by Dürer: 10fr+5fr, Praying hands. 15fr+7fr, Old man of Antwerp.

1955, Dec. 10 **Engr.** ***Perf. 13***

B105 SP54	5fr + 3fr dk grn	.40	*.50*
B106 SP54	10fr + 5fr ol grn	.70	*1.00*
B107 SP54	15fr + 7fr ol bis	.90	*1.40*
	Nos. B105-B107 (3)	2.00	*2.90*

The surtax was for public assistance.

First Aid Station, Saarbrücken, 1870 — SP55

1956, May 7

B108 SP55	15fr + 5fr dk brn	.25	*.50*

The surtax was for the Red Cross.

"Victor of Benevent" SP56

Winterberg Monument SP57

1956, July 25 **Unwmk.** ***Perf. 13***

B109 SP56	12fr + 3fr dk yel grn & bl grn	.30	*.50*
B110 SP56	15fr + 5fr brn vio & brn	.30	*.50*

Melbourne Olympics, 11/22-12/8/56.

1956, Oct. 29

B111 SP57	5fr + 2fr green	.20	*.20*
B112 SP57	12fr + 3fr red lilac	.20	*.30*
B113 SP57	15fr + 5fr brown	.20	*.40*
	Nos. B111-B113 (3)	.60	*.90*

The surtax was for the rebuilding of monuments.

"La Belle Ferronnière" by da Vinci — SP58

Designs: 10fr + 5fr, "Saskia" by Rembrandt. 15fr+7fr, "Family van Berchem," by Frans Floris. (Detail: Woman playing Spinet.)

1956, Dec. 10

B114 SP58	5fr + 3fr deep blue	.20	*.20*
B115 SP58	10fr + 5fr deep claret	.20	*.30*
B116 SP58	15fr + 7fr dark green	.25	*.60*
	Nos. B114-B116 (3)	.65	*1.10*

The surtax was for charitable works.

German Administration

Miner with Drill — SP59

"The Fox who Stole the Goose" — SP60

6fr+4fr, Miner. 15fr+7fr, Miner and conveyor. 30fr+10fr, Miner and coal elevator.

Wmk. 304

1957, Oct. 1 **Litho.** ***Perf. 14***

B117 SP59	6fr + 4fr bis brn & blk	.20	*.20*
B118 SP59	12fr + 6fr blk & yel grn	.20	*.20*
B119 SP59	15fr + 7fr blk & red	.25	*.35*
B120 SP59	30fr + 10fr blk & bl	.35	*.50*
	Nos. B117-B120 (4)	1.00	*1.25*

The surtax was to finance young peoples' study trip to Berlin.

1958, Apr. 1 **Wmk. 304** ***Perf. 14***

15fr+7fr, "A Hunter from the Palatinate."

B121 SP60	12fr + 6fr brn red, grn & blk	.20	*.20*
B122 SP60	15fr + 7fr grn, red, blk & gray	.20	*.30*

The surtax was to finance young peoples' study trip to Berlin.

Friedrich Wilhelm Raiffeisen SP61

Dairy Maid SP62

Designs: 15fr+7fr, Girl picking grapes. 30fr+10fr, Farmer with pitchfork.

1958, Oct. 1 **Wmk. 304** ***Perf. 14***

B123 SP61	6fr + 4fr gldn brn & dk brn	.20	.20
B124 SP62	12fr + 6fr grn, red & yel	.20	.20
B125 SP62	15fr + 7fr red, yel & bl	.35	*.40*
B126 SP62	30fr + 10fr bl & ocher	.40	*.60*
	Nos. B123-B126 (4)	1.15	*1.40*

AIR POST STAMPS

Airplane over Saarbrücken — AP1

Perf. 13½

1928, Sept. 19 **Unwmk.** **Photo.**

C1 AP1	50c brown red	2.50	2.00
C2 AP1	1fr dark violet	4.00	2.75

For overprints see Nos. C5, C7.

Saarbrücken Airport and Church of St. Arnual — AP2

1932, Apr. 30

C3 AP2	60c orange red	4.00	3.00
C4 AP2	5fr dark brown	30.00	*65.00*

For overprints see Nos. C6, C8.

Nos. C1-C4 Overprinted like Nos. 139-154 in Various Colors

1934, Nov. 1 ***Perf. 13½, 13½x13***

C5 AP1	50c brn red (R)	3.25	*4.75*
C6 AP2	60c org red (O)	2.40	*2.25*
C7 AP1	1fr dk vio (V)	5.00	*6.50*
C8 AP2	5fr dk brn (Br)	6.25	*9.00*
	Nos. C5-C8 (4)	16.90	*22.50*

French Protectorate

Shadow of Plane over Saar River AP3

Unwmk.

1948, Apr. 1 **Engr.** ***Perf. 13***

C9 AP3	25fr red	2.50	3.00
C10 AP3	50fr dk Prus grn	1.40	1.50
C11 AP3	200fr rose car	13.00	*26.00*
	Nos. C9-C11 (3)	16.90	*30.50*
	Set, never hinged	27.50	

Symbols of the Council of Europe AP4

1950, Aug. 8 **Photo.** ***Perf. 13½***

C12 AP4	200fr red brown	85.00	*190.00*
	Never hinged	150.00	

Saar's admission to the Council of Europe.

AIR POST SEMI-POSTAL STAMP

French Protectorate

Flood Scene SPAP1

Perf. 13½x13

1948, Oct. 12 **Photo.** **Unwmk.**

CB1 SPAP1	25fr + 25fr sep	9.00	*160.00*
	Never hinged	20.00	
a.	Souvenir sheet of 1	150.00	*1,500.*
	Never hinged	350.00	

The surtax was for flood relief.

OFFICIAL STAMPS

Regular Issue of 1922-1923 Overprinted Diagonally in Red or Blue

DIENSTMARKE

Perf. 12½x13½, 13½x12½

1922-23 **Unwmk.**

O1	A19	3c ol grn & straw (R)	.50	*19.00*
O2	A20	5c org & blk (R)	.20	*.25*
O3	A21	10c bl grn (R)	.25	.20
O4	A19	15c dp brn (Bl)	.25	.20
O5	A19	15c org (Bl) ('23)	1.50	.30
O6	A22	20c dk bl & lem (R)	.25	.20
O7	A22	20c brt bl & straw (R) ('23)	1.50	.30
O8	A22	25c red & yel (Bl)	2.25	.60
O9	A22	25c mag & straw (Bl) ('23)	1.75	.30
O10	A23	30c car & yel (Bl)	.25	.20
O11	A24	40c brn & yel (Bl)	.30	.20
O12	A25	50c dk bl & straw (R)	.30	.20
O13	A24	75c dp grn & straw (R)	11.00	18.00
O14	A24	75c blk & straw (R) ('23)	3.00	1.50
O15a	A26	1fr brn red (Bl)	9.00	1.50
		Nos. O1-O15a (15)	32.30	*42.95*

Inverted overprints exist on 10c, 20c, 30c, 50c, 1fr. Double overprints exist on #O4, O6, 1fr.

Regular Issue of 1927-30 Overprinted in Various Colors

DIENSTMARKE

1927-34 *Perf. 13½*

O16 A31 10c dp brn (Bl) ('34) 1.25 1.60
O17 A32 15c ol blk (Bl) ('34) 1.25 *4.75*
O18 A32 20c brn org (Bk) ('31) 1.25 1.10
O19 A32 25c bluish sl (Bl) 1.60 *4.00*
O20a A31 30c ol grn (C) 1.25 .25
O21 A32 40c ol brn (C) 1.25 .20
O22 A32 50c mag (Bl) 2.50 .20
O23 A35 60c red org (Bk) ('30) .80 .20
O24 A32 75c brn vio (C) 1.60 .50
O25 A35 1fr vio (RO) 1.60 .25
O26 A36 2fr brn red (Bl) 1.60 .25
Nos. O16-O26 (11) 15.95 *13.30*

The overprint listed is at a 23 to 25-degree angle. Also at 32-degree angle on Nos. O20-O22, O24-O26.

The overprint on Nos. O16 and O20 is known only inverted. Nos. O21-O26 exist with double overprint.

French Protectorate

Arms — O1

1949, Oct. 1 Engr. *Perf. 14x13*

O27 O1 10c deep carmine .20 *11.00*
O28 O1 30c blue black .20 *12.00*
O29 O1 1fr Prus green .20 .20
O30 O1 2fr orange red .85 .55
O31 O1 5fr blue .25 .20
O32 O1 10fr black .40 .50
O33 O1 12fr red violet 3.25 *3.75*
O34 O1 15fr indigo .40 .20
O35 O1 20fr green .90 .55
O36 O1 30fr violet rose 1.10 *2.00*
O37 O1 50fr purple 1.10 *1.90*
O38 O1 100fr red brown 40.00 *100.00*
Nos. O27-O38 (12) 48.85 *132.85*
Set, never hinged 100.00

ST. CHRISTOPHER

sānt 'kris-tə-fər

LOCATION — Island in the West Indies, southeast of Puerto Rico
GOVT. — A Presidency of the former Leeward Islands Colony
AREA — 68 sq. mi.
POP. — 18,578 (estimated)
CAPITAL — Basseterre

Stamps of St. Christopher were discontinued in 1890 and replaced by those of Leeward Islands. For later issues, inscribed "St. Kitts-Nevis" or "St. Christopher-Nevis-Anguilla," see St. Kitts-Nevis.

12 Pence = 1 Shilling

Queen Victoria — A1

Wmk. Crown and C C (1)

1870, Apr. 1 Typo. *Perf. 12½*

1 A1 1p dull rose 55.00 40.00
2 A1 1p lilac rose 42.50 24.00
3 A1 6p green 90.00 14.00
Nos. 1-3 (3) 187.50 78.00

1875-79 *Perf. 14*

4 A1 1p lilac rose 57.50 10.00
b. Half used as ½p on cover 1,250.
5 A1 2½p red brown ('79) 175.00 *225.00*
6 A1 4p blue ('79) 140.00 13.50
7 A1 6p green 50.00 6.00
a. Horiz. pair, imperf. vert. —
Nos. 4-7 (4) 422.50 254.50

For surcharges see Nos. 18-20.

1882-90 Wmk. Crown and C A (2)

8 A1 ½p green 1.00 1.25
9 A1 1p rose 1.00 2.00
a. Half used as ½p on cover —
10 A1 1p lilac rose 475.00 67.50
a. Diagonal half used as ½p on cover —
11 A1 2½p red brown 175.00 55.00
a. 2½p deep red brown 200.00 65.00
12 A1 2½p ultra ('84) 1.75 1.90
13 A1 4p blue 375.00 27.50
14 A1 4p gray ('84) 1.25 .90
15 A1 6p olive brn ('90) 80.00 *290.00*
16 A1 1sh violet ('87) 85.00 60.00
a. 1sh bright mauve ('90) 75.00 125.00
Nos. 8-16 (9) 1,195. 506.05

For surcharges see Nos. 17, 21-23.

No. 9 Bisected and Handstamp Surcharged in Black

1885, Mar.

17 A1 ½p on half of 1p 24.00 35.00
b. Inverted surcharge 210.00 110.00
c. Unsevered pair 100.00 *110.00*
d. As "c," one surcharge inverted 350.00 250.00
e. Double surcharge — —

No. 7 Surcharged in Black:

Nos. 18, 21

No. 19

No. 20

1884-86 **Wmk. 1**

18 A1 1p on 6p green ('86) 16.00 25.00
a. Inverted surcharge *5,250.*
b. Double surcharge 1,300.
19 A1 4p on 6p green 55.00 45.00
a. Period after "PENCE" 55.00 45.00
b. Double surcharge *1,600.*
20 A1 4p on 6p green ('86) 47.50 77.50
a. Without period after "d" 175.00 225.00
b. Double surcharge *1,450.* *1,500.*
Nos. 18-20 (3) 118.50 147.50

Value for No. 18b is for stamp with pen cancellation or with violet handstamp (revenue cancels).

Nos. 8 and 12 Surcharged in Black Like No. 18 or:

No. 22

ONE PENNY.

No. 23

1887-88 **Wmk. 2**

21 A1 1p on ½p green 27.50 37.50
22 A1 1p on 2½p ('88) 50.00 50.00
a. Inverted surcharge *7,500.* *5,250.*
23 A1 1p on 2½p ('88) *11,000.* *9,000.*

Nos. 22-23 may have been printed using the same type. The bar on No. 22 is done by hand. No. 23 probably is a sheet that was missed when the bars were added.

Antigua No. 18 was used in St. Christopher in 1890. It is canceled "A12" instead of "A02." Values: used $125, on cover $750.

ST. HELENA

sānt 'he-lə-nə

LOCATION — Island in the Atlantic Ocean, 1,200 miles west of Angola
GOVT. — British Crown Colony
AREA — 47 sq. mi.
POP. — 7,145 (?) (1999 est.)
CAPITAL — Jamestown

12 Pence = 1 Shilling
20 Shillings = 1 Pound
100 Pence = 1 Pound (1971)

Catalogue values for unused stamps in this country are for Never Hinged items, beginning with Scott 128 in the regular postage section, Scott B1 in the semi-postal section and Scott J1 in the postage due section.

Values for unused stamps are for examples with original gum as defined in the catalogue introduction. Very fine examples of Nos. 2-7, 11-39a and 47-47b will have perforations touching the design on one or more sides due to the narrow spacing of the stamps on the plates. Stamps with perfs clear of the design on all four sides are scarce and will command higher prices.

Watermark

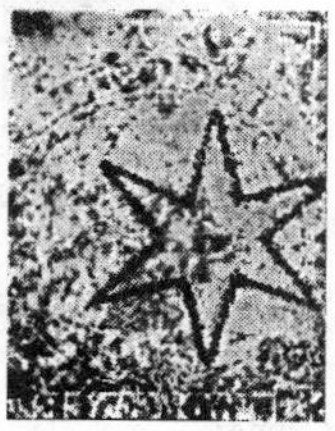

Wmk. 6- Star

Queen Victoria — A1

1856, Jan. Wmk. 6 Engr. *Imperf.*

1 A1 6p blue 500.00 175.00

For types surcharged see Nos. 8-39, 47.

1861 *Clean-Cut Perf. 14 to 15½*

2 A1 6p blue 1,600. 275.00

1863 *Rough Perf. 14 to 15½*

2B A1 6p blue 400.00 125.00

1873-74 Wmk. 1 *Perf. 12½*

3 A1 6p dull blue 550.00 100.00
4 A1 6p ultra ('74) 350.00 82.50

1879 *Perf. 14x12½*

5 A1 6p gray blue 275.00 42.50

1889 *Perf. 14*

6 A1 6p gray blue 325.00 50.00

1889 Wmk. Crown and C A (2)

7 A1 6p gray 10.00 5.50

Type of 1856 Surcharged

ONE PENNY **ONE PENNY**

a b

1863 Wmk. 1 *Imperf.*

Long Bar, 16, 17, 18 or 19mm

8 A1(a) 1p on 6p brown red (surch. 17mm) 110.00 *160.00*
a. Double surcharge 5,500. 2,750.
b. Surcharge omitted *13,500.*
9 A1(a) 1p on 6p brown red (surch. 19mm) 110.00 *150.00*
10 A1(b) 4p on 6p carmine 500.00 240.00
b. Double surcharge *10,000.* *8,500.*

1864-73 *Perf. 12½*

11 A1(a) 1p on 6p brn red 30.00 22.50
a. Double surcharge *5,750.*
12 A1(b) 1p on 6p brn red ('71) 65.00 16.00
a. Blue black surcharge *1,150.* *800.00*
13 A1(b) 2p on 6p yel ('73) 72.50 35.00
a. Blue black surcharge *6,000.* *3,500.*
14 A1(b) 3p on 6p dk vio ('73) 70.00 42.50
15 A1(b) 4p on 6p car 115.00 40.00
a. Double surcharge *5,500.*
16 A1(b) 1sh on 6p grn (bar 16 to 17mm) 175.00 22.50
a. Double surcharge *18,000.*
17 A1(b) 1sh on 6p dp grn (bar 18mm) ('73) 300.00 14.00
a. Blue black surcharge —

1868

Short Bar, 14 or 15mm

18 A1(a) 1p on 6p brn red 125.00 45.00
a. Imperf., pair 7,500.
b. Double surcharge —
19 A1(b) 2p on 6p yellow 140.00 57.50
a. Imperf., pair 17,000.
20 A1(b) 3p on 6p dk vio 67.50 45.00
a. Double surcharge 6,750.
b. Imperf., pair 1,700.
21 A1(b) 4p on 6p car (words 18mm) 75.00 45.00
a. Double surcharge *5,000.*
b. Imperf., pair 19,000.
22 A1(b) 4p on 6p car (words 19mm) 180.00 110.00
a. Words double, 18mm and 19mm *16,000.* *11,000.*
b. Imperf. —
23 A1(a) 1sh on 6p yel grn 400.00 125.00
a. Double surcharge *12,000.*
b. Pair, one without surcharge *12,000.*
24 A1(a) 5sh on 6p org 35.00 52.50

No. 22 exists with surcharge omitted.

1882 *Perf. 14x12½*

25 A1(a) 1p on 6p brown red 55.00 13.50
26 A1(b) 2p on 6p yellow 75.00 45.00
27 A1(b) 3p on 6p violet 170.00 65.00
28 A1(b) 4p on 6p carmine (words 16mm) 80.00 50.00

1883 *Perf. 14*

29 A1(a) 1p on 6p brown red 70.00 13.50
30 A1(b) 2p on 6p yellow 80.00 20.00
31 A1(a) 1sh on 6p yel grn 18.00 11.00

1882 *Perf. 14x12½*

Long Bar, 18mm

32 A1(b) 1sh on 6p dp grn 350.00 20.00

1884-94 Wmk. 2 *Perf. 14*

Short Bar, 14 or 14½mm

33 A1(b) ½p on 6p grn (words 17mm) 6.50 8.00
a. ½p on 6p emer, blurred print (words 17mm) ('84) 6.00 8.00
b. Double surcharge 1,200. 1,200.
34 A1(b) ½p on 6p grn (words 15mm) ('94) 1.10 1.40
35 A1(a) 1p on 6p red ('87) 2.50 2.00
36 A1(b) 2p on 6p yel ('94) 1.25 3.50
37 A1(b) 3p on 6p dp vio ('87) 2.75 3.00
a. 3p on 6p red violet 4.50 6.50
b. Double surcharge,#37a *9,000.* *6,000.*
c. Double surcharge, #37 *9,000.*
38 A1(b) 4p on 6p pale brn (words 16½mm; '90) 13.50 20.00
a. 4p on 6p dk brn (words 17mm; '94) 16.00 8.00
b. With thin bar below thick one 500.00

1894

Long Bar, 18mm

39 A1(b) 1sh on 6p yel grn 30.00 20.00
a. Double surcharge *4,000.*

See note after No. 47.

Queen Victoria — A3

1890-97 Typo. *Perf. 14*

40 A3 ½p green ('97) 3.25 4.25
41 A3 1p rose ('96) 8.75 1.00
42 A3 1½p red brn & grn 4.75 6.50
43 A3 2p yellow ('96) 5.25 9.00
44 A3 2½p ultra ('96) 6.50 9.50
45 A3 5p violet ('96) 11.00 25.00
46 A3 10p brown ('96) 16.50 *45.00*
Nos. 40-46 (7) 56.00 *100.25*

Type of 1856 Surcharged

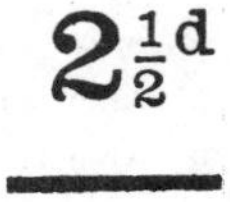

1893 Engr. Wmk. 2

47	A1	2½p on 6p blue	2.00	5.00
a.		Double surcharge	15,000.	
b.		Double impression	6,250.	

In 1905 remainders of Nos. 34-47 were sold by the postal officials. They are canceled with bars, arranged in the shape of diamonds, in purple ink. No such cancellation was ever used on the island and the stamps so canceled are of slight value. With this cancellation removed, these remainders are sometimes offered as unused. Some have been recanceled with a false dated postmark.

King Edward VII — A5

1902 Typo. Wmk. 2

48	A5	½p green	1.50	1.10
49	A5	1p carmine rose	4.25	.85

Government House — A6

"The Wharf" — A7

1903, June Wmk. 1

50	A6	½p gray grn & brn	1.75	2.25
51	A7	1p carmine & blk	1.25	.50
52	A6	2p ol grn & blk	5.25	1.50
53	A7	8p brown & blk	15.00	32.50
54	A6	1sh org buff & brn	15.00	35.00
55	A7	2sh violet & blk	42.50	75.00
		Nos. 50-55 (6)	80.75	146.75

A8

1908, May Wmk. 3

56	A8	2½p ultra	1.40	1.50
57	A8	4p black & red, *yel*	1.50	8.00
58	A8	6p dull violet	3.50	15.00
		Nos. 56-58 (3)	6.40	24.50

Wmk. 2

60	A8	10sh grn & red, *grn*	175.00	225.00

Nos. 57 and 58 exist on both ordinary and chalky paper; No. 56 on ordinary and No. 60 on chalky paper.

Government House — A9

"The Wharf" — A10

1912-16 Ordinary Paper Wmk. 3

61	A9	½p green & blk	1.25	7.50
62	A10	1p carmine & blk	1.40	1.40
a.		1p scarlet & black ('16)	20.00	32.50
63	A10	1½p orange & blk	2.25	4.50
64	A9	2p gray & black	2.25	1.40
65	A10	2½p ultra & blk	1.90	4.50
66	A9	3p vio & blk, *yel*	1.90	4.00
67	A10	8p dull vio & blk	5.25	40.00
68	A9	1sh black, *green*	7.50	27.50
69	A10	2sh ultra & blk, *bl*	25.00	65.00
70	A10	3sh violet & blk	45.00	105.00
		Nos. 61-70 (10)	93.70	260.80

See Nos. 75-77.

A11

A12

Die I

For description of dies I and II see back of this section of the Catalogue.

1912

Chalky Paper

71	A11	4p black & red, *yel*	7.25	22.50
72	A11	6p dull vio & red vio	3.75	8.00

1913

Ordinary Paper

73	A12	4p black & red, *yel*	5.25	2.25
74	A12	6p dull vio & red vio	11.00	22.50

1922 Wmk. 4

75	A10	1p green	1.00	21.00
76	A10	1½p rose red	7.00	22.50
77	A9	3p ultra	14.50	42.50
		Nos. 75-77 (3)	22.50	86.00

Badge of the Colony — A13

1922-27 Wmk. 4

Chalky Paper

79	A13	½p black & gray	1.00	1.40
80	A13	1p grn & blk	1.50	1.00
81	A13	1½p rose red	2.25	9.75
82	A13	2p pale gray & gray	2.50	1.60
83	A13	3p ultra	1.75	3.25
84	A13	5p red & grn, *emer*	2.50	4.50
85	A13	6p red vio & blk	3.25	6.50
86	A13	8p violet & blk	2.75	5.25
87	A13	1sh dk brn & blk	5.00	7.25
88	A13	1sh6p grn & blk, *emer*	12.00	37.50
89	A13	2sh ultra & vio, *bl*	13.50	30.00
90	A13	2sh6p car & blk, *yel*	11.00	40.00
91	A13	5sh grn & blk, *yel*	32.50	60.00
92	A13	7sh6p orange & blk	65.00	95.00
93	A13	10sh ol grn & blk	100.00	125.00
94	A13	15sh vio & blk, *bl*	925.00	1,325.
		Nos. 79-93 (15)	256.50	428.00

Nos. 88, 90, and 91 are on ordinary paper.

Wmk. 3

Chalky Paper

95	A13	4p black, *yel*	6.00	7.00
96	A13	1sh6p bl grn & blk, *grn*	20.00	45.00
97	A13	2sh6p car & blk, *yel*	24.00	47.50
98	A13	5sh grn & blk, *yel*	37.50	70.00
99	A13	£1 red vio & blk, *red*	400.00	425.00
		Nos. 95-99 (5)	487.50	594.50

Issued: ½p, 1½p, 2p, 3p, 4p, 8p, 2/23; 5p, #88-91, 1927; others, 6/22.

Centenary Issue

Lot and Lot's Wife — A14

Plantation; Queen Victoria and Kings William IV, Edward VII, George V A15

Map of the Colony A16

Quay, Jamestown A17

View of James Valley — A18

View of Jamestown A19

View of Mundens A20

St. Helena — A21

View of High Knoll — A22

Badge of the Colony A23

Perf. 12

1934, Apr. 23 Engr. Wmk. 4

101	A14	½p dk vio & blk	.55	.60
102	A15	1p green & blk	.70	.85
103	A16	1½p red & blk	2.25	2.75
104	A17	2p orange & blk	1.75	1.90
105	A18	3p blue & blk	1.50	5.00
106	A19	6p lt blue & blk	3.00	3.50
107	A20	1sh dk brn & blk	6.50	18.00
108	A21	2sh6p car & blk	32.50	45.00
109	A22	5sh choc & blk	70.00	80.00
110	A23	10sh red vio & black	190.00	225.00
		Nos. 101-110 (10)	308.75	382.60

Common Design Types pictured following the introduction.

Silver Jubilee Issue

Common Design Type

1935, May 6 *Perf. 13½x14*

111	CD301	1½p car & dk blue	.60	2.00
112	CD301	2p gray blk & ultra	1.40	1.00
113	CD301	6p indigo & grn	6.00	3.75
114	CD301	1sh brt vio & ind	7.00	9.25
		Nos. 111-114 (4)	15.00	16.00
		Set, never hinged	30.00	

Coronation Issue

Common Design Type

1937, May 19

115	CD302	1p deep green	.20	.20
116	CD302	2p deep orange	.20	.20
117	CD302	3p bright ultra	.30	.30
		Nos. 115-117 (3)	.70	.70
		Set, never hinged	2.00	

Badge of the Colony — A24

1938-40 *Perf. 12½*

118	A24	½p purple	.20	.20
119	A24	1p dp green	9.50	3.00
119A	A24	1p org yel ('40)	.20	.20
120	A24	1½p carmine	.20	.20
121	A24	2p orange	.20	.20
122	A24	3p ultra	47.50	27.50
122A	A24	3p gray ('40)	.20	.25
122B	A24	4p ultra ('40)	.90	.25
123	A24	6p gray blue	.90	.40
123A	A24	8p olive ('40)	1.75	1.10
124	A24	1sh sepia	.45	.55
125	A24	2sh6p deep claret	8.00	3.00
126	A24	5sh brown	10.00	7.00
127	A24	10sh violet	10.00	10.00
		Nos. 118-127 (14)	90.00	53.85
		Set, never hinged	160.00	

Issue dates: May 12, 1938, July 8, 1940.
See Nos. 136-138.

Catalogue values for unused stamps in this section, from this point to the end of the section, are for Never Hinged items.

Peace Issue

Common Design Type

Perf. 13½x14

1946, Oct. 21 Wmk. 4 Engr.

128	CD303	2p deep orange	.20	.20
129	CD303	4p deep blue	.20	.20

Silver Wedding Issue

Common Design Types

1948, Oct. 20 Photo. *Perf. 14x14½*

130	CD304	3p black	.25	.25

Engr.; Name Typo.

Perf. 11½x11

131	CD305	10sh blue violet	20.00	30.00

UPU Issue

Common Design Types

Engr.; Name Typo. on 4p, 6p

1949, Oct. 10 *Perf. 13½, 11x11½*

132	CD306	3p rose carmine	.25	.25
133	CD307	4p indigo	3.75	1.00
134	CD308	6p olive	.55	1.00
135	CD309	1sh slate	.45	1.25
		Nos. 132-135 (4)	5.00	3.50

George VI Type of 1938

1949, Nov. 1 Engr. *Perf. 12½*

Center in Black

136	A24	1p blue green	.60	.80
137	A24	1½p carmine rose	.60	.80
138	A24	2p carmine	.60	.80
		Nos. 136-138 (3)	1.80	2.40

Coronation Issue

Common Design Type

1953, June 2 *Perf. 13½x13*

139	CD312	3p purple & black	1.00	.80

Badge of the Colony A25

A26

A27

Designs: 1p, Flax plantation. 1½p, Heart-shaped waterfall. 2p, Lace making. 2½p, Drying flax. 3p, Wire bird. 4p, Flagstaff and barn. 6p, Donkeys carrying flax. 7p, Map. 1sh, Entrance, government offices. 2sh 6p, Cutting flax. 5sh, Jamestown. 10sh, Longwood house.

1953, Aug. 4 *Perf. 13½x14, 14x13½*

Center and Denomination in Black

140	A25	½p	emerald	.30	.20
141	A25	1p	dark green	.20	.20
142	A26	1½p	red violet	1.60	.50
143	A25	2p	rose lake	.45	.25
144	A25	2½p	red	.35	.30
145	A25	3p	brown	3.00	.30
146	A25	4p	deep blue	.35	.35
147	A25	6p	purple	.35	.30
148	A25	7p	gray	.60	1.00
149	A25	1sh	dk car rose	.35	.35
150	A25	2sh 6p	violet	12.00	3.75
151	A25	5sh	chocolate	16.00	8.00
152	A25	10sh	orange	37.50	22.00
			Nos. 140-152 (13)	73.05	37.50

Perf. 11½

1956, Jan. 3 Wmk. 4 Engr.

153	A27	3p dk car rose & blue	.20	.20
154	A27	4p redsh brown & blue	.35	.35
155	A27	6p purple & blue	.55	.55
		Nos. 153-155 (3)	1.10	1.10

Cent. of the 1st St. Helena postage stamp.

Arms of East India Company A28

Designs: 6p, Dutton's ship "London" off James Bay. 1sh, Memorial stone from fort built by Governor Dutton.

Perf. 12½x13

1959, May 5 Wmk. 314

156	A28	3p rose & black	.20	.20
157	A28	6p gray & yellow green	.45	.45
158	A28	1sh orange & black	.65	.65
		Nos. 156-158 (3)	1.30	1.30

300th anniv. of the landing of Capt. John Dutton on St. Helena and of the 1st settlement.

Cape Canary A29

Elizabeth II A30

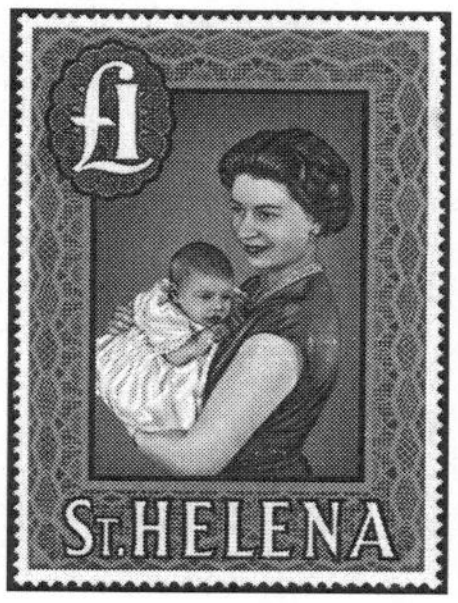

Queen and Prince Andrew A31

Designs: 1p, Cunning fish, horiz. 2p, Brittle starfish, horiz. 4½p, Redwood flower. 6p, Red fody (Madagascar weaver). 7p, Trumpetfish, horiz. 10p, Keeled feather starfish, horiz. 1sh, Gumwood flowers. 1sh6p, Fairy tern. 2sh6p, Orange starfish, horiz. 5sh, Night-blooming cereus. 10sh, Deepwater bull's-eye, horiz.

Perf. 11½x12, 12x11½

1961, Dec. 12 Photo. Wmk. 314

159	A29	1p	multicolored	.20	.20
160	A29	1½p	multicolored	.25	.20
161	A29	2p	gray & red	.20	.20
162	A30	3p	dk blue, rose & grnsh blue	.40	.35
163	A29	4½p	slate, brn & grn	.50	.35
164	A29	6p	cit, brn & dp car	2.00	.40
165	A29	7p	vio, blk & red brn	.40	.40
166	A29	10p	blue & dp cl	.70	.65
167	A29	1sh	red brn, grn & yel	.70	.65
168	A29	1sh6p	gray bl & blk	5.00	1.75
169	A29	2sh6p	grnsh bl, yel & red	3.75	2.75
170	A29	5sh	grn, brn & yel	7.50	4.25
171	A29	10sh	gray bl, blk & sal	10.50	9.50

Perf. 14x14½

172	A31	£1	turq blue & choc	20.00	22.50
			Nos. 159-172 (14)	52.10	44.15

For overprints see Nos. 176-179.

Freedom from Hunger Issue

Common Design Type

1963, June 4 *Perf. 14x14½*

173	CD314	1sh6p ultra	3.00	2.50

Red Cross Centenary Issue

Common Design Type

Wmk. 314

1963, Sept. 2 Litho. *Perf. 13*

174	CD315	3p black & red	.30	.30
175	CD315	1sh6p ultra & red	3.50	3.50

Nos. 159, 162, 164 and 168 Overprinted: "FIRST LOCAL POST / 4th JANUARY 1965"

Perf. 11½x12, 12x11½

1965, Jan. 4 Photo. Wmk. 314

176	A29	1p	multicolored	.20	.20
177	A30	3p	dk bl, rose & grnsh bl	.20	.20
178	A29	6p	cit, brn & dp car	.25	.20
179	A29	1sh6p	gray blue & blk	.35	.20
			Nos. 176-179 (4)	1.00	.80

Establishment of the 1st internal postal service on the island.

ITU Issue

Common Design Type

Perf. 11x11½

1965, May 17 Litho. Wmk. 314

180	CD317	3p ultra & gray	.30	.30
181	CD317	6p red lil & blue grn	.70	.30

Intl. Cooperation Year Issue

Common Design Type

1965, Oct. 25 Litho. *Perf. 14½*

182	CD318	1p blue grn & claret	.20	.20
183	CD318	6p lt violet & green	1.00	.20

Churchill Memorial Issue

Common Design Type

1966, Jan. 24 Photo. *Perf. 14*

Design in Black, Gold and Carmine Rose

184	CD319	1p	bright blue	.20	.20
185	CD319	3p	green	.40	.40
186	CD319	6p	brown	.55	.55
187	CD319	1sh6p	violet	.85	.85
			Nos. 184-187 (4)	2.00	2.00

World Cup Soccer Issue

Common Design Type

1966, July 1 Litho. *Perf. 14*

188	CD321	3p multicolored	.40	.30
189	CD321	6p multicolored	1.00	.30

WHO Headquarters Issue

Common Design Type

1966, Sept. 20 Litho. *Perf. 14*

190	CD322	3p	multicolored	1.00	.20
191	CD322	1sh6p	multicolored	2.75	1.50

UNESCO Anniversary Issue

Common Design Type

1966, Dec. 1 Litho. *Perf. 14*

192	CD323	3p	"Education"	.50	.45
193	CD323	6p	"Science"	1.00	.80
194	CD323	1sh6p	"Culture"	3.50	3.25
			Nos. 192-194 (3)	5.00	4.50

Badge of St. Helena — A32

Perf. 14½x14

1967, May 5 Photo. Wmk. 314

195	A32	1sh dk grn & multi	.30	.30
196	A32	2sh6p blue & multi	.70	.70
a.		Carmine omitted	450.00	

St. Helena's New Constitution.

The Great Fire of London A33

3p, Three-master Charles. 6p, Boats bringing new settlers to shore. 1sh6p, Settlers at work.

Perf. 13½x13

1967, Sept. 4 Engr. Wmk. 314

197	A33	1p	black & carmine	.20	.20
198	A33	3p	black & vio blue	.20	.20
199	A33	6p	black & dull violet	.20	.20
200	A33	1sh6p	black & ol green	.30	.20
			Nos. 197-200 (4)	.90	.80

Tercentenary of the arrival of settlers from London after the Great Fire of Sept. 2-4, 1666.

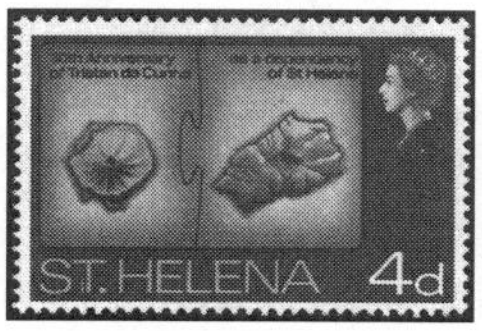

Maps of Tristan da Cunha and St. Helena A34

Designs: 8p, 2sh3p, Maps of St. Helena and Tristan da Cunha.

Perf. 14x14½

1968, June 4 Photo. Wmk. 314

Maps in Sepia

201	A34	4p	dp red lilac	.20	.20
202	A34	8p	olive	.20	.25
203	A34	1sh9p	deep ultra	.20	.35
204	A34	2sh3p	Prus blue	.25	.35
			Nos. 201-204 (4)	.85	1.15

30th anniv. of Tristan da Cunha as a Dependency of St. Helena.

Sir Hudson Lowe A35

1sh6p, 2sh6p, Sir George Bingham.

Perf. 13½x13

1968, Sept. 4 Litho. Wmk. 314

205	A35	3p	multicolored	.20	.20
206	A35	9p	multicolored	.20	.20
207	A35	1sh6p	multicolored	.20	.20
208	A35	2sh6p	multicolored	.30	.30
			Nos. 205-208 (4)	.90	.90

Abolition of slavery in St. Helena, 150th anniv.

Road Construction — A36

Designs: 1p, Electricity development. 1½p, Dentist. 2p, Pest control. 3p, Apartment houses in Jamestown. 4p, Pasture and livestock improvement. 6p, School children listening to broadcast. 8p, Country cottages. 10p, New school buildings. 1sh, Reforestation. 1sh6p, Heavy lift crane. 2sh6p, Playing children in Lady Field Children's Home. 5sh, Agricultural training. 10sh, Ward in New General Hospital. £1, Lifeboat "John Dutton."

Wmk. 314

1968, Nov. 4 Litho. *Perf. 13½*

209	A36	½p	multicolored	.20	.20
210	A36	1p	multicolored	.20	.20
211	A36	1½p	multicolored	.20	.20
212	A36	2p	multicolored	.20	.20
213	A36	3p	multicolored	.20	.20
214	A36	4p	multicolored	.20	.20
215	A36	6p	multicolored	.20	.20
216	A36	8p	multicolored	.25	.25
217	A36	10p	multicolored	.30	.30
218	A36	1sh	multicolored	.40	.40
219	A36	1sh6p	multicolored	.50	.50
220	A36	2sh6p	multicolored	.95	.95
221	A36	5sh	multicolored	1.60	1.60
222	A36	10sh	multicolored	3.25	3.25
223	A36	£1	multicolored	8.50	8.50
			Nos. 209-223 (15)	17.15	17.15

See Nos. 244-256.

Brig Perseverance, 1819 — A37

Ships: 8p, M.S. Dane, 1857. 1sh9p, S.S. Llandovery Castle, 1925. 2sh3p, M.S. Good Hope Castle, 1969.

1969, Apr. 19 Litho. *Perf. 13½*

224	A37	4p	violet & multi	.30	.30
225	A37	8p	ocher & multi	.45	.45
226	A37	1sh9p	ver & multi	.60	.60
227	A37	2sh3p	dk blue & multi	.65	.65
			Nos. 224-227 (4)	2.00	2.00

Issued in recognition of St. Helena's dependence on sea mail.

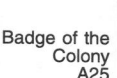

Surgeon and Officer (Light Company) 20th Foot, 1816 — A38

British Uniforms: 6p, Warrant Officer and Drummer, 53rd Foot, 1815. 1sh8p, Drum Major, 66th Foot, 1816, and Royal Artillery Officer, 1820. 2sh6p, Private 91st Foot and 2nd Corporal, Royal Sappers and Miners, 1832.

Perf. 14x14½

1969, Sept. 3 Litho. Wmk. 314

228	A38	6p	red & multi	.50	.50
229	A38	8p	blue & multi	.65	.65
230	A38	1sh8p	green & multi	.65	.65
231	A38	2sh6p	gray & multi	.65	.65
			Nos. 228-231 (4)	2.45	2.45

Charles Dickens, "The Pickwick Papers" A39

Dickens and: 8p, "Oliver Twist." 1sh6p, "Martin Chuzzlewit." 2sh6p, "Bleak House."

Perf. 13½x13

1970, June 9 Litho. Wmk. 314

232	A39	4p	dk brown & multi	.20	.20
233	A39	8p	slate & multi	.40	.20
234	A39	1sh6p	multicolored	.65	.25
235	A39	2sh6p	multicolored	1.40	.35
			Nos. 232-235 (4)	2.65	1.00

Charles Dickens (1812-70), English novelist.

Mouth to Mouth Resuscitation — A40

Centenary of British Red Cross Society: 9p, Girl in wheelchair and nurse. 1sh9p, First aid. 2sh3p, British Red Cross Society emblem.

1970, Sept. 15 *Perf. 14½*

236	A40	6p	bister, red & blk	.20	.20
237	A40	9p	lt blue grn, red & blk	.20	.20
238	A40	1sh9p	gray, red & blk	.25	.20
239	A40	2sh3p	pale vio, red & blk	.35	.30
			Nos. 236-239 (4)	1.00	.90

A41

A42

Regimental Emblems: 4p, Officer's Shako Plate, 20th Foot, 1812-16. 9p, Officer's breast plate, 66th Foot, before 1818. 1sh3p, Officer's full dress shako, 91st Foot, 1816. 2sh11p, Ensign's shako, 53rd Foot, 1815.

Wmk. 314

1970, Nov. 2 Litho. *Perf. 14½*

240	A41	4p	multicolored	.20	.20
241	A41	9p	red & multi	.40	.40
242	A41	1sh3p	dk gray & multi	.65	.65
243	A41	2sh11p	dk gray grn & multi	1.00	1.00
			Nos. 240-243 (4)	2.25	2.25

See Nos. 263-270, 273-276.

Type of 1968
"P" instead of "d"

1971, Feb. 15 Litho. *Perf. 13½*

244	A36	½p	like #210	.20	.20
245	A36	1p	like #211	.20	.20
246	A36	1½p	like #212	.20	.20
247	A36	2p	like #213	.30	.30
a.			Perf. 14½ ('75)	.55	.55
248	A36	2½p	like #214	.35	.35
249	A36	3½p	like #215	.45	.45
250	A36	4½p	like #216	.55	.55
251	A36	5p	like #217	.70	.70
252	A36	7½p	like #218	.90	.90
253	A36	10p	like #219	1.00	1.00
254	A36	12½p	like #220	1.40	1.40
255	A36	25p	like #221	2.75	2.75
256	A36	50p	like #222	12.50	12.50
			Nos. 244-256 (13)	21.50	21.50

The paper of Nos. 244-256 is thinner than the paper of Nos. 209-223 and No. 223 (£1) has been reprinted in slightly different colors.

Perf. 14x14½

1971, Apr. 5 Litho. Wmk. 314

St. Helena, from Italian Miniature, 1460

257	A42	2p	violet blue & multi	.20	.20
258	A42	5p	multicolored	.25	.25
259	A42	7½p	multicolored	.40	.40
260	A42	12½p	olive & multi	.65	.65
			Nos. 257-260 (4)	1.50	1.50

Easter 1971.

Napoleon, after J. L. David, and Tomb in St. Helena A43

34p, Napoleon, by Hippolyte Paul Delaroche.

1971, May 5 *Perf. 13½*

261	A43	2p	multicolored	.25	.20
262	A43	34p	multicolored	2.75	2.10

Sesquicentennial of the death of Napoleon Bonaparte (1769-1821).

Military Type of 1970

1½p, Sword Hilt, Artillery Private, 1815. 4p, Baker rifle, socket bayonet, c. 1816. 6p, Infantry officer's sword hilt, 1822. 22½p, Baker rifle, light sword bayonet, c. 1823.

1971, Nov. 10 *Perf. 14½*

263	A41	1½p	green & multi	.75	.20
264	A41	4p	gray & multi	1.00	.35
265	A41	6p	purple & multi	1.00	.45
266	A41	22½p	multicolored	1.75	1.50
			Nos. 263-266 (4)	4.50	2.50

1972, June 19

Designs: 2p, Royal Sappers and Miners breastplate, 1823. 5p, Infantry sergeant's pike, 1830. 7½p, Royal Artillery officer's breastplate, 1830. 12½p, English military pistol, 1800.

267	A41	2p	multicolored	.50	.20
268	A41	5p	plum & black	.75	.50
269	A41	7½p	dp blue & multi	1.00	.60
270	A41	12½p	olive & multi	1.00	2.00
			Nos. 267-270 (4)	3.25	3.30

Silver Wedding Issue, 1972
Common Design Type

Design: Queen Elizabeth II, Prince Philip, St. Helena plover and white fairy tern.

1972, Nov. 20 Photo. *Perf. 14x14½*

271	CD324	2p	sl grn & multi	.20	*.35*
272	CD324	16p	rose brn & multi	.55	*.75*

Military Type of 1970

Designs: 2p, Shako, 53rd Foot, 1815. 5p, Band and Drums sword hilt, 1830. 7½p, Royal Sappers and Miners officers' hat, 1830. 12½p, General's sword hilt, 1831.

1973, Sept. 20 Litho. *Perf. 14½*

273	A41	2p	dull brown & multi	.85	.50
274	A41	5p	multicolored	1.00	1.00
275	A41	7½p	olive grn & multi	1.40	1.25
276	A41	12½p	lilac & multi	1.75	1.50
			Nos. 273-276 (4)	5.00	4.25

Princess Anne's Wedding Issue
Common Design Type

1973, Nov. 14 Wmk. 314 *Perf. 14*

277	CD325	2p	multicolored	.20	.20
278	CD325	18p	multicolored	.30	.30

Westminster and Claudine Beached During Storm, 1849 — A45

Designs: 4p, East Indiaman True Briton, 1790. 6p, General Goddard in action off St. Helena, 1795. 22½p, East Indiaman Kent burning in Bay of Biscay, 1825.

Perf. 14½x14

1973, Dec. 17 Litho. Wmk. 314

279	A45	1½p	multicolored	.25	*.45*
280	A45	4p	multicolored	.45	*.70*
281	A45	6p	multicolored	.45	*.70*
282	A45	22½p	multicolored	2.10	*2.25*
			Nos. 279-282 (4)	3.25	4.10

Tercentenary of the East India Company Charter.

UPU Emblem, Ships A46

Design: 25p, UPU emblem and letters.

1974, Oct. 15 *Perf. 14½x14*

283	A46	5p	blue & multi	.20	.20
284	A46	25p	red & multi	.80	.80
a.			Souvenir sheet of 2, #283-284	1.00	*1.25*

Centenary of Universal Postal Union.

Churchill and Blenheim Palace — A47

25p, Churchill, Tower Bridge & Thames.

1974, Nov. 30 Wmk. 373 *Perf. 14½*

285	A47	5p	black & multi	.20	.20
286	A47	25p	black & multi	.80	.80
a.			Souvenir sheet of 2, #285-286	1.00	*2.00*

Sir Winston Churchill (1874-1965).

Capt. Cook and Jamestown — A48

5p, Capt. Cook and "Resolution," vert.

Perf. 14x13½, 13½x14

1975, July 14 Litho.

287	A48	5p	multicolored	.75	.35
288	A48	25p	multicolored	1.25	*2.10*

Return of Capt. James Cook to St. Helena, bicent.

Mellissia Begonifolia — A49

Designs: 5p, Mellissius adumbratus (insect). 12p, Aegialitis St. Helena (bird), horiz. 25p, Scorpaenia mellissii (fish), horiz.

1975, Oct. 20 Wmk. 373 *Perf. 13*

289	A49	2p	gray & multi	.20	.20
290	A49	5p	gray & multi	.25	.25
291	A49	12p	gray & multi	.60	.60
292	A49	25p	gray & multi	.70	.70
			Nos. 289-292 (4)	1.75	1.75

Centenary of the publication of "St. Helena," by John Charles Melliss.

Pound Note A50

Design: 33p, 5-pound note.

1976, Apr. 15 Wmk. 314 *Perf. 13½*

293	A50	8p	claret & multi	.35	.35
294	A50	33p	multicolored	.90	.90

First issue of St. Helena bank notes.

St. Helena No. 8 — A51

Designs: 8p, St. Helena No. 80, vert. 25p, Freighter Good Hope Castle.

Perf. 13½x14, 14x13½

1976, May 4 Litho. Wmk. 373

295	A51	5p	buff, brown & blk	.20	.20
296	A51	8p	lt grn, grn & blk	.25	.25
297	A51	25p	multicolored	.55	.80
			Nos. 295-297 (3)	1.00	1.25

Festival of stamps 1976. For souvenir sheet containing No. 297 see Ascension No. 214a.

High Knoll, by Capt. Barnett A52

Views on St. Helena, lithographs: 3p, Friar Rock, by G. H. Bellasis, 1815. 5p, Column Lot, by Bellasis. 6p, Sandy Bay Valley, by H. Salt, 1809. 8p, View from Castle terrace, by Bellasis. 9p, The Briars, 1815. 10p, Plantation House, by J. Wathen, 1821. 15p, Longwood House, by Wathen, 1821. 18p, St. Paul's Church, by Vincent Brooks. 26p, St. James's Valley, by Capt. Hastings, 1815. 40p, St. Matthew's Church, Longwood, by Brooks. £1, St. Helena and sailing ship, by Bellasis. £2, Sugar Loaf Hill, by Wathen, 1821.

Wmk. 373

1976, Nov. 28 Litho. *Perf. 14*

Size: 38½x25mm

298	A52	1p	multicolored	.20	*.85*
299	A52	3p	multicolored	.20	*.85*
300	A52	5p	multicolored	.20	*.85*
301	A52	6p	multicolored	.20	*.85*
302	A52	8p	multicolored	.20	*.85*
303	A52	9p	multicolored	.20	*.85*
304	A52	10p	multicolored	.25	*.55*
305	A52	15p	multicolored	.35	*.50*
306	A52	18p	multicolored	.45	*1.00*
307	A52	26p	multicolored	.65	*.85*
308	A52	40p	multicolored	.85	*1.50*

Size: 47½x35mm

Perf. 13½

309 A52 £1 multicolored 2.25 3.00
310 A52 £2 multicolored 4.50 5.00
Nos. 298-310 (13) 10.50 17.50

Issue dates: 1p, 3p, 5p, 8p, 10p, 18p, 26p, 40p, £1, Sept. 28; others Nov. 23.
1p, 10p and £2 reissued inscribed 1982.
For overprints see Nos. 376-377.

Royal Party Leaving St. Helena, 1947 — A53

15p, Queen's scepter, dove. 26p, Prince Philip paying homage to the Queen.

1977, Feb. 7 Wmk. 373 *Perf. 13*

311 A53 8p multicolored .20 .20
312 A53 15p multicolored .25 *.30*
313 A53 26p multicolored .30 *.50*
Nos. 311-313 (3) .75 1.00

25th anniv. of the reign of Elizabeth II.

Halley's Comet, from Bayeux Tapestry A54

8p, 17th cent. sextant. 27p, Edmund Halley and Halley's Mount, St. Helena.

1977, Aug. 23 Litho. *Perf. 14*

314 A54 5p multicolored .45 .45
315 A54 8p multicolored .55 .55
316 A54 27p multicolored 1.25 1.25
Nos. 314-316 (3) 2.25 2.25

Edmund Halley's visit to St. Helena, 300th anniv.

Elizabeth II Coronation Anniversary Issue

Common Design Types

Souvenir Sheet

Unwmk.

1978, June 2 Litho. *Perf. 15*

317 Sheet of 6 1.75 1.75
a. CD326 25p Black dragon of Ulster .30 .30
b. CD327 25p Elizabeth II .30 .30
c. CD328 25p Sea Lion .30 .30

No. 317 contains 2 se-tenant strips of Nos. 317a-317c, separated by horizontal gutter.

St. Helena, 17th Century Engraving — A55

Designs: 5p, 9p, 15p, Various Chinese porcelain and other utensils salvaged from wreck. 8p, Bronze cannon. 20p, Dutch East Indiaman.

Wmk. 373

1978, Aug. 14 Litho. *Perf. 14½*

318 A55 3p multicolored .20 .20
319 A55 5p multicolored .20 .20
320 A55 8p multicolored .25 .25
321 A55 9p multicolored .30 .30
322 A55 15p multicolored .35 .35
323 A55 20p multicolored .50 .50
Nos. 318-323 (6) 1.80 1.80

Wreck of the Witte Leeuw, 1613.

"Discovery" A56

Capt. Cook's voyages: 8p, Cook's portable observatory. 12p, Pharnaceum acidum (plant), after sketch by Joseph Banks. 25p, Capt. Cook, after Flaxman/Wedgwood medallion.

1979, Feb. 19 Litho. *Perf. 11*

324 A56 3p multicolored .20 .20
325 A56 8p multicolored .30 .25
326 A56 12p multicolored .50 .45

Litho.; Embossed

327 A56 25p multicolored 1.00 .85
Nos. 324-327 (4) 2.00 1.75

St. Helena No. 176 A57

5p, Rowland Hill and his signature. 20p, St. Helena No. 8. 32p, St. Helena No. 49.

1979, Aug. 20 Litho. *Perf. 14*

328 A57 5p multi, vert. .20 .20
329 A57 8p multi .20 .20
330 A57 20p multi .30 .30
331 A57 32p multi .40 .40
Nos. 328-331 (4) 1.10 1.10

Sir Rowland Hill (1795-1879), originator of penny postage.

Seale's Chart, 1823 — A58

8p, Jamestown & Inclined Plane, 1829. 50p, Inclined Plane (stairs), 1979.

1979, Dec. 10 Litho. *Perf. 14*

332 A58 5p multi .20 .20
333 A58 8p multi .20 .20
334 A58 50p multi, vert. .60 .60
Nos. 332-334 (3) 1.00 1.00

Inclined Plane, 150th anniversary.

Tomb of Napoleon I, 1848 — A59

Empress Eugenie: 8p, Landing at St. Helena. 62p, Visiting Napoleon's tomb.

1980, Feb. 23 Litho. *Perf. 14½*

335 A59 5p multicolored .20 .20
336 A59 8p multicolored .20 .20
337 A59 62p multicolored 1.10 1.10
a. Souvenir sheet of 3, #335-337 1.50 1.50
Nos. 335-337 (3) 1.50 1.50

Visit of Empress Eugenie (widow of Napoleon III) to St. Helena, centenary.

East Indiaman, London 1980 Emblem — A60

1980, May 6 Litho. *Perf. 14½*

338 A60 5p shown .20 .20
339 A60 8p "Dolphin" postal stone .20 .20
340 A60 47p Jamestown castle postal stone .85 .85
a. Souvenir sheet of 3, #338-340 1.25 1.25
Nos. 338-340 (3) 1.25 1.25

London 1980 Intl. Stamp Exhib., May 6-14.

Queen Mother Elizabeth Birthday Issue

Common Design Type

1980, Aug. 18 Litho. *Perf. 14*

341 CD330 24p multicolored .60 .60

The Briars, 1815 A61

1980, Nov. 17 Litho. *Perf. 14*

342 A61 9p shown .25 .25
343 A61 30p Wellington, by Goya, vert. .80 .80

Duke of Wellington's visit to St. Helena, 175th anniv. Nos. 342-343 issued in sheets of 10 with gutter giving historical background.

Redwood Flower A62

1981, Jan. 5 *Perf. 13½*

344 A62 5p shown .20 .20
345 A62 8p Old father-live-forever .20 .20
346 A62 15p Gumwood .30 .30
347 A62 27p Black cabbage .55 .55
Nos. 344-347 (4) 1.25 1.25

John Thornton's Map of St. Helena, 1700 — A63

1981, May 22 Litho. *Perf. 14½*

348 A63 5p Reinel Portolan Chart, 1530 .20 .20
349 A63 8p shown .20 .20
350 A63 20p St. Helena, 1815 .40 .40
351 A63 30p St. Helena, 1817 .60 .60
Nos. 348-351 (4) 1.40 1.40

Souvenir Sheet

352 A63 24p Gastaldi's map of Africa, 16th cent. .75 .75

Royal Wedding Issue

Common Design Type

Wmk. 373

1981, July 22 Litho. *Perf. 14*

353 CD331 14p Bouquet .20 .20
354 CD331 29p Charles .50 .50
355 CD331 32p Couple .50 .50
Nos. 353-355 (3) 1.20 1.20

Charonia Variegata — A64

Traffic Guards Taking Oath — A65

1981, Sept. 10 Litho. *Perf. 14*

356 A64 7p shown .20 .20
357 A64 10p Cypraea spurca sanctahelenae .30 .30
358 A64 25p Janthina janthina .75 .75
359 A64 53p Pinna rudis 1.65 1.65
Nos. 356-359 (4) 2.90 2.90

1981, Nov. 5

360 A65 7p shown .20 .20
361 A65 11p Posting signs .25 .25
362 A65 25p Animal care .55 .55
363 A65 50p Duke of Edinburgh 1.10 1.10
Nos. 360-363 (4) 2.10 2.10

Duke of Edinburgh's Awards, 25th anniv.

St. Helena Dragonfly — A66

1982, Jan. 4 Litho. *Perf. 14½*

364 A66 7p shown .20 .20
365 A66 10p Burchell's beetle .30 .30
366 A66 25p Cockroach wasp .70 .70
367 A66 32p Earwig .95 .95
Nos. 364-367 (4) 2.15 2.15

See Nos. 386-389.

Sesquicentennial of Charles Darwin's Visit — A67

1982, Apr. 19 Litho. *Perf. 14*

368 A67 7p Portrait .20 .20
369 A67 14p Flagstaff Hill, hammer .45 .45
370 A67 25p Ring-necked pheasants .75 .75
371 A67 29p Beagle .90 .90
Nos. 368-371 (4) 2.30 2.30

Princess Diana Issue

Common Design Type

1982, July 1 Litho. *Perf. 14*

372 CD333 7p Arms .20 .20
373 CD333 11p Honeymoon .25 .25
374 CD333 29p Diana .65 .65
375 CD333 55p Portrait 1.25 1.25
Nos. 372-375 (4) 2.35 2.35

Nos. 305, 307 Overprinted: "1st PARTICIPATION / COMMONWEALTH GAMES 1982"

1982, Oct. 25 Litho. *Perf. 14*

376 A52 15p multicolored .35 .35
377 A52 26p multicolored .65 .65

Scouting Year A68

1982, Nov. 29

378 A68 3p Baden-Powell, vert. .20 .20
379 A68 11p Campfire .25 .25
380 A68 29p Canon Walcott, vert. .70 .70

381 A68 59p Thompsons Wood camp 1.40 1.40
Nos. 378-381 (4) 2.55 2.55

Coastline from Jamestown — A69

1983, Jan.

382 A69 7p King and Queen Rocks, vert. .20 .20
383 A69 11p Turk's Cap, vert. .20 .20
384 A69 29p shown .65 .65
385 A69 55p Munden's Point 1.40 1.40
Nos. 382-385 (4) 2.45 2.45

Insect Type of 1982

1983, Apr. 22 Litho. *Perf. 14½*

386 A66 11p Death's-head hawk-moth .25 .25
387 A66 15p Saldid-shore bug .35 .35
388 A66 29p Click beetle .65 .65
389 A66 59p Weevil 1.25 1.25
Nos. 386-389 (4) 2.50 2.50

Local Fungi A70

Wmk. 373

1983, June 16 Litho. *Perf. 14*

390 A70 11p Coriolus versicolor, vert. .25 .25
391 A70 15p Pluteus brunneisucus, vert. .40 .40
392 A70 29p Polyporus induratus .75 .75
393 A70 59p Coprinus angulatus, vert. 1.50 1.50
Nos. 390-393 (4) 2.90 2.90

Local Birds — A71

Christmas 1983 — A72

1983, Sept. 12 Litho. *Perf. 14x14½*

394 A71 7p Padda oryzivora .25 .20
395 A71 15p Foudia madagascariensis .55 .40
396 A71 33p Estrilda astrild 1.25 .90
397 A71 59p Serinus flaviventris 2.10 1.65
Nos. 394-397 (4) 4.15 3.15

Souvenir Sheet

1983, Oct. 17 Litho. *Perf. 14x13½*

Stained Glass, Parish Church of St. Michael.

398 Sheet of 10 4.50 3.50
a. A72 10p multicolored .30 .25
b. A72 15p multicolored .50 .40

Sheet contains strips of 5 of 10p and 15p with center margin telling St. Helena story.

See Nos. 424-427, 442-445.

150th Anniv. of the Colony — A73

1984, Jan. 3 Litho. *Perf. 14*

399 A73 1p No. 101 .20 .20
400 A73 3p No. 102 .20 .20
401 A73 6p No. 103 .20 .20
402 A73 7p No. 104 .20 .20
403 A73 11p No. 105 .25 .25
404 A73 15p No. 106 .35 .35
405 A73 29p No. 107 .70 .70
406 A73 33p No. 109 .80 .80
407 A73 59p No. 110 1.40 1.40
408 A73 £1 No. 108 2.25 2.25
409 A73 £2 New coat of arms 4.75 4.75
Nos. 399-409 (11) 11.30 11.30

Visit of Prince Andrew A74

1984, Apr. 4 Litho. *Perf. 14*

410 A74 11p Andrew, Invincible .30 .30
411 A74 60p Andrew, Herald 1.50 1.50

Lloyd's List Issue

Common Design Type

1984, May *Perf. 14½x14*

412 CD335 10p St. Helena, 1814 .25 .25
413 CD335 18p Solomon's facade .40 .40
414 CD335 25p Lloyd's Coffee House .60 .60
415 CD335 50p Papanui, 1898 1.25 1.25
Nos. 412-415 (4) 2.50 2.50

New Coin Issue A75

1984, July *Perf. 14*

416 A75 10p 2p, Donkey .25 .25
417 A75 15p 5p, Wire bird .40 .40
418 A75 29p 1p, Yellowfin tuna .80 .80
419 A75 50p 10p, Arum lily 1.40 1.40
Nos. 416-419 (4) 2.85 2.85

Centenary of Salvation Army in St. Helena — A76

1984, Sept. Litho. Wmk. 373

420 A76 7p Secretary Rebecca Fuller, vert. .20 .20
421 A76 11p Meals on Wheels service .35 .35
422 A76 25p Jamestown SA Hall .70 .70
423 A76 60p Hymn playing, clock tower 1.75 1.75
Nos. 420-423 (4) 3.00 3.00

Stained Glass Windows Type of 1983

1984, Nov. 9

424 A72 6p St. Helena visits prisoners .20 .20
425 A72 10p Betrothal of St. Helena .30 .30
426 A72 15p Marriage of St. Helena & Constantius .40 .40
427 A72 33p Birth of Constantine .90 .90
Nos. 424-427 (4) 1.80 1.80

Queen Mother 85th Birthday Issue

Common Design Type

Perf. 14½x14

1985, June 7 Litho. Wmk. 384

428 CD336 11p Portrait, age 2 .25 .25
429 CD336 15p Queen Mother, Elizabeth II .35 .35
430 CD336 29p Attending ballet, Covent Garden .65 .65
431 CD336 55p Holding Prince Henry 1.40 1.40
Nos. 428-431 (4) 2.65 2.65

Souvenir Sheet

432 CD336 70p Queen Mother and Ford V8 Pilot 2.25 2.25

Marine Life — A78

Perf. 13x13½

1985, July 12 Litho. Wmk. 373

433 A78 7p Rock bullseye .20 .20
434 A78 11p Mackerel .30 .30
435 A78 15p Skipjack tuna .50 .50
436 A78 33p Yellowfin tuna 1.25 1.25
437 A78 50p Stump 1.75 1.75
Nos. 433-437 (5) 4.00 4.00

Audubon Birth Bicent. A79

Portrait of naturalist and his illustrations of American bird species.

1985, Sept. 2 *Perf. 14*

438 A79 11p John Audubon, vert. .35 .35
439 A79 15p Common gallinule .45 .45
440 A79 25p Tropic bird .80 .80
441 A79 60p Noddy tern 2.00 2.00
Nos. 438-441 (4) 3.60 3.60

Stained Glass Windows Type of 1983

Christmas: 7p, St. Helena journeys to the Holy Land. 10p, Zambres slays the bull. 15p, The bull restored to life, conversion of St. Helena. 60p, Resurrection of the corpse, the true cross identified.

1985, Oct. 14

442 A72 7p multicolored .20 .20
443 A72 10p multicolored .30 .30
444 A72 15p multicolored .45 .45
445 A72 60p multicolored 1.75 1.75
Nos. 442-445 (4) 2.70 2.70

Society Banners A80

Designs: 10p, Church Provident Society for Women. 11p, Working Men's Christian Assoc. 25p, Church Benefit Society for Children. 29p, Mechanics & Friendly Benefit Society. 33p, Ancient Order of Foresters.

Perf. 13x13½

1986, Jan. 7 Wmk. 384

446 A80 10p multicolored .30 .30
447 A80 11p multicolored .30 .30
448 A80 25p multicolored .70 .70
449 A80 29p multicolored .80 .80
450 A80 33p multicolored .90 .90
Nos. 446-450 (5) 3.00 3.00

Queen Elizabeth II 60th Birthday

Common Design Type

Designs: 10p, Making 21st birthday broadcast, royal tour of South Africa, 1947. 15p, In robes of state, Throne Room, Buckingham Palace, Silver Jubilee, 1977. 20p, Onboard HMS Implacable, en route to South Africa, 1947. 50p, State visit to US, 1976. 65p, Visiting Crown Agents' offices, 1983.

1986, Apr. 21 *Perf. 14½*

451 CD337 10p scarlet, blk & sil .25 .25
452 CD337 15p ultra & multi .40 .40
453 CD337 20p green, blk & sil .50 .50
454 CD337 50p violet & multi 1.25 1.25
455 CD337 65p rose vio & multi 1.60 1.60
Nos. 451-455 (5) 4.00 4.00

For overprints see Nos. 488-492.

Halley's Comet — A81

Designs: 9p, Site of Halley's observatory on St. Helena. 12p, Edmond Halley, astronomer. 20p, Halley's planisphere of the southern stars. 65p, Voyage to St. Helena on the Unity.

1986, May 15 Wmk. 373 *Perf. 14½*

456 A81 9p multicolored .40 .40
457 A81 12p multicolored .50 .50
458 A81 20p multicolored .60 .60
459 A81 65p multicolored 1.60 1.60
Nos. 456-459 (4) 3.10 3.10

Royal Wedding Issue, 1986

Common Design Type

Designs: 10p, Informal portrait. 40p, Andrew in dress uniform at parade.

Wmk. 384

1986, July 23 Litho. *Perf. 14*

460 CD338 10p multicolored .20 .20
461 CD338 40p multicolored .90 .90

Explorers and Ships — A82

Designs: 1p, James Ross (1800-62), Erebus. 3p, Robert FitzRoy (1805-65), Beagle. 5p, Adam Johann von Krusenstern (1770-1846), Nadezhda, Russia. 9p, William Bligh (1754-1817), Resolution. 10p, Otto von Kotzebue (1786-1846), Rurik, Germany. 12p, Philip Carteret (1639-82), Swallow. 15p, Thomas Cavendish (c.1560-92), Desire. 20p, Louis-Antoine de Bougainville (1729-1811), La Boudeuse, France. 25p, Fyodor Petrovitch Litke (1797-1882), Seniavin, Russia. 40p, Louis Isidore Duperrey (1786-1865), La Coquille, France. 60p, John Byron (1723-86), Dolphin. £1, James Cook, Endeavour. £2, Jules Dumont d'Urville (1790-1842), L'Astrolabe, France.

Wmk. 384

1986, Sept. 22 Litho. *Perf. 14½*

462 A82 1p red brown .20 .20
463 A82 3p bright ultra .20 .20
464 A82 5p olive green .20 .20
465 A82 9p deep claret .25 .25
466 A82 10p sepia .30 .30
467 A82 12p brt blue green .30 .30
468 A82 15p brown lake .40 .40
469 A82 20p sapphire .55 .55
470 A82 25p red brown .70 .70
471 A82 40p myrtle green 1.10 1.10
472 A82 60p brown 1.60 1.60
473 A82 £1 Prussian blue 2.75 2.75
474 A82 £2 bright violet 5.50 5.50
Nos. 462-474 (13) 14.05 14.05

Ships of Royal Visitors A83

Portraits and vessels: 9p, Prince Edward, HMS Repulse, 1925. 13p, King George VI, HMS Vanguard, 1947. 38p, Prince Philip, HMY Britannia, 1957. 45p, Prince Andrew, HMS Herald, 1984.

1987, Feb. 16 Wmk. 373 *Perf. 14*

475 A83	9p multicolored	.40	.40
476 A83	13p multicolored	.60	.60
477 A83	38p multicolored	1.75	1.75
478 A83	45p multicolored	2.00	2.00
	Nos. 475-478 (4)	4.75	4.75

Rare Plants — A84

1987, Aug. 3 *Perf. 14½x14*

479 A84	9p St. Helena tea plant	.45	.45
480 A84	13p Baby's toes	.70	.70
481 A84	38p Salad plant	2.00	2.00
482 A84	45p Scrubwood	2.25	2.25
	Nos. 479-482 (4)	5.40	5.40

Marine Mammals A85

Wmk. 384

1987, Oct. 24 Litho. *Perf. 14*

483 A85	9p Lesser rorqual	.50	.50
484 A85	13p Risso's dolphin	.75	.75
485 A85	45p Sperm whale	2.75	2.75
486 A85	60p Euphrosyne dolphin	3.75	3.75
	Nos. 483-486 (4)	7.75	7.75

Souvenir Sheet

487 A85	75p Humpback whale	4.50	4.50

Nos. 451-455 Ovptd. "40TH WEDDING ANNIVERSARY" in Silver.

Wmk. 384

1987, Dec. 9 Litho. *Perf. 14½*

488 CD337	10p scarlet, blk & sil	.25	.25
489 CD337	15p ultra & multi	.35	.35
490 CD337	20p green, blk & sil	.55	.55
491 CD337	50p violet & multi	1.25	1.25
492 CD337	65p rose vio & multi	1.60	1.60
	Nos. 488-492 (5)	4.00	4.00

Australia Bicentennial A86

Ships and signatures: 9p, HMS Defence, 1691, and William Dampier. 13p, HMS Resolution, 1775, and James Cook. 45p, HMS Providence, 1792, and William Bligh. 60p, HMS Beagle, 1836, and Charles Darwin.

Wmk. 384

1988, Mar. 1 Litho. *Perf. 14½*

493 A86	9p multicolored	.40	.40
494 A86	13p multicolored	.60	.60
495 A86	45p multicolored	2.25	2.25
496 A86	60p multicolored	2.75	2.75
	Nos. 493-496 (4)	6.00	6.00

Christmas — A87

Rare Plants — A88

Religious paintings by unknown artists: 5p, The Holy Family with Child. 20p, Madonna. 38p, The Holy Family with St. John. 60p, The Holy Virgin with the Child.

Wmk. 373

1988, Oct. 11 Litho. *Perf. 14*

497 A87	5p multicolored	.20	.20
498 A87	20p multicolored	.65	.65
499 A87	38p multicolored	1.25	1.25
500 A87	60p multicolored	1.90	1.90
	Nos. 497-500 (4)	4.00	4.00

Lloyds of London, 300th Anniv.

Common Design Type

Designs: 9p, Underwriting room, 1886. 20p, Edinburgh Castle. 45p, Bosun Bird. 60p, Spangereid on fire off St. Helena, 1920.

Wmk. 384

1988, Nov. 1 Litho. *Perf. 14*

501 CD341	9p multi	.25	.25
502 CD341	20p multi, horiz.	.60	.60
503 CD341	45p multi, horiz.	1.40	1.40
504 CD341	60p multi	1.75	1.75
	Nos. 501-504 (4)	4.00	4.00

1989, Jan. 6 *Perf. 14*

505 A88	9p Ebony	.30	.30
506 A88	20p St. Helena lobelia	.70	.70
507 A88	45p Large bellflower	1.50	1.50
508 A88	60p She cabbage tree	2.00	2.00
	Nos. 505-508 (4)	4.50	4.50

Flags and Military Uniforms, 1815 — A89

Designs: 9p, Soldier, 53rd Foot. 13p, Officer, 53rd Foot. 20p, Royal marine. 45p, Officer, 66th Foot. 60p, Soldier, 66th Foot.

1989, June 5 Litho. *Perf. 14*

509	Strip of 5	5.00	5.00
a.	A89 9p multicolored	.30	.30
b.	A89 13p multicolored	.45	.45
c.	A89 20p multicolored	.70	.70
d.	A89 45p multicolored	1.50	1.50
e.	A89 60p multicolored	2.00	2.00

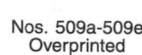

Nos. 509a-509e Overprinted

1989, July 7 Litho. *Perf. 14*

510	Strip of 5	5.00	5.00
a.	A89 9p multicolored	.30	.30
b.	A89 13p multicolored	.45	.45
c.	A89 20p multicolored	.70	.70
d.	A89 45p multicolored	1.50	1.50
e.	A89 60p multicolored	2.00	2.00

PHILEXFRANCE '89.

New Central (Prince Andrew) School A90

1989, Aug. 24 *Perf. 14½*

511 A90	13p Agriculture	.50	.50
512 A90	20p Literacy	.75	.75
513 A90	25p Building exterior	.95	.95
514 A90	60p Campus	2.25	2.25
	Nos. 511-514 (4)	4.45	4.45

Christmas — A91

10p, The Madonna with the Pear, by Durer. 20p, The Holy Family Under the Apple Tree, by Rubens. 45p, The Virgin in the Meadow, by Raphael. 60p, The Holy Family with Saint John, by Raphael.

1989, Oct. 10 Wmk. 373 *Perf. 14*

515 A91	10p multicolored	.30	.30
516 A91	20p multicolored	.65	.65
517 A91	45p multicolored	1.40	1.40
518 A91	60p multicolored	1.90	1.90
	Nos. 515-518 (4)	4.25	4.25

Early Vehicles A92

1989, Dec. 1 Wmk. 384 *Perf. 14½*

519 A92	9p 1930 Chevrolet	.30	.30
520 A92	20p 1929 Austin Seven	.65	.65
521 A92	45p 1929 Morris Cowley	1.40	1.40
522 A92	60p 1932 Sunbeam	1.90	1.90
	Nos. 519-522 (4)	4.25	4.25

Souvenir Sheet

523 A92	£1 Ford Model A	3.00	3.00

Farm Animals — A93

1990, Feb. 1 Litho. *Perf. 14*

524 A93	9p Sheep	.30	.30
525 A93	13p Pigs	.40	.40
526 A93	45p Cow, calf	1.40	1.40
527 A93	60p Geese	1.90	1.90
	Nos. 524-527 (4)	4.00	4.00

Great Britain No. 2 A94

Exhibition emblem and: 20p, Great Britain No. 1. 38p, Mail delivery to branch p.o. 45p, Main p.o., mail van.

1990, May 3 Wmk. 373

528 A94	13p shown	.40	.40
529 A94	20p multicolored	.70	.70
530 A94	38p multicolored	1.25	1.25
531 A94	45p multicolored	1.40	1.40
	Nos. 528-531 (4)	3.75	3.75

Stamp World London '90, 150th anniv. of the Penny Black.

Queen Mother, 90th Birthday

Common Design Types

1990, Aug. 4 Wmk. 384 *Perf. 14x15*

532 CD343	25p As Duchess of York, 1923	1.00	1.00

Perf. 14½

533 CD344	£1 Visiting communal feeding center, 1940	3.75	3.75

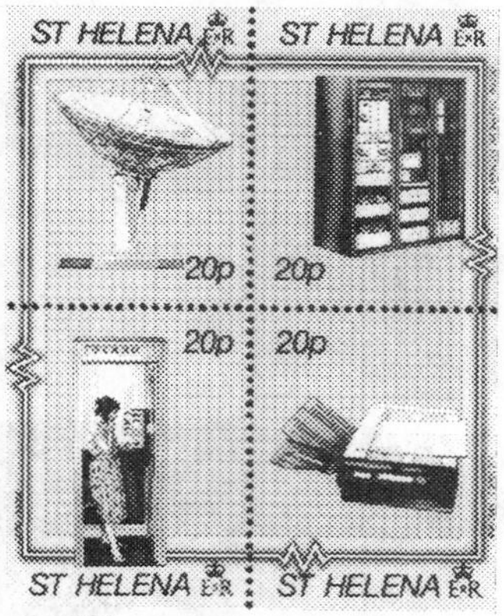

Telecommunications — A95

1990, July 28 Wmk. 373 *Perf. 14*

534 A95	Block of 4	3.50	3.50
a.-d.	20p any single	.80	.80

Dane, 1857 — A96

Designs: 20p, RMS St. Helena offloading cargo. 38p, Launching new RMS St. Helena, 1989. 45p, Duke of York launching new RMS St. Helena. £1, New RMS St. Helena.

1990, Sept. 13 *Perf. 14½*

535 A96	13p multicolored	.45	.45
536 A96	20p multicolored	.75	.75
537 A96	38p multicolored	1.40	1.40
538 A96	45p multicolored	1.65	1.65
	Nos. 535-538 (4)	4.25	4.25

Souvenir Sheet

539 A96	£1 multicolored	4.50	4.50

See Ascension Nos. 493-497, Tristan da Cunha Nos. 482-486.

Christmas — A97

Parish Churches.

1990, Oct. 18 *Perf. 13*

540 A97	10p Baptist Chapel, Sandy Bay	.35	.35
541 A97	13p St. Martin in the Hills	.45	.45
542 A97	20p St. Helena and the Cross	.65	.65
543 A97	38p St. James Church	1.40	1.40
544 A97	45p St. Paul's Church	1.65	1.65
	Nos. 540-544 (5)	4.50	4.50

Removal of Napoleon's Body from St. Helena, 150th Anniv. — A98

Designs: 13p, Funeral cortege, Jamestown wharf. 20p, Moving coffin to *Belle Poule,* James Bay. 38p, Transfer of coffin from *Belle Poule* to *Normandie,* Cherbourg. 45p, Napoleon's Tomb, St. Helena.

1990, Dec. 15 Wmk. 373 *Perf. 14*

545 A98 13p green & black .45 .45
546 A98 20p blue & black .75 .75
547 A98 38p violet & black 1.40 1.40
548 A98 45p multicolored 1.65 1.65
Nos. 545-548 (4) 4.25 4.25

A99

A100

Military Uniforms 1897: 13p, Officer, Leicestershire Regiment. 15p, Officer, York and Lancaster Regiment. 20p, Color Sergeant, Leicestershire Regiment. 38p, Drummer/Flautist, York and Lancaster Regiment. 45p, Lance Corporal, York and Lancaster Regiment.

1991, May 2

549 A99 13p multicolored .55 .55
550 A99 15p multicolored .60 .60
551 A99 20p multicolored .85 .85
552 A99 38p multicolored 1.65 1.65
553 A99 45p multicolored 1.90 1.90
Nos. 549-553 (5) 5.55 5.55

Elizabeth & Philip, Birthdays
Common Design Types

1991, July 1 Wmk. 384 *Perf. 14½*

554 CD345 25p multicolored .85 .85
555 CD346 25p multicolored .85 .85
a. Pair, #554-555 + label 1.75 1.75

1991, Nov. 2 Wmk. 373 *Perf. 14*

Christmas (Paintings): 10p, Madonna and Child, Titian. 13p, Holy Family, Mengs. 20p, Madonna and Child, Dyce. 38p, Two Trinities, Murillo. 45p, Virgin and Child, Bellini.

556 A100 10p multicolored .35 .35
557 A100 13p multicolored .45 .45
558 A100 20p multicolored .65 .65
559 A100 38p multicolored 1.40 1.40
560 A100 45p multicolored 1.65 1.65
Nos. 556-560 (5) 4.50 4.50

Phila Nippon '91 — A101

Motorcycles: 13p, Matchless 346cc (ohv), 1947. 20p, Triumph Tiger 100, 500cc, 1950. 38p, Honda CD 175cc, 1967. 45p, Yamaha DTE 400, 1976. 65p, Suzuki RM 250cc, 1984.

Perf. 14x14½
1991, Nov. 16 Litho. Wmk. 384

561 A101 13p multicolored .45 .45
562 A101 20p multicolored .75 .75
563 A101 38p multicolored 1.40 1.40
564 A101 45p multicolored 1.65 1.65
Nos. 561-564 (4) 4.25 4.25

Souvenir Sheet

565 A101 65p multicolored 3.50 3.50

Discovery of America, 500th Anniv. — A102

Wmk. 373
1992, Jan. 24 Litho. *Perf. 14*

566 A102 15p STV Eye of the Wind .55 .55
567 A102 25p STV Soren Larsen .95 .95
568 A102 35p Santa Maria, Nina & Pinta 1.25 1.25
569 A102 50p Columbus, Santa Maria 1.75 1.75
Nos. 566-569 (4) 4.50 4.50

World Columbian Stamp Expo '92, Chicago and Genoa '92 Intl. Philatelic Exhibitions.

Queen Elizabeth II's Accession to the Throne, 40th Anniv.
Common Design Type

1992, Feb. 6

570 CD349 11p multicolored .45 .45
571 CD349 15p multicolored .55 .55
572 CD349 25p multicolored .95 .95
573 CD349 35p multicolored 1.40 1.40
574 CD349 50p multicolored 1.90 1.90
Nos. 570-574 (5) 5.25 5.25

Liberation of Falkland Islands, 10th Anniv. — A103

Designs: No. 579a, 13p + 3p, like No. 575. b, 20p + 4p, like No. 576. c, 38p + 8p, like No. 577. d, 45p + 8p, like No. 578.

1992, June 12

575 A103 13p HMS Ledbury .50 .50
576 A103 20p HMS Brecon .75 .75
577 A103 38p RMS St. Helena 1.50 1.50
578 A103 45p First mail drop, 1982 1.75 1.75
Nos. 575-578 (4) 4.50 4.50

Souvenir Sheet

579 A103 Sheet of 4, #a.-d. 5.00 5.00

Surtax for Soldiers', Sailors' and Airmens' Families Association.

Christmas — A104

Children in scenes from Nativity plays: 13p, Angel, shepherds. 15p, Magi, shepherds. 20p, Joseph, Mary. 45p, Nativity scene.

1992, Oct. 12 Wmk. 384

580 A104 13p multicolored .50 .50
581 A104 15p multicolored .60 .60
582 A104 20p multicolored .80 .80
583 A104 45p multicolored 1.75 1.75
Nos. 580-583 (4) 3.65 3.65

Anniversaries — A105

Designs: 13p, Man broadcasting at radio station. 20p, Scouts marching in parade. 38p, Breadfruit, HMS Providence, 1792. 45p, Governor Colonel Brooke, Plantation House.

1992, Dec. 4 Wmk. 373 *Perf. 14½*

584 A105 13p multicolored .45 .45
585 A105 20p multicolored .75 .75
586 A105 38p multicolored 1.40 1.40
587 A105 45p multicolored 1.65 1.65
Nos. 584-587 (4) 4.25 4.25

Radio St. Helena, 25th anniv. (#584). Scouting on St. Helena, 75th anniv. (#585). Captain Bligh's visit, 200th anniv. (#586). Plantation House, 200th anniv. (#587).

Flowers — A106

Perf. 14½x14
1993, Mar. 19 Litho. Wmk. 384

588 A106 9p Moses in the bulrush .30 .30
589 A106 13p Periwinkle .50 .50
590 A106 20p Everlasting flower .70 .70
591 A106 38p Cigar plant 1.25 1.25
592 A106 45p Lobelia erinus 1.50 1.50
Nos. 588-592 (5) 4.25 4.25

See Nos. 635-640.

Wirebird A107

Wmk. 373
1993, Aug. 16 Litho. *Perf. 13½*

593 A107 3p Adult with eggs .30 .20
594 A107 5p Male, brooding female .50 .20
595 A107 12p Downy young, adult 1.25 .40
596 A107 25p Two immature birds 2.50 .80
597 A107 40p Adult in flight 1.25 1.25
598 A107 60p Immature bird 1.75 1.75
Nos. 593-598 (6) 7.55 4.60

Birds A108

1993, Aug. 26 *Perf. 14½*

599 A108 1p Swainson's canary .20 .20
600 A108 3p Chuckar partridge .20 .20
601 A108 11p Pigeon .25 .25
602 A108 12p Waxbill .30 .30
603 A108 15p Common myna .35 .35
604 A108 18p Java sparrow .45 .45
605 A108 25p Red-billed tropicbird .65 .65
606 A108 35p Maderian storm petrel .90 .90
607 A108 75p Madagascar fody 2.10 2.10
a. Souvenir sheet of 1 2.25 2.25
608 A108 £1 Common fairy tern 2.75 2.75
609 A108 £2 Southern giant petrel 5.25 5.25
610 A108 £5 Wirebird 14.00 14.00
Nos. 599-610 (12) 27.40 27.40

Nos. 599-604, 607, 610 are vert.
No. 607a for Hong Kong '97. Issued: 2/3/97.
See No. 691.

Christmas — A109

Toys: 12p, Teddy bear, soccer ball. 15p, Sailboat, doll. 18p, Paint palette, rocking horse. 25p, Kite, airplane. 60p, Guitar, roller skates.

1993, Oct. 1 *Perf. 13½x14*

611 A109 12p multicolored .35 .35
612 A109 15p multicolored .45 .45
613 A109 18p multicolored .50 .50
614 A109 25p multicolored .70 .70
615 A109 60p multicolored 1.75 1.75
Nos. 611-615 (5) 3.75 3.75

Flowers — A110

Photographs: No. 616a, Arum lily. No. 617a, Ebony. No. 618a, Shell ginger.
Nos. 616b-618b: Child's painting of same flower as in "a."

1994, Jan. 6 Wmk. 384 *Perf. 14*

616 A110 12p Pair, #a.-b. .65 .65
617 A110 25p Pair, #a.-b. 1.40 1.40
618 A110 35p Pair, #a.-b. 1.90 1.90

Pets — A111

Designs: 12p, Abyssinian guinea pig. 25p, Common tabby cat. 53p, Plain white, black rabbits. 60p, Golden labrador.

1994, Feb. 18 Wmk. 373 *Perf. 14½*

619 A111 12p multicolored .45 .45
620 A111 25p multicolored .90 .90
621 A111 53p multicolored 1.90 1.90
622 A111 60p multicolored 2.00 2.00
Nos. 619-622 (4) 5.25 5.25

Hong Kong '94.

Fish — A112

12p, Springer's blenny. 25p, Bastard five finger. 53p, Deepwater gurnard. 60p, Green fish.

1994, June 6 Wmk. 384 *Perf. 14*

623 A112 12p multicolored .35 .35
624 A112 25p multicolored .75 .75
625 A112 53p multicolored 1.65 1.65
626 A112 60p multicolored 1.75 1.75
Nos. 623-626 (4) 4.50 4.50

Butterflies A113

1994, Aug. 9 Wmk. 373

627 A113 12p Lampides boeticus .35 .35
628 A113 25p Cynthia cardui .75 .75
629 A113 53p Hypolimnas bolina 1.65 1.65
630 A113 60p Danaus chrysippus 1.75 1.75
Nos. 627-630 (4) 4.50 4.50

Christmas Carols — A114

Designs: 12p, "Silent night, holy night..." 15p, "While shepherds watched..." 25p, "Away in a manger..." 38p, "We three kings..." 60p, Angels from the realms of glory.

1994, Oct. 6

631	A114	12p multicolored	.50	.50
632	A114	15p multicolored	.65	.65
633	A114	25p multicolored	1.00	1.00
634	A114	38p multicolored	1.65	1.65
635	A114	60p multicolored	2.50	2.50
		Nos. 631-635 (5)	6.30	6.30

Flower Type of 1993

Wmk. 384

1994, Dec. 15 Litho. *Perf. 14½*

636	A106	12p Honeysuckle	.35	.35
637	A106	15p Gobblegheer	.45	.45
638	A106	25p African lily	.80	.80
639	A106	38p Prince of Wales feathers	1.25	1.25
640	A106	60p St. Johns lily	1.90	1.90
		Nos. 636-640 (5)	4.75	4.75

Emergency Services — A115

Wmk. 384

1995, Feb. 2 Litho. *Perf. 14*

641	A115	12p Fire engine	.40	.40
642	A115	25p Inshore rescue craft	.80	.80
643	A115	53p Police, rural patrol	1.65	1.65
644	A115	60p Ambulance	1.90	1.90
		Nos. 641-644 (4)	4.75	4.75

Harpers Earth Dam Project A116

Designs: a, Site clearance. b, Earthworks in progress. c, Laying the outlet pipe. d, Revetment block protection. e, Completed dam, June 1994.

Wmk. 373

1995, Apr. 6 Litho. *Perf. 14½*

645	A116	25p Strip of 5, #a.-e.	4.00	4.00

No. 645 is a continuous design.

End of World War II, 50th Anniv.

Common Design Types

Designs: No. 646, CS Lady Denison Pender. No. 647, HMS Dragon. No. 648, RFA Darkdale. No. 649, HMS Hermes. No. 650, St. Helena Rifles on parade. No. 651, Gov. Maj. W.J. Bain Gray during Victory Parade. No. 652, 6-inch gun, Ladder Hill. No. 653, Signal Station, flag hoist signalling VICTORY.

No. 654, Reverse of War Medal 1939-45.

1995, May 8 Wmk. 373 *Perf. 14*

646	CD351	5p multicolored	.20	.20
647	CD351	5p multicolored	.20	.20
a.		Pair, #646-647	.40	.30
648	CD351	12p multicolored	.50	.40
649	CD351	12p multicolored	.50	.40
a.		Pair, #648-649	1.00	.80
650	CD351	25p multicolored	.95	.75
651	CD351	25p multicolored	.95	.75
a.		Pair, #650-651	1.90	1.50
652	CD351	53p multicolored	2.00	1.65
653	CD351	53p multicolored	2.00	1.65
a.		Pair, #652-653	4.00	3.25
		Nos. 646-653 (8)	7.30	6.00

Souvenir Sheet

654	CD352	£1 multicolored	4.00	3.25

Invertebrates — A117

Designs: 12p, Blushing snail. 25p, Golden sail spider. 53p, Spiky yellow woodlouse. 60p, St. Helena shore crab. £1, Giant earwig.

1995, Aug. 29 Wmk. 373 *Perf. 14*

655	A117	12p multicolored	.40	.40
656	A117	25p multicolored	.80	.80
657	A117	53p multicolored	1.75	1.75
658	A117	60p multicolored	2.00	2.00
		Nos. 655-658 (4)	4.95	4.95

Souvenir Sheet

659	A117	£1 multicolored	3.25	3.25

Souvenir Sheet

Orchids — A118

a, Epidendrum ibaguense. b, Vanda Miss Joquim.

Perf. 14½x14

1995, Sept. 1 Wmk. 384

660	A118	50p Sheet of 2, #a.-b.	2.00	2.00

Singapore '95.

Christmas A119

Children's drawings: 12p, Christmas Eve in Jamestown. 15p, Santa, musicians. 25p, Party at Blue Hill Community Center. 38p, Santa walking in Jamestown. 60p, RMS St. Helena.

Perf. 14x14½

1995, Oct. 17 Litho. Wmk. 373

661	A119	12p multicolored	.40	.40
662	A119	15p multicolored	.45	.45
663	A119	25p multicolored	.75	.75
664	A119	38p multicolored	1.25	1.25
665	A119	60p multicolored	1.90	1.90
		Nos. 661-665 (5)	4.75	4.75

Union Castle Mail Ships A120

Wmk. 384

1996, Jan. 8 Litho. *Perf. 14*

666	A120	12p Walmer Castle, 1915	.40	.40
667	A120	25p Llangibby Castle, 1934	.80	.80
668	A120	53p Stirling Castle, 1940	1.75	1.75
669	A120	60p Pendennis Castle, 1965	1.90	1.90
		Nos. 666-669 (4)	4.85	4.85

See Nos. 707-710.

Radio, Cent. A121

Designs: 60p, Telecommunications equipment on St. Helena. £1, Marconi aboard yacht, Elettra.

Wmk. 373

1996, Mar. 28 Litho. *Perf. 13½*

670	A121	60p multicolored	1.75	1.75
671	A121	£1 multicolored	3.00	3.00

Queen Elizabeth II, 70th Birthday

Common Design Type

Various portraits of Queen, scenes of St. Helena: 15p, Jamestown. 25p, Prince Andrew School. 53p, Castle entrance. 60p, Plantation house.

£1.50, Queen wearing tiara, formal dress.

Perf. 14x14½

1996, Apr. 22 Litho. Wmk. 384

672	CD354	15p multicolored	.50	.50
673	CD354	25p multicolored	.80	.80
674	CD354	53p multicolored	1.75	1.75
675	CD354	60p multicolored	2.00	2.00
		Nos. 672-675 (4)	5.05	5.05

Souvenir Sheet

676	CD354	£1.50 multicolored	4.75	4.75

CAPEX '96 A122

Postal transport: 12p, Mail airlifted to HMS Protector, 1964. 25p, First local post delivery, motorscooter, 1965. 53p, Mail unloaded at Wideawake Airfield, Ascension Island. 60p, Mail received at St. Helena.

£1, LMS Jubilee Class 4-6-0 locomotive No. 5624 "St. Helena."

Wmk. 384

1996, June 8 Litho. *Perf. 14*

677	A122	12p multicolored	.40	.40
678	A122	25p multicolored	.85	.85
679	A122	53p multicolored	1.75	1.75
680	A122	60p multicolored	2.00	2.00
		Nos. 677-680 (4)	5.00	5.00

Souvenir Sheet

681	A122	£1 multicolored	3.25	3.25

Napoleonic Sites A123

Wmk. 373

1996, Aug. 12 Litho. *Perf. 14½*

682	A123	12p Mr. Porteous' House	.40	.40
683	A123	25p Briars Pavillion	.85	.85
684	A123	53p Longwood House	1.75	1.75
685	A123	60p Napoleon's Tomb	2.00	2.00
		Nos. 682-685 (4)	5.00	5.00

Christmas A124

Flowers: 12p, Frangipani. 15p, Bougainvillaea. 25p, Jacaranda. £1, Pink periwinkle.

Wmk. 373

1996, Oct. 1 Litho. *Perf. 14½*

686	A124	12p multicolored	.40	.40
687	A124	15p multicolored	.50	.50
688	A124	25p multicolored	.80	.80
689	A124	£1 multicolored	3.25	3.25
		Nos. 686-689 (4)	4.95	4.95

Endemic Plants — A125

Designs: a, Black cabbage tree. b, Whitewood. c, Tree fern. d, Dwarf jellico. e, Lobelia. f, Dogwood.

1997, Jan. 17 *Perf. 14½x14*

690	A125	25p Sheet of 6, #a.-f.	5.00	5.00

Bird Type of 1993

Souvenir Sheet

Wmk. 373

1997, June 20 Litho. *Perf. 14½*

691	A108	75p like No. 610	2.50	2.50

Return of Hong Kong to China, July 1, 1997.

Discovery of St. Helena, 500th Anniv. (in 2002) — A126

20p, Discovery by Joao da Nova, May 21, 1502. 25p, 1st inhabitant, Don Fernando Lopez, 1515. 30p, Landing by Thomas Cavendish, 1588. 80p, Ship, Royal Merchant, 1591.

1997, May 29 *Perf. 14*

692	A126	20p multicolored	.65	.65
693	A126	25p multicolored	.85	.85
694	A126	30p multicolored	1.00	1.00
695	A126	80p multicolored	2.60	2.60
		Nos. 692-695 (4)	5.10	5.10

See Nos. 712-715, 736-739, 755-758.

Queen Elizabeth II and Prince Philip, 50th Wedding Anniv. — A127

#696, Queen, Prince coming down steps, royal visit, 1947. #697, Wedding portrait. #698, Wedding portrait, diff. #699, Queen receiving flowers, royal visit, 1947. #700, Royal visit, 1957. #701, Queen, Prince waving from balcony on wedding day.

£1.50, Queen, Prince riding in open carriage.

Wmk. 384

1997, July 10 Litho. *Perf. 13½*

696		10p multicolored	.35	.35
697		10p multicolored	.35	.35
a.	A127	Pair, #696-697	.70	.70
698		15p multicolored	.50	.50
699		15p multicolored	.50	.50
a.	A127	Pair, #698-699	1.00	1.00
700		50p multicolored	1.75	1.75
701		50p multicolored	1.75	1.75
a.	A127	Pair, #700-701	3.50	3.50
		Nos. 696-701 (6)	5.20	5.20

Souvenir Sheet

Perf. 14x14½

702	A127	£1.50 multi, horiz.	5.00	5.00

Christmas — A128

Perf. 13½x14

1997, Sept. 29 Litho. Wmk. 384

703 A128 15p Flowers .50 .50
704 A128 20p Calligraphy .70 .70
705 A128 40p Camping 1.25 1.25
706 A128 75p Entertaining 2.50 2.50
Nos. 703-706 (4) 4.95 4.95

Duke of Edinburgh's Award in St. Helena, 25th anniv.

Union Castle Mail Ships Type of 1996

Wmk. 384

1998, Jan. 2 Litho. *Perf. 14*

707 A120 20p Avondale Castle, 1900 .65 .65
708 A120 25p Dunnottar Castle, 1936 .85 .85
709 A120 30p Llandovery Castle, 1943 1.00 1.00
710 A120 80p Good Hope Castle, 1977 2.60 2.60
Nos. 707-710 (4) 5.10 5.10

Diana, Princess of Wales (1961-97)

Common Design Type

a, Wearing hat. b, In white pin-striped suit jacket. c, In green jacket. d, Wearing choker necklace.

Perf. 14½x14

1998, Apr. 4 Litho. Wmk. 373

711 CD355 30p Sheet of 4, #a.-d. 4.75 4.75

No. 711 sold for £1.20 + 20p, with surtax from international sales being donated to Princess Diana Memorial Fund and surtax from national sales being donated to designated local charity.

Discovery of St. Helena, 500th Anniv. Type of 1997

17th Century events, horiz.: 20p, Fortifying and planting, 1659. 25p, Dutch invasion, 1672. 30p, English recapture, 1673. 80p, Royal Charter, 1673.

Wmk. 384

1998, July 2 Litho. *Perf. 14*

Size: 39x26mm

712 A126 20p multicolored .65 .65
713 A126 25p multicolored .80 .80
714 A126 30p multicolored 1.00 1.00
715 A126 80p multicolored 2.50 2.50
Nos. 712-715 (4) 4.95 4.95

Maritime Heritage — A129

Ships: 10p, HMS Desire, 1588. 15p, Dutch ship, "White Leeuw," 1602. 20p, HMS Swallow, HMS Dolphin, 1751. 25p, HMS Endeavour, 1771. 30p, HMS Providence, 1792. 35p, HMS St. Helena, 1815. 40p, HMS Northumberland, 1815. 50p, Russian brig, "Rurik," 1815. 75p, HMS Erebus, 1826. 80p, Pole junk, "Keying," 1847. £2, La Belle Poule, 1840. £5, HMS Rattlesnake, 1861.

Perf. 13½x14

1998, Aug. 25 Litho. Wmk. 373

716 A129 10p multicolored .35 .35
717 A129 15p multicolored .50 .50
718 A129 20p multicolored .65 .65
719 A129 25p multicolored .80 .80
720 A129 30p multicolored 1.00 1.00
721 A129 35p multicolored 1.10 1.10
722 A129 40p multicolored 1.25 1.25
723 A129 50p multicolored 1.60 1.60
724 A129 75p multicolored 2.50 2.50
725 A129 80p multicolored 2.50 2.50
726 A129 £2 multicolored 6.50 6.50
727 A129 £5 multicolored 16.00 16.00
Nos. 716-727 (12) 34.75 34.75

Christmas A130

Island crafts: 15p, Metal work. 20p, Wood turning. 30p, Inlaid woodwork. 85p, Hessian and seedwork.

1998, Sept. 28 *Perf. 14*

728 A130 15p multicolored .50 .50
729 A130 20p multicolored .65 .65
730 A130 30p multicolored 1.00 1.00
731 A130 85p multicolored 2.75 2.75
Nos. 728-731 (4) 4.90 4.90

Souvenir Sheet

H. M. Bark Endeavour at Anchor, 1771 — A131

Illustration reduced.

Perf. 13½x14

1999, Mar. 5 Litho. Wmk. 373

732 A131 £1.50 multicolored 1.75 1.75

Australia '99 World Stamp Expo.

Wedding of Prince Edward and Sophie Rhys-Jones

Common Design Type

Perf. 13¾x14

1999, June 15 Litho. Wmk. 384

733 CD356 30p Separate portraits 1.00 1.00
734 CD356 £1.30 Couple 4.25 4.25

Souvenir Sheet

PhilexFrance '99, World Philatelic Exhibition — A132

Illustration reduced.

1999, July 2 *Perf. 14*

735 A132 £1.50 #261 4.75 4.75

Discovery of St. Helena, 500th Anniv. Type of 1997

Designs, horiz: 20p, Jamestown fortification. 25p, First safe roadway up Ladder Hill, 1718. 30p, Governor Skottowe with Captain Cook. 80p, Presentation of sword of honor to Governor Brooke, 1799.

Perf. 14¼x14

1999, July 12 Litho. Wmk. 373

736 A126 20p multicolored .65 .65
737 A126 25p multicolored .80 .80
738 A126 30p multicolored 1.00 1.00
739 A126 80p multicolored 2.60 2.60
Nos. 736-739 (4) 5.05 5.05

Queen Mother's Century

Common Design Type

Queen Mother: 15p, With King George VI visiting St. Helena. 25p, With King George VI inspecting bomb damage at Buckingham Palace. 30p, With Prince Andrew, 97th birthday. 80p, As commandant-in-chief of Royal Air Force Central Flying School.

£1.50, With family at coronation of King George VI.

Wmk. 384

1999, Sept. 3 Litho. *Perf. 13½*

740 CD358 15p multicolored .50 .50
741 CD358 25p multicolored .80 .80
742 CD358 30p multicolored 1.00 1.00
743 CD358 80p multicolored 2.60 2.60
Nos. 740-743 (4) 4.90 4.90

Souvenir Sheet

744 CD358 £1.50 multicolored 5.00 5.00

Cable & Wireless, Cent. A133

Wmk. 373

1999, Nov. 26 Litho. *Perf. 14*

745 A133 20p Cable, communication equipment .65 .65
746 A133 25p CS Seine .80 .80
747 A133 30p CS Anglia .95 .95
748 A133 80p Headquarters 2.60 2.60
Nos. 745-748 (4) 5.00 5.00

Souvenir Sheet

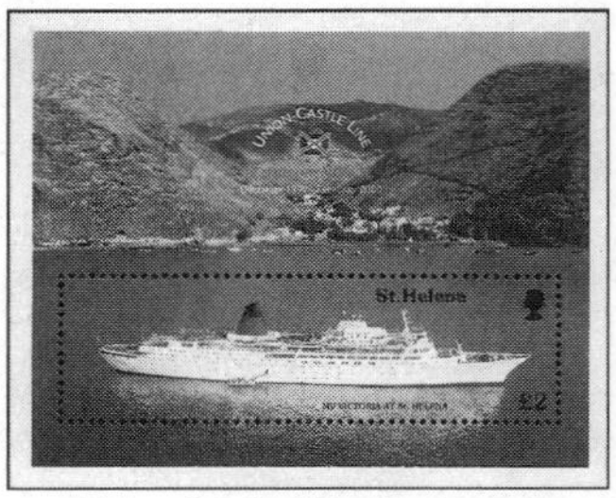

Union-Castle Line Centenary Voyage — A134

1999, Dec. 23 *Perf. 13x13¾*

749 A134 £2 multicolored 6.50 6.50

British Monarchs — A135

Designs: a, Edward VI. b, James I. c, William III, Mary II. d, George II. e, Victoria. f, George VI.

Wmk. 373

2000, Feb. 29 Litho. *Perf. 14*

750 A135 30p Sheet of 6, #a.-f. 5.75 5.75

The Stamp Show 2000, London.

Boer War, Cent. A136

Designs: 15p, Distillation plant, Ruperts. 25p, Camp, Broadbottom. 30p, Committee of Boer prisoners. 80p, Boer General Piet Cronjé, prisoner at Kent Cottage.

Wmk. 373

2000, Apr. 10 Litho. *Perf. 14*

751-754 A136 Set of 4 4.50 4.50

Discovery of St. Helena, 500th Anniv. Type of 1997

Designs: 20p, Withdrawal of the East India Company, 1833, horiz. 25p, Abolition of slavery, 1832, horiz. 30p, Napoleon arrives in 1815, departs in 1840, horiz. 80p, Chief Dinizulu, 1890, horiz.

2000, May 23 Wmk. 373 *Perf. 13¾*

755-758 A126 Set of 4 4.50 4.50

Souvenir Sheet

Royal Birthdays A137

No. 759: a, Princess Margaret, 70th birthday. b, Prince Andrew, 40th birthday. c, Prince William, 18th birthday. d, Princess Anne, 50th birthday. e, Queen Mother, 100th birthday.

2000, Aug. 4 Wmk. 384 *Perf. 14*

759 Sheet of 5 4.50 4.50
a.-d. A137 25p Any single .75 .75
e. A137 50p multi 1.50 1.50

No. 759e is 42x56mm.

Christmas Pantomimes A138

a, Beauty and the Beast. b, Puss in Boots. c, Little Red Riding Hood. d, Jack and the Beanstalk. e, Snow White and the Seven Dwarfs.

Wmk. 373

2000, Oct. 10 Litho. *Perf. 13*

760 Strip of 5 3.00 3.00
a.-e. A138 20p Any single .60 .60

Souvenir Sheet

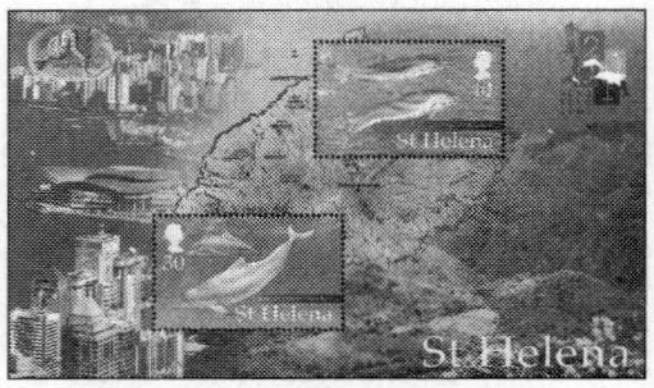

New Year 2001 (Year of the Snake) — A139

No. 761: a, 30p, Chinese white dolphin. b, 40p, Striped dolphin.
Illustration reduced.

Wmk. 373

2001, Feb. 1 Litho. *Perf. 14½*

761 A139 Sheet of 2, #a-b 2.00 2.00

Hong Kong 2001 Stamp Exhibition.

Age of Victoria — A140

Designs: 10p, St. Helena #1. 15p, Visit of HMS Beagle, 1836. 20p, Jamestown, horiz. 25p, Queen Victoria, horiz. 30p, Diamond Jubilee, horiz. 50p, Lewis Carroll.

£1.50, Coffee receives award at the Great Exhibition.

Wmk. 373

2001, May 24 Litho. *Perf. 14*

762-767 A140 Set of 6 4.25 4.25

Souvenir Sheet

768 A140 £1.50 multi 4.25 4.25

Discovery of St. Helena, 500th Anniv. Type of 1997

Designs, horiz.: 20p, World Wars I and II. 25p, Schools. 30p, Flax industry. 80p, RMS St. Helena.

2001, June 19 *Perf. 14x14¾*

769-772 A126 Set of 4 4.50 4.50

World War II Royal Navy Ships A141

HMS: 15p, Dunedin. 20p, Repulse. 25p, Nelson. 30p, Exmoor. 40p, Eagle. 50p, Milford.

2001, Sept. 20				***Perf. 14***
773-778	A141	Set of 6	5.25	5.25

Tammy Wynette (1942-98), American Singer A142

Wynette and Christmas carols: 10p, It Came Upon a Midnight Clear. 15p, Joy to the World. 20p, Away in the Manger. 30p, Silent Night.

Wmk. 373

2001, Oct. 11	**Litho.**			***Perf. 14***
779-782	A142	Set of 4	2.25	2.25

Souvenir Sheet

783	A142	£1.50 Portrait, vert.	4.50	4.50

Napoleon Bonaparte's Early Years — A143

Napoleon: 20p, As young man. 25p, At military school. 30p, At dance. 80p, With family.

2001, Nov. 1				***Perf. 13¾x14***
784-787	A143	Set of 4	4.50	4.50

Reign Of Queen Elizabeth II, 50th Anniv. Issue

Common Design Type

Designs: Nos. 788, 792a, 20p, Princess Elizabeth with Princess Margaret. Nos. 789, 792b, 25p, Wearing tiara. Nos. 790, 792c, 30p, With Princes Andrew and Edward, 1967. Nos. 791, 792d, 80p, In 1999. No. 792e, 50p, 1955 portrait by Annigoni (38x50mm).

Perf. 14¼x14½, 13¾ (#792e)

2002, Feb. 6	**Litho.**	**Wmk. 373**		
	With Gold Frames			
788-791	CD360	Set of 4	4.50	4.50

Souvenir Sheet

Without Gold Frames

792	CD360	Sheet of 5, #a-e	6.00	6.00

Birdlife International A144

Wirebird: 10p, With beak open. 15p, Running, vert. 25p, Looking left with beak closed, vert. 30p, In flight. 80p, Looking right with beak closed.

Perf. 14¼x13¾, 13¾x14¼

2002, Apr. 15				**Litho.**
793	A144	10p multi	.30	.30
a.		Perf. 14¼	.30	.30
794	A144	15p multi	.45	.45
a.		Perf. 14¼	.45	.45
795	A144	30p multi	.85	.85
a.		Perf. 14¼	.85	.85
796	A144	80p multi	2.40	2.40
a.		Perf. 14¼	2.40	2.40
		Nos. 793-796 (4)	4.00	4.00

Souvenir Sheet

Perf. 14¼

797	A144	Sheet, #793a-796a, 797a	4.75	4.75
a.		25p multi	.75	.75

SEMI-POSTAL STAMPS

Catalogue values for unused stamps in this section are for Never Hinged items.

Tristan da Cunha Nos. 46, 49-51 Overprinted "ST. HELENA / Tristan Relief" and Surcharged with New Value and "+"

Perf. 12½x13

1961, Oct. 12		**Wmk. 314**		**Engr.**
B1	A3	2½c + 3p		*425.00*
B2	A3	5c + 6p		*450.00*
B3	A3	7½c + 9p		*500.00*
B4	A3	10c + 1sh		*625.00*
		Nos. B1-B4 (4)	*4,750.*	*1,950.*

Withdrawn from sale Oct. 19.

POSTAGE DUE STAMPS

Catalogue values for unused stamps in this section are for Never Hinged items.

Map — D1

Perf. 15x14

1986, June 9	**Litho.**	**Wmk. 384**		
		Background Color		
J1	D1	1p tan	.20	.20
J2	D1	2p orange	.20	.20
J3	D1	5p vermilion	.20	.20
J4	D1	7p violet	.20	.20
J5	D1	10p chalky blue	.25	.25
J6	D1	25p dull yellow grn	.65	.65
		Nos. J1-J6 (6)	1.70	1.70

WAR TAX STAMPS

WAR TAX

ONE PENNY

No. 62a Surcharged

1916		**Wmk. 3**		***Perf. 14***
MR1	A10	1p + 1p scarlet & blk	.80	.60
a.		Double surcharge		*9,500.*

WAR TAX

1d

No. 62 Surcharged

1919				
MR2	A10	1p + 1p carmine & blk	.40	.40

ST. KITTS

sānt 'kits

LOCATION — West Indies southeast of Puerto Rico
GOVT. — With Nevis, Associated State in British Commonwealth
AREA — 65 sq. mi.
POP. — 31,824 (1991)
CAPITAL — Basseterre

See St. Christopher for stamps used in St. Kitts until 1890. From 1890 until 1903, stamps of the Leeward Islands were used. From 1903 until 1956, stamps of St. Kitts-Nevis and Leeward Islands were used concurrently. See St. Kitts-Nevis for stamps used through June 22, 1980, after which St. Kitts and Nevis pursued separate postal administrations.

100 Cents = 1 Dollar

Catalogue values for all unused stamps in this country are for Never Hinged items.

Watermark

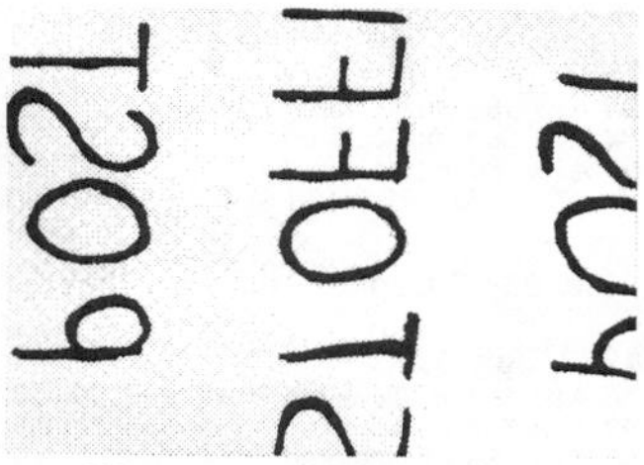

Wmk. 380- "POST OFFICE"

St. Kitts-Nevis Nos. 357-369 Ovptd.

Perf. 14½x14

1980, June 23	**Litho.**	**Wmk. 373**		
25	A61	5c multicolored	.20	.20
26	A61	10c multicolored	.20	.20
27	A61	12c multicolored	.50	.60
28	A61	15c multicolored	.20	.20
29	A61	25c multicolored	.20	.20
30	A61	30c multicolored	.20	.20
31	A61	40c multicolored	.20	.20
32	A61	45c multicolored	.45	.20
33	A61	50c multicolored	.20	.20
34	A61	55c multicolored	.20	.20
35	A61	$1 multicolored	.20	.25
36	A61	$5 multicolored	.75	1.00
37	A61	$10 multicolored	1.25	2.00
		Nos. 25-37 (13)	4.75	5.65

All but 12c, 45c, 50c, exist unwatermarked. About the same values.

Ships A2

1980, Aug. 8				***Perf. 13½***
38	A2	4c HMS *Vanguard*, 1762	.20	.20
39	A2	10c HMS *Boreas*, 1787	.20	.20
40	A2	30c HMS *Druid*, 1827	.20	.20
41	A2	55c HMS *Winchester*, 1831	.20	.20
42	A2	$1.50 *Philosopher*, 1857	.45	.30
43	A2	$2 S.S. *Contractor*, 1930	.65	.40
		Nos. 38-43 (6)	1.90	1.50

Nos. 38-43 not issued without overprint. The 4c, and possibly others, exist without the overprint.

Queen Mother, 80th Birthday — A3

1980, Sept. 4				***Perf. 14***
44	A3	$2 multicolored	.45	.45

Christmas — A4

1980, Nov. 10				***Perf. 14½***
45	A4	5c Magi following star	.20	.20
46	A4	15c Shepherds, star	.20	.20
47	A4	30c Bethlehem, star	.20	.20
48	A4	$4 Adoration of the Magi	.50	.50
		Nos. 45-48 (4)	1.10	1.10

Birds — A5

Military Uniforms — A6

1981		**Wmk. 373**		***Perf. 13½x14***
49	A5	1c Frigatebird	.20	.20
50	A5	4c Rusty-tailed fly-catcher	.20	.20
51	A5	5c Purple-throated carib	.20	.20
52	A5	6c Burrowing owl	.20	.20
53	A5	8c Purple martin	.20	.20
54	A5	10c Yellow-crowned night heron	.20	.20
		Perf. 14		
		Size: 38x25mm		
55	A5	15c Bananaquit	.20	.20
56	A5	20c Scaly-breasted thrasher	.20	.20
57	A5	25c Grey kingbird	.20	.20
58	A5	30c Green-throated carib	.20	.20
59	A5	40c Ruddy turnstone	.25	.25
60	A5	45c Black-faced grass-quit	.30	.30
61	A5	50c Cattle egret	.30	.30
62	A5	55c Brown pelican	.30	.30
63	A5	$1 Lesser Antillean bullfinch	.60	.60
64	A5	$2.50 Zenaida dove	1.50	1.50
65	A5	$5 Sparrow hawk	3.00	3.00
66	A5	$10 Antillean crested hummingbird	6.00	6.00
		Nos. 49-66 (18)	14.25	14.25

Issued: #51, 54-66, Feb. 5; others, May 30.

Nos. 49-66 exist with "1982" imprint, issued June 8, 1982. The 1981 set has no imprint.

For overprints see Nos. 112-122.

1981-83 ***Perf. 14½***

Foot Regiments: 5c, Battalion Company sergeant, 3rd Regiment, c. 1801. 15c, Light Company private, 15th Regiment, c. 1814. No. 69, Battalion Company officer, 45th Regiment, 1796-7. No. 70, Officer, 15th Regiment, c. 1780. No. 71, Officer, 9th Regiment, 1790. No. 72, Light Company officer, 5th Regiment, c. 1822. No. 73, Grenadier, 38th Regiment, 1751. No. 74, Battalion Company officer, 11th Regiment, c. 1804.

67	A6	5c multi	.20	.20
68	A6	15c multi ('83)	.20	.20
69	A6	30c multi	.20	.20
70	A6	30c multi ('83)	.20	.20
71	A6	55c multi	.20	.20
72	A6	55c multi ('83)	.30	.30
73	A6	$2.50 multi	.45	.45
74	A6	$2.50 multi ('83)	1.25	1.25
		Nos. 67-74 (8)	3.00	3.00

Issued: 3/5/81; 5/25/83.

Prince Charles, Lady Diana, Royal Yacht Charlotte A6a

Prince Charles and Lady Diana — A6b

Illustration A6b is greatly reduced.

1981, June 23 ***Perf. 14***

75	A6a	55c Saudadoes	.20	.20
76	A6b	55c Couple	.20	.20
a.		Bklt. pane of 4, perf. 12½x12, unwmkd.	.90	
77	A6a	$2.50 The Royal George	.70	.70
78	A6b	$2.50 like 55c	.70	.70
a.		Bklt. pane of 2, perf. 12½x12, unwmkd.	1.65	
79	A6a	$4 HMY Britannia	1.10	1.10
80	A6b	$4 like 55c	1.10	1.10
		Nos. 75-80 (6)	4.00	4.00

Souvenir Sheet

1981, Dec. 14 ***Perf. 12½x12***

81 A6b $5 like 55c 2.75 2.75

Wedding of Prince Charles and Lady Diana Spencer. Nos. 76a, 78a issued Nov. 19, 1981.

Natl. Girl Guide Movement, 50th Anniv. — A7

Christmas — A8

Designs: 5c, Miriam Pickard, 1st Guide commissioner. 30c, Lady Baden-Powell's visit, 1964. 55c, Visit of Princess Alice, 1960. $2, Thinking-Day Parade, 1980s.

1981, Sept. 21

82	A7	5c multicolored	.20	.20
83	A7	30c multicolored	.20	.20
84	A7	55c multicolored	.20	.20
85	A7	$2 multicolored	.70	.70
		Nos. 82-85 (4)	1.30	1.30

1981, Nov. 30

Stained-glass windows.

86	A8	5c Annunciation	.20	.20
87	A8	30c Nativity, baptism	.20	.20
88	A8	55c Last supper, crucifixion	.20	.20
89	A8	$3 Appearance before Apostles, ascension to heaven	.80	.80
		Nos. 86-89 (4)	1.40	1.40

Brimstone Hill Seige, Bicent. — A9

1982, Mar. 15

90	A9	15c Adm. Samuel Hood	.20	.20
91	A9	55c Marquis de Bouille	.30	.30

Souvenir Sheet

92 A9 $5 Battle scene 2.00 2.00

No. 92 has multicolored margin picturing battle scene. Size: 96x71mm.

21st Birthday of Princess Diana, July 1 — A10

15c, Alexandra of Denmark, Princess of Wales, 1863. 55c, Paternal arms of Alexandra. $6, Diana.

1982, June 22 ***Perf. 13½x14***

93	A10	15c multicolored	.20	.20
94	A10	55c multicolored	.30	.30
95	A10	$6 multicolored	2.50	2.50
		Nos. 93-95 (3)	3.00	3.00

Nos. 93-95 Ovptd. ROYAL BABY

1982, July 12

96	A10	15c multicolored	.20	.20
97	A10	55c multicolored	.30	.30
98	A10	$6 multicolored	2.50	2.50
		Nos. 96-98 (3)	3.00	3.00

Birth of Prince William of Wales.

Scouting, 75th Anniv. — A11

Merit badges.

1982, Aug. 18 ***Perf. 14x13½***

99	A11	5c Nature	.20	.20
100	A11	55c Rescue	.25	.25
101	A11	$2 First aid	.90	.90
		Nos. 99-101 (3)	1.35	1.35

Christmas — A12

Children's drawings.

1982, Oct. 20

102	A12	5c shown	.20	.20
103	A12	55c Nativity	.20	.20
104	A12	$1.10 Three Kings	.20	.20
105	A12	$3 Annunciation	.30	.30
		Nos. 102-105 (4)	.90	.90

A13

Commonwealth Day: 55c, Cruise ship Stella Oceanis docked. $2, RMS Queen Elizabeth 2 anchored in harbor off St. Kitts.

1983, Mar. 14 ***Perf. 14***

106	A13	55c multicolored	.20	.20
107	A13	$2 multicolored	.45	.45

Boys' Brigade, Cent. — A14

Designs: 10c, Sir William Smith, founder. 45c, Brigade members outside Sandy Point Methodist Church. 50c, Drummers. $3, Badge.

1983, July 27

108	A14	10c multicolored	.30	.30
109	A14	45c multicolored	.45	.45
110	A14	50c multicolored	.45	.45
111	A14	$3 multicolored	.80	.80
		Nos. 108-111 (4)	2.00	2.00

Nos. 51, 55-59 and 62-66 Ovptd.

a

b

1983, Sept. 19

112	A5(a)	5c multicolored	.20	.20
a.		Local overprint	2.25	2.25
113	A5(b)	15c multicolored	.20	.20
114	A5(b)	20c multicolored	.20	.20
115	A5(b)	25c multicolored	.20	.20
116	A5(b)	30c multicolored	.20	.20
117	A5(b)	40c multicolored	.25	.25
118	A5(b)	55c multicolored	.35	.35
119	A5(b)	$1 multicolored	.60	.60
120	A5(b)	$2.50 multicolored	1.65	1.65
121	A5(b)	$5 multicolored	3.00	3.00
122	A5(b)	$10 multicolored	6.25	6.25
		Nos. 112-122 (11)	13.10	13.10

Nos. 113-122 have "1982" imprint. Nos. 113, 116, 118-122 exist without imprint. No. 112 is without imprint. No. 112 with imprint is twice the value.

No. 112a has serifed letters and reads down on imprinted stamp. Exists reading up and without imprint.

Manned Flight Bicent. — A15

Designs: 10c, *Montgolfiere,* 1783, vert. 45c, Sikorsky *Russian Knight,* 1913. 50c, Lockheed TriStar. $2.50, Bell XS-1, 1947.

1983, Sept. 28 **Wmk. 380**

123	A15	10c multicolored	.20	.20
124	A15	45c multicolored	.20	.20
125	A15	50c multicolored	.20	.20
126	A15	$2.50 multicolored	.40	.40
a.		Souvenir sheet of 4, #123-126	1.00	1.00
		Nos. 123-126 (4)	1.00	1.00

1st Flight of a 4-engine aircraft, May 1913 (45c); 1st manned supersonic aircraft, 1947 ($2.50).

Christmas — A16

1983, Nov. 7

127	A16	15c shown	.20	.20
128	A16	30c Shepherds	.20	.20
129	A16	55c Mary, Joseph	.20	.20
130	A16	$2.50 Nativity	.30	.30
a.		Souvenir sheet of 4, #127-130	.75	.75
		Nos. 127-130 (4)	.90	.90

Batik Art A17

1984-85

131	A17	15c Country bus	.20	.20
132	A17	40c Donkey cart	.25	.20
133	A17	45c Parrot, vert.	.25	.20
134	A17	50c Man under palm tree, vert.	.20	.20
135	A17	60c Rum shop, cyclist	.40	.20
136	A17	$1.50 Fruit seller, vert.	.25	*.50*
137	A17	$3 Butterflies, vert.	.50	*1.25*
138	A17	$3 S.V. Polynesia	1.00	*1.75*
		Nos. 131-138 (8)	3.00	4.50

Issued: 15c, 40c, 60c, #138, 2/6/85; others, 1/30/84.

Marine Life A18

1984, July 4

139	A18	5c Cushion star	.20	.20
140	A18	10c Rough file shell	.20	.20
a.		Wmk. 384 ('86)	.20	.20
141	A18	15c Red-lined cleaning shrimp	.20	.20
142	A18	20c Bristleworm	.20	.20
143	A18	25c Flamingo tongue	.25	.20
144	A18	30c Christmas tree worm	.30	.30
145	A18	40c Pink-tipped anemone	.35	.35
146	A18	50c Smallmouth grunt	.45	.45
147	A18	60c Glasseye snapper	.60	.60
a.		Wmk. 384 ('88)	.80	.80
148	A18	75c Reef squirrelfish	.70	.70
149	A18	$1 Sea fans, flamefish	.90	.90
150	A18	$2.50 Reef butter-flyfish	2.25	2.25
151	A18	$5 Black soldierfish	4.50	4.50
a.		Wmk. 384 ('88)	6.25	6.25
152	A18	$10 Cocoa damselfish	9.50	9.50
a.		Wmk. 384 ('88)	13.00	13.00
		Nos. 139-152 (14)	20.60	20.55

Nos. 149-152 vert.

#140a has "1986" imprint; also exists with "1988" imprint. #147a, 151a, 152a have "1988" imprint.

4-H in St. Kitts, 25th Anniv. A19

1984, Aug. 15

153	A19	30c Agriculture	.20	.20
154	A19	55c Animal husbandry	.35	.35
155	A19	$1.10 Pledge, flag, youths	.60	.60
156	A19	$3 Parade	1.10	1.10
		Nos. 153-156 (4)	2.25	2.25

1st Anniv. of Independence — A20

15c, Construction of Royal St. Kitts Hotel. 30c, Folk dancers. $1.10, O Land of Beauty, vert. $3, Sea, palm trees, map, vert.

1984, Sept. 18

157 A20	15c multicolored	.20	.20
158 A20	30c multicolored	.25	.25
159 A20	$1.10 multicolored	.45	.45
160 A20	$3 multicolored	1.10	1.10
	Nos. 157-160 (4)	2.00	2.00

Christmas — A21

1984, Nov. 1

161 A21 15c	Opening gifts	.20	.20
162 A21 60c	Caroling	.45	.45
163 A21 $1	Nativity	.70	.70
164 A21 $2	Leaving church	1.40	1.40
	Nos. 161-164 (4)	2.75	2.75

Ships A22

1985, Mar. 27 ***Perf. 13½x14***

165 A22 40c	Tropic Jade	.45	.45
166 A22 $1.20	Atlantic Clipper	1.40	1.40
167 A22 $2	M.V. Cunard Countess	2.25	2.25
168 A22 $2	Mandalay	2.25	2.25
	Nos. 165-168 (4)	6.35	6.35

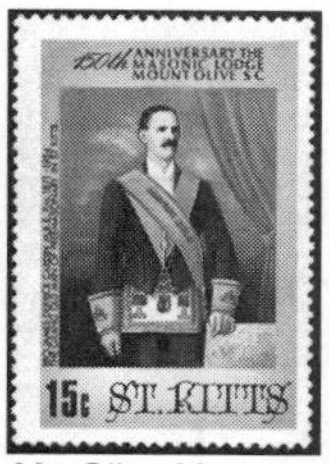

Mt. Olive Masonic Lodge, 150th Anniv. — A23

Christmas — A24

Designs: 15c, James Derrick Cardin (1871-1954). 75c, Lodge banner. $1.20, Compass, Bible, square, horiz. $3, Charter, 1835.

1985, Nov. 9 ***Perf. 15***

169 A23	15c multicolored	.60	.60
170 A23	75c multicolored	1.25	1.25
171 A23	$1.20 multicolored	1.25	1.25
172 A23	$3 multicolored	1.90	1.90
	Nos. 169-172 (4)	5.00	5.00

1985, Nov. 27 **Unwmk.**

173 A24 10c	Map of St. Kitts	.35	.35
174 A24 40c	Golden Hind	.65	.65
175 A24 60c	Sir Francis Drake	.65	.65
176 A24 $3	Drake's shield of arms	.85	2.75
	Nos. 173-176 (4)	2.50	4.40

Visit of Sir Francis Drake to St. Kitts, 400th anniv.

Queen Elizabeth II, 60th Birthday — A25

Designs: 10c, With Prince Philip. 20c, Walking with government officials. 40c, Riding horse in parade. $3, Portrait.

1986, July 9 ***Perf. 14***

177 A25	10c multicolored	.20	.20
178 A25	20c multicolored	.20	.20
179 A25	40c multicolored	.35	.35
180 A25	$3 multicolored	2.25	2.25
	Nos. 177-180 (4)	3.00	3.00

For overprints see Nos. 185-188.

Common Design Types pictured following the introduction.

Royal Wedding Issue, 1986

Common Design Type

Designs: 15c, Prince Andrew and Sarah Ferguson, formal engagement announcement. $2.50, Prince Andrew in military dress uniform.

Perf. 14½x14

1986, July 23 **Wmk. 384**

181 CD338	15c multicolored	.20	.20
182 CD338	$2.50 multicolored	1.25	1.25

Agriculture Exhibition — A26

Children's drawings: 15c, Family farm, by Kevin Tatem, age 14. $1.20, Striving for growth, by Alister Williams, age 19.

1986, Sept. 18 ***Perf. 13½x14***

183 A26	15c multicolored	.20	.20
184 A26	$1.20 multicolored	1.25	1.25

Nos. 177-180 Ovptd. "40th ANNIVERSARY / U.N. WEEK 19-26 OCT." in Gold

1986, Oct. 22 **Unwmk.** ***Perf. 14***

185 A25	10c multicolored	.20	.20
186 A25	20c multicolored	.20	.20
187 A25	40c multicolored	.30	.30
188 A25	$3 multicolored	1.90	*2.25*
	Nos. 185-188 (4)	2.60	2.95

World Wildlife Fund — A27

Various green monkeys, Cercopithecus aethiops sabaeus.

1986, Dec. 1

189 A27	15c multi	*2.50*	*.75*
190 A27	20c multi, diff.	*2.75*	*.75*
191 A27	60c multi, diff.	*6.00*	*4.50*
192 A27	$1 multi, diff.	*6.50*	*9.00*
	Nos. 189-192 (4)	17.75	15.00

Auguste Bartholdi — A28

Statue of Liberty, Cent. — A29

1986, Dec. 17 ***Perf. 14x14½, 14½x14***

193 A28	40c shown	.30	.30
194 A28	60c Torch, head, 1876-78	.45	.45
195 A28	$1.50 Warship Isere, France	1.00	*1.25*
196 A28	$3 Delivering statue, 1884	1.25	*2.50*
	Nos. 193-196 (4)	3.00	4.50

Souvenir Sheet

197 A29	$3.50 Head	2.40	*2.40*

Nos. 194-195 horiz.

British and French Uniforms — A30

Sugar Cane Industry — A31

Designs: No. 198, Officer, East Norfolk Regiment, 1792. No. 199, Officer, De Neustrie Regiment, 1779. No. 200, Sergeant, Third Foot the Buffs, 1801. No. 201, Artillery officer, 1812. No. 202, Private, Light Company, 5th Foot Regiment, 1778. No. 203, Grenadier, Line Infantry, 1796.

1987, Feb. 25 ***Perf. 14½***

198	A30 15c multicolored	.50	.20
199	A30 15c multicolored	.50	.20
200	A30 40c multicolored	.90	.55
201	A30 40c multicolored	.90	.55
202	A30 $2 multicolored	1.60	*2.75*
203	A30 $2 multicolored	1.60	*2.75*
a.	Souvenir sheet of 6, #198-203	7.25	7.25
	Nos. 198-203 (6)	6.00	7.00

1987, Apr. 15 ***Perf. 14***

No. 204: a, Warehouse. b, Barns. c, Steam emitted by processing plant. d, Processing plant. e, Field hands.

No. 205a, Locomotive. b, Locomotive and tender. c, Open cars. d, Empty and loaded cars, tractor. e, Loading sugar cane.

204	Strip of 5	1.00	1.00
a.-e.	A31 15c any single	.20	.20
205	Strip of 5	2.00	2.00
a.-e.	A31 75c any single	.35	.35

Visiting Aircraft A32

Perf. 14x14½

1987, June 24 **Wmk. 373**

206 A32	40c L-1011-500 Tri-Star	.40	.40
207 A32	60c BAe Super 748	.70	.70
208 A32	$1.20 DHC-6 Twin Otter	1.40	1.40
209 A32	$3 Aerospatiale ATR-42	3.25	3.25
	Nos. 206-209 (4)	5.75	5.75

Fungi — A33

Carnival Clowns — A34

1987, Aug. 26 **Wmk. 384** ***Perf. 14***

210 A33	15c Hygrocybe occidentalis	.75	.75
211 A33	40c Marasmius haematocephalus	1.25	.50
212 A33	$1.20 Psilocybe cubensis	2.75	*3.00*
213 A33	$2 Hygrocybe acutoconica	3.50	*3.75*
214 A33	$3 Boletellus cubensis	4.25	*5.00*
	Nos. 210-214 (5)	12.50	13.00

1987, Oct. 28 ***Perf. 14½***

215 A34	15c multi	.25	.25
216 A34	40c multi, diff.	.50	.50
217 A34	$1 multi, diff.	1.25	1.25
218 A34	$3 multi, diff.	2.75	2.75
	Nos. 215-218 (4)	4.75	4.75

Christmas 1987. See Nos. 235-238.

Flowers — A35

1988, Jan. 20

219 A35	15c Ixora	.20	.20
220 A35	40c Shrimp plant	.45	.45
221 A35	$1 Poinsettia	1.10	1.10
222 A35	$3 Honolulu rose	3.25	3.25
	Nos. 219-222 (4)	5.00	5.00

Tourism A36

1988, Apr. 20 **Wmk. 373**

223 A36	60c Ft. Thomas Hotel	.75	.75
224 A36	60c Fairview Inn	.75	.75
225 A36	60c Frigate Bay Beach Hotel	.75	.75
226 A36	60c Ocean Terrace Inn	.75	.75
227 A36	$3 The Golden Lemon	2.25	2.25
228 A36	$3 Royal St. Kitts Casino and Jack Tar Village	2.25	2.25
229 A36	$3 Rawlins Plantation Hotel and Restaurant	2.25	2.25
	Nos. 223-229 (7)	9.75	9.75

See Nos. 239-244.

Leeward Islands Cricket Tournament, 75th Anniv. — A37

Independence, 5th Anniv. — A38

Designs: 40c, Leeward Islands Cricket Assoc. emblem, ball and wicket. $3, Cricket match at Warner Park.

1988, July 13 *Perf. 13x13½*

230 A37 40c multicolored 1.50 .30
231 A37 $3 multicolored 3.75 3.75

1988, Sept. 19 Wmk. 384 *Perf. 14½*

Designs: 15c, Natl. flag. 60c, Natl. coat of arms. $5, Princess Margaret presenting the Nevis Constitution Order to Prime Minister Simmonds, Sept. 19, 1983.

232 A38 15c shown .30 .30
233 A38 60c multicolored .70 .70

Souvenir Sheet

234 A38 $5 multicolored 3.25 3.25

Christmas Type of 1987

Carnival clowns.

1988, Nov. 2 Wmk. 373

235 A34 15c multi .20 .20
236 A34 40c multi, diff. .20 .20
237 A34 80c multi, diff. .35 .35
238 A34 $3 multi, diff. 1.50 1.50
Nos. 235-238 (4) 2.25 2.25

Tourism Type of 1988

Wmk. 384

1989, Jan. 25 Litho. *Perf. 14*

239 A36 20c Old Colonial House .20 .20
240 A36 20c Georgian House .20 .20
241 A36 $1 Romney Manor .75 .75
242 A36 $1 Lavington Great House .75 .75
243 A36 $2 Treasury Building 1.00 *1.50*
244 A36 $2 Government House 1.00 *1.50*
Nos. 239-244 (6) 3.90 4.90

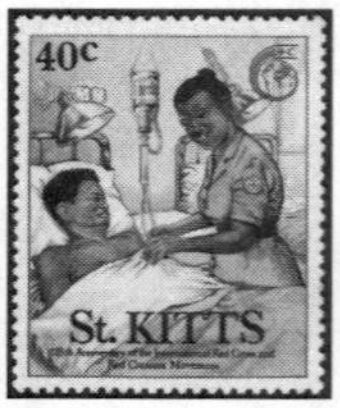

Intl. Red Cross and Red Crescent Organizations, 125th Annivs. (in 1988) — A39

Perf. 14x14½

1989, May 8 Litho. Wmk. 384

245 A39 40c shown .25 .25
246 A39 $1 Ambulance .75 .75
247 A39 $3 Anniv. emblem 2.25 2.25
Nos. 245-247 (3) 3.25 3.25

Moon Landing, 20th Anniv.

Common Design Type

Apollo 13: 10c, Lunar rover at Taurus-Littrow landing site. 20c, Fred W. Haise Jr., John L. Swigert Jr., and James A. Lovell Jr. $1, Mission emblem. $2, Splashdown in the South Pacific. $5, Buzz Aldrin disembarking from the lunar module, Apollo 11 mission.

1989, July 20 *Perf. 14*

Size of Nos. 249-250: 29x29mm

248 CD342 10c multicolored .20 .20
249 CD342 20c multicolored .20 .20
250 CD342 $1 multicolored .75 .75
251 CD342 $2 multicolored 1.50 1.50
Nos. 248-251 (4) 2.65 2.65

Souvenir Sheet

252 CD342 $5 multicolored 4.50 4.50

Souvenir Sheet

Conflict on the Champ-de-Mars — A40

1989, July 7

253 A40 $5 multicolored 3.75 3.75

PHILEXFRANCE '89, French revolution bicent.

Outline Map of St. Kitts — A41

1989 *Perf. 15x14*

255 A41 10c purple & blk .20 .20
256 A41 15c red & blk .20 .20
257 A41 20c org brn & blk .20 .20
259 A41 40c bister & blk .25 .25
261 A41 60c blue & blk .35 .35
265 A41 $1 green & blk .50 .50
Nos. 255-265 (6) 1.70 1.70

This is an expanding set. Numbers will change if neccessary.

Discovery of America, 500th Anniv. (in 1992) A42

Designs: 15c, Galleon passing St. Kitts during Columbus's 2nd voyage, 1493. 80c, Coat of arms and map of 4th voyage. $1, Navigational instruments, c. 1500. $5, Exploration of Cuba and Hispaniola during Columbus's 2nd voyage, 1493-1496.

1989, Nov. 8 Wmk. 384 *Perf. 14*

269 A42 15c multicolored 1.25 .25
270 A42 80c multicolored 2.50 1.75
271 A42 $1 multicolored 2.50 1.75
272 A42 $5 multicolored 7.25 9.75
Nos. 269-272 (4) 13.50 13.50

World Stamp Expo '89 A43

Exhibition emblem, flags and: 15c, Poinciana tree. 40c, Ft. George Citadel, Brimstone Hill. $1, Light Company private, 5th Foot Regiment, 1778. $3, St. George's Anglican Church.

1989, Nov. 17 Wmk. 373

273 A43 15c multicolored .20 .20
274 A43 40c multicolored .55 .55
275 A43 $1 multicolored 1.40 1.40
276 A43 $3 multicolored 4.00 4.00
Nos. 273-276 (4) 6.15 6.15

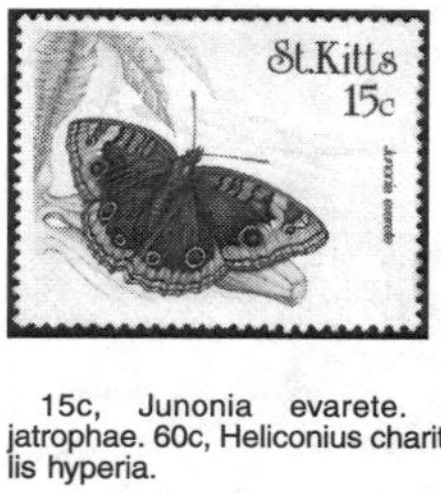

Butterflies A45

15c, Junonia evarete. 40c, Anartia jatrophae. 60c, Heliconius charitonius. $3, Biblis hyperia.

Wmk. 373

1990, June 6 Litho. *Perf. 13½*

277 A45 15c multicolored .20 .20
278 A45 40c multicolored .45 .45
279 A45 60c multicolored .70 .70
280 A45 $3 multicolored 3.50 3.50
Nos. 277-280 (4) 4.85 4.85

Nos. 277-280 with EXPO '90 Emblem Added to Design

1990, June 6

281 A45 15c multicolored .20 .20
282 A45 40c multicolored .40 .40
283 A45 60c multicolored .60 .60
284 A45 $3 multicolored 3.25 3.25
Nos. 281-284 (4) 4.45 4.45

Expo '90, International Garden and Greenery Exposition, Osaka, Japan.

Cannon on Brimstone Hill, 300th Anniv. — A46

15c, 40c, View of Brimstone Hill. 60c, Fort Charles under bombardment. $3, Men firing cannon.

1990 June 30 Wmk. 384 *Perf. 14*

285 A46 15c multicolored .20 .20
286 A46 40c multicolored .35 .35
287 A46 60c multicolored .50 .50
288 Pair 3.00 3.00
a. A46 60c multicolored .50 .50
b. A46 $3 multicolored 2.50 2.50
Nos. 285-288 (4) 4.05 4.05

No. 288 has a continuous design.

Souvenir Sheet

Battle of Britain, 50th Anniv. — A47

1990, Sept. 15

289 Sheet of 2 7.00 7.00
a.-b. A47 $3 any single 3.50 3.50

Ships A48

1990, Oct. 10 Wmk. 373

294 A48 10c Romney .20 .20
a. Wmk. 384 .20 .20
295 A48 15c Baralt .20 .20
296 A48 20c Wear .20 .20
297 A48 25c Sunmount .20 .20
298 A48 40c Inanda .20 .20
299 A48 50c Alcoa Partner .25 .25
300 A48 60c Dominica .30 .30
301 A48 80c CGM Provence .45 .45
302 A48 $1 Director .50 .50
303 A48 $1.20 Typical barque, 1860-1880 .65 .65
304 A48 $2 Chignecto 1.10 1.10
305 A48 $3 Berbice 1.65 1.65
a. Souvenir sheet of 1 2.25 2.25
306 A48 $5 Vamos 2.75 2.75
307 A48 $10 Federal Maple 5.25 5.25
Nos. 294-307 (14) 13.90 13.90

No. 305a issued 2/3/97 for Hong Kong '97.

Christmas — A49

Traditional games.

1990, Nov. 14 *Perf. 14*

308 A49 10c Single fork .20 .20
309 A49 15c Boulder breaking .20 .20
310 A49 40c Double fork .30 .30
311 A49 $3 Run up 2.25 2.25
Nos. 308-311 (4) 2.95 2.95

Flowers — A50

Natl. Census — A51

Perf. 14x13½, 13½x14

1991, May 8 Litho. Wmk. 373

312 A50 10c White periwinkle, horiz. .20 .20
313 A50 40c Pink oleander, horiz. .40 .40
314 A50 60c Pink periwinkle .55 .55
315 A50 $2 White oleander 1.75 1.75
Nos. 312-315 (4) 2.90 2.90

1991, May 13 Wmk. 384 *Perf. 14*

316 A51 15c multicolored .20 .20
317 A51 $2.40 multicolored 2.25 2.25

Elizabeth & Philip, Birthdays

Common Design Types

Wmk. 384

1991, June 17 Litho. *Perf. 14½*

318 CD346 $1.20 multicolored 1.00 1.00
319 CD345 $1.80 multicolored 1.75 1.75
a. Pair, #318-319 + label 2.75 2.75

Fish A52

1991, Aug. 28 Wmk. 373 *Perf. 14*

320 A52 10c Nassau grouper .20 .20
321 A52 60c Hogfish .60 .60
322 A52 $1 Red hind .95 .95
323 A52 $3 Porkfish 2.75 2.75
Nos. 320-323 (4) 4.50 4.50

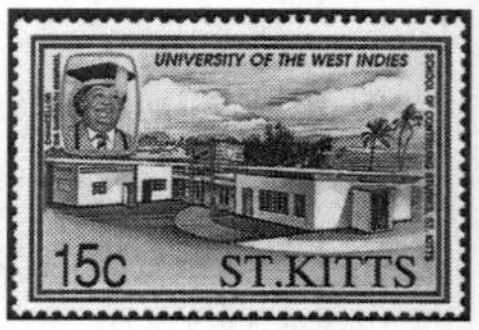

University of the West Indies A53

Designs: 15c, Chancellor Sir Shridath Ramphal, School of Continuing Studies, St. Kitts. 50c, Administration Bldg., Cave Hill Campus, Barbados. $1, Engineering Bldg., St. Augustine Campus, Trinidad & Tobago. $3, Ramphal, Mona Campus, Jamaica.

1991, Sept. 25 Wmk. 384

324 A53 15c multicolored .20 .20
325 A53 50c multicolored .45 .45
326 A53 $1 multicolored .95 .95
327 A53 $3 multicolored 2.75 2.75
Nos. 324-327 (4) 4.35 4.35

Christmas — A54

Various scenes of traditional play, "The Bull."

1991, Nov. 6 Wmk. 373

328 A54 10c multicolored .20 .20
329 A54 15c multicolored .20 .20
330 A54 60c multicolored .45 .45
331 A54 $3 multicolored 2.25 2.25
Nos. 328-331 (4) 3.10 3.10

Queen Elizabeth II's Accession to the Throne, 40th Anniv.
Common Design Type

1992, Feb. 6 Wmk. 384

332 CD349 10c multicolored .20 .20
333 CD349 40c multicolored .35 .35
334 CD349 60c multicolored .50 .50
335 CD349 $1 multicolored .90 .90

Wmk. 373

336 CD349 $3 multicolored 2.50 2.50
Nos. 332-336 (5) 4.45 4.45

St. Kitts and Nevis Red Cross Society, 50th Anniv. A55

10c, Map of St. Kitts & Nevis. 20c, St. Kitts & Nevis flag. 50c, Red Cross House, St. Kitts. $2.40, Jean-Henri Dunant, founder of Red Cross.

Perf. 13½x14

1992, May 8 Litho. Wmk. 373

337 A55 10c multicolored .20 .20
338 A55 20c multicolored .20 .20
339 A55 50c multicolored .65 .65
340 A55 $2.40 multicolored 2.25 2.25
Nos. 337-340 (4) 3.30 3.30

Discovery of America, 500th Anniv. — A56

1992, July 6 *Perf. 13*

341 A56 $1 Coming ashore .90 .90
342 A56 $2 Natives, ships 1.75 1.75

Organization of East Caribbean States.

A57

Christmas — A58

Designs: 25c, Fountain, Independence Square. 50c, Berkeley Memorial drinking fountain and clock. 80c, Sir Thomas Warner's tomb. $2, War Memorial.

1992, Aug. 19 *Perf. 12½x13*

343 A57 25c multicolored .20 .20
344 A57 50c multicolored .40 .40
345 A57 80c multicolored .70 .70
346 A57 $2 multicolored 1.65 1.65
Nos. 343-346 (4) 2.95 2.95

1992, Oct. 28 Wmk. 384 *Perf. 14½*

Stained glass windows: 20c, Mary and Joseph. 25c, Shepherds. 80c, Three Wise Men. $3, Mary, Joseph and Christ Child.

347 A58 20c multicolored .20 .20
348 A58 25c multicolored .20 .20
349 A58 80c multicolored .65 .65
350 A58 $3 multicolored 2.75 2.75
Nos. 347-350 (4) 3.80 3.80

Royal Air Force, 75th Anniv.
Common Design Type

Designs: 25c, Short Singapore III. 50c, Bristol Beaufort. 80c, Westland Whirlwind. $1.60, English Electric Canberra.

No. 355a, Handley Page 0/400. b, Fairey Long Range Monoplane. c, Vickers Wellesley. d, Sepecat Jaguar.

Wmk. 373

1993, Apr. 1 Litho. *Perf. 14*

351 CD350 25c multicolored .25 .25
352 CD350 50c multicolored .50 .50
353 CD350 80c multicolored .80 .80
354 CD350 $1.60 multicolored 1.65 1.65
Nos. 351-354 (4) 3.20 3.20

Miniature Sheet

355 CD350 $2 Sheet of 4, #a.-d. 6.00 6.00

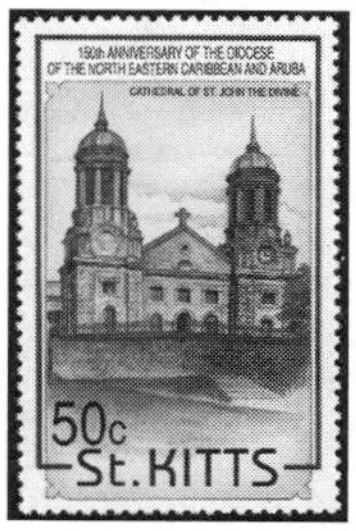

Diocese of the Northeastern Caribbean and Aruba, 150th Anniv. — A59

Coronation of Queen Elizabeth II, 40th Anniv. — A60

Designs: 25c, Diocesan Conference, Basseterre, horiz. 50c, Cathedral of St. John the Divine. 80c, Diocesan coat of arms and motto, horiz. $2, First Bishop, Right Reverend Daniel G. Davis.

Perf. 13½x14, 14x13½

1993, May 21 Litho. Wmk. 384

356 A59 25c multicolored .20 .20
357 A59 50c multicolored .45 .45
358 A59 80c multicolored .75 .75
359 A59 $2 multicolored 1.90 1.90
Nos. 356-359 (4) 3.30 3.30

1993, June 2 *Perf. 14½x14*

Royal regalia and stamps of St. Kitts-Nevis: 10c, Eagle-shaped ampulla, #119. 25c, Anointing spoon, #334. 80c, Tassels, #333. $2, Staff of Scepter with the Cross, #354a-354c.

360 A60 10c multicolored .30 .40
361 A60 25c multicolored .40 .40
362 A60 80c multicolored 1.00 1.00
363 A60 $2 multicolored 2.25 2.25
Nos. 360-363 (4) 3.95 4.05

Girls' Brigade Intl., Cent. — A61

1993, July 1 *Perf. 13½x14*

364 A61 80c Flags .55 .55
365 A61 $3 Badge, coat of arms 2.10 2.10

Independence, 10th Anniv. — A62

Designs: 20c, Flag, map of St. Kitts and Nevis, plane, ship and island scenes. 80c, Natl. arms, independence emblem. $3, Natl. arms, map.

Wmk. 373

1993, Sept. 10 Litho. *Perf. 14*

366 A62 20c multicolored .20 .20
367 A62 80c multicolored .55 .55
368 A62 $3 multicolored 2.00 2.00
Nos. 366-368 (3) 2.75 2.75

Christmas — A63

Prehistoric Aquatic Reptiles — A64

Perf. 13½x14

1993, Nov. 16 Litho. Wmk. 373

369 A63 25c Roselle .20 .20
370 A63 50c Poinsettia .30 .30
371 A63 $1.60 Snow on the Mountain 1.00 1.00
Nos. 369-371 (3) 1.50 1.50

Wmk. 384

1994, Feb. 18 Litho. *Perf. 14*

Designs: a, Mesosaurus. b, Placodus. c, Liopleurodon. d, Hydrotherosaurus. e, Caretta.

372 A64 $1.20 Strip of 5, #a.-e. 4.50 4.50
373 A64 $1.20 #372 ovptd. with Hong Kong '94 emblem 4.50 4.50

Souvenir Sheet

Treasury Building, Cent. — A65

Wmk. 373

1994, Mar. 21 Litho. *Perf. 13½*

374 A65 $10 multicolored 7.50 7.50

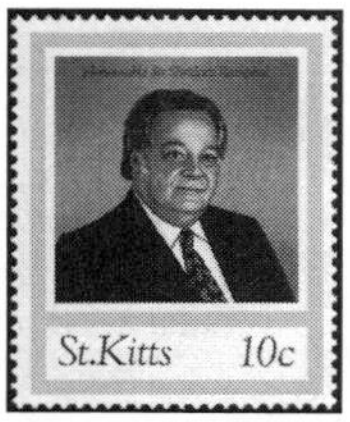

Order of the Caribbean Community A66

First award recipients: Nos. 375a, 376a, Sir Shridath Ramphal, statesman, Guyana. Nos. 375b, 376b, Emblem of the Order. Nos. 375c, 376c, Derek Walcott, writer, St. Lucia. Nos. 375d, 376d, William Demas, economist, Trinidad and Tobago.

Wmk. 373

1994, July 13 Litho. *Perf. 14*

375 A66 10c Strip of 5, #a, b, c, b, d .40 .40
376 A66 $1 Strip of 5, #a, b, c, b, d 3.75 3.75

CARICOM, 20th anniv. (#375b, 376b).

Christmas — A67

1994, Oct. 31

377 A67 25c Carol singing .20 .20
378 A67 25c Opening presents .20 .20
379 A67 80c Carnival .60 .60
380 A67 $2.50 Nativity 1.90 1.90
Nos. 377-380 (4) 2.90 2.90

Intl. Year of the Family.

Green Turtle A68

Wmk. 373

1995, Feb. 27 Litho. *Perf. 14*

381 A68 10c shown .30 .30
382 A68 40c On beach .40 .40
383 A68 50c Laying eggs .55 .55
384 A68 $1 Hatchlings 1.00 1.00
a. Strip of 4, #381-384 2.25 2.25

World Wildlife Fund.
No. 384a issued in sheets of 16 stamps.

First St. Kitts Postage Stamp, 125th Anniv. A69

St. Christopher #1 at left and: 25c, St. Christopher #1. 80c, St. Kitts-Nevis #72. $2.50, St. Kitts-Nevis #91. $3, St. Kitts-Nevis #119.

Wmk. 373

1995, Apr. 10 Litho. *Perf. 13½*

385 A69 25c multicolored .20 .20
386 A69 80c multicolored .60 .60
387 A69 $2.50 multicolored 1.90 1.90
388 A69 $3 multicolored 2.25 2.25
Nos. 385-388 (4) 4.95 4.95

End of World War II, 50th Anniv.
Common Design Types

Designs: 20c, Caribbean Regiment, North Africa. 50c, TBM Avengers on anti-submarine patrol. $2, Spitfire MkVb. $8, US destroyer escort on anti-submarine duty.

$3, Reverse of War Madal 1939-45.

Wmk. 373

1995, May 8 Litho. *Perf. 13½*

389 CD351 20c multicolored .20 .20
390 CD351 50c multicolored .40 .40
391 CD351 $2 multicolored 1.50 1.50
392 CD351 $8 multicolored 6.00 6.00
Nos. 389-392 (4) 8.10 8.10

Souvenir Sheet

Perf. 14

393 CD352 $3 multicolored 2.25 2.25

SKANTEL, 10th Anniv. — A70

Designs: 10c, Satellite transmission. 25c, Telephones, computer. $2, Transmission tower, satellite dish. $3, Satellite dish silhouetted against sun.

1995, Sept. 27 ***Perf. 13½x14***

394	A70	10c	multicolored	.20	.20
395	A70	25c	multicolored	.20	.20
396	A70	$2	multicolored	1.50	1.50
397	A70	$3	multicolored	2.25	2.25
			Nos. 394-397 (4)	4.15	4.15

UN, 50th Anniv.
Common Design Type

Designs: 40c, Energy, clean environment. 50c, Coastal, ocean resources. $1.60, Solid waste management. $2.50, Forestry reserves.

1995, Oct. 24 ***Perf. 13½x13***

398	CD353	40c	multicolored	.30	.30
399	CD353	50c	multicolored	.40	.40
400	CD353	$1.60	multicolored	1.25	1.25
401	CD353	$2.50	multicolored	2.00	2.00
			Nos. 398-401 (4)	3.95	3.95

FAO, 50th Anniv. A71

Designs: 25c, Vegetables. 50c, Glazed carrots, West Indian peas & rice. 80c, Tania, Cassava plants. $1.50, Waterfall, Green Hill Mountain.

1995, Nov. 13 ***Perf. 13½***

402	A71	25c	multicolored	.20	.20
403	A71	50c	multicolored	.40	.40
404	A71	80c	multicolored	.60	.60
405	A71	$1.50	multicolored	1.10	1.10
			Nos. 402-405 (4)	2.30	2.30

Sea Shells — A72

a, Flame helmet. b, Triton's trumpet. c, King helmet. d, True tulip. e, Queen conch.

Wmk. 373

1996, Jan. 10 **Litho.** ***Perf. 13***

406	A72	$1.50	Strip of 5, #a.-e.	5.50	5.50

CAPEX '96 — A73

Leeward Islands LMS Jubilee Class 4-6-0 Locomotives: 10c, No. 45614. $10, No. 5614.

Perf. 13½x14

1996, June 8 **Litho.** **Wmk. 373**

407	A73	10c	multicolored	.20	.20

Souvenir Sheet

Perf. 14x15

408	A73	$10	multicolored	7.50	7.50

No. 408 is 48x31mm.

A74

A75

Modern Olympic Games, Cent.: 10c, Runner, St. Kitts & Nevis flag. 25c, High jumper, US flag. 80c, Runner, Olympic flag. $3, Athens Games poster, 1896.
$6, Olympic torch.

Wmk. 384

1996, June 30 **Litho.** ***Perf. 14***

409	A74	10c	multicolored	.20	.20
410	A74	25c	multicolored	.20	.20
411	A74	80c	multicolored	.60	.60
412	A74	$3	multicolored	2.25	2.25
			Nos. 409-412 (4)	3.25	3.25

Souvenir Sheet

413	A74	$6	multicolored	4.50	4.50

Olymphilex '96 (#413).

1996, Nov. 1 **Wmk. 373**

Defense Force, Cent.: 10c, Volunteer rifleman, 1896. 50c, Mounted infantry, 1911. $2, Bandsman, 1940-60. $2.50, Modern uniform, 1996.

414	A75	10c	multicolored	.20	.20
415	A75	50c	multicolored	.40	.40
416	A75	$2	multicolored	1.50	1.50
417	A75	$2.50	multicolored	1.90	1.90
			Nos. 414-417 (4)	4.00	4.00

Christmas — A76

Paintings: 15c, Holy Virgin and Child, by Anais Colin, 1844. 25c, Holy Family, After Rubens. 50c, Madonna with the Goldfinch, by Krause on porcelain after Raphael, 1507. 80c, Madonna on Throne with Angels, by unknown Spanish, 17th cent.

1996, Dec. 9

418	A76	15c	multicolored	.20	.20
419	A76	25c	multicolored	.20	.20
420	A76	50c	multicolored	.40	.40
421	A76	80c	multicolored	.60	.60
			Nos. 418-421 (4)	1.40	1.40

Fish A77

a, Princess parrot fish. b, Yellowbelly hamlet. c, Coney. d, Clown wrasse. e, Doctor fish. f, Squirrelfish. g, Queen angelfish. h, Spanish hogfish. i, Red hind. j, Red grouper. k, Yellowtail snapper. l, Mutton hamlet.

1997, Apr. 24 ***Perf. 13½***

422	A77	$1	Sheet of 12, #a.-l.	9.00	9.00

Queen Elizabeth II and Prince Philip, 50th Wedding Anniv. — A78

Designs: No. 423, Queen. No. 424, Prince riding with Royal Guard. No. 425, Queen riding in carriage. No. 426, Prince Philip. No. 427, Early photo of Queen, Prince. No. 428, Prince riding horse.
Queen, Prince riding in open carriage, horiz.

Wmk. 373

1997, July 10 **Litho.** ***Perf. 13½***

423	A78	10c	multicolored	.20	.20
424	A78	10c	multicolored	.40	.40
a.			Pair, #423-424	.20	.20
425	A78	25c	multicolored	.20	.20
426	A78	25c	multicolored	.20	.20
a.			Pair, #425-426	.40	.40
427	A78	$3	multicolored	2.25	2.25
428	A78	$3	multicolored	2.25	2.25
a.			Pair, #427-428	4.50	4.50
			Nos. 423-428 (6)	5.50	5.50

Souvenir Sheet

Perf. 14x14½

429	A78	$6	multicolored	4.50	4.50

Christmas — A79

Churches: No. 430, Zion Moravian. No. 431, Wesley Methodist. $1.50, St. Georges Anglican. $15, Co-Cathedral of the Immaculate Conception.

Perf. 13½x14

1997, Oct. 31 **Litho.** **Wmk. 384**

430	A79	10c	multi	.20	.20
431	A79	10c	multi	.20	.20
432	A79	$1.50	multi, vert.	1.00	1.00
433	A79	$15	multi, vert.	9.50	9.50
			Nos. 430-433 (4)	10.90	10.90

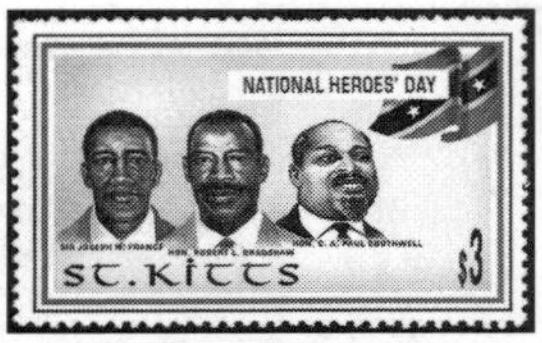

Natl. Heroes' Day — A80

#434, Robert L. Bradshaw (1916-78), 1st premier of St. Kitts, Nevis, & Anguilla. #435, Joseph N. France, trade unionist. #436, C.A. Paul Southwell (1913-79), 1st chief minister of St. Kitts, Nevis, & Anguilla. $3, France, Bradshaw, & Southwell.

1997, Sept. 16 ***Perf. 13½***

434	A80	25c	multi, vert.	.20	.20
435	A80	25c	multi, vert.	.20	.20
436	A80	25c	multi, vert.	.20	.20
437	A80	$3	multi	2.40	2.40
			Nos. 434-437 (4)	3.00	3.00

Diana, Princess of Wales (1961-97)
Common Design Type

#438: a, like #437A. b, Wearing red jacket. c, Wearing white dress. d, Holding flowers.

Perf. 14½x14

1998, Mar. 31 **Litho.** **Wmk. 373**

437A	CD355	30c	Wearing white hat	.25	.25

Sheet of 4

438	CD355	$1.60	Sheet of 4, #a.-d.	4.75	4.75

No. 438 sold for $6.40 + 90c, with surtax from international sales being donated to Princess Diana Memorial Fund and surtax from national sales being donated to designated local charity.

Butterflies A81

Designs: 10c, Common long-tail skipper. 15c, White peacock. 25c, Caribbean buckeye. 30c, Red rim. 40c, Cassius blue. 50c, Flambeau. 60c, Lucas's blue. 90c, Cloudless sulphur. $1, Monarch. $1.20, Fiery skipper. $1.60, Zebra. $3, Southern dagger tail. $5, Polydamus swallowtail. $10, Tropical checkered skipper.

Perf. 14¼x14½

1997, Dec. 29 **Litho.** **Wmk. 373**

439	A81	10c	multicolored	.20	.20
439a			"S" in "Proteus" to left of midline of leaf above	.20	.20
440	A81	15c	multicolored	.20	.20
441	A81	25c	multicolored	.20	.25
442	A81	30c	multicolored	.25	.30
443	A81	40c	multicolored	.25	.30
444	A81	50c	multicolored	.30	.35
445	A81	60c	multicolored	.40	.40
446	A81	90c	multicolored	.65	.65
447	A81	$1	multicolored	.65	.70
448	A81	$1.20	multicolored	.80	.80
449	A81	$1.60	multicolored	1.10	1.10
450	A81	$3	multicolored	2.00	2.00
450a			"S" in "$" same size as numeral	2.25	2.25
451	A81	$5	multicolored	3.25	3.25
451a			Inscribed "Polydamas"	3.75	3.75
452	A81	$10	multicolored	6.50	6.50
452a			"S" in "$" same size as numeral	7.50	7.50
			Nos. 439-452 (17)	22.95	23.20

Nos. 439a, 450a, 451a and 452a have other minor design differences.

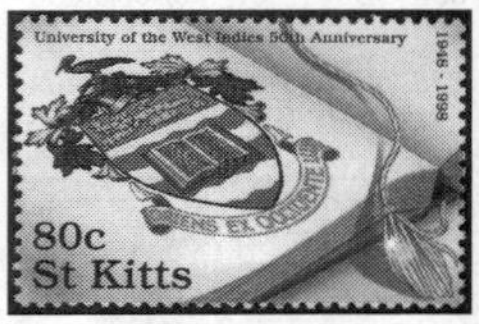

University of West Indies, 50th Anniv. A82

Perf. 13½x13

1998, July 20 **Litho.** **Wmk. 373**

453	A82	80c	shown	.60	.60
454	A82	$2	Arms, mortarboard	1.50	1.50

Carnival Santa A83

Wmk. 373

1998, Oct. 30 **Litho.** ***Perf. 14***

455	A83	80c	shown	.60	.60
456	A83	$1.20	With two dancers	.85	.85

UPU, 125th Anniv. — A84

Wmk. 373

1999, Mar. 5 **Litho.** ***Perf. 14***

457	A84	30c	shown	.25	.25
458	A84	90c	Map of St. Kitts	.70	.70

Birds of the Eastern Caribbean A85

Designs: a, Caribbean martin. b, Spotted sandpiper. c, Sooty tern. d, Red-tailed hawk. e, Trembler. f, Belted kingfisher. g, Black-billed duck. h, Yellow warbler. i, Blue-headed hummingbird. j, Antillean euphonia. k, Fulvous whistling duck. l, Mangrove cuckoo. m, Carib grackle. n, Caribbean elaenia. o, Common ground dove. p, Forest thrush.

Wmk. 373

1999, Apr. 27 **Litho.** ***Perf. 14***

459	A85	80c	Sheet of 16, #a.-p.	9.50	9.50

IBRA '99.

1st Manned Moon Landing, 30th Anniv.

Common Design Type

Designs: 80c, Lift-off. 90c, In lunar orbit. $1, Aldrin deploying scientific equipment. $1.20, Heat shield burns on re-entry.
$10, Earth as seen from moon.

Perf. 14x13¾

1999, July 20 Litho. Wmk. 384

460 CD357	80c	multicolored	.60	.60
461 CD357	90c	multicolored	.65	.65
462 CD357	$1	multicolored	.75	.75
463 CD357	$1.20	multicolored	.90	.90
		Nos. 460-463 (4)	2.90	2.90

Souvenir Sheet

Perf. 14

464 CD357	$10	multicolored	7.50	7.50

No. 464 contains one 40mm circular stamp.

Christmas — A86

Wmk. 373

1999, Oct. 29 Litho. *Perf. 13¾*

465 A86 10c shown		.20	.20
466 A86 30c 3 musicians		.20	.20
467 A86 80c 6 musicians		.55	.55
468 A86 $2 4 musicians, diff.		1.40	1.40
	Nos. 465-468 (4)	2.35	2.35

Children's Drawings Celebrating the Millennium — A87

1999, Dec. 29 Litho. *Perf. 14*

469 A87 10c by Adom Taylor		.20	.20
470 A87 30c by Travis Liburd		.20	.20
471 A87 50c by Darren Moses		.40	.40
472 A87 $1 by Pierre Liburd		.75	.75
	Nos. 469-472 (4)	1.55	1.55

Carifesta VII — A88

Designs: 30c, Festival participants. 90c, Emblem. $1.20, Dancer, vert.

Wmk. 373

2000, Aug. 30 Litho. *Perf. 14*

473 A88 30c multi		.25	.25
474 A88 90c multi		.65	.65
475 A88 $1.20 multi		.90	.90
	Nos. 473-475 (3)	1.80	1.80

Railroads in American Civil War — A89

No. 476, $1.20, horiz.: a, Engine 133. b, Quigley. c, Colonel Holobird. d, Engine 150. e, Doctor Thompson. f, Engine 156.
No. 477, $1.20, horiz.: a, Governor Nye. b, Engine 31. c, C. A. Henry. d, Engine 152. e, Engine 116. f, Job Terry.
No. 478, $1.60, horiz.: a, Dover. b, Scout. c, Baltimore & Ohio Railroad locomotive. d, John M. Forbes. e, Edward Kidder. f, William W. Wright.
No. 479, $1.60, horiz.: a, Engine 83. b, General. c, Engine 38. d, Texas. e, Engine 162. f, Christopher Adams, Jr.
No. 480, $5, Ulysses S. Grant. No. 481, $5, George B. McClellan. No. 482, $5, Herman Haupt. No. 483, $5, Robert E. Lee.

Unwmk.

2001, Feb. 19 Litho. *Perf. 14*

Sheets of 6, #a-f

476-479 A89	Set of 4	25.00	25.00

Souvenir Sheets

480-483 A89	Set of 4	15.00	15.00

Flora & Fauna — A90

No. 484, $1.20 - Flowers: a, Heliconia. b, Anthurium. c, Oncidium splendidum. d, Trumpet creeper. e, Bird of paradise. f, Hibiscus.
No. 485, $1.20: a, Bananaquit. b, Anthurium (hills and clouds in background). c, Common dolphin. d, Horse mushroom. e, Green anole. f, Monarch butterfly.
No. 486, $1.60 - Birds: a, Laughing gull. b, Sooty tern. c, White-tailed tropicbird. d, Painted bunting. e, Belted kingfisher. f, Yellow-bellied sapsucker.
No. 487, $1.60 - Butterflies: a, Figure-of-eight. b, Banded king shoemaker. c, Orange theope. d, Grecian shoemaker. e, Clorinde. f, Small lace-wing.
No. 488, $1.60, horiz.: a, Beaugregory. b, Banded butterflyfish. c, Cherubfish. d, Rock beauty. e, Red snapper. f, Leatherback turtle.
No. 489, $5, Leochilus carinatus. No. 489, $5, Iguana, horiz. No. 490, $5, Ruby-throated hummingbird, horiz. No. 491, $5, Common morpho, horiz.
No. 493, $5, Redband parrotfish, horiz.

2001, Mar. 12 *Perf. 14*

Sheets of 6, #a-f

484-488 A90	Set of 5	32.25	32.25

Souvenir Sheets

489-493 A90	Set of 5	18.75	18.75

Compare No. 490 with No. 520.

2001 Census — A91

Designs: 30c, People in house. $3, People, barn, silos.

2001, Apr. 18 Litho. *Perf. 14½x14¼*

494-495 A91	Set of 2	2.50	2.50

Queen Victoria (1819-1901) — A92

No. 496: a, At coronation. b, In wedding gown. c, With Prince Albert visiting wounded Crimean War veterans. d, With Prince Albert, 1854.
$5, Wearing crown.

2001, Apr. 26 *Perf. 14*

496 A92 $2 Sheet of 4, #a-d		6.00	6.00

Souvenir Sheet

497 A92 $5 black		3.75	3.75

No. 496 contains four 28x42mm stamps.

Monet Paintings — A93

No. 498, horiz.: a, On the Coast of Trouville. b, Vétheuil in Summer. c, Field of Yellow Iris Near Giverny. d, Coastguard's Cottage at Varengeville.
$5, Poplars on the Banks of the Epte, Seen From the Marshes.

2001, July 16 *Perf. 13¾*

498 A93 $2 Sheet of 4, #a-d		6.00	6.00

Souvenir Sheet

499 A93 $5 multi		3.75	3.75

Giuseppe Verdi (1813-1901), Opera Composer — A94

No. 500 - Scenes from the Sicilian Vespers: a, French soldiers in Palermo (all standing). b, French soldiers in Palermo (some seated). c, Costume design. d, Sicilian people and French soldiers
$5, Montserrat Caballé.

2001, July 16 *Perf. 14*

500 A94 $2 Sheet of 4, #a-d		6.00	6.00

Souvenir Sheet

501 A94 $5 multi		3.75	3.75

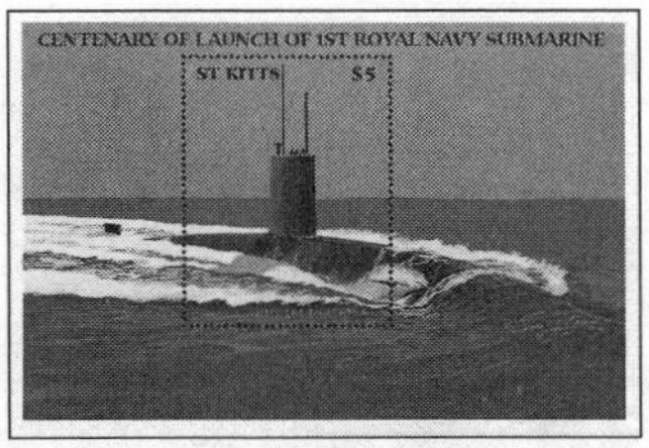

Royal Navy Submarines, Cent. — A95

No. 502, horiz.: a, A Class submarine. b, HMS Dreadnaught battleship. c, HMS Amethyst. d, HMS Barnham. e, HMS Exeter. f, HMS Eagle.
$5, HMS Dreadnaught submarine.

2001, July 16 *Perf. 14*

502 A95 $1.40 Sheet of 6, #a-f		6.25	6.25

Souvenir Sheet

503 A95 $5 multi		3.75	3.75

No. 502 contains six 42x28mm stamps.

Queen Elizabeth II, 75th Birthday — A96

No. 504: a, In blue hat, holding flowers. b, In flowered hat, looking right. c, In blue hat and coat. d, In flowered hat, looking left.
$5, On horse.

2001, July 16

504 A96 $2 Sheet of 4, #a-d		6.00	6.00

Souvenir Sheet

505 A96 $5 multi		3.75	3.75

Phila Nippon '01, Japan — A97

Woodcuts: 50c, Hatsufunedayu as a Tatebina, by Shigenobu. 80c, Samurai Kodenji as Tsuyu No Mae, by Kiyonobu I. $1, Senya Nakamura as Tokonatsu, by Kiyomasu I. $1.60, Sumida River, by Shunsho. $2, Wrestler, Kuemon Yoba, by Shun-ei. $3, Two Actors in Roles, by Kiyonobu Torii I.
$5, Full Length Actor Protraits, by Shun-ei.

2001, July 16 *Perf. 12x12¼*

506-511 A97	Set of 6	6.75	6.75

Souvenir Sheet

512 A97 $5 multi		3.75	3.75

Mao Zedong (1893-1976) — A98

No. 514: a, In 1926. b, In 1945 (green background). c, In 1945 (lilac background). $3, Undated picture.

2001, July 16 Litho. *Perf. 13¾*

513	A98 $2 Sheet of 3, #a-c		4.50	4.50

Souvenir Sheet

514	A98 $3 multi		2.25	2.25

Flora & Fauna — A99

No. 515, $1.20 - Birds: a, Trembler. b, White-tailed tropicbird. c, Red-footed booby. d, Red-legged thrush. e, Painted bunting. f, Bananaquit.

No. 516, $1.20 - Orchids: a, Maxillaria cucullata. b, Cattleya dowiana. c, Rossioglossum grande. d, Aspasia epidendroides. e, Lycaste skinneri. f, Cattleya percivaliana.

No. 517, $1.60 - Butterflies: a, Orange-barred sulphur. b, Giant swallowtail. c, Orange theope. d, Blue night. e, Grecian shoemaker. f, Cramer's mesene.

No. 518, $1.60 - Mushrooms: a, Pholiota spectabilis. b, Flammula penetrans. c, Ungulina marginata. d, Collybia iocephala. e, Amanita muscaria. f, Corinus comatus.

No. 519, $1.60, horiz. - Whales: a, Killer.whale b, Cuvier's beaked whale. c, Humpback whale. d, Sperm whale. e, Blue whale. f, Whale shark.

No. 520, $5, Ruby-throated hummingbird. No. 521, $5, Psychilis atropurpurea. No. 522, $5, Figure-of-eight butterfly. No. 523, $5, Lepiota procera. No. 524, $5, Sei whale, horiz.

2001, Sept. 18 *Perf. 14*

Sheets of 6, #a-f

515-519	A99 Set of 5	32.50	32.50

Souvenir Sheets

520-524	A99 Set of 5	19.00	19.00

Compare No. 520 with No. 490.

Christmas and Carnival — A100

Designs: 10c, Angel, Christmas tree. 30c, Fireworks. 80c, Wreath, dove, bells, candy cane. $2, Steel drums.

2001, Nov. 26

525-528	A100 Set of 4	2.40	2.40

Reign of Queen Elizabeth II, 50th Anniv. — A101

No. 529: a, Ceremonial coach. b, Prince Philip. c, Queen and Queen Mother. d, Queen wearing tiara.
$5, Queen and Prince Philip.

2002, Feb. 6 *Perf. 14¼*

529	A101 $2 Sheet of 4, #a-d	6.00	6.00

Souvenir Sheet

530	A101 $5 multi	3.75	3.75

OFFICIAL STAMPS

Nos. 28-37 Ovptd. "OFFICIAL"

Perf. 14½x14

1980, June 23 Litho. Wmk. 373

O1	A61	15c	multicolored	.20	.20
O2	A61	25c	multicolored	.20	.20
O3	A61	30c	multicolored	.20	.20
O4	A61	40c	multicolored	.20	.20
O5	A61	45c	multicolored	.20	.20
O6	A61	50c	multicolored	.20	.20
O7	A61	55c	multicolored	.20	.20
O8	A61	$1	multicolored	.30	.30
O9	A61	$5	multicolored	1.50	1.50
O10	A61	$10	multicolored	2.75	2.75
		Nos. O1-O10 (10)		5.95	5.95

Unwmk.

O2a	A61	25c	.25	.20
O3a	A61	30c	.50	.35
O4a	A61	40c	11.50	10.75
O7a	A61	55c	.75	.55
O8a	A61	$1	1.25	.90
O9a	A61	$5	3.75	4.00
O10a	A61	$10	4.50	5.75
		Nos. O2a-O10a (7)	22.50	22.50

Nos. 55-66 Ovptd. "OFFICIAL"

1981, Feb. 5 *Perf. 14*

O11	A5	15c	multicolored	.20	.20
O12	A5	20c	multicolored	.20	.20
O13	A5	25c	multicolored	.25	.20
O14	A5	30c	multicolored	.25	.20
O15	A5	40c	multicolored	.30	.20
O16	A5	45c	multicolored	.40	.20
O17	A5	50c	multicolored	.40	.20
O18	A5	55c	multicolored	.50	.25
O19	A5	$1	multicolored	.75	.50
O20	A5	$2.50	multicolored	1.50	1.10
O21	A5	$5	multicolored	2.75	2.25
O22	A5	$10	multicolored	5.00	4.50
		Nos. O11-O22 (12)		12.50	10.00

Nos. 75-80 Ovptd. or Surcharged "OFFICIAL" in Ultra or Black

1983, Feb. 2

O23	A66	45c	on $2.50 No. 77	.25	.25
O24	A67	45c	on $2.50 No. 78	.45	.40
O25	A66	55c	No. 75	.25	.25
O26	A67	55c	No. 76	.50	.45
O27	A66	$1.10	on $4 No. 79 (B)	.50	*.60*
O28	A67	$1.10	on $4 No. 80 (B)	1.00	1.00
		Nos. O23-O28 (6)		2.95	2.95

Nos. 141-152 Ovptd. "OFFICIAL"

1984, July 4 Wmk. 380

O29	A18	15c	multicolored	.20	.20
O30	A18	20c	multicolored	.20	.20
O31	A18	25c	multicolored	.25	.25
O32	A18	30c	multicolored	.30	.30
O33	A18	40c	multicolored	.40	.40
O34	A18	50c	multicolored	.50	.50
O35	A18	60c	multicolored	.60	.60
O36	A18	75c	multicolored	.75	.75
O37	A18	$1	multicolored	1.10	1.10
O38	A18	$2.50	multicolored	2.50	2.50
O39	A18	$5	multicolored	5.25	5.25
O40	A18	$10	multicolored	10.00	10.00
		Nos. O29-O40 (12)		22.05	22.05

ST. KITTS-NEVIS

sānt 'kits-'nē-vəs

(St. Christopher-Nevis-Anguilla)

LOCATION — West Indies southeast of Puerto Rico
GOVT. — Associated State in British Commonwealth
AREA — 153 sq. mi.
POP. — 43,309, excluding Anguilla (1991)
CAPITAL — Basseterre, St. Kitts

St. Kitts-Nevis was one of the presidencies of the former Leeward Islands colony until it became a colony itself in 1956. In 1967 Britain granted internal self-government.

See "St. Christopher" for stamps used in St. Kitts before 1890. From 1890 until 1903, stamps of the Leeward Islands were used. From 1903 until 1956, stamps of St. Kitts-Nevis and Leeward Islands were used concurrently.

Starting in 1967, issues of Anguilla are listed under that heading. Starting in 1980 stamps inscribed St. Kitts or Nevis are listed under those headings.

12 Pence = 1 Shilling
20 Shillings = 1 Pound
100 Cents = 1 Dollar (1951)

Catalogue values for unused stamps in this country are for Never Hinged items, beginning with Scott 91 in the regular postage section and Scott O1 in the officials section.

Columbus Looking for Land — A1

Medicinal Spring — A2

Wmk. Crown and C A (2)

1903 Typo. *Perf. 14*

1	A1	½p	green & violet	1.25	.55
2	A2	1p	car & black	2.75	.20
3	A1	2p	brown & violet	2.00	*8.50*
4	A1	2½p	ultra & black	12.50	3.25
5	A2	3p	org & green	6.25	*20.00*
6	A1	6p	red violet & blk	2.75	*22.50*
7	A1	1sh	orange & green	5.00	*10.00*
8	A2	2sh	black & green	10.00	16.00
9	A1	2sh6p	violet & blk	15.00	*35.00*
10	A2	5sh	ol grn & gray vio	40.00	*50.00*
		Nos. 1-10 (10)		97.50	*166.00*

1905-18 Wmk. 3

11	A1	½p	green & violet	2.75	*4.25*
12	A1	½p	green	.60	.40
13	A2	1p	carmine & blk	.90	.90
14	A2	1p	carmine	1.00	.25
15	A1	2p	brown & violet	4.25	1.25
16	A1	2½p	ultra & blk	8.50	7.00
17	A1	2½p	ultra	1.25	.50
18	A2	3p	orange & green	3.00	3.00
19	A1	6p	red vio & gray blk ('08)	7.25	*22.50*
a.		6p	purple & gray ('08)	5.00	*12.50*
20	A1	1sh	org & grn ('09)	10.50	*14.00*
21	A2	5sh	ol grn & gray vio ('18)	17.50	*55.00*
		Nos. 11-21 (11)		57.50	*109.05*

Nos. 13, 19a and 21 are on chalky paper only and Nos. 15, 18 and 20 are on both ordinary and chalky paper.

For stamp and type overprinted see #MR1-MR2.

King George V — A3

A4

1920-22

Ordinary Paper

24	A3	½p	green	.90	1.10
25	A4	1p	carmine	1.10	.55
26	A3	1½p	orange	.70	.70
27	A4	2p	gray	3.00	*4.25*
28	A3	2½p	ultramarine	1.40	*3.00*

Chalky Paper

29	A4	3p	vio & dull vio, *yel*	1.65	*4.25*
30	A3	6p	red vio & dull vio	2.00	*5.25*
31	A4	1sh	blk, *gray grn*	2.25	*6.00*
32	A3	2sh	ultra & dull vio, *blue*	9.00	*18.00*
33	A4	2sh	6p red & blk, *blue*	9.00	*20.00*
34	A3	5sh	red & grn, *yel*	10.00	*32.50*
35	A4	10sh	red & grn, *grn*	27.50	*45.00*
36	A3	£1	blk & vio, *red* ('22)	190.00	*250.00*
		Nos. 24-36 (13)		258.50	*390.60*

1921-29 Wmk. 4

Ordinary Paper

37	A3	½p	green	1.10	1.10
38	A4	1p	rose red	.45	.25
39	A4	1p	dp violet ('22)	3.00	.65
40	A3	1½p	rose red ('25)	2.25	*2.50*
41	A3	1½p	fawn ('28)	.55	.25
42	A4	2p	gray	.35	*.50*
43	A3	2½p	ultra ('22)	1.25	1.25
44	A3	2½p	brown ('22)	1.50	*7.25*

Chalky Paper

45	A4	3p	ultra ('22)	.60	*3.50*
46	A4	3p	vio & dull vio, *yel*	.55	*3.50*
47	A3	6p	red vio & dull vio ('24)	2.40	*4.50*
48	A4	1sh	black, *grn* ('29)	3.25	*5.25*
49	A3	2sh	ultra & vio, *bl* ('22)	7.00	*19.00*
50	A4	2sh6p	red & blk, *bl* ('27)	11.50	*24.00*
51	A3	5sh	red & grn, *yel* ('29)	32.50	*52.50*
		Nos. 37-51 (15)		68.25	*126.00*

No. 43 exists on ordinary and chalky paper.

Caravel in Old Road Bay — A5

1923 Wmk. 4

52	A5	½p	green & blk	2.10	*2.50*
53	A5	1p	violet & blk	4.25	1.90
54	A5	1½p	carmine & blk	4.25	*7.50*
55	A5	2p	dk gray & blk	3.25	2.75
56	A5	2½p	brown & blk	5.25	*10.00*
57	A5	3p	ultra & blk	3.50	*7.50*
58	A5	6p	red vio & blk	9.00	*16.00*
59	A5	1sh	ol grn & blk	13.00	*16.00*
60	A5	2sh	ultra & blk, *bl*	37.50	*45.00*
61	A5	2sh6p	red & blk, *blue*	45.00	*62.50*
62	A5	10sh	red & blk, *emer*	240.00	*325.00*

Wmk. 3

63	A5	5sh red & blk, *yel*	62.50	*175.00*
64	A5	£1 vio & blk, *red*	800.00	*1,250.*
		Nos. 52-63 (12)	429.60	*671.65*

Tercentenary of the founding of the colony of St. Kitts (or St. Christopher).

Common Design Types pictured following the introduction.

Silver Jubilee Issue
Common Design Type
Inscribed "St. Christopher and Nevis"
Perf. 11x12

1935, May 6 Engr. Wmk. 4

72	CD301	1p car & dk blue	.40	*.60*
73	CD301	1½p gray blk & ultra	.55	*.65*
74	CD301	2½p ultra & brown	1.40	.75
75	CD301	1sh brn vio & ind	4.25	*10.00*
		Nos. 72-75 (4)	6.60	*12.00*
		Set, never hinged	12.50	

Coronation Issue
Common Design Type
Inscribed "St. Christopher and Nevis"

1937, May 12 ***Perf. 13½x14***

76	CD302	1p carmine	.20	.20
77	CD302	1½p brown	.20	.20
78	CD302	2½p bright ultra	.35	.30
		Nos. 76-78 (3)	.75	.70
		Set, never hinged	1.25	

George VI
A6

Medicinal Spring
A7

Columbus Looking for Land — A8

Map Showing Anguilla
A9

Perf. 13½x14 (A6, A9), 14 (A7, A8)

1938-48 Typo.

79	A6	½p green	.20	.20
80	A6	1p carmine	.20	.20
81	A6	1½p orange	.20	.20
82	A7	2p gray & car	.25	.25
83	A6	2½p ultra	.25	.25
84	A7	3p car & pale lilac	.35	.35
85	A8	6p rose lil & dull grn	1.40	1.10
86	A7	1sh green & gray blk	.90	.90
87	A7	2sh6p car & gray blk	3.00	2.50
88	A8	5sh car & dull grn	3.00	3.00

Typo., Center Litho.
Chalky Paper

89	A9	10sh brt ultra & blk	13.00	*21.00*
90	A9	£1 brown & blk	18.00	*22.50*
		Nos. 79-90 (12)	40.75	*52.45*
		Set, never hinged	70.00	

Issued: ½, 1, 1½, 2½p, 8/15/38; 2p, 1941; 3, 6p, 2, 5sh, 1942; 1sh, 1943; 10sh, £1, 9/1/48.
For types overprinted see Nos. 99-104.

1938, Aug. 15 ***Perf. 13x11½***

82a	A7	2p	7.25	2.75
84a	A7	3p	1.40	1.25
85a	A8	6p	1.40	1.25
86a	A7	1sh	2.75	1.75
87a	A7	2sh6p	9.25	7.50
88a	A8	5sh	35.00	*18.00*
		Nos. 82a-88a (6)	57.05	*32.50*

Catalogue values for unused stamps in this section, from this point to the end of the section, are for Never Hinged items.

Peace Issue
Common Design Type
Inscribed "St. Kitts-Nevis"

1946, Nov. 1 Engr. ***Perf. 13½x14***

91	CD303	1½p deep orange	.20	.20
92	CD303	3p carmine	.20	.20

Silver Wedding Issue
Common Design Types
Inscribed: "St. Kitts-Nevis"

1949, Jan. 3 Photo. ***Perf. 14x14½***

93	CD304	2½p bright ultra	.20	.20

Engraved; Name Typographed
Perf. 11½x11

94	CD305	5sh rose carmine	5.50	*4.25*

UPU Issue
Common Design Types
Inscribed: "St. Kitt's-Nevis"
Engr.; Name Typo. on 3p, 6p

1949, Oct. 10 ***Perf. 13½, 11x11½***

95	CD306	2½p ultra	.20	.20
96	CD307	3p deep carmine	.20	.20
97	CD308	6p red lilac	.50	.40
98	CD309	1sh blue green	.80	.70
		Nos. 95-98 (4)	1.70	1.50

Types of 1938 Overprinted in Black or Carmine:

ANGUILLA ANGUILLA

TERCENTENARY 1650-1950
On A6

TERCENTENARY 1650—1950
On A7-A8

Perf. 13½x14, 13x12½

1950, Nov. 10 Wmk. 4

99	A6	1p carmine	.20	.20
100	A6	1½p orange	.20	.20
a.		Wmk. 4a (error)	600.00	
101	A6	2½p ultra	.20	.20
102	A7	3p car & pale lilac	.20	.20
103	A8	6p rose lil & dl grn	.25	.25
104	A7	1sh grn & gray blk (C)	.40	.40
		Nos. 99-104 (6)	1.45	1.45

300th anniv. of the settlement of Anguilla.

University Issue
Common Design Types
Inscribed: "St. Kitts-Nevis"
Perf. 14x14½

1951, Feb. 16 Engr. Wmk. 4

105	CD310	3c org yel & gray blk	.20	.20
106	CD311	12c red violet & aqua	.60	.60

St. Christopher-Nevis-Anguilla

Bath House and Spa, Nevis — A10

Map — A11

Designs: 2c, Warner Park, St. Kitts. 4c, Brimstone Hill, St. Kitts. 5c, Nevis. 6c, Pinney's Beach, Nevis. 12c, Sir Thomas Warner's Tomb. 24c, Old Road Bay, St. Kitts. 48c, Picking Cotton. 60c, Treasury, St. Kitts. $1.20, Salt Pond, Anguilla. $4.80, Sugar Mill, St. Kitts.

1952, June 14 ***Perf. 12½***

107	A10	1c ocher & dp grn	.20	.20
108	A10	2c emerald	.20	.20
109	A11	3c purple & red	.20	.20
110	A10	4c red	.20	.20
111	A10	5c gray & ultra	.30	.30
112	A10	6c deep ultra	.40	.40
113	A11	12c redsh brn & dp blue	.60	.60
114	A10	24c car & gray blk	.90	.70
115	A10	48c vio brn & ol bister	2.50	2.50
116	A10	60c dp grn & och	2.50	2.50
117	A10	$1.20 dp ultra & dp green	6.00	6.00
118	A10	$4.80 car & emer	14.00	14.00
		Nos. 107-118 (12)	28.00	27.80

Coronation Issue
Common Design Type

1953, June 2 ***Perf. 13½x13***

119	CD312	2c brt green & blk	.25	.20

Types of 1952 with Portrait of Queen Elizabeth II

½c, Salt Pond, Anguilla. 8c, Sombrero Lighthouse. $2.40, Map of Anguilla & Dependencies.

1954-57 Engr. ***Perf. 12½***

120	A10	½c gray olive ('56)	.25	.20
121	A10	1c ocher & dp grn	.20	.20
a.		Horiz. pair, imperf. vert.		
122	A10	2c emerald	.35	.20
123	A11	3c purple & red	.55	.20
124	A10	4c red	.20	.20
125	A10	5c gray & ultra	.20	.20
126	A10	6c deep ultra	.35	.25
127	A11	8c dark gray ('57)	2.50	.25
128	A11	12c redsh brn & dp blue	.20	.25
129	A10	24c carmine & blk	.20	.45
130	A10	48c brn & ol bister	.50	1.25
131	A10	60c dp grn & ocher	4.75	1.65
132	A10	$1.20 dp ultra & dp green	15.00	2.75
133	A10	$2.40 red org & blk ('57)	8.50	4.25
134	A10	$4.80 car & emer	11.00	11.00
		Nos. 120-134 (15)	44.75	23.30

Issued: 24c-$1.20, $4.80, 12/1/54; ½c, 7/3/56; 8c, $2.40, 2/1/57; others, 3/1/54.

Alexander Hamilton and Nevis Scene
A12

1957, Jan. 11 ***Perf. 12½***

135	A12	24c dp ultra & yellow grn	.35	.20

Bicent. of the birth of Alexander Hamilton.

West Indies Federation
Common Design Type
Perf. 11½x11

1958, Apr. 22 Engr. Wmk. 314

136	CD313	3c green	.35	.35
137	CD313	6c blue	.60	.60
138	CD313	12c carmine rose	1.25	1.25
		Nos. 136-138 (3)	2.20	2.20

Federation of the West Indies, Apr. 22, 1958.

Stamp of Nevis, 1861
A13

Designs (Stamps of Nevis, 1861 issue): 8c, 4p stamp. 12c, 6p stamp. 24c, 1sh stamp.

1961, July 15 ***Perf. 14***

139	A13	2c green & brown	.20	.20
140	A13	8c blue & pale brown	.20	.20
141	A13	12c carmine & gray	.25	.25
142	A13	24c orange & green	.50	.50
		Nos. 139-142 (4)	1.15	1.15

Centenary of the first stamps of Nevis.

Red Cross Centenary Issue
Common Design Type

1963, Sept. 2 Litho. ***Perf. 13***

143	CD315	3c black & red	.20	.20
144	CD315	12c ultra & red	.60	.60

New Lighthouse, Sombrero — A14

Loading Sugar Cane, St. Kitts
A15

Designs: 2c, Pall Mall Square, Basseterre. 3c, Gateway, Brimstone Hill Fort, St. Kitts. 4c, Nelson's Spring, Nevis. 5c, Grammar School, St. Kitts. 6c, Mt. Misery Crater, St. Kitts. 10c, Hibiscus. 15c, Sea Island cotton, Nevis. 20c, Boat building, Anguilla. 25c, White-crowned pigeon. 50c, St. George's Church tower, Basseterre. 60c, Alexander Hamilton. $1, Map of St. Kitts-Nevis. $2.50, Map of Anguilla. $5, Arms of St. Christopher-Nevis-Anguilla.

1963, Nov. 20 Photo. ***Perf. 14***

145	A14	½c blue & dk brn	.20	.20
146	A15	1c multicolored	.20	.20
147	A14	2c multicolored	.20	.20
a.		Yellow omitted	150.00	
148	A14	3c multicolored	.20	.20
149	A15	4c multicolored	.20	.20
150	A15	5c multicolored	.20	.20
151	A15	6c multicolored	.20	.20
152	A15	10c multicolored	.20	.20
153	A14	15c multicolored	.20	.20
154	A15	20c multicolored	.30	.20
155	A14	25c multicolored	.35	.20
156	A15	50c multicolored	.80	.30
157	A14	60c multicolored	.90	.35
158	A14	$1 multicolored	1.65	.50
159	A15	$2.50 multicolored	3.00	3.00
160	A14	$5 multicolored	5.00	4.50
		Nos. 145-160 (16)	13.80	10.85

For overprints see Nos. 161-162.

1967-69 Wmk. 314 Sideways

145a	A14	½c ('69)	.20	*1.00*
147b	A14	2c	.20	.20
148a	A14	3c ('68)	.25	.20
153a	A14	15c ('68)	.60	.30
155a	A14	25c ('68)	1.90	.20
158a	A14	$1 ('68)	5.75	4.00
		Nos. 145a-158a (6)	8.90	5.90

Nos. 148 and 155 Overprinted: "ARTS / FESTIVAL / ST. KITTS / 1964"

1964, Sept. 14

161	A14	3c multicolored	.20	.20
162	A14	25c multicolored	.30	.30

ITU Issue
Common Design Type
Perf. 11x11½

1965, May 17 Litho. Wmk. 314

163	CD317	2c bister & rose red	.20	.20
164	CD317	50c grnsh blue & ol	.75	.75

Intl. Cooperation Year Issue
Common Design Type

1965, Oct. 25 ***Perf. 14½***

165	CD318	2c blue grn & claret	.20	.20
166	CD318	25c lt violet & green	.45	.45

Churchill Memorial Issue
Common Design Type

1966, Jan. 24 Photo. ***Perf. 14***
Design in Black, Gold and Carmine Rose

167	CD319	½c bright blue	.20	.20
168	CD319	3c green	.20	.20
169	CD319	15c brown	.30	.30
170	CD319	25c violet	.60	.60
		Nos. 167-170 (4)	1.30	1.30

Royal Visit Issue
Common Design Type

1966, Feb. 14 Litho. ***Perf. 11x12***

171	CD320	3c violet blue	.20	.20
172	CD320	25c dk carmine rose	.65	.65

World Cup Soccer Issue
Common Design Type

1966, July 1 Litho. ***Perf. 14***

173	CD321	6c multicolored	.20	.20
174	CD321	25c multicolored	.50	.50

Festival Emblem With Dolphins — A16

Unwmk.

1966, Aug. 15 Photo. *Perf. 14*

175	A16	3c gold, grn, yel & blk	.20	.20
176	A16	25c silver, grn, yel & blk	.30	.30

Arts Festival of 1966.

WHO Headquarters Issue

Common Design Type

1966, Sept. 20 Litho. *Perf. 14*

177	CD322	3c multicolored	.20	.20
178	CD322	40c multicolored	.40	.40

UNESCO Anniversary Issue

Common Design Type

1966, Dec. 1 Litho. *Perf. 14*

179	CD323	3c "Education"	.20	.20
180	CD323	6c "Science"	.20	.20
181	CD323	40c "Culture"	.50	.50
		Nos. 179-181 (3)	.90	.90

Independent State

Government Headquarters, Basseterre — A17

Designs: 10c, Flag and map of Anguilla, St. Christopher and Nevis. 25c, Coat of Arms.

Wmk. 314

1967, July 1 Photo. *Perf. 14½*

182	A17	3c multicolored	.20	.20
183	A17	10c multicolored	.20	.20
184	A17	25c multicolored	.30	.30
		Nos. 182-184 (3)	.70	.70

Achievement of independence, Feb. 27, 1967.

Charles Wesley, Cross and Palm — A18

3c, John Wesley. 40c, Thomas Coke.

1967, Dec. 1 Litho. *Perf. 13x13½*

185	A18	3c dp lilac, dp car & blk	.20	.20
186	A18	25c ultra, grnsh blue & blk	.20	.20
187	A18	40c ocher, yellow & blk	.30	.30
		Nos. 185-187 (3)	.70	.70

Attainment of autonomy by the Methodist Church in the Caribbean and the Americas, and for the opening of headquarters near St. John's, Antigua, May 1967.

Cargo Ship and Plane A19

Perf. 13½x13

1968, July 30 Litho. Wmk. 314

188	A19	25c multicolored	.25	.25
189	A19	50c brt blue & multi	.55	.55

Issued to publicize the organization of the Caribbean Free Trade Area, CARIFTA.

Martin Luther King, Jr. — A20

Mystical Nativity, by Botticelli — A21

Perf. 12x12½

1968, Sept. 30 Litho. Wmk. 314

190	A20	50c multicolored	.35	.35

Dr. Martin Luther King, Jr. (1929-68), American civil rights leader.

Perf. 14½x14

1968, Nov. 27 Photo. Wmk. 314

Christmas (Paintings): 25c, 50c, The Adoration of the Magi, by Rubens.

191	A21	12c brt violet & multi	.20	.20
192	A21	25c multicolored	.20	.20
193	A21	40c gray & multi	.20	.20
194	A21	50c crimson & multi	.30	.30
		Nos. 191-194 (4)	.90	.90

Snook A22

Fish: 12c, Needlefish (gar). 40c, Horse-eye jack. 50c, Red snapper. The 6c is misinscribed "tarpon."

Perf. 14x14½

1969, Feb. 25 Photo. Wmk. 314

195	A22	6c brt green & multi	.20	.20
196	A22	12c blue & multi	.25	.25
197	A22	40c gray blue & multi	.35	.35
198	A22	50c multicolored	.45	.45
		Nos. 195-198 (4)	1.25	1.25

Arms of Sir Thomas Warner and Map of Islands — A23

Designs: 25c, Warner's tomb in St. Kitts. 40c, Warner's commission from Charles I.

1969, Sept. 1 Litho. *Perf. 13½*

199	A23	20c multicolored	.20	.20
200	A23	25c multicolored	.20	.20
201	A23	40c multicolored	.25	.25
		Nos. 199-201 (3)	.65	.65

Issued in memory of Sir Thomas Warner, first Governor of St. Kitts-Nevis, Barbados and Montserrat.

Adoration of the Kings, by Jan Mostaert — A24

Christmas (Painting): 40c, 50c, Adoration of the Kings, by Geertgen tot Sint Jans.

1969, Nov. 17 *Perf. 13½*

202	A24	10c olive & multi	.20	.20
203	A24	25c violet & multi	.20	.20
204	A24	40c yellow grn & multi	.20	.20
205	A24	50c maroon & multi	.20	.20
		Nos. 202-205 (4)	.80	.80

Pirates Burying Treasure, Frigate Bay — A25

Caravels, 16th Century A26

Designs: 1c, English two-decker, 1650. 2c, Flags of England, Spain, France, Holland and Portugal. 3c, Hilt of 17th cent. rapier. 5c, Henry Morgan and fire boats. 6c, The pirate L'Ollonois and a carrack (pirate vessel). 10c, Smugglers' ship. 15c, Spanish 17th cent. piece of eight and map of Caribbean. 20c, Garrison and ship cannon and map of Spanish Main. 25c, Humphrey Cole's astrolabe, 1574. 50c, Flintlock pistol and map of Spanish Main. 60c, Dutch Flute (ship). $1, Capt. Bartholomew Roberts and document with death sentence for his crew. $2.50, Railing piece (small cannon), 17th cent. and map of Spanish Main. $5, Francis Drake, John Hawkins and ships. $10, Edward Teach (Blackbeard) and his capture.

Wmk. 314 Upright (A25), Sideways (A26)

1970, Feb. 1 Litho. *Perf. 14*

206	A25	½c multicolored	.20	.20
207	A25	1c multicolored	.35	.20
208	A25	2c multicolored	.20	.20
209	A25	3c multicolored	.20	.20
210	A26	4c multicolored	.20	.20
211	A26	5c multicolored	.35	.20
212	A26	6c multicolored	.35	.20
213	A26	10c multicolored	.35	.20
214	A25	15c *Hispanianum*	2.25	.45
215	A25	15c *Hispaniarum*	.80	.20
216	A26	20c multicolored	.40	.20
217	A25	25c multicolored	.45	.20
218	A26	50c multicolored	.90	.85
219	A25	60c multicolored	2.25	.75
220	A25	$1 multicolored	2.25	.75
221	A26	$2.50 multicolored	2.00	*3.00*
222	A26	$5 multicolored	3.00	*4.75*
		Nos. 206-222 (17)	16.50	12.75

Coin inscription was misspelled on No. 214, corrected on No. 215 (issued Sept. 8).

Wmk. 314 Sideways (A25), Upright (A26)

1973-74

206a	A25	½c multicolored	.20	*.75*
208a	A25	2c multicolored	.20	*.75*
209a	A25	3c multicolored	.20	*.75*
211a	A26	5c multicolored	.30	*.75*
212a	A26	6c multicolored	.30	*.50*
213a	A26	10c multicolored	.45	*.50*
215a	A25	15c multicolored	.55	*.75*
216a	A26	20c multicolored	.65	*.90*
217a	A25	25c multicolored	.70	*1.25*
218a	A26	50c multicolored	1.00	*1.25*
220a	A25	$1 multicolored	2.25	*3.00*
222A	A26	$10 multi ('74)	17.50	*12.50*
		Nos. 206a-220a,222A (12)	24.30	23.65

Issue dates: $10, Nov. 16; others, Sept. 12.

1975-77 Wmk. 373

207b	A25	1c multi ('77)	.20	.20
209b	A25	3c multi ('76)	.20	.20
210b	A26	4c multi ('76)	.20	.20
211b	A26	5c multicolored	.20	.35
212b	A26	6c multicolored	.80	.20
213b	A26	10c multi ('76)	.30	.20
215b	A25	15c multi ('76)	.35	.20
216b	A26	20c multicolored	2.25	4.00
219b	A25	60c multi ('76)	6.25	1.40
220b	A25	$1 multi ('77)	6.25	2.00
		Nos. 207b-220b (10)	17.00	8.95

Pip Meeting Convict, from "Great Expectations" — A27

Designs: 20c, Miss Havisham from "Great Expectations." 25c, Dickens' birthplace, Portsmouth, vert. 40c, Charles Dickens, vert.

Perf. 13x13½, 13½x13

1970, May 1 Litho. Wmk. 314

223	A27	4c gold, Prus blue & brn	.20	.20
224	A27	20c gold, claret & brn	.20	.20
225	A27	25c gold, olive & brn	.20	.20
226	A27	40c dk blue, gold & brn	.20	*.40*
		Nos. 223-226 (4)	.80	1.00

Charles Dickens (1812-70), English novelist.

Local Steel Band A28

25c, Local string band. 40c, "A Midsummer Night's Dream," 1963 performance.

1970, Aug. 1 *Perf. 13½*

227	A28	20c multicolored	.20	.20
228	A28	25c multicolored	.20	.20
229	A28	40c multicolored	.20	.20
		Nos. 227-229 (3)	.60	.60

Issued to publicize the 1970 Arts Festival.

St. Christopher No. 1 and St. Kitts Post Office, 1970 — A29

Designs: 20c, 25c, St. Christopher Nos. 1 and 3. 50c, St. Christopher No. 3 and St. Kitts postmark, Sept. 2, 1871.

Wmk. 314

1970, Sept. 14 Litho. *Perf. 14½*

230	A29	½c green & rose	.20	.20
231	A29	20c vio bl, rose & grn	.20	.20
232	A29	25c brown, rose & grn	.20	.20
233	A29	50c black, grn & dk red	.30	.30
		Nos. 230-233 (4)	.90	.90

Centenary of stamps of St. Christopher.

Holy Family, by Anthony van Dyck — A30

Christmas: 3c, 40c, Adoration of the Shepherds, by Frans Floris.

1970, Nov. 16 *Perf. 14*

234	A30	3c multicolored	.20	.20
235	A30	20c ocher & multi	.20	.20
236	A30	25c dull red & multi	.20	.20
237	A30	40c green & multi	.20	.20
		Nos. 234-237 (4)	.80	.80

Monkey Fiddle A31

Flowers: 20c, Mountain violets. 30c, Morning glory. 50c, Fringed epidendrum.

1971, Mar. 1 Litho. *Perf. 14*

238	A31	½c multicolored	.20	.20
239	A31	20c multicolored	.20	.20
240	A31	30c multicolored	.20	.20
241	A31	50c multicolored	.40	*.60*
		Nos. 238-241 (4)	1.00	1.20

Chateau de Poincy, St. Kitts — A32

Designs: 20c, Royal poinciana. 50c, De Poincy's coat of arms, vert.

1971, June 1 Litho. Wmk. 314

242	A32	20c green & multi	.20	.20
243	A32	30c dull yellow & multi	.20	.20
244	A32	50c brown & multi	.20	.20
		Nos. 242-244 (3)	.60	.60

Philippe de Longvilliers de Poincy became first governor of French possessions in the Antilles in 1639.

East Yorks A33

Designs: 20c, Royal Artillery. 30c, French Infantry. 50c, Royal Scots.

1971, Sept. 1 *Perf. 14*

245	A33	½c black & multi	.20	.20
246	A33	20c black & multi	.35	.30
247	A33	30c black & multi	.55	.45
248	A33	50c black & multi	.90	.75
		Nos. 245-248 (4)	2.00	1.70

Siege of Brimstone Hill, 1782.

Crucifixion, by Quentin Massys — A34

Perf. 14x13½

1972, Apr. 1 Litho. Wmk. 314

249	A34	4c brick red & multi	.20	.20
250	A34	20c gray green & multi	.20	.20
251	A34	30c dull blue & multi	.20	.20
252	A34	40c lt brown & multi	.25	.25
		Nos. 249-252 (4)	.85	.85

Easter 1972.

Madonna and Child, by Bergognone A35

Paintings: 20c, Adoration of the Kings, by Jacopo da Bassano, horiz. 25c, Adoration of the Shepherds, by Il Domenichino. 40c, Madonna and Child, by Fiorenzo di Lorenzo.

1972, Oct. 2 *Perf. 13½x14, 14x13½*

253	A35	3c gray green & multi	.20	.20
254	A35	20c deep plum & multi	.20	.20
255	A35	25c sepia & multi	.20	.20
256	A35	40c red & multi	.25	.25
		Nos. 253-256 (4)	.85	.85

Christmas 1972.

Silver Wedding Issue, 1972

Common Design Type

Queen Elizabeth II, Prince Philip, pelicans.

1972, Nov. 20 Photo. *Perf. 14x14½*

257	CD324	20c car rose & multi	.25	.25
258	CD324	25c ultra & multi	.35	.35

Warner Landing at St. Kitts — A36

Designs: 25c, Settlers growing tobacco. 40c, Building fort at "Old Road." $2.50, Warner's ship off St. Kitts, Jan. 28, 1623.

1973, Jan. 28 Litho. *Perf. 14x13½*

259	A36	4c pink & multi	.20	.20
260	A36	25c brown & multi	.20	.20
261	A36	40c blue & multi	.25	.25
262	A36	$2.50 multicolored	1.00	1.00
		Nos. 259-262 (4)	1.65	1.65

350th anniversary of the landing of Sir Thomas Warner at St. Kitts.

For overprints see Nos. 266-269.

The Last Supper, by Juan de Juanes — A37

Easter (The Last Supper, by): 4c, Titian, vert. 25c, ascribed to Roberti, vert.

Perf. 14x13½, 13½x14

1973, Apr. 16 Photo. Wmk. 314

263	A37	4c blue black & multi	.20	.20
264	A37	25c multicolored	.20	.20
265	A37	$2.50 purple & multi	.85	.85
		Nos. 263-265 (3)	1.25	1.25

Nos. 259-262 Overprinted:

VISIT OF
H. R. H. THE PRINCE OF WALES 1973

1973, May 31 Litho. *Perf. 14x13½*

266	A36	4c pink & multi	.20	.20
267	A36	25c brown & multi	.20	.20
268	A36	40c blue & multi	.20	.20
269	A36	$2.50 multicolored	.40	.40
		Nos. 266-269 (4)	1.00	1.00

Visit of Prince Charles, May 1973.

Harbor Scene and St. Kitts-Nevis No. 3 — A38

25c, Sugar mill and #2. 40c, Unloading of boat and #1. $2.50, Rock carvings and #5.

1973, Oct. 1 Litho. *Perf. 13½x14*

270	A38	4c salmon & multi	.20	.20
271	A38	25c lt blue & multi	.35	.35
272	A38	40c multicolored	.70	.70
273	A38	$2.50 multicolored	2.25	2.25
a.		Souvenir sheet of 4, #270-273	3.50	3.50
		Nos. 270-273 (4)	3.50	3.50

70th anniv. of 1st St. Kitts-Nevis stamps.

Princess Anne's Wedding Issue

Common Design Type

1973, Nov. 14 *Perf. 14*

274	CD325	25c brt green & multi	.20	.20
275	CD325	40c citron & multi	.20	.20

Virgin and Child, by Murillo — A39

Christ Carrying Cross, by Sebastiano del Piombo — A40

Christmas (Paintings): 40c, Holy Family, by Anton Raphael Mengs. 60c, Holy Family, by Sassoferrato. $1, Holy Family, by Filippino Lippi, horiz.

1973, Dec. 1 Litho. *Perf. 14x13½*

276	A39	4c brt blue & multi	.20	.20
277	A39	40c orange & multi	.20	.20
278	A39	60c multicolored	.25	.25
279	A39	$1 multicolored	.35	.35
		Nos. 276-279 (4)	1.00	1.00

1974, Apr. 8 *Perf. 13*

Easter: 25c, Crucifixion, by Goya. 40c, Trinity, by Diego Ribera. $2.50, Burial of Christ, by Fra Bartolomeo, horiz.

280	A40	4c olive & multi	.20	.20
281	A40	25c lt blue & multi	.20	.20
282	A40	40c purple & multi	.20	.20
283	A40	$2.50 gray & multi	1.25	1.25
		Nos. 280-283 (4)	1.85	1.85

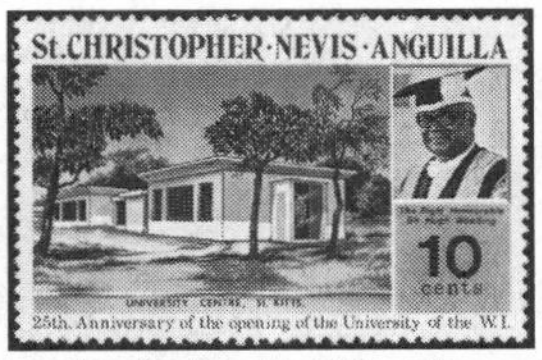

University Center, St. Kitts, Chancellor Hugh Wooding — A41

1974, June 1 *Perf. 13½*

284	A41	10c blue & multi	.20	.20
285	A41	$1 pink & multi	.20	.20
a.		Souvenir sheet of 2, #284-285	.50	.50

University of the West Indies, 25th anniv.

Nurse Explaining Family Planning — A42

Designs: 4c, Globe and hands reaching up, vert. 40c, Family, vert. $2.50, WPY emblem and scale balancing embryo and world.

Wmk. 314

1974, Aug. 5 Litho. *Perf. 14*

286	A42	4c blk, blue & brn	.20	.20
287	A42	25c multicolored	.20	.20
288	A42	40c multicolored	.20	.20
289	A42	$2.50 lilac & multi	.30	.30
		Nos. 286-289 (4)	.90	.90

Family planning and World Population Week, Aug. 4-10.

Churchill as Lieutenant, 21st Lancers — A43

Knight of the Garter — A44

Designs: 25c, Churchill as Prime Minister. 60c, Churchill Statue, Parliament Square, London.

1974, Nov. 30

290	A43	4c dull violet & multi	.20	.20
291	A43	25c yellow & multi	.20	.20
292	A44	40c lt blue & multi	.20	.20
293	A44	60c lt blue & multi	.25	.25
a.		Souvenir sheet of 4, #290-293	.90	.90
		Nos. 290-293 (4)	.85	.85

Sir Winston Churchill (1874-1965).

Souvenir Sheets

Boeing 747 over St. Kitts-Nevis — A45

1974, Dec. 16 *Perf. 14x13½*

294	A45	40c multicolored	.30	.30
295	A45	45c multicolored	.40	.40

Opening of Golden Rock Intl. Airport.

The Last Supper, by Doré — A46

Easter: 25c, Jesus mocked. 40c, Jesus falling beneath the Cross. $1, Raising the Cross. Designs based on Bible illustrations by Paul Gustave Doré (1833-1883).

1975, Mar. 24 ***Perf. 14½***

296	A46	4c ultra & multi	.20	.20
297	A46	25c lt blue & multi	.20	.20
298	A46	40c bister & multi	.20	.20
299	A46	$1 salmon pink & multi	.25	.25
		Nos. 296-299 (4)	.85	.85

ECCA Headquarters, Basseterre, and Map of St. Kitts — A47

Designs: 25c, Specimen of $1 note, issued by ECCA. 40c, St. Kitts half dollar, 1801, and $4 coin, 1875. 45c, Nevis "9 dogs" coin, 1801, and 2c, 5c, coins, 1975.

Perf. 13½x14

1975, June 2 **Wmk. 373**

300	A47	12c orange & multi	.20	.20
301	A47	25c olive & multi	.20	.20
302	A47	40c vermilion & multi	.20	.20
303	A47	45c brt blue & multi	.20	.20
		Nos. 300-303 (4)	.80	.80

East Caribbean Currency Authority Headquarters, Basseterre, opening.

Evangeline Booth, Salvation Army — A48

Colfer Swinging Club — A49

Designs (IWY Emblem and): 25c, Sylvia Pankhurst, suffragette. 40c, Marie Curie, scientist. $2.50, Lady Annie Allen, teacher.

Perf. 14x14½

1975, Sept. 15 **Litho.** **Wmk. 314**

304	A48	4c orange brn & blk	.35	.20
305	A48	25c lilac pur & blk	.40	.20
306	A48	40c blue, vio bl & blk	2.25	.70
307	A48	$2.50 yellow brn & blk	1.75	*3.50*
		Nos. 304-307 (4)	4.75	4.60

International Women's Year 1975.

1975, Nov. 1 ***Perf. 14***

308	A49	4c rose red & blk	.75	.20
309	A49	25c yellow & blk	1.10	.20
310	A49	40c emerald & blk	1.40	.35
311	A49	$1 blue & blk	2.00	2.00
		Nos. 308-311 (4)	5.25	2.75

Opening of Frigate Bay Golf Course.

St. Paul, by Sacchi Pier Francesco A50

Christmas (Paintings, details): 40c, St. James, by Bonifazio di Pitati. 45c, St. John, by Pier Francesco Mola. $1, Virgin Mary, by Raphael.

Wmk. 373

1975, Dec. 1 **Litho.** ***Perf. 14***

312	A50	25c ultra & multi	.20	.20
313	A50	40c multicolored	.50	.50
314	A50	45c red brown & multi	.55	.55
315	A50	$1 gold & multi	1.25	1.25
		Nos. 312-315 (4)	2.50	2.50

Virgin Mary — A51

The Last Supper — A52

Stained Glass Windows: No. 317, Christ on the Cross. No. 318, St. John. 40c, The Last Supper (different). $1, Baptism of Christ.

Perf. 14x13½

1976, Apr. 14 **Litho.** **Wmk. 373**

316		4c black & multi	.20	.20
317		4c black & multi	.20	.20
318		4c black & multi	.20	.20
a.	A51	Triptych, #316-318	.20	.20

Perf. 14½

319	A52	25c black & multi	.25	.25
320	A52	40c black & multi	.40	.40
321	A52	$1 black & multi	.75	.75
		Nos. 319-321 (3)	1.40	1.40

Easter 1976. No. 318a has continuous design.

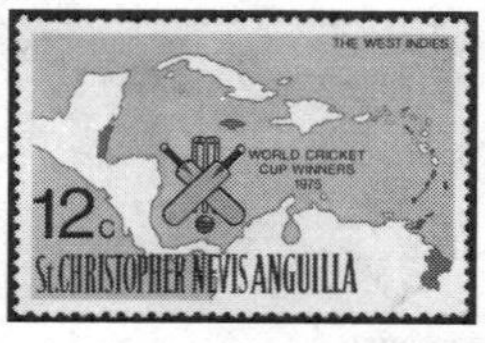

Map of West Indies, Bats, Wicket and Ball A52a

Prudential Cup — A52b

Unwmk.

1976, July 8 **Litho.** ***Perf. 14***

322	A52a	12c lt blue & multi	.45	.35
323	A52b	40c lilac rose & blk	1.40	1.00
a.		Souvenir sheet of 2, #322-323	3.75	3.75

World Cricket Cup, won by West Indies Team, 1975.

Crispus Attucks and Boston Massacre — A53

Designs: 40c, Alexander Hamilton and Battle of Yorktown. 45c, Thomas Jefferson and Declaration of Independence. $1, George Washington and Crossing of the Delaware.

1976, July 26 **Litho.** **Wmk. 373**

324	A53	20c gray & multi	.20	.20
325	A53	40c gray & multi	.25	.25
326	A53	45c gray & multi	.25	.25
327	A53	$1 gray & multi	.50	.50
		Nos. 324-327 (4)	1.20	1.20

American Bicentennial.

Nativity, Sforza Book of Hours — A54

Queen Planting Tree, 1966 Visit — A55

Christmas (Paintings): 40c, Virgin and Child, by Bernardino Pintoricchio. 45c, Our Lady of Good Children, by Ford Maddox Brown. $1, Christ Child, by Margaret W. Tarrant.

1976, Nov. 1 ***Perf. 14***

328	A54	20c purple & multi	.20	.20
329	A54	40c dk blue & multi	.20	.20
330	A54	45c multicolored	.20	.20
331	A54	$1 multicolored	.40	.40
		Nos. 328-331 (4)	1.00	1.00

1977, Feb. 7 **Litho.** ***Perf. 14x13½***

Designs: 55c, The scepter. $1.50, Bishops paying homage to the Queen.

332	A55	50c multicolored	.20	.20
333	A55	55c multicolored	.20	.20
334	A55	$1.50 multicolored	.30	.30
		Nos. 332-334 (3)	.70	.70

25th anniv. of the reign of Elizabeth II.

Christ on the Cross, by Niccolo di Liberatore — A56

Easter: 30c, Resurrection (Imitator of Mantegna). 50c, Resurrection, by Ugolino, horiz. $1, Christ Rising from Tomb, by Gaudenzio.

Wmk. 373

1977, Apr. 1 **Litho.** ***Perf. 14***

335	A56	25c yellow & multi	.20	.20
336	A56	30c deep blue & multi	.20	.20
337	A56	50c olive green & multi	.20	.20
338	A56	$1 red & multi	.25	.25
		Nos. 335-338 (4)	.85	.85

Estridge Mission A57

20c, Mission emblem. 40c, Basseterre Mission.

1977, June 27 **Litho.** ***Perf. 12½***

339	A57	4c blue & black	.20	.20
340	A57	20c multicolored	.20	.20
341	A57	40c orange yel & blk	.20	.20
		Nos. 339-341 (3)	.60	.60

Bicentenary of Moravian Mission.

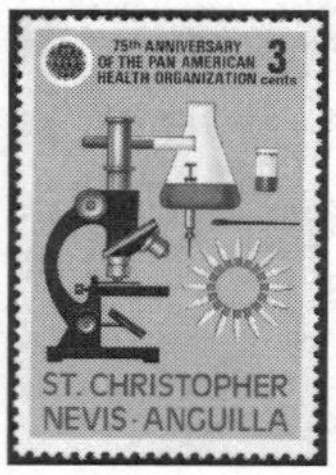

Microscope, Flask, Syringe — A58

12c, Blood, fat, nerve cells. 20c, Symbol of community participation. $1, Inoculation.

1977, Oct. 11 **Litho.** ***Perf. 14***

342	A58	3c multicolored	.20	.20
343	A58	12c multicolored	.20	.20
344	A58	20c multicolored	.20	.20
345	A58	$1 multicolored	1.00	1.00
		Nos. 342-345 (4)	1.60	1.60

Pan American Health Organization, 75th anniversary (PAHO).

Three Kings — A59

Green Monkey and Young — A60

Christmas, Stained-glass Windows, Chartres Cathedral: 4c, Nativity, West Window. 40c, Virgin and Child. $1, Virgin and Child, Rose Window.

1977, Nov. 15 **Wmk. 373**

346	A59	4c multicolored	.20	.20
347	A59	6c multicolored	.20	.20
348	A59	40c multicolored	.30	.30
349	A59	$1 multicolored	.55	.55
		Nos. 346-349 (4)	1.25	1.25

Wmk. 373

1978, Apr. 15 **Litho.** ***Perf. 14½***

Green Monkeys: 5c, $1.50, Mother and young sitting on branch. 55c, like 4c.

350	A60	4c multicolored	.20	.20
351	A60	5c multicolored	.20	.20
352	A60	55c multicolored	.60	.20
353	A60	$1.50 multicolored	1.25	1.40
		Nos. 350-353 (4)	2.25	2.00

Elizabeth II Coronation Anniversary Issue

Common Design Types

Souvenir Sheet

Unwmk.

1978, Apr. 21 Litho. *Perf. 15*

354	Sheet of 6	1.00	1.00
a.	CD326 $1 Falcon of Edward III	.20	.20
b.	CD327 $1 Elizabeth II	.20	.20
c.	CD328 $1 Pelican	.20	.20

No. 354 contains 2 se-tenant strips of Nos. 354a-354c, separated by horizontal gutter with commemorative and descriptive inscriptions and showing central part of coronation procession with coach.

Tomatoes A61

Designs: 2c, Defense Force band. 5c, Radio and TV station. 10c, Technical College. 12c, TV assembly plant. 15c, Sugar cane harvest. 25c, Craft Center. 30c, Cruise ship. 40c, Sea crab and lobster. 45c, Royal St. Kitts Hotel and golf course. 50c, Pinneys Beach, Nevis. 55c, New Runway at Golden Rock. $1, Cotton pickers. $5, Brewery. $10, Pineapples and peanuts.

Perf. 14½x14

1978, Sept. 8 Wmk. 373

355	A61	1c	multicolored	.20	.20
356	A61	2c	multicolored	.20	.20
357	A61	5c	multicolored	.20	.20
358	A61	10c	multicolored	.20	.20
359	A61	12c	multicolored	.20	.20
360	A61	15c	multicolored	.20	.20
361	A61	25c	multicolored	.20	.20
362	A61	30c	multicolored	1.00	.20
363	A61	40c	multicolored	.35	.20
364	A61	45c	multicolored	2.75	.20
365	A61	50c	multicolored	.35	.20
366	A61	55c	multicolored	.70	.20
367	A61	$1	multicolored	.40	.30
368	A61	$5	multicolored	.90	1.50
369	A61	$10	multicolored	1.75	3.25
			Nos. 355-369 (15)	9.60	7.45

For overprints see Nevis #100-112, O1-O10.

Investiture — A62

King Bringing Gift — A63

Designs: 10c, Map reading. 25c, Pitching tent. 40c, Cooking. 50c, First aid. 55c, Rev. W. A. Beckett, founder of Scouting in St. Kitts.

Wmk. 373

1978, Oct. 9 Litho. *Perf. 13½*

370	A62	5c	multicolored	.20	.20
371	A62	10c	multicolored	.20	.20
372	A62	25c	multicolored	.25	.25
373	A62	40c	multicolored	.35	.35
374	A62	50c	multicolored	.50	.50
375	A62	55c	multicolored	.50	.50
			Nos. 370-375 (6)	2.00	2.00

50th anniversary of St. Kitts-Nevis Scouting.

1978, Dec. 1 *Perf. 14x13½*

Christmas: 15c, 30c, King bringing gift, diff. $2.25, Three Kings paying homage to Infant Jesus.

376	A63	5c	multicolored	.20	.20
377	A63	15c	multicolored	.20	.20
378	A63	30c	multicolored	.20	.20
379	A63	$2.25	multicolored	.40	.40
			Nos. 376-379 (4)	1.00	1.00

Canna Coccinea — A64

Flowers: 30c, Heliconia bihai. 55c, Ruellia tuberosa. $1.50, Gesneria ventricosa.

1979, Mar. 19 *Perf. 14*

380	A64	5c	multicolored	.20	.20
381	A64	30c	multicolored	.35	.35
382	A64	55c	multicolored	.45	.45
383	A64	$1.50	multicolored	.75	*1.10*
			Nos. 380-383 (4)	1.75	2.10

See Nos. 393-396.

Rowland Hill and St. Christopher No. 1 — A65

Rowland Hill and: 15c, St. Kitts-Nevis #233. 50c, Great Britain #4. $2.50, St. Kitts-Nevis #64.

Wmk. 373

1979, July 2 Litho. *Perf. 14½*

384	A65	5c	multicolored	.20	.20
385	A65	15c	multicolored	.20	.20
386	A65	50c	multicolored	.25	.25
387	A65	$2.50	multicolored	.45	.45
			Nos. 384-387 (4)	1.10	1.10

Sir Rowland Hill (1795-1879), originator of penny postage.

The Woodman's Daughter, by Millais — A66

Paintings by John Everett Millais and IYC Emblem: 25c, Cherry Ripe. 30c, The Rescue, horiz. 55c, Bubbles. $1, Christ in the House of His Parents.

1979, Nov. 12 Litho. *Perf. 14*

388	A66	5c	multicolored	.20	.20
389	A66	25c	multicolored	.25	.25
390	A66	30c	multicolored	.25	.25
391	A66	55c	multicolored	.30	.30
			Nos. 388-391 (4)	1.00	1.00

Souvenir Sheet

392	A66	$1	multicolored	1.00	1.00

Christmas 1979; Intl. Year of the Child.

Flower Type of 1979

Flowers: 4c, Clerodendrum aculeatum. 55c, Inga laurina. $1.50, Epidendrum difforme. $2, Salvia serontina.

1980, Feb. 4 Litho. *Perf. 14*

393	A64	4c	multicolored	.35	.20
394	A64	55c	multicolored	.50	.30
395	A64	$1.50	multicolored	1.40	1.25
396	A64	$2	multicolored	1.25	1.75
			Nos. 393-396 (4)	3.50	3.50

Nevis Lagoon, London 1980 Emblem — A67

1980, May 6 Litho. *Perf. 13½*

397	A67	5c	shown	.20	.20
398	A67	30c	Fig Tree Church, vert.	.20	.20
399	A67	55c	Nisbet Plantation	.35	.35
400	A67	$3	Lord Nelson, by Fuger, vert.	1.90	1.90
			Nos. 397-400 (4)	2.65	2.65

Souvenir Sheet

401	A67	75c	Nelson Falling, by D. Dighton	1.25	.75

London 80 Intl. Phil. Exhib., May 6-14; Lord Nelson, (1758-1805).

WAR TAX STAMPS

No. 12 Overprinted

1916 Wmk. 3 *Perf. 14*

MR1	A1	½p green	.60	.50

Type of 1905-18 Issue Overprinted

1918

MR2	A1	1½p orange	.60	.60

OFFICIAL STAMPS

Catalogue values for unused stamps in this section are for Never Hinged items.

Nos. 359, 361, 363-369 Overprinted: OFFICIAL

Perf. 14½x14

1980 Litho. Wmk. 373

O1	A61	12c	multicolored	1.10	.90
O2	A61	25c	multicolored	.20	.20
O3	A61	40c	multicolored	.55	.45
O4	A61	45c	multicolored	2.00	.40
O5	A61	50c	multicolored	.40	.35
O6	A61	55c	multicolored	.40	.40
O7	A61	$1	multicolored	1.00	*2.00*
O8	A61	$5	multicolored	1.10	*2.25*
O9	A61	$10	multicolored	2.25	*3.00*
			Nos. O1-O9 (9)	9.00	9.95

ST. LUCIA

sānt 'lü-shə

LOCATION — Island in the West Indies, one of the Windward group

GOVT. — Independent state in British Commonwealth

AREA — 240 sq. mi.

POP. — 154,020 (1999 est.)

CAPITAL — Castries

The British colony of St. Lucia became an associated state March 1, 1967, and independent in 1979.

12 Pence = 1 Shilling

100 Cents = 1 Dollar (1949)

Catalogue values for unused stamps in this country are for Never Hinged items, beginning with Scott 127 in the regular postage section, Scott C1 in the air post section, Scott J3 in the postage due section, and Scott O1 in the officials section.

Watermarks

Wmk. 5- Small Star

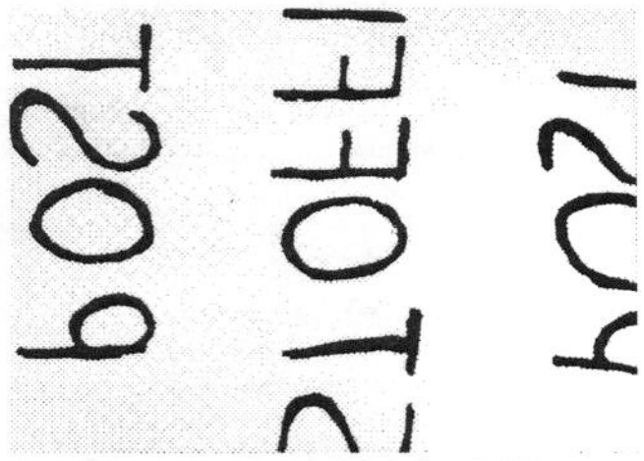

Wmk. 380- "POST OFFICE"

Values for unused stamps are for examples with original gum as defined in the catalogue introduction. Very fine examples of Nos. 1-26 will have perforations touching the design on at least one side due to the narrow spacing of the stamps on the plates. Stamps with perfs clear of the framelines on all four sides are very scarce and will command higher prices.

Queen Victoria — A1

Perf. 14 to 16

1860, Dec. 18 Engr. Wmk. 5

1	A1	(1p) rose red	100.00	75.00
a.		Double impression	*1,600.*	
b.		Horiz. pair, imperf vert.	—	
2	A1	(4p) deep blue	250.00	225.00
a.		Horiz. pair, imperf vert.	—	
3	A1	(6p) green	375.00	225.00
a.		Horiz. pair, imperf vert.	—	
		Nos. 1-3 (3)	725.00	525.00

For types overprinted see #15, 17, 19-26.

1863 Wmk. 1 *Perf. 12½*

4	A1	(1p) lake	50.00	*70.00*
5	A1	(4p) slate blue	125.00	110.00
6	A1	(6p) emerald	180.00	160.00
		Nos. 4-6 (3)	355.00	340.00

Nos. 4-6 exist imperforate on stamp paper, from proof sheets.

1864

7	A1	(1p) black	15.00	10.00
8	A1	(4p) yellow	120.00	45.00
a.		(4p) olive yellow	250.00	70.00
b.		(4p) lemon yellow	*1,350.*	
9	A1	(6p) violet	80.00	32.50
a.		(6p) lilac	160.00	37.50
b.		(6p) deep lilac	85.00	30.00
10	A1	(1sh) red orange	200.00	37.50
a.		(1sh) orange	225.00	37.50
c.		Horiz. pair, imperf between	—	
		Nos. 7-10 (4)	415.00	125.00

Nos. 7-10 exist imperforate on stamp paper, from proof sheets.

Perf. 14

11	A1	(1p) deep black	16.00	13.50
a.		Horiz. pair, imperf between	—	

12 A1 (4p) yellow 70.00 22.50
a. (4p) olive yellow 175.00 75.00
13 A1 (6p) pale lilac 60.00 22.50
a. (6p) deep lilac 60.00 30.00
b. (6p) violet 160.00 55.00
14 A1 (1sh) deep orange 120.00 16.00
a. (1sh) orange 180.00 27.50
Nos. 11-14 (4) 266.00 74.50

Type of 1860 Surcharged in Black or Red:

a

b

1881

15 A1(a) ½p green 55.00 *75.00*
17 A1(b) 2½p scarlet 29.00 20.00

1883-84 Wmk. Crown and CA (2)

19 A1(a) ½p green 15.00 *24.00*
20 A1(a) 1p black (R) 21.00 12.50
a. Half used as ½p on cover *2,500.*
21 A1(a) 4p yellow 200.00 27.50
22 A1(a) 6p violet 35.00 30.00
23 A1(a) 1sh orange 240.00 150.00
Nos. 19-23 (5) 511.00 244.00

1884 ***Perf. 12***

24 A1(a) 4p yellow 300.00 32.50

Half
penny

1885 Wmk. 1 ***Perf. 12½***

25 A1 ½p emerald 60.
26 A1 6p slate blue 1,600.

Nos. 25 and 26 were prepared for use but not issued.

A5

Die B

For explanation of dies A and B see back of this section of the Catalogue.

1883-98 Typo. Wmk. 2 ***Perf. 14***

27 A5 ½p green ('91) 1.75 .90
a. Die A ('83) 5.50 3.50
28 A5 1p rose (die A) ('83) 27.50 16.00
29 A5 1p lilac ('91) 1.75 .50
a. Die A ('86) 4.00 *5.50*
b. Die A, imperf., pair 750.00
30 A5 2p ultra & brn org ('98) 1.25 1.00
31 A5 2½p ultra ('91) 2.50 .90
a. Die A ('83) 25.00 2.25
32 A5 3p lilac & grn ('91) 3.25 *5.50*
a. Die A ('86) 82.50 16.00
33 A5 4p brown ('93) 2.50 *3.25*
a. Die A ('85) 22.50 3.50
b. Die A, imperf., pair 1,050.
34 A5 6p vio (die A; '85) *250.00* *275.00*
a. Imperf., pair 1,800.
35 A5 6p lil & bl (die A; '86) 5.00 *7.50*
a. Die B ('91) 19.00 18.00
36 A5 1sh brn org (die A) ('85) 350.00 140.00
37 A5 1sh lil & red ('91) 3.50 *7.50*
a. Die A ('86) 80.00 27.50
38 A5 5sh lil & org ('91) 37.50 *110.00*
39 A5 10sh lil & blk ('91) 75.00 *120.00*
Nos. 27-39 (13) 761.50 688.05

Nos. 32, 32a, 35a and 33a Surcharged in Black:

No. 40

No. 41

No. 42

1892

40 A5 ½p on 3p lil & grn 52.50 21.00
a. Die A 100.00 70.00
b. Dbl. surch., die B 800.00 725.00
c. Invtd. surch., die B 1,850. 675.00
d. Triple surch., one on back *1,500.*
41 A5 ½p on half of 6p lilac & blue 16.00 12.50
a. Slanting serif 175.00 150.00
c. Without the bar of "½" 175.00 160.00
d. "2" of "½" omitted 400.00 425.00
e. Surcharged sideways 750.00
f. Double surcharge 500.00 500.00
g. Triple surcharge *800.00*
42 A5 1p on 4p brown 5.00 *7.00*
b. Double surcharge 175.00
c. Inverted surcharge 875. 575.00
Nos. 40-42 (3) 73.50 40.50

No. 40 is found with wide or narrow "O" in "ONE," and large or small "A" in "HALF." The narrow "O" and small "A" varieties are worth about 3 times the normal No. 40.

Edward VII
A9

The Pitons
A10

Numerals of 3p, 6p, 1sh and 5sh of type A9 are in color on plain tablet.

1902-03 **Typo.**

43 A9 ½p violet & green 2.00 1.25
44 A9 1p violet & car rose 3.75 .50
46 A9 2½p violet & ultra 13.50 4.75
47 A9 3p violet & yellow 3.75 *7.25*
48 A9 1sh green & black 9.00 *18.00*
Nos. 43-48 (5) 32.00 *31.75*

Wmk. 1 sideways

1902, Dec. 16 **Engr.**

49 A10 2p brown & green 8.50 6.00

Fourth centenary of the discovery of the island by Columbus.

1904-05 Typo. Wmk. 3

50 A9 ½p violet & green 3.25 .25
51 A9 1p violet & car rose 4.50 .85
52 A9 2½p violet & ultra 8.00 1.00
53 A9 3p violet & yellow 3.25 2.50
54 A9 6p vio & dp vio ('05) 10.50 *12.50*
55 A9 1sh green & blk ('05) 23.00 16.00
56 A9 5sh green & car ('05) 47.50 *110.00*
Nos. 50-56 (7) 100.00 143.10

#50, 51, 52, 54 are on both ordinary and chalky paper. #55 is on chalky paper only.

1907-10

57 A9 ½p green 1.75 .85
58 A9 1p carmine 4.00 .40
59 A9 2½p ultra 3.75 1.50

Chalky Paper

60 A9 3p violet, *yel* ('09) 2.00 *10.50*
61 A9 6p violet & red violet 5.00 *17.00*
a. 6p violet & dull vio ('10) 15.00 *13.00*
62 A9 1sh black, *grn* ('09) 3.50 *7.25*
63 A9 5sh green & red, *yel* 55.00 *62.50*
Nos. 57-63 (7) 75.00 *100.00*

King George V
A11 A12

Numerals of 3p, 6p, 1sh and 5sh of type A11 are in color on plain tablet.

For description of dies I and II see back of this section of the Catalogue.

Die I

1912-19

Ordinary Paper

64 A11 ½p deep green .70 .25
65 A11 1p scarlet .55 .35
a. 1p carmine .55 .25
66 A12 2p gray ('13) 2.00 *2.75*
67 A11 2½p ultra 3.00 2.00

Chalky Paper

Numeral on White Tablet

68 A11 3p violet, *yel* 1.25 *1.40*
a. Die II 7.50 *14.50*
69 A11 6p vio & red vio 2.00 *6.00*
70 A11 1sh black, *green* 2.75 *3.75*
a. 1sh black, *bl grn, ol* back 5.00 *6.00*
71 A11 1sh fawn 7.75 *30.00*
72 A11 5sh green & red, *yel* 22.50 *52.50*
Nos. 64-72 (9) 42.50 *99.00*

A13

A14

1913-14

Chalky Paper

73 A13 4p scar & blk, *yel* 2.50 *4.50*
74 A14 2sh6p black & red, *bl* 20.00 *25.00*

Surface-colored Paper

75 A13 4p scar & blk, *yel* 1.00 *1.75*

Die II

1921-24 **Wmk. 4**

Ordinary Paper

76 A11 ½p green .25 .20
77 A11 1p carmine 5.75 *8.00*
78 A11 1p dk brn ('22) .60 .20
79 A13 1½p rose red ('22) .40 *1.25*
80 A12 2p gray .30 .20
81 A11 2½p ultra 2.50 *1.75*
82 A11 2½p orange ('24) 7.75 *30.00*
83 A11 3p ultra ('22) 3.50 *10.00*

Chalky Paper

84 A11 3p violet, *yel* .60 *8.00*
85 A13 4p scar & blk, *yel* ('24) .80 *1.60*
86 A11 6p vio & red vio 1.40 *3.25*
87 A11 1sh fawn 1.40 *2.25*
88 A14 2sh6p blk & red, *bl* ('24) 13.00 *17.00*
89 A11 5sh grn & red, *yel* 32.50 *50.00*
Nos. 76-89 (14) 70.75 *133.70*

Common Design Types pictured following the introduction.

Silver Jubilee Issue

Common Design Type

1935, May 6 Engr. ***Perf. 13½x14***

91 CD301 ½p green & blk .25 .30
92 CD301 2p gray blk & ultra .50 .45
93 CD301 2½p blue & brn 1.00 .75
94 CD301 1sh brt vio & ind 3.25 *6.50*
Nos. 91-94 (4) 5.00 8.00
Set, never hinged 12.00

Port Castries
A15

Columbus Square, Castries
A16

Ventine Falls
A17

Soldiers' Monument
A19

Fort Rodney, Pigeon Island
A18

Government House
A20

Seal of the Colony
A21

1936, Mar. 1 ***Perf. 14***

Center in Black

95 A15 ½p light green .20 .40
a. Perf. 13x12 1.50 *4.00*
96 A16 1p dark brown .35 .20
a. Perf. 13x12 2.25 1.40
97 A17 1½p carmine .50 .25
a. Perf. 12x13 6.00 2.75
98 A15 2p gray .40 .20
99 A16 2½p blue .40 .20
100 A17 3p dull green 1.25 .60
101 A15 4p brown .30 *.80*
102 A16 6p orange .85 .85
103 A18 1sh light blue, perf. 13x12 1.25 *1.50*
104 A19 2sh6p ultra 6.25 *12.00*
105 A20 5sh violet 7.75 *18.00*
106 A21 10sh car rose, perf. 13x12 40.00 *57.50*
Nos. 95-106 (12) 59.50 *92.50*

Nos. 95a, 96a and 97a are coils.
Issue date: Nos. 95a, 96a, Apr. 8.

Coronation Issue

Common Design Type

1937, May 12 ***Perf. 11x11½***

107 CD302 1p dark purple .20 .20
108 CD302 1½p dark carmine .25 .25
109 CD302 2½p deep ultra .25 .25
Nos. 107-109 (3) .70 .70
Set, never hinged 1.25

King George VI — A22

Columbus Square, Castries
A23

Government House
A24

The Pitons
A25

Loading Bananas
A26

Arms of the Colony — A27

Perf. 12½ (#110-111, 1½p-3½p, 8p, 3sh, 5sh, £1), 12 (6p, 1sh, 2sh, 10sh)

1938-48

110 A22 ½p green ('43) .20 .20
a. Perf. 14½x14 .65 .20
111 A22 1p deep violet .20 .20
a. Perf. 14½x14 .75 .65

112 A22 1p red, Perf. 14½x14 ('47) .20 .20
a. Perf. 12½ .20 .20
113 A22 1½p carmine ('43) .20 .20
a. Perf. 14½x14 1.00 .35
114 A22 2p gray ('43) .20 .20
a. Perf. 14½x14 .75 *1.00*
115 A22 2½p ultra ('43) .20 .20
a. Perf. 14½x14 1.50 .20
116 A22 2½p violet ('47) .20 .20
117 A22 3p red org ('43) .20 .20
a. Perf. 14½x14 .20 .20
118 A22 3½p brt ultra ('47) .20 .20
119 A23 6p magenta ('48) .60 .40
a. Perf. 13½ 2.00 1.50
120 A22 8p choc ('46) 1.50 .25
121 A24 1sh lt brn ('48) .25 .20
a. Perf. 13½ .50 .40
122 A25 2sh red vio & sl bl 2.25 1.10
123 A22 3sh brt red vio ('46) 5.00 2.50
124 A26 5sh rose vio & blk 8.75 5.75
125 A27 10sh black, *yel* 2.75 *8.00*
126 A22 £1 sepia ('46) 6.75 7.00
Nos. 110-126 (17) 29.65 27.00
Set, never hinged 55.00

See Nos. 135-148.

Catalogue values for unused stamps in this section, from this point to the end of the section, are for Never Hinged items.

Peace Issue
Common Design Type
Perf. 13½x14

1946, Oct. 8 Wmk. 4 Engr.
127 CD303 1p lilac .20 .20
128 CD303 3½p deep blue .45 .45

Silver Wedding Issue
Common Design Types

1948, Nov. 26 Photo. *Perf. 14x14½*
129 CD304 1p scarlet .20 .20

Engraved; Name Typographed
Perf. 11½x11
130 CD305 £1 violet brown 15.00 30.00

UPU Issue
Common Design Types
Engr.; Name Typo. on 6c, 12c.
Perf. 13½, 11x11½

1949, Oct. 10 Wmk. 4
131 CD306 5c violet .20 .20
132 CD307 6c deep orange 1.25 1.00
133 CD308 12c red lilac .25 .25
134 CD309 24c blue green .55 .30
Nos. 131-134 (4) 2.25 1.75

Types of 1938
Values in Cents and Dollars

1949, Oct. 1 Engr. *Perf. 12½*
135 A22 1c green .20 .20
a. Perf. 14 1.25 .40
136 A22 2c rose lilac .20 .20
a. Perf. 14½x14 2.00 1.75
137 A22 3c red .20 *.50*
138 A22 4c gray .20 .20
a. Perf. 14½x14 *4,000.*
139 A22 5c violet .20 .20
140 A22 6c red orange .20 *.50*
141 A22 7c ultra 1.75 1.25
142 A22 12c rose lake 4.75 1.00
a. Perf. 14½x14 ('50) 450.00 300.00
143 A22 16c brown 2.25 .20

Perf. 11½
144 A27 24c Prus blue .30 .20
145 A27 48c olive green 1.75 .80
146 A27 $1.20 purple 2.50 *5.75*
147 A27 $2.40 blue green 3.50 *14.00*
148 A27 $4.80 dark car rose 7.00 15.00
Nos. 135-148 (14) 25.00 40.00

Nos. 144 to 148 are of a type similar to A27, but with the denomination in the top corners and "St. Lucia" at the bottom.

For overprints see Nos. 152-155.

University Issue
Common Design Types
Perf. 14x14½

1951, Feb. 16 Wmk. 4
149 CD310 3c red & gray black .35 .35
150 CD311 12c brn car & blk .65 .65

Phoenix Rising from Burning Buildings — A28

Engr. & Typo.

1951, June 19 *Perf. 13½x13*
151 A28 12c deep blue & carmine .40 .35

Reconstruction of Castries.

Nos. 136, 138, 139 and 142 Overprinted in Black

N E W 1 9 5 1
CONSTITUTION

1951, Sept. 25 *Perf. 12½*
152 A22 2c rose lilac .30 .30
153 A22 4c gray .30 .30
154 A22 5c violet .30 .30
155 A22 12c rose lilac .35 .35
Nos. 152-155 (4) 1.25 1.25

Adoption of a new constitution for the Windward Islands, 1951.

Coronation Issue
Common Design Type

1953, June 2 Engr. *Perf. 13½x13*
156 CD312 3c carmine & black .45 .45

Queen Elizabeth II A29

Arms of St. Lucia A30

1953-54 Engr. *Perf. 14½x14*
157 A29 1c green .20 .20
158 A29 2c rose lilac .20 .20
159 A29 3c red .20 .20
160 A29 4c gray .20 .20
161 A29 5c violet .20 .20
162 A29 6c orange .20 .20
163 A29 8c rose lake .35 .20
164 A29 10c ultra .20 .20
165 A29 15c brown .35 .20

Perf. 11x11½
166 A30 25c Prus blue .40 .20
167 A30 50c brown olive 4.50 .50
168 A30 $1 blue green 4.50 2.25
169 A30 $2.50 dark car rose 5.50 4.25
Nos. 157-169 (13) 17.00 9.00

Issued: 2c, 10/28; 4c, 1/7/54; 1c, 5c, 4/1/54; others, 9/2/54.

West Indies Federation
Common Design Type
Perf. 11½x11

1958, Apr. 22 Wmk. 314
170 CD313 3c green .35 .20
171 CD313 6c blue .60 *.95*
172 CD313 12c carmine rose .80 .35
Nos. 170-172 (3) 1.75 1.50

16th Century Ship and Pitons — A31

St. Lucia Stamp of 1860 — A32

1960, Jan. 1 *Perf. 12½x13*
173 A31 8c carmine rose .25 .25
174 A31 10c orange .30 .30
175 A31 25c dark blue .70 .70
Nos. 173-175 (3) 1.25 1.25

Granting of new constitution.

1960, Dec. 18 Engr. *Perf. 13½*
176 A32 5c ultra & red brown .20 .20
177 A32 16c yel grn & blue blk .65 *1.00*
178 A32 25c carmine & green .65 .30
Nos. 176-178 (3) 1.50 1.50

Centenary of St. Lucia's first postage stamps.

Freedom from Hunger Issue
Common Design Type

1963, June 4 Photo. *Perf. 14x14½*
179 CD314 25c green .60 .60

Red Cross Centenary Issue
Common Design Type
Wmk. 314

1963, Sept. 2 Litho. *Perf. 13*
180 CD315 4c black & red .20 .20
181 CD315 25c ultra & red 1.00 1.00

A33

A34

Fishing Boats, Soufrière Bay — A35

Designs: 15c, Pigeon Island. 25c, Reduit Beach. 35c, Castries Harbor. 50c, The Pitons. $1, Vigie Beach, vert. $2.50, Queen Elizabeth II, close-up.

Wmk. 314

1964, Mar. 1 Photo. *Perf. 14½*
182 A33 1c dark car rose .20 .20
183 A33 2c violet .35 .35
184 A33 4c brt blue green .35 .35
185 A33 5c slate blue .20 .20
186 A33 6c brown .45 *.60*
187 A34 8c lt blue & multi .20 .20
188 A34 10c multicolored .20 .20
189 A35 12c multicolored .40 .75
190 A35 15c blue & ocher .25 .20
a. Wmkd. sideways ('68) .20 .20
191 A35 25c multicolored .40 .20
192 A35 35c dk blue & buff .65 .20
193 A35 50c brt blue, blk & yel .90 .20
194 A35 $1 multicolored 2.00 .90
195 A34 $2.50 multicolored 3.25 2.25
Nos. 182-195 (14) 9.80 6.80

For overprints see Nos. 215-225.

Shakespeare Issue
Common Design Type

1964, Apr. 23 *Perf. 14x14½*
196 CD316 10c bright green .40 .25

ITU Issue
Common Design Type
Perf. 11x11½

1965, May 17 Litho. Wmk. 314
197 CD317 2c red lilac & brt pink .20 .20
198 CD317 50c lilac & yel grn 1.30 1.30

Intl. Cooperation Year Issue
Common Design Type

1965, Oct. 25 Wmk. 314 *Perf. 14½*
199 CD318 1c blue grn & claret .20 .20
200 CD318 25c lt violet & grn .50 .50

Churchill Memorial Issue
Common Design Type

1966, Jan. 24 Photo. *Perf. 14*
Design in Black, Gold and Carmine Rose
201 CD319 4c bright blue .20 .20
202 CD319 6c green .20 .20
203 CD319 25c brown .40 .40
204 CD319 35c violet .60 .60
Nos. 201-204 (4) 1.40 1.40

Royal Visit Issue
Common Design Type

1966, Feb. 4 Litho. *Perf. 11x12*
205 CD320 4c violet blue .25 .25
206 CD320 25c dk carmine rose .85 .85

World Cup Soccer Issue
Common Design Type

1966, July 1 Litho. *Perf. 14*
207 CD321 4c multicolored .25 .25
208 CD321 25c multicolored .65 .65

WHO Headquarters Issue
Common Design Type

1966, Sept. 20 Litho. *Perf. 14*
209 CD322 4c multicolored .20 .20
210 CD322 25c multicolored .40 .30

UNESCO Anniversary Issue
Common Design Type

1966, Dec. 1 Litho. *Perf. 14*
211 CD323 4c "Education" .20 .20
212 CD323 12c "Science" .30 .30
213 CD323 25c "Culture" .60 .60
Nos. 211-213 (3) 1.10 1.10

Associated State
Nos. 183, 185-194 Overprinted in Red: "STATEHOOD / 1st MARCH 1967"

Wmk. 314

1967, Mar. 1 Photo. *Perf. 14½*

215	A33	2c violet	.30	.20
216	A33	5c slate blue	.20	.20
217	A33	6c brown	.20	.20
218	A34	8c lt blue & multi	.30	.20
219	A34	10c multicolored	.40	.20
220	A35	12c multicolored	.30	.20
221	A35	15c blue & ocher	.90	.50
222	A35	25c multicolored	.40	.40
223	A35	35c dk blue & buff	.75	.55
224	A35	50c multicolored	.75	.75
225	A35	$1 multicolored	.75	.75
		Nos. 215-225 (11)	5.25	4.15

The 1c and $2.50, similarly overprinted, were not sold to the public at the post office but were acknowledged belatedly (May 10) by the government and declared valid. The 1c, 6c and $2.50 overprints exist in black as well as red. No. 213 also exists with this overprint in blue and in black.

Madonna and Child with St. John, by Raphael — A36

Cricket Batsman and Gov. Frederick Clarke — A37

1967, Oct. 16 Wmk. 314 *Perf. 14½*

227	A36	4c black, gold & multi	.20	.20
228	A36	25c multicolored	.30	.20

Christmas 1967.

Perf. 14½x14

1968, Mar. 8 Photo. Wmk. 314

229	A37	10c multicolored	.20	.20
230	A37	35c multicolored	.55	.55

Visit of the Marylebone Cricket Club to the West Indies, Jan.-Feb. 1968.

"Noli me Tangere," by Titian — A38

Martin Luther King, Jr. — A39

Easter: 10c, 25c, The Crucifixion, by Raphael.

1968, Mar. 25 *Perf. 14½*

231	A38	10c multicolored	.20	.20
232	A38	15c multicolored	.20	.20
233	A38	25c multicolored	.20	.20
234	A38	35c multicolored	.20	.20
		Nos. 231-234 (4)	.80	.80

Perf. 13½x14

1968, July 4 Photo. Wmk. 314

235	A39	25c dp blue, blk & brn	.20	.20
236	A39	35c violet, blk & brn	.20	.20

Dr. Martin Luther King, Jr. (1929-68), American civil rights leader.

Virgin and Child in Glory, by Murillo — A40

Christmas: 10c, 35c, Virgin and Child, by Bartolomé E. Murillo.

Perf. 14½x14

1968, Oct. 17 Photo. Wmk. 314

237	A40	5c dark blue & multi	.20	.20
238	A40	10c multicolored	.20	.20
239	A40	25c red brown & multi	.25	.25
240	A40	35c deep blue & multi	.25	.25
		Nos. 237-240 (4)	.90	.90

Purple-throated Carib — A41

Birds: 15c, 35c, St. Lucia parrot.

1969, Jan. 10 Litho. *Perf. 14½*

241	A41	10c multicolored	.55	.55
242	A41	15c multicolored	.70	.70
243	A41	25c multicolored	1.00	1.00
244	A41	35c multicolored	1.25	1.25
		Nos. 241-244 (4)	3.50	3.50

Ecce Homo, by Guido Reni — A42

Painting: 15c, 35c, The Resurrection, by Il Sodoma (Giovanni Antonio de Bazzi).

Perf. 14½x14

1969, Mar. 20 Photo. Wmk. 314

245	A42	10c purple & multi	.20	.20
246	A42	15c green & multi	.20	.20
247	A42	25c black & multi	.25	.25
248	A42	35c ocher & multi	.25	.25
		Nos. 245-248 (4)	.90	.90

Easter 1969.

Map of Caribbean — A43

Design: 25c, 35c, Clasped hands and arrows with names of CARIFTA members.

1969, May 29 Wmk. 314 *Perf. 14*

249	A43	5c violet blue & multi	.20	.20
250	A43	10c deep plum & multi	.20	.20
251	A43	25c ultra & multi	.20	.20
252	A43	35c green & multi	.20	.20
		Nos. 249-252 (4)	.80	.80

First anniversary of CARIFTA (Caribbean Free Trade Area).

Silhouettes of Napoleon and Josephine — A44

Perf. 14½x13

1969, Sept. 22 Photo. Unwmk.

Gold Inscription; Gray and Brown Medallions

253	A44	15c dull blue	.20	.20
254	A44	25c deep claret	.20	.20
255	A44	35c deep green	.20	.20
256	A44	50c yellow brown	.20	*.50*
		Nos. 253-256 (4)	.80	1.10

Napoleon Bonaparte, 200th birth anniv.

Madonna and Child, by Paul Delaroche — A45

Christmas: 10c, 35c, Holy Family, by Rubens.

Perf. 14½x14

1969, Oct. 27 Photo. Wmk. 314

Center Multicolored

257	A45	5c dp rose lil & gold	.20	.20
258	A45	10c Prus blue & gold	.20	.20
259	A45	25c maroon & gold	.25	.25
260	A45	35c dp yel grn & gold	.25	.25
		Nos. 257-260 (4)	.90	.90

House of Assembly — A46

Queen Elizabeth II, by A. C. Davidson-Houston A47

2c, Roman Catholic Cathedral. 4c, Castries Boulevard. 5c, Castries Harbor. 6c, Sulphur springs. 10c, Vigie Airport. 12c, Reduit beach. 15c, Pigeon Island. 25c, The Pitons & sailboat. 35c, Marigot Bay. 50c, Diamond Waterfall. $1, St. Lucia flag & motto. $2.50, Coat of arms. $10, Map of St. Lucia.

Wmk. 314 Sideways, Upright (#271-274)

1970-73 Litho. *Perf. 14½*

261	A46	1c multicolored	.20	.20
262	A46	2c multicolored	.20	.20
a.		Wmk. upright	.55	.55
263	A46	4c multicolored	1.10	.20
a.		Wmk. upright	1.00	1.00
264	A46	5c multicolored	1.75	.20
265	A46	6c multicolored	.20	.20
266	A46	10c multicolored	1.40	.20
267	A46	12c multicolored	.20	.20
268	A46	15c multicolored	.35	.20
269	A46	25c multicolored	.90	.20
270	A46	35c multicolored	.45	.20
271	A47	50c multicolored	.80	.80
272	A47	$1 multicolored	.45	*.70*
273	A47	$2.50 multicolored	.60	*1.75*
274	A47	$5 multicolored	1.40	*3.75*
274A	A47	$10 multicolored	6.00	*8.50*
		Nos. 261-274A (15)	16.00	17.50

Issued: #261-274, Feb. 1, 1970; #274A, Dec. 3, 1973; #262a, 263a, Mar. 15, 1974.

1975, July 28 Wmk. 373

263b	A46	4c multicolored	.65	1.90
264a	A46	5c multicolored	.85	.95
266a	A46	10c multicolored	1.10	1.25
268a	A46	15c multicolored	1.90	1.90
		Nos. 263b-268a (4)	4.50	6.00

The Three Marys at the Tomb, by Hogarth — A48

25c, The Sealing of the Tomb. $1, The Ascension. The designs are from the altarpiece painted by William Hogarth for the Church of St. Mary Redcliffe in Bristol, 1755-56.

Roulette 8½xPerf. 12½

1970, Mar. 7 Litho. Wmk. 314

Size: 27x54mm

275	A48	25c dark brown & multi	.20	.25
276	A48	35c dark brown & multi	.20	.25

Size: 38x54mm

277	A48	$1 dark brown & multi	.35	.40
a.		Triptych (#275-277)	1.75	1.75

Easter 1970.

Nos. 275-277 printed se-tenant in sheets of 30 (10 triptychs) with the center $1 stamp 10mm raised compared to the flanking 25c and 35c stamps.

Charles Dickens and Characters from his Works — A49

1970, June 8 Wmk. 314 *Perf. 14*

278	A49	1c brown & multi	.20	.20
279	A49	25c Prus blue & multi	.25	.25
280	A49	35c brown red & multi	.30	.30
281	A49	50c red lilac & multi	.35	*.60*
		Nos. 278-281 (4)	1.10	1.35

Charles Dickens (1812-70), English novelist.

Nurse Holding Red Cross Emblem A50

15c, 35c, British, St. Lucia & Red Cross flags.

Perf. 14½x14

1970, Aug. 18 Litho. Wmk. 314

282	A50	10c multicolored	.20	.20
283	A50	15c multicolored	.20	.20
284	A50	25c buff & multi	.30	.30
285	A50	35c multicolored	.40	.40
		Nos. 282-285 (4)	1.10	1.10

Centenary of British Red Cross Society.

Madonna with the Lilies, by Luca della Robbia A51

Lithographed and Embossed

1970, Nov. 16 Unwmk. *Perf. 11*

286 A51 5c dark blue & multi	.20	.20
287 A51 10c violet blue & multi	.20	.20
288 A51 35c car lake & multi	.35	.20
289 A51 40c deep green & multi	.35	.35
Nos. 286-289 (4)	1.10	.95

Christmas 1970.

Christ on the Cross, by Rubens — A52

Easter: 15c, 40c, Descent from the Cross, by Peter Paul Rubens.

Perf. 14x13½

1971, Mar. 29 Litho. Wmk. 314

290 A52 10c dull green & multi	.20	.20
291 A52 15c dull red & multi	.20	.20
292 A52 35c brt blue & multi	.35	.20
293 A52 40c multicolored	.35	.35
Nos. 290-293 (4)	1.10	.95

Moule à Chique Lighthouse — A53

Design: 25c, Beane Field Airport.

1971, Apr. 30 *Perf. 14½x14*

294 A53 5c olive & multi	.30	.20
295 A53 25c bister & multi	.60	.20

Opening of Beane Field Airport.

View of Morne Fortune (Old Days) — A54

The "a" stamp shows an old print (as shown) and the "b" stamp a contemporary photograph of the same view (plain frame). 10c, Castries City. 25c, Pigeon Island. 50c, View from Government House.

Perf. 13½x14

1971, Aug. 10 Litho. Wmk. 314

296 A54 5c Pair, #a.-b.	.20	.20
297 A54 10c Pair, #a.-b.	.25	.25
298 A54 25c Pair, #a.-b.	.55	.55
299 A54 50c Pair, #a.-b.	1.00	1.00
Nos. 296-299 (4)	2.00	2.00

Virgin and Child, by Verrocchio — A55

Virgin and Child painted by: 10c, Paolo Moranda. 35c, Giovanni Battista Cima. 40c, Andrea del Verrocchio.

1971, Oct. 15 *Perf. 14*

304 A55 5c green & multi	.20	.20
305 A55 10c brown & multi	.20	.20
306 A55 35c ultra & multi	.25	.25
307 A55 40c red & multi	.35	.35
Nos. 304-307 (4)	1.00	1.00

Christmas 1971.

St. Lucia, School of Dolci, and Arms — A56

1971, Dec. 13 *Perf. 14x14½*

308 A56 5c gray & multi	.20	.20
309 A56 10c lt green & multi	.20	.20
310 A56 25c tan & multi	.30	.20
311 A56 50c lt blue & multi	.55	.50
Nos. 308-311 (4)	1.25	1.10

National Day.

Lamentation, by Carracci A57

Easter: 25c, 50c, Angels Weeping over Body of Jesus, by Guercino.

1972, Feb. 15 Wmk. 314

312 A57 10c lt violet & multi	.20	.20
313 A57 25c ocher & multi	.25	.20
314 A57 35c ultra & multi	.30	.20
315 A57 50c lt green & multi	.50	.50
Nos. 312-315 (4)	1.25	1.10

Teachers' College and Science Building — A58

15c, University Center and coat of arms. 25c, Secondary School. 35c, Technical College.

1972, Apr. 18 Litho. *Perf. 14*

316 A58 5c multicolored	.20	.20
317 A58 15c multicolored	.20	.20
318 A58 25c multicolored	.20	.20
319 A58 35c multicolored	.20	.20
Nos. 316-319 (4)	.80	.80

Opening of Morne Educational Complex.

Steam Conveyance Co. Stamp and Map of St. Lucia — A59

Designs: 10c, Castries Harbor and 3c stamp. 35c, Soufriere Volcano and 1c stamp. 50c, One cent, 3c, 6c stamps.

1972, June 22 *Perf. 14½*

320 A59 5c yellow & multi	.20	.20
321 A59 10c violet blue & multi	.25	.20
322 A59 35c car rose & multi	.70	.20
323 A59 50c emerald & multi	1.10	1.10
Nos. 320-323 (4)	2.25	1.70

Centenary of St. Lucia Steam Conveyance Co. Ltd. postal service.

Holy Family, by Sebastiano Ricci — A60

1972, Oct. 18 *Perf. 14½x14*

324 A60 5c dk brown & multi	.20	.20
325 A60 10c green & multi	.20	.20
326 A60 35c carmine & multi	.25	.20
327 A60 40c dk blue & multi	.35	.20
Nos. 324-327 (4)	1.00	.80

Christmas 1972.

Silver Wedding Issue, 1972

Common Design Type

Design: Queen Elizabeth II, Prince Philip, St. Lucia coat of arms and St. Lucia parrot.

1972, Nov. Photo. *Perf. 14x14½*

328 CD324 15c car rose & multi	.20	.20
329 CD324 35c olive & multi	.30	.30

Weekday Headdress A61

Arms of St. Lucia A62

Women's Headdresses: 10c, For church wear. 25c, Unmarried girl. 50c, Formal occasions.

1973, Feb. 1 Wmk. 314 *Perf. 13*

330 A61 5c multicolored	.20	.20
331 A61 10c dark gray & multi	.20	.20
332 A61 25c multicolored	.25	.20
333 A61 50c slate blue & multi	.35	*.75*
Nos. 330-333 (4)	1.00	1.35

Coil Stamps

1973, Apr. 19 Litho. *Perf. 14½x14*

334 A62 5c gray olive	.20	*.60*
a. Watermark sideways ('76)	.60	*1.50*
335 A62 10c blue	.20	*.60*
a. Watermark sideways ('76)	.60	*1.50*
336 A62 25c claret	.20	*.60*
a. Watermark sideways ('76)	14.00	

H.M.S. St. Lucia A63

Designs: Old Sailing ships.

1973, May 24 Litho. *Perf. 13½x14*

337 A63 15c shown	.20	.20
338 A63 35c "Prince of Wales"	.35	.35
339 A63 50c "Oliph Blossom"	.45	.45
340 A63 $1 "Rose"	1.00	1.00
a. Souv. sheet of 4, #337-340, perf. 15	2.10	2.10
Nos. 337-340 (4)	2.00	2.00

Banana Plantation and Flower — A64

Designs: 15c, Aerial spraying. 35c, Washing and packing bananas. 50c, Loading.

1973, July 26 Litho. *Perf. 14*

341 A64 5c multicolored	.20	.20
342 A64 15c multicolored	.25	.20
343 A64 35c multicolored	.35	.20
344 A64 50c multicolored	.85	.75
Nos. 341-344 (4)	1.65	1.35

Banana industry.

Madonna and Child, by Carlo Maratta — A65

Christmas (Paintings): 15c, Virgin in the Meadow, by Raphael. 35c, Holy Family, by Angelo Bronzino. 50c, Madonna of the Pear, by Durer.

1973, Oct. 17 Litho. *Perf. 14x13½*

345 A65 5c citron & multi	.20	.20
346 A65 15c ultra & multi	.20	.20
347 A65 35c dp green & multi	.25	.20
348 A65 50c red & multi	.35	.25
Nos. 345-348 (4)	1.00	.85

Princess Anne's Wedding Issue

Common Design Type

1973, Nov. 14 Wmk. 314 *Perf. 14*

349 CD325 40c gray green & multi	.20	.20
350 CD325 50c lilac & multi	.20	.20

The Betrayal of Christ, by Ugolino — A66

Easter (Paintings by Ugolino, 14th Cent.): 35c, The Way to Calvary. 80c, Descent from the Cross. $1, Resurrection.

1974, Apr. 1 *Perf. 13½x13*

351 A66 5c ocher & multi	.20	.20
352 A66 35c ocher & multi	.25	.20
353 A66 80c ocher & multi	.25	.20
354 A66 $1 ocher & multi	.30	.30
a. Souvenir sheet of 4, #351-354	1.60	1.60
Nos. 351-354 (4)	1.00	.90

3 Escalins, 1798 — A67

Baron de Laborie, 1784 — A68

Pieces of Eight: 35c, 6 escalins, 1798. 40c, 2 livres 5 sols, 1813. $1, 6 livres 15 sols, 1813.

1974, May 20 *Perf. 13½*

355 A67 15c lt olive & multi	.25	.25
356 A67 35c multicolored	.25	.25
357 A67 40c green & multi	.35	.35
358 A67 $1 brown & multi	.60	.60
a. Souvenir sheet of 4, #355-358	1.75	1.75
Nos. 355-358 (4)	1.45	1.45

Coins of Old St. Lucia.

Wmk. 314

1974, Aug. 29 Litho. *Perf. 14½*

Portraits: 35c, Sir John Moore, Lieutenant Governor, 1796-97. 80c, Major General Sir

Dudley St. Leger Hill, 1834-37. $1, Sir Frederick Joseph Clarke, 1967-71.

359	A68	5c ocher & multi	.20	.20
360	A68	35c brt blue & multi	.20	.20
361	A68	80c violet & multi	.20	.20
362	A68	$1 multicolored	.25	.25
a.		Souvenir sheet of 4, #359-362	1.00	1.00
		Nos. 359-362 (4)	.85	.85

Past Governors of St. Luicia.

Virgin and Child, by Verrocchio — A69

Christmas (Virgin and Child): 35c, by Andrea della Robbia. 80c, by Luca della Robbia. $1, by Antonio Rossellino.

1974, Nov. 13 Wmk. 314 *Perf. 13½*

363	A69	5c gray & multi	.20	.20
364	A69	35c pink & multi	.20	.20
365	A69	80c brown & multi	.20	.20
366	A69	$1 olive & multi	.25	.25
a.		Souvenir sheet of 4, #363-366	1.25	*2.50*
		Nos. 363-366 (4)	.85	.85

Churchill and Gen. Montgomery — A70

Design: $1, Churchill and Pres. Truman.

1974, Nov. 30 *Perf. 14*

367	A70	5c multicolored	.20	.20
368	A70	$1 multicolored	.40	.40

Sir Winston Churchill (1874-1965).

Crucifixion, by Van der Weyden — A71

Easter: 35c, "Noli me Tangere," by Julio Romano. 80c, Crucifixion, by Fernando Gallego. $1, "Noli me Tangere," by Correggio.

Perf. 14x13½

1975, Mar. 27 Wmk. 314

369	A71	5c brown & multi	.20	.20
370	A71	35c ultra & multi	.20	.20
371	A71	80c red brown & multi	.25	.25
372	A71	$1 green & multi	.35	.35
		Nos. 369-372 (4)	1.00	1.00

Nativity — A72

Adoration of the Kings — A73

#375, Virgin & Child. #376, Adoration of the Shepherds. 40c, Nativity. $1, Virgin & Child with Sts. Catherine of Alexandria and Siena.

Wmk. 314

1975, Dec. Litho. *Perf. 14½*

373	A72	5c lilac rose & multi	.20	.20
374	A73	10c yellow & multi	.20	.20
375	A73	10c yellow & multi	.20	.20
376	A73	10c yellow & multi	.20	.20
a.		Strip of 3, #374-376	.40	.40
377	A72	40c yellow & multi	.40	.40
378	A72	$1 blue & multi	.85	.85
a.		Souv. sheet of 3, #373, 377-378	1.00	*1.25*
		Nos. 373-378 (6)	2.05	2.05

Christmas 1975.

"Hanna," First US Warship — A74

Revolutionary Era Ships: 1c, "Prince of Orange," British packet. 2c, "Edward," British sloop. 5c, "Millern," British merchantman. 15c, "Surprise," Continental Navy lugger. 35c, "Serapis," British warship. 50c, "Randolph," first Continental Navy frigate. $1, Frigate "Alliance."

Perf. 14½

1976, Jan. 26 Litho. Unwmk.

379-386	A74	Set of 8	6.00	3.50
386a		Souv. sheet, #383-386, perf. 13	4.00	*6.00*

American Bicentennial.

Laughing Gull — A75

Birds: 2c, Little blue heron. 4c, Belted kingfisher. 5c, St. Lucia parrot. 6c, St. Lucia oriole. 8c, Brown trembler. 10c, American kestrel. 12c, Red-billed tropic bird. 15c, Common gallinule. 25c, Brown noddy. 35c, Sooty tern. 50c, Osprey. $1, White-breasted thrasher. $2.50, St. Lucia black finch. $5, Rednecked pigeon. $10, Caribbean elaenia.

Wmk. 314 (1c); 373 (others)

1976, May 7 Litho. *Perf. 14½*

387	A75	1c gray & multi	.30	*1.00*
388	A75	2c gray & multi	.30	*1.00*
389	A75	4c gray & multi	.35	*1.00*
390	A75	5c gray & multi	1.75	1.00
391	A75	6c gray & multi	1.25	1.00
392	A75	8c gray & multi	1.40	*1.75*
393	A75	10c gray & multi	1.25	.40
394	A75	12c gray & multi	1.90	*2.40*
395	A75	15c gray & multi	1.25	.20
396	A75	25c gray & multi	1.75	1.75
397	A75	35c gray & multi	3.00	1.25
398	A75	50c gray & multi	6.00	3.25
399	A75	$1 gray & multi	3.75	3.25
400	A75	$2.50 gray & multi	6.75	6.25
401	A75	$5 gray & multi	7.25	4.25
402	A75	$10 gray & multi	6.75	*7.75*
		Nos. 387-402 (16)	45.00	37.50

Map of West Indies, Bats, Wicket and Ball A75a

Prudential Cup — A75b

1976, July 19 Unwmk. *Perf. 14*

403	A75a	50c lt blue & multi	1.00	1.00
404	A75b	$1 lilac rose & black	2.00	2.00
a.		Souvenir sheet of 2, #403-404	4.25	*5.50*

World Cricket Cup, won by West Indies Team, 1975.

Arms of H.M.S. Ceres — A76

Madonna and Child, by Murillo — A77

Coats of Arms of Royal Naval Ships: 20c, Pelican. 40c, Ganges. $2, Ariadne.

1976, Sept. 6 Wmk. 373 *Perf. 14½*

405	A76	10c gold & multi	.40	.40
406	A76	20c gold & multi	.70	.70
407	A76	40c gold & multi	1.00	1.00
408	A76	$2 gold & multi	2.40	2.40
		Nos. 405-408 (4)	4.50	4.50

1976, Nov. 15 Litho. *Perf. 14½*

Paintings: 20c, Virgin and Child, by Lorenzo Costa. 50c, Madonna and Child, by Adriaea Isenbrandt. $2, Madonna and Child with St. John, by Murillo. $2.50, Like 10c.

409	A77	10c multicolored	.20	.20
410	A77	20c multicolored	.20	.20
411	A77	50c multicolored	.25	.25
412	A77	$2 multicolored	.90	.90
		Nos. 409-412 (4)	1.55	1.55

Souvenir Sheet

413	A77	$2.50 multicolored	1.50	1.50

Christmas.

Elizabeth II, "Palms and Water" — A78

Wmk. 373

1977, Feb. 7 Litho. *Perf. 14½*

414	A78	10c multicolored	.20	.20
415	A78	20c multicolored	.20	.20
416	A78	40c multicolored	.20	.20
417	A78	$2 multicolored	.40	.40
		Nos. 414-417 (4)	1.00	1.00

Souvenir Sheet

418	A78	$2.50 multicolored	.75	*1.50*

25th anniv. of the reign of Elizabeth II.

Scouts of Tapion School — A79

Nativity, by Giotto — A80

1c, Sea Scouts, St. Mary's College. 2c, Scout giving oath. 10c, Tapion School Cub Scouts. 20c, Venture Scout, Soufrière. 50c, Scout from Gros Islet Division. $1, $2.50, Boat drill, St. Mary's College.

1977, Oct. 17 Unwmk. *Perf. 15*

419	A79	½c multicolored	.20	.20
420	A79	1c multicolored	.20	.20
421	A79	2c multicolored	.20	.20
422	A79	10c multicolored	.20	.20
423	A79	20c multicolored	.20	.20
424	A79	50c multicolored	.50	.50
425	A79	$1 multicolored	1.00	1.00
		Nos. 419-425 (7)	2.50	2.50

Souvenir Sheet

426	A79	$2.50 multicolored	2.00	2.00

6th Caribbean Boy Scout Jamboree, Kingston, Jamaica, Aug. 5-14.

1977, Oct. 31 Litho. *Perf. 14*

Christmas (Virgin and Child by): 1c, Fra Angelico. 2c, El Greco. 20c, Caravaggio. 50c, Velazquez. $1, Tiepolo. $2.50, Adoration of the Kings, by Tiepolo.

427-433	A80	Set of 7	3.50	3.50

Suzanne Fourment in Velvet Hat, by Rubens — A81

Rubens Paintings: 35c, Rape of the Sabine Women (detail). 50c, Ludovicus Nonnius, portrait. $2.50, Minerva Protecting Pax from Mars (detail).

Perf. 14x14½

1977, Nov. 28 Litho. Wmk. 373

434	A81	10c multicolored	.20	.20
435	A81	35c multicolored	.20	.20
436	A81	50c multicolored	.25	.25
437	A81	$2.50 multicolored	1.25	1.25
a.		Souv. sheet, #434-437, perf. 15	2.00	2.00
		Nos. 434-437 (4)	1.90	1.90

Peter Paul Rubens (1577-1640).

Yeoman of the Guard and Life Guard A82

Dress Uniforms: 20c, Groom and postilion. 50c, Footman and coachman. $3, State trumpeter and herald. $5, Master of the Queen's House and Gentleman at Arms.

Unwmk.

1978, June 2 Litho. *Perf. 14*

438	A82	15c multicolored	.20	.20
439	A82	20c multicolored	.20	.20
440	A82	50c multicolored	.30	.30
441	A82	$3 multicolored	2.00	2.00
		Nos. 438-441 (4)	2.70	2.70

Souvenir Sheet

442	A82	$5 multicolored	3.00	3.00

25th anniv. of coronation of Elizabeth II.

Nos. 438-441 exist in miniature sheets of 3 plus label, perf. 12.

Queen Angelfish A83

Tropical Fish: 20c, Four-eyed butterflyfish. 50c, French angelfish. $2, Yellowtail damselfish. $2.50, Rock beauty.

1978, June 19 Litho. *Perf. 14½*

443	A83	10c multicolored	.20	.20
444	A83	20c multicolored	.20	.20
445	A83	50c multicolored	.45	.45
446	A83	$2 multicolored	1.75	1.75
		Nos. 443-446 (4)	2.60	2.60

Souvenir Sheet

447	A83	$2.50 multicolored	2.50	2.50

French Grenadier, Map of Battle — A84

30c, British Grenadier & Bellin map of St. Lucia, 1762. 50c, British fleet opposing French landing & map of coast from Gros Islet to Cul-de-Sac. $2.50, Light infantrymen & Gen. James Grant.

1978, Nov. 15 Litho. *Perf. 14*

448	A84	10c multicolored	.20	.20
449	A84	30c multicolored	.25	.25
450	A84	50c multicolored	.40	.40
451	A84	$2.50 multicolored	2.00	2.00
		Nos. 448-451 (4)	2.85	2.85

Bicent. of Battle of St. Lucia (Cul-de-Sac).

Annunciation A85

Christmas: 55c, 80c, Adoration of the Kings.

Perf. 14x14½

1978, Dec. 4 Wmk. 373

452	A85	30c multicolored	.25	.25
453	A85	50c multicolored	.35	.35
454	A85	55c multicolored	.40	.40
455	A85	80c multicolored	.55	.55
		Nos. 452-455 (4)	1.55	1.55

Independent State

Hewanorra Airport A86

Independence: 30c, New coat of arms. 50c, Government house and Allen Lewis, first Governor General. $2, Map of St. Lucia, French, St. Lucia and British flags.

1979, Feb. 22 Litho. *Perf. 14*

456	A86	10c multicolored	.20	.20
457	A86	30c multicolored	.20	.20
458	A86	50c multicolored	.30	.30
459	A86	$2 multicolored	1.25	1.25
a.		Souvenir sheet of 4, #456-459	2.00	2.00
		Nos. 456-459 (5)	1.95	1.95

Paul VI and John Paul I A87

Pope Paul VI and: 30c, Pres. Anwar Sadat of Egypt. 50c, Secretary General U Thant and UN emblem. 55c, Prime Minister Golda Meir of Israel. $2, Martin Luther King, Jr.

1979, May 7 Litho. *Perf. 14*

460	A87	10c multicolored	.20	.20
461	A87	30c multicolored	.25	.25
462	A87	50c multicolored	.40	.40
463	A87	55c multicolored	.45	.45
464	A87	$2 multicolored	1.75	1.75
		Nos. 460-464 (5)	3.05	3.05

In memory of Popes Paul VI and John Paul I.

Jersey Cows A88

Agricultural Diversification: 35c, Fruits and vegetables. 50c, Waterfall (water conservation). $3, Coconuts, copra industry.

1979, July 2 Litho. *Perf. 14*

465	A88	10c multicolored	.20	.20
466	A88	35c multicolored	.30	.30
467	A88	50c multicolored	.40	.40
468	A88	$3 multicolored	2.50	2.50
		Nos. 465-468 (4)	3.40	3.40

Lindbergh's Route over St. Lucia, Puerto Rico-Paramaribo — A89

1979, Nov. Litho. *Perf. 14*

469	A89	10c Lindbergh, hydroplane	.20	.20
470	A89	30c shown	.25	.25
471	A89	50c Landing at La Toc	.40	.40
472	A89	$2 Flight covers	1.65	1.65
		Nos. 469-472 (4)	2.50	2.50

Lindbergh's inaugural airmail flight (US-Guyana) via St. Lucia, 50th anniversary.

Prince of Saxony, by Cranach the Elder — A90

IYC (Emblem and): 50c, Infanta Margarita, by Velazquez. $2, Girl Playing Badminton, by Jean Baptiste Chardin. $2.50, Mary and Francis Wilcox, by Stock. $5, Two Children, by Pablo Picasso.

1979, Dec. 6 Litho. *Perf. 14*

473	A90	10c multicolored	.20	.20
474	A90	50c multicolored	.40	.40
475	A90	$2 multicolored	1.65	1.65
476	A90	$2.50 multicolored	2.00	2.00
		Nos. 473-476 (4)	4.25	4.25

Souvenir Sheet

477	A90	$5 multicolored	3.50	3.50

A91

A92

Maltese Cross Cancels and: 10c, Penny Post notice, 1839. 50c, Hill's original stamp design. $2, St. Lucia #1. $2.50, Penny Black. $5, Hill portrait.

1979, Dec. 10

478	A91	10c multicolored	.20	.20
479	A91	50c multicolored	.30	.30
480	A91	$2 multicolored	1.25	1.25
481	A91	$2.50 multicolored	1.50	1.50
		Nos. 478-481 (4)	3.25	3.25

Souvenir Sheet

482	A91	$5 multicolored	3.00	3.00

Sir Rowland Hill (1793-1879), originator of penny postage.

Nos. 478-481 also issued in sheets of 5 plus label, perf. 12x12½.

1980, Jan. 14

IYC Emblem, Virgin and Child Paintings by: 10c, Virgin and Child, by Bernardino Fungi, IYC emblem. 50c, Carlo Dolci. $2, Titian. $2.50, Giovanni Bellini.

483	A92	10c multicolored	.20	.20
484	A92	50c multicolored	.40	.40
485	A92	$2 multicolored	1.65	1.65
486	A92	$2.50 multicolored	2.00	2.00
a.		Souvenir sheet of 4, #483-486	4.50	4.50
		Nos. 483-486 (4)	4.25	4.25

Christmas 1979; Intl. Year of the Child.

St. Lucia Conveyance Co. Ltd. Stamp, 1873 A92a

London 1980 Emblem and Covers: 30c, "Assistance" 1p postmark, 1879. 50c, Postage due handstamp, 1929. $2, Postmarks on 1844 cover.

Wmk. 373

1980, May 6 Litho. *Perf. 14*

487	A92a	10c multicolored	.20	.20
488	A92a	30c multicolored	.20	.20
489	A92a	50c multicolored	.35	.35
490	A92a	$2 multicolored	1.40	1.40
a.		Souvenir sheet of 4, #487-490	2.50	2.50
		Nos. 487-490 (4)	2.15	2.15

London 1980 Intl. Stamp Exhib., May 6-14.

Intl. Year of the Child — A93

Space scenes. 1c, 4c, 5c, 10c, $2, $2.50 horiz.

1980, May 29 Litho. *Perf. 11*

491	A93	½c Mickey on rocket	.20	.20
492	A93	1c Donald Duck spacewalking	.20	.20
493	A93	2c Minnie Mouse on moon	.20	.20
494	A93	3c Goofy hitch hiking	.20	.20
495	A93	4c Goofy on moon	.20	.20
496	A93	5c Pluto digging on moon	.20	.20
497	A93	10c Donald Duck, space creature	.20	.20
498	A93	$2 Donald Duck paddling satellite	2.00	2.00
499	A93	$2.50 Mickey Mouse in lunar rover	2.50	2.50
		Nos. 491-499 (9)	5.90	5.90

Souvenir Sheet

500	A93	$5 Goofy on moon	4.00	4.00

Queen Mother Elizabeth, 80th Birthday A94

1980, Aug. 4 Litho. *Perf. 14*

501	A94	10c multicolored	.20	.20
502	A94	$2.50 multicolored	1.75	1.75

Souvenir Sheet

Perf. 12½x12

503	A94	$3 multicolored	2.00	2.00

HS-748 on Runway, St. Lucia Airport, Hewanorra — A95

Wmk. 373

1980, Aug. 11 Litho. *Perf. 14½*

504	A95	5c shown	.20	.20
505	A95	10c DC-10, St. Lucia Airport	.20	.20
506	A95	15c Bus, Castries	.20	.20
507	A95	20c Refrigerator ship	.20	.20
508	A95	25c Islander plane	.20	.20
509	A95	30c Pilot boat	.20	.20
510	A95	50c Boeing 727	.40	.40
511	A95	75c Cruise ship	.55	.55
512	A95	$1 Lockheed Tristar, Piton Mountains	.75	.75
513	A95	$2 Cargo ship	1.50	1.50
514	A95	$5 Boeing 707	3.75	3.75
515	A95	$10 Queen Elizabeth 2	7.25	7.25
		Nos. 504-515 (12)	15.40	15.40

For surcharges see Nos. 531-533.

1984, May 15 Wmk. 380

507a	A95	20c	.20	.20
508a	A95	25c	.20	.20
509a	A95	30c	.20	.20
512a	A95	$1	.75	.75
513a	A95	$2	1.50	1.50
515a	A95	$10	7.25	7.25
		Nos. 507a-515a (6)	10.10	10.10

Shot Put, Moscow '80 Emblem — A96

1980, Sept. 22 Litho. *Perf. 14*

516	A96	10c shown	.20	.20
517	A96	50c Swimming	.25	.25
518	A96	$2 Gymnastics	1.10	1.10
519	A96	$2.50 Weight lifting	1.40	1.40
		Nos. 516-519 (4)	2.95	2.95

Souvenir Sheet

520	A96	$5 Passing the torch	2.75	2.75

22nd Summer Olympic Games, Moscow, July 19-Aug. 3.

A97

A98

1980, Sept. 30 *Perf. 14*

521	A97	10c Palms, coast at dusk	.20	.20
522	A97	50c Rocky shore	.25	.25
523	A97	$2 Sand beach	1.10	1.10
524	A97	$2.50 Pitons at sunset	1.40	1.40
		Nos. 521-524 (4)	2.95	2.95

Souvenir Sheet

525	A97	$5 Two-master	2.75	2.75

Rotary International, 75th Anniversary.

1980, Oct. 23 Litho. *Perf. 14*

Nobel Prize Winners: 10c, Sir Arthur Lewis, Economics. 50c, Martin Luther King, Jr., peace, 1964. $2, Ralph Bunche, peace, 1950. $2.50, Albert Schweitzer, peace, 1952. $5, Albert Einstein, physics, 1921.

526 A98 10c multicolored .20 .20
527 A98 50c multicolored .30 .30
528 A98 $2 multicolored 1.25 1.25
529 A98 $2.50 multicolored 1.65 1.65
Nos. 526-529 (4) 3.40 3.40

Souvenir Sheet

530 A98 $5 multicolored 3.25 3.25

Nos. 506-507, 510 Surcharged:

1980, Nov. 3 Litho. *Perf. 14½*

531 A95 $1.50 on 15c multi 1.50 1.50
532 A95 $1.50 on 20c multi 1.50 1.50
533 A95 $1.50 on 50c multi 1.50 1.50
Nos. 531-533 (3) 4.50 4.50

Nativity, by Battista — A99

Angel and Citizens of St. Lucia — A100

Christmas: 30c, Adoration of the Kings, by Bruegel the Elder. $2, Adoration of the Shepherds, by Murillo.

1980, Dec. 1 *Perf. 14*

534 A99 10c multicolored .20 .20
535 A99 30c multicolored .25 .25
536 A99 $2 multicolored 1.50 1.50
Nos. 534-536 (3) 1.95 1.95

Souvenir Sheet

537 Sheet of 3 2.00 2.00
a. A100 $1 any single .65 .65

Agouti — A101

1981, Jan. 19 Litho. *Perf. 14*

538 A101 10c shown .20 .20
539 A101 50c St. Lucia parrot .40 .40
540 A101 $2 Purple-throated carib 1.50 1.50
541 A101 $2.50 Fiddler crab 1.90 1.90
Nos. 538-541 (4) 4.00 4.00

Souvenir Sheet

542 A101 $5 Monarch butterfly 4.00 4.00

Royal Wedding Issue
Common Design Type

1981, June 16 Litho. *Perf. 14*

543 CD331 25c Couple .20 .20
544 CD331 50c Clarence House .30 .30
545 CD331 $4 Charles 2.50 2.50
Nos. 543-545 (3) 3.00 3.00

Souvenir Sheet

546 CD331 $5 Glass coach 4.50 4.50

Nos. 543-545 also printed in sheets of 5 plus label, perf. 12, in changed colors.

549 CD331 Booklet 8.75 8.75
a. Pane of 1, $5, Couple 3.50 3.50
b. Pane of 6 (3x50c, Diana, 3x$2, Charles) 5.25 5.25

A102

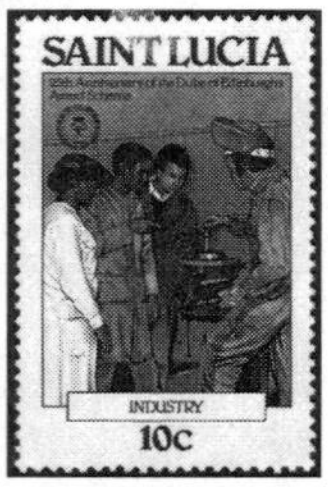

A103

Picasso Birth Centenary: 30c, The Cock. 50c, Man with Ice Cream. 55c, Woman Dressing her Hair. $3, Seated Woman. $5, Night Fishing at Antibes.

1981, May Litho. *Perf. 14*

550 A102 30c multicolored .20 .20
551 A102 50c multicolored .35 .35
552 A102 55c multicolored .40 .40
553 A102 $3 multicolored 2.00 2.00
Nos. 550-553 (4) 2.95 2.95

Souvenir Sheet

554 A102 $5 multicolored 4.00 4.00

Wmk. 373

1981, Sept. 28 Litho. *Perf. 14½*

555 A103 10c Industry .20 .20
556 A103 35c Community service .35 .35
557 A103 50c Hikers .50 .50
558 A103 $2.50 Duke of Edinburgh 2.50 2.50
Nos. 555-558 (4) 3.55 3.55

Duke of Edinburgh's Awards, 25th anniv.

Intl. Year of the Disabled A104

1981, Oct. 30 Litho. *Perf. 14*

559 A104 10c Louis Braille .20 .20
560 A104 50c Sarah Bernhardt .30 .30
561 A104 $2 Joseph Pulitzer 1.25 1.25
562 A104 $2.50 Henri de Toulouse-Lautrec 1.65 1.65
Nos. 559-562 (4) 3.40 3.40

Souvenir Sheet

563 A104 $5 Franklin D. Roosevelt 3.50 3.50

A105 A107

A106

Christmas: Adoration of the King Paintings.

1981, Dec. 15

564 A105 10c Sfoza .20 .20
565 A105 30c Orcanga .25 .25
566 A105 $1.50 Gerard 1.10 1.10
567 A105 $2.50 Foppa 1.90 1.90
Nos. 564-567 (4) 3.45 3.45

1981, Dec. 29 Unwmk.

568 A106 10c No. 1 .20 .20
569 A106 30c No. 251 .35 .35
570 A106 50c No. 459 .55 .55
571 A106 $2 UPU, St. Lucia flags 2.25 2.25
Nos. 568-571 (4) 3.35 3.35

Souvenir Sheets

572 A106 $5 GPO, Castries 3.75 3.75

First anniv. of UPU membership.

Unwmk.

1981, Dec. 11 Litho. *Perf. 14*

1980s Decade for Women (Paintings of Women by Women): 10c, Fanny Travis Cochran, by Cecilia Beaux. 50c, Women with Dove, by Marie Laurencin. $2, Portrait of a Young Pupil of David. $2.50, Self-portrait, by Rosalba Carriera. $5, Self-portrait, by Elisabeth Vigee-Le Brun.

573 A107 10c multicolored .20 .20
574 A107 50c multicolored .35 .35
575 A107 $2 multicolored 1.50 1.50
576 A107 $2.50 multicolored 1.75 1.75
Nos. 573-576 (4) 3.80 3.80

Souvenir Sheet

577 A107 $5 multicolored 3.50 3.50

1982 World Cup Soccer A108

Designs: Various soccer players.

1982, Feb. 15 Litho. *Perf. 14½*

578 A108 10c multicolored .20 .20
579 A108 50c multicolored .40 .40
580 A108 $2 multicolored 1.50 1.50
581 A108 $2.50 multicolored 1.90 1.90
Nos. 578-581 (4) 4.00 4.00

Souvenir Sheet

582 A108 $5 multicolored 3.50 3.50

Battle of the Saints Bicentenary — A109

Wmk. 373

1982, Apr. 13 Litho. *Perf. 14*

583 A109 10c Pigeon Isld. .20 .20
584 A109 35c Battle .30 .30
585 A109 50c Admirals Rodney, DeGrasse .40 .40
586 A109 $2.50 Map 1.90 1.90
a. Souvenir sheet of 4, #583-586 4.50 4.50
Nos. 583-586 (4) 2.80 2.80

Scouting Year — A110

Christmas 1982 — A111

1982, Aug. 4 Litho. *Perf. 14*

587 A110 10c Map reading .20 .20
588 A110 50c First aid .40 .40
589 A110 $1.50 Camping 1.25 1.25
590 A110 $2.50 Campfire sing 2.00 2.00
Nos. 587-590 (4) 3.85 3.85

Princess Diana Issue
Common Design Type
Perf. 14½x14

1982, Sept. 1 Unwmk.

591 CD332 50c Leeds Castle .35 .35
592 CD332 $2 Diana 1.40 1.40
593 CD332 $4 Wedding 2.75 2.75
Nos. 591-593 (3) 4.50 4.50

Souvenir Sheet

594 CD332 $5 Diana, diff. 3.50 3.50

Wmk. 373

1982, Nov. 10 Litho. *Perf. 14*

Paintings: 10c, Adoration of the Kings, by Brueghel the Elder. 30c, Nativity, by Lorenzo Costa. 50c, Virgin and Child, Fra Filippo Lippi. 80c, Adoration of the Shepherds, by Nicolas Poussin.

595 A111 10c multicolored .20 .20
596 A111 30c multicolored .25 .25
597 A111 50c multicolored .40 .40
598 A111 80c multicolored .60 .60
Nos. 595-598 (4) 1.45 1.45

A111a

1983, Mar. 14 Litho.

599 A111a 10c Twin Peaks .20 .20
600 A111a 30c Beach .30 .30
601 A111a 50c Banana harvester .45 .45
602 A111a $2 Flag 1.75 1.75
Nos. 599-602 (4) 2.70 2.70

Commonwealth day.

Crown Agents Sesquicentennial A112

Wmk. 373

1983, Apr. 1 Litho. *Perf. 14½*

603 A112 10c Headquarters, London .20 .20
604 A112 15c Road construction .20 .20
605 A112 50c Map .40 .40
606 A112 $2 First stamp 1.65 1.65
Nos. 603-606 (4) 2.45 2.45

World Communications Year — A113

Unwmk.
1983, July 12 Litho. *Perf. 15*

607	A113	10c	Shipboard inter-communication	.20	.20
608	A113	50c	Air-to-air	.45	.45
609	A113	$1.50	Satellite	1.40	1.40
610	A113	$2.50	Computer com-munications	2.25	2.25
			Nos. 607-610 (4)	4.30	4.30

Souvenir Sheet

611 A113 $5 Weather satellite 4.25 4.25

Coral Reef Fish A114

1983, Aug. 23

612	A114	10c	Longspine squir-relfish	.20	.20
613	A114	50c	Banded butter-flyfish	.50	.50
614	A114	$1.50	Blackbar soldierfish	1.40	1.40
615	A114	$2.50	Yellowtail snap-pers	2.25	2.25
			Nos. 612-615 (4)	4.35	4.35

Souvenir Sheet

616 A114 $5 Red hind 4.50 4.50

For overprint see No. 800.

Locomotives — A115

Perf. 12½
1983, Oct. 13 Litho. Unwmk.
Se-tenant Pairs, #a.-b.
a.-Side and front views.
b.-Action scene.

617	A115	35c	Princess Coro-nation	.45	.45
618	A115	35c	Duke of Suther-land	.45	.45
619	A115	50c	Leeds United	.60	.60
620	A115	50c	Lord Nelson	.60	.60
621	A115	$1	Bodmin	1.25	1.25
622	A115	$1	Eton	1.25	1.25
623	A115	$2	Flying Scotsman	2.50	2.50
624	A115	$2	Stephenson's Rocket	2.50	2.50
			Nos. 617-624 (8)	9.60	9.60

See Nos. 674-679, 711-718, 774-777, 807-814.

Virgin and Child Paintings by Raphael — A115a

Wmk. 373
1983, Oct. 24 Litho. *Perf. 14*

629	A115a	10c	Niccolini-Cowper Madonna	.20	.20
630	A115a	30c	Holy Family with a Palm Tree	.20	.20
631	A115a	50c	Sistine Madonna	.30	.30
632	A115a	$5	Alba Madonna	3.00	3.00
			Nos. 629-632 (4)	3.70	3.70

Christmas.

Battle of Waterloo, King George III — A116

#633a, 633b, shown. #634a, George III, diff. #634b, Kew Palace. #635a, Arms of Elizabeth I. #635b, Elizabeth I. #636a, Arms of George III. #636b, George III, diff. #637a, Elizabeth I, diff. #637b, Hatfield Palace. #638a, Spanish Armada. #638b, Elizabeth, I, diff.

Perf. 12½
1984, Mar. 13 Litho. Unwmk.

633	A116	5c	Pair, #a.-b.	.20	.20
634	A116	10c	Pair, #a.-b.	.20	.20
635	A116	35c	Pair, #a.-b.	.40	.40
636	A116	60c	Pair, #a.-b.	.60	.60
637	A116	$1	Pair, #a.-b.	1.00	1.00
638	A116	$2.50	Pair, #a.-b.	2.50	2.50
			Nos. 633-638 (6)	4.90	4.90

Unissued 30c, 50c, $1, $2.50 and $5 values became available with the liquidation of the printer.

Colonial Building, Late 19th Cent. — A118

Local Architecture. 10c, vert.

Perf. 14x13½, 13½x14
1984, Apr. 6 Wmk. 380

645	A118	10c	Buildings, mid-19th cent.	.20	.20
646	A118	45c	shown	.35	.35
647	A118	65c	Wooden chattel, early 20th cent.	.50	.50
648	A118	$2.50	Treasury, 1906	1.90	1.90
			Nos. 645-648 (4)	2.95	2.95

For overprints see Nos. 796, 801.

Logwood Tree and Blossom — A118a

Perf. 13½x14, 14x13½
1984, June 12 Wmk. 380

649	A118a	10c	shown	.20	.20
650	A118a	45c	Calabash	.35	.35
651	A118a	65c	Gommier, vert.	.50	.50
652	A118a	$2.50	Rain tree	1.90	1.90
			Nos. 649-652 (4)	2.95	2.95

For overprint see No. 802.

Automobiles — A119

Perf. 12½
1984, June 25 Litho. Unwmk.
Se-tenant Pairs, #a.-b.
a.-Side and front views.
b.-Action scene.

653	A119	5c	Bugatti 57SC, 1939	.20	.20
654	A119	10c	Chevrolet Bel Air, 1957	.20	.20
655	A119	$1	Alfa Romeo, 1930	1.25	1.25
656	A119	$2.50	Duesenberg, 1932	3.00	3.00
			Nos. 653-656 (4)	4.65	4.65

See Nos. 686-693, 739-742, 850-855.

Endangered Reptiles — A120

Wmk. 380
1984, Aug. 8 Litho. *Perf. 14*

661	A120	10c	Pygmy gecko	.20	.20
662	A120	45c	Maria Isld. ground lizard	.35	.35
663	A120	65c	Green iguana	.50	.50
664	A120	$2.50	Couresse snake	1.90	1.90
			Nos. 661-664 (4)	2.95	2.95

For overprint see No. 797.

Leaders of the World, 1984 Olympics — A121

#665a, Volleyball. #665b, Volleyball, diff.. #666a, Women's hurdles. #666b, Men's hurdles. #667a, Showjumping. #667b, Dressage. #668a, Women's gymnastics. #668b, Men's gymnastics.

Perf. 12½
1984, Sept. 21 Litho. Unwmk.

665	A121	5c	Pair, #a.-b.	.20	.20
666	A121	10c	Pair, #a.-b.	.20	.20
667	A121	65c	Pair, #a.-b.	.80	.80
668	A121	$2.50	Pair, #a.-b.	3.00	3.00
			Nos. 665-668 (4)	4.20	4.20

Locomotive Type of 1983
1984, Sept. 21 Litho. *Perf. 12½*
Se-tenant Pairs, #a.-b.
a.-Side and front views.
b.-Action scene.

674	A115	1c	TAW 2-6-2T, 1897	.20	.20
675	A115	15c	Crocodile 1-C.C.-1, 1920	.20	.20
676	A115	50c	The Countess 0.6.0T, 1903	.55	.55
677	A115	75c	Class GE6/6C.C., 1921	.85	.85
678	A115	$1	Class P8, 4.6.0, 1906	.55	.55
679	A115	$2	Der Alder 2.2.2., 1835	2.25	2.25
			Nos. 674-679 (6)	4.60	4.60

Automobile Type of 1983
1984, Dec. 19 Litho. *Perf. 12½*
Se-tenant Pairs, #a.-b.
a.-Side and front views.
b.-Action scene.

686	A119	10c	Panhard and Levassor, 1889	.20	.20
687	A119	30c	N.S.U. R0-80 Saloon, 1968	.35	.35
688	A119	55c	Abarth, Balbero, 1958	.65	.65
689	A119	65c	TRV Vixen 2500M, 1972	.75	.75
690	A119	75c	Ford Mustang Convertible, 1965	.90	.90
691	A119	$1	Ford Model T, 1914	1.25	1.25
692	A119	$2	Aston Martin DB3S, 1954	2.50	2.50
693	A119	$3	Chrysler Imperi-al CG, 1931	3.50	3.50
			Nos. 686-693 (8)	10.10	10.10

Christmas — A122

Abolition of Slavery, 150th Anniv. — A123

Wmk. 380
1984, Oct. 31 Litho. *Perf. 14*

702	A122	10c	Wine glass	.20	.20
703	A122	35c	Altar	.30	.30
704	A122	65c	Creche	.55	.55
705	A122	$3	Holy family, ab-stract	2.50	2.50
a.			Souvenir sheet of 4, #702-705	3.50	3.50
			Nos. 702-705 (4)	3.55	3.55

1984, Dec. 12 Litho. *Perf. 14*

Engraving details, Natl. Archives, Castries: 10c, Preparing manioc. 35c, Working with cassava flour. 55c, Cooking, twisting and drying tobacco. $5, Tobacco production, diff.

706	A123	10c	bright buff & blk	.20	.20
707	A123	35c	bright buff & blk	.25	.25
708	A123	55c	bright buff & blk	.40	.40
709	A123	$5	bright buff & blk	3.50	3.50
			Nos. 706-709 (4)	4.35	4.35

Souvenir Sheet

710			Sheet of 4	5.00	5.00
a.	A123		10c like No. 706	.20	.20
b.	A123		35c like No. 707	.25	.25
c.	A123		55c like No. 708	.40	.40
d.	A123		$5 like No. 709	3.50	3.50

#710a-710d se-tenant in continuous design.

Locomotive Type of 1983
1985, Feb. 4 Unwmk. *Perf. 12½*
Se-tenant Pairs, #a.-b.
a.-Side and front views.
b.-Action scene.

711	A115	5c	J.N.R. Class C-53, 1928, Japan	.20	.20
712	A115	15c	Heavy L, 1885, India	.20	.20
713	A115	35c	QGR Class B18¼, 1926, Australia	.50	.50
714	A115	60c	Owain Glyndwr, 1923, U.K.	.80	.80
715	A115	75c	Lion, 1838, U.K.	1.05	1.05
716	A115	$1	Coal Engine, 1873, U.K.	1.40	1.40

717 A115 $2 No. 2238 Class Q6, 1921, U.K. 2.50 2.50
718 A115 $2.50 Class H, 1920, U.K. 3.25 3.25
Nos. 711-718 (8) 9.90 9.90

Girl Guides, 75th Anniv. — A124

1985, Feb. 21 Wmk. 380 *Perf. 14*

727 A124 10c multicolored .20 .20
728 A124 35c multicolored .30 .30
729 A124 65c multicolored .60 .60
730 A124 $3 multicolored 2.75 2.75
Nos. 727-730 (4) 3.85 3.85

For overprint see No. 795.

Butterflies — A125

#731a, Clossiana selene. #731b, Inachis io. #732a, Philaethria werneckei. #732b, Catagramma sorana. #733a, Kallima inachus. #733b, Hypanartia paullus. #734a, Morpho rhetenor helena. #734b, Ornithoptera meridionalis.

1985, Feb. 28 Unwmk. *Perf. 12½*

731 A125 15c Pair, #a.-b. .20 .20
732 A125 40c Pair, #a.-b. .60 .60
733 A125 60c Pair, #a.-b. .80 .80
734 A125 $2.25 Pair, #a.-b. 3.00 3.00
Nos. 731-734 (4) 4.60 4.60

Automobile Type of 1983

1985, Mar. 29

Se-tenant Pairs

739 A119 15c 1940 Hudson Eight, US .20 .20
740 A119 50c 1937 KdF, Germany .70 .70
741 A119 $1 1925 Kissel Goldbug, US 1.40 1.40
742 A119 $1.50 1973 Ferrari 246GTS, Italy 1.90 1.90
Nos. 739-742 (4) 4.20 4.20

Military Uniforms — A126

Designs: 5c, Grenadier, 70th Foot Reg., c. 1775. 10c, Grenadier Co. Officer, 14th Foot Reg., 1780. 20c, Battalion Co. Officer, 46th Foot Reg., 1781. 25c, Officer, Royal Artillery Reg., c. 1782. 30c, Officer, Royal Engineers Corps., 1782. 35c, Battalion Co. Officer, 54th Foot Reg., 1782. 45c, Grenadier Co. Private, 14th Foot Reg., 1782. 50c, Gunner, Royal Artillery Reg., 1796. 65c, Battalion Co. Private, 85th Foot Reg., c. 1796. 75c, Battalion Co. Private, 76th Foot Reg., 1796. 90c, Battalion Co. Private, 81st Foot Reg., c. 1796. $1, Sergeant, 74th (Highland) Foot Reg., 1796. $2.50, Private, Light Co., 93rd Foot Reg., 1803. $5, Battalion Co. Private, 1st West India Reg., 1803. $15, Officer, Royal Artillery Reg., 1850.

1985, May 7 Wmk. 380 *Perf. 15*

747 A126 5c multicolored .20 .20
748 A126 10c multicolored .20 .20
749 A126 20c multicolored .20 .20
750 A126 25c multicolored .20 .20
a. Wmk. 384 ('88) .25 .25
751 A126 30c multicolored .25 .25
752 A126 35c multicolored .30 .30
753 A126 45c multicolored .35 .35
754 A126 50c multicolored .40 .40
755 A126 65c multicolored .55 .55
756 A126 75c multicolored .65 .65
757 A126 90c multicolored .75 .75
758 A126 $1 multicolored .80 .80
759 A126 $2.50 multicolored 2.00 2.00
760 A126 $5 multicolored 4.00 4.00
761 A126 $15 multicolored 10.50 10.50
Nos. 747-761 (15) 21.35 21.35

Nos. 749-750 reissued inscribed 1986, Nos. 747-750, 1989.
See Nos. 876-879.

1987 Unwmk.

747a A126 5c .20 .20
748a A126 10c .20 .20
751a A126 30c .25 .25
753a A126 45c .35 .35
754a A126 50c .40 .40
759a A126 $2.50 2.00 2.00
760a A126 $5 4.00 4.00
Nos. 747a-760a (7) 7.40 7.40

Issued: #747a-748a, 2/24; #751a-760a, 3/16. Dated 1986.

1989 Wmk. 384

747b A126 5c .20 .20
748b A126 10c .20 .20
749a A126 20c .20 .20

World War II Aircraft A127

1985, May 30 Unwmk. *Perf. 12½*

Se-tenant Pairs, #a.-b.

a.-Action scene.

b.-Bottom, front and side views.

762 A127 5c Messerschmitt 109-E .20 .20
763 A127 55c Avro 683 Lancaster Mark I Bomber .75 .75
764 A127 60c North American P.51-D Mustang .80 .80
765 A127 $2 Supermarine Spitfire Mark II 2.50 2.50
Nos. 762-765 (4) 4.25 4.25

Nature Reserves A128

Birds in habitats: 10c, Frigate bird, Frigate Island Sanctuary. 35c, Mangrove cuckoo, Savannes Bay, Scorpion Island. 65c, Yellow sandpiper, Maria Island. $3, Audubon's shearwater, Lapins Island.

1985, June 20 Wmk. 380 *Perf. 15*

770 A128 10c multicolored .20 .20
771 A128 35c multicolored .30 .30
772 A128 65c multicolored .55 .55
773 A128 $3 multicolored 2.75 2.75
Nos. 770-773 (4) 3.80 3.80

Locomotive Type of 1983

1985, June 26 Unwmk. *Perf. 12½*

Se-tenant Pairs, #a.-b.

a.-Side and front views.

b.-Action scene.

774 A115 10c No. 28 Tender engine, 1897, U.K. .20 .20
775 A115 30c No. 1621 Class M, 1893, U.K. .40 .40
776 A115 75c Class Dunalastair, 1896, U.K. .95 .95
777 A115 $2.50 Big Bertha No. 2290, 1919, U.K. 3.00 3.00
Nos. 774-777 (4) 4.55 4.55

Queen Mother, 85th Birthday — A129

#782a, 787a, Facing right. #782b, 787b, Facing left. #783a, Facing right. #783b, Facing left. #784a, 788a, Facing right. #784b, 788b, Facing front. #785a, Facing front. #785b, Facing left. #786a, Facing right. #786b, Facing left.

1985, Aug. 16

782 A129 40c Pair, #a.-b. .60 .60
783 A129 75c Pair, #a.-b. 1.10 1.10
784 A129 $1.10 Pair, #a.-b. 1.60 1.60
785 A129 $1.75 Pair, #a.-b. 2.25 2.25
Nos. 782-785 (4) 5.55 5.55

Souvenir Sheets of 2

786 A129 $2 #a.-b. 2.50 2.50
787 A129 $3 #a.-b. 4.50 4.50
788 A129 $6 #a.-b. 9.00 9.00

For overprints see No. 799.

Intl. Youth Year — A130

Abstracts, by Lyndon Samuel — A131

Illustrations by local artists: 10c, Youth playing banjo, by Wayne Whitfield. 45c, Riding tricycle, by Mark D. Maragh. 75c, Youth against landscape, by Bartholemew Eugene. $3.50, Abstract, by Lyndon Samuel.

1985, Sept. 5 Wmk. 380 *Perf. 15*

791 A130 10c multicolored .20 .20
792 A130 45c multicolored .40 .40
793 A130 75c multicolored .75 .75
794 A130 $3.50 multicolored 3.00 3.00
Nos. 791-794 (4) 4.35 4.35

Souvenir Sheet

795 A131 $5 multicolored 4.00 4.00

Intl. Youth Year.

Stamps of 1983-85 Ovptd. "CARIBBEAN ROYAL VISIT 1985" in Two or Three Lines

Perfs. as Before

1985, Nov. Wmk. as Before

796 A124 35c #728 1.00 1.00
797 A118 65c #647 1.75 1.75
798 A120 65c #663 1.75 1.75
799 A129 $1.10 #784a-784b 6.00 6.00
800 A114 $2.50 #615 6.50 6.50
801 A118 $2.50 #648 6.50 6.50
802 A119 $2.50 #652 6.50 6.50
Nos. 796-802 (7) 30.00 30.00

Masquerade Figures — A132

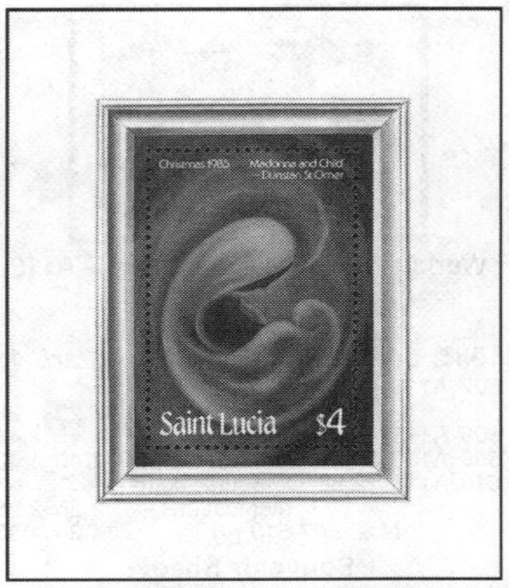

Madonna and Child, by Dunstan St. Omer — A133

Unwmk.

1985, Dec. 23 Litho. *Perf. 15*

803 A132 10c Papa Jab .20 .20
804 A132 45c Paille Bananne .35 .35
805 A132 65c Cheval Bois .50 .50
Nos. 803-805 (3) 1.05 1.05

Miniature Sheet

806 A133 $4 multi 3.00 3.00

Christmas 1985.

Locomotive Type of 1983

1986, Jan. 17 *Perf. 12½x13*

Se-tenant Pairs, #a.-b.

a.-Side and front views.

b.-Action scene.

807 A115 5c 1983 MWCR Rack Loco Tip Top, US .20 .20
808 A115 15c 1975 BR Class 87 Stephenson Bo-Bo, UK .20 .20
809 A115 30c 1901 Class D No. 737, UK .35 .35
810 A115 60c 1922 No. 13 2-Co-2, UK .70 .70
811 A115 75c 1954 BR Class EM2 Electra Co-Co, UK .85 .85
812 A115 $1 1922 City of Newcastle, UK 1.25 1.25
813 A115 $2.25 1930 DRG Von Kruckenberg, Propeller-driven Rail Car, Germany 2.75 2.75
814 A115 $3 1893 JNR No. 860, Japan 3.50 3.50
Nos. 807-814 (8) 9.80 9.80

Miniature Sheets

Cook-out — A134

Designs: No. 823b, Scout sign. No. 824a, Wicker basket, weavings. No. 824b, Lady Olave Baden-Powell, Girl Guides founder.

1986, Mar. 3 Litho. *Perf. 13x12½*

823 Sheet of 2 5.50 5.50
a.-b. A134 $4 any single 2.75 2.75
824 Sheet of 2 8.00 8.00
a.-b. A134 $6 any single 4.00 4.00

Scouting anniv., Girl Guides 75th anniv. Exist with plain or decorative border.

A135

Queen Elizabeth II, 60th Birthday — A136

Various photographs.

Perf. 13x12½, 12½x13, 14x15 (A136)

1986

825 A135 5c Pink hat .20 .20
826 A136 10c Visiting Marian Home .20 .20
827 A136 45c Mindoo Phillip Park speech .30 .30
828 A136 50c Opening Leon Hess School .35 .35
829 A135 $1 Princess Elizabeth .65 .65
830 A135 $3.50 Blue hat 2.25 2.25
831 A136 $5 Government House 3.25 3.25
832 A135 $6 Canberra, 1982, vert. 3.75 3.75
Nos. 825-832 (8) 10.95 10.95

Souvenir Sheets

833 A136 $7 HMY Britannia, Castries Harbor 4.50 4.50
834 A135 $8 Straw hat 5.25 5.25

Issue dates: Nos. 825, 829-830, 832, Apr. 21; Nos. 826-828, 831, 833, June 14.

State Visit of Pope John Paul II A137

1986, July 7 ***Perf. 14x15, 15x14***

835 A137 55c Kissing the ground .40 .40
836 A137 60c St. Joseph's Convent .45 .45
837 A137 80c Cathedral, Castries .60 .60
Nos. 835-837 (3) 1.45 1.45

Souvenir Sheet

838 A137 $6 Pope 4.50 4.50

Nos. 837-838 vert.

Wedding of Prince Andrew and Sarah Ferguson — A138

#839a, Sarah, vert. #839b, Andrew, vert. #840a, Couple. #840b, Andrew, Nancy Reagan.

1986, July 23 ***Perf. 12½***

839 A138 80c Pair, #a.-b. 1.25 1.25
840 A138 $2 Pair, #a.-b. 3.00 3.00

#840a-840b show Westminster Abbey in LR.

US Peace Corps in St. Lucia, 25th Anniv. A139

1986, Sept. 25 **Litho.** ***Perf. 14***

843 A139 80c Technical instruction .60 .60
844 A139 $2 Pres. Kennedy, vert. 1.50 1.50
845 A139 $3.50 Natl. crests, corps emblem 2.60 2.60
Nos. 843-845 (3) 4.70 4.70

Wedding of Prince Andrew and Sarah Ferguson — A140

1986, Oct. 15 ***Perf. 15***

846 A140 50c Andrew .40 .40
847 A140 80c Sarah .60 .60
848 A140 $1 At altar .75 .75
849 A140 $3 In open carriage 2.25 2.25
Nos. 846-849 (4) 4.00 4.00

Souvenir Sheet

849A A140 $7 Andrew, Sarah 5.25 5.25

Automobile Type of 1983

1986, Oct. 23 **Litho.** ***Perf. 12½x13***

Se-tenant Pairs, #a.-b.

a.-Side and front views.

b.-Action scene.

850 A119 20c 1969 AMC AMX, US .20 .20
851 A119 50c 1912 Russo-Baltique, Russia .60 .60
852 A119 60c 1932 Lincoln KB, US .70 .70
853 A119 $1 1933 Rolls Royce Phantom II Continental, UK 1.25 1.25
854 A119 $1.50 1939 Buick Century, US 1.75 1.75
855 A119 $3 1957 Chrysler 300 C, US 3.50 3.50
Nos. 850-855 (6) 8.00 8.00

Chak-Chak Band — A141

1986, Nov. 7 ***Perf. 15***

862 A141 15c shown .20 .20
863 A141 45c Folk dancing .35 .35
864 A141 80c Steel band .60 .60
865 A141 $5 Limbo dancer 3.75 3.75
Nos. 862-865 (4) 4.90 4.90

Souvenir Sheet

866 A141 $10 Gros Islet 7.50 7.50

Christmas A142

Churches: 10c, St. Ann Catholic, Mon Repos. 40c, St. Joseph the Worker Catholic, Gros Islet. 80c, Holy Trinity Anglican, Castries. $4, Our Lady of the Assumption Catholic, Soufriere, vert. $7, St. Lucy Catholic, Micoud.

1986, Nov.

867 A142 10c multicolored .20 .20
868 A142 40c multicolored .30 .30
869 A142 80c multicolored .60 .60
870 A142 $4 multicolored 3.00 3.00
Nos. 867-870 (4) 4.10 4.10

Souvenir Sheet

871 A142 $7 multicolored 5.25 5.25

Map of St. Lucia — A143

Perf. 14x14½

1987, Feb. 24 **Litho.** **Wmk. 373**

872 A143 5c beige & blk .20 .20
a. Wmk. 384 ('89) .20 .20
873 A143 10c pale yel grn & blk .20 .20
a. Wmk. 384 ('89) .20 .20
874 A143 45c orange & blk .35 .35
875 A143 50c pale violet & blk .35 .35
Nos. 872-875 (4) 1.10 1.10

#872-873 exist inscribed 1988, #875 1989. Issued: #872a, 873a, Apr. 12. See #937.

Uniforms Type of 1985

Designs: 15c, Battalion company private, 2nd West India Regiment, 1803. 60c, Battalion company officer, 5th Regiment of Foot, 1778. 80c, Battalion company officer, 27th (or Inniskilling) Regiment of Foot, c. 1780. $20, Grenadier company private, 46th Regiment of Foot, 1778.

1987, Mar. 16 **Unwmk.** ***Perf. 15***

876 A126 15c multicolored .20 .20
877 A126 60c multicolored .40 .40
878 A126 80c multicolored .55 .55
879 A126 $20 multicolored 13.75 13.75
Nos. 876-879 (4) 14.90 14.90

Dated 1986. #876, 879 exist dated 1989.

1988 **Wmk. 384**

876a A126 15c .20 .20
877a A126 60c .40 .40
878a A126 80c .55 .55
879a A126 $20 14.00 14.00
Nos. 876a-879a (4) 15.15 15.15

A144

Statue of Liberty, Cent. — A145

1987, Apr. 29 **Wmk. 373** ***Perf. 14½***

880 A144 15c Statue, flags .20 .20
881 A144 80c Statue, ship .60 .60
882 A144 $1 Statue, Concorde jet .75 .75
883 A144 $5 Statue, flying boat 3.75 3.75
Nos. 880-883 (4) 5.30 5.30

Souvenir Sheet

884 A145 $6 Statue, New York City 4.50 4.50

Maps, Surveying Instruments A147

Wmk. 384

1987, Aug. 31 **Litho.** ***Perf. 14***

888 A147 15c 1775 .20 .20
889 A147 60c 1814 .45 .45
890 A147 $1 1888 .75 .75
891 A147 $2.50 1987 1.90 1.90
Nos. 888-891 (4) 3.30 3.30

First cadastral survey of St. Lucia.

Victoria Hospital, Cent. — A148

#894a, Ambulance, nurse, 1987. #894b, Nurse, hammock, 1913. #895a, Hospital, 1987. #895b, Hospital, 1887.

Wmk. 384

1987, Nov. 4 **Litho.** ***Perf. 14½***

894 A148 $1 Pair, #a.-b. 1.50 1.50
895 A148 $2 Pair, #a.-b. 3.00 3.00

Souvenir Sheet

896 A148 $4.50 Main gate, 1987 3.35 3.35

Christmas A149

Paintings (details) by unidentified artists.

1987, Nov. 30

897 A149 15c The Holy Family .20 .20
898 A149 50c Adoration of the Shepherds .40 .40
899 A149 60c Adoration of the Magi .45 .45
900 A149 90c Madonna and Child .70 .70
Nos. 897-900 (4) 1.75 1.75

Souvenir Sheet

901 A149 $6 Holy Family 4.50 4.50

World Wildlife Fund — A150

American Indian Artifacts — A151

Amazonian parrots, Amazona versicolor.

Wmk. 384

1987, Dec. 18 Litho. *Perf. 14*

902 A150 15c multi .20 .20
903 A150 35c multi, diff. .25 .25
904 A150 50c multi, diff. .40 .40
905 A150 $1 multi, diff. .75 .75
Nos. 902-905 (4) 1.60 1.60

Wmk. 384

1988, Feb. 12 Litho. *Perf. 14½*

906 A151 25c Carib clay zemi .20 .20
907 A151 30c Troumassee cylinder .25 .25
908 A151 80c Three-pointer stone .60 .60
909 A151 $3.50 Dauphine petroglyph 2.60 2.60
Nos. 906-909 (4) 3.65 3.65

St. Lucia Cooperative Bank, 50th Anniv. — A152

Perf. 15x14

1988, Apr. 29 Litho. Wmk. 373

910 A152 10c Coins, banknotes .20 .20
911 A152 45c Branch in Castries .35 .35
912 A152 60c like 45c .45 .45
913 A152 80c Branch in Vieux Fort .60 .60
Nos. 910-913 (4) 1.60 1.60

Cable and Wireless in St. Lucia, 50th Anniv. A153

Designs: 15c, Rural telephone exchange. 25c, Antique and modern telephones. 80c, St. Lucia Teleport (satellite dish). $2.50, Map of Eastern Caribbean microwave communications system.

Wmk. 384

1988, June 10 Litho. *Perf. 14*

914 A153 15c multicolored .20 .20
915 A153 25c multicolored .20 .20
916 A153 80c multicolored .60 .60
917 A153 $2.50 multicolored 1.90 1.90
Nos. 914-917 (4) 2.90 2.90

Cent. of the Methodist Church in St. Lucia — A154

Wmk. 384

1988, Aug. 15 Litho. *Perf. 14½*

918 A154 15c Altar, window .20 .20
919 A154 80c Chancel .60 .60
920 A154 $3.50 Exterior 2.60 2.60
Nos. 918-920 (3) 3.40 3.40

Tourism — A155

Lagoon and: 10c, Tourists, gourmet meal. 30c, Beverage, tourists. 80c, Tropical fruit. $2.50, Fish and chef. $5.50, Market.
Illustration reduced.

Perf. 14x13½

1988, Sept. 15 Litho. Wmk. 384

921 A155 Strip of 4 2.75 2.75
a. 10c multicolored .20 .20
b. 30c multicolored .22 .22
c. 80c multicolored .60 .60
d. $2.50 multicolored 1.85 1.85

Souvenir Sheet

922 A155 $5.50 multicolored 4.00 4.00

Lloyds of London, 300th Anniv.

Common Design Type

Designs: 10c, San Francisco earthquake, 1906. 60c, Castries Harbor, horiz. 80c, *Lady Nelson,* sunk off Castries Harbor, 1942, horiz. $2.50, Castries on fire, 1948.

Wmk. 373

1988, Oct. 17 Litho. *Perf. 14*

923 CD341 10c multicolored .20 .20
924 CD341 60c multicolored .45 .45
925 CD341 80c multicolored .60 .60
926 CD341 $2.50 multicolored 1.85 1.85
Nos. 923-926 (4) 3.10 3.10

A156

A157

Christmas: Flowers.

Perf. 14½x14

1988, Nov. 22 Litho. Wmk. 384

927 A156 15c Snow on the mountain .20 .20
928 A156 45c Christmas candle .35 .35
929 A156 60c Balisier .45 .45
930 A156 80c Poinsettia .60 .60
Nos. 927-930 (4) 1.60 1.60

Souvenir Sheet

931 A156 $5.50 Flower arrangement 4.00 4.00

Perf. 13½x13

1989, Feb. 22 Wmk. 373

Natl. Independence, 10th Anniv.: 15c, Princess Alexandra presenting constitution to Prime Minister Compton. 80c, Sulfur springs geothermal well. $1, Sir Arthur Lewis Community College. $2.50, Pointe Seraphine tax-free shopping center. $5, Emblem.

932 A157 15c Nationhood .20 .20
933 A157 80c Development .60 .60
934 A157 $1 Education .75 .75
935 A157 $2.50 Progress 1.90 1.90
Nos. 932-935 (4) 3.45 3.45

Souvenir Sheet

936 A157 $5 With Confidence We Progress 3.75 3.75

Map Type of 1987

Perf. 14x14½

1989, Mar. 17 Litho. Wmk. 373

937 A143 $1 scarlet & black .75 .75

Indigenous Mushrooms A158

Perf. 14½x14

1989, May 22 Litho. Wmk. 384

938 A158 15c Gerronema citrinum .20 .20
939 A158 25c Lepiota spiculata .20 .20
940 A158 50c Calocybe cyanocephala .40 .40
941 A158 $5 Russula puiggarii 3.75 3.75
Nos. 938-941 (4) 4.55 4.55

PHILEXFRANCE '89, French Revolution Bicent. — A159

Views of St. Lucia and text: 10c, Independence day announcement, vert. 60c, French revolutionary flag at Morne Fortune, 1791. $1, "Men are born and live free and equal in rights," vert. $3.50, Captain La Crosse's arrival at Gros Islet, 1792.

Wmk. 373

1989, July 14 Litho. *Perf. 14*

942 A159 10c multicolored .20 .20
943 A159 60c multicolored .50 .50
944 A159 $1 multicolored .75 .75
945 A159 $3.50 multicolored 2.60 2.60
Nos. 942-945 (4) 4.05 4.05

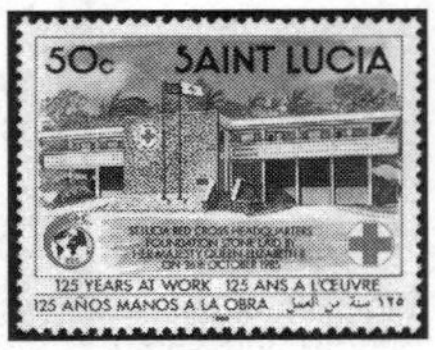

Intl. Red Cross, 125th Anniv. A160

1989, Oct. 10 Wmk. 384 *Perf. 14½*

946 A160 50c Natl. headquarters .40 .40
947 A160 80c Seminar in Castries, 1987 .60 .60
948 A160 $1 Ambulance .75 .75
Nos. 946-948 (3) 1.75 1.75

Christmas Lanterns Shaped Like Buildings A161

1989, Nov. 17 *Perf. 14x14½*

949 A161 10c multi .20 .20
950 A161 50c multi, diff. .40 .40
951 A161 90c multi, diff. .70 .70
952 A161 $1 multi, diff. .75 .75
Nos. 949-952 (4) 2.05 2.05

Trees In Danger of Extinction — A162

1990 Wmk. 384 *Perf. 14*

953 A162 10c Chinna .20 .20
954 A162 15c Latanier .20 .20
955 A162 20c Gwi gwi .20 .20
956 A162 25c L'encens .20 .20
957 A162 50c Bois lele .40 .40
958 A162 80c Bois d'amande .60 .60
959 A162 95c Mahot piman grand bois .70 .70
960 A162 $1 Balata .75 .75
961 A162 $1.50 Pencil cedar 1.10 1.10
962 A162 $2.50 Bois cendre 1.75 1.75
963 A162 $5 Lowye cannelle 3.75 3.75
964 A162 $25 Chalantier grand bois 18.50 18.50
Nos. 953-964 (12) 28.35 28.35

Issued: 20c, 25c, 50c, $25, 2/21; 10c, 15c, 80c, $1.50, 4/12; 95c, $1, $2.50, $5, 6/25.
For overprints see Nos. 971, O28-O39.

1992-95 Wmk. 373 *Perf. 14*

953a A162 10c .20 .20
954a A162 15c .20 .20
955a A162 20c ('95) .20 .20
956a A162 25c ('94) .20 .20
957a A162 50c .40 .40
Nos. 953a-957a (5) 1.20 1.20

#953a, 957a exist dated 1993; #953a, 954a, 957a, 1994; #955a, 1990.

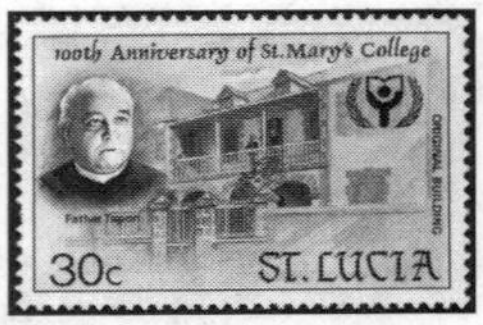

Centenary of St. Mary's College, Intl. Literacy Year — A163

Designs: 30c, Father Tapon, original building. 45c, Rev. Brother Collins, current building. 75c, Students in literacy class. $2, Door to knowledge, children.

1990, June 6 Wmk. 373

965 A163 30c multicolored .22 .22
966 A163 45c multicolored .35 .35
967 A163 75c multicolored .55 .55
968 A163 $2 multicolored 1.50 1.50
Nos. 965-968 (4) 2.62 2.62

Queen Mother, 90th Birthday

Common Design Types

1990, Aug. 3 Wmk. 384 *Perf. 14x15*

969 CD343 50c Coronation, 1937 .40 .40

Perf. 14½

970 CD344 $5 Arriving at theater, 1949 3.75 3.75

No. 963 Overprinted

1990, Aug. 13 *Perf. 14*

971 A162 $5 multicolored 3.75 3.75

Intl. Garden and Greenery Exposition, Osaka, Japan.

Christmas — A164

Butterflies — A166

Boats A165

Paintings: 10c, Adoration of the Magi by Rubens. 30c, Adoration of the Shepherds by Murillo. 80c, Adoration of the Magi by Rubens, diff. $5, Adoration of the Shepherds by Champaigne.

1990, Dec. 3 *Perf. 14*

972 A164 10c multicolored .20 .20
973 A164 30c multicolored .25 .25
974 A164 80c multicolored .65 .65
975 A164 $5 multicolored 3.75 3.75
Nos. 972-975 (4) 4.85 4.85

1991, Mar. 27 Wmk. 373 *Perf. 14½*

Various boats.

976 A165 50c multicolored .40 .40
977 A165 80c multicolored .65 .65
978 A165 $1 multicolored .80 .80
979 A165 $2.50 multicolored 2.00 2.00
Nos. 976-979 (4) 3.85 3.85

Souvenir Sheet

980 A165 $5 multicolored 3.75 3.75

Wmk. 373

1991, Aug. 15 Litho. *Perf. 14*

981 A166 60c Polydamas swallowtail .50 .50
982 A166 80c St. Christopher's hairstreak .65 .65
983 A166 $1 St. Lucia mestra .80 .80
984 A166 $2.50 Godman's hairstreak 2.00 2.00
Nos. 981-984 (4) 3.95 3.95

Christmas A167

Perf. 14x14½

1991, Nov. 20 Litho. Wmk. 384

985 A167 10c Jacmel Church .20 .20
986 A167 15c Red Madonna, vert. .20 .20
987 A167 80c Monchy Church .55 .55
988 A167 $5 Blue Madonna, vert. 3.45 3.45
Nos. 985-988 (4) 4.40 4.40

Atlantic Rally for Cruisers A168

Designs: 60c, Cruisers crossing Atlantic, map. 80c, Cruisers tacking.

1991, Dec. 10 Wmk. 384 *Perf. 14*

989 A168 60c multicolored .40 .40
990 A168 80c multicolored .55 .55

Discovery of America, 500th Anniv. — A169

Wmk. 373

1992, July 6 Litho. *Perf. 13*

991 A169 $1 Coming ashore .70 .70
992 A169 $2 Natives, ships 1.40 1.40

Organization of East Caribbean States.

Contact with New World A170

1992, Aug. 4 *Perf. 13½*

993 A170 15c Amerindians .20 .20
994 A170 40c Juan de la Cosa, 1499 .30 .30
995 A170 50c Columbus, 1502 .35 .35
996 A170 $5 Gimie, Dec. 13th 3.45 3.45
Nos. 993-996 (4) 4.30 4.30

Christmas A171

Paintings: 10c, Virgin and Child, by Delaroche. 15c, The Holy Family, by Rubens. 60c, Virgin and Child, by Luini. 80c, Virgin and Child, by Sassoferrato.

Wmk. 373

1992, Nov. 9 Litho. *Perf. 14½*

997 A171 10c multicolored .20 .20
998 A171 15c multicolored .20 .20
999 A171 60c multicolored .40 .40
1000 A171 80c multicolored .55 .55
Nos. 997-1000 (4) 1.35 1.35

Anti-Drugs Campaign — A172

Perf. 13½x14

1993, Feb. 1 Litho. Wmk. 373

1001 A172 $5 multicolored 2.80 2.80

Gros Piton from Delcer, Choiseul, by Dunstan St. Omer A173

Paintings: 75c, Reduit Bay, by Derek Walcott. $5, Woman and Child at River, by Nancy Cole Auguste.

1993, Nov. 1 Wmk. 373 *Perf. 13*

1002 A173 20c multicolored .20 .20
1003 A173 75c multicolored .40 .40
1004 A173 $5 multicolored 2.75 2.75
Nos. 1002-1004 (3) 3.35 3.35

Christmas A174

Details of paintings: 15c, The Madonna of the Rosary, by Murillo. 60c, The Madonna and Child, by Van Dyck. 95c, The Annunciation, by Champaigne.

1993, Dec. 6 *Perf. 14*

1005 A174 15c multicolored .20 .20
1006 A174 60c multicolored .45 .45
1007 A174 95c multicolored .70 .70
Nos. 1005-1007 (3) 1.35 1.35

A175

A176

1994, July 25 *Perf. 13*

1008 A175 20c multicolored .20 .20

Souvenir Sheet

1009 A175 $5 multicolored 3.75 3.75

Abolition of Slavery on St. Lucia, bicent.

1994, Dec. 9 *Perf. 12½x13*

Christmas (Flowers): 20c, Euphorbia pulcherrima. 75c, Heliconia rostrata. 95c, Alpinia purpurata. $5.50, Anthurium andreanum.

1010 A176 20c multicolored .20 .20
1011 A176 75c multicolored .55 .55
1012 A176 95c multicolored .70 .70
1013 A176 $5.50 multicolored 4.00 4.00
Nos. 1010-1013 (4) 5.45 5.45

Battle of Rabot, Bicent. A177

1995, Apr. 28 *Perf. 13½*

1014 A177 20c Map of island .20 .20
1015 A177 75c Rebelling slaves .55 .55
1016 A177 95c Battle scene .70 .70
Nos. 1014-1016 (3) 1.45 1.45

Souvenir Sheet

Perf. 13

1017 A177 $5.50 Battle map 4.00 4.00

End of World War II, 50th Anniv.

Common Design Types

Designs: 20c, ATS women in Britain. 75c, German U-boat off St. Lucia. 95c, Caribbean regiment, North Africa. $1.10, Presentation Spitfire Mk V.

$5.50, Reverse of War Medal 1939-45.

Wmk. 373

1995, May 8 Litho. *Perf. 13½*

1018 CD351 20c multicolored .20 .20
1019 CD351 75c multicolored .55 .55
1020 CD351 95c multicolored .70 .70
1021 CD351 $1.10 multicolored .80 .80
Nos. 1018-1021 (4) 2.25 2.25

Souvenir Sheet

Perf. 14

1022 CD352 $5.50 multicolored 4.00 4.00

UN, 50th Anniv.

Common Design Type

10c, Puma helicopter. 65c, Renault truck. $1.35, Transall C160. $5, Douglas DC3.

Wmk. 373

1995, Oct. 24 Litho. *Perf. 14*

1023 CD353 10c multicolored .20 .20
1024 CD353 65c multicolored .50 .50
1025 CD353 $1.35 multicolored 1.00 1.00
1026 CD353 $5 multicolored 3.75 3.75
Nos. 1023-1026 (4) 5.45 5.45

Christmas — A178

Flowers: 15c, Eranthemum nervosum. 70c, Bougainvillea. $1.10, Allamanda cathartica. $3, Hibiscus rosa sinensis.

Wmk. 373

1995, Nov. 20 Litho. *Perf. 13*

1027 A178 15c multicolored .20 .20
1028 A178 70c multicolored .50 .50
1029 A178 $1.10 multicolored .80 .80
1030 A178 $3 multicolored 2.25 2.25
Nos. 1027-1030 (4) 3.75 3.75

Carnival — A179

Water — A180

Wmk. 384

1996, Feb. 16 Litho. *Perf. 14*

1031 A179 20c Calypso king .20 .20
1032 A179 65c Carnival band .50 .50
1033 A179 95c King of the band .70 .70
1034 A179 $3 Carnival queen 2.25 2.25
Nos. 1031-1034 (4) 3.65 3.65

1996, Mar. 5 Wmk. 373

1035 A180 20c Muddy stream .20 .20
1036 A180 65c Clear stream .50 .50
1037 A180 $5 Modern dam 3.75 3.75
Nos. 1035-1037 (3) 4.45 4.45

Tourism A181

Designs: 65c, Market. 75c, Riding horses on beach. 95c, Outdoor wedding ceremony. $5, Annual Intl. Jazz Festival.

Wmk. 373

1996, May 13 Litho. *Perf. 14*

1038-1041 A181 Set of 4 5.50 5.50

Modern Olympic Games, Cent. — A182

#1042a, Early runner. #1042b, Modern runner. #1043a, Two sailboats. #1043b, Four sailboats.

Wmk. 373

1996, July 19 Litho. *Perf. 14*

1042 A182 15c Pair, #a.-b. .25 .25
1043 A182 75c Pair, #a.-b. 1.10 1.10

Nos. 1042-1043 have continuous designs.

Flags & Ships A183

Flag, ship: 10c, Spanish Royal banner, 1502, Spanish caravel. 15c, Skull & crossbones, 1550, pirate carrack. 20c, Royal Netherlands, 1660, Dutch 80-gun ship. 25c, Union flag, 1739, Royal Navy 64-gun ship.

40c, French Imperial, 1750, French 74-gun ship. 50c, Martinique & St. Lucia, 1766, French brig. 55c, British White Ensign, 1782, Royal Navy Frigate Squadron. 65c, British Red Ensign, 1782, Battle of the Saints. 75c, British Blue Ensign, 1782, RN brig. 95c, Fench Tricolor, 1792, French 38-gun frigate. $1. British Union, 1801, West Indies Grand Fleet. $2.50, Confederate, 1861, CSA steam/sail armed cruiser. $5, Canada, 1915-19, Canadian V & W class destroyer. $10, US, 1942-48, Fletcher class destroyer. $25, National, cruise ship.

Perf. 14x15

1996-97 Litho. Wmk. 384

1046	A183	10c multi	.20	.20
a.	Wmk. 373		.20	.20
1047	A183	15c multi	.20	.20
a.	Wmk. 373		.20	.20
1048	A183	20c multi	.20	.20
a.	Wmk. 373		.20	.20
1049	A183	25c multi	.20	.20
1050	A183	40c multi	.30	.30
1051	A183	50c multi	.40	.40
a.	Wmk. 373		.40	.40
1052	A183	55c multi	.40	.40
1053	A183	65c multi	.50	.50
a.	Wmk. 373		.50	.50
1054	A183	75c multi	.55	.55
1055	A183	95c multi	.70	.70
1056	A183	$1 multi	.75	.75
a.	Wmk. 373		.75	.75
1057	A183	$2.50 multi	1.85	1.85
1058	A183	$5 multi	3.75	3.75
1059	A183	$10 multi	7.50	7.50
a.	Wmk. 373		7.50	7.50
1060	A183	$25 multi	18.75	18.75
	Nos. 1046-1060 (15)		36.25	36.25

#1046a-1048a, 1051a are inscribed "1998." Nos. 1053a, 1056a, 1059a are inscribed "2001." No. 1048a exists dated "2001."

Issued: 10c, 15c, 20c, 25c, 40c, 9/16/96; 50c, 55c, 65c, 75c, 95c, 11/18/96; $1, $2.50, $5, $10, $25, 1/8/97; #1046a, 1047a, 1048a, 1051a, 7/12/98; #1053a, 1056a, 1059a, 4/2001.

Nos. 1046-1049 exist dated "2000."

Christmas — A184

Flowers: 20c, Cordia sebestena. 75c, Cryptostegia grandiflora. 95c, Hibiscus elatus. $5, Caularthron bicornutum.

Wmk. 384

1996, Dec. 1 Litho. *Perf. 14*

1061-1064	A184 Set of 4	5.00	5.00

Queen Elizabeth II and Prince Philip, 50th Wedding Anniv. — A185

#1068a, Queen. #1068b, Prince with horses. #1069a, Prince. #1069b, Queen riding in carriage. #1070a, Queen, Prince. #1070b, Princess Anne riding horse.

$5, Queen, Prince riding in open carriage, horiz.

Perf. 14½x14

1997, July 10 Litho. Wmk. 384

1068	A185	75c Pair, #a.-b.	1.10	1.10
1069	A185	95c Pair, #a.-b.	1.40	1.40
1070	A185	$1 Pair, #a.-b.	1.50	1.50
	Nos. 1068-1070 (3)		4.00	4.00

Souvenir Sheet

Perf. 14x14½

1071	A185	$5 multicolored	3.50	3.50

Disasters — A186

20c, MV St. George capsizes, 1935. 55c, SS Belle of Bath founders. $1, SS Ethelgonda runs aground, 1897. $2.50, Hurrincane devastation, 1817.

1997, July 14 *Perf. 14x15*

1072-1075	A186 Set of 4	3.00	3.00

Events of 1797 — A187

Designs: 20c, Taking of Praslin. 55c, Battle of Dennery. 70c, Peace. $3, Brigands join 1st West India Regiment.

Wmk. 373

1997, Aug. 15 Litho. *Perf. 14*

1076-1079	A187 Set of 4	3.25	3.25

Christmas — A188

Church art: 20c, Roseau Church. 60c, Altar piece, Regional Seminary, Trinidad. 95c, Our Lady of the Presentation, Trinidad. $5, The Four Days of Creation.

Perf. 14x15

1997, Dec. 1 Litho. Wmk. 384

1080-1083	A188 Set of 4	5.00	5.00

Diana, Princess of Wales (1961-97) — A189

1998, Jan. 19 Litho. *Perf. 14*

1084	A189 $1 multicolored	.75	.75

No. 1084 was issued in sheets of 9.

CARICOM, 25th Anniv. — A190

20c, Errol Barrow, Forbes Burnham, Dr. Eric Williams, Michael Manley signing CARICOM Treaty, 1973. 75c, CARICOM flag, St. Lucia Natl. flag.

Wmk. 373

1998, July 1 Litho. *Perf. 13½*

1085	A190	20c multicolored	.20	.20
1086	A190	75c multicolored	.55	.55

Birds — A191

Designs: 70c, St. Lucia oriole. 75c, Lesser Antillean pewee. 95c, Bridled quail dove. $1.10, Semper's warbler.

1998, Oct. 23 Wmk. 373 *Perf. 14*

1087-1090	A191 70c Set of 4	2.75	2.75

Universal Delcaration of Human Rights, 50th Anniv. — A192

Various butterflies, chains or rope.

1998, Oct. 28

1091	A192	20c multicolored	.20	.20
1092	A192	65c multicolored	.50	.50
1093	A192	70c multicolored	.55	.55
1094	A192	$5 multicolored	3.75	3.75
	Nos. 1091-1094 (4)		5.00	5.00

Christmas — A193

Flowers: 20c, Tabebuia serratifolia. 50c, Hibiscus sabdariffa. 95c, Euphorbia leucocephala. $2.50, Calliandra slaneae.

Wmk. 373

1998, Nov. 27 Litho. *Perf. 14*

1095-1098	A193 20c Set of 4	3.25	3.25

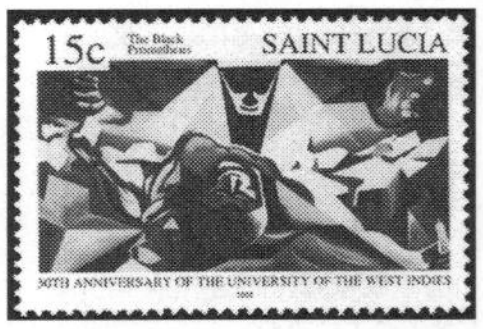

University of West Indies, 50th Anniv. A194

15c, The Black Prometheus. 75c, Sir Arthur Lewis, Sir Arthur Lewis College. $5, The Pitons.

1998, Nov. 30

1099	A194	15c multicolored	.20	.20
1100	A194	75c multicolored	.60	.60
1101	A194	$5 multicolored	3.75	3.75
	Nos. 1099-1101 (3)		4.55	4.55

Wildlife A195

Designs: 20c, Saint Lucia tree lizard. 75c, Boa constrictor. 95c, Leatherback turtle. $5, Saint Lucia whiptail.

Wmk. 373

1999, July 15 Litho. *Perf. 13½*

1102-1105	A195 Set of 4	5.25	5.25

UPU, 125th Anniv. A196

Wmk. 373

1999, Oct. 9 Litho. *Perf. 14*

1106	A196	20c Mail steamer "Tees"	.20	.20
1107	A196	65c Sikorsky S.38	.50	.50
1108	A196	95c Mail ship "Lady Drake"	.70	.70
1109	A196	$3 DC-10	2.25	2.25
	Nos. 1106-1109 (4)		3.65	3.65

Souvenir Sheet

Perf. 14¼

1110	A196	$5 Heinrich von Stephan	3.50	3.50

Stamp inscription on #1107 is misspelled. #1110 contains one 30x38mm stamp.

Christmas and Millennium — A197

Designs: 20c, Nativity. $1, Cathedral of the Immaculate Conception.

Perf. 13¾x14

1999, Dec. 14 Litho. Wmk. 373

1111	A197	20c multi	.20	.20
1112	A197	$1 multi	.70	.70

Independence, 21st Anniv. — A198

20c, Vintage badge of the colony. 75c, 1939 badge. 95c, 1967 arms. $1, 1979 arms.

Perf. 14x13¾

2000, Feb. 29 Litho. Wmk. 373

1113	A198	20c multi	.20	.20
1114	A198	75c multi	.55	.55
1115	A198	95c multi	.70	.70
1116	A198	$1 multi	.75	.75
	Nos. 1113-1116 (4)		2.20	2.20

Historical Views A199

Designs: 20c, Fort sugar factory, 1886-1941. 60c, Coaling at Port Castries, 1885-1940. $1, Fort Rodney, Pigeon Island, 1780-1861. $5, Military hospital ruins, Pigeon Island, 1824-1861.

Wmk. 373

2000, Sept. 4 Litho. *Perf. 14*

1117-1120	A199 Set of 4	5.00	5.00

First Municipality of Castries, 150th Anniv. — A200

Designs: 20c, Old Castries Market. 75c, Central Library. 95c, Port Castries. $5, Mayors Henry H. Breen, Joseph Desir.

Perf. 13¼x13½

2000, Oct. 9 Litho. Wmk. 373

1121-1124 A200 Set of 4 5.25 5.25

Girl Guides in St. Lucia, 75th Anniv. A201

Guides: 70c, Marching in brown uniforms. $1, Marching in blue uniforms. $2.50, At campground.

2000, Oct. 16

1125-1127 A201 Set of 3 3.25 3.25

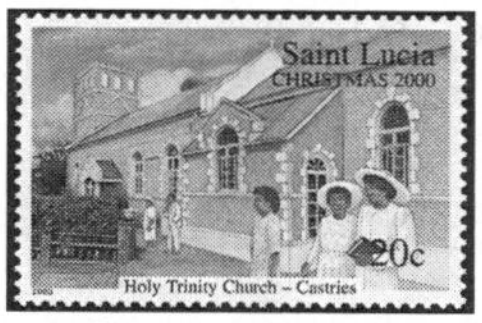

Christmas — A202

Churches: 20c, Holy Trinity, Castries. 50c, St. Paul's, Vieux-Fort. 95c, Christ, Soufriere. $2.50, Grace, River D'Oree.

2000, Nov. 22 ***Perf. 14***

1128-1131 A202 Set of 4 3.25 3.25

Worldwide Fund for Nature (WWF) — A203

Birds: #1132, 20c, White breasted thrasher. #1133, 20c, St. Lucia black finch. #1134, 95c, St. Lucia oriole. #1135, 95c, Forest thrush.

Wmk. 373

2001, Jan. 2 Litho. ***Perf. 14***

1132-1135 A203 Set of 4 1.75 1.75
1135a Strip of 4, #1132-1135 1.75 1.75

Jazz Festival, 10th Anniv. — A204

Designs: 20c, Crowd, stage. $1, Crowd, stage, ocean. $5, Musicians.

Perf. 13¾x14

2001, May 3 Litho. Wmk. 373

1136-1138 A204 Set of 3 4.75 4.75

Civil Administration, Bicent. — A205

Designs: 20c, British flag, island, ship. 65c, French flag, Napoleon Bonaparte, signing of the Treaty of Amiens. $1.10, British flag, King George III, ships. $3, Island map, King George IV.

Perf. 14x13¾

2001, Sept. 24 Litho. Unwmk.

1139-1142 A205 Set of 4 3.75 3.75

Christmas — A206

Various stained glass windows: 20c, 95c, $2.50.

2001, Dec. 7 Wmk. 373 ***Perf. 13½***

1143-1145 A206 Set of 3 2.75 2.75

Reign Of Queen Elizabeth II, 50th Anniv. Issue

Common Design Type

Designs: Nos. 1146, 1150a, 25c, Princess Elizabeth, 1927. Nos. 1147, 1150b, 65c, Wearing hat. Nos. 1148, 1150c, 75c, In 1947. Nos. 1149, 1150d, 95c, In 1996. No. 1150e, $5, 1955 portrait by Annigoni (38x50mm).

Perf. 14¼x14½, 13¾ (#1150e)

2002, Feb. 6 Litho. Wmk. 373

With Gold Frames

1146-1149 CD360 Set of 4 2.00 2.00

Souvenir Sheet

Without Gold Frames

1150 CD360 Sheet of 5, #a-e 5.75 5.75

AIR POST STAMP

Catalogue values for unused stamps in this section are for Never Hinged items.

Map of St. Lucia — AP1

Perf. 14½x14

1967, Mar. 1 Photo. Unwmk.

C1 AP1 15c blue .30 .30

St. Lucia's independence.
Exists imperf. and also in souvenir sheet.

POSTAGE DUE STAMPS

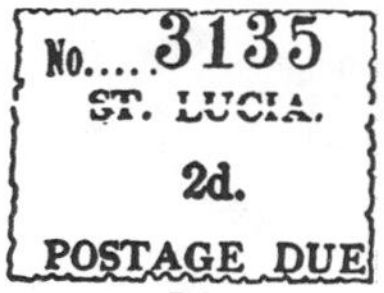

D1

D2

Type I - "No." 3mm wide (shown).
Type II - "No." 4mm wide.

Rough Perf. 12

1931 Unwmk. Typeset

J1 D1 1p blk, *gray bl*, type I 4.00 3.50
 a. Type II 7.50 8.00
J2 D1 2p blk, *yel*, type I 10.00 6.00
 a. Type II 15.00 16.00
 b. Vertical pair, imperf. btwn. *4,000.*

The serial numbers are handstamped. Type II has round "o" and period. Type I has tall "o" and square period.

Catalogue values for unused stamps in this section, from this point to the end of the section, are for Never Hinged items.

1933-47 Typo. Wmk. 4 ***Perf. 14***

J3	D2	1p black	4.25	*3.00*
J4	D2	2p black	14.00	*5.00*
J5	D2	4p black ('47)	4.25	*6.25*
J6	D2	8p black ('47)	4.25	*7.50*
		Nos. J3-J6 (4)	26.75	*21.75*

Issue date: June 28, 1947.

Values in Cents

1949, Oct. 1

J7	D2	2c black	.25	.25
J8	D2	4c black	.50	.50
J9	D2	8c black	1.00	1.00
J10	D2	16c black	1.75	1.75
		Nos. J7-J10 (4)	3.50	3.50

Values are for examples on chalky paper. Regular paper examples are worth more.

Wmk. 4a (error)

J7a	D2	2c	30.00
J8a	D2	4c	35.00
J9a	D2	8c	67.50
J10a	D2	16c	82.50
		Nos. J7a-J10a (4)	215.00

1965, Mar. 9 Wmk. 314

J11 D2 2c black .80 *3.00*
J12 D2 4c black .95 *5.00*

In the 2c center the "c" is heavier and the period bigger.

Nos. J9-J12 exist with overprint "Statehood/1st Mar. '67" in red.

Arms of St. Lucia — D3

1981, Aug. 4 Litho. Wmk. 373

J13	D3	5c red brown	.20	.20
J14	D3	15c green	.20	.20
J15	D3	25c deep orange	.20	.20
J16	D3	$1 dark blue	.55	.55
		Nos. J13-J16 (4)	1.15	1.15

1990 Wmk. 384 ***Perf. 15x14***

J17	D3	5c red brown	.20	.20
J18	D3	15c green	.20	.20
J19	D3	25c deep orange	.20	.20
J20	D3	$1 dark blue	.75	.75
		Nos. J17-J20 (4)	1.35	1.35

WAR TAX STAMPS

No. 65 Overprinted

1916 Wmk. 3 ***Perf. 14***

MR1 A11 1p scarlet 3.50 5.00
 a. Double overprint 400.00 *450.00*
 b. 1p carmine 27.50 30.00

Overprinted **WAR TAX**

MR2 A11 1p scarlet .20 .20

OFFICIAL STAMPS

Catalogue values for unused stamps in this section are for Never Hinged items.

Nos. 504-515 Overprinted

Wmk. 373

1983, Oct. 13 Litho. ***Perf. 14½***

O1	A95	5c multicolored	.20	.20
O2	A95	10c multicolored	.20	.20
O3	A95	15c multicolored	.20	.20
O4	A95	20c multicolored	.20	.20
O5	A95	25c multicolored	.20	.20
O6	A95	30c multicolored	.25	.25
O7	A95	50c multicolored	.40	.40
O8	A95	75c multicolored	.60	.60
O9	A95	$1 multicolored	.75	.75
O10	A95	$2 multicolored	1.50	1.50
O11	A95	$5 multicolored	3.75	3.75
O12	A95	$10 multicolored	7.50	7.50
		Nos. O1-O12 (12)	15.75	15.75

Nos. 747-761 Ovptd.

1985, May 7 Litho. ***Perf. 15***

O13	A126	5c multicolored	.20	.20
O14	A126	10c multicolored	.20	.20
O15	A126	20c multicolored	.20	.20
O16	A126	25c multicolored	.20	.20
O17	A126	30c multicolored	.20	.20
O18	A126	35c multicolored	.20	.20
O19	A126	45c multicolored	.30	.30
O20	A126	50c multicolored	.30	.30
O21	A126	65c multicolored	.40	.40
O22	A126	75c multicolored	.45	.45
O23	A126	90c multicolored	.55	.55
O24	A126	$1 multicolored	.60	.60
O25	A126	$2.50 multicolored	1.50	1.50
O26	A126	$5 multicolored	3.00	3.00
O27	A126	$15 multicolored	7.50	7.50
		Nos. O13-O27 (15)	15.80	15.80

Nos. 953-964 Ovptd.

1990, Feb. 21 Wmk. 384 ***Perf. 14***

O28	A162	10c multicolored	.20	.20
O29	A162	15c multicolored	.20	.20
O30	A162	20c multicolored	.20	.20
O31	A162	25c multicolored	.20	.20
O32	A162	50c multicolored	.40	.40
O33	A162	80c multicolored	.60	.60
O34	A162	95c multicolored	.70	.70
O35	A162	$1 multicolored	.75	.75
O36	A162	$1.50 multicolored	1.10	1.10
O37	A162	$2.50 multicolored	1.75	1.75
O38	A162	$5 multicolored	3.75	3.75
O39	A162	$25 multicolored	18.50	18.50
		Nos. O28-O39 (12)	28.35	28.35

Issued: 20c, 25c, 50c, $25, 2/21; 10c, 15c, 80c, $1.50, 4/12; 95c, $1, $2.50, $5, 6/25.

STE.-MARIE DE MADAGASCAR

sānt-mə-rē-də-,mad-ə-'gas-kər

LOCATION — An island off the east coast of Madagascar
GOVT. — French Possession
AREA — 64 sq. mi.
POP. — 8,000 (approx.)

In 1896 Ste.-Marie de Madagascar was attached to the colony of Madagascar for administrative purposes.

100 Centimes = 1 Franc

Navigation and Commerce — A1

1894 Unwmk. Typo. *Perf. 14x13½*
Name of Colony in Blue or Carmine

1	A1	1c black, *lil bl*	.75	.85
2	A1	2c brown, *buff*	.90	1.00
3	A1	4c claret, *lavender*	3.00	2.50
4	A1	5c green, *grnsh*	6.50	5.00
5	A1	10c black, *lavender*	7.50	5.25
6	A1	15c blue	17.50	15.00
7	A1	20c red, *green*	15.00	11.00
8	A1	25c black, *rose*	12.50	9.00
9	A1	30c brown, *bister*	8.00	7.00
10	A1	40c red, *straw*	8.50	8.00
11	A1	50c carmine, *rose*	32.50	25.00
12	A1	75c violet, *org*	52.50	32.50
13	A1	1fr brnz grn, *straw*	32.50	20.00
		Nos. 1-13 (13)	197.65	142.10

Perf. 13½x14 stamps are counterfeits.

These stamps were replaced by those of Madagascar.

ST. PIERRE & MIQUELON

sānt-'pi,ə,r and 'mik-ə-,län

LOCATION — Two small groups of islands off the southern coast of Newfoundland
GOVT. — Formerly a French colony, now a Department of France
AREA — 93 sq. mi.
POP. — 6,966 (1999 est.)
CAPITAL — St. Pierre

The territory of St. Pierre and Miquelon became a Department of France in July 1976.

100 Centimes = 1 Franc
100 Cents = 1 Euro (2002)

Catalogue values for unused stamps in this country are for Never Hinged items, beginning with Scott 300 in the regular postage section, Scott B13 in the semi-postal section, Scott C1 in the airpost section, and Scott J68 in the postage due section.

Stamps of French Colonies Handstamp Surcharged in Black

05
spm

1885 Unwmk. *Imperf.*

1	A8	05c on 40c ver, *straw*	60.00	32.50
2	A8	10c on 40c ver, *straw*	16.00	15.00
a.		"M" inverted	*150.00*	*110.00*
3	A8	15c on 40c ver, *straw*	17.50	14.50
		Nos. 1-3 (3)	93.50	62.00

Nos. 2 and 3 exist with "SPM" 17mm wide instead of 15½mm.

Nos. 1-3 exist with surcharge inverted and with it doubled.

Handstamp Surcharged in Black

b: 05 / SPM

c: 25 / S P M

d: 25 / S P M

1885

4	A8 (b)	05c on 35c blk, *yel*	85.00	65.00
5	A8 (b)	05c on 75c car, *rose*	225.00	150.00
6	A8 (b)	05c on 1fr brnz grn, *straw*	17.50	14.00
7	A8 (c)	25c on 1fr brnz grn, *straw*	*7,500.*	*1,600.*
8	A8 (d)	25c on 1fr brnz grn, *straw*	*1,800.*	*1,200.*

Nos. 7 and 8 exist with surcharge inverted, and with it vertical. No. 7 exists with "S P M" above "25" (the handstamping was done in two steps).

1885 *Perf. 14x13½*

9	A9 (c)	5c on 2c brn, *buff*	*4,750.*	*1,750.*
10	A9 (d)	5c on 4c cl, *lav*	375.00	200.00
11	A9 (b)	05c on 20c red, *grn*	22.50	22.50

No. 9 surcharge is always inverted. No. 10 exists with surcharge inverted.

P D / 5

1886, Feb. Typo. *Imperf.*
Without Gum

12	A15	5c black	850.00
13	A15	10c black	900.00
14	A15	15c black	750.00
		Nos. 12-14 (3)	2,500.

"P D" are the initials for "Payé a destination." Excellent forgeries exist.

Stamps of French Colonies Surcharged in Black

e: 15 c. / SPM

f: 15 c. / SPM

1891 *Perf. 14x13½*

15	A9 (e)	15c on 30c brn, *bis*	29.00	24.00
a.		Inverted surcharge	*175.00*	*125.00*
16	A9 (e)	15c on 35c blk, *org*	475.00	375.00
a.		Inverted surcharge	*475.00*	*425.00*
17	A9 (f)	15c on 35c blk, *org*	1,200.	750.00
a.		Inverted surcharge	*1,750.*	*1,200.*
18	A9 (e)	15c on 40c red, *straw*	75.00	50.00
a.		Inverted surcharge	*160.00*	*160.00*

Stamps of French Colonies Overprinted in Black or Red

ST - PIERRE M-on

1891, Oct. 15

19	A9	1c blk, *lil bl*	7.50	6.00
a.		Inverted overprint	*18.00*	*18.00*
20	A9	1c blk, *lil bl* (R)	7.00	7.00
a.		Inverted overprint	*13.00*	*13.00*
21	A9	2c brn, *buff*	7.50	6.00
a.		Inverted overprint	*18.00*	*18.00*
22	A9	2c brn, *buff* (R)	17.50	17.50
a.		Inverted overprint	*42.50*	*42.50*
23	A9	4c claret, *lav*	7.50	6.00
a.		Inverted overprint	*21.00*	*21.00*
24	A9	4c claret, *lav* (R)	15.00	14.00
a.		Inverted overprint	*32.50*	*32.50*
25	A9	5c grn, *grnsh*	7.50	6.00
a.		Double surcharge	*70.00*	
26	A9	10c blk, *lav*	25.00	19.00
a.		Inverted overprint	*50.00*	*50.00*
27	A9	10c blk, *lav* (R)	12.00	12.00
a.		Inverted overprint	*32.50*	*32.50*
28	A9	15c blk, *blue*	17.00	11.00
29	A9	20c red, *grn*	47.50	45.00
30	A9	25c blk, *rose*	19.00	15.00
31	A9	30c brn, *bis*	75.00	65.00
32	A9	35c vio, *org*	350.00	275.00
33	A9	40c red, *straw*	50.00	45.00
a.		Double surcharge	*140.00*	
34	A9	75c car, *rose*	75.00	60.00
a.		Inverted overprint	*125.00*	*125.00*
35	A9	1fr brnz grn, *straw*	60.00	45.00
a.		Inverted overprint	*125.00*	*100.00*
		Nos. 19-35 (17)	800.00	654.50

Numerous varieties of mislettering occur in the preceding overprint: "S," "ST," "P," "M," "ON," or "-" missing; "-" instead of "ON"; "=" instead of "-" These varieties command values double or triple those of normal stamps.

Surcharged in Black

1 / ST - PIERRE M-on / cent.

1891-92

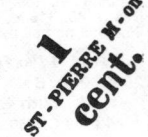

36	A9	1c on 5c grn, *grnsh*	6.00	5.50
37	A9	1c on 10c blk, *lav*	7.00	6.00
38	A9	1c on 25c blk, *rose* ('92)	5.50	5.00
39	A9	2c on 10c blk, *lav*	5.50	5.00
a.		Double surcharge	*70.00*	
40	A9	2c on 15c bl	5.00	5.00
41	A9	2c on 25c blk, *rose* ('92)	5.00	5.00
42	A9	4c on 20c red, *grn*	5.00	5.00
43	A9	4c on 25c blk, *rose* ('92)	5.00	5.00
a.		Double surcharge	*70.00*	
44	A9	4c on 30c brn, *bis*	13.00	11.00
45	A9	4c on 40c red, *straw*	17.00	10.00
		Nos. 36-45 (10)	74.00	62.50

See note after No. 35.

Surcharged

j: ST - PIERRE M-on

k: ST - PIERRE M-on / 1

1892, Nov. 4

46	A9 (j)	1c on 5c grn, *grnsh*	8.75	8.75
47	A9 (j)	2c on 5c grn, *grnsh*	8.75	8.75
48	A9 (j)	4c on 5c grn, *grnsh*	8.75	8.75
49	A9 (k)	1c on 25c blk, *rose*	5.75	5.75
50	A9 (k)	2c on 25c blk, *rose*	5.75	5.75
51	A9 (k)	4c on 25c blk, *rose*	5.75	5.75
		Nos. 46-51 (6)	43.50	43.50

See note after No. 35.

Postage Due Stamps of French Colonies Overprinted in Red

T / ST - PIERRE M-on / P

1892, Dec. 1 *Imperf.*

52	D1	10c black	22.50	22.50
53	D1	20c black	16.00	16.00
54	D1	30c black	17.50	17.50
55	D1	40c black	17.50	17.50
56	D1	60c black	75.00	75.00

Black Overprint

57	D1	1fr brown	110.00	110.00
58	D1	2fr brown	175.00	175.00
59	D1	5fr brown	325.00	325.00
		Nos. 52-59 (8)	758.50	758.50

See note after No. 35. "T P" stands for "Timbre Poste."

Navigation and Commerce — A16

1892-1908 Typo. *Perf. 14x13½*

60	A16	1c blk, *lil bl*	.60	.60
61	A16	2c brown, *buff*	.65	.65
62	A16	4c claret, *lav*	1.25	1.25
63	A16	5c green, *grnsh*	2.00	1.50
64	A16	5c yel grn ('08)	2.25	1.50
65	A16	10c black, *lav*	4.00	3.50
66	A16	10c red ('00)	4.00	1.00
67	A16	15c bl, quadrille paper	6.00	2.25
68	A16	15c gray, *lt gray* ('00)	60.00	35.00
69	A16	20c red, *grn*	16.00	12.00
70	A16	25c black, *rose*	6.00	1.25
71	A16	25c blue ('00)	10.00	6.00
72	A16	30c brown, *bis*	6.00	3.50
73	A16	35c blk, *yel* ('06)	4.50	4.00
74	A16	40c red, *straw*	5.00	4.00
75	A16	50c car, *rose*	30.00	25.00
76	A16	50c brown, *az* ('00)	20.00	18.00
77	A16	75c violet, *org*	17.00	15.00
78	A16	1fr brnz grn, *straw*	15.00	10.00
		Nos. 60-78 (19)	210.25	146.00

Perf. 13½x14 stamps are counterfeits.
For surcharges and overprints see Nos. 110-120, Q1-Q2.

Fisherman A17

Fulmar Petrel A18

Fishing Schooner A19

1909-30

79	A17	1c org red & ol	.20	.20
80	A17	2c olive & dp bl	.20	.20
81	A17	4c violet & ol	.30	.30
82	A17	5c bl grn & ol grn	.55	.20
83	A17	5c blue & blk ('22)	.30	.30
84	A17	10c car rose & red	.55	.45
85	A17	10c bl grn & ol grn ('22)	.30	.30
86	A17	10c bister & mag ('25)	.30	.30
86A	A17	15c dl vio & rose ('17)	.45	.20
87	A17	20c bis brn & vio brn	.70	.60
88	A18	25c dp blue & blue	2.40	1.10
89	A18	25c ol brn & bl grn ('22)	.70	.55
90	A18	30c org & vio brn	1.25	1.00
91	A18	30c rose & dull red ('22)	.85	.85
92	A18	30c red brn & bl ('25)	.55	.55
93	A18	30c gray grn & bl grn ('26)	.70	.70
94	A18	35c ol grn & vio brn	.45	.30
95	A18	40c vio brn & ol grn	2.25	1.25
96	A18	45c violet & ol grn	.55	.45
97	A18	50c olive & ol grn	1.10	.85
98	A18	50c bl & pale bl ('22)	.85	.85
99	A18	50c yel brn & mag ('25)	.70	.70
100	A18	60c dk bl & ver ('25)	.70	.70
101	A18	65c vio & org brn ('28)	1.25	1.10
102	A18	75c brown & olive	1.10	.85
103	A18	90c brn red & org red ('30)	21.00	21.00
104	A19	1fr ol grn & dp bl	2.75	1.50
105	A19	1.10fr bl grn & org red ('28)	3.00	2.75
106	A19	1.50fr bl & dp bl ('30)	8.75	8.25
107	A19	2fr violet & brn	3.00	1.75
108	A19	3fr red violet ('30)	9.75	9.50

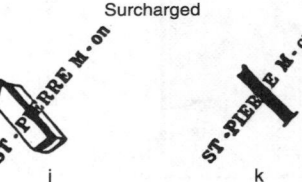

109	A19	5fr vio brn & ol grn	7.50	5.50
		Nos. 79-109 (32)	75.00	65.00

For overprints and surcharges see Nos. 121-131, 206C-206D, B1-B2, Q3-Q5.

Stamps of 1892-1906 Surcharged in Carmine or Black

05 n **10** o

1912

110	A16	5c on 2c brn, *buff*	1.50	1.50
111	A16	5c on 4c claret, *lav* (C)	.40	.40
112	A16	5c on 15c blue (C)	.40	.40
113	A16	5c on 20c red, *grn*	.40	.40
114	A16	5c on 25c blk, *rose* (C)	.40	.40
115	A16	5c on 30c brn, *bis* (C)	.50	.50
116	A16	5c on 35c blk, *yel* (C)	1.00	1.00
117	A16	10c on 40c red, *straw*	.40	.40
118	A16	10c on 50c car, *rose*	.50	.50
119	A16	10c on 75c dp vio, *org*	1.50	1.50
120	A16	10c on 1fr brnz grn, *straw*	2.00	2.00
		Nos. 110-120 (11)	9.00	9.00

Two spacings between the surcharged numerals are found on Nos. 110 to 120.

Stamps and Types of 1909-17 Surcharged with New Value and Bars in Black, Blue (Bl) or Red

1924-27

121	A17	25c on 15c dl vio & rose ('25)	.35	.35
a.		Double surcharge	100.00	
b.		Triple surcharge	100.00	
122	A19	25c on 2fr vio & lt brn (Bl)	.35	.35
123	A19	25c on 5fr brn & ol grn (Bl)	.35	.35
a.		Triple surcharge	100.00	
124	A18	65c on 45c vio & ol grn ('25)	1.10	1.10
125	A18	85c on 75c brn & ol ('25)	1.10	1.10
126	A18	90c on 75c brn red & dp org ('27)	1.75	1.75
127	A19	1.25fr on 1fr dk bl & ultra (R) ('26)	1.60	1.60
128	A19	1.50fr on 1fr ultra & dk bl ('27)	2.00	2.00
129	A19	3fr on 5fr ol brn & red vio ('27)	1.90	1.90
130	A19	10fr on 5fr ver & ol grn ('27)	11.00	11.00
131	A19	20fr on 5fr vio & ver ('27)	16.00	16.00
		Nos. 121-131 (11)	37.50	37.50

Common Design Types pictured following the introduction.

Colonial Exposition Issue

Common Design Types

1931, Apr. 13 Engr. *Perf. 12½*

Name of Country in Black

132	CD70	40c deep green	3.00	3.00
133	CD71	50c violet	3.00	3.00
134	CD72	90c red orange	3.00	3.00
135	CD73	1.50fr dull blue	3.00	3.00
		Nos. 132-135 (4)	12.00	12.00

Map and Fishermen — A20

Lighthouse and Fish — A21

Fishing Steamer and Sea Gulls — A22

Perf. 13½x14, 14x13½

1932-33 Typo.

136	A20	1c red brn & ultra	.20	.20
137	A21	2c blk & dk grn	.20	.20
138	A22	4c mag & ol brn	.20	.20
139	A22	5c vio & dk brn	.20	.20
140	A21	10c red brn & blk	.35	.35
141	A21	15c dk blue & vio	.85	.85
142	A20	20c blk & red org	.85	.85
143	A20	25c lt vio & lt grn	.85	.85
144	A22	30c ol grn & bl grn	.95	.95
145	A22	40c dp bl & dk brn	.95	.95
146	A21	45c ver & dp grn	.95	.95
147	A21	50c dk brn & dk grn	.95	.95
148	A22	65c ol brn & org	1.10	1.10
149	A20	75c grn & red org	1.10	1.10
150	A20	90c dull red & red	1.10	1.10
151	A22	1fr org brn & org red	.95	.95
152	A20	1.25fr dp bl & lake ('33)	1.25	1.25
153	A20	1.50fr dp blue & blue	1.10	1.10
154	A22	1.75fr blk & dk brn ('33)	1.40	1.40
155	A22	2fr bl blk & Prus bl	6.25	6.25
156	A21	3fr dp grn & dk brn	7.50	7.50
157	A21	5fr brn red & dk brn	18.00	18.00
158	A22	10fr dk grn & vio	47.50	47.50
159	A20	20fr ver & dp grn	47.50	47.50
		Nos. 136-159 (24)	142.25	142.25

For overprints and surcharges see Nos. 160-164, 207-221.

Nos. 147, 149, 153-154, 157 Overprinted in Black, Red or Blue

JACQUES CARTIER

JACQUES CARTIER

1534 - 1934 p

1534-1934 q

1934, Oct. 18

160	A21(p)	50c (Bk)	2.75	2.75
161	A20(q)	75c (Bk)	3.00	3.00
162	A20(p)	1.50fr (Bk)	3.50	3.50
163	A22(p)	1.75fr (R)	4.00	4.00
164	A21(p)	5fr (Bl)	22.50	22.50
		Nos. 160-164 (5)	35.75	35.75

400th anniv. of the landing of Jacques Cartier.

Paris International Exposition Issue

Common Design Types

1937 *Perf. 13*

165	CD74	20c deep violet	1.00	1.00
166	CD75	30c dark green	1.00	1.00
167	CD76	40c carmine rose	1.00	1.00
168	CD77	50c dk brown & blue	1.00	1.00
169	CD78	90c red	1.00	1.00
170	CD79	1.50fr ultra	1.00	1.00
		Nos. 165-170 (6)	6.00	6.00

Colonial Arts Exhibition Issue

Souvenir Sheet

Common Design Type

1937 *Imperf.*

171	CD78	3fr dark ultra	17.50	17.50

Dog Team A23

Port St. Pierre A24

Tortue Lighthouse A25

Soldiers' Bay at Langlade A26

1938-40 Photo. *Perf. 13½x13*

172	A23	2c dk blue green	.20	.20
173	A23	3c brown violet	.20	.20
174	A23	4c dk red violet	.20	.20
175	A23	5c carmine lake	.20	.20
176	A23	10c bister brown	.20	.20
177	A23	15c red violet	.35	.35
178	A23	20c blue violet	.50	.50
179	A23	25c Prus blue	1.50	1.50
180	A24	30c dk red violet	.35	.35
181	A24	35c deep green	.50	.50
182	A24	40c slate blue ('40)	.20	.20
183	A24	45c dp grn ('40)	.30	.30
a.		Value omitted	55.00	
184	A24	50c carmine rose	.50	.50
185	A24	55c Prus blue	2.40	2.40
186	A24	60c violet ('39)	.35	.35
187	A24	65c brown	3.75	3.75
188	A24	70c org yel ('39)	.50	.50
189	A25	80c violet	1.00	1.00
190	A25	90c ultra ('39)	.50	.50
191	A25	1fr brt pink	7.50	7.50
192	A25	1fr pale ol grn ('40)	.50	.50
193	A25	1.25fr brt rose ('39)	1.25	1.25
194	A25	1.40fr dk brown ('40)	.60	.60
195	A25	1.50fr blue green	.70	.70
196	A25	1.60fr rose violet ('40)	.60	.60
197	A25	1.75fr deep blue	2.10	2.10
198	A26	2fr rose violet	.50	.50
199	A26	2.25fr brt blue ('39)	.70	.70
200	A26	2.50fr org yel ('40)	.70	.70
201	A26	3fr gray brown	.60	.60
202	A26	5fr henna brown	.70	.70
203	A26	10fr dk bl, *bluish*	1.10	1.10
204	A26	20fr slate green	1.25	1.25
		Nos. 172-204 (33)	32.50	32.50

For overprints and surcharges see Nos. 222-255, 260-299, B9-B10.

New York World's Fair Issue

Common Design Type

1939, May 10 Engr. *Perf. 12½x12*

205	CD82	1.25fr carmine lake	1.25	1.25
206	CD82	2.25fr ultra	1.25	1.25

For overprints and surcharges see Nos. 256-259.

Lighthouse on Cliff — A27

1941 Engr. *Perf. 12½x12*

206A	A27	1fr dull lilac	.55
206B	A27	2.50fr blue	.55

Nos. 206A-206B were issued by the Vichy government and were not placed on sale in the colony.

Stamps of types A23 and A26 without "RF" monogram were issued in 1941-1944 by the Vichy government, but were not sold in the colony.

Free French Administration

The circumstances surrounding the overprinting and distribution of these stamps were most unusual. Practically all of the stamps issued in small quantities, with the exception of Nos. 260-299, were obtained by speculators within a few days after issue. At a later date, the remainders were taken over by the Free French Agency in Ottawa, Canada, by whom they were sold at a premium for the benefit of the Syndicat des Oeuvres Sociales. Large quantities appeared on the market in 1991, including many "errors." More may exist.

Excellent counterfeits of these surcharges and overprints are known.

Nos. 86 and 92 Overprinted in Black

FRANCE LIBRE

a

F. N. F. L.

1942 Unwmk. *Perf. 14x13½*

206C	A17	10c	1,000.	1,000.
206D	A18	30c	1,000.	1,000.

The letters "F. N. F. L." are the initials of "Forces Navales Francaises Libres" or "Free French Naval Forces."

Same Overprint in Black on Nos. 137-139, 145-148, 151, 154-155, 157

207	A21	2c	200.00	200.00
208	A22	4c	40.00	40.00
208A	A22	5c	600.00	600.00
209	A22	40c	12.00	12.00
210	A21	45c	125.00	125.00
211	A21	50c	10.50	10.50
212	A22	65c	30.00	30.00
213	A22	1fr	275.00	275.00
214	A22	1.75fr	7.50	7.50
215	A22	2fr	11.00	11.00
216	A22	5fr	250.00	250.00

Nos. 142, 149, 152-153 Overprinted in Black

FRANCE LIBRE F N F L

Perf. 13½x14

216A	A20	20c	300.00	300.00
217	A20	75c	16.00	16.00
218	A20	1.25fr	13.50	13.50
218A	A20	1.50fr	350.00	350.00

On Nos. 152, 149 Surcharged with New Value and Bars

219	A20	10fr on 1.25fr	27.50	27.50
220	A20	20fr on 75c	35.00	35.00

No. 154 Surcharged in Red

5 fr

FRANCE LIBRE

F. N. F. L.

Perf. 14x13½

221	A22	5fr on 1.75fr	10.00	10.00

Stamps of 1938-40 Overprinted type "a" in Black

Perf. 13½x13

222	A23	2c dk blue grn	300.00	300.00
223	A23	3c brown vio	90.00	90.00
224	A23	4c dk red vio	60.00	60.00
225	A23	5c car lake	675.00	675.00
226	A23	10c bister brn	7.50	7.50
227	A23	15c red violet	1,100.	1,100.
228	A23	20c blue violet	125.00	125.00
229	A23	25c Prus blue	8.50	8.50
230	A24	35c deep green	575.00	575.00
231	A24	40c slate blue	11.00	11.00
232	A24	45c deep green	12.00	12.00
233	A24	55c Prus blue	*6,500.*	*6,500.*
234	A24	60c violet	425.00	425.00
235	A24	65c brown	15.00	15.00
236	A24	70c orange yel	25.00	25.00
237	A25	80c violet	275.00	275.00
238	A25	90c ultra	12.50	12.50
239	A25	1fr pale ol grn	16.00	16.00
240	A25	1.25fr brt rose	12.50	12.50
241	A25	1.40fr dark brown	10.50	10.50
242	A25	1.50fr blue green	575.00	575.00
243	A25	1.60fr rose violet	11.00	11.00
244	A26	2fr rose violet	47.50	47.50
245	A26	2.25fr brt blue	11.50	11.50
246	A26	2.50fr orange yel	15.00	15.00
247	A26	3fr gray brown	*7,500.*	*7,500.*
248	A26	5fr henna brn	*1,500.*	*1,500.*
248A	A26	20fr slate green	700.00	700.00

Nos. 176, 190 Surcharged in Black

FRANCE LIBRE

F. N. F. L.

20 c

249	A23	20c on 10c	7.00	7.00
250	A23	30c on 10c	5.75	5.75
251	A25	60c on 90c	6.25	6.25
252	A25	1.50fr on 90c	8.50	8.50
253	A23	2.50fr on 10c	10.50	10.50
254	A23	10fr on 10c	35.00	35.00
255	A25	20fr on 90c	35.00	35.00
		Nos. 249-255 (7)	108.00	108.00

New York World's Fair Issue
Overprinted type "a" in Black

Perf. 12½x12

256	CD82	1.25fr car lake	9.00	9.00
257	CD82	2.25fr ultra	9.00	9.00

Nos. 205-206 Surcharged

2 fr 50
FRANCE LIBRE
F. N. F. L.

258	CD82	2.50fr on 1.25fr	10.50	10.50
259	CD82	3fr on 2.25fr	10.50	10.50

Stamps of 1938-40 Overprinted in Carmine

Noël 1941
FRANCE LIBRE
F. N. F. L.

1941 ***Perf. 13½x13***

260	A23	10c bister brn	20.00	20.00
261	A23	20c blue violet	20.00	20.00
262	A23	25c Prus blue	20.00	20.00
263	A24	40c slate blue	20.00	20.00
264	A24	45c deep green	20.00	20.00
265	A24	65c brown	20.00	20.00
266	A24	70c orange yel	20.00	20.00
267	A25	80c violet	20.00	20.00
268	A25	90c ultra	20.00	20.00
269	A25	1fr pale ol grn	20.00	20.00
270	A25	1.25fr brt rose	20.00	20.00
271	A25	1.40fr dk brown	20.00	20.00
272	A25	1.60fr rose violet	22.50	22.50
273	A25	1.75fr brt blue	22.50	22.50
274	A26	2fr rose violet	22.50	22.50
275	A26	2.25fr brt blue	22.50	22.50
276	A26	2.50fr orange yel	22.50	22.50
277	A26	3fr gray brown	22.50	22.50

Same Surcharged in Carmine with New Values

278	A23	10fr on 10c bister brn	37.50	37.50
279	A25	20fr on 90c ultra	37.50	37.50
		Nos. 260-279 (20)	450.00	450.00

Stamps of 1938-40 Overprinted in Black

280	A23	10c bister brn	26.00	26.00
281	A23	20c blue violet	26.00	26.00
282	A23	25c Prus blue	26.00	26.00
283	A24	40c slate blue	26.00	26.00
284	A24	45c deep green	26.00	26.00
285	A24	65c brown	26.00	26.00
286	A24	70c orange yel	26.00	26.00
287	A25	80c violet	26.00	26.00
288	A25	90c ultra	26.00	26.00
289	A25	1fr pale ol grn	26.00	26.00
290	A25	1.25fr brt rose	26.00	26.00
291	A25	1.40fr dk brown	26.00	26.00
292	A25	1.60fr rose violet	26.00	26.00
293	A25	1.75fr brt blue	475.00	475.00
294	A26	2fr rose vio	26.00	26.00
295	A26	2.25fr brt blue	26.00	26.00
296	A26	2.50fr orange yel	26.00	26.00
297	A26	3fr gray brown	26.00	26.00

Same Surcharged in Black with New Values

298	A23	10fr on 10c bister brn	75.00	75.00
299	A25	20fr on 90c ultra	75.00	75.00
		Nos. 280-299 (20)	1,067.	1,067.

Christmas Day plebiscite ordered by Vice Admiral Emile Henri Muselier, commander of the Free French naval forces (Nos. 260-299).

Catalogue values for unused stamps in this section, from this point to the end of the section, are for Never Hinged items.

St. Malo Fishing Schooner A28

1942 **Photo.** ***Perf. 14x14½***

300	A28	5c dark blue	.20	.20
301	A28	10c dull pink	.20	.20
302	A28	25c brt green	.20	.20
303	A28	30c slate black	.20	.20
304	A28	40c brt grnsh blue	.20	.20
305	A28	60c brown red	.30	.20
306	A28	1fr dark violet	.40	.25
307	A28	1.50fr brt red	1.00	.85
308	A28	2fr brown	.40	.35
309	A28	2.50fr brt ultra	1.00	.85
310	A28	4fr dk orange	.60	.40
311	A28	5fr dp plum	.60	.40
312	A28	10fr lt ultra	1.00	.85
313	A28	20fr dark green	1.25	1.10
		Nos. 300-313 (14)	7.55	6.25

Nos. 300, 302, 309 Surcharged in Carmine or Black

50c

1945

314	A28	50c on 5c (C)	.20	.20
315	A28	70c on 5c (C)	.20	.20
316	A28	80c on 5c (C)	.35	.30
317	A28	1.20fr on 5c (C)	.35	.30
318	A28	2.40fr on 25c	.35	.30
319	A28	3fr on 25c	.50	.45
320	A28	4.50fr on 25c	1.00	.80
321	A28	15fr on 2.50fr (C)	1.25	1.00
		Nos. 314-321 (8)	4.20	3.55

Eboue Issue
Common Design Type

1945 **Engr.** ***Perf. 13***

322	CD91	2fr black	.70	.40
323	CD91	25fr Prussian green	1.90	.85

Nos. 322 and 323 exist imperforate.

Soldiers' Bay — A29

Fishing Industry Symbols A30

Fishermen A31

Weighing the Catch A32

Fishing Boat and Dinghy A33

Storm-swept Coast — A34

1947, Oct. 6 **Engr.** ***Perf. 12½***

324	A29	10c chocolate	.20	.20
325	A29	30c violet	.20	.20
326	A29	40c rose lilac	.20	.20
327	A29	50c intense blue	.20	.20
328	A30	60c carmine	.50	.20
329	A30	80c brt ultra	.70	.30
330	A30	1fr dk green	.70	.30
331	A31	1.20fr blue grn	.60	.30
332	A31	1.50fr black	.60	.40
333	A31	2fr red brown	.60	.40
334	A32	3fr rose violet	2.00	1.25
335	A32	3.60fr dp brown org	1.50	.80
336	A32	4fr sepia	1.75	.80
337	A33	5fr orange	1.60	1.25
338	A33	6fr blue	1.75	1.25
339	A33	10fr Prus green	2.50	1.65
340	A34	15fr dk slate grn	3.50	2.50
341	A34	20fr vermilion	4.75	2.75
342	A34	25fr dark blue	5.75	3.25
		Nos. 324-342 (19)	29.60	18.20

Imperforates
Most stamps of St. Pierre and Miquelon from 1947 onward exist imperforate in issued and trial colors, and also in small presentation sheets in issued colors.

Silver Fox — A35

1952, Oct. 10 **Unwmk.** ***Perf. 13***

343	A35	8fr dk brown	5.25	1.00
344	A35	17fr blue	6.75	1.50

Military Medal Issue
Common Design Type

1952, Dec. 15 **Engr. & Typo.**

345	CD101	8fr multicolored	10.00	4.50

Fish Freezing Plant A36

1955-56 **Engr.**

346	A36	30c ultra & dk blue	.60	.30
347	A36	50c gray, blk & sepia	.60	.30
348	A36	3fr purple	1.25	.60
349	A36	40fr Prussian blue	3.00	1.50
		Nos. 346-349 (4)	5.45	2.70

Issued: 40fr, July 4; others, Oct. 22, 1956.

FIDES Issue

Fish Freezer "Le Galantry" A37

Perf. 13x12½

1956, Mar. 15 **Unwmk.**

350	A37	15fr blk brn & chestnut	4.00	2.00

See note in Common Design section after CD103.

Codfish A38

4fr, 10fr, Lighthouse and fishing fleet.

1957, Nov. 4 ***Perf. 13***

351	A38	40c dk brn & grnsh bl	.40	.20
352	A38	1fr brown & green	.55	.25
353	A38	2fr indigo & dull blue	.80	.45
354	A38	4fr maroon, car & pur	2.00	1.00
355	A38	10fr grnsh bl, dk bl & brn	2.25	1.10
		Nos. 351-355 (5)	6.00	3.00

Human Rights Issue
Common Design Type

1958, Dec. 10 **Engr.** ***Perf. 13***

356	CD105	20fr red brn & dk blue	2.50	.90

Flower Issue
Common Design Type

1959 **Photo.** ***Perf. 12½x12***

357	CD104	5fr Spruce	2.25	1.50

Ice Hockey A39

Mink A40

1959, Oct. 7 **Engr.** ***Perf. 13***

358	A39	20fr multicolored	2.50	.50

1959, Oct. 7 **Engr.** ***Perf. 13***

359	A40	25fr ind, yel grn & brn	3.50	.70

Cypripedium Acaule — A41

Eider Ducks — A42

Flower: 50fr, Calopogon pulchellus.

1962, Apr. 24 **Unwmk.** ***Perf. 13***

360	A41	25fr grn, org & car rose	4.00	.50
361	A41	50fr green & car lake	5.00	.90
		Nos. 360-361,C24 (3)	*17.50*	2.90

1963, Mar. 4 ***Perf. 13***

Birds: 1fr, Rock ptarmigan. 2fr, Ringed plovers. 6fr, Blue-winged teal.

362	A42	50c blk, ultra & ocher	.40	.20
363	A42	1fr red brn, ultra & rose	.75	.20
364	A42	2fr blk, dk bl & bis	1.25	.25
365	A42	6fr multicolored	3.00	.60
		Nos. 362-365 (4)	5.40	1.25

Albert Calmette A43

1963, Aug. 5 **Engr.**

366	A43	30fr dk brn & dk blue	8.00	.90

Albert Calmette, bacteriologist, birth cent.

Red Cross Centenary Issue
Common Design Type

1963, Sept. 2 **Unwmk.** ***Perf. 13***

367	CD113	25fr ultra, gray & car	8.00	.65

Human Rights Issue
Common Design Type

1963, Dec. 10 **Unwmk.** ***Perf. 13***

368	CD117	20fr org, bl & dk brn	4.50	.65

Philatec Issue
Common Design Type

1964, Apr. 4 **Engr.**

369	CD118	60fr choc, grn & dk bl	7.50	2.25

Rabbits A44

1964, Sept. 28 ***Perf. 13***

370	A44	3fr shown	1.50	.20
371	A44	4fr Fox	1.50	.20
372	A44	5fr Roe deer	3.00	.35
373	A44	34fr Charolais bull	10.00	1.25
		Nos. 370-373 (4)	16.00	2.00

Airport and Map of St. Pierre and Miquelon A45

40fr, Television tube and tower, map. 48fr, Map of new harbor of St. Pierre.

1967 Engr. *Perf. 13*

374	A45	30fr ind, bl & dk red	6.00	.55
375	A45	40fr sl grn, ol & dk red	6.00	.60
376	A45	48fr dk red, brn & sl bl	9.00	.85
		Nos. 374-376 (3)	21.00	2.00

Issued: 30fr, 10/23; 40fr, 11/20; 48fr, 9/25.

WHO Anniversary Issue

Common Design Type

1968, May 4 Engr. *Perf. 13*

377	CD126	10fr multicolored	7.50	.55

René de Chateaubriand and Map of Islands — A46

Designs: 4fr, J. D. Cassini and map. 15fr, Prince de Joinville, Francois F. d'Orleans (1818-1900), ships and map. 25fr, Admiral Gauchet, World War I warship and map.

1968, May 20 Photo. *Perf. 12½x13*

378	A46	4fr multicolored	3.50	.55
379	A46	6fr multicolored	4.00	.60
380	A46	15fr multicolored	7.00	.80
381	A46	25fr multicolored	8.00	1.25
		Nos. 378-381 (4)	22.50	3.20

Human Rights Year Issue

Common Design Type

1968, Aug. 10 Engr. *Perf. 13*

382	CD127	20fr bl, ver & org yel	7.00	.45

Belle Rivière, Langlade A47

Design: 15fr, Debon Brook, Langlade.

1969, Apr. 30 Engr. *Perf. 13*

Size: 36x22mm

383	A47	5fr bl, slate grn & brn	3.00	.30
384	A47	15fr brn, bl & dl grn	4.00	.45
		Nos. 383-384,C41-C42 (4)	*37.00*	9.75

Treasury A48

Designs: 25fr, Scientific and Technical Institute of Maritime Fishing. 30fr, Monument to seamen lost at sea. 60fr, St. Christopher College.

1969, May 30 Engr. *Perf. 13*

385	A48	10fr brt bl, cl & blk	3.00	.25
386	A48	25fr dk bl, brt bl & brn red	6.50	.45
387	A48	30fr blue, grn & gray	7.50	.60
388	A48	60fr brt bl, brn red & blk	12.00	1.00
		Nos. 385-388 (4)	29.00	2.30

Ringed Seals A49

Designs: 3fr, Sperm whales. 4fr, Pilot whales. 6fr, Common dolphins.

1969, Oct. 6 Engr. *Perf. 13*

389	A49	1fr lil, vio brn & red brn	2.50	.40
390	A49	3fr bl grn, ind & red	2.50	.40
391	A49	4fr ol, gray grn & mar	4.25	.55
392	A49	6fr brt grn, pur & red	6.00	.65
		Nos. 389-392 (4)	15.25	2.00

L'Estoile and Granville, France A50

40fr, "La Jolie" & St. Jean de Luz, France, 1750. 48fr, "Le Juste" & La Rochelle, France, 1860.

1969, Oct. 13 Engr. *Perf. 13*

393	A50	34fr grn, mar & slate grn	*12.00*	.90
394	A50	40fr brn red, lem & sl grn	*20.00*	1.50
395	A50	48fr multicolored	*26.00*	1.60
		Nos. 393-395 (3)	*58.00*	4.00

Historic ships connecting St. Pierre and Miquelon with France.

ILO Issue

Common Design Type

1969, Nov. 24

396	CD131	20fr org, gray & ocher	7.00	.55

UPU Headquarters Issue

Common Design Type

1970, May 20 Engr. *Perf. 13*

397	CD133	25fr dk car, brt bl & brn	8.25	.55
398	CD133	34fr maroon, brn & gray	14.00	.70

Rowers and Globe — A51

1970, Oct. 13 Photo. *Perf. 12½x12*

399	A51	20fr lt grnsh bl & brn	13.00	.45

World Rowing Championships, St. Catherine.

Blackberries A52

1970, Oct. 20 Engr. *Perf. 13*

400	A52	3fr shown	1.25	.20
401	A52	4fr Strawberries	1.25	.25
402	A52	5fr Raspberries	2.00	.30
403	A52	6fr Blueberries	3.25	.40
		Nos. 400-403 (4)	7.75	1.15

Ewe and Lamb A53

30fr, Animal quarantine station. 34fr, Charolais bull. 48fr, Refrigeration ship slaughterhouse.

1970 Engr. *Perf. 13*

404	A53	15fr plum, grn & olive	*7.00*	.45
405	A53	30fr sl, bis brn & ap grn	*11.00*	.45
406	A53	34fr red lil, org brn & emer	*17.50*	1.25
407	A53	48fr multicolored	*14.00*	.85
		Nos. 404-407 (4)	*49.50*	3.00

Issue dates: 48fr, Nov. 10; others, Dec. 8.

Saint François d'Assise 1900 A54

Ships: 35fr, Sainte Jehanne, 1920. 40fr, L'Aventure, 1950. 80fr, Commandant Bourdais, 1970.

1971, Aug. 25

408	A54	30fr Prus bl & hn brn	*22.50*	3.00
409	A54	35fr Prus bl, lt grn & ol brn	*29.00*	3.50
410	A54	40fr sl grn, bl & dk brn	*40.00*	5.00
411	A54	80fr dp grn, bl & blk	*50.00*	7.00
		Nos. 408-411 (4)	*141.50*	18.50

Deep-sea fishing fleet.

"Aconit" and Map of Islands — A55

1971, Sept. 27 Engr. *Perf. 13*

412	A55	22fr shown	*22.50*	.80
413	A55	25fr Alysse	*27.50*	1.40
414	A55	50fr Mimosa	*35.00*	1.60
		Nos. 412-414 (3)	*85.00*	3.80

Rallying of the Free French forces, 30th anniv.

Ship's Bell — A56

St. Pierre Museum: 45fr, Old chart and sextants, horiz.

1971, Oct. 25 Photo. *Perf. 12½x13*

415	A56	20fr gray & multi	*11.00*	.55
416	A56	45fr red brn & multi	*22.50*	.70

De Gaulle Issue

Common Design Type

Designs: 35fr, Gen. de Gaulle, 1940. Pres. de Gaulle, 1970.

1971, Nov. 9 Engr. *Perf. 13*

417	CD134	35fr vermilion & blk	*15.00*	1.50
418	CD134	45fr vermilion & blk	*22.50*	2.00

Haddock A57

Fish: 3fr, Hippoglossoides platessoides. 5fr, Sebastes mentella. 10fr, Codfish.

1972, Mar. 7

419	A57	2fr vio bl, ind & pink	3.25	.40
420	A57	3fr grn & gray olive	6.25	.50
421	A57	5fr Prus bl & brick red	4.50	.60
422	A57	10fr grn & slate grn	11.00	.85
		Nos. 419-422 (4)	25.00	2.35

Oldsquaws — A58

Birds: 10c, 70c, Puffins. 20c, 90c, Snow owl. 40c, like 6c. Identification of birds on oldsquaw and puffin stamps transposed.

1973, Jan. 1 Engr. *Perf. 13*

423	A58	6c Prus bl, pur & brn	1.00	.20
424	A58	10c Prus bl, blk & org	1.50	.20
425	A58	20c ultra, bis & dk vio	2.00	.20
426	A58	40c pur, sl grn & brn	3.50	.40
427	A58	70c brt grn, blk & org	5.50	.55
428	A58	90c Prus bl, bis & pur	6.50	.90
		Nos. 423-428 (6)	20.00	2.45

Indoor Swimming Pool — A59

Design: 1fr, Cultural Center of St. Pierre.

1973, Sept. 25 Engr. *Perf. 13*

429	A59	60c brn, brt bl & dk car	4.00	.35
430	A59	1fr bl grn, ocher & choc	6.00	.60

Opening of Cultural Center of St. Pierre.

Map of Islands, Weather Balloon and Ship, WMO Emblem A60

1974, Mar. 23 Engr. *Perf. 13*

431	A60	1.60fr multicolored	9.00	1.25

World Meteorological Day.

Gannet Holding Letter — A61

1974, Oct. 9 Engr. *Perf. 13*

432	A61	70c blue & multi	4.00	.50
433	A61	90c red & multi	5.00	.60

Centenary of Universal Postal Union.

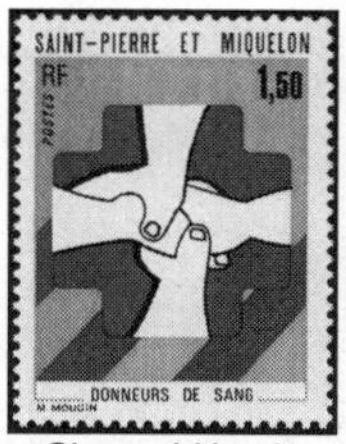

Clasped Hands over Red Cross — A62

Hands Putting Money into Fish-shaped Bank — A63

1974, Oct. 15 Photo. *Perf. 12½x13*

434	A62	1.50fr multicolored	9.00	.70

Honoring blood donors.

1974, Nov. 15 Engr. *Perf. 13*

435	A63	50c ocher & vio bl	5.00	.35

St. Pierre Savings Bank centenary.

Church of St. Pierre and Seagulls A64

Designs: 10c, Church of Miquelon and fish. 20c, Church of Our Lady of the Sailors, and fishermen.

1974, Dec. 9 Engr. *Perf. 13*

436 A64	6c multicolored	1.60	.20
437 A64	10c multicolored	2.75	.20
438 A64	20c multicolored	3.75	.35
	Nos. 436-438 (3)	8.10	.75

Danaus Plexippus A65

Design: 1fr, Vanessa atalanta, vert.

1975, July 17 Litho. *Perf. 12½*

439 A65	1fr blue & multi	*9.50*	.60
440 A65	1.20fr green & multi	*13.00*	.70

Pottery — A66

Mother and Child, Wood Carving — A67

1975, Oct. 2 Engr. *Perf. 13*

441 A66	50c ol, brn & choc	3.50	.45
442 A67	60c blue & dull yel	5.00	.45

Local handicrafts.

Pointe Plate Lighthouse and Murres A68

10c, Galantry lighthouse and Atlantic puffins. 20c, Cap Blanc lighthouse, whale and squid.

1975, Oct. 21

443 A68	6c vio bl, blk & lt grn	*1.75*	.20
444 A68	10c lil rose, blk & dk ol	*3.00*	.20
445 A68	20c blue, indigo & brn	*4.25*	.40
	Nos. 443-445 (3)	*9.00*	.80

Georges Pompidou (1911-74), Pres. of France — A68a

1976, Feb. 17 Engr. *Perf. 13*

446 A68a	1.10fr brown & slate	5.50	.60

Georges Pompidou (1911-1974), President of France.

Washington and Lafayette, American Flag — A69

1976, July 12 Photo. *Perf. 13*

447 A69	1fr multicolored	5.00	.60

American Bicentennial.

Woman Swimmer and Maple Leaf — A70

70c, Basketball and maple leaf, vert.

1976, Aug. 10 Engr. *Perf. 13*

448 A70	70c multicolored	*4.00*	.40
449 A70	2.50fr multicolored	*8.00*	1.25

21st Olympic Games, Montreal, Canada, July 17-Aug. 1.

Vigie Dam — A71

1976, Sept. 7 Engr. *Perf. 13*

450 A71	2.20fr multicolored	6.50	1.25

Croix de Lorraine — A72

Fishing Vessels: 1.40fr, Goelette.

1976, Oct. 5 Photo. *Perf. 13*

451 A72	1.20fr multicolored	6.75	.70
452 A72	1.40fr multicolored	8.00	1.00

France Nos. 1783-1784, 1786-1789, 1794, 1882, 1799, 1885, 1802, 1889, 1803-1804 and 1891 Ovptd. "SAINT PIERRE / ET / MIQUELON"

1986, Feb. 4 Engr. *Perf. 13*

453 A915	5c	dark green	.25	.20
454 A915	10c	dull red	.20	.20
455 A915	20c	brt green	.20	.20
456 A915	30c	orange	.20	.20
457 A915	40c	brown	.20	.20
458 A915	50c	lilac	.20	.20
459 A915	1fr	olive green	.25	.25
460 A915	1.80fr	emerald	.60	.50
461 A915	2fr	brt yellow grn	.60	.50
462 A915	2.20fr	red	.65	.55
463 A915	3fr	chocolate brn	.90	.80
464 A915	3.20fr	sapphire	1.00	.85
465 A915	4fr	brt carmine	1.25	1.00
466 A915	5fr	gray blue	1.50	1.40
467 A915	10fr	purple	3.00	2.75
		Nos. 453-467 (15)	11.00	9.80

Discovery of St. Pierre & Miquelon by Jacques Cartier, 450th Anniv. — A73

1986, June 11 Engr. *Perf. 13*

476 A73	2.20fr sep, sage grn & redsh brn	1.25	.65

Statue of Liberty, Cent. — A74

1986, July 4

477 A74	2.50fr Statue, St. Pierre Harbor	1.50	.70

Fishery Resources A75

Holy Family, Stained Glass by J. Balmet A76

1986-89 Engr. *Perf. 13*

478 A75	1fr	bright red	.50	.30
479 A75	1.10fr	brt orange	.40	.35
480 A75	1.30fr	dark red	.40	.40
481 A75	1.40fr	violet	.70	.45
482 A75	1.40fr	dark red	.50	.45
483 A75	1.50fr	brt ultra	.60	.50
484 A75	1.60fr	emerald grn	.60	.50
485 A75	1.70fr	green	.60	.55
		Nos. 478-485 (8)	4.30	3.50

Issued: 1fr, #481, 10/22; 1.10fr, 1.50fr, 10/14/87; 1.30fr, 1.60fr, 8/7/88; #482, 1.70fr, 7/14/89.

1986, Dec. 10 Litho. *Perf. 13*

486 A76	2.20fr multicolored	1.20	.70

Christmas.

Hygrophorus Pratensis — A77

1987-90 Engr. *Perf. 12½*

487 A77	2.50fr shown	.75	.75
488 A77	2.50fr Russula paludosa britz	.85	.85
489 A77	2.50fr Tricholoma virgatum	.80	.80
490 A77	2.50fr Hydnum repandum	.85	.85
	Nos. 487-490 (4)	3.25	3.25

Issued: #487, Feb. 14; #488, Jan. 29, 1988; #489, Jan. 28, 1989; #490, Jan. 17, 1990.

Dr. François Dunan (1884-1961), Clinic — A78

1987, Apr. 29 Engr. *Perf. 13*

491 A78	2.20fr brt bl, blk & dk red brn	1.00	.70

Transat Yacht Race, Lorient to St. Pierre to Lorient A79

1987, May 16

492 A79	5fr dp ultra, dk rose brn & brt bl	2.25	2.00

Visit of Pres. Mitterand A80

1987, May 29 Litho. *Perf. 12½x13*

493 A80	2.20fr dull ultra, gold & scar	1.40	.70

Marine Slip, Cent. A81

1987, June 20 Litho. *Perf. 13*

494 A81	2.50fr pale sal & dk red brn	1.25	.65

Stern Trawler La Normande — A82

1987-91 Photo.

495 A82	3fr shown	2.25	1.25
496 A82	3fr Le Marmouset	1.25	.95
497 A82	3fr Tugboat Le Malabar	1.00	.95
498 A82	3fr St. Denis, St. Pierre	1.40	1.25
499 A82	3fr Cryos	1.25	1.10
	Nos. 495-499 (5)	7.15	5.50

Issued: #495, 10/14; #496, 9/28/88; #497, 11/2/89; #498, 10/24/90; #499, 11/6/91.

This is an expanding set. Numbers will change when complete.

St. Christopher and the Christ Child, Stained Glass Window and Scout Emblem — A83

1987, Dec. 9 Litho. *Perf. 13*

503 A83	2.20fr multicolored	1.25	.80

Christmas, Scout movement in St. Pierre & Miquelon, 50th anniv.

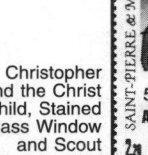

The Great Barachoise Nature Reserve — A84

1987, Dec. 16 Engr. *Perf. 13x12½*

504 A84 3fr Horses, waterfowl 1.50 1.50
505 A84 3fr Waterfowl, seals 1.50 1.50
a. Pair, #504-505 + label 3.25 3.25

No. 505a is in continous design.

1988, Nov. 2

506 A84 2.20fr Ross Cove .75 .75
507 A84 13.70fr Cap Perce 4.75 4.75
a. Pair, #506-507 + label 5.75 5.75

No. 507a is in continous design.

1988 Winter Olympics, Calgary A86

1988, Mar. 5 Engr. *Perf. 13*

508 A86 5fr brt ultra & dark red 1.90 1.90

Louis Thomas (1887-1976), Photographer — A87

1988, May 4 Engr. *Perf. 13*

509 A87 2.20fr blk, dk ol bis & Prus bl .85 .70

France No. 2105 Overprinted "ST-PIERRE ET MIQUELON"

1988, July 25 Engr. *Perf. 13*

510 A1107 2.20fr ver, blk & violet blue 1.25 .70

Seizure of Schooner Nellie J. Banks, 50th Anniv. A88

1988, Aug. 7

511 A88 2.50fr brn, vio blue & brt blue 1.25 .75

The Nellie J. Banks was seized by Canada for carrying prohibited alcohol in 1938.

Christmas — A89

1988, Dec. 17 Litho. *Perf. 13*

512 A89 2.20fr multicolored 1.00 .70

Judo Competitions in St. Pierre & Miquelon, 25th Anniv. — A90

1989, Mar. 4 Engr. *Perf. 13*

513 A90 5fr brn org, blk & yel grn 1.75 1.60

French Revolution Bicent.; 40th Anniv. of the UN Declaration of Human Rights (in 1988) — A91

1989 Engr. *Perf. 12½x13*

514 A91 2.20fr Liberty .80 .75
515 A91 2.20fr Equality .80 .75
516 A91 2.20fr Fraternity .80 .75
Nos. 514-516 (3) 2.40 2.25

Issued: #514, 3/22; #515, 5/3; #516, 6/17.

Souvenir Sheet

French Revolution, Bicent. — A92

Designs: a, Bastille, liberty tree. b, Bastille, ship. c, Building, revolutionaries raising flag and liberty tree. d, Revolutionaries, building with open doors.

1989, July 14 Engr. *Perf. 13*

517 A92 Sheet of 4 + 2 labels 7.50 6.50
a.-d. 5fr any single 1.90 1.60

Heritage of Ile aux Marins — A93

Designs: 2.20fr, Coastline, ships in harbor, girl in boat, fish. 13.70fr, Coastline, ships in harbor, boy flying kite from boat, map of Ile aux Marins.

1989, Sept. 9 Engr. *Perf. 13x12½*

518 A93 2.20fr multi 1.00 .70
519 A93 13.70fr multi 4.50 4.25
a. Pair, #518-519 + label 6.00

Nos. 519a is in continuous design.

George Landry and Bank Emblem A95

1989, Nov. 8 Engr. *Perf. 13*

520 A95 2.20fr bl & golden brn .80 .75

Bank of the Islands, cent.

Christmas — A96

1989, Dec. 2 Litho. *Perf. 13*

521 A96 2.20fr multicolored .80 .75

France Nos. 2179-2182, 2182A-2186, 2188-2189, 2191-2194, 2204B, 2331, 2333-2334, 2336-2339, 2342 Ovptd. "ST-PIERRE / ET / MIQUELON"

1990-96 Engr. *Perf. 13*

522	A1161	10c	brn blk	.20	.20
523	A1161	20c	light grn	.20	.20
524	A1161	50c	bright vio	.20	.20
525	A1161	1fr	orange	.35	.35
526	A1161	2fr	apple grn	.70	.70
527	A1161	2fr	blue	.75	.75
528	A1161	2.10fr	green	.75	.75
529	A1161	2.20fr	green	.80	.80
530	A1161	2.30fr	red	.80	.80
531	A1161	2.40fr	emerald	.85	.85
532	A1161	2.50fr	red	1.00	1.00
533	A1161	2.70fr	emerald	1.10	1.10
534	A1161	3.20fr	bright bl	1.10	1.10
535	A1161	3.40fr	blue	1.25	1.25
536	A1161	3.50fr	apple grn	1.25	1.25
537	A1161	3.80fr	brt pink	1.40	1.40
538	A1161	3.80fr	blue	1.60	1.60
539	A1161	4fr	brt lil rose	1.50	1.50
540	A1161	4.20fr	rose lilac	1.60	1.60
541	A1161	4.40fr	blue	1.50	1.50
542	A1161	4.50fr	magenta	1.90	1.90
543	A1161	5fr	dull blue	1.75	1.75
544	A1161	10fr	violet	3.50	3.50
544A	A1161	(2.50fr)	red	.95	.95
	Nos. 522-544A (24)			27.00	27.00

Booklet Stamps

Self-Adhesive

Die Cut

545 A1161 2.50fr red 1.00 1.00
a. Booklet pane of 10 9.50
545B A1161 (2.80fr) red 1.10 1.10
a. Booklet pane of 10 11.00

Issued: 2.30fr, 1/2/90; 2.10fr, 2/5/90; 10c, 20c, 50c, 3.20fr, #537, 4/17/90; 1fr, 5fr, #526, 10fr, 7/16/90; #532, 2.20fr, 12/21/91; 3.40fr, 4fr, 1/8/92; #545, 2/8/92; 4.20fr, 1/13/93; #544A, 7/5/93; 2.40fr, 3.50fr, 4.40fr, #545B, 10/6/93; #527, 8/17/94; #538, 4/10/96; 2.70fr, 4.50fr, 6/12/96.

A97

A98

1990, June 18 *Perf. 13*

546 A97 2.30fr Charles de Gaulle .80 .80

De Gaulle's call for French Resistance, 50th anniv.

1990, Nov. 22

547 A98 1.70fr red, claret & blue .70 .70
548 A98 2.30fr red, claret & blue .95 .95
a. Pair, #547-548 + label 1.65 1.65

25 Kilometer Race of Miquelon A99

1990, June 23

549 A99 5fr Runner, map 1.75 1.75

Micmac Canoe, 1875 A100

1990, Aug. 15 Engr. *Perf. 13x13½*

550 A100 2.50fr multicolored .95 .95

Views of St. Pierre — A101

Harbor scene.

1990, Oct. 24 Engr. *Perf. 13x12½*

551 A101 2.30fr bl, grn & brn .90 .90
552 A101 14.50fr bl, grn & brn 5.75 5.75
a. Pair, #551-552 + label 6.75 6.75

No. 552a is in continous design.

Christmas — A103

1990, Dec. 15 **Litho.**

553 A103 2.30fr multicolored .95 .95

Papilio Brevicaudata A104

1991-92 **Litho.** ***Perf. 13***

554 A104 2.50fr multicolored .95 .95

Perf. 12

555 A104 3.60fr Aeshna Eremita, Nuphar Variegatum 1.40 1.40

Issued: 2.50fr, Jan. 16; 3.60fr, Mar. 4, 1992.
This is an expanding set. Numbers will change again if necessary.

Marine Tools, Sailing Ship A105

Litho. & Engr.

1991, Mar. 6 ***Perf. 13***

559 A105 1.40fr yellow & green .55 .55
560 A105 1.70fr yellow & red .65 .65

Scenic Views A106

Designs: Nos. 548, 552, Saint Pierre. Nos. 549, 553, Ile aux Marins. Nos. 550, 554, Langlade. Nos. 551, 555, Miquelon.

1991, Apr. 17 **Engr.** ***Perf. 13***

561 A106 1.70fr blue .65 .65
562 A106 1.70fr blue .65 .65
563 A106 1.70fr blue .65 .65
564 A106 1.70fr blue .65 .65
a. Strip of 4, #561-564 2.60 2.60
565 A106 2.50fr red .95 .95
566 A106 2.50fr red .95 .95
567 A106 2.50fr red .95 .95
568 A106 2.50fr red .95 .95
a. Strip of 4, #565-568 4.00 4.00
Nos. 561-568 (8) 6.40 6.40

Lyre Music Society, Cent. — A107

1991, June 21 **Engr.** ***Perf. 13***

569 A107 2.50fr multicolored .85 .85

Newfoundland Crossing by Rowboat "Los Gringos" — A108

1991, Aug. 3 **Engr.** ***Perf. 13x12½***

570 A108 2.50fr multicolored .85 .85

Basque Sports A109

1991, Aug. 24 ***Perf. 13***

571 A109 5fr red & green 1.75 1.75

Natural Heritage — A110

2.50fr, Fishermen. 14.50fr, Shoreline, birds.

1991, Oct. 18 **Engr.** ***Perf. 13x12½***

572 A110 2.50fr multicolored .90 .90
573 A110 14.50fr multicolored 5.00 5.00
a. Pair, #572-573 + label 6.00 6.00

No. 573a is in continuous design.

Central Economic Cooperation Bank, 50th Anniv. — A111

1991, Dec. 2 **Engr.** ***Perf. 13x12½***

574 A111 2.50fr 1941 100fr note 1.00 1.00

Christmas A112

1991, Dec. 21 **Litho.** ***Perf. 13***

575 A112 2.50fr multicolored 1.00 1.00

Christmas Day Plebiscite, 50th anniv.

Vice Admiral Emile Henri Muselier (1882-1965), Commander of Free French Naval Forces — A113

1992, Jan. 8 **Litho.** ***Perf. 13***

576 A113 2.50fr multicolored 1.10 1.00

1992 Winter Olympics, Albertville A114

1992, Feb. 8 **Engr.** ***Perf. 13***

577 A114 5fr vio bl, blue & mag 1.90 1.90

Caulking Tools, Bow of Ship A115

Litho. & Engr.

1992, Apr. 1 ***Perf. 13x12½***

578 A115 1.50fr pale bl gray & brn .55 .55
579 A115 1.80fr pale bl gray & bl .65 .65

Lighthouses — A116

Designs: a, Galantry. b, Feu Rouge. c, Pointe-Plate. d, Ile Aux Marins.

1992, July 8 **Litho.** ***Perf. 13***

580 A116 2.50fr Strip of 4, #a.-d. 5.00 4.00

Natural Heritage — A117

1992, Sept. 9 **Engr.** ***Perf. 13x12½***

581 A117 2.50fr Langlade 1.25 1.25
582 A117 15.10fr Doulisie Valley 7.50 7.50
a. Pair, #581-582 + label 8.75 8.75

No. 582a is in continuous design.
See Nos. 593-594, 605-606.

Discovery of America, 500th Anniv. — A118

Photo. & Engr.

1992, Oct. 12 ***Perf. 13x12½***

583 A118 5.10fr multicolored 2.00 2.00

Le Baron de L'Esperance — A119

1992, Nov. 18 **Engr.** ***Perf. 13***

584 A119 2.50fr claret, brn & bl .95 .95

Christmas — A120

1992, Dec. 9 **Litho.** ***Perf. 13***

585 A120 2.50fr multicolored 1.00 .90

Commander R. Birot (1906-1942) — A121

1993, Jan. 13

586 A121 2.50fr multicolored 1.00 .90

Deep Sea Diving A122

1993, Feb. 10 **Engr.** ***Perf. 12***

587 A122 5fr multicolored 2.00 1.75

A123

A124

Monochamus Scutellatus, Cichorium Intybus.

1993, Mar. 10 **Litho.** ***Perf. 13½x13***

588 A123 3.60fr multicolored 1.25 1.25

See No. 599.

1993, Apr. 7 **Litho.** ***Perf. 13½x13***

Slicing cod.

589 A124 1.50fr green & multi .55 .55
590 A124 1.80fr red & multi .70 .70

Move to the Magdalen Islands, Quebec, by Miquelon Residents, Bicent. — A125

1993, June 9 Engr. *Perf. 13*
591 A125 5.10fr brn, bl & grn 2.00 1.50

Fish A126

Designs: a, Capelin. b, Ray. c, Halibut (fletan). d, Toad fish (crapaud).

1993, July 30 Photo. *Perf. 13*
592 A126 2.80fr Strip of 4, #a.-d. 4.25 3.75

Natl. Heritage Type of 1992

1993, Aug. 18 Engr. *Perf. 13x12½*
593 A117 2.80fr Miquelon 1.25 1.00
594 A117 16fr Otter pool 6.25 5.75
a. Pair, #593-594 + label 7.50 6.75

No. 594a is a continuous design.

Commissioner's Residence — A127

1993, Oct. 6 Engr. *Perf. 13*
595 A127 3.70fr multicolored 1.25 .90

Christmas A128

1993, Dec. 13 Litho. *Perf. 13*
596 A128 2.80fr multicolored 1.25 .95

Commander Louis Blaison (1906-1942), Submarine Surcouf — A129

1994, Jan. 12 Litho. *Perf. 13*
597 A129 2.80fr multicolored 1.00 .90

Petanque World Championships — A130

1994, Feb. 9 Engr. *Perf. 12½x12*
598 A130 5.10fr multicolored 2.00 1.75

Insect and Flower Type of 1993

Cristalis tenax, taraxacum officinale, horiz.

1994, Mar. 9 Litho. *Perf. 13x13½*
599 A123 3.70fr multicolored 1.40 1.25

Drying Codfish, 1905 A131

1994 Litho. *Perf. 13*
600 A131 1.50fr blk & bl grn .55 .55
601 A131 1.80fr multicolored .65 .65

Issued: 1.50fr, 5/4/94; 1.80fr, 4/6/94.

Women's Right to Vote, 50th Anniv. A132

1994, Apr. 21
602 A132 2.80fr multicolored 1.00 1.00

Hospital Ship St. Pierre, Cent. A133

1994, July 2
603 A133 2.80fr multicolored 1.00 1.00

Souvenir Sheet

Ships A134

Designs: a, Miquelon. b, Isle of St. Pierre. c, St. George XII. d, St. Eugene IV.

1994, July 6 *Perf. 12*
604 Sheet of 4 6.00 6.00
a.-b. A134 2.80fr any single 1.00 1.00
c.-d. A134 3.70fr any single 1.50 1.50

See No. 628.

Natural Heritage Type of 1992

1994, Aug. 17 Engr. *Perf. 13*
605 A117 2.80fr Woods 1.10 1.10
606 A117 16fr "The Hat" 6.50 6.50
a. Pair, #605-606 + label 7.75 5.00

Parochial School A135

1994, Oct. 5 Engr. *Perf. 13*
607 A135 3.70fr multicolored 1.40 1.10

Stamp Show A136

1994, Oct. 15
608 A136 3.70fr grn, yel & bl 1.50 1.10

Chirstmas A137

1994, Nov. 23 Litho. *Perf. 13*
609 A137 2.80fr multicolored 1.25 1.10

Louis Pasteur (1822-95) A138

1995, Jan. 11 Litho. *Perf. 13*
610 A138 2.80fr multicolored 1.25 1.10

Triathlon A139

1995, Feb. 8 Engr. *Perf. 12*
611 A139 5.10fr multicolored 2.25 2.00

A140

A141

Dicranum Scoparium & Cladonia Cristatella.

1995, Mar. 8 Litho. *Perf. 13*
612 A140 3.70fr multicolored 1.60 1.50

See Nos. 625, 635.

1995, Apr. 5 Litho. *Perf. 13½x13*

Cooper and his tools.

613 A141 1.50fr black & multi .65 .65
614 A141 1.80fr red & multi .75 .75

Shellfish A142

a, Snail. b, Crab. c, Scallop. d, Lobster.

1995, July 5 Litho. *Perf. 13*
616 Strip of 4 4.75 4.75
a.-d. A142 2.80fr any single 1.25 1.25

Geological Mission — A143

Designs: 2.80fr, Rugged terrain along shoreline, diagram of mineral location, zircon. 16fr, Geological map, terrain.

1995, Aug. 16 Engr. *Perf. 13x12½*
617 A117 2.80fr multicolored 1.25 1.25
618 A117 16fr multicolored 6.75 6.75
a. Pair, #617-618 + label 8.00 8.00

Sister Cesarine (1845-1922), St. Joseph de Cluny — A144

1995, Sept. 6 Litho. *Perf. 13*
619 A144 1.80fr multicolored .90 .75

The Francoforum Public Building — A145

1995, Oct. 4 Engr.
620 A145 3.70fr multicolored 1.50 1.00

Christmas — A146

Design: 2.80fr, Toys in store window.

1995, Nov. 22 Litho. *Perf. 13*
621 A146 2.80fr multicolored 1.25 .75

Charles de Gaulle (1890-1970) A147

1995, Nov. 9 Litho. *Perf. 13x13½*
622 A147 14fr multicolored 5.75 5.00

Commandant Jean Levasseur (1909-47) — A148

1996, Jan. 10 ***Perf. 13***
623 A148 2.80fr multicolored 1.25 1.25

Boxing
A149

1996, Feb. 7 **Engr.** ***Perf. 12x12½***
624 A149 5.10fr multicolored 2.25 2.25

Plant Type of 1995

Design: Cladonia verticillata and polytrichum juniperinum.

1996, Mar. 13 **Litho.** ***Perf. 13***
625 A140 3.70fr multicolored 1.60 1.60

Blacksmiths and Their Tools
A150

1996, Apr. 10
626 A150 1.50fr black & multi .65 .65
627 A150 1.80fr red & multi .75 .75

Ship Type of 1994

Designs: a, Radar II. b, SPM Roro. c, Pinta. d, Pascal Anne.

1996, July 10 **Litho.** ***Perf. 13***
628 Sheet of 4 5.00 5.00
a.-d. A134 3fr Any single 1.25 1.25

Aerial View of Miquelon — A151

Designs: 3fr, "Le Cap," mountains, buildings. 15.50fr, "Le Village," buildings.

1996, Aug. 14 **Engr.** ***Perf. 13x12½***
629 A151 3fr multicolored 1.25 1.25
630 A151 15.50fr multicolored 6.50 6.50
a. Pair, #629-630 + label 7.75 7.75

Customs House, Cent.
A152

1996, Oct. 9 **Engr.** ***Perf. 12½x13***
631 A152 3.80fr blue & black 1.50 1.50

Fall Stamp Show — A153

1996, Nov. 6 **Litho.** ***Perf. 13***
632 A153 1fr multicolored .40 .40

Christmas — A154

1996, Nov. 20 **Litho.** ***Perf. 13***
633 A154 3fr multicolored 1.25 1.25

Constant Colmay (1903-65)
A155

1997, Jan. 8 **Litho.** ***Perf. 13***
634 A155 3fr multicolored 1.25 1.25

Flora and Fauna Type of 1995

Design: Phalacrocorax carbo, sedum rosea.

1997, Mar. 12 **Litho.** ***Perf. 13***
635 A140 3.80fr multicolored 1.50 1.50

Maritime Heritage
A156

Designs: 1.70fr, Man in doorway of salt house. 2fr, Boat, naval architect's drawing.

1997, Apr. 9 **Litho.** ***Perf. 13***
636 A156 1.70fr multicolored .70 .70
637 A156 2fr multicolored .80 .80

Volleyball
A157

Litho. & Engr.

1997, Apr. 9 ***Perf. 12***
638 A157 5.20fr multicolored 2.10 2.10

Fish
A158

a, Shark. b, Salmon. c, Poule d'eau. d, Mackerel.

1997, July 9 **Litho.** ***Perf. 13***
639 A158 3fr Strip of 4, #a.-d. 4.75 4.75

Bay, Headlands — A159

3fr, Basque Cape. 15.50fr, Diamant.

1997, Aug. 13 ***Perf. 13x12***
640 A159 3fr multicolored 1.00 1.00
641 A159 15.50fr multicolored 5.25 5.25
a. Pair #640-641 + label 6.25 6.25

France Nos. 2589-2603 Ovptd. "ST. PIERRE / ET / MIQUELON"

1997-98		**Engr.**		***Perf. 13***	
642	A1409	10c	brown	.20	.20
643	A1409	20c	brt blue grn	.20	.20
644	A1409	50c	purple	.20	.20
645	A1409	1fr	bright org	.35	.35
646	A1409	2fr	bright blue	.70	.70
647	A1409	2.70fr	bright green	.90	.90
648	A1409	(3fr)	red	1.00	1.00
649	A1409	3.50fr	apple green	1.25	1.25
650	A1409	3.80fr	blue	1.25	1.25
651	A1409	4.20fr	dark orange	1.50	1.50
652	A1409	4.40fr	blue	1.60	1.60
653	A1409	4.50fr	bright pink	1.60	1.60
654	A1409	5fr	brt grn bl	1.75	1.75
655	A1409	6.70fr	dark green	2.40	2.40
656	A1409	10fr	violet	3.50	3.50
	Nos. 645-656 (12)			17.80	17.80

Issued: 2.70fr, (3fr), 3.80fr, 8/13/97; 10c, 20c, 50c, 3.50fr, 4.40fr, 10fr, 10/8/97; 1fr, 2fr, 4.20fr, 4.50fr, 5fr, 6.70fr, 1/7/98.

See No. 664 for self-adhesive (3fr).

Post Office Building
A160

1997, Oct. 8 **Engr.** ***Perf. 13***
657 A160 3.80fr multicolored 1.40 1.40

Christmas — A161

1997, Nov. 19 **Litho.** ***Perf. 13***
658 A161 3fr multicolored 1.10 1.10

Alain Savary (1918-88), Governor, Territorial Deputy
A162

1998, Jan. 7 **Litho.** ***Perf. 13***
659 A162 3fr multicolored 1.10 1.10

1998 Winter Olympic Games, Nagano
A163

1998, Feb. 11 **Engr.** ***Perf. 12***
660 A163 5.20fr Curling 1.90 1.90

Flora and Fauna
A164

1998, Mar. 11 **Photo.** ***Perf. 13***
661 A164 3.80fr multicolored 1.40 1.40

Ice Workers
A165

1998, Apr. 8 **Litho.**
662 A165 1.70fr shown .60 .60
663 A165 2fr Cutting ice from lake .75 .75

France Nos. 2604, 2620 Ovptd. "ST. PIERRE / ET / MIQUELON"

Die Cut x Serpentine Die Cut

1998, Apr. 8 **Engr.**

Self-Adhesive

664 A1409 (3fr) red 1.00 1.00
a. Booklet pane of 10 10.00

No. 664a is a complete booklet. The peelable backing serves as a booklet cover.

1998, May 13 ***Perf. 13***
665 A1424 3fr red & blue 1.00 1.00

Houses
A166

a, Gray. b, Yellow, red roof. c, Pink. d, White, red roof.

1998, July 8 **Litho.** ***Perf. 13***
666 A166 3fr Strip of 4, #a.-d. 4.25 4.25

French in North America — A167

1998, Sept. 30 **Engr.** ***Perf. 13x12½***
670 A167 3fr multicolored 1.10 1.10

Cape Blue Natl. Park — A168

Designs: 3fr, Point Plate Lighthouse, shoreline. 15.50fr, Cape Blue.

1998, Sept. 30 ***Perf. 13x12***
671 A168 3fr multicolored 1.25 1.25
672 A168 15.50fr multicolored 5.75 5.75
a. Pair, #671-672 + label 7.00 7.00

France, 1998 World Cup Soccer Champions — A169

1998, Oct. 21 **Litho.** ***Perf. 13***
673 A169 3fr multicolored 1.10 1.10

Memorial to War Dead — A170

1998, Nov. 11 **Engr.**
674 A170 3.80fr multicolored 1.40 1.40

Christmas — A171

1998, Nov. 18 **Litho.**
675 A171 3fr multicolored 1.10 1.10

Emile Letournel (1927-94), Orthopedic Surgeon, Traumatologist — A172

1999, Jan. 6 **Engr.** ***Perf. 13***
676 A172 3fr multicolored 1.10 1.10

Painting, "The Beach at Fisherman Island," by Patrick Guillaume — A173

1999, Feb. 10 **Litho.**
677 A173 5.20fr multicolored 1.90 1.90

See No. 692.

La Plate-Bière — A174

1999, Mar. 10 **Litho.** ***Perf. 13***
678 A174 3.80fr Rubus chamaemorus 1.25 1.25

See No. 693.

Horseshoeing — A175

1.70fr, Horse, blacksmith and his tools. 2fr, Applying horseshoes in blacksmith's shop.

1999, Apr. 7 **Litho.** ***Perf. 13***
679 A175 1.70fr multicolored .55 .55
680 A175 2fr multicolored .65 .65

France No. 2691 Ovptd. "ST. PIERRE / ET / MIQUELON"

1999, Apr. 10 **Engr.**
681 A1470 3fr red & blue 1.00 1.00

Value is shown in both francs and euros on No. 681.

France No. 2691A Overprinted "ST. PIERRE / ET / MIQUELON"

Die Cux x Serpentine Die Cut 7

1999, Apr. 5 **Engr.**

Self-Adhesive

681A A1470 3fr red & blue 1.00 1.00
b. Booklet of 10 10.00

First Stamps of France, 150th Anniv. — A176

a, France #3, St. Pierre & Miquelon #9, 79. b, #145, 270. c, #C21, C36. d, #476, 676.

1999, June 23 **Litho.** ***Perf. 13***
682 A176 3fr Sheet of 4, #a.-d. 4.25 4.25

PhilexFrance '99, World Philatelic Exhibition.

Ships — A177

a, Bearn. b, Pro Patria. c, Erminie. d, Colombier.

1999, July 7 **Litho.** ***Perf. 13x13½***
683 A177 3fr Sheet of 4, #a.-d. 4.25 4.25

General de Gaulle Place — A178

1999, Aug. 11 **Engr.** ***Perf. 13x12¼***
684 A178 3fr Cars, yield sign 1.00 1.00
685 A178 15.50fr Docked boats 5.50 5.50
a. Pair, #684-685 + label 6.50 6.50

Visit of Pres. Jacques Chirac, Sept. 1999 — A179

1999, Sept. 7 **Litho.** ***Perf. 13¼x13***
686 A179 3fr multicolored 1.00 1.00

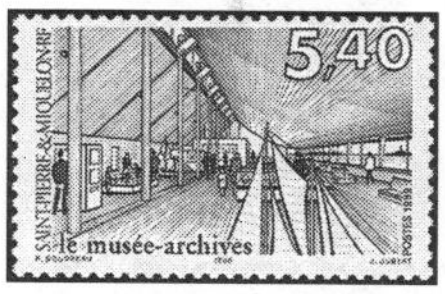

Archives — A180

1999, Oct. 6 **Engr.** ***Perf. 13x12¾***
687 A180 5.40fr deep rose lilac 1.75 1.75

Christmas — A181

1999, Nov. 17 **Litho.** ***Perf. 13***
688 A181 3fr multi .95 .95

Year 2000 — A182

2000, Jan. 12 **Litho.** ***Perf. 13¼x13***
689 A182 3fr multi .95 .95

Whales — A183

Designs: 3fr, Megaptera novaeangliae. 5.70fr, Balaenoptera physalus.

2000, Jan. **Engr.** ***Perf. 13x12¾***
690 A183 3fr blk & Prus bl .95 .95
691 A183 5.70fr Prus grn & blk 1.75 1.75

Painting Type of 1999

2000, Feb. 9 **Litho.** ***Perf. 13***
692 A173 5.20fr Les Graves 1.50 1.50

Plant Type of 1999

2000, Mar. 8
693 A174 3.80fr Vaccinium vitis-idaea 1.10 1.10

Wood Gatherer — A184

Vignette colors: 1.70fr, Blue. 2fr, Brown.

2000, Apr. 5 **Engr.**
694-695 A184 Set of 2 1.00 1.00

Millennium — A185

No. 696: a, Lobstermen on Newfoundland coast, 1904. b, Women on shore, 1905. c, World War I conscripts on ship Chicago, 1915. d, Soldiers in action at Souain Hill, 1915. e, Men walking on ice, 1923. f, Unloading cases of champagne to be smuggled to US, 1925. g, St. Pierre & Miquelon Pavilion at Colonial Expostion in Paris, 1931. h, Alcohol smugglers, 1933. i, Adm. Emile Muselier inspecting troops on ship Mimosa, 1942. j, World War II soldiers crossing bridge, 1945.

No. 697: a, Fishery employees, 1951. b, Fishing trawler, 1960. c, Visit of Gen. Charles de Gaulle, 1967. d, First television images, 1967. e, Port facilities, 1970. f, New high school, 1977. g, Resumption of stamp issuing, 1986. h, Voyage fo Eric Tabarly, 1987. i, Exclusive Economic Zone, 1992. j, New airport, 1999.

2000 **Litho.** ***Perf. 13x13¼***
696 Sheet of 10 8.00 8.00
a.-j. A185 3fr Any single .80 .80
697 Sheet of 10 5.00 5.00
a.-j. A185 2fr Any single .50 .50

Issue: No. 696, 6/21; No. 697, 12/6.

The Inger — A186

2000, Oct. 4 **Engr.** ***Perf. 13x13¼***
698 A186 5.40fr green 1.40 1.40

Boathouses in November — A187

2000, Oct. 4 ***Perf. 13x12¼***
699 Pair + central label 4.75 4.75
a. A187 3fr Hill .75 .75
b. A187 15.50fr Church 4.00 4.00

Christmas — A188

2000, Nov. 15 **Litho.** ***Perf. 13¼x13***
700 A188 3fr multi .80 .80

New Year 2001 — A189

2000, Dec. 27 **Litho.** ***Perf. 13x12¾***
701 A189 3fr multi .90 .90

Whale Type of 2000

Designs: 3fr, Orcinus orca. 5.70fr, Globicephala melaena.

2001, Jan. 24 Engr. ***Perf. 13x12¾***

702-703	A183	Set of 2	2.40	2.40

Landscape A190

2001, Jan. 21 Litho. ***Perf. 13***

704	A190	5.20fr multi	1.40	1.40

Plant Type of 1999

2001, Mar. 23 Litho. ***Perf. 13***

705	A174	3.80fr Vaccinium oxycoccos	1.00	1.00

Hay Gatherers A191

Denomination colors: 1.70fr, Red brown. 2fr, Lilac.

2001, Apr. 18

706-707	A191	Set of 2	.95	.95

Seasons A192

Designs: No. 708, 3fr, Autumn. No. 709, 3fr, Winter.

2001, June 20

708-709	A192	Set of 2	1.50	1.50

See Nos. 714-715.

Vestibules — A193

No. 710: a, Guillou House. b, Jugan House. c, Ile-aux-Marins town hall. d, Vogé House.

2001, July 25

710	Horiz. strip of 4	3.25	3.25
a.-d.	A193 3fr Any single	.80	.80

Anse du Gouvernement — A194

Houses and: a, Boat. b, Rocks near shore.

2001, Sept. 12 Engr. ***Perf. 13x12¼***

711	Horiz. pair, #a-b, + central label	5.50	5.50
a.-b.	A194 10fr Any single	2.75	2.75

Saint Pierre Pointe Blanche — A195

2001, Sept. 26 Litho. ***Perf. 13***

712	A195	5fr multi	1.40	1.40

The Marie-Thérèse — A196

2001, Sept. 26 Engr. ***Perf. 13x13¼***

713	A196	5.40fr green	1.40	1.40

Seasons Type of 2001

Designs: No. 714, 3fr, Spring. No. 715, 3fr, Summer.

2001, Oct. 17 Litho. ***Perf. 13***

714-715	A192	Set of 2	1.60	1.60

Commander Jacques Pepin Lehalleur (1911-2000) A197

2001, Nov. 14

716	A197	3fr multi	.80	.80

Christmas — A198

2001, Nov. 28

717	A198	3fr multi	.80	.80

SEMI-POSTAL STAMPS

Regular Issue of 1909-17 Surcharged in Red

✚ 5c

1915-17 Unwmk. ***Perf. 14x13½***

B1	A17	10c + 5c car rose & red	.80	.80
B2	A17	15c + 5c dl vio & rose ('17)	.80	.80

Curie Issue

Common Design Type

1938, Oct. 24 Engr. ***Perf. 13***

B3	CD80	1.75fr + 50c brt ultra	7.50	7.50

French Revolution Issue

Common Design Type

1939, July 5 Photo.

Name and Value Typo. in Black

B4	CD83	45c + 25c green	8.00	8.00
B5	CD83	70c + 30c brown	8.00	8.00
B6	CD83	90c + 35c red org	8.00	8.00
B7	CD83	1.25fr + 1fr rose pink	8.00	8.00
B8	CD83	2.25fr + 2fr blue	8.00	8.00
		Nos. B4-B8 (5)	40.00	40.00

Common Design Type and

Sailor of Landing Force — SP1

Dispatch Boat "Ville d'Ys" SP2

1941 Photo. ***Perf. 13½***

B8A	SP1	1fr + 1fr red	1.25
B8B	CD86	1.50fr + 3fr maroon	1.25
B8C	SP2	2.50fr + 1fr blue	1.25
		Nos. B8A-B8C (3)	3.75

Nos. B8A-B8C were issued by the Vichy government, and were not placed on sale in the colony.

Nos. 206A-206B were surcharged "OEUVRES COLONIALES" and surtax (including change of denomination of the 2.50fr to 50c). These were issued in 1944 by the Vichy government and not placed on sale in the colony.

Nos. 239, 246 With Additional Surcharge in Carmine

\+ 50c

ŒUVRES SOCIALES

✚

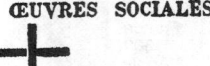

1942 Unwmk. ***Perf. 13½x13***

B9	A25	1fr + 50c	30.00	30.00
B10	A26	2.50fr + 1fr	30.00	30.00

Catalogue values for unused stamps in this section, from this point to the end of the section, are for Never Hinged items.

Red Cross Issue

Common Design Type

1944 ***Perf. 14½x14***

B13	CD90	5fr + 20fr dp ultra	1.00	1.00

Surtax for the French Red Cross and national relief.

Tropical Medicine Issue

Common Design Type

1950, May 15 Engr. ***Perf. 13***

B14	CD100	10fr + 2fr red brn & red	6.25	4.25

The surtax was for charitable work.

AIR POST STAMPS

Catalogue values for unused stamps in this section are for Never Hinged items.

Common Design Type

Perf. 14½x14

1942, Aug. 17 Photo. Unwmk.

C1	CD87	1fr dark orange	.45	.40
C2	CD87	1.50fr bright red	.55	.50
C3	CD87	5fr brown red	.80	.70
C4	CD87	10fr black	1.00	.90
C5	CD87	25fr ultra	1.10	1.00
C6	CD87	50fr dark green	1.75	1.50
C7	CD87	100fr plum	2.25	2.00
		Nos. C1-C7 (7)	7.90	7.00

Victory Issue

Common Design Type

1946, May 8 Engr. ***Perf. 12½***

C8	CD92	8fr deep claret	1.25	1.25

Chad to Rhine Issue

Common Design Types

1946, June 6

C9	CD93	5fr brown red	1.00	1.00
C10	CD94	10fr lilac rose	1.00	1.00
C11	CD95	15fr gray blk	1.50	1.50
C12	CD96	20fr violet	1.60	1.60
C13	CD97	25fr chocolate	2.25	2.25
C14	CD98	50fr grnsh blk	2.25	2.25
		Nos. C9-C14 (6)	9.60	9.60

Plane, Sailing Vessel and Coast — AP2

AP3

AP4

1947, Oct. 6

C15	AP2	50fr yel grn & rose	5.75	1.50
C16	AP3	100fr dk blue grn	10.00	2.25
C17	AP4	200fr bluish blk & brt rose	13.00	3.25
		Nos. C15-C17 (3)	28.75	7.00

UPU Issue

Common Design Type

1949, Oct. 1 Engr. ***Perf. 13***

C18	CD99	25fr multicolored	12.00	6.00

Liberation Issue

Common Design Type

1954, June 8

C19	CD102	15fr sepia & red	8.50	5.00

10th anniversary of the liberation of France.

Plane over St. Pierre Harbor — AP6

1956, Oct. 22

C20	AP6	500fr ultra & indigo	42.50	17.50

Dog and Village — AP7

Design: 100fr, Caravelle over archipelago.

1957, Nov. 4 Unwmk. ***Perf. 13***

C21	AP7	50fr gray, brn blk & bl	35.00	17.50
C22	AP7	100fr black & gray	14.00	7.00

Anchors and Torches — AP8

1959, Sept. 14 Engr. *Perf. 13*
C23 AP8 200fr dk pur, grn & cl 11.50 6.50

Approval of the constitution and the vote which confirmed the attachment of the islands to France.

Pitcher Plant — AP9

1962, Apr. 24 Unwmk. *Perf. 13*
C24 AP9 100fr green, org & car *8.50* 1.50

Gulf of St. Lawrence and Submarine "Surcouf" — AP10

Perf. 13½x12½
1962, July 24 Photo.
C25 AP10 500fr dk red & bl 100.00 75.00

20th anniv. of St. Pierre & Miquelon's joining the Free French.

Telstar Issue
Common Design Type

1962, Nov. 22 Engr. *Perf. 13*
C26 CD111 50fr Prus grn & bis 5.00 2.25

Arrival of Governor Dangeac, 1763 — AP11

1963, Aug. 5 Unwmk. *Perf. 13*
C27 AP11 200fr dk bl, sl grn & brn 19.50 8.50

Bicentenary of the arrival of the first French governor.

Jet Plane and Map of Maritime Provinces and New England — AP12

1964, Sept. 28 Engr. *Perf. 13*
C28 AP12 100fr choc & Prus bl 11.00 6.00

Inauguration of direct airmail service between St. Pierre and New York City.

ITU Issue
Common Design Type

1965, May 17
C29 CD120 40fr org brn, dk bl & lil rose 19.00 8.50

French Satellite A-1 Issue
Common Design Type

Designs: 25fr, Diamant rocket and launching installations. 30fr, A-1 satellite.

1966, Jan. 24 Engr. *Perf. 13*
C30 CD121 25fr dk brn, dk bl & rose cl 4.75 2.00
C31 CD121 30fr dk bl, rose cl & dk brn 4.75 2.00
a. Strip of 2, #C30-C31 + label 10.00 4.50

French Satellite D-1 Issue
Common Design Type

1966, May 23 Engr. *Perf. 13*
C32 CD122 48fr brt grn, ultra & rose claret 7.00 3.75

Arrival of Settlers — AP13

1966, June 22 Photo. *Perf. 13*
C33 AP13 100fr multicolored 11.00 5.00

150th anniv. of the return of the islands of St. Pierre and Miquelon to France.

Front Page of Official Journal and Printing Presses — AP14

1966, Oct. 20 Engr. *Perf. 13*
C34 AP14 60fr dk bl, lake & dk pur 10.50 4.00

Centenary of the Government Printers and the Official Journal.

Map of Islands, Old and New Fishing Vessels — AP15

Design: 100fr, Cruiser Colbert, maps of Brest, St. Pierre and Miquelon.

1967, July 20 Engr. *Perf. 13*
C35 AP15 25fr dk bl, gray & crim 19.00 12.00
C36 AP15 100fr multicolored 35.00 22.50

Visit of President Charles de Gaulle.

Speed Skater and Olympic Emblem — AP16

60fr, Ice hockey goalkeeper.

1968, Apr. 22 Photo. *Perf. 13*
C37 AP16 50fr ultra & multi 7.50 3.00
C38 AP16 60fr green & multi 8.50 4.50

10th Winter Olympic Games, Grenoble, France, Feb. 6-18.

War Memorial, St. Pierre — AP17

1968, Nov. 11 Photo. *Perf. 12½*
C39 AP17 500fr multicolored 22.50 10.00

World War I armistice, 50th anniv.

Concorde Issue
Common Design Type

1969, Apr. 17 Engr. *Perf. 13*
C40 CD129 34fr dk brn & olive 24.00 5.00

Scenic Type of Regular Issue, 1969.

Designs: 50fr, Grazing horses, Miquelon. 100fr, Gathering driftwood on Mirande Beach, Miquelon.

1969, Apr. 30 Engr. *Perf. 13*
Size: 47½x27mm
C41 A47 50fr ultra, brn & olive *11.00* 3.00
C42 A47 100fr dk brn, bl & sl *19.00* 6.00

L'Esperance Leaving Saint-Malo, 1600 — AP18

1969, June 16 Engr. *Perf. 13*
C43 AP18 200fr blk, grn & dk red *45.00* 17.50

Pierre Loti and Sailboats — AP19

1969, June 23
C44 AP19 300fr lemon, choc & Prus bl 50.00 20.00

Loti (1850-1923), French novelist and naval officer.

EXPO Emblem and "Mountains" by Yokoyama Taikan — AP20

34fr, Geisha, rocket and EXPO emblem, vert.

1970, Sept. 8 Engr. *Perf. 13*
C45 AP20 34fr dp cl, ol & ind 15.00 6.00
C46 AP20 85fr org, ind & car 22.50 12.50

EXPO '70 Intl. Exposition, Osaka, Japan, Mar. 15-Sept. 13.

Etienne François Duke of Choiseul and his Ships — AP21

Designs: 50fr, Jacques Cartier, ship and landing party. 60fr, Sebastien Le Gonrad de Sourdeval, ships and map of islands.

1970, Nov. 25
Portrait in Lake
C47 AP21 25fr lilac & Prus bl *17.50* 6.00
C48 AP21 50fr sl grn & red lil *22.50* 8.00
C49 AP21 60fr red lil & sl grn *27.50* 11.00
Nos. C47-C49 (3) *67.50* 25.00

De Gaulle, Cross of Lorraine, Sailor, Soldier, Coast Guard — AP22

1972, June 18 Engr. *Perf. 13*
C50 AP22 100fr lil, brn & grn 22.50 12.00

Charles de Gaulle (1890-1970), French pres.

Louis Joseph de Montcalm — AP23

Designs: 2fr, Louis de Buade Frontenac, vert. 4fr, Robert de La Salle.

1973, Jan. 1
C51 AP23 1.60fr multicolored 7.50 3.00
C52 AP23 2fr multicolored 8.50 4.00
C53 AP23 4fr multicolored 15.00 7.00
Nos. C51-C53 (3) 31.00 14.00

Transall C 160 over St. Pierre — AP24

1973, Oct. 16 Engr. *Perf. 13*
C54 AP24 10fr multicolored *35.00* 12.00

Arms and Map of Islands, Fish and Bird — AP25

1974, Nov. 5 Photo. *Perf. 13*
C55 AP25 2fr gold & multi 12.00 4.00

Copernicus, Kepler, Newton and Einstein — AP26

1974, Nov. 26 **Engr.**

C56	AP26	4fr multicolored	14.00	6.00

Nicolaus Copernicus (1473-1543), Polish astronomer.

Type of 1909, Cod and ARPHILA Emblem AP27

1975, Aug. 5 **Engr.** ***Perf. 13***

C57	AP27	4fr ultra, red & indigo	*16.00*	7.50

ARPHILA 75, International Philatelic Exhibition, Paris, June 6-16.

Judo, Maple Leaf, Olympic Rings AP28

1975, Nov. 18 **Engr.** ***Perf. 13***

C58	AP28	1.90fr red, blue & vio	*7.00*	4.00

Pre-Olympic Year.

Concorde — AP29

1976, Jan. 21 **Engr.** ***Perf. 13***

C59	AP29	10fr red, blk & slate	24.00	13.00

1st commercial flight of supersonic jet Concorde from Paris to Rio, Jan. 21.

A. G. Bell, Telephone and Satellite AP30

1976, June 22 **Litho.** ***Perf. 12½***

C60	AP30	5fr vio bl, org & red	8.00	5.00

Centenary of first telephone call by Alexander Graham Bell, Mar. 10, 1876.

Aircraft — AP31

1987, June 30 **Engr.** ***Perf. 13***

C61	AP31	5fr Hawker-Siddeley H. S. 748, 1987	1.90	1.90
C62	AP31	10fr Latecoere 522, 1939	3.50	3.50

Hindenburg — AP32

10fr, Douglas DC3, 1948-1988. 20fr, Piper Aztec.

1988-89 **Engr.** ***Perf. 13***

C63	AP32	5fr multicolored	1.40	1.40
C64	AP32	10fr multicolored	3.00	3.00
C65	AP32	20fr multicolored	6.50	6.50
		Nos. C63-C65 (3)	10.90	10.90

Issued: 20fr, May 31, 1989; others, June 22.

Flying Flea, Bird — AP33

1990, May 16 **Engr.**

C66	AP33	5fr multicolored	1.75	1.75

Piper Tomahawk — AP34

1991, May 29 **Engr.** ***Perf. 13***

C67	AP34	10fr multicolored	4.00	4.00

Radio-controlled Model Airplanes — AP35

1992, May 6

C68	AP35	20fr brown, red & org	8.00	8.00

Migratory Birds — AP36

1993-97 ***Perf. 13x12½***

C69	AP36	5fr Shearwater (Puffin)	1.90	1.90
C70	AP36	10fr Golden plover	3.75	3.75

Perf. 13x13½

C71	AP36	10fr Arctic Tern	4.25	4.25

Perf. 13

C72	AP36	15fr Courlis	6.25	6.25
C73	AP36	5fr Peregrine falcon, vert.	2.00	2.00
		Nos. C69-C73 (5)	18.15	18.15

Issued: #C69-C70, 5/12; #C71, 5/10/95; #C72, 5/15/96; #C73, 5/28/97.

Disappearance of the Flight of Nungesser and Coli, 70th Anniv. — AP37

1997, June 11

C74	AP37	14fr blk, grn bl & brn	5.50	5.50

Bald Eagle — AP38

1998-2001 **Engr.** ***Perf. 13***

C74A	AP38	5fr Buzzard	1.25	1.25
C75	AP38	10fr shown	3.50	3.50
C75A	AP38	15fr Heron	3.75	3.75
C76	AP38	20fr Wild duck	7.25	7.25

Issued: 5fr, 12/13/00; 10fr, 5/6; 15fr, 4/23/01; 20fr, 5/5/99.

AIR POST SEMI-POSTAL STAMPS

Stamps of the design shown above and stamp of Cameroun type V10 inscribed "St. Pierre-et-Miquelon" were issued in 1942 by the Vichy Government, but were not placed on sale in the Colony.

POSTAGE DUE STAMPS

Postage Due Stamps of French Colonies Overprinted in Red

ST - PIERRE M - on

1892 **Unwmk.** ***Imperf.***

J1	D1	5c black	47.50	47.50
J2	D1	10c black	12.00	12.00
J3	D1	15c black	12.00	12.00
J4	D1	20c black	12.00	12.00
J5	D1	30c black	12.00	12.00
J6	D1	40c black	12.00	12.00
J7	D1	60c black	47.50	47.50

Black Overprint

J8	D1	1fr brown	110.00	110.00
J9	D1	2fr brown	110.00	110.00
		Nos. J1-J9 (9)	375.00	375.00

These stamps exist with and without hyphen. See note after No. 59.

Postage Due Stamps of France, 1893-1924, Overprinted

SAINT-PIERRE
-ET-
MIQUELON

1925-27 ***Perf. 14x13½***

J10	D2	5c blue	.30	.30
J11	D2	10c dark brown	.30	.30
J12	D2	20c olive green	.50	.45
J13	D2	25c rose	.50	.45
J14	D2	30c red	.80	.65
J15	D2	45c blue green	.80	.65
J16	D2	50c brown vio	1.50	1.40
J17	D2	1fr red brn, *straw*	2.00	1.90
J18	D2	3fr magenta ('27)	7.00	6.25

Surcharged

SAINT-PIERRE
-ET-MIQUELON
2
francs
à percevoir

J19	D2	60c on 50c buff	1.40	1.40
J20	D2	2fr on 1fr red	2.25	2.25
		Nos. J10-J20 (11)	17.35	16.00

Newfoundland Dog — D3

1932, Dec. 5 **Typo.**

J21	D3	5c dk blue & blk	1.00	1.00
J22	D3	10c green & blk	1.00	1.00
J23	D3	20c red & blk	1.20	1.20
J24	D3	25c red vio & blk	1.30	1.30
J25	D3	30c orange & blk	2.50	2.50
J26	D3	45c lt blue & blk	3.25	3.25
J27	D3	50c blue grn & blk	5.50	5.50
J28	D3	60c brt rose & blk	7.75	7.75
J29	D3	1fr yellow brn & blk	16.00	16.00
J30	D3	2fr dp violet & blk	25.00	25.00
J31	D3	3fr dk brown & blk	30.00	30.00
		Nos. J21-J31 (11)	94.50	94.50

For overprints and surcharge see Nos. J42-J46.

Codfish — D4

1938, Nov. 17 **Photo.** ***Perf. 13***

J32	D4	5c gray black	.20	.20
J33	D4	10c dk red violet	.20	.20
J34	D4	15c slate green	.20	.20
J35	D4	20c deep blue	.20	.20
J36	D4	30c rose carmine	.30	.30
J37	D4	50c dk blue green	.40	.40
J38	D4	60c dk blue	.50	.50
J39	D4	1fr henna brown	1.00	1.00
J40	D4	2fr gray brown	2.00	2.00
J41	D4	3fr dull violet	3.50	3.50
		Nos. J32-J41 (10)	8.50	8.50

For overprints see Nos. J48-J67.

Type of Postage Due Stamps of 1932 Overprinted in Black

FRANCE LIBRE
F. N. F. L.

1942 **Unwmk.** ***Perf. 14x13½***

J42	D3	25c red vio & blk	190.00	190.00
J43	D3	30c orange & blk	190.00	190.00
J44	D3	50c blue grn & blk	850.00	850.00
J45	D3	2fr dp vio & bl blk	30.00	30.00

Same Surcharged in Black

3 fr
FRANCE LIBRE
F. N. F. L.

J46	D3	3fr on 2fr dp vio & blk, "F.N.F.L." omitted	12.00	12.00
a.		With "F.N.F.L."	7.00	7.00
		Nos. J42-J46 (5)	1,272.	1,272.

Postage Due Stamps of 1938 Overprinted in Black

NOËL 1941
F N F L

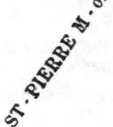

1942 ***Perf. 13***

J48	D4	5c gray black	14.00	14.00
J49	D4	10c dk red violet	14.00	14.00
J50	D4	15c slate green	14.00	14.00
J51	D4	20c deep blue	14.00	14.00
J52	D4	30c rose carmine	14.00	14.00
J53	D4	50c dk blue green	27.50	27.50
J54	D4	60c dark blue	60.00	60.00
J55	D4	1fr henna brown	70.00	70.00
J56	D4	2fr gray brown	75.00	75.00
J57	D4	3fr dull violet	82.50	82.50
		Nos. J48-J57 (10)	385.00	385.00

Christmas Day plebiscite ordered by Vice Admiral Emile Henri Muselier, commander of the Free French naval forces.

Postage Due Stamps of 1938 Overprinted in Black

FRANCE LIBRE F N F L

1942

J58	D4	5c gray black	30.00	30.00
J59	D4	10c dk red violet	6.00	6.00
J60	D4	15c slate green	6.00	6.00
J61	D4	20c deep blue	6.00	6.00
J62	D4	30c rose carmine	6.00	6.00
J63	D4	50c dk blue green	6.00	6.00
J64	D4	60c dark blue	7.50	7.50
J65	D4	1fr henna brown	15.00	15.00
J66	D4	2fr gray brown	17.50	17.50
J67	D4	3fr dull violet	400.00	400.00
		Nos. J58-J67 (10)	500.00	500.00

Catalogue values for unused stamps in this section, from this point to the end of the section, are for Never Hinged items.

Arms and Fishing Schooner — D5

1947, Oct. 6 **Engr.** ***Perf. 13***

J68	D5	10c deep orange	.20	.20
J69	D5	30c deep ultra	.20	.20
J70	D5	50c dk blue green	.20	.20
J71	D5	1fr deep carmine	.25	.20
J72	D5	2fr dk green	.30	.20
J73	D5	3fr violet	1.00	.45
J74	D5	4fr chocolate	1.00	.45
J75	D5	5fr yellow green	1.00	.45
J76	D5	10fr black brown	1.25	.60
J77	D5	20fr orange red	1.60	.80
		Nos. J68-J77 (10)	7.00	3.75

Newfoundland Dog — D6

1973, Jan. 1 **Engr.** ***Perf. 13***

J78	D6	2c brown & blk	.60	.25
J79	D6	10c purple & blk	.90	.40
J80	D6	20c grnsh bl & blk	1.50	.90
J81	D6	30c dk car & blk	3.00	2.00
J82	D6	1fr blue & blk	6.50	5.00
		Nos. J78-J82 (5)	12.50	8.55

France Nos. J106-J115 Overprinted "ST - PIERRE ET MIQUELON" Reading Up in Red

1986, Sept. 15 **Engr.** ***Perf. 13***

J83	D8	10c multicolored	.20	.20
J84	D8	20c multicolored	.20	.20
J85	D8	30c multicolored	.20	.20
J86	D8	40c multicolored	.20	.20
J87	D8	50c multicolored	.30	.20
J88	D8	1fr multicolored	.40	.30
J89	D8	2fr multicolored	.70	.60
J90	D8	3fr multicolored	1.10	.90
J91	D8	4fr multicolored	1.40	1.25
J92	D8	5fr multicolored	1.60	1.50
		Nos. J83-J92 (10)	6.30	5.55

PARCEL POST STAMPS

No. 65 Overprinted **COLIS POSTAUX**

1901 **Unwmk.** ***Perf. 14x13½***

Q1	A16	10c black, *lavender*	80.00	60.00
a.		Inverted overprint		

No. 66 Overprinted **Colis Postaux**

Q2	A16	10c red	11.00	10.00

Nos. 84 and 87 Overprinted

Colis Postaux

1917-25

Q3	A17	10c	1.50	1.50
a.		Double overprint		
Q4	A17	20c ('25)	1.25	1.25
a.		Double overprint	85.00	85.00

No. Q4 with Additional Overprint in Black **FRANCE LIBRE F. N. F. L.**

1942

Q5	A17	20c	550.00	550.00

ST. THOMAS AND PRINCE ISLANDS

sānt-'täm-əs and 'prin‸t‸s 'ī-lənds

Democratic Republic of Sao Tome and Principe

LOCATION — Two islands in the Gulf of Guinea, 125 miles off the west coast of Africa
GOVT. — Republic
AREA — 387 sq. mi.
POP. — 154,878 (1999 est.)
CAPITAL — Sao Tome

This colony of Portugal became a province, later an overseas territory, and achieved independence on July 12, 1975.

1000 Reis = 1 Milreis
100 Centavos = 1 Escudo (1913)
100 Cents = 1 Dobra (1977)

Catalogue values for unused stamps in this country are for Never Hinged items, beginning with Scott 353 in the regular postage section, Scott J52 in the postage due section, and Scott RA4 in the postal tax section.

Portuguese Crown — A1

King Luiz — A2

5, 25, 50 REIS:
Type I - "5" is upright.
Type II - "5" is slanting.

10 REIS:
Type I - "1" has short serif at top.
Type II - "1" has long serif at top.

40 REIS:
Type I - "4" is broad.
Type II - "4" is narrow.

Perf. 12½, 13½

1869-75 **Unwmk.** **Typo.**

1	A1	5r black, I	2.00	1.90
a.		Type II	2.00	1.90
2	A1	10r yellow, I	14.00	8.50
a.		Type II	17.50	10.50
3	A1	20r bister	3.50	2.75
4	A1	25r rose, I	1.25	1.10
a.		25r red	4.50	1.50
5	A1	40r blue ('75), I	4.75	3.50
a.		Type II	5.50	4.50
6	A1	50r gray grn, II	9.00	7.00
a.		Type I	15.00	14.00
7	A1	100r gray lilac	6.00	5.50
8	A1	200r red orange ('75)	8.25	6.25
9	A1	300r chocolate ('75)	8.25	7.00
		Nos. 1-9 (9)	57.00	43.50

1881-85

10	A1	10r gray grn, I	8.00	6.75
a.		Type II	9.50	6.00
b.		Perf. 13½, I	11.00	8.00
11	A1	20r car rose ('85)	3.50	3.00
12	A1	25r vio ('85), II	2.25	1.75
13	A1	40r yel buff, II	5.00	4.00
a.		Perf. 13½	6.00	4.50
14	A1	50r dk blue, I	2.50	2.25
a.		Type II	2.50	2.25
		Nos. 10-14 (5)	21.25	17.75

For surcharges and overprints see Nos. 63-64, 129-129B, 154.

Nos. 1-14 have been reprinted on stout white paper, ungummed, with rough perforation 13½, also on ordinary paper with shiny white gum and clean-cut perforation 13½ with large holes.

Typo., Head Embossed

1887 ***Perf. 12½, 13½***

15	A2	5r black	3.75	2.50
16	A2	10r green	4.25	2.50
17	A2	20r brt rose	4.25	3.00
a.		Perf. 12½	55.00	55.00
18	A2	25r violet	4.25	1.60
19	A2	40r brown	4.25	2.25
20	A2	50r blue	4.25	2.50
21	A2	100r yellow brn	4.25	2.00
22	A2	200r gray lilac	15.00	10.50
23	A2	300r orange	15.00	10.50
		Nos. 15-23 (9)	59.25	37.35

For surcharges and overprints see Nos. 24-26, 62, 65-72, 130-131, 155-158, 234-237.

Nos. 15, 16, 19, 21, 22, and 23 have been reprinted in paler colors than the originals, with white gum and cleancut perforation 13½. Value $1.50 each.

Nos. 16-17, 19 Surcharged:

5 rèis

a

b

c

1889-91 **Without Gum**

24	A2(a)	5r on 10r	35.00	20.00
25	A2(b)	5r on 20r	25.00	20.00
26	A2(c)	50r on 40r ('91)	225.00	70.00
		Nos. 24-26 (3)	285.00	110.00

Varieties of Nos. 24-26, including inverted and double surcharges, "5" inverted, "Cinoc" and "Cinco," were deliberately made and unofficially issued.

King Carlos

A6 A7

1895 **Typo.** ***Perf. 11½, 12½***

27	A6	5r yellow	.80	.60
28	A6	10r red lilac	1.25	1.00
29	A6	15r red brown	1.40	1.10
30	A6	20r lavender	1.50	1.10
31	A6	25r green	1.50	.75
32	A6	50r light blue	1.60	.70
a.		Perf. 13½	2.00	1.50
33	A6	75r rose	3.75	3.25
34	A6	80r yellow grn	8.00	6.25
35	A6	100r brn, *yel*	3.50	3.00
36	A6	150r car, *rose*	6.00	5.00
37	A6	200r dk bl, *bl*	7.75	6.50
38	A6	300r dk bl, *sal*	8.50	7.75
		Nos. 27-38 (12)	45.55	37.00

For surcharges and overprints see Nos. 73-84, 132-137, 159-165, 238-243, 262-264, 268-274.

1898-1903 ***Perf. 11½***

Name and Value in Black except 500r

39	A7	2½r gray	.30	.25
40	A7	5r orange	.30	.25
41	A7	10r lt green	.40	.30
42	A7	15r brown	2.00	1.75
43	A7	15r gray grn ('03)	1.10	1.10
44	A7	20r gray violet	.90	.50
45	A7	25r sea green	.70	.25
46	A7	25r carmine ('03)	1.10	.30
47	A7	50r blue	1.00	.50
48	A7	50r brown ('03)	4.50	4.50
49	A7	65r dull blue ('03)	11.00	9.00
50	A7	75r rose	10.00	6.50
51	A7	75r red lilac ('03)	2.50	1.40
52	A7	80r brt violet	5.00	5.00
53	A7	100r dk blue, *bl*	3.00	2.00
54	A7	115r org brn, *pink* ('03)	10.00	8.00
55	A7	130r brn, *straw* ('03)	10.00	6.00
56	A7	150r brn, *buff*	5.00	2.25
57	A7	200r red lil, *pnksh*	6.00	2.75
58	A7	300r dk blue, *rose*	8.00	5.00
59	A7	400r dull bl, *straw*('03)	13.00	8.50
60	A7	500r blk & red, *bl*('01)	10.00	5.00
61	A7	700r vio, *yelsh*('01)	16.00	12.00
		Nos. 39-61 (23)	121.80	83.10

For overprints and surcharges see Nos. 86-105, 116-128, 138-153, 167-169, 244-249, 255-261, 265-267.

Stamps of 1869-95 Surcharged in Red or Black

1902

On Stamp of 1887

62	A2	130r on 5r blk (R)	6.00	5.00
a.		Perf. 13½	32.50	32.50

On Stamps of 1869

63	A1	115r on 50r grn	10.00	7.50
64	A1	400r on 10r yel	25.00	12.00
a.		Double surcharge	75.00	50.00

On Stamps of 1887

65	A2	65r on 20r rose	6.25	4.50
a.		Perf. 13½	8.50	7.00
66	A2	65r on 25r violet	4.50	4.00
a.		Inverted surcharge	35.00	25.00
67	A2	65r on 100r yel brn	4.50	4.75
68	A2	115r on 10r blue grn	4.50	4.00
69	A2	115r on 300r orange	4.50	4.00
70	A2	130r on 200r gray lil	6.00	5.00
71	A2	400r on 40r brown	8.00	7.00
72	A2	400r on 50r blue	14.00	12.00
a.		Perf. 13½	110.00	90.00

On Stamps of 1895

73	A6	65r on 5r yellow	5.00	3.00
74	A6	65r on 10r red vio	5.00	3.00
75	A6	65r on 15r choc	5.00	3.00
76	A6	65r on 20r lav	5.00	3.00
77	A6	115r on 25r grn	5.00	3.00
78	A6	115r on 150r car, *rose*	5.00	3.00
79	A6	115r on 200r bl, *bl*	5.00	3.00
80	A6	130r on 75r rose	5.00	3.00
81	A6	130r on 100r brn, *yel*	5.00	3.50
a.		Double surcharge	30.00	20.00
82	A6	130r on 300r bl, *sal*	5.00	3.00
83	A6	400r on 50r lt blue	1.10	.95
a.		Perf. 13½	2.00	1.60
84	A6	400r on 80r yel grn	2.00	1.50

On Newspaper Stamp No. P12

85	N3	400r on 2½r brown	1.10	.95
a.		Double surcharge		
		Nos. 62-85 (24)	147.45	103.65

Reprints of Nos. 63, 64, 67, 71, and 72 have shiny white gum and clean-cut perf. 13½.

Stamps of 1898 Overprinted

1902

86	A7	15r brown	2.00	1.50
87	A7	25r sea green	2.00	1.25
88	A7	50r blue	2.25	1.25
89	A7	75r rose	5.00	3.50
		Nos. 86-89 (4)	11.25	7.50

No. 49 Surcharged in Black

1905

90	A7	50r on 65r dull blue	3.25	2.75

Stamps of 1898-1903 Overprinted in Carmine or Green

1911

91	A7	2½r gray	.25	.20
a.		Inverted overprint	15.00	11.00
92	A7	5r orange	.25	.20
93	A7	10r lt green	.25	.20
a.		Inverted overprint	15.00	12.00
94	A7	15r gray green	.25	.20
95	A7	20r gray violet	.25	.20
96	A7	25r carmine (G)	.60	.20
97	A7	50r brown	.30	.20
a.		Inverted overprint	15.00	12.00
98	A7	75r red lilac	.40	.20
99	A7	100r dk bl, *bl*	.75	.50
a.		Inverted overprint	17.50	14.00
100	A7	115r org brn, *pink*	1.50	.95
101	A7	130r brown, *straw*	1.50	.95
102	A7	200r red lil, *pnksh*	6.00	4.25
103	A7	400r dull blue, *straw*	2.00	1.00
104	A7	500r blk & red, *bl*	2.00	1.00
105	A7	700r violet, *yelsh*	2.00	1.00
		Nos. 91-105 (15)	18.30	11.25

King Manuel II — A8

Overprinted in Carmine or Green

1912 ***Perf. 11½, 12***

106	A8	2½r violet	.20	.20
a.		Double overprint	16.00	16.00
b.		Double overprint, one inverted	25.00	
107	A8	5r black	.20	.20
108	A8	10r gray green	.20	.20
a.		Double overprint	14.00	14.00
109	A8	20r carmine (G)	1.00	.75
110	A8	25r violet brn	.60	.45
111	A8	50r dk blue	.60	.55
112	A8	75r bister brn	.90	.55
113	A8	100r brn, *lt grn*	1.10	.50
114	A8	200r dk grn, *sal*	2.00	1.40
115	A8	300r black, *azure*	2.00	2.00
		Nos. 106-115 (10)	8.80	6.80

Stamps of 1898-1905 Overprinted in Black

1913

On Stamps of 1898-1903

116	A7	2½r gray	1.00	1.00
a.		Inverted overprint	15.00	15.00
b.		Double overprint	12.00	12.00
117	A7	5r orange	1.40	1.00
118	A7	15r gray green	22.50	17.50
a.		Inverted overprint	75.00	
119	A7	20r gray violet	1.50	1.50
a.		Inverted overprint	15.00	
120	A7	25r carmine	8.00	4.50
a.		Inverted overprint	30.00	
b.		Double overprint	30.00	
121	A7	75r red lilac	5.00	5.00
122	A7	100r bl, *bluish*	8.50	7.50
123	A7	115r org brn, *pink*	37.50	35.00
a.		Double overprint	75.00	60.00
124	A7	130r brn, *straw*	13.00	13.00
125	A7	200r red lil, *pnksh*	20.00	13.00
126	A7	400r dl bl, *straw*	14.00	12.50
127	A7	500r blk & red, *gray*	35.00	42.50
128	A7	700r vio, *yelsh*	47.50	40.00
		Nos. 116-128 (13)	214.90	194.00

On Provisional Issue of 1902

129	A1	115r on 50r grn	110.00	85.00
a.		Inverted overprint		
129B	A1	400r on 10r yel	600.00	500.00
130	A2	115r on 10r blue grn	2.75	2.50
a.		Inverted overprint	25.00	
131	A2	400r on 50r blue	75.00	75.00
132	A6	115r on 25r grn	2.00	1.75
a.		Inverted overprint	20.00	
133	A6	115r on 150r car, *rose*	42.50	40.00
a.		Inverted overprint	20.00	
134	A6	115r on 200r bl, *bl*	2.50	2.00
135	A6	130r on 75r rose	2.25	2.00
a.		Inverted overprint	25.00	
136	A6	400r on 50r lt bl	4.00	4.00
a.		Perf. 13½	20.00	10.00
137	A6	400r on 80r yel grn	5.00	4.25

Same Overprint on Nos. 86, 88, 90

138	A7	15r brown	2.00	1.75
139	A7	50r blue	2.25	2.00
140	A7	50r on 65r dl bl	16.00	12.00
		Nos. 138-140 (3)	20.25	15.75

No. 123-125, 130-131 and 137 were issued without gum.

Stamps of 1898-1905 Overprinted in Black

On Stamps of 1898-1903

141	A7	2½r gray	.60	.50
a.		Inverted overprint	9.00	
b.		Double overprint	11.00	11.00
c.		Double overprint inverted	30.00	
142	A7	5r orange	27.50	22.50
143	A7	15r gray green	1.75	1.50
a.		Inverted overprint	25.00	
144	A7	20r gray violet	250.00	200.00
a.		Inverted overprint	500.00	
145	A7	25r carmine	37.50	27.50
a.		Inverted overprint	75.00	
146	A7	75r red lilac	2.75	2.25
a.		Inverted overprint	5.00	
147	A7	100r blue, *bl*	2.25	1.75
148	A7	115r org brn, *pink*	10.00	8.00
a.		Inverted overprint	25.00	
149	A7	130r brown, *straw*	8.00	7.00
a.		Inverted overprint	25.00	
150	A7	200r red lil, *pnksh*	2.50	1.75
a.		Inverted overprint	10.00	
151	A7	400r dull bl, *straw*	10.00	8.00
152	A7	500r blk & red, *gray*	9.00	8.50
153	A7	700r violet, *yelsh*	9.00	8.50

On Provisional Issue of 1902

154	A1	115r on 50r green	200.00	150.00
155	A2	115r on 10r bl grn	2.50	2.25
156	A2	115r on 300r org	250.00	125.00
157	A2	130r on 5r black	300.00	125.00
158	A2	400r on 50r blue	200.00	90.00
159	A6	115r on 25r green	2.00	1.75
160	A6	115r on 150r car, *rose*	2.50	2.25
a.		"REPUBLICA" inverted	20.00	
161	A6	115r on 200r bl, *bl*	2.50	2.25
162	A6	130r on 75r rose	2.25	2.00
a.		Inverted surcharge	20.00	
163	A6	130r on 100r brn, *yel*	600.00	500.00
164	A6	400r on 50r lt bl	3.50	3.00
a.		Perf. 13½	17.50	6.00
165	A6	400r on 80r yel grn	2.50	2.25
166	N3	400r on 2½r brn	2.00	1.75

Same Overprint on Nos. 86, 88, 90

167	A7	15r brown	1.50	1.25
a.		Inverted overprint	20.00	
168	A7	50r blue	1.50	1.25
a.		Inverted overprint	20.00	
169	A7	50r on 65r dull bl	2.25	1.50
		Nos. 167-169 (3)	5.25	4.00

Most of Nos. 141-169 were issued without gum.

Common Design Types pictured following the introduction.

Vasco da Gama Issue of Various Portuguese Colonies Surcharged as

On Stamps of Macao

170	CD20	¼c on ½a bl grn	1.60	1.40
171	CD21	½c on 1a red	1.60	1.40
172	CD22	1c on 2a red vio	1.60	1.40
173	CD23	2½c on 4a yel grn	1.60	1.40
174	CD24	5c on 8a dk bl	1.90	1.60
175	CD25	7½c on 12a vio brn	3.00	3.00
176	CD26	10c on 16a bis brn	1.90	1.60
177	CD27	15c on 24a bister	1.90	1.60
		Nos. 170-177 (8)	15.10	13.40

On Stamps of Portuguese Africa

178	CD20	¼c on 2½r bl grn	1.10	1.00
179	CD21	½c on 5r red	1.10	1.00
180	CD22	1c on 10r red vio	1.10	1.00
181	CD23	2½c on 25r yel grn	1.10	1.00
182	CD24	5c on 50r dk bl	1.10	1.00
183	CD25	7½c on 75r vio brn	2.10	2.00
184	CD26	10c on 100r bis brn	1.10	1.00
185	CD27	15c on 150r bister	1.40	1.00
		Nos. 178-185 (8)	10.10	9.00

On Stamps of Timor

186	CD20	¼c on ½a bl grn	1.40	1.25
187	CD21	½c on 1a red	1.40	1.25
188	CD22	1c on 2a red vio	1.40	1.25
a.		Double surcharge	30.00	
189	CD23	2½c on 4a yel grn	1.40	1.25
190	CD24	5c on 8a dk bl	1.75	1.60
191	CD25	7½c on 12a vio brn	2.50	2.50
192	CD26	10c on 16a bis brn	1.40	1.40
193	CD27	15c on 24a bister	1.40	1.40
		Nos. 186-193 (8)	12.65	11.90
		Nos. 170-193 (24)	37.85	34.30

Ceres — A9

1914-26 Typo. ***Perf. 12x11½, 15x14***

Name and Value in Black

194	A9	¼c olive brown	.20	.20
195	A9	½c black	.20	.20
196	A9	1c blue green	.50	.40
197	A9	1c yellow grn ('22)	.20	.20
198	A9	1½c lilac brn	.30	.20
199	A9	2c carmine	.20	.20
200	A9	2c gray ('26)	.20	.20
201	A9	2½c lt violet	.20	.20
202	A9	3c orange ('22)	.20	.20
203	A9	4c rose ('22)	.20	.20
204	A9	4½c gray ('22)	.20	.20
205	A9	5c deep blue	.45	.35
206	A9	5c brt blue ('22)	.20	.20
207	A9	6c lilac ('22)	.20	.20
208	A9	7c ultra ('22)	.20	.20
209	A9	7½c yellow brn	.25	.20
210	A9	8c slate	.25	.20
211	A9	10c orange brn	.30	.25
212	A9	12c blue green ('22)	.40	.40
213	A9	15c plum	1.50	1.25
214	A9	15c brn rose ('22)	.25	.20
215	A9	20c yellow green	1.25	.75
216	A9	24c ultra ('26)	3.00	2.00
217	A9	25c choc ('26)	3.00	2.00
218	A9	30c brown, *grn*	1.75	1.40
219	A9	30c gray grn ('22)	.40	.30
220	A9	40c brown, *pink*	1.75	1.40
221	A9	40c turq bl ('22)	.40	.30
222	A9	50c orange, *sal*	4.00	3.00
223	A9	50c lt violet ('26)	.40	.30
224	A9	60c dk blue ('22)	.40	.30
225	A9	60c rose ('26)	1.50	.75
226	A9	80c brt rose ('22)	1.60	.50
227	A9	1e green, *blue*	4.00	3.00
228	A9	1e pale rose ('22)	2.50	1.40
229	A9	1e blue ('26)	2.00	1.00
230	A9	2e dk violet ('22)	2.75	1.50
231	A9	5e buff ('26)	11.50	7.50
232	A9	10e pink ('26)	19.00	14.00
233	A9	20e pale turq ('26)	60.00	40.00
		Nos. 194-233 (40)	127.80	87.25

Perforation and paper variations command a premium for some of Nos. 194-233.

For surcharges see Nos. 250-253, 281-282.

Preceding Issues Overprinted in Carmine

1915

On Provisional Issue of 1902

234	A2	115r on 10r green	1.75	1.60
235	A2	115r on 300r org	1.75	1.75
236	A2	130r on 5r black	4.00	2.75
237	A2	130r on 200r gray lil	1.40	1.25
238	A6	115r on 25r green	.60	.40
239	A6	115r on 150r car, *rose*	.60	.40
240	A6	115r on 200r bl, *bl*	.60	.40
241	A6	130r on 75r rose	.60	.40
242	A6	130r on 100r brn, *yel*	1.10	1.25
243	A6	130r on 300r bl, *sal*	1.00	.75

Same Overprint on Nos. 88 and 90

244	A7	50r blue	.70	.55
245	A7	50r on 65r dull bl	.70	.55
		Nos. 234-245 (12)	14.80	12.05

No. 86 Overprinted in Blue and Surcharged in Black

1919

246	A7	2½c on 15r brown	.60	.55

No. 91 Surcharged in Black

247	A7	½c on 2½r gray	3.00	2.75
248	A7	1c on 2½r gray	2.25	2.00
249	A7	2½c on 2½r gray	1.10	.65

No. 194 Surcharged in Blue

250	A9	½c on ¼c ol brn	2.00	1.75
251	A9	2c on ¼c ol brn	2.25	1.90
252	A9	2½c on ¼c ol brn	6.00	5.00

No. 201 Surcharged in Black

253	A9	4c on 2½c lt vio	.90	.75
		Nos. 246-253 (8)	18.10	15.35

Nos. 246-253 were issued without gum.

Stamps of 1898-1905 Overprinted in Green or Red

1920

On Stamps of 1898-1903

255	A7	75r red lilac (G)	.55	.50
256	A7	100r blue, *blue* (R)	.80	.75
257	A7	115r org brn, *pink* (G)	2.00	1.40
258	A7	130r brn, *straw* (G)	80.00	50.00
259	A7	200r red lil, *pnksh* (G)	2.00	1.00
260	A7	500r blk, & red, *gray* (G)	1.50	1.00
261	A7	700r vio, *yelsh* (G)	2.00	1.25

On Stamps of 1902

262	A6	115r on 25r grn (R)	1.00	.60
263	A6	115r on 200r bl, *bl* (R)	1.50	1.00
264	A6	130r on 75r rose (G)	2.00	1.50

On Nos. 88-89

265	A7	50r blue (R)	1.50	1.10
266	A7	75r rose (G)	10.00	7.00

On No. 90

267	A7	50r on 65r dl bl (R)	12.00	7.00
		Nos. 255-257,259-267 (12)	36.85	24.10

Nos. 238-243 Surcharged in Blue or Red

1923 **Without Gum**

268	A6	10c on 115r on 25r (Bl)	.70	.50
269	A6	10c on 115r on 150r (Bl)	.70	.50
270	A6	10c on 115r on 200r (R)	.70	.50
271	A6	10c on 130r on 75r (Bl)	.70	.50
272	A6	10c on 130r on 100r (Bl)	.70	.50
273	A6	10c on 130r on 300r (R)	.70	.50
		Nos. 268-273 (6)	4.20	3.00

Nos. 268-273 are usually stained and discolored.

Nos. 84-85 Surcharged

1925

274 A6 40c on 400r on 80r yel grn .90 .45
275 N3 40c on 400r on 2½r brn .90 .45

Nos. 228 and 230 Surcharged

1931

281 A9 70c on 1e pale rose 2.00 1.25
282 A9 1.40e on 2e dk vio 2.75 2.50

Ceres — A11

Perf. 12x11½

1934 Typo. Wmk. 232

283 A11 1c bister .20 .20
284 A11 5c olive brown .20 .20
285 A11 10c violet .20 .20
286 A11 15c black .20 .20
287 A11 20c gray .20 .20
288 A11 30c dk green .20 .20
289 A11 40c red orange .20 .20
290 A11 45c brt blue .30 .35
291 A11 50c brown .20 .20
292 A11 60c olive grn .30 .35
293 A11 70c brown org .30 .35
294 A11 80c emerald .30 .35
295 A11 85c deep rose 1.25 1.10
296 A11 1e maroon .55 .45
297 A11 1.40e dk blue 1.40 1.40
298 A11 2e dk violet 1.40 1.25
299 A11 5e apple green 4.50 2.50
300 A11 10e olive bister 10.00 5.00
301 A11 20e orange 40.00 20.00
Nos. 283-301 (19) 61.90 34.70

Common Design Types
Inscribed "S. Tomé"

1938 Unwmk. *Perf. 13½x13*
Name and Value in Black

302 CD34 1c gray green .20 .20
303 CD34 5c orange brown .20 .20
304 CD34 10c dk carmine .20 .20
305 CD34 15c dk violet brn .20 .20
306 CD34 20c slate .20 .20
307 CD35 30c rose violet .20 .20
308 CD35 35c brt green .20 .20
309 CD35 40c brown .20 .20
310 CD35 50c brt red vio .20 .20
311 CD36 60c gray black .20 .20
312 CD36 70c brown violet .20 .20
313 CD36 80c orange .25 .20
314 CD36 1e red 1.25 .60
315 CD37 1.75e blue 1.10 .80
316 CD37 2e brown car 12.00 4.00
317 CD37 5e olive green 12.00 5.00
318 CD38 10e blue violet 15.00 6.00
319 CD38 20e red brown 22.50 7.00
Nos. 302-319 (18) 66.30 25.80

Marble Column and Portuguese Arms with Cross — A12

1938 *Perf. 12½*

320 A12 80c blue green 1.50 1.00
321 A12 1.75e deep blue 6.00 3.00
322 A12 20e brown 32.50 16.00
Nos. 320-322 (3) 40.00 20.00

Visit of the President of Portugal in 1938.

Common Design Types
Inscribed "S. Tomé e Principe"

1939 *Perf. 13½x13*
Name and Value in Black

323 CD34 1c gray grn .20 .20
324 CD34 5c orange brn .20 .20
325 CD34 10c dk carmine .20 .20
326 CD34 15c dk vio brn .20 .20
327 CD34 20c slate .30 .20
328 CD35 30c rose violet .20 .20
329 CD35 35c brt green .20 .20
330 CD35 40c brown .30 .20
331 CD35 50c brt red vio .30 .20
332 CD36 60c gray black .30 .20
333 CD36 70c brown violet .30 .20
334 CD36 80c orange .30 .20
335 CD36 1e red .60 .45
336 CD37 1.75e blue 1.00 .45
337 CD37 2e brown car 1.60 1.10
338 CD37 5e olive green 4.00 2.00
339 CD38 10e blue violet 9.75 3.00
340 CD38 20e red brown 13.50 4.00
Nos. 323-340 (18) 33.45 13.40

— A13

UPU Symbols — A14

Designs: 5c, Cola Nuts. 10c, Breadfruit. 30c, Annona. 50c, Cacao pods. 1e, Coffee. 1.75e, Dendem. 2e, Avocado. 5e, Pineapple. 10e, Mango. 20e, Coconuts.

1948 Litho. *Perf. 14½*

341 A13 5c black & yellow .30 .30
342 A13 10c black & buff .40 .30
343 A13 30c indigo & gray 1.50 1.25
344 A13 50c brown & yellow 1.50 1.25
345 A13 1e red & rose 3.00 1.75
346 A13 1.75e blue & gray 4.00 3.25
347 A13 2e black & grn 3.00 1.50
348 A13 5e brown & lil rose 7.00 4.00
349 A13 10e black & pink 10.00 7.50
350 A13 20e black & gray 35.00 20.00
a. Sheet of 10, #341-350 90.00 90.00
Nos. 341-350 (10) 65.70 41.10

No. 350a sold for 42.50 escudos.

Lady of Fatima Issue
Common Design Type

1948, Dec. Unwmk.

351 CD40 50c purple 5.25 4.50

Catalogue values for unused stamps in this section, from this point to the end of the section, are for Never Hinged items.

1949 Unwmk. *Perf. 14*

352 A14 3.50e black & gray 6.50 4.00

UPU, 75th anniv.

Holy Year Issue
Common Design Types

1950 *Perf. 13x13½*

353 CD41 2.50e blue 2.75 1.50
354 CD42 4e orange 4.50 3.50

Holy Year Extension Issue
Common Design Type

1951 *Perf. 14*

355 CD43 4e indigo & bl gray + label 2.75 2.00

Stamp without label attached sells for less.

Medical Congress Issue
Common Design Type

1952 *Perf. 13½*

356 CD44 10c Clinic .30 .30

Joao de Santarem — A15

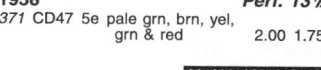

Jeronymos Convent A16

Portraits: 30c, Pero Escobar. 50c, Fernao de Po 1e, Alvaro Esteves. 2e, Lopo Goncalves. 3.50e, Martim Fernandes.

1952 Unwmk. Litho. *Perf. 14*
Centers Multicolored

357 A15 10c cream & choc .20 .20
358 A15 30c pale grn & dk grn .20 .20
359 A15 50c gray & dk gray .20 .20
360 A15 1e gray bl & dk bl .60 .20
361 A15 2e lil gray & vio brn .45 .20
362 A15 3.50e buff & choc .60 .20
Nos. 357-362 (6) 2.25 1.20

For overprints and surcharges see Nos. 423, 425, 428-429, 432, 450-457, 474-481.

1953 *Perf. 13x13½*

363 A16 10c dk brown & gray .20 .20
364 A16 50c brn org & org .50 .40
365 A16 3e blue blk & gray blk 2.00 .80
Nos. 363-365 (3) 2.70 1.40

Exhib. of Sacred Missionary Art, Lisbon, 1951.

Stamp Centenary Issue

Stamp of Portugal and Arms of Colonies — A17

1953 Photo. *Perf. 13*

366 A17 50c multicolored .75 .60

Centenary of Portugal's first postage stamps.

Presidential Visit Issue

Map and Plane — A18

1954 Typo. & Litho. *Perf. 13½*

367 A18 15c blk, bl, red & grn .20 .20
368 A18 5e brown, green & red 1.10 .80

Visit of Pres. Francisco H. C. Lopes.

Sao Paulo Issue
Common Design Type

1954 Litho.

369 CD46 2.50e bl, gray bl & blk .55 .35

Fair Emblem, Globe and Arms — A19

1958 Unwmk. *Perf. 12x11½*

370 A19 2.50e multicolored .60 .50

World's Fair at Brussels.

Tropical Medicine Congress Issue
Common Design Type

Design: Cassia occidentalis.

1958 *Perf. 13½*

371 CD47 5e pale grn, brn, yel, grn & red 2.00 1.75

Compass Rose — A20

Going to Church — A21

1960 Litho. *Perf. 13½*

372 A20 10e gray & multi 1.00 .40

500th death anniv. of Prince Henry the Navigator.

1960 *Perf. 14½*

373 A21 1.50e multicolored .40 .30

10th anniv. of the Commission for Technical Co-operation in Africa South of the Sahara (C.C.T.A.).

Sports Issue
Common Design Type

Sports: 50c, Angling. 1e, Gymnast on rings. 1.50e, Handball. 2e, Sailing. 2.50e, Sprinting. 20e, Skin diving.

1962, Jan. 18 Litho. *Perf. 13½*
Multicolored Design

374 CD48 50c gray green .20 .20
a. "$50 CORREIOS" omitted 50.00
375 CD48 1e lt lilac .60 .25
376 CD48 1.50e salmon .65 .25
377 CD48 2e blue .75 .35
378 CD48 2.50e gray green 1.00 .50
379 CD48 20e dark blue 3.00 1.60
Nos. 374-379 (6) 6.20 3.15

On No. 374a, the blue impression, including imprint, is missing.
For overprint see No. 449.

Anti-Malaria Issue
Common Design Type

Design: Anopheles gambiae.

1962 Unwmk. *Perf. 13½*

380 CD49 2.50e multicolored 1.10 .80

Airline Anniversary Issue
Common Design Type

1963 Unwmk. *Perf. 14½*

381 CD50 1.50e pale blue & multi .60 .50

National Overseas Bank Issue
Common Design Type

Design: Francisco de Oliveira Chamico.

1964, May 16 *Perf. 13½*

382 CD51 2.50e multicolored .70 .50

ITU Issue
Common Design Type

1965, May 17 Litho. *Perf. 14½*

383 CD52 2.50e tan & multi 1.50 1.00

Infantry Officer, 1788 — A22

35c, Sergeant with lance, 1788. 40c, Corporal with pike, 1788. 1e, Private with musket, 1788. 2.50e, Artillery officer, 1806. 5e, Private, 1811. 7.50e, Private, 1833. 10e, Lancer officer, 1834.

1965, Aug. 24 Litho. *Perf. 13½*

384 A22 20c multicolored .20 .20
385 A22 35c multicolored .20 .20
386 A22 40c multicolored .30 .20
387 A22 1e multicolored 1.10 .50
388 A22 2.50e multicolored 1.10 .50
389 A22 5e multicolored 1.60 1.25
390 A22 7.50e multicolored 2.00 1.90
391 A22 10e multicolored 2.50 2.00
Nos. 384-391 (8) 9.00 6.75

For overprints and surcharges see Nos. 424, 426-427, 435, 458-463, 482-485, 489-490.

National Revolution Issue
Common Design Type

Design: 4e, Arts and Crafts School and Anti-Tuberculosis Dispensary.

1966, May 28 Litho. *Perf. 11½*

392 CD53	4e multicolored	.75	.50

Navy Club Issue
Common Design Type

Designs: 1.50e, Capt. Campos Rodrigues and ironclad corvette Vasco da Gama. 2.50e, Dr. Aires Kopke, microscope and tsetse fly.

1967, Jan. 31 Litho. *Perf. 13*

393 CD54	1.50e multicolored	.90	.50
394 CD54	2.50e multicolored	1.40	.75

Valinhos Shrine, Children and Apparition A23

Cabral Medal, from St. Jerome's Convent A24

1967, May 13 Litho. *Perf. 12½x13*

395 A23	2.50e multicolored	.30	.25

50th anniv. of the apparition of the Virgin Mary to 3 shepherd children, Lucia dos Santos, Francisco and Jacinta Marto, at Fatima.

1968, Apr. 22 Litho. *Perf. 14*

396 A24	1.50e blue & multi	.45	.30

500th birth anniv. of Pedro Alvares Cabral, navigator who took possession of Brazil for Portugal.

Admiral Coutinho Issue
Common Design Type

Design: 2e, Adm. Coutinho, Cago Coutinho Island and monument, vert.

1969, Feb. 17 Litho. *Perf. 14*

397 CD55	2e multicolored	.50	.35

Vasco da Gama's Fleet — A25

Manuel Portal of Guarda Episcopal See — A26

1969, Aug. 29 Litho. *Perf. 14*

398 A25	2.50e multicolored	.75	.50

Vasco da Gama (1469-1524), navigator.

Administration Reform Issue
Common Design Type

1969, Sept. 25 Litho. *Perf. 14*

399 CD56	2.50e multicolored	.50	.35

For overprint see No. 430.

1969, Dec. 1 Litho. *Perf. 14*

400 A26	4e multicolored	.50	.35

500th birth anniv. of King Manuel I.

Pero Escobar, Joao de Santarem and Map of Islands — A27

Pres. Américo Rodrigues Thomaz — A28

1970, Jan. 25 Litho. *Perf. 14*

401 A27	2.50e lt blue & multi	.35	.30

500th anniv. of the discovery of St. Thomas and Prince Islands.

1970 Litho. *Perf. 12½*

402 A28	2.50e multicolored	.35	.30

Visit of Pres. Américo Rodrigues Thomaz of Portugal.

Marshal Carmona Issue
Common Design Type

Antonio Oscar Carmona in dress uniform.

1970, Nov. 15 Litho. *Perf. 14*

403 CD57	5e multicolored	.75	.55

Coffee Plant and Stamps — A29

Descent from the Cross — A30

Designs: 1.50e, Postal Administration Building and stamp No. 1, horiz. 2.50e, Cathedral of St. Thomas and stamp No. 2.

1970, Dec. *Perf. 13½*

404 A29	1e multicolored	.25	.20
405 A29	1.50e multicolored	.35	.20
406 A29	2.50e multicolored	.60	.20
	Nos. 404-406 (3)	1.20	.60

Centenary of St. Thomas and Prince Islands postage stamps.

1972, May 25 Litho. *Perf. 13*

407 A30	20e lilac & multi	2.50	1.90

4th centenary of publication of The Lusiads by Luiz Camoens.

Olympic Games Issue
Common Design Type

Track and javelin, Olympic emblem.

1972, June 20 *Perf. 14x13½*

408 CD59	1.50e multicolored	.35	.25

Lisbon-Rio de Janeiro Flight Issue
Common Design Type

Design: 2.50e, "Lusitania" flying over warship at St. Peter Rocks.

1972, Sept. 20 Litho. *Perf. 13½*

409 CD60	2.50e multicolored	.35	.25

WMO Centenary Issue
Common Design Type

1973, Dec. 15 Litho. *Perf. 13*

410 CD61	5e dull grn & multi	.60	.50

For overprint see No. 434.

Republic

Flags of Portugal and St. Thomas & Prince A31

1975, July 12 Litho. *Perf. 13½*

411 A31	3e gray & multi	.25	.20
412 A31	10e yellow & multi	.85	.55
413 A31	20e lt blue & multi	1.60	1.10
414 A31	50e salmon & multi	3.50	2.25
	Nos. 411-414 (4)	6.20	4.10

Argel Agreement, granting independence, Argel, Sept. 26, 1974.
For overprints see Nos. 675-678.

Man and Woman with St. Thomas & Prince Flag A32

1975, Dec. 21

415 A32	1.50e pink & multi	.20	.20
416 A32	4e multicolored	.30	.25
417 A32	7.50e org & multi	.60	.40
418 A32	20e blue & multi	1.40	.95
419 A32	50e ocher & multi	3.75	2.40
	Nos. 415-419 (5)	6.25	4.20

Proclamation of Independence, 12/7/75.

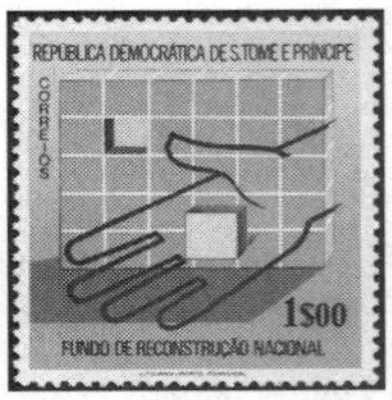
Chart and Hand — A33

1975, Dec. 21 Litho. *Perf. 13½*

420 A33	1e ocher & multi	.20	.20
421 A33	1.50e multicolored	.20	.20
422 A33	2.50e orange & multi	.30	.20
	Nos. 420-422 (3)	.70	.60

National Reconstruction Fund.

Stamps of 1952-1973 Overprinted

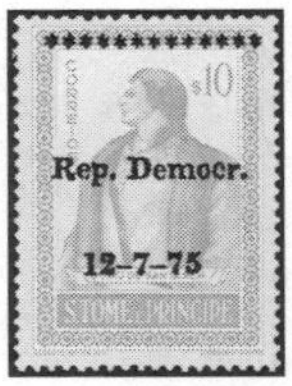

1977 Litho. *Perf. 13½, 14, 13*

423 A15	10c multi (#357)		
424 A22	20c multi (#384)		
425 A15	30c multi (#358)		
426 A22	35c multi (#385)		
427 A22	40c multi (#386)		
428 A15	50c multi (#359)		
429 A15	1e multi (#360)		
430 CD56	2.50e multi (#399)		
431 A27	2.50e multi (#401)		
432 A15	3.50e multi (#362)		
433 A26	4e multi (#400)		
434 CD61	5e multi (#410)		
435 A22	7.50e multi (#390)		
436 A20	10e multi (#372)		
	Nos. 423-436 (14)	15.00	

The 10c, 30c, 50c, 1e, 3.50e, 10e issued with glassine interleaving stuck to back.

Pres. Manuel Pinto da Costa and Flag A34

Designs: 3.50e, 4.50e, Portuguese Governor handing over power. 12.50e, like 2e.

1977, Jan. *Perf. 13½*

437 A34	2e yellow & multi	.20	.20
438 A34	3.50e blue & multi	.25	.20
439 A34	4.50e red & multi	.35	.20
440 A34	12.50e multicolored	.90	.40
	Nos. 437-440 (4)	1.70	1.00

1st anniversary of independence.

Some of the sets that follow may not have been issued by the government.

Peter Paul Rubens (1577-1640), Painter — A35

Details from or entire paintings: 1e (60x44mm), Diana and Calixto, horiz. 5e (60x36mm), The Judgement of Paris, horiz. 10e (60x28mm), Diana and her Nymphs Surprised by Fauns, horiz. 15e (40x64mm), Andromeda and Perseus. 20e (40x64mm), The Banquet of Tereo. 50e (32x64mm) Fortuna.

No. 447a, 20e, (30x40mm) like #445. No. 447b, 75e, (40x30mm) The Banquet of Tereo, diff.

1977, June 28 Litho. *Perf. 13½*

441 A35	1e multicolored		
442 A35	5e multicolored		
443 A35	10e multicolored		
444 A35	15e multicolored		
445 A35	20e multicolored		
446 A35	50e multicolored		
	Nos. 441-446 (6)	6.00	

Souvenir Sheet
Perf. 14

447 A35	Sheet of 2, #a.-b.	6.00	

See type A40 for Rubens stamps without "$" in denomination.

Ludwig van Beethoven — A36

Designs: a, 20e, Miniature, 1802, by C. Hornemann. b, 30e, Life mask, 1812, by F. Klein. c, 50e, Portrait, 1818, by Ferdinand Schimon.

1977, June 28 *Perf. 13½*

448 A36	Strip of 3, #a.-c.	6.00	

For overprint see No. 617.

No. 379 Ovptd. "Rep. Democr. / 12-7-77"

1977, July 12

449 CD48	20e multicolored	75.00	

Pairs of Nos. 358-359, 357, 362, 384-386 Overprinted Alternately in Black

a

b

1977, Oct. 19 Litho. ***Perf. 14, 13½***

450 A15(a) 3e on 30c multi
451 A15(b) 3e on 30c multi
452 A15(a) 5e on 50c multi
453 A15(b) 5e on 50c multi
454 A15(a) 10e on 10c multi
455 A15(b) 10e on 10c multi
456 A15(a) 15e on 3.50e multi
457 A15(b) 15e on 3.50e multi
458 A22(a) 20e on 20c multi
459 A22(b) 20c on 20c multi
460 A22(a) 35e on 35c multi
461 A22(b) 35e on 35c multi
462 A22(a) 40e on 40c multi
463 A22(b) 40e on 40c multi
Nos. 450-463 (14) 15.00

Centenary of membership in UPU. Overprints "a" and "b" alternate in sheets. Nos. 450-457 issued with glassine interleaving stuck to back.

These overprints exist in red on Nos. 452-453, 458-463 and on 1e on 10c, 3.50e and 30e on 30c. Value, set $200.

Mao Tse-tung (1893-1976), Chairman, People's Republic of China — A37

1977, Dec. Litho. ***Perf. 13½x14***

464 A37 50d multicolored 5.50
a. Souvenir sheet 7.50

For overprint see No. 597.

Lenin — A38

Russian Supersonic Plane — A39

Designs: 40d, Rowing crew. 50d, Cosmonaut Yuri A. Gagarin.

1977, Dec. ***Perf. 13½x14, 14x13½***

465 A38 15d multicolored .75
466 A39 30d multicolored 1.50
467 A39 40d multicolored 2.00
468 A38 50d red & black 2.50
a. Sheet of 4, #465-468
Nos. 465-468 (4) 6.75

60th anniv. of Russian October Revolution.
For overprints see Nos. 592-595.

Paintings by Rubens — A40

Designs: 5d, 70d, Madonna and Standing Child. 10d, Holy Family. 25d, Holy Family, diff. 50d, Madonna and Child.

1977, Dec. ***Perf. 13½, 13½x14 (50d)***
Size: 31x47mm (50d)

469 A40 5d multicolored
470 A40 10d multicolored
471 A40 25d multicolored
472 A40 50d multicolored
473 A40 70d multicolored
a. Sheet of 4, #469-471, #473 12.00
Nos. 469-473 9.00

Pairs of Nos. 357-359, 362, 384-385 Surcharged

c

#475

#477

#479

#481

#483, 485

1978, May 25 ***Perf. 14½, 13½***

474 A15 (a) 3d on 30c #358
475 A15 3d on 30c #358
a. Pair, #474-475
476 A15 (a) 5d on 50c #359
477 A15 5d on 50c #359
a. Pair, #476-477
478 A15 (a) 10d on 10c #357
479 A15 10d on 10c #357
a. Pair, #478-479
480 A15 (a) 15d on 3.50e #362
481 A15 15d on 3.50e #362
a. Pair, #480-481
482 A22 (a) 20d on 20c #384
483 A22 20d on 20c #384
a. Pair, #482-483
484 A22 (a) 35d on 35c #385
485 A22 35d on 35c #385
a. Pair, #484-485
Nos. 474-485 (12) 15.00

Overprints for each denomination alternate on sheet. Nos. 474-481 issued with glassine interleaving stuck to back.

Flag of St. Thomas and Prince Islands — A41

Designs: Nos. 487, 487a, Map of Islands, vert. No. 488, Coat of arms, vert.

1978, July 12 ***Perf. 14x13½, 13½x14***

486 A41 5d multi .40
487 A41 5d multi .40
a. Souvenir sheet, 50d 4.25
488 A41 5d multi .40
a. Strip of 3, #486-488 1.25

Third anniversary of independence. Printed in sheets of 9. No. 487a contains one imperf. stamp.

No. 386 Surcharged

1978, Sept. 3 Litho. ***Perf. 13½***

489 A22 40d on 40e #386
490 A22 40d on 40e #386
Nos. 489-490 (2) 5.00

Membership in United Nations, 3rd anniv.

Miniature Sheets

Tahitian Women with Fan, by Paul Gauguin A42

#491: b, Still Life, by Matisse. c, Barbaric Tales, by Gauguin. d, Portrait of Armand Roulin, by Van Gogh. e, Abstract, by Georges Braque.

#492: a, 20d, like #491c. b, 30d, Horsemen on the Beach, by Gauguin.

1978, Nov. 1 ***Perf. 14***

491 A42 10d Sheet of 9, #e., 2 each #a.-d. 6.00

Imperf

492 A42 Sheet of 3, #491a, 492a-492b 4.00

Intl. Philatelic Exhibition, Essen.
No. 492 has simulated perfs and exists with green margin and without simulated perfs and stamps in different order.

Miniature Sheet of 12

UPU, Centennial A43

Designs: Nos. 493a, Emblem, yellow & black. b, Emblem, green & black. c, Emblem, blue & black. d, Emblem, red & black. e, Concorde, balloon. f, Sailing ship, satellite. g, Monorail, stagecoach. h, Dirigible, steam locomotive. 50d, like #487g.

1978, Nov. 1 ***Perf. 14***

493 A43 #a.-d., 2 ea, #e.-h. 12.00
a.-d. 5d any single
e.-h. 15d any single

Souvenir Sheet

494 A43 50d multicolored 15.00

For overprint see No. 706.

Miniature Sheets

New Currency, Ist Anniv. — A44

Obverse and reverse of bank notes: #a, 1000d. b, 50d. c, 500d. d, 100d. e, Obverse of 50c, 1d, 2d, 5d, 10d, 20d coins.

1978, Dec. 15 ***Perf. 13½***
Sheets of 9

495 A44 5d #e., 2 each #a.-d.
496 A44 8d #e., 2 each #a.-d.
Nos. 495-496 (2) 5.00

World Cup Soccer Championships, Argentina — A45

Various soccer plays: No. 497a, Two players in yellow shirts, one in blue. b, Two players in blue shirts, one in white. c, Six players, referee. d, Two players. No. 498a, Seven players. b, Two players at goal. c, Six players.

1978, Dec. 15 ***Perf. 14***

497 A45 3d Block of 4, #a.-d.
498 A45 25d Strip of 3, #a.-c.
Nos. 497-498 (2) 6.00

Souvenir sheets of one exist.

Overprinted with Names of Winning Countries

No. 499b, ITALIA, 1934/38. c, BRASIL, 1958/62/70. d, ALEMANIA 1954/74. No. 500a, INGLATERRA, 1966. b, Vencedores 1978 / 1o ARGENTINA / 2o HOLANDA / 3o BRASIL. c, ARGENTINA 1978.

1979, June 1 Litho. ***Perf. 14***

499 A45 3d Block of 4, #a.-d.
500 A45 25d Strip of 3, #a.-c.
Nos. 499-500 6.50

Souvenir sheets of one exist.

Butterflies A46

Flowers — A47

Designs: 50c, Charaxes odysseus. 1d, Crinum giganteum. No. 503a, Quisqualis indicia.

b, Tecoma stans. c, Nerium oleander. d, Pyrostegia venusta. 10d, Hypolimnas salmacis thomensis. No. 505a, Charaxes monteiri, male. b, Charaxes monteiri, female. c, Papillio leonidas thomasius. d, Crenis boisduvali insularis. 25d, Asystasia gangetica. No. 507, Charaxes varanes defulvata. Nos. 508, Hibiscus mutabilis.

Perf. 15, 15x14½ (#503), 14½x15 (#505)

1979, June 8

501 A46 50c multicolored
502 A47 1d multicolored
503 A47 8d Block of 4, #a.-d.
504 A46 10d multicolored
505 A46 11d Block of 4, #a.-d.
506 A47 25d multicolored
Nos. 501-506 (12) 9.00

Souvenir Sheets

Perf. 15

507 A46 50d multicolored 9.00

Imperf

508 A47 50d multicolored *6.00*

No. 508 contains one 30x46mm stamp with simulated perforations.

Intl. Communications Day — A48

1979, July 6 ***Perf. 13***

509 A48 1d shown
510 A48 11d CCIR emblem
a. Pair, #509-510 + label
511 A48 14d Syncom, 1963
512 A48 17d Symphony, 1975
a. Pair, #511-512 + label
Nos. 509-512 (4) 6.00

Intl. Advisory Council on Radio Commmunications (CCIR), 50th anniv. (#510).

Intl. Year of the Child A49

Designs: 1d, Child's painting of bird. 7d, Young Pioneers. 14d, Children coloring on paper. 17d, Children eating fruit. 50d, Children from different countries joining hands.

1979, July 6

513 A49 1d multicolored
514 A49 7d multicolored
515 A49 14d multicolored
516 A49 17d multicolored

Size: 100x100mm

Imperf

517 A49 50d multicolored
Nos. 513-517 (5) 6.00

Souvenir Sheets

Sir Rowland Hill, 1795-1879 — A50

1979, Sept. 15 ***Perf. 15***

518 A50 25d DC-3 Dakota *15.00*

Perf. 14

519 A50 25d Graf Zeppelin, vert. *15.00*

1st Air Mail Flight, Lisbon to St. Thomas & Prince, 30th anniv. (#518), Brasiliana '79 Intl. Philatelic Exhibition and 18th UPU Congress (#519).

See Nos. 528-533 for other stamps inscribed "Historia da Aviancao."

For overprint see No. 700.

Albrecht Durer, 450th Death Anniv. — A51

Portraits: No. 520, Willibald Pirckheimer. No. 521, Portrait of a Negro. 1d, Portrait of a Young Man, facing right. 7d, Adolescent boy. 8d, The Negress Catherine. No. 525, Girl with Braided Hair. No. 526, Self-portrait as a Boy. No. 527, Feast of the Holy Family.

1979 ***Perf. 14***

Background Color

520 A51 50c blue green
521 A51 50c orange
522 A51 1d blue
523 A51 7d brown
524 A51 8d red
525 A51 25d lilac
Nos. 520-525 (6) 9.00

Souvenir Sheets

Perf. 13½

526 A51 25d lil, buff & blk 6.00

Perf. 13½x14

527 A51 25d blk, lil & buff 6.00

Christmas, Intl. Year of the Child (#527). No. 527 contains one 35x50mm stamp.

Issued: #520-526, Nov. 29; #527, Dec. 25.

For overprint see No. 591.

History of Aviation A52

1979, Dec. 21 ***Perf. 15***

528 A52 50c Wright Flyer I
529 A52 1d Sikorsky VS 300
530 A52 5d Spirit of St. Louis
531 A52 7d Dornier DO X
532 A52 8d Santa Cruz Fairey III D
533 A52 17d Space Shuttle
Nos. 528-533 (6) 5.00

See No. 518 for souvenir sheet inscribed "Historia da Aviancao."

History of Navigation A53

1979, Dec. 21

534 A53 50c Caravel, 1460
535 A53 1d Portuguese galleon, 1560
536 A53 3d Sao Gabriel, 1497
537 A53 5d Caravelao Navio Dos
538 A53 8d Caravel Redonda, 1512
539 A53 25d Galley Fusta, 1540
Nos. 534-539 (6) 5.00

Size: 129x98mm

Imperf

540 A53 25d Map of St. Thomas & Prince, 1602 4.00

Birds — A54

1979, Dec. 21 ***Perf. 14***

541 A54 50c Serinus rufobrunneus
542 A54 50c Euplectes aureus
543 A54 1d Alcedo leucogaster nais
544 A54 7d Dreptes thomensis
545 A54 8d Textor grandis
546 A54 100d Speirops lugubris
Nos. 541-546 (6) 6.00

Souvenir Sheet

Perf. 14½

547 A54 25d Treron S. thomae 4.00

No. 546 is airmail.

Fish A55

1979, Dec. 28 ***Perf. 14***

548 A55 50c Cypselurus lineatus
549 A55 1d Canthidermis maculatus
550 A55 5d Diodon hystrix
551 A55 7d Ostracion tricornis
552 A55 8d Rhinecanthus aculeatus
553 A55 50d Chaetodon striatus
Nos. 548-553 (6) 6.50

Souvenir Sheet

Perf. 14½

554 A55 25d Holocentrus axensionis 5.50

No. 553 is airmail.

Balloons — A56

Designs: 50c, Blanchard, 1784. 1d, Lunardi II, 1785. 3d, Von Lutgendorf, 1786. 7d, John Wise "Atlantic," 1859. 8d, Salomon Anree "The Eagle," 1896. No. 560, Stratospheric balloon of Prof. Piccard, 1931. No. 560A, Indoor demonstration of hot air balloon, 1709, horiz.

1979, Dec. 28 ***Perf. 15***

555 A56 50c multicolored
556 A56 1d multicolored
557 A56 3d multicolored
558 A56 7d multicolored
559 A56 8d multicolored
560 A56 25d multicolored
Nos. 555-560 (6) 6.50

Souvenir Sheet

Perf. 14

560A A56 25d multicolored 6.00

No. 560A contains one 50x38mm stamp.

Dirigibles A57

Designs: 50c, Dupuy de Lome, 1872. 1d, Paul Hanlein, 1872. 3d, Gaston brothers, 1882. 7d, Willows II, 1909. 8d, Ville de Lucerne, 1910. 17d, Mayfly, 1910.

1979, Dec. 28 ***Perf. 15***

561 A57 50c multicolored
562 A57 1d multicolored
563 A57 3d multicolored
564 A57 7d multicolored
565 A57 8d multicolored
566 A57 17d multicolored
Nos. 561-456 (6) 6.50

1980 Olympics, Lake Placid & Moscow A58

Olympic Venues: 50c, Lake Placid, 1980. Nos. 568, 572a, Mexico City, 1968. Nos. 569, 572b, Munich, 1972. Nos. 570, 572c, Montreal, 1976. Nos. 571, 572d, Moscow, 1980.

1980, June 13 **Litho.** ***Perf. 15***

567 A58 50c multicolored
568 A58 11d multicolored
569 A58 11d multicolored
570 A58 11d multicolored
571 A58 11d multicolored
Nos. 567-571 (5) 4.00

Souvenir Sheet

572 A58 7d Sheet of 4, #a.-d. 5.00

Proclamation Type of 1975 and

Sir Rowland Hill (1795-1879) — A59

Sir Rowland Hill and: 50c, #1. 1d, #415. 8d, #411. No. 571, #449. No. 572, #418.

1980, June 1 ***Perf. 15***

573 A59 50c multicolored
574 A59 1d multicolored
575 A59 8d multicolored
576 A59 20d multicolored
Nos. 573-576 (4) 4.00

Souvenir Sheet

Imperf

577 A32 20d multicolored 4.00

No. 577 contains one 38x32mm stamp with simulated perforations.

Moon Landing, 10th Anniv. (in 1979) A60

50c, Launch of Apollo 11, vert. 1d, Astronaut on lunar module ladder, vert. 14d, Setting up research experiments. 17d, Astronauts, experiment. 25d, Command module during reentry.

1980, June 13 ***Perf. 15***

578 A60 50c multicolored
579 A60 1d multicolored
580 A60 14d multicolored
581 A60 17d multicolored
Nos. 578-581 (4) 8.00

Souvenir Sheet

582 A60 25d multicolored 6.50

Miniature Sheet

Independence, 5th Anniv. — A61

#583: a, US #1283B. b, Venezuela #C942. c, Russia #3710. d, India #676. e, T. E. Lawrence (1888-1935). f, Ghana #106. g, Russia #2486. h, Algeria #624. i, Cuba #1318. j, Cape Verde #366. k, Mozambique #617. l, Angola #601. 25d, King Amador.

1980, July 12 ***Perf. 13***

583 A61 5d Sheet of 12, #a.-l. + 13 labels 15.00

Souvenir Sheet

Perf. 14

584 A61 25d multicolored 5.00

No. 584 contains one 35x50mm stamp. For overprint see No. 596.

No. 527 Ovptd. "1980" on Stamp and Intl. Year of the Child emblem in Sheet Margin

1980, Dec. 25 ***Perf. 14***

591 A51 25d on No. 527 6.00

Christmas.

Nos. 465-468a Overprinted in Black or Silver

1981, Feb. 2 ***Perf. 13½x14, 14x13½***

592 A38 15d on #465 (S)
593 A39 30d on #466 (S)
594 A39 40d on #467
595 A38 50d on #468
a. on No. 468a 16.00
Nos. 592-595 (4) 11.00

No. 584 Ovptd. with UN and Intl. Year of the Child emblems and Three Inscriptions

1981, Feb. 2 ***Perf. 14***

596 A61 25d on No. 584 5.00

Nos. 464-464a Ovptd. in Silver and Black "UNIAO / SOVIETICA / VENCEDORA / 1980" with Olympic emblem and "JOGOS OLIMPICOS DE MOSCOVO 1980"

1981, May 15 ***Perf. 13½x14***

597 A37 50d on #464 6.00
a. on #464a 8.00

Mammals — A65

1981, May 22 ***Perf. 14***

598 A65 50c Crocidura thomensis
599 A65 50c Mustela nivalis
600 A65 1d Viverra civetta
601 A65 7d Hipposioleros fuliginosus
602 A65 8d Rattus norvegicus
603 A65 14d Eidolon helvum
Nos. 598-603 (6) 6.50

Souvenir Sheet

Perf. 14½

604 A65 25d Cercopithecus mona 5.00

Shells — A66

No. 611: a, 10d, Bolinus cornutus, diff. b, 15d, Conus genuanus.

1981, May 22 ***Perf. 14***

605 A66 50c Haxaplex hoplites
606 A66 50c Bolinus cornutus
607 A66 1d Cassis tessellata
608 A66 1.50d Harpa doris
609 A66 11d Strombus latus
610 A66 17d Cymbium glans
Nos. 605-610 (6) 6.50

Souvenir Sheet

Perf. 14½

611 A66 Sheet of 2, #a.-b. 6.00

Johann Wolfgang von Goethe (1749-1832), Poet — A67

Design: 75d, Goethe in the Roman Campagna, by Johann Heinrich W. Tischbein.

1981, Nov. 14 ***Perf. 14***

612 A67 25d multicolored 4.00

Souvenir Sheet

613 A67 75d multicolored 4.00

PHILATELIA '81, Frankfurt/Main, Germany.

Tito — A68

1981, Nov. 14 ***Perf. 12½x13***

614 A68 17d Wearing glasses
615 A68 17d shown
a. Sheet of 2, #614-615
Nos. 614-615 (2) 3.00

Souvenir Sheet

Perf. 14x13½

616 A68 75d In uniform 4.00

Nos. 614-615 issued in sheets of 4 each plus label. For overprints see Nos. 644-646.

No. 448 Ovptd. in White

1981, Nov. 28 ***Perf. 13½***

617 A36 Strip of 3, #a.-c. 6.00

Wedding of Prince Charles and Lady Diana.

On No. 617 the white overprint was applied by a thermographic process producing a shiny, raised effect.

Overprint exists in gold, same value.

World Chess Championships — A69

Chess pieces: No. 618, Egyptian. No. 619, Two Chinese, green. No. 620, Two Chinese, red. No. 621, English. No. 622, Indian. No. 623, Scandinavian. 75d, Khmer.

No. 624: a, Anatoly Karpov. b, Victor Korchnoi.

1981, Nov. 28 **Litho.** ***Perf. 14***

618 A69 1.50d multicolored
619 A69 1.50d multicolored
620 A69 1.50d multicolored
621 A69 1.50d multicolored
622 A69 30d multicolored
623 A69 30d multicolored
624 A69 30d Pair, #a.-b.
Nos. 618-624 (7) 6.00

Souvenir Sheet

625 A69 75d multicolored 6.50

Nos. 618-623 exist in souvenir sheets of one. No. 624 exists in souvenir sheet with simulated perfs. Nos. 618-625 exist imperf.

No. 624 Ovptd. in red "ANATOLIJ KARPOV / Campeao Mundial / de Xadrez 1981"

1981, Dec. 10 ***Perf. 14***

627 A69 30d Pair, #a.-b. 4.00

Exists in souvenir sheet with simulated perfs or imperf.

Pablo Picasso — A70

Paintings: 14d, The Old and the New Year.

No. 629: a, Young Woman. b, Child with Dove. c, Paul de Pierrot with Flowers. d, Francoise, Claude, and Paloma.

No. 630: a, Girl. b, Girl with Doll. 75d, Father, Mother and Child.

1981, Dec. 10 ***Perf. 14x13½***

628 A70 14d multicolored
629 A70 17d Strip of 4, #a.-d.
630 A70 20d Pair, #a.-b.
Nos. 628-630 (3) 7.00

Souvenir Sheet

Perf. 13½

631 A70 75d multicolored 15.00

Intl. Year of the Child. Christmas (#628, 631). No. 630 is airmail.

Nos. 628, 629a-629d, 630a-630b exist in souvenir sheets of one. No. 631 contains one 50x60mm stamp.

See Nos. 683-685.

Intl. Year of the Child — A71

Paintings: No. 632: a, Girl with Dog, by Thomas Gainsborough. b, Miss Bowles, by Sir Joshua Reynolds. c, Sympathy, by Riviere. d, Master Simpson, by Devis. e. Two Boys with Dogs, by Gainsborough.

No. 633: a, Girl feeding cat. b, Girl wearing cat mask. c, White cat. d, Cat wearing red bonnet. e, Girl teaching cat to read.

No. 634: a, Boy and Dog, by Picasso. b, Clipper, by Picasso.

No. 635: a, Two white cats. b, Himalayan cat.

1981, Dec. 30 ***Perf. 14***

632 A71 1.50d Strip of 5, #a.-e.
633 A71 1.50d Strip of 5, #a.-e.
634 A71 50d Pair, #a.-b.
635 A71 50d Pair, #a.-b. + label
Nos. 632-635 (14) 15.00

Souvenir Sheets

Perf. 13½

636 A71 75d Girl with dog 7.50
637 A71 75d Girl with cat 7.50

Nos. 636-637 contain one 30x40mm stamp.

2nd Central Africa Games, Luanda, Angola — A73

No. 638: a, Shot put. b, Discus. c, High jump. d, Javelin.

50d, Team handball. 75d, Runner.

1981, Dec. 30 ***Perf. 13½x14***

638 A73 17d Strip of 4, a.-d.
639 A73 50d multicolored
Nos. 638-639 (5) 6.75

Souvenir Sheet

640 A73 75d multicolored 7.00

World Food Day — A74

No. 641: a, Ananas sativus. b, Colocasia esculenta. c, Artocarbus altilis.

No. 642: a, Mangifera indica. b, Theobroma cacao. c, Coffea arabica. 75d, Musa sapientum.

1981, Dec. 30

641 A74 11d Strip of 3, #a.-c.
642 A74 30d Strip of 3, #a.-c.
Nos. 641-642 (6) 6.00

Souvenir Sheet

643 A74 75d multicolored 4.00

Nos. 614-616 Ovptd. in Black

1982, May 25 ***Perf. 12½x13***

644 A68 17d on #614
645 A68 17d on #615
a. On #615a 8.00
Nos. 644-645 (2) 6.00

Souvenir Sheet

Perf. 14

646 A68 75d on #616 8.00

World Cup Soccer Championships, Spain — A75

Emblem and: No. 647: a, Goalie in blue shirt jumping to catch ball. b, Two players, yellow, red shirts. c, Two players, black shirts. d, Goalie in green shirtcatching ball.

No. 648: a, Player dribbling. b, Goalie facing opponent.

No. 649, Goalie catching ball from emblem in front of goal. No. 650, Like #649 with continuous design.

1982, June 21 ***Perf. 13½x14***

647 A75 15d Strip of 4, #a.-d.
648 A75 25d Pair, #a.-b.
Nos. 647-648 (6) 7.50

Souvenir Sheets

649 A75 75d multicolored
650 A75 75d multicolored
Nos. 649-650 (2) 7.50

Nos. 648a-648b are airmail. Nos. 647a-647d, 648a-648b exist in souvenir sheets of one.

A76 A77

Transportation: No. 651, Steam locomotive, TGV train. No. 652, Propeller plane and Concorde.

1982, June 21 ***Perf. 12½x13***

651 A76 15d multicolored
652 A76 15d multicolored
a. Souv. sheet of 2, #651-652 15.00
Nos. 651-652 (2) 12.00

PHILEXFRANCE '82.

1982, July 31

653 A77 25d multicolored 6.00

Robert Koch, discovery of tuberculosis bacillus, cent.

Goethe, 150th Anniv. of Death A78

1982, July 31 ***Perf. 13x12½***

654 A78 50d multicolored 6.00

Souvenir Sheet

655 A78 10d like #654 6.00

A79 A80

1982, July 31 ***Perf. 12½x13***

656 A79 75d multicolored 5.00

Souvenir Sheet

657 A79 10d Sheet of 1 6.00
657A A79 10d Sheet of 2, purple & multi 7.50

Princess Diana, 21st birthday. No. 657A exists with red violet inscriptions and different central flower.

1982, July 31

Boy Scouts, 75th Anniv.: 15d, Cape of Good Hope #178-179. 30d, Lord Baden-Powell, founder of Boy Scouts.

658 A80 15d multicolored
659 A80 30d multicolored
a. Souv. sheet, #658-659 + label 7.00
Nos. 658-659 (2) 5.00

Nos. 658-659 exits in sheets of 4 each plus label.

A81 A82

Caricatures by Picasso - #660: a, Musicians. b, Stravinsky.

1982, July 31

660 A81 30d Pair, #a.-b. 5.00

Souvenir Sheet

661 A81 5d like #660b 10.00

Igor Stravinsky (1882-1971), composer.

1982, July 31

George Washington, 250th Anniv. of Birth: Nos. 662, 663b, Washington, by Gilbert Stuart. Nos. 663, 663c, Washington, by Roy Lichtenstein.

662 A82 30d multicolored
663 A82 30d blk & pink
Nos. 662-663 (2) 5.00

Souvenir Sheet

663A A82 5d Sheet of 2, #b.-c. 10.00

Dinosaurs — A83

1982, Nov. 30 ***Perf. 14x13½***

664 A83 6d Parasaurolophus
665 A83 16d Stegosaurus
666 A83 16d Triceratops
667 A83 16d Brontosaurus
668 A83 16d Tyrannosaurus rex
669 A83 50d Dimetrodon
Nos. 664-669 (6) 10.00

Souvenir Sheet

a, 25d, Pteranodon. b, 50d, Stenopterygius.

670 A83 Sheet of 2, #a.-b. 7.50

Charles Darwin, cent. of death (#670).

Explorers A84

Departure of Marco Polo from Venice — A85

Explorers and their ships: 50c, Thor Heyerdahl, Kon-tiki.

No. 672: a, Magellan, Carrack. b, Drake, Golden Hind. c, Columbus, Santa Maria. d, Leif Eriksson, Viking longship.

50d, Capt. Cook, Endeavour.

1982, Dec. 21 **Litho.**

671 A84 50c multicolored
672 A84 18d Strip of 4, #a.-d.
673 A84 50d multicolored
Nos. 671-673 (6) 7.50

Souvenir Sheet

674 A85 75d multicolored 4.00

Nos. 411-414 Ovptd. with Assembly Emblem and "2o ANIVERSARIO DA 1a ASSEMBLEIA DA J.M.L.S.T.P." in Silver

1982, Dec. 24 ***Perf. 13½x14***

675 A31 3d on #411
676 A31 10d on #412
677 A31 20d on #413
678 A31 50d on #414
Nos. 675-678 (4) 6.00

MLSTP 3rd Assembly A86

1982, Dec. 24 ***Perf. 13½x14***

679 A86 8d bl & multi
680 A86 12d grn & multi
681 A86 16d brn org & multi
682 A86 30d red lilac & multi
Nos. 679-682 (4) 6.00

Picasso Painting Type of 1981

Designs: No. 683a, Lola. b, Aunt Pepa. c, Mother. d, Lola with Mantilla.

No. 684: a, Corina Romeu. b, The Aperitif. 75d, Holy Family in Egypt, horiz.

1982, Dec. 24

683 A70 18d Strip of 4, #a.-d.
684 A70 25d Pair, #a.-b.
Nos. 683-684 (6) 7.00

Souvenir Sheet

Perf. 14x13½

685 A70 75d multicolored 50.00

Intl. Women's Year (#683-684), Christmas (#685).

Locomotives — A87

9d, Class 231K, France, 1941.

No. 687: a, 1st steam locomotive, Great Britain, 1825. b, Class 59, Africa, 1947. c, William Mason, US, 1850. d, Mallard, Great Britain, 1938.

50d, Henschel, Portugal, 1929. 75d, Locomotive barn, Swindon, Great Britain.

1982, Dec. 31 ***Perf. 14x13½***

686 A87 9d multicolored
687 A87 16d Strip of 4, #a.-d.
688 A87 50d multicolored
Nos. 686-688 (6) 7.50

Souvenir Sheet

689 A87 75d multicolored 4.00

Easter — A88

Paintings: No. 690: a, St. Catherine, by Raphael. b, St. Margaret, by Raphael.

No. 691: a, Young Man with a Pointed Beard, by Rembrandt. b, Portrait of a Young Woman, by Rembrandt.

No. 692: a, Rondo (Dance of the Italian Peasants), by Rubens, horiz. b, The Garden of Love, by Rubens, horiz.

No. 693, Samson and Delilah, by Rubens. No. 694, Descent from the Cross, by Rubens.

No. 695: a, Elevation of the Cross, by Rembrandt. b, Descent from the Cross, by Rembrandt.

Nos. 696a, 697, The Crucifixion, by Raphael. Nos. 696b, 698, The Transfiguration, by Raphael.

1983, May 9 ***Perf. 13½x14, 14x13½***

690 A88 16d Pair, #a.-b.
691 A88 16d Pair, #a.-b.
692 A88 16d Pair, #a.-b.
693 A88 18d multicolored
694 A88 18d multicolored
695 A88 18d Pair, #a.-b.
696 A88 18d Pair, #a.-b.
Nos. 690-696 (12) 25.00

Souvenir Sheets

697 A88 18d vio & multi 10.00
698 A88 18d multicolored 10.00

Souvenir sheets containing Nos. 690a-690b, 691a-691b, 692a-692b, 693, 694, 695a-695b exist.

BRASILIANA '83, Rio de Janeiro — A89

Santos-Dumont dirigibles: No. 699a, #5. b, #14 with airplane.

1983, July 29 **Litho.** ***Perf. 13½***

699 A89 25d Pair, #a.-b. 3.00

First manned flight, bicent.

No. 519 Overprinted with Various Designs

1983, July 29 **Litho.** ***Perf. 14***

Souvenir Sheet

700 A50 25d multicolored 100.00

BRASILIANA '83.

First Manned Flight, Bicent. — A90

No. 701: a, Wright Flyer No. 1, 1903. b, Alcock & Brown Vickers Vimy, 1919.
No. 702: a, Bleriot monoplane, 1909. b, Boeing 747, 1983.
No. 703: a, Graf Zeppelin, 1929. b, Montgolfiere brother's balloon, 1783. No. 704, Pierre Tetu-Brissy. 60d, Flight of Vincent Lunardi's second balloon, vert.

1983, Sept. 16 ***Perf. 14x13½***

701 A90 18d Pair, #a.-b.
702 A90 18d Pair, #a.-b.
703 A90 20d Pair, #a.-b.
704 A90 20d multicolored
Nos. 701-704 (7) 7.50

Souvenir Sheet

Perf. 13½x14

705 A90 60d multicolored 4.00

Individual stamps from Nos. 701-704 exist in souvenir sheets of 1.

Nos. 493e, 493a, 493e (#706a) and 493g, 493c, 493g (#706b) Ovptd. in Gold with UPU and Philatelic Salon Emblems and:
"SALON DER PHILATELIE ZUM / XIX WELTPOSTKONGRESS / HAMBURG 1984" Across Strips of Three Stamps
Nos. 493f, 493b, 493f (#706c) 493h, 493d, 493h (#706d) Ovptd. in Gold with UPU and Philatelic Salon Emblems and:
"19TH CONGRESSO DA / UNIAO POSTAL UNIVERSAL / HAMBURGO 1984" Across Strips of Three Stamps

1983, Dec. 24 ***Perf. 14***

706 A43 Sheet of 12, #a.-d. *15.00*

Overprint is 91x30mm. Exists imperf with silver overprint.

Christmas — A91

Paintings: No. 707, Madonna of the Promenade, 1518, by Raphael. No. 708, Virgin of Guadalupe, 1959, by Salavador Dali.

1983, Dec. 24 ***Perf. 12½x13***

707 A91 30d multicolored
708 A91 30d multicolored
Nos. 707-708 (2) 6.00

Nos. 707-708 exist in souvenir sheets of 1.

Automobiles — A92

#709: a, Renault, 1912. b, Rover Phaeton, 1907.
#710: a, Morris, 1913. b, Delage, 1910.
#711: a, Mercedes Benz, 1927. b, Mercedes Coupe, 1936.
#712: a, Mercedes Cabriolet, 1924. b, Mercedes Simplex, 1902.
75d, Peugeot Daimler, 1894.

1983, Dec. 28 ***Perf. 14x13½***

709 A92 12d Pair, #a.-b.
710 A92 12d Pair, #a.-b.
711 A92 20d Pair, #a.-b.
712 A92 20d Pair, #a.-b.
Nos. 709-712 (8) 9.00

Souvenir Sheet

713 A92 75d multicolored 5.00

Nos. 709-712 exist as souvenir sheets. No. 713 contains one 50x41mm stamp.

Medicinal Plants — A93

1983, Dec. 28 ***Perf. 13½***

714 A93 50c Cymbopogon citratus
715 A93 1d Adenoplus breviflorus
716 A93 5.50d Bryophillum pinatum
717 A93 15.50d Buchholzia coriacea
718 A93 16d Hiliotropium indicum
719 A93 20d Mimosa pigra
720 A93 46d Piperonia pallucila
721 A93 50d Achyranthes aspera
Nos. 714-721 (8) 9.00

1984 Olympics, Sarajevo and Los Angeles A94

#722, Pairs' figure skating.
#723: a, Downhill skiing. b, Speed skating. c, Ski jumping.
#724, Equestrian.
#725: a, Cycling. b, Rowing. c, Hurdling.
#726: a, Bobsled. b, Women's archery.

1983, Dec. 29 ***Perf. 13½x14***

722 A94 16d multicolored
723 A94 16d Strip of 3, #a.-c.
724 A94 18d multicolored
725 A94 18d Strip of 3, #a.-c.
Nos. 722-725 (8) 7.50

Souvenir Sheet

726 A94 30d Sheet of 2, #a.-b. 4.00

Souvenir sheets of 2 exist containing Nos. 722 and 723b, 723a and 723c, 724 and 725b, 725a and 725c.

Birds — A95

50c, Spermestes cucullatus. 1d, Xanthophilus princeps. 1.50d, Thomasophantes sanctithomae. 2d, Quelea erythrops. 3d, Textor velatus peixotoi. 4d, Anabathmis hartlaubii. 5.50d, Serinus mozambicus santhome. 7d, Estrilda astrild angolensis. 10d,Horizorhinus dohrni. 11d, Zosterops ficedulinus. 12d, Prinia molleri. 14d, Chrysococcyx cupreus insularum. 15.50d, Halcyon malimhicus dryas. 16d, Turdus olivaceofuscus. 17d, Oriolus crassirostris. 18.50d, Dicrurus modestus. 20d, Columba thomensis. 25d, Stigmatopelia senegalensis thome. 30d, Chaetura thomensis. 42d, Onychognatus fulgidus. 46d, Lamprotornis ornatus. 100d, Tyto alba thomenis.

1983, Dec. 30 ***Perf. 13½***

727 A95 50c multi
728 A95 1d multi
729 A95 1.50d multi
730 A95 2d multi
731 A95 3d multi
732 A95 4d multi
733 A95 5.50d multi
734 A95 7d multi
735 A95 10d multi

Size: 30x43mm

736 A95 11d multi
737 A95 12d multi
738 A95 14d multi
739 A95 15.50d multi
740 A95 16d multi
741 A95 17d multi
742 A95 18.50d multi
743 A95 20d multi
744 A95 25d multi

Size: 31x47mm

Perf. 13½x14

745 A95 30d multi
746 A95 42d multi
747 A95 46d multi
748 A95 100d multi
Nos. 727-748 (22) 25.00

Souvenir Sheet

ESPANA '84, Madrid — A96

Paintings: a, 15.50d, Paulo Riding Donkey, by Picasso. b, 16d, Abstract, by Miro. c, 18.50d, My Wife in the Nude, by Dali.

1984, Apr. 27 ***Perf. 13½x14***

749 A96 Sheet of 3, #a.-c. 6.00

LUBRAPEX '84, Lisbon — A97

Children's drawings: 16d, Children watching play. 30d, Adults.

1984, May 9 ***Perf. 13½***

750 A97 16d multicolored
751 A97 30d multicolored
Nos. 750-751 (2) 5.00

Intl. Maritime Organization, 25th Anniv. — A98

Ships: Nos. 752a, 753a, Phoenix, 1869. 752b, 753b, Hamburg, 1893. 752c, 753c, Prince Heinrich, 1900.
No. 754: a, Leopold, 1840. b, Stadt Schaffhausen, 1851. c, Crown Prince, 1890. d, St. Gallen, 1905.
No. 755: a, Elise, 1816. b, De Zeeuw, 1824. c, Friedrich Wilhelm, 1827. d, Packet Hansa.
No. 756: a, Savannah, 1818. b, Chaperone, 1884. c, Alida, 1847. d, City of Worcester, 1881.
No. 757, Ferry, Lombard Bridge, Hamburg, c. 1900. No. 758, Train, coaches on bridge, c. 1880, vert. No. 759, Windmill, bridge, vert. No. 760, Queen of the West. No. 761, Bremen. No. 762, Union.

1984, June 19 Litho. ***Perf. 14x13½***

752 A98 50c Strip of 3, #a.-c.
753 A98 50c Strip of 3, #a.-c.
754 A98 7d Piece of 4, #a.-d.
e. Souv. sheet of 2, #754a-754b
f. Souv. sheet of 2, #754c-754d
755 A98 8d Piece of 4, #a.-d.
e. Souv. sheet of 2, #755a-755b
f. Souv. sheet of 2, #755c-755d
756 A98 15.50d Piece of 4, #a.-d.
e. Souv. sheet of 2, #756a, 756d
f. Souv. sheet of 2, #756b-756c
Nos. 752-756 (5) 13.50
Nos. 754e-754f, 755e-755f, 756e-756f (6) 55.00

Souvenir Sheets

Perf. 14x13½, 13½x14

757 A98 10d multicolored
758 A98 10d multicolored
759 A98 10d multicolored

Perf. 13½

760 A98 15d multicolored
761 A98 15d multicolored
762 A98 15d multicolored
Nos. 757-762 (6) 45.00

Nos. 757-759 exist imperf in different colors. Nos. 760-762 contain one 60x33mm stamp each. Nos. 753a-753c have UPU and Hamburg Philatelic Salon emblems and are additionally inscribed "PARTICIPACAO DE S. TOME E PRINCIPE / NO CONGRESSO DA U.P.U. EM HAMBURGO."
Sheets containing Nos. 754-756 contain one label.

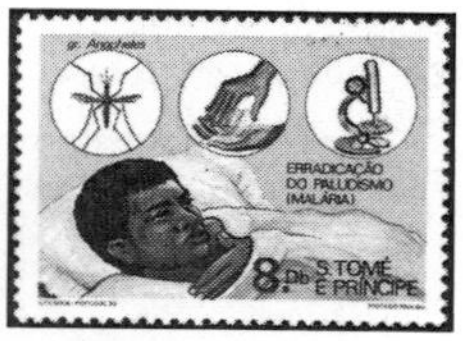

Natl. Campaign Against Malaria A99

1984, Sept. 30 ***Perf. 13½***

764 A99 8d Malaria victim
765 A99 16d Mosquito, DDT, vert.
766 A99 30d Exterminator, vert.
Nos. 764-766 (3) 6.00

A100

A101

World Food Day: 8d, Emblem, animals, produce. 16d, Silhouette, animals. 46d, Plowed field, produce. 30d, Tractor, field, produce, horiz.

1984, Oct. 16

767 A100 8d multicolored
768 A100 16d multicolored
769 A100 46d multicolored
Nos. 767-769 (3) 6.00

Souvenir Sheet

770 A100 30d multicolored 4.00

1984, Nov. 5

Mushrooms: 10d, Coprinus micaceus. 20d, Amanita rubescens. 30d, Armillariella mellea. 50d, Hygrophorus chrysodon, horiz.

771 A101 10d multicolored
772 A101 20d multicolored
773 A101 30d multicolored
Nos. 771-773 (3) 6.00

Souvenir Sheet

774 A101 50d multicolored 4.00

Christmas A102

Designs: 30d, Candles, offering, stable. 50d, Stable, Holy Family, Kings.

1984, Dec. 25
775 A102 30d multicolored 2.00

Souvenir Sheet

776 A102 50d multicolored 3.00

No. 776 contains one 60x40mm stamp.

Conference of Portuguese Territories in Africa A103

1985, Feb. 14
777 A103 25d multicolored 2.00

Reinstatement of Flights from Lisbon to St. Thomas, 1st Anniv. — A104

Designs: 25d, Douglas DC-3, map of northwest Africa. 30d, Air Portugal Douglas DC-8. 50d, Fokker Friendship.

1985, Dec. 6 Litho. *Perf. 13½*
778 A104 25d multicolored
779 A104 30d multicolored
Nos. 778-779 (2) 3.00

Souvenir Sheet

779A A104 50d multicolored 3.00

Flowers — A105

Mushrooms A106

1985, Dec. 30 *Perf. 11½x12*
780 A105 16d Flowering cactus
781 A105 20d Sunflower
782 A105 30d Porcelain rose
Nos. 780-782 (3) 3.00

1986, Sept. 18 *Perf. 13½*
783 A106 6d Fistulina hepatica
784 A106 25d Collybia butyracea
785 A106 30d Entoloma clypeatum
Nos. 783-785 (3) 10.00

Souvenir Sheet

786 A106 75d Cogumelos II 10.00

No. 786 exists with margins trimmed on four sides removing the control number.

Miniature Sheet

World Cup Soccer, Mexico A107

#787: a, Top of trophy. b, Bottom of trophy. c, Interior of stadium. d, Exterior of stadium.

1986, Oct. 1
787 A107 25d Sheet of 4, #a.-d. 10.00

For overprints see Nos. 818-818A.

Miniature Sheet

1988 Summer Olympics, Seoul A108

Seoul Olympic Games emblem, and: No. 788a, Map of North Korea. b, Torch. c, Olympic flag, map of South Korea. d, Text.

1986, Oct. 2
788 A108 25d Sheet of 4, #a.-d. 10.00

Halley's Comet — A109

Designs: No. 789a, 5d, Challenger space shuttle, 1st launch. b, 6d, Vega probe. c, 10d, Giotto probe. d, 16d, Comet over Nuremberg, A.D. 684.
90d, Comet, Giotto probe, horiz.

1986, Oct. 27
789 A109 Sheet of 4, #a.-d.+5 labels 10.00

Souvenir Sheet

790 A109 90d multicolored 8.00

Automobiles — A110

Designs: No. 791a, 50c, Columbus Monument, Barcelona. b, 6d, Fire engine ladder truck, c. 1900. c, 16d, Fire engine, c. 1900. d, 30d, Fiat 18 BL Red Cross ambulance, c. 1916.

1986, Nov. 1
791 A110 Sheet of 4, #a.-d.+5 labels 10.00

Railway Stations and Signals A111

Designs: 50c, London Bridge Station, 1900. 6d, 100-300 meter warning signs. 20d, Signal lamp. 50d, St. Thomas & Prince Station.

1986, Nov. 2 *Perf. 13½*
792 A111 50c multicolored
793 A111 6d multicolored
794 A111 20d multicolored
Nos. 792-794 (3) 6.00

Souvenir Sheet

795 A111 50d multicolored 6.00

LUBRAPEX '86, Brazil — A112

Exhibition emblem and: No. 796a, 1d, Line fisherman on shore. b, 1d, Line fisherman in boat. c, 2d, Net fisherman. d, 46d, Couple trap fishing, lobster.

1987, Jan. 15
796 A112 Sheet of 4, #a.-d.+2 labels 5.00

Intl. Peace Year A113

Designs: 8d, Mahatma Gandhi. 10d, Martin Luther King, Jr. 16d, Red Cross, Intl. Peace Year, UN, UNESCO, Olympic emblems and Nobel Peace Prize medal. 20d, Albert Luthuli. 75d, Peace Dove, by Picasso.

1987, Jan. 15
797 A113 8d bl, blk & pur
798 A113 10d bl, blk & grn
799 A113 16d multicolored
800 A113 20d multicolored
Nos. 797-800 (4) 6.00

Souvenir Sheet

801 A113 75d multicolored 6.00

Christmas 1986 — A114

Paintings by Albrecht Durer: No. 802a, 50c, Virgin and Child. b, 1d, Madonna of the Carnation. c, 16d, Virgin and Child, diff. d, 20d, The Nativity. 75d, Madonna of the Goldfinch.

1987, Jan. 15
802 A114 Strip of 4, #a.-d. 6.00

Souvenir Sheet

803 A114 75d multicolored 6.00

Fauna and Flora — A115

Birds: a, 1d, Agapornis fischeri. b, 2d, Psittacula krameri. c, 10d, Psittacus erithacus. d, 20d, Agapornis personata psittacidae.
Flowers: e, 1d, Passiflora caerulea. f, 2d, Oncidium nubigenum. g, 10d, Heliciontia wagneriana. h, 20d, Guzmania liguiata.
Butterflies: i, 1d, Aglais urticae. j, 2d, Pieris brassicae. k, 10d, Fabriciana niobe. l, 20d, Zerynthia polyxena.
Dogs: m, 1d, Sanshu. n, 2d, Hamiltonstovare. o, 10d, Gran spitz. p, 20d, Chowchow.

1987, Oct. 15 *Perf. 14x13½*
804 A115 Sheet of 16, #a.-p. 20.00

Sports Institute, 10th Anniv. — A116

No. 805: a, 50c, Three athletes. b, 20d, Map of St. Thomas and Prince, torchbearers. c, 30d, Volleyball, soccer, team handball and basketball players.
50d, Bjorn Borg.

1987, Oct. 30
805 A116 Strip of 3, #a.-c. 3.00

Souvenir Sheet
Perf. 13½x14

806 A116 50d Sheet of 1 + label 3.00

Miniature Sheet

Discovery of America, 500th Anniv. (in 1992) — A117

Emblem and: No. 807: a, 15d, Columbus with globe, map and arms. b, 20d, Battle between Spanish galleon and pirate ship. c, 20d, Columbus landing in New World. 100d, Model ship, horiz.

1987, Nov. 3 *Perf. 13½x14*
807 A117 Sheet of 3, #a.-c. + 3 labels 3.50

Souvenir Sheet
Perf. 14x13½

808 A117 100d multicolored 5.50

Mushrooms — A118

Designs: No. 809a, 6d, Calocybe ionides. b, 25d, Hygrophorus coccineus. c, 30d, Boletus versipellis. 35d, Morchella vulgaris, vert.

1987, Nov. 10 *Perf. 14x13½*
809 A118 Strip of 3, #a.-c. 4.00

Souvenir Sheet
Perf. 13½x14

810 A118 35d multicolored 6.00

Locomotives — A119

No. 811: a, 5d, Jung, Germany. b, 10d, Mikado 2413. c, 20d, Baldwin, 1920. 50d, Pamplona Railroad Station, 1900.

1987, Dec. 1 Litho. *Perf. 14x13½*

811 A119 Strip of 3, #a.-c. *3.00*

Souvenir Sheet

812 A119 50d multicolored *3.50*

Miniature Sheet

Christmas A120

Paintings of Virgin and Child by: No. 813a, 1d, Botticelli. b, 5d, Murillo. c, 15d, Raphael. d, 20d, Memling.
50d, Unkmown artist, horiz.

1987, Dec. 20 *Perf. 13½x14*

813 A120 Sheet of 4, #a.-d. *2.50*

Souvenir Sheet

Perf. 14x13½

814 A120 50d multicolored *3.50*

World Boy Scout Jamboree, Australia, 1987-88 — A121

1987, Dec. 30 *Perf. 14x13½*

815 A121 50c multicolored *3.00*

Russian October Revolution, 70th Anniv. A122

1988 Litho. *Perf. 12*

816 A122 25d Lenin addressing revolutionaries 1.25

Souvenir Sheet

Lubrapex '88 — A123

1988, May *Perf. 14x13½*

817 A123 80d Trolley *6.00*

Nos. 787a-787d Ovptd. "CAMPEONATO MUNDIAL / DE FUTEBOL MEXICO '86 / ALEMANHA / SUBCAMPIAO" in Silver (#818) or Same with "ARGENTINA / CAMPIAO" Instead in Gold (#818A) Across Four Stamps

1988, Aug. 15 *Perf. 13½*

818 A107 25d Block of 4 (S) 25.00
818A A107 25d Block of 4 (G) 25.00

Medicinal Plants - A123a

Mushrooms - A123b

Medicinal plants: No. 819a, 5d, Datura metel. b, 5d, Salaconta. c, 5d, Cassia occidentalis. d, 10d, Solanum ovigerum. e, 20d, Leonotis nepetifolia.
Mushrooms: No. 820a, 10d, Rhodopaxillus nudus. b, 10d, Volvaria volvacea. c, 10d, Psalliota bispora. d, 10d, Pleurotus ostreatus. e, 20d, Clitocybe geotropa.

1988, Oct. 26 *Perf. 13½x14*

819 A123a Strip of 5, #a.-e. *4.50*
820 A123b Strip of 5, #a.-e. *6.00*

Souvenir Sheets

821 A123a 35d Hiersas durero *4.00*
822 A123b 35d Mushroom on wood *4.00*

Miniature Sheets of 4

Passenger Trains - A123c

No. 823: a, Swiss Federal Class RE 6/6, left. b, Class RE 6/6, right.
No. 824: a, Japan Natl. Class EF 81, left. b, Class EF 81, right.
No. 825: a, German Electric E 18, 1930, left. b, E 18, 1930, right.
60d, Japan Natl. Class 381 Electric.

1988, Nov. 4 *Perf. 14x13½*

823 A123c 10d 2 ea #a.-b. + 2 labels
824 A123c 10d 2 ea #a.-b. + 2 labels
825 A123c 10d 2 ea #a.-b. + 2 labels
Nos. 823-825 (12) *8.00*

Souvenir Sheet

826 A123c 60d multicolored *6.00*

Butterflies - A123d

Various flowers and: No. 827a, White and brown spotted butterfly. b, Dark brown and white butterfly, flower stigma pointing down. c, Brown and white butterfly, flower stigma pointing down.
50d, Brown, white and orange butterly.

1988, Nov. 25 *Perf. 13½x14*

827 A123d 10d Strip of 3, #a.-c. *3.50*

Souvenir Sheet

828 A123d 50d multicolored *5.50*

Ferdinand von Zeppelin (1838-1917) - A123e

Berlin, 750th Anniv. - A123f — A123f

No. 829: a, Sailing ship, dirigible L23. b, Dirigibles flying over British merchant ships. c, Rendezvous of zeppelin with Russian ice breaker Malygin.
No. 830: a, Airship Le Jeune at mooring pad, Paris, 1903, vert. b, von Zeppelin, vert.

Perf. 14x13½, 13½x14

1988, Nov. 25

829 A123e 10d Strip of 3, #a.-c.
830 A123e 10d Pair, #a.-b.
Nos. 829-830 (5) *7.00*

Souvenir Sheet

831 A123f 50d multicolored 9.00

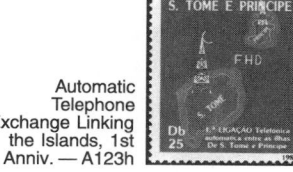

Natl. Arms — A123g

Automatic Telephone Exchange Linking the Islands, 1st Anniv. — A123h

1988, Dec. 15 *Perf. 13½*

832 A123g 10d multicolored *1.00*
833 A123h 25d multicolored *1.50*

Olympics Games, Seoul, Barcelona and Albertville — A123i

World Cup Soccer Championships, Italy, 1990 — A123j

#834, View of Barcelona, Cobi. #835, Barcelona Games emblem. #836, Gold medal from 1988 Seoul games. #837, Emblems of 1988 & 1992 games. #838, Bear on skis, Albertville, 1992. #839, Soccer ball. #840, Italy '90 Championships emblem. #841, World Cup Trophy. #842, Transfer of Olympic flag during Seoul closing ceremony. #843, Olympic pins. #844, like #838. #845, Soccer balls as hemispheres of globe.

1988, Dec. 15 *Perf. 14x13½, 13½x14*

834 A123i 5d multi
835 A123i 5d multi, vert.
836 A123i 5d multi, vert.
837 A123i 5d multi
838 A123i 5d grn & multi
839 A123j 5d multi
840 A123j 5d multi, vert.
841 A123j 5d multi, vert.
Nos. 834-841 (8) *8.00*

Souvenir Sheets

Perf. 14x13½

842 A123i 50d multi *7.50*
843 A123i 50d multi *7.50*
844 A123i 50d blue & multi *7.50*
845 A123j 50d multi *7.50*

No. 842 exists with Olympic emblems in gold or silver. No. 845 exists with marginal inscriptions in gold or silver. See Nos. 876-877 for souvenir sheets similar in design to No. 840.

Intl. Boy Scout Jamboree, Australia, 1987-88 - A123k

#846: a, Campfire. b, Scout emblem, pitched tents, flag. c, Scout emblem, tent flaps, flag, axe.
110d, Trefoil center point, horiz.

1988, Dec. 15 *Perf. 13½x14*

846 A123k 10d Strip of 3, #a.-c. *5.00*

Souvenir Sheet

Perf. 14x13½

847 A123k 110d multicolored *10.00*

Intl. Red Cross, 125th Anniv. - A123m

No. 848: a, 50c, Patient in hospital. b, 5d, Transporting victims. c, 20d, Instructing workers. 50d, Early mail train, horiz.

1988, Dec. 15 *Perf. 13½x14*

848 A123m Strip of 3, #a.-c. *4.00*

Souvenir Sheet

Perf. 14x13½

849 A123m 50d multicolored *7.50*

No. 848c is airmail.

Miniature Sheet

Christmas - A123n

#850: a, 10d, Madonna and Child with St. Anthony Abbot and the Infant Baptism, by Titian. b, 10d, Madonna and Child with St. Catherine and a Rabbit, by Titian. c, 10d, Nativity Scene, by Rubens. d, 30d, Adoration of the Magi, by Rubens.
50d, The Annunciation (detail), by Titian, vert.

1988, Dec. 23 ***Perf. 14x13½***
850 A123n Sheet of 4, #a.-d. *6.00*

Souvenir Sheet
Perf. 13½x14
851 A123n 50d multicolored *5.00*

Titian, 500th anniv. of birth. Country name does not appear on No. 850d.

French Revolution, Bicent. — A123o

Designs: No. 852, Eiffel Tower, Concorde, stylized doves, flag. No. 853 Eiffel Tower, flag, stylized doves. No. 854, Eiffel Tower, flag, stylized doves, TGV train, vert. 50d, TGV train.

Perf. 14x13½, 13½x14
1989, July 14 **Litho.**
852 A123o 10d multicolored
853 A123o 10d multicolored
854 A123o 10d multicolored
Nos. 852-854 (3) *3.00*

Souvenir Sheet
855 A123o 50d multicolored *4.00*

Fruit — A123p

1989, Sept. 15 ***Perf. 13½x14***
856 A123p 50c Chapu-chapu
857 A123p 1d Guava
858 A123p 5d Mango
859 A123p 10d Carambola
860 A123p 25d Nona
861 A123p 50d Avacado
862 A123p 50d Cajamanga

Perf. 14x13½
863 A123p 60d Jackfruit
864 A123p 100d Cacao
865 A123p 250d Bananas
866 A123p 500d Papaya
Nos. 856-866 (11) *15.00*

Souvenir Sheet
Perf. 13½x14
867 A123p 1000d Pomegranate *10.00*

Nos. 863-866 are horiz.

Orchids A123q

Designs: No. 868, Dendrobium phalaenopsis. No. 869, Catteleya granulosa. 50d, Diothonea imbricata and maxillaria eburnea.

1989, Oct. 15 ***Perf. 13½x14***
868 A123q 20d multicolored
869 A123q 20d multicolored
Nos. 868-869 (2) *3.00*

Souvenir Sheet
870 A123q 50d multicolored *3.50*

Hummingbirds — A124

Designs: No. 871, Topaza bella, Sappho sparganura, vert. No. 872, Petasophores anais. No. 873, Lophornis adorabilis, Chalcostigma herrani, vert. 50d, Oreotrochilus chimborazo.

1989, Oct. 15 ***Perf. 13½x14, 14x13½***
871 A124 20d multicolored
872 A124 20d multicolored
873 A124 20d multicolored
Nos. 871-873 (3) *4.00*

Souvenir Sheet
Perf. 14x13½
874 A124 50d multicolored *3.50*

Miniature Sheet

1990 World Cup Soccer Championships, Italy — A125

Program covers: No. 875: a, 10d, Globe and soccer ball, 1962. b, 10d, Foot kicking ball, 1950. c, 10d, Abstract design, 1982. d, 20d, Player kicking ball, 1934.
No. 876: a, Character emblem, horiz. b, USA 94, horiz. 50d, like #876a, horiz.

1989, Oct. 24 ***Perf. 13½x14***
875 A125 Block of 4, #a.-d. *4.00*

Souvenir Sheets
Perf. 14x13½
876 A125 25d Sheet of 2, #a.-b.
877 A125 50d blue & multi
Nos. 876-877 (2) *15.00*

1992 Summer Olympics, Barcelona — A126

1989, Oct. 24 ***Perf. 13½x14, 14x13½***
878 A126 5d Tennis, vert.
879 A126 5d Basketball, vert.
880 A126 5d Running
881 A126 35d Baseball, vert.
Nos. 878-881 (4) *4.00*

Souvenir Sheet
Perf. 14x13½
882 A126 50d Sailing *8.00*

Nos. 878-881 exist in souvenir sheets of one. No country name on souvenir sheet of one of No. 878.

Locomotives — A127

1989, Oct. 27 ***Perf. 14x13½, 13½x14***
884 A127 20d Japan
885 A127 20d Philippines
886 A127 20d Spain, vert.
887 A127 20d India
888 A127 20d Asia
Nos. 884-888 (5) *7.50*

Souvenir Sheets
889 A127 50d Garratt, Africa
890 A127 50d Trans-Gabon, vert.
Nos. 889-890 (2) *10.00*

Nos. 884-888 exist in souvenir sheets of one.

Ships A128

#891, Merchant ships at sea, 16th cent. #892, Caravels, merchant ships in harbor, 16th cent. #893, 3 merchant ships at sea, 18th cent. #894, War ships, 18th cent. #895, 4 merchant ships, 18th cent. #896, Passenger liner, Port of Hamburg. #897, German sailing ship, 17th cent.

1989, Oct. 27 ***Perf. 14x13½***
891 A128 20d multicolored
892 A128 20d multicolored
893 A128 20d multicolored
894 A128 20d multicolored
895 A128 20d multicolored
Nos. 891-895 (5) *7.00*

Souvenir Sheets
896 A128 50d multicolored *4.00*

Perf. 13½x14
897 A128 50d multi, vert. *4.00*

Discovery of America, 500th anniv., in 1992 (#891-895) and Hamburg, 800th anniv. (#891-897).
Nos. 891-895 exist in souvenir sheets of one.

Butterflies A129

1989, Dec. 20 ***Perf. 13½x14***
898 A129 20d Tree bark
899 A129 20d Leaves
900 A129 20d Flowers
901 A129 20d Bird
902 A129 20d Blades of grass
Nos. 898-902 (5) *7.50*

Souvenir Sheet
903 A129 100d yel, brn & multi *8.00*

Nos. 898-902 exist in souvenir sheets of one.

African Development Bank, 25th Anniv. — A130

1989, Dec. 20 ***Perf. 13½x14***
904 A130 25d blk, lt bl & grn *2.00*

World Telecommunications Day — A131

1989, Dec. 20 ***Perf. 14x13½***
905 A131 60d multicolored *5.00*

Souvenir Sheet
Perf. 13½x14
906 A131 100d Early Bird satellite, vert. *10.00*

Christmas A132

Paintings: No. 907, Adoration of the Magi (detail), by Durer. No. 908, Young Virgin Mary, by Titian. No. 909, Adoration of the King, by Rubens. No. 910, Sistine Madonna, by Raphael. 100d, Madonna and Child Surrounded by Garland and Boy Angels, by Rubens.

1989, Dec. 23 ***Perf. 13½x14***
907 A132 25d multicolored
908 A132 25d multicolored
909 A132 25d multicolored
910 A132 25d multicolored
Nos. 907-910 (4) *8.00*

Souvenir Sheet
911 A132 100d multicolored *8.00*

Nos. 907-910 exist in souvenir sheets of one.

Expedition of Sir Arthur Eddington to St. Thomas and Prince, 70th Anniv. A133

Designs: No. 912, Albert Einstein with Eddington. No. 913, Locomotive on Prince Island. No. 914, Roca Sundy railway station.

1990 **Litho.** ***Perf. 13½***
912 A133 60d multicolored
913 A133 60d multicolored
914 A133 60d multicoloed
a. Souvenir sheet of 3, #912-914 *22.50*
Nos. 912-914 (3) *16.00*

Souvenir Sheet

Independence, 15th Anniv. — A134

Designs: a, Map, arms. b, Map, birds carrying envelope. c, Flag.

1990, July 12 *Perf. 13½*

916 A134 50d Sheet of 3, #a.-c. 8.00

Orchids — A135

1990, Sept. 15 **Litho.** *Perf. 13½*

917 A135 20d Eulophia guineensis

918 A135 20d Ancistrochilus

919 A135 20d Oeceoclades maculata

920 A135 20d Vanilla imperialis

921 A135 20d Ansellia africana

Nos. 917-921 (4) 6.00

Souvenir Sheets

Perf. 14x13½

922 A135 50d Angraecum distichum, horiz.

923 A135 50d Polystachya affinis, horiz.

Nos. 922-923 (2) 7.00

Expo '90, Intl. Garden and Greenery Exposition, Osaka.

Locomotives — A136

1990, Sept. 28 *Perf. 14x13½*

924 A136 5d Bohemia, 1923-41

925 A136 20d W. Germany, 1951-56

926 A136 25d Mallet, 1896-1903

927 A136 25d Russia, 1927-30

928 A136 25d England, 1927-30

Nos. 924-928 (5) 6.00

Souvenir Sheets

929 A136 50d Camden-Amboy, 1834-38 6.00

930 A136 50d Stockton-Darlington, 1825 6.00

Souvenir Sheet

Iberoamericana '90 Philatelic Exposition — A137

1990, Oct. 7

931 A137 300d Armas Castle 20.00

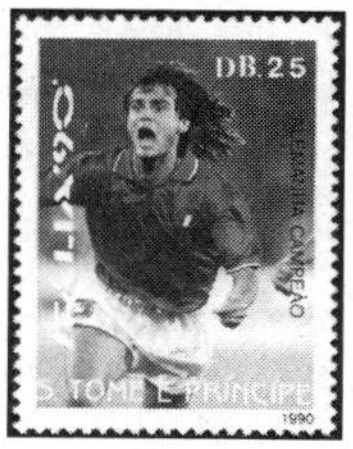

1990 World Cup Soccer Championships, Italy — A138

#932, German team with World Cup Trophy. #933, 2 players with ball. #934, 3 players with ball. #935, Italian player. #936, US Soccer Federation emblem and team members. #937, World Cup Trophy.

1990, Oct. 15 *Perf. 13½*

932 A138 25d multicolored

933 A138 25d multicolored

934 A138 25d multicolored

935 A138 25d multicolored

Nos. 932-935 (4) 8.00

Souvenir Sheets

Perf. 14x13½

936 A138 50d multi, horiz.

937 A138 50d multi, horiz.

Nos. 936-937 (2) 8.00

Mushrooms A139

1990, Nov. 2 *Perf. 13½x14*

938 A139 20d Boletus aereus

939 A139 20d Coprinus micaceus

940 A139 20d Pholiota spectabilis

941 A139 20d Krombholzia aurantiaca

942 A139 20d Stropharia aeruginosa

Nos. 938-942 (5) 8.00

Souvenir Sheets

Perf. 14x13½

943 A139 50d Hypholoma capnoides

944 A139 50d Pleurotus ostreatus

Nos. 943-944 (2) 12.00

Nos. 943-944 horiz. See Nos. 1014-1020.

Butterflies — A140

1990, Nov. 2 *Perf. 14x13½, 13½x14*

945 A140 15d Megistanis baeotus

946 A140 15d Ascia vamillae

947 A140 15d Danaus chrysippus

948 A140 15d Morpho menelaus

949 A140 15d Papilio rutulus, vert.

950 A140 25d Papilio paradiesa

Nos. 945-950 (6) 9.00

Souvenir Sheets

951 A140 50d Parnassius clodius, vert.

952 A140 50d Papilio macmaon, vert.

Nos. 951-952 (2) 9.00

Presenting Gifts to the Newborn King — A141

Christmas: No. 954, Nativity scene. No. 955, Adoration of the Magi. No. 956, Flight into Egypt. No. 957, Adoration of the Magi, diff. No. 958, Portrait of Artist's Daughter Clara (detail), by Rubens, horiz.

1990, Nov. 30 *Perf. 13½x14*

953 A141 25d multicolored

954 A141 25d multicolored

955 A141 25d multicolored

956 A141 25d multicolored

Nos. 953-956 (4) 8.00

Souvenir Sheets

957 A141 50d multicolored

Perf. 14x13½

958 A141 50d multicolored

Nos. 957-958 (2) 8.50

Death of Rubens, 350th anniv. (#958).

Anniversaries and Events A142

1990, Dec. 15 *Perf. 13½x14*

959 A142 20d shown 2.00

Souvenir Sheets

Perf. 14x13½, 13½x14 (#962, 964)

960 A142 50d Oath of Confederation

961 A142 50d Pointed roof

962 A142 50d William Tell statue, vert.

963 A142 50d Brandenburg Gate

964 A142 50d Penny Black, vert.

965 A142 50d 100d bank note

Nos. 960-965 (6) 22.50

Swiss Confederation, 700th anniv. (#959-962). Brandenburg Gate, 200th anniv. (#963). First postage stamp, 150th anniv. (#964). Independence of St. Thomas and Prince, 15th anniv. (#965).

Paintings — A143

#966, The Bathers, by Renoir. #967, Girl Holding Mirror for Nude, by Picasso. #968, Nude, by Rubens. #969, Descent from the Cross (detail), by Rubens. #970, Nude, by Titian. #971, Landscape, by Durer. #972, Rowboats, by Van Gogh. #973, Nymphs, by Titian. #974, Bather, by Titian. #975, Postman Joseph Roulin (detail), by Van Gogh. #976, The Abduction of the Daughters of Leucippus, by Rubens. #977, Nude, by Titian, diff.

1990, Dec. 15 *Perf. 14x13½, 13½x14*

966 A143 10d multi

967 A143 10d multi, vert.

968 A143 10d multi, vert.

969 A143 10d multi, vert.

970 A143 10d multi, vert.

971 A143 20d multi

972 A143 20d multi

973 A143 25d multi

974 A143 25d multi, vert.

Nos. 966-974 (9) 15.00

Souvenir Sheets

Perf. 13½x14

975 A143 50d multi, vert. 8.00

976 A143 50d multi, vert. 8.00

977 A143 50d multi, vert. 8.00

Rubens, 350th anniv. of death (#968-969, 976). Titian, 500th anniv. of death (#970, 973-974, 977). Van Gogh, centennial of death (#972, 975).

See No. 958 for other souvenir sheet for Rubens death anniv.

Flora and Fauna — A144

Designs: 1d, Gecko. 5d, Cobra. 10d, No. 980, Sea turtle. No. 981, Fresh water turtle. No. 982, Civet. 70d, Civet in tree. No. 984, Civet with young. No. 985, Civet in den.

Psittacus erithacus: 80d, In tree, vert. 100d, On branch with wings spread, vert. 250d, Feeding young, vert. No. 989, Three in flight, vert.

1991, Feb. 2 *Perf. 14x13½*

978 A144 1d multicolored

979 A144 5d multicolored

980 A144 10d multicolored

981 A144 50d multicolored

982 A144 50d multicolored

983 A144 70d multicolored

984 A144 75d multicolored

985 A144 75d multicolored

Perf. 13½x14

986 A144 80d multicolored

987 A144 100d multicolored

988 A144 250d multicolored

989 A144 500d multicolored

Nos. 978-989 (12) 18.00

Souvenir Sheets

990 A144 500d Orchid, vert. 9.00

991 A144 500d Rose, vert. 9.00

See Nos. 1054I-1054L.

Locomotives — A145

1991, May 7 *Perf. 14x13½, 13½x14*

992 A145 75d shown

993 A145 75d North America, vert.

994 A145 75d Germany, vert.

995 A145 75d New Delhi, vert.

996 A145 75d Brazil, vert.

997 A145 200d Two leaving terminal

Nos. 992-997 (6) 4.00

Souvenir Sheets

998 A145 500d Engine 120, vert. 7.00

999 A145 500d Engine 151-001 7.00

Birds — A146

1991, July 8 ***Perf. 13½x14***

1000 A146 75d Psittacula kuhlii
1001 A146 75d Plydolophus rosaceus
1002 A146 75d Falco tinnunculus
1003 A146 75d Platycercus palliceps
1004 A146 200d Marcrocercus aracanga
Nos. 1000-1004 (5) 8.00

Souvenir Sheets

1005 A146 500d Ramphastos culmenatus
1006 A146 500d Strix nyctea
Nos. 1005-1006 (2) 16.00

Paintings A147

50d, Venus and Cupid, by Titian. #1008, Horse's Head (detail), by Rubens. #1009, Child's face (detail), by Rubens. 100d, Spanish Woman, by Picasso. 200d, Man with Christian Flag, by Titian. #1012, Study of a Negro, by Rubens. #1013, Madonna and Child, by Raphael.

1991, July 31

1007 A147 50d multicolored
1008 A147 75d multicolored
1009 A147 75d multicolored
1010 A147 100d multicolored
1011 A147 200d multicolored
Nos. 1007-1011 (5) 8.00

Souvenir Sheets

1012 A147 500d multicolored
1013 A147 500d multicolored
Nos. 1012-1013 (2) 16.00

Mushroom Type of 1990

1991, Aug. 30

1014 A139 50d Clitocybe geotropa
1015 A139 50d Lepiota procera
1016 A139 75d Boletus granulatus
1017 A139 125d Coprinus comatus
1018 A139 200d Amanita rubescens
Nos. 1014-1018 (5) 8.00

Souvenir Sheets

1019 A139 500d Armillariella mellea

Perf. 14x13½

1020 A139 500d Nictalis parasitica, horiz.
Nos. 1019-1020 (2) 16.00

Flowers A148

#1022, Zan tedeschia elliotiana. #1023, Cyrtanthes pohliana. #1024, Phalaenopsis lueddemanniana. #1025, Haemanthus katharinae. 500d, Arundina graminifolia.

1991, Sept. 9 ***Perf. 13½x14***

1021 A148 50d shown
1022 A148 50d multicolored
1023 A148 100d multicolored
1024 A148 100d multicolored
1025 A148 200d multicolored
Nos. 1021-1025 (5) 8.00

Souvenir Sheet

1026 A148 500d multicolored 8.00

Souvenir Sheet

Iberoamericano '92 Intl. Philatelic Exhibition — A149

1991, Oct. 11 Litho. ***Perf. 14x13½***

1027 A149 800d multicolored 5.00

Discovery of America, 500th Anniv. (in 1992) — A150

1991, Oct. 12 ***Perf. 13½x14***

1028 A150 50d Columbus
1029 A150 50d Sailing ship
1030 A150 75d Sailing ship, diff.
1031 A150 125d Landing in New World
1032 A150 200d Pointing the way
Nos. 1028-1032 (5) 10.00

Souvenir Sheet

Perf. 14x13½

1033 A150 500d Columbus' fleet, horiz. 10.00

Butterflies — A151

1991, Oct. 16 ***Perf. 14x13½***

1034 A151 125d Limentis popul
1035 A151 125d Pavon inachis io
Nos. 1034-1035 (2) 5.00

Souvenir Sheet

Perf. 13½x14

1036 A151 500d Zerynthia polyxena 8.00

Phila Nippon '91.

1991, Nov. 15 ***Perf. 14x13½***

1037 A151 125d Macaon papilio machaon
1038 A151 125d Gran pavon
1039 A151 125d Pavon inachis io, diff.
1040 A151 125d Artia caja
Nos. 1037-1040 (4) 8.00

Souvenir Sheet

Perf. 13½x14

1041 A151 500d Unnamed butterfly, vert. 8.00

Christmas.

Landmarks — A152

Landmarks of France: No. 1042, Ile de France, vert. No. 1043, Chenonceau Castle. No. 1044, Azay-le-Rideau Castle. No. 1045, Chambord Castle. No. 1046, Chaumont Castle. No. 1047, Fountainebleau Palace.

Perf. 13½x14, 14x13½

1991, Nov. 15

1042-1047 A152 25d Set of 6 8.00

Souvenir Sheet

1048 A152 500d Paris map, 1615 5.00

French National Exposition.

Souvenir Sheet

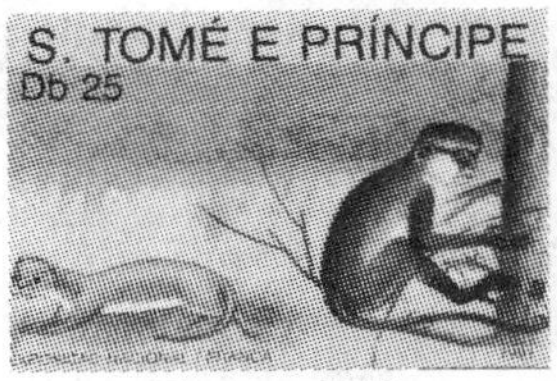

Fauna — A153

Animals and birds: a, Weasel, monkey. b, Civet, rats. c, Goat, cow. d, Rabbits, wildcat. e, Parrot, black bird. f, White bird, multicolored bird.

1991, Nov. 15 ***Perf. 14x13½***

1049 A153 25d Sheet of 6, #a.-f. 8.00

French National Exposition.

Express Mail Service from St. Thomas and Prince — A154

1991 Litho. ***Perf. 14***

1050 A154 3000d multicolored 15.00

Souvenir Sheets

1991 Intl. Olympic Committee Session, Birmingham — A154a

Designs: No. 1050A, IOC emblem, Birmingham Session. No. 1050B, 1998 Winter Olympics emblem, Nagano. No. 1050C, 1998 Winter Olympics mascot.

1992 Litho. ***Perf. 14***

1050A A154a 800d multi
1050B A154a 800d multi
1050C A154a 800d multi
Nos. 1050A-1050C (3) 16.00

Souvenir Sheet

IBEREX '91 — A154b

1992

1050D A154b 800d multi 10.00

Souvenir Sheets

1992 Winter Olympics, Albertville — A154c

1992

1050E A154c 50d Olympic medals, Set of 4, a.-d. 40.00

No. 1050E exists as four souvenir sheets with pictures of different medalists in sheet margins: a., Blanca Fernandez, Spain; b., Alberto Tomba, Italy; c., Mark Kirchner, Germany; d., Torgny Mogren, Norway.

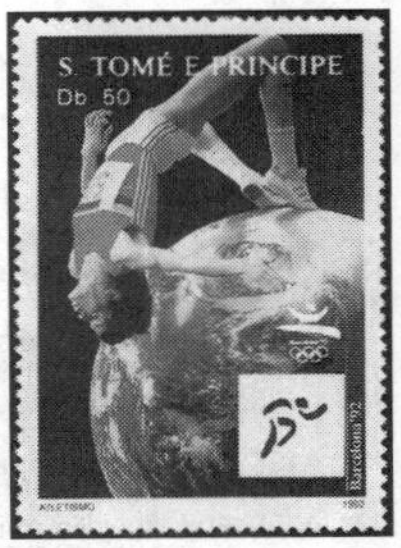

1992 Summer Olympics, Barcelona A154d

View of earth from space with: No. 1050F, High jumper. No. 1050G, Roller hockey player. No. 1050H, Equestrian. No. 1050I, Kayaker. No. 1050J, Weight lifter. No. 1050K, Archer. No. 1050L, Michael Jordan, horiz.

1992

1050F-1050K A154d 50d Set of 6 5.00

Souvenir Sheet

1050L A154d 50d multicolored 8.00

Whales — A155

Designs: No. 1051, Orcinus orca. No. 1052, Orcinus orca, two under water. No. 1053, Pseudoraca crassidens. No. 1054, Pseudoraca crassidens, three under water.

1992 Litho. ***Perf. 14***

1051-1054 A155 450d Set of 4 20.00

World Wildlife Fund.

Visit of Pope John Paul II - A155a

c, Flags, Pope. d, Church with two steeples. e, Church, diff.
f, Pope, vert. g, Church, blue sky, vert. h, Church, closer view, vert.

1992, Apr. 19 Litho. ***Perf. 14***

Sheets of 4

1054A A155a 200d #d.-e., 2 #c
1054B A155a 200d #g.-h., 2 #f
Set 20.00

Flora and Fauna Type of 1991

Designs: No. 1054I, 1000d, Brown & white bird, vert. No. 1054J, 1500d, Yellow flower, vert. No. 1054K, 2000d, Red flower, vert. No. 1054L, 2500d, Black bird, vert.

1992, Apr. 19
1054I-1054L A144 Set of 4 35.00

UN Conference on Environmental Development, Rio — A155b

Designs: 65d, Rain forest. 110d, Walruses. 150d, Raptor. 200d, Tiger. 275d, Elephants.
No. 1054R, Panda, horiz. No. 1054S, Zebras, horiz.

1992, June 6 Litho. *Perf. 14*
1054M-1054Q A155b Set of 5 15.00

Souvenir Sheets

1054R-1054S A155b 800d multi 15.00

Souvenir Sheet

Olymphilex '92 — A156

Olympic athletes: a, Women's running. b, Women's gymnastics. c, Earvin "Magic" Johnson.

1992, July 29
1055 A156 300d Sheet of 3, #a.-c. 8.00

Mushrooms A157

75d, Leccinum ocabrum. 100d, Amanita spissa, horiz. 125d, Strugilomyces floccopus. 200d, Suillus luteus. 500d, Agaricus siluaticus. #1061, Amanita pantherma, horiz. #1062, Agaricus campestre.

1992, Sept. 5 *Perf. 14*
1056 A157 75d multicolored
1057 A157 100d multicolored
1058 A157 125d multicolored
1059 A157 200d multicolored
1060 A157 500d multicolored
Nos. 1056-1060 (5) 8.00

Souvenir Sheets

Perf. 14x13½, 13½x14

1061 A157 1000d multicolored
1062 A157 1000d multicolored
Nos. 1061-1062 (2) 16.00

Birds — A158

Designs: 75d, Paradisea regie, pipra rupicole. 100d, Trogon pavonis. 125d, Paradisea apoda. 200d, Pavocriotctus. 500d, Ramphatos maximus. No. 1068, Woodpecker. No. 1069, Picus major.

1992, Sept. 15 *Perf. 14*
1063 A158 75d multicolored
1064 A158 100d multicolored
1065 A158 125d multicolored
1066 A158 200d multicolored
1067 A158 500d multicolored
Nos. 1063-1067 (5) 8.00

Souvenir Sheets

Perf. 13½x14

1068 A158 1000d multicolored
1069 A158 1000d multicolored
Nos. 1068-1069 (2) 16.00

Marcelo da Veiga (1892-1976), Writer — A159

Designs: a, 10d. b, 40d. c, 50d. d, 100d.

1992, Oct. 3 *Perf. 13½*
1070 A159 Sheet of 4, #a.-d. 3.00

Locomotives — A160

Designs: 75d, 100d, 125d, 200d, 500d, Various locomotives. No. 1076, Steam train arriving at station. No. 1077, Engineer, stoker in locomotive cab.

1992, Oct. 3 *Perf. 14x13½*
1071 A160 75d black
1072 A160 100d black
1073 A160 125d black
1074 A160 200d black
1075 A160 500d black
Nos. 1071-1075 (5) 8.00

Souvenir Sheets

1076 A160 1000d black
1077 A160 1000d black
Nos. 1076-1077 (2) 16.00

Butterflies and Moths — A161

75d, Chelonia purpurea. 100d, Hoetera philocteles. 125d, Attacus pavonia major. 200d, Ornithoptera urvilliana. 500d, Acherontia atropos. No. 1083, Peridromia amphinome, vert. No. 1084, Uramia riphacus, vert.

1992, Oct. 18 *Perf. 14x13½*
1078 A161 75d multicolored
1079 A161 100d multicolored
1080 A161 125d multicolored
1081 A161 200d multicolored
1082 A161 500d multicolored
Nos. 1078-1082 (5) 8.00

Souvenir Sheets

Perf. 13½x14

1083 A161 1000d multicolored
1084 A161 1000d multicolored
Nos. 1083-1084 (2) 16.00

1992, 1996 Summer Olympics, Barcelona and Atlanta — A162

50d, Wind surfing. #1086, Wrestling. #1087, Women's 4x100 meters relay. #1088, Swimming. #1089, Equestrian, vert. #1090, Field hockey. #1091, Men's 4x100 meters relay, vert. #1092, Mascots for Barcelona and Atlanta. #1093, Opening ceremony, Barcelona.
#1094, Atlanta '96 Emblem, vert. #1095, Archer lighting Olympic Flame with flaming arrow, vert. #1096, Transfer of Olympic Flag, closing ceremony, vert. #1097, Gymnastics. #1098, Tennis players.

1992, Oct. 1 Litho. *Perf. 14*
1085 A162 50d multicolored 30.00
1086 A162 300d multicolored 30.00
1087 A162 300d multicolored 30.00
1088 A162 300d multicolored 30.00
1089 A162 300d multicolored 30.00
1090 A162 300d multicolored 30.00
1091 A162 300d multicolored 30.00
1092 A162 300d multicolored 30.00
1093 A162 300d multicolored 30.00
Set, Nos. 1085-1093 (9) 30.00

Souvenir Sheets

1094 A162 800d multicolored 8.00
1095 A162 1000d multicolored 10.00
1096 A162 1000d multicolored 10.00

Perf. 13½

1097 A162 1000d multicolored 16.00

Perf. 14

1098 A162 1000d multicolored 10.00

Butterflies A163

Flowers A164

Designs: No. 1099, White butterfly. No. 1100, Black and orange butterfly. No. 1101, Pink flower, black, white, red and blue butterfly. No. 1102, Black and white butterfly on right side of flower stem. No. 1103, Yellow and black butterfly. 2000d, Iris flower, black butterfly wing, horiz.

1993, May 26 Litho. *Perf. 14*
1099-1103 A163 500d Set of 5 12.00

Souvenir Sheet

1104 A163 2000d multi 15.00

1993, June 18
1105 A164 500d Fucinho de porco
1106 A164 500d Heliconia
1107 A164 500d Gravo nacional
1108 A164 500d Tremessura
1109 A164 500d Anturius
Nos. 1105-1109 (5) 12.00

Souvenir Sheet

1110 A164 2000d Girassol 12.00

Miniature Sheet

Union of Portuguese Speaking Capitals A165

Designs: a, 100d, Emblem. b, 150d, Grotto. c, 200d, Statue of Christ the Redeemer, Rio de Janeiro. d, 250d, Skyscraper. e, 250d, Monument. f, 300d, Building with pointed domed roof. g, 350d, Municipal building. h, 400d, Square tower. i, 500d, Residence, flag, truck.

1993, July 30
1111 A165 Sheet of 9, #a.-i. 7.00

Brasiliana '93.

Birds — A166

Designs: No. 1112, Cecia. No. 1113, Suisui. No. 1114, Falcon. No. 1115, Parrot. No. 1116, Heron.
No. 1117, Macaw, toucan, horiz.

1993, June 15 Litho. *Perf. 14*
1112-1116 A166 500d Set of 5 *18.50*

Souvenir Sheet

1117 A166 1000d multi *7.50*

Dinosaurs — A167

#1118, Lystrosaurus. #1119, Patagosaurus. #1120, Shonisaurus ictiosaurios, vert. #1121, Dilophosaurus, vert. #1122, Dicraeosaurus, vert. #1123, Tyrannosaurus rex, vert.

1993, July 21
1118-1123 A167 500d Set of 6 *15.00*

Souvenir Sheets

1124 A167 1000d Protoavis
1125 A167 1000d Brachiosaurus
Nos. 1124-1125 (2) *15.00*

Mushrooms A168

#1126, Agrocybe aegerita. #1127, Psalliota arvensis. #1128, Coprinus comatus. #1129, Hygrophorus psittacinus. #1130, Amanita caesarea.

#1131, Ramaria aurea. #1132, Pluteus murinus, horiz.

1993, May 25 Litho. *Perf. 14*

1126-1130 A168 800d Set of 5 *15.00*

Souvenir Sheets

1131-1132 A168 2000d Set of 2 *15.00*

Locomotives — A169

#1133-1137, Various views of small diesel locomotive.

#1138-1139, Various steam locomotives, vert.

1993, June 16

1133-1137 A169 800d Set of 5 *20.00*

Souvenir Sheets

1138-1139 A169 2000d Set of 2 *20.00*

1994 World Cup Soccer Championships, US — A170

Designs: No. 1140, Team photo. Nos. 1141-1147, Players in action.

No. 1148, Fans, faces painted as flags. No. 1149, Stylized player.

1993, July 6

1140-1147 A170 800d Set of 8 *20.00*

Souvenir Sheets

1148-1149 A170 2000d Set of 2 *20.00*

UPU Congress — A171

1993, Aug. 16

1150 A171 1000d shown 6.00

Souvenir Sheet

1151 A171 2000d Ship 10.00

1996 Summer Olympics, Atlanta — A172

#1152, Fencing. #1153, Women's running. #1154, Water polo. #1155, Soccer. #1156, Men's running. #1157, Boxing. #1158, Wrestling. #1159, High jump.

#1160, Shooting, vert. #1161, Sailing, vert. #1162, Equestrian, vert. #1163, Kayak, vert.

1993, Oct. 19 Litho. *Perf. 13½x14*

1152-1159 A172 800d Set of 8 40.00

Souvenir Sheets

1160-1163 A172 2000d multi 40.00

1994 World Cup Soccer Championships, US — A173

1994, Jan. 12 *Perf. 14*

1164 A173 500d blk, bl & red 2.50

Issued in miniature sheets of 4.

Miniature Sheets of 8 & 9

Movie Stars — A174

#1165a, James Dean. b, Bette Davis. c, Elvis Presley. d, Humphrey Bogart. e, John Lennon. f, Marilyn Monroe. g, Birthday cake. h, Audrey Hepburn.

#1166a-1166i, Various portraits of Elvis Presley.

#1167a-1167i, Various portraits of Marilyn Monroe.

#1168, James Dean, diff. #1169, Elvis Presley, diff. #1169A, Marilyn Monroe.

1994, Feb. 15

1165 A174 10d #a.-h. 5.00

1166-1167 A174 10d #a.-i. 5.00

Souvenir Sheets

1168-1169 A174 50d multi 5.00

1169A A174 2000d multi 15.00

Souvenir Sheet

Sydney 2000 — A175

1994, June 8

1170 A175 3000d multicolored 15.00

Signing of Argel Accord, 20th Anniv. A175a

1994 Litho. *Perf. 14*

1170A A175a 250d multi 20.00

Nos. 860, 979 Surcharged

d

Nos. 856, 979 Surcharged

e

Methods and Perfs as Before

1995, Mar. 2

1170B A123p(d) 100d on 25d #860 — —

1170E A123p(e) 350d on 50c #856 — —

1170I A144(d) 400d on 5d #979 — —

1170J A144(e) 400d on 5d #979 — —

Numbers have been reserved for additional surcharges. The editors would like to examine any examples.

Butterflies A176

#1171, Timeleoa maqulata-formosana. #1172, Morfho cypris. #1173, Thais polixena. #1174, Argema moenas. #1175, Leptocircus megus-ennius.

2000d, Armandia lidderdalei.

1995, May 10 Litho. *Perf. 14*

1171-1175 A176 1200d Set of 5 16.00

Souvenir Sheet

1176 A176 2000d multi 8.00

Flowering Fruits, Orchids A177

Flowering fruits: #1177, 350d, Pessego. #1178, 370d, Untue. #1179, 380d, Pitanga. #1180, 800d, Morango. #1181, 1000d, Izaquente.

Orchids: No. 1182, Max. houtteana. No. 1183, Max. marginata.

1995, June 6

1177-1181 A177 Set of 5 16.00

Souvenir Sheets

1182-1183 A177 2000d each 16.00

Mushrooms A179

Designs: No. 1185, Lactarius deliciosus. No. 1186, Marasmius oreades. No. 1187, Boletus edulis. No. 1188, Boletus aurantiacus. No. 1189, Lepiota procera. No. 1190, Cortinarius praestans.

No. 1191, Chantharellus cibarius. No. 1192, Lycoperdon pyriforme, horiz.

1995, Nov. 2 Litho. *Perf. 14*

1185-1190 A179 1000d Set of 6 16.00

Souvenir Sheets

1191-1192 A179 2000d each 16.00

UN, 50th Anniv. — A180

Traditional handicrafts made from palm leaves: No. 1193, 350d, Baskets. No. 1194, 350d, Brooms. No. 1195, 400d, Lamp shades. No. 1196, 500d, Klissakli, mussuá. No. 1197, 500d, Pávu. No. 1198, 1000d, Vámplêgá.

1995, June 20 Litho. *Perf. 13½x14*

1193-1198 A180 Set of 6 24.00

Trains — A181

Locomotives: No. 1199, Steam, "#100." No. 1200, Steam, "#778." No. 1201, G. Thommen steam. No. 1202, Steam "#119," vert. No. 1203, Mt. Washington cog railway. No. 1204, Electric.
No. 1205, Electric train on snow-covered mountain, vert. No. 1206, Electric train car with door open, vert.

1995, July 24 ***Perf. 14x13½, 13½x14***
1199-1204 A181 1000d Set of 6 16.00

Souvenir Sheets
1205-1206 A181 2000d multi 16.00

See Nos. 1280-1286.

Dogs & Cats A182

No. 1207: Various dogs. b, d, f, h, vert.
No. 1208: Various cats. b, d, f, h, vert.
No. 1209, St. Bernard, German shepherd. No. 1210, Beagle, vert. No. 1211, Cat, kittens. No. 1212, Kitten on top of mother, vert.

1995, Aug. 12 ***Perf. 14***
1207-1208 A182 1000d Sheets of 9, #a.-i. 10.00

Souvenir Sheets
1209-1212 A182 2000d multicolored 16.00

New Year 1996 (Year of the Rat) A183

Various species of rats, mice.

1995, Oct. 28
1213 A183 100d Sheet of 9, #a.-i. 6.00

Motion Pictures, Cent. — A184

Movie posters from: No. 1214: a, Gone with the Wind. b, Stagecoach. c, Tarzan and His Mate. d, Oregon Trail. e, The Oklahoma Kid. f, King Kong. g, A Lady Fights Back. h, Steamboat Around the Bend. i, Wee Willie Winkie.
No. 1215, Bring 'Em Back Alive. No. 1216 Indian chief.

1995, May 10 **Litho.** ***Perf. 14***
1214 A184 1000d Sheet of 9, #a.-i. 16.00

Souvenir Sheets
1215-1216 A184 2000d multi 16.00

Horses A185

Designs: No. 1217, Various horses.
No. 1218, Painting of Indian on horse, wild horses, horiz. No. 1219, City scene, horses, carriage, horiz.

1995, May 16
1217 A185 1000d Sheet of 9, #a.-i. 16.00

Souvenir Sheets
1218-1219 A185 2000d multi 16.00

Nos. 1218-1219 each contain one 50x35mm stamp.

Souvenir Sheet

Euro '96, European Soccer Championships, Great Britain — A186

Illustration reduced.

1995, July 2 ***Perf. 13½x14***
1220 A186 2000d multicolored 8.00

Souvenir Sheet

Protection of World's Endangered Species — A187

Illustration reduced.

1995, July 6 ***Perf. 14***
1221 A187 2000d multicolored 5.00

Mushrooms — A188

Designs: No. 1222a, Xerocomus rubellus. b, Rozites caperata. c, Cortinarius violaceus. d, Pholiota flammans. e, Lactarius volemus. f, Cortinarius (yellow). g, Cartinarius (blue). h, Higroforo. i, Boletus chrysenteron.
No. 1223, Amanita muscaria, vert. No. 1224, Russula cyanoxantha, vert.

1995, Nov. 2
1222 A188 1000d Sheet of 9, #a.-i. 16.00

Souvenir Sheets
1223-1224 A188 2000d multi 16.00

Details or Entire Paintings A189

No. 1225: a, Aurora and Cefalo. b, Madonna and Child with St. John as a Boy. c, Romulus and Remus. d, Lamentation over the Dead Christ. e, Vison of All Saints Day. f, Perseus and Andromeda. g. The Scent. h, The Encounter in Lyon. i, The Art School of Rubens-Bildern.
No. 1226, Statue of Ceres. No. 1227, Flight into Egypt, horiz.
All but #1225g (Jan Brueghel the Elder) and 1225i are by Rubens.

1995, Sept. 27 **Litho.** ***Perf. 14***
1225 A189 1000d Sheet of 9, #a.-i. 20.00

Souvenir Sheets
1226-1227 A189 2000d each 20.00

Greenpeace, 25th Anniv. — A190

Designs: No. 1237, Potto. No. 1238, Iguana. No. 1239, Tiger. No. 1240, Lion.
50d, Elephant, horiz.

1996, Aug. 5 **Litho.** ***Perf. 14***
1237-1240 A190 50d Set of 4 20.00

Souvenir Sheet
1241 A190 50d multicolored 6.00

Dogs & Cats A191

Nos. 1242a-1242i: Various pictures of dogs with cats, kittens.
Nos. 1243a-1243i, vert.: Various close-up pictures of different breeds of dogs.
No. 1244, Labrador retriever. No. 1245, Bird, woman's eye, vert. No. 1246, Two kittens. No. 1247, Collie, vert. No. 1248, Poodle, vert. No. 1249, Pit bull terrier, vert. No. 1250, Brown and white terrier, vert.

1995, Aug. 12 **Litho.** ***Perf. 14***

Sheets of 9
1242-1243 A191 1000d #a.-i., ea 16.00

Souvenir Sheets
1244-1250 A191 2000d each 16.00

Orchids A192

No. 1251: a, Findlayanum. b, Stan. c, Cruentum. d, Trpla suavis. e, Lowianum. f, Gratiosissimum. g, Cyrtorchis monteirae. h, Sarcanthus birmanicus. i, Loddigesii.
No. 1252, Barkeria Skinneri. No. 1253, Dendrobium nobile.

1995, Sept. 12
1251 A192 1000d Sheet of 9, #a.-i. 16.00

Souvenir Sheets
1252-1253 A192 2000d multi 16.00

Paintings, Drawings by Durer, Rubens — A193

Designs: No. 1254, Soldier on Horseback, by Durer, vert. No. 1255, Archangel St. Michael Slaying Satan, by Rubens, vert. No. 1256, Nursing Madonna in Half Length, by Durer, vert. No. 1257, Head of a Deer, by Durer, vert. No. 1258, View of Innsbruck from the North, by Durer. No. 1259, Madonna Nursing on a Grassy Bench, by Durer, vert. No. 1260, Helene Fourment and Her Children, by Rubens, vert. No. 1261, Adam and Eve, by Durer, vert.
No. 1262, A Young Hare, by Durer, vert. No. 1263, Mills on a River Bank, by Durer. No. 1264, Holy Family with a Basket, by Rubens, vert. No. 1265, The Annunciation, by Rubens, vert.

1995, Dec. 16 **Litho.** ***Perf. 14***
1254-1261 A193 750d Set of 8 20.00

Souvenir Sheets
1262-1265 A193 2000d each 20.00

Christmas.

Independence, 20th Anniv. — A194

1996, July 12 **Litho.** ***Perf. 13½***
1266 A194 350d multicolored 5.00

1996 Summer Olympic Games, Atlanta — A195

Various shells.

1996, Jan. 10 **Litho.** ***Perf. 14***
1267-1271 A195 1000d Set of 5 16.00

Souvenir Sheet
1272 A195 2000d multicolored 16.00

Anniversaries and Events — A196

1996, Aug. 2 ***Perf. 14x13½***

1273 A196 500d multicolored 6.00

UNICEF, 50th anniv., Alfred Nobel, 150th anniv. of birth, Phila-Seoul 96, KOREA 2002, 1996 Summer Olympic Games, Atlanta.

UNESCO A197

Butterflies: No. 1274, Papilio weiskei. No. 1275, Heliconius melpomene. No. 1276, Papilio arcas-mylotes. No. 1277, Mesomenia cresus. No. 1278, Catagramma iyca-satrana.
No. 1279, Lemonius sudias.

1996, Sept. 10 ***Perf. 13½x14***

1274-1278 A197 1000d Set of 5 16.00

Souvenir Sheet

1279 A197 2000d multicolored 10.00

Train Type of 1995

No. 1280, SNCF. No. 1281, CN. No. 1282, White locomotive. No. 1283, Green locomotive. No. 1284, Train in city.
No. 1285, Modern train. No. 1286, Old train.

1996, Oct. 7 ***Perf. 14***

1280-1284 A181 1000d Set of 5 16.00

Souvenir Sheets

1285-1286 A181 2000d each 20.00

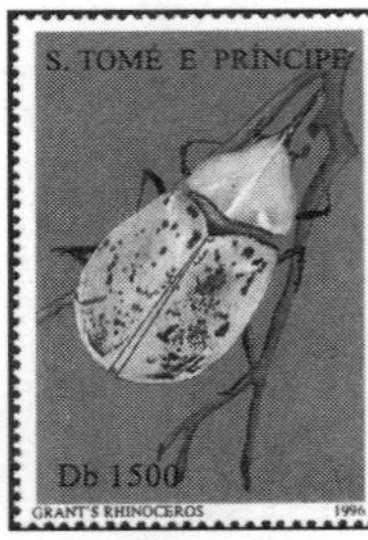

Beetles A198

#1287: a, Grant's rhinoceros. b, Emerald-colored. c, California laurel borer. d, Giant stag.
#1288, Maple borer. #1289, Arizona june.

1996, Nov. 7 ***Perf. 13½x14***

1287 A198 1500d Sheet of 4, #a.-d. 15.00

Souvenir Sheets

1288-1289 A198 2000d each 20.00

Plants, Orchids A199

No. 1290: a, Eryngium fortidum. b, Ocimum viride. c, Piper umbellatum. d, Phal. mariae. e, Odm. chiriquense. f, Phal. gigantea. g, Abutilon grandiflorum. h, Aframomium danielli. i, Chemopodium ambrosiodes.
No. 1291, Crinum jacus. No. 1292, Oncoba apinosa forsk. No. 1293, Z. mackai. No. 1294, Aspasia principissa.

1996, Oct. 14

1290 A199 1000d Sheet of 9, #a.-i. 12.00

Souvenir Sheets

1291-1294 A199 2000d each 20.00

Nos. 857-858 Surcharged

Nos. 736-737, 744, 746, 748 Surcharged in Blue or Black

Perfs. & Printing Methods as Before

1996?

1295 A123p 350d on 1d #857
1295A A123p 400d on 5d #858
1296 A95 1000d on 11d #736 (Bl)
1297 A95 1000d on 12d #737 (Bl)
1298 A95 1000d on 42d #746
1299 A95 2500d on 25d #744 (Bl)
1300 A95 2500d on 100d #748 (Bl)
Set 250.00

Musicians, Musical Instruments A200

"The Beatles" - #1301: a, John Lennon. b, Paul McCartney. c, George Harrison. d, Ringo Starr.
Traditional instruments - #1302: a, Animal horn. b, Flutes. c, Tambourine, drum, sticks. d, Canza.
No. 1303, Guitar, Elvis Presley (in sheet margin). No. 1304, Maraca, Antonio Machin.

1996, Nov. 19 Litho. ***Perf. 13½x14***

Sheets of 4

1301-1302 A200 1500d #a.-d., ea 10.00

Souvenir Sheets

1303-1304 A200 2000d each 20.00

Fish A201

#1305: a, Sailfish. b, Barracuda. c, Cod. d, Atlantic mackerel.
#1306, Bluefin tuna. #1307, Squirrelfish.

1996, Dec. 10 ***Perf. 14x13½***

1305 A201 1500d Sheet of 4, #a.-d. 15.00

Souvenir Sheets

1306-1307 A201 2000d each 20.00

No. 988 Surcharged in Dark Blue

Methods and Perfs as Before

1997, Apr. 16

1307A A144 1000d on 250d multi 25.00

Diana, Princess of Wales (1961-97) — A202

No. 1308: Various portraits, vert.
100d, Diana talking with her sons (in sheet margin), vert. 500d, Portrait. 2000d, Diana, Mother Teresa (in sheet margin), vert.

1997 **Litho.** ***Perf. 14***

1308 A202 10d Sheet of 9, #a.-i. 4.00

Souvenir Sheets

Perf. 13½x14, 14x13½

1309 A202 100d multicolored 6.00
1310 A202 500d gold & multi 8.00
1311 A202 2000d gold & multi 16.00

Issued: #1308, 100d, 500d, 10/15/97; 2000d, 10/20/97.

Souvenir Sheet

Michael Schumacher, World Champion Formula I Driver — A203

Illustration reduced.

1997, Dec. 12 ***Perf. 14***

1312 A203 500d multicolored 10.00

Souvenir Sheets

Titanic — A205

Designs: No. 1319, 2000d, Captain and Titanic (multicolored). No. 1320, 2000d, Captain and Titanic (black).

1998, July 1 **Litho.** ***Perf. 14x13¾***

1319-1320 A205 Set of 2

Numbers are reserved for two additional items in this set. The editors would like to examine any examples.

Expo '98, Lisbon — A206

Sea around the islands: No. 1326, Man fishing from shore. No. 1327, Man in small sailboat, sharks in water below. No. 1328, Flying fish. No. 1329, Diver connecting line on sea bottom. No. 1330, Man paddling boat, turtle, fish below.
8000d, Map of St. Thomas & Prince, vert.

1998 **Litho.** ***Perf. 14***

1326-1330 A206 3500d Set of 5 16.00

Souvenir Sheet

1331 A206 8000d multicolored 20.00

2nd AICEP Philatelic Exhibition — A207

Traditional food: No. 1332, Feijao de coco, coconuts. No. 1333, Cooked bananas, fruit, wine. No. 1334, Molho no fogo, fish, fruit, wine. No. 1335, Calulu, fruits, vegetables, wine. No. 1336, Izaquente de acucar, sugar beet.
7000d, Pot cooking over open fire, vert.

1998, Aug. 1

1332-1336 A207 3500d Set of 5 16.00

Souvenir Sheet

1337 A207 7000d multicolored 20.00

Souvenir Sheet

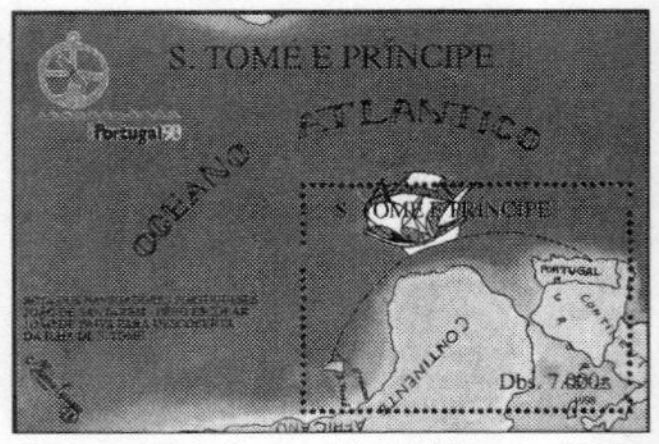

Portugal 98 Stamp Exhibition — A210

1998, Sept. 4 **Litho.** ***Perf. 14x13¾***

1342 A210 7000d Ship on map 15.00

Two stamps were issued with the souvenir sheet. The editors would like to examine them.

Nos. 728, 735, 739 Surcharged

Methods and Perfs as Before

1999, Nov.

1361	A95	5000d on 15.50d #739	*10.00*	*10.00*
1362	A95	7000d on 10d #735	*15.00*	*15.00*
1363	A95	10,000d on 1d #728	*20.00*	*20.00*
		Nos. 1361-1363 (3)	45.00	45.00

Christmas — A211

Designs: Nos. 1364, 1367, 5000d, Adoration of the Shepherds. Nos. 1365, 1368, 6000d, Presentation of Jesus in the Temple. Nos. 1366, 1369, 10,000d, Flight Into Egypt.

1999, Dec. 23 Litho. *Perf. 12¾x13*

1364-1366	A211	Set of 3	*6.50*	*6.50*

Souvenir Sheets

1367-1369	A211	Set of 3	*6.50*	*6.50*

Stamps on Nos. 1367-1369 have continuous designs.

Souvenir Sheet

Independence, 25th Anniv. — A213

No. 1371: a, 5000d, Mountain, bird. b, 6000d, Stylized mountains, birds, flag. c, 7000d, Mountains, "25," flag. d, 10,000d, Mountain, bird, diff.

2000, July 12 Litho. *Perf. 12¾*

1371	A213	Sheet of 4, #a-f	6.75	6.75

Nos. 746, 748 Surcharged

Methods & Perfs as Before

2000, Aug. 7

1372	A95	5000d on 42d multi	1.60	1.60
1373	A95	5000d on 100d multi	1.60	1.60

2000 Summer Olympics, Sydney — A214

Olympic rings and: 5000d, Runner, stadium, kangaroos, bird. 7000d, Runner, Sydney Opera House, kangaroos, emu.

15,000d, Sydney Harbour Bridge, Opera House, kangaroo, horiz.

2000, Sept. 14 Litho. *Perf. 12¾*

1374-1375	A214	Set of 2	4.00	4.00

Souvenir Sheet

Perf. 13

1376	A214	15,000d multi	5.00	5.00

Souvenir Sheet

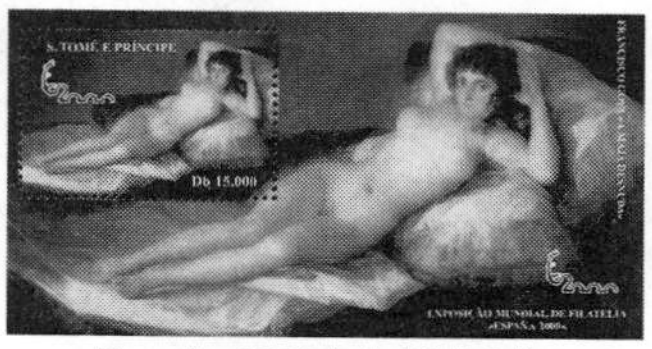

España 2000 Intl. Philatelic Exhibition — A215

2000, Oct. 6 *Perf. 12¾*

1377	A215	15,000d multi	3.25	3.25

Holy Year 2000 — A216

Designs: No. 1381a, 3000d, God, the Father. No. 1381b, 5000d, St. Anne, Virgin Mary, infant Jesus. Nos. 1378, 1381c, 6000d, St. Thomas. No. 1381d, 6000d, Processional cross. Nos. 1379, 1381e, 7000d, Altarpiece. Nos. 1380, 1381f, 8000d, Cathedral.

2000, Dec. 21 *Perf. 12¾*

With "Natal 2000" Inscription

1378-1380	A216	Set of 3	6.00	6.00

Without "Natal 2000" Inscription

1381	A216	Sheet of 6, #a-f	11.50	11.50
g.		Souvenir sheet, #1381a-1381b, 1381d-1381e, perf. 12	7.00	7.00

Rosa de Porcellana A218

Flower in: Nos. 1391, 5000d, 1393a, 7000d, Pink. Nos. 1392, 5000d, 1393b, 8000d, Red.

2001, Apr. 12 Litho. *Perf. 13¾x14*

1391-1392	A218	Set of 2	2.75	2.75

Souvenir Sheet

1393	A218	Sheet of 2, #a-b	4.00	4.00

Butterflies A219

Designs: No. 1394, 3500d, Graphium leonidas (brown frame). No. 1395, 5000d, Acraea newtoni (bright red frame). No. 1396, 6000d, Papilio bromius (bright red frame). No. 1397, 7500d, Papilio dardanos (brown frame).

No. 1398: a, 3500d, Graphium leonidas (orange frame). b, 5000d, Acraea newtoni (dark red frame). c, 6000d, Papilio bromius (dark red frame). d, 7500d, Papilio dardanos (orange frame).

15,000d, Euchloron megaera serrei.

2001, July 15 *Perf. 13¼x13½*

1394-1397	A219	Set of 4	5.75	5.75

Souvenir Sheets

1398	A219	Sheet of 4, #a-d	5.75	5.75
1399	A219	15,000d multi	4.00	4.00

Worldwide Fund for Nature (WWF) A220

Lepidochelys olivacea: 3500d, One swimming. 5000d, Two swimming. 6000d, Three leaving water. 7500d, Three hatchlings in sand.

2001, Oct.

1400-1403	A220	Set of 4	4.75	4.75

Nos. 1400-1403 were each issued in sheets of four. The margin of each of the four stamps on the sheets differs.

AIR POST STAMPS

Common Design Type
Inscribed "S. Tomé"

1938 *Perf. 13½x13*

Name and Value in Black

C1	CD39	10c red orange	30.00	22.50
C2	CD39	20c purple	15.00	11.00
C3	CD39	50c orange	1.50	1.25
C4	CD39	1e ultra	2.50	2.00
C5	CD39	2e lilac brown	3.75	3.00
C6	CD39	3e dark green	5.75	4.00
C7	CD39	5e red brown	7.50	6.50
C8	CD39	9e rose carmine	8.50	6.50
C9	CD39	10e magenta	9.50	6.50
		Nos. C1-C9 (9)	84.00	63.25

Common Design Type
Inscribed "S. Tomé e Principe"

1939 Engr. Unwmk.

Name and Value Typo. in Black

C10	CD39	10c scarlet	.50	.25
C11	CD39	20c purple	.50	.25
C12	CD39	50c orange	.50	.25
C13	CD39	1e deep ultra	.50	.25
C14	CD39	2e lilac brown	1.50	1.10
C15	CD39	3e dark green	2.00	1.25
C16	CD39	5e red brown	3.00	1.75
C17	CD39	9e rose carmine	5.00	2.50
C18	CD39	10e magenta	6.00	2.50
		Nos. C10-C18 (9)	19.50	10.10

No. C16 exists with overprint "Exposicao International de Nova York, 1939-1940" and Trylon and Perisphere.

POSTAGE DUE STAMPS

"S. Thomé" — D1

1904 Unwmk. Typo. *Perf. 12*

J1	D1	5r yellow green	.55	.55
J2	D1	10r slate	.65	.65
J3	D1	20r yellow brown	.65	.65
J4	D1	30r orange	1.00	.65
J5	D1	50r gray brown	1.75	1.40
J6	D1	60r red brown	2.50	1.60
J7	D1	100r red lilac	3.00	1.75
J8	D1	130r dull blue	4.00	3.25
J9	D1	200r carmine	4.50	3.50
J10	D1	500r gray violet	8.00	5.00
		Nos. J1-J10 (10)	26.60	19.00

Overprinted in Carmine or Green

1911

J11	D1	5r yellow green	.25	.25
J12	D1	10r slate	.25	.25
J13	D1	20r yellow brown	.25	.25
J14	D1	30r orange	.25	.25
J15	D1	50r gray brown	.25	.25
J16	D1	60r red brown	.55	.55
J17	D1	100r red lilac	.70	.70
J18	D1	130r dull blue	.70	.70
J19	D1	200r carmine (G)	.70	.70
J20	D1	500r gray violet	1.10	1.10
		Nos. J11-J20 (10)	5.00	5.00

Nos. J1-J10 Overprinted in Black

1913 Without Gum

J21	D1	5r yellow green	3.75	3.75
J22	D1	10r slate	5.00	4.50
J23	D1	20r yellow brown	2.50	2.50
J24	D1	30r orange	2.50	2.50
J25	D1	50r gray brown	2.50	2.50
J26	D1	60r red brown	3.00	3.00
J27	D1	100r red lilac	5.00	4.00
J28	D1	130r dull blue	35.00	35.00
a.		Inverted overprint	70.00	70.00
J29	D1	200r carmine	50.00	50.00
J30	D1	500r gray violet	75.00	40.00
		Nos. J21-J30 (10)	184.25	147.75

Nos. J1-J10 Overprinted in Black

1913 Without Gum

J31	D1	5r yellow green	3.00	3.00
a.		Inverted overprint	40.00	40.00
J32	D1	10r slate	4.00	4.00
J33	D1	20r yellow brown	3.00	3.00
J34	D1	30r orange	3.00	3.00
a.		Inverted overprint	40.00	
J35	D1	50r gray brown	3.00	3.00
J36	D1	60r red brown	4.00	4.00
J37	D1	100r red lilac	4.00	4.00
J38	D1	130r dull blue	4.00	4.00
J39	D1	200r carmine	7.00	6.00
J40	D1	500r gray violet	17.00	15.00
		Nos. J31-J40 (10)	52.00	49.00

No. J5 Overprinted "Republica" in Italic Capitals like Regular Issue in Green

1920 Without Gum

J41	D1	50r gray brn	40.00	35.00

"S. Tomé" — D2

1921 Typo. *Perf. 11½*

J42	D2	½c yellow green	.20	.20
J43	D2	1c slate	.20	.20
J44	D2	2c orange brown	.20	.20
J45	D2	3c orange	.20	.20
J46	D2	5c gray brown	.20	.20
J47	D2	6c lt brown	.20	.20
J48	D2	10c red violet	.20	.20
J49	D2	13c dull blue	.25	.20

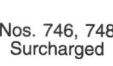

J50 D2 20c carmine .25 .20
J51 D2 50c gray .35 .40
Nos. J42-J51 (10) 2.25 2.20

In each sheet one stamp is inscribed "S. Thomé" instead of "S. Tomé." Value, set of 10, $60.

Catalogue values for unused stamps in this section, from this point to the end of the section, are for Never Hinged items.

Common Design Type
Photo. & Typo.
1952 Unwmk. *Perf. 14*
Numeral in Red, Frame Multicolored

J52 CD45 10c chocolate .30 .30
J53 CD45 30c red brown .30 .30
J54 CD45 50c dark blue .30 .30
J55 CD45 1e dark blue .50 .50
J56 CD45 2e olive green .75 .75
J57 CD45 5e black brown 2.00 2.00
Nos. J52-J57 (6) 4.15 4.15

NEWSPAPER STAMPS

N1

N2

Perf. 11½, 12½ and 13½
1892 Without Gum Unwmk.
Black Surcharge

P1 N1 2½r on 10r green 95.00 55.00
P2 N1 2½r on 20r rose 125.00 57.50
P3 N2 2½r on 10r green 125.00 57.50
P4 N2 2½r on 20r rose 125.00 57.50
Nos. P1-P4 (4) 470.00 227.50

Green Surcharge

P5 N1 2½r on 5r black 67.50 30.00
P6 N1 2½r on 20r rose 125.00 57.50
P8 N2 2½r on 5r black 125.00 60.00
P9 N2 2½r on 10r green 125.00 62.50
P10 N2 2½r on 20r rose 125.00 77.50
Nos. P5-P10 (5) 567.50 287.50

Both surcharges exist on No. 18 in green.

N3

d

1893 Typo. *Perf. 11½, 13½*
P12 N3 2½r brown .45 .40

For surcharges and overprints see Nos. 85, 166, 275, P13.

No. P12 Overprinted Type "d" in Blue
1899
Without Gum
P13 N3 2½r brown 25.00 16.00

POSTAL TAX STAMPS

Pombal Issue
Common Design Types
1925 Unwmk. *Perf. 12½*

RA1 CD28 15c orange & black .45 .45
RA2 CD29 15c orange & black .45 .45
RA3 CD30 15c orange & black .45 .45
Nos. RA1-RA3 (3) 1.35 1.35

Certain revenue stamps (5e, 6e, 7e, 8e and other denominations) were surcharged in 1946 "Assistencia," 2 bars and new values (1e or 1.50e) and used as postal tax stamps.

Catalogue values for unused stamps in this section, from this point to the end of the section, are for Never Hinged items.

PT1

1948-58 Typo. *Perf. 12x11½*
Denomination in Black

RA4 PT1 50c yellow grn 4.00 1.10
RA5 PT1 1e carmine rose 4.25 1.50
RA6 PT1 1e emerald ('58) 1.75 .75
RA7 PT1 1.50e bister brown 2.50 1.90
Nos. RA4-RA7 (4) 12.50 5.25

Denominations of 2e and up were used only for revenue purposes. No. RA6 lacks "Colonia de" below coat of arms.

Type of 1958 Surcharged

m

n

1964-65 Typo. *Perf. 12x11½*
RA8 PT1(m) 1e on 5e org yel 12.00 12.00
RA9 PT1(n) 1e on 5e org yel ('65) 4.50 4.50

The basic 5e orange yellow does not carry the words "Colonia de."

No. RA6 Surcharged: "Um escudo"
1965
RA10 PT1 1e emerald 2.00 2.00

Type of 1948 Surcharged

1965 Typo. *Perf. 12x11½*
RA11 PT1 1e emerald .40 .40

POSTAL TAX DUE STAMPS

Pombal Issue
Common Design Types
1925 Unwmk. *Perf. 12½*

RAJ1 CD28 30c orange & black .75 .75
RAJ2 CD29 30c orange & black .75 .75
RAJ3 CD30 30c orange & black .75 .75
Nos. RAJ1-RAJ3 (3) 2.25 2.25

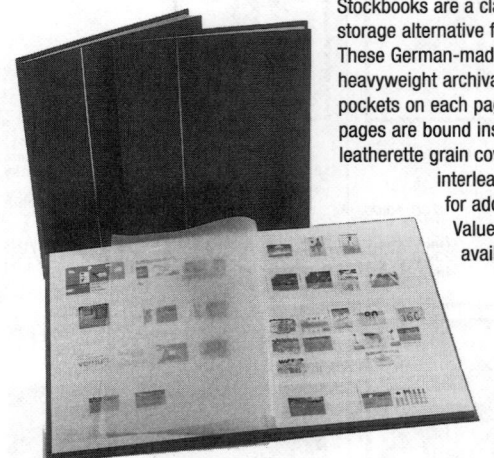

ST. VINCENT

sānt 'vin‿t‿-sənt

LOCATION — Island in the West Indies
GOVT. — Independent state in the British Commonwealth
AREA — 150 sq. mi.
POP. — 120,519 (1999 est.)
CAPITAL — Kingstown

The British colony of St. Vincent became an associated state in 1969 and independent in 1979.

12 Pence = 1 Shilling
20 Shillings = 1 Pound
100 Cents = 1 Dollar (1949)

Catalogue values for unused stamps in this country are for Never Hinged items, beginning with Scott 152 in the regular postage section, Scott B1 in the semi-postal section, and Scott O1 in the officials section.

Values for unused stamps are for examples with original gum as defined in the catalogue introduction. Early stamps were spaced extremely narrowly on the plates, and the perforations were applied irregularly.

Therefore, very fine examples of Nos. 1-28, 30-39 will have perforations that cut into the design slightly on one or more sides.

Also, very fine examples of Nos. 40-53, 55-60 will have perforations touching the design on at least one side.

These stamps with perfs clear of the design on all four sides, especially Nos. 1-28, 30-39, are extremely scarce and command substantially higher prices.

Watermark

Wmk. 5- Small Star

Queen Victoria — A1

1861 Engr. Unwmk. *Perf. 14 to 16*

1	A1	1p rose	—	—
a.		Imperf., pair	310.00	
c.		Horiz. pair, imperf. vert.	—	
1B	A1	6p yellow green	*7,250.*	250.00

Perfs on Nos. 1-1B are not clean cut. See Nos. 2-3 for rough perfs.

1862-66 *Rough Perf. 14 to 16*

2	A1	1p rose	37.50	13.50
a.		Horiz. pair, imperf. vert.	400.00	
3	A1	6p dark green	60.00	17.50
a.		Imperf., pair	750.00	
b.		Horiz. pair, imperf. between	2,750.	*3,750.*
4	A1	1sh slate ('66)	275.00	125.00
		Nos. 2-4 (3)	372.50	156.00

1863-69 *Perf. 11 to 13*

5	A1	1p rose	32.50	15.00
6	A1	4p blue ('66)	290.00	110.00
a.		Horiz. pair, imperf. vert.		
7	A1	4p orange ('69)	300.00	150.00
8	A1	6p deep green	225.00	60.00
8A	A1	1sh slate ('66)	*2,750.*	1,350.
9	A1	1sh indigo ('69)	300.00	100.00
10	A1	1sh brown ('69)	400.00	175.00

Perf. 11 to 13x14 to 16

11	A1	1p rose	*3,600.*	1,250.
12	A1	1sh slate	225.00	125.00

Rough Perf. 14 to 16

1871-78 Wmk. 5

13	A1	1p black	45.00	12.50
a.		Vert. pair, imperf. btwn.	*5,750.*	
14	A1	6p dk blue green	275.00	70.00

Clean-Cut Perf. 14 to 16

14A	A1	1p black	35.00	10.00
14B	A1	6p dp bl grn	600.00	40.00
c.		6p dull blue green	750.00	40.00
15	A1	6p pale yel green ('78)	650.00	32.50
15A	A1	1sh vermilion ('77)		*13,500.*

For surcharge see No. 30.

Perf. 11 to 13

16	A1	4p dk bl ('77)	450.00	90.00
17	A1	1sh deep rose ('72)	750.00	135.00
18	A1	1sh claret ('75)	575.00	225.00

Perf. 11 to 13x14 to 16

20	A1	1p black	60.00	9.00
a.		Horiz. pair, imperf. btwn.		*5,000.*
21	A1	6p pale yel grn ('77)	450.00	50.00
22	A1	1sh lilac rose ('72)	*5,500.*	350.00
23	A1	1sh vermilion ('77)	800.00	100.00
a.		Horiz. pair, imperf. vert.		

See Nos. 25-28A, 36-39, 42-53. For surcharges see Nos. 30, 32-33, 40, 55-60.

Victoria
A2

Seal of Colony
A3

1880-81 *Perf. 11 to 13*

24	A2	½p orange ('81)	8.00	4.50
25	A1	1p gray green	125.00	7.50
26	A1	1p drab ('81)	700.00	13.50
27	A1	4p ultra ('81)	1,000.	110.00
a.		Horiz. pair, imperf. btwn.		
28	A1	6p yellow green	425.00	60.00
28A	A1	1sh vermilion	625.00	55.00
29	A3	5sh rose	1,250.	1,350.

No. 29 is valued well centered with design well clear of the perfs.

See #35, 41, 54, 598. For surcharges see #31-33.

No. 14B Bisected and Surcharged in Red

d.
1

1880, May *Perf. 14 to 16*

30	A1	1p on half of 6p	450.00	300.00
a.		Unsevered pair	1,250.	900.00

No. 28 Bisected and Surcharged in Red

d
1
2

1881, Sept. 1

31	A1	½p on half of 6p yel grn ('81)	160.	160.
a.		Unsevered pair	400.00	400.00
b.		"1" with straight top	900.	
c.		Without fraction bar, pair, #31, 31c	4,500.	*5,500.*

Nos. 28 and 28A Surcharged in Black:

ONE PENNY
c

4d
d

1881, Nov. *Perf. 11 to 13*

32	A1(c)	1p on 6p yel green	400.	300.
33	A1(d)	4p on 1sh ver	1,350.	700.

1883-84 Wmk. 2 *Perf. 12*

35	A2	½p green ('84)	70.00	25.00
36	A1	4p ultra	375.00	22.50
37	A1	4p dull blue ('84)	1,075.	325.00
38	A1	6p yellow grn	325.00	300.00
39	A1	1sh orange ver	120.00	55.00
a.		Imperf., pair		

The ½p orange, 1p rose red, 1p milky blue and 5sh carmine lake were never placed in use. Some authorities believe them to be color trials.

Nos. 35-60 may be found watermarked with single straight line. This is from the frame which encloses each group of 60 watermark designs.

Type of A1 Surcharged in Black

e

2½ PENCE

1883 *Perf. 14*

40	A1	2½p on 1p lake	11.50	1.75

1883-97

41	A2	½p green ('85)	.90	.50
42	A1	1p drab	40.00	1.75
43	A1	1p rose red ('85)	2.75	1.00
44	A1	1p pink ('86)	4.50	2.75
45	A1	2½p brt blue ('97)	2.75	2.75
46	A1	4p ultra	375.00	32.50
47	A1	4p red brown ('85)	850.00	22.50
48	A1	4p lake brn ('86)	45.00	2.50
49	A1	4p yellow ('93)	1.75	*5.50*
a.		4p olive yellow	350.00	350.00
50	A1	5p gray brn ('97)	5.50	*17.50*
51	A1	6p violet ('88)	125.00	*150.00*
52	A1	6p red violet ('91)	2.00	*8.50*
53	A1	1sh org ver ('91)	6.00	10.00
54	A3	5sh car lake ('88)	27.50	*50.00*

Grading footnote after No. 29 applies equally to Nos. 54-54a.

For other shades, see the *Scott Classic Catalogue.*

No. 40 Resurcharged in Black

1d

1885, Mar.

55	A1	1p on 2½p on 1p lake	20.00	15.00

Copies with 3-bar cancel are proofs.

Stamps of Type A1 Surcharged in Black or Violet:

2½d.
g

5 PENCE
h

i

FIVE PENCE

1890-91

56	A1(e)	2½p on 1p brt blue	1.25	.50
a.		2½p on 1p milky blue	22.50	4.75
b.		2½p on 1p gray blue	17.50	1.75
57	A1(g)	2½p on 4p vio brn ('90)	70.00	*90.00*
a.		Without fraction bar	300.00	*350.00*

1892-93

58	A1(h)	5p on 4p lake brn (V)	14.50	*26.00*
59	A1(j)	5p on 6p dp lake ('93)	1.00	*1.75*
a.		5p on 6p carmine lake	20.00	*30.00*
b.		Double surcharge	4,000.	3,500.

1897

60	A1(j)	3p on 1p lilac	6.00	*17.50*

Victoria
A13

Edward VII
A14

Numerals of 1sh and 5sh, type A13, and of 2p, 1sh, 5sh and £1, type A14, are in color on plain tablet.

1898 Typo. *Perf. 14*

62	A13	½p lilac & grn	2.40	1.40
63	A13	1p lil & car rose	3.75	.80
64	A13	2½p lilac & ultra	3.75	2.00
65	A13	3p lilac & ol grn	3.75	*9.00*
66	A13	4p lilac & org	3.75	*13.50*
67	A13	5p lilac & blk	7.50	*13.50*
68	A13	6p lilac & brn	13.50	*27.50*
69	A13	1sh grn & car rose	15.00	*45.00*
70	A13	5sh green & ultra	70.00	*125.00*
		Nos. 62-70 (9)	123.40	*237.70*

1902

71	A14	½p violet & green	2.00	.60
72	A14	1p vio & car rose	2.50	.30
73	A14	2p violet & black	2.00	2.25
74	A14	2½p violet & ultra	3.75	3.00
75	A14	3p violet & ol grn	3.00	2.50
76	A14	6p violet & brn	10.00	*27.50*
77	A14	1sh grn & car rose	17.00	*47.50*
78	A14	2sh green & violet	24.00	*50.00*
79	A14	5sh green & ultra	60.00	*100.00*
		Nos. 71-79 (9)	124.25	*233.65*

1904-11 Wmk. 3

Chalky Paper

82	A14	½p vio & grn	5.00	1.25
83	A14	1p vio & car rose	17.00	.20
84	A14	2½p vio & ultra	13.00	*22.50*
85	A14	6p vio & brn	13.00	*22.50*
86	A14	1sh grn & car rose	13.50	*27.50*
87	A14	2sh vio & bl, *bl*	19.00	*25.00*
88	A14	5sh grn & red, *yel*	14.50	*30.00*
89	A14	£1 vio & blk, *red*	275.00	*325.00*
		Nos. 82-88 (7)	95.00	*128.95*

#82, 83 and 86 also exist on ordinary paper.

Issued: 1p, 1904, ½p, 6p, 1905; 2½p, 1906; 1sh, 1908; 2sh, 5sh, 1909; £1, July 22, 1911.

"Peace and Justice"
A15 A16

1907 Engr.

Ordinary Paper

90	A15	½p yellow green	1.10	1.00
91	A15	1p carmine	2.25	.90
92	A15	2p orange	.75	*4.50*
93	A15	2½p ultra	14.00	*10.50*
94	A15	3p dark violet	3.75	*15.00*
		Nos. 90-94 (5)	21.85	*31.90*

1909

Without Dot under "d"

95	A16	1p carmine	1.50	.50
96	A16	6p red violet	6.75	*25.00*
97	A16	1sh black, *green*	4.75	8.50
		Nos. 95-97 (3)	13.00	*34.00*

1909-11

With Dot under "d"

98	A16	½p yellow grn ('10)	1.25	.55
99	A16	1p carmine	1.25	.20
100	A16	2p gray ('11)	2.75	7.25
101	A16	2½p ultra	5.50	3.00
102	A16	3p violet, *yel*	2.00	*4.75*
103	A16	6p red violet	3.25	*4.25*
		Nos. 98-103 (6)	16.00	*20.00*

King George V — A17

1913-14 *Perf. 14*

104	A17	½p gray green	.20	.20
105	A17	1p carmine	.20	.20
106	A17	2p gray	1.25	*10.00*
107	A17	2½p ultra	.50	.35
108	A17	3p violet, *yellow*	1.00	*3.75*
109	A17	4p red, *yellow*	.65	*1.50*
110	A17	5p olive green	2.00	*9.50*
111	A17	6p claret	1.25	*3.25*
112	A17	1sh black, *green*	1.50	*2.75*
113	A17	1sh bister ('14)	2.50	*14.50*
114	A16	2sh vio & ultra	7.00	*19.00*
115	A16	5sh dk grn & car	15.00	*35.00*
116	A16	£1 black & vio	80.00	*125.00*
		Nos. 104-116 (13)	113.05	*225.00*

Issued: 5p, 11/7; #113, 5/1/14; others, 1/1/13.

For overprints see Nos. MR1-MR2.

No. 112 Surcharged in Carmine

ONE
PENNY.

1915

117 A17 1p on 1sh black, *grn*	7.00	20.00
a. "PENNY" & bar double	750.00	
b. Without period	14.00	
c. "ONE" omitted	900.00	
d. "ONE" double	750.00	

Space between surcharge lines varies from 8 to 10mm.

1921-32 Wmk. 4

118 A17 ½p green	.20	.20
119 A17 1p rose red	.20	.75
120 A17 1½p yel brn ('32)	.80	.20
121 A17 2p gray	.35	.25
122 A17 2½p ultra ('26)	.55	.45
123 A17 3p ultra	2.25	*5.00*
124 A17 3p vio, *yel* ('27)	.50	*1.40*
125 A17 4p red, *yel* ('30)	1.50	*4.50*
126 A17 5p olive green	.45	*4.50*
127 A17 6p claret ('27)	.55	*3.00*
128 A17 1sh bister	1.00	*17.50*
129 A16 2sh brn vio & ultra	4.50	*12.50*
130 A16 5sh dk grn & car	11.25	*27.50*
131 A16 £1 blk & vio ('28)	90.00	*110.00*
Nos. 118-131 (14)	114.10	*187.75*

Common Design Types pictured following the introduction.

Silver Jubilee Issue
Common Design Type

1935, May 6 Perf. 11x12

134 CD301 1p car & dk blue	.30	*1.40*
135 CD301 1½p gray blk & ultra	.35	*2.75*
136 CD301 2½p ultra & brn	1.10	*2.75*
137 CD301 1sh brn vio & ind	3.25	2.75
Nos. 134-137 (4)	5.00	9.65
Set, never hinged	12.00	

Coronation Issue
Common Design Type

1937, May 12 Perf. 11x11½

138 CD302 1p dark purple	.20	.20
139 CD302 1½p dark carmine	.25	.25
140 CD302 2½p deep ultra	.30	*1.00*
Nos. 138-140 (3)	.75	1.45
Set, never hinged	1.00	

Seal of the Colony — A18

Young's Island and Fort Duvernette — A19

Kingstown and Fort Charlotte — A20

Villa Beach — A21

Victoria Park, Kingstown — A22

1938-47 Wmk. 4 Perf. 12

141 A18 ½p grn & brt bl	.20	.20
142 A19 1p claret & blue	.20	.20
143 A20 1½p scar & lt grn	.20	.20
144 A18 2p black & green	.30	.20
145 A21 2½p pck bl & ind	.20	.20
145A A22 2½p choc & grn ('47)	.20	.20
146 A18 3p dk vio & org	.20	.20
146A A21 3½p dp bl grn & ind ('47)	.35	.50
147 A18 6p claret & blk	.60	.25
148 A22 1sh green & vio	.60	.45
149 A18 2sh dk vio & brt blue	3.50	.85
149A A18 2sh6p dp bl & org brn ('47)	.60	1.75
150 A18 5sh dk grn & car	6.00	2.50
150A A18 10sh choc & dp vio ('47)	2.25	*9.00*
151 A18 £1 black & vio	9.50	*12.00*
Nos. 141-151 (15)	24.90	*28.70*
Set, never hinged	40.00	

Issue date: Mar. 11, 1938.
See Nos. 156-169, 180-184.

Catalogue values for unused stamps in this section, from this point to the end of the section, are for Never Hinged items.

Peace Issue
Common Design Type

1946, Oct. 15 Engr. Perf. 13½x14

152 CD303 1½p carmine	.20	.20
153 CD303 3½p deep blue	.20	.20

Silver Wedding Issue
Common Design Types

1948, Nov. 30 Photo. Perf. 14x14½

154 CD304 1½p scarlet	.20	.20

Engraved; Name Typographed
Perf. 11½x11

155 CD305 £1 red violet	17.50	18.00

Types of 1938

1949, Mar. 26 Engr. Perf. 12

156 A18 1c grn & brt bl	.20	*1.25*
157 A19 2c claret & bl	.20	*.50*
158 A20 3c scar & lt grn	.45	*.65*
159 A18 4c gray blk & grn	.40	.20
160 A22 5c choc & grn	.20	.20
161 A18 6c dk vio & org	.45	*.95*
162 A21 7c pck blue & ind	4.50	.95
163 A18 12c claret & blk	.50	.20
164 A22 24c green & vio	.50	.50
165 A18 48c dk vio & brt bl	2.50	2.10
166 A18 60c dp bl & org brn	1.90	*3.25*
167 A18 $1.20 dk grn & car	4.75	3.75
168 A18 $2.40 choc & dp vio	6.75	*8.50*
169 A18 $4.80 gray blk & vio	11.50	*17.00*
Nos. 156-169 (14)	34.80	40.00

For overprints see Nos. 176-179.

UPU Issue
Common Design Types
Engr.; Name Typo. on 6c, 12c
Perf. 13½, 11x11½

1949, Oct. 10 Wmk. 4

170 CD306 5c blue	.20	.20
171 CD307 6c dp rose violet	.45	.90
172 CD308 12c red lilac	.25	.90
173 CD309 24c blue green	1.00	.25
Nos. 170-173 (4)	1.90	2.25

University Issue
Common Design Types

1951, Feb. 16 Engr. Perf. 14x14½

174 CD310 3c red & blue green	.60	.60
175 CD311 12c rose lilac & blk	.60	*1.00*

Nos. 158-160 and 163 Overprinted in Black

NEW CONSTITUTION 1951

1951, Sept. 21 Perf. 12

176 A20 3c scarlet & lt grn	.20	.20
177 A18 4c gray blk & grn	.20	.20
178 A22 5c chocolate & grn	.20	.20
179 A18 12c claret & blk	.40	.40
Nos. 176-179 (4)	1.00	1.00

Adoption of a new constitution for the Windward Islands, 1951.

Type of 1938-47

1952

180 A18 1c gray black & green	.20	.20
181 A18 3c dk violet & orange	.20	.20
182 A18 4c green & brt blue	.20	.20
183 A20 6c scarlet & dp green	.20	.20
184 A21 10c peacock blue & indigo	.35	.35
Nos. 180-184 (5)	1.15	1.15

Coronation Issue
Common Design Type

1953, June 2 Perf. 13½x13

185 CD312 4c dk green & blk	.70	.50

Elizabeth II — A23

Seal of Colony — A24

Perf. 13x14

1955, Sept. 16 Wmk. 4 Engr.

186 A23 1c orange	.20	.20
187 A23 2c violet blue	.20	.20
188 A23 3c gray	.20	.20
189 A23 4c dk red brown	.20	.20
190 A23 5c scarlet	.20	.20
191 A23 10c purple	.25	.20
192 A23 15c deep blue	.35	.40
193 A23 20c green	.50	.20
194 A23 25c brown black	.90	.20

Perf. 14

195 A24 50c chocolate	1.60	1.75
196 A24 $1 dull green	4.75	1.25
197 A24 $2.50 deep blue	16.00	9.00
Nos. 186-197 (12)	25.35	14.00

West Indies Federation
Common Design Type
Perf. 11½x11

1958, Apr. 22 Wmk. 314

198 CD313 3c green	.30	.25
199 CD313 6c blue	.40	.50
200 CD313 12c carmine rose	.80	1.00
Nos. 198-200 (3)	1.50	1.75

Freedom from Hunger Issue
Common Design Type

1963, June 4 Photo. Perf. 14x14½

201 CD314 8c lilac	.90	.50

Red Cross Centenary Issue
Common Design Type

1963, Sept. 2 Litho. Perf. 13

202 CD315 4c black & red	.25	.20
203 CD315 8c ultra & red	.65	.65

Types of 1955
Perf. 13x14

1964-65 Wmk. 314 Engr.

205 A23 1c orange	.20	.20
206 A23 2c violet blue	.20	.20
207 A23 3c gray	.50	.40
208 A23 5c scarlet	.30	.30
209 A23 10c purple	.40	.30
a. Perf. 12½	.25	.25
210 A23 15c deep blue	.80	.55
a. Perf. 12½	.45	.30
211 A23 20c green	.60	.50
a. Perf. 12½	7.50	2.00
212 A23 25c brown black	1.10	.85
a. Perf. 12½	1.10	.85

Perf. 14

213 A24 50c chocolate ('65)	4.75	3.75
a. Perf. 12½	5.00	7.00
Nos. 205-213 (9)	8.85	7.05

Scout Emblem and Merit Badges — A25

1964, Nov. 23 Litho. Perf. 14

216 A25 1c dk brn & brt yel grn	.20	.20
217 A25 4c dk red brn & brt bl	.20	.20
218 A25 20c dk violet & orange	.35	.20
219 A25 50c green & red	.65	.40
Nos. 216-219 (4)	1.40	1.00

Boy Scouts of St. Vincent, 50th anniv.

Breadfruit and Capt. Bligh's Ship "Providence" — A26

Designs: 1c, Tropical fruit. 25c, Doric temple and pond, vert. 40c, Blooming talipot palm and Doric temple, vert.

Perf. 14½x13½, 13½x14½

1965, Mar. 23 Photo. Wmk. 314

220 A26 1c dk green & multi	.20	.20
221 A26 4c lt & dk brn grn & yel	.20	.20
222 A26 25c blue, grn & bister	.25	.20
223 A26 40c dk blue & multi	.50	.75
Nos. 220-223 (4)	1.15	1.35

Bicentenary of the Botanic Gardens.

ITU Issue
Common Design Type

1965, May 17 Litho. Perf. 11x11½

224 CD317 4c blue & yel grn	.20	.20
225 CD317 48c yellow & orange	.80	.70

Boat Building, Bequia A27

Woman Carrying Bananas — A28

Designs: 2c, Friendship Beach, Bequia. 3c, Terminal building. 5c, Crater Lake. 6c, Rock carvings, Carib Stone. 8c, Arrowroot. 10c, Owia saltpond. 12c, Ship at deep water wharf. 20c, Sea Island cotton. 25c, Map of St. Vincent and neighboring islands. 50c, Breadfruit. $1, Baleine Falls. $2.50, St. Vincent parrot. $5, Coat of arms.

Perf. 14x13½, 13½x14

1965-67 Photo. Wmk. 314

226 A27 1c (BEOUIA)	.20	.75
226A A27 1c (BEQUIA)	.50	.25
227 A27 2c lt ultra, grn, yel & red	.20	.20
228 A27 3c red, yel & brn	.25	.20
229 A28 4c brown, ultra & yel	.75	.25
a. Wmkd. sideways	.50	.20
230 A27 5c pur, bl, yel & grn	.20	.20
231 A28 6c sl grn, yel & gray	.20	.30
232 A28 8c pur, yel & grn	.25	.20
233 A27 10c org brn, yel & bluish grn	.25	.20
234 A27 12c grnsh bl, yel & pink	.55	.20
235 A28 20c brt yel, grn, pur & brn	.25	.20
236 A28 25c ultra, grn & vio blue	.30	.20
237 A28 50c grn, yel & bl	.35	.25
238 A28 $1 vio bl, lt grn & dk sl grn	3.00	.25
239 A28 $2.50 pale lilac & multi	14.00	4.00
240 A28 $5 dull vio blue & multi	3.75	6.50
Nos. 226-240 (16)	25.00	14.15

Issued: #226A, 8/8/67; others, 8/16/65.
For overprint see No. 270.

Churchill Memorial Issue
Common Design Type

1966, Jan. 24 Perf. 14
Design in Black, Gold and Carmine Rose

241 CD319 1c bright blue	.20	.20
242 CD319 4c green	.20	.20
243 CD319 20c brown	.40	.40
244 CD319 40c violet	.75	.75
Nos. 241-244 (4)	1.55	1.55

Royal Visit Issue
Common Design Type

1966, Feb. 4 Litho. *Perf. 11x12*

Portrait in Black

245	CD320	4c	violet blue	.50	.20
246	CD320	25c	dk carmine rose	2.50	1.50

WHO Headquarters Issue
Common Design Type

1966, Sept. 20 Litho. *Perf. 14*

247	CD322	4c	multicolored	.20	.20
248	CD322	25c	multicolored	1.00	.75

UNESCO Anniversary Issue
Common Design Type

1966, Dec. 1 Litho. *Perf. 14*

249	CD323	4c	"Education"	.20	.20
250	CD323	8c	"Science"	.45	.20
251	CD323	25c	"Culture"	1.50	.75
			Nos. 249-251 (3)	2.15	1.15

View of Mt. Coke Area A29

Designs: 8c, Kingstown Methodist Church. 25c, First license to perform marriage, May 15, 1867. 35c, Arms of Conference of the Methodist Church in the Caribbean and the Americas.

Perf. 14x14½

1967, Dec. 1 Photo. Wmk. 314

252	A29	2c	multicolored	.20	.20
253	A29	8c	multicolored	.20	.20
254	A29	25c	multicolored	.25	.20
255	A29	35c	multicolored	.30	.20
			Nos. 252-255 (4)	.95	.80

Attainment of autonomy by the Methodist Church in the Caribbean and the Americas, and opening of headquarters near St. John's, Antigua, May 1967.

For overprints see Nos. 268-269, 271.

Caribbean Meteorological Institute, Barbados — A30

Perf. 14x14½

1968, June 28 Photo. Wmk. 314

256	A30	4c	cerise & multi	.20	.20
257	A30	25c	vermilion & multi	.20	.20
258	A30	35c	violet blue & multi	.25	.20
			Nos. 256-258 (3)	.65	.60

Issued for World Meteorological Day.

Martin Luther King, Jr. and Cotton Pickers A31

Perf. 13½x13

1968, Aug. 28 Litho. Wmk. 314

259	A31	5c	violet & multi	.20	.20
260	A31	25c	gray & multi	.25	.25
261	A31	35c	brown red & multi	.35	.25
			Nos. 259-261 (3)	.80	.70

Dr. Martin Luther King, Jr. (1929-68), American civil rights leader.

Scales of Justice and Human Rights Flame — A32

Carnival Costume — A33

3c, Speaker addressing demonstrators, horiz.

Perf. 13x14, 14x13

1968, Nov. 1 Photo. Unwmk.

262	A32	3c	orange & multi	.20	.20
263	A32	35c	grnsh blue & vio blue	.35	.20

International Human Rights Year.

1969, Feb. 17 Litho. *Perf. 14½*

5c, Sketch of a steel bandsman. 8c, Revelers, horiz. 25c, Queen of Bands & attendants.

264	A33	1c	multicolored	.20	.20
265	A33	5c	red & dark brown	.20	.20
266	A33	8c	multicolored	.20	.20
267	A33	25c	multicolored	.40	.25
			Nos. 264-267 (4)	1.00	.85

St. Vincent Carnival celebration, Feb. 17.

Nos. 252-253, 236 and 255 Overprinted: "METHODIST / CONFERENCE / MAY / 1969"

Perf. 14x14½, 13½x14

1969, May 14 Photo. Wmk. 314

268	A29	2c	multicolored	.20	.20
269	A29	8c	multicolored	.20	.20
270	A28	25c	multicolored	.20	.20
271	A29	35c	multicolored	1.50	*2.00*
			Nos. 268-271 (4)	2.10	2.60

1st Caribbean Methodist Conf. held outside Antigua.

"Strength in Unity" — A34

5c, 25c, Map of the Caribbean, vert.

Perf. 13½x13, 13x13½

1969, July 1 Litho.

272	A34	2c	orange, yel & blk	.20	.20
273	A34	5c	lilac & multi	.20	.20
274	A34	8c	emerald, yel & blk	.20	.20
275	A34	25c	blue & multi	.50	.30
			Nos. 272-275 (4)	1.10	.90

1st anniv. of CARIFTA (Caribbean Free Trade Area.)

Flag and Arms of St. Vincent — A35

Designs: 10c, Uprising of 1795. 50c, Government House.

Perf. 14x14½

1969, Oct. 27 Photo. Wmk. 314

276	A35	4c	deep ultra & multi	.20	.20
277	A35	10c	olive & multi	.20	.20
278	A35	50c	orange, gray & blk	.65	.50
			Nos. 276-278 (3)	1.05	.90

Green Heron A36

Birds: ½c, House wren, vert. 2c, Bullfinches. 3c, St. Vincent parrots. 4c, St. Vincent solitaire, vert. 5c, Scalynecked pigeon, vert. 6c, Bananaquits. 8c, Purple-throated Carib. 10c, Mangrove cuckoo, vert. 12c, Black hawk, vert. 20c, Bare-eyed thrush. 25c, Hooded tanager. 50c, Blue-hooded euphonia. $1, Barn owl, vert. $2.50, Yellow-bellied elaenia, vert. $5, Ruddy quail-dove.

Wmk. 314 Upright on ½c, 4c, 5c, 10c, 12c, 50c, $5, Sideways on Others

1970, Jan. 12 Photo. *Perf. 14*

279	A36	½c	multicolored	.20	.20
280	A36	1c	multicolored	.20	.20
281	A36	2c	multicolored	.20	.20
282	A36	3c	multicolored	.20	.20
283	A36	4c	multicolored	.20	.20
284	A36	5c	multicolored	1.25	.65
285	A36	6c	multicolored	.40	.35
286	A36	8c	multicolored	.40	.25
287	A36	10c	multicolored	.45	.35
288	A36	12c	multicolored	.60	.40
289	A36	20c	multicolored	.80	.50
290	A36	25c	multicolored	.80	.50
291	A36	50c	multicolored	1.25	.75
292	A36	$1	multicolored	3.25	1.50
293	A36	$2.50	multicolored	6.50	4.00
294	A36	$5	multicolored	16.00	10.00
			Nos. 279-294 (16)	32.70	20.25

See #379-381. For surcharges see #364-366.

Wmk. 314 Upright on 2c, 3c, 6c, 20c, Sideways on Others

1973

281a	A36	2c	multicolored	.35	*.40*
282a	A36	3c	multicolored	.35	*.40*
283a	A36	4c	multicolored	.35	.35
284a	A36	5c	multicolored	.35	.20
285a	A36	6c	multicolored	.50	*.55*
287a	A36	10c	multicolored	.50	.20
288a	A36	12c	multicolored	.75	.55
289a	A36	20c	multicolored	.85	.35
			Nos. 281a-289a (8)	4.00	3.00

DHC6 Twin Otter A37

20th anniv. of regular air services: 8c, Grumman Goose amphibian. 10c, Hawker Siddeley 748. 25c, Douglas DC-3.

Perf. 14x13

1970, Mar. 13 Litho. Wmk. 314

295	A37	5c	lt blue & multi	.20	.20
296	A37	8c	lt green & multi	.20	.20
297	A37	10c	pink & multi	.40	.25
298	A37	25c	yellow & multi	1.00	.65
			Nos. 295-298 (4)	1.80	1.30

Nurse and Children A38

Red Cross and: 5c, First aid. 12c, Volunteers. 25c, Blood transfusion.

1970, June 1 Photo. *Perf. 14*

299	A38	3c	blue & multi	.20	.20
300	A38	5c	yellow & multi	.20	.20
301	A38	12c	lt green & multi	.30	.20
302	A38	25c	pale salmon & multi	.60	.55
			Nos. 299-302 (4)	1.30	1.15

Centenary of British Red Cross Society.

St. George's Cathedral — A39

Designs: ½c, 50c, Angel and Two Marys at the Tomb, stained glass window, vert. 25c, St. George's Cathedral, front view, vert. 35c, Interior with altar.

Perf. 14x14½, 14½x14

1970, Sept. 7 Litho. Wmk. 314

303	A39	½c	multicolored	.20	.20
304	A39	5c	multicolored	.20	.20
305	A39	25c	multicolored	.25	.20
306	A39	35c	multicolored	.30	.25
307	A39	50c	multicolored	.40	.30
			Nos. 303-307 (5)	1.35	1.15

St. George's Anglican Cathedral, 150th anniv.

Virgin and Child, by Giovanni Bellini — A40

Christmas: 25c, 50c, Adoration of the Shepherds, by Louis Le Nain, horiz.

1970, Nov. 23 Litho. Wmk. 314

308	A40	8c	brt violet & multi	.20	.20
309	A40	25c	crimson & multi	.20	.20
310	A40	35c	yellow grn & multi	.25	.20
311	A40	50c	sapphire & multi	.40	.30
			Nos. 308-311 (4)	1.05	.90

Post Office and St. Vincent No. 1B A41

New Post Office and: 4c, $1, St. Vincent No. 1. 25c, as 2c.

1971, Mar. 29 *Perf. 14½x14*

312	A41	2c	violet & multi	.20	.20
313	A41	4c	olive & multi	.20	.20
314	A41	25c	brown org & multi	.20	.20
315	A41	$1	lt green & multi	.65	.50
			Nos. 312-315 (4)	1.25	1.10

110th anniv. of 1st stamps of St. Vincent.

National Trust Emblem, Fish and Birds — A42

Designs: 30c, 45c, Cannon at Ft. Charlotte.

Perf. 13½x14

1971, Aug. 4 Litho. Wmk. 314

316	A42	12c	emerald & multi	.20	.20
317	A42	30c	lt blue & multi	.40	.35
318	A42	40c	brt pink & multi	.60	.40
319	A42	45c	black & multi	.80	.60
			Nos. 316-319 (4)	2.00	1.55

Publicity for the National Trust (for conservation of wild life and historic buildings).

Holy Family with Angels (detail), by Pietro da Cortona
A43

Christmas: 5c, 25c, Madonna Appearing to St. Anthony, by Domenico Tiepolo, vert.

1971, Oct. 6 ***Perf. 14x14½, 14½x14***

320 A43 5c rose & multi .20 .20
321 A43 10c lt green & multi .20 .20
322 A43 25c lt blue & multi .20 .20
323 A43 $1 yellow & multi .75 .55
Nos. 320-323 (4) 1.35 1.15

Careening — A44

Designs: 5c, 20c, Seine fishermen. 6c, 50c, Map of Grenadines. 15c, as 1c.

1971, Nov. 25 ***Perf. 14x13½***

324 A44 1c dp ver & multi .20 .20
325 A44 5c blue & multi .20 .20
326 A44 6c yel grn & multi .20 .20
327 A44 15c org brn & multi .35 .25
328 A44 20c yellow & multi .40 .30
329 A44 50c blue, blk & plum 1.00 .85
a. Souvenir sheet of 6, #324-329 10.50 9.25
Nos. 324-329 (6) 2.35 2.00

The Grenadines of St. Vincent tourist issue.

Grenadier Company Private, 1764 — A45

Designs: 30c, Battalion Company officer, 1772. 50c, Grenadier Company private, 1772.

1972, Feb. 14 ***Perf. 14x13½***

330 A45 12c gray violet & multi .75 .60
331 A45 30c gray blue & multi 2.00 1.50
332 A45 50c dark gray & multi 3.50 2.75
Nos. 330-332 (3) 6.25 4.85

Breadnut — A46

Flowers of St. Vincent — A47

1972, May 16 **Litho.** ***Perf. 14x13½***

333 A46 3c shown .20 .20
334 A46 5c Papaya .20 .20
335 A46 12c Rose apples .40 .30
336 A46 25c Mangoes 1.10 .75
Nos. 333-336 (4) 1.90 1.45

1972, July 31 **Litho.** ***Perf. 13½x13***

337 A47 1c Candlestick Cassia .20 .20
338 A47 30c Lobster claw .35 .30
339 A47 40c White trumpet .40 .35
340 A47 $1 Flowers, Soufriere tree 1.10 .75
Nos. 337-340 (4) 2.05 1.60

Sir Charles Brisbane, Arms of St. Vincent — A48

Designs: 30c, Sailing ship "Arethusa." $1, Sailing ship "Blake."

1972, Sept. 29 **Wmk. 314** ***Perf. 13½***

341 A48 20c yel, brn & gold .45 .35
342 A48 30c lilac & multi .45 .40
343 A48 $1 multicolored 1.75 1.50
a. Souvenir sheet of 3, #341-343 6.00 6.00
Nos. 341-343 (3) 2.65 2.25

Bicentenary of the birth of Sir Charles Brisbane, naval hero, governor of St. Vincent.

Silver Wedding Issue, 1972
Common Design Type

Design: Queen Elizabeth II, Prince Philip, arrowroot plant, breadfruit foliage and fruit.

1972, Nov. 20 **Photo.** ***Perf. 14x14½***

344 CD324 30c rose brn & multi .20 .20
345 CD324 $1 multicolored .45 .30

Columbus Sighting St. Vincent — A49

12c, Caribs watching Columbus' ships. 30c, Christopher Columbus. 50c, Santa Maria.

1973, Jan. 18 **Litho.** ***Perf. 13***

346 A49 5c multicolored .20 *.25*
347 A49 12c multicolored .35 .25
348 A49 30c multicolored 1.10 .75
349 A49 50c multicolored 2.25 2.00
Nos. 346-349 (4) 3.90 3.25

475th anniversary of Columbus's Third Voyage to the West Indies.

The Last Supper — A50

Perf. 14x13½

1973, Apr. 19 **Litho.** **Wmk. 314**

350 A50 15c red & multi .20 .20
351 A50 60c red & multi .35 .30
352 A50 $1 red & multi .55 .50
a. Strip of 3, #350-352 1.00 1.00

Easter.

William Wilberforce and Slave Auction Poster — A51

40c, Slaves working on sugar plantation. 50c, Wilberforce & medal commemorating 1st anniversary of abolition of slavery.

1973, July 11 ***Perf. 14x13½***

353 A51 30c multicolored .20 .20
354 A51 40c multicolored .25 .20
355 A51 50c multicolored .45 .35
Nos. 353-355 (3) .90 .75

140th anniv. of the death of William Wilberforce (1759-1833), member of British Parliament who fought for abolition of slavery.

Families — A52

Design: 40c, Families and "IPPF."

1973, Oct. 3 ***Perf. 14½***

356 A52 12c multicolored .20 .20
357 A52 40c multicolored .50 .35

Intl. Planned Parenthood Assoc., 21st anniv.

Princess Anne's Wedding Issue
Common Design Type

1973, Nov. 14 ***Perf. 14***

358 CD325 50c slate & multi .20 .20
359 CD325 70c gray green & multi .25 .20

Administration Buildings, Mona University — A53

Designs: 10c, University Center, Kingstown. 30c, Mona University, aerial view. $1, Coat of arms of University of West Indies.

1973, Dec. 13 ***Perf. 14½x14, 14x14½***

360 A53 5c multicolored .20 .20
361 A53 10c multicolored .20 .20
362 A53 30c multicolored .20 .20
363 A53 $1 multicolored .40 .25
Nos. 360-363 (4) 1.00 .85

University of the West Indies, 25th anniv.

Nos. 291, 286 and 292 Surcharged

1973, Dec. 15 **Photo.** ***Perf. 14***

364 A36 30c on 50c multi .30 .20
365 A36 40c on 8c multi .45 .30
366 A36 $10 on $1 multi 10.75 8.50
Nos. 364-366 (3) 11.50 9.00

The position of the surcharge and shape of obliterating bars differs on each denomination.

Descent from the Cross — A54

Easter: 30c, Descent from the Cross. 40c, Pietà. $1, Resurrection. Designs are from sculptures in Victoria and Albert Museum, London, and Provincial Museum, Valladolid (40c).

1974, Apr. 10 **Litho.** ***Perf. 13½x13***

367 A54 5c multicolored .20 .20
368 A54 30c multicolored .20 .20
369 A54 40c multicolored .20 .20
370 A54 $1 multicolored .30 .20
Nos. 367-370 (4) .90 .80

"Istra" A55

1974, June 28 ***Perf. 14½***

371 A55 15c shown .20 .20
372 A55 20c "Oceanic" .20 .20
373 A55 30c "Alexander Pushkin" .35 .25
374 A55 $1 "Europa" 1.00 .60
a. Souvenir sheet of 4, #371-374 1.75 1.50
Nos. 371-374 (4) 1.75 1.25

Cruise ships visiting Kingstown.

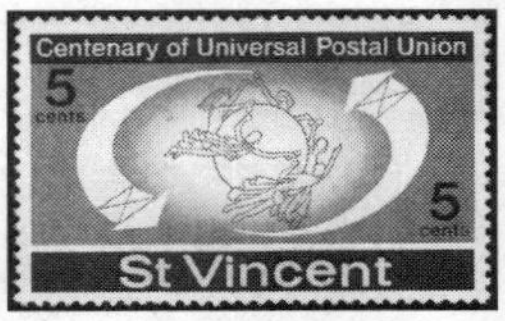

Arrows Circling UPU Emblem A56

UPU, cent.: 12c, Post horn and globe. 60c, Target over map of islands, hand canceler. 90c, Goode's map projection.

1974, July 25 ***Perf. 14½***

375 A56 5c violet & multi .20 .20
376 A56 12c ocher, green & blue .20 .20
377 A56 60c blue green & multi .30 .25
378 A56 90c red & multi .50 .40
Nos. 375-378 (4) 1.20 1.05

Bird Type of 1970

Birds: 30c, Royal tern. 40c, Brown pelican, vert. $10, Magnificent frigate bird, vert.

Wmk. 314 Sideways on 40c, $10, Upright on 30c

1974, Aug. 29 **Litho.** ***Perf. 14½***

379 A36 30c multicolored 2.00 .75
380 A36 40c multicolored 2.00 .75
381 A36 $10 multicolored 13.00 10.00
Nos. 379-381 (3) 17.00 11.50

Scout Emblem and Badges — A57

Churchill as Prime Minister — A58

Perf. 13½x14

1974, Oct. 9 Wmk. 314

385	A57	10c lilac & multi	.20	.20
386	A57	25c bister & multi	.25	.20
387	A57	45c gray & multi	.40	.30
388	A57	$1 multicolored	.80	.60
		Nos. 385-388 (4)	1.65	1.30

St. Vincent Boy Scouts, 60th anniversary.

1974, Nov. 28 *Perf. 14½x14*

Designs (Churchill as): 35c, Lord Warden of the Cinque Ports. 45c, First Lord of the Admiralty. $1, Royal Air Force officer.

389	A58	25c multicolored	.20	.20
390	A58	35c multicolored	.20	.20
391	A58	45c multicolored	.20	.20
392	A58	$1 multicolored	.40	.30
		Nos. 389-392 (4)	1.00	.90

Sir Winston Churchill (1874-1965), birth centenary. Sheets of 30 in 2 panes of 15 with inscribed gutter between.

A59

A60

1974, Dec. 5 *Perf. 12x12½*

393	A59	3c like 8c	.20	.20
394	A59	3c like 35c	.20	.20
395	A60	3c like 45c	.20	.20
396	A60	3c like $1	.20	.20
a.		Strip of 4, #393-396	.20	.20
397	A59	8c Shepherds	.20	.20
398	A59	35c Virgin, Child and Star	.20	.20
399	A60	45c St. Joseph, Ass & Ox	.25	.20
400	A60	$1 Three Kings	.50	.30
		Nos. 393-400 (8)	1.95	1.70

Christmas. Nos. 396a, 397-400 have continuous picture.

Giant Mask and Dancers — A61

Designs: 15c, Pineapple dancers. 25c, Giant bouquet. 35c, Girl dancers. 45c, Butterfly dancers. $1.25, Sun and moon dancers and float.

Wmk. 314

1975, Feb. 7 Litho. *Perf. 14*

401	A61	1c multicolored	.20	.20
a.		Bklt. pane of 2 + label	.25	
b.		Bklt. pane of 3, #401, 403, 405	.60	
402	A61	15c multicolored	.20	.20
a.		Bklt. pane of 3, #402, 404, 406	1.50	
403	A61	25c multicolored	.20	.20
404	A61	35c multicolored	.20	.20
405	A61	45c multicolored	.20	.20
406	A61	$1.25 multicolored	.50	.35
a.		Souvenir sheet of 6, #401-406	1.75	1.25
		Nos. 401-406 (6)	1.50	1.35

Kingstown carnival 1975.

French Angelfish — A62

Designs: Fish and whales.

Two types of $2.50:
I - Line to fish's mouth.
II - Line removed (1976).

Wmk. 373

1975, Apr. 10 Litho. *Perf. 14*

407	A62	1c shown	.20	.20
408	A62	2c Spotfin butterflyfish	.20	.20
409	A62	3c Horse-eyed jack	.20	.20
410	A62	4c Mackerel	.20	.20
411	A62	5c French grunts	.20	.20
412	A62	6c Spotted goatfish	.20	.20
413	A62	8c Ballyhoos	.20	.20
414	A62	10c Sperm whale	.20	.20
415	A62	12c Humpback whale	.20	.20
416	A62	15c Cowfish	.35	.25
417	A62	20c Queen angelfish	.30	.25
418	A62	25c Princess parrotfish	.35	.25
419	A62	35c Red hind	.60	.35
420	A62	45c Atlantic flying fish	.60	.45
421	A62	50c Porkfish	.70	.60
422	A62	$1 Queen triggerfish	1.50	1.10
423	A62	$2.50 Sailfish, type I	3.25	2.25
a.		Type II	3.00	1.25
424	A62	$5 Dolphinfish	7.00	4.50
425	A62	$10 Blue marlin	12.00	9.25
		Nos. 407-425 (19)	28.45	21.05

The 4c, 10c, 20c, $1, were reissued with "1976" below design; 1c, 2c, 3c, 5c, 6c, 8c, 12c, 50c, $10, with "1977" below design; 10c with "1978" below design.

No. 423a issued 7/12/76.

See #472-474. For surcharges and overprints see #463-464, 499-500, 502-503, 572-581, 584-586.

Cutting Bananas — A63

Banana industry: 35c, La Croix packing station. 45c, Women cleaning and packing bananas. 70c, Freighter loading bananas.

1975, June 26 Wmk. 314 *Perf. 14*

426	A63	25c blue & multi	.20	.20
427	A63	35c blue & multi	.20	.20
428	A63	45c carmine & multi	.25	.20
429	A63	70c carmine & multi	.40	.30
		Nos. 426-429 (4)	1.05	.90

Snorkel Diving — A64

Designs: 20c, Aquaduct Golf Course. 35c, Steel band at Mariner's Inn. 45c, Sunbathing at Young Island. $1.25, Yachting marina.

Wmk. 373

1975, July 31 Litho. *Perf. 13½*

430	A64	15c multicolored	.20	.20
431	A64	20c multicolored	.40	.20
432	A64	35c multicolored	.65	.25
433	A64	45c multicolored	.75	.30
434	A64	$1.25 multicolored	2.00	.75
		Nos. 430-434 (5)	4.00	1.70

Tourist publicity.

Presidents Washington, John Adams, Jefferson and Madison — A65

US Presidents: 1c, Monroe, John Quincy Adams, Jackson, Van Buren. 1½c, Wm. Harrison, Tyler, Polk, Taylor. 5c, Fillmore, Pierce, Buchanan, Lincoln. 10c, Johnson, Grant, Hayes, Garfield. 25c, Arthur, Cleveland, Benjamin Harrison, McKinley. 35c, Theodore Roosevelt, Taft, Wilson, Harding. 45c, Coolidge, Hoover, Franklin D. Roosevelt, Truman. $1, Eisenhower, Kennedy, Lyndon B. Johnson, Nixon. $2, Ford and White House.

1975, Sept. 11 Unwmk. *Perf. 14½*

435	A65	½c violet & blk	.20	.20
436	A65	1c green & black	.20	.20
437	A65	1½c rose lilac & blk	.20	.20
438	A65	5c yellow grn & blk	.20	.20
439	A65	10c ultra & blk	.20	.20
440	A65	25c ocher & blk	.20	.20
441	A65	35c brt blue & blk	.20	.20
442	A65	45c carmine & blk	.20	.20
443	A65	$1 orange & blk	.30	.25
444	A65	$2 lt olive & blk	.60	.45
a.		Souvenir sheet of 10, #435-444 + 2 labels	2.75	2.75
		Nos. 435-444 (10)	2.50	2.30

Bicentenary of American Independence. Each issued in sheets of 10 stamps and 2 labels picturing the White House, Capitol, Mt. Vernon, etc.

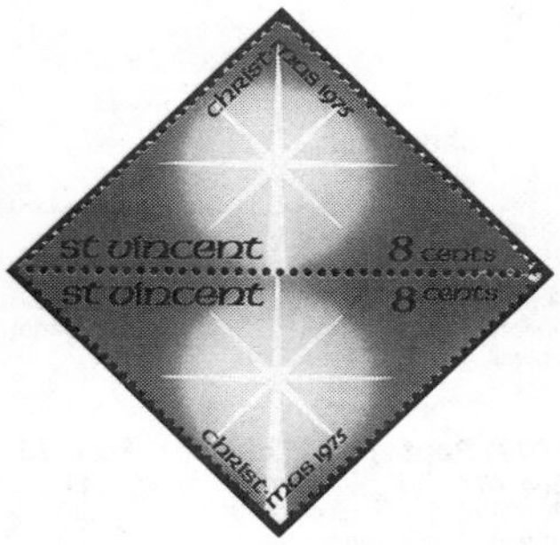

Nativity — A66

#445a, 8c, Star of Bethlehem. #445b, 45c, Shepherds. #445c, $1, Kings. #445d, 35c, Nativity.

Wmk. 314

1975, Dec. 4 Litho. *Perf. 14*

Se-tenant Pairs, #a.-b.

a.-Top stamp.

b.-Bottom stamp.

445	A66	3c Triangular block of 4, #a.-d.	.45	.45
446	A66	8c Pair, #a.-b.	.20	.20
447	A66	35c Pair, #a.-b.	.35	.20
448	A66	45c Pair, #a.-b.	.35	.30
449	A66	$1 Pair, #a.-b.	.65	.60
		Nos. 445-449 (5)	2.00	1.75

Christmas. No. 445 has continuous design.

Carnival Costumes — A68

Designs: 2c, Humpty-Dumpty people. 5c, Smiling faces (masks). 35c, Dragon worshippers. 45c, Duck costume. $1.25, Bumble bee dance.

Perf. 13x13½

1976, Feb. 19 Litho. Wmk. 373

457	A68	1c carmine & multi	.20	.20
a.		Bklt pane of 2, #457-458 + label	.20	
458	A68	2c black & multi	.20	.20
a.		Bklt. pane of 3, #458-460	.50	
459	A68	5c lt blue & multi	.20	.20
460	A68	35c lt blue & multi	.20	.20
a.		Bklt. pane of 3, #460-462	1.75	
461	A68	45c black & multi	.25	.20
462	A68	$1.25 carmine & multi	.50	.30
		Nos. 457-462 (6)	1.55	1.30

Kingstown carnival 1976.

Nos. 409 and 421 Surcharged with New Value and Bar

1976, Apr. 8 Wmk. 314 *Perf. 14*

463	A62	70c on 3c multi	.65	*1.00*
464	A62	90c on 50c multi	.65	*1.25*

Yellow Hibiscus and Blue-headed Hummingbird A69

Designs: 10c, Single pink hibiscus and crested hummingbird. 35c, Single white hibiscus and purple-throated carib. 45c, Common red hibiscus and blue-headed hummingbird. $1.25, Single peach hibiscus and green-throated carib.

1976, May 20 Litho. Wmk. 373

465	A69	5c multicolored	.20	.20
466	A69	10c multicolored	.40	.30
467	A69	35c multicolored	1.25	1.00
468	A69	45c multicolored	2.00	1.50
469	A69	$1.25 multicolored	6.00	3.75
		Nos. 465-469 (5)	9.85	6.75

Map of West Indies, Bats, Wicket and Ball A69a

Prudential Cup — A69b

1976, Sept. 16 Unwmk. *Perf. 14*

470	A69a	15c lt blue & multi	.60	.30
471	A69b	45c lilac rose & blk	1.40	1.00

World Cricket Cup, won by West Indies Team, 1975.

Fish Type of 1975

1976, Oct. 14 Wmk. 373 *Perf. 14*

472	A62	15c Skipjack	.20	.20
473	A62	70c Albacore	.65	.65
474	A62	90c Pompano	.75	.75
		Nos. 472-474 (3)	1.60	1.60

The 15c exists dated "1977."
For overprints see Nos. 501, 582-583.

St. Mary's R.C. Church, Kingstown — A70

Christmas: 45c, Anglican Church, Georgetown. 50c, Methodist Church, Georgetown. $1.25, St. George's Anglican Cathedral, Kingstown.

1976, Nov. 18 Litho. *Perf. 14*

475	A70	35c multicolored	.20	.20
476	A70	45c multicolored	.20	.20
477	A70	50c multicolored	.20	.20
478	A70	$1.25 multicolored	.55	.55
		Nos. 475-478 (4)	1.15	1.15

Barrancoid Pot-stand, c. 450 A.D. — A71

Designs (National Trust Emblem and): 45c, National Museum. 70c, Carib stone head, c. 1510. $1, Ciboney petroglyph, c. 4000 B.C.

1976, Dec. 16 *Perf. 13½*

479 A71	5c	multicolored	.20	.20
480 A71	45c	multicolored	.20	.20
481 A71	70c	multicolored	.30	.30
482 A71	$1	multicolored	.40	.40
		Nos. 479-482 (4)	1.10	1.10

Carib Indian art and establishment of National Museum in Botanical Gardens, Kingstown.

Kings William I, William II, Henry I, Stephen A72

Kings and Queens of England: 1c, Henry II, Richard I, John, Henry III. 1½c, Edward I, II, III, Richard II. 2c, Henry IV, V, VI, Edward IV. 5c, Edward V, Richard III, Henry VII, VIII. 10c, Edward VI, Lady Jane Grey, Mary I, Elizabeth I. 25c, James I, Charles I, II, James II. 35c, William III, Mary II, Anne, George I. 45c, George II, III, IV. 75c, William IV, Victoria, Edward VII. $1, George V, Edward VIII, George VI. $2, Elizabeth II, coronation.

Wmk. 373

1977, Feb. 7 Litho. *Perf. 13½*

483 A72	½c	multicolored	.20	.20
a.		Bklt. pane of 4, #483-486	2.25	
484 A72	1c	multicolored	.20	.20
485 A72	1½c	multicolored	.20	.20
486 A72	2c	multicolored	.20	.20
487 A72	5c	multicolored	.20	.20
a.		Bklt. pane of 4, #487-490	2.25	
488 A72	10c	multicolored	.20	.20
489 A72	25c	multicolored	.20	.20
490 A72	35c	multicolored	.20	.20
491 A72	45c	multicolored	.20	.20
a.		Bklt. pane of 4, #491-494	2.25	
492 A72	75c	multicolored	.20	.20
493 A72	$1	multicolored	.25	.20
494 A72	$2	multicolored	.40	.20
a.		Souv. sheet of 12, #483-494, perf. 14½x14	1.25	2.25
		Nos. 483-494 (12)	2.65	2.40

25th anniv. of the reign of Elizabeth II. Nos. 483a, 487a and 491a are unwmkd. See No. 508.

Bishop Alfred P. Berkeley, Bishop's Miters — A73

15c, Grant of Arms to Bishopric, 1951, & names of former Bishops. 45c, Coat of arms & map of Diocese. $1.25, Interior of St. George's Anglican Cathedral & Bishop G. C. M. Woodroffe.

Wmk. 373

1977, May 12 Litho. *Perf. 13½*

495 A73	15c	multicolored	.20	.20
496 A73	35c	multicolored	.20	.20
497 A73	45c	multicolored	.20	.20
498 A73	$1.25	multicolored	.40	*.50*
		Nos. 495-498 (4)	1.00	1.10

Diocese of the Windward Islands, centenary.

Nos. 411, 414, 472, 417, 422 Overprinted in Black or Red: "CARNIVAL 1977/ JUNE 25TH - JULY 5TH"

1977, June 2 Litho. *Perf. 14*

499 A62	5c	multi	.20	.20
500 A62	10c	multi (R)	.20	.20
501 A62	15c	multi (R)	.20	.20
502 A62	20c	multi (R)	.20	.20
503 A62	$1	multi	.65	.65
		Nos. 499-503 (5)	1.45	1.45

St. Vincent Carnival, June 25-July 5.
5c, 15c dated "1977," 10c, 20c, $1 "1976."

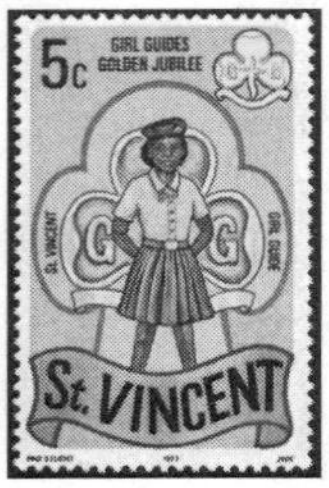

Girl Guide and Emblem — A74

"While Shepherds Watched" A75

Designs: 15c, Early Guide's uniform, Ranger, Brownie and Guide. 20c, Guide uniforms, 1917 and 1977. $2, Lady Baden-Powell, World Chief Guide, 1930-1977.

Wmk. 373

1977, Sept. 1 Litho. *Perf. 13½*

504 A74	5c	multicolored	.20	.20
505 A74	15c	multicolored	.20	.20
506 A74	20c	multicolored	.20	.20
507 A74	$2	multicolored	.40	*.65*
		Nos. 504-507 (4)	1.00	1.25

St. Vincent Girl Guides, 50th anniversary.

No. 494 with Additional Inscription: "CARIBBEAN / VISIT 1977"

1977, Oct. 27

508 A72	$2	multicolored	.40	.40

Caribbean visit of Queen Elizabeth II.

1977, Nov. Litho. *Perf. 13x11*

Christmas: 10c, "Fear not" said He. 15c, David's Town. 25c, The Heavenly Babe. 50c, Thus Spake and Seraph. $1.25, All Glory be to God.

509 A75	5c	buff & multi	.20	.20
510 A75	10c	buff & multi	.20	.20
511 A75	15c	buff & multi	.20	.20
512 A75	25c	buff & multi	.20	.20
513 A75	50c	buff & multi	.20	.20
514 A75	$1.25	buff & multi	.30	*.50*
a.		Souv. sheet, #509-514, perf. 13½	1.00	*1.25*
		Nos. 509-514 (6)	1.30	1.50

Map of St. Vincent — A76

Perf. 14½x14

1977-78 Litho. Wmk. 373

515 A76	20c	dk bl & lt bl ('78)	.20	.20
516 A76	40c	salmon & black	.30	.30
517 A76	40c	car, sal & ocher ('78)	.25	.25
		Nos. 515-517 (3)	.75	.75

Issued: #516, 11/30; #515, 517, 1/31.
For types surcharged see Nos. B1-B4.

Painted Lady and Bougainvillea — A77

Butterflies and Bougainvillea: 25c, Silver spot. 40c, Red anartia. 50c, Mimic. $1.25, Giant hairstreak.

1978, Apr. 6 Litho. *Perf. 14*

523 A77	5c	multicolored	.20	.20
524 A77	25c	multicolored	.35	.20
525 A77	40c	multicolored	.45	.20
526 A77	50c	multicolored	.50	.20
527 A77	$1.25	multicolored	1.00	.45
		Nos. 523-527 (5)	2.50	1.25

Westminster Abbey — A78

Cathedral: 50c, Gloucester. $1.25, Durham. $2.50, Exeter.

Perf. 13x13½

1978, June 2 Litho. Wmk. 373

528 A78	40c	multicolored	.20	.20
529 A78	50c	multicolored	.20	.20
530 A78	$1.25	multicolored	.20	.20
531 A78	$2.50	multicolored	.20	.20
a.		Souv. sheet, #528-531, perf. 13½x14	.75	*1.00*
		Nos. 528-531 (4)	.80	.80

25th anniv. of coronation of Queen Elizabeth II. Nos. 528-531 issued in sheets of 10.
#528-531 also exist in booklet panes of two.

Rotary Emblem A79

Emblems: 50c, Lions Intl. $1, Jaycees.

Wmk. 373

1978, July 13 Litho. *Perf. 14½*

532 A79	40c	brown & multi	.20	.20
533 A79	50c	dark green & multi	.20	.20
534 A79	$1	crimson & multi	.35	.35
		Nos. 532-534 (3)	.75	.75

Service clubs aiding in development of St. Vincent.

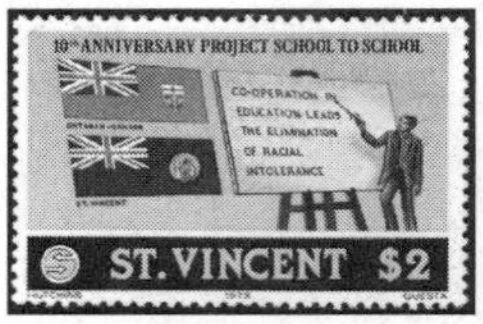

Flags of Ontario and St. Vincent, Teacher A80

Design: 40c, Flags of St. Vincent and Ontario, teacher pointing to board, vert.

1978, Sept. 7 Litho. *Perf. 14*

535 A80	40c	multicolored	.20	.20
536 A80	$2	multicolored	.45	*.60*

School to School Project between children of Ontario, Canada, and St. Vincent, 10th anniversary.

Arnos Vale Airport A81

40c, Wilbur Wright landing Flyer I. 50c, Flyer I airborne. $1.25, Orville Wright and Flyer I.

1978, Oct. 19 *Perf. 14½*

537 A81	10c	multicolored	.20	.20
538 A81	40c	multicolored	.20	.20
539 A81	50c	multicolored	.20	.20
540 A81	$1.25	multicolored	.40	.40
		Nos. 537-540 (4)	1.00	1.00

75th anniversary of 1st powered flight.
For overprint see No. 568.

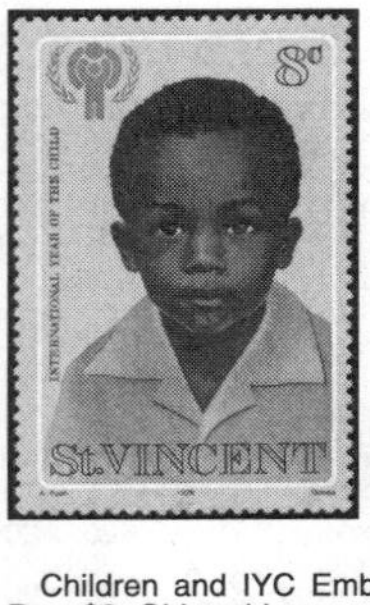

Vincentian Boy, IYC Emblem — A82

Children and IYC Emblem: 20c, Girl. 50c, Boy. $2, Girl and boy.

1979, Feb. 14 Litho. *Perf. 14x13½*

541 A82	8c	multicolored	.20	.20
542 A82	20c	multicolored	.20	.20
543 A82	50c	multicolored	.20	.20
544 A82	$2	multicolored	.40	.40
		Nos. 541-544 (4)	1.00	1.00

International Year of the Child.

Rowland Hill A83

50c, Great Britain #1-2. $3, St. Vincent #1-1B.

1979, May 31 Litho. *Perf. 14*

545 A83	40c	multicolored	.20	.20
546 A83	50c	multicolored	.20	.20
547 A83	$3	multicolored	.60	.60
a.		Souvenir sheet of 6	1.75	1.75
		Nos. 545-547 (3)	1.00	1.00

Sir Rowland Hill (1795-1879), originator of penny postage.
No. 547a contains Nos. 545-547 and Nos. 560, 561 and 565.

Buccament Cancellations, Map of St. Vincent — A84

Cancellations and location of village.

1979, Sept. 1 Litho. *Perf. 14*

548 A84	1c	shown	.20	.20
549 A84	2c	Sion Hill	.20	.20
550 A84	3c	Cumberland	.20	.20
551 A84	4c	Questelles	.20	.20
552 A84	5c	Layou	.20	.20
553 A84	6c	New Ground	.20	.20
554 A84	8c	Mesopotamia	.20	.20
555 A84	10c	Troumaca	.20	.20
556 A84	12c	Arnos Vale	.20	.20
557 A84	15c	Stubbs	.20	.20
558 A84	20c	Orange Hill	.20	.20
559 A84	25c	Calliaqua	.20	.20
560 A84	40c	Edinboro	.30	.20
561 A84	50c	Colonarie	.30	.20
562 A84	80c	Babou St. Vincent	.45	.30
563 A84	$1	Chateaubelair	.45	.45
564 A84	$2	Kingstown	.55	*.70*
565 A84	$3	Barrouallie	.65	*1.00*
566 A84	$5	Georgetown	.90	*1.75*
567 A84	$10	Kingstown	1.75	*3.00*
		Nos. 548-567 (20)	7.75	10.00

See No. 547a.
The 5c, 10c, 25c reissued inscribed 1982.
Singles of #562-564 from #601a are inscribed 1980.

No. 537 Overprinted in Red: "ST. VINCENT AND THE GRENADINES AIR SERVICE 1979"

1979, Aug. 6 Litho. *Perf. 14½*

568 A81	10c	multicolored	.20	.20

St. Vincent and Grenadines air service inauguration.

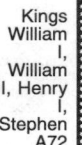

Independent State

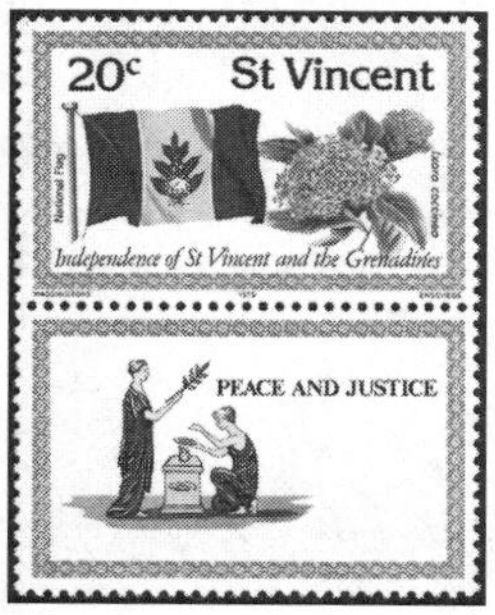

St. Vincent Flag, Ixora Coccinea A85

Designs: 50c, House of Assembly, ixora stricta. 80c, Prime Minister R. Milton Cato.

1979, Oct. 27 ***Perf. 12½x12***

569	A85	20c multi + label	.20	.20
570	A85	50c multi + label	.25	.20
571	A85	80c multi + label	.40	.25
		Nos. 569-571 (3)	.85	.65

Independence of St. Vincent.

Nos. 407, 410-416, 418, 421, 473-474, 422-423, 425 Overprinted in Black: "INDEPENDENCE 1979"

1979, Oct. 27 **Litho.** ***Perf. 14½***

572	A62	1c	multicolored	.20	.20
573	A62	4c	multicolored	.20	.20
574	A62	5c	multicolored	.20	.20
575	A62	6c	multicolored	.20	.20
576	A62	8c	multicolored	.20	.20
577	A62	10c	multicolored	.25	.20
578	A62	12c	multicolored	.25	.20
579	A62	15c	multicolored	.20	.20
580	A62	25c	multicolored	.20	.20
581	A62	50c	multicolored	.40	.30
582	A62	70c	multicolored	.70	.35
583	A62	90c	multicolored	.70	.40
584	A62	$1	multicolored	.70	.40
585	A62	$2.50	multicolored	1.10	1.00
586	A62	$10	multicolored	2.50	*3.75*
			Nos. 572-586 (15)	8.00	8.00

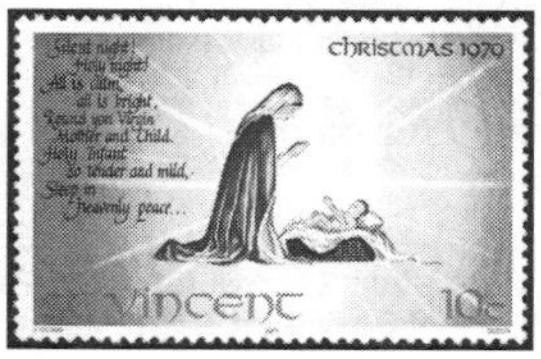

Silent Night Text, Virgin and Child A86

Silent Night Text and: 20c, Infant Jesus and angels. 25c, Shepherds. 40c, Angel. 50c, Angels holding Jesus. $2, Nativity.

1979, Nov. 1 ***Perf. 13½x14***

587	A86	10c multicolored	.20	.20
588	A86	20c multicolored	.20	.20
589	A86	25c multicolored	.20	.20
590	A86	40c multicolored	.20	.20
591	A86	50c multicolored	.20	.20
592	A86	$2 multicolored	.30	.30
a.		Souvenir sheet of 6, #587-592	1.00	*1.25*
		Nos. 587-592 (6)	1.30	1.30

Christmas.

Oleander and Wasp — A87

Oleander and Insects: 10c, Beetle. 25c, Praying mantis. 50c, Green guava beetle. $2, Citrus weevil.

1979, Dec. 13 **Litho.** ***Perf. 14***

593	A87	5c multicolored	.20	.20
594	A87	10c multicolored	.20	.20
595	A87	25c multicolored	.20	.20
596	A87	50c multicolored	.20	.20
597	A87	$2 multicolored	.50	.50
		Nos. 593-597 (5)	1.30	1.30

Type of 1880
Souvenir Sheet

1980, Feb. 28 **Litho.** ***Perf. 14x13½***

598		Sheet of 3	1.00	1.00
a.		A3 50c brown	.20	.20
b.		A3 $1 dark green	.30	.30
c.		A3 $2 dark blue	.60	.60

Coat of arms stamps centenary; London 1980 Intl. Stamp Exhibition, May 6-14.

London '80 Intl. Stamp Exhibition, May 6-14 — A88

Wmk. 373

1980, Apr. 24 **Litho.** ***Perf. 14***

599	A88	80c Queen Elizabeth II	.20	.20
600	A88	$1 GB #297, SV #190	.25	.25
601	A88	$2 Unissued stamp, 1971	.55	.55
a.		Souv. sheet, #562-564, 599-601	1.00	*1.75*
		Nos. 599-601 (3)	1.00	1.00

Steel Band A89

a, shown. b, Drummers, dancers.

1980, June 12 **Litho.** ***Perf. 14***

602	A89	20c Pair, #a.-b.	.35	*.75*

Kingstown Carnival, July 7-8.

Soccer, Olympic Rings — A90

1980, Aug. 7 ***Perf. 13½***

604	A90	10c shown	.20	.20
605	A90	60c Bicycling	.25	.25
606	A90	80c Women's basket-ball	.40	.30
607	A90	$2.50 Boxing	.40	*1.00*
		Nos. 604-607 (4)	1.25	1.75

Sport for all.
For surcharges see Nos. B5-B8.

Agouti A91

1980, Oct. 2 **Litho.** ***Perf. 14x14½***

608	A91	25c shown	.20	.20
609	A91	50c Giant toad	.20	.20
610	A91	$2 Mongoose	.60	.60
		Nos. 608-610 (3)	1.00	1.00

Map of North Atlantic showing St. Vincent — A92

Maps showing St. Vincent: 10c, World. $1, Caribbean. $2, St. Vincent, sail boats, plane.

1980, Dec. 4 **Litho.** ***Perf. 13½x14***

611	A92	10c multicolored	.20	.20
612	A92	50c multicolored	.20	.20
613	A92	$1 multicolored	.30	.20
614	A92	$2 multicolored	.55	.30
a.		Souv. sheet of 1, perf. 14	.80	.80
		Nos. 611-614 (4)	1.25	.90

Ville de Paris in Battle of the Saints, 1782 — A93

Wmk. 373

1981, Feb. 19 **Litho.** ***Perf. 14***

615	A93	50c shown	.45	.25
616	A93	60c Ramillies lost in storm, 1782	.55	.40
617	A93	$1.50 Providence, 1793	1.25	*1.60*
618	A93	$2 Mail Packet Dee, 1840	1.75	*2.00*
		Nos. 615-618 (4)	4.00	4.25

A94

#619a, Arrowroot processing. #619b, Arrowroot Cultivation. #620a, Banana packing plant. #620b, Banana cultivation. #621a, Copra drying frames. #621b, Coconut plantation. #622a, Cocoa beans. #622b, Cocoa cultivation.

Wmk. 373

1981, May 21 **Litho.** ***Perf. 14***

619	A94	25c Pair, #a.-b.	.20	.20
620	A94	50c Pair, #a.-b.	.45	.60
621	A94	60c Pair, #a.-b.	.45	.60
622	A94	$1 Pair, #a.-b.	.65	1.00
		Nos. 619-622 (4)	1.75	2.40

Prince Charles, Lady Diana, Royal Yacht Charlotte A94a

Prince Charles and Lady Diana — A94b

Illustration A94b is reduced.

Wmk. 380

1981, July 13 **Litho.** ***Perf. 14***

627	A94a	60c Couple, Isa-bella	.20	.20
a.		Bklt. pane of 4, perf. 12	.60	
628	A94b	60c Couple	.20	.20
629	A94a	$2.50 Alberta	.70	.70
630	A94b	$2.50 like #628	.70	.70
a.		Bklt. pane of 2, perf. 12	1.00	
631	A94a	$4 Britannia	1.25	1.25
632	A94b	$4 like #628	1.25	1.25
		Nos. 627-632 (6)	4.30	4.30

Royal wedding. Each denomination issued in sheets of 7 (6 type A94a, 1 type A94b).
For surcharges and overprints see Nos. 891-892, O1-O6.

Souvenir Sheet

1981 **Litho.** ***Perf. 12***

632A	A95b	$5 Couple	1.40	1.40

A94b

Kingstown General Post Office A95

Wmk. 373

1981, Sept. 1 **Litho.** ***Perf. 14***

633	A95	$2 Pair, #a.-b.	1.10	*1.75*

UPU membership centenary.

First Anniv. of UN Membership A96

Wmk. 373

1981, Sept. 1 **Litho.** ***Perf. 14***

634A	A96	$1.50 Flags	.35	.35
634B	A96	$2.50 Prime Minister Cato	.55	.55

"The People that Walked in Darkness . . ." — A97

1981, Nov. 19 **Litho.** ***Perf. 12***

635	A97	50c shown	.20	.20
636	A97	60c Angel	.20	.20
637	A97	$1 "My soul . . ."	.25	.25
638	A97	$2 Flight into Egypt	.50	.50
a.		Souvenir sheet of 4, #635-638	1.25	*1.50*
		Nos. 635-638 (4)	1.15	1.15

Christmas. For surcharge see No. 674.

Re-introduction of Sugar Industry, First Anniv. — A98

1982, Apr. 5 **Litho.** ***Perf. 14***

639	A98	50c Boilers	.20	.20
640	A98	60c Drying plant	.25	.25
641	A98	$1.50 Gearwheels	.50	.50
642	A98	$2 Loading sugar cane	.90	.90
		Nos. 639-642 (4)	1.85	1.85

50th Anniv. of Airmail Service A99

1982, July 29 **Litho.** ***Perf. 14***

643	A99	50c DH Moth, 1932	.50	.35
644	A99	60c Grumman Goose, 1952	.60	.40

645 A99 $1.50 Hawker-Siddeley 748, 1968 1.40 *1.50*
646 A99 $2 Britten-Norman Islander, 1982 2.00 *2.25*
Nos. 643-646 (4) 4.50 4.50

21st Birthday of Princess Diana, July 1 — A99a

Wmk. 380

1982, June Litho. *Perf. 14*

647 A99a 50c Augusta of Saxe, 1736 .35 .35
648 A99a 60c Saxe arms .40 .40
649 A99a $6 Diana 2.00 2.00
Nos. 647-649 (3) 2.75 2.75

For overprints see Nos. 652-654.

Scouting Year — A100

1982, July 15 Wmk. 373

650 A100 $1.50 Emblem .75 *1.00*
651 A100 $2.50 "75" 1.25 *1.75*

For overprints see Nos. 890, 893.

Nos. 647-649 Overprinted: "ROYAL BABY"

1982, July Wmk. 380

652 A99a 50c multicolored .20 .30
653 A99a 60c multicolored .20 .30
654 A99a $6 multicolored .85 *1.25*
Nos. 652-654 (3) 1.25 1.85

Birth of Prince William of Wales, June 21.

Carnival A101

1982, June 10 Litho. *Perf. 13½*

655 A101 50c Butterfly float .25 .25
656 A101 60c Angel dancer, vert. .30 .30
657 A101 $1.50 Winged dancer, vert. .70 .70
658 A101 $2 Eagle float 1.00 1.00
Nos. 655-658 (4) 2.25 2.25

Cruise Ships A103

Wmk. 373

1982, Dec. 29 Litho. *Perf. 14*

662 A103 45c Geestport .30 .30
663 A103 60c Stella Oceanis .40 .40
664 A103 $1.50 Victoria 1.00 1.00
665 A103 $2 QE 2 1.40 1.40
Nos. 662-665 (4) 3.10 3.10

Pseudocorynactis Caribbeorum — A104

Sea Horses and Anemones. 60c, $1.50, $2 vert.

1983, Jan. 12 Wmk. 373 *Perf. 12*

666 A104 50c shown .75 .75
667 A104 60c Actinoporus elegans .90 .90
668 A104 $1.50 Arachnanthus nocturnus 1.60 1.60
669 A104 $2 Hippocampus reidi 1.75 1.75
Nos. 666-669 (4) 5.00 5.00

For overprint see No. 886.

Commonwealth Day — A104a

Wmk. 373

1983, Mar. 14 Litho. *Perf. 14*

670 A104a 45c Map .30 .30
671 A104a 60c Flag .40 .40
672 A104a $1.50 Prime Minister Cato .65 .65
673 A104a $2 Banana industry .90 .90
Nos. 670-673 (4) 2.25 2.25

No. 635 Surcharged

Wmk. 373

1983, Apr. 26 Litho. *Perf. 12*

674 A97 45c on 50c multi .45 .35

A104b

A105

Wmk. 373

1983, July 6 Litho. *Perf. 12*

675 A104b 45c Handshake .20 *.30*
676 A104b 60c Emblem .25 *.35*
677 A104b $1 Map .55 *.75*
678 A104b $2 Flags 1.00 *1.25*
Nos. 675-678 (4) 2.00 2.65

10th anniv. of Chaguaramas (Caribbean Free Trade Assoc.)

Perf. 12x11½

1983, Oct. 6 Litho. Wmk. 373

679 A105 45c Founder William A. Smith .30 .30
680 A105 60c Boy, officer .40 .40
681 A105 $1.50 Emblem 1.00 1.00
682 A105 $2 Community service 1.40 1.40
Nos. 679-682 (4) 3.10 3.10

Boys' Brigade, cent. For overprint see #887.

Christmas — A106

1983, Nov. 15 Litho. *Perf. 12*

683 A106 10c Shepherds at Watch .20 .20
684 A106 50c The Angel of the Lord .40 .40
685 A106 $1.50 A Glorious Light 1.15 1.15
686 A106 $2.40 At the Manger 2.00 2.00
a. Souvenir sheet of 4, #683-686 3.75 3.75
Nos. 683-686 (4) 3.75 3.75

Classic Cars A107

1983, Nov. 9 Litho. *Perf. 12½*

Se-tenant Pairs, #a.-b.

a.-Side and front views.

b.-Action scene.

687 A107 10c Ford Model T .20 .20
688 A107 60c Supercharged Cord .50 .50
689 A107 $1.50 Mercedes-Benz 1.40 1.40
690 A107 $1.50 Citroen Open Tourer 1.40 1.40
691 A107 $2 Ferrari Boxer 1.90 1.90
692 A107 $2 Rolls-Royce Phantom 1.90 1.90
Nos. 687-692 (6) 7.30 7.30

See #773-777, 815-822, 906-911.

Locomotives Type of 1985

1983, Dec. 8 Litho. *Perf. 12½x13*

Se-tenant Pairs, #a.-b.

a.-Side and front views.

b.-Action scene.

699 A120 10c King Henry VIII .20 .20
700 A120 10c Royal Scots Greys .20 .20
701 A120 25c Hagley Hall .20 .20
702 A120 50c Sir Lancelot .40 .40
703 A120 60c B12 Class .50 .50
704 A120 75c No. 1000 Deeley Compound .65 .65
705 A120 $2.50 Cheshire 2.00 2.00
706 A120 $3 Bulleid Austerity 2.50 2.50
Nos. 699-706 (8) 6.65 6.65

Fort Duvernette A108

Perf. 14x14½

1984, Feb. 13 Litho. Wmk. 380

715 A108 35c View .25 .25
716 A108 45c Wall, flag .35 .35
717 A108 $1 Canon .70 .70
718 A108 $3 Map 2.30 2.30
Nos. 715-718 (4) 3.60 3.60

Flowering Trees — A109

Perf. 13½x14

1984, Apr. 2 Litho. Wmk. 373

719 A109 5c White frangipani .20 .20
720 A109 10c Genip .20 .20
721 A109 15c Immortelle .20 .20
722 A109 20c Pink poui .20 .20
723 A109 25c Buttercup .20 .20
724 A109 35c Sandbox .25 .25
725 A109 45c Locust .35 .35
726 A109 60c Colville's glory .45 .45
727 A109 75c Lignum vitae .55 .55
728 A109 $1 Golden shower .75 .75
729 A109 $5 Angelin 3.60 3.60
730 A109 $10 Roucou 7.25 7.25
Nos. 719-730 (12) 14.20 14.20

World War I Battle Scene, King George V A110

#732a, Battle of Bannockburn. #732b, Edward II. #733a, George V. #733b, York Cottage, Sandringham. #734a, Edward II. #734b, Berkeley Castle. #735a, Arms of Edward II. #735b, Edward II. #736a, Arms of George V. #736b, George V.

1984, Apr. 25 Litho. *Perf. 13x12½*

731 A110 1c Pair, #a.-b. .20 .20
732 A110 5c Pair, #a.-b. .20 .20
733 A110 60c Pair, #a.-b. .90 .90
734 A110 75c Pair, #a.-b. 1.25 1.25
735 A110 $1 Pair, #a.-b. 1.50 1.50
736 A110 $4 Pair, #a.-b. 5.50 5.50
Nos. 731-736 (6) 9.55 9.55

Carnival A112

Wmk. 380

1984, June 25 Litho. *Perf. 14*

743 A112 35c Musical fantasy .25 .25
744 A112 45c African woman .35 .35
745 A112 $1 Market woman .75 .75
746 A112 $3 Carib hieroglyph 2.25 2.25
Nos. 743-746 (4) 3.60 3.60

Locomotives Type of 1985

1984, July 27 Litho. *Perf. 12½*

Se-tenant Pairs, #a.-b.

a.-Side and front views.

b.-Action scene.

747 A120 1c Liberation Class 141R, 1945 .20 .20
748 A120 2c Dreadnought Class 50, 1967 .20 .20
749 A120 3c No. 242A1, 1946 .20 .20
750 A120 50c Dean Goods, 1883 .50 .50
751 A120 75c Hetton Colliery, 1822 .65 .65
752 A120 $1 Penydarren, 1804 1.00 1.00
753 A120 $2 Novelty, 1829 1.90 1.90
754 A120 $3 Class 44, 1925 3.25 3.25
Nos. 747-754 (8) 7.90 7.90

Slavery Abolition Sesquicentennial — A113

1984, Aug. 1 Litho. *Perf. 14*

761 A113 35c Hoeing .25 .25
762 A113 45c Gathering sugar cane .35 .35
763 A113 $1 Cutting sugar cane .75 .75
764 A113 $3 Abolitionist William Wilberforce 2.25 2.25
Nos. 761-764 (4) 3.60 3.60

1984 Summer Olympics — A114

#765a, Judo. #765b, Weight lifting. #766a, Bicycling (facing left). #766b, Bicycling (facing right). #767a, Swimming (back stroke). #767b, Breast stroke. #768a, Running (start). #768b, Running (finish).

1984, Aug. 30 Unwmk. *Perf. 12½*

765 A114 1c Pair, #a.-b. .20 .20
766 A114 3c Pair, #a.-b. .20 .20
767 A114 60c Pair, #a.-b. .60 .60
768 A114 $3 Pair, #a.-b. 3.00 3.00
Nos. 765-768 (4) 4.00 4.00

Car Type of 1983

1984, Oct. 22 Litho. *Perf. 12½*
Se-tenant Pairs, #a.-b.
a.-Side and front views.
b.-Action scene.

773 A107 5c Austin-Healey Sprite, 1958 .20 .20
774 A107 20c Maserati, 1971 .20 .20
775 A107 55c Pontiac GTO, 1964 .50 .50
776 A107 $1.50 Jaguar, 1957 1.25 1.25
777 A107 $2.50 Ferrari, 1970 2.25 2.25
Nos. 773-777 (5) 4.40 4.40

Military Uniforms — A115

1984, Nov. 12 Wmk. 380 *Perf. 14*

783 A115 45c Grenadier, 1773 .30 .30
784 A115 60c Grenadier, 1775 .45 .45
785 A115 $1.50 Grenadier, 1768 1.15 1.15
786 A115 $2 Battalion Co. Officer, 1780 1.50 1.50
Nos. 783-786 (4) 3.40 3.40

Locomotives Type of 1985

1984, Nov. 21 Litho. *Perf. 12½x13*
Se-tenant Pairs, #a.-b.
a.-Side and front views.
b.-Action scene.

787 A120 5c 1954 R.R. Class 20, Zimbabwe .20 .20
788 A120 40c 1928 Southern Maid, U.K. .45 .45
789 A120 75c 1911 Prince of Wales, U.K. .85 .85
790 A120 $2.50 1935 D.R.G. Class 05, Germany 2.75 2.75
Nos. 787-790 (4) 4.25 4.25

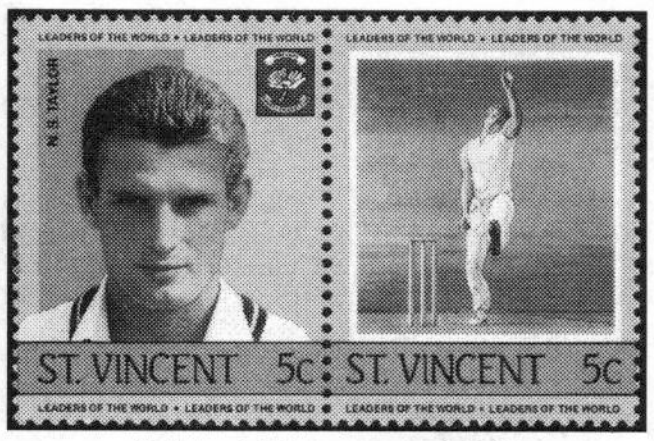

Cricket Players — A116

1985, Jan. 7 Litho. *Perf. 12½*
Se-tenant Pairs, #a.-b.

795 A116 5c N.S. Taylor, portrait .20 .20
796 A116 35c T.W. Graveney with bat .40 .40
797 A116 50c R.G.D. Willis at wicket .60 .60
798 A116 $3 S.D. Fletcher at wicket 3.50 3.50
Nos. 795-798 (4) 4.70 4.70

Orchids — A117

1985, Jan. 31 Litho. *Perf. 14*

803 A117 35c Epidendrum ciliare .25 .25
804 A117 45c Ionopsis utricularioides .35 .35
805 A117 $1 Epidendrum secundum .75 .75
806 A117 $3 Oncidium altissimum 2.25 2.25
Nos. 803-806 (4) 3.60 3.60

Audubon Birth Bicent. — A118

Illustrations of North American bird species by artist/naturalist John J. Audubon: #807a, Brown pelican. #807b, Green heron. #808a, Pileated woodpecker. #808b, Common flicker. #809a, Painted bunting. #809b, White-winged crossbill. #810a, Red-shouldered hawk. #810b, Crested caracara.

1985, Feb. 7 Litho. *Perf. 12½*

807 A118 15c Pair, #a.-b. .20 .20
808 A118 40c Pair, #a.-b. .50 .50
809 A118 60c Pair, #a.-b. .70 .70
810 A118 $2.25 Pair, #a.-b. 2.75 2.75
Nos. 807-810 (4) 4.15 4.15

Car Type of 1983

1c, 1937 Lancia Aprilia, Italy. 25c, 1922 Essex Coach, US. 55c, 1973 Pontiac Firebird Trans Am, US. 60c, 1950 Nash Rambler, US. $1, 1961 Ferrari Tipo 156, Italy. $1.50, 1967 Eagle-Weslake Type 58, US. $2, 1953 Cunningham C-5R, US.

1985
a.-Side and front views.
b.-Action scene.

815-821 A107 Set of 7 pairs 5.75 5.75

Souvenir Sheet of 4

822 A107 #a.-d. 10.00 10.00

#822 contains a pair of $4 stamps like #820 (#a.-b.), and a pair of $5 stamps like #819 (#c.-d.).
Issued: 1c, 55c, $2, 3/11; others, 6/7.

Herbs and Spices — A119

1985, Apr. 22 *Perf. 14*

829 A119 25c Pepper .20 .20
830 A119 35c Sweet marjoram .30 .30
831 A119 $1 Nutmeg .75 .75
832 A119 $3 Ginger 2.25 2.25
Nos. 829-832 (4) 3.50 3.50

Locomotives of the United Kingdom — A120

1985, Apr. 26 *Perf. 12½*
Se-tenant Pairs, #a.-b.
a.-Side and front views.
b.-Action scene.

833 A120 1c 1913 Glen Douglas .20 .20
834 A120 10c 1872 Fenchurch Terrier .20 .20
835 A120 40c 1870 No. 1 Stirling Single .35 .35
836 A120 60c 1866 No. 158A .55 .55
837 A120 $1 1893 No. 103 Class Jones Goods .90 .90
838 A120 $2.50 1908 Great Bear 2.50 2.50
Nos. 833-838 (6) 4.70 4.70

See #699-706, 747-754, 787-790, 849-860, 961-967.

Traditional Instruments — A121

1985, May 16 *Perf. 15*

845 A121 25c Bamboo flute .20 .20
846 A121 35c Quatro .30 .30
847 A121 $1 Bamboo base, vert. .75 .75
848 A121 $2 Goat-skin drum, vert. 1.50 1.50
a. Sheet of 4, #845-848 2.75 2.75
Nos. 845-848 (4) 2.75 2.75

Locomotives Type of 1985

1985, June 27 *Perf. 12½*
Se-tenant Pairs, #a.-b.
a.-Side and front views.
b.-Action scene.

849 A120 5c 1874 Loch, U.K. .20 .20
850 A120 30c 1919 Class 47XX, U.K. .30 .30
851 A120 60c 1876 P.L.M. Class 121, France .60 .60
852 A120 75c 1927 D.R.G. Class 24, Germany .70 .70
853 A120 $1 1889 No. 1008, U.K. 1.00 1.00
854 A120 $2.50 1926 S.R. Class PS-4, US 2.50 2.50
Nos. 849-854 (6) 5.30 5.30

Queen Mother, 85th Birthday — A122

#861a, 867a, Facing right. #861b, 867b, Facing left. #862a, 866a, Facing right. #862b, 866b, Facing left. #863a, Facing right. #863b, Facing left. #864a, Facing front. #864b, Facing left. #865a, Facing right. #865b, Facing front.

1985

861 A122 35c Pair, #a.-b. .30 .30
862 A122 85c Pair, #a.-b. .70 .70
863 A122 $1.20 Pair, #a.-b. 1.10 1.10
864 A122 $1.60 Pair, #a.-b. 1.50 1.50
Nos. 861-864 (4) 3.60 3.60

Souvenir Sheets of 2

865 A122 $2.10 #a.-b. 2.50 2.50
866 A122 $3.50 #a.-b. 3.75 3.75
867 A122 $6 #a.-b. 6.25 6.25

Issued: #861-865, 8/9; #866-867, 12/19.
For overprints see No. 888.

Elvis Presley (1935-77), American Entertainer — A123

#874a, 878a, In concert. #874b, 878b, Facing front. #875a, 879a, In concert. #875b, 879b, Facing left. #876a, 880a, In concert. #876b, 880b, Facing front. #877a, 881a, Wearing leather jacket. #877b, 881b, Facing left.

1985, Aug. 16

874 A123 10c Pair, #a.-b. .20 .20
875 A123 60c Pair, #a.-b. .70 .70
876 A123 $1 Pair, #a.-b. 1.25 1.25
877 A123 $5 Pair, #a.-b. 6.00 6.00
Nos. 874-877 (4) 8.15 8.15

Souvenir Sheets of 4

878 A123 30c #a.-b. .80 .80
879 A123 50c #a.-b. 1.20 1.20
880 A123 $1.50 #a.-b. 3.50 3.50
881 A123 $4.50 #a.-b. 10.00 10.00

Nos. 878-881 contain two of each stamp. Two $4 "stamps" were not issued.
For other Presley souvenir sheet see No. 1567. For overprints see Nos. 1009-1016.

Flour Milling A124

1985, Oct. 17 Wmk. 373 *Perf. 15*

882 A124 20c Conveyor from elevators .20 .20
883 A124 30c Roller mills .20 .20
884 A124 75c Office .55 .55
885 A124 $3 Bran finishers 2.25 2.25
Nos. 882-885 (4) 3.20 3.20

Nos. 667, 680, 862, 650, 631-632, 651 Ovptd. "CARIBBEAN / ROYAL VISIT / -1985-" or Surcharged with 3 Black Bars and New Value in Black

1985, Oct. 27 *Perfs. as Before*

886 A104 60c multi *1.25 1.25*
887 A105 60c multi *1.25 1.25*
888 A122 85c Pair, #a.-b. *4.00 4.00*
890 A100 $1.50 multi *3.50 3.50*
891 A94a $1.60 on $4 *3.75 3.75*
892 A94b $1.60 on $4 *3.75 3.75*
893 A100 $2.50 multi *5.75 5.75*
Nos. 886-893 (7) *23.25 23.25*

Michael Jackson (b. 1960), American Entertainer — A125

#894a, Portrait. #894b, On stage. #895a, Singing. #895b, Portrait. #896a, Black jacket. #896b, Red jacket. #897a, Portrait. #897b, Wearing white glove.

1985, Dec. 2 *Perf. 12½*

894 A125 60c Pair, #a.-b. .60 .60
895 A125 $1 Pair, #a.-b. 1.00 1.00
896 A125 $2 Pair, #a.-b. 2.00 2.00
897 A125 $5 Pair, #a.-b. 5.50 5.50
Nos. 894-897 (4) 9.10 9.10

Souvenir Sheets of 4
Perf. 13x12½

898 A125 45c #a.-b. .90 .90
899 A125 90c #a.-b. 1.90 1.90
900 A125 $1.50 #a.-b. 3.00 3.00
901 A125 $4 #a.-b. 8.25 8.25

#898-901 contain two of each stamp.

Christmas A126

Children's drawings: 25c, Serenade, 75c, Poinsettia. $2.50, Jesus, Our Master.

1985, Dec. 9 **Wmk. 373** *Perf. 14*

903 A126 25c multicolored .20 .20
904 A126 75c multicolored .55 .55
905 A126 $2.50 multicolored 1.90 1.90
Nos. 903-905 (3) 2.65 2.65

Car Type of 1983

30c, 1916 Cadillac Type 53, US. 45c, 1939 Triumph Dolomite, UK. 60c, 1972 Panther J-72, UK. 90c, 1967 Ferrari 275 GTB/4, Italy. $1.50, 1953 Packard Caribbean, US. $2.50, 1931 Bugatti Type 41 Royale, France.

1986, Jan. 27 *Perf. 12½*
a.-Side and front views.
b.-Action scene.

906-911 A107 Set of 6 pairs 7.50 7.50

Halley's Comet A127

Wmk. 380

1986, Apr. 14 **Litho.** *Perf. 15*

918 A127 45c shown .35 .35
919 A127 60c Edmond Halley .45 .45
920 A127 75c Newton's reflector telescope .55 .55
921 A127 $3 Local astronomer 2.25 2.25
a. Souvenir sheet of 4, #918-921 3.60 3.60
Nos. 918-921 (4) 3.60 3.60

Souvenir Sheets of 2

Scouting Movement, 75th Anniv. — A127a

American flag & Girl Guides or Boy Scouts emblem and: #922b, Scout sign, handshake. #922c, Paintbrushes, pallet. #922d, Knots. #922e, Lord Baden-Powell.

1986, Feb. 25 **Litho.** *Perf. 13x12½*

922 A127a $5 #b.-c. 4.50 4.50
922A A127a $6 #d.-e. 5.50 5.50

"Capex '87" overprints on this issue were not authorized.

Elizabeth II Wearing Crown Jewels — A128

Elizabeth II at Victoria Park A129

Various portraits.

1986, Apr. 21 **Wmk. 373** *Perf. 12½*

923 A128 10c multicolored .20 .20
924 A128 90c multicolored .55 .55
925 A128 $2.50 multicolored 1.50 1.50
926 A128 $8 multi, vert. 5.00 5.00
Nos. 923-926 (4) 7.25 7.25

Souvenir Sheet

927 A128 $10 multicolored 6.25 6.25

Perf. 15x14

1986, June 14 **Wmk. 373**

Designs: No. 928, with Prime Minister Mitchell. No. 929, Arriving at Port Elizabeth. No. 930, at Independence Day Parade.

928 A129 45c multicolored .35 .35
929 A129 60c multicolored .45 .45
930 A129 75c multicolored .55 .55
931 A129 $2.50 multicolored 1.90 1.90
Nos. 928-931 (4) 3.25 3.25

Souvenir Sheet

932 A129 $3 multicolored 2.25 2.25

Queen Elizabeth II, 60th birthday.

Discovery of America, 500th Anniv. (1992) — A130

#936a, Fleet. #936b, Columbus. #937a, At Spanish Court. #937b, Ferdinand, Isabella. #938a, Fruit, Santa Maria. #938b, Fruit.

1986, Jan. 23 **Litho.** *Perf. 12½*

936 A130 60c Pair, #a.-b. .90 .90
937 A130 $1.50 Pair, #a.-b. 2.25 2.25
938 A130 $2.75 Pair, #a.-b. 4.00 4.00
Nos. 936-938 (3) 7.15 7.15

Souvenir Sheet

939 A130 $6 Columbus, diff. 4.50 4.50

1986 World Cup Soccer Championships, Mexico — A131

1986, May 7 **Litho.** *Perf. 15*

940 A131 1c Emblem .20 .20
941 A131 2c Mexico .20 .20
942 A131 5c Mexico, diff. .20 .20
943 A131 5c Hungary vs. Scotland .20 .20
944 A131 10c Spain vs. Scotland .20 .20
945 A131 30c England vs. USSR .20 .20
946 A131 45c Spain vs. France .30 .30
947 A131 $1 England vs. Italy .60 .60

Perf. 13½
Size: 56x36mm

948 A131 75c Mexico .40 .40
949 A131 $2 Scotland 1.25 1.25
550 A131 $4 Spain 2.50 2.50
951 A131 $5 England 3.00 3.00
Nos. 940-951 (12) 9.25 9.25

1986, July 7 **Souvenir Sheets**

952 A131 $1.50 like #950 .65 .65
953 A131 $1.50 like #941 .65 .65
954 A131 $2.25 like #949 .95 .95
955 A131 $2.50 like #948 1.00 1.00
956 A131 $3 like #946 1.10 1.10
957 A131 $5.50 like #951 2.50 2.50
Nos. 952-957 (6) 6.85 6.85

Nos. 941-944, 946-947, vert.

Wedding of Prince Andrew and Sarah Ferguson — A132

A132a

#958a, Andrew. #958b, Sarah. #959a, Andrew, horiz. #959b, Andrew, Nancy Reagan, horiz.
Illustration A132a reduced.

1986 **Litho.** *Perf. 12½x13, 13x12½*

958 A132 60c Pair, #a.-b. .70 .70
959 A132 $2 Pair, #a.-b. 2.50 2.50
960 A132a $10 In coach 6.00 6.00
Nos. 958-960 (3) 9.20 9.20

Issued: $10, Nov.; others, July 23.
For overprints see Nos. 976-977.

A number of unissued items, imperfs., part perfs., missing color varieties, etc., were made available when the Format International inventory was liquidated.

Locomotives Type of 1985

Designs: 30c, 1926 JNR ABT Rack & Adhesion Class ED41 BZZB, Japan. 50c, 1883 Chicago RR Exposition, The Judge, 1A Type, US. $1, 1973 BM & LPRR E60C Co-Co, US. $3, 1972 GM (EMD) SD40-2 Co-Co, US.

1986, July *Perf. 12½x13*
a.-Side and front views.
b.-Action scene.

961 A120 30c Pair, #a.-b. .35 .35
962 A120 50c Pair, #a.-b. .60 .60
963 A120 $1 Pair, #a.-b. 1.25 1.25
964 A120 $3 Pair, #a.-b. 3.50 3.50
Nos. 961-964 (4) 5.70 5.70

Trees — A133

1986, Sept. *Perf. 14*

968 A133 10c Acrocomia aculeata .20 .20
969 A133 60c Pithecellobium saman .45 .45
970 A133 75c Tabebuia pallida .55 .55
971 A133 $3 Andira inermis 2.25 2.25
Nos. 968-971 (4) 3.45 3.45

Anniversaries — A134

1986, Sept. 30

972 A134 45c Cadet Force emblem, vert. .35 .35
973 A134 60c Grimble Building, GHS .45 .45
974 A134 $1.50 GHS class 1.10 1.10
975 A134 $2 Cadets in formation 1.50 1.50
Nos. 972-975 (4) 3.40 3.40

St. Vincent Cadet Force, 50th anniv., and Girls' High School, 75th anniv.

Nos. 958-959 Overprinted "Congratulations to T.R.H. The Duke & Duchess of York" in Silver

Perf. 12½x13, 13x12½

1986, Oct. **Litho.**

976 A132 60c Pair, #a.-b. .90 .90
977 A132 $2 Pair, #a.-b. 3.00 3.00

Stamps of the same denomination also exist printed tete-beche.

The Legend of King Arthur — A134a

1986, Nov. 3 *Perf. 14*

979 A134a 30c King Arthur .20 .20
979A A134a 45c Merlin raises Arthur .30 .30
979B A134a 60c Arthur pulls Excalibur from stone .35 .35
979C A134a 75c Camelot .45 .45
979D A134a $1 Lady of the Lake .60 .60
979E A134a $1.50 Knights of the Round Table .90 .90
979F A134a $2 Holy Grail 1.20 1.20
979G A134a $5 Sir Lancelot 3.00 3.00
Nos. 979-979G (8) 7.00 7.00

A134b

Statue of Liberty, Cent. — A135

Various views of the statue.

1986, Nov. 26 Litho. *Perf. 14*

980	A134b	15c	multicolored	.20	.20
980A	A134b	25c	multicolored	.20	.20
980B	A134b	40c	multicolored	.25	.25
980C	A134b	55c	multicolored	.35	.35
980D	A134b	75c	multicolored	.50	.50
980E	A134b	90c	multicolored	.60	.60
980F	A134b	$1.75	multicolored	1.10	1.10
980G	A134b	$2	multicolored	1.25	1.25
980H	A134b	$2.50	multicolored	1.65	1.65
980I	A134b	$3	multicolored	1.90	1.90
			Nos. 980-980I (10)	8.00	8.00

Souvenir Sheets

981	A135	$3.50	multicolored	2.25	2.25
982	A135	$4	multicolored	2.50	2.50
983	A135	$5	multicolored	3.00	3.00

Fresh-water Fishing — A136

#984a, Tri tri fishing. #984b, Tri tri. #985a, Crayfishing. #985b, Crayfish.

1986, Dec. 10 *Perf. 15*

984	A136	75c	Pair, #a.-b.	1.10	1.10
985	A136	$1.50	Pair, #a.-b.	2.25	2.25

1987 Wimbledon Tennis Championships A137

Natl. Child Survival Campaign A138

1987, June 22 *Perf. 13x12½*

988	A137	40c	Hana Mandlikova	.25	.25
989	A137	60c	Yannick Noah	.35	.35
990	A137	80c	Ivan Lendl	.50	.50
991	A137	$1	Chris Evert Lloyd	.60	.60
992	A137	$1.25	Steffi Graf	.75	.75
993	A137	$1.50	John McEnroe	.95	.95
994	A137	$1.75	Martina Navratilova	1.10	1.10
995	A137	$2	Boris Becker	1.25	1.25
			Nos. 988-995 (8)	5.75	5.75

Souvenir Sheet

996			Sheet of 2	3.50	3.50
a.	A137	$2.25	like $2	1.75	1.75
b.	A137	$2.25	like $1.75	1.75	1.75

1987, June 10 *Perf. 14x14½*

997	A138	10c	Growth monitoring	.20	.20
998	A138	50c	Oral rehydration therapy	.40	.40
999	A138	75c	Breast-feeding	.60	.60
1000	A138	$1	Universal immunization	.75	.75
			Nos. 997-1000 (4)	1.95	1.95

For overprints see Nos. 1040-1043.

Carnival, 10th Anniv. A139

Designs: 20c, Queen of the Bands, Miss Prima Donna 1986. 45c, Donna Young, Miss Carival 1985. 55c, M. Haydock, Miss. St. Vincent and the Grenadines 1986.

1987, June 29 *Perf. 12½x13*

1001	A139	20c	multicolored	.20	.20
1002	A139	45c	multicolored	.35	.35
1003	A139	55c	multicolored	.40	.40
1004	A139	$3.70	multicolored	2.75	2.75
			Nos. 1001-1004 (4)	3.70	3.70

Nos. 874-881 Overprinted "THE KING OF ROCK AND ROLL LIVES FOREVER . AUGUST 16TH" and "1977-1987" (Nos. 1009-1012) or "TENTH ANNIVERSARY" (Nos. 1013-1016)

1987, Aug. 26 Litho. *Perf. 12½*

1009	A123	10c	Pair, #a.-b.	.20	.20
1010	A123	60c	Pair, #a.-b.	.80	.80
1011	A123	$1	Pair, #a.-b.	1.25	1.25
1012	A123	$5	Pair, #a.-b.	6.50	6.50
			Nos. 1009-1012 (4)	8.75	8.75

Souvenir Sheets of 4

1013	A123	30c	#a.-b.	.90	.90
1014	A123	50c	#a.-b.	1.50	1.50
1015	A123	$1.50	#a.-b.	4.50	4.50
1016	A123	$4.50	#a.-b.	13.00	13.00

Nos. 1013-1016 contain two of each stamp.

Portrait of Queen Victoria, 1841, by R. Thorburn A140

Portraits and photographs: 75c, Elizabeth and Charles, 1948. $1, Coronation, 1953. $2.50, Duke of Edinburgh, 1948. $5, Elizabeth, c. 1980. $6, Elizabeth and Charles, 1948, diff.

1987, Nov. 20 Litho. *Perf. 12½x13*

1017	A140	15c	multicolored	.20	.20
1018	A140	75c	multicolored	.45	.45
1019	A140	$1	multicolored	.60	.60
1020	A140	$2.50	multicolored	1.50	1.50
1021	A140	$5	multicolored	3.00	3.00
			Nos. 1017-1021 (5)	5.75	5.75

Souvenir Sheet

1022	A140	$6	multicolored	4.50	4.50

Sesquicentennial of Queen Victoria's accession to the throne, wedding of Queen Elizabeth II and Prince Philip, 40th anniv.

Nos. 997-1000 Ovptd. "WORLD POPULATION / 5 BILLION / 11TH JULY 1987"

1987, July 11 Litho. *Perf. 14x14½*

1040	A138	10c	on No. 997	.20	.20
1041	A138	50c	on No. 998	.40	.40
1042	A138	75c	on No. 999	.60	.60
1043	A138	$1	on No. 1000	.75	.75
			Nos. 1040-1043 (4)	1.95	1.95

Automobile Centenary — A143

Automotive pioneers and vehicles: $1, $3, Carl Benz (1844-1929) and the Velocipede, patented 1886. $2, No. 1049, Enzo Ferrari (b. 1898) and 1966 Ferrari Dino 206SP. $4, $6, Charles Rolls (1877-1910), Sir Henry Royce (1863-1933) and 1907 Rolls Royce Silver Ghost. No. 1047, $8, Henry Ford (1863-1947) and Model T Ford.

1987, Dec. 4 *Perf. 13x12½*

1044	A143	$1	multicolored	.65	.65
1045	A143	$2	multicolored	1.10	1.10
1046	A143	$4	multicolored	2.25	2.25
1047	A143	$5	multicolored	3.00	3.00
			Nos. 1044-1047 (4)	7.00	7.00

Souvenir Sheets

1048	A143	$3	like No. 1044	2.25	2.25
1049	A143	$5	like No. 1045	3.75	3.75
1050	A143	$6	like No. 1046	4.50	4.50
1051	A143	$8	like No. 1047	6.00	6.00
			Nos. 1048-1051 (4)	16.50	16.50

Soccer Teams — A144

1987, Dec. 4

1052	A144	$2	Derby County	1.10	1.10
1053	A144	$2	Leeds United	1.10	1.10
1054	A144	$2	Tottenham Hotspur	1.10	1.10
1055	A144	$2	Manchester United	1.10	1.10
1056	A144	$2	Everton	1.10	1.10
1057	A144	$2	Liverpool	1.10	1.10
1058	A144	$2	Portsmouth	1.10	1.10
1059	A144	$2	Arsenal	1.10	1.10
			Nos. 1052-1059 (8)	8.80	8.80

A145

A Christmas Carol, by Charles Dickens (1812-1870) — A147

Portrait of Dickens as left page of book and various scenes from novels as right page of book.

1987, Dec. 17 *Perf. 14x14½*

Se-tenant Pairs

1061	A145	6c	Mr. Fezziwig's Ball	.20	.20
1062	A145	25c	Ghost of Christmases to Come	.40	.40
1063	A145	50c	The Cratchits	.75	.75
1064	A145	75c	Carolers	1.10	1.10
			Nos. 1061-1064 (4)	2.45	2.45

Souvenir Sheet

1065	A147	$5	Reading book to children	3.75	3.75

Eastern Caribbean Currency — A148

Various Eastern Caribbean coins (Nos. 1069-1081) and banknotes (Nos. 1082-1086) in denominations equaling that of the stamp on which they are pictured.

1987-89 Litho. *Perf. 15*

1069	A148	5c	multicolored	.20	.20
1070	A148	6c	multicolored	.20	.20
1071	A148	10c	multicolored	.20	.20
1072	A148	12c	multicolored	.20	.20
1073	A148	15c	multicolored	.20	.20
1074	A148	20c	multicolored	.20	.20
1075	A148	25c	multicolored	.20	.20
1076	A148	30c	multicolored	.25	.25
1077	A148	35c	multicolored	.30	.30
1078	A148	45c	multicolored	.35	.35
1079	A148	50c	multicolored	.40	.40
1080	A148	65c	multicolored	.50	.50
1081	A148	75c	multicolored	.60	.60
1082	A148	$1	multi, horiz.	.75	.75
1083	A148	$2	multi, horiz.	1.50	1.50
1084	A148	$3	multi, horiz.	2.25	2.25
1085	A148	$5	multi, horiz.	3.75	3.75
1086	A148	$10	multi, horiz.	7.50	7.50

Perf. 14

1086A	A148	$20	multi, horiz.	15.00	15.00
			Nos. 1069-1086A (19)	34.55	34.55

Issued: $20, Nov. 7, 1989; others, Dec. 11.

1991 *Perf. 12*

1071a	A148	10c	.20
1073a	A148	15c	.20
1074a	A148	20c	.20
1075a	A148	25c	.20
1078a	A148	45c	.30
1079a	A148	50c	.35
1080a	A148	65c	.45
1081a	A148	75c	.55
1082a	A148	$1	.70
1083a	A148	$2	1.40
1085a	A148	$5	3.50
		Nos. 1071a-1085a (11)	8.05

This perf may not have been issued in St. Vincent.

1991 *Perf. 14*

1071b	A148	10c	.20	.20
1073b	A148	15c	.20	.20
1074b	A148	20c	.20	.20
1075b	A148	25c	.20	.20
1078b	A148	45c	.30	.30
1079b	A148	50c	.35	.35
1080b	A148	65c	.45	.45
1081b	A148	75c	.55	.55
1082b	A148	$1	.70	.70
1083b	A148	$2	1.40	1.40
1085b	A148	$5	3.50	3.50
		Nos. 1071b-1085b (11)	8.05	8.05

US Constitution Bicentennial A149

Christopher Columbus's fleet: 15c, Santa Maria. 75c, Nina and Pinta. $1, Hour glass, compass. $1.50, Columbus planting flag of Spain on American soil. $3, Arawak natives. $4, Parrot, hummingbird, corn, pineapple, eggs. $5, $6, Columbus, Spanish royal coat of arms and caravel.

1988, Jan. 11 *Perf. 14½x14*

1087	A149	15c	multicolored	.20	.20
1088	A149	75c	multicolored	.60	.60
1089	A149	$1	multicolored	.75	.75

1090 A149 $1.50 multicolored 1.25 1.25
1091 A149 $3 multicolored 2.25 2.25
1092 A149 $4 multicolored 3.00 3.00
Nos. 1087-1092 (6) 8.05 8.05

Souvenir Sheets

Perf. 14x14½, 14½x14

1093 A149 $5 multicolored 3.75 3.75
1093A A149 $6 multicolored 4.50 4.50

US Constitution, bicent.; 500th anniv. of the discovery of America (in 1992).

Brown Pelican — A150

1988, Feb. 15 ***Perf. 14***
1094 A150 45c multicolored .35 .35

See No. 1298.

A151

Tourism — A152

1988, Feb. 22 **Litho.** ***Perf. 15***
1095 A151 10c Windsurfing, diff., vert. .20 .20
1096 A151 45c Scuba diving, vert. .35 .35
1097 A151 65c shown .50 .50
1098 A151 $5 Chartered ship 3.75 3.75
Nos. 1095-1098 (4) 4.80 4.80

Souvenir Sheet

Perf. 13x12½

1099 A152 $10 shown 7.50 7.50

A153

Destruction of the Spanish Armada by the English, 400th Anniv. — A154

16th cent. ships and artifacts: 15c, Nuestra Senora del Rosario, Spanish Chivalric Cross. 75c, Ark Royal, Armada medal. $1.50, English fleet, 16th cent. navigational instrument. $2, Dismasted galleon, cannon balls. $3.50, English fireships among the Armada, firebomb. $5, Revenge, Drake's drum. $8, Shoreline sentries awaiting the outcome of the battle.

1988, July 29 **Litho.** ***Perf. 12½***
1100 A153 15c multicolored .20 .20
1101 A153 75c multicolored .45 .45
1102 A153 $1.50 multicolored 1.00 1.00
1103 A153 $2 multicolored 1.25 1.25
1104 A153 $3.50 multicolored 2.00 2.00
1105 A153 $5 multicolored 3.00 3.00
Nos. 1100-1105 (6) 7.90 7.90

Souvenir Sheet

1106 A154 $8 multicolored 5.00 5.00

Cricket Players A156

1988, July 29 **Litho.** ***Perf. 14½x14***
1108 A156 15c D.K. Lillee .20 .20
1109 A156 50c G.A. Gooch .40 .40
1110 A156 75c R.N. Kapil Dev .60 .60
1111 A156 $1 S.M. Gavaskar .75 .75
1112 A156 $1.50 M.W. Gatting 1.15 1.15
1113 A156 $2.50 Imran Khan 1.90 1.90
1114 A156 $3 I.T. Botham 2.25 2.25
1115 A156 $4 I.V.A. Richards 3.00 3.00
Nos. 1108-1115 (8) 10.25 10.25

A souvenir sheet containing a $2 stamp like No. 1115 and a $3.50 stamp like No. 1114 was not issued by the post office.

1988 Summer Olympics, Seoul A158

1988, Dec. 7 **Litho.** ***Perf. 14***
1116 A158 10c Running .20 .20
1117 A158 50c Long jump, vert. .40 .40
1118 A158 $1 Triple jump .75 .75
1119 A158 $5 Boxing, vert. 3.75 3.75
Nos. 1116-1119 (4) 5.10 5.10

Souvenir Sheet

1120 A158 $10 Torch 7.50 7.50

1st Participation of St. Vincent athletes in the Olympics.

For overprints see Nos. 1346-1351.

Christmas — A159

Walt Disney characters: 1c, Minnie Mouse in freight car. 2c, Morty and Ferdy in open rail car. 3c, Chip 'n Dale in open boxcar. 4c, Huey, Dewey, Louie and reindeer. 5c, Donald and Daisy Duck aboard dining car. 10c, Gramma Duck conducting chorus including Scrooge McDuck, Goofy and Clarabelle Cow. $5, No. 1127, Mickey Mouse in locomotive. $6, Santa Claus in caboose. No. 1129, Mickey, Minnie Mouse and nephews in train station, vert. No. 1130, Characters riding carousel, vert.

Perf. 14x13½, 13½x14

1988, Dec. 23 **Litho.**
1121-1128 A159 Set of 8 9.25 9.25

Souvenir Sheets

1129-1130 A159 $5 Set of 2 7.50 7.50

Babe Ruth (1895-1948), American Baseball Star — A160

1988, Dec. 7 **Litho.** ***Perf. 14***
1131 A160 $2 multicolored 1.50 1.50

India '89, Jan. 20-29, New Delhi — A161

Exhibition emblem and Walt Disney characters: 1c, Mickey Mouse as snake charmer, Minnie Mouse as dancer. 2c, Goofy tossing rings at a chowsingha antelope. 3c, Mickey, Minnie, blue peacock. 5c, Goofy and Mickey as miners, Briolette diamond. 10c, Goofy as count presenting Orloff Diamond to Catherine the Great of Russia (Clarabelle Cow). 25c, Regent Diamond and Donald Duck as Napoleon (portrait) in the Louvre. $4, Minnie as Queen Victoria, Mickey as King Albert, crown bearing the Kohinoor Diamond. $5, Mickey and Goofy on safari. No. 1140, Mickey as Nehru, riding an elephant. No. 1141, Mickey as postman delivering Hope Diamond to the Smithsonian Institute.

1989, Feb. 7 **Litho.** ***Perf. 14***
1132-1139 A161 Set of 8 8.00 8.00

Souvenir Sheets

1140-1141 A161 $6 Set of 2 9.00 9.00

Entertainers of the Jazz and Big Band Eras — A162

Designs: 10c, Harry James (1916-83). 15c, Sidney Bechet (1897-1959). 25c, Benny Goodman (1909-86). 35c, Django Reinhardt (1910-53). 50c, Lester Young (1909-59). 90c, Gene Krupa (1909-73). $3, Louis Armstrong (1900-71). $4, Duke Ellington (1899-1974). No. 1150, Charlie Parker, Jr. (1920-55). No. 1151, Billie Holiday (1915-59).

1989, Apr. 3 **Litho.** ***Perf. 14***
1142-1149 A162 Set of 8 7.00 7.00

Souvenir Sheets

1150-1151 A162 $5 Set of 2 7.50 7.50

Holiday misspelled "Holliday" on No. 1151.

Miniature Sheet

Noah's Ark — A163

Designs: a, Clouds, 2 birds at right. b, Rainbow, 4 clouds. c, Ark. d, Rainbow, 3 clouds. e, Clouds, 2 birds at left. f, African elephant facing right. g, Elephant facing forward. h, Leaves on tree branch. i, Kangaroos. j, Hummingbird facing left, flower. k, Lions. l, White-tailed deer. m, Koala at right. n, Koala at left. o, Hummingbird facing right, flower. p, Flower, toucan facing left. q, Toucan facing right. r, Camels. s, Giraffes. t, Sheep. u, Ladybugs. v, Butterfly (UR). w, Butterfly (LL). x, Snakes. y, Dragonflies.

1989, Apr. 10 ***Perf. 14***
1152 A163 Sheet of 25 7.50 7.50
a.-y. 40c any single .30 .30

Easter A164

Paintings by Titian: 5c, Baptism of Christ. 30c, Temptation of Christ. 45c, Ecce Homo. 65c, Noli Me Tangere. 75c, Christ Carrying the Cross. $1, Christ Crowned with Thorns. $4, Lamentation Over Christ. $5, The Entombment. No. 1161, Pieta. No. 1162, The Deposition.

1989, Apr. 17 ***Perf. 13½x14***
1153-1160 A164 Set of 8 9.30 9.30

Souvenir Sheets

1161-1162 A164 $6 Set of 2 9.00 9.00

Telstar II and Cooperation in Space — A165

15c, Recovery of astronaut L. Gordon Cooper, Mercury 9/Faith 7 mission. 35c, Satellite transmission of Martin Luther King's civil rights march address, 1963. 40c, US shuttle STS-7, 1st use of Canadarm, deployment & recovery of a W. German free-flying experiment platform. 50c, Satellite transmission of the 1964 Olympics, Innsbruck (speed skater). 60c, Vladimir Remek of Czechoslovakia, 1st non-Soviet cosmonaut, 1978. $1, CNES Hermes space plane, France, ESA emblem, Columbus space station. $3, Satellite transmission of Pope John XXIII (1881-1963) blessing crowd at the Vatican. $4, Ulf Merbold, W. Germany, 1st non-American astronaut, 1983. #1171, Launch of Telstar II, 5/7/63. #1172, 1975 Apollo-Soyuz mission members shaking hands.

1989, Apr. 26 **Litho.** ***Perf. 14***
1163-1170 A165 Set of 8 7.60 7.60

Souvenir Sheets

1171-1172 A165 $5 Set of 2 7.50 7.50

Cruise Ships A166

1989, Apr. 21 **Litho.** ***Perf. 14***
1173 A166 10c Ile de France .20 .20
1174 A166 40c Liberte .30 .30
1175 A166 50c Mauretania .40 .40
1176 A166 75c France .55 .55
1177 A166 $1 Aquitania .75 .75
1178 A166 $2 United States 1.50 1.50
1179 A166 $3 Olympic 2.25 2.25
1180 A166 $4 Queen Elizabeth 3.00 3.00
Nos. 1173-1180 (8) 8.95 8.95

Souvenir Sheets

1181 A166 $6 Queen Mary 4.50 4.50
1182 A166 $6 QE 2 4.50 4.50

Nos. 1181-1182 contain 84x28mm stamps.
For overprints see Nos. 1352-1361.

Souvenir Sheet

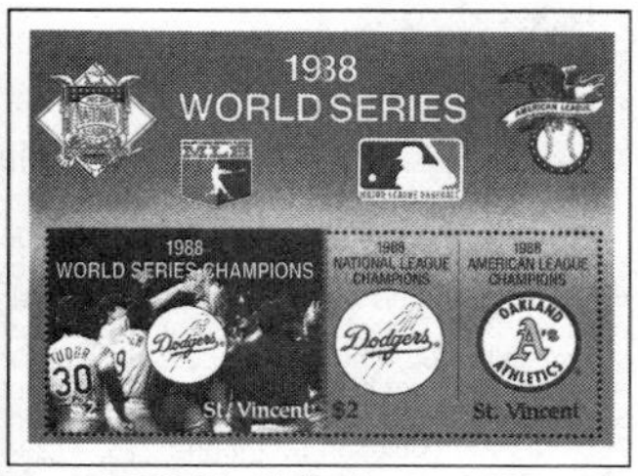

1988 World Series — A167

Designs: a, Dodgers emblem and players celebrating victory. b, Emblems of the Dodgers and the Oakland Athletics.

1989, May 3 Litho. *Perf. 14x13½*
1183 Sheet of 2 3.00 3.00
a.-b. A167 $2 any single 1.50 1.50

World Wildlife Fund, St. Vincent Parrots A168

Indigenous Birds — A169

1989, Apr. 5 *Perf. 14*
1184 A168 10c Parrot's head .20 .20
1185 A168 20c Parrot's wing span .20 .20
1186 A169 25c Mistletoe bird .20 .20
1187 A168 40c Parrot feeding, vert. .30 .30
1188 A168 70c Parrot on rock, vert. .50 .50
1189 A169 75c Crab hawk .60 .60
1190 A169 $2 Coucou 1.50 1.50
1191 A169 $3 Prince bird 2.25 2.25
Nos. 1184-1191 (8) 5.75 5.75

Souvenir Sheets

1192 A169 $5 Doctor bird 3.75 3.75
1193 A169 $5 Soufrieres, vert. 3.75 3.75

Fan Paintings — A170

By Hiroshige unless otherwise stated: 10c, Autumn Flowers in Front of the Full Moon. 40c, Hibiscus. 50c, Iris. 75c, Morning Glories. $1, Dancing Swallows. $2, Sparrow and Bamboo. $3, Yellow Bird and Cotton Rose. $4, Judos Chrysanthemums in a deep ravine in China. No. 1202, Rural Cottages in Spring, by Sotatsu. No. 1203, The Six Immortal Poets Portrayed as Cats, by Kuniyoshi.

1989, July 6 Litho. *Perf. 14x13½*
1194-1201 A170 Set of 8 9.00 9.00

Souvenir Sheets

1202-1203 A170 $6 Set of 2 9.00 9.00

Hirohito (1901-89) and enthronement of Akihito as emperor of Japan.

First Moon Landing, 20th Anniv. A171

Apollo 11 Mission: 35c, Columbia command module. 75c, Lunar module Eagle landing. $1, Rocket launch. No. 1207a, Buzz Aldrin conducting solar wind experiments. No. 1207b, Lunar module on plain. No. 1207c, Earthrise. No. 1207d, Neil Armstrong. No. 1208, Separation of lunar and command modules. No. 1209a, Command module. No. 1209b, Lunar module. $6, Armstrong preparing to take man's 1st step onto the Moon.

1989, Sept. 11 *Perf. 14*
1204 A171 35c multicolored .30 .30
1205 A171 75c multicolored .55 .55
1206 A171 $1 multicolored .75 .75
1207 Strip of 4 6.00 6.00
a.-d. A171 $2 any single 1.50 1.50
1208 A171 $3 multicolored 2.25 2.25
Nos. 1204-1208 (5) 9.85 9.85

Souvenir Sheets

1209 Sheet of 2 4.50 4.50
a.-b. A171 $3 any single 2.25 2.25
1210 A171 $6 multicolored 4.50 4.50

No. 1207 has continuous design.

Players Elected to the Baseball Hall of Fame — A172

1989 All-Star Game, July 11, Anaheim, California — A173

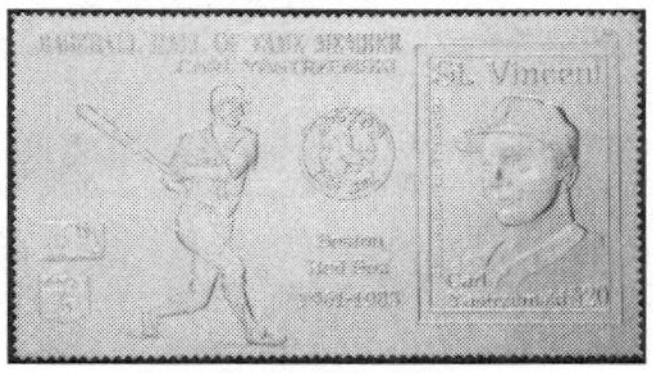

Baseball Hall of Fame Members — A173a

Rookies and Team Emblems A174

Rookies of the Year, Most Valuable Players and Cy Young Award Winners A175

1989, July 23 Litho. *Perf. 14*
1211 A172 $2 Cobb, 1936 1.50 1.50
1212 A172 $2 Mays, 1979 1.50 1.50
1213 A172 $2 Musial, 1969 1.50 1.50
1214 A172 $2 Bench, 1989 1.50 1.50
1215 A172 $2 Banks, 1977 1.50 1.50
1216 A172 $2 Schoendienst, 1989 1.50 1.50
1217 A172 $2 Gehrig, 1939 1.50 1.50
1218 A172 $2 Robinson, 1962 1.50 1.50
1219 A172 $2 Feller, 1962 1.50 1.50
1220 A172 $2 Williams, 1966 1.50 1.50
1221 A172 $2 Yastrzemski, 1989 1.50 1.50
1222 A172 $2 Kaline, 1980 1.50 1.50
Nos. 1211-1222 (12) 18.00 18.00

"Yastrzemski" is misspelled on No. 1221.

Size: 116x82mm

Imperf

1223 A173 $5 multicolored 3.75 3.75

1989 Embossed *Perf. 13*

No. 1223A, Johnny Bench. No. 1223B, Carl Yastrzemski. No. 1223C, Ernie Banks. No. 1223D, Willie Mays. No. 1223E, Al Kaline. No. 1223F, Ty Cobb. No. 1223G, Ted Williams. No. 1223H, Red Schoendienst. No. 1223I, Jackie Robinson. No. 1223J, Lou Gehrig. No. 1223K, Bob Feller. No. 1223L, Stan Musial.

1223A-1223L A173a $20 Set of 12, gold

Miniature Sheets

No. 1224: a, Dante Bichette, 1989. b, Carl Yastrzemski, 1961. c, Randy Johnson, 1989. d, Jerome Walton, 1989. e, Ramon Martinez, 1989. f, Ken Hill, 1989. g, Tom McCarthy, 1989. h, Gaylord Perry, 1963. i, John Smoltz, 1989.

No. 1225: a, Bob Milacki, 1989. b, Babe Ruth, 1915. c, Jim Abbott, 1989. d, Gary Sheffield, 1989. e, Gregg Jeffries, 1989. f, Kevin Brown, 1989. g, Cris Carpenter, 1989. h, Johnny Bench, 1968. i, Ken Griffey Jr., 1989.

No. 1226: a, Chris Sabo, 1988 Natl. League Rookie of the Year. b, Walt Weiss, 1988 American League Rookie of the Year. c, Willie Mays, 1951 Rookie of the Year. d, Kirk Gibson, 1988 Natl. League Most Valuable Player. e, Ted Williams, Most Valuable Player of 1946 and 1949. f, Jose Canseco, 1988 American League Most Valuable Player. g, Gaylord Perry, Cy Young winner for 1972 and 1978. h, Orel Hershiser, 1988 National League Cy Young winner. i, Frank Viola, 1988 American League Cy Young winner.

Perf. 13½

1224 Sheet of 9 4.00 4.00
a.-i. A174 60c any single .40 .40
1225 Sheet of 9 4.00 4.00
a.-i. A174 60c any single .40 .40
1226 Sheet of 9 4.00 4.00
a.-i. A175 60c any single .40 .40

For surcharges see Nos. B9-B11.

French Revolution Bicent., PHILEXFRANCE '89 — A176

French governors and ships.

1989, July 7 Litho. *Perf. 13½x14*
1227 A176 30c Goelette .25 .25
1228 A176 55c Corvette .40 .40
1229 A176 75c Fregate 36 .60 .60
1230 A176 $1 Vaisseau 74 .75 .75
1231 A176 $3 Ville de Paris 2.25 2.25
Nos. 1227-1231 (5) 4.25 4.25

Souvenir Sheet

1232 A176 $6 Map 4.50 4.50

Miniature Sheet

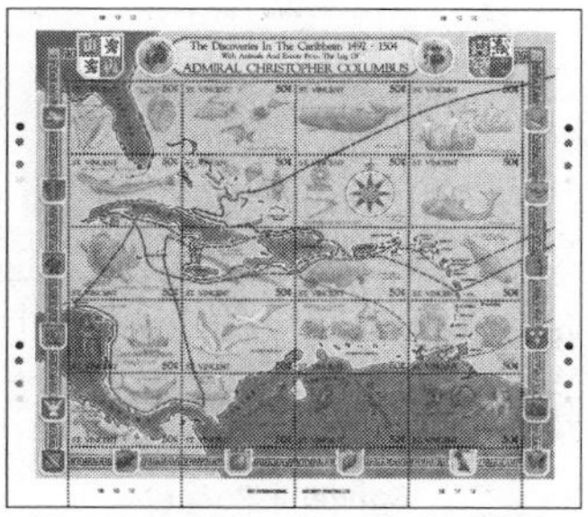

Discovery of the New World, 500th Anniv. (in 1992) — A177

Designs: a, Map of Florida, queen conch and West Indian purpura. b, Caribbean reef fish. c, Sperm whale. d, Columbus's fleet. e, Cuba, Isle of Pines, remora. f, The Bahamas, Turks & Caicos Isls., Columbus raising Spanish flag. g, Navigational instruments. h, Sea monster. i, Kemp's Ridley turtle, Cayman Isls. j, Jamaica, parts of Cuba and Hispaniola, magnificent frigatebird. k, Caribbean manatee, Hispaniola, Puerto Rico, Virgin Isls. l, Caribbean Monk seal, Anguilla and Caribbean isls. m, Mayan chief, galleon, dugout canoe. n, Masked boobies. o, Venezuelan village on pilings and the Netherlands Antilles. p, Atlantic wing oyster, lion's paw scallop, St. Vincent, Grenada, Trinidad & Tobago, Barbados. q, Panama, great hammerhead and mako sharks. r, Brown pelican, Colombia, Hyacinthine macaw. s, Venezuela, Indian bow and spear hunters. t, Capuchin and squirrel monkeys.

1989, Aug. 31 *Perf. 14*
1233 A177 Sheet of 20 9.50 9.50
a.-t. 50c any single .45 .45

Major League Baseball: Los Angeles Dodgers — A178

No. 1234: a, Jay Howell, Alejandro Pena. b, Mike Davis, Kirk Gibson. c, Fernando Valenzuela, John Shelby. d, Jeff Hamilton, Franklin Stubbs. e, Dodger Stadium. f, Ray Searage, John Tudor. g, Mike Sharperson, Mickey Hatcher. h, Coaches Amalfitano, Cresse, Ferguson, Hines, Mota, Perranoski, Russell. i, John Wetteland, Ramon Martinez.

No. 1235: a, Tim Belcher, Tim Crews. b, Orel Hershiser, Mike Morgan. c, Mike Scioscia, Rick Dempsey. d, Dave Anderson, Alfredo Griffin. e, Team emblem. f, Kal Daniels, Mike Marshall. g, Eddie Murray, Willie Randolph. h, Manager Tom Lasorda, Jose Gonzalez. i, Lenny Harris, Chris Gwynn, Billy Bean.

1989, Sept. 23 *Perf. 12½*
1234 Sheet of 9 4.00 4.00
a.-i. A178 60c any single .40 .40
1235 Sheet of 9 4.00 4.00
a.-i. A178 60c any single .40 .40

See Nos. 1344-1345.

1990 World Cup Soccer Championships, Italy — A179

1989, Oct. 16 Litho. *Perf. 14*
1236 A179 10c shown .20 .20
1237 A179 55c Youth soccer teams .40 .40

1238 A179 $1 Natl. team .75 .75
1239 A179 $5 Trophy winners 3.75 3.75
Nos. 1236-1239 (4) 5.10 5.10

Souvenir Sheets

1240 A179 $6 Youth soccer team 4.50 4.50
1241 A179 $6 Natl. team, diff. 4.50 4.50

Fauna and Flora A180

1989, Nov. 1

1242 A180 65c St. Vincent parrot .50 .50
1243 A180 75c Whistling warbler .60 .60
1244 A180 $5 Black snake 3.75 3.75
Nos. 1242-1244 (3) 4.85 4.85

Souvenir Sheet

1245 A180 $6 Volcano plant, vert. 4.50 4.50

Butterflies A181

1989, Oct. 16 ***Perf. 14x14½, 14½x14***

1246 A181 6c Little yellow .20 .20
1247 A181 10c Orion .20 .20
1248 A181 15c American painted lady .20 .20
1249 A181 75c Cassius blue .60 .60
1250 A181 $1 Polydamus swallowtail .75 .75
1251 A181 $2 Guaraguao skipper 1.50 1.50
1252 A181 $3 The Queen 2.25 2.25
1253 A181 $5 Royal blue 3.75 3.75
Nos. 1246-1253 (8) 9.45 9.45

Souvenir Sheets

1254 A181 $6 Monarch 4.50 4.50
1255 A181 $6 Barred sulphur 4.50 4.50

Exhibition Emblem, Disney Characters and US Natl. Monuments A182

Designs: 1c, Seagull Monument, UT. 2c, Lincoln Memorial, Washington, DC. 3c, Crazy Horse Memorial, SD. 4c, Uncle Sam Wilson, Troy, NY. 5c, Benjamin Franklin Natl. Memorial, Philadelphia, PA. 10c, Statue of George Washington, Federal Hall, NY. $3, John F. Kennedy's birthplace, Brookline, MA. $6, George Washington's home, Mount Vernon, VA. No. 1264, Mt. Rushmore, SD. No. 1265, Stone Mountain, GA.

1989, Nov. 17 ***Perf. 13½x14***

1256-1263 A182 Set of 8 8.00 8.00

Souvenir Sheets

1264-1265 A182 $5 Set of 2 7.50 7.50

World Stamp Expo '89.

Souvenir Sheet

The Washington Monument, Washington, DC — A183

1989, Nov. 17 Litho. ***Perf. 14***

1266 A183 $5 multicolored 3.75 3.75

World Stamp Expo '89.

Miniature Sheets

Major League Baseball — A184

Players, owners and commissioner.

No. 1267: a, Early Wynn. b, Cecil Cooper. c, Joe DiMaggio. d, Kevin Mitchell. e, Tom Browning. f, Bobby Witt. g, Tim Wallach. h, Bob Gibson. i, Steve Garvey.

No. 1268: a, Rick Sutcliffe. b, A. Bartlett Giamatti, commissioner. c, Cory Snyder. d, Rollie Fingers. e, Willie Hernandez. f, Sandy Koufax. g, Carl Yastrzemski. h, Ron Darling. i, Gerald Perry.

No. 1269: a, Mike Marshall. b, Tom Seaver. c, Bob Milacki. d, Dave Smith. e, Robin Roberts. f, Kent Hrbek. g, Bill Veeck, owner. h, Carmelo Martinez. i, Rogers Hornsby.

No. 1270: a, Barry Bonds. b, Jim Palmer. c, Lou Boudreau. d, Ernie Whitt. e, Jose Canseco. f, Ken Griffey, Jr. g, Johnny Vander Meer. h, Kevin Seitzer. i, Dave Dravecky.

No. 1271: a, Glenn Davis. b, Nolan Ryan. c, Hank Greenberg. d, Richie Allen. e, Dave Righetti. f, Jim Abbott. g, Harold Reynolds. h, Dennis Martinez. i, Rod Carew.

No. 1272: a, Joe Morgan. b, Tony Fernandez. c, Ozzie Guillen. d, Mike Greenwell. e, Bobby Valentine. f, Doug DeCinces. g, Mickey Cochrane. h, Willie McGee. i, Von Hayes.

No. 1273: a, Frank White. b, Brook Jacoby. c, Boog Powell. d, Will Clark. e, Ray Kroc, owner. f, Fred McGriff. g, Willie Stargell. h, John Smoltz. i, B. J. Surhoff.

No. 1274: a, Keith Hernandez. b, Eddie Mathews. c, Tom Paciorek. d, Alan Trammell. e, Greg Maddux. f, Ruben Sierra. g, Tony Oliva. h, Chris Bosio. i, Orel Hershiser.

No. 1275: a, Casey Stengel. b, Jim Rice. c, Reggie Jackson. d, Jerome Walton. e, Bob Knepper. f, Andres Galarraga. g, Christy Mathewson. h, Willie Wilson. i, Ralph Kiner.

1989, Nov. 30 ***Perf. 12½***

Sheets of 9

1267 A184 30c #a.-j. 2.00 2.00
1268 A184 30c #a.-j. 2.00 2.00
1269 A184 30c #a.-j. 2.00 2.00
1270 A184 30c #a.-j. 2.00 2.00
1271 A184 30c #a.-j. 2.00 2.00
1272 A184 30c #a.-j. 2.00 2.00
1273 A184 30c #a.-j. 2.00 2.00
1274 A184 30c #a.-j. 2.00 2.00
1275 A184 30c #a.-j. 2.00 2.00

No. 1268d is incorrectly inscribed "Finger." Cochrane is misspelled "Cochpane" on No. 1272g.

See No. 1277.

Miniature Sheet

Achievements of Nolan Ryan, American Baseball Player — A185

Portrait and inscriptions: a, 383 League-leading strikeouts, 1973. b, No hitter, Kansas City Royals, May 15, 1973. c, No hitter, Detroit Tigers, July 15, 1973. d, No hitter, Minnesota Twins, Sept. 28, 1974. e, No hitter, Baltimore Orioles, June 1, 1975. f, No hitter, Los Angeles Dodgers, Sept. 26, 1981. g, Won 100+ games in both leagues. h, Struck out 200+ batters in 13 seasons. i, 5000th Strikeout, Aug. 22, 1989, Arlington, Texas.

1989, Nov. 30 Litho. ***Perf. 12½***

1276 Sheet of 9 13.50 13.50
a.-i. A185 $2 any single 1.50 1.50

For overprints see Nos. 1336-1337.

1989, Nov. 30 Litho. ***Perf. 12½***

1277 A184 30c Mike Greenwell, Boston Red Sox .25 .25

No. 1277 issued in sheets of 9.

Coat of Arms, No. 570 — A186

Boy Scouts and Girl Guides — A187

1989, Dec. 20 ***Perf. 14***

1278 A186 65c multicolored .50 .50

Souvenir Sheet

1279 A186 $10 multicolored 7.50 7.50

Independence, 10th anniv.

1989, Dec. 20 ***Perf. 14***

Lord or Lady Baden-Powell and various scouts or girl guides.

1280 A187 35c Boy's modern uniform .30 .30
1281 A187 35c Guide, ranger, brownie .30 .30
1282 A187 55c Boy's old uniform .40 .40
1283 A187 55c Mrs. Jackson .40 .40
1284 A187 $2 75th anniv. emblem 1.50 1.50
1285 A187 $2 Mrs. Russell 1.50 1.50
Nos. 1280-1285 (6) 4.40 4.40

Souvenir Sheets

1286 A187 $5 Canoeing, merit badges 3.75 3.75
1287 A187 $5 Flag-raising, Camp Yourumei, 1985 3.75 3.75

Christmas — A188

Paintings by Da Vinci and Botticelli: 10c, The Adoration of the Magi (holy family), by Botticelli. 25c, The Adoration of the Magi (witnesses). 30c, The Madonna of the Magnificat, by Botticelli. 40c, The Virgin and Child with St. Anne and St. John the Baptist, by Da Vinci. 55c, The Annunciation (angel), by Da Vinci. 75c, The Annunciation (Madonna). $5, #1294, Madonna of the Carnation, by Da Vinci. $6, The Annunciation, by Botticelli. #1296, The Virgin of the Rocks, by Da Vinci. #1297, The Adoration of the Magi, by Botticelli.

1989, Dec. 20 ***Perf. 14***

1288-1295 A188 Set of 8 10.00 10.00

Souvenir Sheets

1296-1297 A188 $5 Set of 2 7.50 7.50

Bird Type of 1988

1989, July 31 Litho. ***Perf. 15x14***

1298 A150 55c St. Vincent parrot .40 .40

Lions Intl. of St. Vincent, 25th Anniv. (in 1989) A189

Services: 10c, Scholarships for the blind, vert. 65c, Free textbooks. 75c, Health education (diabetes). $2, Blood sugar testing machines. $4, Publishing and distribution of pamphlets on drug abuse.

1990, Mar. 5 Litho. ***Perf. 14***

1303-1307 A189 Set of 5 5.75 5.75

World War II A190

Historic events: 5c, Defeat of the Graf Spee, 12/13-17/39. 10c, Charles De Gaulle calls the French Resistance to arms, 6/18/40. 15c, The British drive the Italian army out of Egypt, 12/15/40. 25c, US destroyer Reuben James torpedoed off Iceland, 10/31/41. 30c, MacArthur becomes allied supreme commander of the southwest Pacific, 4/18/42. 40c, US forces attack Corregidor, 2/16/45. 55c, HMS King George V engages the Bismarck, 5/27/41. 75c, US fleet enters Tokyo Harbor, 8/27/45. $5, Russian takeover of Berlin completed, 5/2/45. $6, #1317, Battle of the Philippine Sea, 6/18/44. #1318, Battle of the Java Sea, 2/28/42.

1990, Apr. 2 ***Perf. 14x13½***

1308-1317 A190 Set of 10 10.50 10.50

Souvenir Sheet

1318 A190 $6 multi 4.50 4.50

Penny Black, 150th Anniv. — A191

Great Britain No. 1 (various plate positions).

1990, May 3 Litho. ***Perf. 14x15***

1319 A191 $2 "NK" 1.50 1.50

1320 A191 $4 "AB" 3.00 3.00

Souvenir Sheet

1321 A191 $6 Simulated #1, "SV" 4.50 4.50

Stamp World London '90 — A192

Walt Disney characters in British military uniforms: 5c, Donald Duck as 18th cent. Admiral. 10c, Huey as Bugler, 68th Light Infantry, 1854. 15c, Minnie Mouse as Drummer, 1st Irish Guards, 1900. 25c, Goofy as Lance Corporal, Seaforth Highlanders, 1944. $1, Mickey Mouse as officer, 58th Regiment, 1879, 1881. $2, Donald Duck as officer, Royal Engineers, 1813. $4, Mickey Mouse as Drum Major, 1914. $5, Goofy as Pipe Sergeant, 1918. No. 1330, Scrooge as Company Clerk and Goofy as King's Lifeguard of Foot. No. 1331, Mickey Mouse as British Grenadier.

1990, May Litho. *Perf. 13½x14*

1322-1329 A192 Set of 8 9.50 9.50

Souvenir Sheets

1330-1331 A192 $6 Set of 2 9.00 9.00

A193

1990, July 5 *Perf. 14*

1332 $2 In robes 1.55 1.55
1333 $2 Queen Mother signing book 1.55 1.55
1334 $2 In fur coat 1.55 1.55
a. A193 Strip of 3, #1332-1334 4.65 4.65
Nos. 1332-1334 (3) 4.65 4.65

Souvenir Sheet

1335 A194 $6 Like No. 1334 4.75 4.75

No. 1276 Overprinted

Miniature Sheets

a

b

1990, July 23 Litho. *Perf. 12½*

Sheets of 9

1336 A185(a) $2 #1336a-1336i 13.50 13.50
1337 A185(b) $2 #1337a-1337i 13.50 13.50

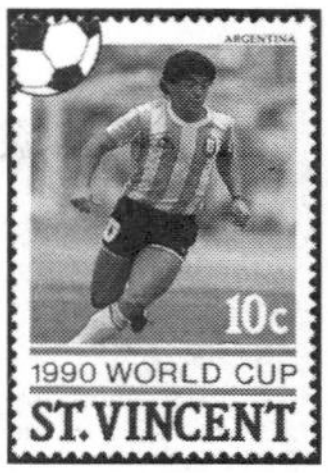

World Cup Soccer Championships, Italy — A195

Players from participating countries.

1990, Sept. 24 Litho. *Perf. 14*

1338 A195 10c Argentina .20 .15
1339 A195 75c Colombia .55 .55
1340 A195 $1 Uruguay .75 .75
1341 A195 $5 Belgium 3.75 3.75
Nos. 1338-1341 (4) 5.25 5.20

Souvenir Sheets

1342 A195 $6 Brazil 4.50 4.50
1343 A195 $6 West Germany 4.50 4.50

Dodger Baseball Type of 1989

No. 1344: a, Hubie Brooks, Orel Hershiser. b, Manager Tom Lasorda, Tim Crews. c, Fernando Valenzuela, Eddie Murray. d, Kal Daniels, Jose Gonzalez. e, Dodger centennial emblem. f, Chris Gwynn, Jeff Hamilton. g, Kirk Gibson, Rick Dempsey. h, Jim Gott, Alfredo Griffin. i, Coaches, Ron Perranoski, Bill Russell, Joe Ferguson, Joe Amalfitano, Mark Cresse, Ben Hines, Manny Mota.

No. 1345: a, Mickey Hatcher, Jay Howell. b, Juan Samuel, Mike Scioscia. c, Lenny Harris, Mike Hartley. d, Ramon Martinez, Mike Morgan. e, Dodger Stadium. f, Stan Javier, Don Aase. g, Ray Searage, Mike Sharperson. h, Tim Belcher, Pat Perry. i, Dave Walsh, Jose Vizcaino, Jim Neidlinger, Jose Offerman, Carlos Hernandez.

Hyphen-hole roulette 7

1990, Sept. 21

1344 Sheet of 9 4.00 4.00
a.-i. A178 60c any single .40 .40
1345 Sheet of 9 4.00 4.00
a.-i. A178 60c any single .40 .40

Nos. 1116-1120 Ovptd. or Similarly

1990, Oct. 18 *Perf. 14*

1346 A158 10c shown .20 .20
1347 A158 50c "CARL / LEWIS / U.S.A." .40 .40
1348 A158 $1 "HRISTO / MARKOV / BULGARIA" .75 .75
1349 A158 $5 "HENRY / MASKE / E. GERMANY" 3.75 3.75
Nos. 1346-1349 (4) 5.10 5.10

Souvenir Sheets

1350 A158 $10 USSR, US medals 7.50 7.50
1351 A158 $10 South Korea, Spain medals 7.50 7.50

Nos. 1173-1182 Overprinted

1990, Oct. 18 Litho. *Perf. 14*

1352 A166 10c *Ile de France* .20 .20
1353 A166 40c *Liberte* .30 .30
1354 A166 50c *Mauretania* .40 .40
1355 A166 75c *France* .55 .55
1356 A166 $1 *Aquitania* .75 .75
1357 A166 $2 *United States* 1.50 1.50
1358 A166 $3 *Olympic* 2.25 2.25
1359 A166 $4 *Queen Elizabeth* 3.00 3.00
Nos. 1352-1359 (8) 8.95 8.95

Souvenir Sheets

1360 A166 $6 *Queen Mary* 4.50 4.50
1361 A166 $6 *QE 2* 4.50 4.50

Overprint on #1360-1361 is 12mm in diameter.

Orchids — A196

Designs: 10c, Dendrophylax funalis, Dimerанda emarginata. 15c, Epidendrum elongatum. 45c, Comparettia falcata. 60c, Brassia maculata. $1, Encyclia cochleata, Encyclia cordigera. $2, Cyrtopodium punctatum. $4, Cattelya labiata. $5, Bletia purpurea. No. 1370, Ionopsis utricularioides. No. 1371, Vanilla planifolia.

1990, Nov. 23

1362-1369 A196 Set of 8 10.00 10.00

Souvenir Sheets

1370-1371 A196 $6 Set of 2 9.00 9.00

Christmas A197

Details from paintings by Rubens: 10c, Miraculous Draught of Fishes. 45c, $2, Crowning of Holy Katherine. 50c, St. Ives of Treguier. 65c, Allegory of Eternity. $1, $4, St. Bavo Receives Monastic Habit of Ghent. $5, Communion of St. Francis. #1380, St. Ives of Treguier (entire). #1381, Allegory of Eternity. #1382, St. Bavo Receives Monastic Habit of Ghent, horiz. #1383, The Miraculous Draft of Fishes, horiz.

1990, Dec. 3 Litho. *Perf. 14*

1372-1379 A197 Set of 8 10.50 10.50

Souvenir Sheets

1380-1383 A197 $6 Set of 4 18.00 18.00

Miniature Sheet

Intl. Literacy Year A198

Canterbury Tales: a, Geoffrey Chaucer (1342-1400), author. b, "When April with his showers sweet..." c, "When Zephyr also has,..." d. "And many little birds make melody..." e, "And palmers to go seeking out strange strands..." f, Quill pen, open book. g, Bluebird in tree. h, Trees, rider's head with white hair. i, Banner on staff. j, Town. k, Rider's head, diff. l, Blackbird in tree. m, Old monk. n, Horse, rider. o, Nun, monk carrying banner. p, Monks. q, White horse, rider. r, Black horse, rider. s, Squirrel. t, Rooster. u, Chickens. v, Rabbit. w, Butterfly. x, Mouse.

1990, Dec. 12 *Perf. 13½*

1384 Sheet of 24 7.20 7.20
a.-x. A198 40c any single .30 .30

Vincent Van Gogh (1853-1890), Painter — A198a

Self-Portraits.

1990, Dec. 17 Litho. *Perf. 13*

1385 A198a 1c 1889 .20 .20
1386 A198a 5c 1886 .20 .20
1387 A198a 10c 1888, with hat & pipe .20 .20
1388 A198a 15c 1888, painting .20 .20
a. Strip of 4, #1385-1388 .30 .30
1389 A198a 20c 1887 .20 .20
1390 A198a 45c 1889, diff. .35 .35
1391 A198a $5 1889, with bandaged ear 3.75 3.75
1392 A198a $6 1887, with straw hat 4.50 4.50
a. Strip of 4, #1389-1392 8.75 8.75
Nos. 1385-1392 (8) 9.60 9.60

Hummel Figurines — A199

1990, Dec. 30 Litho. *Perf. 14*

1393 A199 10c Photographer .20 .20
1394 A199 15c Boy with ladder & rope .20 .20
1395 A199 40c Pharmacist .30 .30
1396 A199 60c Boy answering telephone .45 .45
1396A A199 $1 Bootmaker .70 .70
1396B A199 $2 Artist 1.50 1.50
1397 A199 $4 Waiter 3.00 3.00
a. Sheet of 4, 15c, 40c, $2, $4 5.00 5.00
1398 A199 $5 Mailman 3.75 3.75
a. Sheet of 4, 10c, 60c, $1, $5 5.00 5.00
Nos. 1393-1398 (8) 10.10 10.10

Souvenir Sheets

Super Bowl Highlights — A200

Designs: Nos. 1400-1424, 1425-1449, Super Bowl I (1967) through Super Bowl XXV (1991). Nos. 1425-1449 picture Super Bowl Program Covers. Nos. 1443, 1449 horiz.

1991, Jan. 15 Litho. *Perf. 13½x14*

1400-1424 A200 Set of 25 18.00 18.00

Size: 99x125mm

Imperf

1425-1449 A200 $2 Set of 25 37.50 37.50

Nos. 1400-1423 contain two 50c stamps printed with continuous design showing game highlights. No. 1424 contains three 50c stamps showing AFC and NFC team helmets and the Vince Lombardi Trophy.

Miniature Sheets

Discovery of America, 500th Anniv. (in 1992) — A201

No. 1450: a, 1c, US #230. b, 2c, US #231. c, 3c, US #232. d, 4c, US #233. e, $10, Sailing ship, parrot. f, 5c, US #234. g, 6c, US #235. h, 8c, US #236. i, 10c, US #237.

No. 1451: a, 15c, US #238. b, 30c, US #239. c, 50c, US #240. d, $1, US #241. e, $10, Compass rose, sailing ship. f, $2, US #242. g, $3, US #243. h, $4, US #244. i, $5, US #245.

No. 1452, Bow of sailing ship. No. 1453, Ship's figurehead.

1991, Mar. 18 Litho. *Perf. 14*

Sheets of 9

1450	A201	#1450a-1450i	7.35	7.35
1451	A201	#1451a-1451i	18.00	18.00

Souvenir Sheets

1452	A201	$6 multicolored	4.50	4.50
1453	A201	$6 multicolored	4.50	4.50

Nos. 1452-1453 each contain one 38x31mm stamp.

Jetsons, The Movie — A202

Hanna-Barbera characters: 5c, Cosmo Spacely, vert. 20c, Elroy, Judy, Astro, Jane & George Jetson, vert. 45c, Judy, Apollo Blue, vert. 50c, Mr. Spacely, George, vert. 60c, George, sprocket factory. $1, Apollo Blue, Judy, Elroy and Grungees. $2, Jane and George in Grungee cavern. $4, George, Elroy, Jane and Little Grungee, vert. $5, Jetsons leaving for Earth, vert. No. 1463, Jetsons in sprocket factory. No. 1464, Jetsons traveling to Orbiting Ore Asteroid.

1991, Mar. 25 Litho. *Perf. 13½*

1454-1462	A202	Set of 9	10.50	10.50

Souvenir Sheets

1463-1464	A202	$6 Set of 2	9.00	9.00

The Flintstones Enjoy Sports — A203

1991, Mar. 25

1465	A203	10c Boxing	.20	.20
1466	A203	15c Soccer	.20	.20
1467	A203	45c Rowing	.35	.35
1468	A203	55c Dinosaur riding	.40	.40
1469	A203	$1 Basketball	.70	.70
1470	A203	$2 Wrestling	1.50	1.50
1471	A203	$4 Tennis	3.00	3.00
1472	A203	$5 Cycling	3.75	3.75
		Nos. 1465-1472 (8)	10.10	10.10

Souvenir Sheets

1473	A203	$6 Baseball, batting	4.50	4.50
1474	A203	$6 Baseball, sliding home	4.50	4.50

Voyages of Discovery A204

5c, Sanger 2. 10c, Magellan probe, 1990. 25c, Buran space shuttle. 75c, American space station. $1, Mars mission, 21st century. $2, Hubble space telescope, 1990. $4, Sailship to Mars. $5, Craf satellite, 2000. #1483, Sailing ship, island hopping. #1484, Sailing ship returning home.

1991, May 13

1475-1482	A204	Set of 8	10.00	10.00

Souvenir Sheets

1483-1484	A204	$6 Set of 2	9.00	9.00

Discovery of America, 500th anniv. (in 1992).

Royal Family Birthday, Anniversary Common Design Type

1991, July Litho. *Perf. 14*

1485	CD347	5c multicolored	.20	.20
1486	CD347	20c multicolored	.20	.20
1487	CD347	25c multicolored	.20	.20
1488	CD347	60c multicolored	.50	.50
1489	CD347	$1 multicolored	.75	.75
1490	CD347	$2 multicolored	1.50	1.50
1491	CD347	$4 multicolored	3.00	3.00
1492	CD347	$5 multicolored	3.75	3.75
		Nos. 1485-1492 (8)	10.10	10.10

Souvenir Sheets

1493	CD347	$5 Elizabeth, Philip	3.75	3.75
1494	CD347	$5 Charles, Diana, sons	3.75	3.75

20c, 25c, $1, Nos. 1492, 1494, Charles and Diana, 10th wedding anniversary. Others, Queen Elizabeth II, 65th birthday.

Miniature Sheets

Japanese Trains A205

Designs: No. 1495a, D51 steam locomotive. b, 9600 steam locomotive. c, Chrysanthemum emblem. d, Passenger coach. e, C57 steam locomotive. f, Oil tank car. g, C53 steam locomotive. h, First steam locomotive. i, C11 steam locomotive.

No. 1496a, Class 181 electric train. b, EH-10 electric locomotive. c, Special Express emblem. d, Sendai City Class 1 trolley. e, Class 485 electric train. f, Sendai City trolley street cleaner. g, Hakari bullet train. h, ED-11 electric locomotive. i, EF-66 electric locomotive.

No. 1497, C55 steam locomotive, vert. No. 1498, Series 400 electric train. No. 1499, C62 steam locomotive, vert. No. 1500, Super Hitachi electric train, vert.

1991, Aug. 12 Litho. *Perf. 14x13½*

1495	A205	75c Sheet of 9, #a.-i.	5.00	5.00
1496	A205	$1 Sheet of 9, #a.-i.	6.75	6.75

Souvenir Sheets

Perf. 13x13½

1497	A205	$6 multicolored	4.50	4.50
1498	A205	$6 multicolored	4.50	4.50
1499	A205	$6 multicolored	4.50	4.50
1500	A205	$6 multicolored	4.50	4.50

Phila Nippon '91. Nos. 1497-1500 each contain 27x44mm or 44x27mm stamps.

Miniature Sheets

Entertainers A206

#1501a-1501i, Various portraits of Madonna.

Italian entertainers: #1502a, Marcello Mastroianni. b, Sophia Loren. c, Mario Lanza (1921-59). d, Federico Fellini. e, Arturo Toscanini (1867-1957). f, Anna Magnani (1908-73). g, Giancarlo Giannini. h, Gina Lollobrigida. i, Enrico Caruso (1873-1921).

#1503a-1503i, Various portraits of John Lennon.

1991, Aug. 22 *Perf. 13*

1501	A206	$1 Sheet of 9, #a.-i.	6.75	6.75
1502	A206	$1 Sheet of 9, #a.-i.	6.75	6.75
1503	A206	$1 +2c, Sheet of 9, #a.-i.	6.90	6.90

Souvenir Sheets

Perf. 12x13

1504	A206	$6 Madonna	4.50	4.50

Perf. 13

1505	A206	$6 Luciano Pavarotti, horiz.	4.50	4.50

No. 1503 is semi-postal with surtax going to the Spirit Foundation.

No. 1504 contains one 28x42mm stamp. Compare with No. 1566. See Nos. 1642-1643, 1729, 2055.

Intl. Literacy Year — A207

Walt Disney characters in "The Prince and the Pauper": 5c, Pauper pals. 10c, Princely boredom. 15c, The valet. 25c, Look alikes. 60c, Trading places. 75c, How to be a prince. 80c, Food for the populace. $1, Captain's plot. $2, Doomed in the dungeon. $3, Looking for a way out. $4, A Goofy jailbreak. $5, Long live the real prince. No. 1518, Crowning the wrong guy. No. 1519, Mickey meets the captain of the guard. No. 1520, Real prince arrives. No. 1521, Seize the guard.

1991, Nov. 18 *Perf. 14x13½*

1506-1517	A207	Set of 12	13.50	13.50

Souvenir Sheets

1518-1521	A207	$6 Set of 4	18.00	18.00

1991, Nov. 18

Walt Disney's "The Rescuers Down Under": 5c, Miss Bianca, Heroine. 10c, Bernard, Shy Hero. 15c, Maitre d'Francois. 25c, Wilbur, the Albatross. 60c, Jake, the Aussie kangaroo mouse. 75c, Bernard, Bianca and Jake in the outback. 80c, Bianca and Bernard. $1, Marahute, the magnificent rare eagle. $2, Cody and Marahute. $3, McLeach and his pet Goanna, Joanna. $4, Frank, the frill-necked lizard. $5, Endangered animals: Red Kangaroo, Krebbs Koala, and Polly Platypus. No. 1534, Cody with the rescuers. No. 1535, Delegates of Intl. Rescue Aid Society. No. 1536, Wilbur's painful touchdown "down under." No. 1537, Wilbur transports Miss Bianca and Bernard to Australia.

1522-1533	A207	Set of 12	13.50	13.50

Souvenir Sheets

1534-1537	A207	$6 Set of 4	18.00	18.00

Brandenburg Gate, Bicent. — A209

50c, Demonstrator with sign. 75c, Soldiers at Berlin Wall. 90c, German flag, shadows on wall. $1, Pres. Gorbachev and Pres. Bush shaking hands. $4, Coat of Arms of Berlin.

1991, Nov. 18 Litho. *Perf. 14*

1538-1541	A209	Set of 4	2.40	2.40

Souvenir Sheet

1542	A209	$4 multi	3.00	3.00

Wolfgang Amadeus Mozart, Death Bicent. A210

Designs: $1, Scene from "Marriage of Figaro." $3, Scene from "The Clemency of Titus." $4, Portrait of Mozart, vert.

1991, Nov. 18

1543	A210	$1 multicolored	.75	.75
1544	A210	$3 multicolored	2.25	2.25

Souvenir Sheet

1545	A210	$4 multicolored	3.00	3.00

17th World Scout Jamboree, Korea — A211

Designs: 65c, Adventure tales around camp fire, vert. $1.50, British defenses at Mafeking, 1900, Cape of Good Hope #179. $3.50, Scouts scuba diving, queen angelfish.

1991, Nov. 18 Litho. *Perf. 14*

1546	A211	65c multicolored	.50	.50
1547	A211	$1.50 multicolored	1.15	1.15
1548	A211	$3.50 multicolored	2.65	2.65
		Nos. 1546-1548 (3)	4.30	4.30

Souvenir Sheet

1549	A211	$5 multicolored	3.75	3.75

Charles de Gaulle, Birth Cent. A212

De Gaulle and: 10c, Free French Forces, 1944. 45c, Churchill, 1944. 75c, Liberation of Paris, 1944.

1991, Nov. 18 Litho. *Perf. 14*

1550	A212	10c multicolored	.20	.20
1551	A212	45c multicolored	.35	.35
1552	A212	75c multicolored	.55	.55
		Nos. 1550-1552 (3)	1.10	1.10

Souvenir Sheet

1553	A212	$5 Portrait	3.75	3.75

Anniversaries and Events — A213

Designs: No. 1554, Woman, flag, map. No. 1555, Steam locomotive. $1.65, Otto Lilienthal, glider in flight. No. 1557, Gottfried Wilhelm Liebniz, mathematician. No. 1558, Street warfare.

1991, Nov. 18

1554	A213	$1.50 multicolored	1.15	1.15
1555	A213	$1.50 multicolored	1.15	1.15
1556	A213	$1.65 multicolored	1.25	1.25
1557	A213	$2 multicolored	1.50	1.50
1558	A213	$2 multicolored	1.50	1.50
		Nos. 1554-1558 (5)	6.55	6.55

Swiss Confedration, 700th anniv. (#1554). Trans-Siberian Railway, 100th anniv. (#1555). First glider flight, cent. (#1556). City of Hanover, 750th anniv. (#1557). Fall of Kiev, Sept. 19, 1941 (#1558).

Miniature Sheet

Heroes of Pearl Harbor A214

Congressional Medal of Honor recipients: a, Myrvyn S. Bennion. b, George H. Cannon. c, John W. Finn. d, Francis C. Flaherty. e, Samuel G. Fuqua. f, Edwin J. Hill. g, Herbert C. Jones. h, Isaac C. Kidd. i, Jackson C. Pharris. j, Thomas J. Reeves. k, Donald K. Ross. l, Robert R. Scott. m, Franklin Van Valkenburgh. n, James R. Ward. o, Cassin Young.

1991, Nov. 18 *Perf. 14½x15*

1559 A214 $1 Sheet of 15, #a.-o. 11.25 11.25

Miniature Sheets

Famous People — A215

Golfers - #1560: a, Player. b, Faldo. c, Ballesteros. d, Hogan. e, Nicklaus. f, Norman. g, Olazabal. h, Bobby Jones.

Statesmen and historical events - #1561: a, Hans-Dietrich Genscher, German Foreign Minister, winged victory symbol. b, Destruction of Berlin Wall. c, Charles de Gaulle delivering radio appeal, Winston Churchill, de Gaulle. d, Dwight D. Eisenhower, de Gaulle, Normandy invasion. e, Brandenburg Gate. f, German Chancellor Helmut Kohl, mayors of East, West Berlin. g, De Gaulle and Konrad Adenauer. h, George Washington and Lafayette, De Gaulle and John F. Kennedy.

Chess masters - #1562: a, Francois Andre Danican Philidor. b, Adolph Anderssen. c, Wilhelm Steinitz. d, Alexander Alekhine. e, Boris Spassky. f, Bobby Fischer. g, Anatoly Karpov. h, Garri Kasparov.

Nobel Prize winners - #1563: a, Einstein, physics. b, Roentgen, physics. c, William Shockley, physics. d, Charles Townes, physics. e, Lev Landau, physics. f, Marconi, physics. g, Willard Libby, chemistry. h, Ernest Lawrence, physics.

Entertainers - #1564: a, Michael Jackson. b, Madonna. c, Elvis Presley. d, David Bowie. e, Prince. f, Frank Sinatra. g, George Michael. h, Mick Jagger.

No. 1565, Roosevelt, de Gaulle, Churchill at Morocco Conf., 1943. No. 1566, Madonna. No. 1567, Elvis Presley.

1991, Nov. 25 **Litho.** *Perf. 14½*

Sheets of 8

1560 A215 $1 #a.-h. 6.00 6.00
1561 A215 $1 #a.-h. 6.00 6.00
1562 A215 $1 #a.-h. 6.00 6.00
1563 A215 $1 #a.-h. 6.00 6.00
1564 A215 $2 #a.-h. 12.00 12.00

Souvenir Sheets

Perf. 14

1565 A215 $6 multicolored 4.50 4.50
1566 A215 $6 multicolored 4.50 4.50
1567 A215 $6 multicolored 4.50 4.50

Nos. 1565-1567 each contain one 27x43mm stamp.

See Nos. 1642-1643, 1729-1730 for more Elvis Presley stamps.

Walt Disney Christmas Cards A216

Designs and year of issue: 10c, Goofy, Mickey and Pluto decorating Christmas tree, 1982. 45c, Mickey, reindeer, 1980. 55c, Christmas tree ornament, 1970. 75c, Baby duck holding 1944 sign, 1943. $1.50, Characters papering globe with greetings, 1941. $2, Lady and the Tramp beside Christmas tree, 1986. $4, Donald, Goofy, Mickey and Pluto reciting "Night Before Christmas," 1977. $5, Mickey in doorway of Snow White's Castle, 1965. No. 1576, People from around the world, 1966. No. 1577, Mickey in balloon basket with people of different countries, 1966.

1991, Dec. 23 *Perf. 13½x14*

1568-1575 A216 Set of 8 11.00 11.00

Souvenir Sheets

1576-1577 A216 $6 Set of 2 9.00 9.00

Environmental Preservation — A217

1992, Jan. **Litho.** *Perf. 14*

1578 A217 10c Kings Hill .20 .20
1579 A217 55c Tree planting .40 .40
1580 A217 75c Botanical Gardens .60 .60
1581 A217 $2 Kings Hill Project 1.50 1.50
Nos. 1578-1581 (4) 2.70 2.70

Queen Elizabeth II's Accession to the Throne, 40th Anniv.
Common Design Type

1992, Feb. 6

1582 CD348 10c multicolored .20 .20
1583 CD348 20c multicolored .20 .20
1584 CD348 $1 multicolored .75 .75
1585 CD348 $5 multicolored 3.75 3.75
Nos. 1582-1585 (4) 4.90 4.90

Souvenir Sheets

1586 CD348 $6 Queen, beach 4.50 4.50
1587 CD348 $6 Queen, harbor 4.50 4.50

Queen Elizabeth II's Acession to the Throne, 40th Anniv. A217a

Designs: No. 1587A, Queen Elizabeth II. No. 1587B, King George VI.

1993, Mar. 2 **Embossed** *Perf. 12*

Without Gum

1587A A217a $5 gold
1587B A217a $5 gold

1992 Winter Olympics, Albertville — A218

1992 Summer Olympics, Barcelona — A219

1992, Apr. 21 **Litho.** *Perf. 14*

1588 A218 10c Women's luge, horiz. .20 .20
1589 A218 15c Women's figure skating .20 .20
1590 A218 25c Two-man bobsled, horiz. .20 .20
1591 A218 30c Mogul skiing .25 .25
1592 A218 45c Nordic combined, horiz. .35 .35
1593 A218 55c Ski jump, horiz. .40 .40
1594 A218 75c Giant slalom, horiz. .60 .60
1595 A218 $1.50 Women's slalom 1.15 1.15
1596 A218 $5 Ice hockey, horiz. 3.75 3.75
1597 A218 $8 Biathlon 6.00 6.00
Nos. 1588-1597 (10) 13.10 13.10

Souvenir Sheets

1598 A218 $6 Downhill skiing 4.50 4.50
1599 A218 $6 Speed skating 4.50 4.50

1992, Apr. 21

10c, Women's synchronized swimming duet, horiz. 15c, High jump. 25c, Small-bore rifle, horiz. 30c, 200-meter run. 45c, Judo. 55c. 200-meter freestyle swimming, horiz. 75c, Javelin. $1.50, Pursuit cycling. $5, Boxing. $8, Women's basketball. #1610, Tennis. #1611, Board sailing.

1600-1609 A219 Set of 10 13.00 13.00

Souvenir Sheets

1610-1611 A219 $15 Set of 2 22.50 22.50

World Columbian Stamp Expo '92, Chicago — A220

Walt Disney characters visiting Chicago area landmarks: 10c, Mickey, Pluto at Picasso Sulpture. 50c, Mickey, Donald admiring Frank Lloyd Wright's Robie House. $1, Gus Gander at Calder Sculpture in Sears Tower. $5, Pluto in Buckingham Memorial Fountain. No. 1616, Mickey painting Minnie at Chicago Art Institute, vert.

1992, Apr. **Litho.** *Perf. 14x13½*

1612-1615 A220 Set of 4 5.00 5.00

Souvenir Sheet

Perf. 13½x14

1616 A220 $6 multi 4.50 4.50

Granada '92 — A221

Walt Disney characters from "The Three Little Pigs" in Spanish military uniforms: 15c, Big Bad Wolf as General of Spanish Moors. 40c, Pig as Captain of Spanish infantry. $2, Pig in Spanish armor, c. 1580. $4, Pig as Spaniard of rank, c. 1550. $6, Little Pig resisting wolf from castle built of stone.

1992, Apr. 28 *Perf. 13½x14*

1622-1625 A221 Set of 4 5.00 5.00

Souvenir Sheet

1626 A221 $6 multi 4.25 4.25

Discovery of America, 500th Anniv. A222

1992, May 22 *Perf. 14*

1632 A222 5c Nina .20 .20
1633 A222 10c Pinta .20 .20
1634 A222 45c Santa Maria .35 .35
1635 A222 55c Leaving Palos, Spain .40 .40
1636 A222 $4 Columbus, vert. 3.00 3.00
1637 A222 $5 Columbus' arms, vert. 3.75 3.75
Nos. 1632-1637 (6) 7.90 7.90

Souvenir Sheet

1638 A222 $6 Map, vert. 4.50 4.50
1639 A222 $6 Sailing ship, vert. 4.50 4.50

World Columbian Stamp Expo '92, Chicago. Nos. 1638-1639 contain one 42x57mm stamp.

Bonnie Blair, US Olympic Speed Skating Champion A223

Designs: No. 1641a, Skating around corner. b, Portrait holding skates. c, On straightaway.

1992, May 25 *Perf. 13½*

1640 A223 $3 multicolored 2.25 2.25

Souvenir Sheet

1641 A223 $2 Sheet of 3, #a.-c. 4.50 4.50

World Columbian Stamp Expo '92. No. 1641b is 48x60mm.

Entertainers Type of 1991

Miniature Sheet

Various portraits of Elvis Presley.

1992, May 25 *Perf. 13½x14*

1642 A206 $1 Sheet of 9, #a.-i. 6.75 6.75

Souvenir Sheet

Perf. 14

1643 A206 $6 multicolored 4.50 4.50

No. 1643 contains one 28x43mm stamp.

See Nos. 1729-1730.

Hummingbirds A224

1992, June 15 *Perf. 14*

1644 A224 5c Rufous-breasted hermit .20 .20
1645 A224 15c Hispaniolan emerald .20 .20
1646 A224 45c Green-throated carib .35 .35
1647 A224 55c Jamaican mango .40 .40
1648 A224 65c Vervain .50 .50
1649 A224 75c Purple-throated carib .58 .58
1650 A224 90c Green mango .70 .70
1651 A224 $1 Bee .80 .80
1652 A224 $2 Cuban emerald 1.55 1.55
1653 A224 $3 Puerto Rican emerald 2.30 2.30
1654 A224 $4 Antillean mango 3.00 3.00
1655 A224 $5 Streamertail 3.75 3.75
Nos. 1644-1655 (12) 14.33 14.33

Souvenir Sheets

1656 A224 $6 Antillean crested 4.50 4.50
1657 A224 $6 Bahama woodstar 4.50 4.50
1658 A224 $6 Blue-headed 4.50 4.50

Genoa '92 Intl. Philatelic Exhibition.

Butterflies A225

5c, Dull astraptes. 10c, White peacock. 35c, Tropic queen. 45c, Polydamas swallowtail.

55c, West Indian buckeye. 65c, Long-tailed skipper. 75c, Tropical checkered skipper. $1, Crimson-banded black. $2, Barred sulphur. $3, Cassius blue. $4, Florida duskywing. $5, Malachite. No. 1671, Cloudless giant sulphur. No. 1672, Julia. No. 1673, Zebra longwing.
5c, 35c, 45c, 65c, $1, $2, $5, #1671 vert,

1992, June 15 Litho. *Perf. 14*

1659-1670 A225 Set of 12 13.75 13.75

Souvenir Sheets

1671-1673 A225 $6 Set of 3 13.50 13.50

Genoa '92.

A226

A227

Medicinal Plants: No. 1674a, Coral vine. b, Cocoplum. c, Angel's trumpet. d, Lime. e, White ginger. f, Pussley. g. Sea grape. h, Indian mulberry. i, Plantain. j, Lignum vitae. k, Periwinkle. l, Guava.

1992, July 22 Litho. *Perf. 14*

Miniature Sheet of 12

1674 A226 75c #a.-l. 6.75 6.75

Souvenir Sheets

1675 A226 $6 Aloe 4.50 4.50
1676 A226 $6 Clove tree 4.50 4.50
1677 A226 $6 Wild sage 4.50 4.50

1992, July 2 Litho. *Perf. 14*

Mushrooms: 10c, Collybia subpruinosa. 15c, Gerronema citrinum. 20c, Amanita antillana. 45c, Dermoloma atrobrunneum. 50c, Inopilus maculosus. 65c, Pulveroboletus brachyspermus. 75c, Mycena violacella. $1, Xerocomus brasiliensis. $2, Amanita ingrata. $3, Leptonia caeruleocaptata. $4, Limacella myochroa. $5, Inopilus magnificus. No. 1690, Limacella guttata. No. 1691, Amanita agglutinata. No. 1692, Trogia buccinalis.

1678-1689 A227 Set of 12 13.50 13.50

Souvenir Sheets

1690-1692 A227 $6 Set of 3 13.50 13.50

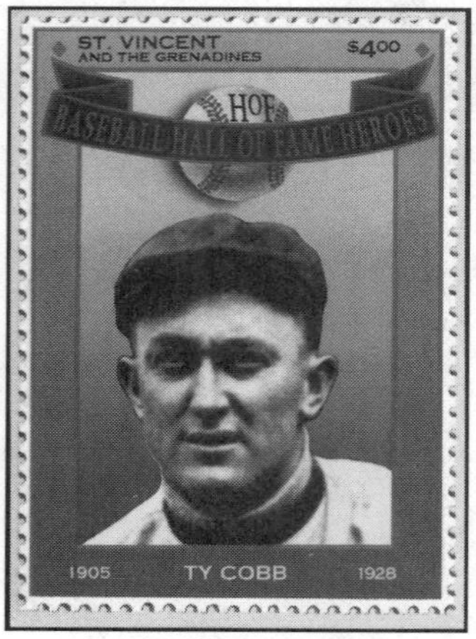

Baseball Players — A228

Designs: #1693, Ty Cobb. #1694, Dizzy Dean. #1695, Bob Feller. #1696, Whitey Ford. #1697, Lou Gehrig. #1698, Rogers Hornsby. #1699, Mel Ott. #1700, Satchel Paige. #1701, Babe Ruth. #1702, Casey Stengel. #1703, Honus Wagner. #1704, Cy Young.

1992, Aug. 5 Litho. *Imperf.*

Self-Adhesive

Size: 64x89mm

1693-1704 A228 $4 Set of 12 36.00

Nos. 1693-1704 printed on thin card and distributed in boxed sets. To affix stamps, backing containing player's statistics must be removed.

A229

A230

1992 Winter Olympic Gold Medalists, Albertville: No. 1705a, Alberto Tomba, Italy, giant slalom. b, Fabrice Guy, France, Nordic combined. c, Patrick Ortlieb, Austria, men's downhill. d, Vegard Ulvang, Norway, cross country. e, Edgar Grospiron, France, freestyle Mogul skiing. f, Kjetil-Andre Aamodt, Norway, super giant slalom. g, Viktor Petrenko, Russia, men's figure skating.

No. 1706a, Kristi Yamaguchi, US, women's figure skating. b, Pernilla Wiberg, Sweden, women's giant slalom. c, Lyubov Yegorova, Unified Team, women's 10-kilometer cross country. d, Josef Polig, Italy, combined Alpine skiing. e, Finn Christian-Jagge, Norway, slalom. f, Kerrin Lee-Gartner, Canada, women's downhill. g, Steffania Belmondo, Italy, women's 30-kilometer cross country.

No. 1707, Alberto Tomba, diff. No. 1708, Kristi Yamaguchi, diff.

1992, Aug. 10 Litho. *Perf. 14*

Sheets of 7

1705 A229 $1 #a.-g. + label 5.25 5.25
1706 A229 $1 #a.-g. + label 5.25 5.25

Souvenir Sheets

1707 A229 $6 multicolored 4.50 4.50
1708 A229 $6 multicolored 4.50 4.50

1992 Litho. *Perf. 14½*

1709 A230 $1 Coming ashore .75 .75
1710 A230 $2 Natives, ships 1.50 1.50

Discovery of America, 500th anniv. Organization of East Caribbean States.

Miniature Sheet

Opening of Euro Disney — A231

Walt Disney movies: #1711a, Pinocchio. b, Alice in Wonderland. c, Bambi. d, Cinderella. e, Snow White and the Seven Dwarfs. f, Peter Pan.

1992 Litho. *Perf. 13*

1711 A231 $1 Sheet of 6, #a.-f. 4.50 4.50

Souvenir Sheet

Perf. 12½

1712 A231 $5 Mickey Mouse 3.75 3.75

Christmas A232

Details or entire paintings of The Nativity by: 10c, Hospitality Refused to the Virgin Mary and Joseph, by Jan Metsys. 40c, Albrecht Durer. 45c, The Nativity, by Geertgen Tot Sint Jans. 50c, The Nativity, by Tintoretto. 55c, Follower of Jan Joest Calcar. 65c, Workshop of Fra Angelico. 75c, Master of the Louvre Nativity. $1, Filippino Lippi. $2, Petrus Christus. $3, Edward Burne-Jones. $4, Giotto. $5, The Birth of Christ, by Domenico Ghirlandaio. No. 1725, Nativity, by Jean Fouquet. No. 1726, Sandro Botticelli. No. 1727, Gerard Horenbout.

1992, Nov. Litho. *Perf. 13½x14*

1713-1724 A232 Set of 11 13.75 13.75

Souvenir Sheets

1725-1727 A232 $6 Set of 3 13.50 13.50

Souvenir Sheet

Jacob Javits Convention Center, NYC — A233

1992, Oct. 28 Litho. *Perf. 14*

1728 A233 $6 multicolored 4.50 4.50

Postage Stamp Mega Event '92, NYC.

No. 1642 Inscribed Vertically "15th Anniversary"

Nos. 1564, 1567 (in margin) Inscribed or Ovptd. "15th Anniversary" and "Elvis Presley's Death / August 16, 1977"

1992, Dec. 15 *Perf. 13½x14*

1729 A206 $1 Sheet of 9, #a.-i. 6.75 6.75

Perf. 14½

1729J A215 $2 Sheet of 8, #k.-r. 12.00 12.00

Perf. 14

1730 A215 $6 Souv. sheet 4.50 4.50

Baseball Players — A234

Members of Baseball Hall Fame — A235

1992, Nov. 9 Litho. *Perf. 14*

1731 A234 $5 Howard Johnson 3.75 3.75
1732 A234 $5 Don Mattingly 3.75 3.75

1992 Summer Olympics, Barcelona.

1992, Dec. 21

Player, year inducted: No. 1733, Roberto Clemente, 1973. No. 1734, Hank Aaron, 1982. No. 1735, Tom Seaver, 1992.

1733 A235 $2 multicolored 1.50 1.50
1734 A235 $2 multicolored 1.50 1.50
1735 A235 $2 multicolored 1.50 1.50
Nos. 1733-1735 (3) 4.50 4.50

Fishing Industry A236

1992, Nov.

1736 A236 5c Fishing with rods .20 .20
1737 A236 10c Inside fishing complex .20 .20
1738 A236 50c Landing the catch .40 .40
1739 A236 $5 Fishing with nets 3.75 3.75
Nos. 1736-1739 (4) 4.55 4.55

Uniting the Windward Islands A237

Children's paintings: 10c, Island coastline. 40c, Four people standing on islands. 45c, Four people standing on beach.

1992, Nov. Litho. *Perf. 14*

1740 A237 10c multicolored .20 .20
1741 A237 40c multicolored .30 .30
1742 A237 45c multicolored .35 .35
Nos. 1740-1742 (3) .85 .85

Miniature Sheets

US Olympic Basketball "Dream Team" A238

#1744: a, Scottie Pippen. b, Earvin "Magic" Johnson. c, Larry Bird. d, Christian Laettner. e, Karl Malone. f, David Robinson.

#1745: a, Michael Jordan. b, Charles Barkley. c, John Stockton. d, Chris Mullin. e, Clyde Drexler. f, Patrick Ewing.

1992, Dec. 22 Litho. *Perf. 14*

1744 A238 $2 Sheet of 6, #a.-f. 9.00 9.00
1745 A238 $2 Sheet of 6, #a.-f. 9.00 9.00

1992 Summer Olympics, Barcelona.

A239

A240

A241

A242

Anniversaries and Events: 10c, Globe and UN emblem. 45c, Zeppelin Viktoria Luise over Kiel Regatta, 1912, vert. 65c, Food products. No. 1749, America's Cup Trophy and Bill Koch, skipper of America 3. No. 1750, Konrad Adenauer, German flag. No. 1751, Adenauer, diff. No. 1752, Snow leopard. $1.50, Caribbean manatee. $2, Humpback whale. No. 1755, Adenauer, John F. Kennedy. No. 1756, Lions Intl. emblem, patient having eye exam. No. 1757, Space shuttle Discovery, vert. No. 1758, Adenauer, Pope John XXIII. $5, Michael Schumacher, race car. $6, Count Zeppelin's first airship over Lake Constance, 1900. No. 1761, Gondola of Graf Zeppelin. No. 1762,

Formula I race car. No. 1763, Sailing ship, steam packet. No. 1764, Adenauer at podium. No. 1765, Woolly spider monkey. No. 1765A, People waving to plane during Berlin airlift.

1992-93 Litho. *Perf. 14*

1746	A239	10c	multi	.20	.20
1747	A239	45c	multi	.35	.35
1748	A242	65c	multi	.50	.50
1749	A239	75c	multi	.60	.60
1750	A239	75c	multi	.60	.60
1751	A239	$1	multi	.75	.75
1752	A239	$1	multi	.75	.75
1753	A239	$1.50	multi	1.15	1.15
1754	A239	$2	multi	1.50	1.50
1755	A239	$3	multi	2.25	2.25
1756	A239	$3	multi	2.25	2.25
1757	A239	$4	multi	3.00	3.00
1758	A239	$4	multi	3.00	3.00
1759	A240	$5	multi	3.75	3.75
1760	A239	$6	multi	4.50	4.50
	Nos. 1746-1760 (15)			25.15	25.15

Souvenir Sheets

1761	A239	$6	multi	4.50	4.50
1762	A240	$6	multi	4.50	4.50
1763	A241	$6	multi	4.50	4.50
1764	A239	$6	multi	4.50	4.50
1765	A239	$6	multi	4.50	4.50
1765A	A239	$6	multi	4.50	4.50

UN Intl. Space Year (#1746, 1757). Count Zeppelin, 75th anniv. of death (#1747, 1760-1761). Intl. Conference on Nutrition, Rome (#1748). America's Cup yacht race (#1749). Konrad Adenauer, 25th death anniv. (#1750-1751, 1755, 1758, 1764). Earth Summit, Rio de Janeiro (#1752-1754, 1765). Lions Intl., 75th anniv. (#1756). Belgian Grand Prix (#1759, 1762). Discovery of America, 500th anniv. (#1763). Konrad Adenauer, 75th death anniv. (#1765A).

Issued: #1747, 1759-1762, Dec; #1763, 10/28/92; #1746, 1749, 1750-1751, 1755-1758, 1764, Dec; #1752-1754, 1765, Dec. 15; #1765A, 6/30/93.

A243

A244

Care Bears Promote Conservation: 75c, Bear, stork. $2, Bear riding in hot air balloon, horiz.

1992, Dec. Litho. *Perf. 14*

1766 A243	75c	multicolored	.60	.60

Souvenir Sheet

1767 A243	$2	multicolored	1.50	1.50

1993 Litho. *Perf. 14*

Elvis Presley (1935-1977): b, Portrait. c, With guitar. d, With microphone.

1767A A244	$1	Strip of 3, #b.-d.	2.25	2.25

Printed in sheets of 9 stamps.

Walt Disney's Beauty and the Beast — A245

Designs: 2c, Gaston. 3c, Belle and her father, Maurice. 5c, Lumiere, Mrs. Potts and Cogsworth. 10c, Philippe. 15c, Beast and Lumiere. 20c, Lumiere and Feather Duster.

No. 1774a, Belle and Gaston. b, Maurice. c, The Beast. d, Mrs. Potts. e, Belle and the Enchanted Vase. f, Belle discovers an Enchanted Rose. g, Belle with wounded Beast. h, Belle. i, Household objects alarmed.

No. 1774k, Belle and Chip. l, Lumiere. m, Cogsworth. n, Armoire. o, Belle and Beast. p, Feather Duster. q, Footstool. r, Belle. All vert.

No. 1775, Belle reading, vert. No. 1776, Lumiere, diff., vert. No. 1776A, Lumiere, Mrs. Potts. No. 1776B, Belle, lake and castle, vert. No. 1776C, The Beast, vert.

Perf. 14x13½, 13½x14

1992, Dec. 15 Litho.

1768	A245	2c	multicolored	.20	.20
1769	A245	3c	multicolored	.20	.20
1770	A245	5c	multicolored	.20	.20
1771	A245	10c	multicolored	.20	.20
1772	A245	15c	multicolored	.20	.20
1773	A245	20c	multicolored	.20	.20
	Nos. 1768-1773 (6)			1.20	1.20

Miniature Sheets of 9, 8

1774	A245	60c	#a.-i.	4.00	4.00
1774J	A245	60c	#k.-r.	4.00	4.00

Souvenir Sheets

1775	A245	$6	multicolored	4.50	4.50
1776	A245	$6	multicolored	4.50	4.50
1776A	A245	$6	multicolored	4.50	4.50
1776B	A245	$6	multicolored	4.50	4.50
1776C	A245	$6	multicolored	4.50	4.50

Louvre Museum, Bicent. A246

Details or entire paintings by Jean-Auguste-Dominique Ingres: No. 1777a, Louis-Francois Bertin. b, The Apotheosis of Homer. c, Joan of Arc. d, The Composer Cherubini with the Muse of Lyric Poetry. e, Mlle Caroline Riviere. f, Oedipus Answers the Sphinx's Riddle. g, Madame Marcotte. h, Mademoiselle Caroline Riviere.

Details or entire paintings by Jean Louis Andre Theodore Gericault (1791-1824): No. 1778a, The Woman with Gambling Mania. b, Head of a White Horse. c, Wounded Cuirassier. d, An Officer of the Cavalry. e, The Vendean. f, The Raft of the Medusa. g-h, The Horse Market (left, right).

Details or entire paintings by Nicolas Poussin (1594-1665): No. 1779a-1779b, The Arcadian Shepherds (left, right). c, Ecstasy of Paul. d-e, The Inspiration of the Poet (left, right). f-g, St. John Baptizing (left, right). h, The Miracle of St. Francis Xavier.

Details or entire paintings by Eustache Le Sueur (1616-1655): No. 1780a-1780b, Melpomene, Erato & Polyhymnia (left, right). By Poussin: c, Christ and Woman Taken in Adultery. d, Spring. e, Autumn. f-h, The Plague of Asdod (left, center, right).

No. 1781a, The Beggars, by Pieter Brueghel, the Elder (1520-1569). b, The Luncheon, by Francois Boucher (1703-1770). c, Louis Guene, Royal Violinist, by Francois Dumont (1751-1831). d, The Virgin of Chancellor Rolin, by Jan Van Eyck. e, Conversation in the Park, by Thomas Gainsborough. f, Lady Alston, by Gainsborough. g, Mariana Waldstein, by Francisco de Goya. h, Ferdinand Guillemardet, by Goya.

No. 1782, The Grand Odalisque, horiz. No. 1783, The Dressing Room of Esther, by Theodore Chasseriau (1819-1856). No. 1784, Liberty Guiding the People, by Eugene Delecroix (1798-1863), horiz.

1993, Apr. 19 *Perf. 12x12½*

Sheets of 8

1777 A246	$1	#a.-h. + label	6.00	6.00
1778 A246	$1	#a.-h. + label	6.00	6.00
1779 A246	$1	#a.-h. + label	6.00	6.00
1780 A246	$1	#a.-h. + label	6.00	6.00
1781 A246	$1	#a.-h. + label	6.00	6.00

Souvenir Sheets

Perf. 14½

1782 A246	$6	multicolored	4.50	4.50
1783 A246	$6	multicolored	4.50	4.50
1784 A246	$6	multicolored	4.50	4.50

Nos. 1783-1784 each contain a 55x88mm or 88x55mm stamp.

Paintings on Nos. 1777d and 1777h were switched.

Numbers have been reserved for two additional souvenir sheets in this set.

Miniature Sheets

A247

A247a

Scenes from Disney Animated Films - A247b

Symphony Hour (1942): No. 1787a, Maestro Mickey. b, Goofy plays a mean horn. c, On first bass with Clara Cluck. d, Stringing along with Clarabelle. e, Donald on drums. f, Clarabelle all fiddled out. g, Donald drumming up trouble. h, Goofy's sour notes. i, Mickey's moment.

No. 1794, Bird's-eye-view of Goofy. No. 1795, Mickey and Macaroni enjoying applause.

The Small One: No. 1791k, Morning comes in Nazareth. l, Good morning, small one. m, Too old to keep. n, Heatbroken. o, Nazareth markplace. p, Auction mockery. q, Off the auction block. r, Lonely and dejected. s, Happy and useful again.

No. 1804, Hard Work in Nazareth. No. 1805, Finding a buyer in Nazareth.

The Three Little Pigs (1933): No. 1792a, Fifer Pig building house of straw. b, Fiddler Pig building house of sticks. c, Practical Pig building house of bricks. d, The Big Bad Wolf. e, Wolf scaring two lazy pigs. f, Wolf blowing down staw house. g, Wolf in sheep's clothing. h, Wolf blowing down twig house. i, Wolf huffs and puffs at brick house.

No. 1806, Animator's sketch of little pig and brick house. No. 1807, Little pigs playing and singing at piano, vert.

How to Play Football (1944): No. 1792k, Cheerleaders. l, Here comes the team. m, In the huddle. n, Who's got the ball? o, Who, me coach? p, Half-time pep talk. q, Another down, and out. r, Only a little injury. s, Up and at 'em.

No. 1807A, Goofy demonstrating how to score touchdown. No. 1807B, Goofy shouting "Hooray for the team," vert.

Rescue Rangers: No. 1793a, Special agents. b, Chip 'n Dale, ready for action. c, Chip 'n Dale on stakeout. d, Gadget in gear. e, Gadget and Monterey Jack rescue Zipper. f, Zipper confers with Monterey Jack. g, Zipper zaps fat cat. h, Team work. i, Innovative Gadget.

No. 1807C, Gadget at controls of Ranger plane, vert. No. 1807D, Dale, vert.

Darkwing Duck: No. 1793k, Darkwing Duck. l, Launchpad McQuack. m, Gosalyn. n, Honker Muddlefoot. o, Tank Muddlefoot. p, Herb & Binkie Muddlefoot. q, Drake Mallard, aka Darkwing Duck. r, Darkwing Duck logo.

No. 1807E, Quarterjack. No. 1807F, Darkwing Duck and Launchpad to the rescue in Ratcatcher.

Clock Cleaners (1937): No. 1788a, Goofy gets in gear. b, Donald on the mainspring. c, Donald in the works. d, Mickey's fine-feathered friend. e, Stork with bundle of joy. f, Father Time. g, Goofy, Mickey leaping upward. h, Donald, Goofy, Mickey out of gear. i, Donald, Goofy, Mickey with headaches.

No. 1796, On the edge of Goofyness. No. 1797, Gonged-out Goofy.

The Art of Skiing (1941): No. 1789a, The ultimate back scratcher. b, Striking a pose. c, And we're off. d, Divided he stands. e, A real twister. f, Hangin' in there. g, Over the hill. h, At the peak of his form. i, Up a tree.

No. 1798, Film poster for Art of Skiing with Goofy slaloming down mountain. No. 1799, Goofy home in bed at last.

Orphan's Benefit (1941): No. 1790a, Mickey introduces Donald. b, Donald recites "Little Boy Blue." c, Orphan mischief. d, Clara Cluck, singing sensation. e, Goofy's debut with Clarabelle. f, Encore for Clara and Mickey. g, A Bronx cheer. h, Donald blows his stack. i, Donald's final bow.

No. 1800, Caveman ballet. No. 1801, Mickey tickles the ivories.

Thru the Mirror (1936): No. 1791a, Mickey steps thru the looking glass. b, Mickey finds a tasty treat. c, Mickey's nutty effect. d, Hats off to Mickey. e, What a card, Mickey. f, Mickey dancing with the Queen Hearts. g, A real two-faced opponent. h, Mickey with a pen mightier than a sword. i, Mickey awake at last.

No. 1802, Mickey's true reflection. No. 1803, Mickey hopping home.

Perf. 14x13½, 13½x14

1992, Dec. 15 Litho.

Sheets of 9 or 8 (#1793J)

1787	A247	60c	#a.-i.	4.00	4.00
1788	A247	60c	#a.-i.	4.00	4.00
1789	A247	60c	#a.-i.	4.00	4.00
1790	A247	60c	#a.-i.	4.00	4.00
1791	A247	60c	#a.-i.	4.00	4.00
1791J	A247a	60c	#k.-s.	4.00	4.00
1792	A247	60c	#a.-i.	4.00	4.00
1792J	A247	60c	#k.-s.	4.00	4.00
1793	A247a	60c	#a.-i.	4.00	4.00
1793J	A247b	60c	#k.-r.	3.60	3.60

Souvenir Sheets

1794	A247	$6	multicolored	4.50	4.50
1795	A247	$6	multicolored	4.50	4.50
1796	A247	$6	multicolored	4.50	4.50
1797	A247	$6	multicolored	4.50	4.50
1798	A247	$6	multicolored	4.50	4.50
1799	A247	$6	multicolored	4.50	4.50
1800	A247	$6	multicolored	4.50	4.50
1801	A247	$6	multicolored	4.50	4.50
1802	A247	$6	multicolored	4.50	4.50
1803	A247	$6	multicolored	4.50	4.50
1804	A247a	$6	multicolored	4.50	4.50
1805	A247a	$6	multicolored	4.50	4.50
1806	A247	$6	multicolored	4.50	4.50
1807	A247	$6	multicolored	4.50	4.50
1807A	A247	$6	multicolored	4.50	4.50
1807B	A247	$6	multicolored	4.50	4.50
1807C	A247a	$6	multicolored	4.50	4.50
1807D	A247a	$6	multicolored	4.50	4.50
1807E	A247b	$6	multicolored	4.50	4.50
1807F	A247b	$6	multicolored	4.50	4.50

See Nos. 2144-2146 for 30c & $3 stamps.

Fish A248

1993, Apr. 1 Litho. *Perf. 14*

1808 A248	5c	Sergeant major	.20	.20
1809 A248	10c	Rainbow parrotfish	.20	.20
1810 A248	55c	Hogfish	.40	.40
1811 A248	75c	Porkfish	.60	.60
1812 A248	$1	Spotfin butterflyfish	.75	.75
1813 A248	$2	Trunkfish	1.50	1.50
1814 A248	$4	Queen triggerfish	3.00	3.00
1815 A248	$5	Queen angelfish	3.75	3.75
	Nos. 1808-1815 (8)		10.40	10.40

Souvenir Sheets

1816 A248	$6	Bigeye, vert.	4.50	4.50
1817 A248	$6	Smallmouth grunt, vert.	4.50	4.50

Birds — A249 Seashells — A250

Designs: 10c, Brown pelican. 25c, Red-necked grebe, horiz. 45c, Belted kingfisher, horiz. 55c, Yellow-bellied sapsucker. $1, Great blue heron. $2, Crab hawk, horiz. $4, Yellow warbler. $5, Northern oriole, horiz. No. 1826,

White ibises, map, horiz. No. 1827, Blue-winged teal, map, horiz.

1993, Apr. 1 Litho. *Perf. 14*

1818-1825 A249 Set of 8 10.00 10.00

Souvenir Sheets

1826-1827 A249 $6 Set of 2 9.00 9.00

1993, May 24 Litho. *Perf. 14*

10c, Hexagonal murex. 15c, Caribbean vase. 30c, Measled cowrie. 45c, Dyson's key-hole limpet. 50c, Atlantic hairy triton. 65c, Orange-banded marginella. 75c, Bleeding tooth. $1, Pink conch. $2, Hawk-wing conch. $3, Music volute. $4, Alphabet cone. $5, Antillean cone. #1840, Flame auger. #1841, Netted olive. #1842, Wide-mouthed purpura. #1840-1842 horiz.

1828-1839 A250 13.50 13.50

Souvenir Sheets

1840-1842 A250 $6 Set of 3 13.50 13.50

Miniature Sheet

Yujiro Ishihara, Actor A251

Various portraits: No. 1843a, $1. b, 55c. c, $1. d, 55c. e, 55c. f, 55c. g, $1. h, 55c. i, $1.
No. 1844a, 55c. b, $1. c, $2. d, $2.
No. 1845a, 55c. b, $2. c, $1. d, $2.
No. 1846a, 55c. b, $2. c, $4.
No. 1847a, 55c. b, $4. c, $4.

1993, May 24 Litho. *Perf. 13½x14*

1843 A251 Sheet of 9, #a.-i. 5.25 5.25

Souvenir Sheets

1844 A251 Sheet of 4, #a.-d. 4.25 4.25

Stamp Size: 32x41mm

Perf. 14½

1845 A251 Sheet of 4, #a.-d. 4.25 4.25

Stamp Size: 60x41mm

Perf. 14x14½

1846 A251 Sheet of 3, #a.-c. 5.00 5.00
1847 A251 Sheet of 3, #a.-c. 6.50 6.50

Automobiles A252

$1, 1932 Ford V8, 1915 Ford Model T, Henry Ford's 1st car. $2, Benz 540K, 1928 Benz Stuttgart, 1908 Benz Racer. $3, 1911 Blitzen Benz, 1905 Benz Tourenwagen, 1894 Benz. $4, 1935 Ford, 1903 Ford A Runabout, 1913 Ford Model T Tourer. #1852, Karl Benz. #1853, Henry Ford.

1993, May Litho. *Perf. 14*

1848-1851 A252 Set of 4 7.50 7.50

Souvenir Sheets

1852-1853 A252 $6 Set of 2 9.00 9.00

First Ford motor, cent. (#1848, 1851, 1853). First Benz motor car, cent. (#1849-1850, 1852).

Miniature Sheet

Coronation of Queen Elizabeth II, 40th Anniv. A253

a, 45c, Official coronation photograph. b, 65c, Opening Parliament, 1980s. c, $2, Coronation ceremony, 1953. d, $4, Queen with her dog, 1970s.
No. 1855, Portrait of Queen as a child.

1993, June 2 Litho. *Perf. 13½x14*

1854 A253 Sheet, 2 ea #a.-d. 11.00 11.00

Souvenir Sheet

Perf. 14

1855 A253 $6 multicolored 4.50 4.50

No. 1855 contains one 28x42mm stamp.

Moths — A254

1993, June 14 Litho. *Perf. 14*

1856 A254 10c Erynnyis ello .20 .20
1857 A254 50c Aellopos tantalus .40 .40
1858 A254 65c Erynnyis alope .50 .50
1859 A254 75c Manduca rustica .55 .55
1860 A254 $1 Xylophanes pluto .75 .75
1861 A254 $2 Hyles lineata 1.50 1.50
1862 A254 $4 Pseudosphinx tetrio 3.00 3.00
1863 A254 $5 Protambulyx strigilis 3.75 3.75
Nos. 1856-1863 (8) 10.65 10.65

Souvenir Sheets

1864 A254 $6 Xylophanes tersa 4.50 4.50
1864A A254 $6 Utetheisa ornatrix 4.50 4.50

A255

A256

Aviation Anniversaries — A257

50c, Supermarine Spitfire. #1866, Graf Zeppelin over Egypt, 1931, Hugo Eckener. #1867, Jean Pierre Blanchard, balloon, George Washington. #1868, De Havilland Mosquito. No. 1869, Eckener, Graf Zeppelin over New York, 1928. $3, Eckener, Graf Zeppelin over Tokyo, 1 929. $4, Philadelphia's Walnut State Prison, balloon lifting off. #1872, Hawker Hurricane. #1873, Hugo Eckener. #1874, Blanchard's Balloon.

1993, June Litho. *Perf. 14*

1865 A255 50c multi .40 .40
1866 A256 $1 multi .75 .75
1867 A257 $1 multi .75 .75
1868 A255 $2 multi 1.50 1.50
1869 A256 $2 multi 1.50 1.50
1870 A256 $3 multi 2.25 2.25
1871 A257 $4 multi 3.00 3.00
Nos. 1865-1871 (7) 10.15 10.15

Souvenir Sheets

1872 A255 $6 multi 4.50 4.50
1873 A256 $6 multi, vert. 4.50 4.50
1874 A257 $6 multi, vert. 4.50 4.50

Royal Air Force, 75th anniv. (#1865, 1868, 1872). Dr. Hugo Eckener, 125th anniv. of birth (#1866, 1869-1870, 1873). First US balloon flight, bicent. (#1867, 1871). Tokyo spelled incorrectly on No. 1870.

Two values and a souvenir sheet commemorating the Wedding of Japan's Crown Prince Naruhito and Masako Owada were printed in 1993 but not accepted by the St. Vincent post office.

1994 Winter Olympics, Lillehammer, Norway — A259

Designs: 45c, Marc Girardelli, silver medalist, giant slalom, 1992. $5, Paul Accola, downhill, 1992. $6, Thommy Moe, downhill, 1992.

1993, June 30 Litho. *Perf. 14*

1878 A259 45c multicolored .35 .35
1879 A259 $5 multicolored 3.75 3.75

Souvenir Sheet

1880 A259 $6 multicolored 4.50 4.50

Picasso (1881-1973) — A260

Paintings: 45c, Massacre in Korea, 1951. $1, Family of Saltimbanques, 1905. $4, La Joie de Vivre, 1946. $6, Woman Eating a Melon and Boy Writing, 1965, vert.

1993, June 30

1881 A260 45c multicolored .35 .35
1882 A260 $1 multicolored .75 .75
1883 A260 $4 multicolored 3.00 3.00
Nos. 1881-1883 (3) 4.10 4.10

Souvenir Sheet

1884 A260 $6 multicolored 4.50 4.50

Willy Brandt (1913-1992), German Chancellor — A261

Designs: 45c, Brandt, Richard Nixon, 1971. $5, Brandt, Robert Kennedy, 1967. $6, Brandt at signing of "Common Declaration," 1973.

1993, June 30

1885 A261 45c multicolored .35 .35
1886 A261 $5 multicolored 3.75 3.75

Souvenir Sheet

1887 A261 $6 multicolored 4.50 4.50

A262 A263

Copernicus: 45c, Astronomical instrument. $4, Space shuttle lift-off. $6, Copernicus.

1993, June 30

1888 A262 45c multicolored .35 .35
1889 A262 $4 multicolored 3.00 3.00

Souvenir Sheet

1890 A262 $6 multicolored 4.50 4.50

1993, June 30

European Royalty: 45c, Johannes, Gloria Thurn & Taxis. 65c, Thurn & Taxis family, horiz. $1, Princess Stephanie of Monaco. $2, Gloria Thurn & Taxis.

1891-1894 A263 Set of 4 3.00 3.00

Inauguration of Pres. William J. Clinton — A264

Designs: $5, Bill Clinton, children. $6, Clinton wearing cowboy hat, vert.

1993, June 30

1895 A264 $5 multicolored 3.75 3.75

Souvenir Sheet

1896 A264 $6 multicolored 4.50 4.50

Polska '93 A265

#1897, Bogusz Church, Gozlin. #1898a, $1, Deux Tetes (Man), by S.I. Witkiewicz, 1920, vert. #1898b, $3, Deux Tetes (Woman), vert. No. 1899, Dancing, by Wladyslaw Roguski, vert.

1993, June 30

1897 A265 $6 multicolored 4.50 4.50
1898 A265 Pair, #a.-b. 3.00 3.00

Souvenir Sheet

1899 A265 $6 multicolored 4.50 4.50

1994 World Cup Soccer Qualifying A266

St. Vincent vs: 5c, Mexico. 10c, Honduras. 65c, Costa Rica. $5, St. Vincent goalkeeper.

1993, Sept. 2
1900-1903 A266 Set of 4 4.25 4.25

Cooperation with Japan — A267

Designs: 10c, Fish delivery van. 50c, Fish aggregation device, vert. 75c, Trawler. $5, Fish complex.

1993, Sept. 2
1904-1907 A267 Set of 4 4.75 4.75

Pope John Paul II's Visit to Denver, CO A268

Design: $6, Pope, Denver skyline, diff.

1993, Aug. 13
1908 A268 $1 multicolored .75 .75

Souvenir Sheet
1909 A268 $6 multicolored 4.50 4.50

No. 1908 issued in sheets of 9.

Miniature Sheet

Corvette, 40th Anniv. — A269

Corvettes: a, 1953. b, 1993, c, 1958, d, 1960. e, "40," Corvette emblem (no car). f, 1961. g, 1963. h, 1968, i, 1973. j, 1975. k, 1982. l, 1984.

1993, Aug. 13 ***Perf. 14x13½***
1910 A269 $1 Sheet of 12, #a.-l. 9.00 9.00

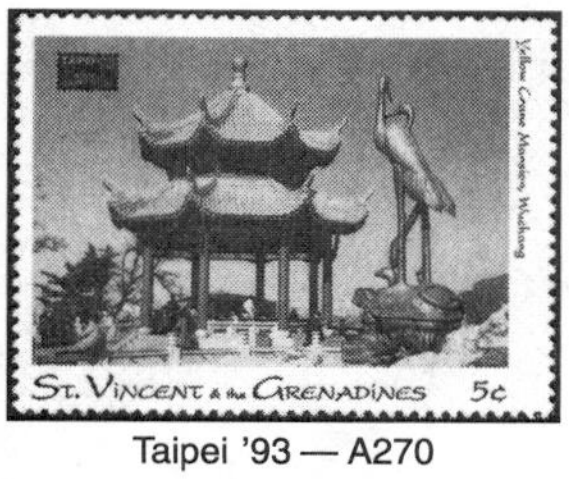

Taipei '93 — A270

Designs: 5c, Yellow Crane Mansion, Wuchang. 10c, Front gate, Chung Cheng Ceremonial Arch, Taiwan. 20c, Marble Peifang, Ming 13 Tombs, Beijing. 45c, Jinxing Den, Beijing. 55c, Forbidden City, Beijing. 75c, Tachih, the Martyr's Shrine, Taiwan. No. 1917, Praying Hall, Xinjiang, Gaochang. No. 1918, Chih Kan Tower, Taiwan. $2, Taihu Lake, Jiangsu. $4, Chengde, Hebei, Pula Si. No. 1921, Kaohsiung, Cheng Ching Lake, Taiwan. No. 1922, Great Wall.

Chinese paintings - #1923: a, Street in Macao, China, by George Chinnery. b, Pair of Birds on Cherry Branch. c, Yellow Dragon Cave, by Patrick Procktor. d, Great Wall of China, by William Simpson. e, Dutch Folly Fort Off Conton, by Chinnery. f, Forbidden City, by Procktor.

Chinese silk paintings: No. 1924a, Rhododendron. b, Irises and bees. c, Easter lily. d, Poinsettia. e, Peach and cherry blossoms. f, Weeping cherry and yellow bird.

Chinese kites - #1925: a, Dragon and tiger fighting. b, Two immortals. c, Five boys playing round a general. d, Zheng Chenggong. e, Nezha stirs up the sea. f, Immortal maiden He.

No. 1926, Giant Buddha, Longmen Caves, Luoyang, Hunan. No. 1927, Guardian and Celestial King, Longmen Caves, Hunan, vert. No. 1928, Giant Buddha, Yungang Caves, Datong, Shanxi, vert.

1993, Aug. 16 Litho. ***Perf. 14x13½***
1911-1922 A270 Set of 12 15.00 15.00

Miniature Sheets of 6
1923 A270 $1.50 #a.-f. 6.75 6.75
1924 A270 $1.50 #a.-f. 6.75 6.75
1925 A270 $1.50 #a.-f. 6.75 6.75

Souvenir Sheets
1926 A270 $6 multicolored 4.50 4.50

Perf. 13½x14
1927 A270 $6 multicolored 4.50 4.50
1928 A270 $6 multicolored 4.50 4.50

No. 1925e issued missing "St." in country name. Some sheets of No. 1925 may have been withdrawn from sale after discovery of error.

With Bangkok '93 Emblem

Designs: 5c, Phra Nakhon Khiri (Rama V's Palace), vert. 10c, Grand Palace, Bangkok. 20c, Rama IX Park, Bangkok. 45c, Phra Prang Sam Yot, Lop Buri. 55c, Dusit Maha Prasad, vert. 75c, Phimai Khmer architecture, Pak Tong Chai. No. 1935, Burmese style Chedi, Mae Hong Son. No. 1936, Antechamber, Central Prang, Prasat Hin Phimai. $2, Brick chedi on laterite base, Si Thep, vert. $4, Isan's Phanom Rung, Korat, vert. No. 1939, Phu Khau Thong, the Golden Mount, Bangkok. No. 1940, Islands, Ang Thong.

Thai Buddha sculpture - #1941: a, Interior of Wat Hua Kuang Lampang, vert. b, Wat Yai Suwannaram, vert. c, Phra Buddha Sihing, City Hall Chapel, vert. d, Wat Ko Keo Suttharam, vert. e, U Thong B image, Wat Ratburana crypt, vert. f, Sri Sakyamuni Wat Suthat, vert.

No. 1942a-1942f: Various details from Mural at Buddhaisawan Chapel.

Thai painting - #1943: a, Untitled, by Arunothai Somsakul. b, Mural at Wat Rajapradit. c, Mural at Wat Phumin (detail). d, Serenity, by Surasit Souakong. e, Scenes of early Bangkok mural (detail). f, Ramayana.

No. 1944, Roof detail of Dusit Mahaprasad, vert. No. 1945, Standing Buddha, Hua Hin, vert. No. 1946, Masked dance.

Perf. 13½x14, 14x13½
1993, Aug. 16 Litho.
1929-1940 A270 5c Set of 12 15.00 15.00

Miniature Sheets of 6
1941 A270 $1.50 #a.-f. 6.75 6.75
1942 A270 $1.50 #a.-f. 6.75 6.75
1943 A270 $1.50 #a.-f. 6.75 6.75

Souvenir Sheets
1944 A270 $6 multicolored 4.50 4.50
1945 A270 $6 multicolored 4.50 4.50
1946 A270 $6 multicolored 4.50 4.50

With Indopex '93 Emblem

Indopex '93 emblem with designs: 5c, Local landmark, Gedung site, 1920. 10c, Masjid Jamik Mosque, Sumenep. 20c, Bromo Caldera, seen from Penanjakan. 45c, Kudus Mosque, Java. 55c, Kampung Naga. 75c, Lower level of Borobudur. No. 1953, Dieng Temple, Dieng Plateau. No. 1954, Temple 1, Gedung Songo group, Semarang. $2, Istana Bogor, 1856. $4, Taman Sari complex, Yogyakarta. $5, #1957, Landscape near Mt. Sumbing, Central Java. $5, #1958, King Adityawarman's Palace, Batusangar.

Paintings - #1959: a, Female Coolies, by Djoko Pekik. b, Family Outing, by Sudjana Kerton. c, My Family, by Pekik. d, Javanese Dancers, by Arthur Melville. e, Leisure Time, by Kerton. f, In the Garden of Eden, by Agus Djaja.

#1960: a, Tayubon, by Pekik. b, Three Dancers, by Nyoman Gunarsa. c, Nursing Neighbor's Baby, by Hendra Gunawan. d, Imagining within a Dialogue, by Sagito. e, Three Balinese Mask Dancers, by Anton H. f, Three Prostitutes, by Gunawan.

Masks - #1961: a, Hanuman. b, Subali/Sugnwa. c, Kumbakarna. d, Sangut. e, Jatayu. f, Rawana.

No. 1962, Relief of Sudamala story, Mt. Lawu. No. 1963, Plaque, 9th Cent., Banyumas, Central Java. No. 1964, Panel from Ramayana reliefs, vert.

1993, Aug. 16 Litho. ***Perf. 14x13½***
1947-1958 A270 Set of 12 15.00 15.00

Minature Sheets of 6
1959 A270 $1.50 #a.-f. 6.75 6.75
1960 A270 $1.50 #a.-f. 6.75 6.75
1961 A270 $1.50 #a.-f. 6.75 6.75

Souvenir Sheets
1962 A270 $6 multicolored 4.50 4.50
1963 A270 $6 multicolored 4.50 4.50

Perf. 13½x14
1964 A270 $6 multicolored 4.50 4.50

Reggie Jackson, Selection to Baseball Hall of Fame — A271

1993, Oct. 4 ***Perf. 14***
1965 A271 $2 multicolored 1.50 1.50

Christmas A272

Details or entire woodcut, The Adoration of the Magi, by Durer: 10c, 35c, 40c, $5.

Details or entire paintings by Rubens: 50c, Holy Family with Saint Francis. 55c, 65c, Adoration of the Shepherds. $1, Holy Family.

No. 1974, The Adoration of the Magi, by Durer, horiz. No. 1975, Holy Family with St. Elizabeth & St. John, by Rubens.

Perf. 13½x14, 14x13½
1993, Nov. 18
1966-1973 A272 Set of 8 7.00 7.00

Souvenir Sheets
1974-1975 A272 $6 each 4.50 4.50

Miniature Sheet

Legends of Country Music A273

Various portraits of: a, f, l, Roy Acuff. b, g, j, Patsy Cline. c, h, i, Jim Reeves. d, e, k, Hank Williams, Sr.

1994, Jan. 17 Litho. ***Perf. 13½x14***
1976 A273 $1 Sheet of 12, #a.-l. 9.00 9.00

Mickey's Portrait Gallery A274

Mickey Mouse as: 5c, Aviator. 10c, Foreign Legionnaire. 15c, Frontiersman. 20c, Best Pals, Mickey, Goofy, Donald. 35c, Horace, Clarabelle. 50c, Minnie, Frankie, Figuro. 75c, Donald, Pluto today. 80c, Party boy Mickey. 85c, Best Friends, Minnie, Daisy. 95c, Mickey's Girl, Minnie. $1, Cool forties Mickey. $1.50, Mickey, "Howdy!", 1950. $2, Totally Mickey. $3, Minnie, Mickey. $4, Congratulations Mickey, birthday cake. $5, Uncle Sam.

No. 1993, Donald Duck, early photo of Mickey, horiz. No. 1994, Minnie disco dancing, horiz. No. 1995, Mickey photographing nephews, horiz. No. 1996, Pluto, Mickey looking at wall of photos.

1994, May 5 Litho. ***Perf. 13½x14***
1977-1992 A274 Set of 16 16.00 16.00

Souvenir Sheets
Perf. 14x13½
1993-1996 A274 $6 Set of 4 18.00 18.00

Breadfruit — A275

Intl. Year of the Family — A276

1994, Jan. Litho. ***Perf. 13½x14***
1997 A275 10c Planting .20 .20
1998 A275 45c Captain Bligh, plant .35 .35
1999 A275 65c Fruit sliced .50 .50
2000 A275 $5 Fruit on branch 3.75 3.75
Nos. 1997-2000 (4) 4.80 4.80

1994, Jan. ***Perf. 14x13½, 13½x14***
2001 A276 10c Outing .20 .20
2002 A276 50c Praying in church .40 .40
2003 A276 65c Working in garden .50 .50
2004 A276 75c Jogging .55 .55
2005 A276 $1 Portrait .75 .75
2006 A276 $2 Running on beach 1.50 1.50
Nos. 2001-2006 (6) 3.90 3.90

Nos. 2001-2004, 2006 are horiz.

Library Service, Cent. A277

1994, Jan. ***Perf. 14x13½***
2007 A277 5c Mobile library .20 .20
2008 A277 10c Old public library .20 .20
2009 A277 $1 Family education .75 .75
2010 A277 $1 Younger, older men .75 .75
Nos. 2007-2010 (4) 1.90 1.90

Barbra Streisand, 1993 MGM Grand Garden Concert — A278

A278a

Illustration A278a reduced.

1994, Jan.
2011 A278 $2 multicolored 1.50 1.50

Embossed

Perf. 12

2011A A278a $20 gold

No. 2011 issued in sheets of 9.

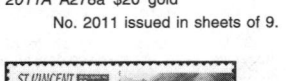

A279

A280

Hong Kong '94 — A281

Hong Kong '94 — A282

Stamps, 19th cent. painting of Hong Kong Harbor: #2012a, Hong Kong #626, ship under sail. #2012b, Ship at anchor, #1548.

Porcelain ware, Qing Dynasty - #2013: a, Bowl with bamboo & sparrows. b, Bowl with flowers of four seasons. c, Bowl with lotus pool & dragon. d, Bowl with landscape. e, Shar-Pei puppies in bowl (not antiquity). f, Covered bowl with dragon & pearls.

Chinese dragon boat races - #2014: a, Dragon boats. b, Tapestry of dragon races. c, Dragon race. d, Dragon boats, diff. e, Chinese crested dog. f, Dragon boats, 4 banners above boats.

Chinese junks - #2015: a, Junk, Hong Kong Island. b, Junk with white sails in harbor. c, Junk with inscription on stern, Hong Kong Island. d, Junk KLN B/G. e, Chow dog, junk. f, Junk with red, white sails, Hong Kong Island.

Chinese seed stitch purses - #2016: a, Vases, fruit on pink purse. b, Peonies, butterflies. c, Vase, fruit on dark blue purse. d, Vases, fruit on light blue purse. e, Fu-dog. f, Flowers.

Chineses pottery - #2017: a, Plate, bird on flowering spray, Qianlong. b, Large dish, Kangxi. c, Egshell plate, cocks on rocky ground, Yongzheng. d, Gladen dish decorated with Qilin curicorn, Yuan. e, Porcelain pug dog. f, Dish with Dutch ship, Uryburg, Qianlong.

Ceramic figures, Qing Dynasty, vert - #2018: a, Waterdropper. b, Two women playing chess. c, Liu-Hai. d, Laughing twins. e, Seated hound. f, Louhan (Ma Ming).

#2019, Dr. Sun Yat-sen. #2020, Chiang Kai-shek.

Dinosaurs - #2021: a, Triceratops. b, Unidentified, vert. c, Apatosaurus (d). d, Stegosaurus, vert.

1994, Feb. 18 ***Perf. 14***

2012 A279 40c Pair, #a.-b. .60 .60

Miniature Sheets of 6

2013	A280	40c #a.-f.	1.90	1.90
2014	A280	40c #a.-f.	1.90	1.90
2015	A280	45c #a.-f.	2.00	2.00
2016	A280	45c #a.-f.	2.00	2.00
2017	A281	50c #a.-f.	2.25	2.25

Perf. 13

2018 A280 50c #a.-f. 2.25 2.25

Souvenir Sheets

2019	A281	$2 multicolored	1.50	1.50
2020	A281	$2 multicolored	1.50	1.50
2021	A282	$1.50 Sheet of 4, #a.-d.	4.50	4.50

No. 2012 issued in sheets of 10 stamps and has a continuous design.

Portions of the design on No. 2021 have been applied by a thermographic process producing a shiny, raised effect.

New Year 1994 (Year of the Dog) (#2013e, 2014e, 2015e, 2016e, 2017e, 2018e). Hong Kong '94 (#2018, 2021).

Miniature Sheet

Hong Kong '94 — A283

Butterflies: a, Blue flasher. b, Tiger swallowtail. c, Lustrous copper. d, Tailed copper. e, Blue copper. f, Ruddy copper. g, Viceroy. h, California sister. i, Mourning cloak. j, Red passion flower. k, Small flambeau. l, Blue wave. m, Chiricahua metalmark. n, Monarch. o, Anise swallowtail. p, Buckeye.

1994, Feb. 18 Litho. ***Perf. 14½***

2022 A283 50c Sheet of 16, #a.-p. 6.00 6.00

A284

A285

Players: No. 2023, Causio. No. 2024, Tardelli. No. 2025, Rossi. No. 2026, Bettega. No. 2027, Platini, Baggio. No. 2028, Cabrini. No. 2029, Scirea. No. 2030, Furino. No. 2031, Kohler. No. 2032, Zoff. No. 2033, Gentile.

$6, Three European Cups won by team, horiz.

1994, Mar. 22 Litho. ***Perf. 14***

2023-2033 A284 $1 Set of 11 8.25 8.25

Souvenir Sheet

2034 A284 $6 multicolored 4.50 4.50

Juventus football (soccer) club of Turin.

1994, Apr. 6 Litho. ***Perf. 14***

Orchids: 10c, Epidendrum ibaguense. 25c, Ionopsis utricularioides. 50c, Brassavola cucullata. 65c, Enclyclia cochleata. $1, Liparis nervosa. $2, Vanilla phaeantha. $4, Elleanthus cephalotus. $5, Isochilus linearis.

No. 2043, Rodriguezia lanceolata. No. 2044, Eulophia alta.

2035-2042 A285 Set of 8 10.00 10.00

Souvenir Sheets

2043-2044 A285 $6 each 4.50 4.50

A286

Dinosaurs — A287

#2045: a, Protoavis (e). b, Pteranodon. c, Quetzalcoatlus (b). d, Lesothosaurus (a, c, e-h). e, Hetrodontosaurus. f, Archaeopteryx (b, e). g, Cearadactylus (f). h, Anchisaurus.

No. 2046: a, Dimorphodon (e). b, Camarasaurus (e, f). c, Spinosaurus (b). d, Allosaurus (a-c, e-h). e, Rhamphorhynchus (a). f, Pteranodon (b). g, Eudimorphodon (c). h, Ornithomimus.

No. 2047: a, Dimorphodon (b). b, Pterodactylus (a). c, Rhamphorhynchus (b). d, Pteranodon. e, Gallimimus. f, Setgosaurus. g, Acanthopholis. h, Trachodon (g). i, Thecodonti (j). j, Ankylosaurus (i). k, Compsognathus. l, Protoceratops.

No. 2048: a, Hesperonis. b, Mesosaurus. c, Plesiosaurus. d, Squalicorax (a). e, Tylosaurus (d, g). f, Plesiosoar. g, Stenopterygius ichthyosaurus (j). h, Stenosaurus (f). i, Eurhinosaurus longirostris (e, f, h, l). j, Cryptocleidus oxoniensis. k, Caturus (h, i, j, l). l, Protostega (k).

No. 2049: a, Quetzalcoatlus. b, Diplodocus (a). c, Spinosaurus (f, g). d, Apatosaurus (c). e, Ornitholestes. f, Lesothosaurus (e). g, Trachodon. h, Protoavis. i, Oviraptor. j, Coelophysis (i). k, Ornitholestes (j). l, Archaeopteryx.

No. 2050, horiz: a, Albertosaurus. b, Chasmosaurus (c). c, Brachiosaurus. d, Coelophysis (e). e, Deinonychus (d). f, Anatosaurus. g, Iguanodon. h, Baryonyx. i, Steneosaurus. j, Nanotyrannus. k, Camptosaurus (j). l, Camarasaurus.

No. 2051, Tyrannosaurus rex. No. 2052: Triceratops, horiz. No. 2053, Pteranodon, diplodocus carnegii, horiz. No. 2054, Styracosaurus.

1994, Apr. 20 Litho. ***Perf. 14***

2045	A286	75c Sheet of 8, #a.-h.	4.50	4.50
2046	A286	75c Sheet of 8, #a.-h.	4.50	4.50

Miniature Sheets of 12

2047-2050 A287 75c #a.-l, each 6.75 6.75

Souvenir Sheets

2051	A286	$6 multi	4.50	4.50
2052-2054	A287	$6 each	4.50	4.50

No. 2048 is horiz.

Entertainers Type of 1991

Miniature Sheet

Various portraits of Marilyn Monroe.

1994, May 16 ***Perf. 13½***

2055 A206 $1 Sheet of 9, #a.-i. 6.75 6.75

1994 World Cup Soccer Championships, US — A288

Team photos: #2056, Colombia. #2057, Romania. #2058, Switzerland. #2059, US. #2060, Brazil. #2061, Cameroon. #2062, Russia. #2063, Sweden. #2064, Bolivia. #2065, Germany. #2066, South Korea. #2067, Spain. #2068, Argentina. #2069, Bulgaria. #2070, Greece. #2071, Nigeria. #2072, Ireland. #2073, Italy. #2074, Mexico. #2075, Norway. #2076, Belgium. #2077, Holland. #2078, Morocco. #2079, Saudi Arabia.

1994 ***Perf. 13½***

2056-2079 A288 50c Set of 24 9.00 9.00

Miniature Sheets of 9

First Manned Moon Landing, 25th Anniv. A289

Famous men, aviation & space scenes: No. 2080a, Fred L. Whipple, Halley's Comet. b, Robert G. Gilruth, Gemini 12. c, George E. Mueller, Ed White walking in space during Gemini 4. d, Charles A. Berry, Johnsville Centrifuge. e, Christopher C. Kraft, Jr., Apollo 4 reentry. f, James A. Van Allen, Explorer I, Van Allen Radiation Belts. g, Robert H. Goddard, Goddard Liquid Fuel Rocket, 1926. h, James E. Webb, Spirit of '76 flight. i, Rocco A. Patrone, Apollo 8 coming home.

No. 2081: a, Walter R. Dornberger, missile launch, 1942. b, Alexander Lippisch, Wolfgang Spate's ME-163B. c, Kurt H. Debus, A4b Launch, 1945. d, Hermann Oberth, Oberth's Spaceship, 1923. e, Hanna Reitsch, Reichenberg (type 2) Piloted Bomb. f, Ernst Stuhlinger, Explorer I, 2nd stage ignition. g, Werner von Braun, Rocket Powered He112. h, Arthur Rudolph, Rudolph Rocket Motor, 1934. i, Willy Ley, Rocket Airplane, Greenwood Lake NY.

No. 2082, Hogler N. Toftoy. No. 2083, Eberhardt Rees.

1994, July 12 ***Perf. 14***

2080-2081 A289 $1 #a.-i, each 6.75 6.75

Souvenir Sheets

2082-2083 A289 $6 each 4.50 4.50

Nos. 2082-2083 each contain one 50x38mm stamp.

D-Day, 50th Anniv. A290

Designs: 40c, Supply armada. $5, Beached cargo ship unloads supplies.

$6, Liberty ship.

1994, July 19 Litho. ***Perf. 14***

2084	A290	40c multicolored	.30	.30
2085	A290	$5 multicolored	3.75	3.75

Souvenir Sheet

2086 A290 $6 multicolored 4.50 4.50

New Year 1994 (Year of the Dog) — A291

Designs: 10c, Yorkshire terrier. 25c, Yorkshire terrier, diff. 50c, Golden retriever. 65c, Bernese mountain dog. $1, Vorstehhund. $2, Tibetan terrier. $4, West highland terrier. $5, Shih tzu.

No. 2095a, Pomeranian. b, English springer spaniel. c, Bearded collie. d, Irish wolfhound. e, Pekingese. f, Irish setter. g, Old English sheepdog. h, Basset hound. i, Cavalier King Charles spaniel. j, Kleiner munsterlander. k, Shetland sheepdog. l, Dachshund.

No. 2096, Afghan hound. No. 2097, German shepherd.

1994, July 21

2087-2094 A291 Set of 8 10.00 10.00

Miniature Sheet of 12

2095 A291 50c #a.-l. 4.50 4.50

Souvenir Sheets

2096-2097 A291 $6 each 4.50 4.50

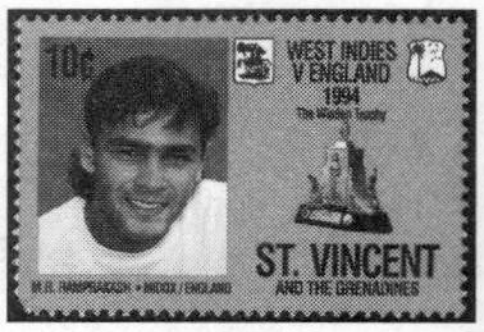

English Touring Cricket, Cent. A292

Designs: 10c, M.R. Ramprakash, England. 30c, P.V. Simmons, W. Indies. $2, Sir. G. St. A. Sobers, W. Indies, vert.

$3, Firsh English team, 1895.

1994, July 25

2098-2100 A292 Set of 3 1.90 1.90

Souvenir Sheet

2101 A293 $3 multicolored 2.25 2.25

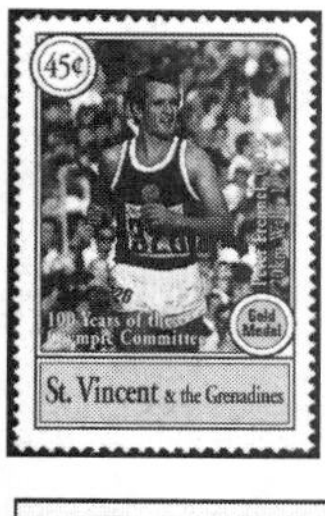

A293

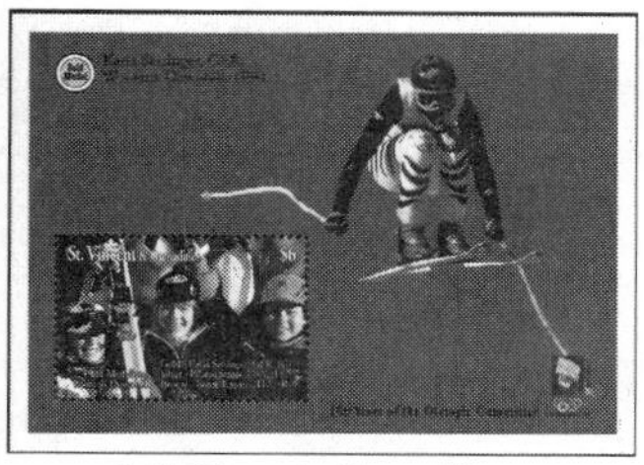

Intl. Olympic Committee, Cent. — A294

Designs: 45c, Peter Frennel, German Democratic Republic, 20k walk, 1972. 50c, Kijung Son, Japan, marathon, 1936. 75c, Jesse Owens, US, 100-, 200-meters, 1936. $1, Greg Louganis, US, diving, 1984, 1988.

$6, Katja Seizinger, Germany, Picabo Street, US, Isolde Kastner, Italy, women's downhill, 1994.

1994, July 25

2102-2105 A293 Set of 4 2.00 2.00

Souvenir Sheet

2106 A294 $6 multicolored 4.50 4.50

PHILAKOREA '94

A295 A296

Designs: 10c, Oryon Waterfall. 45c, Outside P'yongyang Indoor Sports Stadium, horiz. 65c, Pombong, Ch'onhwadae. 75c, Uisangdae, Naksansa. $1, Buddha of the Sokkuram Grotto, Kyangju, horiz. $2, Moksogwon, horiz.

Nos. 2113a-2113h, Various letter pictures, eight panel screen, 18th cent. Choson Dynasty.

Letter pictures, 19th cent. Choson Dynasty: No. 2114a, Fish. No. 2114b, Birds. Nos. 2114c-2114d, 2114h, Various bookshelf pictures. Nos. 2114e-2114g, Various designs from six-panel screen.

No. 2115, Hunting scene, embroidery on silk, Choson Dynasty, horiz. No. 2116, Chongdong Mirukbul.

1994, July 25 ***Perf. 14***

2107-2112 A295 Set of 6 3.75 3.75

Miniature Sheets of 8

Perf. 13½

2113-2114 A296 50c #a.-h. 3.00 3.00

Souvenir Sheets

Perf. 14

2115-2116 A295 $4 each 3.00 3.00

Miniature Sheet of 9

Star Trek, The Next Generation, 7th Anniv. A297

A297a

Designs: No. 2117a, Capt. Picard. b, Cmdr. Riker. c, Lt. Cmdr. Data. d, Lt. Worf. e, Cast members. f, Dr. Crusher. g, Lt. Yar, Lt. Worf. h, Q. i, Counselor Troi.

$10, Cast members, horiz.

$20, Starship Enterprise, Capt. Picard.

Illustration A297a reduced.

1994, June 27 Litho. ***Perf. 14x13½***

2117 A297 $2 #a.-i. 14.00 14.00

Souvenir Sheet

Perf. 14x14½

2118 A297 $10 multicolored 5.75 5.75

No. 2117e exists in sheets of 9. No. 2118 contains one 60x40mm stamp.

Litho. & Embossed

1994, May ***Perf. 9***

2118A A297a $20 gold & multi

Intl. Year of the Family A298

1994 ***Perf. 14***

2119 A298 75c multicolored .55 .55

Order of the Caribbean Community — A299

First award recipients: $1, Sir Shridath Ramphal, statesman, Guyana, vert. $2, Derek Walcott, writer, St. Lucia, vert. $5, William Demas, economist, Trinidad and Tobago.

1994, Sept. 1

2120-2122 A299 Set of 3 6.00 6.00

Miniature Sheets of 6 or 12

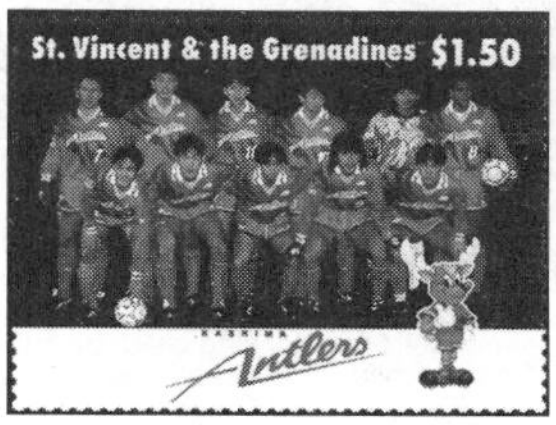

Japanese Soccer — A300

Team photos: No. 2123a, Kahsima Antlers. b, JEF United. c, Red Diamonds. d, Verdy Yomiuri. e, Nissan FC Yokohama Marinos. f, AS Flugels. g, Bellmare. h, Shimizu S-pulse. i, Jubilo Iwata. j, Nogoya Grampus Eight. k, Panasonic Gamba Osaka. l, Sanfrecce Hiroshima FC.

Jubilo Iwata, action scenes: Nos. 2124a, c-d, 55c. b, e, $1.50. f, $3, Team picture.

Red Diamonds, action scenes: Nos. 2125a, c-d, 55c. b, e, $1.50. f, $3, Team pictue.

Nissan FC Yokohama Marinos, action scenes: Nos. 2126a, c-d, 55c. b, e, $1.50. f, $3, Team picture.

Verdy Yomiuri, action scenes: Nos. 2127a, c-d, 55c. b, e, $1.50. f, $3, Team picture.

Nagoya Grampus eight, action scenes: Nos. 2128a, c-d, 55c. b, e, $1.50. f, $3, Team picture.

Kashima Antlers, action scenes: Nos. 2129a, c-d, 55c. b, e, $1.50. f, $3, Team picture.

JEF United, action scenes: Nos. 2130a, c-d, 55c. b, e, $1.50. f, $3, Team picture.

AS Flugels, action scenes: Nos. 2131a, c-d, 55c. b, e, $1.50. f, $3, Team picture.

Bellmare, action scenes: Noa. 2132a, c-d, 55c. b, e, $1.50. f, $3, Team picture.

Sanfrecce Hiroshima FC, action scenes: Nos. 2133a, c-d, 55c. b, e, $1.50. f, $3, Team picture.

Shimizu S-pulse, action scenes: Nos. 2134a, c-d, 55c. b, e, $1.50. f, $3, Team picture.

Panasonic Gamba Isajam, action scenes: Nos. 2135a, c-d, 55c. b, e, $1.50. f, $3, Team picture.

League All-Stars: No. 2136a, $1.50, League emblem. b, 55c, Shigetatsu Matsunaga. c, 55c, Masami Ihara. d, $1.50, Takumi Horiike. e, 55c, Shunzoh Ohno. f, 55c, Luiz Carlos Pereira. g, 55c, Tetsuji Hashiratani. h, 55c, Carlos Alberto Souza Dos Santos. i, $1.50, Rui Ramos. j, 55c, Yasuto Honda. k, 55c, Kazuyoshi Miura. l, $1.50, Ramon Angel Diaz.

1994, July 1 ***Perf. 14x13½***

2123 A300 #a.-l. 7.75 7.75

2124-2135 A300 #a.-f., each 5.75 5.75

Perf. 13½x14

2136 A300 #a.-l., vert. 7.75 7.75

Christmas A301

Illustrations from Book of Hours, by Jean de Berry: 10c, The Annunciation, angel kneeling. 45c, The Visitation. 50c, The Nativity, Madonna seeing infant. 65c, The Purification of the Virgin. 75c, Presentation of Jesus in the Temple. $5, Flight into Egypt.

$6, Adoration of the Magi.

1994 Litho. ***Perf. 13½x14***

2137-2142 A301 Set of 6 5.75 5.75

Souvenir Sheet

2143 A301 $6 multicolored 4.50 4.50

Miniature Sheet

Nos. 1792, 1806-1807 with New Denominations and Added Inscription

1995, Jan. 24 ***Perf. 14x13½***

2144 A247 30c Sheet of 9, #a.-i. 2.00 2.00

Souvenir Sheets

2145 A247 $3 multi (#1806) 2.25 2.25

2146 A247 $3 multi (#1807) 2.25 2.25

Nos. 2144-2146 are inscribed with emblem for "New Year 1995, Year of the Pig."

ICAO, 50th Anniv. A302

Designs: 10c, Bequia Airport. 65c, Union Island. 75c, Liat 8-100, E.T. Joshua Airport. No. 2150, $1, Airplanes, ICAO emblem. No. 2151, $1, J.F. Mitchell Airport, Bequia.

1994, Dec. 1 Litho. ***Perf. 14***

2147-2151 A302 Set of 5 2.75 2.75

Miniature Sheets of 9

Cats A303

Parrots — A304

Cats: No. 2152a, Snowshoe. b, Abyssinian. c, Ocicat. d, Tiffany (e, h). e, Russian blue. f, Siamese. g, Bi-color. h, Malayan. i, Manx.

Parrots: No. 2153a, Mealy Amazon. b, Nanday conure. c, Black-headed caique. d, Scarlet macaw (g). e, Red-masked conure. f, Blue-headed parrot. g, Hyacinth macaw. h, Sun conure. i, Blue & yellow macaw.

#2154, White-eared conure. #2155, Birman.

1995, Apr. 25 Litho. ***Perf. 14***

2152-2153 A303 $1 #a.-i., each 6.75 6.75

Souvenir Sheets

2154 A304 $5 multicolored 3.75 3.75

2155 A304 $6 multicolored 4.50 4.50

A305

Birds A306

World Wildlife Fund, masked booby: No. 2156: a, One standing. b, Two birds. c, One nesting. d, One stretching wings.

No. 2157: a, Greater egret. b, Roseate spoonbill. c, Ring-billed gull. d, Ruddy quail-dove. e, Royal tern. f, Killdeer. g, Osprey. h, Frigatebird. i, Masked booby. j, Green-backed heron. k, Cormorant. l, Brown pelican.

No. 2158, Flamingo, vert. No. 2159, Purple gallinule, vert.

1995, May 2

2156 A305 75c Strip of 4, #a.-d. 2.25 2.25

Miniature Sheet of 12

2157 A306 75c #a.-l. 6.75 6.75

Souvenir Sheets

2158 A306 $5 multicolored 3.75 3.75

2159 A306 $6 multicolored 4.50 4.50

No. 2156 is a continuous design and was issued in sheets of 3.

Miniature Sheets of 6 and 8

VE Day, 50th Anniv. A307

No. 2159A: b, Douglas Devastator. c, Doolittle's B25 leads raid on Tokyo. d, Curtis Helldiver. e, USS Yorktown. f, USS Wasp. g, USS Lexington sinks.

No. 2160: a, US First Army nears the Rhine. b, Last V2 rocket fired at London, Mar. 1945. c, 8th Air Force B24 Liberators devastate industrial Germany. d, French Army advances on Strasbourg. e, Gloster Meteor, first jet aircraft to enter squadron service. f, Berlin burns from both air and ground bombardments. g, Soviet tanks on Unter Den Linden near Brandenburg Gate. h, European war is won.

No. 2161, Pilot in cockpit of Allied bomber.

No. 2161A, Ships in Pacific, sunset.

1995, May 8 Litho. ***Perf. 14***

2159A A307 $2 #b.-g. + label 9.25 9.25

2160 A307 $2 #a.-h. + label 12.00 12.00

Souvenir Sheets

2161-2161A A307 $6 each 4.50 4.50

No. 2161 contains one 57x43mm stamp.

A308

UN, 50th anniv.: a, Globe, dove. b, Lady Liberty. c, UN Headquarters. $6, Child.

1995, May 5
2162 A308 $2 Strip of 3, #a.-c. 4.50 4.50

Souvenir Sheet

2163 A308 $6 multicolored 4.50 4.50

No. 2162 is a continuous design and was issued in miniature sheets of 3.

A309

1995, May 5

18th World Scout Jamboree, Holland: $1, Natl. Scout flag. $4, Lord Baden Powell. $5, Scout handshake.

No. 2167, Scout sign. No. 2168, Scout salute.

1995
2164-2166 A309 Set of 3 7.50 7.50

Souvenir Sheets

2167-2168 A309 $6 each 4.50 4.50

Yalta Conference, 50th Anniv. A310

$50, like #2169. Illustration reduced.

1995, May 8 Litho. *Perf. 14*
2169 A310 $1 multicolored .75 .75

Litho. & Embossed

Perf. 9

2169A A310 $50 gold & multi

No. 2169 was issued in sheets of 9.

New Year 1995 (Year of the Boar) — A311

Stylized boars: a, blue green & multi. b, brown & multi. c, red & multi. $2, Two boars, horiz.

1995, May 8
2170 A311 75c Strip of 3, #a.-c. 1.75 1.75

Souvenir Sheet

2171 A311 $2 multicolored 1.50 1.50

No. 2170 was issued in sheets of 3.

FAO, 50th Anniv. — A312

1995, May 8

Designs: a, Girl holding plate, woman with bowl. b, Stirring pot of food. c, Working in fields of grain.

$6, Infant.

1995, May 8
2172 A312 $2 Strip of 3, #a.-c. 4.50 4.50

Souvenir Sheet

2173 A312 $6 multicolored 4.50 4.50

No. 2172 is a continuous design and was issued in sheets of 3.

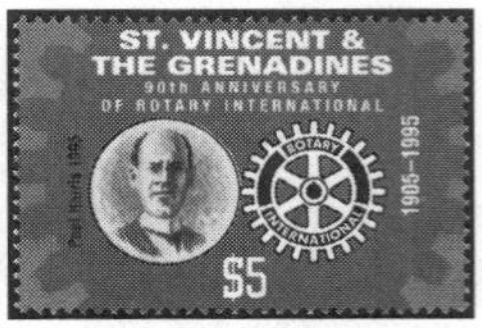

Rotary Intl., 90th Anniv. A313

Designs: $5, Paul Harris, Rotary emblem. $6, St. Vincent flag, Rotary emblem.

1995, May 8
2174 A313 $5 multicolored 3.75 3.75

Souvenir Sheet

2175 A313 $6 multicolored 4.50 4.50

Queen Mother, 95th Birthday A314

Designs: a, Drawing, b, Wearing blue hat. c, Formal portrait. d, Wearing lavender outfit.

$6, Wearing crown jewels, yellow dress.

1995, May 8 *Perf. 13½x14*
2176 A314 $1.50 Block or strip of 4, #a.-d. 4.50 4.50

Souvenir Sheet

2177 A314 $6 multicolored 4.50 4.50

No. 2176 was issued in sheet of 2.

Miniature Sheets

Marine Life A315

No. 2178, vert: a, Humpback whale (b, d, e, f, i). b, Green turtle (c). c, Bottlenosed dolphin (f). d, Monk seal (e). e, Krill. f, Blue shark. g, Striped pork fish. h, Chaelodon sedentarius (e, g). i, Ship wreck, bottom of sea.

No. 2179: a, Pomacentrus leucostictus (b). b, Pomacanthus arcuatus (d). c, Microspathodon chrysurus (d). d, Chaetodon capistratus.

No. 2180, Physalia physalis, vert. No. 2181, Sea anemones, vert.

1995, May 23 *Perf. 14*
2178 A315 90c Sheet of 9, #a.-i. 6.25 6.25
2179 A315 $1 Sheet of 4, #a.-d. 4.25 4.25

Souvenir Sheets

2180-2181 A315 $6 each 4.50 4.50

1995 Special Olympics World Games, Connecticut A316

A316a

Illustration A316a reduced.

1995, July 6
2182 A316 $1 blk, yel & bl .75 .75

Embossed

Perf. 9

2182A A316a $20 gold

No. 2182 issued in sheets of 9.

Miniature Sheet of 6

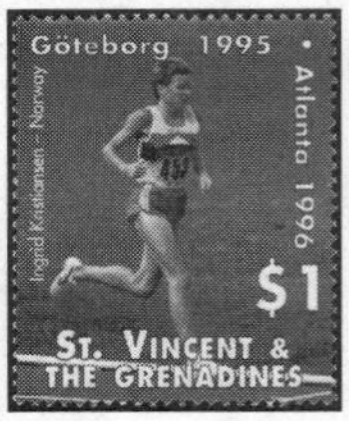

1995 IAAF World Track & Field Championships, Gothenburg & 1996 Summer Olympics, Atlanta — A317

No. 2183: a, Ingrid Kristiansen, Norway. b, Trine Hattestad, Norway. c, Grete Waitz, Norway. d, Vebjorn Rodal, Norway. e, Geir Moen, Norway. f, Steinar Hoen, Norway, horiz.

1995, July 31 Litho. *Perf. 14*
2183 A317 $1 #a.-f. 4.50 4.50

A318 A319

Designs: 15c, Breast, bowl of food, horiz. 20c, Expressing milk, cup, spoon. 90c, Drawing of mother breastfeeding child, by Picasso. $5, Mother, child, olive wreath.

1995, Aug. 4
2184-2187 A318 Set of 4 4.75 4.75

WHO, UNICEF Baby Friendly Program.

1995, Aug. 8

Designs: 10c, Leeward Coast, horiz. 15c, Feeder roads project, horiz. 25c, Anthurium andraeanum, horiz. 50c, Coconut palm. 65c, Housing scene, Fairhall, horiz.

2188-2192 A319 Set of 5 1.25 1.25

Caribbean Development Bank, 25th anniv.

Fudo Myoou (God of Fire), Woodprint, by Shunichi Kadowaki — A320

1995, July 1 Litho. *Perf. 14*
2193 A320 $1.40 multicolored 1.10 1.10

A321

Nolan Ryan, Baseball Player — A322

Designs: No. 2194, Nolan Ryan Foundation emblem. No. 2195, Emblem of major league All Star Game, Arlington,TX.

Portraits of Ryan: No. 2196a, In NY Mets uniform. b, With western hat, dog. c, In Texas Rangers' cap. d, Throwing football. e, With son. f, Laughing, without hat. g, With family. h, Wearing Houston Astros cap.

Ryan in Rangers' uniform: No. 2197a, Blue outfit. b, "34" on front. c, Looking left. d, After pitch looking forward. e, After pitch looking left. f, With bloody lip. g, Ready to pitch ball. h, Holding up cap.

$6, Being carried by team mates.

$30, Ready to pitch (illustration reduced).

1995, Aug. 1 *Perf. 13½x14*
2194 A321 $1 multicolored .75 .75
2195 A321 $1 multicolored .75 .75
a. Pair, #2194-2195 1.50 1.50

Miniature Sheets of 9

2196 A321 $1 #a.-h. + #2194 6.75 6.75
2197 A321 $1 #a.-h. + #2195 6.75 6.75

Souvenir Sheet

2198 A321 $6 multicolored 4.50 4.50

Litho. & Embossed

Perf. 9

2199 A322 $30 gold & multi

Nos. 2194-2195 were issued in sheets containing 5 #2194, 4 #2195.

Miniature Sheets of 6 or 8

1996 Summer Olympics, Atlanta — A323

No. 2200: a, Jean Shiley, US. b, Ruth Fuchs, Germany. c, Alessandro Andrei, Italy. d, Dorando Pietri, Italy. e, Heide Rosendahl, Germany. f, Mitsuoki Watanabe, Japan. g, Yasuhiro Yamashita, Japan. h, Dick Fosbury, US.

No. 2201: a, Long jump. b, Hurdles. c, Sprint. d, Marathon. e, Gymnastics. f, Rowing.

No. 2202, Magic Johnson. No. 2203, Swimmer's hand, horiz.

1995, Aug. 24 Litho. *Perf. 14*

2200 A323 $1 #a.-h. 6.00 6.00
2201 A323 $2 #a.-f. 9.00 9.00

Souvenir Sheets

2202-2203 A323 $5 each 3.75 3.75

Miniature Sheet

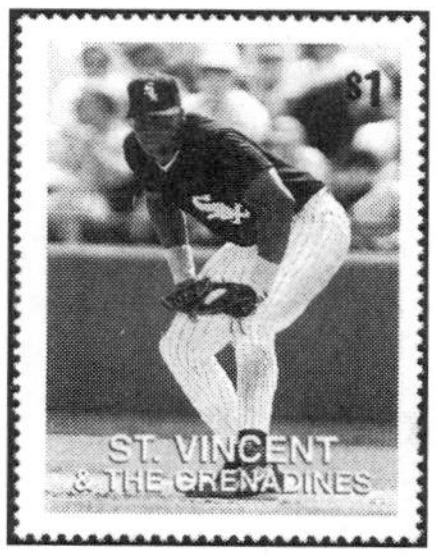

Stars of American League Baseball A324

A324a

#2204, Different portraits of: a, e, i, Frank Thomas, Chicago White Sox. b, f-g, Cal Ripken, Jr., Baltimore Orioles. c-d, h, Ken Griffey, Jr., Seattle Mariners.
No. 2204J, Ken Griffey, Jr. No. 2204K, Cal Ripken, Jr. No. 2204L, Frank Thomas.
Illustration A324a reduced.

1995, Sept. 6 Litho. *Perf. 14*

2204 A324 $1 Sheet of 9, #a.-i. 6.75 6.75

Litho. & Embossed
Perf. 9

2204J-2204L A324a $30 Set of 3, gold & multi

Miniature Sheets of 6 or 9

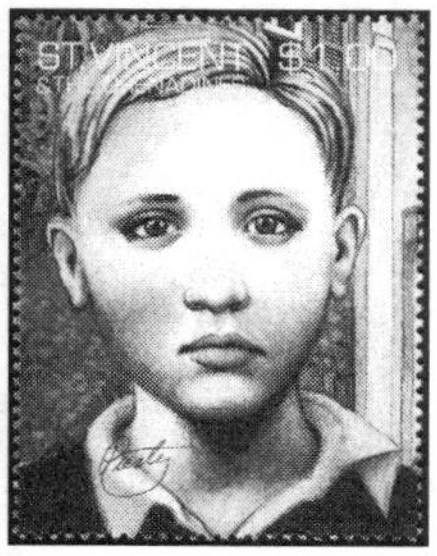

Entertainers A325

#2205-2206: Portraits of Elvis Presley.
#2207: Portraits of John Lennon.
#2208-2210: Portraits of Marilyn Monroe.
#2211, Presley, diff. #2212, Lennon, diff. #2213, Monroe, in black. #2214, Monroe, in red.

1995, Sept. 18 *Perf. 13½x14*

2205 A325 $1 #a.-f. 4.50 4.50
2206-2210 A325 $1 #a.-i., each 6.75 6.75

Souvenir Sheets

2211-2214 A325 $6 each 4.50 4.50

No. 2208 has serifs in lettering. No. 2209 has pink lettering.

Elvis Presley — A325a

$30, Marilyn Monroe. Illustration reduced.
Illustration reduced.

1995 Litho. & Embossed *Perf. 9*

2214A A325a $20 gold & multi
2214B A325a $30 gold & multi

Miniature Sheet

Passenger Trains — A326

Designs: No. 2215a, German Federal Railway ET4-03, high speed four car electric. b, Tres Grande Vitesse (TGV), France. c, British Railways Class 87 electric. d, Beijing locomotive, Railways of the People's Republic of China. e, American Amtrak turbo. f, Swedish State Railways class RC4 electric.
$6, Eurostar.

1995, Oct. 3 *Perf. 14*

2215 A326 $1.50 Sheet of 6, #a.-f. 5.25 5.25

Souvenir Sheet

2216 A326 $6 multicolored 4.50 4.50

No. 2216 contains one 85x28mm stamp.

Miniature Sheets of 12

Nobel Prize Fund Established, Cent. — A327

Recipients: No. 2217a, Heinrich Böll, literature, 1972. b, Walther Bothe, physics, 1954. c, Richard Kuhn, chemistry, 1938. d, Hermann Hesse, literatrue, 1946. e, Knut Hamsun, literature, 1920. f, Konrad Lorenz, medicine, 1973. g, Thomas Mann, literature, 1929. h, Fridtjof Nansen, peace, 1922. i, Fritz Pregl, chemistry, 1923. j, Christian Lange, peace, 1921. k, Otto Loewi, medicine, 1936. l, Erwin Schrodinger, physics, 1933.
No. 2218: a, Giosue Carducci, literature, 1906. b, Wladyslaw Reymont, literature, 1924. c, Ivan Bunin, literature, 1933. d, Pavel Cherenkov, physics, 1958. e, Ivan Pavlov, medicine, 1904. f, Pyotr Kapitza, physics, 1978. g, Lev Landau, physics, 1962. h, Daniel Bovet, medicine, 1957. i, Henryk Sienkiewicz, literature, 1905. j, Aleksandr Prokhorov, physics, 1964. k, Julius Wagner von Jauregg, medicine, 1927. l, Grazia Deledda, literature, 1926.
No. 2219: a, Bjornstjerne Bjornson, literature, 1903. b, Frank Kellogg, peace, 1929. c, Gustav Hertz, physics, 1925. d, Har Gobind Khorana, medicine, 1968. e, Kenichi Fukui, chemistry, 1981. f, Henry Kissinger, peace, 1973. g, Martin Luther King, Jr., peace, 1964. h, Odd Hassel, chemistry, 1969. i, Polykarp Kusch, physics, 1955. j, Ragnar Frisch, economics, 1969. k, Willis E. Lamb, Jr., physics, 1955. l, Sigrid Undset, literature, 1928.
No. 2220: a, Robert Barany, medicine, 1914. b, Ernest Walton, physics, 1951. c, Alfred Fried, peace, 1911. d, James Franck, physics, 1925. e, Werner Forssmann, medicine, 1956. f, Yasunari Kawabata, literature, 1968. g, Wolfgang Pauli, physics, 1945. h, Jean-Paul Sartre, literature, 1964. i, Aleksandr Solzhenitsyn, literature, 1970. j, Hermann Staudinger, chemistry, 1953. k, Igor Tamm, physics, 1958. l, Samuel Beckett, literature, 1969.
No. 2221, Adolf Windaus, chemistry, 1928. No. 2222, Hideki Yukawa, physics, 1949. No. 2223, Bertha von Suttner, peace, 1905. No. 2224, Karl Landsteiner, medicine, 1930.

1995, Oct. 2 Litho. *Perf. 14*

2217-2220 A327 $1 #a.-l., each 9.00 9.00

Souvenir Sheets

2221-2224 A327 $6 each 4.50 4.50

Miniature Sheet

Classic Cars A328

No. 2225: a, 1931 Duesenberg Model J. b, 1913 Sleeve-valve Minerva. c, 1933 Delage D.8. SS. d, 1931-32 Bugatti Royale, Coupe De Ville chassis 41111. e, 1926 Rolls Royce 7668CC Phantom 1 Landauette. f, 1927 Mercedes Benz S26/120/180 PS.
$5, Hispano-Suiza Type H6B tulipwood-bodied roadster by Neuport.

1995, Oct. 3

2225 A328 $1.50 Sheet of 6, #a.-f. 6.75 6.75

Souvenir Sheet

2226 A328 $5 multicolored 3.75 3.75

Singapore '95 (#2225). No. 2226 contains one 85x28mm stamp.

Miniature Sheet

Sierra Club, Cent. — A329

#2227: a, Gray wolf in front of trees. b. Gray wolf pup. c, Gray wolf up close. d, Hawaiian goose. e, Two Hawaiian geese. f, Jaguar. g, Lion-tailed macaque. h, Sand cat. i, Three sand cats.
#2228, horiz.: a, Orangutan swinging from tree. b, Orangutan facing forward. c, Orangutan looking left. d, Jaguar on rock. e, Jaguar up close. f, Sand cats. g, Hawaiian goose. h, Three lion-tailed macaques. i, Lion-tailed macaque.

1995, Dec. 1 Litho. *Perf. 14*

2227 A329 $1 Sheet of 9, #a.-i. 6.75 6.75
2228 A329 $1 Sheet of 9, #a.-i. 6.75 6.75

Miniature Sheet

Natural Wonders of the World A330

No. 2229: a, Nile River. b, Yangtze River. c, Niagara Falls. d, Victoria Falls. e, Grand Canyon, US. f, Sahara Desert, Algeria. g, Kilimanjaro, Tanzania. h, Amazon river.
No. 2230, Haleakala Crater, Hawaii.

1995, Dec. 1

2229 A330 $1.10 Sheet of 8, #a.-h. 6.75 6.75

Souvenir Sheet

2230 A330 $6 multicolored 4.50 4.50

Disney Christmas — A331

Antique Disney toys: 1c, Lionel Santa car. 2c, Mickey Mouse "Choo Choo." 3c, Minnie Mouse pram. 5c, Mickey Mouse circus pull toy. 10c, Mickey, Pluto wind-up cart. 25c, Mickey Mouse mechanical motorcycle. $3, Lionel's Mickey Mouse handcar. $5, Casey Jr. Disneyland Express.
No. 2239, Silver Link, Mickey the Stoker. No. 2240, Mickey, Streamliner Engine.

1995, Dec. 7 *Perf. 13½x14*

2231-2238 A331 Set of 8 6.50 6.50

Souvenir Sheets

2239-2240 A331 $6 each 4.50 4.50

Crotons A331a

Codiaeum variegatum: 10c, Mons florin. 15c, Prince of Monaco. 20c, Craigii. 40c, Gloriosum. 50c, Ebureum, vert. 60c, Volutum ramshorn. 70c, Narrenii, vert. 90c, Undutatum, vert. $1, Caribbean. $1.10, Gloriosa. $1.40, Katonii. $2, Appleleaf. $5, Tapestry. $10, Cornutum. $20, Puntatum aureum.

1996, Jan. 1 Litho. *Perf. 14*

2240A	A331a	10c	multi	.20	.20
2240B	A331a	15c	multi	.20	.20
2240C	A331a	20c	multi	.20	.20
2240D	A331a	40c	multi	.30	.30
2240E	A331a	50c	multi	.40	.40
2240F	A331a	60c	multi	.45	.45
2240G	A331a	70c	multi	.55	.55
2240H	A331a	90c	multi	.70	.70
2240I	A331a	$1	multi	.75	.75
2240J	A331a	$1.10	multi	.85	.85
2240K	A331a	$1.40	multi	1.00	1.00
2240L	A331a	$2	multi	1.50	1.50
2240M	A331a	$5	multi	3.75	3.75
2240N	A331a	$10	multi	7.50	7.50
2240O	A331a	$20	multi	15.00	15.00
	Nos. 2240A-2240O (15)			33.35	33.35

New Year 1996 (Year of the Rat) — A332

Stylized rats, Chinese inscriptions within checkered squares, #2241-2242: a, lilac & multi. b, orange & multi. c, pink & multi.
$2, orange, green & black.

1996, Jan. 2 Litho. *Perf. 14½*

2241 A332 75c Strip of 3, #a.-c. 1.75 1.75

Miniature Sheet

2242 A332 $1 Sheet of 3, #a.-c. 2.25 2.25

Souvenir Sheet

2243 A332 $2 multicolored 1.50 1.50

No. 2241 was issued in sheets of 9 stamps.

Miniature Sheets of 9

A333

Star Trek, 30th Anniv. — A333a

#2244: a, Spock. b, Kirk. c, Uhura. d, Sulu. e, Starship Enterprise. f, McCoy. g, Scott. h, Kirk, McCoy, Spock. i, Chekov.
#2245: a, Spock holding up hand in Vulcan greeting. b, Kirk, Spock in "A Piece of the Action." c. Captain Kirk. d, Kirk, "The Trouble with Tribbles." e, Crew, "City on the Edge of Forever." f, Uhura, Sulu, "Mirror, Mirror." g, Romulans, "Balance of Terror." h, Building exterior. i, Khan, "Space Seed."
$6, Spock, Uhura.
$30, Spock, Kirk, McCoy, Scott, Starship Enterprise.
Illustration A333a reduced.

1996, Jan. 4 ***Perf. 13½x14***

2244-2245 A333 $1 #a-i., each 6.75 6.75

Souvenir Sheet

2246 A333 $6 multicolored 4.50 4.50

Litho. & Embossed

Perf. 9

2246A A333a $30 gold & multi

Miniature Sheets

Disney Characters in Various Occupations — A334

Merchants: No. 2247: a, Stamp dealer. b, At supermarket. c, Car salesman. d, Florist. e, Fast food carhop. f, Street vendor. g, Gift shop. h, Hobby shop owner. i, Bakery.

Transport workers: No. 2248: a, Delivery service. b, Truck driver. c, Airplane crew. d, Railroad men. e, Bus driver. f, Tour guide. g, Messenger service. h, Trolley conductor. i, Air traffice controller.

Law & order: No. 2249: a, Postal inspector. b, Traffic cop. c, Private detectives. d, Highway patrol. e, Justice of the peace. f, Security guard. g, Judge and lawyer. h, Sheriff. i, Court stenographer.

Sports professionals: No. 2250: a, Basketball player. b, Referee. c, Track coach. d, Ice skater. e, Golfer and caddy. f, Sportscaster. g, Tennis champs. h, Football coach. i, Race car driver.

Scientists: No. 2251: a, Paleontologist. b, Archaeologist. c, Inventor. d, Astronaut. e, Chemist. f, Engineer. g, Computer graphics. h, Astronomer. i, Zoologist.

School of education, vert: No. 2252: a, Classroom teacher. b, Nursery school teacher. c, Band teacher. d, Electronic teacher. e, School psychologist. f, School principal. g, Professor. h, Graduate.

Sea & shore workers: No. 2253: a, Ship builders. b, Fisherman. c, Pearl diver. d, Underwater photographer. e, Bait & tackle shop owner. f, Bathing suit covergirls. g, Marine life painter. h, Lifeguard. i, Lighthouse keeper.

No. 2254, Donald in ice cream parlor. No. 2255, Goofy as an oceanographer. No. 2256, Grandma, Grandpa, Daisy Duck as jury, vert. No. 2257, Donald as deep sea treasure hunter, vert. No. 2258, Minnie as librarian, vert. No. 2259, Mickey, ducks, as cheerleaders, vert. No. 2260, Mickey as seaman, vert.

1996, Jan. 8 ***Perf. 14x13½, 13½x14***

Sheets of 9 or 8

2247	A334	10c	#a.-i.	.70	.70
2248	A334	50c	#a.-i.	3.50	3.50
2249	A334	75c	#a.-i.	5.00	5.00
2250	A334	90c	#a.-i.	6.00	6.00
2251	A334	95c	#a.-i.	6.50	6.50
2252	A334	$1.10	#a.-h.	6.75	6.75
2253	A334	$1.20	#a.-i.	8.25	8.25

Souvenir Sheets

2254-2260 A334 $6 each 4.50 4.50

#2248-2253 exist in sheets of 7 or 8 10c stamps + label. The label replaces the following stamps: #2248e, 2249e, 2250e, 2251e, 2252d, 2253e. The sheets had limited release on Dec. 3, 1996.

Miniature Sheets

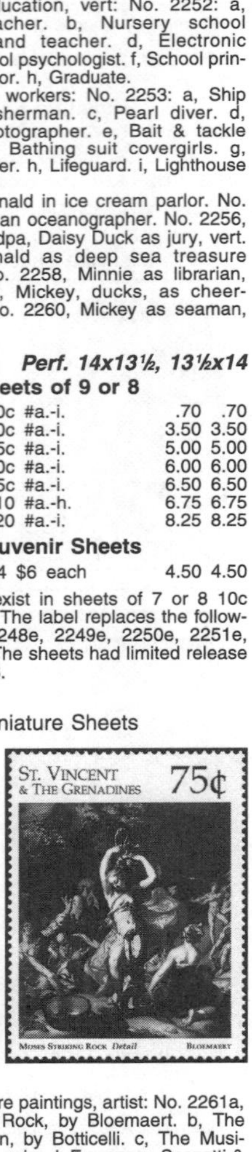

Paintings from Metropolitan Museum of Art — A335

Details or entire paintings, artist: No. 2261a, Moses Striking Rock, by Bloemaert. b, The Last Communion, by Botticelli. c, The Musicians, by Caravaggio. d, Francesco Sassetti & Son, by Ghirlandaio. e, Pepito Costa y Bunells, by Goya. f, Saint Andrew, by Martini. g, The Nativity, by a follower of van der Weyden. h, Christ Blessing, by Solario.

By Cézanne: No. 2262a, Madame Cézanne. b, Still Life with Apples and Pears. c, Man in a Straw Hat. d, Still Life with a Ginger Jar. e, Madame Cézanne in a Red Dress. f, Still Life. g, Dominique Aubert. h, Still Life, diff. i, The Card Players.

No. 2263a, Bullfight, by Goya. b, Portrait of a Man, by Frans Hals. c, Mother and Son, by Sully. d, Portrait of a Young Man, by Memling. e, Maltilde Stoughton de Jaudenes, by Stuart. f, Josef de Jaudenes y Nebot, by Stuart. g, Mont Sainte-Victore, by Cézanne. h, Gardanne, by Cézanne. i, The Empress Eugenie, by Winterhalter.

No. 2264a, The Dissolute Household, by Steen. b, Portrait of Gerard de Lairesse, by Rembrandt. c, Juan de Pareja, by Velázquez. d, Curiosity, by G. Ter Borch. e, The Companions of Rinaldo, by Poussin. f, Don Gaspar de Guzman, by Velázquez. g, Merry Company on a Terrace, by Steen. h, Pilate Washing Hands, by Rembrandt. i, Portrait of a Man, by Van Dyck.

No. 2265, Hagar in Wilderness, by Corot. No. 2266, Young Ladies from the Village, by Courbet. No. 2267, Two Young Peasant Women, by Pissaro. No. 2268, Allegory of the Planets and Continents, by Tiepolo.

1996, Feb. 1 **Litho.** ***Perf. 14***

Sheets of 8 or 9

2261	A335	75c	#a.-h.+label	4.50	4.50
2262	A335	90c	#a.-i.	6.00	6.00
2263	A335	$1	#a.-i.	6.75	6.75
2264	A335	$1.10	#a.-i.	7.50	7.50

Souvenir Sheets

2265-2268 A335 $6 each 4.50 4.50

Nos. 2265-2268 each contain one 81x53mm stamp.

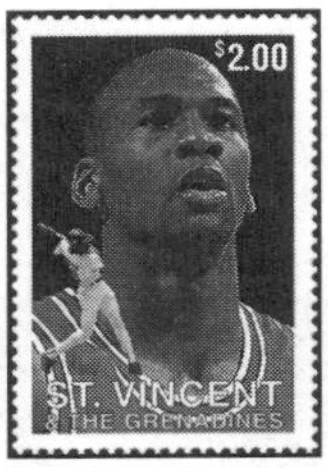

Michael Jordan, Basketball Player - A355a

Perf. 14, Imperf. (#2268Ac)

1996, Apr. 17 **Litho.**

2268A Sheet of 17, 16 #b, 1 #c 29.00 29.00

b.	A335a $2 shown	1.50	1.50
c.	A335a $6 Portrait, up close	4.50	4.50

No. 2268Ac is 68x100mm and has simulated perforations.

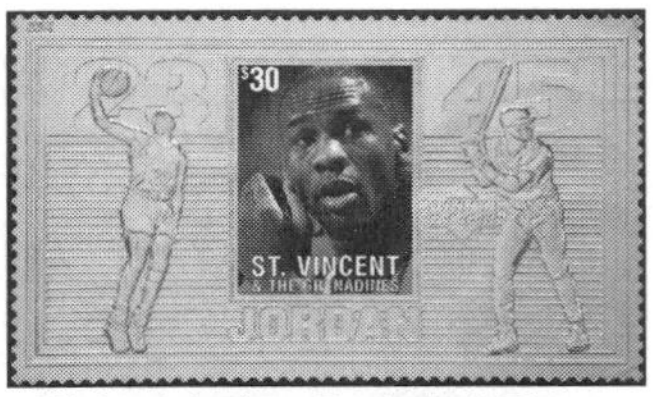

Michael Jordan, Basketball Player, Baseball Player — A335b

No. 2268E, Jordan as basketball player. Illustration reduced.

Litho. & Embossed

1996, Apr. 17 ***Perf. 9***

2268D A335b $30 gold & multi

2268E A335b $30 gold & multi

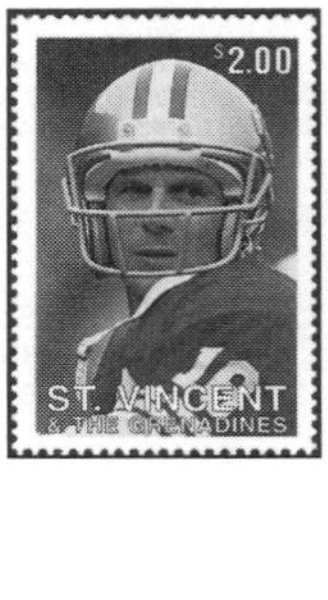

Joe Montana, Football Player — A335c

Perf. 14, Imperf. (#2268Fh)

1996, Apr. 17 **Litho.**

2268F Sheet of 17, 16 #g, 1 #h 29.00 29.00

g.	A335c $2 shown	1.50	1.50
h.	A335c $6 In action	4.50	4.50

No. 2268Fh is 68x100mm and has simulated perforations.

Joe Montana, Football Player — A335d

j, In red jersey. k, In white jersey.

1996, Apr. 17

Sheet of 2

2268I A335d $15 #j.-k., gold & multi

Lou Gehrig and Cal Ripken, Jr., Baseball Ironmen — A336

Illustration reduced.

1995 **Litho. & Embossed** ***Perf. 9***

2269 A336 $30 gold & multi

A336a

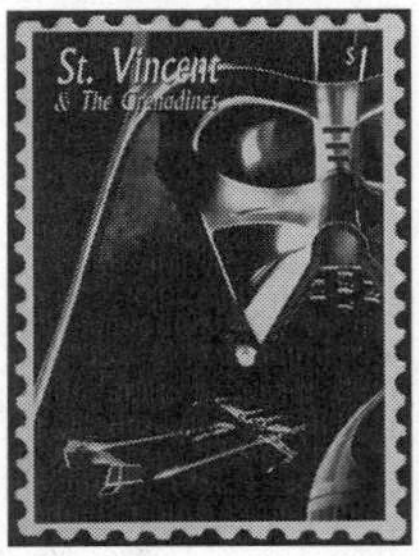

A337

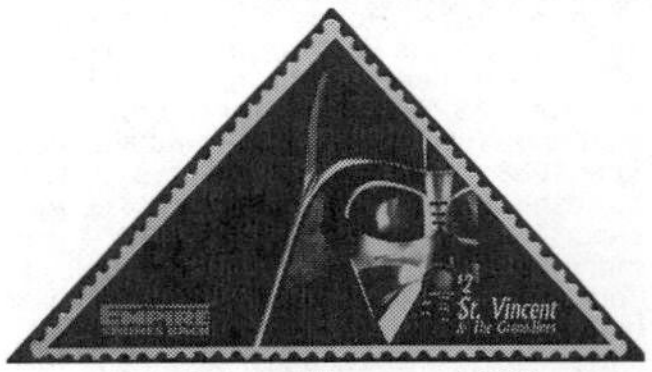

Star Wars Trilogy — A338

#2269: b, In Space Bar. c, Luke, Emperor. d, X-Wing Fighter. e, Star Destroyers. f, Cloud City. g, Speeders on Forest Moon.

Nos. 2270, 2273a, Darth Vader, "Star Wars," 1977. Nos. 2271, 2273c, Yoda, "Return of the Jedi," 1983. Nos. 2272, 2273b, Storm troopers, "The Empire Strikes Back," 1980.

No. 2274, Darth Vader, "Star Wars," 1977. No. 2275, Yoda, "Return of the Jedi," 1983. No. 2276, Storm Trooper, "The Empire Strikes Back," 1980.

Illustration A338 reduced.

1996, Mar. 19 **Litho.** ***Perf. 14***

2269A A336a 35c Sheet of 6, #b.-g. 1.60 1.60

Self-Adhesive

Serpentine Die Cut 6

2270	A337	$1	sil & multi	.75	.75
2271	A337	$1	sil & multi	.75	.75
2272	A337	$1	sil & multi	.75	.75

Souvenir Sheet

Serpentine Die Cut 9

2273 A338 $2 Sheet of 3, #a.-c. 4.50 4.50

Litho. & Embossed

Perf. 9

2274-2276 A337 $30 gold & multi

Nos. 2270-2272 were issued in sheets of 3 each arranged in alternating order.

Nos. 2274-2276 also exist in silver & multi.

Issued: Nos. 2274-2276, 11/18/95; others 3/19/96.

Butterflies — A339

70c, Anteos menippe. $1, Eunica alcmena. $1.10, Doxocopa lavinia. $2, Tithorea tarricina.

No. 2281: a, Papilio lycophron. b, Prepona buckleyana. c, Parides agavus. d, Papilio cacicus. e, Euryades duponchelli. f, Diaethria dymena. g, Orimba jansoni. h, Polystichtis siaka. i, Papilio machaonides.

$5, Adelpha abia. $6, Themone pais.

1996, Apr. 15 **Litho.** ***Perf. 14***

2277-2280 A339 Set of 4 3.60 3.60

2281 A339 90c Sheet of 9, #a.-i. 6.00 6.00

Souvenir Sheets

2282	A339	$5	multicolored	3.75	3.75
2283	A339	$6	multicolored	4.50	4.50

Queen Elizabeth II, 70th Birthday — A340

Designs: a, Portrait. b, In robes of Order of the Garter. c, Wearing red coat, hat.

$6, Waving from balcony, horiz.

1996, June 12 **Litho.** ***Perf. 13½x14***

2284 A340 $2 Strip of 3, #a.-c. 4.50 4.50

Souvenir Sheet

Perf. 14x13½

2285 A340 $6 multicolored 4.50 4.50

No. 2284 was issued in sheets of 9 stamps.

Birds A341

Designs: 60c, Coereba flaveola. $1, Myadestes genibarbis. $1.10, Tangara cucullata. $2, Eulampis jugularis.

No. 2290: a, Progne subis. b, Buteo platypterus. c, Phaethon lepturus. d, Himantopus himantopus. e, Sterna anaethetus. f, Euphonia musica. g, Arenaria interpres. h, Sericotes holosericeus. i, Nyctanassa violacea.

$5, Dendrocygna autumnalis, vert.. $6, Amazona guildingii.

1996, July 11 ***Perf. 14***

2286-2289 A341 Set of 4, vert. 3.50 3.50

Miniature Sheet

2290 A341 $1 Sheet of 9, #a.-i. 6.80 6.80

Souvenir Sheets

2291	A341	$5	multi, vert.	3.80	3.80
2292	A341	$6	multi, vert.	4.50	4.50

Radio, Cent. A342

Entertainers: 90c, Walter Winchell. $1, Fred Allen. $1.10, Hedda Hopper. $2, Eve Arden. $6, Major Bowes.

1996, July 11 ***Perf. 13½x14***
2293-2296 A342 Set of 4 3.75 3.75

Souvenir Sheet

2297 A342 $6 multicolored 4.50 4.50

UNICEF, 50th Anniv. A343

Designs: $1, Boy raising arm. $1.10, Children reading. $2, Girl, microscope. $5, Boy.

1996, July 11 ***Perf. 14***
2298-2300 A343 Set of 3 3.25 3.25

Souvenir Sheet

2301 A343 $5 multicolored 3.80 3.80

Chinese Animated Films — A344

Nos. 2302, 2304: Various characters from "Uproar in Heaven."
Nos. 2303, 2305: Various characters from "Nezha Conquers the Dragon King."

1996, May 10 **Litho.** ***Perf. 12***

Strips of 5

2302-2303 A344 15c #a.-e., each .55 .55

Souvenir Sheets

2304-2305 A344 75c vert., each .55 .55

Nos. 2302-2303 each were issued in a sheet of 10 stamps. CHINA '96, 9th Asian Intl. Philatelic Exhibition.

Jerusalem, 3000th Anniv. — A345

Designs: $1, Knesset. $1.10, Montefiore Windmill. $2, Shrine of the Book. $5, Jerusalem of Gold.

1996, July 11 **Litho.** ***Perf. 14***
2306-2308 A345 Set of 3 3.25 3.25

Souvenir Sheet

2309 A345 $5 multicolored 3.75 3.75

1996 Summer Olympic Games, Atlanta A346

20c, Maurice King, weight lifter, vert. 70c, Eswort Coombs, 400-meter relay, vert. No. 2312, 90c, Runners, Olympia, 530BC. No. 2313, 90c, Pamenos Ballantyne, Benedict Ballantyne, runners, vert. $1, London landmarks, 1908 Olympics, Great Britain. No. 2315, $1.10, Rodney "Chang" Jack, soccer player, vert. No. 2316, $1.10, Dorando Pietri, marathon runner, London, 1908, vert. $2, Yachting.
Past winners, event: No. 2318, vert: a, Vitaly Shcherbo, gymnastics. b, Fu Mingxia, diving. c, Wilma Rudolph, track & field. d, Rafer Johnson, decathlon. e, Teofilo Stevenson, boxing. f, Babe Didrikson, track & field. g, Kyoko Iwasaki, swimming. h, Yoo Namkyu, table tennis. i, Michael Gross, swimming.
No. 2319: a, Chuhei Nambu, triple jump. b, Duncan McNaughton, high jump. c, Jack Kelly, single sculls. d, Jackie Joyner-Kersee, heptathlon. e, Tyrell Biggs, boxing. f, Larisa Latynina, gymnastics. g, Bob Garrett, discus. h, Paavo Nurmi, 5000-meters. i, Eric Lemming, javelin.
No. 2320: a, Yasuhiro Yamashita, judo. b, Peter Rono, 1500-meters. c, Aleksandr Kourlovitch, weight lifting. d, Juha Tiainen, hammer throw. e, Sergei Bubka, pole vault. f, Q. F. Newall, women's archery. g, Nadia Comaneci, gymnastics. h, Carl Lewis, long jump. i, Bob Mathias, decathlon.
Sporting events, vert.: No. 2321a, Women's archery. b, Gymnastics. c, Basketball. d, Soccer. e, Water polo. f, Baseball. g, Kayak. h, Fencing. i, Cycling.
No. 2322, Olympic Flag. No. 2323, Carl Lewis, runner, vert. No. 2324, Alexander Ditiatin, gymnastics, 1980. No. 2325, Hannes Kolehmainen, marathon runner.

1996, July 19
2310-2317 A346 Set of 8 6.00 6.00

Sheets of 9

2318-2321 A346 $1 #a.-i., each 6.75 6.75

Souvenir Sheets

2322-2325 A346 $5 each 3.75 3.75

St. Vincent Olympic Committee (#2310-2311, 2313, 2315).

Disney's "The Hunchback of Notre Dame" A347

No. 2326: a, Quasimodo. b, Phoebus. c, Laverne, Hugo. d, Clopin. e, Frollo. f, Esmeralda. g, Victor. h, Djali.
No. 2327, Esmeralda, Quasimodo, horiz. No. 2328, Esmeralda, Phoebus, horiz.

1996, July 25 ***Perf. 13½x14***
2326 A347 $1 Sheet of 8, #a.-h. 6.00 6.00

Souvenir Sheets

Perf. 14X13½

2327-2328 A347 $6 each 4.50 4.50

Fish A348

Designs: 70c, French angelfish. 90c, Red-spotted hawkfish. $1.10, Spiny puffer. $2, Gray triggerfish.
No. 2333: a, Barred hamlet. b, Flamefish. c, Longsnout butterflyfish. d, Fairy basslet. e, Redtail parrotfish. f, Blackbar soldierfish. g, Threespot damselfish. h, Candy basslet. i, Spotfin hogfish.
No. 2334: a, Equetus lanceolatus. b, Acanthurus coeruleus. c, Lutjanus analis. d, Hippocampus hudsonius. e, Serranus annularis. f, Squatina dumerili. g, Muraena miliaris. h, Bolbometopon bicolor. i, Tritonium nodiferum.
$5, Queen triggerfish. $6, Blue marlin.

1996, Aug. 10 ***Perf. 14***
2329-2332 A348 Set of 4 3.60 3.60

Sheets of 9

2333-2334 A348 $1 #a.-i., each 6.75 6.75

Souvenir Sheets

2335 A348 $5 multicolored 3.75 3.75
2336 A348 $6 multicolored 4.50 4.50

Flowers A349

70c, Beloperone guttata. $1, Epidendrum elongatum. $1.10, Pettrea volubilis. $2, Oncidium altrissimum.
No. 2341: a, Datura candida. b, Amherstia nobilis. c, Ipomoea acuminata. d, Bougainvillea glabra. e, Cassia alata. f, Cordia sebestena. g, Opuntia dilenii. h, Cryptostegia grandiflora. i, Rodriguezia lanceolata.
No. 2342, Acalypha hispida. No. 2343, Hibiscus rosa-sinensis.

1996, Aug. 15
2337-2340 A349 Set of 4 3.60 3.60
2341 A349 90c Sheet of 9, #a.-i. 6.00 6.00

Souvenir Sheets

2342 A349 $5 multicolored 3.75 3.75

Perf. 14x13½

2343 A349 $5 multicolored 3.75 3.75

John F. Kennedy (1917-63) — A350

No. 2344a: , As young boy. b, Proclamation to send man to the moon. c, With Caroline, Jackie. d, Inauguration. e, Giving speech. f, On PT 109. g, With Jackie. h, Funeral procession, portrait. i, Guard, Eternal Flame.
No. 2345: a, With family on yacht. b, On yacht. c, On yacht holding sail. d, "JFK," portrait. e, Talking to astronauts in space. f, Younger picture in uniform. g, Portrait. h, Riding in motorcade. i, Giving speech, US flag.
No. 2346: a, Up close picture. b, In front of house at Hyannis Port. c, Memorial plaque, picture. d, Photograph among crowd. e, Portrait, flag. f, Rocket, portrait. g, Signing document. h, Martin Luther King, John F. Kennedy, Robert F. Kennedy. i, Painting looking down toward microphones.
No. 2347: a, Photograph with Jacqueline greeting people. b, Formal oval-shaped portrait. c, Photograph. d, With family. e, Space capsule, painting. f, Addressing UN. g, In rocking chair. h, Seated at desk, dignitaries. i, Holding telephone, map.

1996, Aug. ***Perf. 14x13½***

Sheets of 9

2344-2347 A350 $1 #a.-i., each 6.75 6.75

Ships A351

No. 2348: a, SS Doric, 1923, Great Britain. b, SS Nerissa, 1926, Great Britain. c, SS Howick Hall, 1910, Great Britain. d, SS Jervis Bay, 1922, Great Britain. e, SS Vauban, 1912, Great Britain. f, MV Orinoco, 1928, Germany.
No. 2349: a, SS Lady Rodney, 1929, Canada. b, SS Empress of Russia, 1913, Canada. c, SS Providence, 1914, France. d, SS Reina Victori-Eugenia, 1913, Spain. e, SS Balmoral Castle, 1910, Great Britain. f, SS Tivives, 1911, US.
No. 2350, SS Imperator, 1913, Germany. No. 2351, SS Aquitania, 1914, Great Britain.

1996, Sept. 5 ***Perf. 14***

Sheets of 6

2348-2349 A351 $1.10 #a.-f., ea 5.00 5.00

Souvenir Sheets

2350-2351 A351 $6 each 4.50 4.50

Elvis Presley's 1st "Hit" Year, 40th Anniv. A352

Various portraits.

1996, Sept. 8 ***Perf. 13½x14***
2352 A352 $2 Sheet of 6, #a.-f. 9.00 9.00

Richard Petty, NASCAR Driving Champion — A353

a, 1990 Pontiac. b, Richard Petty. c, 1972 Plymouth. d, 1974 Dodge.
$5, 1970 Plymouth Superbird. $6, 1996 STP 25th Anniversary Pontiac.

1996, Sept. 26 ***Perf. 14***
2353 A353 $2 Sheet of 4, #a.-d. 6.00 6.00

Souvenir Sheets

2354 A353 $5 multicolored 3.75 3.75
2355 A353 $6 multicolored 4.50 4.50

No. 2354 contains one 85x28mm stamp.

Sandy Koufax, Baseball Pitcher — A354

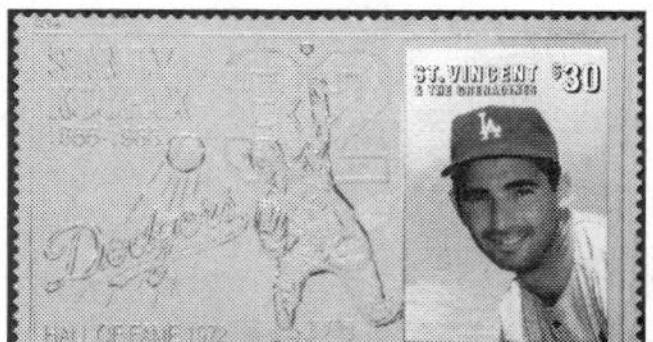

A354a

No. 2356: a.-c., Various action shots. Illustration A354a reduced.

Perf. 14, Imperf. (#2356d)

1996, Sept. 26

2356	Sheet of 17	28.50	28.50
a.-c.	A354 $2 each	1.50	1.50
d.	A354 $6 Portrait	4.50	4.50

Litho. & Embossed

Perf. 9

2356E A354a $30 gold & multi

No. 2356 contains 6 #2356a, 5 each #2356b, 2356c and 1 #2356d. No. 2356d is 70x103mm and has simulated perforations.

Cadet Force, 60th Anniv. — A355

Insignia and: 70c, 2nd Lt. D.S. Cozier, founder. 90c, Cozier, first 12 cadets, 1936.

1996, Oct. 23 Litho. *Perf. 14x13½*

2357 A355 70c multicolored .55 .55
2358 A355 90c multicolored .70 .70

Christmas A356

Details or entire paintings: 70c, Virgin and Child, by Memling. 90c, St. Anthony, by Memling. $1, Madonna and Child, by Bouts. $1.10, Virgin and Child, by Lorenzo Lotto. $2, St. Roch, by Lotto. $5, St. Sebastian, by Lotto.

No. 2365, Virgin and Child with St. Roch and St. Sebastian, by Lotto. No. 2366, Virgin and Child with St. Anthony and a Donor, by Memling.

1996, Nov. 14 *Perf. 13½x14*

2359-2364 A356 Set of 6 8.00 8.00

Souvenir Sheets

2365-2366 A356 $5 each 3.75 3.75

Disney's "The Hunchback of Notre Dame" — A357

Designs: Various scenes from film.

No. 2370, Quasimodo, Phoebus, Esmeralda. No. 2371, Esmeralda, vert. No. 2372, Quasimodo, citizens, vert.

1996, Dec. 12 Litho. *Perf. 13½x14*

2367 A357 10c Sheet of 6, #a.-f., vert. .45 .45

Perf. 14x13½

2368 A357 30c Sheet of 9, #a.-i. 2.00 2.00
2369 A357 $1 Sheet of 9, #a.-i. 6.75 6.75

Souvenir Sheets

2370-2372 A357 $6 each 4.50 4.50

Sylvester Stallone in Movie "Rocky IV" — A358

1996 Litho. *Perf. 14*

2373 A358 $2 Sheet of 3 4.50 4.50

A359

New Year 1997 (Year of the Ox) — A359a

Stylized oxen, Chinese inscriptions within checkered squares: Nos. 2374a, 2375a, pale orange, pale lilac & black. Nos. 2374b, 2375b, green, violet & black. Nos. 2374c, 2375c, tan, pink & black.

Illustration A359a reduced.

1997, Jan. 2 *Perf. 14½*

2374 A359 75c Strip of 3, #a.-c. 1.70 1.70
2375 A359 $1 Sheet of 3, #a.-c. 2.25 2.25

Souvenir Sheet

2376 A359 $2 orange, yellow & blk 1.50 1.50

Litho. & Embossed

Perf. 9

2376A A359a $30 gold & multi

No. 2374 was issued in sheets of 9 stamps.

Star Trek Voyager A360

No. 2377: a, Lt. Tuvak. b, Kes. c, Lt. Paris. d, The Doctor. e, Capt. Janeway. f, Lt. Torres. g, Neelix. h, Ens. Kim. i, Cdr. Chakotay.

$6, Cast of characters.

1997, Jan. 23 Litho. *Perf. 14*

2377 A360 $2 Sheet of 9, #a.-i. 13.50 13.50

Souvenir Sheet

2378 A360 $2 multicolored 4.50 4.50

No. 2378 contains one 29x47mm stamp.

A361

A362

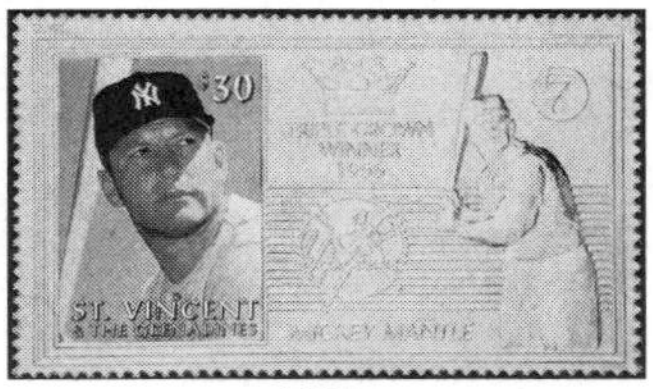

A361a

Mickey Mantle (1931-95), baseball player.

Illustration A361a reduced.

Perf. 14, Imperf. (#2379b)

1997, Jan. 23

2379 Sheet of 17, 16 #2379a, 1 #2379b 28.50 28.50
a. A361 $2 shown 1.50 1.50
b. A361 $6 Portrait holding bat 4.50 4.50

Litho. & Embossed

Perf. 9

2379C A361a $30 gold & multi

No. 2379b is 70x100mm.

Perf. 14x14½, Imperf. (#2380q)

1997, Jan. 23

Black Baseball Players: a, Frank Robinson. b, Satchel Paige. c, Billy Williams. d, Reggie Jackson. e, Roberto Clemente. f, Ernie Banks. g, Hank Aaron. h, Roy Campanella. i, Willie McCovey. j, Monte Irvin. k, Willie Stargell. l, Rod Carew. m, Ferguson Jenkins. n, Bob Gibson. o, Lou Brock. p, Joe Morgan. q, Jackie Robinson.

2380 Sheet of 17 16.50 16.50
a.-p. A362 $1 each .75 .75
q. A362 $6 Portrait 4.50 4.50

No. 2380q is 66x100mm and has simulated perforations.

Souvenir Sheet

Chongqing Dazu Stone Carving — A363

Illustration reduced.

1996, May 20 Litho. *Perf. 12*

2381 A363 $2 multicolored 1.50 1.50

China '96.

No. 2381 was not available until March 1997.

Hong Kong Changeover — A364

A364a

Flags of Great Britain, Peoples' Republic of China and panoramic view of Hong Kong: Nos. 2382a-2382e, In daytime. Nos. 2382f-2382j, At night.

Market scene: No. 2383: a, Vendors, corner of building. b, People strolling. c, Man choosing items to purchase.

Buddhist religious ceremony: No. 2384a, Fruit, incense pot, torch. b, Monk at fire. c, Flower.

Lantern ceremony: No. 2385: a, Boy, girl. b, Couple on bridge. c, Girls with lanterns.

Illustration A364a reduced.

1997, Feb. 12 *Perf. 14*

2382 A364 90c Sheet of 10, #a.-j. 6.75 6.75

Sheets of 3

Perf. 13

2383-2385 A364 $2 #a.-c., ea 4.50 4.50

Litho. & Embossed

Perf. 9

2385D A364a $30 gold & multi

Hong Kong '97.

Nos. 2383-2385 each contain 3 35x26mm stamps.

UNESCO, 50th Anniv. — A365

World Heritage Sites: 70c, Lord Howe Islands, Australia, vert. 90c, Uluru-Kata Tjuta Natl. Park, Australia, vert. $1, Kakadu Natl. Park, Australia, vert. $1.10, Te Wahipounamu, New Zealand, vert. $2, $5, vert., Tongariro Natl. Park, New Zealand.

Various sites in Greece, vert - #2392: a, Monastery of Rossanou, Meteora. b, f, h, Painted ceiling, interior, Mount Athos Monastery. c, Monastery Osios Varlaam, Meteora. d, Ruins in Athens. e, Museum of the Acropolis. g, Mount Athos.

Various sites in Japan, vert - #2393: a, Himeji-Jo. b, Temple Lake, Gardens, Kyoto. c, Kyoto. d, Buddhist Temple of Ninna-Ji. e, View of city of Himeji-Jo. f, Forest, Shirakami-Sanchi. g, h, Forest, Yakushima.

No. 2394, vert: a, City of San Gimignano, Italy. b, Cathedral of Santa Maria Asunta, Pisa, Italy. c, Cathedral of Santa Maria Fiore, Florence, Italy. d, Archaeological site, Valley of the Boyne, Ireland. e, Church of Saint-Savin-Sur-Gartempe, France. f, g, h, City of Bath, England.

No. 2395: a, Trinidad, Valley de los Ingenios, Cuba. b, City of Zacatecas, Mexico. c, Lima, Peru. d, Ruins of Monastery, Paraguay. e, Mayan Ruins, Copan, Honduras.

Various sites in China - No. 2396: a, Palace, Wudang Mountains, Hubei Province. b, Cave Sanctuaries, Mogao. c, House, Desert of Taklamakan. d, e, Great Wall.

Nos. 2397a-2397e: Various sites in Quedlinberg, Germany.

No. 2398, Monastery of Meteora, Greece. No. 2399, Wailing Wall, Jerusalem. No. 2400, Quedlinburg, Germany. No. 2401, Oasis, Dunbuang, China. No. 2402, Himeji-Jo, Japan. No. 2403, Great Wall, China. No. 2404, City of Venice, Italy.

Perf. 13½x14, 14x13½

1997, Mar. 24 Litho.

2386-2391 A365 Set of 6 8.00 8.00

Sheets of 8 + Label

2392-2394 A365 $1.10 #a.-h., ea 6.60 6.60

Sheets of 5 + Label

2395-2397 A365 $1.50 #a.-e., ea 5.75 5.75

Souvenir Sheets

2398-2404 A365 $5 each 3.75 3.75

Telecommunications in St. Vincent, 125th Anniv. — A366

Designs: 5c, Microwave radio relay tower, Dorsetshire Hill. 10c, Cable & wireless headquarters, Kingstown. 20c, Microwave relay tower, vert. 35c, Cable & wireless complex, Arnos Vale. 50c, Cable & wireless tower, Mt. St. Andrew. 70c, Cable ship. 90c, Eastern telecommunication network, 1872. $1.10, Telegraph map of world, 1876.

Perf. 14x14½, 14½x14

1997, Apr. 3 Litho.

2405-2412 A366 Set of 8 3.00 3.00

Birds of the World — A367 Water Birds — A368

Designs: 60c, Smooth-billed ani. 70c, Belted kingfisher. 90c, Blackburnian warbler. $1.10, Blue tit. $2, Chaffinch. $5, Ruddy turnstone.

No. 2419: a, Blue grosbeak. b, Bananaquit. c, Cedar waxwing. d, Ovenbird. e, Hooded warbler. f, Flicker.

No. 2420: a, Song thrush. b, Robin. c, Blackbird. d, Great spotted woodpecker. e, Wren. f, Kingfisher.

No. 2421, St. Vincent parrot. No. 2422, Tawny owl.

1997, Apr. 7 ***Perf. 14***

2413-2418 A367 Set of 6 7.75 7.75
2419 A367 $1 Sheet of 6, #a.-f. 4.50 4.50
2420 A367 $2 Sheet of 6, #a.-f. 9.00 9.00

Souvenir Sheets

2421-2422 A367 $5 each 3.75 3.75

1997, Apr. 7 ***Perf. 15***

Designs: 70c, Mandarin duck, horiz. 90c, Green heron, horiz. $1, Drake ringed teal, horiz. $1.10, Blue-footed boobies, horiz. $2, Australian jacana. $5, Reddish egret.

No. 2429: a, Crested auklet. b, Whiskered auklet. c, Pigeon guillemot. d, Adelie penguins. e, Rockhopper penguin. f, Emperor penguin.

No. 2430, Snowy egrets, horiz. No. 2431, Flamingos, horiz.

2423-2428 A368 Set of 6 8.00 8.00
2429 A368 $1.10 Sheet of 6, #a.-f. 5.00 5.00

Souvenir Sheet

2430-2431 A368 $5 each 3.75 3.75

Jackie Robinson (1919-72) A369

A369a

Illustration A369a reduced.

Serpentine Die Cut 7

1997, Jan. 23 **Litho.**

Self-Adhesive

2432 A369 $1 multicolored .75 .75

Litho. & Embossed

Perf. 9

2432A A369a $30 gold & multi

No. 2432 was issued in sheets of 3 and was not available until June 1997.

Queen Elizabeth II, Prince Philip, 50th Wedding Anniv. A370

No. 2433: a, Queen. b, Royal arms. c, Portrait of Queen, Prince. d, Queen, Prince, crowd. e, Buckingham Palace. f, Prince.

$5, Queen seated in wedding gown, crown.

1997, June 3 **Litho.** ***Perf. 14***

2433 A370 $1.10 Sheet of 6, #a.-f. 5.00 5.00

Souvenir Sheet

2434 A370 $5 multicolored 3.75 3.75

Paintings by Hiroshige (1797-1858) A371

No. 2435: a, Furukawa River, Hiroo. b, Chiyogaike Pond, Meguro. c, New Fuji, Meguro. d, Moon-Viewing Point. e, Ushimachi, Takanawa. f, Original Fuji, Meguro.

No. 2436, Gotenyama, Shinagawa. No. 2437, Shinagawa Susaki.

1997, June 3 ***Perf. 13½x14***

2435 A371 $1.50 Sheet of 6, #a.-f. 6.75 6.75

Souvenir Sheets

2436-2437 A371 $5 each 4.50 4.50

Paul Harris (1868-1947), Founder of Rotary Intl. — A372

$2, World Community Service, blankets from Japan donated to Thai children, Harris.

$5, Rotary Intl. Pres. Luis Vincente Giay, US Pres. Jimmy Carter, Rotary award recipient.

1997, June 3 ***Perf. 14***

2438 A372 $2 multicolored 1.50 1.50

Souvenir Sheet

2439 A372 $5 multicolored 3.75 3.75

Heinrich von Stephan (1831-97) A373

Portraits of Von Stephan and: a, Bicycle postman, India, 1800's. b, UPU emblem. c, Zebu-drawn post carriage, Indochina.

$5, Post rider, Indochina.

1997, June 3

2440 A373 $2 Sheet of 3, #a.-c. 4.50 4.50

Souvenir Sheet

2441 A373 $5 gray brown 3.75 3.75

PACIFIC 97.

Chernobyl Disaster, 10th Anniv. A374

Designs: No. 2442, Chabad's Children of Chernobyl. No. 2443, UNESCO.

1997, June 3 **Litho.** ***Perf. 13½x14***

2442 A374 $2 multicolored 1.50 1.50
2443 A374 $2 multicolored 1.50 1.50

Grimm's Fairy Tales A375

Mother Goose — A376

Scenes showing "Old Sultan:" No. 2444: a, With woman, man. b, On hillside. c, With wolf. No. 2446, Man, Old Sultan, girl.

Scenes from "The Cobbler and the Elves:" No. 2445: a, Cobbler. b, Elves. c, Cobbler holding elf. No. 2447, Elf.

No. 2448, Curly-Locks sewing.

1997, June 3 ***Perf. 13½x14***

Sheets of 3

2444-2445 A375 $2 #a.-c., each 4.50 4.50

Souvenir Sheets

2446-2447 A375 $5 each 3.75 3.75

Perf. 14

2448 A376 $5 multicolored 3.75 3.75

Numbers have been reserved for two additional souvenir sheets with this set.

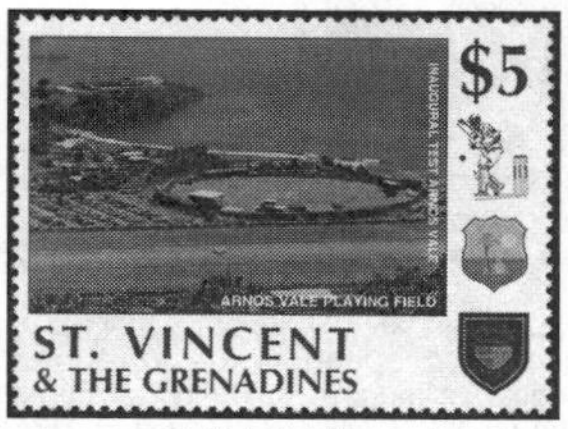

Inaugural Cricket Test, Arnos Vale — A377

Designs: 90c, Alphonso Theodore Roberts (1937-96), vert. $5, Arnos Vale Playing field.

Perf. 13½x14, 14x13½

1997, June 20 **Litho.**

2451 A377 90c multicolored .70 .70
2452 A377 $5 multicolored 3.75 3.75

1998 World Cup Soccer Championships, France — A378

Players: 70c, Beckenbauer, W. Germany. 90c, Moore, England. $1, Lato, Poland. $1.10, Pele, Brazil. $2, Maier, W. Germany. $10, Eusebio, Portugal.

Scenes from England's victory, 1966: No. 2459: a, Stadium. b, c, d, e, f, h, Various action scenes. g, Coming from field, holding trophy.

Action scenes from various finals: No 2460: a, c, Argentina, W. Germany, 1986. b, e, England, W. Germany, 1966. d, Italy, W. Germany, 1982. f, g, Argentina, Holland, 1978. h, W. Germany, Holland, 1974.

Players, vert.: No. 2461: a, Bergkamp, Holland. b, Seaman, England. c, Schmeichel, Denmark. d, Ince, England. e, Futre, Portugal. f, Ravanelli, Italy. g, Keane, Ireland. h, Gascoigne, England.

Action scenes from Argentina v. Holland, 1978, vert.: No. 2462a-2462h.

No. 2463, Ally McCoist, Scotland, vert. No. 2464, Salvatori Schillaci, Italy, vert. No. 2465, Mario Kempes, Argentina, vert. No. 2466, Paulao, Angola.

Perf. 14x13½, 13½x14

1997, Aug. 26 **Litho.**

2453-2458 A378 Set of 6 4.25 4.25

Sheets of 8 + Label

2459-2462 A378 $1 #a.-h., each 6.00 6.00

Souvenir Sheets

2463-2466 A378 $5 each 3.75 3.75

Vincy Mas Carnival, 20th Anniv. A379

10c, Mardi Gras Band, "Cinemas." 20c, Queen of the Bands, J. Ballantyne. 50c, Queen of the Bands, vert. 70c, King of the Bands, "Conquistadore." 90c, Starlift Steel Orchestra, Panorama Champs. $2, Frankie McIntosh, musical arranger, vert.

1997, July 24 ***Perf. 14½x14, 14x14½***

2467-2472 A379 Set of 6 3.30 3.30

Sierra Club, Cent. A380

No. 2473: a, Snow leopard. b, Polar bear. c, d, Isle Royale Natl. Park. e, f, Denali Natl. Park. g, h, i, Joshua Tree Natl. Park.

No. 2474, vert: a, b, c, Mountain gorilla. d, e, Snow leopard. f, g, Polar bear. h, Denali Natl. Park. i, Isle Royale Nat. Park.

No. 2475, vert: a, b, c, Sifaka. d, e, Peregrine falcon. f, Galapagos tortoise. g, h, African Rain Forest. i, China's Yellow Mountains.

No. 2476: a, b, c, Red panda. d, Peregrine falcon. e, f, Galapagos tortoise. g, African Rain Forest. h, i, China's Yellow Mountains.

No. 2477: a, Mountain lion. b, c, Siberian tiger. d, Red wolf. e, Black bear. f, i, Wolong Natl. Reserve. g, h, Belize Rain Forest.

No. 2478, vert: a, Siberian tiger. b, c, Mountain lion. d, e, Black bear. f, g, Red wolf. h, Belize Rain Forest. i, Wolong Natl. Reserve.

No. 2479, vert: a, b, c, Indri. d, e, Gopher tortoise. f, g, Black-footed ferret. h, Haleakala Natl. Park. i, Grand Teton Natl. Park.

No. 2480: a, Black-footed ferret. b, Gopher tortoise. c, d, Grand Teton Natl. Park. e, f, Haleakala Natl. Park. g, h, i, Madagascar Rain Forest.

Scenes in Olympic Natl. Park: No. 2481, Lake, trees. No. 2482, Mountain summit. No. 2483, Snow-topped mountains.

1997, Sept. 18 ***Perf. 14***

Sheets of 9

2473 A380 20c #a.-i. 1.40 1.40
2474 A380 40c #a.-i. 2.75 2.75
2475 A380 50c #a.-i. 3.40 3.40
2476 A380 60c #a.-i. 4.00 4.00
2477 A380 70c #a.-i. 4.75 4.75
2478 A390 90c #a.-i. 6.00 6.00
2479 A380 $1 #a.-i. 6.75 6.75
2480 A380 $1.10 #a.-i. 7.50 7.50

Souvenir Sheets

2481-2483 A380 $5 each 3.75 3.75

Deng Xiaoping (1904-97), Chinese Leader — A381

Various portraits: No. 2484, Dark brown. No. 2485, Dark blue. No. 2486, Black.
No. 2487, Deng Xiaoping, Zhuo Lin, horiz.

1997, June 3 Litho. *Perf. 14*

Sheets of 4

2484-2486 A381 $2 #a.-d., each 6.00 6.00

Souvenir Sheet

2487 A381 $5 multicolored 3.75 3.75

Montreal Protocol on Substances that Deplete Ozone Layer, 10th Anniv. — A382

1997, Sept. 16

2488 A382 90c multicolored .70 .70

A383

A384

Orchids: 90c, Rhyncholaelia digbyana. $1, Laeliocattleya. $1.10, Doritis pulcherrima. $2, Phalaenopsis.

No. 2493: a, Eulophia speciosa. b, Aerangis rhodosticta. c, Angraecum infundibularea. d, Calanthe sylvatica. e, Phalaenopsis mariae. f, Paphiopedilum insigne. g, Dendrobium nobile. h, Aerangis kotschyana. i, Cyrtorchis chailluana.

No. 2494, Brassavola nodosa. No. 2495, Sanguine broughtonia.

1997, Sept. 18

2489-2492 A383 Set of 4 3.75 3.75
2493 A383 $1 Sheet of 9, #a.-i. 6.75 6.75

Souvenir Sheets

2494-2495 A383 $5 each 3.75 3.75

Nos. 2494-2495 each contain one 51x38mm stamp.

1997

Close-up portraits: No. 2496: a, Wearing tiara. b, Black dress. c, Blue dress. d, Denomination in black.

No. 2497: a, White collar. b, Sleeveless. c, Black dress, holding flowers. d, Blue collar, flowers.

No. 2498, Blue dress. No. 2499, White collar.

Sheets of 4

2496-2497 A384 $2 #a.-d., each 6.00 6.00

Souvenir Sheets

2498-2499 A384 $6 each 3.75 3.75

Diana, Princess of Wales (1961-97).

Sinking of RMS Titanic, 85th Anniv. — A385

Sections of the ship: a, 1st funnel. b, 2nd, 3rd funnels. c, 4th funnel. d, Upper decks. e, Stern.

1997, Nov. 5 Litho. *Perf. 14*

2500 A385 $1 Sheet of 5, #a.-e. 3.75 3.75

A386

A387

1997 Inductions, Rock & Roll Hall of Fame, Cleveland, OH: $1, Exterior view. $1.50, Stylized guitar, "the house that rock built."

1997, Nov. 5

2501 A386 $1 multicolored .75 .75
2502 A386 $1.50 multicolored 1.15 1.15

Nos. 2501-2502 were each issued in sheets of 8.

1997, Nov. 5

"The Doors" album covers: 90c, Morrison Hotel, 1970. 95c, Waiting for the Sun, 1968. $1, L.A. Woman, 1971. $1.10, The Soft Parade, 1969. $1.20, Strange Days, 1967. $1.50, The Doors, 1967.

2503-2508 A387 Set of 6 5.00 5.00

Nos. 2503-2508 were each issued in sheets of 8.

20th Cent. Artists — A388

Opera singers: No. 2509: a, Lily Pons (1904-76). b, Donizetti's "Lucia Di Lammermoor," Lily Pons. c, Bellini's "I Puritani," Maria Callas. d, Callas (1923-77). e, Beverly Sills (b. 1929). f, Donizetti's "Daughter of the Regiment," Sills. g, Schoenberg's "Erwartung," Jessye Norman. h, Norman (b.1945).

No. 2510: a, Enrico Caruso (1873-1921). b, Verdi's "Rigoletto," Caruso. c, "The Seven Hills of Rome," Mario Lanza. d, Lanza (1921-59). e, Luciano Pavarotti (b. 1935). f, Donizetti's "Elixer of Love," Pavarotti. g, Puccini's "Tosca," Placido Domingo. h, Domingo (b. 1941).

Artists, sculptures: No. 2511: a, Constantin Brancusi (1876-1957). b, "The New Born," Brancusi, 1920. c, "Four Elements," Alexander Calder, 1962. d, Calder (1898-1976). e, Isamu Noguchi (1904-88). f, "Dodge Fountain," Noguchi, 1975. g, "The Shuttlecock," Claes Oldenburg, 1994. h, Oldenburg (b. 1929).

1997, Nov. 5

Sheets of 8

2509-2511 A388 $1.10 #a.-h., ea 6.50 6.50

Size: Nos. 2509b-2509c, 2509f-2509g, 2510b-2510c, 2510f-2510g, 2511b-2511c, 2511f-2511g, 53x38mm.

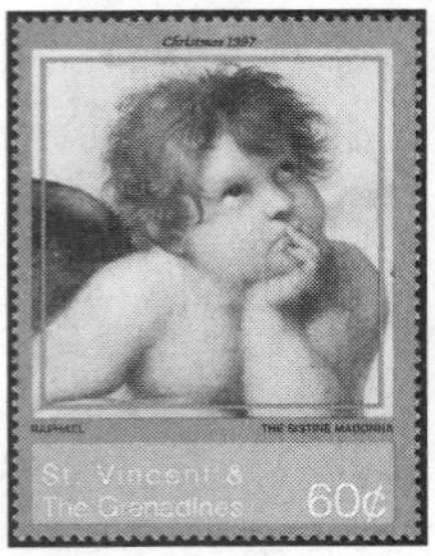

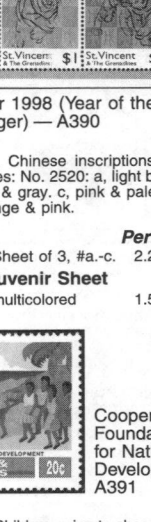

Christmas A389

Paintings (entire or details), or sculptures: 60c, The Sistine Madonna, by Raphael. 70c, Angel, by Edward Burne-Jones. 90c, Cupid, by Etienne-Maurice Flaconet. $1, Saint Michael, by Hubert Gerhard. $1.10, Apollo and the Horae, by Tiepolo. $2, Madonna in a Garland of Flowers, by Rubens and Bruegel the Elder.

No. 2518, The Sacrifice of Isaac, by Tiepolo, horiz. No. 2519, Madonna in a Garland of Flowers, by Rubens and Bruegel the Elder.

1997, Nov. 26

2512-2517 A389 Set of 6 6.25 6.25

Souvenir Sheets

2518-2519 A389 $5 each 3.75 3.75

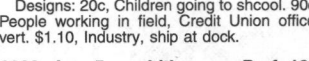

New Year 1998 (Year of the Tiger) — A390

Stylized tigers, Chinese inscriptions within checkered squares: No. 2520: a, light brown & pale olive. b, tan & gray. c, pink & pale violet.
$2, yellow orange & pink.

1998, Jan. 5 *Perf. 14½*

2520 A390 $1 Sheet of 3, #a.-c. 2.25 2.25

Souvenir Sheet

2521 A390 $2 multicolored 1.50 1.50

Cooperative Foundation for Natl. Development A391

Designs: 20c, Children going to shcool. 90c, People working in field, Credit Union office, vert. $1.10, Industry, ship at dock.

1998, Jan. 5 Litho. *Perf. 13½*

2522-2524 A391 Set of 3 2.10 2.10

Jazz Entertainers — A392

Designs: a, King Oliver. b, Louis Armstrong. c, Sidney Bechet. d, Nick Larocca. e, Louis Prima. f, Buddy Bolden.

1998, Feb. 2 *Perf. 14x13½*

2525 A392 $1 Sheet of 6, #a.-f. 4.50 4.50

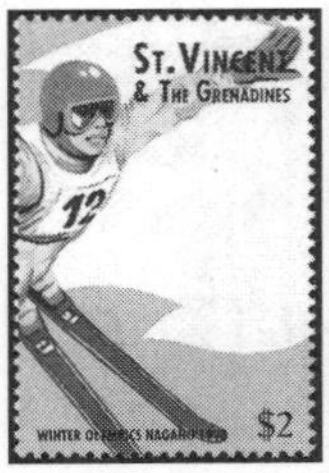

1998 Winter Olympic Games, Nagano
A393 A394

Designs, horiz: 70c, Ice hockey. $1.10, Bobsled. $2, Pairs figure skating. $2, Skier, vert.

Medalists: No. 2530: a, Bjorn Daehlie. b, Gillis Grafstrom. c, Sonja Henie. d, Ingemar Stenmark. e, Christian Jagge. f, Tomas Gustafson. g, Johann Olav Koss. h, Thomas Wassberg.

Olympic rings in background: No. 2531: a, Downhill skier. b, Woman figure skater. c, Ski jumper. d, Speed skater. e, 4-Man bobsled team. f, Cross country country skier.

Olympic flame in background: No. 2532: a, Downhill skier. b, Bobsled. c, Ski jumper. d, Slalom skier. e, Luge. f, Biathlon.

No. 2533, Slalom skiing. No. 2534, Hockey player, horiz.

1998, Feb. 2 *Perf. 14*

2526-2529 A393 Set of 4 4.50 4.50
2530 A394 $1.10 Sheet of 8, #a.-h. 6.50 6.50

Sheets of 6

2531-2532 A393 $1.50 #a.-f., ea 6.75 6.75

Souvenir Sheets

2533-2534 A393 $5 each 3.75 3.75

Butterflies A395

20c, Amarynthis meneria. 50c, Papillo polyxenes. 70c, Emesis fatima, vert. $1, Anartia amathea.

No. 2539, vert: a, Heliconius erato. b, Danaus plexippus. c, Papillo phorcas. d, Morpho pelaides. e, Pandoriana pandora. f, Basilarchia astyanax. g, Vanessa cardui. h, Colobura dirce. i, Heraclides cresphontes.

No. 2540, Colias eurytheme. No. 2541, Everes comyntas.

1998, Feb, 23 *Perf. 13½*

2535-2538 A395 Set of 4 1.80 1.80
2539 A395 $1 Sheet of 9, #a.-i. 6.75 6.75

Souvenir Sheets

2540-2541 A395 $6 each 4.50 4.50

Endangered Fauna — A396

50c, Anegada rock iguana. 70c, Jamaican swallowtail. 90c, Blossom bat. $1, Solenodon. $1.10, Hawksbill turtle. $2, West Indian whistling duck.

No. 2548: a, Roseate spoonbill. b, Golden swallow. c, Short-snouted spinner dolphin. d, Queen conch. e, West Indian manatee. f, Loggerhead turtle.

No. 2549: a, Magnificent frigatebird. b, Humpback whale. c, Southern dagger-tail. d, St. Lucia whiptail e, St. Lucia oriole. f, Green turtle.

No. 2550, St. Vincent parrot. No. 2551, Antiguan racer.

1998, Feb. 23 *Perf. 13*

2542-2547 A396 Set of 6 4.75 4.75

Sheets of 6

2548-2549 A396 $1.10 #a.-f., ea 5.00 5.00

Souvenir Sheets

2550-2551 A396 $5 each 3.75 3.75

Mushrooms A397

Designs: 10c, Gymnopilus spectabilis. 20c, Entoloma lividium. 70c, Pholiota flammans. 90c, Panaeolus semiovatus. $1, Stropharia rugosoannulata. $1.10, Tricholoma sulphureum.

No. 2558: a, Amanita caesarea. b, Amanita muscaria. c, Aminita ovoidea. d, Amanita phalloides. e, Amanitopsis inaurata. f, Amanitopsis vaginata. g, Psalliota campestris, alfalfa butterfly. h, Psalliota arvenis. i, Coprinus comatus.

No. 2559: a, Coprinus picaceus. b, Stropharia umbonatescens. c, Hebeloma crustuliniforme, figure-of-eight butterfly. d, Cortinarius collinitus. e, Cortinarius violaceus, common dotted butterfly. f, Cortinarius armillatus. g, Tricholoma aurantium. h, Russula virescens. i, Clitocybe infundibuliformis.

No. 2560, Hygrocybe conica. No. 2561, Amanita caesarea.

1998, Feb. 23 Litho. *Perf. 13½*

2552-2557 A397 Set of 6 3.00 3.00
2558 A397 $1 Sheet of 9, #a.-i. 6.75 6.75
2559 A397 $1.10 Sheet of 9, #a.-i. 7.50 7.50

Souvenir Sheets

2560-2561 A397 $6 each 4.50 4.50

Mickey Mouse, 70th Birthday — A398

Designs: 2c, Wake up, Mickey. 3c, Morning run. 4c, Getting ready. 5c, Eating breakfast. 10c, School "daze." 65c, Time out for play. $3, Volunteer worker. $4, A date with Minnie. $5, Ready for bed.

Weekly hi-lites from "Mickey Mouse Club," vert: a, The opening march. b, Monday, fun with music day. c, Tuesday, guest star day. d, Wednesday, anything can happen day. e, Thursday, circus day. f, Friday, talent round up day.

Mickey Mouse: No. 2572, Reading, vert. No. 2573, Playing piano, vert. No. 2574, Blowing trumpet. No. 2575, On the Internet, vert.

Perf. 14x13½, 13½x14

1998, Mar. 23 Litho.

2562-2570 A398 Set of 9 9.75 9.75
2571 A398 $1.10 Sheet of 6, #a.-f. 5.00 5.00

Souvenir Sheets

2572 A398 $5 multicolored 3.75 3.75
2573-2575 A398 $6 each 4.50 4.50

Winnie the Pooh — A399

Scenes from animated films: a, Pooh looking out open window. b, Eeyore, Kanga, Roo. c, Pooh getting honey from tree. d, Rabbit, Pooh stuck in entrance to Rabbit's house. e, Christopher Robin pulling Pooh from Rabbit's house, Owl. f, Piglet sweeping leaves. g, Pooh sleeping. h, Eeyore. i, Tigger on top of Pooh.

No. 2577, Tigger, Pooh, Piglet.

1998, Mar. 23 *Perf. 14x13½*

2576 A399 $1 Sheet of 9, #a.-i. 6.75 6.75

Souvenir Sheet

2577 A399 $6 multicolored 4.50 4.50

Dogs — A400

Designs: 70c, Australian terrier. 90c, Bull mastiff. $1.10, Pomeranian. $2, Dandie dinmont terrier.

No. 2582, horiz: a, Tyrolean hunting dog. b, Papillon. c, Fox terriers. d, Bernese mountain dog. e, King Charles spaniel. f, German shepherd.

No. 2583, horiz: a, Beagle. b, German shepherd. c, Pointer. d, Vizsla. e, Bulldog. f, Shetland sheepdogs.

No. 2584, Scottish terrier, wooden deck, grass. No. 2585, Scottish terrier, grass, trees.

1998, Apr. 21 *Perf. 14*

2578-2581 A400 Set of 4 3.50 3.50

Sheets of 6

2582-2583 A400 $1.10 #a.-f., ea 5.00 5.00

Souvenir Sheets

2584-2585 A400 $6 each 4.50 4.50

Nos. 2306-2309 Ovptd.

1998, May 19 Litho. *Perf. 14*

2586-2588 A345 Set of 3 3.25 3.25

Souvenir Sheet

2589 A345 $5 multicolored 3.75 3.75

No. 2589 contains overprint "ISRAEL 98 - WORLD STAMP EXHIBITION / TEL-AVIV 13-21 MAY 1998" in sheet margin.

Trains A401

10c, LMS Bahamas No. 5596. 20c, Ex-Mza 1400. 50c, Mallard. 70c, Monarch 0-4-4 OT. 90c, Big Chief. $1.10, Duchess of Rutland LMS No. 6228.

No. 2596: a, Hadrian Flyer. b, Highland Jones Goods No. 103. c, Blackmore Vale No. 34023. d, Wainwright SECR No. 27. e, Stepney Brighton Terrier. f, RENFE Freight train No. 040 2184. g, Calbourne No. 24. h, Clun Castle 1950.

No. 2597: a, Ancient Holmes J36 060. b, Patentee 2-2-2. c, Kingfisher. d, St. Pierre No. 23. e, SAR Class 19c 4-8-2. f, SAR 6J 4-6-0. g, Evening Star No. 92220. h, Old No. 1.

No. 2598, King George V No. 6000 BR. No. 2599, Caledonia.

1998, June 2 Litho. *Perf. 14*

2590-2595 A401 Set of 6 2.60 2.60

Sheets of 8

2596-2597 A401 $1.10 #a.-h., ea 6.75 6.75

Souvenir Sheets

2598-2599 A401 $5 each 3.75 3.75

UNESCO Intl. Year of the Ocean A402

Marine life: 70c, Beluga whale. 90c, Atlantic manta. $1.10, Forceps butterfly fish, copperband butterfly fish, moorish idol. $2, Octopus.

No. 2604, vert: a, Harlequin wrasse. b, Blue sturgeon fish. c, Spotted trunkfish. d, Regal angelfish. e, Porcupine fish. f, Clownfish, damselfish. g, Lion fish. h, Moray eel. i, French angelfish.

No. 2605, vert: a, Lemonpeel angelfish. b, Narwhal. c, Panther grouper. d, Fur seal. e, Spiny boxfish. f, Loggerhead turtle. g, Qpah. h, Clown triggerfish. i, Bighead searobin.

No. 2606, Seahorse, vert. No. 2607, Australian sea dragon, vert.

1998, July 1

2600-2603 A402 Set of 4 3.50 3.50

Sheets of 9

2604-2605 A402 $1 #a.-i., each 6.75 6.75

Souvenir Sheets

2606-2607 A402 $5 each 3.75 3.75

Birds A403

50c, Cock of the rock, vert. 60c, Quetzal, vert. 70c, Wood stork, vert. No. 2611, 90c, St. Vincent parrot, vert. No. 2612, 90c, Toucan. $1, Greater bird of paradise. $1.10, Sunbittern. $2, Green honeycreeper.

#2616, vert.: a, Racquet-tailed motmot. b, Red-billed quelea. c, Leadbeater's cockatoo. d, Scarlet macaw. e, Bare-throated bellbird. f, Tucaman Amazon parrot. g, Black-lored red tanager. h, Fig parrot. i, St. Vincent Amazon parrot. j, Peach-faced love birds. k, Blue fronted Amazon parrot. l, Yellow billed Amazon parrot.

No. 2617, Hyacinth macaw, vert. No. 2618, Blue-headed hummingbird, vert.

1998, June 16 Litho. *Perf. 14*

2608-2615 A403 Set of 8 5.75 5.75

Sheet of 12

2616 A403 90c Sheet of 12, #a.-l. 8.25 8.25

Souvenir Sheets

2617-2618 A403 $5 each 3.75 3.75

No. 2611 has different style of lettering.

Diana, Princess of Wales (1961-97) — A404

#2619, Diana in orange jacket. #2620, Diana in blue blouse. Illustration reduced.

Litho. & Embossed

1998, Aug. 1 *Die Cut 7½*

2619 A404 $20 gold & multi
2620 A404 $20 gold & multi

CARICOM, 25th Anniv. — A405

1998, July 4 Litho. *Perf. 13½*

2621 A405 $1 multicolored .75 .75

Enzo Ferrari (1898-1988), Automobile Manufacturer — A406

Classic Ferraris - #2622: a, 365 GTS. b, Testarossa. c, 365 GT4 BB.

$6, Dino 206 GT.

1998, Sept. 15 Litho. *Perf. 14*

2622 A406 $2 Sheet of 3, #a.-c. 4.50 4.50

Souvenir Sheet

2623 A406 $6 multicolored 4.50 4.50

No. 2623 contains one 91x35mm stamp.

Paintings by Pablo Picasso (1881-1973) — A407

Designs: $1.10, Landscape, 1972. No. 2625, $2, The Kiss, 1969. No. 2626, $2, The Death of the Female Torero, 1933.

$5, Flute Player, 1962, vert.

1998, Sept. 15 *Perf. 14½*

2624-2626 A407 Set of 3 4.00 4.00

Souvenir Sheet

2627 A407 $5 multicolored 3.75 3.75

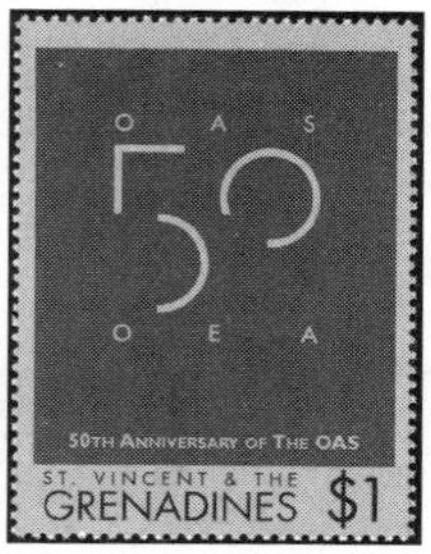

Organization of American States, 50th Anniv. A408

1998, Sept. 15 Litho. *Perf. 13½*

2628 A408 $1 multicolored .75 .75

Diana, Princess of Wales (1961-97) A409

1998, Sept. 15 *Perf. 14½*

2629 A409 $1.10 multicolored .85 .85

Souvenir Sheet

Self-Adhesive

Serpentine Die Cut Perf. 11½

Size: 53x65mm

2630 A409 $8 Diana, buildings

No. 2629 was issued in sheets of 6. Soaking in water may affect the image of No. 2630.

Mahatma Gandhi (1869-1948) A411

$5, Seated at table with officials, horiz.

1998, Sept. 15 *Perf. 14*

2631 A411 $1 shown .75 .75

Souvenir Sheet

2632 A411 $5 multicolored 3.75 3.75

No. 2631 was issued in sheets of 4.

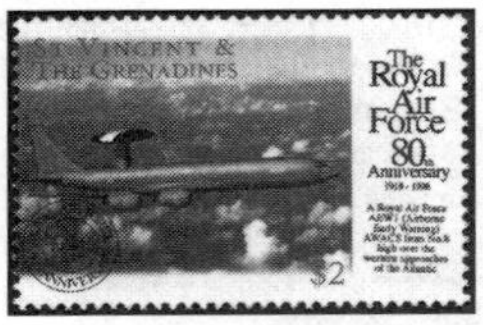

Royal Air Force, 80th Anniv. A412

No. 2633: a, AEW1 AWACS. b, BAe Eurofighter EF2000. c, Sepcat Jaguar GR1A. d, BAe Hawk T1A.

No. 2634: a, Two Sepcat Jaguar GR1s. b, Panavia Tornado F3. c, Three BAe Harrier GR7s. d, Panavia Tornado F3 IDV.

No. 2635, Mosquito, Eurofighter. No. 2636, Hawk's head, hawk, biplane. No. 2637, Biplane, hawk in flight. No. 2638, Vulcan B2, Eurofighter.

1998, Sept. 15 *Perf. 14*

Sheets of 4

2633-2634 A412 $2 #a.-d., each 6.00 6.00

Souvenir Sheets

2635-2638 A412 $6 each 4.50 4.50

1998 World Scout Jamboree, Chile — A413

No. 2639: a, Astronaut John Glenn receives Silver Buffalo award, 1965. b, Herb Shriner learns knot tying at 1960 Natl. Jamboree. c, "Ready to go" Boy Scouts break camp, 1940's.

$5, Lord Robert Baden-Powell (1857-1941), vert.

1998, Sept. 15

2639 A413 $2 Sheet of 3, #a.-c. 4.50 4.50

Souvenir Sheet

2640 A413 $5 multicolored 3.75 3.75

Ancient Order of Foresters Friendly Society, Court Morning Star 2298, Cent. — A414

Designs: 10c, Bro. H.E.A. Daisley, PCR. 20c, R.N. Jack, PCR. 50c, Woman, man shaking hands, emblem. 70c, Symbol of recognition. 90c, Morning Star Court's headquarters.

1998, Oct. 29 **Litho.** *Perf. 13½*

2641-2645 A414 Set of 5 1.75 1.75

RMS Titanic — A415

Illustration reduced.

Die Cut 7½

1998, Oct. 29 **Embossed**

2646 A415 $20 gold

Christmas A418

Domestic cats: 20c, Bi-color longhair. 50c, Korat. 60c, Seal-point Siamese. 70c, Red self longhair. 90c, Black longhair. $1.10, Red tabby exotic shorthair.

No. 2653, Seal-point colorpoint. No. 2654, Toirtoiseshell shorthair.

1998, Dec. **Litho.** *Perf. 14*

2647-2652 A418 Set of 6 3.00 3.00

Souvenir Sheets

2653-2654 A418 $5 each 3.75 3.75

A419

No. 2655: a, Woman playing flute. b, Hildegard holding tablets. c, Woman playing violin. d, Pope Eugenius. e, Bingen, site of Hildegard's convent. f, Portrait.

$5, Portrait, diff.

1998, Dec. 15 **Litho.** *Perf. 14*

2655 A419 $1.10 Sheet of 6, #a.-f. 5.00 5.00

Souvenir Sheet

2656 A419 $5 multicolored 3.75 3.75

Hildegard von Bingen (1098?-1179).

A420

1999, Jan. 4 **Litho.** *Perf. 14½*

Stylized rabbits: a, Looking right. b, Looking forward. c, Looking left.

$2, like #2657b.

2657 A420 $1 Sheet of 3, #a.-c. 2.25 2.25

Souvenir Sheet

2658 A420 $2 multicolored 1.50 1.50

New Year 1999 (Year of the Rabbit).

Queen Elizabeth II and Prince Philip, 50th Wedding Anniv. (in 1997) — A421

Illustration reduced.

Litho. & Embossed

1999, Jan. 5 ***Die Cut Perf. 6***

Without Gum

2659 A421 $20 gold & multi

Disney Characters in Winter Sports A422

Wearing checkered outfits - #2660: a, Minnie. b, Mickey. c, Goofy. d, Donald. e, Mickey (goggles on head). f, Daisy.

Wearing brightly-colored outfits - # 2661: a, Daisy. b, Mickey. c, Mickey, Goofy. d, Goofy. e, Minnie. f, Donald.

Wearing red, purple & yellow - #2662: a, Mickey. b, Goofy. c, Donald. d, Goofy, Mickey. e, Goofy (arms over head). f, Minnie.

No. 2663, Mickey in checkered outfit. No. 2664, Goofy eating ice cream cone, Mickey, horiz. No. 2665, Mickey in red, purple & yellow.

1999, Jan. 21 **Litho.** *Perf. 13½x14*

Sheets of 6

2660-2662 A422 $1.10 #a.-f., ea 5.00 5.00

Souvenir Sheets

2663-2665 A422 $5 each 3.75 3.75

Mickey Mouse, 70th anniv.

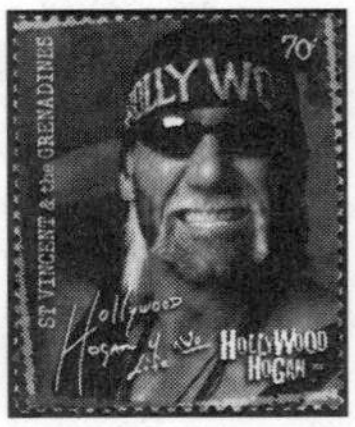

World Championship Wrestling A423

Designs: a, Hollywood Hogan. b, Sting. c, Bret Hart. d, the Giant. e, Kevin Nash. f, Randy Savage. g, Diamond Dallas Page. h, Bill Goldberg.

1999, Jan. 25 **Litho.** *Perf. 13*

2666 A423 70c Sheet of 8, #a.-h. 4.25 4.25

Australia '99, World Stamp Expo A424

Prehistoric animals: 70c, Plateosaurus. 90c, Euoplacephalus. $1.10, Pachycephalosaurus. $1.40, Dilophosaurus.

No. 2671: a, Struthiomimus. b, Indricotherium. c, Giant moa. d, Deinonychus. e, Sabre tooth cat. f, Dawn horse. g, Peittacosaurus. h, Giant ground sloth. i, Wooly rhinoceros. j, Mosasaur. k, Mastodon. l, Syndoyceras.

No. 2672: a, Rhamphorhynchus. b, Pteranodon. c, Archaeopterix. d, Dimetrodon. e, Stegosaurus. f, Parasaurolophus. g, Iguanadon. h, Triceratops. i, Tyrannosaurus. j, Ichthyosaurus. k, Plesiosaurus. l, Hersperonis.

No. 2273, Diplodocus. No. 2674, Wooly mammoth, vert.

1999, Mar. 1 **Litho.** *Perf. 14*

2667-2670 A424 Set of 4 4.25 4.25

Sheets of 12

2671 A424 70c #a.-l. 6.50 6.50
m. As #2671, imperf. 6.50 6.50
2672 A424 90c #a.-l. 8.25 8.25
m. As #2672, imperf. 8.25 8.25

Souvenir Sheets

2673-2674 A424 $5 each 3.75 3.75
2673a-2674a Imperf., each 3.75 3.75

Flora and Fauna A425

Designs: 10c, Acacia tree, elephant. 20c, Green turtle, coconut palm. 25c, Mangrove tree, white ibis. 50c, Tiger swallowtail, ironweed. 70c, Eastern box turtle, jack-in-the-pulpit, vert. 90c, Praying mantis, milkweed, vert. $1.10, Zebra finch, bottle brush, vert. $1.40, Koala, gum tree, vert.

No. 2683, vert: a, Red tailed hawk, ocitillo. b, Morning dove, organ pipe cactus. c, Paloverde tree, burrowing owl. d, Cactus wren, saguaro cactus. e, Ocitillo, puma. f, Organ pipe cactus, gray fox. g, Coyete, prickly pear cactus. h, Saguaro cactus, gila woodpecker. i, Collared lizard, barrel cactus. j, Cowblinder cactus, gila monster. k, Hedgehog cactus, roadrunner. l, Saguaro cactus, jack rabbit.

No. 2684, vert: a, Strangler fig, basilisk lizard. b, Macaw, kapok trees. c, Cecropia tree, howler monkey. d, Cecropia tree, toucan. e, Arrrow poison frog, bromiliad. f, Rattlesnake orchid, heliconius phyllis. g, Tree fern, bat eating hawk. h, Jaguar, tillandsia. i, Margay, sierra palm. j, Lesser bird of paradise, aristolchia. k, Parides, erythrina. l, Fer-de-lance, zebra plant.

No. 2685, Alligator, water lilies. No. 2686, Riuolis, hummingbird.

1999, Apr. 12 **Litho.** *Perf. 14*

2675-2682 A425 Set of 8 3.75 3.75

Sheets of 12

2683-2684 A425 70c #a.-l., each 6.50 6.50

Souvenir Sheets

2685-2686 A425 $5 each 3.75 3.75

Aviation History A426

Designs: 60c, Montgolfier balloon, 1783, vert. 70c, Lilienthal glider, 1894. 90c, Zeppelin. $1, Wright brothers, 1903.

No. 2691: a, DH-4 bomber. b, Sopwith Camel. c, Sopwith Dove. d, Jeannin Stahl Taube. e, Fokker DR-1 triplane. f, Albatros Diva. g, Sopwith Pup. h, Spad XIII Smith IV.

No. 2692: a, M-130 Clipper. b, DC-3, 1937. c, Beech Staggerwing CVR FT C-17L. d, Hughes H-1 racer. e, Gee Bee Model R-1, 1932. f, Lockheed Sirius Tingmissartoq. g, Fokker T-2, 1923. h, Curtiss CW-16E Floatplane.

No. 2693, Bleriot XI crossing English Channel, 1914. No. 2694, Le Bandy airship, 1903.

1999, Apr. 26

2687-2690 A426 Set of 4 2.50 2.50

Sheets of 8

2691-2692 A426 $1.10 #a.-h., ea 6.75 6.75

Souvenir Sheets

2693-2694 A426 $5 each 3.75 3.75

'N Sync, Musical Group — A427

1999, May 4 **Litho.** *Perf. 12½*

2695 A427 $1 multicolored .75 .75

No. 2695 was issued in sheets of 8.

History of Space Exploration, 1609-2000 — A428

Designs: 20c, Galileo, 1609. 50c, Konstantin Tsiolkovsky, 1903. 70c, Robert H. Goddard, 1926. 90c, Sir Isaac Newton, 1668, vert.

No. 2700: a, Luna 9, 1959. b, Soyuz 11, 1971. c, Mir Space Station, 1996. d, Sputnik 1, 1957. e, Apollo 4, 1967. f, Bruce McCandless, 1984. g, Sir William Herschel, telescope, 1781. h, John Glenn, 1962. i, Space Shuttle Columbia, 1981.

No. 2701, vert: a, Yuri Gargarin, 1962. b, Lunar Rover, 1971. c, Mariner 10, 1974-75. d, Laika, 1957. e, Neil A. Armstrong, 1969. f, Skylab Space Station, 1973. g, German V-2 Rocket, 1942. h, Gemini 4, 1965. i, Hubble Telescope, 1990.

No. 2702, vert: a, Explorer, 1958. b, Lunokhod Explorer, 1970. c, Viking Lander, 1975. d, R7 Rocket, 1957. e, Edward H. White, 1965. f, Salyut 1, 1971. g, World's oldest observatory. h, Freedom 7, 1961. i, Ariane Rocket, 1980's.

No. 2703, Atlantis docking with Space Station Mir, 1995. No. 2704, Saturn V, 1969, vert.

1999, May 6 *Perf. 14*

2696-2699 A428 Set of 4 1.75 1.75

Sheets of 9

2700-2702 A428 $1 #a.-i., each 6.75 6.75

Souvenir Sheets

2703-2704 A428 $5 each 3.75 3.75

Johann Wolfgang von Goethe (1749-1832), Poet — A430

No. 2709: a, Faust Dying in the Arms of the Lemures. b, Portraits of Goethe, Friederich von Schiller (1759-1805). c, The Immortal Spirit of Faust is Carried Aloft.
No. 2710: a, Faust and Helena with Their Son, Euphonon. b, Mephistopheles Leading the Lemures to Faust.
No. 2711, The Immortal soul of Faust, vert. No. 2712, Portrait of Goethe, vert.

1999, June 25 Litho. *Perf. 14*

Sheets of 3

2709 A430 $3 #a.-c.	6.75	6.75
2710 A430 $3 #a.-b. + #2709b	6.75	6.75

Souvenir Sheets

2711-2712 A430 $5 each	3.75	3.75

Paintings, by Hokusai (1760-1849) A431

#2713: a, Landscape with a Hundred Bridges (large mountain). b, Sea Life (turtle, head LL). c, Landscape with a Hundred Bridges (large bridge in center). d, A View of Aoigaoka Waterfall in Edo. e, Sea Life (crab). f, Women on the Beach at Enoshima.
#2714: a, Admiring the Irises at Yatsuhashi (large tree). b, Sea Life (turtle, head UL). c, Admiring the Irises at Yatsuhashi (peak of bridge). d, Pilgrims Bathing in Roben Waterfall. e, Sea Life (turtle, head UR). f, Farmers Crossing a Suspension Bridge.
#2715, In the Horse Washing Waterfall. #2716, A Fisherman at Kajikazawa.

1999, June 25 *Perf. 13¾*

Sheets of 6

2713-2714 A431 $1.10 #a.-f., ea	5.00	5.00

Souvenir Sheet

2715-2716 A431 $5 each	3.75	3.75

Wedding of Prince Edward and Sophie Rhys-Jones A432

No. 2717: a, Edward. b, Sophie, Edward. c, Sophie.
$6, Couple, horiz.

1999, June 19 Litho. *Perf. 13½*

2717 A432 $3 Sheet of 3, #a.-c.	6.75	6.75

Souvenir Sheet

2718 A432 $6 multicolored	4.50	4.50

IBRA '99, World Philatelic Exhibition, Nuremberg — A433

Design: $1, Krauss-Maffei V-200 diesel locomotive, Germany, 1852.
Illustration reduced.

1999, June 25 *Perf. 14*

2720 A433 $1 multicolored	.75	.75

A 90c value was issued.

Souvenir Sheets

PhilexFrance '99, World Philatelic Exhibition — A434

Locomotives: No. 2721, Pacific, 1930's. No. 2722, Quadrt, electric hight-speed, 1940.
Illustration reduced.

1999, June 25 *Perf. 13¾*

2721-2722 A434 $6 each	4.50	4.50

A435

A436

Children - #2723: a, Tyreek Isaacs. b, Fredique Isaacs. c, Jerome Burke III. d, Kelisha Roberts.
#2724: a, Girl with braided hair. b, Girl wearing hat. c, Girl holding kitten.
$5, Girl with bow in hair.

1999, June 25 *Perf. 14*

2723 A435 90c Sheet of 4, #a.-d.	2.75	2.75
2724 A435 $3 Sheet of 3, #a.-c.	6.75	6.75

Souvenir Sheet

2725 A435 $5 multicolored	3.75	3.75

UN Convention on Rights of the Child, 10th anniv.

1999, June 25

Intl. Year of Older Persons - No. 2726: a, I.M. Pei. b, Billy Graham. c, Barbara Cartland. d, Mike Wallace. e, Jeanne Moreau. f, B.B. King. g, Elie Wiesel. h, Arthur Miller. i, Colin Powell. j, Jack Palance. k, Neil Simon. l, Eartha Kitt.
No. 2727: a, Thomas M. Saunders J.P. b, Mother Sarah Baptiste, M.B.E. c, Sir Sydney Gun-Munro MD, KF, GCMG. d, Dr. Earle Kirby, JP, OBE.

2726 A436 70c Sheet of 12, #a.-l.	6.25	6.25
2727 A436 $1.10 Sheet of 4, #a.-d.	3.25	3.25

World Teachers' Day — A437

No. 2728: a, Henry Alphaeus Robertson. b, Yvonne C. E. Francis-Gibson. c, Edna Peters. d, Christopher Wilberforce Prescod.

1999, Oct. 5 Litho. *Perf. 14¾*

2728 A437 $2 Sheet of 4, #a.-d.	6.00	6.00

A438

Queen Mother (b. 1900) — A439

Gold Frames

No. 2729: a, In 1909. b, With King George VI, Princess Elizabeth, 1930. c, At Badminton, 1977. d, In 1983.
$6, In 1987. $20, Close-up.

1999, Oct. 18 Litho. *Perf. 14*

2729 A438 $2 Sheet of 4, #a.-d., + label	6.00	6.00

Souvenir Sheet

Perf. 13¾

2730 A438 $6 multicolored	4.50	4.50

No. 2730 contains one 38x50mm stamp.
See Nos. 3010-3011.

Litho. & Embossed

1999, Aug. 4 *Die Cut 9x8¾*

Size: 55x93mm

2731 A439 $20 gold & multi		

Christmas A440

Designs: 20c, The Resurrection, by Albrecht Dürer. 50c, Christ in Limbo, by Dürer. 70c, Christ Falling on the Way to Calvary, by Raphael. 90c, St. Ildefonso with the Madonna and Child, by Peter Paul Rubens. $5, The Crucifixion, by Raphael.
$6,The Sistine Madonna, by Raphael.

1999, Nov. 22 Litho. *Perf. 13¾*

2732-2736 A440 Set of 5	5.50	5.50

Souvenir Sheet

2737 A440 $6 multicolored	4.50	4.50

UPU, 125th Anniv. A441

Designs: a, Mail coach. b, Intercontinental sea mail. c, Concorde.

1999, Dec. 7 *Perf. 14*

2738 A441 $3 Sheet of 3, #a.-c.	6.75	6.75

Paintings A442

Various paintings making up a photomosaic of the Mona Lisa.

1999, Dec. 7 *Perf. 13¼*

2739 A442 $1.10 Sheet of 8, #a.-h.	6.50	6.50

See #2744, 2816.

A443

Millennium: No. 2740, Clyde Tombaugh discovers Pluto, 1930.
No. 2741 - Highlights of the 1930s: a, Mahatma Gandhi's Salt March, 1930. b, Like #2740, with colored margin. c, Empire State Building opens, 1931. d, Spain becomes a republic, 1931. e, Franklin D. Roosevelt launches New Deal, 1933. f, Reichstag burns in Germany, 1933. g, Mao Zedong leads China's revolution, 1934. h, Spanish Civil War led by Francisco Franco, 1936. i, Edward VIII abdicates, 1936. j, Diego Rivera, 50th birthday, 1936. k, Golden Gate Bridge opens, 1937. l, First atomic reaction achieved, 1939. m, World War II begins, 1939. n, Television debuts at New York World's Fair, 1939. o, Selection of Dalai Lama, 1939. p, Hindenburg explodes, 1937 (60x40mm). q, Igor Sikorsky builds first practical helicopter, 1939.
No. 2742 - Sculptures by: a, Elizabeth Murray. b, Alexander Calder. c, Charles William Moss. d, Gaston Lachaise. e, Claes Oldenburg. f, Louise Bourgeois. g, Duane Hanson. h, Brancusi. i, David Smith. j, Dan Flavin. k, Boccioni. l, George Segal. m, Lucas Samaras. n, Marcel Duchamp. o, Isamu Noguchi. p, Donald Judd (60x40mm). q, Louise Nevelson.

1999, Dec. 7 Litho. *Perf. 13¼x13*

2740 A443 60c multicolored	.45	.45

Sheets of 17

Perf. 12¾x12½

2741 A443 60c #a.-q. + label	7.50	7.50
2742 A443 60c #a.-q. + label	7.50	7.50

Inscription on No. 2742e is misspelled. A number has been reserved for an additional sheet in this set.
See No. 2764.

Painting Type of 1999

Various flowers making up a photomosaic of Princess Diana.

1999, Dec. 31 Litho. *Perf. 13¾*

2744 A442 $1 Sheet of 8, #a.-h.	6.00	6.00

A444

2000, Feb. 5 Litho. *Perf. 14¾*

New Year 2000 (Year of the Dragon), Background colors - No. 2745: a, Blue and red lilac.

b, Salmon pink and olive. c, Brick red and lilac rose.
$4, Brown and dull green.

2745 A444 $2 Sheet of 3, #a.-c. 4.50 4.50

Souvenir Sheet

2746 A444 $4 multi 3.00 3.00

Marine Life — A445

50c, High hat. 90c, Spotfin hogfish. $1, Royal gramma. $2, Queen angelfish.

No. 2751: a, Sergeant major. b, Hawksbill turtle, whale's tail. c, Horse-eyed jacks, rear of turtle. d, Two horse-eyed jacks, humpback whale. e, Three horse-eyed jacks, head of humpback whale. f, Black-cap gramma. g, Common dolphins. h, French grunts, with Latin inscription. i, Barracuda. j, Bottlenosed dolphin. k, Sea horse. l, Southern stingray, French grunt. m, French grunts, no Latin inscription. n, Indigo hamlet. o, Basking shark. p, Nassau grouper. q, Nurse shark, ribbonfish. r, Southern stingray. s, Southern stingray, blue shark. t, Spanish hogfish.

No. 2752, Rock beauties. No. 2753, Banded butterflyfish.

2000, Feb. 28 Litho. *Perf. 14*

2747-2750 A445 Set of 4 3.25 3.25

Sheet of 20

2751 A445 50c #a.-t. 7.50 7.50

Souvenir Sheets

2752-2753 A445 $5 each 3.75 3.75

Fish A446

10c, Stoplight parrotfish. 20c, Spotfin hogfish. 70c, Beaugregory. 90c, Porkfish. $1, Barred hamlet. $1.40, Queen triggerfish.

No. 2760: a, French angelfish. b, Smooth trunkfish. c, Sargassum triggerfish. d, Indigo hamlet. e, Yellowheaded jawfish. f, Peppermint bass.

No. 2761: a, Porcupine fish. b, Blue tang. c, Bluehead wrasse. d, Juvenile queen angelfish. e, Sea horse. f, Small mouth grunt.

No. 2762, Pygmy angelfish. No. 2763, Four-eye butterflyfish.

2000, Feb. 28

2754-2759 A446 Set of 6 3.25 3.25

Sheets of 6, #a.-f.

2760-2761 A446 $1.10 each 5.00 5.00

Souvenir Sheets

2762-2763 A446 $5 each 3.75 3.75

Millennium Type of 1999

Highlights of 1900-1950: a, Sigmund Freud publishes "Interpretation of Dreams." b, First long distance wireless transmission. c, First powered airplane flight. d, Einstein proposes theory of relativity. e, Henry Ford unveils Model T. f, Alfred Wegener develops theory of continental drift. g, World War I begins. h, 1917 Russian revolution. i, James Joyce publishes "Ulysses." j, Alexander Fleming discovers penicillin. k, Edwin Hubble determines universe is expanding. l, Mao Zedong leads "Long March." m, Alan Turing develops theory of digital computing. n, Discovery of fission. o, World War II begins. p, Allied leaders meet at Yalta. q, Mahatma Gandhi and Jawaharlal Nehru celebrate India's independence. r, Invention of the transistor.

2000, Mar. 13 *Perf. 12½*

2764 A443 20c Sheet of 18, a.-r. + label 2.75 2.75

Date on No. 2764a is incorrect.

Paintings of Anthony Van Dyck A447

No. 2765: a, Robert Rich, 2nd Earl of Warwick. b, James Stuart, Duke of Lennox and Richmond. c, Sir John Suckling. d, Sir Robert Shirley. e, Teresia, Lady Shirley. f, Thomas Wentworth, 1st Earl of Strafford.

No. 2766: a, Thomas Wentworth, Earl of Strafford, in Armor. b, Lady Anne Carr, Countess of Bedford. c, Portrait of a Member of the Charles Family. d, Thomas Howard, 2nd Earl of Arundel. e, Diana Cecil, Countess of Oxford. f, The Violincellist.

No. 2767: a, The Apostle Peter. b, St. Matthew. c, St. James the Greater. d, St. Bartholomew. e, The Apostle Thomas. f, The Apostle Jude (Thaddeus).

No. 2768: a, The Vision of St. Anthony. b, The Mystic Marriage of St. Catherine. c, The Vision of the Blessed Herman Joseph. d, Madonna and Child Enthroned with Sts. Rosalie, Peter and Paul. e, St. Rosalie Interceding for the Plague-stricken of Palermo. f, Francesco Orero in Adoration of the Crucifixion in the Presence of Sts. Frances and Bernard.

No. 2769, William Feilding, 1st Earl of Denbigh. No. 2770, The Mystic Marriage of St. Catherine, diff. No. 2771, St. Augustine in Ecstasy, horiz.

2000 Litho. *Perf. 13¾*

Sheets of 6, #a.-f.

2765-2768 A447 $1 each 4.50 4.50

Souvenir Sheets

2769-2771 A447 $5 each 3.75 3.75

Orchids A448

Designs: 70c, Brassavola nodosa. 90c, Bletia purpurea. $1.40, Brassavola cucullata.

No. 2775, vert.: a, Oncidium urophyllum. b, Oeceoclades maculata. c, Vanilla planifolia. d, Isolhilus linearis. e, Ionopsis utricularioides. f, Nidema boothii.

No. 2776, vert.: a, Cyrtopodium punctatum. b, Dendrophylax funalis. c, Dichaea hystricina. d, Cyrtopodium andersonii. e, Epidendrum secundum. f, Dimerandra emarginata.

No. 2777, vert.: a, Brassavola cordata. b, Brassia caudata. c, Broughotnia sanguinea. d, Comparettia falcata. e, Clowesia rosea. f, Caularthron bicornutum.

No. 2778, Neocogniauxia hexaptera, vert. No. 2779, Epidendrum altissimum, vert.

2000, May Litho. *Perf. 14*

2772-2774 A448 Set of 3 2.25 2.25

Sheets of 6, #a.-f.

2775-2777 A448 $1.50 each 6.75 6.75

Souvenir Sheets

2778-2779 A448 $5 each 3.75 3.75

The Stamp Show 2000, London.

Prince William, 18th Birthday — A449

No. 2780: a, Wearing checked suit. b, Wearing scarf. c, Wearing solid suit. d, Wearing sweater.
$5, Wearing suit with boutonniere.
Illustration reduced.

2000, June 21 Litho. *Perf. 14*

2780 A449 $1.40 Sheet of 4, #a-d 4.25 4.25

Souvenir Sheet

Perf. 13¾

2781 A449 $5 multi 3.75 3.75

No. 2780 contains four 28x42mm stamps.

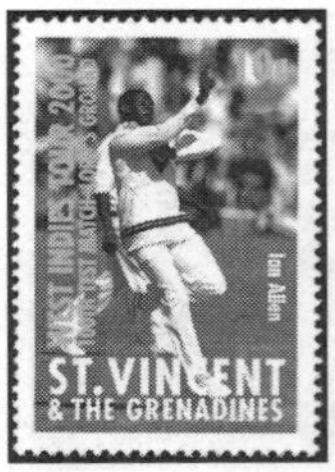

100th Test Match at Lord's Ground — A450

10c, Ian Allen. 20c, T. Michael Findlay. $1.10, Winston Davis. $1.40, Nixon McLean. $5, Lord's Ground, horiz.

2000, June 26 *Perf. 14*

2782-2785 A450 Set of 4 2.10 2.10

Souvenir Sheet

2786 A450 $5 multi 3.75 3.75

First Zeppelin Flight, Cent. — A451

No. 2787: a, LZ-6. b, LZ-127. c, LZ-129.
$5, LZ-9.
Illustration reduced.

2000, June 26

2787 A451 $3 Sheet of 3, #a-c 6.75 6.75

Souvenir Sheet

2788 A451 $5 multi 3.75 3.75

No. 2787 contains 39x24mm stamps.

Berlin Film Festival, 50th Anniv. — A452

No. 2789: a, Pane, Amore e Fantasia. b, Richard III. c, Smultronstället (Wild Strawberries). d, The Defiant Ones. e, The Living Desert. f, A Bout de Souffle.
$5, Jean-Luc Godard.
Illustration reduced.

2000, June 26

2789 A452 $1.40 Sheet of 6, #a-f 6.25 6.25

Souvenir Sheet

2790 A452 $5 multi 3.75 3.75

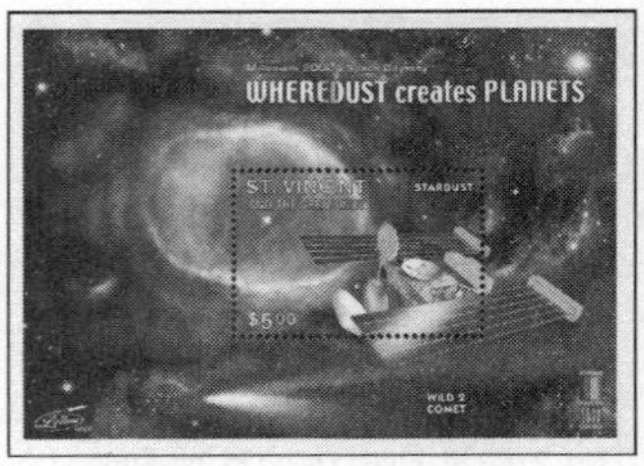

Space — A453

No. 2791: a, Comet Hale-Bopp, Calisto. b, Galileo probe. c, Ulysses probe. d, Pioneer 11. e, Voyager 1. f, Pioneer 10.

No. 2792: a, Voyager 2, Umbriel. b, Pluto Project. c, Voyager 1, purple background. d, Oort cloud. e, Pluto, Kuiper Express. f, Voayger 2 near Neptune.

No. 2793: a, Cassini probe. b, Pioneer 11. c, Voyager 1, green background. d, Huygens. e, Deep Space IV Champollion. f, Voyager 2.

No. 2794, Stardust. No. 2795, Pluto Project, diff.

Illustration reduced.

2000, June 26

Sheets of 6, #a-f

2791-2793 A453 $1.50 each 6.75 6.75

Souvenir Sheets

2794-2795 A453 $5 each 3.75 3.75

World Stamp Expo 2000, Anaheim.

Souvenir Sheets

2000 Summer Olympics, Sydney — A454

No. 2796: a, Mildred Didrikson. b, Pommel horse. c, Barcelona Stadium and Spanish flag. d, Ancient Greek horse racing.
Illustration reduced.

2000, June 26

2796 A454 $2 Sheet of 4, #a-d 6.00 6.00

Albert Einstein (1879-1955) — A455

No. 2797: a, Wearing green sweater. b, Wearing blue sweater. c, Wearing black sweater.
Illustration reduced.

2000, June 26

2797 A455 $2 Sheet of 3, #a-c 4.50 4.50

Public Railways, 175th Anniv. — A456

No. 2798: a, Locomotion No. 1, George Stephenson. b, John Bull.
Illustration reduced.

2000, June 26

2798 A456 $3 Sheet of 2, #a-b 4.50 4.50

Mario Andretti, Automobile Racer — A457

No. 2799: a, In car, without helmet. b, In white racing uniform. c, With hands in front of face. d, In car, with helmet. e, In white, standing in front of car. f, With trophy. g, In red racing uniform. h, Close-up.
$5, With trophy, diff.
Illustration reduced.

2000, July 6 ***Perf. 12x12¼***

2799 A457 $1.10 Sheet of 8, #a-h 6.50 6.50

Souvenir Sheet

Perf. 13¾

2800 A457 $5 multi 3.75 3.75

Souvenir Sheets

Monty Python's Flying Circus, 30th Anniv. (in 1999) — A458

No. 2801: a, Michael Palin. b, Eric Idle. c, John Cleese. d, Graham Chapman. e, Terry Gilliam. f, Terry Jones.
Illustration reduced.

2000, July 6 ***Perf. 12x12¼***

2801 A458 $1.40 Sheet of 6, #a-f 6.25 6.25

Jazz — A459

No. 2802: a, Clarinetist. b, Pianist. c, Trumpeter. d, Guitarist. e, Bassist. f, Saxophonist.
Illustration reduced.

2000, July 6 ***Perf. 14***

2802 A459 $1.40 Sheet of 6, #a-f 6.25 6.25

Female Recording Groups of the 1960s — A460

No. 2803, Portraits of the members of The Chantels (green background). No. 2804, Portraits of the members of The Marvelettes (blue background)

2000, July 6

Sheets of 5, #a-e

2803-2804 A460 $1.40 each 5.25 5.25

Barbara Taylor Bradford, Writer — A461

Illustration reduced.

2000, July 6 ***Perf. 12x12¼***

2805 A461 $5 multi 3.75 3.75

Betty Boop — A462

No. 2806: a, As Jill, with Jack. b, With three blind mice. c, Jumping over candlestick. d, As fiddler in Hey, Diddle, Diddle. e, On back of Mother Goose. f, As Little Miss Muffet. g, With three cats. h, As candlestick maker, with butcher and baker. i, As Little Jack Horner.

No. 2807, As the Woman Who Lived In a Shoe. No. 2808, As Little Bo Peep.
Illustration reduced.

2000, July 6 ***Perf. 13¾***

2806 A462 $1 Sheet of 9 #a-i 6.75 6.75

Souvenir Sheets

2807-2808 A462 $5 each 3.75 3.75

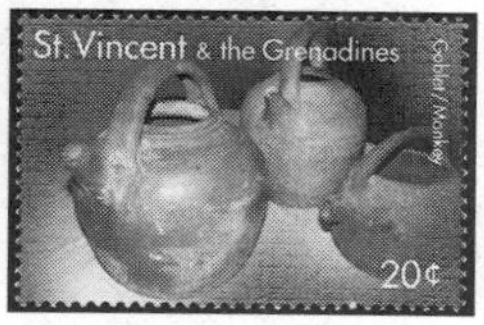

Artifacts A463

Designs: 20c, Goblet. 50c, Goose. 70c, Boley and calabash. $1, Flat iron.

2000, Aug. 21 **Litho.** ***Perf. 14***

2809-2812 A463 Set of 4 1.75 1.75

Flowers — A464

No. 2813: a, Pink ginger lily. b, Thumbergia grandiflora. c, Red ginger lily. d, Madagascar jasmine. e, Cluster palm. f, Red torch lily. g, Salvia splendens. h, Balsam apple. i, Rostrata.
No. 2814, Red flamingo. No. 2815, Balsam apple, horiz.
Illustration reduced.

2000, Aug. 21

2813 A464 90c Sheet of 9, #a-i 6.00 6.00

Souvenir Sheet

2814-2815 A464 $5 Set of 2 7.50 7.50

Paintings Type of 1999

Various pictures of flowers making up a photomosaic of the Queen Mother.

2000, Sept. 5 ***Perf. 13¾***

2816 A442 $1 Sheet of 8, #a-h 6.00 6.00
i. As No. 2816, imperf. 6.00 6.00

Magician David Copperfield — A465

No. 2817: a, Head of Copperfield. b, Copperfield's body. c, Copperfield's body vanishing. d, Copperfield's body vanished.

2000 ***Perf. 14***

2817 A465 $1.40 Sheet of 4, #a-d 4.25 4.25

Local Musicians — A466

Designs: No. 2818, $1.40, Horn player with striped shirt. No. 2819, $1.40, Horn player, diff. No. 2820, $1.40, Pianist. No. 2821, $1.40, Fiddler.

2000, Oct. 16 **Litho.** ***Perf. 14***

2818-2821 A466 Set of 4 4.25 4.25

Blues Musicians — A467

No. 2822, $1.40: a, Bessie Smith. b, Willie Dixon. c, Gertrude "Ma" Rainey. d, W. C. Handy. e, Leadbelly. f, Big Bill Broonzy.
No. 2823, $1.40: a, Ida Cox. b, Lonnie Johnson. c, Muddy Waters. d, T-Bone Walker. e, Howlin' Wolf. f, Sister Rosetta Tharpe.
No. 2824, Robert Johnson. No. 2825, Billie Holiday.
Illustration reduced.

2000, Oct. 16

Sheets of 6, #a-f

2822-2823 A467 Set of 2 12.50 12.50

Souvenir Sheets

2824-2825 A467 Set of 2 7.50 7.50

World at War — A468

No. 2826: a, USS Shaw explodes at Pearl Harbor. b, B-24s bomb Ploesti oil fields. c, Soviet T-34 tank moves towards Berlin. d, USS New Jersey off coast of North Korea. e, F-86 Sabre over North Korea. f, USS Enterprise off the Indochina coast. g, B-52 over Viet Nam. h, M-113 tank in Viet Nam.
No. 2827: a, Israeli F-4 Phantoms in action in Six-day War. b, Egyptian T-72 tank destroyed, Six-day War. c, Egyptian SAM-6 missiles, Yom Kippur War. d, Israeli M-48 tanks in desert, Yom Kippur War. e, HMS Hermes, Falkand Islands War. f, British AV-8 harriers in action, Falkland Islands War. g, Iraqi Scud missile launcher in desert, Gulf War. h, M1-A1 Abrams tanks in desert, Gulf War.
No. 2828, Israeli F-4s bomb SAM sites, Yom Kippur War. No. 2829 B-52 bomber, Pershing II missile.
Illustration reduced.

2000, Oct. 16

Sheets of 8, #a-h

2826-2827 A468 $1 Set of 2 12.00 12.00

Souvenir Sheets

2828-2829 A468 $5 Set of 2 7.50 7.50

No. 2829 contains one 56x42mm stamp.

Independence, 21st Anniv. — A469

Designs: 10c, Government House. 15c, First session of Parliament, 1998. 50c, House of Assembly. $2, Financial Complex.

2000, Oct. 27 Litho. *Perf. 14*

2830-2833 A469 Set of 4 2.00 2.00

Birds — A470

Designs: 50c, Blue and gold macaw. 90c, English fallow budgerigar. $1, Barraband parakeet. $2, Dominat pied blue.

No. 2838, $2: a, English short-faced tumbler. b, Diamond dove. c, Norwich cropper.

No. 2839, $2: a, Scarlet macaw. b, Blue-fronted Amazon. c, Buffon's macaw.

No. 2840, $2: a, Stafford canary. b, Masked lovebird. c, Parisian full canary.

No. 2841, $2, horiz.: a, Canada goose. b, Mandarin duck. c, Gouldian finch.

No. 2842, $5, Common peafowl, horiz. No. 2843, $5, Budgerigar, horiz.

2000, Nov. 15

2834-2837 A470 Set of 4 3.25 3.25

Sheets of 3, #a-c

2838-2841 A470 Set of 4 18.00 18.00

Souvenir Sheets

2842-2843 A470 Set of 2 7.50 7.50

Shirley Temple in Rebecca of Sunnybrook Farm — A471

No. 2844, horiz.: a, With man in dark suit. b, With man and woman. c, With woman wearing glasses. d, with blonde woman. e, With man in white hat. f, With three women.

No. 2845: a, At microphone, wearing checked coat and hat. b, Wearing straw hat. c, At microphone, no hat. d, With woman wearing glasses.

No. 2846, With Bill Robinson.

2000, Nov. 29 *Perf. 13¾*

Sheets of 6 and 4

2844 A471 90c #a-f 4.00 4.00
2845 A471 $1.10 #a-d 3.25 3.25

Souvenir Sheet

2846 A471 $1.10 multi .85 .85

Queen Mother, 100th Birthday — A472

2000, Sept. 5 Litho. *Perf. 14*

2847 A472 $1.40 multi 1.00 1.00

Printed in sheets of 6.

Christmas — A473

20c, Angel looking right. 70c, Two angels, orange background. 90c, Two angels, blue background. #2851, $5, Angel looking left.

No. 2852, Angel, yellow background.

2000, Dec. 7

2848-2851 A473 Set of 4 5.00 5.00

Souvenir Sheet

2852 A473 $5 multi 3.75 3.75

Battle of Britain, 60th Anniv. — A474

No. 2853, 90c: a, Junkers Ju87. b, Two Gloster Gladiators flying left. c, Messerschmitt BF109. d, Heinkel He111 bomber, British fighter. e, Three Hawker Hurricanes. f, Two Bristol Blenheims. g, Two Supermarine Spitfires and ground. h, Messerschmitt BF110.

No. 2854, 90c: a, Two Spitfires, flying left. b, Spitfire. c, Dornier DO217. d, Two Gladiators flying right. e, Four Hurricanes. f, Junkers Ju87 Stuka. g, Two Spitfires flying right. h, Junkers Ju88.

#2855, $5, Spitfire. #2856, $5, Hurricane.

Illustration reduced.

2000, Dec. 18 *Perf. 14¼x14½*

Sheets of 8, #a-h

2853-2854 A474 Set of 2 10.50 10.50

Souvenir Sheets

Perf. 14¼

2855-2856 A474 Set of 2 7.50 7.50

New Year 2001 (Year of the Snake) — A475

No. 2857: a, Blue and light blue background. b, Purple and pink background. c, Green and light green background.

2001, Jan. 2 Litho. *Perf. 13x13¼*

2857 A475 $1 Sheet of 3, #a-c 2.25 2.25

Souvenir Sheet

2858 A475 $2 shown 1.50 1.50

Paintings of Peter Paul Rubens in the Prado A476

Designs: 10c, Three women and dog from Diana the Huntress. 90c, Adoration of the Magi. $1, Woman and two dogs from Diana the Huntress.

No. 2862, $2: a, Heraclitus, the Mournful Philosopher. b, Heraclitus, close-up. c, Anne of Austria, Queen of France, close-up. d, Anne of Austria.

No. 2863, $2: a, Prometheus Carrying Fire. b, Vulcan Forging Jupiter's Thunderbolt. c, Saturn Devouring One of His Sons. d, Polyphemus.

No. 2864, $2: a, St. Matthias. b, The Death of Seneca. c, Maria de'Medici, Queen of France. d, Achilles Discovered by Ulysses.

No. 2865, $5, The Judgment of Solomon. No. 2866, $5, The Holy Family with St. Anne.

2001, Jan. 2 *Perf. 13¾*

2859-2861 A476 Set of 3 1.50 1.50

Sheets of 4, #a-d

2862-2864 A476 Set of 3 18.00 18.00

Souvenir Sheets

2865-2866 A476 Set of 2 7.50 7.50

Rijksmuseum, Amsterdam, Bicent. — A477

No. 2867, $1.40: a, The Spendthrift, by Thomas Asselijn. b, The Art Gallery of Jan Gildermeester Jansz, by Adriaan de Lelie. c, The Rampoortje, by Wouter Johannes van Troostwijk. d, Winter Landscape, by Barend Cornelis Koekkoek. e, Man with white headdress from The Procuress, by Dirck van Baburen. f, Man and woman from The Procuress.

No. 2868, $1.40: a, A Music Party, by Rembrandt. b, Rutger Jan Schimmelpennick and Family, by Pierre Paul Prud'hon. c, Tobit and Anna With a Kid, by Rembrandt. d, The Syndics of the Amsterdam Goldsmiths' Guild, by Thomas de Keyser. e, Portrait of a Lady, by de Keyser. f, Marriage Portrait of Isaac Massa and Beatrix van der Laen, by Frans Hals.

No. 2869, $1.40: a, The Concert, by Hendrick ter Brugghen. b, Vertumnus and Pomona, by Paulus Moreelse. c, Standing couple from Dignified Couples Courting, by Willem Buytewech. d, The Sick Woman, by Jan Steen. e, Seated couple from Dignified Couples Courting. f, Don Ramón Satué, by Francisco de Goya.

No. 2870, $5, Donkey Riding on the Beach, by Isaac Lazarus Israels. No. 2871, $5, The Stone Bridge, by Rembrandt, horiz. No. 2872, $5, Child with Dead Peacocks, by Rembrandt, horiz.

2001, Jan. 15 *Perf. 13¾*

Sheets of 6, #a-f

2867-2869 A477 Set of 3 19.00 19.00

Souvenir Sheets

2870-2872 A477 Set of 3 11.00 11.00

Birds of Prey A478

Designs: 10c, Barred owl. No. 2874, 90c, Lammergeier. $1, California condor. $2, Mississippi kite.

No. 2877, 90c: a, Crested caracara. b, Boreal owl. c, Harpy eagle. d, Oriental bay owl. e, Hawk owl. f, Laughing falcon.

No. 2878, $1.10: a, Bateleur. b, Hobby. c, Osprey. d, Goshawk. e, African fish eagle. f, Egyptian vulture.

No. 2879, $5, Great gray owl. No. 2880, $5, American kestrel.

2001, Feb. 13 *Perf. 14*

2873-2876 A478 Set of 4 3.00 3.00

Sheets of 6, #a-f

2877-2878 A478 Set of 2 9.00 9.00

Souvenir Sheets

2879-2880 A478 Set of 2 7.50 7.50

Hong Kong 2001 Stamp Exhibition (Nos. 2877-2880).

Owls — A479

Designs: 10c, Eagle. 20c, Barn. 50c, Great gray. 70c, Long-eared. 90c, Tawny. $1, Hawk.

No. 2887, horiz.: a, Ural. b, Tengmalm's. c, Marsh. d, Brown fish. e, Little. f, Short-eared.

No. 2888, $5, Hume's. No. 2889, $5, Snowy.

2001, Feb. 13

2881-2886 A479 Set of 6 2.50 2.50
2887 A479 $1.40 Sheet of 6, #a-f 6.25 6.25

Souvenir Sheets

2888-2889 A479 Set of 2 7.50 7.50

Pokémon — A480

No. 2890: a, Kadabra. b, Spearow. c, Kakuna. d, Koffing. e, Tentacruel. f, Cloyster.

2001, Feb. 13 ***Perf. 13¾***
2890 A480 90c Sheet of 6, #a-f 4.00 4.00

Souvenir Sheet

2891 A480 $3 Meowth 2.25 2.25

UN Women's Human Rights Campaign — A481

Woman: 90c, With bird and flame. $1, With necklace.

2001, Mar. 8 ***Perf. 14***
2892-2893 A481 Set of 2 1.40 1.40

Mushrooms — A482

Designs: 20c, Amanita fulva. 90c, Hygrophorus speciosus. $1.10, Amanita phalloides. $2, Cantharellus cibarius.

No. 2898, $1.40: a, Amanita muscaria. b, Boletus zelleri. c, Coprinus picaceus. d, Stroharia aeruginosa. e, Lepista nuda. f, Hygrophorus conicus.

No. 2899, $1.40: a, Lactarius deliciosus. b, Hygrophorus psittacinus. c, Tricholomopsis rutilans. d, Hygrophorus coccineus. e, Collybia iocephala. f, Gyromitra esculenta.

No. 2900, $1.40: a, Lactarius peckii. b, Lactarius rufus. c, Cortinarius elatior. d, Boletus luridus. e, Russula cyanoxantha. f, Craterellus cornopioioles.

No. 2901, $5, Cyathus olla. No. 2902, $5, Lycoperdon pyriforme, horiz. No. 2903, $5, Pleurotus ostreatus, horiz.

Perf. 13½x13¼, 13¼x13½

2001, Mar. 15
2894-2897 A482 Set of 4 3.25 3.25

Sheets of 6, #a-f

2898-2900 A482 Set of 3 19.00 19.00

Souvenir Sheets

2901-2903 A482 Set of 3 11.00 11.00

A484

A485

Butterflies and Moths A486

Designs: No. 2904, 10c, Tiger. No. 2905, 20c, Figure-of-eight. No. 2906, 50c, Mosaic. No. 2907, 90c, Monarch. No. 2908, $1, Blue-green reflector. No. 2909, $2, Blue tharops.

No. 2910, 10c, Eunica alemena. No. 2911, 70c, Euphaedra medon. No. 2912, 90c, Prepona praeneste. No. 2913, $1, Gold-banded forester.

No. 2914, 20c, Ancycluris formosissima. No. 2915, 50c, Callicore cynosura. No. 2916, 70c, Nessaea obrinus. No. 2917, $2, Eunica alemena.

No. 2918, 90c: a, Orange theope. b, Blue night. c, Small lace-wing. d, Grecian shoemaker. e, Clorinde. f, Orange-barred sulphur.

No. 2919, $1.10: a, Atala. b, Giant swallowtail. c, Banded king shoemaker. d, White peacock. e, Cramer's mesene. f, Polydamas swallowtail.

No. 2920, 90c: a, Cepora aspasia. b, Morpho aega. c, Mazuca amoeva. d, Beautiful tiger. e, Gold-drop helicopsis. f, Esmerelda.

No. 2921, $1.10: a, Lilac nymph. b, Ruddy dagger wing. c, Tiger pierid. d, Orange forester. e, Prepona deiphile. f, Phoebus avellaneda.

No. 2922, $1: a, Calisthenia salvinii flying downward. b, Perisama vaninka. c, Malachite. d, Diaethria aurelia. e, Perisama conplandi. f, Cramer's mesene. g, Calisthenia salvinii flying upward. h, Carpella districata.

No. 2923, $1: a, Euphaedra heophron. b, Milionia grandis. c, Ruddy dagger wiry. d, Bocotus bacotus. e, Cream spot tiger moth. f, Yellow tiger moth. g, Baorisa hiroglyphica. h, Jersey tiger.

No. 2924, $5, Small flambeau. No. 2925, $5, Common morpho, vert. No. 2926, $5, Heliconius sapho. No. 2927, $5 Ornate moth. No. 2928, $5, Hewitson's blue hair streak. No. 2929, $5, Anaxita drucei.

Perf. 13¼x13½, 13½x13¼

2001 **Litho.**
2904-2909 A484 Set of 6 3.50 3.50
2910-2913 A485 Set of 4 2.00 2.00
2914-2917 A486 Set of 4 2.50 2.50

Sheets of 6, #a-f

2918-2919 A484 Set of 2 9.00 9.00
2920-2921 A485 Set of 2 9.00 9.00

Sheets of 8, #a-h

2922-2923 A486 Set of 2 12.00 12.00

Souvenir Sheets

2924-2925 A484 Set of 2 7.50 7.50
2926-2927 A485 Set of 2 7.50 7.50
2928-2929 A486 Set of 2 7.50 7.50

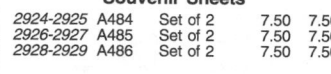

Giuseppe Verdi (1813-1901), Opera Composer — A487

No. 2930: a, Mario Del Monico, Raina Kabaivanska in Othello. b, 1898 Costume design for Iago. c, 1898 costume design for Othello. d, Anna Tomowa-Sintow as Desdemona.

$5, Nicolai Ghiaurov in Othello.

2001, June 12 **Litho.** ***Perf. 14***
2930 A487 $2 Sheet of 4, #a-d 6.00 6.00

Souvenir Sheet

2931 A487 $5 multi 3.75 3.75

Toulouse-Lautrec Paintings — A488

No. 2932: a, Portrait of Comtesse Adèle-Zoé de Toulouse-Lautrec. b, Carmen. c, Madame Lily Grenier.

$5, Jane Avril.

2001, June 12 ***Perf. 13¾***
2932 A488 $3 Sheet of 3, #a-c 6.75 6.75

Souvenir Sheet

2933 A488 $5 multi 3.75 3.75

Mao Zedong (1893-1976) — A489

No. 2934: a, In 1924. b, In 1938. c, In 1945. $5, Undated portrait.

2001, June 12
2934 A489 $2 Sheet of 3, #a-c 4.50 4.50

Souvenir Sheet

2935 A489 $5 multi 3.75 3.75

Queen Victoria (1819-1901) — A490

No. 2936: a, As young lady in dark blue dress. b, In white dress. c, With flowers in hair. d, Wearing crown. e, Wearing black dress, facing forward. f, With gray hair.

$5, Sky in background.

2001, June 12 ***Perf. 14***
2936 A490 $1.10 Sheet of 6, #a-f 5.00 5.00

Souvenir Sheet

Perf. 13¾

2937 A490 $5 multi 3.75 3.75

No. 2936 contains six 28x42mm stamps.

Queen Elizabeth II, 75th Birthday — A491

No. 2938: a, With gray hat. b, In gray jacket, no hat. c, In dark blue dress. d, Wearing tiara. e, With blue hat. f, With green hat.

$5, In uniform.

2001, June 12 ***Perf. 14***
2938 A491 $1.10 Sheet of 6, #a-f 5.00 5.00

Souvenir Sheet

Perf. 13¾

2939 A491 $5 multi 3.75 3.75

No. 2938 contains six 28x42mm stamps.

Monet Paintings — A492

Designs: No. 2940, $2, Venice at Dusk (shown). No. 2941, $2, Regatta at Argenteuil. No. 2942, $2, Grain Stacks, End of Summer, Evening Effect. No. 2943, $2, Impression, Sunrise.

$5, Parisians Enjoying the Parc Monceau, vert.

2001, June 12 ***Perf. 13¾***
2940-2943 A492 Set of 4 6.00 6.00

Souvenir Sheet

2944 A492 $5 multi 3.75 3.75

Phila Nippon '01, Japan A493

Designs: 10c, The Courtesan Sumimoto of the Okanaya, by Koryusai Isoda. 15c, Oiran at Shinto Shrine - Shotenyama, by Kiyonaga. No. 2947, 20c, Two Girls on a Veranda, by Kiyonaga. No. 2948, 20c, Rooster, from A Variety of Birds, by Hoen Nishiyama, horiz. 50c, On Banks of the Sumida, by Kiyonaga. 70c, Three ducks, from A Variety of Birds, horiz. 90c, Seven ducks, from A Variety of Birds, horiz. $1, Three pigeons and other birds from A Variety of Birds. horiz. $1.10, Two birds, from A Variety of Birds, horiz. $2, Five birds, from A Variety of Birds.

No. 2955, $1.40 - Paintings by Eishi: a, Toriwagi, Geisha of Kanaya, Writing. b, Courtesan Preparing for Doll Festival. c, Two Court Ladies in a Garden. d, Lady With a Lute.

No. 2956, $1.40 - Portraits by Sharaku: a, Oniji Otani II as Edohei, a Yakko. b, Hanshiro Iwai IV. c, Kikunojo Segawa. d, Komazo Ichikawa II.

No. 2957, $1.40 - Paintings by Harunobu Suzuki: a, 6 Tama Rivers, Girls by Lespedeza Bush in Moonlight. b, Warming Sake with Maple Leaves. c, Young Samurai on Horseback. d, 6 Tamu Rivers, Ide No Tamagawa.

No. 2958, $1.40 - Paintings by Harunobu Suzuki: a, Girl on River Bank. b, Horseman Guided by Peasant Girl. c, Komachi Praying for Rain. d, Washing Clothes in the Stream.

No. 2959, $5, Peasants Ferried Across Sumida, by Hokkei. No. 2960. $5, Shadows on the Shoji, by Kikugawa. No. 2961, $5, Boy Spying on Lovers, by Suzuki. No. 2962, $5, Tayu Komurasaki and Hanamurasaki of the Kado Tamaya, by Masanobu Kitao. No. 2963, $5, Gathering Lotus Flowers, by Suzuki.

2001, June 12 Litho. *Perf. 13¾*

2945-2954 A493 Set of 10 5.25 5.25

Sheets of 4, #a-d

2955-2958 A493 Set of 4 17.00 17.00

Souvenir Sheets

2959-2963 A493 Set of 5 19.00 19.00

Dale Earnhardt (1951-2001), Stock Car Racer — A494

Designs: a, Dale Earnhardt, Jr. b, Dale and Dale, Jr. with trophy. c, Dale. d, Dale with trophy. e, Dale and Dale, Jr. embracing. f, Dale Jr. with trophy.

2001, July 16

2964 A494 $2 Sheet of 6, #a-f + label 9.00 9.00

Wedding of Norwegian Prince Haakon and Mette-Marie Tjessem Hoiby — A495

2001, Aug. 1 *Perf. 14*

2965 A495 $5 multi 3.75 3.75

Printed in sheets of 4.

Dinosaurs and Prehistoric Animals — A496

Designs: 10c, Mammoth. 20c, Pinacosaurus. No. 2968, 90c, Oviraptor. $1, Centrosaurus. No. 2970, $1.40, Protoceratops. $2, Bactrosaurus.

No. 2972, 90c: a, Saltasaurus. b, Apatosaurus. c, Brachiosaurus. d, Troodon. e, Deinonychus. f, Segnosaurus.

No. 2973, 90c: a, Iguanodon. b, Hypacrosaurus. c, Ceratosaurus. d, Hypsilophodon. e, Herrerasaurus. f, Velociraptor.

No. 2974, $1.40: a, Pteranodon. b, Archaeopteryx. c, Eudimorphodon. d, Shonisaurus. e, Elasmosaurus. f, Kronosaurus.

No. 2975, $1.40: a, Allosaurus. b, Dilophosaurus. c, Lambeosaurus. d, Coelophysis. e, Ornitholestes. f, Eustreptospondylus.

No. 2976, $5, Stegosaurus. No. 2977, $5, Triceratops. No. 2978, $5, Parasaurolophus, vert. No. 2979, $5, Tyrannosaurus, vert.

2001, Oct. 15 Litho. *Perf. 14x13¾*

2966-2971 A496 Set of 6 4.25 4.25

Sheets of 6, #a-f

2972-2975 A496 Set of 4 21.00 21.00

Souvenir Sheets

Perf. 13¾

2976-2979 A496 Set of 4 15.00 15.00

Nos. 2976-2977 each contain one 50x38mm stamp; Nos. 2978-2979 each contain one 38x50mm stamp.

Photomosaic of Queen Elizabeth II — A497

2001, Nov. 12 *Perf. 14*

2980 A497 $1 multi .75 .75

Printed in sheets of 8.

2002 World Cup Soccer Championships, Japan and Korea — A498

Players and flags - No. 2981, $1.40: a, Hong Myung-Bo, Korea. b, Hidetoshi Nakata, Japan. c, Ronaldo, Brazil. d, Paolo Maidini, Italy. e, Peter Schmeichel, Denmark. f, Raul Blanco, Spain.

No. 2982, $1.40: a, Kim Bong Soo, Korea. b, Masami Ihara, Japan. c, Marcel Desailly, France. d, David Beckham, England. e, Carlos Valderrama, Colombia. f, George Popescu, Romania.

No. 2983, $5, Seoul World Cup Stadium. No. 2984, $5, International Yokohama Stadium.

2001, Nov. 29

Sheets of 6, #a-f

2981-2982 A498 Set of 2 12.50 12.50

Souvenir Sheets

2983-2984 A498 Set of 2 7.50 7.50

Nos. 2983-2984 each contain one 63x31mm stamp.

Attack on Pearl Harbor, 60th Anniv. — A499

No. 2985, $1.40, horiz.: a, Japanese bombing Pearl Harbor. b, Japanese pilot ties on a hachimaki. c, Emperor Hirohito. d, Japanese Adm. Isoroku Yamamoto. e, Japanese fighter planes from aircraft carrier Akagi. f, Japanese Zero plane.

No. 2986, $1.40, horiz.: a, Japanese fighter from the Kaga over Ewa Marine Base. b, Hero Dorie Miller downing four Japanese planes. c, Battleship USS Nevada sinking. d, American sailors struggle on the USS Oklahoma. e, Japanese plane takes off from the Akagi. f, Rescue during bombing.

No. 2987, $5, Dorie Miller receiving navy Cross from Adm. Chester Nimitz. No. 2988, $5, Second wave of attack at Wheeler Field, horiz.

2001, Dec. 7

Sheets of 6, #a-f

2985-2986 A499 Set of 2 12.50 12.50

Souvenir Sheets

2987-2988 A499 Set of 2 7.50 7.50

Pres. John F. Kennedy — A500

Pres. Kennedy - No. 2989, $1.40: a, With John, Jr. b, With Jacqueline (red dress). c, With Caroline. d, With family, 1963. e, With Jacqueline, at sea. f, With Jacqueline (white dress).

No. 2990, $1.40: a, At 1956 Democratic Convention. b, Campaigning with Jacqueline, 1959. c, At White House, 1960. d, With brother Robert. e, Announcing Cuban blockade, 1962. f, John Jr. saluting father's casket.

No. 2991, $5, Portrait with violet background. No. 2992, $5, Portrait with green background.

2001, Dec. 7

Sheets of 6, #a-f

2989-2990 A500 Set of 2 12.50 12.50

Souvenir Sheets

2991-2992 A500 Set of 2 7.50 7.50

Princess Diana (1961-97) — A501

Flowers and Diana: a, In gray suit. b, In pink dress. c, With tiara.

$5, With tirara and high-necked gown.

2001, Dec. 7

2993 A501 $1.40 Sheet, 2 each #a-c 6.25 6.25

Souvenir Sheet

2994 A501 $5 multi 3.75 3.75

Moths A502

Designs: 70c, Croker's frother. 90c, Virgin tiger moth. $1, Leopard moth. $2, Fiery campylotes.

No. 2999, $1.40: a, Buff-tip. b, Elephant hawkmoth. c, Streaked sphinx. d, Cizara hawkmoth. e, Hakea moth. f, Boisduval's autumnal moth.

No. 3000, $1.40: a, Eyespot anthelid. b, Collenette's variegated browntail. c, Common epicoma moth. d, Staudinger's longtail. e, Green silver lines. f, Salt marsh moth.

No. 3001, $5, Gypsy moth. No. 3002, Orizaba silkmoth caterpillar.

2001, Dec. 10

2995-2998 A502 Set of 4 3.50 3.50

Sheets of 6, #a-f

2999-3000 A502 Set of 2 12.50 12.50

Souvenir Sheets

3001-3002 A502 Set of 2 7.50 7.50

Christmas — A503

Paintings: 10c, Madonna and Child, by Francesco Guardi. 20c, The Immaculate Conception, by Giovanni Battista Tiepolo. 70c, Adoration of the Magi, by Tiepolo. 90c, The Virgin, by Tintoretto. $1.10, The Annunciation, by Veronese. $1.40 Madonna della Quaglia, by Antonio Pisanello.

$5, Madonna and Child Appear to St. Philip Neri, by Tiepolo.

2001, Dec. 12

3003-3008 A503 Set of 6 3.25 3.25

Souvenir Sheet

3009 A503 $5 multi 3.75 3.75

Queen Mother Type of 1999 Redrawn

No. 3010: a, In 1909. b, With King George, Princess Elizabeth, 1930. c, At Badminton, 1977. d, In 1983.

$6, In 1987.

2001, Dec. 13 *Perf. 14*

Yellow Orange Frames

3010 A438 $2 Sheet of 4, #a-d, + label 6.00 6.00

Souvenir Sheet

Perf. 13¾

3011 A438 $6 multi 4.50 4.50

Queen Mother's 101st birthday. No. 3010 contains one 38x50mm stamp with a greener background than that found on No. 2730. Sheet margins of Nos. 3010-3011 lack embossing and gold arms and frames found on Nos. 2729-2730.

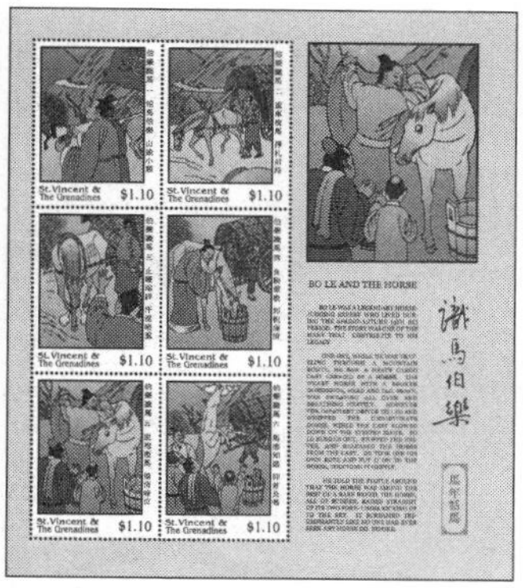

New Year 2002 (Year of the Horse) — A504

Scenes from Bo Le and the Horse: a, Man pointing at horse. b, Horse pulling cart. c, Horse snorting. d, Horse drinking. e, Man putting robe on horse. f, Horse rearing.

2001, Dec. 17 *Perf. 13¾*

3012 A504 $1.10 Sheet of 6, #a-f 5.00 5.00

Tourism A505

Designs: 20c, Vermont Nature Trails. 70c, Tamarind Beach Hotel, horiz. 90c, Tobago Cays, horiz. $1.10, Trinity Falls.

2001, Dec. 31 *Perf. 14*

Stamps + labels

3013-3016 A505 Set of 4 2.25 2.25

Fauna — A506

No. 3017, $1.40, vert.: a, Bumble bee. b, Green darner dragonfly. c, Small lace-wing. d, Black widow spider. e, Praying mantis. f, Firefly.

No. 3018, $1.40: a, Caspian tern. b, White-tailed tropicbird. c, Black-necked stilt. d, Black-billed plover. e, Black-winged stilt. f, Ruddy turnstone.

No. 3019, $5, Blue night butterfly. No. 3020, $5, Brown pelican, vert.

2001, Dec. 10 **Litho.** *Perf. 14*

Sheets of 6, #a-f

3017-3018 A506 Set of 2 12.50 12.50

Souvenir Sheets

3019-3020 A506 Set of 2 7.50 7.50

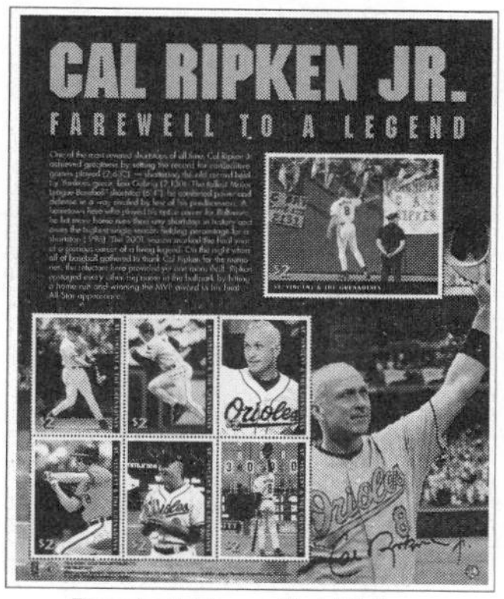

Baseball Player Cal Ripken, Jr. — A507

No. 3021: a, Hitting ball. b, Running. c, Without hat. d, Batting (orange shirt). e, Holding trophy. f, Waving hat. g, Greeting fans (68x56mm).

$6, Wearing batting helmet.

2001, Dec. 27 *Perf. 13¼*

3021 A507 $2 Sheet of 7, #a-g 10.50 10.50

Souvenir Sheet

Perf. 13x13¼

3022 A507 $6 multi 4.50 4.50

No. 3022 contains one 36x56mm stamp.

United We Stand — A508

2001, Dec. 28 *Perf. 14*

3023 A508 $2 multi 1.50 1.50

SEMI-POSTAL STAMPS

Catalogue values for unused stamps in this section are for Never Hinged items.

Map Type of 1977-78 Overprinted: "SOUFRIERE / RELIEF / FUND 1979" and New Values, "10c+5c" etc.

Litho. and Typo.

1979 **Wmk. 373** *Perf. 14½x14*

B1	A76	10c + 5c multi	.20	.20
B2	A76	50c + 25c multi	.35	.35
B3	A76	$1 + 50c multi	.70	.70
B4	A76	$2 + $1 multi	1.40	1.40
		Nos. B1-B4 (4)	2.65	2.65

The surtax was for victims of the eruption of Mt. Soufrière.

Nos. 604-607 Surcharged: "HURRICANE / RELIEF / 50c"

1980, Aug. 7 **Litho.** *Perf. 13½*

B5	A90	10c + 50c multi	.30	.30
B6	A90	60c + 50c multi	.55	.55
B7	A90	80c + 50c multi	.65	.65
B8	A90	$2.50 + 50c multi	1.50	1.50
		Nos. B5-B8 (4)	3.00	3.00

Surtax was for victims of Hurricane Allen.

Nos. 1224-1226 Surcharged "CALIF EARTHQUAKE RELIEF" on 1 or 2 Lines and "+10c"

1989, Nov. 17 **Litho.** *Perf. 13½x14*

B9	Sheet of 9	4.50	4.50
a.-i.	A174 60c +10c #1224a-1224i	.50	.50
B10	Sheet of 9	4.50	4.50
a.-i.	A174 60c +10c #1225a-1225i	.50	.50
B11	Sheet of 9	4.50	4.50
a.-i.	A175 60c +10c #1226a-1226i	.50	.50

WAR TAX STAMPS

No. 105 Overprinted **WAR STAMP.**

Type I - Words 2 to 2½mm apart.
Type II - Words 1½mm apart.
Type III - Words 3½mm apart.

1916 **Wmk. 3** *Perf. 14*

MR1	A17 1p car, type III	2.50	3.00
a.	Double ovpt., type III	175.00	200.00
b.	1p carmine, type I	2.25	1.75
c.	Comma after "STAMP", type I	7.50	10.00
d.	Double overprint, type I	150.00	150.00
e.	1p carmine, type II	80.00	80.00

Overprinted **WAR STAMP**

MR2 A17 1p carmine .35 .25

OFFICIAL STAMPS

Catalogue values for unused stamps in this section are for Never Hinged items.

Nos. 627-632 Ovptd. "OFFICIAL"

1982, Nov. **Litho.** *Perf. 14*

O1	A94a	60c	Couple, Isabella	.30	.30
O2	A94b	60c	Couple	.30	.30
O3	A94a	$2.50	Couple, Alberta	.80	.80
O4	A94b	$2.50	Couple	1.25	1.25
O5	A94a	$4	Couple, Britannia	1.50	1.50
O6	A94b	$4	Couple	1.75	1.75
			Nos. O1-O6 (6)	5.90	5.90

ST. VINCENT GRENADINES

sānt ˈvin,t,-sənt grə-ˈnā-də

LOCATION — Group of islands south of St. Vincent

CAPITAL — None

St. Vincent's portion of the Grenadines includes Bequia, Canouan, Mustique, Union and a number of smaller islands.

Catalogue values for unused stamps in this area are for Never Hinged items.

All stamps are designs of St. Vincent unless otherwise noted or illustrated.

See St. Vincent Nos. 324-329a for six stamps and a souvenir sheet issued in 1971 inscribed "The Grenadines of St. Vincent."

Princess Anne's Wedding Issue

Common Design Type

1973, Nov. 14 **Litho.** *Perf. 14*

1	CD325	25c green & multi	.20	.20
2	CD325	$1 org brn & multi	.50	.50

Common Design Types pictured following the introduction.

Bird Type of 1970 and St. Vincent Nos. 281a-285a, 287a-289a Overprinted

a

b

1974 **Photo.** **Wmk. 314** *Perf. 14*

3	A36(a)	1c	multicolored	.20	.20
4	A36(a)	2c	multicolored	.20	.20
5	A36(b)	2c	multicolored	.40	.40
6	A36(a)	3c	multicolored	.20	.20
7	A36(b)	3c	multicolored	.40	.40
8	A36(a)	4c	multicolored	.20	.20
9	A36(a)	5c	multicolored	.20	.20
10	A36(a)	6c	multicolored	.20	.20
11	A36(a)	8c	multicolored	.20	.20
12	A36(a)	10c	multicolored	.20	.20
13	A36(a)	12c	multicolored	.25	.20
14	A36(a)	20c	multicolored	.40	.25
15	A36(a)	25c	multicolored	.40	.25
16	A36(a)	50c	multicolored	.80	.45
17	A36(a)	$1	multicolored	1.25	.85
18	A36(a)	$2.50	multicolored	1.25	1.10
19	A36(a)	$5	multicolored	2.25	2.00
			Nos. 3-19 (17)	9.00	7.50

Nos. 8-9, 12-13, 17-18 vert.
Issue dates: #5, 7, June 7; others, Apr. 24.

Maps of Islands — G1

Perf. 13x12½

1974, May 9 **Litho.** **Wmk. 314**

20	G1	5c	Bequia	.20	.20
21	G1	15c	Prune	.20	.20
22	G1	20c	Mayreau	.20	.20
23	G1	30c	Mustique	.20	.20
24	G1	40c	Union	.20	.20
24A	G1	$1	Canouan	.20	.20
			Nos. 20-24A (6)	1.20	1.20

No. 20 has no inscription at bottom. No. 84 is dated "1976."

See Nos. 84-111.

UPU Type of 1974

2c, Arrows circling UPU emblem. 15c, Post horn, globe. 40c, Target over map of islands, hand canceler. $1, Goode's map projection.

1974, July 25 **Litho.** *Perf. 14½*

25-28 A56 Set of 4 .85 .80

Bequia Island G2

Designs: 5c, Boat building. 30c, Careening at Port Elizabeth. 35c, Admiralty Bay. $1, Fishing Boat Race.

1974

29-32 G2 Set of 4 .85 .80

Shells
G3

Designs: 1c, Atlantic thorny oyster. 2c, Zigzag scallop. 3c, Reticulated helmet. 4c, Music volute. 5c, Amber pen shell. 6c, Angular triton. 8c, Flame helmet. 10c, Caribbean olive. 12c, Common sundial. 15c, Glory of the atlantic cone. 20c, Flame auger. 25c King venus. 35c. Long-spined star-shell. 45c, Speckled tellin. 50c, Rooster tail conch. $1, Green star-shell. $2.50, Incomparable cone. $5, Rough file clam. $10, Measled cowrie.

1974-76 **Wmk. 373**

33-51 G3 Set of 19 19.00 19.00

Issued: #33-50, 11/27/74; #51, 7/12/76.
#36-40, 43, 45, 47-48, exist dated "1976," #40, 42-45, 49-50 dated "1977."

Churchill Type

Churchill as: 5c, Prime Minister. 40c, Lord Warden of the Cinque Ports. 50c, First Lord of the Admiralty. $1, Royal Air Force officer.

1974, Nov. 28

52-55 A58 Set of 4 .90 .90

Mustique Island
G4

1975, Feb. 27 **Wmk. 373**

56 G4 5c Cotton House .20 .20
57 G4 35c Blue Waters, Endeavour .20 .20
58 G4 45c Endeavour Bay .20 .20
59 G4 $1 Gelliceaux Bay .35 .35
Nos. 56-59 (4) .95 .95

Butterflies
G5

1975, May 15 ***Perf. 14***

60 G5 3c Soldier martinique .30 .30
61 G5 5c Silver-spotted flambeau .40 .40
62 G5 35c Gold rim .80 .80
63 G5 45c Bright blue, Donkey's eye 1.00 1.00
64 G5 $1 Biscuit 1.50 1.50
Nos. 60-64 (5) 4.00 4.00

Views of Petit St. Vincent
G6

1975, July 24 ***Perf. 14½***

65 G6 5c Resort pavilion .20 .20
66 G6 35c Harbor .20 .20
67 G6 45c Jetty .20 .20
68 G6 $1 Sailing in coral lagoon .35 .35
Nos. 65-68 (4) .95 .95

Christmas — G7

Island churches: 5c, Ecumenical Church, Mustique. 25c, Catholic Church, Union. 50c, Catholic Church, Bequia. $1, Anglican Church, Bequia.

1975, Nov. 20 **Wmk. 314**

69-72 G7 Set of 4 .90 .90

Union Island
G8

1976, Feb. 26 **Wmk. 373** ***Perf. 13½***

73 G8 5c Sunset .20 .20
74 G8 35c Customs and post office .20 .20
75 G8 45c Anglican Church .20 .20
76 G8 $1 Mail boat .30 .30
Nos. 73-76 (4) .90 .90

Staghorn Coral — G9

1976, May 13 ***Perf. 14½***

77 G9 5c shown .20 .20
78 G9 35c Elkhorn coral .25 .20
79 G9 45c Pillar coral .25 .20
80 G9 $1 Brain coral .40 .25
Nos. 77-80 (4) 1.10 .85

US Bicentennial Coins — G10

1976, July 15 ***Perf. 13½***

81 G10 25c Washington quarter .20 .20
82 G10 50c Kennedy half dollar .20 .20
83 G10 $1 Eisenhower dollar .30 .30
Nos. 81-83 (3) .70 .70

St. Vincent Grenadines Map Type

Bequia Island

, 1976, Sept. 23 **Litho.** ***Perf. 14***

84 G1 5c grn, brt grn & blk .20 .20
85 G1 10c multicolored .20 .20
a. Bklt. pane of 3, 2 #84, 85 .25 .25
86 G1 35c multicolored .20 .20
a. Bklt. pane of 3, 2 #85, 86 .35 .35
87 G1 45c multicolored .25 .25
a. Bklt. pane of 3, #84, 85, 87 .40 .40
b. Bklt. pane of 3, 2 #86, 87 .60 .60
Nos. 84-87 (4) .85 .85

For previous 5c see No. 20.

Canouan Island

1976, Sept. 23

88 G1 5c multicolored .20 .20
89 G1 10c multicolored .20 .20
a. Bklt. pane of 3, 2 #88, 89 .25 .25
90 G1 35c multicolored .20 .20
a. Bklt. pane of 3, 2 #89, 90 .35 .35
91 G1 45c multicolored .25 .25
a. Bklt. pane of 3, #88-89, 91 .40 .40
b. Bklt. pane of 3, 2 #90, 91 .60 .60
Nos. 88-91 (4) .85 .85

Mayreau Island

1976, Sept. 23

92 G1 5c multicolored .20 .20
93 G1 10c multicolored .20 .20
a. Bklt. pane of 3, 2 #92, 93 .25 .25
94 G1 35c multicolored .25 .20
a. Bklt. pane of 3, 2 #93, 94 .35 .35
95 G1 45c multicolored .25 .25
a. Bklt. pane of 3, #92-93, 95 .40 .40
b. Bklt. pane of 3, 2 #94, 95 .60 .60
Nos. 92-95 (4) .85 .85

Mustique Island

1976, Sept. 23

96 G1 5c multicolored .20 .20
97 G1 10c multicolored .20 .20
a. Bklt. pane of 3, 2 #96, 97 .25 .25
98 G1 35c multicolored .20 .20
a. Bklt. pane of 3, 2 #97, 98 .35 .35
99 G1 45c multicolored .25 .25
a. Bklt. pane of 3, #96-97, 99 .40 .40
b. Bklt. pane of 3, 2 #98, 99 .60 .60
Nos. 96-99 (4) .85 .85

Petit St. Vincent

1976, Sept. 23

100 G1 5c multicolored .20 .20
101 G1 10c multicolored .20 .20
a. Bklt. pane of 3, 2 #100, 101 .25 .25
102 G1 35c multicolored .20 .20
a. Bklt. pane of 3, 2 #101, 102 .35 .35
103 G1 45c multicolored .25 .25
a. Bklt. pane of 3, #100-101, 103 .40 .40
b. Bklt. pane of 3, 2 #102, 103 .60 .60
Nos. 100-103 (4) .85 .85

Prune Island

1976, Sept. 23

104 G1 5c multicolored .20 .20
105 G1 10c multicolored .20 .20
a. Bklt. pane of 3, 2 #104, 105 .25 .25
106 G1 35c multicolored .20 .20
a. Bklt. pane of 3, 2 #105, 106 .35 .35
107 G1 45c multicolored .25 .25
a. Bklt. pane of 3, #104-105, 107 .40 .40
b. Bklt. pane of 3, 2 #106, 107 .60 .60
Nos. 104-107 (4) .85 .85

Union Island

1976, Sept. 23

108 G1 5c multicolored .20 .20
109 G1 10c multicolored .20 .20
a. Bklt. pane of 3, 2 #108, 109 .25 .25
110 G1 35c multicolored .20 .20
a. Bklt. pane of 3, 2 #109, 110 .35 .35
111 G1 45c multicolored .25 .25
a. Bklt. pane of 3, #108-109, 111 .40 .40
b. Bklt. pane of 3, 2 #110, 111 .60 .60
Nos. 108-111 (4) .85 .85

Mayreau Island
G11

Designs: 5c, Station Hill school, post office. 35c, Church at Old Wall. 45c, Cruiser at anchor, La Souciere. $1, Saline Bay.

1976, Dec. 2 ***Perf. 14½***

112-115 G11 Set of 4 .70 .50

Queen Elizabeth II, Silver Jubilee — G12

Coins: 25c, Coronation Crown. 50c, Silver Wedding Crown. $1, Silver Jubilee Crown.

1977, Mar. 3

116-118 G12 Set of 3 .50 .40

Fiddler Crab
G13

1977, May 19

119 G13 5c shown .20 .20
120 G13 35c Ghost crab .20 .20
121 G13 50c Blue crab .30 .30
122 G13 $1.25 Spiny lobster .70 .70
Nos. 119-122 (4) 1.40 1.40

Prune Island
G14

1977, Aug. 25

123 G14 5c Snorkel diving .20 .20
124 G14 35c Palm Island Resort .20 .20
125 G14 45c Casuarina Beach .20 .20
126 G14 $1 Palm Island Beach Club .30 .30
Nos. 123-126 (4) .90 .90

Map Type of 1977 Overprinted

Perf. 14½x14

1977, Oct. 31 **Wmk. 314**

127 A76 40c multicolored (R) .20 .20
128 A76 $2 multicolored (B) .60 .60

Canouan Island
G15

1977, Dec. 8 **Wmk. 373** ***Perf. 14½***

129 G15 5c Clinic, Charlestown .20 .20
130 G15 35c Town jetty, Charlestown .20 .20
131 G15 45c Mailboat, Charlestown .20 .20
132 G15 $1 Grand Bay .35 .35
Nos. 129-132 (4) .95 .95

Birds and Eggs
G16

1c, Tropical Mockingbird. 2c, Mangrove cuckoo. 3c, Osprey. 4c, Smooth bellied ani. 5c, House wren. 6c, Bananaquit. 8c, Carib grackle. 10c, Yellow bellied elaenia. 12c, Collared plover. 15c, Cattle egret. 20c, Red footed booby. 25c, Red-billed tropic bird. 40c, Royal tern. 50c, Rusty tailed flycatcher. 80c, Purple gallinule. $1, Broad winged hawk. $2, Common ground dove. $3, Laughing gull. $5, Brown noddy. $10, Grey kingbird.

1978, May 11 ***Perf. 13x12***

133-152 G16 15.00 15.00

#139, 143, 149 exist imprinted "1979," #137-138, 140, 142, 144 imprinted "1980."
Nos. 147-148 imprinted "1979" are from No. 175a. Nos. 145-146, 150 imprinted "1980" are from No. 189a.
For surcharge see No. 266.

Elizabeth II Coronation Anniv. Type

Cathedrals.

1978, June 2 ***Perf. 13½***

153 A78 5c Worcester .20 .20
154 A78 40c Coventry .20 .20
155 A78 $1 Winchester .20 .20
156 A78 $3 Chester .25 .25
a. Souv. sheet, #153-156, perf. 14 .70 .70
Nos. 153-156 (4) .85 .85

Turtles
G17

1978, July 20 ***Perf. 14***

157 G17 5c Green turtle .20 .20
158 G17 40c Hawksbill turtle .20 .20
159 G17 50c Leatherback turtle .25 .25
160 G17 $1.25 Loggerhead turtle .65 .65
Nos. 157-160 (4) 1.30 1.30

Christmas G18

Christmas scenes and verses from the carol "We Three Kings of Orient Are".

1978, Nov. 2
161 G18 5c Three kings following star .20 .20
162 G18 10c Gold .20 .20
163 G18 25c Frankincense .20 .20
164 G18 50c Myrrh .20 .20
165 G18 $2 With infant Jesus .35 .35
a. Souvenir sheet of 5 + label, #161-165 .70 *1.00*
Nos. 161-165 (5) 1.15 1.15

Sailing Yachts — G19

1979
166 G19 5c multicolored .20 .20
167 G19 40c multi, diff. .20 .20
168 G19 50c multi, diff. .20 .20
169 G19 $2 multi, diff. .75 .75
Nos. 166-169 (4) 1.35 1.35

Wildlife Type of 1980

1979, Mar. 8 *Perf. 14½*
170 A91 20c Green iguana .20 .20
171 A91 40c Manicou .20 .20
172 A91 $2 Red-legged tortoise .85 .85
Nos. 170-172 (3) 1.25 1.25

Sir Rowland Hill Type of 1979

Designs: 80c, Sir Rowland Hill. $1, Great Britain Types A1 and A5 with "A10" (Kingstown, St. Vincent) cancel. $2, St. Vincent #41 & 43 with Bequia cancel.

1979, May 21 *Perf. 13x12*
173 A83 80c multicolored .20 .20
174 A83 $1 multicolored .25 .25
175 A83 $2 multicolored .40 .40
a. Souv. sheet, #173-175, 147-149 1.50 1.50
Nos. 173-175 (3) .85 .85

IYC Type of 1979

Children and IYC emblem: 6c, Boy. 40c, Girl. $1, Boy, diff. $3, Girl and boy.

1979, Oct. 24 *Perf. 14x13½*
176 A82 6c multicolored .20 .20
177 A82 40c multicolored .20 .20
178 A82 $1 multitolored .20 .20
179 A82 $3 multicolored .50 .50
Nos. 176-179 (4) 1.10 1.10

Independence Type of 1979

Designs: 5c, National flag, Ixora salici-folia. 40c, House of Assembly, Ixora odorata. $1, Prime Minister R. Milton Cato, Ixora jayanica.

1979, Oct. 27 *Perf. 12½x12*
180-182 A85 Set of 3 .75 .75

Printed se-tenant with label inscribed "Independence of St. Vincent and the Grenadines."

False Killer Whale G20

1979, Jan. 25 *Perf. 14*
183 G20 10c shown .60 .60
184 G20 50c Spinner dolphin .65 .65
185 G20 90c Bottle nosed dolphin .75 .75
186 G20 $2 Blackfish 2.25 2.25
Nos. 183-186 (4) 4.25 4.25

London '80 Type

1980, Apr. 24 *Perf. 13x12*
187 A88 40c Queen Elizabeth II .20 .20
188 A88 50c St. Vincent #227 .20 .20
189 A88 $3 #1-2 .60 .60
a. Souvenir sheet of 6, #187-189, 145-146, 150 2.75 2.50
Nos. 187-189 (3) 1.00 1.00

Olympics Type of 1980

1980, Aug. 7 *Perf. 13½*
190 A90 25c Running .20 .20
191 A90 50c Sailing .20 .20
192 A90 $1 Long jump .20 .20
193 A90 $2 Swimming .40 .40
Nos. 190-193 (4) 1.00 1.00

Christmas G21

Scenes and verse from the carol "De Borning Day."

1980, Nov. 13 *Perf. 14*
194 G21 5c multicolored .20 .20
195 G21 50c multicolored .20 .20
196 G21 60c multicolored .20 .20
197 G21 $1 multicolored .20 .20
198 G21 $2 multicolored .25 .25
a. Souvenir sheet of 5 + label, #194-198 .85 *1.25*
Nos. 194-198 (5) 1.05 1.05

Bequia Island G22

1981, Feb. 19 *Perf. 14½*
199 G22 50c P.O., Port Elizabeth .20 .20
200 G22 60c Moonhole .20 .20
201 G22 $1.50 Fishing boats, Admiralty Bay .30 .30
202 G22 $2 Friendship Rose at jetty .45 .45
Nos. 199-202 (4) 1.15 1.15

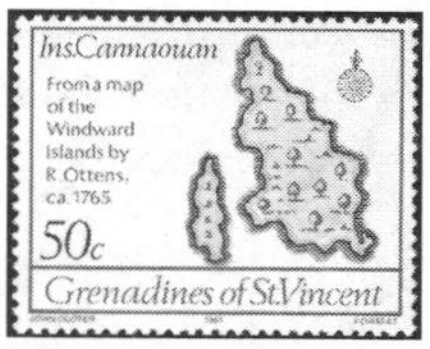

Map by R. Ottens, c. 1765 — G23

Maps: Nos. 204, 206 by J. Parsons, 1861. No. 208, by T. Jefferys, 1763.

1981, Apr. 2 *Perf. 14*
203 G23 50c Ins. Cannaouan .30 .30
204 G23 50c Cannouan Island .30 .30
a. Pair, #203-204 .60 .60
205 G23 60c Ins. Moustiques .30 .30
206 G23 60c Mustique Island .30 .30
a. Pair, #205-206 .60 .60
207 G23 $2 Ins. Bequia .50 .50
208 G23 $2 Bequia Island .50 .50
a. Pair, #207-208 1.00 1.00
Nos. 203-208 (6) 2.20 2.20

Royal Wedding Types

1981, July 17 **Wmk. 380**
209 A94a 50c Couple, the Mary .20 .20
a. Booklet pane of 4, perf. 12 .60 .60
210 A94b 50c Couple .20 .20
211 A94a $3 Couple, the Alexandra .90 .90
212 A94b $3 like #210 .90 .90
a. Booklet pane of 2, perf. 12 2.00 2.00
213 A94a $3.50 Couple, the Brittania 1.10 1.10
214 A94b $3.50 like #210 1.10 1.10
Nos. 209-214 (6) 4.40 4.40

Each denomination issued in sheets of 7 (6 type A94a, 1 type A94b).
For surcharges see Nos. 507-508.

Souvenir Sheet

1981 *Perf. 12*
215 A94b $5 like #210 1.00 1.00

Bar Jack G25

1981, Oct. 9 **Wmk. 373** *Perf. 14*
218 G25 10c shown .20 .20
219 G25 50c Tarpon .35 .35
220 G25 60c Cobia .45 .45
221 G25 $2 Blue marlin 1.10 1.10
Nos. 218-221 (4) 2.10 2.10

Ships G26

1982, Jan. 28 *Perf. 14x13½*
222 G26 1c Experiment .20 .20
223 G26 3c Lady Nelson .20 .20
224 G26 5c Daisy .20 .20
225 G26 6c Carib canoe .20 .20
226 G26 10c Hairoun Star .30 .30
227 G26 15c Jupiter .40 .40
228 G26 20c Christina .40 .40
229 G26 25c Orinoco .55 .55
230 G26 30c Lively .55 .55
231 G26 50c Alabama .75 .75
232 G26 60c Denmark .85 .85
233 G26 75c Santa Maria 1.00 1.00
234 G26 $1 Baffin 1.10 1.10
235 G26 $2 QE 2 1.60 1.60
236 G26 $3 Britannia 1.60 1.60
237 G26 $5 Geeststar 1.60 1.60
238 G26 $10 Grenadines Star 2.75 2.75
Nos. 222-238 (17) 14.25 14.25

For overprint see No. 509.

G27

G29

1982, Apr. 5 *Perf. 14*
239 G27 10c Prickly pear fruit .20 .20
240 G27 50c Flower buds .30 .30
241 G27 $1 Flower .50 .50
242 G27 $2 Cactus 1.25 1.25
Nos. 239-242 (4) 2.25 2.25

Princess Diana Type of Kiribati

1982, July 1 **Wmk. 380** *Perf. 14*
243 A99a 50c Anne Neville .20 .20
244 A99a 60c Arms of Anne Neville .20 .20
245 A99a $6 Diana, Princess of Wales .60 .60
Nos. 243-245 (3) 1.00 1.00

For overprints see Nos. 248-262.

1982, July 1 **Wmk. 373** *Perf. 14½*
246 G29 $1.50 Old, new uniforms .60 .60
247 G29 $2.50 Lord Baden-Powell 1.00 1.00

75th anniversary of Boy Scouts.

Nos. 243-245 Ovptd. "ROYAL BABY / BEQUIA"

1982, July 19 **Wmk. 380** *Perf. 14*
248 A99a 50c multicolored .20 .20
249 A99a 60c multicolored .20 .20
250 A99a $6 multicolored .60 .60
Nos. 248-250 (3) 1.00 1.00

"ROYAL BABY / CANOUAN"

1982, July 19
251 A99a 50c multicolored .20 .20
252 A99a 60c multicolored .20 .20
253 A99a $6 multicolored .60 .60
Nos. 251-253 (3) 1.00 1.00

"ROYAL BABY / MAYREAU"

1982, July 19
254 A99a 50c multicolored .20 .20
255 A99a 60c multicolored .20 .20
256 A99a $6 multicolored .60 .60
Nos. 254-256 (3) 1.00 1.00

"ROYAL BABY / MUSTIQUE"

1982, July 19
257 A99a 50c multicolored .20 .20
258 A99a 60c multicolored .20 .20
259 A99a $6 multicolored .60 .60
Nos. 257-259 (3) 1.00 1.00

"ROYAL BABY / UNION"

1982, July 19
260 A99a 50c multicolored .20 .20
261 A99a 60c multicolored .20 .20
262 A99a $6 multicolored .60 .60
Nos. 260-262 (3) 1.00 1.00

Christmas Type of 1981

1982, Nov. 18 *Perf. 13½*
263 A97 10c Mary and Joseph at inn .20 .20
264 A97 $1.50 Animals of stable .45 .45
265 A97 $2.50 Nativity .60 .60
a. Souvenir sheet of 3, #263-265 1.10 1.10
Nos. 263-265 (3) 1.25 1.25

No. 146 Surcharged

Perf. 13x12

1983, Apr. 26 **Wmk. 373**
266 G16 45c on 50c multicolored .35 .35

Union Island G30

1983, May 12 *Perf. 13½*
267 G30 50c Power Station, Clifton .20 .20
268 G30 60c Sunrise, Clifton Harbor .20 .20
269 G30 $1.50 School, Ashton .45 .45
270 G30 $2 Frigate Rock, Conch Shell Beach .65 .65
Nos. 267-270 (4) 1.50 1.50

Treaty of Versailles, Bicent. — G31

1983, Sept. 15 *Perf. 14½x14*
271 G31 45c British warship .20 .20
272 G31 60c American warship .30 .30
273 G31 $1.50 US troops, flag .65 .65

274 G31 $2 British troops in battle .95 .95
Nos. 271-274 (4) 2.10 2.10

200 Years of Manned Flight
G32

Designs: 45c, Montgolfier balloon 1783, vert. 60c, Ayres Turbo-thrush Commander. $1.50, Lebaudy "1" dirigible. $2, Space shuttle Columbia.

1983, Sept. 15 ***Perf. 14***

275 G32 45c multicolored .20 .20
276 G32 60c multicolored .20 .20
277 G32 $1.50 multicolored .45 .45
278 G32 $2 multicolored .65 .65
a. Souvenir sheet of 4, #275-278 1.75 1.75
Nos. 275-278 (4) 1.50 1.50

British Monarch Type of 1984

#279a, Arms of Henry VIII. #279b, Henry VIII. #280a, Arms of James I. #280b, James I. #281a, Henry VIII. #281b, Hampton Court. #282a, James I. #282b, Edinburgh Castle. #283a, Mary Rose. #283b, Henry VIII, Portsmouth harbor. #284a, Gunpowder Plot. #284b, James I & Gunpowder Plot.

1983, Oct. 25 Unwmk. ***Perf. 12½***

279 A110 60c Pair, #a.-b. .30 .30
280 A110 60c Pair, #a.-b. .30 .30
281 A110 75c Pair, #a.-b. .30 .30
282 A110 75c Pair, #a.-b. .30 .30
283 A110 $2.50 Pair, #a.-b. .90 .90
284 A110 $2.50 Pair, #a.-b. .90 .90
Nos. 279-284 (6) 3.00 3.00

Old Coinage — G33

1983, Dec. 1 Wmk. 373 ***Perf. 14***

291 G33 20c Quarter and half dollar, 1797 .20 .20
292 G33 45c Nine bitts, 1811-14 .20 .20
293 G33 75c Six and twelve bitts, 1811-14 .25 .25
294 G33 $3 Sixty six shillings, 1798 .85 .85
Nos. 291-294 (4) 1.50 1.50

Locomotives Type of 1985

1984-87 Litho. Unwmk. ***Perf. 12½***

Se-tenant Pairs, #a.-b.

a.-Side and front views.

b.-Action scene.

295 A120 1c 1948 Class C62, Japan .20 .20
296 A120 1c 1898 P.L.M. Grosse C, France .20 .20
297 A120 5c 1892 Class D13, US .20 .20
298 A120 5c 1903 Class V, UK .20 .20
299 A120 10c 1980 Class 253, UK .20 .20
300 A120 10c 1968 Class 581, Japan .20 .20
301 A120 10c 1874 1001 Class, UK .30 .30
302 A120 10c 1977 Class 142, DDR .30 .30
303 A120 15c 1899 T-9 Class, UK .20 .20
304 A120 15c 1932 Class C12, Japan .20 .20
305 A120 15c 1897 Class T15, Germany .30 .30
306 A120 20c 1808 Catch-me-who-can, UK .30 .30
307 A120 35c 1900 Claud Hamilton Class, UK .25 .25
308 A120 35c 1948 Class E10, Japan .30 .30
309 A120 35c 1937 Coronation Class, UK .30 .30
310 A120 40c 1936 Class 231, Algeria .40 .40
311 A120 40c 1927 Class 4P, UK .50 .50
312 A120 40c 1979 Class 120, Germany .50 .50
313 A120 45c 1941 Class J, US .30 .30
314 A120 45c 1900 Class 13, UK .40 .40
315 A120 50c 1913 Slieve Gullion Class S, UK .40 .40
316 A120 50c 1929 Class A3, UK .60 .60
317 A120 50c 1954 Class X, Australia .60 .60
318 A120 60c 1895 Class D16, US .30 .30
319 A120 60c 1904 J. B. Earle, UK .40 .40
320 A120 60c 1879 Halesworth, UK .40 .40
321 A120 60c 1930 Class V1, UK .60 .60
322 A120 60c 1986 Class 59, UK .60 .60
323 A120 70c 1935 Class E18, Germany .40 .40
324 A120 75c 1923 Class D50, Japan .40 .40
325 A120 75c 1859 Problem Class, UK .40 .40
326 A120 75c 1958 Class 40, UK .60 .60
327 A120 75c 1875 Class A, US .60 .60
328 A120 $1 1907 Star Class, British .40 .40
329 A120 $1 1898 Lyn, UK .40 .40
330 A120 $1 1961 Western Class, UK .50 .50
331 A120 $1 1958 Warship Class 42, UK .60 .60
332 A120 $1 1831 Samson Type, US .60 .60
333 A120 $1.20 1854 Hayes, US .60 .60
334 A120 $1.25 1902 Class P-69, US .60 .60
335 A120 $1.50 1865 Talyllyn, UK .50 .50
336 A120 $1.50 1899 Drummond's Bug, UK .50 .50
337 A120 $1.50 1913 Class 60-3 Shay, US .80 .80
338 A120 $1.50 1938 Class H1-d, Canada .80 .80
339 A120 $2 1890 Class 2120, Japan .80 .80
340 A120 $2 1951 Clan Class, UK .60 .60
341 A120 $2 1934 Pioneer Zephyr, US .90 .90
342 A120 $2.50 1948 Blue Peter, UK .50 .50
343 A120 $2.50 1874 Class Beattie Well Tank, UK 1.40 1.40
344 A120 $3 1906 Cardean, UK .70 .70
345 A120 $3 1840 Fire Fly, UK 1.00 1.00
a. Souvenir sheet of 4, #324, 345 3.75
346 A120 $3 1884 Class 1800, Japan .60 .60
Nos. 295-346 (52) 24.85 24.85

Issued: #297, 299, 303, 307, 313, 318, 328, 342, 3/15/84; #295, 298, 306, 308, 319, 329, 335, 344, 10/9/84; #296, 304, 324, 345, 1/31/85; #300, 310, 315, 343, 5/17/85; #309, 323, 333, 339, 9/16/85; #305, 314, 320, 325, 330, 336, 340, 346, 3/14/86; #301, 311, 316, 321, 326, 331, 334, 337, 5/5/87; #302, 312, 317, 322, 327, 332, 338, 341, 8/26/87.

Spotted Eagle Ray
G34

Wmk. 380

1984, Apr. 26 Litho. ***Perf. 14***

399 G34 45c shown .20 .20
400 G34 60c Queen trigger fish .20 .20
401 G34 $1.50 White spotted file fish .50 .50
402 G34 $2 Schoolmaster .70 .70
Nos. 399-402 (4) 1.60 1.60

For overprint see No. 504.

Cricket Players Type of 1985

1984-85 Unwmk. ***Perf. 12½***

Pairs, #a.-b.

403 A116 1c R. A. Woolmer, portrait .20 .20
404 A116 3c K. S. Ranjitsinhji, portrait .20 .20
405 A116 5c W. R. Hammond, in action .20 .20
406 A116 5c S. F. Barnes, portrait .20 .20
407 A116 30c D. L. Underwood, in action .30 .30
408 A116 30c R. Peel, in action .25 .25
409 A116 55c M. D. Moxon, in action .25 .25
410 A116 60c W. G. Grace, portrait .40 .40
411 A116 60c L. Potter, portrait .25 .25
412 A116 $1 E. A. E. Baptiste, portrait .40 .40
413 A116 $1 H. Larwood, in action .30 .30
414 A116 $2 A. P. E. Knott, portrait .45 .45
415 A116 $2 Yorkshire & Kent county cricket clubs .40 .40
416 A116 $2.50 Sir John Berry Hobbs, portrait .45 .45
417 A116 $3 L. E. G. Ames, in action .60 .60
Nos. 403-417 (15) 4.85 4.85

Size of stamps in No. 415: 58x38mm.

Issued: #403, 407, 410, 412, 414, 417, 8/16/84; #406, 408, 413, 416, 11/2/84; #409, 411, 415, 2/22/85.

Canouan Island
G35

1984, Sept. 3 Wmk. 380

433 G35 35c Junior secondary school .20 .20
434 G35 45c Police station .20 .20
435 G35 $1 Post office .45 .45
436 G35 $3 Anglican church 1.25 1.25
Nos. 433-436 (4) 2.10 2.10

Night-blooming Flowers — G36

1984, Oct. 15

437 G36 35c Lady of the night .25 .25
438 G36 45c Four o'clock .30 .30
439 G36 75c Mother-in-law's tongue .50 .50
440 G36 $3 Queen of the night 2.00 2.00
Nos. 437-440 (4) 3.05 3.05

Car Type of 1983

1984-86 Unwmk. ***Perf. 12½***

Se-tenant Pairs, #a.-b.

a.-Side and front views.

b.-Action scene.

441 A107 5c 1959 Facel Vega, France .20 .20
442 A107 5c 1903 Winton, Britain .20 .20
443 A107 15c 1914 Mercedes-Benz, Germany .20 .20
444 A107 25c 1936 BMW, Germany .20 .20
445 A107 45c 1954 Rolls Royce, Britain .20 .20
446 A107 50c 1934 Frazer Nash, Britain .30 .30
447 A107 60c 1931 Invicta, Britain .30 .30
448 A107 60c 1974 Lamborghini, Italy .20 .20
449 A107 $1 1959 Daimler, Britain .30 .30
450 A107 $1 1932 Marmon, US .30 .30
451 A107 $1.50 1966 Brabham Repco, Britain .30 .30
452 A107 $1.75 1968 Lotus Ford .30 .30
453 A107 $3 1949 Buick, US .60 .60
454 A107 $3 1927 Delage, France .50 .50
Nos. 441-454 (14) 4.10 4.10

Issued: #441, 444, 446, 453, 11/28/84; #442, 447, 449, 451, 4/9/85; #443, 445, 448, 450, 452, 454, 2/20/86.

Stamps issued 2/20/86 not inscribed "Leaders of the World."

Christmas Type of 1983

Wmk. 380

1984, Dec. 3 Litho. ***Perf. 14½***

469 A106 20c Three wise men, star .20 .20
470 A106 45c Journeying to Bethlehem .20 .20
471 A106 $3 Presenting gifts .60 .60
a. Souvenir sheet of 3, #469-471 1.40 1.40
Nos. 469-471 (3) 1.00 1.00

Shellfish
G37

1985, Feb. 11 ***Perf. 14***

472 G37 25c Caribbean king crab .25 .25
473 G37 60c Queen conch .40 .40
474 G37 $1 White sea urchin .50 .50
475 G37 $3 West Indian top shell .95 .95
Nos. 472-475 (4) 2.10 2.10

Flowers — G38

#476a, Cypripedium calceolus. #476b, Gentiana asclepiadea. #477a, Clianthus formosus. #477b, Celmisia coriacea. #478a, Erythronium americanum. #478b, Laelia anceps. #479a, Leucadendron discolor. #479b, Meconopsis horridula.

1985, Mar. 13 Unwmk. ***Perf. 12½***

476 G38 5c Pair, #a.-b. .20 .20
477 G38 55c Pair, #a.-b. .30 .30
478 G38 60c Pair, #a.-b. .30 .30
479 G38 $2 Pair, #a.-b. .70 .70
Nos. 476-479 (4) 1.50 1.50

Water Sports
G39

1985, May 9 Wmk. 380 ***Perf. 14***

484 G39 35c Windsurfing .25 .25
485 G39 45c Water skiing .25 .25
486 G39 75c Scuba diving .25 .25
487 G39 $3 Deep sea fishing .50 .50
Nos. 484-487 (4) 1.25 1.25

Tourism.

Fruits and Blossoms
G40

1985, June 24 ***Perf. 15***

488 G40 30c Passion fruit .20 .20
489 G40 75c Guava .40 .40
490 G40 $1 Sapodilla .60 .60
491 G40 $2 Mango 1.10 1.10
a. Souvenir sheet of 4, #488-491, perf. 14½x15 2.75 2.75
Nos. 488-491 (4) 2.30 2.30

For overprint see No. 503.

Queen Mother Type of 1985

#496a, Facing right. #496b, Facing forward. #497a, Facing right. #497b, Facing left. #498a, Facing right. #498b, Facing forward. #499a, Facing right. #499b, Facing left. #500a, As girl facing forward. #500b, Facing left.

1985, July 31 Unwmk. ***Perf. 12½***

496 A122 40c Pair, #a.-b. .20 .20
497 A122 75c Pair, #a.-b. .35 .35
498 A122 $1.10 Pair, #a.-b. .35 .35
499 A122 $1.75 Pair, #a.-b. .35 .35
Nos. 496-499 (4) 1.25 1.25

Souvenir Sheet of 2

500 A122 $2 Pair, #a.-b. .85 .85

Souvenir sheets containing two $4 or two $5 stamps exist.

Nos. 213-214, 236, 399, 488, and 496-497 Overprinted or Surcharged "CARIBBEAN ROYAL VISIT 1985" in 1, 2 or 3 Lines

Perfs., Wmks. as Before

1985, Oct. 27

503	G40	30c On #488	*1.00*	*1.00*
504	G37	45c On #399	*1.25*	*1.25*
505	A122	$1.10 On #496	*2.25*	*2.25*
506	A122	$1.10 On #497	*2.25*	*2.25*
507	A94a	$1.50 On $3.50, #213	*2.50*	*2.50*
508	A94b	$1.50 On $3.50, #214	*18.00*	*18.00*
509	G26	$3 On #236	*2.75*	*2.75*
		Nos. 503-509 (7)	*30.00*	*30.00*

Traditional Dances G41

1985, Dec. 16 Unwmk. *Perf. 15*

510	G41	45c Donkey man	.20	.20
511	G41	75c Cake dance, vert.	.30	.30
512	G41	$1 Bois-bois man, vert.	.45	.45
513	G41	$2 Maypole dance	.85	.85
		Nos. 510-513 (4)	1.80	1.80

Queen Elizabeth II 60th Birthday Type

5c, Elizabeth II. $1, At Princess Anne's christening. $4, As Princess. $6, In Canberra, 1982, vert. $8, Elizabeth II with crown.

1986, Apr. 21 *Perf. 12½*

514-517	A128	Set of 4	2.75	2.75

Souvenir Sheet

518	A128	$8 multi	3.25	3.25

Handicrafts — G41a

Wmk. 380

1986, Apr. 22 Litho. *Perf. 15*

519	G41a	10c Dolls	.20	.20
520	G41a	60c Basketwork	.20	.20
521	G41a	$1 Scrimshaw	.35	.35
522	G41a	$3 Model boat	1.10	1.10
		Nos. 519-522 (4)	1.85	1.85

World Cup Soccer Championship, Mexico — G42

Perf. 12½, 15 (#525-528)

1986, May 7 Unwmk.

523	G42	1c Uruguayan team	.20	.20
524	G42	10c Polish team	.20	.20
525	G42	45c Bulgarian player	.25	.25
526	G42	75c Iraqi player	.30	.30
527	G42	$1.50 S. Korean player	.70	.70
528	G42	$2 N. Ireland player	.75	.75
529	G42	$4 Portuguese team	1.00	1.00
530	G42	$5 Canadian team	1.10	1.10
		Nos. 523-530 (8)	4.50	4.50

Souvenir Sheets

531	G42	$1 like #529	.40	.40
532	G42	$3 like #523	1.25	1.25

Size: Nos. 525-528, 25x40mm.

Fungi — G43

Wmk. 380

1986, May 23 Litho. *Perf. 14*

533	G43	45c Marasmius pallescens	*2.00*	*2.00*
534	G43	60c Leucocoprinus fragilissimus	*2.25*	*2.25*
535	G43	75c Hygrocybe occidentalis	*2.50*	*2.50*
536	G43	$3 Xerocomus hypoxanthus	*7.25*	*7.25*
		Nos. 533-536 (4)	14.00	14.00

Royal Wedding Type of 1986

#539a, Sarah, Diana. #539b, Andrew. #540a, Anne, Andrew, Charles, Margaret, horiz. #540b, Sarah, Andrew, horiz.

1986 Unwmk. *Perf. 12½*

539	A132	60c Pair, #a.-b.	.40	.40
540	A132	$2 Pair, #a.-b.	1.25	1.25

Souvenir Sheet

541	A132a	$8 Andrew, Sarah, in coach	3.50	3.50

Issued: #539-540, July 18; #541, Oct. 15.

Nos. 539-540 Ovptd. in Silver "Congratulations to TRH The Duke & Duchess of York" in 3 Lines

1986, Oct. 15

542	A132	60c Pair, #a.-b.	.60	.60
543	A132	$2 Pair, #a.-b.	2.25	2.25

Dragonflies — G44

1986, Nov. 19 *Perf. 15*

546	G44	45c Brachymesia furcata	.20	.20
547	G44	60c Lepthemis vesiculosa	.25	.25
548	G44	75c Perithemis domitta	.30	.30
549	G44	$2.50 Tramea abdominalis, vert.	.95	.95
		Nos. 546-549 (4)	1.70	1.70

Statue of Liberty Type

Souvenir Sheets

Each stamp shows different views of Statue of Liberty and a different US president in the margin.

1986, Nov. 26 *Perf. 14*

550	A135	$1.50 multicolored	.60	.60
551	A135	$1.75 multicolored	.70	.70
552	A135	$2 multicolored	.80	.80
553	A135	$2.50 multicolored	1.00	1.00
554	A135	$3 multicolored	1.10	1.10
555	A135	$3.50 multicolored	1.40	1.40
556	A135	$5 multicolored	1.90	1.90
557	A135	$6 multicolored	2.25	2.25
558	A135	$8 multicolored	3.25	3.25
		Nos. 550-558 (9)	13.00	13.00

Birds of Prey — G45

Christmas — G46

1986, Nov. 26 Litho.

560	G45	10c Sparrow hawk	.20	.20
561	G45	45c Black hawk	.30	.30
562	G45	60c Duck hawk	.35	.35
563	G45	$4 Fish hawk	2.50	2.50
		Nos. 560-563 (4)	3.35	3.35

1986, Nov. 26

564	G46	45c Santa playing drums	.25	.25
565	G46	60c Santa wind surfing	.30	.30
566	G46	$1.25 Santa water skiing	.80	.80
567	G46	$2 Santa limbo dancing	1.25	1.25
a.		Souvenir sheet of 4, #564-567	2.75	2.75
		Nos. 564-567 (4)	2.60	2.60

Queen Elizabeth II, 40th Wedding Anniv. Type of 1987

1987, Oct. 15 *Perf. 12½*

568	A140	15c Elizabeth, Charles	.20	.20
569	A140	45c Victoria, Albert	.20	.20
570	A140	$1.50 Elizabeth, Philip	.55	.55
571	A140	$3 Elizabeth, Philip, diff.	1.10	1.10
572	A140	$4 Elizabeth, portrait	1.50	1.50
		Nos. 568-572 (5)	3.55	3.55

Souvenir Sheet

573	A140	$6 Elizabeth as Princess	2.50	2.50

Victoria's accession to the throne, 150th anniv.

Marine Life G48

1987, Dec. 17 *Perf. 15*

574	G48	45c Banded coral shrimp	.25	.25
575	G48	50c Arrow crab, flamingo tongue	.30	.30
576	G48	65c Cardinal fish	.40	.40
577	G48	$5 Moray eel	3.25	3.25
		Nos. 574-577 (4)	4.20	4.20

Souvenir Sheet

578	G48	$5 Puffer fish	3.25	3.25

America's Cup Yachts — G49

1988, Mar. 31 *Perf. 12½*

579	G49	50c Australia IV	.20	.20
580	G49	65c Crusader II	.25	.25
581	G49	75c New Zealand K27	.30	.30
582	G49	$2 Italia	.85	.85
583	G49	$4 White Crusader	1.75	1.75
584	G49	$5 Stars and Stripes	2.25	2.25
		Nos. 579-584 (6)	5.60	5.60

Souvenir Sheet

585	G49	$1 Champosa V	.80	.80

Bequia Regatta G50

1988, Mar. 31 *Perf. 15*

586	G50	5c Seine boats	.20	.20
587	G50	50c Friendship Rose	.20	.20
588	G50	75c Fishing boats	.30	.30
589	G50	$3.50 Yacht racing	1.50	1.50
		Nos. 586-589 (4)	2.20	2.20

Souvenir Sheet

Perf. 12½

590	G50	$8 Port Elizabeth	5.25	5.25

Tourism — G51

Aircraft of Mustique Airways, Genadine Tours.

1988, May 26 *Perf. 14x13½*

591	G51	15c multicolored	.20	.20
592	G51	65c multi, diff.	.25	.25
593	G51	75c multi, diff.	.30	.30
594	G51	$5 multi, diff.	2.00	2.00
		Nos. 591-594 (4)	2.75	2.75

Souvenir Sheet

595	G51	$10 Waterfall, vert.	6.00	6.00

No. 595 contains one 35x56mm stamp.

Great Explorers G52

Designs: 15c, Vitus Bering and the St. Peter. 75c, Bering and pancake ice. $1, David Livingstone and the Ma-Robert. $2, Livingstone meeting Henry M. Stanley. $3, John Speke (1827-1864) and Sir Richard Burton (1821-1890) welcomed at Tabori. $3.50, Speke, Burton at Lake Victoria. $4, Crewman of Christopher Columbus spotting land. $4.50, Columbus, exchange of gifts. $5, Sextant. $6, Columbus' ship landing in Bahamas, 1492.

1988, July 29 *Perf. 14*

596-603	G52	Set of 8	4.50	4.50

Souvenir Sheets

604	G52	$5 multi	2.00	2.00
605	G52	$6 multi	2.25	2.25

Nos. 602-603, 605 picture 500th anniversary discovery of America emblem.

A number of unissued items, imperfs., part perfs., missing color varieties, etc., were made available when the Format International inventory was liquidated.

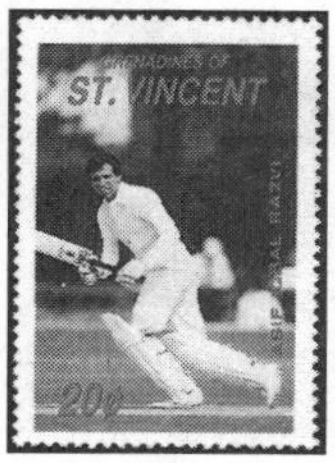

Cricketers — G53

1988, July 29 *Perf. 15*

606	G53	20c A. I. Razvi	.20	.20
607	G53	45c R. J. Hadlee	.25	.25
608	G53	75c M. D. Crowe	.50	.50
609	G53	$1.25 C. H. Lloyd	.80	.80
610	G53	$1.50 A. R. Boarder	.95	.95
611	G53	$2 M. D. Marshall	1.25	1.25
612	G53	$2.50 G. A. Hick	1.50	1.50
613	G53	$3.50 C. G. Greenidge, horiz.	2.25	2.25
		Nos. 606-613 (8)	7.70	7.70

A $3 souvenir sheet in the design of the $2 stamp was not a postal issue according to the St. Vincent P.O.

Tennis Type of 1987

1988, July 29 ***Perf. 12½***

614 A137 15c Pam Shriver, horiz. .20 .20
615 A137 50c Kevin Curran .20 .20
616 A137 75c Wendy Turnbull .30 .30
617 A137 $1 Evonne Cawley .40 .40
618 A137 $1.50 Ilie Nastase, horiz. .60 .60
619 A137 $2 Billie Jean King .80 .80
620 A137 $3 Bjorn Borg 1.25 1.25
621 A137 $3.50 Virginia Wade 1.40 1.40
Nos. 614-621 (8) 5.15 5.15

Souvenir Sheet

622 Sheet of 2 2.75 2.75
a. A137 $2.25 Stefan Edberg 1.25 1.25
b. A137 $2.25 Steffi Graf 1.25 1.25

No. 616 inscribed "Turnball" in error.

India '89, International Stamp Exhibition, New Dehli — G54

Disney characters and sites in India.

1989, Feb. 7 ***Perf. 14x13½***

623 G54 1c Fatehpur Sikri .20 .20
624 G54 2c Palace on Wheels .20 .20
625 G54 3c Old fort, Delhi .20 .20
626 G54 5c Pinjore Gardens .20 .20
627 G54 10c Taj Mahal .20 .20
628 G54 25c Chandni Chowk .20 .20
629 G54 $4 Agra Fort, Jaipur 2.50 2.50
630 G54 $5 Gandhi Memorial 3.50 3.50
Nos. 623-630 (8) 7.20 7.20

Souvenir Sheets

631 G54 $6 Qutab Minar, vert. 4.00 4.00
632 G54 $6 Palace of the Winds 4.00 4.00

Japanese Art Type

Paintings: 5c, The View at Yotsuya, by Hokusai. 30c, Landscape at Ochanomizu, by Hokuju. 45c, Itabashi, by Eisen. 65c, Early Summer Rain, by Kunisada. 75c, High Noon at Kasumigaseki, by Kuniyoshi. $1, The Yoshiwara Embankment by Moonlight, by Kuniyoshi. $4, The Bridge of Boats at Sano, by Hokusai. $5, Lingering Snow on Mount Hira, by Kunitora. No. 641, Colossus of Rhodes, by Kunitora. No. 642, Shinobazu Pond, by Kokan.

1989, July 6 ***Perf. 14x13½***

633-640 A170 Set of 8 9.40 9.40

Souvenir Sheets

641 A170 $6 multicolored 4.50 4.50
642 A170 $6 multicolored 4.50 4.50

Miniature Sheet

1990 World Cup Soccer Championships, Italy — G55

Soccer players and landmarks: a, Mt. Vesuvius. b, The Colosseum. c, Venice. d, Roman Forum. e, Leaning Tower of Pisa. f, Florence. g, The Vatican. h, The Pantheon.

1989, July 10 ***Perf. 14***

643 Sheet of 8 9.00 9.00
a.-h. G55 $1.50 any single 1.10 1.10

Discovery of America 500th Anniv. Type of Antigua & Barbuda

UPAE emblem and American Indians: 25c, Smoking tobacco. 75c, Rolling tobacco. $1, Body painting. No. 647a, Starting campfire. No. 647b, Woman drinking from bowl. No. 647c, Woman frying grain or corn patties. No. 647d, Adult resting in hammock using stone mortar and pestle. $4, Smoothing wood. No. 649, Chief. No. 650, Fishing with bow and arrow.

1989, Oct. 2 **Litho.** ***Perf. 14***

644 A196 25c multicolored .20 .20
645 A196 75c multicolored .60 .60
646 A196 $1 multicolored .75 .75
647 Strip of 4 4.50 4.50
a.-d. A196 $1.50 any single 1.10 1.10
648 A196 $4 multicolored 3.00 3.00
Nos. 644-648 (5) 9.05 9.05

Souvenir Sheets

649 A196 $6 multicolored 4.50 4.50
650 A196 $6 multicolored 4.50 4.50

No. 647 has continuous design.

1st Moon Landing Type

Designs: 5c *Columbia* command module. 40c, Neil Armstrong saluting flag on the Moon. 55c. Command module over Moon. 65c, *Eagle* liftoff from Moon. 70c, *Eagle* on the Moon. $1, Command module re-entering Earth's atmosphere. $3, Apollo 11 mission emblem. $5, Armstrong and Buzz Aldrin walking on the Moon. No. 659, Apollo 11 launch, vert. No. 660, Splashdown.

1989, Oct. 2 ***Perf. 14***

651-658 A171 Set of 8 8.50 8.50

Souvenir Sheets

659 A171 $6 multi, vert. 4.50 4.50
660 A171 $6 multi 4.50 4.50

Butterflies G56

1989, Oct. 16 **Litho.** ***Perf. 14x14½***

661 G56 5c Southern dagger tail .20 .20
662 G56 30c Androgeus swallowtail .25 .25
663 G56 45c Clench's hairstreak .35 .35
664 G56 65c Buckeye .50 .50
665 G56 75c Venezuelan sulphur .60 .60
666 G56 $1 Mimic .75 .75
667 G56 $4 Common longtail skipper 3.00 3.00
668 G56 $5 Carribean buckeye 3.75 3.75
Nos. 661-668 (8) 9.40 9.40

Souvenir Sheets

669 G56 $6 Flambeau 4.50 4.50
670 G56 $6 Queen, large orange sulphur, Ramsden's giant white 4.50 4.50

Flora — G57

1989, Nov. 1 **Litho.** ***Perf. 14***

671 G57 80c Solanum urens .60 .60
672 G57 $1.25 Passiflora andersonii .95 .95
673 G57 $1.65 Miconia andersonii 1.25 1.25
674 G57 $1.85 Pitcairnia sulphurea 1.40 1.40
Nos. 671-674 (4) 4.20 4.20

Christmas — G58

Walt Disney characters and classic automobiles.

1989, Dec. 20 ***Perf. 14x13½, 13½x14***

675 G58 5c 1907 Rolls-Royce .20 .20
676 G58 10c 1897 Stanley Steamer .20 .20
677 G58 15c 1904 Darracq Genevieve .20 .20
678 G58 45c 1914 Detroit Electric Coupe .35 .35
679 G58 55c 1896 Ford .40 .40
680 G58 $2 1904 REO Runabout 1.50 1.50
681 G58 $3 1899 Winton Mail Truck 2.25 2.25
682 G58 $5 1893 Duryea Car 3.75 3.75
Nos. 675-682 (8) 8.85 8.85

Souvenir Sheets

683 G58 $6 1912 Pope-Hartford 4.50 4.50
684 G58 $6 1908 Buick Model 10 4.50 4.50

Nos. 683-684 vert.

Battles of World War II G59

10c, 1st Battle of Narvik, 4/10/40. 15c, Allies land at Anzio, 1/22/44. 20c, Battle of Midway, 6/4/42. 45c, Allies launch offensive on Gustav Line, 5/11/44. 55c, Allies take over zones in Berlin, 7/3/45. 65c, Battle of the Atlantic, 3/1-20/43. 90c, Allies launch final phase of North African Campaign, 4/22/43. $3, US forces land on Guam, 7/21/44. $5, US 7th Army meets the 3rd Army across the Rhine, 3/26/45. #694, Battle of Leyte Gulf, 10/23/44. #695, The Dambusters Raid, 5/16/43.

1990, Apr. 2 **Litho.** ***Perf. 14***

685-694 G59 Set of 10 13.00 13.00

Souvenir Sheet

695 G59 $6 multi 4.50 4.50

Penny Black, 150th Anniv. — G60

$1, Stamp World London '90 emblem. $5, Negative image of the Penny Black. $6, Penny Black with non-existent letters.

1990, May 3 ***Perf. 14x15***

696 G60 $1 pale rose & blk .75 .75
697 G60 $5 pale violet & blk 3.50 3.50

Souvenir Sheet

698 G60 $6 dull blue & blk 4.50 4.50

Stamp World London '90.

Disney Characters Portraying Shakespearian Roles — G61

Designs: 20c, Goofy as Marc Antony in "Julius Caesar." 30c, Clarabelle Cow as nurse in "Romeo and Juliet." 45c, Pete as Falstaff in "Henry IV." 50c, Minnie Mouse as Portia in "The Merchant of Venice." $1, Donald Duck holding head of Yorick in "Hamlet." $2, Daisy Duck as Ophelia in "Hamlet." $4, Donald and Daisy Duck as Benedick and Beatrice in "Much Ado About Nothing." $5, Minnie Mouse and Donald Duck as Katherine and Petruchio in "The Taming of the Shrew." No. 707, Mickey and Minnie Mouse portraying Romeo and Juliet. No. 708, Clarabelle Cow as Titania in "A Midsummer Night's Dream."

1990, May ***Perf. 14x13½***

699-706 G61 Set of 8 10.00 10.00

Souvenir Sheets

707 G61 $6 multi 4.50 4.50
708 G61 $6 multi 4.50 4.50

World Cup Soccer Championships, Italy — G62

World Cup Trophy and players from participating countries.

1990, Sept. 24 **Litho.** ***Perf. 14***

709 G62 25c Scotland .20 .20
710 G62 50c Egypt .40 .40
711 G62 $2 Austria 1.50 1.50
712 G62 $4 United States 3.00 3.00
Nos. 709-712 (4) 5.10 5.10

Souvenir Sheets

713 G62 $6 Holland 4.50 4.50
714 G62 $6 England 4.50 4.50

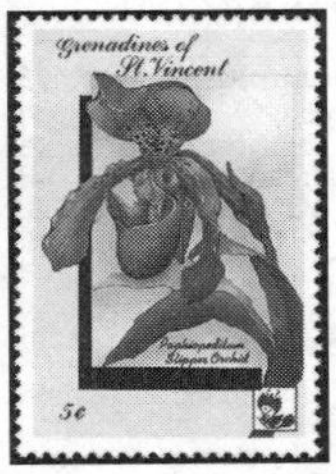

Orchids — G63

Designs: 5c, Paphiopedilum. 25c, Dendrobium phalaenopsis, Cymbidium. 30c, Miltonia candida. 50c, Epidendrum ibaguense, Cymbidium Elliot Rogers. $1, Rossioglassum grande. $2, Phalaenopsis Elisa Chang Lou, Masdevallia coccinea. $4, Cypripedium accale, Cypripedium calceolus. $5, Orchis spectabilis. No. 723, Epidendrum ibaguense, Phalaenopsis. No. 724, Dendrobium anosmum.

1990, Nov. 23 **Litho.** ***Perf. 14***

715-722 G63 Set of 8 10.00 10.00

Souvenir Sheets

723 G63 $6 multi 4.50 4.50
724 G63 $6 multi 4.50 4.50

Expo '90, Intl. Garden and Greenery Exposition, Osaka, Japan.

Birds G64

1990, Nov. 26

725 G64 5c Common ground dove .20 .20
726 G64 25c Purple martin .20 .20
727 G64 45c Painted bunting .35 .35
728 G64 55c Blue-hooded euphonia .40 .40
729 G64 75c Blue-gray tanager .55 .55
730 G64 $1 Red-eyed vireo .75 .75
731 G64 $2 Palm chat 1.50 1.50
732 G64 $3 North American jacana 2.25 2.25
733 G64 $4 Green-throated carib 3.00 3.00
734 G64 $5 St. Vincent parrot 3.75 3.75
Nos. 725-734 (10) 12.95 12.95

Souvenir Sheets

735 Sheet of 2 4.50 4.50
a. G64 $3 Bananaquit 2.25 2.25
b. G64 $3 Magnificent frigatebird 2.25 2.25
736 G64 $6 Red-legged honeycreeper 4.50 4.50

Queen Mother 90th Birthday Type

Photographs: Nos. 737a-737i, From 1900-1929. Nos. 738a-738i, From 1930-1959. Nos. 739a-739i, From 1960-1989. Nos. 740-748, Enlarged photographs used for Nos. 737-739.

1991, Feb. 14 **Litho.** ***Perf. 14***

Miniature Sheets of 9, #a.-i.

737 A193 $2 blue & multi 13.50 13.50
738 A193 $2 pink & multi 13.50 13.50
739 A193 $2 green & multi 13.50 13.50

Souvenir Sheets

740 A193 $5 like #737a 3.75 3.75
741 A193 $5 like #737f 3.75 3.75
742 A193 $5 like #737h 3.75 3.75

743 A193 $5 like #738b 3.75 3.75
744 A193 $5 like #738f 3.75 3.75
745 A193 $5 like #738g 3.75 3.75
746 A193 $5 like #739b 3.75 3.75
747 A193 $5 like #739d 3.75 3.75
748 A193 $5 like #739h 3.75 3.75

Paintings by Vincent Van Gogh — G65

Designs: 5c, View of Arles with Irises in the Foreground. 10c, View of Saintes-Maries, vert. 15c, An Old Woman of Arles, vert. 20c, Orchard in Blossom, Bordered by Cypresses. 25c, Three White Cottages in Saintes-Maries. 35c, Boats at Saintes-Maries-De-La-Mer. 40c, Interior of a Restaurant in Arles. 45c, Peasant Woman, vert. 55c, Self-Portrait, Sept. 1888, vert. 60c, A Pork Butcher's Shop Seen From a Window, vert. 75c, The Night Cafe in Arles. $1, Portrait of Milliet, Second Lieutenant of the Zouaves, vert. $2, The Cafe Terrace on the Place Du Forum Arles, at Night, vert. $3, The Zouave, vert. $4, Two Lovers (Fragment), vert. No. 764, Still Life: Blue Enamel Coffeepot, Earthenware and Fruit. No. 765, Street in Saintes-Maries. No. 766, A Lane Near Arles. No. 767, Harvest at La Crau, with Montmajour in the Background. No. 768, The Sower.

1991, June 10 Litho. *Perf. 13½*
749-764 G65 Set of 16 14.50 14.50

Size: 102x76mm

Imperf

765-766 G65 $5 Set of 2 7.50 7.50
767-768 G65 $6 Set of 2 9.00 9.00

Royal Family Birthday, Anniversary
Common Design Type

1991, July 5 Litho. *Perf. 14*
769 CD347 10c multicolored .20 .20
770 CD347 15c multicolored .20 .20
771 CD347 40c multicolored .30 .30
772 CD347 50c multicolored .40 .40
773 CD347 $1 multicolored .75 .75
774 CD347 $2 multicolored 1.50 1.50
775 CD347 $4 multicolored 3.00 3.00
776 CD347 $5 multicolored 3.75 3.75
Nos. 769-776 (8) 10.10 10.10

Souvenir Sheets

777 CD347 $5 Henry, William, Charles, Diana 3.75 3.75
778 CD347 $5 Elizabeth, Andrew, Philip 3.75 3.75

10c, 50c, $1, Nos. 776-777, Charles and Diana, 10th wedding anniversary. Others, Queen Elizabeth II, 65th birthday.

Phila Nippon '91 G66

Japanese locomotives: 10c, First Japanese steam. 25c, First American steam locomotive in Japan. 35c, Class 8620 steam. 50c, C53 steam. $1, DD-51 diesel. $2, RF 22327 electric. $4, EF-55 electric. $5, EF-58 electric. No. 787, Class 9600 steam, vert. No. 788, Class 4100 steam, vert. No. 789, C57 steam, vert. No. 790, C62 steam, vert.

1991, Aug. 12 Litho. *Perf. 14x13½*
779-786 G66 Set of 8 10.00 10.00

Souvenir Sheets

Perf. 12x13

787-790 G66 $6 Set of 4 18.00 18.00

Brandenburg Gate Type

Designs: 45c, Brandenburg Gate and Soviet Pres. Mikhail Gorbachev. 65c, Sign. 80c, Statue, soldier escaping through barbed wire. No. 794, Berlin police insignia. No. 795, Berlin coat of arms.

1991, Nov. 18 Litho. *Perf. 14*
791 A209 45c multicolored .35 .35
792 A209 65c multicolored .50 .50
793 A209 80c multicolored .60 .60
Nos. 791-793 (3) 1.45 1.45

Souvenir Sheets

794 A209 $5 multicolored 3.75 3.75
795 A209 $5 multicolored 3.75 3.75

Wolfgang Amadeus Mozart Type

Portrait of Mozart and: $1, Scene from "Abduction from the Seraglio." $3, Dresden, 1749. No. 799, Portrait, vert. No. 800, Bust, vert.

1991, Nov. 18 Litho. *Perf. 14*
797 A210 $1 multicolored .75 .75
798 A210 $3 multicolored 2.25 2.25

Souvenir Sheets

799 A210 $5 multicolored 3.75 3.75
800 A210 $5 multicolored 3.75 3.75

Boy Scout Type

Designs: $2, Scout delivering mail and Czechoslovakian (local) scout stamp. $4, Cog train, Boy Scouts on Mt. Snowdon, Wales, vert. Nos. 803-804, Emblem of World Scout Jamboree, Korea.

1991, Nov. 18 Litho. *Perf. 14*
801 A211 $2 multicolored 1.50 1.50
802 A211 $4 multicolored 3.00 3.00

Souvenir Sheets

803 A211 $5 tan & multi 3.75 3.75
804 A211 $5 violet blue & multi 3.75 3.75

Lord Robert Baden-Powell, 50th death anniv. and 17th World Scout Jamboree, Korea.

De Gaulle Type

Designs: 60c, De Gaulle in Djibouti, 1959. No. 807, In military uniform, vert. No. 808, Portrait as President.

1991, Nov. 18 Litho. *Perf. 14*
806 A212 60c .45 .45

Souvenir Sheets

807 A212 $5 multicolored 3.75 3.75
808 A212 $5 multicolored 3.75 3.75

A number has been reserved for additional value in this set.

Anniversaries and Events Type

Designs: $1.50, Otto Lilienthal, aviation pioneer. No. 810, Train in winter, vert. No. 811, Trans-Siberian Express Sign. No. 812, Man and woman celebrating. No. 813, Woman and man wearing hats. No. 814, Georg Ludwig Friedrich Laves, architect of Hoftheater, Hanover. No. 815, Locomotive, Trans-Siberian Railway, vert. No. 816, Cantonal arms of Appenzell and Thurgau. No. 817, Hanover, 750th anniv.

1991, Nov. 18 Litho. *Perf. 14*
809 A213 $1.50 multicolored 1.15 1.15
810 A213 $1.75 multicolored 1.30 1.30
811 A213 $1.75 multicolored 1.30 1.30
812 A213 $2 multicolored 1.50 1.50
813 A213 $2 multicolored 1.50 1.50
814 A213 $2 multicolored 1.50 1.50
Nos. 809-814 (6) 8.25 8.25

Souvenir Sheets

815 A213 $5 multicolored 3.75 3.75
816 A213 $5 multicolored 3.75 3.75
817 A213 $5 multicolored 3.75 3.75

First glider flight, cent. (#809). Trans-Siberian Railway, cent. (#810-811, 815). Swiss Confederation, 700th anniv. (#812-813, 816). City of Hanover, 750th anniv. (#814, 817). No. 815 contains one 42x58mm stamp.

Pearl Harbor Type of 1991
Miniature Sheet

Designs: a, Japanese submarines and aircraft leave Truk to attack Pearl Harbor. b, Japanese flagship, Akagi. c, Nakajima B5N2 Kate, attack leader. d, Torpedo bombers attack battleship row. e, Ford Island Naval Air Station. f, Doris Miller earns Navy Cross. g, USS West Virginia and USS Tennessee ablaze. h, USS Arizona destroyed. i, USS New Orleans. j, Pres. Roosevelt declares war.

1991, Nov. 18 *Perf. 14½x15*
818 A214 $1 Sheet of 10, #a.-j. 7.50 7.50

Disney Christmas Card Type

Card design and year of issue: 10c, Mickey in sleigh pulled by Pluto, 1974. 55c, Donald, Pluto, and Mickey watching marching band, 1961. 65c, Greeting with stars, 1942. 75c, Mickey, Donald watch Merlin create a snowman, 1963. $1.50, Mickey placing wreath on door, 1958. $2, Mickey as Santa beside fireplace, 1957. $4, Mickey manipulating "Pinnochio" for friends. $5, Prince Charming and Cinderella dancing beside Christmas tree, 1987. No. 827, Snow White, 1957, vert. No. 828, Santa riding World War II bomber, 1942, vert.

1991, Nov. 18 *Perf. 14x13½,13½x14*
819-826 A216 Set of 8 11.00 11.00

Souvenir Sheets

827-828 A216 $6 Set of 2 9.00 9.00

Nos. 819-826 are horiz.

Queen Elizabeth II's Accession to the Throne, 40th Anniv.
Common Design Type

1992, Feb. 6 Litho. *Perf. 14*
829 CD348 15c multicolored .20 .20
830 CD348 45c multicolored .35 .35
831 CD348 $2 multicolored 1.50 1.50
832 CD348 $4 multicolored 3.00 3.00
Nos. 829-832 (4) 5.05 5.05

Souvenir Sheets

833 CD348 $6 Queen at left, beach 4.50 4.50
834 CD348 $6 Queen at right, building 4.50 4.50

World Columbian Stamp Expo Type

Walt Disney characters as famous Chicagoans: 10c, Mickey as Walt Disney walking past birthplace. 50c, Donald Duck and nephews sleeping in George Pullman's railway cars. $1, Daisy Duck as Jane Addams in front of Hull House. $5, Mickey as Carl Sandburg. No. 839, Grandma McDuck as Mrs. O'Leary with her cow, vert.

1992, Apr. Litho. *Perf. 14x13½*
835 A220 10c multicolored .20 .20
836 A220 50c multicolored .35 .35
837 A220 $1 multicolored .75 .75
838 A220 $5 multicolored 3.75 3.75
Nos. 835-838 (4) 5.05 5.05

Souvenir Sheet

Perf. 13½x14

839 A220 $6 multicolored 4.50 4.50

Nos. 840-844 have not been used.

Granada '92 Type

Walt Disney characters as Spanish explorers in New World: 15c, Aztec King Goofy giving treasure to Big Pete as Hernando Cortes. 40c, Mickey as Hernando de Soto discovering Mississippi River. $2, Goofy as Vasco Nunez de Balboa discovering Pacific Ocean. $4, Donald Duck as Francisco Coronado discovering Rio Grande. $6, Mickey as Ponce de Leon discovering Fountain of Youth.

1992, Apr. *Perf. 14x13½*
845 A221 15c multicolored .20 .20
846 A221 40c multicolored .35 .35
847 A221 $2 multicolored 1.50 1.50
848 A221 $4 multicolored 3.00 3.00
Nos. 845-848 (4) 5.05 5.05

Souvenir Sheet

Perf. 13½x14

849 A221 $6 multicolored 4.50 4.50

Nos. 850-854 have not been used.

Discovery of America, 500th Anniv. Type

10c, King Ferdinand & Queen Isabella. 45c, Santa Maria & Nina in Acul Bay, Haiti. 55c, Santa Maria, vert. $2, Columbus' fleet departing Canary Islands, vert. $4, Sinking of Santa Maria off Hispanola. $5, Nina and Pinta returning to Spain. #861, Columbus' fleet during night storm. #862, Columbus landing on San Salvador.

1992, May 22 Litho. *Perf. 14*
855-860 A222 Set of 6 9.00 9.00

Souvenir Sheets

861-862 A222 $6 Set of 2 9.00 9.00

World Columbian Stamp Expo '92, Chicago.

Mushrooms — G67

Designs: 10c, Entoloma bakeri. 15c, Hydropus paraensis. 20c, Leucopaxillus gracillimus. 45c, Hygrotrama dennisianum. 50c, Leucoagaricus hortensis. 65c, Pyrrhoglossum pyrrhum. 75c, Amanita craeoderma. $1, Lentinus bertieri. $2, Dennisiomyces griseus. $3, Xerulina asprata. $4, Hygrocybe acutoconica. $5, Lepiota spiculata. No. 879, Pluteus crysophlebius. No. 880, Lepiota volvatua. No. 881, Amanita lilloi.

1992, July 2
867-878 G67 Set of 12 13.00 13.00

Souvenir Sheets

879-881 G67 $6 each 4.50 4.50

Butterfly Type of 1992

15c, Nymphalidae paulogramma 20c, Heliconius cydno. 30c, Ithomiidae eutresis hypereia. 45c, Eurytides Columbus koll, vert. 55c, Papilio ascolius. 75c, Anaea pasibula. 80c, Heliconius doris. $1, Nymphalidae persisama pitheas. $2, Nymphalidae batesia hypochlora. $3, Heliconius erato. $4, Elzunia cassandrina. $5, Ithomiidae sais. #894, Pieridae dismorphia orise. #895, Nymphalidae podotricha. #896, Oleria tigilla.

1992, June 15 Litho. *Perf. 14*
882-893 A225 Set of 12 13.75 13.75

Souvenir Sheets

894-896 A225 $6 Set of 3 13.50 13.50

Genoa '92.

Hummingbirds Type of 1992

5c, Antillean crested, female, horiz. 10c, Blue-tailed emerald, female. 35c, Antillean mango, male, horiz. 45c, Antillean mango, female, horiz. 55c, Green-throated carib, horiz. 65c, Green violet-ear. 75c, Blue-tailed emerald, male, horiz. $1, Purple throated carib. $2, Copper-rumped, horiz. $3, Rufous-breasted hermit. $4, Antillean crested, male. $5, Green breasted mango, male. #909, Blue-tailed emerald. #910, Antillean mango, diff. #911, Antillean crested, male, diff.

1992, July 7 Litho. *Perf. 14*
897-908 A224 Set of 12 14.00 14.00

Souvenir Sheets

909-911 A224 $6 Set of 3 13.50 13.50

Genoa '92.

Discovery of America Type

1992 Litho. *Perf. 14½*
912 A230 $1 Coming ashore .75 .75
913 A230 $2 Natives, ships 1.50 1.50

Organization of East Caribbean States.

Summer Olympics Type

10c, Volleyball, vert. 15c, Men's floor exercise. 25c, Cross-country skiing, vert. 30c, 110-meter hurdles. 45c, 120-meter ski jump. 55c, Women's 4x100-meter relay, vert. 75c, Triple jump, vert. 80c, Mogul skiing, vert. $1, 100-meter butterfly. $2, Tornado class yachting. $3, Decathlon. $5, Equestrian jumping. #926, Ice hockey. #927, Single luge. #928, Soccer.

1992, Apr. 21 Litho. *Perf. 14*
914 A219 10c multicolored .20 .20
915 A219 15c multicolored .20 .20
916 A218 25c multicolored .20 .20
917 A219 30c multicolored .25 .25
918 A218 45c multicolored .35 .35
919 A219 55c multicolored .40 .40
920 A219 75c multicolored .60 .60
921 A218 80c multicolored .60 .60
922 A219 $1 multicolored .75 .75
923 A219 $2 multicolored 1.50 1.50
924 A219 $3 multicolored 2.25 2.25
925 A219 $5 multicolored 3.75 3.75
Nos. 914-925 (12) 11.05 11.05

Souvenir Sheets

926 A218 $6 multicolored 4.50 4.50
927 A218 $6 multicolored 4.50 4.50
928 A219 $6 multicolored 4.50 4.50

Christmas Art Type

Details or entire paintings: 10c, Our Lady with St. Roch & St. Anthony of Padua, by Giorgione. 40c, St. Anthony of Padua, by Master of the Emboridered Leaf. 45c, Madonna & Child in a Landscape, by Orazio Gentileschi. 50c, Madonna & Child with St. Anne, by Leonardo da Vinci. 55c, The Holy Family, by Giuseppe Maria Crespi. 65c, Madonna & Child, by Andrea Del Sarto. 75c, Madonna & Child with Sts. Lawrence & Julian, by Gentile da Fabriano. $1, Virgin & Child, by School of Parma. $2, Madonna with the Iris in the style of Durer. $3, Virgin & Child with St. Jerome & St. Dominic, by Filippino Lippi. $4, Rapolano Madonna, by Ambrogio Lorenzetti. $5, The Virgin & Child with Angels in a Garden with a

Rose Hedge, by Stefano da Verona. #941, Virgin & Child with St. John the Baptist, by Botticelli. #942, Madonna & Child with St. Anne, by Leonardo da Vinci. #943, Madonna & Child with Grapes, by Lucas Cranach the Elder.

1992, Nov. Litho. *Perf. 13½x14*

929-940	A232	Set of 12	14.00	14.00

Souvenir Sheets

941-943	A232	$6 Set of 3	13.50	13.50

Anniversaries and Events — G68

Designs: 10c, Nina in the harbor of Baracoa. No. 948, Columbus' fleet at sea. No. 949, America 3, US and Il Moro, Italy. No. 945, Zeppelin LZ3, 1907. No. 946, Blind man with guide dog, vert. No. 947, Guide dog. No. 950, German flag, natl. arms, Konrad Adenauer. No. 951, Hands breaking bread, vert. $2, Mars, Voyager 2. $3, Berlin airlift, Adenauer. No. 954, Wolfgang Amadeus Mozart, Constanze, vert. No. 955, Adenauer, Cologne after World War II. No. 956, Zeppelin LZ 37 shot down over England, World War I. $5, Buildings in Germany, Adenauer. No. 958, Scene from "Don Giovanni," vert. No. 959, Columbus looking through telescope. No. 960, Count Ferdinand von Zeppelin, facing right. No. 960A, Count Ferdinand von Zeppelin, facing left. No. 961, Mars Observer. No. 962, Adenauer with hand on face, vert. No. 963, Adenauer, diff.

1992, Dec. *Perf. 14*

944	G68	10c multicolored	.20	.20
945	G68	75c multicolored	.60	.60
946	G68	75c multicolored	.60	.60
947	G68	75c multicolored	.60	.60
948	G68	$1 multicolored	.75	.75
949	G68	$1 multicolored	.75	.75
950	G68	$1 multicolored	.75	.75
951	G68	$1 multicolored	.75	.75
952	G68	$2 multicolored	1.50	1.50
953	G68	$3 multicolored	2.25	2.25
954	G68	$4 multicolored	3.00	3.00
955	G68	$4 multicolored	3.00	3.00
956	G68	$4 multicolored	3.00	3.00
957	G68	$5 multicolored	3.75	3.75
		Nos. 944-957 (14)	21.50	21.50

Souvenir Sheets

958-963	G68	$6 each	4.50	4.50

Discovery of America, 500th anniv. (#944, 948, 959). Count Zeppelin, 75th death anniv. (#945, 956, 960-960A). Lions Intl., 75th anniv. (#946-947). Konrad Adenauer, 25th death anniv. (#950, 953, 955, 957, 962-963).America's Cup yacht race (#949). Intl. Conference on Nutrition, Rome (#951). Intl. Space Year (#952, 961). Wolfgang Amadeus Mozart, bicent. of death (in 1991) (#954, 958).

Issued: #945, 956, 960-960A, 12/15; others, Dec.

Miniature Sheets

Walt Disney's Tales of Uncle Scrooge — G69

Goldilocks (Daisy Duck) and the Three Bears: No. 964a, Comes upon the house. b, Finds three bowls of soup. c, Finds three chairs. d, Ventures upstairs. e, Tries Papa Bear's bed. f, Falls asleep in Baby Bear's bed. g, The Three Bears return home. h, Baby Bear finds Goldilocks in his bed. i, Goldilocks awakens.

No. 970, The Three Bears in the forest, vert. No. 971, Goldilocks runs home.

The Princess (Minnie Mouse) and the Pea: No. 965a, Prince Mickey in search of a bride. b, Princess Minnie caught in a storm. c, Queen Clarbelle meets the princess. d, Royal family entertains Princess Minnie. e, Queen places a pea on the mattress. f, Mattresses upon mattresses. g, Princess Minnie at her bed-chamber. h, Princess Minnie very tired the next morning. i, A true princess for a real prince.

No. 972, Prince Mickey's useless search for a true princess. No. 973, Mickey's royal family lived happily ever after.

Little Red Riding Hood (Minnie Mouse): No. 966a, Off to Grandmother's. b, Stopping for flowers. c, Followed by the wolf. d, Frightened by the wolf. e, Wolf charges into Grandmother's house. f, Little Red Riding Hood at Grandmother's door. g, "What big teeth you have." h, Calling woodsman for help. i, Woodsman to the rescue.

No. 974, Little Riding Hood on the way to Grandmother's, vert. No. 975, A happy ending.

Hop O'-My-Thumb (Mickey, Minnie, family): No. 967a, Poor woodcutter without food for his children. b, Pebbles to find way back. c, Sadly leaving children's forest. d, Surveying from tree top. e, Ogress sends boys to bed. f, Ogre and his magic seven-league boots. g, Ogre chasing boys. h, Taking the magic seven-league boots. i, Running to Royal Palace.

No. 976, Boy of woodcutter with bag over shoulder. No. 977, Woodcutter's family reunited.

Pied Piper of Hamelin (Donald, Mickey and friends): No. 968a, Mayor (Donald) offers reward. b, Piper Mickey accepts the challenge. c, Piper leads rats to the river. d, Piper promises revenge. Children follow Piper outside village gates. f, Mayor and townspeople watch from above. g, Children follow Piper through countryside. h, Children pass through the cavern. i, All closed off from Hamelin, except for one.

No. 978, Pied Piper leading rats past town square. No. 979, Piper Mickey encouraging children in land of sweets, vert.

Puss in Boots (Goofy, Donald and friends): No. 969a, Gift for the king. b, Puss brings Marquis of Carabas to bathe in river. c, Puss calls for king's help. d, King introduces his daughter (Daisy Duck). e, Puss and reapers. f, Puss received by the Ogre. g, Ogre changed into a lion. h, Ogre changed into a mouse. i, Puss shows off Marquis' castle.

No. 980, Miller's estate, Donald with cat, Puss, donkey. No. 981, Marriage of Marquis of Carabis to daughter of the king, vert.

Perf. 14x13½, 13½x14

1992, Dec. 15 Litho.

964	G69	60c Sheet of 9, #a.-i.	4.25	4.25
965	G69	60c Sheet of 9, #a.-i.	4.25	4.25
966	G69	60c Sheet of 9, #a.-i.	4.25	4.25
967	G69	60c Sheet of 9, #a.-i.	4.25	4.25
968	G69	60c Sheet of 9, #a.-i.	4.25	4.25
969	G69	60c Sheet of 9, #a.-i.	4.25	4.25

Souvenir Sheets

Perf. 13½x14, 14x13½

970-981	G69	$6 each	4.50	4.50

Disney Animated Films Type

Miniature Sheets

Duck Tales (Donald Duck and family): No. 982: a, Scrooge McDuck, Launchpad. b, Scrooge reads treasure map. c, Collie Baba's treasure revealed. d, Webby finds magic lamp. e, Genie and new masters. f, Webby gets her wish. g, Scrooge McDuck, Genie. h, Retrieving the magic lamp. i, Villain Merlock, Genie.

No. 984, Webby's tea party, vert. No. 985, Treasure of the lost lamp, vert.

Darkwing Duck: No. 983: a, Darkwing Duck. b, Tuskerninni. c, Megavolt. d, Bushroot. e, Steelbeak. f, Eggman. g, Agent Gryzlikoff. h, Director J. Gander Hooter.

No. 985A, Gosalyn. No. 985B, Honker, horiz.

Perf. 14x13½, 13½x14

1992, Dec. 15 Litho.

982	A247a	60c Sheet of 9, #a.-i.	4.00	4.00
983	A247b	60c Sheet of 8, #a.-h.	3.60	3.60

Souvenir Sheets

984	A247a	$6 multicolored	4.50	4.50
985	A247a	$6 multicolored	4.50	4.50
985A	A247b	$6 multicolored	4.50	4.50
985B	A247b	$6 multicolored	4.50	4.50

Miniature Sheets

G71

Disney Animated Films — G72

The Great Mouse Detective: No. 986: a, Olivia and Flaversham. b, Olivia's mechanical mouse. c, Ratigan's evil scheme. d, Ratigan and Mechanical Mouse Queen. e, Fidget pens ransom note. f, Basil studies clues. g, Fidget holds Olivia captive. h, Ratigan in disguise. i, Basil and Dr. Dawson, crime stoppers.

Oliver & Company: No. 987: a, Dodger. b, Oliver. c, Dodger and Oliver. d, Oliver introduced to the Company. e, Oliver meets Fagin. f, Fagin's bedtime story hour. g, Oliver sleeping with Dodger. h, Fagin's trike. i, Georgette and Tito.

The Legend of Sleepy Hollow: No. 988: a, Ichabod Crane comes to town. b, Ichabod meets Katrina Van Tassel. c, Schoolmaster Ichabod Crane. d, Ichabod and rival, Brom Bones. e, Ichabod and Katrina at Halloween dance. f, Ichabod is scared of ghosts. g, Ichabod in Sleepy Hollow. h, Ichabod and his horse. i, Meeting the Headless Horseman.

No. 989, Detective Basil holding pipe. No. 990, Detective Basil holding magnifying glass. No. 991, Oliver. No. 992, Oliver and kittens. No. 993, Ichabod Crane, children praying, vert. No. 994, Headless Horseman.

Perf. 14x13½, 13½x14

1992, Dec. 15 Litho.

986	G71	60c Sheet of 9, #a.-i.	4.00	4.00
987	G71	60c Sheet of 9, #a.-i.	4.00	4.00
988	G72	60c Sheet of 9, #a.-i.	4.00	4.00

Souvenir Sheets

989-994	G71	$6 each	4.50	4.50

Elvis Presley Type of 1993

Designs: a, Portrait. b, With guitar. c, With microphone.

1993 Litho. *Perf. 14*

1001	A244	$1 Strip of 3, #a.-c.	2.25	2.25

Printed in sheets of 9 stamps.

Medicinal Plants — G73

Designs: 5c, Oleander. 10c, Beach morning glory. 30c, Calabash. 45c, Porita tree. 55c, Cashew. 75c, Prickly pear. $1, Shell ginger. $1.50, Avocado. $2, Mango. $3, Blood flower. $4, Sugar apple. $5, Barbados lily.

1994, May 20 Litho. *Perf. 13½x13*

1002-1013	G73	Set of 12	14.00	14.00

Diana, Princess of Wales (1961-97)
G74 G75

1997 Litho. *Perf. 14*

1015	G74	$1 multicolored	.75	.75
1016	G75	$1 multicolored	.75	.75

Each issued in sheets of 6.

Paintings Type of 1999

Various pictures of flowers making up a photomosaic of the Queen Mother. Stamps inscribed "Mustique."

2000, Sept. 5 *Perf. 13¾*

1017	A442	$1 Sheet of 8, #a-h	6.00	6.00
i.		As No. 1017, imperf.	6.00	6.00

Queen Mother Type of 2000 Inscribed "Canouan"

2000, Sept. 5 Litho. *Perf. 14*

1018	A472	$1.40 multi	1.00	1.00

Issued in sheets of 6.

SEMI-POSTAL STAMPS

Nos. 190-193 Surcharged

1980, Aug. 7 Litho. *Perf. 13½*

B1	A90	25c + 50c Running	.20	.20
B2	A90	50c + 50c Sailing	.20	.20
B3	A90	$1 + 50c Long jump	.20	.20
B4	A90	$2 + 50c Swimming	.35	.35
		Nos. B1-B4 (4)	.95	.95

OFFICIAL STAMPS

Nos. 209-214 Ovptd. "OFFICIAL"

1982, Oct. 11

O1	A66	50c on No. 209	.20	.20
O2	A67	50c on No. 210	.20	.20
O3	A66	$3 on No. 211	.90	.90
O4	A67	$3 on No. 212	.90	.90
O5	A66	$3.50 on No. 213	1.10	1.10
O6	A67	$3.50 on No. 214	1.10	1.10
		Nos. O1-O6 (6)	4.40	4.40

BEQUIA

All stamps are types of St. Vincent ("A" illustration letter), St. Vincent Grenadines ("G" illustration letter) or Bequia ("B" illustration letter).

"Island" issues are listed separately beginning in 1984. See St. Vincent Grenadines Nos. 84-111, 248-262 for earlier issues.

Locomotive Type of 1985

1984-87 Litho. Unwmk. *Perf. 12½*

Se-tenant Pairs, #a.-b.

a.-Side and front views.

b.-Action scene.

1	A120	1c 1942 Challenger Class, US	.20	.20
2	A120	1c 1908 S3/6, Germany	.20	.20
3	A120	5c 1944 2900 Class, US	.20	.20
4	A120	5c 1903 Jersey Lily, UK	.20	.20
5	A120	10c 1882 Gladstone Class, UK	.20	.20
6	A120	10c 1909 Thundersley, UK	.20	.20
7	A120	15c 1860 Ser Class 118, UK	.20	.20
8	A120	25c 1893 No. 999 NY Central & Hudson River, US	.20	.20
9	A120	25c 1921 Class G2, UK	.20	.20
10	A120	25c 1902 Jr. Class 6400, Japan	.20	.20
11	A120	25c 1877 Class G3, Germany	.20	.20
12	A120	35c 1945 Niagara Class, US	.25	.25
13	A120	35c 1938 Manor Class, UK	.25	.25
14	A120	40c 1880 Class D VI, Germany	.25	.25
15	A120	45c 1914 K4 Class, US	.30	.30
16	A120	50c 1960 Class U25B, US	.35	.35
17	A120	55c 1921 Stephenson, UK	.40	.40
18	A120	55c 1909 Class H4, US	.40	.40

19 A120 60c 1922 Baltic, UK .40 .40
20 A120 60c 1903 J.R. 4500, Japan .40 .40
21 A120 60c 1915 Class LS .40 .40
22 A120 75c 1841 Borsig, Germany .50 .50
23 A120 75c 1943 Royal Scot, UK .50 .50
24 A120 75c 1961 Krauss-Maffei, US .50 .50
25 A120 $1 1928 River IRT, UK .70 .70
26 A120 $1 1890 Electric, UK .70 .70
27 A120 $1 1934 A.E.C., UK .70 .70
28 A120 $1.50 1929 No. 10000, UK 1.00 1.00
29 A120 $2 1904 City Class, UK 1.40 1.40
30 A120 $2 1901 No. 737, UK 1.40 1.40
31 A120 $2 1847 Cornwall, UK 1.40 1.40
32 A120 $2.50 1938 Duke Dog Class, UK 1.75 1.75
33 A120 $2.50 1881 Ella, UK 1.75 1.75
34 A120 $3 1910 George V Class, UK 2.00 2.00
Nos. 1-34 (34) 19.90 19.90

Issued: #1, 3, 5, 8, 12, 15, 28-29, 2/22/84; #2, 4, 6, 13, 22, 25, 32, 34, 11/26/84; #9, 17, 19, 30, 2/1/85; #10, 18, 20, 23, 26, 33, 8/14/85; #7, 11, 14, 16, 21, 24, 27, 31, 11/16/87.

Stamps issued 11/16/87 are not inscribed "Leaders of the World."

St. Vincent Grenadines Nos. 222-238 Ovptd. "BEQUIA"

Perf. 14x13½

1984, Aug. 23 Wmk. 373

69 G26 1c on No. 222 .20 .20
70 G26 3c on No. 223 .20 .20
71 G26 5c on No. 224 .20 .20
72 G26 6c on No. 225 .20 .20
73 G26 10c on No. 226 .20 .20
74 G26 15c on No. 227 .20 .20
75 G26 20c on No. 228 .20 .20
76 G26 25c on No. 229 .20 .20
77 G26 30c on No. 230 .20 .20
78 G26 50c on No. 231 .30 .30
79 G26 60c on No. 232 .40 .40
80 G26 75c on No. 233 .50 .50
81 G26 $1 on No. 234 .65 .65
82 G26 $2 on No. 235 1.25 1.25
83 G26 $3 on No. 236 2.00 2.00
84 G26 $5 on No. 237 3.25 3.25
85 G26 $10 on No. 238 6.75 6.75
Nos. 69-85 (17) 16.90 16.90

Car Type of 1983

1984-87 Unwmk. *Perf. 12½*

Se-tenant Pairs, #a.-b.

a.-Side and front views.

b.-Action scene.

***1953 Cadillac, US\20—20**

87 A107 5c 1932 Fiat, Italy .20 .20
88 A107 5c 1968 Excalibur, US .20 .20
89 A107 5c 1952 Hudson, US .20 .20
90 A107 10c 1924 Leyand, UK .20 .20
91 A107 20c 1911 Marmon, US .20 .20
92 A107 20c 1950 Alfa Romeo, Italy .20 .20
93 A107 20c 1968 Ford Escort, UK .20 .20
94 A107 20c 1939 Maserati 8 CTF, Italy .20 .20
95 A107 25c 1963 Ford, UK .20 .20
96 A107 25c 1958 Vanwall, UK .20 .20
97 A107 25c 1910 Stanley, US .20 .20
98 A107 35c 1948 Ford Wagon, US .25 .25
99 A107 40c 1936 Auto Union, Germany .30 .30
100 A107 45c 1907 Chadwick, US .35 .35
101 A107 50c 1924 Lanchester, UK .40 .40
102 A107 50c 1957 Austin-Healy, UK .40 .40
103 A107 60c 1935 Brewster-Ford, US .45 .45
104 A107 60c 1942 Willys Jeep, US .45 .45
105 A107 65c 1929 Isotta, Italy .50 .50
106 A107 75c 1940 Lincoln, US .60 .60
107 A107 75c 1964 Bluebird II, UK .60 .60
108 A107 75c 1948 Moore-Offenhauser, US .60 .60
109 A107 75c 1936 Ford, UK .60 .60
110 A107 80c 1936 Mercedes Benz, Germany .65 .65
111 A107 90c 1928 Mercedes Benz SSK, Germany .70 .70
112 A107 $1 1907 Rolls Royce, UK .75 .75
113 A107 $1 1955 Citroen, France .75 .75
114 A107 $1 1936 Fiat, Italy .75 .75
115 A107 $1 1922 Dusenberg, US .75 .75
116 A107 $1 1957 Pontiac Bonneville, US .75 .75
117 A107 $1.25 1916 Hudson Super Six, US 1.00 1.00
118 A107 $1.25 1977 Coyote Ford, US 1.00 1.00
119 A107 $1.50 1960 Porsche, Germany 1.25 1.25
120 A107 $1.50 1970 Plymouth, US 1.25 1.25
121 A107 $1.75 1933 Stutz, US 1.35 1.35
122 A107 $2 1910 Benz-Blitzen, Germany 1.60 1.60
123 A107 $2 1933 Napier Railton, UK 1.60 1.60
124 A107 $2.50 1978 BMW, Germany 2.00 2.00
125 A107 $3 1912 Hispano Suiza, Spain 2.40 2.40
126 A107 $3 1954 Mercedes Benz, Germany 2.40 2.40
127 A107 $3 1927 Stutz Black Hawk, US 2.40 2.40
Nos. 86-127 (42) 31.25 31.25

Issued: #86, 99, 112, 119, 9/14; #87, 90-91, 95, 106, 113, 124-125, 12/19; #88, 96, 101, 114, 117, 122, 6/25/85; #92, 100, 120, 123, 9/26/85; #97, 102, 105, 107, 115, 126, 1/29/86; #93, 103, 108, 111, 116, 127, 12/23/86; #89, 94, 98, 104, 109-110, 118, 121, 7/22/87.

Beginning on Sept. 26, 1985, this issue is not inscribed "Leaders of the World."

1984 Summer Olympics — B1

#170a, Men's gymnastics. #170b, Women's gymnastics. #171a, Men's javelin. #171b, Women's javelin. #172a, Women's basketball. #172b, Men's basketball. #173a, Women's long jump. #173b, Men's long jump.

1984, Sept. 14 *Perf. 12½*

170 B1 1c Pair, #a.-b. .20 .20
171 B1 10c Pair, #a.-b. .20 .20
172 B1 60c Pair, #a.-b. .50 .50
173 B1 $3 Pair, #a.-b. 2.25 2.25
Nos. 170-173 (4) 3.15 3.15

Dogs — B2

#178a, Hungarian Kuvasz. #178b, Afghan. #179a, Whippet. #179b, Bloodhound. #180a, Cavalier King Charles Spaniel. #180b, German Shepherd. #181a, Pekinese. #181b, Golden Retriever.

1985, Mar. 14 *Perf. 12½*

178 B2 25c Pair, #a.-b. .20 .20
179 B2 35c Pair, #a.-b. .30 .30
180 B2 55c Pair, #a.-b. .45 .45
181 B2 $2 Pair, #a.-b. 1.60 1.60
Nos. 178-181 (4) 2.55 2.55

World War II Warships B3

1985, Apr. 29 *Perf. 12½*

Se-tenant Pairs, #a.-b.

a.-Side and top views.

b.-Action scene.

186 B3 15c HMS Hood .20 .20
187 B3 50c HMS Duke of York .25 .25
188 B3 $1 KM Admiral Graf Spee .35 .35
189 B3 $1.50 USS Nevada .55 .55
Nos. 186-189 (4) 1.35 1.35

St. Vincent Grenadines Flower Type

#194a, Primula veris. #194b, Pulsatilla vulgaris. #195a, Lapageria rosea. #195b, Romneya coulteri. #196a, Anigozanthos manglesii. #196b, Metrosideros collina. #197a, Protea laurifolia. #197b, Thunbergia grandiflora.

1985, May 31 *Perf. 12½*

194 G38 10c Pair, #a.-b. .20 .20
195 G38 20c Pair, #a.-b. .20 .20
196 G38 70c Pair, #a.-b. .50 .50
197 G38 $2.50 Pair, #a.-b. 1.75 1.75
Nos. 194-197 (4) 2.65 2.65

Queen Mother Type of 1985

Hat: #206a, 212a, Blue. #206b, 212b, Violet. #207a, 211a, Blue. #207b, 211b, Tiara. #208a, Blue. #208b, White. #209a, Blue. #209b, Pink. #210a, Hat. #210b, Tiara.

1985, Aug. 29 *Perf. 12½*

206 A122 20c Pair, #a.-b. .20 .20
207 A122 65c Pair, #a.-b. .50 .50
208 A122 $1.35 Pair, #a.-b. 1.00 1.00
209 A122 $1.80 Pair, #a.-b. 1.40 1.40
Nos. 206-209 (4) 3.10 3.10

Souvenir Sheets of 2

210 A122 $2.05 #a.-b. 1.60 1.60
211 A122 $3.50 #a.-b. 2.75 2.75
212 A122 $6 #a.-b. 4.75 4.75

Queen Elizabeth II Type of 1986

Various portraits.

1986, Apr. 21

213 A128 5c multicolored .20 .20
214 A128 75c multicolored .30 .30
215 A128 $2 multicolored .80 .80
216 A128 $8 multicolored, vert. 3.25 3.25
Nos. 213-216 (4) 4.55 4.55

Souvenir Sheet

217 A128 $10 multicolored 4.00 4.00

B4

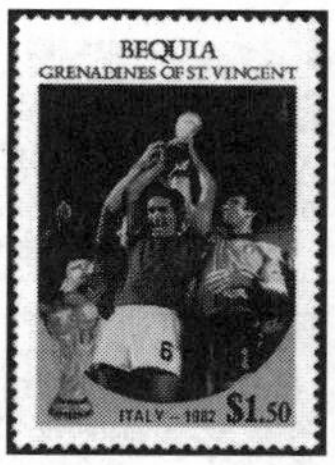

World Cup Soccer Championships, Mexico, 1986 — B5

1986 July 3 *Perf. 12¼, 15 (B5)*

218 B4 1c South Korean team .20 .20
219 B4 2c Iraqi team .20 .20
220 B4 5c Algerian team .20 .20
221 B4 10c Bulgaria vs. France .20 .20
222 B5 45c Belgium .20 .20
223 B4 60c Danish team .30 .30
224 B4 75c Italy vs. W. Germany .35 .35
225 B4 $1.50 USSR vs. England .65 .65
226 B5 $1.50 Italy, 1982 champions .65 .65
227 B5 $2 W. Germany .95 .95
228 B5 $3.50 N. Ireland 1.65 1.65
229 B4 $6 England 2.75 2.75
Nos. 218-229 (12) 8.30 8.30

Souvenir Sheets

230 B4 $1 like No. 219 .45 .45
231 B4 $1.75 like No. 221 .85 .85

Royal Wedding Type of 1986

1986, July 15 *Perf. 12½x13, 13x12½*

232 A132 60c Andrew .25 .25
233 A132 60c Andrew in helicopter .25 .25
234 A132 $2 Andrew in crowd .75 .75
235 A132 $2 Andrew, Sarah .75 .75
Nos. 232-235 (4) 2.00 2.00

Souvenir Sheet

236 A132a $8 Andrew, Sarah in coach 3.25 3.25

Nos. 234-235 horiz.

Railway Engineers and Locomotives — B6

Designs: $1, Sir Daniel Gooch, Fire Fly Class, 1840. $2.50, Sir Nigel Gresley, A4 Class, 1938. $3, Sir William Stanier, Coronation Class, 1937. $4, Oliver V. S. Bulleid, Battle of Britain Class, 1946.

1986, Sept. 30 *Perf. 13x12½*

237-240 B6 Set of 4 5.00 5.00

Nos. 232-235 Ovptd. "Congratulations to TRH The Duke & Duchess of York" in 3 Lines

1986 *Perf. 12½x13, 13x12½*

241 A132 60c on No. 232 .25 .25
242 A132 60c on No. 233 .25 .25
243 A132 $2 on No. 234 .75 .75
244 A132 $2 on No. 235 .75 .75
Nos. 241-244 (4) 2.00 2.00

Royalty Portrait Type

Portraits and photographs: 15c, Queen Victoria, 1841. 75c, Elizabeth, Charles, 1948. $1, Coronation, 1953. $2.50, Duke of Edinburgh, 1948. $5, Elizabeth c. 1980. $6, Elizabeth, Charles, 1948, diff.

1987, Oct. 15 *Perf. 12½x13*

245-249 A140 Set of 5 2.50 2.50

Souvenir Sheet

250 A140 $6 multi 3.00 3.00

Great Explorers Type of St. Vincent Grenadines

Designs: 15c, Gokstad, ship of Leif Eriksson (c. 1000). 50c, Eriksson and bearing dial. $1.75, The Mathew, ship of John Cabot. $2, Cabot, quadrant. $2.50, The Trinidad, ship of Ferdinand Magellan. $3, Arms, portrait of Christopher Columbus. $3.50, Columbus' ship Santa Maria. $4, Magellan, globe. $5, Anchor, long boat, ship.

1988, July 11 Litho. *Perf. 14*

251-258 G52 Set of 8 11.75 11.75

Souvenir Sheet

259 G52 $5 multi 3.50 3.50

Tennis Type of 1987

1988, July 29 *Perf. 13x13½*

260 A137 15c Anders Jarryd .20 .20
261 A137 45c Anne Hobbs .25 .25
262 A137 80c Jimmy Connors .50 .50
263 A137 $1.25 Carling Bassett .75 .75
264 A137 $1.75 Stefan Edberg, horiz. 1.00 1.00
265 A137 $2.00 Gabriela Sabatini, horiz. 1.20 1.20
266 A137 $2.50 Mats Wilander 1.50 1.50
267 A137 $3.00 Pat Cash 1.80 1.80
Nos. 260-267 (8) 7.20 7.20

No. 263 inscribed "Carlene Basset" instead of "Carling Bassett."

An unissued souvenir sheet exists.

French Revolution Bicentennial B7

1c, Grandma Duck as French peasant woman. 2c, Donald & Daisy celebrating liberty. 3c, Minnie as Marie Antoinette. 4c, Clarabelle & patriotic chair. 5c, Goofy in Republican citizen's costume. 10c, Mickey & Donald planting liberty tree. $5, #274, Horace taking Tennis Court Oath. $6, Grand Master Mason McDuck. #276, Dancing the Carmagnole. #277, Philosophers at Cafe La Procope.

1989, July 7 ***Perf. 13½x14***

268-275 B7 Set of 8 7.50 7.50

Souvenir Sheets

276-277 B7 $5 Set of 2 6.00 6.00

Anniversaries and Events Type

$5, Otto Lililienthal, aviation pioneer.

1991, Nov. 18 **Litho.** ***Perf. 14***

278 A213 $5 multicolored 3.75 3.75

Japanese Attack on Pearl Harbor, 50th Anniv. B8

Designs: 50c, Kate from second-wave over Hickam Field. $1, B17 sights Zeros in Pearl Harbor attack. $5, Firefighters rescue sailors from blazing USS Tennessee.

1991, Nov. 18

287 B8 50c multicolored .40 .40
288 B8 $1 multicolored .75 .75

Souvenir Sheet

289 B8 $5 multicolored 3.75 3.75

Wolfgang Amadeus Mozart, Death Bicentennial — B9

Mozart and: 10c, Piccolo. 75c, Piano. $4, Violotta.

No. 293, Mozart's last composition, Lacrimosa from the Requiem Mass. No. 294, Bronze of Mozart by Adrien-Etienne Gaudez, vert. No. 295, Score of opening of the "Paris" symphony, K297.

1991 **Litho.** ***Perf. 14***

290-292 B9 Set of 3 3.75 3.85

Souvenir Sheets

293-295 B9 $6 Set of 3 13.50 13.50

Nos. 293-295 each contain one 57x42mm or 42x57mm stamp.

Boy Scout Type

50c, Lord Baden-Powell, killick hitch knot. $1, Baden-Powell, clove hitch knot. $2, Drawing of Boy Scout by Baden-Powell, vert. $3, American 1st Class Scout badge, vert. $6, Baden-Powell, Lark's head knot.

1991

296-299 A211 Set of 4 4.90 4.90

Souvenir Sheet

300 A211 $6 multicolored 4.50 4.50

Diana, Princess of Wales, (1961-97) — B10

1997, Dec. 10 **Litho.** ***Perf. 14***

301 B10 $1 multicolored .75 .75

No. 301 was issued in sheets of 6.

Paintings Type of 1999

Various pictures of flowers making up a photomosaic of the Queen Mother.

2000, Sept. 5 ***Perf. 13¾***

302 A442 $1 Sheet of 8, #a-h 6.00 6.00
i. As No. 302, imperf. 6.00 6.00

Worldwide Fund for Nature (WWF) B11

Leatherback turtle: a, Three on beach. b, One coming ashore. c, One in water. d, One digging nest.

2001, Dec. 10 **Litho.** ***Perf. 14***

303 B11 $1.40 Vert or horiz. strip of 4, #a-d 4.25 4.25

UNION ISLAND

All stamps are types of St. Vincent ("A" illustration letter), St. Vincent Grenadines ("G" illustration letter) or Union ("U" illustration letter).

"Island" issues are listed separately beginning in 1984. See St. Vincent Grenadines Nos. 84-111, 248-262 for earlier issues.

British Monarch Type of 1984

#1a, Battle of Hastings. #1b, William the Conqueror. #2a, William the Conqueror. #2b, Abbaye Aux Dames. #3a, Skirmish at Dunbar. #3b, Charles II. #4a, Arms of William the Conqueror. #4b, William the Conqueror. #5a, Charles II. #5b, St. James Palace. #6a, Arms of Charles II. #6b, Charles II, Great Fire of London.

Perf. 12½

1984, Mar. 29 **Litho.** **Unwmk.**

1 A110 1c Pair, #a.-b. .20 .20
2 A111 5c Pair, #a.-b. .20 .20
3 A110 10c Pair, #a.-b. .20 .20
4 A110 20c Pair, #a.-b. .20 .20
5 A111 60c Pair, #a.-b. .50 .50
6 A111 $3 Pair, #a.-b. 2.25 2.25
Nos. 1-6 (6) 3.55 3.55

Locomotives Type of 1985

1984-87 ***Perf. 12½***

Se-tenant Pairs, #a.-b.

a.-Side and front views.

b.-Action scene.

13 A120 5c 1813 Puffing Billy, UK .20 .20
14 A120 5c 1911 Class 9N, UK .20 .20
15 A120 5c 1882 Class Skye Bogie, UK .20 .20
16 A120 10c 1912 Class G8, Germany .20 .20
17 A120 15c 1954 Class 65.10, Germany .20 .20
18 A120 15c 1900 Castle Class, UK .20 .20
19 A120 15c 1887 Spinner Class 25, UK .20 .20
20 A120 15c 1951 Fell #10100, UK .20 .20
21 A120 20c 1942 Class 42, Germany .20 .20
22 A120 20c 1951 Class 5MT, UK .20 .20
23 A120 25c 1929 P.O. Rebuilt Class 3500, France .20 .20
24 A120 25c 1886 Class 123, UK .20 .20
25 A120 30c 1976 Class 56, UK .25 .25
26 A120 30c 1897 Class G5, US .25 .25
27 A120 40c 1947 9400 Class, UK .30 .30
28 A120 45c 1888 Sir Theodore, UK .35 .35
29 A120 45c 1929 Class Z, UK .35 .35
30 A120 45c 1896 Atlantic City RR, US .35 .35
31 A120 50c 1906 45xx Class, UK .40 .40
32 A120 50c 1912 Class D15, UK .40 .40
33 A120 50c 1938 Class U4-b, Canada .40 .40
34 A120 60c 1812 Prince Regent, UK .45 .45
35 A120 60c 1920 Butler Henderson, UK .45 .45
36 A120 60c 1889 Elidir, UK .45 .45
37 A120 60c 1934 7200 Class, UK .45 .45
38 A120 60c 1911 Class Z, UK .45 .45
39 A120 75c 1938 Class C, Australia .60 .60
40 A120 75c 1879 Sir Haydn, UK .60 .60
41 A120 75c 1850 Aberdeen No. 26, UK .60 .60
42 A120 75c 1883 Class Y14, UK .60 .60
43 A120 75c 1915 River Class, UK .60 .60
44 A120 $1 1936 D51 Class, Japan .75 .75
45 A120 $1 1837 L&B Bury, UK .75 .75
46 A120 $1 1903 Class 900, US .75 .75
47 A120 $1 1904 Class H-20, US .75 .75
48 A120 $1 1905 Class L, UK .75 .75
49 A120 $1.50 1952 Class 4, UK 1.10 1.10
50 A120 $1.50 1837 Campbell's 8-Wheeler, US 1.10 1.10
51 A120 $1.50 1934 Class GG1, US 1.10 1.10
52 A120 $2 1924 Class 01, Germany 1.50 1.50
53 A120 $2 1920 Gordon Highlander, UK 1.50 1.50
54 A120 $2 1969 Metroliner Railcar, US 1.50 1.50
55 A120 $2 1951 Class GP7, US 1.50 1.50
56 A120 $2.50 1873 Hardwicke Precedent Class, UK 1.75 1.75
57 A120 $2.50 1899 Highflyer Class, UK 1.75 1.75
58 A120 $3 1925 Class U1, UK 2.25 2.25
59 A120 $3 1880 Class 7100, Japan 2.25 2.25
60 A120 $3 1972 Gas Turbine Prototype, France 2.25 2.25
Nos. 13-60 (48) 34.00 34.00

Issued: #13, 34, 44, 52, 8/9/84; #14, 16, 21, 23, 39, 45, 56, 58, 12/18/84; #15, 31, 35, 53, 3/25/85; #17, 25, 28, 36, 40, 49, 57, 59, 1/31/86; #18, 29, 37, 41, 46, 50, 54, 60, 12/23/86; #19, 24, 27, 32, 38, 42, 47, 55, 9/87; #20, 22, 26, 308, 33, 43, 48, 51, 12/4/87.

Beginning on Jan. 31, 1986, this issue is not inscribed "Leaders of the World."

St. Vincent Grenadines Nos. 222-238 Overprinted "UNION ISLAND"

Perf. 14x13½

1984, Aug. 23 **Wmk. 373**

109 G26 1c on No. 222 .20 .20
110 G26 3c on No. 223 .20 .20
111 G26 5c on No. 224 .20 .20
112 G26 6c on No. 225 .20 .20
113 G26 10c on No. 226 .20 .20
114 G26 15c on No. 227 .20 .20
115 G26 20c on No. 228 .20 .20
116 G26 25c on No. 229 .20 .20
117 G26 30c on No. 230 .20 .20
118 G26 50c on No. 231 .35 .35
119 G26 60c on No. 232 .40 .40
120 G26 75c on No. 233 .45 .45
121 G26 $1 on No. 234 .70 .70
122 G26 $2 on No. 235 1.40 1.40
123 G26 $3 on No. 236 2.00 2.00
124 G26 $5 on No. 237 3.40 3.40
125 G26 $10 on No. 238 6.50 6.50
Nos. 109-125 (17) 17.00 17.00

Cricket Players Type of 1985

1984, Nov. **Unwmk.** ***Perf. 12½***

Pairs, #a.-b.

126 A116 1c S. N. Hartley .20 .20
127 A116 10c G. W. Johnson .20 .20
128 A116 15c R. M. Ellison .20 .20
129 A116 55c C. S. Cowdrey .40 .40
130 A116 60c K. Sharp .50 .50
131 A116 75c M. C. Cowdrey, in action .60 .60
132 A116 $1.50 G. R. Dilley, in action 1.25 1.25
133 A116 $3 R. Illingworth, in action 2.25 2.25
Nos. 126-133 (8) 5.60 5.60

Classic Car Type of 1983

1985-86 ***Perf. 12½***

Se-tenant Pairs, #a.-b.

a.-Side and front views.

b.-Action scene.

142 A107 1c 1963 Lancia, Italy .20 .20
143 A107 5c 1895 Duryea, US .20 .20
144 A107 10c 1970 Datsun, Japan .20 .20
145 A107 10c 1962 BRM, UK .20 .20
146 A107 50c 1927 Amilcar, France .35 .35
147 A107 55c 1929 Duesenberg, US .40 .40
148 A107 60c 1913 Peugeot, France .50 .50
149 A107 60c 1938 Lagonda, UK .50 .50
150 A107 60c 1924 Fiat, Italy .50 .50
151 A107 75c 1957 Alfa Romeo, Italy .60 .60
152 A107 75c 1957 Panhard, France .60 .60
153 A107 75c 1954 Porsche, Germany .60 .60
154 A107 90c 1904 Darraco, France .70 .70
155 A107 $1 1927 Daimler, UK .85 .85
156 A107 $1 1949 Oldsmobile, US .85 .85
157 A107 $1 1934 Chrysler, US .85 .85
158 A107 $1.50 1965 MG, UK 1.25 1.25
159 A107 $1.50 1922 Fiat, Italy 1.25 1.25
160 A107 $1.50 1934 Bugatti, France 1.25 1.25
161 A107 $2 1963 Watson/Meyer-Drake, US 1.60 1.60
162 A107 $2.50 1917 Locomobile, US 2.00 2.00
163 A107 $3 1928 Ford, US 2.50 2.50
Nos. 142-163 (22) 17.95 17.95

Issued: #142, 146, 151, 162, 1/4/85; #143, 148, 155, 158, 5/20/85; #144, 147, 149, 152, 154, 156, 159, 161, 7/15/85; #145, 150, 153, 157, 160, 163, 7/30/86.

Beginning on 7/30/86, this issue is not inscribed "Leaders of the World."

Birds — U1

#186a, Hooded warbler. #186b, Carolina wren. #187a, Song sparrow. #187b, Black-headed grosbeak. #188a, Scarlet tanager. #188b, Lazuli bunting. #189a, Sharp-shinned hawk. #189b, Merlin.

1985, Feb. ***Perf. 12½***

186 U1 15c Pair, #a.-b. .20 .20
187 U1 50c Pair, #a.-b. .40 .40
188 U1 $1 Pair, #a.-b. .80 .80
189 U1 $1.50 Pair, #a.-b. 1.25 1.25
Nos. 186-189 (4) 2.65 2.65

Butterflies — U2

#194a, Cynthia cardui. #194b, Zerynthia rumina. #195a, Byblia ilithyia. #195b, Papilio machaon. #196a, Carterocephalus palaemon. #196b, Acraea anacreon. #197a, Anartia amathea. #197b, Salamis temora.

1985, Apr. 15

194	U2	15c Pair, #a.-b.	.20	.20
195	U2	25c Pair, #a.-b.	.20	.20
196	U2	75c Pair, #a.-b.	.60	.60
197	U2	$2 Pair, #a.-b.	1.60	1.60
		Nos. 194-197 (4)	2.60	2.60

Queen Mother Type of 1985

85th birthday - Hats: #206a, Mortarboard. #206b,Blue . #207a, Turquoise. #207b, Blue. #208a, 212a, Without hat. #208b, 212b, White. #209a, 211a, White hat, violet feathers. #209b, 211b, Blue. #210a, Crown. #210b, Hat.

1985, Aug. 19

206	A122	55c Pair, #a.-b.	.40	.40
207	A122	70c Pair, #a.-b.	.50	.50
208	A122	$1.05 Pair, #a.-b.	.70	.70
209	A122	$1.70 Pair, #a.-b.	1.25	1.25
		Nos. 206-209 (4)	2.85	2.85

Souvenir Sheets of 2

210	A122	$1.95 #a.-b.	1.50	1.50
211	A122	$2.25 #a.-b.	1.60	1.60
212	A122	$7 #a.-b.	5.00	5.00

Elizabeth II 60th Birthday Type of 1986

Designs: 10c, Wearing scarf. 60c, Riding clothes. $2, Wearing crown and jewels. $8, In Canberra, vert. $10, Holding flowers.

1986, Apr. 21

213-216	A128	10c Set of 4	4.50	4.50

Souvenir Sheet

217	A128	$10 multi	4.00	4.00

U3

World Cup Soccer Championships, Mexico — U4

1986, May 7 ***Perf. 12½ (U3), 15 (U4)***

218	U3	1c Moroccan team	.20	.20
219	U3	10c Argentinian team	.20	.20
220	U4	30c Algerian player	.20	.20
221	U3	75c Hungarian team	.30	.30
222	U3	$1 Russian team	.45	.45
223	U4	$2.50 Belgian player	1.10	1.10
224	U4	$3 French player	1.25	1.25
225	U4	$6 W. German player	2.50	2.50
		Nos. 218-225 (8)	6.20	6.20

Souvenir Sheets

226	U3	$1.85 like No. 222	.85	.85
227	U3	$2 like No. 219	.85	.85

Souvenir sheets contain one 60x40mm stamp.

Prince Andrew Royal Wedding Type

1986, July 15 ***Perf. 12½x13, 13x12½***

228	A132	60c Andrew with cap	.25	.25
229	A132	60c Andrew, diff.	.25	.25
230	A132	$2 Sarah Ferguson	.75	.75
231	A132	$2 Sarah, Andrew	.75	.75
		Nos. 228-231 (4)	2.00	2.00

Nos. 228-231 Overprinted in Silver "CONGRATULATIONS TO T.R.H. THE DUKE & DUCHESS OF YORK" in 3 Lines

1986, Oct.

232	A132	60c on No. 228	.25	.25
233	A132	60c on No. 229	.25	.25
234	A132	$2 on No. 230	.75	.75
235	A132	$2 on No. 231	.75	.75
		Nos. 232-235 (4)	2.00	2.00

Queen Elizabeth II Wedding Anniv. Type of St. Vincent Grenadines

1987, Oct. 15 ***Perf. 12½***

236	G47	15c like No. 568	.20	.20
237	G47	45c like No. 569	.25	.25
238	G47	$1.50 like No. 570	.70	.70
239	G47	$3 like No. 571	1.40	1.40
240	G47	$4 like No. 572	1.75	1.75
		Nos. 236-240 (5)	4.30	4.30

U5

Disney characters in various French vehicles: 1c, 1893 Peugeot. 2c, 1890-91 Panhard-Levassor. 3c, 1910 Renault. 4c, 1919 Citroen. 5c, 1878 La Mancelle. 10c, 1891 De Dion Bouton Quadricycle. $5, 1896 Leon Bollee Trike. No. 248, 1911 Brasier Coupe. No. 249, French road race. No. 250, 1769, Cugnot's artillery tractor.

1989, July 7 ***Perf. 14x13½***

241-250	U5	Set of 10	18.00	18.00

PHILEXFRANCE '89.

Diana, Princess of Wales (1961-97) — U6

1997 **Litho.** ***Perf. 14***

251	U6	$1 multicolored	.75	.75

No. 251 was issued in sheets of 6.

Paintings Type of 1999

Various pictures of flowers making up a photomosaic of the Queen Mother.

2000, Sept. 5 ***Perf. 13¾***

252	A442	$1 Sheet of 8, #a-h	6.00	6.00
l.		As No. 252, imperf.	6.00	6.00

EL SALVADOR

ˈel-sal-və-ˌdor

LOCATION — On the Pacific coast of Central America, between Guatemala, Honduras and the Gulf of Fonseca
GOVT. — Republic
AREA — 8,236 sq. mi.
POP. — 5,839,079 (1999 est.)

CAPITAL — San Salvador

8 Reales = 100 Centavos = 1 Peso
100 Centavos = 1 Coló

Catalogue values for unused stamps in this country are for Never Hinged items, beginning with Scott 589 in the regular postage section, Scott C85 in the airpost section, and Scott O362 in the official section.

Watermarks

Wmk. 117- Liberty Cap

Position of wmk. on reprints

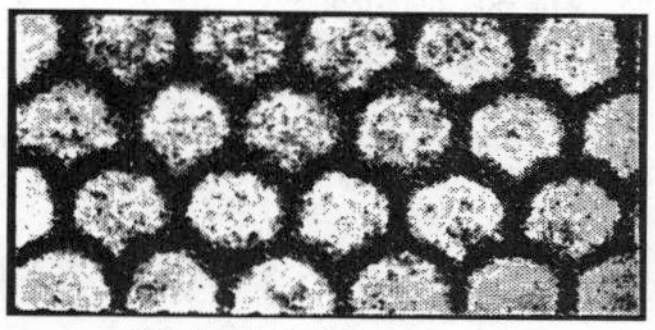
Wmk. 172- Honeycomb

Wmk. 173- S

Wmk. 240- REPUBLICA DE EL SALVADOR in Sheet

Wmk. 269- REPUBLICA DE EL SALVADOR

Volcano San Miguel — A1

1867 **Unwmk.** **Engr.** ***Perf. 12***

1	A1	½r blue	.55	*.70*
2	A1	1r red	.55	.55
3	A1	2r green	2.40	*2.75*
4	A1	4r bister	4.50	3.50
		Nos. 1-4 (4)	8.00	7.50

Nos. 1-4 when overprinted "Contra Sello" and shield with 14 stars, are telegraph stamps. For similar overprint see Nos. 5-12.
Counterfeits exist.

Nos. 1-4 Handstamped

1874

5	A1	½r blue	6.50	3.50
6	A1	1r red	6.50	3.50
7	A1	2r green	6.50	3.50
8	A1	4r bister	19.00	17.50
		Nos. 5-8 (4)	38.50	28.00

Nos. 1-4 Handstamped

9	A1	½r blue	3.75	2.00
10	A1	1r red	3.75	2.00
11	A1	2r green	3.75	2.00
12	A1	4r bister	7.50	5.00
		Nos. 9-12 (4)	18.75	11.00

The overprints on Nos. 5-12 exist double. Counterfeits are plentiful.

Coat of Arms
A2 A3

A4

A5

A6

1879 **Litho.** ***Perf. 12½***

13	A2	1c green	2.00	.90
a.		Invtd. "V" for 2nd "A" in "SALVADOR"	4.00	2.00
b.		Invtd. "V" for "A" in "REPUBLICA"	4.00	2.00
c.		Invtd. "V" for "A" in "UNIVERSAL"	4.00	2.00
14	A3	2c rose	2.75	1.50
a.		Invtd. scroll in upper left corner	8.00	5.00
15	A4	5c blue	5.00	1.25
a.		5c ultra	8.00	4.00
16	A5	10c black	10.00	3.50
17	A6	20c violet	16.00	10.00
		Nos. 13-17 (5)	35.75	17.15

There are fifteen varieties of the 1c and 2c, twenty-five of the 5c and five each of the 10 and 20c.

In 1881 the 1c, 2c and 5c were redrawn, the 1c in fifteen varieties and the 2c and 5c in five varieties each.

No. 15 comes in a number of shades from light to dark blue.

These stamps, when overprinted "Contra sello" and arms, are telegraph stamps.

Counterfeits of No. 14 exist.

For overprints see Nos. 25D-25E, 28A-28C.

Allegorical Figure of El Salvador — A7

Volcano — A8

1887 **Engr.** ***Perf. 12***

18	A7	3c brown	.40	.20
a.		Imperf., pair	2.50	2.50
19	A8	10c orange	3.00	.90

For surcharges and overprints see Nos. 25, 26C-28, 30-32.

A9

A10

1888 *Rouletted*

20	A9	5c deep blue	.40	.35

For overprints see Nos. 35-36.

1889 *Perf. 12*

21	A10	1c green	.20	
22	A10	2c scarlet	.20	

Same Overprinted with Heavy Bar Obliterating "UNION POSTAL DEL"

23	A10	1c green	.30	.25
24	A10	2c scarlet	.30	

Nos. 21, 22 and 24 were never placed in use.
For overprints see Nos. 26, 29.

No. 18 Surcharged **1 centavo**

Type I - thick numerals, heavy serifs.
Type II - thin numerals, straight serifs.

25	A7	1c on 3c brn, type II	.65	.50
a.		Double surcharge	1.50	
b.		Triple surcharge	3.50	
c.		Type I	.65	

The 1c on 2c scarlet is bogus.

Handstamped **1889.**

1889

Violet Handstamp

25D	A2	1c green	12.50	12.50
25E	A6	20c violet	30.00	30.00
26	A10	1c green, #23	1.00	.90
26C	A7	1c on 3c, #27	20.00	20.00
27	A7	3c brown	1.00	.90
28	A8	10c orange	5.00	4.00

Black Handstamp

28A	A2	1c green	15.00	14.00
28B	A3	2c rose	17.50	17.50
28C	A6	20c violet	30.00	30.00
29	A10	1c green, #23	1.25	1.00
30	A7	3c brown	1.25	1.00
31	A7	1c on 3c, #27	17.50	17.50
32	A8	10c orange	4.50	3.50

Rouletted

Black Handstamp

35	A9	5c deep blue	1.25	.75

Violet Handstamp

36	A9	5c deep blue	1.25	.75

The 1889 handstamps as usual, are found double, inverted, etc. Counterfeits are plentiful.

A13

A14

1890 **Engr.** *Perf. 12*

38	A13	1c green	.20	.20
39	A13	2c bister brown	.20	.20
40	A13	3c yellow	.20	.20
41	A13	5c blue	.20	.20
42	A13	10c violet	.20	.20
43	A13	20c orange	.20	.20
44	A13	25c red	.50	*1.00*
45	A13	50c claret	.20	*.65*
46	A13	1p carmine	.20	*1.50*
		Nos. 38-46 (9)	2.10	*4.35*

The issues of 1890 to 1898 inclusive were printed by the Hamilton Bank Note Co., New York, to the order of N. F. Seebeck, who held a contract for stamps with the government of El Salvador. This contract gave the right to make reprints of the stamps and such were subsequently made in some instances, as will be found noted in italic type.

Used values of 1890-1898 issues are for stamps with genuine cancelations applied while the stamps were valid. Various counterfeit cancellations exist.

1891

47	A14	1c vermilion	.20	.20
48	A14	2c yellow green	.20	.20
49	A14	3c violet	.20	.20
50	A14	5c carmine lake	1.00	*2.00*
51	A14	10c blue	.20	.20
52	A14	11c violet	.20	.20
53	A14	20c green	.20	*.30*
54	A14	25c yellow brown	.20	*.40*
55	A14	50c dark blue	.20	*.90*
56	A14	1p dark brown	.20	*1.50*
		Nos. 47-56 (10)	2.80	*6.10*

For surcharges see Nos. 57-59.
Nos. 47 and 56 have been reprinted in thick toned paper with dark gum.

A15

Nos. 48, 49 Surcharged in Black or Violet:

UN CENTAVO
b

5 CENTAVOS
c

1891

57	A15	1c on 2c yellow grn	2.25	2.00
a.		Inverted surcharge	4.00	
58	A14 (b)	1c on 2c yellow grn	1.60	1.40
59	A14 (c)	5c on 3c violet	4.00	3.25
		Nos. 57-59 (3)	7.85	6.65

Landing of Columbus — A18

1892 **Engr.**

60	A18	1c blue green	.35	.20
61	A18	2c orange brown	.35	.20
62	A18	3c ultra	.35	.20
63	A18	5c gray	.35	.20
64	A18	10c vermilion	.35	.20
65	A18	11c brown	.35	.35
66	A18	20c orange	.35	.35
67	A18	25c maroon	.35	*.55*
68	A18	50c yellow	.35	*1.10*
69	A18	1p carmine lake	.35	*1.90*
		Nos. 60-69 (10)	3.50	*5.25*

400th anniversary of the discovery of America by Columbus.

Nos. 63, 66-67 Surcharged

Nos. 70, 72

Nos. 73-75

Surcharged in Black, Red or Yellow

1892

70	A18	1c on 5c gray (Bk) (down)	1.00	.65
a.		Surcharge reading up	1.75	1.10
72	A18	1c on 5c gray (R) (up)	1.00	.80
a.		Surcharge reading down		
73	A18	1c on 20c org (Bk)	1.25	.75
a.		Inverted surcharge	3.50	2.50
b.		"V" of "CENTAVO" inverted	3.50	2.50
		Nos. 70-73 (3)	3.25	2.20

Similar Surcharge in Yellow or Blue, "centavo" in lower case letters

74	A18	1c on 25c mar (Y)	1.50	1.25
a.		Inverted surcharge	2.50	2.50
75	A18	1c on 25c mar (Bl)	*200.00*	*200.00*
a.		Double surcharge (Bl + Bk)	*225.00*	*225.00*

Counterfeits exist of Nos. 75 and 75a. Nos. 75, 75a have been questioned.

Pres. Carlos Ezeta — A21

1893 **Engr.**

76	A21	1c blue	.20	.20
77	A21	2c brown red	.20	.20
78	A21	3c purple	.20	.20
79	A21	5c deep brown	.20	.20
80	A21	10c orange brown	.20	.20
81	A21	11c vermilion	.20	*.25*
82	A21	20c green	.20	*.30*
83	A21	25c dk olive gray	.20	*.40*
84	A21	50c red orange	.20	*.50*
85	A21	1p black	.20	*.75*
		Nos. 76-85 (10)	2.00	*3.20*

For surcharge see No. 89.

Founding City of Isabela — A22

Columbus Statue, Genoa — A23

Departure from Palos — A24

1893

86	A22	2p green	.75	—
87	A23	5p violet	.75	
88	A24	10p orange	.75	
		Nos. 86-88 (3)	2.25	

Discoveries by Columbus. No. 86 is known on cover, but experts are not positive that Nos. 87 and 88 were postally used.

No. 77 Surcharged "UN CENTAVO"

1893

89	A21	1c on 2c brown red	.50	.40
a.		"CENTNVO"	3.00	2.50

Liberty — A26

Columbus before Council of Salamanca A27

Columbus Protecting Indian Hostages A28

Columbus Received by Ferdinand and Isabella A29

1894, Jan.

91	A26	1c brown	.20	.20
92	A26	2c blue	.20	.20
93	A26	3c maroon	.20	.20
94	A26	5c orange brn	.20	.20
95	A26	10c violet	.20	.20
96	A26	11c vermilion	.20	*.25*
97	A26	20c dark blue	.20	*.30*
98	A26	25c orange	.20	*.40*
99	A26	50c black	.20	*.65*
100	A26	1p slate blue	.20	*.90*
101	A27	2p deep blue	.75	
102	A28	5p carmine lake	.75	
103	A29	10p deep brown	.75	
		Nos. 91-103 (13)	4.25	
		Nos. 91-100 (10)		*3.50*

Nos. 101-103 for the discoveries by Columbus. Experts are not positive that these were postally used.

No. 96 Surcharged **1 Centavo**

1894, Dec.

104	A26	1c on 11c vermilion	1.50	.65
a.		"Ccntavo"	*40.00*	*40.00*
b.		Double surcharge		

Coat of Arms
A31 A32

Arms Overprint in Second Color
Various Frames

1895, Jan. 1

105	A31	1c olive & green	.20	.20
106	A31	2c dk green & bl	.20	.20
a.		2c dark green & green	1.00	.85
107	A31	3c brown & brown	.20	.20
108	A31	5c blue & brown	.20	.20
109	A31	10c orange & brn	.20	*.25*
110	A31	12c magenta & brn	.20	*.30*
111	A31	15c ver & ver	.20	*.35*
112	A31	20c yellow & brn	.20	*.40*
a.		Inverted overprint	2.00	
113	A31	24c violet & brn	.20	*.45*
114	A31	30c dp blue & blue	.20	*.50*
115	A31	50c carmine & brn	.20	*.65*
116	A31	1p black & brn	.20	*.90*
		Nos. 105-116 (12)	2.40	*4.60*

As printed, Nos. 105-116 portrayed Gen. Antonio Ezeta, brother of Pres. Carlos Ezeta. Before issuance, Ezeta's overthrow caused the government to obliterate his features with the national arms overprint. The 3c, 10c, 30c exist without overprint. Value $1 each.
Reprints of 2c are in dark yellow green on thick paper. Value 20 cents.

Various Frames

1895 **Engr.** *Perf. 12*

117	A32	1c olive	.55	.50
118	A32	2c dk blue grn	.20	.20
119	A32	3c brown	.20	.20
120	A32	5c blue	.20	.20
121	A32	10c orange	.65	.30
122	A32	12c claret	.65	.30
123	A32	15c vermilion	.20	*.30*

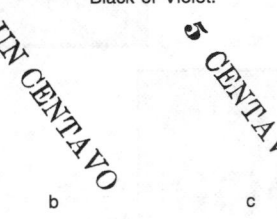

124	A32	20c	deep green	.20	*.50*
125	A32	24c	violet	.20	*.50*
126	A32	30c	deep blue	.20	*.45*
127	A32	50c	carmine lake	1.25	*1.25*
128	A32	1p	gray black	1.50	*1.75*
			Nos. 117-128 (12)	6.00	*6.45*

The reprints are on thicker paper than the originals, and many of the shades differ. Value 15c each.

Nos. 122, 124-126 Surcharged in Black or Red:

UN
centavo

1895

129	A32	1c on 12c claret (Bk)		1.00	.90
130	A32	1c on 24c violet		1.00	.90
131	A32	1c on 30c dp blue		1.00	.90
132	A32	2c on 20c dp green		1.00	.90
133	A32	3c on 30c dp blue		1.25	1.10
a.		Double surcharge		4.50	
		Nos. 129-133 (5)		5.25	4.70

"Peace" — A45

1896, Jan. 1 Engr. Unwmk.

134	A45	1c	blue	.20	.20
135	A45	2c	dark brown	.20	.20
136	A45	3c	blue green	.20	.20
137	A45	5c	brown olive	.20	.20
138	A45	10c	yellow	.20	.20
139	A45	12c	dark blue	.75	.90
140	A45	15c	brt ultra	.20	*.20*
a.		15c	light violet	1.10	*2.00*
141	A45	20c	magenta	.65	.50
142	A45	24c	vermilion	.20	*.25*
143	A45	30c	orange	.20	*.40*
144	A45	50c	black brn	.20	*.50*
145	A45	1p	rose lake	.20	*.90*
			Nos. 134-145 (12)	3.40	*4.65*

The frames of Nos. 134-145 differ slightly on each denomination.

For overprints see Nos. O1-O12, O37-O48.

Wmk. 117

145B	A45	2c	dark brown	.20	.20

The 1c, 2c, 12c, 20c, 30c, 50c and 1p on unwatermarked paper and the 2c on watermarked have been reprinted. The paper is thicker than that of the originals and the shades are different. The watermark is always upright on original stamps of Salvador, sideways on the reprints. Value 15c each.

Coat of Arms — A46

"White House" — A47

Locomotive A48

Mt. San Miguel A49

Ocean Steamship
A50 A51

Post Office A52

Lake Ilopango A53

Atehausillas Waterfall A54

Coat of Arms A55

Coat of Arms A56

Columbus A57

1896

146	A46	1c	emerald	.20	.20
147	A47	2c	lake	.20	.20
148	A48	3c	yellow brn	.20	.20
149	A49	5c	deep blue	.20	.20
150	A50	10c	brown	.20	.20
151	A51	12c	slate	.20	*.20*
152	A52	15c	blue green	.20	*.25*
153	A53	20c	carmine rose	.20	*.30*
154	A54	24c	violet	*.20*	*.40*
155	A55	30c	deep green	.20	.40
156	A56	50c	orange	.20	*.40*
157	A57	100c	dark blue	.20	*.90*
			Nos. 146-157 (12)	2.40	*3.85*

Nos. 146-157 exist imperf.

Unwmk.

157B	A46	1c	emerald	.20	.20
157C	A47	2c	lake	.20	.20
157D	A48	3c	yellow brn	.20	.20
157E	A49	5c	deep blue	.20	.20
157F	A50	10c	brown	.20	.20
157G	A51	12c	slate	.20	.20
157I	A52	15c	blue green	.25	.20
157J	A53	20c	carmine rose	.20	*.45*
157K	A54	24c	violet	.50	*.80*
157M	A55	30c	deep green	.20	*.55*
157N	A56	50c	orange	.20	*.55*
157O	A57	100c	dark blue	.20	*1.00*
			Nos. 157B-157O (12)	2.75	*4.75*

See Nos. 159-170L. For surcharges and overprints see Nos. 158, 158D, 171-174C, O13-O36, O49-O72, O79-O126.

The 15c, 30c, 50c and 100c have been reprinted on watermarked and the 1c, 2c, 3c, 5c, 12c, 20c, 24c and 100c on unwatermarked paper. The papers of the reprints are thicker than those of the originals and the shades are different. Value, set of 12, $1.20.

Black Surcharge on Nos. 154, 157K

Quince
centavos

1896 Wmk. 117

158	A54	15c on 24c violet	4.00	4.00
a.		Double surcharge		
b.		Inverted surcharge	8.50	

Unwmk.

158D	A54	15c on 24c violet	4.00	3.00

Exist spelled "Qnince."

Types of 1896

1897 Engr. Wmk. 117

159	A46	1c	scarlet	*.20*	*.20*
160	A47	2c	yellow grn	.20	.20
161	A48	3c	bister brn	.20	.20
162	A49	5c	orange	.20	.20
163	A50	10c	blue grn	.20	.20
164	A51	12c	blue	.40	.30
165	A52	15c	black	2.50	2.00
166	A53	20c	slate	.20	.20
167	A54	24c	yellow	.20	.25
168	A55	30c	rose	.20	.20
169	A56	50c	violet	.20	.50
170	A57	100c	brown lake	2.50	2.00
			Nos. 159-170 (12)	7.20	6.45

Unwmk.

170A	A46	1c	scarlet	.20	.20
170B	A47	2c	yellow grn	.20	.20
170C	A48	3c	bister brn	.20	.20
170D	A49	5c	orange	.20	.20
170E	A50	10c	blue grn	.75	.50
170F	A51	12c	blue	.75	.75
170G	A52	15c	black	2.00	2.00
170H	A53	20c	slate	.20	*.25*
170I	A54	24c	yellow	.20	*.50*
170J	A55	30c	rose	1.90	1.25
170K	A56	50c	violet	.90	.90
170L	A57	100c	brown lake	6.25	6.25
			Nos. 170A-170L (12)	13.75	13.20

The 1c, 2c, 3c, 5c, 12c, 15c, 50c and 100c have been reprinted on watermarked and the entire issue on unwatermarked paper. The papers of the reprints are thicker than those of the originals. Value, set of 20, $2.

Surcharged in Red or Black

TRECE
centavos

1897 Wmk. 117

171	A54	13c on 24c yel (R)	2.50	2.50
172	A55	13c on 30c rose (Bk)	2.50	2.50
173	A56	13c on 50c vio (Bk)	2.50	2.50
174	A57	13c on 100c brn lake (Bk)	2.50	2.50

Unwmk.

174A	A54	13c on 24c yel (R)	2.50	2.50
174B	A55	13c on 30c rose (Bk)	2.50	2.50
174C	A56	13c on 50c vio (Bk)	2.50	2.50
		Nos. 171-174C (7)	17.50	17.50

Coat of Arms of "Republic of Central America" — A59

ONE CENTAVO:

Originals: The mountains are outlined in red and blue. The sea is represented by short red and dark blue lines on a light blue background.

Reprints: The mountains are outlined in red only. The sea is printed in green and dark blue, much blurred.

FIVE CENTAVOS:

Originals: The sea is represented by horizontal and diagonal lines of dark blue on a light blue background.

Reprints: The sea is printed in green and dark blue, much blurred. The inscription in gold is in thicker letters.

1897 Litho.

175	A59	1c bl, gold, rose & grn	.50	*1.50*
176	A59	5c rose, gold, bl & grn	.50	*1.50*

Forming of the "Republic of Central America."

For overprints see Nos. O73-O76.

Stamps of type A59 formerly listed as "Type II" are now known to be reprints.

Allegory of Central American Union — A60

1898 Engr. Wmk. 117

177	A60	1c	orange ver	.20	.20
178	A60	2c	rose	.20	.20
179	A60	3c	pale yel grn	.20	.20
180	A60	5c	blue green	.20	.20
181	A60	10c	gray blue	.20	.20
182	A60	12c	violet	.20	.25
183	A60	13c	brown lake	.20	.20
184	A60	20c	deep blue	.20	*.30*
185	A60	24c	deep ultra	.20	*.35*
186	A60	26c	bister brn	.20	*.40*
187	A60	50c	orange	.20	*.75*
188	A60	1p	yellow	.20	*1.00*
			Nos. 177-188 (12)	2.40	*4.25*

For overprints and surcharges see Nos. 189-198A, 224-241, 269A-269B, O129-O142.

The entire set has been reprinted on unwatermarked paper and all but the 12c and 20c on watermarked paper. The shades of the reprints are not the same as those of the originals, and the paper is thicker. Value, set of 22, $2.25.

No. 180 Overprinted Vertically, up or down in Black, Violet, Red, Magenta and Yellow

Transito
Territorial

1899

189	A60	5c blue grn (Bk)	7.50	6.25
a.		Italic 3rd "r" in "Territorial"	12.50	12.50
b.		Double ovpt. (Bk + Y)	37.50	37.50
190	A60	5c blue grn (V)	*82.50*	*82.50*
191	A60	5c blue grn (R)	*70.00*	*70.00*
191A	A60	5c blue grn (M)	*70.00*	*70.00*
191B	A60	5c blue grn (Y)	*75.00*	*75.00*
		Nos. 189-191B (5)	*305.00*	*303.75*

Counterfeits exist.

Nos. 177-184 Overprinted in Black

1899

192	A60	1c	orange ver	1.00	.50
193	A60	2c	rose	1.25	1.00
194	A60	3c	pale yel grn	1.25	.50
195	A60	5c	blue green	1.25	.50
196	A60	10c	gray blue	2.00	1.25
197	A60	12c	violet	3.25	2.50
198	A60	13c	brown lake	3.25	2.00
198A	A60	20c	deep blue	100.00	100.00
			Nos. 192-198A (8)	113.25	108.25

Counterfeits exist of the "wheel" overprint used in 1899-1900.

Ceres ("Estado") — A61

Inscribed: "Estado de El Salvador"

1899 Unwmk. Litho. *Perf. 12*

199	A61	1c	brown	.20
200	A61	2c	gray green	.20
201	A61	3c	blue	.20
202	A61	5c	brown org	.20
203	A61	10c	chocolate	.20
204	A61	12c	dark green	.20
205	A61	13c	deep rose	.20
206	A61	24c	light blue	.20
207	A61	26c	carmine rose	.20
208	A61	50c	orange red	.20
209	A61	100c	violet	.20
			Nos. 199-209 (11)	2.20

#208-209 were probably not placed in use.

For overprints and surcharges see Nos. 210-223, 242-252D, O143-O185.

Same, Overprinted

Red Overprint

210	A61	1c	brown	50.00	32.50

Blue Overprint

211	A61	1c	brown	.50	.20
212	A61	5c	brown org	.50	.20
212A	A61	10c	chocolate	5.00	3.50

Black Overprint

213	A61	1c	brown	.50	.20
214	A61	2c	gray grn	.75	.20
215	A61	3c	blue	.75	.25
216	A61	5c	brown org	.35	.20
217	A61	10c	chocolate	.50	.20
218	A61	12c	dark green	1.25	.50
219	A61	13c	deep rose	1.10	.65
220	A61	24c	light blue	12.50	10.00
221	A61	26c	car rose	3.25	2.00
222	A61	50c	orange red	3.25	2.75
223	A61	100c	violet	3.25	3.25
			Nos. 213-223 (11)	27.45	20.20

"Wheel" overprint exists double and triple.

No. 177 Handstamped

1900

1900 Wmk. 117

224	A60	1c orange ver	1.00	1.00

No. 177 Overprinted

1900

225	A60	1c orange ver	12.50	12.50

Stamps of 1898 Surcharged in Black

1900
1 centavo

1900

226	A60	1c on 10c gray blue	5.00	4.25
a.		Inverted surcharge	7.50	6.50
227	A60	1c on 13c brn lake	*275.00*	

228 A60 2c on 12c vio 17.50 12.50
a. "eentavo"
b. Inverted surcharge
c. "centavos" 30.00
d. As "c," double surcharge
e. Vertical surcharge
229 A60 2c on 13c brn lake 2.00 1.75
a. "eentavo" 3.25 2.75
b. Inverted surcharge 5.00 4.00
c. "1900" omitted
230 A60 2c on 20c dp blue 2.00 2.00
a. Inverted surcharge 3.25 3.25
230B A60 2c on 26c bis brn *175.00 175.00*
231 A60 3c on 12c vio *37.50 37.50*
a. "eentavo"
b. Inverted surcharge *35.00 35.00*
c. Double surcharge
232 A60 3c on 50c org 10.00 10.00
a. Inverted surcharge 10.00 10.00
233 A60 5c on 12c vio
234 A60 5c on 24c ultra 11.00 11.00
a. "eentavo"
b. "centavos" 11.00
235 A60 5c on 26c bis brn *37.50 37.50*
a. Inverted surcharge *35.00 35.00*
236 A60 5c on 1p yel 15.00 15.00
a. Inverted surcharge 15.00 15.00

With Additional Overprint in Black

237 A60 2c on 12c vio 2.50 2.50
a. Inverted surcharge 2.50 2.50
b. "eentavo" 8.00
c. "centavos" (plural) 75.00
d. "1900" omitted
237H A60 2c on 13c brn lake
238 A60 3c on 12c vio 42.50 42.50
a. "eentavo" 35.00 35.00
239 A60 5c on 26c bis brn 67.50 67.50
a. Inverted surcharge

Vertical Surcharge "Centavos" in the Plural

240 A60 2c on 12c vio 95.00 95.00
b. Without wheel
240A A60 5c on 24c dp ultra 95.00 95.00

With Additional Overprint in Black

241 A60 5c on 12c vio 17.50 17.50
a. Surcharge reading downward

Counterfeits exist of the surcharges on Nos. 226-241 and the "wheel" overprint on Nos. 237-239, 241.

Same Surcharge on Stamps of 1898 Without Wheel

1900 **Unwmk.**

242 A61 1c on 13c dp rose .40 .40
a. Inverted surcharge .75 .75
b. "eentavo" .75 .75
c. "ecntavo" 1.25 .75
d. "1 centavo 1" 4.00 3.00
e. Double surcharge
243 A61 2c on 12c dk grn 1.75 1.25
a. Inverted surcharge 2.50 2.50
b. "eentavo"
244 A61 2c on 13c dp rose 1.00 .75
a. "eentavo" 1.25 1.25
b. "ecntavo" 1.40 1.40
c. Inverted surcharge
245 A61 3c on 12c dk grn 1.00 .85
a. Inverted surcharge 2.00 1.50
b. "eentavo" 4.00 4.00
c. Double surcharge 2.00
Nos. 242-245 (4) 4.15 3.25

With Additional Overprint in Black

246 A61 1c on 2c gray grn .25 .20
a. "eentavo" .90 .65
b. Inverted surcharge 4.00 3.00
247 A61 1c on 13c dp rose 1.00 .85
a. "eentavo" 4.00
b. "1 centavo 1"
248 A61 2c on 12c dk grn 1.40 1.00
a. "eentavo" 4.00
b. Inverted surcharge 1.25 1.25
c. Double surcharge 2.00
249 A61 2c on 13c dp rose 42.50
a. "eentavo"
b. Double surcharge 75.00 75.00
250 A61 3c on 12c dk grn 1.40 .90
a. Inverted surcharge 1.50 1.25
b. "eentavo" 2.50 2.25
c. Date double 4.00
251 A61 5c on 24c lt bl 2.50 1.25
a. "eentavo" 4.00 4.00
252 A61 5c on 26c car rose 1.10 1.00
a. Inverted surcharge 4.00 2.50
b. "eentavo" 1.75 1.50
252D A61 5c on 1c on 26c car rose
Nos. 246-248,250-252 (6) 7.65 5.20

Counterfeits exist of the surcharges on Nos. 242-252D and the "wheel" overprint on Nos. 246-252D.

Ceres ("Republica") — A63

There are two varieties of the 1c, type A63, one with the word "centavo" in the middle of the label (#253, 263, 270, 299, 305, 326), the other with "centavo" nearer the left end than the right (#270, 299, 305, 326).

The stamps of type A63 are found in a great variety of shades. Stamps of type A63 without handstamp were not regularly issued.

Handstamped in Violet or Black

Inscribed: "Republica de El Salvador"

1900

253 A63 1c blue green .20 .20
a. 1c yellow green .20 .20
254 A63 2c rose .30 .20
255 A63 3c gray black .20 .20
256 A63 5c pale blue .50 .35
a. 5c deep blue .50 .35
257 A63 10c deep blue .60 .45
258 A63 12c yel green .60 .45
259 A63 13c yel brown .50 .45
260 A63 24c gray 4.00 4.00
261 A63 26c yel brown 1.75 1.75
262 A63 50c rose red 1.75 1.50
Nos. 253-262 (10) 10.40 9.55

For overprints and surcharges see Nos. 263-269, 270-282, 293A-311B, 317, 326-335, O223-O242, O258-O262, O305-O312.

Handstamped in Violet or Black

263 A63 1c lt green 1.75 1.75
264 A63 2c pale rose 1.75 1.75
265 A63 3c gray black 1.75 .75
266 A63 5c slate blue 1.75 .50
267 A63 10c deep blue 50.00 42.50
268 A63 13c yellow brn 12.50 8.75
269 A63 50c dull rose 1.75 1.75
Nos. 263-269 (7) 71.25 57.75

Handstamped on 1898 Stamps

Wmk. 117

269A A60 2c rose 30.00 30.00
269B A60 10c gray blue 30.00 30.00

The overprints on Nos. 253 to 269B are handstamped and, as usual with that style of overprint, are to be found double, inverted, omitted, etc.

Stamps of Type A63 Overprinted in Black

1900 **Unwmk.**

270 A63 1c light green .20 .20
271 A63 2c rose .20 .20
272 A63 3c gray black .20 .20
273 A63 5c pale blue .20 .20
a. 5c dark blue .20 .20
274 A63 10c deep blue .40 .20
a. 10c pale blue .30 .20
275 A63 12c light green .40 .30
276 A63 13c yellow brown .20 .20
277 A63 24c gray .40 .40
278 A63 26c yellow brown .50 .50
Nos. 270-278 (9) 2.70 2.40

This overprint is known double, inverted, etc.

Nos. 271-273 Surcharged in Black

1902

280 A63 1c on 2c rose 2.75 2.25
281 A63 1c on 3c black 2.00 1.40
282 A63 1c on 5c blue 1.25 1.00
Nos. 280-282 (3) 6.00 4.65

Morazán Monument — A64

Perf. 14, 14½

1903 **Engr.** **Wmk. 173**

283 A64 1c green .35 .20
284 A64 2c carmine .35 .20
285 A64 3c orange .80 .50
286 A64 5c dark blue .35 .20
287 A64 10c dull violet .35 .20
288 A64 12c slate .40 .20
289 A64 13c red brown .40 .20
290 A64 24c scarlet 2.50 1.25
291 A64 26c yellow brn 2.50 1.25
292 A64 50c bister 1.25 .75
293 A64 100c grnsh blue 3.75 2.50
Nos. 283-293 (11) 13.00 7.45

For surcharges and overprint see Nos. 312-316, 318-325, O253.

Stamps of 1900 with Shield in Black Overprinted:

1905 (5¾x13½mm) — a
1905 (5x14¾mm) — b
(4½x16mm) — c 1905
(4½x13½mm) — d 1905
(5x14½mm) — e 1905

1905-06 **Unwmk.** ***Perf. 12***

Blue Overprint

293A A63 (a) 2c rose
294 A63 (a) 3c gray blk 4.00 3.00
a. Without shield
295 A63 (a) 5c blue 4.50 3.00

Purple Overprint

296 A63 (b) 3c gray blk (Shield in pur) 4.50 4.00
296A A63 (b) 5c bl (Shield in pue) 3.25 3.00
297 A63 (b) 3c gray blk 6.00 4.50
298 A63 (b) 5c blue 4.00 3.00

Black Overprint

298A A63 (b) 5c blue

Blue Overprint

299 A63 (c) 1c green 4.50 3.00
299B A63 (c) 2c rose .40 .35
c. "1905" vert. .80
300 A63 (c) 5c blue 1.25 .60
301 A63 (c) 10c deep blue .75 .60

Black Overprint

302 A63 (c) 2c rose 3.00 1.50
303 A63 (c) 5c blue 12.50 12.50
304 A63 (c) 10c deep blue 4.00 3.50

Blue Overprint

305 A63 (d) 1c green 5.00 3.50
306 A63 (d) 2c rose, ovpt. vert. 3.00 1.50
a. Overprint horiz.
306B A63 (d) 3c gray black 5.00 1.75
307 A63 (d) 5c blue 2.50 1.00

Blue Overprint

311 A63 (e) 2c rose 2.50 2.00
a. Without shield 4.00 3.00

Black Overprint

311B A63 (e) 5c blue 20.00 19.00
Nos. 293-311B (20) 94.40 73.80

These overprints are found double, inverted, omitted, etc. Counterfeits exist.

Regular Issue of 1903 Surcharged with New Values:

UN CENTAVO
f

5 CENTAVOS
g

1 1

1 CENTAVO 1
h

1905-06 **Wmk. 173** ***Perf. 14, 14½***

Black Surcharge

312 A64 (f) 1c on 2c car .40 .25
a. Double surcharge 3.00 3.00

Red Surcharge

312B A64 (g) 5c on 12c slate .75 .50
c. Double surcharge
d. Black surcharge 3.50 3.50
e. As "d," double surcharge

Blue Handstamped Surcharge

313 A64 (h) 1c on 2c car .25 .20
314 A64 (h) 1c on 10c vio .20 .20
315 A64 (h) 1c on 12c sl ('06) 1.00 .50
316 A64 (h) 1c on 13c red brn 4.00 3.25

No. 271 with Handstamped Surcharge in Blue

Unwmk.

317 A63 (h) 1c on 2c rose 42.50 37.50
Nos. 312-317 (7) 49.10 42.40

The "h" is handstamped in strips of four stamps each differing from the others in the size of the upper figures of value and in the letters of the word "CENTAVO," particularly in the size of the "N" and the "O" of that word. The surcharge is known inverted, double, etc.

Regular Issue of 1903 with Handstamped Surcharge:

i 5 5
5 5
5 5
5 5 5 5
j k

Wmk. 173

Red Handstamped Surcharge

318 A64 (i) 5c on 12c slate 2.25 1.50
319 A64 (j) 5c on 12c slate 2.25 1.75
a. Blue surcharge

Blue Handstamped Surcharge

320 A64 (k) 5c on 12c slate 2.00 1.75
Nos. 318-320 (3) 6.50 5.00

One or more of the numerals in the handstamped surcharges on Nos. 318, 319 and 320 are frequently omitted, inverted, etc.

Surcharged:

1 1
6 6

6 CENTAVOS 6
l

m

Blue Handstamped Surcharge

321 A64 (l) 6c on 12c slate .50 .30
322 A64 (l) 6c on 13c red brn 1.00 .40

Red Handstamped Surcharge

323 A64 (l) 6c on 12c slate 17.50 12.00

Type "l" is handstamped in strips of four varieties, differing in the size of the numerals and letters. The surcharge is known double and inverted.

Black Surcharge

324 A64 (m) 1c on 13c red brn 1.50 1.00
a. Double surcharge 4.00 3.00
b. Right "1" & dot omitted
c. Both numerals omitted
325 A64 (m) 3c on 13c red brn .50 .40

Stamps of 1900, with Shield in Black, Overprinted — n 01905

1905 **Unwmk.** ***Perf. 12***

Blue Overprint

326 A63 (n) 1c green 4.50 3.25
a. Inverted overprint
327 A63 (n) 2c rose 3.25 3.25
a. Vertical overprint 6.00 5.00
327B A63 (n) 3c black 30.00 27.50
327C A63 (n) 5c blue 12.50 10.00
328 A63 (n) 10c deep blue 6.00 4.50

Black Overprint

328A A63 (n) 10c deep blue 7.50 4.50
Nos. 326-328A (6) 63.75 53.00

Counterfeits of Nos. 326-335 abound.

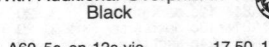

Stamps of 1900, with Shield in Black Surcharged or Overprinted:

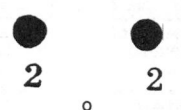

1906

2 2
o

p 1906

1906 q

1906

Blue and Black Surcharge

329	A63 (o)	2c on 26c brn org	.50	.40
a.		"2" & dot double	7.50	7.50
330	A63 (o)	3c on 26c brn org	4.00	3.25
a.		"3" & dot double		

Black Surcharge or Overprint

331	A63 (o)	3c on 26c brn org	3.00	2.50
a.		Disks & numerals omitted		
b.		"3" and disks double		
c.		"1906" omitted		
333	A63 (p)	10c deep blue	1.75	1.40
334	A63 (q)	10c deep blue	1.25	1.25
334A	A63 (q)	26c brown org	22.50	20.00
b.		"1906" in blue		

No. 257 Overprinted in Black

335	A63 (q)	10c dp bl (Shield in violet)	17.50	15.00
a.		Overprint type "p"		
		Nos. 329-335 (7)	50.50	43.80

There are numerous varieties of these surcharges and overprints.

Pres. Pedro José Escalón — A65

1906 **Engr.** ***Perf. 11½***

Glazed Paper

336	A65	1c green & blk	.20	.20
a.		Thin paper	.75	.20
337	A65	2c red & blk	.20	.20
338	A65	3c yellow & blk	.20	.20
339	A65	5c ultra & blk	.20	.20
a.		5c dark blue & black	.20	.20
340	A65	6c carmine & blk	.20	.20
341	A65	10c violet & blk	.20	.20
342	A65	12c violet & blk	.20	.20
343	A65	13c dk brn & blk	.20	.20
345	A65	24c carmine & blk	.35	.35
346	A65	26c choc & blk	.35	.35
347	A65	50c yellow & blk	.35	.45
348	A65	100c blue & blk	*3.00*	*3.00*
		Nos. 336-348 (12)	*5.65*	*5.75*

All values of this set are known imperforate but are not believed to have been issued in this condition.

See Nos. O263-O272. For overprints and surcharges see Nos. 349-354.

The entire set has been reprinted. The shades of the reprints differ from those of the originals, the paper is thicker and the perforation 12. Value, set of 12, $1.20.

Nos. 336-338 Overprinted in Black

1907

349	A65	1c green & blk	.25	.20
a.		Shield in red	3.50	
350	A65	2c red & blk	.25	.20
a.		Shield in red	3.50	
351	A65	3c yellow & blk	.25	.20
		Nos. 349-351 (3)	.75	.60

Reprints of Nos. 349 to 351 have the same characteristics as the reprints of the preceding issue. Value, set of 3, 15c.

Stamps of 1906 Surcharged with Shield and

1

352	A65	1c on 5c ultra & blk	.20	.20
a.		1c on 5c dark blue & black	.20	.20
b.		Inverted surcharge	.35	.35
c.		Double surcharge	.45	.45
352D	A65	1c on 6c rose & blk	.20	.20
e.		Double surcharge	1.25	1.25
353	A65	2c on 6c rose & blk	2.00	1.00
354	A65	10c on 6c rose & blk	.50	.35
		Nos. 352-354 (4)	2.90	1.75

The above surcharges are frequently found with the shield double, inverted, or otherwise misplaced.

National Palace — A66

Overprinted with Shield in Black

1907 **Engr.** **Unwmk.**

Paper with or without colored dots

355	A66	1c green & blk	.20	.20
356	A66	2c red & blk	.20	.20
357	A66	3c yellow & blk	.20	.20
358	A66	5c blue & blk	.20	.20
a.		5c ultramarine & black	.20	.20
359	A66	6c ver & blk	.20	.20
a.		Shield in red	3.25	
360	A66	10c violet & blk	.20	.20
361	A66	12c violet & blk	.20	.20
362	A66	13c sepia & blk	.20	.20
363	A66	24c rose & blk	.20	.20
364	A66	26c yel brn & blk	.30	.20
365	A66	50c orange & blk	.50	.35
a.		50c yellow & black	3.50	
366	A66	100c turq bl & blk	1.00	.50
		Nos. 355-366 (12)	3.60	2.85

Most values exist without shield, also with shield inverted, double, and otherwise misprinted. Many of these were never sold to the public.

See 2nd footnote following No. 421.

See Nos. 369-373, 397-401. For surcharges and overprints see Nos. 367-368A, 374-77, 414-421, 443-444, J71-J74, J76-J80, O329-O331.

No. 356 With Additional Surcharge in Black

UN CENTAVO

1908

367	A66	1c on 2c red & blk	.25	.25
a.		Double surcharge	1.00	1.00
b.		Inverted surcharge	.50	.50
c.		Double surcharge, one inverted	.50	.50
d.		Red surcharge		

Same Surcharged in Black or Red

UN CENTAVO

368	A66	1c on 2c	*19.00*	*17.50*
368A	A66	1c on 2c (R)	*27.50*	*25.00*

Counterfeits exist of the surcharges on Nos. 368-368A.

Type of 1907

1909 **Engr.** **Wmk. 172**

369	A66	1c green & blk	.20	.20
370	A66	2c rose & blk	.20	.20
371	A66	3c yellow & blk	.25	.20
372	A66	5c blue & blk	.25	.20
373	A66	10c violet & blk	.30	.20
		Nos. 369-373 (5)	1.20	1.00

The note after No. 366 will apply here also.

Nos. 355, 369 Overprinted in Red

1821
15 septiembre
1909

1909, Sept. **Unwmk.**

374	A66	1c green & blk	2.25	1.10
a.		Inverted overprint	10.00	

Wmk. 172

375	A66	1c green & blk	1.75	1.40
a.		Inverted overprint		

88th anniv. of El Salvador's independence.

Nos. 362, 364 Surcharged

2
CENTAVOS
1909

1909 **Unwmk.**

376	A66	2c on 13c sep & blk	1.50	1.25
a.		Inverted surcharge		
377	A66	3c on 26c yel brn & blk	1.75	1.40
a.		Inverted surcharge		

A67

A68

Design: Pres. Fernando Figueroa.

1910 **Engr.** **Wmk. 172**

378	A67	1c sepia & blk	.20	.20
379	A67	2c dk grn & blk	.20	.20
380	A67	3c orange & blk	.20	.20
381	A67	4c carmine & blk	.20	.20
a.		4c scarlet & black	.20	.20
382	A67	5c purple & blk	.20	.20
383	A67	6c scarlet & blk	.20	.20
384	A67	10c purple & blk	.20	.20
385	A67	12c dp bl & blk	.20	.20
386	A67	17c ol grn & blk	.20	.20
387	A67	19c brn red & blk	.20	.20
388	A67	29c choc & blk	.20	.20
389	A67	50c yellow & blk	.20	.20
390	A67	100c turq bl & blk	.20	.20
		Nos. 378-390 (13)	2.60	2.60

1911 **Unwmk.**

5c, José Matías Delgado. 6c, Manuel José Arce. 12c, Centenary Monument.

Paper with colored dots

391	A68	5c dp blue & brn	.20	.20
392	A68	6c orange & brn	.20	.20
393	A68	12c violet & brn	.20	.20

Wmk. 172

394	A68	5c dp blue & brn	.20	.20
395	A68	6c orange & brn	.20	.20
396	A68	12c violet & brn	.20	.20
		Nos. 391-396 (6)	1.20	1.20

Centenary of the insurrection of 1811.

Palace Type of 1907 without Shield

1911

Paper without colored dots

397	A66	1c scarlet	.20	.20
398	A66	2c chocolate	.30	.30
a.		Paper with brown dots		
399	A66	13c deep green	.20	.20
400	A66	24c yellow	.20	.20
401	A66	50c dark brown	.20	.20
		Nos. 397-401 (5)	1.10	1.10

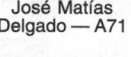

José Matías Delgado — A71

Manuel José Arce — A72

Francisco Morazán A73

Rafael Campo A74

Trinidad Cabañas A75

Monument of Gerardo Barrios A76

Centenary Monument A77

National Palace A78

Rosales Hospital — A79

Coat of Arms — A80

1912 **Unwmk.** ***Perf. 12***

402	A71	1c dp bl & blk	.20	.20
403	A72	2c bis brn & blk	.25	.20
404	A73	5c scarlet & blk	.25	.20
405	A74	6c dk grn & blk	.20	.20
406	A75	12c ol grn & blk	1.00	.20
407	A76	17c violet & slate	.60	.20
408	A77	19c scar & slate	1.25	.30
409	A78	29c org & slate	1.50	.30
410	A79	50c blue & slate	1.75	.45
411	A80	1col black & slate	2.50	1.00
		Nos. 402-411 (10)	9.50	3.25

Juan Manuel Rodríguez A81

Pres. Manuel E. Araujo A82

1914 ***Perf. 11½***

412	A81	10c orange & brn	2.50	.75
413	A82	25c purple & brn	2.50	.75

Type of 1907 without Shield Overprinted in Black

1915

1915

Paper overlaid with colored dots

414	A66	1c gray green	.20	.20
415	A66	2c red	.20	.20
416	A66	5c ultra	.20	.20
417	A66	6c pale blue	.20	.20
418	A66	10c yellow	.60	.30
419	A66	12c brown	.50	.20
420	A66	50c violet	.20	.20
421	A66	100c black brn	1.40	1.40
		Nos. 414-421 (8)	3.50	2.90

Varieties such as center omitted, center double, center inverted, imperforate exist with or without date, inverted, date double, etc., but are believed to be entirely unofficial.

Preceding the stamps with the "1915" overprint a quantity of stamps of this type was overprinted with the letter "S." Evidence is lacking that they were ever placed in use. The issue was demonetized in 1916.

National Theater — A83

Various frames.

1916 **Engr.** ***Perf. 12***

431	A83	1c deep green	.20	.20
432	A83	2c vermilion	.20	.20
433	A83	5c deep blue	.20	.20
434	A83	6c gray violet	.25	.20
435	A83	10c black brn	.25	.20
436	A83	12c violet	2.50	.50
437	A83	17c orange	.35	.20
438	A83	25c dk brown	.80	.20
439	A83	29c black	5.00	.75
440	A83	50c slate	2.50	1.50
		Nos. 431-440 (10)	12.25	4.15

Watermarked letters which occasionally appear are from the papermaker's name.

For surcharges and overprints see Nos. 450-455, 457-466, O332-O341.

Nos. O324-O325 with "OFICIAL" Barred out in Black

1917

441	O3	2c red	.45	.45
a.		Double bar		
442	O3	5c ultramarine	.50	.35
a.		Double bar		

Regular Issue of 1915 Overprinted "OFICIAL" and Re-overprinted In Red

CORRIENTE

443	A66	6c pale blue	.65	.50
a.		Double bar		
444	A66	12c brown	.85	.65
a.		Double bar		
b.		"CORRIENTE" inverted		

Same Overprint in Red On Nos. O323-O327

445	O3	1c gray green	1.75	1.25
a.		"CORRIENTE" inverted		
b.		Double bar		
c.		"CORRIENTE" omitted		
446	O3	2c red	1.75	1.25
a.		Double bar		
447	O3	5c ultra	9.00	6.00
a.		Double bar, both in black		
448	O3	10c yellow	1.00	.50
a.		Double bar		
b.		"OFICIAL" and bar omitted		
449	O3	50c violet	.50	.50
a.		Double bar		
		Nos. 443-449 (7)	15.50	10.65

Nos. O334-O335 Overprinted or Surcharged in Red:

Corriente
a

1 1 CORRIENTE 1
Un Centavo
b

450	A83 (a)	5c deep blue	1.50	1.00
a.		"CORRIENTE" double		
451	A83 (b)	1c on 6c gray vio	1.00	.75
a.		"CORRIERTE"		
b.		"CORRIENRE"	5.00	
c.		"CORRIENTE" double		

No. 434 Surcharged in Black

1
1 CENTAVO 1

1918

452	A83	1c on 6c gray vio	1.75	1.00
a.		Double surcharge		
b.		Inverted surcharge		

No. 434 Surcharged in Black

1
1 Centavo *1*

1918

453	A83	1c on 6c gray vio	1.50	.75
a.		"Centado"	2.25	1.50
b.		Double surcharge	2.50	1.75
c.		Inverted surcharge		

No. 434 Surcharged in Black or Red

I CENTAVO I

454	A83	1c on 6c gray vio	4.00	3.25
a.		Double surcharge		
b.		Inverted surcharge	5.00	5.00
455	A83	1c on 6c gray vio (R)	4.00	3.25
a.		Double surcharge		
b.		Inverted surcharge	5.00	5.00
		Nos. 454-455 (2)	8.00	6.50

Counterfeits exist of Nos. 454-455.

Pres. Carlos Meléndez — A85

1919 **Engr.**

456	A85	1col dk blue & blk	.50	.50

For surcharge see No. 467.

No. 437 Surcharged in Black

1
1 Centavo 1

1919

457	A83	1c on 17c orange	.25	.25
a.		Inverted surcharge	1.00	1.00
b.		Double surcharge	1.00	1.00

Nos. 435-436, 438, 440 Surcharged in Black or Blue

1920-21

458	A83	1c on 12c violet	.20	.20
a.		Double surcharge	1.00	1.00
459	A83	2c on 10c dk brn	.25	.20
460	A83	5c on 50c slate ('21)	.40	.20
461	A83	6c on 25c dk brn (Bl) ('21)	.40	.20

Same Surch. in Black on No. O337

462	A83	1c on 12c violet	1.00	1.00
a.		Double surcharge		
		Nos. 458-462 (5)	2.25	1.80

No. 460 surcharged in yellow and 461 surcharged in red are essays.

No. 462 is due to some sheets of Official Stamps being mixed with the ordinary 12c stamps at the time of surcharging. The error stamps were sold to the public and used for ordinary postage.

Surcharged in Red, Blue or Black:

15c Types:

15 I · 15 II · 15 III · 15 IV

463	A83	15c on 29c blk (III) ('21)	1.00	.40
a.		Double surcharge	2.00	
b.		Type I	1.50	1.00
c.		Type II	1.00	.75
d.		Type IV	2.50	
464	A83	26c on 29c blk (Bl)	1.00	.60
a.		Double surcharge		
466	A83	35c on 50c slate (Bk)	1.00	.60
467	A85	60c on 1col dk bl & blk (R)	.30	.25
		Nos. 463-467 (4)	3.30	1.85

Surcharge on No. 464 differs from 15c illustration in that bar at bottom extends across stamp and denomination includes "cts." One stamp in each row of ten of No. 464 has the "t" of "cts" inverted and one stamp in each row of No. 466 has the letters "c" in "cinco" larger than the normal.

Setting for No. 467 includes three types of numerals and "CENTAVOS" measuring from 16mm to 20mm wide.

No. 464 surcharged in green or yellow and the 35c on 29c black are essays.

A93

1921

468	A93	1c on 1c ol grn	.20	.20
a.		Double surcharge	.75	
469	A93	1c on 5c yellow	.20	.20
a.		Inverted surcharge		
b.		Double surcharge		
470	A93	1c on 10c blue	.20	.20
a.		Double surcharge	.50	
471	A93	1c on 25c green	.20	.20
a.		Double surcharge		
472	A93	1c on 50c olive	.20	.20
a.		Double surcharge		
473	A93	1c on 1p gray blk	.20	.20
a.		Double surcharge		
		Nos. 468-473 (6)	1.20	1.20

The frame of No. 473 differs slightly from the illustration.

Setting includes many wrong font letters and numerals.

Francisco Menéndez
A94

Manuel José Arce
A95

Confederation Coin — A96

Delgado Addressing Crowd — A97

Coat of Arms of Confedera-tion
A98

Francisco Morazán
A99

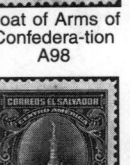

Independence Monument
A100

Columbus
A101

1921 **Engr.** ***Perf. 12***

474	A94	1c green	.25	.20
475	A95	2c black	.25	.20
476	A96	5c orange	1.00	.20
477	A97	6c carmine rose	.50	.20
478	A98	10c deep blue	.50	.20
479	A99	25c olive grn	2.50	.20
480	A100	60c violet	6.00	.50
481	A101	1col black brn	10.00	.75
		Nos. 474-481 (8)	21.00	2.45

For overprints and surcharges see Nos. 481A-485, 487-494, 506, O342-O349.

Nos. 474-477 Overprinted in Red, Black or Blue

a

b

1921

481A	A94 (a)	1c green (R)	5.00	4.00
481B	A95 (a)	2c black (R)	5.00	4.00
481C	A96 (b)	5c orange (Bk)	5.00	4.00
481D	A97 (b)	6c car rose (Bl)	5.00	4.00
		Nos. 481A-481D (4)	20.00	16.00

Centenary of independence.

No. 477 Surcharged:

5
a 5 5

5
b

1923

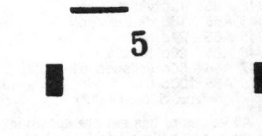

482	A97 (a)	5c on 6c	.35	.20
483	A97 (b)	5c on 6c	.30	.20
484	A97 (b)	20c on 6c	.35	.25
		Nos. 482-484 (3)	1.00	.65

Nos. 482-484 exist with double surcharge.

No. 475 Surcharged in Red

10

1923

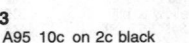

485	A95	10c on 2c black	.50	.20

José Simeón Cañas y Villacorta — A102

1923 Engr. *Perf. 11½*

486 A102 5c blue .50 .30

Centenary of abolition of slavery.
For surcharge see No. 571.

Nos. 479, 481 Surcharged in Red or Black

6 Seis centavos 6

1924 *Perf. 12*

487 A99 1c on 25c ol grn (R) .20 .20
a. Numeral at right inverted
b. Double surcharge
488 A99 6c on 25c ol grn (R) .20 .20
489 A99 20c on 25c ol grn (R) .50 .25
490 A101 20c on 1col blk brn (Bk) .65 .35
Nos. 487-490 (4) 1.55 1.00

Nos. 476, 478 Surcharged:

1924

491 A96 1c on 5c orange (Bk) .35 .20
492 A98 6c on 10c dp bl (R) .35 .20

Nos. 491-492 exist with double surcharge.
A stamp similar to No. 492 but with surcharge "6 centavos 6" is an essay.

No. 476 Surcharged

2
Dos centavos

493 A96 2c on 5c orange .40 .35
a. Top ornament omitted 2.00 2.00
Nos. 491-493 (3) 1.10 .75

No. 480 Surcharged:

1924

Red Surcharge

494 A100 5c on 60c violet 4.25 3.75
a. "1781" for "1874" 10.00 8.75
b. "1934" for "1924" 10.00 8.75

Universal Postal Union, 50th anniversary.
This stamp with black surcharge is an essay. Copies have been passed through the post.

Daniel Hernández Monument A106

National Gymnasium A107

Atlacatl — A108

Conspiracy of 1811 — A109

Bridge over Lempa River — A110

Map of Central America — A111

Balsam Tree — A112

Tulla Serra — A114

Columbus at La Rábida — A115

Coat of Arms — A116

Photogravure; Engraved (35c, 1col)

1924-25 *Perf. 12½; 14 (35c, 1col)*

495 A106 1c red violet .20 .20
496 A107 2c dark red .25 .20
497 A108 3c chocolate .20 .20
498 A109 5c olive blk .20 .20
499 A110 6c grnsh blue .25 .20
500 A111 10c orange .60 .20
a. "ATLANT CO" 5.50 5.50
501 A112 20c deep green 1.00 .25
502 A114 35c scar & grn 2.50 .35
503 A115 50c orange brown 2.00 .30
504 A116 1col grn & vio ('25) 3.00 .30
Nos. 495-504 (10) 10.20 2.40

For overprints and surcharges see Nos. 510-511, 520-534, 585, C1-C10, C19, O350-O361, RA1-RA4.

No. 480 Surcharged in Red

1925, Aug. *Perf. 12*

506 A100 2c on 60c violet 1.25 1.25

City of San Salvador, 400th anniv.
The variety with dates in black is an essay.

View of San Salvador — A118

1925 Photo. *Perf. 12½*

507 A118 1c blue .65 .65
508 A118 2c deep green .65 .65
509 A118 3c Mahogany red .65 .65
Nos. 507-509 (3) 1.95 1.95

#506-509 for the 4th centenary of the founding of the City of San Salvador.

Black Surcharge

1928, July 17

510 A111 3c on 10c orange .75 .50
a. "ATLANT CO" 12.50 12.50

Industrial Exhibition, Santa Ana, July 1928.

Red Surcharge

1928

511 A109 1c on 5c olive black .25 .20
a. Bar instead of top left "1" .40 .25

Pres. Pío Romero Bosque, Salvador, and Pres. Lázaro Chacón, Guatemala A121

1929 Litho. *Perf. 11½*

Portraits in Dark Brown

512 A121 1c dull violet .35 .25
a. Center inverted 11.50 11.50
513 A121 3c bister brn .35 .25
a. Center inverted 35.00 35.00
514 A121 5c gray grn .35 .25
515 A121 10c orange .35 .25
Nos. 512-515 (4) 1.40 1.00

Opening of the international railroad connecting El Salvador and Guatemala.
Nos. 512-515 exist imperforate. No. 512 in the colors of No. 515.

Tomb of Menéndez A122

1930, Dec. 3

516 A122 1c violet 3.00 2.50
517 A122 3c brown 3.00 2.50
518 A122 5c dark green 3.00 2.50
519 A122 10c yellow brn 3.00 2.50
Nos. 516-519 (4) 12.00 10.00

Centenary of the birth of General Francisco Menéndez.

Stamps of 1924-25 Issue Overprinted **1932**

1932 *Perf. 12½, 14*

520 A106 1c deep violet .20 .20
521 A107 2c dark red .20 .20
522 A108 3c chocolate .30 .20
523 A109 5c olive blk .30 .20
524 A110 6c deep blue .35 .20
525 A111 10c orange 1.00 .20
a. "ATLANT CO" 7.50 6.25
526 A112 20c deep green 1.50 .45
527 A114 35c scar & grn 2.25 .75
528 A115 50c orange brown 3.00 1.00
529 A116 1col green & vio 5.00 2.25
Nos. 520-529 (10) 14.10 5.65

Values are for the overprint measuring 7½x3mm. It is found in two other sizes: 7½x3¼mm and 8x3mm.

Types of 1924-25 Surcharged with New Values in Red or Black

1934 *Perf. 12½*

530 A109 2(c) on 5c grnsh blk .20 .20
a. Double surcharge
531 A111 3(c) on 10c org (Bk) .25 .20
a. "ATLANT CO" 4.00 4.00

Nos. 503, 504, 502 Surcharged with New Values in Black

Perf. 12½, 14½

532 A115 2(c) on 50c .30 .20
a. Double surcharge 3.00
533 A116 8(c) on 1col .20 .20
534 A114 15(c) on 35c .30 .20
Nos. 530-534 (5) 1.25 1.00

Police Barracks — A123

Two types of the 2c:
Type I - The clouds have heavy lines of shading.
Type II - The lines of shading have been removed from the clouds.

Wmk. 240

1934-35 Litho. *Perf. 12½*

535 A123 2c gray brn, type I .20 .20
a. 2c brown, type II .20 .20
536 A123 5c car, type II .20 .20
537 A123 8c lt ultra, type II .20 .20
Nos. 535-537,C33-C35 (6) 3.10 1.75

Discus Thrower A124

1935, Mar. 16 Engr. Unwmk.

538 A124 5c carmine 2.00 1.65
539 A124 8c blue 2.25 1.90
540 A124 10c orange yel 2.75 2.00
541 A124 15c bister 3.25 2.25
542 A124 37c green 4.00 3.25
Nos. 538-542,C36-C40 (10) 47.75 36.55

3rd Central American Games.

Same Overprinted in Black **HABILITADO**

1935, June 27

543 A124 5c carmine 2.75 2.00
544 A124 8c blue 4.00 2.00
545 A124 10c orange yel 4.00 2.50
546 A124 15c bister 4.00 2.50
547 A124 37c green 6.50 4.00
Nos. 543-547,C41-C45 (10) 62.75 39.75

Flag of El Salvador A125

Tree of San Vicente A126

1935, Oct. 26 Litho. Wmk. 240

548 A125 1c gray blue .20 .20
549 A125 2c black brn .20 .20
550 A125 3c plum .20 .20
551 A125 5c rose carmine .25 .20
552 A125 8c ultra .30 .20
553 A125 15c fawn .40 .25
Nos. 548-553,C46 (7) 2.05 1.45

1935, Dec. 26

Numerals in Black, Tree in Yellow Green

554 A126 2c black brn .50 .25
555 A126 3c dk blue grn .50 .30
556 A126 5c rose red .50 .35
557 A126 8c dark blue .50 .40
558 A126 15c brown .50 .50
Nos. 554-558,C47-C51 (10) 6.50 5.30

Tercentenary of San Vicente.

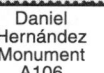

Volcano of Izalco — A127

Wharf at Cutuco — A128

Doroteo Vasconcelos A129

Parade Ground A130

Dr. Tomás G. Palomo — A131

Sugar Mill — A132

Coffee at Pier — A133

Gathering Balsam — A134

Pres. Manuel E. Araujo — A135

1935, Dec. Engr. Unwmk.

559	A127	1c deep violet	.20	.20
560	A128	2c chestnut	.20	.20
561	A129	3c green	.20	.20
562	A130	5c carmine	.40	.20
563	A131	8c dull blue	.20	.20
564	A132	10c orange	.25	.20
565	A133	15c dk olive bis	.40	.20
566	A134	50c indigo	2.00	1.25
567	A135	1col black	5.00	3.00
		Nos. 559-567 (9)	8.85	5.65

Paper has faint imprint "El Salvador" on face.

For surcharges and overprint see Nos. 568-570, 573, 583-584, C52.

Stamps of 1935 Surcharged with New Value in Black

1938 *Perf. 12½*

568	A130	1c on 5c carmine	.20	.20
569	A132	3c on 10c orange	.20	.20
570	A133	8c on 15c dk ol bis	.20	.20
		Nos. 568-570 (3)	.60	.60

No. 486 Surcharged with New Value in Red

1938 *Perf. 11½*

571 A102 3c on 5c blue .25 .25

Centenary of the death of José Simeón Cañas, liberator of slaves in Latin America.

Map of Flags of US and El Salvador — A136

Engraved and Lithographed

1938, Apr. 21 *Perf. 12*

572 A136 8c multicolored .50 .50

US Constitution, 150th anniv. See #C61.

No. 560 Surcharged with New Value in Black

1938 *Perf. 12½*

573 A128 1c on 2c chestnut .20 .20

Indian Sugar Mill — A137

Designs: 2c, Indian women washing. 3c, Indian girl at spring. 5c, Indian plowing. 8c, Izote flower. 10c, Champion cow. 20c, Extracting balsam. 50c, Maquilishuat in bloom. 1col, Post Office, San Salvador.

1938-39 Engr. *Perf. 12*

574	A137	1c dark violet	.20	.20
575	A137	2c dark green	.20	.20
576	A137	3c dark brown	.25	.20
577	A137	5c scarlet	.25	.20
578	A137	8c dark blue	1.25	.20
579	A137	10c yel org ('39)	2.00	.20
580	A137	20c bis brn ('39)	1.75	.20
581	A137	50c dull blk ('39)	2.25	.45
582	A137	1col black ('39)	2.00	.75
		Nos. 574-582 (9)	10.15	2.60

For surcharges & overprints see #591-592, C96.

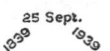

25 Sept.
1839 1939

Nos. 566-567, 504 Surcharged in Red

BATALLA
SAN PEDRO PERULAPAN
₡ 0.50

1939, Sept. 25 *Perf. 12½, 14*

583	A134	8c on 50c indigo	.30	.20
584	A135	10c on 1col blk	.45	.20
585	A116	50c on 1col grn & vio	2.75	2.10
		Nos. 583-585 (3)	3.50	2.50

Battle of San Pedro Perulapán, 100th anniv.

Sir Rowland Hill — A146

1940, Mar. 1 *Perf. 12½*

586	A146	8c dk bl, lt bl & blk	5.50	1.75
		Nos. 586,C69-C70 (3)	24.00	14.00

Postage stamp centenary.

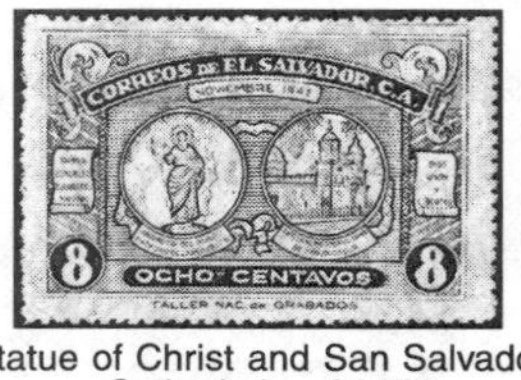
Statue of Christ and San Salvador Cathedral — A147

A148

Wmk. 269

1942, Nov. 23 Engr. *Perf. 14*

587 A147 8c deep blue .50 .20

Souvenir Sheet

Imperf

Without Gum

Lilac Tinted Paper

588	A148	Sheet of 4	15.00	15.00
a.		8c deep blue	3.75	3.75
b.		30c red orange	3.75	3.75

Nos. 587-588 commemorate the first Eucharistic Congress of Salvador. See No. C85.

No. 588 contains two No. 587 and two No. C85, imperf.

Catalogue values for unused stamps in this section, from this point to the end of the section, are for Never Hinged items.

Cuscatlán Bridge, Pan-American Highway — A149

Arms Overprint at Right in Carmine

Perf. 12½

1944, Nov. 24 Unwmk. Engr.

589 A149 8c dk blue & blk .25 .20

See No. C92.

Gen. Juan José Canas — A150

1945, June 9

590 A150 8c blue .40 .20

No. 575 Surcharged in Black

1 1
a *b*

1944-46

591	A137(a)	1(c) on 2c dk grn	.20	.20
592	A137(b)	1(c) on 2c dk grn ('46)	.20	.20

Lake of Ilopango A151

Ceiba Tree A152

Water Carriers — A153

1946-47 Litho. Wmk. 240

593	A151	1c blue ('47)	.25	.20
594	A152	2c lt bl grn ('47)	.25	.20
595	A153	5c carmine	.25	.20
		Nos. 593-595 (3)	.75	.60

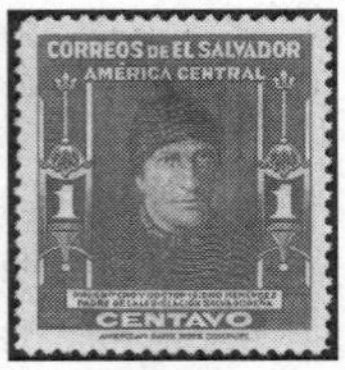
Isidro Menéndez A154

2c, Cristano Salazar. 3c, Juan Bertis. 5c, Francisco Duenas. 8c, Ramon Belloso. 10c, Jose Presentacion Trigueros. 20c, Salvador Rodriguez Gonzalez. 50c, Francisco Castaneda. 1col, David Castro.

1947 Unwmk. Engr. *Perf. 12*

596	A154	1c car rose	.20	.20
597	A154	2c dp org	.20	.20
598	A154	3c violet	.20	.20
599	A154	5c slate gray	.20	.20
600	A154	8c dp bl	.20	.20
601	A154	10c bis brn	.20	.20
602	A154	20c green	.30	.20
603	A154	50c black	.65	.30
604	A154	1col scarlet	1.40	.40
		Nos. 596-604 (9)	3.55	2.10

For surcharges and overprints see Nos. 621-626, 634, C118-C120, O362-O368.

Manuel José Arce — A163

1948, Feb. 25 *Perf. 12½*

605	A163	8c deep blue	.30	.20
		Nos. 605,C108-C110 (4)	3.00	2.00

President Roosevelt Presenting Awards for Distinguished Service — A164

President Franklin D. Roosevelt A165

A166

Designs: 8c, Pres. and Mrs. Roosevelt. 15c, Mackenzie King, Roosevelt and Winston Churchill. 20c, Roosevelt and Cordell Hull. 50c, Funeral of Pres. Roosevelt.

1948, Apr. 12
Various Frames; Center in Black

606 A164	5c dk bl	.20	.20
607 A164	8c green	.20	.20
608 A165	12c violet	.20	.20
609 A164	15c vermilion	.25	.20
610 A164	20c car lake	.30	.20
611 A164	50c gray	.70	.45
	Nos. 606-611,C111-C117 (13)	10.85	7.45

Souvenir Sheet
Perf. 13½

612 A166 1col ol grn & brn 2.25 1.50

3rd anniv. of the death of F. D. Roosevelt.

Torch and Winged Letter A167

Perf. 12½
1949, Oct. 9 Unwmk. Engr.

613 A167 8c blue .65 .40
Nos. 613,C122-C124 (4) 16.00 12.30

75th anniv. of the UPU.

Workman and Soldier Holding Torch — A168

Wreath and Open Book — A169

1949, Dec. 15 Litho. *Perf. 10½*

614 A168 8c blue .30 .25
Nos. 614,C125-C129 (6) 6.50 5.00

Revolution of Dec. 14, 1948, 1st anniv.

Perf. 11½
1952, Feb. 14 Photo. Unwmk.
Wreath in Dark Green

615 A169	1c yel grn	.20	.20
616 A169	2c magenta	.20	.20
617 A169	5c brn red	.20	.20
618 A169	10c yellow	.20	.20
619 A169	20c gray grn	.20	.20
620 A169	1col dp car	1.00	.75
	Nos. 615-620,C134-C141 (14)	8.25	5.75

Constitution of 1950.

Nos. 598, 600 and 603 Surcharged with New Values in Various Colors

1952-53 *Perf. 12½*

621 A154	2c on 3c vio (C)	.20	.20
622 A154	2c on 8c dp bl (C)	.20	.20
623 A154	3c on 8c dp bl (G)	.20	.20
624 A154	5c on 8c dp bl (O)	.20	.20
625 A154	7c on 8c dp bl (Bk)	.20	.20
626 A154	10c on 50c blk (O) ('53)	.20	.20
	Nos. 621-626 (6)	1.20	1.20

Nos. C106 and C107 Surcharged and "AEREO" Obliterated in Various Colors

1952-53 Wmk. 240

627 AP31	2c on 12c choc (Bl)	.20	.20
628 AP32	2c on 14c dk bl (R) ('53)	.20	.20
629 AP31	5c on 12c choc (Bl)	.20	.20
630 AP32	10c on 14c dk bl (C)	.20	.20
	Nos. 627-630 (4)	.80	.80

José Marti — A170

Perf. 10½
1953, Feb. 27 Litho. Unwmk.

631 A170	1c rose red	.25	.20
632 A170	2c bl grn	.25	.20
633 A170	10c dk vio	.25	.20
	Nos. 631-633,C142-C144 (6)	2.60	1.35

José Marti, Cuban patriot, birth cent.

No. 598 Overprinted in Carmine — "IV Congreso Médico Social Panamericano 15 / 19 Abril, 1953"

1953, June 19 *Perf. 12½*

634 A154 3c violet .20 .20

4th Pan-American Congress of Social Medicine, San Salvador, April 16-19, 1953. See #C146.

Signing of Act of Independence A171

Capt. Gen. Gerardo Barrios — A172

1953, Sept. 15 Litho. *Perf. 11½*

635 A171	1c rose pink	.20	.20
636 A171	2c dp bl grn	.20	.20
637 A171	3c purple	.20	.20
638 A171	5c dp bl	.20	.20
639 A171	7c lt brn	.20	.20
640 A171	10c ocher	.20	.20
641 A171	20c dp org	.60	.20
642 A171	50c green	.80	.30
643 A171	1col gray	1.60	.90
	Nos. 635-643,C147-C150 (13)	5.75	3.70

Act of Independence, Sept. 15, 1821.

1953, Dec. 1 *Perf. 11½*

Portrait: 3c, 7c, 10c, 22c, Francisco Morazan, (facing left).

Black Overprint ("C de C")

644 A172	1c green	.20	.20
645 A172	2c blue	.20	.20
646 A172	3c green	.20	.20
647 A172	5c carmine	.20	.20
648 A172	7c blue	.20	.20
649 A172	10c carmine	.25	.20
650 A172	20c violet	.25	.20
651 A172	22c violet	.40	.20
	Nos. 644-651 (8)	1.90	1.60

The overprint "C de C" is a control indicating "Tribunal of Accounts." A double entry of this overprint occurs twice in each sheet of each denomination.

For overprint see No. 729.

Coastal Bridge A173

Motherland and Liberty A174

Census Allegory — A175

Balboa Park — A176

Designs: Nos. 654, 655, National Palace. Nos. 659, 665, Izalco Volcano. Nos. 660, 661, Guayabo dam. No. 666, Lake Ilopango. No. 669, Housing development. Nos. 670, 673, Coast guard boat. No. 671, Modern highway.

Perf. 11½
1954, June 1 Unwmk. Photo.

652 A173	1c car rose & brn	.20	.20
653 AP43	1c ol & bl gray	.20	.20
654 A173	1c pur & pale lil	.20	.20
655 A173	2c yel grn & lt gray	.20	.20
656 A174	2c car lake	.20	.20
657 A175	2c org red	.20	.20
658 AP44	3c maroon	.20	.20
659 A173	3c bl grn & bl	.20	.20
660 A174	3c dk gray & vio	.20	.20
661 A174	5c red vio & vio	.20	.20
662 AP44	5c emerald	.20	.20
663 A176	7c magenta & buff	.20	.20
664 AP43	7c bl grn & gray bl	.20	.20
665 A173	7c org brn & org	.20	.20
666 A173	10c car lake	.20	.20
667 AP46	10c red, dk brn & bl	.20	.20
668 A174	10c dk bl grn	.20	.20
669 A174	20c org & cr	.30	.20
670 A173	22c gray vio	.30	.25
671 A176	50c dk gray & brn	.65	.30
672 AP46	1col brn org, dk brn & bl	1.25	.75
673 A173	1col brt bl	1.25	.50
	Nos. 652-673 (22)	7.15	5.40
	Nos. 652-673,C151-C165 (37)	17.15	10.55

For surcharges & overprints see #692-693, 736, C193.

Capt. Gen. Gerardo Barrios — A177

Coffee Picker — A178

Wmk. 269
1955, Dec. 20 Engr. *Perf. 12½*

674 A177	1c red	.20	.20
675 A177	2c yel grn	.30	.25
676 A177	3c vio bl	.30	.25
677 A177	20c violet	.35	.30
	Nos. 674-677,C166-C167 (6)	1.70	1.50

Perf. 13½
1956, June 20 Litho. Unwmk.

678 A178	3c bis brn	.20	.20
679 A178	5c red org	.20	.20
680 A178	10c dk bl	.20	.20
681 A178	2col dk red	1.60	1.00
	Nos. 678-681,C168-C172 (9)	6.70	4.30

Centenary of Santa Ana Department.
For overprint see No. C187.

Map of Chalatenango — A179

1956, Sept. 14

682 A179	2c blue	.20	.20
683 A179	7c rose red	.30	.25
684 A179	50c yel brn	.50	.30
	Nos. 682-684,C173-C178 (9)	3.25	2.60

Centenary of Chalatenango Department (in 1955).
For surcharge see No. 694.

Coat of Arms of Nueva San Salvador — A180

Wmk. 269
1957, Jan. 3 Engr. *Perf. 12½*

685 A180	1c rose red	.20	.20
686 A180	2c green	.20	.20
687 A180	3c violet	.20	.20
688 A180	7c red org	.35	.20
689 A180	10c ultra	.20	.20
690 A180	50c pale brn	.35	.20
691 A180	1col dl red	.65	.55
	Nos. 685-691,C179-C183 (12)	5.50	3.70

Centenary of the founding of the city of Nueva San Salvador (Santa Tecla).
For surcharges and overprints see Nos. 695-696, 706, 713, C194-C195, C197-C199.

Nos. 664-665, 683 and 688 Surcharged with New Value in Black

1957 Unwmk. Photo. *Perf. 11½*

692 A173 6c on 7c bl grn & gray bl .30 .30
693 A173 6c on 7c org brn & org .30 .30

1957 Litho. *Perf. 13½*

694 A179 6c on 7c rose red .20 .20

Wmk. 269
1957-58 Engr. *Perf. 12½*

695 A180	5c on 7c red org ('58)	.25	.20
696 A180	6c on 7c red org	.30	.20
	Nos. 692-696 (5)	1.35	1.20

El Salvador Intercontinental Hotel — A181

Perf. 11½
1958, June 28 Unwmk. Photo.
Granite Paper
Vignette in Green, Dark Blue & Red

697 A181	3c brown	.20	.20
698 A181	6c crim rose	.20	.20
699 A181	10c brt bl	.20	.20
700 A181	15c brt grn	.20	.20
701 A181	20c lilac	.30	.20
702 A181	30c brt yel grn	.40	.25
	Nos. 697-702 (6)	1.50	1.25

Presidents Eisenhower and Lemus and Flags — A182

1959, Dec. 14 Granite Paper
Design in Ultramarine, Dark Brown, Light Brown and Red

703	A182	3c pink	.20	.20
704	A182	6c green	.20	.20
705	A182	10c crimson	.30	.20
		Nos. 703-705,C184-C186 (6)	1.45	1.20

Visit of Pres. José M. Lemus of El Salvador to the US, Mar. 9-21.

No. 686 Overprinted: "5 Enero 1960 XX Aniversario Fundacion Sociedad Filatelica de El Salvador"

1960 Wmk. 269 Engr. *Perf. 12½*

706	A180	2c green	.20	.20

Philatelic Association of El Salvador, 20th anniv.

Apartment Houses A183

1960 Unwmk. Photo. *Perf. 11½*
Multicolored Centers; Granite Paper

707	A183	10c scarlet	.20	.20
708	A183	15c brt pur	.20	.20
709	A183	25c brt yel grn	.25	.20
710	A183	30c Prus bl	.25	.20
711	A183	40c olive	.35	.25
712	A183	80c dk bl	.75	.75
		Nos. 707-712 (6)	2.00	1.80

Issued to publicize the erection of multifamily housing projects in 1958.
For surcharges see Nos. 730, 733.

No. 686 Surcharged with New Value

1960 Wmk. 269 Engr. *Perf. 12½*

713	A180	1c on 2c grn	.20	.20

Poinsettia — A184

Perf. 11½
1960, Dec. Unwmk. Photo.
Granite Paper
Design in Slate Green, Red and Yellow

714	A184	3c yellow	.20	.20
715	A184	6c salmon	.20	.20
716	A184	10c grnsh bl	.30	.20
717	A184	15c pale vio bl	.30	.20
		Nos. 714-717,C188-C191 (8)	2.50	1.80

Miniature Sheet

718	A184	40c silver	.65	.50

Nos. 718 and C192 exist with overprints for: 1- 1st Central American Philatelic Cong., July, 1961. 2- Death of General Barrios, 96th anniv. 3- Cent. of city of Ahuachapan. 4- Football (soccer) games. 5- 4th Latin American Cong. of Pathological Anatomy and 10th Central American Medical Cong., Dec., 1963. 6- Alliance for Progress, 2nd anniv.
For surcharge see No. C196.

Fathers Nicolas, Vicente and Manuel Aguilar A185

Parish Church, San Salvador, 1808 A186

Designs: 5c, 6c, Manuel José Arce, José Matias Delgado and Juan Manuel Rodriguez. 10c, 20c, Pedro Pablo Castillo, Domingo Antonio de Lara and Santiago José Celis. 50c, 80c, Monument to the Fathers, Plaza Libertad.

Perf. 11½
1961, Nov. 5 Unwmk. Photo.

719	A185	1c gray & dk brn	.20	.20
720	A185	2c rose & dk brn	.20	.20
721	A185	5c pale brn & dk ol grn	.20	.20
722	A185	6c brt pink & dk brn	.20	.20
723	A185	10c bl & dk brn	.20	.20
724	A185	20c vio & dk brn	.30	.20
725	A186	30c brt bl & vio	.40	.20
726	A186	40c brn org & sep	.55	.20
727	A186	50c bl grn & sep	.75	.40
728	A186	80c gray & ultra	1.25	.75
		Nos. 719-728 (10)	4.25	2.75

Sesquicentennial of the first cry for Independence in Central America.
For surcharges and overprints see Nos. 731-732, 734-735, 737, 760, 769, 776.

No. 651 Overprinted: "III Exposición Industrial Centroamericana Diciembre de 1962"

1962, Dec. 21 Litho. *Perf. 11½*

729	A172	22c violet	.28	.20
		Nos. 729,C193-C195 (4)	2.78	1.95

3rd Central American Industrial Exposition.

Nos. 708, 726-728 and 673 Surcharged

1962-63 Photo.

730	A183	6c on 15c ('63)	.25	.20
731	A186	6c on 40c ('63)	.25	.20
732	A186	6c on 50c ('63)	.25	.20
733	A183	10c on 15c	.30	.20
734	A186	10c on 50c ('63)	.30	.20
735	A186	10c on 80c ('63)	.30	.20
736	A173	10c on 1col ('63)	.30	.20
		Nos. 730-736 (7)	1.95	1.40

Surcharge includes bars on Nos. 731-734, 736; dot on Nos. 730, 735.

No. 726 Overprinted in Arc: "CAMPAÑA MUNDIAL CONTRA EL HAMBRE"

1963, Mar. 21

737	A186	40c brn org & sepia	.70	.40

FAO "Freedom from Hunger" campaign.

Coyote A187

Christ on Globe — A188

2c, Spider monkey, vert. 3c, Raccoon. 5c, King vulture, vert. 6c, Brown coati. 10c, Kinkajou.

1963 Photo. *Perf. 11½*

738	A187	1c lil, blk, ocher & brn	.20	.20
739	A187	2c lt grn & blk	.20	.20
740	A187	3c fawn, dk brn & buff	.20	.20
741	A187	5c gray grn, ind, red & buff	.20	.20
742	A187	6c rose lil, blk, brn & buff	.20	.20
743	A187	10c lt bl, brn & buff	.20	.20
		Nos. 738-743,C200-C207 (14)	4.45	3.20

1964-65 *Perf. 12x11½*

744	A188	6c bl & brn	.20	.20
745	A188	10c bl & bis	.20	.20
		Nos. 744-745,C208-C209 (4)	.80	.80

Miniature Sheets
Imperf

746	A188	60c bl & brt pur	.60	.60
a.		Marginal ovpt. La Union	1.25	1.25
b.		Marginal ovpt. Usulutan	1.25	1.25
c.		Marginal ovpt. La Libertad	1.25	1.25

2nd Natl. Eucharistic Cong., San Salvador, Apr. 16-19.
Nos. 746a, 746b and 746c commemorate the centenaries of the Departments of La Union, Usulután and La Libertad.
Issued: #744-746, Apr. 16, 1964; #746a-746b, June 22, 1965; #746c, Jan. 28, 1965.
See #C210. For overprints see #C232, C238.

Pres. John F. Kennedy A189

Perf. 11½x12
1964, Nov. 22 Unwmk.

747	A189	6c buff & blk	.20	.20
748	A189	10c tan & blk	.20	.20
749	A189	50c pink & blk	.50	.25
		Nos. 747-749,C211-C213 (6)	1.75	1.25

Miniature Sheet
Imperf

750	A189	70c dp grn & blk	.65	.50

President John F. Kennedy (1917-1963).
For overprints & surcharge see #798, 843, C259.

Water Lily — A190

1965, Jan. 6 Photo. *Perf. 12x11½*

751	A190	3c shown	.20	.20
752	A190	5c Maquilishuat	.20	.20
753	A190	6c Cinco negritos	.20	.20
754	A190	30c Hortensia	.20	.20
755	A190	50c Maguey	.60	.20
756	A190	60c Geranium	.65	.20
		Nos. 751-756,C215-C220 (12)	3.85	2.50

For overprints and surcharges see Nos. 779, C243, C348-C349.

ICY Emblem A191

1965, Apr. 27 Photo. *Perf. 11½x12*
Design in Brown and Gold

757	A191	5c dp yel	.20	.20
758	A191	6c dp rose	.20	.20
759	A191	10c gray	.20	.20
		Nos. 757-759,C221-C223 (6)	1.30	1.20

International Cooperation Year.
For overprints see #764, 780, C227, C244, C312.

No. 728 Overprinted in Red: "Ier. Centenario Muerte / Cap. Gral. Gerardo Barrios / 1865 1965 / 29 de Agosto"

1965 Unwmk. *Perf. 11½*

760	A186	80c gray & ultra	.65	.50
a.		"Garl." instead of "Gral."	1.00	1.00

Capt. Gen. Gerardo Barrios, death cent.

Gavidia A192

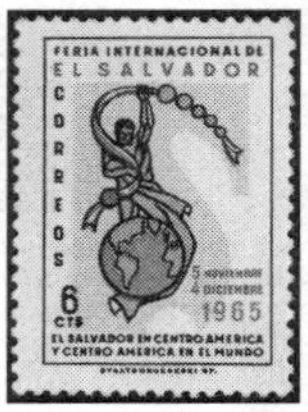

Fair Emblem — A193

Perf. 11½x12
1965, Sept. 24 Photo. Unwmk.
Portrait in Natural Colors

761	A192	2c blk & rose vio	.20	.20
762	A192	3c blk & org	.20	.20
763	A192	6c blk & lt ultra	.20	.20
		Nos. 761-763,C224-C226 (6)	2.30	1.50

Francisco Antonio Gavidia, philosopher.
For surcharges see Nos. 852-853.

No. 759 Overprinted in Carmine: "1865 / 12 de Octubre / 1965 / Dr. Manuel Enrique Araujo"

1965, Oct. 12

764	A191	10c brn, gray & gold	.20	.20

Centenary of the birth of Manuel Enrique Araujo, president of Salvador, 1911-1913. See No. C227.

1965, Nov. 5 Photo. *Perf. 12x11½*

765	A193	6c yel & multi	.20	.20
766	A193	10c multi	.20	.20
767	A193	20c pink & multi	.20	.20
		Nos. 765-767,C228-C230 (6)	4.70	3.45

Intl. Fair of El Salvador, Nov. 5-Dec. 4.
For overprints and surcharge see Nos. 784, C246, C311, C323.

WHO Headquarters, Geneva — A194

1966, May 20 Photo. Unwmk.

768	A194	15c beige & multi	.20	.20

Inauguration of WHO Headquarters, Geneva. See No. C231. For overprints and surcharges see Nos. 778, 783, 864, C242, C245, C322.

No. 728 Overprinted in Red: "Mes de Conmemoracion / Civica de la Independencia / Centroamericana / 19 Sept. / 1821 1966"

1966, Sept. 19 Photo. *Perf. 11½*

769	A186	80c gray & ultra	.50	.50

Month of civic commemoration of Central American independence.

UNESCO Emblem A195

1966, Nov. 4 Unwmk. *Perf. 12*

770	A195	20c gray, blk & vio bl	.20	.20
771	A195	1col emer, blk & vio bl	.85	.40
		Nos. 770-771,C233-C234 (4)	2.95	1.80

20th anniv. of UNESCO.
For surcharges see Nos. 853A, C352.

Map of Central America, Flags and Cogwheels A196

1966, Nov. 27 Litho. *Perf. 12*

772	A196	6c multi	.20	.20
773	A196	10c multi	.20	.20
		Nos. 772-773,C235-C237 (5)	1.30	1.15

2nd Intl. Fair of El Salvador, Nov. 5-27.

José Simeon Cañas Pleading for Indian Slaves — A197

1967, Feb. 18 Litho. *Perf. 11½*

774 A197 6c yel & multi .20 .20
775 A197 10c lil rose & multi .20 .20
Nos. 774-775,C239-C240 (4) 1.15 .95

Father José Simeon Cañas y Villacorta, D.D. (1767-1838), emancipator of the Central American slaves.

For surcharges see #841A-842, 891, C403-C405.

No. 726 Overprinted in Red: "XV Convención de Clubes / de Leones, Región de / El Salvador-11 y 12 / de Marzo de 1967"

1967 Photo.

776 A186 40c brn org & sepia .50 .25

Issued to publicize the 15th Convention of Lions Clubs of El Salvador, March 11-12.

Volcano San Miguel A198

1967, Apr. 14 Photo. *Perf. 13*

777 A198 70c lt rose lilac & brn 1.00 .60

Centenary of stamps of El Salvador.

See No. C241. For surcharges see Nos. 841, C320, C350.

No. 768 Overprinted in Red: "VIII CONGRESO / CENTROAMERICANO DE / FARMACIA Y BIOQUIMICA / 5 di 11 Noviembre de 1967"

1967, Oct. 26 Photo. *Perf. 12x11½*

778 A194 15c multi .20 .20

8th Central American Congress for Pharmacy and Biochemistry. See No. C242.

No. 751 Overprinted in Red: "I Juegos / Centroamericanos y del / Caribe de Basquetbol / 25 Nov. al 3 Dic. 1967"

1967, Nov. 15

779 A190 3c dl grn, brn, yel & org .20 .20

First Central American and Caribbean Basketball Games, 11/25-12/3. See #C243.

No. 757 Overprinted in Carmine: "1968 / AÑO INTERNACIONAL DE / LOS DERECHOS HUMANOS"

1968, Jan. 2 Photo. *Perf. 11½x12*

780 A191 5c dp yel, brn & gold .20 .20

Intl. Human Rights Year. See #C244.

Weather Map, Satellite and WMO Emblem A199

1968, Mar. 25 Photo. *Perf. 11½x12*

781 A199 1c multi .20 .20
782 A199 30c multi .30 .20

World Meteorological Day, Mar. 25.

No. 768 Overprinted in Red: "1968 / XX ANIVERSARIO DE LA / ORGANIZACION MUNDIAL / DE LA SALUD"

1968, Apr. 7 *Perf. 12x11½*

783 A194 15c multi .20 .20

20th anniv. of WHO. See No. C245.

No. 765 Overprinted in Red: "1968 / Año / del Sistema / del Crédito / Rural"

1968, May 6 Photo. *Perf. 12x11½*

784 A193 6c yellow & multi .20 .20

Rural credit system. See No. C246.

Alberto Masferrer A200

Scouts Helping to Build — A201

1968, June 22 Litho. *Perf. 12x11½*

785 A200 2c multi .20 .20
786 A200 6c multi .20 .20
787 A200 25c vio & multi .30 .20
Nos. 785-787,C247-C248 (5) 1.10 1.00

Centenary of the birth of Alberto Masferrer, philosopher and scholar.

For surcharges and overprints see Nos. 819, 843A, 890, C297.

1968, July 26 Litho. *Perf. 12*

788 A201 25c multi .25 .20

Issued to publicize the 7th Inter-American Boy Scout Conference, July-Aug., 1968. See No. C249.

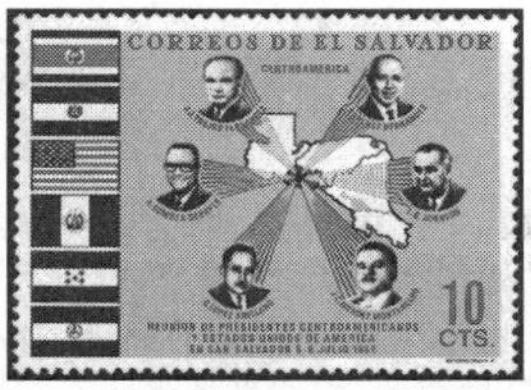

Map of Central America, Flags and Presidents of US, Costa Rica, Salvador, Guatemala, Honduras and Nicaragua — A202

1968, Dec. 5 Litho. *Perf. 14½*

789 A202 10c tan & multi .20 .20
790 A202 15c multi .20 .20
Nos. 789-790,C250-C251 (4) 1.35 1.10

Meeting of Pres. Lyndon B. Johnson with the presidents of the Central American republics (J. J. Trejos, Costa Rica; Fidel Sanchez Hernandez, Salvador; J. C. Mendez Montenegro, Guatemala; Osvaldo López Arellano, Honduras; Anastasio Somoza Debayle, Nicaragua), San Salvador, July 5-8, 1968.

Heliconius Charithonius — A203

Various Butterflies.

1969 Litho. *Perf. 12*

791 A203 5c bluish lil, blk & yel .20 .20
792 A203 10c beige & multi .20 .20
793 A203 30c lt grn & multi .25 .20
794 A203 50c tan & multi .40 .20
Nos. 791-794,C252-C255 (8) 11.50 7.35

For surcharge see No. C353.

Red Cross Activities A204

1969 Litho. *Perf. 12*

795 A204 10c lt bl & multi .20 .20
796 A204 20c pink & multi .20 .20
797 A204 40c lil & multi .25 .20
Nos. 795-797,C256-C258 (6) 5.00 3.80

50th anniv. of the League of Red Cross Societies.

No. 749 Overprinted in Green: "Alunizaje / Apolo-11 / 21 Julio / 1969"

1969, Sept. Photo. *Perf. 11½x12*

798 A189 50c pink & blk .40 .30

Man's first landing on the moon, July 20, 1969. See note after US No. C76.

The same overprint in red brown and pictures of the landing module and the astronauts on the moon were applied to the margin of No. 750.

See No. C259.

Social Security Hospital A205

1969, Oct. 24 Litho. *Perf. 11½*

799 A205 6c multi .20 .20
800 A205 10c multi, diff. .20 .20
801 A205 30c multi, diff. .30 .20
Nos. 799-801,C260-C262 (6) 7.40 4.60

For surcharges see Nos. 857, C355.

ILO Emblem — A206

1969 Litho. *Perf. 13*

802 A206 10c yel & multi .20 .20

50th anniv. of the ILO. See No. C263.

Chorros Spa A207

Views: 40c, Jaltepeque Bay. 80c, Fountains, Amapulapa Spa.

1969, Dec. 19 Photo. *Perf. 12x11½*

803 A207 10c blk & multi .20 .20
804 A207 40c blk & multi .30 .25
805 A207 80c blk & multi .65 .50
Nos. 803-805,C264-C266 (6) 2.15 1.75

Tourism.

Euchroma Gigantea — A208

Insects: 25c, Grasshopper. 30c, Digger wasp.

1970, Feb. 24 Litho. *Perf. 11½x11*

806 A208 5c lt bl & multi .20 .20
807 A208 25c dl yel & multi .20 .20
808 A208 30c dl rose & multi .25 .20
Nos. 806-808,C267-C269 (6) 8.00 5.10

For surcharges see Nos. C371-C373.

Map and Arms of Salvador, National Unity Emblem A209

1970, Apr. 14 Litho. *Perf. 14*

809 A209 10c yel & multi .20 .20
810 A209 40c pink & multi .50 .20
Nos. 809-810,C270-C271 (4) 1.70 1.00

Salvador's support of universal human rights. For overprints and surcharge see Nos. 823, C301, C402.

Soldiers with Flag A210

Design: 30c, Anti-aircraft gun.

1970, May 7 *Perf. 12*

811 A210 10c green & multi .20 .20
812 A210 30c lemon & multi .30 .20
Nos. 811-812,C272-C274 (5) 1.50 1.00

Issued for Army Day, May 7.

For overprints see Nos. 836, C310.

National Lottery Headquarters A211

1970, July 15 Litho. *Perf. 12*

813 A211 20c lt vio & multi .20 .20

National Lottery centenary. See No. C291.

UN and Education Year Emblems A212

1970, Sept. 11 Litho. *Perf. 12*

814 A212 50c multi .40 .20
815 A212 1col multi .85 .45
Nos. 814-815,C292-C293 (4) 3.05 1.85

Issued for International Education Year.

Map of Salvador, Globe and Cogwheels A213

1970, Oct. 28 Litho. *Perf. 12*

816 A213 5c pink & multi .20 .20
817 A213 10c buff & multi .20 .20
Nos. 816-817,C294-C295 (4) 1.00 .80

4th International Fair, San Salvador.

Beethoven — A214

1971, Feb. 22 Litho. *Perf. 13½*
818 A214 50c ol, brn & yel .50 .20

Second International Music Festival. See No. C296. For overprint see No. 833.

No. 787 Overprinted: "Año / del Centenario de la / Biblioteca Nacional / 1970"

1970, Nov. 25 *Perf. 12x11½*
819 A200 25c vio & multi .20 .20

Cent. of the National Library. See No. C297.

Maria Elena Sol — A215

Pietà>, by Michelangelo A216

1971, Apr. 1 Litho. *Perf. 14*
820 A215 10c lt grn & multi .20 .20
821 A215 30c multi .20 .20
Nos. 820-821,C298-C299 (4) 1.05 .90

Maria Elena Sol, Miss World Tourism, 1970-71. For overprint see No. 832.

1971, May 10
822 A216 10c salmon & vio brn .20 .20

Mother's Day, 1971. See No. C300.

No. 810 Overprinted in Red

1971, July 6 Litho. *Perf. 14*
823 A209 40c pink & multi .35 .20

National Police, 104th anniv. See #C301.

Tiger Sharks — A217

1971, July 28
824 A217 10c shown .20 .20
825 A217 40c Swordfish .20 .20
Nos. 824-825,C302-C303 (4) 1.25 1.15

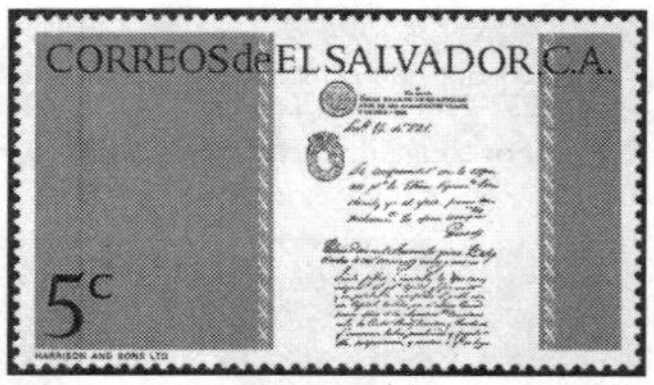

Declaration of Independence — A218

Designs: Various sections of Declaration of Independence of Central America.

1971 *Perf. 13½x13*
826 A218 5c yel grn & blk .20 .20
827 A218 10c brt rose & blk .20 .20
828 A218 15c dp org & blk .20 .20
829 A218 20c dp red lil & blk .20 .20
Nos. 826-829,C304-C307 (8) 2.15 1.80

Sesquicentennial of independence of Central America.
For overprints see Nos. C321, C347.

Izalco Church A219

Design: 30c, Sonsonate Church.

1971, Aug. 21 Litho. *Perf. 13x13½*
830 A219 20c blk & multi .20 .20
831 A219 30c pur & multi .30 .20
Nos. 830-831,C308-C309 (4) 1.25 .95

No. 821 Overprinted in Carmine: "1972 Año de Turismo / de las Américas"

1972, Nov. 15 Litho. *Perf. 14*
832 A215 30c multi .20 .20

Tourist Year of the Americas, 1972.

No. 818 Overprinted in Red

1973, Feb. 5 Litho. *Perf. 13½*
833 A214 50c ol, brn & yel .25 .20

3rd Intl. Music Festival, Feb. 9-25. See No. C313.

Lions International Emblem A220

1973, Feb. 20 Litho. *Perf. 13*
834 A220 10c pink & multi .20 .20
835 A220 25c lt bl & multi .20 .20
Nos. 834-835,C314-C315 (4) .90 .80

31st Lions International District "D" Convention, San Salvador, May 1972.

No. 812 Overprinted: "1923 1973 / 50 AÑOS FUNDACION / FUERZA AEREA"

1973, Mar. 20 Litho. *Perf. 12*
836 A210 30c lem & multi .20 .20

50th anniversary of Salvadorian Air Force.

Hurdling A221

1973, May 21 Litho. *Perf. 13*
837 A221 5c shown .20 .20
838 A221 10c High jump .20 .20
839 A221 25c Running .20 .20
840 A221 60c Pole vault .30 .25
Nos. 837-840,C316-C319 (8) 3.70 2.85

20th Olympic Games, Munich, Aug. 26-Sept. 11, 1972.

No. 777 Surcharged:

1973, Dec. Photo. *Perf. 13*
841 A198 10c on 70c multi .20 .20

See No. C320.

Nos. 774, C240 Surcharged with New Value and Overprinted "1823-1973 / 150 Aniversario Liberación / Esclavos en Centroamérica"

1973-74 Litho. *Perf. 11½*
841A A197 5c on 6c multi ('74) .20 .20
842 A197 10c on 45c multi .20 .20

Sesquicentennial of the liberation of the slaves in Central America. On No. 841A two bars cover old denomination. On No. 842 "Aereo" is obliterated with a bar and old denomination with two bars.

Nos. 747 and 786 Surcharged:

1974 Photo. *Perf. 11½x12*
843 A189 5c on 6c buff & blk .20 .20

Litho. *Perf. 12x11½*
843A A200 5c on 6c multi .20 .20

No. 843A has one obliterating rectangle and sans-serif "5."
Issued: #843, Apr. 22; #843A, June 21.

Rehabilitation Institute Emblem A222

1974, Apr. 30 Litho. *Perf. 13*
844 A222 10c multi .20 .20

10th anniversary of the Salvador Rehabilitation Institute. See No. C324.

INTERPOL Headquarters, Saint-Cloud, France — A223

1974, Sept. 2 Litho. *Perf. 12½*
845 A223 10c multi .20 .20

50th anniv. of Intl. Criminal Police Organization (INTERPOL). See No. C341.

UN and FAO Emblems A224

1974, Sept. 2 Litho. *Perf. 12½*
846 A224 10c bl, dk bl & gold .20 .20

World Food Program, 10th anniv. See #C342.

25c Silver Coin, 1914 A225

1974, Nov. 19 Litho. *Perf. 12½x13*
848 A225 10c shown .20 .20
849 A225 15c 50c silver, 1953 .20 .20
850 A225 25c 25c silver, 1943 .20 .20
851 A225 30c 1c copper, 1892 .20 .20
Nos. 848-851,C343-C346 (8) 2.30 1.80

No. 763 Surcharged

1974, Oct. 14 Photo. *Perf. 11½x12*
852 A192 5c on 6c multi .20 .20

12th Central American and Caribbean Chess Tournament, Oct. 1974.

No. 762 and 771 Surcharged

1974-75 *Perf. 11½x12, 12*
853 A192 10c on 3c multi .20 .20
853A A195 25c on 1col multi ('75) .20 .20

Bar and surcharge on one line on No. 853A.
Issued: #853, Dec. 19; #853A, Jan. 13.

UPU Emblem A226

1975, Jan. 22 Litho. *Perf. 13*
854 A226 10c bl & multi .20 .20
855 A226 60c bl & multi .25 .30
Nos. 854-855,C356-C357 (4) .90 .90

Cent. of UPU.

Acajutla Harbor
A227

1975, Feb. 17

856 A227 10c blue & multi .20 .20

See No. C358.

No. 799 Surcharged

1975 Litho. *Perf. 11½*

857 A205 5c on 6c multi .20 .20

Central Post Office, San Salvador
A228

1975, Apr. 25 Litho. *Perf. 13*

858 A228 10c bl & multi .20 .20

See No. C359.

Map of Americas and El Salvador, Trophy
A229

1975, June 25 Litho. *Perf. 12½*

859 A229 10c red org & multi .20 .20
860 A229 40c yel & multi .25 .25
Nos. 859-860,C360-C361 (4) 1.15 1.05

El Salvador, site of 1975 Miss Universe Contest.

Claudia Lars, Poet, and IWY Emblem — A230

1975, Sept. 4 Litho. *Perf. 12½*

861 A230 10c yel & bl blk .20 .20
Nos. 861,C362-C363 (3) .60 .60

Intl. Women's Year 1975.

Nurses Attending Patient
A231

1975, Oct. 24 Litho. *Perf. 12½*

862 A231 10c lt grn & multi .20 .20

Nurses' Day. See No. C364. For overprint see No. 868.

Congress Emblem — A232

1975, Nov. 19 Litho. *Perf. 12½*

863 A232 10c yel & multi .20 .20

15th Conference of Inter-American Federation of Securities Enterprises, San Salvador, Nov. 16-20. See No. C365.

No. 768 Overprinted in Red: "XVI / CONGRESO MEDICO / CENTROAMERICANO / SAN SALVADOR, / EL SALVADOR, / DIC. 10-13, 1975"

1975, Nov. 26 Photo. *Perf. 12x11½*

864 A194 15c beige & multi .20 .20

16th Central American Medical Congress, San Salvador, Dec. 10-13.

Flags of Participants, Arms of Salvador
A233

1975, Nov. 28 Litho. *Perf. 12½*

865 A233 15c blk & multi .20 .20
866 A233 50c brn & multi .20 .20
Nos. 865-866,C366-C367 (4) .85 .80

8th Ibero-Latin-American Dermatological Congress, San Salvador, Nov. 28-Dec. 3.

Jesus and Caritas Emblem — A234

1975, Dec. 18 Litho. *Perf. 13½*

867 A234 10c dull red & maroon .20 .20

7th Latin American Charity Congress, San Salvador, Nov. 1971. See No. C368.

No. 862 Overprinted: "III CONGRESO / ENFERMERIA / CENCAMEX 76"

1976, May 10 Litho. *Perf. 12½*

868 A231 10c lt grn & multi .20 .20

CENCAMEX 76, 3rd Nurses' Congress.

Map of El Salvador
A235

1976, May 18

869 A235 10c vio bl & multi .20 .20

10th Congress of Revenue Collectors (Centro Interamericano de Administradores Tributarios, CIAT), San Salvador, May 16-22. See No. C382.

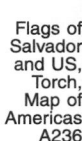

Flags of Salvador and US, Torch, Map of Americas
A236

The Spirit of '76, by Archibald M. Willard — A237

1976, June 30 Litho. *Perf. 12½*

870 A236 10c yel & multi .20 .20
871 A237 40c multi .20 .20
Nos. 870-871,C383-C384 (4) 4.35 3.10

American Bicentennial.

American Crocodile — A238

1976, Sept. 23 Litho. *Perf. 12½*

872 A238 10c shown .20 .20
873 A238 20c Green iguana .20 .20
874 A238 30c Iguana .25 .25
Nos. 872-874,C385-C387 (6) 1.50 1.50

Post-classical Vase, San Salvador
A239

Pre-Columbian Art: 15c, Brazier with classical head, Tazumal. 40c, Vase with classical head, Tazumal.

1976, Oct. 11 Litho. *Perf. 12½*

875 A239 10c multi .20 .20
876 A239 15c multi .20 .20
877 A239 40c multi .30 .30
Nos. 875-877,C388-C390 (6) 1.85 1.55

For overprint see No. C429.

Fair Emblem
A240

1976, Oct. 25 Litho. *Perf. 12½*

878 A240 10c multi .20 .20
879 A240 30c gray & multi .25 .25
Nos. 878-879,C391-C392 (4) 1.20 1.05

7th Intl. Fair, Nov. 5-22.

Child under Christmas Tree — A241

1976, Dec. 16 Litho. *Perf. 11*

880 A241 10c yel & multi .20 .20
881 A241 15c buff & multi .20 .20
882 A241 30c vio & multi .25 .25
883 A241 40c pink & multi .30 .30
Nos. 880-883,C393-C396 (8) 2.65 2.10

Christmas 1976.

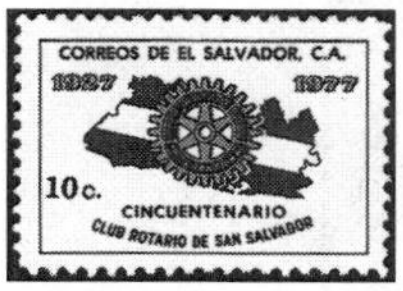

Rotary Emblem, Map of Salvador
A242

1977, June 20 Litho. *Perf. 11*

884 A242 10c multi .20 .20
885 A242 15c multi .20 .20
Nos. 884-885,C397-C398 (4) 1.40 1.10

San Salvador Rotary Club, 50th anniversary.

Cerron Grande Hydroelectric Station — A243

Designs: No. 887, 15c, Central sugar refinery, Jiboa. 30c, Radar station, Izalco, vert.

1977, June 29 *Perf. 12½*

886 A243 10c multi .20 .20
887 A243 10c multi .20 .20
888 A243 15c multi .20 .20
889 A243 30c multi .25 .20
Nos. 886-889,C399-C401 (7) 2.05 1.60

Industrial development. Nos. 886-889 have colorless overprint in multiple rows: GOBIERNO DEL SALVADOR.

Nos. 785 and 774 Surcharged with New Value and Bar

1977, June 30 *Perf. 12x11½, 11½*

890 A200 15c on 2c multi .20 .20
891 A197 25c on 6c multi .20 .20

Microphone, ASDER Emblem — A244

1977, Sept. 14 Litho. *Perf. 14*

892 A244 10c multi .20 .20
893 A244 15c multi .20 .20
Nos. 892-893,C406-C407 (4) .80 .80

Broadcasting in El Salvador, 50th anniversary (Asociacion Salvadoreño de Empresa Radio).

Wooden Drum
A245

Design: 10c, Flute and recorder.

1978, Aug. 29 Litho. *Perf. 12½*

894 A245 5c multi .20 .20
895 A245 10c multi .20 .20
Nos. 894-895,C433-C435 (5) 1.60 1.20

For surcharge see No. C492.

"Man and Engineering" A246

1978, Sept. 12 Litho. *Perf. 13½*
896 A246 10c multi .20 .20

4th National Engineers' Congress, San Salvador, Sept. 18-23. See No. C436.

Izalco Station A247

1978, Sept. 14 *Perf. 12½*
897 A247 10c multi .20 .20

Inauguration of Izalco satellite earth station, Sept. 15, 1978. See No. C437.

Fair Emblem A248

1978, Oct. 30 Litho. *Perf. 12½*
898 A248 10c multi .20 .20
899 A248 20c multi .20 .20
Nos. 898-899,C440-C441 (4) .80 .80

8th Intl. Fair, Nov. 3-20.

Henri Dunant, Red Cross Emblem A249

1978, Oct. 30 *Perf. 11*
900 A249 10c multi .20 .20

Henri Dunant (1828-1910), founder of the Red Cross. See No. C442.

World Map and Cotton Boll A250

1978, Nov. 22 *Perf. 12½*
901 A250 15c multi .20 .20

Intl. Cotton Consulting Committee, 37th Meeting, San Salvador, 11/27-12/2. See #C443.

Nativity, Stained-glass Window A251

1978, Dec. 5 Litho. *Perf. 12½*
902 A251 10c multi .20 .20
903 A251 15c multi .20 .20
Nos. 902-903,C444-C445 (4) 1.40 1.10

Christmas 1978.

Athenaeum Coat of Arms — A252

1978, Dec. 20 Litho. *Perf. 14*
904 A252 5c multi .20 .20

Millennium of Castilian language. See No. C446.

Postal Service and UPU Emblems A253

1979, Apr. 2 Litho. *Perf. 14*
905 A253 10c multi .20 .20

Centenary of Salvador's membership in Universal Postal Union. See No. C447.

"75," Health Organization and WHO Emblems — A254

1979, Apr. 7 *Perf. 14x14½*
906 A254 10c multi .20 .20

Pan-American Health Organization, 75th anniversary. See No. C448.

Flame and Pillars — A255

1979, May 25 Litho. *Perf. 12½*
907 A255 10c multi .20 .20
908 A255 15c multi .20 .20
Nos. 907-908,C449-C450 (4) 1.40 1.10

Social Security 5-year plan, 1978-1982.

Pope John Paul II, Map of Americas A256

1979, July 12 Litho. *Perf. 14½x14*
909 A256 10c multi .20 .20
910 A256 20c multi .20 .20
Nos. 909-910,C454-C455 (4) 4.90 3.20

Mastodon A257

1979, Sept. 7 Litho. *Perf. 14*
911 A257 10c shown .20 .20
912 A257 20c Saber-toothed tiger .20 .20
913 A257 30c Toxodon .25 .25
Nos. 911-913,C458-C460 (6) 2.65 2.05

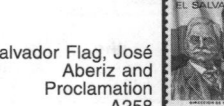

Salvador Flag, José Aberiz and Proclamation A258

1979, Sept. 14 *Perf. 14½x14*
914 A258 10c multi .20 .20

National anthem centenary. See No. C461.

Cogwheel around Map of Americas A259

1979, Oct. 19 Litho. *Perf. 14½x14*
915 A259 10c multi .20 .20

8th COPIMERA Congress (Mechanical, Electrical and Allied Trade Engineers), San Salvador, Oct. 22-27. See No. C462.

Children of Various Races, IYC Emblem A260

Children and Nurses, IYC Emblem A261

1979, Oct. 29 *Perf. 14x14½, 14½x14*
916 A260 10c multi .20 .20
917 A261 15c multi .20 .20

International Year of the Child.

Map of Central and South America, Congress Emblem — A262

1979, Nov. 1 Litho. *Perf. 14½x14*
918 A262 10c multi .20 .20

5th Latin American Clinical Biochemistry Cong., San Salvador, 11/5-10. See #C465.

Coffee Bushes in Bloom, Coffee Association Emblem A263

Salvador Coffee Assoc., 50th Anniv.: 30c, Planting coffee bushes, vert. 40c, Coffee berries.

1979, Dec. 18 *Perf. 14x14½, 14½x14*
919 A263 10c multi .20 .20
920 A263 30c multi .25 .25
921 A263 40c multi .30 .30
Nos. 919-921,C466-C468 (6) 2.55 1.95

Children, Dove and Star — A264

1979, Dec. 18 *Perf. 14½x14*
922 A264 10c multi .20 .20

Christmas 1979.

Hoof and Mouth Disease Prevention A265

1980, June 3 Litho. *Perf. 14½x14*
923 A265 10c multi .20 .20

See No. C469.

Anadara Grandis A266

1980, Aug. 12 *Perf. 14x14½*
924 A266 10c *shown* .20 .20
925 A266 30c *Ostrea iridescens* .25 .25
926 A266 40c *Turitello leucostoma* .30 .30
Nos. 924-926,C470-C473 (7) 2.45 2.10

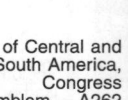

Quetzal (Pharomachrus mocino) — A267

1980, Sept. 10 Litho. *Perf. 14x14½*

927 A267 10c shown .20 .20
928 A267 20c Penelopina nigra .20 .20
Nos. 927-928,C474-C476 (5) 1.60 1.25

Local Snakes A268

1980, Nov. 12 Litho. *Perf. 14x14½*

929 A268 10c Tree snake .20 .20
930 A268 20c Water snake .20 .20
Nos. 929-930,C477-C478 (4) 1.00 .85

A269

A270

1980, Nov. 26 Litho. *Perf. 14*

931 A269 15c multi .20 .20
932 A269 20c multi .20 .20
Nos. 931-932,C479-C480 (4) 1.40 1.05

Corporation of Auditors, 50th anniv.

1980, Dec. 5 Litho. *Perf. 14*

933 A270 5c multi .20 .20
934 A270 10c multi .20 .20
Nos. 933-934,C481-C482 (4) 1.10 .90

Christmas.

A271

A272

Dental association emblems.

1981, June 18 Litho. *Perf. 14*

935 A271 15c lt yel grn & blk .20 .20

Dental Society of Salvador, 50th anniv.; Odontological Federation of Central America and Panama, 25th anniv. See No. C494.

1981, Aug. 14 Litho. *Perf. 14x14½*

Design: Hands reading braille book.

936 A272 10c multi .20 .20
Nos. 936,C495-C498 (5) 2.20 1.60

Intl. Year of the Disabled.

A273

A274

1981, Aug. 28 Litho. *Perf. 14x14½*

937 A273 10c multi .20 .20

Roberto Quinonez Natl. Agriculture College, 25th anniv. See No. C499.

1981, Sept. 16 Litho. *Perf. 14x14½*

938 A274 10c multi .20 .20

World Food Day. See No. C500.

1981 World Cup Preliminaries — A275

1981, Nov. 27 Litho. *Perf. 14x14½*

939 A275 10c shown .20 .20
940 A275 40c Cup soccer ball, flags .30 .25
Nos. 939-940,C505-C506 (4) 1.30 1.05

Salvador Lyceum (High School), 100th Anniv. — A276

1981, Dec. 17 Litho. *Perf. 14*

941 A276 10c multi .20 .20

See No. C507.

Pre-Columbian Stone Sculptures A277

1982, Jan. 22 Litho. *Perf. 14*

942 A277 10c Axe with bird's head .20 .20
943 A277 20c Sun disc .20 .20
944 A277 40c Stele Carving with effigy .30 .30
Nos. 942-944,C508-C510 (6) 1.80 1.55

Scouting Year — A278

1982, Mar. 17 Litho. *Perf. 14½x14*

945 A278 10c shown .20 .20
946 A278 30c Girl Scout helping woman .25 .25
Nos. 945-946,C511-C512 (4) 1.05 .90

Armed Forces A279

1982, May 7 Litho. *Perf. 14x13½*

947 A279 10c multi .20 .20

See No. C514.

1982 World Cup A280

1982, July 14 *Perf. 14x14½*

948 A280 10c Team, emblem .20 .20
Nos. 948,C518-C520 (4) 2.50 1.75

10th International Fair — A281

1982, Oct. 14 Litho. *Perf. 14*

949 A281 10c multi .20 .20

See No. C524.

Christmas 1982 — A282

1982, Dec. 14 Litho. *Perf. 14*

950 A282 5c multi .20 .20

See No. C528.

Dancers, Pre-Colombian Ceramic Design — A283

1983, Feb. 18 Litho. *Perf. 14*

951 A283 10c shown .20 .20
952 A283 20c Sower .20 .20
953 A283 25c Flying Man .20 .20
954 A283 60c Hunters .50 .50
955 A283 60c Hunters, diff. .50 .50
a. Pair, #954-955 1.00 1.00
956 A283 1col Procession .80 .80
957 A283 1col Procession, diff. .80 .80
a. Pair, #956-957 1.60 1.60
Nos. 951-957 (7) 3.20 3.20

Nos. 953-957 airmail. #955a, 957a have continuous designs.

Visit of Pope John Paul II — A284

1983, Mar. 4 Litho. *Perf. 14*

958 A284 25c shown .20 .20
959 A284 60c Monument to the Divine Savior, Pope .50 .40

Salvadoran Air Force, 50th Anniv. A285

1983, Mar. 24 Litho. *Perf. 14*

960 A285 10c Ricardo Aberle .20 .20
961 A285 10c Air Force Emblem .20 .20
962 A285 10c Enrico Massi .20 .20
a. Strip of 3, #960-962 .25 .25
963 A285 10c Juan Ramon Munes .20 .20
964 A285 10c American Air Force Cooperation Emblem .20 .20
965 A285 10c Belisario Salazar .20 .20
a. Strip of 3, #963-965 .25 .25

Arranged se-tenant horizontally with two Nos. 960 or 963 at left and two Nos. 962 or 965 at right.

A286

Local butterflies.

1983, May 31 Litho. *Perf. 14*

966 A286 Pair .20 .20
a. 5c Papilio torquatus .20 .20
b. 5c Metamorpha steneles .20 .20
967 A286 Pair .20 .20
a. 10c Papilio torquatus, diff. .20 .20
b. 10c Anaea marthesia .20 .20
968 A286 Pair .25 .25
a. 15c Prepona brooksiana .20 .20
b. 15c Caligo atreus .20 .20
969 A286 Pair .40 .40
a. 25c Morpho peleides .20 .20
b. 25c Dismorphia praxinoe .20 .20
970 A286 Pair .80 .80
a. 50c Morpho polyphemus .40 .40
b. 50c Metamorphia epaphus .40 .40
Nos. 966-970 (5) 1.85 1.85

A287

1983, June 23 Litho. *Perf. 14*

971 A287 75c multi .60 .50

Simon Bolivar, 200th birth anniv.

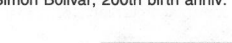

A288

A289

1983, July 21 Litho. *Perf. 14*

972 A288 10c Dr. Jose Mendoza, college emblem .20 .20

Salvador Medical College, 40th anniv.

Perf. 13½x14, 14x13½

1983, Oct. 30 Litho.

973 A289 10c multi .20 .20
974 A289 50c multi, horiz. .40 .40

Centenary of David J. Guzman national museum. 50c airmail.

World Communications Year — A290

10c, Gen. Juan Jose Canas, Francisco Duenas (organizers of 1st natl. telegraph service), Morse key, 1870. 25c, Mailman delivering letters. 50c, Post Office sorting center, San Salvador. 25c, 50c airmail.

Perf. 14x13½, 13½x14

1983, Nov. 23 Litho.

975 A290 10c multi .20 .20
976 A290 25c multi, vert. .20 .20
977 A290 50c multi .40 .30
Nos. 975-977 (3) .80 .70

A291

A292

Perf. 13½x14, 14x13½

1983, Nov. 30

978 A291 10c Dove over globe .20 .20
979 A291 25c Creche figures, horiz. .20 .20

Christmas. 25c is airmail.

1983, Dec. 13

980 A292 10c Vehicle exhaust .20 .20
981 A292 15c Fig tree .20 .20
982 A292 25c Rodent .20 .20
Nos. 980-982 (3) .60 .60

Environmental protection. 15c, 25c airmail.

Philatelists' Day A293

Corn — A294

1984, Jan. 5 *Perf. 14x13½*

983 A293 10c No. 1 .20 .20

1984, Feb. 21 Litho. *Perf. 14½x14*

984 A294 10c shown .20 .20
985 A294 15c Cotton .20 .20
986 A294 25c Coffee beans .20 .20
987 A294 50c Sugar cane .20 .20
988 A294 75c Beans .30 .25
989 A294 1col Agave .40 .30
990 A294 5col Balsam 2.00 1.50
Nos. 984-990 (7) 3.50 2.85

See Nos. 1047-1051.

Caluco Church, Sonsonate A295

1984, Mar. 30 *Perf. 14x13½*

991 A295 5c shown .20 .20
992 A295 10c Salcoatitan, Sonsonate .20 .20
993 A295 15c Huizucar, La Libertad .20 .20
994 A295 25c Santo Domingo, Sonsonate .20 .20
995 A295 50c Pilar, Sonsonate .20 .20
996 A295 75c Nahuizalco, Sonsonate .30 .25
Nos. 991-996 (6) 1.30 1.25

Nos. 993-996 airmail.

Central Reserve Bank of Salvador, 50th Anniv. A296

1984, July 17 Litho. *Perf. 14x14½*

997 A296 10c First reserve note .20 .20
998 A296 25c Bank, 1959 .20 .20

25c airmail.

1984 Summer Olympics A297

1984, July 20 *Perf. 14x13½, 13½x14*

999 A297 10c Boxing .20 .20
1000 A297 25c Running, vert. .20 .20
1001 A297 40c Bicycling .20 .20
1002 A297 50c Swimming .20 .20
1003 A297 75c Judo, vert. .30 .25
1004 A297 1col Pierre de Coubertin .40 .30
Nos. 999-1004 (6) 1.50 1.35

Nos. 1000-1004 airmail.
For surcharge see No. C536A.

Govt. Printing Office Building Opening A298

1984, July 27 *Perf. 14x13½*

1005 A298 10c multi .20 .20

5th of November Hydroelectric Plant — A299

Designs: 55c, Cerron Grande Plant. 70c, Ahuachapan Geothermal Plant. 90c, Mural. 2col, 15th of September Plant. 7c, 90c, 2 col airmail.

1984, Sept. 13 Litho. *Perf. 14x14½*

1006 A299 20c multi .20 .20
1007 A299 55c multi .25 .20
1008 A299 70c multi .30 .25
1009 A299 90c multi .35 .30
1010 A299 2col multi .80 .60
Nos. 1006-1010 (5) 1.90 1.55

Boys Playing Marbles A300

1984, Oct. 16 *Perf. 14½x14*

1011 A300 55c shown .25 .20
1012 A300 70c Spinning top .30 .25
1013 A300 90c Flying kite .35 .30
1014 A300 2col Top, diff. .80 .60
Nos. 1011-1014 (4) 1.70 1.35

11th International Fair — A301

1984, Oct. 31 Litho. *Perf. 14x14½*

1015 A301 25c shown .20 .20
1016 A301 70c Fairgrounds .30 .25

70c airmail.

Los Chorros Tourist Center A302

1984, Nov. 23 Litho. *Perf. 14x14½*

1017 A302 15c shown .20 .20
1018 A302 25c Plaza las Americas .20 .20
1019 A302 70c El Salvador International Airport .30 .20
1020 A302 90c El Tunco Beach .35 .30
1021 A302 2col Sihuatehuacan Tourist Center .80 .60
Nos. 1017-1021 (5) 1.85 1.50

The Paper of Papers, 1979, by Roberto A. Galicia (b. 1945) A302a

Paintings by natl. artists: 20c, The White Nun, 1939, by Salvador Salazar Arrue (b. 1899), vert. 70c, Supreme Elegy to Masferrer, 1968, by Antonio G. Ponce (b. 1938), vert. 90c, Transmutation, 1979, by Armando Solis (b. 1940). 2 col, Figures at Theater, 1959, by Carlos Canas (b. 1924), vert.

1984, Dec. 10 Litho. *Perf. 14*

1021A A302a 20c multi .20 .20
1021B A302a 55c multi .25 .20
1021C A302a 70c multi .30 .25
1021D A302a 90c multi .35 .25
1021E A302a 2col multi .75 .60
Nos. 1021A-1021E (5) 1.85 1.50

Nos. 1021B-1021E are airmail. 70c and 2col issued with overprinted silver bar and corrected inscription in black; copies exist without overprint.

Christmas 1984 — A303

1984, Dec. 19 Litho.

1022 A303 25c Glass ornament .20 .20
1023 A303 70c Ornaments, dove .30 .25

No. 1023 airmail.

Birds — A304

1984, Dec. 21 Litho. *Perf. 14½x14*

1024 A304 15c Lepidocolaptes affinis .20 .20
1025 A304 25c Spodiornis rusticus barriliensis .20 .20
1026 A304 55c Claravis mondetoura .25 .20
1027 A304 70c Hylomanes momotula .30 .25
1028 A304 90c Xenotriccus callizonus .35 .30
1029 A304 1col Cardellina rubrifrons .45 .35
Nos. 1024-1029 (6) 1.75 1.50

Nos. 1026-1029 airmail.

Salvador Bank Centenary A305

1985, Feb. 6 Litho. *Perf. 14*

1030 A305 25c Stock certificate .20 .20

Mortgage Bank, 50th Anniv. — A306

1985, Feb. 20 Litho. *Perf. 14*

1031 A306 25c Mortgage .20 .20

Intl. Youth Year A307

1985, Feb. 28 Litho. *Perf. 14*

1032 A307 25c IYY emblem .20 .20
1033 A307 55c Woodcrafting .25 .20
1034 A307 70c Professions symbolized .30 .25
1035 A307 1.50col Youths marching .60 .45
Nos. 1032-1035 (4) 1.35 1.10

Nos. 1033-1035 airmail.

Archaeology A308

1985, Mar. 6 Litho. *Perf. 14½x14*

1036 A308 15c Pre-classical figure .20 .20
1037 A308 20c Engraved vase .20 .20
1038 A308 25c Post-classical ceramic .20 .20
1039 A308 55c Post-classical figure .25 .20
1040 A308 70c Late post-classical deity .30 .25
1041 A308 1col Late post-classical figure .40 .30
Nos. 1036-1041 (6) 1.55 1.35

Souvenir Sheet

Rouletted 13½

1042 A308 2col Tazumal ruins, horiz. .80 .60

Nos. 1039-1041 airmail. No. 1042 has enlargement of stamp design in margin.

Natl. Red Cross, Cent. A309

1985, Mar. 13 Litho. *Perf. 14*

1043 A309 25c Anniv. emblem vert. .20 .20
1044 A309 55c Sea rescue .20 .20
1045 A309 70c Blood donation service .25 .20
1046 A309 90c First aid, ambulance, vert. .35 .25
Nos. 1043-1046 (4) 1.00 .85

Nos. 1044-1046 are airmail.

Agriculture Type of 1984

1985 *Perf. 14½x14*

1047 A294 55c Cotton .20 .20
1048 A294 70c Corn .25 .20
1049 A294 90c Sugar cane .35 .25
1050 A294 2col Beans .75 .60
1051 A294 10col Agave 4.00 3.00
Nos. 1047-1051 (5) 5.55 4.25

Issued: 55c, 70c, 90c, 4/4; 2col, 10col, 9/4.

Child Survival A310

Children's drawings.

1985, May 3 Litho. *Perf. 14x14½*

1052 A310 25c Hand, houses .20 .20
1053 A310 55c House, children .20 .20
1054 A310 70c Boy, girl holding hands .25 .20
1055 A310 90c Oral vaccination .35 .30
Nos. 1052-1055 (4) 1.00 .90

Nos. 1053-1055 are airmail.

Salvador Army A311

1985, May 17 *Perf. 14*

1056 A311 25c Map .20 .20
1057 A311 70c Recruit, natl. flag .25 .20

No. 1057 is airmail.

Inauguration of Pres. Duarte, 1st Anniv. — A312

1985, June 28 *Perf. 14½x14*

1058 A312 25c Flag, laurel, book .20 .20
1059 A312 70c Article I, Constitution .25 .20

Inter-American Development Bank, 25th Anniv. — A313

25c, Central Hydro-electric Dam, power station. 70c, Map of Salvador. 1col, Natl. arms.

1985, July 5 *Perf. 14x13½*

1060 A313 25c multi .20 .20
1061 A313 70c multi .25 .20
1062 A313 1col multi .40 .30
Nos. 1060-1062 (3) .85 .70

Nos. 1061-1062 are airmail.

Fish A314

1985, Sept. 30 *Perf. 14x14½*

1064 A314 25c Cichlasoma trimaculatum .20 .20
1065 A314 55c Rhamdia guatemalensis .20 .20
1066 A314 70c Poecilia sphenops .25 .20
1067 A314 90c Cichlasoma nigrofasciatum .35 .30
1068 A314 1col Astyanax fasciatus .40 .30
1069 A314 1.50col Dormitator latifrons .60 .40
Nos. 1064-1069 (6) 2.00 1.60

Nos. 1065-1069 are airmail.

UNFAO, 40th Anniv. — A315

1985, Oct. 16 *Perf. 14½x14*

1070 A315 20c Cornucopia .20 .20
1071 A315 40c Centeotl, Nahuat god of corn .20 .20

Dragonflies A316

25c, Cordulegaster godmani mclachlan. 55c, Libellula herculea karsch. 70c, Cora marina selys. 90c, Aeshna cornigera braver. 1col, Mecistogaster ornata rambur. 1.50col, Hetaerina smaragdalis de marmels.

1985, Dec. 9 *Perf. 14x14½*

1072 A316 25c multi .20 .20
1073 A316 55c multi .20 .20
1074 A316 70c multi .25 .20
1075 A316 90c multi .35 .30
1076 A316 1col multi .40 .30
1077 A316 1.50col multi .60 .40
Nos. 1072-1077 (6) 2.00 1.60

Nos. 1073-1077 are airmail.
For surcharge see No. C544.

Summer, 1984, by Roberto Huezo (b.1947) A317

Paintings by natl. artists: 25c, Profiles, 1978, by Rosa Mena Valenzuela (b. 1924), vert. 70c, The Deliverance, 1984, by Fernando Llort (b. 1949). 90c, Making Tamale, 1975, by Pedro A. Garcia (b. 1930). 1col, Warm Presence, 1984, by Miguel A. Orellana (b. 1929), vert. Nos. 1079-1082 are airmail.

1985, Dec. 18 *Perf. 14*

1078 A317 25c multi .20 .20
1079 A317 55c multi .20 .20
1080 A317 70c multi .25 .20
1081 A317 90c multi .35 .25
1082 A317 1col multi .40 .30
Nos. 1078-1082 (5) 1.40 1.15

San Vincente de Austria y Lorenzana City, 350th Anniv. A318

1985, Dec. 20

1083 A318 15c Tower, vert. .20 .20
1084 A318 20c Cathedral .20 .20

Intl. Peace Year 1986 — A319

1986, Feb. 21 Litho. *Perf. 14*

1085 A319 15c multi .20 .20
1086 A319 70c multi .50 .40

Postal Code Inauguration — A320

1986, Mar. 14 Litho. *Perf. 14x14½*

1087 A320 20c Domestic mail .20 .20
1088 A320 25c Intl. mail .20 .20

Radio El Salvador, 60th Anniv. A321

1986, Mar. 21

1089 A321 25c Microphone .20 .20
1090 A321 70c Map .50 .40

No. 1090 is airmail.

Mammals A322

1986, May 30 Litho. *Perf. 14x14½*

1091 A322 15c Felis wiedii .20 .20
1092 A322 20c Tamandua tetradactyla .20 .20
1093 A322 1col Dasypus novemcinctus .80 .60
1094 A322 2col Pecarii tajacu 1.60 1.25
Nos. 1091-1094 (4) 2.80 2.25

Nos. 1093-1094 are airmail.

1986 World Cup Soccer Championships, Mexico — A323

Designs: 70c, Flags, mascot. 1col, Players, Soccer Cup, vert. 2col, Natl. flag, player dribbling, vert. 5col, Goal, emblem.

1986, June 6 *Perf. 14x14½, 14½x14*

1095 A323 70c multi .55 .40
1096 A323 1col multi .80 .60
1097 A323 2col multi 1.60 1.25
1098 A323 5col multi 4.00 3.00
Nos. 1095-1098 (4) 6.95 5.25

Teachers — A324

1986, June 30 Litho. *Perf. 14½x14*

1099 20c Dario Gonzalez .20 .20
1100 20c Valero Lecha .20 .20
a. A324 Pair, #1099-1100 .20 .20
1101 40c Marcelino G. Flamenco .20 .20
1102 40c Camilo Campos .20 .20
a. A324 Pair, #1101-1102 .40 .30
1103 70c Saul Flores .30 .25
1104 70c Jorge Larde .30 .25
a. A324 Pair, #1103-1104 .65 .50
1105 1col Francisco Moran .50 .35
1106 1col Mercedes M. De Luarca .50 .35
a. A324 Pair, #1105-1106 1.00 .70
Nos. 1099-1106 (8) 2.40 2.00

Nos. 1103-1106 are airmail.

Pre-Hispanic Ceramic Seal, Cara Sucia, Ahuachapan, Tlaloc Culture (300 B.C.-A.D. 1200) — A325

1986, July 23 Litho. *Perf. 13½*

1107	A325	25c org & brn	.20	.20
1108	A325	55c grn, org & brn	.25	.20
1109	A325	70c pale gray, org & brn	.30	.25
1110	A325	90c pale yel, org & brn	.45	.30
1111	A325	1col pale grn, org & brn	.50	.35
1112	A325	1.50col pale pink, org & brn	.70	.50
		Nos. 1107-1112 (6)	2.40	1.80

Nos. 1108-1112 are airmail.

World Food Day A326

1986, Oct. 30 Litho. *Perf. 14x14½*

1113	A326	20c multi	.20	.20

Flowers A327

1986, Sept. 30 *Perf. 14*

1114	A327	20c Spathiphyllum phryniifolium, vert.	.20	.20
1115	A327	25c Asclepias curassavica	.20	.20
1116	A327	70c Tagetes tenuifolia	.30	.25
1117	A327	1col Ipomoea tiliacea, vert.	.50	.35
		Nos. 1115-1117 (3)	1.00	.80

Nos. 1116-1117 are airmail.

Christmas A328

Perf. 14x14½, 14½x14

1986, Dec. 10 Litho.

1118	A328	25c Candles, vert.	.20	.20
1119	A328	70c Doves	.30	.25

No. 1119 is airmail.

Crafts A329

1986, Dec. 18

1120	A329	25c Basket-making	.20	.20
1121	A329	55c Ceramicware	.25	.20
1122	A329	70c Guitars, vert.	.30	.25
1123	A329	1col Baskets, diff.	.50	.35
		Nos. 1120-1123 (4)	1.25	1.00

Christmas A330

Paintings: 25c, Church, by Mario Araujo Rajo, vert. 70c, Landscape, by Francisco Reyes.

1986, Dec. 22

1124	A330	25c multi	.20	.20
1125	A330	70c multi	.30	.25

No. 1125 is airmail.

Promotion of Philately A331

1987, Mar. 10 Litho. *Perf. 14½x14*

1126	A331	25c multi	.20	.20

Intl. Aid Following Earthquake, Oct. 10, 1986 — A332

1987, Mar. 25

1127	A332	15c multi	.20	.20
1128	A332	70c multi	.30	.25
1129	A332	1.50col multi	.70	.50
1130	A332	5col multi	2.40	1.75
		Nos. 1127-1130 (4)	3.60	2.70

Orchids — A333

1987, June 8 Litho. *Perf. 14½x14*

1131		20c Maxillaria tenuifolia	.20	.20
1132		20c Ponthieva maculata	.20	.20
a.	A333	Pair, #1131-1132	.20	.20
1133		25c Meiracyllium trinasutum	.20	.20
1134		25c Encyclia vagans	.20	.20
a.	A333	Pair, #1133-1134	.25	.20
1135		70c Encyclia cochleata	.30	.25
1136		70c Maxillaria atrata	.30	.25
a.	A333	Pair, #1135-1136	.65	.50
1137		1.50col Sobrialia xantholeuca	.70	.50
1138		1.50col Encyclia microcharis	.70	.50
a.	A333	Pair, #1137-1138	1.40	1.00
		Nos. 1131-1138 (8)	2.80	2.30

#1133-1138 horiz. #1135-1138 are airmail.

Teachers — A334

Designs: No. 1139, C. de Jesus Alas, music. No. 1140, Luis Edmundo Vasquez, medicine. No. 1141, David Rosales, law. No. 1142, Guillermo Trigueros, medicine. No. 1143, Manuel Farfan Castro, history. No. 1144, Iri Sol, voice. No. 1145, Carlos Arturo Imendia, primary education. No. 1146, Benjamin Orozco, chemistry.

1987, June 30 Litho. *Perf. 14½x14*

1139		15c greenish blue & blk	.20	.20
1140		15c greenish blue & blk	.20	.20
a.	A334	Pair, #1139-1140	.20	.20
1141		20c beige & blk	.20	.20
1142		20c beige & blk	.20	.20
a.	A334	Pair, #1141-1142	.20	.20
1143		70c yel org & blk	.30	.25
1144		70c yel org & blk	.30	.25
a.	A334	Pair, #1143-1144	.65	.50
1145		1.50col lt blue grn & blk	.70	.50
1146		1.50col lt blue grn & blk	.70	.50
a.	A334	Pair, #1145-1146	1.40	1.00
		Nos. 1139-1146 (8)	2.80	2.30

Nos. 1143-1146 are airmail.

10th Pan American Games, Indianapolis — A335

1987, July 31 *Perf. 14½x14, 14x14½*

1147		20c Emblem, vert.	.20	.20
1148		20c Table tennis, vert.	.20	.20
a.	A335	Pair, #1147-1148	.20	.20
1149		25c Wrestling	.20	.20
1150		25c Fencing	.20	.20
a.	A335	Pair, #1149-1150	.25	.20
1151		70c Softball	.30	.25
1152		70c Equestrian	.30	.25
a.	A335	Pair, #1151-1152	.65	.50
1153		5col Weight lifting, vert.	2.40	1.75
1154		5col Hurdling, vert.	2.40	1.75
a.	A335	Pair, #1153-1154	5.00	3.50
		Nos. 1147-1154 (8)	6.20	4.80

Nos. 1149-1153 are horizontal.
Nos. 1151-1154 are airmail.

Prior Nicolas Aguilar (1742-1818) A336

Famous men: 20c, Domingo Antonio de Lara (1783-1814), aviation pioneer. 70c, Juan Manuel Rodrigues (1771-1837), president who abolished slavery. 1.50col, Pedro Pablo Castillo (1780-1814), patriot.

1987, Sept. 11 Litho. *Perf. 14½x14*

1155	A336	15c multi	.20	.20
1156	A336	20c multi	.20	.20
1157	A336	70c multi	.30	.25
1158	A336	1.50col multi	.70	.50
		Nos. 1155-1158 (4)	1.40	1.15

Nos. 1157-1158 are airmail.

World Food Day A337

1987, Oct. 16 *Perf. 14x14½*

1159	A337	50c multi	.25	.20

Paintings by Salarrue A338

Perf. 14½x14, 14x14½

1987, Nov. 30

1160	A338	25c Self-portrait	.20	.20
1161	A338	70c Lake	.30	.25

#1161 is airmail. See #1186-1189.

Christmas 1987 A339

25c, Virgin of Perpetual Sorrow, stained-glass window. 70c, The Three Magi, figurines.

1987, Nov. 18 *Perf. 14x14½*

1162	A339	25c multi	.20	.20
1163	A339	70c multi	.30	.25

No. 1163 is airmail.

Pre-Columbian Musical Instruments — A340

Designs: 20c, Pottery drum worn around neck. No. 1165, Frieze picturing pre-Columbian musicians, from a Salua culture ceramic vase, c. 700-800 A.D. (left side), vert. No. 1166, Frieze (right side), vert. 1.50col, Conch shell trumpet.

Perf. 14x14½, 14½x14

1987, Dec. 14 Litho.

1164	A340	20c multi	.20	.20
1165	A340	70c multi	.30	.25
1166	A340	70c multi	.30	.25
a.		Pair, #1165-1166	.65	.55
1167	A340	1.50col multi	.70	.50
		Nos. 1164-1167 (4)	1.50	1.20

Nos. 1165-1167 are airmail. No. 1166a has a continuous design.

Promotion of Philately A341

1988, Jan. 20 Litho. *Perf. 14*

1168	A341	25c multi	.20	.20

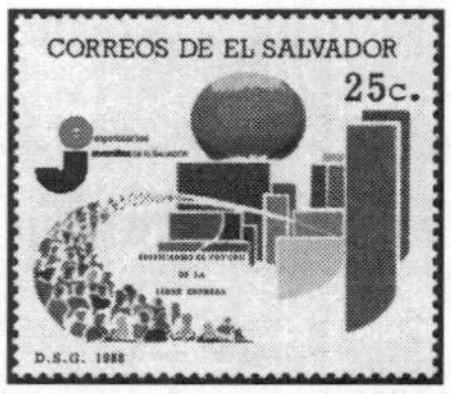

Young Entrepreneurs of El Salvador — A342

1988 *Perf. 14x14½*

1169	A342	25c multi	.20	.20

St. John Bosco (1815-88) A343

1988, Mar. 15 Litho. *Perf. 14x14½*
1170 A343 20c multi .20 .20

Environmental Protection — A344

1988, June 3 Litho. *Perf. 14x14½*
1171 A344 20c Forests .20 .20
1172 A344 70c Forests and rivers .35 .30

No. 1172 is airmail.

1988-1992 Summer Olympics, Seoul and Barcelona A345

1988, Aug. 31 Litho. *Perf. 13½*
1173 A345 1col High jump
1174 A345 1col Javelin
1175 A345 1col Shooting
1176 A345 1col Wrestling
1177 A345 1col Basketball
a. Strip of 5, Nos. 1173-1177
b. Min. sheets of 5 + 5 labels

Souvenir Sheets

1178 A345 2col Torch

Printed in sheets of 10 containing 2 each Nos. 1173-1177.

No. 1177b exists in 2 forms: 1st contains labels picturing 1988 Summer Games emblem or character trademark; 2nd contains labels picturing the 1992 Summer Games emblem or character trademark.

No. 1178 exists in 2 forms: 1st contains 1988 Games emblem; 2nd 1992 Games emblem.

Some, or all, of this issue seem not to have been available to the public.

World Food Day A346

1988, Oct. 11 Litho. *Perf. 14x14½*
1179 A346 20c multi .20 .20

13th Intl. Fair, Nov. 23-Dec. 11 — A347

1988, Oct. 25 *Perf. 14½x14*
1180 A347 70c multi .35 .30

Child Protection A348

1988, Nov. 10
1181 A348 15c Flying kite .20 .20
1182 A348 20c Child hugging adult's leg .20 .20

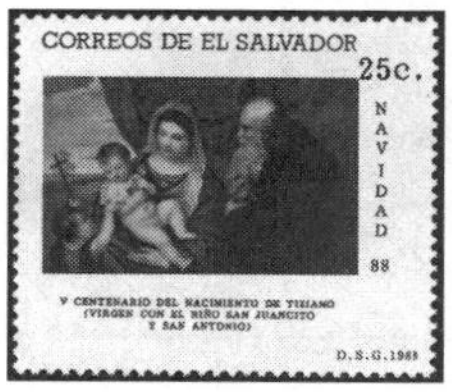

Christmas A349

Paintings by Titian: 25c, *Virgin and Child with the Young St. John and St. Anthony.* 70c, *Virgin and Child in Glory with St. Francis and St. Alvise,* vert.

Perf. 14x14½, 14½x14
1988, Nov. 15
1183 A349 25c multi .20 .20
1184 A349 70c multi .35 .30

70c is airmail.

Return to Moral Values A350

1988, Nov. 22 *Perf. 14½x14*
1185 A350 25c multi .20 .20

Art Type of 1987

Paintings by Salvadoran artists: 40c, *Esperanza de los Soles,* by Victor Rodriguez Preza. 1col, *Shepherd's Song,* by Luis Angel Salinas, horiz. 2col, *Children,* by Julio Hernandez Aleman, horiz. 5col, *El Nino de Las Alcancias,* by Camilo Minero. Nos. 1187-1189 are airmail.

Perf. 14½x14, 14x14½
1988, Nov. 30
1186 A338 40c multi .20 .20
1187 A338 1col multi .50 .40
1188 A338 2col multi 1.00 .75
1189 A338 5col multi 2.50 1.90
Nos. 1186-1189 (4) 4.20 3.25

A351

Discovery of America, 500th Anniv. (in 1992) — A352

Ruins and artifacts: a, El Tazumul. b, Multicolored footed bowl. c, San Andres. d, Two-color censer. e, Sihuatan. f, Carved head of the God of Lluvia. g, Cara Sucia. h, Man-shaped vase. i, San Lorenzo. j, Multicolored pear-shaped vase. 2col, Christopher Columbus.

1988, Dec. 21 *Perf. 14x14½*
1190 Sheet of 10 5.00 3.75
a.-j. A351 1col any single .50 .40

Souvenir Sheet
Roulette 13½

1191 A352 2col vermilion 1.00 .75

UN Declaration of Human Rights, 40th Anniv. A353

1988, Dec. 9 *Perf. 14½x14, 14x14½*
1192 A353 25c Family, map, emblem, vert. .20 .20
1193 A353 70c shown .35 .30

70c is airmail.

World Wildlife Fund — A354

Felines: a, *Felis wiedii* laying on tree branch. b, *Felis wiedii* sitting on branch. c, *Felis pardalis* laying in brush. d, *Felis pardalis* standing on tree branch.

1988 *Perf. 14½x14*
1194 Strip of 4 .80 .60
a.-b. A354 25c any single .20 .20
c.-d. A354 55c any single .30 .20

World Meteorological Organization, 40th Anniv. — A355

1989, Feb. 3 Litho. *Perf. 14½x14*
1195 A355 15c shown .20 .20
1196 A355 20c Wind gauge .20 .20

Meteorology in El Salvador, cent.

Promotion of Philately A356

1989, Mar. 15 Litho. *Perf. 14½x14*
1197 A356 25c Philatelic Soc. emblem .20 .20

See No. 1230.

Natl. Fire Brigade, 106th Anniv. A357

1989, June 19 Litho. *Perf. 14x14½*
1198 A357 25c Fire truck .20 .20
1199 A357 70c Firemen .35 .30

French Revolution, Bicent. A358

1989, July 12
1200 A358 90c Anniv. emblem .45 .35
1201 A358 1col Storming of the Bastille .50 .40

Souvenir Sheets

Stamps on Stamps A359

Statues of Queen Isabella and Christopher Columbus — A360

Designs: a, #88. b, #101. c, #86. d, #102. e, #87. f, #103.

1989, May 31 Litho. *Perf. 14x14½*
Miniature Sheet

1202 Sheet of 6 1.25 .90
a.-f. A359 50c any single .20 .20

Souvenir Sheet
Rouletted 13½

1203 A360 2col shown .80 .60

Discovery of America, 500th anniv. (in 1992).

No. 1203 exists in two forms: margin pictures Natl. Palace with either 500th anniv. emblem or anniv. emblem and "92" at lower right.

Signing Act of Independence — A361

1989, Sept. 1 *Perf. 14x14½*
1204 A361 25c shown .20 .20
1205 A361 70c Flag, natl. seal, heroes .30 .20

Natl. independence, 168th anniv. No. 1205 is airmail.

Demographic Assoc., 27th Anniv. — A362

1989, July 26

1206	A362	25c multi	.20	.20

1990 World Cup Soccer Championships, Italy — A363

Soccer ball, flags of Salvador and: No. 1207, US No. 1208, Guatemala. No. 1209, Costa Rica. No. 1210, Trinidad & Tobago. 55c, Trinidad & Tobago, Guatemala, US, Costa Rica. 1col, Soccer ball, Cuscatlan Stadium.

1989, Sept. 1 Litho. ***Perf. 14x14½***

1207	A363	20c shown	.20	.20
1208	A363	20c multicolored	.20	.20
a.		Pair, #1207-1208	.20	.20
1209	A363	25c multicolored	.20	.20
1210	A363	25c multicolored	.20	.20
a.		Pair, #1209-1210	.25	.25
1211	A363	55c multicolored	.25	.20
1212	A363	1col multicolored	.50	.35
		Nos. 1207-1212 (6)	1.55	1.35

Beatification of Marcellin Champagnat, Founder of the Marist Brothers Order — A364

1989, Sept. 28

1213	A364	20c multicolored	.20	.20

America Issue A365

UPAE emblem and pre-Columbian artifacts: 25c, *The Cultivator,* rock painting. 70c, Ceramic urn.

1989, Oct. 12

1214	A365	25c multicolored	.20	.20
1215	A365	70c multicolored	.35	.30

World Food Day A366

Perf. 14x14½, 14½x14

1989, Oct. 16 Litho.

1216	A366	15c shown	.20	.20
1217	A366	55c Aspects of agriculture, vert.	.30	.20

Children's Rights A367

1989, Oct. 26 Litho. ***Perf. 14½x14***

1218	A367	25c multicolored	.20	.20

Creche Figures A368

1989, Dec. 1

1219	A368	25c shown	.20	.20
1220	A368	70c Holy Family, diff.	.35	.30

Christmas.

Birds of Prey A369

1989, Dec. 20 ***Perf. 14½x14, 14x14½***

1221	A369	70c *Sarcoramphus papa*	.35	.30
1222	A369	1col *Polyborus plancus*	.50	.40
1223	A369	2col *Accipiter striatus*	1.00	.75
1224	A369	10col *Glaucidium brasilianum*	5.00	3.75
		Nos. 1221-1224 (4)	6.85	5.20

Nos. 1221 and 1223 vert.

Tax Court, 50th Aniv. A370

1990, Jan. 12 Litho. ***Perf. 14x14½***

1225	A370	50c multicolored	.20	.20

Lord Baden-Powell, 133rd Birth Anniv. — A371

1990, Feb. 23 ***Perf. 14½x14***

1226	A371	25c multicolored	.20	.20

Intl. Women's Day — A372

1990, Mar. 8 Litho. ***Perf. 14½x14***

1227	A372	25c multicolored	.20	.20

Type of 1989 and

Hour Glass — A373

1990 ***Perf. 14½x14***

1228	A373	25c multicolored	.20	.20
1229	A373	55c multicolored	.22	.20

Souvenir Sheet

Rouletted 13½ with Simulated Perfs.

1230	A356	2col blk & pale blue	.80	.60

Philatelic Soc., 50th anniv. Nos. 1229-1230 are airmail.

Fight Against Addictions A375

1990, Apr. 26 Litho. ***Perf. 14x14½***

1231	A375	20c Alcohol	.20	.20
1232	A375	25c Smoking	.20	.20
1233	A375	1.50col Drugs	.60	.40
		Nos. 1231-1233 (3)	1.00	.80

No. 1233 is airmail.

La Prensa, 75th Anniv. — A376

1990, May 14 Litho. ***Perf. 14½x14***

1234	A376	15c multicolored	.20	.20
1235	A376	25c "75," newspaper	.20	.20

A377

World Cup Soccer Championships, Italy — A378

Soccer player and flags of: No. 1236, Argentina, USSR, Cameroun, Romania. No. 1237, Italy, US, Austria, Czechoslovakia. No. 1238, Brazil, Costa Rica, Sweden, Scotland. No. 1239, Germany, United Arab Emirates, Yugoslavia, Colombia. No. 1240, Belgium, Spain, Korea, Uruguay. No. 1241, England, Netherlands, Ireland, Egypt.

1990, June 15 ***Perf. 14x14½***

1236	A377	55c multicolored	.25	.20
1237	A377	55c multicolored	.25	.20
1238	A377	70c multicolored	.35	.25
1239	A377	70c multicolored	.35	.25
1240	A377	1col multicolored	.50	.40
1241	A377	1col multicolored	.50	.40
1242	A378	1.50col multicolored	.80	.55
		Nos. 1236-1242 (7)	3.00	2.25

For surcharge see No. 1245.

Christopher Columbus A379

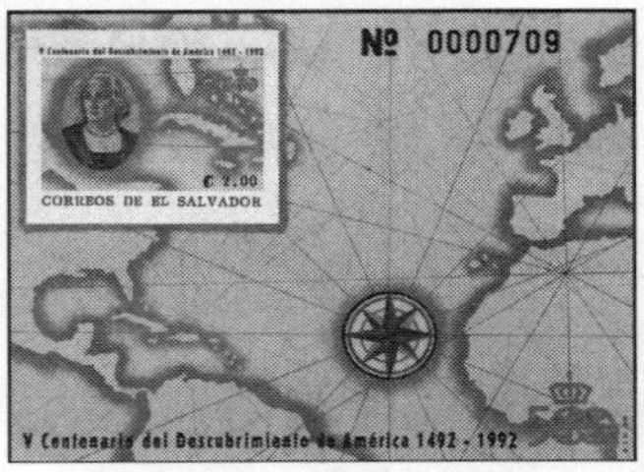

Columbus, Map — A380

Stained glass window: b, Queen Isabella. c, Columbus' Arms. d, Discovery of America 500th anniv. emblem. e, One boat of Columbus' fleet. f, Two boats.

1990, July 30 Litho. ***Perf. 14***

Miniature Sheet

1243		Sheet of 6	3.00	2.25
a.-f.		A379 1col any single	.50	.40

Souvenir Sheet

Rouletted 13 1/2

1244	A380	2col multicolored	1.10	.80

See Nos. 1283-1284.

No. 1239 Surcharged in Black

1991, Feb. Litho. ***Perf. 14x14½***

1245	A377	90c on 70c multi	.45	.25

World Summit for Children A381

1990, Sept. 25 ***Perf. 14½x14***

1246 A381 5col blk, gold & dk bl 2.75 2.00

First Postage Stamps, 150th Anniv. A382

a, Sir Rowland Hill. b, Penny Black. c, No. 21. d, Central Post Office. e, No. C124.

1990, Oct. 5 **Litho.** ***Perf. 14***

1247 Sheet of 5 + label 4.75 3.50
a.-e. A382 2col any single .95 .70

World Food Day — A383

1990, Oct. 16 **Litho.** ***Perf. 14***

1248 A383 5col multicolored 2.40 1.75

San Salvador Electric Light Co., Cent. A384

1990, Oct. 30

1249 A384 20c shown .20 .20
1250 A384 90c Lineman, power lines .45 .35

America Issue A385

1990, Oct. 11 **Litho.** ***Perf. 14x14½***

1251 A385 25c Chichontepec Volcano .20 .20
1252 A385 70c Lake Coatepeque .35 .25

Chamber of Commerce, 75th Anniv. A386

1990, Nov. 22

1253 A386 1 col blk, gold & bl .50 .35

Traffic Safety — A387

Design: 40c, Intersection, horiz.

Perf. 14½x14, 14x14½

1990, Nov. 13

1254 A387 25c multicolored .20 .20
1255 A387 40c multicolored .20 .20

Butterflies A388

Perf. 14x14½, 14½x14

1990, Nov. 28

1256 A388 15c Eurytides calliste .20 .20
1257 A388 20c Papilio garamas amerias .20 .20
1258 A388 25c Papilio garamas .20 .20
1259 A388 55c Hypanartia godmani .30 .20
1260 A388 70c Anaea excellens .35 .30
1261 A388 1col Papilio pilumnus .50 .40
Nos. 1256-1261 (6) 1.75 1.50

Souvenir Sheet

Roulette 13½

1262 A388 2col Anaea proserpina 1.00 .80

Nos. 1259-1261 are vert.

University of El Salvador, 150th Anniv. — A389

1991, Feb. 27 **Litho.** ***Perf. 14½x14***

1263 A389 25c shown .20 .20
1264 A389 70c Sun, footprints, hand .35 .30
1265 A389 1.50col Dove, globe .75 .65
Nos. 1263-1265 (3) 1.30 1.15

Christmas A390

Perf. 14x14½, 14½x14

1990, Dec. 7 **Litho.**

1266 A390 25c shown .20 .20
1267 A390 70c Nativity, vert. .35 .30

Month of the Elderly A391

1991, Jan. 31 ***Perf. 14½x14***

1268 A391 15c purple & blk .20 .20

Restoration of Santa Ana Theater A392

1991, Apr. 12 ***Perf. 14***

1269 A392 20c Interior .20 .20
1270 A392 70c Exterior .35 .30

Amphibians — A393

Designs: 25c, Smilisca baudinii. 70c, Eleutherodactylus rugulosus. 1col, Plectrohyla guatemalensis. 1.50col, Agalychnis moreletii.

1991, May 29 **Litho.** ***Perf. 14x14½***

1271 A393 25c multicolored .20 .20
1272 A393 70c multicolored .35 .30
1273 A393 1col multicolored .50 .40
1274 A393 1.50col multicolored .75 .65
Nos. 1271-1274 (4) 1.80 1.55

Aid for Children's Village A394

Designs: 90c, Children playing outdoors.

1991, June 21 **Litho.** ***Perf. 14x14½***

1275 A394 20c multicolored .20 .20
1276 A394 90c multicolored .40 .35

United Family A395

1991, June 28 **Litho.** ***Perf. 14½x14***

1277 A395 50c multicolored .25 .20

Birds — A396

1991, Aug. 30

1278 A396 20c Melanotis hypoleucus .20 .20
1279 A396 25c Agelaius phoeniceus .20 .20
1280 A396 70c Campylorhynchus rufinucha .35 .30
1281 A396 1col Cissilopha melanocyanea .50 .40
1282 A396 5col Chiroxiphia linearis 2.40 1.75
Nos. 1278-1282 (5) 3.65 2.85

Discovery of America, 500th Anniv. Type of 1990

No. 1283: a, Hourglass, chart. b, Chart, ship's sails. c, Sailing ship near Florida. d, Corner of chart, ships. e, Compass rose, Cuba, Yucatan Peninsula. f, South America, "500" emblem. No. 1284, Sail, landfall.

1991, Sept. 16 **Litho.** ***Perf. 14***

Miniature Sheet

1283 A379 1col Sheet of 6, #a.-f. 3.00 1.50

Souvenir Sheet

Rouletted 6½

1284 A380 2col multicolored 1.00 .50

America Issue A397

Designs: 25c, Battle of Acaxual. 70c, First missionaries in Cuzcatlan.

1991, Oct. 11 **Litho.** ***Perf. 14x14½***

1285 A397 25c multicolored .20 .20
1286 A397 70c multicolored .35 .30

World Food Day — A398

1991, Oct. 16 ***Perf. 14½x14***

1287 A398 50c multicolored .25 .20

Wolfgang Amadeus Mozart, Death Bicent. A399

1991, Oct. 23 ***Perf. 14x14½***

1288 A399 1col multicolored .50 .40

Christmas A400

Perf. 14½x14, 14x14½

1991, Nov. 13 **Litho.**

1289 A400 25c Nativity scene, vert. .20 .20
1290 A400 70c Children singing .40 .30

Total Solar Eclipse, July 11 — A401

1991, Dec. 17 ***Perf. 14x14½***

1291 70c shown .40 .30
1292 70c Eastern El Salvador .40 .30
a. A401 Pair, #1291-1292 .80 .60

No. 1292a has continous design.

Red Cross Life Guards A402

1992, Feb. 28 Litho. *Perf. 14x14½*

1293 A402 3col Rescue 1.50 1.10
1294 A402 4.50col Swimming competition 2.25 1.70

Lions Clubs in El Salvador, 50th Anniv. — A403

1992, Mar. 13 *Perf. 14½x14*

1295 A403 90c multicolored .45 .35

Protect the Environment A404

Designs: 60c, Man riding bicycle. 80c, Children walking outdoors. 1.60col, Sower in field. 3col, Clean water. 2.20col, Natural foods. 5col, Recycling center. 10col, Conservation of trees and nature. 25col, Wildlife protection.

1992, Apr. 6 Litho. *Perf. 14x14½*

1298 A404 60c multi .30 .25
1299 A404 80c multi .40 .30
1300 A404 1.60col multi .80 .60
1302 A404 2.20col multi 1.10 .85
1303 A404 3col multi 1.50 1.10
1304 A404 5col multi 2.50 1.90
1305 A404 10col multi 5.00 3.75
1307 A404 25col multi 12.50 9.50
Nos. 1298-1307 (8) 24.10 18.25

This is an expanding set. Numbers may change.

Physicians A405

80c, Dr. Roberto Orellana Valdes. 1col, Dr. Carlos Gonzalez Bonilla. 1.60col, Dr. Andres Gonzalo Funes. 2.20col, Dr. Joaquin Coto.

1992, Apr. 30 *Perf. 14½x14*

1308 A405 80c multicolored .40 .30
1309 A405 1col multicolored .50 .40
1310 A405 1.60col multicolored .80 .60
1311 A405 2.20col multicolored 1.10 .85
Nos. 1308-1311 (4) 2.80 2.15

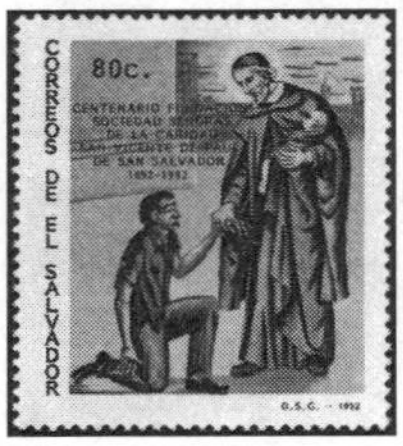

Women's Auxiliary of St. Vincent de Paul Society, Cent. — A406

1992, Mar. 10 Litho. *Perf. 14½x14*

1312 A406 80c multicolored .45 .40

Population and Housing Census A407

80c, Globe showing location of El Salvador.

1992, June 29 Litho. *Perf. 14½x14*

1313 A407 60c multicolored .35 .30
1314 A407 80c multicolored .45 .40

1992 Summer Olympics, Barcelona A408

1992, July 17 Litho. *Perf. 14½x14*

1315 A408 60c Hammer throw .35 .30
1316 A408 80c Volleyball .45 .40
1317 A408 90c Shot put .75 .60
1318 A408 2.20col Long jump 1.25 .65
1319 A408 3col Vault 1.75 .85
1320 A408 5col Balance beam 3.00 1.50
Nos. 1315-1320 (6) 7.55 4.30

Simon Bolivar A409

1992, July 24

1321 A409 2.20col multicolored 1.25 .65

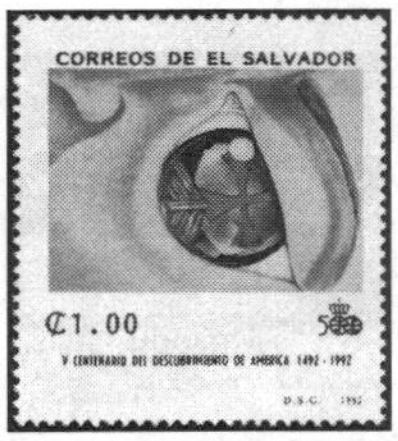

A410

Discovery of America, 500th Anniv. — A411

Designs: No. 1322, European and Amerindian faces. No. 1323, Ship in person's eye. No. 1324, Ship at sea. No. 1325, Ship, satellite over Earth. 3col, Cross, Indian pyramid.

1992, Aug. 28 Litho. *Perf. 14x14½*

1322 A410 1col multicolored .60 .30
1323 A410 1col multicolored .60 .30

Perf. 14½x14

1324 A410 1col multicolored .60 .30
1325 A410 1col multicolored .60 .30
a. Min. sheet, 2 each #1322-1325 4.75 2.40
Nos. 1322-1325 (4) 2.40 1.20

Souvenir Sheet

Rouletted 13½

1326 A411 3col multicolored 1.75 .85

Immigrants to El Salvador A412

Designs: No. 1327, Feet walking over map. No. 1328, Footprints leading to map.

1992, Sept. 16 Litho. *Perf. 14x14½*

1327 A412 2.20col multicolored 1.10 .60
1328 A412 2.20col multicolored 1.10 .60
a. Pair, #1327-1328 2.25 1.25

General Francisco Morazan (1792-1842) A413

1992, Sept. 28 *Perf. 14½x14*

1329 A413 1col multicolored .60 .30

Association of Salvadoran Broadcasters A414

1992, Oct. 3

1330 A414 2.20col multicolored 1.10 .60

Salvadoran Radio Day, Intl. Radio Day.

Discovery of America, 500th Anniv. A415

1992, Oct. 13 Litho. *Perf. 14x14½*

1331 A415 80c Indian artifacts .45 .25
1332 A415 2.20col Map, ship 1.25 .60

Exfilna '92 — A416

1992, Oct. 22 *Perf. 14x14½*

1333 A416 5col multicolored 2.75 1.40

Discovery of America, 500th Anniv.

Peace in El Salvador A417

1992, Oct. 30

1334 A417 50c black, blue & yellow .30 .20

Christmas A418

Perf. 14x14½, 14½x14

1992, Nov. 23 Litho.

1335 A418 80c shown .45 .25
1336 A418 2.20col Nativity, vert. 1.25 .60

Wildlife A419

Designs: 50c, Tapirus bairdii. 70c, Chironectes minimus. 1col, Eira barbara. 3col, Felis yagouaroundi. 4.50col, Odocoileus virginianus.

1993, Jan. 15 Litho. *Perf. 14x14½*

1337 A419 50c multicolored .30 .20
1338 A419 70c multicolored .40 .20
1339 A419 1col multicolored .60 .30
1340 A419 3col multicolored 1.75 .85
1341 A419 4.50col multicolored 2.50 1.25
Nos. 1337-1341 (5) 5.55 2.80

Month of the Elderly A420

Design: 2.20col, Boy, old man holding tree.

1993, Jan. 27

1342 A420 80c black .45 .25
1343 A420 2.20col multicolored 1.25 .60

Agape Social Welfare Organization — A421

Designs: a, Divine Providence Church. b, People, symbols of love and peace.

1993, Mar. 4 Litho. *Perf. 14x14½*

1344 A421 1col Pair, #a.-b. .45 .25

Secretary's Day A422

1993, Apr. 26 Litho. *Perf. 14x14½*

1345 A422 1col multicolored .45 .25

Benjamin Bloom Children's Hospital A423

1993, June 18 Litho. *Perf. 14x14½*

1346 A423 5col multicolored 2.25 1.10

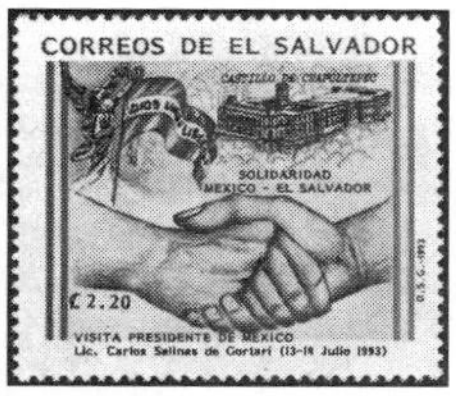

Visit by Mexican President Carlos Salinas de Gortari A424

1993, July 14

1347 A424 2.20col multicolored 1.00 .50

Aquatic Birds A425

1993, Sept. 28 Litho. *Perf. 14x14½*

1348 A425 80c Casmerodius albus .20 .20
1349 A425 1col Mycteria americana .25 .20
1350 A425 2.20col Ardea herodias .45 .25
1351 A425 5col Ajaja ajaja 1.10 .60
Nos. 1348-1351 (4) 2.00 1.25

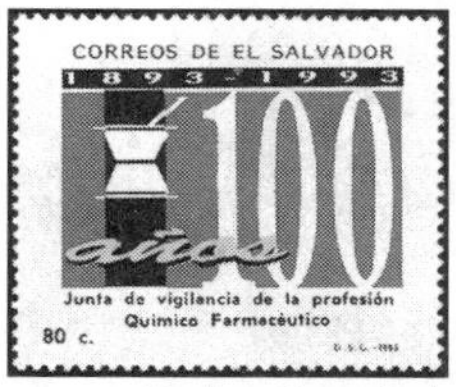

Pharmacy Review Commission, Cent. — A426

1993, Oct. 6

1352 A426 80c multicolored .20 .20

America Issue A427

Endangered species: 80c, Dasyprocta punctata. 2.20col, Procyon lotor.

1993, Oct. 11 Litho. *Perf. 14x14½*

1353 A427 80c multicolored .20 .20
1354 A427 2.20col multicolored .50 .25

Fifth Central America Games A428

50c, Mascot, torch. 1.60col, Emblem. 2.20col, Mascot, map of Central America. 4.50col, Map of El Salvador, mascot.

Perf. 14½x14, 14x14½

1993, Oct. 29 Litho.

1355 A428 50c multi .20 .20
1356 A428 1.60col multi .40 .20
1357 A428 2.20col multi, horiz. .50 .25
1358 A428 4.50col multi, horiz. 1.00 .50
Nos. 1355-1358 (4) 2.10 1.15

Miniature Sheet

Medicinal Plants — A429

Designs: a, Solanum mammosum. b, Hamelia patens. c, Tridex procumbens. d, Calea urticifolia. e, Ageratum conyzoides. f, Pluchea odorata.

1993, Dec. 10 Litho. *Perf. 14½x14*

1359 A429 1col Sheet of 6, #a.-f. 1.25 .65

Christmas A430

1993, Nov. 23 *Perf. 14x14½*

1360 A430 80c Holy Family .30 .20
1361 A430 2.20col Nativity Scene .85 .40

Alberto Masferrer (1868-1932), Writer — A431

1993, Nov. 30

1362 A431 2.20col multicolored .85 .40

Intl. Year of the Family — A432

1994, Feb. 28 Litho. *Perf. 14½x14*

1363 A432 2.20col multicolored .85 .40

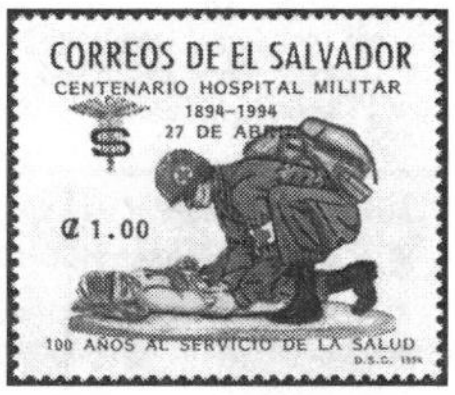

Military Hospital, Cent. A433

1994, Apr. 27 Litho. *Perf. 14*

1364 A433 1col shown .25 .20
1365 A433 1col Hospital building .25 .20

City of Santa Ana, Cent. — A434

Designs: 60c, Arms of Department of Santa Ana. 80c, Inscription honoring heroic deeds of 44 patriots.

1994, Apr. 29 Litho. *Perf. 14*

1366 A434 60c multicolored .20 .20
1367 A434 80c multicolored .20 .20

1994 World Cup Soccer Championships, US — A435

Soccer plays, flags from: 60c, Romania, Colombia, Switzerland, US. 80c, Sweden, Cameroun, Russia, Brazil. 1col, South Korea, Spain, Bolivia, Germany. 2.20col, Bulgaria, Nigeria, Greece, Argentina. 4.50col, Mexico, Norway, Ireland, Italy. 5col, Saudi Arabia, Netherlands, Morocco, Belgium.

1994, June 6 Litho. *Perf. 14*

1368 A435 60c multicolored .20 .20
1369 A435 80c multicolored .20 .20
1370 A435 1col multicolored .25 .20
1371 A435 2.20col multicolored .45 .25
1372 A435 4.50col multicolored 1.00 .50
1373 A435 5col multicolored 1.10 .55
Nos. 1368-1373 (6) 3.20 1.90

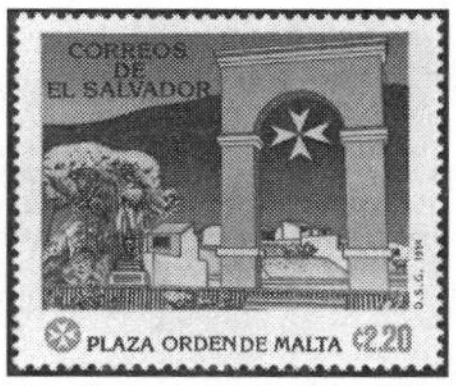

Plaza of Sovereign Military Order of Malta A436

1994, June 24 Litho. *Perf. 14*

1374 A436 2.20col multicolored .50 .25

Traditions A437

Designs: 1col, Tiger and deer dance. 2.20col, Spotted bull dance.

1994, June 30

1375 A437 1col multicolored .20 .20
1376 A437 2.20col multicolored .50 .25

Nutritional Plants — A438

1994, Aug. 29 Litho. *Perf. 14*

1377 A438 70c Capsicum annuum .20 .20
1378 A438 80c Theobroma cacao .20 .20
1379 A438 1col Ipomoea batatas .25 .20
1380 A438 5col Chamaedorea tepejilote 1.10 .55
Nos. 1377-1380 (4) 1.75 1.15

Postal Transport Vehicles A439

1994, Oct. 11 Litho. *Perf. 14*

1381 A439 80c Jeep .40 .20
1382 A439 2.20col Train 1.10 .55

America issue.

22nd Bicycle Race of El Salvador A440

1994, Oct. 26

1383 A440 80c multicolored .40 .20

16th Intl. Fair of El Salvador A441

1994, Oct. 31

1384 A441 5col multicolored 2.50 1.25

Christmas A442

1994, Nov. 16

1385 A442 80c shown .40 .20
1386 A442 2.20col Magi, Christ child 1.10 .55

Beetles A443

1994, Dec. 16 Litho. *Perf. 14*

1387 A443 80c Cotinis mutabilis .20 .20
1388 A443 1col Phyllophaga .20 .20
1389 A443 2.20col Galofa .50 .25
1390 A443 5col Callipogon barbatus 1.10 .55
Nos. 1387-1390 (4) 2.00 1.20

Salvadoran Culture Center, 40th Anniv. — A444

1995, Mar. 24 Litho. *Perf. 14½x14*

1391	A444	70c shown	.20	.20
1392	A444	1col "40" emblem	.25	.20

Ceramic Treasures Archeological Site — A445

Designs: 60c, Cup. 70c, Three-footed earthen dish. 80c, Two-handled jar. 2.20col, Long-necked jar. 4.50col, Excavation structure #3. 5col, Excavation structure #4.

1995, Apr. 26 Litho. *Perf. 14½x14*

1393	A445	60c multicolored	.30	.20
1394	A445	70c multicolored	.40	.20
1395	A445	80c multicolored	.45	.25
1396	A445	2.20col multicolored	1.10	.55
1397	A445	4.50col multicolored	2.50	1.25
1398	A445	5col multicolored	2.75	1.25
		Nos. 1393-1398 (6)	7.50	3.70

Fr. Isidro Menendez (1795-1858), Physician A446

1995, May 19

1399	A446	80c multicolored	.45	.25

Central America, SA, 80th Anniv. — A447

Designs: 80c, Insuring the future of children. 2.20col, Child wearing costume.

1995, July 7 Litho. *Perf. 14*

1400	A447	80c multicolored	.40	.20
1401	A447	2.20col multicolored	1.10	.55

Sacred Heart College, Cent. A448

1995, July 26 *Perf. 14x14½*

1402	A448	80c multicolored	.40	.20

FAO, 50th Anniv. — A449

1995, Aug. 16 Litho. *Perf. 14½x14*

1403	A449	2.20col multicolored	1.10	.55

Tourism A450

Designs: 50c, Los Almendros Beach, Sonsonate. 60c, Green Lagoon, Apaneca. 2.20col, Guerrero Beach, La Union. 5col, Usulutan Volcano.

1995, Aug. 30 *Perf. 14x14½*

1404	A450	50c multicolored	.25	.20
1405	A450	60c multicolored	.30	.20
1406	A450	2.20col multicolored	1.10	.55
1407	A450	5col multicolored	2.75	1.25
		Nos. 1404-1407 (4)	4.40	2.20

Orchids A451

#1408, Pleurothallis glandulosa. #1409, Pleurothallis grobyi. #1410, Pleurothallis fuegii. #1411, Lemboglossum stellatum. #1412, Lepanthes inaequalis. #1413, Pleurothallis hirsuta. #1414, Hexadesmia micrantha. #1415, Pleurothallis segoviense. #1416, Stelis aprica. #1417, Platystele stenostachya. #1418, Stelis barbata. #1419, Pleurothallis schiedeii.

1995, Sept. 28 Litho. *Perf. 14½x14*

1408	A451	60c multicolored	.30	.20
1409	A451	60c multicolored	.30	.20
a.		Pair, #1408-1409	.60	.30
1410	A451	70c multicolored	.40	.20
1411	A451	70c multicolored	.40	.20
1412	A451	1col multicolored	.55	.30
1413	A451	1col multicolored	.55	.30
1414	A451	3col multicolored	1.60	.80
1415	A451	3col multicolored	1.60	.80
1416	A451	4.50col multicolored	2.50	1.25
1417	A451	4.50col multicolored	2.50	1.25
a.		Pair, #1416-1417	5.00	2.50
1418	A451	5col multicolored	2.75	1.40
1419	A451	5col multicolored	2.75	1.40
		Nos. 1408-1419 (12)	16.20	8.30

America Issue — A452

Martins: 80c, Chloroceryle aenea. 2.20col, Chloroceryle americana.

1995, Oct. 11

1420	A452	80c multicolored	.40	.20
1421	A452	2.20col multicolored	1.25	.60

UN, 50th Anniv. — A453

Design: 2.20col, Hands of different races holding UN emblem, "50."

1995, Oct. 23

1422	A453	80c multicolored	.40	.20
1423	A453	2.20col multicolored	1.25	.60

Christmas A454

1995, Nov. 17 Litho. *Perf. 14½x14*

1424	A454	80c shown	.40	.20
1425	A454	2.20col Families, clock tower	1.25	.60

Miniature Sheet

Fauna A455

Designs: a, Bubo virginianus. b, Potos flavus. c, Porthidium godmani. d, Felis pardalis (f). e, Dellathis bifurcata. f, Felis concolor (h). g, Mazama americana. h, Leptophobia aripa. i, Bolitoglossa salvinii. j, Eugenes fulgens (h, i).

1995, Nov. 24 *Perf. 14x14½*

1426	A455	80c Sheet of 10, #a.-j.	4.00	2.00

Independence, 174th Anniv. — A456

Designs: 80c, Natl. arms, export products, money, textile workers, pharmaceuticals. 25col, Crates of products leaving El Salvador.

1995, Sept. 14 *Perf. 14½x14*

1427	A456	80c shown	.40	.20
1428	A456	25col multicolored	13.00	7.50

2nd Visit of Pope John Paul II — A457

5.40col, Pope John Paul II, Metropolitan Cathedral.

1996, Feb. 8 Litho. *Perf. 14½x14*

1429	A457	1.50col multicolored	.90	.45
1430	A457	5.40col multicolored	3.25	1.60

ANTEL, Telecommunications Workers' Day — A458

1.50col, Satellite dish, hand holding cable fibers. 5col, Three globes, telephone receiver.

Perf. 14x14½, 14½x14

1996, Apr. 27 Litho.

1431	A458	1.50col multi	.90	.45
1432	A458	5col multi, vert.	3.00	1.50

City of San Salvador, 450th Anniv. A459

Designs: 2.50col, Spanish meeting natives. 2.70col, Diego de Holguin, first mayor, mission. 3.30col, Old National Palace. 4col, Heroe's Boulevard, modern view of city.

1996, Mar. 27 *Perf. 14x14½*

1433	A459	2.50col multicolored	1.50	.80
1434	A459	2.70col multicolored	1.75	.85
1435	A459	3.30col multicolored	2.00	1.00
1436	A459	4col multicolored	2.50	1.25
		Nos. 1433-1436 (4)	7.75	3.90

Natl. Artists, Entertainers A460

Designs: 1col, Rey Avila (1929-95). 1.50col, María Teresa Moreira (1934-95). 2.70col, Francisco Antonio Lara (1900-89). 4col, Carlos Alverez Pineda (1928-93).

1996, May 17 Litho. *Perf. 14½x14*

1437	A460	1col multicolored	.60	.30
1438	A460	1.50col multicolored	.90	.45
1439	A460	2.70col multicolored	1.50	.75
1440	A460	4col multicolored	2.25	1.10
		Nos. 1437-1440 (4)	5.25	2.60

YSKL Radio, 40th Anniv. A461

1996, May 24 *Perf. 14x14½*

1441	A461	1.40col multicolored	.85	.40

1996 Summer Olympic Games, Atlanta A462

Early Greek athletes: 1.50col, Discus thrower. 3col, Jumper. 4col, Wrestlers. 5col, Javelin thrower.

1996, July 3 Litho. *Perf. 14*

1442 A462 1.50col multicolored .90 .45
1443 A462 3col multicolored 1.75 .90
1444 A462 4col multicolored 2.40 1.25
1445 A462 5col multicolored 3.00 1.50
Nos. 1442-1445 (4) 8.05 4.10

Birds A463

Designs: a, Pheucticus ludovicianus. b, Tyrannus forficatus. c, Dendroica petechia. d, Falco sparverius. e, Icterus galbula.

1996, Aug. 9 Litho. *Perf. 14x14½*

1446 A463 1.50col Strip of 5, #a.-e. 4.50 2.25

Diaro de Hoy Newspaper, 60th Anniv. — A464

1996, Sept. 20

1447 A464 5.20col multicolored 3.00 1.50

Channel 2 Television Station, 30th Anniv. — A465

1996, Sept. 27 *Perf. 14½x14*

1448 A465 10col multicolored 5.75 3.00

UNICEF, 50th Anniv. A466

1996, Oct. 4 *Perf. 14x14½*

1449 A466 1col multicolored .60 .30

Traditional Costumes A467

America issue: 1.50col, Blouse, short flannel skirt, Nahuizalco. 4col, Blouse, long skirt, Panchimalco.

1996, Oct. 11 *Perf. 14½x14*

1450 A467 1.50col multicolored .90 .45
1451 A467 4col multicolored 2.25 1.10

Christmas A468

Designs: 2.50col, Night scene of homes, Christmas tree, church. 4col, Day scene of people celebrating outside homes, church.

1996, Nov. 28 Litho. *Perf. 14½x14*

1452 A468 2.50col multicolored 1.50 .75
1453 A468 4col multicolored 2.25 1.10

Constitution Day — A469

1996, Dec. 19 Litho. *Perf. 14½x14*

1454 A469 1col multicolored .60 .30

Marine Life — A470

a, Nasolamia velox. b, Scomberomorus sierra. c, Delphinus delphis. d, Eretmochelys imbricata. e, Epinephelus labriformis. f, Pomacanthus zonipectus. g, Scarus perrico. h, Hippocampus ingens.

1996, Dec. 17

1455 A470 1col Sheet of 8, #a.-h. 4.50 2.25

Jerusalem, 3000th Anniv. A471

1996, Dec. 5 Litho. *Perf. 14x14½*

1456 A471 1col multicolored .60 .30

El Mundo Newspaper, 30th Anniv. A472

1997, Feb. 6 Litho. *Perf. 14x14½*

1457 A472 10col multicolored 5.75 3.00

Exfilna '97 — A473

1997, Feb. 21

1458 A473 4col Baldwin 58441, 1925 2.25 1.25

Carmelite Order of San Jose, 80th Anniv. A474

Design: Mother Clara Maria of Jesus Quiros.

1997, Mar. 19

1459 A474 1col multicolored .60 .30

American School, 50th Anniv. — A475

1997, Apr. 10 *Perf. 14½x14*

1460 A475 25col multicolored 14.50 7.25

Tropical Fruit A476

No. 1461: a, Annona diversifolia. b, Anacardium occidentale. c, Cucumis melo. d, Pouteria mammosa.
4col, Carica papaya.

1997, May 28 Litho. *Perf. 14x14½*

1461 A476 1.50col Sheet of 4, #a.-d. 3.50 3.50

Souvenir Sheet

Rouletted 13½

1462 A476 4col multicolored 2.25 2.25

Lions Club in El Salvador, 55th Anniv. A476a

1997, Aug. 15 Litho. *Perf. 14*

1463 A476a 4col multicolored 2.25 1.10

Montreal Protocol on Substances that Deplete Ozone Layer, 10th Anniv. — A477

1997, Aug. 28 Litho. *Perf. 14*

1464 A477 1.50col shown .90 .45
1465 A477 4col Boy drinking water 2.25 1.10

Inter-American Water Day (#1465).

Miguel de Cervantes Saavedra (1547-1616), Writer — A478

1997, Sept. 26 Litho. *Perf. 14*

1466 A478 4col multicolored 2.25 1.10

Independence Day — A479

1997, Sept. 10 Litho. *Perf. 14x14½*

1467 A479 2.50col shown 1.40 .70
1468 A479 5.20col Flag, children, dove 2.75 1.40

Scouting in El Salvador, 75th Anniv. — A480

1997, Oct. 3 *Perf. 14½x14*

1469 A480 1.50col multicolored .90 .45

Life of a Postman A481

America issue: 1col, Postman delivering mail. 4col, Postman on motor scooter, dog.

1997, Oct. 10 Litho. *Perf. 14½x14*

1470 A481 1col multicolored .60 .30
1471 A481 4col multicolored 2.40 1.25

ACES (Automobile Club of El Salvador), 26th Anniv. A482

1997, Oct. 28 *Perf. 14x14½*

1472 A482 10col multicolored 5.75 3.00

Christmas — A483

Children's paintings: No. 1473, Outdoor scene. No. 1474, Indoor scene.

1997, Nov. 20 Litho. *Perf. 14*

1473	1.50col multicolored	.85	.45
1474	1.50col multicolored	.85	.45
a.	A483 Pair, #1473-1474	1.75	.90

Salesian Order in El Salvador, Cent. A484

Designs: a, Map, St. John Bosco (1715-88). b, St. Cecilia College. c, San Jose College, priest. d, Ricaldone, students working with machinery. e, Maria Auxiliadora Church. f, City of St. John Bosco, students working with electronic equipment.

1997, Dec. 6

1475 A484 1.50col Sheet of 6, #a.-f. 2.75 1.40

Antique Automobiles — A485

Designs: a, 1946 Standard. b, 1936 Chrysler. c, 1954 Jaguar. d, 1930 Ford. e, 1953 Mercedes Benz. f, 1956 Porsche.

1997, Dec. 17

1476 A485 2.50col Sheet of 6, #a.-f. 4.50 2.25

St. Joseph Missionaries, 125th Anniv. — A486

1col, Image, Church of St. Joseph, Ahuachapan. 4col, Jose M. Vilaseca, Cesarea Esparza.

1998, Jan. 23 Litho. *Perf. 14*

1477	A486 1col multicolored	.30	.20
1478	A486 4col multicolored	1.25	.60

New Intl. Airport A487

1998, Mar. 17 Litho. *Perf. 14*

1479 A487 10col multicolored 3.00 1.50

Organization of American States, 50th Anniv. — A488

1998, May 29 Litho. *Perf. 14½x14*

1480 A488 4col multicolored 1.25 .60

1998 World Cup Soccer Championships, France — A489

Soccer player, Paris landmarks: a, Sacre Coeur. b, Eiffel Tower. c, Louvre. d, Notre Dame.

4col, Soccer ball, Arc d'Triumphe, horiz.

1998, May 13

1481 A489 1.50col Strip of 4, #a.-d. 1.75 .90

Souvenir Sheet

Rouletted 13½

1482 A489 4col multicolored 1.25 .60

El Salvador, 1997 Champions of the 6th Central American Games A490

Designs inside medals: No. 1483, Women's gymnastics, weight lifting, judo. No. 1484, Discus, volleyball, women's basketball. No. 1485, Swimming, tennis, water polo. No. 1486, Gymnastics, wrestling, shooting.

1998, July 17 Litho. *Perf. 14*

1483	A490 1.50col multicolored	.45	.20
1484	A490 1.50col multicolored	.45	.20
1485	A490 1.50col multicolored	.45	.20
1486	A490 1.50col multicolored	.45	.20
	Nos. 1483-1486 (4)	1.80	.80

Dr. Jose Gustavo Guerrero (1876-1958), President of the World Court — A491

1998, July 22 Litho. *Perf. 14*

1487 A491 1col multicolored .25 .20

18th International Fair — A492

1998, Aug. 28

1488 A492 4col multicolored 1.25 .60

Painting of the Death of Manuel José Arce, Soldier, Politician A493

1998, Sept. 1

1489 A493 4col multicolored 1.25 .60

Hummingbirds and Flowers — A494

a, Archilochus colubris. b, Amazilia rutila. c, Hylocharis eliciae. d, Colibri thalassinus. e, Campylopterus hemileucurus. f, Lampornis amethystinus.

1998, Sept. 7

1490 A494 1.50col Sheet of 6, #a.-f. 2.75 1.40

House Social Fund, 25th Anniv. — A495

1998, Sept. 29 Litho. *Perf. 14*

1491 A495 10col multicolored 3.00 1.50

Natl. Archives, 50th Anniv. — A496

1998, Oct. 2

1492 A496 1.50col multicolored .45 .25

Famous Women A497

America issue: 1col, Alice Lardé de Venturino. 4col, Maria de Baratta.

1998, Oct. 12

1493	A497 1col multicolored	.30	.20
1494	A497 4col multicolored	1.25	.65

Christmas A498

Children's drawings: 1col, Clock tower, nativity scene. 4col, Pageant players as angels, Holy Family parading to church, nativity scene.

1998, Nov. 24 Litho. *Perf. 14*

1495	A498 1col multicolored	.30	.20
1496	A498 4col multicolored	1.25	.60

World Stamp Day A499

1998, Nov. 27 Litho. *Perf. 14*

1497 A499 1col multicolored .35 .20

Salvadoran Air Force, 75th Anniv. — A500

Designs: a, C47T transport plane. b, TH-300 helicopter. c, UH-1H helicopter. d, Dragonfly bomber.

1998, Dec. 1 Litho. *Perf. 14¼*

1498 A500 1.50col Strip of 4, #a.-d. 1.75 .90

Traditional Foods A501

Designs: a, Ensalada de papaya y pacaya. b, Sopa de mondongo. c, Camarones en alhuaiste. d, Buñuelos en miel de panela. e, Refresco de ensalada. f, Ensalada de aguacate. g, Sopa de arroz aguado con chipilín. h, Plato típico salvadoreño. i, Empanadas de plátano. j, Horchata.

1998, Dec. 9 Litho. *Perf. 14*

1499 A501 1.50col Block of 10, #a.-j. 4.50 2.25

Roberto D'Aubisson Signing New Constitution, 1983 — A502

1998, Dec. 15 Litho. *Perf. 14x14¼*

1503 A502 25col multicolored 7.25 3.50

First Natl. Topical Philatelic Exhibition A503

Salvador Railway Company Steamship Service.

1999, Feb. 19 Litho. *Perf. 14*

1504 A503 2.50col multicolored .60 .30

Introduction of Television, 40th Anniv. — A504

1999, Feb. 24

1505 A504 4col multicolored .90 .45

European Union Cooperation with El Salvador — A505

1999, May 7 Litho. *Perf. 14x14¼*

1506 A505 5.20col shown 1.50 .75
1507 A505 10col Hands clasped 3.00 1.50

Water Birds A506

No. 1508: a, Gallinula chlorupus. b, Porphyrula martinica. c, Pardirallus maculatus. d, Anas discors. e, Dendrocygna autumnalis. f, Fulica americana. g, Jacana spinosa. h, Perzana carolina. i, Aramus guarauna. j, Oxyura dominica.
4col, Aythya affinis.

1999, Apr. 22 *Perf. 14x14¼*

1508 A506 1col Block of 10, #a.-j. 3.00 1.50

Souvenir Sheet

Rouletted 8¾

1509 A506 4col multicolored .95 .50

Bats A507

Designs: a, Glossophaga soricina. b, Desmodus rotundus. c, Noctilio leporinus. d, Vampyrum spectrum. e, Ectophilla alba. f, Myotis nigricans.

1999, June 30 Litho. *Perf. 14x14½*

1510 A507 1.50col Sheet of 6, #a.-f. 2.50 1.25

Visit of US Pres. William J. Clinton — A508

Designs: a, Seals, flags of El Salvador, US. b, Pres. Francisco Flores of El Salvador, Pres. Clinton.

1999, May 19 *Perf. 14¼*

1511 A508 5col Pair, #a.-b. 3.00 1.50

Quality Control Institute, 20th Anniv. — A509

1999, May 20 *Perf. 14¼*

1512 A509 5.40col multicolored 1.60 .80

Geothermic Energy A510

1999, July 16 Litho. *Perf. 14x14½*

1513 A510 1col Drilling tower .30 .20
1514 A510 4col Power station 1.25 .60

Exports A511

1999, July 21 *Perf. 14½x14*

1515 A511 4col multicolored 1.25 .60

Salvadoran Journalists' Association A512

1999, July 30 *Perf. 14x14½*

1516 A512 1.50col multicolored .45 .25

Cattleya Orchids A513

Designs: a, Skinneri var. alba. b, Skinneri var. coerulea. c, Skinneri. d, Guatemalensis. e, Aurantiaca var. flava. f, Aurantiaca.

1999, Aug. 25

1517 A513 1.50col Sheet of 6, #a.-f. + 4 labels 2.50 1.25

Toño Salazar, Caricaturist A514

Designs: a, Self-portrait. b, Salarrué. c, Claudia Lars. d, Fancisco Gavidia. e, Miguel Angel Asturias.

1999, Aug. 31

1518 A514 1.50col Strip of 5, #a.-e. 2.25 1.10

Central American Nutrition Institute A515

1999, Sept. 14 Litho. *Perf. 14x14½*

1519 A515 5.20col Children, food 1.40 .70
1520 A515 5.40col Food 1.50 .75

Armed Forces, 175th Anniv. — A516

1999, Sept. 24 *Perf. 14¼x14*

1521 A516 1col Gens. Arce & Barrios .30 .20
1522 A516 1.50col Soldier, flag .45 .20

Intl. Year of Older Persons A517

1999, Oct. 8

1523 A517 10col multicolored 2.75 1.40

America Issue, A New Millennium Without Arms — A518

1999, Oct. 12

1524 A518 1col Dove, children .30 .20
1525 A518 4col "No Guns" sign 1.10 .55

UPU, 125th Anniv. — A519

Designs: a, UPU emblem. b, Mail, jeep, ship, airplane, computer.

1999, Oct. 22

1526 A519 4col Pair, #a.-b. 2.25 1.10

Christmas — A520

Paintings by - #1527: a, Delmy Guandique. b, Margarita Orellana.
No. 1528: a, Lolly Sandoval. b, José Francisco Guadrón.

1999, Nov. 4

1527 A520 1.50col Pair, #a.-b. .85 .45
1528 A520 4col Pair, #a.-b. 2.25 1.10

Inter-American Development Bank, 40th Anniv. — A521

1999, Nov. 24 Litho. *Perf. 14¼x14*

1529 A521 25col multi 7.00 3.50

Woodpeckers A522

Designs: a, Melanerpes aurifrons. b, Piculus rubiginosus. c, Sphyrapicus varius. d, Dryocopus lineatus. e, Melanerpes formicivorus.

1999, Dec. 3

1530 A522 1.50col Vert. strip of 5, #a.-e. 2.10 1.00

Salvadoran Coffee Assoc., 70th Anniv. A523

1999, Dec. 7 *Perf. 14x14¼*

1531 A523 10col multi 2.75 1.40

Millennium A524

2000, Jan. 6 *Perf. 14¼x14*

1532 A524 1.50col multi .45 .20

Fireman's Foundation, 25th Anniv. — A525

Designs: 2.50col, Fireman rescuing child. 25col, Emblem.

2000, Jan. 17 Litho. *Perf. 14¼x14*

1533 A525 2.50col multi .70 .35
1534 A525 25col multi 7.00 3.50

Faith and Happiness Foundation, 30th Anniv. — A526

2000, Feb. 10

1535 A526 1col multi		.30	.20

Millennium A527

#1536: a, El Tazumal Mayan pyramid. b, Christopher Columbus and ships. c, Spanish soldier, native. d, Independence.

#1537: a, Salvadoran White House, 1890. b, Shoppers at street market, 1920. c, Trolley and Nuevo Mundo Hotel, 1924. d, Automobiles on South 2nd Avenue, San Salvador, 1924.

2000 ***Perf. 14x14¼***

Sheets of 4

1536 A527 1.50col #a.-d.		1.75	.90
1537 A527 1.50col #a-d+2 labels		1.60	.80

Issued: #1536, 3/16; #1537, 6/16.

No. 1536 includes two labels.

El Imposible Natl. Park — A528

No. 1538: a, Gate. b, Ocelot (tigrillo). c, Paca (tepezcuintle). d, Venado River waterfalls. e, Black curassow (pajuil). f, Tree with yellow leaves. g, Orchid (flor de encarnación). h, Honeycreeper (torogoz). i, Bird with purple head (siete colores). j, Vegetation near cliff. k, Interpretation center. l, Bird with black and yellow plumage (payasito). m, Frog. n, Mushrooms (hongos). o, Red flower (guaco de tierra). p, Green toucan. q, Hillside foliage. r, Agouti (cotuza). s, Ant bear (oso hormiguero). t, Cascaddes of El Imposible.

2000, Apr. 28 ***Perf. 14¼x14***

1538	Sheet of 20	5.50	2.75
a.-t.	A528 1col Any single	.25	.20

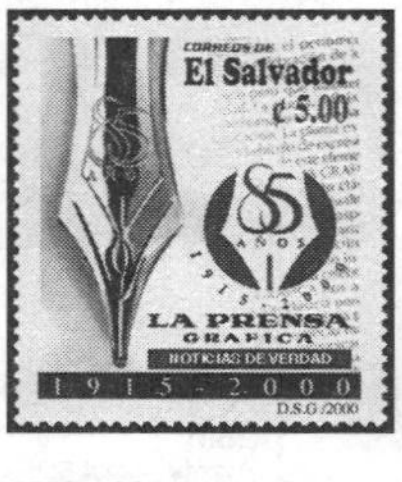

La Prensa Grafica, 85th Anniv. — A529

2000, May 9

1539 A529 5col multi		1.40	.70

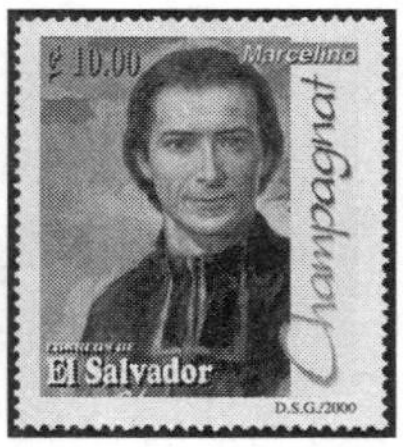

Canonization of Marcelino Champagnat (1789-1840) A530

2000, June 2

1540 A530 10col multi		2.75	1.40

2000 Summer Olympics, Sydney A531

No. 1541: a, Runners. b, Gymnast. c, High jumper. d, Weight lifter. e, Fencer. f, Cyclist. g, Swimmer. h, Shooter. i, Archer. j, Judo.

2000, July 20 ***Perf. 14x14¼***

1541	Sheet of 10	2.75	1.40
a.-j.	A531 1col Any single	.25	.20

Trains A532

No. 1542: a, Baldwin locomotive Philadelphia 58441. b, General Electric locomotive series 65k-15. c, Train car. d, Presidential coach car.

2000, Aug. 3

1542	Vert. strip of 4	1.60	.80
a.-d.	A532 1.50col Any single	.40	.20

block>

World Post Day — A533

2000, Oct. 9 **Litho.** ***Perf. 14¼x14***

1543 A533 5col multi		1.40	.70

Christmas Tree Ornaments A534

No. 1544: a, Snowman. b, Bells. c, Striped pendants. d, Candy cane. e, Candles. f, Sleigh. g, Gifts. h, Santa Claus. i, Santa's hat. j, Santa's boot.

2000, Nov. 9

1544	Block of 10	2.75	1.40
a.-j.	A534 1col Any single	.25	.20

Art by Expatriates A535

Art by: a, Roberto Mejía Ruíz. b, Alex Cuchilla. c, Nicolas Fredy Shi Quán. d, José Bernardo Pacheco. e, Oscar Soles.

2000, Dec. 4 ***Perf. 14x14¼***

1545	Horiz. strip of 5	5.00	2.50
a.-e.	A535 4col Any single	1.00	.50

Pets A536

No. 1546: a, 1.50col, Dogs. b, 1.50col, Dog and cat.

No. 1547: a, 2.50col, Parakeets. b, 2.50col, Dogs, diff.

2001, Feb. 28 **Litho.** ***Perf. 14x14¼***

Vert. Pairs, #a-b

1546-1547 A536	Set of 2	1.90	.95

Starting with Nos. 1546-1547, stamps also show denominations in US dollars.

Saburo Hirao Park, 25th Anniv. A537

Designs: 5col, Playground. 25col, Bridge in gardens.

2001, Mar. 14

1548-1549 A537	Set of 2	7.00	3.50

Claudia Lars (1899-1974), Salvadoran Writer, and Federico Proaño (1848-94), Ecuadoran Writer — A538

2001, Aug. 28 **Litho.** ***Perf. 14x14¼***

1550 A538 10col multi		2.40	1.25

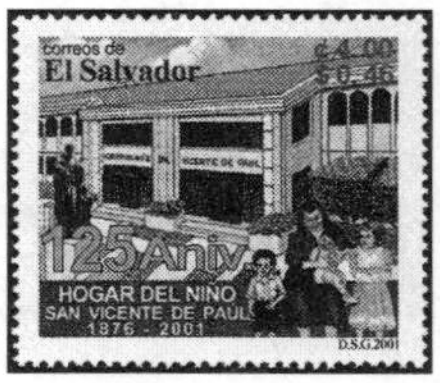

St. Vincent de Paul Children's Home, 125th Anniv. A539

2001, Oct. 26

1551 A539 4col multi		.95	.45

Mushrooms A540

No. 1552: a, Lactaius indigo. b, Pleurotus ostreatus. c, Ramaria sp. d, Clavaria vermicularis.

No. 1553: a, Amanita muscaria. b, Phillipsia sp. c, Russula emetica. d, Geastrum triplex.

2001 ***Perf. 14¼x14***

1552	Horiz. strip of 4	1.40	.70
a.-d.	A540 1.50col Any single	.35	.20
1553	Horiz. strip of 4	4.00	2.00
a.-d.	A540 4col Any single	1.00	.50

AIR POST STAMPS

Regular Issue of 1924-25 Overprinted in Black or Red

Servicio Aéreo

First Printing.

15c on 10c: "15 QUINCE 15" measures 22½mm.

20c: Shows on the back of the stamp an albino impression of the 50c surcharge.

25c on 35c: Original value canceled by a long and short bar.

40c on 50c: Only one printing.

50c on 1col: Surcharge in dull orange red.

Perf. 12½, 14

1929, Dec. 28 **Unwmk.**

C1	A112 20c dp green (Bk)	3.25	3.25
a.	Red overprint	600.00	600.00

Counterfeits exist of No. C1a.

With Additional Surcharge of New Values and Bars in Black or Red

C3	A111 15c on 10c orange	.50	.50
a.	"ALTANT CO"	14.00	14.00
C4	A114 25c on 35c scar & grn	1.25	1.25
a.	Bars inverted	7.50	7.50
C5	A115 40c on 50c org brn	.50	.35
C6	A116 50c on 1col grn & vio (R)	8.00	6.50
	Nos. C1-C6 (5)	13.50	11.85

Second Printing.

15c on 10d: "15 QUINCE 15" measures 20½mm.

20c: Has not the albino impression on the back of the stamp.

25c on 35c: Original value cancelled by two bars of equal length.

50c on 1col: Surcharge in carmine rose.

1930, Jan. 10

C7	A112 20c deep green	.45	.45
C8	A111 15c on 10c org	.45	.45
a.	"ATLANT CO"	17.50	
b.	Double surcharge	10.00	
c.	As "a," double surcharge	75.00	
d.	Pair, one without surcharge	*175.00*	
C9	A114 25c on 35c scar & grn	.40	.40
C10	A116 50c on 1col grn & vio (C)	.90	.90
a.	Without bars over "UN COLON"	2.50	
b.	As "a," without block over "1"	2.50	
	Nos. C7-C10 (4)	2.20	2.20

Numerous wrong font and defective letters exist in both printings of the surcharges.

No. C10 with black surcharge is bogus.

Mail Plane over San Salvador AP1

1930, Sept. 15 **Engr.** ***Perf. 12½***

C11	AP1 15c deep red	.20	.20
C12	AP1 20c emerald	.20	.20
C13	AP1 25c brown violet	.20	.20
C14	AP1 40c ultra	.30	.20
	Nos. C11-C14 (4)	.90	.80

Simón Bolivar — AP2

1930, Dec. 17 Litho. *Perf. 11½*

C15	AP2	15c deep red	3.75	3.50
a.		"15" double	82.50	
C16	AP2	20c emerald	3.75	3.50
C17	AP2	25c brown violet	3.75	3.50
a.		Vert. pair, imperf. btwn.	110.00	
b.		Imperf., pair		
C18	AP2	40c dp ultra	3.75	3.50
		Nos. C15-C18 (4)	15.00	14.00

Centenary of death of Simón Bolivar. Counterfeits of Nos. C15-C18 exist.

No. 504 Overprinted in Red

1931, June 29 Engr. *Perf. 14*

C19	A116	1col green & vio	2.50	2.00

Tower of La Merced Church — AP3

1931, Nov. 5 Litho. *Perf. 11½*

C20	AP3	15c dark red	2.50	2.00
a.		Imperf., pair	50.00	
C21	AP3	20c blue green	2.50	2.00
C22	AP3	25c dull violet	2.50	2.00
a.		Vert. pair, imperf. btwn.	110.00	
C23	AP3	40c ultra	2.50	2.00
a.		Imperf., pair	60.00	
		Nos. C20-C23 (4)	10.00	8.00

120th anniv. of the 1st movement toward the political independence of El Salvador. In the tower of La Merced Church (AP3) hangs the bell which José Matias Delgado-called the Father of his Country-rang to initiate the movement for liberty.

José Matias Delgado AP4

Airplane and Caravels of Columbus AP5

1932, Nov. 12 Wmk. 271 *Perf. 12½*

C24	AP4	15c dull red & vio	.75	.75
C25	AP4	20c blue grn & bl	1.00	1.00
C26	AP4	25c dull vio & brn	1.00	1.00
C27	AP4	40c ultra & grn	1.25	1.25
		Nos. C24-C27 (4)	4.00	4.00

1st centenary of the death of Father José Matías Delgado, who is known as the Father of El Salvadoran Political Emancipation.

Nos. C24-C27 show cheek without shading in the 72nd stamp of each sheet.

1933, Oct. 12 Wmk. 240 *Perf. 13*

C28	AP5	15c red orange	2.00	1.40
C29	AP5	20c blue green	2.00	1.40
C30	AP5	25c lilac	2.00	1.40
C31	AP5	40c ultra	2.00	1.40
C32	AP5	1col black	2.00	1.40
		Nos. C28-C32 (5)	10.00	7.00

Saling of Chistopher Columbus from Palos, Spain, for the New World, 441st anniv

Police Barracks Type

1934, Dec. 16 *Perf. 12½*

C33	A123	25c lilac	.40	.20
C34	A123	30c brown	.60	.30
a.		Imperf., pair	42.50	
C35	A123	1col black	1.50	.65
		Nos. C33-C35 (3)	2.50	1.15

Runner AP7

1935, Mar. 16 Engr. Unwmk.

C36	AP7	15c carmine	3.00	2.75
C37	AP7	25c violet	3.00	2.75
C38	AP7	30c brown	2.50	2.00
C39	AP7	55c blue	15.00	10.00
C40	AP7	1col black	10.00	8.00
		Nos. C36-C40 (5)	33.50	25.50

Third Central American Games.

For overprints and surcharge see Nos. C41-C45, C53.

Same Overprinted in Black HABILITADO

1935, June 27

C41	AP7	15c carmine	3.00	1.25
C42	AP7	25c violet	3.00	1.25
C43	AP7	30c brown	3.00	1.25
C44	AP7	55c blue	22.50	15.00
C45	AP7	1col black	10.00	8.00
		Nos. C41-C45 (5)	41.50	26.75

Flag of El Salvador Type

1935, Oct. 26 Litho. Wmk. 240

C46	A125	30c black brown	.50	.20

Tree of San Vicente Type

1935, Dec. 26 *Perf. 12½*

Numerals in Black, Tree in Yellow Green

C47	A126	10c orange	.80	.70
C48	A126	15c brown	.80	.70
C49	A126	20c dk blue grn	.80	.70
C50	A126	25c dark purple	.80	.70
C51	A126	30c black brown	.80	.70
		Nos. C47-C51 (5)	4.00	3.50

Tercentenary of San Vicente.

No. 565 Overprinted in Red AEREO

1937 Engr. Unwmk.

C52	A133	15c dk olive bis	.20	.20
a.		Double overprint	25.00	

30

No. C44 Surcharged in Red

C53	AP7	30c on 55c blue	1.75	.75

Panchimalco Church — AP10

1937, Dec. 3 Engr. *Perf. 12*

C54	AP10	15c orange yel	.20	.20
C55	AP10	20c green	.20	.20
C56	AP10	25c violet	.20	.20
C57	AP10	30c brown	.20	.20
C58	AP10	40c blue	.20	.20
C59	AP10	1col black	.90	.25
C60	AP10	5col rose carmine	3.00	2.00
		Nos. C54-C60 (7)	4.90	3.25

US Constitution Type of Regular Issue

1938, Apr. 22 Engr. & Litho.

C61	A136	30c multicolored	.60	.50

José Simeón Cañas y Villacorta — AP12

1938, Aug. 18 Engr.

C62	AP12	15c orange	.75	.75
C63	AP12	20c brt green	.90	.75
C64	AP12	30c redsh brown	.90	.75
C65	AP12	1col black	3.00	2.50
		Nos. C62-C65 (4)	5.55	4.75

José Simeón Cañas y Villacorta (1767-1838), liberator of slaves in Central America.

Golden Gate Bridge, San Francisco Bay — AP13

1939, Apr. 14 *Perf. 12½*

C66	AP13	15c dull yel & blk	.20	.20
C67	AP13	30c dk brown & blk	.25	.20
C68	AP13	40c dk blue & blk	.35	.20
		Nos. C66-C68 (3)	.80	.60

Golden Gate Intl. Exposition, San Francisco.

For surcharges see Nos. C86-C91.

Sir Rowland Hill Type

1940, Mar. 1 Engr.

C69	A146	30c dk brn, buff & blk	5.00	1.75
C70	A146	80c org red & blk	13.50	10.50

Centenary of the postage stamp. Covers postmarked Feb. 29 were predated. Actual first day was Mar. 1.

Map of the Americas, Figure of Peace, Plane — AP15

1940, May 22 *Perf. 12*

C71	AP15	30c brown & blue	.25	.20
C72	AP15	80c dk rose & blk	.50	.40

Pan American Union, 50th anniversary.

Coffee Tree in Bloom — AP16

Coffee Tree with Ripe Berries — AP17

1940, Nov. 27

C73	AP16	15c yellow orange	1.00	.20
C74	AP16	20c deep green	1.25	.20
C75	AP16	25c dark violet	1.50	.40
C76	AP17	30c copper brown	2.00	.20
C77	AP17	1col black	6.00	.45
		Nos. C73-C77 (5)	11.75	1.45

Juan Lindo, Gen. Francisco Mallespin and New National University of El Salvador — AP18

Designs (portraits changed): 40c, 80c, Narciso Monterey and Antonio José Canas. 60c, 1col, Isidro Menéndez and Chrisanto Salazar.

1941, Feb. 16 *Perf. 12½*

C78	AP18	20c dk grn & rose lake	.80	.50
C79	AP18	40c ind & brn org	.80	.50
C80	AP18	60c dl pur & brn	.80	.50
C81	AP18	80c hn brn & dk bl grn	2.00	1.40
C82	AP18	1col black & org	2.00	1.40
C83	AP18	2col yel org & rose vio	2.00	1.40
a.		Min. sheet of 6, #C78-C83, perf. 11½	9.25	9.25
		Nos. C78-C83 (6)	8.40	5.70

Centenary of University of El Salvador.

Stamps from No. C83a, perf. 11½, sell for about the same values as the perf. 12½ stamps.

Catalogue values for unused stamps in this section, from this point to the end of the section, are for Never Hinged items.

Map of El Salvador AP20

Wmk. 269

1942, Nov. 25 Engr. *Perf. 14*

C85	AP20	30c red orange	.50	.30
a.		Horiz. pair, imperf. between	100.00	

1st Eucharistic Cong. of El Salvador. See #588.

Nos. C66 to C68 Surcharged with New Values in Dark Carmine **15**

1943 Unwmk. *Perf. 12½*

C86	AP13	15c on 15c dl yel & blk	.30	.20
C87	AP13	20c on 30c dk brn & blk	.40	.30
C88	AP13	25c on 40c dk bl & blk	.65	.50
		Nos. C86-C88 (3)	1.35	1.00

Nos. C66 to C68 Surcharged with New Values in Dark Carmine **15**

1944

C89	AP13	15c on 15c dl yel & blk	.30	.20
C90	AP13	20c on 30c dk brn & blk	.50	.30
C91	AP13	25c on 40c dk bl & blk	.65	.30
		Nos. C89-C91 (3)	1.45	.80

Bridge Type of Regular Issue Arms Overprint at Right in Blue Violet

1944, Nov. 24 Engr.

C92	A149	30c crim rose & blk	.30	.20

No. C92 exists without overprint, but was not issued in that form.

Presidential Palace AP22

National Theater AP23

National Palace AP24

1944, Dec. 22 ***Perf. 12½***

C93 AP22 15c red violet .20 .20
C94 AP23 20c dk blue grn .20 .20
C95 AP24 25c dull violet .20 .20
Nos. C93-C95 (3) .60 .60

For surcharge and overprint see Nos. C145-C146.

No. 582 Overprinted in Red **Aéreo**

1945, Aug. 23 ***Perf. 12***

C96 A137 1col black .60 .20

Juan Ramon Uriarte — AP25

Wmk. 240

1946, Jan. 1 Typo. ***Perf. 12½***

C97 AP25 12c dark blue .20 .20
C98 AP25 14c deep orange .20 .20

Mayan Pyramid, St. Andrés Plantation AP26

Municipal Children's Garden, San Salvador AP27

Civil Aeronautics School, Ilopango Airport AP28

1946, May 1 **Unwmk.**

C99 AP26 30c rose carmine .20 .20
C100 AP27 40c deep ultra .20 .20
C101 AP28 1col black .85 .30
Nos. C99-C101 (3) 1.25 .70

For surcharge see No. C121.

Alberto Masferrer — AP29

1946, July 19 Litho. Wmk. 240

C102 AP29 12c carmine .20 .20
C103 AP29 14c dull green .20 .20
a. Imperf., pair 10.00

Souvenir Sheets

AP30

Designs: 40c, Charles I of Spain. 60c, Juan Manuel Rodriguez. 1col, Arms of San Salvador. 2col, Flag of El Salvador.

Perf. 12, Imperf.

1946, Nov. 8 Engr. Unwmk.

C104 AP30 Sheet of 4 2.50 2.50
a. 40c brown .40 .40
b. 60c carmine .40 .40
c. 1col green .40 .40
d. 2col ultramarine .40 .40

4th cent. of San Salvador's city charter. The imperf. sheets are without gum.

Felipe Soto — AP31

Alfredo Espino — AP32

Wmk. 240

1947, Sept. 11 Litho. ***Perf. 12½***

C106 AP31 12c chocolate .20 .20
C107 AP32 14c dark blue .20 .20

For surcharges see Nos. 627-630.

Arce Type of Regular Issue

1948, Feb. 26 Engr. Unwmk.

C108 A163 12c green .20 .20
C109 A163 14c rose carmine .25 .20
C110 A163 1col violet 2.25 1.40
Nos. C108-C110 (3) 2.70 1.80

Cent. of the death of Manuel José Arce (1783-1847). "Father of Independence" and 1st pres. of the Federation of Central America.

Roosevelt Types of Regular Issue

Designs: 12c, Pres. Franklin D. Roosevelt. 14c, Pres. Roosevelt presenting awards for distinguished service. 20c, Roosevelt and Cordell Hull. 25c, Pres. and Mrs. Roosevelt. 1col, Mackenzie King, Roosevelt and Winston Churchill. 2col, Funeral of Pres. Roosevelt. 4col, Pres. and Mrs. Roosevelt.

1948, Apr. 12 Engr. ***Perf. 12½***

Various Frames, Center in Black

C111 A165 12c green .35 .25
C112 A164 14c olive .35 .25
C113 A164 20c chocolate .35 .25
C114 A164 25c carmine .35 .25
C115 A164 1col violet brn 1.35 .75
C116 A164 2col blue violet 2.25 1.25
Nos. C111-C116 (6) 5.00 3.00

Souvenir Sheet

Perf. 13½

C117 A166 4col gray & brn 4.00 3.00

Nos. 599, 601 and 604 Overprinted in Carmine or Black **Aéreo**

1948, Sept. 7 ***Perf. 12½***

C118 A154 5c slate gray .20 .20
C119 A154 10c bister brown .20 .20
C120 A154 1col scarlet (Bk) 1.20 .50
Nos. C118-C120 (3) 1.60 .90

No. C99 Surcharged in Black

1949, July 23

C121 AP26 10(c) on 30c rose car .20 .20

UPU Type of Regular Issue

1949, Oct. 9 Engr. ***Perf. 12½***

C122 A167 5c brown .35 .20
C123 A167 10c black .50 .20
C124 A167 1col purple 14.50 11.50
Nos. C122-C124 (3) 15.35 11.90

Flag and Arms of El Salvador — AP38

1949, Dec. 15 ***Perf. 10½***

Flag and Arms in Blue, Yellow and Green

C125 AP38 5c ocher .20 .20
C126 AP38 10c dk green .20 .20
a. Yellow omitted 20.00
C127 AP38 15c violet .25 .20
C128 AP38 1col rose .55 .40
C129 AP38 5col red violet 5.00 3.75
Nos. C125-C129 (5) 6.20 4.75

1st anniv. of the Revolution of 12/14/48.

Isabella I of Spain — AP39

Flag, Torch and Scroll — AP40

1951, Apr. 28 Litho. Unwmk.

Background in Ultramarine, Red and Yellow

C130 AP39 10c green .30 .20
C131 AP39 20c purple .30 .20
a. Horiz. pair, imperf. between 25.00
C132 AP39 40c rose carmine .35 .20
C133 AP39 1col black brown 1.25 .50
Nos. C130-C133 (4) 2.20 1.10

500th anniv. of the birth of Queen Isabella I of Spain. Nos. C130-C133 exist imperforate.

1952, Feb. 14 Photo. ***Perf. 11½***

Flag in Blue

C134 AP40 10c brt blue .20 .20
C135 AP40 15c chocolate .20 .20
C136 AP40 20c deep blue .20 .20
C137 AP40 25c gray .20 .20
C138 AP40 40c purple .30 .20
C139 AP40 1col red orange .65 .35
C140 AP40 2col orange brn 2.25 1.75
C141 AP40 5col violet blue 2.25 .90
Nos. C134-C141 (8) 6.25 4.00

Constitution of 1950.

Marti Type of Regular Issue Inscribed "Aereo"

1953, Feb. 27 Litho. ***Perf. 10½***

C142 A170 10c dk purple .25 .20
C143 A170 20c dull brown .35 .20
C144 A170 1col dull orange 1.25 .35
Nos. C142-C144 (3) 1.85 .75

No. C95 Surcharged "C 0.20" and Obliterations in Red

1953, Mar. 20 ***Perf. 12½***

C145 AP24 20c on 25c dl vio .30 .20

No. C95 Overprinted in Carmine

"IV Congreso Medico Social Panamericano 16 / 19 Abril, 1953"

1953, June 19

C146 AP24 25c dull violet .40 .20

See note after No. 634.

Bell Tower, La Merced Church AP42

1953, Sept. 15 ***Perf. 11½***

C147 AP42 5c rose pink .20 .20
C148 AP42 10c dp blue grn .20 .20
C149 AP42 20c blue .20 .20
C150 AP42 1col purple .95 .50
Nos. C147-C150 (4) 1.55 1.10

132nd anniv. of the Act of Independence, Sept. 15, 1821.

Postage Types and

Fishing Boats — AP43

Gen. Manuel José Arce — AP44

ODECA Officials and Flag AP46

#C155, National Palace. #C157, Coast guard boat. #C158, Lake Ilopango. #C160, Guayabo dam. #C161, Housing development. #C162, Modern highway. #C164, Izalco volcano.

Perf. 11½

1954, June 1 Unwmk. Photo.

C151 AP43 5c org brn & cr .20 .20
C152 A175 5c brt carmine .20 .20
C153 AP44 10c gray blue .25 .20
C154 A176 10c pur & lt brn .25 .20
C155 AP43 10c ol & bl gray .25 .20
C156 AP46 10c bl grn, dk grn & bl .25 .20
C157 AP43 10c rose carmine .30 .20
C158 AP43 15c dk gray .35 .20
C159 A173 20c pur & gray .40 .20
C160 AP46 25c bl grn & bl .45 .20
C161 AP46 30c mag & sal .50 .20
C162 A176 40c brt org & brn .60 .25
C163 A174 80c red brown 1.40 .90
C164 AP43 1col magenta & sal 1.60 .90
C165 A174 2col orange 3.00 .90
Nos. C151-C165 (15) 10.00 5.15

Barrios Type of Regular Issue

Wmk. 269

1955, Dec. 20 Engr. ***Perf. 12½***

C166 A177 20c brown .25 .25
C167 A177 30c dp red lilac .30 .25

Santa Ana Type of Regular Issue

Perf. 13½

1956, June 20 Unwmk. Litho.

C168 A178 5c orange brown .20 .20
C169 A178 10c green .20 .20
C170 A178 40c red lilac .25 .20
C171 A178 80c emerald .60 .35
C172 A178 5col gray blue 3.25 1.75
Nos. C168-C172 (5) 4.50 2.70

For overprint see No. C187.

Chalatenango Type of Regular Issue

1956, Sept. 14

C173 A179 10c brt rose .20 .20
C174 A179 15c orange .20 .20
C175 A179 20c lt olive grn .20 .20
C176 A179 25c dull purple .30 .20
C177 A179 50c orange brn .50 .40
C178 A179 1col brt vio bl .85 .65
Nos. C173-C178 (6) 2.25 1.85

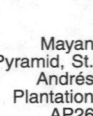

Nueva San Salvador Type

Wmk. 269

1957, Jan. 3 Engr. *Perf. 12½*

C179 A180 10c pink .20 .20
C180 A180 20c dull red .20 .20
C181 A180 50c pale org red .30 .20
C182 A180 1col lt green .75 .35
C183 A180 2col orange red 1.90 1.00
Nos. C179-C183 (5) 3.35 1.95

For overprints see Nos. C195, C198.

Lemus' Visit Type of Regular Issue

Perf. 11½

1959, Dec. 14 Unwmk. Photo.

Granite Paper

Design in Ultramarine, Dark Brown Light Brown and Red

C184 A182 15c red .20 .20
C185 A182 20c green .25 .20
C186 A182 30c carmine .30 .20
Nos. C184-C186 (3) .75 .60

No. C169 Overprinted in Red: "ANO MUNDIAL DE LOS REFUGIADOS 1959-1960"

1960, Apr. 7 Litho. *Perf. 13½*

C187 A178 10c green .25 .20

World Refugee Year, 7/1/59-6/30/60.

Poinsettia Type of Regular Issue

Perf. 11½

1960, Dec. 17 Unwmk. Photo.

Granite Paper

Design in Slate Green, Red and Yellow

C188 A184 20c rose lilac .30 .20
C189 A184 30c gray .30 .20
C190 A184 40c light gray .35 .20
C191 A184 50c salmon pink .55 .40
Nos. C188-C191 (4) 1.50 1.00

Miniature Sheet

Imperf

C192 A184 60c gold .65 .35

See note after No. 718.
For surcharge see No. C196.

Nos. 672, 691 and C183 Overprinted: "III Exposición Industrial Centroamericana Diciembre de 1962" with "AEREO" Added on Nos. 672, 691

1962, Dec. 21 *Perf. 11½, 12½*

C193 A174 1col brn org, dk brn & bl 1.00 .75
C194 A180 1col dull red .50 .35
C195 A180 2col orange red 1.00 .65
Nos. C193-C195 (3) 2.50 1.75

3rd Central American Industrial Exposition.
For surcharges see Nos. C197, C199.

Nos. C189, C194, C182 and C195 Surcharged

1963

C196 A184 10c on 30c multi .20 .20
C197 A180 10c on 1col dl red .20 .20
C198 A180 10c on 1col lt grn 1.10 .25
C199 A180 10c on 2col org red 1.10 .25
Nos. C196-C199 (4) 2.60 .90

Surcharges include: "X" on No. C196; two dots and bar at bottom on No. C197. Heavy bar at bottom on No. C198. On No. C199, the four-line "Exposition" overprint is lower than on No. C195.

Turquoise-browed Motmot — AP49

Birds: 5c, King vulture (vert., like No. 741). 6c, Yellow-headed parrot, vert. 10c, Spotted-breasted oriole. 30c, Greattailed grackle. 40c, Great curassow, vert. 50c, Magpie-jay. 80c, Golden-fronted woodpecker, vert.

1963 Unwmk. Photo. *Perf. 11½*

Birds in Natural Colors

C200 AP49 5c gray grn & blk .20 .20
C201 AP49 6c tan & blue .20 .20
C202 AP49 10c lt bl & blk .20 .20
C203 AP49 20c gray & brn .25 .20
C204 AP49 30c ol bis & blk .35 .20
C205 AP49 40c pale & dk vio .50 .20
C206 AP49 50c lt grn & blk .55 .25
C207 AP49 80c vio bl & blk 1.00 .55
Nos. C200-C207 (8) 3.25 2.00

Eucharistic Congress Type

1964-65 *Perf. 12x11½*

C208 A188 10c slate grn & bl .20 .20
C209 A188 25c red & blue .20 .20

Miniature Sheets

Imperf

C210 A188 80c blue & green .65 .65
a. Marginal ovpt. La Union .85 .85
b. Marginal ovpt. Usulutan .85 .85
c. Marginal ovpt. La Libertad .85 .85

See note after No. 746.
Issued: #C208-C210, Apr. 16, 1964; #C210a-C210b, June 22, 1965; #210c, Jan. 28, 1965.
For overprints see Nos. C232, C238.

Kennedy Type of Regular Issue

1964, Nov. 22 *Perf. 11½x12*

C211 A189 15c gray & blk .20 .20
C212 A189 20c sage grn & blk .25 .20
C213 A189 40c yellow & blk .40 .20
Nos. C211-C213 (3) .85 .60

Miniature Sheet

Imperf

C214 A189 80c grnsh bl & blk 1.00 .75

For overprint see No. C259.

Flower Type of Regular Issue

1965, Jan. 6 Photo. *Perf. 12x11½*

C215 A190 10c Rose .20 .20
C216 A190 15c Platanillo .20 .20
C217 A190 25c San Jose .20 .20
C218 A190 40c Hibiscus .25 .20
C219 A190 45c Veranera .40 .20
C220 A190 70c Fire flower .55 .30
Nos. C215-C220 (6) 1.80 1.30

For overprint and surcharges see Nos. C243, C348-C349.

ICY Type of Regular Issue

Perf. 11½x12

1965, Apr. 27 Photo. Unwmk.

Design in Brown and Gold

C221 A191 15c light blue .20 .20
C222 A191 30c dull lilac .20 .20
C223 A191 50c ocher .30 .20
Nos. C221-C223 (3) .70 .60

For overprints see Nos. C227, C244, C312.

Gavidia Type of Regular Issue

1965, Sept. 24 Photo. Unwmk.

Portraits in Natural Colors

C224 A192 10c black & green .20 .20
C225 A192 20c black & bister .25 .20
C226 A192 1col black & rose 1.25 .50
Nos. C224-C226 (3) 1.70 .90

No. C223 Overprinted in Green: "1865 / 12 de Octubre / 1965 / Dr. Manuel Enrique Araujo"

1965, Oct. 12 *Perf. 11½x12*

C227 A191 50c brn, ocher & gold .45 .40

See note after No. 764.

Fair Type of Regular Issue

1965, Nov. 5 *Perf. 12x11½*

C228 A193 20c blue & multi .20 .20
C229 A193 80c multi .65 .40
C230 A193 5col multi 3.25 2.25
Nos. C228-C230 (3) 4.10 2.85

For overprint see No. C311.

WHO Type of Regular Issue

1966, May 20 Photo. Unwmk.

C231 A194 50c multicolored .40 .20

For overprints see Nos. C242, C245.

No. C209 Overprinted in Dark Green: "1816 1966 / 150 años / Nacimiento / San Juan Bosco"

1966, Sept. 3 Photo. *Perf. 12x11½*

C232 A188 25c red & blue .30 .25

150th anniv. of the birth of St. John Bosco (1815-88), Italian priest, founder of the Salesian Fathers and Daughters of Mary.

UNESCO Type of Regular Issue

1966, Nov. 4 Photo. *Perf. 12*

C233 A195 30c tan, blk & vio bl .30 .20
C234 A195 2col emer, blk & vio bl 1.60 1.00

For surcharge see No. C352.

Fair Type of Regular Issue

1966, Nov. 27 Litho. *Perf. 12*

C235 A196 15c multicolored .20 .20
C236 A196 20c multicolored .20 .20
C237 A196 60c multicolored .50 .35
Nos. C235-C237 (3) .90 .75

No. C209 Overprinted: "IX-Congreso / Interamericano / de Educacion / Católica / 4 Enero 1967"

1967, Jan. 4 Photo. *Perf. 12x11½*

C238 A188 25c red & blue .30 .25

Issued to publicize the 9th Inter-American Congress for Catholic Education.

Cañas Type of Regular Issue

1967, Feb. 18 Litho. *Perf. 11½*

C239 A197 5c multicolored .20 .20
C240 A197 45c lt bl & multi .55 .35

For surcharges see Nos. C403-C405.

Volcano Type of Regular Issue

1967, Apr. 14 Photo. *Perf. 13*

C241 A198 50c ol gray & brn .50 .25

For surcharges see Nos. C320, C350

No. C231 Overprinted in Red: "VIII CONGRESO / CENTROAMERICANO DE / FARMACIA & B10QUIMICA / 5 di 11 Noviembre de 1967"

1967, Oct. 26 Photo. *Perf. 12x11½*

C242 A194 50c multicolored .45 .40

Issued to publicize the 8th Central American Congress for Pharmacy and Biochemistry.

No. C217 Overprinted in Red: "I Juegos / Centroamericanos y del / Caribe de Basquetbol / 25 Nov. al 3 Dic. 1967"

1967, Nov. 15

C243 A190 25c bl, yel & grn .25 .25

First Central American and Caribbean Basketball Games, Nov. 25-Dec. 3.

No. C222 Overprinted in Carmine: "1968 / AÑO INTERNACIONAL DE / LOS DERECHOS HUMANOS"

1968, Jan. 2 Photo. *Perf. 11½x12*

C244 A191 30c dl lil, brn & gold .40 .30

International Human Rights Year 1968.

No. C231 Overprinted in Red: "1968 / XX ANIVERSARIO DE LA / ORGANIZACION MUNDIAL / DE LA SALUD"

1968, Apr. 7 *Perf. 12x11½*

C245 A194 50c multicolored .50 .50

20th anniv. of WHO.

No. C229 Overprinted in Red: "1968 / Año / del Sistema / del Crédito / Rural"

1968, May 6 Photo. *Perf. 12x11½*

C246 A193 80c multicolored .65 .50

Rural credit system.

Masferrer Type of Regular Issue

1968, June 22 Litho. *Perf. 12x11½*

C247 A200 5c brown & multi .20 .20
C248 A200 15c green & multi .20 .20

For overprint see No. C297.

Scouts Hiking AP50

1968, July 26 Litho. *Perf. 12*

C249 AP50 10c multicolored .20 .20

Issued to publicize the 7th Inter-American Boy Scout Conference, July-Aug., 1968.

Presidents' Meeting Type

1968, Dec. 5 Litho. *Perf. 14½*

C250 A202 20c salmon & multi .20 .20
C251 A202 1col lt blue & multi .75 .50

Butterfly Type of Regular Issue

Designs: Various butterflies.

1969 Litho. *Perf. 12*

C252 A203 20c multi .20 .20
C253 A203 1col multi .65 .35
C254 A203 2col multi 1.60 1.00
C255 A203 10col gray & multi 8.00 5.00
Nos. C252-C255 (4) 10.45 6.55

For surcharge see No. C353.

Red Cross, Crescent and Lion and Sun Emblems AP51

1969 Litho. *Perf. 11*

C256 AP51 30c yellow & multi .25 .20
C257 AP51 1col multicolored .85 .50
C258 AP51 4col multicolored 3.25 2.50
Nos. C256-C258 (3) 4.35 3.20

League of Red Cross Societies, 50th anniv.
For surcharges see Nos. C351, C354.

No. C213 Overprinted in Green: "Alunizaje / Apolo-11 / 21 Julio / 1969"

1969, Sept. Photo. *Perf. 11½x12*

C259 A189 40c yellow & blk .30 .30

Man's 1st landing on the moon, July 20, 1969. See note after US No. C76.
The same overprint in red brown and pictures of the landing module and the astronauts on the moon were applied to the margin of No. C214.

Hospital Type of Regular Issue

Benjamin Bloom Children's Hospital.

1969, Oct. 24 Litho. *Perf. 11½*

C260 A205 1col multi .85 .50
C261 A205 2col multi 1.60 1.00
C262 A205 5col multi 4.25 2.50
Nos. C260-C262 (3) 6.70 4.00

For surcharge see No. C355.

ILO Type of Regular Issue

1969 Litho. *Perf. 13*

C263 A206 50c lt bl & multi .40 .20

Tourist Type of Regular Issue

Views: 20c, Devil's Gate. 35c, Ichanmichen Spa. 60c, Aerial view of Acajutla Harbor.

1969, Dec. 19 Photo. *Perf. 12x11½*

C264 A207 20c black & multi .20 .20
C265 A207 35c black & multi .30 .20
C266 A207 60c black & multi .50 .40
Nos. C264-C266 (3) 1.00 .80

Insect Type of Regular Issue, 1970

1970, Feb. 24 Litho. *Perf. 11½x11*

C267 A208 2col Bee 1.60 1.00
C268 A208 3col Elaterida 2.50 1.50
C269 A208 4col Praying mantis 3.25 2.00
Nos. C267-C269 (3) 7.35 4.50

For surcharges see Nos. C371-C373.

Human Rights Type of Regular Issue

20c, 80c, Map and arms of Salvador and National Unity emblem similar to A209, but vert.

1970, Apr. 14 Litho. *Perf. 14*

C270 A209 20c blue & multi .20 .20
C271 A209 80c blue & multi .80 .40

For overprint & surcharge see #C301, C402.

Army Type of Regular Issue

Designs: 20c, Fighter plane. 40c, Gun and crew. 50c, Patrol boat.

1970, May 7 *Perf. 12*

C272 A210 20c gray & multi .20 .20
C273 A210 40c green & multi .35 .20
C274 A210 50c blue & multi .45 .20
Nos. C272-C274 (3) 1.00 .60

For overprint see No. C310.

Brazilian Team, Jules Rimet Cup — AP52

Soccer teams and Jules Rimet Cup.

1970, May 25 Litho. *Perf. 12*

C275 AP52 1col Belgium	1.00	.65
C276 AP52 1col Brazil	1.00	.65
C277 AP52 1col Bulgaria	2.00	1.00
C278 AP52 1col Czechoslovakia	1.00	.65
C279 AP52 1col Germany (Fed. Rep.)	1.00	.65
C280 AP52 1col Britain	1.00	.65
C281 AP52 1col Israel	1.00	.65
C282 AP52 1col Italy	1.00	.65
C283 AP52 1col Mexico	1.00	.65
C284 AP52 1col Morocco	1.00	.65
C285 AP52 1col Peru	1.00	.65
C286 AP52 1col Romania	1.00	.65
C287 AP52 1col Russia	1.00	.65
C288 AP52 1col Salvador	1.00	.65
C289 AP52 1col Sweden	1.00	.65
C290 AP52 1col Uruguay	1.00	.65
Nos. C275-C290 (16)	17.00	10.75

9th World Soccer Championships for the Jules Rimet Cup, Mexico City, 5/30-6/21/70.

For overprints see Nos. C325-C340.

Lottery Type of Regular Issue

1970, July 15 Litho. *Perf. 12*

C291 A211 80c multi .65 .25

Education Year Type of Regular Issue

1970, Sept. 11 Litho. *Perf. 12*

C292 A212 20c pink & multi .20 .20
C293 A212 2col buff & multi 1.60 1.00

Fair Type of Regular Issue

1970, Oct. 28 Litho. *Perf. 12*

C294 A213 20c multi .25 .20
C295 A213 30c yel & multi .35 .20

Music Type of Regular Issue

Johann Sebastian Bach, harp, horn, music.

1971, Feb. 22 Litho. *Perf. 13½*

C296 A214 40c gray & multi .40 .20

For overprint see No. C313.

No. C247 Overprinted: "Año / del Centenario de la / Biblioteca Nacional / 1970"

1970, Nov. 25 *Perf. 12x11½*

C297 A200 5c brn & multi .20 .20

Miss Tourism Type of Regular Issue

1971, Apr. 1 Litho. *Perf. 14*

C298 A215 20c lil & multi .20 .20
C299 A215 60c gray & multi .45 .30

Pietà Type of Regular Issue

1971, May 10

C300 A216 40c lt yel grn & vio brn .30 .20

No. C270 Overprinted in Red Like No. 823

1971, July 6 Litho. *Perf. 14*

C301 A209 20c bl & multi .20 .25

Fish Type of Regular Issue

30c, Smalltooth sawfish. 1col, Atlantic sailfish.

1971, July 28

C302 A217 30c lilac & multi .20 .25
C303 A217 1col multi .65 .50

Independence Type of Regular Issue

Designs: Various sections of Declaration of Independence of Central America.

1971 Litho. *Perf. 13½x13*

C304 A218 30c bl & blk .20 .20
C305 A218 40c brn & blk .30 .20
C306 A218 50c yel & blk .35 .25
C307 A218 60c gray & blk .50 .35
a. Souvenir sheet of 8 1.75 1.60
Nos. C304-C307 (4) 1.35 1.00

No. C307a contains 8 stamps with simulated perforations similar to Nos. 826-829, C304-C307.

For overprints see Nos. C311, C347.

Church Type of Regular Issue

15c, Metapan Church. 70c, Panchimalco Church.

1971, Aug. 21 Litho. *Perf. 13x13½*

C308 A219 15c ol & multi .20 .20
C309 A219 70c multi .55 .35

No. C274 Overprinted in Red

1971, Oct. 12 Litho. *Perf. 12*

C310 A210 50c bl & multi .40 .30

National Navy, 20th anniversary.

No. C229 Overprinted: "V Feria / Internacional / 3-20 Noviembre / de 1972"

1972, Nov. 3 Photo. *Perf. 12x11½*

C311 A193 80c multi .90 .50

5th Intl. Fair, El Salvador, Nov. 3-20.

No. C223 Overprinted in Red

1972, Nov. 30 Photo. *Perf. 11½x12*

C312 A191 50c ocher, brn & gold .40 .30

30th anniversary of the Inter-American Institute for Agricultural Sciences.

No. C296 Overprinted

1973, Feb. 5 Litho. *Perf. 13½*

C313 A214 40c gray & multi .30 .25

3rd International Music Festival, Feb. 9-29.

Lions Type of Regular Issue

Designs: 20c, 40c, Map of El Salvador and Lions International Emblem.

1973, Feb. 20 Litho. *Perf. 13*

C314 A220 20c gray & multi .20 .20
C315 A220 40c multi .30 .20

Olympic Type of Regular Issue

Designs: 20c, Javelin, women's. 80c, Discus, women's. 1col, Hammer throw. 2col, Shot put.

1973, May 21 Litho. *Perf. 13*

C316 A221 20c lt grn & multi .20 .20
C317 A221 80c sal & multi .55 .35
C318 A221 1col ultra & multi .65 .55
C319 A221 2col multi 1.40 .90
Nos. C316-C319 (4) 2.80 2.00

No. C241 Surcharged Like No. 841

1973, Dec. Photo. *Perf. 13*

C320 A198 25c on 50c multi .20 .20

No. C307a Overprinted: "Centenario / Cuidad / Santiago de Maria / 1874 1974"

Souvenir Sheet

1974, Mar. 7 Litho. *Imperf.*

C321 A218 Sheet of 8 1.00 1.00

Centenary of the City Santiago de Maria. The overprint is so arranged that each line appears on a different pair of stamps.

No. C231 Surcharged in Red

1974, Apr. 22 Photo. *Perf. 12x11½*

C322 A194 25c on 50c multi .20 .20

No. C229 Surcharged

1974, Apr. 24

C323 A193 10c on 80c multi .20 .20

Rehabilitation Type

1974, Apr. 30 Litho. *Perf. 13*

C324 A222 25c multi .20 .20

Nos. C275-C290 Overprinted

1974, June 4 Litho. *Perf. 12*

C325 AP52 1col Belgium	.65	.50
C326 AP52 1col Brazil	.65	.50
C327 AP52 1col Bulgaria	.65	.50
C328 AP52 1col Czech.	.65	.50
C329 AP52 1col Germany	.65	.50
C330 AP52 1col Britain	.65	.50
C331 AP52 1col Israel	.65	.50
C332 AP52 1col Italy	.65	.50
C333 AP52 1col Mexico	.65	.50
C334 AP52 1col Morocco	.65	.50
C335 AP52 1col Peru	.65	.50
C336 AP52 1col Romania	.65	.50
C337 AP52 1col Russia	.65	.50
C338 AP52 1col Salvador	.65	.50
C339 AP52 1col Sweden	.65	.50
C340 AP52 1col Uruguay	.65	.50
Nos. C325-C340 (16)	10.40	8.00

World Cup Soccer Championship, Munich, June 13-July 7.

INTERPOL Type of 1974

1974, Sept. 2 Litho. *Perf. 12½*

C341 A223 25c multi .20 .20

FAO Type of 1974

1974, Sept. 2 Litho. *Perf. 12½*

C342 A224 25c bl, dk bl & gold .20 .20

Coin Type of 1974

1974, Nov. 19 Litho. *Perf. 12½x13*

C343 A225 20c 1p silver, 1892 .20 .20
C344 A225 40c 20c silver, 1828 .30 .20
C345 A225 50c 20p gold, 1892 .50 .25
C346 A225 60c 20col gold, 1925 .50 .35
Nos. C343-C346 (4) 1.50 1.00

No. C307a Overprinted: "X ASAMBLEA GENERAL DE LA CONFERENCIA / INTERAMERICANA DE SEGURIDAD SOCIAL Y XX / REUNION DEL COMITE PERMANENTE INTERAMERICANO / DE SEGURIDAD SOCIAL, 24 -- 30 NOVIEMBRE 1974"

1974, Nov. 18 Litho. *Imperf.*

Souvenir Sheet

C347 A218 Sheet of 8 1.75 1.75

Social Security Conference, El Salvador, Nov. 24-30. The overprint is so arranged that each line appears on a different pair of stamps.

Issues of 1965-69 Surcharged

a

b

c

d

1974-75

C348 A190(a) 10c on 45c #C219	.20	.20
C349 A190(a) 10c on 70c #C220	.20	.20
C350 A198(b) 10c on 50c #C241	.20	.20
C351 AP51(d) 25c on 1col #C257	.20	.20
C352 A195(c) 25c on 2col #C234 ('75)	.30	.20
C353 A203(d) 25c on 2col #C254 ('75)	.20	.20
C354 AP51(d) 25c on 4col #C258	.20	.20
C355 A205(d) 25c on 5col #C262	.20	.20
Nos. C348-C355 (8)	1.70	1.60

No. C353 has new value at left and 6 vertical bars. No. C355 has 7 vertical bars.

UPU Type of 1975

1975, Jan. 22 Litho. *Perf. 13*

C356 A226 25c bl & multi .20 .20
C357 A226 30c bl & multi .25 .20

Acajutla Harbor Type of 1975

1975, Feb. 17

C358 A227 15c bl & multi .20 .20

Post Office Type of 1975

1975, Apr. 25 Litho. *Perf. 13*

C359 A228 25c bl & multi .20 .20

Miss Universe Type of 1975

1975, June 25 *Perf. 12½*

C360 A229 25c multi .20 .20
C361 A229 60c lil & multi .50 .40

Women's Year Type and

IWY Emblem — AP53

1975, Sept. 4 Litho. *Perf. 12½*
C362 A230 15c bl & bl blk .20 .20
C363 AP53 25c yel grn & blk .20 .20

International Women's Year 1975.

Nurse Type of 1975

1975, Oct. 24 Litho. *Perf. 12½*
C364 A231 25c lt blue & multi .20 .20

Printers' Congress Type

1975, Nov. 19 Litho. *Perf. 12½*
C365 A232 30c green & multi .25 .25

Dermatologists' Congress Type

1975, Nov. 28
C366 A233 20c blue & multi .20 .20
C367 A233 30c red & multi .25 .20

Caritas Type of 1975

1975, Dec. 18 Litho. *Perf. 13½*
C368 A234 20c bl & vio bl .20 .20

UNICEF Emblem — AP54

1975, Dec. 18
C369 AP54 15c lt grn & sil .20 .20
C370 AP54 20c dl rose & sil .20 .20

UNICEF, 25th anniv. (in 1971).

Nos. C267-C269 Surcharged

1976, Jan. 14 *Perf. 11½x11*
C371 A208 25c on 2col multi .20 .20
C372 A208 25c on 3col multi .20 .20
C373 A208 25c on 4col multi .20 .20
Nos. C371-C373 (3) .60 .60

Caularthron Bilamellatum AP55

Designs: Orchids.

1976, Feb. 19 Litho. *Perf. 12½*
C374 AP55 25c *shown* .20 .20
C375 AP55 25c *Oncidium oliganthum* .20 .20
C376 AP55 25c *Epidendrum radicans* .20 .20
C377 AP55 25c *Epidendrum vitellinum* .20 .20
C378 AP55 25c *Cyrtopodium punctatum* .20 .20
C379 AP55 25c *Pleurothallis schiedei* .20 .20
C380 AP55 25c *Lycaste cruenta* .20 .20
C381 AP55 25c *Spiranthes speciosa* .20 .20
Nos. C374-C381 (8) 1.60 1.60

CIAT Type of 1976

1976, May 18 Litho. *Perf. 12½*
C382 A235 50c org & multi .40 .20

Bicentennial Types of 1976

1976, June 30 Litho. *Perf. 12½*
C383 A236 25c multi .20 .20
C384 A237 5col multi 3.75 2.50

Reptile Type of 1976

Reptiles: 15c, Green fence lizard. 25c, Basilisk. 60c, Star lizard.

1976, Sept. 23 Litho. *Perf. 12½*
C385 A238 15c multi .20 .20
C386 A238 25c multi .20 .20
C387 A238 60c multi .45 .45
Nos. C385-C387 (3) .85 .85

Archaeology Type of 1976

Pre-Columbian Art: 25c, Brazier with pre-classical head, El Trapiche. 50c, Kettle with pre-classical head, Atiquizaya. 70c, Classical whistling vase, Tazumal.

1976, Oct. 11 Litho. *Perf. 12½*
C388 A239 25c multi .20 .20
C389 A239 50c multi .40 .25
C390 A239 70c multi .55 .40
Nos. C388-C390 (3) 1.15 .85

For overprint see No. C429.

Fair Type of 1976

1976, Oct. 25 Litho. *Perf. 12½*
C391 A240 25c multi .20 .20
C392 A240 70c yel & multi .55 .40

Christmas Type of 1976

1976, Dec. 16 Litho. *Perf. 11*
C393 A241 25c bl & multi .20 .20
C394 A241 50c multi .40 .25
C395 A241 60c multi .50 .30
C396 A241 75c red & multi .60 .40
Nos. C393-C396 (4) 1.70 1.15

Rotary Type of 1977

1977, June 20 Litho. *Perf. 11*
C397 A242 25c multi .20 .20
C398 A242 1col multi .80 .50

Industrial Type of 1977

Designs: 25c, Radar station, Izalco (vert.). 50c, Central sugar refinery, Jiboa. 75c, Cerron Grande hydroelectric station.

1977, June 29 *Perf. 12½*
C399 A243 25c multi .20 .20
C400 A243 50c multi .40 .20
C401 A243 75c multi .60 .40
Nos. C399-C401 (3) 1.20 .80

Nos. C399-C401 have colorless overprint in multiple rows: GOBIERNO DEL SALVADOR.

Nos. C271 and C239 Surcharged with New Value and Bar

1977 *Perf. 14, 11½*
C402 A209 25c on 80c multi .20 .20
C403 A197 30c on 5c multi .25 .20
C404 A197 40c on 5c multi .30 .20
C405 A197 50c on 5c multi .40 .25
Nos. C402-C405 (4) 1.15 .85

Broadcasting Type of 1977

1977, Sept. 14 Litho. *Perf. 14*
C406 A244 20c multi .20 .20
C407 A244 25c multi .20 .20

Symbolic Chessboard and Emblem — AP56

1977, Oct. 20 Litho. *Perf. 11*
C408 AP56 25c multi .20 .20
C409 AP56 50c multi .40 .25

El Salvador's victory in International Chess Olympiad, Tripoli, Libya, Oct. 24-Nov. 15, 1976.

Soccer AP57

Boxing AP58

1977, Nov. 16 Litho. *Perf. 16*
C410 AP57 10c shown .20 .20
C411 AP57 10c Basketball .20 .20
C412 AP57 15c Javelin .20 .20
C413 AP57 15c Weight lifting .20 .20
C414 AP57 20c Volleyball .20 .20
C415 AP58 20c shown .20 .20
C416 AP57 25c Baseball .20 .20
C417 AP58 25c Softball .20 .20
C418 AP58 30c Swimming .25 .20
C419 AP58 30c Fencing .25 .20
C420 AP58 40c Bicycling .30 .25
C421 AP58 50c Rifle shooting .40 .30
C422 AP58 50c Women's tennis .40 .30
C423 AP57 60c Judo .50 .35
C424 AP58 75c Wrestling .60 .40
C425 AP58 1col Equestrian hurdles .80 .50
C426 AP58 1col Woman gymnast .80 .50
C427 AP58 2col Table tennis 1.60 1.00
Nos. C410-C427 (18) 7.50 5.60

Size: 100x119mm

C428 AP57 5col Games' poster 4.00 4.00

2nd Central American Olympic Games, San Salvador, Nov. 25-Dec. 4.

No. C390 Overprinted in Red: "CENTENARIO / CIUDAD DE / CHALCHUAPA / 1878-1978"

1978, Feb. 13 Litho. *Perf. 12½*
C429 A239 70c multi .55 .55

Centenary of Chalchuapa.

Map of South America, Argentina '78 Emblem AP59

1978, Aug. 15 Litho. *Perf. 11*
C430 AP59 25c multi .20 .20
C431 AP59 60c multi .50 .40
C432 AP59 5col multi 4.00 3.00
Nos. C430-C432 (3) 4.70 3.60

11th World Cup Soccer Championship, Argentina, June 1-25.

Musical Instrument Type

Designs: 25c, Drum, vert. 50c, Hollow rattles. 80c, Xylophone.

1978, Aug. 29 *Perf. 12½*
C433 A245 25c multi .20 .20
C434 A245 50c multi .40 .20
C435 A245 80c multi .60 .40
Nos. C433-C435 (3) 1.20 .80

For surcharge see No. C492.

Engineering Type of 1978

1978, Sept. 12 Litho. *Perf. 13½*
C436 A246 25c multi .20 .20

Izalco Station Type of 1978

1978, Sept. 14 *Perf. 12½*
C437 A247 75c multi .60 .40

Softball, Bat and Globes AP60

1978, Oct. 17 Litho. *Perf. 12½*
C438 AP60 25c pink & multi .20 .20
C439 AP60 1col yel & multi .80 .50

4th World Softball Championship for Women, San Salvador, Oct. 13-22.

Fair Type, 1978

1978, Oct. 30 Litho. *Perf. 12½*
C440 A248 15c multi .20 .20
C441 A248 25c multi .20 .20

Red Cross Type, 1978

1978, Oct. 30 Litho. *Perf. 11*
C442 A249 25c multi .20 .20

Cotton Conference Type, 1978

1978, Nov. 22 *Perf. 12½*
C443 A250 40c multi .30 .20

Christmas Type, 1978

1978, Dec. 5 Litho. *Perf. 12½*
C444 A251 25c multi .20 .20
C445 A251 1col multi .80 .50

Athenaeum Type 1978

1978, Dec. 20 Litho. *Perf. 14*
C446 A252 25c multi .20 .20

UPU Type of 1979

1979, Apr. 2 Litho. *Perf. 14*
C447 A253 75c multi .60 .40

Health Organization Type

1979, Apr. 7 *Perf. 14x14½*
C448 A254 25c multi .20 .20

Social Security Type of 1979

1979, May 25 Litho. *Perf. 12½*
C449 A255 25c multi .20 .20
C450 A255 1col multi .80 .50

Games Emblem AP61

1979, July 12 Litho. *Perf. 14½x14*
C451 AP61 25c multi .20 .20
C452 AP61 40c multi .30 .20
C453 AP61 70c multi .50 .40
Nos. C451-C453 (3) 1.00 .80

8th Pan American Games, Puerto Rico, July 1-15.

For surcharge see No. C493.

Pope John Paul II Type of 1979

60c, 5col, Pope John Paul II & pyramid.

1979, July 12
C454 A256 60c multi, horiz. .50 .30
C455 A256 5col multi, horiz. 4.00 2.50

"25," Family and Map of Salvador — AP62

1979, May 14 Litho. *Perf. 14x14½*
C456 AP62 25c blk & bl .20 .20
C457 AP62 60c blk & lil rose .50 .35

Social Security, 25th anniversary.

Pre-Historic Animal Type

1979, Sept. 7 Litho. *Perf. 14*
C458 A257 15c Mammoth .20 .20
C459 A257 25c Giant anteater, vert. .20 .20
C460 A257 2 col Hyenas 1.60 1.00
Nos. C458-C460 (3) 2.00 1.40

National Anthem Type, 1979

1979, Sept. 14 *Perf. 14½x14*
C461 A258 40c Jose Aberiz, score .30 .20

COPIMERA Type, 1979

1979, Oct. 19 Litho. ***Perf. 14½x14***

C462 A259 50c multi .40 .25

Circle Dance, IYC Emblem AP63

Children's Village and IYC Emblems AP64

1979, Oct. 29 ***Perf. 14½x14, 14x14½***

C463 AP63 25c multi .20 .20
C464 AP64 30c vio & blk .25 .20

International Year of the Child.

Biochemistry Type of 1979

1979, Nov. 1 Litho. ***Perf. 14½x14***

C465 A262 25c multi .20 .20

Coffee Type of 1979

Designs: 50c, Picking coffee. 75, Drying coffee beans. 1col, Coffee export.

1979, Dec. 18 ***Perf. 14x14½, 14½x14***

C466 A263 50c multi .40 .25
C467 A263 75c multi .60 .40
C468 A263 1 col multi .80 .55
Nos. C466-C468 (3) 1.80 1.20

Hoof and Mouth Disease Type

1980, June 3 Litho. ***Perf. 14½x14***

C469 A265 60c multi .50 .30

Shell Type of 1980

1980, Aug. 12 ***Perf. 14x14½***

C470 A266 15c *Hexaplex regius* .20 .20
C471 A266 25c *Polinices helicoides* .20 .20
C472 A266 75c *Jenneria pustulata* .50 .40
C473 A266 1 col *Pitar lupanaria* .80 .55
Nos. C470-C473 (4) 1.70 1.35

Birds Type

1980, Sept. 10 Litho. ***Perf. 14x14½***

C474 A267 25c Aulacorhynchus prasinus .20 .20
C475 A267 50c Strix varia fulvescens .40 .25
C476 A267 75c Myadestes unicolor .60 .40
Nos. C474-C476 (3) 1.20 .85

Snake Type of 1980

1980, Nov. 12 Litho. ***Perf. 14x14½***

C477 A268 25c Rattlesnake .20 .20
C478 A268 50c Coral snake .40 .25

Auditors Type

1980, Nov. 26 Litho. ***Perf. 14***

C479 A269 50c multi .40 .25
C480 A269 75c multi .60 .40

Christmas Type

1980, Dec. 5 Litho. ***Perf. 14***

C481 A270 25c multi .20 .20
C482 A270 60c multi .50 .30

Intl. Women's Decade, 1976-85 — AP65

1981, Jan. 30 ***Perf. 14½x14***

C483 AP65 25c olive green & blk .20 .20
C484 AP65 1 col orange & black .80 .50

Protected Animals AP66

1981, Mar. 20 Litho. ***Perf. 14x14½***

C485 AP66 25c Ateles geoffroyi .20 .20
C486 AP66 40c Lepisosteus tropicus .30 .20
C487 AP66 50c Iguana iguana .40 .25
C488 AP66 60c Eretmochelys imbricata .50 .35
C489 AP66 75c Spizaetus ornatus .60 .40
Nos. C485-C489 (5) 2.00 1.40

Heinrich von Stephan, 150th Birth Anniv. — AP67

1981, May 18 Litho. ***Perf. 14½x14***

C490 AP67 15c multi .20 .20
C491 AP67 2 col multi 1.60 1.00

Nos. C435, C453 Surcharged

Perf. 12½, 14½x14

1981, May 18 Litho.

C492 A245 50c on 80c, #C435 .40 .25
C493 AP61 1 col on 70c, #C453 .80 .55

Dental Associations Type

1981, June 18 Litho. ***Perf. 14***

C494 A271 5 col bl & blk 4.00 3.00

IYD Type of 1981

1981, Aug. 14 Litho. ***Perf. 14x14½***

C495 A272 25c like #936 .20 .20
C496 A272 50c Emblem .40 .25
C497 A272 75c like #936 .60 .40
C498 A272 1 col like # C496 .80 .55
Nos. C495-C498 (4) 2.00 1.40

Quinonez Type

1981, Aug. 28 Litho. ***Perf. 14x14½***

C499 A273 50c multi .40 .25

World Food Day Type

1981, Sept. 16 Litho. ***Perf. 14x14½***

C500 A274 25c multi .20 .20

Land Registry Office, 100th Anniv. — AP68

1981, Oct. 30 Litho. ***Perf. 14x14½***

C501 AP68 1 col multi .80 .55

TACA Airlines, 50th Anniv. AP69

1981, Nov. 10 Litho. ***Perf. 14***

C502 AP69 15c multi .20 .20
C503 AP69 25c multi .20 .20
C504 AP69 75c multi .60 .40
Nos. C502-C504 (3) 1.00 .80

World Cup Preliminaries Type

1981, Nov. 27 Litho. ***Perf. 14x14½***

C505 A275 25c Like No. 939 .20 .20
C506 A275 75c Like No. 940 .60 .40

Lyceum Type

1981, Dec. 17 Litho. ***Perf. 14***

C507 A276 25c multi .20 .20

Sculptures Type

1982, Jan. 22 Litho. ***Perf. 14***

C508 A277 25c Palm leaf with effigy .20 .20
C509 A277 30c Jaguar mask .25 .20
C510 A277 80c Mayan flint carving .65 .45
Nos. C508-C510 (3) 1.10 .85

Scouting Year Type of 1982

1982, Mar. 17 Litho. ***Perf. 14½x14***

C511 A278 25c Baden-Powell .20 .20
C512 A278 50c Girl Scout, emblem .40 .25

TB Bacillus Cent. — AP70

Symbolic Design — AP71

1982, Mar. 24 ***Perf. 14***

C513 AP70 50c multi .40 .25

Armed Forces Type of 1982

1982, May 7 Litho. ***Perf. 14x13½***

C514 A279 25c multi .20 .20

1982, May 14 ***Perf. 14***

C515 AP71 75c multi .60 .40

25th anniv. of Latin-American Tourist Org. Confederation (COTAL).

14th World Telecommunications Day — AP72

1982, May 17 ***Perf. 14x14½***

C516 AP72 15c multi .20 .20
C517 AP72 2col multi 1.60 1.00

World Cup Type of 1982

1982, July 14

C518 A280 25c Team, emblem .20 .20
C519 A280 60c Map, cup .50 .35

Size: 67x47mm

Perf. 11½

C520 A280 2col Team, emblem, diff. 1.60 1.00

1982 World Cup — AP73

Flags or Arms of Participating Countries; #C521a, C522a, Italy. #C521b, C522c, Germany. #C521c, C522e, Argentina. #C521d, C522m, England. #C521e, C522o, Spain. #C521f, C522q, Brazil. #C521g, C522b, Poland. #C521h, C522d, Algeria. #C521i, C522f, Belgium. #C521j, C522n, France. #C521k, C522p, Honduras. #C521l, C522r, Russia. #C521m, C522g, Peru. #C521n, C522i, Chile. #C521o, C522k, Hungary. #C521p, C522s, Czechoslovakia. #C521q, C522u, Yugoslavia. #C521r, C522w, Scotland. #C521s, C522h, Cameroun. #C521t, C522j, Austria. #C521u, C522l, Salvador. #C521v, C522t, Kuwait. #C521w, C522v, Ireland. #C521x, C522x, New Zealand.

1982, Aug. 26

C521 Sheet of 24 3.00
a.-x. AP73 15c Flags .20 .20
C522 Sheet of 24 5.00
a.-x. AP73 25c Arms .20 .20

Salvador Team, Cup, Flags — AP74

1982, Aug. 26 Litho. ***Perf. 11½***

C523 AP74 5col multi 4.00 2.50

International Fair Type

1982, Oct. 14 Litho. ***Perf. 14***

C524 A281 15c multi .20 .20

World Food Day — AP75

1982, Oct. 21 Litho. ***Perf. 14***

C525 AP75 25c multi .20 .20

St. Francis of Assisi, 800th Birth Anniv. AP76

Natl. Labor Campaign AP77

1982, Nov. 10 Litho. ***Perf. 14***

C526 AP76 1col multi .80 .60

1982, Nov. 30 Litho. ***Perf. 14x14½***

C527 AP77 50c multi .40 .25

Christmas Type

1982, Dec. 14 Litho. ***Perf. 14***

C528 A282 25c multi, horiz. .20 .20

Salvadoran Paintings AP78

#C529, The Pottery of Paleca, by Miguel Ortiz Villacorta. #C530, The Rural School, by Luis Caceres Madrid. #C531, To the Wash, by Julia Diaz. #C532, "La Pancha" by Jose Mejia Vides. #C533, Boats Near The Beach, by Raul Elas Reyes. #C534, The Muleteers, by Canjura.

Perf. 14x13½, 13½x14

1983, Oct. 18 Litho.

C529 AP78 25c multi .20 .20
C530 AP78 25c multi .20 .20
a. Pair, #C529-C530 .40 .30
C531 AP78 75c multi, vert. .60 .40
C532 AP78 75c multi, vert. .60 .40
a. Pair, #C531-C532 1.25 .80
C533 AP78 1col multi, vert. .80 .55
C534 AP78 1col multi, vert. .80 .55
a. Pair, #C533-C534 1.60 1.10
Nos. C529-C534 (6) 3.20 2.30

Fishing Industry AP79

1983, Dec. 20 Litho. *Perf. 14½x14*

C535 AP79 25c Fisherman .20 .20
C536 AP79 75c Feeding fish .60 .40

No. 999 Surcharged

1985, Apr. 10 Litho. *Perf. 14*

C536A A297 1col on 10c multi .80 .50

Natl. Constitution, Cent. — AP80

1986, Aug. 29 Litho. *Perf. 14*

C537 AP80 1col multi .50 .35

Hugo Lindo (1917-1985), Writer — AP81

1986, Nov. 10 Litho. *Perf. 14½x14*

C538 AP81 1col multi .50 .35

Central American Economic Integration Bank, 25th Anniv. AP82

1986, Nov. 20

C539 AP82 1.50col multi .70 .50

12th Intl. Fair, Feb. 14-Mar. 1 AP83

1987, Jan. 20 Litho. *Perf. 14½x14*

C540 AP83 70c multi .35 .25

Intl. Year of Shelter for the Homeless AP84

Perf. 14x14½, 14½x14

1987, July 15 Litho.

C541 AP84 70c shown .35 .25
C542 AP84 1col Emblem, vert. .45 .35

Miniature Sheet

Discovery of America, 500th Anniv. (in 1992) AP85

15th cent. map of the Americas (details) and: a, Ferdinand. b, Isabella. c, Caribbean. d, Ships, coat of arms. e, Base of flagstaff. f, Ships. g, Pre-Columbian statue. h, Compass. i, Anniv. emblem. j, Columbus rose.

1987, Dec. 21 Litho. *Perf. 14*

C543 Sheet of 10 4.50 3.50
a.-j. AP85 1col any single .45 .35

No. 1075 Surcharged

1988, Oct. 28 Litho. *Perf. 14x14½*

C544 A316 5col on 90c multi 2.50 1.75

PRENFIL '88, Nov. 25-Dec. 2, Buenos Aire.

Organization of American States 18th General Assembly, Nov. 14-19 — AP86

1988, Nov. 19

C545 AP86 70c multi .40 .30

Handicapped Soccer Championships — AP87

1990, May 2 Litho. *Perf. 14½x14*

C546 AP87 70c multicolored .35 .25

REGISTRATION STAMPS

Gen. Rafael Antonio Gutiérrez — R1

1897 Engr. Wmk. 117 *Perf. 12*

F1 R1 10c dark blue 125.00
F2 R1 10c brown lake .20

Unwmk.

F3 R1 10c dark blue .20
F4 R1 10c brown lake .20

Nos. F1 and F3 were probably not placed in use without the overprint "FRANQUEO OFICIAL" (Nos. O127-O128).

The reprints are on thick unwatermarked paper. Value, set of 2, 16c.

ACKNOWLEDGMENT OF RECEIPT STAMPS

AR1

1897 Engr. Wmk. 117 *Perf. 12*

H1 AR1 5c dark green .20

Unwmk.

H2 AR1 5c dark green .20

No. H2 has been reprinted on thick paper. Value 15c.

POSTAGE DUE STAMPS

D1

1895 Unwmk. Engr. *Perf. 12*

J1 D1 1c olive green .20 .20
J2 D1 2c olive green .20 .20
J3 D1 3c olive green .20 .20
J4 D1 5c olive green .20 .20
J5 D1 10c olive green .20 .20
J6 D1 15c olive green .20 .20
J7 D1 25c olive green .20 .20
J8 D1 50c olive green .20 .25
Nos. J1-J8 (8) 1.60 1.65

See Nos. J9-J56. For overprints see Nos. J57-J64, O186-O214.

1896 Wmk. 117

J9 D1 1c red .20 .20
J10 D1 2c red .20 .20
J11 D1 3c red .20 .25
J12 D1 5c red .20 .25
J13 D1 10c red .20 .25
J14 D1 15c red .20 .30
J15 D1 25c red .20 .30
J16 D1 50c red .20 .35
Nos. J9-J16 (8) 1.60 2.10

Unwmk.

J17 D1 1c red .20 .20
J18 D1 2c red .20 .20
J19 D1 3c red .20 .20
J20 D1 5c red .20 .20
J21 D1 10c red .20 .20
J22 D1 15c red .20 .20
J23 D1 25c red .20 .20
J24 D1 50c red .20 .20
Nos. J17-J24 (8) 1.60 1.60

Nos. J17-J24 exist imperforate.

1897

J25 D1 1c deep blue .20 .20
J26 D1 2c deep blue .20 .20
J27 D1 3c deep blue .20 .20
J28 D1 5c deep blue .20 .20
J29 D1 10c deep blue .20 .20
J30 D1 15c deep blue .20 .20
J31 D1 25c deep blue .20 .20
J32 D1 50c deep blue .20 .20
Nos. J25-J32 (8) 1.60 1.60

1898

J33 D1 1c violet .20
J34 D1 2c violet .20
J35 D1 3c violet .20
J36 D1 2c violet .20
J37 D1 10c violet .20
J38 D1 15c violet .20
J39 D1 25c violet .20
J40 D1 50c violet .20
Nos. J33-J40 (8) 1.60

Reprints of Nos. J1 to J40 are on thick paper, often in the wrong shades and usually with the impression somewhat blurred. Value, set of 40, $2, watermarked or unwatermarked.

1899 Wmk. 117 Sideways

J41 D1 1c orange .20
J42 D1 2c orange .20
J43 D1 3c orange .20
J44 D1 5c orange .20
J45 D1 10c orange .20
J46 D1 15c orange .20
J47 D1 25c orange .20
J48 D1 50c orange .20
Nos. J41-J48 (8) 1.60

Unwmk.

Thick Porous Paper

J49 D1 1c orange .20
J50 D1 2c orange .20
J51 D1 3c orange .20
J52 D1 5c orange .20
J53 D1 10c orange .20
J54 D1 15c orange .20
J55 D1 25c orange .20
J56 D1 50c orange .20
Nos. J49-J56 (8) 1.60

Nos. J41-J56 were probably not put in use without the wheel overprint.

Nos. J49-J56 Overprinted in Black

1900

J57 D1 1c orange .50
J58 D1 2c orange .50
J59 D1 3c orange .50
J60 D1 5c orange .75
J61 D1 10c orange 1.00
J62 D1 15c orange 1.00
J63 D1 25c orange 1.25
J64 D1 50c orange 1.50
Nos. J57-J64 (8) 7.00

See note after No. 198A.

Morazán Monument — D2

Perf. 14, 14½

1903 Engr. Wmk. 173

J65 D2 1c yellow green 1.25 1.00
J66 D2 2c carmine 2.00 1.50
J67 D2 3c orange 2.00 1.50
J68 D2 5c dark blue 2.00 1.50
J69 D2 10c dull violet 2.00 1.50
J70 D2 25c blue green 2.00 1.50
Nos. J65-J70 (6) 11.25 8.50

Nos. 355, 356, 358 and 360 Overprinted **DEFICIENCIA DE FRANQUEO**

1908 Unwmk. *Perf. 11½*

J71 A66 1c green & blk .40 .35
J72 A66 2c red & blk .30 .25
J73 A66 5c blue & blk .75 .50
J74 A66 10c violet & blk 1.10 1.00

Same Overprint on No. O275

J75 O3 3c yellow & blk .75 .65
Nos. J71-J75 (5) 3.30 2.75

Nos. 355-358, 360 Overprinted

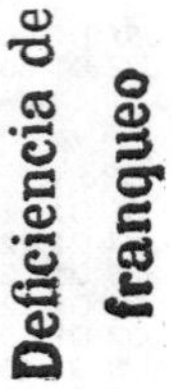

J76	A66	1c green & blk	.25	.25
J77	A66	2c red & blk	.30	.30
J78	A66	3c yellow & blk	.35	.35
J79	A66	5c blue & blk	.50	.50
J80	A66	10c violet & blk	1.00	1.00
		Nos. J76-J80 (5)	2.40	2.40

It is now believed that stamps of type A66, on paper with Honeycomb watermark, do not exist with genuine overprints of the types used for Nos. J71-J80.

Pres. Fernando Figueroa — D3

1910 Engr. Wmk. 172

J81	D3	1c sepia & blk	.20	.20
J82	D3	2c dk grn & blk	.20	.20
J83	D3	3c orange & blk	.20	.20
J84	D3	4c scarlet & blk	.20	.20
J85	D3	5c purple & blk	.20	.20
J86	D3	12c deep blue & blk	.20	.20
J87	D3	24c brown red & blk	.20	.20
		Nos. J81-J87 (7)	1.40	1.40

OFFICIAL STAMPS

Overprint Types

a

Nos. 134-157O Overprinted Type a

1896 Unwmk. *Perf. 12*

O1	A45	1c blue	.20	
O2	A45	2c dk brown	.20	
a.		Double overprint		
O3	A45	3c blue grn	.30	
O4	A45	5c brown ol	.20	
O5	A45	10c yellow	.20	
O6	A45	12c dk blue	.20	
O7	A45	15c blue vio	.20	
O8	A45	20c magenta	.30	
O9	A45	24c vermilion	.20	
O10	A45	30c orange	.30	
O11	A45	50c black brn	.20	
O12	A45	1p rose lake	.20	
		Nos. O1-O12 (12)	2.70	

The 1c has been reprinted on thick unwatermarked paper. Value 15c.

Wmk. 117

O13	A46	1c emerald	.20	
O14	A47	2c lake	.20	
O15	A48	3c yellow brn	.20	
a.		Inverted overprint	1.00	
O16	A49	5c dp blue	.20	
O17	A50	10c brown	.20	
a.		Inverted overprint	1.25	
O18	A51	12c slate	.20	
O19	A52	15c blue grn	.20	
O20	A53	20c car rose	.20	
a.		Inverted overprint		
O21	A54	24c violet	.20	
O22	A55	30c dp green	.20	
O23	A56	50c orange	.20	
O24	A57	100c dk blue	.20	
		Nos. O13-O24 (12)	2.40	

Unwmk.

O25	A46	1c emerald	.20	
a.		Double overprint		
O26	A47	2c lake	.20	
O27	A48	3c yellow brn	.20	
O28	A49	5c dp blue	.85	
O29	A50	10c brown	.20	
a.		Inverted overprint		
O30	A51	12c slate	.20	
O31	A52	15c blue grn	.20	
O32	A53	20c car rose	.20	
a.		Inverted overprint		
O33	A54	24c violet	.40	
O34	A55	30c dp green	.20	
O35	A56	50c orange	.85	
O36	A57	100c dk blue	1.10	
		Nos. O25-O36 (12)	4.80	

The 3, 5, 10, 12, 15, 20, 24, 30 and 100c have been reprinted on thick unwatermarked paper and the 15c, 50c and 100c on thick watermarked paper. Value, set of 12, $1.20.

Nos. 134-145 Handstamped Type b in Black or Violet

b

1896

O37	A45	1c blue	7.50	
O38	A45	2c dk brown	7.50	
O39	A45	3c blue green	7.50	
O40	A45	5c brown olive	7.50	
O41	A45	10c yellow	8.75	
O42	A45	12c dk blue	11.50	
O43	A45	15c blue violet	11.50	
O44	A45	20c magenta	11.50	
O45	A45	24c vermilion	11.50	
O46	A45	30c orange	11.50	
O47	A45	50c black brown	15.00	
O48	A45	1p rose lake	15.00	
		Nos. O37-O48 (12)	126.25	

Reprints of the 1c and 2c on thick paper exist with this handstamp. Value, set of 2, 20c.

Forged overprints exist of Nos. O37-O78, O103-O126 and of the higher valued stamps of O141-O214.

Nos. 146-157F, 157I-157O, 158D Handstamped Type b in Black or Violet

1896 Wmk. 117

O49	A46	1c emerald	6.25	
O50	A47	2c lake	6.25	
O51	A48	3c yellow brn	6.25	
O52	A49	5c deep blue	6.25	
O53	A50	10c brown	6.25	
O54	A51	12c slate	10.00	
O55	A52	15c blue green	11.50	
O56	A53	20c carmine rose	11.50	
O57	A54	24c violet	11.50	
O58	A55	30c deep green	11.50	
O59	A56	50c orange	11.50	
O60	A57	100c dark blue	11.50	
		Nos. O49-O60 (12)	110.25	

Unwmk.

O61	A46	1c emerald	6.25	
O62	A47	2c lake	6.25	
O63	A48	3c yellow brn	6.25	
O64	A49	5c deep blue	6.25	
O65	A50	10c brown	8.75	
O66	A52	15c blue green	11.50	
O67	A58	15c on 24c vio	11.50	
O68	A53	20c carmine rose	11.50	
O69	A54	24c violet	11.50	
O70	A55	30c deep green	11.50	
O71	A56	50c orange	12.50	
O72	A57	100c dark blue	12.50	
		Nos. O61-O72 (12)	116.25	

Nos. 175-176 Overprinted Type a in Black

1897

O73	A59	1c bl, gold, rose & grn	.25	
O74	A59	5c rose, gold, bl & grn	.25	

These stamps were probably not officially issued.

Nos. 175-176 Handstamped Type b in Black or Violet

1900

O75	A59	1c bl, gold, rose & grn	17.50	
O76	A59	5c rose, gold, bl & grn	17.50	

Nos. 159-170L Overprinted Type a in Black

1897 Wmk. 117

O79	A46	1c scarlet	.20	
O80	A47	2c yellow green	1.25	
O81	A48	3c bister brown	.50	
O82	A49	5c orange	.20	.20
O83	A50	10c blue green	.20	
O84	A51	12c blue	.25	
O85	A52	15c black	.25	.50
O86	A53	20c slate	.20	
O87	A54	24c yellow	.20	
a.		Inverted overprint		
O88	A55	30c rose	.50	
O89	A56	50c violet	1.25	1.00
O90	A57	100c brown lake	1.75	
		Nos. O79-O90 (12)	6.75	

Unwmk.

O91	A46	1c scarlet	.20	
O92	A47	2c yellow green	.30	
O93	A48	3c bister brown	.20	
O94	A49	5c orange	.20	.20
O95	A50	10c blue green	.65	
O96	A51	12c blue	.65	
O97	A52	15c black	.75	
O98	A53	20c slate	.20	.35
O99	A54	24c yellow	.20	.35
O100	A55	30c rose	.20	.35
O101	A56	50c violet	.65	
O102	A57	100c brown lake	.40	1.00
		Nos. O91-O102 (12)	4.60	

All values have been reprinted on thick paper without watermark and the 1c, 12c, 15c and 100c on thick paper with watermark. Value, set of 16, $1.60.

Nos. 159-170L Handstamped Type b in Violet or Black

1897 Wmk. 117

O103	A46	1c scarlet	7.50	
O104	A47	2c yellow green	7.50	
O105	A48	3c bister brown	7.50	
O106	A49	5c orange	7.50	
O107	A50	10c blue green	8.75	
O108	A51	12c blue		
O109	A52	15c black		
O110	A53	20c slate	15.00	
O111	A54	24c yellow	17.50	
O112	A55	30c rose		
O113	A56	50c violet		
O114	A57	100c brown lake		

Unwmk.

O115	A46	1c scarlet	7.50	
O116	A47	2c yellow grn	7.50	
O117	A48	3c bister brn	7.50	
O118	A49	5c orange	7.50	
O119	A50	10c blue green	7.50	
O120	A51	12c blue		
O121	A52	15c black		
O122	A53	20c slate		
O123	A54	24c yellow		
O124	A55	30c rose	15.00	
O125	A56	50c violet		
O126	A57	100c brown lake	17.50	

Reprints of the 1 and 15c on thick watermarked paper and the 12, 30, 50 and 100c on thick unwatermarked paper are known with this overprint. Value, set of 6, 60c.

Nos. F1, F3 Overprinted Type a in Red

Wmk. 117

O127	R1	10c dark blue	.20	

Unwmk.

O128	R1	10c dark blue	.20	

The reprints are on thick paper. Value 15c.
Originals of the 10c brown lake Registration Stamp and the 5c Acknowledgment of Receipt stamp are believed not to have been issued with the "FRANQUEO OFICIAL" overprint. They are believed to exist only as reprints.

Nos. 177-188 Overprinted Type a

1898 Wmk. 117

O129	A60	1c orange ver	.20	
O130	A60	2c rose	.20	
O131	A60	3c pale yel grn	1.40	
O132	A60	5c blue green	.20	
O133	A60	10c gray blue	.20	
O134	A60	12c violet	1.40	
O135	A60	13c brown lake	.20	
O136	A60	20c deep blue	.20	
O137	A60	24c ultra	.20	
O138	A60	26c bister brn	.20	
O139	A60	50c orange	.20	
O140	A60	1p yellow	.20	
		Nos. O129-O140 (12)	4.80	

Reprints of the above set are on thick paper. Value, set of 12, $1.20, with or without watermark.

No. 177 Handstamped Type b in Violet

O141	A60	1c orange ver	30.00	

No. O141 with Additional Overprint Type c in Black

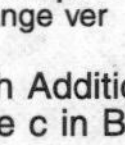

c

Type "c" is called the "wheel" overprint.

O142	A60	1c orange ver		

Counterfeits exist of the "wheel" overprint.

Nos. 204-205, 207 and 209 Overprinted Type a

1899 Unwmk.

O143	A61	12c dark green		
O144	A61	13c deep rose		
O145	A61	26c carmine rose		
O146	A61	100c violet		

Nos. O143-O144 Punched With Twelve Small Holes

O147	A61	12c dark green		
O148	A61	13c deep rose		

Official stamps punched with twelve small holes were issued and used for ordinary postage.

Nos. 199-209 Overprinted

d

1899

Blue Overprint

O149	A61	1c brown	.20	
O150	A61	2c gray green	.20	
O151	A61	3c blue	.20	
O152	A61	5c brown orange	.20	
O153	A61	10c chocolate	.20	
O154	A61	13c deep rose	.20	
O155	A61	26c carmine rose	.20	
O156	A61	50c orange red	.20	
O157	A61	100c violet	.20	

Black Overprint

O158	A61	3c blue	.20	
O159	A61	12c dark green	.20	
O160	A61	24c lt blue	.20	
		Nos. O149-O160 (12)	2.40	

#O149-O160 were probably not placed in use.

With Additional Overprint Type c in Black

O161	A61	1c brown	.40	.35
O162	A61	2c gray green	.60	.50
O163	A61	3c blue	.40	.35
O164	A61	5c brown org	.40	.35
O165	A61	10c chocolate	.50	.40
O166	A61	12c dark green		
O167	A61	13c deep rose	1.00	.85
O168	A61	24c lt blue	15.00	15.00
O169	A61	26c carmine rose	1.00	.60
O170	A61	50c orange red	1.00	.85
O171	A61	100c violet	1.25	.85
		Nos. O161-O165,O167-O171 (10)	21.55	20.10

Nos. O149-O155, O159-O160 Punched With Twelve Small Holes

Blue Overprint

O172	A61	1c brown	2.75	1.00
O173	A61	2c gray green	3.25	1.00
O174	A61	3c blue	4.50	3.75
O175	A61	5c brown org	6.00	3.00
O176	A61	10c chocolate	7.50	5.00
O177	A61	13c deep rose	7.50	3.75
O177A	A61	24c lt blue		
O178	A61	26c carmine rose	75.00	35.00

Black Overprint

O179	A61	12c dark green	6.00	4.50
		Nos. O172-O177,O178-O179 (8)	112.50	57.00

It is stated that Nos. O172-O214 inclusive were issued for ordinary postage and not for use as official stamps.

Nos. O161-O167, O169 Overprinted Type c in Black

O180	A61	1c brown	1.25	1.10
O180A	A61	2c gray green		
O181	A61	3c blue		
O182	A61	5c brown orange	1.25	
O182A	A61	10c chocolate		
O182B	A61	12c dark green		
O183	A61	13c deep rose	4.00	2.00
O184	A61	26c carmine rose		

Overprinted Types a and e in Black

e

O185	A61	100c violet		

Nos. J49-J56 Overprinted Type a in Black

1900

O186	D1	1c orange	22.50	
O187	D1	2c orange	22.50	
O188	D1	3c orange	22.50	
O189	D1	5c orange	22.50	
O190	D1	10c orange	22.50	
O191	D1	15c orange	50.00	

O192 D1 25c orange 50.00
O193 D1 50c orange 50.00
Nos. O186-O193 (8) 262.50

Nos. O194-O189, O191-O193 Overprinted Type c in Black

O194 D1 1c orange
O195 D1 2c orange 12.50
O196 D1 3c orange
O197 D1 5c orange
O198 D1 15c orange 12.50
O199 D1 25c orange 15.00
O200 D1 50c orange 140.00

Nos. O186-O189 Punched With Twelve Small Holes

O201 D1 1c orange 25.00
O202 D1 2c orange 25.00
O203 D1 3c orange 25.00
O204 D1 5c orange 25.00
Nos. O201-O204 (4) 100.00

Nos. O201-O204 Overprinted Type c in Black

O205 D1 1c orange 9.00 6.50
O206 D1 2c orange 6.50
O207 D1 3c orange 6.50
O208 D1 5c orange 9.00 6.50

Overprinted Type a in Violet and Type c in Black

O209 D1 2c orange 12.50
a. Inverted overprint
O210 D1 3c orange
O211 D1 10c orange 3.00

Nos. O186-O188 Handstamped Type e in Violet

O212 D1 1c orange 9.00 7.50
O213 D1 2c orange 9.00 7.50
O214 D1 3c orange 9.00 9.00
Nos. O212-O214 (3) 27.00 24.00

See note after No. O48.

Type of Regular Issue of 1900 Overprinted Type a in Black

O223 A63 1c lt green .35 .35
a. Inverted overprint
O224 A63 2c rose .40 .35
a. Inverted overprint 1.75
O225 A63 3c gray black .25 .25
a. Overprint vertical
O226 A63 5c blue .25 .25
O227 A63 10c blue .70 .70
a. Inverted overprint
O228 A63 12c yellow grn .70 .70
O229 A63 13c yellow brn .70 .70
O230 A63 24c gray black .50 .70
O231 A63 26c yellow brn 25.00 20.00
a. Inverted overprint
O232 A63 50c dull rose
a. Inverted overprint
Nos. O223-O231 (9) 28.85 24.00

Nos. O223-O224, O231-O232 Overprinted in Violet

f

O233 A63 1c lt green 4.75 4.00
O234 A63 2c rose 25.00
a. "FRANQUEO OFICIAL" invtd.
O235 A63 26c yellow brown .50 .50
O236 A63 50c dull rose .75 .55

Nos. O223, O225-O228, O232 Overprinted in Black

g

O237 A63 1c lt green 5.00 5.00
O238 A63 3c gray black
O239 A63 5c blue
O240 A63 10c blue
O241 A63 12c yellow green

Violet Overprint

O242 A63 50c dull rose 10.00

The shield overprinted on No. O242 is of the type on No. O212.

O1

1903 Wmk. 173 *Perf. 14, 14½*

O243 O1 1c yellow green .35 .25
O244 O1 2c carmine .35 .20
O245 O1 3c orange 1.00 .85
O246 O1 5c dark blue .35 .20
O247 O1 10c dull violet .50 .35
O248 O1 13c red brown .50 .35
O249 O1 15c yellow brown 3.25 1.75
O250 O1 24c scarlet .35 .35
O251 O1 50c bister .50 .35
O252 O1 100c grnsh blue .50 .75
Nos. O243-O252 (10) 7.65 5.40

For surcharges see Nos. O254-O257.

No. 285 Handstamped Type b in Black

1904

O253 A64 3c orange 35.00

2 2

Nos. O246-O248 Surcharged in Black

1905

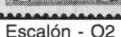

O254 O1 2c on 5c dark blue 3.25 2.75
O255 O1 3c on 5c dark blue
a. Double surcharge
O256 O1 3c on 10c dl vio 9.00 6.00
O257 O1 3c on 13c red brn .85 .70

A 2c surcharge of this type exists on No. O247.

No. O225 Overprinted in Blue

1905 — a
1905 — b

1905 Unwmk.

O258 A63(a) 3c gray black 2.00 1.75
O259 A63(b) 3c gray black 1.75 1.50

Nos. O224-O225 Overprinted in Blue

1906 — c
1906 — d

1906

O260 A63(c) 2c rose 11.25 10.00
O261 A63(c) 3c gray black 1.25 1.00
a. Overprint "1906" in blk
O262 A63(d) 3c gray black 1.40 1.25
Nos. O260-O262 (3) 13.90 12.25

Escalón - O2

National Palace — O3

1906 Engr. *Perf. 11½*

O263 O2 1c green & blk .20 .20
O264 O2 2c carmine & blk .20 .20
O265 O2 3c yellow & blk .20 .20
O266 O2 5c blue & blk .20 .30
O267 O2 10c violet & blk .20 .20
O268 O2 13c dk brown & blk .20 .20
O269 O2 15c red org & blk .20 .20
O270 O2 24c carmine & blk .25 .20
O271 O2 50c orange & blk .25 *.65*
O272 O2 100c dk blue & blk .25 *2.00*
Nos. O263-O272 (10) 2.15 *4.35*

The centers of these stamps are also found in blue black.

Nos. O263 to O272 have been reprinted. The shades differ, the paper is thicker and the perforation 12. Value, set of 10, 50c.

1908

O273 O3 1c green & blk .20 .20
O274 O3 2c red & blk .20 .20
O275 O3 3c yellow & blk .20 .20
O276 O3 5c blue & blk .20 .20
O277 O3 10c violet & blk .20 .20
O278 O3 13c violet & blk .20 .20
O279 O3 15c pale brn & blk .20 .20
O280 O3 24c rose & blk .20 .20
O281 O3 50c yellow & blk .20 .20
O282 O3 100c turq blue & blk .20 .20
Nos. O273-O282 (10) 2.00 2.00

For overprints see Nos. 441-442, 445-449, J75, O283-O292, O323-O328.

Nos. O273-O282 Overprinted Type g in Black

O283 O3 1c green & blk .85
O284 O3 2c red & blk 1.00
O285 O3 3c yellow & blk 1.00
O286 O3 5c blue & blk 1.25
O287 O3 10c violet & blk 1.25
O288 O3 13c violet & blk 1.50
O289 O3 15c pale brn & blk 1.50
O290 O3 24c rose & blk 2.00
O291 O3 50c yellow & blk 2.50
O292 O3 100c turq & blk 3.00
Nos. O283-O292 (10) 15.85

Pres. Figueroa — O4

1910 Engr. Wmk. 172

O293 O4 2c dk green & blk .20 .20
O294 O4 3c orange & blk .20 .20
O295 O4 4c scarlet & blk .20 .20
a. 4c carmine & black
O296 O4 5c purple & blk .20 .20
O297 O4 6c scarlet & blk .20 .20
O298 O4 10c purple & blk .20 .20
O299 O4 12c dp blue & blk .20 .20
O300 O4 17c olive grn & blk .20 .20
O301 O4 19c brn red & blk .20 .20
O302 O4 29c choc & blk .20 .20
O303 O4 50c yellow & blk .20 .20
O304 O4 100c turq & blk .20 .20
Nos. O293-O304 (12) 2.40 2.40

Regular Issue, Type A63, Overprinted or Surcharged:

OFICIAL — a
OFICIAL 3 — b
OFICIAL UN COLON — c

1911 Unwmk.

O305 A63(a) 1c lt green .20 .20
O306 A63(b) 3c on 13c yel brn .20 .20
O307 A63(b) 5c on 10c dp bl .20 .20
O308 A63(a) 10c deep blue .20 .20
O309 A63(a) 12c lt green .20 .20
O310 A63(a) 13c yellow brn .20 .20
O311 A63(b) 50c on 10c dp bl .20 .20
O312 A63(c) 1col on 13c yel brn .20 .20
Nos. O305-O312 (8) 1.60 1.60

O5

O6

1914 Typo. *Perf. 12*

Background in Green, Shield and "Provisional" in Black

O313 O5 2c yellow brn .20 .20
O314 O5 3c yellow .20 .20
O315 O5 5c dark blue .20 .20
O316 O5 10c red .20 .20
O317 O5 12c green .20 .20
O318 O5 17c violet .20 .20
O319 O5 50c brown .20 .20
O320 O5 100c dull rose .20 .20
Nos. O313-O320 (8) 1.60 1.60

Stamps of this issue are known imperforate or with parts of the design omitted or misplaced. These varieties were not regularly issued.

1914 Typo.

O321 O6 2c blue green .20 .20
O322 O6 3c orange .20 .20

Type of Official Stamps of 1908 With Two Overprints

1915 OFICIAL

1915

O323 O3 1c gray green .30 .25
a. "1915" double
b. "OFICIAL" inverted
O324 O3 2c red .30 .25
O325 O3 5c ultra .30 .25
O326 O3 10c yellow .30 .25
a. Date omitted
O327 O3 50c violet .55 .50
O328 O3 100c black brown 1.25 1.00
Nos. O323-O328 (6) 3.00 2.50

Same Overprint on #414, 417, 429

O329 A66 1c gray green 1.60 1.60
O330 A66 6c pale blue .50 .40
a. 6c ultramarine
O331 A66 12c brown .60 .60
Nos. O329-O330 (2) 2.10 2.00

\# O323-O327, O329-O331 exist imperf.

Nos. O329-O331 exist with "OFICIAL" inverted and double. See note after No. 421.

Nos. 431-440 Overprinted in Blue or Red OFICIAL

1916

O332 A83 1c deep green .20 .20
O333 A83 2c vermilion .35 .20
O334 A83 5c dp blue (R) .25 .20
O335 A83 6c gray vio (R) .20 .20
O336 A83 10c black brown .20 .20
O337 A83 12c violet .40 .25
O338 A83 17c orange .20 .20
O339 A83 25c dark brown .20 .20
O340 A83 29c black (R) .20 .20
O341 A83 50c slate (R) .20 .20
Nos. O332-O341 (10) 2.40 2.05

Nos. 474-481 Overprinted

OFICIAL — a
OFICIAL — b

1921

O342 A94(a) 1c green .20 .20
O343 A95(a) 2c black .20 .20
a. Inverted overprint
O344 A96(b) 5c orange .20 .20
O345 A97(a) 6c carmine rose .20 .20
O346 A98(a) 10c deep blue .20 .20
O347 A99(a) 25c olive green .50 .25
O348 A100(a) 60c violet .60 .50
O349 A101(a) 1col black brown .65 .65
Nos. O342-O349 (8) 2.75 2.40

Nos. 498 and 500 Overprinted in Black or Red OFICIAL

1925

O350 A109 5c olive black .35 .20
O351 A111 10c orange (R) .50 .20
a. "ATLANT CO" 7.50 6.25

Inverted overprints exist.

Regular Issue of 1924-25 Overprinted in Black or Red OFICIAL

1927

O352 A106 1c red violet .20 .20
O353 A107 2c dark red .40 .25
O354 A109 5c olive blk (R) .40 .25
O355 A110 6c dp blue (R) 3.00 2.50
O356 A111 10c orange .50 .30
a. "ATLANT CO" 12.50 11.50
O357 A116 1col grn & vio (R) 1.50 1.00
Nos. O352-O357 (6) 6.00 4.50

Inverted overprints exist on 1c, 2c, 5c, 10c.

Regular Issue of 1924-25 Overprinted in Black OFICIAL

1932 *Perf. 12½*

O358 A106 1c deep violet .20 .20
O359 A107 2c dark red .40 .20
O360 A109 5c olive black .20 .20

O361	A111	10c orange	.70	.30
a.		"ATLANT CO"	14.00	12.50
		Nos. O358-O361 (4)	1.50	.90

Catalogue values for unused stamps in this section, from this point to the end of the section, are for Never Hinged items.

Regular Issue of 1947 Overprinted in Black or Red **OFICIAL**

1948 Unwmk. Engr. *Perf. 12*

O362	A154	1c car rose	42.50	22.50
O363	A154	2c deep org	42.50	22.50
O364	A154	5c slate gray (R)	42.50	22.50
O365	A154	10c bis brn (R)	42.50	22.50
O366	A154	20c green (R)	42.50	22.50
O367	A154	50c black (R)	42.50	22.50
		Nos. O362-O367 (6)	255.00	135.00

No. 602 Surcharged in Carmine and Black

1964(?)

O368 A154 1c on 20c green

The X's are black, the rest carmine.

PARCEL POST STAMPS

Mercury PP1

1895 Unwmk. Engr. *Perf. 12*

Q1	PP1	5c brown orange	.25
Q2	PP1	10c dark blue	.25
Q3	PP1	15c red	.25
Q4	PP1	20c orange	.25
Q5	PP1	50c blue green	.25
		Nos. Q1-Q5 (5)	1.25

POSTAL TAX STAMPS

Nos. 503, 501 Surcharged **EDIFICIOS POSTALES 1**

1931 Unwmk. *Perf. 12½*

RA1	A115	1c on 50c org brn	.20	.20
a.		Double surcharge	2.00	2.00
RA2	A112	2c on 20c dp grn	.20	.20

Nos. 501, 503 Surcharged **EDIFICIOS POSTALES ₡ 0.01**

RA3	A112	1c on 20c dp grn	.20	.20
RA4	A115	2c on 50c org brn	.20	.20
a.		Without period in "0.02"	1.25	

The use of these stamps was obligatory, in addition to the regular postage, on letters and other postal matter. The money obtained from their sale was to be used to erect a new post office in San Salvador.

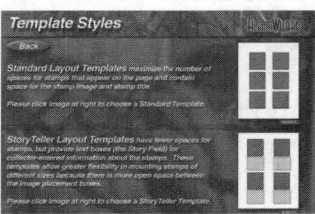

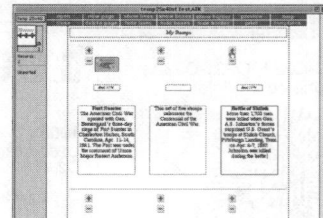

SAMOA

sə-ˈmō-ə

(Western Samoa)

LOCATION — Archipelago in the south Pacific Ocean, east of Fiji
GOVT. — Independent state; former territory mandated by New Zealand
AREA — 1,093 sq. mi.
POP. — 161,298 (1991)
CAPITAL — Apia

In 1861-99, Samoa was an independent kingdom under the influence of the US, to which the harbor of Pago Pago had been ceded, and that of Great Britain and Germany. In 1898 a disturbance arose, resulting in the withdrawal of Great Britain, and the partitioning of the islands between Germany and the US. Early in World War I the islands under German domination were occupied by New Zealand troops and in 1920 the League of Nations declared them a mandate to New Zealand. Western Samoa became independent Jan. 1, 1962.

12 Pence = 1 Shilling
20 Shillings = 1 Pound
100 Pfennig = 1 Mark (1900)
100 Sene (Cents) = 1 Tala (Dollar) (1967)

Catalogue values for unused stamps in this country are for Never Hinged items, beginning with Scott 191 in the regular postage section, Scott B1 in the semi-postal section and Scott C1 in the air post section.

Watermarks

Wmk. 61- N Z and Star Close Together

Wmk. 62- N Z and Star Wide Apart

On watermark 61 the margins of the sheets are watermarked "NEW ZEALAND POSTAGE" and parts of the double-lined letters of these words are frequently found on the stamps. It occasionally happens that a stamp shows no watermark whatever.

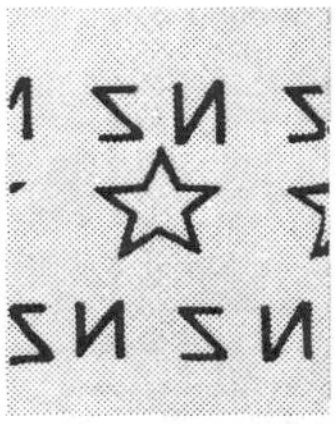

Wmk. 253- Multiple N Z and Star

Wmk. 355- Kava Bowl and WS, Multiple

Issues of the Kingdom

A1

Type I - Line above "X" is usually unbroken. Dots over "SAMOA" are uniform and evenly spaced. Upper right serif of "M" is horizontal.
Type II - Line above "X" is usually broken. Small dot near upper right serif of "M."
Type III - Line above "X" roughly retouched. Upper right serif of "M" bends down.
Type IV - Speck of color on curved line below center of "M."

Perf. 12, 12½

1877-82 Litho. Unwmk.

1 A1 1p blue (III) ('79) 22.50 40.00
 a. 1p ultra (III) ('79) 30.00 40.00
 b. 1p ultra (II) ('78) 90.00 90.00
 c. 1p ultra (I) ('77) 250.00 100.00
2 A1 2p lil rose (IV) ('82) 35.00
3 A1 3p ver (III) ('79) 45.00 70.00
 a. 3p brt scarlet (III) 45.00 80.00
 b. 3p scarlet (II) ('77) 300.00 125.00
 c. 3p deep scarlet (I) ('77) 275.00 125.00
4 A1 6p violet (III) ('79) 42.50 50.00
 a. 6p violet (II) ('78) 165.00 85.00
 b. 6p violet (I) ('77) 275.00 110.00
5 A1 9p yel brn (IV) ('80) 62.50 *125.00*
 a. 9p orange brown (IV) ('80) 62.50 *125.00*
6 A1 1sh org yel (II) ('78) 90.00 90.00
 a. 1sh dull yellow (II) ('77) *150.00* *125.00*
7 A1 2sh dp brn (III) ('79) 140.00 250.00
 a. 2sh red brown (II) ('78) 275.00 190.00
 b. 2sh brown (II) ('78) 300.00 350.00
8 A1 5sh deep green (III) ('79) 375.00 550.00
 a. 5sh yel grn (III) ('79) 400.00 600.00
 b. 5sh gray green (II) ('78) *1,350.* *1,250.*

The 1p often has a period after "PENNY." The 2p was never placed in use since the Samoa Express service was discontinued late in 1881.

Imperforates of this issue are proofs.

Sheets of the first issue were not perforated around the outer sides. All values except the 2p were printed in sheets of 10 (2x5). The 1p, 3p and 6p type I and the 1p type III were also printed in sheets of 20 (4x5), and six stamps on each of these sheets were perforated all around. These are the only varieties of the original stamps which have not one or two imperforate edges. The 2p was printed in sheets of 21 (3x7) and five stamps in the second row were perforated all around. The 2p was also reprinted in sheets of 40, which are much more common than the sheets of 21.

Reprints are of type IV and nearly always perforated on all sides. They have a spot of color at the edge of the panel below the "M." This spot is not on any originals except the 9p, the original of which may be distinguished by having a rough blind perf. 12. The 2p does show a spot of color.

Forgeries exist.

Palms
A2

King Malietoa Laupepa
A3

1895-99 Typo. Wmk. 62 *Perf. 11*

9 A2 ½p brown vio 1.75 1.75
10 A2 ½p green ('99) 1.50 *1.75*
11 A2 1p green 3.00 1.75
12 A2 1p red brown ('99) 1.50 *1.75*
13 A2 2p brt yellow 5.00 4.50
14 A3 2½p rose 1.75 *4.50*
15 A3 2½p blk, perf. 10x11 ('96) 1.40 *3.00*
 a. Perf. 11 65.00 *65.00*
16 A2 4p blue 7.00 2.00
17 A2 6p maroon 7.00 3.00
18 A2 1sh rose 7.00 3.75
19 A2 2sh6p red violet 10.00 *7.50*
 c. Vert. pair, imperf. btwn. 350.00
 Nos. 9-19 (11) 46.90 35.25

1886-92 *Perf. 12½*

9a A2 ½p brown violet 17.00 *42.50*
11a A2 1p green 7.00 *15.00*
13a A2 2p orange 20.00 8.50
14a A3 2½p rose ('92) *22.50* *4.75*
16a A2 4p blue 35.00 8.50
17a A2 6p maroon 2000.00 1000.00
18a A2 1sh rose 65.00 8.00
 c. Diagonal half used as 6p on cover 300.00
19a A2 2sh6p purple 52.50 60.00
 Nos. 9a-16a,18a-19a (7) 219.00 147.25

1887-92 *Perf. 12x11½*

9b A2 ½p brown violet 3.25 3.25
11b A2 1p green 20.00 1.40
13b A2 2p brown orange 25.00 1.75
14b A3 2½p rose ('92) 75.00 3.50
16b A2 4p blue 130.00 5.00
17b A2 6p maroon 22.50 10.00
18b A2 1sh rose *225.00* *5.00*
19b A2 2sh6p red violet 350.00 *8.50*
 Nos. 9b-19b (8) 850.75 38.40

Three forms of watermark 62 are found on stamps of type A2:
1 - Wide "N Z" and wide star, 6mm apart (used 1886-87).
2 - Wide "N Z" and narrow star, 4mm apart (1890).
3 - Narrow "NZ" and narrow star, 7mm apart (1890-1900). The 2½p has only the 3rd form.
For surcharges or overprints on stamps or types of design A2 see Nos. 20-22, 24-38.

No. 16b Handstamp Surcharged in Black or Red:

a

b

c

1893 *Perf. 12x11½*

20 A2(a) 5p on 4p blue 47.50 45.00
21 A2(b) 5p on 4p blue 90.00 *100.00*
22 A2(c) 5p on 4p blue (R) 22.50 *30.00*
 Nos. 20-22 (3) 160.00 *175.00*

As the surcharges on Nos. 20-21 were handstamped in two steps and on No. 22 in three steps, various varieties exist.

Flag Design — A7

1894-95 Typo. *Perf. 11½x12*

23 A7 5p vermilion 25.00 3.00
 a. Perf. 11 ('95) 15.00 7.00

Types of 1887-1895 Surcharged in Blue, Black, Red or Green:

1½p, 2½p

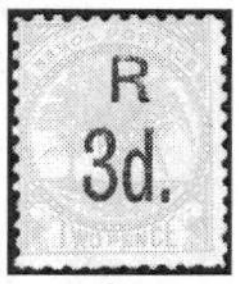

3p

1895 *Perf. 11*

24 A2 1½p on 2p orange (Bl) 2.25 *5.50*
 a. 1½p on 2p brn org, perf 12x11½ (bl) 7.50 5.50
 b. 1½p on 2p yellow, "2" ends with vertical stroke 2.50 *22.50*
25 A2 3p on 2p orange (Bk) 7.50 *9.50*
 a. 3p on 2p brn org, perf. 12x11½ (Bk) 35.00 8.50
 b. 3p on 2p yel, perf. 11 (Bk) 80.00 60.00
 c. Vert. pair, imperf. btwn. 375.00

1898-1900 *Perf. 11*

26 A2 2½p on 1sh rose (Bk) 6.00 *12.00*
 a. Double surcharge 425.00
27 A2 2½p on 2sh6p vio (Bk) 6.50 *13.50*
28 A2 2½p on 1p bl grn (R) .70 *2.50*
 a. Inverted surcharge *350.00*
29 A2 2½p on 1sh rose (R) 6.00 *12.00*
30 A2 3p on 2p org (G) 1.75
 Nos. 26-30 (5) 20.95

No. 30 was a reissue, available for postage. The surcharge is not as tall as the 3p surcharge illustrated, which is the surcharge on No. 25.

Stamps of 1886-99 Overprinted in Red or Blue

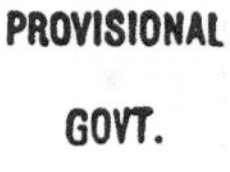

1899

31 A2 ½p green (R) .90 *2.00*
32 A2 1p red brown (Bl) 2.00 *4.25*
33 A2 2p orange (R) 1.75 *4.75*
 a. 2p yellow 1.50 *5.50*
34 A2 4p blue (R) .60 *6.00*
35 A7 5p scarlet (Bl) 2.00 *5.50*
36 A2 6p maroon (Bl) 1.10 *5.00*
37 A2 1sh rose (Bl) 1.40 *16.00*
38 A2 2sh6p violet (R) 4.25 *16.50*
 Nos. 31-38 (8) 14.00 *60.00*

In 1900 the Samoan islands were partitioned between the US and Germany. The part which became American has since used US stamps.

Issued under German Dominion

Stamps of Germany Overprinted

1900 Unwmk. *Perf. 13½x14½*

51 A10 3pf dark brown 7.50 *10.50*
52 A10 5pf green 10.00 *13.50*
53 A11 10pf carmine 7.50 *13.50*
54 A11 20pf ultra 15.00 *22.50*
55 A11 25pf orange 30.00 *60.00*
56 A11 50pf red brown 30.00 *55.00*
 Nos. 51-56 (6) 75.50 *135.50*

Kaiser's Yacht "Hohenzollern"
A12 A13

1900 Typo. *Perf. 14*

57 A12 3pf brown .80 .80
58 A12 5pf green .80 .80
59 A12 10pf carmine .80 .80
60 A12 20pf ultra .80 *1.60*
61 A12 25pf org & blk, *yel* .85 *9.25*
62 A12 30pf org & blk, *sal* 1.00 *8.00*
63 A12 40pf lake & blk 1.00 *9.25*
64 A12 50pf pur & blk, *sal* 1.00 *10.00*
65 A12 80pf lake & blk, *rose* 2.10 *22.50*

Engr.

66 A13 1m carmine 2.50 *47.50*
67 A13 2m blue 2.50 *47.50*
68 A13 3m black vio 5.25 *110.00*
69 A13 5m slate & car 100.00 *400.00*
 Nos. 57-69 (13) 111.00 *549.70*

1915 Wmk. 125 Typo. *Perf. 14*

70 A12 3pf brown 1.00
71 A12 5pf green 1.25
72 A12 10pf carmine 1.25

Perf. 14½x14

Engr.

73 A13 5m slate & car 20.00

Nos. 70-73 were never put in use.

Issued under British Dominion

#57-69 Surcharged:

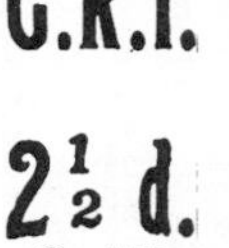

On A12

On A13

1914 Unwmk. *Perf. 14*

101 A12 ½p on 3pf brown 22.50 9.00
 a. Double surcharge 600.00 450.00
 b. Fraction bar omitted 50.00 30.00
 c. Comma after "I" 550.00 375.00
102 A12 ½p on 5pf green 45.00 10.00
 a. Double surcharge 600.00 450.00
 b. Fraction bar omitted 110.00 55.00
 d. Comma after "I" 325.00 225.00
103 A12 1p on 10pf car 90.00 40.00
 a. Double surcharge 600.00 450.00
104 A12 2½p on 20pf ultra 35.00 450.00
 a. Fraction bar omitted 70.00 37.50
 b. Inverted surcharge 725.00 650.00
 c. Double surcharge 600.00 500.00
 d. Commas after "I" 375.00 310.00
105 A12 3p on 25pf org & blk, *yel* 50.00 40.00
 a. Double surcharge 700.00 550.00
 b. Comma after "I" 4,000. 800.00
106 A12 4p on 30pf org & blk, *sal* 100.00 62.50

107 A12 5p on 40pf lake & blk 100.00 70.00
108 A12 6p on 50pf pur & blk, *sal* 60.00 35.00
a. Inverted "9" for "6" 165.00 110.00
b. Double surcharge 750.00 700.00
109 A12 9p on 80pf lake & blk, *rose* 200.00 100.00

Perf. 14½x14

110 A13 1sh on 1m car ("1 Shillings.") 3,000. *3,500.*
a. "1 Shilling." *9,500.* *7,000.*
111 A13 2sh on 2m blue 3,000. 2,750.
112 A13 3sh on 3m blk vio 1,200. 1,000.
a. Double surcharge *7,500.* *8,500.*
113 A13 5sh on 5m slate & car 1,000. 900.00

G.R.I. stands for Georgius Rex Imperator. The 3d on 30pf and 4d on 40pf were produced at a later time.

Stamps of New Zealand Overprinted in Red or Blue:

k

m

Perf. 14, 14x13½, 14x14½

1914, Sept. 29 **Wmk. 61**

114 A41(k) ½p yel grn (R) .60 .25
115 A42(k) 1p carmine .60 .25
116 A41(k) 2p mauve (R) .75 *.80*
117 A22(m) 2½p blue (R) 1.40 *1.50*
118 A41(k) 6p car rose, perf. 14x14½ 1.40 *1.50*
a. Perf. 14x13½ 17.00 20.00
119 A41(k) 1sh vermilion 4.25 *13.50*
Nos. 114-119 (6) 9.00 *17.75*

Overprinted Type "m"

1914-25 ***Perf. 14, 14½x14***

120 PF1 2sh blue (R) 5.50 *7.00*
121 PF1 2sh6p brown (Bl) 5.00 *8.50*
122 PF1 3sh vio (R) ('22) 13.50 *40.00*
123 PF1 5sh green (R) 12.00 *11.00*
124 PF1 10sh red brn (Bl) 20.00 *27.50*
125 PF2 £1 rose (Bl) 55.00 *50.00*
126 PF2 £2 vio (R) ('25) 400.00
Nos. 120-126 (7) 511.00
Nos. 120-125 (6) *144.00*

Postal use of the £2 is questioned.

Overprinted Type "k"

Perf. 14x13½, 14x14½

1916-19 **Typo.**

127 A43 ½p yellow grn (R) .50 *.60*
128 A47 1½p gray blk (R) ('17) .40 .20
129 A47 1½p brn org (R) ('19) .30 .25
130 A43 2p yellow (R) ('18) 1.25 .20
131 A43 3p chocolate (Bl) 1.25 *9.50*

Engr.

132 A44 2½p dull blue (R) .55 .25
133 A45 3p violet brn (Bl) .50 *.75*
134 A45 6p carmine rose (Bl) 1.50 *2.25*
135 A45 1sh vermilion (Bl) 1.75 1.00
Nos. 127-135 (9) 8.00 15.00

Overprinted Type "k"

On New Zealand Victory Issue of 1919

1920, June ***Perf. 14***

136 A48 ½p yellow grn (R) 2.75 *5.00*
137 A49 1p carmine (Bl) 2.25 *4.50*
138 A50 1½p brown org (R) 1.25 *5.75*
139 A51 3p black brn (Bl) 6.75 *7.50*
140 A52 6p purple (R) 3.50 *5.50*
141 A53 1sh vermilion (Bl) 11.50 9.25
Nos. 136-141 (6) 28.00 37.50

British Flag and Samoan House — A22

1921, Dec. 23 **Engr.** ***Perf. 14x13½***

142 A22 ½p green 3.50 *1.50*
a. Perf. 14x14½ 1.50 *5.00*
143 A22 1p lake 3.75 .25
a. Perf. 14x14½ 2.50 .50
144 A22 1½p orange brn, perf. 14x14½ .60 *7.25*
a. Perf. 14x13½ 4.00 *8.00*
145 A22 2p yel, perf. 14x14½ 1.90 1.50
a. Perf. 14x13½ 5.00 1.50
146 A22 2½p dull blue 1.50 *5.75*
147 A22 3p dark brown 1.50 *4.00*
148 A22 4p violet 1.50 *2.50*
149 A22 5p brt blue 1.50 *5.00*
150 A22 6p carmine rose 1.50 *4.00*
151 A22 8p red brown 1.50 *7.25*
152 A22 9p olive green 1.75 *18.00*
153 A22 1sh vermilion 1.50 *18.00*
Nos. 142-153 (12) 22.00 *75.00*

For overprints see Nos. 163-165.

New Zealand Nos. 182-183 Overprinted Type "m" in Red

1926-27 ***Perf. 14½x14***

154 A56 2sh dark blue 5.00 *12.00*
a. 2sh blue ('27) 10.00 *35.00*
155 A56 3sh deep violet 11.00 *30.00*
a. 3sh violet ('27) 45.00 *75.00*

Issued: 2sh, Nov.; 3sh, Oct.; #154a, 155a, 11/10.

New Zealand Postal-Fiscal Stamps, Overprinted Type "m" in Blue or Red

1932, Aug. ***Perf. 14***

156 PF5 2sh6p brown 15.00 *35.00*
157 PF5 5sh green (R) 22.50 *37.50*
158 PF5 10sh lake 45.00 *80.00*
159 PF5 £1 pink 55.00 *100.00*
160 PF5 £2 violet (R) *650.00*
161 PF5 £5 dk bl (R) *1,600.*
Nos. 156-159 (4) 137.50 *252.50*

See Nos. 175-180, 195-202, 216-219.

Silver Jubilee Issue

Stamps of 1921 Overprinted in Black

1935, May 7 ***Perf. 14x13½***

163 A22 1p lake .40 *.50*
a. Perf. 14x14½ *80.00* *140.00*
164 A22 2½p dull blue .85 *1.00*
165 A22 6p carmine rose 3.25 *3.50*
Nos. 163-165 (3) 4.50 5.00

25th anniv. of the reign of George V.

Western Samoa

Samoan Girl and Kava Bowl — A23

View of Apia — A24

River Scene — A25

Samoan Chief and Wife — A26

Samoan Canoe and House — A27

"Vailima," Stevenson's Home — A28

Stevenson's Tomb — A29

Lake Lanuto'o — A30

Falefa Falls — A31

Perf. 14x13½, 13½x14

1935, Aug. 7 **Engr.** **Wmk. 61**

166 A23 ½p yellow grn .20 .20
167 A24 1p car lake & blk .20 .20
168 A25 2p red org & blk, perf. 14 .40 .40
a. Perf. 13½x14 3.50 *4.00*
169 A26 2½p dp blue & blk .25 .25
170 A27 4p blk brn & dk gray .50 .50
171 A28 6p plum .50 .50
172 A29 1sh brown & violet .80 .80
173 A30 2sh red brn & yel grn 1.25 1.25
174 A31 3sh org brn & brt bl 2.00 2.00
Nos. 166-174 (9) 6.10 6.10

See Nos. 186-188.

Postal-Fiscal Stamps of New Zealand Overprinted in Blue or Carmine

1935 ***Perf. 14***

175 PF5 2sh6p brown 5.50 *15.00*
176 PF5 5sh green 9.50 *20.00*
177 PF5 10sh dp carmine 47.50 *60.00*
178 PF5 £1 pink 57.50 *90.00*
179 PF5 £2 violet (C) 140.00 *290.00*
180 PF5 £5 dk bl (C) 240.00 *525.00*
Nos. 175-180 (6) 500.00 *1,000.*

See Nos. 195-202, 216-219.

Samoan Coastal Village — A32

Map of Western Samoa — A33

Samoan Dancing Party A34

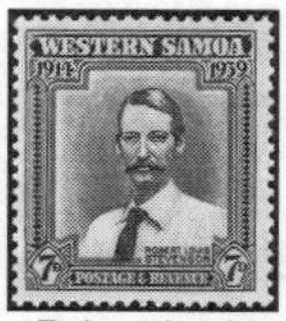

Robert Louis Stevenson A35

Perf. 13½x14

1939, Aug. 29 **Engr.** **Wmk. 253**

181 A32 1p scar & olive .25 .25
182 A33 1½p copper brn & bl .50 .50
183 A34 2½p dk blue & brn 1.00 1.00

Perf. 14x13½

184 A35 7p dp sl grn & vio 2.75 2.00
Nos. 181-184 (4) 4.50 3.75
Set, never hinged 7.75

25th anniv. of New Zealand's control of the mandated territory of Western Samoa.

Samoan Chief — A36

1940, Sept. 2 ***Perf. 14x13½***

185 A36 3p on 1½p brown .20 .20
Never hinged .30

Issued only with surcharge. Examples without surcharge are from printer's archives.

Types of 1935 and A37

Apia Post Office — A37

1944-49 **Wmk. 253** ***Perf. 14***

186 A23 ½p yellow green .20 11.50
187 A25 2p red orange & blk 1.40 4.00
188 A26 2½p dp blue & blk ('48) 2.40 19.00

Perf. 13½x14

189 A37 5p dp ultra & ol brn ('49) .75 .50
Nos. 186-189 (4) 4.75 35.00
Set, never hinged 7.50

Issue date: 5p, June 8.

Catalogue values for unused stamps in this section, from this point to the end of the section, are for Never Hinged items.

Peace Issue

New Zealand Nos. 248, 250, 254, and 255 Overprinted in Black or Blue

WESTERN SAMOA
p

WESTERN SAMOA
q

1946, June 1 ***Perf. 13x13½, 13½x13***

191 A94(p) 1p emerald .20 .20
192 A96(q) 2p rose violet (Bl) .20 .20
193 A100(p) 6p org red & red brn .20 .20
194 A101(p) 8p brn lake & blk (Bl) .20 .20
Nos. 191-194 (4) .80 .80

Stamps and Type of New Zealand, 1931-50 Overprinted Like Nos. 175-180 in Blue or Carmine

1945-50 **Wmk. 253** ***Perf. 14***

195 PF5 2sh6p brown 4.00 *10.00*
196 PF5 5sh green 6.50 *12.00*
197 PF5 10sh car ('48) 19.00 17.00
198 PF5 £1 pink ('48) 75.00 *125.00*
199 PF5 30sh choc ('48) 125.00 *200.00*
200 PF5 £2 violet (C) 140.00 *225.00*
201 PF5 £3 lt grn ('50) 175.00 *300.00*
202 PF5 £5 dk bl (C) ('50) 300.00 *400.00*

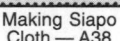

Making Siapo Cloth — A38

Thatching Hut — A40

Western Samoa and New Zealand Flags, Village A39

Samoan Chieftainess — A41

Designs: 2p, Western Samoa seal. 3p, Aleisa Falls (actually Malifa Falls). 5p, Manumea (tooth-billed pigeon). 6p, Fishing canoe. 8p, Harvesting cacao. 2sh, Preparing copra.

Perf. 13, 13½x13

1952, Mar. 10 Engr. Wmk. 253

203	A38	½p org brn & claret	.20	*1.25*
204	A39	1p green & olive	.20	.20
205	A38	2p deep carmine	.20	.20
206	A39	3p indigo & blue	.40	.20
207	A38	5p dk grn & org brn	5.50	.35
208	A39	6p dp rose pink & bl	.75	.20
209	A39	8p rose carmine	.30	.25
210	A40	1sh blue & brown	.20	.20
211	A39	2sh yellow brown	1.00	.40
212	A41	3sh ol gray & vio brn	2.50	2.50
		Nos. 203-212 (10)	11.25	5.75

Coronation Issue

Types of New Zealand 1953

1953, May 25 Photo. *Perf. 14x14½*

214	A113	2p brown	.35	.35
215	A114	6p slate black	1.10	1.10

Type of New Zealand 1944-52 Overprinted in Blue or Carmine

WESTERN

SAMOA

Wmk. 253

1955, Nov. 14 Typo. *Perf. 14*

216	PF5	5sh yellow green	9.50	*16.00*
217	PF5	10sh carmine rose	9.50	*21.00*
218	PF5	£1 dull rose	16.00	*30.00*
219	PF5	£2 violet (C)	70.00	*125.00*
		Nos. 216-219 (4)	105.00	*192.00*

Redrawn Types of 1952 and

Map of Western Samoa and Mace A42

Designs: 4p, as 1p. 6p, as 2p.

Inscribed: "Fono Fou 1958" and "Samoa I Sisifo"

Perf. 13½x13, 13

1958, Mar. 21 Engr. Wmk. 253

220	A39	4p rose carmine	.20	.20
221	A38	6p dull purple	.20	.20
222	A42	1sh light violet blue	.70	.30
		Nos. 220-222 (3)	1.10	.70

Independent State

Samoa College A43

Designs: 1p, Woman holding ceremonial mat, vert. 3p, Public Library. 4p, Fono House (Parliament). 6p, Map of Western Samoa, ship and plane. 8p, Faleolo airport. 1sh, Talking chief with fly whisk, vert. 1sh3p, Government House, Vailima. 2sh6p, Flag of Western Samoa. 5sh, State Seal.

Wmk. 253

1962, July 2 Litho. *Perf. 13½*

223	A43	1p car & brown	.20	.20
224	A43	2p org, lt grn, red & brown	.20	.20
225	A43	3p blue, grn & brn	.20	.20
226	A43	4p dk grn, bl & car	.35	.35
227	A43	6p yel, grn & ultra	.45	.45
228	A43	8p blue & emerald	.55	.55
229	A43	1sh brt grn & brn	.85	.85
230	A43	1sh3p blue & emerald	1.10	1.10
231	A43	2sh6p vio blue & red	1.65	1.65
232	A43	5sh olive gray, red & dk blue	4.00	4.00
		Nos. 223-232 (10)	9.55	9.55

Western Samoa's independence. See #242-247.

Tupua Tamasese Mea'ole, Malietoa Tanumafili II and Seal — A44

1963, Oct. 1 Photo. *Perf. 14*

233	A44	1p green & blk	.20	.20
234	A44	4p dull blue & blk	.20	.20
235	A44	8p carmine rose & blk	.20	.20
236	A44	2sh orange & blk	.20	.20
		Nos. 233-236 (4)	.80	.80

First anniversary of independence.

Signing of Western Samoa-New Zealand Friendship Treaty A45

1964, Sept. 1 Unwmk. *Perf. 13½*

237	A45	1p multicolored	.20	.20
238	A45	8p multicolored	.20	.20
239	A45	2sh multicolored	.25	.20
240	A45	3sh multicolored	.25	*.35*
		Nos. 237-240 (4)	.90	.95

2nd anniv. of the signing of the Treaty of Friendship between Western Samoa and New Zealand. Signers: J. B. Wright, N. Z. High Commissioner for Western Pacific, and Fiame Mata'afa, Prime Minister of Western Samoa.

Type of 1962

Wmk. 355

1965, Oct. 4 Litho. *Perf. 13½*

242	A43	1p carmine & brn	.40	*1.00*
243	A43	3p blue, grn & brn	35.00	7.00
244	A43	4p dk grn, bl & car	.40	*1.00*
245	A43	6p yel, grn & ultra	.45	.45
246	A43	8p blue & emerald	.55	.20
247	A43	1sh brt green & brn	.70	*1.00*
		Nos. 242-247 (6)	37.50	10.65

For surcharge see No. B1.

Aerial View of Deep-Sea Wharf A46

8p, 2sh, View of Apia harbor & deep-sea wharf.

1966, Mar. 2 Photo. *Perf. 13½*

251	A46	1p multicolored	.20	.20
252	A46	8p multicolored	.20	.20
253	A46	2sh multicolored	.30	.25
254	A46	3sh multicolored	.50	.35
		Nos. 251-254 (4)	1.20	1.00

Opening of Western Samoa's first deep-sea wharf at Apia.

Inauguration of WHO Headquarters, Geneva — A47

Design: 4p, 1sh, WHO building and flag.

1966, July 4 Photo. Wmk. 355

255	A47	3p gray, ultra & bister	.20	.20
256	A47	4p multicolored	.30	.30
257	A47	6p lt ol grn, pur & grn	.40	.40
258	A47	1sh multicolored	.85	.85
		Nos. 255-258 (4)	1.75	1.75

Tuatagaloa L.S., Minister of Justice A48

Designs: 8p, F.C.F. Nelson, Minister of Works, Marine and Civil Aviation. 2sh, To'omata T. L., Minister of Lands. 3sh, Fa'alava'au Galu, Minister of Post Office, Radio and Broadcasting.

Perf. 14½x14

1967, Jan. 16 Photo. Wmk. 355

259	A48	3p violet & sepia	.20	.20
260	A48	8p blue & sepia	.20	.20
261	A48	2sh lt olive grn & sepia	.30	.30
262	A48	3sh lilac rose & sepia	.50	.50
		Nos. 259-262 (4)	1.20	1.20

Fifth anniversary of Independence.

Samoan Fales, 1900, and Fly Whisk A49

1sh, Fono House (Parliament) and mace.

1967, May 16 *Perf. 14½*

263	A49	8p multicolored	.30	.30
264	A49	1sh multicolored	.40	.40

Centenary of Mulinu'u as Government Seat.

Wattled Honey-Eater — A50

Birds of Western Samoa: 2s, Pacific pigeon. 3s, Samoan starling. 5s, Samoan broadbill. 7s, Red-headed parrot finch. 10s, Purple swamp hen. 20s, Barn owl. 25s, Tooth-billed pigeon. 50s, Island thrush. $1, Samoan fantail. $2, Mao (gymnomyza samoensis). $4, Samoan white-eye (zosterops samoensis).

Perf. 14x14½

1967, July 10 Photo. Wmk. 355

Birds in Natural Colors

Size: 37x24mm

265	A50	1s black & lt brown	.20	.20
266	A50	2s lt ultra, blk & brn org	.20	.20
267	A50	3s blk, lt brn & emer	.20	.20
268	A50	5s lilac, blk & vio bl	.20	.20
269	A50	7s blk, vio bl & gray	.20	.20
270	A50	10s Prus blue & blk	.20	.20
271	A50	20s dk gray & blue	1.75	.35
272	A50	25s pink, blk & dk grn	.50	.20
273	A50	50s brn, blk & lt ol grn	.50	.25
274	A50	$1 yellow & black	.80	1.75

1969 Size: 43x28mm *Perf. 13½*

274A	A50	$2 blk & lt grnsh bl	3.75	6.25
274B	A50	$4 dp orange & blk	47.50	35.00
		Nos. 265-274B (12)	56.00	45.00

For surcharge see No. 294.

Child Care A51

Designs: 7s, Leprosarium. 20s, Mobile X-ray unit. 25s, Apia Hospital.

1967, Dec. 1 Litho. *Perf. 14*

275	A51	3s multicolored	.20	.20
276	A51	7s multicolored	.20	.20
277	A51	20s multicolored	.40	.40
278	A51	25s multicolored	.50	.50
		Nos. 275-278 (4)	1.30	1.30

South Pacific Health Service.

Thomas Trood A52

Portraits: 7s, Dr. Wilhelm Solf. 20s, John C. Williams. 25s, Fritz Marquardt.

1968, Jan. 1 Unwmk. *Perf. 13½*

279	A52	2s multicolored	.20	.20
280	A52	7s multicolored	.20	.20
281	A52	20s multicolored	.30	.30
282	A52	25s multicolored	.40	.40
		Nos. 279-282 (4)	1.10	1.10

Sixth anniversary of independence.

Samoan Agricultural Development A53

Perf. 13x12½

1968, Feb. 15 Photo. Wmk. 355

283	A53	3s Cocoa	.20	.20
284	A53	5s Breadfruit	.20	.20
285	A53	10s Copra	.30	.30
286	A53	20s Bananas	.40	.40
		Nos. 283-286 (4)	1.10	1.10

Curio Vendors, Pago Pago A54

20s, Palm trees at the shore. 25s, A'Umi Beach.

Perf. 14½x14

1968, Apr. 22 Photo. Wmk. 355

287	A54	7s multicolored	.20	.20
288	A54	20s multicolored	.35	.35
289	A54	25s multicolored	.40	.40
		Nos. 287-289 (3)	.95	.95

South Pacific Commission, 21st anniv.

Bougainville and Compass Rose — A55

Designs: 3s, Map showing Western Samoa Archipelago and Bougainville's route. 20s, Bougainvillea. 25s, Bougainville's ships La Boudeuse and L'Etoile.

1968, June 10 Litho. *Perf. 14*

290	A55	3s brt blue & blk	.20	.20
291	A55	7s ocher & blk	.20	.20
292	A55	20s grnsh blk, brt rose & grn	.50	.50
293	A55	25s brt lil, vio, blk & org	.65	.65
		Nos. 290-293 (4)	1.55	1.55

200th anniv. of the visit of Louis Antoine de Bougainville (1729-1811) to Samoa.

No. 270 Surcharged with New Value, Three Bars and: "1928-1968 / KINGSFORD-SMITH / TRANSPACIFIC FLIGHT"

1968, June 13 Photo. *Perf. 14x14½*

294	A50	20s on 10s multicolored	.35	.35

40th anniv. of the 1st Transpacific flight under Capt. Charles Kingsford-Smith (Oakland, CA to Brisbane, Australia, via Honolulu and Fiji).

Human Rights Flame and Globe A56

Perf. 14½x14

1968, Aug. 26 Photo. Wmk. 355

295 A56 7s multicolored .20 .20
296 A56 20s multicolored .35 .35
297 A56 25s multicolored .45 .45
Nos. 295-297 (3) 1.00 1.00

International Human Rights Year, 1968.

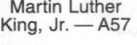

Martin Luther King, Jr. — A57

Polynesian Madonna — A58

1968, Sept. 23 Litho. *Perf. 14*

298 A57 7s green & black .20 .20
299 A57 20s brt rose lil & blk .40 .40

Rev. Dr. Martin Luther King, Jr. (1929-68), American civil rights leader.

1968, Oct. 12 Wmk. 355

300 A58 1s olive & multi .20 .20
301 A58 3s multicolored .20 .20
302 A58 20s crimson & multi .20 .20
303 A58 30s dp orange & multi .40 .40
Nos. 300-303 (4) 1.00 1.00

Christmas 1968.

Frangipani — A59

Flowers: 7s, Chinese hibiscus, vert. 20s, Red ginger, vert. 30s, Canangium odoratum.

1969, Jan. 20 Unwmk. *Perf. 14*

304 A59 2s brt blue & multi .45 .45
305 A59 7s multicolored .70 .70
306 A59 20s yellow & multi 1.25 1.25
307 A59 30s multicolored 1.60 1.60
Nos. 304-307 (4) 4.00 4.00

Seventh anniversary of independence.

R. L. Stevenson and Silver from "Treasure Island" — A60

Robert Louis Stevenson and: 7s, Stewart and Balfour on the moor from "Kidnapped," 20s, "Doctor Jekyll and Mr. Hyde." 22s, Archie Weir and Christiana Elliot from "Weir of Hermiston."

Perf. 14x13½

1969, Apr. 21 Litho. Wmk. 355

308 A60 3s gray & multi .40 .40
309 A60 7s gray & multi .40 .40
310 A60 20s gray & multi .60 .60
311 A60 22s gray & multi .60 .60
Nos. 308-311 (4) 2.00 2.00

75th anniv. of the death of Robert Louis Stevenson, who is buried in Samoa.

Weight Lifting — A61

Perf. 13½x13

1969, July 21 Photo. Unwmk.

312 A61 3s shown .20 .20
313 A61 20s Sailing .30 .30
314 A61 22s Boxing .40 .40
Nos. 312-314 (3) .90 .90

3rd Pacific Games, Port Moresby, Papua and New Guinea, Aug. 13-23.

American Astronaut on Moon, Splashdown and Map of Samoan Islands — A62

1969, July 24 Photo.

315 A62 7s red, blk, silver & grn .20 .20
316 A62 20s car, blk, sil & ultra .40 .40

US astronauts. See note after US No. C76.

Holy Family by El Greco A63

Christmas (Paintings): 1s, Virgin and Child, by Murillo. 20s, Nativity, by El Greco. 30s, Virgin and Child (from Adoration of the Kings), by Velazquez.

1969, Oct. 13 Unwmk. *Perf. 14*

317 A63 1s gold, red & multi .20 .20
318 A63 3s gold, red & multi .20 .20
319 A63 20s gold, red & multi .35 .35
320 A63 30s gold, red & multi .55 .55
a. Souvenir sheet of 4, #317-320 2.00 2.00
Nos. 317-320 (4) 1.30 1.30

Seventh Day Adventists' Sanatorium, Apia — A64

7s, Father Louis Violette, R. C. Cathedral, Apia. 20s, Church of Latter Day Saints (Mormon), Tuasivi, Safotulafai, vert. 22s, John Williams, London Missionary Soc. Church, Sapapali'i.

1970, Jan. 19 Litho. Wmk. 355

321 A64 2s brown, blk & gray .20 .20
322 A64 7s violet, blk & bister .20 .20
323 A64 20s rose, blk & lt violet .35 .35
324 A64 22s olive, blk & bister .40 .40
Nos. 321-324 (4) 1.15 1.15

Eighth anniversary of independence.

U.S.S. Nipsic A65

Designs: 5s, Wreck of German ship Adler. 10s, British ship Calliope in storm. 20s, Apia after hurricane.

1970, Apr. 27 *Perf. 13½x14*

325 A65 5s multicolored .40 .40
326 A65 7s multicolored .50 .50
327 A65 10s multicolored .85 .85
328 A65 20s multicolored 1.65 1.65
Nos. 325-328 (4) 3.40 3.40

The great Apia hurricane of 1889.

Cook Statue, Whitby, England — A66

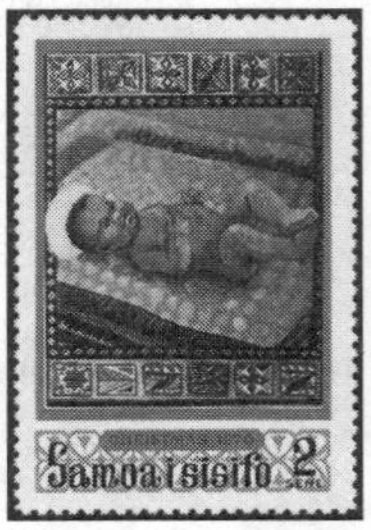

"Peace for the World" by Frances B. Eccles — A67

Designs: 1s, Kendal's chronometer and Cook's sextant. 20s, Capt. Cook bust, in profile. 30s, Capt. Cook, island scene and "Endeavour," horiz.

Perf. 14x14½

1970, Sept. 14 Litho. Wmk. 355

Size: 25x41mm

329 A66 1s silver, dp car & blk .20 .20
330 A66 2s multicolored .25 .20
331 A66 20s gold, black & ultra 2.25 1.50

Perf. 14½x14

Size: 83x25mm

332 A66 30s multicolored 3.25 2.25
Nos. 329-332 (4) 5.95 4.15

Bicentenary of Capt. James Cook's exploration of South Pacific.

Perf. 13½

1970, Oct. 26 Photo. Unwmk.

Christmas: 3s, Samoan coat of arms and Holy Family, by Werner Erich Jahnke. 20s, Samoan Mother and Child, by F. B. Eccles. 30s, Prince of Peace, by Sister Melane Fe'ao.

333 A67 2s gold & multi .20 .20
334 A67 3s gold & multi .20 .20
335 A67 20s gold & multi .50 .50
336 A67 30s gold & multi .70 .70
a. Souvenir sheet of 4, #333-336 1.75 1.75
Nos. 333-336 (4) 1.60 1.60

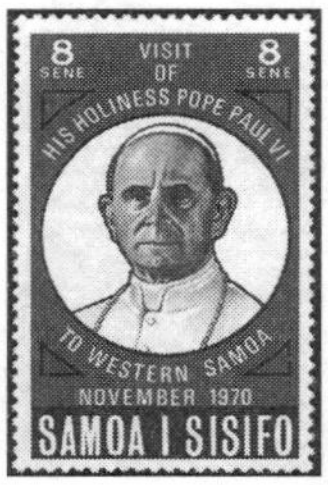

Pope Paul VI — A68

Lumberjack A69

Wmk. 355

1970, Nov. 29 Litho. *Perf. 14*

337 A68 8s Prus blue & black .20 .20
338 A68 20s deep plum & black .45 .45

Visit of Pope Paul VI, Nov. 29, 1970.

Perf. 14x13½, 13½x14

1971, Feb. 1 Litho. Unwmk.

8s, Woman and tractor in clearing, horiz. 20s, Log and saw carrier, horiz. 22s, Logging and ship.

339 A69 3s multicolored .20 .20
340 A69 8s multicolored .20 .20
341 A69 20s multicolored .35 .35
342 A69 22s multicolored .45 .45
Nos. 339-342 (4) 1.20 1.20

Development of the timber industry on Savaii Island by the American Timber Company of Potlatch.

Souvenir Sheet

Longboat in Apia Harbor; Samoa #3 and US #3 — A70

1971, Mar. 12 Photo. *Perf. 11½*

Granite Paper

343 A70 70s blue & multi 2.00 2.00

INTERPEX, 13th Intl. Stamp Exhib., NYC, Mar. 12-14.

Siva Dance A71

Tourist Publicity: 7s, Samoan cricket game. 8s, Hideaway Resort Hotel. 10s, Aggie Grey and Aggie's Hotel.

Wmk. 355

1971, Aug. 9 Litho. *Perf. 14*

344 A71 5s orange brn & multi .45 .45
345 A71 7s orange brn & multi .60 .60
346 A71 8s orange brn & multi .75 .75
347 A71 10s orange brn & multi .90 .90
Nos. 344-347 (4) 2.70 2.70

A72

A73

Samoan Legends, carved by Sven Ortquist: 3s, Queen Salamasina. 8s, Lu and his sacred hens (Samoa). 10s, God Tagaloa fishing Samoan islands of Upolu and Savaii from the sea. 22s, Mt. Vaea and Pool of Tears.

1971, Sept. 20

348 A72 3s dark violet & multi .20 .20
349 A72 8s multicolored .20 .20
350 A72 10s dark blue & multi .25 .25
351 A72 22s dark blue & multi .65 .65
Nos. 348-351 (4) 1.30 1.30

See Nos. 399-402.

1971, Oct. 4 *Perf. 14x13½*

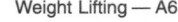

Christmas: 2s, 3s, Virgin and Child, by Giovanni Bellini. 20c, 30c, Virgin and Child with

St. Anne and St. John the Baptist, by Leonardo da Vinci.

352 A73 2s blue & multi .20 .20
353 A73 3s black & multi .20 .20
354 A73 20s yellow & multi .55 .55
355 A73 30s dark red & multi .80 .80
Nos. 352-355 (4) 1.75 1.75

Samoan Islands, Scales of Justice A74

1972, Jan. 10 Photo. *Perf. 11½x12*
356 A74 10s light blue & multi .35 .35

1st So. Pacific Judicial Conf., Samoa, Jan. 1972.

Asau Wharf, Savaii A75

Designs: 8s, Parliament Building. 10s, Mothers' Center. 22s, Portraits of Tupua Tamasese Mea'ole and Malietoa Tanumafili II, and view of Vailima.

Perf. 13x13½
1972, Jan. 10 Litho. Wmk. 355
357 A75 1s bright pink & multi .20 .20
358 A75 8s lilac & multi .20 .20
359 A75 10s green & multi .25 .25
360 A75 22s multicolored .60 .60
Nos. 357-360 (4) 1.25 1.25

10th anniversary of independence.

Commission Members' Flags — A76

Sunset and Ships — A77

Designs: 7s, Afoafouvale Misimoa, Secretary-General, 1970-71 and Commission flag. 8s, Headquarters Building, Noumea, New Caledonia, horiz. 10s, Flag of Samoa, flag and map of South Pacific Commission area, horiz.

1972, Mar. 17 *Perf. 14x13½, 13½x14*
361 A76 3s ultra & multi .20 .20
362 A76 7s yellow, black & ultra .25 .25
363 A76 8s multicolored .30 .30
364 A76 10s lt green & multi .35 .35
Nos. 361-364 (4) 1.10 1.10

South Pacific Commission, 25th anniv.

1972, June 14 *Perf. 14½*

Designs: 8s, Sailing ships Arend, Thienhoven and Africaansche Galey in storm. 10s, Outrigger canoe and Roggeveen's ships. 30s, Hemispheres with exploration route and map of Samoan Islands. All horiz.

365 A77 2s car rose & multi .20 .20
366 A77 8s violet blue & multi .40 .30
367 A77 10s ultra & multi .45 .40

Size: 85x25mm
368 A77 30s ocher & multi 2.00 1.10
Nos. 365-368 (4) 3.05 2.00

250th anniv. of Jacob Roggeveen's Pacific voyage and discovery of Samoa in June 1722.

Bull Conch A78

1972-75 Litho. *Perf. 14½*
Size: 41x24mm
369 A78 1s shown .20 .20
370 A78 2s Rhinoceros beetle .20 .20
371 A78 3s Skipjack (fish) .20 .20
372 A78 4s Painted crab .20 .20
373 A78 5s Butterflyfish .20 .20
374 A78 7s Samoan monarch .20 .20
375 A78 10s Triton shell .20 .20
376 A78 20s Jewel beetle .45 .45
377 A78 50s Spiny lobster 1.25 1.25

Perf. 14x13½
Size: 29x45mm
378 A78 $1 Hawk moth 2.25 2.25
378A A78 $2 Green turtle 4.50 4.50
378B A78 $4 Black marlin 9.25 9.25
378C A78 $5 Green tree lizard 12.00 12.00
Nos. 369-378C (13) 31.10 31.10

Issued: 1s-$1, Oct. 18, 1972; $2, June 18, 1973; $4, Mar. 27, 1974; $5, June 30, 1975.

Ascension, Stained Glass Window — A79

Stained Glass Windows in Apia Churches: 4s, Virgin and Child. 10s, St. Andrew blessing Samoan canoe. 30s, The Good Shepherd.

Perf. 14x14½
1972, Nov. 1 Wmk. 355
379 A79 1s ocher & multi .20 .20
380 A79 4s gray & multi .20 .20
381 A79 10s dull green & multi .30 .30
382 A79 30s blue & multi .90 .90
a. Souvenir sheet of 4, #379-382 1.65 1.65
Nos. 379-382 (4) 1.60 1.60

Christmas.

Scouts Saluting Flag, Emblems A80

1973, Jan. 29 *Perf. 14*
383 A80 2s shown .20 .20
384 A80 3s First aid .20 .20
385 A80 8s Pitching tent .40 .40
386 A80 20s Action song 1.00 1.00
Nos. 383-386 (4) 1.80 1.80

Boy Scouts of Samoa.

Apia General Hospital — A81

"A Prince is Born," by Jahnke — A82

WHO, 25th anniv.: 8s, Baby clinic. 20s, Filariasis research. 22s, Family welfare.

1973, Aug. 20 Wmk. 355
387 A81 2s green & multi .20 .20
388 A81 8s multicolored .25 .25
389 A81 20s brown & multi .55 .55
390 A81 22s vermilion & multi .65 .65
Nos. 387-390 (4) 1.65 1.65

1973, Oct. 15 Litho. *Perf. 14*

Christmas: 4s, "Star of Hope," by Fiasili Keil. 10s, "Mother and Child," by Ernesto Coter. 30s, "The Light of the World," by Coter.

391 A82 3s blue & multi .20 .20
392 A82 4s purple & multi .20 .20
393 A82 10s red & multi .30 .30
394 A82 30s blue & multi .95 .95
a. Souvenir sheet of 4, #391-394 2.00 2.00
Nos. 391-394 (4) 1.65 1.65

Boxing and Games' Emblem A83

1974, Jan. 24
395 A83 8s shown .20 .20
396 A83 10s Weight lifting .30 .30
397 A83 20s Lawn bowling .65 .65
398 A83 30s Stadium .90 .90
Nos. 395-398 (4) 2.05 2.05

10th British Commonwealth Games, Christchurch, New Zealand, Jan. 24-Feb. 2.

Legends Type of 1971

Samoan Legends, Wood Carvings by Sven Ortquist: 2s, Tigilau and dove. 8s, Pili with his sons and famous fish net. 20s, The girl Sina and the eel which became the coconut tree. 30s, Nafanua who returned from the spirit world to free her village.

1974, Aug. 13 Wmk. 355 *Perf. 14*
399 A72 2s lemon & multi .20 .20
400 A72 8s rose red & multi .20 .20
401 A72 20s yellow grn & multi .65 .65
402 A72 30s lt violet & multi .95 .95
Nos. 399-402 (4) 2.00 2.00

Faleolo Airport — A84

Designs: 20s, Apia Wharf. 22s, Early post office, Apia. 50s, William Willis, raft "Age Unlimited" and route from Callao, Peru, to Tully, Western Samoa.

1974, Sept. 4 Unwmk. *Perf. 13½*
Size: 47x29mm
403 A84 8s multicolored .20 .20
404 A84 20s multicolored .45 .45
405 A84 22s multicolored .60 .60

Size: 86x29mm
406 A84 50s multicolored 1.25 1.25
a. Souvenir sheet of 1, perf. 13 1.75 1.75
Nos. 403-406 (4) 2.50 2.50

Cent. of UPU. The 8s is inscribed "Air Mail"; 20s, "Sea Mail"; 22s, "Raft Mail."

Holy Family, by Sebastiano — A85

Christmas: 4s, Virgin and Child with Saints, by Lotto. 10s, Virgin and Child with St. John, by Titian. 30s, Adoration of the Shepherds, by Rubens.

1974, Nov. 18 Litho. *Perf. 13x13½*
407 A85 3s ocher & multi .20 .20
408 A85 4s fawn & multi .20 .20
409 A85 10s dull green & multi .25 .25
410 A85 30s blue & multi .80 .80
a. Souvenir sheet of 4, #407-410 1.40 1.40
Nos. 407-410 (4) 1.45 1.45

Winged Passion Flower A86

20s, Gardenias, vert. 22s, Lecythidaceae, vert. 30s, Malay apple.

Wmk. 355
1975, Jan. 17 Litho. *Perf. 14½*
411 A86 8s dull yellow & multi .25 .25
412 A86 20s pale pink & multi .55 .55
413 A86 22s pink & multi .60 .60
414 A86 30s lt green & multi .85 .85
Nos. 411-414 (4) 2.25 2.25

Joyita Loading at Apia A87

Designs: 8s, Joyita, Samoa and Tokelau Islands. 20s, Joyita sinking, Oct. 1955. 22s, Rafts in storm. 50s, Plane discovering wreck.

1975, Mar. 14 Photo. *Perf. 13*
415 A87 1s multicolored .20 .20
416 A87 8s multicolored .20 .20
417 A87 20s multicolored .45 .45
418 A87 22s multicolored .55 .55
419 A87 50s multicolored 1.25 1.25
a. Souvenir sheet of 5, #415-419 2.75 2.75
Nos. 415-419 (5) 2.65 2.65

17th INTERPEX Phil. Exhib., NYC, 3/14-16.

Pate Drum — A88

Mother and Child, by Meleane Fe'ao — A89

1975, Sept. 30 Litho. *Perf. 14½x14*
420 A88 8s shown .20 .20
421 A88 20s Lali drum .50 .50
422 A88 22s Logo drum .55 .55
423 A88 30s Pu shell horn .75 .75
Nos. 420-423 (4) 2.00 2.00

1975, Nov. 25 Litho. Wmk. 355

Christmas (Paintings): 4s, Christ Child and Samoan flag, by Polataia Tuigamala. 10s, "A

Star is Born," by Iosua Toafa. 30s, Mother and Child, by Ernesto Coter.

424 A89 3s multicolored .20 .20
425 A89 4s multicolored .20 .20
426 A89 10s multicolored .25 .25
427 A89 30s multicolored .75 .75
a. Souvenir sheet of 4, #424-427 1.40 1.40
Nos. 424-427 (4) 1.40 1.40

Boston Massacre, by Paul Revere — A90

8s, Declaration of Independence, by John Trumbull. 20s, The Sinking of the Bonhomme Richard, by J. L. G. Ferris. 22s, Wm. Pitt Addressing House of Commons, by R. A. Hickel. 50s, Battle of Princeton, by William Mercer.

Perf. 13½x14

1976, Jan. 20 Litho. Wmk. 355

428 A90 7s salmon & multi .20 .20
429 A90 8s green & multi .25 .25
430 A90 20s lilac & multi .60 .60
431 A90 22s blue & multi .65 .65
432 A90 50s yellow & multi 1.50 1.50
a. Souvenir sheet of 5, #428-432 + label 5.50 5.50
Nos. 428-432 (5) 3.20 3.20

Bicentenary of American Independence.

Mullet Fishing A91

1976, Apr. 27 Litho. *Perf. 14½*

433 A91 10s shown .20 .20
434 A91 12s Fish traps .25 .25
435 A91 22s Fishermen .45 .45
436 A91 50s Net fishing 1.00 1.00
Nos. 433-436 (4) 1.90 1.90

Souvenir Sheet

Samoan $100 Gold Coin with Paul Revere and US Map — A92

Unwmk.

1976, May 29 Photo. *Perf. 13*

437 A92 $1 green & gold 3.00 3.00

American Bicentennial and Interphil 76 Intl. Phil. Exhib., Philadelphia, PA, May 29-June 6.

Boxing A93

12s, Wrestling. 22s, Javelin. 50s, Weight lifting.

Perf. 14½x14

1976, June 21 Litho. Wmk. 355

438 A93 10s black & multi .20 .20
439 A93 12s dark brown & multi .25 .25
440 A93 22s dark purple & multi .45 .45
441 A93 50s dark blue & multi 1.10 1.10
Nos. 438-441 (4) 2.00 2.00

21st Olympic Games, Montreal, Canada, July 17-Aug. 1.

Mary and Joseph on Road to Bethlehem A94

Christmas: 5s, Adoration of the Shepherds. 22s, Nativity. 50s, Adoration of the Kings.

1976, Oct. 18 Litho. *Perf. 14x13½*

442 A94 3s multicolored .20 .20
443 A94 5s multicolored .20 .20
444 A94 22s multicolored .45 .45
445 A94 50s multicolored 1.25 1.25
a. Souvenir sheet of 4, #442-445 2.50 2.50
Nos. 442-445 (4) 2.10 2.10

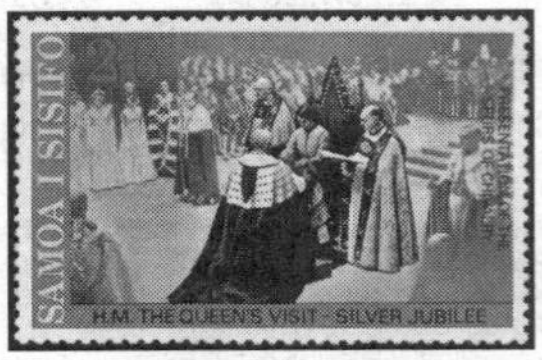

Presentation of the Spurs of Chivalry — A95

Designs: 12s, Queen and view of Apia. 32s, Royal Yacht Britannia and Queen. 50s, Queen leaving Westminster Abbey.

Perf. 13½x14

1977, Feb. 11 Wmk. 355

446 A95 12s multicolored .20 .20
447 A95 26s multicolored .35 .35
448 A95 32s multicolored .55 .55
449 A95 50s multicolored .85 .85
Nos. 446-449 (4) 1.95 1.95

25th anniv. of the reign of Elizabeth II.

Lindbergh and Spirit of St. Louis A96

Designs: 22s, Map of transatlantic route and plane. 24s, Spirit of St. Louis in flight. 26s, Spirit of St. Louis taking off.

1977, May 20 Litho. *Perf. 14*

450 A96 22s multicolored .35 .35
451 A96 24s multicolored .40 .40
452 A96 26s multicolored .45 .45
453 A96 50s multicolored .85 .85
a. Souvenir sheet of 4, #450-453 2.50 2.50
Nos. 450-453 (4) 2.05 2.05

Charles A. Lindbergh's solo transatlantic flight from New York to Paris, 50th anniv.

Apia Automatic Telephone Exchange — A97

Designs: 13s, Mulinuu radio terminal. 26s, Old wall and new dial telephones. 50s, Global communications (2 telephones and globe).

1977, July 11 Litho. *Perf. 14*

454 A97 12s multicolored .20 .20
455 A97 13s multicolored .20 .20
456 A97 26s multicolored .45 .45
457 A97 50s multicolored .80 .80
Nos. 454-457 (4) 1.65 1.65

Telecommunications.

Samoa No. 3 and First Mail Notice — A98

13s, Samoa #4 & 1881 cover. 26s, Samoa #1 & Chief Post Office, Apia. 50s, Samoa #4 7 schooner "Energy," which carried 1st mail.

1977, Aug. 29 Wmk. 355 *Perf. 13½*

458 A98 12s multicolored .20 .20
459 A98 13s multicolored .20 .20
460 A98 26s multicolored .40 .40
461 A98 50s multicolored .80 .80
Nos. 458-461 (4) 1.60 1.60

Samoan postage stamp centenary.

Nativity — A99

Christmas: 6s, People bringing gifts to Holy Family in Samoan hut. 26s, Virgin and Child. 50s, Stars over Christ Child.

1977, Oct. 11 Litho. *Perf. 14*

462 A99 4s multicolored .20 .20
463 A99 6s multicolored .20 .20
464 A99 26s multicolored .35 .35
465 A99 50s multicolored 1.25 1.25
a. Souvenir sheet of 4, #462-465 2.00 2.00
Nos. 462-465 (4) 2.00 2.00

Polynesian Airlines' Boeing 737 — A100

Aviation Progress: 24s, Kitty Hawk. 26s, Kingsford-Smith Fokker. 50s, Concorde.

Unwmk.

1978, Mar. 21 Litho. *Perf. 14*

466 A100 12s multicolored .20 .20
467 A100 24s multicolored .45 .45
468 A100 26s multicolored .50 .50
469 A100 50s multicolored .95 .95
a. Souvenir sheet of 4, #466-469, perf. 13½ 3.00 3.00
Nos. 466-469 (4) 2.10 2.10

Turtle Hatchery, Aleipata — A101

$1, Hawksbill turtle & Wildlife Fund emblem.

1978, Apr. 14 Wmk. 355 *Perf. 14½*

470 A101 24s multicolored *1.00 1.00*
471 A101 $1 multicolored *4.25 4.25*

Project to replenish endangered hawksbill turtles.

Common Design Types pictured following the introduction.

Elizabeth II Coronation Anniversary Issue

Souvenir Sheet

Common Design Types

1978, Apr. 21 Unwmk. *Perf. 15*

472 Sheet of 6 3.00 3.00
a. CD326 26s King's lion .45 .45
b. CD327 26s Elizabeth II .45 .45
c. CD328 26s Pacific pigeon .45 .45

No. 472 contains 2 se-tenant strips of Nos. 472a-472c, separated by horizontal gutter with commemorative and descriptive inscriptions and showing central part of coronation procession with coach.

Souvenir Sheet

Canadian and Samoan Flags — A102

Wmk. 355

1978, June 9 Litho. *Perf. 14½*

473 A102 $1 multicolored 2.25 2.25

CAPEX Canadian Intl. Phil. Exhib., Toronto, June 9-18.

Capt. James Cook — A103

Designs: 24s, Cook's cottage, now in Melbourne, Australia. 26s, Old drawbridge over River Esk, Whitby, 1766-1833. 50s, Resolution and map of Hawaiian Islands.

1978, Aug. 28 Litho. *Perf. 14½x14*

474 A103 12s multicolored .25 .25
475 A103 24s multicolored .55 .55
476 A103 26s multicolored .70 .70
477 A103 50s multicolored 1.40 1.40
Nos. 474-477 (4) 2.90 2.90

A104

A105

Cowrie Shells: 1s, Thick-edged Cowrie. 2s, Isabella cowrie. 3s, Money cowrie. 4s, Eroded cowrie. 6s, Honey cowrie. 7s, Banded cowrie. 10s, Globe cowrie. 11s, Mole cowrie. 12s, Children's cowrie. 13s, Flag cone. 14s, Soldier cone. 24s, Cloth-of-gold cone. 26s, Lettered cone. 50s, Tiled cone. $1, Black marble cone. $2, Marlin-spike auger. $3, Scorpion spider conch. $5, Common harp.

1978-80 Photo. Unwmk. *Perf. 12½*

Size: 31x24mm

Granite Paper

478 A104 1s multicolored .20 .20
479 A104 2s multicolored .20 .20
480 A104 3s multicolored .20 .20
481 A104 4s multicolored .20 .20
482 A104 6s multicolored .20 .20
483 A104 7s multicolored .20 .20
484 A104 10s multicolored .20 .20
485 A104 11s multicolored .20 .20
486 A104 12s multicolored .20 .20

487 A104 13s multicolored .20 .20
488 A104 14s multicolored .20 .20
489 A104 24s multicolored .25 .25
490 A104 26s multicolored .25 .25
491 A104 50s multicolored .45 .45
492 A104 $1 multicolored .90 .90

Perf. 11½

Size: 36x26mm

493 A104 $2 multi ('79) 1.75 1.75
494 A104 $3 multi ('79) 3.00 3.00
494A A104 $5 multi ('80) 7.50 7.50
Nos. 478-494A (18) 16.30 16.30

Issue dates: 1s-12s, Sept. 15. 13s-$1, Nov. 20. $2, $3, July 18. $5, Aug. 26.

Wmk. 355

1978, Nov. 6 Litho. *Perf. 14*

Works by Dürer: 4s, The Virgin in Glory. 6s, Nativity. 26s, Adoration of the Kings. 50s, Annunciation.

495 A105 4s lt brown & blk .20 .20
496 A105 6s grnsh blue & blk .20 .20
497 A105 26s violet blue & blk .40 .40
498 A105 50s purple & blk .80 .80
a. Souvenir sheet of 4, #495-498 1.75 1.75
Nos. 495-498 (4) 1.60 1.60

Christmas and for 450th death anniv. of Albrecht Dürer.

Boy Carrying Coconuts A106

Designs: 24s, Children leaving church on White Sunday. 26s, Children pumping water. 50s, Girl playing ukulele.

1979, Apr. 10 Litho. *Perf. 14*

499 A106 12s multicolored .20 .20
500 A106 24s multicolored .40 .40
501 A106 26s multicolored .45 .45
502 A106 50s multicolored .95 .95
Nos. 499-502 (4) 2.00 2.00

International Year of the Child.

Charles W. Morgan A107

1979, May 29 Litho. *Perf. 13½*

503 A107 12s multicolored .30 .30
504 A107 14s Lagoda .40 .40
505 A107 24s James T. Arnold .65 .65
506 A107 50s Splendid 1.40 1.40
Nos. 503-506 (4) 2.75 2.75

See Nos. 521-524, 543-546.

Saturn V Launch — A108

Penny Black, Hill Statue — A109

Designs: 14s, Landing module and astronaut on moon, horiz. 24s, Earth seen from moon. 26s, Astronaut on moon, horiz. 50s, Lunar and command modules. $1, Command module after splashdown, horiz.

Perf. 14½x14, 14x14½

1979, June 20 Litho. Wmk. 355

507 A108 12s multicolored .20 .20
508 A108 14s multicolored .20 .20
509 A108 24s multicolored .30 .30
510 A108 26s multicolored .35 .35
511 A108 50s multicolored .65 .65
512 A108 $1 multicolored 1.40 1.40
a. Souvenir sheet 1.75 1.75
Nos. 507-512 (6) 3.10 3.10

1st moon landing, 10th anniv.

1979, Aug. 27 *Perf. 14*

24s, Great Britain #2 with Maltese Cross postmark. 26s, Penny Black and Rowland Hill. $1, Great Britain #2 and Hill statue.

513 A109 12s multicolored .20 .20
514 A109 24s multicolored .25 .25
515 A109 26s multicolored .30 .30
516 A109 $1 multicolored 1.10 1.10
a. Souvenir sheet of 4, #513-516 1.90 1.90
Nos. 513-516 (4) 1.85 1.85

Sir Rowland Hill (1795-1879), originator of penny postage.

Anglican Church, Apia A110

Samoan Churches: 6s, Congregational Christian Church, Leulumoega. 26s, Methodist Church, Piula. 50s, Protestant Church, Apia.

1979, Oct. 22 Photo. *Perf. 12x11½*

517 A110 4s lt blue & blk .20 .20
518 A110 6s lt yellow grn & blk .20 .20
519 A110 26s dull yellow & blk .40 .40
520 A110 50s lt lilac & blk .75 .75
a. Souvenir sheet of 4, #517-520 1.40 1.40
Nos. 517-520 (4) 1.55 1.55

Christmas.

Ship Type of 1979

Wmk. 355

1980, Jan. 22 Litho. *Perf. 14*

521 A107 12s William Hamilton .25 .25
522 A107 14s California .30 .30
523 A107 24s Liverpool II .55 .55
524 A107 50s Two Brothers 1.10 1.10
Nos. 521-524 (4) 2.20 2.20

Map of Samoan Islands, Rotary Emblem A111

Missionary Flag, John Williams, Plaque — A112

Flag-raising Memorial — A113

1980, Mar. 26 Photo. *Perf. 14*

525 A111 12s shown .20 .20
526 A112 13s shown .20 .20
527 A112 14s German flag, Dr. Wilhelm Solf, plaque .20 .20
528 A113 24s shown .35 .35
529 A113 26s Williams Memorial, Savai'i .40 .40
530 A111 50s Emblem, Paul P. Harris, founder .70 .70
Nos. 525-530 (6) 2.05 2.05

Rotary Intl., 75th anniv. (A111); arrival of Williams, missionary in Samoa, 150th anniv. (13s, 26s); raising of the German flag, 80th anniv. (14s, 24s).

Souvenir Sheet

Village and Long Boat — A114

Wmk. 355

1980, May 6 Litho. *Perf. 14*

531 A114 $1 multicolored 2.00 2.00

London 80 Intl. Phil. Exhib., May 6-14.

Queen Mother Elizabeth Birthday Issue

Common Design Type

1980, Aug. 4 Litho.

532 CD330 50s multicolored .70 .70

Souvenir Sheet

Samoa No. 239, ZEAPEX Emblem — A115

Unwmk.

1980, Aug. 23 Litho. *Perf. 14*

533 A115 $1 multicolored 2.00 2.00

ZEAPEX '80, New Zealand International Stamp Exhibition, Auckland, Aug. 23-31.

Afiamalu Satellite Earth Station A116

14s, Station, diff. 24s, Station, map of Samoa. 50s, Satellite sending waves to earth. $2, Samoa #536, Sydpex '80 emblem.

1980, Sept. 17 Litho. *Perf. 11½*

Granite Paper

534 A116 12s multicolored .20 .20
535 A116 14s multicolored .20 .20
536 A116 24s multicolored .30 .30
537 A116 50s multicolored .70 .70
Nos. 534-537 (4) 1.40 1.40

Souvenir Sheet

1980, Sept. 29 *Imperf.*

538 A116 $2 multicolored 2.25 2.25

Sydpex '80 Natl. Phil. Exhib., Sydney.

The Savior, by John Poynton — A117

Christmas (Paintings by Local Artists): 14s, Madonna and Child, by Lealofi F. Siaopo. 27s, Nativity, by Pasila Feata. 50s, Yuletide, by R.P. Aiono.

Wmk. 355

1980, Oct. 28 Litho. *Perf. 14*

539 A117 8s multicolored .20 .20
540 A117 14s multicolored .20 .20
541 A117 27s multicolored .30 .30
542 A117 50s multicolored .50 .50
a. Souvenir sheet of 4, #539-542 1.40 1.40
Nos. 539-542 (4) 1.20 1.20

Ship Type of 1979

1981, Jan. 26 Litho. *Perf. 13½*

543 A107 12s Ocean .25 .25
544 A107 18s Horatio .40 .40
545 A107 27s Calliope .60 .60
546 A107 32s Calypso .70 .70
Nos. 543-546 (4) 1.95 1.95

Pres. Franklin Roosevelt and Hyde Park Home A118

IYD: Scenes of Franklin D. Roosevelt.

Wmk. 355

1981, Apr. 29 Litho. *Perf. 14*

547 A118 12s shown .20 .20
548 A118 18s Inauguration .20 .20
549 A118 27s Pres. & Mrs. Roosevelt .25 .25
550 A118 32s Atlantic convoy (Lend Lease Bill) .30 .30
551 A118 38s With stamp collection .35 .35
552 A118 $1 Campobello House .85 .85
Nos. 547-552 (6) 2.15 2.15

Hotel Tusitala — A119

Perf. 14½x14

1981, June 29 Litho. Wmk. 355

553 A119 12s shown .20 .20
554 A119 18s Apia Harbor .20 .20
555 A119 27s Aggie Grey's Hotel .30 .30
556 A119 32s Ceremonial kava preparation .35 .35
557 A119 54s Piula Pool .60 .60
Nos. 553-557 (5) 1.65 1.65

Royal Wedding Issue

Common Design Type

Wmk. 355

1981, July 22 Litho. *Perf. 14*

558 CD331 18s Bouquet .20 .20
559 CD331 32s Charles .20 .20
560 CD331 $1 Couple .65 .65
Nos. 558-560 (3) 1.05 1.05

Tattooing Instruments A120

1981, Sept. 29 Litho. *Perf. 13½x14*

561 Strip of 4 1.75 1.75
a. A120 12s shown .20 .20
b. A120 18s 1st stage .20 .20
c. A120 27s Later stage .30 .30
d. A120 $1 Tattooed man 1.10 1.10

Christmas — A121

1981, Nov. 30 Litho. *Perf. 13½*

562 A121 11s Milo tree blossom .20 .20
563 A121 15s Copper leaf .20 .20
564 A121 23s Yellow allamanda .25 .25
565 A121 $1 Mango blossom 1.10 1.10
a. Souvenir sheet of 4, #562-565 2.25 2.25
Nos. 562-565 (4) 1.75 1.75

Souvenir Sheet

Philatokyo '81 Intl. Stamp Exhibition — A122

1981, Oct. 9 Litho. *Perf. 14x13½*
566 A122 $2 multicolored 2.25 2.25

250th Birth Anniv. of George Washington A123

1982, Feb. 26 Litho. *Perf. 14*
567 A123 23s Pistol .25 .25
568 A123 25s Mt. Vernon .30 .30
569 A123 34s Portrait .45 .45
Nos. 567-569 (3) 1.00 1.00

Souvenir Sheet

570 A123 $1 Taking oath 1.25 1.25

20th Anniv. of Independence — A124

1982, May 24 Litho. *Perf. 13½x14*
571 A124 18s Freighter Forum Samoa .25 .25
572 A124 23s Jet, routes .30 .30
573 A124 25s Natl. Provident Fund building .35 .35
574 A124 $1 Intl. subscriber dialing system 1.25 1.25
Nos. 571-574 (4) 2.15 2.15

Scouting Year A125

1982, July 20 Wmk. 355 *Perf. 14½*
575 A125 5s Map reading .20 .20
576 A125 38s Salute .50 .50
577 A125 44s Rope bridge .60 .60
578 A125 $1 Troop 1.10 1.10
a. Souvenir sheet 1.50 1.50
Nos. 575-578 (4) 2.40 2.40

No. 578a contains one stamp similar to No. 578, 48x36mm.

12th Commonwealth Games, Brisbane, Australia, Sept. 30-Oct. 9 — A126

Perf. 14x14½

1982, Sept. 20 Wmk. 373
579 A126 23s Boxing .25 .25
580 A126 25s Hurdles .30 .30
581 A126 34s Weightlifting .40 .40
582 A126 $1 Lawn bowling 1.00 1.00
Nos. 579-582 (4) 1.95 1.95

Christmas A127

Children's Drawings: 11s, 15s, Flight into Egypt diff. 38s, $1, Virgin and Child, diff.

1982, Nov. 15 Litho. Wmk. 355
583 A127 11s multicolored .20 .20
584 A127 15s multicolored .20 .20
585 A127 38s multicolored .50 .50
586 A127 $1 multicolored 1.10 1.10
a. Souvenir sheet of 4, #583-586 2.00 2.00
Nos. 583-586 (4) 2.00 2.00

Commonwealth Day — A128

Perf. 13½x14

1983, Feb. 23 Litho. Wmk. 373
587 A128 14s Map .20 .20
588 A128 29s Flag .35 .35
589 A128 43s Harvesting copra .50 .50
590 A128 $1 Malietoa Tanumafili II 1.10 1.10
Nos. 587-590 (4) 2.15 2.15

Manned Flight Bicentenary and 50th Anniv. of Douglas Aircraft A129

a, DC-1. b, DC-2. c, DC-3. d, DC-4. e, DC-5. f, DC-6. g, DC-7. h, DC-8. i, DC-9. j, DC-10.

Wmk. 373

1983, June 7 Litho. *Perf. 14*
591 Sheet of 10 4.00 4.00
a.-j. A129 32s any single .40 .40

7th South Pacific Games, Apia — A130

Local Fruit — A131

1983, Aug. 29 Litho. *Perf. 14x14½*
592 A130 8s Pole vault .20 .20
593 A130 15s Basketball .20 .20
594 A130 25c Tennis .25 .25
595 A130 32s Weightlifting .35 .35
596 A130 35s Boxing .35 .35
597 A130 46s Soccer .50 .50
598 A130 48s Golf .55 .55
599 A130 56s Rugby .60 .60
Nos. 592-599 (8) 3.00 3.00

Perf. 14x13½

1983-84 Litho. Wmk. 373
600 A131 1s Limes .20 .20
601 A131 2s Star fruit .20 .20
602 A131 3s Mangosteen .20 .20
603 A131 4s Lychee .20 .20
604 A131 7s Passion fruit .20 .20
605 A131 8s Mangoes .20 .20
606 A131 11s Papaya .20 .20
607 A131 13s Pineapple .20 .20
608 A131 14s Breadfruit .20 .20
609 A131 15s Bananas .20 .20
610 A131 21s Cashew nut .25 .25
611 A131 25s Guava .30 .30
612 A131 32s Water Melon .35 .35
613 A131 48s Sasalapa .55 .55
614 A131 56s Avocado .65 .65
615 A131 $1 Coconut 1.10 1.10

Perf. 13½
616 A131 $2 Apples ('84) 2.25 2.25
617 A131 $4 Grapefruit ('84) 4.50 4.50
618 A131 $5 Oranges ('84) 5.50 5.50
Nos. 600-618 (19) 17.45 17.45

Issued: 1s-15s, 9/28; 21s-$1, 11/30; $2-$5, 4/11.

For overprint see No. 628.

Miniature Sheet

Boys' Brigade Centenary — A132

1983, Oct. 10 *Perf. 14½*
619 A132 $1 multicolored 1.00 1.00

Togitogiga Falls, Upolu A133

Wmk. 373

1984, Feb. 15 Litho. *Perf. 14*
620 A133 25s shown .25 .25
621 A133 32s Lano Beach, Savai'i .30 .30
622 A133 48s Mulinu'u Point, Upolu .45 .45
623 A133 56s Nu'utele Isld. .50 .50
Nos. 620-623 (4) 1.50 1.50

Lloyd's List Issue

Common Design Type

Perf. 14½x14

1984, May 24 Litho. Wmk. 373
624 CD335 32s Apia Harbor .30 .30
625 CD335 48s Apia hurricane, 1889 .50 .50
626 CD335 60s Forum Samoa .60 .60
627 CD335 $1 Matua 1.00 1.00
Nos. 624-627 (4) 2.40 2.40

No. 615 Overprinted: "19th U.P.U. CONGRESS / HAMBURG 1984"

1984, June 7 *Perf. 14x13½*
628 A131 $1 multicolored 1.25 1.25

Los Angeles Coliseum — A134

1984, June 26 Litho. *Perf. 14½*
629 A134 25s shown .25 .25
630 A134 32s Weightlifting .35 .35
631 A134 48s Boxing .55 .55
632 A134 $1 Running 1.10 1.10
a. Souvenir sheet of 4, #629-632 2.25 2.25
Nos. 629-632 (4) 2.25 2.25

1984 Summer Olympics and Samoa's first Olympic participation.

Souvenir Sheet

Ausipex '84 — A135

1984, Sept. 21 Litho. *Perf. 14*
633 A135 $2.50 Nomad N24 3.25 3.25

Christmas — A136

The Three Virtues, by Raphael.

1984, Nov. 7 *Perf. 14½x14*
634 A136 25s Faith .25 .25
635 A136 35s Hope .30 .30
636 A136 $1 Charity .95 .95
a. Souvenir sheet of 3, #634-636 1.50 1.50
Nos. 634-636 (3) 1.50 1.50

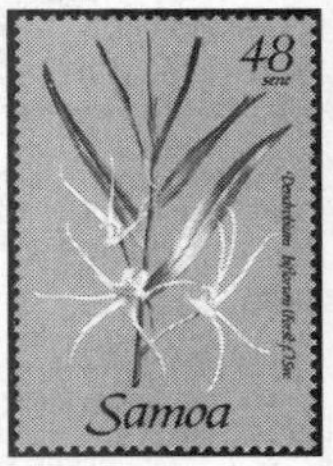

Orchids — A137

Unwmk.

1985, Jan. 23 Litho. *Perf. 14*
637 A137 48s Dendrobium biflorum .75 .45
638 A137 56s Dendrobium vaupelianum kraenzl .90 .90
639 A137 67s Glomera montana 1.10 1.10
640 A137 $1 Spathoglottis plicata 1.65 1.65
Nos. 637-640 (4) 4.40 4.10

Vintage Automobiles — A138

Wmk. 373

1985, Mar. 26 Litho. *Perf. 14*
641 A138 48s Ford Model A, 1903 .65 .65
642 A138 56s Chevrolet Tourer, 1912 .75 .75
643 A138 67s Morris Oxford, 1913 .85 .85
644 A138 $1 Austin Seven, 1923 1.40 .95
Nos. 641-644 (4) 3.65 3.20

Fungi — A139

1985, Apr. 17 Litho. *Perf. 14½*
645 A139 48s Dictyophora indusiata .70 .70
646 A139 56s Ganoderma tornatum .85 .85

647 A139 67s Mycena chlorophos .95 .95
648 A139 $1 Mycobonia flava 1.50 1.50
Nos. 645-648 (4) 4.00 4.00

Queen Mother 85th Birthday
Common Design Type
Perf. 14½x14

1985, June 7 Litho. Wmk. 384
649 CD336 32s Photo., age 9 .30 .30
650 CD336 48s With Prince William at christening of Prince Henry .50 .50
651 CD336 56s At Liverpool street station .60 .60
652 CD336 $1 Holding Prince Henry 1.00 1.00
Nos. 649-652 (4) 2.40 2.40

Souvenir Sheet
653 CD336 $2 Arriving at Tattenham corner station 2.00 2.00

Souvenir Sheet

EXPO '85, Tsukuba, Japan — A140

Unwmk.
1985, Aug. 26 Litho. *Perf. 14*
654 A140 $2 Emblem, elevation map 1.75 1.75

Intl. Youth Year — A141

Christmas 1985 — A142

Portions of world map and: a, Emblem, map of No. America, Europe and Africa. b, Hands reaching high. c, Arms reaching, hands limp. d, Hands clenched. e, Emblem and map of Africa, Asia and Europe.

1985, Sept. 18 Wmk. 373
655 Strip of 5 2.75 2.75
a.-e. A141 60s any single .55 .55

1985, Nov. 5 Unwmk. *Perf. 14x14½*

Illustrations by Millicent Sowerby from A Child's Garden of Verses, by Robert Louis Stevenson.

656 A142 32s System .30 .30
657 A142 48s Time to Rise .40 .40
658 A142 56s Auntie's skirts .50 .50
659 A142 $1 Good Children .90 .90
a. Souvenir sheet of 4, #656-659 2.10 2.10
Nos. 656-659 (4) 2.10 2.10

Butterflies A143

1986, Feb. 13 Wmk. 384 *Perf. 14½*
660 A143 25s Hypolimnas bolina inconstans .40 .40
661 A143 32s Anapheis java sparrman .50 .50
662 A143 48s Deudorix epijarbas doris .70 .70
663 A143 56s Badamia exclamationis .85 .85
664 A143 60s Tirumala hamata mellitula 1.00 1.00
665 A143 $1 Catochrysops taitensis 1.75 1.75
Nos. 660-665 (6) 5.20 5.20

Halley's Comet A144

Designs: 32s, Comet over Apia. 48s, Edmond Halley, astronomer. 60s, Comet orbiting the Earth. $2, Giotto space probe under construction at British Aerospace.

1986, Mar. 24
666 A144 32s multicolored .30 .30
667 A144 48s multicolored .40 .40
668 A144 60s multicolored .55 .55
669 A144 $2 multicolored 1.75 1.75
Nos. 666-669 (4) 3.00 3.00

Queen Elizabeth II 60th Birthday
Common Design Type

Designs: 32s, Engagement to the Duke of Edinburgh, 1947. 48s, State visit to US, 1976. 56s, Attending outdoor ceremony, Apia, 1977. 67s, At Badminton Horse Trials, 1978. $2, Visiting Crown Agents' offices, 1983.

1986, Apr. 21
670 CD337 32s scarlet, blk & sil .30 .30
671 CD337 48s ultra & multi .40 .40
672 CD337 56s green & multi .50 .50
673 CD337 67s violet & multi .60 .60
674 CD337 $2 rose violet & multi 1.75 1.75
Nos. 670-674 (5) 3.55 3.55

AMERIPEX '86, Chicago, May 22-June 1 — A145

1986, May 22 Unwmk.
675 A145 48s USS Vincennes .40 .40
676 A145 56s Sikorsky S-42 .50 .50
677 A145 60s USS Swan .55 .55
678 A145 $2 Apollo 10 splashdown 1.75 1.75
Nos. 675-678 (4) 3.20 3.20

Souvenir Sheet

Vailima, Estate of Novelist Robert Louis Stevenson, Upolu Is. — A146

1986, Aug. 4 Litho. *Perf. 13½*
679 A146 $3 multicolored 3.25 3.25

STAMPEX '86, Adelaide, Aug. 4-10.

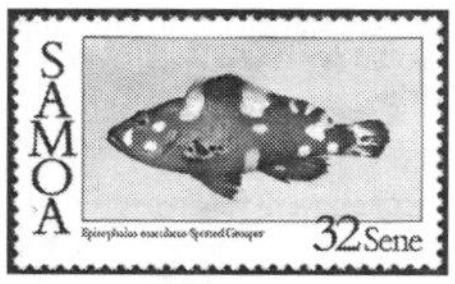

Fish A147

Unwmk.
1986, Aug. 13 Litho. *Perf. 14*
680 A147 32s Spotted grouper .30 .30
681 A147 48s Sabel squirrelfish .45 .45
682 A147 60s Lunartail grouper .55 .55
683 A147 67s Longtail snapper .70 .70
684 A147 $1 Berndt's soldierfish 1.10 1.10
Nos. 680-684 (5) 3.10 3.10

US Peace Corps in Samoa, 25th Anniv. A148

Statesmen: Vaai Kolone of Samoa, Ronald Reagan of US and: 45s, Fiame Mata'afa, John F. Kennedy (1961) and Parliament House. 60s, Jules Grevy, Grover Cleveland (1886) and the Statue of Liberty.

1986, Dec. 1 *Perf. 14½*
685 A148 45s multicolored .40 .40
686 A148 60s multicolored .55 .55
a. Souvenir sheet of 2, #685-686 2.00 2.00

Christmas, Statue of Liberty, cent.

Natl. Independence, 25th Anniv. — A149

Perf. 14x14½
1987, Feb. 16 Litho. Unwmk.
687 A149 15s Map, hibiscus .20 .20
688 A149 45s Parliament .65 .65
689 A149 60s Rowing race, 1987 .80 .80
690 A149 70s Dove .90 .90
691 A149 $2 Prime minister, flag 2.50 2.50
Nos. 687-691 (5) 5.05 5.05

Nos. 687-690 vert.

Marine Life A150

1987, Mar. 31
692 A150 45s Gulper .45 .45
693 A150 60s Hatchet-fish .60 .60
694 A150 70s Angler .70 .70
695 A150 $2 Gulper, diff. 1.90 1.90
Nos. 692-695 (4) 3.65 3.65

Souvenir Sheet

CAPEX '87 — A151

1987, June 13 *Perf. 14½*
696 A151 $3 Logger, construction workers 2.75 2.75

Landscapes — A152

1987, July 29 *Perf. 14*
697 A152 45s Lefaga Beach, Upolu .40 .40
698 A152 60s Vaisala Beach, Savaii .55 .55
699 A152 70s Solosolo Beach, Upolu .65 .65
700 A152 $2 Neiafu Beach, Savaii 1.90 1.90
Nos. 697-700 (4) 3.50 3.50

Australia Bicentennial A153

Explorers of the Pacific: 40s, Abel Tasman (c. 1603-1659), Dutch navigator, discovered Tasmania, 1642. 45s, James Cook. 80s, Count Louis-Antoine de Bougainville (1729-1811), French navigator, discovered Bougainvelle Is., largest of the Solomon Isls., 1768. $2, Comte de La Perouse (1741-1788), French navigator, discovered La Perouse Strait.

1987, Sept. 30 Litho. *Perf. 14½*
701 A153 40s multicolored .35 .35
702 A153 45s multicolored .45 .45
703 A153 80s multicolored .80 .80
704 A153 $2 multicolored 1.90 1.90
a. Souvenir sheet of 1 1.90 1.90
Nos. 701-704 (4) 3.50 3.50

No. 704a Ovptd. with HAFNIA '87 Emblem in Scarlet

1987, Oct. 16
705 A153 $2 multicolored 2.00 2.00

Christmas 1987 — A154

1987, Nov. 30 *Perf. 14*
706 A154 40s Christmas tree .35 .35
707 A154 45s Going to church .45 .45
708 A154 50s Bamboo fire-gun .50 .50
709 A154 80s Going home .75 .75
Nos. 706-709 (4) 2.05 2.05

Australia Bicentennial A155

a, Samoan natl. crest, Australia Post emblem. b, Two jets, postal van. c, Loading airmail. d, Jet, van, postman. e, Congratulatory aerogramme.

1988, Jan. 27 *Perf. 14½*
710 Strip of 5 3.00 3.00
a.-e. A155 45s any single .60 .60

Faleolo Intl. Airport A156

Perf. 13x13½
1988, Mar. 24 Litho. Unwmk.
711 A156 40s Terminal, Boeing 727 .40 .40
712 A156 45s Boeing 727, Fuatino .45 .45
713 A156 60s So. Pacific Is. N43SP, terminal .60 .60
714 A156 70s Air New Zealand Boeing 737 .70 .70
715 A156 80s Tower, jet .80 .80
716 A156 $1 Hawaian Air DC-9, VIP house 1.00 1.00
Nos. 711-716 (6) 3.95 3.95

EXPO '88, Brisbane, Australia A157

1988, Apr. 27 ***Perf. 14½***

717 A157 45s Island village display .45 .45
718 A157 70s EXPO complex, monorail and flags .70 .70
719 A157 $2 Map 2.00 2.00
Nos. 717-719 (3) 3.15 3.15

Souvenir Sheet

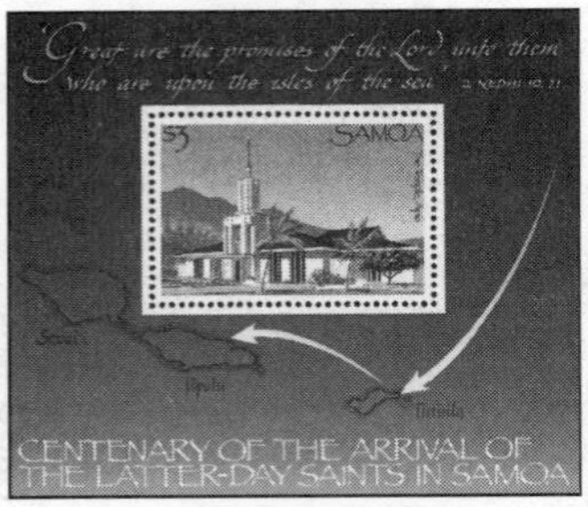

Arrival of the Latter Day Saints in Samoa, Cent. — A158

1988, June 9 **Litho.** ***Perf. 13½***

720 A158 $3 The Temple, Apia 3.00 3.00

1988 Summer Olympics, Seoul — A159

Birds — A160

1988, Aug. 10 **Litho.** ***Perf. 14***

721 A159 15s Running .20 .20
722 A159 60s Weight lifting .60 .60
723 A159 80s Boxing .80 .80
724 A159 $2 Olympic Stadium 2.00 2.00
a. Souvenir sheet of 4, #721-724 3.55 3.55
Nos. 721-724 (4) 3.60 3.60

1988-89 **Unwmk.** ***Perf. 13½***

725 A160 10s Polynesian triller .20 .20
726 A160 15s Samoan wood rail .20 .20
727 A160 20s Flat-billed kingfisher .20 .20
728 A160 25s Samoan fantail .25 .25
729 A160 35s Scarlet robin .35 .35
730 A160 40s Mao .40 .40
731 A160 50s Cardinal honey-eater .50 .50
732 A160 65s Samoan whistler .60 .60
733 A160 75s Many-colored fruit dove .75 .75
734 A160 85s White-throated pigeon .80 .80

Perf. 14

Size:45x39mm

735 A160 75s Silver gull .75 .75
736 A160 85s Great frigatebird .80 .80
737 A160 90s Eastern reef heron .85 .85
738 A160 $3 Short-tailed albatross 3.00 3.00
739 A160 $10 Common fairy tern 9.25 9.25
740 A160 $20 Shy albatross 19.00 19.00
Nos. 725-740 (16) 37.90 37.90

Issue dates: #725-734, 8/17/88; #735-738, 2/28/89; #739-740, 7/31/89.

Conservation — A161

1988, Oct. 25 ***Perf. 14***

741 A161 15s Forests, vert. .20 .20
742 A161 40s Culture, vert. .40 .40
743 A161 45s Wildlife, vert. .45 .45
744 A161 50s Water .50 .50
745 A161 60s Marine resources .60 .60
746 A161 $1 Land and soil .95 .95
Nos. 741-746 (6) 3.10 3.10

Christmas A162

Orchids — A163

Designs: 15s, 40s, Congregational Church of Jesus, Apia. 40s, Roman Catholic Church, Leauvaa. 45s, Congregational Christian Church, Moataa. $2, Baha'i Temple, Vailima.

Perf. 14x14½

1988, Nov. 14 **Litho.** **Unwmk.**

747 A162 15s multicolored .20 .20
748 A162 40s multicolored .40 .40
749 A162 45s multicolored .45 .45
750 A162 $2 multicolored 2.00 2.00
a. Souvenir sheet of 4, #747-750 3.00 3.00
Nos. 747-750 (4) 3.05 3.05

1989, Jan. 31 **Litho.** ***Perf. 14***

751 A163 15s Phaius flavus .20 .20
752 A163 45s Calanthe triplicata .65 .65
753 A163 60s Luisia teretifolia .85 .85
754 A163 $3 Dendrobium mohlianum 4.50 4.50
Nos. 751-754 (4) 6.20 6.20

Apia Hurricane, 1889 A164

1989, Mar. 16 **Litho.** **Unwmk.**

755 Strip of 4 4.50 4.50
a. A164 50s SMS Eber .55 .55
b. A164 65s SMS Olga .70 .70
c. A164 85s SMS Calliope .95 .95
d. A164 $2 SMS Vandalia 2.25 2.25
e. Souv. sheet of 2, #c.-d., imperf. 4.00 4.00

World Stamp Expo '89.
#755e, issued Nov. 17, is wmk. 355.

Intl. Red Cross and Red Crescent Organizations, 125th Annivs. — A165

1989, May 15 ***Perf. 14½x14***

756 A165 50s Youths in parade .45 .45
757 A165 65s Blood donation .60 .60
758 A165 75s First Aid .70 .70
759 A165 $3 Volunteers 2.75 2.75
Nos. 756-759 (4) 4.50 4.50

Moon Landing, 20th Anniv.
Common Design Type

Apollo 14: 18s, Saturn-Apollo vehicle and mobile launcher. 50s, Alan Shepard, Stuart Roosa and Edgar Mitchell. 65s, Mission emblem. $2, Tracks of the modularised equipment transporter. $3, Buzz Aldrin and American flag raised on the Moon, Apollo 11 mission.

1989, July 20 **Wmk. 384** ***Perf. 14***
Size of Nos. 761-762: 29x29mm

760 CD342 18s multicolored .20 .20
761 CD342 50s multicolored .45 .45
762 CD342 65s multicolored .60 .60
763 CD342 $2 multicolored 1.75 1.75
Nos. 760-763 (4) 3.00 3.00

Souvenir Sheet

764 CD342 $3 multicolored 2.75 2.75

"Roosa" is misspelled on No. 761.

Christmas A166

Perf. 13½x13

1989, Nov. 1 **Litho.** **Unwmk.**

765 A166 18s Joseph and Mary .20 .20
766 A166 50s Shepherds .45 .45
767 A166 55s Animals .50 .50
768 A166 $2 Three kings 1.75 1.75
Nos. 765-768 (4) 2.90 2.90

Local Transport — A167

Designs: 18s, Pao pao (outrigger canoe). 55s, Fautasi (longboat). 60s, Polynesian Airlines propeller plane. $3, Lady Samoa ferry.

1990, Jan. 31 **Unwmk.** ***Perf. 14x15***

769 A167 18s multicolored .20 .20
770 A167 55s multicolored .45 .45
771 A167 60s multicolored .55 .55
772 A167 $3 multicolored 2.60 2.60
Nos. 769-772 (4) 3.80 3.80

Otto von Bismarck, Brandenburg Gate — A168

1990, May 3 ***Perf. 14x13½***

773 A168 75s shown .65 .65
774 A168 $3 SMS Adler 2.50 2.50
a. Pair, #773-774 3.25 3.25

Opening of the Berlin Wall, 1989, and cent. of the Treaty of Berlin (in 1989). No. 774a has a continuous design.

Great Britain No. 1 and Alexandra Palace — A169

Illustration reduced.

1990, May 3

775 A169 $3 multicolored 2.50 2.50

Stamp World London '90 and 150th anniv. of the Penny Black.

Tourism A170

1990, July 30 **Litho.** ***Perf. 14***

776 A170 18s Visitors Bureau .20 .20
777 A170 50s Samoa Village Resorts .45 .45
778 A170 65s Aggies Hotel .60 .60
779 A170 $3 Tusitala Hotel 2.75 2.75
Nos. 776-779 (4) 4.00 4.00

Souvenir Sheet

No. 240, Exhibition Emblem — A171

1990, Aug. 24 **Litho.** ***Perf. 13***

780 A171 $3 multicolored 2.30 2.30

World Stamp Exhib., New Zealand 1990.

Christmas — A172

Paintings of Madonna and Child.

1990, Oct. 31 ***Perf. 12½***

781 A172 18s Bellini .20 .20
782 A172 50s Bouts .45 .45
783 A172 55s Correggio .50 .50
784 A172 $3 Cima 2.75 2.75
Nos. 781-784 (4) 3.90 3.90

The 55s is "The School of Love," not "Madonna of the Basket."

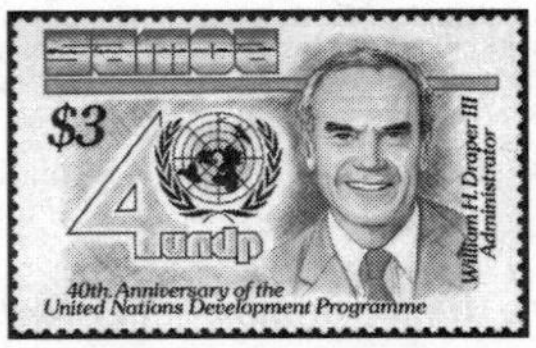

UN Development Program, 40th Anniv. — A173

1990, Nov. 26 ***Perf. 13½***

785 A173 $3 multicolored 2.75 2.75

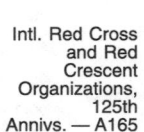

Parrots
A174

1991, Apr. 8 Litho. *Perf. 13½*

786 A174 18s Black-capped lory .20 .20
787 A174 50s Eclectus parrot .55 .55
788 A174 65s Scarlet macaw .70 .70
789 A174 $3 Palm cockatoo 3.25 3.25
Nos. 786-789 (4) 4.70 4.70

Elizabeth & Philip, Birthdays
Common Design Types
Wmk. 384

1991, June 17 Litho. *Perf. 14½*

790 CD346 75s multicolored .60 .60
791 CD345 $2 multicolored 1.65 1.65
a. Pair, #790-791 + label 2.25 2.25

Souvenir Sheet

1991 Rugby World Cup — A175

1991, Oct. 12 Litho. *Perf. 14½*

792 A175 $5 multicolored 5.00 5.00

Christmas
A176

Orchids and Christmas carols: 20s, O Come All Ye Faithful. 60s, Joy to the World. 75s, Hark! the Herald Angels Sing. $4, We Wish You a Merry Christmas.

1991, Oct. 31 Litho. *Perf. 14½*

793 A176 20s multicolored .20 .20
794 A176 60s multicolored .55 .50
795 A176 75s multicolored .70 .70
796 A176 $4 multicolored 3.50 3.50
Nos. 793-796 (4) 4.95 4.90

See Nos. 815-818, 836-840.

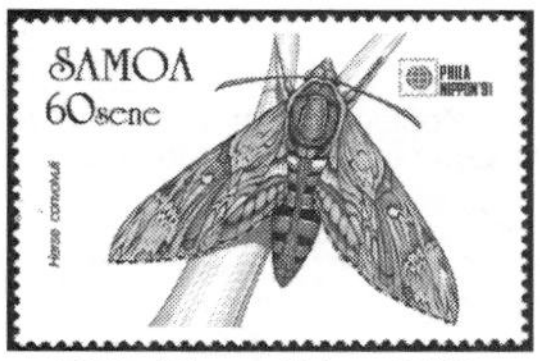

Phila Nippon '91 — A177

Samoan hawkmoths: 60s, Herse convolvuli. 75s, Gnathothlibus erotus. 75s, Hippotion celerio. $3, Cephonodes armatus.

1991, Nov. 16 *Perf. 13½x14*

797 A177 60s multicolored .60 .60
798 A177 75s multicolored .75 .75
799 A177 85s multicolored .90 .90
800 A177 $3 multicolored 3.00 3.00
Nos. 797-800 (4) 5.25 5.25

Independence, 30th Anniv. — A178

1992, Jan. 8 Litho. *Perf. 14*

801 A178 50s Honor guard .40 .40
802 A178 65s Siva scene .50 .50
803 A178 $1 Parade float .80 .80
804 A178 $3 Raising flag 2.50 2.50
Nos. 801-804 (4) 4.20 4.20

Queen Elizabeth II's Accession to the Throne, 40th Anniv.
Common Design Type

1992, Feb. 6 Wmk. 384

805 CD349 20s multicolored .20 .20
806 CD349 60s multicolored .50 .50
807 CD349 75s multicolored .60 .60
808 CD349 85s multicolored .70 .70

Wmk. 373

809 CD349 $3 multicolored 2.50 2.50
Nos. 805-809 (5) 4.50 4.50

Souvenir Sheet

Discovery of America, 500th Anniv. — A179

1992, Apr. 17 Unwmk. *Perf. 14½*

810 A179 $4 No. 1 3.25 3.25

World Columbian Stamp Expo '92, Granada '92 and Genoa '92 Philatelic Exhibitions.

1992 Summer Olympics, Barcelona — A180

1992, July 28 Wmk. 373 *Perf. 14*

811 A180 60s Weight lifting .50 .50
812 A180 75s Boxing .65 .65
813 A180 85s Running .75 .75
814 A180 $3 Stadium, statue 2.60 2.60
Nos. 811-814 (4) 4.50 4.50

Christmas Type of 1991

Christmas carol, orchid: 50s, "God rest you, merry gentlemen...," liparis layardii. 60s, "While shepherds watched...," corymborkis veratrifolia. 75s, "Away in a manger...," phaius flavus. $4, "O little town...," bulbophyllum longifolium.

1992, Oct. 28 Litho. *Perf. 14½*

815 A176 50s multicolored .45 .45
816 A176 60s multicolored .50 .50
817 A176 75s multicolored .65 .65
818 A176 $4 multicolored 3.50 3.50
Nos. 815-818 (4) 5.10 5.10

Fish
A182

1993, Mar. 17 Litho. *Perf. 14*

819 A182 60s Batfish .55 .55
820 A182 75s Lined surgeonfish .65 .65
821 A182 $1 Red-tail snapper .90 .90
822 A182 $3 Long-nosed emperor 2.75 2.75
Nos. 819-822 (4) 4.85 4.85

World Cup Seven-a-Side Rugby Championships, Scotland — A183

60s, Team performing traditional dance. 75c, Two players. 85c, Player. $3, Edinburgh Castle.

1993, May 12 *Perf. 13½x14*

823 A183 60s multi .50 .50
824 A183 75s multi, vert. .60 .60
825 A183 85s multi, vert. .70 .70
826 A183 $3 multi 2.25 2.25
Nos. 823-826 (4) 4.05 4.05

Bats
A184

1993, June 10 *Perf. 14x14½*

827 A184 20s Two hanging .20 .20
828 A184 50s Two flying .40 .40
829 A184 60s Three flying .50 .50
830 A184 75s One on flower .55 .55
Nos. 827-830 (4) 1.65 1.65

World Wildlife Fund.

Souvenir Sheet

Taipei '93, Asian Intl. Invitation Stamp Exhibition — A185

Illustration reduced.

1993, Aug. 16 Litho. *Perf. 14*

831 A185 $5 multicolored 4.00 4.00

World Post Day
A186

Designs: 60s, Globe, letter, flowers. 75s, Customers at Post Office. 85s, Black, white hands exchanging letter. $4, Globe, national flags, letter.

1993, Oct. 8 Litho. *Perf. 14*

832 A186 60s multicolored .45 .45
833 A186 75s multicolored .55 .55
834 A186 85s multicolored .65 .65
835 A186 $4 multicolored 3.00 3.00
Nos. 832-835 (4) 4.65 4.65

Christmas Type of 1991

Flowers, Christmas carol: 20s, "Silent Night! Holy Night!..." 60s, "As with gladness men of old..." 75s, "Mary had a Baby, Yes Lord..." $1.50, "Once in Royal David's City..." $3, "Angels, from the realms of Glory..."

Perf. 14½

1993, Nov. 1 Litho. Unwmk.

836 A176 20s multicolored .20 .20
837 A176 60s multicolored .45 .45
838 A176 75s multicolored .55 .55
839 A176 $1.50 multicolored 1.10 1.10
840 A176 $3 multicolored 2.25 2.25
Nos. 836-840 (5) 4.55 4.55

Corals
A187

1994, Feb. 18 Litho. *Perf. 14*

841 A187 20s Alveropora allingi .20 .20
842 A187 60s Acropora polystoma .45 .45
843 A187 90s Acropora listeri .70 .70
844 A187 $4 Acropora grandis 3.00 3.00
Nos. 841-844 (4) 4.35 4.35

Ovptd. with Hong Kong '94 Emblem

1994, Feb. 18

845 A187 20s on #841 .20 .20
846 A187 60s on #842 .45 .45
847 A187 90s on #843 .70 .70
848 A187 $4 on #844 3.00 3.00
Nos. 845-848 (4) 4.35 4.35

Manu Samoa Rugby Team
A188

Designs: 70s, Management. 90s, Test match with Wales. 95s, Test match with New Zealand. $4, Apia Park Stadium.

1994, Apr. 11 Litho. *Perf. 14*

849 A188 70s multicolored .50 .50
850 A188 90s multicolored .65 .65
851 A188 95s multicolored .70 .70
852 A188 $4 multicolored 3.00 3.00
Nos. 849-852 (4) 4.85 4.85

Souvenir Sheet

PHILAKOREA '94 — A189

Butterflies: $5, White caper, glasswing. Illustration reduced.

1994, Aug. 16 Litho. *Perf. 13*

853 A189 $5 multicolored 4.00 4.00

Teuila Tourism Festival
A190

1994, Sept. 22 Litho. *Perf. 13½*

854 A190 70s Singers .55 .55
855 A190 90s Fire dancer .70 .70
856 A190 95s Parade float .75 .75
857 A190 $4 Police band 3.25 3.25
Nos. 854-857 (4) 5.25 5.25

A191

A192

1994, Nov. 21 ***Perf. 14***

858 A191 70s Schooner Equator .55 .55
859 A191 90s Portrait .70 .70
860 A191 $1.20 Tomb, Mount Vaea .95 .95
861 A191 $4 Vailima House, horiz. 3.25 3.25
Nos. 858-861 (4) 5.45 5.45

Robert Louis Stevenson (1850-94), writer.

1994, Nov. 30

Children's Christmas paintings: 70s, Father Christmas. 95s, Nativity. $1.20, Picnic. $4, Greetings.

862 A192 70s multicolored .55 .55
863 A192 95s multicolored .75 .75
864 A192 $1.20 multicolored .95 .95
865 A192 $4 multicolored 3.25 3.25
Nos. 862-865 (4) 5.50 5.50

Scenic Views A193

Designs: 5s, Lotofaga Beach, Aleipata. 10s, Nuutele Island. 30s, Satuiatua, Savaii. 50s, Sinalele, Aleipata. 60s, Paradise Beach, Lefaga. 70s, Houses, Piula Cave. 80s, Taga blowholes. 90s, View from east coast road. 95s, Canoes, Leulumoega. $1, Parliament Building.

1995 **Litho.** ***Perf. 14½x13***

866 A193 5s multicolored .20 .20
867 A193 10s multicolored .20 .20
871 A193 30s multicolored .25 .25
874 A193 50s multicolored .40 .40
875 A193 60s multicolored .50 .50
876 A193 70s multicolored .55 .55
877 A193 80s multicolored .65 .65
878 A193 90s multicolored .70 .70
879 A193 95s multicolored .75 .75
880 A193 $1 multicolored .80 .80
Nos. 866-880 (10) 5.00 5.00

Issued: Nos. 866-867, 871, 874-880, 3/29/95. This is an expanding set. Numbers may change.

1995 World Rugby Cup Championships, South Africa — A194

Designs: 70s, Players under age 12. 90s, Secondary Schools' rugby teams. $1, Manu Samoa test match with New Zealand. $4, Ellis Park Stadium, Johannesburg.

1995, May 25 **Litho.** ***Perf. 14x13½***

886 A194 70s multicolored .55 .55
887 A194 90s multicolored .70 .70
888 A194 $1 multicolored .80 .80
889 A194 $4 multicolored 3.25 3.25
Nos. 886-889 (4) 5.30 5.30

End of World War II, 50th Anniv.
Common Design Types

Designs: 70s, OS2U Kingfisher over Faleolo Air Base. 90s, F4U Corsair, Faleolo Air Base. 95s, US troops in landing craft. $3, US Marines landing on Samoan beach. $4, Reverse of War Medal 1939-45.

1995, May 31 **Litho.** ***Perf. 13½***

890 CD351 70s multicolored .55 .55
891 CD351 90s multicolored .70 .70
892 CD351 95s multicolored .75 .75
893 CD351 $3 multicolored 2.50 2.50
Nos. 890-893 (4) 4.50 4.50

Souvenir Sheet
Perf. 14

894 CD352 $4 multicolored 3.25 3.25

Year of the Sea Turtle — A195

1995, Aug. 24 **Litho.** ***Perf. 13x13½***

895 A195 70s Leatherback .55 .55
896 A195 90s Loggerhead .70 .70
897 A195 $1 Green turtle .80 .80
898 A195 $4 Pacific Ridley 3.25 3.25
Nos. 895-898 (4) 5.30 5.30

Souvenir Sheet

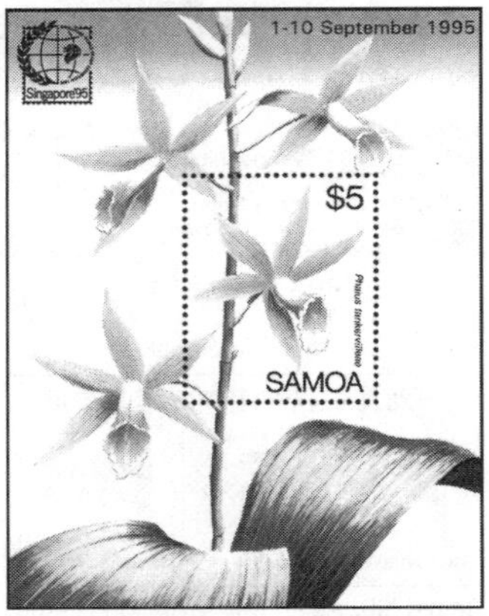

Singapore '95 — A196

1995, Sept. 1 ***Perf. 14***

899 A196 $5 Phaius tankervilleae 4.00 4.00

See No. 935.

UN, 50th Anniv.
Common Design Type

70s, Mobile hospital. 90s, Bell Sioux helicopter. $1, Bell 212 helicopter. $4, RNZAF Andover.

Unwmk.

1995, Oct. 24 **Litho.** ***Perf. 14***

900 CD353 70s multicolored .55 .55
901 CD353 90s multicolored .70 .70
902 CD353 $1 multicolored .80 .80
903 CD353 $4 multicolored 3.25 3.25
Nos. 900-903 (4) 5.30 5.30

A197

A198

1995, Nov. 15 ***Perf. 14½***

904 A197 25s Madonna & Child .20 .20
905 A197 70s Wise Man .55 .55
906 A197 90s Wise Man, diff. .70 .70
907 A197 $5 Wise Man, diff. 4.00 4.00
Nos. 904-907 (4) 5.45 5.45

Christmas.

1996, Jan. 26 **Litho.** ***Perf. 14***

Importance of Water: 70s, Waterfall, bird, woman, hands. 90s, Girl standing under fountain, "WATER FOR LIFE." $2, Outline of person's head containing tree, birds, waterfall, girl. $4, Community receiving water from protected watersheds.

908 A198 70s multicolored .55 .55
909 A198 90s multicolored .70 .70
910 A198 $2 multicolored 1.50 1.50
911 A198 $4 multicolored 3.00 3.00
Nos. 908-911 (4) 5.75 5.75

Queen Elizabeth II, 70th Birthday
Common Design Type

Various portraits of Queen, Samoan scenes: 70s, Apia, Main Street. 90s, Neiafu beach. $1, Official residence of Head of State. $3, Parliament Building.
$5, Queen wearing tiara, formal dress.

Perf. 14½

1996, Apr. 22 **Litho.** **Unwmk.**

912 CD354 70s multicolored .55 .55
913 CD354 90s multicolored .75 .75
914 CD354 $1 multicolored .80 .80
915 CD354 $3 multicolored 2.50 2.50
Nos. 912-915 (4) 4.60 4.60

Souvenir Sheet

916 CD354 $5 multicolored 4.25 4.25

Souvenir Sheet

Moon Festival — A199

Illustration reduced.

1996, May 18 **Litho.** ***Perf. 14***

917 A199 $2.50 multicolored 2.00 2.00

CHINA '96.

Souvenir Sheet

63rd Session of African-Carribean-Pacific-European Union Council of Ministers — A200

Illustration reduced.

1996, June 19 **Litho.** ***Perf. 13½***

918 A200 $5 multicolored 4.00 4.00

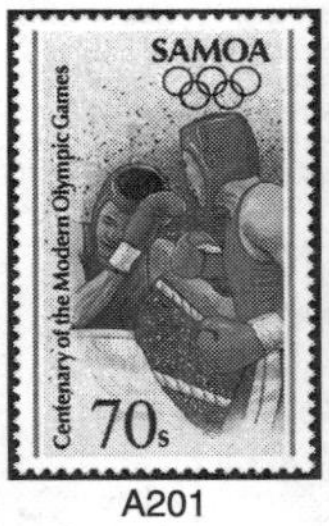

A201

A202

1996, July 15 **Litho.** ***Perf. 13½***

919 A201 70s Boxing .60 .60
920 A201 90s Running .75 .75
921 A201 $1 Weight lifting .80 .80
922 A201 $4 Javelin 3.25 3.25
Nos. 919-922 (4) 5.40 5.40

1996 Summer Olympic Games, Atlanta.

1996, Sept. 13 **Litho.** ***Perf. 14***

923 A202 60s Logo .50 .50
924 A202 70s Pottery .60 .60
925 A202 80s Stained glass .65 .65
926 A202 90s Dancing .75 .75
927 A202 $1 Wood carving .80 .80
928 A202 $4 Samoan chief 3.25 3.25
Nos. 923-928 (6) 6.55 6.55

7th Pacific Festival of Arts, Apia.

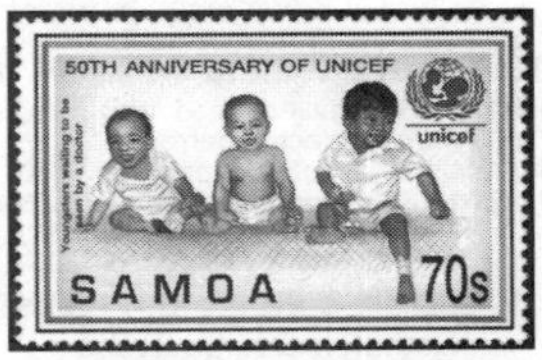

UNICEF, 50th Anniv. — A203

70s, Children in doctor's waiting room. 90s, Children in hospital undergoing treatment. $1, Child receiving injection. $4, Mothers, children playing.

1996, Oct. 24 **Litho.** ***Perf. 14***

929 A203 70s multicolored .60 .60
930 A203 90s multicolored .75 .75
931 A203 $1 multicolored .80 .80
932 A203 $4 multicolored 3.25 3.25
Nos. 929-932 (4) 5.40 5.40

Souvenir Sheet

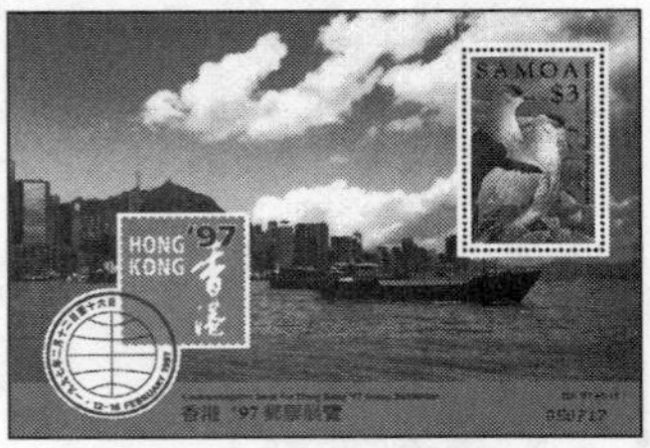

Many-Colored Fruit Dove — A204

Illustration reduced.

1997, Feb. 3 **Litho.** ***Perf. 14***

933 A204 $3 multicolored 2.50 2.50

Hong Kong '97. See No. 962.

Souvenir Sheet

1st US Postage Stamps, 150th Anniv., 1st Samoan Postage Stamps, 120th Anniv. — A205

1997, May 29 **Litho.** ***Perf. 14½***

934 A205 $5 US #2, Samoa #1 4.25 4.25

PACIFIC 97.

Phaius Tankervilleae Type of 1995
Souvenir Sheet
Wmk. 373

1997, June 20 **Litho.** ***Perf. 14½***

935 A196 $2.50 multicolored 2.00 2.00

Return of Hong Kong to China, July 1, 1997.

Queen Elizabeth II & Prince Philip, 50th Wedding Anniv. — A206

#936, Queen. #937, Prince at reins of team, Royal Windsor Horse Show, 1996. #938, Queen, horse. #939, Prince laughing, horse show, 1995. #940, Zara Philips, Balmoral 1993, Prince Philip. #941, Queen, Prince William.
$5, Queen, Prince, Royal Ascot 1988.

1997, July 10 Unwmk. *Perf. 13*

936 A206 70s multicolored .60 .60
937 A206 70s multicolored .60 .60
a. Pair, #936-937 1.20 1.20
938 A206 90s multicolored .75 .75
939 A206 90s multicolored .75 .75
a. Pair, #938-939 1.50 1.50
940 A206 $1 multicolored .80 .80
941 A206 $1 multicolored .80 .80
a. Pair, #940-941 1.60 1.60
Nos. 936-941 (6) 4.30 4.30

Souvenir Sheet

942 A206 $5 multicolored 4.00 4.00

Greenpeace, 26th Anniv. — A207

Dolphins: 50s, #947a, Jumping out of water. 60s, #947b, Two swimming right. 70s, #947c, Two facing front. $1, #947d, With mouth open out of water.

1997, Sept. 17 Litho. *Perf. 13½x14*

943 A207 50s multicolored .40 .40
944 A207 60s multicolored .50 .50
945 A207 70s multicolored .60 .60
946 A207 $1 multicolored .80 .80
Nos. 943-946 (4) 2.30 2.30

Miniature Sheet

947 A207 $1.25 Sheet of 4, #a.-d. 4.00 4.00

Christmas A208

1997, Nov. 26 Litho. *Perf. 14*

948 A208 70s Bells .60 .60
949 A208 80s Ornament .65 .65
950 A208 $2 Candle 1.65 1.65
951 A208 $3 Star 2.50 2.50
Nos. 948-951 (4) 5.40 5.40

Mangroves A209

Bruguiera gymnorrhiza: 70s, Fruit on trees. 80s, Saplings. $2, Roots. $4, Tree at water's edge.

1998, Feb. 26 Litho. *Perf. 13½*

952 A209 70s multicolored .60 .60
953 A209 80s multicolored .65 .65
954 A209 $2 multicolored 1.50 1.50
955 A209 $4 multicolored 3.25 3.25
Nos. 952-955 (4) 6.00 6.00

Diana, Princess of Wales (1961-97)
Common Design Type

#956: a, Up close portrait. b, Wearing checkered jacket. c, In red dress. d, Holding flowers.

Perf. 14½x14

1998, Mar. 31 Litho. Unwmk.

955A CD355 50s like #956a 1.00 1.00

Sheet of 4

956 CD355 $1.40 #a.-d. 12.75 12.75

No. 956 sold for $5.60 + 75c, with surtax from international sales being donated to the Princess Diana Memorial Fund and surtax from national sales being donated to designated local charity.

Royal Air Force, 80th Anniversary
Common Design Type of 1993
Re-Inscribed

70s, Westland Wallace. 80s, Hawker Fury. $2, Vickers Varsity. $5, BAC Jet Provost.
No. 961: a, Norman-Thompson N.T.2b. b, Nieuport 27 Scout. c, Miles Magister. d, Bristol Bombay.

1998, Apr. 1 *Perf. 13½*

957 CD350 70s multicolored .60 .60
958 CD350 80s multicolored .65 .65
959 CD350 $2 multicolored 1.60 1.60
960 CD350 $5 multicolored 4.00 4.00
Nos. 957-960 (4) 6.85 6.85

Miniature Sheet

961 CD350 $2 Sheet of 4, #a.-d. 6.50 6.50

Many-Colored Fruit Dove Type of 1997

1998, Sept. 1 Litho. *Perf. 14*

962 A204 25s multicolored .20 .20

Christmas Ornaments — A210

1998, Nov. 16 Litho. *Perf. 14*

963 A210 70s Star .60 .60
964 A210 $1.05 Bell .85 .85
965 A210 $1.40 Ball 1.10 1.10
966 A210 $5 Cross 4.00 4.00
Nos. 963-966 (4) 6.55 6.55

Australia '99, World Stamp Expo A211

Boats: 70s, Dugout canoe. 90s, Tasman's ships Heemskerck & Zeehaen, 1642. $1.05, HMS Resolution, HMS Adventure, 1773. $6, New Zealand scow schooner, 1880.

1999, Mar. 19 Litho. *Perf. 14*

967 A211 70s multicolored .50 .50
968 A211 90s multicolored .60 .60
969 A211 $1.05 multicolored .70 .70
970 A211 $6 multicolored 4.00 4.00
Nos. 967-970 (4) 5.80 5.80

Wedding of Prince Edward and Sophie Rhys-Jones
Common Design Type

1999, June 19 Litho. *Perf. 14*

971 CD356 $1.50 Separate portraits 1.00 1.00
972 CD356 $6 Couple 4.00 4.00

1st Manned Moon Landing, 30th Anniv.
Common Design Type

70s, Lift-off. 90s, Lunar module separates from Service module. $3, Aldrin deploys solar wind experiment. $5, Parachutes open.
$5, Earth as seen from moon.

Perf. 14x13¾

1999, July 20 Litho. Wmk. 384

973 CD357 70s multicolored .45 .45
974 CD357 90s multicolored .60 .60
975 CD357 $3 multicolored 2.00 2.00
976 CD357 $5 multicolored 3.25 3.25
Nos. 973-976 (4) 6.30 6.30

Souvenir Sheet
Perf. 14

977 CD357 $5 multicolored 3.25 3.25

No. 977 contains one 40mm circular stamp.

Queen Mother's Century
Common Design Type

Queen Mother: 70s, Talking to tenants of bombed apartments, 1940. 90s, At garden party, South Africa. $2, Reviewing scouts at Windsor. $6, With Princess Eugenie, 98th birthday.
$5, With film showing Charlie Chaplin.

Perf. 13½

1999, Aug. 24 Litho. Unwmk.

978 CD358 70s multicolored .50 .50
979 CD358 90s multicolored .60 .60
980 CD358 $2 multicolored 1.40 1.40
981 CD358 $6 multicolored 4.00 4.00
Nos. 978-981 (4) 6.50 6.50

Souvenir Sheet

982 CD358 $5 multicolored 3.25 3.25

Christmas and Millennium — A212

Perf. 13½x13¼

1999, Nov. 30 Litho. Unwmk.

983 A212 70s Hibiscus .45 .45
984 A212 90s Poinsettia .60 .60
985 A212 $2 Christmas cactus 1.40 1.40
986 A212 $6 Flag, Southern Cross 4.00 4.00
Nos. 983-986 (4) 6.45 6.45

Millennium — A213

Unwmk.

2000, Jan. 1 Litho. *Perf. 14*

987 A213 70s shown .45 .45
988 A213 70s Rocks .45 .45
a. Pair, #987-988 .90 .90

Sesame Street — A214

No. 989: a, The Count. b, Ernie. c, Grover. d, Cookie Monster and Prairie Dawn. e, Elmo, Ernie and Zoe. f, Big Bird. g, Telly. h, Magician. i, Oscar the Grouch.
$3, Cookie Monster.
Illustration reduced.

Perf. 14½x14¾

2000, Mar. 22 Litho.

989 A214 90s Sheet of 9, #a-i 4.75 4.75

Souvenir Sheet

990 A214 $3 multi 1.75 1.75

Fire Dancers — A215

Various dancers. Denominations: 25s, 50s, 90s, $1, $4.

2001, Sept. 3 Litho. *Perf. 13x13¼*

991-995 A215 Set of 5 3.75 3.75

Butterflies — A216

Serpentine Die Cut

2001, Dec. 12 Litho.

Self-Adhesive

996 Horiz. strip of 5 4.75
a. A216 70s Vagrans egista .40 .40
b. A216 $1.20 Jamides bochus .70 .70
c. A216 $1.40 Papilio godeffroyi .80 .80
d. A216 $2 Achraea andromacha 1.10 1.10
e. A216 $3 Eurema hecabe 1.75 1.75

Intl. Year of Ecotourism — A217

Designs: 60s, Snorkelers. 95s, Kayakers. $1.90, Village, chidren, craftsman. $3, Bird watchers.

2002, Feb. 27 *Perf. 13¼*

997-1000 A217 Set of 4 3.75 3.75
1000a Horiz strip of 4, #997-1000 + central label 3.75 3.75

SEMI-POSTAL STAMP

Catalogue values for unused stamps in this section are for Never Hinged items.

No. 246 Surcharged: "HURRICANE RELIEF / 6d"

Wmk. 355

1966, Sept. 1 Litho. *Perf. 13½*

B1 A43 8p + 6p blue & emerald .25 .25

Surtax for aid to plantations destroyed by the hurricane of Jan. 29, 1966.

AIR POST STAMPS

Catalogue values for unused stamps in this section are for Never Hinged items.

Red-tailed Tropic Bird — AP1

Wmk. 355

1965, Dec. 29 Photo. *Perf. 14½*

C1	AP1	8p shown	.25	.25
C2	AP1	2sh Flying fish	.65	.65

Sir Gordon Taylor's Bermuda Flying Boat "Frigate Bird III" — AP2

Designs: 7s, Polynesian Airlines DC-3. 20s, Pan American Airways "Samoan Clipper." 30s, Air Samoa Britten-Norman "Islander."

Perf. 13½x13

1970, July 27 Photo. Unwmk.

C3	AP2	3s multicolored	.20	.20
C4	AP2	7s multicolored	.30	.30
C5	AP2	20s multicolored	.90	.90
C6	AP2	30s multicolored	1.40	1.40
		Nos. C3-C6 (4)	2.80	2.80

Hawker Siddeley 748 — AP3

Planes at Faleolo Airport: 10s, Hawker Siddeley 748 in the air. 12s, Hawker Siddeley 748 on ground. 22s, BAC 1-11 planes on ground.

1973, Mar. 9 *Perf. 11½*

Granite Paper

C7	AP3	8s multicolored	.30	.30
C8	AP3	10s multicolored	.40	.40
C9	AP3	12s multicolored	.45	.45
C10	AP3	22s multicolored	.85	.85
		Nos. C7-C10 (4)	2.00	2.00

SAN MARINO

ˌsan mə-ˈrē-ˌnō

LOCATION — Eastern Italy, about 20 miles inland from the Adriatic Sea
GOVT. — Republic
AREA — 24.1 sq. mi.
POP. — 25,061 (1999 est.)
CAPITAL — San Marino

100 Centesimi = 1 Lira
100 Cents = 1 Euro (2002)

Catalogue values for unused stamps in this country are for Never Hinged items, beginning with Scott 412 in the regular postage section, Scott B39 in the semi-postal section, Scott C97 in the airpost section, Scott E26 in the special delivery section, and Scott Q40 in the parcel post section.

Watermarks

Wmk. 140- Crown

Wmk. 174- Coat of Arms

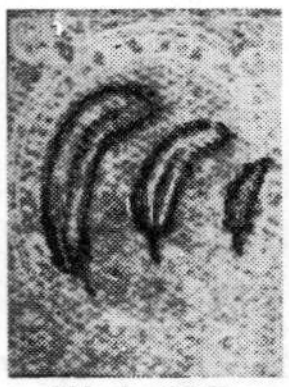

Wmk. 217- Three Plumes

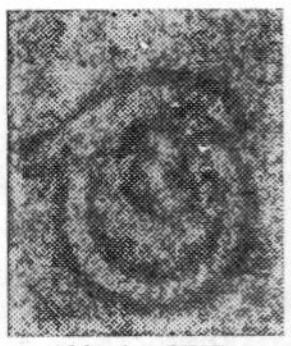

Wmk. 277- Winged Wheel

Wmk. 303- Multiple Stars

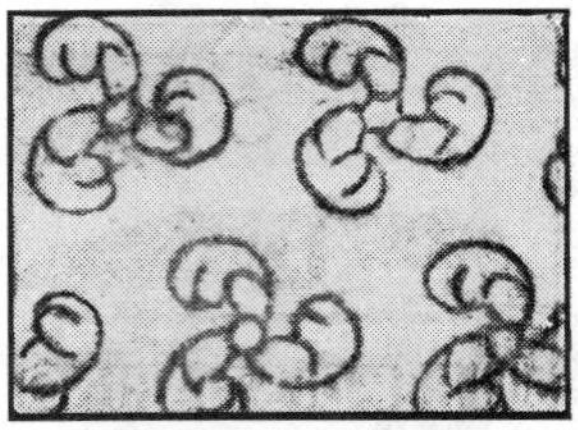

Wmk. 339- Triskelion

Numeral — A1

Coat of Arms — A2

1877-99 Typo. Wmk. 140 *Perf. 14*

1	A1 2c green		10.00	3.25
2	A1 2c blue ('94)		6.25	3.75
3	A1 2c claret ('95)		5.00	4.50
4	A2 5c orange ('90)		85.00	7.50
5	A2 5c olive grn ('92)		3.75	1.75
6	A2 5c green ('99)		3.00	2.50
7	A2 10c ultra		100.00	10.00
	a. 10c blue ('90)		450.00	57.50
8	A2 10c dk green ('92)		3.75	2.25
9	A2 10c claret ('99)		3.00	2.50
10	A2 15c claret ('94)		90.00	25.00
11	A2 20c vermilion		15.00	3.25
12	A2 20c lilac ('95)		3.50	3.25
13	A2 25c maroon ('90)		85.00	10.00
14	A2 25c blue ('99)		3.00	3.25
15	A2 30c brown		575.00	37.50
16	A2 30c org yel ('92)		3.75	3.25
17	A2 40c violet		575.00	37.50
18	A2 40c dk brown ('92)		3.75	3.25
19	A2 45c gray grn ('92)		3.75	3.25
20	A2 65c red brown ('92)		3.75	3.25
21	A2 1 l car & yel ('92)		1,100.	260.00
22	A2 1 l lt blue ('95)		900.	225.00
23	A2 2 l brn & yel ('94)		35.00	32.50
24	A2 5 l vio & grn ('94)		95.00	87.50

See Nos. 911-915.

Nos. 7a, 15, 11 Surcharged in Black Cmi. 5

1892

25	A2 5c on 10c blue	50.00	8.75
a.	Inverted surcharge	55.00	11.50
b.	5c on 10c ultramarine	*19,000.*	*3,375.*
c.	As "b," inverted surcharge	—	
d.	Double surcharge, one inverted	—	—
e.	Pair, one without surcharge	750.00	
e.	Pair, one without surcharge, surcharge inverted	750.00	
26	A2 5c on 30c brown	200.00	40.00
a.	Inverted surcharge	210.00	47.50
b.	Double surch., one inverted	210.00	62.50
c.	Double invtd. surcharge	210.00	62.50
27	A2 10c on 20c ver	37.50	3.75
a.	Inverted surcharge	40.00	5.00
b.	Double surch., one inverted	40.00	8.25
c.	Double surcharge	40.00	8.25
	Nos. 25-27 (3)	287.50	52.50

Ten to twelve varieties of each surcharge.

No. 11 Surcharged 10 10

28	A2 10c on 20c ver	190.00	5.00

Government Palace and Portraits of Regents, Tonnini and Marcucci
A6 A7

Portraits of Regents and View of Interior of Palace — A8

Wmk. 174

1894, Sept. 30 Litho. *Perf. 15½*

29	A6 25c blue & dk brn	2.25	1.00
30	A7 50c dull red & dk brn	20.00	3.00
31	A8 1 l green & dk brown	11.50	3.50
	Nos. 29-31 (3)	33.75	7.50

Opening of the new Government Palace and the installation of the new Regents.

Statue of Liberty — A9

Wmk. 140

1899-1922 Typo. *Perf. 14*

32	A9 2c brown	1.25	.75
33	A9 2c claret ('22)	.20	.20
34	A9 5c brown org	2.40	1.75
35	A9 5c olive grn ('22)	.20	.20
36	A9 10c brown org ('22)	.20	.20
37	A9 20c dp brown ('22)	.20	.20
38	A9 25c ultra ('22)	.60	.60
39	A9 45c red brown ('22)	1.25	1.25
	Nos. 32-39 (8)	6.30	5.15

Numeral of Value — A10

Mt. Titano — A11

1903-25 *Perf. 14, 14½x14*

40	A10 2c violet	7.25	3.50
41	A10 2c org brn ('21)	.40	.40
42	A11 5c blue grn	3.50	1.50
43	A11 5c olive grn ('21)	.40	.40
44	A11 5c red brn ('25)	.20	.20
45	A11 10c claret	3.50	1.50
46	A11 10c brown org ('21)	.40	.40
47	A11 10c olive grn ('25)	.20	.20
48	A11 15c blue grn ('22)	.40	.40
49	A11 15c brown vio ('25)	.20	.20
50	A11 20c brown orange	70.00	20.00
51	A11 20c brown ('21)	.40	.40
52	A11 20c blue grn ('25)	.20	.20
53	A11 25c blue	7.50	3.50
54	A11 25c gray ('21)	.40	.40
55	A11 25c violet ('25)	.20	.20
56	A11 30c brown red	3.50	*4.50*
57	A11 30c claret ('21)	.40	.40
58	A11 30c orange ('25)	8.50	1.25
59	A11 40c orange red	7.00	5.50
60	A11 40c dp rose ('21)	.40	.40
61	A11 40c brown ('25)	.20	.20
62	A11 45c yellow	5.50	5.50
63	A11 50c brown vio ('23)	1.00	*1.50*
64	A11 50c gray blk ('25)	.20	.20
65	A11 60c brown red ('25)	.50	.25
66	A11 65c chocolate	5.50	5.50
67	A11 80c blue ('21)	2.00	2.00
68	A11 90c brown ('23)	2.00	2.00
69	A11 1 l olive green	15.00	9.00
70	A11 1 l ultra ('21)	.40	.40
71	A11 1 l lt blue ('25)	.50	.25
72	A11 2 l violet	425.00	125.00
73	A11 2 l orange ('21)	9.75	10.00
74	A11 2 l lt green ('25)	3.50	3.50
75	A11 5 l slate	92.50	90.00
76	A11 5 l ultra ('25)	10.00	9.50
	Nos. 40-76 (37)	688.50	310.25

For overprints and surcharges see Nos. 77, 93-96, 103, 107, 188-189, B1-B2, E2, E4.

No. 50 Surcharged

1905, Sept. 1

77	A11 15c on 20c brown org	4.50	1.50
a.	Large 5 in 1905 on level with 9	30.00	19.00

Coat of Arms
A12 A13

Two types:
I - Width 18½mm.
II - Width 19mm.

1907-10 Unwmk. Engr. *Perf. 12*

78	A12 1c brown, II ('10)	1.10	.55
a.	Type I	2.00	.80
79	A13 15c gray, I	9.00	1.40
a.	Type II ('10)	110.00	7.25

No. 79a Surcharged in Brown

1918, Mar. 15

80	A13 20c on 15c gray	1.40	1.25

St. Marinus — A14

Perf. 14½x14, 14x14½

1923, Aug. 11 Typo. Wmk. 140

81	A14 30c dark brown	.40	.40

San Marino Intl. Exhib. of 1923. Proceeds from the sale of this stamp went to a mutual aid society.

Italian Flag and Views of Arbe and Mt. Titano A15

1923, Aug. 6

82	A15 50c olive green	.40	.40

Presentation to San Marino of the Italian flag which had flown over the island of Arbe, the birthplace of the founder of San Marino. Inscribed on back: "V. Moraldi dis. Blasi inc. Petiti impr.-Roma."

Mt. Titano and Sword — A16

1923, Sept. 29 *Perf. 14x14½*

83	A16	1 l dark brown	7.00	7.00

In honor of the San Marino Volunteers who were killed or wounded in WWI.

Giuseppe Garibaldi A17

Allegory-San Marino Sheltering Garibaldi A18

1924, Sept. 25 *Perf. 14*

84	A17	30c dark violet	1.50	1.50
85	A17	50c olive brown	1.75	1.75
86	A17	60c dull red	2.25	2.25
87	A18	1 l deep blue	3.50	3.50
88	A18	2 l gray green	4.00	4.00
		Nos. 84-88 (5)	13.00	13.00

75th anniv. of Garibaldi's taking refuge in San Marino.

Semi-Postal Stamps of 1918 Surcharged with New Values and Bars

1924, Oct. 9

89	SP1	30c on 45c yel brn & blk	.75	.75

Surcharged

LIRE UNA

▪▪▪▪▪▪▪▪▪▪▪▪▪▪▪▪▪▪▪▪▪▪▪▪

90	SP2	60c on 1 l bl grn & blk	4.50	4.50
91	SP2	1 l on 2 l vio & blk	11.00	11.00
92	SP2	2 l on 3 l red brn & blk	8.50	8.50
		Nos. 89-92 (4)	24.75	24.75

Nos. 67 and 68 Surcharged in Black or Red

Lire 1,20

1926, July 1

93	A11	75c on 80c blue	.75	.75
94	A11	1.20 l on 90c brown	.75	.75
95	A11	1.25 l on 90c brn (R)	2.00	2.00
96	A11	2.50 l on 80c blue (R)	4.00	4.00
		Nos. 93-96 (4)	7.50	7.50

Antonio Onofri — A19

A20

Unwmk.

1926, July 29 **Engr.** *Perf. 11*

97	A19	10c dk blue & blk	.20	.20
98	A19	20c olive grn & blk	.35	.35
99	A19	45c dk vio & blk	.25	.25
100	A19	65c green & blk	.25	.25
101	A19	1 l orange & blk	2.75	2.75
102	A19	2 l red vio & blk	2.75	2.75
		Nos. 97-102 (6)	6.55	6.55

For surcharges see Nos. 104-106, 181-182.

Special Delivery Stamp No. E2 surcharged with New Value and Bars

Perf. 14½x14

1926, Nov. 25 **Wmk. 140**

103	A20	1.85 l on 60c violet	.40	.40

Nos. 101 and 102 Surcharged **1,25**

1927, Mar. 10 **Unwmk.** *Perf. 11*

104	A19	1.25 l on 1 l	2.75	2.75
105	A19	2.50 l on 2 l	5.25	5.25
106	A19	5 l on 2 l	24.00	24.00
		Nos. 104-106 (3)	32.00	32.00

Type of Special Delivery Stamp of 1923 Surcharged

1927, Sept. 15 **Wmk. 140** *Perf. 14*

107	A11	1.75 l on 50c on 25c vio	.50	.50

The 50c on 25c violet was not issued without 1.75-lire surcharge.

War Memorial A21

Unwmk.

1927, Sept. 28 **Engr.** *Perf. 12*

108	A21	50c brown violet	1.00	1.00
109	A21	1.25 l blue	1.50	1.50
110	A21	10 l gray	13.50	13.50
		Nos. 108-110 (3)	16.00	16.00

Erection of a cenotaph in memory of the San Marino volunteers in WWI.

Capuchin Church and Convent A22

Design: 2.50 l, 5 l, Death of St. Francis.

1928, Jan. 2

111	A22	50c red	11.50	3.00
112	A22	1.25 l dp blue	4.50	4.50
113	A22	2.50 l dk brown	4.50	4.50
114	A22	5 l dull violet	15.00	13.50
		Nos. 111-114 (4)	35.50	25.50

7th centenary of the death of St. Francis of Assisi.
For surcharges see Nos. 183-184.

The Rocca (State Prison) A24

Government Palace A25

Statue of Liberty — A26

1929-35 **Wmk. 217**

115	A24	5c vio brn & ultra	1.00	.50
116	A24	10c bl gray & red vio	1.25	.75
117	A24	15c dp org & emer	1.00	.50
118	A24	20c dk bl & org red	1.00	.50
119	A24	25c grn & gray blk	1.00	.50
120	A24	30c gray brn & red	1.00	.50
121	A24	50c red vio & ol gray	1.00	.50
122	A24	75c dp red & gray blk	1.00	.50
123	A25	1 l dk brn & emer	1.00	.50
124	A25	1.25 l dk blue & blk	1.00	.50
125	A25	1.75 l green & org	2.50	1.25
126	A25	2 l bl gray & red	1.25	.75
127	A25	2.50 l car rose & ultra	1.25	.75
128	A25	3 l dp org & bl	1.25	.75
129	A25	3.70 l ol blk & red brn ('35)	1.25	.75
130	A26	5 l dk vio & dk grn	2.00	1.75
131	A26	10 l bis brn & dk bl	5.25	5.25
132	A26	15 l green & red vio	37.50	37.50
133	A26	20 l dk bl & red vio	190.00	190.00
		Nos. 115-133 (19)	252.50	244.00

General Post Office — A27

San Marino-Rimini Electric Railway — A28

1932, Feb. 4

134	A27	20c blue green	6.00	4.50
135	A27	50c dark red	9.00	7.50
136	A27	1.25 l dark blue	140.00	80.00
137	A27	1.75 l dark brown	67.50	40.00
138	A27	2.75 l dark violet	27.50	18.00
		Nos. 134-138 (5)	250.00	150.00

Opening of new General Post Office.
For surcharges see Nos. 151-160.

1932, June 11

139	A28	20c deep green	1.00	1.00
140	A28	50c dark red	1.25	1.25
141	A28	1.25 l dark blue	4.00	4.00
142	A28	5 l deep brown	32.50	30.00
		Nos. 139-142 (4)	38.75	36.25

Opening of the new electric railway between San Marino and Rimini.

Giuseppe Garibaldi — A29

Garibaldi's Arrival at San Marino — A30

1932, July 30

143	A29	10c violet brown	1.75	.65
144	A29	20c violet	1.75	.65
145	A29	25c green	1.75	.65
146	A29	50c yellow brn	3.25	1.90
147	A30	75c dark red	5.00	3.75
148	A30	1.25 l dark blue	9.00	7.50
149	A30	2.75 l brown org	27.50	19.00
150	A30	5 l olive green	175.00	175.00
		Nos. 143-150 (8)	225.00	209.10

Garibaldi (1807-1882), Italian patriot.

Nos. 138 and 137 Surcharged

1933, May 27

151	A27	25c on 2.75 l	3.75	3.75
152	A27	50c on 1.75 l	7.25	7.25
153	A27	75c on 2.75 l	16.00	16.00
154	A27	1.25 l on 1.75 l	190.00	190.00
		Nos. 151-154 (4)	217.00	217.00

Convention of philatelists, San Marino, May 28.

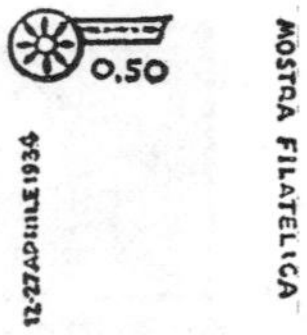

Nos. 134-137 Surcharged in Black

1934, Apr. 12

155	A27	25c on 1.25 l	1.00	1.00
156	A27	50c on 1.75 l	2.00	2.00
157	A27	75c on 50c	4.50	4.50
158	A27	1.25 l on 20c	17.00	17.00
		Nos. 155-158 (4)	24.50	24.50

San Marino's participation (with a philatelic pavilion) in the 15th annual Trade Fair at Milan, Apr. 12-27.

Nos. 136 and 138 Surcharged Wheel and New Value

1934, Apr. 12

159	A27	3.70 l on 1.25 l	40.00	40.00
160	A27	3.70 l on 2.75 l	47.50	47.50

Ascent to Mt. Titano A31

Unwmk.

1935, Feb. 7 Engr. *Perf. 14*

161	A31	5c choc & blk	.20	.20
162	A31	10c dk vio & blk	.20	.20
163	A31	20c orange & blk	.20	.20
164	A31	25c green & blk	.20	.20
165	A31	50c olive bis & blk	.20	.20
166	A31	75c brown red & blk	1.50	1.50
167	A31	1.25 l blue & blk	3.00	3.00
		Nos. 161-167 (7)	5.50	5.50

12th anniv. of the founding of the Fascist Movement.

Melchiorre Delfico — A32

Statue of Delfico — A33

1935, Apr. 15 Wmk. 217 *Perf. 12*

Center in Black

169	A32	5c brown lake	.60	.50
170	A32	7½c lt brown	.60	.50
171	A32	10c dk blue grn	.60	.50
172	A32	15c rose carmine	7.25	2.40
173	A32	20c orange	1.25	1.00
174	A32	25c green	1.25	1.00
175	A33	30c dull violet	1.25	1.00
176	A33	50c olive green	2.40	2.40
177	A33	75c red	6.00	6.00
178	A33	1.25 l dark blue	2.00	1.75
179	A33	1.50 l dk brown	32.50	27.50
180	A33	1.75 l brown org	45.00	42.50
		Nos. 169-180 (12)	100.70	87.05

Melchiorre Delfico (1744-1835), historian.
For surcharges see Nos. 202, 277.

Nos. 99-100 Surcharged in Black

Nos. 112-113 Surcharged in Black

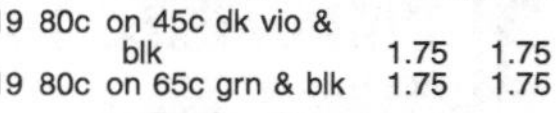

1936 Unwmk. *Perf. 11*

181	A19	80c on 45c dk vio & blk	1.75	1.75
182	A19	80c on 65c grn & blk	1.75	1.75

Perf. 12

183	A22	2.05 l on 1.25 l	4.50	4.50
184	A22	2.75 l on 2.50 l	14.00	14.00
		Nos. 181-184 (4)	22.00	22.00

Issued: #181-182, 4/14; #183-184, 8/23.

Souvenir Sheet

Design from Base of Roman Column — A34

1937, Aug. 23 Engr. Wmk. 217

185	A34	5 l steel blue	9.75	9.75

Unveiling of the Roman Column at San Marino. The date "1636 d. F. R." means the 1,636th year since the founding of the republic.

No. 185 was privately surcharged "+ 10 L 1941."

Souvenir Sheets

Abraham Lincoln — A35

1938, Apr. 7 Wmk. 217 *Perf. 13*

186	A35	3 l dark blue	1.25	1.25
187	A35	5 l rose red	14.50	14.50

Dedication of a Lincoln bust, Sept. 3, 1937.

No. 49 and Type of 1925 Surcharged with New Value in Black

1941 Wmk. 140 *Perf. 14*

188	A11	10c on 15c brown vio	.20	.20
189	A11	10c on 30c brown org	.50	.50

Flags of Italy and San Marino — A36

Harbor of Arbe A37

1942 Photo.

190	A36	10c yel brn & brn org	.20	.20
191	A36	15c brn & red brn	.20	.20
192	A36	20c gray grn & gray blk	.20	.20
193	A36	25c green & blue	.20	.20
194	A36	50c brn red & brn	.20	.20
195	A36	75c red & gray blk	.20	.20
196	A37	1.25 l bl & gray bl	.20	.20
197	A37	1.75 l brn & grnsh blk	.20	.20
198	A37	2.75 l bis brn & gray bl	.25	.25
199	A37	5 l green & brown	1.50	1.50
		Nos. 190-199 (10)	3.35	3.35

Return of the Italian flag to Arbe.

No. 190 Surcharged in Black

1942, July 30

200	A36	30c on 10c	.20	.20

Rimini-San Marino Stamp Day, Aug. 3.

No. 192 Surcharged with New Value and Bars in Black

1942, Sept. 14

201	A36	30c on 20c	.20	.20

No. 177 Surcharged with New Value in Black

1942, Sept. 28 Wmk. 217 *Perf. 12*

202	A33	20 l on 75c red & blk	8.50	8.50

Printing Press and Newspaper A38

Newspapers A39

Wmk. 140

1943, Apr. 12 Photo. *Perf. 14*

203	A38	10c deep green	.20	.20
204	A38	15c bister	.20	.20
205	A38	20c dk orange brn	.20	.20
206	A38	30c dk rose vio	.20	.20
207	A38	50c blue black	.20	.20
208	A38	75c red orange	.20	.20
209	A39	1.25 l blue	.20	.20
210	A39	1.75 l deep violet	.20	.20
211	A39	5 l slate	.55	.25
212	A39	10 l dark brown	2.40	2.40
		Nos. 203-212 (10)	4.55	4.25

Nos. 206 and 207 Overprinted in Red

1943, July 1

213	A38	30c dk rose vio	.20	.20
214	A38	50c blue black	.20	.20

Rimini-San Marino Stamp Day, July 5.

A40

A41

Overprinted in Black: "28 LVGLIO 1943 1642 F. R."

1943, Aug. 27

215	A40	5c brown	.20	.20
216	A40	10c orange red	.20	.20
217	A40	20c ultra	.20	.20
218	A40	25c deep green	.20	.20
219	A40	30c brown carmine	.20	.20
220	A40	50c deep violet	.20	.20
221	A40	75c car rose	.20	.20
222	A41	1.25 l sapphire	.20	.20
223	A41	1.75 l red org	.20	.20
224	A41	2.75 l dk red brn	.20	.20
225	A41	5 l green	.45	.45
226	A41	10 l violet	.75	.75
227	A41	20 l slate blue	1.90	1.90
		Nos. 215-227,C26-C33 (21)	11.10	11.10

This series was prepared for the 20th anniv. of fascism, but as Mussolini was overthrown July 25, 1943, it was overprinted for the downfall of fascism.

Overprint on Nos. 222-227 adds "d." before "F.R."

Exist without overprint. Value of set $16.

A42

A43

Overprinted "Governo Provvisorio" in Black

1943, Aug. 27

228	A42	5c brown	.20	.20
229	A42	10c orange red	.20	.20
230	A42	20c ultra	.20	.20
231	A42	25c deep green	.20	.20
232	A42	30c brown carmine	.20	.20
233	A42	50c deep violet	.20	.20
234	A42	75c carmine rose	.20	.20
235	A43	1.25 l sapphire	.20	.20
236	A43	1.75 l red orange	.20	.20
237	A43	5 l green	.45	.45
238	A43	20 l slate blue	1.25	1.25
		Nos. 228-238,C34-C39 (17)	6.65	6.65

Souvenir Sheets

A44

Perf. 14, Imperf.

1945, Mar. 15 Photo. Unwmk.

239	A44	Sheet of 3	75.00	75.00
a.		10 l dull blue	20.00	20.00
b.		15 l dull green	20.00	20.00
c.		25 l dull red brown	20.00	20.00

Sheets contain a papermaker's watermark, "Hammermill Bond, Made in U.S.A."

Nos. 239, 241 and C40 were issued to commemorate the 50th anniv. of the reconstruction of the Government Palace.

Government Palace — A45

1945, Mar. 15 Wmk. 140 Perf. 14

241	A45	25 l brown violet	3.75	3.75

Coat of Arms of Faetano — A46

Coats of Arms: 20c, 60c, 25 l, Montegiardino. 40c, 5 l, 50 l, San Marino. 80c, 2 l-4 l, Fiorentino. 10 l, Borgomaggiore. 20 l, Serravalle.

1945-46 Wmk. 277

242	A46	10c dark blue	.20	.20
243	A46	20c vermilion	.20	.20
244	A46	40c deep orange	.20	.20
245	A46	60c slate black	.20	.20
246	A46	80c dark green	.20	.20
247	A46	1 l dk car rose	.20	.20
248	A46	1.20 l deep violet	.20	.20
249	A46	2 l chestnut	.20	.20
250	A46	3 l dp blue ('46)	.20	.20
250A	A46	4 l red org ('46)	.20	.20
251	A46	5 l dark brown	.25	.25
251A	A46	15 l dp blue ('46)	1.00	1.00

Lithographed and Engraved

252	A46	10 l brt red & brown	1.00	1.00
253	A46	20 l brt red & ultra	2.75	2.75
254	A46	20 l org brn & ultra ('46)	5.50	5.50
a.		Vert. pair, imperf. btwn.	300.00	
255	A46	25 l hn brn & ultra ('46)	5.00	5.00

Size: 22x27mm

256	A46	50 l ol brn & ultra ('46)	7.50	7.50
		Nos. 242-256 (17)	25.00	25.00

Nos. 252-256 are in sheets of 10 (2x5). Values: Nos. 252, 254-255, $60 each. No. 253, $90, No. 256, $200.

For surcharges see Nos. 258-259, B26.

"Dawn of New Hope" — A52

Engr. & Litho.

1946 Unwmk. Perf. 14

257	A52	100 l dull yel & brn vio	5.25	5.25
j.		Vert. pair, imperf. btwn.	350.00	

UN Relief and Rehabilitation Administration. Sheets of 10 with blue coat of arms in top margin.

Franklin D. Roosevelt and Flags of San Marino and US — A52a

Designs: 1 l, 50 l, Quotation on Liberty, from Franklin D. Roosevelt. 2 l, 100 l, Roosevelt portrait, vert. 5 l, 15 l, Roosevelt and flags (as shown).

Wmk. 277

1947, May 3 Photo. Perf. 14

257A	A52a	1 l bister & brn	.20	.20
257B	A52a	2 l blue & sepia	.20	.20
257C	A52a	5 l violet & multi	.20	.20
257D	A52a	15 l green & multi	.20	.20
257E	A52a	50 l vermilion & brn	.40	.40
257F	A52a	100 l violet & sepia	.70	.70
		Nos. 257A-257F,C51A-C51H (14)	17.20	17.20

For surcharges see #257G-257I, C51I-C51K.

Nos. 257A-257C Surcharged with New Value

1947, June 16

257G	A52a	3 l on 1 l	.25	.25
257H	A52a	4 l on 2 l	.25	.25
257I	A52a	6 l on 5 l	.25	.25
		Nos. 257G-257I,C51I-C51K (6)	1.50	1.50

No. 250A Surcharged with New Value in Black

1947, June 16 Wmk. 277

258	A46	6(l) on 4 l red org	.20	.20

No. 250A Surcharged in Black

259	A46	21 l on 4 l red org	.50	.50

"St. Marinus Raising the Republic" by Girolamo Batoni — A53

Wmk. 217

1947, July 18 Engr. Perf. 12

260	A53	1 l brt grn & vio	.20	.20
261	A53	2 l purple & olive	.20	.20
262	A53	4 l vio brn & dk bl grn	.20	.20
263	A53	10 l org & bl blk	.20	.20
264	A53	25 l carmine & purple	.50	.50
265	A53	50 l dk bl grn & brn	10.50	10.50
		Nos. 260-265,C52-C53 (8)	14.00	14.00

For overprints and surcharges see Nos. 294-295, B27-B38, C56.

United States 1847 Stamp A54

United States Stamps of 1847 and 1869 A55

A56

Wmk. 277

1947, Dec. 24 Photo. Perf. 14

266	A54	1 l red vio & dk brn	.20	.20
267	A55	3 l sl gray, dp ultra & car	.20	.20
268	A54	6 l dp bl & dk gray grn	.20	.20
269	A56	15 l vio, dp ultra & car	.20	.20
270	A55	35 l dk brn, dp ultra & car	.60	.60
271	A56	50 l sl grn, dp ultra & car	.85	.85
		Nos. 266-271,C55 (7)	7.75	7.75

1st United States postage stamps, cent.

Laborer and San Marino Flag A57

1948, June 3

272	A57	5 l brown	.20	.20
273	A57	8 l green	.20	.20
274	A57	30 l crimson	.20	.20
275	A57	50 l red brn & rose lil	.65	.65

Engr.

276	A57	100 l dk bl & dp vio	26.00	26.00
		Nos. 272-276 (5)	27.25	27.25

See Nos. 373-374.

No. 172 Surcharged with New Value and Ornaments in Black

1948 Wmk. 217 Perf. 12

277	A32	100 l on 15c	32.50	32.50

Government Palace — A58

Mt. Titano, Distant View — A59

Various Views of San Marino.

1949-50 Wmk. 277 Photo. Perf. 14

278	A58	1 l black & blue	.20	.20
279	A58	2 l violet & car	.20	.20
280	A58	3 l violet & ultra	.20	.20
281	A58	4 l black & vio	.20	.20
282	A58	5 l violet & brn	.20	.20
283	A58	6 l dp blue & sep	.50	.25
284	A59	8 l blk brn & yel brn	.30	.20
285	A59	10 l brn blk & bl	.35	.20
286	A58	12 l brt rose & vio	1.10	.50
287	A58	15 l vio & brt rose	2.75	.85
288	A58	20 l dp bl & brn ('50)	8.00	1.10
289	A58	35 l green & violet	5.75	2.50
290	A58	50 l brt rose & yel brn	2.75	.90
291	A58	55 l dp bl & dl grn ('50)	35.00	20.00

Perf. 14x13½

Engr.

292	A59	100 l blk brn & dk grn	45.00	32.50
293	A59	200 l dp blue & brn	47.50	*50.00*
		Nos. 278-293 (16)	150.00	110.00

Nos. 260 and 261 Overprinted in Black

Giornata Filatelica
San Marino-Riccione
28-6-1949

1949, June 28 Wmk. 217

294	A53	1 l brt green & vio	.20	.20
295	A53	2 l purple & olive	.20	.20

San Marino-Riccione Stamp Day, June 28.

Francesco Nullo — A60

1 l, 20 l, Francesco Nullo. 2 l, 5 l, Anita Garibaldi. 3 l, 50 l, Giuseppe Garibaldi. 4 l, 15 l, Ugo Bassi.

Wmk. 277

1949, July 31 Photo. Perf. 14

Size: 22x28mm

296	A60	1 l blk & car lake	.20	.20
297	A60	2 l red brn & blue	.20	.20
298	A60	3 l car lake & dk grn	.20	.20
299	A60	4 l violet & dk brn	.20	.20

Size: 26½x36½mm

300	A60	5 l purple & dk brn	.20	.20
301	A60	15 l car lake & gray bl	.50	.50
302	A60	20 l violet & car lake	1.00	1.00
303	A60	50 l red brn & violet	10.00	10.00
		Nos. 296-303 (8)	12.50	12.50

Centenary of Garibaldi's escape to San Marino.

See Nos. C57-C61, 404-410.

Stagecoach on Road from San Marino — A61

1949, Dec. 29 Engr.

304	A61	100 l blue & gray vio	7.00	7.00
		Sheet of 6	110.00	110.00

UPU, 75th anniversary.

A62

A63a

A63

Perf. 13½x14, 14x13½

1951, Mar. 15 Engr. Wmk. 277

Sky and Cross in Carmine

305	A62	25 l dk brn & red vio	4.25	4.25
306	A63	75 l org brn & dk brn	5.75	5.75
307	A63a	100 l dk brn & gray blk	7.00	7.00
		Nos. 305-307 (3)	17.00	17.00

Issued to honor the San Marino Red Cross.

Christopher Columbus A64

Designs: 2 l, 25 l, Columbus on his ship. 3 l, 10 l, 20 l, Landing of Columbus. 4 l, 15 l, 80 l, Pioneers trading with Indians. 5 l, 200 l, Columbus and map of Americas.

1952, Jan. 28 Photo. Perf. 14

308	A64	1 l brn org & dk grn	.20	.20
309	A64	2 l dk brown & vio	.20	.20
310	A64	3 l violet & dk brn	.20	.20
311	A64	4 l blue & org brn	.20	.20
312	A64	5 l grn & dk bl grn	.30	.30
313	A64	10 l dk brown & blk	.40	.40
314	A64	15 l carmine & blk	.60	.60

Engr.

315 A64 20 l dp bl & dk bl grn .90 .90
316 A64 25 l vio brn & blk brn 3.50 3.50
317 A64 60 l choc & vio bl 5.00 5.00
318 A64 80 l gray & blk 15.00 15.00
319 A64 200 l Prus grn & dp ultra 27.50 27.50
Nos. 308-319,C80 (13) 70.00 70.00

Issued to honor Christopher Columbus.

Type of 1952 in New Colors Overprinted in Black or Red — FIERA DI TRIESTE 1952

1952, June 29 **Photo.**

320 A64 1 l vio & dk brn .20 .20
321 A64 2 l carmine & blk .20 .20
322 A64 3 l grn & dk bl grn (R) .20 .20
323 A64 4 l dk brn & blk .20 .20
324 A64 5 l purple & vio .20 .20
325 A64 10 l bl & org brn (R) 1.00 1.00
326 A64 15 l org brn & blue 2.75 2.75
Nos. 320-326,C81 (8) 22.75 22.75

4th Intl. Sample Fair of Trieste.

Discobolus — A65

Tennis A66

Model Airplane — A67

Designs: 3 l, Runner. 4 l, Cyclist. 5 l, Soccer. 25 l, Shooting. 100 l, Roller skating.

1953, Apr. 20 **Wmk. 277** ***Perf. 14***

327 A65 1 l dk brn & blk .20 .20
328 A66 2 l black & brown .20 .20
329 A65 3 l blk & grnsh bl .20 .20
330 A66 4 l blk & brt bl .20 .20
331 A66 5 l dk brn & sl grn .20 .20
332 A67 10 l dp blue & crim .20 .20
333 A67 25 l blk & dk brn 1.10 1.10
334 A66 100 l dk brn & slate 4.25 4.25
Nos. 327-334,C90 (9) 35.55 35.55

See No. 438.

Type of 1953 Overprinted in Black — GIORNATA FILATELICA S. MARINO • RICCIONE 24 AGOSTO 1953

1953, Aug. 24

335 A66 100 l grn & dk bl grn 9.50 9.50

San Marino-Riccione Stamp Day, Aug. 24.

Narcissus A68

Flowers: 2 l, Tulips. 3 l, Oleanders. 4 l, Cornflowers. 5 l, Carnations. 10 l, Irises. 25 l, Cyclamen. 80 l, Geraniums. 100 l, Roses.

1953, Dec. 28 **Photo.**

336 A68 1 l multicolored .20 .20
337 A68 2 l multicolored .20 .20
338 A68 3 l multicolored .20 .20
339 A68 4 l multicolored .20 .20
340 A68 5 l multicolored .20 .20
341 A68 10 l multicolored .20 .20
342 A68 25 l multicolored 1.40 1.40
343 A68 80 l multicolored 8.00 8.00
344 A68 100 l multicolored 13.50 13.50
Nos. 336-344 (9) 24.10 24.10

Walking Racer — A69

Fencing A70

Sports: 3 l, Boxing. 4 l, 200 l, 250 l, Gymnastics. 5 l, Motorcycling. 8 l, Javelin-throwing. 12 l, Automobiling. 25 l, Wrestling. 80 l, Walk racer.

1954-55 **Photo.** **Wmk. 277**

345 A69 1 l violet & cer .20 .20
346 A70 2 l dk grn & vio .20 .20
347 A70 3 l brn & brn org .20 .20
348 A69 4 l dk bl & brt bl .20 .20
349 A70 5 l dk grn & dk brn .20 .20
350 A70 8 l lil rose & pur .20 .20
351 A70 12 l black & crim .20 .20
352 A69 25 l bl & dk bl grn .20 .20
353 A69 80 l dk bl & brt grn .40 .40
354 A69 200 l violet & brn 2.25 2.25

Perf. 12½x13

Engr.

355 A69 250 l multi ('55) 19.00 19.00
Sheet of 4 (#355) 160.00 160.00
Nos. 345-355 (11) 23.25 23.25

A71

A72

Liberty statue and Government palace.

1954, Dec. 16 ***Perf. 13x13½***

356 A71 20 l choc & blue .20 .20
357 A71 60 l car & dk grn .75 .75
Nos. 356-357,C92 (3) 1.85 1.85

1955, Aug. 27 **Wmk. 303** ***Perf. 14***

358 A72 100 l gray blk & bl 2.50 2.50
Never hinged 3.75

7th San Marino-Riccione Stamp Fair. See No. 385.

Murata Nuova Bridge — A73

View of La Rocca — A74

Design: 15 l, Government Palace.

1955, Nov. 15 ***Perf. 14***

Size: 22x27½mm; 27½x22mm

359 A73 5 l blue & brown .20 .20
360 A74 10 l org & bl grn .20 .20
361 A74 15 l Prus grn & car .20 .20
362 A73 25 l dk brn & vio .20 .20
363 A74 35 l vio & red car .20 .20
Nos. 359-363 (5) 1.00 1.00
Set, never hinged 1.00

See Nos. 386-388, 636-638.

Ice Skater — A75

Skier A76

3 l, 50 l, Tobogganing. 4 l, Skier going downhill. 5 l, 100 l, Ice Hockey player. 10 l, Girl ice skater.

1955, Dec. 15 **Wmk. 303** ***Perf. 14***

364 A75 1 l brown & yellow .20 .20
365 A76 2 l brt blue & red .20 .20
366 A76 3 l blk brn & lt brn .20 .20
367 A75 4 l brown & green .20 .20
368 A76 5 l ultra & sal pink .20 .20
369 A75 10 l ultra & pink .20 .20
370 A76 25 l gray blk & red .65 .65
371 A76 50 l brown & indigo 1.40 1.40
372 A76 100 l blk & Prus grn 3.25 3.25
Nos. 364-372,C95 (10) 16.00 16.00
Set, never hinged 30.00

7th Winter Olympic Games at Cortina d'Ampezzo, Jan. 26-Feb. 5, 1956.
For surcharge see No. C96.

Type of 1948 Inscribed: "50th Anniversario Arengo 25 Marzo 1906"

1956, Mar. 24 **Wmk. 303** ***Perf. 14***

373 A57 50 l sapphire 4.00 5.00
Never hinged 5.00

50th anniv. of the meeting of the heads of families (Arengo), the beginning of the democratic era in San Marino.

Type of 1948 inscribed: "Assistenza Invernale"

1956, Mar. 24 **Photo.**

374 A57 50 l dark green 4.00 5.00
Never hinged 5.00

Issued to publicize the Winterhelp charity.

Pointer and Arms A77

Dogs: 2 l, Russian greyhound. 3 l, Sheep dog. 4 l, English greyhound. 5 l, Boxer. 10 l, Great Dane. 25 l, Irish setter. 60 l, German shepherd. 80 l, Scotch collie. 100 l, Hunting hound.

1956, June 8 **Wmk. 303** ***Perf. 14***

375 A77 1 l ultra & brown .20 .20
376 A77 2 l car lake & bl gray .20 .20
377 A77 3 l ultra & brown .20 .20
378 A77 4 l grnsh bl & gray vio .20 .20
379 A77 5 l car lake & dk brn .20 .20
380 A77 10 l ultra & brown .20 .20
381 A77 25 l dk blue & multi .20 .20
382 A77 60 l car lake & multi 1.40 1.40
383 A77 80 l dk blue & multi 1.75 1.75
384 A77 100 l car lake & multi 2.75 2.75
Nos. 375-384 (10) 7.30 7.30
Set, never hinged 26.00

Sailboat Type of 1955

1956 **Wmk. 303** ***Perf. 14***

385 A72 100 l brown & bl grn 1.50 1.75
Never hinged 2.00

8th San Marino-Riccione Stamp Fair.

Types of 1955 with added inscription: "Congresso Internaz. Periti Filatelici San Marino-Salsomaggiore 6-8 Ottobre 1956."

Designs: 20 l, La Rocca. 80 l, Murata Nuova Bridge. 100 l, Government palace.

1956, Oct. 6 ***Perf. 14***

Size: 26x36mm; 36x26mm

386 A74 20 l blue & brown .45 .30
387 A73 80 l vio & red car 1.75 1.40
388 A74 100 l org & bl grn 1.90 1.65
Nos. 386-388 (3) 4.10 3.35
Set, never hinged 5.25

Intl. Philatelic Cong., San Marino, 10/6-8.

Street and Borgo Maggiore Church — A78

Hospital Street — A79

Views: 3 l, Gate tower. 20 l, Covered Market of Borgo Maggiore. 125 l, View from South Bastion.

1957, May 9 **Photo.** **Wmk. 303**

389 A78 2 l dk grn & rose red .20 .20
390 A78 3 l blue & brown .20 .20
391 A78 20 l dk blue green .20 .20
392 A79 60 l brn & blue vio .75 .65

Engr.

393 A78 125 l dk blue & blk .30 .25
Nos. 389-393 (5) 1.65 1.50
Set, never hinged 2.00

See Nos. 473-476, 633-635.

Daisies and View of San Marino — A80

Flowers: 2 l, Primrose. 3 l, Lily. 4 l Orchid. 5 l, Lily of the Valley. 10 l, Poppy. 25 l, Pansy. 60 l, Gladiolus. 80 l, Wild Rose. 100 l, Anemone.

Wmk. 303

1957, Aug. 31 **Photo.** ***Perf. 14***

Flowers in Natural Colors

394 A80 1 l dk vio blue .20 .20
395 A80 2 l dk vio blue .20 .20
396 A80 3 l dk vio blue .20 .20
397 A80 4 l dk vio blue .20 .20
398 A80 5 l dk vio blue .20 .20
399 A80 10 l blue, buff & lilac .20 .20
400 A80 25 l blue, yel & lilac .20 .20
401 A80 60 l blue, yel & dl red brn .30 .25
402 A80 80 l blue & dl red brn .40 .35
403 A80 100 l bl, yel & dl red brn .90 .90
Nos. 394-403 (10) 3.00 2.90
Set, never hinged 3.25

Type of 1949 Inscribed: "Commemorazione 150 Nascita G. Garibaldi."

Portraits: 2 l, 50 l, Anita Garibaldi. 3 l, 25 l, Francesco Nullo. 5 l, 100 l, Giuseppe Garibaldi. 15 l, Ugo Bassi.

1957, Dec. 12 **Wmk. 303** ***Perf. 14***

Size: 22x28mm

404 A60 2 l vio & dull bl .20 .20
405 A60 3 l lake & dk grn .20 .20
406 A60 5 l brn & ol gray .20 .20

Size: 26½x37mm

407 A60 15 l blue & vio .20 .20
408 A60 25 l green & dk gray .20 .30
409 A60 50 l violet & brn .85 1.50
410 A60 100 l brown & vio .85 1.50
Nos. 404-410 (7) 2.70 4.10
Set, never hinged 3.50

Nos. 409-410 are printed se-tenant.
Birth of Giuseppe Garibaldi, 150th anniv.

Panoramic View A81

1958, Feb. 27 Engr. *Perf. 14*

411	A81	500 l	green & blk	42.50	42.50
			Never hinged	60.00	
			Sheet of 6	375.00	375.00
			Never hinged	450.00	

Catalogue values for unused stamps in this section, from this point to the end of the section, are for Never Hinged items.

Fair Emblem and San Marino Peaks — A82

1958, Apr. 12 Photo. *Perf. 14*

412	A82	40 l	yel green & brn	.20	.20
413	A82	60 l	brt blue & mar	.20	.20

World's Fair, Brussels, Apr. 17-Oct. 19.

Madonna and Fair Entrance A83

Design: 60 l, View of Fair Grounds.

1958, Apr. 12

414	A83	15 l	yellow, grn & bl	.20	.20
415	A83	60 l	green & rose red	.55	.45
			Nos. 414-415,C97 (3)	2.35	2.25

San Marino's 10th participation in the Milan Fair.

Wheat — A84

Designs: 2 l, 125 l, Corn. 3 l, 80 l, Grapes. 4 l, 25 l, Peaches. 5 l, 40 l, Plums.

1958, Aug. 30 Wmk. 303 *Perf. 14*

416	A84	1 l	dk blue & yel org	.20	.20
417	A84	2 l	dk grn & red org	.20	.20
418	A84	3 l	blue & ocher	.20	.20
419	A84	4 l	green & rose car	.20	.20
420	A84	5 l	blue, yel & grn	.20	.20
421	A84	15 l	ultra & brn org	.20	.20
422	A84	25 l	multicolored	.20	.20
423	A84	40 l	multicolored	.20	.20
424	A84	80 l	multicolored	1.10	.45
425	A84	125 l	bl, grn & org ver	3.50	1.75
			Nos. 416-425 (10)	6.20	3.80

Bay and Stamp of Naples A85

1958, Oct. 8 Photo.

426	A85	25 l	lilac & red brn	.25	.20

Cent. of the stamps of Naples. See No. C100.

Pierre de Coubertin — A86

Portraits: 3 l, Count Alberto Bonacossa. 5 l, Avery Brundage. 30 l, Gen. Carlo Montu. 60 l, J. Sigfrid Edstrom. 80 l, Henri de Baillet Latour.

1959, May 19 Wmk. 303 *Perf. 14*

427	A86	2 l	brn org & blk	.20	.20
428	A86	3 l	lilac & gray brn	.20	.20
429	A86	5 l	blue & dk grn	.20	.20
430	A86	30 l	violet & blk	.20	.20
431	A86	60 l	dk grn & gray brn	.20	.20
432	A86	80 l	car rose & dp grn	.20	.20
			Nos. 427-432,C106 (7)	4.45	2.05

Leaders of the Olympic movement; 1960 Olympic Games, Rome.
See Nos. 1060-1062.

Lincoln and his Praise of San Marino, May 7, 1861 A87

Lincoln Portraits and: 10 l, Map of San Marino. 15 l, Government palace. 70 l, San Marino peaks, vert.

1959, July 1 *Perf. 14*

433	A87	5 l	brown & blk	.20	.20
434	A87	10 l	blue grn & ultra	.20	.20
435	A87	15 l	gray & green	.20	.20

Perf. 13x13½

Engr.

436	A87	70 l	violet	.45	.45
			Nos. 433-436,C108 (5)	3.45	3.15

Birth sesquicentennial of Abraham Lincoln.

Arch of Augustus, Rimini, and Romagna ½b Stamp A88

1959, Aug. 29 Photo. *Perf. 14*

437	A88	30 l	black & brown	.20	.20

Centenary of the first stamps of Romagna. See No. C109.

Type of 1953 Inscribed: "Universiade Torino"

1959, Aug. 29 Wmk. 303 *Perf. 14*

438	A65	30 l	red orange	.60	.40

Turin University Sports Meet, 8/27-9/6.

Messina Cathedral Portal and Stamp of Sicily 1859 — A89

Stamp of Sicily and: 2 l, Greek temple, Selinus. 3 l, Erice Church. 4 l, Temple of Concordia, Agrigento. 5 l, Ruins of Castor and Pollux Temple, Agrigento. 25 l, San Giovanni degli Eremiti Church. 60 l, Greek theater, Taormina, horiz.

1959, Oct. 16

439	A89	1 l	ocher & dk brn	.20	.20
440	A89	2 l	olive & dk red	.20	.20
441	A89	3 l	blue & slate	.20	.20
442	A89	4 l	red & brown	.20	.20
443	A89	5 l	dull bl & rose lil	.20	.20
444	A89	25 l	multicolored	.25	.20
445	A89	60 l	multicolored	.25	.20
			Nos. 439-445,C110 (8)	2.15	2.00

Centenary of stamps of Sicily.

Golden Oriole A90

Nightingale A91

Shot Put A92

Birds: 3 l, Woodcock. 4 l, Hoopoe. 5 l, Red-legged partridge. 10 l, Goldfinch. 25 l, European Kingfisher. 60 l, Ringnecked pheasant. 80 l, Green woodpecker. 110 l, Red-breasted flycatcher.

1960, Jan. 28 Photo. *Perf. 14*

Centers in Natural Colors

446	A90	1 l	blue	.20	.20
447	A91	2 l	green & red	.20	.20
448	A90	3 l	green & red	.20	.20
449	A91	4 l	dk green & red	.20	.20
450	A90	5 l	dark green	.20	.20
451	A91	10 l	blue & red	.20	.20
452	A91	25 l	grnsh blue	.40	.20
453	A90	60 l	blue & red	1.10	1.00
454	A91	80 l	Prus blue & red	2.00	1.90
455	A91	110 l	blue & red	10.00	2.25
			Nos. 446-455 (10)	14.70	6.55

1960, May 23 Wmk. 303 *Perf. 14*

Sports: 2 l, Gymnastics. 3 l, Walking. 4 l, Boxing. 5 l, Fencing, horiz. 10 l, Bicycling. 15 l, Hockey, horiz. 25 l, Rowing, horiz. 60 l, Soccer. 110 l, Equestrian, horiz.

456	A92	1 l	car rose & vio	.20	.20
457	A92	2 l	gray & org	.20	.20
458	A92	3 l	brn ol & pur	.20	.20
459	A92	4 l	rose red & brn	.20	.20
460	A92	5 l	brown & blue	.20	.20
461	A92	10 l	red brn & bl	.20	.20
462	A92	15 l	emer & lilac	.20	.20
463	A92	25 l	bl grn & org	.20	.20
464	A92	60 l	dp grn & org	.20	.20
465	A92	110 l	emer, red & blk	.30	.20
			Set of 3 souvenir sheets	5.50	5.50
			Nos. 456-465,C111-C114 (14)	3.00	2.80

17th Olympic Games, Rome, 8/25-9/11.

Souvenir sheets are: (1.) Sheet of 4, one each of 1 l, 2 l, 3 l and 60 l, all printed in deep green and brown. (2.) Sheet of 4, one each of 4 l and 10 l plus a 20 l and 40 l in designs of Nos. C111-C112 but without "Posta Aerea" inscribed-all 4 printed in rose red and brown. (3.) Sheet of 6, one each of 5 l, 15 l, 25 l and 110 l plus an 80 l and 125 l in designs of Nos. C113-C114 but without "Posta Aerea"- all 6 printed in emerald and brown.

Mt. Titano — A93

Founder Melvin Jones and Lions Headquarters — A94

60 l, Government Palace and statue of Liberty. 115 l, Clarence L. Sturm, president. 150 l, Finis E. Davis, vice president.

1960, July 1 Photo. Wmk. 303

466	A93	30 l	red brn & dk bl	.20	.20
467	A94	45 l	bl vio & bis brn	.50	.50
468	A93	60 l	dull rose & bl	.20	.20
469	A94	115 l	green & blk	.50	.50
470	A94	150 l	brn & dk bl	3.50	2.75
			Nos. 466-470,C115 (6)	9.90	8.15

Lions Intl.; founding of the Lions Club of San Marino.

Beach of Riccione and San Marino Peaks A95

1960, Aug. 27 *Perf. 14*

471	A95	30 l	multicolored	.35	.20

12th San Marino-Riccione Stamp Day, Aug. 27. See No. C116.

Boy with Basket of Fruit, by Caravaggio — A96

1960, Dec. 29 Wmk. 303 *Perf. 14*

472	A96	200 l	multicolored	6.50	4.75

350th anniversary of the death of Michelangelo da Caravaggio (Merisi), painter.

Types of 1957

Views: 1 l, Hospital street. 4 l, Government building. 80 l, Gate tower. 115 l, Covered market of Borgo Maggiore.

1961, Feb. 16 *Perf. 14*

473	A79	1 l	dk blue grn	.20	.20
474	A78	4 l	dk blue & blk	.20	.20
475	A78	30 l	brt vio & brn	.40	.20
476	A78	115 l	brown & blue	.20	.20
			Nos. 473-476 (4)	1.00	.80

Hunting Roebuck A97

Hunting Scenes (16th-18th century): 2 l, Falconer, vert. 3 l, Wild boar hunt. 4 l, Duck shooting with crossbow. 5 l, Stag hunt. 10 l, Mounted falconer, vert. 30 l, Hunter with horn and dogs. 60 l, Hunter with rifle and dog, vert. 70 l, Hunter and beater. 115 l, Duck hunt.

Wmk. 303

1961, May 4 Photo. *Perf. 14*

477	A97	1 l	lil rose & vio bl	.20	.20
478	A97	2 l	gray, dk red & blk	.20	.20
479	A97	3 l	red org, brn & blk	.20	.20
480	A97	4 l	lt bl, red & blk	.20	.20
481	A97	5 l	yellow grn & brn	.20	.20
482	A97	10 l	org, blk, brn & vio	.20	.20
483	A97	30 l	yel, bl & dk grn	.20	.20
484	A97	60 l	ocher, brn, blk & red	.20	.20
485	A97	70 l	green, blk & car	.25	.25
486	A97	115 l	brt pink, blk & dk bl	.40	.40
			Nos. 477-486 (10)	2.25	2.25

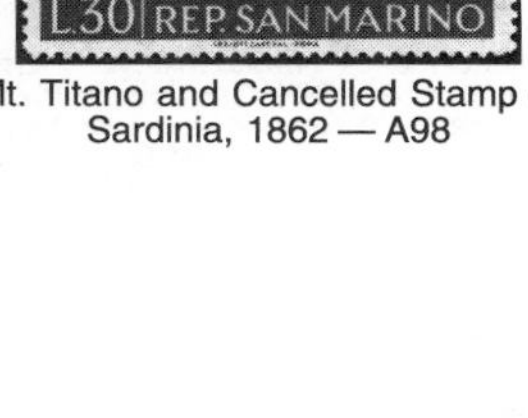

Mt. Titano and Cancelled Stamp of Sardinia, 1862 — A98

Photogravure and Embossed

1961, Sept. 5 Wmk. 303 *Perf. 13*

487	A98	30 l	multicolored	.50	.50
488	A98	70 l	multicolored	1.00	1.00
489	A98	200 l	multicolored	.50	.50
			Nos. 487-489 (3)	2.00	2.00

Cent. of Independence Phil. Exhib., Turin, 1961.

Europa Issue, 1961

View of San Marino A99

Wmk. 339

1961, Oct. 20 Photo. *Perf. 13*

490	A99	500 l	brn & blue grn	*25.00*	*25.00*
			Sheet of 6	*150.00*	*150.00*

King Enzo's Palace and Neptune Fountain, Bologna — A100

Views of Bologna: 70 l, Loggia dei Mercanti. 100 l, Two Towers.

1961, Nov. 25 Wmk. 339 *Perf. 14*

491	A100	30 l	grnsh bl & blk	.20	.20
492	A100	70 l	dk ol grn & blk	.20	.20
493	A100	100 l	red brown & blk	.20	.20
			Nos. 491-493 (3)	.60	.60

Bophilex, philatelic exhibition, Bologna.

Duryea, 1892 A101

Automobiles (pre-1910): 2 l, Panhard-Levassor. 3 l, Peugeot. 4 l, Daimler. 5 l, Fiat, vert. 10 l, Decauville. 15 l, Wolseley. 20 l, Benz. 25 l, Napier. 30 l, White, vert. 50 l, Oldsmobile. 70 l, Renault, vert. 100 l, Isotta Fraschini. 115 l, Bianchi. 150 l, Alfa.

1962, Jan. 23 Wmk. 303 *Perf. 14*

494	A101	1 l	red brn & bl	.20	.20
495	A101	2 l	ultra & org brn	.20	.20
496	A101	3 l	black, brn & org	.20	.20
497	A101	4 l	gray & dk red	.20	.20
498	A101	5 l	violet & org	.20	.20
499	A101	10 l	black & org	.20	.20
500	A101	15 l	black & ver	.20	.20
501	A101	20 l	black & ultra	.20	.20
502	A101	25 l	gray & org	.20	.20
503	A101	30 l	black & ocher	.20	.20
504	A101	50 l	black & brt pink	.20	.20
505	A101	70 l	black, gray & grn	.20	.20
506	A101	100 l	black, yel & car	.20	.20
507	A101	115 l	blk, org & bl grn	.20	.20
508	A101	150 l	multicolored	.30	.30
			Nos. 494-508 (15)	3.10	3.10

Wright Plane, 1904 A102

Historic Planes (1907-1910): 2 l, Ernest Archdeacon. 3 l, Albert and Emile Bonnet-Labranche. 4 l, Glenn Curtiss. 5 l, Farman. 10 l, Louis Bleriot. 30 l, Hubert Latham. 60 l, Alberto Santos Dumont. 70 l, Alliott Verdon Roe. 115 l, Faccioli.

Wmk. 339

1962, Apr. 4 Photo. *Perf. 14*

509	A102	1 l	blk & dull yel	.20	.20
510	A102	2 l	red brn & grn	.20	.20
511	A102	3 l	red brn & gray grn	.20	.20
512	A102	4 l	brown & blk	.20	.20
513	A102	5 l	magenta & blue	.20	.20
514	A102	10 l	ocher & bl grn	.20	.20
515	A102	30 l	ocher & ultra	.20	.20
516	A102	60 l	black & ocher	.20	.20
517	A102	70 l	dp orange & blk	.40	.40
518	A102	115 l	blk, grn & ocher	.50	.50
			Nos. 509-518 (10)	2.50	2.50

Mountaineer Descending A103

Designs: 2 l, View of Sassolungo. 3 l, Mt. Titano. 4 l, Three Peaks of Javaredo. 5 l, Matterhorn. 15 l, Skier on downhill run. 30 l, Climbing an overhang. 40 l, Cutting steps in ice. 85 l, Giant's Tooth. 115 l, Mt. Titano.

1962, June 14 Wmk. 339 *Perf. 14*

519	A103	1 l	bis brn & blk	.20	.20
520	A103	2 l	Prus grn & blk	.20	.20
521	A103	3 l	lilac & blk	.20	.20
522	A103	4 l	brt bl & blk	.20	.20
523	A103	5 l	dp org & blk	.20	.20
524	A103	15 l	org yel & blk	.20	.20
525	A103	30 l	carmine & blk	.20	.20
526	A103	40 l	grnsh bl & blk	.20	.20
527	A103	85 l	lt green & blk	.20	.20
528	A103	115 l	vio bl & blk	.20	.20
			Nos. 519-528 (10)	2.00	2.00

Hunter with Dog A104

Modern Hunting Scenes: 2 l, Hound master on horseback, vert. 3 l, Duck hunt. 4 l, Stag hunt. 5 l, Partridge hunt. 15 l, Lapwing (hunt). 50 l, Wild duck hunt. 70 l, Duck hunt from boat. 100 l, Boar hunt. 150 l, Pheasant hunt, vert.

1962, Aug. 25 Photo. *Perf. 14*

529	A104	1 l	brown & yel grn	.20	.20
530	A104	2 l	dk bl & org	.20	.20
531	A104	3 l	blk & Prus bl	.20	.20
532	A104	4 l	black & brown	.20	.20
533	A104	5 l	brn & yel grn	.20	.20
534	A104	15 l	blk & org brn	.20	.20
535	A104	50 l	brn, dp grn & blk	.20	.20
536	A104	70 l	grn, sal pink & blk	.20	.20
537	A104	100 l	blk, brick red & sep	.20	.20
538	A104	150 l	grn, lil & blk	.20	.20
			Nos. 529-538 (10)	2.00	2.00

Europa Issue, 1962

Mt. Titano and "Europa" A105

1962, Oct. 25 Wmk. 339

539	A105	200 l	gray & car	1.00	1.00
			Sheet of 6	9.50	9.50

Egyptian Cargo Ship A106

Ancient Ships: 2 l, Greece, 2nd Cent. B.C. 3 l, Roman galley. 4 l, Vikings, 10th Cent. 5 l, "Santa Maria," 1492. 10 l, Cypriote galleon, vert. 30 l, Galley, 1600. 60 l, "Sovereign of the Seas," 1637, vert. 70 l, Danish ship, 1750, vert. 115 l, Frigate, 1850.

1963, Jan. 10

540	A106	1 l	blue & org yel	.20	.20
541	A106	2 l	mag, tan & brn	.20	.20
542	A106	3 l	brown & lil rose	.20	.20
543	A106	4 l	vio brn & gray	.20	.20
544	A106	5 l	brown & yellow	.20	.20
545	A106	10 l	brn & brt yel grn	.20	.20
546	A106	30 l	blk, bl & sep	.60	.45
547	A106	60 l	lt vio bl & yel grn	.30	.30
548	A106	70 l	blk, gray & dl red	.40	.40
549	A106	115 l	blk, brn & gray bl	2.50	1.40
			Nos. 540-549 (10)	5.00	3.75

Lady with Veil, by Raphael — A107

Jousting with "Saracen," Arezzo — A108

Paintings by Raphael: 70 l, Self-portrait. 100 l, St. Barbara from Sistine Madonna. 200 l, Portrait of a Young Woman (Maddalena Strozzi).

Wmk. 339

1963, Mar. 28 Photo. *Perf. 14*

Size: 26½x37mm

550	A107	30 l	multicolored	.20	.20
551	A107	70 l	multicolored	.25	.20
552	A107	100 l	multicolored	.35	.20

Size: 26½x44mm

553	A107	200 l	multicolored	.20	.20
			Nos. 550-553 (4)	1.00	.80

1963, June 22 Wmk. 339 *Perf. 14*

Medieval "Knightly Games": 2 l, French knights, horiz. 3 l, Crossbow contest. 4 l, English knight receiving lance, horiz. 5 l, Tournament, Florence. 10 l, Jousting with "Quintana," Ascoli Piceno. 30 l, "Quintana," Foligno, horiz. 60 l, Race through Siena. 70 l, Tournament, Malpaga, horiz. 115 l, Knights challenging.

554	A108	1 l	lilac rose	.20	.20
555	A108	2 l	slate	.20	.20
556	A108	3 l	black	.20	.20
557	A108	4 l	violet	.20	.20
558	A108	5 l	rose violet	.20	.20
559	A108	10 l	dull green	.20	.20
560	A108	30 l	red brown	.20	.20
561	A108	60 l	Prus green	.20	.20
562	A108	70 l	brown	.20	.20
563	A108	115 l	black	.20	.20
			Nos. 554-563 (10)	2.00	2.00

Butterfly — A109

St. Marinus Statue, Government Palace — A110

Various butterflies. 70 l, 115 l, horiz.

Wmk. 339

1963, Aug. 31 Photo. *Perf. 14*

564	A109	25 l	multicolored	.20	.20
565	A109	30 l	multicolored	.20	.20
566	A109	60 l	multicolored	.20	.20
567	A109	70 l	multicolored	.25	.20
568	A109	115 l	multicolored	.55	.35
			Nos. 564-568 (5)	1.40	1.15

1963, Aug. 31

569	A110	100 l	shown	.20	.20
570	A110	100 l	Modern fountain	.20	.20

San Marino-Riccione Stamp Fair.

Europa Issue, 1963

Flag and "E" — A111

1963, Sept. 21 Wmk. 339 *Perf. 14*

571	A111	200 l	blue & brn org	.30	.30

Women's Hurdles A112

Sports: 2 l, Pole vaulting, vert. 3 l, Women's relay race. 4 l, Men's high jump. 5 l, Soccer. 10 l, Women's high jump. 30 l, Women's discus throw, vert. 60 l, Women's javelin throw. 70 l, Water polo. 115 l, Hammer throw.

1963, Sept. 21

572	A112	1 l	org & red brn	.20	.20
573	A112	2 l	lt grn & dk brn	.20	.20
574	A112	3 l	bl & dk brn	.20	.20
575	A112	4 l	dp bl & dk brn	.20	.20
576	A112	5 l	red & dk brn	.20	.20
577	A112	10 l	lil rose & claret	.20	.20
578	A112	30 l	gray & red brn	.20	.20
579	A112	60 l	brt yel & dk brn	.20	.20
580	A112	70 l	brt bl & dk brn	.20	.20
581	A112	115 l	grn & dk brn	.20	.20
			Nos. 572-581 (10)	2.00	2.00

Publicity for 1964 Olympic Games.

Modern Pentathlon A113

Designs: 1 l, Runner, vert. 2 l, Woman gymnast, vert. 3 l, Basketball, vert. 5 l, Dual rowing. 15 l, Broad jumper. 30 l, Swimmer in racing dive. 70 l, Woman sprinter. 120 l, Bicycle racers, vert. 150 l, Fencers, vert.

Inscribed "Tokio, 1964"

1964, June 25 Wmk. 339 *Perf. 14*

582	A113	1 l	brn & yel grn	.20	.20
583	A113	2 l	blk & red brn	.20	.20
584	A113	3 l	blk & brown	.20	.20
585	A113	4 l	blk & org red	.20	.20
586	A113	5 l	blk & brt bl	.20	.20
587	A113	15 l	dk brn & org	.20	.20
588	A113	30 l	dk vio & bl	.20	.20
589	A113	70 l	red brn & grn	.20	.20
590	A113	120 l	brn & brt bl	.20	.20
591	A113	150 l	blk & crimson	.20	.20
			Nos. 582-591 (10)	2.00	2.00

18th Olympic Games, Tokyo, Oct. 10-25.

Same Inscribed "Verso Tokio"

1964, June 25 Photo.

592	A113	30 l	indigo & lilac	.20	.20
593	A113	70 l	brn & Prus grn	.20	.20

"Verso Tokyo" Stamp Exhibition at Rimini, Italy, June 25-July 6.

Murray-Blenkinsop Locomotive, 1812 — A114

History of Locomotive: 2 l, Puffing Billy, 1813. 3 l, Locomotion I, 1825. 4 l, Rocket, 1829. 5 l, Lion, 1838. 15 l, Bayard, 1839. 20 l, Crampton, 1849. 50 l, Little England, 1851. 90 l, Spitfire, c. 1860. 110 l, Rogers, c. 1865.

1964, Aug. 29 Wmk. 339 *Perf. 14*

594 A114	1 l	blk & buff	.20	.20
595 A114	2 l	blk & green	.20	.20
596 A114	3 l	blk & rose lilac	.20	.20
597 A114	4 l	blk & yellow	.20	.20
598 A114	5 l	blk & salmon	.20	.20
599 A114	15 l	blk & yel grn	.20	.20
600 A114	20 l	blk & dp pink	.20	.20
601 A114	50 l	blk & pale bl	.20	.20
602 A114	90 l	blk & yel org	.20	.20
603 A114	110 l	blk & brt bl	.35	.35
		Nos. 594-603 (10)	2.15	2.15

Baseball Players A115

1964, Aug. 29 Photo.

604 A115	30 l	shown	.20	.20
605 A115	70 l	Pitcher	.20	.20

8th European Baseball Championship, Milan.

Europa Issue, 1964

"E" and Globe A116

1964, Oct. 15 Wmk. 339 *Perf. 14*

606 A116	200 l	dk blue & red	.80	.80

President John F. Kennedy (1917-1963) — A117

130 l, Kennedy and American flag, vert.

1964, Nov. 22 Photo. *Perf. 14*

607 A117	70 l	multicolored	.20	.20
608 A117	130 l	multicolored	.20	.20

Start of Bicycle Race from Government Palace — A118

Rooks on Chessboard A120

Brontosaurus — A119

Designs: 70 l, Cyclists (going right) and view of San Marino. 200 l, Cyclists (going left) and view of San Marino.

1965, May 15 Photo. Wmk. 339

609 A118	30 l	sepia	.20	.20
610 A118	70 l	deep claret	.20	.20
611 A118	200 l	rose red	.20	.20
		Nos. 609-611 (3)	.60	.60

48th Bicycle Tour of Italy.

1965, June 30 Wmk. 339 *Perf. 14*

Dinosaurs: 2 l, Brachiosaurus, vert. 3 l, Pteranodon. 4 l, Elasmosaurus. 5 l, Tyrannosaurus. 10 l, Stegosaurus. 75 l, Thaumatosaurus victor. 100 l, Iguanodon. 200 l, Triceratops.

612 A119	1 l	dk brn & emer	.20	.20
613 A119	2 l	blk & sl bl	.20	.20
614 A119	3 l	sl grn, ol grn & yel	.20	.20
615 A119	4 l	brn & slate bl	.20	.20
616 A119	5 l	claret & grn	.20	.20
617 A119	10 l	claret & grn	.30	.30
618 A119	75 l	dk bl & bl grn	.30	.30
619 A119	100 l	green & claret	.30	.30
620 A119	200 l	brown & grn	.35	.35
		Nos. 612-620 (9)	2.25	2.25

Europa Issue, 1965

1965, Aug. 28 Photo. *Perf. 14*

621 A120	200 l	brown & multi	.45	.45

Dante by Gustave Doré A121

Doré's Illustrations for Divina Commedia: 90 l, Charon ferrying boat across Acheron. 130 l, Eagle carrying Dante from Purgatory to Paradise. 140 l, Dante with Beatrice examined by Sts. Peter, James and John on faith.

Perf. 14x14½

1965, Nov. 20 Engr. Wmk. 339

Center in Brown Black

622 A121	40 l	indigo	.20	.20
623 A121	90 l	car rose	.20	.20
624 A121	130 l	red brown	.20	.20
625 A121	140 l	ultra	.20	.20
		Nos. 622-625 (4)	.80	.80

Dante Alighieri (1265-1321), poet.

Stylized Peaks, Flags of Italy and San Marino A122

1965, Nov. 25 Photo. *Perf. 14*

626 A122	115 l	grn, red, ocher & bl	.20	.20

Visit of Giuseppe Saragat, president of Italy.

Trotter A123

Horses: 20 l, Cross Country, vert. 40 l, Hurdling. 70 l, Gallop. 90 l, Steeplechase. 170 l, Polo, vert.

Perf. 14x13, 13x14

1966, Feb. 28 Photo. Wmk. 339

627 A123	10 l	multicolored	.20	.20
628 A123	20 l	multicolored	.20	.20
629 A123	40 l	multicolored	.20	.20
630 A123	70 l	multicolored	.20	.20
631 A123	90 l	multicolored	.20	.20
632 A123	170 l	multicolored	.20	.20
		Nos. 627-632 (6)	1.20	1.20

Scenic Types of 1955-57

5 l, Hospital Street. 10 l, Gate tower. 15 l, View from South Bastion. 40l, Murata Nuova Bridge. 90 l, View of La Rocca. 140 l, Government Palace.

1966, Mar. 29 Wmk. 339 *Perf. 14*

633 A79	5 l	blue & brn	.20	.20
634 A78	10 l	dk sl grn & bl grn	.20	.20
635 A78	15 l	dk brn & vio	.20	.20
636 A73	40 l	dk pur & brick red	.20	.20
637 A74	90 l	blk & dull bl	.20	.20
638 A74	140 l	violet & org	.20	.20
		Nos. 633-638 (6)	1.20	1.20

"Bella" by Titian A124

Titian Paintings: 90 l, 100 l, Details from "The Education of Love." 170 l, Detail from "Sacred and Profane Love."

1966, June 16 Wmk. 339 *Perf. 14*

639 A124	40 l	multicolored	.20	.20
640 A124	90 l	multicolored	.20	.20
641 A124	100 l	multicolored	.20	.20
642 A124	170 l	multicolored	.20	.20
		Nos. 639-642 (4)	.80	.80

Stone Bass A125

Fish: 2 l, Cuckoo wrasse. 3 l, Dolphin. 4 l, John Dory. 5 l, Octopus, vert. 10 l, Orange scorpionfish. 40 l, Electric ray, vert. 90 l, Jellyfish, vert. 115 l, Sea Horse, vert. 130 l, Dentex.

Perf. 14x13½, 13½x14

1966, Aug. 27 Photo. Wmk. 339

643 A125	1 l	multicolored	.20	.20
644 A125	2 l	multicolored	.20	.20
645 A125	3 l	multicolored	.20	.20
646 A125	4 l	multicolored	.20	.20
647 A125	5 l	multicolored	.20	.20
648 A125	10 l	multicolored	.20	.20
649 A125	40 l	multicolored	.20	.20
650 A125	90 l	multicolored	.20	.20
651 A125	115 l	multicolored	.20	.20
652 A125	130 l	multicolored	.20	.20
		Nos. 643-652 (10)	2.00	2.00

Europa Issue, 1966

Our Lady of Europe A126

1966, Sept. 24 Wmk. 339 *Perf. 14*

653 A126	200 l	multicolored	.20	.20

Peony and Mt. Titano — A127

Flowers and Various Views of Mt. Titano: 10 l, Bell flowers. 15 l, Pyrenean poppy. 20 l, Purple nettle. 40 l, Day lily. 140 l, Gentian. 170 l, Thistle.

Wmk. 339

1967, Jan. 12 Photo. *Perf. 14*

654 A127	5 l	multicolored	.20	.20
655 A127	10 l	multicolored	.20	.20
656 A127	15 l	multicolored	.20	.20
657 A127	20 l	multicolored	.20	.20
658 A127	40 l	multicolored	.20	.20
659 A127	140 l	multicolored	.20	.20
660 A127	170 l	multicolored	.20	.20
		Nos. 654-660 (7)	1.40	1.40

St. Marinus — A128

The Return of the Prodigal Son — A129

Design: 170 l, St. Francis. The paintings are by Giovanni Francesco Barbieri (1591-1666).

Wmk. 339

1967, Mar. 16 Photo. *Perf. 14*

661 A128	40 l	multicolored	.20	.20
662 A128	170 l	multicolored	.20	.20
663 A129	190 l	multicolored	.20	.20
a.		Strip of 3, #661-663	.40	.40

Map Showing Members of CEPT — A130

Amanita Caesarea — A131

Europa Issue, 1967

1967, May 5 Wmk. 339 *Perf. 14*
664 A130 200 l sl grn & brn org .50 .50

1967, June 15 Photo. *Perf. 14*

Various Mushrooms.

665 A131 5 l multicolored .20 .20
666 A131 15 l multicolored .20 .20
667 A131 20 l multicolored .20 .20
668 A131 40 l multicolored .20 .20
669 A131 50 l multicolored .20 .20
670 A131 170 l multicolored .20 .20
Nos. 665-670 (6) 1.20 1.20

Amiens Cathedral A132

Designs: 40 l, Siena Cathedral. 80 l, Toledo Cathedral. 90 l, Salisbury Cathedral. 170 l, Cologne Cathedral.

Wmk. 339

1967, Sept. 21 Engr. *Perf. 14*
671 A132 20 l dk vio, *bister* .20 .20
672 A132 40 l slate grn, *bis* .20 .20
673 A132 80 l slate bl, *bis* .20 .20
674 A132 90 l sepia, *bis* .20 .20
675 A132 170 l deep plum, *bis* .20 .20
Nos. 671-675 (5) 1.00 1.00

Crucifix of Santa Croce, by Cimabue A133

1967, Dec. 5 Wmk. 339 *Perf. 15*
676 A133 300 l brn & vio blue .30 .30

The Crucifix of Santa Croce, by Giovanni Cimabue (1240-1302), was severely damaged in the Florentine flood of Nov. 1966.

Coat of Arms — A134

Coats of Arms: 3 l, Penna Rossa. 5 l, Fiorentino. 10 l, Montecerreto. 25 l, Serravalle. 35 l, Montegiardino. 50 l, Faetano. 90 l, Borgo Maggiore. 180 l, Montelupo. 500 l, State arms of San Marino.

Perf. 13x13½

1968, Mar. 14 Litho. Wmk. 339
677 A134 2 l multi .20 .20
678 A134 3 l multi .20 .20
679 A134 5 l multi .20 .20
680 A134 10 l multi .20 .20
681 A134 25 l multi .20 .20
682 A134 35 l multi .20 .20
683 A134 50 l multi .20 .20
684 A134 90 l multi .20 .20
685 A134 180 l multi .20 .20
686 A134 500 l multi .25 .20
Nos. 677-686 (10) 2.05 2.00

Common Design Types pictured following the introduction.

Europa Issue, 1968
Common Design Type

1968, Apr. 29 Engr. *Perf. 14x13½*
Size: 37x27½mm
687 CD11 250 l claret brown .40 .40

"Battle of San Romano" (Detail), by Paolo Uccello — A135

Designs: Details from "The Battle of San Romano," by Paolo Uccello (1397-1475).

Photogravure and Engraved

1968, June 14 Wmk. 339 *Perf. 14*
688 A135 50 l pale lil & blk .20 .20
689 A135 90 l pale lil & blk, vert. .20 .20
690 A135 130 l pale lil & blk .20 .20
691 A135 230 l pale pink & blk .20 .20
Nos. 688-691 (4) .80 .80

The Mystic Nativity, by Botticelli, Detail A136

Wmk. 339

1968, Dec. 5 Engr. *Perf. 14*
692 A136 50 l dark blue .20 .20
693 A136 90 l deep claret .20 .20
694 A136 180 l sepia .20 .20
Nos. 692-694 (3) .60 .60

Christmas.

"Peace" by Lorenzetti A137

Designs: 80 l, "Justice." 90 l, "Moderation." 180 l, View of Siena, 14th century, horiz. All designs are from the "Good Government" frescoes by Ambrogio Lorenzetti in the Town Hall of Siena.

Wmk. 339

1969, Feb. 13 Engr. *Perf. 14*
695 A137 50 l dark blue .20 .20
696 A137 80 l brown .20 .20
697 A137 90 l dk blue vio .20 .20
698 A137 180 l magenta .20 .20
Nos. 695-698 (4) .80 .80

Young Soldier, by Bramante — A138

Designs: 90 l, Old Soldier, by Bramante. Designs are from murals in the Pinakotheke of Brear, Milan.

1969, Apr. 28 Photo. *Perf. 14*
699 A138 50 l multicolored .20 .20
700 A138 90 l multicolored .20 .20

Bramante (1444-1514), Italian architect and painter.

Europa Issue, 1969
Common Design Type

1969, Apr. 28 Engr. *Perf. 14x13*
Size: 37x27mm
701 CD12 50 l dull green .20 .20
702 CD12 180 l rose claret .20 .20

Charabanc A139

Coaches, 19th Century: 10 l, Barouche. 25 l, Private drag. 40 l, Hansom cab. 50 l, Curricle. 90 l, Wagonette. 180 l, Spider phaeton.

Perf. 14½x14

1969, June 25 Photo. Unwmk.
703 A139 5 l blk, ocher & dk bl .20 .20
704 A139 10 l blk, grn & pur .20 .20
705 A139 25 l dk grn, pink & brn .20 .20
706 A139 40 l ind, lil & lt brn .20 .20
707 A139 50 l blk, dl yel & dk bl .20 .20
708 A139 90 l blk, yel grn & brn .20 .20
709 A139 180 l multi .20 .20
Nos. 703-709 (7) 1.40 1.40

Pier at Rimini A140

Paintings by R. Viola: 20 l, Mt. Titano. 200 l, Pier at Riccione, horiz.

1969, Sept. 17 Unwmk. *Perf. 14*
710 A140 20 l multicolored .20 .20
711 A140 180 l multicolored .20 .20
712 A140 200 l multicolored .20 .20
Nos. 710-712 (3) .60 .60

"Faith" by Raphael — A141

Designs: 180 l, "Hope" by Raphael. 200 l, "Charity" by Raphael.

Perf. 13½x14

1969, Dec. 10 Engr. Wmk. 339
713 A141 20 l dl pur & sal .20 .20
714 A141 180 l dl pur & lt grn .20 .20
715 A141 200 l dp pur & bis .20 .20
Nos. 713-715 (3) .60 .60

Signs of the Zodiac A142

Perf. 14x13½

1970, Feb. 18 Photo. Unwmk.
716 A142 1 l Aries .20 .20
717 A142 2 l Taurus .20 .20
718 A142 3 l Gemini .20 .20
719 A142 4 l Cancer .20 .20
720 A142 5 l Leo .20 .20
721 A142 10 l Virgo .20 .20
722 A142 15 l Libra .20 .20
723 A142 20 l Scorpio .20 .20
724 A142 70 l Sagittarius .20 .20
725 A142 90 l Capricorn .20 .20
726 A142 100 l Aquraius .20 .20
727 A142 180 l Pisces .20 .20
Nos. 716-727 (12) 2.40 2.40

Fleet in Bay of Naples, by Peter Brueghel, the Elder — A143

Unwmk.

1970, Apr. 30 Photo. *Perf. 14*
728 A143 230 l multi .25 .25

10th Europa Phil. Exhib., Naples, May 2-10.

Europa Issue, 1970
Common Design Type

1970, Apr. 30 *Perf. 14x13½*
Size: 36x27mm
729 CD13 90 l brt yel grn & red .20 .20
730 CD13 180 l ocher & red .20 .20

St. Francis' Gate and Rotary Emblem — A144

Woman with Mandolin, by Tiepolo — A145

220 l, Rocca (State Prison) and Rotary emblem.

1970, June 25 Photo. *Perf. 13½x14*
731 A144 180 l multi .25 .25
732 A144 220 l multi .30 .30

65th anniv. of Rotary Intl.; 10th anniv. of the San Marino Rotary Club.

1970, Sept. 10 Unwmk. *Perf. 14*

Paintings by Tiepolo: 180 l, Woman with Parrot. 220 l, Rinaldo and Armida Surprised, horiz.

Size: 26½x37½mm
733 A145 50 l multi .20 .20
734 A145 180 l multi .20 .20

Size: 56x37½mm
735 A145 220 l multi .30 .30
a. Strip of 3, #733-735 .65 .65

Giambattista Tiepolo (1696-1770), Venetian painter.

Black Pete — A146

Walt Disney and Jungle Book Scene A147

Disney Characters: 2 l, Gyro Gearloose. 3 l, Pluto. 4 l, Minnie Mouse. 5 l, Donald Duck. 10 l, Goofy. 15 l, Scrooge McDuck. 50 l, Huey, Louey and Dewey. 90 l, Mickey Mouse.

Perf. 13x14, 14x13

1970, Dec. 22 **Photo.**

736	A146	1 l	multi	.20	.20
737	A146	2 l	multi	.20	.20
738	A146	3 l	multi	.20	.20
739	A146	4 l	multi	.20	.20
740	A146	5 l	multi	.20	.20
741	A146	10 l	multi	.20	.20
742	A146	15 l	multi	.20	.20
743	A146	50 l	multi	.20	.20
744	A146	90 l	multi	.20	.20
745	A147	220 l	multi	3.50	3.50
			Nos. 736-745 (10)	5.30	5.30

Walt Disney (1901-66), cartoonist & film maker.

Customhouse Dock, by Canaletto — A148

Paintings by Canaletto: 180 l, Grand Canal between Balbi Palace and Rialto Bridge. 200 l, St. Mark's and Doges' Palace.

1971, Mar. 23 **Unwmk.** ***Perf. 14***

746	A148	20 l	multi	.20	.20
747	A148	180 l	multi	.25	.25
748	A148	200 l	multi	.85	.85
			Nos. 746-748 (3)	1.30	1.30

Save Venice campaign.

Europa Issue, 1971

Common Design Type

1971, May 29 ***Perf. 13½x14***

Size: 27½x23mm

749	CD14	50 l	org & blue	.20	.20
750	CD14	90 l	blue & org	.20	.20

Congress Emblem and Hall, San Marino Flag — A149

Design: 90 l, Detail from Government Palace door, Congress and San Marino emblems, vert.

1971, May 29 **Photo.** ***Perf. 12***

751	A149	20 l	violet & multi	.20	.20
752	A149	90 l	olive & multi	.20	.20
753	A149	180 l	multi	.20	.20
			Nos. 751-753 (3)	.60	.60

Italian Philatelic Press Union Congress, San Marino, May 29-30.

Duck-shaped Jug with Flying Lasa — A150

Etruscan Art, 6th-3rd Centuries B.C.: 80 l, Head of Mercury, vert. 90 l, Sarcophagus of a married couple, vert. 180 l, Chimera.

Photo. & Engr.

1971, Sept. 16 ***Perf. 14***

754	A150	50 l	blk & org	.20	.20
755	A150	80 l	blk & lt grn	.20	.20
756	A150	90 l	blk & lt bl	.20	.20
757	A150	180 l	blk & org	.20	.20
			Nos. 754-757 (4)	.80	.80

Tiger Lily A151

Venus, by Botticelli A152

1971, Dec. 2 **Photo.** ***Perf. 11½***

758	A151	1 l	shown	.20	.20
759	A151	2 l	Phlox	.20	.20
760	A151	3 l	Carnations	.20	.20
761	A151	4 l	Globe flowers	.20	.20
762	A151	5 l	Thistles	.20	.20
763	A151	10 l	Peonies	.20	.20
764	A151	15 l	Hellebore	.20	.20
765	A151	50 l	Anemones	.20	.20
766	A151	90 l	Gaillardia	.20	.20
767	A151	220 l	Asters	.20	.20
			Nos. 758-767 (10)	2.00	2.00

1972, Feb. 23 ***Perf. 14, 13x14 (180 l)***

Details from La Primavera, by Sandro Botticelli: 180 l, Three Graces. 220 l, Spring.

Sizes: 50 l, 220 l, 21x37mm; 180 l, 27x37mm

768	A152	50 l	gold & multi	.20	.20
769	A152	180 l	gold & multi	.20	.20
770	A152	220 l	gold & multi	.40	.40
			Nos. 768-770 (3)	.80	.80

Europa Issue 1972

Common Design Type

1972, Apr. 27 ***Perf. 11½***

Granite Paper

Size: 22½x33mm

771	CD15	50 l	org & multi	.20	.20
772	CD15	90 l	lt bl & multi	.20	.20

St. Marinus Taming Bear A153

Designs: 55 l, Donna Felicissima asking St. Marinus for mercy for her sons. 100 l, St. Marinus turning archers to stone. 130 l, Felicissima giving mountains to St. Marinus to establish Republic.

Photo. & Engr.

1972, Apr. 27 ***Perf. 14***

773	A153	25 l	dl yel & blk	.20	.20
774	A153	55 l	sal pink & blk	.20	.20
775	A153	100 l	dl bl & blk	.20	.20
776	A153	130 l	citron & blk	.20	.20
			Nos. 773-776 (4)	.80	.80

Allegories of San Marino after 16th century paintings.

Italian House Sparrow — A154

1972, June 30 **Photo.** ***Perf. 11½***

Granite Paper

777	A154	1 l	shown	.20	.20
778	A154	2 l	Firecrest	.20	.20
779	A154	3 l	Blue tit	.20	.20
780	A154	4 l	Ortolan bunting	.20	.20
781	A154	5 l	White-spotted bluethroat	.20	.20
782	A154	10 l	Bullfinch	.20	.20
783	A154	25 l	Linnet	.20	.20
784	A154	50 l	Black-eared wheater	.20	.20
785	A154	90 l	Sardinian warbler	.20	.20
786	A154	220 l	Greenfinch	.20	.20
			Nos. 777-786 (10)	2.00	2.00

Young Man, Heart, Emblem — A155

Italian Philatelic Federation Emblem — A156

Design: 90 l, Heart disease victim, horiz.

Perf. 13½x14, 14x13½

1972, Aug. 26

787	A155	50 l	lt bl & multi	.20	.20
788	A155	90 l	ocher & multi	.20	.20

World Heart Month.

1972, Aug. 26 ***Perf. 13½x14***

789	A156	25 l	gold & ultra	.20	.20

Honoring veterans of Philately.

5c Coin, 1864 A157

Coins: 10 l, 10c coin, 1935. 15 l, 1 lira, 1906. 20 l, 5 lire, 1898. 25 l, 5 lire, 1937. 50 l, 10 lire, 1932. 55 l, 20 lire, 1938. 220 l, 20 lire, 1925.

1972, Dec. 15 **Litho.** ***Perf. 12½x13***

790	A157	5 l	gray, blk & brn	.20	.20
791	A157	10 l	org, blk & sil	.20	.20
792	A157	15 l	brt rose, blk & sil	.20	.20
793	A157	20 l	lil, blk & sil	.20	.20
794	A157	25 l	vio, blk & sil	.20	.20
795	A157	50 l	brt bl, blk & sil	.20	.20
796	A157	55 l	ocher, blk & sil	.20	.20
797	A157	220 l	emer, blk & gold	.20	.20
			Nos. 790-797 (8)	1.60	1.60

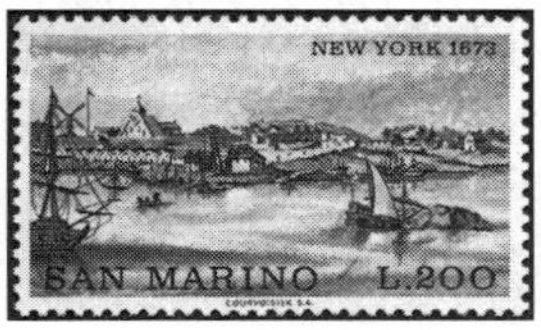

New York, 1673 A158

300 l, View of New York from East River, 1973.

1973, Mar. 9 **Photo.** ***Perf. 11½***

Granite Paper

798	A158	200 l	bis, och & ol grn	.20	.20
799	A158	300 l	bl, lil & blk	.45	.45
a.			Pair, #798-799	.65	.65

New York, 300th anniv. Printed checkerwise.

Rotary Press, San Marino Towers — A159

Gymnasts and Olympic Rings — A160

1973, May 10 **Photo.** ***Perf. 13x14***

800	A159	50 l	multi	.20	.20

Tourist Press Congress, San Marino.

1973, May 10 **Unwmk.**

801	A160	100 l	grn & multi	.20	.20

5th Youth Games.

Europa Issue 1973

Common Design Type

1973, May 10 ***Perf. 11½***

Size: 32½x23mm

802	CD16	20 l	salmon & multi	.20	.20
803	CD16	180 l	lt bl & multi	.40	.40

Grapes — A161

1973, July 11 **Photo.** ***Perf. 11½***

804	A161	1 l	shown	.20	.20
805	A161	2 l	Tangerines	.20	.20
806	A161	3 l	Apples	.20	.20
807	A161	4 l	Plums	.20	.20
808	A161	5 l	Strawberries	.20	.20
809	A161	10 l	Pears	.20	.20
810	A161	25 l	Cherries	.20	.20
811	A161	50 l	Pomegranate	.20	.20
812	A161	90 l	Apricots	.20	.20
813	A161	220 l	Peaches	.20	.20
			Nos. 804-813 (10)	2.00	2.00

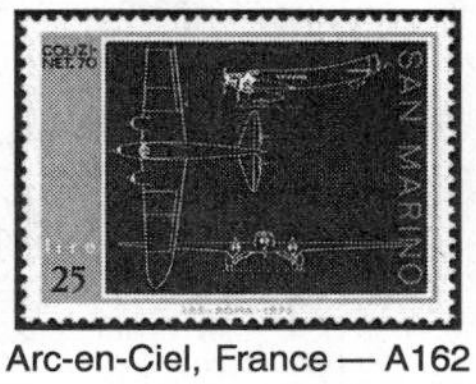

Arc-en-Ciel, France — A162

Famous Aircraft: 55 l, Macchi Castoldi, Italy. 60 l, Antonov, USSR. 90 l, Spirit of St. Louis, US. 220 l, Handley Page, Great Britain.

1973, Aug. 31 **Photo.** ***Perf. 14x13½***

814	A162	25 l	ocher, vio bl & gold	.20	.20
815	A162	55 l	gray, vio bl & gold	.20	.20
816	A162	60 l	rose, vio bl & gold	.20	.20
817	A162	90 l	lem, vio bl & gold	.20	.20
818	A162	220 l	org, vio bl & gold	.20	.20
			Nos. 814-818 (5)	1.00	1.00

Crossbowman, Serravalle Castle — A163

Attendants, by Gentile Fabriano — A164

Designs: 10 l, Crossbowman, Pennarossa Castle. 15 l, Drummer, Montegiardino Castle. 20 l, Trumpeter, Fiorentino Castle. 30 l, Crossbowman, Borga Maggiore Castle. 50 l, Trumpeter, Guaita Castle. 80 l, Crossbowman, Faetano Castle. 200 l, Crossbowman, Montelupo Castle.

1973, Nov. 7 Photo. *Perf. 13½*

819	A163	5 l black & multi	.20	.20
820	A163	10 l black & multi	.20	.20
821	A163	15 l black & multi	.20	.20
822	A163	20 l black & multi	.20	.20
823	A163	30 l black & multi	.20	.20
824	A163	40 l black & multi	.20	.20
825	A163	50 l black & multi	.20	.20
826	A163	80 l black & multi	.20	.20
827	A163	200 l black & multi	.20	.20
		Nos. 819-827 (9)	1.80	1.80

San Marino victories in the Crossbow Tournament, Massa Marittima, July 15, 1973.

1973, Dec. 19 Photo. *Perf. 11½*

Christmas: Details from Adoration of the Kings, by Gentile Fabriano (1370-1427).

828	A164	5 l shown	.20	.20
829	A164	30 l King	.20	.20
830	A164	115 l King	.20	.20
831	A164	250 l Horses	.20	.20
		Nos. 828-831 (4)	.80	.80

Shield, 16th Century A165

16th Century Armor: 5 l, Round shield. 10 l, German full armor. 15 l, Helmet with intricate etching. 20 l, Horse's head armor "Massimiliano." 30 l, Decorated helmet with Sphinx statuette on top. 50 l, Pommeled sword and gauntlets. 80 l, Sparrow-beaked helmet. 250 l, Sforza round shield.

Engr. & Litho.

1974, Mar. 12 *Perf. 13*

832	A165	5 l blk, lt grn & buff	.20	.20
833	A165	10 l blk, buff & bl	.20	.20
834	A165	15 l blk, bl & ultra	.20	.20
835	A165	20 l blk, tan & ultra	.20	.20
836	A165	30 l blk & lt bl	.20	.20
837	A165	50 l blk, rose & ultra	.20	.20
838	A165	80 l blk, gray & grn	.20	.20
839	A165	250 l blk & yel	.20	.20
		Nos. 832-839 (8)	1.60	1.60

Head of Woman, by Emilio Greco — A166

Europa: 200 l, Nude, by Emilio Greco (head shown on 100 l).

Engr. & Litho.

1974, May 9 *Perf. 13x14*

840	A166	100 l buff & blk	.20	.20
841	A166	200 l pale grn & blk	.30	.30

Yachts at Riccione and San Marino Peaks A167

1974, July 18 Photo. *Perf. 11½*

Granite Paper

842	A167	50 l ultra & multi	.20	.20

26th San Marino-Riccione Stamp Day.

Arms of Lucia — A168

Coats of arms of participating cities.

1974, July 18 *Perf. 12*

843	A168	15 l shown	.45	.45
844	A168	20 l Massa Marittima	.45	.45
845	A168	50 l San Marino	.45	.45
846	A168	115 l Gubbio	.45	.45
847	A168	300 l Lucca	.45	.45
a.		Strip of 5, #843-847	2.25	2.25

9th Crossbow Tournament, San Marino.

UPU Emblem — A169

1974, Oct. 9 Photo. *Perf. 11½*

Granite Paper

848	A169	50 l multi	.20	.20
849	A169	90 l grn & multi	.20	.20

Centenary of Universal Postal Union.

Mt. Titano and Hymn by Tommaseo A170

Niccolo Tommaseo A171

1974, Dec. 12 Photo. *Perf. 13½x14*

850	A170	50 l lt grn, blk & red	.20	.20
851	A171	150 l yel, grn & blk	.20	.20

Tommaseo (1802-1874), Italian writer.

Virgin and Child, 14th Century Wood Panel — A172

1974, Dec. 12 *Perf. 11½*

852	A172	250 l gold & multi	.30	.30

Christmas.

"Refuge in San Marino" — A173

1975, Feb. 20 Photo. *Perf. 13½x14*

853	A173	50 l multi	.20	.20

Flight of 100,000 refugees from Romagna to San Marino, 30th anniversary.

Musicians, from Leopard Tomb, Tarquinia — A174

Etruscan Art: 30 l, Chariot race, from Tomb on the Hill, Chiusi. 180 l, Achilles and Troilus, from Bulls' Tomb, Tarquinia. 220 l, Dancers, from Triclinium Tomb, Tarquinia.

Litho. & Engr.

1975, Feb. 20 *Perf. 14*

854	A174	20 l multi	.20	.20
855	A174	30 l multi	.20	.20
856	A174	180 l multi	.20	.20
857	A174	220 l multi	.25	.25
		Nos. 854-857 (4)	.85	.85

Europa Issue 1975

St. Marinus, by Guercino (Francesco Barbieri)

A175 A176

1975, May 14 Photo. *Perf. 11½*

Granite Paper

858	A175	100 l multi	.20	.20
859	A176	200 l multi	.25	.25

The Lamentation, by Giotto — A177

Frescoes by Giotto (details): 40 l, Mary and Jesus (Flight into Egypt). 50 l, Heads of four angels (Flight into Egypt). 100 l, Mary Magdalene (Noli Me Tangere), horiz. 500 l, Angel and the elect (Last Judgment), horiz.

1975, July 10 Photo. *Perf. 11½*

Granite Paper

860	A177	10 l gold & multi	.20	.20
861	A177	40 l gold & multi	.20	.20
862	A177	50 l gold & multi	.20	.20
863	A177	100 l gold & multi	.20	.20
864	A177	500 l gold & multi	.45	.45
		Nos. 860-864 (5)	1.25	1.25

Holy Year.

Tokyo, 1835, Woodcut by Hiroshige — A178

300 l, Tokyo, Business District, 1975.

1975, Sept. 5 Photo. *Perf. 11½*

Granite Paper

865	A178	200 l multi	.25	.25
866	A178	300 l multi	.40	.40
a.		Pair, #865-866	.65	.65

Printed checkerwise.

Aphrodite A179

1975, Sept. 19 Photo. *Perf. 11½*

867	A179	50 l vio, blk & gray	.20	.20

Europa '75 Philatelic Exhibition, Naples.

Multiple Crosses A180

1975, Sept. 19

868	A180	100 l blk, dp org & vio	.20	.20

EUROCOPHAR Intl. Pharmaceutical Cong.

Christmas — A181

Christmas: Paintings by Michelangelo: 50 l, Angel. 100 l, Head of Virgin. 250 l, Doni Madonna.

1975, Dec. 3 Photo. *Perf. 11½*

Granite Paper

869		50 l multi	.20	.20
870		100 l multi	.20	.20
871		250 l multi	.30	.30
a.	A181	Strip of 3, #869-871	.50	.50

Woman on Balcony, by Gentilini — A183

Two Women, by Gentilini A184

230 l, Woman (same as right head on 150 l) & IWY emblem, by Franco Gentilini.

1975, Dec. 3
Granite Paper

872 A183 70 l bl & multi .20 .20
873 A184 150 l multi .20 .20
874 A183 230 l multi .25 .25
Nos. 872-874 (3) .65 .65

International Women's Year.

Modesty, by Emilio Greco — A185

Capitol, Washington, D.C. — A186

"Civic Virtues": 20 l, Temperance. 50 l, Fortitude. 100 l, Altruism. 150 l, Hope. 220 l, Prudence. 250 l, Justice. 300 l, Faith. 500 l, Honesty. 1000 l, Industry. Designs show drawings of women's heads by Emilio Greco.

1976, Mar. 4 Photo. *Perf. 11½*
Granite Paper

875 A185 10 l buff & blk .20 .20
876 A185 20 l pink & blk .20 .20
877 A185 50 l grnsh & blk .20 .20
878 A185 100 l salmon & blk .20 .20
879 A185 150 l lilac & blk .20 .20
880 A185 220 l gray & blk .20 .20
881 A185 250 l yel & multi .20 .20
882 A185 300 l gray & blk .30 .30
883 A185 500 l yel & blk .40 .40
884 A185 1000 l gray & blk 1.25 1.25
Nos. 875-884 (10) 3.35 3.35

See Nos. 900-905, 931-933.

1976, May 29 Photo. *Perf. 11½*

Arms of San Marino and: 150 l, Statue of Liberty. 180 l, Independence Hall, Philadelphia.

885 A186 70 l multi .20 .20
886 A186 150 l multi .20 .20
887 A186 180 l multi .20 .20
Nos. 885-887 (3) .60 .60

American Bicentennial.

Montreal Olympic Games Emblem A187

1976, May 29

888 A187 150 l crimson & blk .20 .20

21st Olympic Games, Montreal, Canada, 7/17-8/1.

Decorated Plate — A188

Europa: 180 l, Seal of San Marino.

1976, July 8 Photo. *Perf. 11½*
Granite Paper

889 A188 150 l multi .20 .20
890 A188 180 l bl, sil & blk .20 .20

"Unity" — A189

"Peaks of San Marino" — A190

1976, July 8 *Perf. 13½x14*

891 A189 150 l vio blk, yel & red .20 .20

United Mutual Aid Society, centenary.

1976, Oct. 14 Photo. *Perf. 13x14*

892 A190 150 l blk & multi .25 .25

ITALIA 76 Intl. Phil. Exhib., Milan, 10/14-24.

Children and UNESCO Emblem A191

1976, Oct. 14 *Perf. 11½*
Granite Paper

893 A191 180 l multi .25 .25
894 A191 220 l multi .25 .25

UNESCO, 30th anniv.

Christmas — A192

Design: 150 l, Annunciation (detail), by Titian. 300 l, Virgin and Child, by Titian.

Litho. & Engr.
1976, Dec. 15 *Perf. 13x14*

895 150 l multi .20 .20
896 300 l multi .45 .45
a. A192 Pair, #895-896 .60 .60

Exhibition Emblem A193

1977, Jan. 28 Photo. *Perf. 11½*
Granite Paper

897 A193 80 l multi .20 .20
898 A193 170 l multi .20 .20
899 A193 200 l multi .20 .20
Nos. 897-899,C133 (4) .80 .80

San Marino 77 Phil. Exhib.

Civic Virtues Type of 1976

70 l, Fortitude. 90 l, Prudence. 120 l, Altruism. 160 l, Temperance. 170 l, Hope. 320 l, Faith.

1977, Apr. 14 Photo. *Perf. 11½*
Granite Paper

900 A185 70 l pink & blk .20 .20
901 A185 90 l buff & blk .20 .20
902 A185 120 l lt bl & blk .20 .20
903 A185 160 l lt grn & blk .20 .20
904 A185 170 l cream & blk .20 .20
905 A185 320 l lil & blk .40 .40
Nos. 900-905 (6) 1.40 1.40

San Marino, after Ghirlandaio A194

Europa: 200 l, San Marino, detail from painting by Guercino.

1977, Apr. 14
Granite Paper

906 A194 170 l multi .20 .20
907 A194 200 l multi .30 .30

Vertical Flying Machine, by da Vinci — A195

Litho. & Engr.
1977, June 6 *Perf. 13x14*

908 A195 120 l multi .20 .20

Centenary of Enrico Forlanini's experiments with vertical flight.

University Square, Bucharest, 1877 — A196

Design: 400 l, National Theater and Intercontinental Hotel, 1977.

1977, June 6 Photo. *Perf. 11½*
Granite Paper

909 A196 200 l bis & multi .30 .30
910 A196 400 l lt bl & multi .40 .40
a. Pair, #909-910 .70 .70

Centenary of Romanian independence. Printed checkerwise.

Type A2 of 1877 — A197

1977, June 15 Engr. *Perf. 15x14½*

911 A197 40 l slate grn .20 .20
912 A197 70 l deep blue .20 .20
913 A197 170 l red .20 .20
914 A197 500 l brown .40 .40
915 A197 1000 l purple .90 .90
Nos. 911-915 (5) 1.90 1.90

Centenary of San Marino stamps.

St. Marinus, by Retrosi — A198

Medicinal Plants — A199

Souvenir Sheet

1977, Aug. 28 Photo. *Perf. 11½*
Granite Paper

916 A198 Sheet of 5 7.50 7.50
a. 1000 l single stamp 1.50 1.50

Centenary of San Marino stamps; San Marino '77 Phil. Exhib., Aug. 28-Sept. 4.

1977, Oct. 19 Photo. *Perf. 11½*

917 A199 170 l multi .20 .20

Congress of Italian Pharmacists' Union. Design shows high mallow, tilia, camomile, borage, centaury and juniper.

Woman Attacked by Octopus, Emblem A200

1977, Oct. 19

918 A200 200 l multi .25 .25

World Rheumatism Year.

Virgin Mary — A201

San Francisco Gate — A202

Christmas: 230 l, Palm, olive and star. 300 l, Angel.

1977, Dec. 5 Photo. *Perf. 11½*

919 A201 170 l sil, gray & blk .20 .20
920 A201 230 l sil, gray & blk .25 .25
921 A201 300 l sil, gray & blk .30 .30
a. Strip of 3, #919-921 .75 .75

1978, May 30 Photo. *Perf. 11½*

Europa: 200 l, Ripa Gate.

922 A202 170 l lt bl & dk bl .25 .25
923 A202 200 l buff & brn .35 .35

Baseball Player and Diamond — A203

Feather, WHO Emblem — A204

1978, May 30

924	A203	90 l multi	.20	.20
925	A203	120 l multi	.20	.20

World Baseball Championships.

1978, May 30

926	A204	320 l multi	.35	.35

Fight against hypertension.

ITU Emblem, Waves Coming from 3 Peaks — A205

1978, July 26 Photo. *Perf. 11½*

927	A205	10 l car & yel	.20	.20
928	A205	200 l vio bl & lt bl	.20	.20

Membership in ITU.

Seagull and Falcon, 3 Peaks A206

1978, July 26

929	A206	120 l multi	.20	.20
930	A206	170 l multi	.20	.20

30th San Marino-Riccione Stamp Day.

Civic Virtues Type of 1976

Drawings by Emilio Greco: 5 l, Wisdom. 35 l, Love. 2000 l, Faithfulness.

1978, Sept. 28 Photo. *Perf. 11½*
Granite Paper

931	A185	5 l lt vio & blk	.20	.20
932	A185	35 l gray & blk	.20	.20
933	A185	2000 l yel & blk	2.00	2.00
		Nos. 931-933 (3)	2.40	2.40

Christmas A207

1978, Dec. 6 Photo. *Perf. 14x13½*

941	A207	10 l Holly leaves	.20	.20
942	A207	120 l Stars	.20	.20
943	A207	170 l Snowflakes	.20	.20
		Nos. 941-943 (3)	.60	.60

Globe and Woman Holding Torch — A208

1978, Dec. 6 *Perf. 11½x12*

944	A208	200 l multi	.20	.20

Universal Declaration of Human Rights, 30th anniversary.

First San Marino Autobus, 1915 A209

Europa: 220 l, Mail coach, 1895.

1979, Mar. 29 Photo. *Perf. 11½x12*

945	A209	170 l multi	.25	.25
946	A209	220 l multi	.55	.55

Albert Einstein (1879-1955), Theoretical Physicist — A210

1979, Mar. 29 *Perf. 11½*

947	A210	120 l gray, lt & dk brn	.20	.20

San Marino Crossbow Federation Emblem — A211

Maigret — A212

1979, July 12 Litho. *Perf. 14x13*

948	A211	120 l multi	.20	.20

14th Crossbow Tournament.

Litho. & Engr.

1979, July 12 *Perf. 13x14*

Fictional Detectives: 80 l, Perry Mason. 150 l, Nero Wolfe. 170 l, Ellery Queen. 220 l, Sherlock Holmes.

949	A212	10 l multi	.20	.20
950	A212	80 l multi	.20	.20
951	A212	150 l multi	.20	.20
952	A212	170 l multi	.20	.20
953	A212	220 l multi	.35	.35
		Nos. 949-953 (5)	1.15	1.15

Girl Holding Bird — A213

IYC Emblem, Paintings by Marina Busignani: 120 l, 170 l, 220 l, Children and birds, diff. 350 l, Mother nursing child.

1979, Sept. 6 Litho. *Perf. 11½*

954	A213	20 l multi	.20	.20
955	A213	120 l multi	.20	.20
956	A213	170 l multi	.20	.20
957	A213	220 l multi	.20	.20
958	A213	350 l multi	.25	.25
		Nos. 954-958 (5)	1.05	1.05

St. Apollonia, 15th Century Woodcut — A214

Chestnut Tree, Deer — A216

Waterskier A215

1979, Sept. 6 Photo.

959	A214	170 l multi	.20	.20

13th Biennial Intl. Congress of Stomatology.

1979, Sept. 6

960	A215	150 l multi	.20	.20

European Waterskiing Championship.

1979, Oct. 25 Photo. *Perf. 11½*

Protected Trees and Animals or Birds: 10 l, Cedar of Lebanon, falcon. 35 l, Dogwood, racoon. 50 l, Banyan, tiger. 70 l, Umbrella pine, hoopoe. 90 l, Siberian spruce, marten. 100 l, Eucalyptus, koala bear. 120 l, Date palm, camel. 150 l, Sugar maple, beaver. 170 l, Adansonia, elephant.

961	A216	5 l multi	.20	.20
962	A216	10 l multi	.20	.20
963	A216	35 l multi	.20	.20
964	A216	50 l multi	.20	.20
965	A216	70 l multi	.20	.20
966	A216	90 l multi	.20	.20
967	A216	100 l multi	.20	.20
968	A216	120 l multi	.20	.20
969	A216	150 l multi	.20	.20
970	A216	170 l multi	.20	.20
		Nos. 961-970 (10)	2.00	2.00

Holy Family, by Antonio Alberto de Ferrara, 15th Century Fresco A217

Christmas (de Ferrara Fresco): 80 l, St. Joseph. 170 l, Infant Jesus. 220 l, One of the Three Kings.

1979, Dec. 6 Photo. *Perf. 12*

971	A217	80 l multi	.20	.20
972	A217	170 l multi	.20	.20
973	A217	220 l multi	.20	.20
974	A217	320 l multi	.40	.40
		Nos. 971-974 (4)	1.00	1.00

Disturbing Muses, by Giorgio de Chirico — A218

1979, Dec.

975	A218	40 l shown	.20	.20
976	A218	150 l Ancient horses	.20	.20
977	A218	170 l Self-portrait	.20	.20
		Nos. 975-977 (3)	.60	.60

Giorgio de Chirico, Italian surrealist painter.

St. Benedict, 15th Century Fresco — A219

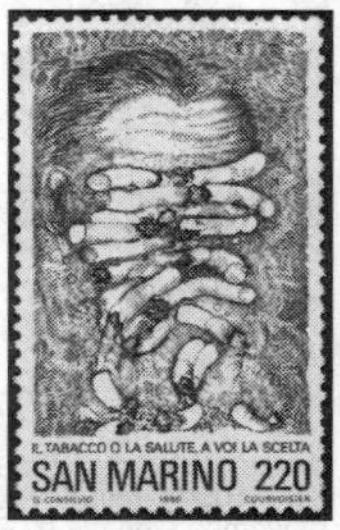

Fight Against Cigarette Smoking — A220

1980, Mar. 27 Photo. *Perf. 12x11½*
Granite Paper

978	A219	170 l multi	.20	.20

St. Benedict of Nursia, 1500th birth anniversary.

1980, Mar. 27

Designs: Sketches of smokers and cigarettes by Giuliana Consilivio.

979	A220	120 l multi	.20	.20
980	A220	220 l multi	.20	.20
981	A220	520 l multi	.60	.60
		Nos. 979-981 (3)	1.00	1.00

Naples, 17th Century Engraving A221

1980, Mar. 27 *Perf. 14x13½*

982	A221	170 l multi	.20	.20

20th Intl. Phil. Exhib., Europa '80, Naples, Apr. 26-May 4.

View of London, 1850 — A222

1980, May 8 *Perf. 11½x12*

983	A222	200 l shown	.25	.25
984	A222	400 l London, 1980	.45	.45
a.		Pair, #983-984	.70	.70

London 1980 Intl. Stamp Exhib., May 6-14. Printed checkerwise.

See Nos. 1001-1002, 1032-1033, 1054-1055, 1069-1070, 1098-1099, 1110-1111, 1141-1142, 1339-1340.

A223

A224

Europa: 170 l, Giovanbattista Belluzzi (1506-54), military architect. 220 l, Antonio Orafo (1460-1552), goldsmith and jeweler.

1980, May 8 ***Perf. 11½***
985 A223 170 l multi .25 .25
986 A223 220 l multi .30 .30

1980, July 7 Photo. ***Perf. 11½***
Granite Paper
987 A224 70 l Bicycling .20 .20
988 A224 90 l Basketball .20 .20
989 A224 170 l Running .20 .20
990 A224 350 l Gymnast .40 .40
991 A224 450 l High jump .40 .40
Nos. 987-991 (5) 1.40 1.40

22nd Summer Olympic Games, Moscow, July 19-Aug. 3.

Ancient Fortifications A225

Weight Lifting A226

Photogravure and Engraved
1980, Sept. 18 ***Perf. 13½x14***
992 A225 220 l multi .25 .25

World Tourism Conf., Manila, Sept. 27.

1980, Sept. 18 Photo. ***Perf. 14x13½***
993 A226 170 l multi .20 .20

European Junior Weight Lifting Championship, Sept.

Robert Stolz, "Philatelic Waltz" Score A227

Photo. & Engr.
1980, Sept. 18 ***Perf. 14***
994 A227 120 l lt bl & blk .20 .20

Robert Stolz (1880-1975) composer.

Madonna of the Harpies, by Andrea Del Sarto — A228

Annunciation by Del Sarto (Details): 250 l, Virgin Mary. 500 l Angel.

1980, Dec. 11 ***Perf. 13½***
995 A228 180 l multi .20 .20
996 A228 250 l multi .20 .20
997 A228 500 l multi .60 .60
Nos. 995-997 (3) 1.00 1.00

Christmas; 450th death anniv. of Del Sarto.

St. Joseph's Eve Bonfire — A229

Intl. Year of the Disabled — A230

Europa Issue 1981
1981, Mar. 24 Photo. ***Perf. 12***
Granite Paper
998 A229 200 l shown .20 .20
999 A229 300 l San Marino Day fireworks .30 .30

1981, May 15 Photo. ***Perf. 11½***
Granite Paper
1000 A230 300 l multi .30 .30

Exhibition Type of 1980

St. Charles' Square, Vienna, by Jakob Alt, 1817.

1981, May 15
Granite Paper
1001 A222 200 l shown .20 .20
1002 A222 300 l Vienna, 1981 .40 .40
a. Pair, #1001-1002 .60 .60

WIPA '81 Intl. Phil. Exhib., Vienna, 5/22-31.

Woman Playing Flute — A232

Grand Prix Motorcycle Race — A233

Drawings based on Roman sculptures.

1981, July 10 Photo. ***Perf. 11½***
Granite Paper
1003 A232 300 l shown .20 .20
1004 A232 550 l Soldier .60 .60
1005 A232 1500 l Shepherd 1.25 1.25
a. Souv. sheet of 3, #1003-1005 2.25 2.25

Virgil's birth bimillennium. No. 1005a has continuous design.

1981, July 10 Litho. ***Perf. 14x15***
1006 A233 200 l multi .25 .25

Natl. Urban Development Plan (Housing) — A234

1981, Sept. 22 Photo.
Granite Paper
1007 A234 20 l shown .20 .20
1008 A234 80 l Parks .20 .20
1009 A234 400 l Energy plants .30 .30
Nos. 1007-1009 (3) .70 .70

European Junior Judo Championship, Oct. 30-Nov. 1 — A235

1981, Sept. 22 Photo. ***Perf. 11½***
Granite Paper
1010 A235 300 l multi .35 .35

World Food Day — A236

1981, Oct. 23
Granite Paper
1011 A236 300 l multi .35 .35

A237

A238

Designs: 150 l, Child Holding a Dove, by Pablo Picasso (1881-1973). 200 l, Homage to Picasso, by Renato Guttuso.

1981, Oct. 23
Granite Paper
1012 A237 150 l multi .20 .20
1013 A237 200 l multi .25 .25

Photo. & Engr.
1981, Dec. 15 ***Perf. 13½***

Christmas; 500th Birth Anniv. of Benvenuto Tisi da Garofalo Adoration of the Kings and St. Bartholomew): 200 l, One of the Three Kings with Goblet, by Garafalo. 300 l, King with a Jar. 600 l, Virgin and Child.

1014 A238 200 l multi .20 .20
1015 A238 300 l multi .25 .25
1016 A238 600 l multi .55 .55
Nos. 1014-1016 (3) 1.00 1.00

Postal Stationery Centenary A239

1982, Feb. 19 Photo. ***Perf. 12***
1017 A239 200 l multi .25 .25

Savings Bank Centenary A240

1982, Feb. 19
1018 A240 300 l multi .25 .25

Europa 1982 — A241

Designs: 300 l, Convocation of the Assembly of Heads of Families, 1906. 450 l, Napoleons's Treaty of Friendship offer, 1797.

1982, Apr. 21 Photo. ***Perf. 11½***
Granite Paper
1019 A241 300 l multi .60 .60
1020 A241 450 l multi .65 .65

Archimedes A242

800th Birth Anniv. of St. Francis of Assisi A243

1982, Apr. 21 Photo. ***Perf. 14x13½***
1021 A242 20 l shown .20 .20
1022 A242 30 l Copernicus .20 .20
1023 A242 40 l Newton .20 .20
1024 A242 50 l Lavoisier .20 .20
1025 A242 60 l Marie Curie .20 .20
1026 A242 100 l Robert Koch .20 .20

Litho. & Engr.
1027 A242 200 l Thomas Edison .20 .20
1028 A242 300 l Guglielmo Marconi .20 .20
1029 A242 450 l Hippocrates .30 .30

Engr.
1030 A242 5000 l Galileo 5.25 5.25
Nos. 1021-1030 (10) 7.15 7.15

See Nos. 1041-1046.

1982, June 10 Photo.
1031 A243 200 l multi .20 .20

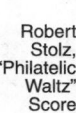

Exhibition Type of 1980

1982, June 10

1032 A222 300 l Notre Dame, 1806 .30 .30
1033 A222 450 l 1982 .45 .45
a. Pair, #1032-1033 .75 .75

PHILEXFRANCE '82 Stamp Exhibition, Paris, June 11-21.

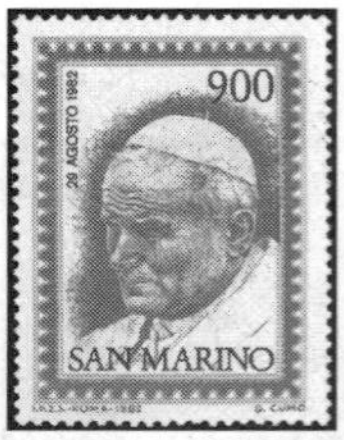

Visit of Pope John Paul II — A245

Natl. Flags of ASCAT Members — A246

1982, Aug. 29 Litho. *Perf. 13½x14*

1034 A245 900 l multi .90 .90

1982, Sept. 1 Photo. *Perf. 11½*
Granite Paper

1035 A246 300 l multi .35 .35

Inaugural Meeting of ASCAT (Assoc. of Editors of Philatelic Catalogues), 1977.

A247

A248

1982, Sept. 1 Unwmk.

1036 A247 700 l blk & red .70 .70

15th Amnesty Intl. Congress, Rimini, Italy, Sept. 9-15.

Photo. & Engr.

1982, Dec. 15 *Perf. 13½*

Christmas: Paintings by Gregorio Sciltian (1900-85).

1037 A248 200 l Angel .20 .20
1038 A248 300 l Virgin and Child .35 .35
1039 A248 450 l Angel, diff. .55 .55
Nos. 1037-1039 (3) 1.10 1.10

Secondary School Centenary A249

Auguste Piccard — A251

3rd Formula One Grand Prix A250

1983, Feb. 24 Photo. *Perf. 13½x14*

1040 A249 300 l Begni Building .35 .35

Scientist Type of 1982

1983, Apr. 21 *Perf. 14x13½*

1041 A242 150 l Alexander Fleming .20 .20
1042 A242 250 l Alessandro Volta .25 .25
1043 A242 350 l Evangelista Torricelli .35 .35
1044 A242 400 l Carolus Linnaeus .40 .40
1045 A242 1000 l Pythagoras 1.00 1.00
1046 A242 1400 l Leonardo da Vinci 1.40 1.40
Nos. 1041-1046 (6) 3.60 3.60

1983, Apr. 20 Photo. *Perf. 14x13½*

1047 A250 50 l multi .20 .20
1048 A250 350 l multi .40 .40

1983, Apr. 20 *Perf. 12x11½*
Granite Paper

1049 A251 400 l Aerostat *.90* .90
1050 A251 500 l Bathyscaph *1.10* 1.10

Europa. Piccard (1884-1962), Swiss scientist.

World Communications Year — A252

1983, Apr. 28 Engr. *Perf. 14x13*

1051 A252 400 l Ham radio operator .40 .40
1052 A252 500 l Mailman .60 .60

Manned Flight Bicentenary A253

Lithographed and Engraved

1983, May 22 *Perf. 13½x14*

1053 A253 500 l Montgolfiere, 1783 .50 .50

Exhibition Type of 1980

Designs: Botafogo Bay and Monte Corcovado, Rio de Janeiro.

1983, July 29 Photo. *Perf. 11½x12*
Granite Paper

1054 A222 400 l 1845 .50 .50
1055 A222 1400 l 1983 1.50 1.50
a. Pair, #1054-1055 2.00 2.00

BRASILIANA '83 Intl. Stamp Show, Rio de Janeiro, July 29-Aug. 7.

20th Anniv. of World Food Program A255

1983, Sept. 29 Photo. *Perf. 14x13½*

1056 A255 500 l multi .50 .50

Christmas A256

Flag-wavers Group, 2nd Anniv. — A257

Paintings, Raphael (1483-1520): 300 l, Our Lady of the Grand Duke. 400 l, Our Lady of the Goldfinch. 500 l, Our Lady of the Chair.

Photo. & Engr.

1983, Dec. 1 *Perf. 13½*

1057 A256 300 l multi .30 .30
1058 A256 400 l multi .40 .40
1059 A256 500 l multi .50 .50
a. Strip of 3, #1057-1059 1.25 1.25

Olympic Type of 1959

IOC Presidents: 300 l, Demetrius Vikelas, 1894-96. 400 l, Lord Killanin. 550 l, Antonio Samaranch, 1984.

1984, Feb. 8 Photo. *Perf. 14x13½*

1060 A86 300 l multi .35 .35
1061 A86 400 l multi .50 .50
1062 A86 550 l multi .70 .70
Nos. 1060-1062 (3) 1.55 1.55

Litho. & Engr.

1984, Apr. 27 *Perf. 13x14*

1063 A257 300 l Flag .35 .35
1064 A257 400 l Flags .45 .45

Europa (1959-1984) A258

1984, Apr. 27 Photo. *Perf. 11½*
Granite Paper

1065 A258 400 l multi *1.00* 1.00
1066 A258 550 l multi *1.50* 1.50

A259

A260

1984, June 14 Photo. *Perf. 13½x14*

1067 A259 450 l multi .55 .55

Motorcross Grand Prix, Baldasserona.

Souvenir Sheet

1984, June 14 Litho. *Perf. 13x14*

1068 Sheet of 2 1.50 1.50
a. A260 550 l Man .55 .55
b. A260 1000 l Woman .95 .95

1984 Summer Olympics.

Exhibition Type of 1980

Ausipex '84: Views of Melbourne. Se-tenant.

1984, Sept. 21 Photo. *Perf. 11½*
Granite Paper

1069 A222 1500 l 1839 1.60 1.60
1070 A222 2000 l 1984 2.10 2.10
a. Pair, #1069-1070 3.75 3.75

Visit of Italian Pres. Pertini A262

1984, Oct. 20 Photo. *Perf. 14x13½*

1071 A262 1950 l multi 1.75 1.75

School and Philately — A263

Christmas A264

Sketches by Jacovitti.

1984, Oct. 30 *Perf. 13½x14*

1072 A263 50 l Universe .20 .20
1073 A263 100 l Evolution .20 .20
1074 A263 150 l Environment .20 .20
1075 A263 200 l Mankind .20 .20
1076 A263 450 l Science .50 .50
1077 A263 550 l Philosophy .70 .70
Nos. 1072-1077 (6) 2.00 2.00

1984, Dec. 5 Litho. *Perf. 13½x14*

Details of Madonna of San Girolamo by Correggio, 1527.

1078 A264 400 l multi .65 .65
1079 A264 450 l multi .70 .70
1080 A264 550 l multi .90 .90
a. Strip of 3, #1078-1080 2.25 2.25

Composers and Music — A265

Olympiad of the Small States, May 23-26 — A266

Europa: 450 l, Johann Sebastian Bach (1685-1750), Toccata and Fugue. 600 l, Vincenzo Bellini (1801-1835), Norma.

1985, Mar. 18 Photo. *Perf. 12*

1081 A265 450 l ocher & gray blk 1.10 1.10
1082 A265 600 l yel grn & gray blk 1.40 1.40

1985, May 16 Litho. *Perf. 13½x14*

Sportphilex '85: Natl. Olympic Committee and Sportphilex '85 emblems, flags of Andorra, Cyprus, Iceland, Liechtenstein, Luxembourg, Malta, Monaco, San Marino.

1083 A266 50 l Diving .20 .20
1084 A266 350 l Running .30 .30
1085 A266 400 l Rifle shooting .35 .35
1086 A266 450 l Cycling .40 .40
1087 A266 600 l Handball .55 .55
Nos. 1083-1087 (5) 1.80 1.80

Emigration A267

Intl. Youth Year — A268

1985, May 16

1088 A267 600 l Birds migrating .60 .60

1985, June 24 Photo. *Perf. 12*
Granite Paper

1089 A268 400 l Boy, dove .45 .45
1090 A268 600 l Girl, dove, horse .65 .65

Helsinki Conference, 10th Anniv. — A269

City Hall, by Renzo Bonelli, Camera Lens. — A270

1985, June 24 *Perf. 13½x14*

1091 A269 600 l Sapling, sun-burst, clouds .70 .70

1985, June 24 *Perf. 13½x14½*

1092 A270 450 l multi .50 .50

Intl. Fed. of Photographic Art, 18th Congress.

World Angling Championships, Arno River, Florence, Sept. 14-15 — A271

1985, Sept. 11 Photo. *Perf. 14½x15*

1093 A271 600 l Hooked fish .70 .70

Alessandro Manzoni (1785-1873), Novelist & Poet — A272

19th century engravings from Manzoni's I Promessi Sposi (1825-27): 400 l, Don Abbondio encounters Don Rodrigo's henchmen. 450 l, The attempt to force the curate to perform a dubious marriage ceremony. 600 l, The Plague at Milan.

1985, Sept. 11 Engr. *Perf. 14x13½*

1094 A272 400 l multi .45 .45
1095 A272 450 l multi .50 .50
1096 A272 600 l multi .70 .70
Nos. 1094-1096 (3) 1.65 1.65

Intl. Feline Fed. Congress A273

Mosaic detail: Cat, Natl. Museum, Naples.

1985, Oct. 25 Photo. *Perf. 12*
Granite Paper

1097 A273 600 l multi .70 .70

Exhibition Type of 1980

ITALIA '85: Views of the Colosseum, Rome.

1985, Oct. 25 *Perf. 11½x12*
Granite Paper

1098 A222 1000 l multi 1.10 1.10
1099 A222 1500 l multi 1.60 1.60
a. Pair, #1098-1099 2.75 2.75

Christmas A275

Photo. & Engr.

1985, Dec. 3 *Perf. 14*

1100 A275 400 l Angel .55 .55
1101 A275 450 l Mother and Child .60 .60
1102 A275 600 l Angel, diff. .80 .80
a. Strip of 3, #1100-1102 1.90 1.90

Hospital, Cailungo A276

1986, Mar. 6 Photo. *Perf. 12x11½*

1103 A276 450 l multi .60 .60
1104 A276 650 l multi .85 .85

Natl. social security org., ISS, 30th anniv., and World Health Day.

Halley's Comet — A277

Designs: 550 l, Giotto space probe. 1000 l, Adoration of the Magi, by Giotto (1276-1337).

1986, Mar. 6 *Perf. 11½x12*

1105 A277 550 l multi .70 .70
1106 A277 1000 l multi 1.25 1.25

Deer — A278

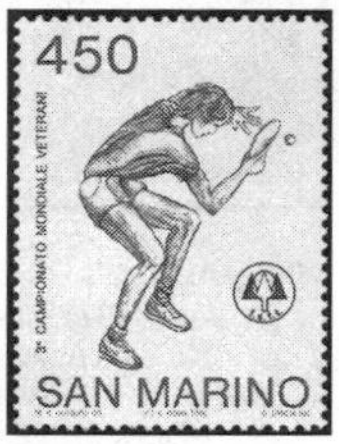

3rd Veterans World Table Tennis Championships A279

Europa Issue 1986

1986, May 22 Photo. *Perf. 13½x14*

1107 A278 550 l shown *5.25 5.25*
1108 A278 650 l Falcon *6.75 6.50*

1986, May 22 Engr.

1109 A279 450 l multicolored .60 .60

AMERIPEX '86, Chicago, May 22-June 1 — A280

Views of Old Water Tower, Chicago: 2000 l, Lithograph, 1870, by Charles Shober. 3000 l, Photograph, 1986.

Perf. 11½x12

1986, May 22 Photo. Unwmk.

1110 A280 2000 l multi 2.25 2.25
1111 A280 3000 l multi 3.50 3.50
a. Pair, #1110-1111 5.75 5.75

Intl. Peace Year — A281

1986, July 10 Photo. *Perf. 11½x12*

1112 A281 550 l multi .65 .65

Souvenir Sheet

Terra Cotta Statuary, Tomb of Emperor Qin Shi Huang Di (259-210 B.C.) — A282

Litho. & Engr.

1986, July 10 *Perf. 13½*

1113 Sheet of 3 4.25 4.25
a. A282 550 l Bearded man .70 .70
b. A282 650 l Horse, horiz. .80 .80
c. A282 2000 l Bearded man, diff. 2.75 2.75

Normalization of diplomatic relations with the People's Republic of China, 15th anniv.

UNICEF, 40th Anniv. — A283

European Boccie Championships A284

1986, Sept 16 Photo. *Perf. 12*

1114 A283 650 l multi .75 .75

1986, Sept. 16 *Perf. 14x15*

1115 A284 550 l multi .65 .65

Choral Society, 25th Anniv. — A285

Christmas A286

Painting (detail): Apollo Dancing with the Muses, by Giulio Romano (1492-1546).

1986, Sept. 16

1116 A285 450 l multi .55 .55

Photo. & Engr.

1986, Nov. 26 *Perf. 14*

Design: Oil on wood triptych, 15th cent., by Hans Memling (1435-1494), Kunsthistorisches Museum, Vienna.

1117 A286 450 l St. John the Baptist .80 .80
1118 A286 550 l Virgin and Child .95 .95
1119 A286 650 l St. John the Evangelist 1.25 1.25
a. Strip of 3, #1117-1119 3.00 3.00

Europa Issue 1987

Our Lady of Consolation Church, Borgomaggiore
A287

Church designed by Giovanni Michelucci, architect: 600 l, Architect's sketch of interior. 700 l, Actual interior.

1987, Mar. 12 Photo. *Perf. 12*

1120	A287	600 l multi	*5.00*	*5.00*
1121	A287	700 l multi	*6.50*	*6.50*

Motoring Events
A288

Designs: 500 l, 80th anniv., Peking-Paris Race. 600 l, 15th San Marino Rally. 700 l, Mille Miglia Race, 60th anniv.

1987, Mar. 12 *Perf. 11½*

1122	A288	500 l multi	.60	.60
1123	A288	600 l multi	.70	.70
1124	A288	700 l multi	.80	.80
		Nos. 1122-1124 (3)	2.10	2.10

Sculptures, Open-air Museum
A289

Seventh Natl. Art Biennale
A290

Perf. 14½x13½

1987, June 13 Photo.

1125	A289	50 l Reffi Busignani	.20	.20
1126	A289	100 l Bini	.20	.20
1127	A289	200 l Guguianu	.25	.25
1128	A289	300 l Berti	.40	.40
1129	A289	400 l Crocetti	.55	.55
1130	A289	500 l Berti, diff.	.70	.70
1131	A289	600 l Messina	.80	.80
1132	A289	1000 l Minguzzi	1.40	1.40
1133	A289	2200 l Greco	3.00	3.00
1134	A289	10000 l Sassu	13.50	13.50
		Nos. 1125-1134 (10)	21.00	21.00

1987, June 13 *Perf. 11½*

Abstract works: 500 l, Dal Diario del Brasile-foresta Vergine, by Emilio Vedova. 600 l, Invenzione Cromatica con Brio, by Corrado Cagli.

Granite Paper

1135	A290	500 l multi	.60	.60
1136	A290	600 l multi	.75	.75

Air Club of San Marino Ultra-lightweight Aircraft — A291

1987, June 13
Granite Paper

1137	A291	600 l multi	.75	.75

Mahatma Gandhi
A292

1987, Aug. 2 Photo. *Perf. 14x13½*

1138	A292	500 l Gandhi Square, bust	.60	.60

A293

A294

1987, Aug. 29 *Perf. 12*
Granite Paper

1139	A293	600 l Olympic emblem, athlete	.90	.90

OLYMPHILEX '87, Rome.

1987, Aug. 29 Granite Paper

1140	A294	700 l ultra, blk & red	.80	.80

First Representation of San Marino at the Mediterranean Games, Syria, Sept. 11-15.

Exhibition Type of 1980

HAFNIA '87: Views of Copenhagen (1836-1986), as seen from the Round Tower.

1987, Oct. 16 Photo. *Perf. 11½x12*
Granite Paper

1141	A222	1200 l multi	1.90	1.90
1142	A222	2200 l multi, diff.	3.50	3.50
a.		Pair, #1141-1142	5.50	5.50

Christmas
A296

High Speed Train — A297

Details from Triptych of Cortona and The Annunciation, by Fra Angelico (c. 1400-1455), Diocesan Museum of Cortona: No. 1143, Angel. No. 1144, Madonna and child. No. 1145, Saint. Printed se-tenant.

Photo. & Engr.

1987, Nov. 12 *Perf. 13½*

1143	A296	600 l multi	1.10	1.10
1144	A296	600 l multi	1.10	1.10
1145	A296	600 l multi	1.10	1.10
a.		Strip of 3, #1143-1145	3.50	3.50

Europa Issue 1988

1988, Mar. 17 Photo. *Perf. 12*
Granite Paper

1146	A297	600 l shown	*4.00*	*4.00*
1147	A297	700 l Fiber optics	*4.50*	*4.50*

Promote Stamp Collecting
A298

Stamps, cancellations, covers: 50 l, Nos. 81, B25 and 859. 150 l, No. C11. 300 l, Nos. 349 and 1006. 350 l, Nos. 944 and 1031. 1000 l, Nos. 303, 1081 and 308.

1988, Mar. 17 *Perf. 11½*
Granite Paper

1148	A298	50 l multi	.20	.20
1149	A298	150 l multi	.20	.20
1150	A298	300 l multi	.40	.40
1151	A298	350 l multi	.50	.50
1152	A298	1000 l multi	1.40	1.40
		Nos. 1148-1152 (5)	2.70	2.70

See Nos. 1179-1183, 1225-1229.

A299

A300

Historic sites and distinguished professors: 550 l, Carlo Malagola. 650 l, Pietro Ellero. 1300 l, Giosue Carducci (1835-1907), professor of literary history, 1861-1904, and Nobel Prize winner for literature, 1906. 1700 l, Giovanni Pascoli (1855-1912), lyric poet, Pascoli's successor as professor at Bologna.

1988, May 7 Photo. *Perf. 13½x14*

1153	A299	550 l multi	.65	.65
1154	A299	650 l multi	.75	.75
1155	A299	1300 l multi	1.60	1.60
1156	A299	1700 l multi	2.00	2.00
		Nos. 1153-1156 (4)	5.00	5.00

Bologna University, 900th anniv.

1988, July 8 Photo. *Perf. 13½x14*

Posters from Fellini Films: 300 l, La Strada. 900 l, La Dolce Vita. 1200 l, Amarcord.

1157	A300	300 l multi	.40	.40
1158	A300	900 l multi	1.25	1.25
1159	A300	1200 l multi	1.75	1.75
		Nos. 1157-1159 (3)	3.40	3.40

Federico Fellini, Italian film director and winner of the 1988 San Marino Prize.

See Nos. 1187-1189, 1202-1204.

Mt. Titano and Sand Dunes of the Adriatic Coast
A301

1988, July 8 *Perf. 14x13½*

1160	A301	750 l multi	.85	.85

40th Stamp Fair, Riccione.

Souvenir Sheet

1988 Summer Olympics, Seoul — A302

1988, Sept. 19 Photo. *Perf. 13½x14*

1161	A302	Sheet of 3	2.75	2.75
a.		650 l Running	.65	.65
b.		750 l Hurdles	.75	.75
c.		1300 l Gymnastics	1.25	1.25

Intl. AIDS Congress, San Marino, Oct. 10-14
A303

1988, Sept. 19 *Perf. 14x13½*

1162	A303	250 l shown	.30	.30
1163	A303	350 l "AIDS"	.40	.40
1164	A303	650 l Virus, knot	.80	.80
1165	A303	1000 l Newspaper	1.25	1.25
		Nos. 1162-1165 (4)	2.75	2.75

Kurhaus Scheveningen, The Hague — A304

1988, Oct. 18 Photo. *Perf. 11½x12*
Granite Paper

1166	A304	1600 l Lithograph, c. 1885	2.00	2.00
1167	A304	3000 l 1988	3.75	3.75
a.		Pair, #1166-1167	5.75	5.75

FILACEPT '88, Holland.

See Nos. 1190-1191.

Christmas
A305

Children's Games — A306

Paintings by Melozzo da Forli (1438-1494): No. 1168, Angel with Violin, Vatican Art Gallery. No. 1169, Angel of the Annunciation, Uffizi Gallery, Florence. No. 1170, Angel with Lute, Vatican Art Gallery.

1988, Dec. 9 Photo. *Perf. 13½*
Size of No. 1169: 21x40mm

1168	A305	650 l multi	1.00	1.00
1169	A305	650 l multi	1.00	1.00
1170	A305	650 l multi	1.00	1.00
a.		Strip of 3, #1168-1168	3.00	3.00

Europa Issue 1989
Souvenir Sheet

1989, Mar. 31 Photo. ***Perf. 13½x14***
1171 Sheet of 2 14.00 14.00
a. A306 650 l Sledding 7.00 7.00
b. A306 750 l Hopscotch 7.00 7.00

Nature Conservation — A307

Illustrations by contest-winning youth: 200 l, Federica Sparagna. 500 l, Giovanni Monteduro. 650 l, Rosa Mannarino.

1989, Mar. 31 ***Perf. 14x13½***
1172 A307 200 l multi .25 .25
1173 A307 500 l multi .65 .65
1174 A307 650 l multi .80 .80
Nos. 1172-1174 (3) 1.70 1.70

Sporting Anniversaries and Events — A308

1989, May 13 Photo. ***Perf. 12***
Granite Paper
1175 A308 650 l Olympics .85 .85
1176 A308 750 l Soccer .95 .95
1177 A308 850 l Tennis 1.10 1.10
1178 A308 1300 l Car racing 1.60 1.60
Nos. 1175-1178 (4) 4.50 4.50

Natl. Olympic Committee, 30th anniv. (650 l); admission of San Marino Soccer Federation to the UEFA and FIFA (750 l); San Marino '89, the tennis grand prix (850 l); Grand Prix of San Marino, Imola (1300 l).

Stamp Collecting Type of 1988

Covers and canceled stamps (postal history): 100 l, No. 916a with Iserravalle cancel, Sept. 1, 1977. 200 l, No. 1151 with Montegiardino cancel, May 3, 1986. 400 l, Italy No. 47 canceled on San Marino parcel card #422, 1895. 500 l, Type SP3 essay proposed by Martin Riester di Parigi, March 1865. 1000 l, Stampless cover, 1862.

1989, May 13 ***Perf. 12***
Granite Paper
1179 A298 100 l multi .20 .20
1180 A298 200 l multi .25 .25
1181 A298 400 l multi .50 .50
1182 A298 500 l multi .60 .60
1183 A298 1000 l multi 1.25 1.25
Nos. 1179-1183 (5) 2.80 2.80

French Revolution, Bicent. — A309

1989, July 7 Litho. ***Perf. 12½x13***
1184 A309 700 l The Tennis Court Oath .80 .80
1185 A309 1000 l Arrest of Louis XVI 1.10 1.10
1186 A309 1800 l Napoleon 2.10 2.10
Nos. 1184-1186 (3) 4.00 4.00

Show Business Type of 1988

Scenes from: 1200 l, *Marguerite et Armand.* 1500 l, *Apollon Musagete.* 1700 l, *Valentino.*

1989, Sept. 18 Photo. ***Perf. 13½x14***
1187 A300 1200 l multi 1.60 1.60
1188 A300 1500 l multi 2.00 2.00
1189 A300 1700 l multi 2.40 2.40
Nos. 1187-1189 (3) 6.00 6.00

Rudolf Nureyev, Russian ballet dancer and winner of the 1989 San Marino Prize.

Exhibition Type of 1988

Views of The Capitol, Washington, DC.: 2000 l, In 1850. 2500 l, In 1989.

1989, Nov. 17 Photo. ***Perf. 11½***
Granite Paper
1190 A304 2000 l multi 2.50 2.50
1191 A304 2500 l multi 3.00 3.00
a. Pair, #1190-1191 5.50 5.50

World Stamp Expo '89.

A310

A311

Christmas: Panels from a Polyptych, c. 1540, by Coda Studio of Rimini, in the Church of the Servants of Mary, Valdragone.

1989, Nov. 17
Size of No. 1193: 50x40mm
Granite Paper
1192 A310 650 l Angel .90 .90
1193 A310 650 l Holy family .90 .90
1194 A310 650 l Praying Madonna .90 .90
a. Strip of 3, #1192-1194 2.75 2.75

1990, Feb. 22 Photo. ***Perf. 13½x14***

Europa: Post offices.

1195 A311 700 l Palazzeto delle Poste, 1842 1.10 1.10
1196 A311 800 l Dogana 1.40 1.40

A312

A313

Design: *The Martyrdom of Saint Agatha,* by Giambattista Tiepolo, and occupation force departing by the Porta del Loco.

1990, Feb. 22 ***Perf. 12***
Granite Paper
1197 A312 3500 l multicolored 3.75 3.75

Liberation from Cardinal Alberoni's occupation force, 250th anniv.

1990, Mar. 23 Photo. ***Perf. 11½x12***
Granite Paper

European Tourism Year: No. 1198, The republic pinpointed on a map of Italy. No. 1199, San Marino atop Mt. Titano in proximity to other cities in the region. No. 1200, Rocca Guaita, San Marino.

1198 A313 600 l shown .65 .65
1199 A313 600 l multicolored .65 .65
1200 A313 600 l multicolored .65 .65
Nos. 1198-1200 (3) 1.95 1.95

See Nos. 1209a, 1260-1262.

Souvenir Sheet

1990 World Cup Soccer Championships, Italy — A314

Various athletes: a, Germany. b, Italy. c, Great Britain. d, Uruguay. e, Brazil. f, Argentina.

1990, Mar. 23 ***Perf. 13½x14***
1201 Sheet of 6 4.00 4.00
a.-f. A314 700 l any single .65 .65

Show Business Type of 1988

Scenes from: 600 l, *Hamlet.* 700 l, *Richard III.* 1500 l, *Marathon Man.*

1990, May 3 Photo. ***Perf. 13½x14***
1202 A300 600 l multi .90 .90
1203 A300 700 l multi 1.00 1.00
1204 A300 1500 l multi 2.10 2.10
Nos. 1202-1204 (3) 4.00 4.00

Sir Laurence Olivier (1907-1989), British actor, winner of the 1990 San Marino Prize. Name misspelled "Lawrence" on the stamps.

President of Italy, State Visit A315

1990, June 11 Litho. ***Perf. 13x12½***
1205 A315 600 l multicolored .70 .70

Statue of Saint Marinus — A316

#1207, Liberty statue. #1208, Government Palace. #1209, Flag of San Marino.

1990, June 11 Photo. ***Perf. 11½***
Granite Paper
Booklet Stamps
1206 A316 50 l multicolored .20 .20
1207 A316 50 l multicolored .20 .20
1208 A316 50 l multicolored .20 .20
1209 A316 50 l multicolored .20 .20
a. Bklt. pane of 7, #1198-1200, perf. 11½ vert., #1206-1209 2.60
Nos. 1206-1209 (4) .80 .80

See Nos. 1256-1259.

Discovery of America, 500th Anniv. (in 1992) A317

1990, Sept. 6 Litho. ***Perf. 13x12½***
1210 A317 1500 l Artifacts, map 1.60 1.60
1211 A317 2000 l Native plants, map 2.10 2.10

See Nos. 1230-1231.

Pinocchio, by Carlo Collodi (1826-1890) A318

Flora and Fauna A319

Cartoon style drawings from Pinocchio.

1990, Sept. 6 Photo. ***Perf. 11½x12***
Granite Paper
1212 A318 250 l shown .30 .30
1213 A318 400 l Geppetto .45 .45
1214 A318 450 l Blue fairy .55 .55
1215 A318 600 l Cat & wolf .70 .70
Nos. 1212-1215 (4) 2.00 2.00

1990, Oct. 31 Photo. ***Perf. 14x13½***

Designs: 200 l, Papilio machaon, Ephedra major. 300 l, Apoderus coryli, Corylus avellana. 500 l, Eliomys quercinus, Quercus ilex. 1000 l, Lacerta viridis, Ophrys bertolonii. 2000 l, Regulus ignicapillus, Pinus nigra.

1216 A319 200 l multicolored .20 .20
1217 A319 300 l multicolored .30 .30
1218 A319 500 l multicolored .55 .55
1219 A319 1000 l multicolored 1.10 1.10
1220 A319 2000 l multicolored 2.10 2.10
Nos. 1216-1220 (5) 4.25 4.25

A320

A321

Christmas: Cuciniello Crib, San Martino Museum of Naples.

1990, Oct. 31 ***Perf. 11½***
Granite Paper
1221 A320 750 l shown 1.50 1.50
1222 A320 750 l Nativity, diff. 1.50 1.50
a. Pair, #1221-1222 3.00 3.00

1991, Feb. 12 Photo. ***Perf. 13½x14***
1223 A321 750 l Ariane 4 rocket *3.75 3.75*
1224 A321 800 l ERS-1 satellite *3.75 3.75*

Europa.

Stamp Collecting Type of 1988

Areas of philately: 100 l, Stamp store. 150 l, Clubs. 200 l, Exhibitions. 450 l, Albums, catalogues. 1500 l, Magazines, books.

1991, Feb. 12 ***Perf. 12***
Granite Paper
1225 A298 100 l multicolored .20 .20
1226 A298 150 l multicolored .20 .20
1227 A298 200 l multicolored .20 .20
1228 A298 450 l multicolored .50 .50
1229 A298 1500 l multicolored 1.75 1.75
Nos. 1225-1229 (5) 2.85 2.85

Italian Philatelic Press Union, 25th anniv. (No. 1229).

Discovery of America Type

1991, Mar. 22 Litho. ***Perf. 13x12½***
1230 A317 750 l Map, instruments .75 .75
1231 A317 3000 l Columbus' fleet 3.25 3.25

1992 Summer Olympics, Barcelona A323

Olympic torch relay.

1991, Mar. 22 ***Perf. 15x14***
1232 A323 400 l Athens .45 .45
1233 A323 600 l San Marino .70 .70
1234 A323 2000 l Barcelona 2.25 2.25
Nos. 1232-1234 (3) 3.40 3.40

Basketball, Cent. — A324

Fauna — A325

Designs: 750 l, James Naismith (1861-1939), creator of basketball, players.

1991, June 4 Photo. *Perf. 13½x14*
1235 A324 650 l multicolored .70 .70
1236 A324 750 l multicolored .80 .80

1991, June 4 *Perf. 14x13½*
1237 A325 500 l House cat .45 .45
1238 A325 550 l Hamster on wheel .55 .55
1239 A325 750 l Great Dane, poodle .75 .75
1240 A325 1000 l Tropical fish 1.00 1.00
1241 A325 1200 l Birds in cage 1.25 1.25
Nos. 1237-1241 (5) 4.00 4.00

Children's Day.
See Nos. 1251-1255.

James Clerk Maxwell (1831-1879), Physicist — A326

1991, Sept. 24 Photo. *Perf. 14x13½*
1242 A326 750 l multicolored 1.10 1.10

Radio, cent. (in 1995).
See Nos. 1263, 1279, 1300.

Souvenir Sheet

Birth of New Europe — A327

Designs: No. 1243a, Dove, broken chains, Brandenburg Gate. b, Pres. Gorbachev, rainbow, Pres. Bush. c, Flower, broken barbed wire, map.

1991, Sept. 24 Litho.
1243 A327 1500 l Sheet of 3, #a.-c. 4.00 4.00

La Rocca fortress — A328

Christmas: Diff. winter views of 10th cent.

1991, Nov. 13 Litho. *Perf. 14½*
1244 A328 600 l multicolored .70 .70
1245 A328 750 l multicolored .90 .90
1246 A328 1200 l multicolored 1.40 1.40
Nos. 1244-1246 (3) 3.00 3.00

No. 1246 is airmail.

Gioacchino Rossini (1792-1868), Composer — A329

Designs: 750 l, Bianca e Falliero, Rossini opera festival 1989. 1200 l, The Barber of Seville, La Scala 1982-83.

1992, Feb. 3 Photo. *Perf. 14x13½*
1247 A329 750 l multicolored .80 .80
1248 A329 1200 l multicolored 1.40 1.40

Discovery of America, 500th Anniv. A330

Designs: 1500 l, Columbus, ships at anchor, natives. 2000 l, Map of voyages.

1992, Feb. 3 Litho. *Perf. 12*
1249 A330 1500 l multicolored 1.75 1.75
1250 A330 2000 l multicolored 2.25 2.25

Fauna Type of 1991

Flora.

1992, Mar. 26 Litho. *Perf. 13½*
1251 A325 50 l Roses .20 .20
1252 A325 200 l House plant .20 .20
1253 A325 300 l Orchids .30 .30
1254 A325 450 l Cacti .50 .50
1255 A325 5000 l Geraniums 6.00 6.00
Nos. 1251-1255 (5) 7.20 7.20

Tourism Types of 1990

Designs: No. 1256, Crossbowman. No. 1257, Tennis player. No. 1258, Motorcyclist. No. 1259, Race car. No. 1260, Couple in moonlight. No. 1261, Man in restaurant. No. 1262, Woman reading beneath umbrella.

1992, Mar. 26 *Perf. 14½x13½*
Booklet Stamps
1256 A316 50 l multicolored .20 .20
1257 A316 50 l multicolored .20 .20
1258 A316 50 l multicolored .20 .20
1259 A316 50 l multicolored .20 .20

Perf. 13½ Vert.
1260 A313 600 l multicolored .95 .95
1261 A313 600 l multicolored .95 .95
1262 A313 600 l multicolored .95 .95
a. Bklt. pane of 7, #1256-1262+label 3.50

Physicist Type of 1991

Design: Heinrich Rudolf Hertz (1857-94).

1992, Mar. 26 Photo. *Perf. 14x13½*
1263 A326 750 l multicolored 1.10 1.10

Radio, cent. (in 1995).

Discovery of America, 500th Anniv. — A331

1992, May 22 Photo. *Perf. 12x11½*
Granite Paper
1264 A331 750 l Globe, ship at sea 1.10 1.10
1265 A331 850 l Ship in egg 1.40 1.40

Europa.

Souvenir Sheet

1992 Summer Olympics, Barcelona — A332

a, Soccer. b, Shooting. c, Swimming. d, Running.

1992, May 22 Litho. *Perf. 14*
1266 A332 1250 l Sheet of 4, #a.-d. 8.00 8.00

Mushrooms — A333

Designs: Nos. 1267, Poisonous mushrooms. No. 1268a, Edible mushrooms in bowl. No. 1268b, Edible mushrooms on table.

1992, Sept. 18 Photo. *Perf. 11½x12*
Granite Paper
1267 A333 Pair .90 .90
a.-b. 250 l any single .45 .45
1268 A333 Pair 1.10 1.10
a.-b. 350 l any single .55 .55

Admission to the UN — A334

Designs: a, Arms of San Marino, buildings. b, UN emblem, buildings.

1992, Sept. 18 Litho. *Perf. 12x12½*
1269 A334 Pair 2.00 2.00
a.-b. 1000 l any single 1.00 1.00

The Sacred Conversation, by Piero della Francesca (1420-1492) A335

Christmas: a, Entire painting. b, Detail of faces. c, Detail of dome.

1992, Nov. 16 Litho. *Perf. 14½*
1270 Triptych 2.50 2.50
a.-c. A335 750 l any single 1.25 1.25

Contemporary Art — A336

Paintings: 750 l, Stars, by Nicola de Maria. 850 l, Abstract face, by Mimmo Paladino.

1993, Jan. 29 Litho. *Perf. 11½*
1271 A336 750 l multicolored .90 .90
1272 A336 850 l multicolored 1.10 1.10

Europa.

1993 Sporting Events — A337

1993, Jan. 29 *Perf. 13½x14*
1273 A337 300 l Tennis .25 .25
1274 A337 400 l Cross-country skiing .40 .40
1275 A337 550 l Women running .55 .55
1276 A337 600 l Fisherman .65 .65
1277 A337 700 l Men running .75 .75
1278 A337 1300 l Sailboat, runners 1.40 1.40
Nos. 1273-1278 (6) 4.00 4.00

No. 1273, Youth Games. No. 1274-1275, European Youth Olympic Days. No. 1276, World Championships for Freshwater Angling Clubs, Ostellato, Italy. No. 1277, Games of Small European Countries, Malta. No. 1278, Mediterranean Games, Roussillon, France.

Physicists Type of 1991

Design: 750 l, Edouard Branly (1844-1940).

1993, Mar. 26 Photo. *Perf. 14x13½*
1279 A326 750 l multicolored 1.00 1.00

Radio, cent. (in 1995).

Souvenir Sheet

Inauguration of State Television — A338

Designs: a, 100-meter finals, World Track Championships, Tokyo, 1991. b, San Marino. c, Neil Armstrong on moon, 1969.

1993, Mar. 26 Litho. *Perf. 13½*
1280 Sheet of 3 5.75 5.75
a.-c. A338 2000 l any single 1.90 1.90

Soaking may affect the hologram on #1280b.

Butterflies A339

1993, May 26 Litho. *Perf. 14x15*
1281 A339 250 l Iphiclides podalirius .40 .40
1282 A339 250 l Colias crocea .40 .40
1283 A339 250 l Nymphalis antiopa .40 .40
1284 A339 250 l Melitaea cinxia .40 .40
a. Block or strip of 4, #1281-1284 1.60 1.60

World Wildlife Fund.

Miniature Sheet

United Europe — A340

Village of Europe: No. 1285a, Denmark. b, England. c, Ireland. d, Luxembourg. e, Germany. f, Netherlands. g, Belgium. h, Portugal. i, Italy. j, Spain. k, France. l, Greece.

1993, May 26 *Perf. 13½x14*

1285 A340 750 l Sheet of 12 10.00 10.00
a. Any single, #a.-l. .80 .80

Famous Men A341

Designs: 550 l, Carlo Goldoni (1707-93), playwright, vert. 650 l, Horace (65-8 BC), poet and satrist, vert. 850 l, Claudio Monteverdi (1567-1643), composer. 1850 l, Guy de Maupassant (1850-93), writer.

1993, Sept. 17 **Litho.** *Perf. 13½x14*

1286	A341	550 l	multicolored	.70	.70
1287	A341	650 l	multicolored	.80	.80
1288	A341	850 l	multicolored	1.00	1.00
1289	A341	1850 l	multicolored	2.25	2.25
			Nos. 1286-1289 (4)	4.75	4.75

Christmas A342

Designs: 600 l, San Marino in winter, vert. Paintings by Gerard van Honthorst: 750 l, Adoration of the Child. 850 l, Adoration of the Shepherds, vert.

1993, Nov. 12 **Litho.** *Perf. 14½*

1290	A342	600 l	multicolored	.70	.70
1291	A342	750 l	multicolored	.90	.90
1292	A342	850 l	multicolored	1.00	1.00
			Nos. 1290-1292 (3)	2.60	2.60

10th Intl. Dog Show A343

Designs: 350 l, Dachshund. 400 l, Afghan hound. 450 l, Belgian tervueren shepherd dog. 500 l, Boston terrier. 550 l, Mastiff. 600 l, Alaskan malamute.

1994, Jan. 31 **Litho.** *Perf. 15x14*

1293	A343	350 l	multicolored	.40	.40
1294	A343	400 l	multicolored	.50	.50
1295	A343	450 l	multicolored	.55	.55
1296	A343	500 l	multicolored	.60	.60
1297	A343	550 l	multicolored	.65	.65
1298	A343	600 l	multicolored	.70	.70
			Nos. 1293-1298 (6)	3.40	3.40

Souvenir Sheet

1994 Winter Olympics, Lillehammer A344

a, 90-meter ski jump. b, Downhill skiing. c, Giant slalom skiing. d, Pairs figure skating.

1994, Jan. 31 *Perf. 13½*

1299 A344 750 l 2 each #a.-d. 6.50 6.50

Physicists Type of 1991

Aleksandr Stepanovich Popov (1859-1905).

1994, Mar. 11 **Photo.** *Perf. 14x13½*

1300 A326 750 l multicolored 1.10 1.10

Radio cent. (in 1995).

Gardens — A345

1994, Mar. 11 **Litho.** *Perf. 13*

1301	A345	100 l	Gate	.20	.20
1302	A345	200 l	Grape arbor	.25	.25
1303	A345	300 l	Well	.35	.35
1304	A345	450 l	Gazebo	.50	.50
1305	A345	1850 l	Pond	2.25	2.25
			Nos. 1301-1305 (5)	3.55	3.55

Intl. Olympic Committee, Cent. A346

1994, Mar. 11 **Photo.** *Perf. 14x13½*

1306 A346 600 l multicolored .80 .80

A347

A348

Various soccer plays: a, Two players, one with #8 on shirt. b, Player in blue shirt kicking ball upward. c, Player heading ball. d, Players, one with #6 on shirt. e, Goal keeper.

1994, May 23 **Litho.** *Perf. 14*

1307 A347 600 l Strip of 5, #a.-e. 3.75 3.75

1994 World Cup Soccer Championships, US. No. 1307 has a continuous design.

1994, May 23

Europa (Ulysses spacecraft and: 750 l, Flight path around Sun and Jupiter. 850 l, Sun.

1308	A348	750 l	multicolored	.75	.75
1309	A348	850 l	multicolored	1.00	1.00

Inauguration of Government Building, Cent. — A349

Designs: 150 l, Exterior in shade, vert. 600 l, Exterior in sunshine, vert. 650 l, Clock tower. 1000 l, Interior.

Perf. 13½x13, 13x13½

1994, Sept. 30 **Litho.**

1310	A349	150 l	multicolored	.20	.20
1311	A349	600 l	multicolored	.70	.70
1312	A349	650 l	multicolored	.85	.85
1313	A349	1000 l	multicolored	1.25	1.25
			Nos. 1310-1313 (4)	3.00	3.00

Dedication of St. Mark's Basilica, 900th Anniv. A350

1994, Oct. 8 **Photo.** *Perf. 13½x13*

1314 A350 750 l multicolored 1.10 1.10
a. Souvenir sheet of 2, tete beche 2.25 2.25

No. 1314 printed with se-tenant label. No. 1314a contains No. 1314 and Italy No. 2003. Only No. 1314 was valid for postage in San Marino.

Touring Club of Italy, Cent. — A351

Vehicles traveling on road in middle of flower field: a, Traffic cop, bus. b, Tandem tanker truck. c, Sailboat, volcano. d, Truck loaded with animals, camper, fish in lake.

1994, Nov. 18 **Litho.** *Perf. 14x13½*

1315 Block of 4 4.50 4.50
a.-d. A351 1000 l any single 1.10 1.10

No. 1315 is a continuous design.

A352

A353

The Enthroned Madonna and Child with Saints, by Giovanni Santi (1440-1494) (Christmas): 600 l, Drummer, piper. 750 l, Madonna and Child. 850 l, Piper, harpist.

1994, Nov. 18 *Perf. 14x15*

1316	A352	600 l	multicolored	.75	.75
1317	A352	750 l	multicolored	.90	.90
1318	A352	850 l	multicolored	1.00	1.00
			Nos. 1316-1318 (3)	2.65	2.65

1995, Feb. 10 **Photo.** *Perf. 13x14*

1319	A353	100 l	Cycling	.20	.20
1320	A353	500 l	Volleyball	.60	.60
1321	A353	650 l	Speed skater	.75	.75
1322	A353	850 l	Runner	1.00	1.00
			Nos. 1319-1322 (4)	2.55	2.55

Sporting Events of 1995: Junior World Cycling Championships, Forli, San Marino (#1319). Volleyball, cent. (#1320). Men's Speed Skating World Championships, Baselga di Pine, Italy (#1321). World Track & Field Championships, Goteborg, Sweden (#1322).

European Nature Conservation Year — A354

Nature scenes with flowers, water: a, Snails, dragonfly, fish. b, Frog, snake. c, Ladybugs, butterfly. d, Ducklings, frog. e, Ducks, snail.

1995, Feb. 10

1323 A354 600 l Strip of 5, #a.-e. 3.50 3.50

No. 1323 is a continuous design.

UN, 50th Anniv. — A355

Designs: 550 l, UN emblem surrounded by people. 600 l, Emblem in center of rose. 650 l, Hourglass shaped from halves of globe. 1200 l, "50," Emblem, rainbow.

1995, Mar. 24 **Litho.** *Perf. 14x15*

1324	A355	550 l	multicolored	.65	.65
1325	A355	600 l	multicolored	.70	.70
1326	A355	650 l	multicolored	.75	.75
1327	A355	1200 l	multicolored	1.40	1.40
			Nos. 1324-1327 (4)	3.50	3.50

Peace & Freedom A356

1995, Mar. 24 *Perf. 15x14*

1328	A356	750 l	shown	.70	.70
1329	A356	850 l	Sheep, meadow	.80	.80

Europa.

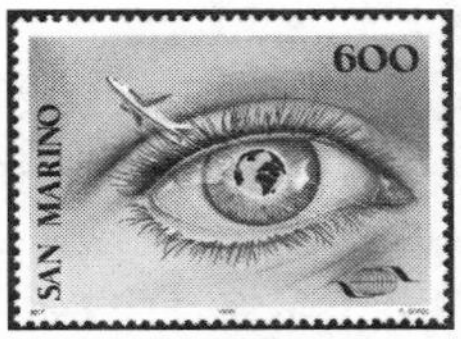

World Tourism Organization, 20th Anniv. — A357

Designs: 750 l, Mt. Titano encircled by five colored lines symbolizing continents. 850 l, Airplane over globe. 1200 l, Five lines encircling earth.

1995, May 5 **Litho.** *Perf. 15x14*

1330	A357	600 l	multicolored	.70	.70
1331	A357	750 l	multicolored	.90	.90
1332	A357	850 l	multicolored	1.00	1.00
1333	A357	1200 l	multicolored	1.40	1.40
			Nos. 1330-1333 (4)	4.00	4.00

Santa Croce Basilica, Florence, 700th Anniv. A358

1200 l, Detail from fresco, The Legend of the True Cross, by Agnolo Gaddi, facade of the basilica. 1250 l, Painting, The Madonna and Child with Saints, by Andrea della Robbia, Santa Croce Cloister, Pazzi Chapel.

1995, May 5

1334 A358 1200 l multicolored 1.50 1.50
1335 A358 1250 l multicolored 1.50 1.50

Radio, Cent. A359

Designs: No. 1336, Stations on radio dial. No. 1337, Guglielmo Marconi (1874-1937), transmitting equipment.

1995, June 8 Litho. *Perf. 14*

1336 A359 850 l multicolored 1.00 1.00
1337 A359 850 l multicolored 1.00 1.00
a. Pair, #1336-1337 2.00 2.00

Printed in sheets of 10 stamps.

See Germany #1900, Ireland #973-974, Italy #2038-2039, Vatican City #978-979.

Miniature Sheet

Motion Picture, Cent. A360

Different frames from films:
The General: a, 1. b, 2. c, 3. d, 4.
Il Gattopardo: e, 1. f, 2. g, 3. h, 4.
Allegro Non Troppo: i, 1. j, 2. k, 3. l, 4.
Braveheart: m, 1. n, 2. o, 3. p, 4.

1995, Sept. 14 Litho. *Perf. 15x14*

1338 Sheet of 16 4.50 4.50
a.-p. A360 250 l any single .25 .25

Exhibition Type of 1980

Qianmen complex of Zhengyangmen Rostrum, Embrasured Watchtower, Beijing: No. 1339, In 1914. No. 1340, In 1995.

1995, Sept. 14 *Perf. 14*

1339 A222 1500 l multicolored 1.60 1.60
1340 A222 1500 l multicolored 1.60 1.60
a. Pair, #1339-1340 3.25 3.25

Beijing '95.

Neri of Rimini, 14th Cent. Artist — A361

Designs: 650 l, The Annunciation.

1995, Nov. 6 Litho. *Perf. 14x15*

1341 A361 650 l multicolored .85 .85

Christmas — A362

Designs: a, Santa, sleigh, reindeer. b, Children, Christmas tree. c, Nativity, star.

1995, Nov. 6 Litho. *Perf. 14x15*

1342 A362 Strip of 3 3.00 3.00
a.-c. 750 l any single 1.00 1.00

No. 1342 is a continuous design.

Express Mail Service A363

1995, Nov. 6 *Perf. 15x14*

1343 A363 6000 l multicolored 7.00 7.00

A364

A365

1996, Feb. 12 Litho. *Perf. 14x15*

1344 A364 100 l Discus .20 .20
1345 A364 500 l Wrestling .55 .55
1346 A364 650 l Athletics .75 .75
1347 A364 1500 l Javelin 1.75 1.75
1348 A364 2500 l Running 2.75 2.75
Nos. 1344-1348 (5) 6.00 6.00

1996 Summer Olympics, Atlanta.

1996, Mar. 22 Photo. *Perf. 12*

Portrait of Mother Teresa of Calcutta, by Gina Lollobrigida.

Granite Paper

1349 A365 750 l multicolored 1.10 1.10

Europa.

China '96 Philatelic Exhibition, Beijing A366

1996, Mar. 22 *Perf. 14x13½*

1350 A366 1250 l multicolored 1.60 1.60

Marco Polo's return from China, 700th anniv. (in 1995).

See Italy No. 2070.

Nature World Exhibition A367

Photographs of wildlife: 50 l, Dolphin. 100 l, Frog. 150 l, Penguins. 1000 l, Butterfly. 3000 l, Ducks.

1996, Mar. 22 *Perf. 12*

Granite Paper

1351 A367 50 l multicolored .20 .20
1352 A367 100 l multicolored .20 .20
1353 A367 150 l multicolored .20 .20
1354 A367 1000 l multicolored 1.10 1.10
1355 A367 3000 l multicolored 3.50 3.50
Nos. 1351-1355 (5) 5.20 5.20

China-San Marino Relations, 25th Anniv. A368

#1356, Great Wall of China. #1357, Wall surrounding Mount Titano, San Marino.

1996, May 6 Litho. *Perf. 12*

1356 A368 750 l multicolored .95 .95
1357 A368 750 l multicolored .95 .95
a. Pair, Nos. 1356-1357 1.90 1.90
b. Souvenir sheet, No. 1357a 2.00 2.00

No. 1357a is a continuous design.

See People's Republic of China Nos. 2675-2676.

Medieval Days Celebration A369

Festival activities: No. 1358, Woman weaving yarn, vert. No. 1359, Potter, vert. No. 1360, Woman making brushes, vert. No. 1361, Man playing checkers, vert. No. 1362, Group blowing trumpets. No. 1363, Group holding banners. No. 1364, Men seated with crossbows. No. 1365, Street performers.

Perf. 14 on 2 Sides

1996, May 6 Litho. & Photo.

Booklet Stamps

1358 A369 750 l multicolored .80 .80
1359 A369 750 l multicolored .80 .80
1360 A369 750 l multicolored .80 .80
1361 A369 750 l multicolored .80 .80
1362 A369 750 l multicolored .80 .80
1363 A369 750 l multicolored .80 .80
1364 A369 750 l multicolored .80 .80
1365 A369 750 l multicolored .80 .80
a. Booklet pane, #1358-1365 6.50
Complete booklet, #1365a 6.50

Festival Bar A370

History of Italian Songs A371

Singer, allegory of song: a, Enrico Caruso, "O Sole Mio." b, Armando Gill, "Come Pioveva." c, Ettore Petrolini, "Gastone." d, Vittorio de Sica, "Parlami D'Amore Mariu." e, Odoardo Spadaro, "La Porti un Bacione a Firenze." f, Alberto Rabagliati, "O Mia Bela Madonina." g, Beniamino Gigli, "Mamma." h, Claudio Villa, "Luna Rossa." i, Secondo Casadei, "Romagna Mia." j, Renato Rascel, "Arrivederci Roma." k, Fred Buscaglione, "Guarda Che Luna." l, Domenico Modugno, "Nel Blu Dipinto di Blu."

1996, May 25 Litho. *Perf. 14x13½*

1366 A370 2000 l shown 2.25 2.25

Granite Paper

Photo.

Perf. 12x11½

1367 A371 750 l Sheet of 12, #a.-l. 11.00 11.00

Gazzetta Dello Sport, Cent. — A372

1996, May 25 *Perf. 12*

Granite Paper

1368 A372 1850 l multicolored 2.10 2.10

UNICEF, 50th Anniv. A373

1996, Sept. 20 Photo. *Perf. 12*

Granite Paper

1369 A373 550 l Hen, chicks .65 .65
1370 A373 1000 l Baby birds 1.10 1.10

UNESCO, 50th Anniv. A374

World Heritage Sites: 450 l, Yellowstone Natl. Park, US. 500 l, Prehistoric caves, Vézère Valley, France. 650 l, Old town center, San Gimignano, Italy. 1450 l, Church of the Wies Pilgrimage, Germany.

1996, Sept. 20

Granite Paper

1371 A374 450 l multicolored .50 .50
1372 A374 500 l multicolored .60 .60
1373 A374 650 l multicolored .75 .75
1374 A374 1450 l multicolored 1.75 1.75
Nos. 1371-1374 (4) 3.60 3.60

Christmas — A375

Scenes looking through windows of a home: a, Playing game underneath Christmas tree. b, Tags draped from holly branch. c, Girl reading book, Santa in sleigh. d, Christmas tree. e, Fruits, candles, nuts. f, Streaking star, snowflakes. g, Toys. h, Presents. i, Santa Claus puppet. j, Nativity. k, Mistletoe. l, Stocking hung by fireplace. m, Family eating, drinking. n, Christmas tree, silhouettes of mother, father, wreath. o, Wreath, silhouettes of children & grandmother, snowman. p, Calendar, champaigne bottle popping cork.

1996, Nov. 8 Photo. *Perf. 14½*

1375 A375 750 l Sheet of 16, #a.-p. 13.50 13.50

Souvenir Sheet

Hong Kong A376

View from harbor: a, 1897. b, 1997.

1997, Feb. 12 Litho. *Perf. 12½*

1376 A376 750 l Sheet of 2, #a.-b. 1.60 1.60

World Alpine Skiing Championships, Sestrière, Italy — A377

Scene of people skiing on mountain: a, Skier jumping left, birds. b, Ski lift, bird in sky. c, Coming down mountain, sleigh. d, Coming down mountain, Sestrière sign.

1997, Feb. 12 *Perf. 12*

Granite Paper

1377 A377 1000 l Block of 4, #a.-d. 4.25 4.25

No. 1377 is a continuous design.

San Marino Townships (Castelli) A378

1997, Mar. 21 Photo. *Perf. 12*
Granite Paper

1378	A378	100 l	Acquaviva	.20	.20
1379	A378	200 l	Borgomaggiore	.20	.20
1380	A378	250 l	Chiesanuova	.25	.25
1381	A378	400 l	Domagnano	.45	.45
1382	A378	500 l	Faetano	.55	.55
1383	A378	550 l	Fiorentino	.60	.60
1384	A378	650 l	Montegiardino	.70	.70
1385	A378	750 l	Serravalle	.80	.80
1386	A378	5000 l	San Marino	5.50	5.50
			Nos. 1378-1386 (9)	9.25	9.25

Stories and Legends — A379

St. Marinus, Mt. Titano: 650 l, St. Marinus talking to bear that killed the mule. 750 l, Mother begging St. Marinus to forgive her son for trying to kill him.

1997, Mar. 21
Granite Paper

1387	A379	650 l	multicolored	.75	.75
1388	A379	750 l	multicolored	.85	.85

Europa.

Sporting Events A380

500 l, Giro d'Italia cycling event. 550 l, 10th Tennis Intl. 750 l, Formula 1 San Marino Grand Prix. 850 l, Republic of San Marino (Soccer) Trophy. 1000 l, Bowls (pétanque) World Championship. 1250 l, Motorcross 250cc World Championship. 1500 l, Mille Miglia classic car spectacle.

1997, May 19 Photo. *Perf. 12*
Granite Paper

1389	A380	500 l	multicolored	.55	.55
1390	A380	550 l	multicolored	.60	.60
1391	A380	750 l	multicolored	.80	.80
1392	A380	850 l	multicolored	.95	.95
1393	A380	1000 l	multicolored	1.10	1.10
1394	A380	1250 l	multicolored	1.40	1.40
1395	A380	1500 l	multicolored	1.60	1.60
			Nos. 1389-1395 (7)	7.00	7.00

5th Intl. Symposium on UFO's and Associated Phenomena A381

1997, May 19
Granite Paper

1396	A381	750 l	multicolored	.90	.90

Trees — A382

50 l, Pinus pinea. 800 l, Quercus pubescens. 1800 l, Juglans regia. 2000 l, Pirus communis.

1997, June 27 Photo. *Perf. 12*
Granite Paper

1397	A382	50 l	multicolored	.20	.20
1398	A382	800 l	multicolored	.90	.90
1399	A382	1800 l	multicolored	2.00	2.00
1400	A382	2000 l	multicolored	2.10	2.10
			Nos. 1397-1400 (4)	5.20	5.20

First Stamps of San Marino, 120th Anniv. — A383

Designs: No. 1401, G. Battista Barbavara di Gravellona, director general of Sardinian Post Office. No. 1402, Enrico Repettati, chief engraver for Officina Carte Valori, Turin. No. 1403, Otto Bickel, German stamp dealer, promoter of San Marino-Philatelist. No. 1404, Alfredo Reffi, San Marino stamp dealer, publisher of post cards, stamp catalogue.

1997, June 27 *Perf. 11½*
Granite Paper

1401	A383	800 l	multicolored	1.00	1.00
1402	A383	800 l	multicolored	1.00	1.00
1403	A383	800 l	multicolored	1.00	1.00
1404	A383	800 l	multicolored	1.00	1.00
a.			Strip of 4, #1401-1404	4.00	4.00

Beatification of Bartolomeo Maria Dal Monte (1726-78) A384

1997, Sept. 18 Photo. *Perf. 12*
Granite Paper

1405	A384	800 l	multicolored	.90	.90

Italian Comic Book Characters A385

Designs: a, "Quadratino," by Antonio Rubino. b, "Signor Bonaventura," by Sergio Tofano. c, "Kit Carson," by Rino Albertarelli. d, "Cocco Bill," by Benito Jacovitti. e, "Tex Willer," by Gian Luigi Bonelli and Arelio Galleppini. f, "Diabolik," by Angela and Luciana Giussani and Franco Paludetti. g, "Valentina," by Guido Crepax. h, "Corto Maltese," by Hugo Pratt. i, "Sturmtruppen," by Franco Bonvicini. j, "Alan Ford," by Max Bunker. k, "Lupo Alberto," by Guido Silvestri. l, "Pimpa," by Francesco Tullio Altan. m, "Bobo," by Sergio Staino. n, "Zanardi," by Andrea Pazienza. o, "Martin Mystère," by Alfredo Castelli and Giancarlo Alessandrini. p, "Dylan Dog," by Tiziano Sclavi and Angelo Stano.

1997, Sept. 18 Granite Paper
Sheet of 16

1406	A385	800 l	#a.-p.	13.00	13.00

Adoration of the Magi, by Georgio Vasari (1511-74) — A386

1997, Nov. 14 Photo. *Perf. 12*
Granite Paper

1407	A386	800 l	multicolored	.85	.85

Volunteer Service, Solidarity A387

Designs: 550 l, St. Francis of Assisi, doves. 650 l, Mariele Ventre, children. 800 l, Children circling hands around world, Zecchino d'Oro song festival.

1997, Nov. 14
Granite Paper

1408	A387	550 l	multicolored	.70	.70
1409	A387	650 l	multicolored	.85	.85
1410	A387	800 l	multicolored	1.00	1.00
			Nos. 1408-1410 (3)	2.55	2.55

Volkswagen Beetle A388

Designs: a, Maggiolino (old Beetle). b, Golf I. c, New Beetle. d, Golf IV.

1997, Nov. 14
Granite Paper

1411	A388	800 l	Sheet of 4, #a.-d.	4.25	4.25

No. 1411 was issued with attached entry form for drawing to win a new Beetle car. Entry form is rouletted at top to separate from bottom of sheet. Values are for sheets with entry form attached.

Ferrari's Formula 1 Race Cars, 50th Anniv. A389

Model number, year: a, 125S, 1947. b, 500F2, 1952. c, 801, 1956. d, 246 Dino, 1958. e, 156, 1961. f, 158, 1964. g, 312T, 1975. h, 312T4, 1979. i, 126C, 1981. j, 156/85, 1985. k, 639, 1989. l, F310, 1996.

1998, Feb. 11 Litho. *Perf. 13*

1412	A389	800 l	Sheet of 12, #a.-l.	11.00	11.00

A390

A391

6th World Day of the Sick: 1500 l, Rainbow pulled over earth by dove.

1998, Feb. 11 *Perf. 14x14½*

1413	A390	650 l	shown	.75	.75
1414	A390	1500 l	multicolored	1.70	1.70

1998, Mar. 31 Litho. *Perf. 14x15*

Europa (Natl. Feasts and Festivals): 650 l, Installation of the Captains Regent. 1200 l, Feast Day of the Republic's Patron Saint.

1415	A391	650 l	multicolored	.75	.75
1416	A391	1200 l	multicolored	1.25	1.25

Giacomo Leopardi (1798-1837), Poet — A392

Words from poem, illustration: 550 l, "The Infinite," 1819, hedges, hill. 650 l, "A Village Saturday," 1829, woman walking. 900 l, "Nocturne of a Wandering Asian Shepherd," 1822-30, man looking at moon. 2000 l, "To Sylvia," woman's face.

1998, Mar. 31 *Perf. 15x14*

1417	A392	550 l	multicolored	.60	.60
1418	A392	650 l	multicolored	.75	.75
1419	A392	900 l	multicolored	1.00	1.00
1420	A392	2000 l	multicolored	2.25	2.25
			Nos. 1417-1420 (4)	4.60	4.60

1998 World Cup Soccer Championships, France — A393

Soccer players: 650 l, At goal. 800 l, In black & yellow, in blue. 900 l, In red, in black & blue.

1998, May 28 Photo. *Perf. 11½x12*
Granite Paper

1421	A393	650 l	multicolored	.75	.75
a.			Booklet pane of 4	3.00	
1422	A393	800 l	multicolored	.85	.85
a.			Booklet pane of 4	3.50	
1423	A393	900 l	multicolored	1.00	1.00
a.			Booklet pane of 4	4.00	
			Complete booklet, #1421a, 1422a, 1423a	11.00	
			Nos. 1421-1423 (3)	2.60	2.60

Emigration A394

Designs: 800 l, People on ship's deck, group photograph in front of Mt. Titano, 3rd class ticket to New York, passport. 1500 l, People at work, work permit, residency permit, pay slip, US dollar.

1998, May 28
Granite Paper

1424	A394	800 l	multicolored	.90	.90
1425	A394	1500 l	multicolored	1.75	1.75

Souvenir Sheet

San Marino Natl. Flag in Space — A395

Designs: a, Launch of US space shuttle. b, Shuttle in orbit, flag of San Marino. c, Earth, space shuttle.

1998, May 28

Granite Paper

1426 A395 2000 l Sheet of 3, #a.-c. 6.75 6.75

A396 A397

Riccione 1998, Intl. Stamp Fair: 800 l, Sun, sail on boat as canceled stamp. 1500 l, Dolphin diving through canceled stamp.

1998, Aug. 28 Photo. *Perf. 12x11½*

Granite Paper

1427 A396 800 l multicolored 1.00 1.00
1428 A396 1500 l multicolored 1.75 1.75

1998, Aug. 28 *Perf. 14½*

Science Fiction: a, Twenty Thousand Leagues Under the Sea, by Jules Verne (1828-1905). b, War of the Worlds, by H.G. Wells (1866-1946). c, Brave New World, by Aldous Huxley (1894-1963). d, 1984, by George Orwell (1903-50). e, Chronicles of the Galaxy, by Isaac Asimov (1920-92). f, City without End, by Clifford D. Simak (1904-88). g, Fahrenheit 451, by Ray Bradbury (b. 1920). h, The Seventh Victim, by Robert Sheckley (b. 1928). i, The Space Merchants, by Frederik Pohl (b. 1919) and C.M. Kornbluth (1923-58). j, Neighbors from the Middle Ages and the Future, by Roberto Vacca (b. 1927). k, Stranger in a Strange Land, by Robert Heinlein (1907-88). l, A Clockwork Orange, by Anthony Burgess (1917-93). m, Drowned World, by James G. Ballard (b. 1930). n, Dune, by Frank Herbert (1920-86). o, 2001, A Space Odessy, by Arthur Clarke (b. 1917). p, Blade Runner (Do Androids Dream of Electric Sheep), by Phillip K. Dick (1928-82).

Granite Paper

1429 A397 800 l Sheet of 16, #a.-p. 15.00 15.00

Italia '98 A398

1998, Oct. 23 Photo. *Perf. 14*

1430 A398 800 l Pope John Paul II .95 .95

See Italy No. 2265, Vatican City No. 1085.

A399 A400

Christmas (Children of different races, Christmas tree made up of Santa Clauses, gifts): a, Boy running left, star on tree. b, Child from tropical region, star on tree. c, Child, rabbit, bottom of tree. d, Dog, girl, bottom of tree.

1998, Oct. 23 *Perf. 12x11½*

Granite Paper

1431 A399 800 l Block of 4, #a.-d. 3.75 3.75

No. 1431 is a continuous design.

1998, Oct. 23

Granite Paper

1432 A400 900 l Woman 1.10 1.10
1433 A400 900 l Man 1.10 1.10
a. Pair, #1432-1433 2.25 2.25

Universal Declaration of Human Rights, 50th Anniv. No. 1433a is a continuous design.

A401

A402

Italia '98: Statue, "Girl," by Emilio Greco.

1998, Oct. 23

Granite Paper

1434 A401 1800 l multicolored 2.25 2.25

Beginning with No. 1435 denominations are shown in euros and lira. For listing purposes we are showing the face value in lira.

1999, Feb. 12 Litho. *Perf. 13½x13*

1999 World Hang Gliding Championships, Italy: 800 l, Hand using feather to write in sky. 1800 l, Man on glider, holding balloon.

1435 A402 800 l multicolored 1.10 1.10
1436 A402 1800 l multicolored 2.40 2.40

Operas in San Marino, 400th Anniv. A403

Opera, composer: a, "L'incoronazione di Poppea," by Monteverdi. b, "Dido and Aeneas," by Purcell. c, "Orpheus and Euridice," by Gluck. d, "Don Giovanni," by Mozart. e, "The Barber of Seville," by Rossini. f, "Norma," by Bellini. g, "Lucia di Lammermour," by Donizetti. h, "Aida," by Verdi. i, "Faust," by Gounod. j, "Carmen," by Bizet. k, "The Ring of the Nibelungen," by Wagner. l, "Boris Godonov," by Mussorgski. m, "Tosca," by Puccini. n, "Love for Three Oranges," by Prokofiev. o, "Porgy and Bess," by Gershwin. p, "West Side Story," by Bernstein.

1999, Feb. 12 *Perf. 13x13½*

Sheet of 16

1437 A403 800 l #a.-p. 17.00 17.00

Bonsai '99, San Marino Bonsai Exhibition A404

50 l, Pinus mugo. 300 l, Olea europaea. 350 l, Pinus silvestris. 500 l, Quercus robar.

1999, Mar. 27 Litho. *Perf. 13x13½*

1438 A404 50 l multicolored .20 .20
1439 A404 300 l multicolored .35 .35
1440 A404 350 l multicolored .40 .40
1441 A404 500 l multicolored .55 .55
Nos. 1438-1441 (4) 1.50 1.50

Mount Titano Natl. Park A405

Europa: 650 l, Walled enclosure, Cesta tower. 1250 l, Eastern slopes, fortress tower.

1999, Mar. 27

1442 A405 650 l multicolored .60 .60
1443 A405 1250 l multicolored 1.25 1.25

1999 World Cycling Championships, Veneto, Italy — A406

1999, Mar. 27

1444 A406 900 l Building, emblem 1.00 1.00
1445 A406 3000 l Colosseum, emblem 3.25 3.25

2nd Roman Republic, Garibaldi's Escape to San Marino, 150th Anniv. A407

1999, May 12 Litho. *Perf. 13x13¼*

1446 A407 1250 l multicolored 1.40 1.40

Council of Europe, 50th Anniv. — A408

1999, May 12 *Perf. 13¼x13*

1447 A408 1300 l multicolored 1.40 1.40

UPU, 125th Anniv. A409

800 l, Text from original UPU Treaty, Swiss Parliament Building, Bern. 3000 l, World map highlighting UPU's 22 founding countries.

1999, May 12 *Perf. 13x13¼*

1448 A409 800 l multicolored .85 .85
1449 A409 3000 l multicolored 3.25 3.25

Holy Year 2000 A410

650 l, Map of route of 15th cent. European pilgrims, Canterbury Cathedral. 800 l, Fresco of priest blessing pilgrim, 11th cent., Reims Cathedral. 900 l, Fresco of hospice welcoming pilgrims, 15th cent., Duomo de Pavia. 1250 l, Bas-relief of pilgrims on the road, Cathedral of Fidenza, 12th cent. 1500 l, View of Rome from Monte Mario, by Sir Charles Eastlake, St. Peter's Basilica, Rome.

1999, June 5

1450 A410 650 l multicolored .70 .70
1451 A410 800 l multicolored .85 .85
1452 A410 900 l multicolored 1.00 1.00
1453 A410 1250 l multicolored 1.40 1.40
1454 A410 1500 l multicolored 1.60 1.60
Nos. 1450-1454 (5) 5.55 5.55

Fauna of San Marino A411

1999, June 5

1455 A411 500 l Lepus europaeus .55 .55
1456 A411 650 l Sciurus vulgaris .70 .70
1457 A411 1100 l Meles meles 1.25 1.25
1458 A411 1250 l Vulpes vulpes 1.40 1.40
1459 A411 1850 l Hystrix cristata 2.00 2.00
Nos. 1455-1459 (5) 5.90 5.90

Architecture — A412

Designs: 50 l, Sant'Agata Feltria, Rocca Fregosa. 250 l, San Leo, Rocca Feltresca. 650 l, Urbino, Ducal Palace. 1300 l, Sassocorvaro, Rocca Ubaldinesca. 6000 l, Montale and Rocca towers, San Marino.

1999, Sept. 20 Litho. *Perf. 13x13¼*

1460 A412 50 l multicolored .20 .20
1461 A412 250 l multicolored .25 .25
1462 A412 650 l multicolored .65 .65
1463 A412 1300 l multicolored 1.40 1.40
1464 A412 6000 l multicolored 6.50 6.50
Nos. 1460-1464 (5) 9.00 9.00

San Marino Red Cross, 50th Anniv. A413

1999, Sept. 20

1465 A413 800 l St. Martin of Tours .90 .90

Souvenir Sheet

Milan Soccer Club, 100th Anniv. — A414

Designs: a, 1901 team, trophy on table. b, Players Gren, Nordahl and Liedholm. c, 1963 team, black and white photograph. d, 1990 team, white shirts. e, 1994 team, hanging banners. f, 1999 team, player holding trophy.

1999, Sept. 20

1466 A414 800 l Sheet of 6, #a.-f. 5.25 5.25

Souvenir Sheet

Audi Automobiles — A415

Designs: a, Horch. b, Audi TT. c, Audi A8. d, Auto Union.

1999, Nov. 5 Litho. *Perf. 13x13¼*

1467 A415 1500 l Sheet of 4, #a.-d. 6.50 6.50

No. 1467 was issued with attached entry form for drawing to win a new Audi A3 car. Entry form is rouletted at top to separate from bottom of sheet. Values are for sheets with entry form attached.

Christmas A416

1999, Nov. 5

1468 A416 800 l multicolored .85 .85

Millennium A417

Designs: a, Tank, soldiers and refugees of World Wars. b, Syringe and vial, MRI machine, DNA molecule. c, Washing machine, subway, Tiffany lamp. d, Radio, telephone operators, person at computer. e, Airplanes, airship, astronaut on moon. f, Pollution. g, Automobiles and truck. h, Atomic diagram, nuclear submarine, mushroom cloud. i, Charlie Chaplin in "Modern Times," comic strip, chair. j, Crossword puzzle, art gallery visitors, car and trailer, people exercising. k, Advertisements and slogans. l, Cyclist, soccer players, stadium.

2000, Feb. 2 Litho. *Perf. 13x13¼*

1469 A417 650 l Sheet of 12, #a.-l. 8.00 8.00

Souvenir Sheet

Holy Year 2000 A418

Designs: a, St. John Lateran Basilica, St. Marinus and Mt. Titano. b, Basilica of St. Paul, statue of St. Marinus, the Rocca. c, Basilica of St. Mary Major, Basilica of San Marino. d, St. Peter's Basilica, St. Marinus.

2000, Feb. 2

1470 A418 1000 l Sheet of 4, #a.-d. 4.00 4.00

A419 A420

Designs: 650 l, Rotary emblem and towers. 800 l, Palace, coat of arms, Statue of Liberty, Rotary emblem.

2000, Apr. 27 Litho. *Perf. 13¼x13*

1471	A419	650 l	multi	.65	.65
1472	A419	800 l	multi	.80	.80

Rotary Club of San Marino, 40th anniv.

2000, Apr. 27

Bologna, European City of Culture: 650 l, Government Palace and Statue of Liberty, San Marino, and Fiera Towers, Bologna. 800 l, Marconi's workbench, radio antenna, Bologna buildings. 1200 l, Microchip, drums, keyboards, Bologna buildings. 1500 l, Still Life, by Giorgio Morandi, antique books, Bologna buildings.

1473	A420	650 l	multi	.65	.65
1474	A420	800 l	multi	.80	.80
1475	A420	1200 l	multi	1.25	1.25
1476	A420	1500 l	multi	1.50	1.50
	Nos. 1473-1476 (4)			4.20	4.20

Community of San Patrignano's Fight Against Drug Abuse — A421

Designs: 650 l, Vincenzo Muccioli, community's founder. 1200 l, Rainbow emblem. 2400 l, Muccioli and community residents.

2000, Apr. 27 *Perf. 13x13¼*

1477	A421	650 l	multi	.65	.65
1478	A421	1200 l	multi	1.25	1.25
1479	A421	2400 l	multi	2.40	2.40
	Nos. 1477-1479 (3)			4.30	4.30

Europa, 2000

Common Design Type

2000, Apr. 27 *Perf. 13¼x13*

1480 CD17 800 l multi .80 .80

Stampin' the Future Children's Stamp Design Contest Winner A422

2000, May 31 *Perf. 13x13¼*

1481 A422 800 l multi .80 .80

Intl. Cycling Union, Cent. A423

2000, May 31

1482 A423 1200 l multi 1.25 1.25

2000 Summer Olympics, Sydney — A424

Designs: a, Dog, butterfly. b, Hippopotamus, penguin. c, Elephant, ladybug. d, Rabbit, snail. Illustration reduced.

2000, May 31 *Perf. 13¼x13*

1483 A424 1000 l Block of 4, #a-d 4.00 4.00

European Convention on Human Rights, 50th Anniv. A425

2000, Sept. 15 Litho. *Perf. 13x13¼*

1484 A425 800 l multi .80 .80

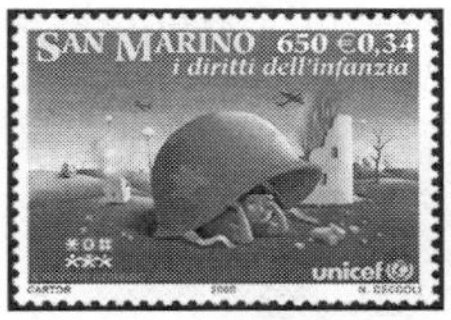

Intl. Rights of the Child Convention, 10th Anniv. A426

Child: 650 l, And army helmet. 800 l, In corner of room. 1200 l, As flower. 1500 l, With book.

2000, Sept. 15

1485-1488 A426 Set of 4 4.00 4.00

Art of the Montefeltro A427

650 l, Basilica of San Marino, Statue of St. Marinus, by Adamo Tadolini. 800 l, Santa Maria d'Antico Church, Madonna and Child statue, by Luca Della Robbia. 1000 l, San Lorenzo Church, church door. 1500 l, Interior and exterior of San Leo Church. 1800 l, Frescoes, Santuario Madonna della Grazie.

2000, Sept. 15

1489-1493 A427 Set of 5 5.75 5.75

Republic of San Marino, 1700th Anniv. — A428

No. 1494: a, Melchiorre Delfico (1744-1835), historian. b, Giuseppe Garibaldi. c, Abraham Lincoln. d, World War II refugees. e, Jewels from Treasure of Domagnano. f, Map after 1643 war. g, Napoleon Bonaparte's offer to extend territory. h, Arengo of 1906. i, Child's head. j, Young man's head. k, Woman's head. l, Old man's head. m, St. Marinus, by Francesco Manzocchi di Forlì, left half of arms. n, Right half of arms, St. Marinus, work attributed to Ghirlandaio. o, St. Marinus, by School of Guercino (blue denomination at top). p, St. Marinus in Glory, by anonymous artist. q, Double throne of Regents. r, Republican statutes, 17th cent. s, Palace Guards on parade. t, Flags of San Marino and other countries.

2000, Nov. 14 Photo. *Perf. 11¾*

1494	Souvenir booklet		21.00	
a.-l.	A428 800 l Any single		.80	.80
m.-t.	A428 1200 l Any single		1.25	1.25
u.	Booklet pane, #1494a-1494d		3.25	
v.	Booklet pane, #1494e-1494h		3.25	
w.	Booklet pane, #1494i-1494l		3.25	
x.	Booklet pane, #1494m-1494p		5.00	
y.	Booklet pane, #1494q-1494t		5.00	

No. 1494 includes an 800 l postal card.

Virgin With the Infant Jesus, by Ludovico Carracci A429

2000, Nov. 14 Litho. *Perf. 13x13½*

1495 A429 800 l multi .80 .80

Christmas.

Souvenir Sheet

Ferrari, 2000 Formula 1 Racing Champion — A430

a, Car on track. b, Car, track wall.

2001, Jan. 10

1496 A430 1500 l #a-b 3.00 3.00

Heritage of the Malatesta Family A431

Sigismondo Malatesta and: 800 l, Malatestian Temple, by Leon Battista Alberti. 1200 l, Pieta by Giovanni Bellini.

2001, Feb. 19 Litho. *Perf. 13x13¼*

1497-1498 A431 Set of 2 1.90 1.90

24 Hours of San Marino Regatta — A432

Hull colors: a, Green. b, Orange. c, Black. d, Brown.

2001, Feb. 19 ***Perf. 13¼x13***
1499 A432 1200 l Block or strip of 4, #a-d 4.50 4.50

Giuseppe Verdi (1813-1901), Composer — A433

Verdi and scenes from operas: a, Nabucco. b, Ernani. c, Rigoletto. d, Il Trovatore. e, La Traviata. f, I Vespri Siciliani. g, Un Ballo in Maschera. h, La Forza del Destino. i, Don Carlos. j, Aida. k, Otello. l, Falstaff.

2001, Feb. 19 ***Perf. 13x13¼***
1500 Sheet of 12 9.00 9.00
a.-l. A433 800 l Any single .75 .75

Europa — A434

Designs: 800 l, Safe in forest. 1200 l, Faucet on mountain.

2001, Apr. 17 **Litho.** ***Perf. 13¼x13***
1501-1502 A434 Set of 2 1.90 1.90

Emigration to the US — A435

Immigrants viewing Statue of Liberty and: 1200 l, Ellis Island Immigration Museum, New York. 2400 l, San Marino Social Club, Detroit.

2001, Apr. 17 ***Perf. 13x13¼***
1503-1504 A435 Set of 2 3.50 3.50

Euroflora 2001, Genoa — A436

Designs: 800 l, Dahlia variabilis, ship. 1200 l, Zantedeschia aethiopica, ship. 1500 l, Helen Troubel rose, ship. 2400 l, Amaryllis hippeastrum, Lanterna.

2001, Apr. 17 ***Perf. 13¼x13***
1505-1508 A436 Set of 4 5.50 5.50

9th Games of the Small European States — A437

No. 1509: a, Bocce, running. b, Swimming. c, Cycling. d, Shooting. e, Judo. f, Tennis, table tennis. g, Basketball and volleyball. h, Mascot carrying torch.

2001, Apr. 17
1509 A437 800 l Sheet of 8, #a-h 6.00 6.00

Opening of New State Museum A438

Various holdings: 550 l, 800 l, 1500 l, 2000 l.

2001, June 23 ***Perf. 13x13¼***
1510-1513 A438 Set of 4 4.25 4.25

UN High Commisioner for Refugees, 50th Anniv. — A439

No. 1514: a, Emblem at bottom. b, Emblem at top.

2001, June 23 ***Perf. 13¼x13***
1514 A439 1200 l Horiz. pair, #a-b 2.10 2.10

Foundation of the Republic, 1700th Anniv. — A440

No. 1515: a, Uninhabited land. b, People on horses. c, Small community. d, Town with highway.
Illustration reduced.

2001, June 23 ***Perf. 13x13¼***
1515 A440 1200 l Block of 4, #a-d 4.25 4.25

Homage to Artist Joseph Beuys A441

2001, Sept. 10
1516 A441 2400 l multi 2.25 2.25

Year of Dialogue Among Civilizations A442

2001, Sept. 10 ***Perf. 13¼x13***
1517 A442 2400 l multi 2.25 2.25

United Mutual Aid Society, 125th Anniv. — A443

Allegory of assistance and: a, Old building. b, Modern building.
Illustration reduced.

2001, Sept. 10 ***Perf. 13x13¼***
1518 A443 1200 l Horiz. pair, #a-b 2.25 2.25

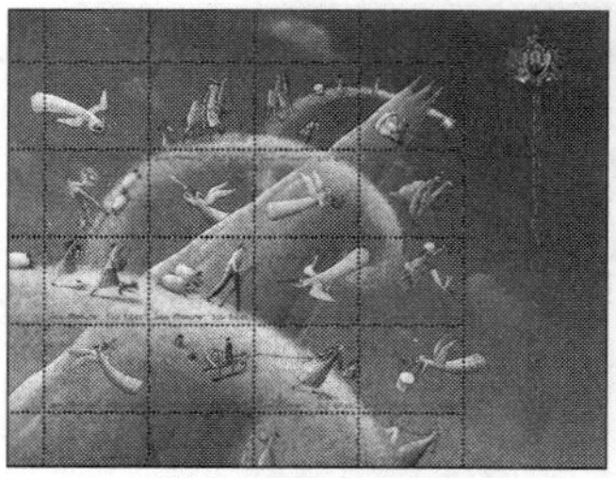

Christmas — A444

No. 1519: a, Angel with lute. b, Woman with basket, Magus on camel. c, Magus on camel, shepherd with sheep, woman with gift. d, Man with gift, castles, star, Holy Family. e, Man with lantern, goose, chicken, sheep. f, Angel with long, thin-mouthed, horn. g, Angel with harp. h, Magus on camel. i, Two women with baskets, dog. j, Shepherd with two sheep. k, Angel with short, wide-mouthed horn. l, Woman with gift, angel with horn. m, Angel with violin. n, Man, sleigh, gifts. o, Woman with gift, pulling sleigh. p, Angel with drum.

2001, Oct. 18 **Litho.** ***Perf. 13***
1519 A444 800 l Sheet of 16, #a-p 12.00 12.00

Introduction of the Euro (in 2002) A445

Map of Europe and: 1200 l, Coins of various countries, 1-euro coin. 2400 l, Banknotes of various countries, 100-euro banknote.

2001, Oct. 18 ***Perf. 13x13¼***
1520-1521 A445 Set of 2 3.50 3.50

100 Cents = 1 Euro (€)

A446

Designs: 1c, Rabbits. 2c, Sunset over San Marino. 5c, Cactus. 10c, Field of grain. 25c, Aerial view of alpine landscape. 50c, Wet olive branches. €1, Sparrows. €5, Baby.

2002, Jan. 16 **Litho.** ***Perf. 13¼x13***

1522	A446	1c	multi	.20	.20
1523	A446	2c	multi	.20	.20
1524	A446	5c	multi	.20	.20
1525	A446	10c	multi	.20	.20
1526	A446	25c	multi	.45	.45
1527	A446	50c	multi	.85	.85
1528	A446	€1	multi	1.75	1.75
1529	A446	€5	multi	8.50	8.50
	Nos. 1522-1529 (8)			12.35	12.35

Manuel Poggiali, 2001 World 125cc Class Motorcycling Champion — A447

No. 1530: a, "2001" at UR. b, "2001" at UL.
Illustration reduced.

2002, Jan. 16 ***Perf. 13x13¼***
1530 A447 62c Horiz. pair, #a-b 2.25 2.25

2002 Winter Olympics, Salt Lake City — A448

No. 1531: a, Dog skiing. b, Hippopotamus skating. c, Rabbit skiing. d, Elephant playing ice hockey.

2002, Jan. 16 ***Perf. 13¼x13***
1531 A448 41c Block of 4, #a-d 3.00 3.00

SEMI-POSTAL STAMPS

Regular Issue of 1903 Surcharged:

1917 **1917**

Pro combattenti **Pro combattenti**

= 25 Cent. **50**

a b

1917, Dec. 15 Wmk. 140 *Perf. 14*

B1 A10(a) 25c on 2c violet 3.75 3.00
B2 A11(b) 50c on 2 l violet 21.00 17.50

Statue of Liberty — SP1

View of San Marino SP2

1918, June 1 Typo.

B3 SP1 2c dl vio & blk .60 .60
B4 SP1 5c bl grn & blk .60 .60
B5 SP1 10c lake & blk .60 .60
B6 SP1 20c brn org & blk .60 .60
B7 SP1 25c ultra & blk .60 .60
B8 SP1 45c yel brn & blk .60 .60
B9 SP2 1 l bl grn & blk 7.25 7.25
B10 SP2 2 l vio & blk 6.75 6.75
B11 SP2 3 l claret & blk 6.75 6.75
Nos. B3-B11 (9) 24.35 24.35

These stamps were sold at an advance of 5c each over face value, the receipts from that source being devoted to the support of a hospital for Italian soldiers.

For surcharges see Nos. 89-92.

Nos. B6-B8 Overprinted

3
Novembre
1918

1918, Dec. 12

B12 SP1 20c brn org & blk 1.10 1.25
B13 SP1 25c ultra & blk 1.10 1.25
B14 SP1 45c yel brn & blk 1.10 1.25

Overprinted **3 Novembre 1918**

B15 SP2 1 l blue grn & blk 2.60 3.25
B16 SP2 2 l violet & blk 6.00 6.50
B17 SP2 3 l claret & blk 6.00 6.50
Nos. B12-B17 (6) 17.90 20.00

Celebration of Italian Victory over Austria.

Inverted overprints were privately produced.

Coat of Arms SP3

Liberty SP4

1923, Sept. 20 Engr.

B18 SP3 5c + 5c olive grn .20 .20
B19 SP3 10c + 5c orange .20 .20
B20 SP3 15c + 5c dk green .20 .20
B21 SP3 25c + 5c brn lake .25 .25
B22 SP3 40c + 5c vio brn 1.75 1.75
B23 SP3 50c + 5c gray 1.10 .20
B24 SP4 1 l + 5c blk & bl 3.00 3.00
Nos. B18-B24 (7) 6.70 5.80

St. Marinus SP5

Wmk. 140

1944, Apr. 25 Photo. *Perf. 14*

B25 SP5 20 l + 10 l gldn brn 1.25 1.25
Sheet of 8 30.0 30.00

The surtax was used for workers' houses. See No. CB1.

No. 256 Surcharged in Red "L. 10"

1946, Aug. 24 Unwmk.

B26 A46 50 l + 10 l 5.00 5.00
Sheet of 10 *575.00 575.00*

Third Philatelic Day, Rimini. The surtax was for the exhibition.

Air Post Types of 1946 Surcharged "CONVEGNO FILATELICO / 30 NOVEMBRE 1946 / + LIRE 25" (or "LIRE 50") in Red or Violet

1946, Nov. 30 Wmk. 277

B26A AP7 3 l + 25 l dk brn (R) .25 .20
B26B AP8 5 l + 25 l red org (V) .25 .20
B26C AP6 10 l + 50 l ultra (R) 2.75 2.50
Nos. B26A-B26C (3) 3.25 2.90

Inscription "Posta Aerea" does not appear on these stamps.

No. 260 Surcharged in Black

1947, Nov. 13 Wmk. 217 *Perf. 12*

B27 A53 1 l + 1 l brt grn & vio .20 .20
B28 A53 1 l + 2 l brt grn & vio .20 .20
B29 A53 1 l + 3 l brt grn & vio .20 .20
B30 A53 1 l + 4 l brt grn & vio .20 .20
B31 A53 1 l + 5 l brt grn & vio .20 .20
a. Strip of 5, #B27-B31 1.00 1.00

Surcharged on No. 261

B32 A53 2 l + 1 l pur & olive .20 .20
B33 A53 2 l + 2 l pur & olive .20 .20
B34 A53 2 l + 3 l pur & olive .20 .20
B35 A53 2 l + 4 l pur & olive .20 .20
B36 A53 2 l + 5 l pur & olive .20 .20
a. Strip of 5, #B32-B36 1.00 1.00

Surcharged on No. 262

B37 A53 4 l + 1 l 2.50 2.50
B38 A53 4 l + 2 l 2.50 2.50
a. Pair, #B37-B38 11.00 11.00
Nos. B27-B38 (12) 7.00 7.00

Surcharges on Nos. B27-B38 are arranged consecutively, changing from ascending to descending order of denomination on alternate rows in the sheet.

Catalogue values for unused stamps in this section, from this point to the end of the section, are for Never Hinged items.

Refugee Boy — SP6

1982, Dec. 15 Photo. *Perf. 11½*

B39 SP6 300 l + 100 l multi .40 .40

Surcharge was for refugee support.

AIR POST STAMPS

View of San Marino AP1

Wmk. 217

1931, June 11 Engr. *Perf. 12*

C1 AP1 50c blue grn 3.75 3.75
C2 AP1 80c red 3.75 3.75
C3 AP1 1 l bister brn 1.25 1.25
C4 AP1 2 l brt violet 1.25 1.25
C5 AP1 2.60 l Prus bl 16.00 16.00
C6 AP1 3 l dk gray 16.00 16.00
C7 AP1 5 l olive grn 1.25 1.25
C8 AP1 7.70 l dk brown 3.75 3.75
C9 AP1 9 l dp orange 3.75 3.75
C10 AP1 10 l dk blue 175.00 175.00
Nos. C1-C10 (10) 225.75 225.75

Exist imperf.

Graf Zeppelin Issue

Stamps of Type AP1 Surcharged in Blue or Black

ZEPPELIN 1933

L. 3.

1933, Apr. 28

C11 AP1 3 l on 50c org 1.25 *45.00*
C12 AP1 5 l on 80c ol grn 22.50 *45.00*
C13 AP1 10 l on 1 l dk bl (Bk) 22.50 *55.00*
C14 AP1 12 l on 2 l yel brn 22.50 *67.50*
C15 AP1 15 l on 2.60 l dl red (Bk) 22.50 *75.00*
C16 AP1 20 l on 3 l bl grn (Bk) 22.50 *87.50*
Nos. C11-C16 (6) 113.75 *375.00*

Exist imperf.

Nos. C1 and C2 Surcharged

1936, Apr. 14

C17 AP1 75c on 50c blue grn 1.25 1.25
C18 AP1 75c on 80c red 6.00 6.00

Nos. C5 and C6 Surcharged with New Value and Bars

1941, Jan. 12

C19 AP1 10 l on 2.60 l 55.00 55.00
C20 AP1 10 l on 3 l 13.50 13.50

View of Arbe — AP2

Wmk. 140

1942, Mar. 16 Photo. *Perf. 14*

C21 AP2 25c brn & gray blk .20 .20
C22 AP2 50c grn & brn .20 .20
C23 AP2 75c gray bl & red brn .20 .20
C24 AP2 1 l ocher & brn .25 .25
C25 AP2 5 l bis brn & bl 3.00 3.00
Nos. C21-C25 (5) 3.85 3.85

Return of the Italian flag to Arbe.

AP3

San Marino Map, Fasces and Wing — AP4

Overprinted "28 LVGLIO 1943 1642 d. F. R." in Black

1943, Aug. 27

C26 AP3 25c yellow org .20 .20
C27 AP3 50c car rose .20 .20
C28 AP3 75c dark brown .20 .20
C29 AP3 1 l dk rose vio .20 .20
C30 AP3 2 l sapphire .20 .20
C31 AP3 5 l orange red .75 .75
C32 AP3 10 l deep green 1.00 1.00
C33 AP3 20 l black 3.25 3.25
Nos. C26-C33 (8) 6.00 6.00

See footnote after No. 227. Nos. C26-C33 exist without overprint (not regularly issued). Value $1,500.

Overprinted "GOVERNO PROVVISORIO"

1943, Aug. 27

C34 AP4 25c yellow org .20 .20
C35 AP4 50c car rose .20 .20
C36 AP4 75c dark brown .20 .20
C37 AP4 1 l dk rose vio .20 .20
C38 AP4 5 l orange red .60 .60
C39 AP4 20 l black 1.75 1.75
Nos. C34-C39 (6) 3.15 3.15

Government Palace — AP5

Planes over Mt. Titano — AP8

Gulls and San Marino Skyline AP6

Plane and View of San Marino AP7

Plane over Globe AP9

1945, Mar. 15 Photo.

C40 AP5 25 l bister brn 2.50 2.50

See note after No. 239.

Photo., Engr. (20 l, 50 l)

1946-47 Unwmk. *Perf. 14*

C41 AP6 25c blue blk .20 .20
C42 AP7 75c red org .20 .20
C43 AP6 1 l brown .20 .20
C44 AP7 2 l dull green .20 .20
C45 AP7 3 l violet .20 .20

C46 AP8 5 l violet blue .20 .20
C47 AP6 10 l crimson .20 .20
C48 AP8 20 l brown lake 1.10 1.10
C49 AP8 35 l orange red 2.40 2.40
C50 AP8 50 l dk yellow grn 3.00 3.00
C51 AP9 100 l sepia ('47) .85 .85
Nos. C41-C51 (11) 8.75 8.75

Some values exist imperforate.
Issue dates: 35 l, Nov. 3, 1946; 100 l, Mar. 27, 1947; others, Aug. 8, 1946.
For surcharges and overprint see Nos. B26A-B26C, C54.

Roosevelt Type of Regular Issue, 1947

F. D. Roosevelt and: 1 l, 31 l, 50 l, Eagle. 2 l, 20 l, 100 l, San Marino arms. 5 l, 200 l, Flags of San Marino and US, vert.

Wmk. 277
1947, May 3 Photo. *Perf. 14*
C51A A52a 1 l dp ultra & sep .20 .20
C51B A52a 2 l org red & sep .20 .20
C51C A52a 5 l multicolored .20 .20
C51D A52a 20 l choc & sep .20 .20
C51E A52a 31 l org & sep .40 .40
C51F A52a 50 l dk car & sep .70 .70
C51G A52a 100 l bl & sepia 1.40 1.40
C51H A52a 200 l multicolored 12.00 12.00
Nos. C51A-C51H (8) 15.30 15.30

Nos. C51A-C51E, C51H exist imperf. Value, set $105.

Nos. C51A-C51C Surcharged

1947, June 16
C51I A52a 3 l on 1 l dp ultra & sep .25 .25
C51J A52a 4 l on 2 l org red & sep .25 .25
C51K A52a 6 l on 5 l multicolored .25 .25
Nos. C51I-C51K (3) .75 .75

St. Marinus Type of Regular Issue, 1947
Wmk. 217
1947, July 18 Engr. *Perf. 12*
Center in Bright Blue
C52 A53 25 l deep orange .70 .70
C53 A53 50 l red brown 1.50 1.50

No. C51 Overprinted in Red

1947, July 18 Unwmk. *Perf. 14*
C54 AP9 100 l sepia .70 .70
a. Double overprint 22.50
b. Inverted overprint 65.00

Rimini Phil. Exhib., July 18-20.

US No. 1 and Mt. Titano AP11

Wmk. 277
1947, Dec. 24 Engr. *Perf. 14*
C55 AP11 100 l dk pur & dk brn 5.50 5.50
a. Imperf. 60.00
Sheet of 10 *1,500.*

1st US postage stamps, cent.

No. 264 Surcharged "POSTA AEREA" and New Value in Black

1948, Oct. 9 Wmk. 217 *Perf. 12*
C56 A53 200 l on 25 l 13.50 13.50

Giuseppe and Anita Garibaldi Entering San Marino — AP12

Wmk. 277
1949, June 28 Photo. *Perf. 14*
Size: 27½x22mm
C57 AP12 2 l brn red & ultra .20 .20
C58 AP12 3 l dk green & sepia .20 .20
C59 AP12 5 l dk bl grn & ultra .20 .20

Size: 37x22mm
C60 AP12 25 l dk green & vio 1.00 1.00
C61 AP12 65 l grnsh blk & gray blk 5.00 5.00
Nos. C57-C61 (5) 6.60 6.60

Garibaldi's escape to San Marino, cent.

Stagecoach on Road from San Marino AP13

1950, Feb. 9 Engr. *Perf. 14*
C62 AP13 200 l deep blue .85 .85
a. Perf. 13½x14 ('51) 1.90 1.90
As "a," sheet of 6 22.50 22.50
b. Imperf ('51) 12.50 12.50
As "b," sheet of 6 140.00 140.00

UPU, 75th anniv. #C62 was issued in sheets of 25; #C62a & C62b in sheets of 6. See #C75.

AP14

AP15

AP16

Various Views of San Marino.

1950, Apr. 12 Photo. *Perf. 14*
Size: 27½x21½mm, 21½x27½mm
C63 AP14 2 l vio & dp grn .20 .20
C64 AP14 3 l blue & brown .20 .20
C65 AP15 5 l brn blk & rose red .20 .20
C66 AP14 10 l grnsh blk & bl .60 .25
C67 AP14 15 l grnsh blk & vio .75 .35

Size: 36x26½mm, 26½x36mm
C68 AP15 55 l dp bl & dp grn 10.50 9.25
C69 AP14 100 l car & gray 8.00 7.25
C70 AP15 250 l violet & brn 32.50 21.00

Engr.
C71 AP16 500 l bl, dk grn & vio brn 35.00 *47.50*
Nos. C63-C71 (9) 87.95 86.20

See No. C78. For overprints and surcharges see Nos. C72-C74, C76, C79.

Types of 1950 Overprinted in Black, Blue or Brown

1950, Apr. 12 Photo.
New Colors; Sizes as Before
C72 AP15 5 l dp bl & dp grn .20 .20
C73 AP14 15 l car & gray (Bl) .35 .30
C74 AP15 55 l vio & brn (Br) 2.10 2.10
Nos. C72-C74 (3) 2.65 2.60

The overprint is arranged differently on each denomination.

San Marino's participation in the 28th Intl. Fair of Milan, Apr., 1950.

Stagecoach Type of 1950
1951, Jan. 31 Engr. *Perf. 13½x14*
C75 AP13 300 l rose brown & brown 12.00 12.00
Sheet of 6 110.00 125.00
a. Imperf. 350.00
Sheet of 6 2,100.

No. C71 Surcharged in Black "Giornata Filatelica San Marino-Riccione 20-8-1951," New Value and Bars

1951, Aug. 20 *Perf. 14*
C76 AP16 300 l on 500 l 18.00 18.00

Flag and Plane AP17

Perf. 13½x14
1951, Nov. 22 Engr. Wmk. 277
C77 AP17 1000 l multi 250.00 250.00
Sheet of 6 *3,500.* *3,500.*

Type of 1950
1951, Apr. 28 Photo. *Perf. 14*
Size: 36x26½mm
C78 AP16 500 l dk grn & brn 62.50 62.50
Sheet of 6 925.00 925.00

No. C70 Surcharged in Black

1951, Dec. 6
C79 AP15 100 l on 250 l 2.00 2.00

Issued to raise funds for flood victims in northern Italy.

Columbus, Globe, Statue of Liberty and Buildings AP18

1952, Jan. 28 Engr.
C80 AP18 200 l dk bl & blk 16.00 16.00

Issued to honor Christopher Columbus.

Type of 1952 Overprinted in Red

FIERA DI TRIESTE
1952

1952, June 29
C81 AP18 200 l blk brn & choc 18.00 18.00

4th Intl. Sample Fair of Trieste.

Cyclamen — AP19

Flowers and Seacoast — AP20

2 l, As #C85-C87 with flowers omitted. 3 l, Rose.

1952, Aug. 25 Photo. *Perf. 10x14*
C82 AP19 1 l pur & lil rose .20 .20
C83 AP19 2 l blue & bl grn .20 .20
C84 AP19 3 l dk brn & red .20 .20

Perf. 14
C85 AP20 5 l rose lil & brn .20 .20
C86 AP20 25 l vio & bl grn .20 .25

Perf. 13
Engr.
C87 AP20 200 l multicolored 22.50 22.50
Sheet of 6, #C87 300.00 300.00
Nos. C82-C87 (6) 23.50 23.55

Riccione Phil. Exhib., Aug. 25, 1952.

Plane Making Photographic Survey — AP21

75 l, Aerial survey, seen through window.

1952, Nov. 17 Photo. *Perf. 14*
C88 AP21 25 l olive green .60 .60
C89 AP21 75 l red brn & pur 2.10 2.10

Aerial photographic survey of San Marino, 1952.

Skier AP22

1953, Apr. 20 Engr.
C90 AP22 200 l bl grn & dk grn 29.00 29.00
Sheet of 6 450.00 450.00

Plane and Arms of San Marino AP23

1954, Apr. 5
C91 AP23 1000 l dk blue & brn 47.50 47.50
Sheet of 6 450.00 450.00

Type of Regular Issue, 1954
1954, Dec. 16 Photo. *Perf. 13*
C92 A71 120 l dp bl & red brn .90 .90

Hurdler AP25

1955, June 26 Wmk. 303 *Perf. 14*
C93 AP25 80 l shown .70 .65
C94 AP25 120 l Relay .70 .70
Set, never hinged 2.75

San Marino's first Intl. Exhib. of Olympic Stamps, June.

Ski Jumper AP26

1955, Dec. 15
C95 AP26 200 l blk & red org 9.50 9.50
Never hinged 22.50

7th Winter Olympic Games at Cortina d'Ampezzo, Jan. 26-Feb. 5, 1956.

No. 372 Overprinted in Upper Right Corner with Plane and "Posta Aerea"

1956, Dec. 10
C96 A76 100 l blk & Prus grn .95 1.25
Never hinged 1.25

Catalogue values for unused stamps in this section, from this point to the end of the section, are for Never Hinged items.

Helicopter, Plane and Modernistic Building — AP27

Wmk. 303
1958, Apr. 12 Photo. *Perf. 14*
C97 AP27 125 l lt blue & brn 1.60 1.60

10th participation in Milan Fair.
See Nos. 414-415.

View of San Marino AP28

Design: 300 l, Road from Mt. Titano.

Wmk. 303
1958, June 23 Engr. *Perf. 13*
C98 AP28 200 l brn & dk blue 2.25 2.25
C99 AP28 300 l magenta & vio 2.25 2.25
a. Strip, Nos. C98, C99 + label 5.50 5.50

Printed in sheets containing 20 each of Nos. C98 and C99 flanking a center label with San Marino coat of arms. Nos. C98 and C99 also come se-tenant in sheet.

Naples Stamps Type of Regular Issue

Design: Bay of Naples and 50g stamp of Naples.

1958, Oct. 8 Photo. *Perf. 14*
C100 A85 125 l brn & red brn 1.25 1.25

Sea Gull AP29

Birds: 10 l, Falcon. 15 l, Mallard. 120 l, Stock dove. 250 l, Barn swallow.

1959, Feb. 12 *Perf. 14*
C101 AP29 5 l green & gray .20 .20
C102 AP29 10 l blue & org brn .20 .20
C103 AP29 15 l red & multi .20 .20
C104 AP29 120 l rose red, yel & gray blk .70 .35
C105 AP29 250 l dp grn, yel & blk 1.90 1.10
Nos. C101-C105 (5) 3.20 2.05

Pierre de Coubertin AP30

Wmk. 303
1959, May 19 Engr. *Perf. 13*
C106 AP30 120 l sepia 3.25 .85

Pierre de Coubertin; 1960 Olympic Games in Rome.

Alitalia Viscount Over San Marino AP31

1959, June 3 Photo. *Perf. 14*
C107 AP31 120 l bright violet 1.10 1.10

First flight San Marino-Rimini-London.

Lincoln Type of Regular Issue, 1959

Design: Abraham Lincoln and San Marino peaks.

1959, July 1 Engr. *Perf. 14x13*
C108 A87 200 l dark blue 2.40 2.10

Romagna Stamps Type

Design: Bologna view, 3b Romagna stamp.

Wmk. 303
1959, Aug. 29 Photo. *Perf. 14*
C109 A88 120 l blk & blue grn 1.60 1.10

Sicily Stamps Type

Design: Fishing boats, Monte Pellegrino and 50g stamp of Sicily, horiz.

1959, Oct. 16
C110 A89 200 l multicolored .65 .60

Olympic Games Type

Sports: 20 l, Basketball. 40 l, Sprint race. 80 l, Swimming, horiz. 125 l, Target shooting, horiz.

1960, May 23 Wmk. 303 *Perf. 14*
C111 A92 20 l lilac .20 .20
C112 A92 40 l bis brn & dk red .20 .20
C113 A92 80 l ultra & buff .20 .20
C114 A92 125 l ver & dk brn .30 .20
Nos. C111-C114 (4) .90 .80

Souvenir sheets are valued and described below No. 465.

Lions Intl. Type

Design: 200 l, Globe and Lions emblem.

1960, July 1 Photo.
C115 A94 200 l ol grn, brn & ultra 5.00 4.00

12th Stamp Fair Type

1960, Aug. 27 Wmk. 303 *Perf. 14*
C116 A95 125 l multicolored 1.10 1.00

Helicopter and Mt. Titano AP32

1961, July 6 Engr. *Perf. 14*
C117 AP32 1000 l rose car 35.00 22.50
Sheet of 6 225.00 140.00

Tupolev TU-104A AP33

Planes: 10 l, Boeing 707, vert. 15 l, Douglas DC-8. 25 l, Boeing 707. 50 l, Vickers Viscount 837. 75 l, Caravelle, vert. 120 l, Vickers VC10. 200 l, D. H. Comet 4C. 300 l, Boeing 727. 500 l, Rolls Royce Dart turbo-prop. 1000 l, Boeing 707.

1963-65 Wmk. 339 Photo. *Perf. 14*
C118 AP33 5 l bl & vio brn .20 .20
C119 AP33 10 l org & dk bl .20 .20
C120 AP33 15 l violet & red .20 .20
C121 AP33 25 l violet & car .20 .20
C122 AP33 50 l grnsh bl & red .20 .20
C123 AP33 75 l emer & dp org .20 .20
C124 AP33 120 l vio bl & red .20 .20
C125 AP33 200 l brt yel & blk .20 .20
C126 AP33 300 l org & blk .20 .20

Perf. 13
C127 AP33 500 l multicolored 2.50 2.50
Sheet of 4 14.00 14.00
C128 AP33 1000 l lil rose, ultra & yel 1.60 1.60
Sheet of 4 15.00 15.00
Nos. C118-C128 (11) 5.90 5.90

Issued: Nos. C118-C126, Dec. 5, 1963. No. C127, Mar. 4, 1965. No. C128, Mar. 12, 1964.

Mt. Titano and Flight Symbolized AP34

1972, Oct. 25 Unwmk. *Perf. 11½*
Granite Paper
C129 AP34 1000 l multi 1.00 .90

Glider AP35

Designs: Each stamp shows a different type of air current in background.

1974, Oct. 9 Photo. *Perf. 11½*
Granite Paper
C130 AP35 40 l multicolored .20 .20
C131 AP35 120 l multicolored .20 .20
C132 AP35 500 l multicolored .30 .30
Nos. C130-C132 (3) .70 .70

50th anniversary of gliding in Italy.

San Marino 77 Type of 1977

1977, Jan. 28 Photo. *Perf. 11½*
C133 A193 200 l multicolored .20 .20

Wright Brothers' Flyer A — AP36

1978, Sept. 28 Photo. *Perf. 11½*
C134 AP36 10 l multicolored .20 .20
C135 AP36 50 l multicolored .20 .20
C136 AP36 200 l multicolored .20 .20
Nos. C134-C136 (3) .60 .60

75th anniversary of first powered flight.

AIR POST SEMI-POSTAL STAMP

View of San Marino APSP1

Wmk. 140
1944, Apr. 25 Photo. *Perf. 14*
CB1 APSP1 20 l + 10 l ol grn 1.25 1.25
Sheet of 8 30.00 30.00

The surtax was used for workers' houses.

SPECIAL DELIVERY STAMPS

SD1

Unwmk.
1907, Apr. 25 Engr. *Perf. 12*
E1 SD1 25c carmine 15.00 7.50

For surcharges see Nos. E3, E5.

Type of Regular Issue of 1903 Overprinted

Perf. 14½x14
1923, May 30 Wmk. 140
E2 A11 60c violet .50 .50

For surcharge see No. 103.

Type of 1907 Issue Surcharged

1923, July 26 *Perf. 14*
E3 SD1 60c on 25c carmine .50 .50
a. Vert. pair, imperf. between 125.00

No. E2 Surcharged

1926, Nov. 25 *Perf. 14½x14*
E4 A11 1.25 l on 60c violet 1.00 1.00

No. E3 Surcharged

L. 1,25

1927, Sept. 15
E5 SD1 1.25 l on 60c on 25c .50 .50
a. Inverted surcharge 72.50
b. Vert. pair, imperf. between 300.00
c. Double surcharge 85.00

Statue of Liberty and View of San Marino — SD2

Wmk. 217
1929, Aug. 29 Engr. *Perf. 12*
E6 SD2 1.25 l green .20 .20

Overprinted in Red UNION POSTALE UNIVERSELLE

E7 SD2 2.50 l deep blue .60 .60

Arms of San Marino
SD3

Wmk. 140

1943, Sept. Photo. *Perf. 14*

E8 SD3 1.25 l green .20 .20
E9 SD3 2.50 l reddish orange .20 .20

View of San Marino
SD4

Pegasus
SD5

1945-46 Photo. Wmk. 140

E12 SD4 2.50 l deep green .20 .20
E13 SD4 5 l deep orange .20 .20

Unwmk.

E14 SD4 5 l carmine rose .70 .50

Wmk. 277

E15 SD4 10 l sapphire ('46) 1.75 1.25

Engr.

Unwmk.

E16 SD5 30 l deep ultra ('46) 4.00 4.00
Nos. E12-E16 (5) 6.85 6.15

See Nos. E22-E23. For surcharges see Nos. E17-E21, E24-E25.

Nos. E14 and E15 Surcharged in Black

1947 Unwmk. *Perf. 14*

E17 SD4 15 l on 5 l car rose .25 .20

Wmk. 277

E18 SD4 15 l on 10 l saph .25 .20

No. E16 Surcharged with New Value and Bars in Carmine

1947-48 Unwmk.

E19 SD5 35 l on 30 l ('48) 18.00 18.00
E20 SD5 60 l on 30 l 3.00 3.00
E21 SD5 80 l on 30 l ('48) 8.50 10.00
Nos. E19-E21 (3) 29.50 31.00

Types of 1945-46

1950, Dec. 11 Photo. Wmk. 277

E22 SD4 60 l rose brown 3.50 3.50
E23 SD5 80 l deep blue 3.50 3.50
Set, never hinged 21.00

Nos. E22-E23 Surcharged with New Value and Three Bars

1957, Dec. 12 *Perf. 14*

E24 SD4 75 l on 60 l rose brn 1.50 1.50
E25 SD5 100 l on 80 l dp blue 1.50 1.50
Set, never hinged 5.00

Catalogue values for unused stamps in this section, from this point to the end of the section, are for Never Hinged items.

Crossbow
SD6

Design: No. E27, "Espresso" at left; crossbow casts two shadows.

1965, Aug. 28 Photo. Wmk. 339

E26 SD6 120 l on 75 l blk, gray & yel .20 .20
E27 SD6 135 l on 100 l blk & org .20 .20

Without Surcharge

Design: 80 l, 100 l, "Espresso" at left; crossbow casts two shadows.

1966, Mar. 29

E28 SD6 75 l blk, gray & yel .20 .20
E29 SD6 80 l blk & lilac .20 .20
E30 SD6 100 l blk & orange .20 .20
Nos. E28-E30 (3) .60 .60

SEMI-POSTAL SPECIAL DELIVERY STAMP

SPSD1

Wmk. 140

1923, Sept. 20 Engr. *Perf. 14*

EB1 SPSD1 60c + 5c brown red .75 .75

POSTAGE DUE STAMPS

D1

Wmk. 140

1897-1920 Typo. *Perf. 14*

J1 D1 5c bl grn & dk brn .20 .20
J2 D1 10c bl grn & dk brn .20 .20
a. Numerals inverted 125.00 —
J3 D1 30c bl grn & dk brn .75 .75
J4 D1 50c bl grn & dk brn 1.25 1.25
a. Numerals inverted 125.00 —
J5 D1 60c bl grn & dk brn 10.50 5.50
J6 D1 1 l claret & dk brn 3.00 3.50
J7 D1 3 l claret & brn ('20) 10.50 11.00
J8 D1 5 l claret & dk brn 45.00 29.00
J9 D1 10 l claret & dk brn 16.00 16.00
Nos. J1-J9 (9) 87.40 67.40

See Nos. J10-J36. For surcharges see Nos. J37-J60, J64.

1924

J10 D1 5c rose & brown .50 .50
J11 D1 10c rose & brown .50 .50
J12 D1 30c rose & brown .75 .75
J13 D1 50c rose & brown 1.25 1.25
J14 D1 60c rose & brown 3.50 3.50
J15 D1 1 l green & brown 6.00 6.00
J16 D1 3 l green & brown 22.50 22.50
J17 D1 5 l green & brown 26.00 26.00
J18 D1 10 l green & brown 160.00 160.00
Nos. J10-J18 (9) 221.00 221.00

1925-39 *Perf. 14*

J19 D1 5c blue & brn .35 .20
a. Numerals inverted 125.00 —
J20 D1 10c blue & brn .35 .20
a. Numerals inverted 125.00 —
J21 D1 15c blue & brn ('39) .20 .20
J22 D1 20c blue & brn ('39) .20 .20
J23 D1 25c blue & brn ('39) .25 .25
J24 D1 30c blue & brn .35 .20
J25 D1 40c blue & brn ('39) 2.50 2.50
J26 D1 50c blue & brn .75 .25
a. Numerals inverted 125.00 —
J27 D1 60c blue & brn 1.50 .60
J28 D1 1 l buff & brn 3.00 .50
J29 D1 2 l buff & brn ('39) 1.50 1.50
J30 D1 3 l buff & brn 50.00 22.50
J31 D1 5 l buff & brn 13.50 3.75
J32 D1 10 l buff & brn 18.00 9.75
J33 D1 15 l buff & brn ('28) 1.50 .85
J34 D1 25 l buff & brn ('28) 27.50 16.00
J35 D1 30 l buff & brn ('28) 6.00 6.00
J36 D1 50 l buff & brn ('28) 7.25 6.75
Nos. J19-J36 (18) 134.70 72.20

Postage Due Stamps of 1925 Surcharged in Black and Silver

1931, May 18

J37 D1 15c on 5c bl & brn .20 .20
J38 D1 15c on 10c bl & brn .20 .20
J39 D1 15c on 30c bl & brn .20 .20
J40 D1 20c on 5c bl & brn .20 .20
J41 D1 20c on 10c bl & brn .20 .20
J42 D1 20c on 30c bl & brn .20 .20
J43 D1 25c on 5c bl & brn 1.00 .75
J44 D1 25c on 10c bl & brn 1.00 .75
J45 D1 25c on 30c bl & brn 7.75 6.00
J46 D1 40c on 5c bl & brn 1.00 .20
J47 D1 40c on 10c bl & brn 1.25 .25
J48 D1 40c on 30c bl & brn 1.25 .25
J49 D1 2 l on 5c bl & brn 32.50 24.00
J50 D1 2 l on 10c bl & brn 67.50 45.00
J51 D1 2 l on 30c bl & brn 45.00 32.50
Nos. J37-J51 (15) 159.45 110.90

Nos. J19, J24-J25, J30, J34, J33, J22 Surcharged in Black

Lire 1

Perf. 14, 14½x14

1936-40 Wmk. 140

J52 D1 10c on 5c ('38) .50 .50
J53 D1 25c on 30c ('38) 7.25 7.25
J54 D1 50c on 5c ('37) 7.25 7.25
J55 D1 1 l on 30c 27.50 5.50
J56 D1 1 l on 40c ('40) 5.00 3.75
J57 D1 1 l on 3 l ('37) 27.50 1.90
J58 D1 1 l on 25 l ('39) 55.00 12.00
J59 D1 2 l on 15 l ('38) 27.50 14.50
J60 D1 3 l on 20c ('40) 21.00 14.00
Nos. J52-J60 (9) 178.50 66.65

Coat of Arms — D6

1939 Typo. *Perf. 14*

J61 D6 5c blue & brown .20 .20

Nos. J61 and J36 Surcharged with New Values and Bars

1940-43

J62 D6 10c on 5c .20 .20
J63 D6 50c on 5c 1.25 .60
J64 D1 25 l on 50 l ('43) 1.75 1.75
Nos. J62-J64 (3) 3.20 2.55

Coat of Arms — D7

Unwmk.

1945, June 7 Photo. *Perf. 14*

J65 D7 5c dk green .20 .20
J66 D7 10c orange brn .20 .20
J67 D7 15c rose red .20 .20
J68 D7 20c dp ultra .20 .20
J69 D7 25c dk purple .20 .20
J70 D7 30c rose lake .20 .20
J71 D7 40c bister .20 .20
J72 D7 50c slate blk .20 .20
J73 D7 60c chestnut .20 .20
J74 D7 1 l dp orange .20 .20
J75 D7 2 l carmine .20 .20
J76 D7 5 l dull violet .20 .20
J77 D7 10 l dark blue .20 .20
J78 D7 20 l dark green 4.50 4.00
J79 D7 25 l red orange 4.50 4.00
J80 D7 50 l dark brown 4.50 4.00
Nos. J65-J80 (16) 16.10 14.60

PARCEL POST STAMPS

These stamps were used by affixing them to the way bill so that one half remained on it following the parcel, the other half staying on the receipt given the sender. Most used halves are right halves. Complete stamps were and are obtainable canceled, probably to order. Both unused and used values are for complete stamps.

PP1

Engraved, Typographed

1928, Nov. 22 Unwmk. *Perf. 12*

Pairs are imperforate between

Q1 PP1 5c blk brn & bl .20 .20
a. Imperf. 40.00
Q2 PP1 10c dk bl & bl .20 .20
Q3 PP1 20c gray blk & bl .20 .20
a. Imperf. 40.00
Q4 PP1 25c car & blue .20 .20
Q5 PP1 30c ultra & blue .20 .20
Q6 PP1 50c orange & bl .20 .20
Q7 PP1 60c rose & blue .20 .20
Q8 PP1 1 l violet & brn .20 .20
a. Imperf. 40.00
Q9 PP1 2 l green & brn .60 .60
Q10 PP1 3 l bister & brn .75 .75
Q11 PP1 4 l gray & brn 1.00 1.00
Q12 PP1 10 l rose lilac & brn 2.40 2.40
Q13 PP1 12 l red brn & brn 8.50 8.50
Q14 PP1 15 l olive grn & brn 13.50 13.50
a. Imperf. 40.00
Q15 PP1 20 l brn vio & brn 21.00 21.00
Nos. Q1-Q15 (15) 49.35 49.35

Halves Used

Q1-Q8 .20
Q9-Q10 .20
Q11 .20
Q12 .35
Q13 .65
Q14 2.75
Q15 3.00

1945-46 Wmk. 140 *Perf. 14*

Pairs are perforated between

Q16 PP1 5c rose vio & red org .20 .20
Q17 PP1 10c red org & blk .20 .20
Q18 PP1 20c dark red & grn .20 .20
Q19 PP1 25c yel & blk .20 .20
Q20 PP1 30c red vio & org red .20 .20
Q21 PP1 50c dull pur & blk .20 .20
Q22 PP1 60c rose lake & blk .20 .20
Q23 PP1 1 l brown & dp bl .20 .20
Q24 PP1 2 l dk brn & dk bl .20 .20
Q25 PP1 3 l olive brn & brn .20 .20
Q26 PP1 4 l blue grn & brn .20 .20
Q27 PP1 10 l bl blk & brt pur .20 .20
Q28 PP1 12 l myr grn & dl bl 3.00 1.40
Q29 PP1 15 l green & purple 1.90 1.40
Q30 PP1 20 l rose lil & brn 1.60 1.40
Q31 PP1 25 l dp car & ultra ('46) 29.00 20.00
Q32 PP1 50 l yel & dp org ('46) 45.00 29.00
Nos. Q16-Q32 (17) 82.90 55.60

Halves Used

Q16-Q27 .20
Q28 .20
Q29 .20
Q30 .20
Q31 .25
Q32 .50

Nos. Q32 and Q31 Surcharged with New Value and Wavy Lines in Black

1948-50

Q33 PP1 100 l on 50 l 42.50 32.50
Half, used 1.00
Q34 PP1 200 l on 25 l ('50) 140.00 90.00
Half, used 1.00

1953, Mar. 5 Wmk. 277 *Perf. 13½*

Pairs Perforated Between

Q35 PP1 10 l dk grn & rose lil 24.00 8.50
Half, used 1.00
Q36 PP1 300 l pur & lake 110.00 82.50
Half, used 1.00

1956 Wmk. 303 *Perf. 13½*

Q37 PP1 10 l gray & brt pur .20 .20
Half, used .20
Q38 PP1 50 l yel & dp org .60 .50
Half, used .20

No. Q38 Surcharged with New Value and Wavy Lines in Black

Q39 PP1 100 l on 50 l .40 .40
Half, used .25

Catalogue values for unused stamps in this section, from this point to the end of the section, are for Never Hinged items.

1960-61

Q40 PP1 300 l violet & brn 35.00 24.00
Half, used .50
Q41 PP1 500 l dk brn & car ('61) 1.50 1.50
Half, used .20

1965-72 Wmk. 339 *Perf. 13½*

Pairs Perforated Between

Q42 PP1 10 l gray & brt pur .20 .20
Q43 PP1 50 l yel & red org .20 .20
Q44 PP1 100 l on 50 l yel & red org .50 .50
Q45 PP1 300 l violet & brown .20 .20
Q46 PP1 500 l brn & red ('72) 3.75 3.75

Q47 PP1 1000 l bl grn & lt red brn ('67) .50 .50
Nos. Q42-Q47 (6) 5.35 5.35

Halves Used

Q42-Q43 .20
Q44-Q45 .20
Q46 .20
Q47 .45

SARAWAK

sə-'rä-ˌwäk

LOCATION — Northwestern part of the island of Borneo, bordering on the South China Sea
GOVT. — Former British Crown Colony
AREA — 48,250 sq. mi. (approx.)
POP. — 1,954,300 (1997 est.)
CAPITAL — Kuching

The last ruling Raja, who retired in 1946 when he ceded Sarawak to the British Crown, was Sir Charles Vyner Brooke, an Englishman. He inherited the title from his father, Sir Charles Johnson Brooke, who in turn received it from his uncle, Sir James Brooke. The title of Raja was conferred on Sir James by Raja Muda Hassim after Sir James had aided him in subduing a rebellion. The title and right of succession were duly recognized by the Sultan of Brunei and by Great Britain.

Sarawak joined the Federation of Malaysia in 1963.

100 Cents = 1 Dollar

Catalogue values for unused stamps in this country are for Never Hinged items, beginning with Scott 155.

Watermarks

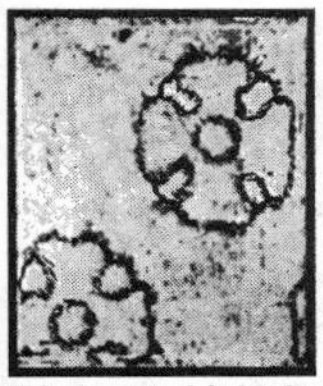

Wmk. 47- Multiple Rosettes

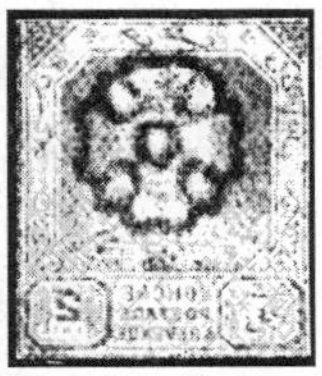

Wmk. 71- Rosette

Wmk. 231- Oriental Crown

Unused examples of Nos. 1-7, 25 and 32-35 are valued without gum. Stamps with original gum are worth more.

Sir James Brooke — A1

Sir Charles Johnson Brooke — A2

Unwmk.

1869, Mar. 1 Litho. *Perf. 11*
1 A1 3c brown, *yellow* 30.00 *210.00*

1871, Jan.
2 A2 3c brown, *yellow* 1.00 *3.00*
a. Vertical pair, imperf between *500.00*
b. Horiz. pair, imperf between *750.00*

No. 2 surcharged "TWO CENTS" is believed to be bogus.

There are a number of varieties including narrow A, "period" after THREE, etc.

Imperfs. of Nos. 1, 2 are proofs.

A papermaker's watermark, "LNL," usually appears once or twice in each pane.

For surcharges see Nos. 25, 32.

1875, Jan. 1 *Perf. 12*
3 A2 2c gray lilac, *lilac* 3.25 *14.00*
4 A2 4c brown, *yellow* 2.00 *2.50*
b. Vertical pair, imperf between *550.00*
5 A2 6c green, *green* 3.00 *3.25*
6 A2 8c blue, *blue* 3.50 *4.00*
7 A2 12c red, *rose* 5.50 *6.50*
Nos. 3-7 (5) 17.25 *30.25*

Nos. 3-7 have each five varieties of the words of value.

Imperfs are proofs.

A papermaker's watermark usually appears once or twice in each pane of Nos. 3-7, "LNT" on No. 5, "LNL" on others.

Some examples of No. 6 have the appearance of being on laid paper, but the lines are accidental and not constant within the sheets.

For surcharges see Nos. 33-35.

Sir Charles Johnson Brooke — A4

1888-97 Typo. *Perf. 14*
8 A4 1c lilac & blk ('92) .95 .50
9 A4 2c lilac & rose .75 1.00
10 A4 3c lilac & blue 1.60 *1.75*
11 A4 4c lilac & yellow 8.50 *30.00*
12 A4 5c lil & grn ('91) 7.25 4.00
13 A4 6c lilac & brown 8.25 *45.00*
14 A4 8c green & car 5.00 2.50
a. 8c green & rose ('97) 15.00 13.50
15 A4 10c grn & vio ('93) 24.00 13.50
16 A4 12c green & blue 5.00 *7.50*
17 A4 16c gray grn & org ('97) 35.00 *57.50*
18 A4 25c green & brown 32.50 *35.00*
19 A4 32c gray grn & blk ('97) 22.50 *40.00*
20 A4 50c gray green ('97) 22.50 *75.00*
21 A4 $1 gray grn & blk ('97) 42.50 *70.00*
Nos. 8-21 (14) 216.30 *383.25*

No. 21 shows the numeral on white tablet.

Three higher values —$2, $5, $10— were prepared but not issued. Value $500 each.

For surcharges see Nos. 22-24, 26-27.

Nos. 14 and 16 Surcharged in Black:

a

No. 23

No. 24 **5c.**

1889-91
22 A4 2c on 8c 3.00 *5.00*
a. Double surcharge 300.00
b. Pair, one without surcharge 2,000.
c. Inverted surcharge 2,000.
23 A4 5c on 12c ('91) 22.00 *35.00*
a. Double surcharge 1,100. *1,100.*
b. Pair, one without surcharge —
c. No period after "C" 22.50 *32.50*
d. Without "C" 325.00 325.00
e. Double surch., one vert. 2,250.
24 A4 5c on 12c ('91) 75.00 *125.00*
a. No period after "C" 70.00 *80.00*
b. Double surcharge 1,100.
c. "C" omitted 425.00 375.00

No. 2 Surcharged in Black

1892, May 23 *Perf. 11*
25 A2 1c on 3c brown, *yel* .70 *1.50*
b. Without bar 150.00
c. Period after "THREE" 20.00 30.00
d. Double surcharge 375.00 375.00
e. Vertical pair, imperf between *475.00*
f. Vertical pair, imperf horiz. *475.00*

Examples of No. 25b must be from the first printing, wherein the bar was applied after the surcharge. Examples of No. 25 with parts of the surcharge and/or bar omitted are stamps that had glue on the face prior to the surcharging operation. The ink was removed when the glue was washed off.

No. 10 Surcharged in Black:

e

f

1892 *Perf. 14*
26 A4(e) 1c on 3c lilac & blue 3.00 *5.00*
a. No period after "cent" 100.00 100.00
27 A4(f) 1c on 3c lil & bl 28.00 24.00
b. Double surcharge 425.00 275.00

Issued: #26, Feb.; #27, Jan. 12.

Sir Charles Johnson Brooke
A11 A12

A13

A14

1895, Jan. 1 Engr. *Perf. 11½, 12*
28 A11 2c red brown 5.75 *7.00*
a. Perf. 12½ 5.75 4.50
b. Vertical pair, imperf between *300.00*
c. Horiz. pair, imperf between *275.00*
d. As "a," horiz. pair, imperf between *325.00*
29 A12 4c black 5.75 2.50
a. Horiz. pair, imperf between *425.00*
30 A13 6c violet 6.00 7.00
31 A14 8c deep green 20.00 6.00
Nos. 28-31 (4) 37.50 22.50

The 2c and 8c imperf are proofs. Perforated stamps of these designs in other colors are color trials.

Stamps of 1871-75 Surcharged in Black or Red

1899 *Perf. 11*
32 A2 2c on 3c brown, *yel* 1.50 1.50
a. Period after "THREE" 40.00 *50.00*
b. Vertical pair, imperf between *800.00*

Perf. 12
33 A2 2c on 12c red, *rose* 2.50 *3.00*
a. Inverted surcharge 900.00 *1,150.*
34 A2 4c on 6c green, *grn* (R) 22.50 *45.00*
a. Inverted surcharge
35 A2 4c on 8c blue, *bl* (R) 3.50 5.75
Nos. 32-35 (4) 30.00 *55.25*

Sir Charles J. Brooke A16

Sir Charles Vyner Brooke A17

1899-1908 Typo. *Perf. 14*
36 A16 1c blue & car ('01) .90 *1.10*
37 A16 2c gray green 1.10 .80
38 A16 3c dull violet ('08) 4.25 .45
39 A16 4c analine car 1.50 .20
40 A16 8c yellow & black 1.50 .70
41 A16 10c ultra 1.75 .75
42 A16 12c light violet 3.75 3.50
43 A16 16c org brn & grn 1.75 1.50
44 A16 20c brn ol & vio ('00) 4.00 3.00
45 A16 25c brown & ultra 2.50 *4.00*
46 A16 50c ol grn & rose 15.50 *18.00*
47 A16 $1 rose & green 50.00 *100.00*
Nos. 36-47 (12) 88.50 *134.00*

A 5c was prepared but not issued. Value $10.

See the *Scott Classic Catalogue*, for listings of shades.

1901 Wmk. 71
48 A16 2c gray green 15.00 10.00

1918-23 Unwmk.
50 A17 1c slate bl & rose 1.00 .20
51 A17 2c deep green 1.50 .20
52 A17 2c violet ('23) 1.50 1.50
53 A17 3c violet brown 2.75 1.00
54 A17 3c deep grn ('22) .85 *1.00*
55 A17 4c carmine rose 2.75 .40
56 A17 4c purple brn ('23) .85 .20
57 A17 5c orange ('23) 1.00 .20
58 A17 6c lake brown ('22) .85 *1.00*
59 A17 8c yellow & blk 8.00 *40.00*
60 A17 8c car rose ('22) 6.00 *22.00*
61 A17 10c ultra 2.25 1.50
a. 10c blue 2.75 1.50
62 A17 10c black ('23) 1.75 *2.00*
63 A17 12c violet 6.00 *16.00*
64 A17 12c ultra ('22) 6.00 *12.00*
65 A17 16c brn & blue grn 4.25 *6.00*
66 A17 20c olive bis & vio 4.50 *6.00*
a. 20c olive green & violet 5.00 *5.00*
67 A17 25c brown & blue 3.25 *6.00*
68 A17 30c bis & gray ('22) 3.00 *3.00*
69 A17 50c olive grn & rose 6.50 *10.00*
70 A17 $1 car rose & grn 14.00 *20.00*
Nos. 50-70 (21) 78.55 *150.20*

In 1918 a supply of the 1c (No. 50) had the value tablet printed, by error, in slate blue instead of rose. It is officially stated that this stamp was never issued and had no franking power. Value $10.

The $1 denomination shows numeral of value in color on white tablet.

Nos. 61 and 63 Surcharged

1st Printing - bars 1¼mm apart.
2nd Printing - Bars ¾mm apart.

1923, Jan.
77 A17 1c on 10c ultra 11.00 *42.50*
a. "cnet" 300.00 *600.00*
b. Bars ¾mm apart 125.00 *200.00*
78 A17 2c on 12c violet 5.00 *30.00*
a. Bars ¾mm apart 60.00 *120.00*

Type of 1918 Issue

1928-29 Typo. Wmk. 47
79 A17 1c slate blue & rose 1.00 .30
80 A17 2c dull violet 1.00 .90
81 A17 3c deep green 1.25 *4.25*
82 A17 4c purple brown 1.50 .20
83 A17 5c orange ('29) 8.25 4.25
84 A17 6c brown lake 1.00 .25
85 A17 8c carmine 2.75 *11.00*
86 A17 10c black 1.75 1.10
87 A17 12c ultra 2.75 *16.00*
88 A17 16c dp brn & bl grn 2.75 *3.50*
89 A17 20c dp olive & vio 2.75 *4.50*
90 A17 25c dk brown & ultra 5.00 *5.00*
91 A17 30c olive bis & gray 4.00 *8.00*
92 A17 50c olive grn & rose 4.75 *8.00*
93 A17 $1 car rose & grn 14.50 *21.00*
Nos. 79-93 (15) 55.00 *88.25*

Sir Charles Vyner Brooke
A18 A19

Wmk. 231

1932, Jan. 1 Engr. *Perf. 12½*
94 A18 1c indigo .65 .40
95 A18 2c dark green .65 .40
96 A18 3c deep violet 2.25 .65
97 A18 4c deep orange 1.00 .25
98 A18 5c brown lake 3.75 .65
99 A18 6c deep red 5.25 *6.00*
100 A18 8c orange yel 3.25 *6.00*
101 A18 10c black 2.25 *3.00*
102 A18 12c violet blue 3.50 *6.00*

103 A18 15c orange brown 4.75 5.00
104 A18 20c violet & org 4.00 6.00
105 A18 25c org brn & yel 8.25 16.00
106 A18 30c org red & ol brn 5.75 16.00
107 A18 50c olive grn & red 7.25 8.75
108 A18 $1 car & green 11.50 22.00
Nos. 94-108 (15) 64.05 97.10

1934-41 Unwmk. Perf. 12

109 A19 1c brown violet .20 .20
110 A19 2c blue green .20 .20
111 A19 2c black ('41) 1.10 1.40
112 A19 3c black .20 .20
113 A19 3c blue grn ('41) 2.60 4.00
114 A19 4c magenta .25 .20
115 A19 5c violet .55 .20
116 A19 6c deep rose .80 .50
117 A19 6c red brn ('41) 3.50 7.00
118 A19 8c red brown .65 .20
119 A19 8c dp rose ('41) 2.60 .20
120 A19 10c red 1.25 .35
121 A19 12c deep ultra 1.60 .25
122 A19 12c orange ('41) 1.75 5.00
123 A19 15c orange 1.90 6.00
124 A19 15c deep blue ('41) 4.00 13.50
125 A19 20c dp rose & olive 1.75 .60
126 A19 25c orange & vio 1.75 1.40
127 A19 30c vio & red brn 1.90 2.25
128 A19 50c red & violet 1.90 .65
129 A19 $1 dk brn & red .70 .65
130 A19 $2 violet & mag 8.00 7.50
131 A19 $3 blue grn & rose 22.50 22.50
132 A19 $4 red & ultra 22.50 25.00
133 A19 $5 red brn & red 22.50 27.50
134 A19 $10 orange & blk 19.00 35.00
Nos. 109-134 (26) 125.65 162.45

Issue dates: May 1, 1934, Mar. 1, 1941.
For overprints see #135-154, 159-173, N1-N22.

Stamps of 1934-41 Overprinted in Black or Red

1945, Dec. 17

135 A19 1c brown violet .30 .40
136 A19 2c black (R) .30 .40
137 A19 3c blue green .30 .40
138 A19 4c magenta .30 .20
139 A19 5c violet (R) .30 .45
140 A19 6c red brown .50 .45
141 A19 8c deep rose 9.00 8.00
142 A19 10c red .40 .45
143 A19 12c orange .65 2.75
144 A19 15c deep blue 1.10 .25
145 A19 20c dp rose & ol 1.60 1.00
146 A19 25c org & vio (R) 1.60 1.50
147 A19 30c vio & red brn 3.00 2.00
148 A19 50c red & violet .90 .25
149 A19 $1 dk brn & red 1.75 .95
150 A19 $2 violet & mag 6.50 6.00
151 A19 $3 bl grn & rose 12.00 26.00
152 A19 $4 red & ultra 18.00 24.00
153 A19 $5 red brn & red 80.00 80.00
154 A19 $10 org & blk (R) 80.00 100.00
Nos. 135-154 (20) 218.50 255.45
Set, never hinged 275.00

Catalogue values for unused stamps in this section, from this point to the end of the section, are for Never Hinged items.

Sir James Brooke, Sir Charles V. Brooke and Sir Charles J. Brooke
A20

1946, May 18

155 A20 8c dark carmine .30 .20
156 A20 15c dark blue .30 1.25
157 A20 50c red & black .60 1.50
158 A20 $1 sepia & black 2.25 10.00
Nos. 155-158 (4) 3.45 12.95

Type of 1934-41 Overprinted in Blue or Red

1947, Apr. 16 Wmk. 4 Perf. 12

159 A19 1c brown violet .20 .30
160 A19 2c black (R) .20 .20
161 A19 3c blue green (R) .20 .20
162 A19 4c magenta .20 .20
163 A19 6c red brown .25 .90
164 A19 8c deep rose .70 .20
165 A19 10c red .25 .20
166 A19 12c orange .25 .90
167 A19 15c deep blue (R) .25 .40
168 A19 20c dp rose & ol (R) 1.50 .50
169 A19 25c orange & vio (R) .50 .25
170 A19 50c red & violet (R) .50 .35
171 A19 $1 dk brown & red .90 .90
172 A19 $2 violet & magenta 1.60 3.25
173 A19 $5 red brown & red 3.50 3.25
Nos. 159-173 (15) 11.00 12.00

Common Design Types pictured following the introduction.

Silver Wedding Issue
Common Design Types

1948, Oct. 25 Photo. Perf. 14x14½

174 CD304 8c scarlet .25 .25

Engraved; Name Typographed
Perf. 11½x11

175 CD305 $5 light brown 30.00 30.00

UPU Issue
Common Design Types
Engr.; Name Typo. on 15c, 25c
Perf. 13½, 11x11½

1949, Oct. 10 Wmk. 4

176 CD306 8c rose carmine 1.00 .60
177 CD307 15c indigo 2.50 1.50
178 CD308 25c green 2.00 1.40
179 CD309 50c violet 2.00 3.50
Nos. 176-179 (4) 7.50 7.00

Troides Brookiana
A21

Western Tarsier — A22

Designs: 3c, Kayan tomb. 4c, Kayan girl and boy. 6c, Bead work. 8c, Dyak dancer. 10c, Scaly anteater. 12c, Kenyah boys. 15c, Fire making. 20c, Kelemantan rice barn. 25c, Pepper vines. 50c, Iban woman. $1, Kelabit smithy. $2, Map of Sarawak. $5, Arms of Sarawak.

Perf. 11½x11, 11x11½

1950, Jan. 3 Engr.

180 A21 1c black .20 .20
181 A22 2c orange red .20 .20
182 A22 3c green .25 .20
183 A22 4c brown .25 .20
184 A22 6c aquamarine .30 .20
185 A21 8c red .45 .30
186 A21 10c orange .50 2.25
187 A21 12c purple 1.65 1.25
188 A21 15c deep blue .50 .25
189 A21 20c red org & brn .85 .50
190 A21 25c carmine & grn .90 .60
191 A22 50c purple & brn 1.40 .20
192 A21 $1 dk brn & bl grn 4.75 1.50
193 A21 $2 rose car & blue 20.00 10.00

Engr. and Typo.

194 A21 $5 dp vio, blk, red & yel 20.00 11.00
Nos. 180-194 (15) 52.20 28.85

1952, Feb. 1

195 A21 10c orange (Map) 1.00 .40

Coronation Issue
Common Design Type

1953, June 3 Engr. Perf. 13½x13

196 CD312 10c ultra & black .80 1.00

Logging — A23

Hornbill
A24

Elizabeth II — A25

Designs: 2c, Young Orangutan. 4c, Kayan Dancing. 8c, Shield with spears. 10c, Kenyah ceremonial carving. 12c, Barong Panau (sailboat). 15c, Turtles. 20c, Melanau basket making. 25c, Astana, Kuching (Governor's Residence). $1, $2, Queen Elizabeth II (Portrait like Fiji A39). $5, Arms.

Perf. 11x11½, 11½x11, 12x12½ (A25)

1955-57 Wmk. 4 Engr.

197 A23 1c green .20 .20
198 A23 2c red orange .20 .25
199 A23 4c brown carmine .45 .20
200 A24 6c greenish blue 3.00 1.50
201 A24 8c rose red .30 .20
202 A24 10c dark green .20 .20
203 A24 12c purple 3.75 .50
204 A24 15c ultra 1.00 .20
205 A24 20c brown & olive 1.00 .25
206 A24 25c brt green & brn 6.50 .25
207 A25 30c violet & red brn 2.50 .20
208 A25 50c car rose & blk 2.10 .30
209 A25 $1 orange brn & grn 4.00 .50
210 A25 $2 green & violet 12.00 2.25

Engr. and Typo.

211 A24 $5 dp vio, blk, red & yel 16.00 7.00
Nos. 197-211 (15) 53.20 14.00

Issued: 30c, 6/1/55; others, 10/1/57.
See Nos. 215-222.

Freedom from Hunger Issue
Common Design Type
Perf. 14x14½

1963, June 4 Photo. Wmk. 314

212 CD314 12c sepia 1.50 .80

STATE OF MALAYSIA
Types of 1955-57
Perf. 11x11½, 11½x11

1964-65 Engr. Wmk. 314

215 A23 1c green .20 .30
216 A23 2c red orange .60 7.00
217 A24 6c green blue 3.75 3.00
218 A24 10c dark green .95 .60
219 A24 12c purple 1.40 6.00
220 A24 15c ultra 1.10 9.00
221 A24 20c brown & olive .40 1.25
222 A24 25c brt grn & brn 1.90 3.00
Nos. 215-222 (8) 10.30 30.15

Issued: 20c, 6/9/64; 2c, 15c, 8/17/65; others, 9/9/64.

Orchid Type of Johore (Malaysia), 1965, with State Crest
Wmk. 338

1965, Nov. 15 Photo. Perf. 14½
Flowers in Natural Colors

228 A14 1c black & lt grnsh bl .20 .50
229 A14 2c black, red & gray .20 .60
230 A14 5c black & Prus blue .40 .20
231 A14 6c black & lt lilac .55 .60
232 A14 10c black & lt ultra .70 .30
233 A14 15c black, lil rose & grn 1.40 .30
234 A14 20c black & brown 1.75 .50
Nos. 228-234 (7) 5.20 3.00

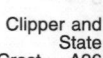

Clipper and State Crest — A26

Perf. 13½x13

1971, Feb. 1 Litho. Unwmk.

235 A26 1c Delias ninus .20 .60
236 A26 2c Danaus melanippus .35 .60
237 A26 5c Parthenos sylvia .70 .20
a. Booklet pane of 4 ('73) 2.25
238 A26 6c Papilio demoleus .90 1.00
239 A26 10c Hebomnia glaucippe .90 .20
a. Booklet pane of 4 ('73) 3.00
240 A26 15c Precis orithya 1.25 .20
a. Booklet pane of 4 ('73) 4.50
241 A26 20c Valeria valeria 1.50 .60
Nos. 235-241 (7) 5.80 3.45

Clipper and New State Crest — A27

Changed Colors, Designs as Before

1977-78 Photo. Unwmk.

242 A27 1c multi ('78) 7.00 8.00
243 A27 2c multi ('78) 6.00 6.00
244 A27 5c multicolored 1.00 .50
245 A27 10c multicolored .65 .20
246 A27 15c multicolored 1.50 .30
247 A27 20c multi ('78) 2.75 1.50
Nos. 242-247 (6) 18.90 16.50

Flower Type of Johore, 1979, with State Crest

1979, Apr. 30 Wmk. 47 Perf. 14½

248 A16 1c multicolored .20 .30
249 A16 2c multicolored .20 .30
250 A16 5c multicolored .20 .20
251 A16 10c multicolored .20 .20
252 A16 15c multicolored .20 .20
253 A16 20c multicolored .20 .20
254 A16 25c multicolored .45 .20
Nos. 248-254 (7) 1.65 1.60

1983-86 Unwmk.

250a A16 5c ('86) 1.00 1.25
251a A16 10c ('85) 1.00 1.10
253a A16 20c 1.00 1.10
Nos. 250a-253a (3) 3.00 3.45

Agriculture and State Arms Type of Johore
Shield Divided into 3 Parts of Different Colors
Wmk. 388

1986, Oct. 25 Litho. Perf. 12

255 A19 1c multicolored .20 .20
256 A19 2c multicolored .20 .20
257 A19 5c multicolored .20 .20
258 A19 10c multicolored .20 .20
259 A19 15c multicolored .20 .20
260 A19 20c multicolored .20 .20
261 A19 30c multicolored .25 .20
Nos. 255-261 (7) 1.45 1.40

Agriculture and Arms Type of Johore
Yellow Shield Divided by Diagonal Bands of Black and Red

1986-96 Litho. Wmk. 388 Perf. 12

262 A19 1c multicolored .20 .20
263 A19 2c multicolored .20 .20
a. Perf. 15x14½ 3.00
264 A19 5c multicolored .20 .20
a. Perf 14 ('96) .90 .20
265 A19 10c multicolored .20 .20
a. Perf. 14 ('95) 2.00
b. Perf. 15x14½ ('95) 2.00
c. Perf. 14x14½ ('96) 4.50 .35
266 A19 15c multicolored .20 .20
267 A19 20c multicolored .20 .20
268 A19 30c multicolored .25 .20
a. Perf. 14 ('94) 1.75 .20
b. Perf. 15x14½ ('94) 4.00 .35
c. Perf. 14x14½ ('94) 4.25 .45
Nos. 262-268 (7) 1.45 1.40

OCCUPATION STAMPS

Issued under Japanese Occupation

府政国帝本日大

Stamps of 1934-41 Handstamped in Violet

1942		Unwmk.		Perf. 12
N1	A19	1c brown violet	45.00	*60.00*
N2	A19	2c blue green	100.00	*140.00*
N3	A19	2c black	100.00	*85.00*
N3A	A19	3c black	*275.00*	*275.00*
N4	A19	3c blue green	60.00	*70.00*
N5	A19	4c magenta	65.00	65.00
N6	A19	5c violet	80.00	65.00
N7	A19	6c deep rose	125.00	90.00
N8	A19	6c red brown	80.00	*65.00*
N8A	A19	8c red brown	*200.00*	*225.00*
N9	A19	8c deep rose	110.00	*110.00*
N10	A19	10c red	75.00	*75.00*
N11	A19	12c deep ultra	165.00	125.00
N12	A19	12c orange	165.00	135.00
N12A	A19	15c orange	*300.00*	*250.00*
N13	A19	15c deep blue	110.00	100.00
N14	A19	20c dp rose & ol	60.00	*80.00*
N15	A19	25c orange & vio	100.00	*80.00*
N16	A19	30c violet & red brn	65.00	*80.00*
N17	A19	50c red & violet	80.00	*80.00*
N18	A19	$1 dk brown & red	100.00	*95.00*
N19	A19	$2 violet & mag	200.00	*190.00*
N19A	A19	$3 blue grn & rose	*800.00*	*900.00*
N20	A19	$4 red & ultra	225.00	*225.00*
N21	A19	$5 red brown & red	225.00	*225.00*
N22	A19	$10 orange & blk	225.00	*225.00*
		Nos. N1-N22 (26)	*4,135.*	*4,115.*

Stamps overprinted with Japanese characters in oval frame or between 2 vertical black lines were not for paying postage.

SASENO

ˈsə-ˈzā-ˌnō

LOCATION — An island in the Adriatic Sea, lying at the entrance of Valona Bay, Albania.
GOVT. — Italian possession
AREA — 2 sq. mi.

Italy occupied this Albanian islet in 1914, and returned it to Albania in 1947.

100 Centesimi = 1 Lira

Used values in italics are for postally used stamps. CTO's or stamps with fake cancels sell for about the same as unused, hinged stamps.

Italian Stamps of 1901-22 Overprinted **SASENO**

1923		Wmk. 140		Perf. 14
1	A48	10c claret	9.00	*14.50*
2	A48	15c slate	9.00	*14.50*
3	A50	20c brown orange	9.00	*14.50*
4	A49	25c blue	9.00	*14.50*
5	A49	30c yellow brown	9.00	*14.50*
6	A49	50c violet	9.00	*14.50*
7	A49	60c carmine	9.00	*14.50*
8	A46	1 l brown & green	9.00	*14.50*
a.		Double overprint	150.00	
		Nos. 1-8 (8)	72.00	*116.00*
		Set, never hinged	140.00	

Superseded by postage stamps of Italy.

SAUDI ARABIA

ˈsau-dē ə-ˈrā-bē-ə

LOCATION — Southwestern Asia, on the Arabian Peninsula between the Red Sea and the Persian Gulf
GOVT. — Kingdom
AREA — 849,400 sq. mi.
POP. — 17,880,000 (1995 est.)
CAPITAL — Riyadh

In 1916 the Grand Sherif of Mecca declared the Sanjak of Hejaz independent of Turkish rule. In 1925, Ibn Saud, then Sultan of the Nejd, captured the Hejaz after a prolonged siege of Jedda, the last Hejaz stronghold.

The resulting Kingdom of the Hejaz and Nejd was renamed Saudi Arabia in 1932.

40 Paras = 1 Piaster = 1 Guerche (Garch, Qirsh)
11 Guerche = 1 Riyal (1928)
110 Guerche = 1 Sovereign (1931)
440 Guerche = 1 Sovereign (1952)
20 Piasters (Guerche) = 1 Riyal (1960)
100 Halalas = 1 Riyal (1976)

Catalogue values for unused stamps in this country are for Never Hinged items, beginning with Scott 178 in the regular postage section, Scott C1 in the airpost section, Scott J28 in the postage due section, Scott O7 in official section, and Scott RA6 in the postal tax section.

Watermarks

Wmk. 337- Crossed Swords and Palm Tree

Watermark lines are thicker than the paper.

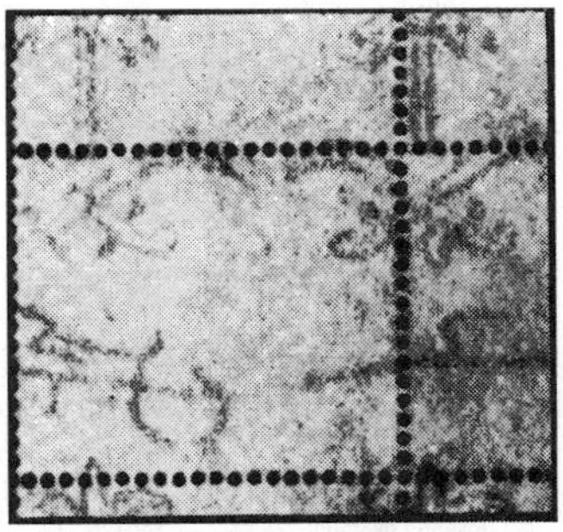

Wmk. 361- Crossed Swords, Palm Tree and Arabic Inscription

HEJAZ

Sherifate of Mecca

Adapted from Carved Door Panels of Mosque El Salih Talay, Cairo — A1

Taken from Page of Koran in Mosque of El Sultan Barquq, Cairo — A2

Taken from Details of an Ancient Prayer Niche in the Mosque of El Amri at Qus in Upper Egypt — A3

Perf. 10, 12

1916, Oct.		Unwmk.		Typo.
L1	A1	¼pi green	40.00	32.50
L2	A2	½pi red	40.00	30.00
a.		Perf. 10	110.00	90.00
L3	A3	1pi blue	11.00	11.00
a.		Perf. 12	140.00	140.00
b.		Perf. 10x12		775.00
		Nos. L1-L3 (3)	91.00	73.50

Exist imperf. Forged perf. exist.

See Nos. L5-L7, L10-L12. For overprints see Nos. L16-L18, L26-L28, L52-L54, L57-L59, L61-L66, L67, L70-L72, L77-L81, 37.

Central Design Adapted from a Koran Design for a Tomb. Background is from Stone Carving on Entrance Arch to the Ministry of Wakfs — A4

1916-17				Roulette 20
L4	A4	⅛pi orange ('17)	3.50	1.40
L5	A1	¼pi green	4.50	1.40
L6	A2	½pi red	5.50	1.40
L7	A3	1pi blue	5.50	1.40
		Nos. L4-L7 (4)	19.00	5.60

See #L9. For overprints & surcharge see #L15a, L16c, L17b, L18d, L25, L51, L56, L69, 33.

Adapted from Stucco Work above Entrance to Cairo R. R. Station A5

Adapted from First Page of the Koran of Sultan Farag — A6

1917				Serrate Roulette 13
L8	A5	1pa lilac brown	2.75	1.40
L9	A4	⅛pi orange	2.75	1.40
L10	A1	¼pi green	2.75	1.40
L11	A2	½pi red	2.75	1.40
L12	A3	1pi blue	2.75	1.40
L13	A6	2pi magenta	18.00	9.00
		Nos. L8-L13 (6)	31.75	16.00

Designs A1-A6 are inscribed "Hejaz Postage."

For overprints and surcharge see #L14-L31, L55-60, L62, L65--L75, L79a-81.

Kingdom of the Hejaz

Stamps of 1917-18 Overprinted in Black, Red or Brown:

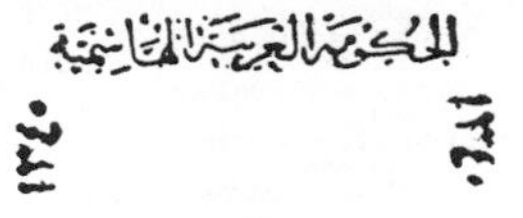

1921, Dec. 21				Serrate Roulette 13
L14	A5	1pa lilac brown	27.50	14.00
L15	A4	⅛pi orange	55.00	16.00
a.		Inverted overprint	90.00	
b.		Double overprint	175.00	
c.		Roulette 20	650.00	
d.		As "c," invtd. overprint	1,500.	*1,400.*
e.		Double overprint, one inverted	425.00	
f.		Double overprint, both inverted	425.00	
L16	A1	¼pi green	11.00	5.50
a.		Inverted overprint	90.00	
b.		Double overprint	175.00	
c.		Roulette 20	650.00	
d.		As "c," invtd. overprint	1,500.	
e.		Double overprint, one inverted	550.00	
f.		Double overprint, both inverted	150.00	
L17	A2	½pi red	14.00	6.75
a.		Inverted overprint	140.00	77.50
b.		Roulette 20	550.00	
c.		Double overprint	425.00	
d		Double overprint, both inverted	425.00	
L18	A3	1pi blue (R)	11.00	6.25
a.		Brown overprint	25.00	18.00
b.		Black overprint	32.50	27.50
c.		As "b," invtd. overprint	350.00	
d.		Roulette 20	625.00	
L19	A6	2pi magenta	16.00	9.00
a.		Double overprint	—	
		Nos. L14-L19 (6)	134.50	57.50

Nos. L15-L17, L18b and L19 exist with date (1340) omitted at left or right side.

Some values exist with gold overprint.

Forgeries of Nos. L14-L23 abound.

No. L14 With Additional Surcharge:

a b

L22	A5(a)	½pi on 1pa	325.00	125.00
L23	A5(b)	1pi on 1pa	325.00	125.00

Stamps of 1917-18 Overprinted in Black

1922, Jan. 7

L24 A5 1pa lilac brown 3.00 2.75
a. Inverted overprint 140.00
b. Double overprint 90.00
c. Double ovpt., one inverted 175.00
L25 A4 ⅛pi orange 9.00 6.25
a. Inverted overprint 90.00
b. Double ovpt., one inverted 175.00
L26 A1 ¼pi green 3.00 2.75
a. Inverted overprint 90.00
b. Double ovpt., one inverted 175.00
L27 A2 ½pi red 2.25 1.75
a. Inverted overprint 90.00
b. Double ovpt., one inverted 175.00
L28 A3 1pi blue 2.25 .80
a. Double overprint 80.00
b. Inverted overprint 140.00
L29 A6 2pi magenta 6.50 5.50
a. Double overprint 140.00

With Additional Surcharge of New Value

L30 A5(a) ½pi on 1pa lil brn 20.00 14.00
L31 A5(b) 1pi on 1pa lil brn 2.25 .90
a. Inverted surcharge 90.00
b. Double surcharge 80.00
c. Dbl. surch., one invtd., ovpt. invtd.
d. Inverted overprint 75.00
e. Inverted overprint and surcharge 210.00
f. Inverted overprint, double surcharge 210.00
g. Words of surcharge transposed 200.00
h. Overprint and surcharge inverted, words of surcharge transposed 400.00
i. Right hand character of surcharge inverted 75.00
Nos. L24-L31 (8) 48.25 34.70

The 1921 and 1922 overprints read: "The Government of Hashemite Arabia, 1340."

The overprint on No. L28 in red is bogus.

Forgeries abound.

Types A7 and A8

Very fine examples will be somewhat off center but perforations will be clear of the framelines.

Arms of Sherif of Mecca — A7

1922, Feb. Typo. *Perf. 11½*

L32 A7 ⅛pi red brown 1.75 .45
L34 A7 ½pi red 1.75 .45
L35 A7 1pi dark blue 1.75 .45
L36 A7 1½pi violet 1.75 .45
L37 A7 2pi orange 1.75 .45
L38 A7 3pi olive brown 1.75 .45
L39 A7 5pi olive green 1.75 .55
Nos. L32-L39 (7) 12.25 3.25

Numerous shades exist. Some values were printed in other colors in 1925 for handstamping by the Nejdi authorities in Mecca. These exist without handstamps.

Exist imperf.

Forgeries exist, usually perf. 11.

Reprints of Nos. L32, L35 exist; paper and shades differ.

See Nos. L48A-L49. For surcharges and overprints see Nos. L40-L48, L76, L82-L159, 7-20, 38A-48, 55A-58A, LJ11-LJ16, LJ26-LJ39, J1-J8, J10-J11, P1-P3, Jordan 64-72, 91, 103-120, J1-J17, O1.

Stamps of 1922 Surcharged with New Values in Arabic:

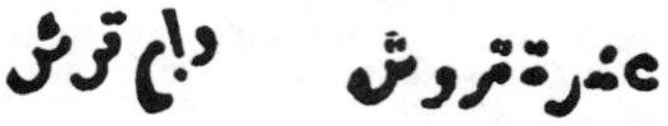

c d

1923

L40 A7(c) ¼pi on ⅛pi org brn 32.50 32.50
a. Double surcharge
b. Double inverted surcharge
c. Double surch., one invtd.
L41 A7(d) 10pi on 5pi ol grn 27.50 27.50
a. Double surch., one invtd.
b. Inverted surcharge

Forgeries exist.

Caliphate Issue

Stamps of 1922 Overprinted in Gold

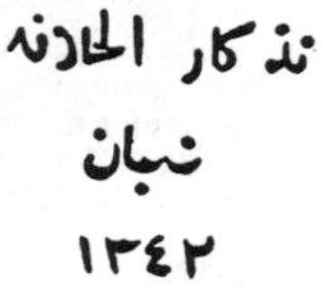

1924

L42 A7 ⅛pi orange brown 3.25
L43 A7 ½pi red 3.25
L44 A7 1pi dark blue 3.25
a. Inverted overprint 200.00
L45 A7 1½pi violet 3.25
L46 A7 2pi orange 3.25
a. Inverted overprint 200.00
L47 A7 3pi olive brown 3.50
L48 A7 5pi olive green 3.50
a. Inverted overprint 200.00
Nos. L42-L48 (7) 23.25

Assumption of the Caliphate by King Hussein in Mar., 1924. The overprint reads "In commemoration of the Caliphate, Shaaban, 1342."

The overprint was typographed in black and dusted with "gold" powder while wet. Inverted overprints on other values are forgeries. So-called black overprints are either forgeries or gold overprints with the gold rubbed off. No genuine black overprints are known.

The overprint is 18-20mm wide. The 1st setting of the ½p is 16mm.

Forgeries exist.

Nos. L43-L44, L46 exist with postage due overprint as on Nos. LJ11-LJ13.

Type of 1922 and

Arms of Sherif of Mecca — A8

1924 *Perf. 11½*

L48A A7 ¼pi yellow green 5.75 5.75
b. Tete beche pair 27.50
L49 A7 3pi brown red 9.00 9.00
a. 3pi dull red 4.50 4.50
L50 A8 10pi vio & dk brn 4.50 4.50
a. Center inverted 55.00 55.00
b. Center omitted 67.50
c. 10pi purple & sepia 4.50 4.50
Nos. L48A-L50 (3) 19.25 19.25

Nos. L48A, L50, L50a exist imperf.

Several printings of Nos. L48A-L50 exist; paper and shades differ.

Forgeries exist, usually perf. 11.

For overprint see Nos. L76A, Jordan 121.

Jedda Issues

Stamps of 1916-17 Overprinted

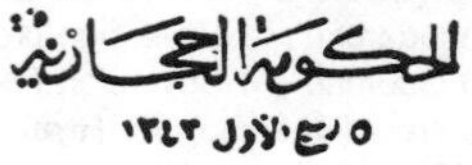

The control overprints on Nos. L51-L159 read: "Hukumat al Hejaziyeh, 5 Rabi al'awwal 1343"

(The Hejaz Government, October 4, 1924). This is the date of the accession of King Ali.

Counterfeits exist of all Jedda overprints.

Jedda issues were also used in Medina and Yambo.

Used values for #L51-L186 and LJ17-LJ39 are for genuine cancels. Privately applied cancels exist for "Mekke" (Mecca, bilingual or all Arabic), Khartoum, Cairo, as well as for Jeddah. Many private cancels have wrong dates, some as early as 1916. These are worth half the used values.

Red Overprint

1925, Jan. *Roulette 20*

L51 A4 ⅛pi orange 14.00 14.00
a. Inverted overprint 90.00
b. Ovptd. on face and back 175.00
c. Normal ovpt. on face, double ovpt. on back 200.00
L52 A1 ¼pi green 14.00 14.00
a. Inverted overprint 60.00
b. Double overprint 55.00
c. Double overprint, one invtd. 140.00
L53 A2 ½pi red 67.50 67.50
a. Inverted overprint 150.00
L54 A3 1pi blue 32.50 32.50
a. Inverted overprint 140.00
b. Double ovpt., one invtd. 125.00
Nos. L51-L53 (3) 95.50 95.50

Serrate Roulette 13

L55 A5 1pa lilac brown 12.50 12.50
a. Inverted overprint 67.50
b. Double overprint 60.00
c. Ovptd. on face and back 175.00
d. Normal ovpt. on face, double ovpt on back 125.00
L56 A4 ⅛pi orange 35.00 35.00
a. Inverted overprint 80.00
L57 A1 ¼pi green 20.00 20.00
a. Pair, one without overprint 1,600.
b. Inverted overprint 45.00
c. Double ovpt., one inverted 275.00
L58 A2 ½pi red 27.50 27.50
a. Inverted overprint 140.00
L59 A3 1pi blue 32.50 32.50
a. Inverted overprint 100.00
L60 A6 2pi magenta 35.00 35.00
a. Inverted overprint 140.00
Nos. L55-L60 (6) 162.50 162.50

Gold Overprint

Roulette 20

L61 A1 ¼pi green, gold on red ovpt. 1,500.
a. Gold on blue ovpt. 3,000. 2,250.

Serrate Roulette 13

L62 A1 ¼pi green, gold on red ovpt. 22.50 22.50
a. Inverted overprint 100.00

The overprint on No. L61 was typographed in red or blue (No. L62 only in red) and dusted with "gold" powder while wet.

Blue Overprint

Roulette 20

L63 A1 ¼pi green 75.00 22.50
a. Inverted overprint 150.00
b. Ovptd. on face and back 175.00
L64 A2 ½pi red, invtd. ovpt. 80.00 80.00
a. Upright overprint 140.00

Serrate Roulette 13

L65 A1 ¼pi green 16.00 16.00
a. Inverted overprint 67.50
b. Vertical overprint 900.00
L66 A2 ½pi red 27.50 27.50
a. Inverted overprint 90.00
L66B A6 2pi mag, invtd. ovpt. 1,400.

Blue overprint on Nos. L4, L8, L9 are bogus.

Same Overprint in Blue on Provisional Stamps of 1922

Overprinted on No. L17

L67 A2 ½pi red 2,500.

Overprinted on Nos. L24-L29

L68 A5 1pa lilac brn 160.00 160.00
L69 A4 ⅛pi orange 2,500. 1,800.
a. Inverted overprint
L70 A1 ¼pi green 65.00 65.00
a. Inverted overprint 725.00
L71 A2 ½pi red 85.00 85.00
a. Inverted overprint 800.00
L72 A3 1pi blue 110.00 110.00
L73 A6 2pi magenta 160.00 160.00
a. Inverted overprint 1,400.

Same Overprint on Nos. L30 and L31

L74 A5(a) ½pi on 1pa 90.00 90.00
L75 A5(b) 1pi on 1pa 75.00 75.00
a. Inverted overprint 575.00

Same Overprint in Blue Vertically, Reading Up or Down, on Stamps of 1922-24

Perf. 11½

L76 A7 ½pi red 900.00 900.00
L76A A8 10pi vio & dk brn 1,800. 1,800.

Nos. L5, L10 Overprinted Reading Up in Blue or Red (Overprint reads up in illustration)

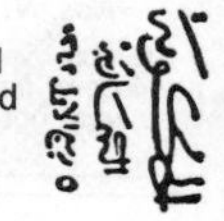

Roulette 20

L77a A1 ¼pi green (Bl) 500.00 500.00
L78 A1 ¼pi green (R) 450.00 450.00

Serrate Roulette 13

L79a A1 ¼pi green (Bl) 300.00 300.00
L80 A1 ¼pi green (R) 60.00 60.00

Overprint Reading Down

Roulette 20

L77 A1 ¼pi green (Bl) 175.00 175.00

Serrate Roulette 13

L79 A1 ¼pi green (Bl) 90.00 90.00
L80a A1 ¼pi green (R) 200.00 200.00

Nos. L10, L32-L39, L48A, L49a, L50 Overprinted

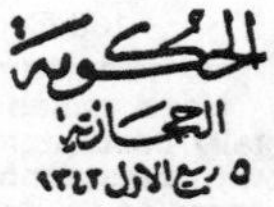

Serrate Roulette 13

Red Overprint (vertical)

L81 A1 ¼pi green 1,200.

Overprint on No. L81 also exists horizontal and inverted.

Perf. 11½

Blue Overprint

L82 A7 ⅛pi red brown 5.50 5.50
a. Inverted overprint 45.00
L83 A7 ½pi red 7.25 7.25
a. Double overprint 67.50
b. Inverted overprint 45.00 45.00
c. Double ovpt., one invtd. 67.50
d. Overprint reading up
L84 A7 1pi dark blue 350.00
a. Inverted overprint 350.00
L85 A7 1½pi violet 11.00 11.00
a. Inverted overprint 45.00 45.00
L86 A7 2pi orange 11.00 11.00
a. Double ovpt., one invtd. 67.50
b. Inverted overprint 45.00
c. Double overprint 67.50
L87 A7 3pi olive brown 9.00 9.00
a. Inverted overprint 45.00
b. Double ovpt., one invtd. 67.50
c. Overprint reading up 160.00
d. Dbl. ovpt., both invtd. 90.00
L88 A7 3pi dull red 11.00 11.00
a. Inverted overprint 45.00
b. Double ovpt., one invtd. 67.50
L89 A7 5pi olive green 11.00 11.00
a. Inverted overprint 45.00

Some values exist in pairs, one without overprint.

Black Overprint

L90 A7 ⅛pi red brown 45.00
a. Inverted overprint 140.00
L91 A7 ½pi red 4.50 4.50
a. Inverted overprint 60.00
L92 A7 1pi dark blue 350.00
a. Inverted overprint 350.00
L93 A7 1½pi violet 12.00 12.00
a. Inverted overprint 67.50
L94 A7 2pi orange 7.25 7.25
a. Inverted overprint 45.00
L95 A7 3pi olive brown 5.50 5.50
a. Inverted overprint 67.50 67.50
L96 A7 3pi dull red 7.25 7.25
a. Inverted overprint 45.00

L97 A7 5pi olive green 9.00 *9.00*
a. Inverted overprint 45.00

Red Overprint

L98 A7 ⅛pi red brn, invtd. *725.00*
L99 A7 ¼pi yellow grn 16.00 *16.00*
a. Tête bêche pair 62.50
b. Inverted overprint 45.00
c. Tête bêche pair, one with inverted overprint 75.00
L100 A7 ½pi red *1,000.* *500.00*
a. Inverted overprint *1,000.* *500.00*
L101 A7 1pi dark blue 8.00 *8.00*
a. Inverted overprint 45.00
b. Double ovpt., one invtd. 32.50
L102 A7 1½pi violet 4.50 *4.50*
a. Inverted overprint 45.00
L103 A7 2pi orange 12.00 *12.00*
a. Inverted overprint 45.00
b. Overprint reading up 160.00
L104 A7 3pi olive brown 12.00 *12.00*
a. Inverted overprint 45.00
L105 A7 3pi dull red, invtd. *1,500.*
L106 A7 5pi olive green 7.25 *7.25*
a. Inverted overprint 45.00
b. Overprint reading up
c. Overprint reading down
L107 A8 10pi vio & dk brn 16.00 *16.00*
a. Inverted overprint 45.00
b. Center inverted 90.00
c. As "b," invtd. ovpt. *140.00*

Nos. L98, L105 with normal overprint are fakes.

Gold Overprint

L108 A7 ⅛pi red brown 27.50 *27.50*
L109 A7 ½pi red 27.50 *27.50*
L110 A7 1pi dark blue 27.50 *27.50*
L111 A7 1½pi violet 110.00 *110.00*
L112 A7 2pi orange 90.00 *90.00*
L113 A7 3pi olive brown 35.00 *35.00*
L114 A7 3pi dull red 100.00 *100.00*
L115 A7 5pi olive green 85.00 *85.00*
Nos. L108-L115 (8) 502.50 *502.50*

Inverted overprints are forgeries.

Same Overprint on Nos. L42-L48

Blue Overprint

L116 A7 ⅛pi red brown 42.50 *42.50*
a. Double ovpt., one invtd. *275.00*
L117 A7 ½pi red 80.00 *80.00*
L118 A7 1pi dark blue 55.00 *55.00*
L119 A7 1½pi violet 65.00 *65.00*
L120 A7 2pi orange 275.00 *275.00*
a. Inverted overprint *425.00*
L121 A7 3pi olive brown 110.00 *110.00*
a. Inverted overprint *175.00*
L122 A7 5pi olive green 37.50 *37.50*
a. Inverted overprint *200.00*
Nos. L116-L122 (7) 665.00 *665.00*

Black Overprint

L123 A7 ⅛pi red brown 42.50 *42.50*
a. Inverted overprint *225.00*
L125 A7 1½pi violet 140.00 *140.00*
a. Inverted overprint *225.00*
L127 A7 3pi olive brown 110.00 *110.00*
a. Inverted overprint *225.00*
L128 A7 5pi olive green 140.00 *140.00*
a. Inverted overprint *225.00*
Nos. L123-L128 (4) 432.50 *432.50*

Red Overprint

L129 A7 1pi dark blue 90.00 *90.00*
L130 A7 1½pi violet 110.00 *110.00*
L131 A7 2pi orange 90.00 *90.00*
Nos. L129-L131 (3) 290.00 *290.00*

Overprints on stamps or in colors other than those listed are forgeries.

Stamps of 1922-24 Surcharged

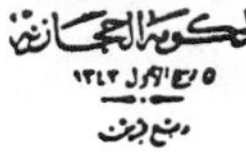

a

and Handstamp Surcharged

b — 1/4pi 

b — 1pi b — 10pi

1925 Litho. *Perf. 11½*

L135 A7 ¼pi on ¼pi on ⅛pi red brn 47.50 *47.50*
b. 1pi on ¼pi on ⅛pi red brown
L136 A7 ¼pi on ¼pi on ½pi red 30.00 *30.00*
c. 1pi on ¼pi on ½pi 55.00 *55.00*
L138 A7 1pi on 1pi on 2pi orange 30.00 *30.00*
a. ¼pi on ¼pi on 2pi org
b. 10pi on 1pi on 2pi org 90.00
c. ¼pi on 1pi on 2pi org 45.00
d. 1pi on ¼pi on 2pi org *90.00*
L139 A7 1pi on 1pi on 3pi ol brn 22.50 *22.50*
L140 A7 1pi on 1pi on 3pi dl red 35.00 *35.00*
b. ¼pi on 1pi on 3pi dl red
L141 A7 10pi on 10pi on 5pi ol grn 16.00 *16.00*
b. 1pi on 10 pi on 5 pi
Nos. L135-L141 (6) 181.00 *181.00*

The printed surcharge (a) reads "The Hejaz Government. October 4, 1924." with new denomination in third line. This surcharge alone was used for the first issue (Nos. L135a-L141a). The new denomination was so small and indistinct that its equivalent in larger characters was soon added by handstamp (b) at bottom of each stamp for the second issue (Nos. L135-L141).

The handstamped surcharge (b) is found double, inverted, etc. It is also known in dark violet.

Without Handstamp "b"

L135a A7 ¼pi on ⅛pi red brn 90.00
L136b A7 ¼pi on ½pi red 90.00
L138e A7 1pi on 2pi orange 90.00
L139a A7 1pi on 3pi olive brn 90.00
L140a A7 1pi on 3pi dull red 90.00
L141a A7 10pi on 5pi olive grn 90.00
Nos. L135a-L141a (6) 540.00

Stamps of 1922-24 Surcharged

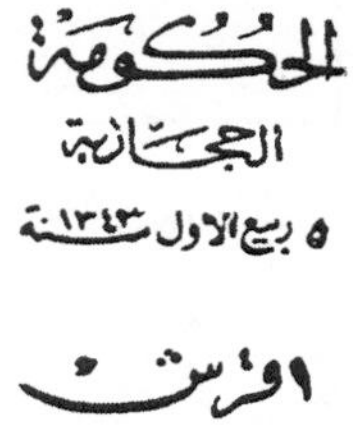

Black Surcharge

L142 A7 ⅛pi on ½pi red 7.25 *7.25*
a. Inverted surcharge 35.00
L143 A7 ¼pi on ½pi red 7.25 *7.25*
a. Inverted surcharge 35.00
L144 A7 1pi on ½pi red 7.25 *7.25*
a. Inverted surcharge 22.50
L145 A7 1pi on 1½pi vio 7.25 *7.25*
a. Inverted surcharge 32.50
L146 A7 1pi on 2pi org 7.25 *7.25*
a. "10pi" 77.50
b. Inverted surcharge 35.00
c. As "a," inverted surcharge 130.00
L147 A7 1pi on 3pi olive brn 7.25 *7.25*
a. "10pi" 67.50
b. Inverted surcharge 45.00
c. As "a," inverted surcharge 130.00
L148 A7 10pi on 5pi olive grn 14.00 *14.00*
a. Inverted surcharge 60.00
Nos. L142-L148 (7) 57.50 *57.50*

Blue Surcharge

L149 A7 ⅛pi on ½pi red 11.00 *11.00*
a. Inverted surcharge 60.00
b. Double surcharge 200.00
L150 A7 ¼pi on ½pi red 11.00 *11.00*
a. Inverted surcharge 45.00
L151 A7 1pi on ½pi red 11.00 *11.00*
a. Inverted surcharge 45.00
b. Double surcharge
L152 A7 1pi on 1½pi vio 11.00 *11.00*
a. Inverted surcharge 60.00
L153 A7 1pi on 2pi org 11.00 *11.00*
a. "10pi" 62.50
b. Inverted surcharge 60.00
L154 A7 1pi on 3pi olive brn 22.50 *22.50*
a. "10pi" 77.50
b. Inverted surcharge 62.50
L155 A7 10pi on 5pi olive grn 25.00 *25.00*
a. Inverted surcharge 55.00
Nos. L149-L155 (7) 102.50 *102.50*

Red Surcharge

L156 A7 1pi on 1½pi vio 22.50 *22.50*
a. Inverted surcharge 72.50
L157 A7 1pi on 2pi org 22.50 *22.50*
a. "10pi" 72.50
b. Inverted surcharge 72.50
L158 A7 1pi on 3pi olive brn 22.50 *22.50*
a. "10pi" 90.00
b. Inverted surcharge 72.50
L159 A7 10pi on 5pi olive grn 22.50 *22.50*
a. Inverted surcharge 72.50
Nos. L156-L159 (4) 90.00 *90.00*
Nos. L142-L159 (18) 250.00 *250.00*

The "10pi" surcharge is found inverted on Nos. L146a, L147a. The existence of genuine inverted "10pi" surcharges on Nos. L153a, L154a, L157a and L158a is in doubt.

The 10pi on 1½pi is bogus.

King Ali Issue

A9

A10

A11

A12

1925, May-June *Perf. 11½*

Black Overprint

L160 A9 ⅛pi chocolate 1.50 *1.50*
L161 A9 ¼pi ultra 1.50 *1.50*
L162 A9 ½pi car rose 1.50 *1.50*
L163 A10 1pi yellow green 1.75 *1.75*
L164 A10 1½pi orange 1.75 *1.75*
L165 A10 2pi blue 2.25 *2.25*
L166 A11 3pi dark green 2.25 *2.25*
L167 A11 5pi orange brn 2.25 *2.25*
L168 A12 10pi red & green 4.50 *4.50*
a. Center inverted 67.50
Nos. L160-L168 (9) 19.25 *19.25*

Red Overprint

L169 A9 ⅛pi chocolate 2.75 *2.75*
L170 A9 ¼pi ultra 1.60 *1.60*
L171 A10 1pi yellow green 2.00 *2.00*
L172 A10 1½pi orange 2.00 *2.00*
L173 A10 2pi deep blue 2.50 *2.50*
L174 A11 3pi dark green 2.75 *2.75*
a. Horiz. pair, imperf. vert.
L175 A11 5pi org brn 2.75 *2.75*
L176 A12 10pi red & green 5.50 *5.50*
Nos. L169-L176 (8) 21.85 *21.85*

Blue Overprint

L177 A9 ⅛pi chocolate 1.75 *1.75*
L179 A9 ½pi car rose 1.75 *1.75*
L180 A10 1pi yellow green 1.75 *1.75*
L181 A10 1½pi orange 1.75 *1.75*
L182 A11 3pi dark green 1.75 *1.75*
L183 A11 5pi orange brn 5.50 *5.50*
L184 A12 10pi red & green 7.25 *7.25*
L185 A12 10pi red & org 275.00
Nos. L177-L184 (7) 21.50 *21.50*

Without Overprint

L186 A12 10pi red & green 6.75 *6.75*
a. Dbl. impression of center *90.00*

The overprint in the tablets on Nos. L160-L185 reads: "5 Rabi al'awwal, 1343" (Oct. 5, 1924), the date of the accession of King Ali.

The tablet overprints vary slightly in size. Each is found reading upward or downward and at either side of the stamp. These control overprints were first applied in Jedda by the government press.

They were later made from new plates by the stamp printer in Cairo. In the Jedda overprint, the bar over the "0" figure extends to the left.

Some values exist with 13m or 15mm instead of 18mm between tablets. They sell for more. The lines of the Cairo overprinting are generally wider, but more lightly printed, usually appearing slightly grayish and the bar is at center right. The Cairo overprints are believed not to have been placed in use.

Imperforates exist.

Nos. L160-L168 are known with the overprints spaced as on type D3 and aligned horizontally.

Copies of these stamps (perforated or imperforate) without the overprint, except No. L186 were not regularly issued and not available for postage.

No. L185 exists only with Cairo overprint. Imperfs of No. L185 sell for much less than No. L185. Fake perfs have been added to the imperfs.

The ¼pi with blue overprint is bogus.

No. L186 in other colors are color trials.

For overprints see #58B-58D, Jordan 122-129.

NEJDI ADMINISTRATION OF HEJAZ

Handstamped in Blue, Red, Black or Violet

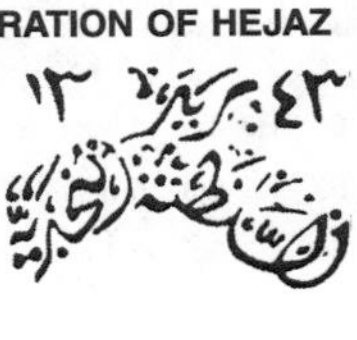

The overprint reads: "1343. Barid al Sultanat an Nejdia" (1925. Post of the Sultanate of Nejd).

The overprints on this and succeeding issues are handstamped and, as usual, are found double, inverted, etc. These variations are scarce.

1925, Mar.-Apr. Unwmk. *Perf. 12*

On Stamp of Turkey, 1915, With Crescent and Star in Red

1 A22 5pa ocher (Bl) 35.00 27.50
2 A22 5pa ocher (R) 22.50 20.00
3 A22 5pa ocher (Bk) 27.50 22.50
4 A22 5pa ocher (V) 22.50 18.00

On Stamp of Turkey, 1913

5 A28 10pa green (Bl) 20.00 16.00
6 A28 10pa green (R) 16.00 12.50

On Stamps of Hejaz, 1922-24
Perf. 11½

7 A7 ⅛pi red brn (R) 22.50 22.50
8 A7 ⅛pi red brn (Bk) 32.50 32.50
9 A7 ⅛pi red brn (V) 22.50 22.50
10 A7 ⅛pi car (R) 27.50 27.50
11 A7 ⅛pi car (Bk) 32.50 32.50
12 A7 ⅛pi car (V) *25.00* *25.00*
13 A7 ½pi red (Bl) 20.00 20.00
14 A7 ½pi red (V) 16.00 16.00
15 A7 1½pi vio (R) 22.50 22.50
16 A7 2pi yel buff (R) 55.00 55.00
a. 2pi orange (R) 35.00
17 A7 2pi yel buff (V) 55.00 55.00
a. 2pi orange (V) 32.50 32.50
18 A7 3pi brn red (Bl) 27.50 27.50
19 A7 3pi brn red (R) 20.00 20.00
20 A7 3pi brn red (V) 22.50 22.50

Many Hejaz stamps of the 1922 type were especially printed for this and following issues. The re-impressions are usually more clearly printed, in lighter shades than the 1922 stamps, and some are in new colors.

Counterfeits exist.

Arabic Inscriptions

R1 R2

On Hejaz Bill Stamp

22 R1 1pi violet (R) 14.00 14.00

On Hejaz Notarial Stamps

23 R2 1pi violet (R) 18.00 18.00
24 R2 2pi blue (R) 27.50 27.50
25 R2 2pi blue (V) 25.00 25.00

For overprint see No. 49.

Locomotive — R3

On Hejaz Railway Tax Stamps

26 R3 1pi blue (R) 35.00 9.00
27 R3 2pi ocher (R) 42.50 14.00
28 R3 2pi ocher (V) 35.00 14.00
29 R3 3pi lilac (R) 35.00 20.00
Nos. 1-20,22-29 (28) 776.50 659.00

There are two types of the basic stamps. The difference is in the locomotive.

For overprints and surcharges see Nos. 34, 50-54, 55, 59-68, J12-J15.

Pilgrimage Issue

Various Stamps Handstamp Surcharged in Blue and Red in Types "a" and "b" and with Tablets with New Values

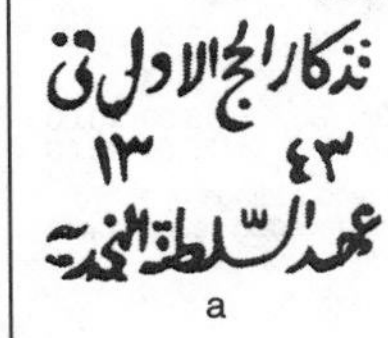 

a b

Surcharge "a" reads: "Tezkar al Hajj al Awwal Fi 'ahd al Sultanat al Nejdia, 1343" (Commemorating the first pilgrimage under the Nejdi Sultanate, 1925).
"b" reads: "Al Arba" (Wednesday.)

1925, July 1 *Perf. 12*

On Stamps of Turkey, 1913

30 A28 1pi on 10pa grn (Bl & R) 67.50 55.00
31 A30 5pi on 1pi bl (Bl & R) 67.50 55.00

On Stamps of Hejaz, 1917-18

Serrate Roulette 13

32 A5 2pi on 1pa lil brn (R & Bl) 85.00 67.50
33 A4 4pi on ⅛pi org (R & Bl) 325.00 325.00

On Hejaz Railway Tax Stamp

Perf. 11½

34 R3 3pi lilac (Bl & R) 67.50 35.00
Nos. 30-34 (5) 612.50 537.50

No. 30 with handstamp "a" in black was a favor item. Nos. 30 and 33 with both handstamps in red is a forgery.

Handstamped in Blue, Red, Black or Violet

This overprint has practically the same meaning as that described over No. 1. The Mohammedan year (1343) is omitted.
This handstamp is said to be in private hands at this time. Extreme caution is advised before buying rare items.

1925, July-Aug. *Perf. 12*

On Stamp of Turkey, 1915, with Crescent and Star in Red

35 A22 5pa ocher (Bl) 22.50 22.50

On Stamps of Turkey, 1913

36 A28 10pa green (Bl) 18.00 18.00
a. Black overprint 72.50

On Stamps of Hejaz, 1922 (Nos. L28-L29)

Serrate Roulette 13

37 A3 1pi blue (R) 55.00 *67.50*
38 A6 2pi magenta (Bl) 55.00 *67.50*

On Stamps of Hejaz, 1922-24

Perf. 11½

38A A7 ⅛pi red brn (Bk) *4,250.*
38B A7 ⅛pi red brn (Bl) *3,500.*
39 A7 ½pi red (Bl) 9.00 9.00
a. Imperf., pair 22.50 22.50
39B A7 ½pi red (Bk) 18.00 18.00
c. Imperf., pair 37.50 37.50
40 A7 1pi gray vio (R) 27.50 27.50
a. 1pi black violet (R) *40.00*
41 A7 1½pi dk red (Bk) 27.50 27.50
a. 1½pi brick red (Bk) 45.00
42 A7 2pi yel buff (Bl) 45.00 45.00
a. 2pi orange (Bl) 55.00 55.00
43 A7 2pi deep vio (Bl) 50.00 50.00
44 A7 3pi brown red (Bl) 27.50 27.50
45 A7 5pi scarlet (Bl) 35.00 35.00
Nos. 35-38,39-45 (12) 390.00 *415.00*

Overprint on Nos. 38A, 39B, 39C is blue-black.
See note above No. 35.

With Additional Surcharge of New Value Typo. in Black:

c: قرش واحد
d: قرش ونصف
e: ، قرشان

Color in parenthesis is that of overprint on basic stamp.

46 A7(c) 1pi on ½pi (Bl) 9.00 1.75
a. Imperf, pair 27.50
b. Ovpt. & surch. inverted
47 A7(d) 1½pi on ½pi (Bl) 13.00 7.25
a. Imperf., pair 27.50
b. Black overprint 18.00
48 A7(e) 2pi on 3pi (Bl) 13.00 13.00
Nos. 46-48 (3) 35.00 22.00

Several variations in type settings of "c," "d" and "e" exist, including inverted letters and values.

On Hejaz Notarial Stamp

49 R2 2pi blue (Bk) 18.00 18.00

On Hejaz Railway Tax Stamps

50 R3 1pi blue (R) 22.50 22.50
51 R3 1pi blue (Bk) 27.50 9.00
52 R3 2pi ocher (Bl) 25.00 9.00
53 R3 3pi lilac (Bl) 20.00 20.00
54 R3 5pi green (Bl) 18.00 18.00
Nos. 49-54 (6) 131.00 96.50

Hejaz Railway Tax Stamp Handstamped in Black

السعوده
السلطنه النجديه

This overprint reads: "Al Saudia. - Al Sultanat al Nejdia." (The Saudi Sultanate of Nejd.)

1925-26

55 R3 1pi blue *160.00*

On Nos. L34, L36-L37, L41

55A A7 ½ pi red *325.00*
56 A7 1½pi violet *325.00*
a. Violet overprint *325.00*
57 A7 2pi orange *325.00*
57A A7 10pi on 5pi ol grn *325.00*

On Nos. L95 and L97

Color in parentheses is that of rectangular overprint on basic stamp

58 A7 3pi olive brn (Bk) *325.00*
58A A7 5pi olive grn (Bk) *325.00*

On Nos. L162-L163, L173

Perf. 11½

58B A9 ½pi car rose (Bk) *325.00*
58C A10 1pi yel grn (Bk) *190.00*
58D A10 2pi blue (R) *325.00*

Nos. 55-58D were provisionally issued at Medina after its capitulation.
This overprint exists on Nos. L160-L161, L164-L172, L174-L175, L180-L183. These 17 are known as bogus items, but may exist genuine.
Lithographed overprints are forgeries.
The illustrated overprint is not genuine.

Medina Issue

Hejaz Railway Tax Stamps Handstamped

and Handstamp Surcharged in Various Colors

The large overprint reads: "The Nejdi Posts - 1344 - Commemorating Medina, the Illustrious." The tablet shows the new value.

1925

59 R3 1pi on 10pi vio (Bk & V) 45.00 55.00
60 R3 2pi on 50pi lt bl (R & Bl) 45.00 55.00
61 R3 3pi on 100pi red brn (Bl & Bk) 45.00 55.00
62 R3 4pi on 500pi dull red (Bl & Bk) 45.00 55.00
63 R3 5pi on 1000pi dp red (Bl & Bk) 45.00 55.00
Nos. 59-63 (5) 225.00 275.00

Jedda Issue

Hejaz Railway Tax Stamps Handstamped and Tablet with New Value in Various Colors

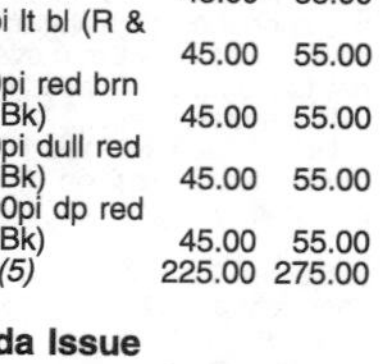

This handstamp reads: "Commemorating Jedda - 1344 - The Nejdi Posts."

1925

64 R3 1pi on 10pi vio (Bk & Bl) 55.00 55.00
65 R3 2pi on 50pi lt bl (R & Bk) 55.00 55.00
66 R3 3pi on 100pi red brn (R & Bl) 55.00 55.00
67 R3 4pi on 500pi dl red (Bk & Bl) 55.00 55.00
68 R3 5pi on 1000pi dp red (Bk & Bl) 55.00 55.00
Nos. 64-68 (5) 275.00 275.00

Nos. 59-63 and 64-68 were prepared in anticipation of the surrender of Medina and Jedda.

Kingdom of Hejaz-Nejd

Arabic Inscriptions and Value — A1

A2

Inscriptions in upper tablets: "Barid al Hejaz wa Nejd" (Posts of the Hejaz and Nejd)

1926, Feb. Typo. Unwmk. *Perf. 11*

69 A1 ¼pi violet 11.00 8.25
70 A1 ½pi gray 11.00 8.25
71 A1 1pi deep blue 14.00 10.00
72 A2 2pi blue green 12.00 8.25
73 A2 3pi carmine 14.00 9.00
74 A2 5pi maroon 7.50 5.75
Nos. 69-74 (6) 69.50 49.50

Nos. 69-71, 74 exist imperf. Value, each $30.
Used values are for favor cancels.

1926, Mar. *Perf. 11*

75 A1 ¼pi orange 5.75 3.25
76 A1 ½pi blue green 2.25 1.40
77 A1 1pi carmine 1.75 1.10
78 A2 2pi violet 2.25 1.40
79 A2 3pi dark blue 2.25 1.40
80 A2 5pi lt brown 5.75 3.25
a. 5pi olive brown
Nos. 75-80 (6) 20.00 11.80

Nos. 75-80 also exist with perf. 14, 14x11, 11x14 and imperf. All of these sell for 10 times the values quoted.
Counterfeits of types A1 and A2 are perf. 11½. They exist with and without overprints.
Types A1 and A2 in colors other than listed are proofs.

Pan-Islamic Congress Issue

Stamps of 1926 Handstamped

1926 *Perf. 11*

92 A1 ¼pi orange 4.75 2.75
93 A1 ½pi blue green 4.75 2.75
94 A1 1pi carmine 4.75 2.75
95 A2 2pi violet 4.75 2.75
96 A2 3pi dark blue 4.75 2.75
97 A2 5pi light brown 4.75 2.75
Nos. 92-97 (6) 28.50 16.50

The overprint reads: "al Mootamar al Islami 20 Zilkada, Sanat 1344." (The Islamic Congress, June 1, 1926.)
See counterfeit note after No. 80.

Tughra of King Abdul Aziz — A3

1926-27 Typo. *Perf. 11½*

98 A3 ⅛pi ocher 3.25 .45
99 A3 ¼pi gray green 3.50 1.10
100 A3 ½pi dull red 3.50 1.10
101 A3 1pi deep violet 3.50 1.10
102 A3 1½pi gray blue 11.00 1.75
103 A3 3pi olive green 9.00 3.50
104 A3 5pi brown orange 18.00 4.00
105 A3 10pi dark brown 55.00 5.50
Nos. 98-105 (8) 106.75 18.50

Inscription at top reads: "Al Hukumat al Arabia" (The Arabian Government). Inscription below tughra reads: "Barid al Hejaz wa Nejd" (Post of the Hejaz and Nejd).

Stamps of 1926-27 Handstamped in Black or Red

1927

107 A3 ⅛pi ocher 11.00 4.50
108 A3 ¼pi gray grn 11.00 4.50
109 A3 ½pi dull red 11.00 4.50
110 A3 1pi deep violet 11.00 4.50
111 A3 1½pi gray bl (R) 11.00 4.50
112 A3 3pi olive green 11.00 4.50
113 A3 5pi brown orange 11.00 4.50
114 A3 10pi dark brown 11.00 4.50
Nos. 107-114 (8) 88.00 36.00

The overprint reads: "In commemoration of the Kingdom of Nejd and Dependencies, 25th Rajab 1345."
Inverted varieties have not been authenticated.

Turkey No. 258 Surcharged in Violet

قرش واحد

1925 *Perf. 12*

115 A28 1g on 10pa green

Similar surcharges of 6g and 20g were made in red, but were not known to have been issued.

A4

A5

1929-30 Typo. *Perf. 11½*

117 A4 1¾g gray blue 18.00 2.25
119 A4 20g violet 22.50 5.00
120 A4 30g green 35.00 11.00

1930 *Perf. 11, 11½*

125 A5 ½g rose 14.00 2.75
126 A5 1½g violet 14.00 1.75
127 A5 1¾g ultra 14.00 2.25
128 A5 3½g emerald 14.00 3.50

Perf. 11

129 A5 5g black brown 22.50 5.50
Nos. 125-129 (5) 78.50 15.75

Anniversary of King Ibn Saud's accession to the throne of the Hejaz, January 8, 1926.

A6

A7

1931-32 *Perf. 11½*

130 A6 ⅛g ocher ('32) 12.50 2.25
131 A6 ¼g blue green 12.50 1.75
133 A6 1¾g ultra 16.00 2.25
Nos. 130-133 (3) 41.00 6.25

1932 *Perf. 11½*

135 A7 ¼g blue green 5.50 1.75
a. Perf 11
136 A7 ½g scarlet 16.00 2.75
a. Perf 11
137 A7 2¼g ultra 37.50 4.50
a. Perf 11
Nos. 135-137 (3) 59.00 9.00

Kingdom of Saudi Arabia

A8

1934, Jan. *Perf. 11½, Imperf.*

138 A8 ⅛g yellow green 7.25 7.25
139 A8 ¼g red 7.25 7.25
140 A8 1½g light blue 14.00 14.00
141 A8 3g blue green 14.00 14.00

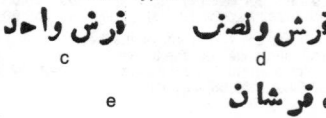

142 A8 3½g ultra 25.00 5.50
143 A8 5g yellow 32.50 27.50
144 A8 10g red orange 60.00
145 A8 20g bright violet 77.50
146 A8 ¼s claret 150.00
147 A8 30g dull violet 90.00
148 A8 ½s chocolate 325.00
149 A8 1s violet brown 675.00
Nos. 138-149 (12) 1,477.

Proclamation of Emir Saud as Heir Apparent of Arabia. Perf. and imperf. stamps were issued in equal quantities.

Favor cancels exist on Nos. 144-149.

Tughra of King Abdul Aziz — A9

1934-57 ***Perf. 11, 11½***

159 A9 ⅛g yellow 3.25 .35
160 A9 ¼g yellow grn 3.25 .35
161 A9 ½g rose red ('43) 2.50 .20
a. ½g dark carmine 12.00 1.40
162 A9 ⅞g lt blue ('56) 4.00 .45
163 A9 1g blue green 3.25 .35
164 A9 2g olive grn ('57) 6.50 1.75
a. 2g olive bister ('57) 25.00 7.25
165 A9 2⅞g violet ('57) 4.00 .45
166 A9 3g ultra ('38) 4.00 .20
a. 3g light blue 20.00 1.75
167 A9 3½g lt ultra 16.00 1.75
168 A9 5g orange 4.00 .45
169 A9 10g violet 14.00 1.40
170 A9 20g purple brn 20.00 .90
a. 20g purple black 20.00 2.25
171 A9 100g red vio ('42) 65.00 4.00
172 A9 200g vio brn ('42) 80.00 5.50
Nos. 159-172 (14) 229.75 18.10

The ½g has two types differing in position of the tughra.

No. 162 measures 31x22mm. No. 164 30½x21½mm. No. 165, 30½x22mm. No. 166 30x21mm. No. 171, 31x22mm. No. 172, 30½x21½mm. Rest of set, 29x20½mm. Grayish paper was used in 1946-49 printings.

No. 168 exists with pin-perf 6.

For overprint see No. J24.

Yanbu Harbor near Radwa — A10

1945 **Typo.** ***Perf. 11½***

173 A10 ½g brt carmine 5.75 .25
174 A10 3g lt ultra 7.50 .90
175 A10 5g purple 22.50 1.10
176 A10 10g dk brown vio 50.00 2.75
Nos. 173-176 (4) 85.75 5.00

Meeting of King Abdul Aziz and King Farouk of Egypt at Jebal Radwa, Saudi Arabia, Jan. 24, 1945.

Catalogue values for unused stamps in this section, from this point to the end of the section, are for Never Hinged items.

Arms of Saudi Arabia and Afghanistan A12

1950, Mar. ***Perf. 11***

178 A12 ½g carmine 6.75 .90
179 A12 3g violet blue 11.00 .90

Visit of Zahir Shah of Afghanistan, March 1950. One 3g in each sheet inscribed POSTFS, value $45.

Old City Walls, Riyadh A13

1950

Center in Red Brown

180 A13 ½g magenta 3.50 .20
181 A13 1g lt blue 6.75 .20
182 A13 3g violet 10.00 .45
183 A13 5g vermilion 22.50 .90
184 A13 10g green 40.00 2.25
a. Singular "guerche" in Arabic 275.00 35.00
Nos. 180-184 (5) 82.75 4.00

50th lunar anniversary of King Ibn Saud's capture of Riyadh, Jan. 16, 1902.

No. 184a: On the 3g, 5g and 10g the currency is expressed in the plural in both French (grouche) and Arabic. One stamp in each sheet of 20 (4x5), position 11, of the 10g shows the Arabic characters in the singular form of "guerche," as on the ½g and 1g.

Arms of Saudi Arabia and Jordan — A14

1951, Nov. ***Perf. 11***

185 A14 ½g carmine 5.75 .90
a. "BOYAUME" 250.00
186 A14 3g violet blue 9.25 1.40
a. "BOYAUME" 250.00

Visit of King Tallal of Jordan, Nov. 1951.

Bedouins and Train — A15

1952, June **Engr.** ***Perf. 12***

187 A15 ½q redsh brown 4.25 .65
188 A15 1q deep green 4.25 .65
189 A15 3q violet 8.50 .45
190 A15 10q rose pink 17.00 3.25
191 A15 20q blue 35.00 6.75
Nos. 187-191 (5) 69.00 11.75

Inaugural trip over the Saudi Government Railroad between Riyadh and Dammam.

Saudi Arabia Arms and Lebanon Emblem — A16

1953, Feb. **Typo.** ***Perf. 11***

192 A16 ½g carmine 4.75 .90
193 A16 3g violet blue 9.50 1.40

Visit of President Camille Chamoun of Lebanon.

Arms of Saudi Arabia and Emblem of Pakistan A17

1953, Mar.

194 A17 ½g dark carmine 6.00 .90
195 A17 3g violet blue 12.50 1.40

Visit of Gov.-Gen. Ghulam Mohammed of Pakistan.

Arms of Saudi Arabia and Jordan — A18

Globe — A18a

1953, July **Unwmk.**

196 A18 ½g carmine 4.50 .90
a. "GOERCHE" 75.00
197 A18 3g violet blue 14.00 1.40

Visit of King Hussein of Jordan, July, 1953.

1955, July **Litho.**

198 A18a ½g emerald 2.50 .45
199 A18a 3g violet 7.00 .90
200 A18a 4g orange 10.00 2.25
Nos. 198-200 (3) 19.50 3.60

Founding of the Arab Postal Union, July 1, 1954.

Ministry of Communications Building, Riyadh — A19

1960, Apr. 12 **Photo.** ***Perf. 13***

201 A19 2p bright blue .65 .20
202 A19 5p deep claret 1.40 .20
203 A19 10p dark green 3.50 .45
Nos. 201-203 (3) 5.55 .85

Arab Postal Union Conference, at Riyadh, Apr. 11. Imperfs. exist.

Arab League Center, Cairo A20

1960, Mar. 22 ***Perf. 13x13½***

204 A20 2p dull grn & blk 1.75 .20

Opening of the Arab League Center and the Arab Postal Museum in Cairo. Exists imperf.

Radio Tower and Waves A21

1960, June 4

205 A21 2p red & black 1.75 .25
206 A21 5p brown blk & mar 2.75 .30
207 A21 10p bluish blk & ultra 4.50 .65
Nos. 205-207 (3) 9.00 1.20

1st international radio station in Saudi Arabia. Imperfs. exist.

Map of Palestine, Refugee Camp and WRY Emblem — A22

1960, Oct. 30 **Litho.** ***Perf. 13***

208 A22 2p dark blue .30 .20
209 A22 8p lilac .30 .20
210 A22 10p green .95 .20
Nos. 208-210 (3) 1.55 .60

World Refugee Year, July 1, 1959-June 30, 1960. Imperfs. exist.

Wadi Hanifa Dam, near Riyadh — A23

Gas-Oil Separating Plant, Buqqa — A24

Type I (Saud Cartouche) (Illustrated over No. 286)

1960-62 **Unwmk.** **Photo.** ***Perf. 14***

Size: 27½x22mm

211 A23 ½p bis brn & org 1.25 .20
212 A23 1p ol bis & pur 1.25 .20
213 A23 2p blue & sepia 1.25 .20
214 A23 3p sepia & blue 1.25 .20
215 A23 4p sepia & ocher 1.25 .20
216 A23 5p blk & dk violet 1.25 .20
217 A23 6p brn blk & car rose ('62) 1.25 .20
a. 6p black & carmine rose 1.50 .35
218 A23 7p red & gray ol 1.25 .20
219 A23 8p dk bl & brn blk 1.25 .30
220 A23 9p org brn & scar 1.25 .30
c. 9p yel brn & metallic red 1.50 .45
221 A23 10p emer grn & mar ('62) 1.50 .35
a. 10p blue green & maroon 1.75 .70
222 A23 20p brown & green 3.50 .35
223 A23 50p black & brown 20.00 1.75
224 A23 75p brown & gray 55.00 2.00
225 A23 100p dk bl & grn bl 50.00 2.25
226 A23 200p lilac & green 77.50 5.75
Nos. 211-226 (16) 220.00 14.65

1960-61

227 A24 ½p maroon & org 1.10 .20
228 A24 1p blue & red org 1.10 .20
229 A24 2p ver & blue 1.10 .20
230 A24 3p lilac & brt grn 1.10 .20
231 A24 4p yel grn & lilac 1.10 .20
232 A24 5p dk gray & brn red 1.10 .20
233 A24 6p brn org & dk vio 1.10 .20
234 A24 7p vio & dull grn 1.10 .20
235 A24 8p blue grn & gray 1.10 .20
236 A24 9p ultra & sepia 3.25 .20
237 A24 10p dk blue & rose 1.75 .35
238 A24 20p org brn & blk 6.25 .45
239 A24 50p red & brn grn 18.00 1.40
240 A24 75p red & blk brn 27.50 2.75
241 A24 100p dk bl & red brn 42.50 2.50
242 A24 200p dk gray & ol grn 72.50 5.75
Nos. 227-242 (16) 181.65 15.20

Nearly all of Nos. 211-242 exist imperf; probably not regularly issued.

See Nos. 258-273, 286-341, 393-450, 461-483.

Dammam Port — A25

Wmk. 337

1961, Aug. 16 **Litho.** ***Perf. 13***

243 A25 3p lilac 1.40 .20
244 A25 6p light blue 1.90 .30
245 A25 8p dark green 3.25 .35
Nos. 243-245 (3) 6.55 .85

Expansion of the port of Dammam. Imperf min. sheets of 4 were for presentation purposes and have wmk. sideways. Value, set $200. Imperforate pairs or margined imperfs with upright watermark come from full sheets not perforated by the print shop.

Globe, Radio and Telegraph A26

Perf. 13x13½

1961, Aug. 7 **Photo.** **Unwmk.**

246 A26 3p dull purple 1.25 .20
247 A26 6p gray black 2.00 .30
248 A26 8p brown 3.25 .50
Nos. 246-248 (3) 6.50 1.00

Arab Union of Telecommunications. Imperfs. exist.

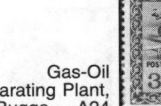

Arab League Building, Cairo — A27

Malaria Eradication Emblem — A28

1962, Apr. 22 Wmk. 337 *Perf. 13*

249	A27	3p olive green	1.10	.20
250	A27	6p carmine rose	2.25	.30
251	A27	8p slate blue	3.50	.35
		Nos. 249-251 (3)	6.85	.85

Arab League Week, Mar. 22-28.

Imperforate or missing-color varieties of Nos. 249-285 and 344-353 were not regularly issued.

1962, May 7 Litho. Wmk. 337

252	A28	3p red org & blue	.75	.20
253	A28	6p emerald & Prus bl	1.10	.25
254	A28	8p black & lil rose	1.75	.40
	a.	Souv. sheet of 3, #252-254, imperf.	14.00	14.00
		Nos. 252-254 (3)	3.60	.85

WHO drive to eradicate malaria.

Nos. 252-254 are known unofficially overprinted with new dates only or with "AIR MAIL" and two plane silhouettes.

A 4p exists as an essay.

Koran A29

1963, Mar. 12 Wmk. 337 *Perf. 11*

255	A29	2½p lilac rose & pink	.90	.20
256	A29	7½p blue & pale grn	1.75	.35
257	A29	9½p green & gray	2.75	.35
		Nos. 255-257 (3)	5.40	.90

First anniversary of the Islamic Institute, Medina. A 3p exists as an essay. Copies of the 2½p exist with virtually all the pink background omitted. No copies are known with the pink completely omitted.

Dam Type of 1960 Redrawn
Type I (Saud Cartouche)

Perf. 13½x13

1963-65 Wmk. 337 Litho.

Size: 28½x23mm

258	A23	½p bis brn & org	9.00	.65

Nos. 258, 264-265 are widely spaced in the sheet, producing large margins.

Perf. 14

Photo.

Size: 27½x22mm

259	A23	½p bis brn & org ('65)	20.00	1.40
260	A23	3p sepia & blue	7.75	.55
261	A23	4p sepia & ocher ('64)	11.00	.70
262	A23	5p black & dk vio	11.00	.70
263	A23	20p dk car & grn	20.00	1.40
		Nos. 258-263 (6)	78.75	5.40

A 1p was prepared but not issued. It is known only imperf.

Gas-Oil Plant Type of 1960 Redrawn
Type I (Saud Cartouche)

Perf. 13½x13

1963-65 Wmk. 337 Litho.

Size: 28½x23mm

264	A24	½p maroon & orange	9.50	.90
265	A24	1p blue & red org ('64)	4.50	.30

Photo.

Perf. 14

Size: 27½x22mm

266	A24	½p mar & org ('64)	9.00	.45
267	A24	1p blue & red org	7.75	.30
268	A24	3p lilac & brt grn	18.00	.90
269	A24	4p yel grn & lilac	11.00	.45
270	A24	5p dk gray & brn red	11.00	.45
271	A24	6p brn org & dk vio ('65)	16.00	.60
272	A24	8p dull grn & blk	27.50	1.10
273	A24	9p blue & sepia	27.50	1.40
		Nos. 264-273 (10)	141.75	6.85

The 3p, 4p and 6p exist imperf.

Hands Holding Wheat Emblem A30

1963, Mar. 21 Litho. *Perf. 11*

274	A30	2½p lilac rose & rose	.90	.20
275	A30	7½p brt lilac & pink	.90	.30
276	A30	9p red brn & lt blue	1.90	.35
		Nos. 274-276 (3)	3.70	.85

FAO "Freedom from Hunger" campaign. The 3p imperf in various colors are essays.

Jet over Dhahran Airport — A31

Flame — A32

1963, July 27 Litho. *Perf. 13*

277	A31	1p blue gray & ocher	.95	.20
278	A31	3½p ultra & emer	1.90	.20
279	A31	6p emerald & rose	3.25	.25
	a.	"Thahran" for "Dharan" in Arabic	5.50	
280	A31	7½p lilac rose & lt bl	3.25	.30
281	A31	9½p ver & dull vio	4.75	.35
		Nos. 277-281 (5)	14.10	1.30

Opening of the US-financed terminal of the Dhahran Airport and inauguration of international jet service

On No. 279a the misspelling consists of an omitted dot over character near top left in one horiz. row of five.

Nos. 277-281 with a second impression of the frame are forgeries.

1964, Apr. Wmk. 337 *Perf. 13x13½*

282	A32	3p lil, pink & Prus bl	2.75	.20
283	A32	6p yel grn, lt bl & Prus bl	3.25	.25
284	A32	9p brn, buff & Prus bl	7.00	.35
		Nos. 282-284 (3)	13.00	.80

15th anniv. of the signing of the Universal Declaration of Human Rights.

The 3p in other colors is an essay.

King Faisal and Arms of Saudi Arabia A33

1964, Nov. Litho. *Perf. 13*

285	A33	4p dk blue & emerald	3.75	.20

Installation of Prince Faisal ibn Abdul Aziz as King, Nov. 2, 1964.

King Saud's Cartouche - Type I

King Faisal's Cartouche - Type II

Redrawn Dam Type of 1960
Type I (Saud Cartouche)

1965-70 Litho. Unwmk. *Perf. 14*

Size: 27x22mm

286	A23	1p ol bis & pur	18.00	.90
287	A23	2p dk blue & sep	3.50	.25
288	A23	3p sepia & blue	2.75	.30
289	A23	4p sepia & ocher	5.00	.30
290	A23	5p blk & dk vio	4.50	.30
291	A23	6p blk & car rose	11.00	.55
292	A23	7p brown & gray	11.00	.30
293	A23	8p dk bl & gray	*60.00*	4.50
294	A23	9p org brn & scar	*55.00*	4.50
295	A23	10p bl grn & mar	*52.50*	2.75
296	A23	11p red & yel grn	4.75	1.75
297	A23	12p org & dk bl	4.75	.30
298	A23	13p dk ol & rose	4.75	.35
299	A23	14p org brn & yel grn	4.75	.35
300	A23	15p sepia & gray grn	4.75	1.75
301	A23	16p dk red & dl vio	6.00	.40
302	A23	17p rose lil & dk bl	6.00	2.00
303	A23	18p green & brt bl	6.00	.40
304	A23	19p black & bister	8.00	.45
305	A23	20p brn & grn	7.75	.90
306	A23	23p mar & lilac	6.50	1.75
307	A23	24p ver & blue	8.00	.55
308	A23	26p olive & yel	10.00	.65
309	A23	27p ultra & red brn	10.00	.65
310	A23	31p gray & dull bl	10.00	.70
311	A23	33p ol grn & lilac	10.00	.70
312	A23	100p dk bl & grnsh bl	*300.00*	*45.00*
313	A23	200p dull lil & grn	*300.00*	*45.00*
		Nos. 286-313 (28)	935.25	118.30

A 50p exists but was never placed in use.

Issue years: 1966, 2p, 4p, 10p-20p, 1968, 6p-9p. 1970, 100p-200p.

Redrawn Gas-Oil Plant Type of 1960
Type I (Saud Cartouche)

1964-70 Litho. Unwmk.

Size: 27x22mm

314	A24	1p bl & red org	7.25	.20
315	A24	2p vermilion & bl	11.00	.20
316	A24	3p lilac & brt grn	4.50	.20
317	A24	4p yel grn & lilac	6.50	.20
318	A24	5p dl gray vio & dk red brn	24.00	1.75
319	A24	6p brn org & dk vio	50.00	4.50
320	A24	7p vio & dull grn	27.50	1.75
321	A24	8p bl grn & gray	6.00	.30
322	A24	9p ultra & sepia	12.50	.70
323	A24	10p dk blue & rose	325.00	32.50
324	A24	11p olive & org	4.00	.30
325	A24	12p bister & grn	4.00	.30
326	A24	13p rose red & dk bl	4.00	.35
327	A24	14p vio & lt brown	5.50	.35
328	A24	15p rose red & sep	6.00	.45
329	A24	16p green & rose red	8.00	.45
330	A24	17p car rose & red brn	12.50	1.40
331	A24	18p gray & ultra	8.00	.55
332	A24	19p brown & yel	8.00	.55
333	A24	20p dull org & dk gray	27.50	1.75
334	A24	23p orange & car	7.25	.65
335	A24	24p emer & org yel	8.00	.70
336	A24	26p lil & red brn	11.00	.70
337	A24	27p ver & dk gray	11.00	.70
338	A24	31p dull grn & car	19.00	1.40
339	A24	33p red brn & gray	17.00	1.40
340	A24	50p red brn & dull grn	*325.00*	*45.00*
341	A24	200p dk gray & ol gray	*325.00*	*45.00*
		Nos. 314-341 (28)	1,285.	144.30

A 100p exists but was never placed in use.

Issue years: 1965, 4p, 8p, 9p, 23p-33p. 1966, 1p, 2p, 5p, 11p-14p, 16p-20p. 1967, 15p. 1968, 6p, 7p. 1969, 50p. 1970, 200p. Others, 1964.

Holy Ka'aba, Mecca — A34

1965, Apr. 17 Wmk. 337 *Perf. 13*

344	A34	4p salmon & blk	3.25	.20
345	A34	6p brt pink & blk	5.00	.25
346	A34	10p yel grn & blk	7.00	.35
		Nos. 344-346 (3)	15.25	.80

Mecca Conf. of the Moslem World League.

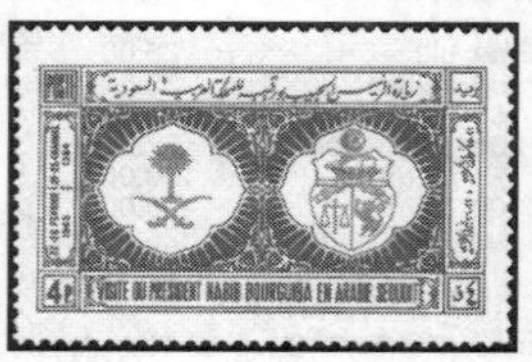

Arms of Saudi Arabia and Tunisia A35

1965, Apr. Litho.

347	A35	4p car rose & silver	2.75	.20
348	A35	8p red lilac & silver	3.50	.35
349	A35	10p ultra & silver	5.00	.35
		Nos. 347-349 (3)	11.25	.90

Visit of Pres. Habib Bourguiba of Tunisia, Feb. 22-26.

Highway, Hejaz Mountains — A36

1965, June 2 Wmk. 337 *Perf. 13*

350	A36	2p red & blk	1.65	.30
351	A36	4p blue & blk	2.50	.35
352	A36	6p lilac & blk	3.50	.45
353	A36	8p brt green & blk	5.00	.55
		Nos. 350-353 (4)	12.65	1.65

Opening of highway from Mecca to Tayif.

ICY Emblem A37

1965, Nov. 13 Unwmk. *Perf. 13*

354	A37	1p yellow & dk brn	1.40	.20
355	A37	2p orange & ol grn	1.40	.20
356	A37	3p lt blue & gray	1.40	.20
357	A37	4p yel grn & dk sl grn	1.40	.20
358	A37	10p orange & magenta	3.50	.45
		Nos. 354-358 (5)	9.10	1.25

International Cooperation Year, 1965.

ITU Emblem, Old and New Communication Equipment — A38

1965, Dec. 22 Litho. *Perf. 13*

359	A38	3p blue & blk	2.00	.20
360	A38	4p lilac & dk grn	2.00	.20
361	A38	8p emerald & dk brn	2.00	.35
362	A38	10p dull org & dk grn	2.00	.35
		Nos. 359-362 (4)	8.00	1.10

Centenary of the ITU.

Library Aflame and Lamp A39

1966, Jan. Litho. *Perf. 12x12½*

363	A39	1p orange	1.40	.20
364	A39	2p dark red	1.40	.20
365	A39	3p red violet	2.00	.20
366	A39	4p violet	2.25	.20
367	A39	5p lilac rose	4.75	.35
368	A39	6p vermilion	8.00	.45
		Nos. 363-368 (6)	19.80	1.60

Burning of the Library of Algiers, June 2, 1962. Nos. 363-368 were withdrawn from sale Jan. 26, 1966, due to incorrect Arabic inscriptions. Later some values were inadvertently again placed in use.

Arab Postal Union Emblem — A40

Dagger in Map of Palestine — A41

1966, Mar. 15 Litho. *Perf. 14*

369	A40	3p dull pur & olive	.90	.20
370	A40	4p deep blue & olive	.90	.20
371	A40	6p maroon & olive	3.50	.25
372	A40	7p deep green & olive	3.50	.35
		Nos. 369-372 (4)	8.80	1.00

10th anniv. (in 1964) of the APU. Printed in sheets of two panes, so horizontal gutter pairs exist.

1966, Mar. 19 Litho. *Perf. 13*

373	A41	2p yel grn & blk	1.50	.20
374	A41	4p lt brown & blk	2.75	.20
375	A41	6p dull blue & blk	4.00	.25
376	A41	8p ocher & blk	5.75	.35
		Nos. 373-376 (4)	14.00	1.00

Deir Yassin massacre, Apr. 9, 1948.

Emblems of World Boy Scout Conference and Saudi Arabian Scout Association A42

1966, Mar. 23 Unwmk.

377	A42	4p yel, blk, grn & gray	4.00	.45
378	A42	8p yel, blk, org & lt bl	4.00	.45
379	A42	10p yel, blk, sal & bl	8.00	.65
		Nos. 377-379 (3)	16.00	1.55

Arab League Rover Moot (Boy Scout Jamboree).

WHO Headquarters, Geneva, and Flag — A43

1966, May Litho. *Perf. 13*

380	A43	4p aqua & multi	1.10	.20
381	A43	6p yel brn & multi	2.25	.25
382	A43	10p pink & multi	4.50	.35
		Nos. 380-382 (3)	7.85	.80

Opening of the WHO Headquarters, Geneva.

UNESCO Emblem — A44

1966, Sept. Unwmk. *Perf. 12*

383	A44	1p apple grn & multi	1.25	.20
384	A44	2p dull org & multi	1.25	.20
385	A44	3p lilac rose & multi	1.75	.20
386	A44	4p pale green & multi	1.75	.20
387	A44	10p gray & multi	2.50	.35
		Nos. 383-387 (5)	8.50	1.15

20th anniv. of UNESCO.

Radio Tower, Telephone and Map of Arab Countries — A45

1966, Nov. 7 Litho. *Perf. 12½*
Design in Black, Carmine & Yellow

388	A45	1p vio blue	1.60	.20
389	A45	2p bluish lilac	1.60	.20
390	A45	4p rose lilac	3.25	.20
391	A45	6p lt olive grn	3.25	.30
392	A45	7p gray green	4.00	.40
		Nos. 388-392 (5)	13.70	1.30

Issued to publicize the 8th Congress of the Arab Telecommunications Union, Riyadh.

Redrawn Dam Type of 1960
Type II (Faisal Cartouche)
(Illustrated over No. 286)

1966-76 Litho. Unwmk. *Perf. 14*
Size: 27x22mm

393	A23	1p ol bis & pur	*160.00*	*22.50*
394	A23	2p dk blue & sep	19.00	1.50
395	A23	3p blk & dk bl	11.00	.80
396	A23	4p sepia & ocher	15.00	.40
397	A23	5p blk & dk vio	40.00	7.50
398	A23	6p blk & car rose	32.50	6.75
399	A23	7p sepia & gray	18.00	1.75
400	A23	8p dk bl & gray	11.00	.45
401	A23	9p org brn & scar	7.50	.80
402	A23	10p bl grn & mar	15.00	1.40
403	A23	11p red & yel grn	11.00	1.40
404	A23	12p org & dk bl	6.50	1.40
405	A23	13p blk & rose	22.50	1.40
406	A23	14p org brn & yel grn	19.00	1.40
407	A23	15p sep & gray grn	19.00	1.75
408	A23	16p dk red & dl vio	27.50	3.25
409	A23	17p rose lil & dk bl	32.50	1.75
410	A23	18p green & brt bl	22.50	2.50
411	A23	19p black & bister	7.25	.80
412	A23	20p brown & grn	72.50	*2.25*
413	A23	23p maroon & lil	*260.00*	*4.50*
414	A23	24p ver & blue	52.50	5.50
415	A23	26p olive & yel	6.75	.70
416	A23	27p ultra & red brn	7.75	.70
417	A23	33p ol grn & lilac	42.50	2.25
419	A23	50p black & brown	*175.00*	*35.00*
420	A23	100p dk bl & grnsh bl	*275.00*	*45.00*
421	A23	200p dull lilac & grn	*275.00*	*72.50*
		Nos. 393-421 (28)	*1,663.*	*227.90*

A 31p has been reported.
Issue years: 1966, 1p. 1967, 2p, 10p. 1968, 3p, 4p, 6p, 7p, 20p; 1969, 5p, 8p. 1970, 9p, 23p; 1972, 12p, 15p, 16p. 1973, 11p; 1974, 17p, 50p-200p; 1975, 13p, 14p, 19p, 24p-33p; 1976, 18p.

Redrawn Gas-Oil Plant Type of 1960
Type II (Faisal Cartouche)

1966-78 Unwmk.
Size: 27x22mm

422	A24	1p bl & red org	35.00	*2.75*
423	A24	2p ver & dull bl	7.00	.30
424	A24	3p lilac & brt grn	14.00	.55
425	A24	4p grn & dull lil	8.00	.30
426	A24	5p dl gray vio & dk red brn	37.50	1.75
427	A24	6p brn org & dull pur	24.00	3.50
428	A24	7p vio & dull grn	32.50	1.75
429	A24	8p bl grn & grnsh gray	5.50	.30
430	A24	9p ultra & sep	3.75	.30
431	A24	10p dk bl & rose	4.50	.55
432	A24	11p olive & org	72.50	7.25
433	A24	12p bister & grn	4.50	.70
434	A24	13p rose red & dk bl	42.50	.30
435	A24	14p vio & lt brn	40.00	2.25
436	A24	15p car & sepia	10.50	.60
437	A24	16p grn & rose red	14.00	.70
438	A24	17p car rose & red brn	10.00	.55
439	A24	18p gray & ultra	14.00	1.50
440	A24	19p brown & yel	16.00	1.50
441	A24	20p brn org & gray	12.00	1.50
442	A24	23p orange & car	20.00	1.75
443	A24	24p emer & org yel	9.00	.70
444	A24	26p lilac & red brn	*175.00*	
445	A24	27p ver & dk gray	35.00	3.50
446	A24	31p green & rose car	11.00	.70
447	A24	33p brown & gray	20.00	1.10
448	A24	50p red brn & dl grn	350.00	*140.00*
449	A24	100p dk bl & red brn	300.00	*40.00*
450	A24	200p dk gray & ol gray	350.00	*57.50*
		Nos. 422-450 (29)	1,677.	

Issue years: 1967, 20p; 1968, 3p, 5p-9p, 15p, 16p; 1969, 100p; 1970, 11p, 14p, 200p; 1973, 13p, 18p, 24p; 1974, 19p, 50p; 1975, 12p, 17p, 27p-33p; 1978, 26p; others, 1966.
No. 442 with a double impression of the frame is a forgery.

Emblem of Saudi Arabian Scout Association A46

Meteorological Instruments and WMO Emblem — A47

1967, Mar. 28 Litho. *Perf. 13½*
Emblem in Green, Red, Yellow & Black

451	A46	1p dk blue & blk	2.00	.20
452	A46	2p blue grn & blk	2.00	.20
453	A46	3p lt blue & blk	3.00	.20
454	A46	4p rose brn & blk	3.75	.20
455	A46	10p brown & blk	8.50	.45
		Nos. 451-455 (5)	19.25	1.25

2nd Arabic League Rover Moot, Mecca, March 13-28.

1967, July Unwmk. *Perf. 13*

456	A47	1p brt magenta	.95	.20
457	A47	2p violet	1.90	.20
458	A47	3p olive	1.90	.20
459	A47	4p blue green	6.00	.20
460	A47	10p blue	8.25	.35
		Nos. 456-460 (5)	19.00	1.15

Issued for World Meteorological Day.

Redrawn Dam Type of 1960
Type II (Faisal Cartouche)

1968-76 Wmk. 361 Litho. *Perf. 14*

461	A23	1p ol bis & pur ('71)	*1,100.*	*275.00*
462	A23	2p dk blue & sep	30.00	*1.75*
463	A23	3p blk & dk bl	20.00	*.95*
464	A23	4p sepia & ocher	175.00	*30.00*
465	A23	5p blk & dk vio	25.00	*1.75*
466	A23	6p blk & car rose	24.00	*1.40*
467	A23	7p sepia & gray	35.00	*2.75*
468	A23	8p dk bl & gray	18.00	.90
469	A23	9p org brn & ver	65.00	*6.25*
470	A23	10p bl grn & mar	45.00	*3.50*
471	A23	11p red & yel grn	55.00	*5.50*
472	A23	12p org & sl bl	50.00	*4.50*
473	A23	13p black & rose	67.50	*6.75*
		Nos. 462-473 (12)	609.50	*66.00*

Issue years: 1968, 2p, 10p; 1969, 3p; 1970, 8p; 1971, 1p, 5p; 1972, 6p, 9p, 11p, 12p; 1973, 4p; 1974, 13p; 1976, 9p.

Redrawn Gas-Oil Plant Type of 1960
Type II (Faisal Cartouche)

1968-76 *Perf. 14*

474	A24	1p bl & red org	9.50	.90
475	A24	2p ver & dl bl	5.75	.45
476	A24	4p grn & dl lil	72.50	*7.25*
477	A24	5p dk brn & red brn ('73)	20.00	1.40
478	A24	6p brn org & dk vio ('73)	25.00	1.75
479	A24	9p dk bl & sep ('76)	40.00	3.50
480	A24	10p dk bl & rose	8.50	.60
481	A24	11p ol & org ('72)	30.00	1.75
482	A24	12p bis & grn ('72)	32.50	2.75
483	A24	23p org & car ('74)	55.00	2.75
		Nos. 474-483 (10)	298.75	23.10

Map Showing Dammam to Jedda Road, and Dates — A48

Wmk. 361
1968, Aug. Litho. *Perf. 14*

484	A48	1p yellow & multi	1.40	.20
485	A48	2p orange & multi	1.40	.20
486	A48	3p multicolored	2.75	.20
487	A48	4p multicolored	2.75	.20
488	A48	10p multicolored	8.00	.35
		Nos. 484-488 (5)	16.30	1.15

Issued to commemorate the completion of the trans-Saudi Arabia highway in 1967.
Several positions in the sheet have the dots representing Dammam and Riyadh omitted. Most had the dots added by pen before issuance.

Prophet's Mosque, Medina — A49

New Arcade, Mecca Mosque — A50

Wmk. 361, 337 (#489, 493)
1968-76 Litho. *Perf. 13½x14*
Design A49

489	A49	1p org & grn ('70)	2.10	.30
490	A49	2p red brn & grn, redrawn ('72)	3.50	.35
a.		2p red brn & grn, wmk. 337	6.25	.30
b.		As "a," redrawn	*175.00*	
491	A49	3p vio & grn ('72)	3.25	.35
a.		3p vio & grn, wmk. 337 ('70)	2.75	.30
492	A49	4p ocher & grn	3.50	.35
a.		Redrawn ('71)	5.50	.45
b.		4p ocher & green, redrawn, wmk. 337	6.25	
493	A49	5p dp lil rose & grn ('71)	7.75	.90
494	A49	6p blk & grn ('73)	9.75	.90
a.		6p gray & green ('76)	18.00	.90
495	A49	10p brown & grn	12.00	.90
a.		Redrawn	9.00	
496	A49	20p dk brn & grn ('70)	15.00	1.75
a.		Redrawn	18.00	
497	A49	50p sepia & grn ('75)	19.00	5.75
498	A49	100p dk bl & grn ('75)	15.00	4.50
499	A49	200p red & grn ('75)	19.00	6.25
		Nos. 489-499 (11)	109.85	22.30

See redrawn note following design A55. No. 494 exists imperf.

Warning: Stamps of design A49 in other colors, double frames, inverted centers or centers omitted are forgeries. They are printed on sheet selvage.

1968-69 Wmk. 361

500	A50	3p dp org & gray ('69)	350.00	90.00
501	A50	4p green & gray	5.75	.45
502	A50	10p mag & gray	8.25	.90

Expansion of Prophet's Mosque — A51

Madayin Saleh — A52

1968-76 **Wmk. 361**

503	A51	1p org & grn ('72)	4.50	.25
504	A51	2p brn & grn ('72)	7.25	.25
505	A51	3p blk & grn ('69)	6.25	.35
b.		3p gray & green ('76)	18.00	1.75
c.		As No. 505, redrawn	4.50	
506	A51	4p org & grn ('70)	6.25	.45
a.		Redrawn	4.50	.45
507	A51	5p red & grn, redrawn ('74)	6.75	.75
508	A51	6p Prus bl & grn ('72)	9.00	.90
509	A51	8p rose red & grn ('76)	22.50	1.75
510	A51	10p brn red & grn ('70)	8.25	.55
b.		10p org & grn, redrawn ('76)	18.00	.90
511	A51	20p vio & grn ('74)	18.00	2.25
		Nos. 503-511 (9)	88.75	7.50

Wmk. 337

503a	A51	1p	5.00	.35
504a	A51	2p ('70)	6.75	.35
b.		As "a," redrawn	35.00	
505a	A51	3p ('71)	7.25	.70
506b	A51	4p Redrawn ('72)	9.00	
507a	A51	5p ('70)	4.50	.45
508a	A51	6p ('72)	6.25	.55
510a	A51	10p ('70)	11.00	.60
c.		As "a," redrawn	18.00	
511a	A51	20p ('72)	8.25	.70
		Nos. 503a-511a (8)	58.00	3.70

See redrawn note following design A55.

1968-75

512	A52	2p ultra & bis brn ('70)	20.00	3.50
513	A52	4p dk & lt brown	5.00	.70
514	A52	7p org & lt brn ('75)	40.00	*9.00*
515	A52	10p sl grn & lt brn	12.50	1.75
516	A52	20p lil rose & brn ('71)	14.00	1.40
		Nos. 512-516 (5)	91.50	*16.35*

Arabian Stallion — A53

Camels and Oil Derrick — A54

517	A53	4p mag & org brn	5.00	.70
518	A53	10p blk & org brn	14.00	2.75
519	A53	14p bl & ocher ('71)	22.50	5.50
520	A53	20p ol grn & ocher ('71)	7.75	1.75
		Nos. 517-520 (4)	49.25	10.70

1969-71

521	A54	4p dk pur & redsh brn ('71)	21.00	3.50
522	A54	10p ultra & hn brn	19.00	2.75

Holy Ka'aba, Mecca — A55

Original

Redrawn

On the original stamps the knob-shaped Arabic letter, located under the two square dots in the middle of the top panel, has a small central dot. The dot often is missing.

On the redrawn stamps the dot has been enlarged into a conspicuous irregular oval. The 3p also has a period added after the value and the 4p has the "4" under the "T" instead of the "S." There are other small differences.

Numeral & "Postage" on Gray Background, 8p on White

1969-75

523	A55	4p dp grn & blk ('70)	7.75	.70
a.		Redrawn, value corner white ('74)	16.00	1.75
b.		Redrawn ('75)	14.00	
524	A55	6p dp lil rose & blk ('71)	4.50	.35
a.		Value corner white ('74)	22.50	2.75
525	A55	8p red & blk ('75)	27.50	2.75
526	A55	10p org & blk ('69)	16.00	1.40
a.		Redrawn, value corner white ('74)	14.00	1.75
b.		Redrawn ('75)	18.00	
		Nos. 523-526 (4)	55.75	5.20

Rover Moot Badge — A56

Perf. 13½x14

1969, Feb. 19 **Litho.** **Wmk. 337**

607	A56	1p orange & multi	1.25	.20
608	A56	4p dull purple & multi	4.00	.20
609	A56	10p orange brn & multi	11.00	.60
		Nos. 607-609 (3)	16.25	1.00

3rd Arab League Rover Moot, Mecca, Feb. 19-Mar. 3.

Traffic Light and Intersection — A57

1969, Feb. **Wmk. 361** ***Perf. 13½***

610	A57	3p dl bl, red & brt bl grn	2.00	.20
a.		3p dull blue, red & gray green	6.00	.90
611	A57	4p org brn, red & gray grn	2.00	.20
612	A57	10p dl pur, red & gray grn	4.00	.45
		Nos. 610-612 (3)	8.00	.85

Issued for Traffic Day.

WHO Emblem — A58

1969, Oct. 20 **Wmk. 337** ***Perf. 14***

613	A58	4p lt bl, vio bl & yel	10.00	.20

20th anniv. (in 1968) of WHO.

Islamic Conference Emblem A59

1970, Mar. 23 **Litho.** **Wmk. 361**

614	A59	4p blue & black	2.40	.20
615	A59	10p yellow bis & blk	3.50	.40

Islamic Conference of Foreign Ministers, Jedda, March 1970.

Open Book and Satellite Earth Receiving Station — A60

Perf. 14x13½

1970, Aug. 1 **Litho.** **Wmk. 337**

616	A60	4p violet bl & multi	4.25	.20
617	A60	10p green & multi	8.50	.45

World Telecommunications Day.

Steel Rolling Mill, Jedda A61

1970, Oct. 26 **Wmk. 337** ***Perf. 13½***

618	A61	3p yellow org & multi	2.50	.20
619	A61	4p violet & multi	3.75	.20
620	A61	10p brt green & multi	6.50	.45
		Nos. 618-620 (3)	12.75	.85

Inauguration of 1st steel mill in Saudi Arabia.

Rover Moot Emblem — A62

1971, Feb. **Litho.** ***Perf. 14***

621	A62	10p brt blue & multi	8.00	.65

4th Arab League Rover Moot, 1971.

Telecommunications Symbol — A63

1971, May 17 **Wmk. 337** ***Perf. 14***

622	A63	4p blue & blk	2.00	.20
623	A63	10p lilac & blk	4.25	.35

World Telecommunications Day.

University Minaret — A64

Arab League Emblem — A65

Wmk. 337; Wmk. 361 (4p)

1971, Aug. **Litho.** ***Perf. 14***

624	A64	3p brt green & black	1.60	.20
625	A64	4p brown & black	3.00	.20
626	A64	10p blue & black	5.75	.45
		Nos. 624-626 (3)	10.35	.85

King Abdul Aziz National University.

1971, Nov. **Wmk. 337** ***Perf. 13½***

627	A65	10p multicolored	5.75	.35

Arab League Week.

Education Year Emblem — A66

OPEC Emblem — A67

1971, Nov. **Litho.**

628	A66	4p apple grn & brn red	5.75	.20

International Education Year 1970.

1971, Dec. ***Perf. 14***

629	A67	4p light blue	6.25	.20

10th anniversary of OPEC (Organization of Petroleum Exporting Countries).

Globe A68

1972, Aug. **Wmk. 361** ***Perf. 14***

630	A68	4p multicolored	5.75	.20

4th World Telecommunications Day.

Telephone — A69

1972, Oct. **Wmk. 337, 361 (5p)**

631	A69	1p red, blk & grn	2.00	.20
632	A69	4p dk grn, blk & grn	2.00	.20
633	A69	5p lil, blk & grn	3.75	.20
634	A69	10p tan, blk & grn	8.00	.40
		Nos. 631-634 (4)	15.75	1.00

Inauguration of automatic telephone system (1969).

Writing Hand — A70

1972, Sept. 8 **Litho.** **Wmk. 361**

635	A70	10p multicolored	7.50	.35

World Literacy Day, Sept. 8.

Holy Ka'aba and Grand Mosque, Mecca A71

Rover Moot Emblem and: 4p, Prophet's Mosque, Medina. 10p, Plains of Arafat.

1973

636 A71	4p lt blue & multi	3.00	.20
637 A71	6p lilac & multi	5.75	.30
638 A71	10p salmon & multi	9.00	.50
	Nos. 636-638 (3)	17.75	1.00

5th Arab League Rover Moot.

Globe and Map of Palestine A71a

1973 Litho. Wmk. 361 *Perf. 14*

639 A71a	4p black, yel & red	3.00	.20
640 A71a	10p blue, yel & red	6.00	.35

Palestine Week.

Leaf and Emblem — A72

1973

641 A72	4p yellow & multi	5.50	.25

International Hydrological Decade 1965-74.

Arab Postal Union Emblem — A73

1973, Dec. Litho. *Perf. 14*

642 A73	4p sepia & multi	4.25	.25
643 A73	10p purple & multi	9.00	.45

25th anniversary (in 1971) of the Conference of Sofar, Lebanon, establishing the Arab Postal Union.

Balloons and Pacifier — A74

1973, Dec.

644 A74	4p lt blue & multi	6.75	.20

Universal Children's Day (stamp dated 1971).

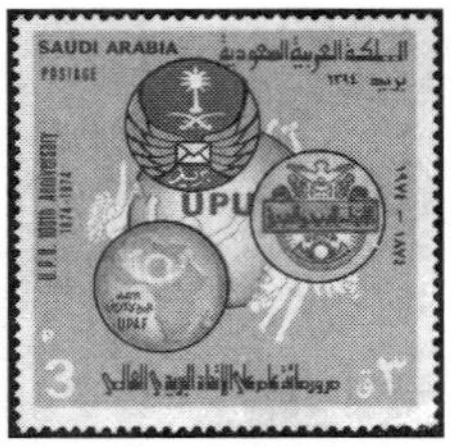

Arab Postal and UPU Emblems A75

1974, July 7 Wmk. 361 *Perf. 14*

645 A75	3p yellow & multi	*40.00*	2.25
646 A75	4p rose & multi	*40.00*	4.50
647 A75	10p lt green & multi	*40.00*	6.75
	Nos. 645-647 (3)	*120.00*	13.50

Centenary of the Universal Postal Union.

Handshake and UNESCO Emblem — A76

1974, May 21 *Perf. 13½*

648 A76	4p orange & multi	2.75	.25
649 A76	10p green & multi	11.00	.65

International Book Year, 1972.

Desalination Plant — A77

1974, Sept. 3 Wmk. 361 *Perf. 14*

650 A77	4p dp orange & bl	2.00	.20
651 A77	6p emerald & vio	4.25	.25
652 A77	10p rose red & blk	6.50	.45
	Nos. 650-652 (3)	12.75	.90

Opening (in 1971) of sea water desalination plant, Jedda.

A78

A79

Design: INTERPOL emblem.

1974, Nov. 1

653 A78	4p ocher & ultra	6.25	.20
654 A78	10p emerald & ultra	12.50	.45

50th anniversary (in 1973) of International Criminal Police Organization.

1974, Oct. 26 Litho. Wmk. 361

APU emblem, tower and letter.

655 A79	4p multicolored	9.00	.20

Arab Consultative Council for Postal Studies, 3rd session.

UPU Headquarters, Bern — A80

1974, Nov. 15 *Perf. 13½*

656 A80	3p orange & multi	2.75	.25
657 A80	4p lilac & multi	5.75	.45
658 A80	10p blue & multi	8.00	1.10
	Nos. 656-658 (3)	16.50	1.80

Opening of new Universal Postal Union Headquarters, Bern, May 1970.

Tank, Planes, Rockets and Flame A81

1974, Dec. 15 *Perf. 14*

659 A81	3p slate & multi	2.00	.20
660 A81	4p brown & multi	4.00	.25
661 A81	10p lilac & multi	11.00	.65
	Nos. 659-661 (3)	17.00	1.10

King Faisal Military Cantonment, 1971.

A82

A84

A83

Red Crescent flower.

1974, Dec. 17 *Perf. 14x14½*

662 A82	4p gray & multi	1.75	.25
663 A82	6p lt green & multi	4.50	.45
664 A82	10p lt blue & multi	9.00	.90
	Nos. 662-664 (3)	15.25	1.60

Saudi Arabian Red Crescent Society, 10th anniversary (in 1973).

1974, Dec. 23 Wmk. 361 *Perf. 14*

Saudi Arabian scout emblem and minarets.

665 A83	4p brown & multi	4.25	.20
666 A83	6p blue blk & multi	8.25	.30
667 A83	10p purple & multi	12.50	.50
	Nos. 665-667 (3)	25.00	1.00

6th Arab League Rover Moot, Mecca.

1975, Mar. 31 *Perf. 14x13½*

Design: Reading braille.

668 A84	4p multicolored	3.50	.25
669 A84	10p multicolored	8.50	.45

Day of the Blind.

Anemometer and Weather Balloon with UN Emblem — A85

Perf. 13½x14

1975, May 8 Litho. Wmk. 361

670 A85	4p multicolored	8.00	.25

Centenary (in 1973) of International Meteorological Cooperation.

King Faisal — A86

Conference Emblem — A87

1975, July 6 Unwmk. *Perf. 14*

671 A86	4p green & rose brn	2.50	.25
672 A86	16p violet & green	3.25	.65
673 A86	23p dk green & vio	6.75	1.10
	Nos. 671-673 (3)	12.50	2.00

Miniature Sheet

Imperf

674 A86	40p Prus bl & ocher	*400.00*	

King Faisal ibn Abdul-Aziz Al Saud (1906-1975). Size of No. 674: 71x80mm.

1975, July 11 *Perf. 14*

675 A87	10p rose brn & blk	4.75	.45

6th Islamic Conference of Foreign Ministers, Jedda, July 12.

Wheat and Sun — A88

1975, Sept. 17 Litho. Wmk. 361

676 A88	4p lilac & multi	2.75	.20
677 A88	10p blue & multi	8.00	.35

Charity Society, 20th anniversary.

Holy Ka'aba, Globe, Clasped Hands — A89

1975, Sept. 17 *Perf. 14*

678 A89 4p olive bis & multi *6.25* .20
679 A89 10p orange & multi *12.50* .35

Conference of Moslem Organizations, Mecca, Apr. 6-10, 1974.

Saudia Tri-Star and DC-3 — A90

1975, Sept. Litho. Unwmk.

680 A90 4p buff & multi *6.25* .25
681 A90 10p lt blue & multi *12.50* .45

Saudia, Saudi Arabian Airline, 30th anniversary.

Conference Centers in Mecca and Riyadh A91

1975, Sept. *Perf. 14*

682 A91 10p multicolored *9.00* .45

Friday Mosque, Medina, and Juwatha Mosque, al-Hasa — A92

1975, Oct. 26 Litho. Unwmk.

683 A92 4p green & multi *5.25* .25
684 A92 10p vermilion & multi *7.25* .45

Ancient Islamic holy places.

FAO Emblem — A93

1975, Oct. 26

685 A93 4p gray & multi 3.50 .20
686 A93 10p buff & multi 11.00 .45

World Food Program, 10th anniversary (in 1973). Stamps are dated 1973.

Conference Emblem — A94

1976, Mar. 20 Unwmk. *Perf. 14*

687 A94 4p multicolored 12.50 .25

Islamic Solidarity Conference of Science and Technology.

Saudi Arabia Map, Transmission Tower, TV Screen — A95

1976, May 26 Litho. *Perf. 14*

688 A95 4p multicolored 16.00 .25

Saudi Arabian television, 10th anniversary.

Grain, Atom Symbol, Graph A96

1976, June 28 Litho. *Perf. 14*

689 A96 20h yellow & multi 3.25 .25
690 A96 50h yellow & multi 5.50 .45

Second Five-year Plan.

Holy Ka'aba A97

Two types:
I - "White" minarets. Gray vignette.
II - Black minarets and vignette. Design redrawn, strengthened, darkened, clarified.

1976-79 Litho. Wmk. 361 *Perf. 14*
Type II

691	A97	5h lilac & blk	.20	.20
692	A97	10h lt violet & blk	.25	.20
693	A97	15h salmon & blk	.35	.20
a.		Type I	4.25	.20
694	A97	20h lt bl & blk, II	3.75	.20
a.		Type I	5.00	.20
695	A97	25h yellow & blk	1.00	.20
696	A97	30h gray grn & blk	1.40	.20
697	A97	35h bister & blk	.80	.20
698	A97	40h lt green & blk	3.25	.20
a.		Type I ('77)	6.00	.30
699	A97	45h dull rose & blk	1.10	.20
700	A97	50h pink & blk	1.00	.20
703	A97	65h gray blue & blk	1.25	.20
710	A97	1r lt yel grn & blk	1.75	.20
711	A97	2r green & black	6.50	.35
		Nos. 691-711 (13)	22.60	2.75

No. 698 imperf exists as an issued error. Value, $110. Nos. 691-711 also exist as imperfs not regularly issued.

Issue years: 20h, 1977; 5h-15h, 25h-50h, 1r, 1978; 65h, 2r, 1979.

See Nos. 872-882, 961-968.

Quba Mosque, Medina, built 622 — A98

1976-77

719 A98 20h orange & blk 2.00 .20
720 A98 50h emer & lilac ('77) 3.75 .20

Reissued in 1978 in different shades. No. 720 exists imperf as an issued error.

Globe, Telephones 1876 and 1976 A100

1976, July 17 Unwmk. *Perf. 13½*

721 A100 50h multicolored *7.25* .30

Centenary of first telephone call by Alexander Graham Bell, Mar. 10, 1876.

Arab Leaders A101

1976, Oct. 30 Litho. *Perf. 14*

722 A101 20h ultra & emerald *5.25* .25

Arab Summit Conference, Riyadh, October. Leaders pictured: Pres. Elias Sarkis, Lebanon; Pres. Anwar Sadat, Egypt; Pres. Hafez al Assad, Syria; King Khalid, Saudi Arabia; Amir Sabah, Kuwait; Yasir Arafat, Palestine Liberation Organization chairman.

WHO Emblem and Eye A102

1976, Nov. 28 Litho. *Perf. 14*

723 A102 20h multicolored *11.00* .20

World Health Day; Prevention of Blindness.

Holy Ka'aba — A103

1976, Nov. 28 Unwmk.

724 A103 20h multicolored *6.75* .20

50th anniversary of installation of new covering of Holy Ka'aba, Mecca.

Conference Emblem A104

Unwmk.

1977, Feb. 18 Litho. *Perf. 14*

725 A104 20h multicolored *7.00* .20

Islamic Jurisprudence Conference, Riyadh, Oct. 24-Nov. 2, 1976.

A105

A106

Design: Sharia College emblem.

1977, Feb. 25 *Perf. 14*

726 A105 4p multicolored *6.25* .20

25th anniversary (in 1974) of the founding of Sharia (Islamic Law) College, Mecca.

1977

727 A106 20h dk brn & brt grn 1.75 .20
a. Incorrect date 15.00
728 A106 80h bl blk & brt grn 3.50 .50
a. Incorrect date 15.00

2nd anniversary of installation of King Khalid ibn Abdul-Aziz. Nos. 727a-728a (illustrated), issued Mar. 3, have incorrect Arabic date in bottom panel, last characters of 2nd and 3rd rows identical "ir." Stamps withdrawn after a few days and replaced Aug. 14 with corrected date, last characters in 3rd row changed to "ro."

Diesel Train and Map of Route A107

1977, May 23 Litho. *Perf. 14*

729 A107 20h multicolored *21.00* .20

Dammam-Riyadh railroad, 25th anniversary.

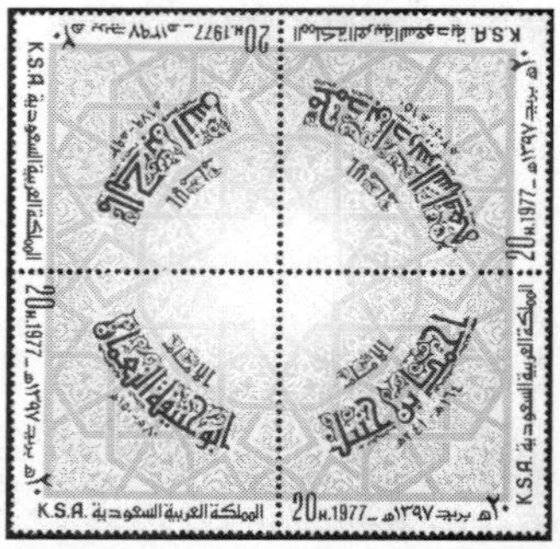

Arabic Ornament and Names — A108

Designs (Names from Left to Right): UL, Malik Ben Anas (715-795). UR, Mohammad Ben Idris Al-Shafi'i (767-820). LL, Abu Hanifa an-Nu'man (699-767). LR, Ahmed Ben Hanbal (780-855).

1977, Aug. 15 Litho. *Perf. 14*

730 A108 Block of 4 *50.00* 3.00
a.-d. 20h, single stamp *4.50* .35

Famous Imams (7th-9th centuries), founders of traditional schools of Islamic jurisprudence. Sheets of 60 stamps (15 blocks).

No. 730 exists with a double impression of the blue color. Stamps with double impressions of the black color are forgeries.

Al Khafji Oil Rig — A109

1976-80 **Wmk. 361**

731	A109	5h vio blue & org	.20	.20
732	A109	10h yel grn & org	.20	.20
733	A109	15h brown & org	.20	.20
734	A109	20h green & org	.20	.20
735	A109	25h dk pur & org	.20	.20
736	A109	30h blue & orange	.25	.20
737	A109	35h sepia & org	.30	.20
738	A109	40h mag & org	.30	.20
a.		40h dull purple & org	175.00	
739	A109	45h violet & orange	.35	.20
740	A109	50h rose & orange	.45	.20
a.		50h dull org & org (error)	67.50	6.75
741	A109	55h grnsh bl & org	20.00	3.50
743	A109	65h sepia & org	1.10	.35
750	A109	1r gray & orange	1.40	.55
751	A109	2r dk vio & org ('80)	3.00	.90
		Nos. 731-751 (14)	28.15	7.30

All values exist with extra dot in Arabic "Al Khafji." The 20h, 25h, 50h, 65h and 1r were retouched to remove the dot.

Color of flame varies from light orange to vermilion. See Nos. 885-892.

No. 737 imperf exists as an issued error. Value, $275. Nos. 731-751 also exist as imperfs not regularly issued.

Mohenjo-Daro Ruins — A110

1977, Oct. 23 **Litho.** **Unwmk.**

761 A110 50h multicolored 7.25 .30

UNESCO campaign to save Mohenjo-Daro excavations in Pakistan.

Idrisi's World Map, 1154 — A111

1977, Nov. 1 **Litho.** ***Perf. 14***

762	A111	20h multicolored	1.75	.20
763	A111	50h multicolored	3.50	.35

First International Symposium on Studies in the History of Arabia at the University of Riyadh, Apr. 23-26, 1977.

King Faisal Specialist Hospital, Riyadh — A112

1977, Nov. 13 **Litho.** **Unwmk.**

764	A112	20h multicolored	2.75	.20
765	A112	50h multicolored	4.50	.35

Conference Emblem — A113

1978, Jan. 24 **Litho.** ***Perf. 14***

766 A113 20h vio blue & yel 3.75 .20

1st World Conf. on Moslem Education.

APU Emblem, Members' Flags A114

1978, Jan. 21

767	A114	20h multicolored	1.50	.20
768	A114	80h multicolored	3.25	.45

25th anniversary of Arab Postal Union.

Taif-Abha-Gizan Highway — A115

1978, Oct. 15 **Litho.** ***Perf. 14***

769	A115	20h multicolored	1.50	.20
770	A115	80h multicolored	3.25	.35

Inauguration of Taif-Abha-Gizan highway.

No. 770 exists with black (road) missing and with black double.

Pilgrims, Mt. Arafat and Holy Ka'aba — A116

Unwmk.

1978, Nov. 6 **Litho.** ***Perf. 14***

771	A116	20h multicolored	1.50	.20
772	A116	80h multicolored	3.25	.35

Pilgrimage to Mecca.

No. 772 exists with inscriptions (black and blue colors) omitted.

Gulf Postal Organization Emblem — A117

1979, Feb. 6 **Litho.** ***Perf. 14***

773	A117	20h multicolored	1.25	.20
774	A117	50h multicolored	2.50	.25

1st Conf. of Gulf Postal Organization, Baghdad.

Saudi Arabia No. 129, King Abdul Aziz ibn Saud A118

Unwmk.

1979, June 4 **Litho.** ***Perf. 14***

775	A118	20h multicolored	1.40	.20
776	A118	50h multicolored	3.00	.25
777	A118	115h multicolored	4.75	.55
		Nos. 775-777 (3)	9.15	1.00

Souvenir Sheet

Imperf

778 A118 100h multicolored *90.00*

1st commemorative stamp, 50th anniv. No. 778 contains one stamp with simulated perforations. Size: 101x76mm.

Crown Prince Fahd A119

1979, June 25 ***Perf. 14***

779	A119	20h multicolored	1.75	.20
780	A119	50h multicolored	3.50	.25

Crown Prince Fahd ibn Abdul Aziz.

Dome of the Rock, Jerusalem A120

1979, July 2 **Wmk. 361**

781 A120 20h multi (shades) 1.60 .25

No. 781 exists with inscriptions (green and mauve colors) omitted.

Imperfs. exist. See No. 866.

Gold Door, Holy Ka'aba — A121

1979, Oct. 13 **Litho.** ***Perf. 14***

782	A121	20h multicolored	1.40	.20
783	A121	80h multicolored	3.00	.35

Installation of new gold doors. Imperfs. exist.

Pilgrims at Holy Ka'aba, Mecca Mosque — A122

1979, Oct. 27

784	A122	20h multicolored	.90	.20
785	A122	50h multicolored	2.40	.25

Pilgrimage to Mecca. Imperfs. exist.

Birds in Trees, IYC Emblem — A123

IYC Emblem and: 50h, Child's drawing.

1980, Feb. 17 **Litho.** ***Perf. 14***

786	A123	20h multicolored	*8.75*	.20
787	A123	50h multicolored	*14.00*	.25

Intl. Year of the Child (1979). Imperfs. exist.

King Abdul Aziz ibn Saud on Horseback, Saudi Flag A124

1980, Apr. 5 **Litho.** ***Perf. 14***

788	A124	20h multicolored	1.25	.20
789	A124	80h multicolored	3.00	.35

Saudi Arabian Army, 80th anniv. (1979). Imperfs. exist.

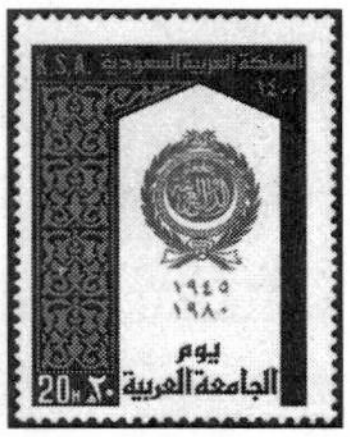

Arab League, 35th Anniversary A125

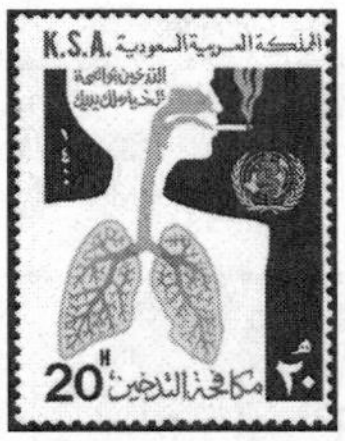

Smoke Entering Lungs, WHO Emblem — A127

International Bureau of Education, 50th Anniversary — A126

1980, Apr. 27 **Litho.** ***Perf. 14***

790 A125 20h multicolored 1.60 .20

Imperfs. exist.

1980, May 4

791 A126 50h multicolored 1.90 .25

Imperfs. exist.

1980, May 20

792	A127	20h shown	1.40	.20
793	A127	50h Cigarette, horiz.	3.25	.25

Anti-smoking campaign. Imperfs. exist.

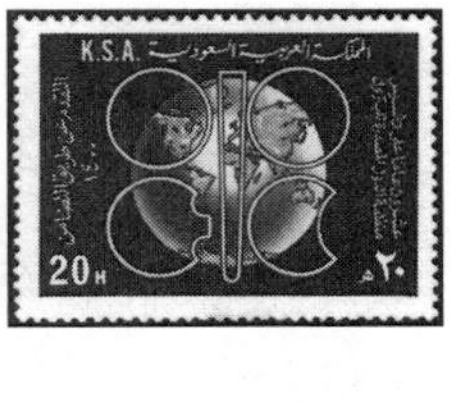

20th Anniversary of OPEC A128

Design: 50h, Workers holding OPEC emblem (Organization of Petroleum Exporting Countries).

1980, Sept. 1 Litho. *Perf. 14*

794	A128 20h multicolored	1.25	.20
795	A128 50h multi, vert.	2.25	.25

Pilgrims Arriving at Jedda Airport A129

1980, Oct. 18

796	A129 20h multicolored	.80	.20
797	A129 50h multicolored	1.60	.25

Pilgrimage to Mecca.

Conference Emblem A130

Holy Ka'aba, Mecca Mosque — A131

1981, Jan. 25 Litho. *Perf. 14*

798	A130 20h shown	.85	.20
799	A131 20h shown	.85	.20
800	A131 20h Prophet's Mosque, Medina	.85	.20
801	A131 20h Dome of the Rock, Jerusalem	.85	.20
	Nos. 798-801 (4)	3.40	.80

Third Islamic Summit Conference, Mecca.

Hegira, 1500th Anniv. A132

1981, Jan. 26

802	A132 20h multicolored	.65	.20
803	A132 50h multicolored	1.25	.25
804	A132 80h multicolored	2.60	.35
	Nos. 802-804 (3)	4.50	.80

Souvenir Sheet

805 A132 300h multicolored

Industry Week A133

1981, Feb. 21

806	A133 20h multicolored	.60	.20
807	A133 80h multicolored	2.00	.35

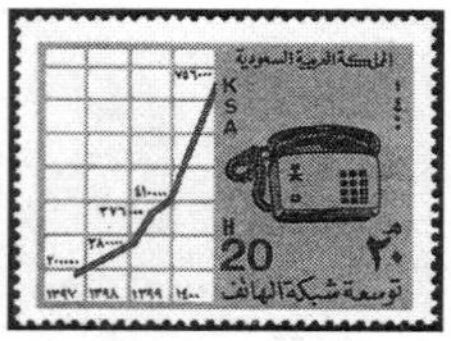
Line Graph and Telephone A134

Map of Saudi Arabia, Microwave Tower A135

1981, Feb. 28

808	A134 20h shown	.30	.20
809	A135 80h shown	2.10	.35
810	A134 115h Earth satellite station	2.40	.45
	Nos. 808-810 (3)	4.80	1.00

Souvenir Sheets

811 A134 100h like #808
812 A135 100h like #809
813 A134 100h like #810

Ministry of Posts and Telecommunications achievements.

Arab City Day — A135a

1981, Apr. 2 Litho. *Perf. 14*

814	A135a 20h multicolored	.35	.20
815	A135a 65h multicolored	1.00	.35
816	A135a 80h multicolored	1.40	.35
817	A135a 115d multicolored	1.90	.55
	Nos. 814-817 (4)	4.65	1.45

Jedda Airport Opening A136

1981, Apr. 12

818	A136 20h shown	.50	.20
819	A136 80h Plane over airport, diff.	2.10	.35

1982 World Cup Soccer Preliminary Games — A137

Intl. Year of the Disabled — A138

1981, July 26 Litho. *Perf. 14*

820	A137 20h multicolored	1.75	.20
821	A137 80h multicolored	3.25	.35

1981, Aug. 5

822	A138 20h Reading braille	1.60	.20
823	A138 50h Man weaving rug	2.50	.25

3rd Five-year Plan (1981-1985) — A139

1981, Sept. 5

824	A139 20h multicolored	1.25	.20

King Abdul Aziz, Map of Saudi Arabia A140

1981, Sept. 23 Litho. *Perf. 14*

825	A140 5h multicolored	.20	.20
826	A140 10h multicolored	.20	.20
827	A140 15h multicolored	.20	.20
828	A140 20h multicolored	.30	.20
829	A140 50h multicolored	.60	.25
830	A140 65h multicolored	.90	.35
831	A140 80h multicolored	2.25	.35
832	A140 115h multicolored	2.75	.50
	Nos. 825-832 (8)	7.40	2.25

Souvenir Sheet

Imperf

833 A140 10r multicolored *72.50*

50th anniv. of kingdom. No. 833 shows king, map, document. Size: 100x75mm.

Pilgrimage to Mecca A141

1981, Oct. 7

834	A141 20h multicolored	1.25	.20
835	A141 65h multicolored	2.50	.35

World Food Day A142

1981, Oct. 16

836	A142 20h multicolored	1.10	.20

2nd Session of the Gulf Cooperative Council Summit Conference, Riyadh, Nov. 10 — A143

1981, Nov. 10 Litho. *Perf. 14*

837	A143 20h multicolored	.60	.20
838	A143 80h multicolored	2.00	.40

King Saud University, 25th Anniv. A144

1982, Mar. 10 Litho. *Perf. 14*

839	A144 20h multicolored	.70	.20
840	A144 50h multicolored	1.50	.25

New Regional Postal Centers A145

1982, July 14 Litho. *Perf. 14*

841	A145 20h Riyadh P.O.	.35	.20
842	A145 65h Jedda	1.10	.35
843	A145 80h Dammam	1.50	.35
844	A145 115h Automated sorting	1.75	.50
	Nos. 841-844 (4)	4.70	1.40

Four 300h souvenir sheets exist in same designs as Nos. 841-844 respectively. Value, $10 each.

Riyadh Television Center — A146

1982, Sept. 4

845	A146 20h multicolored	1.10	.20

25th Anniv. of King's Soccer Cup A147

1982, Sept. 8

846	A147 20h multicolored	.75	.20
847	A147 65h multicolored	1.60	.30

30th Anniv. of Arab Postal Union A148

1982, Sept. 8

848	A148 20h Emblem	.70	.20
849	A148 65h Map, vert.	1.60	.35

Pilgrimage to Mecca A149

1982, Sept. 26

850	A149 20h multicolored	.70	.20
851	A149 50h multicolored	1.60	.25

World Standards Day A150

1982, Oct. 14

852	A150 20h multicolored	1.25	.20

World Food Day A151

1982, Oct. 16

853 A151 20h multicolored 1.10 .20

Coronation of King Fahd, June 14, 1982 A152

Installation of Crown Prince Abdullah, June 14, 1982 A153

1983, Feb. 12 Litho. *Perf. 14*

854	A152	20h	multicolored	.30	.20
855	A153	20h	multicolored	.30	.20
856	A152	50h	multicolored	.60	.25
857	A153	50h	multicolored	.60	.25
858	A152	65h	multicolored	.90	.30
859	A153	65h	multicolored	.90	.30
860	A152	80h	multicolored	1.10	.35
861	A153	80h	multicolored	1.10	.35
862	A152	115h	multicolored	1.60	.55
863	A153	115h	multicolored	1.60	.55
			Nos. 854-863 (10)	9.00	3.30

Two one-stamp souvenir sheets contain Nos. 862-863, perf. 12½.

6th Anniv. of United Arab Shipping Co. — A154

Various freighters.

1983, Aug. 9 Litho. *Perf. 14*

864 A154 20h multicolored .40 .20
865 A154 65h multicolored 1.75 .20

Dome of the Rock, Jerusalem A155

1983, Sept. Wmk. 361 *Perf. 12*

866 A155 20h multicolored .65 .20

See No. 781.

Pilgrimage to Mecca A156

1983, Sept. 16 Litho. *Perf. 14*

867 A156 20h brt blue & multi .35 .20
868 A156 65h dk black & multi 1.25 .20

World Communications Year — A157

1983, Oct. 8 Litho. *Perf. 14*

869 A157 20h Post and UPU emblems .25 .20
870 A157 80h Telephone and ITU emblems 1.25 .25

Holy Ka'ba Type of 1976
Type II

Perf. 14x13½

1982-86 Litho. Wmk. 361

Size: 26x21mm

872	A97	10h	lt vio & blk ('83)	.20	.20
874	A97	20h	lt blue & blk	.20	.20
880	A97	50h	pink & blk ('83)	.45	.20
881	A97	65h	gray bl & blk	.60	.20
882	A97	1r	lt yel grn & blk	1.40	.20

Perf. 13½

874c	A97	20h	lt blue & blk	.25	.20
880a	A97	50h	pink & blk ('83)	.45	.20
881a	A97	65h	gray bl & blk	.60	.20
882a	A97	1r	lt yel grn & blk	1.40	.20

Perf. 12

873	A97	15h	sal & blk ('85)	.20	.20
874a	A97	20h	lt blue & blk ('84)	.20	.20
880b	A97	50h	pink & blk ('86)	.30	.20
881b	A97	65h	gray bl & blk ('84)	.60	.20
882b	A97	1r	lt yel grn & blk ('83)	1.40	.20

Perf. 12

Unwmk.

872a	A97	10h	lt vio & blk ('87)	.20	.20
874b	A97	20h	lt blue & blk	.20	.20
881c	A97	65h	gray bl & blk ('84)	.60	.20
882c	A97	1r	lt yel grn & blk ('85)	1.40	.20

Counterfeits of the 1r are perf. 11.

Al Khafji Oil Rig Type of 1976

Perf. 14x13½

1982-84 Litho. Wmk. 361

Size: 26x21mm

885	A109	5h	vio bl & org	.20	.20
886	A109	10h	yel grn & org	.20	.20
887	A109	15h	bis brn & org	.20	.20
888	A109	20h	green & org	.20	.20
889a	A109	65h	dk pur & org ('00)	.35	.35
890	A109	50h	rose & org	.30	.20
891a	A109	65h	sepia & orange	2.75	1.40
892	A109	1r	gray & org	.60	.30

Perf. 13½

885a	A109	5h		.20	.20
886a	A109	10h		.20	.20
887a	A109	15h		.20	.20
888a	A109	20h		.20	.20
890a	A109	50h		.30	.20
891	A109	65h	sepia & org ('84)	.35	.20
892a	A109	1r		.55	.30

1983 *Perf. 12*

886b	A109	10h		.20	.20
887b	A109	15h		.20	.20
888b	A109	20h		.20	.20
889	A109	25h	dk pur & org	.20	.20
890b	A109	50h		.30	.20
891b	A109	65h		.35	.20
892b	A109	1r		.45	.30

Opening of King Khalid International Airport — A158

1983, Nov. 16 Litho. *Perf. 13½x14*

893 A158 20h shown .45 .20
894 A158 65h blue & multi 1.40 .20

World Food Day — A159

1983, Nov. 29 Litho. *Perf. 14*

895 A159 20h Wheat, Irrigation, Silos .45 .20

Aqsa Mosque, Jerusalem A160

1983, Dec. 13 Litho. *Perf. 14*

896 A160 20h multicolored .45 .20

Old and Modern Riyadh — A161

Shobra Palace, Taif — A162

Old and New Jedda (Waterfront) — A163

Damman — A164

1984-95 Litho. Wmk. 361 *Perf. 12*

897	A161	20h	lilac rose & multi	.20	.20
898	A162	20h	Prus grn & multi	.20	.20
899	A161	50h	black & multi	.30	.20
900	A162	50h	brown & multi	.65	.35

Unwmk.

901	A161	50h	multicolored	.45	.25
902	A162	50h	multicolored	.65	.35
903	A163	50h	multicolored	.90	.45
904	A164	50h	green & multi	.40	.25
905	A161	75h	green & multi	.65	.35
906	A162	75h	multicolored	.65	.35
907	A163	75h	pink & multi	.90	.45
908	A164	75h	blue & multi	.60	.35
909	A161	150h	pink & multi	1.50	.75
910	A162	150h	green & multi	1.50	.75
911	A163	150h	green & multi	1.60	.75
911A	A164	150h	red lilac & multi	1.25	.60
			Nos. 897-911A (16)	12.40	6.60

Issued: #897, 6/27/84; #898, 10/13/84; #899, 8/29/84; #900, 3/10/87; #910, 9/3/87; #902, 11/3/87; #909, 5/4/88; #903, 911, 1/31/89; #906, 1990; #901, 907, 1991; #905, 1992; #904, 908, 911A, 1995.

Estate Development Fund, 10th Anniv. — A165

1984, July 28 Unwmk.

912 A165 20h multicolored .45 .20

Opening of Solar Village, near Al-Eyenah A166

1984, Aug. 14 Litho. *Perf. 12*

913 A166 20h multicolored .35 .20
914 A166 80h Stylized sun, solar panels 1.10 .25

Imperf

Size: 81x81mm

915 A166 100h like 20h 12.50
916 A166 100h like 80h 12.50

Pilgrimage to Mecca — A167

Al-Kheef Mosque: 65h, Aerial view.

1984, Sept. 4 Litho. *Perf. 14*

917 A167 20h brown & multi .45 .20

Perf. 12

918 A167 65h olive gray & multi 1.40 .20

Participation of Saudi Arabian Soccer Team in 1984 Olympics — A168

1984, Sept. 25 Litho. *Perf. 12*

919 A168 20h blue & multi .35 .20
920 A168 115h green & multi 1.10 .35

"Games" and "Olympiad" are misspelled on both stamps.

World Food Day A169

1984, Oct. 16 Litho. *Perf. 12*

921 A169 20h multicolored .40 .20

Beginning with Nos. 922-923 some issues are printed in sheets that have labels inscribed in Arabic. Generally there are from 2 to 6 labels per sheet. Stamps with label attached command a premium.

90th Anniv. International Olympic Committee — A170

1984, Dec. 23 Litho. *Perf. 12*

922 A170 20h multicolored .25 .20
923 A170 50h multicolored 1.40 .20

Launch of ARABSAT — A171

1985, Feb. 9 Litho. *Perf. 12*

924 A171 20h ARABSAT, view of Earth 1.75 .20

7th Holy Koran Competition — A172

1985, Feb. 10 Litho. *Perf. 12*

925 A172 20h multicolored .35 .20
926 A172 65h multicolored .90 .20

4th Five-Year Development Plan, 1985-1990 — A173

Portrait of King Fahd, industry emblems and: 20h, Dhahran Harbor, Jubail. 50h, Television tower, earth receiver, microwave tower. 65h, Agriculture. 80h, Harbor, Yanbu.

1985, Mar. 23 Litho. *Perf. 13x12*

927 A173 20h multicolored .35 .20
928 A173 50h multicolored .90 .20
929 A173 65h multicolored 1.10 .20
930 A173 80h multicolored 1.50 .25
a. Block of 4, #927-930 4.25 .75

Intl. Youth Year A174

1985, May 4 *Perf. 12*

931 A174 20h multicolored .30 .20
932 A174 80h multicolored 1.00 .25

Self-sufficiency in Wheat Production A175

1985, May 4

933 A175 20h multicolored .45 .20

East-West Pipeline — A176

1985, June 9

934 A176 20h Tanker loading berth, Yanbu .40 .20
935 A176 65h Pipeline, map 1.25 .20

Shuttle Launch — A177

Shuttle, Missions Emblem — A178

1985, July 7

936 A177 20h multicolored .40 .20
937 A178 115h multicolored 2.00 .35

Prince Sultan Ibn Salman Al-Saud, 1st Arab-Moslem astronaut, on Discovery 51-G.

UN, 40th Anniv. A179

1985, July 15

938 A179 20h multicolored .55 .20

Highway, Map, Holy Ka'aba in Mecca to Prophet's Mosque in Medina — A180

1985, July 22

939 A180 20h multicolored .35 .20
940 A180 65h multicolored .90 .20

Mecca-Medina Highway opening, 10/11/84.

Post Code Inauguration — A181

1985, July 24

941 A181 20h Covers .45 .20

1984 Asian Soccer Cup Victory A182

1985, July 30

942 A182 20h multicolored .25 .20
943 A182 65h multicolored .65 .20
944 A182 115h multicolored 1.60 .35
Nos. 942-944 (3) 2.50 .75

Pilgrimage to Mecca — A183

1985, Aug. 25 Litho. *Perf. 12*

945 A183 10h multicolored .20 .20
946 A183 15h multicolored .20 .20
947 A183 20h multicolored .30 .20
948 A183 65h multicolored .70 .20
Nos. 945-948 (4) 1.40 .80

1st Gulf Olympics Day, Riyadh, May 2 A184

1985, Sept. 8

949 A184 20h multicolored .35 .20
950 A184 115h multicolored 1.75 .35

World Food Day A185

1985, Oct. 16

951 A185 20h multicolored .45 .20
952 A185 65h multicolored 1.50 .20

King Abdul Aziz, Masmak Fort and Horsemen — A186

1985, Dec. 1

953 A186 15h multicolored .20 .20
954 A186 20h multicolored .20 .20
955 A186 65h multicolored .70 .20
956 A186 80h multicolored .90 .25
Nos. 953-956 (4) 2.00 .85

Intl. Conference on the History of King Abdul Aziz Al-Sa'ud, Riyadh. An imperf. souvenir sheet showing smaller versions of Nos. 953-956 and the conference emblem exists. Sold for 10r.

King Fahd Koran Publishing Center, Medina — A187

1985, Dec. 18

957 A187 20h multicolored .20 .20
958 A187 65h multicolored .95 .20

OPEC, 25th Anniv. A188

1985, Dec. 24

959 A188 20h multicolored .25 .20
960 A188 65h multicolored 1.40 .20

Holy Ka'aba Type of 1976
Type II
Booklet Stamps

1986, Feb. 17 Litho. *Perf. 12*
Size: 29x19mm

961 A97 10h lt vio & blk
a. Booklet pane of 4 22.50
965 A97 20h bluish grn & blk
968 A97 50h pink & black
a. Bklt. pane of 4, #961, 2 #965, #968 35.00

Due to vending machine breakdowns, distribution of this set has been very limited. The government does have stocks of these stamps but they are not currently being sold.

A189

A191

A190

1986, Jan. 8 Litho. *Perf. 12*

971 A189 20h multicolored .90 .20

Intl. Peace Year.

1986, Mar. 24 *Perf. 14, 12 (65h)*

972 A190 20h multicolored .45 .20
a. Perf. 12 .45 .20
973 A190 65h multicolored .90 .20

Riyadh Municipality, 50th aAnniv.

1986, Apr. 21 *Perf. 12*

974 A191 20h multicolored .45 .20
975 A191 50h multicolored .90 .20

UN child survival campaign.

General Establishment for Electric Power, 10th Anniv. — A192

1986, Apr. 26

976	A192	20h	multicolored	.25	.20
977	A192	65h	multicolored	.90	.20

Continental Maritime Cable Inauguration — A193

1986, June 1 Litho. *Perf. 12*

978	A193	20h	multicolored	.45	.20
979	A193	50h	multicolored	.90	.20

Natl. Guard Housing Project, Riyadh, Inauguration — A194

1986, July 19

980	A194	20h	multicolored	.35	.20
981	A194	65h	multicolored	1.10	.20

Islamic Arch, Holy Ka'aba — A195

1986-98 Litho. *Perf. 12*

984	A195	30h	blk & bluish grn	.20	.20
985	A195	40h	black & lilac rose	.25	.20
986	A195	50h	black & brt green	.65	.35
987	A195	75h	black & Prus bl	.80	.40
a.			Perf. 13½x14	.65	.35
987B	A195	100h	black & red		
988	A195	100h	blk & bl green	.90	.45
989	A195	150h	black & rose lilac	1.60	.80
a.			Perf. 13½x14	1.40	.70
990	A195	2r	blk & vio blue	1.75	.90
			Nos. 984-990 (7)	6.15	3.30

Issued: 30h, 40h, 8/5; 75h, 150h, 7/30/90; 50h, 10/9/90; #987a, 6/13/92; #989a, 6/6/92; 2r, 4/99; #987B, 988, 9/21/96.

This is an expanding set. Numbers may change.

Pilgrimage to Mecca — A196

Designs of: a, A116. b, A129. c, A156. d, A149. e, A141. f, A122. g, A183. h, A167.

1986, Aug. 13 Litho. *Perf. 12*

1002	Block of 8		*11.00*	*11.00*
a.-h.	A196 20h, any single			

Discovery of Oil, 50th Anniv. — A197

World Food Day — A198

1986, Sept. 16

1003	A197	20h	Well, refinery	.45	.20
1004	A197	65h	Well, map	1.40	.20

Because of difficulty in separation most copies have damaged perfs.

1986, Oct. 18

1005	A198	20h	shown	.20	.20
1006	A198	115h	Stylized plant	1.00	.35

Massacre of Palestinian Refugees, Sept. 17, 1982 — A199

1986, Nov. 1 Litho. *Perf. 12*

1007	A199	80h	multicolored	.70	.35
1008	A199	115h	multicolored	1.10	.55

Definitive stamps generally do not have an official date of issue. Any dates shown probably reflect sales at the Riyadh or Dammam post offices only.

Saudi Universities

Imam Mohammed ibn Saud — A200

Umm al-Qura — A201

King Saud — A202

King Fahd Petroleum and Minerals — A203

King Faisal — A204

King Abdul Aziz — A205

Medina Islamic — A206

1986-91

1009	A200	15h	sage grn & blk	.20	.20
1010	A200	20h	ultra & black	.20	.20
1011	A200	50h	ultra & black	.40	.25
1012	A200	65h	brt bl & blk	.50	.25
1013	A200	75h	brt bl & blk	.65	.35
1014	A200	100h	rose & black	.70	.35
1015	A200	150h	rose cl & blk	1.25	.60
1016	A201	50h	ultra & black	.50	.30
1017	A201	65h	brt bl & blk	.65	.25
1018	A201	75h	brt bl & blk	.65	.35
1019	A201	100h	dull rose & blk	1.00	.50
1020	A201	150h	rose cl & blk	1.50	.75
1021	A202	50h	ultra & black	.55	.30
1022	A202	75h	brt bl & blk	.65	.35
1023	A202	100h	dull rose & blk	1.00	.50
1024	A202	150h	rose cl & blk	1.40	.65
1025	A203	50h	ultra & black	.40	.25
1026	A203	75h	brt bl & blk	.65	.35
1027	A203	150h	rose cl & blk	1.25	.60
1028	A204	50h	ultra & black	.40	.25
1029	A204	75h	brt bl & blk	.65	.35
1030	A204	150h	rose cl & blk	1.40	.45
1031	A205	50h	ultra & black	.40	.25
1032	A205	75h	brt bl & blk	.65	.40
1033	A205	150h	rose cl & blk	1.40	.65
1034	A206	50h	ultra & black	.45	.20
1035	A206	75h	brt bl & blk	.55	.35
1036	A206	150h	rose cl & blk	1.25	.25
			Nos. 1009-1036 (28)	21.35	10.50

Issued: #1009-1010, 1012, 1014, 11/26; #1019, 3/29; #1023, 7/22; #1016, 1020, 8/8; #1015, 1027, 1036, 1/31/89; #1011, 1025, 1028, 1031, 2/25/89; #1017, 3/89; #1024, 1030, 1033, 4/29/89; #1034, 7/4/89; #1021, 1989; #1013, 1018, 1026, 1990; #1022, 1029, 1032, 1035, 1991.

Saudi-Bahrain Highway Inauguration — A207

1986, Nov. 26 *Perf. 14*

1039	Strip of 2	1.40	.20
a.-b.	A207 20h any single	.65	.20

Printed se-tenant in a continuous design.

1st Modern Olympic Games, Athens, 90th Anniv. A208

1986, Dec. 27

1040	A208	20h	multicolored	.40	.20
1041	A208	100h	multicolored	2.25	.35

General Petroleum and Minerals Organization (Petromin), 25th Anniv. — A209

Unwmk.

1987, Feb. 23 Litho. *Perf. 12*

1042	A209	50h	multicolored	.50	.25
1043	A209	100h	multicolored	1.00	.50

Restoration and Expansion of Quba Mosque, Medina — A210

Design: View of mosque and model of expanded mosque.

1987, Mar. 21

1044	A210	50h	multicolored	.60	.25
1045	A210	75h	multicolored	.90	.35

Vocational Training A211

Designs: a, Welding. b, Drill press operation. c, Lathe operation. d, Electrician.

Unwmk.

1987, Apr. 8 Litho. *Perf. 12*

1046	Block of 4	5.00	2.50
a.-d.	A211 50h any single	1.25	.60

Cairo Exhibition A212

Design: Desert fortifications in silhouette, Riyadh television tower, King Khalid Intl. Airport hangars and pyramid of Giza.

Unwmk.

1987, June 17 Litho. *Perf. 12*

1047	A212	50h	multicolored	.60	.30
1048	A212	75h	multicolored	1.00	.40

A213

Inauguration of King Fahd Telecommunications Center, Jedda — A214

1987, July 21

1049 A213 50h multicolored .60 .30
1050 A214 75h multicolored 1.00 .40

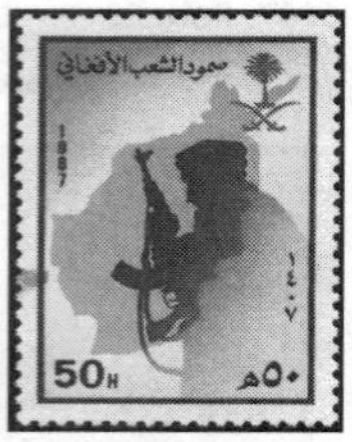

Afghan Resistance Movement A215

1987, July 25

1051 A215 50h multicolored .55 .30
1052 A215 100h multicolored .95 .50

Pilgrimage to Mecca — A216

Design: View of Ihram and Meqat Wadi Muhrim Mosque from Wadi Muhrim Meqat.

1987, Aug. 3

1053 A216 50h multicolored .60 .30
1054 A216 75h multicolored .90 .40
1055 A216 100h multicolored 1.10 .55
Nos. 1053-1055 (3) 2.60 1.25

Home for Disabled Children, 1st Anniv. — A217

1987, Oct. 3

1056 A217 50h multicolored .50 .25
1057 A217 75h multicolored .80 .35

World Post Day — A218

1987, Oct. 10

1058 A218 50h multicolored .50 .30
1059 A218 150h multicolored 1.40 .70

World Food Day A219

1987, Oct. 17

1060 A219 50h multicolored .60 .25
1061 A219 75h multicolored .90 .35

Social Welfare Society, 25th Anniv. — A220

Dome of the Rock — A221

1987, Oct. 26

1062 A220 50h multicolored .65 .30
1063 A220 100h multicolored 1.25 .55

1987, Dec. 5

1064 A221 75h multicolored 1.50 .40
1065 A221 150h multicolored 3.00 .75

Restoration and Expansion of the Prophet's Mosque, Medina — A222

1987, Dec. 15 ***Perf. 14***

1066 A222 50h multicolored .60 .25
1067 A222 75h multicolored .90 .35
1068 A222 150h multicolored 1.75 .70
Nos. 1066-1068 (3) 3.25 1.30

An imperf. 300h souvenir sheet exists.

Battle of Hattin, 800th Anniv. A223

Warriors in silhouette and Dome of the Rock.

1987, Dec. 21 ***Perf. 12***

1069 A223 75h multicolored 1.50 .35
1070 A223 150h multicolored 3.00 .75

Saladin's conquest of Jerusalem.

A224

A225

1987, Dec. 26

1071 A224 50h multicolored .60 .30
1072 A224 75h multicolored 1.00 .40

8th session of the Supreme Council of the Gulf Cooperation Council.

1988, Feb. 13 **Litho.** ***Perf. 12***

1073 A225 50h multicolored .85 .45
1074 A225 75h multicolored 1.25 .65

3rd Regional Highways Conf. of the Middle East.

A226

Inauguration of King Fahd Intl. Stadium — A227

1988, Mar. 2

1075 A226 50h multicolored .65 .30
1076 A227 150h multicolored 2.00 .85

Blood Donation — A228

1988, Apr. 13 **Litho.** ***Perf. 12***

1077 A228 50h multicolored .65 .30
1078 A228 75h multicolored .85 .40

WHO, 40th Anniv. — A229

1988, Apr. 7

1079 A229 50h multicolored .75 .30
1080 A229 75h multicolored .85 .40

King Fahd, Custodian of the Holy Mosques — A230

King Fahd and mosques at Medina and Mecca.

1988, Apr. 23 **Litho.** ***Perf. 12***

1081 A230 50h multicolored .45 .25
1082 A230 75h multicolored .65 .35
1083 A230 150h multicolored 1.40 .65
Nos. 1081-1083 (3) 2.50 1.25

A 75h souvenir sheet exists containing an enlarged version of No. 1082. Sold for 3r.

Environmental Protection A231

1988, June 5

1084 A231 50h multicolored .60 .25
1085 A231 75h multicolored 1.00 .35

Palestinian Uprising, Gaza and the West Bank A232

1988, July 10

1086 A232 75h multicolored 1.10 .40
1087 A232 150h multicolored 2.00 .75

Pilgrimage to Mecca — A233

1988, July 23 **Litho.** ***Perf. 12***

1088 A233 50h multicolored .85 .30
1089 A233 75h multicolored 1.25 .45

World Food Day A234

1988, Oct. 16 **Litho.** ***Perf. 12***

1090 A234 50h multicolored .70 .25
1091 A234 75h multicolored 1.10 .40

Qiblatain Mosque Expansion — A235

1988, Nov. 9

1092 A235 50h multicolored .70 .25
1093 A235 75h multicolored 1.10 .40

5th World Youth Soccer Championships, Riyadh, Dammam, Jedda and Taif — A250

1989, Feb. 16 **Litho.** ***Perf. 12***

1094 A250 75h multicolored .65 .25
1095 A250 150h multicolored 1.25 .50

World Health Day — A251

1989, Apr. 8 Litho. *Perf. 12*

1096 A251 50h multicolored .80 .25
1097 A251 75h multicolored 1.25 .40

Sea Water Desalination Plant — A252

1989, May 30 Litho. *Perf. 12*

1098 A252 50h multicolored .50 .30
1099 A252 75h multicolored .80 .45

Proclamation of the State of Palestine, Nov. 15, 1988 — A253

1989, June 6 Litho. *Perf. 12*

1100 A253 50h multicolored .65 .20
1101 A253 75h multicolored 1.00 .25

Pilgrimage to Mecca — A254

Design: Al-Tan'eem Mosque, Mecca.

1989, July 12 Litho. *Perf. 12*

1102 A254 50h multicolored .60 .20
1103 A254 75h multicolored .95 .25

World Food Day A255

1989, Oct. 16 Litho. *Perf. 12*

1104 A255 75h multicolored .55 .35
1105 A255 150h multicolored 1.10 .70

Holy Mosque Expansion — A256

1989, Dec. 30 Litho. *Perf. 12*

1106 A256 50h multicolored .55 .25
1107 A256 75h multicolored .80 .40
1108 A256 150h multicolored 1.50 .80
Nos. 1106-1108 (3) 2.85 1.45

An imperf souvenir sheet containing an enlarged version of design A256 exists. Sold for 5r.

Youth Soccer Cup Championships A257

UNESCO World Literacy Year — A258

1989, Dec. 20

1109 A257 75h multicolored .80 .35
1110 A257 150h multicolored 1.60 .75

1990, Jan. 9

1111 A258 50h multicolored .70 .30
1112 A258 75h multicolored 1.00 .40

World Health Day — A259

Unwmk.

1990, Apr. 7 Litho. *Perf. 12*

1113 A259 75h multicolored .80 .35
1114 A259 150h multicolored 1.60 .70

Flowers — A262

1990

1115 Sheet of 21 8.50
a.-u. A262 50h any single .40 .20
1116 Sheet of 21 12.50
a.-u. A262 75h any single .55 .30
1117 Sheet of 21 24.00
a.-u. A262 150h any single 1.10 .60
Nos. 1115-1117 (3) 45.00

21 Different species pictured on the sheets. Issued: 50h, 75h, Feb. 6; 150h, Jan. 17.

Islamic Conference, 20th Anniv. — A263

1990, Feb. 7 Litho. *Perf. 12*

1118 A263 75h blue & multi .50 .25
1119 A263 150h gray & multi 1.00 .50

Islamic Heritage A264

Designs: b, Arabic script in rectangle. c, Circular design. d, Mosque and minaret.

1990, July 29

1120 Block of 4 3.25 1.90
a.-d. A264 75h any single .80 .45

Horses A265

1990, Apr. 14

Color of Horse

1121 Block of 4 3.50 1.25
a. A265 50h white, red tassels on bridle .85 .30
b. A265 50h black .85 .30
c. A265 50h white, brown bridle .85 .30
d. A265 50h chestnut .85 .30
1122 A265 50h like #1121d .60 .30
1123 A265 75h like #1121b .90 .45
1124 A265 100h like #1121a 1.25 .60
1125 A265 150h like #1121c 1.75 .90
Nos. 1121-1125 (5) 8.00 3.50

No. 1121 has white border on two sides. Nos. 1122-1125 have white border on four sides.

Pilgrimage to Mecca — A266

1990, June 28

1126 A266 75h multicolored .80 .40
1127 A266 150h multicolored 1.60 .80

Television Tower — A267

1990, July 21

1128 A267 75h multicolored .80 .40
1129 A267 150h multicolored 1.60 .80

Saudi Arabian Airlines Route Map A268

1990, Sept. 3

1130 A268 75h Global routes .60 .35
1131 A268 75h Domestic routes .60 .35
a. Pair, #1130-1131 1.25 .75
1132 A268 150h like #1130 1.25 .75
1133 A268 150h like #1131 1.25 .75
a. Pair, #1132-1133 2.50 1.50
Nos. 1130-1133 (4) 3.70 2.20

World Food Day A269

1990, Oct. 16 Litho. *Perf. 12*

1134 A269 75h multicolored .75 .40
1135 A269 150h multicolored 1.50 .75

Organization of Petroleum Exporting Countries (OPEC), 30th Anniv. — A270

1990, Sept. 26

1136 A270 75h multicolored 1.00 .40
1137 A270 150h multicolored 2.00 .75

Fifth Five Year Development Plan — A271

Designs: a, Oil refinery, irrigation, and oil storage tanks. b, Radio tower, highway, and mine. c, Monument, sports stadium, and vocational training. d, Television tower, environmental protection, and modern architecture.

1990, Oct. 30

1138 A271 75h Block of 4, #a.-d. 4.00 1.50

Battle of Badr, 624 — A272

1991, Apr. 3 Litho. *Perf. 12*

1139 A272 75h org, dk grn & grn .70 .35
1140 A272 150h lt bl, dk bl & grn 1.40 .70

A273

A274

1991, Apr. 9

1141 A273 75h multicolored .70 .35
1142 A273 150h multicolored 1.40 .70

World Health Day.

1991 Litho. *Perf. 12*

Animals: a, k, Impala. b, l, Ibex. c, m, Oryx. d, n, Fox. e, o, Bat. f, p, Hyena. g, q, Cat. h, r, Dugong. i, s, Leopard.

Blocks of 9

1143 A274 25h Block, #a.-i. 2.50 1.25
1144 A274 50h Block, #a.-i. 4.75 2.50
1145 A274 75h Block, #a.-i. 7.25 3.75

1146	A274	100h	Block, #a.-i.	9.50	4.75
1146J	A274	150h	Block, #k.-s.	15.00	11.00
t.			Perf 14x13½	15.00	11.00
			Nos. 1143-1146J (5)	39.00	23.25

Issued: #1143-1146, May 1; #1146J, Dec. 1. No. 1146J exists imperf.

Pilgrimage to Mecca — A275

1991, June 20 Litho. *Perf. 14*

1147	A275	75h	blue & multi	.70	.35
1148	A275	150h	green & multi	1.40	.70

World Telecommunications Day — A276

1991, June 3 *Perf. 12*

1149	A276	75h	multicolored	.70	.35
1150	A276	150h	multicolored	1.40	.70

A277

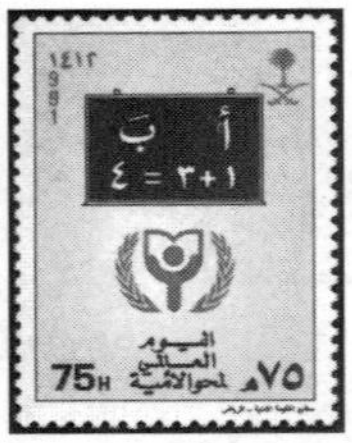

A278

1991, May 11

1151	A277	75h	multicolored	.80	.50
1152	A277	150h	multicolored	1.75	1.00

Liberation of Kuwait.

1991, Sept. 8 Litho. *Perf. 12*

1153	A278	75h	blue & multi	1.00	.50
1154	A278	150h	buff & multi	2.00	1.00

Literacy Day.

A279

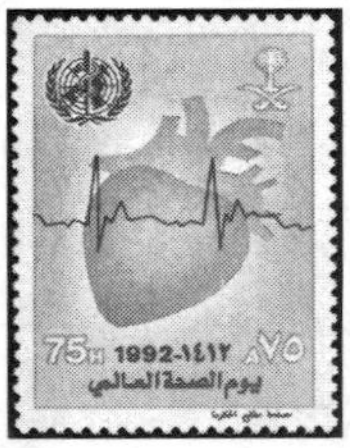

A281

A280

1991, Oct. 16 Litho. *Perf. 12*

1155	A279	75h	green & multi	.70	.40
1156	A279	150h	orange & multi	1.40	.80

World Food Day.

1991, Dec. 7

1157	A280	75h	green & multi	.80	.40
1158	A280	150h	dk blue & multi	1.60	.80

Childrens' Day.

1992, Apr. 8 Litho. *Perf. 12*

1159	A281	75h	lt blue & multi	.75	.40
1160	A281	150h	lt org & multi	1.50	.75

World Health Day.

War Between the Arabs of Medina and Mecca, 624-630 A282

1992, Apr. 18

1161	A282	75h	lt org & grn	.70	.40
1162	A282	150h	lt bl, dk bl & grn	1.40	.75

Pilgrimage to Mecca A283

Unwmk.

1992, June 9 Litho. *Perf. 12*

1163	A283	75h	lt blue & multi	.75	.40
1164	A283	150h	lt orange & multi	1.50	.75

Population and Housing Census — A284

1992, Sept. 26 Litho. *Perf. 14*

1165	A284	75h	blue & multi	.55	.35
1166	A284	150h	org yel & multi	1.10	.70

World Food Day A285

1992, Oct. 17 *Perf. 12*

1167	A285	75h	Vegetables	.70	.35
1168	A285	150h	Fruits	1.40	.70

Consultative Council — A286

Document: d, g, 12 lines. e, h, 13 lines. f, i, 11 lines. 5r, Scrolls of 12, 11, & 13 lines.

1992, Dec. 12 Litho. *Perf. 12*

1168A	A286	75h	Strip of 3, #d.-f.	1.75	1.00
1168B	A286	150h	Strip of 3, #g.-i.	3.50	2.00

Imperf

Size: 120x79mm

1168C	A286	5r	multicolored	17.00	8.50

Birds — A287

a, k, Woodpecker. b, l, Arabian bustard. c, m, Lark. d, n, Turtle dove. e, o, Heron. f, p, Partridge. g, q, Hoopoe. h, r, Falcon. i, s, Houbara bustard. Illustration reduced.

1992-97 *Perf. 14x13½*

Blocks of 9

1169	A287	25h	#a.-i.	2.25	2.25
j.			Perf. 12, #k.-s.		
1170	A287	50h	#a.-i.		
j.			Perf. 12, #k.-s.		
1171	A287	75h	#a.-i.	6.75	3.25
j.			Perf. 12, #k.-s.		
1172	A287	100h	#a.-i.	8.00	4.00
j.			Perf. 12, #k.-s.	8.00	4.00
1173	A287	150h	#a.-i.	13.00	6.50
j.			Perf. 12, #k.-s.	13.00	6.50
			Nos. 1169-1173 (4)	30.00	16.00

Issued: 150h, 3/18/92; 75h, 7/14/92; 100h, 3/1/93; 25h, 50h, 11/6/94; #1171j, 1173j, 8/94; 1169j, 1996; 1170j, 1997(?).

World Health Day A288

1993, Apr. 7 Litho. *Perf. 12*

1175	A288	75h	red & multi	.70	.35
1175A	A288	150h	blue & multi	1.40	.70

King Fahd Championship Soccer Cup — A289

1993, Mar. 15

1176	A289	75h	green & multi	.70	.35
1176A	A289	150h	rose red & multi	1.40	.70

Pilgrimage to Mecca — A290

1993, May 30 Litho. *Perf. 12*

1177	A290	75h	green & multi	.60	.35
1178	A290	150h	blue & multi	1.10	.70

Intl. Telecommunications Day — A291

1993, May 17

Inscription Color

1179	A291	75h	dark blue	.60	.35
1180	A291	150h	red lilac	1.10	.70

Battle of Alkandk A292

1993, May 15

1181	A292	75h	lt org & grn	.60	.35
1182	A292	150h	lt bl, dk bl & grn	1.10	.70

World Food Day — A293

1993, Dec. 14 Litho. *Perf. 12*

1183	A293	75h	black & multi	.70	.35
1184	A293	150h	red & multi	1.40	.70

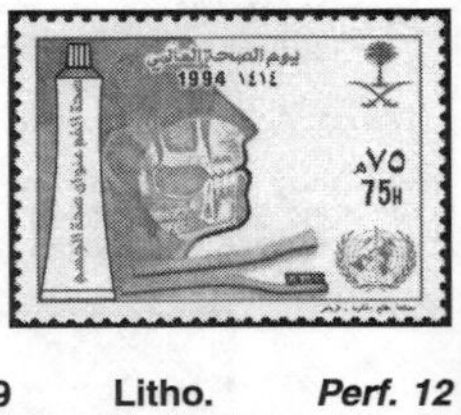

World Dental Health Day A294

1994, Apr. 9 Litho. *Perf. 12*

1185	A294	75h	multicolored	.70	.35
1186	A294	150h	multicolored	1.40	.70

Intl. Olympic Committee, Cent. A295

1994, Apr. 23 Litho. *Perf. 12*

1187	A295	75h	blue & multi	.70	.35
1188	A295	150h	red & multi	1.40	.70

Battle of Kaben A296

1994, June 14 Litho. *Perf. 12*

1189 A296 75h bister & green .70 .35
1190 A296 150h sil, bl & grn 1.40 .70

Pilgrimage to Mecca — A297

1994, May 14

1191 A297 75h green & multi .55 .35
1192 A297 150h red & multi 1.10 .70

Consultative Council — A298

Design: 150h, Different view of building, inscription tablet at right.

1994, July 12 Litho. *Perf. 12*

1193 A298 75h multicolored .70 .35
1194 A298 150h multicolored 1.40 .70
a. Souv. sheet of 2, #1193-1194, imperf.

No. 1194a sold for 5r.

A299

1994 World Soccer Cup Championships, US — A300

1994, June 18

1195 A299 75h multicolored .70 .35
1196 A300 150h multicolored 1.40 .70

King Abdul Aziz Port, Dammam — A301

1994-95 Litho. *Perf. 12*

1198 A301 25h multicolored .50 .25
1199 A301 50h multicolored .50 .25
1200 A301 75h multicolored .70 .35
1201 A301 100h multicolored .90 .45
1202 A301 150h multicolored 1.40 .70
Nos. 1198-1202 (5) 4.00 2.00

Issued: 75h, 8/22/94; 150h, 11/5/94; 100h, 3/11/95; 50h, 11/28/95; 25h, 12/27/95; .

This is an expanding set. Numbers may change.

A304

World Food Day A305

1994, Oct. 16 Litho. *Perf. 12*

1212 A304 75h Green house .70 .35
1213 A305 150h Foods 1.40 .70

A306

Arab League, 50th Anniv. A307

1995, Mar. 25 Litho. *Perf. 12*

1214 A306 75h multicolored .60 .35
1215 A307 150h multicolored 1.25 .70

A308

UN, 50th Anniv. — A309

1995, Feb. 19

1216 A308 75h multicolored .70 .35
1217 A309 150h multicolored 1.40 .70

Refugee Care A310

1995, Apr. 9 Litho. *Perf. 12*

1218 A310 75h green & multi .60 .35
1219 A310 150h tan & multi 1.25 .70

Pilgrimage to Mecca A311

1995, May 3 Litho. *Perf. 12*

1220 A311 75h blue & multi .60 .35
1221 A311 150h tan & multi 1.25 .70

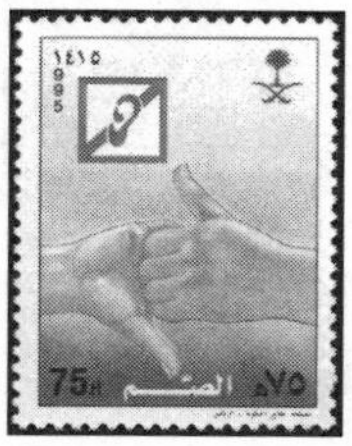

Deaf Week — A312

1995, May 3 Litho. *Perf. 12*

1222 A312 75h shown .70 .35
1223 A312 150h Hand sign, ear 1.40 .70

Saudi Arabian Airlines, 50th Anniv. A313

1995, Aug. 21

1224 A313 75h Anniv. emblem, vert. .70 .35
1225 A313 150h shown 1.40 .70

FAO, 50th Anniv. — A314

1995, Oct. 16 Litho. *Perf. 12*

1226 A314 75h shown .70 .35
1227 A314 150h Emblem over globe 1.40 .70

Jeddah Port — A315

1996 Litho. *Perf. 12*

1228 A315 25h multicolored .25 .20
1229 A315 50h multicolored .50 .25
1230 A315 75h multicolored .75 .40
1230A A315 100h multicolored 1.25 1.25
1230B A315 150h multicolored

Issued: 25h and 50h, 1/27/96; 75h, 2/7/96; 100h, 11/25/96; 150h, 3/30/96.

1996 Summer Olympics, Atlanta A316

1996, June 23

1231 A316 150h orange & multi 1.50 .75
1232 A316 2r blue & multi 2.00 1.00

Pilgrimage to Mecca — A317

1996, Apr. 21

1233 A317 150h black & multi 1.50 .75
1234 A317 2r rose red & multi 2.00 1.00
1235 A317 3r green & multi 3.00 1.50
Nos. 1233-1235 (3) 6.50 3.25

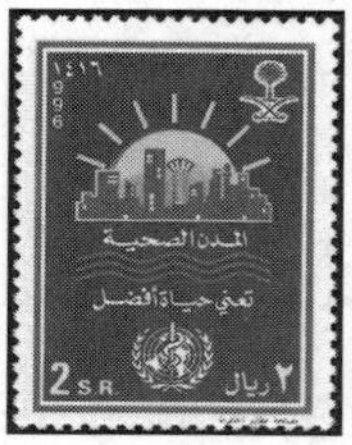

World Health Organization A318

1996, July 21 Litho. *Perf. 12*

1236 A318 2r green & multi 1.75 .90
1237 A318 3r red & multi 2.75 1.40

FAO, 50th Anniv. A319

1996, Oct. 22 Litho. *Perf. 12*

1238 A319 2r blue & multi 1.90 .90
1239 A319 3r red & multi 2.75 1.40

UNICEF, 50th Anniv. A320

1996, Nov. 12

1240 A320 150h buff & multi 1.40 .70
1241 A320 2r blue & multi 1.90 .90

King Abdul Aziz Research Center, 25th Anniv. A321

1996, Dec. 25 Litho. *Perf. 12*

1242 A321 150h brown & multi 1.40 .70
1243 A321 2r green & multi 1.90 .95

Rabigh Steam Power Plant A322

Designs: 150h, Power plant. 2r, Power plant, electrical power lines.

1996, Dec. 26

1244 A322 150h multicolored 1.40 .70

Size: 51x26mm

1245 A322 2r multicolored 1.90 .95

Yanbu Port — A323

1996 Litho. *Perf. 12*

1245A A323 50h multicolored
1246 A323 2r multicolored 1.90 .95

Issued: 1245A, 12/21; 1246 11/25.
See No. 1273.

Opening Mecca A324

1997, Jan. 30

1247 A324 1r brt grn & multi .95 .45
1248 A324 2r lt yel grn & multi 1.90 .95

King Fahd, Birthday A325

1997, Feb. 26

1249 A325 100h green & multi .95 .45
1250 A325 150h pink & multi 1.40 .70
1251 A325 2r tan & multi 1.90 .95
Nos. 1249-1251 (3) 4.25 2.10

An imperf souvenir sheet containing an enlarged version of design A325 exists. Sold for 5r.

Jubail Port — A326

1996-97

1251A A326 50h multicolored .55 .30
1251B A326 100h multicolored .55 .25
1252 A326 150h multicolored .75 .40
1252A A326 2r multicolored 1.90 .95
1252B A326 4r multicolored 2.25 1.10
Nos. 1251A-1252B (5) 6.00 3.00

Issued: 50h, 10/17/96; 100h, 6/29/96; 150h, 7/8/96; 2r, 9/97(?); 4r, 7/24/96.

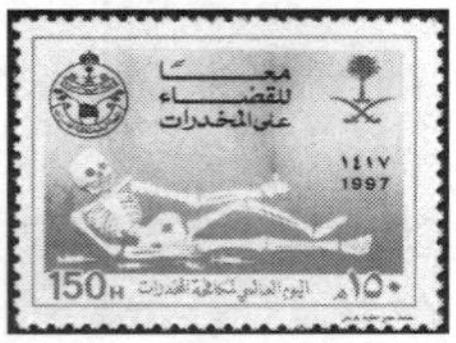

Campaign Against Use of Illegal Drugs A327

1997, Mar. 2

1253 A327 150h blue & multi 1.40 .70
1254 A327 2r red & multi 1.90 .95

Battle of Kayban A328

1997, Mar. 19 Litho. *Perf. 12*

1255 A328 150h multicolored 1.40 .70
1256 A328 2r multicolored 1.90 .95

World Health Day A329

1997, May 9 Litho. *Perf. 14*

1257 A329 150h multicolored 1.40 .70
1258 A329 2r multicolored 1.90 .95

A330

Al-Hijjah A331

1997, Apr. 29

1259 A330 1r multicolored .95 .45
1260 A331 2r multicolored 1.90 .95

King Fahd Natl. Library A332

1997, June 24 Litho. *Perf. 12*

1261 A332 1r shown .95 .45
1262 A332 2r Open book 1.90 .95

A333

A334

1997, July 5

1263 A333 150h Emblem, rays 1.40 .70
1264 A333 2r shown 1.90 .95

King Abdul Aziz Public Library.

1997, June 29 Litho. *Perf. 12*

1265 A334 1r red & multi .95 .50
1266 A334 2r green & multi 1.90 .95

Montreal Protocol on Substances that Deplete Ozone Layer, 10th anniv.

3rd GCC Stamp Exhibition, Riyadh A335

1997, Sept. 28 Litho. *Perf. 12*

1267 A335 1r multicolored 1.00 .50

Prince Salman Center — A336

1997, July 12 Litho. *Perf. 12*

1268 A336 1r multicolored 1.00 .50

Battle of Tabuk A337

1997, Aug. 12 Litho. *Perf. 12*

1269 A337 1r multicolored .95 .50

World Food Day — A338

1998, Feb. 9

1270 A338 2r multicolored 1.90 1.00

Disabled Persons Day — A339

Al Hijjah — A340

1998, May 3 Litho. *Perf. 12*

1271 A339 1r multicolored .95 .50

1998, May 17

1272 A340 2r multicolored 1.90 .95

Yanbu Port Type of 1997

1996, Sept. 3 Litho. *Perf. 12*

1273 A323 100h multicolored .95 .45
1273A A323 150h multi
1273B A323 4r multi

Issued: 150h, 8/28/96; 4r, 11/8/97.

WHO, 50th Anniv. — A341

Dam — A342

1998, May 31

1274 A341 1r multicolored .95 .45

1998, May 17

1275 A342 1r multicolored .95 .45

A343

A344

1998, July 12 Litho. *Perf. 12*

1276 A343 1r multicolored .90 .45

Islamic Organization for Education and Science.

1998, Oct. 7

1277 A344 2r multicolored 1.75 .90

Arabic Stamp Day.

A345

KSA, Cent. A346

Designs: No. 1278, Forts. No. 1279, Military equipment. No. 1280, Entrance to fort, vert. 2r, King Fahd, KSA emblem, outline of map of Saudi Arabia, vert.

1999, Jan 22 Litho. *Perf. 12*

1278 A345 1r multicolored .90 .45
1279 A346 1r multicolored .90 .45
1280 A345 1r multicolored .90 .45
1281 A345 2r multicolored 1.75 .90
Nos. 1278-1281 (4) 4.45 2.25

#1278-1279 exist imperf in souvenir sheets of 1. There are some color variations. #1280-1281 exist imperf in a souvenir sheet of 2. The three sheets sold for 5r each.

King Fahd Intl. Airport — A347

1999, Feb. 6
1282 A347 1r multicolored .85 .45

Size: 26x38mm

1283 A347 2r Jet, control tower 1.75 .85

Development of Palce of Justice Area - A348

1999, Jan. 22
1284 A348 1r multicolored .90 .45

Exists imperf in a souvenir sheet of 1. It sold for 5r.

World Food Day — A348a

1999, Mar. 16 Litho. *Perf. 12*
1285 A348a 1r multicolored .90 .45

Al-Hijjah — A349

1999, Mar. 18 Litho. *Perf. 12*
1286 A349 2r multicolored 1.75 .85

A350

A351

1999, Mar. 6
1287 A350 1r multicolored .90 .45

Kingdom of Saudi Arabia, cent. Exists in an imperf. souvenir sheet of 1. It sold for 5r.

1999, May 22 Litho. *Perf. 12*
1288 A351 1r Traffic signals .90 .45

Academy for Security Sciences — A352

1999, May 29 Litho. *Perf. 12*
1289 A352 150h multicolored 1.40 .70

Intl. Holy Koran Competition — A353

1999, Oct. 32 Litho. *Perf. 12*
1290 A353 1r multicolored .90 .45

UPU, 125th Anniv. — A354

1999, Oct. 26 Litho. *Perf. 12*
1291 A354 1r multi .90 .45

World Meteorological Organization, 50th Anniv. — A355

2000, Mar. 23 Litho. *Perf. 12*
1292 A355 1r multi .90 .45

Flowers Type of 1990

Designs like Nos. 1115a-1115u.

2000, Feb. 1 Litho. *Perf. 12*
1292A Block of 21
b.-v. A262 1r Any single

Pilgrimage to Mecca A356

2000, Mar. 11 *Perf. 14x14¼*
1293 A356 1r black & multi .80 .40
1294 A356 2r red & multi 1.50 .75

Scouting — A357

2000, July 18 Litho. *Perf. 14*
1295 A357 1r multi .75 .35

Riyadh, Arabian Cultural Capital, 2000 — A358

2000, July 4 Litho. *Perf. 14*
1296 A358 1r multi

Water Conservation A359

2000, June 18
1297 A359 1r multi

Consultative Council, 75th Anniv. — A360

2000, June 7
1298 A360 1r multi

UN High Commissioner for Refugees, 50th Anniv. — A361

2000, Sept. 23
1299 A361 2r multi 1.50 .75

Jizan Port — A362

2000, Sept. 16 Litho. *Perf. 14*
1299A A362 50h multi .40 .40
1299B A362 1r multi
1300 A362 2r multi 1.60 1.60

King Abdul Aziz City for Science and Technology A363

2000, Oct. 28
1301 A363 1r multi .75 .35

King Khalid University A364

2000, Dec. 5 *Perf. 14*
1302 A364 1r multi .75 .35

Buraydah — A365

2000 *Perf. 13¾x14*
1303 A365 50h blue & multi
1304 A365 1r grn & multi
1305 A365 2r blk & multi

Buraydah — A366

2000-01 *Perf. 13¾x14*
1306 A366 50h blue & multi
1307 A366 1r grn & multi
1308 A366 2r blk & multi

No. 1308 issued 2/2/01.

King Fahd Printing Press A367

Denomination color: 50h, Pink. 1r, Blue. 2r, Black.

2001, Apr. 25 Litho. *Perf. 14*
1309-1311 A367 Set of 3

A368

2001, Apr. 28
1312 A368 1r multi

Pilgrimage to Mecca — A369

No. 1313: a, Mosque, tower at center, b, Holy Ka'aba. c, Mosque, tower at left and center. d, Mosque, tower and two men at left. e, Mosque, tower at right, mountain in background. f, Mosque, tower and five pilgrims at left. g, Mosque, tower at right. h, Mosque, orange background.

2001, May 1 ***Perf. 13¾x14***

1313	A369	1r Block of 8, #a-h	6.25	6.25

Palestinian Intifada A370

Designs: 1r, Map of Israel, Palestinian boy and father. 2r, Barbed wire, boy and father, vert.

2001, May 15 **Litho.** ***Perf. 14***

1314-1315	A370	Set of 2	2.60	2.60

A souvenir sheet containing an imperforate 49x36mm example of No. 1314 sold for 5r.

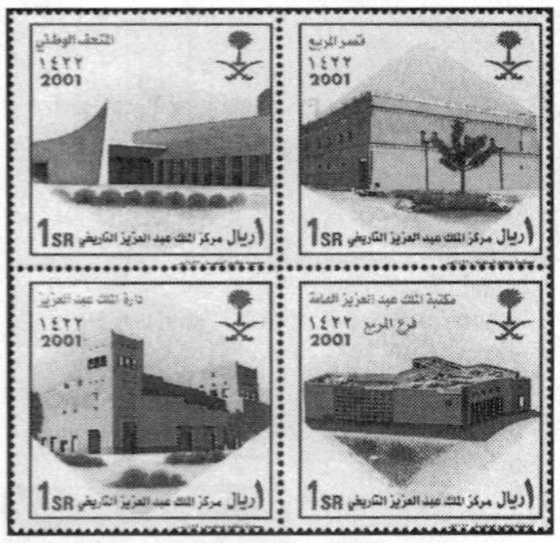

King Abdul Aziz Historical Center — A371

No. 1316: a, Building with curved, pointed wall. b, Building with one tree in front. c, Building with towers. d, Aerial view of building. Illustration reduced.

2001, Aug. 15

1316	A371	1r Block of 4, #a-d	3.25	3.25

World Teacher's Day — A372

2001, Oct. 10

1317	A372	1r multi	.75	.75

Paintings A373

No. 1318: a, Abstract cityscape in green and yellow. b, Horse and geometric designs. c, Building windows. d, Landscape in yellow, orange and brown. e, Building with blue sky.

2001, Oct. 15

1318		Horiz. strip of 5	4.00	4.00
a.-e.	A373	1r Any single	.80	.80

AIR POST STAMPS

Catalogue values for unused stamps in this section are for Never Hinged items.

Airspeed Ambassador Airliner — AP1

1949-58 **Unwmk.** **Typo.** ***Perf. 11***

C1	AP1	1g blue green	2.00	.20
C2	AP1	3g ultra	2.50	.20
a.		3g blue ('58)	10.50	.90
C3	AP1	4g orange	2.50	.20
C4	AP1	10g purple	7.00	.20
C5	AP1	20g brn vio ('58+)	6.25	.20
a.		20g chocolate ('49)	12.50	.45
C6	AP1	100g violet rose	62.50	6.25
		Nos. C1-C6 (6)	82.75	7.25

Imperfs. exist, not regularly issued.
The 1st printings are on grayish paper and sell for more.
No. C3 exists with pin-perf 6.
+ The date for No. C5 is not definite.

Saudi Airlines Convair 440 — AP2

Type I (Saud Cartouche)
(Illustrated over No. 286)

1960-61 **Photo.** ***Perf. 14***

C7	AP2	1p dull pur & grn	.55	.20
C8	AP2	2p grn & dull pur	.55	.20
C9	AP2	3p brn red & bl	.55	.20
C10	AP2	4p bl & dull pur	.55	.20
C11	AP2	5p grn & rose red	.55	.20
C12	AP2	6p ocher & slate	.90	.20
C13	AP2	8p rose & gray ol	1.10	.20
C14	AP2	9p purple & red brn	1.60	.20
C15	AP2	10p blk & dl red brn	4.50	.40
C16	AP2	15p bl & bis brn	4.50	.20
C17	AP2	20p bis brn & emer	4.50	.35
C18	AP2	30p sep & Prus grn	11.00	.90
C19	AP2	50p green & indigo	22.50	.65
C20	AP2	100p gray & dk brn	45.00	1.75
C21	AP2	200p dk vio & black	67.50	2.75
		Nos. C7-C21 (15)	165.85	8.60

Nos. C7-C18 exist imperf., probably not regularly issued.

1963-64 **Photo.** **Wmk. 337**
Size: 27½x22mm

C24	AP2	1p lilac & green	2.25	.20
C25	AP2	2p green & dull pur	8.50	.20
C26	AP2	4p blue & dull pur	3.25	.20
C27	AP2	6p ocher & slate	8.50	.70
C28	AP2	8p rose & gray olive	16.00	1.40
C29	AP2	9p pur & red brn ('64)	11.00	.90
		Nos. C24-C29 (6)	49.50	3.60

Redrawn
Perf. 13½x13
1964 **Wmk. 337** **Litho.**
Size: 28½x23mm

C30	AP2	3p brn red & dull bl	4.75	.45
C31	AP2	10p blk & dk red brn	7.50	.70
C32	AP2	20p bis brn & emer	16.00	1.60
		Nos. C30-C32 (3)	28.25	2.75

Nos. C30-C32 are widely spaced in the sheet, producing large margins.

Saudi Airline Boeing 720-B Jet — AP3

Type I (Saud Cartouche)
(Illustrated over No. 286)

1965-70 **Unwmk.** **Litho.** ***Perf. 14***

C33	AP3	1p lilac & green	80.00	2.75
C34	AP3	2p grn & dull pur	2,750.	90.00
C35	AP3	3p rose lil & dull bl	9.50	.20
C36	AP3	4p blue & dull pur	5.50	.20
C37	AP3	5p ol & rose red	1,800.	400.00
C38	AP3	6p ocher & slate	100.00	1.75
C39	AP3	7p rose & ol gray	6.25	.35
C40	AP3	8p rose & gray ol	80.00	1.75
C41	AP3	9p purple & red brn	5.25	.30
C42	AP3	10p blk & dk red brn	80.00	5.50
C43	AP3	11p green & bister	80.00	18.00
C44	AP3	12p orange & gray	5.50	.30
C45	AP3	13p dk green & yel grn	4.25	.30
C46	AP3	14p dk blue & org	4.25	.35
C47	AP3	15p blue & bis brn	75.00	5.50
C48	AP3	16p black & ultra	6.25	.45
C49	AP3	17p bister & sepia	5.00	.35
C50	AP3	18p dk bl & yel grn	5.00	.35
C51	AP3	19p car & dp org	5.50	.45
C52	AP3	20p bis brn & emer	140.00	6.25
C53	AP3	23p olive & bister	150.00	11.00
C54	AP3	24p dk blue & sep	5.00	.45
C55	AP3	26p ver & blue grn	5.00	.45
C56	AP3	27p ol brn & ap grn	5.75	.45
C57	AP3	31p car rose & rose red	7.25	.55
C58	AP3	33p red & dull pur	9.50	.55

The 50p, 100p and 200p exist but were not placed in use.
Issue years: 1966, 1p, 3p, 7p, 10p, 12p-14p, 16p-19p; 1969, 5p, 11p; 1970, 2p, 6p, 8p, 15p, 20p; others, 1965.

Type II (Faisal Cartouche)

1966-78 **Unwmk.** **Litho.** ***Perf. 14***

C59	AP3	1p dull pur & grn	20.00	.90
C60	AP3	2p green & dull pur	20.00	1.40
C61	AP3	3p brn red & dull bl	20.00	.45
C62	AP3	4p blue & dull pur	10.00	.25
C63	AP3	5p ol & rose red	1,800.	450.00
C64	AP3	6p ocher & slate	125.00	9.00
C65	AP3	7p rose & ol gray	57.50	6.25
C66	AP3	8p rose & gray ol	77.50	11.00
C67	AP3	9p purple & red brn	5.00	.55
C68	AP3	10p blk & dull red brn	16.00	.90
C69	AP3	11p green & bister	12.00	.45
C70	AP3	12p orange & gray	45.00	3.50
C71	AP3	13p dk grn & yel grn	14.00	.90
C72	AP3	14p dk blue & org	13.00	1.50
C73	AP3	15p blue & bis brn	11.00	.70
C74	AP3	16p black & ultra	16.00	2.75
C75	AP3	17p bister & sepia	14.00	1.40
C76	AP3	18p dk bl & yel grn	13.00	2.25
C77	AP3	19p carmine & org	18.00	.90
C78	AP3	20p brn & brt grn	175.00	12.50
C79	AP3	23p olive & bister	22.50	2.75
C80	AP3	24p dk blue & blk	27.50	2.75
C83	AP3	31p car rose & rose red		—
C84	AP3	33p red & dull pur	11.00	.45
C85	AP3	50p emer & ind	575.00	175.00
C86	AP3	100p gray & dk brn	775.00	275.00
C87	AP3	200p dk vio & blk	900.00	175.00

The existence of 26p and 27p denominations has been reported.
The status of the 31p has been questioned. If it exists it may not have been issued.
Issue years: 1968, 4p, 33p; 1969, 7p; 1970, 8p, 9p, 20p; 1971, 13p, 16p; 1974, 50p, 200p; 1975, 12p, 14p, 15p, 17p, 19p, 24p; 1976, 18p; 1978, 31p, 100p; others, 1966.

1968-71 **Wmk. 361** **Litho.** ***Perf. 14***

C88	AP3	1p lilac & green	6.00	.20
C89	AP3	2p green & lilac	7.50	.20
C90	AP3	3p rose lil & dull bl	35.00	1.75
C91	AP3	4p blue & dull pur	9.50	1.10
C92	AP3	7p rose & gray	9.50	1.50
C93	AP3	8p red & gray ol	37.50	6.00
C94	AP3	9p pur & red brn	52.50	7.25
C95	AP3	10p blk & dull red brn	32.50	3.50
		Nos. C88-C95 (8)	190.00	21.50

Issue years: 1969, 3p, 10p; 1970, 4p; 1971, 7p-9p; others, 1968.

Falcon — AP4

Perf. 13½x14
1968-71 **Litho.** **Wmk. 361**

C96	AP4	1p green & red brn	10.00	.20
C97	AP4	4p dk red & red brn	150.00	11.00
C98	AP4	10p blue & red brn	18.00	2.75
C99	AP4	20p green & red brn ('71)	32.50	5.50
		Nos. C96-C99 (4)	210.50	19.45

Nine other denominations were printed but are not known to have been issued.

HEJAZ POSTAGE DUE STAMPS

From Old Door at El Ashraf Barsbai in Shari el Ashrafiya, Cairo — D1

Serrate Roulette 13
1917, June 27 **Typo.** **Unwmk.**

LJ1	D1	20pa red	2.75	2.00
LJ2	D1	1pi blue	2.75	2.00
LJ3	D1	2pi magenta	2.75	2.00
		Nos. LJ1-LJ3 (3)	8.25	6.00

For overprints see Nos. LJ4-LJ10, LJ17-LJ25, J9,

a

b

Nos. LJ1-LJ3 Overprinted Type "a" in Black or Red

1921, Dec.

LJ4	D1	20pa red	18.00	2.75
a.		Double overprint, one at left	140.00	
b.		Overprint at left	30.00	20.00
LJ5	D1	1pi blue (R)	5.50	3.50
LJ6	D1	1pi bl, ovpt. at left	27.50	18.00
a.		Overprint at right	27.50	32.50
LJ7	D1	2pi magenta	10.00	7.25
a.		Double overprint, one at left	62.50	
b.		Overprint at left	27.50	
		Nos. LJ4-LJ7 (4)	61.00	31.50

Nos. LJ1-LJ3 Overprinted Type "b" in Black

1922, Jan.

LJ8 D1 20pa red 22.50 27.50
a. Overprint at left 35.00
LJ9 D1 1pi blue 3.25 3.25
a. Overprint at left 45.00
LJ10 D1 2pi magenta 3.25 3.25
a. Overprint at left 32.50
Nos. LJ8-LJ10 (3) 29.00 34.00

Regular issue of 1922 Overprinted

Black Overprint

1923 ***Perf. 11½***

LJ11 A7 ½pi red 3.50 1.40
a. Inverted overprint 50.00
LJ12 A7 1pi dark blue 6.50 1.40
a. Inverted overprint 80.00
b. Double overprint 125.00
LJ13 A7 2pi orange 3.50 1.75
a. Inverted overprint 47.50
Nos. LJ11-LJ13 (3) 13.50 4.55

1924

Blue Overprint

LJ14 A7 ½pi red 16.00 2.75
a. Inverted overprint 80.00
LJ15 A7 1pi dark blue 35.00 2.75
a. Inverted overprint 100.00
LJ16 A7 2pi orange 27.50 4.50
a. Inverted overprint 80.00
Nos. LJ14-LJ16 (3) 78.50 10.00

This overprint reads "Mustahaq" (Due).

Jedda Issues

Nos. LJ1-LJ3 Overprinted in Red or Blue (Overprint reads up in illustration)

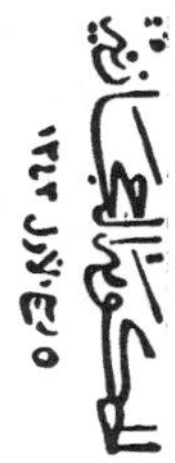

Jedda issues were also used in Medina and Yambo. **Used values for #L51-L186 and LJ17-LJ39 are for genuine cancels. Privately applied cancels exist for "Mekke" (Mecca, bilingual or all Arabic), Khartoum, Cairo, as well as for Jeddah. Many private cancels have wrong dates, some as early as 1916. These are worth half the used values.**

1925, Jan. ***Serrate Roulette 13***

LJ17 D1 20pa red (R) 350.00 *350.00*
LJ19 D1 1pi blue (R) 18.00 *18.00*
LJ20 D1 1pi blue (Bl) 25.00 *25.00*
LJ21 D1 2pi mag (Bl) 14.00 *14.00*

Overprint Reading Down

LJ17a D1 20pa *550.00 550.00*
LJ18 D1 20pa red (Bl) *450.00*
LJ19a D1 1pi 18.00 *18.00*
LJ20a D1 1pi 67.50 *80.00*
LJ21a D1 2pi 60.00 *60.00*

Nos. LJ1-LJ3 Overprinted in Blue or Red

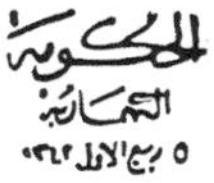

1925

LJ22 D1 20pa red (Bl) 425.00 *425.00*
a. Inverted overprint 325.00 *325.00*
LJ24 D1 1pi blue (R) 22.50 *27.50*
a. Inverted overprint 32.50 *32.50*
LJ25 D1 2pi magenta (Bl) 18.00 *18.00*
a. Inverted overprint 35.00 *45.00*
b. Double overprint 350.00

No. LJ2 with this overprint in blue is bogus.

Regular Issues of 1922-24 Overprinted

a

and Handstamped

b

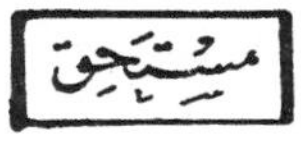

1925 ***Perf. 11½***

LJ26 A7 ⅛pi red brown 18.00 *18.00*
LJ27 A7 ½pi red 25.00 *25.00*
LJ28 A7 1pi dark blue 18.00 *18.00*
LJ29 A7 1½pi violet 18.00 *18.00*
LJ30 A7 2pi orange 20.00 *20.00*
LJ31 A7 3pi olive brown 20.00 *20.00*
LJ32 A7 3pi dull red 45.00 *45.00*
LJ33 A7 5pi olive green 20.00 *20.00*
LJ34 A7 10pi vio & dk brn 25.00 *25.00*
Nos. LJ26-LJ34 (9) 209.00 *209.00*

The printed overprint *(a)*, consisting of the three top lines of Arabic, was used alone for the first issue (Nos. LJ26a-LJ34a). The "postage due" box was so small and indistinct that its equivalent in larger characters was added by boxed handstamp *(b)* at bottom of each stamp for the second issue (Nos. LJ26-LJ34). The handstamped overprint *(b)* is found double, inverted, etc. It is also known in dark violet.

Counterfeits exist of both overprint and handstamp.

Without Boxed Handstamp "b"

LJ26a A7 ⅛pi red brown 42.50
LJ27a A7 ½pi red 42.50
LJ28a A7 1pi dark blue 42.50
LJ29a A7 1½pi violet 42.50
LJ30a A7 2pi orange 42.50
LJ31a A7 3pi olive brown 42.50
LJ32a A7 3pi dull red 42.50
LJ33a A7 5pi olive green 55.00
LJ34a A7 10pi vio & dk brn 55.00
Nos. LJ26a-LJ34a (9) 407.50

Regular Issue of 1922 Overprinted

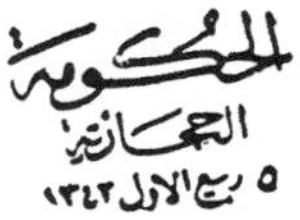

and Handstamped

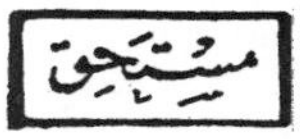

LJ35 A7 ½pi red *140.00 140.00*
LJ36 A7 1½pi violet *140.00 140.00*
a. Overprint in red, boxed handstamp violet *1,400.*
LJ37 A7 2pi orange *175.00 175.00*
LJ38 A7 3pi olive brown *140.00 140.00*
LJ39 A7 5pi olive green *140.00 140.00*
Nos. LJ35-LJ39 (5) *735.00 735.00*

Counterfeits exist of Nos. LJ4-LJ39.

Arabic Numeral of Value
D2 D3

1925, May-June ***Perf. 11½***

LJ40 D2 ½pi light blue 2.75
LJ41 D2 1pi orange 2.75
LJ42 D2 2pi lt brown 2.75
LJ43 D2 3pi pink 2.75
Nos. LJ40-LJ43 (4) 11.00

Nos. LJ40-LJ43 exist imperforate. Impressions in colors other than issued are trial color proofs.

Black Overprint

1925

LJ44 D3 ½pi light blue 2.75
LJ45 D3 1pi orange 2.75
LJ46 D3 2pi light brown 2.75
LJ47 D3 3pi pink 3.50
Nos. LJ44-LJ47 (4) 11.75

Nos. LJ44-LJ47 exist with either Jedda or Cairo overprints and the tablets normally read upward. Values are for Cairo overprints; Jedda overprints sell for more.

Red Overprint

LJ48 D3 ½pi light blue 3.50
LJ49 D3 1pi orange 3.50
LJ50 D3 2pi light brown 3.50
LJ51 D3 3pi pink 3.50

Blue Overprint

LJ52 D3 ½pi light blue 3.50
LJ53 D3 1pi orange 3.50
LJ54 D3 2pi light brown 3.50
LJ55 D3 3pi pink 3.50
Nos. LJ40-LJ55 (16) 50.75

Red and blue overprints are from Cairo. Nos. LJ44-LJ55 exist imperf.

NEJDI ADMINISTRATION OF HEJAZ POSTAGE DUE STAMPS

Nos. LJ11-LJ16 Handstamped in Blue, Red or Black

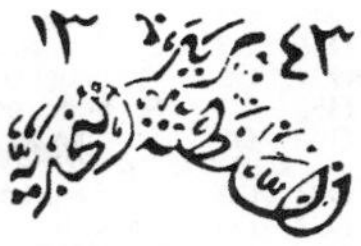

1925, Apr.-June Unwmk. ***Perf. 11½***

J1 A7 ½pi red (Bl) 27.50 27.50
J2 A7 1pi lt blue (R) 55.00 55.00
a. 1pi dark blue (R) 35.00 35.00
J3 A7 2pi yel buff (Bl) 55.00 55.00
a. 2pi orange (Bl) 47.50 47.50
Nos. J1-J3 (3) 137.50 137.50

The original boxed overprint is printed on Nos. J1, J2a and J3a. Nos. J2-J3 are overprinted on a new printing of the basic stamps with handstamped boxed overprints.

Same, with Postage Due Overprint in Blue

J4 A7 ½pi red (Bl) *140.00*
J5 A7 1pi dk blue (R) —
J6 A7 2pi orange (Bl) *175.00*

On Hejaz Stamps of 1922-24

Handstamped in Blue

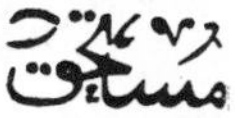

J7 A7 ½pi red (Bl & Bl) 16.00 16.00
J8 A7 3pi brn red (Bl & Bl) 19.00 19.00

Handstamped in Blue, Black or Violet

See note before No. 35.

On Hejaz No. LJ9

Serrate Roulette 13½

J9 D1 1pi blue (V) 60.00 27.50

Same Overprint on Hejaz Stamps of 1924 with additional Handstamp in Black, Blue or Red

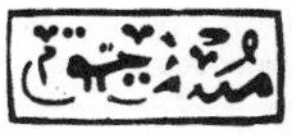

Perf. 11½

J10 A7 3pi brn red (Bl & Bk) 11.00 11.00
J11 A7 3pi brn red (Bk & Bl) 11.00 11.00

Same Handstamps on Hejaz Railway Tax Stamps

J12 R3 1pi blue (Bk & R) 12.00 12.00
J13 R3 2pi ocher (Bl & Bk) 12.00 12.00
J14 R3 5pi green (Bk & R) 20.00 20.00
J15 R3 5pi green (V & BK) 20.00 9.00
Nos. J10-J15 (6) 86.00 75.00

The second handstamp, which is struck on the lower part of the Postage Due Stamps, is the word Mustahaq (Due) in various forms.

#J13 exists with 2nd handstamp in blue.

Hejaz-Nejd

D1

1926 Typo. ***Perf. 11***

J16 D1 ½pi carmine 4.00 .65
J17 D1 2pi orange 4.00 .65
J18 D1 6pi light brown 4.00 .65
Nos. J16-J18 (3) 12.00 1.95

Nos. J16-J18 exist with perf. 14, 14x11 and 11x14, and imperf. These sell for six times the values quoted.

Nos. J16-J18 in colors other than listed (both perf. and imperf.) are proofs.

Counterfeit note after No. 80 also applies to Nos. J16-J21.

Pan-Islamic Congress Issue

Postage Due Stamps of 1926 Handstamped like Regular Issue

J19 D1 ½pi carmine 5.50 4.50
J20 D1 2pi orange 5.50 4.50
J21 D1 6pi light brown 5.50 4.50
Nos. J19-J21 (3) 16.50 13.50

D2

1927 ***Perf. 11½***

J22 D2 1pi slate 18.00 .45
a. Inscription reads "2 piastres" in upper right circle 175.00 100.00
J23 D2 2pi dark violet 5.75 .45

Saudi Arabia

Saudi Arabia No. 161 Handstamped in Black

1935

J24 A9 ½g dark carmine 225.00

Two types of overprint.

D3

1937-39 **Unwmk.**

J25 D3 ½g org brn ('39) 12.00 12.00
J26 D3 1g light blue 12.00 12.00
J27 D3 2g rose vio ('39) 17.00 8.00
Nos. J25-J27 (3) 41.00 32.00

Catalogue values for unused stamps in this section, from this point to the end of the section, are for Never Hinged items.

D4

1961 Litho. ***Perf. 13x13½***

J28 D4 1p purple 5.00 5.00
J29 D4 2p green 8.50 4.00
J30 D4 4p rose red 10.00 10.00
Nos. J28-J30 (3) 23.50 19.00

The use of Postage Due stamps ceased in 1963.

OFFICIAL STAMPS

Official stamps were normally used only on external correspondence.

O1

O2

1939 Unwmk. Typo. *Perf. 11½*

O1	O1	3g deep ultra	3.00	1.40
		Perf. 11, 11½		
O2	O1	5g red violet	3.75	1.75
		Perf. 11		
O3	O1	20g brown	8.00	3.50
O4	O1	50g blue green	15.00	7.25
O5	O1	100g olive grn	62.50	32.50
O6	O1	200g purple	50.00	22.50
		Nos. O1-O6 (6)	142.25	68.90

Catalogue values for unused stamps in this section, from this point to the end of the section, are for Never Hinged items.

1961 Litho. *Perf. 13x13½*
Size: 18x22-22½mm

O7	O2	1p black	.90	.20
O8	O2	2p dark green	1.50	.30
O9	O2	3p bister	1.75	.35
O10	O2	4p dark blue	2.25	.45
O11	O2	5p rose red	2.75	.55
O12	O2	10p maroon	4.75	1.75
O13	O2	20p violet blue	8.25	3.25
O14	O2	50p dull brown	22.50	9.00
O15	O2	100p dull green	40.00	16.00
		Nos. O7-O15 (9)	84.65	31.85

Nos. O8, O10-O15 exist imperf., probably not regularly issued.

1964-65 Wmk. 337 *Perf. 13½x13*
Size: 21x26mm

O16	O2	1p black	.90	.35
O17	O2	2p green ('65)	1.75	.70
O18	O2	3p bister	6.25	2.50
O19	O2	4p dark blue	4.50	1.75
O20	O2	5p rose red	5.50	1.10
		Nos. O16-O20 (5)	18.90	6.40

1965-70 Wmk. 337 Typo. *Perf. 11*

O21	O2	1p dark brown	3.50	1.40
O22	O2	2p green	3.50	1.40
O23	O2	3p bister	3.50	1.40
O24	O2	4p dark blue	3.50	1.40
O25	O2	5p deep orange	6.75	1.75
O26	O2	6p red lilac	6.75	1.75
O27	O2	7p emerald	6.75	1.75
O28	O2	8p car rose	6.75	1.75
O29	O2	9p red	*75.00*	
O30	O2	10p red brown	27.50	1.75
O31	O2	11p pale green	*55.00*	
O32	O2	12p violet	*275.00*	
O33	O2	13p blue	9.00	2.75
O34	O2	14p purple	9.00	2.75
O35	O2	15p orange	*90.00*	
O36	O2	16p black	*90.00*	
a.		"19" instead of "16"	*450.00*	
O37	O2	17p gray green	*90.00*	
O38	O2	18p yellow	*90.00*	
O39	O2	19p dp red lilac	*90.00*	
O39A	O2	20p lt blue green		
O40	O2	23p ultra	*225.00*	
O41	O2	24p yellow green	*90.00*	
O42	O2	26p bister	*90.00*	
O43	O2	27p pale lilac	*90.00*	
O44	O2	31p pale salmon	*140.00*	
O45	O2	33p yellow green	*90.00*	
O46	O2	50p olive bister	*350.00*	
O47	O2	100p ol gray ('70)	*800.00*	
		Nos. O21-O39,O40-O47 (27)	*2,816.*	

Nos. O21-O28, O30 and O33-O34 were released to the philatelic trade in 1964. Nos. O21-O47 were printed from new plates; lines of the design are heavier. The numerals have been enlarged and the P's are smaller. Head of "P" 2mm wide on 1964-65 issue, 1mm wide on 1965-70 issue.

O3

Wmk. 361, 337 (7p, 8p, 9p, 11p, 12p, 23p)

1970-72 Litho. *Perf. 13½x14*

O48	O3	1p red brown	2.75	.90
O49	O3	2p deep green	2.75	.90
O50	O3	3p rose red	3.50	1.40
O51	O3	4p bright blue	4.50	1.75
O52	O3	5p brick red	4.50	1.75
O53	O3	6p orange	4.50	1.75
a.		Wmk. 337	*175.00*	*45.00*
O54	O3	7p deep salmon	*175.00*	
O55	O3	8p violet		
O56	O3	9p dk blue grn		
O57	O3	10p blue	6.25	2.75
a.		Wmk. 337		
O58	O3	11p olive green		
O58A	O3	12p black brown		
O59	O3	20p gray violet	14.00	4.50
a.		Wmk. 337	*175.00*	*90.00*
O59B	O3	23p ocher ('72)	*375.00*	
O60	O3	31p deep plum	*45.00*	*18.00*
O61	O3	50p light brown	*700.00*	
O62	O3	100p green	*700.00*	

Use of official stamps ceased in 1974.

NEWSPAPER STAMPS

Nos. 8, 9 and 14 with Additional Overprint in Black

1925 Unwmk. *Perf. 11½*

P1	A7	⅛pi red brown (Bk)	*1,800.*	*1,800.*
P2	A7	⅛pi red brown (V)	*1,400.*	*900.*
P3	A7	½pi red (V)	*2,750.*	*1,800.*

Overprint reads: "Matbu'a" (Newspaper), but these stamps were normally used for regular postage. Counterfeits exist.

The status of this set in question. The government may have declared it to be unauthorized.

POSTAL TAX STAMPS

PT1

1934, May 15 Unwmk. *Perf. 11½*

RA1	PT1	⅛g scarlet	*175.00*	4.50

No. RA1 collected a "war tax" to aid wounded of the 1934 Saudi-Yemen war.

Nos. RA2-RA8 raised funds for the Medical Aid Society.

General Hospital, Mecca PT2

1936, Oct.
Size: 37x20mm

RA2	PT2	⅛g scarlet	*625.00*	9.00

Type of 1936, Redrawn

1937-42
Size: 30½x18mm

RA3	PT2	⅛g scarlet	60.00	.90
a.		⅛g rose ('39)	*110.00*	1.75
b.		⅛g rose car, perf. 11 ('42)	*175.00*	*6.75*

General Hospital, Mecca — PT3

1943 Typo. *Perf. 11½, 11*
Grayish Paper

RA4	PT3	⅛g car rose	*35.00*	.20
a.		⅛g scarlet	*35.00*	.20

The 1g green and 5g indigo were not for postal use.

See Nos. RA5-RA8.

Map of Saudi Arabia Type I (Flag inscriptions intact) — PT4

Type II (Flag inscriptions scratched out)

1946 Unwmk. *Perf. 11½*

RA4B	PT4	½g magenta (II)	16.00	.90
c.		Type I	55.00	.90
d.		Type I, perf. 11	45.00	9.00
e.		Type II, perf. 11	67.50	

Return of King Ibn Saud from Egypt.

This stamp was required on all mail during Jan.-July.

Type of 1943, Redrawn

1948-53 Litho. *Perf. 10*

RA5	PT3	⅛g rose brn ('53)	*20.00*	.20
c.		Perf. 11x10	*27.50*	2.75

Catalogue values for unused stamps in this section, from this point to the end of the section, are for Never Hinged items.

1950 *Rouletted*

RA6	PT3	⅛g red brown	5.50	.20
a.		⅛g rose	7.25	.20
b.		⅛g carmine	9.00	.25

All lines in lithographed design considerably finer; some shading in center eliminated.

Type of 1943

1955-56 Photo. *Perf. 11*

RA7	PT3	⅛g rose car	8.00	.20
RA8	PT3	¼g car rose ('56)	4.75	.20

The tax on postal matter was discontinued in May, 1964.

Coat of Arms, Waves and View — PT5

Wmk. 361

1974, Oct. Litho. *Perf. 14*

RA9	PT5	1r blue & multi	*110.00*	

Obligatory on all mailed entries in a government television contest during month of Ramadan in 1974 and 1975. The tax aided a benevolent society.

SCHLESWIG

'shles-ˌwig

LOCATION — In the northern part of the former Schleswig-Holstein Province, in northern Germany.

Schleswig was divided into North and South Schleswig after the Versailles Treaty, and plebiscites were held in 1920. North Schleswig (Zone 1) voted to join Denmark, South Schleswig to stay German.

100 Pfennig = 1 Mark
100 Ore = 1 Krone

Watermark

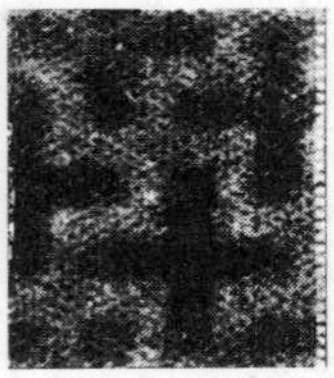
Wmk. 114-Multiple Crosses

Plebiscite Issue

Arms — A11

View of Schleswig A12

Perf. 14x15

1920, Jan. 25 Typo. Wmk. 114

1	A11	2½pf gray	.20	*.20*
2	A11	5pf green	.20	*.20*
3	A11	7½pf yellow brown	.20	*.20*
4	A11	10pf deep rose	.20	*.20*
5	A11	15pf red violet	.20	*.20*
6	A11	20pf deep blue	.20	*.20*
7	A11	25pf orange	.30	*.20*
8	A11	35pf brown	.35	*.30*
9	A11	40pf violet	.30	*.20*
10	A11	75pf greenish blue	.35	*.30*
11	A12	1m dark brown	.35	*.30*
12	A12	2m deep blue	.50	*.40*
13	A12	5m green	1.00	*.70*
14	A12	10m red	1.75	*1.40*
		Nos. 1-14 (14)	6.10	*5.00*
		Set, never hinged	14.00	

The colored portions of type A11 are white, and the white portions are colored, on Nos. 7-10.

Types of 1920 Overprinted in Blue

1920, May 20

15	A11	1o dark gray	.20	*.75*
16	A11	5o green	.20	*.35*
17	A11	7o yellow brn	.20	*.75*
18	A11	10o rose red	.20	*.75*
19	A11	15o lilac rose	.20	*.75*
20	A11	20o dark blue	.20	*1.25*
21	A11	25o orange	.20	*4.50*
22	A11	35o brown	.70	*7.75*
23	A11	40o violet	.25	*2.50*
24	A11	75o greenish blue	.35	*4.50*
25	A12	1k dark brown	.50	*7.00*
26	A12	2k deep blue	4.25	*27.50*
27	A12	5k green	2.75	*27.50*
28	A12	10k red	6.25	*52.50*
		Nos. 15-28 (14)	16.45	*138.35*
		Set, never hinged	62.50	

OFFICIAL STAMPS

Nos. 1-14 Overprinted **C·I·S**

1920 Wmk. 114 *Perf. 14x15*

O1	A11	2½pf gray	52.50	*77.50*
O2	A11	5pf green	52.50	*90.00*
O3	A11	7½pf yellow brn	52.50	*77.50*
O4	A11	10pf deep rose	52.50	*97.50*
O5	A11	15pf red violet	35.00	*50.00*
O6	A11	20pf dp blue	52.50	*55.00*
O7	A11	25pf orange	100.00	*140.00*
a.		Inverted overprint	*900.00*	
O8	A11	35pf brown	100.00	*140.00*
O9	A11	40pf violet	90.00	82.50
O10	A11	75pf grnsh blue	100.00	*210.00*
O11	A12	1m dark brown	100.00	*210.00*
O12	A12	2m deep blue	150.00	*225.00*
O13	A12	5m green	225.00	*350.00*
O14	A12	10m red	425.00	*525.00*
		Nos. O1-O14 (14)	1,587.	*2,330.*
		Set, never hinged	3,100.	

The letters "C.I.S." are the initials of "Commission Interalliée Slesvig," under whose auspices the plebiscites took place.

Counterfeit overprints exist.

SENEGAL

ˌse-ni-ˈgäl

LOCATION — West coast of Africa, bordering on the Atlantic Ocean
GOVT. — Republic
AREA — 76,000 sq. mi.
POP. — 10,051,930 (1999 est.)
CAPITAL — Dakar

The former French colony of Senegal became part of French West Africa in 1943. The Republic of Senegal was established Nov. 25, 1958. From Apr. 4, 1959, to June 20, 1960, the Republic of Senegal and the Sudanese Republic together formed the Mali Federation. After its breakup, Senegal resumed issuing its own stamps in 1960.

100 Centimes = 1 Franc

Catalogue values for unused stamps in this country are for Never Hinged items, beginning with Scott 195 in the regular postage section, Scott B16 in the in the semi-postal section, Scott C26 in the airpost section, Scott CB2 in the airpost semi-postal section, Scott J32 in the postage due section, and Scott O1 in the official section.

French Colonies Nos. 48, 49, 51, 52, 55, Type A9, Surcharged:

55555
a b c d e

1887 Unwmk. *Perf. 14x13½*

Black Surcharge

1	(a)	5c on 20c red, *grn*	140.00	140.00
a.		Double surcharge		
2	(b)	5c on 20c red, *grn*	200.00	200.00
3	(c)	5c on 20c red, *grn*	600.00	600.00
4	(d)	5c on 20c red, *grn*	175.00	175.00
5	(e)	5c on 20c red, *grn*	275.00	275.00
6	(a)	5c on 30c brn, *bis*	225.00	225.00
7	(b)	5c on 30c brn, *bis*	800.00	800.00
8	(d)	5c on 30c brn, *bis*	300.00	275.00
		Nos. 1-8 (8)	2,715.	2,690.

See Madagascar #6-7 for stamps with surcharge like "d" on 10c and 25c stamps.

10101010
f g h i

9	(f)	10c on 4c cl, *lav*	75.00	75.00
10	(g)	10c on 4c cl, *lav*	125.00	125.00
11	(h)	10c on 4c cl, *lav*	50.00	*60.00*
12	(i)	10c on 4c cl, *lav*	55.00	55.00
a.		"1" without top stroke		
13	(f)	10c on 20c red, *grn*	400.00	400.00
14	(g)	10c on 20c red, *grn*	475.00	475.00
15	(h)	10c on 20c red, *grn*	375.00	375.00
16	(i)	10c on 20c red, *grn*	*2,500.*	*2,500.*
17	(j)	10c on 20c red, *grn*	450.00	450.00
18	(k)	10c on 20c red, *grn*	1,400.	1,400.
19	(l)	10c on 20c red, *grn*	425.00	425.00
20	(m)	10c on 20c red, *grn*	425.00	425.00

15151515
n o p q

1515151515
r s t u

1515
v w

21	(n)	15c on 20c red, *grn*	57.50	57.50
22	(o)	15c on 20c red, *grn*	50.00	50.00
23	(p)	15c on 20c red, *grn*	40.00	40.00
24	(q)	15c on 20c red, *grn*	75.00	75.00
25	(r)	15c on 20c red, *grn*	45.00	45.00
26	(s)	15c on 20c red, *grn*	45.00	45.00
27	(t)	15c on 20c red, *grn*	125.00	125.00
28	(u)	15c on 20c red, *grn*	45.00	45.00
29	(v)	15c on 20c red, *grn*	55.00	55.00
30	(w)	15c on 20c red, *grn*	240.00	240.00
		Nos. 21-30 (10)	777.50	777.50

Counterfeits exist of Nos. 1-34.

Surcharged:

1892

Black Surcharge

31	A9	75c on 15c blue	325.	125.
32	A9	1fr on 5c grn, *grnsh*	375.	140.

"SENEGAL" in Red

33	A9	75c on 15c blue	*8,000.*	*3,250.*
34	A9	1fr on 5c grn, *grnsh*	*3,750.*	*850.*

Navigation and Commerce — A24

1892-1900 Typo. *Perf. 14x13½*

Name of Colony in Blue or Carmine

35	A24	1c blk, *lil bl*	.70	.65
36	A24	2c brn, *buff*	1.40	1.25
37	A24	4c claret, *lav*	1.40	1.10
38	A24	5c grn, *grnsh*	1.60	1.25
39	A24	5c yel grn ('00)	1.40	.75
40	A24	10c blk, *lav*	5.00	3.75
41	A24	10c red ('00)	3.25	1.00
42	A24	15c bl, quadrille paper	8.00	1.25
43	A24	15c gray ('00)	3.50	1.25
44	A24	20c red, *grn*	6.75	3.75
45	A24	25c blk, *rose*	11.50	4.25
46	A24	25c blue ('00)	25.00	21.00
47	A24	30c brn, *bis*	11.00	5.25
48	A24	40c red, *straw*	14.00	11.50
49	A24	50c car, *rose*	25.00	17.50
50	A24	50c brn, *az* ('00)	30.00	26.00
51	A24	75c vio, *org*	12.50	12.00
52	A24	1fr brnz grn, *straw*	13.00	11.50
		Nos. 35-52 (18)	175.00	125.00

Perf. 13½x14 stamps are counterfeits.
For surcharges see Nos. 53-56, 73-78.

Stamps of 1892 Surcharged:

5 10

1903

53	A24	5c on 40c red, *straw*	7.50	7.50
54	A24	10c on 50c car, *rose*	11.00	11.00
55	A24	10c on 75c vio, *org*	10.00	10.00
56	A24	10c on 1fr brnz grn, *straw*	55.00	55.00
		Nos. 53-56 (4)	83.50	83.50

General Louis Faidherbe A25

Oil Palms — A26

Dr. Noel Eugène Ballay — A27

1906 Typo.

"SÉNÉGAL" in Red or Blue

57	A25	1c slate	.45	.40
a.		"SENEGAL" omitted	75.00	75.00
58	A25	2c choc (R)	.60	.55
58A	A25	2c choc (Bl)	1.25	1.10
59	A25	4c choc, *gray bl*	.80	.80
60	A25	5c green	1.50	.45
61	A25	10c car (Bl)	5.00	.45
a.		"SENEGAL" omitted	300.00	300.00
62	A25	15c violet	4.00	2.25
63	A26	20c blk, *az*	4.25	2.25
64	A26	25c bl, *pnksh*	1.40	1.00
65	A26	30c choc, *pnksh*	3.50	3.00
66	A26	35c blk, *yellow*	15.00	1.50
67	A26	40c car, *az* (Bl)	5.25	4.50
67A	A26	45c choc, *grnsh*	13.00	8.25
68	A26	50c dp violet	5.00	4.25
69	A26	75c bl, *org*	4.25	2.25
70	A27	1fr blk, *azure*	16.00	11.00
71	A27	2fr blue, *pink*	22.50	16.00
72	A27	5fr car, *straw* (Bl)	42.50	40.00
		Nos. 57-72 (18)	146.25	100.00

Stamps of 1892-1900 Surcharged in Carmine or Black

05 10

1912

73	A24	5c on 15c gray (C)	.50	.50
74	A24	5c on 20c red, *grn*	.60	.60
75	A24	5c on 30c brn, *bis* (C)	.60	.60
76	A24	10c on 40c red, *straw*	.70	.70
77	A24	10c on 50c car, *rose*	1.75	1.75
78	A24	10c on 75c vio, *org*	3.25	3.25
		Nos. 73-78 (6)	7.40	7.40

Two spacings between the surcharged numerals found on Nos. 73 to 78.

Senegalese Preparing Food A28

1914-33 Typo.

79	A28	1c ol brn & vio	.20	.20
80	A28	2c black & blue	.20	.20
81	A28	4c gray & brn	.20	.20
82	A28	5c yel grn & bl grn	.30	.20
83	A28	5c blk & rose ('22)	.20	.20
84	A28	10c org red & rose	.60	.20
85	A28	10c yel grn & bl grn ('22)	.20	.20
86	A28	10c red brn & bl ('25)	.20	.20
87	A28	15c red org & brn vio ('17)	.20	.20
88	A28	20c choc & blk	.20	.20
89	A28	20c grn & bl grn ('26)	.20	.20
90	A28	20c db & lt bl ('27)	.30	.30
91	A28	25c ultra & bl	.60	.30
92	A28	25c red & blk ('22)	.30	.20
93	A28	30c black & rose	.40	.20
94	A28	30c red org & rose ('22)	.30	.20
95	A28	30c gray & bl ('26)	.30	.20
96	A28	30c dl grn & dp grn ('28)	.40	.30
97	A28	35c orange & vio	.40	.30
98	A28	40c violet & grn	.50	.30
99	A28	45c bl & ol brn	.95	.85
100	A28	45c rose & bl ('22)	.50	.20
101	A28	45c rose & ver ('25)	.50	.35
102	A28	45c ol brn & org ('28)	2.50	1.75
103	A28	50c vio brn & bl	.95	.70
104	A28	50c ultra & bl ('22)	1.25	1.10
105	A28	50c red org & grn ('26)	.30	.20
106	A28	60c vio, *pnksh* ('26)	.30	.20
107	A28	65c rose red & dp grn ('28)	.95	.85
108	A28	75c gray & rose	.60	.45
109	A28	75c dk bl & lt bl ('25)	.60	.45
110	A28	75c rose & gray bl ('26)	.95	.35
111	A28	90c brn red & rose ('30)	3.75	3.00
112	A28	1fr violet & blk	.70	.45
113	A28	1fr blue ('26)	.60	.45
114	A28	1fr blk & gray bl ('26)	1.10	.35
115	A28	1.10fr bl grn & blk ('28)	2.50	2.00
116	A28	1.25fr dp grn & dp org ('33)	.80	.70
117	A28	1.50fr dk bl & bl ('30)	1.90	1.75
118	A28	1.75fr dk brn & Prus bl ('33)	4.75	.70
119	A28	2fr carmine & bl	2.10	1.50
120	A28	2fr lt bl & brn ('22)	1.75	.55
121	A28	3fr red vio ('30)	2.75	1.40
122	A28	5fr green & vio	3.25	1.00
		Nos. 79-122 (44)	42.50	25.80

Nos. 79, 82, 84 and 97 are on both ordinary and chalky paper.
For surcharges see Nos. 123-137, B1-B2.

No. 108 and Type of 1914 Surcharged:

60 60

1922-25

123	A28	60c on 75c vio, *pnksh*	.65	.65
124	A28	65c on 15c red org & dl vio ('25)	.85	.85
125	A28	85c on 15c red org & dl vio ('25)	.85	.85
126	A28	85c on 75c ('25)	.85	.85

No. 87 Surcharged in Various Colors

0,01 0,01

1922

127	A28	1c on 15c (Bk)	.45	.45
128	A28	2c on 15c (Bl)	.45	.45
129	A28	4c on 15c (G)	.45	.45
130	A28	5c on 15c (R)	.45	.45
		Nos. 123-130 (8)	5.00	5.00

Stamps and Type of 1914 Surcharged with New Value and Bars in Black or Red

1924-27

131	A28	25c on 5fr grn & vio	.35	.30
132	A28	90c on 75c brn red & cer ('27)	.60	.55
a.		Double surcharge	90.00	90.00
133	A28	1.25fr on 1fr bl & lt bl (R) ('26)	.35	.30
134	A28	1.50fr on 1fr dk bl & ultra ('27)	.45	.35
135	A28	3fr on 5fr mag & ol brn ('27)	1.25	.50
136	A28	10fr on 5fr dk bl & red org ('27)	5.00	2.00
137	A28	20fr on 5fr vio & ol bis ('27)	6.00	5.00
		Nos. 131-137 (7)	14.00	9.00

Common Design Types pictured following the introduction

Colonial Exposition Issue

Common Design Types

Name of Country Typographed in Black

1931 Engr. *Perf. 12½*

138	CD70	40c deep green	1.75	1.75
139	CD71	50c violet	1.75	1.75
140	CD72	90c red orange	1.75	1.75
a.		"SENEGAL" double	100.00	100.00
141	CD73	1.50fr dull blue	1.75	1.75
		Nos. 138-141 (4)	7.00	7.00

Faidherbe Bridge, St. Louis A29

Diourbel Mosque A30

1935-40 *Perf. 12½x12*

142	A29	1c violet blue	.20	.20
143	A29	2c brown	.20	.20
144	A29	3c violet ('40)	.20	.20
145	A29	4c gray blue	.20	.20
146	A29	5c orange red	.20	.20
147	A29	10c violet	.20	.20
148	A29	15c black	.20	.20
149	A29	20c dk carmine	.20	.20
150	A29	25c black brn	.20	.20
151	A29	30c green	.20	.20
152	A29	40c rose lake	.20	.20
153	A29	45c dk blue grn	.20	.20
154	A30	50c red orange	.20	.20
155	A30	60c violet ('40)	.20	.20
156	A30	65c dk violet	.20	.20
157	A30	70c red brn ('40)	.30	.30
158	A30	75c brown	.40	.40
159	A30	90c rose car	1.50	.90
160	A30	1fr violet	6.25	1.25
161	A30	1.25fr redsh brn	.70	.40
162	A30	1.25fr rose car ('39)	.50	.50
163	A30	1.40fr dk bl grn ('40)	.40	.40
164	A30	1.50fr dk blue	.20	.20
165	A30	1.60fr pck bl ('40)	.40	.40
166	A30	1.75fr dk blue grn	.20	.20
167	A30	2fr blue	.30	.20
168	A30	3fr green	.30	.20
169	A30	5fr black brn	.50	.30
170	A30	10fr rose lake	.80	.50
171	A30	20fr grnsh slate	.85	.50
		Nos. 142-171 (30)	16.60	9.65

Nos. 143, 148 and 156 surcharged with new values are listed under French West Africa.

For surcharges see Nos. B9, B11-B12.

Paris International Exposition Issue
Common Design Types

1937 *Perf. 13*
172 CD74 20c deep violet .50 .50
173 CD75 30c dark green .50 .50
174 CD76 40c car rose .55 .55
175 CD77 50c dark brown .65 .65
176 CD78 90c red .70 .70
177 CD79 1.50fr ultra 1.10 1.10
Nos. 172-177 (6) 4.00 4.00

Colonial Arts Exhibition Issue
Souvenir Sheet
Common Design Type

1937 Unwmk. ***Imperf.***
178 CD76 3fr rose violet 3.50 3.50

Senegalese Woman — A31

1938-40 ***Perf. 12x12½, 12½x12***
179 A31 35c green .40 .25
180 A31 55c chocolate .40 .35
181 A31 80c violet .70 .25
182 A31 90c lt rose vio ('39) .30 .30
183 A31 1fr car lake 1.50 .65
184 A31 1fr cop brn ('40) .20 .20
185 A31 1.75fr ultra .50 .25
186 A31 2.25fr ultra ('39) .40 .40
187 A31 2.50fr black ('40) .70 .70
Nos. 179-187 (9) 5.10 3.35

For surcharge see No. B10.

Caillié Issue
Common Design Type

1939 Engr. ***Perf. 12½x12***
188 CD81 90c org brn & org .35 .35
189 CD81 2fr brt vio .50 .50
190 CD81 2.25fr ultra & dk bl .50 .50
Nos. 188-190 (3) 1.35 1.35

For No. 188 surcharged 20fr and 50fr, see French West Africa.

New York World's Fair Issue
Common Design Type

1939 ***Perf. 12½x12***
191 CD82 1.25fr car lake .35 .35
192 CD82 2.25fr ultra .35 .35

Diourbel Mosque and Marshal Pétain A32

1941 Engr.
193 A32 1fr green .30
194 A32 2.50fr blue .30

Nos. 193-194 were issued by the Vichy government, but it is doubtful whether they were placed on sale in Senegal.

Stamps of types A29, A30 and A31, without "RF," were issued in 1943 by the Vichy Government, but were not placed on sale in the colony.

See French West Africa No. 69 for additional stamp inscribed "Senegal" and "Afrique Occidentale Francaise."

Catalogue values for unused stamps in this section, from this point to the end of the section, are for Never Hinged items.

Republic

Roan Antelope — A33

Animals: 10fr, Savannah buffalo, horiz. 15fr, Wart hog. 20fr, Giant eland. 25fr, Bushbuck, horiz. 85fr, Defassa waterbuck.

1960 Unwmk. Engr. ***Perf. 13***
195 A33 5fr brn, grn & claret .20 .20
196 A33 10fr grn & brn .20 .20
197 A33 15fr blk, claret & org brn .20 .20
198 A33 20fr brn, grn, ocher & sal .25 .20
199 A33 25fr brn, lt grn & org .35 .20
200 A33 85fr brn, grn, olive & bis 1.10 .50
Nos. 195-200 (6) 2.30 1.50

Imperforates
Most Senegal stamps from 1960 onward exist imperforate in issued and trial colors, and also in small presentation sheets in issued colors.

Allegory of Independent State — A34

1961, Apr. 4
201 A34 25fr bl, choc & grn .25 .20

Independence Day, Apr. 4.

Wrestling A35

1fr, Pirogues racing. 2fr, Horse race. 30fr, Male tribal dance. 45fr, Lion game.

1961, Sept. 30 ***Perf. 13***
202 A35 50c ol, bl & choc .20 .20
203 A35 1fr grn, bl & maroon .20 .20
204 A35 2fr ultra, bis & sepia .20 .20
205 A35 30fr carmine & claret .30 .20
206 A35 45fr indigo & brn org .40 .25
Nos. 202-206 (5) 1.30 1.05

UN Headquarters, New York and Flag — A36

1962, Jan. 6 Engr. ***Perf. 13***
207 A36 10fr grn, ocher & car .20 .20
208 A36 30fr car, ocher & grn .30 .20
209 A36 85fr grn, ocher & car .70 .40
Nos. 207-209 (3) 1.20 .80

1st anniv. of Senegal's admission to the United Nations, Sept. 28, 1960.

Map of Africa, ITU Emblem and Man with Telephone A37

1962, Jan. 22 Photo. ***Perf. 12½x12***
210 A37 25fr blk, grn, red & ocher .25 .20

Meeting of the Commission for the Africa Plan of the ITU, Dakar.

African and Malgache Union Issue
Common Design Type

1962, Sept. 8 Unwmk.
211 CD110 30fr grn, bluish grn, red & gold .40 .35

Boxing — A38

Charaxes Varanes — A40

UPU Monument, Bern A39

15fr, Diving, horiz. 20fr, High jump, horiz. 25fr, Soccer. 30fr, Basketball. 85fr, Running.

1963, Apr. 11 Engr. ***Perf. 13***
Athletes in Dark Brown
212 A38 10fr ver & emer .20 .20
213 A38 15fr dk bl & bis .20 .20
214 A38 20fr ver & dk bl .20 .20
215 A38 25fr grn & dk bl .25 .20
216 A38 30fr ver & grn .35 .20
217 A38 85fr vio bl .90 .60
Nos. 212-217 (6) 2.10 1.60

Friendship Games, Dakar, Apr. 11-21.

1963, June 14 Unwmk. ***Perf. 13***
218 A39 10fr grn & ver .20 .20
219 A39 15fr dk bl & red brn .20 .20
220 A39 30fr red brn & dk bl .35 .25
Nos. 218-220 (3) .75 .65

2nd anniv. of Senegal's admission to the UPU.

1963, July 20 Photo. ***Perf. 12½x13***

Butterflies: 45fr, Papilio nireus. 50fr, Colotis danae. 85fr, Epiphora bauhiniae. 100fr, Junonia hierta. 500fr, Danaus chrysippus.

Butterflies in Natural Colors
221 A40 30fr bl gray & blk .60 .20
222 A40 45fr org & blk .80 .25
223 A40 50fr brt yel & blk .90 .30
224 A40 85fr red & blk 1.40 .55
225 A40 100fr bl & blk 1.60 .65
226 A40 500fr emer & blk 6.25 2.25
Nos. 221-226 (6) 11.55 4.20

Prof. Gaston Berger (1896-1960), Philosopher, and Owl — A41

1963, Nov. 13 ***Perf. 12½x12***
227 A41 25fr multi .25 .20

Scales, Globe, Flag and UNESCO Emblem A42

1963, Dec. 10
228 A42 60fr multi .55 .30

15th anniv. of the Universal Declaration of Human Rights.

Flag, Mother and Child — A43

1963, Dec. 21 ***Perf. 12x12½***
229 A43 25fr multi .30 .25

Issued for the Senegalese Red Cross.

Dredging of Titanium-bearing Sand — A44

Designs: 10fr, Titanium extraction works. 15fr, Cement works at Rufisque. 20fr, Phosphate quarry at Pallo. 25fr, Extraction of phosphate ore at Taiba. 85fr, Mineral dock, Dakar.

1964, July 4 Engr. ***Perf. 13***
230 A44 5fr grnsh bl, car & dk brn .20 .20
231 A44 10fr ocher, grn & ind .20 .20
232 A44 15fr dk bl, brt grn & dk brn .20 .20
233 A44 20fr ultra, ol & pur .20 .20
234 A44 25fr dk bl, yel & blk .25 .20
235 A44 85fr bl, red & brn .80 .40
Nos. 230-235 (6) 1.85 1.40

Cooperation Issue
Common Design Type

1964, Nov. 7 Engr. ***Perf. 13***
236 CD119 100fr dk grn, dk brn & car .90 .60

St. Theresa's Church, Dakar A45

10fr, Mosque, Touba. 15fr, Mosque, Dakar, vert.

1964, Nov. 28 Unwmk. ***Perf. 13***
237 A45 5fr bl, grn & red brn .20 .20
238 A45 10fr dk bl, ocher & blk .20 .20
239 A45 15fr brn, bl & sl grn .20 .20
Nos. 237-239 (3) .60 .60

Leprosy Examination — A46

Leprosarium, Peycouk Village — A47

1965, Jan. 30 Engr. *Perf. 13*

240 A46 20fr brn red, grn & blk .25 .20
241 A47 65fr org, dk bl & grn .65 .40

Issued to publicize the fight against leprosy.

Upper Casamance Region — A48

Views: 30fr, Sangalkam. 45fr, Forest along Senegal River.

1965, Feb. 27 Unwmk. *Perf. 13*

242 A48 25fr red brn, sl bl & grn .25 .20
243 A48 30fr indigo & lt brn .25 .20
244 A48 45fr yel grn, red brn & dk brn .40 .20
Nos. 242-244,C41 (4) 1.90 1.00

Abdoulaye Seck A49

Berthon-Ader Telephone A51

General Post Office, Dakar A50

1965, Apr. 24 Unwmk. *Perf. 13*

245 A49 10fr dk brn & blk .20 .20
246 A50 15fr brn & dk sl grn .20 .20

1965, May 17 Engr.

Designs: 60fr, Cable laying ship "Alsace." 85fr, Picard's cable relay for submarine telegraph.

247 A51 50fr bl grn & org brn .50 .30
248 A51 60fr mag & dk bl .60 .40
249 A51 85fr ver, bl & red brn .90 .50
Nos. 247-249 (3) 2.00 1.20

ITU, centenary.

Plowing with Ox Team A52

Designs: 60fr, Harvesting millet, vert. 85fr, Men working in rice field.

1965, July 3 Unwmk. *Perf. 13*

250 A52 25fr dk ol grn, brn & pur .25 .20
251 A52 60fr ind, sl grn & dk brn .55 .25
252 A52 85fr dp car, sl grn & brt grn .80 .35
Nos. 250-252 (3) 1.60 .80

Gorée Sailboat A53

Cashew — A54

Designs: 20fr, Large Seumbediou canoe. 30fr, Fadiouth one-man canoe. 45fr, One-man canoe on Senegal River.

1965, Aug. 7 Photo. *Perf. 12½x13*

253 A53 10fr multi .20 .20
254 A53 20fr multi .20 .20
255 A53 30fr multi .30 .20
256 A53 45fr multi .40 .25
Nos. 253-256 (4) 1.10 .85

1965 Photo. *Perf. 12½*

257 A54 10fr shown .20 .20
258 A54 15fr Papaya .20 .20
259 A54 20fr Mango .20 .20
260 A54 30fr Peanuts .30 .20
Nos. 257-260 (4) .90 .80

Issued: 10fr, 15fr, 20fr, Nov. 6. 30fr, Dec. 18.

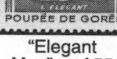

"Elegant Man" — A55

Drummer and Map of Africa — A56

Dolls of Gorée: 2fr, "Elegant Woman." 3fr, Woman peddling fruit. 4fr, Woman pounding grain.

1966, Jan. 22 Engr. *Perf. 13*

261 A55 1fr brn, rose car & ultra .20 .20
262 A55 2fr brn, bl & org .20 .20
263 A55 3fr brn, red & bl .20 .20
264 A55 4fr brn, lil & emer .20 .20
Nos. 261-264 (4) .80 .80

1966

15fr, Sculpture; mother & child. #267, Music; stringed instrument. 75fr, Dance; carved antelope headpiece (Bambara). 90fr, Ideogram.

265 A56 15fr dk red brn, bl & ocher .20 .20
266 A56 30fr brn, red & grn .30 .20
267 A56 30fr dk red brn, bl & yel .30 .20
268 A56 75fr dk red brn, bl & blk .70 .40
269 A56 90fr dk red brn, org & sl grn .90 .55
a. Souv. sheet of 4, #265, 267-269 2.50 2.50
Nos. 265-269 (5) 2.40 1.55

Intl. Negro Arts Festival, Dakar, Apr. 1-24. Issued: #266, 2/5; others, 4/2. See #364.

Fish — A57

1966, Feb. 26 Photo. *Perf. 12½x13*

270 A57 20fr Tuna .25 .20
271 A57 30fr Merou .35 .20
272 A57 50fr Girella .55 .30
273 A57 100fr Parrot fish 1.10 .50
Nos. 270-273 (4) 2.25 1.20

Arms of Senegal — A58

Flowers — A59

1966, July 2 Litho. *Perf. 13x12½*

274 A58 30fr multi .25 .20

1966, Nov. 19 Photo. *Perf. 11½*

275 A59 45fr Mexican poppy .40 .20
276 A59 55fr Mimosa .50 .20
277 A59 60fr Haemanthus .60 .25
278 A59 90fr Baobab .80 .35
Nos. 275-278 (4) 2.30 1.00

Harbor, Gorée Island A60

Designs: 25fr, S.S. France in roadstead, Dakar and seagulls. 30fr, Hotel and tourist village, N'Gor. 50fr, Hotel and bay, N'Gor.

1966, Dec. 25 Engr. *Perf. 13*

279 A60 20fr mar & vio bl .20 .20
280 A60 25fr red, grn & blk .25 .20
281 A60 30fr dk red & dp bl .25 .20
282 A60 50fr brn, sl grn & emer .45 .20
Nos. 279-282 (4) 1.15 .80

Laying Urban Water Pipes A61

Symbolic Water Cycle — A62

20fr, Cattle at water trough. 50fr, Village well.

1967, Mar. 25 Engr. *Perf. 13*

283 A61 10fr org brn, grn & dk bl .20 .20
284 A61 20fr grn, brt bl & org brn .25 .20

Typo.

Perf. 13x14

285 A62 30fr sky bl, blk & org .35 .20

Engr.

Perf. 13

286 A62 50fr brn red, brt bl & bis .55 .20
Nos. 283-286 (4) 1.35 .80

Intl. Hydrological Decade (UNESCO), 1965-74.

Lions Emblem A63

1967, May 27 Photo. *Perf. 12½x13*

287 A63 30fr lt ultra & multi .30 .20

50th anniversary of Lions International.

Blaise Diagne A64

1967, June 10 Engr. *Perf. 13*

288 A64 30fr ocher, sl grn & dk red brn .30 .20

Blaise Diagne (1872-1934), member of French Chamber of Deputies and Colonial Minister.

For surcharge see No. 380.

City Hall and Arms, Dakar A65

1967, June 10

289 A65 90fr bl, dk grn & blk .80 .40

Eagle and Antelope Carvings — A66

150fr, Flags, maple leaf and EXPO '67 emblem.

1967, Sept. 2 Photo. *Perf. 13x12½*

290 A66 90fr red & blk .60 .30
291 A66 150fr red & multi 1.00 .50

EXPO '67 Intl. Exhib., Montreal, 4/28-10/27.

International Tourist Year Emblem — A67

Tourist Photographing Hippopotamus and Siminti Hotel — A68

1967, Oct. 7 Typo. *Perf. 14x13*

292 A67 50fr blk & bl .55 .40

Perf. 13

Engr.

293 A68 100fr blk, sl grn & ocher 1.10 .50

International Tourist Year.

Monetary Union Issue

Common Design Type

1967, Nov. 4 Engr. *Perf. 13*

294 CD125 30fr multi .25 .20

West African Monetary Union, 5th anniv.

Lyre-shaped Megalith, Kaffrine — A69

70fr, Ancient covered bowl, Bandiala.

1967, Dec. 2 Engr. *Perf. 13*

295 A69 30fr grn, grnsh bl & red brn .25 .20
296 A69 70fr red brn, ocher & brt bl .60 .25

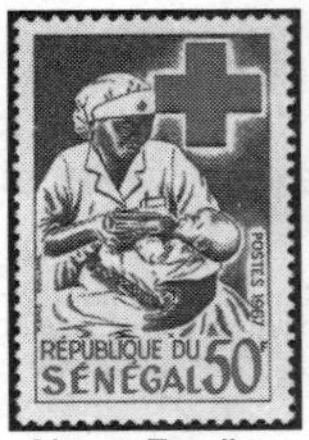

Nurse Feeding Child — A70

Human Rights Flame — A71

1967, Dec. 23

297 A70 50fr bl grn, red & red brn .45 .25

Issued for the Senegalese Red Cross.

1968, Jan. 20 Photo. *Perf. 13x12½*

298 A71 30fr brt grn & gold .30 .20

International Human Rights Year.

Parliament, Dakar A72

1968, Apr. 16 Photo. *Perf. 12½x13*

299 A72 30fr car rose .25 .20

Inter-Parliamentary Union Meeting, Dakar.

Pied Kingfisher — A73

Goose Barnacles A74

10fr, Green lobster. 15fr, African jacana. 20fr, Sea cicada. 35fr, Shrimp. 70fr, African anhinga.

1968-69 Photo. *Perf. 11½*

Dated "1968" or (70fr) "1969"

Granite Paper

300 A73 5fr brn & multi .20 .20
301 A74 10fr red & multi .20 .20
302 A73 15fr yel & multi .20 .20
303 A74 20fr ultra & multi .20 .20
304 A74 35fr car rose & ol grn .30 .20
305 A73 70fr Prus bl & multi .65 .35
306 A74 100fr yel grn & multi .90 .50
Nos. 300-306 (7) 2.65 1.85

Issued: 5fr, 7/13/68; 15fr, 12/21/68; 70fr, 4/26/69; others 5/18/68. See #C53-C57.

Steer and Hypodermic Syringe — A75

1968, Aug. 17 Engr. *Perf. 13*

307 A75 30fr dk grn, dp bl & brn red .25 .20

Campaign against cattle plague.

Boy and WHO Emblem — A76

Bambara Antelope Symbol — A77

1968, Nov. 16 Engr. *Perf. 13*

308 A76 30fr blk, grn & car .25 .20
309 A76 45fr red brn, grn & blk .40 .20

WHO, 20th anniversary.

1969, Jan. 13 Engr. *Perf. 13*

Design: 30fr, School of Medicine and Pharmacology, Dakar, horiz.

310 A77 30fr emer, brt bl & ind .25 .20
311 A77 50fr red, gray ol & bl grn .40 .20

6th Medical Meeting, Dakar, Jan. 13-18.

Panet, Camels and Mogador-St. Louis Route — A78

1969, Feb. 15 Engr. *Perf. 13*

312 A78 75fr ultra, Prus bl & brn .60 .25

Leopold Panet (1819-1859), first explorer of the Mauritanian Sahara.

ILO Emblem A79

1969, May 3 Photo. *Perf. 12½x13*

313 A79 30fr blk & grnsh bl .25 .20
314 A79 45fr blk & dp car .40 .20

ILO, 50th anniversary.

Arms of Casamance A80

Mahatma Gandhi A81

Design: 20fr, Arms of Gorée Island.

1969, July 26 Litho. *Perf. 13½*

315 A80 15fr rose & multi .20 .20
316 A80 20fr bl & multi .20 .20

Development Bank Issue

Common Design Type

1969, Sept. 10 Engr. *Perf. 13*

317 CD130 30fr gray, grn & ocher .25 .20
318 CD130 45fr brn, grn & ocher .40 .20

1969, Oct. 2 Engr. *Perf. 13*

319 A81 50fr multi .50 .50
a. Miniature sheet of 4 2.25 2.25

Mohandas K. Gandhi (1869-1948), leader in India's fight for independence.

Rotary Emblem and Symbolic Ship — A82

1969, Nov. 29 Photo. *Perf. 12½x13*

320 A82 30fr ultra, yel & blk .35 .20

Dakar Rotary Club, 30th anniversary.

ASECNA Issue

Common Design Type

1969, Dec. 12 Engr. *Perf. 13*

321 CD132 100fr dark gray .65 .35

Niokolo-Koba Campsite — A83

Tourism: 20fr, Cape Skiring, Casamance. 35fr, Elephants at Niokolo-Koba National Park. 45fr, Millet granaries, pigs and boats, Fadiouth Island.

1969, Dec. 27

322 A83 20fr bl, red brn & ol .20 .20
323 A83 30fr bl, red brn & ocher .25 .20
324 A83 35fr grnsh bl, blk & ocher .30 .20
325 A83 45fr vio bl & hn brn .35 .20
Nos. 322-325 (4) 1.10 .80

Bottle-nosed Dolphins A84

Lenin (1870-1924) A85

1970, Feb. 21 Photo. *Perf. 12x12½*

326 A84 50fr dl bl, blk & red .40 .20

1970, Apr. 22 Photo. *Perf. 11½*

327 A85 30fr brn, buff & ver .25 .20

Souvenir Sheet

Perf. 12x11½

327A A85 50fr brn, buff & ver .40 .20

No. 327A contains one 32x48mm stamp.

UPU Headquarters Issue

Common Design Type

1970, May 20 Engr. *Perf. 13*

328 CD133 30fr dk red, ind & dp cl .25 .20
329 CD133 45fr dl brn, dk car & bl grn .40 .20

Textile Plant, Thies — A86

Design: 45fr, Fertilizer plant, Dakar.

1970, Nov. 21 Engr. *Perf. 13*

330 A86 30fr grn, brt bl & brn red .25 .20
331 A86 45fr brn red & brt bl .40 .20

Industrialization of Senegal.

Boy Scouts — A87

Three Heads and Sun — A88

Design: 100fr, Lord Baden-Powell, map of Africa with Dakar, and fleur-de-lis.

1970, Dec. 11 Photo. *Perf. 11½*

332 A87 30fr multi .25 .20
333 A87 100fr multi .80 .40

1st African Boy Scout Conf., Dakar, Dec. 11-14.

1970, Dec. 19 Engr. *Perf. 13*

Design: 40fr, African man and woman, globe with map of Africa.

334 A88 25fr ultra, org & vio brn .25 .20
335 A88 40fr brn ol, dk brn & org .45 .20

International Education Year.

Senegal Arms — A89

Refugees and UN Emblem A90

1970-76 Photo. *Perf. 12*

336 A89 30fr yel grn & multi .20 .20
336A A89 35fr brt pink & multi ('71) .25 .20
b. Bklt. pane of 10 ('72) 2.50
336C A89 50fr bl & multi ('75) .25 .20
336D A89 65fr lil rose & multi ('76) .30 .20
Nos. 336-336D (4) 1.00 .80

The booklet pane has a control number in the margin.

See No. 654.

1971, Jan. 16 *Perf. 12½x12*

337 A90 40fr ver, blk, yel & grn .35 .20

High Commissioner for Refugees, 20th anniversary. See No. C94.

Mare "Mbayang" A91

Horses: 25fr, Mare Madjiguene. 100fr, Stallion Pass. 125fr, Stallion Pepe.

1971 Photo. *Perf. 11½*

338 A91 25fr multi .20 .20
339 A91 40fr multi .35 .20
340 A91 100fr multi .70 .40
341 A91 125fr multi .90 .40
Nos. 338-341 (4) 2.15 1.20

Improvements in horse breeding.

For surcharge see No. 392.

UN Emblem, Black and White Children
A92

Globe and Telephone
A94

UN Emblem, Four Races
A93

Perf. 13x12½, 12½x11

1971, Mar. 21 **Litho.**

342 A92 30fr multi .25 .20
343 A93 50fr multi .40 .20

Intl. Year against Racial Discrimination.

1971, May 17 **Engr.** ***Perf. 13***

Design: 40fr, Radar, satellite, orbits.

344 A94 30fr pur, grn & brn .25 .20
345 A94 40fr Prus bl, dk brn & red brn .30 .20

3rd World Telecommunications Day.

Drummer (Hayashida) — A95

50fr, Dwarf Japanese quince and grape hyacinth. 65fr, Judo. 75fr, Mt. Fuji.

1971, Aug. 7 **Photo.** ***Perf. 13½***

346 A95 35fr lt ultra & multi .30 .20
347 A95 50fr yel & multi .50 .20
348 A95 65fr dp org & multi .65 .25
349 A95 75fr grn & multi .80 .35
Nos. 346-349 (4) 2.25 1.00

13th Boy Scout World Jamboree, Asagiri Plain, Japan, Aug. 2-10.

Map of West Africa with Senegal, UNICEF Emblem
A97

100fr, Nurse, children, UNICEF emblem.

1971, Oct. 30 ***Perf. 12½***

352 A97 35fr dl bl, org & blk .25 .20
353 A97 100fr multi .80 .40

UNICEF, 25th anniv.

Basketball and Games' Emblem — A98

40fr, Basketball. 75fr, Emblem.

1971, Dec. 24 **Photo.** ***Perf. 13½x13***

354 A98 35fr lt vio & multi .30 .20
355 A98 40fr emer & multi .35 .20
356 A98 75fr ocher & multi .65 .40
Nos. 354-356 (3) 1.30 .80

6th African Basketball Championships, Dakar, Dec. 25, 1971-Jan. 2, 1972.

"The Exile of Albouri" — A99

Design: 40fr, "The Merchant of Venice."

1972, Mar. 25 ***Perf. 13x12½***

357 A99 35fr dk red & multi .30 .20
358 A99 40fr dk red & multi .40 .20

Intl. Theater Day. See No. C112.

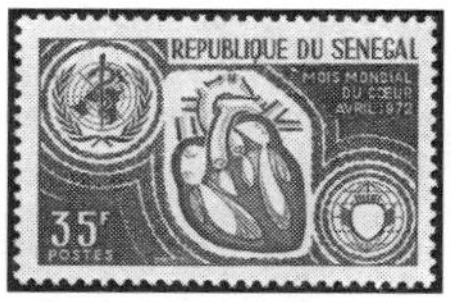

WHO Emblem and Heart
A100

Design: 40fr, Physician with patient, WHO emblem and electrocardiogram.

1972, Apr. 7 **Engr.** ***Perf. 13***

359 A100 35fr brt bl & red brn .25 .20
360 A100 40fr slate grn & brn .30 .20

"Your heart is your health," World Health Month.

Containment of the Desert, Environment Emblem — A101

1972, June 3 **Photo.** ***Perf. 13x12½***

361 A101 35fr multi .30 .20

UN Conference on Human Environment, Stockholm, June 5-16. See No. C113.

Tartarin Shooting the Lion — A102

Design: 100fr, Alphonse Daudet.

1972, June 24 **Engr.** ***Perf. 13***

362 A102 40fr brt grn, rose car & brn .35 .20
363 A102 100fr Prus bl, bl & brn .80 .35

Alphonse Daudet (1840-1897), French novelist, and centenary of the publication of his "Tartarin de Tarascon."

Souvenir Sheet

Stringed Instrument — A103

1972, July 1 **Engr.** ***Perf. 11½***

364 A103 150fr rose red 1.25 1.00

Belgica 72, Intl. Phil. Exhib., Brussels, June 24-July 9. No. 364 contains one stamp in design similar to No. 267.

Wrestling, Olympic Rings — A104

1972, July 22 **Photo.** ***Perf. 14x13½***

365 A104 15fr shown .20 .20
366 A104 20fr 100-meter dash .20 .20
367 A104 100fr Basketball .65 .35
368 A104 125fr Judo .80 .40
Nos. 365-368 (4) 1.85 1.15

Souvenir Sheet

Perf. 13½x14½

369 A104 240fr Torchbearer and Munich 1.90 1.60

20th Olympic Games, Munich, 8/26-9/11.

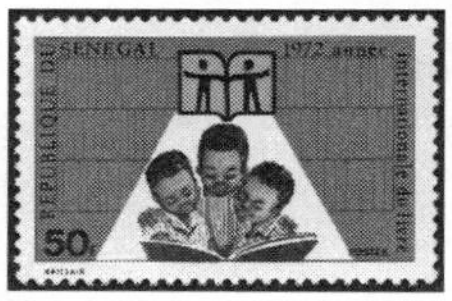

Book Year Emblem, Children Reading
A105

Senegalese Fashion — A106

1972, Sept. 16 **Photo.** ***Perf. 13***

370 A105 50fr gray & multi .40 .20

International Book Year.

1972-76 **Engr.**

371 A106 25fr black .20 .20
a. Booklet pane of 5 1.60
b. Booklet pane of 10 3.50
372 A106 40fr brt ultra .25 .20
a. Booklet pane of 5 2.50
b. Booklet pane of 10 5.50
372C A106 60fr brt grn ('76) .35 .20
372D A106 75fr lil rose .50 .20
Nos. 371-372D (4) 1.30 .80

See Nos. 563-573, 1153-1164, 1249-1257D, 1345B.

Aleksander Pushkin
A107

Amphicrasphedum Murrayanum
A108

1972, Oct. 28 **Photo.** ***Perf. 11½***

373 A107 100fr salmon & purple .80 .40

Aleksander Pushkin (1799-1837), Russian writer.

West African Monetary Union Issue

Common Design Type

Design: 40fr, African couple, city, village and commemorative coin.

1972, Nov. 2 **Engr.** ***Perf. 13***

374 CD136 40fr ol brn, bl & gray .30 .20

1972-73 **Photo.** ***Perf. 11½***

Marine Life: 10fr, Pterocanium tricolpum. 15fr, Ceratospyris polygona. 20fr, Cortiniscus typicus. 30fr, Theopera cortina.

375 A108 5fr multi .20 .20
376 A108 10fr multi .20 .20
377 A108 15fr multi .20 .20
378 A108 20fr multi .20 .20
379 A108 30fr multi .20 .20
Nos. 375-379,C115-C118 (9) 3.10 2.20

Issued: #375-377, 11/25/72; #378-379, 7/28/73.

No. 288 Surcharged in Vermilion

1872-1972
100F

1972, Dec. 9 **Engr.** ***Perf. 13***

380 A64 100fr on 30fr multi .60 .30

Blaise Diagne (1872-1934).

Melchior — A109

Black and White Men Carrying Emblem — A110

1972, Dec. 23 **Photo.** ***Perf. 13x13½***

381 A109 10fr shown .20 .20
382 A109 15fr Caspar .20 .20
383 A109 40fr Balthasar .25 .20
384 A109 60fr Joseph .30 .20
385 A109 100fr Virgin and Child .50 .30
a. Strip of 5, #381-385 1.30 1.00

Christmas. No. 385a has continuous design, showing traditional Gorée dolls.

Europafrica Issue

1973, Jan. 20 **Engr.** ***Perf. 13***

386 A110 65fr blk & grn .40 .25

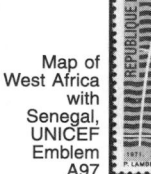

Radar Station, Gandoul
A111

1973, May 17 **Engr.** ***Perf. 13***
387 A111 40fr multi .25 .20

Phases of Solar Eclipse
A112

Designs: 65fr, Moon between earth and sun casting shadow on earth. 150fr, Diagram of areas of partial and total eclipse, satellite in space.

1973, June 30 **Photo.** ***Perf. 13x14***
388 A112 35fr dk bl & multi .25 .20
389 A112 65fr dk bl & multi .40 .25
390 A112 150fr dk bl & multi .90 .55
Nos. 388-390 (3) 1.55 1.00

Total solar eclipse over Africa, June 30.

Men Holding Torch over Africa — A113

1973, July 7 ***Perf. 12½x13***
391 A113 75fr multi .40 .30

Org. for African Unity, 10th anniv.

No. 338 Surcharged with New Value, 2 Bars, and Overprinted in Ultramarine: "SECHERESSE / SOLIDARITE AFRICAINE"

1973, July 21 **Photo.** ***Perf. 11½***
392 A91 100fr on 25fr multi .60 .40

African solidarity in drought emergency.

African Postal Union Issue
Common Design Type

1973, Sept. 12 **Engr.** ***Perf. 13***
393 CD137 100fr dk grn, vio & dk red .60 .30

Child, Map of Senegal, WMO Emblem
A114

1973, Sept. 22
394 A114 50fr multi .30 .20

Intl. meteorological cooperation, cent.

INTERPOL Headquarters, Paris — A115

1973, Oct. 6 **Engr.** ***Perf. 13***
395 A115 75fr ultra, bis & slate grn .40 .25

50th anniv. of Intl. Criminal Police Org.

Souvenir Sheet

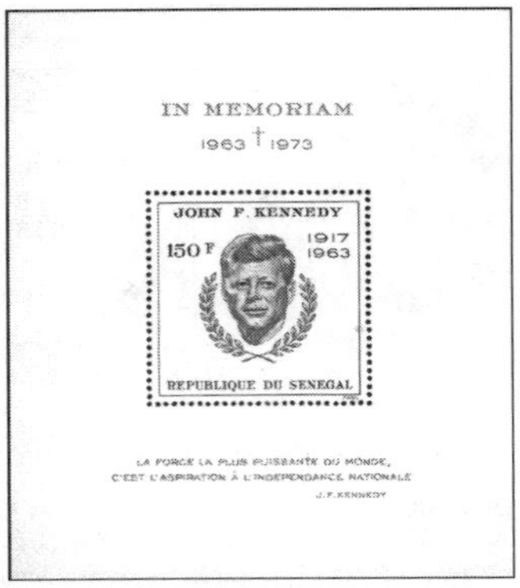

John F. Kennedy (1917-1963) — A116

1973, Nov. 22 **Engr.** ***Perf. 13***
396 A116 150fr ultra 1.00 1.00

Amilcar Cabral — A117

Victorious Athletes and Flag — A118

1973, Dec. 15 **Photo.** ***Perf. 12½x13***
397 A117 75fr multi .40 .35

Cabral (1924-1973), leader of anti-Portuguese guerrilla movement in Portuguese Guinea.

1974, Apr. 6 **Photo.** ***Perf. 12½x13***
398 A118 35fr shown .25 .20
399 A118 40fr Folk theater .30 .20

National Youth Week.

Soccer Cup, Yugoslavia-Brazil Game, Our Lady's Church, Munich — A119

Soccer Cup and Games: 40fr, Australia-Germany (Fed. Rep.) and Belltower, Hamburg. 65fr, Netherlands-Uruguay and Tower, Hanover. 70fr, Zaire-Italy and Church, Stuttgart.

1974, June 29 **Photo.** ***Perf. 13x14***
400 A119 25fr car & multi .20 .20
401 A119 40fr car & multi .25 .20
402 A119 65fr car & multi .40 .20
403 A119 70fr car & multi .40 .20
Nos. 400-403 (4) 1.25 .80

World Cup Soccer Championship, Munich, June 13-July 7.
For surcharge see No. 406.

UPU Emblem, Envelopes and Means of Transportation — A120

1974, Oct. 9 **Engr.** ***Perf. 13***
404 A120 100fr multi .60 .40

Centenary of Universal Postal Union.

Fair Emblem — A121

1974, Nov. 28 **Engr.** ***Perf. 12½x13***
405 A121 100fr bl, org & dk brn .55 .35

Dakar International Fair.

No. 401 Surcharged in Black on Gold

1975, Feb. 1 **Photo.** ***Perf. 13x14***
406 A119 200fr on 40fr multi 1.10 .65

World Cup Soccer Championships, 1974, victory of German Federal Republic.

Pres. Senghor and King Baudouin — A122

1975, Feb. 28 **Photo.** ***Perf. 13x13½***
407 A122 65fr lil & dk bl .35 .20
408 A122 100fr org & grn .55 .35

Visit of King Baudouin of Belgium.

ILO Emblem
A123

1975, Apr. 30 **Photo.** ***Perf. 13½x13***
409 A123 125fr multi .65 .40

International Labor Festival.

Globe, Stamp, Letters, España 75 Emblem — A124

1975, June 6 **Engr.** ***Perf. 13***
410 A124 55fr indigo, grn & red .30 .20

Espana 75 Intl. Phil. Exhib., Madrid, 4/4-13.

Apollo of Belvedere, Arphila 75 Emblem, Stamps — A125

1975, June 6
411 A125 95fr dk brn, brn & bis .50 .35

Arphila 75 International Philatelic Exhibition, Paris, June 6-16.

Professional Instruction — A126

1975, June 28 **Engr.** ***Perf. 13***
412 A126 85fr multi .45 .25

Dr. Albert Schweitzer (1875-1965), Medical Missionary, Lambarene Hospital — A127

1975, July 5
413 A127 85fr grn & vio brn .45 .25

Senegalese Soldier, Batallion Flag, Map of Sinai — A128

1975, July 10 **Litho.** ***Perf. 12½***
414 A128 100fr multi .75 .35

Senegalese Battalion of the UN' Sinai Service, 1973-74.

Women and Child — A129

55fr, Women pounding grain, vert.

1975, Oct. 18 **Photo.** ***Perf. 13½***
415 A129 55fr silver & multi .30 .20
416 A129 75fr silver & multi .40 .20

International Women's Year.

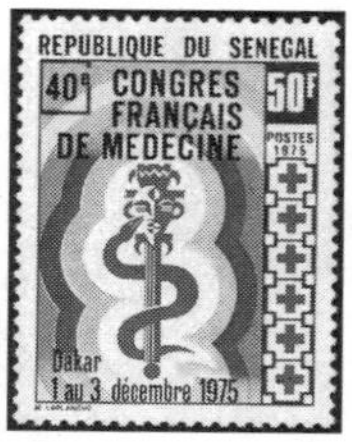

Staff of Aesculapius and African Mask — A130

1975, Dec. 1 Photo. *Perf. 12½x13*
417 A130 50fr multi .25 .20

40th French Medical Cong., Dakar, Dec. 1-3.

Map of Africa with Senegal and Namibia, UN Emblem A131

1976, Jan. 5 Photo. *Perf. 13*
418 A131 125fr vio bl & multi .65 .35

International Human Rights and Namibia Conference, Dakar, Jan. 5-8.

Sailfish Fishing A132

200fr, Racing yachts & Oceanexpo 75 emblem.

1976, Jan. 28 Photo. *Perf. 13½x13*
419 A132 140fr multi .70 .40
420 A132 200fr multi 1.10 .55

Oceanexpo 75, 1st Intl. Oceanographic Exhib., Okinawa, July 20, 1975-Jan. 1976.

Servals — A133

Designs: 3fr, Black-tailed godwits. 4fr, River hogs. 5fr, African fish eagles. No. 425, Okapis. No. 426, Sitatungas.

1976, Feb. 26 Photo. *Perf. 13*
421 A133 2fr gold & multi .20 .20
422 A133 3fr gold & multi .20 .20
423 A133 4fr gold & multi .20 .20
424 A133 5fr gold & multi .20 .20
425 A133 250fr gold & multi 1.40 .65
426 A133 250fr gold & multi 1.40 .65
a. Strip of 2, #425-426 + label 3.00
Nos. 421-426 (6) 3.60 2.10

Basse Casamance National Park.
See Nos. 473-478.

A. G. Bell, Telephone, ITU Emblem — A134

1976, Mar. 31 Litho. *Perf. 12½x13*
427 A134 175fr multi .90 .40

Centenary of first telephone call by Alexander Graham Bell, Mar. 10, 1876.

Map of African French-speaking Countries — A135

1976, Apr. 12 Litho. *Perf. 13½*
428 A135 60fr yel grn & multi .35 .20

Scientific and Cultural Meeting of the African Dental Association, Dakar, Apr. 12-17.

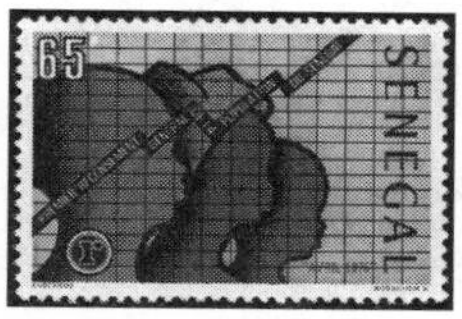

Family and Graph A136

1976, Apr. 26
429 A136 65fr multi .35 .20

1st population census in Senegal, Apr. 1976.

Thomas Jefferson and 13-star Flag — A137

1976, June 19 Engr. *Perf. 13*
430 A137 50fr bl, red & blk .25 .20

American Bicentennial.

Planting Seedlings — A138

1976, Aug. 21 Litho. *Perf. 12*
431 A138 60fr yel & multi .35 .20

Reclamation of Sahel region.

Campfire A139

Jamboree Emblem, Map of Africa — A140

1976, Aug. 30 Litho. *Perf. 12½*
432 A139 80fr multi .40 .35
433 A140 100fr multi .55 .40

1st All Africa Scout Jamboree, Sherehills, Jos, Nigeria, Apr. 2-8, 1977.

A140a

1976 Summer Olympics, Montreal — A140b

1976, Sept. 11 Litho. *Perf. 13½*
433A A140a 5fr Swimming
433B A140a 10fr Weightlifting
433C A140a 15fr Hurdles, horiz.
433D A140a 20fr Equestrian, horiz.
433E A140a 25fr Steeplechase, horiz.
433F A140a 50fr Wrestling
433G A140a 60fr Field hockey
433H A140a 65fr Track
433I A140a 70fr Women's gymnastics
433J A140a 100fr Cycling, horiz.
433K A140a 400fr Boxing
433L A140a 500fr Judo

Litho. & Embossed

433M A140b 1000fr Basketball

Souvenir Sheet

433Q A140b 1000fr Boxers, city skyline

Nos. 433K-433Q are airmail.

Mechanized Tomato Harvest — A141

1976, Oct. 23 Photo. *Perf. 13*
434 A141 180fr multi 1.00 .40

Map of Dakar and Gorée A142

Designs: 60fr, Star over Africa. 70fr, Students in laboratory and library. 200fr, Handshake over world map, Pres. Senghor.

1976, Oct. 9 Litho. *Perf. 13½x14*
435 A142 40fr multi .20 .20
436 A142 60fr multi .20 .20
437 A142 70fr multi .20 .20
438 A142 200fr multi .60 .55
Nos. 435-438 (4) 1.20 1.15

70th birthday of Pres. Leopold Sedar Senghor.

Scroll with Map of Africa, Senegalese People — A143

1977, Jan. 8 *Perf. 12½*
439 A143 60fr multi .35 .20

Day of the Black People.

Joe Frazier and Muhammad Ali — A144

Design: 60fr, Ali and Frazier in ring, vert.

1977, Jan. 7 Photo. *Perf. 13x13½*
440 A144 60fr blue & blk .65 .20
441 A144 150fr emerald & blk 1.20 .40

World boxing champion Muhammad Ali.

Dancer and Musician A145

Festival Emblem and: 75fr, Wood carving and masks. 100fr, Dancers and ancestor statuette.

1977, Feb. 10 Litho. *Perf. 12½*
442 A145 50fr yellow & multi .25 .20
443 A145 75fr green & multi .40 .20
444 A145 100fr rose & multi .55 .25
Nos. 442-444 (3) 1.20 .65

2nd World Black and African Festival, Lagos, Nigeria, Jan. 15-Feb. 12.

Cogwheels and Symbols of Industry — A146

1977, Mar. 28 Engr. *Perf. 13*
445 A146 70fr yel grn & ocher .40 .20

Dakar Industrial Zone, 1st anniversary.

Burning Match and Burnt Trees — A147

60fr, Burnt trees and house, fire-truck, horiz.

1977, Apr. 30 Litho. *Perf. 12½*

446 A147 40fr green & multi	.20	.20
447 A147 60fr slate & multi	.35	.20

Prevention of forest fires.

Drummer, Telephone, Agriculture and Industry — A148

Electronic Tree and ITU Emblem — A149

1977, May 17 Litho. *Perf. 13*

448 A148 80fr multi	.35	.25
449 A149 100fr multi	.40	.25

World Telecommunications Day.

Symbol of Language Studies — A150

Sassenage Castle, Grenoble — A151

Perf. 12x12½, 12½

1977, May 21 Litho.

450 A150 65fr multi	25	.20
451 A151 250fr multi	1.00	.65

10th anniv. of Intl. French Language Council.

Woman in Boat, Wooden Shoe A152

Design: 125fr, Senegalese woman, symbolic tulip and stamp, vert.

1977, June 4 *Perf. 13½x14, 14x13½*

452 A152 50fr blue grn & multi	.25	.20
453 A152 125fr ocher & multi	.65	.35

Amphilex '77 International Philatelic Exhibition, Amsterdam, May 26-June 5.

Adult Reading Class A153

Design: 65fr, Man learning to read.

1977, Sept. 10 Litho. *Perf. 12½*

454 A153 60fr multi	.35	.20
455 A153 65fr multi	.40	.20

National Literacy Week, Sept. 8-14.

A154

A155

Paintings: 20fr, Mercury, by Rubens. 25fr, Daniel in the Lions' Den, by Peter Paul Rubens (1577-1640). 40fr, The Empress, by Titian (1477-1576). 60fr, Flora, by Titian. 65fr, Jo, the Beautiful Irish Woman, by Gustave Courbet (1819-1877). 100fr, The Painter's Studio, by Courbet.

1977, Nov. Photo. *Perf. 13x13½*

456 A154 20fr multi	.20	.20
457 A154 25fr multi	.20	.20
458 A154 40fr multi	.20	.20
459 A154 60fr multi	.30	.20
460 A154 65fr multi	.35	.20
461 A154 100fr multi	.55	.25
Nos. 456-461 (6)	1.80	1.25

1977, Dec. 22 Litho. *Perf. 12½*

Christmas: 20fr, Adoration by People of Various Races. 25fr, Decorated arch and procession. 40fr, Christmas tree, mother and child. 100fr, Adoration of the Kings, horiz.

462 A155 20fr multi	.20	.20
463 A155 25fr multi	.20	.20
464 A155 40fr multi	.20	.20
465 A155 100fr multi	.55	.25
Nos. 462-465 (4)	1.15	.85

Regatta at Soumbedioun A156

Tourism: 10fr, Senegalese wrestlers. 65fr, Regatta at Soumbedioun. 100fr, Dancers.

1978, Jan. 7 Litho. *Perf. 12½*

466 A156 10fr multi	.20	.20
467 A156 30fr multi	.20	.20
468 A156 65fr multi, horiz.	.35	.20
469 A156 100fr multi, horiz.	.55	.25
Nos. 466-469 (4)	1.30	.85

Acropolis, Athens, and African Buildings A157

1978, Jan. 30

470 A157 75fr multi	.40	.20

UNESCO campaign to save world's cultural heritage.

Solar-powered Pump, Field and Sheep — A158

Energy in Senegal: 95fr, Pylon bringing electricity to villages and factories.

1978, Feb. 25

471 A158 50fr multi	.25	.20
472 A158 95fr multi	.50	.25

Park Type of 1976

5fr, Caspian terns in flight, royal terns on ground. 10fr, Pink-backed pelicans. 15fr, Wart hog & gray heron. 20fr, Greater flamingoes, nests, eggs & young. #477, Gray heron & royal terns. #478, Abyssinian ground hornbill & wart hog.

1978, Apr. 22 Photo. *Perf. 13*

473 A133 5fr gold & multi	.20	.20
474 A133 10fr gold & multi	.20	.20
475 A133 15fr gold & multi	.20	.20
476 A133 20fr gold & multi	.20	.20
477 A133 150fr gold & multi	1.00	.65
478 A133 150fr gold & multi	1.00	.65
a. Strip of 2, #477-478 + label	2.00	
Nos. 473-478 (6)	2.80	2.10

Salum Delta National Park.

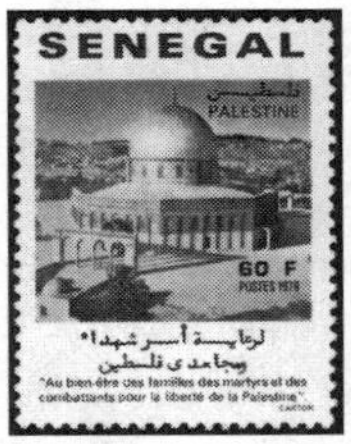

Dome of the Rock, Jerusalem A159

1978, May 15 Litho. *Perf. 12½*

479 A159 60fr multi	.40	.20

Palestinian fighters and their families.

Vaccination, Dr. Jenner, WHO Emblem — A160

1978, June 3

480 A160 60fr multi	.40	.20

Eradication of smallpox.

Soccer, Flags: Argentina, Hungary, France, Italy — A161

Mahatma Gandhi — A162

Soccer, Cup, Argentina '78 Emblem and Flags of: 40fr, No. 486a, Poland, German Democratic Rep., Tunisia, Mexico. 65fr, 125fr, Austria, Spain, Sweden, Brazil. 75fr, No. 484, Netherlands, Iran, Peru, Scotland. 150fr, like 25fr.

1978, June 24 Photo. *Perf. 13*

481 A161 25fr multi	.20	.20
482 A161 40fr multi	.20	.20
483 A161 65fr multi	.30	.20
484 A161 100fr multi	.50	.25
Nos. 481-484 (4)	1.20	.85

Souvenir Sheets

485 Sheet of 2	1.10	
a. A161 75fr multi	.40	
b. A161 125fr multi	.65	
486 Sheet of 2	1.40	
a. A161 100fr multi	.50	
b. A161 150fr multi	.75	

11th World Cup Soccer Championship, Argentina, June 1-25.

1978, June 27 *Perf. 12*

Design: 150fr, No. 489a, Martin Luther King. No. 489b, like 125fr.

487 A162 125fr multi	.95	.35
488 A162 150fr multi	1.25	.40

Souvenir Sheet

489 Sheet of 2	3.50	
a. A162 200fr multi	1.60	
b. A162 200fr multi	1.60	

Mahatma Gandhi and Martin Luther King, advocates of non-violence.

Homes and Industry — A163

1978, Aug. 5 Litho. *Perf. 12½*

490 A163 110fr multi	.70	.30

3rd Intl. Fair, Dakar, Nov. 28-Dec. 10.

Wright Brothers and Flyer — A164

Designs: 150fr, like 75fr. 100fr, 250fr, Yuri Gagarin and spacecraft. 200fr, 300fr, US astronauts Frank Borman, William Anders, James Lovell Jr. and spacecraft.

1978, Sept. 25 Litho. *Perf. 13½x14*

491 A164 75fr multi	.50	.20
492 A164 100fr multi	.60	.25
493 A164 200fr multi	1.40	.55
Nos. 491-493 (3)	2.50	1.00

Souvenir Sheet

494 Sheet of 3	4.00	
a. A164 150fr multi	.60	
b. A164 250fr multi	1.40	
c. A164 300fr multi	2.00	

75th anniv. of 1st powered flight; 10th anniv. of the death of Yuri Gagarin, first man in space; 10th anniv. of Apollo 8 flight around moon.

Henri Dunant (1828-1910), Founder of Red Cross, and Patients — A165

Design: 20fr, Henri Dunant, First Aid station, Red Cross flag.

1978, Oct. 28 Photo. *Perf. 11½*

495 A165 5fr brt blue & red .20 .20
496 A165 20fr multi .20 .20

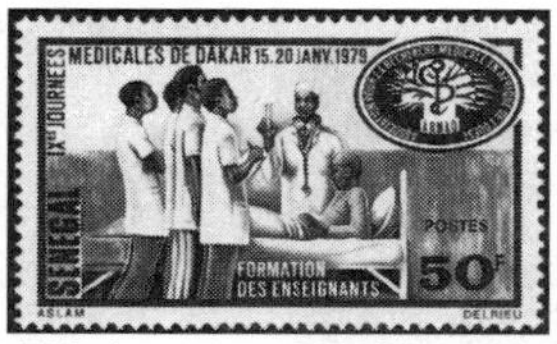

Bedside Lecture and Emblem — A166

100fr, Pollution, fish and mercury bottles.

1979, Jan. 15 Litho. *Perf. 13½x13*

497 A166 50fr multi .35 .20
498 A166 100fr multi .65 .25

9th Medical Days, Dakar, Jan. 15-20.

Map of Senegal with Shortwave Stations A167

60fr, Children on vacation, ambulance, soccer player. 65fr, Rural mobile post office.

1978, Dec. 27 Litho. *Perf. 13½x13*

499 A167 50fr multi .35 .20
500 A167 60fr multi .40 .20
501 A167 65fr multi .40 .20
Nos. 499-501 (3) 1.15 .60

Achievements of postal service.

Farmer A168

Design: 150fr, Factories, communication, transportation, fish, physician and worker.

1979, Feb. 17 Litho. *Perf. 12½*

502 A168 30fr multi .20 .20
503 A168 150fr multi 1.00 .40

Pride in workmanship.

Children's Village and Children — A169

Design: 60fr, Different view of village.

1979, Mar. 30 *Perf. 12x12½*

504 A169 40fr multi .25 .20
505 A169 60fr multi .40 .20

Children's SOS villages.

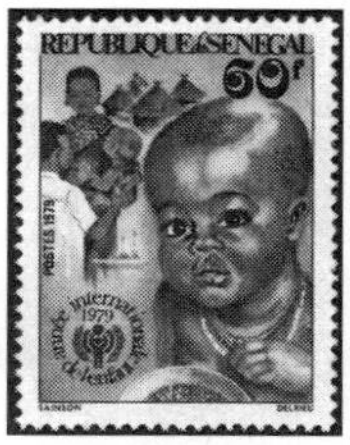

Infant, Physician Vaccinating Child, IYC Emblem — A170

65fr, Boys with book, globe, IYC emblem.

1979, Apr. 24 Litho. *Perf. 13½x13*

506 A170 60fr multi .40 .20
507 A170 65fr multi .40 .20

International Year of the Child.

Drum, Carrier Pigeon, Satellite — A171

Design: 60fr, Baobab tree and flower, Independence monument with lion, vert.

1979, June 8 *Perf. 12½x13*

Size: 36x48mm

508 A171 60fr multi .40 .20

Perf. 12½

Size: 36x36mm

509 A171 150fr multi 1.00 .40

Philexafrique II, Libreville, Gabon, June 8-17. Nos. 508, 509 each printed with labels showing UAPT '79 emblem.

People Walking through Open Book A172

1979, Sept. 15 Photo. *Perf. 11½x12*

510 A172 250fr multi 1.90 .65

Intl. Bureau of Education, Geneva, 50th anniv.

Sir Rowland Hill (1795-1879), Originator of Penny Postage, Type AP3 with Exhibition Cancel — A173

1979, Oct. 9 *Perf. 11½*

511 A173 500fr multi 3.50 1.40

Black Trees, by Hundertwasser A174

Litho. & Engr.

1979, Dec. 10 *Perf. 13½x14*

512 A174 60fr shown .40 .20
a. Souvenir sheet of 4 1.90 .80
513 A174 100fr Head of a man .65 .25
a. Souvenir sheet of 4 3.00 1.25
514 A174 200fr Rainbow windows 1.40 .55
a. Souvenir sheet of 4 5.75 2.25
Nos. 512-514 (3) 2.45 1.00

Paintings by Friedensreich Hundertwasser, pseudonym of Friedrich Stowasser (b. 1928).

Running, Championship Emblem A175

1980, Jan. 14 Litho. *Perf. 13*

515 A175 20fr shown .20 .20
516 A175 25fr Javelin .20 .20
517 A175 50fr Relay race .35 .20
518 A175 100fr Discus .80 .25
Nos. 515-518 (4) 1.55 .85

1st African Athletic Championships.

Mudra Afrique Arts Festival A176

1980, Mar. 22 Photo. *Perf. 14*

519 A176 50fr Musicians .35 .20
520 A176 100fr Dancers, festival building .65 .25
521 A176 200fr Drummer, dancers 1.40 .55
Nos. 519-521 (3) 2.40 1.00

Lions Emblem, Map of Dakar Harbor A177

1980, May 17 Litho. *Perf. 13*

522 A177 100fr multi .80 .25

22nd Cong., Lions Intl. District 403, Dakar.

Chimpanzees — A178

1980, June 2 Photo. *Perf. 13½*

523 A178 40fr shown .25 .20
524 A178 60fr Elephants .40 .20
525 A178 65fr Derby's elands .40 .20
526 A178 100fr Hyenas .65 .30
527 Pair 2.50 1.10
a. A178 200fr Herd 1.25 .55
b. A178 200fr Guest house 1.25 .55
Nos. 523-527 (5) 4.20 2.00

Souvenir Sheet

528 Sheet of 4 4.00 1.40
a. A178 125fr like #523 1.00 .35
b. A178 125fr like #524 1.00 .35
c. A178 125fr like #525 1.00 .35
d. A178 125fr like #526 1.00 .35

Niokolo Koba National Park. No. 527 printed in continuous design with label showing location of park.

Tree Planting Year — A179

1980, June 27 Litho. *Perf. 13*

529 A179 60fr multi .40 .20
530 A179 65fr multi .40 .20

Rural Women Workers A180

Rural women workers. 50fr, 200fr, horiz.

1980, July 19

531 A180 50fr multi .35 .20
532 A180 100fr multi .65 .25
533 A180 200fr multi 1.40 .55
Nos. 531-533 (3) 2.40 1.00

Wrestling, Moscow '80 Emblem — A181

1980, Aug. 21 *Perf. 14½*

534 A181 60fr shown .40 .20
535 A181 65fr Running .40 .20
536 A181 70fr Sports, map showing Moscow .45 .20
537 A181 100fr Judo .80 .25
538 A181 200fr Basketball 1.60 .55
Nos. 534-538 (5) 3.65 1.40

Souvenir Sheet

539 Sheet of 2 1.50
a. A181 75fr like #534 .50 .25
b. A181 125fr like #535 .80 .35
540 Sheet of 2 1.50
a. A181 75fr like #527 .50 .25
b. A181 125fr like #538 .80 .35

22nd Summer Olympic Games, Moscow, July 19-Aug. 3.

Caspian Tern and Sea Gulls, Kalissaye Bird Sanctuary A182

National Park Wildlife: 70fr, Laughing gulls and Hansel's tern, Barbarie Spit. 85fr, Turtle and crab, Madeleine Islands. 150fr, Cormorant, Madeleine Islands.

1981, Jan. 31 Litho. *Perf. 14½x14*

541 A182 50fr multi .50 .20
542 A182 70fr multi .65 .20
543 A182 85fr multi .75 .25
544 A182 150fr multi 1.25 .35
Nos. 541-544 (4) 3.15 1.00

Souvenir Sheet

545 Sheet of 4 4.00 1.40
a. A182 125fr like #541 1.00 .35
b. A182 125fr like #542 1.00 .35
c. A182 125fr like #543 1.00 .35
d. A182 125fr like #544 1.00 .35

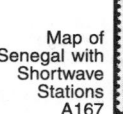

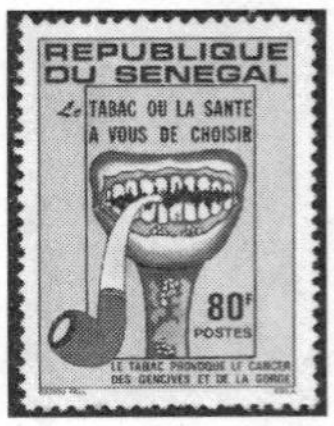

Anti-Tobacco Campaign — A183

1981, June 20 Litho. *Perf. 13*

546 A183 75fr Healthy people .50 .20
547 A183 80fr shown .55 .25

4th Intl. Dakar Fair, Nov. 25-Dec. 7 A184

1981, Sept. 19 Litho. *Perf. 12½*

548 A184 80fr multi .55 .25

Natl. Hero Lat Dior A185

1982, Jan. 11 Photo. *Perf. 14*

549 A185 80fr Portrait, vert. .55 .25
550 A185 500fr Battle 3.50 1.40

Local Flora — A186

1982, Feb. 1 *Perf. 11½*

551 A186 50fr Nymphaea lotus .35 .20
552 A186 75fr Strophanthus sarmentosus .50 .20
553 A186 200fr Crinum moorei 1.40 .55
554 A186 225fr Cochlospermum tinctorium 1.50 .60
Nos. 551-554 (4) 3.75 1.55

Inscribed 1981.

Euryphrene Senegalensis — A187

1982, Feb. 27 Litho. *Perf. 14*

555 A187 45fr shown .30 .20
556 A187 55fr Hypolimnas salmacis .40 .20
557 A187 75fr Cymothoe caenis .50 .20
558 A187 80fr Precis cebrene .55 .25
Nos. 555-558 (4) 1.75 .85

Souvenir Sheet

Perf. 14½

559 Sheet of 4 6.00 2.00
a. A187 100fr like 45fr .65 .25
b. A187 150fr like 55fr 1.00 .40
c. A187 200fr like 75fr 1.40 .55
d. A187 250fr like 80fr 1.60 .65

Destructive Insects — A188

Banner and Stamp — A189

Various insects. 80fr, 100fr horiz.

1982, Apr. 7 Litho. *Perf. 14*

560 A188 75fr multi .50 .20
561 A188 80fr multi .55 .25
562 A188 100fr multi .65 .25
Nos. 560-562 (3) 1.70 .70

Fashion Type of 1972

1982-93 Engr. *Perf. 13*

563 A106 5fr Prus blue .20 .20
564 A106 10fr dull red .20 .20
565 A106 15fr orange .20 .20
566 A106 20fr dk purple .20 .20
567 A106 30fr henna brn .20 .20
568 A106 45fr orange yellow .35 .20
569 A106 50fr bright magenta .40 .20
570 A106 90fr brt carmine .25 .20
571 A106 125fr ultramarine .95 .50
572 A106 145fr orange .75 .35
573 A106 180fr gray blue 1.40 .70
Nos. 563-573 (11) 5.10 3.15

Issued: 5, 10, 15, 20, 30fr, Apr. 30; 90fr, Dec., 1984; 180fr, 1991; 45, 50, 125fr, 1993; 145fr, 1995.

1982, Dec. 30 Photo. *Perf. 13*

575 A189 100fr shown .50 .25
576 A189 500fr Stamp, arrows 3.00 1.40

PHILEXFRANCE Intl. Stamp Exhibition, Paris, June 11-21.

Senegambia Confederation, Feb. 1 — A190

1982, Nov. 15 Litho. *Perf. 12½*

577 A190 225fr Map, flags 1.00 .65
578 A190 350fr Arms 1.60 1.00

Local Birds — A191

1982 World Cup — A192

1982, Dec. 1 Photo. *Perf. 11½*

Granite Paper

579 A191 45fr Godwit .30 .20
580 A191 75fr Jabiru .50 .20
581 A191 80fr Francolin .55 .30
582 A191 500fr Eagle 3.50 1.40
Nos. 579-582 (4) 4.85 2.10

1982, Dec. 11 Litho. *Perf. 12½x13*

583 A192 30fr Player .20 .20
584 A192 50fr Player, diff. .35 .20
585 A192 75fr Ball .50 .20
586 A192 80fr Cup .55 .25
Nos. 583-586 (4) 1.60 .85

Souvenir Sheets

Perf. 12½

587 A192 75fr like 30fr .50 .25
588 A192 100fr like 50fr .65 .35
589 A192 150fr like 75fr 1.00 .50
590 A192 200fr like 80fr 1.40 .65
Nos. 587-590 (4) 3.55 1.75

A193

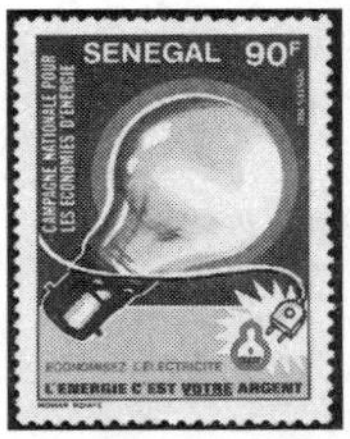

A194

Designs: 60fr, Exhibition poster, viewers, horiz. 70fr, Simulated butterfly stamps. 90fr, Simulated stamps under magnifying glass. 95fr, Coat of Arms over Exhibition Building.

1983, Aug. 6 Litho. *Perf. 12½*

591 A193 60fr multi .20 .20
592 A193 70fr multi .25 .20
593 A193 90fr multi .25 .20
594 A193 95fr multi .30 .20
Nos. 591-594 (4) 1.00 .80

Dakar '82 Stamp Exhibition.

1983, Oct. 25 Litho. *Perf. 12½x13*

595 A194 90fr Electricity .30 .20
596 A194 95fr Gasoline .30 .20
597 A194 260fr Coal, wood .90 .40
Nos. 595-597 (3) 1.50 .80

Energy conservation.

Namibia Day — A195

1983, Nov. 14 Litho. *Perf. 13½x13*

598 A195 90fr Torch .30 .20
599 A195 95fr Chain, fist .30 .20
600 A195 260fr Woman bearing torch .90 .40
Nos. 598-600 (3) 1.50 .80

West African Monetary Union, 20th Anniv. — A196

Dakar Alizes Rotary Club, First Anniv. — A197

Designs: 60fr, Mask emblem, Ziguinchor Agency building, Dakar, horiz. 65fr, Monetary Union headquarters, emblem.

Perf. 13½x13, 13x13½

1983, Nov. 28

601 A196 60fr multi .20 .20
602 A196 65fr multi .20 .20

1983, Dec. 5 *Perf. 13x13½*

603 A197 70fr green & multi .25 .20
604 A197 500fr blue & multi 1.60 .80

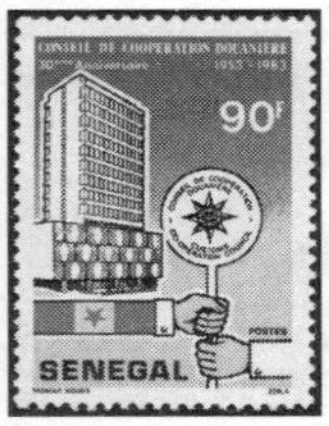

Customs Cooperation Council, 30th Anniv. — A198

Economic Comm. for Africa, 25th Anniv. — A199

1983, Dec. 23 *Perf. 12½x13*

605 A198 90fr multi .30 .20
606 A198 300fr multi 1.00 .50

1984, Jan. 10 *Perf. 12½*

607 A199 90fr multi .30 .20
608 A199 95fr multi .30 .20

SOS Children's Village A200

1984, Mar. 29 *Perf. 13½x13, 13x13½*

609 A200 90fr Village .30 .20
610 A200 95fr Mother & child, vert. .30 .20
611 A200 115fr Brothers & sisters .40 .20
612 A200 260fr House, vert. .90 .40
Nos. 609-612 (4) 1.90 1.00

Scouting Year A201

1984, May 28 Litho. *Perf. 13*

613 A201 60fr Sign .20 .20
614 A201 70fr Emblem .25 .20
615 A201 90fr Scouts .25 .20
616 A201 95fr Baden-Powell .30 .20
Nos. 613-616 (4) 1.00 .80

1984 Olympic Games — A202

1984, July 28 Litho. *Perf. 13*

617 A202 90fr Javelin .30 .20
618 A202 95fr Hurdles .35 .20
619 A202 165fr Soccer .55 .30
Nos. 617-619 (3) 1.20 .70

Souvenir Sheet

Perf. 13x12½

620 Sheet of 3 1.90 1.00
a. A202 125fr like 90fr .40 .20
b. A202 175fr like 95fr .60 .30
c. A202 250fr like 165fr .80 .45

World Food Day A203

Perf. 13x12½, 12½x13

1984, Dec. 16 — Litho.

621 A203 65fr Food production .20 .20
622 A203 70fr Cooking, vert. .20 .20
623 A203 225fr Dining .60 .30
Nos. 621-623 (3) 1.00 .70

No. 612 Overprinted "AIDE AU SAHEL 84"

1984, Dec. — *Perf. 13x13½*

624 A200 260fr multi .70 .35

Drought relief.

UNESCO World Heritage Campaign — A204

Water Emergency Plan — A205

1984, Dec. 6 — Litho. — *Perf. 13½*

625 A204 90fr William Ponty School .25 .20
626 A204 95fr Island map, horiz. .25 .20
627 A204 250fr History Museum .65 .35
628 A204 500fr Slave Prison, horiz. 1.40 .65
Nos. 625-628 (4) 2.55 1.40

Souvenir Sheet

Perf. 13x12½, 12½x13

629 Sheet of 4 3.50 1.90
a. A204 125fr like No. 625 .30 .20
b. A204 150fr like No. 626 .40 .20
c. A204 325fr like No. 627 .90 .40
d. A204 675fr like No. 628 1.90 .90

Restoration of historic sites, Goree Island.

1985, Mar. 28 — *Perf. 13x12½, 12½x13*

630 A205 40fr Well and pump .20 .20
631 A205 50fr Spigot and crops .20 .20
632 A205 90fr Water tanks, livestock .25 .20
633 A205 250fr Women at well .65 .40
Nos. 630-633 (4) 1.30 1.00

Nos. 631-633 horiz.

World Communications Year — A206

Designs: 95fr, Maps of Africa and Senegal, transmission tower. 350fr, Globe, pigeon with letter.

1985, Apr. 13 — Litho. — *Perf. 13*

634 A206 90fr multi .25 .20
635 A206 95fr multi .25 .20
636 A206 350fr multi .90 .45
Nos. 634-636 (3) 1.40 .85

Traditional Musical Instruments — A207

50fr, Gourd fiddle, bamboo flute. 85fr, Drums, stringed instrument. 125fr, Musician playing balaphone, drums. 250fr, Rabab, shawm & single-string fiddles.

1985, May 4 — *Perf. 12½x13, 13x12½*

637 A207 50fr multi .20 .20
638 A207 85fr multi .25 .20
639 A207 125fr multi .35 .20
640 A207 250fr multi .65 .40
Nos. 637-640 (4) 1.45 1.00

Nos. 638-640 vert. For surcharge see No. 676.

PHILEXAFRICA '85, Lome, Togo, Nov. 16-24 — A208

1985, Oct. 21 — *Perf. 13*

641 A208 100fr Political and civic education .35 .20
642 A208 125fr Vocational training .40 .20
643 A208 150fr Culture, space exploration .55 .25
644 A208 175fr Self-sufficiency in food production .60 .35
Nos. 641-644 (4) 1.90 1.00

Intl. Youth Year A209

1985, Nov. 30 — *Perf. 14*

645 A209 40fr Vocational training .20 .20
646 A209 50fr Communications .20 .20
647 A209 90fr World peace .30 .20
648 A209 125fr Cultural exchange .40 .20
Nos. 645-648 (4) 1.10 .80

Senegal Arms Type of 1970

1985, Dec. — Litho. — *Perf. 13*

Background Color

654 A89 95fr bright orange .35 .20

Fishing at Kayar A210

1986, Jan. 28 — Litho. — *Perf. 14*

659 A210 40fr Hauling boat .20 .20
660 A210 50fr Women on beach .25 .20
661 A210 100fr Fisherman, catch .50 .25
662 A210 125fr Women buying fish .70 .35
663 A210 150fr Unloading fish .80 .40
Nos. 659-663 (5) 2.45 1.40

Nos. 661-662 vert.

Folk Costumes — A211

1985, Dec. 28 — Litho. — *Perf. 13½*

664 A211 40fr multi .20 .20
665 A211 95fr multi, vert., diff. .35 .20
666 A211 100fr multi, vert., diff. .40 .20
667 A211 150fr multi, vert., diff. .55 .30
Nos. 664-667 (4) 1.50 .90

Coiffures — A212

1986 Africa Soccer Cup, Cairo — A213

1986, Mar. 3 — *Perf. 13*

668 A212 90fr Perruque, Ceeli .50 .25
669 A212 125fr Ndungu, Kearly, Rasta .70 .35
670 A212 250fr Jamono Kura, Kooraa 1.40 .70
671 A212 300fr Mbaram, Jeere 1.60 .80
Nos. 668-671 (4) 4.20 2.10

1986, Mar. 7 — *Perf. 13½*

672 A213 115fr Soccer ball, flags .65 .30
673 A213 125fr Athlete, map .70 .35
674 A213 135fr Pyramid, heraldic lion .75 .40
675 A213 165fr Flag, lions, map .90 .45
Nos. 672-675 (4) 3.00 1.50

No. 638 Surcharged with Lions Intl. Emblem, Two Bars, and "Ve CONVENTION / MULTI-DISTRICT / 403 / 8-10 / MAI / 1986" in Dark Ultramarine

1986, May 8 — Litho. — *Perf. 13x12½*

676 A207 165fr on 85fr multi 1.00 .50

World Wildlife Fund — A214

Ndama gazelles.

1986, June 30 — *Perf. 13*

677 A214 15fr multi .20 .20
678 A214 45fr multi .25 .20
679 A214 85fr multi .50 .25
680 A214 125fr multi .70 .35
Nos. 677-680 (4) 1.65 1.00

UN Child Survival Campaign — A215

1986, Sept. 5 — Litho. — *Perf. 14*

681 A215 50fr Immunization .30 .20
682 A215 85fr Nutrition .50 .25

1986 World Cup Soccer Championships, Mexico — A216

Various plays, world cup and artifacts: 125fr, Ceremonial vase. 135fr, Mayan mask, Palenque. 165fr, Gold breastplate. 340fr, Porcelain mask, Teofihuacan, 7th cent. B.C.

1986, Nov. 17 — *Perf. 12½x12*

683 A216 125fr multi .80 .40
684 A216 135fr multi .85 .40
685 A216 165fr multi 1.10 .55
686 A216 340fr multi 2.25 1.10
Nos. 683-686 (4) 5.00 2.45

Nos. 683-686 Overprinted "ARGENTINE 3 / R.F.A. 2" in Scarlet

1986, Nov. 17

687 A216 125fr multi .80 .40
688 A216 135fr multi .85 .45
689 A216 165fr multi 1.10 .55
690 A216 340fr multi 2.25 1.10
Nos. 687-690 (4) 5.00 2.50

Guembeul Nature Reserve A217

1986, Dec. 4 — Litho. — *Perf. 13½*

691 A217 50fr Ostriches .30 .20
692 A217 65fr Kob antelopes .40 .20
693 A217 85fr Giraffes .50 .25
694 A217 100fr Ostrich, buffalo, kob, giraffe .55 .30
695 A217 150fr Buffaloes .85 .40
Nos. 691-695 (5) 2.60 1.35

Christmas A218

1986, Dec. 22 — Litho. — *Perf. 14*

696 A218 70fr Puppet, vert. .40 .20
697 A218 85fr Folk musicians .50 .25
698 A218 150fr Outdoor celebration, vert. .80 .40
699 A218 250fr Boy praying, creche 1.40 .70
Nos. 696-699 (4) 3.10 1.55

Inscribed 1985.

Statue of Liberty, Cent. — A219

1986, Dec. 30 — Litho. — *Perf. 12½*

700 A219 225fr multi 1.25 .65

Marine Life A220

1987, Jan. 2 — *Perf. 14*

701 A220 50fr Jellyfish, coral .30 .20
702 A220 85fr Sea urchin, starfish .50 .25
703 A220 100fr Spiny lobster .55 .30
704 A220 150fr Dolphin .85 .40
705 A220 200fr Octopus 1.10 .60
Nos. 701-705 (5) 3.30 1.75

Senegal Stamp Cent. — A221

1987, Apr. 8 — *Perf. 13*

706 A221 100fr Intl. express mail .55 .30
707 A221 130fr #37 .75 .40
708 A221 140fr Similar to #201 .80 .40
709 A221 145fr #151, similar to #154 .80 .40
710 A221 320fr #27 1.75 .90
Nos. 706-710 (5) 4.65 2.40

Designs of Nos. 37, 151 and 27 same as originally released but perfs simulated.

For overprint see No. 784.

Paris-Dakar Rally — A222

1987, Jan. 22 *Perf. 14*

711 A222 115fr Motorcycle, truck, vert. .65 .30
712 A222 125fr Official, race .70 .35
713 A222 135fr Sabine, truck .80 .40
714 A222 340fr Eiffel Tower, Dakar huts, vert. 2.00 .95
Nos. 711-714 (4) 4.15 2.00

Homage to Thierry Sabine. Inscribed 1986.

Ferlo Nature Reserve — A223

1987, Feb. 5 *Perf. 13½*

715 A223 55fr Antelope .30 .20
716 A223 70fr Ostrich .40 .20
717 A223 85fr Warthog .50 .25
718 A223 90fr Elephant .50 .25
Nos. 715-718 (4) 1.70 .90

Inscribed 1986.

Agena-Gemini 8 Link-up in Outer Space, 20th Anniv. — A224

1987, Feb. 27 Litho. *Perf. 13*

719 A224 320fr multi 1.75 .90

Souvenir Sheet

Perf. 12½

720 A224 500fr multi 2.75 1.40

Nos. 719-720 inscribed 1986 and have erroneous "10e Anniversaire" inscription.

Solidarity Against South African Apartheid — A225

1987, July 31 Litho. *Perf. 13*

721 A225 130fr shown .85 .40
722 A225 140fr Mandela, hand, broken chain, vert. .90 .45
723 A225 145fr Mandela, dove, death .95 .50
Nos. 721-723 (3) 2.70 1.35

Inscribed 1986.

Intelsat, 20th Anniv. A226

1987, Aug. 31 *Perf. 14*

724 A226 50fr Emblem .30 .20
725 A226 125fr Satellite .85 *.40*
726 A226 150fr Emblem, globe 1.00 .50
727 A226 200fr Earth, satellite in space 1.40 .70
Nos. 724-727 (4) 3.55 1.80

Inscribed 1985. Nos. 726-727 vert.

West African Union, 10th Anniv. — A227

Dakar Rotary Club, 45th Anniv. — A228

1987, Sept. 7

728 A227 40fr shown .30 .20
729 A227 125fr Emblem, handshake .90 .45

Inscribed 1985.

1987, Sept. 29 *Perf. 13*

730 A228 500fr multi 3.50 1.75

Inscribed 1985.

United Nations, 40th Anniv. — A229

1987, Oct. 8 *Perf. 14*

731 A229 85fr Emblem, NYC office .60 .30
732 A229 95fr Emblem .70 .35
733 A229 150fr Hands, emblem 1.10 .55
Nos. 731-733 (3) 2.40 1.20

Inscribed 1985.

Cathedral of African Memory, 50th Anniv. A230

130fr, Statue of saint, Fr. Daniel Brottier, vert.

1987, Oct. 16 *Perf. 12½x13, 13x12½*

734 A230 130fr multi .95 .50
735 A230 140fr multi 1.00 .50

Inscribed 1986.

Lat Dior, King of Cayor (d. 1887) A231

1987, Oct. 27 Litho. *Perf. 14*

736 A231 130fr Battle of Dekhele .95 .50
737 A231 160fr Lat Dior 1.25 .60

World Food Day A232

1987, Oct. 30 Litho. *Perf. 12½*

738 A232 130fr Earth storing grain, vert. .90 .45
739 A232 140fr shown 1.00 .50
740 A232 145fr Emblem, vert. 1.00 .50
Nos. 738-740 (3) 2.90 1.45

Inscribed 1986.

A233

Fauna, Bassa Casamance Natl. Park — A234

1987, Nov. 9 *Perf. 13*

741 A233 115fr Felis servaline .85 .40
742 A233 135fr Galagoides demidovii .95 .50
743 A233 150fr Potamochoerus porcus 1.10 .55
744 A233 250fr Panthera pardus 1.75 .90
745 A234 300fr Aigrette 2.10 1.10
746 A234 300fr Guepier 2.10 1.10
a. Pair, #745-746 + label 4.25 2.25
Nos. 741-746 (6) 8.85 4.55

Inscribed 1986. No. 745-746 has continuous design with corner label picturing map of Senegal with park highlighted.

Traditional Wrestling — A235

Birds in Djoudj Natl. Park — A236

Various moves.

1987, Nov. 30 Litho. *Perf. 14*

747 A235 115fr multi, horiz. .80 .40
748 A235 125fr multi, diff., horiz. .90 .45
749 A235 135fr multi, diff. .95 .50
750 A235 165fr multi, diff. 1.25 .65
Nos. 747-750 (4) 3.90 2.00

1987, Dec. 4

751 A236 115fr Stork .80 .40
752 A236 125fr Pink flamingos, horiz. .90 .45
753 A236 135fr White pelicans, horiz. .95 .55
754 A236 300fr Pelicans in water 2.10 1.10
755 A236 350fr like 125fr, horiz. 2.50 1.25
756 A236 350fr like 135fr, horiz. 2.50 1.25
a. Pair, #755-756 + label 5.00 2.50
Nos. 751-756 (6) 9.75 5.00

Christmas A237

Designs: 145fr, Youth dreaming of presents. 150fr, Madonna and child. 180fr, Holy Family, congregation praying. 200fr, Holy Family, candle and Christmas tree.

1987, Dec. 24 *Perf. 12½x13*

757 A237 145fr multi 1.00 .50
758 A237 150fr multi 1.10 .55
759 A237 180fr multi 1.25 .65
760 A237 200fr multi 1.50 .70
Nos. 757-760 (4) 4.85 2.40

Dakar Intl. Fair, 10th Anniv. (in 1985) — A238

1988, Feb. 27 Litho. *Perf. 13*

761 A238 125fr multi .90 .45

Inscribed 1985.

Fish — A239

1988, Feb. 29 Litho. *Perf. 13*

762 A239 5fr Amelurus nebulosus .20 .20
763 A239 100fr Heniochus acuminatus .70 .35
764 A239 145fr Anthias anthias 1.10 .50
765 A239 180fr Cyprinus carpio 1.25 .65
Nos. 762-765 (4) 3.25 1.70

World Meteorology Day — A240

1988, Mar. 15 *Perf. 13½*

766 A240 145fr multi 1.00 .50

Paris-Dakar Rally, 10th Anniv. (in 1987) — A241

Various motorcycle and automobile entries in desert settings.

1988 *Perf. 13*

767 A241 145fr Motorcycle 1.00 .50
768 A241 180fr Race car 1.25 .65
769 A241 200fr Race car, truck 1.40 .70
770 A241 410fr Thierry Sabine 3.00 1.50
Nos. 767-770 (4) 6.65 3.35

Inscribed 1987. For surcharge see No. 1051.

Mollusks
A242

1988, Apr. 20 *Perf. 12½*

771 A242 10fr Squid .20 .20
772 A242 20fr Donax trunculus .20 .20
773 A242 145fr Achatina fulica, vert. 1.00 .50
774 A242 165fr Helix nemoralis 1.25 .60
Nos. 771-774 (4) 2.65 1.50

1988 African Soccer Cup Championships, Rabat — A243

1988, May 10 **Litho.** *Perf. 13*

775 A243 80fr Cameroun (winner) .55 .30
776 A243 100fr Kick, CAF emblem .70 .35
777 A243 145fr Map, players, final score 1.00 .50
778 A243 180fr Trophy 1.25 .60
Nos. 775-778 (4) 3.50 1.75

Nos. 776-778 vert.

US Peace Corps in Senegal, 25th Anniv. — A244

1988, May 11 **Litho.** *Perf. 13*

779 A244 190fr multi 1.25 .60

Marine Flora — A245

1988, June 13 **Litho.** *Perf. 12½*

780 A245 10fr Dictyota atomaria .20 .20
781 A245 65fr Agarum gmelini .45 .25
782 A245 145fr Saccorrhiza bulbosa .95 .50
783 A245 180fr Rhodymenia palmetta 1.25 .60
Nos. 780-783 (4) 2.85 1.55

Inscribed 1987.

No. 710 Overprinted

1988, Aug. 27 **Litho.** *Perf. 13*

784 A221 320fr multi 2.25 1.10

Stamp Fair, Riccione, Aug. 27-29, 1988. Stamp incorrectly overprinted "89," instead of "88."

ENDA — A246

1988 **Litho.** *Perf. 13*

785 A246 125fr Thierno Saidou Nourou Tall Center .80 .40

1988 Summer Olympics, Seoul — A247

1988, Sept. 17 **Litho.** *Perf. 13*

786 A247 5fr shown .20 .20
787 A247 75fr Running, swimming, soccer .50 .25
788 A247 300fr Character trademark, torch 2.00 1.00
789 A247 410fr Emblems, running 2.75 1.40
Nos. 786-789 (4) 5.45 2.85

Industries A248

Indigenous Flowers — A250

Postcards, c. 1900 — A249

1988, Nov. 7 **Litho.** *Perf. 13*

790 A248 5fr Phosphate, Thies .20 .20
791 A248 20fr I.C.S. .20 .20
792 A248 145fr Seib Mill, Diourbel .90 .45
793 A248 410fr Mbao refinery 2.50 1.25
Nos. 790-793 (4) 3.80 2.10

1988, Nov. 26

20fr, Boys, Government Palace. 145fr, Wrestlers, St. Louis Great Mosque. 180fr, Dakar Depot, young woman in folk costume. 200fr, Governor's Residence, housewife using mortar & pestle.

794 A249 20fr red brn & blk .20 .20
795 A249 145fr red brn & blk .90 .45
796 A249 180fr red brn & blk 1.10 .60
797 A249 200fr red brn & blk 1.25 .65
Nos. 794-797 (4) 3.45 1.90

1988, Dec. 4 *Perf. 13x12½*

798 A250 20fr Packia biglobosa .20 .20
799 A250 60fr Eurphorbia pulcherrima .40 .20
800 A250 65fr Cyrtosperma senegalense .40 .20
801 A250 410fr Bombax costatum 2.50 1.25
Nos. 798-801 (4) 3.50 1.85

11th Paris-Dakar Rally A251

1989, Jan. 13 **Litho.** *Perf. 13½*

802 A251 10fr Mask, vehicle, Eiffel Tower .20 .20
803 A251 145fr Helmet, desert scene .95 .50
804 A251 180fr Turban, rallyist in desert 1.25 .60
805 A251 220fr Thierry Sabine 1.50 .70
Nos. 802-805 (4) 3.90 2.00

For surcharge see No. 1050.

Tourism A252

1989, Feb. 15 *Perf. 13*

806 A252 10fr Teranga .20 .20
807 A252 80fr Campement .50 .25
808 A252 100fr Saly .65 .30
809 A252 350fr Dior 2.25 1.10
Nos. 806-809 (4) 3.60 1.85

Inscribed 1988.

Tourism — A253

1989, Mar. 11

810 A253 130fr Natl. tourism emblem, vert. .85 .40
811 A253 140fr Visiting rural community .95 .45
812 A253 145fr Sport fishing .95 .50
813 A253 180fr Water skiing, polo 1.25 .65
Nos. 810-813 (4) 4.00 2.00

Inscribed 1987.

French Revolution, Bicent. — A254

Designs: 180fr, Governor's Palace, St. Louis. 220fr, Declaration of Human Rights and Citizenship, vert. 300fr, Flag, revolutionaries.

1989, May 24 **Litho.** *Perf. 13*

814 A254 180fr shown 1.10 .55
815 A254 220fr multi 1.25 .65
816 A254 300fr multi 1.75 .90
Nos. 814-816 (3) 4.10 2.10

PHILEXFRANCE '89 — A255

1989, July 7 **Litho.** *Perf. 13x12½*

817 A255 10fr shown .20 .20
818 A255 25fr Simulated stamp, map of France .20 .20
819 A255 75fr Exhibit .45 .25
820 A255 145fr Affixing stamp .85 .35
Nos. 817-820 (4) 1.70 1.00

Antoine de Saint-Exupery (1900-1944), French Aviator and Writer — A256

Scenes from novels: 180fr, *Southern Courier,* 1929. 220fr, *Night flier,* 1931. 410fr, *Bomber pilot,* 1942.

1989, Aug. 30 **Litho.** *Perf. 13*

821 A256 180fr multi 1.10 .60
822 A256 220fr multi 1.40 .70
823 A256 410fr multi 2.75 1.40
Nos. 821-823 (3) 5.25 2.70

No. 785 Surcharged in Bright Green

1989 **Litho.** *Perf. 13*

824 A246 555fr on 125fr multi 4.00 2.00

3rd Francophone Summit on the Arts and Culture — A257

Designs: 5fr, Palette, quill pen in ink pot, dancer, vert. 30fr, Children reading. 100fr, Architecture, women, Earth. 200fr, Artist sketching, easel, gear wheels, chemist, computer operator.

1989 *Perf. 13x13½, 13½x13*

825 A257 5fr multicolored .20 .20
826 A257 30fr multicolored .25 .20
827 A257 100fr multicolored .70 .35
828 A257 200fr multicolored 1.40 .70
Nos. 825-828 (4) 2.55 1.45

Pottery A258

1989, Nov. 1 *Perf. 13*

829 A258 15fr shown .20 .20
830 A258 30fr Potter, three-handled urn .30 .20
831 A258 75fr Vases .50 .25
832 A258 145fr Woman carrying pottery 1.00 .50
Nos. 829-832 (4) 2.00 1.15

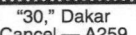

"30," Dakar Cancel — A259

Natl. Archives, 75th Anniv. — A260

30fr, Telephone handset, map. 180fr, Map, simulated stamp, phone handset. 220fr, Telecommunications satellite, globe, map.

1989, Oct. 9 *Perf. 13½*

833	A259	25fr	multicolored	.20	.20
834	A259	30fr	multicolored	.25	.20
835	A259	180fr	multicolored	1.25	.60
836	A259	220fr	multicolored	1.50	.80
			Nos. 833-836 (4)	3.20	1.80

Conference of Postal and Telecommunication Administrations of West African Nations (CAPTEAO), 30th anniv.

1989, Oct. 23 *Perf. 11½*

Designs: 15fr, Stacks, postal card of 1922. 40fr, Document, 1825. 145fr, Document, Archives building. 180fr, Tome.

837	A260	15fr	multicolored	.20	.20
838	A260	40fr	multicolored	.30	.20
839	A260	145fr	multicolored	1.10	.50
840	A260	180fr	multicolored	1.25	.60
			Nos. 837-840 (4)	2.85	1.50

Jawarharlal Nehru, 1st Prime Minister of Independent India — A261

1989, Nov. 14 *Perf. 13*

841	A261	220fr	Portrait, vert.	1.50	.80
842	A261	410fr	shown	2.90	1.45

Marine Life A262

1989, Nov. 27

843	A262	10fr	*Grapsus grapsus*	.20	.20
844	A262	60fr	*Hippocampus guttulatus*	.45	.25
845	A262	145fr	*Lepas anatifera*	1.00	.50
846	A262	220fr	Beach flea	1.50	.80
			Nos. 843-846 (4)	3.15	1.75

Children's March to the Sanctuary A263

1989, Dec. 9 **Litho.** *Perf. 13½*

847	A263	145fr	shown	1.00	.50
848	A263	180fr	Church	1.25	.60

Pilgrimage to Notre Dame de Popenguine, cent.

Birds A263a

Designs: 10fr, *Phalacrocovax carbolucidus, Anhinga rufa.* 45fr, *Lavius cirrocephalus.* 100fr, Dwarf bee-eater, *Lophogetus occipitalis.* 180fr, *Egretta gularis.*

1989, Dec. 11 *Perf. 13*

849	A263a	10fr	multicolored	.20	.20
850	A263a	45fr	multicolored	.30	.20
851	A263a	100fr	multicolored	.70	.35
852	A263a	180fr	multicolored	1.25	.65
			Nos. 849-852 (4)	2.45	1.40

Natl. parks: Djoudj (10fr), Langue de Barbarie (45fr), Basse Casamance (100fr) and Saloum (180fr).

Christmas A264

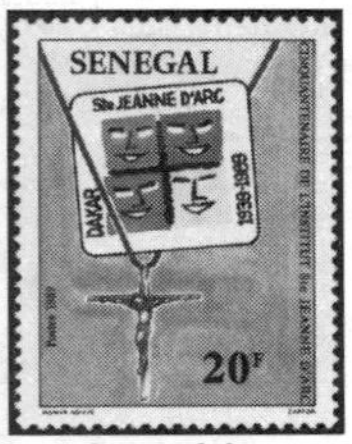

Joan of Arc Institute, 50th Anniv. A265

1989, Dec. 22 **Litho.** *Perf. 13*

853	A264	10fr	shown	.20	.20
854	A264	25fr	Teddy bear	.20	.20
855	A264	30fr	Manger	.30	.20
856	A264	200fr	Mother and child	1.40	.70
			Nos. 853-856 (4)	2.10	1.30

1989, Dec. 26 *Perf. 13½*

857	A265	20fr	shown	.20	.20
858	A265	500fr	Institute	3.50	3.50

Flight of the 1st Seaplane, Mar. 28, 1910 — A266

Perf. 13x12½, 12½x13

1989, Dec. 30 **Litho.**

859	A266	125fr	shown	.90	.45
860	A266	130fr	Seaplane, Fabre	.90	.45
861	A266	475fr	Fabre, schematic of aircraft, vert.	3.50	1.75
			Nos. 859-861 (3)	5.30	2.65

Souvneir Sheet

862	A266	700fr	like 475fr, vert.	5.00	2.50

Henri Fabre (1882-1984), aviator.

1992 Summer Olympics, Barcelona — A267

Various athletes and monuments or architecture.

1990, Jan. 8 *Perf. 12½*

863	A267	10fr	Basketball	.20	.20
864	A267	130fr	High jump	.90	.45
865	A267	180fr	Discus	1.25	.60
866	A267	190fr	Running	1.40	.70
867	A267	315fr	Tennis	2.25	1.10
868	A267	475fr	Equestrian	3.25	1.60
			Nos. 863-868 (6)	9.25	4.65

Souvenir Sheet

869	A267	600fr	Soccer	4.25	2.10

Fight AIDS Worldwide A268

1989, Dec. 1 **Litho.** *Perf. 13½*

870	A268	5fr	shown	.20	.20
871	A268	100fr	Umbrella	.70	.35
872	A268	145fr	Fist crushing virus	1.00	.50
873	A268	180fr	Hammering away at virus	1.25	.65
			Nos. 870-873 (4)	3.15	1.70

12th Paris-Dakar Rally — A269

1990, Jan. 16 *Perf. 13*

874	A269	20fr	shown	.20	.20
875	A269	25fr	Motorcycle	.25	.20
876	A269	180fr	Trophy winner, crowd	1.25	.60
877	A269	200fr	Thierry Sabine	1.40	.70
			Nos. 874-877 (4)	3.10	1.70

1990 World Cup Soccer Championships, Italy — A270

Various athletes and: 45fr, Trophy, the Piazza Della Signoria, Florence. 140fr, Piazza Navona, Rome. 180fr, *The Virgin with St. Anne and the Infant Jesus,* by Leonardo da Vinci. 220fr, Portrait of Giuseppe Garibaldi (1807-1882), Risorgimento Museum, Turin. 300fr, *The Sistine Madonna,* by Raphael. 415fr, *The Virgin and Child,* by Daniele da Volterra. 700fr, Columbus Monument, Milan.

1990, Jan. 31 **Litho.** *Perf. 13x12½*

878	A270	45fr	multicolored	.30	.20
879	A270	140fr	multicolored	1.00	.50
880	A270	180fr	multicolored	1.25	.65
881	A270	220fr	multicolored	1.60	.80
882	A270	300fr	multicolored	2.10	1.10
883	A270	415fr	multicolored	3.00	1.50
			Nos. 878-883 (6)	9.25	4.75

Souvenir Sheet

Nos. 878-883 exist in souvenir sheets of 1.

884	A270	700fr	multicolored	5.00	2.50

1990 African Soccer Cup Championships, Algeria — A271

1990, Mar. 2 **Litho.** *Perf. 13*

885	A271	20f	shown	.20	.20
886	A271	60f	Goalie	.45	.25
887	A271	100f	Exchange of flags	.75	.40
888	A271	500f	Ball, trophy	3.75	1.90
			Nos. 885-888 (4)	5.15	2.75

Postal Services A272

1990, Apr. 30 **Litho.** *Perf. 13*

889	A272	5fr	Facsimile transmission	.20	.20
890	A272	15fr	Express mail	.20	.20
891	A272	100fr	Postal money orders	.75	.40
892	A272	180fr	CNE	1.25	.65
			Nos. 889-892 (4)	2.40	1.45

A273

A274

1990, May 31 *Perf. 13½*

893	A273	145fr	shown	1.00	.50
894	A273	180fr	Hand, wreath, envelope	1.25	.65

Multinational Postal School, 20th anniv.

1990, May 31

895	A274	5fr	shown	.20	.20
896	A274	500fr	Family	3.75	1.50

S.O.S. Children's Village appeal for aid.

Boy Scouts A275

Scouting emblems and: 30fr, Camping. 100fr, Hiking at lakeshore. 145fr, Following trail. 200fr, Scout, vert.

1990, Nov. 5 **Litho.** *Perf. 11½*

897	A275	30fr	multicolored	.25	.20
898	A275	100fr	multicolored	.90	.45
899	A275	145fr	multicolored	1.25	.65
900	A275	200fr	multicolored	1.75	.85
			Nos. 897-900 (4)	4.15	2.15

Medicinal Plants — A276

1990, Nov. 30 *Perf. 13x13½*

901	A276	95fr	Cassia tora	.85	.40
902	A276	105fr	Tamarindus indica	.95	.45

903 A276 125fr Cassia occidentalis 1.10 .55
904 A276 175fr Leptadenia hastata 1.50 .75
Nos. 901-904 (4) 4.40 2.15

A277

A278

1990, Dec. 24 Litho. *Perf. 13½*
905 A277 25fr shown .20 .20
906 A277 145fr Angel, stars, people 1.25 .65
907 A277 180fr Adoration of the Magi 1.60 .80
908 A277 200fr Animals, baby in manger 1.75 .85
Nos. 905-908 (4) 4.80 2.50

Christmas.

1991, Jan. 2 Litho. *Perf. 13x12½*
909 A278 180fr multicolored 1.50 .80

Intl. Red Cross, 125th Anniv., Senegalese Red Cross, 25th anniv. No. 909 inscribed 1988.

Paris-Dakar Rally — A279

1991, Jan. 17
910 A279 15fr shown .20 .20
911 A279 125fr Car, motorcycle 1.10 .55
912 A279 180fr Car racing in water 1.50 .80
913 A279 220fr Two motorcycles, beach 1.90 .95
Nos. 910-913 (4) 4.70 2.50

Reptiles A280

1991, Jan. 31 *Perf. 13½x13*
914 A280 15fr Python sebae .20 .20
915 A280 60fr Chelonia mydas .55 .30
916 A280 100fr Crocolylus niloticus .90 .45
917 A280 180fr Chameleo senegalensis 1.50 .80
Nos. 914-917 (4) 3.15 1.75

Inscribed 1990.

African Film Festival A281

Designs: 30fr, Sphinx, slave house, cave paintings, tomb of Mohammed. 60fr, Dogon mask, mosque of Dioulasso, drawing of Osiris, man on camel. 100fr, Ruins, drum, statue of scribe, camels. 180fr, mask, mosque of Djenne, pyramids, Moroccan architecture.

1991, Feb. 23 *Perf. 11½*
918 A281 30fr org & multi .25 .20
919 A281 60fr org & multi .50 .25
920 A281 100fr org & multi .90 .45
921 A281 180fr org & multi 1.50 .80
Nos. 918-921 (4) 3.15 1.70

Alfred Nobel (1833-1896), Industrialist — A282

Designs: 145fr, Drawing of Nobel.

1991, Mar. 29 Litho. *Die Cut*
Self-adhesive
922 A282 145fr multi, vert. 1.10 .55
923 A282 180fr shown 1.40 .65

Antelope — A283

1991, Apr. 24 Litho. *Perf. 13½x13*
924 A283 5fr Ouerbia ourebi .20 .20
925 A283 10fr Gazella dorcas .20 .20
926 A283 180fr Kobos kob kob 1.40 .70
927 A283 555fr Alcelaphus bucelaphus major 4.00 2.00
Nos. 924-927 (4) 5.80 3.10

Trees A284

1991, May 30 *Perf. 13½x13, 13x13½*
928 A284 90fr Ancardium occidentalus .65 .35
929 A284 100fr Mangifera indica .75 .40
930 A284 125fr Borassus flabellifer, vert. .95 .50
931 A284 145fr Elaeis guineensis, vert. 1.10 .55
Nos. 928-931 (4) 3.45 1.80

Christopher Columbus — A285

100fr, Meeting Haitian natives. 145fr, Columbus' personal coat of arms, vert. 180fr, Santa Maria, Columbus. 200fr, 220fr, Columbus, ships. 500fr, Details of voyages. 625fr, Columbus at chart table.

1991, July 8 Litho. *Perf. 13*
932 A285 100fr multicolored .75 .40
a. Sheet of 1, perf. 12½ .75 .40
933 A285 145fr multicolored 1.10 .55
a. Sheet of 1, perf. 12½ 1.10 .55
934 A285 180fr multicolored 1.40 .65
a. Sheet of 1, perf. 12½ 1.40 .65
935 A285 200fr multicolored 1.50 .75
a. Sheet of 1, perf. 12½ 1.50 .75
936 A285 220fr multicolored 1.60 .80
a. Sheet of 1, perf. 12½ 1.60 .80
937 A285 500fr multicolored 3.75 1.90
a. Sheet of 1, perf. 12½ 3.75 1.90
938 A285 625fr multicolored 4.75 2.25
a. Sheet of 1, perf. 12½ 4.75 2.25
Nos. 932-938 (7) 14.85 7.30

Tourism A286

Designs: 10fr, Canoe excursion, Basse-Casamance. 25fr, Shore at Boufflers Hotel, Goree Island. 30fr, Huts built on stilts, Fadiouth Island. 40fr, Salt collecting on lake.

1991, July 30 Litho. *Perf. 13*
939 A286 10fr multicolored .20 .20
940 A286 25fr multicolored .20 .20
941 A286 30fr multicolored .25 .20
942 A286 40fr multicolored .35 .20
Nos. 939-942 (4) 1.00 .80

Dated 1989.

Louis Armstrong, Jazz Musician, 20th Death Anniv. — A287

1991, Oct. 7 *Perf. 13½*
943 A287 10fr shown .20 .20
944 A287 145fr Singing 1.25 .60
945 A287 180fr With trumpets 1.50 .75
946 A287 220fr Playing trumpet 1.75 .90
Nos. 943-946 (4) 4.70 2.45

Yuri Gagarin, First Man in Space, 30th Anniv. — A288

Various portraits of Gagarin with Vostok I in Earth orbit.

1991, Nov. 25 Litho. *Perf. 13½*
947 A288 15fr multicolored .20 .20
948 A288 145fr multicolored 1.25 .60
949 A288 180fr multicolored 1.50 .75
950 A288 220fr multicolored 1.75 .90
Nos. 947-950 (4) 4.70 2.45

Rural Water Supply Project — A289

6th Islamic Summit — A290

1991, Dec. 2 Litho. *Perf. 13½*
951 A289 30fr Bowl of water .25 .20
952 A289 145fr Water faucet, huts 1.25 .65
953 A289 180fr Dripping faucet, flags 1.60 .80
954 A289 220fr Water tower, huts 1.90 .95
Nos. 951-954 (4) 5.00 2.60

1991, Dec. 9
955 A290 15fr shown .25 .20
956 A290 145fr Upraised hands 1.25 .65
957 A290 180fr Congress Center, Dakar 1.60 .80
958 A290 220fr Grand Mosque, Dakar 1.90 .95
Nos. 955-958 (4) 5.00 2.60

A291

A292

Basketball, Cent.: 145fr, Player dribbling ball. 180fr, Couple holding trophy. 220fr, Lion, basketball, trophies.

1991, Dec. 21 Litho. *Perf. 13½*
959 A291 125fr multicolored 1.00 .50
960 A291 145fr multicolored 1.25 .60
961 A291 180fr multicolored 1.50 .75
962 A291 220fr multicolored 1.75 .90
Nos. 959-962 (4) 5.50 2.75

1991, Dec. 24 Litho. *Perf. 13½*
963 A292 5fr Jesus .20 .20
964 A292 145fr Madonna and Child 1.25 .60
965 A292 160fr Angels 1.40 .70
966 A292 220fr Christ Child, animals 1.90 .95
Nos. 963-966 (4) 4.75 2.45

Christmas. For surcharge see No. 975.

A293

A294

A293a

Musical score and: 5fr, Bust of Mozart. 150fr, Mozart conducting. 180fr, Mozart at piano. 220fr, Portrait.

1991, Dec. 31
967 A293 5fr multicolored .25 .20
968 A293 150fr multicolored 1.25 .65
969 A293 180fr multicolored 1.60 .80
970 A293 220fr multicolored 1.90 .95
Nos. 967-970 (4) 5.00 2.60

Wolfgang Amadeus Mozart, death bicent.

1991? Litho. *Perf. 13½*

Mermoz and: 145fr, Outline maps of South America, Africa. 180fr, Airplane. 200fr, Aiplane in flight.

970A A293a 15fr multicolored
970B A293a 145fr multicolored
970C A293a 180fr multicolored
970D A293a 200fr multicolored

Jean Mermoz (1901-36), pilot.

Nos. 970A-970D exist in imperf. souvenir sheets of 1.

1992, Jan. 12 Litho. *Perf. 13½*

971 A294	10fr	shown	.20	.20
972 A294	145fr	Map, soccer balls	1.25	.60
973 A294	200fr	Lion, trophy	1.60	.85
974 A294	220fr	Players	1.75	.90
		Nos. 971-974 (4)	4.80	2.55

18th African Soccer Cup Championships.

No. 965 Surcharged

1992, Feb. 19 Litho. *Perf. 13½*

975 A292 180fr on 160fr 1.50 .75

Natl. Parks A295

1992, Mar. 20 *Perf. 13½x13*

976 A295	10fr	Delta Du Saloum	.20	.20
977 A295	125fr	Djoudj	1.00	.50
978 A295	145fr	Niokolo-Koba	1.25	.60
979 A295	220fr	Basse Casamance	1.75	.90
		Nos. 976-979 (4)	4.20	2.20

Senegal's Participation in Gulf War — A296

Designs: 30fr, Oil wells, flag and missiles. 145fr, Oil wells, soldier. 180fr, Holy Ka'aba, soldier with gun. 220fr, Peace dove with flag, map.

1992, Apr. 4 *Perf. 13½*

980 A296	30fr	multicolored	.25	.20
981 A296	145fr	multicolored	1.25	.60
982 A296	180fr	multicolored	1.50	.75
983 A296	220fr	multicolored	1.75	.90
		Nos. 980-983 (4)	4.75	2.45

Fish Industry A297

Stylized designs: 5fr, Catching fish. 60fr, Retail outlets. 100fr, Processing plant. 150fr, Packaging.

1992, Apr. 6 Litho. *Perf. 13½*

984 A297	5fr	multicolored	.20	.20
985 A297	60fr	multicolored	.55	.30
986 A297	100fr	multicolored	.90	.45
987 A297	150fr	multicolored	1.25	.65
		Nos. 984-987 (4)	2.90	1.60

Tourism — A298

1992, May 5 *Perf. 13½x13*

988 A298	5fr	Niokolo complex	.20	.20
989 A298	10fr	Casamance River	.20	.20
990 A298	150fr	Dakar region	1.25	.65
991 A298	200fr	Saint-Louis excursion	1.75	.95
		Nos. 988-991 (4)	3.40	2.00

Planting Trees A299

Various designs showing children planting trees.

1992, May 29 *Perf. 13½x13, 13x13½*

992 A299	145fr	multi	1.25	.65
993 A299	180fr	multi	1.60	.80
994 A299	200fr	multi	1.75	.90
995 A299	220fr	multi, vert.	1.90	.95
		Nos. 992-995 (4)	6.50	3.30

Public Works Projects A300

Various scenes of people cleaning and repairing public walkways.

Perf. 13½x13, 13x13½

1992, June 1 Litho.

996 A300	25fr	multi	.25	.20
997 A300	145fr	multi	1.25	.65
998 A300	180fr	multi, vert.	1.60	.80
999 A300	220fr	multi, vert.	2.00	1.00
		Nos. 996-999 (4)	5.10	2.65

Children's Rights — A301

1992, June 12 *Perf. 13*

1000 A301	20fr	Education	.20	.20
1001 A301	45fr	Guidance	.40	.20
1002 A301	165fr	Instruction	1.40	.70
1003 A301	180fr	Health care	1.60	.80
		Nos. 1000-1003 (4)	3.60	1.90

African Integration A302

1992, June 29 Litho. *Perf. 13*

1004 A302	10fr	Free trade	.20	.20
1005 A302	30fr	Youth activities	.25	.20
1006 A302	145fr	Communications	1.25	.60
1007 A302	220fr	Women's movements	2.00	1.00
		Nos. 1004-1007 (4)	3.70	2.00

1992 Summer Olympics, Barcelona A303

Blue Train — A304

1992, July 25 Litho. *Perf. 13½*

1008 A303	145fr	Map, horiz.	1.10	.55
1009 A303	180fr	Runner	1.40	.70
1010 A303	200fr	Sprinter, horiz.	1.50	.75
1011 A303	300fr	Torch bearer	2.25	1.10
		Nos. 1008-1011 (4)	6.25	3.10

1992, Aug. 3

1012 A304	70fr	shown	.55	.30
1013 A304	145fr	Train yard	1.10	.55
1014 A304	200fr	Train, passengers	1.50	.75
1015 A304	220fr	Station	1.60	.85
		Nos. 1012-1015 (4)	4.75	2.45

Intl. Maritime Heritage Year — A305

25fr, Map of Antarctica. 100fr, Ocean, sea life. 180fr, Man addressing UN. 220fr, Hands holding globe, flags, ship, fish.

1992, Sept. 4

1016 A305	25fr	multi, horiz.	.20	.20
1017 A305	100fr	multi	.75	.35
1018 A305	180fr	multi	1.40	.65
1019 A305	220fr	multi	1.60	.80
		Nos. 1016-1019 (4)	3.95	2.00

Corals A306

Various coral formations.

Perf. 13½x13, 13x13½

1992, Sept. 18 Litho.

1020 A306	50fr	multicolored	.40	.20
1021 A306	100fr	multicolored	.85	.40
1022 A306	145fr	multi, vert.	1.25	.60
1023 A306	220fr	multicolored	1.75	.90
		Nos. 1020-1023 (4)	4.25	2.10

Konrad Adenauer (1876-1967) — A307

Designs: 5fr, Portrait, vert. 145fr, Schaumburg Palace, Bonn. 180fr, Hands clasped. 220fr, Map of West Germany.

Perf. 13x13½, 13½x13

1992, Sept. 30 Litho.

1024 A307	5fr	multicolored	.20	.20
1025 A307	145fr	multicolored	1.25	.60
1026 A307	180fr	multicolored	1.50	.75
1027 A307	220fr	multicolored	1.75	.90
		Nos. 1024-1027 (4)	4.70	2.45

Shellfish — A308

1992, Oct. 1 Litho. *Perf. 13½*

1028 A308	20fr	Crab	.20	.20
1029 A308	30fr	Spider crab	.25	.20
1030 A308	180fr	Lobster	1.40	.70
1031 A308	200fr	Shrimp	1.50	.75
		Nos. 1028-1031 (4)	3.35	1.85

Fruit-bearing Plants — A309

1992, Oct. 16 Litho. *Perf. 13x13½*

1032 A309	10fr	Parkia biglobosa	.20	.20
1033 A309	50fr	Balanites aegyptiaca	.45	.20
1034 A309	200fr	Parinari macrophylla	1.60	.70
1035 A309	220fr	Opuntiatuna	1.75	.90
		Nos. 1032-1035 (4)	4.00	2.00

John Glenn's Orbital Flight, 30th Anniv. — A310

15fr, Astronaut in spacesuit, flag, map, spacecraft, horiz. 145fr, American flag, Glenn, horiz. 180fr, Flag, lift-off of rocket, Glenn in spacesuit, horiz. 200fr, Astronaut in spacesuit, spacecraft.

1992, Nov. 30 Litho. *Perf. 13½*

1036 A310	15fr	multicolored	.20	.20
1037 A310	145fr	multicolored	1.10	.60
1038 A310	180fr	multicolored	1.40	.70
1039 A310	200fr	multicolored	1.60	.80
		Nos. 1036-1039 (4)	4.30	2.30

Maps Featuring Bakari II — A311

100fr, Map from Spanish Atlas, 1375. 145fr, Stone head, Vera Cruz, Mexico, world map, 1413.

1992, Dec. 2 *Perf. 13*

1040 A311	100fr	multicolored	.80	.40
1041 A311	145fr	multicolored	1.25	.60

No. 1041 issued only with black bar obliterating "Mecades."

Biennial of Dakar — A312

Christmas A313

20fr, Picture frame. 50fr, Puppet head, stage. 145fr, Open book. 220fr, Musical instrument.

1992, Dec. 14 ***Perf. 13½***

1042 A312 20fr multicolored .20 .20
1043 A312 50fr multicolored .40 .20
1044 A312 145fr multicolored 1.10 .60
1045 A312 220fr multicolored 1.75 .90
Nos. 1042-1045 (4) 3.45 1.90

1992, Dec. 24 ***Perf. 13½***

Designs: 15fr, Children dancing around large ornament, horiz. 145fr, Christmas tree. 180fr, Jesus Christ. 200fr, Santa Claus.

1046 A313 15fr multicolored .20 .20
1047 A313 145fr multicolored 1.10 .60
1048 A313 180fr multicolored 1.40 .70
1049 A313 200fr multicolored 1.60 .80
Nos. 1046-1049 (4) 4.30 2.30

Nos. 770, 804 Surcharged in Red

1993, Jan. 17 **Litho.** ***Perf. 13½***

1050 A251 145fr on 180fr #804 1.10 .60

Perf. 13

1051 A241 220fr on 410fr #770 1.75 .90

Size and location of surcharge varies.

Environmental Protection — A314

Accident Prevention A315

Designs: 20fr, Medical clinic. 25fr, Preventing industrial accidents. 145fr, Preventing chemical spills. 200fr, Red Cross helicopter, airline crash.

Perf. 13 (#1052, 1055), 13½

1993, Mar. 22 **Litho.**

1052 A314 20fr multicolored .20 .20
1053 A315 25fr multicolored .20 .20
1054 A315 145fr multicolored 1.10 .60
1055 A314 200fr multicolored 1.60 .80
Nos. 1052-1055 (4) 3.10 1.80

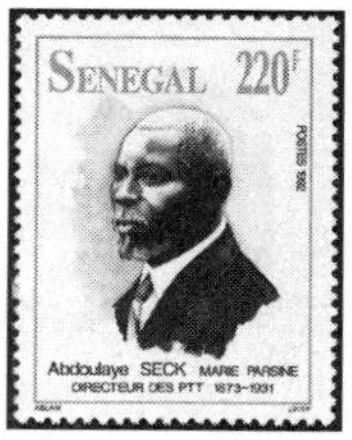

Abdoulaye Seck Marie Parsine (1873-1931), PTT Director — A316

1993, Apr. 21 **Litho.** ***Perf. 13½***

1056 A316 220fr multicolored 1.75 .90

Wild Animals A317

30fr, Crocuta crocuta. 50fr, Panthera leo. 70fr, Panthera pardus. 150fr, Giraffa camelopardalis peratta, vert. 180fr, Cervus.

1993, Nov. 26 **Litho.** ***Perf. 13½***

1057 A317 30fr multicolored .20 .20
1058 A317 50fr multicolored .20 .20
1059 A317 70fr multicolored .25 .20
1060 A317 150fr multicolored .55 .30
1061 A317 180fr multicolored .70 .35
Nos. 1057-1061 (5) 1.90 1.25

Christmas A318

Designs: 80fr, Two children seated by Christmas tree. 145fr, Santa holding presents, three children. 150fr, Girl, Santa with present.

1993, Dec. 24 **Litho.** ***Perf. 13x13½***

1062 A318 5fr multicolored .20 .20
1063 A318 80fr multicolored .30 .20
1064 A318 145fr multicolored .55 .30
1065 A318 150fr multicolored .60 .30
Nos. 1062-1065 (4) 1.65 1.00

Paris-Dakar Rally, 16th Anniv. — A319

Designs: 145fr, Truck, car, motorcycle racing by tree. 180fr, Racing through desert, men with camel. 220fr, Car, truck, village.

1994, Jan. 5 ***Perf. 13½***

1066 A319 145fr multicolored .55 .30
1067 A319 180fr multicolored .70 .35
1068 A319 220fr multicolored .90 .45
Nos. 1066-1068 (3) 2.15 1.10

Assassination of John F. Kennedy, 30th Anniv. — A320

1993, Dec. 31 **Litho.** ***Perf. 13***

1069 A320 80fr shown .30 .20
1070 A320 555fr Kennedy, White House 2.25 1.10

Fishing Industry A321

5fr, Drying eels. 90fr, Sifting for shellfish. 100fr, Salting fish. 200fr, Cooking fish.

1994, Feb. 28

1071 A321 5fr multicolored .20 .20
1072 A321 90fr multicolored .35 .20
1073 A321 100fr multicolored .40 .20
1074 A321 200fr multicolored .80 .40
Nos. 1071-1074 (4) 1.75 1.00

Flowers — A321a

Design: 100fr, Erythrina senegalensis. 145fr, Spathodea campanulata.

Perf. 13¼x13½; 13½

1994, Feb. 28 **Litho.**

1074B A321a 100fr multi
1074C A321a 145fr multi

Three additional stamps were released in this set. The editors would like to examine them.

Conservation of the Seashore — A322

Stylized designs: 5fr, Halting removal of sand. 75fr, Fight against drifting sand dunes. 100fr, Dams, dikes against beach erosion. 200fr, Healthy, aesthetic environment.

1994, Mar. 7

1075 A322 5fr multicolored .20 .20
1076 A322 75fr multicolored .30 .20
1077 A322 100fr multicolored .40 .20
1078 A322 200fr multicolored .80 .40
Nos. 1075-1078 (4) 1.70 1.00

Save the Elephant A323

1994, Apr. 18

1079 A323 30fr shown .20 .20
1080 A323 60fr Elephant in "SOS" .25 .20
1081 A323 90fr Elephants forming "SOS" .35 .20
1082 A323 145fr Elephant, tusks .60 .30
Nos. 1079-1082 (4) 1.40 .90

Arrival of Portuguese in Senegal, 550th Anniv. A324

1994, Nov. 17 **Litho.** ***Perf. 12***

1083 A324 175fr multicolored .80 .40

See Portugal No. 2036.

A325

A326

Shells: 20fr, Murex saxatilis, horiz. 45fr, Nerita senegalensis. 75fr, Polymita picea, horiz. 175fr, Scalaria pretiosa. 215fr, Conus gloria maris.

1994, Oct. 3 **Litho.** ***Perf. 13½***

1084 A325 20fr multicolored .20 .20
1085 A325 45fr multicolored .20 .20
1086 A325 75fr multicolored .30 .20
1087 A325 175fr multicolored .75 .40
1088 A325 215fr multicolored .95 .50
Nos. 1084-1088 (5) 2.40 1.50

1994, Nov. 4

1089 A326 175fr multi, horiz. .75 .40
1090 A326 215fr multi, horiz. .95 .50
1091 A326 275fr multicolored 1.25 .60
1092 A326 290fr multi, diff. 1.25 .65
Nos. 1089-1092 (4) 4.20 2.15

Intl. Olympic Committee, Cent.

Wild Animals A327

1994, Oct. 28 **Litho.** ***Perf. 13½***

1093 A327 60fr Canis aureus .30 .20
1094 A327 70fr Aonyx capensis .30 .20
1095 A327 100fr Herpestes ichneumon .45 .25
1096 A327 175fr Manis gigantea .75 .40
1097 A327 215fr Varanus niloticus .95 .45
Nos. 1093-1097 (5) 2.75 1.50

Lions Club Intl., 13th Multidistrict Convention, Dakar — A328

1994, May 5 **Litho.** ***Perf. 13½x13***

1098 A328 30fr shown .20 .20
1099 A328 60fr Emblem, butterfly .30 .20
1100 A328 175fr Emblem, "L's" .85 .40
1101 A328 215fr Colors, emblem 1.00 .50
Nos. 1098-1101 (4) 2.35 1.30

African Children's Day A329

UNICEF emblem and: 175fr, Children playing. 215fr, Family, huts.

1994, June 16 Litho. *Perf. 13½*

1102	A329	175fr multicolored	.80	.40
1103	A329	215fr multicolored	1.00	.50

1994 World Cup Soccer Championships, US — A330

Designs: 45fr, Flags of participants, soccer ball, vert. 175fr, Top of globe, bottom of soccer ball, vert. 215fr, Player. 665fr, Two players.

1994, June 17

1104	A330	45fr multicolored	.20	.20
1105	A330	175fr multicolored	.80	.40
1106	A330	215fr multicolored	1.00	.50
1107	A330	665fr multicolored	3.00	1.50
		Nos. 1104-1107 (4)	5.00	2.60

UPU Congress, Seoul — A331

1994, Aug. 16 Litho. *Perf. 13½x13*

1108	A331	10fr Rainbow		

Numbers have been reserved for three more values in this set. The editors would like to examine them.

UPU Congress Type of 1994

1994, Aug. 16 Litho. *Perf. 13½x13*

1110	A331	260fr Stylized stamp		

Two additional stamps were released in this set. The editors would like to examine them.

Intl. Year of the Family A333

UN emblem and: 5fr, People of different races, national flags, peace dove, globe, sun. 175fr, Globe, flags, people. 215fr, Globe, mother & child. 290fr, Buildings, family, dove, sun, globe.

1994, Aug. 19 *Perf. 13½x13*

1113	A333	5fr multicolored	.20	.20
1114	A333	175fr multicolored	.80	.40
1115	A333	215fr multicolored	1.00	.50
1116	A333	290fr multicolored	1.40	.70
		Nos. 1113-1116 (4)	3.40	1.80

10th Toulouse to Saint-Louis Air Rally — A334

1994, Apr. 10 *Perf. 13½*

1117	A334	100fr Breguet 14	.50	.25
1118	A334	145fr Guillaumet	.65	.35
1119	A334	180fr Jean Mermoz	.85	.40
1120	A334	220fr Saint-Exupery	1.00	.50
		Nos. 1117-1120 (4)	3.00	1.50

Dated 1993.

Christmas — A335

175fr, Santa Claus, Christ, children, presents. 215fr, Christmas trees, religious scenes. 275fr, Magi, Christ Child. 290fr, Madonna & Child.

Perf. 13x13½, 13½x13

1994, Nov. 24

1121	A335	175fr multi, vert.	.80	.40
1122	A335	215fr multi, vert.	1.00	.50
1123	A335	275fr multi	1.25	.65
1124	A335	290fr multi, vert.	1.40	.70
		Nos. 1121-1124 (4)	4.45	2.25

Historical Sites — A336

Designs: 100fr, Goree Chateau. 175fr, Soudan Mansion. 215fr, Goree Island. 275fr, Pinet Laprade fort, Sedhiou.

1994, Mar. 20 Litho. *Perf. 13½x13*

1125	A336	100fr multicolored	.45	.20
1126	A336	175fr multicolored	.80	.40
1127	A336	215fr multicolored	1.00	.50
1128	A336	275fr multicolored	1.25	.65
		Nos. 1125-1128 (4)	3.50	1.75

Kallisaye Natl. Park A337

Water birds: 100fr, Ardea melanocephala, vert. 275fr, Sterna caspia, vert. 290fr, Egretta gularis, vert. 380fr, Pelecanus rufescens.

1995, Feb. 2 *Perf. 13½*

1129	A337	100fr multicolored	.45	.20
1130	A337	275fr multicolored	1.25	.65
1131	A337	290fr multicolored	1.40	.70
1132	A337	380fr multicolored	1.75	.85
		Nos. 1129-1132 (4)	4.85	2.40

Dinosaurs A338

1995, Jan. 27

1133	A338	100fr Diplodocus	.45	.20
1134	A338	175fr Brontosaurus	.75	.40
1135	A338	215fr Triceratops	1.00	.50
1136	A338	290fr Stegosaurus	1.40	.70
1137	A338	300fr Tyrannosaurus	1.40	.70
		Nos. 1133-1137 (5)	5.00	2.50

House of Slaves, Goree A339

1994 Litho. *Perf. 13½*

1138	A339	500fr multicolored	2.50	1.25

Flowers — A340

Designs: 30fr, Bombax costatum. 75fr, Allamanda cathartica. 100fr, Catharantus roseus. 1000fr, Clerodendron speciossimum.

1995, Apr. 9

1139	A340	30fr multicolored	.20	.20
1140	A340	75fr multicolored	.40	.20
1141	A340	100fr multicolored	.50	.25
1142	A340	1000fr multicolored	5.00	2.50
		Nos. 1139-1142 (4)	6.10	3.15

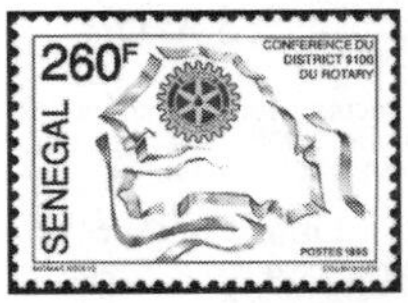

A341

A342

1995, May 11 Litho. *Perf. 11½*

1143	A341	260fr shown	1.25	.65
1144	A341	275fr Emblem, dove	1.40	.70

District 9100 Conference of Rotary, Intl.

1995, June 17

Map of Africa with countries highlighted, native item or animal: 10fr, Sudan, musical instrument. 15fr, Dahomey (Benin), huts, canoes. 30fr, Ivory Coast, elephant. 70fr, Mauritania, camel. 175fr, Guinea, string instrument, bananas. 180fr, Upper Volta (Burkina Faso), ox, vegetables, drum. 215fr, Niger, Cross of Agadès. 225fr, Senegal, lions.

1145	A342	10fr multicolored	.20	.20
1146	A342	15fr multicolored	.20	.20
1147	A342	30fr multicolored	.20	.20
1148	A342	70fr multicolored	.35	.20
1149	A342	175fr multicolored	.90	.45
1150	A342	180fr multicolored	.95	.45
1151	A342	215fr multicolored	1.10	.55
1152	A342	225fr multicolored	1.25	.60
		Nos. 1145-1152 (8)	5.15	2.85

Fashion Type of 1972

1995, June 30 *Perf. 13½x13*

Size: 21x26mm

1153	A106	5fr light brown	.20	.20
1154	A106	10fr bright green	.20	.20
1155	A106	20fr henna brown	.20	.20
1156	A106	25fr olive	.20	.20
1157	A106	30fr light olive	.20	.20
1158	A106	40fr yellow green	.20	.20
1159	A106	100fr slate blue	.50	.25
1160	A106	150fr deep blue	.75	.35
1161	A106	175fr dull brown	.90	.45
1162	A106	200fr black	1.00	.50
1163	A106	250fr red	1.25	.60
1164	A106	275fr rose carmine	1.40	.80
		Nos. 1153-1164 (12)	7.00	4.15

Economic Community of West African States (ECOWAS), 20th Anniv. — A343

Designs: 175fr, Satellite dish, telephone, computer, map, dam, vert. 215fr, Flags of member nations, fruits, vegetables.

1995, Sept. 11 Litho. *Perf. 13½*

1165	A343	175fr multicolored	.90	.45
1166	A343	215fr multicolored	1.10	.55

Louis Pasteur (1822-95) — A345

275fr, Holding vial. 500fr, In laboratory.

1995, Sept. 28 Litho. *Perf. 11½*

1168	A345	275fr multicolored	1.25	.60
1169	A345	500fr multicolored	2.25	1.25

Motion Pictures, Cent. A346

Early developments by Lumiere Brothers: 100fr, Scene from "The Water Sprinkler." 200fr, First pulbic showing of motion picture. 250fr, Auguste, Louis Lumiere watching picture of train arriving at station. 275fr, Demonstrating cinematography.

1995, Oct. 2 *Perf. 13½*

1170	A346	100fr multicolored	.45	.20
1171	A346	200fr multicolored	.90	.45
1172	A346	250fr multicolored	1.10	.55
1173	A346	275fr multicolored	1.25	.60
		Nos. 1170-1173 (4)	3.70	1.80

FAO, 50th Anniv. A347

Designs: 175fr, Farmer, oxen. 215fr, Technician, bringing water to arid regions. 260fr, Gathering fish. 275fr, Nutrition of infants.

1995, Oct. 16

1174	A347	175fr multicolored	.80	.40
1175	A347	215fr multicolored	.95	.50
1176	A347	260fr multicolored	1.10	.55
1177	A347	275fr multicolored	1.25	.60
		Nos. 1174-1177 (4)	4.10	2.05

A348

A349

1995, Oct. 24 *Perf. 11½*

1178	A348	275fr shown	1.25	.60
1179	A348	1000fr Building	4.25	2.00

UN, 50th anniv.

1995, Nov. 2

1180	A349	150fr shown	.70	.35
1181	A349	500fr Contestants	2.25	1.10

La Francophonie, 25th anniv.

Wild Animals A350

Designs: a, 90fr, Syncerus nanus savanensis. b, 150fr, Phacochoerus aethiopicus. c, 175fr, Tragelaphus scriptus. d, 275fr, Goechelone sulcata. e, 300fr, Hystrix cristata.

1995, Nov. 13 ***Perf. 13½***

1182 A350 Strip of 5, #a.-e. 4.50 2.25

Endangered Birds — A351

1995, Nov. 30 ***Perf. 13½x13***

1183 A351 90fr Hydroprogne caspia .40 .20
1184 A351 145fr Gelochelidon nilotica .65 .30
1185 A351 150fr Sterna maxima .70 .35
1186 A351 180fr Sterna hirunda .80 .40
Nos. 1183-1186 (4) 2.55 1.25

Butterflies A352

Designs: 45fr, Meganostoma eurydice. 100fr, Luehdorfia japonica. 200fr, Hebomoia glaucippe. 220fr, Aglais urticae.

1995, Dec. 4 ***Perf. 13***

1187 A352 45fr multicolored .20 .20
1188 A352 100fr multicolored .45 .20
1189 A352 200fr multicolored .90 .45
1190 A352 220fr multicolored 1.00 .50
Nos. 1187-1190 (4) 2.55 1.35

Tourism A353

1995, Dec. 28 ***Perf. 13½***

1191 A353 100fr Bassari Festival .45 .20
1192 A353 175fr Baawnaan, vert. .80 .40
1193 A353 220fr Traditional huts 1.00 .50
1194 A353 500fr Turu 2.25 1.10
Nos. 1191-1194 (4) 4.50 2.20

A354

A355

Paris-Granada-Dakar Rally, 17th Anniv.: 215fr, Car, silhouettes of three people. 275fr, Man racing on motorcycle, vert. 290fr, Car under Eiffel Tower, car racing toward finish line. 665fr, Two cars going over hill.

1996, Jan. 16 **Litho.** ***Perf. 11½***

1195 A354 215fr multicolored 1.10 .60
1196 A354 275fr multicolored 1.50 .75
1197 A354 290fr multicolored 1.60 .80
1198 A354 665fr multicolored 3.50 1.75
Nos. 1195-1198 (4) 7.70 3.90

1996, Feb.2

Flowers: 175fr, Gossypium barbadense. 275fr, Hibiscus sabdariffa. 290fr, Hibiscus asper. 500fr, Nymphaea lotus.

1199 A355 175fr multicolored .95 .45
1200 A355 275fr multicolored 1.50 .75
1201 A355 290fr multicolored 1.60 .80
1202 A355 500fr multicolored 2.75 1.40
Nos. 1199-1202 (4) 6.80 3.40

Sports A356

1996, Mar. 29 **Litho.** ***Perf. 11½***

1203 A356 125fr Boxing .65 .35
1204 A356 215fr Judo 1.10 .60
1205 A356 275fr Javelin 1.50 .75
1206 A356 320fr Discus 1.75 .90
Nos. 1203-1206 (4) 5.00 2.60

Art by Serge Correa, Hall of Pearls A357

1996,Apr. 18

1207 A357 260fr Corridor 1 1.25 .70
1208 A357 320fr Symphony 1 1.75 .85

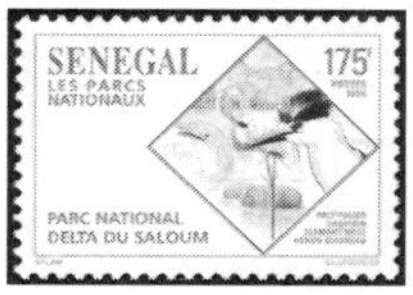

National Parks A358

Designs: 175fr, Dolphin, flamingo, heron, Saloum Delta. 200fr, Chimpanzee, giraffe, elephant, Niokolo-Koba. 220fr, Crustaceans, bird in cave, Madeleine Island. 275fr, Abyssinia hornbill, crocodile, hippopotamus, Basse Casamance.

1996, Mar. 4

1209 A358 175fr multicolored .95 .50
1210 A358 200fr multicolored 1.10 .55
1211 A358 220fr multicolored 1.25 .60
1212 A358 275fr multicolored 1.50 .75
Nos. 1209-1212 (4) 4.80 2.40

Intl. Olympic Committee, Cent. A359

1996, July 1 **Litho.** ***Perf. 12½***

1213 A359 215fr multicolored 1.25 .60

1996 Summer Olympic Games, Atlanta A360

1996, July 15 ***Perf. 13***

1214 A360 10fr Swimming .20 .20
1215 A360 80fr Gymnastics .40 .20
1216 A360 175fr Running 1.00 .50
1217 A360 260fr Hurdles 1.40 .70
Nos. 1214-1217 (4) 3.00 1.60

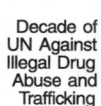

Decade of UN Against Illegal Drug Abuse and Trafficking A361

215fr, UN emblem, hand holding red stop sign, drug paraphernalia.

1996, June 21 ***Perf. 13½***

1218 A361 175fr multicolored .95 .50
1219 A361 215fr multicolored 1.10 .60

Red Cross of Senegal — A362

1996, Oct. 21 ***Perf. 12½***

1220 A362 275fr multicolored 1.50 .75

Primates A363

Designs: 10fr, Cercopithecus aethiops. 30fr, Erthrocebus patas. 90fr, Cercopithecus campbelli. 215fr, Pantroglodytes verus. 260fr, Papio papio.

1996, Nov. 29 **Litho.** ***Perf. 13x13½***

1221 A363 10fr multicolored .20 .20
1222 A363 30fr multicolored .20 .20
1223 A363 90fr multicolored .35 .20
1224 A363 215fr multicolored .85 .45
1225 A363 260fr multicolored 1.00 .50
a. Strip of 5, #1221-1225 2.50 1.25

UNICEF, 50th Anniv. A364

1996, Dec. 11 ***Perf. 13½x13***

1226 A364 75fr shown .30 .20
1227 A364 275fr Child, diff. 1.25 .60

19th Dakar-Agades-Dakar Rally — A365

25fr, Semi-truck. 75fr, Man pushing car, figure of man. 215fr, Race car. 300fr, Man on motorcycle.

1997, Jan. 19 **Litho.** ***Perf. 13x13½***

1228 A365 25fr multicolored .20 .20
1229 A365 75fr multicolored .30 .20
1230 A365 215fr multicolored .90 .45
1231 A365 300fr multicolored 1.25 .65
Nos. 1228-1231 (4) 2.65 1.50

Trees — A366

Designs: 80fr, Faidherbia albida. 175fr, Eucalyptus. 220fr, Khaya senegalensis. 260fr, Casuarina equisetifolia.

1997, Mar. 31

1232 A366 80fr multicolored .35 .20
1233 A366 175fr multicolored .75 .35
1234 A366 220fr multicolored .90 .45
1235 A366 260fr multicolored 1.00 .50
Nos. 1232-1235 (4) 3.00 1.50

Birds — A367

25fr, Platalea leucorodia. 70fr, Leptilos crumeniferus. 175fr, Balcarica pavonina. 215fr, Ephippiarhychus senegalensis. 220fr, Numenius arquata.

1997, Feb. 28

1236 A367 25fr multicolored .20 .20
1237 A367 70fr multicolored .30 .20
1238 A367 175fr multicolored .75 .35
1239 A367 215fr multicolored .90 .45
1240 A367 220fr multicolored .95 .50
a. Strip of 5, #1236-1240 3.00 1.50

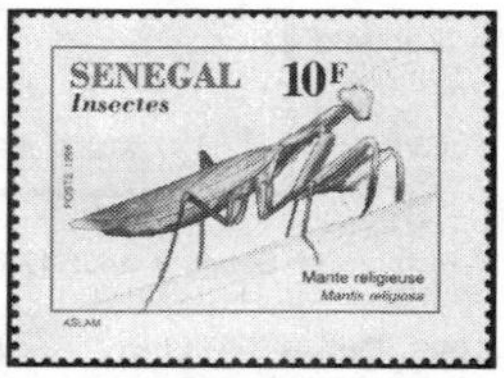

Insects A368

Designs: 10fr, Mantis religiosa. 50fr, Forficula auricularia. 75fr, Schistocerca gregaria. 215fr, Cicindela lunulata. 220fr, Gryllus campestris.

1997, Jan. 31 ***Perf. 13½x13***

1241 A368 10fr multicolored .20 .20
1243 A368 50fr multicolored .20 .20
1244 A368 75fr multicolored .30 .20
1245 A368 215fr multicolored .90 .45
1246 A368 220fr multicolored .95 .45
a. Strip of 5, #1241-1246 2.40 1.25

Postal officials in Senegal have declared Greenpeace sheets of nine with values of 250fr and 425fr "fake" and "illegal".

Cheikh Anta Diop (1923-86), Historian — A369

Diop: 175fr, And Egyptian hieroglyphs, Sphinx. 215fr, Performing carbon 14 test.

1996, Feb. 26 **Litho.** ***Perf. 13¼***

1247-1248 A369 Set of 2 1.50 1.50

Fashion Type of 1972

1996-97 **Engr.** ***Perf. 13½x14***

Size: 21x26mm

1249 A106 15fr green

Perf. 13½x13

1250 A106 50fr green .20 .20
1251 A106 60fr olive grn
1251A A108 70fr olive green
1253 A106 190fr olive green
1254 A106 215fr dark blue .80 .40
1255 A106 240fr brown
1256 A106 260fr red brown 1.00 .50
1256A A106 300fr red lilac
1256B A106 320fr rose lilac
1257 A106 350fr henna brown

1257B A106 410fr lake
1257C A106 500fr brn violet
1257D A106 1000fr carmine

Issued: 50fr, 70fr, 215fr, 260fr, 4/13; 190fr, 240fr, 300fr, 350fr, 1000fr, 6/97.
Additional stamps were released in this set. The editors would like to examine them. Numbers will change if necessary.

Third World A370

Design: 500fr, Hot air balloon in flight.

1996, Apr. 13 Litho. *Perf. 13½*
1258 A370 215fr shown .75 .40
1259 A370 500fr multicolored 1.75 .90

See Mali Nos. 812-813.

Pres. Leopold Senghor, 90th Birthday A371

Pictures of Senghor and: 175fr, Map of Senegal. 275fr, Quotation, vert.

1996, Oct. 9 Litho. *Perf. 13¼*
1260-1261 A371 Set of 2 1.75 1.75

Niokolo-Badiar Natl. Park — A372

Designs: 30fr, Haliaetus vacifer. 90fr, Hippopotamus amphibius. 240fr, Loxindonta africana oxyotis. 300fr, Taurotragus derbianus.

1997, July 21 Litho. *Perf. 13½x13*
1262 A372 30fr multicolored .20 .20
1263 A372 90fr multicolored .40 .20
1264 A372 240fr multicolored 1.00 .50
1265 A372 300fr multicolored 1.25 .65
Nos. 1262-1265 (4) 2.85 1.55

Shells A373

Designs: a, 15fr, Cassis tesselata. b, 40fr, Pugilina meria. c, 190fr, Cyprea mappa. d, 200fr, Natica adansoni. e, 300fr, Bullia miran.

1997, Aug. 19 *Perf. 13x13½*
1266 A373 Strip of 5, #a.-e. 3.00 1.50

Wild Animals A374

a, 25fr, African buffaloes. b, 90fr, Gazelles. c, 100fr, Gnu. d, 200fr, Wild dogs. e, 240fr, Cheetah.

1997, June 27
1267 A374 Strip of 5, #a.-e. 2.75 1.40

Goree Island A375

1997, May 30 *Perf. 13½*
1268 A375 180fr multicolored .75 .40

No. 1268 is dated 1992 and has word "almadies" obliterated.

Dakar-Dakar Rally, 20th Anniv. — A376

Designs: 20fr, Truck traveling across Sahel. 45fr, Motorcycle arriving at Lake Rose. 190fr, Sports utility vehicle crossing Mauritanian Desert. 240fr, Car at Senegal River.

1998, Jan. 1 Litho. *Perf. 13½x13*
1269 A376 20fr multicolored .20 .20
1270 A376 45fr multicolored .20 .20
1271 A376 190fr multicolored .80 .40
1272 A376 240fr multicolored 1.00 .50
Nos. 1269-1272 (4) 2.20 1.30

Food Day A377

190fr, Receiving grain through cereal bank. 200fr, Proper nutrition for women.

1997, Oct. 16
1273 A377 190fr multicolored .80 .40
1274 A377 200fr multicolored .85 .45

A378 A379

Masks: 45fr, Planche, Burkina Faso. 90fr, Kpeliyehe, Ivory Coast. 200fr, Nimba, Guinea Bissau. 240fr, Walu, Mali. 300fr, Dogon, Mali.

1997, Nov. 28
1275 A378 45fr multicolored .20 .20
1276 A378 90fr multicolored .45 .20
1277 A378 200fr multicolored .85 .40
1278 A378 240fr multicolored 1.00 .50
1279 A378 300fr multicolored 1.25 .65
a. Strip of 5, #1275-1279 3.75 1.90

1997 *Perf. 11½*
1280 A379 310fr multicolored 1.25 .65

Heinrich von Stephan (1831-97).

Vasco de Gama (1460-1524), Expedition Around Cape of Good Hope, 500th Anniv. A380

De Gama and: 40fr, Route of spices. 75fr, Port of Zanzibar. 190fr, Caravel revolution. 200fr, Maps being printed.

1997, Nov. 22
1281 A380 40fr multicolored .20 .20
1282 A380 75fr multicolored .30 .20
1283 A380 190fr multicolored .80 .40
1284 A380 200fr multicolored .85 .40
Nos. 1281-1284 (4) 2.15 1.20

Trains A381

Designs: 15fr, CC2400. 90fr, Loco-tractor. 100fr, Mountain train. 240fr, Maquinista. 310fr, Freight train, series 151-A.

1997, Dec. 16 *Perf. 13x13½*
1285 A381 15fr multicolored .20 .20
1286 A381 90fr multicolored .40 .20
1287 A381 100fr multicolored .45 .25
1288 A381 240fr multicolored 1.00 .50
1289 A381 310fr multicolored 1.25 .65
a. Strip of 5, #1285-1289 3.25 1.65

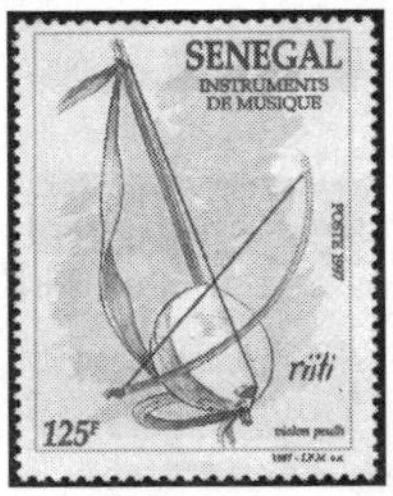

Musical Instruments A382

1997, Nov. 22 *Perf. 13x13½*
1290 A382 125fr Riiti .55 .25
1291 A382 190fr Kora .80 .40
1292 A382 200fr Fama .85 .45
1293 A382 240fr Dioung dioung 1.00 .50
Nos. 1290-1293 (4) 3.20 1.60

World Wildlife Fund A383

Profelis aurata: 100fr, Climbing on tree limb. 240fr, Lying on tree limb. 300fr, Two cubs.

1997, Dec. 24 Litho. *Perf. 11½*
1294 A383 45fr multicolored .20 .20
1295 A383 100fr multicolored .40 .20
1296 A383 240fr multicolored 1.00 .50
1297 A383 300fr multicolored 1.25 .65
Nos. 1294-1297 (4) 2.85 1.55

SOS Children's Village, Ziguinchor A384

1998, Jan. 14 Litho. *Perf. 11½*
1298 A384 190fr shown .80 .40
1299 A384 240fr Child, buildings 1.00 .50

Club Aldiana, 25th Anniv. — A385

Designs: 290fr, Hut, people at market, mother and baby. 320fr, People on boats, woman in traditional dress, fish in basket.

1998, Jan. 12 *Perf. 13½*
1300 A385 290fr multicolored 1.10 .60
1301 A385 320fr multicolored 1.25 .65

Diana, Princess of Wales (1967-97) A386

Various portraits.

1998
1302 A386 240fr like #1304g 1.00 .50

Sheets of 9

1303 A386 200fr #a.-i. 7.50 3.75
1304 A386 250fr #a.-i. 9.50 4.75

Nos. 1303-1304 are continuous designs.

Souvenir Sheets

1305 A386 1000fr Portrait 4.25 2.10
1306 A386 1500fr With her sons 6.25 3.25
1307 A386 2000fr Wearing tiara 8.25 4.25

1998 World Cup Soccer Cup Championships, France — A387

Designs: 25fr, Soccer players. 50fr, Player's legs kicking ball. 150fr, Mascot, ball in air. 300fr, Country flags in shape of soccer players.

1998, June 10 Litho. *Perf. 13x13½*
1308 A387 25fr multicolored .20 .20
1309 A387 50fr multicolored .20 .20
1310 A387 150fr multicolored .60 .25
1311 A387 300fr multicolored 1.00 .50
Nos. 1308-1311 (4) 2.00 1.15

Henriette Bathily Women's Museum A388

1998, May 16 Litho. *Perf. 13*
1312 A388 190fr shown .75 .35
1313 A388 270fr Emblem at right 1.00 .50

Abolition of Slavery, 150th Anniv. — A389

Designs: 20fr, Slavery Museum, Goree. 40fr, Frederick Douglass. 190fr, Mother, child. 290fr, Victor Schoelcher.

1998, Apr. 27

1314	A389	20fr multicolored	.20	.20
1315	A389	40fr multicolored	.20	.20
1316	A389	190fr multicolored	.70	.35
1317	A389	290fr multicolored	1.10	.55
		Nos. 1314-1317 (4)	2.20	1.30

SOS Children's Village — A390

Children's drawings: 30fr, House, car. 50fr, shown. 180fr, Sun, flowers. 300fr, Lakes, trees.

1998, June 16

1318	A390	30fr multicolored	.20	.20
1319	A390	50fr multicolored	.20	.20
1320	A390	180fr multicolored	.70	.35
1321	A390	300fr multicolored	1.10	.55
		Nos. 1318-1321 (4)	2.20	1.30

Navigational Aids — A391

Designs: 50fr, Red buoy. 100fr, Mamelles Lighthouse. 190fr, Lighted buoy. 240fr, Port entrance lighthouse.

1998, July 3 ***Perf. 12***

1322	A391	50fr multicolored	.20	.20
1323	A391	100fr multicolored	.40	.20
1324	A391	190fr multicolored	.70	.35
1325	A391	240fr multicolored	.90	.45
		Nos. 1322-1325 (4)	2.20	1.20

21st Paris-Dakar Rally — A392

Designs: 150fr, Race car broken down, hood up, helicopter, rescue van. 175fr, Man with shovels, vehicle stuck in sand, helicopter. 240fr, Motorcycles racing, one down, camel. 290fr, Motorcycle racing, man walking, vehicle broken down.

1999, Jan. 17 **Litho.** ***Perf. 11½***

1326	A392	150fr multicolored	.55	.30
1327	A392	175fr multicolored	.65	.35
1328	A392	240fr multicolored	.90	.45
1329	A392	290fr multicolored	1.00	.50
		Nos. 1326-1329 (4)	3.10	1.60

Women's Hair Styles, Headdresses A393

Designs: 100fr, Long hair over shoulders. 240fr, Shorter hair. 300fr, Head wrapped.

1998, Nov. 30

1330	A393	40fr red brn & blk	.20	.20
1331	A393	100fr brt grn & blk	.35	.20
1332	A393	240fr violet & black	.90	.45
1333	A393	300fr blue & black	1.10	.55
		Nos. 1330-1333 (4)	2.55	1.40

Endangering Marine Fauna A394

Designs: 50fr, Intensive net fishing. 100fr, Sewage and pollutants in sea. 310fr, Use of dynamite for fishing. 365fr, Oil slicks released from tanker ships.

1998, Dec. 29

1334	A394	50fr multicolored	.20	.20
1335	A394	100fr multicolored	.35	.20
1336	A394	310fr multicolored	1.10	.55
1337	A394	365fr multicolored	1.25	.65
		Nos. 1334-1337 (4)	2.90	1.60

Intl. Year of the Ocean A395

1998, Oct. 30 ***Perf. 13x13½***

1338	A395	190fr shown	.70	.35
1339	A395	790fr Sea life, diff.	2.75	1.50

Universal Declaration of Human Rights, 50th Anniv. A396

1998, Dec. 9

1340	A396	200fr Prisoner	.75	.40
1341	A396	350fr Free people	1.25	.65

Hotel Palm Beach, Voyages of Fram, 50th Anniv. A397

Designs: 240fr, Huts, trees, aerial view of hotel grounds. 300fr, Woman braiding another's hair, beach at hotel.

1998, Nov. 6 **Litho.** ***Perf. 13½x13***

1342	A397	240fr multicolored	.90	.45
1343	A397	300fr multicolored	1.10	.55

Italia '98 Intl. Philatelic Exhibition — A398

Design: Leaning Tower of Pisa.

1998, Oct. 23

1344	A398	290fr multicolored	1.00	.50

Souvenir Sheet

Ferrari Automobiles, 50th Anniv. — A399

1998, Oct. 23 **Litho.** ***Perf. 13½***

1345	A399	1000fr multicolored	3.50	3.50

Italia '98.

Fashion Type of 1972

1998 **Engr.** ***Perf. 13½x13***

Size: 21x26mm

1345B A106 290fr violet

Two additional stamps were issued in this set. The editors would like to examine any examples.

Souvenir Sheet

De Tomaso Automobiles, 40th Anniv. — A400

Automobile colors: a, black, shown. b, silver. c, black, diff. d, red.

1999, Feb. 28 **Litho.** ***Perf. 12¼***

1346	A400	250fr Sheet of 4, #a.-d.	3.50	3.50

Italia '98. Dated 1998.

Actors & Actresses A401

No. 1347: a, Romy Schneider. b, Yves Montand. c, Catherine Deneuve. d, Gina Lollobrigida. e, Marcello Mastroianni. f, Sophia Loren. g, Frank Sinatra. h, Dean Martin. i, Marilyn Monroe.

1500fr, Monroe, diff. 2000fr, Mastroianni, diff.

1999, Feb. 28 **Litho.** ***Perf. 12x12¼***

1347	A401	200fr Sheet of 9, #a.-i.	6.00	6.00

Souvenir Sheets

Perf. 13½

1348	A401	1500fr multicolored	5.00	5.00
1349	A401	2000fr multicolored	6.75	6.75

Italia '98. Dated 1998.

Elvis Presley A402

Various portraits.

1999, Feb. 28 **Litho.** ***Perf. 12x12¼***

1350	A402	250fr Sheet of 9, #a.-i.	7.75	7.75

Dated 1998.

A sheet similar to No. 1350 exists. Stamps are perf 13¼ and have Italia '98 logo. The top margins of the sheet are not inscribed.

PhilexFrance 99 — A403

1999, July 2 **Litho.** ***Perf. 13***

1351	A403	240fr multicolored	*1.00*	*1.00*

No. 1351 has a holographic image. Soaking in water may affect hologram.

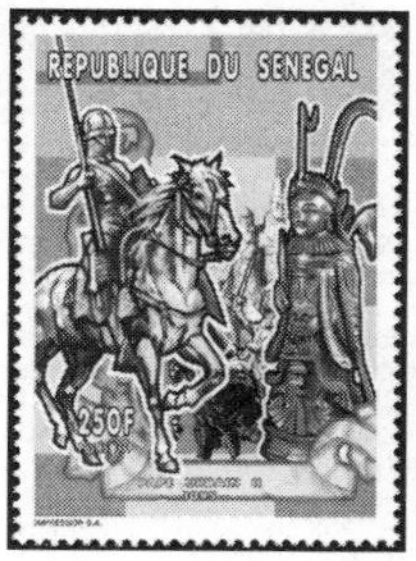

Chess Pieces and Scenes of the Crusades A404

Designs: No. 1353, Pope Urban II, 1053.

No. 1354: a, Muslim army. b, Bishopric of St. George. c, Army of Karbuqha. d, Muslim troops attacking Christians. e, Baldwin I, King of Jerusalem. f, Christian Army. g, Third crusade, Richard the Lion-Hearted. h, Capture of Acre, 1191. i, Crusaders leave for Jaffa, 1191.

No. 1355: a, Pope Urban II, diff. b, Peter the Hermit. c, Byzantine Emperor Alexius. d, People's Crusade, 1096. e, Godfrey of Bouillon. f, Crusaders at Constantinople, 1097. g, Knights of St. John. h, Crusaders cross Alps. i, Capture of Jerusalem.

No. 1356: a, Chateau-gaillard of Richard the Lion-Hearted. b, Capture of Arsuf, 1191. c, Truce between Richard the Lion-Hearted and Saladin, 1192. d, Arrival of Louis IX at Damietta, 1248. e, Children's Crusade. f, Capture of Louis IX. g, Flood at El Mansurah. h, Treaty between Sultan al-Kamil and Frederick II. i, Monks record history of Crusades.

1999, July 16 **Litho.** ***Perf. 13½***

1353	A404	250fr multicolored	1.00	1.00

Sheets of 9

1354	A404	200fr #a.-i.	7.50	7.50
1355	A404	250fr #a.-i.	9.25	9.25
1356	A404	400fr #a.-i.	15.00	15.00

Athletes — A405

No. 1357, Jackie Robinson with bat behind back. No. 1358, Muhammad Ali, arm raised by referee.

No. 1359: a-h, various portraits of Jackie Robinson.

No. 1360: a-h, various portraits of Muhammad Ali.

1000fr, Muhammad Ali in robe. 1500fr, Close-up of Jackie Robinson like No. 1359g. No. 1363, Robinson at bat. No. 1364, Ali with both fists clenched.

1999, July 16 Litho. *Perf. 13½*

1357 A405	250fr multicolored	1.00	1.00
1358 A405	300fr multicolored	1.25	1.25

Sheets of 9

1359 A405	250fr #1357, 1359a.-h.	9.25	9.25
1360 A405	300fr #1358, 1360a.-h.	11.50	11.50

Souvenir Sheets

1361 A405	1000fr multicolored	4.25	4.25
1362 A405	1500fr multicolored	6.25	6.25
1363 A405	2000fr multicolored	8.25	8.25
1364 A405	2000fr multicolored	8.25	8.25

Nos. 1361-1364 each contain one 36x42mm stamp.

Sports A405a

Designs: 200fr, Ayrton Senna, Formula 1 racing champion. 300fr, Ludger Beerbaum, equestrian competitor, vert. 400fr, Pete Sampras, tennis player, vert.

No. 1366 - Formula 1 racing champions: a, Juan Manuel Fangio. b, Alberto Ascari. c, Graham Hill. d, Jim Clark. e, Jack Brabham. f, Jackie Stewart. g, Niki Lauda. h, Like No. 1365, no white margin. i, Alain Prost.

No. 1367 - Equestrian competitors, vert.: a, Martin Schaudt. b, Klaus Balkenhol. c, Nadine Capellman-Biffar. d, Willi Melliger. e, Like No. 1365A, without printer's name at LL. f, Ulrich Kirchhoff. g, Sally Clark. h, Bettina Overesch-Boker. i, Karen O'Conner.

No. 1368 - Tennis and table tennis players, vert.: a, Liu Guoliang. b, Martina Hingis. c, Deng Yaping. d, Andre Agassi. e, Jean-Philippe Gatien. f, Anna Kournikova. g, Mikael Appelgren. h, Like No. 1365B, no white margin. i, Jan-Ove Waldner.

1500fr, German Equestrian jumping team. No. 1370, Ayrton Senna. No. 1370A, Table tennis players Vladimir Samsonov, Deng Yaping, Jörg Rosskopf.

1999, July 16 Litho. *Perf. 13½*

1365-1365B A405a	Set of 3	3.75	3.75

Sheets of 9, #a-i

1366 A405a	200fr multi	7.50	7.50
1367 A405a	300fr multi	11.00	11.00
1368 A405a	400fr multi	15.00	15.00

Souvenir Sheets

1369 A405a	1500fr multi	6.25	6.25
1370 A405a	2000fr multi	8.00	8.00
1370A A405a	2000fr multi	8.00	8.00

Transportation — A406

Designs: 250fr, Sailboat of Sir Thomas Lipton. 300fr, Sinking of Titanic. 325fr, Bentley coupe. 350fr, Prussian locomotive. 375fr, Ducati Motorcycle. 500fr, Concorde.

1999, July 23 Litho. *Perf. 13½*

1371 A406	250fr multicolored	1.00	1.00
1372 A406	300fr multicolored	1.25	1.25
1373 A406	325fr multicolored	1.40	1.40
1374 A406	350fr multicolored	1.40	1.40
1375 A406	375fr multicolored	1.50	1.50
1376 A406	500fr multicolored	2.00	2.00
	Nos. 1371-1376 (6)	8.55	8.55

See Nos. 1385-1399.

Intl. Year of Older Persons A407

30fr, Picture in book. 150fr, Man with mallet. 290fr, Musicians. 300fr, Scientists, vert.

Perf. 13¼x13, 13x13¼

1999, Aug. 10 Litho.

1377 A407	30fr multicolored	.20	.20
1378 A407	150fr multicolored	.60	.60
1379 A407	290fr multicolored	1.10	1.10
1380 A407	300fr multicolored	1.25	1.25
	Nos. 1377-1380 (4)	3.15	3.15

Mushrooms A408

Scouting emblem and: 60fr, "Amanite phalloide." 175fr, Coprinus atramantarius. 220fr, "Amanite vireuse." 250fr, Agaricus campester.

Perf. 13¼x13½

1999, Aug. 27 Litho.

1381 A408	60fr multicolored	.25	.25
1382 A408	175fr multicolored	.70	.70
1383 A408	220fr multicolored	.90	.90
1384 A408	250fr multicolored	1.00	1.00
	Nos. 1381-1384 (4)	2.85	2.85

Transportation Type of 1999

No. 1385 - Boats and ships: a, France. b, United States. c, Finnjet. d, Chusan. e, Sheers. f, Vendredi 13. g, Like No. 1371 without white margin. h, Pen Duick 11. i, Jester.

No. 1386 - Titanic: a, Construction. b, Launching. c, Departing. d, At start of voyage. e, Collision with iceberg. f, Like No. 1372 without white margin. g, Exploration of wreckage. h, Bow, passengers. i, Captain Edward John Smith.

No. 1387 - Automobiles: a, Duryea. b, Menon. c, Petite Renault. d, Zero Fiat. e, Spa. f, Packard. g, Like No. 1373 without white margin. h, Mercedes-Benz. i, Morris Minor.

No. 1388 - Trains: a, Mikado. b, 241P. c, Ten-wheeler. d, The Milwaukee. e, Class 1.S. f, Prussian locomotive G12. g, Like No. 1374 without white margin. h, KK-SEB Series 310. i, Outrance.

No. 1389 - Motorcycles and bicycles: a, Brooklands. b, Moto Brough Superior. c, 1903 race. d, Like No. 1375 without inscription at LL. e, Dave Thorpe Moto-cross Yamaha. f, Kevin Schwantz Moto Suzuki. g, Michaux bicycle. h, Racing bicycle with helmeted rider. i, Women on bicycles.

No. 1390 - Rockets, vert.: a, R.D. 107, USSR. b, Soyuz, USSR. c, Proton, USSR. d, Atlas-Centaur, US. e, Atlas-Agena, US. f, Atlas-Mercury, US. g, Titan 2, US. h, Juno 2, US. i, Saturn 1, US.

No. 1391 - Express trains: a, Acela, US. b, Class 332, Great Britain. c, ICE, Germany. d, TEE, Luembourg. e, Nevada Super Speed, US. f, Inter City 250, Great Britain. g, Korean High Speed. h, Eurostar, France & Great Britain. i, Thalys PBA, France.

No. 1392 - Supersonic aircraft or prototypes: a, SR-71. b, Maglifter. c, S.M. d, Super Concorde. e, TU-144. f, Boeing X. g, X-33. h, Like No. 1376 without white margin. i, X-34.

1000fr, Eric Tabarly and Pen Duick IV. No. 1394, Marc Seguin, arrival of train at Mont-Saint-Michel, vert. No. 1395, Walter P. Chrysler, 1924 Chrysler. No. 1396, Etienne Chambron, TGV trains, vert. No. 1397, Bobby Julich on racing bicycle. No. 1398, Concorde, diff. 2500fr, Neil Armstrong.

1999, July 23 Litho. *Perf. 13½*

Sheets of 9

1385 A406	250fr #a.-i.	9.25	9.25
1386 A406	300fr #a.-i.	11.00	11.00
1387 A406	325fr #a.-i.	12.00	12.00
1388 A406	350fr #a.-i.	13.00	13.00
1389 A406	375fr #a.-i.	14.00	14.00
1390 A406	400fr #a.-i.	15.00	15.00
1391 A406	450fr #a.-i.	17.00	17.00
1392 A406	500fr #a.-i.	18.00	18.00

Souvenir Sheets

1393 A406	1000fr multicolored	4.25	4.25
1394 A406	1500fr multicolored	5.50	5.50
1395 A406	1500fr multicolored	6.00	6.00
1396 A406	2000fr multicolored	8.25	8.25
1397 A406	2000fr multicolored	8.25	8.25
1398 A406	2000fr multicolored	8.25	8.25
1399 A406	2500fr multicolored	10.50	10.50

No. 1390 contains nine 35x50mm stamps. Nos. 1393, 1395, 1397-1399 each contain one 50x35 stamp. Nos. 1394 and 1396 each contain one 35x50mm stamp.

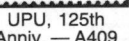

UPU, 125th Anniv. — A409

Mother Teresa — A411

First Manned Moon Landing, 30th Anniv. — A410

UPU emblem and: 270fr, Rainbows, envelope. 350fr, "125."

1999, Oct. 9 Litho. *Perf. 11½x11¾*

1400 A409	270fr multi	1.10	1.10
1401 A409	350fr multi	1.40	1.40

1999, Oct. 9 *Perf. 13½x13, 13x13½*

Designs: 25fr, Two astronauts on moon, flag. 145fr, Neil Armstrong, flag, astronaut on moon, vert. 180fr, Astronaut, flag, rocket, vert. 500fr, Astronaut on moon, space shuttle, vert.

1402 A410	25fr multi	.20	.20
1403 A410	145fr multi	.60	.60
1404 A410	180fr multi	.70	.70
1405 A410	500fr multi	2.00	2.00
	Nos. 1402-1405 (4)	3.50	3.50

1999, Oct. 9 *Perf. 11½x11¾*

Mother Teresa and: 75fr, Child, facing away. 100fr, Three children. 290fr, Priest. 300fr, Child.

1406 A411	75fr multi	.25	.25
1407 A411	100fr multi	.40	.40
1408 A411	290fr multi	1.10	1.10
1409 A411	300fr multi	1.25	1.25
	Nos. 1406-1409 (4)	3.00	3.00

Awarding of Nobel Peace Prize to Mother Teresa, 20th anniv.

Fauna A412

Designs: 60fr, Hippotragus equinus. 90fr, Haematopus ostralegus. 300fr, Dendrocygna viduada. 320fr, Demochelys coriacea.

1999, Oct. 9 *Perf. 13½x13*

1410 A412	60fr multi	.25	.25
1411 A412	90fr multi	.35	.35
1412 A412	300fr multi	1.25	1.25
1413 A412	320fr multi	1.25	1.25
	Nos. 1410-1413 (4)	3.10	3.10

Paintings by Paul Cézanne — A413

Various paintings.

1999 *Perf. 13¼*

1414 A413	200fr Sheet of 9, #a.-i.	8.00	8.00

Betty Boop — A414

Designs: No. 1415, 250fr, With red guitar. No. 1416, 250fr, With microphone. No. 1417, 400fr, On chair.

No. 1418, 250fr: a, With saxophone. b, With tambourine. c, Like #1415 (continuous design). d, With pink guitar. e, On piano keys. f, With drumsticks. g, With earphones. h, Like #1416 (continuous design). i, With purple jacket.

No. 1419, 400fr: a, With red dress. b, With flowers. c, With blue pants. d, With purple dress. e, Like #1417 (continuous design). f, With black pants. g, With ankh earrings. h, With black dress. i, With purple shirt and pants.

No. 1420, 1000fr, With saxophone. No. 1421, 1500fr, With red dress. No. 1422, 2000fr, With purple shirt.

1999 Litho. *Perf. 13¼*

1415-1417 A414	Set of 3	3.75	3.75

Sheets of 9, #a-i

1418-1419 A414	Set of 2	24.00	24.00

Souvenir Sheets

1420-1422 A414	Set of 3	12.00	12.00

Actors and Actresses — A415

No. 1423, 250fr: a, Clark Gable. b, Rudolph Valentino. c, Errol Flynn. d, Cary Grant. e, Robert Taylor. f, Gary Cooper. g, James Dean. h, Humphrey Bogart. i, Marlon Brando.

No. 1424, 425fr: a, Grace Kelly. b, Marilyn Monroe. c, Audrey Hepburn. d, Greta Garbo. e, Jean Harlow. f, Loretta Young. g, Jane Russell. h, Dorothy Lamour. i, Veronica Lake.

No. 1425, 450fr: a, Ginger Rogers, Fred Astaire. b, Cary Grant, Katharine Hepburn, James Stewart. c, Melvyn Douglas, Greta Garbo. d, Vivien Leigh, Clark Gable. e, Burt Lancaster, Deborah Kerr. f, Humphrey Bogart, Lauren Bacall. g, Steve McQueen, Jacqueline

Bisset. h, Gene Kelly, Rita Hayworth. i, Ingrid Bergman, Cary Grant.

1999 Sheets of 9, #a-i

1423-1425 A415 Set of 3 32.50 32.50

I Love Lucy — A416

Designs: No. 1426, 300fr, Fred, Ethel and Lucy with chick boxes. No. 1427, 300fr, Lucy reading murder mystery, vert.

No. 1428: a, Ethel, Lucy holding box. b, Ricky, Lucy, Fred and Ethel. c, Fred, Ethel and Lucy standing. d, Lucy with chicks. e, Fred, Ethel, Lucy and Ricky at table. f, Ethel and Lucy bending over. g, Lucy. h, Lucy, Ethel and Fred at table.

No. 1429, vert. - Lucy with: a, Telephone. b, Green dress. c, Black vest. d, Black hair bow. e, Spoon and bottle. f, Salad. g, Lilac jacket. h, Tan coat.

No. 1430, 1000fr, Lucy holding box, vert. No. 1431, 2000fr, Lucy holding bag, vert.

1999

1426-1427 A416 Set of 2 2.40 2.40

1428 A416 300fr Sheet of 9, #1426, 1428a-1428h 11.00 11.00

1429 A416 300fr Sheet of 9, #1427, 1429a-1429h 11.00 11.00

Souvenir Sheets

1430-1431 A416 Set of 2 12.00 12.00

The Three Stooges — A417

Designs: No. 1432, Larry with scissors, Curly, Moe with drill.

No. 1433: a, Larry and Moe on bed. b, Larry, Moe, Curly in police uniforms. c, Moe, Larry on telephone. d, Larry and Moe with scissors, Curly. e, Larry, Curly, Moe behind operating room equipment. f, Moe on floor, Larry, Curly. g, Moe, Curly, Larry with ladder. h, Moe with plank, Larry, Curly.

No. 1434, 1000fr, Moe with feathers in hair, Curly, vert. No. 1435, 1500fr, Curly with hat, vert.

1999

1432 A417 400fr multi 1.60 1.60

1433 A417 400fr Sheet of 9, #1432, 1433a-1433h 14.50 14.50

Souvenir Sheets

1434-1435 A417 Set of 2 10.00 10.00

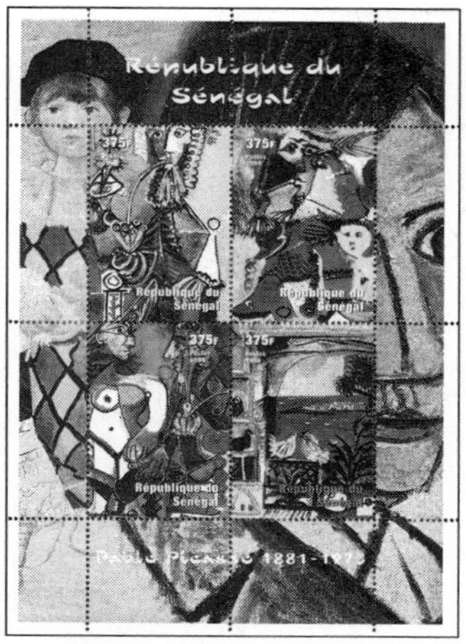

Picasso Paintings — A418

No. 1436: a, Country name in yellow, denomination at UL. b, Country name in white. c, Country name in yellow, denomination at UR. d, Country name in red.

1999

1436 A418 375fr Sheet of 4, #a-d 5.50 5.50

22nd Paris-Cairo-Dakar Rally — A419

Designs: 75fr, Motorcycles, car, truck, helicopter, Pyramids. 100fr, Cars, truck, Sphinx, Pyramid, camel and driver. 220fr, Motorcycle, truck, helicopter. 320fr, Camel and driver, motorcycle, car, Pyramids.

2000 Litho. *Perf. 11¾x11½*

1437-1440 A419 Set of 4 2.00 2.00

World Meteorological Organization, 50th Anniv. A420

Designs: 100fr, Satellite dish, map, weather station. 790fr, Weather measuring equipment, vert.

2000 *Perf. 11¾x11½, 11½x11¾*

1441-1442 A420 Set of 2 2.50 2.50

23rd Paris-Cairo-Dakar Rally — A421

Stylized head and: 190fr, Motorcyclist. 220fr, Facial features with text, vert. 240fr, Camel, vert. 790fr, Car.

Perf. 13½x13¼, 13¼x13½

2001, Jan. 6

1443-1446 A421 Set of 4 4.00 4.00

Advent of New Millennium A422

Millennium emblem and: 20fr, National Festival of Arts and Culture. 100fr, Pan-African Plastic Arts. 150fr, National Heritage Day. 300fr, Goree Memorial, horiz.

2001, Feb. 13 *Perf. 13½x13, 13x13½*

1447-1450 A422 Set of 4 1.60 1.60

Dated 2000.

2000 Summer Olympics, Sydney — A423

Designs: 40fr, Swimming, weight lifting. 80fr, Taekwondo. 240fr, 200-meter race. 290fr, Handball.

2001, Feb. 28 *Perf. 13¼x13½*

1451-1454 A423 Set of 4 1.75 1.75

Dated 2000.

Kermel Artisan Market — A424

Building and: 50fr, Woman, flowers. 90fr, Mask, drum. 250fr, Masks, bowls, horiz. 350fr, Woman, carvings.

Perf. 13¼x13½, 13½x13¼

2001, Mar. 15

1455-1458 A424 Set of 4 1.60 1.60

Medicinal Plants — A425

Designs: 240fr, Maytenus senegalensis. 320fr, Boscia senegalensis. 350fr, Euphorbia hirta. 500fr, Guierra senegalensis.

2001, Apr. 16 Litho. *Perf. 13¼x13*

1459-1462 A425 Set of 4 4.00 4.00

19th Lions Intl. Convention, Dakar A426

Lions Intl. emblem and: 190fr, People in canoe, map of Senegal. 300fr, Lion, vert.

Perf. 13½x13¼, 13¼x13½

2001, May 21

1463-1464 A426 Set of 2 1.40 1.40

UN High Commissioner for Refugees, 50th Anniv. — A427

Emblem and: 240fr, Tank, refugees. 320fr, Refugee, globe, vert.

Perf. 13½x13¼, 13¼x13½

2001, June 20

1465-1466 A427 Set of 2 1.60 1.60

SEMI-POSTAL STAMPS

No. 84 Surcharged in Red ✚5c

1915 Unwmk. *Perf. 14x13½*

B1 A28 10c + 5c org red & rose .60 .60

No. B1 is on both ordinary and chalky paper.

Same Surcharge on No. 87

1918

B2 A28 15c + 5c red org & brn vio .70 .70

Curie Issue

Common Design Type

1938 Engr. *Perf. 13*

B3 CD80 1.75fr + 50c brt ultra 6.50 6.50

French Revolution Issue

Common Design Type

Photo., Name & Value Typo. in Black

1939

B4 CD83 45c + 25c green 4.50 4.50

B5 CD83 70c + 30c brown 4.50 4.50

B6 CD83 90c + 35c red org 4.50 4.50

B7 CD83 1.25fr + 1fr rose pink 4.50 4.50

B8 CD83 2.25fr + 2fr blue 4.50 4.50

Nos. B4-B8 (5) 22.50 22.50

Stamps of 1935-38 Surcharged in Red or Black

SECOURS
+ 1 fr.
NATIONAL

1941 *Perf. 12x12½, 12*

B9 A30 50c + 1fr red org .60

B10 A31 80c + 2fr vio (R) 2.25

B11 A30 1.50fr + 2fr dk bl 3.00

B12 A30 2fr + 3fr blue 3.00

Nos. B9-B12 (4) 8.85

Common Design Type and

Bambara Sharpshooter SP1

Colonial Soldier SP2

1941 Photo. *Perf. 13½*

B13 SP1 1fr + 1fr red .55

B14 CD86 1.50fr + 3fr maroon .55

B15 SP2 2.50fr + 1fr blue .55

Nos. B13-B15 (3) 1.65

The surtax was for the defense of the colonies.

Nos. B13-B15 were issued by the Vichy government, but it is doubtful whether they were placed in use in Senegal.

Stamps of type A32 surcharged "OEUVRES COLONIALES" and new values were issued in 1944 by the Vichy Government, but were not placed on sale in the colony.

Catalogue values for unused stamps in this section, from this point to the end of the section, are for Never Hinged items.

Republic

Anti-Malaria Issue

Common Design Type

Perf. 12½x12

1962, Apr. 7 Engr. Unwmk.

B16 CD108 25fr + 5fr brt grn .40 .40

Freedom from Hunger Issue
Common Design Type

1963, Mar. 21 *Perf. 13*
B17 CD112 25fr + 5fr dp vio, grn & brn .35 .35

AIR POST STAMPS

Landscape AP1

Caravan AP2

Perf. 12½x12, 12x12½
1935 **Engr.** **Unwmk.**
C1 AP1 25c dk brown .20 .20
C2 AP1 50c red orange .40 .30
C3 AP1 1fr rose lilac .20 .20
C4 AP1 1.25fr yellow grn .20 .20
C5 AP1 2fr blue .20 .20
C6 AP1 3fr olive grn .20 .20
C7 AP2 3.50fr violet .20 .20
C8 AP2 4.75fr orange .50 .30
C9 AP2 6.50fr dk blue .60 .45
C10 AP2 8fr black 1.25 .85
C11 AP2 15fr rose lake .75 .45
Nos. C1-C11 (11) 4.70 3.55

No. C8 surcharged "ENTR' AIDE FRANCAIS + 95f 25" in green, red violet or blue, was never issued in this colony.

Common Design Type
1940 **Engr.** *Perf. 12½x12*
C12 CD85 1.90fr ultra .25 .25
C13 CD85 2.90fr dk red .25 .25
C14 CD85 4.50fr dk gray grn .35 .35
C15 CD85 4.90fr yellow bis .40 .40
C16 CD85 6.90fr dp orange .40 .40
Nos. C12-C16 (5) 1.65 1.65

Common Design Types
1942
C17 CD88 50c car & bl .20
C18 CD88 1fr brn & blk .25
C19 CD88 2fr dk grn & red brn .25
C20 CD88 3fr dk bl & scar .60
C21 CD88 5fr vio & brn red .35

Frame Engr., Center Typo.
C22 CD89 10fr ultra, ind & hn .35
C23 CD89 20fr rose car, mag & choc .45
C24 CD89 50fr yel grn, dl grn & yel .90 1.25

Engr. & Photo.
Size: 47x26mm
C25 CD88 100fr dk red & bl 1.50 2.50
Nos. C17-C25 (9) 4.85

There is doubt whether Nos. C17 to C23 were officially placed in use.

Catalogue values for unused stamps in this section, from this point to the end of the section, are for Never Hinged items.

Republic

Abyssinian Roller — AP3

Designs: 50fr, Carmine bee-eater, vert. 200fr, Violet touraco, vert. 250fr, Red bishop, vert. 500fr, Fish eagle, vert.

Perf. 12½x13, 13x12½
1960-63 **Photo.** **Unwmk.**
Birds in Natural Colors
C26 AP3 50fr blk & gray bl ('61) .65 .20
C27 AP3 100fr blk, yel & lil 1.40 .45
C28 AP3 200fr blk, grn & bl ('61) 2.50 1.50
C29 AP3 250fr blk & pale grn ('63) 3.50 1.90
C30 AP3 500fr blk & bl 8.50 2.50
Nos. C26-C30 (5) 16.55 6.55

Air Afrique Issue
Common Design Type

1962, Feb. 17 **Engr.** *Perf. 13*
C31 CD107 25fr vio brn, sl grn & ocher .30 .20

African Postal Union Issue
Common Design Type

1963, Sept. 8 **Photo.** *Perf. 12½*
C32 CD114 85fr choc, ocher & red .65 .40

Air Afrique Issue, 1963
Common Design Type

1963, Nov. 19 **Unwmk.** *Perf. 13x12*
C33 CD115 50fr multicolored .70 .50

Independence Monument — AP4

1964, Apr. 4 **Photo.** *Perf. 12x13*
C34 AP4 300fr ultra, tan, ocher & grn 2.00 1.00

Symbolic European and African Cities — AP5

1964, Apr. 18 **Engr.** *Perf. 13*
C35 AP5 150fr grn, brn red & blk 1.60 1.00

Congress of the Intl. Federation of Twin Cities, Dakar.

Europafrica Issue, 1964

Peanuts, Globe, Factory, Figures of "Africa," and "Europe" — AP6

1964, July 20 **Photo.** *Perf. 13x12*
C36 AP6 50fr multicolored .65 .50

See note after Madagascar No. 357.

Basketball AP7

Launching of Syncom 2 — AP8

1964, Aug. 22 **Engr.** *Perf. 13*
C37 AP7 85fr shown .65 .40
C38 AP7 100fr Pole vault .90 .50

18th Olympic Games, Tokyo, Oct. 10-25.

1964, Oct. 24 **Unwmk.** *Perf. 13*
C39 AP8 150fr grn, red brn & ultra 1.10 .55

Communication through space.

Pres. John F. Kennedy (1917-1963) AP9

Mother and Child, Globe and Emblems AP10

1964, Dec. 5 **Photo.** *Perf. 13*
C40 AP9 100fr brt yel, dk grn & brn red .90 .75
a. Souvenir sheet of 4 4.00 4.00

Scenic Type of Regular Issue, 1965

View: 100fr, Shore of Gambia River in Eastern Senegal.

1965, Feb. 27 **Engr.** *Perf. 13*
Size: 48x27mm
C41 A48 100fr brn blk, grn & bis 1.00 .40

1965, Sept. 25 **Unwmk.** *Perf. 13*
C42 AP10 50fr choc, brt bl & grn .45 .25

International Cooperation Year.

A-1 Satellite and Earth — AP11

Designs: No. C44, Diamant rocket. 90fr, Scout rocket and FR-1 satellite.

1966, Feb. 19 **Engr.** *Perf. 13*
C43 AP11 50fr yel brn, dk grn & blk .40 .20
C44 AP11 50fr Prus bl, lt red brn & car rose .40 .20
C45 AP11 90fr dk red brn, dk gray & Prus bl .80 .40
Nos. C43-C45 (3) 1.60 .80

French achievements in space.

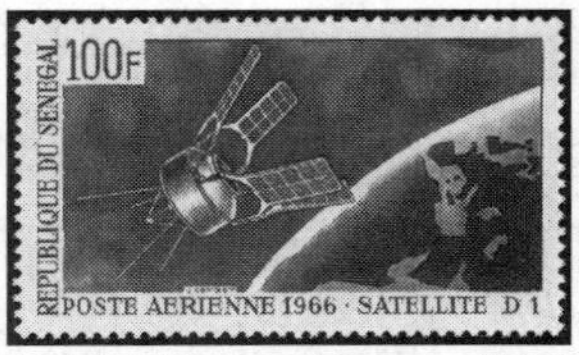

D-1 Satellite over Globe — AP12

1966, June 11 **Engr.** *Perf. 13*
C46 AP12 100fr dk car, sl & vio 1.00 .55

Launching of the D-1 satellite at Hammaguir, Algeria, Feb. 17, 1966.

Air Afrique Issue, 1966
Common Design Type

1966, Aug. 31 **Photo.** *Perf. 13*
C47 CD123 30fr red brn, blk & lem .30 .20

Mermoz Plane "Arc-en-Ciel" — AP13

Jean Mermoz — AP14

Designs: 35fr, Latecoére 300 "Croix du Sud." 100fr, Map showing last flight from Dakar to Brazil.

1966, Dec. 7 **Engr.** *Perf. 13*
C48 AP13 20fr bl, rose lil & indigo .25 .20
C49 AP13 35fr slate, brn & grn .35 .20
C50 AP13 100fr grn, lt grn & mar 1.00 .40
C51 AP14 150fr blk, ultra & mar 1.50 .70
Nos. C48-C51 (4) 3.10 1.50

Jean Mermoz (1901-36), French aviator, on the 30th anniv. of his last flight.

Dakar-Yoff Airport — AP15

1967, Apr. 22 Engr. *Perf. 13*

C52 AP15 200fr red brn, ind & brt bl 1.10 .40

Knob-billed Goose — AP16

Flowers and Birds: 100fr, Mimosa. 150fr, Flowering cactus. 250fr, Village weaver. 500fr, Bateleur.

1967-69 Photo. *Perf. 11½*

Granite Paper

Dated "1967"

C53 AP16 100fr gray, yel & grn 1.10 .45
C54 AP16 150fr multicolored 1.60 .65

Dated "1969"

C55 AP16 250fr gray & multi 2.00 1.00

Dated "1968"

C56 AP16 300fr brt bl & multi 3.00 1.25
C57 AP16 500fr orange & multi 4.25 1.90
Nos. C53-C57 (5) 11.95 5.25

Issued: 100fr, 150fr, 6/24/67; 500fr, 7/13/68; 300fr, 12/21/68; 250fr, 4/26/69.

The Girls from Avignon, by Picasso AP17

1967, July 22 *Perf. 12x13*

C59 AP17 100fr multicolored 1.25 .80

African Postal Union Issue, 1967

Common Design Type

1967, Sept. 9 Engr. *Perf. 13*

C60 CD124 100fr brt grn, vio & car lake .90 .45

Konrad Adenauer AP18

Weather Balloon, Vegetation and WMO Emblem — AP19

1968, Feb. 17 Photo. *Perf. 12½*

C61 AP18 100fr dk red, ol & blk 1.10 .55
a. Souvenir sheet of 4 4.50 4.50

Konrad Adenauer (1876-1967), chancellor of West Germany (1949-63).

1968, Mar. 23 Engr. *Perf. 13*

C62 AP19 50fr blk, ultra & bl grn .45 .25

8th World Meteorological Day, Mar. 23.

19th Olympic Games, Mexico City, Oct. 12-27 — AP20

1968, Oct. 12 Engr. *Perf. 13*

C63 AP20 20fr Hurdling .20 .20
C64 AP20 30fr Javelin .25 .20
C65 AP20 50fr Judo .40 .20
C66 AP20 75fr Basketball .60 .25
Nos. C63-C66 (4) 1.45 .85

PHILEXAFRIQUE Issue

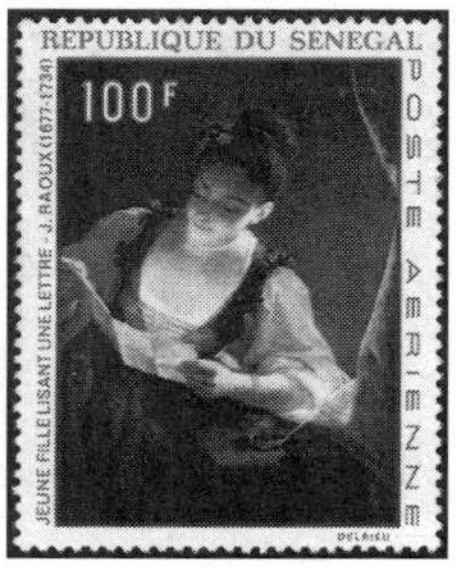

Young Woman Reading Letter, by Jean Raoux AP21

1968, Oct. 26 Photo. *Perf. 12½*

C67 AP21 100fr buff & multi 1.10 1.00

PHILEXAFRIQUE, Phil. Exhib. in Abidjan, Feb. 14-23, 1969. Printed with alternating buff label.

2nd PHILEXAFRIQUE Issue

Common Design Type

Senegal #160 and Boulevard, Dakar.

1969, Feb. 14 Engr. *Perf. 13*

C68 CD128 50fr grn, gray & pur .60 .50

Tourist Emblem with Map of Africa and Dove — AP22

1969 Photo. *Perf. 13*

C69 AP22 100fr red, lt grn & lt bl .70 .35

Year of African Tourism, 1969.

Pres. Lamine Gueye (1891-1968) AP23

Design: 45fr, Pres. Gueye wearing fez.

1969, June 10 Photo. *Perf. 12½*

C70 AP23 30fr brn, org & blk .25 .20
C71 AP23 45fr brn, lt grnsh bl & blk .35 .20
a. Min. sheet, 2 ea #C70-C71 1.25 1.25

"Transmission of Thought" Tapestry by Ousmane Faye — AP24

Fari, Tapestry by Allaye N'Diaye — AP25

1969, Oct. 25 Photo. *Perf. 12½*

C72 AP24 25fr multicolored .25 .20

Perf. 12x12½

C73 AP25 50fr multicolored .45 .25

Europafrica Issue

Baila Bridge — AP26

1969, Nov. 15 Photo. *Perf. 13x12*

C74 AP26 100fr multicolored .70 .40

Emile Lécrivain, Plane and Toulouse-Dakar Route — AP27

1970, Jan. 31 Engr. *Perf. 13*

C75 AP27 50fr grn, slate & rose brn .40 .25

40th anniv. of the disappearance of the aviator Emile Lécrivain (1897-1929).

René Maran, Martinique AP28

Portraits: 45fr, Marcus Garvey, Jamaica. 50fr, Dr. Price Mars, Haiti.

1970, Mar. 21 Photo. *Perf. 12½*

C76 AP28 30fr red brn, lt grn & blk .25 .20
C77 AP28 45fr blue, pink & blk .40 .20
C78 AP28 50fr grn, buff & blk .50 .20
Nos. C76-C78 (3) 1.15 .60

Issued to honor prominent Negro leaders.

"One People, One Purpose, One Faith" AP29

1970, Apr. 3 Photo. *Perf. 11½*

C79 AP29 500fr gold & multi 4.00 1.90
a. Souvenir sheet 4.50 4.50

10th anniv. of independence. No. C79 sold for 600fr.

Bay of Naples and Dakar Post Office — AP30

1970, May 2 Photo. *Perf. 13x12½*

C80 AP30 100fr multicolored .80 .55

10th Europa Phil. Exhib., Naples, May 2-10.

Blue Cock, by Mamadou Niang AP31

Tapestries: 45fr, Fairy. 75fr, "Lunaris," by Jean Lurçat.

1970, June 20 Photo. *Perf. 12½x12*

C81 AP31 30fr black & multi .20 .20
C82 AP31 45fr dk red brn & multi .30 .20
C83 AP31 75fr yellow & multi .50 .30
Nos. C81-C83 (3) 1.00 .70

Head of the Courtesan Nagakawa, by Chobunsai Yeishi, and Mt. Fuji, by Hokusai — AP32

EXPO Emblem and: 25fr, Woman Playing Guitar, by Hokusai, and Sun Tower, vert. 150fr, "One of the Present-day Beauties of Nanboku" by Katsukawa Shuncho, vert.

1970, July 18 Engr. *Perf. 13*

C84 AP32 25fr red & green .20 .20
C85 AP32 75fr yel grn, dk bl & red brn .55 .25
C86 AP32 150fr bl, red brn & ocher 1.10 .55
Nos. C84-C86 (3) 1.85 1.00

EXPO '70 Intl. Exhib., Osaka, Japan, Mar. 15-Sept. 13.

Tuna, Processing Plant and Ship — AP33

Urban Development in Dakar — AP34

1970, Aug. 22 Engr. *Perf. 13*

C87 AP33 30fr dl red, blk & brt bl .25 .20
C88 AP34 100fr chocolate & grn .70 .40

Progress in industrialization and urbanization in Dakar.

Beethoven; Napoleon and Allegory of Eroica Symphony AP35

Design: 100fr, Beethoven holding quill.

1970, Sept. 26 Engr. *Perf. 13*

C89 AP35 50fr ol, brn & ocher .50 .25
C90 AP35 100fr Prus grn & dp claret 1.00 .50

Ludwig van Beethoven (1770-1827), composer.

Globe, Scales and Women of Four Races — AP36

1970, Oct. 24 Engr. *Perf. 13*

C91 AP36 100fr grn, ocher & red .90 .55

25th anniversary of United Nations.

De Gaulle, Map of Africa, Symbols — AP37

Phillis Wheatley, American Poet — AP39

"A Roof for Every Refugee" — AP38

100fr, Charles de Gaulle & map of Senegal.

1970, Dec. 31 Photo. *Perf. 12½*

C92 AP37 50fr multicolored .45 .35
C93 AP37 100fr blue & multi 1.00 .65

Honoring Pres. Charles de Gaulle as liberator of the colonies.

1971, Jan. 16

C94 AP38 100fr multicolored .80 .40

High Commissioner for Refugees, 20th anniv.

1971, Apr. 10 Photo. *Perf. 12½*

Prominent Blacks: 40fr, James E. K. Aggrey, Methodist missionary, Ghana. 60fr, Alain Le Roy Locke, American educator. 100fr, Booker T. Washington, American educator.

C95 AP39 25fr multicolored .20 .20
C96 AP39 40fr blk, bl & bis .30 .20
C97 AP39 60fr blk, bl & emer .45 .20
C98 AP39 100fr blk, bl & red .70 .40
Nos. C95-C98 (4) 1.65 1.00

Napoleon as First Consul, by Ingres AP40

Designs: 25fr, Napoleon in 1809, by Robert Lefevre. 35fr, Napoleon on his death bed, by Georges Rouget. 50fr, Awakening into Immortality, sculpture by Francois Rude.

1971, June 19 Photo. *Perf. 13*

C99 AP40 15fr gold & multi .25 .20
C100 AP40 25fr gold & multi .40 .25
C101 AP40 35fr gold & multi .45 .35
C102 AP40 50fr gold & multi .65 .60
Nos. C99-C102 (4) 1.75 1.40

Napoleon Bonaparte (1769-1821).

Gamal Abdel Nasser — AP41

Alfred Nobel — AP41a

1971, July 17 *Perf. 12½*

C103 AP41 50fr multicolored .40 .20

Nasser (1918-1970), President of Egypt.

1971, Sept. 25 Photo. *Perf. 13½x13*

C103A AP41a 100fr multicolored .80 .45

Alfred Nobel (1833-1896), inventor of dynamite who established the Nobel Prizes.

Iranian Flag and Senegal Coat of Arms — AP42

1971, Oct. 15 *Perf. 13x12½*

C104 AP42 200fr multicolored 1.50 .65

2500th anniversary of the founding of the Persian empire by Cyrus the Great.

African Postal Union Issue, 1971

Common Design Type

Design: 100fr, Arms of Senegal and UAMPT Building, Brazzaville, Congo.

1971, Nov. 13 *Perf. 13x13½*

C105 CD135 100fr blue & multi .70 .30

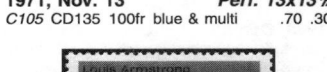

Louis Armstrong (1900-1971), American Jazz Musician — AP43

1971, Nov. 27 Photo. *Perf. 12½*

C106 AP43 150fr gold & dk brn 1.25 .80

Sapporo Olympic Emblem and Speed Skating — AP44

Sapporo '72 Emblem and: 10fr, Bobsledding. 125fr, Skiing.

1972, Jan. 22 *Perf. 13*

C107 AP44 5fr multicolored .20 .20
C108 AP44 10fr multicolored .20 .20
C109 AP44 125fr multicolored .90 .40
Nos. C107-C109 (3) 1.30 .80

11th Winter Olympic Games, Sapporo, Japan, Feb. 3-13.

Fonteghetto della Farina, by Canaletto — AP45

Design: 100fr, San Giorgio Maggiore, by Giovanni Antonio Guardi, vert.

1972, Feb. 26

C110 AP45 50fr gold & multi .40 .20
C111 AP45 100fr gold & multi .80 .40

UNESCO campaign to save Venice.

Theater Type of Regular Issue

150fr, Daniel Sorano as Shylock, vert.

1972, Mar. 25 Photo. *Perf. 12½x13*

C112 A99 150fr multicolored 1.40 .70

Environment Type of Regular Issue

100fr, Protection of the ocean (oil slick).

1972, June 3 Photo. *Perf. 13x12½*

C113 A101 100fr multicolored .80 .45

Emperor Haile Selassie, Ethiopian and Senegalese Flags — AP46

1972, July 23 Photo. *Perf. 13½x13*

C114 AP46 100fr gold & multi .80 .40

80th birthday of Emperor Haile Selassie of Ethiopia.

Swordfish — AP47

Designs: 65fr, Killer whale. 75fr, Rhincodon. 125fr, Common rorqual (whale).

1972-73 Photo. *Perf. 11½*

C115 AP47 50fr multi .35 .20
C116 AP47 65fr multi .40 .20
C117 AP47 75fr multi .45 .25
C118 AP47 125fr multi .90 .55
Nos. C115-C118 (4) 2.10 1.20

Issued: #C115, C118, 11/25/72; #C116-C117, 7/28/73.

Palace of the Republic — AP48

1973, Apr. 3 Photo. *Perf. 13*

C119 AP48 100fr multi .60 .35

Hotel Teranga, Dakar — AP49

1973, May 26 Photo. *Perf. 13*
C120 AP49 100fr multi .60 .35

Emblem of African Lions Club — AP50

1973, June 2
C121 AP50 150fr multi 1.00 .65

15th Congress of Lions Intl., District 403, Dakar, June 1-2.

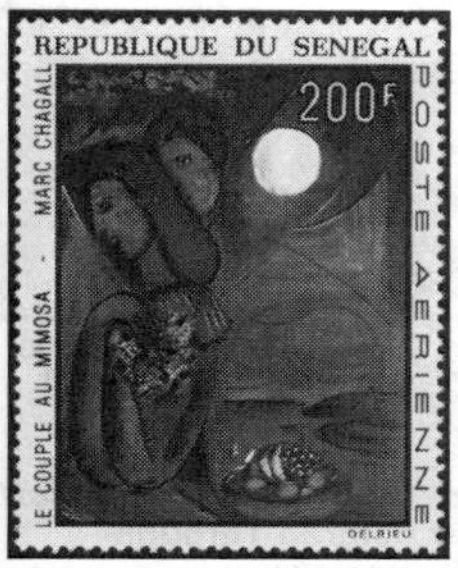

"Couple with Mimosa," by Marc Chagall AP51

1973, Aug. 11 Photo. *Perf. 13*
C122 AP51 200fr multi 1.90 .90

Map of Italy with Riccione AP52

Human Rights Flame and People AP54

Raoul Follereau and World Map — AP53

1973, Aug. 25 Engr.
C123 AP52 100fr dk grn, red & pur .60 .40

Intl. Phil. Exhib., Riccione 1973.

1973, Dec. 22 Engr. *Perf. 13*

100fr, Dr. Armauer G. Hansen & leprosy bacilli.

C124 AP53 40fr sl grn, pur & red brn .25 .20
C125 AP53 100fr sl grn, mag & plum .65 .40

Centenary of the discovery of the Hansen bacillus, the cause of leprosy.

1973, Dec. 15 Photo. *Perf. 13½*

65fr, Human Rights flame and drummer.

C126 AP54 35fr grn & multi .20 .20
C127 AP54 65fr org & multi .25 .25

25th anniv. of the Universal Declaration of Human Rights.

Men of Four Races, Arms of Dakar, Congress Emblem — AP55

50fr, Key joining twin cities & emblem, vert.

1973, Dec. 26 Photo.
C128 AP55 50fr org & multi .35 .20
C129 AP55 125fr red & multi .80 .45

8th Congress of the World Federation of Twin Cities, Dakar, Dec. 26-29.

Finfoots — AP56

1974, Feb. 9 Photo. *Perf. 13*
C130 AP56 1fr shown .20 .20
C131 AP56 2fr Spoonbills .20 .20
C132 AP56 3fr Crested cranes .20 .20
C133 AP56 4fr Egrets .20 .20
C134 AP56 250fr Flamingos 1.40 .90
C135 AP56 250fr Flamingos 1.40 .90
a. Strip of 2 + label 3.00
Nos. C130-C135 (6) 3.60 2.60

Djoudj Park bird sanctuary. Denomination in gold on No. C134, in black on No. C135.

Tiger Attacking Wild Horse, by Delacroix — AP57

Design: 200fr, Tiger Hunt, by Eugéne Delacroix (1798-1863).

1974, Mar. 23 Photo. *Perf. 13*
C136 AP57 150fr gold & multi .90 .60
C137 AP57 200fr gold & multi 1.25 .65

Intl. Fair, Dakar — AP57a

1974, Nov. 28 Embossed *Perf. 10½*
C137A AP57a 350fr silver
C137B AP57a 1500fr gold

Soyuz and Apollo, Space Docking Emblem — AP58

1975, May 23 Engr. *Perf. 13*
C138 AP58 125fr multi .50 .35

US-USSR space cooperation.
For overprint see No. C140.

Senegal Type D6, Tuscany Type A1, Map of Italy AP59

1975, Aug. 23 Engr. *Perf. 13*
C139 AP59 125fr org, vio & dk red .65 .35

Intl. Phil. Exhib., Riccione 1975.

No. C138 Overprinted: "JONCTION / 17 Juil. 1975"

1975, Oct. 21 Engr. *Perf. 13*
C140 AP58 125fr multi .50 .35

Apollo-Soyuz link-up in space, July 17, 1975.

Boston Massacre — AP60

Design: 500fr, Lafayette, Washington, Rochambeau and Battle of Yorktown.

1975, Dec. 20 Engr. *Perf. 13*
C141 AP60 250fr ultra, red & brn 1.40 .65
C142 AP60 500fr bl & ver 2.50 1.40

American Bicentennial.

Concorde and Map — AP61

1976, Jan. 21 Litho. *Perf. 13*
C143 AP61 300fr multi 1.60 .80

First commercial flight of supersonic jet Concorde, Paris to Rio de Janeiro, Jan. 21.
For overprint see No. C145.

2nd Intl. Fair, Dakar — AP61a

1976, Dec. 3 Embossed *Perf. 10½*
C143A AP61a 500fr silver
C143B AP61a 1500fr gold

Spaceship and Control Room — AP62

1977, June 25 Litho. *Perf. 12½*
C144 AP62 300fr multi 1.60 .80

Viking space mission to Mars.

No. C143 Overprinted in Red: "22.11.77 / PARIS NEW-YORK"

1977, Nov. 22 *Perf. 13*
C145 AP61 300fr multi 1.60 .80

Concorde, 1st commercial flight, Paris-New York.

Evolution of Fishing — AP62a

Designs: 10fr, Fishermen hauling in netted catch. 15fr, Two fishermen in canoe. 20fr, Ship, man holding fish. 25fr, Fisherman holding net.

1977 Litho. *Perf. 12¾*
C145A AP62a 5fr shown — —
C145B AP62a 10frmulti — —
C145C AP62a 15frmulti — —
C145D AP62a 20frmulti — —
C145E AP62a 25frmulti — —
Nos. C145A-C145E (0) .00 .00

Philexafrique II-Essen Issue
Common Design Types

Designs: No. C146, Lion & Senegal #C28. No. C147, Capercaillie & Schleswig-Holstein #1.

1978, Nov. 1 Litho. *Perf. 12½*
C146 CD138 100fr multi .65 .30
C147 CD139 100fr multi .65 .30
a. Pair, #C146-C147 1.30 .60

J. Dabry, L. Gimie, and J. Mermoz, Airplane, Map of Route (St. Louis-Natal) — AP63

1980, Dec. Photo. *Perf. 13*
C148 AP63 300fr multi 2.25 .80

1st airmail crossing of So. Atlantic, 50th anniv.

1st Transatlantic Commercial Airmail Flight, 55th Anniv. — AP64

1985, May 12 Litho. *Perf. 13*
C149 AP64 250fr multi .65 .35

Clement Ader (1841-1926), Engineer and Aviation Pioneer — AP65

Ader and: 145fr, Automobile, microphone. 180fr, 615fr, 940fr, Bat-winged steam powered airplane.

1991, June 7 Litho. *Perf. 13*

C150 AP65 145fr multicolored 1.10 .55
C151 AP65 180fr multicolored 1.40 .65
C152 AP65 615fr multi, vert. 4.50 2.25
Nos. C150-C152 (3) 7.00 3.45

Souvenir Sheet

C153 AP65 940fr multi, vert. 7.00 3.50

AIR POST SEMI-POSTAL STAMPS

French Revolution Issue
Common Design Type

1939 Unwmk. Photo. *Perf. 13*
Name and Value Typo. in Orange

CB1 CD83 4.75 + 4fr brn blk 7.50 7.50

Surtax used for the defense of the colonies.

Stamps of types of Dahomey V1, V2, V3, and V4 inscribed "Sénégal" were issued in 1942 by the Vichy Government, but were not placed on sale in the colony.

Catalogue values for unused stamps in this section, from this point to the end of the section, are for Never Hinged items.

Republic

Nile Gods Uniting Upper and Lower Egypt (Abu Simbel) — SPAP1

1964, Mar. 7 Engr. *Perf. 13*

CB2 SPAP1 25fr + 5fr Prus bl, red brn & sl grn .80 .60

UNESCO campaign to save historic monuments in Nubia.

POSTAGE DUE STAMPS

Postage Due Stamps of French Colonies Surcharged **10**

1903 Unwmk. *Imperf.*

J1 D1 10c on 50c lilac 55.00 55.00
J2 D1 10c on 60c brown, *buff* 55.00 55.00
J3 D1 10c on 1fr rose, *buff* 300.00 300.00
Nos. J1-J3 (3) 410.00 410.00

D2

D3

1906 Typo. *Perf. 14x13½*

J4 D2 5c green, *grnsh* 3.00 3.00
J5 D2 10c red brown 3.50 3.50
J6 D2 15c dark blue 4.25 4.00
J7 D2 20c black, *yellow* 4.75 4.00
J8 D2 30c red, *straw* 5.50 4.75
J9 D2 50c violet 6.00 4.75
J10 D2 60c black, *buff* 7.50 7.50
J11 D2 1fr black, *pinkish* 12.50 12.50
Nos. J4-J11 (8) 47.00 44.00

1914

J12 D3 5c green .20 .20
J13 D3 10c rose .25 .20
J14 D3 15c gray .25 .25
J15 D3 20c brown .50 .30
J16 D3 30c blue .85 .60
J17 D3 50c black 1.10 .80
J18 D3 60c orange 1.25 1.10
J19 D3 1fr violet 1.40 1.10
Nos. J12-J19 (8) 5.80 4.55

Type of 1914 Issue Surcharged **2F.**

1927

J20 D3 2fr on 1fr lilac rose 3.25 3.25
J21 D3 3fr on 1fr orange brown 3.25 3.25

D4

1935 Engr. *Perf. 12½x12*

J22 D4 5c yellow green .20 .20
J23 D4 10c red orange .20 .20
J24 D4 15c violet .20 .20
J25 D4 20c olive green .20 .20
J26 D4 30c reddish brown .20 .20
J27 D4 50c rose lilac .40 .40
J28 D4 60c orange .80 .80
J29 D4 1fr black .60 .60
J30 D4 2fr dark blue .60 .60
J31 D4 3fr dark carmine .60 .60
Nos. J22-J31 (10) 4.00 4.00

Catalogue values for unused stamps in this section, from this point to the end of the section, are for Never Hinged items.

Republic

D5

Lion — D6

1961, Feb. 20 Typo. *Perf. 14x13½*

J32 D5 1fr orange & red .20 .20
J33 D5 2fr ultra & red .20 .20
J34 D5 5fr brown & red .20 .20
J35 D5 20fr green & red .50 .50
J36 D5 25fr red lilac & red .55 .55
Nos. J32-J36 (5) 1.65 1.65

1966-83 Typo. *Perf. 14x13*
Lion in Gold

J37 D6 1fr red & black .20 .20
J38 D6 2fr yel brn & black .20 .20
J39 D6 5fr red lilac & black .20 .20
J40 D6 10fr brt blue & black .20 .20
J41 D6 20fr emerald & black .30 .30
J42 D6 30fr gray & black .55 .55
J43 D6 60fr blue & black .30 .30
J44 D6 90fr rose & black .40 .40
Nos. J37-J44 (8) 2.35 2.35

Issued: 1fr-30fr, 12/1/66; others, 10/1983.

OFFICIAL STAMPS

Catalogue values for unused stamps in this section are for Never Hinged items.

Arms — O1

Baobab Tree — O2

Perf. 14x13½
1961, Sept. 18 Typo. Unwmk.
Denominations in Black

O1 O1 1fr sepia & bl .20 .20
O2 O1 2fr dk bl & org .20 .20
O3 O1 5fr maroon & grn .20 .20
O4 O1 10fr ver & bl .20 .20
O5 O1 25fr vio bl & ver .35 .20
O6 O1 50fr ver & gray .65 .35
O7 O1 85fr lilac & org 1.25 .60
O8 O1 100fr ver & yel grn 1.60 .90
Nos. O1-O8 (8) 4.65 2.85

1966-77 Typo. *Perf. 14x13*

O9 O2 1fr yel & blk .20 .20
O10 O2 5fr org & blk .20 .20
O11 O2 10fr red & blk .20 .20
O12 O2 20fr dp red lil & blk .20 .20
O13 O2 25fr dp lil & blk ('75) .20 .20
O14 O2 30fr bl & blk .30 .20
O15 O2 35fr bl & blk ('73) .40 .20
O16 O2 40fr grnsh bl & blk ('75) .25 .20
O17 O2 55fr emer & blk .65 .45
O18 O2 60fr emer & blk ('77) .30 .20
O19 O2 90fr dk bl grn & blk 1.00 .25
O20 O2 100fr brn & blk 1.25 .25
Nos. O9-O20 (12) 5.15 2.75

See Nos. O22-O25.

No. O17 Surcharged with New Value and Two Bars

1969

O21 O2 60fr on 55fr emer & blk 1.00 .20

1983, Oct. Typo. *Perf. 14x13*

O22 O2 90fr dk grn & blk .40 .20

"90F" is shorter and wider than on Nos. O9-O22.

1991 Litho. *Perf. 13*

O23 O2 50fr red & blk .40 .20
O24 O2 145fr brt grn & blk 1.25 .60
O25 O2 180fr org yel & blk 1.50 .75
Nos. O23-O25 (3) 3.15 1.55

This is an expanding set. Numbers will change if necessary.

SENEGAMBIA & NIGER

ˌse-nə-ˈgam-bē-ə and ˈnī-jər

A French Administrative unit for the Senegal and Niger possessions in Africa during the period when the French possessions in Africa were being definitely divided into colonies and protectorates. The name was dropped in 1904 when this territory was consolidated with part of French Sudan, under the name Upper Senegal and Niger.

100 Centimes = 1 Franc

Navigation and Commerce — A1

1903 Unwmk. Typo. *Perf. 14x13½*
Name of Colony in Blue or Carmine

1 A1 1c black, *lil bl* 1.00 1.00
2 A1 2c brown, *buff* 1.25 1.25
3 A1 4c claret, *lav* 3.25 3.25
4 A1 5c yel grn 4.25 4.25
5 A1 10c red 4.75 4.75
6 A1 15c gray 9.00 9.00
7 A1 20c red, *green* 8.50 8.50
8 A1 25c blue 12.00 12.00
9 A1 30c brn, *bister* 11.00 11.00
10 A1 40c red, *straw* 15.00 15.00
11 A1 50c brn, *azure* 30.00 30.00
12 A1 75c deep vio, *org* 32.50 32.50
13 A1 1fr brnz grn, *straw* 42.50 42.50
Nos. 1-13 (13) 175.00 175.00

Perf. 13½x14 stamps are counterfeits.

SERBIA

ˈsər-bē-ə

LOCATION — In southeastern Europe, bounded by Romania and Bulgaria on the east, the former Austro-Hungarian Empire on the north, Greece on the south, and Albania and Montenegro on the west
GOVT. — Kingdom
AREA — 18,650 sq. mi.
POP. — 2,911,701 (1910)
CAPITAL — Belgrade

Following World War I, Serbia united with Montenegro, Bosnia and Herzegovina, Croatia, Dalmatia and Slovenia to form the kingdom (later republic) of Yugoslavia.

100 Paras = 1 Dinar

Coat of Arms — A1

Prince Michael (Obrenovich III) — A2

1866 Unwmk. Typo. *Imperf.*
Paper colored Through

1 A1 1p dk green, *dk vio rose* 45.00

Surface Colored Paper, Thin or Thick

2 A1 1p dk green, *lil rose* 50.00
a. 1p olive green, *rose* 50.00
b. 1p yel grn, *pale rose* (thick paper) 300.00
3 A1 2p red brown, *lilac* 60.00
a. 2p red brn, *lil gray* (thick paper) 250.00
b. 2p dl grn, *lil gray* (thick paper) 800.00
Nos. 1-3 (3) 155.00

Vienna Printing
Perf. 12

4 A2 10p orange 750.00 500.00
5 A2 20p rose 425.00 17.50
6 A2 40p blue 475.00 125.00
a. Half used as 20p on cover
Nos. 4-6 (3) 1,650. 642.50

Belgrade Printing
Perf. 9½

7 A2 1p green 15.00
8 A2 2p bister brn 22.50
9 A2 20p rose 15.00 15.00
a. Pair, imperf. between
10 A2 40p ultra 160.00 175.00
a. Half used as 20p on cover
Nos. 7-10 (4) 212.50

Pelure Paper

11 A2 10p orange 65.00 70.00
12 A2 20p rose 60.00 8.75
a. Pair, imperf. between
13 A2 40p ultra 35.00 25.00
a. Pair, imperf. between
b. Half used as 20p on cover
Nos. 11-13 (3) 160.00 103.75

Nos. 1-3, 7-8, 14-16, 25-26 were used only as newspaper tax stamps.

1868-69 Ordinary Paper *Imperf.*

14 A2 1p green 35.00
a. 1p olive green ('69) *2,000.*
15 A2 2p brown 50.00
a. 2p bister brown ('69) 160.00

Counterfeits of type A2 are common.

Prince Milan (Obrenovich IV)

A3 A4

Perf. 9½, 12 and Compound

1869-78

16	A3	1p yellow	3.75	95.00
17	A3	10p red brown	7.50	3.75
a.		10p yellow brown	350.00	35.00
18	A3	10p orange ('78)	1.25	3.25
19	A3	15p orange	85.00	15.00
20	A3	20p gray blue	1.50	2.50
a.		20p ultramarine	3.25	2.00
b.		Half used as 10p on cover		
21	A3	25p rose	1.50	5.75
22	A3	35p lt green	3.00	3.50
23	A3	40p violet	1.50	2.75
a.		Half used as 20p on cover		
24	A3	50p blue green	5.00	3.75
		Nos. 16-24 (9)	110.00	135.25

The first setting, which included all values except No. 18, had the stamps 2-2½mm apart.

A new setting, introduced in 1878, had the stamps 3-4mm apart, providing wider margins. Only Nos. 17, 18, 20 and 21 exist in this new setting, which differs also in shades from the earlier setting.

The narrow-spaced Nos. 17, 20 and 21 are rarer, especially unused, as are the early shades of Nos. 23 and 24.

All values except Nos. 19 and 24 are known in various partly perforated varieties.

Counterfeits exist.

See No. 25.

1872-79 ***Imperf.***

25	A3	1p yellow	4.50	8.75
a.		Tête bêche pair		
26	A4	2p blk, thin paper ('79)	.50	.50
a.		Thick paper ('73)	1.50	10.00

Used value of No. 26 is for canceled-to-order.

King Milan I — A5

King Alexander (Obrenovich V) — A6

1880 ***Perf. 13x13½***

27	A5	5p green	.50	.20
a.		5p olive green	475.00	2.00
28	A5	10p rose	1.50	.20
29	A5	20p orange	.50	.20
a.		20p yellow	3.00	1.25
30	A5	25p ultra	1.00	.75
a.		25p blue	1.25	.75
31	A5	50p brown	1.00	3.75
a.		50p brown violet	140.00	3.00
32	A5	1d violet	6.75	6.00
		Nos. 27-32 (6)	11.25	11.10

1890

33	A6	5p green	.20	.20
34	A6	10p rose red	.50	.20
35	A6	15p red violet	.50	.20
36	A6	20p orange	.35	.20
37	A6	25p blue	.60	.25
38	A6	50p brown	2.00	2.00
39	A6	1d dull lilac	7.50	6.25
		Nos. 33-39 (7)	11.65	9.30

King Alexander — A7

1894-96 ***Perf. 13x13½***

Granite Paper

40	A7	5p green	3.25	.20
a.		Perf. 11½	3.50	.40
41	A7	10p car rose	3.50	.20
b.		Perf. 11½	45.00	.75
42	A7	15p violet	5.00	.20
43	A7	20p orange	52.50	.50
a.		Half used as 10p on cover		375.00
44	A7	25p blue	10.50	.20
45	A7	50p brown	11.00	.45
46	A7	1d dk green	1.50	2.50
47	A7	1d red brn, *bl* ('96)	11.00	3.75
		Nos. 40-47 (8)	98.25	8.00

1898-1900 ***Perf. 13x13½, 11½***

Ordinary Paper

48	A7	1p dull red	.25	.25
49	A7	5p green	1.50	.20
50	A7	10p rose	42.50	.20
51	A7	15p violet	7.00	.20
52	A7	20p orange	6.25	.25
53	A7	25p deep blue	7.00	.30
54	A7	50p brown	12.50	3.00
		Nos. 48-54 (7)	77.00	4.40

Nos. 49-54 exist imperf.

Nos. 49-51, 53 and 56-57 exist with perf. 13x13½x11½x13½.

Type of 1900 Stamp Surcharged **10 ПАРА**

1900

56	A7	10p on 20p rose	2.50	.20

Same, Surcharged **10 ПАРА**

1901

57	A7	10p on 20p rose	1.75	.20
58	A7	15p on 1d red brn, *bl*	3.75	1.00
a.		Inverted surcharge	100.00	110.00

King Alexander (Obrenovich V)

A8 A9

1901-03 **Typo.** ***Perf. 11½***

59	A8	5p green	.20	.20
60	A8	10p rose	.20	.20
61	A8	15p red violet	.20	.20
62	A8	20p orange	.20	.20
63	A8	25p ultra	.20	.20
64	A8	50p bister	.20	.20
65	A9	1d brown	.70	.60
66	A9	3d brt rose	6.75	5.75
67	A9	5d deep violet	5.25	5.75
		Nos. 59-67 (9)	13.90	13.30

Counterfeits of Nos. 66-67 exist. Nos. 59-67 imperf. value of set of pairs, $100.

Arms of Serbia on Head of King Alexander — A10

Two Types of the Overprint

Type I - Overprint 12mm wide. Bottom of mantle defined by a single line. Wide crown above shield.

Type II - Overprint 10mm wide. Double line at bottom of mantle. Smaller crown above shield.

Arms Overprinted in Blue, Black, Red and Red Brown

1903-04 **Type I** ***Perf. 13½***

68	A10	1p red lil & blk (Bl)	.50	.50
a.		Inverted overprint	10.00	
69	A10	5p yel grn & blk (Bl)	.35	.20
70	A10	10p car & blk (Bk)	.20	.20
a.		Double overprint	8.75	
71	A10	15p ol gray & blk (Bk)	.20	.20
a.		Double overprint	8.75	
72	A10	20p org & blk (Bk)	.25	.20
73	A10	25p bl & blk (Bk)	.25	.20
a.		Double overprint	10.00	
74	A10	50p gray & blk (R)	2.50	.65

There were two printings of the type I overprint on Nos. 68-74, one typographed and one lithographed.

Type II

75	A10	1d bl grn & blk (Bk)	7.50	2.50

#68-75 with overprint omitted, value, set $75.

Perf. 11½

Type I

75A	A10	5p (Bl)	.25	.35
75B	A10	50p (R)	.75	2.00
75C	A10	1d (Bk)	1.50	4.00

Type II

76	A10	3d vio & blk (R Br)	1.50	1.75
a.		Perf. 13½	90.00	90.00
77	A10	5d lt brn & blk (Bl)	1.50	2.00

Type I With Additional Surcharge **1 ПАРА 1**

78	A10	1p on 5d (R)	.75	2.75
a.		Perf. 13½	275.00	275.00
		Nos. 68-78 (14)	18.00	17.50

Karageorge and Peter I — A11

Insurgents, 1804 A12

1904 **Typo.**

79	A11	5p yellow green	.20	.20
80	A11	10p rose red	.20	.20
81	A11	15p red violet	.35	.30
82	A11	25p blue	.50	.35
83	A11	50p gray brown	.60	.60
84	A12	1d bister	1.00	1.25
85	A12	3d blue green	2.00	3.50
86	A12	5d violet	2.50	4.00
		Nos. 79-86 (8)	7.35	10.40

Centenary of the Karageorgevich dynasty and the coronation of King Peter. Counterfeits of Nos. 79-86 exist.

King Peter I Karageorgevich

A13 A14

Perf. 11½, 12x11½

1905 **Wove Paper**

87	A13	1p gray & blk	.20	.20
88	A13	5p yel grn & blk	.50	.20
89	A13	10p red & blk	1.50	.20
90	A13	15p red lil & blk	1.75	.20
91	A13	20p yellow & blk	3.00	.20
92	A13	25p ultra & blk	4.25	.20
93	A13	30p sl grn & blk	2.50	.20
94	A13	50p dk brown & blk	3.00	.20
95	A13	1d bister & blk	.60	.25
96	A13	3d blue grn & blk	.60	.60
97	A13	5d violet & blk	2.50	1.90
		Nos. 87-97 (11)	20.40	4.35

Counterfeits of Nos. 87-97 abound.

The stamps of this issue may be found on both thick and thin paper.

1908 **Laid Paper**

98	A13	1p gray & blk	.25	.20
99	A13	5p yel grn & blk	2.25	.20
100	A13	10p red & blk	6.75	.20
101	A13	15p red lilac & blk	6.75	.20
102	A13	20p yellow & blk	7.25	.20
103	A13	25p ultra & blk	6.75	.20
104	A13	30p gray grn & blk	10.00	.20
105	A13	50p dk brn & blk	13.00	.60
		Nos. 98-105 (8)	53.00	2.00

Nos. 90, 98-100, 102-104 are known imperforate but are not believed to have been issued in this condition.

Values of Nos. 98-105 are for horizontally laid paper. Four values also exist on vertically laid paper (1p, 5p, 10p, 30p).

1911-14

Thick Wove Paper

108	A14	1p slate green	.20	.20
109	A14	2p dark violet	.20	.20
110	A14	5p green	.20	.20
111	A14	5p pale yel grn ('14)	.20	.20
112	A14	10p carmine	.20	.20
113	A14	10p red ('14)	.20	.20
114	A14	15p red violet	.20	.20
115	A14	15p slate blk ('14)	.20	.20
a.		15p red (error)		
116	A14	20p yellow	.20	.20
117	A14	20p brown ('14)	.40	.20
118	A14	25p deep blue	.30	.20
119	A14	25p indigo ('14)	.20	.20
120	A14	30p blue green	.20	.20
121	A14	30p olive grn ('14)	.20	.20
122	A14	50p dk brown	.20	.20
123	A14	50p brn red ('14)	.20	.20
124	A14	1d orange	15.00	25.00
125	A14	1d slate ('14)	2.00	2.75
126	A14	3d lake	27.50	77.50
127	A14	3d olive yel ('14)	77.50	475.00
128	A14	5d violet	27.50	42.50
129	A14	5d dk violet ('14)	2.00	14.00
		Nos. 108-129 (22)	155.00	

Counterfeits exist.

King Peter and Military Staff — A15

1915 ***Perf. 11½***

132	A15	5p yellow green	.20	—
133	A15	10p scarlet	.20	—
134	A15	15p slate	3.75	
135	A15	20p brown	.60	
136	A15	25p blue	7.50	
137	A15	30p olive green	5.00	
138	A15	50p orange brown	20.00	
		Nos. 132-138 (7)	37.25	

Nos. 134-138 were prepared but not issued for postal use. Instead they were permitted to be used as wartime emergency currency. Some are known imperf. The 15p also exists in blue; value $250.

POSTES SERBES

Stamps of France, 1900-1907, with this handstamped control were issued in 1916-1918 by the Serbian Postal Bureau, in the Island of Corfu, during a temporary shortage of Serbian stamps. On the 1c to 35c, the handstamp covers 2 or 3 stamps. It was applied after the stamps were on the cover, and frequently no further cancellation was used.

King Peter and Prince Alexander — A16

1918-20 **Typo.** ***Perf. 11, 11½***

155	A16	1p black	.20	.20
156	A16	2p olive brown	.20	.20
157	A16	5p apple green	.20	.20
158	A16	10p red	.20	.20
159	A16	15p black brown	.20	.20
160	A16	20p red brown	.20	.20
161	A16	20p violet ('20)	1.10	.60
162	A16	25p deep blue	.20	.20
163	A16	30p olive green	.20	.20
164	A16	50p violet	.20	.20
165	A16	1d violet brown	.25	.20
166	A16	3d slate green	.75	.60
167	A16	5d red brown	1.25	.80
		Nos. 155-167 (13)	5.15	4.00

#157-160, 164 exist imperf. Value each $6.

1920 **Pelure Paper** ***Perf. 11½***

169	A16	1p black	.20	.20
170	A16	2p olive brown	.20	.20

POSTAGE DUE STAMPS

Coat of Arms

D1 D2

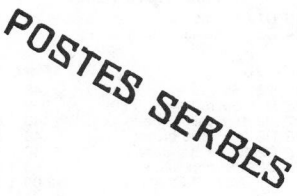

1895 Unwmk. Typo. *Perf. 13x13½*

Granite Paper

J1	D1	5p red lilac	2.50	.80
J2	D1	10p blue	2.50	.20
J3	D1	20p orange brown	30.00	5.00
J4	D1	30p green	.20	.35
J5	D1	50p rose	.30	.40
a.		Cliché of 5p in plate of 50p	75.00	*95.00*
		Nos. J1-J5 (5)	35.50	6.75

No. J1 exists imperf. Value $35.

1898-1904

Ordinary Paper

J6	D1	5p magenta ('04)	.70	.70
J7	D1	20p brown	3.00	.70
a.		Tête bêche pair	150.00	*150.00*
J8	D1	20p dp brn ('04)	3.00	.70
		Nos. J6-J8 (3)	6.70	2.10

1906 Granite Paper *Perf. 11½*

J9	D1	5p magenta	5.25	1.00

1909

Laid Paper

J10	D1	5p magenta	.60	.60
J11	D1	10p pale blue	3.00	1.60
J12	D1	20p pale brown	.40	.40
		Nos. J10-J12 (3)	4.00	2.60

1914

White Wove Paper

J13	D1	5p rose	.25	.50
J14	D1	10p deep blue	3.75	6.25

1918-20 *Perf. 11*

J15	D2	5p red	.40	.85
J16	D2	5p red brown ('20)	.40	.85
J17	D2	10p yellow green	.40	.85
J18	D2	20p olive brown	.40	.85
J19	D2	30p slate green	.40	.85
J20	D2	50p chocolate	.80	1.25
		Nos. J15-J20 (6)	2.80	5.50

NEWSPAPER STAMPS

N1

Overprinted with Crown-topped Shield in Black

1911 Unwmk. Typo. *Perf. 11½*

P1	N1	1p gray	.45	.45
P2	N1	5p green	.45	.45
P3	N1	10p orange	.45	.45
a.		Cliché of 1p in plate of 10p	200.00	
P4	N1	15p violet	.45	.45
P5	N1	20p yellow	.45	.45
a.		Cliché of 50p in plate of 20p	75.00	*125.00*
P6	N1	25p blue	.50	.50
P7	N1	30p slate	5.25	5.25
P8	N1	50p brown	4.50	4.50
P9	N1	1d bister	4.50	4.50
P10	N1	3d rose red	4.50	4.50
P11	N1	5d gray vio	4.50	4.50
		Nos. P1-P11 (11)	26.00	26.00

ISSUED UNDER AUSTRIAN OCCUPATION

100 Heller = 1 Krone

Stamps of Bosnia, 1912-14, Overprinted

1916 Unwmk. *Perf. 12½*

1N1	A23	1h olive green	1.60	2.25
1N2	A23	2h brt blue	1.60	2.25
1N3	A23	3h claret	1.60	1.75
1N4	A23	5h green	.40	.45
1N5	A23	6h dk gray	.80	1.50
1N6	A23	10h rose carmine	.40	.40
1N7	A23	12h dp olive grn	.80	1.50
1N8	A23	20h orange brown	.50	.90
1N9	A23	25h ultra	.50	.80
1N10	A23	30h orange red	.50	.80
1N11	A24	35h myrtle grn	.50	.80
1N12	A24	40h dk violet	.50	.80
1N13	A24	45h olive brown	.50	.80
1N14	A24	50h slate blue	.50	.80
1N15	A24	60h brown violet	.50	.80
1N16	A24	72h dark blue	.50	.80
1N17	A25	1k brn vio, *straw*	.70	1.00
1N18	A25	2k dk gray, *bl*	.70	1.00
1N19	A26	3k carmine, *grn*	.70	1.00
1N20	A26	5k dk vio, *gray*	.70	1.00
1N21	A25	10k dk ultra, *gray*	10.00	19.00
		Nos. 1N1-1N21 (21)	24.50	40.40

Stamps of Bosnia, 1912-14, Overprinted "SERBIEN" Horizontally at Bottom

1916

1N22	A23	1h olive green	6.75	8.00
1N23	A23	2h bright blue	6.75	8.00
1N24	A23	3h claret	6.75	8.00
1N25	A23	5h green	.50	.65
1N26	A23	6h dark gray	6.75	8.00
1N27	A23	10h rose carmine	.50	.65
1N28	A23	12h dp olive grn	6.75	8.00
1N29	A23	20h orange brn	6.75	8.00
1N30	A23	25h ultra	6.75	8.00
1N31	A23	30h orange red	6.75	8.00
1N32	A24	35h myrtle green	6.75	8.00
1N33	A24	40h dark violet	6.75	8.00
1N34	A24	45h olive brown	6.75	8.00
1N35	A24	50h slate blue	6.75	8.00
1N36	A24	60h brown violet	6.75	8.00
1N37	A24	72h dark blue	6.75	8.00
1N38	A25	1k brn vio, *straw*	14.00	19.00
1N39	A25	2k dk gray, *bl*	16.00	19.00
1N40	A26	3k carmine, *grn*	18.00	19.00
1N41	A26	5k dk vio, *gray*	27.50	30.00
1N42	A25	10k dk ultra, *gray*	42.50	45.00
		Nos. 1N22-1N42 (21)	213.50	245.30

Nos. 1N22-1N42 were prepared in 1914, at the time of the 1st Austrian occupation of Serbia. They were not issued at that time because of the retreat. The stamps were put on sale in 1916, at the same time as Nos. 1N1-1N21.

ISSUED UNDER GERMAN OCCUPATION

In occupied Serbia, authority was ostensibly in the hands of a government created by the former Yugoslav General, Milan Nedich, supported by the Chetniks, a nationalist organization which turned fascist. Actually the German military ran the country.

Types of Yugoslavia, 1939-40, Overprinted in Black

1941 Unwmk. Typo. *Perf. 12½*

Paper with colored network

2N1	A16	25p blk (*lt grn*)	.20	*1.25*
2N2	A16	50p org (*pink*)	.20	.25
2N3	A16	1d yel grn (*lt grn*)	.20	.25
2N4	A16	1.50d red (*pink*)	.20	.25
2N5	A16	2d dp mag (*pink*)	.20	.25
2N6	A16	3d dl red brn (*pink*)	.90	*5.00*
2N7	A16	4d ultra (*lt grn*)	.20	*.75*
2N8	A16	5d dk bl (*lt grn*)	.50	*2.00*
2N9	A16	5.50d dk vio brn (*pink*)	.50	*2.00*
2N10	A16	6d sl bl (*pink*)	.50	*2.00*
2N11	A16	8d sep (*lt grn*)	.70	*3.00*
2N12	A16	12d brt vio (*lt grn*)	.75	*3.00*
2N13	A16	16d dl vio (*pink*)	1.10	*10.00*
2N14	A16	20d bl (*lt grn*)	1.10	*12.50*
2N15	A16	30d brt pink (*lt grn*)	5.75	*75.00*
		Nos. 2N1-2N15 (15)	13.00	*117.50*

Double overprints exist on 50p, 1d, 5d, 5.50d and 12d. Value, each $125 to $250.

Stamps of Yugoslavia, 1939-40, Overprinted in Black

Paper with colored network

2N16	A16	25p blk (*lt grn*)	.20	3.75
2N17	A16	50p org (*pink*)	.20	*.75*
2N18	A16	1d yel grn (*lt grn*)	.20	*.50*
2N19	A16	1.50d red (*pink*)	.20	*.75*
2N20	A16	2d dp mag (*pink*)	.20	*.50*
2N21	A16	3d dl red brn (*pink*)	.30	*3.00*
2N22	A16	4d ultra (*lt grn*)	.20	*.50*
2N23	A16	5d dk bl (*lt grn*)	.20	*1.25*
2N24	A16	5.50d dk vio brn (*pink*)	.45	*3.00*
2N25	A16	6d sl bl (*pink*)	.45	*3.00*
2N26	A16	8d sep (*lt grn*)	.65	*3.75*
2N27	A16	12d brt vio (*lt grn*)	1.10	*3.75*
2N28	A16	16d dl vio (*pink*)	1.10	*12.50*
2N29	A16	20d bl (*lt grn*)	1.10	*20.00*
2N30	A16	30d brt pink (*lt grn*)	5.75	*65.00*
		Nos. 2N16-2N30 (15)	12.30	*122.00*

Lazaritza Monastery — OS1

Ruins of Manassia Monastery OS4

Designs: 1d, Kalenica Monastery. 1.50d, Ravanica Monastery. 3d, Ljubostinja Monastery. 4d, Sopocane Monastery. 7d, Tsitsa Monastery. 12d, Goriak Monastery. 16d, Studenica Monastery.

1942-43 Typo. *Perf. 11½*

2N31	OS1	50p brt violet	.20	.20
2N32	OS1	1d red	.20	.20
2N33	OS1	1.50d red brn	.75	*2.00*
2N34	OS1	1.50d green ('43)	.20	.20
2N35	OS4	2d dl rose violet	.20	.20
2N36	OS4	3d brt blue	.75	*2.00*
2N37	OS4	3d rose pink ('43)	.20	.20
2N38	OS4	4d ultra	.20	.20
2N39	OS4	7d dk slate grn	.20	.20
2N40	OS1	12d lake	.20	*1.25*
2N41	OS1	16d grnsh blk	1.00	*1.50*
		Nos. 2N31-2N41 (11)	4.10	*8.15*

For surcharges see Nos. 2NB29-2NB37.

Post Rider — OS10

Post Wagon — OS11

9d, Mail train. 30d, Mail truck. 50d, Mail plane.

1943, Oct. 15 Photo. *Perf. 12½*

2N42	OS10	3d copper red & gray lilac	.40	*1.00*
2N43	OS11	8d vio rose & gray	.40	*1.00*
2N44	OS10	9d dk bl grn & sep	.40	*1.00*
2N45	OS10	30d chnt & sl grn	.40	*1.00*
2N46	OS10	50d dp bl & red brn	.40	*1.00*
		Nos. 2N42-2N46 (5)	2.00	*5.00*

Centenary of postal service in Serbia. Printed in sheets of 24 containing 4 of each stamp and 4 labels.

OCCUPATION SEMI-POSTAL STAMPS

Smederevo Fortress on the Danube OSP1

Refugees OSP2

Perf. 11½x12½

1941, Sept. 22 Typo. Unwmk.

2NB1	OSP1	50p + 1d dk brn	.35	*.65*
2NB2	OSP2	1d + 2d dk gray grn	.35	*.85*
2NB3	OSP2	1.50d + 3d dp cl	.65	*1.50*
a.		Perf. 12½	4.00	*6.25*
2NB4	OSP1	2d + 4d dk bl	.95	*2.00*
		Nos. 2NB1-2NB4 (4)	2.30	*5.00*

Souvenir Sheets

2NB5		Sheet of 2	40.00	*100.00*
a.	OSP2	1d + 49d rose lake	6.75	*17.50*
b.	OSP1	2d + 48d gray	6.75	*17.50*

Imperf

2NB6		Sheet of 2	40.00	*100.00*
a.	OSP2	1d + 49d gray	6.75	*17.50*
b.	OSP1	2d + 48d rose lake	6.75	*17.50*

The surtax aided the victims of an explosion at Smederevo and was used for the reconstruction of the town.

Christ and Virgin Mary — OSP4

a

b

1941, Dec. 5 Photo. *Perf. 11½*

With Rose Burelage

2NB7	OSP4	50p + 1.50d brn red	.35	*3.75*
2NB8	OSP4	1d + 3d sl grn	.35	*3.75*
2NB9	OSP4	2d + 6d dp red	.35	*3.75*
2NB10	OSP4	4d + 12d dp bl	.35	*3.75*
		Nos. 2NB7-2NB10 (4)	1.40	*15.00*

With Symbol "a" Outlined in Cerise

2NB7a	OSP4	50p	10.00	*37.50*
2NB8a	OSP4	1d	10.00	*37.50*
2NB9a	OSP4	2d	10.00	*37.50*
2NB10a	OSP4	4d	10.00	*37.50*
		Nos. 2NB7a-2NB10a (4)	40.00	*150.00*

With Symbol "b" Outlined in Cerise

2NB7b	OSP4	50p	10.00	*37.50*
2NB8b	OSP4	1d	10.00	*37.50*
2NB9b	OSP4	2d	10.00	*37.50*
2NB10b	OSP4	4d	10.00	*37.50*
		Nos. 2NB7b-2NB10b (4)	40.00	*150.00*

Without Burelage

2NB7c	OSP4	50p	1.50	*12.00*
2NB8c	OSP4	1d	1.50	*12.50*
2NB9c	OSP4	2d	1.50	*12.50*
2NB10c	OSP4	4d	1.50	*12.50*
		Nos. 2NB7c-2NB10c (4)	6.00	*49.50*

These stamps were printed in sheets of 50, in 2 panes of 25. In the panes, #8, 12, 13, 14, 18, forming a cross, are without burelage. #7, 17 are type "a," #9, 19 type "b." 16 of the 25 stamps have overall burelage.

Surtax aided prisoners of war.

1942, Mar. 26

Thicker Paper, Without Burelage

2NB11	OSP4	50p + 1.50d brn	.60	*2.75*
2NB12	OSP4	1d + 3d bl grn	.60	*2.75*
2NB13	OSP4	2d + 6d mag	.60	*2.75*
2NB14	OSP4	4d + 12d ultra	.60	*3.00*
		Nos. 2NB11-2NB14 (4)	2.40	*11.25*

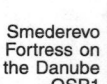

OSP5

OSP6

OSP7

OSP8

Designs: Anti-Masonic symbolisms.

1942, Jan. 1

2NB15	OSP5	50p + 50p yel brn	.25	*.65*
2NB16	OSP6	1d + 1d dk grn	.25	*.65*
2NB17	OSP7	2d + 2d rose car	.45	*1.25*
2NB18	OSP8	4d + 4d indigo	.45	*1.25*
		Nos. 2NB15-2NB18 (4)	1.40	*3.80*

Anti-Masonic Exposition of Oct. 22, 1941. The surtax was used for anti-Masonic propaganda.

Mother and Children — OSP9

1942

2NB19	OSP9	2d + 6d brt pur	1.10	*2.50*
2NB20	OSP9	4d + 8d dp bl	1.10	*2.50*
2NB21	OSP9	7d + 13d dk bl grn	1.10	*2.50*
2NB22	OSP9	20d + 40d dp rose lake	1.10	*2.50*
		Nos. 2NB19-2NB22 (4)	4.40	*10.00*

Nos. 2NB19-2NB22 were issued in sheets of 16 consisting of a block of four of each denomination. The surtax aided war orphans.

Broken Sword — OSP10

Wounded Flag-bearer OSP11

Designs: 1.50d+48.50d, Broken sword. 3d+5d, 2d+48d, Wounded soldier. 3d+47d, Wounded flag-bearer. 4d+10d, 4d+46d, Tending casualty.

1943

2NB23	OSP10	1.50d + 1.50d dk brn	.55	*1.25*
2NB24	OSP11	2d + 3d dk bl grn	.55	*1.25*
2NB25	OSP11	3d + 5d dp rose vio	.80	*2.00*
2NB26	OSP10	4d + 10d dp bl	1.25	*3.00*
		Nos. 2NB23-2NB26 (4)	3.15	*7.50*

Souvenir Sheets
Thick Paper

2NB27	Sheet of 2	27.50	*550.00*
a.	OSP10 1.50d + 48.50d dk brn	10.00	*225.00*
b.	OSP10 4d + 46d dp bl	10.00	*225.00*
2NB28	Sheet of 2	27.50	*550.00*
a.	OSP11 2d + 48d dk bl grn	10.00	*225.00*
b.	OSP11 3d + 47d dp rose vio	10.00	*225.00*

The sheets measure 150x110mm. The surtax aided war victims.

За пострадале
од англо-америчког
терор. бомбардовања
Ниша — 20-X-1943

+ 9

Stamps of 1942-43 Surcharged in Black

1943, Dec. 11
Pale Green Burelage

2NB29	OS1	50p + 2d brt vio	.20	*2.50*
2NB30	OS1	1d + 3d red	.20	*2.50*
2NB31	OS1	1.50d + 4d dp grn	.20	*2.50*
2NB32	OS4	2d + 5d dl rose vio	.20	*2.50*
2NB33	OS4	3d + 7d rose pink	.20	*2.50*
2NB34	OS4	4d + 9d ultra	.20	*2.50*
2NB35	OS4	7d + 15d dk sl grn	.55	*2.50*
2NB36	OS1	12d + 25d lake	.55	*12.50*
2NB37	OS1	16d + 33d grnsh blk	.95	*12.50*
		Nos. 2NB29-2NB37 (9)	3.25	*42.50*

The surtax aided victims of the bombing of Nisch.

OCCUPATION AIR POST STAMPS

Types of Yugoslavia, 1937-40, Overprinted in Carmine or Maroon

Nos. 2NC1-2NC3, 2NC5-2NC7, 2NC9

SERBIEN

Nos. 2NC4, 2NC8, 2NC10

SERBIEN

1941 **Unwmk.** ***Perf. 12½***
Paper with colored network

2NC1	AP6	50p brown	3.00	*25.00*
2NC2	AP7	1d yellow grn	3.00	*25.00*
2NC3	AP8	2d blue gray	3.00	*25.00*
2NC4	AP9	2.50d rose red (M)	3.00	*25.00*
2NC5	AP6	5d brown vio	3.00	*25.00*
2NC6	AP7	10d brn lake (M)	3.00	*25.00*
2NC7	AP8	20d dk green	3.00	*25.00*
2NC8	AP9	30d ultra	3.00	*25.00*
2NC9	AP10	40d Prus grn & pale grn (C)	6.75	*125.00*
2NC10	AP11	50d sl bl & gray bl (C)	8.50	*190.00*
		Nos. 2NC1-2NC10 (10)	39.25	*515.00*

Nos. 2NC1-2NC2 exist without network.

Same Surcharged in Maroon or Carmine with New Values and Bars
Without colored network

2NC11	AP7	1d on 10d	2.25	*15.00*
2NC12	AP8	3d on 20d	2.25	*15.00*
2NC13	AP9	6d on 30d	2.25	*15.00*
2NC14	AP10	8d on 40d	2.50	*30.00*
2NC15	AP11	12d on 50d	5.00	*75.00*
		Nos. 2NC11-2NC15 (5)	14.25	*150.00*

Regular Issue of Yugoslavia, 1939-40, Surcharged in Black

14 СРБИЈА

1942
Green Network

2NC16	A16	2d on 2d dp mag	.20	*1.25*
2NC17	A16	4d on 4d ultra	.20	*1.25*
2NC18	A16	10d on 12d brt vio	.20	*2.00*
2NC19	A16	14d on 20d blue	.20	*2.00*
2NC20	A16	20d on 30d brt pink	.45	*10.00*
		Nos. 2NC16-2NC20 (5)	1.25	*16.50*

OCCUPATION POSTAGE DUE STAMPS

Types of Yugoslavia Similar to OD3-OD4 Overprinted

1941 **Unwmk.** **Typo.** ***Perf. 12½***

2NJ1	OD3	50p violet	.65	*3.75*
2NJ2	OD3	1d lake	.65	*3.75*
2NJ3	OD3	2d dark blue	.65	*3.75*
2NJ4	OD3	3d red	.95	*5.00*
2NJ5	OD4	4d lt blue	1.25	*12.50*
2NJ6	OD4	5d orange	1.25	*12.50*
2NJ7	OD4	10d violet	2.75	*25.00*
2NJ8	OD4	20d green	8.00	*75.00*
		Nos. 2NJ1-2NJ8 (8)	16.15	*141.25*

OD3

OD4

1942 ***Perf. 12½***

2NJ9	OD3	1d maroon & grn	.30	*1.25*
2NJ10	OD3	2d dk blue & red	.30	*1.25*
2NJ11	OD3	3d vermilion & bl	.55	*2.50*
2NJ12	OD4	4d blue & red	.55	*2.50*
2NJ13	OD4	5d orange & bl	.60	*3.00*
2NJ14	OD4	10d violet & red	.70	*7.50*
2NJ15	OD4	20d green & red	3.00	*22.50*
		Nos. 2NJ9-2NJ15 (7)	6.00	*40.50*

OD5

2NJ16	OD5	50p black	.20	*1.25*
2NJ17	OD5	3d violet	.20	*1.25*
2NJ18	OD5	4d blue	.20	*1.25*
2NJ19	OD5	5d dk slate grn	.20	*1.25*
2NJ20	OD5	6d orange	.35	*3.75*
2NJ21	OD5	10d red	.60	*6.25*
2NJ22	OD5	20d ultra	1.75	*15.00*
		Nos. 2NJ16-2NJ22 (7)	3.50	*30.00*

OCCUPATION OFFICIAL STAMP

OOS1

1943 **Unwmk.** **Typo.** ***Perf. 12½***

2NO1	OOS1	3d red lilac	1.00	*1.50*

SEYCHELLES

sā-'shel͵z͵

LOCATION — A group of islands in the Indian Ocean, off the coast of Africa north of Madagascar.
GOVT. — Republic
AREA — 175 sq. mi.
POP. — 79,164 (1999 est.)
CAPITAL — Victoria

The islands were attached to the British colony of Mauritius from 1810 to 1903, when they became a separate colony. Seychelles achieved internal self-government in October 1975 and independence on June 29, 1976.

100 Cents = 1 Rupee

Catalogue values for unused stamps in this country are for Never Hinged items, beginning with Scott 149 in the regular postage section and Scott J1 in the postage due section.

Watermark

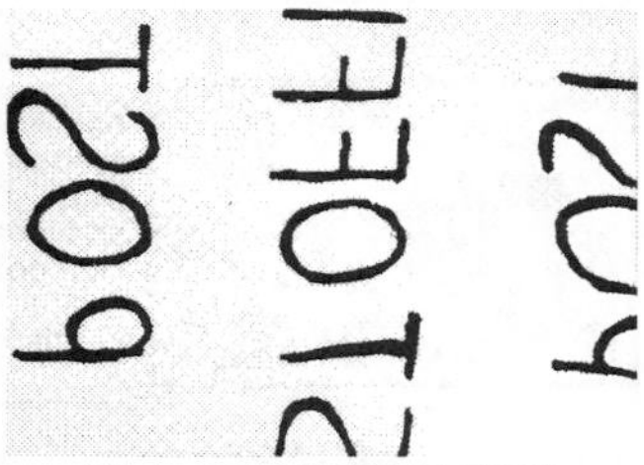

Wmk. 380- "POST OFFICE"

Queen Victoria — A1

Two dies of 2c, 4c, 8c, 10c, 13c, 16c:

Die I - Shading lines at right of diamond in tiara band.
Die II - No shading lines in this rectangle.

1890-1900 Typo. Wmk. 2 Perf. 14

1 A1 2c grn & rose (II) 2.00 .90
a. Die I 2.10 *8.00*
2 A1 2c org brn & grn ('00) 1.85 .75
3 A1 3c dk vio & org ('93) 1.40 .30
4 A1 4c car rose & grn (II) 2.00 1.00
a. Die I 17.50 *10.00*
5 A1 6c car rose ('00) 3.00 *.40*
6 A1 8c brn vio & ultra (II) 5.00 1.50
a. 8c brn vio & bl (I) 6.00 *3.00*
7 A1 10c ultra & brn (II) 6.00 3.00
a. 10c bl & brn (I) 5.00 *12.00*
8 A1 12c ol gray & grn ('93) 2.10 .60
9 A1 13c slate & blk (II) 2.25 1.75
a. Die I 5.00 *10.00*
10 A1 15c ol grn & vio ('93) 4.00 2.00
11 A1 15c ultra ('00) 3.50 3.00
12 A1 16c org brn & bl (I) 3.75 3.75
a. 16c org brn & ultra (II) 35.00 10.00
13 A1 18c ultra ('97) 3.75 .90
14 A1 36c brn & rose ('97) 17.50 3.75
15 A1 45c brn & rose ('93) 20.00 27.50
16 A1 48c ocher & green 17.50 15.00
17 A1 75c yel & pur ('00) 42.50 60.00
18 A1 96c violet & car 42.50 *45.00*
19 A1 1r vio & red ('97) 12.00 4.00
20 A1 1.50r blk & rose ('00) 50.00 70.00
21 A1 2.25r vio & grn ('00) 75.00 *75.00*
Nos. 1-21 (21) 317.60 320.10

Numerals of 75c, 1r, 1.50r and 2.25r of type A1 are in color on plain tablet.
For surcharges see Nos. 22-37.

Surcharged in Black

1893

22 A1 3c on 4c car rose & green (II) 50.00 1.10
a. Inverted surcharge 300.00 *325.00*
b. Double surcharge 475.00
d. Pair, one without surcharge *5,000.*
23 A1 12c on 16c org brn & ultra (II) 4.25 1.10
a. 12c on 16c org brn & bl (I) 1.50 *3.25*
b. Inverted surcharge (I) 425.00 325.00
d. Double surcharge (I) *4,250.* *4,500.*
e. Double surcharge (II) 3,750 3,750
24 A1 15c on 16c org brn & ultra (II) 5.25 2.25
a. 15c on 16c org brn & bl (I) 8.50 12.50
b. Inverted surcharge (I) 300.00 350.00
c. Inverted surcharge (II) 750.00 800.00
d. Double surcharge (I) 650.00 650.00
e. Double surcharge (II) 1,000. 1,000.
f. Triple surcharge (II) *3,750.*
25 A1 45c on 48c ocher & grn 11.00 5.00
26 A1 90c on 96c vio & car 24.00 24.00
Nos. 22-26 (5) 94.50 33.45

No. 15 Surcharged in Black

1896

27 A1 18c on 45c brn & rose 7.50 3.00
a. Double surcharge 1,300. 1,300.
b. Triple surcharge *1,500.*
28 A1 36c on 45c brn & rose 10.50 *42.50*
a. Double surcharge 1,250.

Surcharged in Black:

1901

29 A1 3c on 10c bl & brn (II) .80 .55
a. Double surcharge 600.00
30 A1 3c on 16c org brn & ultra (II) 1.50 *2.75*
a. "3 cents" omitted (II) 500.00 500.00
b. Inverted surcharge (II) 600.00 600.00
c. Double surcharge (II) 650.00
31 A1 3c on 36c brn & rose .40 .70
a. Without bars
b. Double surcharge 700.00 *825.00*
c. "3 cents" omitted 550.00 600.00
32 A1 6c on 8c brn vio & ultra (II) .80 *2.50*
a. Inverted surcharge 600.00 *700.00*
Nos. 29-32 (4) 3.50 *6.50*

Stamps of 1890-1900 Surcharged

1902, June

33 A1 2c on 4c car rose & grn (II) 1.50 2.25
34 A1 30c on 75c yel & pur 1.25 *3.25*
a. Narrow "0" in "30" 20.00 *40.00*
35 A1 30c on 1r vio & red 4.00 *19.00*
a. Narrow "0" in "30" 40.00 *87.50*
b. Double surcharge *1,250.*
36 A1 45c on 1r vio & red 3.25 *19.00*
37 A1 45c on 2.25r vio & grn 35.00 *32.50*
a. Narrow "5" in "45" 150.00 225.00
Nos. 33-37 (5) 45.00 *76.00*

King Edward VII — A6

Numerals of 75c, 1.50r and 2.25r of type A6 are in color on plain tablet.

1903, May 26 Typo. Wmk. 2

38 A6 2c red brn & grn 1.50 1.00
39 A6 3c green .85 *1.00*
40 A6 6c carmine rose 1.90 .75
41 A6 12c ol gray & grn 2.00 *2.25*
42 A6 15c ultra 3.50 1.75
43 A6 18c pale yel grn & rose 3.50 *5.25*
44 A6 30c purple & grn 5.50 *9.00*
45 A6 45c brown & rose 5.75 *9.00*
46 A6 75c yel & pur 8.50 *22.50*
47 A6 1.50r black & rose 34.00 *57.50*
48 A6 2.25r red vio & grn 23.00 *70.00*
Nos. 38-48 (11) 90.00 *180.00*

Nos. 42-43, 45 Surcharged

1903

49 A6 3c on 15c .75 *2.75*
50 A6 3c on 18c 2.25 *26.00*
51 A6 3c on 45c 2.50 *3.25*
Nos. 49-51 (3) 5.50 *32.00*

Type of 1903

1906 Wmk. 3

52 A6 2c red brn & grn 1.25 *3.50*
53 A6 3c green 1.25 1.25
54 A6 6c car rose 1.50 .65
55 A6 12c ol gray & grn 2.50 2.25
56 A6 15c ultra 2.75 *1.60*
57 A6 18c pale yel grn & rose 2.75 *5.25*
58 A6 30c purple & grn 5.25 *6.50*
59 A6 45c brown & rose 2.75 *5.25*
60 A6 75c yellow & pur 7.50 *45.00*
61 A6 1.50r black & rose 45.00 *50.00*
62 A6 2.25r red vio & grn 27.50 *47.50*
Nos. 52-62 (11) 100.00 *168.75*

King George V
A7 A8

Numerals of 75c, 1.50r and 2.25r of type A7 are in color on plain tablet.

1912 Perf. 14

63 A7 2c org brn & grn .35 *3.00*
64 A7 3c green .40 .40
65 A7 6c car rose 5.00 3.50
66 A7 12c ol gray & grn .85 2.75
67 A7 15c ultra 1.40 .35
68 A7 18c pale yel grn & rose 1.25 *3.25*
69 A7 30c purple & grn 4.50 .95
70 A7 45c brown & rose 2.25 *24.00*
71 A7 75c yellow & pur 3.50 *4.25*
72 A7 1.50r black & rose 15.00 .65
73 A7 2.25r violet & grn 27.50 1.90
Nos. 63-73 (11) 62.00 45.00

Die I

For description of dies I and II see back of this section of the Catalogue.
The 5c of type A8 has a colorless numeral on solid-color tablet. Numerals of 9c, 20c, 25c, 50c, 75c, and 1r to 5r of type A8 are in color on plain tablet.

1917-20

74 A8 2c org brn & grn .20 *1.90*
75 A8 3c green .75 *.95*
76 A8 5c brown ('20) .90 *4.50*
77 A8 6c carmine rose .60 *1.10*
78 A8 12c gray .45 *.70*
79 A8 15c ultra .55 *1.10*
80 A8 18c violet, *yel* 2.00 *15.00*
a. Die II ('20) 1.00 *14.00*
81 A8 25c blk & red, *yel* ('20) 1.90 *21.00*
a. Die II ('20) 1.50 *9.00*
82 A8 30c dull vio & ol grn 1.90 *6.25*
83 A8 45c dull vio & org 2.50 *27.50*
84 A8 50c dull vio & blk ('20) 2.50 *17.00*
85 A8 75c blk, *bl grn*, ol back 2.75 *10.50*
a. 75c blk, *emer* (Die II) ('20) 5.00 *17.50*
86 A8 1r dl vio & red ('20) 13.00 *32.50*
87 A8 1.50r vio & bl, *bl* 12.50 *40.00*
a. Die II ('20) 10.00 *30.00*
88 A8 2.25r gray grn & dp vio 27.50 *95.00*
89 A8 5r gray grn & ultra ('20) 65.00 *150.00*
Nos. 74-89 (16) 135.00 *425.00*

Die II

1921-32 Wmk. 4

Ordinary Paper

91 A8 2c org brn & grn .20 .20
92 A8 3c green .20 .20
93 A8 3c black ('22) .35 .35
94 A8 4c green ('22) .50 *2.00*
95 A8 4c ol grn & rose red ('28) 2.50 *12.00*
96 A8 5c dk brown 1.25 *4.50*
97 A8 6c car rose 1.25 *6.50*
98 A8 6c violet ('22) .30 .20
99 A8 9c rose red ('27) 1.00 *3.25*
100 A8 12c gray .50 .20
a. Die I ('32) 7.50 .65
101 A8 12c carmine ('22) .35 .25
102 A8 15c ultra 5.00 *44.00*
103 A8 15c yellow ('22) .80 *2.00*
104 A8 18c violet, *yel* 1.50 *9.00*
105 A8 20c ultra ('22) .90 .30

Chalky Paper

106 A8 25c blk & red, *yel* ('22) 1.50 *8.00*
107 A8 30c dull vio & ol grn 1.25 *11.50*
108 A8 45c dull vio & org .95 *4.00*
109 A8 50c dull vio & blk .95 *1.75*
110 A8 75c blk, *emerald* 7.75 *17.00*
111 A8 1r dull vio & red 10.00 *14.50*
a. Die I ('32) 11.00 *30.00*
112 A8 1.50r vio & bl, *bl* 10.00 *17.00*
113 A8 2.25r green & vio 12.50 *11.50*
114 A8 5r green & ultra 65.00 *105.00*
Nos. 91-114 (24) 126.50 *275.20*

Common Design Types pictured following the introduction.

Silver Jubilee Issue

Common Design Type

1935, May 6 Engr. *Perf. 11x12*

118 CD301 6c black & ultra .75 *1.50*
119 CD301 12c indigo & green 2.25 .75
120 CD301 20c ultra & brown 2.00 .50
121 CD301 1r brn vio & indigo 5.00 *9.00*
Nos. 118-121 (4) 10.00 *11.75*

Coronation Issue

Common Design Type

1937, May 12 *Perf. 11x11½*

122 CD302 6c olive green .20 .20
123 CD302 12c deep orange .20 .20
124 CD302 20c deep ultra .30 .30
Nos. 122-124 (3) .70 .70

Coco-de-mer Palm — A9

Seychelles Giant Tortoise — A10

Fishing Canoe — A11

Perf. 13½x14½, 14½x13½

1938-41 Photo. Wmk. 4

125 A9 2c violet brown .35 .20
126 A10 3c green 2.40 1.00
127 A10 3c orange .40 .25
128 A11 6c orange 2.40 2.00
129 A11 6c green 1.00 .25
130 A9 9c rose red 3.50 *1.65*
131 A9 9c peacock blue 1.75 .30
132 A10 12c violet 13.00 1.00
133 A10 15c copper red 2.00 .20
134 A9 18c rose lake 2.00 .45
135 A11 20c bright blue 14.50 4.00
136 A11 20c ocher 1.60 .35
137 A9 25c ocher 20.00 11.00
138 A10 30c rose lake 20.00 7.25
139 A9 30c bright blue 1.60 .40
140 A11 45c brown 3.50 .60
141 A9 50c dull violet 1.50 .30
142 A10 75c gray blue 29.00 30.00
143 A10 75c dull violet 2.25 .45
144 A11 1r yellow green 35.00 37.50
145 A11 1r gray 2.75 .60
146 A9 1.50r ultra 5.00 1.10

147 A10 2.25r olive bister 6.50 3.00
148 A11 5r copper red 3.00 2.50
Nos. 125-148 (24) 175.00 106.35

Issued: #126, 128, 132, 135, 137, 1/1; #125, 130, 138, 140-142, 144, 146-148, 2/10; others, 8/8/41.

See Nos. 158-169, 174-188.

Catalogue values for unused stamps in this section, from this point to the end of the section, are for Never Hinged items.

Peace Issue
Common Design Type
Perf. 13½x14
1946, Sept. 23 Engr. Wmk. 4
149 CD303 9c light blue .20 .20
150 CD303 30c dark blue .20 .20

Silver Wedding Issue
Common Design Types
1948, Nov. 11 Photo. *Perf. 14x14½*
151 CD304 9c bright ultra .20 .20

Engraved; Name Typographed
Perf. 11½x11
152 CD305 5r rose carmine 11.00 *22.50*

UPU Issue
Common Design Types
Perf. 13½, 11x11½
1949, Oct. 10 Engr.
153 CD306 18c red violet .20 .20
154 CD307 50c dp rose violet 1.75 .75
155 CD308 1r gray .35 .35
156 CD309 2.25r olive .45 *.75*
Nos. 153-156 (4) 2.75 2.05

Types of 1938-41 Redrawn and

Sailfish — A12

Map — A13

Perf. 14½x13½, 13½x14½
1952, Mar. 3 Photo. Wmk. 4
157 A12 2c violet .50 .55
158 A10 3c orange .50 .25
159 A9 9c peacock blue .50 *1.00*
160 A11 15c yellow green .35 *.60*
161 A13 18c rose lake 1.00 .25
162 A11 20c ocher 1.00 .60
163 A10 25c bright red .65 .80
164 A12 40c ultra .75 .75
165 A11 45c violet brown .65 .25
166 A9 50c brt violet 1.10 .55
167 A13 1r gray 2.50 1.90
168 A9 1.50r brt blue 5.50 *8.25*
169 A10 2.25r olive bister 8.00 *8.25*
170 A13 5r copper red 8.50 *10.00*
171 A12 10r green 16.00 *21.00*
Nos. 157-171 (15) 47.50 55.00

The redrawn design shows a new portrait of King George VI surmounted by crown, as on type A12.
Nos. 157-170 exist with watermark 4a.

Coronation Issue
Common Design Type
1953, June 2 Engr. *Perf. 13½x13*
172 CD312 9c dark blue & blk .50 .50

Types of 1938-52 with Portrait of Queen Elizabeth II
Perf. 14½x13½, 13½x14½
1954-56 Photo.
173 A12 2c violet .20 .20
174 A10 3c orange .20 .20
175 A9 9c peacock blue .20 .20
176 A9 10c blue ('56) .40 *1.00*
177 A11 15c yellow grn .25 .20
178 A13 18c rose lake .20 .20
179 A11 20c ocher .40 .20
180 A10 25c bright red .50 .75
181 A13 35c mag ('56) 2.25 .90
182 A12 40c ultra .25 .25
183 A11 45c violet brn .20 .20
184 A9 50c brt violet .25 .20
185 A11 70c vio brn ('56) 4.25 1.10
186 A13 1r gray .45 .40
187 A9 1.50r brt blue 2.75 *3.25*
188 A10 2.25r olive bister 2.75 *3.25*
189 A13 5r copper red 14.50 8.00
190 A12 10r green 22.50 17.50
Nos. 173-190 (18) 52.50 38.00

Issued: 10c, 35c, 70c, 9/15/56; others, 2/1/54.

For surcharge see No. 193.

"Stone of Possession" A14

Flying Fox A15

Perf. 14½x14
1956, Nov. 15 Wmk. 4
191 A14 40c ultra .20 .20
192 A14 1r gray black .30 .30

Bicentenary of French colonization.

No. 183 Surcharged "5 cents" and Bars
1957, Sept. 16 *Perf. 13½x14½*
193 A11 5c on 45c violet brn .25 .25
a. Double surcharge 325.00
b. Thick bars omitted 650.00

The "c," "e" or "s" of surcharge may be found in italic.

1957, Oct. 25 *Perf. 14½x13½*
194 A15 5c light violet .60 .20

Mauritius Stamp of 1859 with Seychelles "B64" Cancellation A16

Engr. & Typo.
Perf. 11½x11
1961, Dec. 11 Wmk. 314
Stamp in Dull Blue & Black
195 A16 10c lilac .20 .20
196 A16 35c dull green .30 .30
197 A16 2.25r orange brown 1.10 1.10
Nos. 195-197 (3) 1.60 1.60

1st post office in Victoria, Seychelles, cent.

Black Parrot — A17

Anse Royal Bay — A18

Designs: 10c, Vanilla. 15c, Fisherman. 20c, Denis Island Lighthouse. 25c, Clock Tower, Victoria. 30c, 35c, Anse Royal Bay. 40c, Government House. 45c, Fishing boat. 50c, Cascade Church. 60c, Flying fox. 70c, 85c, Sailfish. 75c, Coco-de-mer palm. 1r, Cinnamon. 1.50r, Copra. 2.25r, Map of Indian Ocean. 3.50r, Settlers' homes. 5r, Regina Mundi Convent. 10r, Badge of Seychelles.

Perf. 14½x13½, 13½x14½
1962-69 Photo. Wmk. 314
Size: 24x31mm, 31x24mm
198 A17 5c multicolored 2.00 .20
a. Wmkd. sideways ('67) .20 .20
199 A17 10c multicolore 1.10 .20
a. Wmkd. sideways ('68) .20 .20
200 A17 15c multicolored .20 .20
201 A17 20c multicolored .20 .20
202 A17 25c multicolored .20 .20
202A A18 30c multicolored 3.00 *3.50*
203 A18 35c multicolored 1.40 1.75
204 A18 40c multicolored .20 *.85*
204A A18 45c multicolore 2.75 *3.50*
205 A17 50c multicolored .35 .20
b. Wmkd. sideways ('69) .80 .80
205A A17 60c multicolored 1.40 .40
206 A17 70c multicolored 4.75 2.50
206A A17 75c multicolored 1.75 *3.25*
206B A17 85c multicolored .70 .35
207 A18 1r multicolored .25 .20
208 A18 1.50r multicolored 4.25 *5.25*
209 A18 2.25r multicolored 4.25 4.25
210 A18 3.50r multicolored 1.75 *4.50*
211 A18 5r multicolored 2.75 2.00

Perf. 13x14
Size: 22½x39mm
212 A17 10r multicolored 10.25 4.00
Nos. 198-212 (20) 43.50 37.50

Issued: 45c, 75c, 8/1/66; #198a, 2/7/67; 30c, 60c, 85c, 7/15/68; others 2/21/62.
The 60c and 85c have watermark sideways.

For surcharges and overprints see Nos. 216-217, 233-236, 241-243.

Freedom from Hunger Issue
Common Design Type
1963, June 4 *Perf. 14x14½*
213 CD314 70c lilac .75 .35

Red Cross Centenary Issue
Common Design Type
1963, Sept. 2 Litho. *Perf. 13*
214 CD315 10c black & red .20 .20
215 CD315 75c ultra & red .70 .60

Nos. 203 and 206 Surcharged with New Value and Bars
Perf. 14x14½, 14½x14
1965, Apr. Photo. Wmk. 314
216 A18 45c on 35c .20 .20
217 A17 75c on 70c .30 .30

ITU Issue
Common Design Type
Perf. 11x11½
1965, June 1 Litho. Wmk. 314
218 CD317 5c orange & vio bl .20 .20
219 CD317 1.50r red lil & apple grn .70 .35

Intl. Cooperation Year Issue
Common Design Type
1965, Oct. 25 *Perf. 14½*
220 CD318 5c blue grn & claret .20 .20
221 CD318 40c lt violet & green .40 .30

Churchill Memorial Issue
Common Design Type
1966, Jan. 24 Photo. *Perf. 14*
Design in Black, Gold and Carmine Rose
222 CD319 5c bright blue .20 .20
223 CD319 15c green .20 .20
224 CD319 75c brown .60 .25
225 CD319 1.50r violet 1.40 .75
Nos. 222-225 (4) 2.40 1.40

World Cup Soccer Issue
Common Design Type
1966, July 1 Litho. *Perf. 14*
226 CD321 15c multicolored .20 .20
227 CD321 1r multicolored .30 .30

WHO Headquarters Issue
Common Design Type
1966, Sept. 20 Litho. *Perf. 14*
228 CD322 20c multicolored .20 .20
229 CD322 50c multicolored .55 .30

UNESCO Anniversary Issue
Common Design Type
1966, Dec. 1 Litho. *Perf. 14*
230 CD323 15c "Education" .20 .20
231 CD323 1r "Science" .30 .30
232 CD323 5r "Culture" 1.25 1.25
Nos. 230-232 (3) 1.75 1.75

Nos. 200, 204A, 206A and 210 Overprinted: "UNIVERSAL / ADULT / SUFFRAGE / 1967"
Perf. 14½x14, 14x14½
1967, Sept. 18 Photo. Wmk. 314
233 A17 15c multicolored .20 .20
234 A18 45c brt blue & yel .20 .20
235 A17 75c multicolored .20 .20
236 A18 3.50r multicolored .40 *.50*
Nos. 233-236 (4) 1.00 1.10

Cowries: Tiger, Mole, Money A19

Sea Shells (ITY Emblem and): 40c, Textile, betulinus and virgin cones. 1r, Arthritic spider conch. 2.25r, Triton and subulate auger.

Perf. 14x13½
1967, Dec. 4 Photo. Wmk. 314
237 A19 15c multicolored .20 .20
238 A19 40c multicolored .25 .25
239 A19 1r multicolored .40 .40
240 A19 2.25r multicolored .65 .65
Nos. 237-240 (4) 1.50 1.50

Issued for International Tourist Year, 1967.

Nos. 204, 204A and 206A Surcharged
Perf. 14x14½, 14½x14
1968, Apr. 16 Photo. Wmk. 314
241 A18 30c on 40c multicolored .20 .20
242 A18 60c on 45c blue & yel .20 .20
243 A17 85c on 75c multicolored .25 .25
Nos. 241-243 (3) .65 .65

The surcharge on No. 241 includes 2 bars; on Nos. 242-243 it includes 3 bars and "CENTS."

Family, Rising Sun and Human Rights Flame A20

Perf. 14½x14
1968, Sept. 2 Litho. Wmk. 314
244 A20 20c chocolate & multi .20 .20
245 A20 50c vio blue & multi .20 .20
246 A20 85c black & multi .20 .20
247 A20 2.25r brown & multi .25 *.75*
Nos. 244-247 (4) .85 1.35

International Human Rights Year.

First Landing on Praslin Island — A21

Designs: 50c, La Digue and La Curieuse at anchor, vert. 85c, Coco-de-mer and black parrot, vert. 2.25r, La Digue and La Curieuse under sail.

Litho.; Head Embossed in Gold
Perf. 14x14½
1968, Dec. 30 Wmk. 314
248 A21 20c multicolored .20 .20
249 A21 50c dk blue, blk & red .25 .25
250 A21 85c rose red & multi .40 .40
251 A21 2.25r ultra & multi 1.90 1.90
Nos. 248-251 (4) 2.75 2.75

Landing on Praslin Island of the Chevalier Marion Dufresne expedition, 200th anniv.

Separation of Rocket and Spacecraft — A22

5c, Launching of Apollo XI, vert. 50c, Landing module & men on the moon. 85c, Seychelles tracking station. 2.25r, Moonscape & earth.

1969, Sept. 9 Litho. *Perf. 13½*
252 A22 5c multicolored .20 .20
253 A22 20c multicolored .20 .20
254 A22 50c multicolored .25 .20

255	A22	85c multicolored	.35	.35
256	A22	2.25r multicolored	.60	*1.25*
		Nos. 252-256 (5)	1.60	2.20

See note after US No. C76.

Lazare Picault Landing in 1741 — A23

History of Seychelles: 10c, US satellite tracking station. 15c, German cruiser Königsberg at Aldabra, 1915. 20c, British fleet refueling, St. Anne, 1939-45. 25c, Ashanti King Prempeh in exile, 1896. 30c, 40c, Stone of Possession placed, 1756. 50c, 65c, Pirates. 60c, Corsairs. 85c, 95c, Jet and airport. 1r, First capitulation of the French to the British, 1794. 1.50r, Battle between the sailing vessels Sybille and Chiffone, 1801. 3.50r, Visit of Duke of Edinburgh, 1956. 5r, Chevalier Queau de Quincy. 10r, Map of Indian Ocean, 1574. 15r, Seychelles coat of arms.

Perf. 13x12½

1969-72 Litho. Wmk. 314

257	A23	5c multicolored	.20	.20
258	A23	10c multicolored	.20	.20
259	A23	15c multicolored	1.50	1.50
260	A23	20c multicolored	.85	.20
261	A23	25c multicolored	.20	.20
262	A23	30c multicolored	.75	*2.75*
262A	A23	40c multicolored	1.40	*1.00*
263	A23	50c multicolored	.25	.25
264	A23	60c multicolored	.75	*1.00*
264A	A23	65c multicolored	4.25	*5.50*
265	A23	85c multicolored	1.50	1.40
265A	A23	95c multicolored	4.50	3.25
266	A23	1r multicolored	.25	.20
267	A23	1.50r multicolored	1.25	*1.50*
268	A23	3.50r multicolored	.75	*1.75*
269	A23	5r multicolored	.75	*2.10*
270	A23	10r multicolored	1.90	*5.00*
271	A23	15r multicolored	2.75	*8.00*
		Nos. 257-271 (18)	24.00	36.00

Issued: 40, 65, 95c, 12/11/72; others, 11/3/69.

For overprints & surcharges see Nos. 294-298, 323-330, 361-369.

St. Anne Island, Ship and Gulls A24

Designs: 50c, Flying fish, island and ship. 85c, Map of Seychelles and compass rose. 3.50r, Anchor, chain on sea bottom.

1970, Apr. 27 ***Perf. 14***

272	A24	20c multicolored	.60	.60
273	A24	50c multicolored	.40	.40
274	A24	85c multicolored	.40	.40
275	A24	3.50r multicolored	.60	.60
		Nos. 272-275 (4)	2.00	2.00

Bicentenary of first settlement on St. Anne.

Girl and Eye Chart A25

Designs: 50c, Infant on scales and milk bottles. 85c, Mother and child, vert. 3.50r, Red Cross branch headquarters.

1970, Aug. 4 Litho. Wmk. 314

276	A25	20c lt blue & multi	.20	.20
277	A25	50c multicolored	.35	.35
278	A25	85c multicolored	.55	.55
279	A25	3.50r multicolored	1.50	1.50
		Nos. 276-279 (4)	2.60	2.60

Centenary of British Red Cross Society.

Pitcher Plant — A26

Flowers: 50c, Wild vanilla. 85c, Tropic-bird flower. 3.50r, Vare hibiscus.

1970, Dec. 29 ***Perf. 14½***

280	A26	20c multicolored	.20	.20
281	A26	50c multicolored	.40	.40
282	A26	85c multicolored	.75	.75
283	A26	3.50r multicolored	3.75	3.75
a.		Souvenir sheet of 4, #280-283	7.50	*12.50*
		Nos. 280-283 (4)	5.10	5.10

Souvenir Sheet

Map Showing Location of Seychelles — A27

Perf. 13½x14

1971, Apr. 20 Litho. Wmk. 314

284	A27	5r yellow grn & multi	7.50	*9.00*

Issued to publicize Seychelles' location.

Consolidated Catalina Amphibian — A28

Designs: 5c, Piper Navajo, vert. 20c, Westland Wessex, vert. 60c, Grumman Albatross amphibian, vert. 85c, "G" class Short Brothers flying boat. 3.50r, Vickers supermarine "Walrus" amphibian.

Perf. 14x14½, 14½x14

1971, June 28 Litho. Wmk. 314

285	A28	5c orange & multi	.20	.20
286	A28	20c purple & multi	.20	.20
287	A28	50c olive & multi	.40	.20
288	A28	60c sepia & multi	.50	.25
289	A28	85c brown & multi	.70	.35
290	A28	3.50r blue & multi	5.25	2.00
		Nos. 285-290 (6)	7.25	3.20

Completion of Seychelles Airport.

Santa Claus, by Jean-Claude Waye Hive — A29

Christmas (Children's Drawings): 15c, Santa Claus riding a tortoise, by Edison Thérésine. 3.50r, Santa Claus on the seashore, by Isabelle Tirant.

1971, Oct. 12 ***Perf. 13½***

291	A29	10c dark blue & multi	.20	.20
292	A29	15c dark green & multi	.20	.20
293	A29	3.50r violet & multi	.60	*.85*
		Nos. 291-293 (3)	1.00	1.25

Nos. 262, 264-265 Surcharged with New Value and 5 Bars

1971, Dec. 21 ***Perf. 13x12½***

294	A23	40c on 30c multicolored	.25	*.40*
295	A23	65c on 60c multicolored	.35	*.75*
296	A23	95c on 85c multicolored	.40	*1.00*
		Nos. 294-296 (3)	1.00	2.15

Nos. 260, 269 Overprinted in Black or Gold: "ROYAL VISIT 1972"

1972, Mar. 21 Litho. Wmk. 314

297	A23	20c multicolored	.20	.20
298	A23	5r multicolored (G)	1.40	*2.00*

Visit of Elizabeth II and Prince Philip.

Brush Warbler — A30

Fireworks — A31

1972, July 15 ***Perf. 14x13½***

299	A30	5c shown	.50	.50
300	A30	20c Scops owl	1.75	.50
301	A30	50c Blue pigeons	1.75	.60
302	A30	65c Magpie robin	2.25	.65
303	A30	95c Paradise fly-catch0rs	2.50	2.25
304	A30	3.50r Kestrel	6.75	*11.00*
a.		Souvenir sheet of 6, #299-304	25.00	25.00
		Nos. 299-304 (6)	15.50	15.50

1972, Sept. 18 Litho. ***Perf. 14***

305	A31	10c shown	.20	.20
306	A31	15c Canoe race, horiz.	.20	.20
307	A31	25c Women in local costumes	.20	.20
308	A31	5r Water-skiing, horiz.	.70	.70
		Nos. 305-308 (4)	1.30	1.30

Seychelles Festival 1972.

Silver Wedding Issue, 1972

Common Design Type

Design: Queen Elizabeth II, Prince Philip, giant tortoise and leaping sailfish.

1972, Nov. 20 Photo. ***Perf. 14x14½***

309	CD324	95c multicolored	.20	.20
310	CD324	1.50r multicolored	.50	.50

Princess Anne's Wedding Issue

Common Design Type

1973, Nov. 14 Litho. ***Perf. 14***

311	CD325	95c ocher & multi	.30	.30
312	CD325	1.50r slate & multi	.30	.30

Soldierfish — A32

Wmk. 314

1974, Mar. 5 Litho. ***Perf. 14***

313	A32	20c shown	.20	.20
314	A32	50c Filefish	.30	.20
315	A32	95c Butterflyfish	.60	.60
316	A32	1.50r Gaterin	1.40	1.75
		Nos. 313-316 (4)	2.50	2.75

Envelope and Globe — A33

UPU, cent.: 50c, Globe with location of Seychelles and radio tower. 95c, Cancellation and globe. 1.50r, "UPU" with emblems.

Perf. 12½x12

1974, Oct. 9 Wmk. 314

317	A33	20c multicolored	.20	.20
318	A33	50c multicolored	.20	.20
319	A33	95c multicolored	.30	.30
320	A33	1.50r multicolored	.50	.50
		Nos. 317-320 (4)	1.20	1.20

Winston Churchill A34

Design: 1.50r, Churchill, different portrait.

1974, Nov. 30 Litho. ***Perf. 14½***

321	A34	95c lt blue & multi	.20	.20
322	A34	1.50r lt green & multi	.35	.35
a.		Souvenir sheet of 2, #321-322	.60	*1.25*

Sir Winston Churchill (1874-1965).

Nos. 260, 263, 265A and 267 Overprinted in Black or Silver

Perf. 13x12½

1975, Feb. 8 Wmk. 314

323	A23	20c multi (B)	.20	.20
324	A23	50c multi (B)	.20	.20
325	A23	95c multi (S)	.25	.25
326	A23	1.50r multi (B)	.35	*.75*
		Nos. 323-326 (4)	1.00	1.40

Visit of cruise ship Queen Elizabeth II, Mahe, Seychelles.

Nos. 260, 264A, 266, 268 Overprinted in Gold

1975, Oct. 1 Litho. Wmk. 314

327	A23	20c multicolored	.20	.20
328	A23	65c multicolored	.25	.25
329	A23	1r multicolored	.35	.35
330	A23	3.50r multicolored	1.10	1.10
		Nos. 327-330 (4)	1.90	1.90

Queen Elizabeth I A35

Portraits: 15c, Gladys Aylward. 20c, Elizabeth Fry. 25c, Emmeline Pankhurst. 65c, Florence Nightingale. 1r, Amy Johnson. 1.50r, Joan of Arc. 3.50r, Eleanor Roosevelt.

Wmk. 314

1975, Dec. 15 Litho. ***Perf. 13½***

331	A35	10c dp brown & multi	.20	.20
332	A35	15c dk brown & multi	.20	.20
333	A35	20c dk green & multi	.20	.20
334	A35	25c purple & multi	.20	.20
335	A35	65c dk blue & multi	.35	.35

336 A35 1r Prus blue & multi .55 .55
337 A35 1.50r dp violet & multi .70 *1.00*
338 A35 3.50r dk olive & multi 1.40 *2.00*
Nos. 331-338 (8) 3.80 4.70

International Women's Year.

Praslin Map and Grand Anse Postmark, 1907 — A36

First Landing, 1609, and James Mancham — A37

Designs: 65c, La Digue map and postmark, 1916. 1r, Partial map of Mahé and Victoria postmark, 1917. 1.50r, Southern part of Mahé and Anse Royale postmark, 1938.

1976, Mar. 30 Wmk. 373 *Perf. 14*

339 A36 20c lt blue & multi .20 .20
340 A36 65c lt blue & multi .30 .30
341 A36 1r lt blue & multi .40 .40
342 A36 1.50r lt blue & multi .60 .60
a. Souvenir sheet of 4, #339-342 2.50 *3.00*
Nos. 339-342 (4) 1.50 1.50

Rural posts of Seychelles.

1976, June 29 *Perf. 14*

Designs: 25c, Stone of Possession. 40c, Arrival of 1st settlers, 1770 (ship). 75c, Le Chevalier Quéau de Quincy. 1r, Sir Bickham Sweet-Escott. 1.25r, Government House. 1.50r, Coat of arms of Internal Self-government. 3.50r, Seychelles flag.

343 A37 20c rose & multi .20 .20
344 A37 25c yellow & multi .20 .20
345 A37 40c lilac & multi .20 .20
346 A37 75c green & multi .30 .30
347 A37 1r salmon & multi .45 .45
348 A37 1.25r multicolored .50 .50
349 A37 1.50r ocher & multi .65 .65
350 A37 3.50r blue & multi 1.50 1.50
Nos. 343-350 (8) 4.00 4.00

Seychelles' independence, June 29, 1976.

Flags of Seychelles and US — A38

US bicent.: 10r, State House, Seychelles, and Independence Hall, Philadelphia.

1976, July 12 Litho.

351 A38 1r blue & multi .25 .25
352 A38 10r red & multi 1.75 *2.50*

Swimming — A39

Designs (Olympic Rings and): 65c, Hockey. 1r, Basketball. 3.50r, Soccer.

1976, July 26 *Perf. 14½*

353 A39 20c vio blue & blk .20 .20
354 A39 65c dk grn, yel grn & blk .40 .20
355 A39 1r brown, grn & blk .40 .20
356 A39 3.50r car rose & blk .60 *1.50*
Nos. 353-356 (4) 1.60 2.10

21st Olympic Games, Montreal, Canada, July 17-Aug. 1.

Seychelles Sunbird — A40

Seychelles Birds (James R. Mancham, Congress Emblem and): 20c, Paradise flycatcher, vert. 1.50r, Gray white-eye. 5r, Black parrot, vert.

Wmk. 373

1976, Nov. 8 Litho. *Perf. 14½*

357 A40 20c multicolored .20 .20
358 A40 1.25r multicolored .80 .65
359 A40 1.50r multicolored 1.00 .85
360 A40 5r multicolored 2.50 *3.00*
a. Souvenir sheet of 4, #357-360 6.75 *8.00*
Nos. 357-360 (4) 4.50 4.70

4th Pan-African Ornithological Cong., Mahe Beach Hotel, Nov. 6-13.

Nos. 260, 263, 265A-266, 268-271, 264A Overprinted or Surcharged: "Independence / 1976"

Perf. 13x12½

1976, Nov. 22 Litho. Wmk. 314

361 A23 20c multicolored .80 *1.25*
362 A23 50c multicolored .75 *1.50*
363 A23 95c multicolored 2.25 1.50
364 A23 1r multicolored .70 *1.50*
365 A23 3.50r multicolored 3.50 3.00
366 A23 5r multicolored 3.00 *4.25*
367 A23 10r multicolored 4.00 *8.25*
368 A23 15r multicolored 4.50 *8.25*
369 A23 25r on 65c multi 5.50 *13.00*
Nos. 361-369 (9) 25.00 42.50

Washington's Inauguration — A41

American Bicentennial: 2c, Jefferson and map of Louisiana Purchase. 3c, Seward and map of Alaska Purchase. 4c, Pony Express, 1860. 5c, Lincoln's Emancipation Proclamation, 1863. 1.50r, Completion of Transcontinental Railroad, 1869. 3.50r, Wright Brothers' 1st flight, 1903. 5r, Ford assembly line, 1913. 10r, Kennedy and Apollo 11 moon landing, 1969. 25r, Declaration of Independence, 1776.

Perf. 14x13½

1976, Dec. 21 Wmk. 373

370 A41 1c rose & plum .20 .20
371 A41 2c lilac & vio .20 .20
372 A41 3c blue & vio bl .20 .20
373 A41 4c yellow & brn .20 .20
374 A41 5c brt yel & grn .20 .20
375 A41 1.50r yel brn & brn .35 .35
376 A41 3.50r brt grn & bl grn .80 .80
377 A41 5r yellow & brn 1.25 1.25
378 A41 10r dull bl & dk bl 2.50 2.50
Nos. 370-378 (9) 5.90 5.90

Souvenir Sheet

379 A41 25r lilac rose & pur 4.75 4.75

Seychelles Islands and Arms — A42

The Orb — A43

Designs: 40c, 5r, 10r, similar to 20c. 1r, St. Edward's Crown. 1.25r, Ampulla and Spoon. 1.50r, Scepter with Cross.

1977, Sept. 5 Litho. *Perf. 14*

380 A42 20c multicolored .20 .20
381 A42 40c multicolored .20 .20
382 A43 50c multicolored .20 .20
383 A43 1r multicolored .20 .20
384 A43 1.25r multicolored .20 .20
385 A43 1.50r multicolored .20 .20
386 A42 5r multicolored .40 .40
387 A42 10r multicolored .85 .85
a. Souv. sheet of 4, #380, 382, 383, 387 1.40 1.40
Nos. 380-387 (8) 2.45 2.45

25th anniv. of reign of Elizabeth II.

Coral Reef — A44

Perf. 14, 14x14½ (40c, 1, 1.25, 1.50r)

1977-91 Litho. Wmk. 373

Sizes: 40c, 1, 1.25, 1.50r, 30x25mm, Others 28x23mm

388 A44 5c Reef fish .20 .20
389 A44 10c Hawksbill turtle .20 .20
390 A44 15c Coco de mer .20 .20
391 A44 20c Wild vanilla .20 .20
392 A44 25c Butterfly .20 .20
393 A44 40c Coral reef .20 .20
394 A44 50c Giant tortoise .20 .20
a. Wmk. 384, perf. 14x14½ .30 .30
395 A44 75c Crayfish .20 .20
396 A44 1r Madagascar cardinal .30 .30
397 A44 1.25r Fairy tern .40 .40
398 A44 1.50r Flying fox .45 .45
398A A44 3r like #399, wmk. 384 1.75 1.75
399 A44 3.50r Green gecko 1.10 1.10

Perf. 13

Size: 27x35mm

400 A44 5r Octopus, vert. 1.60 1.60
401 A44 10r Tiger cowrie, vert. 3.25 3.25
402 A44 15r Pitcher plant, vert. 4.75 4.75
403 A44 20r Arms, vert. 6.50 6.50
Nos. 388-403 (17) 21.70 21.70

Issued: 40c, 1r, 1.25r, 1.50r, 10/31/77; #394a, 398A, 11/1991; others, 1978.

Reissued dated "1979" below design: 10, 15, 25, 40, 50, 75c, 1r, 1.50r. Dated "1981": 40c. Dated "1982": 40c.

For surcharge and overprint see #446, 605.

Denomination "R" Instead of "Re." or "Rs."

Perf. 14x14½, 14 (1.10r)

1981, Jan. 6 Litho.

Sizes: 1.10r, 28x23mm, Others, 30x25mm

403A A44 1r like No. 396 .30 .30
403B A44 1.10r like No. 399 .35 .35
403C A44 1.25r like No. 397 .40 .40
i. Wmk. 384 ('89) .45 .45
403D A44 1.50r like No. 398 .45 .45

Perf. 13

403E A44 5r like No. 400 1.60 1.60
j. Perf. 14x14½, Wmk 384 ('90) 2.00 2.00
403F A44 10r like No. 401 3.25 3.25
403G A44 15r like No. 402 4.75 4.75
403H A44 20r like No. 403 6.50 6.50
Nos. 403A-403H (8) 17.60 17.60

Reissued dated "1981" below design: 1.50r. Dated "1982": 1r, 1.50r. Dated "1985": 5r, Dated "1986": 1r, Dated "1990": 1r, Dated "1991": 1r, 1.50r.

See No. 576 for No. 403C with commemorative inscription.

Cruiser Aurora, Star and Flag — A45

1977, Nov. 7 Unwmk. *Perf. 12*

404 A45 1.50r red, black & gold .65 .65
a. Souvenir sheet 1.40 1.40

60th anniv. of Russian Oct. Revolution.

St. Roch Roman Catholic Church, Bel Ombre — A46

Christmas: 1r, Anglican Cathedral, Victoria. 1.50r, R. C. Cathedral, Victoria. 5r, St. Mark's Anglican Church, Praslin.

Perf. 13½x14

1977, Dec. 5 Wmk. 373

405 A46 20c multicolored .20 .20
406 A46 1r multicolored .20 .20
407 A46 1.50r multicolored .20 .20
408 A46 5r multicolored .50 .50
Nos. 405-408 (4) 1.10 1.10

Calendar Page, June 5, 1977 — A47

Edward VII, George V, George VI — A48

1.25r, Hands holding rifle, torch & Seychelles flag. 1.50r, Fisherman & farmer holding hands. 5r, Soldiers & waving children.

Perf. 14x13½

1978, June 5 Litho. Wmk. 373

409 A47 40c multicolored .20 .20
410 A47 1.25r multicolored .20 .20
411 A47 1.50r multicolored .20 .20
412 A47 5r multicolored .60 .60
Nos. 409-412 (4) 1.20 1.20

First anniversary of Liberation Day.

1978, Aug. 21 Litho. *Perf. 14*

Designs: 1.50r, Queens Victoria and Elizabeth II. 3r, Queen Victoria Monument, Seychelles. 5r, Queen's Building, Victoria, Seychelles.

413 A48 40c multicolored .20 .20
414 A48 1.50r multicolored .20 .20
415 A48 3r multicolored .25 .25
416 A48 5r multicolored .35 .35
a. Souvenir sheet of 4, #413-416 .95 .95
Nos. 413-416 (4) 1.00 1.00

25th anniv. of coronation of Elizabeth II.

Gardenia from Aride Island — A49

Designs (Coat of Arms and): 1.25r, Magpie robin of Fregate Island. 1.50r, Seychelles paradise flycatchers. 5r, Green turtle.

Perf. 13½x14

1978, Oct. 16 Litho. Wmk. 373

417 A49 40c multicolored .20 .20
418 A49 1.25r multicolored .45 .45
419 A49 1.50r multicolored .55 .55
420 A49 5r multicolored 2.25 2.25
Nos. 417-420 (4) 3.45 3.45

"Stone of Possession" — A50

1978, Dec. 15 Litho. Perf. 13½

421 A50 20c shown .20 .20
422 A50 1.25r Map, 1782 .20 .20
423 A50 1.50r Clock tower .20 .20
424 A50 5r Pierre Poivre .40 .40
Nos. 421-424 (4) 1.00 1.00

Bicentennary of the founding of Victoria.

Seychelles Fody — A51 Patrice Lumumba — A52

Birds: No. 426, Green-backed heron. No. 427, Seychelles bulbul. No. 428, Seychelles cave swiftlets. No. 429, Grayheaded lovebirds.

1979, Feb. 27 Litho. Perf. 14

425 A51 2r multicolored .80 .80
426 A51 2r multicolored .80 .80
427 A51 2r multicolored .80 .80
428 A51 2r multicolored .80 .80
429 A51 2r multicolored .80 .80
a. Strip of 5, #425-429 4.00 4.00
Nos. 425-429 (5) 4.00 4.00

1979, June 5 Litho. Perf. 14½

African Liberation Heroes: 2r, Kwame Nkrumah. 2.25r, Dr. Eduardo Mondlane. 5r, Amilcar Cabral.

430 A52 40c violet & blk .20 .20
431 A52 2r dark blue & blk .20 .20
432 A52 2.25r orange brn & blk .25 .25
433 A52 5r olive grn & blk .55 .55
Nos. 430-433 (4) 1.20 1.20

Coat of Arms, Rowland Hill, Seychelles No. 412 — A53

Coat of Arms, Hill, Seychelles stamps: 2.25r, No. 301. 3r, No. 205. 5r, No. 4.

1979, Aug. Litho. Perf. 14x14½

434 A53 40c multicolored .20 .20
435 A53 2.25r multicolored .40 .40
436 A53 3r multicolored .55 .55
Nos. 434-436 (3) 1.15 1.15

Souvenir Sheet

437 A53 5r multicolored 1.00 1.00

Sir Rowland Hill (1795-1879), originator of penny postage.

Schoolboy, IYC Emblem — A54

IYC Emblem and: 2.25r, Children. 3r, Boy with ball, vert. 5r, Girl with puppet, vert.

Perf. 14½x14, 14x14½

1979, Oct. 25 Litho.

438 A54 40c multicolored .20 .20
439 A54 2.25r multicolored .20 .20
440 A54 3r multicolored .25 .25
441 A54 5r multicolored .45 .45
Nos. 438-441 (4) 1.10 1.10

International Year of the Child.

Three Kings Bearing Gifts A55

Christmas (Stained Glass Windows): 20c, Angel, vert. 2.25r, Virgin and Child, vert. 5r, Flight into Egypt.

1979, Dec. 3 Litho. Perf. 14½

442 A55 20c multicolored .20 .20
443 A55 2.25r multicolored .35 .35
444 A55 3r multicolored .45 .45
Nos. 442-444 (3) 1.00 1.00

Souvenir Sheet

445 A55 5r multicolored .85 .85

No. 399 Surcharged

Wmk. 373

1979, Dec. 7 Litho. Perf. 14

446 A44 1.10r on 3.50r multicolored .35 .35

Seychelles Kestrel — A56

Seychelles Kestrel: a, shown. b, Pair. c, Female, eggs. d, Mother and chick. e, Chicks nesting.

1980, Feb. 29 Litho. Perf. 14

447 Strip of 5 4.75 4.75
a.-e. A56 2r any single .95 .95

See Nos. 468, 483.

50-Rupee Bank Note, London 1980 Emblem — A57

Sprinting, Moscow '80 Emblem — A58

New Currency: 40c, 1.50r, horiz.

1980, Apr. 18 Litho. Perf. 14

448 A57 40c multicolored .20 .20
449 A57 1.50r multicolored .30 .30
450 A57 2.25r multicolored .45 .45
451 A57 5r multicolored .90 .90
a. Souvenir sheet of 4, #448-451 1.90 1.90
Nos. 448-451 (4) 1.85 1.85

London 1980 Intl. Stamp Exhib., May 6-14.

1980, June 13 Perf. 14½

452 A58 40c shown .20 .20
453 A58 2.25r Weight lifting .25 .25
454 A58 3r Boxing .35 .35
455 A58 5r Yachting 1.10 1.10
a. Souvenir sheet of 4, #452-455 2.25 2.25
Nos. 452-455 (4) 1.90 1.90

22nd Summer Olympic Games, Moscow, July 19-Aug. 3.

Boeing 747 A59

1980, Aug. 22 Litho. Perf. 14

456 A59 40c shown .20 .20
457 A59 2.25r Tour bus .35 .35
458 A59 3r Ocean liner, pirogue .50 .50
459 A59 5r Tour motor boat .85 .85
Nos. 456-459 (4) 1.90 1.90

World Tourism Conf., Manila, Sept. 27.

Female Coco-de-Mer Palm Tree — A60

1980, Oct. 31 Litho. Perf. 14

460 A60 40c shown .20 .20
461 A60 2.25r Male tree .40 .40
462 A60 3r Bowls .55 .55
463 A60 5r Gourds, canoes .90 .90
a. Souvenir sheet of 4, #460-463 2.75 2.75
Nos. 460-463 (4) 2.05 2.05

Vasco da Gama's San Gabriel, 1497 A61

Wmk. 373

1981, Feb. Litho. Perf. 14½

464 A61 40c shown .20 .20
465 A61 2.25r Mascarenhas' Caravel, 1505 .60 .60
466 A61 3.50r Darwin's Beagle, 1831 .95 .95
467 A61 5r Queen Elizabeth 2, 1968 1.25 1.25
a. Souvenir sheet of 4, #464-467 3.00 3.00
Nos. 464-467 (4) 3.00 3.00

Bird Type of 1980

1981, Apr. 10 Litho. Perf. 14

468 Strip of 5, multi 4.50 4.50
a. A56 2r Male fairy tern .90 .90
b. A56 2r Pair .90 .90
c. A56 2r Female .90 .90
d. A56 2r Female, diff. .90 .90
e. A56 2r Adult bird, chick .90 .90

Prince Charles, Lady Diana, Royal Yacht Charlotte A61a

Prince Charles and Lady Diana — A61b

Illustration A61b is reduced.

Wmk. 380

1981, June 23 Litho. Perf. 14

469 A61a 1.50r Couple, Victoria & Albert I .30 .30
a. Bklt. pane of 4, perf. 12 1.00
470 A61b 1.50r Couple .30 .30
471 A61a 5r Cleveland 1.00 1.00
472 A61b 5r like #470 1.00 1.00
a. Bklt. pane of 2, perf. 12 1.60
473 A61a 10r Britannia 2.10 2.10
474 A61b 10r like #470 2.10 2.10
Nos. 469-474 (6) 6.80 6.80

Each denomination issued in sheets of 7 (6 type A61a, 1 type A61b).

For surcharges see Nos. 528-533.

Souvenir Sheet

1981 Litho. Perf. 12

474A A61b 7.50r Couple 2.10 2.10

Seychelles Intl. Airport, 10th Anniv. — A62

Wmk. 373

1981, July 27 Litho. Perf. 14½

475 A62 40c Britten-Norman Islander .20 .20
476 A62 2.25r Britten-Norman Trislander .55 .55
477 A62 3.50r Vickers VC-10 .80 .80
478 A62 5r Boeing 747 1.10 1.10
Nos. 475-478 (4) 2.65 2.65

A63 A65

Designs: Various flying foxes.

1981, Oct. 9 Litho. Perf. 14

479 A63 40c multicolored .20 .20
480 A63 2.25r multicolored .55 .55
481 A63 3r multicolored .70 .70
482 A63 5r multicolored 1.25 1.25
a. Souvenir sheet, #479-482 3.50 3.50
Nos. 479-482 (4) 2.70 2.70

Bird Type of 1980

a, Male Chinese bittern. b, Female. c, Hen on nest. d, Nest, eggs. e, Hen, chicks.

Wmk. 373

1982, Feb. 4 Litho. Perf. 14

483 Strip of 5 10.00 10.00
a.-e. A56 3r any single 2.00 2.00

1982, Apr. 22 Litho. Perf. 14½

487 A65 40c Map of Silhouette Island and La Digue .20 .20

488 A65 1.50r Denis & Bird Islds. .30 .30
489 A65 2.75r Curieuse Isld., Praslin .60 .60
490 A65 7r Mahe 1.40 1.40
a. Souvenir sheet of 4, #487-490 3.75 3.75
Nos. 487-490 (4) 2.50 2.50

5th Anniv. of Liberation A66

1982, June 5 ***Perf. 14***

491 A66 40c Bookmobile .20 .20
492 A66 1.75r Mobile dental clinic .30 .30
493 A66 2.75r Farming .50 .50
494 A66 7r Construction site 1.40 1.40
a. Souvenir sheet of 4, #491-494 4.25 4.25
Nos. 491-494 (4) 2.40 2.40

Tourist Board Emblem A67

Tourism: Hotels.

1982, Sept. 1

495 A67 1.75r Northolme .40 .40
496 A67 1.75r Reef .40 .40
497 A67 1.75r Barbarons Beach .40 .40
498 A67 1.75r Coral Strand .40 .40
499 A67 1.75r Beau Vallon Bay .40 .40
500 A67 1.75r Fisherman's Cove .40 .40
501 A67 1.75r Mahe Beach, shown .40 .40
502 A67 1.75r Island scene .40 .40
Nos. 495-502 (8) 3.20 3.20

Tata Bus A68

Wmk. 373

1982, Nov. 18 Litho. *Perf. 14*

503 A68 20c shown .20 .20
504 A68 1.75r Mini moke .35 .35
505 A68 2.75r Ox cart .55 .55
506 A68 7r Truck 1.40 1.40
Nos. 503-506 (4) 2.50 2.50

World Communications Year — A69

1983, Feb. 25

507 A69 40c Radio control room .20 .20
508 A69 2.75r Satellite earth station .60 .60
509 A69 3.50r TV control room .70 .70
510 A69 5r Postal services 1.00 1.00
Nos. 507-510 (4) 2.50 2.50

Commonwealth Day — A70

1983, Mar. 14

511 A70 40c Agricultural research .20 .20
512 A70 2.75r Food processing plant .45 .45
513 A70 3.50r Fishing industry .60 .60
514 A70 7r Flag 1.25 1.25
Nos. 511-514 (4) 2.50 2.50

Denis Isld. Lighthouse, 1910 — A71

1983, July 14 ***Perf. 14x13½***

515 A71 40c shown .20 .20
516 A71 2.75r Seychelles Hospital, 1924 .35 .35
517 A71 3.50r Supreme Court, 1894 .50 .50
518 A71 7r State House, 1911 .95 .95
a. Souvenir sheet of 4, #515-518 4.50 4.50
Nos. 515-518 (4) 2.00 2.00

Manned Flight Bicentenary — A72

1983, Sept. 15 ***Perf. 14***

519 A72 40c Royal Vauxhall balloon, 1836 .20 .20
520 A72 1.75r DeHavilland D.H.-50j .50 .50
521 A72 2.75r Grumman Albatross .75 .75
522 A72 7r Sweavingen Merlin 1.90 1.90
Nos. 519-522 (4) 3.35 3.35

First Intl. Air Seychelles Flight — A73

1983, Oct. 26 **Litho.**

523 A73 2r DC10 aircraft .65 .65

Paintings, Marianne North — A74

1983, Nov. 17 Litho. *Perf. 14*

524 A74 40c Swamp Plant and Moorhen .20 .20
525 A74 1.75r Wormia flagellaria .50 .50
526 A74 2.75r Asiatic Pancratium .80 .80
527 A74 7r Pitcher Plant 2.00 2.00
a. Souvenir sheet of 4, #524-527 4.50 4.50
Nos. 524-527 (4) 3.50 3.50

Nos. 469-474 Surcharged

Wmk. 380

1983, Dec. 28 Litho. *Perf. 14*

528 A61a 50c on 1.50r multi .20 .20
529 A61b 50c on 1.50r multi .20 .20
530 A61a 2.25r on 5r multi .75 .75
531 A61b 2.25r on 5r multi .75 .75
532 A61a 3.75r on 10r multi 1.25 1.25
533 A61b 3.75r on 10r multi 1.25 1.25
Nos. 528-533 (6) 4.40 4.40

Handicrafts — A75

Wmk. 373

1984, Feb. 29 Litho. *Perf. 14*

534 A75 50c Coconut kettle .20 .20
535 A75 2r Scarf, doll .60 .60
536 A75 3r Coconut-fiber roses .90 .90
537 A75 10r Carved fishing boat, doll 2.75 2.75
Nos. 534-537 (4) 4.45 4.45

Lloyd's List Issue

Common Design Type

1984, May 21 Litho. *Perf. 14½x14*

538 CD335 50c Port Victoria .20 .20
539 CD335 2r Steamship, 1930s .60 .60
540 CD335 3r Cruise liner .90 .90
541 CD335 10r Ennerdale 2.75 2.75
Nos. 538-541 (4) 4.45 4.45

People's United Party, 20th Anniv. A76

1984, June 2 Litho. *Perf. 14*

542 A76 50c Original headquarters .20 .20
543 A76 2r Liberation statue, vert. .60 .60
544 A76 3r New headquarters .90 .90
545 A76 10r Pres. Rene, vert. 2.75 2.75
Nos. 542-545 (4) 4.45 4.45

Souvenir Sheet

UPU Congress — A77

1984, June 18 ***Perf. 14½***

546 A77 5r No. 156 1.50 1.50

1984 Summer Olympics A78

1984, July 28 ***Perf. 14***

547 A78 50c Long jump .20 .20
548 A78 2r Boxing .55 .55
549 A78 3r Diving .80 .80
550 A78 10r Weight lifting 2.75 2.75
a. Souvenir sheet of 4, #547-550 4.25 4.25
Nos. 547-550 (4) 4.30 4.30

Scuba Diving A79

1984, Sept. 24

551 A79 50c shown .20 .20
552 A79 2r Paragliding .70 .70
553 A79 3r Sailing 1.00 1.00
554 A79 10r Water skiing 3.25 3.25
Nos. 551-554 (4) 5.15 5.15

Whale Conservation — A80

1984, Nov. **Litho.**

555 A80 50c Humpback whale .25 .25
556 A80 2r Sperm whale 1.00 1.00
557 A80 3r Right whale 1.50 1.50
558 A80 10r Blue whale 5.25 5.25
Nos. 555-558 (4) 8.00 8.00

Audubon Birth Bicent. — A81

EXPO '85, Tsukuba — A82

Bare-legged scops owls.

1985, Mar. 11 Litho. *Perf. 14*

559 A81 50c multicolored .20 .20
560 A81 2r multicolored .70 .70
561 A81 3r multicolored 1.00 1.00
562 A81 10r multicolored 3.50 3.50
Nos. 559-562 (4) 5.40 5.40

Wmk. 373

1985, Mar. 15 Litho. *Perf. 14*

563 A82 50c Giant tortoise .20 .20
564 A82 2r Fairy tern .60 .60
565 A82 3r Wind surfing .80 .80
566 A82 5r Coco de mer 1.40 1.40
a. Souvenir sheet of 4, #563-566 3.00 3.00
Nos. 563-566 (4) 3.00 3.00

See No. 604.

Queen Mother 85th Birthday

Common Design Type

Perf. 14½x14

1985, June 7 Litho. Wmk. 384

567 CD336 50c Queen Elizabeth, 1930 .20 .20
568 CD336 2r With grandchildren, 1970 .60 .60
569 CD336 3r 75th birthday celebration .90 .90
570 CD336 5r Holding Prince Henry 1.50 1.50
Nos. 567-570 (4) 3.20 3.20

Souvenir Sheet

571 CD336 10r Exiting from helicopter 3.00 3.00

2nd Indian Ocean Islands Games A83

1985, Aug. 24

572 A83 50c Boxing .20 .20
573 A83 2r Soccer .55 .55
574 A83 3r Swimming .80 .80
575 A83 10r Wind surfing 2.75 2.75
Nos. 572-575 (4) 4.30 4.30

A83a

A84

1985, Nov. 1 **Wmk. 384**
576 A83a 1.25r Fairy tern .35 .35

Air Seychelles 1st Airbus.

1985, Nov. 28
577 A84 50c Agriculture .20 .20
578 A84 2r Construction .55 .55
579 A84 3r Carpentry .80 .80
580 A84 10r Science education 2.75 2.75
Nos. 577-580 (4) 4.30 4.30

Intl. Youth Year.

Vintage Cars A85

1985, Dec. 18
581 A85 50c 1919 Ford Model T .20 .20
582 A85 2r 1922 Austin Seven .60 .60
583 A85 3r 1924 Morris Bull-nose Oxford .85 .85
584 A85 10r 1929 Humber Cou-pe 3.00 3.00
Nos. 581-584 (4) 4.65 4.65

Halley's Comet — A86

1986, Feb. **Wmk. 384** ***Perf. 14x14½***
585 A86 50c Transit instrument .20 .20
586 A86 2r Quadrant .60 .60
587 A86 3r Trajectory diagram .85 .85
588 A86 10r Edmond Halley 3.00 3.00
Nos. 585-588 (4) 4.65 4.65

Giselle, Performed by the Ballet Louvre, Apr. 4-8 — A87

Wmk. 384

1986, Apr. 4 **Litho.** ***Perf. 14***
589 A87 2r Heroine .60 .60
590 A87 3r Hero .90 .90

Souvenir Sheet

591 A87 10r United 3.00 3.00

First ballet performed in the Seychelles.

Queen Elizabeth II 60th Birthday
Common Design Type

Designs: 50c, Marrying the Duke of Edinburgh, 1947. 1.25r, Silver Jubilee celebration. 2r, Greeting child aboard the Britannia, Qatar Harbor. 3r, State opening of Parliament, 1982. 5r, Visiting Crown Agents' offices, 1983.

1986, Apr. 21 ***Perf. 14½***
592 CD337 50c scarlet, blk & sil .20 .20
593 CD337 1.25r ultra & multi .40 .40
594 CD337 2r green & multi .60 .60
595 CD337 3r violet & multi .90 .90
596 CD337 5r rose vio & multi 1.50 1.50
Nos. 592-596 (5) 3.60 3.60

For overprints see Nos. 625-629.

AMERIPEX '86, Inter-island Communications — A88

Wmk. 384

1986, May 22 **Litho.** ***Perf. 14***
597 A88 50c La Digue Ferry .20 .20
598 A88 2r Phone booth, vert. .60 .60
599 A88 3r Victoria P.O., vert. .95 .95
600 A88 7r Air Seychelles tris-lander 2.25 2.25
Nos. 597-600 (4) 4.00 4.00

Coptic Catholic Knights of Malta Celebration Day — A89

Perf. 14½x14

1986, June 7 **Litho.** **Wmk. 384**
601 A89 5r Natl. arms, assoc. emblem 1.50 1.50
a. Souvenir sheet of 1 1.65 1.65

Royal Wedding Issue, 1986
Common Design Type

2r, Informal portrait. 10r, Andrew, helicopter.

1986, July 23 **Litho.** ***Perf. 14***
602 CD338 2r multicolored .60 .60
603 CD338 10r multicolored 3.00 3.00

Tsukuba Expo Type of 1985
Souvenir Sheet

Wmk. 384

1986, July 12 **Litho.** ***Perf. 14***
604 Sheet of 4 3.00 3.00
a. A82 50c multicolored .20 .20
b. A82 2r multicolored .55 .55
c. A82 3r multicolored .80 .80
d. A82 5r multicolored 1.40 1.40

No. 604 inscribed "Seychelles Philatelic Exhibition-Tokyo-1986" and printed without EXPO '85 emblem on margin or on individual stamps. Nos. 604a-604d inscribed "1986."

No. 396 Overprinted

Perf. 14½x14

1986, Oct. 28 **Wmk. 373**
605 A44 1r multicolored .30 .30

Intl. Creole Day.

State Visit of Pope John Paul II — A90

Pope and: 50c, Seychelles Airport. 2r, Cathedral. 3r, Baie Lazare parish church. 10r, People's Stadium.

1986, Dec. 1 **Wmk. 384** ***Perf. 14½***
606 A90 50c multicolored .20 .20
607 A90 2r multicolored .70 .70
608 A90 3r multicolored 1.00 1.00
609 A90 10r multicolored 3.25 3.25
a. Souvenir sheet of 4, #606-609 5.00 5.00
Nos. 606-609 (4) 5.15 5.15

Butterflies — A91

Wmk. 384

1987, Feb. 18 **Litho.** ***Perf. 14½***
610 A91 1r Melanitis leda .40 .40
611 A91 2r Phalanta philiberti .75 .75
612 A91 3r Danaus chrysippus 1.10 1.10
613 A91 10r Euploea mitra 3.50 3.50
Nos. 610-613 (4) 5.75 5.75

Seashells — A92

Liberation, 10th Anniv. — A93

1987, May 7 **Wmk. 373**
614 A92 1r Gloripallium pallium .40 .40
615 A92 2r Spondylus aurantius .75 .75
616 A92 3r Harpa ventricosa, Lioconcha ornata 1.10 1.10
617 A92 10r Strombus lentigi-nosus 3.50 3.50
Nos. 614-617 (4) 5.75 5.75

Perf. 14x14½, 14½x14

1987, June 5 **Wmk. 384**
618 A93 1r Liberation monu-ment .30 .30
619 A93 2r Hospital, horiz. .60 .60
620 A93 3r Orphanage, horiz. .90 .90
621 A93 10r Fish monument 3.00 3.00
Nos. 618-621 (4) 4.80 4.80

Natl. Banking Cent. — A94

1987, June 25 ***Perf. 14½x14***
622 A94 1r Savings Bank, Pras-lin .30 .30
623 A94 2r Development Bank .60 .60
624 A94 10r Central Bank 3.00 3.00
Nos. 622-624 (3) 3.90 3.90

Nos. 592-596 Ovptd. in Silver

Wmk. 384

1987, Dec. 9 **Litho.** ***Perf. 14½***
625 CD337 50c scar, blk & sil .20 .20
626 CD337 1.25r ultra & multi .40 .40
627 CD337 2r green & multi .70 .70
628 CD337 3r violet & multi 1.00 1.00
629 CD337 5r rose vio & multi 1.75 1.75
Nos. 625-629 (5) 4.05 4.05

Fishing Industry A95

Wmk. 384

1987, Dec. 11 **Litho.** ***Perf. 14***
630 A95 50c Tuna cannery .20 .20
631 A95 2r Fishing trawler .65 .65
632 A95 3r Weighing fish 1.00 1.00
633 A95 10r Hauling catch from net 3.50 3.50
Nos. 630-633 (4) 5.35 5.35

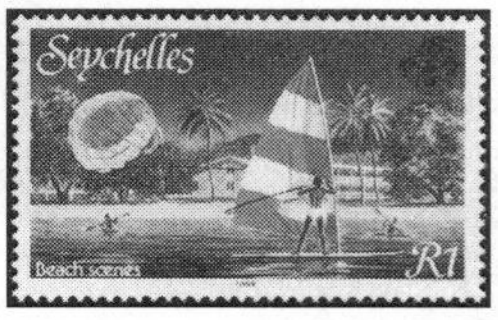

Beach Scenes A96

Wmk. 384

1988, Feb. 9 **Litho.** ***Perf. 14½***
634 A96 1r Para-sailing, wind-surfing, kayaks .30 .30
635 A96 2r Boating .65 .65
636 A96 3r Yacht at anchor .95 .95
637 A96 10r Hotel, cabanas 3.00 3.00
Nos. 634-637 (4) 4.90 4.90

Green Turtles — A97

A98

No. 638, Newly hatched turtles headed toward ocean. No. 639, Offspring hatching. No. 640, Female emerging from ocean. No. 641, Female laying eggs in sand. Stamps of same denomination printed se-tenant in a continuous design.

1988, Apr. 22 **Wmk. 373**
638 A97 2r multicolored .75 .75
639 A97 2r multicolored .75 .75
640 A97 3r multicolored 1.10 1.10
641 A97 3r multicolored 1.10 1.10
Nos. 638-641 (4) 3.70 3.70

1988, July 29 **Wmk. 384** ***Perf. 14½***

Designs: 1r, No. 647a, Shot put. Nos. 643, 647b, High jump. 3r, No. 647c, Medal winner, grandstand and flags. 4r, No. 647d, Running. 5r, No. 647e, Javelin. 10r, Tennis.

642 A98 1r multicolored .30 .30
643 A98 2r multicolored .60 .60
644 A98 3r multicolored .90 .90
645 A98 4r multicolored 1.25 1.25
646 A98 5r multicolored 1.40 1.40
647 Strip of 5 3.00 3.00
a.-e. A98 2r any single .60 .60
Nos. 642-647 (6) 7.45 7.45

Souvenir Sheet
Wmk. 373

648 A98 10r multicolored 3.75 3.75

No. 647 has a continuous design.
1988 Summer Olympics, Seoul, (1r-5r). Intl. Tennis Fed., 75th anniv. (10r). No. 648 contains one stamp, size: 28x39mm.

Lloyds of London, 300th Anniv.
Common Design Type

Designs: 1r, Leadenhall Street, London, 1928. 2r, Cinq Juin, horiz. 3r, Queen Elizabeth II, horiz. 10r, Explosion of the Hindenburg, Lakehurst, New Jersey, 1937.

Wmk. 384
1988, Sept. 30 Litho. *Perf. 14*

649 CD341 1r multicolored .40 .40
650 CD341 2r multicolored .70 .70
651 CD341 3r multicolored 1.00 1.00
652 CD341 10r multicolored 3.50 3.50
Nos. 649-652 (4) 5.60 5.60

Defense Forces Day, 1st Anniv. A99

1988, Nov. 25 Litho. Wmk. 373

653 A99 1r Motorcycle police .40 .40
654 A99 2r Air force helicopter .70 .70
655 A99 3r Navy patrol boat 1.00 1.00
656 A99 10r Tank 3.50 3.50
Nos. 653-656 (4) 5.60 5.60

Christmas A100

Illustrations by local artists.

1988, Dec. 1 Litho. Wmk. 373

657 A100 50c Selwyn Hoareau .20 .20
658 A100 2r Robin Leste .70 .70
659 A100 3r France Anacoura 1.10 1.10
660 A100 10r Andre McGaw 3.75 3.75
Nos. 657-660 (4) 5.75 5.75

Orchids A101

Wmk. 384
1988, Dec. 21 Litho. *Perf. 14*

661 A101 1r Dendrobium, vert. .40 .40
662 A101 2r Arachnis hybrid .75 .75
663 A101 3r Vanda caerulea, vert. 1.10 1.10
664 A101 10r Dendrobium phalaenopsis 3.75 3.75
Nos. 661-664 (4) 6.00 6.00

Jawaharlal Nehru (1889-1964), 1st Prime Minister of Independent India A102

1989, Mar. 30 *Perf. 13½*

665 A102 2r India Type A409 .75 .75
666 A102 10r Portrait 3.75 3.75

People's United Party (SPUP), 25th Anniv. — A103

1989, June 5 *Perf. 14*

667 A103 1r Rally, old office .40 .40
668 A103 2r Maison Du Peuple .75 .75
669 A103 3r Pres. Rene, banner, torch 1.10 1.10
670 A103 10r Torch, flag, Rene 3.75 3.75
Nos. 667-670 (4) 6.00 6.00

Moon Landing, 20th Anniv.
Common Design Type

Apollo 15: 1r, Saturn 5 lift-off. 2r, David R. Scott, Alfred M. Worden and James B. Irwin. 3r, Mission emblem. 5r, Irwin salutes flag in front of the Hadley Delta. 10r, Buzz Aldrin about to step onto the Moon, Apollo 11 mission.

1989, July 20
Size of Nos. 677-678: 29x29mm

676 CD342 1r multicolored .35 .35
677 CD342 2r multicolored .70 .70
678 CD342 3r multicolored 1.10 1.10
679 CD342 5r multicolored 1.75 1.75
Nos. 676-679 (4) 3.90 3.90

Souvenir Sheet

680 CD342 10r multicolored 3.65 3.65

Intl. Red Cross and Red Crescent Organizations, 125th Annivs. — A104

1989, Sept. 12 *Perf. 14½*

681 A104 1r Ambulance, 1870 .40 .40
682 A104 2r H.M. Hospital Ship Liberty, 1914-18 .80 .80
683 A104 3r Sunbeam Standard Army Ambulance, 1914-18 1.25 1.25
684 A104 10r The White Train, 1899-1902 4.00 4.00
Nos. 681-684 (4) 6.45 6.45

Island Birds — A105

1989, Oct. 16 *Perf. 14½x14*

685 A105 50c Black parrot .25 .25
686 A105 2r Sooty tern .85 .85
687 A105 3r Magpie robin 1.40 1.40
688 A105 5r Roseate tern 2.25 2.25
a. Souvenir sheet of 4, #685-688 4.75 4.75
Nos. 685-688 (4) 4.75 4.75

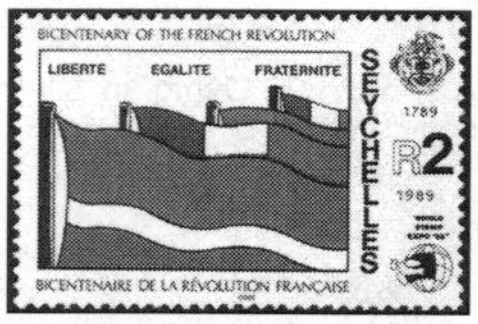

French Revolution Bicent., World Stamp Expo '89 — A106

1989, Nov. 17 *Perf. 14*

689 A106 2r Flags .70 .70
690 A106 5r Storming of the Bastille 1.75 1.75

Souvenir Sheet

691 A106 10r Raising French flag, Seychelles, 1791 3.50 3.50

African Development Bank, 25th Anniv. — A107

Orchids — A108

1r, Beau Vallon School, horiz. 2r, Fishing Authority headquarters, horiz. 3r, Variola. 10r, Deneb.

1989, Dec. 29 Wmk. 384

692 A107 1r multicolored .35 .35
693 A107 2r multicolored .70 .70
694 A107 3r multicolored 1.00 1.00
695 A107 10r multicolored 3.50 3.50
Nos. 692-695 (4) 5.55 5.55

1990, Jan. 26

696 A108 1r Disperis tripetaloides .35 .35
697 A108 2r Vanilla phalaenopsis .70 .70
698 A108 3r Angraecum eburneum superbum 1.00 1.00
699 A108 10r Polystachya concreta 3.50 3.50
Nos. 696-699 (4) 5.55 5.55

Expo '90 (International Garden & Greenery Exposition), Japan — A109

Designs: 2r, Fumiyo Sako. 3r, Coco-de-mer, male and female plants. 5r, Pitcher plant, Aldabra lily. 7r, Gardenia, Arms of Seychelles.

1990, June 8 Litho. Wmk. 373

700 A109 2r multicolored .75 .75
701 A109 3r multicolored 1.00 1.00
702 A109 5r multicolored 1.75 1.75
703 A109 7r multicolored 2.50 2.50
a. Souvenir sheet of 4, #700-703 6.00 6.00
Nos. 700-703 (4) 6.00 6.00

Penny Black 150th Anniv., Stamp World London '90 A110

Exhibition emblem and stamps on stamps: 1r, Seychelles #38, Great Britain #80 canceled. 2r, Seychelles #81, Great Britain #64 canceled. 3r, Seychelles #74, Great Britain #62 canceled. 5r, Seychelles #2, Great Britain #3 canceled. 10r, Seychelles #197, Great Britain #1 canceled.

1990, May 3 *Perf. 12½*

704 A110 1r multicolored .35 .35
705 A110 2r multicolored .70 .70
706 A110 3r multicolored 1.00 1.00
707 A110 5r multicolored 1.75 1.75
Nos. 704-707 (4) 3.80 3.80

Souvenir Sheet

708 A110 10r multicolored 3.50 3.50

Boeing 767-200ER A111

Perf. 14½x14½
1990, July 27 Litho. Wmk. 384

709 A111 3r multicolored 1.00 1.00

Printed in panes of 10 (2 strips of 5 separated by pictorial gutter).

Queen Mother, 90th Birthday
Common Design Types

1990, Aug. 4 Wmk. 384 *Perf. 14x15*

710 CD343 2r Queen Elizabeth in coronation robes, 1937 .70 .70

Perf. 14½

711 CD344 10r Visiting workshops, 1947 3.50 3.50

A112

A113

1990, Sept. 8 Wmk. 373 *Perf. 14*

712 A112 1r Blackboard .35 .35
713 A112 2r Reading mail .70 .70
714 A112 3r Reading directions 1.10 1.10
715 A112 10r Crossword puzzle 3.50 3.50
Nos. 712-715 (4) 5.65 5.65

Intl. Literacy Year.

1990, Oct. 27 *Perf. 13½x14*

Various Sega Dancers: a, Pink and white skirt, white blouse. b, Yellow dress. c, Blue, sky blue and pink dress. d, Yellow, green and pink dress. e, White and pink skirt, green blouse.

716 Strip of 5 3.50 3.50
a.-e. A113 2r any single .70 .70

Festival Kreol 1990.

First Regional Seminar, Indian Ocean Petroleum Exploration A114

1990, Dec. 10 Wmk. 384 *Perf. 14½*

717 A114 3r Beach 1.10 1.10
718 A114 10r Geological map 3.75 3.75

Orchids — A115

1991, Feb. 1 *Perf. 14*

719 A115 1r Bulbophyllum intertextum .35 .35
720 A115 2r Agrostophyllum occidentale .70 .70
721 A115 3r Vanilla planifolia 1.10 1.10
722 A115 10r Malaxis seychellarum 3.50 3.50
Nos. 719-722 (4) 5.65 5.65

Elizabeth & Philip, Birthdays
Common Design Types

1991, June 17 *Perf. 14½*

723 CD345 4r multicolored 1.50 1.50
724 CD346 4r multicolored 1.50 1.50
a. Pair, #723-724 + label 3.00 3.00

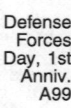

Butterflies A116

Perf. 14½x14

1991, Nov. 15 Litho. Wmk. 373

725	A116	1.50r Precis rhadama	.60	.60
726	A116	3r Lampides boeticus	1.10	1.10
727	A116	3.50r Zizeeria knysna	1.40	1.40
728	A116	10r Phalanta phalanta aethiopica	4.00	4.00
		Nos. 725-728 (4)	7.10	7.10

Souvenir Sheet

729	A116	10r Eagris sabadius	4.00	4.00

Phila Nippon '91.

Christmas A117

Woodcuts: 50c, The Holy Virgin, Joseph, the Holy Child and St. John by Raphael, engraved by S. Vouillemont. 1r, The Holy Virgin, the Child and an Angel by Van Dyck, engraved by A. Blooting. 2r, The Holy Family, St. John and St. Anna by Rubens, engraved by Lucas Vorsterman. 7r, The Holy Family, an Angel and St. Catherine, painting and engraving by Cornelius Bloemaert.

1991, Dec. 2 Wmk. 384 *Perf. 14*

730	A117	50c multicolored	.20	.20
731	A117	1r multicolored	.40	.40
732	A117	2r multicolored	.80	.80
733	A117	7r multicolored	2.75	2.75
		Nos. 730-733 (4)	4.15	4.15

Queen Elizabeth II's Accession to the Throne, 40th Anniv.

Common Design Type

1992, Feb. 6 Wmk. 373

734	CD349	1r multicolored	.40	.40
735	CD349	1.50r multicolored	.55	.55
736	CD349	3r multicolored	1.10	1.10
737	CD349	3.50r multicolored	1.25	1.25
738	CD349	5r multicolored	1.90	1.90
		Nos. 734-738 (5)	5.20	5.20

Flora and Fauna A118

Designs: 10c, Brush warbler. 25c, Bronze gecko, vert. 50c, Seychelles tree frog. 1r, Seychelles splendid palm, vert. 1.50r, Seychelles skink, vert. 2r, Giant tenebrionid beetle. 3r, Seychelles sunbird. 3.50r, Seychelles killifish. 4r, Magpie robin. 5r, Seychelles vanilla, vert. 10r, Tiger chameleon. 15r, Coco-de-mer, vert. 25r, Paradise flycatcher, vert. 50r, Giant tortoise.

Wmk. 373

1993, Mar. 1 Litho. *Perf. 13½*

739	A118	10c multicolored	.20	.20
740	A118	25c multicolored	.20	.20
741	A118	50c multicolored	.20	.20
742	A118	1r multicolored	.35	.35
743	A118	1.50r multicolored	.55	.55
744	A118	2r multicolored	.80	.80
745	A118	3r multicolored	1.10	1.10
746	A118	3.50r multicolored	1.40	1.40
747	A118	4r multicolored	1.50	1.50
748	A118	5r multicolored	1.90	1.90
749	A118	10r multicolored	3.75	3.75
750	A118	15r multicolored	5.75	5.75
751	A118	25r multicolored	9.50	9.50
752	A118	50r multicolored	18.00	18.00
		Nos. 739-752 (14)	45.20	45.20

#742, 748-749, 751-752 exist inscribed "1994;" #739-741, 744, 750 "1996;" #745, "1998;" #739, 741-743, 745-46 "2000."

First Visit to Seychelles by Archbishop of Canterbury — A119

Archbishop and: 3r, Anglican Cathedral, Victoria. 10r, Air France, Air Seychelles airplanes.

1993, June 8 *Perf. 13½*

753	A119	3r multicolored	1.10	1.10
754	A119	10r multicolored	3.75	3.75

4th Indian Ocean Island Games — A120

1993, Aug. 21 *Perf. 14½*

755	A120	1.50r Running	.60	.60
756	A120	3r Soccer	1.10	1.10
757	A120	3.50r Cycling	1.40	1.40
758	A120	10r Sailing	3.75	3.75
		Nos. 755-758 (4)	6.85	6.85

Telecommunications, Cent. — A121

Designs: 1r, Cable ship Scotia, Victoria, 1893. 3r, Eastern Telegraph Company's Office, Victoria, 1904. 4r, HF Transmitting Station, operational 1971. 10r, New Telecoms House, Victoria, 1993.

1993, Nov. 12 *Perf. 13*

759	A121	1r multicolored	.40	.40
760	A121	3r multicolored	1.25	1.25
761	A121	4r multicolored	1.60	1.60
762	A121	10r multicolored	4.00	4.00
		Nos. 759-762 (4)	7.25	7.25

Zil Elwannyen Sesel Nos. 59, 61, 63, 64 Surcharged

1994, Feb. 18 *Perf. 14x14½*

763	A9	1r on 2.10r #59	.40	.40
764	A9	1.50r on 2.75r #61	.55	.55
765	A9	3.50r on 7r #63	1.40	1.40
766	A9	10r on 15r #64	3.75	3.75
		Nos. 763-766 (4)	6.10	6.10

Hong Kong '94. Size and location of surcharge varies.

Butterflies A122

1994, Aug. 16 Wmk. 384 *Perf. 14*

767	A122	1.50r Eurema floricola	.60	.60
768	A122	3r Coeliades forestan	1.25	1.25
769	A122	3.50r Borbo borbonica	1.40	1.40
770	A122	10r Zizula hylax	4.00	4.00
		Nos. 767-770 (4)	7.25	7.25

A123

A124

1995, Sept. 26 Wmk. 373

771	A123	1.50r Age 9	.65	.65
772	A123	3r Wedding day	1.25	1.25
773	A123	3.50r 1936 Portrait	1.50	1.50
774	A123	10r 1975 Photograph	4.25	4.25
		Nos. 771-774 (4)	7.65	7.65

Queen Mother, 95th birthday.

Wmk. 384

1996, July 12 Litho. *Perf. 14*

Black Paradise Flycatcher.

775	A124	1r Female on branch	.40	.40
776	A124	1r Male in flight	.40	.40
777	A124	1r Male on branch	.40	.40
778	A124	1r Female, young	.40	.40
a.		Strip of 4, #775-778	1.60	1.60

Souvenir Sheet

779	A124	10r Female, male birds	4.00	4.00

World Wildlife Fund.

Stamps in No. 778a may be out of Scott number sequence.

A125

A126

1996, July 15

780	A125	50c Swimming	.20	.20
781	A125	1.50r Running	.55	.55
782	A125	3r Sailing	1.25	1.25
783	A125	5r Boxing	2.00	2.00
		Nos. 780-783 (4)	4.00	4.00

Modern Olympic Games, cent.

Wmk. 373

1996, Aug. 19 Litho. *Perf. 14*

784	A126	3r shown	1.25	1.25
785	A126	10r Portrait up close	4.00	4.00

Archbishop Makarios of Cyprus, Exiled in Seychelles, 40th anniv.

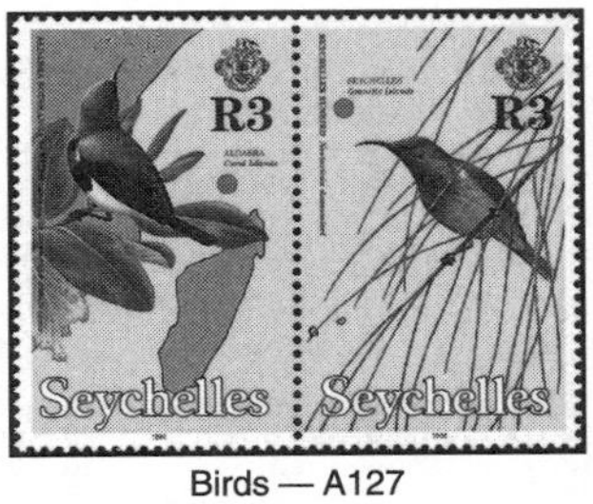
Birds — A127

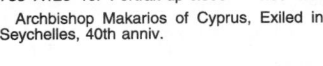

#786, Aldabra souimanga sunbird. #787, Seychelles sunbird. #788, Aldabra blue pigeon. #789, Seychelles blue pigeon. #790, Aldabra red headed fody. #791, Seychelles fody. #792, Aldabra white-eye. #793, Seychelles white-eye.

Wmk. 373

1996, Nov. 11 Litho. *Perf. 14½*

786		3r multicolored	1.10	1.10
787		3r multicolored	1.10	1.10
a.		A127 Pair, #786-787	2.25	2.25
788		3r multicolored	1.10	1.10
789		3r multicolored	1.10	1.10
a.		A127 Pair, #788-789	2.25	2.25
790		3r multicolored	1.10	1.10
791		3r multicolored	1.10	1.10
a.		A127 Pair, #790-791	2.25	2.25
792		3r multicolored	1.10	1.10
793		3r multicolored	1.10	1.10
a.		A127 Pair, #792-793	2.25	2.25
		Nos. 786-793 (8)	8.80	8.80

Zil Elwannyen Sesel No. 58 Surcharged

1997, Feb. 12 *Perf. 14x14½*

794	A9	1.50r on 2r	.60	.60

Hong Kong '97.

Queen Elizabeth II and Prince Philip, 50th Wedding Anniv. — A128

Designs: No. 795, Queen in red & white dress. No. 796, Prince driving four-in-hand team. No. 797, Prince in business suit. No. 798, Queen, horse. No. 799, Prince Charles, Princess Anne. No. 800, Prince, Queen.

10r, Queen and Prince in open carriage, horiz.

Wmk. 373

1997, Nov. 20 Litho. *Perf. 13*

795		1r multicolored	.40	.40
796		1r multicolored	.40	.40
a.		A128 Pair, #795-796	.80	.80
797		1.50r multicolored	.60	.60
798		1.50r multicolored	.60	.60
a.		A128 Pair, #797-798	1.25	1.25
799		3r multicolored	1.25	1.25
800		3r multicolored	1.25	1.25
a.		A128 Pair, #799-800	2.50	2.50
		Nos. 795-800 (6)	4.50	4.50

Souvenir Sheet

801	A128	10r multicolored	4.00	4.00

Diana, Princess of Wales (1961-97)

Common Design Type

Designs: a, In red dress. b, Wearing white blouse, printed vest. c, In blue dress, flowers. d, Wearing white dress.

Perf. 14½x14

1998, Mar. 31 Litho. Wmk. 373

802	CD355	3r Sheet of 4, #a.-d.	5.50	5.50

No. 802 sold for 12r + 3r, with surtax from international sales being donated to the Princess Diana Memorial Fund and surtax from national sales being donated to designated local charity.

Intl. Year of the Ocean — A129

Designs: a, Blue and yellow fish. b, School of gold-colored fish. c, Lionfish. d, Various small fish. e, Anemones. f, Turtle.

1998 Litho. *Perf. 14*

803	A129	3r Strip of 6, #a.-f.	6.50	6.50
		Complete booklet, 2 #803	13.00	

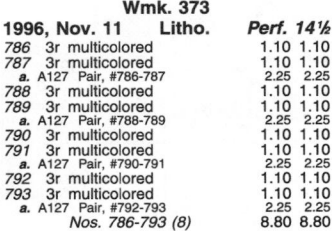

Australia '99, World Stamp Expo A130

18th Cent. ships: 1.50r, Vierge du Cap, 1721. 3r, Elizabeth, 1741. 3.50r, Curieuse, 1768. 10r, Le Flèche, 1801.
20r, The Cheval Marin, 1774, vert.

1999 Litho. Wmk. 384 *Perf. 14*

804 A130	1.50r multicolored	.60	.60
805 A130	3r multicolored	1.10	1.10
806 A130	3.50r multicolored	1.25	1.25
807 A130	10r multicolored	3.75	3.75
	Nos. 804-807 (4)	6.70	6.70

Souvenir Sheet

808 A130	20r multicolored	7.50	7.50

Nos. 804-807 each issued with se-tenant label.

Wedding of Prince Edward and Sophie Rhys-Jones A131

Wmk. 373

1999, Sept. 1 Litho. *Perf. 13¼*

809 A131	3r shown	1.10	1.10
810 A131	15r In carriage	4.00	4.00

Christmas and Millennium A132

1r, Cathedral of the Immaculate Conception. 1.50r, Fairy tern. 2.50r, Dolphin. 10r, Comet.

Perf. 14x14½

1999, Dec. 14 Litho. Wmk. 373

811 A132	1r multi	.35	.35
812 A132	1.50r multi	.55	.55
813 A132	2.50r multi	.90	.90
814 A132	10r multi	3.75	3.75
	Nos. 811-814 (4)	5.55	5.55

Queen Mother, 100th Birthday — A133

Designs: 3r, As child. 5r, As young woman. 7r, With King George VI. 10r, As old woman.

Wmk. 373

2000, Aug. 4 Litho. *Perf. 14¼*

815 A133	3r multi	1.10	1.10
816 A133	5r multi	1.75	1.75
817 A133	7r multi	2.50	2.50
818 A133	10r multi	3.50	3.50
	Nos. 815-818 (4)	8.85	8.85

Anniversaries — A134

Designs: 1r, Arrival of the Jacobin deportees, 200th anniv. 1.50r, Victoria as capital of Seychelles, 160th anniv. 3r, Arrival of Father Leon Des Avanchers, 150th anniv. 3.50r, Victoria Fountain, cent., vert. 5r, Botanical Gardens, cent. 10r, Independence, 25th anniv., vert.

Wmk. 373

2001, July 25 Litho. *Perf. 14*

819-824 A134	Set of 6	8.25	8.25

Nos. 819 and 824 lack Age of Victoria emblem.

Ducks A135

Designs: No. 825, 3r, Garganey. No. 826, 3r, Northern shoveler. No. 827, 3r, Ruddy shelduck. No. 828, 3r, White-faced whistling duck.

Wmk. 384

2001, Oct. 4 Litho. *Perf. 14*

825-828 A135	Set of 4	4.25	4.25

Birdlife International World Bird Festival — A136

Seychelles Scops owl: a, In flight. b, In tree. c, Standing on branch, vert. d, Standing on tip of broken branch, vert. e, Standing on branch.

Perf. 14¼x14½, 14½x14¼

2001, Oct. 4

829 A136	3r Sheet of 5, #a-e	5.25	5.25

POSTAGE DUE STAMPS

Catalogue values for unused stamps in this section are for Never Hinged items.

D1

Engr.; Denomination Typo. in Carmine

1951, Mar. 1 Wmk. 4 *Perf. 11½*

J1 D1	2c carmine	1.50	*3.25*
J2 D1	3c blue green	1.50	*3.25*
J3 D1	6c ocher	1.00	*1.60*
J4 D1	9c brown orange	1.25	*5.00*
J5 D1	15c purple	1.50	*6.25*
J6 D1	18c deep blue	1.90	*7.00*
J7 D1	20c black brown	2.00	*8.25*
J8 D1	30c red brown	2.50	*10.50*
	Nos. J1-J8 (8)	13.15	*45.10*

Engr.; Denomination Typo.

1964-65 Wmk. 314

J9 D1	2c carmine	.80	.80
J10 D1	3c green & red	2.50	2.50

Issue dates: July 7, 1964, Sept. 14, 1965.

Dated "1980"

1980 Litho. *Perf. 14*

J11 D1	5c lilac rose & red	.20	.20
J12 D1	10c dk green & red	.20	.20
J13 D1	15c bister & red	.20	.20
J14 D1	20c brown org & red	.20	.20
J15 D1	25c violet & red	.20	.20
J16 D1	75c dk red brown & red	.25	.25
J17 D1	80c dk blue & red	.30	.30
J18 D1	1r claret & red	.30	.30
	Nos. J11-J18 (8)	1.85	1.85

ZIL ELWANNYEN SESEL

LOCATION — South of Seychelles

The islands of Aldabra, Farquhar and Des Roches. Formerly part of the British Indian Ocean Territory.

Catalogue values for unused stamps in this country are for Never Hinged items.

Type of Seychelles, 1977-78

Perf. 14, 14½x14 (40c, 1r, 1.25r, 1.50r)

1980-81 Litho. Wmk. 373

Size: 30x26mm (40c, 1r, 1.25r, 1.50r)

1 A44	5c Reef fish	.20	.25
2 A44	10c Hawksbill turtle	.20	.25
3 A44	15c Coco-de-mer	.20	.25
4 A44	20c Wild vanilla	.25	.25
5 A44	25c Butterfly	1.00	.25
6 A44	40c Coral reef	.35	.25
7 A44	50c Giant tortoise	.35	.25
8 A44	75c Crayfish	.45	.25
9 A44	1r Madagascar fody	1.25	.40
10 A44	1.10r Green gecko	.50	.40
11 A44	1.25r Fairy tern	1.50	.45
12 A44	1.50r Flying fox	.60	.35

Size: 27x35mm

13 A44	5r Octopus, vert.	.85	.75
a.	Perf. 13 ('81)	1.25	1.25
14 A44	10r Giant tiger cowrie, vert.	1.00	1.25
a.	Perf. 13 ('81)	2.00	2.00
15 A44	15r Pitcher plant, vert.	1.25	2.00
a.	Perf. 13 ('81)	3.00	3.00
16 A44	20r Natl. arms, vert.	1.25	2.75
a.	Perf. 13 ('81)	4.00	4.00
	Nos. 1-16 (16)	11.20	10.35

Nos. 1-12 exist with 1981 imprint.

Traveling Post Office A1

1980, Oct. 24 *Perf. 14*

17 A1	1.50r Cinq Juin	.40	.30
18 A1	2.10r Canceling letters	.50	.40
19 A1	5r Map	1.00	.90
	Nos. 17-19 (3)	1.90	1.60

The 5r showing Agalega as part of the Seychelles was not issued.

Marine Life — A2

1980, Nov. 28

20 A2	1.50r Yellowfin Tuna	.40	.30
21 A2	2.10r Blue marlin	.50	.40
22 A2	5r Sperm whale	1.00	.90
	Nos. 20-22 (3)	1.90	1.60

Royal Wedding Types of Seychelles

1981, June 23 Wmk. 380 *Perf. 14*

23 A61a	40c Royal Escape	.20	.20
a.	Bklt. pane of 4, perf. 12½x12, unwmkd.	.45	.45
24 A61b	40c Couple	.40	.40
25 A61a	5r Victoria & Albert II	.75	.75
26 A61b	5r like #24	1.25	1.25
a.	Bklt pane of 2, perf. 12½x12, unwmkd.	2.50	2.50
27 A61a	10r Britannia	1.50	1.50
28 A61b	10r like #24	2.50	2.50
	Nos. 23-28 (6)	6.60	6.60

Souvenir Sheet

Perf. 12½x12

29 A61b	7.50r like #24	2.00	2.00

Each denomination issued in sheets of 7 (6 type A61a, 1 type A61b).
For surcharges see Nos. 70-75.

Wildlife A3

1981, Dec. 11 Wmk. 373 *Perf. 14*

30 A3	1.40r Wright's skink	.35	.35
31 A3	2.25r Tree frog	.50	.50
32 A3	5r Robber crab	1.00	1.00
	Nos. 30-32 (3)	1.85	1.85

Workboats — A4

1982, Mar. 11 *Perf. 14x14½*

33 A4	1.75r Cinq Juin	.50	.40
34 A4	2.10r Junon	.60	.50
35 A4	5r Diamond M. Dragon	.70	.60
	Nos. 33-35 (3)	1.80	1.50

Mailboats A5

1982, July 22 Wmk. 373 *Perf. 14*

36 A5	40c Paulette	.35	.25
37 A5	1.75r Janette	.50	.50
38 A5	2.75r Lady Esme	.65	.70
39 A5	3.50r Cinq Juin	.70	.85
	Nos. 36-39 (4)	2.20	2.30

Aldabra, World Heritage Site — A6

1982, Nov. 19

40 A6	40c Birds flying over island	.20	.20
41 A6	2.75r Map	.70	.70
42 A6	7r Giant tortoises	1.90	1.90
	Nos. 40-42 (3)	2.80	2.80

Wildlife A7

1983, Feb. 25 *Perf. 14x14½*

43 A7	1.75r Red land crab	.55	.55
44 A7	2.75r Black terrapin	.90	.90
45 A7	7r Madagascar green gecko	2.25	2.25
	Nos. 43-45 (3)	3.70	3.70

Maps — A8

1983, Apr. 27 *Perf. 14½*

46 A8	40c Poivre Island, Ile du Sud	.20	.20
47 A8	1.50r Ile des Roches	.50	.50
48 A8	2.75r Astove Island	.90	.90
49 A8	7r Coetivy Island	2.25	2.25
a.	Souvenir sheet of 4, #46-49	4.00	4.00
	Nos. 46-49 (4)	3.85	3.85

Birds — A9

Perf. 14x14½

1983, July 13 **Wmk. 373**

50 A9 5c Aldabra brush warbler .20 .20
51 A9 10c Barred ground dove .20 .20
52 A9 15c Aldabra nightjar .20 .20
53 A9 20c Malagasy grass warbler .20 .20
54 A9 25c Aldabra white-eye .20 .20
55 A9 40c Aldabra fody .20 .20
56 A9 50c Aldabra rail .20 .20
57 A9 75c Aldabra bulbul .25 .25
58 A9 2r Dimorphic little egret .60 .60
59 A9 2.10r Aldabra sunbird .65 .65
60 A9 2.50r Aldabra turtle dove .80 .80
61 A9 2.75r Aldabra sacred ibis .90 .90

Perf. 14½x14

62 A9 3.50r Aldabra coucal 1.10 1.10
63 A9 7r Aldabra kestrel 2.25 2.25
64 A9 15r Aldabra blue pigeon 5.00 5.00
65 A9 20r Greater flamingo 6.25 6.25
Nos. 50-65 (16) 19.20 19.20

Nos. 62-65 vert. See Nos. 96-100. For surcharges see Seychelles Nos. 763-766.

World Tourism Day A10

1983, Sept. 27 ***Perf. 14***

66 A10 50c Windsurfing .20 .20
67 A10 2r Hotel .60 .60
68 A10 3r Beach .95 .95
69 A10 10r Sunset 3.25 3.25
Nos. 66-69 (4) 5.00 5.00

Nos. 23-28 Surcharged

1983 **Wmk. 380** ***Perf. 14***

70 A61a 30c on 40c multi .20 .20
71 A61b 30c on 40c multi .20 .20
72 A61a 2r on 5r multi .65 .65
73 A61b 2r on 5r multi .65 .65
74 A61a 3r on 10r multi .95 .95
75 A61b 3r on 10r multi .95 .95
Nos. 70-75 (6) 3.60 3.60

Each denomination issued in sheets of 7 (6 type A61a, 1 type A61b).

Aldabra Post Office, Reopening — A11

1984, Mar. 30 **Wmk. 373** ***Perf. 14***

76 A11 50c Map, postmark .20 .20
77 A11 2.75r Aldabra rail .85 .85
78 A11 3r Giant tortoise .95 .95
79 A11 10r Red-footed booby 3.25 3.25
Nos. 76-79 (4) 5.25 5.25

Game Fishing A12

1984, May 31

80 A12 50c Fishing boat .20 .20
81 A12 2r Hooked fish, vert. .65 .65
82 A12 3r Weighing catch, vert. .90 .90
83 A12 10r Fishing boat, stern view 3.25 3.25
Nos. 80-83 (4) 5.00 5.00

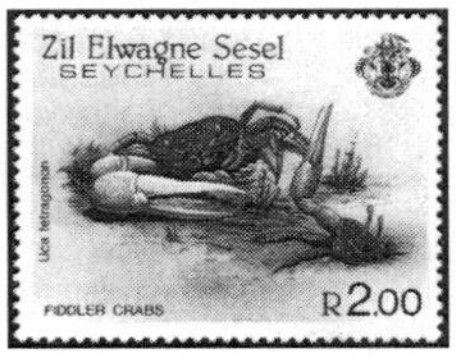

Crabs A13

1984, Aug. 24 ***Perf. 14½***

84 A13 50c Giant hermit crab .20 .20
85 A13 2r Fiddler crabs .65 .65
86 A13 3r Ghost crab .90 .90
87 A13 10r Spotted pebble crab 3.25 3.25
Nos. 84-87 (4) 5.00 5.00

Constellations A14

Mushrooms A15

1984, Oct. 16 ***Perf. 14***

88 A14 50c Orion .20 .20
89 A14 2r Cygnus .65 .65
90 A14 3r Virgo .90 .90
91 A14 10r Scorpio 3.25 3.25
Nos. 88-91 (4) 5.00 5.00

Wmk. 373

1985, Jan. 31 **Litho.** ***Perf. 14***

92 A15 50c Lenzites elegans .20 .20
93 A15 2r Xylaria telfairei .55 .55
94 A15 3r Lentinus sajor-caju .80 .80
95 A15 10r Hexagonia tenuis 2.75 2.75
Nos. 92-95 (4) 4.30 4.30

Bird Type of 1983
Inscribed "Zil Elwannyen Sesel"
Wmk. 373, 384 (5c)

1985-88 ***Perf. 14x14½***

96 A9 5c Like #50 ('88) .20 .20
97 A9 10c Like #51 .20 .20
a. Wmk. 384 ('88) .20 .20
98 A9 25c Like #54 .20 .20
99 A9 50c Like #56 ('87) .20 .20
a. Wmk. 384 ('88) .20 .20
100 A9 2r Like #58 .55 .55
a. Wmk. 384 ('88) .55 .55
Nos. 96-100 (5) 1.35 1.35

No. 97 exists with 1987 imprint, No. 100a with 1990 imprint.

Common Design Types pictured following the introduction.

Queen Mother 85th Birthday
Common Design Type
Perf. 14½x14

1985, June 1 **Wmk. 384**

101 CD336 1r Coronation portrait .25 .25
102 CD336 2r With Princess Anne .55 .55
103 CD336 3r Wearing tiara .80 .80
104 CD336 5r Holding Prince Henry 1.40 1.40
Nos. 101-104 (4) 3.00 3.00

Souvenir Sheet

105 CD336 10r In river taxi, Venice 2.75 2.75

World Wildlife Fund A16

1985, Sept. 27 ***Perf. 14***

106 A16 50c Giant tortoise .20 .20
107 A16 75c Tortoises crossing stream .20 .20
108 A16 1r Three tortoises .25 .25
109 A16 2r Tortoise facing right .55 .55
Nos. 106-109 (4) 1.20 1.20

Souvenir Sheet
Perf. 13x13½

110 A16 10r Two tortoises 2.75 2.75

See Nos. 131-134.

Famous Visitors A17

Visitors and their ships: 50c, Phoenician trader, 600 B.C. 2r, Sir Hugh Scott, HMS Sealark, 1908. 10r, Vasco de Gama, Sao Gabriel, 1502.

1985, Oct. 25 **Wmk. 373** ***Perf. 14***

111 A17 50c multicolored .20 .20
112 A17 2r multicolored .55 .55
113 A17 10r multicolored 2.75 2.75
Nos. 111-113 (3) 3.50 3.50

Queen Elizabeth II, 60th Birthday
Common Design Type

Designs: 75c, As princess. 1r, With Prince Philip. 1.50r, Wearing blue cape. 3.75r, Portrait. 5r, Wearing red hat.

Perf. 14½x14

1986, Apr. 21 **Wmk. 384**

114 CD337 75c scar, blk & sil .20 .20
115 CD337 1r blue & multi .25 .25
116 CD337 1.50r grn & multi .40 .40
117 CD337 3.75r vio & multi 1.00 1.00
118 CD337 5r rose vio & multi 1.40 1.40
Nos. 114-118 (5) 3.25 3.25

For overprints see Nos. 135-139.

Royal Wedding
Common Design Type

3r, Sarah Ferguson, Prince Andrew. 7r, Andrew.

1986, July 23 ***Perf. 14***

119 CD338 3r multicolored .70 .70
120 CD338 7r multicolored 1.60 1.60

Coral — A18

Flowers — A19

Continuous design: a, Acropora palifera, Tubastraea coccinea. b, Echinopora lamellosa, Favia pallida. c, Sarcophyton sp, Porites lutea. d, Goniopora sp, Goniastrea retiformis. e, Tubipora musica, Fungia fungites.

1986, Sept. 17

121 A18 2r Strip of 5, #a.-e. 2.75 2.75

1986, Nov. 12

122 A19 50c Hibiscus tiliaceus .20 .20
123 A19 2r Crinum angustum .55 .55
124 A19 3r Phaius tetragonus .80 .80
125 A19 10r Rothmannia annae 2.75 2.75
Nos. 122-125 (4) 4.30 4.30

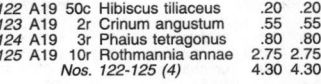

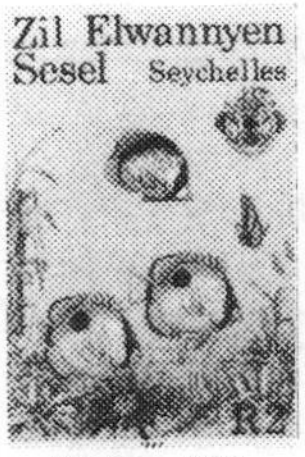

Fish — A20

Trees — A21

Continuous design: a, Chaetodon unimaculatus. b, Ostorhincus fleurieu. c, Platax orbicularis. d, abudefduf annulatus. e, Chaetodon lineolatus.

1987, Mar. 26

126 A20 2r Strip of #126a-126e 2.75 2.75

1987, Aug. 26 ***Perf. 14½***

127 A21 1r Coconut .25 .25
128 A21 2r Mangrove .55 .55
129 A21 3r Pandanus palm .80 .80
130 A21 5r Indian almond 1.40 1.40
Nos. 127-130 (4) 3.00 3.00

Nos. 106-110 Redrawn
World Wildlife Fund Emblem without Circle

1987, Sept. 9 **Wmk. 384** ***Perf. 14***

131 A16 50c multicolored .20 .20
132 A16 75c multicolored .20 .20
133 A16 1r multicolored .25 .25
134 A16 2r multicolored .55 .55
Nos. 131-134 (4) 1.20 1.20

Nos. 114-118 Ovptd. in Silver
"40TH WEDDING ANNIVERSARY"

1987, Dec. 9 ***Perf. 14½x14***

135 CD337 75c scar, blk & sil .20 .20
136 CD337 1r blue & multi .30 .30
137 CD337 1.50r grn & multi .45 .45
138 CD337 3.75r vio & multi 1.10 1.10
139 CD337 5r rose vio & multi 1.50 1.50
Nos. 135-139 (5) 3.55 3.55

Mai Valley Tropical Forest — A22

Continuous design: b, Trunk of palm tree at right. c, Bamboo.

1987, Dec. 16 ***Perf. 14***

140 A22 3r Strip of 3, #a.-c. 2.75 2.75

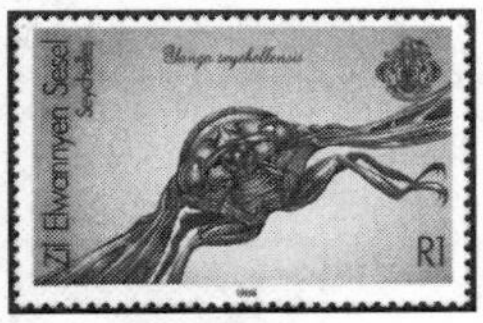

Insects A23

1988, July 28 **Wmk. 373**

141 A23 1r Yanga seychellensis 1.00 .65
142 A23 2r Belenois aldabraensis 1.75 1.00
143 A23 3r Polyspilota seychelliana 2.00 1.50
144 A23 5r Polposipus herculeanus 2.50 2.00
Nos. 141-144 (4) 7.25 5.15

Souvenir Sheet

1988 Summer Olympics, Seoul — A24

1988, Aug. 31 **Wmk. 384**

145 A24 10r multicolored 3.00 3.00

Lloyds' of London, 300th Anniv.
Common Design Type

Designs: 1r, Lloyd's building, 1988. 2r, Cable ship Retriever, horiz. 3r, Chantel, horiz. 5r, Torrey Canyon aground off Cornwall, 1967.

1988, Oct. 28 **Wmk. 373**

146 CD341 1r multicolored .30 .30
147 CD341 2r multicolored .60 .60
148 CD341 3r multicolored .90 .90
149 CD341 5r multicolored 1.50 1.50
Nos. 146-149 (4) 3.30 3.30

Christmas — A25

Perf. 13½x14, 14x13½

1988, Nov. 18 Wmk. 384

150 A25 1r Santa, toys in canoe .30 .30
151 A25 2r Church, vert. .60 .60
152 A25 3r Santa riding bird, vert. .90 .90
153 A25 5r Sleigh over island 1.50 1.50
Nos. 150-153 (4) 3.30 3.30

Moon Landing, 20th Anniv.
Common Design Type

Apollo 18: 1r, Firing room, Launch Control Center. 2r, Astronauts Slayton, Stafford, Brand and cosmonauts Leonov and Kubasov. 3r, Mission emblem. 5r, Apollo and Soyuz docking in space. 10r, Apollo 11 lifted aboard USS Hornet.

Perf. 14x13½, 14 (#155-156)

1989, July 20

Size of Nos. 155-156: 29x29mm

154 CD342 1r multicolored .40 .40
155 CD342 2r multicolored .75 .75
156 CD342 3r multicolored 1.10 1.10
157 CD342 5r multicolored 1.75 1.75
Nos. 154-157 (4) 4.00 4.00

Souvenir Sheet

158 CD342 10r multicolored 3.75 3.75

Poisonous Plants — A26

1989, Oct. 9 *Perf. 14*

159 A26 1r Dumb cane .40 .40
160 A26 2r Star of Bethlehem .75 .75
161 A26 3r Indian licorice 1.10 1.10
162 A26 5r Black nightshade 1.75 1.75
Nos. 159-162 (4) 4.00 4.00

See Nos. 173-176.

Creole Cooking — A27

1989, Dec. 18

163 A27 1r Tec-tec broth .40 .40
164 A27 2r Pilaf a la Seychelloise .75 .75
165 A27 3r Mullet grilled in banana leaves 1.10 1.10
166 A27 5r Daube 1.75 1.75
a. Souvenir sheet of 4, #163-166 4.00 4.00
Nos. 163-166 (4) 4.00 4.00

No. 166a has continuous design.

Stamp World London '90 A28

Designs: 1r, #22. 2r, #13. 3r, #61. 5r, #32.

Wmk. 373

1990, May 3 Litho. *Perf. 12½*

167 A28 1r multicolored .35 .35
168 A28 2r multicolored .70 .70
169 A28 3r multicolored 1.00 1.00
170 A28 5r multicolored 1.75 1.75
a. Souvenir sheet of 4, #167-170 4.00 4.00
Nos. 167-170 (4) 3.80 3.80

Queen Mother 90th Birthday
Common Design Types

Designs: 2r, As Duchess of York with infant Elizabeth. 10r, With King George VI viewing bomb-damaged London, 1940.

1990, Aug. 4 Wmk. 384 *Perf. 14x15*

171 CD343 2r multi .70 .70

Perf. 14½

172 CD344 10r yel brn & blk 3.50 3.50

Poisonous Plants Type of 1989

Wmk. 373

1990, Nov. 5 Litho. *Perf. 12½*

173 A26 1r Ordeal plant .35 .35
174 A26 2r Thorn apple .70 .70
175 A26 3r Strychnine tree 1.00 1.00
176 A26 5r Bwa zasmen 1.75 1.75
Nos. 173-176 (4) 3.80 3.80

Elizabeth & Philip, Birthdays
Common Design Types

Wmk. 384

1991, June 17 Litho. *Perf. 14½*

177 CD345 4r multicolored 2.00 2.00
178 CD346 4r multicolored 2.00 2.00
a. Pair, #177-178 + label 4.00 4.00

Shipwrecks — A29

Wmk. 373

1991, Oct. 28 Litho. *Perf. 14*

179 A29 1.50r St. Abbs, 1860 .55 .55
180 A29 3r Norden, 1862 1.10 1.10
181 A29 3.50r Clan Mackay, 1894 1.25 1.25
182 A29 10r Glenlyon, 1905 3.50 3.50
Nos. 179-182 (4) 6.40 6.40

Queen Elizabeth II's Accession to the Throne, 40th Anniv.
Common Design Type

1992, Feb. 6

183 CD349 1r multicolored .40 .40
184 CD349 1.50r multicolored .55 .55
185 CD349 3r multicolored 1.10 1.10
186 CD349 3.50r multicolored 1.25 1.25
187 CD349 5r multicolored 1.90 1.90
Nos. 183-187 (5) 5.20 5.20

Aldabra World Heritage Site, 10th Anniv. — A30

Designs: 1.50r, Lomatopyllum aldabrense. 3r, Dryolimnas cuvieri aldabranus. 3.50r, Birgus latro. 10r, Dicrurus aldabranus.

1992, Nov. 19 *Perf. 14½*

188 A30 1.50r multicolored .60 .60
189 A30 3r multicolored 1.25 1.25
190 A30 3.50r multicolored 1.50 1.50
191 A30 10r multicolored 4.00 4.00
Nos. 188-191 (4) 7.35 7.35

SHANGHAI

shaŋ-'hī

LOCATION — A city on the Whangpoo River, Kiangsu Province, China
POP. — 3,489,998

A British settlement was founded there in 1843 and by agreement with China settlements were established by France and the United States. Special areas were set aside for the foreign settlements and a postal system independent of China was organized which was continued until 1898.

16 Cash = 1 Candareen
100 Candareens = 1 Tael
100 Cents = 1 Dollar (1890)

Watermark

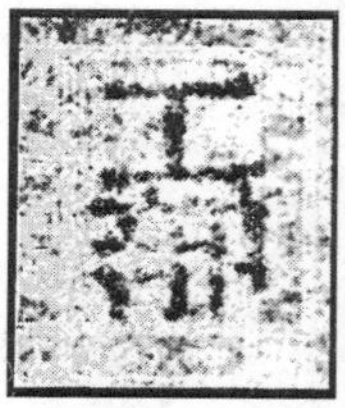
Wmk. 175- Kung Pu (Municipal Council)

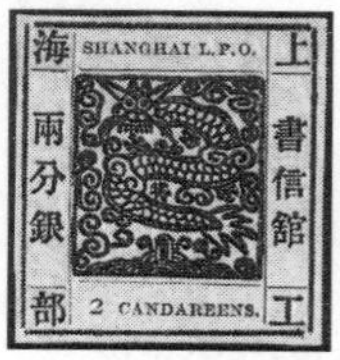

Dragon — A1

1865-66 Unwmk. Typo. *Imperf.*

Antique Numerals

Roman "I" in "I6"

"Candareens" Plural

Wove Paper

1 A1 2ca black 300.00 2,000.
a. Pelure paper 450.00
2 A1 4ca yellow 300.00 3,000.
a. Pelure paper 600.00 —
b. Double impression —
3 A1 8ca green 300.00 3,500.
a. 8ca yellow green 350.00 —
4 A1 16ca scarlet 700.00 4,500.
a. 16ca vermilion 625.00
b. Pelure paper 800.00
Nos. 1-4 (4) 1,600.

No. 1: top character of three in left panel as illustrated. No. 5: top character is two horiz. lines.

Nos. 2, 3: center character of three in left panel as illustrated. Nos. 6, 7: center character much more complex.

Antique Numerals

"Candareens" Plural

Pelure Paper

5 A1 2ca black 300.00
a. Wove paper 250.00
6 A1 4ca yellow 500.00 —
7 A1 8ca deep green 500.00 —
Nos. 5-7 (3) 1,300.

Antique Numerals

"Candareen" Singular

Laid Paper

8 A1 1ca blue 300.00 3,500.
9 A1 2ca black 3,000.
10 A1 4ca yellow 700.00
Nos. 8-10 (3) 4,000.

Wove Paper

11 A1 1ca blue 275.00 4,500.
12 A1 2ca black 575.00 3,000.
13 A1 4ca yellow 500.00 —
14 A1 8ca olive green 500.00 —
15 A1 16ca vermilion 275.00 —
a. "1" of "16" omitted —
Nos. 11-15 (5) 2,125.

Roman "I," Antique "2"

"Candareens" Plural Except on 1ca

Wove Paper

16 A1 1ca blue 600.00 3,000.
17 A1 12ca fawn 350.00
18 A1 12ca chocolate 350.00
Nos. 16-18 (3) 1,300.

Antique Numerals

"Candareens" Plural Except on 1ca

Wove Paper

19 A1 1ca indigo, pelure paper 250.00 2,000.
a. 1ca blue, wove paper 3,500.
20 A1 3ca orange brown 225.00 1,800.
a. Pelure paper 300.00
21 A1 6ca red brown 140.00
22 A1 6ca fawn 400.00 —
23 A1 6ca vermilion 200.00
24 A1 12ca orange brown 110.00
25 A1 16ca vermilion 140.00 700.00
a. "1" of "16" omitted 450.00
Nos. 19-25 (7) 1,465.

Examples of No. 22 usually have the straight lines cutting through the paper.

Antique Numerals

Roman "I"

"Candareens" Plural Except on 1ca

Laid Paper

26 A1 1ca blue —
27 A1 2ca black 4,500.
28 A1 3ca red brown — —

Examples of No. 28 usually have the straight lines cutting through the paper.

Modern Numerals

"Candareen" Singular

29 A1 1ca slate blue 200.00 2,000.
a. 1ca dark blue 150.00 —
30 A1 3ca red brown 125.00

"Candareens" Plural Except the 1c

31 A1 2ca gray 175.00
32 A1 3ca red brown 150.00 2,000.

Coarse Porous Wove Paper

33a A1 1ca blue 150.00
34a A1 2ca black 190.00
b. Grayish paper 250.00
35a A1 3ca red brown 125.00
36a A1 4ca yellow 300.00
37a A1 6ca olive green 175.00 —
38a A1 8ca emerald 200.00 —
39a A1 12ca orange vermilion 150.00 —
40a A1 16ca red 225.00 800.00
41a A1 16ca red brown 175.00 800.00
Nos. 33a-41a (9) 1,690.

Chinese characters change on same denomination stamps.

Nos. 1, 2, 11 and 32 exist on thicker paper, usually toned. Most authorities consider these four stamps and Nos. 33a-41a to be official reprints made to present sample sets to other post offices. The tone in this paper is an acquired characteristic, due to various causes. Many shades and minor varieties exist of Nos. 1-41a.

A2

A3

A4

A5

1866 Litho. *Perf. 12*

42 A2 2c rose 8.50 *11.00*
43 A3 4c lilac 20.00 20.00
44 A4 8c gray blue 20.00 *21.00*
45 A5 16c green 60.00 *70.00*
Nos. 42-45 (4) 108.50 122.00

Nos. 42-45 imperf. are proofs. See No. 50. For surcharges see Nos. 51-61, 67.

A6

A7

A8

A9

1866 *Perf. 15*

46 A6 1ca brown 6.00 5.50
a. "CANDS" 55.00 50.00

47 A7 3ca orange 22.50 *27.50*
48 A8 6ca slate 22.50 *27.50*
49 A9 12ca olive gray 55.00 *60.00*
Nos. 46-49 (4) 106.00 120.50

See Nos. 69-77. For surcharges see Nos. 62-66, 68, 78-83.

1872
50 A2 2c rose 75.00 *100.00*

Handstamp Surcharged in Blue, Red or Black

a

1873 ***Perf. 12***
51 A2 1ca on 2c rose 27.50 *32.50*
52 A3 1ca on 4c lilac 16.00 *18.00*
53 A3 1ca on 4c lilac (R) *1,500.* *1,500.*
54 A3 1ca on 4c lilac (Bk) 20.00 *27.50*
55 A4 1ca on 8c gray bl 22.50 *25.00*
56 A4 1ca on 8c gray bl (R) *3,250.* *3,250.*
57 A5 1ca on 16c green *2,500.* *2,500.*
58 A5 1ca on 16c green (R) *3,500.* *3,500.*

Perf. 15
59 A2 1ca on 2c rose 35.00 *40.00*

1875 ***Perf. 12***
60 A2 3ca on 2c rose 65. 65.
61 A5 3ca on 16c green *1,100.* *1,100.*

Perf. 15
62 A7 1ca on 3ca orange *3,500.* *3,500.*
63 A8 1ca on 6ca slate 250. 250.
64 A8 1ca on 6ca slate (R) *2,300.* *2,300.*
65 A9 1ca on 12ca ol gray 225. 225.
66 A9 1ca on 12ca ol gray (R) *2,250.* *2,250.*
67 A2 3ca on 2c rose 200. 200.
68 A9 3ca on 12ca olive gray *5,500.* *5,500.*

Counterfeits exist of Nos. 51-68.

Types of 1866

1875 ***Perf. 15***
69 A6 1ca yel, *yel* 22.50 22.50
70 A7 3ca rose, *rose* 20.00 *22.50*

Perf. 11½
71 A6 1ca yel, *yel* 325.00 325.00

1876 ***Perf. 15***
72 A6 1ca yellow 5.50 *6.50*
73 A7 3ca rose 37.50 *45.00*
74 A8 6ca green 65.00 65.00
75 A9 9ca blue 82.50 82.50
76 A9 12ca light brown 110.00 110.00
Nos. 72-76 (5) 300.50 309.00

1877 **Engr.** ***Perf. 12½***
77 A6 1ca rose 900.00 *1,000.*

Stamps of 1875-76 Surcharged type "a" in Blue or Red

1877 **Litho.** ***Perf. 15***
78 A7 1ca on 3ca rose, *rose* 200. 200.
79 A7 1ca on 3ca rose 40. 40.
80 A8 1ca on 6ca green 50. 50.
81 A9 1ca on 9ca blue 175. 175.
82 A9 1ca on 12ca lt brn 850. 850.
83 A9 1ca on 12ca lt brn (R) *3,000.* *3,000.*

Counterfeits exist of Nos. 78-83.

A11

A12

A13

A14

1877 ***Perf. 15***
84 A11 20 cash blue violet 10.00 *12.00*
a. 20 cash violet 9.00 9.00
85 A12 40 cash rose 10.00 9.00
86 A13 60 cash green 11.00 11.00
87 A14 80 cash blue 20.00 18.00
88 A14 100 cash brown 16.00 *22.50*
Nos. 84-88 (5) 67.00 72.50

Handstamp Surcharged in Blue

b

1879 ***Perf. 15***
89 A12 20 cash on 40c rose 17.00 17.00
90 A14 60 cash on 80c blue 24.00 *30.00*
91 A14 60 cash on 100c brn 24.00 *30.00*
Nos. 89-91 (3) 65.00 77.00

Types of 1877

1880 ***Perf. 11½***
92 A11 20 cash violet 5.00 *5.50*
93 A12 40 cash rose 7.50 6.50
94 A13 60 cash green 2.75 2.75
95 A14 80 cash blue 8.00 *9.50*
96 A14 100 cash brown 9.50 *10.50*

Perf. 15x11½
97 A11 20 cash lilac 30.00 *32.50*
Nos. 92-97 (6) 62.75 67.25

Surcharged type "b" in Blue

1884 ***Perf. 11½***
98 A12 20 cash on 40c rose 13.00 9.00
99 A14 60 cash on 80c blue 15.00 *18.00*
100 A14 60 cash on 100c brn 18.00 18.00
Nos. 98-100 (3) 46.00 45.00

Types of 1877

1884
101 A11 20 cash green 5.00 *6.00*

1885 ***Perf. 15***
102 A11 20 cash green 2.75 *3.00*
103 A12 40 cash brown 3.50 *3.75*
104 A13 60 cash violet 7.00 *8.25*
a. 60 cash red violet 11.00 *17.00*
105 A14 80 cash buff 7.00 6.00
106 A14 100 cash yellow 8.00 *10.00*

Perf. 11½x15
107 A11 20 cash green 3.50 *6.00*
108 A13 60 cash red vio 7.00 7.00
Nos. 102-108 (7) 38.75 44.00

Surcharged type "b" in Blue

1886 ***Perf. 15***
109 A14 40 cash on 80c buff 4.25 3.75
110 A14 60 cash on 100c yel 5.75 5.00

Types of 1877

1888 ***Perf. 15***
111 A11 20 cash gray 3.25 3.25
112 A12 40 cash black 3.25 *4.25*
113 A13 60 cash rose 4.50 4.25
a. Third character at left lacks dot at top 6.25 *7.00*
114 A14 80 cash green 4.50 *5.25*
115 A14 100 cash lt blue 6.50 *7.50*
Nos. 111-115 (5) 22.00 24.50

#106, 103, 105 Handstamp Surcharged in Blue or Red Type "b" or:

c

d

1888 ***Perf. 15***
116 A14(b) 40 cash on 100c 4.50 *6.00*
117 A14(b) 40 cash on 100c (R) 5.00 *6.00*
118 A12(c) 20 cash on 40c 10.00 10.00
119 A14(c) 20 cash on 80c 2.50 2.50
120 A12(d) 20 cash on 40c 11.00 *12.00*
Nos. 116-120 (5) 33.00 36.50

Inverted surcharges exist on Nos. 116-120; double on Nos. 116, 119, 120; omitted surcharges paired with normal stamp on Nos. 116, 119.

Handstamp Surcharged in Black and Red (100 cash) or Red (20 cash)

e

1889 **Unwmk.**
121 A14(e) 100 cash on 20c on 100c yel 45.00 35.00
a. Without the surcharge "100 cash" 275.00 —
b. Blue & red surcharge
122 A14(c) 20 cash on 80c grn 6.00 6.00
123 A14(c) 20 cash on 100c bl 5.00 *6.00*
Nos. 121-123 (3) 56.00 47.00

Counterfeits exist of Nos. 116-123.

1889 **Wmk. 175** ***Perf. 15***
124 A11 20 cash gray 2.00 2.00
125 A12 40 cash black 3.00 3.00
126 A13 60 cash rose 3.50 *4.00*
a. Third character at left lacks dot at top 6.50 *7.00*

Perf. 12
127 A14 80 cash green 3.25 *4.00*
128 A14 100 cash dk bl 9.00 8.00
Nos. 124-128 (5) 20.75 21.00

Nos. 124-126 are sometimes found without watermark. This is caused by the sheet being misplaced in the printing press, so that the stamps are printed on the unwatermarked margin of the sheet.

Shield with Dragon Supporters — A20

1890 **Unwmk.** **Litho.** ***Perf. 15***
129 A20 2c brown 1.75 *2.25*
130 A20 5c rose 4.00 4.00
131 A20 15c blue 5.00 5.00

Nos. 129-131 imperforate are proofs.

Wmk. 175
132 A20 10c black 5.50 5.50
133 A20 15c blue 11.00 11.00
134 A20 20c violet 4.50 *5.00*
Nos. 129-134 (6) 31.75 32.75

See Nos. 135-141. For surcharges and overprints see Nos. 142-152, J1-J13.

1891 ***Perf. 12***
135 A20 2c brown 2.00 2.00
136 A20 5c rose 3.50 3.50

1892
137 A20 2c green 1.25 1.10
138 A20 5c red 3.00 2.75
139 A20 10c orange 8.50 *10.00*
140 A20 15c violet 5.00 *6.00*
141 A20 20c brown 6.00 6.00
Nos. 137-141 (5) 23.75 25.85

No. 130 Handstamp Surcharged in Blue

2 Cts.
時先式
f

1892 **Unwmk.** ***Perf. 15***
142 A20 2c on 5c rose 37.50 25.00

Counterfeits exist of Nos. 142-152.

Stamps of 1892 Handstamp Surcharged in Blue:

銀分半
HALF
CENT.
g

銀分壹
ONE
CENT.
h

1893 **Wmk. 175** ***Perf. 12***
143 A20 ½c on 15c violet 5.00 5.00
144 A20 1c on 20c brown 5.00 5.00
a. ½c on 20c brown (error) *4,000.*

Surcharged in Blue or Red (#152) on Halves of #136 (#145-147), #138 (#148-150), #135 (#151), #137 (#152):

½Ct. ½Ct. ½Ct. 1Ct.
i j k m

145 A20(i) ½c on half of 5c 5.00 4.00
146 A20(j) ½c on half of 5c 7.00 5.50
147 A20(k) ½c on half of 5c 75.00 65.00
148 A20(i) ½c on half of 5c 5.00 3.50
149 A20(j) ½c on half of 5c 7.00 5.50
150 A20(k) ½c on half of 5c 75.00 65.00
151 A20(m) 1c on half of 2c 2.00 2.00
c. Dbl. surch., one in green *325.00*
d. Dbl. surch., one in black *325.00*
152 A20(m) 1c on half of 2c 11.00 10.00
Nos. 145-152 (8) 187.00 160.50

The ½c surcharge setting of 20 (2x10) covers a vertical strip of 10 unsevered stamps, with horizontal gutter midway. This setting has 11 of type "i," 8 of type "j" and 1 of type "k." Nos. 145-152 are perforated vertically down the middle.

Inverted surcharges exist on Nos. 145-151. Double surcharges, one inverted, are also found in this issue.

Handstamped provisionals somewhat similar to Nos. 145-152 were issued in Foochow by the Shanghai Agency.

Coat of Arms — A24

Mercury — A26

1893 **Litho.** ***Perf. 13½x14***
Frame Inscriptions in Black
153 A24 ½c orange, typo. .30 .25
a. ½c orange, litho. 5.00 5.00
154 A24 1c brown, typo. .30 .25
a. 1c brown, litho. 5.00 5.00
155 A24 2c vermilion 10.00 10.00
a. Imperf.
156 A24 5c blue .30 .25
a. Black inscriptions inverted 650.00
157 A24 10c grn, typo. & litho. 3.25 *4.00*
a. 10c green, litho. 10.00 *12.00*
158 A24 15c yellow .45 .40
159 A24 20c lil, typo. & litho. 2.75 *3.50*
a. 20c lilac, litho. 6.00 6.00
Nos. 153-159 (7) 17.35 18.65

On Nos. 157 and 159, frame inscriptions are lithographed, rest of design typographed.

See Nos. 170-172. For overprints and surcharges see Nos. 160-166, 168-169.

Stamps of 1893 Overprinted in Black

1893, Dec. 14
160 A24 ½c orange & blk .30 .30
161 A24 1c brown & blk .35 .35
a. Double overprint 25.00 25.00
162 A24 2c vermilion & blk .75 .75
a. Inverted overprint 55.00
163 A24 5c blue & black 3.00 *3.50*
a. Inverted overprint 110.00
164 A24 10c green & blk 7.00 *8.00*
165 A24 15c yellow & blk 3.50 3.50
166 A24 20c lilac & blk 6.00 *6.50*
Nos. 160-166 (7) 20.90 22.90

50th anniv. of the first foreign settlement in Shanghai.

1893, Nov. 11 **Litho.** ***Perf. 13½***
167 A26 2c vermilion & black .40 *.60*

Nos. 158 and 159 Handstamp Surcharged in Black

1896 ***Perf. 13½x14***

168	A24	4c on 15c yellow & blk	5.50	5.50
169	A24	6c on 20c lilac & blk (#159)	5.50	5.50
a.		On #159a	30.00	25.00

Surcharge occurs inverted or double on Nos. 168-169.

Arms Type of 1893

1896

170	A24	2c scarlet & blk	.30	*1.40*
a.		Black inscriptions inverted	140.00	
171	A24	4c orange & blk, *yel*	2.00	*3.25*
172	A24	6c car & blk, *rose*	1.25	*3.75*
		Nos. 170-172 (3)	3.55	8.40

POSTAGE DUE STAMPS

Postage Stamps of 1890-92 Handstamped in Black, Red or Blue

Postage Due.

1892 **Unwmk.** ***Perf. 15***

J1	A20	2c brown (Bk)	250.00	*275.00*
J2	A20	5c rose (Bk)	3.50	*5.00*
J3	A20	15c blue (Bk)	22.50	22.50

Wmk. 175

J4	A20	10c black (R)	7.50	*8.00*
J5	A20	15c blue (Bk)	8.00	*10.00*
J6	A20	20c violet (Bk)	4.00	*5.00*
		Nos. J1-J6 (6)	295.50	325.50

1892-93 ***Perf. 12***

J7	A20	2c brown (Bk)	1.75	1.75
J8	A20	2c brown (Bl)	1.40	*2.00*
J9	A20	5c rose (Bl)	2.75	*3.00*
J10	A20	10c orange (Bk)	65.00	*70.00*
J11	A20	10c orange (Bl)	3.50	*8.00*
J12	A20	15c violet (R)	10.00	10.00
J13	A20	20c brown (R)	9.00	9.00
		Nos. J7-J13 (7)	93.40	103.75

D2

1893 **Litho.** ***Perf. 13½***

J14	D2	½c orange & blk	.55	.55

Perf. 14x13½

J15	D2	1c brown & black	.55	.55
J16	D2	2c vermilion & black	.55	.55
J17	D2	5c blue & black	.90	.90
J18	D2	10c green & black	1.25	1.25
J19	D2	15c yellow & black	1.25	1.25
J20	D2	20c violet & black	1.25	1.25
		Nos. J14-J20 (7)	6.30	6.30

Stamps of Shanghai were discontinued in 1898.

SHARJAH & DEPENDENCIES

'shär-jə

LOCATION — Oman Peninsula, Arabia, on Persian Gulf
GOVT. — Sheikdom under British protection
POP. — 5,000 (estimated)
CAPITAL — Sharjah

The dependencies on the Gulf of Oman are Dhiba, Khor Fakkan, and Kalba.

Sharjah is one of six Persian Gulf sheikdoms to join the United Arab Emirates which proclaimed independence Dec. 2, 1971. See United Arab Emirates.

100 Naye Paise = 1 Rupee

Catalogue values for all unused stamps in this country are for Never Hinged items.

Sheik Saqr bin Sultan al Qasimi, Flag and Map — A1

Malaria Eradication Emblem — A2

Perf. 14½x14

1963, July 10 **Photo.** **Unwmk.**
Black Portrait and Inscriptions; Lilac Rose Flag

1	A1	1np lt bl grn & pink	.20	.20
2	A1	2np grnsh bl & sal	.20	.20
3	A1	3np violet & yel	.20	.20
4	A1	4np emerald & gray	.20	.20
5	A1	5np aqua & lt grn	.20	.20
6	A1	6np dl grn & brt yel	.20	.20
7	A1	8np Prus bl & bis	.20	.20
8	A1	10np aqua & tan	.20	.20
9	A1	16np ultra & bis	.20	.20
10	A1	20np lt vio & lem	.20	.20
11	A1	30np rose lil & brt yel grn	.25	.25
12	A1	40np dk bl & yel grn	.30	.30
13	A1	50np green & fawn	.40	.40
14	A1	75np ultra & fawn	.60	.60
15	A1	100np ol bis & rose	.75	.75
		Nos. 1-15 (15)	4.30	4.30

1963, Aug. 8

16	A2	1np grnsh blue	.20	.20
17	A2	2np dull blue	.20	.20
18	A2	3np violet blue	.20	.20
19	A2	4np emerald	.20	.20
20	A2	90np yellow brown	.50	.50
		Nos. 16-20 (5)	1.30	1.30

Miniature Sheet

Imperf

21	A2	100np bright blue	.80	.80

WHO drive to eradicate malaria. No. 21 contains one 39x67mm stamp.

See Nos. C1-C6. For surcharge and overprints see Nos. 35, C7-C12, O1-O9.

Red Crescent and Sheik — A3

1963, Aug. 25 ***Perf. 14x14½***

22	A3	1np purple & red	.20	.20
23	A3	2np brt green & red	.20	.20
24	A3	3np dark blue & red	.20	.20
25	A3	4np dark green & red	.20	.20
26	A3	5np dark brown & red	.20	.20
27	A3	85np green & red	.40	.40
		Nos. 22-27 (6)	1.40	1.40

Miniature Sheet

Imperf

28	A3	100np plum & red	1.00	1.00

Cent. of the Intl. Red Cross. Imperfs. exist. No. 28 contains one 67x39m stamp.

Nos. 36-40 and No. 20 Surcharged

Nos. 29-34

No. 35

1963, Oct. 6 **Photo.** ***Perf. 14½x14***

29	A4	10np on 1np brt grn	.20	.20
30	A4	20np on 2np red brn	.30	.30
31	A4	30np on 3np ol grn	.45	.45
32	A4	40np on 4np dp ultra	.60	.60
33	A4	75np on 90np carmine	1.00	1.00
34	A4	80np on 90np carmine	1.25	1.25
35	A2	1r on 90np yel brn	1.60	1.60
		Nos. 29-35 (7)	5.40	5.40

Due to a stamp shortage the surcharged set appeared before the commemorative issue.

Wheat Emblem and Hands with Broken Chains — A4

1963, Oct. 15 ***Perf. 14½x14***

36	A4	1np brt green	.20	.20
37	A4	2np red brown	.20	.20
38	A4	3np olive green	.20	.20
39	A4	4np deep ultra	.20	.20
40	A4	90np carmine	.40	.40
		Nos. 36-40 (5)	1.20	1.20

Miniature Sheet

Imperf

41	A4	100np purple	.50	.50

"Freedom from Hunger" campaign of the FAO. Imperfs. exist. No. 41 contains one 39x67mm stamp.

For surcharges see Nos. 29-34.

Orbiting Astronomical Observatory — A5

Satellites: 2np, Nimbus weather satellite. 3np, Pioneer V space probe. 4np, Explorer XIII. 5np, Explorer XII. 35np, Relay satellite. 50np, Orbiting Solar Observatory.

1964, Feb. 5 **Photo.** ***Perf. 14***

42	A5	1np blue	.20	.20
43	A5	2np red brn & yel grn	.20	.20
44	A5	3np blk & grnsh bl	.20	.20
45	A5	4np lemon & blk	.20	.20
46	A5	5np brt pur & lem	.20	.20
47	A5	35np grnsh bl & pur	.50	.50
48	A5	50np ol grn & redsh brn	.70	.70
		Nos. 42-48 (7)	2.20	2.20

Space research. A 100np imperf. souvenir sheet shows various satellites, the Earth and stars. Colors: dark blue, gold, green & pink. Size: 112x80mm.

Runner — A6

1964, Mar. 3 **Unwmk.**

49	A6	1np shown	.20	.20
50	A6	2np Discus	.20	.20
51	A6	3np Hurdler	.20	.20
52	A6	4np Shot put	.20	.20
53	A6	20np High jump	.20	.20
54	A6	30np Weight lifting	.20	.20
55	A6	40np Javelin	.25	.25
56	A6	1r Diving	.65	.65
		Nos. 49-56 (8)	2.10	2.10

18th Olympic Games, Tokyo, Oct. 10-25, 1964. An imperf. souvenir sheet contains one 1r stamp similar to No. 56. Size of stamp: 67x67mm, size of sheet: 102x102mm.

Girl Scouts A7

1964, June 30 ***Perf. 14x14½***

57	A7	1np grnsh gray	.20	.20
58	A7	2np emerald	.20	.20
59	A7	3np brt blue	.20	.20
60	A7	4np brt violet	.20	.20
61	A7	5np carmine rose	.20	.20
62	A7	2r dark red brown	4.00	2.00
		Nos. 57-62 (6)	5.00	3.00

An imperf. souvenir sheet contains one 2r bright red stamp. Size of stamp: 67x40mm. Size of sheet: 102½x76mm.

Sharjah Boy Scout — A8

Marching Scouts With Drummers — A9

Designs: 3np, 2r, Boy Scout portrait.

Perf. 14½x14, 14x14½

1964, June 30 Photo. Unwmk.

63	A8	1np gray green	.20	.20
64	A9	2np emerald	.20	.20
65	A8	3np brt blue	.20	.20
66	A8	4np brt violet	.30	.25
67	A9	5np brt carmine rose	.40	.35
68	A8	2r dk red brown	3.75	1.00
		Nos. 63-68 (6)	5.05	2.20

Issued to honor the Sharjah Boy Scouts. An imperf. souvenir sheet exists with one 2r bright red stamp in design of No. 68. Size of stamp: 39½x67mm. Size of sheet: 77x103mm.

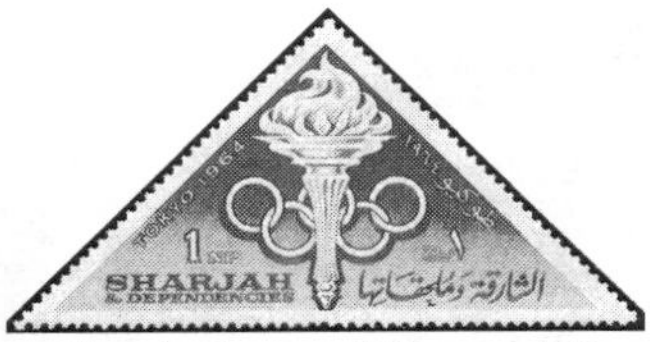

Olympic Torch and Rings — A10

1964, Oct. 15 Litho. *Perf. 14*

69	A10	1np olive green	.20	.20
70	A10	2np ultra	.20	.20
71	A10	3np orange brown	.20	.20
72	A10	4np blue green	.20	.20
73	A10	5np dark violet	.20	.20
74	A10	40np brt blue	.25	.20
75	A10	50np dark red brown	.40	.25
76	A10	2r bister	1.60	1.00
		Nos. 69-76 (8)	3.25	2.45

18th Olympic Games, Tokyo, Oct. 10-25. An imperf. souvenir sheet exists with one 2r yellow green stamp. Size of stamp: 82mm at base. Size of sheet: 107x76mm.

Early Telephone — A11

Designs: No. 78, Modern telewriter. No. 79, 1895 car. No. 80, American automobile, 1964. No. 81, Early X-ray. No. 82, Modern X-ray. No. 83, Mail coach. No. 84, Telstar and Delta rocket. No. 85, Sailing vessel. No. 86, Nuclear ship "Savannah." No. 87, Early astronomers. No. 88, Jodrell Bank telescope. No. 89, Greek messengers. No. 90, Relay satellite, Delta rocket and globe. No. 91, Early flying machine. No. 92, Caravelle plane. No. 93, Persian water wheel. No. 94, Hydroelectric dam. No. 95, Old steam locomotive. No. 96, Diesel locomotive.

Unwmk.

1965, Apr. 23 Litho. *Perf. 14*

77	A11	1np rose red & blk	.20	.20
78	A11	1np rose red & blk	.20	.20
79	A11	2np orange & indigo	.20	.20
80	A11	2np orange & indigo	.20	.20
81	A11	3np dk brn & emer	.20	.20
82	A11	3np emer & dk brn	.20	.20
83	A11	4np yel grn & dk vio	.20	.20
84	A11	4np dk vio & yel grn	.20	.20
85	A11	5np bl grn & brn	.20	.20
86	A11	5np bl grn & brn	.20	.20
87	A11	30np gray & bl	.20	.20
88	A11	30np blue & gray	.20	.20
89	A11	40np vio bl & yel	.30	.20
90	A11	40np vio bl & yel	.30	.20
91	A11	50np blue & sepia	.40	.20
92	A11	50np blue & sepia	.40	.20
93	A11	75np brt grn & dk brn	.60	.30
94	A11	75np brt grn & dk brn	.60	.30
95	A11	1r yellow & vio bl	.75	.35
96	A11	1r yellow & vio bl	.75	.35
		Nos. 77-96 (20)	6.50	4.50

Issued to show progress in science, transport and communications. Each two stamps of same denomination are printed se tenant. Two imperf. souvenir sheets exist. One contains one each of Nos. 89-90 and the other, of Nos. 95-96. Size: 102x75mm.

Stamps of Sharjah & Dependencies were replaced in 1972 by those of United Arab Emirates.

AIR POST STAMPS

Type of Regular Issue, 1963 with Flying Hawk and "Air Mail" in English and Arabic Added

Perf. 14½x14

1963, July 10 Photo. Unwmk.

Black Portrait and Inscriptions; Lilac Rose Flag

C1	A1	1r ultra & fawn	.40	.40
C2	A1	2r lt violet & lemon	.70	.70
C3	A1	3r dl grn & brt yel	1.00	1.00
C4	A1	4r grnsh bl & sal	1.40	1.40
C5	A1	5r emerald & gray	1.60	1.60
C6	A1	10r olive bis & rose	3.50	3.50
		Nos. C1-C6 (6)	8.60	8.60

Nos. C1-C6 Overprinted

1964, Apr. 7

Black Portrait and Inscriptions; Lilac Rose Flag

C7	A1	1r ultra & fawn	1.10	1.10
C8	A1	2r lt violet & lem	2.10	2.10
C9	A1	3r dull grn & brt yel	4.25	4.25
C10	A1	4r grnsh blue & sal	5.50	5.50
C11	A1	5r emerald & gray	7.50	7.50
C12	A1	10r olive bis & rose	12.00	12.00
		Nos. C7-C12 (6)	32.45	32.45

Pres. John F. Kennedy (1917-63).

World Map and Flame AP1

1964, Apr. 15 *Perf. 14x14½*

C13	AP1	50np red brown	.20	.20
C14	AP1	1r purple	.40	.40
C15	AP1	150np Prus green	.60	.60
		Nos. C13-C15 (3)	1.20	1.20

Issued for Human Rights Day. An imperf. souvenir sheet contains one 3r carmine rose stamp. Size of stamp: 67x40mm. Size of sheet: 89x64mm.

View of Khor Fakkan — AP2

Designs: 20np, Beni Qatab Bedouin camp near Dhaid. 30np, Oasis of Dhaid. 40np, Kalba Castle. 75np, Sharjah street with wind tower. 100np, Sharjah Fortress.

1964, Aug. 13 Photo. Unwmk.

C16	AP2	10np multi	.20	.20
C17	AP2	20np multi	.20	.20
C18	AP2	30np multi	.20	.20
C19	AP2	40np multi	.20	.20
C20	AP2	75np multi	.25	.20
C21	AP2	100np multi	.40	.20
		Nos. C16-C21 (6)	1.45	1.20

Unisphere and Sheik Saqr — AP3

J. F. Kennedy, Statue of Liberty — AP4

20np, Offshore oil rig. 1r, New York skyline.

Perf. 14½x14

1964, Sept. 5 Photo. Unwmk.

Size: 26x45mm

C22	AP3	20np multi	.20	.20
C23	AP3	40np multi	.20	.20

Size: 86x45mm

C24	AP3	1r multi, horiz.	.40	.40
a.		Strip of 3, Nos. C22-C24	.60	.60

New York World's Fair, 1964-65.

An imperf. souvenir sheet exists with one 40np stamp in AP3 design. Size of stamp: 40x68mm. Size of sheet: 76x108mm.

1964, Nov. 22 *Perf. 14x13½*

C25	AP4	40np multicolored	.75	.75
C26	AP4	60np multicolored	1.25	1.25
C27	AP4	100np multicolored	2.00	2.00
		Nos. C25-C27 (3)	4.00	4.00

Pres. John F. Kennedy. A souvenir sheet contains one each of Nos. C25-C27, imperf. Size: 107x76mm.

Rock Dove AP5

Birds: 40np, 2r, Red jungle fowl. 75np, 3r, Hoopoe.

Perf. 14x14½

1965, Feb. 20 Photo. Unwmk.

C28	AP5	30np gray & multi	.20	.20
C29	AP5	40np multicolored	.20	.20
C30	AP5	75np brt blue & multi	.25	.20
C31	AP5	150np blue & multi	1.40	.20
C32	AP5	2r multicolored	1.50	.25
C33	AP5	3r red & multi	4.50	.40
		Nos. C28-C33 (6)	8.05	1.45

OFFICIAL STAMPS

Nos. 7-15 Overprinted

Perf. 14½x14

1965, Jan. 13 Photo. Unwmk.

O1	A1	8np multi	.20	.20
O2	A1	10np multi	.20	.20
O3	A1	16np multi	.20	.20
O4	A1	20np multi	.20	.20
O5	A1	30np multi	.20	.20
O6	A1	40np multi	.20	.20
O7	A1	50np multi	.20	.20
O8	A1	75np multi	.35	.35
O9	A1	100np multi	.50	.50
		Nos. O1-O9 (9)	2.25	2.25

SIBERIA

sī-ˈbir-ē-ə

LOCATION — A vast territory of Russia lying between the Ural Mountains and the Pacific Ocean.

The anti-Bolshevist provisional government set up at Omsk by Adm. Aleksandr V. Kolchak issued Nos. 1-10 in 1919. The monarchist, anti-Soviet government in Priamur province issued Nos. 51-118 in 1921-22.

(Stamps of the Czechoslovak Legion are listed under Czechoslovakia.)

100 Kopecks = 1 Ruble

Russian Stamps of 1909-18 Surcharged

a

b

On Stamps of 1909-12

1919 Unwmk. *Perf. 14x14½*

Wove Paper

Lozenges of Varnish on Face

1	A14(a)	35k on 2k dull grn	.55	*2.75*
a.		Inverted surcharge	27.50	
b.		"5" omitted	*80.00*	
c.		Double surcharge	—	
2	A14(a)	50k on 3k car	.55	*2.75*
a.		Inverted surcharge	35.00	
3	A14(a)	70k on 1k dl org yel	.80	*5.50*
a.		Inverted surcharge	27.50	
4	A15(b)	1r on 4k car	.90	*2.75*
a.		Dbl. surch., one inverted	110.00	*110.00*
b.		Inverted surcharge	55.00	
c.		Double surcharge	80.00	
5	A14(b)	3r on 7k blue	1.50	*5.50*
a.		Double surcharge	27.50	*27.50*
b.		Inverted surcharge	22.50	*22.50*
c.		Pair, one without surcharge	—	
d.		"3" omitted	—	
6	A11(b)	5r on 14k dk bl & car	2.75	*14.00*
a.		Double surcharge	22.50	*22.50*
b.		Inverted surcharge	22.50	*22.50*

On Stamps of 1917

Imperf

7	A14(a)	35k on 2k gray grn	.90	*5.50*
a.		Inverted surcharge	*80.00*	
8	A14(a)	50k on 3k red	.90	*5.50*
a.		Inverted surcharge	100.00	
b.		Double surcharge	—	
9	A14(a)	70k on 1k orange	.75	*5.50*
a.		Inverted surcharge	35.00	
b.		Dbl. surch., one inverted	—	
10	A15(b)	1r on 4k car	4.50	*7.75*
		Nos. 1-10 (10)	14.10	*57.50*

Nos. 1-10, were first issued in Omsk during the regime of Admiral Kolchak. Later they were used along the line of the Trans-Siberian railway to Vladivostok.

Some experts question the postal use of most off-cover canceled copies of Nos. 1-10.

25P 1-

Similar surcharges, handstamped as above are bogus.

Priamur Government Issues

Nikolaevsk Issue

A5

A6

A7

Russian Stamps Handstamp Surcharged or Overprinted

On Stamps of 1909-17

1921 Unwmk. *Perf. 14x14½, 13½*

No.	Type	Description	Unused	Used
51	A5	10k on 4k carmine	*110.00*	
52	A5	10k on 10k dark blue	*1,200.*	
53	A6	15k on 14k dk blue & car	*125.00*	
54	A6	15k on 15k red brn & dp bl	*70.00*	
55	A6	15k on 35k red brn & grn	*80.00*	
56	A6	15k on 50k brn vio & grn	*75.00*	
57	A6	15k on 70k brn & red org	*200.00*	
58	A7	15k on 1r brn & org	*175.00*	
59	A5	on 20k dl bl & dk car	*175.00*	
60	A5	on 20k on 14k dk bl & car (#118)	*160.00*	
a.		15k on 20k on 14k dk bl & car (error)	—	
61	A7	20k on 3½r mar & lt grn	*200.00*	
62	A7	20k on 5r ind, grn & lt bl	*850.00*	
63	A7	20k on 7r dk grn & pink	*400.00*	

Nos. 59-60 are overprinted with initials but original denominations remain.

A 10k on 5k claret (Russia No. 77) and a 15k on 20k blue & carmine (Russia No. 82a) were not officially issued. Some authorities consider them bogus.

No evidence found of genuine usage of #51-72.

Reprints exist.

On Semi-Postal Stamp of 1914

No.	Type	Description	Unused	Used
64	SP6	20k on 3k mar & gray grn, *pink*	*775.00*	

On Stamps of 1917

Imperf

No.	Type	Description	Unused	Used
65	A5	10k on 1k orange	*55.00*	
66	A5	10k on 2k gray green	*60.00*	
67	A5	10k on 3k red	*60.00*	
68	A5	10k on 5k claret	*700.00*	
69	A6	15k on 1r pale brn, brn & red org	*80.00*	
70	A7	20k on 1r pale brn, brn & red org	*140.00*	
71	A7	20k on 3½r mar & lt grn	*260.00*	
72	A7	20k on 7r dk grn & pink	*500.00*	

The letters of the overprint are the initials of the Russian words for "Nikolaevsk on Amur Priamur Provisional Government."

As the surcharges on Nos. 51-72 are handstamped, a number exist inverted or double.

A 20k blue & carmine (Russia No. 126) with Priamur overprint and a 15k on 20k (Russia No. 126) were not officially issued. Some authorities consider them bogus.

No evidence found of genuine usage of #51-72.

Stamps of Far Eastern Republic Overprinted

1922

No.	Type	Description	Unused	Used
78	A2	2k gray green	25.00	25.00
a.		Inverted overprint	125.00	
79	A2a	4k rose	25.00	25.00
a.		Inverted overprint	*110.00*	
80	A2	5k claret	25.00	25.00
81	A2a	10k blue	25.00	25.00
		Nos. 78-81 (4)	100.00	100.00

Anniv. of the overthrow of the Bolshevik power in the Priamur district.

The letters of the overprint are the initials of "Vremeno Priamurski Pravitel'stvo" i.e. Provisional Priamur Government, 26th May.

Russian Stamps of 1909-21 Overprinted in Dark Blue or Vermilion

On Stamps of 1909-18

1922 *Perf. 14x14½*

No.	Type	Description	Unused	Used
85	A14	1k dull org yel	45.00	50.00
86	A14	2k dull green	80.00	65.00
87	A14	3k carmine	25.00	30.00
88	A15	4k carmine	12.50	15.00
89	A14	5k dk claret	25.00	27.50
90	A14	7k blue (V)	25.00	27.50
91	A15	10k dark blue (V)	35.00	40.00
92	A11	14k dk bl & car	45.00	55.00
93	A11	15k red brn & dp bl	12.50	15.00
94	A8	20k dl bl & dk car	12.50	15.00
95	A11	20k on 14k dk bl & car	100.00	100.00
96	A11	25k dl grn & dk vio (V)	25.00	30.00
97	A11	35k red brn & grn	7.50	10.00
a.		Inverted overprint	80.00	
98	A8	50k brn vio & grn	12.50	15.00
99	A11	70k brn & red org	25.00	30.00
		Nos. 85-99 (15)	487.50	525.00

On Stamps of 1917

Imperf

No.	Type	Description	Unused	Used
100	A14	1k orange	4.25	5.00
a.		Inverted overprint	65.00	85.00
101	A14	2k gray green	9.00	9.00
102	A14	3k red	12.00	12.00
103	A15	4k carmine	65.00	65.00
104	A14	5k claret	19.00	15.00
105	A11	15k red brn & dp bl	110.00	100.00
106	A8	20k blue & car	47.50	40.00
107	A9	1r pale brn, brn & red org	14.00	15.00
		Nos. 100-107 (8)	280.75	261.00

On Stamps of Siberia, 1919

Perf. 14½x15

No.	Type	Description	Unused	Used
108	A14	35k on 2k green	60.00	60.00

Imperf

No.	Type	Description	Unused	Used
109	A14	70k on 1k orange	85.00	85.00

On Stamps of Far Eastern Republic, 1921

No.	Type	Description	Unused	Used
110	A2	2k gray green	6.00	5.50
111	A2a	4k rose	6.00	5.50
112	A2	5k claret	6.00	5.50
a.		Inverted overprint	100.00	
113	A2a	10k blue (R)	4.00	3.50
		Nos. 109-113 (5)	107.00	105.00

Same, Surcharged with New Values

No.	Type	Description	Unused	Used
114	A2	1k on 2k gray grn	4.00	3.50
115	A2a	3k on 4k rose	4.00	3.50

The overprint is in a rectangular frame on stamps of 1k to 10k and 1r; on the other values the frame is omitted. It is larger on the 1 ruble than on the smaller stamps.

The overprint reads "Priamurski Zemski Krai," Priamur Rural Province.

Far Eastern Republic Nos. 30-32 Overprinted in Blue

Perf. 14½x15

No.	Type	Description	Unused	Used
116	A14	35k on 2k green	5.00	6.50

Imperf

No.	Type	Description	Unused	Used
117	A14	35k on 2k green	90.00	110.00
118	A14	70k on 1k orange	8.25	11.50
		Nos. 116-118 (3)	103.25	128.00

Counterfeits of Nos. 51-118 abound.

SIERRA LEONE

sē-ˌer-ə lē-ˈōn

LOCATION — West coast of Africa, between Guinea and Liberia
GOVT. — Republic in British Commonwealth
AREA — 27,925 sq. mi.
POP. — 5,296,651 (1999 est.)
CAPITAL — Freetown

Sierra Leone was a British colony and protectorate. In 1961 it became fully independent, remaining within the Commonwealth. It became a republic April 19, 1971.

12 Pence = 1 Shilling
20 Shillings = 1 Pound
100 Cents = 1 Leone (1964)

Catalogue values for unused stamps in this country are for Never Hinged items, beginning with Scott 186 in the regular postage section and Scott C1 in the air post section.

Watermark

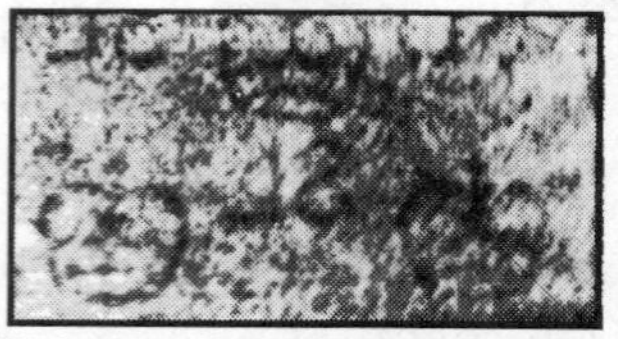

Wmk. 336- St. Edwards Crown & SL, Multiple

Queen Victoria
A1 A2

1859-74 Unwmk. Typo. *Perf. 14*

No.	Type	Description	Unused	Used
1	A1	6p bright violet ('74)	37.50	27.50
a.		6p dull violet ('59)	200.00	50.00
b.		6p gray lilac ('65)	225.00	40.00

1872 *Perf. 12½*

No.	Type	Description	Unused	Used
5	A1	6p violet	325.00	55.00

1872 Wmk. 1 Sideways *Perf. 12½*

No.	Type	Description	Unused	Used
6	A2	1p rose	67.50	27.50
8	A2	3p yellow buff	110.00	35.00
9	A2	4p blue	140.00	37.50
10	A2	1sh yellow green	325.00	50.00

1873 Wmk. 1 Upright

No.	Type	Description	Unused	Used
6a	A2	1p	80.00	30.00
7	A2	2p magenta	110.00	45.00
8a	A2	3p	500.00	80.00
9a	A2	4p	250.00	47.50
10a	A2	1sh	375.00	90.00

1876-96 Wmk. 1 Upright *Perf. 14*

No.	Type	Description	Unused	Used
11	A2	½p bister	1.90	5.75
12	A2	1p rose	45.00	10.00
13	A2	1½p violet ('77)	45.00	6.00
14	A2	2p magenta	50.00	3.75
15	A2	3p yellow buff	45.00	4.00
16	A2	4p blue	110.00	6.50
17	A1	6p brt violet ('85)	52.50	22.50
a.		Half used as 3p on cover		2,500.
18	A1	6p violet brn ('90)	12.50	13.00
19	A1	6p brown vio ('96)	2.00	6.25
20	A2	1sh green	55.00	6.50
		Nos. 11-20 (10)	418.90	84.25

For surcharge see No. 32.

1883-93 Wmk. Crown and C A (2)

No.	Type	Description	Unused	Used
21	A2	½p bister	19.00	45.00
22	A2	½p dull green ('84)	.40	.75
23	A2	1p carmine ('84)	2.00	.75
a.		1p rose carmine	27.50	8.00
b.		1p rose	200.00	35.00
24	A2	1½p violet ('93)	2.25	5.50
25	A2	2p magenta	45.00	7.00
26	A2	2p slate ('84)	24.00	2.25
27	A2	2½p ultra ('91)	6.75	.80
28	A2	3p org yel ('92)	2.00	6.75
29	A2	4p blue	825.00	27.50
30	A2	4p bister ('84)	1.50	1.00
31	A2	1sh org brn ('88)	15.00	10.00
		Nos. 21-28,30-31 (10)	117.90	79.80

For surcharge see No. 33.

HALF
PENNY

Nos. 13 and 24 Surcharged in Black

1893 Wmk. 1

No.	Type	Description	Unused	Used
32	A2	½p on 1½p violet	450.00	*475.00*
a.		"PFNNY"	2,000.	*2,500.*

Wmk. 2

No.	Type	Description	Unused	Used
33	A2	½p on 1½p violet	2.75	3.00
a.		"PFNNY"	72.50	*65.00*
b.		Inverted surcharge	100.00	100.00
c.		Same as "a," inverted	1,800.	
d.		Double surcharge	*1,000.*	

A4

1896-97

No.	Type	Description	Unused	Used
34	A4	½p lilac & grn ('97)	1.00	1.75
35	A4	1p lilac & car	1.00	1.25
36	A4	1½p lilac & blk ('97)	2.75	11.50
37	A4	2p lilac & org	2.25	5.00
38	A4	2½p lilac & ultra	1.40	1.00
39	A4	3p lilac & sl ('97)	6.50	6.50
40	A4	4p lilac & car ('97)	8.00	12.50
41	A4	5p lilac & blk	8.75	11.00
42	A4	6p lilac ('97)	6.50	15.00
43	A4	1sh green & blk	5.75	15.00
44	A4	2sh green & ultra	22.50	32.50
45	A4	5sh green & car	47.50	110.00
46	A4	£1 violet, *red*	140.00	350.00
		Nos. 34-46 (13)	253.90	573.00

Numerals of Nos. 39-46 of type A4 are in color on plain tablet.

A5

A6

2½d. a — 2½d. b — 2½d. c — 2½d. d — 2½d. e — 2½d. f

1897 Wmk. C A over Crown (46)

No.	Type	Description	Unused	Used
47	A5	1p lilac & grn	2.00	2.25
a.		Double overprint	*1,300.*	*1,300.*
48	A6(a)	2½p on 3p lil & grn	12.50	*13.00*
a.		Double surcharge	*16,000.*	
49	A6(b)	2½p on 3p	60.00	*65.00*
50	A6(c)	2½p on 3p	160.00	*170.00*
51	A6(d)	2½p on 3p	275.00	*350.00*
52	A6(a)	2½p on 6p lil & grn	10.00	*12.50*
53	A6(b)	2½p on 6p	45.00	*50.00*
54	A6(c)	2½p on 6p	110.00	110.00
55	A6(d)	2½p on 6p	225.00	*250.00*
56	A6(a)	2½p on 1sh lilac	95.00	75.00
57	A6(b)	2½p on 1sh lilac	1,100.	1,100.
58	A6(c)	2½p on 1sh lilac	450.00	450.00
59	A6(e)	2½p on 1sh lilac	1,750.	2,000.
59A	A6(f)	2½p on 1sh lilac	1,350.	1,350.
60	A6(a)	2½p on 2sh lilac	1,700.	1,800.
61	A6(b)	2½p on 2sh lilac	*16,000.*	
62	A6(c)	2½p on 2sh lilac	*8,500.*	*9,500*
63	A6(e)	2½p on 2sh lilac	*35,000.*	*40,000*
63A	A6(f)	2½p on 2sh lilac	*35,000.*	*40,000*

The words "POSTAGE AND REVENUE" on Nos. 56-63A are set in two lines and overprinted below instead of above "2½d."

The "d" in type "f" is 3½mm wide; that in type "a" is 3mm.

Very fine examples of Nos. 47-63A will have perforations touching the frameline on one or more sides.

Nos. 56-59A are often found discolored. Such copies sell for about half the values quoted.

King Edward VII — A7

Numerals of 3p to £1 of type A7 are in color on plain tablet.

1903 Wmk. Crown and C A (2)

64	A7	½p	violet & grn	3.00	4.00
65	A7	1p	violet & car	1.50	1.00
66	A7	1½p	violet & blk	1.25	8.50
67	A7	2p	violet & brn org	3.00	13.50
68	A7	2½p	violet & ultra	3.75	7.00
69	A7	3p	violet & gray	7.25	11.00
70	A7	4p	violet & car	5.75	12.00
71	A7	5p	violet & blk	6.50	27.50
72	A7	6p	violet & dull vio	9.00	13.00
73	A7	1sh	green & blk	11.50	40.00
74	A7	2sh	green & ultra	32.50	42.50
75	A7	5sh	green & car	55.00	80.00
76	A7	£1	violet, *red*	160.00	190.00
			Nos. 64-76 (13)	300.00	450.00

1904-05 Wmk. 3

Chalky Paper

77	A7	½p	violet & grn	4.50	2.25
78	A7	1p	violet & car	.75	.25
79	A7	1½p	violet & blk	2.50	7.50
80	A7	2p	violet & brn org	4.00	3.00
81	A7	2½p	violet & ultra	4.00	1.75
82	A7	3p	violet & gray	19.00	3.00
83	A7	4p	violet & car	5.00	5.50
84	A7	5p	violet & blk	10.00	16.00
85	A7	6p	violet & dl vio	4.50	3.00
86	A7	1sh	green & blk	7.00	8.00
87	A7	2sh	green & ultra	12.00	18.00
88	A7	5sh	green & car	30.00	45.00
89	A7	£1	violet, *red*	200.00	200.00
			Nos. 77-89 (13)	303.25	313.25

The 1p also exists on ordinary paper.

1907-10

Ordinary Paper

90	A7	½p	green	.40	.25
91	A7	1p	carmine	6.00	.25
92	A7	1½p	orange ('10)	.48	1.25
93	A7	2p	gray	.70	1.25
94	A7	2½p	ultra	1.75	1.10

Chalky Paper

95	A7	3p	violet, *yel*	5.00	2.50
96	A7	4p	blk & red, *yel*	2.00	1.00
97	A7	5p	vio & ol grn	5.00	3.50
98	A7	6p	vio & red vio	3.00	4.50
99	A7	1sh	black, *green*	5.00	4.00
100	A7	2sh	vio & bl, *bl*	14.00	12.00
101	A7	5sh	grn & red, *yel*	25.00	35.00
102	A7	£1	vio & blk, *red*	150.00	160.00
			Nos. 90-102 (13)	218.33	226.60

The 3p also exists on ordinary paper.

King George V and Seal of the Colony
A8 A9
Die I

For description of dies I and II see back of this volume.

Numerals of 3p, 4p, 5p, 6p and 10p of type A8 are in color on plain tablet. Numerals of 7p and 9p are on solid-color tablet.

1912-24 Ordinary Paper Wmk. 3

103	A8	½p	green	1.00	2.00
104	A8	1p	scarlet	1.00	.80
a.			1p carmine	1.25	.20
105	A8	1½p	orange	1.00	1.50
106	A8	2p	gray	1.00	.20
107	A8	2½p	ultra	6.50	2.00

Chalky Paper

108	A9	3p	violet, *yel*	2.50	2.75
109	A8	4p	blk & red, *yel*	1.25	7.00
a.			Die II ('24)	4.00	5.00
110	A8	5p	violet & ol grn	.85	4.25
111	A8	6p	vio & red vio	3.00	4.25
112	A8	7p	violet & org	1.90	7.00
113	A8	9p	violet & blk	4.50	9.00
114	A8	10p	violet & red	3.00	15.00
115	A9	1sh	black, *green*	3.50	3.75
a.			1sh black, *emerald*		165.00
116	A9	2sh	vio & ultra, *bl*	7.50	4.50
117	A9	5sh	grn & red, *yel*	9.00	21.00
118	A9	10sh	grn & red, *grn*	42.50	150.00
119	A9	£1	vio & blk, *red*	110.00	90.00
120	A9	£2	violet & ultra	500.00	600.00
121	A9	£5	gray grn & org	1,200.	—
			Nos. 103-119 (17)	200.00	325.00

The status of #115a has been questioned.

Die II

1921-27 Wmk. 4

Ordinary Paper

122	A8	½p	green	1.10	.40
123	A8	1p	violet ('26)	2.50	.20
a.			Die I ('24)	1.25	2.00
124	A8	1½p	scarlet	1.10	1.00
125	A8	2p	gray ('22)	.75	.20
126	A8	2½p	ultra	.85	3.75
127	A8	3p	ultra ('22)	.85	.75
128	A8	4p	blk & red, *yel*	1.50	3.00
129	A8	5p	vio & ol grn	.70	.70

Chalky Paper

130	A8	6p	dp vio & red vio	1.10	2.00
131	A8	7p	vio & org ('27)	2.40	13.00
132	A8	9p	dl vio & blk ('22)	2.40	9.25
133	A8	10p	violet & red	2.50	17.00
134	A9	1sh	blk, *emerald*	5.75	5.50
135	A9	2sh	vio & ultra, *bl*	8.25	7.75
136	A9	5sh	grn & red, *yel*	8.25	35.00
137	A9	10sh	grn & red, *grn*	65.00	125.00
138	A9	£2	violet & ultra	450.00	600.00
139	A9	£5	gray grn & org	1,000.	1,500.
			Nos. 122-137 (16)	105.00	224.50

Rice Field — A10

Palms and Kola Tree — A11

1932, Mar. 1 Engr. *Perf. 12½*

140	A10	½p	green	.20	.20
141	A10	1p	dk violet	.20	.20
142	A10	1½p	rose car	.30	1.00
143	A10	2p	yellow brn	.30	.20
144	A10	3p	ultra	.75	1.00
145	A10	4p	orange	.75	2.25
146	A10	5p	olive green	.75	1.25
147	A10	6p	light blue	.75	1.25
148	A10	1sh	red brown	2.50	3.00

Perf. 12

149	A11	2sh	dk brown	6.00	8.25
150	A11	5sh	indigo	10.00	14.00
151	A11	10sh	deep green	40.00	85.00
152	A11	£1	deep violet	77.50	125.00
			Nos. 140-152 (13)	140.00	242.60

Wilberforce Issue

Arms of Sierra Leone — A12

Slave Throwing Off Shackles — A13

Map of Sierra Leone — A14

Old Slave Market, Freetown A15

Fruit Seller — A16

Government Sanatorium — A17

Bullom Canoe — A18

Punting near Banana Islands — A19

Government Buildings, Freetown A20

Old Slavers' Resort, Bunce Island — A21

African Elephant — A22

George V A23

Freetown Harbor — A24

1933, Oct. 2

153	A12	½p	deep green	.40	1.00
154	A13	1p	brown & blk	.35	.20
155	A14	1½p	orange brn	4.00	3.75
156	A15	2p	violet	2.50	.20
157	A16	3p	ultra	2.00	1.60
158	A17	4p	dk brown	6.50	8.50
159	A18	5p	red brn & sl grn	6.50	13.50
160	A19	6p	dp org & blk	6.50	6.75
161	A20	1sh	dk violet	5.25	14.50
162	A21	2sh	bl & dk brn	21.00	35.00
163	A22	5sh	red vio & blk	125.00	140.00
164	A23	10sh	green & blk	140.00	200.00
165	A24	£1	yel & dk vio	350.00	350.00
			Nos. 153-165 (13)	670.00	775.00

Abolition of slavery in the British colonies and cent. of the death of William Wilberforce, English philanthropist and agitator against the slave trade.

Common Design Types pictured following the introduction.

Silver Jubilee Issue

Common Design Type

1935, May 6 *Perf. 11x12*

166	CD301	1p	black & ultra	.85	2.00
167	CD301	3p	ultra & brown	.90	7.00
168	CD301	5p	indigo & green	1.25	7.00
169	CD301	1sh	brown vio & ind	5.00	4.00
			Nos. 166-169 (4)	8.00	20.00

Coronation Issue

Common Design Type

1937, May 12 *Perf. 11x11½*

170	CD302	1p	deep orange	.25	.25
171	CD302	2p	dark violet	.30	.30
172	CD302	3p	deep ultra	.40	1.00
			Nos. 170-172 (3)	.95	1.55
			Set, never hinged	2.25	

Freetown Harbor A25

Rice Harvesting A26

1938-44 *Perf. 12½*

173	A25	½p	green & blk	.20	.20
174	A25	1p	dp cl & blk	.20	.20
175	A26	1½p	rose red	12.00	.60
175A	A26	1½p	red vio ('41)	.20	.50
176	A26	2p	red violet	24.00	1.50
176A	A26	2p	dark red ('41)	.20	.85
177	A25	3p	ultra & blk	.20	.30
178	A25	4p	red brn & blk	.45	2.25
179	A26	5p	olive green	3.00	3.00
180	A26	6p	gray	.45	.30
181	A25	1sh	ol grn & blk	.90	.40
181A	A26	1sh3p	org yel ('44)	.20	.30
182	A25	2sh	sepia & blk	2.50	1.60
183	A26	5sh	red brown	5.75	4.25
184	A26	10sh	emerald	9.50	6.25
185	A25	£1	dk blue	10.00	15.00
			Nos. 173-185 (16)	69.75	37.50
			Set, never hinged	105.00	

Catalogue values for unused stamps in this section, from this point to the end of the section, are for Never Hinged items.

Peace Issue

Common Design Type

Perf. 13½x14

1946, Oct. 1 Engr. Wmk. 4

186	CD303	1½p	lilac	.20	.20
187	CD303	3p	bright ultra	.20	.20

Silver Wedding Issue

Common Design Types

1948, Dec. 1 Photo. *Perf. 14x14½*

188	CD304	1½p	brt red violet	.20	.20

Engraved; Name Typographed

Perf. 11½x11

189	CD305	£1	dark blue	15.00	16.00

UPU Issue

Common Design Types

Engr.; Name Typo. on 3p, 6p

1949, Oct. 10 *Perf. 13½, 11x11½*

190	CD306	1½p	rose violet	.20	.25
191	CD307	3p	indigo	.35	1.25
192	CD308	6p	gray	.60	1.50
193	CD309	1sh	olive	1.00	.75
			Nos. 190-193 (4)	2.15	3.75

Coronation Issue

Common Design Type

1953, June 2 Engr. *Perf. 13½x13*

194	CD312	1½p	purple & black	.25	.25

Cape Lighthouse A27

Cotton Tree, Freetown — A28

1p, Queen Elizabeth II Quay. 1½d, Piassava workers. 3p, Rice harvesting. 4p, Iron ore production, Marampa. 6p, Whale Bay, York Village. 1sh, Bullom boat. 1sh3p, Map of Sierra Leone & plane. 2sh6p, Orugu Bridge. 5sh, Kuranko chief. 10sh, Law Courts, Freetown. £1, Government House.

Perf. 13 (A27), 13½ (A28)

1956, Jan. 2 Engr. Wmk. 4

Center in Black

195	A27	½p	lt violet	.70	1.00
196	A27	1p	reseda	.70	.20
197	A27	1½p	ultra	1.25	2.50
198	A28	2p	lt brown	.55	.20
199	A28	3p	ultra	.95	.20
a.		Perf 13x13½		1.40	6.00
200	A27	4p	gray blue	1.90	.65
201	A27	6p	violet	.75	.20
202	A28	1sh	carmine	.95	.20
203	A27	1sh3p	gray brown	8.25	.20
204	A28	2sh6p	brown org	10.50	4.00
205	A28	5sh	green	1.75	1.25
206	A27	10sh	red violet	2.75	1.90
207	A27	£1	orange	9.00	12.00
			Nos. 195-207 (13)	40.00	24.50

For surcharges and overprints see Nos. 242-247, 251-253, 255-256, 319, 322, C1-C7, C13.

Independent State

Carrying Oil Palm Fruit — A29

Diamond Miner and Badge A30

Badge and: 1½p, 5sh, Bundu mask. 2p, 10sh, Bishop Crowther and Old Fourah Bay College. 3p, 6p, Sir Milton Margai. 4p, 1sh3p, Lumley Beach, Freetown. £1, Bugler.

Perf. 13x13½, 13½x13

1961, Apr. 27 Engr. Wmk. 336

208	A29	½p	blue grn & dk brn	.20	.20
209	A30	1p	gray grn & brn org	1.10	.20
210	A29	1½p	green & blk	.20	.20
211	A29	2p	vio blue & blk	.20	.20
212	A30	3p	brn org & ultra	.20	.20
213	A30	4p	rose red & grnsh bl	.20	.20
214	A30	6p	lilac & gray	.20	.20
215	A29	1sh	org & dk brn	.30	.20
216	A30	1sh3p	vio & grnsh bl	.30	.20
217	A30	2sh6p	black & grn	2.50	.25
218	A29	5sh	rose red & blk	.90	1.10
219	A29	10sh	emerald & blk	.95	*1.10*
220	A29	£1	carmine & yel	6.75	3.25
			Nos. 208-220 (13)	14.00	7.50

Sierra Leone's Independence.

For surcharges see Nos. 254, 274, 279-280, 285-286, 290-291, 294, 296, 299, C10, C29-C31, C132-C133.

Royal Charter, 1799 — A31

House of Representatives, Freetown, 1924 — A32

Designs: 4p, King's Yard Gate, Freetown, 1817. 1sh3p, Yacht "Britannia."

1961, Nov. 25 Engr. Wmk. 336

221	A31	3p	vermilion & blk	.20	.20
222	A31	4p	violet & blk	.25	.25
223	A32	6p	orange & blk	.30	.30
224	A32	1sh3p	blue & blk	.60	.60
			Nos. 221-224 (4)	1.35	1.35

Visit of Elizabeth II to Sierra Leone, Nov., 1961.

For overprints and surcharges see Nos. 272, 278, C8-C9, C11-C12.

Malaria Eradication Emblem — A33

1962, Apr. 7 ***Perf. 11x11½***

225	A33	3p	crimson	.20	.20
226	A33	1sh3p	green	.40	.40

WHO drive to eradicate malaria.

Fireball Lily — A34

Jina Gbo — A35

Plants: 1½p, Stereospermum. 2p, Black-eyed Susan. 3p, Beniseed. 4p, Blushing hibiscus. 6p, Climbing lily. 1sh, Beautiful crinum. 1sh3p, Bluebells. 2sh6p, Broken hearts. 5sh, Ra-ponthi. 12sh, Blue plumbago. £1, African tulip tree.

1963, Jan. 1 Photo. ***Perf. 14***

Flowers in Natural Colors

227	A34	½p	olive brown	.20	.20
228	A35	1p	org ver & dk red	.20	.20
229	A34	1½p	green	.20	.20
230	A35	2p	lemon	.20	.20
231	A34	3p	dark green	.20	.20
232	A34	4p	lt violet blue	.20	.20
233	A35	6p	indigo	.20	.20
234	A34	1sh	brt yel grn & red	.40	.25
235	A35	1sh3p	dk yellow grn	.50	.25
236	A34	2sh6p	dk gray	1.00	.70
237	A34	5sh	deep violet	1.50	1.25
238	A34	10sh	red lilac	3.25	2.75
239	A35	£1	bright blue	8.50	6.75
			Nos. 227-239 (13)	16.55	13.35

For surcharges see Nos. 271, 273, 276-277, 283-284, 289, 295, 300-305, 317-318, 320-321, 329-332, C37-C41, C57-C60, C134.

Wheat Emblem, Grain Bin and Threshing Machine A36

1sh3p, Bullom woman examining onion crop.

Perf. 11½x11

1963, Mar. 21 Engr. Wmk. 336

240	A36	3p	orange yel & blk	.20	.20
241	A36	1sh3p	green & brown	.40	.40

FAO "Freedom from Hunger" campaign.

For surcharges see Nos. 275, C28.

Nos. 195, 197 and 199 Surcharged in Red, Brown, Orange, Violet or Blue:

On A27

On A28

Perf. 13, 13½

1963, Apr. 27 Wmk. 4

Center in Black

242	A27	3p	on ½p lt vio (R)	.20	.20
243	A27	4p	on 1½p ultra (Br)	.20	.20
244	A27	6p	on ½p lt vio (O)	.20	.20
245	A28	10p	on 3p ultra (R)	.30	.30
246	A28	1sh6p	on 3p ultra (V)	.40	.40
247	A28	3sh6p	on 3p ultra (Bl)	.85	.85
			Nos. 242-247 (6)	2.15	2.15

Type "a" exists in two settings, varying in the width of the line "19 Progress 63." In each sheet of 60, this line measures 19½-21mm on 55 stamps, and 17½-18mm on 5 stamps. See Nos. C1-C7.

Centenary Emblem — A37

Design: 6p, Red Cross. 1sh3p, Centenary Emblem with curved-lines background.

Perf. 11x11½

1963, Nov. 1 Engr. Wmk. 336

248	A37	3p	purple & red	.20	.20
249	A37	6p	black & red	.20	.20
250	A37	1sh3p	dark green & red	.30	.30
			Nos. 248-250 (3)	.70	.70

Centenary of International Red Cross.

For surcharge see No. C56.

Nos. 199, 197, 216 and 195 Overprinted or Surcharged in Pink, Red, Violet or Brown

1853–1859–1963
Oldest Postal Service
Newest G.P.O.
in West Africa

4d.

Perf. 13, 13½, 13½x13

1963, Nov. 4 Engr. Wmk. 4

Center in Black except No. 254

251	A28	3p	(P)	.20	.20
252	A27	4p	on 1½p (R)	.20	.20
253	A27	9p	on 1½p (V)	.20	.20
254	A30	1sh	on 1sh3p (R)	.20	.20
255	A27	1sh6p	on ½p (P)	.30	.30
256	A28	2sh	on 3p (Br)	.35	.35
			Nos. 251-256,C8-C13 (12)	12.75	12.75

Oldest postal service (1st stamps in 1859) and the newest GPO in West Africa. Overprint in 5 lines on Nos. 251 and 256. A number of surcharge varieties and errors exist.

Map and Lion of Sierra Leone — A38

Engraved and Lithographed

1964, Feb. 10 Unwmk. ***Die Cut***

Self-adhesive

257	A38	1p	multicolored	.20	.20
258	A38	3p	multicolored	.20	.20
259	A38	4p	multicolored	.20	.20
260	A38	6p	multicolored	.20	.20
261	A38	1sh	multicolored	.20	.20
262	A38	2sh	multicolored	.30	.30
263	A38	5sh	multicolored	.80	.80
			Nos. 257-263,C14-C20 (14)	5.85	5.85

New York World's Fair, 1964-65.

For surcharges see Nos. 288, 297, 335 and note under No. 299.

"John F. Kennedy, American Patriot, World Humanitarian" A39

1964, May 11

Self-adhesive

264	A39	1p	multicolored	.20	.20
265	A39	3p	multicolored	.20	.20
266	A39	4p	multicolored	.20	.20
267	A39	6p	multicolored	.20	.20
268	A39	1sh	multicolored	.20	.20
269	A39	2sh	multicolored	.35	.35
270	A39	5sh	multicolored	.95	.95
			Nos. 264-270,C21-C27 (14)	6.80	6.80

For surcharges see Nos. 281-282, 287, 292-293, 298, 333, 336, and note under No. 299.

Issues of 1961-63 Surcharged in Red, Black, Dark Blue, Violet or Orange

1964, Aug. 4

271	A35	1c on 6p (#233) (R)	.20	.20
272	A31	2c on 3p (#221)	.20	.20
273	A34	3c on 3p (#231)	.20	.20
274	A29	5c on ½p (#208) (DB)	.20	.20
275	A36	8c on 3p (#240) (R)	.20	.20
276	A35	10c on 1sh3p (#235) (R)	.30	.25
277	A34	15c on 1sh (#234)	.40	.40
278	A32	25c on 6p (#223) (V)	.60	.60
279	A30	50c on 2sh6p (#217) (O)	1.20	1.20
		Nos. 271-279,C28-C31 (13)	5.70	5.65

Issues of 1961-64 Surcharged in Black or Gold

1965, Jan. 20

280	A30	1c on 3p (#212)	.20	.20
281	A39	2c on 1p (#264)	.20	.20
282	A39	4c on 3p (#265)	.20	.20
283	A35	5c on 2p (#230)	.20	.20
284	A34	1 le on 5sh (#237) (G)	2.50	2.50
285	A29	2 le on £1 (#220)	5.25	5.25
		Nos. 280-285 (6)	8.55	8.55

The surcharges on Nos. 284-285 are given in numerals and spelled out in two lines; numeral on Nos. 280-283.

Issues of 1961-64 Surcharged in Red, Black, Orange, Blue or Pink

1965, Apr.

286	A29	1c on 1½p (#210) (R)	.20	.20
287	A39	2c on 3p (#265)	.20	.20
288	A38	2c on 4p (#259)	.20	.20
289	A35	3c on 1p (#228)	.20	.20
290	A29	3c on 2p (#211) (O)	.20	.20

291	A30	5c on 1sh3p (#216) (O)	.20	.20
292	A39	15c on 6p (#267)	.95	.95
293	A39	15c on 1sh (#268) (O)	1.65	1.65
294	A30	20c on 6p (#214) (O)	.40	.40
295	A35	25c on 6p (#233) (R)	.55	.55
296	A30	50c on 3p (#212) (R)	1.10	1.10
297	A38	60c on 5sh(#263) (Bl)	2.50	2.50
298	A39	1 le on 4p (#266) (P)	3.25	3.25
299	A29	2 le on £1 (#220) (Bl)	6.00	6.00
		Nos. 286-299 (14)	17.60	17.60

Additional surcharges exist: "1c" on Nos. 260, 262, 269-270. See note after No. C41 for airmails. Value $4 each.

For surcharges see Nos. 333, 335-336.

Nos. 228, 231, 234, 235, 232, 237 Surcharged

Designs of Surcharge: Nos. 301, 304, Sir Milton Margai. Nos. 302, 305, Sir Winston Churchill.

Wmk. 336

1965, May 19 Photo. *Perf. 14*

300	A35	2c on 1p multi	.20	.20
301	A34	3c on 3p multi	.20	.20
302	A34	10c on 1sh multi	.30	.30
303	A35	20c on 1sh3p multi	.55	.55
304	A34	50c on 4p multi	1.25	1.25
305	A34	75c on 5sh multi	2.25	2.25
		Nos. 300-305,C37-C41 (11)	14.35	14.35

For surcharges see Nos. 329-332.

Cola Nut and Plant — A40

Coat of Arms A41

Typographed; Embossed on Silver Foil

1965 Unwmk. *Die Cut*

Self-adhesive

310	A40	1c multicolored	.20	.20
311	A40	2c multicolored	.20	.20
312	A40	3c multicolored	.20	.20
313	A40	4c multicolored	.30	.30
314	A40	5c multicolored	.30	.30

Engr.; Embossed on Paper

315	A41	20c multi, *cream*	.75	.60
316	A41	50c multi, *cream*	2.00	1.75
		Nos. 310-316,C53-C55 (10)	6.80	6.40

Various advertisements printed on peelable paper backing. Nos. 310-316 have side tabs for handling and come packed in boxes of 100. Nos. 310-312 and 314 were released during November due to a stamp shortage; official release date for set, Dec. 17, 1965. See #338-356, C67, C97. For surcharges see #334, 337, 364-368.

Nos. 197-198, and 232-234, 236 Surcharged with New Value in Black or Ultramarine and Overprinted: "FIVE YEARS / INDEPENDENCE / 1961-1966"

1966, Apr. 27 Wmk. 4, 336

317	A35	1c on 6p multi	.20	.20
318	A34	2c on 4p multi	.20	.20
319	A27	3c on 1½p ultra & blk (U)	.20	.20
320	A34	8c on 1sh multi (U)	.20	.20
321	A34	10c on 2sh6p multi (U)	.20	.20
322	A28	20c on 2p lt brown (U)	.40	.40
		Nos. 317-322,C56-C60 (11)	6.10	6.10

5th anniv. of independence. The surcharge on No. 317 includes an "X" over old denomination.

Lion's Head Coin — A42

Designs: 2c, 3c, ¼ Golde coin. 5c, 8c, ½ Golde coin. 25c, 1 le, 1 Golde coin. (3c, 8c, 1 le, Map of Sierra Leone.)

Litho.; Embossed on Gilt Foil

1966, Nov. 12 Unwmk. *Die Cut*

Self-adhesive

Diameter: 2c, 3c, 38mm; 5c, 8c, 54mm; 25c, 1 le, 82mm

323	A42	2c orange & dp plum	.20	.20
324	A42	3c red lilac & emerald	.20	.20
325	A42	5c vio blue & red org	.20	.20
326	A42	8c black & Prus blue	.20	.20
327	A42	25c emerald & violet	.35	.35
328	A42	1 le red & orange	1.75	1.75
		Nos. 323-328,C61-C66 (12)	8.40	8.40

1st gold coinage of Sierra Leone. Advertising printed on paper backing.

Nos. 297-298, 303-305 and 316 Surcharged in Red, Silver, Violet, Green, Blue or Black:

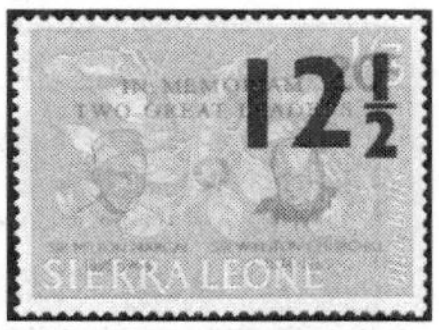

on A34, A35

on A38, A39

on A41

1967, Dec. 2

329	A34	6½c on 75c on 5sh (R)	.30	.30
330	A34	7½c on 75c on 5sh (S)	.30	.30
331	A34	9½c on 50c on 4p (G)	.40	.40
332	A35	12½c on 20c on 1sh3p (V)	.50	.50
333	A39	17½c on 1 le on 4p (Bl)	3.50	3.50
334	A41	17½c on 50c	3.50	3.50
335	A38	18½c on 60c on 5sh	10.00	10.00
336	A39	18½c on 1 le on 4p	3.50	3.50
337	A41	25c on 50c	1.00	1.00
		Nos. 329-337,C67-C69 (12)	24.90	24.90

Self-adhesive & Die Cut

Nos. 338-421 are self-adhesive and die cut.

Cola Nut Type of 1965

Typographed; Embossed on White Paper

1967-68 Unwmk.

White Numeral Tablet

338	A40	½c brt car, grn & yel	.20	.20
339	A40	1c brt car, grn & yel	.20	.20
340	A40	1½c orange, grn & yel	.20	.20
341	A40	2c brt car, grn & yel	.25	.25
342	A40	2½c emer, bl grn & yel	.40	.40
343	A40	3c brt car, grn & yel	.25	.25
344	A40	3½c olive, rose & ultra	.25	.25
345	A40	4½c gray ol, grn & yel	.40	.40
346	A40	5c brt car, grn & yel	.40	.40
347	A40	5½c red brn, grn & yel	.45	.45
		Nos. 338-347 (10)	3.00	3.00

Advertisements printed on peelable backing except on the 2c, 3c, 3½c and 5c.

Colored Numeral Tablet

348	A40	½c brt car, grn & yel	.20	.20
349	A40	1c brt car, grn & yel	.20	.20
350	A40	2c pink, brn & car	.20	.20
351	A40	2c brt car, grn & yel	.75	.60
352	A40	2½c bl grn, vio & org	1.00	.75
353	A40	2½c emer, bl grn & yel	.30	.20
354	A40	3c brt car, grn & yel	.20	.20
355	A40	3½c lilac rose, grn & yel	.30	.30
356	A40	4c brt car, grn & yel	.25	.25
		Nos. 348-356 (9)	3.40	2.90

Nos. 344, 348-354 issued in 1968.

Advertisements printed on peelable backing on the 3½c and 4c.

Map of Africa Showing Rhodesia A43

Each denomination shows map of Africa with map of one of the following countries—Portuguese Guinea, South Africa, Mozambique, Rhodesia, South West Africa or Angola.

1968, Sept. 25 Unwmk. Litho.

357	A43	½c multicolored	.20	.20
358	A43	2c multicolored	.20	.20
359	A43	2½c multicolored	.20	.20
360	A43	3½c multicolored	.20	.20
361	A43	10c multicolored	.40	.40
362	A43	11½c multicolored	.45	.45
363	A43	15c multicolored	.60	.60
		Nos. 357-363 (7)	2.25	2.25
		7 Strips of 6 (1 of each design) (42)	11.40	

Intl. Human Rights Year. Sheets of 30 have 5 horizontal rows containing one stamp of each design. Advertisements printed on peelable backing.

See #C72-C78. For surcharges see #C106-C111.

No. 316 Surcharged

Engraved; Embossed on Paper

1968, Nov. 30

364	A41	6½c on 50c multi	.20	.20
365	A41	17½c on 50c multi	.30	.30
366	A41	22½c on 50c multi	.40	.40
367	A41	28½c on 50c multi	.50	.50
368	A41	50c on 50c multi	.85	.85
		Nos. 364-368,C79-C83 (10)	4.65	4.65

19th Olympic Games, Mexico City, 10/12-27.

Sierra Leone Type A1, 1859 A44

2c, Design A40, 2c, 1965. 3½c, #220. 5c, #315. 12½c, #189. 1 le, Design A9, #2, 1912.

1969, Mar. 1 Litho.

369	A44	1c multicolored	.20	.20
370	A44	2c multicolored	.20	.20
371	A44	3½c multicolored	.20	.20
372	A44	5c multicolored	.20	.20
373	A44	12½c multicolored	.40	.40
374	A44	1 le multicolored	4.75	4.75
		Nos. 369-374,C84-C89 (12)	25.25	25.25

5th anniv. of free-form self-adhesive postage stamps. Various advertisements printed on peelable paper backing. No. 369 has side tab for handling and comes packed in boxes of 50. Nos. 370-374 are without side tabs and come 20 stamps attached to one sheet.

Globe, Freighter, Flags of Sierra Leone and Japan — A45

Map of Europe and Africa, Freighter, Flags of Sierra Leone and Netherlands — A46

Anvil Shape with Flags of Sierra Leone and: 3½c, Union Jack. 10c, 50c, West Germany. 18½c, Netherlands.

1969, July 10

375	A45	1c multicolored	.20	.20
376	A46	2c multicolored	.20	.20
377	A46	3½c multicolored	.20	.20
378	A46	10c multicolored	.20	.20
379	A46	18½c multicolored	.30	.30
380	A46	50c multicolored	.80	.80
		Nos. 375-380,C90-C95 (12)	7.80	7.80

Completion of the Pepel Port iron ore carrier terminal. Various advertisements printed on peelable paper backing. No. 375 has side tab for handling and comes packed in boxes of 50. Nos. 376-380 are without side tabs and come 20 stamps attached to one sheet.

African Development Bank Emblem — A47

Lithographed; Gold Impressed

1969, Sept. 10

381 A47 3½c lt blue, grn & gold .30 .30

5th anniv. of the African Development Bank. Advertising printed on peelable paper backing, 20 imperf. stamps to a sheet of backing, roulette 10. See No. C96.

Diamond and Boy Scout Emblem A48

1969, Dec. 6 **Litho.**

382 A48 1c multicolored .20 .20
383 A48 2c multicolored .20 .20
384 A48 3½c multicolored .20 .20
385 A48 4½c multicolored .25 .20
386 A48 5c multicolored .30 .30
387 A48 75c multicolored 10.00 8.00
Nos. 382-387,C100-C105 (12) 123.50 91.20

60th anniv. of the Sierra Leone Boy Scouts. Various advertising printed on peelable paper backing. No. 382 has side tab for handling and comes packed in boxes of 100. Nos. 383-387 are without side tabs and come 20 stamps attached to one sheet.

EXPO '70 Emblems, Torii, Maps of Sierra Leone and Japan — A49

1970, June 22

388 A49 2c multicolored .20 .20
389 A49 3½c multicolored .20 .20
390 A49 10c multicolored .20 .20
391 A49 12½c multicolored .30 .30
392 A49 20c multicolored .45 .45
393 A49 45c multicolored 1.00 1.00
Nos. 388-393,C112-C117 (12) 13.05 13.05

EXPO '70 Intl. Exhib., Osaka, Japan, Mar. 15-Sept. 13. Various advertising printed on peelable paper backing.

Diamond A50

Palm Kernel — A51

Lithographed and Embossed

1970, Oct. 3 **Unwmk.**

Light Blue Background

394 A50 1c carmine & blk .20 .20
395 A50 1½c brt green & car .20 .20
396 A50 2c lilac & yel grn .20 .20
397 A50 2½c ocher & dk bl .20 .20
398 A50 3c vio bl & org red .25 .25
399 A50 3½c dk blue & grn .30 .30
400 A50 4c olive & ultra .30 .30
401 A50 5c black & lilac .30 .30

Orange Brown Background

402 A51 6c bright green .30 .30
403 A51 7c rose lilac .45 .45
404 A51 8½c orange .50 .50
405 A51 9c lilac .50 .50
406 A51 10c dark blue .55 .55
407 A51 11½c blue .75 .75
408 A51 18½c yellow green 1.10 1.10
Nos. 394-408,C118-C124 (22) 28.60 24.80

Advertisements printed on peelable paper backing. Packed in boxes of 500.

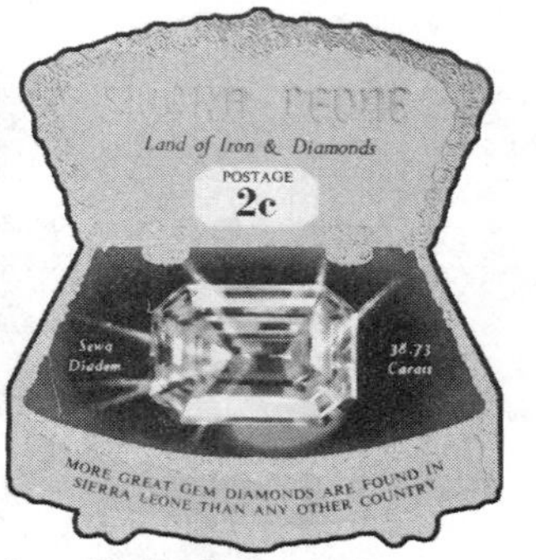

Sewa Diadem in Jewelry Box — A52

1970, Dec. 30

409 A52 2c multicolored .20 .20
410 A52 3½c multicolored .20 .20
411 A52 10c multicolored .35 .35
412 A52 12½c multicolored .45 .45
413 A52 40c multicolored 1.50 1.35
414 A52 1 le multicolored 7.50 5.00
Nos. 409-414,C125-C130 (12) 39.20 30.55

Diamond industry. Advertisement printed on peelable paper backing. Sheets of 20.

Traffic Pattern — A53

1971, Mar. 1 **Litho.**

415 A53 3½c orange & vio blue .25 .25

Right hand traffic change-over. See No. C131. Advertisements printed on peelable paper backing.

Flag and Lion's Head — A54

Litho.; Embossed in Silver

1971, Apr. 27

416 A54 2c multicolored .20 .20
417 A54 3½c multicolored .20 .20
418 A54 10c multicolored .20 .20
419 A54 12½c multicolored .20 .20
420 A54 40c multicolored .80 .80
421 A54 1 le multicolored 1.75 1.75
Nos. 416-421,C137-C142 (12) 12.20 12.20

10th anniversary of independence. Advertisements printed on peelable paper backing. Stamps are in shape of Sierra Leone map.

Pres. Siaka Stevens — A55

1972 **Litho.** ***Perf. 13***

422 A55 1c pink & multi .20 .20
423 A55 2c violet & multi .20 .20
424 A55 4c lt ultra & multi .20 .20
425 A55 5c buff & multi .20 .20
426 A55 7c rose & multi .20 .20
427 A55 10c olive & multi .20 .20
428 A55 15c emerald & multi .25 .25
429 A55 18c yellow & multi .30 .30
430 A55 20c lt blue & multi .35 .35
431 A55 25c orange & multi .40 .40
432 A55 50c brt green & multi .90 .90
433 A55 1 le multicolored 1.60 1.60
434 A55 2 le red org & multi 3.25 3.25
435 A55 5 le multicolored 8.50 8.50
Nos. 422-435 (14) 16.75 16.75

Shades from later printings are found on several denominations including 1c, 2c, 7c, 10c, 1 le, 2 le.

Guma Valley Dam and Bank Emblem — A56

1975, Jan. 14 **Litho.** ***Perf. 13½***

436 A56 4c multicolored *125.00* *82.50*

African Development Bank, 10th anniversary. See No. C143.

Pres. Siaka Stevens and Opening of Congo Bridge — A57

1975, Aug. 24 **Litho.** ***Perf. 13x13½***

437 A57 5c multicolored *11.00* *11.00*

Congo Bridge opening and Pres. Siaka Stevens' 70th birthday. See No. C144.

Pres. Tolbert and Stevens, Hands across Mano River — A58

1975, Oct. 3 **Litho.** ***Perf. 13x13½***

438 A58 4c multicolored 1.40 1.40

Mano River Union Agreement between Liberia and Sierra Leone, signed Oct. 3, 1973. See No. C145.

Mohammed Ali Jinnah, Flags of Sierra Leone and Pakistan — A59

Elizabeth II — A60

1977, Jan. 28 **Litho.** ***Perf. 13 rough***

439 A59 30c multicolored .80 .80

Mohammed Ali Jinnah (1876-1948), First Governor General of Pakistan.

1977, Nov. 28 **Litho.** ***Perf. 12½x12***

440 A60 5c multicolored .20 .20
441 A60 1 le multicolored 1.40 1.40

25th anniv. of the reign of Elizabeth II.

Fourah Bay College — A61

Design: 20c, Old College, vert.

Perf. 12x12½, 12½x12

1977, Dec. 19 **Litho.**

442 A61 5c multicolored .20 .20
443 A61 20c multicolored .35 .35

Fourah Bay College, Mt. Aureol, Freetown, founded 1827.

St. Edward's Crown and Scepters — A62

Designs: 50c, Elizabeth II in coronation coach. 1 le, Elizabeth II and Prince Philip on coronation day.

1978, Sept. 14 **Litho.** ***Perf. 14½x14***

444 A62 5c multicolored .20 .20
445 A62 50c multicolored .60 .60
446 A62 1 le multicolored 1.10 1.10
Nos. 444-446 (3) 1.90 1.90

25th anniv. of coronation of Elizabeth II.

Fig Tree Blue A63

Butterflies: 15c, Narrow blue-banded swallowtail. 25c, Pirate. 1 le, African giant swallowtail.

1979, Apr. 9 Litho. *Perf. 14½*

447 A63 5c multicolored .20 .20
448 A63 15c multicolored .35 .35
449 A63 25c multicolored .60 .60
450 A63 1 le multicolored 2.50 2.50
Nos. 447-450 (4) 3.65 3.65

Child, IYC and SOS Emblems — A64

Designs (Emblems and): 27c, Girl and infant. 1 le, Mother and infant.

Perf. 14x13½

1979, Aug. 13 Litho. Wmk. 373

451 A64 5c multicolored .20 .20
452 A64 27c multicolored .55 .55
453 A64 1 le multicolored 2.25 2.25
a. Souvenir sheet of 1 2.50 2.50
Nos. 451-453 (3) 3.00 3.00

Intl. Year of the Child and 30th anniv. of SOS villages (villages for homeless children).

Presidents Stevens and Tolbert, Pigeon Post, Mano River — A65

1979, Oct. 3 *Perf. 13½*

454 A65 5c multicolored .20 .20
455 A65 22c multicolored .30 .30
456 A65 27c multicolored .40 .40
457 A65 35c multicolored .45 .45
458 A65 1 le multicolored 1.40 1.40
a. Souvenir sheet of 1 1.40 1.40
Nos. 454-458 (5) 2.75 2.75

Mano River Union, 5th anniv.; Postal Union, 1st anniv.

Sierra Leone No. 9, Hill — A66

1979, Dec. 19 Litho. *Perf. 14½x14*

459 A66 10c Grt. Britain #6 .20 .20
460 A66 15c shown .25 .25
461 A66 50c Sierra Leone #220 .90 .90
Nos. 459-461 (3) 1.35 1.35

Souvenir Sheet

462 A66 1 le Sierra Leone #119 1.25 1.25

Sir Rowland Hill (1795-1879), originator.

Touraco A67

1980, Jan. 29 *Perf. 14*

463 A67 1c shown .20 .20
464 A67 2c Olive-bellied sunbird .20 .20
465 A67 3c Black-headed oriole .20 .20
466 A67 5c Spur-winged goose .20 .20
467 A67 7c White-bellied didric cuckoo .20 .20
468 A67 10c Gray parrot, vert. .20 .20
469 A67 15c African blue quail, vert. .30 .30
470 A67 20c West African wood owl, vert. .40 .40
471 A67 30c Blue plantain eater, vert. .60 .60
472 A67 40c Nigerian blue-breasted kingfisher, vert. .75 .75
473 A67 50c Black crake, vert. 1.10 1.10
474 A67 1 le Hartlaub's duck 2.00 2.00
475 A67 2 le Black bee-eater 4.00 4.00
476 A67 5 le Denham's bustard 10.00 10.00
Nos. 463-476 (14) 20.35 20.35

Reissues: Nos. 464-476 inscribed 1982. Nos. 463-464, 466, 468-473, 475-476 inscribed 1983.

For surcharges see Nos. 632-636. For overprints see Nos. 637-638.

Rotary Intl., 75th Anniv. A68

1980, Feb. 23 *Perf. 14*

477 A68 5c orange & multi .20 .20
478 A68 27c red & multi .35 .35
479 A68 50c green & multi .70 .70
480 A68 1 le blue & multi 1.40 1.40
Nos. 477-480 (4) 2.65 2.65

Mail Ship "Maria," 1884, London '80 Emblem A69

1980, May 6 Litho. *Perf. 14*

481 A69 6c shown .20 .20
482 A69 31c "Tarquah," 1902 .45 .45
483 A69 50c "Aureol," 1951 .75 .75
484 A69 1 le "Africa Palm," 1974 1.50 1.50
Nos. 481-484 (4) 2.90 2.90

London 80 Intl. Stamp Exhib., May 6-14.

Conf. Emblem — A70

1980, July 1 Litho. *Perf. 14½*

485 A70 20c multicolored .25 .25
486 A70 1 le multicolored 1.25 1.25

17th African Summit Conf., Freetown, July 1-4.

Small Striped Swordtail — A71

1980, Oct. 6 Litho. *Perf. 14*

487 A71 5c shown .20 .20
488 A71 27c Pearl charaxes .45 .45
489 A71 35c White barred charaxes .55 .55
490 A71 1 le Zaddach's forester 1.65 1.65
Nos. 487-490 (4) 2.85 2.85

Freetown Airport — A72

1980, Dec. 5 Litho. *Perf. 13½*

491 A72 6c shown .20 .20
492 A72 26c Mammy Yoko Hotel .30 .30
493 A72 31c Freetown Cotton Tree .35 .35
494 A72 40c Beindomgo Falls .50 .50
495 A72 50c Water skiing .60 .60
496 A72 1 le Elephant 1.25 1.25
Nos. 491-496 (6) 3.20 3.20

Servals — A73

Cats and Kittens: No. 498, Serval kittens. No. 500a, African golden cats. No. 502a, Leopards. No. 504a, Lions. Pairs have continuous design.

1981, Feb. 23 Litho. *Perf. 14*

497 A73 6c multicolored .20 .20
498 A73 6c multicolored .20 .20
a. Pair, #497-498 .20 .20
499 A73 31c multicolored .45 .45
500 A73 31c multicolored .45 .45
a. Pair, #499-500 .90 .90
501 A73 50c multicolored .75 .75
502 A73 50c multicolored .75 .75
a. Pair, #501-502 1.50 1.50
503 A73 1 le multicolored 1.50 1.50
504 A73 1 le multicolored 1.50 1.50
a. Pair, #503-504 3.00 3.00
Nos. 497-504 (8) 5.80 5.80

Ambulance Clinic — A74

Wmk. 373

1981, Apr. 18 Litho. *Perf. 14½*

505 A74 6c Soldiers, vert. .20 .20
506 A74 31c shown .50 .50
507 A74 40c Traffic policeman, vert. .70 .70
508 A74 1 le Coast Guard ship 1.60 1.60
Nos. 505-508 (4) 3.00 3.00

Anniv.: independence, 20th; republic, 10th.

Royal Wedding Issue

Common Design Type

1981 Litho. *Perf. 12, 14*

509 CD331 31c Bouquet .60 .60
510 CD331 35c Sandringham .70 .70
511 CD331 45c Charles .95 .95
512 CD331 60c Charles 1.25 1.25
513 CD331 70c like 35c 1.50 1.50
514 CD331 1 le Couple 2.00 2.00
515 CD331 1.30 le Charles 2.50 2.50
516 CD331 1.50 le Couple 3.00 3.00
517 CD331 2 le Couple 4.00 4.00
Nos. 509-517 (9) 16.50 16.50

Souvenir Sheet

518 CD331 3 le Royal landau 5.00 5.00

31c, 45c, 1 le, 3 le issued July 22, perf. 14. 35c, 60c, 1.50 le issued in sheets of 5 plus label; perf. 12, Sept. 9. 70c, 1.30 le, 2 le issued in booklets only, perf. 14.

For surcharges see #540-546, 714, 716, 721.

Soccer Player — A75

Wmk. 373

1981, Sept. 30 Litho. *Perf. 14*

519 A75 6c shown .20 .20
520 A75 31c Boys planting trees .45 .45
521 A75 1 le Duke of Edinburgh 1.50 1.50
522 A75 1 le Pres. Stevens 1.50 1.50
Nos. 519-522 (4) 3.65 3.65

Duke of Edinburgh's Awards and Pres. Steven's Awards, 25th anniv.

Pineapples — A76

Woman Tending Rice Plants — A77

Perf. 14, 14½ (A77)

1981 Litho. Wmk. 373

523 A76 6c shown .20 .20
524 A77 6c Peanuts for export .20 .20
525 A76 31c Peanuts .50 .50
526 A77 31c Crushing, eating cassava .50 .50
527 A76 50c Cassava fruits .85 .85
528 A77 50c shown .85 .85
529 A76 1 le Rice plants 1.60 1.60
530 A77 1 le Men tending pineapple plants 1.60 1.60
Nos. 523-530 (8) 6.30 6.30

World Food Day. Issue dates: Nos. 523, 525, 527, 529, Oct. 16; others, Nov. 2.

Princess Diana Issue

Common Design Type

1982, July Litho. *Perf. 14½*

531 CD332 31c Caernarvon Castle .50 .50
532 CD332 50c Honeymoon .85 .85
533 CD332 2 le Wedding 3.00 3.00
Nos. 531-533 (3) 4.35 4.35

Souvenir Sheet

534 CD332 3 le Diana 4.75 4.75

Also issued in sheetlets of 5 + label.

For overprints and surcharges see Nos. 552-555, 713, 715, 717-720, 722-723.

Scouting Year A78

1982, Aug. 23 *Perf. 14*

535 A78 20c Studying animal husbandry .30 .30
536 A78 50c Botanical study .85 .85
537 A78 1 le Baden-Powell 1.60 1.60
538 A78 2 le Fishing at campsite 3.00 3.00
Nos. 535-538 (4) 5.75 5.75

Souvenir Sheet

539 A78 3 le Raising flag 4.75 4.75

For surcharges see Nos. 694-698.

Nos. 509-512, 514, 516, 518 Surcharged

1982, Aug. 30 Wmk. 373

540 CD331 50c on 31c 1.60 1.60
541 CD331 50c on 35c 1.60 1.60
542 CD331 50c on 45c 1.60 1.60
543 CD331 50c on 60c 1.60 1.60
544 CD331 90c on 1 le 2.75 2.75
545 CD331 2 le on 1.50 le 6.00 6.00
Nos. 540-545 (6) 15.15 15.15

Souvenir Sheet

546 CD331 3.50 le on 3 le 6.00 6.00

1982 World Cup — A79

Designs: Various soccer players.

1982, Sept. 7

547 A79 20c multicolored .35 .35
548 A79 30c multicolored .50 .50
549 A79 1 le multicolored 1.75 1.75
550 A79 2 le multicolored 3.25 3.25
Nos. 547-550 (4) 5.85 5.85

Souvenir Sheet

551 A79 3 le multicolored 4.75 4.75

For overprints see Nos. 561-565.

Nos. 531-534 Overprinted: "ROYAL BABY/ 21.6.82"

1982, Oct. 15 Litho. *Perf. 14½*

552 CD332 31c multicolored .50 .50
553 CD332 50c multicolored .85 .85
554 CD332 2 le multicolored 3.00 3.00
Nos. 552-554 (3) 4.35 4.35

Souvenir Sheet

555 CD332 3 le multicolored 4.75 4.75

Birth of Prince William of Wales, June 21. Also issued in sheetlets of 5 + label.
For surcharges see #715, 719-720, 723.

George Washington — A80

Various paintings of Washington. 31c, 1 le, vert.

1982, Oct. 30 Litho. *Perf. 14*

556 A80 6c multicolored .20 .20
557 A80 31c multicolored .45 .45
558 A80 50c multicolored .75 .75
559 A80 1 le multicolored 1.50 1.50
Nos. 556-559 (4) 2.90 2.90

Souvenir Sheet

560 A80 2 le multicolored 3.00 3.00

Nos. 547-551 Overprinted with Finalists and Score

1982, Nov. 9 *Perf. 14*

561 A79 20c multicolored .30 .30
562 A79 30c multicolored .45 .45
563 A79 1 le multicolored 1.50 1.50
564 A79 2 le multicolored 2.75 2.75
Nos. 561-564 (4) 5.00 5.00

Souvenir Sheet

565 A79 3 le multicolored 4.25 4.25

Italy's victory in 1982 World Cup.

Christmas — A81

Stained-glass Windows, St. George's Cathedral, Freetown.

1982, Nov. 18 *Perf. 14*

566 A81 6c Temptation of Christ .20 .20
567 A81 31c Baptism of Christ .45 .45
568 A81 50c Annunciation .75 .75
569 A81 1 le Nativity 1.50 1.50
Nos. 566-569 (4) 2.90 2.90

Souvenir Sheet

570 A81 2 le Mary and Joseph 3.00 3.00

Charles Darwin (1809-82) A82

1982, Dec. 10

571 A82 6c Long-snouted crocodile .20 .20
572 A82 31c Rainbow lizard .50 .50
573 A82 50c River turtle .90 .90
574 A82 1 le Chameleon 1.75 1.75
Nos. 571-574 (4) 3.35 3.35

Souvenir Sheet

575 A82 2 le Royal python, vert. 3.25 3.25

500th Birth Anniv. of Raphael — A83

School of Athens, Fresco, Vatican. Nos. 576-579 show details.

1983, Jan. 28 Litho. *Perf. 14*

576 A83 6c Diogenes .20 .20
577 A83 31c Euclid, Ptolemy .45 .45
578 A83 50c Euclid and his Students .75 .75
579 A83 2 le Pythagoras, Heraclitus 3.00 3.00
Nos. 576-579 (4) 4.40 4.40

Souvenir Sheet

580 A83 3 le Entire painting 4.50 4.50

A83a

1983, Mar. 14 Litho. *Perf. 14*

581 A83a 6c Agricultural training .20 .20
582 A83a 10c Tourism development .20 .20
583 A83a 50c Broadcast training .75 .75
584 A83a 1 le Airport services 1.50 1.50
Nos. 581-584 (4) 2.65 2.65

Commonwealth Day.

25th Anniv. of Economic Commission for Africa — A84

1983, Apr. 29 Litho. *Perf. 13½x13*

585 A84 1 le multicolored 1.40 1.40

Endangered Chimpanzees, World Wildlife Fund Emblem — A85

Various chimpanzees from Outamba-Kilimi Natl. Park. 10c, 31c, vert.

1983, May Litho. *Perf. 14*

586 A85 6c multicolored .20 .20
587 A85 10c multicolored .25 .25
588 A85 31c multicolored .70 .70
589 A85 60c multicolored 1.50 1.50
Nos. 586-589 (4) 2.65 2.65

Souvenir Sheet

590 A85 3 le Elephants 4.00 4.00

World Communications Year — A86

1983, July 14 *Perf. 14*

591 A86 6c Traditional communications .20 .20
592 A86 10c Mano River mail .20 .20
593 A86 20c Satellite ground station .30 .30
594 A86 1 le English packet, 1805 1.50 1.50
Nos. 591-594 (4) 2.20 2.20

Souvenir Sheet

595 A86 2 le Map, phone, envelope 3.00 3.00

Manned Flight Bicentenary — A87

1983, Aug. 31 Litho. *Perf. 14*

596 A87 6c Montgolfiere, 1783, vert. .20 .20
597 A87 20c Deutschland blimp, 1897 .35 .35
598 A87 50c Norge I blimp, North Pole, 1926 .80 .80
599 A87 1 le Cape Sierra sport balloon, Freetown, 1983, vert. 1.65 1.65
Nos. 596-599 (4) 3.00 3.00

Souvenir Sheet

600 A87 2 le Futuristic airship 2.75 2.75

Walt Disney, Space Ark Fantasy — A88

1983, Nov.

601 A88 1c Hippopotamus, Huey, Dewey and Louie .20 .20
602 A88 1c Mickey Mouse and Snake .20 .20
603 A88 3c Elephant and Donald Duck .20 .20
604 A88 3c Zebra and Goofy .20 .20
605 A88 10c Lion and Ludwig von Drake .20 .20
606 A88 10c Rhinoceros and Goofy .20 .20
607 A88 2 le Giraffe and Mickey Mouse 1.75 1.75
608 A88 3 le Monkey and Donald Duck 2.50 2.50
Nos. 601-608 (8) 5.45 5.45

Souvenir Sheet

609 A88 5 le Mickey Mouse and animals 4.50 4.50

10th Anniv. of Mano River Union A89

1984, Feb. 8 Litho. *Perf. 15*

610 A89 6c Teaching Program graduates .20 .20
611 A89 25c Emblem .20 .20
612 A89 31c Map, presidents .25 .25
613 A89 41c Guinea Accession signing .35 .35
a. Souvenir sheet of 1 .50 .50
Nos. 610-613 (4) 1.00 1.00

23rd Olympic Games, Los Angeles, July 28-Aug. 12 — A90

1984, Mar. 15 *Perf. 14*

614 A90 90c Gymnastics .65 .65
615 A90 1 le Hurdles .70 .70
616 A90 3 le Javelin 2.25 2.25
Nos. 614-616 (3) 3.60 3.60

Souvenir Sheet

617 A90 7 le Boxing 5.25 5.25

For surcharges see Nos. 699-702.

Apollo 11, 15th Anniv. — A91

1984, May 14 Litho. *Perf. 14*

618 A91 50c Lift off .40 .40
619 A91 75c Lunar landing .60 .60
620 A91 1.25 le 1st step on moon 1.00 1.00
621 A91 2.50 le Walking on moon 2.00 2.00
Nos. 618-621 (4) 4.00 4.00

Souvenir Sheet

622 A91 5 le TV transmission, horiz. 4.00 4.00

UPU Congress A92

1984, June 19

623 A92 4 le Concorde 2.75 2.75

Souvenir Sheet

624 A92 4 le UPU emblem, von Stephan 2.75 2.75

UN Decade for African Transportation — A93

Various cars.

1984, July 16 *Perf. 14½x15*

625	A93	12c	Citroen	.20	.20
626	A93	60c	Locomobile	.50	.50
627	A93	90c	AC Ace	.65	.65
628	A93	1 le	Vauxhall Prince Henry	.80	.80
629	A93	1.50 le	Delahaye-185	1.25	1.25
630	A93	2 le	Mazda	1.60	1.60
			Nos. 625-630 (6)	5.00	5.00

Souvenir Sheet

Perf. 15

631	A93	6 le	Volkswagon Beetle	5.00	5.00

Nos. 466, 468, 475 Surcharged

Wmk. 373

1984, Aug. 3 **Litho.** *Perf. 14*

632	A67	25c on 10c multi	.20	.20
633	A67	40c on 10c multi	.30	.30
634	A67	50c on 2 le multi	.50	.50
635	A67	70c on 5c multi	.55	.55
636	A67	10 le on 5c multi	8.00	8.00
		Nos. 632-636 (5)	9.55	9.55

#473, 476 Ovptd.: "AUSIPEX 84"

Wmk. 373

1984, Aug. 22 **Litho.** *Perf. 14*

637	A67	50c multicolored	.40	.40
638	A67	5 le multicolored	4.00	4.00

Portuguese Caravel Da Sintra — A94

1984

639	A94	2c	shown	.20	.20
640	A94	5c	Merlin of Bristol	.20	.20
641	A94	10c	Golden Hind	.20	.20
642	A94	15c	Interloper Morduant	.20	.20
643	A94	20c	Navy Board Transport Atlantic	.20	.20
644	A94	25c	Navy Vessel Lapwing	.20	.20
645	A94	30c	Brig Traveller	.20	.20
646	A94	40c	Schooner Amistad	.25	.25
647	A94	50c	Teazer	.30	.30
648	A94	70c	Cable Ship Scotia	.45	.45
649	A94	1 le	Alecto	.60	.60
650	A94	2 le	Blonde	1.25	1.25
651	A94	5 le	Fox	3.25	3.25
652	A94	10 le	Mail ship Accra	6.50	6.50
			Nos. 639-652 (14)	14.00	14.00

Issued: #639-649, 9/5; #650-651, 10/9; 10 le, 11/7.

See #739-740. For surcharges see #809-812.

1985 *Perf. 12½x12*

639a	A94	2c	.20	.20
640a	A94	5c	.20	.20
641a	A94	10c	.20	.20
643a	A94	20c	.20	.20
644a	A94	25c	.20	.20
645a	A94	30c	.20	.20
646a	A94	40c	.20	.20
647a	A94	50c	.20	.20
648a	A94	70c	.20	.20
649a	A94	1 le	.25	.25
650a	A94	2 le	.50	.50
651a	A94	5 le	1.25	1.25
652a	A94	10 le	2.50	2.50
		Nos. 639a-652a (13)	6.30	6.30

125th Anniv. of Sierra Leone Postage Stamps A95

1984, Oct. 9

653	A95	50c	Mail messenger, No. 2	.30	.30
654	A95	2 le	Post Master receiving letters, No. 2	1.25	1.25
655	A95	3 le	Cover	2.00	2.00
			Nos. 653-655 (3)	3.55	3.55

Souvenir Sheet

656	A95	5 le	Penny Black, No. 2	3.25	3.25

50th Anniv. of Donald Duck — A95a

1984, Nov. **Litho.** *Perf. 14x13½*

657	A95a	1c	Wise Little Hen	.20	.20
658	A95a	2c	Boat Builders	.20	.20
659	A95a	3c	Three Caballeros	.20	.20
660	A95a	4c	Mathematic Land	.20	.20
661	A95a	5c	Mickey Mouse Club	.20	.20
662	A95a	10c	On Parade	.20	.20
663	A95a	1 le	Don Donald	.80	.80
663A	A95a	2 le	Donald gets drafted, p. 12½x12	1.60	1.60
664	A95a	4 le	Tokyo Disneyland	3.25	3.25
			Nos. 657-664 (9)	6.85	6.85

Souvenir Sheet

665	A95a	5 le	Sketches	4.00	4.00

Christmas — A96

Mother and Child paintings.

1984, Nov. 28 *Perf. 14*

666	A96	20c	Pisanello	.20	.20
667	A96	1 le	Memling	.70	.70
668	A96	2 le	Raphael	1.40	1.40
669	A96	3 le	van der Werff	2.00	2.00
			Nos. 666-669 (4)	4.30	4.30

Souvenir Sheet

670	A96	6 le	Picasso	4.25	4.25

Songbirds A97

1985, Jan. 31 **Litho.**

671	A97	40c	Straw-tailed whydah	.40	.40
672	A97	90c	Spotted flycatcher	.95	.95
673	A97	1.30 le	Garden warbler	1.40	1.40
674	A97	3 le	Speke's weaver	3.00	3.00
			Nos. 671-674 (4)	5.75	5.75

Souvenir Sheet

675	A97	5 le	Great gray shrike	5.00	5.00

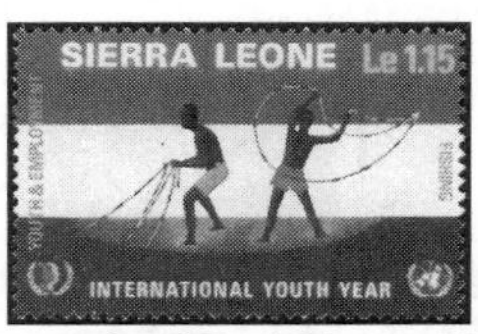

International Youth Year — A98

1985, Feb. 14 **Litho.**

676	A98	1.15 le	Fishing	1.10	1.10
677	A98	1.50 le	Timber	1.40	1.40
678	A98	2.15 le	Rice farming	2.00	2.00
			Nos. 676-678 (3)	4.50	4.50

Souvenir Sheet

679	A98	5 le	Diamond polishing	4.50	4.50

Intl. Civil Aviation Org., 40th Anniv. A100

Early aviators and their aircraft: 70c, Eddie Rickenbacker, Spad XIII (1918). 1.25 le, Samuel P. Langley, Aerodrome No. 5. 1.30 le, Orville and Wilbur Wright, Flyer 1. 2 le, Charles Lindbergh, Spirit of St. Louis.

1985, Feb. 28 **Litho.** *Perf. 14*

680	A100	70c	multicolored	.60	.60
681	A100	1.25 le	multicolored	1.10	1.10
682	A100	1.30 le	multicolored	1.10	1.10
683	A100	2 le	multicolored	1.90	1.90
			Nos. 680-683 (4)	4.70	4.70

Souvenir Sheet

684	A100	5 le	Jet over Freetown	4.50	4.50

Easter A101

Religious paintings: Nos. 685, 687, 689 by Botticelli (1445-1510). Nos. 686, 688 by Velazquez (1599-1660).

1985, Apr. 29

685	A101	45c	The Temptation of Christ	.20	.20
686	A101	70c	Christ at the Column	.25	.25
687	A101	1.55 le	Pieta	.55	.55
688	A101	10 le	Christ on the Cross	4.00	4.00
			Nos. 685-688 (4)	5.00	5.00

Souvenir Sheet

689	A101	12 le	Man of Sorrows	4.75	4.75

Queen Mother, 85th Birthday — A102

Designs: 1 le, Queen Mother at St. Peter's Cathedral, London, vert. 1.70 le, With Double Star at Sandown Racetrack. 10 le, Attending the gala ballet at Covent Garden, 1971, vert. 12 le, With Princess Anne at Ascot, vert.

1985, July 8 **Litho.** *Perf. 14*

690	A102	1 le	multicolored	.30	.30
691	A102	1.70 le	multicolored	.60	.60
692	A102	10 le	multicolored	3.25	3.25
			Nos. 690-692 (3)	4.15	4.15

Souvenir Sheet

693	A102	12 le	multicolored	4.00	4.00

Nos. 535-539 Surcharged "75th Anniversary / of Girl Guides," Black Bar and New Value

1985, July 25

694	A78	70c on 20c multi	.60	.60
695	A78	1.30 le on 50c multi	1.25	1.25
696	A78	5 le on 1 le multi	.90	.90
697	A78	7 le on 2 le multi	1.75	1.75
		Nos. 694-697 (4)	4.50	4.50

Souvenir Sheet

698	A78	15 le on 3 le multi	5.00	5.00

Nos. 614-617 Surcharged with Winners Names, Country, "Gold Medal," Black Bar and New Value

1985, July 25

699	A90	2 le on 90c Ma Yanhonjg, China	.65	.65
700	A90	4 le on 1 le E. Moses, USA	1.25	1.25
701	A90	8 le on 3 le A. Haerkoenen, Finland	2.50	2.50
		Nos. 699-701 (3)	4.40	4.40

Souvenir Sheet

702	A90	15 le on 7 le M. Taylor, USA	4.75	4.75

1905 Chater-Lea, Hill Station House — A103

Designs: 2 le, Honda XR 350 R, QE II Quay. 4 le, Kawasaki Vulcan, Bo Clock Tower. 5 le, Harley-Davidson Electra-Glide, Makeni. 12 le, 1893 Millet.

1985, Aug. 15

703	A103	1.40 le	multicolored	.45	.45
704	A103	2 le	multicolored	.65	.65
705	A103	4 le	multicolored	1.25	1.25
706	A103	5 le	multicolored	1.60	1.60
			Nos. 703-706 (4)	3.95	3.95

Souvenir Sheet

707	A103	12 le	multicolored	4.00	4.00

Motorcycle cent., Decade for African Transport.

A104 Christmas — A105

1985, Sept. 3

708	A104	70c	Viola pomposa	.25	.25
709	A104	3 le	Spinet	1.00	1.00
710	A104	4 le	Lute	1.25	1.25
711	A104	5 le	Oboe	1.60	1.60
			Nos. 708-711 (4)	4.10	4.10

Souvenir Sheet

712	A104	12 le	Portrait	4.00	4.00

Johann Sebastian Bach (1685-1750), composer. Nos. 708-712 show music from "Clavier Ubang."

Nos. 510, 512, 516, 531-534, 552-555 Surcharged

1985, Sept. 30 *Perfs. as Before*

Designs CD331-CD332

713	70c on 31c #531	.50	.50
714	1.30 le on 60c #512	.90	.90
715	1.30 le on 31c #552	.90	.90
716	2 le on 35c #510	1.25	1.25
717	4 le on 50c #532	2.75	2.75
718	5 le on 2 le #533	3.25	3.25
719	5 le on 50c #553	3.25	3.25
720	7 le on 2 le #554	4.50	4.50
721	8 le on 1.50 le #516	5.50	5.50
	Nos. 713-721 (9)	22.80	22.80

Souvenir Sheets

722	15 le on 3 le #534	7.00	7.00
723	15 le on 3 le #555	7.00	7.00

1985, Oct. 18 **Litho.** *Perf. 14*

Madonna and child paintings by: 70c, Carlo Crivelli (c. 1430-1494). 3 le, Dirk Bouts (c. 1400-1475). 4 le, Antonello de Messina (c. 1430-1479). 5 le, Stefan Lochner (c. 1400-1451). 12 le, Miniature from the Book of Kells, 9th cent., Ireland.

724	A105	70c	multicolored	.25	.25
725	A105	3 le	multicolored	1.00	1.00
726	A105	4 le	multicolored	1.25	1.25
727	A105	5 le	multicolored	1.60	1.60
			Nos. 724-727 (4)	4.10	4.10

Miniature Sheet

728	A105	12 le	multicolored	4.00	4.00

Jacob and Wilhelm Grimm, Fabulists — A106

Mark Twain, American Humorist A107

Walt Disney characters acting out Twain quotes (A107) or in Rumpelstiltskin (A106).

1985, Oct. 30 Litho. *Perf. 14*

729 A106	70c multicolored	.25	.25
730 A106	1.30 le multicolored	.40	.40
731 A107	1.50 le multicolored	.45	.45
732 A106	2 le multicolored	.55	.55
733 A107	3 le multicolored	.85	.85
734 A107	4 le multicolored	1.25	1.25
735 A107	5 le multicolored	1.40	1.40
736 A106	10 le multicolored	2.75	2.75
	Nos. 729-736 (8)	7.90	7.90

Souvenir Sheets

737 A106 15 le multicolored 4.25 4.25
738 A107 15 le multicolored 4.25 4.25

Nos. 731, 733-735 bear the Intl. Youth Year emblem.

Ship Type of 1984

1985, Nov. 15

739 A94 15 le Favourite 4.50 4.50
740 A94 25 le Euryalus 7.50 7.50

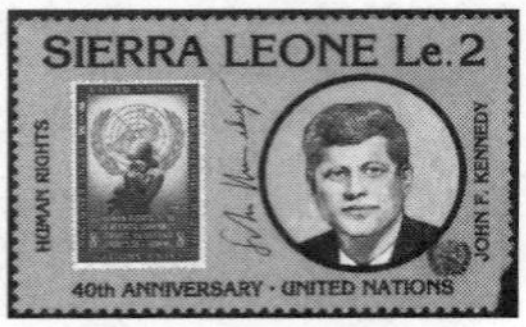

UN, 40th Anniv. A108

Stamps of UN and famous men: 2 le, No. 30, Kennedy. 4 le, No. 59, Einstein. 7 le, No. 44, Maimonides (1135-1204), medieval Judaic scholar. 12 le, Martin Luther King, Jr. (1929-1968), civil rights leader, vert.

1985, Nov. 28 Litho. *Perf. 14½*

741 A108 2 le multicolored .65 .65
742 A108 4 le multicolored 1.25 1.25
743 A108 7 le multicolored 2.25 2.25
Nos. 741-743 (3) 4.15 4.15

Souvenir Sheet

744 A108 12 le multicolored 4.00 4.00

1986 World Cup Soccer Championships A109

Statue of Liberty, Cent. — A110

Various soccer plays.

1986, Mar. 3 *Perf. 14*

745 A109 70c multicolored .30 .30
746 A109 3 le multicolored 1.10 1.10
747 A109 4 le multicolored 1.50 1.50
748 A109 5 le multicolored 1.90 1.90
Nos. 745-748 (4) 4.80 4.80

Souvenir Sheet

749 A109 12 le multicolored 4.50 4.50

For overprints and surcharges see Nos. 788-792.

1986, Mar. 11

New York City: 40c, Times Square, 1905. 70c, Times Square, 1986. 1 le, Tally Ho Coach, c. 1880, horiz. 10 le, Liberty Lines express bus, 1986. 12 le, Statue of Liberty.

750 A110 40c multicolored .20 .20
751 A110 70c multicolored .20 .20
752 A110 1 le multicolored .35 .35
753 A110 10 le multicolored 2.25 2.25
Nos. 750-753 (4) 3.00 3.00

Souvenir Sheet

754 A110 12 le multicolored 3.25 3.25

A111

Halley's Comet — A112

15c, Johannes Kepler (1571-1630), German astronomer, & Paris Observatory. 50c, US space shuttle landing, 1985. 70c, Bayeux Tapestry (detail), 1066 sighting. 10 le, Arthurian magician, Merlin, sights comet, 530. 12 le, Comet over Sierra Leone.

1986, Apr. 1

755 A111 15c multicolored .20 .20
756 A111 50c multicolored .20 .20
757 A111 70c multicolored .25 .25
758 A111 10 le multicolored 3.25 3.25
Nos. 755-758 (4) 3.90 3.90

Souvenir Sheet

759 A112 12 le multicolored 2.75 2.75

For overprints and surcharges see Nos. 813-817.

Queen Elizabeth II, 60th Birthday
Common Design Type

1986, Apr. 21

760 CD339 10c Cranwell, 1951 .20 .20
761 CD339 1.70 le Garter Ceremony .45 .45
762 CD339 10 le Braemar Games, 1970 2.10 2.10
Nos. 760-762 (3) 2.75 2.75

Souvenir Sheet

763 CD339 12 le Windsor Castle, 1943 2.25 2.25

For surcharges see Nos. 793-795.

AMERIPEX '86 — A113

Locomotives.

1986, May 22

764 A113 50c Hiawatha, Milwaukee .90 .90
765 A113 2 le The Rocket, Rock Is. 1.60 1.60
766 A113 4 le Prospector, Rio Grande 2.50 2.50
767 A113 7 le Daylight, So. Pacific 3.00 3.00
Nos. 764-767 (4) 8.00 8.00

Souvenir Sheet

768 A113 12 le Broadway, Pennsylvania 4.00 4.00

Royal Wedding Issue, 1986
Common Design Type

Designs: 10c, Prince Andrew and Sarah Ferguson. 1.70 le, Andrew with shotgun. 10 le, Andrew saluting. 12 le, Couple, diff.

1986, July 23

769 CD340 10c multi .20 .20
770 CD340 1.70 le multi .35 .35
771 CD340 10 le multi 1.60 1.60
Nos. 769-771 (3) 2.15 2.15

Souvenir Sheet

772 CD340 12 le multi 2.25 2.25

For surcharges see Nos. 796-798.

Indigenous Flowers — A114

1986, Aug. 25 Litho. *Perf. 15*

773 A114 70c Monodora myristica .20 .20
774 A114 1.50 le Gloriosa simplex .25 .25
775 A114 4 le Mussaenda erythrophylla .40 .40
776 A114 6 le Crinum ornatum .60 .60
777 A114 8 le Bauhinia purpurea .70 .70
778 A114 10 le Bombax costatum .85 .85
779 A114 20 le Hibiscus rosa-sinensis 1.50 1.50
780 A114 30 le Cassia fistula 2.00 2.00
Nos. 773-780 (8) 6.50 6.50

Souvenir Sheets

781 A114 40 le Clitoria ternatea 3.00 3.00
782 A114 40 le Plumbago auriculata 3.00 3.00

US Peace Corps in Sierra Leone, 25th Anniv. A115

1986, Aug. 26 Litho. *Perf. 14*

783 A115 10 le multi 1.10 1.10

Intl. Peace Year A116

1986, Sept. 1

784 A116 1 le Transportation .35 .35
785 A116 2 le Education .50 .50
786 A116 5 le Communications .90 .90
787 A116 10 le Fishing 1.75 1.75
Nos. 784-787 (4) 3.50 3.50

Nos. 745-749 Ovptd. or Surcharged "WINNERS / Argentina 3 / West Germany 2" in Gold

1986, Sept. 15 *Perf. 14*

788 A109 70c multi .30 .30
789 A109 3 le multi .70 .70
790 A109 4 le multi .75 .75
791 A109 40 le on 5 le multi 6.25 6.25
Nos. 788-791 (4) 8.00 8.00

Souvenir Sheet

792 A109 40 le on 12 le multi 3.75 3.75

Nos. 760, 762-763 Surcharged in Silver or Black

1986, Sept. 15

793 CD339 70c on 10c multi .50 .20
794 CD339 45 le on 10 le multi 4.00 4.00

Souvenir Sheet

795 CD339 50 le on 12 le (B) 3.25 3.25

Nos. 769, 771-772 Surcharged in Silver

1986, Sept. 15

796 CD340 70c on 10c multi .20 .20
797 CD340 45 le on 10 le multi 2.50 2.50

Souvenir Sheet

798 CD340 50 le on 12 le multi 3.75 3.75

STOCKHOLMIA '86 — A117

Disney characters in Mother Goose fairy tales.

1986, Sept. 22 *Perf. 11*

799 A117 70c Jack and Jill .20 .20
800 A117 1 le Wee Willie Winkie .20 .20
801 A117 2 le Little Miss Muffet .20 .20
802 A117 4 le Old King Cole .50 .50
803 A117 5 le Mary Quite Contrary .65 .65
804 A117 10 le Little Bo Peep 1.00 1.00
805 A117 25 le Polly Put the Kettle On 2.50 2.50
806 A117 35 le Rub-a-Dub-Dub 3.25 3.25
Nos. 799-806 (8) 8.50 8.50

Souvenir Sheets

807 A117 40 le Old Woman in the Shoe 4.00 4.00
808 A117 40 le Simple Simon 4.00 4.00

Nos. 639, 645-646 and 648 Surcharged

1986, Oct. 15

809 A94 30 le on 2c multi 2.75 2.75
810 A94 40 le on 30c multi 3.00 3.00
811 A94 45 le on 40c multi 3.50 3.50
812 A94 50 le on 70c multi 3.50 3.50
Nos. 809-812 (4) 12.75 12.75

Nos. 755-759 Ovptd. or Surcharged with Halley's Comet Emblem in Black or Silver

1986, Oct. 15

813 A111 50c multi .20 .20
814 A111 70c multi .20 .20
815 A111 1.50 le on 15c multi .20 .20
816 A111 45 le on 10 le multi 4.25 4.25
Nos. 813-816 (4) 4.85 4.85

Souvenir Sheet

817 A112 50 le on 12 le multi (S) 4.25 4.25

Christmas A118

Paintings by Titian: 70c, Virgin and Child with St. Dorothy. $1.50 le, The Gypsy Madonna, vert. 20 le, The Holy Family. 30 le, Virgin and Child in an Evening Landscape, vert. 40 le, Madonna with the Pesaro Family.

1986, Nov. 17 Litho. *Perf. 14*

818 A118	70c	multi	.20	.20
819 A118	1.50 le	multi	.20	.20
820 A118	20 le	multi	2.50	2.50
821 A118	30 le	multi	3.25	3.25
		Nos. 818-821 (4)	6.15	6.15

Souvenir Sheet

822 A118	40 le	multi	9.00	9.00

Statue of Liberty, Cent. A119

Pictures of the statue by Peter B. Kaplan before and after renovation. Nos. 823, 825-826, 828-829, 831, vert.

1987, Jan. 2 *Perf. 14*

823 A119	70c	Torch assembly	.20	.20
824 A119	1.50 le	Liberty holding torch	.20	.20
825 A119	2 le	Torch assembly, diff.	.20	.20
826 A119	3 le	Man, torch	.20	.20
827 A119	4 le	Crown	.20	.20
828 A119	5 le	Lighting of the statue	.25	.25
829 A119	10 le	Lighting, diff.	.50	.50
830 A119	25 le	Liberty Is.	1.25	1.25
831 A119	30 le	Face	1.50	1.50
		Nos. 823-831 (9)	4.50	4.50

UNICEF, 40th Anniv. A120

1987, Mar. 18 Litho. *Perf. 14*

832 A120	10 le	multi	.80	.80

Nomoli Soapstone Sculpture — A121

Tall Ship in Harbor, Freetown — A122

1987, Jan. 2 *Perf. 15*

833 A121	2 le	shown	.20	.20
834 A121	5 le	King's Yard Gate, 1817	.30	.30

Souvenir Sheet

835 A122	60 le	shown	3.50	3.50

First settlement of liberated slaves returned to the African continent by the British, Freetown, bicent.

America's Cup — A123

Constellation, 1964 — A124

1987, June 15 Litho. *Perf. 14*

836 A123	1 le	USA, 1987	.20	.20
837 A123	1.50 le	New Zealand, 1987	.20	.20
838 A123	2.50 le	French Kiss, 1987	.20	.20
839 A123	10 le	Stars & Stripes, 1987	.90	.90
840 A123	15 le	Australia II, 1983	1.25	1.25
841 A123	25 le	Freedom, 1980	2.00	2.00
842 A123	30 le	Kookaburra III, 1987	2.00	2.00
		Nos. 836-842 (7)	6.75	6.75

Souvenir Sheet

843 A124	50 le	shown	3.00	3.00

Nos. 837, 839 and 842 horiz.
For overprint see No. 964.

CAPEX '87 — A125

Disney characters, Canadian sights.

1987, June 15 *Perf. 11*

849 A125	2 le	Parliament	.20	.20
850 A125	5 le	Totem poles	.40	.40
851 A125	10 le	Perce Rock	.65	.65
852 A125	20 le	Canadian Rockies	1.00	1.00
853 A125	25 le	Old Quebec City	1.25	1.25
854 A125	45 le	Aurora Borealis	1.90	1.90
855 A125	50 le	Yukon P.O.	2.10	2.10
856 A125	75 le	Niagara Falls	3.50	3.50
		Nos. 849-856 (8)	11.00	11.00

Souvenir Sheets

857 A125	100 le	Exploring Newfoundland	4.75	4.75
858 A125	100 le	Calgary Exhibition and Stampede	4.75	4.75

Butterflies — A126

1988 Summer Olympics, Seoul — A127

1987, Aug. 4 *Perf. 14*

859 A126	10c	Blue salamis	1.40	.50
860 A126	20c	Pale-tailed blue	1.40	.50
861 A126	40c	Acraea swallowtail	1.40	.50
862 A126	1 le	Broad blue-banded swallowtail	1.40	.50
863 A126	2 le	Giant blue swallowtail	1.40	.50
864 A126	3 le	Blood-red cymothoe	1.75	.75
865 A126	5 le	Green-spotted swallowtail	1.75	.75
866 A126	10 le	Small-striped swordtail	2.75	1.00
867 A126	20 le	Congo long-tailed blue	5.25	2.50
868 A126	25 le	Blue monarch	5.50	3.00
869 A126	30 le	Black and yellow swallowtail	5.50	3.25
870 A126	45 le	Western blue charaxes	9.25	4.50
871 A126	60 le	Violet-washed charaxes	2.25	*4.50*
872 A126	75 le	Orange admiral	2.75	*4.00*
873 A126	100 le	Blue-patched judy	3.75	*7.50*
		Nos. 859-873 (15)	47.50	34.25

Nos. 859-864 exist with 1989 date, No. 871 with 1990.
See Nos. 1257-1260, 1332A-1332I.

1988-89 *Perf. 12x12½*

859a A126	10c		.60	.20
860a A126	20c		.90	.20
861a A126	40c		.90	.20
862a A126	1 le		.90	.20
863a A126	2 le		1.10	.20
864a A126	3 le		1.10	.20
865a A126	5 le		1.10	.20
866a A126	10 le		1.10	.40
867a A126	20 le		1.40	.80
868a A126	25 le		1.40	1.00
869a A126	30 le		1.50	1.25
870a A126	45 le		1.75	1.75
873a A126	100 le		6.25	5.00
		Nos. 859a-873a (13)	20.00	11.60

1987, Aug. 10

874 A127	5 le	Cycling	.25	.25
875 A127	10 le	Equestrian	.50	.50
876 A127	45 le	Running	2.25	2.25
877 A127	50 le	Tennis	2.50	2.50
		Nos. 874-877 (4)	5.50	5.50

Souvenir Sheet

878 A127	100 le	Gold medal, map	5.50	5.50

Works of Art by Marc Chagall, (1887-1985) A128

1987, Aug. 17 *Perf. 14*

879 A128	3 le	The Quarrel, 1911-1912	.20	.20
880 A128	5 le	Rebecca Giving Abraham's Servant a Drink	.25	.25
881 A128	10 le	The Village	.45	.45
882 A128	20 le	Ida at the Window, 1924	.70	.70
883 A128	25 le	Promenade, 1913	1.00	1.00
884 A128	45 le	Peasants	2.40	2.40
885 A128	50 le	Turquoise Plate	2.75	2.75
886 A128	75 le	Cemetery Gate, 1917	3.75	3.75
		Nos. 879-886 (8)	11.50	11.50

Size: 111x95mm

Imperf

887 A128	100 le	Wedding Feast, Stravinsky's Ballet, 1945	6.00	6.00
888 A128	100 le	The Falling Angel	6.00	6.00

Nos. 879-886 printed in sheets of 10 (5x2). Stamp selvage inscribed with name of painting.

Transportation Innovations — A129

1987, Aug. 28 *Perf. 15*

889 A129	3 le	Apollo 8, 1968, vert.	.20	.20
890 A129	5 le	Blanchard's Balloon, 1793	.20	.20
891 A129	10 le	Lockheed Vega, 1932	.40	.40
892 A129	15 le	Vicker's Vimy, 1919	.60	.60
893 A129	20 le	Tank Mk1, c. 1918	.85	.85
894 A129	25 le	Sikorsky VS-300, 1939	1.00	1.00
895 A129	30 le	Flyer 1, 1903	1.25	1.25
896 A129	35 le	Bleriot XI, 1909	1.40	1.40
897 A129	40 le	Paraplane, 1983, vert.	1.60	1.60
898 A129	50 le	Daimler's motorcycle, 1885	2.00	2.00
		Nos. 889-898 (10)	9.50	9.50

Rhinegold Express, Ireland (1st Electric Railroad, 1884) — A129a

1987, Aug. 28 Litho. *Perf. 15*

898A A129a	100 le	multi	5.25	5.25

Wimbledon Tennis Champions — A130

2 le, Evonne Goolagong, Australia. 5 le, Martina Navratilova, US-Czechoslovakia. 10 le, Jimmy Connors, US. 15 le, Bjorn Borg, Sweden. 30 le, Boris Becker, West Germany. 40 le, John McEnroe, US. 50 le, Chris Evert Lloyd, US. 75 le, Virgina Wade, Great Britain. #907, Steffi Graf, German Open 1986. #908, Boris Becker.

1987, Sept. 4 *Perf. 14*

899 A130	2 le	multicolored	.25	.25
900 A130	5 le	multicolored	.50	.50
901 A130	10 le	multicolored	.75	.75
902 A130	15 le	multicolored	1.00	1.00
903 A130	30 le	multicolored	2.00	2.00
904 A130	40 le	multicolored	2.25	2.25
905 A130	50 le	multicolored	2.50	2.50
906 A130	75 le	multicolored	3.25	3.25
		Nos. 899-906 (8)	12.50	12.50

Souvenir Sheets

907 A130	100 le	multicolored	6.50	6.50
908 A130	100 le	multicolored	6.50	6.50

For overprints see Nos. 965, 1023-1024.

Discovery of America, 500th Anniv. (in 1992) A131

5 le, Ducats, Santa Maria, Issac Abravanel (1437-1508), fund raiser. 10 le, Astrolabe, Pinta, Abraham Zacuto (1452-1515), astronomer. 45 le, Maravedis (coins), Nina, Luis de Santangel (1448-1498), fund raiser. 50 le, Tobacco leaves, plant, Luis de Torres (1453-1522), translator.

1987, Sept. 11

909 A131 5 le multicolored .75 .75
910 A131 10 le multicolored 1.00 1.00
911 A131 45 le multicolored 3.00 3.00
912 A131 50 le multicolored 3.50 3.50
Nos. 909-912 (4) 8.25 8.25

Souvenir Sheet

913 A131 100 le Columbus, map 4.50 4.50

For overprint see No. 966.

Fauna and Flora A132

1987, Sept. 15

914 A132 3 le Cotton tree .20 .20
915 A132 5 le Dwarf crocodile .20 .20
916 A132 10 le Kudu .40 .40
917 A132 20 le Yellowbells .80 .80
918 A132 25 le Hippopotamus 1.00 1.00
919 A132 45 le Comet orchid 1.75 1.75
920 A132 50 le Baobab tree 2.00 2.00
921 A132 75 le Elephant 3.00 3.00
Nos. 914-921 (8) 9.35 9.35

Souvenir Sheets

922 A132 100 le Banana, papaya, coconut, pineapple 3.50 3.50
923 A132 100 le Leopard 3.50 3.50

16th World Scout Jamboree, Australia, 1987-88 A133

Scouts, jamboree emblem, map of Australia and: 5 le, Ayers Rock. 15 le, Sailing. 40 le, Sydney skyline. 50 le, Sydney harbor bridge, opera house. 100 le, Flags of Sierra Leone, Australia and Scouts.

1987, Oct. 5 Litho. *Perf. 15*

924 A133 5 le multicolored .30 .30
925 A133 15 le multicolored .65 .65
926 A133 40 le multicolored 1.40 1.40
927 A133 50 le multicolored 2.40 2.40
Nos. 924-927 (4) 4.75 4.75

Souvenir Sheet

928 A133 100 le multicolored 4.50 4.50

1.50 le stamps like the 50 le were printed but not issued.

US Constitution Bicentennial — A134

Designs: 5 le, White House. 10 le, George Washington. 30 le, Patrick Henry. 65 le, New Hampshire state flag. 100 le, John Jay.

1987, Nov. 9 *Perf. 14*

929 A134 5 le multi .20 .20
930 A134 10 le multi, vert. .70 .70
931 A134 30 le multi, vert. 1.10 1.10
932 A134 65 le multi 2.25 2.25
Nos. 929-932 (4) 4.25 4.25

Souvenir Sheet

933 A134 100 le multi, vert. 3.75 3.75

Tokyo Disneyland, 5th Anniv. — A135

Disney animated characters and attractions at Tokyo Disneyland.

1987, Dec. 9 Litho. *Perf. 14*

934 A135 20c Space Mountain .20 .20
935 A135 40c Country Bear Jamboree .20 .20
936 A135 80c Mickey Mouse Review .20 .20
937 A135 1 le Mark Twain's River Boat .20 .20
938 A135 2 le Western River Railroad .20 .20
939 A135 3 le Pirates of the Caribbean .20 .20
940 A135 10 le Big Thunder Mountain train .65 .65
941 A135 20 le It's a Small World 1.40 1.40
942 A135 30 le Park entrance 2.00 2.00
Nos. 934-942 (9) 5.25 5.25

Souvenir Sheet

943 A135 65 le Cinderella's Castle 6.00 6.00

Mickey Mouse, 60th anniv.

Christmas — A136

Paintings by Titian: 2 le, The Annunciation. 10 le, Madonna and Child with Saints. 20 le, Madonna and Child with Saints Ulfus and Brigid. 35 le, Madonna of the Cherries. 65 le, Pesaro Altarpiece, vert.

1987, Dec. 21

944 A136 2 le multicolored .25 .25
945 A136 10 le multicolored .85 .85
946 A136 20 le multicolored 1.40 1.40
947 A136 35 le multicolored 2.50 2.50
Nos. 944-947 (4) 5.00 5.00

Souvenir Sheet

948 A136 65 le multicolored 4.75 4.75

40th Wedding Anniv. of Queen Elizabeth II and Prince Philip A137

Mushrooms A138

1988, Feb. 15 Litho. *Perf. 14*

949 A137 2 le Ceremony, 1947 .25 .25
950 A137 3 le Elizabeth, Charles, 1948 .25 .25
951 A137 10 le Elizabeth, Anne, Charles, c. 1950 .50 .50
952 A137 50 le Elizabeth, c. 1970 2.50 2.50
Nos. 949-952 (4) 3.50 3.50

Souvenir Sheet

953 A137 65 le Wedding portrait 3.50 3.50

1988, Feb. 29

954 A138 3 le Russula cyanoxantha .20 .20
955 A138 10 le Lycoperdon perlatum .90 .90
956 A138 20 le Lactarius deliciosus 1.75 1.75
957 A138 30 le Boletus edulis 2.75 2.75
Nos. 954-957 (4) 5.60 5.60

Miniature Sheet

958 A138 65 le Amanita muscaria 5.75 5.75

Fish A139

1988, Apr. 13 *Perf. 15*

959 A139 3 le Golden pheasant .30 .30
960 A139 10 le Banded toothcarp .60 .60
961 A139 20 le Jewel fish 1.00 1.00
962 A139 35 le Butterfly fish 1.60 1.60
Nos. 959-962 (4) 3.50 3.50

Miniature Sheet

963 A139 65 le African longfin 4.00 4.00

Nos. 841, 903 and 911 Ovptd. for Philatelic Exhibitions in Black

a

b

c

1988, Apr. 19 Litho. *Perf. 14*

964 A123(a) 25 le multicolored 1.60 1.60
965 A130(b) 30 le multicolored 1.90 1.90
966 A131(c) 45 le multicolored 2.50 2.50
Nos. 964-966 (3) 6.00 6.00

Intl. Fund for Agricultural Development (IFAD), 10th Anniv. — A140

1988, May 3 Litho. *Perf. 14*

967 A140 3 le Cocoa, coffee .20 .20
968 A140 15 le Tropical fruit .80 .80
969 A140 25 le Rice harvest 1.50 1.50
Nos. 967-969 (3) 2.50 2.50

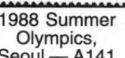

1988 Summer Olympics, Seoul — A141

Birds — A142

1988, June 15

970 A141 3 le Basketball .20 .20
971 A141 10 le Judo .40 .40
972 A141 15 le Gymnastics .55 .55
973 A141 40 le Synchronized swimming 1.60 1.60
Nos. 970-973 (4) 2.75 2.75

Souvenir Sheet

974 A141 65 le Torch-bearer 2.25 2.25

1988, June 25

975 A142 3 le Swallow-tailed bee-eater .85 .85
976 A142 5 le Tooth-billed barbet 1.10 1.10
977 A142 8 le African golden oriole 1.40 1.40
978 A142 10 le Red bishop 1.40 1.40
979 A142 12 le Red-billed shrike 1.40 1.40
980 A142 20 le European bee-eater 1.60 1.60
981 A142 35 le Barbary shrike 2.25 2.25
982 A142 40 le Black-headed oriole 2.50 2.50
Nos. 975-982 (8) 12.50 12.50

Souvenir Sheets

983 A142 65 le Saddlebill stork 2.50 2.50
984 A142 65 le Purple heron 2.50 2.50

Merchant Marine A143

1988, July 1

985 A143 3 le Aureol .70 .70
986 A143 10 le Dunkwa 1.90 1.90
987 A143 15 le Melampus 2.40 2.40
988 A143 30 le Dumbaia 3.00 3.00
Nos. 985-988 (4) 8.00 8.00

Souvenir Sheet

989 A143 65 le Loading containers 3.25 3.25

Paintings by Titian A144

1 le, The Concert, 1512. 2 le, Philip II of Spain, c. 1550-51. 3 le, St. Sebastian, c. 1520-22. 5 le, Martyrdom of St. Peter Martyr, c. 1528-30. 15 le, St. Jerome, 1560. 20 le, St. Mark Enthroned with Saints Cosmas and Damian, Roch & Sebastian, c. 1508-09. 25 le, Portrait of a Young Man, 1506. 30 le, St. Jerome in Penitence, 1555. #998, Self-portrait, 1567. #999, Orpheus and Eurydice, 1508.

1988, Aug. 22 Litho. *Perf. 13½x14*

990 A144 1 le multicolored .20 .20
991 A144 2 le multicolored .20 .20
992 A144 3 le multicolored .25 .25
993 A144 5 le multicolored .35 .35
994 A144 15 le multicolored .85 .85
995 A144 20 le multicolored 1.00 1.00
996 A144 25 le multicolored 1.25 1.25
997 A144 30 le multicolored 1.40 1.40
Nos. 990-997 (8) 5.50 5.50

Souvenir Sheets

998 A144 50 le multicolored 2.75 2.75
999 A144 50 le multicolored 2.75 2.75

John F. Kennedy A145

Kennedy half-dollar and space achievements: 3 le, Recovery of a Mercury capsule by the US Navy. 5 le, Splashdown and recovery of Liberty Bell 7, July 21, 1961, piloted by Virgil "Gus" Grissom, vert. 15 le, Launch of Freedom 7, piloted by Alan B. Shepherd, May 5, 1961, vert. 40 le, Friendship 7 in orbit, piloted by John Glenn, Feb. 20, 1962. 65 le, Kennedy, speech excerpt.

1988, Sept. 26 Litho. *Perf. 14*

1000 A145 3 le multicolored .25 .25
1001 A145 5 le multicolored .40 .40
1002 A145 15 le multicolored 1.25 1.25
1003 A145 40 le multicolored 1.60 1.60
Nos. 1000-1003 (4) 3.50 3.50

Souvenir Sheet

1004 A145 65 le multicolored 2.75 2.75

Intl. Red Cross and Red Crescent Organizations, 125th Annivs. — A146

1988, Nov. 1

1005 A146 3 le Africa food relief .65 .65
1006 A146 10 le Battle of Solferino 2.10 2.10
1007 A146 20 le WWII Pacific 2.75 2.75
1008 A146 40 le WWI Europe 3.50 3.50
Nos. 1005-1008 (4) 9.00 9.00

Souvenir Sheet

Size: 41x28mm

1009 A146 65 le Alfred Nobel, Dunant, horiz. 3.75 3.75

Miniature Sheet

Christmas, Mickey Mouse 60th Anniv. — A147

Walt Disney characters dancing: No. 1010a, Huey, Dewey and Louie. No. 1010b, Clarabelle Cow. No. 1010c, Goofy. No. 1010d, Scrooge McDuck and Grandma Duck. No. 1010e, Donald Duck. No. 1010f, Daisy Duck. No. 1010g, Minnie Mouse. No. 1010h, Mickey Mouse. No. 1011, Dance, c. 1920. No. 1012, Dance, c. 1950.

1988, Dec. 1 ***Perf. 13½x14***

1010 A147 Sheet of 8 7.00 7.00
a.-h. 10 le any single .70 .70

Souvenir Sheets

1011 A147 70 le multicolored 4.50 4.50
1012 A147 70 le multicolored 4.50 4.50

Christmas A148

Paintings by Rubens (details): 3 le, Adoration of the Magi (Virgin and Child). 3.60 le, Adoration of the Shepherds (shepherds and child). 5 le, Adoration of the Magi (Magi). 10 le, Adoration of the Shepherds (Virgin and Child). 20 le, Virgin and Child Surrounded by Flowers. 40 le, St. Gregory the Great and Other Saints (Virgin and Child). 60 le, Adoration of the Magi, (Virgin, Child and Magi), diff. 80 le, Madonna and Child with Saints. No. 1021, St. Gregory the Great and Other Saints. No. 1022, Virgin and Child Enthroned with Saints.

1988, Dec. 15 Litho. ***Perf. 13½x14***

1013 A148 3 le multicolored .20 .20
1014 A148 3.60 le multicolored .20 .20
1015 A148 5 le multicolored .30 .30
1016 A148 10 le multicolored .45 .45
1017 A148 20 le multicolored .85 .85
1018 A148 40 le multicolored 1.75 1.75
1019 A148 60 le multicolored 2.50 2.50
1020 A148 80 le multicolored 3.25 3.25
Nos. 1013-1020 (8) 9.50 9.50

Souvenir Sheets

1021 A148 100 le multicolored 4.50 4.50
1022 A148 100 le multicolored 4.50 4.50

No. 907 Ovptd. "GRAND SLAM WINNER" in Gold

1989, Jan. 16 ***Perf. 14***

Souvenir Sheets

1023A-1023D A130 100 le Set of 4 4.50 4.50

Gold marginal overprints: No. 1023A, "AUSTRALIAN OPEN / JANUARY 11-24, 1988 / GRAF v EVERET / 6-1 / 7-6." 1023B, "FRENCH OPEN / MAY 23-JUNE 5, 1988 / GRAF v ZVEREVA / 6-0 / 6-0." 1023C, "WIMBLEDON / JUNE 20-JULY 4, 1988 / GRAF v NAVRATILOVA / 5-7 / 6-2 / 6-1." 1023D, "U.S. OPEN / AUGUST 29-SEPTEMBER 11, 1988 / GRAF v SABATINI / 6-3 / 3-6 / 6-1."

No. 907 Ovptd. "GOLD MEDALIST" in Gold

1989, Jan. 16 Litho. ***Perf. 14***

1024 A130 100 le multi 4.50 4.50

Marginal overprint: "SEOUL OLYMPICS 1988 / GRAF v SABATINI / 6-3 / 6-3."

Medalists of the 1988 Summer Olympics, Seoul A149

Designs: 3 le, Christian Schenk, German Democratic Republic, decathlon. 6 le, Hitoshi Saito, Japan, heavyweight judo. 10 le, Jutta Niehaus, Federal Republic of Germany, women's road race. 15 le, Tomas Lange, German Democratic Republic, single sculls. 20 le, Matthew Biondi, US, 50m and 100m freestyle. 30 le, Carl Lewis, US, 100m sprint. 40 le, Nicole Uphoff, Federal Republic of Germany, individual dressage. 50 le, Andras Sike, Hungary, 126-pound Greco-Roman wrestling. No. 1033, Gold medal, five-ring emblem. No. 1034, Torch, five-ring emblem.

1989, Apr. 28 Litho. ***Perf. 14***

1025 A149 3 le multicolored .60 .60
1026 A149 6 le multicolored .75 .75
1027 A149 10 le multicolored 1.25 1.25
1028 A149 15 le multicolored 1.25 1.25
1029 A149 20 le multicolored 1.25 1.25
1030 A149 30 le multicolored 1.60 1.60
1031 A149 40 le multicolored 1.90 1.90
1032 A149 50 le multicolored 1.90 1.90
Nos. 1025-1032 (8) 10.50 10.50

Souvenir Sheets

1033 A149 100 le multicolored 4.75 4.75
1034 A149 100 le multicolored 4.75 4.75

Name of athlete not inscribed on No. 1031.

1990 World Cup Soccer Championships, Italy — A150

1989, May 8

1035 A150 3 le Brazil vs. Sweden .20 .20
1036 A150 6 le Germany vs. Hungary .30 .30
1037 A150 8 le England vs. Germany .40 .40
1038 A150 10 le Argentina vs. The Netherlands .50 .50
1039 A150 12 le Brazil vs. Czechoslovakia .60 .60
1040 A150 20 le Germany vs. The Netherlands 1.00 1.00
1041 A150 30 le Italy vs. Germany 1.50 1.50
1042 A150 40 le Brazil vs. Italy 2.00 2.00
Nos. 1035-1042 (8) 6.50 6.50

Souvenir Sheets

1043 A150 100 le Uruguay vs. Brazil 3.50 3.50
1044 A150 100 le Argentina vs. Germany 3.50 3.50

Mano River Union, 15th Anniv. A151

Designs: 1 le, Sierra Leone-Guinea postal service. 3 le, Presidents Momoh, Conte of Guinea and Doe of Liberia. 10 le, Freetown-Monrovia Highway under construction. 15 le, Presidents signing the Communique at a 1988 summit.

1989, May 19 ***Perf. 14***

1045 A151 1 le multicolored .35 .35
1046 A151 3 le multicolored .65 .65
1047 A151 10 le multicolored 1.00 1.00
Nos. 1045-1047 (3) 2.00 2.00

Souvenir Sheet

1048 A151 15 le multicolored 1.50 1.50

Ahmadiyya Muslim Centenary Thanksgiving Celebrations A152

1989, June 8

1049 A152 3 le black & brt blue .25 .25

Miniature Sheets

Shakespeare's 425th Birth Anniv. — A153

Scenes from the playwright's works.

No. 1050: a, Richard III. b, Othello (Desdemona and two men). c, The Two Gentlemen of Verona. d, Macbeth (chamber). e, Hamlet. f, Taming of the Shrew (scene with dog). g, The Merry Wives of Windsor. h, Henry IV (assembly room).

No. 1051: a, Macbeth (horsemen). b, Romeo and Juliet. c, Merchant of Venice. d, As You Like It. e, Taming of the Shrew (ruined meal). f, King Lear. g, Othello (death scene). h, Henry IV (street scene).

1989, May 30 ***Perf. 13***

1050 Sheet of 8 + label 5.50 5.50
a.-h. A153 15 le any single .60 .60
1051 Sheet of 8 + label 5.50 5.50
a.-h. A153 15 le any single .60 .60

Souvenir Sheets

1052 A153 100 le Portrait 5.00 5.00
1053 A153 100 le Portrait, coat of arms 5.00 5.00

Nos. 1050-1051 contain center label picturing Shakespeare's portrait (No. 1050) or his birthplace in Stratford (No. 1051).

Paintings by Takeuchi Seiho (1864-1942) — A154

Designs: 3 le, Lapping Waves. 6 le, Hazy Moon, vert. 8 le, Passing Spring, vert. 10 le, Mackerels. 12 le, Calico Cat. 30 le, The First Time To Be a Model, vert. 40 le, Kingly Lion. 75 le, After a Shower, vert. No. 1062, Domesticated Monkeys and Rabbits. No. 1063, Dozing in the Midst of All the Chirping, vert.

Perf. 14x13½, 13½x14

1989, July 3 Litho.

1054 A154 3 le multicolored .20 .20
1055 A154 6 le multicolored .25 .25
1056 A154 8 le multicolored .30 .30
1057 A154 10 le multicolored .35 .35
1058 A154 12 le multicolored .40 .40
1059 A154 30 le multicolored 1.00 1.00
1060 A154 40 le multicolored 1.50 1.50
1061 A154 75 le multicolored 2.75 2.75
Nos. 1054-1061 (8) 6.75 6.75

Souvenir Sheets

1062 A154 150 le multicolored 4.50 4.50
1063 A154 150 le multicolored 4.50 4.50

Hirohito (1901-89) and enthronement of Akihito as emperor of Japan.

See Nos. 1098-1129.

PHILEXFRANCE '89, French Revolution Bicent. — A155

Famous people, sites, exhibition and anniv. emblems: 6 le, Robespierre (1758-94), the Bastille. 20 le, Georges Jacques Danton (1759-94), the Louvre. 45 le, Marie Antoinette (1755-93), Notre Dame Cathedral interior. 80 le, Louis XVI (1754-93), Palace of Versailles. 150 le, Revolutionaries in Paris, vert.

1989, July 14 Litho. ***Perf. 14***

1064 A155 6 le multicolored .45 .45
1065 A155 20 le multicolored .90 .90
1066 A155 45 le multicolored 1.40 1.40
1067 A155 80 le multicolored 2.50 2.50
Nos. 1064-1067 (4) 5.25 5.25

Souvenir Sheet

1068 A155 150 le multicolored 4.50 4.50

Miniature Sheets

Space Exploration — A156

Satellites, probes and spacecraft.

No. 1069: a, Sputnik, 1957. b, Telstar, 1962. c, Rendezvous of Gemini 6 and 7, 1965. d, Yuri Gagarin, 1st man in space, 1961. e, Mariner, 1964. f, Surveyor on Mars, 1966. g, US-Canadian Alouette satellite, 1962. h, Edward White, 1st American to walk in space, 1965. i, OGO-4 satellite, 1967.

No. 1070: a, Buzz Aldrin on the Moon, Apollo 11 mission, 1969. b, Apollo 15 mission lunar rover. c, Apollo 15 crew member. d, Conducting experiments on the lunar surface. e, Splitrock, Valley of Taurus-Littrow. f, Saluting the flag, Apollo 15 lunar module. g, Solar wind experiment. h, Lunar rover, diff. i, Apollo command module.

No. 1071: a, Module separation. b, Docking maneuvers. c, Lunar module in space. d, Second stage separation. e, Module transposition. f, Lunar module controlled descent, Moon's surface. g, Apollo 11 liftoff, 1969. h, Lunar module separates from command module. i, Neil Armstrong's first step on the Moon.

No. 1072: a, Mariner-Mars, 1971. b, Mariner 10, 1973. c, Viking, 1975. d, Skylab, 1974. e, Soyuz-Salyut, 1974. f, Viking robot craft, 1974. g, Pioneer 2, 1973. h, Apollo-Soyuz, 1975. i, Pioneer-Venus, 1978.

No. 1073: a, Apollo 17 lunar module, 1972. b, Command module jettison of service module before reentry. c, Soyuz 11, 1971. d, Lunar module liftoff. e, U.S. Navy recovery operation. f, Mars 2, 1971. g, Command module in docking position. h, Luna 17, 1970. i, Mars 3, 1971.

No. 1074: a, Voyager 1 and 2, 1977. b, Columbia space shuttle, 1981. c, Mir space station, 1986. d, IUE-Ultraviolet Explorer, US, U.K. and the European Space Agency, 1978. e, Astronaut operating out of shuttle cargo bay, 1983. f, Magellan, 1989. g, Soyuz-Salyut, 1978. h, STS-10, 1984. i, Shuttle, space telescope, 1989.

No. 1075, Spacelab. No. 1076, Future space station. No. 1077, Voyager.

1989, July 20 Litho. *Perf. 14*

1069 Sheet of 9 3.75 3.75
a.-i. A156 10 le any single .40 .40
1070 Sheet of 9 3.75 3.75
a.-i. A156 10 le any single .40 .40
1071 Sheet of 9 3.75 3.75
a.-i. A156 10 le any single .40 .40
1072 Sheet of 9 5.50 5.50
a.-i. A156 15 le any single .60 .60
1073 Sheet of 9 5.50 5.50
a.-i. A156 15 le any single .60 .60
1074 Sheet of 9 5.50 5.50
a.-i. A156 15 le any single .60 .60

Souvenir Sheets

1075 A156 100 le multicolored 5.00 5.00
1076 A156 100 le multicolored 5.00 5.00
1077 A156 100 le multicolored 5.00 5.00

Nos. 1069f is incorrectly inscribed "Mars" instead of "Moon."

Orchids — A157 Butterflies — A158

1989, Sept. 8 Litho. *Perf. 14*

1078 A157 3 le Bulbophyllum barbigerum .60 .60
1079 A157 6 le Bulbophyllum falcatum .90 .90
1080 A157 12 le Habenaria macrara 1.25 1.25
1081 A157 20 le Eurychone rothchildiana 1.50 1.50
1082 A157 50 le Calyptrochilum christyanum 2.25 2.25
1083 A157 60 le Bulbophyllum distans 2.75 2.75
1084 A157 70 le Eulophia guineensis 2.75 2.75
1085 A157 80 le Diaphananthe pellucida 3.00 3.00
Nos. 1078-1085 (8) 15.00 15.00

Souvenir Sheets

1086 A157 100 le Cyrtorchis arcuata 8.50 8.50
1087 A157 100 le Butterflies, Eulophia cucullata 8.50 8.50

1989, Sept. 11

1088 A158 6 le Salamis temora .90 .90
1089 A158 12 le Pseudacraea lucretia 1.25 1.25
1090 A158 18 le Charaxes boueti 1.60 1.60
1091 A158 30 le Graphium antheus 2.25 2.25
1092 A158 40 le Colotis protomedia 2.75 2.75
1093 A158 60 le Asterope pechueli 3.25 3.25
1094 A158 72 le Coenura aurantiaca 3.50 3.50
1095 A158 80 le Precis octavia 3.50 3.50
Nos. 1088-1095 (8) 19.00 19.00

Souvenir Sheets

1096 A158 100 le Charaxes cithaeron 8.50 8.50
1097 A158 100 le Euphaedra themis 8.50 8.50

Nos. 1088-1090, 1095 and 1097 horiz.

Art Type of 1989

Paintings by Hiroshige in the series Fifty-three Stations on the Tokaido: No. 1098, Coolies Warming Themselves at Hamamatsu. No. 1099, Imakiri Ford at Maisaka. No. 1100, Pacific Ocean Seen from Shirasuka. No. 1101, Futakawa Street Singers. No. 1102, Repairing Yoshida Castle. No. 1103, The Inn at Akasaka. No. 1104, The Bridge to Okazaki. No. 1105, Samurai's Wife Entering Narumi. No. 1106, Harbour at Kuwana. No. 1107, Autumn in Ishiyakushi. No. 1108, Snowfall at Kameyama. No. 1109, The Frontier Station of Seki. No. 1110, Teahouse at Sakanoshita. No. 1111, Kansai Houses at Minakushi. No. 1112, Kusatsu Station. No. 1113, Ferry to Kawasaki. No. 1114, The Hilly Town of Hodogaya. No. 1115, Lute Players at Fujisawa. No. 1116, Mild Rainstorm at Oiso. No. 1117, Lake Ashi and Mountains of Hakone. No. 1118, Twilight at Numazu. No. 1119, Mount Fuji From Hara. No. 1120, Samurai's Children Riding Through Yoshiwara. No. 1121, Mountain Pass at Yui. No. 1122, Harbour at Ejiri. No. 1123, Stopping at Fujieda. No. 1124, Misty Kanaya on the Oi River. No. 1125, The Bridge to Kakegawa. No. 1126, Teahouse at Fukuroi. No. 1127, The Ford at Mistuke. No. 1128, Sanjo Bridge in Kyoto. No. 1129, Nibonbashi Bridge in Edo.

1989, Nov. 13 Litho. *Perf. 14x13½*

1098-1127 A154 25 le Set of 30 27.50 27.50

Souvenir sheets

1128-1129 A154 120 le each 4.00 4.00

Hirohito (1901-1989) and enthronement of Akihito as emperor of Japan.

Souvenir Sheet

Jefferson Memorial, Washington, DC — A159

1989, Nov. 17 Litho. *Perf. 14*

1136 A159 100 le multicolored 2.00 2.00

World Stamp Expo '89.

Endangered Species — A160

1989, Nov. 29 *Perf. 14*

1137 A160 6 le Humpback whale .20 .20
1138 A160 9 le Formosan sika deer .25 .25
1139 A160 16 le Spanish lynx .45 .45
1140 A160 20 le Goitered gazelle .60 .60
1141 A160 30 le Japanese sea lion .90 .90
1142 A160 50 le Long-eared owl 1.50 1.50
1143 A160 70 le Chinese copper pheasant 2.10 2.10
1144 A160 100 le Siberian tiger 3.00 3.00
Nos. 1137-1144 (8) 9.00 9.00

Souvenir Sheets

1145 A160 150 le Mauritius kestrel falcon 5.75 5.75
1146 A160 150 le Crested ibis 5.75 5.75

World Stamp Expo '89.

Christmas — A161

Disney characters and classic automobiles: 3 le, 1934 Phantom II Rolls-Royce Roadstar. 6 le, 1935 Mercedes-Benz 500K. 10 le, 1938 Jaguar SS-100. 12 le, 1941 Jeep. 20 le, 1937 Buick Roadmaster Sedan Model 91. 30 le, 1948 Tucker. 40 le, 1933 Alfa Romeo. 50 le, 1937 Cord. No. 1155, 1938 Fiat Topolino. No. 1156, 1931 Pontiac Model 401, 1929 Pontiac Landau.

1989, Dec. 18 *Perf. 14x13½*

1147 A161 3 le multicolored .60 .60
1148 A161 6 le multicolored .75 .75
1149 A161 10 le multicolored .90 .90
1150 A161 12 le multicolored 1.00 1.00
1151 A161 20 le multicolored 1.40 1.40
1152 A161 30 le multicolored 1.60 1.60
1153 A161 40 le multicolored 1.75 1.75
1154 A161 50 le multicolored 2.00 2.00
Nos. 1147-1154 (8) 10.00 10.00

Souvenir Sheets

1155 A161 100 le multicolored 4.00 4.00
1156 A161 100 le multicolored 4.00 4.00

Christmas — A162

Religious paintings by Rembrandt: 3 le, Adoration of the Magi. 6 le, The Holy Family with a Cat. 10 le, The Holy Family with Angels. 15 le, Simeon in the Temple. 30 le, The Circumcision. 90 le, The Holy Family. 100 le, The Visitation. 120 le, The Flight into Egypt. No. 1165, The Adoration of the Shepherds. No. 1166, The Presentation of Jesus in the Temple.

1989, Dec. 22 *Perf. 14*

1157 A162 3 le multicolored .40 .40
1158 A162 6 le multicolored .50 .50
1159 A162 10 le multicolored .70 .70
1160 A162 15 le multicolored .85 .85
1161 A162 30 le multicolored 1.25 1.25
1162 A162 90 le multicolored 2.40 2.40
1163 A162 100 le multicolored 2.40 2.40
1164 A162 120 le multicolored 2.50 2.50
Nos. 1157-1164 (8) 11.00 11.00

Souvenir Sheets

1165 A162 150 le multicolored 3.25 3.25
1166 A162 150 le multicolored 3.25 3.25

Miniature Sheets

Exploration of Mars — A163

No. 1167: a, Kepler. b, Galileo. c, Drawings by Huygens in 1672 and Schiaparelli in 1886. d, Sir W. Herschel. e, Percival Lowell in Arizona, 1896-1907. f, Mars. g, Mariner 4, 1965. h, Mars 2, 1971. i, Mars 3, 1971.

No. 1168: a, Mariner 9, 1971. b, Mariner 9, Phobos. c, Cydonia Region. d, South polar cap. e, Profile of Mars. f, Polar cap, diff. g, Nix Olympica. h, Grand Canyon of Mars. i, North Pole.

No. 1169: a, Olympus Mons. b, Viking 1, July 1976. c, Viking 2 releases Lander, Sept. 1976. d, Lander entering Mars's atmosphere. e, Parachute deployed. f, Terminal descent. g, Viking Lander on Mars. h, Soil sampler (robotic arm). i, Soil Sampler (US flag, machine).

No. 1170: a, Martian dusk. b, Project Deimos. c, Exploration of Mars (astronauts surveying land). d, Return to Rombus. e, US rocket bound for Mars. f, Spacecraft bound for Mars. g, Spacecraft in Martian orbit. h, Mission to Mars (astronauts weightless in spacecraft cabin). i, Space station.

No. 1171, "The Face," Mars.

1990 Litho. *Perf. 14*

1167 Sheet of 9 25.00 25.00
a.-i. A163 175 le any single 2.75 2.75
1168 Sheet of 9 25.00 25.00
a.-i. A163 175 le any single 2.75 2.75
1169 Sheet of 9 25.00 25.00
a.-i. A163 175 le any single 2.75 2.75
1170 Sheet of 9 25.00 25.00
a.-i. A163 175 le any single 2.75 2.75

Souvenir Sheet

1171 A163 150 le multicolored 2.50 2.50
1171A A163 150 le Space station 2.50 2.50

Issued: No. 1171A, Dec. 24; others, Jan. 15.

Extreme speculation has occured with this issue, centered around No. 1171, the face on Mars stamp.

World War II — A164

USAF aircraft.

1990, Feb. 5 Litho. *Perf. 14*

1172 A164 1 le Doolittle Raid B-25 .20 .20
1173 A164 2 le B-24 Liberator .20 .20
1174 A164 3 le A-20 Boston .20 .20
1175 A164 9 le P-38 Lightning .30 .30
1176 A164 12 le B-26 .35 .35
1177 A164 16 le B-17 F .50 .50
1178 A164 50 le B-25 D Mitchell 1.50 1.50
1179 A164 80 le Boeing B-29 2.40 2.40
1180 A164 90 le B-17 G 2.75 2.75
1181 A164 100 le The Enola Gay 3.00 3.00
Nos. 1172-1181 (10) 11.40 11.40

Souvenir Sheets

1182 A164 150 le B-25, USS Hornet 4.50 4.50
1183 A164 150 le B-17 G 4.50 4.50

Stage and Screen Roles Played by Sir Laurence Olivier (1907-1989) — A165

1990, Apr. 27

1184 A165 3 le Antony & Cleopatra, 1951 .20 .20
1185 A165 9 le Henry V, 1943 .20 .20
1186 A165 16 le Oedipus, 1945 .30 .30
1187 A165 20 le Wuthering Heights, 1939 .40 .40
1188 A165 30 le Marathon Man, 1976 .60 .60
1189 A165 70 le Othello, 1964 1.40 1.40
1190 A165 175 le Beau Geste, 1929 3.50 3.50
1191 A165 200 le Richard III, 1956 4.00 4.00
Nos. 1184-1191 (8) 10.60 10.60

Souvenir Sheets

1192 A165 250 le The Battle of Britain, 1969 5.00 5.00
1193 A165 250 le Hamlet, 1947 5.00 5.00

Walt Disney Characters, Settings in Sierra Leone — A166

1990, Apr. 23

1194 A166 3 le Bauxite mine .20 .20
1195 A166 6 le Panning for gold .20 .20
1196 A166 10 le Lungi Intl. Airport .25 .25
1197 A166 12 le Old Fourah Bay College .30 .30
1198 A166 16 le Mining bauxite .40 .40
1199 A166 20 le Rice harvest .50 .50
1200 A166 30 le The Cotton Tree .75 .75
1201 A166 100 le Rutile Mine 2.50 2.50
1202 A166 200 le Fishing at Goderich 5.00 5.00
1203 A166 225 le Bintumani Hotel 5.50 5.50
Nos. 1194-1203 (10) 15.60 15.60

Souvenir Sheets

1204	A166	250 le	Market Place, King Jimmy	5.00	5.00
1205	A166	250 le	Diamond mining	5.00	5.00

Penny Black, 150th Anniv. — A167

1990, May 3 ***Perf. 14***

1206	A167	50 le	deep ultra	1.00	1.00
1207	A167	100 le	violet brown	2.50	2.50

Souvenir Sheet

1208	A167	250 le	black	5.00	5.00

World Cup Soccer Championships, Italy — A168

Team photographs.

1990, May 11 **Litho.** ***Perf. 14***

1209	A168	15 le	Colombia	.25	.25
1210	A168	15 le	United Arab Emirates	.25	.25
1211	A168	15 le	South Korea	.25	.25
1212	A168	15 le	Cameroun	.25	.25
1213	A168	15 le	Costa Rica	.25	.25
1214	A168	15 le	Romania	.25	.25
1215	A168	15 le	Yugoslavia	.25	.25
1216	A168	15 le	Egypt	.25	.25
1217	A168	30 le	Netherlands	.50	.50
1218	A168	30 le	Uruguay	.50	.50
1219	A168	30 le	USSR	.50	.50
1220	A168	30 le	Czechoslovakia	.50	.50
1221	A168	30 le	Scotland	.50	.50
1222	A168	30 le	Belgium	.50	.50
1223	A168	30 le	Austria	.50	.50
1224	A168	30 le	Sweden	.50	.50
1225	A168	45 le	W. Germany	.75	.75
1226	A168	45 le	England	.75	.75
1227	A168	45 le	United States	.75	.75
1228	A168	45 le	Ireland	.75	.75
1229	A168	45 le	Spain	.75	.75
1230	A168	45 le	Brazil	.75	.75
1231	A168	45 le	Italy	.75	.75
1232	A168	45 le	Argentina	.75	.75
			Nos. 1209-1232 (24)	12.00	12.00

No. 1209 spelled "Columbia," No. 1218 "Uraguay," No. 1220 "Czecheslovakia" on stamps.

Great Crested Grebe A169

1990, June 4

1233	A169	3 le	shown	.20	.20
1234	A169	6 le	Green woodhoopoe	.20	.20
1235	A169	10 le	African jacana	.20	.20
1236	A169	12 le	Avocet	.20	.20
1237	A169	20 le	African finfoot	.35	.35
1238	A169	80 le	Glossy ibis	1.40	1.40
1239	A169	150 le	Hamerkop	2.50	2.50
1240	A169	200 le	Greater honey guide	3.25	3.25
			Nos. 1233-1240 (8)	8.30	8.30

Souvenir Sheets

1241	A169	250 le	Painted snipe	4.25	4.25
1242	A169	250 le	Palm swift	4.25	4.25

Mickey as Yeoman Warder A170

Disney characters: 6 le, Scrooge as lamplighter. 12 le, Knight Goofy. 15 le, Clarabell as Anne Boleyn. 75 le, Minnie Mouse as Queen Elizabeth I. 100 le, Donald Duck as chimmey sweep. 125 le, Pete as King Henry VIII. 150 le, May dancers in Salisbury. No. 1251, Boadicea, Queen of the Iceni. No. 1252, Lawyers at Parliament House.

1990, June 6 ***Perf. 13½x14***

1243	A170	3 le	multicolored	.20	.20
1244	A170	6 le	multicolored	.20	.20
1245	A170	12 le	multicolored	.20	.20
1246	A170	15 le	multicolored	.25	.25
1247	A170	75 le	multicolored	1.25	1.25
1248	A170	100 le	multicolored	1.75	1.75
1249	A170	125 le	multicolored	2.25	2.25
1250	A170	150 le	multicolored	2.50	2.50
			Nos. 1243-1250 (8)	8.60	8.60

Souvenir Sheets

1251	A170	250 le	multicolored	4.50	4.50
1252	A170	250 le	multicolored	4.50	4.50

Queen Mother, 90th Birthday — A171

1990, July 5 ***Perf. 14***

1253	75 le	shown	1.25	1.25
1254	75 le	Wearing black hat	1.25	1.25
1255	75 le	Wearing yellow hat	1.25	1.25
a.		A171 Strip of 3, #1253-1255	3.75	3.75
		Nos. 1253-1255 (3)	3.75	3.75

Souvenir Sheet

1256	A170	250 le	Like No. 1252	4.50	4.50

Butterfly Type of 1987

1990 ***Perf. 12½x11½***

1257	A126	3 le	like No. 861	.20	.20
1258	A126	9 le	like No. 864	.20	.20
1259	A126	12 le	like No. 859	.20	.20
1260	A126	16 le	like No. 860	.30	.30
			Nos. 1257-1260 (4)	.90	.90

Inscribed 1989.

Miniature Sheet

Wildlife A172

Designs: No. 1261a, Golden cat. b, White-backed night heron. c, Bateleur eagle. d, Marabou stork. e, White-faced whistling duck. f, Aardvark. g, Royal antelope. h, Pygmy hippopotamus. i, Leopard. j, Sacred ibis. k, Mona monkey. l, Darter. m, Chimpanzee. n, African elephant. o, Potto. p, African manatee. q, African fish eagle. r, African spoonbill.

1990, Sept. 24 **Litho.** ***Perf. 14***

1261		Sheet of 18	7.50	7.50
a.-r.		A172 25 le any single	.40	.40

Souvenir Sheet

1262	A172	150 le	Crowned eagle, vert.	2.50	2.50

No. 1261 printed in continuous design showing map of Sierra Leone in background.

A173

A174

Carousel animals.

1990, Oct. 22 **Litho.** ***Perf. 14***

1263	A173	5 le	Rabbit	.20	.20
1264	A173	10 le	Horse with panther saddle	.20	.20
1265	A173	20 le	Ostrich	.30	.30
1266	A173	30 le	Zebra	.50	.50
1267	A173	50 le	White horse	.80	.80
1268	A173	80 le	Sea monster	1.25	1.25
1269	A173	100 le	Giraffe	1.60	1.60
1270	A173	150 le	Armored horse	2.40	2.40
1271	A173	200 le	Camel	3.25	3.25
			Nos. 1263-1271 (9)	10.50	10.50

Souvenir Sheets

1272	A173	300 le	Centaur, Lord Baden-Powell	4.75	4.75
1273	A173	300 le	Horse head	4.75	4.75

1990, Nov. 12 **Litho.** ***Perf. 14***

1274	A174	5 le	Men's 100-meter race	.20	.20
1275	A174	10 le	Men's 4x400-meter relay	.20	.20
1276	A174	20 le	Men's 100-meter race, diff.	.30	.30
1277	A174	30 le	Weight lifting	.50	.50
1278	A174	40 le	Freestyle wrestling	.65	.65
1279	A174	80 le	Water polo	1.25	1.25
1280	A174	150 le	Women's gymnastics	2.40	2.40
1281	A174	200 le	Cycling	3.25	3.25
			Nos. 1274-1281 (8)	8.75	8.75

Souvenir Sheets

1282	A174	400 le	Boxing	6.50	6.50
1283	A174	400 le	Olympic flag	6.50	6.50

1992 Summer Olympics, Barcelona.

Christmas A175

Paintings: 10 le, The Holy Family Resting by Rembrandt. 20 le, The Holy Family with St. Elizabeth by Andrea Mantegna. 30 le, Virgin and Child with an Angel by Correggio. 50 le, The Annunciation by Bernardo Strozzi. 100 le, Madonna and Child Appearing to St. Anthony by Filippino Lippi. 175 le, Virgin and Child by Giovanni Boltraffio. 200 le, The Esterhazy Madonna by Raphael. 300 le, Coronation of Mary by Orcagna. No. 1292, Adoration of the Shepherds by Bronzino. No. 1293, Adoration of the Shepherds by Gerard David.

1990, Dec. 17 ***Perf. 13***

1284	A175	10 le	multicolored	.20	.20
1285	A175	20 le	multicolored	.30	.30
1286	A175	30 le	multicolored	.50	.50
1287	A175	50 le	multicolored	.80	.80
1288	A175	100 le	multicolored	1.60	1.60
1289	A175	175 le	multicolored	2.75	2.75
1290	A175	200 le	multicolored	3.25	3.25
1291	A175	300 le	multicolored	4.75	4.75
			Nos. 1284-1291 (8)	14.15	14.15

Souvenir Sheets

1292	A175	400 le	multicolored	6.50	6.50
1293	A175	400 le	multicolored	6.50	6.50

Christmas A176

Walt Disney characters in "The Night Before Christmas."

No. 1294a, 'Twas the night. . . b, Not a creature. . . c, The stockings were hung. . . d, And Mama in her kerchief. . . e, When out on the lawn. . . f, I sprang from my bed. . . g, Away to the window. . . h, Tore open the shutter. . .

No. 1295a, The moon on the breast. . . b, When what to my wondering. . . c, With a little old driver. . . d, More rapid than eagles. . . e, To the top of the porch. . . f, And then in a twinkling. . . g, As I drew in my head. . . h, He was dressed. . .

No. 1296a, A bundle of toys. . . b, The stump of a pipe. . . c, He had a broad face. . . d, He was chubby and plump. . . e, A wink of his eye. . . f, Then turned with a jerk. . . g, And giving a nod. . . h, He sprang to his sleigh. . .

No. 1297, The children were nestled. . . No. 1298, His eyes, how they twinkled. . . No. 1299, He spoke not a word. . . No. 1300, And he whistled. . . No. 1301, As dry leaves. . . No. 1302, But I heard him exclaim. . .

1990, Dec. 17 **Litho.** ***Perf. 13***

Miniature Sheets of 8

1294	A176	50 le	#a.-h.	4.50	4.50
1295	A176	75 le	#a.-h.	6.75	6.75
1296	A176	100 le	#a.-h.	9.00	9.00

Souvenir Sheets

1297	A176	400 le	multi	4.50	4.50
1298	A176	400 le	multi, horiz.	4.50	4.50
1299	A176	400 le	multi	4.50	4.50
1300	A176	400 le	multi, horiz.	4.50	4.50
1301	A176	400 le	multi, horiz.	4.50	4.50
1302	A176	400 le	multi	4.50	4.50

Peter Paul Rubens (1577-1640), Painter A177

Entire paintings or different details from: 5 le, Helena Fourment as Hagar in the Wilderness. 10 le, Isabella Brant. 20 le, 60 le, Countess of Arundel and Her Party. 80 le, Nicolaas Rockox. 100 le, Adriana Perez. 150 le, George Villiers, Duke of Buckingham. 300 le, Countess of Buckingham. No. 1311, Veronica Spinola Dorio. No. 1312, Giovanni Carlo Dorio.

1990, Dec. 24 ***Perf. 14***

1303	A177	5 le	multicolored	.20	.20
1304	A177	10 le	multicolored	.20	.20
1305	A177	20 le	multicolored	.30	.30
1306	A177	60 le	multicolored	.95	.95
1307	A177	80 le	multicolored	1.25	1.25
1308	A177	100 le	multicolored	1.60	1.60
1309	A177	150 le	multicolored	2.40	2.40
1310	A177	300 le	multicolored	4.75	4.75
			Nos. 1303-1310 (8)	11.65	11.65

Souvenir Sheets

1311	A177	350 le	multicolored	5.50	5.50
1312	A177	350 le	multicolored	5.50	5.50

Mushrooms — A178

Designs: 3 le, Chlorophyllum molybdites. 5 le, Lepista nuda. 10 le, Clitocybe nebularis.

15 le, Cyathus striatus. 20 le, Bolbitius vitellinus. 25 le, Leucoagaricus naucinus. 30 le, Suillus luteus. 40 le, Podaxis pistillaris. 50 le, Oudemansiella radicata. 60 le, Phallus indusiatus. 80 le, Macrolepiota rhacodes. 100 le, Mycena pura. 150 le, Volvariella volvacea. 175 le, Omphalotus olearius. 200 le, Sphaerobolus stellatus. 250 le, Schizophyllum commune. No. 1329, Agaricus campestris. No. 1330, Hypholama fasciculare. No. 1331, Suillus granulatus. No. 1332, Psilocybe coprophila.

1990, Dec. 31 ***Perf. 14***

1313 A178 3 le multicolored .20 .20
1314 A178 5 le multicolored .20 .20
1315 A178 10 le multicolored .20 .20
1316 A178 15 le multicolored .25 .25
1317 A178 20 le multicolored .30 .30
1318 A178 25 le multicolored .40 .40
1319 A178 30 le multicolored .50 .50
1320 A178 40 le multicolored .65 .65
1321 A178 50 le multicolored .80 .80
1322 A178 60 le multicolored .95 .95
1323 A178 80 le multicolored 1.25 1.25
1324 A178 100 le multicolored 1.60 1.60
1325 A178 150 le multicolored 2.40 2.40
1326 A178 175 le multicolored 2.75 2.75
1327 A178 200 le multicolored 3.25 3.25
1328 A178 250 le multicolored 4.00 4.00
Nos. 1313-1328 (16) 19.70 19.70

Souvenir Sheets

1329-1332 A178 350 le each 5.50 5.50

Butterfly Type of 1987
"Sierra Leone" in Blue

1990(?) **Litho.**

1332A A126 50c like #861 .20 .20
1332B A126 2 le like #863
1332C A126 5 le like #865
1332D A126 10 le like #866
1332E A126 30 le like #864
1332F A126 50 le like No. 859
1332G A126 60 le like #871
1332H A126 80 le like No. 860
1332I A126 300 le like No. 869

Issued: 2, 5, 10, 30, 60 le, 1990(?), perf. 14; 50c, 50, 80, 300 le, Aug, 1991, perf. 12½x11½;

Nos. 1332A, 1332F, 1332H-1332I inscribed 1990.

Easter
A179

Entire works or details from paintings by Rubens: 10 le, Flight of St. Barbara. 20 le, No. 1341, The Last Judgement. 30 le, St. Gregory of Nazianzus. 50 le, Doubting Thomas. 80 le, No. 1342, The Way to Calvary. 100 le, St. Gregory with Sts. Domitilla, Maurus and Papianus. 175 le, Sts. Gregory, Maurus and Papianus. 300 le, Christ and the Penitent Sinners.

1991, Apr. 8 **Litho.** ***Perf. 13½x14***

1333 A179 10 le multicolored .20 .20
1334 A179 20 le multicolored .30 .30
1335 A179 30 le multicolored .50 .50
1336 A179 50 le multicolored .80 .80
1337 A179 80 le multicolored 1.25 1.25
1338 A179 100 le multicolored 1.60 1.60
1339 A179 175 le multicolored 2.75 2.75
1340 A179 300 le multicolored 4.75 4.75
Nos. 1333-1340 (8) 12.15 12.15

Souvenir Sheets

1341-1342 A179 400 le each 6.50 6.50

Phila Nippon '91 — A180

Japanese locomotives: 10 le, Class 1400 steam. 20 le, Streamlined C55 steam. 30 le, ED17 electric. 60 le, EF13 electric. 100 le, Baldwin Mikado steam. 150 le, C62 steam. 200 le, KiHa 81 class diesel. 300 le, Class 8550 steam. No. 1351, Hikari bullet train. No. 1352, Class 7000 electric. No. 1353, D51 steam. No. 1354, Class 9600 steam.

1991, May 13 **Litho.** ***Perf. 14***

1343 A180 10 le multicolored .20 .20
1344 A180 20 le multicolored .30 .30
1345 A180 30 le multicolored .50 .50
1346 A180 60 le multicolored .95 .95
1347 A180 100 le multicolored 1.60 1.60
1348 A180 150 le multicolored 2.40 2.40
1349 A180 200 le multicolored 3.25 3.25
1350 A180 300 le multicolored 4.75 4.75
Nos. 1343-1350 (8) 13.95 13.95

Souvenir Sheets

1351-1354 A180 400 le each 6.50 6.50

Fish — A181

1991, June 3 **Litho.** ***Perf. 14***

1355 A181 10 le Aphyosemion ghana .20 .20
1356 A181 20 le Black-lipped panchax .25 .25
1357 A181 30 le Peter's killie .35 .35
1358 A181 60 le Micro-walkeri killie .70 .70
1359 A181 100 le Butterfly fish 1.25 1.25
1360 A181 150 le Green panchax 1.75 1.75
1361 A181 200 le Six-barred panchax 2.40 2.40
1362 A181 300 le Banded puffer 3.50 3.50
Nos. 1355-1362 (8) 10.40 10.40

Souvenir Sheets

1363 A181 400 le Spotfin synodontis 4.75 4.75
1364 A181 400 le Two-striped panchax 4.75 4.75

Paintings by Vincent Van Gogh — A182

Designs: 10c, The Langlois Bridge at Arles. 50c, Trees in the Garden of Saint-Paul Hospital, vert. 1 le, Wild Flowers and Thistles in a Vase, vert. 2 le, Still Life: Vase with Oleanders and Books. 5 le, Farmhouses in a Wheat Field Near Arles. 10 le, Self-Portrait, Sept. 1889, vert. 20 le, Portrait of Patience Escalier, vert. 30 le, Portrait of Doctor Felix Rey, vert. 50 le, The Iris, vert. 60 le, The Shepherdess, vert. 80 le, Vincent's House in Arles (The Yellow House). 100 le, The Road Menders. 150 le, The Garden of Saint-Paul Hospital, vert. 200 le, View of the Church of Saint-Paul-De-Mausole. 250 le, Seascape at Saintes-Maries. 300 le, Pieta, vert. No. 1381, Church at Auvers Sur Dise, vert. No. 1382, Vineyards with a View of Auvers. No. 1383, The Trinquetaille Bridge. No. 1384, Two Poplars on a Road Through the Hills, vert. No. 1385, Haystacks in Provence. No. 1386, The Garden of Saint-Paul Hospital, diff.

1991, June 28 **Litho.** ***Perf. 13½***

1365 A182 10c multicolored .20 .20
1366 A182 50c multicolored .20 .20
1367 A182 1 le multicolored .20 .20
1368 A182 2 le multicolored .20 .20
1369 A182 5 le multicolored .20 .20
1370 A182 10 le multicolored .20 .20
1371 A182 20 le multicolored .25 .25
1372 A182 30 le multicolored .35 .35
1373 A182 50 le multicolored .60 .60
1374 A182 60 le multicolored .70 .70
1375 A182 80 le multicolored .95 .95
1376 A182 100 le multicolored 1.25 1.25
1377 A182 150 le multicolored 1.75 1.75
1378 A182 200 le multicolored 2.40 2.40
1379 A182 250 le multicolored 3.00 3.00
1380 A182 300 le multicolored 3.50 3.50
Nos. 1365-1380 (16) 15.95 15.95

Size: 102x76mm

Imperf

1381-1386 A182 400 le each 4.75 4.75

Royal Family Birthday, Anniversary
Common Design Type

1991, July 5 **Litho.** ***Perf. 14***

1387 CD347 10 le multi .20 .20
1388 CD347 20 le multi .30 .30
1389 CD347 30 le multi .50 .50
1390 CD347 80 le multi 1.25 1.25
1391 CD347 100 le multi 1.60 1.60
1392 CD347 200 le multi 3.25 3.25
1393 CD347 250 le multi 4.00 4.00
1394 CD347 300 le multi 4.75 4.75
Nos. 1387-1394 (8) 15.85 15.85

Souvenir Sheets

1395 CD347 400 le Elizabeth, Philip 6.50 6.50
1396 CD347 400 le Charles, Diana, sons 6.50 6.50

10 le, 30 le, 200 le, 250 le, No. 1395, Queen Elizabeth II, 65th birthday. Others, Charles and Diana, 10th wedding anniversary.

Butterflies
A183

1991, Aug. 5 **Litho.** ***Perf. 14x13½***

1397 A183 10 le Coppery swallowtail .20 .20
1398 A183 30 le Orange forester .35 .35
1399 A183 50 le Large striped swordtail .60 .60
1400 A183 60 le Lilac beauty .75 .75
1401 A183 80 le African leaf .95 .95
1402 A183 100 le Blue diadem 1.25 1.25
1403 A183 200 le Beautiful monarch 2.50 2.50
1404 A183 300 le Veined swallowtail 3.50 3.50
Nos. 1397-1404 (8) 10.10 10.10

Souvenir Sheets

Perf. 13x12

1405 A183 400 le Blue banded nymph 4.80 4.80
1406 A183 400 le Western red charaxes 2.75 2.75
1407 A183 400 le Broad-bordered grass yellow 2.75 2.75
1408 A183 400 le African clouded yellow 3.25 3.25

While numbers 1406-1407 have the same issue date as Nos. 1397-1405, the dollar value of Nos. 1406-1407 was lower when they were released. While No. 1408 has the same issue date as Nos. 1397-1407, the value of No. 1408 was different when released.

World War II Motion Pictures
A184

Designs: 2 le, To Hell and Back, Audie Murphy. 5 le, Attack, Jack Palance. 10 le, Mrs. Miniver, Greer Garson and Walter Pidgeon. 20 le, The Guns of Navarone. 30 le, The Great Dictator, Paulette Goddard and Charlie Chaplin. 50 le, The Train. 60 le, The Diary of Anne Frank. 80 le, The Bridge on the River Kwai, William Holden. 100 le, Lifeboat, Alfred Hitchcock, Tallulah Bankhead. 200 le, Sands of Iwo Jima, John Wayne. 300 le, Thirty Seconds Over Tokyo, Van Johnson and Spencer Tracy. 350 le, Casablanca, Humphrey Bogart and Ingrid Bergman. No. 1421, Twelve O'Clock High, Gregory Peck. No. 1422, Tora! Tora! Tora!. No. 1423, Patton, George C. Scott.

1991, Oct. 14 **Litho.** ***Perf. 14***

1409 A184 2 le multicolored .20 .20
1410 A184 5 le multicolored .20 .20
1411 A184 10 le multicolored .20 .20
1412 A184 20 le multicolored .25 .25
1413 A184 30 le multicolored .35 .35
1414 A184 50 le multicolored .60 .60
1415 A184 60 le multicolored .70 .70
1416 A184 80 le multicolored .95 .95
1417 A184 100 le multicolored 1.25 1.25
1418 A184 200 le multicolored 2.40 2.40
1419 A184 300 le multicolored 3.50 3.50
1420 A184 350 le multicolored 4.25 4.25
Nos. 1409-1420 (12) 14.85 14.85

Souvenir Sheets

1421 A184 450 le multicolored 5.50 5.50
1422 A184 450 le multicolored 5.50 5.50
1423 A184 450 le multicolored 5.50 5.50

Miniature Sheets

Botanic Gardens — A185

Munich Botanic Garden: No. 1424a, Meissen China ornament. b, Masdevallia. c, White Egyptian lotus. d, French marigold. e, Pitcher plant. f, The Palm House. g, Dog's tooth violet. h, Passion flower. i, Hedge rose. j, Sensitive plant. k, Pitcher plant, diff. l, Trillium. m, Wild plantain. n, German primrose. o, Tulip. p, Spring walk.

Kyoto Botanic Garden: No. 1425a, Flowering cherry. b, Gardenia. c, The Domed Conservatory. d, Chrysanthemums. e, Bleeding heart. f, Hibiscus. g, Hiryu azalea. h, Sweet honeysuckle. i, Goldband lily. j, Non-traditional garden art. k, Viburnum. l, Japanese iris. m, Orchid. n, Hydrangea. o, View of Kyoto Botanic Garden. p, Camelia.

Brooklyn Botanic Garden: No. 1426a, The Palm House. b, Kurume azalea. c, Southern magnolia. d, Oleander. e, Chinese wisteria. f, Sourwood tree. g, Cattleya orchid. h, Gingko tree. i, Japanese Hill and Pond Garden. j, Rose. k, German iris. l, East Indian lotus. m, Speciosum lily. n, Lilac. o, Rose bay. p, Cranford Rose Garden.

No. 1427, Rhododendron, Munich, horiz. No. 1428, Chrysanthemum, Kyoto, horiz. No. 1429, Magnolia soulangeana, Brooklyn, horiz.

1991, Oct. 28

Sheets of 16

1424 A185 60 le #a.-p. 11.50 11.50
1425 A185 60 le #a.-p. 11.50 11.50
1426 A185 60 le #a.-p. 11.50 11.50

Souvenir Sheets

1427-1429 A185 600 le each 7.25 7.25

Christmas
A186

Details from paintings or engravings by Albrecht Durer: 6 le, Mary being Crowned by Two Angels. 60 le, St. Christopher. 80 le, Virgin and Child. 100 le, Madonna and Child (Virgin with the Pear). 200 le, Madonna and Child. 300 le, The Virgin in Half-Length. 700 le, The Madonna with the Siskin. No. 1437, The Feast of the Rose Garlands. No. 1438, Virgin and Child with St. Anne.

1991, Dec. 9 **Litho.** ***Perf. 12***

1430 A186 6 le pink & black .20 .20
1431 A186 60 le blue & black .50 .50
1432 A186 80 le multicolored .65 .65
1433 A186 100 le multicolored .80 .80
1434 A186 200 le multicolored 1.60 1.60
1435 A186 300 le multicolored 2.40 2.40
1436 A186 700 le multicolored 5.50 5.50
Nos. 1430-1436 (7) 11.65 11.65

Souvenir Sheets

Perf. 14½

1437-1438 A186 600 le each 4.75 4.75

Wolfgang Amadeus Mozart, Death Bicent.
A187

Mozart and: 50 le, National Theatre, Prague. 100 le, St. Peter's Abbey, Salzburg. 500 le, Scene from opera, "Idomeneo."

1991, Dec. 20 *Perf. 14*

1439 A187 50 le multicolored .40 .40
1440 A187 100 le multicolored .80 .80
1441 A187 500 le multicolored 4.00 4.00
Nos. 1439-1441 (3) 5.20 5.20

Souvenir Sheet

1442 A187 600 le Bust, vert. 4.75 4.75

17th World Scout Jamboree, Korea A188

Designs: 250 le, Scouts learning to sail. 300 le, Lord Robert Baden-Powell, founder. 400 le, Scouts playing baseball. 750 le, Jamboree emblem, vert.

1991, Dec. 20

1443 A188 250 le multicolored 2.00 2.00
1444 A188 300 le multicolored 2.40 2.40
1445 A188 400 le multicolored 3.25 3.25
Nos. 1443-1445 (3) 7.65 7.65

Souvenir Sheet

1446 A188 750 le multicolored 6.00 6.00

Miniature Sheet

Attack on Pearl Harbor, 50th Anniv. A189

Designs: a, Japanese D3A1 Val dive bomber. b, Plane amid rising smoke over Ford Island. c, Battleships ablaze. d, Naval station, three planes. e, Drydock ablaze, tank farm. f, Two Vals over water, ships. g, USS Utah and Ford Island installations ablaze, ship underway. h, Installations on Ford Island ablaze. i, US P-40 Warhawk fighter plane. j, Two Japanese torpedo bombers, plane on fire falling from sky. k, Three Japanese bombers over Pearl City. l, Two Japanese bombers diving on four ships, one burning ship. m, Japanese plane on fire. n, Two Japanese planes. o, One Japanese plane over Waipio Peninsula.

1991, Dec. 20 *Perf. 14½x15*

1447 A189 75 le Sheet of 15, #a.-o. 9.00 9.00

Walt Disney Christmas Cards — A190

Designs and year of issue: 12 le, Mickey and Donald decorating tree, 1952. 30 le, Characters surrounding book with "Alice in Wonderland", 1950. 60 le, Dwarf asleep with hare and tortoise, 1938. 75 le, Minnie, Donald, Mickey and Pluto mailing Christmas card, 1936. 100 le, Costumed characters in front of Magic Kingdom, 1984. 125 le, Mickey singing, Donald's nephews and Pluto reading 20,000 Leagues Under the Sea, 1954. 150 le, 101 Dalmations with season's greetings, 1960. 200 le, Donald and Mickey among gifts, 1948. 300 le, Mickey, Minnie at home for Christmas, 1983. 400 le, Donald and ducks preparing for Christmas watching Mickey Mouse Club, 1956. Characters on parade with Christmas cheer. 500 le, Disney characters, 50th birthday of Walt Disney Productions, 1972. No. 1460, Map of Magic Kingdom, 1955, vert. No. 1461, Seven dwarfs in bobsled, 1959, vert. No. 1462, Alice in Wonderland at tea party, 1950, vert.

1991, Dec. 24 **Litho.** *Perf. 14x13½*

1448 A190 12 le multicolored .20 .20
1449 A190 30 le multicolored .20 .20
1450 A190 60 le multicolored .35 .35
1451 A190 75 le multicolored .40 .40
1452 A190 100 le multicolored .55 .55
1453 A190 125 le multicolored .75 .75
1454 A190 150 le multicolored .85 .85
1455 A190 200 le multicolored 1.25 1.25
1456 A190 300 le multicolored 1.75 1.75
1457 A190 400 le multicolored 2.25 2.25
1458 A190 500 le multicolored 2.75 2.75
1459 A190 600 le multicolored 3.25 3.25
Nos. 1448-1459 (12) 14.55 14.55

Souvenir Sheets

Perf. 13½x14

1460-1462 A190 900 le each 5.25 5.25

Disney Characters on World Tour A192

Designs: 6 le, Chiquita Minnie in Central America. 10 le, Gold Medal Goofy in Ancient Greece. 20 le, Donald, Daisy having Flamenco Fun in Spain. 30 le, Goofy guarding Donald at London's Buckingham Palace. 50 le, Mickey and Minnie dressed in Paris originals. 100 le, Goofy with mountain goat in Switzerland. 200 le, Daisy, Minnie as luau ladies in Hawaii. 350 le, Mickey, Donald and Goofy as ancient Egyptian comic strips, horiz. 500 le, Daisy and Minnie as can-can dancers in Paris, horiz. No. 1479, Mickey playing bagpipes in Scotland. No. 1480, Goofy fishes from Donald's gondola in Venice, Italy. No. 1481, Mickey and Goofy taking crash course in Greek.

Perf. 13x13½, 13½x13

1992, Feb. **Litho.**

1470 A192 6 le multicolored .20 .20
1471 A192 10 le multicolored .20 .20
1472 A192 20 le multicolored .20 .20
1473 A192 30 le multicolored .25 .25
1474 A192 50 le multicolored .40 .40
1475 A192 100 le multicolored .80 .80
1476 A192 200 le multicolored 1.60 1.60
1477 A192 350 le multicolored 2.75 2.75
1478 A192 500 le multicolored 4.00 4.00
Nos. 1470-1478 (9) 10.40 10.40

Souvenir Sheets

1479-1481 A192 700 le each 5.50 5.50

Queen Elizabeth II's Accession to the Throne, 40th Anniv.

Common Design Type

1992, Feb. 6 **Litho.** *Perf. 14*

1482 CD348 60 le multicolored .50 .50
1483 CD348 100 le multicolored .80 .80
1484 CD348 300 le multicolored 2.40 2.40
1485 CD348 400 le multicolored 3.25 3.25
Nos. 1482-1485 (4) 6.95 6.95

Souvenir Sheets

1486 CD348 700 le Queen, hillside 5.50 5.50
1487 CD348 700 le Queen, houses 5.50 5.50

Spanish Art — A193

Paintings by Francisco de Zurbaran: 1 le, The Visit of St. Thomas Aquinas to St. Bonaventure. 10 le, St. Gregory. 30 le, St. Andrew. 50 le, St. Gabriel the Archangel. 60 le, The Blessed Henry Suso. 100 le, St. Lucy. 300 le, St. Casilda. 400 le, St. Margaret of Antioch. 500 le, St. Apollonia. 600 le, St. Bonaventure at the Council of Lyons. 700 le, St. Bonaventure on His Bier. 800 le, The Martyrdom of St. James (detail). No. 1496, St. Hugh in the Refectory, horiz. No. 1497, The Martyrdom of St. James. No. 1497A, The Young Virgin.

1992, May 25 **Litho.** *Perf. 13*

1487A A193 1 le multi .20 .20
1488 A193 10 le multi .20 .20
1489 A193 30 le multi .25 .25
1490 A193 50 le multi .40 .40
1491 A193 60 le multi .45 .45
1491A A193 100 le multi .50 .50
1491B A193 300 le multi 1.50 1.50
1492 A193 400 le multi 3.00 3.00
1493 A193 500 le multi 4.00 4.00
1494 A193 600 le multi 4.75 4.75
1495 A193 700 le multi 3.50 3.50
1495A A193 800 le multi 4.00 4.00

Size: 120x95mm

Imperf

1496 A193 900 le multi 7.25 7.25
1497 A193 900 le multi 6.75 6.75
1497A A193 900 le multi 4.75 4.75
Nos. 1487A-1497A (15) 41.50 41.50

Granada '92.

While Nos. 1487A-1497A all have the same issue date, the dollar value of Nos. 1487A, 1489-1490, 1491A-1491B, 1492, 1495, 1497-1497A was lower when they were released.

Prehistoric Animals — A194

Designs: No. 1498a, Rhamphorhynchus. b, Pteranodon. c, Dimorphodon. d, Pterodactyl. e, Archaeopteryx. f, Iguanodon. g, Hypsilophodon. h, Nothosaurus. i, Brachiosaurus. j, Kentrosaurus. k, Plesiosaurus. l, Trachodon. m, Hesperornis. n, Henodus. o, Steneosaurus. p, Stenopterygius. q, Eurhinosaurus r, Placodus. s, Mosasaurus. t, Mixosaurus. No. 1499, Herperornis, diff.

1992, June 8 *Perf. 14*

1498 A194 50 le Sheet of 20, #a.-t. 8.00 8.00

Souvenir Sheet

1499 A194 50 le multicolored .40 .40

"Sierra Leone" is 22mm wide on No. 1499.

A195

A196

Tropical Birds: 30 le, Greater flamingo. 50 le, White-crested hornbill. 100 le, Verreaux's touraco. 170 le, Yellow-spotted barbet. 200 le, African spoonbill. 250 le, Saddlebill stork. 300 le, Red-headed lovebird. 600 le, Yellow-billed barbet. No. 1508, Fire-bellied woodpecker. No. 1509, Swallow-tailed bee-eater.

1992, July 20 **Litho.** *Perf. 14*

1500 A195 30 le multi .25 .25
1501 A195 50 le multi .40 .40
1502 A195 100 le multi .50 .50
1503 A195 170 le multi .90 .90
1504 A195 200 le multi 1.50 1.50
1505 A195 250 le multi 1.25 1.25
1506 A195 300 le multi 1.60 1.60
1507 A195 600 le multi 4.75 4.75
Nos. 1500-1507 (8) 11.15 11.15

Souvenir Sheets

1508 A195 1000 le multi 7.75 7.75
1509 A195 1000 le multi 5.25 5.25

While Nos. 1500-1509 all have the same release date, the value of Nos. 1502-1503, 1505-1506, 1509 was lower when they were released.

1992 **Litho.** *Perf. 14*

1992 Summer Olympics, Barcelona: 10 le, Marathon. 20 le, Gymnastics, parallel bars. 30 le, Discus. 50 le, 110-meter hurdles, horiz. 60 le, Women's long jump. 100 le, Gymnastics, floor exercise, horiz. 200 le, Windsurfing. 300 le, Road race cycling. 400 le, Weight lifting. 900 le, Soccer, horiz.

1510 A196 10 le multicolored .20 .20
1511 A196 20 le multicolored .20 .20
1512 A196 30 le multicolored .25 .25
1513 A196 50 le multicolored .35 .35
1514 A196 60 le multicolored .45 .45
1515 A196 100 le multicolored .75 .75
1516 A196 200 le multicolored 1.50 1.50
1517 A196 300 le multicolored 2.25 2.25
1518 A196 400 le multicolored 3.00 3.00
Nos. 1510-1518 (9) 8.95 8.95

Souvenir Sheet

1519 A196 900 le multicolored 6.75 6.75

1992 Winter Olympics, Albertville A197

Designs: 250 le, Women's biathlon, vert. 500 le, Speed skating, vert. 600 le, Men's downhill skiing. No. 1523, Men's single luge. No. 1524, Ice dancing, vert.

1992, Sept. 8 **Litho.** *Perf. 14*

1520 A197 250 le multicolored 1.25 1.25
1521 A197 500 le multicolored 2.60 2.60
1522 A197 600 le multicolored 3.00 3.00
Nos. 1520-1522 (3) 6.85 6.85

Souvenir Sheets

1523-1524 A197 900 le each 4.75 4.75

Discovery of America, 500th Anniv. A198

Designs: 300 le, Ferdinand, Isabella, Columbus. 500 le, Landing in New World. 900 le, Columbus, vert.

1992, Oct. **Litho.** *Perf. 14*

1525 A198 300 le multicolored 1.60 1.60
1526 A198 500 le multicolored 2.60 2.60

Souvenir Sheet

1527 A198 900 le multicolored 4.75 4.75

Birds — A199

Designs: 50c, Pygmy goose. 1 le, Spotted eagle owl. 2 le, Verreaux's touraco. 5 le, Saddlebill stork. 10 le, African golden oriole. 20 le, Malachite kingfisher. 30 le, Fire-crowned bishop. 40 le, Fire-bellied woodpecker. 50 le, Red-billed fire-finch. 80 le, Blue fairy flycatcher. 100 le, Crested malimbe. 150 le, Vitelline masked weaver. 170 le, Blue plantain-eater. 200 le, Superb sunbird. 250 le, Swallow-tailed bee-eater. 300 le, Cabani's yellow bunting. 500 le, Crocodile bird. 750 le, White-faced owl. 1000 le, Blue cuckoo-shrike. 2000 le, Bare-headed rock-fowl. 3000 le, Red-tailed buzzard.

1992-93 **Litho.** *Perf. 14x15*

1528 A199 50c multi .20 .20
1529 A199 1 le multi .20 .20
1530 A199 2 le multi .20 .20
1531 A199 5 le multi .20 .20
1532 A199 10 le multi .20 .20
1533 A199 20 le multi .20 .20
1534 A199 30 le multi .20 .20
1535 A199 40 le multi .20 .20
1536 A199 50 le multi .25 .25
1537 A199 80 le multi .40 .40
1538 A199 100 le multi .50 .50
1539 A199 150 le multi .80 .80
1540 A199 170 le multi .90 .90
1541 A199 200 le multi 1.00 1.00
1542 A199 250 le multi 1.25 1.25
1543 A199 300 le multi 1.60 1.60
1544 A199 500 le multi 2.75 2.75
1545 A199 750 le multi 4.00 4.00
1546 A199 1000 le multi 5.25 5.25
1546A A199 2000 le multi 16.00 16.00
1546B A199 3000 le multi 15.75 15.75
Nos. 1528-1546B (21) 52.05 52.05

#1536, 1538-1539, 1541, 1543 exist inscribed 1994; #1538, 1541, 1543-1544, 1546, 1546B inscribed 1996; #1536, 1538, 1541-1544 inscribed 1997; #1538, 1541, 1543, 1546 inscribed 1999; #1538, 1541-1546B 2000.

Issued: #1528-1546, 9/92; #1546A-1546B, 1993.

See Nos. 2152-2155.

Model Trains
A200

Lionel models: No. 1547a, Pennsylvania RR GG-1 electric #6-18306, O gauge, 1992. b, Wabash RR Hudson #8610, O gauge, 1985. c, Locomotive #1911, standard gauge, 1911. d, Chesapeake & Ohio 4-4-2 #6-18627, O gauge, 1992. e, Gang car #50, O gauge, 1954. f, #8004, 1980 model of Rock Island & Peoria RR engine built for Columbian Exposition of 1893, O gauge. g, Western Maryland RR Shay #6-18023, O gauge, 1992. h, (Kenner-Parker) Boston & Albany Hudson #784, O gauge, 1986. i, Locomotive #6, standard gauge, 1906.

No. 1548a, Pennsylvania RR Torpedo #238EW, O gauge, 1936. b, Denver & Rio Grande Western Alco Pa No. 6-18107, O gauge, 1992. c, #408E Locomotive, standard gauge, 1930. d, Mickey Mouse 60th birthday boxcar No. 19241, O gauge, 1991. e, Polished brass locomotive, No. 54, standard gauge, 1913. f, Broadway limited #392E, standard gauge, 1936. g, Great Northern RR EP-5 #18302, O gauge, 1988. h, 4-4-0 Locomotive #6, standard gauge, 1918. i, 4-4-4 Locomotive No. 400E, standard gauge, 1933.

No. 1549a, Special F-3 diesel engine, O gauge, 1947. b, Pennsylvannia RR GE 44-ton switcher #6-18905, O gauge, 1992. c, #1 trolley, standard gauge, 1913. d, Seaboard RR freight diesel, O gauge, 1958. e, Pennsylvania S-2 turbine, O gauge, 1991. f, Western Pacific RR GP-9 diesel #6-18822, O gauge, 1992. g, #10 with Ives plates transition model, standrad gauge, 1929. h, 4-4-4 locomotive #400E, standard gauge, 1931. i, #384E, standard gauge, 1928.

No. 1550, Hudson No. 8210 Special, O gauge. No. 1551, #381E, standard gauge, 1928. No. 1552, 2-Rail electric model #300 trolley with converse body, 2⅞-inch gauge.

1992, Nov. 23 Litho. *Perf. 14*

Sheets of 9

1547 A200	150 le #a.-i.		7.00	7.00
1548 A200	170 le #a.-i.		8.00	8.00
1549 A200	170 le #a.-i.		8.00	8.00

Souvenir Sheets

Perf. 13

1550-1552 A200	1000 le each	5.25	5.25

Genoa '92 (#1547-1549). Nos. 1550-1552 contains one 51x39mm stamp.

Walt Disney Characters in Christmas Scenes
A201

1992, Nov. 16 *Perf. 13½x14*

1553 A201	10 le Minnie & Chip	.20	.20
1554 A201	20 le Goofy as Santa	.20	.20
1555 A201	30 le Daisy, Minnie	.20	.20
1556 A201	50 le Mickey, Goofy	.25	.25
1557 A201	80 le Pete	.40	.40
1558 A201	100 le Donald Duck	.50	.50
1559 A201	150 le Morty & Ferdie	.80	.80
1560 A201	200 le Mickey	1.00	1.00
1561 A201	300 le Goofy with ornament	1.60	1.60
1562 A201	500 le Chip & Dale	2.60	2.60
1563 A201	600 le Donald & Dale	3.25	3.25
1564 A201	800 le Huey, Dewey & Louie	4.25	4.25
Nos. 1553-1564 (12)		15.25	15.25

Souvenir Sheets

1565 A201	900 le Mickey Mouse	4.75	4.75

Perf. 14x13½

1566 A201	900 le Angel with Chip, horiz.	4.75	4.75
1567 A201	900 le Mickey & Minnie, horiz.	4.75	4.75

Mickey Mouse Magazines and Books
A202

10 le, Magazine cover, Mar. 1936, v. 1, #6. 20 le, Magazine cover, June 1936, v. 1, #9. 30 le, Magazine cover, Nov. 1936, v. 2, #2. 40 le, Magazine cover, Aug. 1937, v. 2, #11. 50 le, Magazine cover, Oct. 1937, v. 2, #13. 60 le, Magazine cover, Dec. 1937, v. 3, #3. 70 le, Magazine cover, Jan. 1938, v. 3, #4. 150 le, Cover, Big Book #4062, 1935. 170 le, Story book cover, 1936. 200 le, Comic book cover, unnumbered. 300 le, Comic book cover, No. 181. 400 le, Comic book cover #194. 500 le, Story book cover, Book 1, 1931. No. 1581, Boys' and Girls' March of Comics cover, 1948. No. 1582, First Mickey Mouse Magazine cover for June-Aug. 1935, v. 1, #1, horiz. No. 1583, Cover of early Mickey Mouse story book published in England, 1933, horiz.

1992 *Perf. 13½x14*

1568 A202	10 le multicolored	.20	.20
1569 A202	20 le multicolored	.20	.20
1570 A202	30 le multicolored	.20	.20
1571 A202	40 le multicolored	.20	.20
1572 A202	50 le multicolored	.30	.30
1573 A202	60 le multicolored	.35	.35
1574 A202	70 le multicolored	.40	.40
1575 A202	150 le multicolored	.80	.80
1576 A202	170 le multicolored	.90	.90
1577 A202	200 le multicolored	1.00	1.00
1578 A202	300 le multicolored	1.60	1.60
1579 A202	400 le multicolored	2.00	2.00
1580 A202	500 le multicolored	2.75	2.75
Nos. 1568-1580 (13)		10.90	10.90

Souvenir Sheets

1581 A202	900 le multicolored	4.75	4.75

Perf. 14x13½

1582 A202	900 le multicolored	4.75	4.75
1583 A202	900 le multicolored	4.75	4.75

Christmas
A203

Details or entire paintings: 1 le, Virgin and Child, by Fiorenzo di Lorenzo. 10 le, Madonna and Child on a Wall, by Circle of Dirk Bouts. 20 le, Virgin and Child with the Flight into Egypt, by Master of Hoogstraeten. 30 le, Madonna and Child before Firescreen, by Master of Flemalle. 50 le, Mary in a Rose Garden, by Hans Memling. 100 le, Virgin Mary and Child, by Lucas Cranach the Elder. 170 le, Virgin and Child, by Rogier van der Weyden. 200 le, Madonna and Saints, by Perugino. 250 le, Madonna Enthroned with Saints Catherine and Barbara, by Master of Hoogstraeten. 300 le, The Virgin in a Rose Arbor, by Stefan Lochner. 500 le, Madonna and Child with Angels, by Sandro Botticelli. 1000 le, Madonna and Child with Young St. John the Baptist, by Fra Bartolemmeo. No. 1596, The Virgin with the Green Cushion, by Andrea Solario. No. 1597, The Virgin and Child, by Jan Gossaert. No. 1598, The Virgin and Child, by Lucas Cranach the Younger.

1992, Dec. 7 Litho. *Perf. 13½x14*

1584 A203	1 le multi	.20	.20
1585 A203	10 le multi	.20	.20
1586 A203	20 le multi	.20	.20
1587 A203	30 le multi	.20	.20
1588 A203	50 le multi	.30	.30
1589 A203	100 le multi	.50	.50
1590 A203	170 le multi	.90	.90
1591 A203	200 le multi	1.00	1.00
1592 A203	250 le multi	1.25	1.25
1593 A203	300 le multi	1.60	1.60
1594 A203	500 le multi	2.75	2.75
1595 A203	1000 le multi	5.25	5.25
Nos. 1584-1595 (12)		14.35	14.35

Souvenir Sheets

1596-1598 A203	900 le each	4.75	4.75

Anniversaries and Events
A204

150 le, Emblems of FAO, ICN, WHO. #1600, Graf Zeppelin. #1601, Cow, emblems, grain stalk. 200 le, Starving child. #1603, Lions Intl. emblem, map. #1604, Cottonwood tree. 300 le, African elephant. 600 le, Space Shuttle. 700 le, Graf Zeppelin LZ 127, specifications. #1608, Astronaut. #1609, Count Zeppelin.

1992, Dec. Litho. *Perf. 14*

1599 A204	150 le multicolored	.80	.80
1600 A204	170 le multicolored	.90	.90
1601 A204	170 le multicolored	.90	.90
1602 A204	200 le multicolored	1.00	1.00
1603 A204	250 le multicolored	1.25	1.25
1604 A204	250 le multicolored	1.25	1.25
1605 A204	300 le multicolored	1.60	1.60
1606 A204	600 le multicolored	3.25	3.25
1607 A204	700 le multicolored	3.65	3.65
Nos. 1599-1607 (9)		14.60	14.60

Souvenir Sheets

1608-1609 A204	900 le each	4.75	4.75

Intl. Conference on Nutrition, Rome (#1599, 1601). Count Zeppelin, 75th anniv. of death (#1600, 1607, 1609). World Health Organization (#1602). Lions Intl., 75th anniv. (#1603). Earth Summit, Rio de Janeiro (#1604-1605). Intl. Space Year (#1606, 1608).

Miniature Sheet

Boxing
A205

Boxing movies, stars: No. 1610a, The Champ, Wallace Beery. b, Golden Boy, William Holden. c, Body and Soul, John Garfield. d, Champion, Kirk Douglas. e, The Set-Up, Robert Ryan. f. Requiem for a Heavyweight, Anthony Quinn. g, Kid Galahad, Elvis Presley. h, Fat City, Jeff Bridges.

No. 1612, Gentlemen Jim, Errol Flynn. No. 1614, Rocky III, Sylvester Stallone.

Boxing champions: No. 1611a, Joe Louis. b, Archie Moore. c, Muhammad Ali. d, George Foreman. e, Joe Frazier. f, Marvin Hagler. g, Sugar Ray Leonard. h, Evander Holyfield.

No. 1613, Muhammad Ali, diff.

1993, Feb. 8 Litho. *Perf. 13½x14*

1610 A205	200 le Sheet of 8, #a.-h.	8.50	8.50
1611 A205	200 le Sheet of 8, #a.-h.	8.50	8.50

Souvenir Sheets

1612-1614 A205	1000 le each	5.25	5.25

Miniature Sheets

Louvre Museum, Bicent.
A206

Details or entire paintings by Eugene Delacroix (1798-1863): Nos. 1615a-1615b, Entry of the Crusaders into Constantinople (left, right). c-d, Jews Purchasing Brides in Morocco (left, right). e-f, The Death of Sardanapalus (left, right). g-h, Liberty Guiding the People (left, right).

No. 1616a, An Orphan at the Cemetery. b-c, Women of Algiers in their Apartment (left, right). d, Dante and Virgil in the Infernal Regions. e, Self-Portrait. f-g, Massacre at Chios (left, right). h, Frederic Chopin.

No. 1617, Rape of the Sabine Women, by Jacques-Louis David (1748-1825).

1993, Mar. 8 Litho. *Perf. 12x12½*

1615 A206	70 le Sheet of 8, #a.-h. + label	3.00	3.00
1616 A206	70 le Sheet of 8, #a.-h. + label	3.00	3.00

Souvenir Sheet

Perf. 14½

1617 A206	900 le multicolored	4.75	4.75

Mushrooms
A207

Butterflies
A208

Designs: 30 le, Amanita flammeola. 50 le, Cantharellus pseudocibarius. 100 le, Volvariella volvacea. 200 le, Termitomyces microcarpus. 300 le, Auricularia auricula. 400 le, Pleurotus tuberregium. 500 le, Schizophyllum commune. 600 le, Termitomyces robustus. No. 1626, Phallus rubicundus. No. 1627, Daldina concentrica.

1993, May 5 *Perf. 14*

1618 A207	30 le multi	.20	.20
1619 A207	50 le multi	.30	.30
1620 A207	100 le multi	.50	.50
1621 A207	200 le multi	1.00	1.00
1622 A207	300 le multi	1.50	1.50
1623 A207	400 le multi	2.10	2.10
1624 A207	500 le multi	2.75	2.75
1625 A207	600 le multi	3.25	3.25
Nos. 1618-1625 (8)		11.60	11.60

Souvenir Sheets

1626-1627 A207	1000 le each	5.25	5.25

1993, May 5

20 le, False acraea. 30 le, Blue temora. 50 le, Foxy charaxes. 100 le, Leaf blue. 150 le, Blue-banded swallowtail. 170 le, African monarch. 200 le, Mountain beauty. 250 le, Gaudy commodore. 300 le, Palla butterfly. 500 le, Pirate butterfly. 600 le, Painted lady. 700 le, Gold-banded forester.

#1640, Blue diadem. #1641, Blue swallowtail. #1642, African leaf butterfly.

1628-1639 A208	Set of 12	16.50	16.50

Souvenir Sheets

1640-1642 A208	1000 le Set of 3	15.50	15.50

Miniature Sheets

Cats — A209

Designs: No. 1643a, Somali. b, Egyptian Mau smoke. c, Chocolate-point Siamese. d, Mi-Ke Japanese bobtail. e, Chinchilla. f, Red Burmese. g, British shorthair brown tabby. h, Blue Persian. i, British silver classic tabby. j, Oriental ebony. k, Red Persian. l, British calico shorthair.

No. 1644a, Black Persian. b, Blue-point Siamese. c, American wirehair. d, Birman. e, Scottish fold (silver tabby). f, American shorthair red tabby. g, Blue & white Persian bicolor. h, Havana brown. i, Norwegian forest cat. j, Brown tortie Burmese. k. Angora. l, Exotic shorthair.

No. 1645, American shorthair blue tabby, horiz. No. 1646, Seal-point colorpoint, horiz.

1993, May 17 Litho. *Perf. 14*

1643 A209	150 le Sheet of 12, #a.-l.	9.50	9.50
1644 A209	150 le Sheet of 12, #a.-l.	9.50	9.50

Souvenir Sheets

1645-1646 A209	1000 le each	5.25	5.25

Nos. 1643-1646 Ovptd. with Hong Kong '94 Emblem

1994	Litho.	Perf. 14	
1643m	On #1643b & in sheet margin	9.50	9.50
1644m	On #1644b & in sheet margin	9.50	9.50
1645a	Ovptd. in sheet margin	5.25	5.25
1646a	Ovptd. in sheet margin	5.25	5.25

Wild Animals A210

1993, June 17

1647	A210	30 le	Gorilla	.20	.20
1648	A210	100 le	Bongo	.50	.50
1649	A210	150 le	Potto	.80	.80
1650	A210	170 le	Chimpanzee	.90	.90
1651	A210	200 le	Dwarf galago	1.00	1.00
1652	A210	300 le	African linsang	1.60	1.60
1653	A210	500 le	Banded duiker	2.75	2.75
1654	A210	750 le	Diana monkey	4.00	4.00
			Nos. 1647-1654 (8)	11.75	11.75

Souvenir Sheets

1655	A210	1200 le	Leopard	6.25	6.25
1656	A210	1200 le	Elephant	6.25	6.25

Flowers A211

30 le, Bleeding-heart vine. 40 le, Passion vine. 50 le, Hydrangea. 60 le, Wax begonia. 100 le, Hibiscus. 150 le, Crape-myrtle. 170 le, Bougainvillea. 200 le, Leadwort. 250 le, Gerbera daisy. 300 le, Black-eyed susan. 500 le, Gloriosa lily. 900 le, Sweet violet. #1669, Gloriosa lily, diff. #1670, Passion vine, diff. #1671, Hibiscus, diff.

1993, July 15 Litho. Perf. 14

1657	A211	30 le	multi	.20	.20
1658	A211	40 le	multi	.20	.20
1659	A211	50 le	multi	.25	.25
1660	A211	60 le	multi	.30	.30
1661	A211	100 le	multi	.50	.50
1662	A211	150 le	multi	.80	.80
1663	A211	170 le	multi	.90	.90
1664	A211	200 le	multi	1.00	1.00
1665	A211	250 le	multi	1.25	1.25
1666	A211	300 le	multi	1.50	1.50
1667	A211	500 le	multi	2.50	2.50
1668	A211	900 le	multi	3.00	3.00
			Nos. 1657-1668 (12)	12.40	12.40

Souvenir Sheets

1669-1671 A211 1200 le each 6.25 6.25

Coronation of Queen Elizabeth II, 40th Anniv. — A212

100 le, Queen, Princess Anne. 200 le, Coronation procession. 600 le, Official coronation photograph. 1500 le, Portrait, by Pietro Annigoni, 1954-55.

1993, Oct. Litho. Perf. 14

1672	A212	100 le	multicolored	.50	.50
1673	A212	200 le	black	1.00	1.00
1674	A212	600 le	multicolored	3.25	3.25
			Nos. 1672-1674 (3)	4.75	4.75

Souvenir Sheet

1675 A212 1500 le multicolored 7.75 7.75

Copernicus (1473-1543) A213

Picasso (1881-1973) A214

250 le, Early telescope. 800 le, Moon's surface.

1993, Oct.

1676	A213	250 le	multicolored	1.25	1.25
1677	A213	800 le	multicolored	4.25	4.25

1993, Oct.

Sculpture: 170 le, Woman with Hat, 1961. Paintings: 200 le, Buste de Femme, 1958. 800 le, Maya with a Doll, 1938. 1000 le, Women of Algiers (after Delacroix), 1955.

1678	A214	170 le	multicolored	.90	.90
1679	A214	200 le	multicolored	1.00	1.00
1680	A214	800 le	multicolored	4.25	4.25
			Nos. 1678-1680 (3)	6.15	6.15

Souvenir Sheet

1681 A214 1000 le multicolored 5.25 5.25

Christmas A215

Details or entire paintings, by Raphael: 50 le, 100 le, No. 1690, Madonna of the Fish. 150 le, Madonna & Child Enthroned with Five Saints. 800 le, The Holy Family with the Lamb.

Details or entire woodcuts, by Durer: 200 le, 250 le, 300 le, The Circumcision. 500 le, No. 1691, Holy Clan with Saints and Two Angels Playing Music.

1993, Dec. Perf. 13½x14

1682	A215	50 le	multi	.25	.25
1683	A215	100 le	multi	.50	.50
1684	A215	150 le	multi	.80	.80
1685	A215	200 le	multi	1.00	1.00
1686	A215	250 le	multi	1.25	1.25
1687	A215	300 le	multi	1.50	1.50
1688	A215	500 le	multi	2.50	2.50
1689	A215	800 le	multi	4.25	4.25
			Nos. 1682-1689 (8)	12.05	12.05

Souvenir Sheets

1690-1691 A215 1200 le each 6.25 6.25

Christmas A216

Disney characters celebrate Christmas: different.

#1700, Santa. #1701, Elves, horiz. #1702, Santa, horiz. #1703, Mickey, Minnie, horiz.

1993, Dec. 17 Perf. 13½x14

1692	A216	50 le	multi	.25	.25
1693	A216	100 le	multi	.50	.50
1694	A216	170 le	multi	.90	.90
1695	A216	200 le	multi	1.00	1.00
1696	A216	250 le	multi	1.25	1.25
1697	A216	500 le	multi	2.50	2.50
1698	A216	600 le	multi	3.00	3.00
1699	A216	800 le	multi	4.25	4.25
			Nos. 1692-1699 (8)	13.65	13.65

Souvenir Sheets

Perf. 13½x14, 14x13½

1700-1703 A216 1200 le each 6.25 6.25

1994 World Cup Soccer Championships, US — A217

Players, country: 30 le, Jose Luis Brown (R), Argentina. 50 le, Gary Lineker, England. 100 le, Carlos Valderrama, Colombia. 250 le, Skuhravy, Czechoslovakia; Marchena, Costa Rica. 300 le, Butragueno, Spain. 400 le, Roger Milla, Cameroun. 500 le, Roberto Donadoni, Italy. 700 le, Enzo Scifo, Belgium.

No. 1712, 1200 le, Socrates, Brazil. No. 1713, 1200 le, Wright, England; Demol, Belgium.

1993 Perf. 13½x14

1704-1711 A217 Set of 8 10.00 10.00

Souvenir Sheets

1712-1713 A217 1200 le each 6.25 6.25

A218

Hong Kong '94 A219

Stamps and: No. 1714, Hong Kong #455, pagoda, Tiger Baum Garden. No. 1715, Ai Par Garden, #1084.

Carved lacquer, Qing Dynasty: No. 1716a, Bowl with "Wan-Sui-Ch'ang-Chun." b, Four-wheeled box. c, Flower container. d, Box with human figure design. e, Shishi dog (not lacquer). f, Persimmon.

1994, Feb. 18 Litho. Perf. 14

1714	A218	200 le	multicolored	1.00	1.00
1715	A218	200 le	multicolored	1.00	1.00
a.			Pair, #1714-1715	2.00	2.00

Miniature Sheet

1716 A219 100 le Sheet of 6, #a.-f. 3.25 3.25

Nos. 1714-1715 issued in sheets of 5 pairs. No. 1715a is a continuous design.

New Year 1994 (Year of the Dog) (#1716e).

Miniature Sheet

New Year 1994 (Year of the Dog) A220

a, 100 le, Pekingese. b, 150 le, Doberman pinscher. c, 200 le, Tibetan terrier. d, 250 le, Weimaraner. e, 400 le, Rottweiler. f, 500 le, Akita. g, 600 le, Schnauzer. h, 1000 le, Tibetan spaniel.

No. 1718, Wire-haired pointing Griffon. No. 1719, Shih Tzu.

1994, June 20 Litho. Perf. 14

1717 A220 Sheet of 8, #a.-h. 13.00 13.00

Souvenir Sheets

1718-1719 A220 1200 le each 4.75 4.75

D-Day, 50th Anniv. A221

Designs: 500 le, British paratroops drop behind enemy lines. 750 le, US paratrooper jumps from C47 transport.

1000 le, C47 Douglas Dakota, paratroops.

1994, July 11 Litho. Perf. 14

1720	A221	500 le	multicolored	2.00	2.00
1721	A221	750 le	multicolored	3.00	3.00

Souvenir Sheet

1722 A221 1000 le multicolored 4.00 4.00

A222

PHILAKOREA '94 — A223

100 le, Traditional wedding, Korea House, Seoul. 400 le, Royal tombs, Koryo Dynasty, Kaesong. 600 le, Terraced farm land, near Chungmu.

Tiger paintings, Choson Dynasty: No. 1726: a, Tiger, cubs, 19th cent. b, Munsa-pasal seated on lion. c, Extinct Korean tiger. d, Tiger, bamboo. e, Tiger guarding 3 cubs, 4 magpies. f, Tiger, 19th cent. g, Mountain Spirit. h, Tiger, bird in tree.

No. 1727, Wall painting of mounted hunters from Tomb of the Dancers of Kungnaesong, Koguryo period.

Perf. 14, 13½ (#1726)

1994, July 11 Litho.

1723-1725 A222 Set of 3 4.50 4.50

Miniature Sheet of 8

1726 A223 200 le #a.-h. 6.50 6.50

Souvenir Sheet

1727 A222 1200 le multicolored 4.75 4.75

Miniature Sheets of 6

First Manned Moon Landing, 25th Anniv. A224

No. 1728: a, Edwin E. Aldrin, Jr. b, Michael Collins. c, Neil A. Armstrong. d, Apollo 11 liftoff. e, Aldrin descending to lunar surface. f, Armstrong, lunar module Eagle reflected in Aldrin's face shield.

No. 1729: a, Aldrin gathering soil samples. b, Eagle with Aldrin deploying solar wind experiment. c, Aldrin, ALSEP & Eagle at Tranquility Base. d, US flag, Aldrin, Tranquility Base. e, Plaque on moon. f, Apollo 11 crew, stamp ceremony.

1000 le, First footprint on moon.

1994, July 11 Perf. 14

1728-1729 A224 200 le #a.-f, ea 4.75 4.75

Souvenir Sheet

1730 A224 1000 le multicolored 4.00 4.00

Miniature Sheet of 6

A225

1994 World Cup Soccer Championships, US — A226

Players: No. 1731a, Kim Ho, South Korea. b, Cobi Jones, US. c, Claudio Suarez, Mexico. d, Tomas Brolin, Sweden. e, Ruud Gullit, Netherlands. f, Andreas Herzog, Austria.
No. 1732, Sierra Leone team. No. 1733, Giants Stadium, New Jersey.

1994, July 15
1731 A225 250 le #a.-f. 6.00 6.00

Souvenir Sheets
1732-1733 A226 1500 le each 6.00 6.00

Birds — A227

250 le, Black kite. 300 le, Superb sunbird. 500 le, Martial eagle. 800 le, Red bishop.
White-necked picathartes: No. 1738a, 50 le, Feeding young. b, 100 le, On brown tree limb. c, 150 le, Two at nest. d, On gray limb, green leaves.
No. 1739, Greater flamingo, vert. No. 1740, White-necked picathartes up close, vert.

1994, Aug. 10
1734-1737 A227 Set of 4 8.50 8.50

Miniature Sheet of 9
1738 A227 3 each, #a.-d. 6.00 6.00

Souvenir Sheets
1739-1740 A227 1200 le each 4.75 4.75

World Wildlife Fund (#1738).

Orchids — A228

Designs: 50 le, Aerangis kotschyana. 100 le, Brachycorythis kalbreyeri. 150 le, Diaphananthe pellucida. 200 le, Eulophia guineensis. 300 le, Eurychone rothschildana. 500 le, Tridactyle tridactylites. 750 le, Cyrtorchis arcuata. 900 le, Ancistrochilus rothschildianus.
No. 1749, Plectrelminthus caudatus. No. 1750, Polystachaya affinis.

1994, Sept. 1
1741-1748 A228 Set of 8 12.00 12.00

Souvenir Sheets
1749-1750 A228 1500 le each 6.00 6.00

Christmas A229

Details or entire paintings: 50 le, The Birth of the Virgin, by Murillo. 100 le, Education of the Virgin, by Murillo. 150 le, Annunciation, by Filippino Lippi. 200 le, Marriage of the Virgin, by Bernard van Orley. 250 le, The Visitation, by Nicolas Vleughels. 300 le, Holy Infant from Castelfranco altarpiece, by Giorgione. 400 le, Adoration of the Magi, Workshop of Bartholome Zeitblom. 600 le, Presentation of Infant Jesus in the Temple, by Memling.
No. 1759, Nativity Altarpiece, by Lorenzo Monado. No. 1760, Allendale Nativity, by Giorgione.

1994, Dec. 1 Litho. *Perf. 13½x14*
1751-1758 A229 Set of 8 6.75 6.75

Souvenir Sheets
1759-1760 A229 1500 le each 5.00 5.00

Intl. Year of the Family A230

1994, Dec. 20 Litho. *Perf. 14*
1761 A230 300 le Working in field 1.00 1.00
1762 A230 350 le At beach 1.10 1.10

Disney Christmas — A231

Designs: 50 le, Mickey's Christmas cat. 100 le, Goofy's Christmas tree, vert. 150 le, Daisy's Christmas gift. 200 le, Donald's Christmas surprise, vert. 250 le, Minnie's Christmas flight. 300 le, Goofy's Christmas snowball, vert. 400 le, Goofy's Christmas letters. 500 le, Christmas sled ride, vert. 600 le, Mickey's Christmas snowman. 800 le, Pluto's Christmas treat, vert.
No. 1773, Goofy hanging outdoor lights. No. 1774, Mickey asleep in chair, vert.

Perf. 14x13½, 13½x14
1995, Jan. 23 Litho.
1763-1772 A231 Set of 10 11.00 11.00

Souvenir Sheets
1773-1774 A231 1500 le each 5.00 5.00

Donald Duck's Gallery of Old Masters A232

Name of painting, inspiration: 50 le, Madonna Duck, Leonardo da Vinci. 100 le, Portrait of a Venetian Duck, Tintoretto. 150 le, Duck with a Glove, Frans Hals. 200 le, Donald with a Pink, Quentin Massys. 250 le, Pinkie Daisy, Sir Thomas Lawrence. 300 le, Donald's Whistling Mother, Whistler. 400 le, El Quacko, El Greco. 500 le, The Noble Snob, Rembrandt. 600 le, The Blue Duck, by Gainsborough. 800 le, Modern Quack, Picasso.
No. 1785, Soup's On, Brueghel. No. 1786, Duck Dancers, Degas, horiz.

1995, Jan. 23 *Perf. 13½x14, 14x13½*
1775-1784 A232 Set of 10 11.00 11.00

Souvenir Sheets
1785-1786 A232 1500 le each 5.00 5.00

Miniature Sheets of 12

Olympic Medal Winners — A233

Summer Olympics: No. 1787a, Ragnar Lundberg, 1952 men's pole vault. b, Karin Janz, 1972 all-round gymnastics. c, Matthias Volz, 1936 gymnastics. d, Carl Lewis, 1988 long jump. e, Sara Simeoni, 1976 high jump. f, Daley Thompson, 1980 decathlon. g, Japan vs. Britain, 1964 soccer. h, Gabriella Dorio, 1984 1500-meters run. i, Daniela Hunger, 1988 200-meters individual medley swimming. j, Kyoko Iwasaki, 1992 200-meters breast stroke. k, Italian team member, 1960 water polo. l, David Wilkie, 1976 200-meters breast stroke.
1994 Winter Olympics, Lillehammer: No. 1788a, Katja Seizinger, downhill skiing. b, Hot air balloon (no medalist). c, Elvis Stojko, figure skating. d, Jens Weissflog, individual large hill ski jump. e, Bjorn Daehlie, 10k cross-country skiing. f, Germany, four-man bobsled. g, Markus Wasmeier, men's super giant slalom. h, Georg Hackl, luge. i, Trovill & Dean, ice dancing. j, Bonnie Blair, speed skating. k, Nancy Kerrigan, figure skating. l, Team Sweden, hockey.
No. 1789, torchbearer, horiz. No. 1790, Oksana Baiul, Nancy Kerrigan, Chen Lu, 1994 figure skating, horiz.

1995, Feb. 6 Litho. *Perf. 14*
1787 A233 75 le #a.-l. 3.00 3.00
1788 A233 200 le #a.-l. 8.00 8.00

Souvenir Sheets
1789-1790 A233 1000 le each 3.50 3.50

Miniature Sheets

Dinosaurs A234

No. 1791: a, Ceratosaurus (d). b, Brachiosaurus. c, Pteranodon (b). d, Stegoceras. e, Saurolophus (h). f, Ornithomumus. g, Compsognathus (j). h, Deinonychus (i). i, Ornitholestes. j, Archaeopteryx. k, Heterodontosaurus (l). l, Lesothosaurus.
No. 1792: a, 100 le, Triceratops. b, 250 le, Protoceratops (c). c, 400 le, Monoclonius (b). d, 800 le, Styracosaurus (c).
No. 1793, Deinonychus. No. 1794, Rhamphorynchus.

1995, May 4 Litho. *Perf. 14*
1791 A234 200 le Sheet of 12, #a.-l. 8.00 8.00
1792 A234 Sheet of 4, #a.-d. 5.25 5.25

Souvenir Sheets
1793-1794 A234 2500 le each 8.25 8.25

Miniature Sheets of 9

Sierra Club, Cent. A235

No. 1795, vert: a, L'Hoest's guenon. b, Black-footed cat. c, Colobus monkey up close. d, Colobus monkey in tree. e, Mandrill facing forward. f, Bonobo with young. g, Bonobo lying down. h, Mandrill facing right. i, Colobus monkey standing.
No. 1796: a, Black-faced impala facing forward. b, Herd of black-faced impala. c, Black-faced impala drinking. d, Bonobo. e, Black-footed cat. f, Black-footed cat up close. g, L'Hoest's guenon. h, L'Hoest's guenon, seated. i, Mandrills.

1995, May 10
1795-1796 A235 150 le #a.-i., ea 4.50 4.50

New Year 1995 (Year of the Boar) A236

Stylized boars: No. 1797a, red & multi, facing left. b, green & multi, facing right. c, green & multi, facing left. d, red & multi, facing right.
500 le, Two boars, vert.

1995, May 8 Litho. *Perf. 14*
1797 A236 100 le Block of 4, #a.-d. 1.25 1.25

Souvenir Sheet
1798 A236 500 le multicolored 1.60 1.60

Miniature Sheets of 9

Singapore '95 — A237

Marine life: No. 1799a, Pufferfish. b, Coral grouper. c, Hawksbill turtle. d, Hogfish. e, Emperor angelfish. f, Butterflyfish. g, Lemon butterflyfish. h, Parrotfish. i, Moray eel.
Water birds, marine life: No. 1800a, Cape pigeons. b, Pelican. c, Puffin. d, Humpback whale. e, Greater shearwater. f, Bottlenose dolphin. g, Gurnard. h, Salmon. i, John dory.
#1801, Surgeonfish. #1802, Angelfish, vert.

1995
1799-1800 A237 300 le #a.-i., each 9.00 9.00

Souvenir Sheet
1801-1802 A237 1500 le each 5.00 5.00

Miniature Sheets of 6 or 8

A238

End of World War II, 50th Anniv. A239

No. 1803: a, USS Idaho. b, HMS Ark Royal. c, Admiral Graf Spee. d, Destroyer. e, HMS Nelson. f, PT 109. g, USS Iowa. h, Bismark.
No. 1804: a, B-17. b, B-25. c, B-24 Liberator. d, USS Missouri. e, A-20 Boston. f, Pennsylvania, Colorado, Louisville, Portland, Columbia enter Lingayen Gulf.
No. 1805, HMS Indomitable launching aircraft. No. 1806, B-29 bomber.

1995, July 10
1803 A238 250 le #a.-h. + label 6.75 6.75
1804 A239 300 le #a.-f. + label 6.00 6.00

Souvenir Sheet
1805 A238 1500 le multicolored 5.00 5.00
1806 A239 1500 le multicolored 5.00 5.00

No. 1805 contains one 57x42mm stamp.

UN, 50th Anniv. — A240

No. 1807: a, 300 le, Dais, UN General Assembly. 400 le, Sec. Gen. U. Thant. 500 le, UN building, dove.
1500 le, Sec. Gen. Dag Hammarskjold.

1995, July 10 Litho. *Perf. 14*
1807 A240 Strip of 3, #a.-c. 4.00 4.00

Souvenir Sheet
1808 A240 1500 le multicolored 5.00 5.00

No. 1807 is a continuous design.

1995 Boy Scout Jamboree, Holland A241

No. 1809: a, 400 le, Natl. flag. b, 500 le, Lord Baden-Powell. c, 600 le, Scout sign.
1500 le, Scout salute.

1995, July 10
1809 A241 Strip of 3, #a.-c. 5.00 5.00

Souvenir Sheet
1810 A241 1500 le multicolored 5.00 5.00

Queen Mother, 95th Birthday A242

No. 1811: a, Drawing. b, Holding bouquet of flowers. c, Formal portrait. d, Without hat.
1500 le, Blue hat, dress.

1995, July 10 ***Perf. 13½x14***
1811 A242 400 le Block or strip of 4, #a.-d. 5.25 5.25

Souvenir Sheet
1812 A242 1500 le multicolored 5.00 5.00

No. 1811 was issued in sheets of 8 stamps.

FAO, 50th Anniv. A243

No. 1813: a, 300 le, Man working with sack of food. b, 400 le, Boy carrying bundle of sticks on head. c, 500 le, Woman holding bowl of fruit.
1500 le, Woman holding baby, vert.

1995, July 10 ***Perf. 14***
1813 A243 Strip of 3, #a.-c. 4.00 4.00

Souvenir Sheet
1814 A243 1500 le multicolored 5.00 5.00

Rotary Intl., 90th Anniv. A244

Designs: 500 le, Natl. flag, Rotary emblem. 1000 le, Paul Harris, Rotary emblem.

1995, July 10
1815 A244 500 le multicolored 1.75 1.75

Souvenir Sheet
1816 A244 1000 le multicolored 3.50 3.50

Miniature Sheets of 8

Singapore '95 — A245

Flora & fauna: No. 1817a, African tulip tree. b, Senegal bush locust. c, Killifish. d, Bird of paradise. e, Mandrill. f, Painted reed frog. g, Large spotted acraea. h, Carmine bee-eater.
No. 1818: a, Flame lily. b, Grants gazelle. c, Dogbane. d, Gold-banded forester. e, Horned chameleon. f, Malachite kingfisher. g, Leaf beetle. h, Acanthus.
No. 1819, Lion. No. 1820, African elephant.

1995, Sept. 5 **Litho.** ***Perf. 14***
1817-1818 A245 300 le #a.-h., each 8.00 8.00

Souvenir Sheets
1819-1820 A245 1500 le each 5.00 5.00

Third UN Decade for Advancement of Women — A246

Designs: 300 le, Development. 500 le, Peace. 700 le, Equality.

1995 **Litho.** ***Perf. 14***
1821-1823 A246 Set of 3 5.00 5.00

Sierra Leone Grammar School, 150th Anniv. A247

1995, Sept. 27 **Litho.** ***Perf. 14***
1824 A247 300 le multicolored 1.00 1.00

Christmas A248

Details or entire paintings: 50 le, Holy Family, by Beccafumi. 100 le, Rest on Flight into Egypt, by Barocci. 150 le, La Vierge, by Bellini. 200 le, The Flight, by d'Arpino. 600 le, Adoration of the Magi, by Francken. 800 le, The Annunciation, by da Conegliano.
No. 1831, Virgin and child, by Cranach. No. 1832, Madonna and Child, by Berlinghiero.

1995, Dec. 1 **Litho.** ***Perf. 13½x14***
1825-1830 A248 Set of 6 6.50 6.50

Souvenir Sheets
1831-1832 A248 1500 le each 5.00 5.00

Disney Christmas A249

Antique Disney toys: 5 le, Mickey Mouse doll. 10 le, Donald rag drum major. 15 le, Donald wind up. 20 le, Toothbrush holder. 25 le, Mickey telephone. 30 le, Walking wind-up. 800 le, Movie projector. 1000 le, Goofy tricycle.
No. 1841, Black Mickey Mouse. No. 1842, First Mickey book.

1995, Dec. 4 ***Perf. 13½x14***
1833-1840 A249 Set of 8 6.50 6.50

Souvenir Sheets
1841-1842 A249 1500 le each 5.00 5.00

Miniature Sheets of 9

Nobel Prize Fund Established, Cent. — A250

Recipients: No. 1843a, Andrew Huxley, medicine, 1963. b, Nelson Mandela, peace, 1993. c, Gabriela Mistral, literature, 1945. d, Otto Diels, chemistry, 1950. e, Hannes Alfven, physics, 1970. f, Wole Soyinka, literature, 1986. g, Hans G. Dehmelt, physics, 1989. h, Desmond Tutu, peace, 1984. i, Leo Esaki, physics, 1973.
No. 1844: a, Maria Goeppert Mayer, physics, 1963. b, Irène Joliot-Curie, chemistry, 1935. c, Mother Teresa, peace, 1979. d, Selma Lagerlöf, literature, 1909. e, Rosalyn Yalow, medicine, 1977. f, Dorothy Hodgkin, chemistry, 1964. g, Rita Levi-Montalcini, medicine, 1986. h, Mairead Corrigan, peace, 1976. i, Betty Williams, peace, 1976.
No. 1845: a, Tobias Asser, peace, 1911. b, Andrei Sakharov, peace, 1975. c, Frederic Passy, peace, 1901. d, Dag Hammarskjöld, peace, 1961. e, Aung San Suu Kyi, peace, 1991. f, Ludwig Quidde, peace, 1927. g, Elie Wiesel, peace, 1986. h, Bertha von Suttner, peace, 1905. i, Dalai Lama, peace, 1989.
No. 1846: a, Richard Zsigmondy, chemistry, 1925. b, Robert Huber, chemistry, 1988. c, Wilhelm Ostwald, chemistry, 1909. d, Johann Deisenhofer, chemistry, 1988. e, Heinrich Wieland, chemistry, 1927. f, Gerhard Herzberg, chemistry, 1971. g, Hans von Euler-Chelpin, chemistry, 1929. h, Richard Willstätter, chemistry, 1915. i, Fritz Haber, chemistry, 1918.
No. 1847, Albert Einstein, physics, 1921. No. 1848, Wilhelm Röentgen, physics, 1901. No. 1849, Sin-Itiro Tomonaga, physics, 1965.

1995, Dec. 29 **Litho.** ***Perf. 14***
1843-1846 A250 250 le #a.-i., each 7.50 7.50

Souvenir Sheets
1847-1849 A250 1500 le each 5.00 5.00

Miniature Sheets of 12

Railways of the World A251

No. 1850: a, Denver and Rio Grande Western. b, Central of Georgia. c, Seaboard Air Line. d, Missouri Pacific Lines. e, Atchison, Topeka and Santa Fe. f, Chicago, Milwaukee, St. Paul and Pacific. g, Texas and Pacific. h, Minneapolis, St. Paul & Sault Saint Marie. (Soo Line). i, Western Pacific. j, Great Northern. k, Baltimore & Ohio. l, Chicago, Rock Island and Pacific.
No. 1851: a, Southern Pacific 4-8-4 "Daylight" express, US. b, Belgian National 4-4-2 express. c, Indian Railways 4-6-2 "WP" express. d, South Australian 4-8-4 express. e, Union Pacific 4-8-8-4 "Big Boy," US. f, UK 4-6-2 "Royal Scot" streamlined. g, German Federal, class 052 2-10-0. h, Japanese National, 4-6-4 express. i, Pennsylvania, 4-4-4-4 streamlined, US. j, East African 4-8-2+2-8-4 Beyer-Garratt. k, Milwaukee Road 4-6-4 "Hiawatha" express, US. l, Paris-Orleans, 4-6-2 Pacific, France.
No. 1852: a, "Eurostar" express. b, ETR 401 Pendolino four-car tilting train, Italy. c, HST 125 inter-city high speed train, UK. d, "Virgin" B-B class high speed diesel-hydraulic express, Spain. e, French Natl. Railways TGV. f, Amtrak "Southwest Chief," US. g, TGV "Atlantique," France. h, "Peloponnese Express," Greece. i, "Shin-Kansen" high-speed electric train, Japan. j, Canadian Natl. turbo train. k, XPT high-speed diesel-electric train, Australia. l, SS1 Co-Co electric locomotive, China.
No. 1853: a, Canadian Natl. U1-F. b, Central Pacific No. 119 at Promontory, US. c, LNER "A4" class streamlined 4-6-2, UK. d, New York Central J32 "Empire State Express," US. e, Canadian Natl. 4-8-4. f, Class 38 Pacific 4-6-2 express, Australia. g, Canadian Pacific 4-6-2 express. h, Southern "West Country" class 4-6-2, UK.i, Norfolk & Western Class J 4-8-4, US. j, RM Class 4-6-0 Pacific, China. k, P-36 class 4-8-4 express, USSR. l, Great Western "King" class 4-6-0, UK.
No. 1853M, British Railways Jubilee class 4-6-0, No. 45627 named "Sierra Leone." No. 1853N, Denver & Rio Grande Western "California Zephyr," US. No. 1853O, 1st train to cross newly opened bridge over Yangtze River, 1968, China. No. 1853P, Beijing-Shanghai Express, China. No. 1853Q, China Railways, "QJ" class 2-10-2.

1995, May 23 **Litho.** ***Perf. 14***
1850-1851 A251 200 le #a.-l., each 8.00 8.00
1852 A251 250 le #a.-l. 10.00 10.00
1853 A251 300 le #a.-l. 12.00 12.00

Souvenir Sheets
1853M-1853Q A251 1500 le each 5.00 5.00

Nos. 1853M-1853Q each contain one 56x43mm stamp. No. 1850 exists with two different top margin inscriptions, "THE COLOURFUL RAILROADS OF NORTH AMERICA" and "THE COLOURFUL RAILROADS OF THE WORLD."

New Year 1996 (Year of the Rat) A252

Different stylized rats: No. 1854a, Facing left, purple & multi. b, Facing right, blue green & multi. c, Facing left, blue green & multi. d, Facing right, blue & multi.
No. 1856, Rat, vert.

1996, Jan. 6
1854 A252 200 le Block of 4, #a.-d. 2.00 2.00

Miniature Sheet of 4
1855 A252 200 le #1854a-1854d 2.00 2.00

Souvenir Sheet
1856 A252 500 le multicolored 1.25 1.25

No. 1854 was issued in sheets of 16 stamps.

Disney Characters as Circus Performers A253

Designs: 100 le, Mickey, the magician. 200 le, Clarabelle Cow, the tightrope walker. 250 le, The clowns, Donald and Huey, Dewey and Louie. 300 le, Donald, the lion tamer. 800 le, Minnie, the bareback rider. 1000 le, Goofy and Minnie, the trapeze artists.
#1863, Mickey, horiz. #1864, Pluto, horiz.

1996, Jan. 29 **Litho.** ***Perf. 14x13½***
1857-1862 A253 Set of 6 6.50 6.50

Souvenir Sheets
Perf. 13½x14½
1863-1864 A253 1500 le each 3.75 3.75

Miniature Sheets of 9

Motion Pictures, Cent. A254

No. 1865: a, Film projector. b, Pete. c, Silver. d, Rin-Tin-Tin. e, King Kong. f, Flipper. g, Jaws. h, Elsa. i, Moby Dick.
Directors or stars, scene from movie: No. 1866: a, Lumière Brothers. b, George Méliès. c, Toshiro Mifune d, Clark Gable, Vivian Leigh, David O. Selznick. e, Fritz Lang, Metropolis. f, Akira Kurosawa, Ran. g, Charlie Chaplin. h, Marlène Dietrich. i, Steven Spielberg, ET.
#1867, Lassie. #1868, Cecil B. de Mille.

1996, Feb. 26 **Litho.** ***Perf. 14***
1865-1866 A254 250 le #a.-i., each 7.50 7.50

Souvenir Sheets
1867-1868 A254 1500 le each 3.75 3.75

Sheets of 8 + label

Paintings from Metropolitan Museum of Art — A255

Entire paintings or details: No. 1869: a, Honfleur, by Jongkind. b, A Boat on the Shore, by Courbet. c, Barges at Pontoise, by Pissarro. d, The Dead Christ with Angels, by Manet. e, Salisbury Cathedral, by Constable. f, A Lady with a Setter Dog, by Eakins. g, Tahitian Women Bathing, by Gaugin. h, Majas on a Balcony, by Goya.

By Renoir: No. 1870: a, In the Meadow. b, By the Seashore. c, Still Life with Peaches and Grapes. d, Marguerite (Margot) Bérard. e, Young Girl in Pink and Black Hat. f, A Waitrress at Duval's Restaurant. g, A Road in Louveciennes. h, Two Young Girls at the Piano.

No. 1871: a, Morning, an Overcast Day, Rouen, by Pissarro. b, The Horse Fair, by Bonheur. c, High Tide: the Bathers, by Homer. d, The Dance Class, by Degas. e, The Brioche, by Manet. f, The Grand Canal, Venice, by Turner. g, St. Tecia Interceding for Plague-stricken Este, by G. B. Tiepolo. h, Bridge at Villeneuve, by Sisley.

No. 1872: a, Madame Charpentier, by Renoir. b, Head of Christ, by Rembrandt. c, The Standard-Bearer, by Rembrandt. d, Girl Asleep, by Vermeer. e, Lady with a Lute, by Vermeer. f, Portrait of a Woman, by Rembrandt. g, La Grenouillère, by Monet. h, Woman with Chrysanthemums, by Degas.

No. 1873, The Death of Socrates, by J.L. David. No. 1874, Battle of Constantine and Licinius, by Rubens. No. 1875, Samson and Delilah, by Rubens. No. 1876, The Emblem of Christ Appearing to Constantine, by Rubens.

1996 Litho. *Perf. 13½x14*

1869-1872 A255 200 le #a.-h., each 4.00 4.00

Souvenir Sheets

Perf. 14

1873-1876 A255 1500 le each 3.75 3.75

Nos. 1873-1876 each contain one 85x57mm.

Nos. 1874-1876 are not in the Metropolitan.

1996 Summer Olympic Games, Atlanta A256

100 le, 1932 Olympic Stadium, Los Angeles. 150 le, Archery. 500 le, Rings (gymnastics). 600 le, Pole vault.

No. 1881: a, Field hockey. b, Swimming. c, Equestrian. d, Boxing. e, Pommel horse. f, 100-meter dash.

1996, June 11 Litho. *Perf. 14*

1877-1880 A256 Set of 4 3.40 3.40

1881 A256 300 le Sheet of 6, #a.-f. 4.50 4.50

Souvenir Sheet

1882 A256 1500 le Runner 3.75 3.75

Queen Elizabeth II, 70th Birthday A257

Designs: a, Portrait. b, Receiving flowers. c, Holding flowers, wearing black hat, coat.

1500 le, Waving from balcony.

1996, July 15 Litho. *Perf. 13½x14*

1886 A257 600 le Strip of 3, #a.-c. 4.50 4.50

Souvenir Sheet

1887 A257 1500 le multicolored 3.75 3.75

No. 1886 was issued in sheets of 9 stamps.

UNICEF, 50th Anniv. A258

Designs: 300 le, Children reading. 400 le, Young man, woman reading. 500 le, Children in class.

1500 le, Children's faces.

1996, July 15 *Perf. 14*

1888-1890 A258 Set of 3 3.00 3.00

Souvenir Sheet

1891 A258 1500 le multicolored 3.75 3.75

Sheets of 12

Cats — A259

No. 1892: a, Abyssinian. b, British tabby. c, Norwegian forest. d, Maine coon. e, Bengal. f, Asian. g, American curl. h, Devon rex. i, Tonkinese. j, Egyptian mau. k, Burmese. l, Siamese.

No. 1893: a, British shorthair. b, Tiffany. c, Birman. d, Somali. e, Malayan. f, Japanese bobtail. g, Himalayan. h, Tortoiseshell. i, Oriental. j, Ocicat. k, Chartreux. l, Ragdoll.

No. 1894, Persian. No. 1895, Burmilla.

1996, June 17

1892-1893 A259 200 le #a.-l., each 6.00 6.00

Souvenir Sheets

1894-1895 A259 2000 le each 5.00 5.00

Mushrooms — A260

50 le, Cinnabar-red chanterelle. 300 le, Larch suillus. 400 le, Yellow more. 500 le, Variable cort.

No. 1900: a, African driver ant, Indigo milky, Marshall's false monarch (e). b, Scally inky cap. c, Pyxie cup (b). d, Barometer earthstar (c), rainbow grasshopper (h). e, Felt-ringed agaricus, long-horned longhorn. f, Spotted mycena. g, Orange latex milky. h, Tawny grissett amanita fulva, lamellicorn larva.

No. 1901: a, Millar tiger, little nest polymore. b, Coral slime. c, Red-gilled cort. d, Parasitic volvamella, veined tiger. e, Onion-stalked lepiota. f, Blusher. g. Orange mock oyster. h, Lizard claw, red and yellow barbet.

No. 1903, Netted rhodotus. No. 1904, Parasitic psathyrella.

1996, June 17

1896-1899 A260 Set of 4 3.25 3.25

Sheets of 8, #a.-h.

1900-1901 A260 250 le each 4.00 4.00

Souvenir Sheets

1902-1903 A260 1500 le each 3.75 3.75

Space Exploration — A261

Designs: a, Pioneer-Venus orbiter, 1986-92. b, Hubble space telescope. c, Voyager probe. d, Space Shuttle Challenger in orbit. e, Pioneer II. f, Mars-Viking 1 lander.

1500 le, Shuttle Challenger landing.

1996

1904 A261 300 le Sheet of 6, #a.-f. 4.50 4.50

Souvenir Sheet

1905 A261 1500 le multicolored 3.75 3.75

Butterflies A262

Designs: 150 le, Charaxes pleione. 200 le, Eurema brigitta. 300 le, Charaxes ameliae. 500 le, Kallimoides rumia.

No. 1910: a, Precis orithya. b, Palla ussheri. c, Junonia orithya. d, Cymothoe sangaris. e, Cyrestis camillus. f, Precis rhadama. g, Precis cebrene. h, Hypolimnas misippus. i, Colotis danae.

No. 1911, Charaxes bohemani. No. 1912, Papilio antimachus.

1996, Aug. 15 Litho. *Perf. 14*

1906-1909 A262 Set of 4 3.00 3.00

1910 A262 250 le Sheet of 9, #a.-i. 5.50 5.50

Souvenir Sheets

1911-1912 A262 1500 le each 3.75 3.75

Flowers — A263

Designs: 150 le, Tulipa. 200 le, Helichrysum bracteatum. 400 le, Viola. 500 le, Phalaenopsis.

No. 1917: a, Fountain. b, Begonia multiflora. c, Narcissus. d, Crocus speciosus. e, Chrysanthemum frutescens. Petunia. f, Cosmos pipinnatus. g, Anemone coronaria. h, Convolvulus minor.

No. 1918: a, Paphiopedilum. b, Cymbidium "Peach bloom." c, Sailboat. d, Miltonia. e, Parides gundalachianus. f, Laeliocatt leya. g, Lycaste aromatica. h, Brassolaeliocatt leya. i, Cymbidium "Southern Lace," Catastica teutila.

No. 1919, Helianthus annuus. No. 1920, Cymbidium "Lucifer."

1996, Aug. 19

1913-1916 A263 Set of 4 3.25 3.25

1917 A263 200 le Sheet of 9, #a.-i. 4.50 4.50

1918 A263 300 le Sheet of 9, #a.-i. 6.75 6.75

Souvenir Sheets

1919-1920 A263 1500 le each 3.75 3.75

Chinese Lunar Calendar A264

Year of the: a, Rat. b, Ox. c, Tiger. d, Hare. e, Dragon. f, Snake. g, Horse. h, Sheep. i, Monkey. j, Rooster. k, Dog. l, Pig.

1996, July 15 Litho. *Perf. 13½x14*

1921 A264 150 le Sheet of 12, #a.-l. 4.50 4.50

Ships A265

No. 1922: a, Clipper ship, "Cutty Sark," 19th cent. b, SS Great Britain, 1846. c, "Dreadnaught," 1906. d, RMS Queen Elizabeth, 1940-72. e, Ocean-going racing yacht, 1962. f, SS United States, 1952. g, Nuclear powered submarine, 1950's. h, Super tanker, 1960's. i, USS Enterprise, 1980s.

No. 1923: a, Greek war galley, 4th cent. BC. b, Roman war galley, 50AD. c, Viking ship, 9th cent. d, Flemish carrack, 15th cent. e, Merchant man, 16th cent. f, Tudor warship, 16th cent. g, Elizabethan galleon, 17th cent. h, Dutch Man of War, 17th cent. i, "Maestrale," Maltese galley, 18th cent.

No. 1924, Cruise ship "Legend of the Seas," 1996 Panama Canal. No. 1925, Egyptian ocean-going ship, 1480BC.

1996, Oct. 29 Litho. *Perf. 14*

Sheets of 9

1922-1923 A265 300 le #a.-i., each 6.75 6.75

Souvenir Sheets

1924-1925 A265 1500 le each 3.75 3.75

Nos. 1924-1925 each contain one 56x43mm stamp.

Christmas A266

Details or entire paintings, by Filippo Lippi: 200 le, Madonna of Humility. 250 le, Coronation of the Virgin. 400 le, 500 le, Annunciation. 600 le, Barbadori Altarpiece. 800 le, Coronation of the Virgin, diff.

Paintings by Rubens: No. 1932, Adoration of the Magi. No. 1933, Holy Family with St. Anne.

1996, Dec. 12 Litho. *Perf. 13½x14*

1926-1931 A266 Set of 6 6.75 6.75

Souvenir Sheets

1932-1933 A266 2000 le each 5.00 5.00

Souvenir Sheets

Fantasies of the Sea — A267

#1934, Sea Dragon's Daughter. #1935, Homo Aquaticus. #1936, Chinese Sea Fairy. #1937, Sea Totem. #1938, The Turtle, horiz. #1939, Mermaid, horiz. #1940, How the Whale Got its Throat, horiz. #1941, Killer Whale Crest. #1942, Aphrodite. #1943, Ship Figurehead. #1944, Lilith. #1945, Queen of the Orkney Islands. #1946, Haida Eagle. #1947, Captain Ahab. #1948, Waskos. #1949, Jonah. #1950, Odysseus. #1951, The Little Mermaid. #1952, Squamish Indians. #1953, Boy on a Dolphin. $1954, Airship to Atlantis. #1955, Sea Bishop. #1956, 20,000 Leagues Under the Sea. #1957, Whale Song. #1958, Arion. #1959, Dragonrider of Pern. #1960, Kelpie. #1961, Natsihlane. #1962, Merman. #1963, Albatross. #1964, City under polar ice melt. #1965, Tom Swift. #1966, The Flying Dutchman, horiz. #1967, Sea Centaur. #1968, Lang (dragon), horiz. #1969, Triton. #1970, Sea Serpent. #1971, Arthropod sea monster.

#1972, The Ancient Mariner. #1973, Poseidon.

1996, Dec. 19 Litho. *Perf. 14*

1934-1973 A267 1500 le each 3.75 3.75

New Year 1997 (Year of the Ox) A268

Various stylized oxen, background color: Nos. 1975-1976: a, purple. b, green. c, blue. d, claret.

800 le, like #1975d, vert.

1997, Jan. 8 Litho. *Perf. 14*

1975 A268 150 le Block of 4, #a.-d. 1.50 1.50
1976 A268 250 le Sheet of 4, #a.-d. 2.50 2.50

Souvenir Sheet

1977 A268 800 le multicolored 2.00 2.00

No. 1975 was issued in sheets of 16 stamps.

Disney's Aladdin in Christmas Scenes A269

Designs: 10 le, Aladdin, Jasmine. 15 le, Santa, Genie. 20 le, Aladdin, Jasmine on magic carpet. 25 le, Genie as Christmas tree. 30 le, Aladdin, Genie "Santa." 100 le, Jasmine, Aladdin, Genie. 800 le, Genie's letter to Santa. 1000 le, Genie's Christmas carol.

No. 1986, Aladdin, Abu. No. 1987, Jasmine, Aladdin, horiz.

1997, Jan. 27 *Perf. 14x13½*

1978-1985 A269 Set of 8 5.00 5.00

Souvenir Sheets

Perf. 14x13½, 13½x14

1986-1987 A269 2000 le each 5.00 5.00

Hong Kong — A270

Panoramic view of Hong Kong: No. 1988, in daytime. No. 1989, at night.

1997, Feb. 12 Litho. *Perf. 14*

Sheets of 4

1988-1989 A270 500 le #a.-d., each 5.25 5.25

UNESCO, 50th Anniv. A271

World Heritage Sites: 60 le, Town of Kizhi Pogost, Russia. 200 le, Durmitor Natl. Park, Yugoslavia. 250 le, City of Nessebar, Bulgaria. 400 le, City of Bukhara, Uzbekistan. 500 le, Monastery of Kiev-Pechersk, Ukraine. 700 le, Mountain Walks, Vlkolinec, Slovakia.

No. 1996: a, Town of Roros, Norway. b, City of Warsaw, Poland. c, Cathedral of Notre Dame, Luxembourg. d, City of Vilnius, Lithuania. e, Jelling, Denmark. f, Old Church of Petäjävesi, Finland. g, Sweden. h, Cathedral City of Bern, Switzerland.

No. 1997: a, Area surrounding Mt. Kilimanjaro, Tanzania. b, Monument, Fasil Ghebbi, Ethiopia. c, Natl. Park, Mt. Ruwenzori, Uganda. d, Abu Simbel, Egypt. e, Tsingy Bemaraha Strict Nature Reserve, Madagascar. f, House, Djenne, Mali. g, Traditional house construction, Ghana. h, Large house, Aromey.

Various views of Himeji-Jo, Japan, vert: No. 1998: a, b, c, d, e.

No. 1999, Natl. Bird Sanctuary, Djudj, Senegal, horiz. No. 2000, Acropolis, Athens, Greece, horiz.

1997, Mar. 24 Litho. *Perf. 13½x14*

1990-1995 A271 Set of 6 5.50 5.50

Sheets of 8 + Label

1996-1997 A271 300 le #a.-h., each 6.00 6.00

Sheet of 5 + Label

1998 A271 500 le #a.-e. 6.25 6.25

Souvenir Sheets

1999-2000 A271 2000 le each 5.00 5.00

Paintings by Hiroshige (1797-1858) A272

No. 2001: a, Hatsune Riding Grounds, Bakuro-cho. b, Mannen Bridge, Fukagawa. c, Ryogoku Bridge and the Great Riverbank. d, Asakusa River, Great Riverbank, Miyato River. e, Silk-goods Lane, Odenma-cho. f, Mokuboji Temple, Uchigawa Inlet, Gozensaihata.

No. 2002, Tsukudajima from Eitai Bridge. No. 2003, Nihonbashi Bridge and Edobashi Bridge.

1997 Litho. *Perf. 13½x14*

2001 A272 400 le Sheet of 6, #a.-f. 6.50 6.50

Souvenir Sheets

2002-2003 A272 1500 le each 3.75 3.75

Chernobyl Disaster, 10th Anniv. A273

Designs: 1000 le, UNESCO. 1500 le, Chabad's Children of Chernobyl.

1997, June 23

2004 A273 1000 le multicolored 2.75 2.75
2005 A273 1500 le multicolored 4.00 4.00

Queen Elizabeth II and Prince Philip, 50th Wedding Anniv. A274

No. 2006: a, Queen. b, Royal arms. c, Black & white photograph, Prince in dress uniform. d, Black & white photograph, Prince in tuxedo, bow tie. e, Palace of Holyroodhouse. f, Prince in hat guiding horses.

1500 le, Queen, Prince in colored photograph.

1997, June 23 *Perf. 14*

2006 A274 400 le Sheet of 6, #a.-f. 6.50 6.50

Souvenir Sheet

2007 A274 1500 le multicolored 4.00 4.00

Return of Hong Kong to China — A275

Designs: 400 le, Flag of China, map of China, Hong Kong, Victoria at night. 500 le, 650 le, Flag of China, July 1, 1997, city scene inside letters spelling "Hong Kong." 550 le, 600 le, Flag of China, Victoria harbor inside letters spelling "Hong Kong '97." 800 le, Victoria harbor, Deng Xiaoping (1904-97).

Illustration reduced.

1997, June 23

2008-2013 A275 Set of 6 9.50 9.50

Nos. 2008-2013 were each issued in sheets of 3.

Souvenir Sheets

Mother Goose — A276

Designs: No. 2014, Three Blind Mice. No. 2015, Woman holding out full skirt as "Myself."

1997, June 23 Litho. *Perf. 14*

2014-2015 A276 1500 le each 4.00 4.00

1998 Winter Olympic Games, Nagano A277

Designs: 250 le, Stadium, Calgary, 1988, American Indian. 300 le, Freestyle aerial skiing, vert. 500 le, Ice hockey, vert. 800 le, Dan Jansen, 1000-meter speed skater, vert.

No. 2022, vert: a, Peggy Fleming, figure skating. b, Japanese ski jumper, Nordic combined. c, 2-man luge, Germany. d, Frank-Peter Roetsch, biathlon, E. Germany.

No. 2023, Jamaican bobsled team, vert. No. 2024, Johann Olav Koss, Norway, vert.

1997, July 16 Litho. *Perf. 14*

2018-2021 A277 Set of 4 5.00 5.00
2022 A276 300 le Strip of 4, #a.-d. 3.25 3.25

Souvenir Sheets

2023-2024 A277 1500 le each 4.00 4.00

No. 2022 was issued in sheets of 8 stamps.

1998 World Cup Soccer Championships, France — A278

Players: 100 le, Stabile, Uruguay. 150 le, Schiavio, Italy. 200 le, Kocsis, Hungary. 250 le, Nejedly, Czechoslovakia. 500 le, Leonidas, Brazil. 600 le, Ademir, Brazil.

No. 2031: a, Dwight Yorke, Trinidad & Tobago. b, Dennis Bergkamp, Holland. c, Steve McManaman, England. d, Ryan Giggs, Wales. e, Romario, Brazil, f, Faustino Asprilla, Colombia. g, Roy Keane, Ireland. h, Peter Schmeichel, Denmark.

No. 2032, Pele, Brazil, horiz. No. 2033, Lato, Poland, horiz.

1997, July 23 *Perf. 13½x14, 14x13½*

2025-2030 A278 Set of 6 4.75 4.75

Sheet of 8

2031 A278 300 le #a.-h. + 2 labels 6.50 6.50

Souvenir Sheets

2032-2033 A278 1500 le each 4.00 4.00

Classic Horror Movies — A279

Lead character, movie: No. 2034: a, Lon Chaney, "Phantom of the Opera," 1934. b, Boris Karloff, "The Mummy," 1932. c, Fredric March, "Dr. Jekyll & Mr. Hyde, " 1932. d, Lon Chaney, Jr., "The Wolf Man," 1941. e, Charles Laughton, "Island of Lost Souls," 1933. f, Lionel Atwill, "Mystery of the Wax Museum, " 1933. g, Bela Lugosi, "Dracula," 1931. h, Vincent Price, "The Haunted Palace," 1963. i, Elsa Lanchester, "Bride of Frankenstein," 1935.

3000 le, Bela Lugosi, Boris Karloff, "Son of Frankenstein," 1939.

1997, Aug. 15 *Perf. 14*

2034 A279 300 le Sheet of 9, #a.-i. 7.25 7.25

Souvenir Sheet

2035 A279 3000 le multicolored 8.00 8.00

Domestic Cats — A280

Designs: 150 le, American short hair tabby. 200 le, British short hair. 500 le, Turkish angora.

No. 2039: a, Chartreux. b, Abyssinian. c, Burmese. d, White angora. e, Japanese bobtail. f, Cymric.

1500 le, Egyptian mau.

1997, Aug. 29

2036-2038 A280 Set of 3 2.25 2.25
2039 A280 400 le Sheet of 6, #a.-f. 6.50 6.50

Souvenir Sheet

2040 A280 1500 le multicolored 4.00 4.00

No. 2040 contains one 64x32mm stamp.

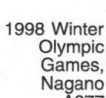

Butterflies
A281

Orchids
A282

Designs: 150 le, Vindula erota. 200 le, Pereutel leucodrosime. 250 le, Dynstor napolean. 300 le, Thauria aliris. 600 le, Papilio aegeus. 800 le, Amblypodia anita. 1500 le, Kallimoides rumia. 2000 le, Papilio dardanas.

No. 2049: a, Lycaena dispar. b, Graphium sarpedon. c, Euploe core. d, Papilio cresphontes. e, Colotis danae. f, Battus philenor.

No. 2050: a, Mylothris chloris. b, Argynnis lathonia. c, Elymnias agondas. d, Palla ussheri. e, Papilio glaucus. f, Cercyonis pegala.

No. 2051, Hebomoia glaucippe, horiz. No. 2052, Colias eurytheme, horiz.

1997, Aug. 1 Litho. *Perf. 14*

2041-2048 A281 Set of 8 15.00 15.00

Sheets of 6

2049 A281 500 le #a.-f. 8.00 8.00
2050 A281 600 le #a.-f. 9.75 9.75

Souvenir Sheets

2051-2052 A281 3000 le each 8.00 8.00

1997, Sept. 1

Designs: 150 le, Ansellia africana. 200 le, Maxillaria praestans. 250 le, Cymbidium mimi. 300 le, Dendrobium bigibbum. 500 le, Encyclia vitellina. 800 le, Epidendrum prismatocarpum.

No. 2059: a, Laelia anceps. b, Paphiopedilum fairrieanum. c, Restrepia lansbergii. d, Yamadara cattleya. e, Cleistes divaricata. f, Calypso bulbosa.

No. 2060, Odontoglossum schlieperianum. No. 2061, Paphiopedilum tonsum.

2053-2058 A282 Set of 6 6.00 6.00
2059 A282 400 le Sheet of 6, #a.-f. 3.25 3.25

Souvenir Sheets

2060-2061 A282 1500 le each 4.00 4.00

Motion Pictures Directed by Alfred Hitchcock
A283

No. 2062: a, Ray Milland in "Dial M for Murder." b, James Stewart, Kim Novak in "Vertigo." c, Cary Grant, Ingrid Bergman in "Notorious." d, John Dall, James Stewart in "Rope." e, Cary Grant in "North by Northwest." f, Grace Kelly, James Stewart in "Rear Window." g, Joan Fontaine, Laurence Olivier in "Rebecca." h, Tippi Hedren in "The Birds." i, Janet Leigh in "Psycho."

1500 le, Alfred Hitchcock.

1997, Aug. 15 Litho. *Perf. 14*

2062 A283 350 le Sheet of 9, #a.-i. 8.50 8.50

Souvenir Sheet

2063 A283 1500 le multicolored 4.00 4.00

Dogs — A284

Designs: 100 le, Shetland sheep dog. 250 le, Alaskan husky. 600 le, Jack Russell terrier.

No. 2067: a, Basset hound. b, Irish setter. c, St. Bernard. d, German shepherd. e, Dalmatian. f, Cocker spaniel.

1500 le, Boxer.

1997, Aug. 29

2064-2066 A284 Set of 3 2.50 2.50
2067 A284 400 le Sheet of 6, #a.-f. 6.50 6.50

Souvenir Sheet

2068 A284 1500 le multicolored 4.00 4.00

No. 2068 contains one 31x63mm stamp.

Disney Christmas Stamps
A285

Designs: 150 le, Huey, Dewey, & Louie. 200 le, Mickey's kids. 250 le, Daisy Duck. 300 le, Minnie. 400 le, Mickey. 500 le, Donald Duck. 600 le, Pluto. 800 le, Goofy.

No. 2077: a, like #2071. b, like #2069. c, like #2074. d, like #2072. e, like #2070. f, like #2073.

No. 2078, Mickey in sleigh. No. 2079, Mickey, Donald, Daisy in Santa suits, horiz.

1997, Oct. 1 *Perf. 13½x14, 14x13½*

2069-2076 A285 Set of 8 8.50 8.50
2077 A285 50 le Sheet of 6, #a.-f. 1.60 1.60

Souvenir Sheets

2078-2079 A285 2000 le multi 5.25 5.25

For overprints see Nos. 2117-2119.

Civilian Airliners
A286

No. 2080: a, SUD Caravelle 6. b, DeHaviland comet. c, Boeing 707. d, Airbus industrie A-300.

No. 2080E: f, Benoist Type XIV. g, Junkers JU52/3m. h, Douglas DC-3. i, Sikorsky S-42.

#2081, Concorde. #2081A, Lockheed L-1649A Starliner.

1997, Oct. 6 *Perf. 14*

2080 A286 600 le Sheet of 4, #a.-d. + label 6.50 6.50
2080E A286 600 le Sheet of 4, #f.-i. + label 6.50 6.50

Souvenir Sheets

2081-2081A A286 2000 le each 5.25 5.25

Nos. 2081-2081A contain one 91x34mm stamp.

Christmas
A287

Entire paintings or details: 100 le, 150 le, The Annunciation, by Titian (diff. details). 200 le, Madonna of Foligno, by Raphael. 250 le, The Annunciation, by Michelino. 500 le, The Prophet Isaiah, by Michelangelo. 600 le, Three Angels, by Master of the Rhenish Housebook.

No. 2088, The Fall of the Rebel Angels, by Peter Bruegel the Elder, horiz. No. 2089, Unidentified painting of Angel pointing hand in air, man with book, horiz.

1997, Dec. 24

2082-2087 A287 Set of 6 4.75 4.75

Souvenir Sheets

2088-2089 A287 2000 le each 5.25 5.25

Diana, Princess of Wales (1961-97) — A288

Various portraits, color of sheet margin: No. 2090, Pale pink. No. 2091, Pale blue. No. 2092, Pale yellow.

No. 2093, Wearing wide-brimmed hat. No. 2094, With Prince Harry (in margin). No. 2095, Helping to feed needy.

1998, Jan. 12 Litho. *Perf. 14*

Sheets of 6, #a.-f.

2090-2092 A288 400 le each 6.50 6.50

Souvenir Sheets

2093-2095 A288 1500 le each 4.00 4.00

New Year 1998 (Year of the Tiger)
A289

Various stylized tigers in: No. 2096: a, purple. b, maroon. c, bright lilac rose. d, orange.

800 le, maroon, vert.

1998, Jan. 26 Litho. *Perf. 14*

2096 A289 250 le Sheet of 4, #a.-d. 2.75 2.75

Souvenir Sheet

2097 A289 800 le red org & multi 2.25 2.25

Flora and Fauna
A290

Designs: 200 le, Metagyrphus nitens, vert. 250 le, Lord Derby's parakeet, vert. 300 le, Narcissus, vert. 400 le, Barbus tetrazona. 500 le, Agalychnis callidryas. 600 le, Wolverine.

No. 2104: a, Japanese white-eyes. b, Rhododendron. c, Slow loris. d, Violet flowers. e, Orthetrum albistylum. f, Coluber jugularis.

No. 2105: a, Cheetah. b, Ornithogalum thyrsoides. c, Ostrich. d, Common chameleon. e, Fennec fox. f, Junonia hierta cebrene.

No. 2106, Tricolored heron, vert. No. 2107, Artheris squamiger.

1998, Aug. 4 Litho. *Perf. 14*

2098-2103 A290 Set of 6 4.50 4.50

Sheets of 6, #a.-f.

2104-2105 A290 450 le each 6.50 6.50

Souvenir Sheets

2106-2107 A290 2000 le each 4.00 4.00

Dinosaurs
A291

Designs: 200 le, Hypsilophodon, vert. 400 le, Lambeosaurus, vert. 500 le, Corythosaurus, vert. 600 le, Stegosaurus, vert. 800 le, Antrodemus.

No. 2113, vert: a, Plateosaurus. b, Tyrannosaurus. c, Brachiosaurus. d, Iguanodon. e, Styracosaurus. f, Hadrosaurus.

No. 2114: a, Tyrannosaurus. b, Tenontosaurus. c, Deinonychus. d, Triceratops. e, Maiasaura. f, Struthiomimus.

No. 2115, Tyrannosaurus. No. 2116, Triceratops.

1998, Aug. 18 Litho. *Perf. 14*

2108-2112 A291 Set of 5 5.00 5.00

Sheets of 6, #a.-f.

2113-2114 A291 500 le each 6.00 6.00

Souvenir Sheets

2115-2116 A291 2000 le each 4.00 4.00

Nos. 2077-2079 Ovptd.

Perf. 13½x14, 14x13½

1998, Aug. 31

2117 A285 50 le Sheet of 6, #a.-f. .60 .60

Souvenir Sheets

2118-2119 A285 2000 le each 4.00 4.00

Emblem and "MICKEY & MINNIE - 70TH ANNIVERSARY" appear in sheet margin on Nos. 2118-2119.

Ships of the World
A292

No. 2120: a, Phoenician, 8th cent. BC. b, Drakkar, 6th cent. c, Carrack, 14th cent. d, Venetian Galley, 16th cent. e, Galeasse, 17th cent. f, Chebeck, 17th cent.

No. 2121: a, Junk, 19th cent. b, HMS Victory, 19th cent. c, Savanna, 19th cent. d, Gaissa, 19th cent. e, Warrior, 19th cent. f, Preussen, 20th cent.

No. 2122, Santa Maria, 1492. No. 2123, Titanic, 1912.

1998, Sept. 1 *Perf. 14*

Sheets of 6, #a.-f.

2120-2121 A292 300 le each 3.50 3.50

Souvenir Sheets

2122-2123 A292 2000 le each 4.00 4.00

Nos. 2122-2123 each contain one 57x43mm stamp.

Disney's The Lion King, Simba's Pride
A293

No. 2124: a, Kiara (with bird). b, Pumbaa. c, Kiara & Kovu. d, Kovu. e, Kiara & Kovu (red background). f, Timon (orange background).

No. 2125: a, Kiara (with butterfly). b, Timon & Pumbaa. c, Kiara. d, Kiara & Kovu (green background). e, Kovu (with bird). f, Kiara & Kovu (pink background).

No. 2126, Pumbaa & Timon. No. 2127, Kiara & Kovu, horiz.

Perf. 13½x14, 14x13½

1998, Sept. 15

Sheets of 6, #a.-f.

2124-2125 A293 500 le each 6.00 6.00

Souvenir Sheets

2126-2127 A293 2500 le each 5.00 5.00

Paintings by Picasso — A294

Paintings: 400 le, Man with Straw Hat and Ice Cream Cone, 1938. 600 le, Woman in Red Armchair, 1932. 800 le, Nude in a Garden, 1934.
2000 le, Child Holding a Dove, 1901.

1998, Dec. 15 Litho. *Perf. 14½*

2128-2130	A294	Set of 3	3.75	3.75

Souvenir Sheet

2131	A294	2000 le multicolored	4.00	4.00

Gandhi — A295

1998, Dec. 15 *Perf. 14*

2132	A295	600 le Portrait	1.25	1.25

Souvenir Sheet

2133	A295	2000 le Close-up	4.00	4.00

No. 2132 printed in sheets of 4.

Royal Air Force, 80th Anniv. A296

No. 2134: a, McDonnell Douglas Phantom FRG2. b, Two Panavia Tornado GR1. c, Jaguar GR1A. d, Hercules C-130.
No. 2135, Eagle, biplane. No. 2136, Lysander, Eurofighter.

1998, Dec. 15

2134	A296	800 le Sheet of 4, #a.-d.	6.50	6.50

Souvenir Sheets

2135-2136	A296	2000 le each	4.00	4.00

19th World Scouting Jamboree, Chile A297

No. 2137: a, Dan Beard, Robert Baden-Powell, 1937. b, Kuwaiti Scouts. c, Scout leader bottle feeding bear cub.
No. 2138, vert.: a, William D. Boyce, Lone Scouts founder. b, Guion S. Bluford. c, Ellison S. Onizuka.
No. 2139, Lord, Lady Robert Baden-Powell. No. 2140, Bear cub drinking from bottle.

1998, Dec. 15

Sheets of 3, #a.-c.

2137-2138	A297	1500 le each	9.00	9.00

Souvenir Sheets

2139-2140	A297	3000 le each	6.00	6.00

Christmas A298

Entire paintings or details: 200 le, Penitent of Mary Magdalen, by Titian. 500 le, Lamentation of Christ, by Veronese. 1500 le, The Building of Noah's Ark, by Guido Reni. 2000 le, Abraham and Isaac, by Rembrandt.
No. 2145, Adoration of the Shepherds, by Bartolomé Estéban Murillo. No. 2146, The Assumption of the Virgin, by Murillo.

1998, Dec. 14 Litho. *Perf. 14*

2141-2144	A298	Set of 4	6.50	6.50

Souvenir Sheets

2145-2146	A298	3000 le each	4.50	4.50

Ferrari Automobiles — A298a

No. 2146A: c, 400 Superamerica. d, 250 GT Lusso. e, 342 America.
2000 le, 330 GTC.
Illustration reduced.

1998, Dec. 15 Litho. *Perf. 14*

2146A	A298a	800 le Sheet of 3, #c-e	3.00	3.00

Souvenir Sheet

2146B	A298a	2000 le multi	2.60	2.60

No. 2146A contains three 39x25mm stamps.

Diana, Princess of Wales (1961-97) — A299

1998, Dec. 15 *Perf. 14½x14*

2147	A299	600 le multicolored	.90	.90

No. 2147 was issued in sheets of 6.

New Year 1999 (Year of the Rabbit) A300

Color of stylized rabbits - #2148: a, red. b, red violet. c, blue. d, light violet.
1500 le, Rabbit, vert.

1998, Dec. 24 *Perf. 14*

2148	A300	700 le Sheet of 4, #a.-d.	4.25	4.25

Souvenir Sheet

2149	A300	1500 le multicolored	2.50	2.50

Paintings by Eugène Delacroix (1798-1863) — A301

Designs: a, Rocks and a Small Valley. b, Jewish Musicians from Magador. c, Moroccans Traveling. d, Women of Algiers in their Apartment. e, Moroccan Military Exercises. f, Arabs Skirmishing in the Mountains. g, Arab Chieftan Reclining on a Carpet. h, Procession in Tangier.
No. 2151, Self-portrait, vert.

1998

2150	A301	400 le Sheet of 8, #a.-h.	5.00	5.00

Souvenir Sheet

2151	A301	400 le multicolored	.65	.65

Bird Type of 1992

Designs: 4000 le, Gray-headed bush-shrike. 5000 le, Black-backed puffback. 6000 le, Crimson-breasted shrike. 10,000 le, Northern shrike.

1999 Litho. *Perf. 14x15*

2152	A199	4000 le multi	5.25	5.25
2153	A199	5000 le multi	6.50	6.50
2154	A199	6000 le multi	7.75	7.75
2155	A199	10,000 le multi	13.00	13.00
		Nos. 2152-2155 (4)	32.50	32.50

Issued: 4000 le, 5000 le, 2/18/99.

Birds, Marine Life — A302

150 le, Powder blue surgeon. 250 le, Frilled anemone. 600 le, Red beard sponge. 800 le, Red-finned batfish.
No. 2160: a, Eastern reef egret. b, Dolphins. c, Sailing ship, Humpback whale. d, Red and green macaw. e, Blue tangs. f, Guitarfish. g, Manatees. h, Hammerhead shark. i, Blue shark. j, Lemon goby, moorish idol. k, Ribbon eels. l, Loggerhead turtle.
Sharks - #2161: a, Blue shark. b, Tiger shark. c, Bull shark. d, Great white. e, Scalloped hammerhead. f, Oceanic whitetip. g, Zebra shark. h, Leopard shark. i, Horn shark.
Dolphins, whales - #2162: a, Hector's dolphin. b, Tucuxi. c, Hourglass dolphin. d, Bottlenose dolphin. e, Gray's beaked whale. f, Bowhead whale. g, Fin whale. h, Gray whale. i, Blue whale.
No. 2163, Purple firefish. No. 2164, Spotted eagle ray. No. 2165, Leatherback turtle.

1999, Feb. 22 *Perf. 14*

2156-2159	A302	Set of 4	2.25	2.25
2160	A302	400 le Sheet of 12, #a.-l.	6.25	6.25

Sheets of 9, #a.-i.

2161-2162	A302	500 le each	5.75	5.75

Souvenir Sheets

2163-2165	A302	3000 le each	4.00	4.00

Intl. Year of the Ocean (#2160-2162, #2164-2165).

Airplanes A303

200 le, Grumman X-29. 300 le, Rocket-powered Bell X-1. 400 le, MiG-21 Fishbed, 1956, USSR. 600 le, Blériot X1 Monoplane, 1909. 800 le, Southern Cross, Fokker F.VII, 1928. 1500 le, Supermarine S.6B.
No. 2172: a, Grumman F3F-1, 1940. b, North American F-86A Sabre Jet, 1949. c, Cessna 377 Super Skymaster. d, F-16 Fighting Falcon, 1973. e, Voyager, Experimental Aircraft, Dick Rutan, Jeana Yeager. f, Fairchild A10A Thunderbolt II, 1975. g, Lockheed Vega, 1933. h, Lockheed Vega, 1930.
No. 2173: a, Sopwith Tabloid, 1914, UK. b, Vickers F.B.5 Gun Bus, 1915. c, Savoia Marchetti S.M. 79-II Sparviero, 1940. d, Mitsubishi A6M3 Zero Sen, 1942. e, Morane-Saulnier L, 1915. f, Shorts 360. g, Tupolev TU-160, 1988. h, Mikoyan-Gurevich MiG-15, 1948.
No. 2174: a, Nieuport 11C. 1, 1915. b, D.H. Vampire N.F. 10, 1951. c, Aerospatiale-Aeritalia ATR 72. d, Fiat CR.32, 1933. e, Curtiss P-6E Hawk, 1932. f, Saab JA 37 Viggen, 1977. g, Piper Pa-46 Malibu. h, F-14 Tomcat.
No. 2175, Spirit of St. Louis. No. 2176, Canadair CL-215.

1999, Mar. 22 Litho. *Perf. 14*

2166-2171	A303	Set of 6	5.50	5.50

Sheets of 8, #a.-h.

2172-2174	A303	600 le each	6.75	6.75

Souvenir Sheets

2175-2176	A303	3000 le each	4.50	4.50

Australia '99 World Stamp Expo A304

Flowers: 150 le, Geranium wallchianum. 200 le, Osmanthus x burkwoodu. 250 le, Iris pallida, vert. 500 le, Rhododendron, vert. 600 le, Rose, vert. 800 le, Papoose, vert. 1500 le, Viola labradorica, vert. 2000 le, Rosa banksiae, vert.
No. 2185: a, Jack snipe. b, Alstroemeria ligtu. c, Lilium (yellow). d, Marjorie fair. e, Aemone coranaria. f, Clematis ranncu.
No. 2186: a, Aquilegiaa olympica. b, Lilium (orange). c, Magnolia grandiflora. d, Polygonatum x hybridum. e, Clematis montana. f, Vinca minor.
No. 2187: a, Colchicum speciosum. b, Scandere. c, Helianthus annuus. d, Lady Kerkrade. e, Clematix x durandil. f, Lilium regale.
No. 2188, vert.: a, Clematis hybrida. b, Cardiospermum halicacabum. c, Fritillaria imperialis. d, Iris ibetidiisima. e, Pyracantina. f, Hepatica transsilvanica.
No. 2189, Clerodendrum trichotomum. No. 2190, Holboellia. No. 2191, Crocus angustifolius, vert. No. 2192, Rubus fruitcosus, vert.

1999, Apr. 14

2177-2184	A304	Set of 8	8.50	8.50

Sheets of 6, #a.-f.

2185-2188	A304	600 le each	5.00	5.00

Souvenir Sheets

2189-2192	A304	4000 le each	5.75	5.75

Birds — A305

Fauna — A306

No. 2193: a, Cattle egret. b, White-fronted bee-eater. c, African gray parrot. d, Cinnamon-chested bee-eater. e, Malachite kingfisher. f, White-throated bee-eater. g, Yellow-billed stork. h, Hildebrandt's starling.
No. 2194: a, Great white pelican. b, Superb starling. c, Red-throated bee-eater. d, Woodland kingfisher. e, Purple swamphen. f, Pied kingfisher. g, African spoonbill. h, Crocodile bird.
No. 2195, African fish-eagle. No. 2196, Richenow's weaver.

1999, May 18 Litho. *Perf. 14*

Sheets of 8, #a.-h.

2193-2194	A305	600 le each	6.50	6.50

Souvenir Sheets

2195-2196	A305	3000 le each	4.00	4.00

1999, May 31 Litho.

Designs: 300 le, Diana monkey. 400 le, Red-vented malimbe. 500 le, Eurasian kestrel. 600 le, Little owl. 800 le, Bush pig. 1500 le, Lion.
No. 2203: a, Flap-necked chameleon. b, Golden oriole (c). c, Europeon bee-eater. d, Leopard. e, Lion (d). f, Chimpanzee (e).
No. 2204: a, Senagal galago. b, Hoopoe. c, Long-tailed pangolin (f). d, Hippopotamus. e, African elephant (d). f, Red-billed hornbill.

No. 2205, West African linsang. No. 2206, Gray parrot.

2197-2202 A306 Set of 6 6.25 6.25

Sheets of 6, #a.-f.

2203-2204 A306 900 le each 7.25 7.25

Souvenir Sheets

2205-2206 A306 3000 le each 4.50 4.50

Queen Mother (b. 1900) — A307

Trains — A308

No. 2207: a, With Duke of York and Princess Elizabeth, 1926. b, In 1979. c, In Nairobi, 1959. d, In 1991.
4000 le, With crown, 1937.

1999, Aug. 4 Litho. *Perf. 14*

Gold Frames

2207 A307 1300 le Sheet of 4, #a.-d. + label 6.75 6.75

Souvenir Sheet

Perf. 13½

2208 A307 4000 le multicolored 5.75 5.75

No. 2208 contains one 38x51mm stamp.
See Nos. 2512-2513.

1999, Aug. 4 *Perf. 14*

Designs: 100 le, Rocket. 150 le, Benguela Railway, horiz. 200 le, Sudan Railways 310 2-8-2, horiz. 250 le, Chicago, Burlington & Quincy Railroad, horiz. 300 le, Terrier, horiz. 400 le, Dublin-Cork Express, horiz. 500 le, George Stephenson, horiz. 600 le, Shay, horiz. 1500 le, South Wind, horiz.

No. 2218, horiz.: a, American. b, Flying Scotsman. c, Lord Nelson. d, Mallard. e, Evening Star. f, Britannia.

No. 2219, horiz.: a, Class 19D 4-8-2. b, Double-headed train. c, Egyptian Railways Bo-Bo. d, GMAM Garratt 4-8-2+2-8-4. e, Passenger train, Rabat. f, Rhodesian Railway 14A Class 2-2 Garratt.

No. 2220, Mountain Class Garratt. No. 2221, Royal train.

2209-2217 A308 Set of 9 4.25 4.25

Sheets of 6, #a.-f.

2218-2219 A308 800 le each 5.00 5.00

Souvenir Sheets

2220-2221 A308 3000 le each 3.25 3.25

Inscription on No. 2218f is misspelled.

Paintings of Fu Baoshi (1904-65) A309

No. 2222: a, Interpretation of a Poem of Shi-Tao. b, Autumn of Ho-Pao. c, Landscape in Rain (bridge). d, Landscape in Rain, diff. e, Landscape in Rain (house on mountain). f, Portrait of To-Fu. g, Classic Lady (trees with leaves). h, Portrait of Li-Pai. i, Sprite of the Mountain. j, Classic Lady (bare trees).

No. 2223: a, 800 le, Four Seasons - Winter, horiz. b, 1500 le, Four Seasons - Summer, horiz.

1999, Aug. 4 *Perf. 12¾*

2222 A309 400 le Sheet of 10, #a.-j. 5.25 5.25

Perf. 13

2223 A309 Sheet of 2, #a.-b. 3.00 3.00

China 1999 World Philatelic Exhibition. No. 2223 contains 51x38mm stamps.

1999 Return of Macao to People's Republic of China — A310

Illustration reduced.

1999, Aug. 4 *Perf. 14*

2224 A310 1200 le multi 1.60 1.60

China 1999 World Philatelic Exhibition. Issued in sheets of 3 stamps.

Hokusai Paintings — A311

#2225: a, Hanging Cloud Bridge. b, Timber Yard by the Tate River. c, Bird Drawings (owl). d, As "c," (ducks). e, Travelers Crossing the Oi River. f, Travelers on the Tokaido Road at Hodogaya.

No. 2226: a, People Admiring Mount Fuji from a Tea House. b, People on a Temple Balcony. c, Sea Life (crustacean). d, Sea Life (clam). e, Pontoon Bridge at Sano in Winter. f, A Shower Below the Summit.

No. 2227, A View of Mount Fuji and Travelers by a Bridge, vert. No. 2228, A Sudden Gust of Wind at Eijiri, vert.

1999, Aug. 4 *Perf. 13¾*

Sheets of 6, #a.-f.

2225-2226 A311 1000 le each 6.50 6.50

Souvenir Sheets

2227-2228 A311 3000 le each 3.25 3.25

Johann Wolfgang von Goethe (1749-1832), German Poet — A312

No. 2229: a, Witch besieges faust. b, Goethe and Friedrich von Schiller. c, Margaret places flowers before the niche of Mater Dolorosa.

No. 2230: a, Helena with her chorus. b, Faust takes a seat beside Helena.

#2231, Angelic spirit. #2232, Ariel, vert.

1999, Aug. 4 *Perf. 14*

Sheets of 3

2229 A312 1600 le #a.-c. 5.00 5.00

2230 A312 1600 le #a.-b, 2229b 5.00 5.00

Souvenir Sheets

2231-2232 A312 3000 le each 3.25 3.25

Souvenir Sheets

PhilexFrance '99 — A313

Designs: No. 2233, Crampton locomotive. No. 2234, De Glehn compound with Lemaitre front end 4-4-2.

1999, Aug. 4 *Perf. 13¾*

2233-2234 A313 3000 le each 3.25 3.25

IBRA '99 — A314

1999 *Perf. 14x14½*

2235 A314 1500 le Class 4-4-0 1.60 1.60

2236 A314 2000 le Class 05 2.10 2.10

Rights of the Child — A315

No. 2237: a, Girl holding candle. b, Two children. c, Girl, diff.
2000 le, Child, horiz.

1999, Aug. 4 Litho. *Perf. 14*

2237 A315 1600 le Sheet of 3, #a.-c. 5.25 5.25

Souvenir Sheet

2238 A315 3000 le multicolored 3.25 3.25

Wedding of Prince Edward and Sophie Rhys-Jones A316

No. 2239: a, Sophie, close-up. b, Edward (shirt and tie). c, Sophie, diff. d, edward, diff.
4000 le, Couple.

1999, Aug. 4 *Perf. 13¾x13¼*

2239 A316 2000 le Sheet of 4, #a.-d. 8.50 8.50

Souvenir Sheet

Perf. 13¼x13¾

2240 A316 4000 le multicolored 4.25 4.25

Birds of Africa A317

No. 2241: a, African paradise monarch. b, Lilac-breasted roller. c, Common Scops owl. d, African emerald cuckoo. e, Blue monarch. f, African golden oriole. g, White-throated bee eater. h, Black-bellied seedcracker. i, Hoopoe.

No. 2242: a, White-faced whistling duck. b, Black-headed heron. c, Black-headed gonolek. d, Malachite kingfisher. e, Fish eagle. f, African spoonbill. g, African skimmer. h, Black heron. i, Allen's gallinule.

No. 2243: a, Scimitarbill. b, Bateleur. c, Black-headed weaver. d, Variable sunbird. e, Blue swallow. f, Black-winged red bishop. g, Namaqua dove. h, Golden-breasted bunting. i, Hartlaub's bustard.

No. 2244: a, Montagu's harrier. b, Booted eagle. c, Yellow crested helmet-shrike. d, Scarlet-tufted malachite sunbird. e, Pin-tailed whydah. f, Red-headed malimbe. g, Western violet-backed sunbird. h, Yellow white eye. i, Brubru.

No. 2245, Rwenzori turaco, vert. No. 2246, African pygmy kingfisher, vert. No. 2247, Gray crowned crane, vert. No. 2248, Shoebill, vert.

1999 Litho. *Perf. 14*

Sheets of 9, #a.-i.

2241-2244 A317 600 le each 5.75 5.75

Souvenir Sheets

2245-2248 A317 4000 le each 4.25 4.25

New Year 2000 (Year of the Dragon) A318

No. 2249 (dragon color): a, Brown red. b, Blue green. c, Bright red. d, Lilac.
4000 le, Red dragon, vert.

2000, Feb. 5 Litho. *Perf. 14*

2249 A318 1500 le Sheet of 4, #a.-d. 6.25 6.25

Souvenir Sheet

2250 A318 4000 le multi 4.25 4.25

Sammy Davis, Jr. — A319

No. 2251: a, As child. b, With motorcycle. c, With red checked shirt. d, With microphone. e, With leg on chair. f, Holding cigarette.
5000 le, With other people.

2000, Mar. 8 *Perf. 13¾*

2251 A319 1000 le Sheet of 6, #a.-f. 6.25 6.25

Souvenir Sheet

2252 A319 5000 le multi 5.25 5.25

Flowers — A320

Various flowers making up a photomosaic of Princess Diana.

2000, Mar. 28

2253 A320 800 le Sheet of 8, #a.-h. 6.50 6.50

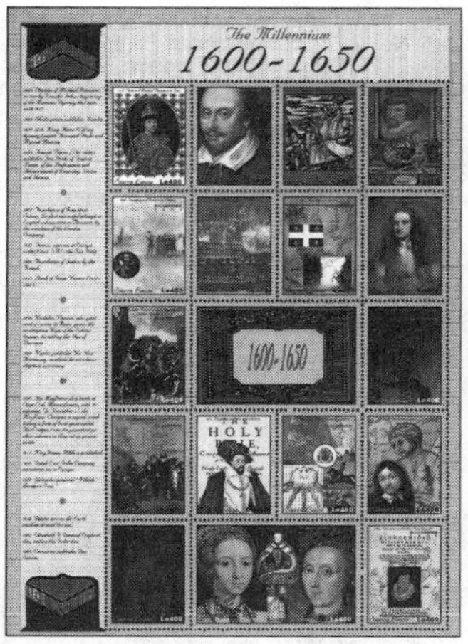

Millennium — A321

Highlights of 1600-1650: a, Election of Michael Romanov as Russian tsar. b, William Shakespeare publishes "Hamlet." c, Kung Hsien paints "Thousand Peaks and Myriad Ravines." d, Francis Bacon publishes his works. e, Founding of Jamestown, Virginia. f, Reign of Louis XIV of France. g, Founding of Quebec. h, Birth of Isaac Newton. i, Nicholas Poussin paints "Rape of the Sabine Women." j, Johannes Kepler publishes "The New Astronomy." k, The Mayflower arrives in America. l, King James Bible is published. m, Dutch East India Company introduces tea to Europe. n, René Descartes develops his philosophy. o, Galileo defends Copernican system. p, Queen Elizabeth I dies (60x40mm). q, Miguel de Cervantes publishes "Don Quixote."

2000, Mar. 28 ***Perf. 12¾x12½***

2254 A321 400 le Sheet of 17, #a.-q., + label 6.75 6.75

Paintings of Anthony Van Dyck — A322

No. 2255: a, Portrait of a Man. b, Anna Wake, Wife of Peter Stevens. c, Peter Stevens. d, Adriaen Stevens. e, Maria Bosschaerts, Wife of Adriaen Stevens. f, Portrait of a Woman.

No. 2256: a, Self-portrait, 1617-18. b, Self-portrait, 1620-21. c, Self-portrait, 1622-23. d, Andromeda Chained to the Rock. e, Self-portrait, late 1620s-early 1630s. f, Mary Ruthven.

No. 2257: a, The Betrayal of Judas (detail of The Taking of Christ.) b, Ecce Homo, 1625-26. c, Christ Carrying the Cross (showing woman with blue garment). d, The Raising of Christ on the Cross. e, The Crucifixion, c. 1627 f, The Lamentation, c. 1616 (actually the "Mocking of Christ").

No. 2258: a, The Taking of Christ. b, The Mocking of Christ. c, Ecce Homo, 1628-32. d, Christ Carrying the Cross (showing poleax). e, The Crucifixion, c. 1629-30. f, The Lamentation 1618-20.

No. 2258G: h, The Duchess of Crowy With Her Son. i, Susanna Fourment and Her Daughter. j, Geronima Brignole-Sale With Her Daughter Maria Aurelia. k, A Woman With Her Daughter. l, A Genoese Noblewoman With Her Child. m, A Genoese Noblewoman (Paola Adorno) and Her Son.

No. 2259, Self-portrait With a Sunflower. No. 2260, Self-portrait with Endymion Porter. No. 2261, Young Woman With a Child. No. 2262, Porzia Imperiale With Her Daughter Maria Francesca. No. 2263, Portrait of a Mother and Her Daughter. No. 2264, A Woman and a Child, horiz.

2000, Apr. 10 ***Perf. 13¾***

Sheets of 6, #a.-f.

2255-2258G A322 1000 le each 6.25 6.25

Souvenir Sheets

2259-2264 A322 5000 le each 5.25 5.25

Easter (Nos. 2257-2258).

Mario Andretti — A323

No. 2265: a, Behind wheel. b, With helmet, facing left. c, In pits. d, In crash. e, Inspecting tire. f, With white shirt. g, Without shirt. h, In car #50.

5000 le, With others in front of old car.

Illustration reduced.

2000, Mar. 28 **Litho.** ***Perf. 13¾***

2265 A323 600 le Sheet of 8, #a-h 5.50 5.50

Souvenir Sheet

2266 A323 5000 le multi 5.50 5.50

Scenes from "The Little Colonel" with Shirley Temple — A324

Temple - No. 2267: a, With Colonel Lloyd (Lionel Barrymore), standing. b, With Walker (Bill Robinson). c, With two children. d, With soldiers. e, With mother (Evelyn Venable), Becky (Hattie McDaniel). f, Hugging Colonel Lloyd.

No. 2268: a, With Becky and Walker. b, With Walker, diff. c, Alone. d, Tugging Colonel Lloyd's coat.

No. 2269, Holding chair.

Illustration reduced.

2000, Mar. 28

Sheets of 6 and 4

2267 A324 1200 le #a-f 8.00 8.00

2268 A324 1500 le #a-d 6.75 6.75

Souvenir Sheet

2269 A324 5000 le multi 5.50 5.50

Parrots — A325

Designs: 200 le, African gray parrot. 1500 le, Sulfur-crested cockatoo, horiz.

No. 2272: a, Monk parakeet. b, Citron-crested cockatoo. c, Queen-of-Bavaria conure. d, Budgerigar. e, Yellow-chevroned parakeet. f, Cockatiel. g, Amazon parrot. h, Sun conure. i, Malabar parakeet.

No. 2273: a, Grand eclectus parrot. b, Sun parakeet. c, Red fan parakeet. d, Fischer's lovebird. e, Blue masked lovebird. f, White belly rosella. g, Plum-headed parakeet. h, Striated lorikeet. i, Gold-mantled rosella.

4000 le, Blue and gold macaw.

2000, May 16 ***Perf. 13¾x14, 14x13¾***

2270-2271 A325 Set of 2 1.90 1.90

Sheets of 9, #a-i

2272-2273 A325 800 le each 8.00 8.00

Souvenir Sheet

2274 A325 4000 multi le 4.50 4.50

The Stamp Show 2000, London (Nos. 2272-2274). Size of stamps: Nos. 2272-2273, 28x42mm; No. 2274, 38x50mm.

Orchids A326

Designs: 300 le, Aeranthes henrici. 500 le, Ophrys apifera. 600 le, Disa crassicornis. 2000 le, Aeranthes grandiflora.

No. 2279: a, Oeleoclades maculata. b, Polystachya campyloglossa. c, Polystachya pubescens. d, Tridactyle bicaudata. e, Angraecum veitcii. f, Sobennikoffia robusta.

No. 2280: a, Aerangis curnowiana. b, Aerangis fastudsa. c, Angraecum magdalenae. d, Angraecum sororium. e, Eulophia speciosa. f, Ansellia africana.

No. 2281, Angraecum compactum. No. 2282, Angraecum eburneum.

2000, May 16 ***Perf. 14***

2275-2278 A326 Set of 4 3.75 3.75

Sheets of 6, #a-f

2279-2280 A326 1100 le each 7.50 7.50

Souvenir Sheets

2281-2282 A326 4000 le each 4.50 4.50

Prince William, 18th Birthday — A327

Various photos.

Illustration reduced.

2000, May 29 ***Perf. 14***

2283 A327 1100 le Sheet of 4, #a-d 5.00 5.00

Souvenir Sheet

Perf. 13¾

2284 A327 5000 le multi 5.50 5.50

No. 2284 contains one 38x50mm stamp.

Souvenir Sheet

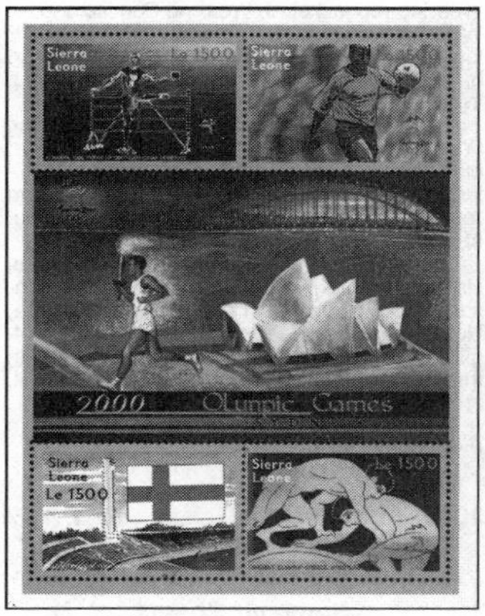

2000 Summer Olympics, Sydney — A328

Designs: a, Hurdler. b, Soccer player. c, Finnish flag, Helsinki Stadium. d, Ancient Greek wrestlers.

Illustration reduced.

2000, May 29 ***Perf. 14***

2285 A328 1500 le Sheet of 4. #a-d 6.75 6.75

First Zeppelin Flight, Cent. — A329

No. 2286: a, LZ-129. b, LZ-4. c, LZ-6. 4000 le, LZ-127.

Illustration reduced.

2000, May 29 ***Perf. 14***

2286 A329 2000 le Sheet of 3, #a-c 6.75 6.75

Souvenir Sheet

Perf. 14¼

2287 A329 4000 le multi 4.50 4.50

Size of stamps: No. 2286, 38x24mm.

Betty Boop — A330

No. 2288: a, Wearing flowered dress. b, Carrying shopping bags. c, Wearing baseball cap. d, Holding shoes. e, Sitting in chair. f, Wearing jacket. g, Playing guitar. h, Holding lasso. i, Holding flower.

No. 2289, Pointing at dog. No. 2290, Riding bicycle.

Illustration reduced.

2000, Mar. 8 **Litho.** ***Perf. 13¾***

2288 A330 800 le Sheet of 9, #a-i 8.25 8.25

Souvenir Sheets

2289-2290 A330 5000 le each 5.75 5.75

I Love Lucy — A331

No. 2291 - Lucy: a, Wearing blue cap. b, With arms in front, with Vitameatavegamin bottle. c, Wearing pink nightgown. d, Wearing pink nightgown, sticking out tongue. e, Wearing blue cap on television screen. f, Holding

bottle near table. g, With arms at side, with bottle. h, Holding bottle near cheek. i, Pouring out liquid in bottle.
No. 2292, Wearing blue cap on television, Desi touching television. No. 2293, Lucy and Fred Mertz.
Illustration reduced.

2000, Mar. 8

2291 A331 800 le Sheet of 9, #a-i 8.25 8.25

Souvenir Sheets

2292-2293 A331 5000 le each 5.75 5.75

Berlin Film Festival, 50th Anniv. — A332

No. 2294: a, Las Palabras de Max. b, Ascendancy. c, Deprisa, Deprisa. d, Die Sehnsucht der Veronika Voss. e, Heartland. f, La Colmena.
5000 le, Las Truchas.
Illustration reduced.

2000, May 29 ***Perf. 14***

2294 A332 1100 le Sheet of 6, #a-f 7.50 7.50

Souvenir Sheet

2295 A332 5000 le multi 5.75 5.75

Souvenir Sheet

Public Railways, 175th Anniv. — A333

No. 2296: a, Locomotion No. 1, George Stephenson. b, James Watt's original design for a separate condenser engine.
Illustration reduced.

2000, May 29

2296 A333 3000 le Sheet of 2, #a-b 7.00 7.00

Souvenir Sheet

Johann Sebastian Bach (1685-1750) — A334

2000, May 29

2297 A334 5000 le multi 5.75 5.75

Sea Birds A335

Designs: 400 le, Herring gull. 600 le, Caspian tern. 800 le, Red phalarope. 2000 le, Magnificent frigatebird.
No. 2302: a, Caspian tern, diff. b, Glaucous gull. c, Northern gannet. d, Long-tailed jaeger. e, Brown pelican. f, Great skua.
No. 2303: a, Wandering albatross. b, Fork-tailed storm petrel. c, Great shearwater. d, Blue-footed booby. e, Great cormorant. f, Atlantic puffin.
No. 2304, Brown booby, vert. No. 2305, Red-tailed tropicbird, vert.

2000, May 16 Litho. ***Perf. 14***

2298-2301 A335 Set of 4 3.75 3.75

Sheets of 6, #a-f

2302-2303 A335 1000 le each 6.00 6.00

Souvenir Sheets

2304-2305 A335 5000 le each 5.00 5.00

Richard Petty, Stock Car Racer — A336

No. 2306: a, Car in pits. b, With family. c, Wearing red jacket. d, Wearing Pontiac cap. e, Wearing white hat, uniform with two STP logos. f, Wearing STP cap. g, Standing in car. h, Profile, wearing STP logos on shoulder. i, Wearing headphones.
No. 2307: a, Holding trophy. b, Wearing Winston cap. c, Wearing black hat. d, Hatless, blue background. e, Wearing shirt with red collar. f, Holding helmet. g, Leaning on blue and red car. h, With arm in car. i, Leaning head out of car.
No. 2308: a, Wearing red shirt, white hat. b, Hatless, orange background. c, Wearing Pontiac cap. d, Strapped in car, without helmet. e, Holding timer. f, Wearing red and blue helmet. g, Wearing white hat, blue uniform. h, With trophy, wearing STP cap. i, With white hat, reclining.
No. 2309, Standing in car, diff. No, 2310, In race, horiz.
Illustration reduced.

2000, Aug. 15 ***Perf. 13¾***

Sheets of 9, #a-i

2306-2308 A336 800 le each 7.00 7.00

Souvenir Sheets

2309-2310 A336 5000 le each 5.00 5.00

Popes — A337

No. 2311: a, Gregory VI (1045-46). b, Celestine V (1294). c, Honorius IV (1285-87). d, Innocent IV (1243-54). e, Innocent VII (1404-06). f, John XXII (1316-34).
No. 2312: a, Martin IV (1281-85). b, Nicholas II (1059-61). c, Nicholas IV (1288-92). d, Urban IV (1261-64). e, Urban V (1362-70). f, Urban VI (1378-89).
No. 2313, Nicholas IV (1288-92), diff. No. 2314, Clement XI (1700-21).
Illustration reduced.

2000, Aug. 21

Sheets of 6, #a-f

2311-2312 A337 1100 le each 6.50 6.50

Souvenir Sheets

2313-2314 A337 5000 le each 5.00 5.00

Monarchs — A338

No. 2315: a, Emperor Hung Wu of China. b, Emperor Hsuan Te of China. c, King Sejong of Korea. d, Emperor T'ung Chih of China. e, Emperor T'ai Tsu (Chao K'uang-yin) of Chin. f, Empress Yung Ching of China.
No. 2316, Kublai Khan of China.
Illustration reduced.

2000, Aug. 21

2315 A338 1100 le Sheet of 6, #a-f 6.50 6.50

Souvenir Sheet

2316 A338 5000 le multi 5.00 5.00

European Soccer Championships — A339

No. 2317 - Germany: a, Worns. b, Team photo. c, Babbel. d, Franz Beckenbauer. e, Selessin Stadium, Liege, Belgium. f, Stefan Kuntz.
No. 2318 - Italy: a, Walter Zenga. b, Team photo. c, Roberto Bettega. d, Totti. e, Philips Stadium, Eindhoven, Netherlands. f, Vieri.
No. 2319 - Portugal: a, Dimas. b, Team photo. c, Pinto. d, Santos. e, Gelredome Stadium, Arnhem, Netherlands. f, Sousa.
No. 2320 - Romania: a, Munteanu. b, Team photo. c, Petre. d, Petrescu. e, Popescu.
No. 2321, German coach Erich Ribbeck, vert. No. 2322, Italian coach Dino Zoff, vert. No. 2323, Portuguese coach Humberto Coelho, vert. No. 2324, Romanian coach Emerich Jenei, vert.
Illustration reduced.

2000, Aug. 21

Sheets of 6, #a-f (#2317-2319); Sheet of 6 #a-e, #2319e (#2320)

2317-2320 A339 1300 le each 7.75 7.75

Souvenir Sheets

2321-2324 A339 5000 le each 5.00 5.00

Souvenir Sheet

Albert Einstein (1879-1955) — A340

illustration reduced.

2000, May 29 Litho. ***Perf. 14***

2325 A340 5000 le multi 5.00 5.00

Apollo-Soyuz Mission, 25th Anniv. — A341

No. 2326, vert.: a, Apollo 18. b, Soyuz 19. c, Apollo and Soyuz docked.
5000 le, Apollo and Soyuz docking.
Illustration reduced.

2000, May 29

2326 A341 1200 le Sheet of 3, #a-c 3.50 3.50

Souvenir Sheet

2327 A341 5000 le multi 5.00 5.00

Queen Mother, 100th Birthday — A342

Litho. & Embossed

2000, Aug. 4 ***Die Cut Perf. 8¾***

Without Gum

2328 A342 18,000 le gold & multi

Dogs and Cats A343

500 le, Bulldog. 800 le, Brown tabby. 1500 le, Burmese. 2000 le, Dachshund.

No. 2333, 1000 le: a, Beagle. b, Scottish terrier. c, Bloodhound. d, Greyhound. e, German shepherd. f, Cocker spaniel.

No. 2334, 1000 le: a, Red tabby stumpy Manx. b, Red self. c, Maine Coon cat. d, Black smoke. e, Chinchilla. f, Russian Blue.

No. 2335, 1100 le: a, Pointer. b, Doberman pinscher. c, Collie. d, Chihuahua. e, Afghan hound. f, Boxer.

No. 2336, 1100 le: a, Singapura. b, Himalayan. c, Abyssinian. d, Black cat. e, Siamese. f, North African wild cat.

No. 2337, 5000 le, Fox terrier, vert. No. 2338, 5000 le, Calico, vert.

2000, Oct. 2 Litho. *Perf. 14*

2329-2332 A343 Set of 4 5.00 5.00

Sheets of 6, #a-f

2333-2336 A343 Set of 4 26.00 26.00

Souvenir Sheets

2337-2338 A343 Set of 2 10.50 10.50

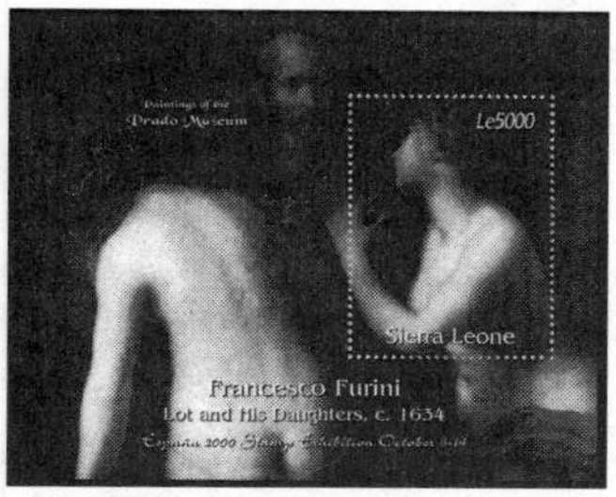

Paintings from the Prado — A344

No. 2339, 1000 le: a, The Transport of Mary Magdalen, by José Antolinez. b, The Holy Family, by Francisco de Goya. c, Our Lady of the Immaculate Conception, by Antolinez. d, Charles IV as Prince, by Anton Raphael Mengs. e, Louis XIII of France, by Philippe de Champaigne. f, Prince Ferdinand VI by Jean Ranc.

No. 2340, 1000 le: a, Adam, by Albrecht Dürer. b, Moor, by Manuel Benedito Vives. c, Eve, by Dürer. d, A Gypsy, by Raimundo Madrazo y Garreta. e, Maria Guerrero, by Joaquin Sorolla y Bastida. f, The Model Aline Masson with a White Mantilla, by Madrazo y Garreta.

No. 2341, 1000 le: a, Figure in yellow robe from Madonna and Child Between Saints Catherine and Ursula, by Giovanni Bellini. b, Madonna and Child from Madonna and Child Between Saints Catherine and Ursula. c, Figure in red robe from Madonna and Child Between Saints Catherine and Ursula. d, Giovanni Mateo Ghiberti, by Bernardino India. e, The Marchioness of Santa Cruz, by Agustín Esteve. f, Self-portrait, by Orazio Borgianni.

No. 2342, 1000 le: a, Mary from The Holy Family with a Bird, by Bartolomé Esteban Murillo. b, Jesus from The Holy Family with a Bird. c, Joseph, from The Holy Family with a Bird. d, Cardinal Carlos de Borja, by Andrea Procaccini. e, St. Dominic de Guzmán, by Claudio Coello. f, Christ Supported by an Angel, by Alonso Cano.

No. 2343, 1000 le: a, Woman from The Seller of Fans, by José del Castillo. b, Allegory of Summer, by Mariano Salvador Maella. c, Man with basket from The Seller of Fans. d, Portrait of a Girl, by Carlos Luis de Ribera y Fieve. e, The Poultry Keeper, by Pensionante del Saraceni. f, The Death of Cleopatra, by Guido Reni.

No. 2344, 1000 le; a, Feliciana Bayeu, by Francisco Bayeu y Subias. b, Tomás de Iriarte by Joaquin Inza. c, St. Elizabeth of Portugal, by Francisco de Zurbarán. d, Christ from The Vision of St. Francis at Porziuncola, by Murillo. e, Monk from The Vision of St. Francis at Porziuncola. f, Woman from The Vision of St. Francis at Porziuncola.

No. 2345, 5000 le, Lot and His Daughters, by Francesco Furini. No. 2346, 5000 le, The Execution of Torrijos and His Companions, by Antonio Gisbert Pérez. No. 2347, 5000 le, the Concert, by Vicente Palmaroli y González. No. 2348, 5000 le, The Finding of Joseph's Cup in Benjamin's Bag, by Jacopo Amiconi. No. 2349, 5000 le, Vulcan's Forge, by Diego Velázquez. No. 2350, 5000 le, The Two Friends, by Joaquin Agrasot y Juan, horiz.

Illustration reduced.

2000, Oct. 6 *Perf. 12x12¼, 12¼x12*

Sheets of 6, #a-f

2339-2344 A344 Set of 6 37.50 37.50

Souvenir Sheets

2345-2350 A344 Set of 6 32.50 32.50

Espana 2000 Intl. Philatelic Exhibition.

Mushrooms — A345

Designs: 600 le, Tuberous polyphore. 900 le, Cultivated agaricus. 1200 le, Scarlet wax cap. 2500 le, Blue-green psilocybe.

No. 2355, 1000 le, vert.: a, Armed stinkhorn. b, Red-staining inocybe. c, Amanitopsis vaginata. d, Inocybe jurana. e, Xerula longipes. f, Tricholoma matsutake.

No. 2356, 1000 le, vert.: a, Orange-staining mycena. b, Russula amoema. c, Cinnabar chanterelle. d, Calodon aurantiacum. e, Lentinus lepidus. f, Gomphidius roseus.

No. 2357, 5000 le, Orange latex lactarius. No. 2358, 5000 le, Common morel, vert.

2000, Oct. 30 Litho. *Perf. 14*

2351-2354 A345 Set of 4 5.50 5.50

Sheets of 6, #a-f

2355-2356 A345 Set of 2 12.50 12.50

Souvenir Sheets

2357-2358 A345 Set of 2 10.50 10.50

Flower Photomosaic Type of 2000

No. 2359, 800 le: Various flowers making up a photomosaic of the Queen Mother.

No. 2360, 900 le: Various photographs of religious scenes making up a photomosaic of Pope John Paul II.

2000, Oct. 30 *Perf. 13¾*

Sheets of 8, #a-h

2359-2360 A320 Set of 2 14.50 14.50

Massacre of Israeli Olympic Athletes, 1972 — A346

No. 2361, horiz.: a, Kahat Shor. b, Andrei Schpitzer. c, Joseph Romano. d, Yaakov Springer. e, Eliazer Halffin. f, Amitsur Shapira. g, Moshe Weinberg. h, Mark Slavin. i, Torchbearer, Israeli flag. j, Joseph Gottfreund. k, Ze'ev Friedman. l, David Berger.

2000, Nov. 9 *Perf. 14*

2361 A346 500 le Sheet of 12, #a-l 6.25 6.25

Souvenir Sheet

2362 A346 5000 le Torchbearer 5.25 5.25

Circus A347

Designs: 800 le, Tightrope rider. 1000 le, Bear and ball. 1500 le, Tiger on ball. 2000 le, Camels.

No. 2367, 1100 le: a, Polar bear on roller. b, Ape. c, Clown, green background. d, Tightrope walker. e, Seals. f, Camel.

No. 2368, 1100 le: a, Clown, brown background. b, Tiger on wires. c, Monkey. d, Dogs. e, Bear on skates. f, Trapeze artists.

No. 2369, 1100 le, vert.: a, Acrobat. b, Giraffe. c, Bear on poles. d, Elephant. e, Horse. f, Fire eater.

No. 2370, 5000 le, Trainer on elephant's trunk, vert. No. 2371, 5000 le, Tiger jumping through flaming hoop, vert. No. 2372, 5000 le, Cannon flyer, vert.

2000, Dec. 1 Litho.

2363-2366 A347 Set of 4 5.75 5.75

Sheets of 6, #a-f

2367-2369 A347 Set of 3 21.00 21.00

Souvenir Sheets

2370-2372 A347 Set of 3 16.00 16.00

Queen Mother, 100th Birthday — A348

2000, Dec. 18

2373 A348 1100 le multi 1.10 1.10

Issued in sheets of 6.

New Year 2001 (Year of the Snake) — A349

No. 2374, horiz.: a, Blue snake. b, Red snake. c, Purple snake. d, Green snake.

2001, Jan. 2

2374 A349 800 le Sheet of 4, #a-d 3.50 3.50

Souvenir Sheet

2375 A349 2500 le Green snake 2.60 2.60

History of the Orient Express — A350

No. 2376, 1000 le: a, First sleeping car, 1872. b, Dining car #193, 1886. c, Dining car #2422, 1913. d, Sleeping car Type S1. e, Metal sleeping car #2645. f, Metal sleeping car #2644, 1922.

No. 2377, 1000 le: a, Dining car, Series #8341. b, Dining car, Series #3342. c, Sleeping car, Series #3312 Type Z. d, Sleeping car, Series #3879, 1950. e, Sleeping car, Series #3311 Type Z. f, Dining car, Series #3785, 1932.

No. 2378, 1100 le: a, Ostend-Vienna. b, Engine East 230, #3175. c, Dual cylinder locomotive. d, Simplon Orient Express, 1919. e, Engine East 220, #2405. f, Caboose of Simplon Express, c. 1906.

No. 2379, 1100 le: a, Sleeping car #507, 1897. b, Sleeping car #438, 1894. c, Sleeping car #313, 1880. d, Sleeping car #190, 1886. e, Sleeping car #102, 1882. f, Sleeping car #77, 1881.

No. 2380, 5000 le, Locomotive. No. 2381, 5000 le, Georges Nagelmackers, vert. No. 2382, 5000 le, Mata Hari, vert. No. 2383, 5000 le, Agatha Christie, vert.

2001, Jan. 15 *Perf. 14*

Sheets of 6, #a-f

2376-2379 A350 Set of 4 26.00 26.00

Souvenir Sheets

2380-2383 A350 Set of 4 21.00 21.00

Reptiles A351

Designs: 250 le, Natal Mixands dwarf chameleon. 400 le, Cape cobra. 500 le, Western sand lizard. 600 le, Pan-hinged terrapin. 800 le, Many-horned adder. 1500 le, Hawequa flat gecko.

No. 2390, 1200 le: a, Reticulated desert lizard. b, Ball python. c, Gaboon viper. d, Dumeril's boa. e, Common egg-eater. f, Helmet turtle.

No. 2391, 1200 le: a, Asian saw-scaled viper. b, Namibian sand snake. c, Angolan garter snake. d, Striped skaapsteker. e, Brown house snake. f, Shield-nosed cobra.

No. 2392, 5000 le, Green water snake. No. 2393, 5000 le, Flap-necked chameleon.

2001, Jan. 15

2384-2389 A351 Set of 6 4.25 4.25

Sheets of 6, #a-f

2390-2391 A351 Set of 2 15.00 15.00

Souvenir Sheets

2392-2393 A351 Set of 2 10.50 10.50

Rijksmuseum, Amsterdam, Bicent. (in 2000) — A352

No. 2394, 1100 le, vert.: a, Gentleman Writing a Letter, by Gabriel Metsu. b, Self-portrait, by Carel Fabritius. c, The Windmill at Wijk bij Duurstede, by Jacob van Ruisdael. d, Bentheim Castle, by van Ruisdael. e, Ships on a Stormy Sea, by Willem van de Velde, the Younger. f, David from David Playing the Harp, by Jan de Bray.

No. 2395, 1100 le, vert.: a, St. Paul from St. Paul Healing the Cripple at Lystra, by Karel Dujardin. b, Two hatless men from The Meagre Company, by Frans Hals and Pieter Codde. c, Man from Elegant Couple in an Interior, by Eglon van der Neer. d, Laid Table With Cheese and Fruit, by Floris van Dijck. e, Bacchanal, by Moses van Uyttenbroeck. f, Kneeling woman from St. Paul Healing the Cripple at Lystra.

No. 2396, 1100 le, vert.: a, Lady Reading a Letter, by Metsu. b, Portrait of Titus, by Rembrandt. c, Portrait of Gerard de Lairesse, by Rembrandt. d, Portrait of a Family in an Interior, by Emanuel de Witte. e, The Letter, by Gerard Terborch. f, Three Women and a Man in a Courtyard Behind a House, by Pieter de Hooch.

No. 2397, 1100 le, vert.: a, Candlebearers from David Playing the Harp. b, Hand of St. Paul from St. Paul Healing the Cripple at Lystra. c, Two men, one with hat, from The Meagre Company. d, The Gray, by Ohilips Wouwerman. e, Couple from Elegant Couple in an Interior. f, The Hut, by Adriaen van de Velde.

No. 2398, 5000 le, Road in the Dunes With a Passenger Coach, by Salomon van Ruysdael. No. 2399, 5000 le, Cows in the Meadow, by Albert Gerard Bilders. No. 2400, 5000 le, Lot and His Daughters, by Hendrick Goltzius. No. 2401, 5000 le, Arrival of Queen Wilhelmina at the Frederiksplein in Amsterdam, by Otto Eerelman.

2001, Jan. 15 *Perf. 13¾*

Sheets of 6, #a-f

2394-2397 A352 Set of 4 27.50 27.50

Souvenir Sheets

2398-2401 A352 Set of 4 21.00 21.00

Battle of Britain, 60th Anniv. — A353

No. 2402, 1000 le: a, Bombed village near London. b, The Underground as a bomb shelter. c, Firemen. d, Home Guard. e, Setting lights out time. f, Pilots resting between flights. g, Brendan "Paddy" Finucane, ace pilot. h, Hawk 75.

No. 2403, 1000 le: a, St. Paul's Cathedral. b, Eastenders leaving London. c, Winston Churchill being cheered by British crew. d, Rescue pilot. e, Boy Scouts helping children. f, Big gunners, 1940. g, Plane spotter lights. h, Survey watchers.

No. 2404, 1000 le: a, Post Office Engineer, WAFF. b, Women munitions workers. c, Churchill as prime minister and defense minister. d, German Dornier DO17. e, Church fires from Nazi bombs, London, 1940. f, All-night raid on London, 1940. g, Lunchtime in the Underground. h, People in the Underground, 1940.

No. 2405, 1000 le: a, London Bridge. b, Surrey Home Guard. c, British Cruiser tank MK III. d, Newfoundland men at the guns, 1940. e, Lady Astor's Constituency hit, 1940. f, Churchill worried with war, 1940. g, Bomb blast at Parliament. h, Development of radar, 1940.

No. 2406, 6000 le, Churchill and wife inspecting harbor damage. No. 2407, 6000 le, London, 1940. No. 2408, 6000 le, British Supermarine Spitfire. No. 2409, 6000 le, Bombing crew preparing for flight, 1940, vert.

2001, Jan. 30 ***Perf. 14***

Sheets of 8, #a-h

2402-2405 A353 Set of 4 35.00 35.00

Souvenir Sheets

2406-2409 A353 Set of 4 25.00 25.00

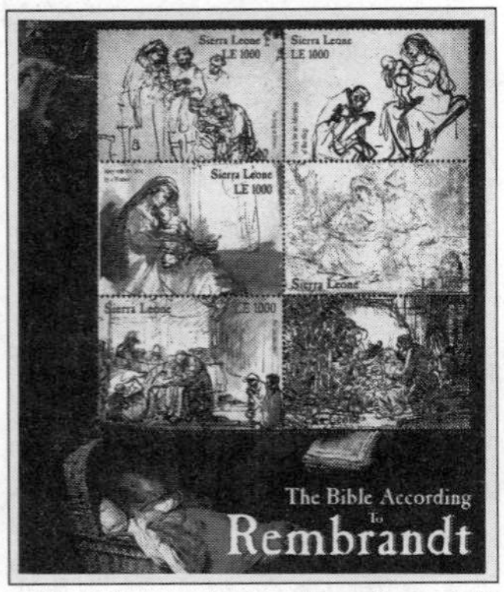

Biblical Scenes by Rembrandt — A354

No. 2410, 1000 le: a, The Song of Simeon. b, Study for Adoration of the Magi. c, Mary With the Child by a Window. d, The Rest on the Flight Into Egypt. e, The Circumcision. f, The Shepherds Worship the Child.

No. 2411, 1000 le: a, The Angel Rises Up in the Flame of Manoah's Sacrifice. b, Tobias Frighterned by the Fish. c, The Angel of the Lord Stands in Balaam's Path. d, The Angel Appears to Hagar in the Desert. e, Jacob's Dream. f, The Healing of Tobit.

No. 2412, 5000 le, Simeon's Prophecy to Mary. No. 2413, 5000 le, The Angel Prevents the Sacrifice of Isaac. No. 2414, 5000 le, The Angel Leaves Tobit and His Family, vert. No. 2415, 5000 le, The Adoration of the Magi, vert.

2001, Feb. 13 ***Perf. 13¾***

Sheets of 6, #a-f

2410-2411 A354 Set of 2 12.50 12.50

Souvenir Sheets

2412-2415 A354 Set of 4 21.00 21.00

Racehorses A355

Designs: 200 le, Native Dancer. 500 le, Citation. 1500 le, Spectre. 2000 le, Carbine.

No. 2420, 1200 le: a, Arkle. b, Golden Miller. c, Phar Lap. d, Battleship. e, Kelso. f, Nijinsky.

No. 2421, 1200 le: a, Red Rum. b, Sir Ken. c, War Admiral. d, Troytown. e, Shergar. f, Allez France.

No. 2422, 5000 le, Cigar. No. 2423, 5000 le, Desert Orchid. No. 2424, 5000 le, Trophy. No. 2425, 5000 le, Horses on turf track, horiz.

2001, Feb. 27 ***Perf. 14***

2416-2419 A355 Set of 4 4.50 4.50

Sheets of 6, #a-f

2420-2421 A355 Set of 2 15.00 15.00

Souvenir Sheets

2422-2425 A355 Set of 4 21.00 21.00

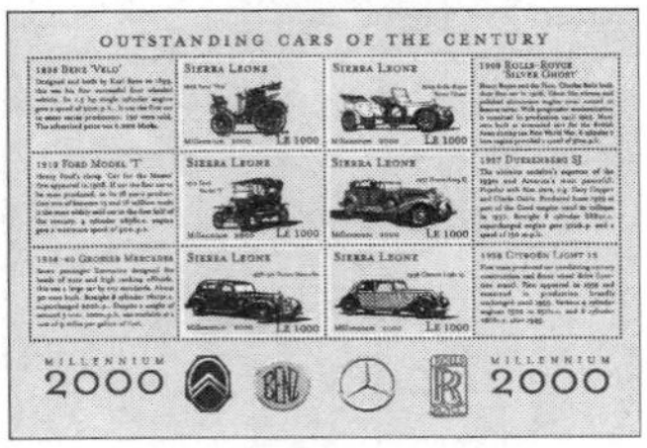

Automobiles — A356

No. 2426, 1000 le: a, 1898 Benz Velo. b, 1909 Rolls-Royce Silver Ghost. c, 1912 Ford Model T. d, 1937 Duesenberg SJ. e, 1938-40 Grosser Mercedes. f, 1938 Citroen Light 15.

No. 2427, 1000 le: a, 1939 Lincoln Zephyr. b, 1947 Volkswagen Beetle. c, 1959 Jaguar Mark II. d, 1968 Ford Shelby Mustang GT500. e, 1987-94 Opel/Vauxhall Senator. f, 2002 Mercedes Maybach.

No. 2428, 5000 le, 1928 Bentley 3-liter short chassis Tourer. No. 2429, 5000 le, 1999 Ferrari 360 Modena.

2001, Apr. 30 ***Perf. 13¾***

Sheets of 6, #a-f, + 6 labels

2426-2427 A356 Set of 2 12.50 12.50

Souvenir Sheets

2428-2429 A356 Set of 2 10.50 10.50

Butterflies A357

Designs: 250 le, Eurema floricola. 400 le, Papilio dardanus. 800 le, Amauris nossima. 1500 le, Gideona lucasi.

No. 2431, 1100 le: a, Papilio dardanus. b, Cymothoe sangaris. c, Epiphora albida. d, African giant swallowtail. e, Papilio nobilis nobilis. f, Charaxes hadnanus.

No. 2432, 1100 le: a, Charaxes lucretia. b, Euxanthe closslex. c, Charaxes phenix. d, Charaxes acraeades. e, Charaxes protoclea azota. f, Charaxes lydiae.

No. 2433, 5000 le, Clotis zoe. No. 2434, 5000 le, Acraea ranaualona, vert.

Perf. 13¼x13½, 13½x13¼

2001, Apr. 30 **Litho.**

2430-2433 A357 Set of 4 3.25 3.25

Sheets of 6, #a-f

2434-2435 A357 Set of 2 14.50 14.50

Souvenir Sheets

2436-2437 A357 Set of 2 11.00 11.00

Queen Elizabeth II, 75th Birthday — A358

No. 2438: a, Wearing hat. b, With infant. c, Wearing crown. d, Wearing black blouse.

2001, June 18 **Litho.** ***Perf. 14***

2438 A358 2000 le Sheet of 4, #a-d 8.25 8.25

Souvenir Sheet

Perf. 13¾

2439 A358 5000 le As older woman 5.25 5.25

No. 2438 contains four 28x42mm stamps.

Japanese Art — A359

Designs: 50 le, Iziu Chinuki No Hi, by Hokkei, horiz. 100 le, A Visit to Enoshima, by Kiyonaga Torii, horiz. 150 le, Inn on a Harbor, by Sadahide, horiz. 200 le, Entrance to Foreigner's Establishment, by Sadahide, horiz. 250 le, Courtesans at Cherry Blossom Time, by Kiyonaga, horiz. 300 le, Cherry Blossom Viewing at Ueno, by Toyohara Chikanobu, horiz. 400 le, A Summer Evening at a Restaurant by the Sumida River, by Torii, horiz. 500 le, Ichikana Yaozo I As Samurai, by Buncho. 600 le, The Actor Nakamura Noshoi II as a Street Walker, by Shunzan Katsukawa. 800 le, Arashi Sangoro II Hosoban, by Shokosai. 1500 le, bando Mitsugoro I by Shunko. No. 2451, 2000 le, Matsumoto Koshiro II, by Masanobu.

No. 2452, 2000 le: a, Nakamura Shikan II and Nakamura Baiko, by Shigeharu. b, Women Making Rice Cakes, by Shunsho. c, Youth Sending Letter by Arrow, by Harushige. d, Woman with green sash from Six Girls, by Eisho.

No. 2453, 2000 le: a, Woman with checked kimono, from Six Girls. b, Courtesan on a Bench, by Eiri. c, Courtesan and Her Two Kamuro, by Suzuki Harunobu. d, Clearing Weather at Awazu, by Shigemasa.

No. 2454, 2000 le - Paintings by Harunobu: a, Promenade. b, Wine Tasters. c, Rain in May. d, Lovers by the Wall.

No. 2455, 2000 le - Paintings by Harunobu: a, Young Woman Attended by Maid. b, Lovers by Lespedeza Bush. c, Girl Contemplating a Landscape. d, Young Man Unrolling a Hanging Scroll.

No. 2456, 5000 le, Searching for the Hermit, by Harunobu. No. 2457, 5000 le, Courtesan and Two Kamuro, by Harunobu. No. 2458, 5000 le, Drying Clothes, by Harunobu. No. 2459, 5000 le, Komachi Praying For Rain, by Harunobu. No. 2460, 5000 le, Girl Contemplating Landscape, by Harunobu.

2001, July 2 ***Perf. 13½***

2440-2451 A359 Set of 12 7.25 7.25

Sheets of 4, #a-d

2452-2455 A359 Set of 4 32.50 32.50

Souvenir Sheets

2456-2460 A359 Set of 5 26.00 26.00

Phila Nippon '01, Japan (#2452-2460).

Marlene Dietrich — A360

No. 2461: a, Looking over shoulder. b, Wearing necklace. c, Wearing coat with flower. d, Holding cigarette.

2001, June 18 **Litho.** ***Perf. 13¾***

2461 A360 2000 le Sheet of 4, #a-d 8.25 8.25

Toulouse-Lautrec Paintings — A361

No. 2462, horiz.: a, A La Mie. b, A Corner of the Moulin de la Gallete. c, The Start of the Quadrille.

5000 le, La Goulue.

2001, June 18

2462 A361 2200 le Sheet of 3, #a-c 7.00 7.00

Souvenir Sheet

2463 A361 5000 le multi 5.25 5.25

Monet Paintings — A362

No. 2464, horiz.: a, The Road to Vétheuil, Winter. b, The Church at Vétheuil, Snow. c, Breakup of the Ice Near Vétheuil. d, The Boulevard de Pontoise at Argenteuil, Snow.

5000 le, Irises by the Pond.

2001, June 18

2464 A362 1500 le Sheet of 4, #a-d 6.25 6.25

Souvenir Sheet

2465 A362 5000 le multi 5.25 5.25

Giuseppe Verdi (1813-1901), Opera Composer — A363

No. 2466: a, Vladimir Popov. b, Enrico Caruso. c, Rudolf Bockelmann. d, Stage.
5000 le, Aprile Millo and Barseq Tumayan.

2001, June 18 ***Perf. 14***

2466 A363 1700 le Sheet of 4, #a-d 7.00 7.00

Souvenir Sheet

2467 A363 5000 le multi 5.25 5.25

Royal Navy Submarines, Cent. — A364

No. 2468: a, C Class submarine. b, HMS Spartan. c, HMS Exeter. d, HMS Chatham. e, HMS Verdun. f, HMS Marlborough.
5000 le, HMS Vanguard.

2001, June 18

2468 A364 1100 le Sheet of 6, #a-f 7.00 7.00

Souvenir Sheet

2469 A364 5000 le multi 5.25 5.25

US Civil War — A365

No. 2470, 2000 le - Generals: a, Ulysses S. Grant. b, John Bell Hood. c, Jeb Stuart. d, Robert E. Lee.
No. 2471, 2000 le: a, Gen. Joshua Chamberlain. b, Gen. Stonewall Jackson. c, Gen. George McClellan. d, Adm. David Farragut.
No. 2472, 2000 le - Battle scenes: a, Shiloh. b, Bull Run. c, Fair Oaks. d, Chattanooga.
No. 2473, 2000 le - Battle scenes: a, Fredericksburg. b, Gettysburg. c, Mobile Bay. d, Fort Sumter.

No. 2474, 5000 le, Gen. William Tecumseh Sherman. No. 2475, 5000 le, Gen. George A. Custer. No. 2476, 5000 le, Battle of Vicksburg. No. 2477, 5000 le, Battle of Antietam.

2001, Aug. 27

Sheets of 4, #a-d

2470-2473 A365 Set of 4 32.50 32.50

Souvenir Sheets

2474-2477 A365 Set of 4 21.00 21.00

Horses in Literature and Mythology — A366

No. 2478, 1100 le: a, Piebald, from National Velvet, by Enid Bagnold. b, Strider, by Leo Tolstoy. c, Black Beauty, by Anna Sewell. d, Red Pony, by John Steinbeck. e, Black Stallion, by Walter Farley. f, Misty of Chincoteague, by Marguerite Henry.
No. 2479, 1100 le: a, Arvak Alsvid. b, Pegasus. c, Sleipnir. d, Veillanfif. e, Grani. f, Galathe, from Troilus and Cressida, by William Shakespeare.
No. 2480, 5000 le, Rocinante, from Don Quixote, by Miguel de Cervantes. No. 2481, 5000 le, Xanthus and Balius.

2001, Feb. 27 **Litho.** ***Perf. 14***

Sheets of 6, #a-f

2478-2479 A366 Set of 2 14.00 14.00

Souvenir Sheets

2480-2481 A366 Set of 2 10.50 10.50

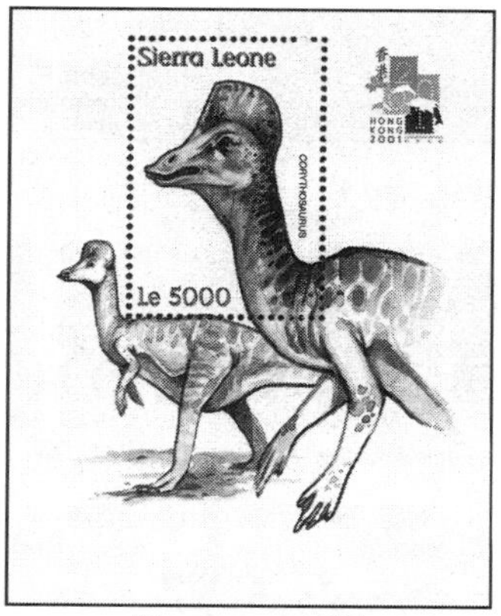

Dinosaurs — A367

No. 2482, 1000 le: a, Acrocanthosaurus. b, Edmontosaurus. c, Archaeopteryx. d, Hadrosaurus. e, Mongolian avimimus. f, Pachyrhinosaurus. g, Iguanodons (with tree trunk). h, Iguanodons, diff.
No. 2483, 1000 le, horiz.: a, Albertosaurus. b, Pteranodon ingens. c, Asiatic iguanodon. d, Sordes. e, Coelophysis. f, Saichania. g, Bactrosaurus. h, Triceratops.
No. 2484, 5000 le, Corythosaurus. No. 2485, 5000 le, Stenonychosaurus.

2001, Mar. 1 ***Perf. 13½***

Sheets of 8, #a-h

2482-2483 A367 Set of 2 17.00 17.00

Souvenir Sheets

2484-2485 A367 Set of 2 10.50 10.50

Hong Kong 2001 Stamp Exhibition.

Butterflies — A368

No. 2486, 1100 le: a, Teinopalpus imperialis. b, Swallowtail. c, Doris. d, Northern Jezebel. e, Beautiful monarch. f, Gaudy commodore.
No. 2487, 1100 le: a, Plain tiger. b, Tiger. c, Morpho cypris. d, Castnia litus. e, Dismorphia nemesis. f, Blue and yellow butterfly (inscribed African violets).
No. 2488, 5000 le, Scarce swallowtail. No. 2489, 5000 le, Clouded yellow, vert.

2001, Apr. 30

Sheets of 6, #a-f

2486-2487 A368 Set of 2 14.50 14.50

Souvenir Sheets

2488-2489 A368 Set of 2 11.00 11.00

Photomosaic of Queen Elizabeth II — A369

2001, June 18 ***Perf. 14***

2490 A369 1000 le multi 1.10 1.10

Printed in sheets of 8.

Mao Zedong (1893-1976) — A370

No. 2492, 1100 le - Map of China and Mao: a, Without hat. b, With green cap. c, With blue cap.
No. 2493, 1100 le - Red frame and Mao with: a, Uniform. b, Shirt with open collar. d, Cap.
No. 2493, 5000 le, Mao wearing black suit. No. 2494, 5000 le, Mao in white.

2001, June 18

Sheets of 3, #a-c

2491-2492 A370 Set of 2 7.00 7.00

Souvenir Sheets

2493-2494 A370 Set of 2 10.50 10.50

Ferrari Automobiles — A371

Designs: 100 le, 2001 360 Challenge. 500 le, 1971 712 Can Am. 600 le, 1970 512M. 1000 le, 1988 F40. 1500 le, 1982 365 GT4/BB. 2000 le, 1972 365 GTB/4.

2001, Oct. 8 ***Perf. 13¾***

2495-2500 A371 Set of 6 6.00 6.00

Souvenir Sheets

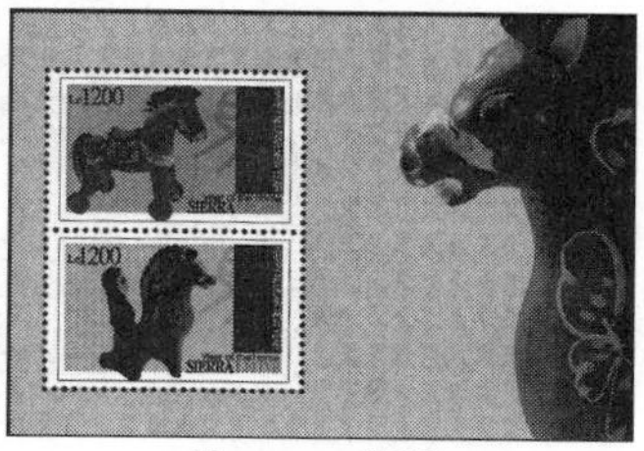

Horses — A372

Chinese Character for Horse — A373

No. 2501: a, Green background. b, Blue background.
No. 2502 - "2002" in: a, Green. b, Red. c, Orange. d, Purple.

2001, Nov. 29 ***Perf. 13***

2501 A372 1200 le Sheet of 2, #a-b 2.50 2.50

Perf. 13x13¼

2502 A373 1200 le Sheet of 4, #a-d 5.00 5.00

New Year 2002 (Year of the Horse).

2002 World Cup Soccer Championships, Japan and Korea — A374

No. 2503, 1400 le: a, Newspaper article, 1950. b, Jules Rimet, 1954. c, Pele and teammates, 1958. d, Vava and Schroiff, 1962. e, Bobby Charlton, 1966. f, Pele, 1970.
No. 2504, 1400 le: a, Daniel Passarella, 1978. b, Karl-Heinz Rummenigge, 1982. c, Diego Maradona, 1986. d, Roger Milla, 1990. e, Romario, 1994. f, Zinedine Zidane, 1998.
No. 2505, 5000 le, Head from Jules Rimet trophy, 1930. No. 2506, 5000 le, Head and globe from World Cup trophy, 2002.

2001, Dec. 7 ***Perf. 13¾x14¼***

Sheets of 6, #a-f

2503-2504 A374 Set of 2 17.00 17.00

Souvenir Sheets

Perf. 14½x14¼

2505-2506 A374 Set of 2 10.00 10.00

Christmas A375

Paintings by Filippo Lippi: 300 le, Madonna of Humility. 600 le, Annunciation. 1500 le,

Annunciation, vert. 2000 le, Adoration of the Child and Saints, vert.
5000 le, Barbadori Altarpeice, vert.

2001, Dec. 26 ***Perf. 14***
2507-2510 A375 Set of 4 4.50 4.50

Souvenir Sheet

2511 A375 5000 le multi 5.00 5.00

Queen Mother Type of 1999 Redrawn

No. 2512: a, With Duke of York and Princess Elizabeth, 1926. b, In 1979. c, In Nairobi, 1959. d, In 1991.
4000 le, With crown, 1937.

2001, Dec. ***Perf. 14***

Yellow Orange Frames

2512 A307 1300 le Sheet of 4, #a-d, + label 5.25 5.25

Souvenir Sheet

Perf. 13¾

2513 A307 4000 le multi 4.00 4.00

Queen Mother's 101st birthday. No. 2513 contains one 38x51mm stamp with a slightly darker backdrop than that found on No. 2208. Sheet margins of Nos. 2512-2513 lack embossing and gold arms and frames found on Nos. 2207-2208.

SOS Children's Village — A376

2002, Jan. 24 ***Perf. 14***
2514 A376 2000 le multi 2.00 2.00

Steam and Electric Inventions and Their Inventors — A377

No. 2515, 1100 le: a, The Rocket steam locomotive, 1829. b, High-speed electric passenger train. c, 1863 Steam pumper. d, Early electric trolley. e, 1893 Steam automobile. f, Electric monorail.
No. 2516, 1100 le: a, Early steam pumper. b, Telephone. c, Steam liner. d, Battery and light bulb. e, 1770 Steam carriage. f, Electric passenger train.
No. 2517, 1100 le: a, Robert Fulton and steamboat. b, Thomas Edison and light bulb. c, 1899 T9 steam locomotive. d, Radio and antennae. e, James Watt, and steam engine diagram. f, Alexander Graham Bell and telephone.
No. 2518, 5000 le, 1899 Steam locomotive. No. 2519, 5000 le, Telephone, radio and light bulb. No. 2520, 5000 le, Benjamin Franklin, vert.

Perf. 13¼x13½, 13½x13¼

2002, Jan. 24

Sheets of 6, #a-f

2515-2517 A377 Set of 3 20.00 20.00

Souvenir Sheets

2518-2520 A377 Set of 3 15.00 15.00

United We Stand — A378

2002, Feb. 6 ***Perf. 13½x13¼***
2521 A378 2000 le multi 2.25 2.25

Reign of Queen Elizabeth II, 50th Anniv. — A379

No. 2522: a, With young Prince Charles and Princess Anne. b, Wearing tiara and stole, looking forward. c, Wearing tiara and stole, looking right. d, Wearing hat.
5000 le, Wearing hat and gloves.

2002, Feb. 6 ***Perf. 14¼***
2522 A379 2000 le Sheet of 4, #a-d 9.00 9.00

Souvenir Sheet

2523 A379 5000 le multi 5.50 5.50

AIR POST STAMPS

Catalogue values for unused stamps in this section are for Never Hinged items.

Independence — Progress Issue

Nos. 197, 199, 204 and 206 Surcharged Like Nos. 242-247 plus "AIRMAIL" in Carmine, Red, Violet, Blue or Orange

Perf. 13, 13½

1963, Apr. 27 Wmk. 4 Engr.

Center in Black

C1 A27 7p on 1½p (C) .20 .20
C2 A27 1sh3p on 1½p (R) .20 .20
C3 A28 2sh6p brn org (V) .40 .40
C4 A28 3sh on 3p (Bl) .40 .40
C5 A28 6sh on 3p (O) .50 .50
C6 A27 11sh on 10sh (C) 1.60 1.60
C7 A27 11sh on £1 (C) 500.00 175.00
Nos. C1-C6 (6) 3.30 3.30

Nos. 221, 224, 213, 223 and 207 Surcharged or Overprinted in Brown, Red, Black, Violet, Ultramarine or Orange

Perf. 13x13½, 13½x13, 13

1963, Nov. 4 Wmk. 4, 336

C8 A31 7p on 3p (Br) .20 .20
C9 A32 1sh3p blue & blk (R) .25 .25
C10 A30 2sh6p on 4p (Bk) .50 .50
C11 A31 3sh on 3p (V) .60 .60
C12 A32 6sh on 6p (U) 1.25 1.25
C13 A27 £1 org & blk (O) 8.50 8.50
Nos. C8-C13 (6) 11.30 11.30

Overprint is in 6 lines on Nos. C8, C11 and C12. A number of surcharge varieties and errors exist.

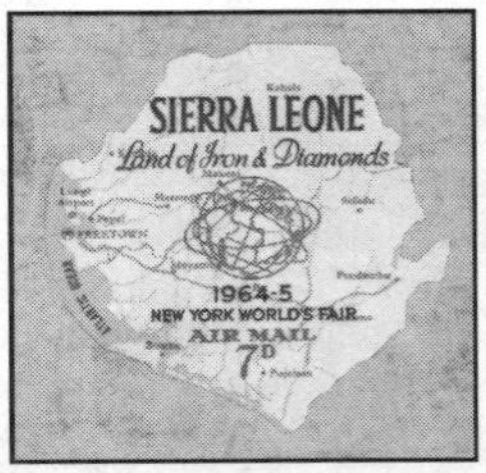

Unisphere and Map of Sierra Leone — AP1

Engraved and Lithographed

1964, Feb. 10 Unwmk. *Die Cut*

Self-adhesive

C14 AP1 7p multicolored .20 .20
C15 AP1 9p multicolored .20 .20
C16 AP1 1sh3p multicolored .20 .20
C17 AP1 2sh6p multicolored .35 .35
C18 AP1 3sh6p multicolored .50 .50
C19 AP1 6sh multicolored .90 .90
C20 AP1 11sh multicolored 1.40 1.40
Nos. C14-C20 (7) 3.75 3.75

New York World's Fair, 1964-65.
For surcharge see No. C33.

John F. Kennedy AP2

1964, May 11

Self-adhesive

C21 AP2 7p multicolored .20 .20
C22 AP2 9p multicolored .20 .20
C23 AP2 1sh3p multicolored .25 .25
C24 AP2 2sh6p multicolored .40 .40
C25 AP2 3sh6p multicolored .60 .60
C26 AP2 6sh multicolored 1.10 1.10
C27 AP2 11sh multicolored 1.75 1.75
Nos. C21-C27 (7) 4.50 4.50

For surcharges see Nos. C32, C34-C36.

Nos. 241, 213, 219 and 218 Surcharged in Dark Blue, Black, Red or Violet Blue

Perf. 11½x11, 13½x13, 13x13½

1964, Aug. 4 Engr. Wmk. 336

C28 A36 7c on 1sh3p (#241) (DB) .25 .25
C29 A30 20c on 4p (#213) .40 .40
C30 A29 30c on 10sh (#219) (R) .70 .70
C31 A29 40c on 5sh (#218) (VB) .85 .85
Nos. C28-C31 (4) 2.20 2.20

Map-shaped Issues of 1964 Surcharged in Red or Black

Engraved and Lithographed

1964-65 Unwmk. *Die Cut*

C32 AP2 7c on 7p (#C21) (R) .20 .20
C33 AP1 7c on 9p (#C15) .85 .85
C34 AP2 60c on 9p (#C22) 1.25 1.25
C35 AP2 1 le on 1sh3p (#C23) (R) 2.00 2.00
C36 AP2 2 le on 11sh (#C27) 4.25 4.25
Nos. C32-C36 (5) 8.55 8.55

Issue dates: Aug. 4, 1964, Nos. C35-C36. Jan. 20, 1965, Nos. C32, C34. April, 1965, No. C33.

Regular Issue of 1963 Surcharged like Nos. 300-305 with "AIRMAIL" added

Wmk. 336

1965, May 19 Photo. *Perf. 14*

Designs of Surcharge: No. C37, C39-C40, Sir Milton Margai and Sir Winston Churchill. No. C38, Margai. No. C41, Churchill.

C37 A35 7c on 2p (#230) .20 .20
C38 A34 15c on ½p (#227) .40 .40
C39 A35 30c on 6p (#233) .75 .75
C40 A35 1 le on £1 (#239) 2.75 2.75
C41 A34 2 le on 10sh (#238) 5.50 5.50
Nos. C37-C41 (5) 9.60 9.60

The portraits and inscription on No. C39 are white, the denomination and "AIRMAIL" are orange.
Ten more surcharges were issued Nov. 9, 1965: "2c" on Nos. C16, C23 and C25. "3c" on Nos. C14 and C22. "5c" on Nos. C17-C19, C24, and C26. Value $4 each.
One further surcharge was issued Jan. 28, 1966: "TWO/Leones" on No. C39. Value $10.

Type of Regular Issue and

Diamond Necklace AP3

Litho.; Reversed Embossing

1965, Dec. 17 Unwmk. *Die Cut*

Self-adhesive

C53 AP3 7c blk, grn, gold & bl .35 .35
C54 AP3 15c blk, brnz, car & bl .75 .75

Engr. and Embossed on Paper

C55 A41 40c multi, *cream* 1.75 1.75
Nos. C53-C55 (3) 2.85 2.85

Various advertisements printed on peelable paper backing. Nos. C54-C55 have side tabs for handling and come packed in boxes of 100. No. C53 is without side tab and comes 25 stamps attached to one sheet.
For overprints and surcharges see Nos. C68-C69, C79-C83.

Nos. 248, 229, 232, 234 and 236 Surcharged and Overprinted: "AIRMAIL/FIVE YEARS/INDEPENDENCE/1961-1966"

1966, Apr. 27 Wmk. 336

C56 A37 7c on 3p pur & red .20 .20
C57 A34 15c on 1sh multi .35 .35
C58 A34 25c on 2sh6p multi .55 .55
C59 A34 50c on 1½p multi 1.10 1.10
C60 A34 1 le on 4p multi 2.50 2.50
Nos. C56-C60 (5) 4.70 4.70

The denomination on No. C60 is spelled out "One Leone."

Self-adhesive & Die Cut
Nos. C61-C131, C135-C142 are self-adhesive and die cut.

Gold Coin Type of Regular Issue

Designs: 7c, 10c, ¼ Golde coin. 15c, 30c, ½ Golde coin. 50c, 2 le, 1 Golde coin. (7c, 15c, 50c, Map of Sierra Leone. 10c, 30c, 2 le, Lion's head.)
Diameter: 7c, 10c, 38mm; 15c, 30c, 54mm; 50c, 2 le, 82mm.

Lithographed; Embossed on Gilt Foil

1966, Nov. 12 Unwmk.

C61 A42 7c red & orange .20 .20
C62 A42 10c dull blue & red .20 .20
C63 A42 15c red & orange .20 .20
C64 A42 30c black & rose lilac .40 .40
C65 A42 50c rose lilac & emer .75 .75
C66 A42 2 le green & black 3.75 3.75
Nos. C61-C66 (6) 5.50 5.50

Advertising printed on paper backing.

Type of Regular Issue, 1965 and No. C55 Surcharged

1967, Dec. 2 Engr. & Embossed

C67	A41	10c multi (red frame), *cream*	.50	.50
a.		Black frame	.50	.50
C68	A41	11½c on 40c multi, *cr*	.40	.40
C69	A41	25c on 40c multi, *cr*	1.00	1.00
		Nos. C67-C69 (3)	1.90	1.90

Eagle — AP4

Embossed Foil on Black Paper

1967, Dec. 2 Unwmk.

C70	AP4	9½c black, gold & red	.75	.75
C71	AP4	15c black, gold & grn	.90	.90

Various advertisements printed on peelable paper backing. See Nos. C98-C99, C118-C124.

Map Type of Regular Issue

Designs: Each denomination shows map of Africa with map of one of the following countries — Portuguese Guinea, South Africa, Mozambique, Rhodesia, South West Africa or Angola. Sheets of 30 (6x5) have 5 horizontal rows containing one stamp of each design.

1968, Sept. 25 Litho.

C72	A43	7½c multicolored	.30	.30
C73	A43	9½c multicolored	.45	.45
C74	A43	14½c multicolored	.65	.65
C75	A43	18½c multicolored	.75	.75
C76	A43	25c multicolored	1.25	1.25
C77	A43	1 le multicolored	7.50	7.50
C78	A43	2 le multicolored	17.50	17.50
		Nos. C72-C78 (7)	28.40	28.40
		7 Strips of 6, 1 of each design (42)	170.40	

No. C55 Overprinted and Surcharged in Red Similar to Nos. 364-368

Engraved and Embossed on Paper

1968, Nov. 30

C79	A41	6½c on 40c multi	.20	.20
C80	A41	17½c on 40c multi	.40	.40
C81	A41	22½c on 40c multi	.40	.40
C82	A41	28½c on 40c multi	.55	.55
C83	A41	40c multicolored	.85	.85
		Nos. C79-C83 (5)	2.40	2.40

Scroll Type of Regular Issue

7½c, #C54. 9½c, #C70. 20c, #C16. 30c, #C26. 50c, #165. 2 le, #207 with "2nd Year of Independence" overprint. All are horiz.

1969, Mar. 1 Litho.

C84	A44	7½c multicolored	.25	.25
C85	A44	9½c multicolored	.30	.30
C86	A44	20c multicolored	.60	.60
C87	A44	30c multicolored	.90	.90
C88	A44	50c multicolored	2.25	2.25
C89	A44	2 le multicolored	15.00	15.00
		Nos. C84-C89 (6)	19.30	19.30

Various advertisements printed on peelable paper backing. No. C84 has side tab for handling and comes packed in boxes of 50. Nos. C85-C89 are without side tabs and come 20 stamps attached to one sheet.

For surcharges see Nos. C135-C136.

Pepel Port Types of Regular Issue

Designs: 7½c, 15c, Globe, tanker, flags of Sierra Leone and Japan. Anvil Shape with Flags of Sierra Leone and: 9½c, 2 le, Union Jack. 25c, Netherlands. 1 le, West Germany.

1969, July 10

C90	A45	7½c multicolored	.20	.20
C91	A46	9½c multicolored	.20	.20
C92	A45	15c multicolored	.25	.25
C93	A46	25c multicolored	.40	.40
C94	A46	1 le multicolored	1.60	1.60
C95	A46	2 le multicolored	3.25	3.25
		Nos. C90-C95 (6)	5.90	5.90

Various advertisements printed on peelable paper backing. No. C90 has side tab for handling and comes packed in boxes of 50. Nos. C91-C95 are without side tabs and come 20 stamps attached to one sheet.

Bank Type of Regular Issue

Lithographed; Gold Impressed

1969, Sept. 10

C96	A47	9½c yel grn, vio & gold	.90	.90

Advertising printed on peelable paper backing; 20 imperf. stamps to a sheet of backing, roulette 10.

Cola Nut Type of Regular Issue and Type of 1967

Typo.; Embossed on White Paper

1969, Sept. 10

C97	A40	7c yel, mar & car	.40	.40

Embossed Foil on Black Paper

C98	AP4	9½c blk, gold & bl	.50	.50
C99	AP4	15c blk, gold & red	.75	.75
		Nos. C97-C99 (3)	1.65	1.65

No. C97 has side tab for handling and comes packed in boxes of 100. Nos. C98-C99 have advertisements printed on peelable paper backing, side tabs and come packed in boxes of 50.

Boy Scout, Lord Baden-Powell and Scout Emblem — AP5

1969, Dec. 6 Litho.

C100	AP5	7½c multicolored	.50	.40
C101	AP5	9½c multicolored	.60	.50
C102	AP5	15c multicolored	1.25	.80
C103	AP5	22c multicolored	2.00	1.40
C104	AP5	55c multicolored	8.00	6.50
C105	AP5	3 le multicolored	100.00	72.50
		Nos. C100-C105 (6)	112.35	82.10

60th anniv. of the Sierra Leone Boy Scouts. Various advertising printed on peelable paper backing. No. C100 has side tab for handling and comes packed in boxes of 100. Nos. C101-C105 are without side tabs and come 20 stamps attached to one sheet.

No. 357 Surcharged "AIRMAIL" and New Denomination in Metallic Emerald, Lilac, Blue, Green, Bronze or Silver

1970, Mar 28

C106	A43	7½c on ½c (E)	.30	.30
C107	A43	9½c on ½c (L)	.40	.40
C108	A43	15c on ½c (Bl)	.55	.55
C109	A43	28c on ½c (G)	1.00	1.00
C110	A43	40c on ½c (Br)	1.75	1.75
C111	A43	2 le on ½c (S)	9.00	9.00
		Nos. C106-C111 (6)	13.00	13.00

See design paragraph over No. 357.

EXPO Type of Regular Issue

Maps of Sierra Leone and Japan.

1970, June 22 Litho.

C112	A49	7½c multicolored	.20	.20
C113	A49	9½c multicolored	.20	.20
C114	A49	15c multicolored	.35	.35
C115	A49	25c multicolored	.70	.70
C116	A49	50c multicolored	1.50	1.50
C117	A49	3 le multicolored	7.75	7.75
		Nos. C112-C117 (6)	10.70	10.70

Various advertising printed on peelable paper backing.

Eagle Type of 1967

1970, Oct. 3 Embossed Foil

C118	AP4	7½c crim & gold	.45	.45
C119	AP4	9½c emer & cop	.55	.50
C120	AP4	15½c grnsh bl & sil	.85	.65
C121	AP4	25c brt red lil & gold	1.40	1.10
C122	AP4	50c gold & emer	2.75	2.25
C123	AP4	1 le silver & dk bl	5.50	4.50
C124	AP4	2 le gold & brt bl	11.00	9.25
		Nos. C118-C124 (7)	22.50	18.70

Advertisements printed on peelable paper backing. Issued in sheets of 10.

"Treasure of Sierra Leone" Diamond — AP6

Lithographed and Embossed

1970, Dec. 30

C125	AP6	7½c multicolored	.20	.20
C126	AP6	9½c multicolored	.30	.30
C127	AP6	15c multicolored	.50	.50
C128	AP6	25c multicolored	.50	.50
C129	AP6	75c multicolored	5.00	4.00
C130	AP6	2 le multicolored	22.50	17.50
		Nos. C125-C130 (6)	29.00	23.00

Diamond industry. Advertisement printed on peelable paper backing. Sheets of 20.

Traffic Type of Regular Issue

1971, Mar. 1 Litho.

C131	A53	9½c vio blue & org	.75	.75

Advertisements printed on peelable paper backing.

Nos. 211, 215, 228 and C87 Surcharged in Dark Red, Dark Blue or Black

a

b

1971, Mar. 1 Engr. Wmk. 336

C132	A29(a)	10c on 2p (DR)	.35	.30
C133	A29(a)	20c on 1sh (DB)	.70	.65

Photo. Perf. 14

C134	A35(a)	50c on 1p (Bk)	1.75	1.50

Unwmk.

Litho. Imperf.

C135	A44(b)	70c on 30c (DB)	2.75	2.50
C136	A44(b)	1 le on 30c (Bk)	4.00	3.25
		Nos. C132-C136 (5)	9.55	8.20

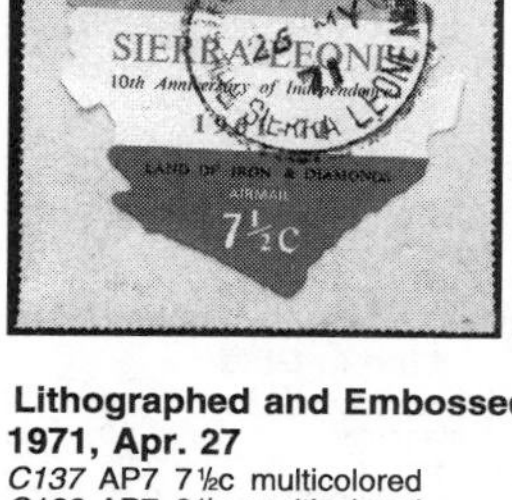

Lion's Head and Bugles AP7

Lithographed and Embossed (Gold)

1971, Apr. 27

C137	AP7	7½c multicolored	.20	.20
C138	AP7	9½c multicolored	.20	.20
C139	AP7	15c multicolored	.25	.25
C140	AP7	25c multicolored	.45	.45
C141	AP7	75c multicolored	1.75	1.75
C142	AP7	2 le multicolored	6.00	6.00
		Nos. C137-C142 (6)	8.85	8.85

10th anniversary of independence. Advertisements printed on peelable paper backing. Stamps are in shape of Sierra Leone map and in flag colors.

Guma Valley Dam and Bank Emblem — AP8

1975, Jan. 14 Litho. Perf. 13½

C143	AP8	15c multicolored	1.00	1.00

African Development Bank, 10th anniv.

Congo River Type of 1975

1975, Aug. 24 Litho. Perf. 13x13½

C144	A57	20c multicolored	.75	.75

Mano River Type of 1975

1975, Oct. 3 Perf. 13x13½

C145	A58	15c multicolored	.60	.60

SINGAPORE

ˈsiŋ-ə-ˌpor

LOCATION — An island just off the southern tip of the Malay Peninsula, south of Johore
GOVT. — Republic in British Commonwealth
AREA — 250 sq. mi.
POP. — 3,531,600 (1999 est.)
CAPITAL — Singapore

Singapore, Malacca and Penang were the British settlements which, together with the Federated Malay States, composed the former colony of Straits Settlements. On April 1, 1946, Singapore became a separate colony when the Straits Settlements colony was dissolved. Malacca and Penang joined the Malayan Union, which was renamed the Federation of Malaya in 1948. In 1959 Singapore became a state with internal self-government.

Singapore joined the Federation of Malaysia in 1963 and withdrew in 1965.

100 Cents = 1 Dollar

Catalogue values for all unused stamps in this country are for Never Hinged items.

Watermark

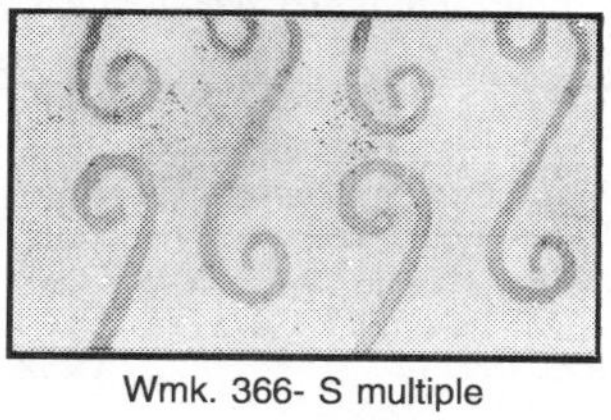

Wmk. 366- S multiple

King George VI — A1

1948 Wmk. 4 Typo. Perf. 14

1	A1	1c black	.20	.20
2	A1	2c orange	.25	.20
3	A1	3c green	.35	.20
4	A1	4c chocolate	.35	.20
6	A1	6c gray	.35	.20
7	A1	8c rose red	.45	.30
9	A1	10c plum	.40	.20

11	A1	15c ultra	2.75	.20
12	A1	20c dk green & blk	1.65	.40
14	A1	25c org & rose lilac	1.50	.20
16	A1	40c dk vio & rose red	7.25	*9.00*
17	A1	50c ultra & black	8.50	.25
18	A1	$1 vio brn & ultra	12.50	.45
19	A1	$2 rose red & emer	72.50	3.00
20	A1	$5 chocolate & emer	150.00	2.75
		Nos. 1-20 (15)	259.00	17.75
		Set, hinged	150.00	

1949-52 ***Perf. 18***

1a	A1	1c black ('52)	.65	.20
2a	A1	2c orange	.80	.20
4a	A1	4c chocolate	.90	.20
5	A1	5c rose violet ('52)	2.75	.20
6a	A1	6c gray ('52)	1.40	.20
8	A1	8c green ('52)	5.00	2.50
9a	A1	10c plum ('50)	.50	.20
10	A1	12c rose red ('52)	5.00	2.50
11a	A1	15c ultra ('50)	13.50	.30
12a	A1	20c dark green & black	3.50	1.25
13	A1	20c ultra ('52)	4.50	.75
14a	A1	25c org & rose lil ('50)	1.00	.20
15	A1	35c dk vio & rose red ('52)	4.50	3.00
16a	A1	40c dk vio & rose red ('51)	32.50	15.00
17a	A1	50c ultra & black ('50)	8.50	.20
18a	A1	$1 violet brown & ultra	15.00	.75
b.		Wmk. 4a (error)	*2,750.*	
19a	A1	$2 rose red & emer ('51)	100.00	3.00
b.		Wmk. 4a (error)	*2,750.*	
20a	A1	$5 choc & emerald ('51)	200.00	3.75
		Nos. 1a-20a (18)	400.00	34.40
		Set, hinged	260.00	

Common Design Types pictured following the introduction.

Silver Wedding Issue

Common Design Types

Inscribed: "Singapore"

1948, Oct. 25 Photo. ***Perf. 14x14½***

21	CD304	10c purple	1.00	.20

Engraved; Name Typographed

Perf. 11½x11

22	CD305	$5 light brown	120.00	27.50

UPU Issue

Common Design Types

Inscribed: "Malaya-Singapore"

Engr.; Name Typo. on 15c, 25c

Perf. 13½, 11x11½

1949, Oct. 10 Wmk. 4

23	CD306	10c rose violet	.75	.25
24	CD307	15c indigo	7.25	1.75
25	CD308	25c orange	7.25	1.25
26	CD309	50c slate	7.25	4.25
		Nos. 23-26 (4)	22.50	6.50

Coronation Issue

Common Design Type

1953, June 2 Engr. ***Perf. 13½x13***

27	CD312	10c magenta & black	1.75	.20

Chinese Sampans — A2

Sir Stamford Raffles Statue — A3

Singapore River — A4

Designs: 2c, Malay kolek. 4c, Twa-kow. 5c, Lombok sloop. 6c, Trengganu pinas. 8c, Palari. 10c, Timber tongkong. 12c, Hylam trader. 20c, Cocos-Keeling schooner. 25c, Argonaut plane. 30c, Oil tanker. 50c, Liner (M.S. Chusan). $5, Arms of Singapore.

Perf. 13½x14½

1955, Sept. 4 Photo. Wmk. 4

28	A2	1c sepia	.20	*.35*
29	A2	2c orange yellow	.20	*.75*
30	A2	4c orange brown	.40	.20
31	A2	5c magenta	.40	.20
32	A2	6c gray blue	.40	.30
33	A2	8c aqua	.95	.50
34	A2	10c dark purple	.50	.20
35	A2	12c rose red	2.00	2.00
36	A2	20c violet blue	2.00	.20
37	A2	25c orange & purple	1.10	.70
38	A2	30c purple & plum	1.60	.20
39	A2	50c bright blue	3.25	.20

Perf. 13½x14, 14x13½

Engr.

40	A3	$1 blue & purple	9.50	.20
41	A4	$2 blue green & red	32.50	1.25

Engr.; Arms Typo.

42	A3	$5 multicolored	65.00	2.75
		Nos. 28-42 (15)	120.00	10.00

For a later printing of the 10c and 50c, plates with finer screen (250) than normal (200) were used.

Singapore Lion and Administrative Center — A5

Perf. 11½x12

1959, June 1 Photo. Wmk. 314

Lion in Gold

43	A5	4c deep rose red	.60	*.65*
44	A5	10c magenta	.90	.35
45	A5	20c ultra	2.25	*2.75*
46	A5	25c yellow green	2.50	2.25
47	A5	30c bright violet	2.50	*3.00*
48	A5	50c bluish gray	3.25	3.00
		Nos. 43-48 (6)	12.00	12.00

New Constitution of Singapore.

State Flag of Singapore A6

1960, June 3 Litho. ***Perf. 13½***

49	A6	4c blue, red & yellow	1.50	.50
50	A6	10c gray, red & yellow	2.50	.75

Issued for National Day, June 3, 1960.

Hands and Map of Singapore A7

1961, June 3 Photo.

51	A7	4c brown, yellow & gray	1.00	.30
52	A7	10c green, yellow & gray	1.25	.45

Issued for National Day, June 3, 1961.

Sea Horse — A8

Malayan Fish: 4c, Tiger barb, horiz. 5c, Anemone fish, horiz. 6c, Archerfish. 10c, Harlequin fish, horiz. 20c, Butterflyfish. 25c, Two-spot gournami, horiz.

Perf. 14½x13½, 13½x14½

1962, Mar. 31 Wmk. 314

53	A8	2c lt grn & red brn	.20	*1.00*
54	A8	4c red orange & blk	.20	*.60*
a.		Black omitted	275.00	
55	A8	5c gray & red org	.20	.20
a.		Red orange omitted	275.00	
b.		Wmkd. sideways ('67)	2.00	2.00
56	A8	6c yellow & blk	.20	*.60*
57	A8	10c dk gray & red org	.40	.20
a.		Red orange omitted	175.00	
b.		Wmkd. sideways ('67)	1.00	.50
58	A8	20c blue & orange	.90	.20
a.		Orange omitted	300.00	
59	A8	25c orange & black	.90	.20
a.		Black omitted	100.00	
b.		Wmkd. sideways ('67)	.85	.25
		Nos. 53-59 (7)	3.00	3.00

For surcharge see No. 370.

Symbolic of Labor's Role in Building the Nation — A9

1962, June 3 Unwmk. ***Perf. 11½***

60	A9	4c brt rose, blk & yel	.75	.35
61	A9	10c brt blue, blk & yel	1.25	.65

Issued for National Day, June 3, 1962.

Vanda Tan Chay Yan — A10

Yellow-Breasted Sunbird — A11

Designs: 1c, Arachnis Maggie Oei, horiz. 12c, Grammatophyllum speciosum. 30c, Vanda Miss Joaquim. 50c, Shama, horiz. $1, White-breasted kingfisher, horiz. $5, White-tailed sea eagle.

Perf. 12½, 13½x13 (50c, $1), 13x13½ ($2, $5)

1963, Mar. 10 Photo. Wmk. 314

Flowers and Birds in Natural Colors

Size: 37x26mm, 26x37mm

62	A10	1c brt pink & ultra	.20	.20
a.		Wmkd. sideways ('67)	.20	.20
63	A10	8c lt blue & mag	.65	.55
64	A10	12c salmon & brown	1.25	.30
65	A10	30c tan & ol green	1.75	.20
a.		tan omitted	75.00	

Size: 35½x25½mm, 25½x35½mm

66	A11	50c yel green & blk	1.90	.20
a.		Wmkd. sideways ('66)	6.00	3.00
67	A11	$1 yellow & blk	5.75	.20
a.		Wmkd. sideways ('67)	10.00	5.00
68	A11	$2 dull blue & blk	11.00	1.10
69	A11	$5 pale blue & blk	32.50	2.75
		Nos. 62-69 (8)	55.00	5.50

See No. 76.

Government Housing Project — A12

1963, June 3 ***Perf. 12½***

70	A12	4c multicolored	.50	.30
71	A12	10c multicolored	.75	.45

Issued for National Day, June 3, 1963.

Folk Dancers — A13

1963, Aug. 8 Photo. ***Perf. 14x14½***

72	A13	5c multicolored	.45	.45

Southeast Asia Cultural Festival.

Workers, Factory and Apartment House A14

Wmk. 314 (30c), Unwmd. (15, 20c)

1966, Aug. 9 Photo. ***Perf. 12½x13***

73	A14	15c ultra & multi	.65	.25
74	A14	20c red & multi	.85	1.00
75	A14	30c yellow & multi	1.25	1.50
		Nos. 73-75 (3)	2.75	2.75

First anniversary of the Republic.

Bird Type of 1963

Design: 15c, Black-naped tern (sterna).

1966, Nov. 9 Wmk. 314 ***Perf. 12½***

Bird in Natural Colors

Size: 26x37mm

76	A11	15c blue & black	1.00	.20
a.		Orange (eye) omitted	25.00	

Marching Women, Chinese Inscription — A15

15c, Malay inscription. 50c, Tamil inscription.

Perf. 14x14½

1967, Aug. 9 Photo. Unwmk.

77 A15 6c lt brown, gray & red .45 .65
78 A15 15c multicolored .65 .20
79 A15 50c multicolored 1.40 1.40
Nos. 77-79 (3) 2.50 2.25

"Build a Vigorous Singapore" campaign.

Buildings and Map of Africa and Southeast Asia — A16

1967, Oct. 7 ***Perf. 14x13½***

Black Overprint

80 A16 10c multicolored .30 .25
81 A16 25c multicolored .70 .90
82 A16 50c multicolored 1.25 1.25
Nos. 80-82 (3) 2.25 2.40

2nd Afro-Asian Housing Cong., Oct. 7-15.
No. 80 exists without overprint.

Map of Singapore and Symbolic Worker — A17

Sword Dance — A18

Stamps are inscribed "Work for Prosperity" in English and: 6c, Chinese. 15c, Malay. 50c, Tamil.

Perf. 13½x14½

1968, Aug. 9 Photo. Unwmk.

83 A17 6c red, black & gold .20 .20
84 A17 15c brt yel grn, blk & gold .40 .35
85 A17 50c brt blue, blk & gold 1.40 1.25
Nos. 83-85 (3) 2.00 1.80

Issued for National Day, 1968.

Wmk. Rectangles (334)

1968 Photo. ***Perf. 14***

Designs: 6c, Lion dance. 10c, Bharatha Natyam, Indian dance. 15c, Tari Payong, Sumatran dance. 20c, Kathak Kali, Indian dance mask. 25c, Lu Chih Shen and Lin Chung, Chinese opera masks. 30c, Dragon dance, horiz. 50c, Tari Lilin, Malayan candle dance. 75c, Tarian Kuda Kepang, Javanese dance. $1, Yao Chi, Chinese opera mask.

86 A18 5c yellow & multi .25 .20
87 A18 6c orange & multi .35 .20
88 A18 10c blue green & multi .50 .20
89 A18 15c lt brown & multi .65 .30
a. Booklet pane of 4 ('69) 2.50
90 A18 20c brown & multi .75 .30
91 A18 25c dp car & multi 1.25 .50
92 A18 30c pink & multi 1.50 .50
93 A18 50c brown org & multi 1.75 1.00
94 A18 75c brt rose & multi 3.00 1.50
95 A18 $1 olive grn & multi 4.00 2.00
Nos. 86-95 (10) 14.00 6.70

Issue dates: 6c, 20c, 30c, 50c, 75c, Dec. 1; 5c, 10c, 15c, 25c, $1, Dec. 29.

1973 ***Perf. 13***

86a A18 5c yellow & multi 6.25 4.00
88a A18 10c blue green & multi 6.25 3.50
90a A18 20c brown & multi 8.00 6.00
91a A18 25c deep car & multi 5.50 5.00
92a A18 30c pink & multi 10.00 7.00
93a A18 50c brown org & multi 11.00 11.50
95a A18 $1 olive green & multi 15.00 9.00
Nos. 86a-95a (7) 62.00 46.00

Cogwheel and Emblem — A19

1969, Apr. 15 Unwmk. ***Perf. 13***

96 A19 15c blue, black & silver .40 .25
97 A19 30c red, black & silver .85 .65
98 A19 75c violet, black & silver 1.50 1.50
Nos. 96-98 (3) 2.75 2.40

25th Plenary Session of the Economic Commission for Asia and the Far East (ECAFE), Singapore, Apr. 15-28.

"Homes for the People" A20

Plane over Docks of Singapore A21

Perf. 13x13½

1969, July 20 Litho. Unwmk.

99 A20 25c emerald & black 1.00 .70
100 A20 50c dark blue & black 1.50 1.25

1960-69 building program of the Housing and Development Board.

1969, Aug. 9 ***Perf. 14x14½***

30c, UN emblem and map of Singapore. 75c, Flags and map of Malaya and Borneo. $1, Uplifted hands and Singapore flag. $5, Tail of Japanese plane and searchlights. $10, Statue of Sir Thomas Stamford Raffles.

101 A21 15c yel, blk & org *2.75* .50
102 A21 30c brt blue & blk *2.75* 1.50
103 A21 75c orange & multi *6.00* 1.75
104 A21 $1 red & black *11.00* 8.75
105 A21 $5 gray, blk & red *40.00* *47.50*
106 A21 $10 emerald & blk *52.50* 50.00
a. Souv. sheet of 6, #101-106 *500.00* 500.00
Nos. 101-106 (6) *115.00* 110.00

Sesquicent. of the founding of Singapore.

Mirudhangam, South Indian Drum — A22

Musical Instruments: 4c, Pi Pa, Chinese, 4 strings, vert. $2, Rebab, Malay violin, 3 strings, vert. $5, Vina, Indian, 7 strings. $10, Ta Ku, Chinese drum.

1969 Photo. Wmk. 366 ***Perf. 13***

107 A22 1c multicolored .20 *2.25*
108 A22 4c multicolored .80 *2.75*
109 A22 $2 multicolored 3.50 1.00
110 A22 $5 multicolored 13.00 1.50
111 A22 $10 multicolored 35.00 15.00
Nos. 107-111 (5) 52.50 22.50

Issued: 1c, 4c, $2, $5, Nov. 10; $10, Dec. 6.

Sea Shells — A23

Designs: 30c, Tropical fish. 75c, Greater flamingo and helmeted hornbill. $1, Orchids.

Perf. 13½

1970, Mar. 15 Unwmk. Litho.

112 A23 15c pale vio & multi .75 .25
113 A23 30c lt blue & multi 2.25 1.00
114 A23 75c yellow & multi 6.00 4.25
115 A23 $1 lt green & multi 7.00 7.00
a. Souvenir sheet of 4, #112-115 25.00 20.00
Nos. 112-115 (4) 16.00 12.50

EXPO '70 International Exposition, Osaka, Japan, Mar. 15-Sept. 13.

Child Playing (Kindergarten) — A24

50c, Sports activities. 75c, Cultural activities.

1970, July Unwmk. ***Perf. 13½***

116 A24 15c deep orange & blk .75 .25
117 A24 50c orange, blk & vio bl 2.50 2.25
118 A24 75c blk & dp lilac rose 3.75 3.50
Nos. 116-118 (3) 7.00 6.00

People's Association, 10th anniversary.

Soldier and Map of Singapore — A25

Map and soldiers in various positions.

1970, Aug. 9 Litho. Unwmk.

119 A25 15c emerald, blk & org 1.25 .20
120 A25 50c org, blk & brt mag 3.75 3.00
121 A25 $1 brt mag, blk & emer 5.00 *7.00*
Nos. 119-121 (3) 10.00 10.20

National military service.

Runners A26

1970, Aug. 23 Photo. ***Perf. 13***

122 A26 10c shown 2.00 2.00
123 A26 15c Swimmers 2.50 2.50
124 A26 25c Badminton 2.75 2.75
125 A26 50c Automobile race 3.25 3.25
a. Strip of 4, #122-125 10.00 10.00

1970 Festival of Sports.

Ship and Emblem of National Line (Neptune Oriental Lines) — A27

Designs: 30c, Ship in first container berth. 75c, Ship repairing and ship building.

1970, Nov. 1 Litho. ***Perf. 12***

126 A27 15c vio bl, lem & red 2.75 2.75
127 A27 30c dp ultra & lemon 5.75 5.75
128 A27 75c red & lemon 9.50 9.50
Nos. 126-128 (3) 18.00 18.00

Singapore shipping industry.

Flags of Commonwealth Nations — A28

Designs: 15c, Circular arrangement of names of Commonwealth members. 30c, Flags arranged in circle. $1, Flags (different arrangement).

1971, Jan. 14 ***Perf. 15x14½***

Size: 46½x31mm

129 A28 15c gold & multi .75 .75
130 A28 30c gold & multi 1.75 1.75
131 A28 75c gold & multi 3.25 3.25

Size: 67x31mm

Perf. 14

132 A28 $1 gold & multi 4.25 4.25
Nos. 129-132 (4) 10.00 10.00

Commonwealth Heads of Government Meeting, Singapore, Jan. 12-14.

Cycle Rickshaws A29

Houses of Worship in Singapore — A30

Perf. 11½

1971, Apr. 4 Unwmk. Litho.

133 A29 15c shown .60 .20
134 A29 20c Sampans .90 .55
135 A29 30c Market place 2.75 1.25

Perf. 13x13½

136 A30 50c Waterfront 3.25 *5.00*
137 A30 75c shown 6.00 *6.50*
Nos. 133-137 (5) 13.50 13.50

Tourist publicity.

Chinese New Year — A31

Singapore Festivals: 30c, Hari Raya Puasa (Moslem). 50c, Deepavali (Hindu). 75c, Christmas.

1971, Aug. 9 Litho. *Perf. 14*

138 A31 15c multicolored 1.00 1.00
139 A31 30c multicolored 2.75 2.75
140 A31 50c multicolored 3.50 3.50
141 A31 75c multicolored 4.75 4.75
a. Souvenir sheet of 4, #138-141 80.00 80.00
Nos. 138-141 (4) 12.00 12.00

Satellite Earth Station, Sentosa Island — A32

No. 143 as 15c, enlarged to cover 4 stamps.

1971, Oct. 23 Unwmk. *Perf. 13½*

142 A32 15c red & multi 5.00 1.50
143 A32 Block of 4 45.00 40.00
a. 30c (yellow numeral) 11.25 10.00
b. 30c (green numeral) 11.25 10.00
c. 30c (rose numeral) 11.25 10.00
d. 30c (orange numeral) 11.25 10.00

Establishment of Singapore's satellite earth station, Sentosa Island.

Singapore River and Fort Canning, 1843-1847 — A33

Views of Singapore, from 19th century art works: 15c, The Padang, 1851. 20c, Waterfront, 1848-1849. 35c, View from Fort Canning, 1846. 50c, View from Mount Wallich, 1857. $1, Waterfront with ships, from the sea, 1861.

1971, Dec. 5 Unwmk. *Perf. 13x12½*

Size: 52x45mm

144 A33 10c gold & multi 2.50 2.50
145 A33 15c gold & multi 3.50 3.50
146 A33 20c gold & multi 4.50 4.50
147 A33 35c gold & multi 8.75 8.75

Perf. 12½x13

Size: 68x47mm

148 A33 50c gold & multi 12.50 12.50
149 A33 $1 gold & multi 16.00 16.00
Nos. 144-149 (6) 47.75 47.75

George V 1c Copper Coin, 1920 A34

Singapore Coins: 35c, Silver dollar, 1969. $1, Gold $150, 1969 commemorative coin for sesquicentennial of founding of Singapore.

1972, June 4 Litho. *Perf. 13½*

150 A34 15c dk grn, dp org & blk 1.25 1.25
151 A34 35c red & black 2.75 2.75
152 A34 $1 ultra, yellow & blk 4.00 4.00
Nos. 150-152 (3) 8.00 8.00

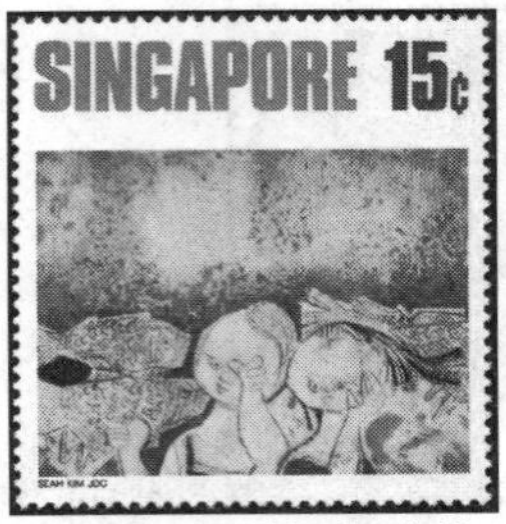

"Moon Festival," by Seah Kim Joo — A35

Paintings by Singapore Artists: 35c, "Complimentary Force," by Thomas Yeo. 50c, "Rhythm in Blue," by Yusman Aman. $1, "Gibbons," by Chen Wen Hsi.

1972, July 9 Litho. *Perf. 12½*

Size: 40x43½mm

153 A35 15c brown org & multi .50 .50

Size: 35½x53½mm

154 A35 35c blue green & multi 1.50 1.50
155 A35 50c dull violet & multi 2.25 2.25

Size: 40x43½mm

156 A35 $1 bister & multi 5.75 5.75
Nos. 153-156 (4) 10.00 10.00

Chinese New Year — A36

Festivals: 35c, Hari Raya Puasa (candles and ornament). 50c, Deepavali (incense and teapot). 75c, Christmas (candle and stained glass window).

1972, Aug. 9 Litho. *Perf. 13x12½*

157 A36 15c deep rose & multi .65 .65
158 A36 35c violet & multi 1.60 1.60
159 A36 50c green & multi 2.00 2.00
160 A36 75c blue & multi 3.25 3.25
Nos. 157-160 (4) 7.50 7.50

Technical and Scientific Training — A37

Designs: 35c, Sport. $1, Art and culture.

1972, Oct. 1 Photo. *Perf. 12*

161 A37 15c orange & multi .75 .75
162 A37 35c blue & multi 1.75 1.75
163 A37 $1 orange & multi 4.50 4.50
Nos. 161-163 (3) 7.00 7.00

Youth of Singapore.

Neptune Ruby A38

1972, Dec. 17 Litho. *Perf. 14x14½*

Size: 42x28½mm

164 A38 15c shown .50 .50

Size: 29½x28½mm

165 A38 75c Maria Rickmers 3.50 3.50
166 A38 $1 Chinese junk 11.00 11.00
a. Souvenir sheet of 3, #164-166 40.00 37.50
Nos. 164-166 (3) 15.00 15.00

Singapore shipping industry.

Quality and Reliability Emblem — A39

Birds, Jurong Bird Park — A40

15c, Emblem & initials of participating organizations: Singapore Institute of Standards & Industrial Research, Singapore Manufacturers' Association, Natl. Trades Union Congress. 75c, Emblem & "Prosperity through Quality & Reliability" in multiple rows. $1, Quality & Reliability emblem.

1973, Feb. 25 Litho. *Perf. 14½x14*

167 A39 15c gold & multi .65 .65
168 A39 35c gold & multi 1.90 1.90
169 A39 75c gold & multi 2.10 2.10
170 A39 $1 gold & multi 2.10 2.10
Nos. 167-170 (4) 6.75 6.75

Prosperity through Quality and Reliability campaign.

1973, Apr. 29 *Perf. 12½*

Landmarks: 35c, Dancers, National Theater. 50c, City Hall and ballplayers. $1, Singapore River with boats and buildings.

171 A40 15c vermilion & blk .90 .90
172 A40 35c dull green & blk 2.10 2.10
173 A40 50c brown & blk 2.75 2.75
174 A40 $1 dark violet & blk 4.25 4.25
Nos. 171-174 (4) 10.00 10.00

Airline Emblems A41

35c, Emblem of Singapore Airlines and intl. destinations. 75c, SIA emblem on stylized tail of Boeing jet. $1, SIA emblems circling globe.

1973, June 24 Litho. *Perf. 13½*

175 A41 10c multicolored .60 .60
176 A41 35c multicolored 1.60 1.60
177 A41 75c multicolored 1.90 1.90
178 A41 $1 multicolored 2.40 2.40
Nos. 175-178 (4) 6.50 6.50

Singapore Intl. Airport at Paya Lebar.

Entertainers A42

Running, Judo, Boxing — A43

Composite of various forms of entertainment.

1973, Aug. 9 Litho. *Perf. 13½x14*

179 A42 10c black & orange red 2.00 2.00
180 A42 35c black & orange red 2.75 2.75
181 A42 50c black & orange red 2.75 2.75
182 A42 75c black & orange red 3.00 3.00
a. Block of 4, #179-182 10.50 10.50

National Day 1973.

1973, Sept. 1 Photo. *Perf. 14*

Designs: 15c, Bicycling, weight lifting, pistol shoot, yachting. 25c, Various balls. 35c, Tennis racket, ball, hockey stick. 50c, Swimming. $1, Singapore National Stadium.

Size: 25x25mm

183 A43 10c gold, silver & ind .55 .55
184 A43 15c gold & dk brown 1.75 1.75
185 A43 25c silver, gold & blk 1.60 1.60
186 A43 35c gold, silver & dk pur 3.00 3.00

Perf. 13x14

Size: 40½x25mm

187 A43 50c gold & multi 2.10 2.10
188 A43 $1 sil, vio bl & emer 3.50 3.50
a. Souvenir sheet of 6, #183-188 35.00 35.00
Nos. 183-188 (6) 12.50 12.50

7th South East Asia (SEAP) Games, Singapore.

Agave A44

Mangosteen A45

Designs: Stylized flowers and fruit.

1973 Photo. *Perf. 13*

189 A44 1c shown .20 .20
190 A44 5c Coleus blumei .20 .20
a. Booklet pane of 10 (4 #190, 4 #191 + 2 #193) 6.00
191 A44 10c Madagascar periwinkle .20 .20
192 A44 15c Sunflower .20 .20
193 A44 20c Dwarf palm .40 .20
194 A44 25c Yellow daisy .45 .20
195 A44 35c Chrysanthemum .75 .40
196 A44 50c Costus 1.10 .20
197 A44 75c Transvaal daisy 1.50 .70
198 A45 $1 shown 2.00 .20
199 A45 $2 Jackfruit 4.25 .75
200 A45 $5 Coconuts 10.50 5.50
201 A45 $10 Pineapple 20.00 11.50
Nos. 189-201 (13) 41.75 20.45

Nos. 189-201 have fluorescent underprint "Singapore" in multiple rows.

Tiger and Orangutans — A46

Tropical Fish — A47

1973, Dec. 16 Litho. *Perf. 13*

202 A46 5c shown .65 .65
203 A46 10c Leopard and deer .35 .35
204 A46 35c Panther and stag 4.50 4.50
205 A46 75c White horse & lion 7.00 7.00
Nos. 202-205 (4) 12.50 12.50

Opening of Singapore Zoo.

1974, Apr. 21 *Perf. 13½x14*

Designs: Various poecilia reticulata fish.

206 A47 5c apple green & multi .70 .70
207 A47 10c pink & multi .70 .70
208 A47 35c brt blue & multi 3.00 3.00
209 A47 $1 brt green & multi 5.25 5.25
Nos. 206-209 (4) 9.65 9.65

Scout Conference Emblem A48

1974, June 9 *Perf. 13½x14½*

210 A48 10c multicolored .25 .25
211 A48 75c multicolored 2.00 2.00

9th Asia-Pacific Boy Scout Conf., Singapore.

UPU Emblem, Circle and "Centenary" Multiple — A49

UPU, cent.: 35c, Circle and UN emblems, multiple. 75c, Circle and pigeons, multiple.

1974, July 7 Litho. *Perf. 14½x13½*

212 A49 10c orange brn & multi .20 .20
213 A49 35c blue & multi .55 .55
214 A49 75c emerald & multi 1.25 1.25
Nos. 212-214 (3) 2.00 2.00

Family — A50

1974, Aug. 9 Litho. *Perf. 13x13½*

215 A50 10c shown .25 .25
216 A50 35c Symbols for male & female .75 .75
217 A50 75c World map and WPY emblem 1.75 1.75
Nos. 215-217 (3) 2.75 2.75

Natl. Day and World Population Year 1974.

"Sun and Tree" — A51

Children's Drawings: 10c, "My Daddy and Mommy." 35c, "A Dump Truck." 50c, "My Aunt."

1974, Oct. 1 Photo. *Perf. 14x13½*

218 A51 5c multicolored .40 .40
219 A51 10c multicolored .40 .40
220 A51 35c multicolored 2.40 2.40
221 A51 50c multicolored 2.50 2.50
a. Souv. sheet, #218-221, perf 13 24.00 24.00
Nos. 218-221 (4) 5.70 5.70

Children's drawings for Children's Day (UNICEF).

Alfresco Dining A52

Tourist publicity: 20c, Singapore River. $1, "Kelong" fish traps.

1975, Jan. 26 Litho. *Perf. 14*

222 A52 15c multicolored .75 .75
223 A52 20c multicolored 1.50 1.50
224 A52 $1 multicolored 4.75 4.75
Nos. 222-224 (3) 7.00 7.00

Prows of Barges and Wave Design A53

25c, Cargo ships & ship's wheel. 50c, Tanker & signal flags. $1, Container ship & propellers.

1975, Mar. 10 Litho. *Perf. 13½*

225 A53 5c multicolored .25 .25
226 A53 25c multicolored 1.75 1.75
227 A53 50c multicolored 2.25 2.25
228 A53 $1 multicolored 3.25 3.25
Nos. 225-228 (4) 7.50 7.50

9th Biennial Conf. of the Intl. Assoc. of Ports and Harbors, Singapore, Mar. 8-15.

Satellite Earth Stations, Sentosa Island — A54

Oil Refinery — A55

Science and Industry: 75c, Brain surgery, Medical Center, Jurong.

1975, June 29 Photo. *Perf. 13½*

229 A54 10c multicolored .25 .25
230 A55 35c multicolored 2.25 2.25
231 A54 75c multicolored 2.50 2.50
Nos. 229-231 (3) 5.00 5.00

"10" and "Homes and Gardens for the People" — A56

Crowned Cranes — A57

Tenth Natl. Day ("10" and): 35c, "Shipping and ship building." 75c, "Communications and technology." $1, "Trade, commerce and industry."

1975, Aug. 9 Litho. *Perf. 13½*

232 A56 10c multicolored .35 .35
233 A56 35c multicolored .90 .90
234 A56 75c multicolored 2.25 2.25
235 A56 $1 multicolored 2.50 2.50
Nos. 232-235 (4) 6.00 6.00

1975, Oct. 5 Litho. *Perf. 14½x13½*

Birds: 10c, Great hornbill. 35c, White-breasted and white-collared kingfishers. $1, Sulphur-crested cockatoo and blue and yellow macaw.

236 A57 5c emerald & multi 1.75 1.75
237 A57 10c emerald & multi 1.75 1.75
238 A57 35c emerald & multi 9.00 9.00
239 A57 $1 emerald & multi 13.50 13.50
Nos. 236-239 (4) 26.00 26.00

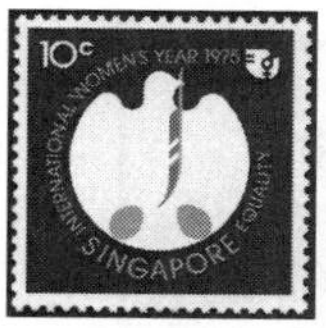

IWY Emblem, Peace Dove as "Equality" — A58

IWY Emblem: 35c, Peace dove with eggs in basket, symbolizing "Development." 75c, Peace dove & young, symbolizing "Peace."

1975, Dec. 7 Litho. *Perf. 13½*

240 A58 10c blk, blue & pink .20 .20
241 A58 35c orange & multi 1.90 1.90
242 A58 75c dp violet & multi 2.40 2.40
a. Souvenir sheet of 3, #240-242 14.00 14.00
Nos. 240-242 (3) 4.50 4.50

International Women's Year 1975.

Yellow Flame — A59

Aranda Hybrid — A60

Wayside Trees: 35c, Cabbage tree. 50c, Rose of India. 75c, Variegated coral tree.

1976, Apr. 18 Litho. *Perf. 14*

243 A59 10c multicolored .50 .50
244 A59 35c multicolored 1.50 1.50
245 A59 50c multicolored 2.25 2.25
246 A59 75c multicolored 4.25 4.25
Nos. 243-246 (4) 8.50 8.50

1976, June 20 Litho. *Perf. 14*

Designs: Varieties of aranda orchids.

247 A60 10c black & multi 1.25 1.25
248 A60 35c black & multi 3.75 3.75
249 A60 50c black & multi 4.50 4.50
250 A60 75c black & multi 5.50 5.50
Nos. 247-250 (4) 15.00 15.00

"10" and Children's Band A61

35c, Running boys. 75c, Dancing children.

1976, Aug. 9 Litho. *Perf. 12½*

251 A61 10c multicolored .25 .25
252 A61 35c multicolored 1.40 1.40
253 A61 75c multicolored 1.60 1.60
Nos. 251-253 (3) 3.25 3.25

Singapore Youth Festival, 10th anniversary.

Queen Elizabeth Walk — A62

Paintings of Old Singapore, c. 1905-10: 50c, The Padang. $1, Raffles Place.

1976, Nov. 14 Litho. *Perf. 14*

254 A62 10c multicolored .50 .50
255 A62 50c multicolored 2.25 2.25
256 A62 $1 multicolored 4.75 4.75
a. Souvenir sheet of 3, #254-256, perf. 13½ 21.00 21.00
Nos. 254-256 (3) 7.50 7.50

Chinese Bridal Costume — A63

Radar, Surface to Air Missile, Soldiers — A64

Designs: 35c, Indian bridal costume. 75c, Malay bridal costume.

1976, Dec. 19 Litho. *Perf. 14½*

257 A63 10c lt green & multi .50 .50
258 A63 35c lilac & multi 1.75 1.75
259 A63 75c yellow & multi 3.75 3.75
Nos. 257-259 (3) 6.00 6.00

1977, Mar. 12 Litho. *Perf. 14½*

50c, Infantry soldiers and tank. 75c, Jet fighter, pilot, telecommunications center.

260 A64 10c multicolored .60 .60
261 A64 50c multicolored 2.40 2.40
262 A64 75c multicolored 3.25 3.25
Nos. 260-262 (3) 6.25 6.25

National Service, 10th anniversary.

Lyrate Cockle A65

Spotted Hermit Crab A66

Sea Shells: 5c, Folded scallop. 10c, Marble cone. 15c, Scorpion conch. 20c, Amplustre bubble. 25c, Spiral Babylon. 35c, Regal thorny oyster. 50c, Winged frog shell. 75c, Troschel's murex.

Marine Life: $2, Stingray. $5, Cuttlefish. $10, Lionfish.

1977 *Perf. 13½*

263 A65 1c orange & multi .65 .65
264 A65 5c orange & multi .20 .20
a. Bklt. pane, 4 #264, 8 #265 3.00
265 A65 10c orange & multi .20 .20
266 A65 15c orange & multi .90 .20
267 A65 20c orange & multi .90 .20
268 A65 25c orange & multi 1.00 .25
269 A65 35c orange & multi 1.25 .75
270 A65 50c orange & multi 1.60 .30
271 A65 75c orange & multi 2.50 .90

Perf. 14

272 A66 $1 multicolored 1.90 .25
273 A66 $2 multicolored 1.90 .50
274 A66 $5 multicolored 3.25 1.00
275 A66 $10 multicolored 6.25 3.00
Nos. 263-275 (13) 22.50 8.40

No. 264a has a large inscribed selvage, the size of 6 stamps.

Issued: #263-271, Apr. 9; others, June 4.

Singapore Harbor Improvements A67

Labor Day: 50c, Construction workers. 75c, Road workers.

1977, May 1 Litho. *Perf. 13x12½*

276 A67 10c multicolored .35 .35
277 A67 50c multicolored 1.25 1.25
278 A67 75c multicolored 1.90 1.90
Nos. 276-278 (3) 3.50 3.50

"Key to Savings" — A68

Grain and Cattle — A69

Designs: 35c, "On-line Banking Service." 75c, "GIRO Service."

1977, July 16 Litho. *Perf. 13*

279 A68 10c multicolored .20 .20
280 A68 35c multicolored .80 .80
281 A68 75c multicolored 2.25 2.25
Nos. 279-281 (3) 3.25 3.25

Centenary of Post Office Savings Bank.

1977, Aug. 8 Litho. *Perf. 14*

10c, Flags of founding members: Thailand, Indonesia, Singapore, Malaysia, Philippines. 75c, Steel, oil & chemical industries.

282 A69 10c multicolored .35 .35
283 A69 35c multicolored .90 .90
284 A69 75c multicolored 2.25 2.25
Nos. 282-284 (3) 3.50 3.50

Association of South East Asian Nations (ASEAN), 10th anniversary.

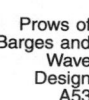

Bus Stop — A70

Children's Drawings: 10c, Chingay procession, vert. 75c, Playground.

1977, Oct. 1 *Perf. 12½*

285 A70 10c multicolored .35 .20
286 A70 35c multicolored 1.00 .65
287 A70 75c multicolored 3.25 1.50
a. Souvenir sheet of 3, #285-287 13.50 13.50
Nos. 285-287 (3) 4.60 2.35

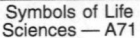

Symbols of Life Sciences — A71

Botanical Gardens — A72

Singapore Science Center: 35c, "Physical sciences." 75c, "Science and technology." $1, Science Center.

1977, Dec. 10 Litho. *Perf. 14½x14*

288 A71 10c multicolored .20 .20
289 A71 35c multicolored .45 .45
290 A71 75c multicolored 1.10 1.10
291 A71 $1 multicolored 1.75 1.75
Nos. 288-291 (4) 3.50 3.50

1978, Apr. 22 Litho. *Perf. 14½*

Singapore Parks and Gardens: 10c, Jurong Bird Park, horiz. 35c, East Coast Lagoon and Park.

292 A72 10c multicolored .20 .20
293 A72 35c multicolored .70 .70
294 A72 75c multicolored 1.60 1.60
Nos. 292-294 (3) 2.50 2.50

Red-whiskered Bulbul — A73

Songbirds: 35c, White eyes. 50c, White-rumped shama. 75c, White-crested laughing thrush.

1978, July 1 Litho. *Perf. 13½*

295 A73 10c multicolored .60 .60
296 A73 35c multicolored 1.75 1.75
297 A73 50c multicolored 1.90 1.90
298 A73 75c multicolored 2.25 2.25
Nos. 295-298 (4) 6.50 6.50

Thian Hock Keng Temple — A74

National Monuments: No. 303a, like No. 299. Nos. 300, 303b, Hajjah Fatimah Mosque. Nos. 301, 303c, Armenian Church. Nos. 302, 303d, Sri Mariamman Temple.

1978, Aug. 9

299 A74 10c tan & multi .50 .50
300 A74 10c green & multi .50 .50
301 A74 10c blue & multi .50 .50
302 A74 10c lilac & multi .50 .50
Nos. 299-302 (4) 2.00 2.00

Souvenir Sheet

303 Sheet of 4 6.00 6.00
a. A74 35c tan & multi 1.00
b. A74 35c green & multi 1.00
c. A74 35c blue & multi 1.00
d. A74 35c lilac & multi 1.00

Map of Proposed Cable Network A75

1978, Oct. 30 Litho. *Perf. 14*

304 A75 10c multicolored .20 .20
305 A75 35c multicolored .60 .60
306 A75 50c multicolored .80 .80
307 A75 75c multicolored 1.40 1.40
Nos. 304-307 (4) 3.00 3.00

ASEAN Submarine Cable Network. Nos. 304-307 printed in sheets of 100. Stamps have perforations around design and around edges. See No. 429a.

Neptune Spinel — A76

Ships: 35c, Neptune Aries. 50c, Arno Temasek. 75c, Neptune Pearl.

1978, Nov. 18 Litho. *Perf. 13½x14*

308 A76 10c multicolored .70 .70
309 A76 35c multicolored 1.75 1.75
310 A76 50c multicolored 1.90 1.90
311 A76 75c multicolored 2.40 2.40
Nos. 308-311 (4) 6.75 6.75

Neptune Oriental Shipping Lines, 10th anniv.

Concorde A77

Aviation Development: 35c, Vickers-Vimy, 1st aircraft to land in Singapore. 50c, Boeing 747B. 75c, Wright Brothers' Flyer I.

1978, Dec. 16 *Perf. 13½*

312 A77 10c yellow green & blk 1.00 1.00
313 A77 35c blue & black 1.00 1.00
314 A77 50c carmine & black 1.40 1.40
315 A77 75c brown & black 1.60 1.60
Nos. 312-315 (4) 5.00 5.00

75th anniversary of 1st powered flight.

Distance Marker in Kilometers — A78

Vanda Orchids — A79

Designs: 35c, Tape measure in centimeters. 75c, Scales in grams and kilograms.

1979, Jan. 24 Litho. *Perf. 13x13½*

316 A78 10c multicolored .25 .25
317 A78 35c multicolored .50 .50
318 A78 75c multicolored 1.00 1.00
Nos. 316-318 (3) 1.75 1.75

Introduction of metric system.

Perf. 14½x14, 14x14½

1979, Apr. 14 Litho.

Varieties of vanda hybrids. 10c, 35c, horiz.

319 A79 10c multicolored .20 .20
320 A79 35c multicolored .55 .55
321 A79 50c multicolored .90 .90
322 A79 75c multicolored 1.10 1.10
Nos. 319-322 (4) 2.75 2.75

Envelope Addressed to Postmaster A80

50c, Envelope addressed to Philatelic Bureau.

1979, July 1 Litho. *Perf. 12½x13*

323 A80 10c orange & multi .20 .20
324 A80 50c dark blue & multi .80 .80

Singapore's postal code system.

Old Phone, Telephone Lines — A81

Designs: 35c, Dial, world map. 50c, Push-button phone, skyline. 75c, Line network.

1979, Oct. 5 Litho. *Perf. 13½*

325 A81 10c multicolored .20 .20
326 A81 35c multicolored .30 .30
327 A81 50c multicolored .45 .45
328 A81 75c multicolored .65 .65
Nos. 325-328 (4) 1.60 1.60

Telephone service centenary.

IYC Emblem, Lanterns Festival A82

IYC Emblem, Children's Drawings: 35c, Singapore Harbor. 50c, "Use Your Hands." 75c, Soccer.

1979, Nov. 10 Litho. *Perf. 13*

329 A82 10c multicolored .20 .20
330 A82 35c multicolored .25 .25
331 A82 50c multicolored .35 .35
332 A82 75c multicolored .55 .55
a. Souvenir sheet of 4, #329-332 5.50 5.50
Nos. 329-332 (4) 1.35 1.35

International Year of the Child.

Botanic Gardens, 120th Anniversary — A83

1979, Dec. 15 *Perf. 13½*

333 A83 10c shown .20 .20
334 A83 50c Gazebo .85 .85
335 A83 $1 Greenhouse 1.75 1.75
Nos. 333-335 (3) 2.80 2.80

Hainan Junk — A84

1980 Litho. *Perf. 14*

336 A84 1c shown .20 .20
337 A84 5c Clipper .20 .20
338 A84 10c Fujian junk .20 .20
a. Booklet pane of 10 1.00
339 A84 15c Golekkan .20 .20
340 A84 20c Palari .20 .20
341 A84 25c East Indiaman .20 .20
342 A84 35c Galleon .30 .20
343 A84 50c Caravel .45 .25
344 A84 75c Jiangsu trader .65 .25

Size: 41½x24½mm

Perf. 13½

345 A84 $1 Coaster .90 .30
346 A84 $2 Oil tanker 1.75 .50
347 A84 $5 Screw steamer 4.50 1.50
348 A84 $10 Paddle wheel steamer 9.00 5.00
Nos. 336-348 (13) 18.75 9.20

Issued: #336-344, Apr. 26; others, Apr. 5.

Straits Settlements No. 1, Old Singapore Map, London 1980 Emblem — A85

London 1980 Emblem and: 35c, Straits Settlements No. 146, letter. $1, Singapore No. 19, map of Straits. $2, Singapore No. 106, letter, 1819.

1980, May 6 Litho. *Perf. 13*

349 A85 10c multicolored .20 .20
350 A85 35c multicolored .30 .30
351 A85 $1 multicolored .65 .65
352 A85 $2 multicolored 1.10 1.10
a. Souvenir sheet of 4, #349-352 3.50 3.50
Nos. 349-352 (4) 2.25 2.25

London 1980 Intl. Stamp Exhib., May 6-14.

Fund Board Emblem, Keys to Retirement — A86

1980, July 1 Litho. *Perf. 13*

353 A86 10c shown .20 .20
354 A86 50c Home ownership savings .35 .35
355 A86 $1 Old age savings .70 .70
Nos. 353-355 (3) 1.25 1.25

Central Provident Fund Board, 25th anniv.

Map Showing Singapore-Indonesia Cable Route — A87

1980, Aug. 8 Litho. *Perf. 14*

356 A87 10c multicolored .20 .20
357 A87 35c multicolored .50 .50
358 A87 50c multicolored .70 .70
359 A87 75c multicolored 1.10 1.10
Nos. 356-359 (4) 2.50 2.50

ASEAN Submarine Cable Network extension. Stamps perforated around design and around edges. See No. 429a.

Fair Emblem A88

1980, Oct. 3 Litho. *Perf. 13*

360 A88 10c multicolored	.20	.20
361 A88 35c multicolored	.40	.40
362 A88 75c multicolored	.90	.90
Nos. 360-362 (3)	1.50	1.50

Asean Trade Fair, Oct. 3-12.

A89

A90

1980, Nov. 2 Litho. *Perf. 13½*

363 A89 10c Flame of the wood	.20	.20
364 A89 35c Golden trumpet	.40	.40
365 A89 50c Sky vine	.50	.50
366 A89 75c Bougainvillea	.80	.80
Nos. 363-366 (4)	1.90	1.90

1981, Jan. 24 Litho. *Perf. 14x14½*

367 A90 10c multicolored	.20	.20
368 A90 35c multicolored	.30	.30
369 A90 75c multicolored	.60	.60
Nos. 367-369 (3)	1.10	1.10

Monetary Authority of Singapore, 10th anniv.

No. 54 Surcharged

Perf. 13½x14½

1981, Mar. 5 Photo. Wmk. 314

370 A8 10c on 4c red org & blk	.30	.30

A91

A92

Unwmk.

1981, Apr. 11 Litho. *Perf. 13*

371 A91 10c Technical Training (Woodworking)	.20	.20
372 A91 35c Building construction	.30	.30
373 A91 50c Electronics	.45	.45
374 A91 75c Precision machinery	.55	.55
Nos. 371-374 (4)	1.50	1.50

1981, Aug. 25 Litho. *Perf. 14*

Sports For All: Various sports.

375 A92 10c multicolored	.35	.35
376 A92 75c multicolored	2.40	2.40
377 A92 $1 multicolored	2.75	2.75
Nos. 375-377 (3)	5.50	5.50

A93

A94

1981, Nov. 24 Litho. *Perf. 14½*

378 A93 10c Man in wheelchair	.20	.20
379 A93 35c Group	.40	.40
380 A93 50c Teacher, student	.60	.60
381 A93 75c Blind communications worker	.80	.80
Nos. 378-381 (4)	2.00	2.00

Intl. Year of the Disabled.

1981, Dec. 29 Litho. *Perf. 14x13½*

382 A94 10c multicolored	.20	.20
383 A94 35c multicolored	.30	.30
384 A94 50c multicolored	.45	.45
385 A94 75c multicolored	.60	.60
386 A94 $1 multicolored	.70	.70
a. Souvenir sheet of 5, #382-386	3.50	3.50
Nos. 382-386 (5)	2.25	2.25

Changi airport opening.

A95

1982, Mar. 3 Litho. *Perf. 14x14½*

387 A95 10c Clipper	.40	.40
388 A95 50c Blue grassy tiger	1.25	1.25
389 A95 $1 Raja Brooke's birdwing	1.75	1.75
Nos. 387-389 (3)	3.40	3.40

A96

A97

1982, June 14 Litho. *Perf. 14*

390 A96 10c multicolored	.20	.20
391 A96 35c multicolored	.50	.50
392 A96 50c multicolored	.65	.65
393 A96 75c multicolored	.90	.90
Nos. 390-393 (4)	2.25	2.25

15th ASEAN Ministerial meeting.

1982, July 9 Litho. *Perf. 12*

394 A97 10c multicolored	.20	.20
395 A97 75c multicolored	.90	.90
396 A97 $1 multicolored	1.40	1.40
Nos. 394-396 (3)	2.50	2.50

1982 World Cup.

Sultan Shoal Lighthouse, 1896 — A98

1982, Aug. 7

397 A98 10c shown	.50	.50
398 A98 75c Horsburgh, 1851	1.50	1.50
399 A98 $1 Raffles, 1855	1.75	1.75
a. Souvenir sheet of 3, #397-399	4.00	4.00
Nos. 397-399 (3)	3.75	3.75

10th Anniv. of PSA Container Terminal A99

1982, Sept. 15 Litho. *Perf. 13½*

400 A99 10c Yard gantry cranes	.20	.20
401 A99 35c Computer	.40	.40
402 A99 50c Freightlifter	.55	.55
403 A99 75c Straddle carrier	.85	.85
Nos. 400-403 (4)	2.00	2.00

Scouting Year — A100

1982, Oct. 15 Litho. *Perf. 14x13½*

404 A100 10c Color guard	.20	.20
405 A100 35c Hiking	.60	.60
406 A100 50c Building tower	.80	.80
407 A100 75c Kayaking	1.25	1.25
Nos. 404-407 (4)	2.85	2.85

Productivity Movement A101

1982, Nov. 17 *Perf. 13½*

408 A101 10c Text	.20	.20
409 A101 35c Housing	.45	.45
410 A101 50c Quality control meeting	.65	.65
411 A101 75c Participation	1.00	1.00
Nos. 408-411 (4)	2.30	2.30

Commonwealth Day — A102

12th Southeast Asia Games — A103

1983, May 14 Litho. *Perf. 13½x13*

412 A102 10c multicolored	.20	.20
413 A102 35c multicolored	.40	.40
414 A102 75c multicolored	.75	.75
415 A102 $1 multicolored	1.00	1.00
Nos. 412-415 (4)	2.35	2.35

1983, May 28 Litho. *Perf. 14x13½*

416 A103 10c Soccer	.20	.20
417 A103 35c Racket games	.35	.35
418 A103 75c Athletics	.75	.75
419 A103 $1 Swimming	1.00	1.00
Nos. 416-419 (4)	2.30	2.30

Neighborhood Watch Safety Campaign A104

1983, June 24 Litho. *Perf. 14*

420 A104 10c Family	.20	.20
421 A104 35c Children	.55	.55
422 A104 75c Community	1.25	1.25
Nos. 420-422 (3)	2.00	2.00

BANGKOK '83 Intl. Stamp Show, Aug. 4-13 — A105

10c, #282-284, statue of King Chulalongkorn (1868-1910). 35c, #304-307, map of southeast Asia. $1, #390-393, Declaration of ASEAN (Assoc. of South East Asian Nations) signatures, 1976.

1983, Aug. 4 Litho. *Perf. 14x14½*

423 A105 10c multicolored	.20	.20
424 A105 35c multicolored	.40	.40
425 A105 $1 multicolored	1.25	1.25
a. Souvenir sheet of 3, #423-425	2.75	2.75
Nos. 423-425 (3)	1.85	1.85

ASEAN Submarine Cable Network A106

1983, Sept. 27 Litho. *Perf. 14*

426 A106 10c multicolored	.20	.20
427 A106 35c multicolored	.45	.45
428 A106 50c multicolored	.65	.65
429 A106 75c multicolored	.95	.95
a. Souv. sheet of 6, #304, 359, 426-429	3.00	3.00
Nos. 426-429 (4)	2.25	2.25

World Communications Year — A107

1983, Nov. 10 Litho. *Perf. 13*

430 A107 10c Telex service	.20	.20
431 A107 35c Telephone numbering plan	.35	.35
432 A107 75c Satellite transmission	.75	.75
433 A107 $1 Sea communications	1.00	1.00
Nos. 430-433 (4)	2.30	2.30

Coastal Birds — A108

Perf. 14½x13½

1984, Mar. 15 Litho.

434 A108 10c Slaty-breasted rail	.20	.20
435 A108 35c Black bittern	.80	.80
436 A108 50c Brahminy kite	1.25	1.25
437 A108 75c Common moorhens	1.75	1.75
Nos. 434-437 (4)	4.00	4.00

Natl. Monuments A109

10c, House of Tan Yeok Nee (merchant), 1885. 35c, Thong Chai Building (former hospital), 1892. 50c, Telok Ayer Market, 1894. $1, Nagore Durgha Muslim Shrine, 1828.

1984, June 7 Litho. *Perf. 12*
438 A109 10c multicolored .20 .20
439 A109 35c multicolored .45 .45
440 A109 50c multicolored .65 .65
441 A109 $1 multicolored 1.40 1.40
Nos. 438-441 (4) 2.70 2.70

A110

A111

1984, Aug. 9 Litho. *Perf. 14*
442 A110 10c No. 121 .20 .20
443 A110 35c No. 377 .40 .40
444 A110 50c No. 99 .55 .55
445 A110 75c No. 243 .80 .80
446 A110 $1 No. 386 1.10 1.10
447 A110 $2 No. 367 2.25 2.25
a. Souvenir sheet of 6, #442-447 7.00 7.00
Nos. 442-447 (6) 5.30 5.30

25th anniv. of self-government.

1984, Oct. 26 Litho. *Perf. 12*

Total Defense: a, This is our country. b, We are one. c, We work together. d, We are prepared. e, We are ready.

448 Strip of 5 .70 .70
a.-e. A111 10c any single .20 .20

Bridges A112

1985, Mar. 15 Engr. *Perf. 14½x14*
449 A112 10c Coleman .20 .20
450 A112 35c Cavenagh .35 .35
451 A112 75c Elgin .85 .85
452 A112 $1 Benjamin Sheares 1.25 1.25
Nos. 449-452 (4) 2.65 2.65

Insects — A113

1985 Litho. *Perf. 13x13½*
453 A113 5c Ceriagrion cerinorubellum .20 .20
454 A113 10c Apis javana .20 .20
455 A113 15c Delta arcuata .20 .20
456 A113 20c Xylocopa caerulea .20 .20
457 A113 25c Donacia javana .25 .25
458 A113 35c Heteroneda reticulata .35 .35
459 A113 50c Catacanthus nigripes .50 .50
460 A113 75c Chremistica pontianaka .75 .75

Litho. & Engr.
Size: 35x30mm

461 A113 $1 Homoeoxipha lycoides 1.00 1.00
462 A113 $2 Traulia azureipennis 2.00 2.00
463 A113 $5 Trithemis aurora 5.00 5.00
464 A113 $10 Scambophyllum sangiunolentum 10.00 10.00
Nos. 453-464 (12) 20.65 20.65

Issued: #453-460, 4/24; #461-464, 6/5.

Redrawn

1986 *Perf. 13x13½*
453a A113 5c 1.90 1.90
454a A113 10c 3.75 3.75
455a A113 15c 5.75 5.75
456a A113 20c 7.75 7.75
457a A113 25c 9.50 9.50
458a A113 35c 13.50 13.50
459a A113 50c 20.00 20.00
460a A113 75c 29.00 29.00
Nos. 453a-460a (8) 91.15 91.15

Singapore is 20½mm long on Nos. 453a-454a; 21mm long on Nos. 453-454. Rock is 1½mm from bottom right on No. 455; 2½mm on No. 455a. Pink flower touches frame on No. 456; is clear of the frame on No. 456a. Feelers indistinct and left one touches frame on No. 457; feelers sharp and left one ends just below frame on No. 457a.

Vein of leaf at lower left stops short of frame on No. 458; vein touches frame on No. 458a. Leaf at top touches frame on No. 459; leaf is below frame on No. 460; wing ends 1½mm above frame on No. 460a. [sic: Leaf at top touches frame on No. 459; leaf is below frame on No. 459a. Wing touches frame at bottom on No. 460; wing ends 1½mm above frame on No. 460a.]

Other differences exist in the position and sharpness of the design and colors.

People's Assoc., 25th Anniv. — A114

Montage of public services.

1985, July 1 *Perf. 13½x14*
465 A114 10c multicolored .20 .20
466 A114 35c multicolored .40 .40
467 A114 50c multicolored .65 .65
468 A114 75c multicolored .90 .90
Nos. 465-468 (4) 2.15 2.15

Public Housing, 25th Anniv. — A115

Modern housing developments.

1985, Aug. 9
469 A115 10c multicolored .20 .20
470 A115 35c multicolored .40 .40
471 A115 50c multicolored .55 .55
472 A115 75c multicolored .85 .85
a. Souv. sheet of 4, #469-472 3.00 3.00
Nos. 469-472 (4) 2.00 2.00

Girl Guides, 75th Anniv. — A116

Activities.

1985, Nov 6 *Perf. 14½x14*
473 A116 10c Brownies .20 .20
474 A116 35c Guides .40 .40
475 A116 50c Seniors .60 .60
476 A116 75c Guide leaders .95 .95
Nos. 473-476 (4) 2.15 2.15

Intl. Youth Year — A117

1985, Dec. 18 *Perf. 13*
477 A117 10c Youth assoc. emblems .20 .20
478 A117 75c Hand, sapling .85 .85
479 A117 $1 Dove, stick figures 1.10 1.10
Nos. 477-479 (3) 2.15 2.15

Indigenous Fruit — A118

Natl. Trade Unions Cong., 25th Anniv. — A119

1986, Feb. 26 Litho. *Perf. 14½x14*
480 A118 10c Psidium guajava .20 .20
481 A118 35c Eugenia aquea .50 .50
482 A118 50c Nephelium lappaceum .65 .65
483 A118 75c Manilkara zapota 1.00 1.00
Nos. 480-483 (4) 2.35 2.35

1986, May 1 *Perf. 13½*

Progress: a, Science and technology. b, Communications. c, Industry. d, Education.

484 Strip of 4 1.00 1.00
a.-d. A119 10c any single .20 .20

Souvenir Sheet

485 Sheet of 4 2.00 2.00
a.-d. A119 35c any single .50 .50

EXPO '86, Vancouver A120

1986, May 2 *Perf. 14½x14*
486 Strip of 3 2.50 2.50
a. A120 50c Calligraphy .55 .55
b. A120 75c Garland making .75 .75
c. A120 $1 Batik printing 1.10 1.10

Economic Development Board, 25th Anniv. — A121

1986, Aug. 1 *Perf. 15*
487 A121 10c Automation .20 .20
488 A121 35c Precision engineering .30 .30
489 A121 50c Electronics .45 .45
490 A121 75c Biotechnology .70 .70
Nos. 487-490 (4) 1.65 1.65

Submarine Cable — A122

1986, Sept. 8 *Perf. 13½*
491 A122 10c multicolored .20 .20
492 A122 35c multicolored .50 .50
493 A122 50c multicolored .70 .70
494 A122 75c multicolored 1.00 1.00
Nos. 491-494 (4) 2.40 2.40

Citizens' Consultative Committees, 21st Anniv. — A123

1986, Oct 15 *Perf. 12*
495 A123 Block of 4 2.50 2.50
a. 10c multicolored .20 .20
b. 35c multicolored .50 .50
c. 50c multicolored .75 .75
d. 75c multicolored 1.10 1.10

Intl. Peace Year — A124

1986, Dec. 17 Litho. *Perf. 14x13½*
496 A124 10c People .20 .20
497 A124 35c Southeast Asia map .45 .45
498 A124 $1 Globe 1.40 1.40
Nos. 496-498 (3) 2.05 2.05

Views of Singapore A125

1986, Feb. 25 *Perf. 12x12½*
499 A125 10c Orchard Road .20 .20
500 A125 50c Central business district .70 .70
501 A125 75c Marina Center, Raffles City .95 .95
Nos. 499-501 (3) 1.85 1.85

Assoc. of Southeast Asian Nations (ASEAN), 20th Anniv. A126

National Service, 20th Anniv. A127

1987, June 15 *Perf. 12*
502 A126 10c multicolored .20 .20
503 A126 35c multicolored .35 .35
504 A126 50c multicolored .55 .55
505 A126 75c multicolored .80 .80
Nos. 502-505 (4) 1.90 1.90

1987, July 1 *Perf. 15x14*

Designs: a, Army. b, Navy. c, Air Force. d, Pledge of Allegiance. e, Singapore Lion.

506 Strip of 4 1.00 1.00
a.-d. A127 10c any single .20 .20
507 Sheet of 5 2.00 2.00
a.-e. A127 35c any single .40 .40

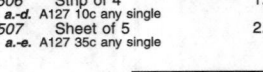

River Life — A128

1987, Sept. 2 *Perf. 14*
508 A128 10c Singapore River .20 .20
509 A128 50c Kallang Basin .65 .65
510 A128 $1 Kranji Reservoir 1.40 1.40
Nos. 508-510 (3) 2.25 2.25

Natl. Museum Cent. A129

Views of the museum and artifacts: 10c, Majapahis gold bracelet, 14th-15th cent. 75c, Ming fluted kendi (water jar). $1, Seventeen-wave kris (sword with silver hilt, sheath), property of Sultan Abdul Jalil Sabat, 1699.

1987, Oct. 12 Litho. *Perf. 13½x14*
511 A129 10c multicolored .20 .20
512 A129 75c multicolored .75 .75
513 A129 $1 multicolored .95 .95
Nos. 511-513 (3) 1.90 1.90

Singapore Science Center, 10th Anniv. A130

Attractions.

1987, Dec. 10 ***Perf. 14½***

514 A130 10c Omni Theater .20 .20
515 A130 35c Omni Planetarium .40 .40
516 A130 75c Cellular model .85 .85
517 A130 $1 Science exhibits 1.10 1.10
Nos. 514-517 (4) 2.55 2.55

Artillery, Cent. A131

Designs: 10c, 155-Gun Howitzer and Khatib Camp, headquarters of the Singapore Gunners. 35c, 25-Pound gun salute and Singapore City Hall. 50c, 4.5-inch Howitzer and Singapore Cricket Club, c. 1928. $1, Ft. Fullerton Drill Hall, c. 1893, and .405 Maxim gun.

1988, Feb. 22 Litho. ***Perf. 13½x14***

518 A131 10c multicolored .20 .20
519 A131 35c multicolored .40 .40
520 A131 50c multicolored .65 .65
521 A131 $1 multicolored 1.25 1.25
Nos. 518-521 (4) 2.50 2.50

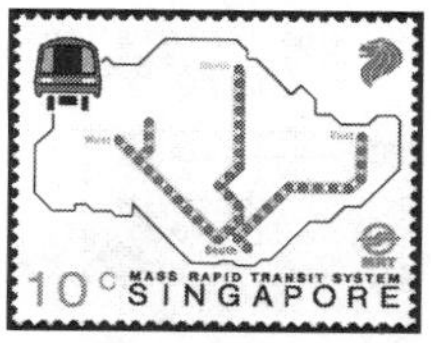

Mass Transit A132

1988, Mar. 12 ***Perf. 14***

522 A132 10c Rail car, map .20 .20
523 A132 50c Elevated train .60 .60
524 A132 $1 Urban subway 1.25 1.25
Nos. 522-524 (3) 2.05 2.05

Natl. Television Broadcast System, 25th Anniv. A133

1988, Apr. 4 Litho. ***Perf. 13½x14***

525 A133 10c shown .20 .20
526 A133 35c Studio .35 .35
527 A133 75c Television, transmission tower .75 .75
528 A133 $1 Screen, satellite dish 1.00 1.00
Nos. 525-528 (4) 2.30 2.30

Public Utilities Board, 25th Anniv. — A134

1988, May 4 Litho. ***Perf. 13½***

529 A134 10c Water works .20 .20
530 A134 50c Electric company .60 .60
531 A134 $1 Fossil fuels 1.25 1.25
a. Souvenir sheet of 3, #529-531 2.25 2.25
Nos. 529-531 (3) 2.05 2.05

Courtesy Campaign, 10th Anniv. — A135

Singa the lion (character trademark) and: 10c, Neighbors. 30c, Store service counter. $1, Helping the elderly.

1988, July 6 Litho. ***Perf. 14½***

532 A135 10c multicolored .20 .20
533 A135 30c multicolored .30 .30
534 A135 $1 multicolored 1.00 1.00
Nos. 532-534 (3) 1.50 1.50

Fire Service, Cent. A136

1988, Nov. 1 Litho. ***Perf. 13½***

535 A136 10c Turntable ladder truck .20 .20
536 A136 $1 1890s Steam pump 2.25 2.25

Port Authority, 25th Anniv. — A137

Various facilities.

1989, Apr. 3 Litho. ***Perf. 14x13½***

537 A137 10c multicolored .20 .20
538 A137 30c multi, diff. .40 .40
539 A137 75c multi, diff. 1.00 1.00
540 A137 $1 multi, diff. 1.40 1.40
Nos. 537-540 (4) 3.00 3.00

Old Chinatown A138

1989, May 17 Litho. ***Perf. 14½***

541 A138 10c Sago St. .20 .20
542 A138 35c Pagoda St. .60 .60
543 A138 75c Trengganu St. 1.25 1.25
544 A138 $1 Temple St. 1.60 1.60
Nos. 541-544 (4) 3.65 3.65

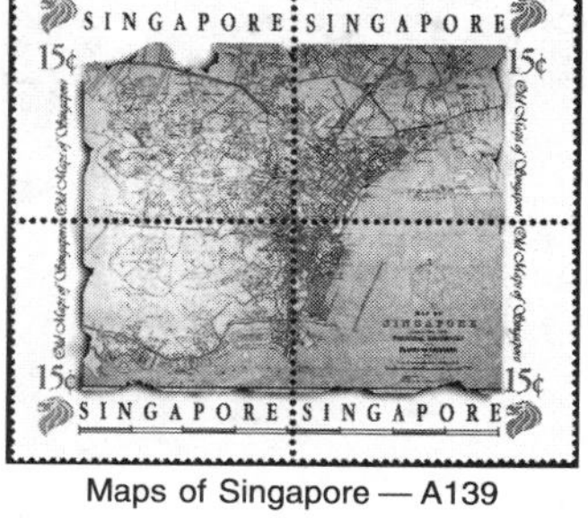

Maps of Singapore — A139

Early 19th cent. map Singapore Showing Principal Residences and Places of Interest: No. 545a, Upper left. No. 545b, Upper right. No. 545c, Lower left. No. 545d, Lower right. (Illustration reduced).

1989, July 26 Litho. ***Perf. 14½***

545 A139 Block of 4 .65 .65
a.-d. 15c any single .20 .20

Size: 33x31mm

Perf. 12½x13

546 A139 50c Singapore and Dependencies .55 .55
547 A139 $1 Plan of the British Settlement 1.10 1.10
Nos. 545-547 (3) 2.30 2.30

Fish — A140

1989, Sept. 6 ***Perf. 14***

548 A140 15c Clown triggerfish .20 .20
549 A140 30c Majestic angelfish .30 .30
550 A140 75c Emperor angelfish .80 .80
551 A140 $1 Royal empress angelfish 1.10 1.10
Nos. 548-551 (4) 2.40 2.40

Festivals — A141

Children's drawings: 15c, *Hari Raya Puasa*, by Loke Yoke Yen. 35c, *Chinese New Year*, by Simon Koh. 75c, *Thaipusam*, by Henry Setiono. $1, *Christmas*, by Wendy Ang Lin.

1989, Oct. 25 Litho. ***Perf. 14½***

552 A141 15c multicolored .20 .20
553 A141 35c multicolored .40 .40
554 A141 75c multicolored .80 .80
555 A141 $1 multicolored 1.10 1.10
a. Souv. sheet of 4, #552-555, perf. 14 2.50 2.50
Nos. 552-555 (4) 2.50 2.50

Singapore Indoor Stadium — A142

1989, Dec. 27 Litho. ***Perf. 14½***

556 A142 30c North entrance .35 .35
557 A142 75c Interior .80 .80
558 A142 $1 East entrance 1.10 1.10
a. Souvenir sheet of 3, #556-558 2.75 2.75
Nos. 556-558 (3) 2.25 2.25

Sports issue.

Lithographs of 19th Cent. Singapore A143

1990, Feb. 21 Litho. ***Perf. 13***

559 A143 15c Singapore River, 1839 .20 .20
560 A143 30c Chinatown, 1837 .30 .30
561 A143 75c Waterfront, 1837 .80 .80
562 A143 $1 View from Ft. Canning, 1824 1.10 1.10
Nos. 559-562 (4) 2.40 2.40

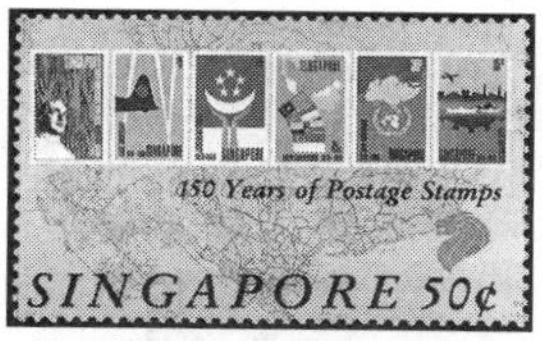

First Postage Stamps, 150th Anniv. — A144

Maps and: 50c, Nos. 101-106. 75c, Cover to Scotland. $1, Cover to Ireland $2, Great Britain Nos. 1, 2.

1990, May 3 Litho. ***Perf. 13½***

563 A144 50c multicolored .50 .50
564 A144 75c multicolored .75 .75
565 A144 $1 multicolored 1.00 1.00
566 A144 $2 multicolored 2.00 2.00
a. Souvenir sheet of 4, #563-566 4.75 4.75
Nos. 563-566 (4) 4.25 4.25

Tourism A145

1990, July 4 ***Perf. 14½***

567 A145 5c Zoo .20 .20
568 A145 15c Resort .20 .20
a. Booklet pane of 10 1.60
569 A145 20c City .25 .25
570 A145 25c Dragon boat race .30 .30
571 A145 30c Hotel .35 .35
572 A145 35c Caged birds .40 .40
573 A145 40c Park .45 .45
574 A145 50c Festival .55 .55
575 A145 75c Building, diff. .85 .85
Nos. 567-575 (9) 3.55 3.55

Independence, 25th Anniv. — A146

1990, Aug. 16 Litho. ***Perf. 14x14½***

576 A146 15c shown .20 .20
a. Booklet pane of 10 1.60
577 A146 35c One Singapore .40 .40
578 A146 75c One hope .85 .85
579 A146 $1 One people 1.10 1.10
Nos. 576-579 (4) 2.55 2.55

Tourism A147

$1, Chinese opera singer, Siong Lim Temple. $2, Malay dancer, Sultan Mosque. $5, Indian dancer, Sri Mariamman Temple. $10, Ballet dancer, Victoria Memorial Hall.

Photo. & Engr.

1990, Oct. 10 ***Perf. 15x14***

580 A147 $1 multicolored 1.40 1.40
581 A147 $2 multicolored 2.75 2.75
582 A147 $5 multicolored 6.75 6.75
583 A147 $10 multicolored 12.00 12.00
Nos. 580-583 (4) 22.90 22.90

Ferns A148

1990, Nov. 14 Litho. *Perf. 14*
584 A148 15c Stag's horn .20 .20
585 A148 35c Maiden hair .40 .40
586 A148 75c Bird's nest .85 .85
587 A148 $1 Rabbit's foot 1.10 1.10
Nos. 584-587 (4) 2.55 2.55

Houses of Worship A149

Designs: 20c, Hong San See Temple, 1912. 50c, Abdul Gattoor Mosque, 1910. 75c, Sri Perumal Temple, 1961. $1, St. Andrew's Cathedral, 1863.

1991, Jan. 23 Litho. *Perf. 14½*
588 20c multicolored .25 .25
589 20c multicolored .25 .25
a. A149 Pair, #588-589 .45 .45
590 50c multicolored .55 .55
591 50c multicolored .55 .55
a. A149 Pair, #590-591 1.10 1.10
592 75c multicolored .80 .80
593 75c multicolored .80 .80
a. A149 Pair, #592-593 1.60 1.60
594 $1 multicolored 1.10 1.10
595 $1 multicolored 1.10 1.10
a. A149 Pair, #594-595 2.25 2.25
Nos. 588-595 (8) 5.40 5.40

Vanda Miss Joaquim — A151

Design: No. 597, Dendrobium Anocha.

1991, Apr. 24 Litho. *Perf. 14*
596 A151 $2 multicolored 2.25 2.25
597 A151 $2 multicolored 2.25 2.25
a. Pair, #596-597 + label 4.50 4.50

Singapore '95 Intl. Philatelic Exhibition.

See Nos. 615-616, 664-665, 685-686, 716-717.

Civilian Airports A152

Designs: 20c, Boeing 747, Changi Terminal II, 1991. 75c, Boeing 747, Changi Terminal I, 1981. $1, Concorde, Paya Lebar, 1955-1981. $2, DC-3, Kallang, 1937-1955.

Perf. 13½x14½
1991, July 1 Litho. & Engr.
598 A152 20c multicolored .25 .25
599 A152 75c multicolored .85 .85
600 A152 $1 multicolored 1.10 1.10
601 A152 $2 multicolored 2.25 2.25
Nos. 598-601 (4) 4.45 4.45

Arachnopsis Eric Holttum A153

Orchids: 30c, Cattleya Meadii. $1, Calanthe vestita.

1991, Aug. 8 Litho. *Perf. 14½x13½*
602 A153 20c multicolored .25 .25
603 A153 30c multicolored .35 .35
604 A153 $1 multicolored 1.10 1.10
Nos. 602-604 (3) 1.70 1.70

Birds — A154

Designs: 20c, Common tailorbird. 35c, Scarlet-backed flowerpecker. 75c, Black-naped oriole. $1, Common tora.

1991, Sept. 19 *Perf. 14*
605 A154 20c multicolored .20 .20
a. Booklet pane of 10 2.25 2.25
606 A154 35c multicolored .40 .40
607 A154 75c multicolored .85 .85
608 A154 $1 multicolored 1.10 1.10
Nos. 605-608 (4) 2.55 2.55

10 Years of Productivity — A155

Phila Nippon '91 — A156

1991, Nov. 1 Litho. *Perf. 14x14½*
609 A155 20c shown .25 .25
610 A155 $1 Construction engineers 1.10 1.10

1991, Nov. 16 *Perf. 14½x14*

Flowers: 30c, Railway creeper. 75c, Asystasia. $1, Singapore rhododendron. $2, Coat buttons.

611 A156 30c multicolored .35 .35
612 A156 75c multicolored .85 .85
613 A156 $1 multicolored 1.10 1.10
614 A156 $2 multicolored 2.25 2.25
a. Souvenir sheet of 4, #611-614 4.75 4.75
Nos. 611-614 (4) 4.55 4.55

Flower Type of 1991

Designs: No. 615, Dendrobium Sharifah Fatimah. No. 616, Phalaenopsis Shim Beauty.

1992, Jan. 22 Litho. *Perf. 14*
615 A151 $2 multicolored 2.25 2.25
616 A151 $2 multicolored 2.25 2.25
a. Pair, #615-616 + label 4.75 4.75
b. Souvenir sheet of 2, #615-616 5.75 5.75

Singapore '95 Intl. Philatelic Exhibition.

Paintings A157

1992, Mar. 11 Litho. *Perf. 14*
617 A157 20c Singapore Waterfront, 1958 .25 .25
618 A157 75c Kampung Hut, 1973 .85 .85
619 A157 $1 Bridge, 1983 1.10 1.10
620 A157 $2 Singapore River, 1984 2.25 2.25
Nos. 617-620 (4) 4.45 4.45

1992 Summer Olympics, Barcelona A158

1992, Apr. 24 *Perf. 14*
621 A158 20c Soccer .30 .30
622 A158 35c Relay races .50 .50
623 A158 50c Swimming .70 .70
624 A158 75c Basketball 1.00 1.00
625 A158 $1 Tennis 1.25 1.25
626 A158 $2 Sailing 2.75 2.75
a. Souvenir sheet of 6, #621-626 7.00 7.00
Nos. 621-626 (6) 6.50 6.50

Costumes, 1910 — A159

1992, Apr. 24 Litho. *Perf. 14½*
627 A159 20c Chinese family .25 .25
628 A159 35c Malay family .45 .45
629 A159 75c Indian family .90 .90
630 A159 $2 Straits Chinese family 2.50 2.50
Nos. 627-630 (4) 4.10 4.10

Natl. Military Forces, 25th Anniv. — A160

Designs: 35c, Frogman with gun, fighter plane, artillery. $1, Fighter, tank, ship.

1992, July 1
631 A160 20c multicolored .25 .25
632 A160 35c multicolored .45 .45
633 A160 $1 multicolored 1.25 1.25
Nos. 631-633 (3) 1.95 1.95

Visit ASEAN Year, 25th Anniv. A161

Designs: 20c, Mask, bird, sea life. 35c, Costumed women. $1, Outdoor scenery.

1992, Aug. 8
634 A161 20c multicolored .25 .25
635 A161 35c multicolored .45 .45
636 A161 $1 multicolored 1.25 1.25
Nos. 634-636 (3) 1.95 1.95

Crabs A162

Designs: 20c, Mosaic crab. 50c, Johnson's freshwater crab. 75c, Singapore freshwater crab. $1, Swamp forest crab.

1992, Aug. 21 *Perf. 14½x15*
637 A162 20c multicolored .25 .25
a. Booklet pane of 10 2.50
638 A162 50c multicolored .60 .60
639 A162 75c multicolored .90 .90
640 A162 $1 multicolored 1.25 1.25
Nos. 637-640 (4) 3.00 3.00

Currency, Notes and Coins — A163

1992, Oct. 2 Litho. *Perf. 14½*
641 20c Coins .25 .25
642 75c Coin, flowers on note .90 .90
643 $1 Boat on note, coins 1.25 1.25
644 $2 Bird on note 2.50 2.50
a. A163 Block of 4, #641-644 4.75 4.75

Wild Animals A164

1993, Jan. 13 Litho. *Perf. 14½x15*
645 A164 20c Sun bear .25 .25
646 A164 30c Orangutan .35 .35
647 A164 75c Slow loris .90 .90
648 A164 $2 Large mouse deer 2.50 2.50
Nos. 645-648 (4) 4.00 4.00

Greetings Stamps — A165

a, Thank you. b, Congratulations. c, Best wishes. d, Happy birthday. e, Get well soon.

Perf. 14½x14 on 3 Sides
1993, Feb. 10
Booklet Stamps
649 A165 20c Strip of 5, #a.-e. 1.25 1.25
f. Booklet pane of 2 #649 2.50 2.50

Preservation of Tanjong Pagar — A166

1993, Mar. 10 Litho. *Perf. 14*
650 A166 20c shown .25 .25
651 A166 30c Building facade, tower .35 .35
652 A166 $2 Aerial view 2.50 2.50
Nos. 650-652 (3) 3.10 3.10

A167

A168

1993, May 29 *Perf. 12x11½*

653 A167 $2 Cranes, by Chen Wen Hsi		2.50	2.50

Indopex '93.

1993, June 12 **Litho.** *Perf. 14*

654 A168 20c Soccer	.25	.25
655 A168 35c Basketball	.45	.45
656 A168 50c Badminton	.60	.60
657 A168 75c Running	.95	.95
658 A168 $1 Water polo	1.25	1.25
659 A168 $2 Yachting	2.50	2.50
Nos. 654-659 (6)	6.00	6.00

17th Sea Games, Singapore.

Butterflies A169

Fruits — A170

1993, Aug. 21 **Litho.** *Perf. 14½*

660 A169 20c Plain tiger	.25	.25
a. Booklet pane of 10	2.50	
661 A169 50c Malay lacewing	.60	.60
662 A169 75c Palm king	.90	.90
663 A169 $1 Banded swallowtail	1.25	1.25
Nos. 660-663 (4)	3.00	3.00

Flower Type of 1991

1993, Aug. 13

Size: 26x34mm

664 A151 $2 Phalaenopsis amabilis	2.50	2.50
665 A151 $2 Vanda sumatrana	2.50	2.50
a. Pair, #664-665 + label	5.00	5.00
b. Souvenir sheet of 2, #664-665, perf. 15x14½	5.00	5.00

Singapore '95 World Stamp Exhibition and Taipei '93, Asian Intl. Invitation Stamp Exhibition (#665b).

1993, Oct. 1 **Litho.** *Perf. 14½x14*

666 A170 20c Papaya	.25	.25
667 A170 35c Pomegranate	.45	.45
668 A170 75c Starfruit	.95	.95
669 A170 $2 Durian	2.50	2.50
a. Souvenir sheet of 4, #666-669	4.50	4.50
Nos. 666-669 (4)	4.15	4.15

Bangkok '93 (#669a).

Chinese Egrets — A171

Designs: 20c, Two, one with bill in water. 25c, Two, one with fish in mouth. 30c, Two facing opposite directions. 35c, In flight.

1993, Nov. 10 **Litho.** *Perf. 13½x14*

670 A171 20c multicolored	*.40*	*.40*
671 A171 25c multicolored	*.55*	*.55*
672 A171 30c multicolored	*.65*	*.65*
673 A171 35c multicolored	*.75*	*.75*
a. Strip of 4, #670-673	*2.50*	*2.50*

World Wildlife Fund.

Palm Tree — A171a

1993, Nov. 24 **Photo.** ***Die Cut***

Self-Adhesive

Booklet Stamp

673B A171a (20c) multicolored	.25	.25
c. Booklet pane of 15	3.75	

By its nature, No. 673c is a complete booklet. The peelable backing serves as a booklet cover.

Marine Life — A172

Perf. 13x13½, 13½x14 (#675B)

1994 **Litho.**

674 A172 5c Tiger cowrie	.20	.20
675 A172 20c Sea fan	.25	.25
a. Booklet pane of 10	2.50	
675B A172 (20c) Blue-spotted stingray	.30	.30
676 A172 25c Tunicate	.35	.35
677 A172 30c Clownfish	.40	.40
678 A172 35c Nudibranch	.45	.45
679 A172 40c Sea urchin	.50	.50
680 A172 50c Soft coral	.65	.65
681 A172 75c Pin cushion star	.95	.95

Litho. & Embossed

Perf. 14 Syncopated Type A (2 Sides)

682 A172 $1 Knob coral	1.40	1.40
683 A172 $2 Mushroom coral	2.75	2.75
684 A172 $5 Bubble coral	7.00	7.00
684A A172 $10 Octopus coral	14.00	14.00
Nos. 674-684A (13)	29.20	29.20

Self-Adhesive

Die Cut Perf. 8½

684B A172 (20c) Blue-spotted stingray	.30	.30
c. Booklet pane of 10	3.00	

Nos. 675B, 684B inscribed "FOR LOCAL ADDRESSES ONLY." By its nature, No. 684c is a complete booklet. The peelable paper backing serves as a booklet cover.

Issued: 5c-75c, 1/12/94; $1-$10, 3/23/94; #675B, 684B, 11/16/94.

See Nos. 816-824.

Flower Type of 1991

Designs: No. 685, Paphiopedilum victoriaregina. No. 686, Dendrobium smillieae.

1994, Feb. 18 **Litho.** *Perf. 14½*

Size: 26x35mm

685 A151 $2 multicolored	2.75	2.75
686 A151 $2 multicolored	2.75	2.75
a. Pair, #685-686 + label	5.50	5.50
b. Souvenir sheet of 2, #685-686	6.00	6.00

Singapore '95 and Hong Kong '94 (#686b).

Spring Festival — A173

1994, May 18 **Litho.** *Perf. 13½*

687 A173 20c Ballet	.30	.30
688 A173 30c Mime, puppets	.40	.40
689 A173 50c Musicians	.70	.70
690 A173 $1 Crafts	1.40	1.40
Nos. 687-690 (4)	2.80	2.80

Operationally Ready Natl. Servicemen, 25th Anniv. — A174

Civilian-soldiers: 20c, Saluting flag, aiming anti-tank missile. 30c, With family, on jungle patrol with automatic rifle. 35c, Reading newspaper, aiming machine gun. 75c, Working with computer, and as commander, looking through binoculars.

1994, July 1 **Litho.** *Perf. 13½*

691 A174 20c multicolored	.30	.30
692 A174 30c multicolored	.45	.45
693 A174 35c multicolored	.50	.50
694 A174 75c multicolored	1.10	1.10
Nos. 691-694 (4)	2.35	2.35

Herons — A175

1994, Aug. 16 **Litho.** *Perf. 14*

695 A175 20c Black-crowned night heron	.30	.30
a. Booklet pane of 10	3.00	
696 A175 50c Little heron	.70	.70
697 A175 75c Purple heron	1.00	1.00
698 A175 $1 Gray heron	1.40	1.40
a. Block of 4, #695-698	3.50	3.50
Nos. 695-698 (4)	3.40	3.40

Greetings Stamps — A175a

#698B, Birthday cake. #698C, Bouquet of flowers. #698D, Gift-wrapped present. #698E, Fireworks. #698F, Balloons.

Die Cut Perf. 11½

1994, Sept. 14 **Litho.**

Self-Adhesive

Booklet Stamps

698B A175a (20c) multicolored	.30	.30
698C A175a (20c) multicolored	.30	.30
698D A175a (20c) multicolored	.30	.30
698E A175a (20c) multicolored	.30	.30
698F A175a (20c) multicolored	.30	.30
g. Bklt. pane, 2 ea #698B-698F	3.00	
Nos. 698B-698F (5)	1.50	1.50

Nos. 698B-693F inscribed "For Local Addresses Only." By its nature, No. 698Fg is a complete booklet. The peelable paper backing serves as a booklet cover. The outside of the cover contains 10 peelable labels.

Modern Singapore, 175th Anniv. — A176

Early, modern scenes: 20c, Schoolchildren reading, graduating seniors. 50c, Horse-drawn carriages, high-speed train. 75c, Small boats, container ship dock. $1, Skyline.

1994, Sept. 30 *Perf. 13½x14*

699 A176 20c multicolored	.30	.30
700 A176 50c multicolored	.70	.70
701 A176 75c multicolored	1.00	1.00
702 A176 $1 multicolored	1.40	1.40
a. Souvenir sheet of 4, #699-702	4.00	4.00
Nos. 699-702 (4)	3.40	3.40

ICAO, 50th Anniv. A177

Designs: 35c, Control tower, passenger jet. 75c, Terminal, Concord jet. $2, Control tower, communication satellite, passenger jet.

1994, Oct. 5 **Litho.** *Perf. 14*

703 A177 20c multicolored	.30	.30
704 A177 35c multicolored	.50	.50
705 A177 75c multicolored	1.10	1.10
706 A177 $2 multicolored	3.00	3.00
Nos. 703-706 (4)	4.90	4.90

Love Stamps — A178

#707, "Love" in three different inscriptions. #708, Spiral of "Love." #709, "Love" on two lines. #710, "Love" in different languages. #711, Geometrical "Love."

Die Cut Perf. 11½

1995, Feb. 8 **Litho.**

Self-Adhesive

Booklet Stamps

707 A178 (20c) multicolored	.30	.30
708 A178 (20c) multicolored	.30	.30
709 A178 (20c) multicolored	.30	.30
710 A178 (20c) multicolored	.30	.30
711 A178 (20c) multicolored	.30	.30
a. Booklet pane, 2 each #707-711	3.00	
Nos. 707-711 (5)	1.50	1.50

Nos. 707-711 inscribed "FOR LOCAL ADDRESSES ONLY." By its nature, No. 711a is a complete booklet. The peelable paper backing serves as a booklet cover. The outside of the cover contains 10 peelable labels.

Meet in Singapore — A179

Scenes in Suntec City: (20c), Intl. Convention & Exhibition Center. 75c, High rise buildings. $1, Temasek Boulevard. $2, Fountain Terrace.

1995, Jan. 11 *Perf. 13½x14*

712 A179 (20c) multicolored	.30	.30
713 A179 75c multicolored	1.10	1.10
714 A179 $1 multicolored	1.50	1.50
715 A179 $2 multicolored	3.00	3.00
Nos. 712-715 (4)	5.90	5.90

Singapore '95. No. 712 inscribed "FOR LOCAL ADDRESSES ONLY."

Souvenir Sheets of 2, #712, 715 Inscribed:

715a	FIP DAY	4.00	4.00
715b	OLYMPIC DAY-YOUTH	4.00	4.00
715c	FIAP DAY	4.00	4.00
715d	LETTER WRITING DAY	4.00	4.00
715e	STAMP COLLECTING DAY	4.00	4.00
715f	SINGAPORE '95 DAY	4.00	4.00
715g	PHILATELIC MUSEUM DAY	4.00	4.00
715h	SINGAPORE POST DAY	4.00	4.00
715i	AWARDS DAY	4.00	4.00
715j	THEMATIC PHILATELY DAY	4.00	4.00

Flower Type of 1991

Designs: No. 716, Vanda Marlie Dolera, No. 717, Vanda limbata.

1995, Mar. 15 **Litho.** *Perf. 14*

716 A151 $2 multicolored	3.00	3.00
717 A151 $2 multicolored	3.00	3.00
a. Pair, #716-717 + label	6.00	6.00
b. Souvenir sheet, #716-717	6.00	6.00
c. Souvenir sheet, #716-717	6.00	6.00

Singapore '95 (#717a-717c).

The margin of No. 717b pictures a chimpanzee in the jungle and No. 717c pictures a fish.

Three limited edition sheets were issued 9/1/95 at the show. They sold for 50, 12.5 and 2.9 times face. Values, $550, $220, $350.

Independence, 30th Anniv. — A180

"My Singapore, My Country, Happy Birthday" in various languages and: 20c, "30" formed in ribbon, vert. 50c, #471, flower. 75c,

#598, Music sheet. $1, Natl. flag, #489, music sheets, vert.

Perf. 14x13½, 13½x14

1995, Apr. 19 **Litho.**

718	A180	(20c) multicolored	.30	.30
719	A180	50c multicolored	.70	.70
720	A180	75c multicolored	1.10	1.10
721	A180	$1 multicolored	1.40	1.40
a.		Souvenir sheet of 4, #718-721	3.75	3.75
		Nos. 718-721 (4)	3.50	3.50

No. 718 inscribed "For Local Addresses Only." No. 721a is a continuous design.

End of World War II, 50th Anniv. A181

Designs: (20c), Crowd celebrating, Straits Settlements #271, vert. 60c, Lord Mountbatten receiving Japanese surrender of Singapore, Straits Settlements #265, vert. 70c, Food kitchen. $2, Police road block.

Perf. 14x13½, 13½x14

1995, June 21 **Litho.**

723	A181	(20c) multicolored	.30	.30
724	A181	60c multicolored	.90	.90
725	A181	70c multicolored	1.00	1.00
726	A181	$2 multicolored	3.00	3.00
		Nos. 723-726 (4)	5.20	5.20

No. 723 inscribed "For Local Addresses Only" and sold for 20c on day of issue.

New Six Digit Postal Code A182

1995, Sept. 1 **Litho.** ***Perf. 14x14½***

727	A182	(20c) shown	.30	.30
728	A182	$2 Six boxes, numbers	3.00	3.00

No. 728 inscribed "For Local Addresses Only."

Philatelic Museum, Singapore A183

Museum building, various stamps, featuring: 20c, #12. 50c, #157. 60c, #661. $2, Displays of stamps.

1995, Aug. 19 ***Perf. 13x13½***

729	A183	(20c) multicolored	.30	.30
730	A183	50c multicolored	.80	.80
731	A183	60c multicolored	.90	.90
732	A183	$2 multicolored	3.00	3.00
		Nos. 729-732 (4)	5.00	5.00

No. 729 inscribed "For Local Addresses Only."

Fish A184

1995, July 19 **Litho.** ***Perf. 13½x14***

733	A184	(20c) Yellow-faced angelfish	.30	.30
		Complete booklet, 10 #733	3.00	
734	A184	60c Harlequin sweetlips	.90	.90
735	A184	70c Lionfish	1.00	1.00
736	A184	$1 Longfin bannerfish	1.50	1.50
		Nos. 733-736 (4)	3.70	3.70

No. 733 inscribed "For Local Addresses Only."

Paintings in Singapore Art Museum A185

Designs: (20c), Tropical Fruits, by Georgette Chen. 30c, Bali Beach, by Cheong Soo Pieng. 70c, Gibbons, by Chen Wen Hsi. $2, Shi (Lion), by Pan Shou (calligraphy).

1995, Oct. 20 **Litho.** ***Perf. 12½***

737	A185	(20c) multicolored	.30	.30
738	A185	30c multicolored	.45	.45
739	A185	70c multicolored	1.00	1.00

Perf. 13½x13

740	A185	$2 multicolored	3.00	3.00
		Nos. 737-740 (4)	4.75	4.75

No. 737 inscribed "For Local Addresses Only." No. 740 is 22½x39mm.

New Year 1996 (Year of the Rat) — A186

1996, Feb. 9 **Litho.** ***Perf. 12***

741	A186	(20c) shown	.25	.25
742	A186	$2 Rat with orange	3.00	3.00

Souvenir Sheet

742A	A186	Sheet of 2, #742, 742Ab	3.25	3.25
b.		22c like #741	.25	.25
c.		As #742A, diff. sheet margin	3.25	3.25
d.		As #742A, diff. sheet margin	3.25	3.25

No. 741 inscribed "For Local Addresses Only."

Sheet margins contain exhibition emblems for: #742A: Indonesia '96; #742Ac, China '96; #742Ad, CAPEX '96.

Issued: #742A, 3/21; #742Ac, 5/18; #742Ad, 6/8.

Architectural Styles — A187

Designs: (20c), Bukit Pasoh, Chinatown. 35c, Jalan Sultan, Kampong Glam. 70c, Dalhousie Lane, Little India. $1, Supreme Court, Civic District.

1996, Jan. 17 ***Perf. 13½x14***

743	A187	(20c) multicolored	.30	.30
744	A187	35c multicolored	.55	.55
745	A187	70c multicolored	1.00	1.00
746	A187	$1 multicolored	1.50	1.50
		Nos. 743-746 (4)	3.35	3.35

No. 743 inscribed "For Local Addresses Only."

Old Maps of Singapore A188

Designs: (20c), Old Straits. 60c, Detail of town. $1, Part of Malay Penisula, Singapore. $2, Town and entrance.

1996, Mar. 13 **Litho.** ***Perf. 12***

747	A188	(20c) multicolored	.30	.30
748	A188	60c multicolored	.90	.90
749	A188	$1 multicolored	1.50	1.50
750	A188	$2 multicolored	3.00	3.00
		Nos. 747-750 (4)	5.70	5.70

No. 747 inscribed "For Local Addresses Only."

Greetings Stamps — A189

Children's drawings about courtesy: (22c), #755Ab, Child telling another to be quiet in library. 35c, Children helping elderly during outdoor activities. 50c, Giving seat at bus stop to expectant mother. 60c, Sharing umbrella. $1, Giving up seat on bus to senior citizen.

Die Cut Perf. 11

1996, July 10 **Litho.**

Self-Adhesive

Booklet Stamps

751	A189	(22c) multicolored	.30	.30
a.		Booklet pane of 10	3.00	
752	A189	35c multicolored	.55	.55
753	A189	50c multicolored	.75	.75
754	A189	60c multicolored	.90	.90
755	A189	$1 multicolored	1.50	1.50
a.		Booklet pane of 10, 5 #751, 2 #752, 1 each #753-755	5.75	
		Nos. 751-755 (5)	4.00	4.00

Souvenir Sheet

755B	A189	Sheet of 5, #752-755, 755Bc	4.00	4.00
c.		22c multicolored	.30	.30

No. 751 inscribed "For Local Addresses Only." By their nature Nos. 751a and 755a are complete booklets. The peelable paper backing serves as a booklet cover. The outside of the cover contains 10 peelable labels.

1996 Summer Olympic Games, Atlanta — A190

Designs: (22c), #759Ab, Board, dinghy sailing. 60c, Soccer, tennis. 70c, Pole vault, hurdles. $2, Diving, swimming.

1996, July 19 **Litho.** ***Perf. 14½***

756	A190	(22c) multicolored	.30	.30
757	A190	60c multicolored	.90	.90
758	A190	70c multicolored	1.00	1.00
759	A190	$2 multicolored	3.00	3.00
		Nos. 756-759 (4)	5.20	5.20

Souvenir Sheet

759A	A190	Sheet of 4, #757-759, 759Ab	5.25	5.25
b.		22c multicolored	.30	.30

No. 756 inscribed "For Local Addresses Only."

Asian Civilizations Museum — A191

(22c), Calligraphy in Caoshu, Ming Dynasty, 17th cent. 60c, Javanese Divination manuscript, Surkarta (Solo), Indonesia, 1842. 70c, Temple hanging, Tamilnadu. South India, 19th cent. $2, Calligraphic implements, Persia and Turkey, 17th-19th cent.

1996, June 5 **Litho.** ***Perf. 13½x14***

760	A191	(22c) multicolored	.30	.30
761	A191	60c multicolored	.90	.90
762	A191	70c multicolored	1.00	1.00
763	A191	$2 multicolored	3.00	3.00
		Nos. 760-763 (4)	5.20	5.20

No. 760 inscribed "For Local Addresses Only."

Care for Nature — A192

Native trees: (22c), Cinnamomum iners. 60c, Hibiscus tiliaceus. 70c, Parkia speciosa. $1, Terminalia catappa.

1996, Sept. 11 **Litho.** ***Perf. 13½***

764	A192	(22c) multicolored	.30	.30
a.		Booklet pane of 10	3.00	
		Complete booklet, #764a	3.00	
765	A192	60c multicolored	.90	.90
766	A192	70c multicolored	1.00	1.00
767	A192	$1 multicolored	1.50	1.50
		Nos. 764-767 (4)	3.70	3.70

No. 764 inscribed "For Local Addresses Only."

Panmen, Suzhou, China — A193

Design: 60c, Singapore waterfront.

1996, Oct. 9 **Litho.** ***Perf. 13x13½***

768	A193	(22c) multicolored	.30	.30
769	A193	60c multicolored	.90	.90

Souvenir Sheet

769A	A193	Sheet of 2, #769, 769Ab	1.25	1.25
b.		22c like #768	.30	.30
c.		As #769A, ovptd. in sheet margin	1.20	1.20

No. 768 inscribed "For Local Addresses Only."

No. 769Ac is ovptd. in sheet margin with violet on gold Singapore-China Stamp Exhibition emblem.

See People's Republic of China Nos. 2733-2734.

First World Trade Organization Ministerial Conference — A194

Illustration reduced.

1996, Nov. 20 **Litho.** ***Perf. 14***

770	A194	(22c) pink, vio & multi	.35	.35
771	A194	60c ver, grn & multi	.90	.90
772	A194	$1 bl, yel org & multi	1.50	1.50
773	A194	$2 grn, car & multi	3.00	3.00
		Nos. 770-773 (4)	5.75	5.75

No. 770 inscribed "For Local Addresses Only."

New Year 1997 (Year of the Ox) A195

Nos. 774, 775, Different stylized oxen.

1997, Jan. 10 ***Perf. 13½x14***

774 A195 (22c) multicolored .35 .35
775 A195 $2 multicolored 3.00 3.00
a. Sheet, 9 each #774-775 32.50
b. Souvenir sheet of #775, #775d 3.50 3.50
c. As "b," diff. sheet margin 3.50 3.50
d. 22c like #774 .35 .35
e. As "b," diff. sheet margin 3.50 3.50

No. 774 inscribed "For Local Addresses Only."

Sheet margin contains exhibition emblem: #775b Hong Kong '97; #775c Pacific '97; #775e Shanghai 1997.

Issued: #775b, 2/12/97; #775c, 5/29/97; #775e, 11/19/97.

Traditional Games
A196

Ground Transportation
A197

1997, Feb. 21 **Litho.** ***Perf. 14½***

776 A196 (22c) Shuttlecock .35 .35
777 A196 35c Marbles .55 .55
778 A196 60c Tops .90 .90
779 A196 $1 Fivestones 1.50 1.50
a. Souvenir sheet of 4, #776-779 3.30 3.30
Nos. 776-779 (4) 3.30 3.30

No. 776 inscribed "For Local Addresses Only." Singpex '97 (#779a).

1997, Mar. 19 ***Perf. 13½***

780 A197 5c Bullock cart .20 .20
781 A197 20c Bicycle .30 .30
782 A197 (22c) Rickshaw .35 .35
783 A197 30c Electric tram .45 .45
784 A197 35c Trolley bus .55 .55
785 A197 40c Trishaw .60 .60
786 A197 50c Vintage car .75 .75
787 A197 60c Horse-drawn carriage .90 .90
788 A197 70c Fire engine 1.00 1.00
Nos. 780-788 (9) 5.10 5.10

Souvenir Sheet

788A A197 Sheet, #780-781, 783-788, 788Ab 5.00 5.00
b. 22c like #782 .35 .35

Self-Adhesive

Serpentine Die Cut Perf. 11½

Booklet Stamp

789 A197 (22c) like #782 .35 .35
a. Booklet pane of 10 3.50

Nos. 782, 789 are inscribed "For Local Addresses Only." Nos. 780, 783-784, 787-788 are horiz.

By its nature No. 789a is a complete booklet. The peelable paper backing serves as a booklet cover.

Litho. & Engr.

1997, Apr. 23 ***Perf. 13***

$1, Taxi. $2, Bus, horiz. $5, Mass rapid transit system. $10, Light rapid transit system, horiz.

Size: 28x35mm (#790, 792), 43x24mm (#791, 793)

790 A197 $1 multicolored 1.50 1.50
791 A197 $2 multicolored 3.00 3.00
792 A197 $5 multicolored 7.50 7.50
793 A197 $10 multicolored 15.00 15.00
a. Souvenir sheet, #790-793 27.50 27.50
Nos. 790-793 (4) 27.00 27.00

Greetings Stamps — A198

Word "Friends" used in making designs: #794, Man's head. #795, Sharing umbrella. #796, Penguins. #797, Butterflies, hand. #798, Coffee cup. #799, Flower. #800, Candle. #801, Tree. #802, Jar holding stars. #803, Two cans connected by string.

Serpentine Die Cut 14½

1997, May 14 **Litho.**

Self-Adhesive

Booklet Stamps

794 A198 (22c) multicolored .35 .35
795 A198 (22c) multicolored .35 .35
796 A198 (22c) multicolored .35 .35
797 A198 (22c) multicolored .35 .35
798 A198 (22c) multicolored .35 .35
a. Booklet pane, 2 each #794-798 3.50
Nos. 794-798 (5) 1.75 1.75
799 A198 (22c) multicolored .35 .35
800 A198 (22c) multicolored .35 .35
801 A198 (22c) multicolored .35 .35
802 A198 (22c) multicolored .35 .35
803 A198 (22c) multicolored .35 .35
a. Booklet pane, 2 each #799-803 3.50
Nos. 799-803 (5) 1.75 1.75

Nos. 794-803 are inscribed "For Local Addresses Only." By their nature Nos. 798a and 803a are complete booklets. The peelable paper backing serves as a booklet cover. The outside cover contains 10 peelable labels.

Upgrading of Public Housing — A199

Designs: (22c) New look for the precinct. 30c, Outdoor facilities. 70c, Landscaped gardens. $1, Additional space, balcony.

1997, July 16 **Litho.** ***Perf. 14***

804 A199 (22c) multicolored .30 .30
805 A199 30c multicolored .40 .40
806 A199 70c multicolored .90 .90
807 A199 $1 multicolored 1.40 1.40
Nos. 804-807 (4) 3.00 3.00

No. 804 is inscribed "For Local Addresses Only."

ASEAN, 30th Anniv. — A200

Designs: (22c), 30 years of "dates," globe, hands clasped, sky. 35c, Southeast Asian cultures. 60c, Satellite dish, circuit board, map of Southeast Asia, sky. $1, Tourist attractions in ASEAN countries.

1997, Aug. 8 **Litho.** ***Perf. 14***

808 A200 (22c) multicolored .30 .30
809 A200 35c multicolored .50 .50
810 A200 60c multicolored .80 .80
811 A200 $1 multicolored 1.40 1.40
Nos. 808-811 (4) 3.00 3.00

No. 808 is inscribed "For Local Addresses Only."

Value is for copy with surrounding selvage.

Protection of the Environment — A201

(22c), Clean Environment. 60c, Clean waters. 70c, Clean air. $1, Clean homes.

1997, Sept. 13 **Litho.** ***Perf. 14x13½***

812 A201 (22c) multicolored .30 .30
a. Booklet pane of 10 3.00
Complete booklet, #812a 3.00

813 A201 60c multicolored .80 .80
814 A201 70c multicolored .90 .90
815 A201 $1 multicolored 1.30 1.30
Nos. 812-815 (4) 3.30 3.30

No. 812 is inscribed "For Local Addresses Only."

Marine Life Type of 1994

1997 **Photo.** ***Perf. 13x13½***

816 A172 5c like #674 .20 .20
816A A172 (20c) like #675B .35 .35
817 A172 25c like #676 .30 .30
818 A172 30c like #677 .40 .40
819 A172 35c like #678 .45 .45
820 A172 40c like #679 .50 .50
821 A172 50c like #680 .65 .65
821A A172 75c like #681 1.25 1.25

Photo. & Embossed

Perf. 14 Syncopated Type A (2 Sides)

822 A172 $1 like #682 1.25 1.25
822A A172 $2 like #683 3.25 3.25
823 A172 $5 like #684 6.25 6.25
824 A172 $10 like #684A 12.50 12.50
Nos. 816-824 (12) 27.35 27.35

No. 816A is inscribed "For Local Addresses Only."

Nos. 822-824 have embossed logo in center of stamp and denomination and country are white. Nos. 682, 684, 684A have embossed lettering for country name and denomination.

Shells of Singapore and Thailand A202

Designs: (22c), Drupa morum. 35c, Nerita chamaeleon. 60c, Littoraria melanostoma. $1, Cryptospira elegans.

1997, Oct. 9 **Litho.** ***Perf. 13x14***

825 A202 (22c) multicolored .30 .30
826 A202 35c multicolored .45 .45
827 A202 60c multicolored .75 .75
828 A202 $1 multicolored 1.25 1.25
Nos. 825-828 (4) 2.75 2.75

Souvenir Sheet

828A A202 Sheet of 4, #826-828, #828Ab 2.75 2.75
b. 22c like #825 .30 .30

No. 825 inscribed "For Local Addresses Only."

See Thailand Nos. 1771-1774.

New Year 1998 (Year of the Tiger) A203

Different stylized tigers.

1998, Jan. 9 **Litho.** ***Perf. 13x14***

829 A203 (22c) multicolored .25 .25
830 A203 $2 multicolored 2.50 2.50
a. Horiz. or vert. pair, #829-830 2.75 2.75
b. Sheet of 9 each, #829-830 27.50 27.50

Souvenir Sheet

830C A203 Sheet of 2, #830, #830Cd 2.75 2.75
d. 22c like #829 .30 .30
e. As #830C, diff. inscription 2.75 2.75

Israel '98 (#830C). Italia '98 (#830Ce).

No. 829 inscribed "For Local Addresses Only."

Stamps in No. 830b are arranged in a checkerboard fashion.

Issued: #830Ce, 10/23/98.

Dinosaurs — A204

Self-Adhesive

831 A204 (22c) Pentaceratops .30 .30
832 A204 (22c) Apatosaurus .30 .30
833 A204 (22c) Albertosaurus .30 .30
a. Pane, 5 each #831-833 4.50
Nos. 831-833 (3) .90 .90

Nos. 831-833 are inscribed "For Local Addresses Only."

A205

A206

Songbirds: (22c), Lesser green leafbird. 60c, Magpie robin. 70c, Straw-headed bulbul. $2, Yellow-bellied prinia.

1998, May 6 **Photo.** ***Perf. 11½***

Granite Paper

834 A205 (22c) multicolored .25 .25
835 A205 60c multicolored .75 .75
836 A205 70c multicolored .85 .85
837 A205 $2 multicolored 2.40 2.40
Nos. 834-837 (4) 4.25 4.25

No. 834 is inscribed "For Local Addresses Only."

Serpentine Die Cut 11

1998, May 20 **Litho.**

"Hello" stamps.

Self-Adhesive

Booklet Stamps

838 A206 (22c) yellow & multi .25 .25
839 A206 (22c) orange & multi .25 .25
840 A206 (22c) green & multi .25 .25
841 A206 (22c) blue & multi .25 .25
842 A206 (22c) black & multi .25 .25
a. Booklet pane, 2 each #838-842 2.50

Nos. 838-842 are inscribed "For Local Addresses Only."

By its nature No. 842a is a complete booklet. The peelable paper backing serves as a booklet cover. The outside cover contains 10 peelable labels.

Fauna from "Fragile Forest," Singapore Zoological Gardens — A207

Serpentine Die Cut 11½

1998, June 5 **Litho.**

Self-Adhesive

Booklet Stamps

843 A207 (22c) Rhino beetle .30 .30
844 A207 (22c) Surinam horned frog .30 .30
845 A207 (22c) Atlas moth .30 .30
846 A207 (22c) Green iguana .30 .30
847 A207 (22c) Giant scorpion .30 .30
a. Booklet, 2 each #843-847 3.00
848 A207 (22c) Hissing cockroach .30 .30
849 A207 (22c) Two-toed sloth .30 .30
850 A207 (22c) Archer fish .30 .30
851 A207 (22c) Cobalt blue tarantula .30 .30
852 A207 (22c) Greater mousedeer .30 .30
a. Booklet, 2 each #848-852 3.00

Nos. 843-852 are inscribed "For Local Addresses Only."

The peelable paper backing of Nos. 847a & 852a serves as a booklet cover. In the margins of Nos. 847a & 852a there is a leaf-shaped scratch-off that reveals an animal.

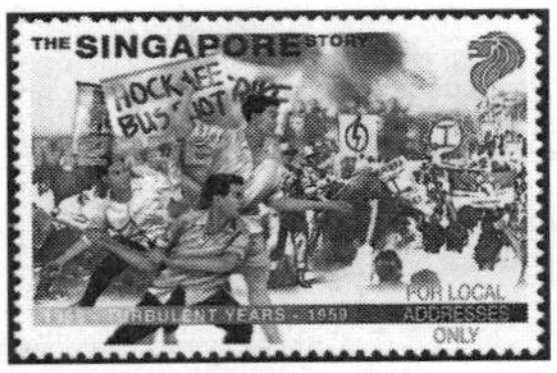

The Singapore Story (Moments in History) — A208

(22c), 22c, "Turbulent years," 1955-59. 60c, "Self-government," 1959-63. $1, "Towards merger and independence," 1961-65. $2, "A nation is born," 1965.

1998 ***Perf. 13x13½***

853 A208 (22c) multicolored .30 .30
854 A208 60c multicolored .75 .75
855 A208 $1 multicolored 1.25 1.25
856 A208 $2 multicolored 2.50 2.50
Nos. 853-856 (4) 4.80 4.80

Souvenir Sheet

857 Souvenir sheet of 4 9.00 9.00
a. 22c multicolored .50 .50
b. 60c multicolored 1.40 1.40
c. $1 multicolored 2.25 2.25
d. $2 multicolored 4.50 4.50

Issued: #853-856, 7/7/98; #857, 7/23/98.

No. 853 is inscribed "For Local Addresses Only." No. 857 has a UV varnish producing a shiny effect on portions of the design. No. 857 sold for $7.

Singpex '98 (#857).

Orchids of Singapore and Australia — A209

1998, Aug. 6 **Photo.** ***Perf. 11½***

858 A209 (22c) Moth orchid .30 .30
859 A209 70c Bamboo orchid .85 .85
860 A209 $1 Tiger orchid 1.25 1.25
861 A209 $2 Cooktown orchid 2.60 2.60
Nos. 858-861 (4) 5.00 5.00

Souvenir Sheet

861A A209 Sheet of 4, #859-861, #861Ab 5.00 5.00
b. 22c like #858 .30 .30

No. 858 is inscribed "For Local Addresses Only."

See Australia Nos. 1681-1684.

Flowers A210

Designs: No. 862, Wedilia trilobata. No. 863, Dillenia suffruticosa. No. 864, Canna hybrid. No. 865, Caesalpinia pulcherrima.

No. 866, Zephyranthes rosea. No. 867, Cassia alata. No. 868, Heliconia rostrata. No. 869, Allamanda cathartica.

1998, Sept. 9 **Litho.** ***Perf. 14***

862 A210 (22c) multicolored .30 .30
863 A210 (22c) multicolored .30 .30
864 A210 (22c) multicolored .30 .30
865 A210 (22c) multicolored .30 .30
a. Strip of 4, #862-865 1.25 1.25
b. Booklet pane, 3 each #864-865, 2 each #862-863 3.00
Complete booklet, #865b 3.00
866 A210 35c multicolored .40 .40
867 A210 35c multicolored .40 .40
868 A210 60c multicolored .70 .70
869 A210 60c multicolored .70 .70
a. Strip of 4, #866-869 2.25 2.25
b. Souvenir sheet of 8, #862-869 3.40 3.40

Stamps in #869b are in pairs, #864-863, 862/865 horiz., #866-867, 868, 869 vert.

A211

Festivals — A212

#870, 874 Eid al-Fitr. #871, 875, Christmas. #872, 876, Chinese New Year. #873, 877, Deepavali.

1998, Oct. 7 **Litho.** ***Perf. 13x14***

870 A211 (22c) multicolored .30 .30
871 A211 (22c) multicolored .30 .30
872 A211 (22c) multicolored .30 .30
873 A211 (22c) multicolored .30 .30
a. Block of 4, #870-873 1.25 1.25
874 A212 30c multicolored .35 .35
875 A212 30c multicolored .35 .35
876 A212 30c multicolored .35 .35
877 A212 30c multicolored .35 .35
Nos. 870-877 (8) 2.60 2.60

Nos. 870-873 are inscribed "For Local Addresses Only."

Serpentine Die Cut

878 A211 (22c) like #870 .30 .30
879 A211 (22c) like #871 .30 .30
880 A211 (22c) like #872 .30 .30
881 A211 (22c) like #873 .30 .30
Nos. 878-881 (4) 1.20 1.20

Historical Buildings — A213

(22c), Parliament House. 70c, Former Convent of the Holy Infant Jesus Chapel. $1, Hill Street Building. $2, Sun Yat Sen Nanyang Memorial Hall.

1998, Nov. 4 ***Perf. 13½***

882 A213 (22c) multicolored .30 .30
883 A213 70c multicolored .90 .90
884 A213 $1 multicolored 1.25 1.25
885 A213 $2 multicolored 2.50 2.50
Nos. 882-885 (4) 4.95 4.95

No. 882 inscribed "For Local Addresses Only."

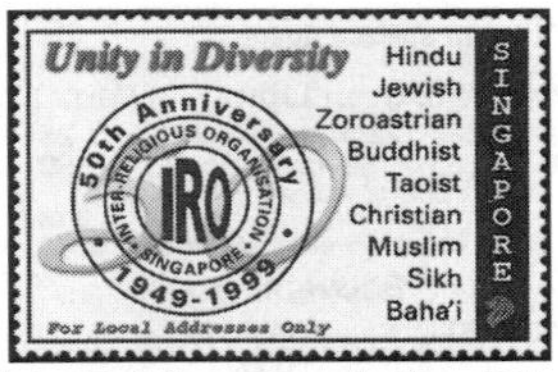

Inter-Religious Organization, 50th Anniv. — A214

1999, Jan. 15 **Litho.** ***Perf. 13x13½***

886 A214 (22c) white & multi .25 .25
887 A214 60c pink & multi .70 .70
888 A214 $1 blue & multi 1.25 1.25
Nos. 886-888 (3) 2.20 2.20

No. 886 is inscribed "For Local Addresses Only."

New Year 1999 (Year of the Rabbit) A215

Various stylized rabbits.

1999, Jan. 15 ***Perf. 14***

889 A215 (22c) multicolored .25 .25
890 A215 $2 multicolored 2.40 2.40
a. Horiz. or vert. pair, #889-890 2.75 2.75
b. Sheet, 9 each #829-830 25.00

Souvenir Sheet

890C Sheet of 2, #890 & 890Cd 2.75 2.75
d. A215 22c like #889 .30 .30
e. As #890C, with PhilexFrance 99 margin 2.75 2.75
f. As #890C, with China 1999 World Phil. Exhib. margin 2.75 2.75

No. 889 is inscribed "For Local Addresses Only."

No. 890C was issued 4/27 for IBRA '99, World Philatelic Exhibition, Nuremberg.

Issued: #890Ce, 7/2/99; #890Cf, 8/21/99.

19th Century Sailing Ships — A216

1999, Mar. 19 **Litho.** ***Perf. 14½***

891 A216 (22c) Clipper .25 .25
892 A216 70c Twakow, vert. .80 .80
893 A216 $1 Fujian junk, vert. 1.25 1.25
894 A216 $2 Golekkan 2.25 2.25
Nos. 891-894 (4) 4.55 4.55

Souvenir Sheet

894A A216 Sheet of 4, #892-894, #894Ab 4.50 4.50
b. 22c like #891 .25 .25

Australia '99 World Stamp Expo (#894A).

No. 891 is inscribed "For Local Address Only."

Greetings Stamps — A217

Expressions of kindness: a, "Think of others." b, "Do not litter." c, "Be kind to animals." d, "Be considerate." e, "Be generous."

Serpentine Die Cut 9½

1999, May 12 **Litho.**

Self-Adhesive

Booklet Stamps

895 A217 (22c) Booklet pane, 2 each #a.-e. 2.25 2.25

Nos. 895a-895e are inscribed "For Local Addresses Only."

No. 895 is a complete booklet. The peelable paper backing serves as a booklet cover. Stamps are printed 2 each #895a-895c on one side, 2 each #895d-895e on the other with 3 labels on each side.

Hong Kong and Singapore Tourism — A218

(22c), Hong Kong Harbor. 35c, Skyline of Singapore. 50c, Giant Buddha, Hong Kong. 60c, Merlion Sentosa Island, Singapore. 70c, Hong Kong Street scene. $1, Bugis Junction, Singapore.

1999, July 1 **Litho.** ***Perf. 13½x13¼***

896 A218 (22c) multicolored .25 .25
897 A218 35c multicolored .40 .40
898 A218 50c multicolored .60 .60
899 A218 60c multicolored .70 .70
900 A218 70c multicolored .85 .85
901 A218 $1 multicolored 1.25 1.25
Nos. 896-901 (6) 4.05 4.05

Souvenir Sheet

902 Sheet of 6, #897-901, #902a 4.00 4.00
a. A218 22c like #896 .25 .25

No. 896 is inscribed for "For Local Addresses Only."

See Hong Kong Nos. 849-854.

Butterflies A219

Perf. 12½x12¾

1999, Aug. 12 **Litho. & Engr.**

903 A219 (22c) Peacock .25 .25
904 A219 70c Blue pansy .85 .85
905 A219 $1 Great egg-fly 1.25 1.25
906 A219 $2 Red admiral 2.40 2.40
Nos. 903-906 (4) 4.75 4.75

Souvenir Sheet

907 A219 Sheet of 4, #904-906, #907a 4.75 4.75
a. A219 22c like #903 .25 .25

No. 903 is inscribed "For Local Addresses Only."

See Sweden No. 2356.

Yusof bin Ishak (1910-70), First President of Singapore A220

Perf. 13¼x13¾

1999, Sept. 9 **Litho. & Engr.**

908 A220 $2 multicolored 2.40 2.40

Amphibians & Reptiles — A221

1999, Oct. 13 **Litho.** ***Perf. 14***

909 A221 (22c) Green turtle .25 .25
Complete booklet, 10 #909 2.50
910 A221 60c Green crested lizard .75 .75
911 A221 70c Copper-cheeked frog .85 .85
912 A221 $1 Water monitor 1.25 1.25
Nos. 909-912 (4) 3.10 3.10

No. 909 inscribed "For Local Addresses Only."

New Parliament House — A222

Perf. 13¼x13¾

1999, Nov. 17 **Litho.**

913 A222 (22c) North view .30 .30
914 A222 60c Northeast view .75 .75
915 A222 $1 Southeast view 1.25 1.25
916 A222 $2 West view 2.50 2.50
Nos. 913-916 (4) 4.80 4.80

#913 inscribed "For Local Address Only."

Singapore in the 20th Century A223

No. 917: a, Colonialism. b, Education. c, Immigration. d, Government. e, Japanese occupation. f, National service. g, Transportation. h, Tourism. i, Housing. j, Economic progress.

Perf. 13¼x12½

1999, Dec. 31 Litho.
917 Sheet of 10 + 5 labels 7.00 7.00
a.-b. A223 (22c) Any single .25 .25
c.-d. A223 35c Any single .40 .40
e.-f. A223 60c Any single .70 .70
g.-h. A223 70c Any single .85 .85
i.-j. A223 $1 Any single 1.25 1.25

Nos. 917a-917b inscribed "For Local Addresses Only."

Millennium — A224

No. 918: a, (22c), Information technology. b, 60c, Arts and culture. c, $1, Heritage. d, $2, Globalization.
Illustration reduced.

2000, Jan. 1 Photo. *Perf. 14¼x14¾*
Granite Paper
918 A224 Horiz. strip of 4, #a-d 4.75 4.75
e. Souvenir sheet, #918 4.75 4.75

No. 918a inscribed "For Local Addresses Only."

New Year 2000 (Year of the Dragon) A225

Dragon: (22c), 22c, Facing left. $2, $10, Facing right.

2000 Litho. *Perf. 13x13¼*
919 A225 (22c) multi .25 .25
920 A225 $2 multi 2.40 2.40
a. Horiz. pair, #919-920 2.75 2.75
b. Souvenir sheet, #920a 2.75 2.75

Souvenir Sheets
921 Sheet of 2, #920, 922a, with Bangkok 2000 margin 2.75 2.75
a. A225 22c multi .25 .25
b. As No. 921, with The Stamp Show 2000 margin 2.75 2.75
c. As No. 921, with Naba 2000 margin 2.75 2.75

Litho. & Embossed
922 A225 $10 gold & multi 12.00 12.00

Issued: No. 920b, 10/30; No. 921, 3/25; No. 921b, 5/22; No. 921c, 6/21; others, 1/1. No. 919 inscribed "For Local Addresses Only."

Post Offices and Cancels A226

Designs: (22c), Original post office, B172 cancel. 60c, General Post Office, c. 1873, 1875 cancel. $1, General Post Office, 1928, 1935 cancel. $2, Singapore Post Center, 1998 cancel.

2000, Mar. 8 Litho. *Perf. 13½*
935 A226 (22c) multi .25 .25
936 A226 60c multi .70 .70
a. Booklet pane, 4 #935, 2 #936 2.40
937 A226 $1 multi 1.10 1.10
938 A226 $2 multi 2.40 2.40
a. Booklet pane, 4 #937, 2 #938 9.25
Complete bklt., #936a, 938a 12.00
Nos. 935-938 (4) 4.45 4.45

Souvenir Sheet
939 A226 Sheet of 4, #936-938, 939a 4.50 4.50
a. A226 22c like No. 935 .25 .25

No. 935 is inscribed "For Local Addresses Only."

Celebrations A227

Designs: No. 940, (22c), Yipee. No. 940A, (22c), Yeah. No. 940B, (22c), Hurray. No. 940C, (22c), Yes. No. 941, (22c), Happy.

Serpentine Die Cut 9½
2000, May 10 Litho.
Self-Adhesive
940-941 A227 Set of 5 1.40 1.40
941a Booklet, 2 each #940-941 2.80

Nos. 940-941 are inscribed "For Local Addresses Only." Eight self-adhesive die cut labels are affixed to the opposite side of the peelable backing paper.

Singapore River A228

No. 942: a, River community, 1920s. b, South Boat Quay, 1930s. c, Social gathering, 1950s. d, Changing skyline, 1980s. e, River Regatta, 1990s. f, At the river mouth, 1900s. g, Stevedores, 1910s. h, Lighters, 1940s. i, Men at work, 1960s. j, Working with cranes, 1970s.

2000, June 21 *Perf. 14*
942 Sheet of 10 5.00 5.00
a.-e. A228 (22c) Any single .25 .25
f.-j. A228 60c Any single .75 .75

Nos. 942a-942e are inscribed "For Local Addresses Only."

Stampin' the Future A229

Children's Stamp Design Contest Winners: (22c), Future lifestyle, art by Liu Jiang Wen. 60c, Future homes, art by Shaun Yew Chuan Bin. $1, Home automation, art by Gwendolyn Soh Shihui. $2, Floating city, art by Dawn Koh.

2000, July 7 Litho. *Perf. 14x12¾*
943-946 A229 Set of 4 4.75 4.75
946a Souvenir sheet, #943-946 4.75 4.75

World Stamp Expo 2000, Anaheim (No. 946a). No. 943 is inscribed "For Local Addresses Only."

Care for Nature A230

No. 947: a, Archer fish. b, Smooth otter. c, Collared kingfisher. d, Orange fiddler crab.

2000, Aug. 11 Photo. *Perf. 14½*
Granite Paper
947 Block of 4 3.00 3.00
a.-b. A230 (22c) Any single .25 .25
c.-d. A230 $1 Any single 1.25 1.25
e. Booklet pane, 5 each #947a, 947b 7.50
Booklet, #947e 7.50
f. Souv. sheet, #947, 947 imperf 6.00 6.00

Nos. 947a-947b are inscribed "For Local Addresses Only."
No. 947f sold for $5.

2000 Summer Olympics, Sydney — A231

Designs: (22c), Swimming and high jump. 60c, Badminton and discus. $1, Soccer and hurdles. $2, Table tennis and gymnastics.

2000, Sept. 15 Litho. *Perf. 13½*
948-951 A231 Set of 4 4.75 4.75

No. 948 is inscribed "For Local Addresses Only."

A232

Festivals and Holidays A233

Designs: Nos. 952, (22c), 956, 30c, Christmas. Nos. 953, (22c), 957, 30c, Eid ul-Fitr. Nos. 954, (22c), 958, 30c, Chinese New Year. Nos. 955, (22c), 959, 30c, Deepavali.

2000, Oct. 11 Litho. *Perf. 13*
952-955 A232 Set of 4 1.00 1.00
956-959 A233 Set of 4 1.40 1.40

Nos. 952-955 are inscribed "For Local Addresses Only."

Festivals and Holidays Type of 2000

Designs: No. 960, (22c), Christmas. No. 961, (22c), Eid ul-Fitr. No. 962, (22c), Chinese New Year. No. 963, (22c), Deepavali.

Serpentine Die Cut 12¾x13¼
2000, Oct. 11 Litho.
Self-Adhesive
960-963 A232 Set of 4 1.00 1.00

Nos. 960-963 inscribed "For Local Addresses Only."

New Year 2001 (Year of the Snake) A234

Designs: (22c), Snake and branch. $2, Two snakes.

2001, Jan. 12 *Perf. 14½x14*
964 A234 (22c) multi .25 .25
965 A234 $2 multi 2.40 2.40
a. Horiz. pair, #964-965 2.75 2.75
b. Souvenir sheet, #964-965, with Hong Kong 2001 margin 2.75 2.75
c. Souvenir sheet, #964-965, with Belgica 2001 margin 2.75 2.75
d. Souvenir sheet, #964-965, with Phila Nippon '01 margin 2.75 2.75

Issued: No. 965c, 6/9; No. 965d, 7/1.

Early Singaporeans A235

Designs: No. 966, $1, Tan Tock Seng (1798-1850), philanthropist. No. 967, $1, P. Govindasamy Pillai (1887-1980), businessman. No. 968, $1, Edwin John Tessensohn (1857-1926), politician. No. 969, $1, Eunos bin Abdullah (1876-1941), politician.

2001, Feb. 28 Photo. *Perf. 11¾*
Granite Paper
966-969 A235 Set of 4 4.75 4.75

Commonwealth Day, 25th Anniv. — A236

Designs: (22c), Co-operation. 60c, Education. $1, Sports. $2, Arts and culture.

2001, Mar. 12 Litho. *Perf. 14x14¼*
970-973 A236 Set of 4 4.25 4.25

No. 970 inscribed "For Local Addresses Only."

Greetings — A237

Serpentine Die Cut 10
2001, Apr. 25 Litho.
Self-Adhesive
974 A237 (22c) Balloons .25 .25
975 A237 (22c) Fireworks .25 .25
976 A237 (22c) Roses .25 .25
977 A237 (22c) Gifts .25 .25
978 A237 (22c) Musical instruments .25 .25
a. Booklet, 2 each #974-978 + 10 labels 2.50
Nos. 974-978 (5) 1.25 1.25

Nos. 974-978 inscribed "For Local Addresses Only."

Singapore Arts Festival — A238

No. 979: a, (22c), "a." b, 60c, "r." c, $1, "t." d, $2, "s."

2001, May 16 *Perf. 14*
979 A238 Block of 4, #a-d 4.25 4.25

No. 979a inscribed "For Local Addresses Only."

Pets — A239

No. 980: a, Fish. b, Cockatoos. c, Chicks. d, Turtle. e, Dog and fish. f, Cat and mice. g, Bird and dog. h, Dog and cat. i, Parrots. j, Cat and rabbit.

2001, July 26 *Perf. 13½*
980 A239 Sheet of 10 5.00 5.00
a.-d. (22c) Any single, 25x25mm .25 .25
e.-f. (22c) Any single, 25x35mm .25 .25
g.-h. 50c Any single, 25x42mm .60 .60
i.-j. $1 Any single, 25x42mm 1.10 1.10

Nos. 980a-980f are inscribed "For Local Addresses Only." Singpex '01.

Frame — A240

Serpentine Die Cut 15x14½

2001, July 26

Self-Adhesive

981 A240 (22c) multi .25 .25

Size: 24x34mm

982 A240 (22c) multi .25 .25
a. Pane, 6 #981, 4 #982 +16 labels 2.50

Nos. 981-982 inscribed "For Local Addresses Only." No. 982a contains three examples of No. 982 with differing white paw prints, and one example without paw print. Singpex '01.

Care for Nature — A241

Orangutans: (22c), Adult hanging on tree. 60c, Two adults. No. 983c, Adult and child. No. 983d, Two adults and child.

2001, Sept. 5 ***Perf. 13½x13***

983 Horiz. strip of 4 3.25 3.25
a. A241 (22c) multi .25 .25
b. A241 60c multi .70 .70
c.-d. A241 $1 Any single 1.10 1.10
e. Souvenir sheet, #983 4.50 4.50

Self-Adhesive

Booklet Stamp

Serpentine Die Cut 12½

984 A241 (22c) multi .25 .25
a. Booklet of 10 2.50

Nos. 983a, 984 inscribed "For Local Addresses Only."

No. 983e sold for $3.90, with 50c of that donated to the Care for Nature Trust Fund.

Flowers A242

Designs: (22c), Melastoma malabathricum. 60c, Leontopodium alpinum. $1, Saraca cauliflora. $2, Gentiana clusii.

2001, Sept. 20 ***Perf. 13¼x12¾***

985-988 A242 Set of 4 4.50 4.50
988a Souvenir sheet, #985-988 4.50 4.50

No. 985 inscribed "For Local Addresses Only." See Switzerland No. 1107.

Tropical Fish — A243

Designs: 5c, Moorish idol. 20c, Threadfin butterflyfish. (22c), Copperband butterflyfish. 30c, Pearlscale butterflyfish. 40c, Rainbow butterflyfish. 50c, Yellow-faced angelfish. 60c, Emperor angelfish. 70c, Striped sailfin tang. 80c, Palette tang.

2001, Oct. 24 ***Perf. 13x13¼***

989 A243 5c multi .20 .20
990 A243 20c multi .20 .20
991 A243 (22c) multi .25 .25
992 A243 30c multi .35 .35
993 A243 40c multi .45 .45
994 A243 50c multi .55 .55
995 A243 60c multi .65 .65
996 A243 70c multi .75 .75
997 A243 80c multi .85 .85
a. Sheet of 9, #989-997 4.25 4.25

Self-Adhesive

Serpentine Die Cut 12½

998 A243 (22c) multi .25 .25
a. Booklet of 10 2.50
Nos. 989-998 (10) 4.50 4.50

Nos. 991, 998 inscribed "For Local Addresses Only."

New Year 2002 (Year of the Horse) A244

Designs: Nos. 999, 1001a, (22c), One horse. Nos. 1000, 1001b, $2, Two horses.

Litho., Litho & Embossed with Foil Application (#1001a, 1001b)

2002, Jan. 10 ***Perf. 13½x13¼***

999-1000 A244 Set of 2 2.50 2.50
1001 Sheet, #1001a-1001b, 8 each #999-1000 22.50 22.50
a. A244 (22c) silver & multi .25 .25
b. A244 $2 gold & multi 2.25 2.25

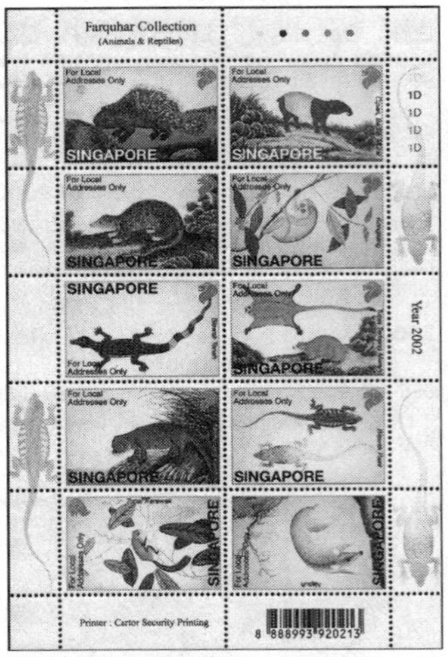

William Farquhar Collection of Natural History Drawings — A245

No. 1002, (22c) - Animals and Reptiles: a, Landak raya. b, Cipan, Badak murai. c, Landak kelubu. d, Kongkang. e, Biawak tanah. f, Tupai terbang merah. g, Memerang kecil. h, Biawak pasir. i, Tupai kerawak, vert. j, Napuh, vert.

No. 1003, (22c) - Fruits and Plants: a, Buah rumenia. b, Manggis hutan. c, Cempedak. d, Bunga dedap. e, Jeringau, vert. f, Rotang, vert. g, Tuba, vert. h, Tebu gagak, vert. i, Temu kunci, vert. j, Rambutan, vert.

No. 1004, (22c) - Birds: a, Burung gaji-gaji. b, Kuau cermin. c, Ayam kolam. d, Kelengking. e, Burung kuang. f, Puhung. g, Burung kunyit, vert. h, Burung pacat sayap biru, vert. i, Burung mural, vert. j, Burung berek-berek, vert.

No. 1005, (22c) - Fish: a, Ikan tenggiri papan. b, Ikan kertang. c, Ikan kakatua. d, Ikan bambangan. e, Ikan parang. f, Ikan buntai pisang. g, Ikan ketang. h, Pari hitam. i, Telinga gajah. j, Ikan babi.

Perf. 13¼x13¾, 13¾x13¼

2002 **Litho.**

Sheets of 10, #a-j

1002-1005 A245 Set of 4 10.00 10.00

Issued: Nos. 1002-1003, 2/20; Nos. 1004-1005, 3/20.

POSTAGE DUE STAMPS

D1

D2

Wmk. 314

1968, Feb. 1 **Litho.** ***Perf. 9***

J1 D1 1c emerald .25 .25
J2 D1 2c red org .35 .35
J3 D1 4c yel org .75 .75
J4 D1 8c brown .90 .90
J5 D1 10c rose mag 2.25 2.25
J6 D1 12c dl vio 1.25 1.25
J7 D1 20c brt bl 2.75 2.75
J8 D1 50c gray grn 6.50 6.50
Nos. J1-J8 (8) 15.00 15.00

1973-77 ***Perf. 13x13½***

J1a D1 1c Unwmkd. ('77) *30.00 30.00*
J3a D1 4c Unwmkd. ('77) *35.00 35.00*
J5a D1 10c 1.00 1.00
b. Unwmkd. ('77) *35.00 35.00*
J7a D1 20c Unwmkd. ('77) *45.00 50.00*
J8a D1 50c *8.00 8.00*
b. Unwmkd. ('77) *55.00 55.00*

1981 **Unwmk.** ***Perf. 12x11½***

J9 D2 1c emerald .20 .20
J10 D2 4c orange .20 .20
J11 D2 10c carmine .55 .55
J12 D2 20c light blue .60 .60
J13 D2 50c light yellow green .85 .85
Nos. J9-J13 (5) 2.40 2.40

1978, Sept. 25 ***Perf. 13x13½***

J9a D2 1c .70 .70
J10a D2 4c .75 .75
J11a D2 10c .80 .80
J12a D2 20c 1.00 1.00
J13a D2 50c 1.75 1.75
Nos. J9a-J13a (5) 5.00 5.00

D3

1989, July 12 **Litho.** ***Perf. 13x13½***

J14 D3 5c red lilac .20 .20
J15 D3 10c red .20 .20
J16 D3 20c light blue .25 .25
J17 D3 50c yellow green .70 .70
J18 D3 $1 brown 1.50 1.50
Nos. J14-J18 (5) 2.85 2.85

Issued: $1, 4/30/93; others, 7/12/89.

1997, Nov. 7 **Litho.** ***Perf. 13x13½***

J19 D3 1c green *75.00*
J20 D3 4c brown orange *75.00*

A small quantity of Nos. J19-J20 were produced, which was sold locally only, in late 1997. Postage due stamps were replaced by machine-generated labels on Dec. 31, 1997.

SLOVAKIA

slō-'vä-kē-ə

LOCATION — Central Europe
GOVT. — Republic
AREA — 18,932 sq. mi.
POP. — 5,396,193 (1999 est.)
CAPITAL — Bratislava

Formerly a province of Czechoslovakia, Slovakia declared its independence in Mar., 1939. A treaty was immediately concluded with Germany guaranteeing Slovakian independence but providing for German "protection" for 25 years.

In 1945 the republic ended and Slovakia again became a part of Czechoslovakia.

On January 1, 1993, Czechoslovakia split into the Czech Republic and Slovakia.

100 Halierov = 1 Koruna

Catalogue values for unused stamps in this country are for never hinged items, beginning with Scott 26 in the regular postage section, Scott B1 in the semi-postal section, Scott C1 in the airmail section, Scott EX1 in the personal delivery section, Scott J1 in the postage due section, and Scott P10 in the newspaper section.

Watermark

Wmk. 263-Double-Barred Cross Multiple

Stamps of Czechoslovakia, 1928-39, Overprinted in Red or Blue

Slovenský štát 1939

1939 ***Perf. 10, 12½, 12x12½***

2 A29 5h dk ultra 1.00 .90
3 A29 10h brown .20 .20
4 A29 20h red (Bl) .20 .20
5 A29 25h green 5.00 4.00
6 A29 30h red vio (Bl) .20 .20
7 A61a 40h dark blue .20 .20
8 A73 50h deep green .20 .20
9 A63 50h deep green .20 .20
10 A63 60h dull violet .20 .20
11 A63 60h dull blue 5.75 *8.75*
12 A60 1k rose lake (Bl) (On No. 212) .20 .20

Overprinted Diagonally

13 A64 1.20k rose lil (Bl) 1.00 1.00
14 A65 1.50k carmine (Bl) 1.00 1.00
15 A79 1.60k ol grn (Bl) 1.75 *2.50*
16 A66 2k dk bl grn 1.75 *2.50*
17 A67 2.50k dark blue .30 *1.00*
18 A68 3k brown .40 *1.00*
19 A69 3.50k dk violet 17.50 *32.50*
20 A69 3.50k dk vio (Bl) 20.00 *50.00*
21 A70 4k dk violet 8.75 *16.00*
22 A71 5k green 9.50 *22.50*
23 A72 10k blue 70.00 *125.00*
Nos. 2-23 (22) 145.30 *270.25*

Excellent counterfeit overprints exist.

Andrej Hlinka
A1 A2

Overprinted in Red or Blue

Perf. 12½

1939, Apr. **Unwmk.** **Photo.**

24 A1 50h dark green (R) .40 .40
a. Perf. 10½ 4.00 2.00
b. Perf. 10½x12½ 20.00 10.00
25 A1 1k dk car rose (Bl) .60 .50
a. Perf. 10½ 650.00 —
Never hinged 850.00
b. Perf. 10½x12½ 25.00 15.00

Catalogue values for unused stamps in this section, from this point to the end of the section, are for Never Hinged items.

1939 **Unwmk.** ***Perf. 12½***

26 A2 5h brt ultra .50 *.45*
27 A2 10h olive green .80 *.65*
a. Perf. 10½x12½ 20.00 9.00
b. Perf. 10½ 17.00 14.00
28 A2 20h orange red .80 *.65*
a. Imperf. .85 *.80*
29 A2 30h dp violet .80 *.65*
a. Imperf. 1.00 *1.25*
b. Perf. 10½x12½ 5.00 *6.25*
c. Perf. 10½ 7.50 *7.00*
30 A2 50h dk green .80 *.65*
31 A2 1k dk carmine rose 1.00 *.65*
32 A2 2.50k brt blue 1.00 *.30*
33 A2 3k black brown 3.00 *.50*
Nos. 26-33 (8) 8.70 *4.50*

On Nos. 32 and 33 a pearl frame surrounds the medallion. See Nos. 55-57, 69.

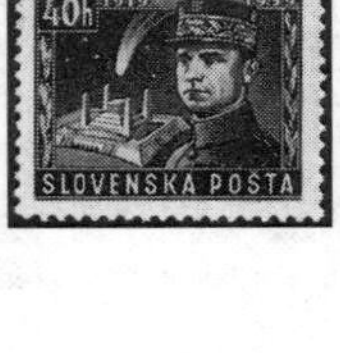

General Stefánik and Memorial Tomb — A3

Rev. Josef Murgas and Radio Towers — A4

1939, May ***Perf. 12½***

Size: 25x20mm

34	A3	40h dark blue	.90	
35	A3	60h slate green	.90	
36	A3	1k gray violet	.90	

Size: 30x23¾mm

37	A3	2k bl vio & sepia	.90	
		Nos. 34-37 (4)	3.60	

20th anniv. of the death of Gen. Milan Stefánik, but not issued.

1939 **Unwmk.**

38	A4	60h purple	.25	.30
39	A4	1.20k slate black	.50	.20

10th anniv. of the death of Rev. Josef Murgas. See No. 65.

Girl Embroidering A5

Woodcutter A6

Girl at Spring — A7

1939-44 **Wmk. 263** ***Perf. 12½***

40	A5	2k dk blue green	6.25	.50
41	A6	4k copper brown	1.40	1.00
42	A7	5k orange red	1.00	.50
a.		Perf. 10 ('44)	1.25	1.00
		Nos. 40-42 (3)	8.65	2.00

Dr. Josef Tiso — A8

Presidential Residence — A9

1939-44 **Wmk. 263** ***Perf. 12½***

43	A8	50h slate green	.45	.30
43A	A8	70h dk red brn ('42)	.30	.20
b.		Perf. 10½ ('44)	.50	.35

See No. 88.

1940, Mar. 14

44	A9	10k deep blue	1.00	.75

Tatra Mountains A10

Krivan Peak A11

Edelweiss in the Tatra Mountains A12

Chamois A13

Church at Javorina — A14

1940-43 **Wmk. 263** ***Perf. 12½***

Size: 17x21mm

45	A10	5h dk olive grn	.25	.20
46	A11	10h deep brown	.20	.20
47	A12	20h blue black	.20	.20
48	A13	25h olive brown	.45	.25
49	A14	30h chestnut brown	.30	.25
a.		Perf. 10½ ('43)	2.50	1.00
		Nos. 45-49 (5)	1.40	1.10

See Nos. 84-87, 103-107.

Hlinka Type of 1939

1940-42 **Wmk. 263** ***Perf. 12½***

55	A2	1k dk car rose	.80	.60
56	A2	2.50k brt blue ('42)	1.00	.75
a.		Perf. 10½	.60	.60
57	A2	3k black brn ('41)	2.00	1.00
a.		Perf. 10½	1.75	.90

On Nos. 56 and 57 a pearl frame surrounds the medallion.

Stiavnica A15

Lietava A16

Spissky Hrad — A17

Bojnice — A18

1941 ***Perf. 12½***

58	A15	1.20k rose lake	.25	.20
59	A16	1.50k rose pink	.25	.20
60	A17	1.60k royal blue	.25	.20
61	A18	2k dk gray green	.25	.20
		Nos. 58-61 (4)	1.00	.80

Slovakian Castles.

S. M. Daxner and Stefan Moyses A19

Andrej Hlinka — A20

1941, May 26 **Photo.** **Wmk. 263**

62	A19	50h olive green	2.25	1.50
63	A19	1k slate blue	8.50	7.25
64	A19	2k black	4.25	3.25
		Nos. 62-64 (3)	15.00	12.00

80th anniv. of the Memorandum of the Slovak Nation.

Murgas Type of 1939

1941 **Wmk. 263**

65	A4	60h purple	.40	.20

1942

69	A20	1.30k dark purple	.45	.20

Post Horn and Miniature Stamp — A21

Philatelist — A22

Philatelist — A23

1942, May 23

70	A21	30h dark green	1.00	.80
71	A22	70h dk car rose	1.00	.80
72	A23	80h purple	1.00	.80
73	A21	1.30k dark brown	1.00	.80
		Nos. 70-73 (4)	4.00	3.20

Natl. Philatelic Exhibition at Bratislava.

On No. 70 the miniature stamp bears the coat-of-arms of Bratislava; on No. 73 it shows the National arms of Slovakia.

St. Stephen's Cathedral, Vienna — A24

1942, Oct. 12 ***Perf. 14***

74	A24	70h blue green	.65	*.75*
75	A24	1.30k olive green	1.10	*1.75*
76	A24	2k sapphire	1.75	*2.50*
		Nos. 74-76 (3)	3.50	*5.00*

European Postal Congress held in Vienna.

Slovakian Educational Society — A25

1942, Dec. 14

77	A25	70h black	.20	.20
78	A25	1k rose red	.20	.20
79	A25	1.30k sapphire	.20	*.20*
80	A25	2k chestnut brown	.25	.20
81	A25	3k dark green	.35	.30
82	A25	4k dull purple	.35	.30
		Nos. 77-82 (6)	1.55	1.40

Slovakian Educational Soc., 150th anniv.

Andrej Hlinka — A26

1943 **Wmk. 263**

83	A26	1.30k brt ultra	.40	.25

See Nos. 93-94A.

Types of 1939-40

1943 **Unwmk.** ***Perf. 12½***

84	A11	10h deep brown	.25	.20
85	A12	20h blue black	.70	.50
86	A13	25h olive brown	.70	.50
87	A14	30h chestnut brown	.50	.35
88	A8	70h dk red brown	.85	.95
		Nos. 84-88 (5)	3.00	2.50

Presov Church — A27

Locomotive A28

Railway Tunnel A29

Viaduct — A30

1943, Sept. 5 ***Perf. 14***

89	A27	70h dk rose violet	.45	.40
90	A28	80h sapphire	.45	.40
91	A29	1.30k black	.45	.40
92	A30	2k dk violet brn	.45	*.40*
		Nos. 89-92 (4)	1.80	1.60

Inauguration of the new railroad line between Presov and Strazske.

Hlinka Type of 1943 and

Ludovit Stur — A31

Martin Razus — A32

1944 **Unwmk.**

93	A31	80h slate green	.25	.20
94	A32	1k brown red	.25	.20
94A	A26	1.30k brt ultra	.20	.20
		Nos. 93-94A (3)	.70	.60

Prince Pribina — A33

Designs: 70h, Prince Mojmir. 80h, Prince Ratislav. 1.30k, King Svatopluk. 2k, Prince Kocel. 3k, Prince Mojmir II. 5k, Prince Svatopluk II. 10k, Prince Braslav.

1944, Mar. 14

95	A33	50h dark green	.20	.20
96	A33	70h lilac rose	.20	.20
97	A33	80h red brown	.20	.20

98 A33 1.30k brt ultra .20 .20
99 A33 2k Prus blue .20 .20
100 A33 3k dark brown .45 .30
101 A33 5k violet .95 .70
102 A33 10k black 2.50 2.00
Nos. 95-102 (8) 4.90 4.00

Scenic Types of 1940

1944, Apr. 1 ***Perf. 14***

Size: 18x23mm

103 A11 10h bright carmine .20 *.20*
104 A12 20h bright blue .20 *.20*
105 A13 25h brown red .20 *.20*
106 A14 30h red violet .20 *.20*
107 A10 50h deep green .20 *.20*
Nos. 103-107 (5) 1.00 *1.00*

5th anniv. of Slovakia's independence.

Symbolic of National Protection A41

President Josef Tiso — A42

1944, Oct. 6 **Wmk. 263**

108 A41 2k green .40 *.60*
109 A41 3.80k red violet .40 *.90*

1945 **Unwmk.**

110 A42 1k orange .55 .40
111 A42 1.50k brown .20 .20
112 A42 2k green .20 *.40*
113 A42 4k rose red .90 .55
114 A42 5k sapphire .80 .40

Wmk. 263

115 A42 10k red violet .60 .40
Nos. 110-115 (6) 3.25 2.35

6th anniv. of the Republic of Slovakia's declaration of independence, Mar. 14, 1939.

Natl. Arms — A50

1993 **Photo. & Engr.** ***Perf. 11½***

150 A50 3k multicolored .50 .30

Engr.

Perf. 12

Size: 30x44mm

151 A50 8k multicolored 4.00 3.00

Issued: 3k, Jan. 2; 8k, Jan. 1. No. 151 does not have black frameline.

Castles & Churches — A51

#152-155 are churches, #156-157 castles.

Perf. 11½x12, 12x11½

1993-95 **Photo. & Engr.**

152 A51 2k Nitra .20 .20
153 A51 3k Banska Bystrica .25 .20
154 A51 5k Ruzomberok, horiz. .40 .20
155 A51 10k Kosice .80 .40
156 A51 30k Zvolen, horiz. 2.50 1.25
157 A51 50k Bratislava 6.50 3.25
Nos. 152-157 (6) 10.65 5.50

Issued: 5k, 10k, 1993; 30k, 9/12/93; 50k, 12/31/93; 3k, 11/15/94; 2k, 3/15/95.

See Nos. 218-227.

St. John Nepomuk, 600th Death Anniv. A57

1993 **Photo. & Engr.** ***Perf. 12x11½***

158 A57 8k multicolored .75 .40

See Czech Republic #2880; Germany #1776.

A58

A59

President Michal Kovac

1993 **Engr.** ***Perf. 12x11½***

159 A58 2k dark gray blue .20 .20
159A A58 3k red brown & red .25 .20

Issued: 2k, 3/2/93; 3k, 11/3/93.

Photo. & Engr.

1993, May 14 ***Perf. 11½***

Trees.

160 A59 3k Quercus robur .25 .20
161 A59 4k Carpinus betulus .35 .20
162 A59 10k Pinus silvestris .85 .40
Nos. 160-162 (3) 1.45 .80

A60

A61

Famous Men: 5k, Jan Levoslav Bella (1843-1936), composer. 8k, Alexander Dubcek (1921-92), politician. 20k, Jan Kollar (1793-1852), writer.

Photo. & Engr.

1993, May 20 ***Perf. 12x11½***

163 A60 5k red brown & blue .75 .40
164 A60 8k brown & lilac red 1.25 .60
165 A60 20k gray blue & orange 3.00 1.50
Nos. 163-165 (3) 5.00 2.50

1993, May 31 **Engr.** ***Perf. 12***

Woman with Pitcher, by Marian Cunderlik.

166 A61 14k multicolored 6.00 5.00

Europa.

Literary Slovak Language, 150th Anniv. A62

Design: 8k, Arrival of St. Cyril and St. Methodius, 1130th Anniv.

Photo. & Engr.

1993, June 22 ***Perf. 12x11½***

167 A62 2k multicolored .20 .20
168 A62 8k multicolored .75 .40

See Czech Republic No. 2886.

A63

A64

Arms of Dubnica nad Vahom.

Photo. & Engr.

1993, July 8 ***Perf. 12x11½***

169 A63 1k multicolored .20 .20

Photo. & Engr.

1993, Sept. 2 ***Perf. 11½***

The Big Pets, by Lane Smith.

170 A64 5k multicolored .45 .20

Bratislava Biennial of Illustrators.

Gavcikovo Dam — A65

Photo. & Engr.

1993, Nov. 12 ***Perf. 11½***

172 A65 10k multicolored 1.25 .60

No. 172 issued se-tenant with label.

Madonna and Child, by J. B. Klemens (1817-83) — A66

Photo. & Engr.

1993, Dec. 1 ***Perf. 11½***

173 A66 2k multicolored .30 .20

Christmas.

Souvenir Sheet

Monument to Gen. Milan Stefanik — A67

1993, Dec. 17 **Engr.** ***Perf. 11½x12***

174 A67 16k multicolored 2.00 1.00

Art from Bratislava Natl. Gallery — A68

Sculpture: 9k, Plough of Springtime, by Josef Kostka.

1993, Dec. 31

175 A68 9k multicolored 1.50 1.00

See Nos. 199-200, 237-238, 255.

A69

A70

Photo. & Engr.

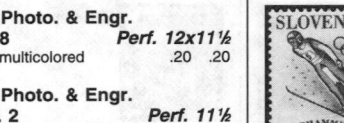

1994, Jan. 26 ***Perf. 11x11½***

176 A69 2k multicolored .20 .20

1994 Winter Olympics, Lillehammer.

Photo. & Engr.

1994, Apr. 29 ***Perf. 11x11½***

177 A70 3k multicolored .25 .20

Intl. Year of the Family.

Jan Andrej Segner (1704-77), Physicist — A71

Design: 9k, Antoine de Saint-Exupery (1900-44), aviator, author.

Photo. & Engr.

1994, May 25 ***Perf. 11½x11***

178 A71 8k red brown & blue .80 .40
179 A71 9k black, blue & pink .90 .45

See Nos. 196-198.

Josef Murgas (1864-1929), Inventor of Radio Transmitters — A72

1994, May 27 **Engr.** ***Perf. 11½***

180 A72 28k multicolored 2.25 1.10

Europa.

A73

A74

Photo. & Engr.

1994, May 31 ***Perf. 11½x11***

181 A73 3k multicolored .25 .20

Intl. Stop Smoking Day.

Photo. & Engr.

1994, June 10 ***Perf. 11½***

182 A74 2k blue, black & green .20 .20

1994 World Cup Soccer Championships, US.

Intl. Olympic Committee, Cent. — A75

Photo. & Engr.

1994, June 23 ***Perf. 12x11½***

183 A75 3k multicolored .40 .20

No. 183 issued with se-tenant label.

Raptors — A76

Photo. & Engr.

1994, July 4 **Perf. 11½x12**

184 A76 4k Aquila chrysaetos .40 .20
185 A76 5k Falco peregrinus .50 .25
186 A76 7k Bubo bubo .70 .35
Nos. 184-186 (3) 1.60 .80

Prince Svatopluk of Moravia (870-894) — A77

1994, July 20 **Engr.** **Perf. 12**

187 A77 12k red brn, buff & blk 1.25 .60

UPU, 120th Anniv. — A78

Photo. & Engr.

1994, Aug. 1 **Perf. 11½x12**

188 A78 8k multicolored .55 .30

Slovak Uprising, 50th Anniv. — A79

Design: 6k, Gen. Rudolf Viest, Gen. Jan. Golian. 8k, French Volunteers' Memorial, Strecno hill.

Photo. & Engr.

1994, Aug. 27 **Perf. 12x11½**

189 A79 6k multicolored .75 .40
190 A79 8k multicolored .75 .40

Nos. 189-190 printed with se-tenant label.

Souvenir Sheet

Janko Matuska, Lyricist, 150th Death Anniv. A80

Design: 34k, Matuska, woman with pitcher, verse of "A Well She Dug."

Photo. & Engr.

1994, Sept. 1 **Perf. 12x11½**

191 A80 34k multicolored 3.25 1.60

Comenius University, 75th Anniv. — A81

Photo. & Engr.

1994, Oct. 18 **Perf. 11½x12**

192 A81 12k multicolored 1.25 .60

Mojmirovce Horse Race, 180th Anniv. A82

1994, Oct. 25 **Perf. 12x11½**

193 A82 2k multicolored .20 .20

St. George's Church, Kostotany pod Tribecom — A83

1994, Nov. 8 **Perf. 11**

194 A83 20k multicolored 1.90 .95

Christmas — A84

1994, Nov. 29 **Perf. 11½**

195 A84 2k multicolored .35 .20

Personalities Type of 1994

Designs: 5k, Chatam Sofer (1762-1839), rabbi. 6k, Wolfgang Kempelen (1734-1804), polytechnician. 10k, Stefan Banic (1870-1941), inventor of aviation parachute.

1994, Dec. 12 **Perf. 11½x11**

196 A71 5k multicolored .50 .25
197 A71 6k multicolored .60 .30
198 A71 10k multicolored 1.00 .50
Nos. 196-198 (3) 2.10 1.05

Bratislava Art Type of 1993

Designs: 7k, Girls, by Janko Alexy, horiz. 14k, The Bulls, by Vincent Hloznik.

Perf. 12x11½, 11½x12

1994, Dec. 15 **Engr.**

199 A68 7k multicolored .70 .35
200 A68 14k multicolored 1.40 .70

Ships — A85

5k, Cargo ship, NL EMS. 8k, Cargo ship, Ryn. 10k, 400-passenger cruise ship.

Photo. & Engr.

1994, Dec. 30 **Perf. 12x11½**

201 A85 5k multicolored .50 .25
202 A85 8k multicolored .75 .40
203 A85 10k multicolored 1.00 .50
Nos. 201-203 (3) 2.25 1.15

Samuel Jurkovic, Founder of of Landlords Assoc., 1845 — A86

Photo. & Engr.

1995, Feb. 8 **Perf. 11½**

204 A86 9k multicolored .65 .35

European Nature Conservation Year — A87

Protected plants: 2k, Ciminalis clusii. 3k, Pulsatilla slavica. 8k, Onosma tornense.

1995, Feb. 28

205 A87 2k multicolored .20 .20
Complete booklet, 10 #205 1.25
206 A87 3k multicolored .20 .20
Complete booklet, 5 #206 1.00
207 A87 8k multicolored .60 .30
Nos. 205-207 (3) 1.00 .70

Slovak Natl. Theatre, 75th Anniv. A88

1995, Feb. 28 **Perf. 12x11½**

208 A88 10k multicolored .70 .35

1995 Group B World Cup Ice Hockey Championships, Bratislava — A89

1995, Mar. 29 **Perf. 11½**

209 A89 5k blue & yellow .35 .20

Bela Bartok (1881-1945), Composer A90

6k, Jan Bahyl (1856-1916), inventor.

Photo. & Engr.

1995, Apr. 20 **Perf. 12x11½**

210 A90 3k multicolored .20 .20
211 A90 6k multicolored .40 .20

Souvenir Sheet

Ludovit Stur (1815-56), Writer — A91

1995, Apr. 20 **Perf. 11½**

212 A91 16k multicolored 1.10 .55

Europa A92

1995, May 5 **Engr.** **Perf. 12**

213 A92 8k multicolored 1.00 .80

Liberation of the Concentration Camps, 50th Anniv. — A93

Photo. & Engr.

1995, May 5 **Perf. 11**

214 A93 12k multicolored .80 .40

Slovak Scouting — A94

1995, May 18 **Perf. 11½x11**

215 A94 5k multicolored 1.00 .30

Visit of Pope John Paul II — A95

1995, May 29 **Engr.**

216 A95 3k red .20 .20
Complete booklet, 10 #216 2.00

Organized Philately in Slovakia, Cent. — A96

Photo. & Engr.

1995, June 1 **Perf. 11½x12**

217 A96 3k blue, black & gray .20 .20
a. Souv. sheet of 2, perf 11½x12 .40 .40

Dunafila '95.

Castles & Churches — A100

Perf. 12x11½, 11½x12 (#218, 225), 11¼x11¾ (#226, 227)

1995-2001 **Photo. & Engr.**

218 A100 50h Bardejov, horiz. .20 .20
219 A100 4k Nova Bana .30 .20
220 A100 4k Presov .20 .20
221 A100 5k Trnava .30 .20
222 A100 7k Martin .40 .20
223 A100 8k Trencin Castle .55 .30
224 A100 9k Zelina .55 .30
225 A100 20k Roznava, horiz. .85 .40
226 A100 40k Plestany, horiz. 1.60 .80
227 A100 50k Komarno 2.10 1.00
Nos. 218-227 (10) 7.05 3.80

Issued: 4k (#219), 6/15/95; 8k, 9/12/95. 9k, 4/15/97. 7k, 7/17/97. 5k. 9/12/98. 4k (#220), 11/3/98. 50h, 2/1/00. 20k, 7/26/00. 40k and 50k, 2001.

UNESCO World Heritage Sites A107

Perf. 11½x12, 12x11½

1995, July 19 **Photo. & Engr.**

228 A107 7k Banska Stiavnica, vert. .50 .25
229 A107 10k Spissky Hrad .70 .35
230 A107 15k Vlkolinec 1.00 .50
Nos. 228-230 (3) 2.20 1.10

Volleyball, Cent. — A108

1995, Aug. 16 ***Perf. 11½***
231 A108 9k multicolored .60 .30

A109

A110

Bratislava Biennial of Illustrators: 2k, Clown, by Lorenzo Mattotti, Italy. 3k, Two characters, by Dusan Kallay, Slovakia.

Photo. & Engr.

1995, Sept. 5 ***Perf. 11½***
232 A109 2k multicolored .20 .20
Complete booklet, 10 #232 1.50
233 A109 3k multicolored .20 .20
Complete booklet, 10 #233 2.00

1995, Sept. 14
234 A110 4k multicolored .30 .20

St. Adalbert Assoc.

The Cleveland Agreement, 80th Anniv. A111

Photo. & Engr.

1995, Oct. 20 ***Perf. 12x11½***
235 A111 5k multicolored .40 .20

UN, 50th Anniv. A112

1995, Oct. 24 **Engr.** ***Perf. 11½x12***
235A A112 8k multicolored .60 .30

Issued in sheets of 8 + 2 labels.

Christmas A113

Photo. & Engr.

1995, Oct. 27 ***Perf. 11½***
236 A113 2k multicolored .20 .20

Bratislava Art Type of 1993

Designs: 8k, The Hlohovec Nativity. 16k, Two Women, by Mikulás Galanda.

Photo. & Engr.

1995, Nov. 30 ***Perf. 11½x12***
237 A68 8k multicolored .55 .30
238 A68 16k multicolored 1.10 .55

Issued in sheets of 4 + 2 labels.

Jozef Cíger-Hronsky (1896-1960) A114

Olympic Games, Cent. A115

4k, Jozef L'udovít Holuby (1836-1923).

Photo. & Engr.

1996, Feb. 15 ***Perf. 11½***
239 A114 3k multicolored .20 .20
240 A114 4k multicolored .25 .20

See Nos. 293-295, 320-322.

1996, Feb. 15
241 A115 9k multicolored .60 .30

Folk Traditions — A116

Easter tradition of dousing women with water

Photo. & Engr.

1996, Mar. 15 ***Perf. 11½***
242 A116 2k multicolored .20 .20

Souvenir Sheet

Year for the Eradication of Poverty — A117

1996, Apr. 15 **Engr.** ***Perf. 12***
243 A117 7k multicolored 1.00 .70

A118

A119

Europa: a, Holding thistle, carduus textorianus marg. b, Portrait, daphne cneorum.

1996, May 3 **Engr.** ***Perf. 11½***
244 A118 8k Pair, #a.-b. 1.00 .50

Izabela Textorisová (1866-1949), Slovakia's 1st female botanist. Issued in sheets of 4.

Souvenir Sheet

Motion Pictures, Cent.: Two frames from 1936 film, Jánosík.

1996, May 15 ***Perf. 11½x12***
245 A119 16k multicolored 1.00 .50

Printed se-tenant with label.

Round Slovakia Cycle Race — A120

1996, May 30 **Engr.** ***Perf. 11½***
246 A120 3k multicolored .20 .20
Complete booklet, 10 #246 2.00

Slovak Perspectives, 150th Anniv. — A121

1996, May 30
247 A121 18k multicolored 1.10 .55

A122

A123

Photo. & Engr.

1996, June 14 ***Perf. 12x11½***
248 A122 6k Coat of arms .40 .20

Town of Senica.

1996, July 16 ***Perf. 11½x12***

Nature protection: No. 249, Ovis musimon. No. 250, Bison bonasus. No. 251, Rupicapra rupicapra.

249 A123 4k multicolored .30 .20
Complete booklet, 10 #249 3.00
250 A123 4k multicolored .30 .20
Complete booklet, 10 #250 3.00
251 A123 4k multicolored .30 .20
Complete booklet, 10 #251 3.00
Nos. 249-251 (3) .90 .60

Splendors of Homeland — A124

Photo. & Engr.

1996, Sept. 25 ***Perf. 11½x12***
252 A124 4k Popradské Lake .30 .20
253 A124 8k Skalnaté Lake .60 .30
254 A124 12k Strbské Lake .90 .45
Nos. 252-254 (3) 1.80 .95

Bratislava Art Type of 1993

The Baroque Chair, by Endre Nemes (1909-85).

1996, Oct. 5 **Engr.** ***Perf. 11½x12***
255 A68 14k multicolored 1.00 .50

See Czech Republic #2995, Sweden #2199. Issued in sheets of 4 + label.

Technological Advances A125

4k, Bratislava-Trnava horse-drawn railway. 6k, Andrej Kvasz's (1883-1974) airplane.

Photo. & Engr.

1996, Oct. 15 ***Perf. 11***
256 A125 4k multicolored .30 .20
Complete booklet, 10 #256 3.00
257 A125 6k multicolored .45 .25
Complete booklet, 10 #257 4.50

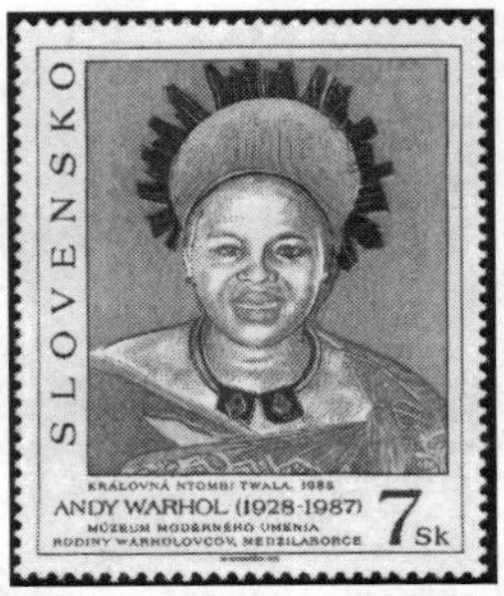

Queen Ntombi Twala, by Andy Warhol (1928-87) — A126

Design: 10k, Suppressed Laughter, by Franz Xaver Messerschmidt (1736-83).

1996 **Engr.** ***Perf. 11½***
258 A126 7k multicolored .45 .20
259 A126 10k multicolored .65 .30

Each issued in sheets of 4.
Issued: 7k, 11/13/96; 10k, 10/5/96.
See #284-286, 311, 314-315, 340-341.

Christmas, Kysuce Village — A127

Photo. & Engr.

1996, Nov. 5 ***Perf. 11½***
260 A127 2k multicolored .20 .20

Michael Martikén, Olympic Gold Medalist, Canoeing A128

Photo. & Engr.

1996, Dec. 18 ***Perf. 12x11½***
261 A128 3k brown & yellow .20 .20

Stamp Day A129

Designs: Unexecuted 1938 stamp design of a woman with patriarchal cross, dove, Martin Benka, stamp designer.

1996, Dec. 18
262 A129 3k violet & buff .20 .20

No. 262 was printed se-tenant with label.

Bishop Stefan Moyses (1797-1869) — A130

Design: 4k, Svetozar Hurban Vajansky (1847-1916), politician.

Photo. & Engr.

1997, Jan. 16 ***Perf. 11½***

263 A130 3k multicolored .25 .20
264 A130 4k multicolored .30 .20

A131

A132

Photo. & Engr.

1997, Jan. 31 ***Perf. 11½***

265 A131 6k multicolored .35 .20

1997 World Biathlon Championships, Osrblie.

Photo. & Engr.

1997, Feb. 15 ***Perf. 11½***

266 A132 3k multicolored .20 .20
Complete booklet, 10 #266 2.00

Folk Tradition of collecting dew.

Franciscan Church, Bratislava, 700th Anniv. A133

Parochial Church, City Arms, Zilina A134

Photo. & Engr.

1997, Mar. 25 ***Perf. 11½x12***

267 A133 16k multicolored 1.00 .50

Radio, Cent. A135

1997, Apr. 15 ***Perf. 12x11½***

269 A135 10k multicolored .60 .30

A136

A137

Europa (Stories and Legends): Miraculous rain near Hron.

1997, May 5 Engr. ***Perf. 12x11½***

270 A136 9k multicolored .55 .30

1997, June 12 Engr. ***Perf. 12x11½***

Limestone Formations: 6k, Domica Cavern, Silická. 8k, Aragonit Cavern, Octiná.

271 A137 6k multicolored .35 .20
272 A137 8k multicolored .50 .25

Souvenir Sheet

Folklore Festival, Vychodná — A138

1997, June 12 **Photo. & Engr.**

273 A138 11k multicolored .65 .35

Triennale of Naive Art, Bratislava A139

Photo. & Engr.

1996, June 26 ***Perf. 12x11½***

274 A139 3k multicolored .20 .20
Complete booklet, 10 #274 2.00

World Year of Slovaks A140

Bratislava Biennale of Illustrators A141

1997, July 17 ***Perf. 11½***

276 A140 9k multicolored .50 .25

Photo. & Engr.

1997, Aug. 5 ***Perf. 11½***

277 A141 3k multicolored .20 .20
Complete booklet, 10 #277 2.00

Water Mill, Jelka — A142

1997, Aug. 5

278 A142 4k multicolored .25 .20
Complete booklet, 10 #278 2.50

A143

A144

Photo. & Engr.

1997, Sept. 1 ***Perf. 11½***

279 A143 4k multicolored .25 .20

Constitution, 5th anniv.

1997, Sept. 17

280 A144 9k multicolored .55 .30

6th Half Marathon World Championships, Kosice.

Mushrooms A145

Designs: #281, Boletus aereus. #282, Morchella esculenta. #283, Catathelasma imperiale.

1997, Sept. 17 ***Perf. 12***

281 A145 9k multicolored .55 .30
282 A145 9k multicolored .55 .30
283 A145 9k multicolored .55 .30
a. Souvenir sheet, #281-283 1.75 .90
Nos. 281-283 (3) 1.65 .90

Art Type of 1996

Designs: 9k, Self-portrait, by Ján Kupecky (1667-1740). 10k, Bojnice Altar, St. Peter and St. Lucia, by Nardo Di Cione, 14th cent., horiz. 12k, Towards the Goal (The Miners), by Koloman Sokol (b. 1902).

1997, Oct. 15 Engr. ***Perf. 11½***

284 A126 9k multicolored .55 .30
285 A126 10k multicolored .60 .30
286 A126 12k multicolored .70 .40
Nos. 284-286 (3) 1.85 1.00

Cernova 1907 A146

Christmas A147

Photo. & Engr.

1997, Oct. 24 ***Perf. 11½x12***

287 A146 4k Lamenting woman, church .30 .20

1997, Nov. 3 ***Perf. 11½***

288 A147 3k Nativity .25 .20

Ondrej Nepala, Figure Skater — A148

A149

1997, Nov. 3

289 A148 5k multicolored .60 .20

Photo. & Engr.

1997, Dec. 1 ***Perf. 11½***

290 A149 4k Resurrection of Christ .25 .20
Complete booklet, 10 #290 2.50

Spiritual renewal. See #301, 327.

Stamp Day — A150

1997, Dec. 18

291 A150 4k dark brown & blue .25 .20
Complete booklet, 9 #291 + 12 labels 2.25

No. 291 was printed se-tenant with label.

Slovak Republic, 5th Anniv. — A151

Photo. & Engr.

1998, Jan. 1 ***Perf. 11½***

292 A151 4k multicolored .25 .20
Complete booklet, 10 #292 2.50

Personality Type of 1996

Writers: No. 293, Martin Rázus (1888-1937), politician. No. 294, Ján Smrek (1898-1982), poet. No. 295, Jozef Skultéty (1853-1948), linquist, editor.

1998, Jan. 19

293 A114 4k multicolored .25 .20
294 A114 4k multicolored .25 .20
295 A114 4k multicolored .25 .20
Nos. 293-295 (3) .75 .60

1998 Winter Olympic Games, Nagano A152

1998, Jan. 19 ***Perf. 12x11½***

296 A152 19k Hockey player 1.10 .55

Folk Tradition, Banishing of Winter — A153

Photo. & Engr.

1998, Mar. 3 ***Perf. 11½***

297 A153 3k multicolored .20 .20
Complete booklet, 10 #297 2.00

Castles A154

1998, Mar. 3

298 A154 6k Budatin .35 .20
299 A154 11k Krásna Horka .65 .30

Souvenir Sheet

300 A154 18k Nitra 1.00 .50

Spiritual Renewal Type of 1997

Design: Descent of the Holy Spirit, flames above peoples' heads.

Photo. & Engr.

1998, May 5 ***Perf. 11½***

301 A149 4k multicolored .25 .20
Complete booklet, 10 #301 2.50

Folklore Festivals — A155

1998, May 5

302 A155 12k Tekov wedding .70 .35

Europa.

A156 A157

Photo. & Engr.

1998, June 1 ***Perf. 11½***

303 A156 3k Child's drawing .20 .20
Complete booklet, 10 #303 2.00

The Children's Center, Ruzomberok.

1998, June 1

Design: Viktor Kolibik (1890-1918), wireworker, leader of revolt.

304 A157 3k multicolored .20 .20

Mutiny at Kragujevac, 80th anniv.

Slovak Uprising of 1848-49
A158

1998, June 1

305 A158 4k multi, with 1 or 2 labels 1.50 .40

Railways in Slovakia, Cent. — A159

Designs: 4k, Bihar steam locomotive. 10k, Lubochna-Mocidla electrified narrow-gauge trolley. 15k, Diesel locomotive.

Photo. & Engr.

1998, Aug. 20 ***Perf. 11½***

306 A159 4k multicolored .50 .20
307 A159 10k multicolored .60 .30
308 A159 15k multicolored .85 .50
Nos. 306-308 (3) 1.95 1.00

Fish
A160

Designs: a, 4k, Umbra krameri. b, 11k, Zingel zingel. c, 16k, Cyprinus carpio.

1998, Sept. 7

Sheet of 3

309 A160 #a.-c. + 3 labels 1.75 .90

Art Type of 1996

1564 Wooden "Pieta" statue, by unknown artist, Sastín.

1998, Sept. 14 ***Perf. 11½x12***

311 A126 18k multicolored 1.00 .50

"No" to Drugs — A161

Photo. & Engr.

1998, Oct. 5 ***Perf. 11x11½***

312 A161 3k multicolored .20 .20

Ektopfilm, Ecology-Related Film Festival, 25th Anniv. — A162

1998, Oct. 5 ***Perf. 11***

313 A162 4k multicolored .20 .20
Complete booklet, 10 #313 2.00

Art Type of 1996

Designs: 10k, Terchova Landscape, by Martin Benka (1888-1971). 12k, Fishermen, by L'udovít Fulla (1902-80).

1998, Oct. 15 **Engr.** ***Perf. 11½x12***

314 A126 10k multicolored .55 .30
315 A126 12k multicolored .65 .35

Adoration of the Magi — A163

1998, Nov. 3 ***Perf. 11x11½***

317 A163 3k Christmas .20 .20
Complete booklet, 10 #317 1.50

Stamp Day
A164

Photo. & Engr.

1998, Dec. 18 ***Perf. 12x11½***

318 A164 4k multi, with 1 or 2 labels .20 .20
Complete booklet, 9 #318 + 12 labels 1.75

19th World Winter Universiad Games, 4th European Youth Olympic Days — A165

Photo. & Engr.

1999, Jan. 12 ***Perf. 12x11½***

319 A165 12k multicolored .60 .30

No. 319 is printed se-tenant with 2 labels.

Personality Type of 1996

Designs: 3k, Matej Bel (1684-1749), teacher, pastor. 4k, Juraj Haulik (1788-1869), 1st cardinal of Croatia. 11k, Pavol Országh-Hviezdoslav (1849-1921), poet, dramatist.

1999, Jan. 28 ***Perf. 11½***

320 A114 3k multicolored .20 .20
321 A114 4k multicolored .20 .20
322 A114 11k multicolored .60 .30
Nos. 320-322 (3) 1.00 .70

UPU, 125th Anniv. — A166 A167

Photo. & Engr.

1999, Mar. 12 ***Perf. 11½***

323 A166 4k multicolored .20 .20
Complete booklet, 10 #323 2.00

Litho. & Engr.

1999, Mar. 12 ***Perf. 11½x12***

Traditional bonnets.

324 A167 4k Cajkov .20 .20
325 A167 15k Helpa .75 .35
326 A167 18k Madunice .90 .45
Nos. 324-326 (3) 1.85 1.00

Nos. 324-326 were each issued in sheets of 10.

Spiritual Renewal Type of 1997

Design: "Transfiguration," by Vincent Hloznik, depicting ascension of Christ.

Photo. & Engr.

1999, May 5 ***Perf. 11½***

327 A149 5k multicolored .25 .20
Complete booklet, 10 #327 2.50

Tatra National Park
A168

1999, May 5 **Engr.** ***Perf. 11½***

328 A168 9k shown .40 .20
329 A168 11k Mountains, diff. .50 .25
a. Pair, #328-329 .90 .45

Europa. No. 329a is a continuous design. Issued in sheets of 8 + label.

Council of Europe, 50th Anniv.
A169

1999, May 5 **Engr.** ***Perf. 12x11½***

330 A169 16k multicolored .75 .75
a. Souvenir sheet of 1 .75 .75

A170 A171

Photo. & Engr.

1999, June 15 ***Perf. 11½x11¾***

331 A170 4k multicolored .20 .20

Slovak Philharmonic Orchestra, 50th anniv.

1999, June 15 ***Perf. 11½***

332 A171 5k multicolored .25 .20

Intl. Year of Older Persons.

Souvenir Sheet

Astronaut Ivan Bella, First Slovak in Space — A172

Illustration reduced.

1999, June 15 ***Perf. 11¾x11½***

333 A172 12k multicolored .55 .30

UPU, 125th Anniv. — A173

Photo. & Engr.

1999, July 15 ***Perf. 11½***

334 A173 12k Zilina University .55 .30
335 A173 16k Globe .75 .75

A174 A175

Photo. & Engr.

1999, Sept. 3 ***Perf. 11¼x11¾***

336 A174 4k multicolored .20 .20

Bratislava Univ. of Fine Arts, 50th anniv.

1999, Sept. 3 ***Perf. 11¼x11½***

337 A175 5k multicolored .25 .20
Complete booklet, 10 #337 2.50

Bratislava Biennale of Illustrators,

Mine Water Pump Invented By Jozef Hell (1713-89)
A176

1999, Sept. 21 ***Perf. 11x11¼***

338 A176 7k sepia & yellow .35 .20

Souvenir Sheet

Birds — A177

a, 14k, Panurus biarmicus. b, 15k, Lanius collurio. c, 16k, Phoenicurus phoenicurus.

Litho. & Engr.

1999, Sept. 21 ***Perf. 11¾***

339 A177 Sheet of 3, #a.-c. 2.25 1.10

Art Type of 1996

Designs: 13k, Malatiná, by Milos Alexander Bazovsky (1899-1968), horiz. 14k, Study of the Blacksmith, by Dominik Skutecky.

1999, Oct. 5 **Engr.** ***Perf. 11¾***

340 A126 13k multicolored .65 .30
341 A126 14k multicolored .70 .35

Each issued in sheets of 4.

Christmas — A178

Photo. & Engr.

1999, Nov. 3 ***Perf. 11¾x11¼***

342 A178 4k multicolored .20 .20
Complete booklet, 10 #342 2.00

Czechoslovakia's "Velvet Revolution," 10th Anniv. — A179

1999, Nov. 17 ***Perf. 12x11¼***
343 A179 5k multicolored .25 .20

Ceramic Urns, Museum of Jewish Culture — A180

Litho. & Engr.

1999, Nov. 23 ***Perf. 11¾***
344 A180 12k 1776 urn .55 .30
345 A180 18k 1734 urn .85 .40
a. Pair, #344-345 1.40 .70

Issued in sheets of 8.
See Israel #1380-1381.

Albín Brunovsky (1935-97), Stamp Designer A181

Photo. & Engr.

1999, Dec. 18 ***Perf. 12x11¼***
346 A181 5k multi .25 .20
Complete booklet, 9 #346 2.25

Stamp Day. Issued se-tenant with label.

Rivers and Gaps — A182

Designs: a, 10k, Dunajec. b, 12k, Váh.

Litho. & Engr.

2000, Jan. 1 ***Perf. 11¾***
347 A182 Pair, #a.-b. 1.00 .50

Issued in sheets of 8.

Famous People — A183

4k, Hana Melickova (1900-78), actress. 5k, Stefan Anián Jedlik (1800-95), inventor.

Photo. & Engr.

2000, Jan. 11 ***Perf. 11½x11¼***
348 A183 4k multi .20 .20
349 A183 5k multi .25 .20

Basketball A184

Easter A186

World Mathematics Year — A185

Photo. & Engr.

2000, Feb. 15 ***Perf. 11¼x11½***
351 A184 4k multi .20 .20

Ruzomberok team, 1999 European Women's Basketball League champions.

2000, Feb. 15 ***Perf. 11¾x11¼***
352 A185 5k multi .25 .20

Juraj Hronec (1881-1959), Stefan Schwarz (1914-96), mathematicians.

2000, Feb. 15 Engr. ***Perf. 11¼x11½***
353 A186 4k brown .20 .20
Complete booklet, 10 #353 2.00

Ján Holly (1785-1849), Poet — A187

Photo. & Engr.

2000, Mar. 24 ***Perf. 11½x11¼***
354 A187 5.50k multi .25 .20

Europa, 2000
Common Design Type

Litho. & Engr.

2000, May 9 ***Perf. 11¾***
355 CD17 12k multi .55 .30

UNICEF A188

Photo. & Engr.

2000, June 1 ***Perf. 11½x11¼***
356 A188 5.50k multi .25 .20

A189

A190

Postman and Austria design A1.

Photo. & Engr.

2000, June 1 ***Perf. 11¼x11¾***
357 A189 10k multi .45 .25

First postage stamp used in Slovakia, 150th anniv.

Perf. 11¾x11¼

2000, June 15 **Engr.**
358 A190 5.50k Pres. Rudolf Schuster .25 .20

2000 Summer Olympics, Sydney — A191

Photo. & Engr.

2000, June 27 ***Perf. 11¼x11½***
359 A191 18k multi + label 1.50 1.00

Organization for Security and Cooperation in Europe, 25th Anniv. — A192

2000, Aug. 18 ***Perf. 11½x11¼***
361 A192 4k black & blue .20 .20

Wooden Bridge, Klukava A193

2000, Sept. 14 ***Perf. 11¼***
362 A193 6k multi .50 .20

Souvenir Sheet

Berries — A194

No. 363: a, 11k, Rubus idaeus. b, 13k, Fragaria vesca. c, 15k, Vaccinium myrtillus.

Litho. & Engr.

2000, Sept. 14 ***Perf. 11¾***
363 A194 Sheet of 3, #a-c 1.60 .80

Holy Year 2000 — A195

Photo. & Engr.

2000, Oct. 5 ***Perf. 11¼x11½***
364 A195 4k multi .20 .20
Booklet, 10 #364 2.00

Postal Agreement with Sovereign Military Order of Malta — A196

2000, Oct. 13 ***Perf. 11¼x11¾***
365 A196 10k multi .45 .20

Art Type of 1996

Designs: 18k, Nativity, from church in Spisska Stara Ves. 20k, Crucifixion, from church in Kocelovce, horiz.

Perf. 11½x11¾, 11¾x11½

2000, Oct. 17 **Engr.**
366-367 A126 Set of 2 1.75 .85

Stamp Day — A197

Illustration reduced.

Photo. & Engr.

2000, Dec. 18 ***Perf. 11¾x11½***
368 A197 5.50k multi + label .25 .20
Booklet, 9 #368 2.25

POFIS, 50th Anniv.

History of Postal Law A198

2000, Dec. 18 **Engr.** ***Perf. 11¾***
369 A198 20k multi .85 .40

Mantel Clock, c. 1780 — A199

Janko Blaho (1901-81), Singer — A200

Photo. & Engr.

2001, Jan. 1 ***Perf. 11¼x11½***
370 A199 13k multi .55 .30

2001, Jan. 15
371 A200 5.50k multi .25 .20

2001 European Figure Skating Championships, Bratislava — A201

2001, Jan. 16
372 A201 16k multi .70 .35

Agricultural Control Institute, 50th Anniv. — A202

2001, Feb. 22 ***Perf. 11¾x11¼***
373 A202 12k multi .50 .25

Traditional Costumes — A203

Designs: 5.50k, Man from Detva. 6k, Woman and child from Detva.

2001, Feb. 22 *Perf. 11¼x11½*

374 A203 5.50k multi		.25	.20
	Booklet, 10 #374	2.50	
375 A203 6k multi		.25	.20
	Booklet, 10 #375	2.50	

Archaeological Sites — A204

No. 376: a, 12k. Havránok. b, 15k, Ducové. Illustration reduced.

2001, Apr. 10 Engr. *Perf. 11¾*

376 A204	Horiz. pair, #a-b	1.10	.55

Europa A205

2001, May 5 Engr. *Perf. 11¾*

379 A205	18k multi	.75	.35

Souvenir Sheet

Princes of Great Moravia — A206

No. 380: a, 6k, Pribina. b, 9k, Rastislav. c, 11k, Kocel. d, 14k, Svatopluk.

Litho. & Engr.

2001, July 4 *Perf. 11¾*

380 A206	Sheet of 4, #a-d	1.75	.90

Souvenir Sheet

Wild Animals — A207

No. 381: a, 14k, Ursus arctos. b, 15k, Canis lupus. c, 16k, Lynx lynx.

2001, July 10 *Perf. 11¾x11½*

381 A207	Sheet of 3, #a-c	2.00	1.00

SEMI-POSTAL STAMPS

Catalogue values for unused stamps in this section are for Never Hinged items.

Josef Tiso — SP1

Wmk. 263

1939, Nov. 6 Photo. *Perf. 12½*

B1 SP1	2.50k + 2.50k royal blue	3.25	*3.50*

The surtax was used for Child Welfare.

Medical Corpsman and Wounded Soldier — SP2

1941, Nov. 10

B2 SP2	50h + 50h dull green	.45	.45
B3 SP2	1k + 1k rose lake	.45	.45
B4 SP2	2k + 1k brt blue	1.60	1.25
	Nos. B2-B4 (3)	2.50	2.15

Mother and Child — SP3

Soldier and Hlinka Youth — SP4

1941, Dec. 10

B5 SP3	50h + 50h dull green	.95	.85
B6 SP3	1k + 1k brown	.95	.85
B7 SP3	2k + 1k violet	.95	.85
	Nos. B5-B7 (3)	2.85	2.55

Surtax for the benefit of child welfare.

1942, Mar. 14

B8 SP4	70h + 1k brown org	.35	.25
B9 SP4	1.30k + 1k brt blue	.35	.25
B10 SP4	2k + 1k rose red	1.10	1.00
	Nos. B8-B10 (3)	1.80	1.50

The surtax aided the Hlinka Youth Society "Hlinkova Mladez."

SP5

SP6

National Costumes — SP7

1943 *Perf. 14*

B11 SP5	50h + 50h dk slate grn	.25	.20
B12 SP6	70h + 1k dp carmine	.25	.20
B13 SP7	80h + 2k dark blue	.35	.35
	Nos. B11-B13 (3)	.85	.75

The surtax was for the benefit of children, the Red Cross and winter relief of the Slovakian popular party.

Infantrymen — SP8

Aviator — SP9

Tank and Gun Crew SP10

1943, July 28

B14 SP8	70h + 2k rose brown	.75	*.90*
B15 SP9	1.30k + 2k sapphire	.75	*.90*
B16 SP10	2k + 2k olive green	.75	*.90*
	Nos. B14-B16 (3)	2.25	2.70

The surtax was for soldiers' welfare.

"The Slovak Language Is Our Life" - L. Stur — SP11

Slovakian National Museum SP12

Slovakian Foundation SP13

Slovakian Peasant — SP14

1943, Oct. 16

B17 SP11	30h + 1k brown red	.45	.35
B18 SP12	70h + 1k slate green	.60	.55
B19 SP13	80h + 2k slate blue	.45	.35
B20 SP14	1.30k + 2k dull brown	.50	.35
	Nos. B17-B20 (4)	2.00	1.60

The surtax was for the benefit of Slovakian cultural institutions.

Soccer Player — SP15

Skier — SP16

Diver — SP17

Relay Race — SP18

1944, Apr. 30 **Unwmk.**

B21 SP15	70h + 70h slate grn	.75	.75
B22 SP16	1k + 1k violet	.75	.75
B23 SP17	1.30k + 1.30k Prus bl	.75	.75
B24 SP18	2k + 2k chnt brn	.75	.75
	Nos. B21-B24 (4)	3.00	*3.00*

Symbolic of National Protection SP19

Children — SP20

1944, Oct. 6 **Wmk. 263**

B25 SP19	70h + 4h sapphire	.75	.75
B26 SP19	1.30k + 4k red brown	.75	.75

The surtax was for the benefit of social institutions.

1944, Dec. 18

B27 SP20	2k + 4k light blue	3.00	*4.00*
a.	Sheet of 8 + Label	50.00	*70.00*

The surtax was to aid social work for Slovak youth.

Red Cross — SP21

Photo. & Engr.

1993, Nov. 15 *Perf. 11x11½*

B28 SP21	3k +1k red & gray blue	.30	.30

Souvenir Sheet

1996 Summer Olympics, Atlanta — SP22

Photo. & Engr.

1996, May 15 ***Perf. 12x11½***

B29	SP22	12k +2k multi	.80	.80

Surcharge for Slovak Olympic Committee.

AIR POST STAMPS

Catalogue values for unused stamps in this section are for Never Hinged items.

Planes over Tatra Mountains
AP1 AP2

Perf. 12½

1939, Nov. 20 **Photo.** **Unwmk.**

C1	AP1	30h	violet	.35	.35
C2	AP1	50h	dark green	.35	.35
C3	AP1	1k	vermilion	.35	.35
C4	AP2	2k	grnsh black	.55	.55
C5	AP2	3k	dark brown	.80	.80
C6	AP2	4k	slate blue	1.60	1.60
			Nos. C1-C6 (6)	4.00	*4.00*

See No. C10.

Plane in Flight — AP3

1940, Nov. 30 **Wmk. 263** ***Perf. 12½***

C7	AP3	5k	dk violet brn	1.40	1.40
C8	AP3	10k	gray black	1.60	1.60
C9	AP3	20k	myrtle green	2.00	2.00
			Nos. C7-C9 (3)	5.00	*5.00*

Type of 1939

1944, Sept. 15 **Wmk. 263**

C10	AP1	1k	vermilion	1.00	1.00

PERSONAL DELIVERY STAMPS

Catalogue values for unused stamps in this section are for Never Hinged items.

PD1

1940 **Wmk. 263** **Photo.** ***Imperf.***

EX1	PD1	50h	indigo & blue	.90	*1.60*
EX2	PD1	50h	carmine & rose	.90	*1.60*

POSTAGE DUE STAMPS

Catalogue values for unused stamps in this section are for Never Hinged items.

D1

Letter, Post Horn — D2

1939 **Unwmk.** **Photo.** ***Perf. 12½***

J1	D1	5h	bright blue	1.00	.55
J2	D1	10h	bright blue	.50	.55
J3	D1	20h	bright blue	.50	.55
J4	D1	30h	bright blue	3.00	1.00
J5	D1	40h	bright blue	.70	.75
J6	D1	50h	bright blue	2.50	.80
J7	D1	60h	bright blue	2.00	.80
J8	D1	1k	dark carmine	14.00	8.25
J9	D1	2k	dark carmine	14.00	2.50
J10	D1	5k	dark carmine	8.00	2.50
J11	D1	10k	dark carmine	55.00	7.50
J12	D1	20k	dark carmine	18.00	9.25
			Nos. J1-J12 (12)	119.20	35.00

1940-41 **Wmk. 263**

J13	D1	5h	bright blue ('41)	.75	.55
J14	D1	10h	bright blue ('41)	.30	.30
J15	D1	20h	bright blue ('41)	.50	.30
J16	D1	30h	bright blue ('41)	4.00	2.00
J17	D1	40h	bright blue ('41)	.60	.55
J18	D1	50h	bright blue ('41)	.75	.95
J19	D1	60h	bright blue	.90	.95
J20	D1	1k	dark carmine ('41)	.90	1.10
J21	D1	2k	dark carmine ('41)	20.00	9.00
J22	D1	5k	dark carmine ('41)	4.00	2.75
J23	D1	10k	dark carmine ('41)	3.00	3.25
			Nos. J13-J23 (11)	35.70	21.70

1942 **Unwmk.** ***Perf. 14***

J24	D2	10h	deep brown	.20	.20
J25	D2	20h	deep brown	.20	.20
J26	D2	40h	deep brown	.20	.20
J27	D2	50h	deep brown	1.00	.60
J28	D2	60h	deep brown	.20	.20
J29	D2	80h	deep brown	.30	.20
J30	D2	1k	rose red	.35	.20
J31	D2	1.10k	rose red	.70	.60
J32	D2	1.30k	rose red	.40	.20
J33	D2	1.60k	rose red	.50	.20
J34	D2	2k	rose red	.70	.20
J35	D2	2.60k	rose red	1.25	1.00
J36	D2	3.50k	rose red	7.75	6.50
J37	D2	5k	rose red	3.00	2.25
J38	D2	10k	rose red	3.25	2.75
			Nos. J24-J38 (15)	20.00	15.50

NEWSPAPER STAMPS

Newspaper Stamps of Czechoslovakia, 1937, Overprinted in Red or Blue

1939, Apr. **Unwmk.** ***Imperf.***

P1	N2	2h	bister brn (Bl)	.30	*.40*
P2	N2	5h	dull blue (R)	.30	*.40*
P3	N2	7h	red org (Bl)	.30	*.40*
P4	N2	9h	emerald (R)	.30	*.40*
P5	N2	10h	henna brn (Bl)	.30	*.40*
P6	N2	12h	ultra (R)	.30	*.40*
P7	N2	20h	dk green (R)	.60	*.85*
P8	N2	50h	dk brown (Bl)	2.00	*2.50*
P9	N2	1k	grnsh gray (R)	10.00	*12.00*
			Nos. P1-P9 (9)	14.40	*17.75*

Excellent counterfeits exist of Nos. P1-P9.

Catalogue values for unused stamps in this section, from this point to the end of the section, are for Never Hinged items.

Arms of Slovakia
N1

Type Block "N" (for "Noviny" - Newspaper)
N2

1939 **Typo.**

P10	N1	2h	ocher	.20	*.20*
P11	N1	5h	ultra	.25	*.40*
P12	N1	7h	red orange	.20	*.30*
P13	N1	9h	emerald	.20	*.30*
P14	N1	10h	henna brown	.95	1.10
P15	N1	12h	dk ultra	.20	*.35*
P16	N1	20h	dark green	.95	1.10
P17	N1	50h	red brown	1.10	1.25
P18	N1	1k	grnsh gray	1.10	1.10
			Nos. P10-P18 (9)	5.15	6.10

1940-41 **Wmk. 263**

P20	N1	5h	ultra	.20	.20
P23	N1	10h	henna brown	.20	.20
P24	N1	15h	brt purple ('41)	.20	.20
P25	N1	20h	dark green	.35	.35
P26	N1	25h	lt blue ('41)	.35	.35
P27	N1	40h	red org ('41)	.35	.35
P28	N1	50h	chocolate	.60	.55
P29	N1	1k	grnsh gray ('41)	.60	.55
P30	N1	2k	emerald ('41)	1.25	1.40
			Nos. P20-P30 (9)	4.10	4.15

1943 **Photo.** **Unwmk.**

P31	N2	10h	green	.20	.20
P32	N2	15h	dark brown	.20	.20
P33	N2	20h	ultra	.30	.30
P34	N2	50h	rose red	.30	.30
P35	N2	1k	slate green	.40	.40
P36	N2	2k	intense blue	.60	.60
			Nos. P31-P36 (6)	2.00	2.00

SLOVENIA

slō-ˈvē-nē-ə

LOCATION — Southeastern Europe
GOVT. — Independent state
AREA — 7,819 sq. mi.
POP. — 1,970,570 (1999 est.)
CAPITAL — Ljubljana

A constitutent republic of Yugoslavia since 1945, Slovenia declared its independence on June 25, 1991.

100 Paras = 1 Dinar
100 Stotin = 1 Tolar

Catalogue values for unused stamps in this country are for Never Hinged items, beginning with Scott 100 in the regular postage section and Scott RA1 in the postal tax section.

Declaration of Independence
A18

1991, June 26 **Litho.** ***Perf. 10½***

100	A18	5d Parliament building	.60	.60

National Arms
A19 A20

1991-92 ***Perf. 14***

Background Color

101	A19	1t	brown	.20	.20
102	A20	1t	brown	.20	.20
103	A20	2t	lilac rose	.20	.20
105	A19	4t	green	.20	.20
106	A20	4t	green	.20	.20
107	A19	5t	salmon	.20	.20
108	A20	5t	salmon	.20	.20
109	A20	6t	yellow	.25	.25
114	A19	11t	orange	.40	.35
115	A20	11t	orange	.25	.20
119	A20	15t	blue	.30	.25
123	A20	20t	purple	.55	.55
126	A20	50t	dark green	.75	.75
131	A20	100t	gray	1.25	1.25
			Nos. 101-131 (14)	5.15	

Issued: #108, 3/6/91; #101, 105, 107, 114, 12/26/91; #102, 6t, 20t, 50t, 100t, 2/12/92; 2t, 15t, #106, 115, 3/16/92.

This is an expanding set. Numbers may change.

1992 Winter Olympics, Albertville — A21

a, 30t, Ski jumper. b, 50t, Alpine skier.

1992, Feb. 8

134	A21	Pair, #a.-b., + 1 or 2 labels	3.50	3.50

Rhomboid stamps issued in sheets of 3 #134 plus 4 labels. See No. 143.

Ljubljana Opera House, Cent.
A22

1992, Mar. 31

135	A22	20t multicolored	.60	.60

Giuseppe Tartini (1692-1770), Italian Violinist and Composer
A23

1992, Apr. 8

136	A23	27t multicolored	.65	.65

Discovery of America, 500th Anniv.
A24

Designs: a, 27t, Map of northwestern Mexico and Gulf of California, Marko Anton Kappus preaching to natives. b, 47t, Map of parts of North and South America, sailing ship.

1992, Apr. 21
137 A24 Pair, #a.-b. 4.25 4.25

Issued in sheets containing 6 No. 137.

Intl. Conference of Interior Designers, Ljubljana — A25

1992, May 17
138 A25 41t multicolored .65 .65

A. M. Slomsek (1800-1862), Bishop of Maribor — A26

Mountain Rescue Service, 80th Anniv. — A27

1992, May 29
139 A26 6t multicolored .25 .25

1992, June 12
140 A27 41t multicolored .65 .65

A28

A29

1992, June 20
141 A28 6t multicolored .25 .25

Ljubljana Boatmen's Competition, 900th anniv.

1992, June 25
142 A29 41t multicolored .65 .65

Independence, 1st anniv.

Olympic Type of 1992

a, 40t, Leon Stukelj, triple medalist in 1924, 1928. b, 46t, Olympic rings, three heads of Apollo.

1992, July 25
143 A21 Pair, #a.-b. +1 or 2 labels 1.75 1.75

1992 Summer Olympics, Barcelona. Rhomboid stamps issued in sheets of 3 #143 plus 4 labels.

World Championship of Registered Dogs, Ljubljana — A30

1992, Sept. 4
144 A30 40t Slovenian sheep dog .70 .65

Marij Kogoj (1892-1956), Composer A31

Self-Portrait, by Matevz Langus (1792-1855), Painter — A32

1992, Sept. 30
145 A31 40t multicolored .70 .65

1992, Oct. 30
146 A32 40t multicolored .70 .65

Christmas A33

Designs: 6t, 7t, Nativity Scene, Ljubljana. 41t, Stained glass window of Madonna and Child, St. Mary's Church, Bovec, vert.

1992
147 A33 6t multicolored .20 .20
147A A33 7t multicolored .20 .20
148 A33 41t multicolored .70 .70
Nos. 147-148 (3) 1.10

Issued: 6t, 41t, Nov. 20. 7t, Dec. 15.

Herman Potocnik, Theoretician of Geosynchronous Satellite Orbit, Birth Cent. — A34

1992, Nov. 27 Litho. *Perf. 14*
149 A34 46t multicolored .70 .60

Prezihov Voranc (1893-1950), Writer — A35

1993, Jan. 22 Litho. *Perf. 14*
150 A35 7t multicolored .20

Rihard Jakopic (1869-1943), Painter — A36

1993, Jan. 22
151 A36 44t multicolored .65 .60

Jozef Stefan (1835-93), Physicist A37

1993, Jan. 22
152 A37 51t multicolored .75 .65

A38

Designs: 1t, Early cake. 2t, Pan pipes. 5t, Kozolec. 6t, Early building. 7t, Zither. 8t, Water mill. 9t, Sled. 10t, Lonceni bajs. 11t, Kraski kos. 12t, Statue of boy on horseback, Ribnica. 20t, Cross-section of house. 44t, Stone building. 50t, Wind-powered pump. 100t, Potica.

1993-94

153	A38	1t multicolored	*.20*	.20
154	A38	2t multicolored	*.20*	.20
155	A38	5t multicolored	*.20*	.20
156	A38	6t multicolored	*.20*	.20
157	A38	7t multicolored	*.20*	.20
158	A38	8t multicolored	*.20*	.20
159	A38	9t multicolored	*.20*	.20
160	A38	10t multicolored	*.20*	.20
160A	A38	11t multicolored	*.20*	.20
160B	A38	12t multicolored	*.25*	.25
161	A38	20t multicolored	*.30*	.30
162	A38	44t multicolored	*.45*	.45
163	A38	50t multicolored	*.60*	.60
164	A38	100t multicolored	*1.10*	1.10
		Nos. 153-164 (14)	*4.50*	

Issued: 1t, 6t, 7t, 44t, 2/18/93; 2t, 5t, 10t, 20t, 50t, 5/14/93; 8t, 9t, 8/25/93; 11t, 12t, 7/8/94.

See #208A-220, 370. For surcharge see #371.

Mountain Climbers A39

1993, Feb. 27
165 A39 7t shown .20 .20
166 A39 44t Route map, mountain .50 .45

Slovenian Alpine Club, centennial (#165). Joza Cop (1893-1975), mountain climber (#166).

A40

A41

1993, Mar. 19
167 A40 7t multicolored .20 .20

Slovenian Post Office, 75th anniv.

1993, Apr. 9 Litho. *Perf. 14*

7t, Altarpiece, by Tintoretto. 44t, Coat of arms.

168 A41 7t multicolored .20 .20
169 A41 44t multicolored .55 .55

Collegiate Church of Novo Mesto, 500th anniv.

Contemporary Art — A42

Europa: 44t, Round Table of Pompeii, by Marij Pregelj (1913-1967). 159t, Little Girl at Play, by Gabrijel Stupica (1913-1990).

1993, Apr. 29 Litho. *Perf. 14*
170 44t multicolored 1.00 1.00
171 159t multicolored 2.50 2.50
a. A42 Pair, #170-171 3.50 3.50

Schwagerina Carniolica — A43

1993, May 7
172 A43 44t multicolored .60 .60

Admission of Slovenia to UN, 1st Anniv. A44

1993, May 21 Litho. *Perf. 14*
173 A44 62t multicolored .90 .90

Mediterranean Youth Games, Agde, France — A45

1993, June 8
174 A45 36t multicolored .45 .45

Battle of Sisak, 400th Anniv. A46

1993, June 22 Litho. *Perf. 14*
175 A46 49t multicolored .60 .60

Aphaenopidius Kamnikensis — A47

Designs: 7t, Monolistra spinosissima. 55t, Proteus anguinus. 65t, Zospeum spelaeum.

1993, July 12 Litho. *Perf. 14*
176 A47 7t multicolored .20 .20
177 A47 40t multicolored .40 .40
178 A47 55t multicolored .60 .60
179 A47 65t multicolored .80 .80
Nos. 176-179 (4) 2.00

A48

A49

1993, July 30
180 A48 65t multicolored .75 .75

World dressage competition.

1993, Oct. 29 Litho. *Perf. 14*

Coats of Arms: 9t, Janez Vajkard Valvasor. 65t, Citizen's Academy of Ljubljana.

181 A49 9t multicolored *.20* .20
182 A49 65t multicolored *.75* .75

Christmas A50

Designs: 9t, Slovenian Family Viewing Nativity, by Maxim Gaspari (1883-1980). 65t, Archbishop Joze Pogacnik (1902-80), writer.

1993, Nov. 15
183 A50 9t multicolored *.20* .20
184 A50 65t multicolored *.75* .75

Famous People — A51

Love — A52

Works by: 8t, Josip Jurcic (1844-81), writer. 9t, Simon Gregorcic (1844-1906), poet. 55t, Stanislav Skrabec (1844-1918), linguist. 65t, Jernej Kopitar (1780-1844), linguist.

1994, Jan. 14 Litho. *Perf. 14*
185 A51 8t multicolored *.20* .20
186 A51 9t multicolored *.20* .20
187 A51 55t multicolored *.60* .60
188 A51 65t multicolored *.65* .65
Nos. 185-188 (4) 1.65

1994, Jan. 25
189 A52 9t multicolored *.20* .20

1994 Winter Olympics, Lillehammer — A53

1994, Feb. 4
190 A53 9t Cross-country skiing *.20*
191 A53 65t Slalom skiing *.60* .60
a. Pair, #190-191 *.75* .75

World Ski Jumping Championships, Planica — A54

1994, Mar. 11 Litho. *Perf. 14*
192 A54 70t multicolored *.75* .75

City of Ljubljana, 850th Anniv. A55

1994, Mar. 25 Litho. *Perf. 14*
193 A55 9t multicolored *.20*

Europa — A56

70t, Janez Puhar, camera. 215t, Moon, Jurij Vega.

1994, Apr. 22
194 A56 70t multicolored *.75* .75
195 A56 215t multicolored *1.90* 1.90
a. Pair, #194-195 *2.75* 2.75

Miniature Sheet

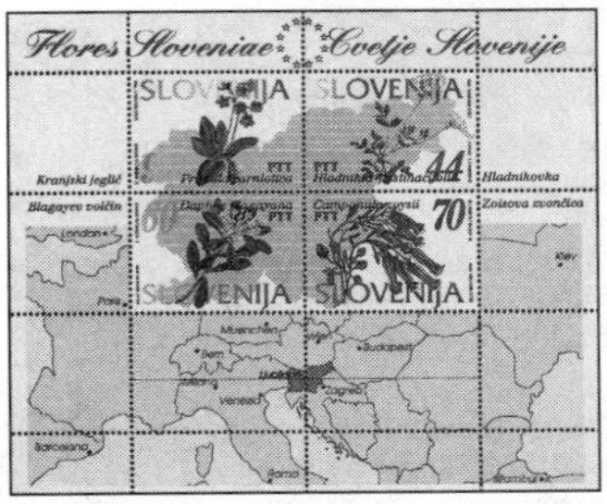

Flowers of Slovenia — A57

Designs: a, 9t, Primula carniolica. b, 44t, Hladnikia pastinacifolia. c, 60t, Daphne blagayana. d, 70t, Campanula zoysii.

1994, May 20 Litho. *Perf. 14*
196 A57 Sheet of 4 + 2 labels *1.75* 1.75

1994 World Cup Soccer Championships, US — A58

1994, June 10
197 A58 44t multicolored *.45* .45

Intl. Olympic Committee, Cent. A59

1994, June 10
198 A59 100t multicolored *1.00* 1.00

Mt. Ojstrica — A60

Max Pletersnik, Professors — A61

1994, July 1 Litho. *Perf. 14*
199 A60 12t multicolored *.20* .20

1994, July 22
200 A61 70t multicolored *.60* .60

First Slovenian-German dictionary published by Max Pletersnik (1840-1932), cent.

Battle of the Frigidus, 1600th Anniv. A62

1994, Sept. 1 Litho. *Perf. 14*
201 A62 60t multicolored *.55* .55

Maribor Post Office, Cent. A63

1994, Sept. 23 Litho. *Perf. 14*
202 A63 70t multicolored *.60* .60

Ljubljana-Novo Mesto Railway, Cent. — A64

1994, Sept. 24 Litho. *Perf. 14*
203 A64 70t Locomotive 5722, 1893 *.60* .60

See Nos. 233, 243, 291, 325, 363.

Philharmonic Assoc., Bicent. — A65

Designs: 12t, Building, Ljubljana. 70t, Beethoven, Brahms, Dvorak, Haydn, Paganini.

1994, Oct. 20
204 A65 12t multicolored *.20*
205 A65 70t multicolored *.55* .55

Black Madonna of Loreto, 700th Anniv. — A66

1994, Nov. 18
206 A66 70t multicolored *.60* .60

Christmas — A67

Intl. Year of the Family — A68

1994, Nov. 18
207 A67 12t multicolored *.20* .20

1994, Nov. 18
208 A68 70t multicolored *.60* .60

Type of 1993

13t, Wind rattle, Prlekija. 14t, Sentjernej pottery cock. 15t, Blast furnace, Zelezniki. 16t, Windmill, Stara Gora. 17t, Corn storage building. 55t, Easter eggs, Bela Krajina. 65t, Cobbler's lamp with glass spheres, Trzic. 70t, Snow skis. 75t, 1812 Iron window lattice, Srednja vas, Bohinj. 80t, Palm Sunday bundle. 90t, Beehive. 200t, "Zajec," insect-shaped bootjack, Dvor. 300t, Slamnati doznjek. 400t, Wine press. 500t, Kumer family's table, Koprivna, Carinthia.

1994-99 Litho. *Perf. 14*
208A A38 13t multicolored .40 .20
208B A38 14t multicolored .20 .20
209 A38 15t multicolored .20 .20
210 A38 16t multicolored .20 .20

210A	A38	17t multicolored	.20	.20
211	A38	55t multicolored	.40	.40
212	A38	65t multicolored	.50	.50
213	A38	70t multicolored	.60	.60
214	A38	75t multicolored	.55	.55
215	A38	80t multicolored	.55	.55
216	A38	90t multicolored	.60	.60
217	A38	200t multicolored	1.25	1.25
218	A38	300t brown	2.50	2.25
219	A38	400t brown & lake	3.25	3.00
220	A38	500t multicolored	3.00	3.00
		Nos. 208A-220 (15)	14.40	13.70

Issued: 300t, 400t, 11/7/94; 70t, 11/16/95; 55t, 65t, 75t, 3/22/96; 80t, 3/20/97; 13t, 14t, 8/8/97; 90t, 5/30/97; 15t, 6/23/98; 200t, 500t, 11/12/98; 16t, 2/5/99; 17t, 5/7/99.

Ljubljana University, 75th Anniv. A69

Design: 70t, Provincial palace buildings, founders, I. Hribar, M. Rostohar, D. Majaron.

1994, Dec. 3 Litho. *Perf. 14*

221 A69 70t multicolored *.60* .60

Postal Service Emblem — A70

1995, Jan. 27

222 A70 13t multicolored *.20* .20

Love — A71

Famous People — A72

1995, Feb. 7

223 A71 20t multicolored *.25* .20

1995, Feb. 7

Works by: 20t, Anton Tomaz Linhart (1756-95), playwright, horiz. No. 225, Ivan Vurnik (1884-1971), architect. No. 226, Lili Novy (1885-1958), poet, horiz.

224 A72 20t multicolored *.20* .20
225 A72 70t multicolored *.55* .55
226 A72 70t multicolored *.55* .55
Nos. 224-226 (3) *1.30*

A73

A74

1995, Mar. 29 Litho. *Perf. 14*

227 A73 13t multicolored *.20* .20

End of World War II, 50th anniv.

1995, Mar. 29

228 A74 70t Karavankina schellwieni *.60* .60

Liberation of the Concentration Camps, 50th Anniv. — A75

Europa: 60t, Skeleton of Death lying on bride. 70t, Nike going from dark to light.

1995, Mar. 29

229 A75 60t multicolored *.60* .60
230 A75 70t multicolored *.75* .75
a. Pair, #229-230 *2.35*

#230a was issued in sheets of 4.

European Nature Conservation Year — A76

1995, Mar. 29

231 A76 70t Triglav Natl. Park *.60* .60

Town of Radovljica, 500th Anniv. A77

1995, June 8 Litho. *Perf. 14*

232 A77 44t multicolored *.40* .40

Railways Type of 1994

Design: 70t, Locomotive KRB 37, Podnart.

1995, June 8

233 A64 70t multicolored *.60* .60

Ljubljana-Jesenice Line, 125th anniv.

Aljaz Tower, Cent. — A78

1995, June 8 *Perf. 13½*

234 A78 100t multicolored *.85* .85

Portions of the design on No. 234 were applied by a thermogrphic process producing a shiny, raised effect.

Endangered Birds — A79

Designs: a, 13t, Falco naumanni. b, 60t, Coracias garrulus. c, 70t, Lanius minor. d, 215t, Emberiza melanocephala.

1995, June 8 *Perf. 14*

235 A79 Block of 4, #a.-d. *3.25* 3.25

Slovenian Boy Scouts A80

1995, Sept. 26 Litho. *Perf. 14*

236 A80 70t multicolored *.60* .60

Comtemporary Art, by France Kralj — A81

1995, Sept. 26

237 A81 60t Death of a Genius, 1921 *.50* .50
238 A81 70t Family of Horses, 1959 *.60* .60
a. Pair, #237-238 *1.10* 1.10

A82

A83

UN, FAO, 50th Anniv.: No. 239, Stylized pictures of food products, faces of people from many nations. No. 240, Black & white figures touching hands, faces of people from many nations.

1995, Sept. 26

239 A82 70t multicolored *.50* .50
240 A82 70t multicolored *.50* .50
a. Pair, #239-240 *1.25* 1.25

Issued in miniature sheets of 4 stamps.

1995, Nov. 16

Christmas (Paintings): 13t, Winter, by Marlenka Stupica. 70t, St. Mary of Succour, Brezje, by Leopold Layer.

241 A83 13t multicolored *.20* .20
a. Booklet pane of 10 + 2 labels *1.50* 1.50
Complete booklet *1.50* 1.50
242 A83 70t multicolored *.60* .60
a. Booklet pane of 10 + 2 labels *6.00* 6.00
Complete booklet *6.00* 6.00

Railways Type of 1994

Design: 70t, Locomotive "Aussee."

1996, Jan. 31 Litho. *Perf. 14*

243 A64 70t multicolored *.60* .60

The Graz-Celje Line, 150th anniv.

St. Gregory's Day — A84

1996, Jan. 31 Litho. *Perf. 14*

244 A84 13t multicolored *.20* .20

Carnival Costumes A85

1996, Jan. 31

245 A85 13t Ptujsko region *.20* .20
246 A85 70t Dravsko region *.50* .50

See Nos. 281-282, 384-385.

Emys Orbicularis A86

World Wildlife Fund: a, 13t, Peeking head out of water. b, 50t, Two young. c, 60t, Adult crawling though water. d, 70t, Laying eggs.

1996, Jan. 31

247 A86 Strip of 4, #a.-d. *2.00* 2.00

No. 247 printed in sheets of 4 vertical or horizontal strips, each having a different order.

Fran Saleski Finzgar (1871-1962), Writer, Priest — A87

1996, Apr. 18 Litho. *Perf. 14*

248 A87 13t multicolored *.20*

A88

1996, Apr. 18

249 A88 65t multicolored *.50* .50

UNICEF, 50th anniv.

A89

1996, Apr. 18

Paintings: 65t, Children on Grass (detail). 75t, Bouquet of Dahlias.

250 65t multicolored .45 .45
251 75t multicolored .55 .55
a. A89 Pair, Nos. 250-251 1.00 1.00

Ivana Kobilca (1861-1926), painter. Issued in sheets of 8 stamps. Europa.

Ita Rina (1907-79), Film Actress A90

1996, Apr. 18

252 A90 100t multicolored .75 .75

Visit of Pope John Paul II, May 17-19 — A91

1996, Apr. 18

253 A91 75t multicolored .50 .50

Souvenir Sheet

254 A91 200t multicolored 1.50 1.50

City of Zagorje ob Savi, 700th Anniv. A92

1996, June 6 **Litho.** ***Perf. 14***

255 A92 24t Gallenberg Castle .25 .25

World Junior Cycling Championships, Novo Mesto — A93

1996, June 6

256 A93 55t multicolored .45 .45

Independence, 5th Anniv. — A94

1996, June 6

257 A94 75t multicolored .60 .60

Mushrooms — A95

Designs: a, 65t, Cantharellus cibarius. b, 75t, Boletus aestivalis.

1996, June 6

258 A95 Sheet of 2, #a.-b. 1.40 1.40

Modern Olympic Games, Cent., 1996 Summer Olympics, Atlanta — A96

Designs: 75t, Iztok Cop, rower; Fredja Marsic, kayaker. 100t, Britta Bilac, high jumper; Brigita Bukovec, hurdler.

1996, June 6

259 A96 75t multicolored .60 .60
260 A96 100t multicolored .80 .80
a. Pair, #259-260+label 1.50 1.50

No. 260a issued in sheets of 6 stamps + 3 labels.

Two versions of the sheet exist. One with white, red & blue flag, the other with white, blue & red flag.

A97

A98

A99

A100

Idrijan Lace
A101 A102

1996, June 21 **Litho.** ***Perf. 14***

261 A97 1t shown .20 .20
262 A97 1t olive gray, diff. .20 .20
a. Pair, #261-262 .20 .20
263 A98 2t shown .20 .20
264 A98 2t carmine, diff. .20 .20
a. Pair, #263-264 .20 .20
265 A99 5t shown .20 .20
266 A99 5t square .20 .20
a. Pair, #265-266 .20 .20
267 A100 12t shown .20 .20
268 A100 12t diamond .20 .20
a. Pair, #267-268 .30 .30
269 A101 13t shown .20 .20
270 A101 13t red, diff. .20 .20
a. Pair, #269-270 .30 .30
271 A102 50t shown .40 .40
272 A102 50t lilac, diff. .40 .40
a. Pair, #272-272 .80 .80
Nos. 261-272 (12) *2.80*

The background of the designs on Nos. 261-272 contain "1996," posthorn, and security lettering that appear under UV light.

See Nos. 297-304.

Modern Cardiology, Cent. — A103

1996, Sept. 6 **Litho.** ***Perf. 14***

273 A103 12t multicolored .20 .20

Grammar School, Novo Mesto, 250th Anniv. A104

1996, Sept. 6

274 A104 55t multicolored .55 .35

Skocjan Caves, Karst Region, UNESCO World Heritage Site A105

1996, Sept. 6

275 A105 55t multicolored .55 .35

Moscon Family Portrait, by Jozef Tominc (1790-1866) — A106

1996, Sept. 6

276 A106 65t multicolored .75 .50

A107

A108

1996, Oct. 18 **Litho.** ***Perf. 14***

277 A107 100t multicolored 1.00 .65

Post Office, Ljubljana, cent.

1996, Oct. 20

278 A108 12t multicolored .20 .20

Introduction of automatic letter sorting machines, Maribor.

A109

Christmas A110

1996, Nov. 20 **Litho.** ***Perf. 14***

279 A109 12t Children sledding .20 .20
a. Booklet pane of 10 1.40
Complete booklet, #279a 1.40
280 A110 65t Nativity .65 .50
a. Booklet pane of 10 6.75
Complete booklet, #280a 6.75

Carnival Costumes Type of 1996

From Cerkno region: 20t, "Ta terjast." 80t, "Pust."

1997, Jan. 21 **Litho.** ***Perf. 14***

281 A85 20t multicolored .20 .20
282 A85 80t multicolored .80 .55

Love A111

1997, Jan. 21 **Litho.** ***Perf. 14***

283 A111 15t multicolored .20 .20

Sneznik Mountain A112

1997, Jan. 21

284 A112 20t multicolored .20 .20

A113

A114

1997, Mar. 27 **Litho.** ***Perf. 14***

285 A113 80t Legend of the Goldenhorn .80 .50

Europa.

1997, Mar. 27

286 A114 80t Wulfenite .80 .50

Endangered Fish — A115

1997, Mar. 27

287 A115 12t Salmo marmoratus .20 .20
288 A115 13t Zingel streber .20 .20
289 A115 80t Vimba vimba .80 .50
290 A115 90t Umbra krameri .95 .60
a. Souvenir sheet, #287-290 2.00 2.00
Nos. 287-290 (4) 2.15 1.50

Railways Type of 1994

Design: 80t, Locomotive SZ 03-002, Ljubljana-Trieste Railway Line, 140th anniv.

1997, May 30 Litho. *Perf. 14*

291 A64 80t multicolored .80 .50

A116

A117

1997, May 30

292 A116 70t multicolored .65 .45

Volunteer fire fighting brigades in Slovenia.

1997, May 30

Famous People: 13t, Matija Cop (1797-1835), literary expert. 24t, Sigismundus Zois (1747-1819), economist, natural scientist. 80t, Bishop Frederic Baraga (1797-1868), missionary, linguist.

293 A117 13t multicolored .20 .20
294 A117 24t multicolored .25 .20
295 A117 80t multicolored .80 .50
Nos. 293-295 (3) 1.25 .90

Souvenir Sheet

4th Meeting of the Presidents of Central European Countries, Piran — A118

Designs: a, 100t, Tartini Square. b, 200t, Coats of arms from eight countries.

1997, June 6

296 A118 Sheet of 2, #a.-b. 3.00 3.00

Idrijan Lace Type of 1996

Shape of lace: No. 297, Flower in center of oval. No. 298, Circular outside with swirl at bottom. No. 299, Butterfly. No. 300, Diamond. No. 301, Square. No. 302, Circle. No. 303, Leaves. No. 304, Tulip.

1997, June 20 Litho. *Perf. 14*

297 A97 10t magenta .20 .20
298 A97 10t magenta .20 .20
a. Pair, #297-298 .25 .25
299 A97 20t violet .20 .20
300 A97 20t violet .20 .20
a. Pair, #299-300 .40 .40
301 A97 44t bright blue .45 .30
302 A97 44t bright blue .45 .30
a. Pair, #301-302 .90 .90
303 A97 100t gray brown 1.00 .60
304 A97 100t gray brown 1.00 .60
a. Pair, #303-304 2.00 2.00
Nos. 299-304 (6) 3.30 2.20

A119

A120

1997, Sept. 9

305 A119 14t multicolored .20 .20

Children's Week.

1997, Sept. 9

306 A120 50t multicolored .50 .35

Return of Primorska, 50th anniv.

France Gorse (1897-1986), Sculptor — A121

1997, Sept. 9

307 A121 70t "Bashful Armor" .70 .45
308 A121 80t "Peasant Woman" .80 .55
a. Pair, #307-308 1.50 1.50

A122

A123

1997, Sept. 9

309 A122 90t multicolored .90 .60

MEJP '97, European Youth Judo Championship.

1997, Nov. 18 Litho. *Perf. 14*

310 A123 90t multicolored .90 .60

Golden Fox World Cup Ski Competition for Women, 35th anniv.

Christmas & New Year A124

Designs: 14t, Children watching birds and snow outside window. 90t, Sculptured Nativity scene, by Liza Hribar (1913-96).

1997, Nov. 18

311 A124 14t multicolored .20 .20
312 A124 90t multicolored .80 .55
a. Booklet pane of 8, 5 #311, 3 #312 3.50
Complete booklet, #312a 3.50

New Mail Center, Ljubljana — A125

1997, Nov. 28

313 A125 30t multicolored .30 .20

Borovo Gostüvanje (Pine Wedding) — A126

20t, Participating "players," tree. 80t, Participants, "bride & groom," top of pine tree.

1998, Jan. 22 Litho. *Perf. 14*

314 A126 20t multicolored .25 .20
315 A126 80t multicolored .75 .50
a. Pair, #314-315 1.00 1.00

See Nos. 338-339.

1998 Winter Olympic Games, Nagano A127

1998, Jan. 22

316 A127 70t Woman skater .65 .45
317 A127 90t Biathlete .90 .55
a. Vert. pair, #316-317 + label 1.60 1.60

Issued in sheets of 6 stamps + 3 labels.

EUROCONTROL (European Organization for Safety of Air Navigation), 35th Anniv. — A128

1998, Jan. 22

318 A128 90t multicolored .90 .60

Louis Adamic (1898-1951), Writer — A129

90t, Francesco Robba (1698-1757), sculptor.

1998, Mar. 25 Litho. *Perf. 14*

319 A129 26t multicolored .25 .20
320 A129 90t multicolored .85 .55

Jurjevanje (Green George's Festival) A130

1998, Mar. 25

321 A130 90t multicolored .90 .60

Europa.

Comic Strip Characters, by Miki Muster — A131

1998, Mar. 25

322 A131 14t Fox .20 .20
323 A131 105t Turtle 1.00 .65
324 A131 118t Wolf 1.10 .70
a. Sheet, 2 each #322-324 4.50 4.50
Nos. 322-324 (3) 2.30 1.55

Railways Type of 1994

Design: Steam locomotive SZ 06-018.

1998, June 10 Litho. *Perf. 14*

325 A64 80t multicolored .80 .50

Boc Mountain, Pulsatilla Grandis — A132

1998, June 10

326 A132 14t multicolored .20 .20

A133

A134

Conifers: a, 14t, Juniperus communis. b, 15t, Picea abies. c, 80t, Pinus nigra. d, 90t, Larix decidua.

1998, June 10

327 A133 Sheet of 4, #a.-d. 2.00 2.00

1998, June 23 Litho. *Perf. 14*

328 A134 15t multicolored .20 .20

Committee for the Protection of Human Rights, 10th anniv.

United Slovenia, 150th Anniv. A135

1998, June 23

329 A135 80t multicolored		.80	.50

Cistercian Order, 900th Anniv. and Sticna Revival, Cent. A136

1998, Sept. 11 Litho. *Perf. 14*

330 A136 14t multicolored	.20	.20

Radio Ljubljana, 70th Anniv. A137

1998, Sept. 11

331 A137 50t Cuckoo	.50	.30

Avgust Cernigoj (1898-1985), Artist — A138

Designs: 70t, Abstract painting, "Banker." 80t, Sculpture, "El."

1998, Sept. 11

332 A138 70t multicolored	.65	.45
333 A138 80t multicolored	.75	.55
a. Pair, #332-333	1.40	1.40

Universal Declaration of Human Rights, 50th Anniv. — A139

1998, Sept. 11

334 A139 100t multicolored	.95	.65

Christmas A140

Designs: 15t, Children walking through snow, candle. 90t, Fresco of "Bow of the Three Wise Men of the East," Church of St. Nicholas, Mace, 1476.

1998, Nov. 12 Litho. *Perf. 14*

335 A140 15t multicolored	.20	.20
a. Booklet pane of 10	1.60	
Complete booklet, #335a	1.60	
336 A140 90t multicolored	.85	.55
a. Bklt. pane, 6 #335, 4 #336	4.50	
Complete booklet, #336a	4.50	

Leon Stukelj, Olympic Gymnastics Champion, 100th Birthday — A141

Designs: a, Portrait. b, As a gymnast. c, With IOC Pres. Juan Antonio Samaranch, horiz. (58x40mm).

1998, Nov. 12

337 A141 100t Sheet of 3, #a.-c.	3.00	3.00

Wedding, Festival Type of 1998

Skoromati carnival mask characters: 20t, Wearing tall hats, Skopit character in black. 80t, Skopit character blowing horn.

1999, Jan. 22 Litho. *Perf. 14*

338 A126 20t multicolored	.25	.20
339 A126 80t multicolored	.75	.50
a. Pair, #338-339	1.00	1.00

Greetings A142

1999, Jan. 22

340 A142 15t multicolored	.20	.20

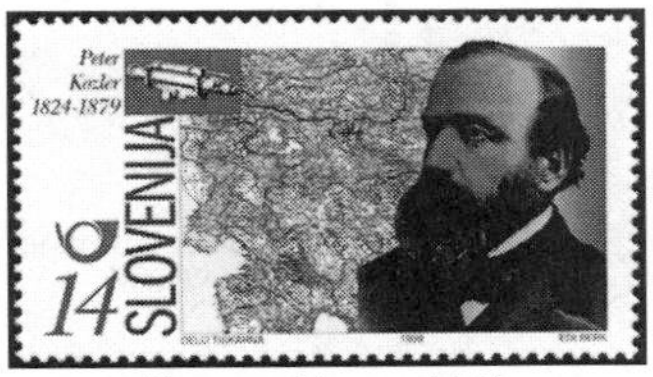

Famous Men — A143

14t, Peter Kozler (1824-79), geographer. 15t, Bozidar Lavric (1899-1961), surgeon. 70t, Rudolf Maister (1874-1934), general, poet. 80t, France Preseren (1800-49), poet.

1999, Jan. 22

341 A143 14t multicolored	.20	.20
342 A143 15t multicolored	.20	.20
343 A143 70t multicolored	.65	.40
344 A143 80t multicolored	.75	.50
Nos. 341-344 (4)	1.80	1.30

Golica Mountain, Narcissus Flowers A144

1999, Mar. 23 Litho. *Perf. 14*

345 A144 15t multicolored	.20	.20

Slovenian Philatelic Assoc., 50th Anniv. — A145

1999, Mar. 23

346 A145 16t Yugoslavia #3L5 & #305	.20	.20

Mercury & Cinnabar, Idrija Mine A146

1999, Mar. 23

347 A146 80t multicolored	.90	.45

Council of Europe, 50th Anniv. A147

1999, Mar. 23

348 A147 80t multicolored	.90	.45

Triglav Natl. Park A148

1999, Mar. 23

349 A148 90t multicolored	1.00	.50

Europa.

5th Rescue Dog World Championships — A149

1999, May 21 Litho. *Perf. 14*

350 A149 80t multicolored	.90	.45

UPU, 125th Anniv. — A150

Designs: 30t, Early postman with backpack. 90t, Astronaut on moon with backpack.

1999, May 21

351 A150 30t multicolored	.60	.30
352 A150 90t multicolored	1.00	.50
a. Pair, #351-352	1.60	.80

Horses A151

Designs: 60t, Slovenian cold-blooded horse. 70t, Ljutomer trotter. 120t, Slovenian warm-blooded horse (show jumper). 350t, Lipizzaner.

1999, May 21

353 A151 60t multicolored	.65	.35
354 A151 70t multicolored	.75	.40
355 A151 120t multicolored	1.25	.65
356 A151 350t multicolored	3.75	1.90
a. Sheet of 4, #353-356	6.50	3.50
Nos. 353-356 (4)	6.40	3.30

Towards A New Millennium — A152

Designs: 20t, Balanced objects. 70t, Roadway, earth. 80t, Cogwheels. 90t, Tree.

1999, Sept. 16 Litho. *Perf. 13¾*

357 A152 20t multicolored	.20	.20
358 A152 70t multicolored	.80	.40
359 A152 80t multicolored	.90	.45
360 A152 90t multicolored	1.00	.50
a. Block of 4, #357-360	3.00	1.50

Bozidar Jakac (1899-1989), Painter — A153

Self-portraits and: 70t, Girl drawing curtain. 80t, Landscape.

1999, Sept. 16

361 A153 70t multicolored	.80	.40
362 A153 80t multicolored	.90	.45
a. Pair, #361-362	1.75	.85

Railway type of 1994

1999, Sept. 16

363 A64 80t multicolored	.90	.45

Rail Line to Ljubljana, 150th anniv.

Bishop Anton M. Slomsek (1800-62) — A154

1999, Sept. 16

364 A154 90t multicolored	1.00	.50

Millennium A155

Christmas — A156

1999, Nov. 18 Litho. *Perf. 14*

365 A155 17t multicolored	.20	.20
a. Booklet pane of 10	2.00	
Complete booklet, #365a	2.00	
366 A155 18t multicolored	.20	.20
367 A156 80t multicolored	.80	.40
a. Booklet pane, 5 #365, 3 #367 + 2 labels	3.50	
Complete booklet, #367a	3.50	
368 A156 90t multicolored	.90	.45
Nos. 365-368 (4)	2.10	1.25

#365 and 367 were issued only in booklets.

Type of 1993

Design: 18t, Accordion.

1999 Litho. *Perf. 14*

370 A38 18t multi .20 .20

Issued: 18t, 12/17/99. This is an continuing set. Numbers may change.

No. 210A Surcharged

2000 Litho. *Perf. 14*

371 A38 19t on 17t multi .20 .20

Issued: No. 371, 4/20/00.

Love — A158

2000, Jan. 20 Litho. *Perf. 14*

383 A158 34t multi .35 .20

Carnival Costume Type of 1996

Pustovi masks: 34t, Two masks, horiz. 80t, Four masks, horiz.

2000, Jan. 20

384 A85 34t multi .35 .20

385 A85 80t multi .80 .40

A159

A160

2000, Jan. 20

386 A159 64t multi .65 .30

Tone Seliskar (1900-69), poet.

2000, Jan. 20

387 A160 120t multi 1.25 .60

Elvira Kralj (1900-78), actress.

Postal Service in Slovenia, 500th Anniv. — A161

2000, Jan. 20

388 A161 500t multi 5.00 2.50

Mt. Storzic A162

2000, Mar. 21 Litho. *Perf. 14*

389 A162 18t multi .20 .20

Return of World War II Exiles A163

2000, Mar. 21

390 A163 25t multi .25 .20

Characters from Children's Books — A164

#391, 394, Pedenjped. #392, 395, Mojca Pokrajculja. #393, 396, Macek Muri.

2000, Mar. 21 *Perf. 14*

391 A164 20t multi .20 .20

392 A164 20t multi .20 .20

393 A164 20t multi .20 .20

Booklet Stamps

Self-Adhesive

Serpentine Die Cut 7½

394 A164 20t multi .20 .20

395 A164 20t multi .20 .20

396 A164 20t multi .20 .20

a. Booklet pane, 3 each #394-396 + 9 labels 1.80

Nos. 391-396 (6) 1.20 1.20

No. 396a is a complete booklet.

Fossils and Minerals A165

2000, Mar. 21 *Perf. 14*

397 A165 80t Trilobite .75 .35

398 A165 90t Dravite .85 .45

Souvenir Sheet

Holy Year 2000 — A166

Illustration reduced.

2000, Mar. 21

399 A166 2000t multi 20.00 10.50

Castles — A167

2000-01 Litho. *Perf. 14*

400 A167 1t Predjama .20 .20

401 A167 1t Velenje .20 .20

a. Pair, #400-401 .20 .20

404 A167 A Ptuj .20 .20

405 A167 A Otocec .20 .20

a. Pair, #404-405 .35 .20

406 A167 B Zuzemberk .20 .20

407 A167 B Turjak .20 .20

a. Pair, #406-407 .35 .20

410 A167 C Dobrovo .80 .40

411 A167 C Breziski .80 .40

a. Pair, #410-411 1.60 .80

412 A167 100t Podsreda .90 .45

413 A167 100t Bled .90 .45

a. Pair, #412-413 1.80 .90

414 A167 D Olimje .85 .45

415 A167 D Murska Sobota .85 .45

a. Pair, #414-415 1.70 .90

Nos. 400-415 (12) 6.30 3.80

Nos. 404-405 each sold for 20t; Nos. 406-407 for 21t; Nos. 410-411 for 95t; Nos. 414-415 for 107t on day of issue.

Issued: Nos. 1t, 100t, 4/20; A, B, 6/23; Nos. 410-411, 414-415, 10/4/01. This is an expanding set.

Fruits, Blossoms and Insects — A168

Designs: No. 416, Apple blossom weevil. No. 417, Apple blossom. No. 418, Apple.

2000, Apr. 20 Litho. *Perf. 13¾*

416 A168 10t multi .20 .20

417 A168 10t multi .20 .20

418 A168 10t multi .20 .20

a. Strip, #416-418 .25 .20

Printed in sheets of 15 stamps + 5 labels. See Nos. 426-428.

Amateur Radio A169

2000, May 9 Litho. *Perf. 14*

419 A169 20t multi .20 .20

Slovenian Team Qualification for European Soccer Championships A170

2000, May 9

420 A170 40t multi .35 .20

2000 Summer Olympics, Sydney A171

2000, May 9

421 A171 80t Sailboats .70 .35

422 A171 90t Sydney Opera House .80 .40

a. Pair, #421-422 1.50 .75

World Environment Day — A172

2000, May 9

423 A172 90t multi .80 .40

Issued in sheets of 10 + 5 labels.

Europa, 2000

Common Design Type

2000, May 9 Litho. *Perf. 14*

424 CD17 90t multi .80 .40

Issued in sheets of 8 + 1 label.

Meteorology A173

2000, May 9 *Perf. 13¾*

425 A173 150t multi 1.40 .70

Issued in sheets of 9 + 1 label.

Fruits, Blossoms and Insects Type of 2000

#426, Cherry blossom. #427, European cherry fruit fly. #428, Cherries.

2000, June 23 Litho. *Perf. 13¾*

426 A168 5t multi .20 .20

427 A168 5t multi .20 .20

428 A168 5t multi .20 .20

a. Strip, #426-428 .20 .20

Printed in sheets of 15 stamps + 5 labels.

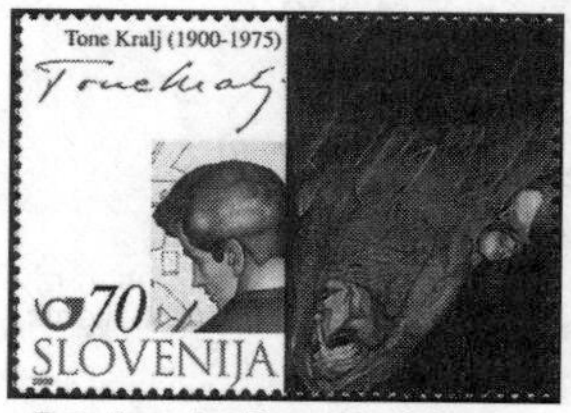

Paintings by Tone Kralj (1900-75) — A174

2000, Sept. 15 Litho. *Perf. 14*

429 Horiz. pair 1.25 .65

a. A174 70t multi .60 .30

b. A174 80t multi, diff. .65 .35

Grape Varieties — A175

Designs: 20t, Zelen. 40t, Ranfol. 80t, Zametovka. 130t, Rumeni Plavec.

2000, Sept. 15

430-433 A175 Set of 4 2.25 1.10

a. Souvenir sheet, #430-433 2.25 1.10

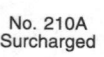

Gold Medalists at 2000 Summer Olympics A176

Winners and events: No. 434, 21t, Iztok Cop, Luka Spik, double sculls. No. 435, 21t, Rajmond Debevec, Men's three-position rifle.

2000, Oct. 16
434-435 A176 Set of 2 .35 .20

First Book Printed in Slovenian, 450th Anniv. — A177

2000, Nov. 21
436 A177 50t multi .45 .20

Christmas A178

Designs: B, Children in snow. 90t, Christ in manger.

2000, Nov. 21
437-438 A178 Set of 2 1.00 .50

No. 437 sold for 21t on day of issue.

Christmas Type of 2000

Designs: B, Children in snow. 90t, Christ in manger.

Serpentine Die Cut 7¼

2000, Nov. 21 Litho.

Booklet Stamps

Self-Adhesive

439 A178 B multi .20 .20
a. Booklet of 10 + 2 labels 2.00
440 A178 90t multi .80 .40
a. Booklet, 6 #439, 4 #440 + 2 labels 4.50

No. 439 sold for 21t on day of issue.

Advent of New Millennium — A179

2000, Nov. 21 Litho. *Perf. 14*
441 A179 40t multi .35 .20

Wedding Greetings A180

2001, Jan. 19 Litho. *Perf. 14*
442 A180 B multi .25 .20

No. 442 sold for 25t on day of issue.

Carnival Masks, Dobrepolje — A181

Mask wearers including: 50t, Woman with flowers. 95t, Woman in box on cart.

2001, Jan. 19
443-444 A181 Set of 2 1.25 .65

Writers — A182

Objects symbolic of writer's works: A, Bucket (Dragotin Kette, 1876-99). 95t, Flowers in jar (Ivan Tavcar, 1851-1923). 107t, Coffee cup (Ivan Cankar, 1876-1918).

2001, Jan. 19
445-447 A182 Set of 3 2.00 1.00

No. 445 sold for 24t on day of issue.

Mt. Jalovec and Triglav Flowers — A183

2001, Mar. 21 Litho. *Perf. 14*
448 A183 B multi .20 .20

No. 448 sold for 25t on day of issue.

Comic Strip Characters by Bozo Kos — A184

Designs: No. 449, B, Cowboy. No. 450, B, Indian.

2001, Mar. 21
449-450 A184 Set of 2 .40 .20

Nos. 449-450 each sold for 25t on day of issue.

Comic Strip Characters Type of 2001

Designs: No. 451, B, Cowboy. No. 452, B, Indian.

Serpentine Die Cut 7¼

2001, Mar. 21 Litho.

Booklet Stamps

Self-Adhesive

451-452 A184 Set of 2 .40 .20
452a Booklet, 4 each #451-452 1.60

Nos. 451-452 each sold for 25t on day of issue.

Fossil and Mineral Type of 2000

No. 453 - Stereoscopic image of fluorite crystal with arrow at: a, Right. b, Left.
107t, Starfish fossil.

2001, Mar. 21 Litho. *Perf. 14*
453 Horiz. pair 1.60 .80
a.-b. A165 95t Any single .80 .40
454 A165 107t Starfish fossil .90 .45

Europe Day A185

2001, Mar. 21
455 A185 221t multi 1.90 .95

Solkan, 1000th Anniv. — A186

2001, Mar. 21
456 A186 261t multi 2.25 1.10

Formation of Liberation Front, 60th Anniv. — A187

2001, Apr. 24 Litho. *Perf. 14*
457 A187 24t multi .20 .20

Independence, 10th Anniv. — A188

2001, May 23
458 A188 100t multi .80 .40

Issued in sheets of 10 + 2 labels.

Europa — A189

2001, May 23
459 A189 107t multi .85 .45

Issued in sheets of 8 + 1 label.

Ljubljana Tram System, Cent. A190

2001, May 23
460 A190 113t multi .90 .45

6th World Maxi Basketball Championships, Ljubljana — A191

2001, May 23
461 A191 261t multi 2.10 1.10

Souvenir Sheet

Apiculture — A192

No. 462: a, 24t, Bee on flower. b, 48t, Queen and drones. c, 95t, Worker bees. d, 170t, Hive and apiary.

2001, May 23
462 A192 Sheet of 4, #a-d 2.75 1.40

Flags of US and Russia, Dragon Bridge, Ljubljana — A193

2001, June 14
463 A193 107t multi .85 .45
a. Souvenir sheet of 1 .85 .45

First meeting of US Pres. George W. Bush and Russian Pres. Vladimir Putin, Brdo Castle, June 16.

Fruit, Blossoms and Insects Type of 2000

Designs: No. 464, Peach blossom. No. 465, Green peach aphid. No. 466, Peach.

2001, July 21 *Perf. 13¾*
464 A168 50t multi .40 .20
465 A168 50t multi .40 .20
466 A168 50t multi .40 .20
a. Strip, #464-466 1.20 .60

Printed in sheets of 15 strips + 5 labels.

Mohorjeve Druzbe Publishing House, 150th Anniv. — A194

2001, Sept. 4 *Perf. 14*
467 A194 B multi .25 .20

No. 467 sold for 27t on day of issue.

Foundation of First Technical High School, Cent. A195

2001, Sept. 21
468 A195 A multi .20 .20

No. 468 sold for 26t on day of issue.

World Animal Day — A196

2001, Sept. 21
469 A196 107t multi .90 .45

Composers — A198

Designs: 95t, Blaz Arnic (1901-70). 107t, Lucijan Marija Skerjanc (1900-73).

2001, Sept. 21 Litho. *Perf. 14*
471-472 A198 Set of 2 1.75 .85

New Year's Greetings A199

Christmas A200

2001, Nov. 16 Litho. *Perf. 14*
473 A199 B multi .25 .20
474 A200 D multi .90 .45

Nos. 473 and 474 sold for 31t and 107t respectively on day of issue.

Love — A201

2002, Jan. 23 Litho. *Perf. 14*
477 A201 B multi .25 .20

No. 477 sold for 31t on day of issue.

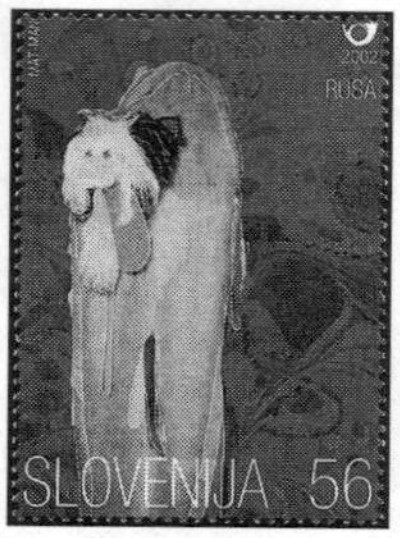

Masks — A202

Designs: 56t, Rusa. 95t, Picek.

2002, Jan. 23
478-479 A202 Set of 2 1.25 .60

Famous Slovenians — A203

Designs: 95t, Joze Plecnik (1872-1957), architect. 107t, Janko Kersnik (1852-97), poet.

2002, Jan. 23
480-481 A203 Set of 2 1.60 .80

2002 Winter Olympics, Salt Lake City — A204

No. 482: a, 95t, Sledder. b, 107t, Skier. Illustration reduced.

2002, Jan. 23
482 A204 Horiz. pair, #a-b, + label 1.60 .80

No. 482 printed in sheets of three pairs. Labels, which have different designs, appear at left and center in other pairs on the sheet.

Type of 1993-94

Designs: B, Easter eggs. D, Ljubljana Palm Sunday bundle.

2002, Feb. 28 *Perf. 14*
483 A38 B multi .25 .20
484 A38 D multi .85 .45

Nos. 483 and 484 sold for 31t and 107t respectively on day of issue.

Insect Fossil A205

2002, Mar. 21
485 A205 C multi .75 .40

No. 485 sold for 95t on day of issue.

Kostanjevica on the Krka, 750th Anniv. A206

2002, Mar. 21
486 A206 D multi .85 .45

No. 486 sold for 107t on day of issue.

Intl. Year of Mountains A207

Flowers and mountains: A, Clematis alpina and Martuljek Group. D, Lilium carniolicum and Mt. Spik.

2002, Mar. 21
487-488 A207 Set of 2 1.10 .55

Nos. 487-488 sold for 30t and 107t respectively on day of issue.

Martin Krpan from Vrh, by Fran Levstik — A208

Designs: No. 489, B, Krpan carrying horse. No. 490, B, Krpan at blacksmith's shop. No. 491, B, Krpan in Ljubljana.

2002, Mar. 21 *Perf. 14*
489-491 A208 Set of 3 .75 .35

Nos. 489-491 each sold for 31t on day of issue.

POSTAL TAX STAMPS

Catalogue values for unused stamps in this section are for Never Hinged items.

Red Cross — PT1

1992, May 8 Litho. *Perf. 14*
RA1 PT1 3t blue, black & red .50 .50

PT2 PT3

1992, June 2 *Perf. 14½x14*
RA2 PT2 3t multicolored .30 .30

Red Cross, Solidarity.

1992, Sept. 14 Litho. *Perf. 14*
RA3 PT3 3t multicolored .25 .25

Stop Smoking Week, Sept. 14-21.

Red Cross — PT4

Rescue Team — PT5

1993, May 8 Litho. *Perf. 14*
RA4 PT4 3.50t blue, black & red .20 .20

1993, June 1
RA5 PT5 3.50t multicolored .20 .20

Anti-Smoking Campaign PT6

1993, Sept. 14 Litho. *Perf. 14*
RA6 PT6 4.50t multicolored .20 .20

PT7

1994, May 8 Litho. *Perf. 14*
RA7 PT7 4.50t multicolored .20 .20

Obligatory on mail May 8-15.

Red Cross Worker, Child — PT8

1994, June 1
RA8 PT8 4.50t multicolored .20 .20

Obligatory on mail June 1-7.

PT9

Red Cross, Solidarity PT10

1995, May 8 Litho. *Perf. 14*
RA9 PT9 6.50t multicolored .20 .20

Obligatory on mail May 8-15.

1995, June 1 Litho. *Perf. 14*
RA10 PT10 6.50t multicolored .20 .20

Obligatory on mail June 1-7.

Red Cross, Solidarity — PT11

1996, May 8 Litho. *Perf. 14*
RA11 PT11 7t multicolored .20 .20

Obligatory on mail May 8-15.

Red Cross, Solidarity PT12

1996, June 1 Litho. *Perf. 14*
RA12 PT12 7t multicolored .20 .20

Obligatory on mail June 1-7.

Red Cross, Solidarity PT13

1997, May 8 Litho. *Perf. 14*
RA13 PT13 7t multicolored .20 .20

Obligatory on mail May 8-14.

Red Cross, Solidarity PT14

1997, June 1 **Litho.** ***Perf. 14***
RA14 PT14 7t multicolored .20 .20
Obligatory on mail June 1-7.

PT15 PT10

1998, May 8 **Litho.** ***Perf. 14***
RA15 PT15 7t black & red .20 .20
Obligatory on mail May 8-14.

Red Cross, Solidarity — PT16

1998, June 1

Design: No. RA16a, "7" at lower left. No. RA16b, "7" at upper right.

RA16 PT16 7t Pair, #a.-b. .20 .20
Obligatory on mail June 1-7.

Red Cross — PT17

1999, May 8 **Litho.** ***Perf. 14***
RA17 PT17 8t black & red .20 .20
Obligatory on mail May 8-15.

Solidarity Type of 1998

a, 9t at LL. b, 9t at UR.

1999, Nov. 1 **Litho.** ***Perf. 14***
RA18 PT16 9t Pair, #a.-b. .20 .20
Obligatory on mail Nov. 1-7.

Red Cross — PT19

2000, May 8 **Litho.** ***Perf. 14***
RA19 PT19 10t blk & red .20 .20
Obligatory on mail May 8-15.

Red Cross Solidarity Type of 1998

No. RA20: a, 10 at LL. b, 10 at UR.

2000, Nov. 1 **Litho.** ***Perf. 14***
RA20 PT16 10t Horiz. pair, #a-b .20 .20
Obligatory on mail Nov. 1-7.

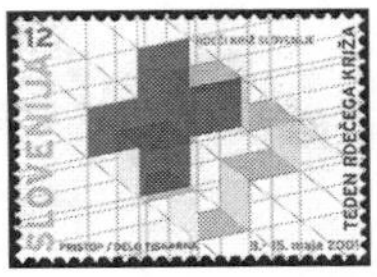

Red Cross — PT20

2001, May 8
RA21 PT20 12t multi .20 .20
Obligatory on mail May 8-15.

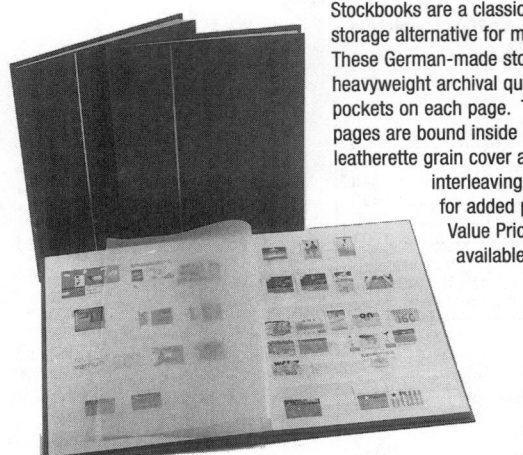

Vol. 5 Number Additions, Deletions & Changes

Number in 2002 Catalogue	Number in 2003 Catalogue
Papua New Guinea	
new	720a
new	867a
Philippines	
restored	8
restored	9
new	34a
new	1699
new	1700
new	1701
new	1702
new	1703
new	1704
new	1705
Poland	
3572 (Oct. Update)	3573
3573 (Oct. Update)	3574
Portuguese Guinea	
new	RA4a
Portuguese India	
new	7A
Russia	
footnote	2930A
footnote	2930Ab
Saar	
1a	1c
1b	1d
2a	2c
3a	3c
4a	4c
4b	4f
5a	5c
6a	6c
6b	6d
7a	7c
8a	8c
9a	9c
11a	11c
12a	12c
13a	13c
15a	15c
new	85b
new	87c
new	92b
new	93a
new	94a
St. Lucia	
new	336a
Saudi Arabia	
new	L61a
Sierra Leone	
1023	1023A-1023D
Slovakia	
221	219
224	223
268	224
275	222
310	221
316	220
350	218
360	225
377 (Jan. Update)	226
378 (Jan. Update)	227

Dies of British Colonial Stamps

DIE A

DIE B

DIE A:
1. The lines in the groundwork vary in thickness and are not uniformly straight.
2. The seventh and eighth lines from the top, in the groundwork, converge where they meet the head.
3. There is a small dash in the upper part of the second jewel in the band of the crown.
4. The vertical color line in front of the throat stops at the sixth line of shading on the neck.

DIE B:
1. The lines in the groundwork are all thin and straight.
2. All the lines of the background are parallel.
3. There is no dash in the upper part of the second jewel in the band of the crown.
4. The vertical color line in front of the throat stops at the eighth line of shading on the neck.

DIE I

DIE II

DIE I:
1. The base of the crown is well below the level of the inner white line around the vignette.
2. The labels inscribed "POSTAGE" and "REVENUE" are cut square at the top.
3. There is a white "bud" on the outer side of the main stem of the curved ornaments in each lower corner.
4. The second (thick) line below the country name has the ends next to the crown cut diagonally.

DIE Ia.	DIE Ib.
1 as die II.	1 and 3 as die II.
2 and 3 as die I.	2 as die I.

DIE II:
1. The base of the crown is aligned with the underside of the white line around the vignette.
2. The labels curve inward at the top inner corners.
3. The "bud" has been removed from the outer curve of the ornaments in each corner.
4. The second line below the country name has the ends next to the crown cut vertically.

British Colonial and Crown Agents Watermarks

Wmk. 1
Crown and C C

Wmk. 2
Crown and C A

Wmk. 3
Multiple Crown and C A

Wmk. 4
Multiple Crown and Script C A

Wmk. 4a

Wmk. 314
St. Edward's Crown and C A Multiple

Wmk. 373

Wmk. 384

Watermarks 1 to 4, 314, 373, and 384, common to many British territories, are illustrated here to avoid duplication.

The letters "CC" of Wmk. 1 identify the paper as having been made for the use of the Crown Colonies, while the letters "CA" of the others stand for "Crown Agents." Both Wmks. 1 and 2 were used on stamps printed by De La Rue & Co.

Wmk. 3 was adopted in 1904; Wmk. 4 in 1921; Wmk. 314 in 1957; Wmk. 373 in 1974; and Wmk. 384 in 1985.

In Wmk. 4a, a non-matching crown of the general St. Edwards type (bulging on both sides at top) was substituted for one of the Wmk. 4 crowns which fell off the dandy roll. The non-matching crown occurs in 1950-52 printings in a horizontal row of crowns on certain regular stamps of Johore and Seychelles, and on various postage due stamps of Barbados, Basutoland, British Guiana, Gold Coast, Grenada, Northern Rhodesia, St. Lucia, Swaziland and Trinidad and Tobago. A variation of Wmk. 4a, with the non-matching crown in a horizontal row of crown-CA-crown, occurs on regular stamps of Bahamas, St. Kitts-Nevis and Singapore.

Wmk. 314 was intentionally used sideways, starting in 1966. When a stamp was issued with Wmk. 314 both upright and sideways, the sideways varieties usually are listed also – with minor numbers. In many of the later issues, Wmk. 314 is slightly visible.

Wmk. 373 is usually only faintly visible.

Illustrated Identifier

This section pictures stamps or parts of stamp designs that will help identify postage stamps that do not have English words on them.

Many of the symbols that identify stamps of countries are shown here as well as typical examples of their stamps.

See the Index and Identifier on the previous pages for stamps with inscriptions such as "sen," "posta," "Baja Porto," "Helvetia," "K.S.A.", etc.

Linn's Stamp Identifier is now available. The 144 pages include more 2,000 inscriptions and over 500 large stamp illustrations. Available from Linn's Stamp News, P.O. Box 29, Sidney, OH 45365-0029.

1. HEADS, PICTURES AND NUMERALS

GREAT BRITAIN

Great Britain stamps never show the country name, but, except for postage dues, show a picture of the reigning monarch.

Victoria

Edward VII George V Edward VIII

George VI

Elizabeth II

Some George VI and Elizabeth II stamps are surcharged in annas, new paisa or rupees. These are listed under Oman.

Silhouette (sometimes facing right, generally at the top of stamp)

The silhouette indicates this is a British stamp. It is not a U.S. stamp.

VICTORIA

Queen Victoria

INDIA

Other stamps of India show this portrait of Queen Victoria and the words "Service" and "Annas."

AUSTRIA

YUGOSLAVIA

(Also BOSNIA & HERZEGOVINA if imperf.)

BOSNIA & HERZEGOVINA

Denominations also appear in top corners instead of bottom corners.

HUNGARY

Another stamp has posthorn facing left

BRAZIL

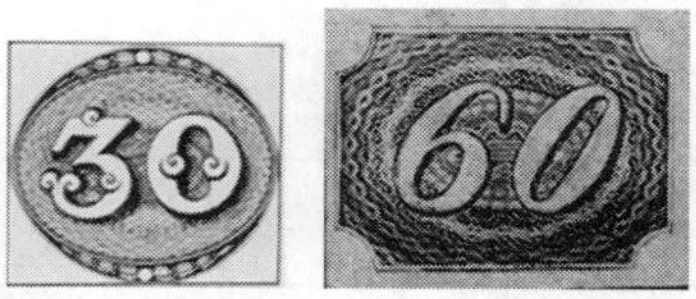

AUSTRALIA

Kangaroo and Emu

GERMANY

Mecklenburg-Vorpommern

SWITZERLAND

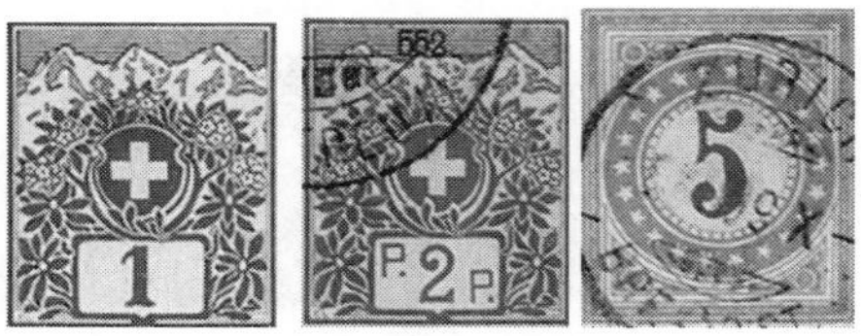

2. ORIENTAL INSCRIPTIONS

CHINA

中 中

Any stamp with this one character is from China (Imperial, Republic or People's Republic). This character appears in a four-character overprint on stamps of Manchukuo. These stamps are local provisionals, which are unlisted. Other overprinted Manchukuo stamps show this character, but have more than four characters in the overprints. These are listed in People's Republic of China.

Some Chinese stamps show the Sun.

中華民國郵票

Most stamps of Republic of China show this series of characters.

Stamps with the China character and this character are from People's Republic of China. 人

Calligraphic form of People's Republic of China

Chinese stamps without China character

REPUBLIC OF CHINA

PEOPLE'S REPUBLIC OF CHINA

Mao Tse-tung

MANCHUKUO

Temple Emperor Pu-Yi

The first 3 characters are common to many Manchukuo stamps.

The last 3 characters are common to other Manchukuo stamps.

Orchid Crest

Manchukuo stamp without these elements

JAPAN

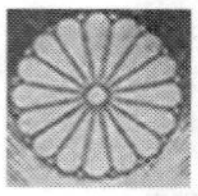

Chrysanthemum Crest Country Name

Japanese stamps without these elements

The number of characters in the center and the design of dragons on the sides will vary.

RYUKYU ISLANDS

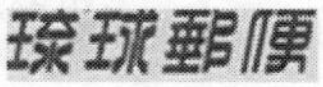

Country Name

PHILIPPINES (Japanese Occupation)

Country Name

NORTH BORNEO (Japanese Occupation)

Indicates Japanese Occupation Country Name

MALAYA (Japanese Occupation)

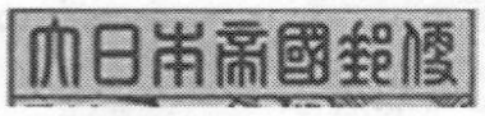

Indicates Japanese Occupation Country Name

BURMA (Japanese Occupation)

Indicates Japanese Occupation Country Name

Other Burma Japanese Occupation stamps without these elements

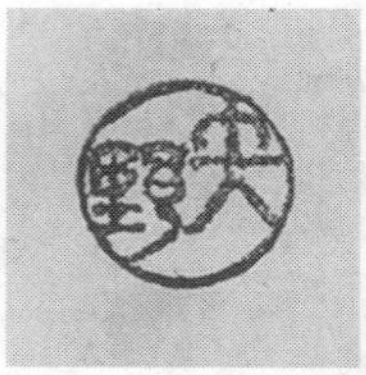

Burmese Script

KOREA

These two characters, in any order, are common to stamps from the Republic of Korea (South Korea) or the unlisted stamps of the People's Democratic Republic of Korea (North Korea).

This series of four characters can be found on the stamps of both Koreas.

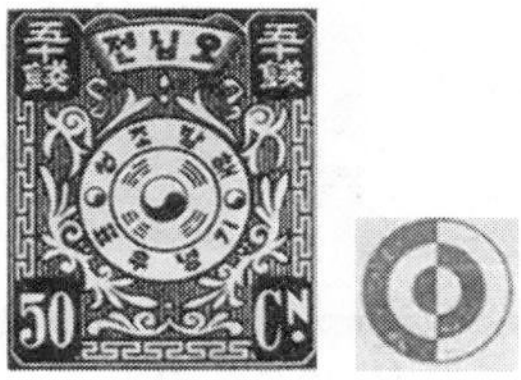

Yin Yang appears on some stamps.

Indicates Republic of Korea (South Korea)

South Korean postage stamps issed after 1952 do not show currency expressed in Latin letters. Stamps wiith "HW," "HWAN," "WON," "WN," "W" or "W" with two lines through it, if not illustrated in listings of stamps before this date, are revenues. North Korean postage stamps do not have currency expressed in Latin letters.

THAILAND

Country Name

King Chulalongkorn

King Prajadhipok and Chao P'ya Chakri

3. CENTRAL AND EASTERN ASIAN INSCRIPTIONS

INDIA - FEUDATORY STATES

Alwar

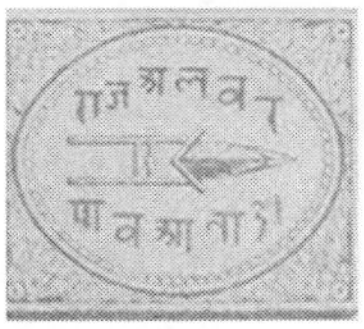

Bhor

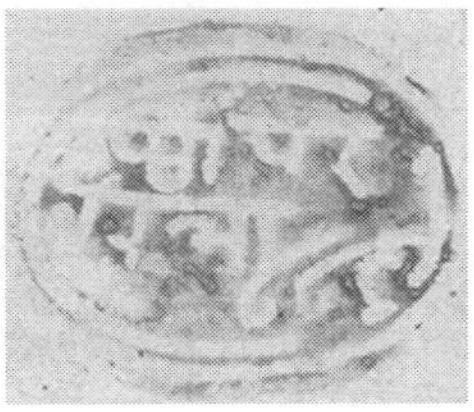

Bundi

Similar stamps come with different designs in corners and differently drawn daggers (at center of circle).

Dhar

Faridkot

Hyderabad

Similar stamps exist with straight line frame around stamp, and also with different central design which is inscribed "Postage" or "Post & Receipt."

Indore

Jhalawar

A similar stamp has the central figure in an oval.

Nandgaon

Nowanuggur

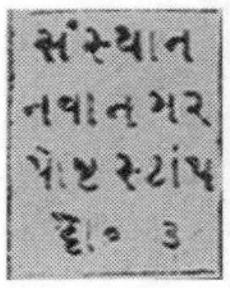

Poonch

Similar stamps exist in various sizes

Rajpeepla

Soruth

BANGLADESH

Country Name

NEPAL

Similar stamps are smaller, have squares in upper corners and have five or nine characters in central bottom panel.

TANNU TUVA

ISRAEL

GEORGIA

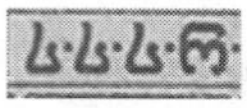

This inscription is found on other pictorial stamps.

Country Name

ARMENIA

The four characters are found somewhere on pictorial stamps. On some stamps only the middle two are found.

4. AFRICAN INSCRIPTIONS

ETHIOPIA

5. ARABIC INSCRIPTIONS

AFGHANISTAN

Many early Afghanistan stamps show Tiger's head, many of these have ornaments protruding from outer ring, others show inscriptions in black.

Arabic Script

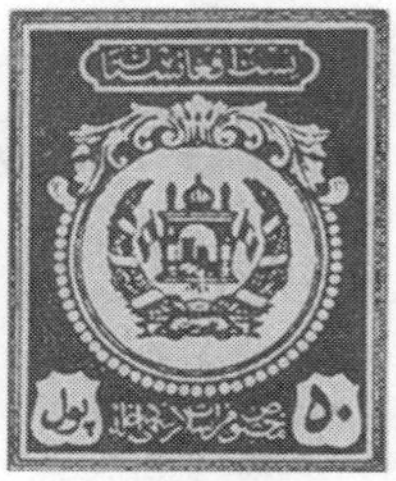

Mosque Gate & Crossed Cannons
The four characters are found somewhere on pictorial stamps. On some stamps only the middle two are found.

BAHRAIN

EGYPT

Postage

INDIA - FEUDATORY STATES

Jammu & Kashmir

Text and thickness of ovals vary. Some stamps have flower devices in corners.

India-Hyderabad

IRAN

Country Name

Royal Crown

Lion with Sword

Symbol

IRAQ

JORDAN

LEBANON

Similar types have denominations at top and slightly different design.

LIBYA

Country Name in various styles

Other Libya stamps show Eagle and Shield (head facing either direction) or Red, White and Black Shield (with or without eagle in center).

SAUDI ARABIA

Tughra (Central design)

Palm Tree and Swords

SYRIA

THRACE

YEMEN

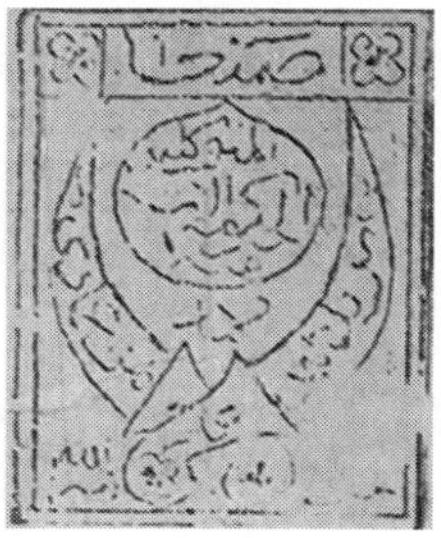

PAKISTAN

PAKISTAN - BAHAWALPUR

Country Name in top panel, star and crescent

TURKEY

Star & Crescent is a device found on many Turkish stamps, but is also found on stamps from other Arabic areas (see Pakistan-Bahawalpur)

Tughra (similar tughras can be found on stamps of Turkey in Asia, Afghanistan and Saudi Arabia)

Mohammed V

Mustafa Kemal

Plane, Star and Crescent

TURKEY IN ASIA

Other Turkey in Asia pictorials show star & crescent.
Other stamps show tughra shown under Turkey.

6. GREEK INSCRIPTIONS

GREECE

Country Name in various styles
(Some Crete stamps overprinted with the Greece country name are listed in Crete.)

Lepta

Drachma Drachmas Lepton

Abbreviated Country Name 

Other forms of Country Name

No country name

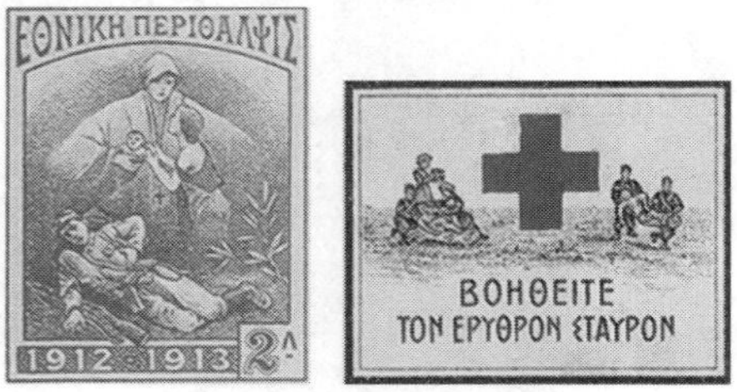

CRETE

Country Name

These words are on other stamps

Grosion

Crete stamps with a surcharge that have the year "1922" are listed under Greece.

EPIRUS

Country Name

IONIAN IS.

7. CYRILLIC INSCRIPTIONS

RUSSIA

Postage Stamp

Imperial Eagle

Postage in various styles

Abbreviation for Kopeck Abbreviation for Ruble Russia

Abbreviation for Russian Soviet Federated Socialist Republic
RSFSR stamps were overprinted (see below)

Abbreviation for Union of Soviet Socialist Republics

This item is footnoted in Latvia

RUSSIA - Army of the North

"OKCA"

RUSSIA - Wenden

RUSSIAN OFFICES IN THE TURKISH EMPIRE

These letters appear on other stamps of the Russian offices.

The unoverprinted version of this stamp and a similar stamp were overprinted by various countries (see below).

ARMENIA

BELARUS

FAR EASTERN REPUBLIC

Country Name

SOUTH RUSSIA

Country Name

FINLAND

Circles and Dots on stamps similar to Imperial Russia issues

BATUM

Forms of Country Name

TRANSCAUCASIAN FEDERATED REPUBLICS

Abbreviation for Country Name

KAZAKHSTAN

ҚАЗАҚСТАН

Country Name

KYRGYZSTAN

КЫРГЫЗСТАН

КЫРГЫЗСТАН Country Name

ROMANIA

TADJIKISTAN

Country Name & Abbreviation

UKRAINE

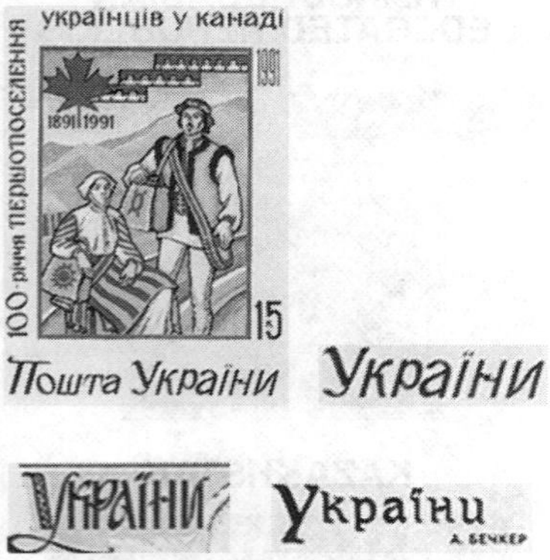

Country Name in various forms

The trident appears on many stamps, usually as an overprint.

Abbreviation for Ukrainian Soviet Socialist Republic

WESTERN UKRAINE

Abbreviation for Country Name

AZERBAIJAN

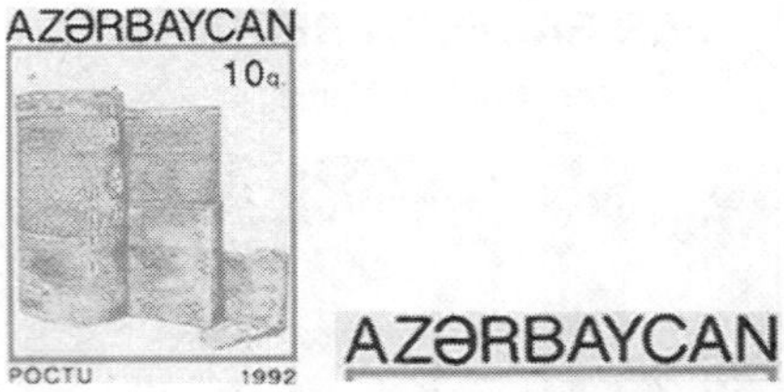

Country Name

Abbreviation for Azerbaijan Soviet Socialist Republic

MONTENEGRO

Country Name in various forms

Abbreviation for country name

No country name (A similar Montenegro stamp without country name has same vignette.)

SERBIA

Country Name in various forms

Abbreviation for country name

No country name

YUGOSLAVIA

Showing country name

No Country Name

MACEDONIA

Country Name

Different form of Country Name

BULGARIA

Country Name Postage

Stotinka

Stotinki (plural) Abbreviation for Stotinki

Country Name in various forms and styles

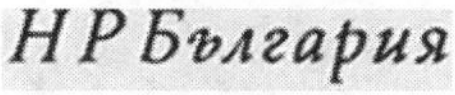

No country name

Abbreviation for Lev, leva

MONGOLIA

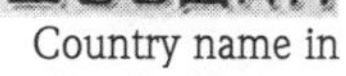

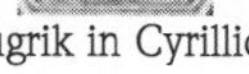

Country name in one word Tugrik in Cyrillic

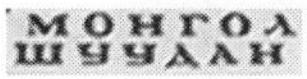

Country name in two words Mung in Cyrillic

Mung in Mongolian

Tugrik in Mongolian

Arms

No Country Name

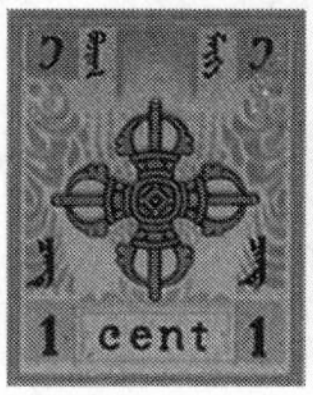

value priced **stockbooks**

Stockbooks are a classic and convenient storage alternative for many collectors. These German-made stockbooks feature heavyweight archival quality paper with 9 pockets on each page. The 8½" x 11⅝" pages are bound inside a handsome leatherette grain cover and include glassine interleaving between the pages for added protection. The Value Priced Stockbooks are available in two page styles, the white page stockbooks feature glassine pockets while the black page variety includes clear acetate pockets

WHITE PAGE STOCKBOOKS GLASSINE POCKETS

ITEM	DESCRIPTION		RETAIL
SW16BL	Blue	16 pages	$5.95
SW16GR	Green	16 pages	$5.95
SW16RD	Red	16 pages	$5.95

BLACK PAGE STOCKBOOKS ACETATE POCKETS

ITEM	COLOR	PAGES	RETAIL
ST16RD	Red	16 pages	$9.95
ST16GR	Green	16 pages	$9.95
ST16BL	Blue	16 pages	$9.95
ST16BK	Black	16 pages	$9.95
ST32RD	Red	32 pages	$14.95
ST32GR	Green	32 pages	$14.95
ST32BL	Blue	32 pages	$14.95
ST32BK	Black	32 pages	$14.95
ST64RD	Red	64 pages	$27.95
ST64GR	Green	64 pages	$27.95
ST64BL	Blue	64 pages	$27.95
ST64BK	Black	64 pages	$27.95

Scott Value Priced Stockbooks are available from your favorite dealer or direct from:

SCOTT®

P.O. Box 828
Sidney OH 45365-0828
www.amosadvantage.com
1-800-572-6885

AMOS
HOBBY PUBLISHING

The black page stockbook is available in three sizes:
16 pages
32 pages
64 pages.

Index and Identifier

All page numbers shown are those in this Volume 5.

Postage stamps that do not have English words on them are shown in the Identifier which begins on page 1010.

Pronunciation Symbols

ə .... banana, collide, abut

'ə, ˌə .... humdrum, abut

ə .... immediately preceding \l\, \n\, \m\, \ŋ\, as in battle, mitten, eaten, and sometimes open \'ō-pᵊm\, lock **and** key \-ᵊŋ-\; immediately following \l\, \m\, \r\, as often in French table, prisme, titre

ər .... further, merger, bird

'ər-, 'ə-r .... as in two different pronunciations of hurry \'hər-ē, 'hə-rē\

a .... mat, map, mad, gag, snap, patch

ā .... day, fade, date, aorta, drape, cape

ä .... bother, cot, and, with most American speakers, father, cart

ȧ .... father as pronounced by speakers who do not rhyme it with *bother*; French patte

aů .... now, loud, out

b .... baby, rib

ch .... chin, nature \'nā-chər\

d .... did, adder

e .... bet, bed, peck

'ē, ˌē .... beat, nosebleed, evenly, easy

ē .... easy, mealy

f .... fifty, cuff

g .... go, big, gift

h .... hat, ahead

hw .... whale as pronounced by those who do not have the same pronunciation for both *whale* and *wail*

i .... tip, banish, active

ī .... site, side, buy, tripe

j .... job, gem, edge, join, judge

k .... kin, cook, ache

k̲ .... German ich, Buch; one pronunciation of loch

l .... lily, pool

m .... murmur, dim, nymph

n .... no, own

ⁿ .... indicates that a preceding vowel or diphthong is pronounced with the nasal passages open, as in French *un bon vin blanc* \œⁿ -bōⁿ -vaⁿ -bläⁿ\

ŋ .... sing \'siŋ\, singer \'siŋ-ər\, finger \'fiŋ-gər\, ink \'iŋk \

ō .... bone, know, beau

ȯ .... saw, all, gnaw, caught

œ .... French boeuf, German Hölle

œ̄ .... French feu, German Höhle

ȯi .... coin, destroy

p .... pepper, lip

r .... red, car, rarity

s .... source, less

sh .... as in shy, mission, machine, special (actually, this is a single sound, not two); with a hyphen between, two sounds as in *grasshopper* \'gras-ˌhä-pər\

t .... tie, attack, late, later, latter

th .... as in thin, ether (actually, this is a single sound, not two); with a hyphen between, two sounds as in *knighthood* \'nīt-ˌhůd\

t̲h̲ .... then, either, this (actually, this is a single sound, not two)

ü .... rule, youth, union \'yün-yən\, few \'fyü\

ů .... pull, wood, book, curable \'kyůr-ə-bəl\, fury \'fyůr-ē\

ue .... German füllen, hübsch

ue̅ .... French rue, German fühlen

v .... vivid, give

w .... we, away

y .... yard, young, cue \'kyü\, mute \'myüt\, union \'yün-yən\

ʸ .... indicates that during the articulation of the sound represented by the preceding character the front of the tongue has substantially the position it has for the articulation of the first sound of *yard*, as in French *digne* \dēnʸ\

z .... zone, raise

zh .... as in vision, azure \'a-zhər\ (actually, this is a single sound, not two); with a hyphen between, two sounds as in *hogshead* \'hȯgz-ˌhed, 'hägz-\

\ .... slant line used in pairs to mark the beginning and end of a transcription: \'pen\

' .... mark preceding a syllable with primary (strongest) stress: \'pen-mən-ˌship\

ˌ .... mark preceding a syllable with secondary (medium) stress: \'pen-mən-ˌship\

\- .... mark of syllable division

( ) .... indicate that what is symbolized between is present in some utterances but not in others: *factory* \'fak-t(ə-)rē\

÷ .... indicates that many regard as unacceptable the pronunciation variant immediately following: *cupola* \'kyü-pə-lə, ÷-ˌlō\

INDEX TO ADVERTISERS – 2003 VOLUME 5

2003
VOLUME 5
DEALER DIRECTORY
YELLOW PAGE LISTINGS

This section of your Scott Catalogue contains advertisements to help you conveniently find what you need, when you need it...!

Whatever Your Needs... Our Members Can Always Help You.

Integrity • Honesty • Expertise Dedication • Hobby Builders Reliability — Since 1914, the reputation of our members has been unexcelled. Over 700 dealer members stand ready to help you.

Here's How:

- **Send an SASE to us now for the complete list of our members** by specialty and location.
- **Visit the ASDA's main website** where you'll not only find a complete list of all of our members, but lots of exciting and helpful information.
- **Selling your stamps?** Send SASE for our free brochure with lots of important tips for selling your collection.
- **Visit StampBourse Online℠**, the ASDA's great sales site on the Internet at: www.asdabourse.com.

www.asdaonline.com

Established 1914

American Stamp Dealers Association, Inc.℠

3-SC School Street
Glen Cove NY 11542
Ph: (516) 759-7000
Fax: (516) 759-7014
www.asdaonline.com
E-mail: asda@erols.com

Accessories

BROOKLYN GALLERY COIN & STAMP
8725 4th Avenue
Brooklyn, NY 11209
718-745-5701
718-745-2775 Fax
Email: info@brooklyngallery.com
Web: www.brooklyngallery.com

Appraisals

CONNEXUS
P.O. Box 819
Snow Camp, NC 27349
336-376-8207 Phone/Fax
Email: Connexus1@world.att.net

Approvals-Personalized WW & U.S.

THE KEEPING ROOM
P.O. Box 257
Trumbull, CT 06611
203-372-8436

Asia

MICHAEL ROGERS, INC.
199 E. Welbourne Ave.
Suite 3
Winter Park, FL 32789
407-644-2290 or 800-843-3751
407-645-4434 Fax
Email: mrogersinc@aol.com
Web: www.michaelrogersinc.com

Asia

THE STAMP ACT
P.O. Box 1136
Belmont, CA 94002
650-592-3315
650-508-8104 Fax
Email: bchang@ix.netcom.com

Auctions

DANIEL F. KELLEHER CO., INC.
24 Farnsworth Street
Suite 605
Boston, MA 02210
617-443-0033
617-443-0789 Fax

JACQUES C. SCHIFF, JR., INC.
195 Main Street
Ridgefield Park, NJ 07660
201-641-5566
From NYC: 662-2777
201-641-5705 Fax

STAMP CENTER/DUTCH COUNTRY AUCTIONS
4115 Concord Pike
Wilmington, DE 19803
302-478-8740
302-478-8779 Fax
Email: scdca@dol.net
Web: www.thestampcenter.com

Auctions - Mail Bid

JAMES J. REEVES, INC.
P.O. Box 219
Huntingdon, PA 16652
800-364-2948 Ext. 302
814-641-2600 Fax
Email: Reeves5@vicon.net
Web: www.jamesjreeves.com
For Supplies: 888-574-6229 or www.supplies.fromjjr.com

Auctions-Public

ALAN BLAIR STAMPS/AUCTIONS
5407 Lakeside Ave.
Suite 4
Richmond, VA 23228
800-689-5602 Phone/Fax
Email: alanblair@prodigy.net

Austria

JOSEPH EDER
P.O. Box 185529
Hamden, CT 06518
203-281-0742
203-230-2410 Fax
Email: j.eder@worldnet.att.net
Web: www.ederstamps.com

British Colonies

EMPIRE STAMP CO.
P.O. Box 19248
Encino, CA 91416
800-616-7278 or 818-225-1181
818-225-1182 Fax
Email: empirestamps@msn.com
Web: www.empirestamps.com

British Commonwealth

JAY'S STAMP CO.
Box 28484
Dept. S
Philadelphia, PA 19149-0184
215-743-0207 Phone/Fax
Email: JASC@Juno.com
Web: www.jaysco.com

British Commonwealth

METROPOLITAN STAMP CO., INC.
P.O. Box 1133
Chicago, IL 60690-1133
815-439-0142
815-439-0143 Fax
Email: metrostamp@aol.com

British Commonwealth

THE BRITISH COMMONWEALTH O•F N•A•T•I•O•N•S

We are active buyers and sellers of stamps and postal history of all areas of pre-1960 British Commonwealth, including individual items, collections or estates. Want lists from all reigns are accepted with references.

"VISIT OUR BOOTH AT MOST MAJOR SHOWS"

L. W. Martin, Jr.

CROWN COLONY STAMPS
P.O. Box 1198
BELLAIRE, TEXAS 77402
PH. (713) 781-6563 • FAX (713) 789-9998
E-mail: crowncolony@compuserve.com

Auctions

Schiff Auctions

Buyers, Auctioneers & Appraisers of U.S. & Worldwide Stamps & Covers

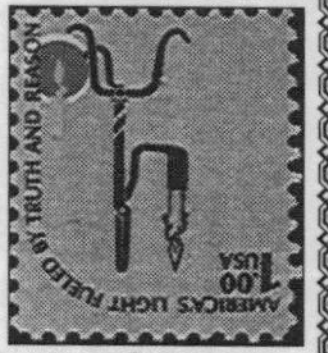

We have been catering to the individual buyer and seller since 1947. Let us put our **55** years of experience to work for you when selling your stamps, covers or your collection. Whether you prefer consigning to public auction or selling outright, call us first. Describe your material before sending. Please include your address and telephone numbers.

CATALOG SUBSCRIPTIONS	N. AMERICA	OVERSEAS
1 Year Catalogs & Prices Realized	$10.00	$18.00
1 Year Catalog Only	$7.50	$15.00
1 Catalog with Prices Realized	$1.50	$2.50
1 Catalog Only	$1.00	$1.50

JACQUES C. SCHIFF, JR., INC.

195 Main St., Ridgefield Park, NJ 07660 USA
Telephone 201-641-5566 from NYC 662-2777
FAX 201-641-5705

OFFICIAL AUCTIONEERS:
AMERIPEX 1986.
WORLD STAMP EXPO 1989.
WORLD COLUMBIAN STAMP EXPO 1992.
AMERICAN PHILATELIC SOCIETY 2000-2001

QUALIFIED AUCTIONEER

British Commonwealth

VICTORIA STAMP CO.
P.O. Box 745
Ridgewood, NJ 07451
201-652-7283
201-612-0024 Fax
Email: VictoriaStampCo@aol.com
Web: www.VictoriaStampCo.com

Central America

GUY SHAW
P.O. Box 10025
Bakersfield, CA 93389
661-834-7135 Phone/Fax
Email: guyshaw@guyshaw.com
Web: www.guyshaw.com

China

MICHAEL ROGERS, INC.
199 E. Welbourne Ave.
Suite 3
Winter Park, FL 32789
407-644-2290 or 800-843-3751
407-645-4434 Fax
Email: mrogersinc@aol.com
Web: www.michaelrogersinc.com

China - Expertising

EXPERTS & CONSULTANTS LTD.
Dr. Shiu - Hon Chan & Mr. K.L. Poon
P.O. Box 9840
General Post Office
HONG KONG
852-2519-6510 Fax
Email: poonchan@netvigator.com

China - Imperial

TREASURE-HUNTERS LTD.
G.P.O. Box 11446
HONG KONG
+852-2507-3773 or
+852-2507-5770
+852-2519-6820 Fax
Email: thunters@netvigator.com
Web: www.treasurehunters.com.hk

Collections

BOB & MARTHA FRIEDMAN
624 Homestead Place
Joliet, IL 60435
815-725-6666
815-725-4134 Fax

DR. ROBERT FRIEDMAN & SONS
2029 West 75th Street
Woodridge, IL 60517
630-985-1515
630-985-1588 Fax

HENRY GITNER PHILATELISTS, INC.
P.O. Box 3077-S
Middletown, NY 10940
845-343-5151 or 800-947-8267
845-343-0068 Fax
Email: hgitner@hgitner.com
Web: www.hgitner.com

Ducks

MICHAEL JAFFE
P.O. Box 61484
Vancouver, WA 98666
360-695-6161 or 800-782-6770
360-695-1616 Fax
Email:
mjaffe@brookmanstamps.com
Web: www.brookmanstamps.com

Ducks - Foreign

METROPOLITAN STAMP CO., INC.
P.O. Box 1133
Chicago, IL 60690-1133
815-439-0142
815-439-0143 Fax
Email: metrostamp@aol.com

France

JOSEPH EDER
P.O. Box 185529
Hamden, CT 06518
203-281-0742
203-230-2410 Fax
Email: j.eder@worldnet.att.net
Web: www.ederstamps.com

German Colonies

COLONIAL STAMP COMPANY
$1 million - photo price list, $5.00
(refundable against purchase)
5757 Wilshire Blvd. PH #8
Los Angeles, CA 90036
323-933-9435
323-939-9930 Fax
Email: gwh225@aol.com
Web: www.colonialstamps.com

JOSEPH EDER
P.O. Box 185529
Hamden, CT 06518
203-281-0742
203-230-2410 Fax
Email: j.eder@worldnet.att.net
Web: www.ederstamps.com

German Occupation

JOSEPH EDER
P.O. Box 185529
Hamden, CT 06518
203-281-0742
203-230-2410 Fax
Email: j.eder@worldnet.att.net
Web: www.ederstamps.com

Germany

JOSEPH EDER
P.O. Box 185529
Hamden, CT 06518
203-281-0742
203-230-2410 Fax
Email: j.eder@worldnet.att.net
Web: www.ederstamps.com

British Commonwealth

The British Empire
(A-Z 1840-1935 Mint & Used)
The Largest & Most Valuable Stock in America.

Want Lists (per Scott or S. G.) prompt expert service, 30 volumes in all price ranges, stocked individually so you can acquire exactly those you need on approval or per quotations (references appreciated). For decades we have had the great pleasure of working closely with our clients in the formation of many fine private or international exhibition standard collections. I will be pleased to place our expertise at your disposal.

British Empire Public Auctions
Please request a complimentary copy

George W. Holschauer
COLONIAL STAMP CO.
5757 WILSHIRE BLVD., PH #8
LOS ANGELES, CA 90036
Ph. (323) 933-9435 • Fax (323) 939-9930
www.colonialstamps.com
CCNY, CSDA, IFSDA, INTERNATIONAL SOCIETY OF APPRAISERS

Aron R. Halberstam Philatelists, Ltd.
POB 150168, Van Brunt Station
Brooklyn, NY 11215-0168, USA
Tel: 718-788-3978 Fax: 718-965-3099
Toll Free: 800-343-1303
E-mail:arh@aronrhalberstam.com

British Commonwealth
Pre-1960

Call or write to request our free Price List, or send us your Want Lists. We are also eager buyers of better Commonwealth singles or sets and collections. Let us know what you have to offer.

Accepted on all orders. Member

Visit our Website: www.aronrhalberstam.com

BRITISH EMPIRE EXCLUSIVELY
Request a catalogue for our next Public Auction.
Please specify your interests.

Want lists invited from serious collectors of the BRITISH EMPIRE. References please.

Selling? Ask us about consigning *your* collection to a future sale.

Victoria Stamp Co.

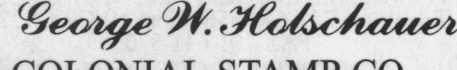

PHOEBE A. MacGILLIVARY
P.O. BOX 745, RIDGEWOOD, NJ 07451
PHONE 201-652-7283 • FAX 201-612-0024
www.VictoriaStampCo.com
Email: VictoriaStampCo@aol.com

Germany- Third Reich

JOSEPH EDER
P.O. Box 185529
Hamden, CT 06518
203-281-0742
203-230-2410 Fax
Email: j.eder@worldnet.att.net
Web: www.ederstamps.com

Great Britain

COLONIAL STAMP COMPANY
5757 Wilshire Blvd. PH #8
Los Angeles, CA 90036
323-933-9435
323-939-9930 Fax
Email: gwh225@aol.com
Web: www.colonialstamps.com

Insurance

COLLECTIBLES INSURANCE AGENCY
P.O. Box 1200 SSC
Westminster, MD 21158
888-837-9537
410-876-9233 Fax
Email:
info@insurecollectibles.com
Web: www.collectinsure.com

Japan

MICHAEL ROGERS, INC.
199 E. Welbourne Ave.
Suite 3
Winter Park, FL 32789
407-644-2290 or 800-843-3751
407-645-4434 Fax
Email: mrogersinc@aol.com
Web: www.michaelrogersinc.com

Korea

MICHAEL ROGERS, INC.
199 E. Welbourne Ave.
Suite 3
Winter Park, FL 32789
407-644-2290 or 800-843-3751
407-645-4434 Fax
Email: mrogersinc@aol.com
Web: www.michaelrogersinc.com

Latin America

GUY SHAW
P.O. Box 10025
Bakersfield, CA 93389
661-834-7135 Phone/Fax
Email: guyshaw@guyshaw.com
Web: www.guyshaw.com

Mail Order

ALMAZ STAMP CO., DEPT. VY
P.O. Box 100-812
Vanderveer Station
Brooklyn, NY 11210
718-241-6360 Phone/Fax

Manchukuo

MICHAEL ROGERS, INC.
199 E. Welbourne Ave.
Suite 3
Winter Park, FL 32789
407-644-2290 or 800-843-3751
407-645-4434 Fax
Email: mrogersinc@aol.com
Web: www.michaelrogersinc.com

Mexico

AMEEN STAMPS
8831 Long Point Road, Suite 204
Houston, TX 77055
713-468-0644
713-468-2420 Fax
Email: rameen@ev1.net

New Issues

DAVIDSON'S STAMP SERVICE
P.O. Box 36355
Indianapolis, IN 46236-0355
317-826-2620
Email: davidson@in.net
Web: www.newstampissues.com

New Issues- Retail

BOMBAY PHILATELIC INC.
P.O. Box 480009
Delray Beach, FL 33448
561-499-7990
561-499-7553 Fax
Email: sales@bombaystamps.com
Web: www.bombaystamps.com

STANLEY M. PILLER
3351 Grand Avenue
Oakland, CA 94610
510-465-8290
510-465-7121 Fax
Email: stmpdlr@aol.com

New Issues- Wholesale

BOMBAY PHILATELIC INC.
P.O. Box 480009
Delray Beach, FL 33448
561-499-7990
561-499-7553 Fax
Email: sales@bombaystamps.com
Web: www.bombaystamps.com

Papua New Guinea

COLONIAL STAMP COMPANY
5757 Wilshire Blvd. PH #8
Los Angeles, CA 90036
323-933-9435
323-939-9930 Fax
Email: gwh225@aol.com
Web: www.colonialstamps.com

Portugal & Colonies

AMEEN STAMPS
8831 Long Point Road, Suite 204
Houston, TX 77055
713-468-0644
713-468-2420 Fax
Email: rameen@ev1.net

Proofs & Essays

HENRY GITNER PHILATELISTS, INC.
P.O. Box 3077-S
Middletown, NY 10940
845-343-5151 or 800-947-8267
845-343-0068 Fax
Email: hgitner@hgitner.com
Web: www.hgitner.com

Publications - Collector

AMERICAN PHILATELIC SOCIETY
Dept. TZ
P.O. Box 8000
State College, PA 16803
814-237-3803
814-237-6128 Fax
Email: flsente@stamps.org
Web: www.stamps.org

Rhodesia

COLONIAL STAMP COMPANY
5757 Wilshire Blvd. PH #8
Los Angeles, CA 90036
323-933-9435
323-939-9930 Fax
Email: gwh225@aol.com
Web: www.colonialstamps.com

Russia

AMEEN STAMPS
8831 Long Point Road, Suite 204
Houston, TX 77055
713-468-0644
713-468-2420 Fax
Email: rameen@ev1.net

Russia - Year Sets

WALLACE STAMPS
Box 82
Port Washington, NY 11050
516-883-5578

Ryukyu Islands

HENRY GITNER PHILATELISTS, INC.
P.O. Box 3077-S
Middletown, NY 10940
845-343-5151 or 800-947-8267
845-343-0068 Fax
Email: hgitner@hgitner.com
Web: www.hgitner.com

St. Christopher

COLONIAL STAMP COMPANY
5757 Wilshire Blvd. PH #8
Los Angeles, CA 90036
323-933-9435
323-939-9930 Fax
Email: gwh225@aol.com
Web: www.colonialstamps.com

St. Helena

COLONIAL STAMP COMPANY
5757 Wilshire Blvd. PH #8
Los Angeles, CA 90036
323-933-9435
323-939-9930 Fax
Email: gwh225@aol.com
Web: www.colonialstamps.com

St. Kitts & Nevis

COLONIAL STAMP COMPANY
5757 Wilshire Blvd. PH #8
Los Angeles, CA 90036
323-933-9435
323-939-9930 Fax
Email: gwh225@aol.com
Web: www.colonialstamps.com

St. Lucia

COLONIAL STAMP COMPANY
5757 Wilshire Blvd. PH #8
Los Angeles, CA 90036
323-933-9435
323-939-9930 Fax
Email: gwh225@aol.com
Web: www.colonialstamps.com

St. Pierre & Miquelon

E. JOSEPH McCONNELL
P.O. Box 683
Monroe, NY 10950
845-496-5916
845-782-0347 Fax
Email: mcconn1@warwick.net
Web: www.EJMcConnell.com

S. SEREBRAKIAN, INC.
P.O. Box 448
Monroe, NY 10950
845-783-9791
845-782-0347 Fax
Email: mcconn1@warwick.net

St. Vincent

COLONIAL STAMP COMPANY
5757 Wilshire Blvd. PH #8
Los Angeles, CA 90036
323-933-9435
323-939-9930 Fax
Email: gwh225@aol.com
Web: www.colonialstamps.com

New Issues

Samoa

COLONIAL STAMP COMPANY
5757 Wilshire Blvd. PH #8
Los Angeles, CA 90036
323-933-9435
323-939-9930 Fax
Email: gwh225@aol.com
Web: www.colonialstamps.com

Sarawak

COLONIAL STAMP COMPANY
5757 Wilshire Blvd. PH #8
Los Angeles, CA 90036
323-933-9435
323-939-9930 Fax
Email: gwh225@aol.com
Web: www.colonialstamps.com

Seychelles

COLONIAL STAMP COMPANY
5757 Wilshire Blvd. PH #8
Los Angeles, CA 90036
323-933-9435
323-939-9930 Fax
Email: gwh225@aol.com
Web: www.colonialstamps.com

Sierra Leone

COLONIAL STAMP COMPANY
5757 Wilshire Blvd. PH #8
Los Angeles, CA 90036
323-933-9435
323-939-9930 Fax
Email: gwh225@aol.com
Web: www.colonialstamps.com

South America

GUY SHAW
P.O. Box 10025
Bakersfield, CA 93389
661-834-7135 Phone/Fax
Email: guyshaw@guyshaw.com
Web: www.guyshaw.com

Stamp Shows

ATLANTIC COAST EXHIBITIONS
Division of Beach Philatelics
42 Baltimore Lane
Palm Coast, FL 32137-8850
386-445-4550
386-447-0811 Fax
Email: mrstamp2@aol.com
Web: www.beachphilatelics.com

STAMP STORES

Arizona

B.J.'S STAMPS
Barbara J. Johnson
6342 W. Bell Road
Glendale, AZ 85308
623-878-2080
623-412-3456 Fax
Email: info@bjstamps.com
Web: www.bjstamps.com

California

ASHTREE STAMP & COIN
2410 N. Blackstone
Fresno, CA 93703
559-227-7167

BROSIUS STAMP & COIN
2105 Main Street
Santa Monica, CA 90405
310-396-7480
310-396-7455 Fax

COLONIAL STAMP CO./BRITISH EMPIRE SPECIALIST
5757 Wilshire Blvd. PH #8 (by appt.)
Los Angeles, CA 90036
323-933-9435
323-939-9930 Fax
Email: gwh225@aol.com
Web: www.colonialstamps.com

NATICK STAMPS & HOBBIES
405 S. Myrtle Avenue
Monrovia, CA 91016
626-305-7333
626-305-7335 Fax
Email: natickco@earthlink.net
Web: www.natickco.com

STANLEY M. PILLER
3351 Grand Avenue
Oakland, CA 94610
510-465-8290
510-465-7121 Fax
Email: stmpdlr@aol.com

Colorado

ACKLEY'S STAMPS
3230 N. Stone Avenue
Colorado Springs, CO 80907
719-633-1153

SHOWCASE STAMPS
3865 Wadsworth
Wheat Ridge, CO 80033
303-425-9252
Email: kbeiner@colbi.net

Florida

Connecticut

MILLER'S STAMP SHOP
41 New London Turnpike
Uncasville, CT 06382
860-848-0468
860-848-1926 Fax
Email: millstamps@aol.com
Web: www.millerstamps.com

SILVER CITY COIN & STAMP
41 Colony Street
Meriden, CT 06451
203-235-7634
203-237-4915 Fax

Florida

BEACH PHILATELICS
Daytona Flea Market (Fri-Sun)
I 95 Exit 87 (Tamoka Farms Rd.)
Corner Shoppes Bldg. - Booths 70-72
Daytona Beach, FL 32119
386-503-6598

CORBIN STAMP & COIN, INC.
108 West Robertson Street
Brandon, FL 33511
813-651-3266

R.D.C. STAMPS
7381 SW 24th Street
Miami, FL 33155-1402
305-264-4213
305-262-2919 Fax
Email: rdcstamps@aol.com

SUN COAST STAMP CO.
3231 Gulf Gate Drive
Suite 102
Sarasota, FL 34231
941-921-9761 or 800-927-3351
941-921-1762 Fax
Email: suncoaststamp@aol.com

WINTER PARK STAMP SHOP
Ranch Mall (17-92)
325 S. Orlando Ave.
Suite 1-2
Winter Park, FL 32789-3608
407-628-1120 or 800-845-1819
407-628-0091 Fax
Email: jim@winterparkstampshop.com
Web: www.winterparkstampshop.com

Georgia

STAMPS UNLIMITED OF GEORGIA
133 Carnegie Way
Room 250
Atlanta, GA 30303
404-688-9161

Illinois

DON CLARK'S STAMPS & COINS
937 1/2 W. Galena Blvd.
Aurora, IL 60506
630-896-4606

DR. ROBERT FRIEDMAN & SONS
2029 West 75th Street
Woodridge, IL 60517
630-985-1515
630-985-1588 Fax

Indiana

KNIGHT STAMP & COIN CO.
237 Main Street
Hobart, IN 46342
219-942-4341 or 800-634-2646
Email: knight@knightcoin.com
Web: www.knightcoin.com

Kentucky

COLLECTORS STAMPS LTD.
4012 Dupont Circle #313
Louisville, KY 40207
502-897-9045
Email: csl@aye.net

Maryland

BALTIMORE COIN & STAMP EXCHANGE
10194 Baltimore National Pike
Unit 104
Ellicott City, MD 21042
410-418-8282
410-418-4813 Fax

BULLDOG STAMP COMPANY
4641 Montgomery Avenue
Bethesda, MD 20814
301-654-1138

Massachusetts

KAPPY'S COINS & STAMPS
534 Washington Street
Norwood, MA 02062
781-762-5552
781-762-3292 Fax
Email: kappyscoins@aol.com

Michigan

THE MOUSE AND SUCH
696 N. Mill Street
Plymouth, MI 48170
734-454-1515

New Jersey

AALLSTAMPS
38 N. Main Street
P.O. Box 249
Milltown, NJ 08850
732-247-1093
732-247-1094 Fax
Email: mail@aallstamps.com
Web: www.aallstamps.com

BERGEN STAMPS & COLLECTIBLES
717 American Legion Drive
Teaneck, NJ 07666
201-836-8987

RON RITZER STAMPS INC.
Millburn Mall
2933 Vauxhall Road
Vauxhall, NJ 07088
908-687-0007
908-687-0795 Fax
Email: ritzerstamps@earthlink.net

TRENTON STAMP & COIN CO.
Thomas DeLuca
Store: Forest Glen Plaza
1804 Route 33
Hamilton Square, NJ 08690
Mail: P.O. Box 8574
Trenton, NJ 08650
800-446-8664
609-587-8664 Fax

STAMP STORES

New York

CHAMPION STAMP CO., INC.
432 West 54th Street
New York, NY 10019
212-489-8130
212-581-8130 Fax
Email: championstamp@aol.com
Web: www.championstamp.com

Ohio

FEDERAL COIN & STAMP EXCHANGE
P.O. Box 14579
401 Euclid Ave.
Suite 45
Cleveland, OH 44114
216-861-1160
216-861-5960 Fax

HILLTOP STAMP SERVICE
Richard A. Peterson
P.O. Box 626
Wooster, OH 44691
330-262-8907 or 330-262-5378
Email: hilltop@bright.net

THE LINK STAMP CO.
3461 E. Livingston Ave.
Columbus, OH 43227
614-237-4125 Phone/Fax
800-546-5726 Phone/Fax

Pennsylvania

LARRY LEE STAMPS
322 S. Front Street
Greater Harrisburg Area
Wormleysburg, PA 17043
717-763-7605
Email: llstamps1@aol.com

PHILLY STAMP & COIN CO., INC.
1804 Chestnut Street
Philadelphia, PA 19103
215-563-7341
215-563-7382 Fax
Email: phillysc@netreach.net
Web:
www.phillystampandcoin.com

Tennessee

HERRON HILL, INC.
5007 Black Road
Suite 140
Memphis, TN 38117
901-683-9644

Virginia

KENNEDY'S STAMPS & COINS
7059 Brookfield Plaza
Springfield, VA 22150
703-569-7300
703-569-7644 Fax
Email: kennedy@patriot.net

LATHEROW & CO., INC.
5054 Lee Hwy.
Arlington, VA 22207
703-538-2727 or 800-647-4624
703-538-5210 Fax

Washington

TACOMA MALL BLVD. COIN & STAMP
5225 Tacoma Mall Blvd. E101
Tacoma, WA 98409
253-472-9632
253-472-8948 Fax
Email: kfeldman01@sprynet.com
Web: www.tmbcoinandstamp.com

Wisconsin

JIM LUKES' STAMP & COIN
815 Jay Street
P.O. Box 1780
Manitowoc, WI 54221
920-682-2324 Phone/Fax

Supplies

GOPHER SUPPLY
2525 Nevada Ave. N
Suite 102
Minneapolis, MN 55427
800-815-3868 or 763-525-1750
763-544-4683 Fax
Web: www.gophersupply.com

Topicals

MINI-ARTS
P.O. Box 457
Estherville, IA 51334
712-362-4710
Email: pmga@rconnect.com
Web:
www.ebaystores.com/miniarts

Topicals - Columbus

MR. COLUMBUS
Box 1492
Fennville, MI 49408
616-543-4755
616-543-3507 Fax
Email: columbus@accn.org

Topicals - Miscellaneous

BOMBAY PHILATELIC INC.
P.O. Box 480009
Delray Beach, FL 33448
561-499-7990
561-499-7553 Fax
Email: sales@bombaystamps.com
Web: www.bombaystamps.com

HENRY GITNER PHILATELISTS, INC.
P.O. Box 3077-S
Middletown, NY 10940
845-343-5151 or 800-947-8267
845-343-0068 Fax
Email: hgitner@hgitner.com
Web: www.hgitner.com

Ukraine

MR. VAL ZABIJAKA
P.O. Box 3711
Silver Spring, MD 20918
301-593-5316 Phone/Fax
Email: bnm123@erols.com

United States

BROOKMAN STAMP CO.
P.O. Box 90
Vancouver, WA 98666
360-695-1391 or 800-545-4871
360-695-1616 Fax
Email:
dave@brookmanstamps.com
Web: www.brookmanstamps.com

DR. ROBERT FRIEDMAN & SONS
2029 West 75th Street
Woodridge, IL 60517
630-985-1515
630-985-1588 Fax

U.S. - Price Lists

ROBERT E. BARKER
P.O. Box 1100
Warren, ME 04864
207-273-6200 or 800-833-0217
207-273-4254 or 888-325-5158
Email: rebarker@rebarker.com
Web: www.rebarker.com

Want Lists

BROOKMAN INTERNATIONAL
P.O. Box 450
Vancouver, WA 98666
360-695-1391 or 800-545-4871
360-695-1616 Fax
Email:
dave@brookmanstamps.com

CHARLES P. SCHWARTZ
P.O. Box 165
Mora, MN 55051
320-679-4705
Email: charlesp@ecenet.com

Want Lists-British Empire 1840-1935 German Colonies/Offices

COLONIAL STAMP COMPANY
5757 Wilshire Blvd. PH #8
Los Angeles, CA 90036
323-933-9435
323-939-9930 Fax
Email: gwh225@aol.com
Web: www.colonialstamps.com

Websites

HENRY GITNER PHILATELISTS, INC.
P.O. Box 3077-S
Middletown, NY 10940
845-343-5151 or 800-947-8267
845-343-0068 Fax
Email: hgitner@hgitner.com
Web: www.hgitner.com

Wholesale

HENRY GITNER PHILATELISTS, INC.
P.O. Box 3077-S
Middletown, NY 10940
845-343-5151 or 800-947-8267
845-343-0068 Fax
Email: hgitner@hgitner.com
Web: www.hgitner.com

Worldwide-Collections

BOB & MARTHA FRIEDMAN
624 Homestead Place
Joliet, IL 60435
815-725-6666
815-725-4134 Fax

Worldwide-Collections

DR. ROBERT FRIEDMAN & SONS
2029 West 75th Street
Woodridge, IL 60517
630-985-1515
630-985-1588 Fax

Worldwide-Year Sets

BOMBAY PHILATELIC INC.
P.O. Box 480009
Delray Beach, FL 33448
561-499-7990
561-499-7553 Fax
Email: sales@bombaystamps.com
Web: www.bombaystamps.com

WALLACE STAMPS
Box 82
Port Washington, NY 11050
516-883-5578

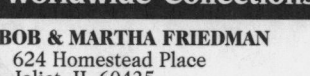

S C O T T ... H I N G C O.

Specialty Series

Scott Publishing Co. produces album pages for more than 120 countries.
Scott Specialty pages are renowned for their quality and detail.
There are spaces for every major variety of postage stamp
within each country or specialty area.

Each space is identified by Scott number and many of the spaces are illustrated.
Pages are printed on one side only on chemically neutral paper
that will not harm your stamps.

Scott Specialty series pages are sold as page units only.
Binders and slipcases are sold separately.

For more information on the entire line of Scott products visit your favorite stamp dealer
or go online at:

www.amosadvantage.com

SCOTT

P.O. Box 828, Sidney OH 45365-0828
1-800-572-6885

AMOS
HOBBY PUBLISHING